Periodical Title Abbreviations: By Abbreviation

Contents

Gale's publications in the acronyms and abbreviations field include:

Acronyms, Initialisms & Abbreviations Dictionary series:

Acronyms, Initialisms & Abbreviations Dictionary (Volume 1). A guide to acronyms, initialisms, abbreviations, and similar contractions, arranged alphabetically by abbreviation.

Reverse Acronyms, Initialisms & Abbreviations Dictionary (Volume 3). A companion to Volume 1 in which terms are arranged alphabetically by meaning of the acronym, initialism, or abbreviation.

Acronyms, Initialisms & Abbreviations Dictionary Subject Guide series:

Computer & Telecommunications Acronyms (Volume 1). A guide to acronyms, initialisms, abbreviations, and similar contractions used in the field of computers and telecommunications in which terms are arranged alphabetically both by abbreviation and by meaning.

Business Acronyms (Volume 2). A guide to business-oriented acronyms, initialisms, abbreviations, and similar contractions in which terms are arranged alphabetically both by abbreviation and by meaning.

International Acronyms, Initialisms & Abbreviations Dictionary series:

International Acronyms, Initialisms & Abbreviations Dictionary (Volume 1). A guide to foreign and international acronyms, initialisms, abbreviations, and similar contractions, arranged alphabetically by abbreviation.

Reverse International Acronyms, Initialisms & Abbreviations Dictionary (Volume 2). A companion to Volume 1, in which terms are arranged alphabetically by meaning of the acronym, initialism, or abbreviation.

Periodical Title Abbreviations series:

Periodical Title Abbreviations: By Abbreviation (Volume 1). A guide to abbreviations commonly used for periodical titles, arranged alphabetically by abbreviation.

Periodical Title Abbreviations: By Title (Volume 2). A guide to abbreviations commonly used for periodical titles, arranged alphabetically by title.

Highlights

Nearly 212,000 Entries
11,700 New Abbreviations
Broad Coverage
Arrangement by Abbreviation

With this edition, the contents of *Periodical Title Abbreviations: By Abbreviation (PTA-A)* have been expanded to a total of over 212,000 entries. This represents a seven percent increase over the previous edition. Abbreviations in all fields have been updated and expanded.

Scope of Coverage

PTA-A helps scholars, academic researchers, information specialists, and librarians to translate magazine, journal, and newspaper title abbreviations into full titles. It is intended to be used neither as an authority file nor as a standard for periodical abbreviations, but merely as a record of the myriad ways in which commonly used indexing and abstracting services abbreviate periodical titles.

Arrangement of Entries

Abbreviated titles are arranged alphabetically in letter-by-letter sequence. If the same abbreviation has more than one meaning, the various translations are then subarranged alphabetically. Should you need to determine quickly if and how a given periodical title has been previously abbreviated, a companion volume is available. *Periodical Title Abbreviations: By Title (PTA-T)* contains essentially the same entries, but arranges them by title, rather than by abbreviation.

Introduction

Periodical Title Abbreviations: By Abbreviation (*PTA-A*) translates magazine, journal, and newspaper title abbreviations into full titles. It does so in response to what has generally been recognized as a major bibliographic obstacle. In spite of attempts by organizations and individuals to prescribe standard periodical abbreviations or rules for constructing periodical abbreviations, the uniform abbreviated citation has remained an admirable but elusive ideal. Many indexing and abstracting services use homegrown abbreviation systems which, more often than not, disregard the efforts of such bodies as the National Clearinghouse for Periodical Title Word Abbreviations-or such documents as the *American Standard for Periodical Title Abbreviations.* As a consequence, the present edition of *PTA-A* is intended to be used neither as an authority file nor as a standard for periodical abbreviations, but merely as a record of the myriad ways in which commonly used indexing and abstracting services abbreviate periodical titles. While it may be vexing to the user of this dictionary that the same title is abbreviated several different ways, and disconcerting that a single abbreviation can stand for more than one title, *Periodical Title Abbreviations: By Abbreviation* is nonetheless intended only as a record of things as they are, not as they "should" be. At the very least, however, it may be hoped that this volume will serve to prevent the creation of additional abbreviations where none are needed.

In those occasional instances where the same abbreviation is used for two or more periodical titles, the user should consult such standard serial sources as the *Union List of Serials, New Serial Titles, Ulrich's International Periodicals Directory,* or *The British Union Catalogue of Periodicals* for the publishing history of the periodical one suspects the abbreviation represents. Normally, when this information is compared with the year and volume of the citation in question, satisfactory identification is possible.

Although some abbreviations from *Chemical Abstracts* appear in *PTA,* many have not been included because of the large number of complicated serial and monographic entries contained in that source. Thus, users will still need to use *Chemical Abstracts Service Source Index* in conjunction with *Periodical Title Abbreviations: By Abbreviation.*

For discussions of the full range of difficulties associated with periodical abbreviations, the reader is directed to the following publications:

Kinney, Mary R., *The Abbreviated Citation-A Bibliographic Problem,* Association of College and Research Libraries Monographs, Number 28, Chicago, American Library Association, 1967.

Alkire, Leland G., "The Initial Problem," *Serials Librarian,* vol. 2, summer 1978: 401-404.

(Excerpts from "The Initial Problem" follow this introduction).

Editorial Policies

In all decisions, the principle of simplicity of use has been kept foremost. In certain indexing services, periodical abbreviations were found to change from one year to the next. While this accounts for the seemingly elegant variation of some abbreviations found in this dictionary, the user should also be aware that several thousand nearly repetitive entries have been eliminated after having been judged to add nothing to the identification process. With these exceptions, and with minor alterations in the interest of uniform format and corrections of typographical errors found in the source materials, the abbreviations and periodical titles reproduced in this dictionary conform to the information found in the source materials.

Like sailors long at sea, who derive great satisfaction from a curious cloud formation or the sight of a bird, those who labor over abbreviation dictionaries look for and celebrate anything which serves to break the monotony. In this work, typographical errors provided occasional diversions; some repeatable and several not. My lightest moment came with the permutation of the *Yen Ching Journal* into the *Wenching Journal.* Many such errors have been eliminated, but no doubt some will remain. Though no work of this sort is ever completely error-proof, those which abide must be laid at my door. I ask only the user's understanding of the difficulties involved in dealing with a dozen or more languages simultaneously, and the problems posed by error-sprinkled source materials.

Suggestions for New Material

As in the past, the users of the *Periodical Title Abbreviations* series remain a valuable source in the identification of abbreviations not yet included in the *PTA* system. Users wishing to suggest new entries may do so by mailing a photocopy of the source of the suggested entries (i.e., the key to abbreviations in an index, abstract, or book), along with a complete bibliographic citation of the publication from which the pages were copied, to:

Leland G. Alkire
Kennedy Library
Eastern Washington University
Cheney, WA 99004

Excerpts from "The Initial Problem"*

In a July 1960 letter to *Science* magazine, a somewhat mournful plea was raised by one J. B. Sykes, in favor of "more sparing use of abbreviations when citing references to periodicals." He rightly saw that abbreviated titles often create some difficulty for the user.

In the years since Sykes' complaint, abbreviated periodical citations have proliferated in a way that has exceeded the expectations of even the most pessimistic of observers. Despite organized and sustained efforts, both before and after 1960, either to abandon outright the use of abbreviated citations or, failing this, to adopt a standardized system of abbreviated periodical titles, we are presently faced with a greater diversity than ever before.

Observers of language, such as George Orwell, Jacques Barzun, and Stephen Leacock, have variously lamented, railed, and poked fun at abbreviated forms. But the battle has been a losing one. In government, business, and academe, an element of gamesmanship has long dictated that those "in-the-know" should speak in direct, if sometimes barbaric sounding terms, such as NASA, NATO, and ICSU. Further, in a kind of variant of punning, we are surrounded by a buzzing swarm of acronyms which not only identifies their users as the *cognoscenti*, but which also implies an element of one-upmanship. Some, like CORE and NOW, are clever and apt, but what was once bright and chic begins to wear thin through overuse. Yet in spite of what, in some quarters, has become a cautionary approach to the short-form phenomenon, it must be admitted that both the acronym and the abbreviation serve as time and space savers in these information-heavy times.

The real trouble with short-form usage lies in the tendency of abbreviated forms to duplicate one another. When we encounter a reference to an organization called AID, we must ask: Does it refer to the Agency for International Development or the Americans of Italian Descent? When such multimeaning abbreviations are used without accompanying definitions or in contexts that leave one in doubt, the result is often a breakdown in basic communication.

Small specialized professional groups are perhaps the greatest purveyors of this sort of noncommunication. Imagine, for a moment, a nonlibrarian, or even a librarian who has been away from the profession for a time, picking up a recent library publication and attempting to negotiate the foaming rapids of OCLC, CONSER, MULS, ISSN, and AACR. They will scarcely find themselves paddling in familiar waters. Indeed, Some would ask if we are not entering a time when professional subspecialists will be decreasingly able to decipher one another's abb pro jarg (abbreviated professional jargon).

Whatever future may await us as librarians, as researchers, and as users of the English language, one thing is clear: The concern of J.B. Sykes in 1960 regarding the problem of abbreviated periodical titles haunts us in ways that are increasingly troublesome. When a reference, periodicals, or interlibrary loan librarian encounters a citation in which the title has been reduced to an abbreviation, AM for example, where does he or she turn? *Acta Musicologia, Atlantic Monthly, Americas,* or any one of the eleven journals to which this abbreviation is commonly applied, all represent logical choices. To use another even more disconcerting example, the abbreviation MHM can mean either *Maryland History Magazine* or *Michigan History Magazine,* depending on the source of the citation. The list of such competitors could be extended indefinitely since tens of thousands of periodicals are currently employed by indexing and abstracting services, as well as by scholarly journals and bibliographies. Many of these publications, as must be obvious by now, employ periodical title abbreviations without regard to how such forms are used elsewhere. This disorderly situation is further compounded by the assumption of scholars, students, and other users that a given abbreviation is not only unique, but that it is part of a generally acknowledged language, which others, particularly librarians, will immediately recognize. Often, because of experience, intuition, and the subject of the article in question, a little detective work will reveal the full title. Yet this work takes time, and inevitably, after a number of such requests, the librarian will draw a blank, particularly when a patron is uncertain as to the origin of the citation.

Attempts to bring order to this disarray have been numerous, if only partially successful, but one can hope, if orderly access to periodical information is seen as a desirable end, that the current proliferation of systems of abbreviation will one day be rationalized and reduced to a single, understandable system.

In the meantime, a few of us continue to recall that moment in the Apollo 12 Moon Mission when Ground Control discovered that a minor equipment failure was caused by something called the Digital Uplink Assembly. When the controllers radioed up that the fault lay with the DUA, the response from the crew of the Apollo 12 was: "What's a DUA?"

*Excerpted by permission of Haworth Press, *Serials Librarian*, vol. 2, summer 1978: 401-404.

User's Guide

Entries are arranged in letter-by-letter sequence, regardless of spacing, punctuation, or capitalization. For sorting purposes, ampersands are translated into 'AND'; hyphenated terms are treated as one word. Articles, conjunctions, and prepositions are not generally considered in the alphabetizing for sorting. If the same abbreviation has more than one meaning, the various translations are then subarranged alphabetically in word-by-word sequence. Entries may contain the following elements:

❶ Abbreviated title   ❷ Complete title

❸ Explanation of acronym within title   ❹ Translation

❺ Sponsoring organization or Publisher   ❻ Place of publication

❶   ❷   ❸   ❹

> **Bol Tec PETROBRAS**—Boletim Tecnico. PETROBRAS [*Petroleo Brasileiro SA*] [*Technical Bulletin. PETROBRAS*] [*Centro de Pesquisas e Desenvolvimento*] [*Rio De Janeiro, Brazil*]

❺   ❻

The completeness of an entry is dependent upon both the nature of the term and the amount of information provided by the source. If additional information becomes available during future research, an entry will be revised.

Major Sources of Abbreviations Contained in Periodical Title Abbreviations Series

Abstract Bulletin of the Institute of Paper Chemistry

ACTFL (American Council on the Teaching of Foreign Languages) Annual Bibliography of Books and Articles on Pedagogy in Foreign Languages

Alternative Press Index

American Journal of Archaeology

American-German Review

American Literature Abstracts

Annee-Philologique

Annual Bibliography of English Language and Literature

Applied Science and Technology Index

Art Index

Arts and Humanities Citation Index

Bibliographic Index

Bibliography of Asian Studies

Bibliography of Corn

Bibliography and Index of Geology

Bibliography of North American Geology

Bibliography of Wheat

Biography Index

Biological and Agricultural Index

Serial Sources for the BIOSIS Data Base

Book Review Digest

Book Review Index

British Education Index

British Technology Index

Business Education Index

Business Periodicals Index

Canadian Periodicals Index

Catholic Periodical Index

Chicorel Index to Mental Health Book Reviews

Christian Periodicals Index

Classified Shakespeare Bibliography

Combined Retrospective Index to Book Reviews in Scholarly Journals

Cumulated Index Medicus

Cumulative Index to Nursing and Allied Health Literature

Current Book Review Citations

Current Index to Statistics

DSH (Deafness, Speech, and Hearing) Abstracts

Education Index

Elsevier Book Series Abbreviations

Engineering Index

English Language Notes

ELH (English Literary History)

Film Literature Index

Forestry Abstracts

French Periodical Index

Geological Literature of North America, 1785-1918

Germanic Review

Harvard Guide to American History

Hospital Literature Index

Humanities Index

IMM (Institute of Mining and Metallurgy) Abstracts

Index of American Periodical Verse

Index Catalogue of Medical and Veterinary Zoology

Index Chemicus

Index of Economic Articles

Index to Legal Periodicals

Index to Little Magazines

Index to Periodicals by and about Negroes

Index to Religious Periodical Literature

Index to Science Fiction Magazines

Industrial Arts Index

INIS (International Nuclear Information System) Authority List for Journal Titles

INSPEC (Information Service for Physics, Electrotechnology, and Control)

Insurance Periodicals Index

International Bibliography of the History of Religions

International Bibliography of Social Sciences: Anthropology

International Bibliography of Social Sciences: Political Science

International Bibliography of Social Sciences: Sociology

International Index

International Nursing Index

Journal of Aesthetics and Art Criticism

Journal of American Folklore

Journal of English and Germanic Philology

Keats-Shelley Journal

Library and Information Science Abstracts

Library Literature

Mathematical Reviews

Metals Abstracts. Annual Index

Numerics

2C Constr Ciudad — 2C. Construccion de la Ciudad
2C Constr Ciudad — 2 [dos] C. Construccion de la Ciudad
2CSAB — Two Complete Science Adventure Books
2 x 2 — Ketto
4 WCJS — Fourth World Congress of Jewish Studies
9th Dist Banker — Ninth District Banker
16th C J — Sixteenth Century Journal
18th C — Eighteenth Century
18th C Life — Eighteenth Century Life
18th C Stud — Eighteenth Century Studies

18th C Theory & Interpretation — Eighteenth Century. Theory and Interpretation
19th C & After — Nineteenth Century and After
19th Cent — Nineteenth Century
19th Cent — Nineteenth Century and After
19th C London — Nineteenth Century [London]
19th C New York — Nineteenth Century [Victorian Society of America, NY]
30s Soc J — Thirties Society Journal
35 mm Photog — 35 mm Photography
35 MM Photogr — Thirty-Five mm (35 mm) Photography
900 Cah Italie & Europe — 900 Cahiers d'Italie et d'Europe

A

A — Adam's Justiciary Reports
A — Admap
A — America
A — Anthropos
A — Antike
A — Antiquity
A — Archiv fuer das Studium der Neueren Sprachen
A — Arthuriana
A — Asia
A — Aufbau
A — [*The*] Australian
A — Buchanan's Reports of the Court of Appeal, Cape
A1 Appl Nat Resour Manage — A1 Applications in Natural Resource Management
A 1888 B — Australia 1888 Bulletin
A 1938-1988 B — Australia 1938-1988 Bicentennial History Project. Bulletin
AA — Abstracts in Anthropology
AA — Acta Archaeologica
AA — Advertising Age
AA — Aegyptologische Abhandlungen
AA — African Abstracts
AA — Alacran Azul
AA — Al Ahram
AA — Album Acoriano
AA — Alttestamentliche Abhandlungen
AA — Amazing Stories. Annual
AA — American Annals of the Deaf
AA — American Anthropologist
AA — American Antiquity
AA — American Archivist
AA — Anecdota Atheniensia et Alia
AA — Anglo-American Magazine
AA — Annales Africaines
AA — Antwerpsch Archievenblad
AA — Apicultural Abstracts
AA — Arbeitsamt
AA — Archaeologischer Anzeiger
AA — Archiv fuer Anthropologie
AA — Ars Aequi; Juridisch Studentenblad
AA — Art and Archaeology
AA — Art and Architecture
AA — Artibus Asiae
AA — Asian Affairs
AA — Athro Arfon
AA — Ausgaben und Abhandlungen aus dem Gebiete der Romanischen Philologie
AA — Aut Aut
AAA — Acta Academiae Aboensis
AAA — Acta Apostolorum Apocrypha
AAA — Acta Archaeologica Academiae Scientiarum Hungaricae
AAA — Aerosol Age
AAA — Al-Alam al-Arabi
AAA — American Arab Affairs
AAA — Annals. American Academy of Political and Social Science
AAA — Annals of Archaeology and Anthropology
AAA — Archaiologika Analekta ex Athenon
AAA — Archives of Asian Art
AAA — Archivio. Alto Adige
AAA — Arquivo de Anatomia e Antropologia
AAA — Art and Archaeology
AAA — Athens Annals of Archaeology
AAA — Atlas Archeologique de l'Algerie
AAAA — Abstracts. Annual Meeting. American Anthropological Association
AAAA — Activities, Adaptation, and Aging
AAAA — Annuaire. Association des Auditeurs et Anciens Auditeurs de l'Academie de DroitInternational a La Haye
AAA/AA — American Anthropologist. American Anthropological Association
AAAB — Annales. Academie Royale d'Archeologie de Belgique
AAABC — Astronomy and Astrophysics. Abstracts
AAAbo — Acta Academiae Aboensis
AA Abo H — Acta Academiae Aboensis. Serie A. Humaniora
AAAC — About Arts and Crafts. Department of Indian and Northern Affairs
AAACCA — Advances in Antimicrobial and Antineoplastic Chemotherapy
AAAd — Antichita Altoadriatiche
AAAd — Archivio. Alto Adige
AAAF — Acta Academiae Aboensis. Humaniora (Finland)
AAAG — Annals. Association of American Geographers
AAAGA — Association of American Geographers. Annals

AAAH — Acta Academiae Aboensis. Series A. Humaniora
AAAH — Acta ad Archaeologiam et Artium Historiam Pertinentia
AAAH — Acta Antique Academiae Scientiarum Hungaricae
AAAHAN — Australian Journal of Experimental Agriculture and Animal Husbandry
AAA Hum — Acta Academiae Aboensis. Series A. Humaniora
AAAIBR — Aspects of Allergy and Applied Immunology
AAAM — American Anthropological Association. Memoirs
AAAM Q Jnl — AAAM [*American Association for Automotive Medicine*] Quarterly Journal
AAAN — Alaska Anthropological Association. Newsletter
AAAN — Atti. Real Accademia di Archeologia, Lettere, e Belle Arti (Napoli)
AAANA7 — Arquivo de Anatomia e Antropologia
AAAPS — Annals. American Academy of Political and Social Science
AAAPSS — Annals. American Academy of Political and Social Science
AAAr — Atti. Accademia degli Arcadi
AAARBK — AGARD [*Advisory Group for Aerospace Research and Development*] Advisory Report
AAAS — Annales Archeologiques Arabes de Syrie
AAAS — Annales Archeologiques Arabes Syriennes
AAASAH — Acta Academiae Aboensis. Series A. Humaniora
AAAS Bull — American Association for the Advancement of Science. Bulletin
AAASH — Acta Antiqua. Academiae Scientiarum Hungaricae
AAAS Publication — American Association for the Advancement of Science. Publication
AAAS/S — Science. American Association for the Advancement of Science
AAAS Selected Symposia Series — American Association for the Advancement of Science. Selected Symposia Series
AAAS Sel Sympos Ser — American Association for the Advancement of Science. Selected Symposia Series
AAAZ — Archaeologischer Anzeiger zur Archaeologischen Zeitung
AAB — Abhandlungen der Deutschen
AAB — Actes de l'Academie des Sciences, Belles Lettres, et Arts de Besancon
AAB — Annuaire. Academie Real de Belgique
AABn — Annales. Academie Royale d'Archeologie de Belgique
AABC — Anecdota quae ex Ambrosianae Bibliothecae Codicibus
AABC — Annals of Applied Biology (Cambridge, England)
AABCAD — Anais. Academia Brasileira de Ciencias
AABEAJ — Acta Anaesthesiologica Belgica
AABIAV — Annals of Applied Biology
Aab Nord Oldknd & Hist — Aarboger for Nordisk Oldkyndighed og Historie
AABO Akad Aarssk — AABO [*Aabo Akademi, Domkyrkotorget*] Akademi. Aarsskrift
AA Bordeaux — Actes. Academie Nationale des Sciences, Belles-Lettres, et Arts de Bordeaux
AAC — Academia (Chile)
AAC — Acta Archaeologica Carpathica
AAC — Acta Archaeologica (Copenhagen)
AAC — Airworthiness Advisory Circular
AAC — Amico dell'Arte Cristiana
AAC — Augmentative and Alternative Communication
A Acad Sci Fenn — Annales Academiae Scientiarum Fennicae
AACC (Am Assoc Cereal Chem) Monogr — AACC (American Association of Cereal Chemists) Monograph
AACCB — All Africa Conference of Churches. Bulletin
A Acc Ital Sci For — Annali. Accademia Italiana di Scienze Forestali
AACCLA Outl — AACLA [*Association of American Chambers of Commerce in Latin America*] Outlook
AACC News — Affirmative Action Coordinating Center. Newsletter
AACC Trans — AACC [*American Association of Cereal Chemists*] Transactions
AACE (Am Assoc Cost Eng) Bull — AACE (American Association of Cost Engineers) Bulletin
AACE Bull — American Association of Cost Engineers. Bulletin
AACFAR — Annales. ACFAS
AACHBY — Acta Arachnologica
Aachen Beitr Baugesch & Heimatkst — Aachener Beitraege fuer Baugeschichte und Heimatkunst
Aachen Kstbl — Aachener Kunstblaetter
Aachen Kuntsbl — Aachener Kuntsblaetter
Aach Kbl — Aachener Kunstblaetter
A A Chron — Arthur Andersen Chronicle
AACIA2 — Advances in Analytical Chemistry and Instrumentation
AACMP — Anales. Academia de Ciencias Morales y Politicas
AACN — Arts and Culture of the North
AACOB — Applied Acoustics
AACOBS Ann Rep — AACOBS [*Australian Advisiory Council on Bibliographical Services*] Annual Report
AA Cos — Atti. Accademia Cosentina

AACPDQ — Archives d'Anatomie et de Cytologie Pathologiques
AACRA — Anesthesia and Analgesia (Cleveland)
AACS — Acta Academiae Catholicae Suecanae
AACSE2 — Advances in Agronomy and Crop Science
A Ac Vel — Acta Academiae Velehradensis
AAD — Army Aviation Digest
AADE J — AADE [*American Association of Dental Editors*] Journal
AAE — AACE [*American Association of Cost Engineers*] Transactions
AAE — Advertising Age Europe
AAe — Analecta Aegyptiaca
AAE — Appointment of Agents. Excise
AAE — Archivio per l'Antropologia e l'Etnologia
A Ae A — Archiv fuer Aegyptische Archaeologie
AAEB — Aus der Arbeit des Evangelischen Bundes
AAEC — Annuario. Accademia Etrusca di Cortona
AAEC Nucl News — AAEC [*Australian Atomic Energy Commission*] Nuclear News
AAEC Nucl News (AU) — AAEC [*Australian Atomic Energy Commission*] Nuclear News (Australia)
AAED — Alcoholism and Alcohol Education
A Aeg — Analecta Aegyptiaca
AAEG — Annuaire. Association pour l'Encouragement des Etudes Grecques en France
A Aeg Arch — Archiv fuer Aegyptische Archaeologie
A Ael — Archaeologia Aeliana
AAEM — Annals of Agricultural and Environmental Medicine
AAEPC — Anales. Asociacion Espanola para el Progreso de las Ciencias
AAERA5 — Alabama. Agricultural Experiment Station. Progress Report Series (Auburn University)
AAES — Abhandlungen des Archaeologischepigraphischen Seminars der Universitaet Wien
AAES — American Archaeological Expedition to Syria. Publication
AAESDA Bul — AAESDA [*Association of Architects, Engineers, Surveyors, and Draughtsmen of Australia*] Bulletin
AAF — Anglo-American Forum
AAF — Archives de l'Art Francais
AAF — Atti. Accademia Fiorentina
AAFBA — Annales Academiae Scientiarum Fennicae. Series A-IV (Biologica)
AAFBAU — Annales Academiae Scientiarum Fennicae. Series A-IV (Biologica)
AAFCAX — Annales Academiae Scientiarum Fennicae. Series A-II (Chemica)
AAFGAB — Annales Academiae Scientiarum Fennicae. Series A-III (Geologica-Geographica)
AAFHB — Academy of American Franciscan History. Bibliography Series
AAFHM — Academy of American Franciscan History. Monograph Series
AAFH/TAM — [*The*] Americas. Academy of American Franciscan History
AAFMBU — Annales Academiae Scientiarum Fennicae. Series A-V (Medica)
AAFPA — Annales Academiae Scientiarum Fennicae. Series A-VI (Physica)
A Afr — Annales Africaines
AAFRA — Arcispedale S. Anna di Ferrara
A Afric — Annales Africaines
A Afrique — Arts d'Afrique
A Afrique Noire — Arts d'Afrique Noire
AAFV — Anuario. Asociacion Francisco de Vitoria
AAG — Abhandlungen. Akademie der Wissenschaften in Goettingen
AAg — Afrique Agriculture
AAG — Anales Academia Geografia e Historia de Guatemala
AAG — Annals of American Geographers
AAG — Archives Andre Gide
AAg — Archivo Agustiniano
AAG Bijdr Afd Agrar Gesch Landbouwhochgeschool Wageningen — AAG Bijdragen. Afdeling Agrarische Geschiedenis de Landbouwhochgeschool te Wageningen
AAGCA4 — Atti. Accademia Gioenia di Scienze Naturali in Catania
AAGEA — Arkhiv Anatomii, Gistologii, i Embriologii
AAGEAA — Arkhiv Anatomii, Gistologii, i Embriologii
A Agn — Annales Agronomiques
AAGNA — Atti. Associazione Genetica Italiana
AAGNA3 — Atti. Associazione Genetica Italiana
AAGRCH — Australia. Commonwealth Scientific and Industrial Research Organisation. Division of Applied Geomechanics. Technical Report
AAGSAI — Annals of Agricultural Science
AAGTCN — Australia. Commonwealth Scientific and Industrial Research Organisation. Division of Applied Geomechanics. Technical Paper
AAGWAU — Acta Agrobotanica
AAH — Acta Antiqua. Academiae Scientiarum Hungaricae
AAH — Archaeologischer Anzeiger (Heidelberg)
AAHA — Archives Alsaciennes d'Histoire de l'Art
AAHAA3 — Australia. Commonwealth Scientific and Industrial Research Organisation. Division of Animal Health. Annual Report
AAhAkBerl — Abhandlungen der Koeniglich Preussischen Akademie der Wissenschaften
AAHA Proc — AAHA (American Animal Hospital Association) Proceedings
AAHC — Anales. Academia de la Historia de Cuba
AAHEAF — Archives d'Anatomie, d'Histologie, et d'Embryologie
AAHG — Anzeiger fuer die Altertumswissenschaft. Herausgegeben von der Oesterreichischen Humanistischen Gesellschaft
AAHPAE — Australia. Commonwealth Scientific and Industrial Research Organisation. Division of Animal Health and Production. Technical Paper
AAHRAK — Arizona. Commission of Agriculture and Horticulture. Annual Report
A A Hung — Acta Archaeologica Academiae Scientiarum Hungaricae
AAI — Atti. Real Accademia d'Italia
AAIM — Atti. Real Accademia d'Italia. Memorie. Classe di Scienze Morali, Storiche, e Filologiche
AAIN — Atti. Real Accademia d'Italia. Notizie degli Scavi di Antichita
A A Intignc — Applied Artificial Intelligence Reporter

AAIR — Atti. Real Accademia d'Italia. Rendiconti. Classe di Scienze Morali e Storiche
AAJ — American Alpine Journal
AAJ — Anatomischer Anzeiger (Jena)
AAJ — Annual. Department of Antiquities of Jordon
AAJ — Australian Anthropological Journal
AAJBDJ — Al-Khalij Al-Arabi
AAJDAI — Archaeologischer Anzeiger. Beiblatt zum Jahrbuch des Kaiserlich Deutschen Archaeologischen Instituts
AAJID — AJRI. American Journal of Reproductive Immunology
AAJID6 — AJRI. American Journal of Reproductive Immunology
AAJNDL — AJNR. American Journal of Neuroradiology
A A Jord — Annual. Department of Antiquities. Jordan
AAJRD — AJR. American Journal of Roentgenology
AAKHD — Arbeiten und Berichte. Arbeitsgemeinschaft Katholischer Homiletiker Deutschlands
AAL — African Affairs (London)
AAL — Annals of Archaeology. University of Liverpool
AAL — Asien, Afrika, Lateinamerika
AAL — Atti. Accademia dei Lincei
AAL — Atti. Accademia Ligure di Scienze e Lettere di Genova
AALB — Australian Administrative Law Bulletin
AALBAQ — Atti. Accademia Nazionale dei Lincei. Memorie. Classe di Scienze Fisiche, Matematiche, e Naturali. Sezione 3a
Aalb B — Aalborg-Bogen
Aalb St — Aalborg Stiftsbog
AALGA7 — Atti. Accademia Ligure di Scienze e Lettere
AALi — Artisan et les Arts Liturgiques
AALIAM — Arcadia, Accademia Letteraria Italiana. Atti e Memorie
AA Lig — Atti. Accademia Ligure di Scienze e Lettere di Genova
AALM — Atti. Reale Accademia dei Lincei. Memorie. Classe di Scienze Morali, Storiche, e Filologiche
AALN — Atti. Reale Accademia dei Lincei. Notizie degli Scavi di Antichita. Classe di Scienze Morali, Storiche, e Filologiche
AALR — Anglo-American Law Review
AALR — Atti. Accademia dei Lincei. Rendiconti. Classe di Scienze Morali, Storiche, e Filologiche
AALR — Australian Argus Law Reports
AALSA9 — Acta Allergologica. Supplementum
AALS News — Association of American Library Schools. Newsletter
AALS Proc — Association of American Law Schools. Proceedings
AALT — Atti. Accademia dei Lincei. Transunti
AALTN — Arctic Aeromedical Laboratory. Technical Note
AALTR — Arctic Aeromedical Laboratory. Technical Report
AAm — Acta Americana
AAM — American Antiquity (Menasha, Wisconsin and Salt Lake City, Utah)
AAM — Annales. Academie de Macon
AAM — Arquivo do Alto Minho
AAM — Arte Antica e Moderna
AAm — Asia and the Americas
AAM — Atti e Memorie. Accademia di Scienze, Lettere, ed Arti di Modena
AAM — Atti e Memorie. Reale Accademia Virgiliana di Scienze, Lettere, ed Arti di Montova
A Amat — Art Amateur
AAMA Tech Adv Com Bull — AAMA [*American Apparel Manufacturers Association*] Technical Advisory Committee. Bulletin
AAMA Tech Adv Comm Res Pap — AAMA [*American Apparel Manufacturers Association*] Technical Advisory Committee. Research Paper
AAMA Wash Let — AAMA [*American Apparel Manufacturers Association*] Washington Letter
AAmb — Analecta Ambrosiana
AAMEA6 — Australasian Annals of Medicine
A Amer Acad Polit Soc Sci — Annals. American Academy of Political and Social Science
A America — Art in America
A America & Elsewhere — Art in America and Elsewhere
A America & Filipinas — Arte en America y Filipinas
AAMFA — Atti. Accademia dei Fisiocritici in Siena. Sezione Medico-Fisica
AAMFA9 — Atti. Accademia dei Fisiocritici in Siena. Sezione Medico-Fisica
AAMGBD — Annales Academiae Medicae Gedanensis
AAMI Technol Assess Rep — AAMI [*Association for the Advancement of Medical Instrumentation*] Technology Assessment Report
AAMLAR — Atti. Accademia Medica Lombarda
AAMMAU — Archives d'Anatomie Microscopique et de Morphologie Experimentale
AAMod — Atti e Memorie. Accademia di Scienze, Lettere, ed Arti di Modena
AAMS — Atti. Accademia Mariana Salesiana
AAMSC — Annals. Academy of Medicine (Singapore)
AAMSDH — Annales Academiae Medicae Stetinensis. Suplement
AAMZ — Abhandlungen. Akademie der Wissenschaften und der Literatur in Mainz
AAMZAZ — Acta Amazonica
AAN — Aanwinsten van de Centrale Bibliotheek
AAn — Acta Antiqua
AAn — American Anthropologist
AAn — American Antiquity
AAN — Ann Arbor News
AAn — Archiv fuer Anthropologie
AAN — Armenian Affairs (New York)
AAN — Atti. Accademia di Scienze Morali e Politiche della Societa Nazionale di Scienze, Lettere, ed Arti di Napoli
AAN — Atti. Accademia Pontaniana
AAN — Atti. Reale Accademia di Archeologia, Lettere, e Belle Arti di Napoli
AAN — Rendiconti. Accademia di Archeologia, Lettere, e Belle Arti di Napoli
AANA J — AANA [*American Association of Nurse Anesthetists*] Journal
AANAL — Anales. Academia Nacional de Artes y Letras
A & A — Antike und Abendland

A & A — Art and Archaeology
A & A — Arta si Arheologia
A & A — Arts and Architecture
A&A — Arts and Artists
A & A — Astronautics and Aeronautics
A & Ant — Art and Antiques
A & Archaeol — Art and Archaeology
A & Archaeol Res Pap — Art and Archaeology Research Papers
A & Archaeol Tech Abstr — Art and Archaeology Technical Abstracts
A & Archit — Art and Architecture
A & Archit — Arts and Architecture
A & Argent — Art et l'Argent
A & Arqueol — Arte e Arqueologia
A & Artistes — Art et les Artistes
A & Artists — Art and Artists
A & Auction — Art and Auction
A & Australia — Art and Australia
A & Cienc — Arte y la Ciencia
A & Crit — Art et la Critique
A & CS — Area and Culture Studies
A & Curiosite — Art et Curiosite
AANDD — Aparatura Naukowa i Dydaktyczna
A & Dec — Art et Decoration
A & Dec — Arts and Decoration
A & Des — Art and Design
A & Dossier — Art et Dossier
A&E — Anthropology and Education Quarterly
A&F — Ardenne et Famenne. Art-Archeologie-Histoire-Folklore
A & Idee — Art et l'Idee
A & Indust — Art and Industry
A & Islam World — Arts and the Islamic World
A&L — Art and Literature
A & Lett — Art and Letters
A & Lett — Arts and Letters
A & Libris — Arte et Libris
A & Lit — Art and Literature
A & M — Archives and Manuscripts
A & Metiers Graph — Arts et Metiers Graphiques
A & NZ Bank Quarterly Surv — Australia and New Zealand Bank. Quarterly Survey
A & Pensee — Arts et Pensee
A & Prog — Art and Progress
A & Publ — Art and Publicity
A and R (JP) — A and R. Analysis and Research (Japan)
A and S — Antiquity and Survival
A & S — Arts and Sciences
A & Stor — Arte e Storia
A & Tech — Art et Technique
A & Text — Art and Text
A & U — Architecture and Urbanism
A & Vie — Art et la Vie
AANEAB — Acta Anaesthesiologica Scandinavica
AANEBC — Archivio per l'Antropologia e la Etnologia
AANFA — Annales de l'Anesthesiologie Francaise
AANIBO — Acta Anaesthesiologica Italica
AANKG — Archiv fuer Alte und Neue Kirchengeschichte
AANL — Atti. Accademia Nazionale dei Lincei
AANLAW — Atti. Accademia Nazionale dei Lincei. Rendiconti. Classe di Scienze Fisiche, Matematiche, e Naturali
AANLM — Atti. Accademia Nazionale dei Lincei. Memorie. Classe de Scienze Morali, Storiche, e Filologiche
AANLN — Atti. Accademia Nazionale dei Lincei. Notizie degle Scavi di Antichita Communicate
AANLR — Atti. Accademia Nazionale dei Lincei. Rendiconti. Classe di Scienze Morali, Storiche, e Filologiche
AANMP — Atti. Accademia Nazionale di Scienze Morali e Politiche (Napoli)
AANNT — AANNT [American Association of Nephrology Nurses and Technicians] Journal
A Annu — Art Annual
AaNo — Aarboeger foer Nordisk Oldkyndighed og Historie
AA Notes — Architectural Association Notes
AAns — Analecta Anselmiana
AANSAJ — Acta Anatomica. Supplementum
AAnt — Acta Antiqua. Academiae Scientiarum Hungaricae
AANT — Arctic Anthropology
A Ant — Ars Antiqua
AANTA — American Antiquity
A Ant & Mod — Arte Antica e Moderna
A Ant H — Acta Antique Academiae Scientiarum Hungaricae
A ANTH — American Anthropologist
AAnth — Archiv fuer Anthropologie
AAnthr — American Anthropologist
A Ant Hung — Acta Antiqua Academiae Scientiarum Hungaricae
AAntHung — Acta Antiqua. Academiae Scientiarum Hungaricae
A Antiqua Acad Sci Hung — Acta Antiqua. Academiae Scientiarum Hungaricae
AAntr — Anales de Antropologia
A Antropol — Anales de Antropologia
AANZ — Archaeologischer Anzeiger zur Archaeologischen Zeitung
A AnZ B — Archaeologischer Anzeiger (Berlin)
AAOF — Annuaire et Memoires. Comite d'Etudes Historiques et Scientifiques de l'AfriqueOccidentale Francaise
AAOHN J — American Association of Occupational Health Nurses. Journal
AAOJ — American Antiquarian and Oriental Journal
AAP — Atti. Accademia di Palermo
AAP — Atti. Accademia Pontaniana

AAP — Atti e Memorie. Reale Accademia di Scienze, Lettere, ed Arti in Padova
AAP — Australia Air Publications
AAPad — Atti e Memorie. Accademia di Padova
AAPal — Atti. Accademia di Scienze, Lettere, ed Arti di Palermo
AAPA Newsl — AAPA [Australian Asphalt Pavement Association] Newsletter
AAPat — Atti e Memorie. Accademia Patavina
AAPB — Australian Prayer Book
AAPBBD — Advances in Aquatic Microbiology
AAPBCE — Archiv fuer Acker- und Pflanzenbau und Bodenkunde
A A Pel — Atti. Reale Accademia Peloritana
AAP Envmt Des — AAP Environment Design
AAPF — Arctos. Acta Philologica Fennica
AAPG — Affirmative Action Planning Guide
AAPG — American Association of Petroleum Geologists. Bulletin
AAPG (Am Assoc Pet Geol) Bull — AAPG (American Association of Petroleum Geologists) Bulletin
AAPGB — American Association of Petroleum Geologists. Bulletin
AAPG Bull — AAPG [American Association of Petroleum Geologists] Bulletin
AAPG Continuing Education — American Association of Petroleum Geologists. Continuing Education
AAPG Explorer — American Association of Petroleum Geologists. Explorer
AAPG Mem — AAPG [American Association of Petroleum Geologists] Memoir
AAPG Memoir — American Association of Petroleum Geologists. Memoir
AAPG Stud Geol — AAPG [American Association of Petroleum Geologists] Studies in Geology
AAPH — Anais. Academia Portuguesa da Historia
AAPJ — Acta Academiae Paedagogicae Jyvaskylaensis
AAPLA — Annales de l'Amelioration des Plantes
AAPLA8 — Annales de l'Amelioration des Plantes
AAPN — Atti. Accademia Pontaniana (Naples)
AAPNL — Atti. Accademia Pontificia dei Nuovi Lincei
AAPODK — Acta Alimentaria Polonica
AAPont — Atti. Accademia Pontaniana
AAPP — Anais da Academia Politecnica do Porto
AaPp — Arbeiten zur Angewandten Psychopathologie
AAPP Abstr — Amino Acids, Peptide, and Protein Abstracts
AAPPCM — Specialist Periodical Reports. Amino-Acids, Peptides, and Proteins
AAPPDN — Australasian Plant Pathology
AAPS — Annals. American Academy of Political and Social Science
AAPSAT — Archives d'Anatomie Pathologique
AAPS Newsletter — Association of American Physicians and Surgeons. Newsletter
AAPSSA — American Academy of Political and Social Science. Annals
AAPSS Mg — American Academy of Political and Social Science. Monographs
AAPTCY — Australia. Commonwealth Scientific and Industrial Research Organisation. Division of Atmospheric Physics. Technical Paper
AAPVA4 — Archives des Recherches Agronomiques et Pastorales au Vietnam
AAPYAD — Annual of Animal Psychology
AAQ — Architectural Association. Quarterly
AAQU-A — Architectural Association. Quarterly
AAR — Affirmative Action Register
AAr — American Artist
AAR — Annales. Academie des Sciences de Russie
AAR — Ann Arbor Review
AAR — Annual Archaeological Report. Ontario Provincial Museum
AAR — Asiatic Annual Register
AAR — Atlas of Australian Resources
AAR — Atti. Reale Accademia d'Italia (Roma). Memorie. Classe di Scienze Morali e Storiche
AARA — Atti. Accademia Roveretana degli Agiati
AARAAJ — Acta Albertina Ratisbonensia
AARAB — Annales. Academie Royale d'Archeologie de Belgique
Aarau Arch Md — Archiv der Medizin, Chirurgie, und Pharmacie. Aarau
Aarau Mt — Mittheilungen der Aargauischen Naturforschenden Gesellschaft. Aarau
Aarb — Aarboger foer Nordisk Oldkyndighed og Historie
AARB — Annuaire. Academie Royale de Belgique
Aarb Aarh St — Aarboger udg af Historish Samfund for Aarhus Stift
Aarb d PT — Aarbog for det Danske Post- og Telegrafvaesen
Aarb n O — Aarboger for Nordisk Oldkyndighed og Historie
Aarb Nor Polarinst — Aarbok. Norsk Polarinstitutt
Aarbog Frederiksborg Amts Hist Samfd — Aarbog for Frederiksborg Amts Historiske Samfund
Aarbok Univ Bergen Mat-Naturvitensk Ser — Aarbok foer Universitetet i Bergen. Matematisk-Naturvitenskapelig Serie
Aarb Pr A — Historisk Samfund for Praesto Amt
AARB Res Rep ARR — AARB [Australian Road Research Board] Research Report ARR
Aarb So A — Aarbog for Historisk Samfund for Soro Amt
AARCDS — University of the Orange Free State. Publication. Series C
AArch — Acta Archaeologica
A Arch — American Archivist
A Arch Acad Sci Hung — Acta Archaeologica. Academiae Scientiarum Hungaricae
AArchAnthr — Annals of Archaeology and Anthropology
A Arch Ar Syr — Annales Archeologiques Arabes Syriennes
A Arch Carpathica — Acta Archaeologica Carpathica
A Archeol Khmers — Art et Archeologie Khmers
AArchHung — Acta Archaeologica. Academiae Scientiarum Hungaricae
A Arch Lodziensia — Acta Archaeologica Lodziensia
A Arch Mus — Istanbul Arkeolji Muezeleri Yiligi
AArchSlov — Acta Archaeologica/Arheoloski Vestnik. Slovenska Akademija
A Arch Stor — Acta Archaeologica Storica
AArchSyr — Annales Archeologiques de Syrie
Aardappelstudiecentrum Kleinhandel — Aardappelstudiecentrum voor de Kleinhandel
Aarde & Vlk — Aarde en haar Volken
AARDS — Australian Advertising Rate and Data Service

AAREA — Anesthesie, Analgesie, Reanimation
AAR Facts — Association of American Railroads. Yearbook of Railroad Facts
AArH — Acta Archaeologica Academiae Scientiarum Hungaricae
A Arh — Arta si Arheologia Revista
Aarhus Univ 50th Anniv Symp Proc — Aarhus University 50th Anniversary Symposium. Proceedings
Aarhus Univ Lab Fys Geogr Skr — Aarhus Universitet. Laboratoriet foer Fysisk Geografi Skrifter
AARL — Australian Academic and Research Libraries
AARLLF — Annuaire de l'Academie Royale de Langue et de Litterature Francaises
AArmL — Annual of Armenian Linguistics
AARN Newsl — AARN [*Alberta Association of Registered Nurses*] Newsletter
AARN News Lett — AARN [*Alberta Association of Registered Nurses*] News Letter
A A Rov — Atti. Accademia Roveretana degli Agiati
AARP — Art and Archaeology. Research Papers
AARR — Association des Amis de Romain Rolland. Bulletin
AARS — Annals of Regional Science
Aarsberet Inst Sterilitetsforsk K Vet Landbohoejsk — Aarsberetning Institut foer Sterilitetsforskning Kongelige Veterinaer og Landbohoejskole
Aarsberetn Foren Norske Fortidsmind Bevar — Aarsberetning fra Foreningen til Norske Fortidsminders Bevaring
Aarsb Jernkontoret — Aarsbok. Jernkontoret
Aarsb K Vetensk Soc Uppsala — Aarsbok. Kungl Vetenskaps-Societeten i Uppsala
Aarsb Soc Sci Fenn — Aarsbok. Societas Scientiarum Fennica
Aarsb Vuosik Soc Sci Fenn — Aarsbok-Vuosikirja. Societas Scientiarum Fennica
Aarsskr K Vet Landbohoejsk (DK) — Aarsskrift den Kongelige Veterinaer og Landbohoejskole (Denmark)
Aarsskr Yearb Annu Jahrb Copenh Vet Landbohojsk — Aarsskrift/Yearbook/Annuaire/Jahrbuch. Copenhagen Veterinaer og Landbohoejskole
Aarst — Aarstiderne
AArt — American Artist
AARTI — Australian Art Index
AARTimes — American Association for Respiratory Therapy. Times
AARV-A — Architectural Review
AAS — Acta Apostolicae Sedis
AAS — American Antiquarian Society. Proceedings
AAS — Annales Archeologiques de Syrie
AAS — Annual Abstracts of Statistics
AaS — Antiquity and Survival
AAS — Artibus Asiae
AAS — Asian and African Studies
AAS — Azia i Afrika Segodnia
AASA — Advances in Alcohol and Substance Abuse
AASAAO — Acta Agriculturae Suecana
AASADR — Advances in Alcohol and Substance Abuse
AAS (Am Astronaut Soc) Sci Technol Ser — AAS (American Astronautical Society) Science and Technology Series
AASB — Annuaire. Academie Real des Sciences, des Lettres, et des Beaux-Arts de Belgique
AASB — Asian and African Studies. Bratislava
AASB — Atti. Accademia delle Scienze. Istituto di Bologna
AASBA — American Astronomical Society. Bulletin
AASC — Acta Agriculturae Scandinavica
AASCAU — Acta Agriculturae Scandinavica
AASF — Annales Academiae Scientiarum Fennicae
AASHAB — Acta Agronomica. Academiae Scientiarum Hungaricae
AASHCD — Aliphatic, Alicyclic, and Saturated Heterocyclic Chemistry
A Asia — Arts of Asia
A/asian Irrigator — Australasian Irrigator and Pasture Improver
A/asian J Philos — Australasian Journal of Philosophy
A Asiatiques — Arts Asiatiques
AASJ — Asian and African Studies (Jerusalem)
AASLA — Atti. Accademia di Scienze, Lettere, ed Arti di Palermo
AASLAN — Atti. Accademia di Scienze, Lettere, ed Arti di Palermo. Parte Prima. Scienze
AASL SLMQ — AASL [*American Association of School Librarians*] School Library Media Quarterly
AASN — Atti. Accademia di Scienze Morali e Politiche di Napoli
AASNAT — Acta Agriculturae Scandinavica. Supplementum
AASO — Annual. American Schools of Oriental Research
AASOR — Annual. American Schools of Oriental Research
AASP — Atti. Accademia di Scienze, Lettere, e Arti di Palermo
AAS Photo-Bull — AAS [*American Astronomical Society*] Photo-Bulletin
AASRA7 — Atti. Accademia delle Scienze di Ferrara
AASRC Newsl — AASRC [*American Association of Small Research Companies*] Newsletter
AASS — Acta Sanctorum
AAS Sci Technol Ser — AAS [*American Astronautical Society*] Science and Technology Series
A Assoc Amer Geogr — Annals. Association of American Geographers
AAST — Atti. Reale Accademia delle Scienze di Torino. Classe di Scienze Morali, Storiche, e Filologiche
AAST — Reale Accademia delle Scienze di Torino. Atti
AASTD — ASSET. Abstracts of Selected Solar Energy Technology
AASTM — Atti. Accademia delle Scienze di Torino. Classe di Scienze Morali, Storiche, e Filologiche
AASU — Acta Academiae Scientiarum Upsaliensis
AASV — Acta Apostolicae Sedis (Cittal del Vaticano)
AASXAP — Acta Anaesthesiologica Scandinavica. Supplementum
AASy — Annales Archeologiques de Syrie
AASYA — Arkiv foer Astronomi
A A Syr — Annales Archeologiques Arabes Syriennes
AASZBW — Acta Agraria et Silvestria. Series Zootechnia

AAT — Atti. Accademia delle Scienze di Torino
AATA — Art and Archaeology. Technical Abstracts
AATAAT — Avances en Alimentacion y Mejora Animal
AATB — Afro-Asian Theatre Bulletin
AATC — Atti e Memorie. Accademia Toscana la Colombaria
AATCC Nat Tech Conf Book Pap — AATCC [*American Association of Textile Chemists and Colorists*] National Technical Conference. Book of Papers
AATCC Symp Coated Fabr Technol — AATCC (American Association of Textile Chemists and Colorists) Symposium. Coated Fabrics Technology
AATCC Symp Coated Fabr Update — AATCC (American Association of Textile Chemists and Colorists) Symposium. Coated Fabrics Update
AATCC Symp Flock Technol — AATCC [*American Association of Textile Chemists and Colorists*] Symposium.Flock Technology
AATCC Symp Text Ind Environ — AATCC [*American Association of Textile Chemists and Colorists*] Symposium.Textile Industry and the Environment
AATCC Text Print Symp — AATCC (American Association of Textile Chemists and Colorists) Textile PrintingSymposium
AATFAA — Atti. Accademia delle Scienze di Torino. I. Classe di Scienze Fisiche, Matematiche, e Naturali
AATFNB — American Association of Teachers of French. National Bulletin
AATMA — Archiwum Automatyki i Telemechaniki
AATNAY — Archivos Argentinos de Tisiologia y Neumonologia
AATSEEL Bull — American Association of Teachers of Slavic and East European Languages. Bulletin
AATSEEL Jour — American Association of Teachers of Slavic and East European Languages. Journal
AAU — Americas
AAU — Archaeologie Austriaca
AAU — Atti. Accademia di Scienze, Lettere, ed Arti di Udine
AAug — Analecta Augustiniana
A Aujourdhui — Art d'Aujourd'hui
AAUPB — American Association of University Professors. Bulletin
AAUPB — Proceedings. Astronomical Society of Australia
AAUP Bul — American Association of University Professors. Bulletin
AAUP Bull — American Association of University Professors. Bulletin
AAus — Americana-Austriaca. Beitraege zur Amerikakunde
A Austr — Archaeologie Austriaca
A Australia — Art in Australia
AAV — Acta Academiae Velehradensis
AAV — Archaeologica Austriaca (Vienna)
AAV — Atti. Accademia di Agricoltura, Scienze, e Lettere di Verona
AAV — Aus Aachens Vorzeit
AAVF — Archiv fuer Anthropologie und Voelkerforschung
AAVN — Australian Audio-Visual News
AAVPC — Annuarium van de Apologetische Vereeniging (Petrus Canisius)
AAVSO Circ — AAVSO [*American Association of Variable Star Observers*] Circular
AAV Today — AAV (Association of Avian Veterinarians) Today
AAW — Afro-Asian Writings
AAW — Annales. Cercle Archeologique du Pays de Waes
AAW — Anzeiger. Akademie der Wissenschaften
AAW — Anzeiger fuer die Altertumswissenschaft
AAW — Aus Allen Welttheilen
AAWA — Afro-Asian and World Affairs
AAWB — Abhandlungen der Academie der Wissenschaften zu Berlin
AAWB — Abhandlungen der Philosophischen-Historischen Klasse. Akademie der Wissenschaften
AAWG — Abhandlungen. Akademie der Wissenschaften in Goettingen
AAWGPh — Abhandlungen. Akademie der Wissenschaften in Goettingen. Philologisch-Historische Klasse
AAWL — Abhandlungen. Akademie der Wissenschaften und der Literatur in Mainz. Geistes- und Sozialwissenschaftliche Klasse
AAWLMMN — Abhandlungen der Akademie der Wissenschaften und der Literatur in Mainz. Mathematisch-Naturwissenschaftliche Klasse
AAWM — Abhandlungen. Akademie der Wissenschaften in Mainz. Geistes- und Sozialwissenschaftliche Klasse
AAWSAU — Abhandlungen. Deutschen Akademie der Wissenschaften zu Berlin
AAWTD2 — Abhandlungen. Akademie der Wissenschaften der DDR. Abteilung Mathematik, Naturwissenschaften, Technik
AAWW — Anzeiger der Akademie der Wissenschaften in Wien
AAWW — Anzeiger. Oesterreichische Akademie der Wissenschaften (Wien). Philosophisch-Historische Klasse
AAWWPH — Anzeiger der Akademie der Wissenschaften in Wien. Philosophisch-Historische Klasse
AAXRAW — ANARE [*Australian National Antarctic Research Expeditions*] Interim Reports. Series A
AAY — American Antiquity
AAYPA — Annals. American Academy of Political and Social Science
AAZPA (Am Assoc Zool Parks Aquariums) Annu Proc — AAZPA (American Association of Zoological Parks and Aquariums) Annual Proceedings
AAZPA (Am Assoc Zool Parks Aquariums) Natl Conf — AAZPA (American Association of Zoological Parks and Aquariums) National Conference
AB — AB Bookman's Weekly
Ab — Abruzzo
AB — Acta Baltica
AB — Actualidad Bibliografica de Filosofia y Teologia
AB — Advocatenblad
AB — African Business
Ab — Al-Abhath
AB — American Bookman
AB — Analecta Biblica
AB — Analecta Bollandiana
AB — Antiquarian Bookman
AB — Archaeologische Bibliographie
AB — Architecture Bulletin
Ab — Artbibliographies Modern

AB — Art Bulletin
AB — Assyriologische Bibliothek
AB — Augustana Bulletin
AB — Australian Boating
AB — Australian Business
Aba — Abaco
ABA — Abacus
ABA — Abhandlungen. Bayerische Akademie der Wissenschaften
ABa — Annee Balzacienne
ABA — Arts-Beaux-Arts
ABA Antitrust L J — American Bar Association. Antitrust Law Journal
ABA Asoc Bibl Antioq Medellin — ABA. Asociacion de Bibliotecarios de Antioquia (Medellin)
ABABA — Annales de Biologie Animale, Biochimie, et Biophysique
ABA Banking J — ABA [*American Bankers Association*] Banking Journal
ABA Bank J — ABA [*American Bankers Association*] Banking Journal
ABABT — Academie des Beaux Arts. Bulletin Trimestriel
ABA Comp L Bull — American Bar Association. Comparative Law Bureau. Annual Bulletin
ABadG — Annalen der Grossherzoglich Badischen Gerichte
ABaeG — Amsterdamer Beitraege zur Aelteren Germanistik
ABAG — Amsterdamer Beitraege zur Aelteren Germanistik
ABAI — Izvestiia na Arkheologicheskiia Institut. Bulgarska Akademiia na Naukite
ABA J — American Bar Association. Journal
ABA Jo — American Bar Association. Journal
ABA Jour — American Bar Association. Journal
Abak Artikulaere Periartikulaere Entzuendungen — Abakterielle, Artikulaere, und Periartikulaere Entzuendungen
ABal — Annee Balzacienne
ABalt-Slav — Acta Baltico-Slavica
A Balzac — Annee Balzacienne
AbAn — Abstracts in Anthropology
AB & LA — Australian Builder and Land Advertiser
AB & P — Australian Bookseller and Publisher
ABAP — Anais. Bibliotecas e Arquivos de Portugal
ABA Sect Antitrust L — American Bar Association. Section of Antitrust Law
ABA Sect Crim L — American Bar Association. Section of Criminal Law
ABA Sect Ins N & CL — American Bar Association. Section of Insurance, Negligence, and Compensation Law
ABA Sect Int & Comp L Bull — American Bar Association. Section of International and Comparative Law. Bulletin
ABA Sect Lab Rel L — American Bar Association. Section of Labor Relations Law
ABA Sect M & NRL — American Bar Association. Section of Mineral and Natural Resources Law
ABA Sect Real Prop L — American Bar Association. Section of Real Property, Probate, and Trust Law. Proceedings
A Basse Normandie — Arte de Basse-Normandie
Ab Atomenergi Rapp AE — Abtiebolaget Atomenergi. Rapport AE
Ab Atomenergi (Stockholm) AE — Aktiebolaget Atomenergi (Stockholm). Rapport AE
Ab Atomenergi (Stockholm) Rapp — Aktiebolaget Atomenergi (Stockholm). Rapport
A Bavar — Ars Bavarica
ABAW — Abhandlungen. Bayerische Akademie der Wissenschaften. Philosophisch-HistorischeKlasse
ABAW — Abhandlungen der Koeniglichen Bayerischen Akademie der Wissenschaften. Mathematisch-Physikalische Klasse
ABAWPH — Abhandlungen der Bayerischen Akademie der Wissenschaften. Philosophisch-Historische Abteilung
ABAWPP — Abhandlungen der Bayerischen Akademie der Wissenschaften. Philosophisch-Philologische Klasse
ABB — Absatzwirtschaft; Zeitschrift fuer Marketing
ABB — Applied Biochemistry and Biotechnology
ABB — Archives et Bibliotheques de Belgique
ABB — Arizona Business
ABB — Australian Bankruptcy Bulletin
ABBA — Abhandlungen der Bayerischen Benedictiner-Akademie
ABBA — Anales. Biblioteca Nacional (Buenos Aires)
ABBACG — Analele. Universitatii Bucuresti. Biologie Animala
ABBADH — Acta Botanica Barcinonensia
ABBBMR — Another Boring Book Bi-Monthly Rag
ABBCM — Arquivo de Beja. Boletim da Camara Municipal
ABBGB — Animal Blood Groups and Biochemical Genetics
ABBIA4 — Archives of Biochemistry and Biophysics
AB Bkman's W — AB Bookman's Weekly
ABBL — Allgemeine Bibliothek der Biblischen Literatur
ABBPA — Acta Biochimica et Biophysica. Academiae Scientiarum Hungaricae
Abbrennstumpf Reib Verw Verfahren Vortr Int DVS Tag — Abbrennstumpf- und Reibschweissen mit Verwandten Verfahren. Vortraege der Internationalen DVS-Tagung
ABB Rev — ABB Review
ABBSAY — Archives Belges de Dermatologie et de Syphiligraphie
ABBU — Altbabylonische Briefe in Umschrift
ABBZAL — Acta Botanica Instituti Botanici. Universitatis Zagrebensis
ABC — Abacus
ABC — Abstracts in Biocommerce
ABC — Al-Bathah
ABC — American Book Collector
ABC — Australian Bankruptcy Cases
ABC — Australian Business Computer
ABCAA — Arquivos Brasileiros de Cardiologia
ABCAAJ — Arquivos Brasileiros de Cardiologia
ABCA Bul — ABCA [*American Business Communication Association*] Bulletin
ABCD — Archives, Bibliotheques, Collections, Documentation
ABCDE News — Association of British Columbia Drama Educators. Newsletter

ABCLA — Annales de Biologie Clinique
ABCLDL — Acta Bioquimica Clinica Latinoamericana
ABC Newsl — International Association of Accident Boards and Commissions. Newsletter
ABC Pol Sci — Advance Bibliography of Contents: Political Science and Government
ABCRA2 — Acta Botanica Croatica
ABCUDE — Acta Botanica Cubana
ABCXA — Annales Biologiques
ABDEB3 — Anais Brasileiros de Dermatologia
ABDMAQ — Archives Belges de Dermatologie
Abdom Imaging — Abdominal Imaging
Abdom Surg — Abdominal Surgery
ABDSAA — Anais Brasileiros de Dermatologia e Sifilografia
ABE — Akron Business and Economic Review
ABEBA — Annales Universitatis Scientiarum Budapestensis de Rolando Eoetvoes Nominatae. Sectio Biologica
A'Beckett — A'Beckett's Reserved Judgements
A'Beckett Res Judg — A'Beckett's Reserved Judgements
A'Beck Judg (Vic) — A'Beckett's Reserved Judgements (Victoria)
A'Beck Judg (Vict) — A'Beckett's Reserved Judgements (Victoria)
A'Beck Res — A'Beckett's Reserved Judgements
A'Beck Res Judg — A'Beckett's Reserved Judgements
A'Beck Res Judgm — A'Beckett's Reserved Judgements
A'Beck RJ (NSW) — A'Beckett's Reserved Judgements (New South Wales)
A'Beck RJ (PP) — A'Beckett's Reserved Judgements (Port Phillip)
ABEEA — Annual Bulletin of the Electric Statistics for Europe
ABEGB — Advances in Biomedical Engineering
ABEGBE — Advances in Biomedical Engineering
Abeille Fr — Abeille de France [*Later, Abeille de France et l'Apiculteur*]
Abeille Fr Apic — Abeille de France et l'Apiculteur
Abeille Med (Paris) — Abeille Medicale (Paris)
Abeill Fr Apicul — Abeille de France et l'Apiculteur
A Beja — Arquivo de Beja
A Belge — Art Belge
ABelges — Archives Belges
ABELL — Annual Bibliography of English Language and Literature
ABENA — Arquivos Brasileiros de Endocrinologia e Metabologia
ABENAY — Arquivos Brasileiros de Endocrinologia e Metabologia
ABE News — Action for Better Education Newsletter
A Ben R — American Benedictine Review
AbEnSt — Abstracts of English Studies
Aberdeens Concr Constr — Aberdeen's Concrete Construction
Aberdeen Univ Rev — Aberdeen University. Review
Aberdeen Univ Stu — Aberdeen University. Studies
Aberdeen U Rev — Aberdeen University Review
Aberdeen U Stud — Aberdeen University Studies
Aberdeen Wkly J — Aberdeen Weekly Journal
Aber Trondhjems Kstforen — Arsberetning, Trondhjems Konstforening
ABes — Academie des Sciences, Belles-Lettres, et Arts de Besancon. Proces-Verbaux et Memoires
ABF — Acta Botanica Fennica
ABF — American Baptist Flag
ABF — Attic Black Figured Vase-Painters
Abfallst Duenger Vortr Generalthema VDLUFA Kongr — Abfallstoffe als Duenger. Moeglichkeiten und Grenzen. Vortraege zum Generalthema des VDLUFA-Kongresses
Abfallwirtsch J — Abfallwirtschafts Journal
Abfallwirtsch Loesungen Kreisebene Abfalltech Kolloq — Abfallwirtschaftliche Loesungen auf Kreisebene. Abfalltechnisches Kolloquium
Abfallwirtsch Loesungen Prax Abfalltech Kolloq — Abfallwirtschaftliche Loesungen fuer die Praxis. Abfalltechnisches Kolloquium
Abfallwirtsch Tech Univ Berlin — Abfallwirtschaft an der Technischen Universitaet Berlin
ABFC — Archivio Storico di Belluno, Feltre, e Cadore
ABFE — Acta Botanica Fennica
ABFEAC — Acta Botanica Fennica
AbFolkSt — Abstracts of Folklore Studies
ABF Research J — American Bar Foundation. Research Journal
ABF Res J — American Bar Foundation. Research Journal
ABF Res Newsl — American Bar Foundation. Research Newsletter
AbFS — Abstracts of Folklore Studies
ABFZA — Analele. Universitatii Bucuresti. Fizica
ABG — Amsterdamer Beitraege zur Alteren Germanistik
ABG — Archiv fuer Begriffsgeschichte
ABGE — Albertan Geographer
ABGLA — Analele. Universitatii Bucuresti. Geologie
ABGMI — Abridged Biography and Genealogy Master Index
Ab G R — Above the Ground Review
Abh — Al-Abhath
Abh Abt Phytomorphogenese — Abhandlungen. Abteilung fuer Phytomorphogenese der Timiriaseff. Instituts fuerBiologie
Abh Abt Phytomorphogenese Timiriaseff Inst Biol — Abhandlungen aus der Abteilung fuer Phytomorphogenese des Timiriaseff-Institutsfuer Biologie am Zentralen Exekutivkomitee der USSR
Abh Acad Berl — Abhandlungen der Koeniglichen Akademie der Wissenschaften in Berlin
Abh Akad Mainz — Abhandlungen der Geistes- und Socialwissenschaftlichen Klasse. Akademie der Wissenschaften und der Literatur in Mainz
Abh Akad Muench — Abhandlungen der Mathematisch-Physikalischen Classe der Koeniglich Bayerischen Akademie der Wissenschaften
Abh Akad Muenchen — Abhandlungen der Mathematisch-Physikalischen Klasse der Koeniglich Bayerischen Akademie der Wissenschaften. Muenchen
Abh Akad Wiss Berlin Phys — Abhandlungen der Koeniglich Preussischen Akademie der Wissenschaften. Physikalisch-Mathematische Classe (Berlin)

Abh Akad Wiss DDR — Abhandlungen der Akademie der Wissenschaften der DDR

Abh Akad Wiss DDR Abt Math Naturwiss Tech — Abhandlungen. Akademie der Wissenschaften der DDR. Abteilung Mathematik, Naturwissenschaften, Technik

Abh Akad Wiss DDR Abt Math Naturwiss Tech 1978 — Abhandlungen. Akademie der Wissenschaften der DDR. Abteilung Mathematik, Naturwissenschaften, Technik. 1978

Abh Akad Wiss DDR Abt Math Naturwiss Tech 1979 — Abhandlungen. Akademie der Wissenschaften der DDR. Abteilung Mathematik, Naturwissenschaften, Technik. 1979

Abh Akad Wiss DDR Abt Math Naturwiss Tech 1981 — Abhandlungen. Akademie der Wissenschaften der DDR. Abteilung Mathematik, Naturwissenschaften, Technik. 1981

Abh Akad Wiss Goettingen Math-Physik Kl — Abhandlungen der Wissenschaften in Goettingen. Mathematisch-Physikalische Klasse

Abh Akad Wiss Goettingen Math-Phys Kl — Abhandlungen. Akademie der Wissenschaften in Goettingen. Mathematisch-Physikalische Klasse

Abh Akad Wiss Goettingen Math Phys Kl Folge 3 — Abhandlungen der Akademie der Wissenschaften in Goettingen. Mathematisch-Physika

Abh Akad Wiss Goettingen Philol Hist Kl — Abhandlungen der Akademie der Wissenschaften in Goettingen. Philologisch-Historische Klasse

Abh Akad Wiss Lit Mainz — Akademie der Wissenschaften und der Literatur. Abhandlungen der Geistes- und Sozialwissenschaftlichen Klasse (Mainz)

Abh Akad Wiss Muenchen — Abhandlungen der Bayerischen Akademie der Wissenschaften. Mathematisch-Naturwissenschaftliche Klasse (Muenchen)

Abh Akad Wiss Muenchen — Abhandlungen der Koeniglich Bayerischen Akademie der Wissenschaften. Mathematisch-Physikalische Klasse

Abh Akad Wiss Muenchen — Abhandlungen der Mathematisch-Physikalischen Classe der Koeniglich Bayerischen Akademie der Wissenschaften (Muenchen)

AbhAkWiss Berlin — Abhandlungen. Deutsche Akademie der Wissenschaften zu Berlin

A Bhandarkar Or Res Inst — Annals. Bhandarkar Oriental Research Institute

Abh & Ber Koen Zool & Anthropol Ethnog Mus Dresden — Abhandlungen und Berichte des Koeniglichen Zoologischen und Anthropologisch-Ethnographischen Museums zu Dresden

Abh & Ber Mus Tierknd & Vlkerknd Dresden — Abhandlungen und Berichte der Museen fuer Tierkunde und Voelkerkunde zu Dresden

Abh & Ber Staatl Mus Vlkernd Dresden — Abhandlungen und Berichte des Staatlichen Museums fuer Voelkerkunde. Dresden

Abhandl Akad Wiss Lit Geistes Sozialwiss Kl — Akademie der Wissenschaften und der Literatur. Abhandlungen der Geistes- und Sozialwissenschaftlichen Klasse

Abhandl Akad Wiss Lit Mainz Math Naturwiss Kl — Abhandlungen. Akademie der Wissenschaften und der Literatur in Mainz. Mathematisch-Naturwissenschaftliche Klasse

Abhandl Bayer Akad Wiss Math Naturwiss Abt — Abhandlungen. Bayerische Akademie der Wissenschaften. Mathematisch-Naturwissenschaftliche Abteilung

Abhandl Bayer Akad Wiss Math Phys Kl — Abhandlungen. Bayerische Akademie der Wissenschaften. Mathematisch-Physikalische Klasse

Abhandl Bayer Akad Wiss Phil Hist Abt — Abhandlungen. Bayerische Akademie der Wissenschaften. Philosophisch-Historische Abteilung

Abhandl Bayer Akad Wiss Phil Philol Hist Kl — Abhandlungen. Bayerische Akademie der Wissenschaften. Philosophisch-Philologische und Historische Klasse

Abhandl Ber Deut Mus — Abhandlungen und Berichte. Deutsches Museum

Abhandl Ber Ver Naturk — Abhandlungen und Berichte des Vereins fuer Naturkunde zu Cassel

Abhandl Braunschweig Wiss Ges — Abhandlungen. Braunschweigische Wissenschaftliche Gesellschaft

Abhandl Deut Akad Wiss Kl Math Phys Tech — Abhandlungen. Deutsche Akademie der Wissenschaften zu Berlin. Klasse fuer Mathematik, Physik, und Technik

Abhandl Deut Akad Wiss Math Naturwiss Kl — Abhandlungen. Deutsche Akademie der Wissenschaften zu Berlin. Mathematisch-Naturwissenschaftliche Klasse

Abhandl Deut Akad Wiss Phil Hist Kl — Abhandlungen. Deutsche Akademie der Wissenschaften zu Berlin. Philosophisch-Historische Klasse

Abhandl Geb Naturwiss — Abhandlungen. Gebiet der Naturwissenschaften

Abhandl Gesamtgeb Med — Abhandlungen aus dem Gesamtgebiete der Medizin

Abhandl Gesch Math Wiss — Abhandlungen zur Geschichte der Mathematischen Wissenschaften mit Einschluss Ihrer Anwendungen

Abhandl Gesch Naturwiss Med — Abhandlungen zur Geschichte der Naturwissenschaften und der Medizin

Abhandl Gesch Veterinaermed — Abhandlungen aus der Geschichte der Veterinaermedizin

Abhandl Ges Wiss Goettingen Math Phys Kl — Abhandlungen. Koenigliche Gesellschaft der Wissenschaften zu Goettingen. Mathematisch-Physikalische Klasse

Abhandl Ges Wiss Goettingen Philol Hist Kl — Abhandlungen. Koenigliche Gesellschaft der Wissenschaften zu Goettingen. Philologisch-Historische Klasse

Abhandl Heidelb Akad — Abhandlungen der Heidelberger Akademie der Wissenschaften. Philosophisch-Historische Klasse

Abhandl Herder-Ges Herder Inst — Abhandlungen der Herder-Gesellschaft und des Herder Instituts zu Riga

Abhandl K Gesell Wiss Goettingen — Abhandlungen der Koeniglichen Gesellschaft der Wissenschaften zu Goettingen

Abhandl Kunde Morgenlandes — Abhandlungen fuer die Kunde des Morgenlandes

Abhandl Med Fak Sun Yatsen-Univ Canton — Abhandlungen der Medizinischen Fakultaet der Sun Yatsen-Universitaet Canton

Abhandl Naturforsch Ges Goerlitz — Abhandlungen der Naturforschenden Gesellschaft zu Goerlitz

Abhandl Naturhist Ges Nuernberg — Abhandlungen der Naturhistorischen Gesellschaft zu Nuernberg

Abhandl Naturwiss Ver Bremen — Abhandlungen Herausgegeben vom Naturwissenschaftlichen Verein zu Bremen

Abhandl Naturw Ver Bremen — Abhandlungen Herausgegeben vom Naturwissenschaftlichen Vereine zu Bremen

Abhandl Preuss Akad Wiss Math Naturwiss Kl — Abhandlungen. Preussische Akademie der Wissenschaften. Mathematisch-Naturwissenschaftliche Klasse

Abhandl Preuss Akad Wiss Phil Hist Kl — Abhandlungen. Preussische Akademie der Wissenschaften. Philosophisch-Historische Klasse

Abhandl Preuss Akad Wiss Phys Math Kl — Abhandlungen. Preussische Akademie der Wissenschaften. Physikalisch-Mathematische Klasse

Abhandl Saechs Akad Wiss Philol Hist Kl — Abhandlungen. Saechsische Akademie der Wissenschaften. Philologisch-Historische Klasse

Abhandl Saechs Ges Wiss Philol Hist Kl — Abhandlungen. Saechsische Gesellschaft der Wissenschaften. Philologisch-Historische Klasse

Abhandl Schlesischen Ges Vaterlaend Cult Geisteswiss Reihe — Abhandlungen. Schlesische Gesellschaft fuer Vaterlaendische Cultur. Geisteswissenschaftliche Reihe

Abhandl Theor Biol — Abhandlungen zur Theoretischen Biologie

Abhandlung Ber Deut Mus — Abhandlungen und Berichte des Deutschen Museums

Abh Arbgem Tier- u Pflageogr — Abhandlungen. Arbeitsgemeinschaft fuer Tier- und Pflanzengeographische Heimatforschung im Saarland

Abh Aus D Ges D Kriminalpsychol — Abhandlungen aus dem Gesamt-Gebiete der Kriminalpsychologie [*Heidelberger Abhandlungen*]

AbhBAW — Abhandlungen. Bayerische Akademie der Wissenschaften

Abh Bay Ak Wiss — Abhandlungen der Bayerischen Akademie der Wissenschaften

Abh Bayer Ak — Abhandlungen der Bayerischen Akademie der Wissenschaften

Abh Bayer Akad Wiss — Abhandlungen der Bayerischen Akademie der Wissenschaften

Abh Bayer Akad Wiss — Abhandlungen der Mathematisch-Physikalischen Classe der Koeniglich Bayerischen Akademie der Wissenschaften

Abh Bayer Akad Wiss Math Naturwiss Abt — Abhandlungen der Bayerischen Akademie der Wissenschaften. Mathematisch-Naturwissenschaftliche Abteilung

Abh Bayer Akad Wiss Math-Naturwiss Kl — Abhandlungen. Bayerische Akademie der Wissenschaften. Mathematisch-Naturwissenschaftliche Klasse

Abh Bayer Akad Wiss Math Phys Kl — Abhandlungen der Bayerischen Akademie der Wissenschaften. Mathematisch-Physikalische Klasse

Abh Bayr — Abhandlungen der Bayerischen Akademie der Wissenschaften

Abh Beob Oekon Ges Bern — Abhandlungen und Beobachtungen Durch Die Oekonomische Gesellschaft zu Bern Gesammelt

Abh Ber Dtsch Mus — Abhandlungen und Berichte. Deutsches Museum

Abh Berl — Abhandlungen der Deutschen Akademie der Wissenschaften zu Berlin

Abh Berl Ak — Abhandlungen der Preussischen Akademie der Wissenschaften zu Berlin

Abh Berl Akad — Abhandlungen der Deutschen Akademie der Wissenschaften zu Berlin

Abh (Berlin) — Abhandlungen (Berlin)

Abh Ber Mus Nat U Heimatk Naturk Vorgesch Magdeburg — Abhandlungen und Berichte aus dem Museum fuer Naturkunde und Vorgeschichte in Magdeburg

Abh Ber Mus Naturk Magdeburg — Abhandlungen und Berichte aus dem Museum fuer Naturkunde und Vorgeschichte in Magdeburg

Abh Ber Mus Volkerk Dresden — Abhandlungen und Berichte des Staatlichen Museums fuer Volkerkunde (Dresden)

Abh Ber Naturkundemus Goerlitz — Abhandlungen und Berichte. Naturkundemuseums Goerlitz

Abh Ber Naturwiss Ges Bayreuth — Abhandlungen und Berichte. Naturwissenschaftliche Gesellschaft Bayreuth

Abh Ber Staat Mus Volk Dres — Abhandlungen und Berichte. Staatlichen Museum fuer Voelkerkunde Dresden

Abh Ber St Mus Miner Geol (Dresden) — Abhandlungen und Berichte. Staatlichen Museum fuer Mineralogie und Geologie (Dresden)

Abh Ber Vereins Naturk Kassel — Abhandlungen und Bericht des Vereins fuer Naturkunde zu Kassel

AbhBMM — Abhandlungen und Berichte des Museums fuer Natur- und Heimatkunde zu Magdeburg

Abh Boehm Ges — Abhandlungen der Boehmischen Gesellschaft der Wissenschaften, nebst der Geschichte derselben

Abh Braunschweig Wiss Gesellsch — Abhandlungen. Braunschweigische Wissenschaftliche Gesellschaft

Abh Braunschw Wiss Ges — Abhandlungen. Braunschweigische Wissenschaftliche Gesellschaft

Abh Chursaechs Weinbauges — Abhandlungen der Chursaechsischen Weinbaugesellschaft

Abh Deut Akad Wiss Berlin — Abhandlungen der Deutschen Akademie der Wissenschaften zu Berlin

Abh Deut Akad Wiss Berlin Kl Math — Abhandlungen. Deutsche Akademie der Wissenschaften zu Berlin. Klasse fuer Mathematik, Physik, und Technik

Abh Deutsch Akad Wiss Berlin Kl Chem — Abhandlungen der Deutschen Akademie der Wissenschaften zu Berlin. Klasse fuer Chemie, Geologie, und Biologie

Abh Deutsch Akad Wiss Berlin Kl Math Phys Tech — Abhandlungen. Deutsche Akademie der Wissenschaften zu Berlin. Klasse fuer Mathematik, Physik, und Technik

Abh Deutsch Ges Wiss Prag Math Naturwiss Kl — Abhandlungen der Deutschen Gesellschaft der Wissenschaften und Kuenste in Prag.Mathematisch-Naturwissenschaftliche Klasse

Abhdl Berlin — Abhandlungen der Deutschen Akademie der Wissenschaften zu Berlin

Abhdl Leipzig — Abhandlungen der Philologisch-Historischen Klasse der Saechsischen Akademie der Wissenschaften (Leipzig)

Abh Dt Naturw Med Ver Boehm — Abhandlungen des Deutschen Naturwissenschaftlich-Medizinischen Vereins fuer Boehmen "Lotos"

Abh Dtsch Akad Naturforsch Leopold — Abhandlungen der Deutschen Akademie der Naturforscher Leopoldina

Abh Dtsch Akad Wiss Berl — Abhandlungen. Deutsche Akademie der Wissenschaften zu Berlin

Abh Dtsch Akad Wiss Berlin — Abhandlungen der Deutschen Akademie der Wissenschaften zu Berlin. Klasse fuer Mathematik und Allgemeine Naturwissenschaften

Abh Dtsch Akad Wiss Berlin Kl Bergbau Huettenwes Montangeol — Abhandlungen. Deutsche Akademie der Wissenschaften zu Berlin. Klasse fuer Bergbau, Huettenwesen, und Montangeologie

Abh Dtsch Akad Wiss Berlin Kl Chem Geol Biol — Abhandlungen. Deutsche Akademie der Wissenschaften zu Berlin. Klasse fuer Chemie, Geologie, und Biologie

Abh Dtsch Akad Wiss Berlin Kl Math Allg Naturwiss — Abhandlungen. Deutsche Akademie der Wissenschaften zu Berlin. Klasse fuer Mathematik und Allgemeine Naturwissenschaften

Abh Dtsch Akad Wiss Berlin Kl Math Phys Tech — Abhandlungen. Deutsche Akademie der Wissenschaften zu Berlin. Klasse fuer Mathematik, Physik, und Technik

Abh Dtsch Akad Wiss Berlin Kl Med — Abhandlungen. Deutsche Akademie der Wissenschaften zu Berlin. Klasse fuer Medizin

Abh Dtsch Akad Wiss Berlin Kl Med Wiss — Abhandlungen der Deutschen Akademie der Wissenschaften zu Berlin. Klasse fuer Medizinische Wissenschaften

Abh Dtsch Akad Wiss Berlin Math Naturwiss Kl — Abhandlungen der Deutschen Akademie der Wissenschaften zu Berlin. Mathematisch-Naturwissenschaftliche Klasse

Abh Dtsch Akad Wiss Berlin Math-Naturwiss Kl — Abhandlungen. Deutsche Akademie der Wissenschaften zu Berlin. Mathematisch-Naturwissenschaftliche Klasse

Abh Dtsch Akad Wiss Berl Kl Chem Geol Biol — Abhandlungen. Deutsche Akademie der Wissenschaften zu Berlin. Klasse fuer Chemie, Geologie, und Biologie

Abh Dtsch Akad Wiss Berl Kl Med — Abhandlungen. Deutsche Akademie der Wissenschaften zu Berlin. Klasse fuer Medizin

Abh Dtsch Kaelte Klimatech Ver — Abhandlungen des Deutschen Kaelte und Klimatechnischen Vereins

Abh Dtsch Kaeltetech Ver — Abhandlungen. Deutscher Kaeltetechnische Verein

Abh Forschungsinst Flugfahrtmater Moscow — Abhandlungen des Forschungsinstituts fuer Flugfahrtmaterialien. Moscow

Abh Fritz Haber Inst Max Planck Ges — Abhandlungen aus dem Fritz-Haber-Institut der Max-Planck-Gesellschaft

Abh Geb Auslandsk — Abhandlungen aus dem Gebiet der Auslandskunde. Reihe C. Naturwissenschaften

Abh Geb Hirnforsch Verhaltenphysiol — Abhandlungen. Gebiet der Hirnforschung und Verhaltensphysiologie

Abh Geburtsh — Abhandlungen aus dem Gebiete der Geburtshilfe und Gynaekologie

Abh Geistes & Sozwiss Kl — Abhandlungen der Geistes- und Sozialwissenschaftlichen Klasse. Akademie der Wissenschaften und der Literatur [*Mainz*]

Abh Geol Bundesanst (Austria) — Abhandlungen der Geologischen Bundesanstalt (Austria)

Abh Geol Dienstes (Berl) — Abhandlungen. Geologischer Dienst (Berlin)

Abh Geol Dienstes Berlin — Abhandlungen des Geologischen Dienstes Berlin

Abh Geol Landesamtes Baden Wuerttemb — Abhandlungen. Geologisches Landesamt in Baden Wuerttemberg

Abh Geol Landesanst DDR — Abhandlungen der Geologischen Landesanstalt (DDR)

Abh Gesamtgeb Hyg — Abhandlungen aus dem Gesamtgebiete der Hygiene

Abh Gesch Med Naturwiss — Abhandlungen zur Geschichte der Medizin und der Naturwiss

Abh Gesch Stadt Augsburg — Abhandlungen zur Geschichte der Stadt Augsburg

Abh Ges Kuenste Batavia — Abhandlungen der Gesellschaft der Kuenste und Wissenschaften in Batavia

Abh Ges Wiss Goett — Abhandlungen der Koeniglichen Gesellschaft der Wissenschaften zu Goettingen

Abh Ges Wiss Goettg — Abhandlungen der Gesellschaft der Wissenschaften zu Goettingen

Abh Ges Wiss Goettingen Math Phys Kl — Abhandlungen der Gesellschaft der Wissenschaften zu Goettingen. Mathematisch-Physikalische Klasse

Abh Goett — Abhandlungen der Akademie der Wissenschaften zu Goettingen

AbhGWG — Abhandlungen. Gesellschaft der Wissenschaften zu Goettingen

Abh Hallischen Naturf Ges — Abhandlungen der Hallischen Naturforschenden Gesellschaft

Abh Heid — Abhandlungen der Heidelberger Akademie der Wissenschaften. Philosophisch-Historische Klasse

Abh Heidelb Ak — Abhandlungen der Heidelberger Akademie der Wissenschaften. Philosophisch-Historische Klasse

Abh Heidelb Akad Wiss — Abhandlungen der Heidelberger Akademie der Wissenschaften

Abh Heidelberg — Abhandlungen der Heidelberger Akademie der Wissenschaften. Philosophisch-Historische Klasse

Abh Heidelberg Akad Wiss — Abhandlungen der Heidelberger Akademie der Wissenschaften

Abh Heidelberg Akad Wiss Philos Hist Kl — Abhandlungen der Heidelberger Akademie der Wissenschaften. Philosophisch-Historische Klasse

Abh Heidelberger Akad Wiss Math Naturwiss Kl — Abhandlungen der Heidelberger Akademie der Wissenschaften. Stiftung Heinrich Lanz. Mathematisch-Naturwissenschaftliche Klasse

Abh Hess Landesamtes Bodenforsch — Abhandlungen des Hessischen Landesamtes fuer Bodenforschung

Abh HGLA — Abhandlungen des Hessischen Geologischen Landesanstalt

Abh Inst Hochspannungstech Elektr Anlagen — Abhandlungen. Institut fuer Hochspannungstechnik und Elektrische Anlagen

Abh Inst Hochspannungstechnik Elektr Anlagen — Abhandlungen. Institut fuer Hochspannungstechnik und Elektrische Anlagen

Abh Inst Metallhuettenwes Elektrometall Tech Hochsch Aachen — Abhandlungen. Institut fuer Metallhuettenwesen und Elektrometallurgie der Technischen Hochschule (Aachen)

Abh Inst Milchwirtsch Zon Stn Milchwirtschaftswes Omsk — Abhandlungen des Instituts fuer Milchwirtschaft und der Zonal Station fuer Milchwirtschaftswesen. Omsk

Abh Int Keram Kongr — Abhandlungen des Internationalen Keramischen Kongresses

Abh Int Pulvermetall Tag — Abhandlungen der Internationalen Pulvermetallurgischen Tagung

Abh Kaiser Wilhelm Inst Eisenforsch Duesseldorf — Abhandlungen aus dem Kaiser-Wilhelm-Institut fuer Eisenforschung zu Duesseldorf

Abh Kaiser Wilhelm Inst Phys Chem Elektrochem — Abhandlungen aus dem Kaiser-Wilhelm-Institut fuer Physikalische Chemie und Elektrochemie

Abh K Bayer Ak Wiss M Ph Kl Muench — Abhandlungen der Koeniglich Bayerischen Akademie der Wissenschaften. Mathematisch-Physikalische Klasse

Abh K Boehm Ges Wiss M N Cl — Abhandlungen der Koeniglichen Boehmischen Gesellschaft der Wissenschaften

Abh K Ges Wiss Goettingen Math Phys Kl — Abhandlungen der K. Gesellschaft der Wissenschaften zu Goettingen. Mathematisch-Physikalische Klasse

Abh Kinderheilkd Ihren Grenzgeb — Abhandlungen aus der Kinderheilkunde und Ihren Grenzgebieten

AbhKM — Abhandlungen fuer die Kunde des Morgenlandes

Abh Koenigl Akad Wiss Berlin — Abhandlungen der Physikalischen Klasse der Koeniglichen Akademie der Wissenschaften zu Berlin

Abh Koenigl Akad Wiss Berlin — Abhandlungen der Physikalisch-Mathematischen Klasse der Koeniglichen Akademie der Wissenschaften zu Berlin

Abh Koenigl Akad Wiss Berlin — Abhandlungen. Koeniglichen Akademie der Wissenschaften in Berlin

Abh Koenigl Boehm Ges Wiss — Abhandlungen. Koeniglichen Boehmischen Gesellschaft der Wissenschaften

Abh Koenigl Ges Wiss Goettingen Math Phys Kl — Abhandlungen der Koeniglichen Gesellschaft der Wissenschaften, Goettingen. Mathematisch-Physikalische Klasse

Abh Koenigl Preuss Akad Wiss Phys Math Cl — Abhandlungen der Koeniglich Preussischen Akademie der Wissenschaften. Physikalisch-Mathematische Classe

Abh Kunde Morgenl — Abhandlungen fuer die Kunde des Morgenlandes

Abh Kurfuerstl Mainz Akad Nuetzl Wiss Erfurt — Abhandlungen der Kurfuerstlich-Mainzischen Akademie Nuetzlicher Wissenschaften zu Erfurt/Nova Acta Academiae Electoralis Moguntinae Scientiar Utilium Quae Erfurti Est

Abh Landesk Prov Westpreussen — Abhandlungen zur Landeskunde der Provinz Westpreussen

Abh Landesmus Naturkd Muenster Westfalen — Abhandlungen. Landesmuseum fuer Naturkunde zu Muenster in Westfalen

Abh Landesmus Prov Westfalen Mus Naturk — Abhandlungen aus dem Landesmuseum der Provinz Westfalen. Museum fuer Naturkunde

Abh Landes Prov Westfalen Mus Naturkd — Abhandlungen. Landesmuseum der Provinz Westfalen. Museum fuer Naturkunde

Abh Landwirtsch Inst Omsk — Abhandlungen des Landwirtschaftlichen Instituts in Omsk

Abh Leipz — Abhandlungen der Philologisch-Historische Klasse der Saechsischen Akademie der Wissenschaften (Leipzig)

Abh Leipzig — Abhandlungen der Philologisch-Historische Klasse der Saechsischen Akademie der Wissenschaften (Leipzig)

Abh Mainz — Abhandlungen der Geistes- und Socialwissenschaftlichen Klasse. Akademie der Wissenschaften und der Literatur in Mainz

Abh Math Nat Cl Boehm Ges Wiss — Abhandlungen der Koeniglichen Boehmischen Gesellschaft der Wissenschaften

Abh Math Naturwiss Kl Akad Wiss Lit Mainz — Abhandlungen der Mathematisch-Naturwissenschaftlichen Klasse. Akademie der Wissenschaften und der Literatur. Mainz

Abh Math Phys Abt Akad Wiss Muenchen — Abhandlungen der Mathematisch-Physikalischen Classe der Koeniglich Bayerischen Akademie der Wissenschaften (Muenchen)

Abh Math Phys Kl Koenigl Saechs Ges Wiss — Abhandlungen der Mathematisch-Physischen Classe der Koeniglich Saechsischen Gesellschaft der Wissenschaften

Abh Math-Phys Kl Saechs Akad Wiss — Abhandlungen. Mathematisch-Physische Klasse der Saechsischen Akademie der Wissenschaften

Abh Math Sem Univ (Hamburg) — Abhandlungen aus dem Mathematischen Seminar der Universitaet (Hamburg)

Abh Meteorol Dienstes DDR — Abhandlungen. Meteorologischer Dienst der Deutschen Demokratischen Republik

Abh Mineral Geol Inst Stephan Tisza Univ Debrecen — Abhandlungen aus dem Mineralogisch-Geologischen Institut der Stephan Tisza-Universitaet in Debrecen

Abh Monatl Mitth Gesamtgeb Naturwiss — Abhandlungen und Monatliche Mittheilungen aus dem Gesammtgebiete der Naturwissenschaften

Abh Muench — Abhandlungen der Bayerischen Akademie der Wissenschaften

Abh Muenchen — Abhandlungen der Bayerischen Akademie der Wissenschaften (Muenchen)

Abh Natf Ges Halle — Abhandlungen der Naturforschenden Gesellschaft. Halle

Abh Naturf Ges Zuerich — Abhandlungen der Naturforschenden Gesellschaft in Zuerich

Abh Naturg — Abhandlungen aus der Naturgeschichte, Praktischen Arzneykunst und Chirurgie, aus den Schriften der Haarlemer und anderer Hollaendischen Gesellschaften

Abh Naturgesch Chem — Abhandlungen zur Naturgeschichte, Chemie, Anatomie, Medicin und Physik, aus denSchriften des Instituts der Kuenste und Wissenschaften zu Bologna

Abh Naturgesch Thiere Pflanzen — Abhandlungen zur Naturgeschichte der Thiere und Pflanzen, Welche Ehemals der Koeniglich Franzoesischen Akademie der Wissenschaften Vorgetragen Wurden

Abh Naturhist Ges Nuernb — Abhandlungen der Naturhistorischen Gesellschaft zu Nuernberg

Abh Naturhist Ges Nuernberg — Abhandlung. Naturhistorische Gesellschaft Nuernberg

Abh Naturwiss Ges Saxonia Gross Neuschoenau — Abhandlungen der Naturwissenschaftlichen Gesellschaft Saxonia zu Gross-und Neuschoenau

Abh Naturwiss Ver Bremen — Abhandlungen. Naturwissenschaftlicher Verein zu Bremen

Abh Naturwiss Vereines Sachsen Halle — Abhandlungen des Naturwissenschaftlichen Vereines fuer Sachsen und Thueringen in Halle

Abh Naturwiss Vereins Magdeburg — Abhandlungen des Naturwissenschaftlichen Vereins zu Magdeburg

Abh Naturwiss Ver Hamb — Abhandlungen. Naturwissenschaftlicher Verein in Hamburg

Abh Naturw Ver Bremen — Abhandlungen. Naturwissenschaftlicher Verein zu Bremen

Abh Naturw Ver Hamburg — Abhandlungen aus dem Gebiete der Naturwissenschaften Herausgegeben von dem Naturwissenschaftlichen Verein in Hamburg

Abh Oekon Inhalts — Abhandlungen Oekonomischen, Technologischen, Naturwissenschaftlichen und Vermischten Inhalts

Abh Pathophysiol Regul — Abhandlungen ueber die Pathophysiologie der Regulationen

Abh Philol Hist Kl Bayer Akad Wiss — Abhandlungen der Philologisch-Historischen Klasse der Bayerischen Akademie der Wissenschaft

Abh Philol Hist Kl Koen Saechs Ges Wiss — Abhandlungen der Philologisch-Historischen Klasse der Koeniglichen Saechsischen Gesellschaft der Wissenschaften

Abh Philos Ges — Abhandlungen zur Philosophie und Ihrer Geschichte

Abh Philos Philol Kl Koen Bayer Akad Wiss — Abhandlungen der Philolosophisch-Philologischen Klasse der Koeniglichen Bayerischen Akademie der Wissenschaften

Abh Phys Kl Koenigl Akad Wiss Berlin — Abhandlungen der Koeniglichen Akademie der Wissenschaften in Berlin

Abh Phys Math Kl Koenigl Akad Wiss Berlin — Abhandlungen der Koeniglichen Akademie der Wissenschaften in Berlin

Abh Preuss Akad Wiss — Abhandlungen der Berliner Akademie der Wissenschaften

Abh Preuss Akad Wiss — Abhandlungen der Koeniglich Preussischen Akademie der Wissenschaften. Physikalisch-Mathematische Classe

Abh Preuss Akad Wiss Math Naturwiss Kl — Abhandlungen. Preussische Akademie der Wissenschaften. Mathematisch-Naturwissenschaftliche Klasse

Abh Preuss Akad Wiss Philol Hist Kl — Abhandlungen der Preussischen Akademie der Wissenschaften. Philologisch-Historische Klasse

Abh Preuss Akad Wiss Phys Math — Abhandlungen der Preussischen Akademie der Wissenschaften. Physikalisch-Mathematische Klasse

Abh Preuss Akad Wiss Phys Math Kl — Abhandlungen. Preussische Akademie der Wissenschaften. Physikalisch-Mathematische Klasse

Abh Preuss Geol Landesanst — Abhandlungen der Preussischen Geologischen Landesanstalt

Abh Privatges Boehmen — Abhandlungen einer Privatgesellschaft in Boehmen, zur Aufnahme der Mathematik, der Vaterlaendischen Geschichte, und der Naturgeschichte

Abh Privatges Naturf Oberdeutschl — Abhandlungen einer Privatgesellschaft von Naturforschern und Oekonomen in Oberheutschland

Abh PTRA — Wissenschaftliche Abhandlungen der Physikalisch-Technischen Reichsanstalt

ABHRAR — Anais Botanicos. Herbario "Barbosa Rodrigues"

Abh Reichsamts Bodenforsch Ger — Abhandlungen des Reichsamts fuer Bodenforschung (Germany)

Abh Reichsstelle Bodenforsch (Ger) — Abhandlungen des Reichsstelle fuer Bodenforschung (Germany)

Abh Rheinisch-Westfael Akad Wiss — Abhandlungen. Rheinisch-Westfaelische Akademie der Wissenschaften

ABHSA — American Behavioral Scientist

Abh Saech Ges Wiss — Abhandlungen der Philologisch-Historische Klasse der Saechsischen Akademie der Wissenschaften

Abh Saechs — Abhandlungen der Philologisch-Historische Klasse der Saechsischen Akademie der Wissenschaften

Abh Saechs Akad Phil — Abhandlungen der Philologisch-Historische Klasse der Saechsischen Akademie der Wissenschaften

Abh Saechs Akad Wiss Leipzig Math-Natur Kl — Abhandlungen. Saechsische Akademie der Wissenschaften zu Leipzig. Mathematisch-Naturwissenschaftliche Klasse

Abh Saechs Akad Wiss Leipzig Math Naturwiss Kl — Abhandlungen. Saechsische Akademie der Wissenschaften zu Leipzig. Mathematisch-Naturwissenschaftliche Klasse

Abh Saechs Akad Wiss Leipzig Philol Hist Kl — Abhandlungen der Saechsischen Akademie der Wissenschaften zu Leipzig. Philologisch-Historische Klasse

Abh Saechs Ges Wiss — Abhandlungen der Mathematisch-Physischen Classe der Koeniglich Saechsischen Gesellschaft der Wissenschaften

Abh Saechs Ges Wiss Leipzig — Abhandlungen der Saechsischen Akademie der Wissenschaften zu Leipzig. Mathematisch-Naturwissenschaftliche Klasse

Abh Schles Gesell — Abhandlungen der Schlesischen Gesellschaft fuer Vaterlaendische Cultur. Abtheilung fuer Naturwissenschaften und Medicin

Abh Senckenb Natf Ges — Abhandlungen der Senckenbergischen Naturforschenden Gesellschaft

Abh Senckenb Naturf — Abhandlungen Herausgegeben von der Senckenbergischen Naturforschenden Gesellschaft

Abh Senckenb Naturforsch Ges — Abhandlungen. Senckenbergische Naturforschende Gesellschaft

Abh Senkenb Ges Frankfurt — Abhandlungen Herausgegeben von der Senkenbergischen Naturforschenden Gesellschaft (Frankfurt)

Abh Staatl Mus Mineral Geol Dresden — Abhandlungen. Staatliches Museum fuer Mineralogie und Geologie zu Dresden

AbhTANT — Abhandlungen zur Theologie des Alten und Neuen Testaments

Abh Th ANT — Abhandlungen zur Theologie des Alten und Neuen Testaments

Abh u Ber Staatl Mus f Voelkerkde Dresden — Abhandlungen und Berichte des Staatlichen Musems fuer Voelkerkunde Dresden

Abh Vereins Forstwiss Ausbild — Abhandlungen des Vereins fuer Forstwissenschaftliche Ausbildung

Abh Vereins Naturwiss Erforsch Niederrheins — Abhandlungen des Vereins fuer Naturwissenschaftliche Erforschung des Niederrheins

Abh Verh Naturwiss Ver Hamb — Abhandlungen und Verhandlungen. Naturwissenschaftlicher Verein in Hamburg

Abh Verh Naturwiss Ver Hamburg — Abhandlungen und Verhandlungen. Naturwissenschaftlicher Verein in Hamburg

Abh Wiss Forschungsinst Konservenind Plovdiv — Abhandlungen. Wissenschaftliches Forschungsinstitut fuer Konservenindustrie. Plovdiv

Abh Zool-Bot Ges Wien — Abhandlungen. Zoologisch-Botanischen Gesellschaft in Wien

Abh zu Gesch d Math — Abhandlungen zur Geschichte der Mathematischen Wissenschaften

Abh zu Gesch d Med — Abhandlungen zur Geschichte der Naturwissenschaften und der Medizin

ABI — Accademia e Biblioteche d'Italia

ABI — Australian Business Index

ABIA — Annual Bibliography of Indian Archaeology

ABIA Assoc Bras Ind Aliment — ABIA. Associacao Brasileira das Industrias da Alimentacao

ABIA SAPRO Bol Inf — ABIA [*Associacao Brasileira das Industrias da Alimentacao*] SAPRO Boletim Informativo

A Bib — Assyriologische Bibliothek

ABIBD — Applied Biochemistry and Biotechnology

Abidjan Univ Ann Sci — Abidjan Universite. Annales. Sciences

ABILAE — Archives de Biologie

ABIM — Abridged Index Medicus

ABIOAN — Acta Biotheoretica

A Biol Colloq Ore St Coll — Annual Biology Colloquium. Oregon State College

ABIP — Australian Books in Print

ABIPB — Proceedings. Australian Biochemical Society

ABIPC — Abstract Bulletin. Institute of Paper Chemistry

ABIRBD — Australia. Commonwealth Scientific and Industrial Research Organisation. Division of Irrigation Research. Report

ABIS — Acta Botanica Islandica

Ab Isl — Abstracta Islamica

ABITA — American Biology Teacher

ABIX — Australian Business Index

ABJCAQ — Annales. Universite d'Abidjan. Serie C. Sciences

ABJOA — American Bee Journal

ABK — Aachener Beitraege zur Komparatistik

ABK — Ajia Bunka

ABKK — Amtliche Berichte. Koenigliche Kunstsammlungen

AbKM — Abhandlungen fuer die Kunde des Morgenlandes

AbKSGW — Abhandlungen. Koenigliche Saechsische Gesellschaft der Wissenschaften

A BI — Advocatenblad

ABL — American Business Law Journal

Abl — Arbeidsblad

ABL — Attic Black Figured Lekythoi

ABL — Business Law Cases for Australia

Ablauf-Planungsforsch — Ablauf- und Planungsforschung

ABI EKD — Amtsblatt der Evangelischen Kirche in Deutschland

Ablex Ser Artif Intell — Ablex Series in Artificial Intelligence

ABLR — Australian Business Law Review

ABLSAG — Archives of Biological Sciences

Ab LSO — Arbok Listasafn Sigurjon Olafsson

ABM — Academie Royale de Belgique

ABM — Art Bibliographies Modern

ABMA — Auctores Britannici Medii Aevi

ABMAE5 — Acta Botanica Malacitana

ABMB — Archives, Bibliotheques, et Musees de Belgique [*Later, Archives et Bibliotheques de Belgique*]

ABM Bol — ABM (Associacao Brasileira de Metais) Boletim

ABM Congr Anu — ABM (Associacao Brasileira de Metais) Congresso Anual

ABME — Archeion ton Byzantinon Mnemeion tes Hellados

ABMEAD — Arquivos Brasileiros de Medicina

ABMEC — Annals of Biomedical Engineering

ABMEEH — Annals of Behavioral Medicine

ABMGA — Acta Biologica et Medica Germanica

ABMH — Archeion ton Byzantinon Mnemeion tes Hellados

ABMHAM — Archives Belges de Medecine Sociale, Hygiene, Medecine du Travail, et Medecine Legale

ABMI — Author Biographies Master Index

AbMilt — Abstracts of Military Bibliography

ABMK — Archiwa, Biblioteki, i Muzea Koscielne

ABMMC — Analele. Universitatii Bucuresti. Matematica-Mecanica

ABM Not — ABM [*Associacao Brasileira de Metais*] Noticiario

ABMPEG — Medica Physica

ABMR — ABM [*Australian Board of Missions*] Review

ABMR — Antiquarian Book Monthly Review

ABM Rev — ABM [*Australian Board of Missions*] Review

ABMSM — Arbeiten der Biologischen Meeresstation am Schwarzen Meer in Varna

ABMXA — Archivos de Biologia y Medicina Experimentales

ABMXA2 — Archivos de Biologia y Medicina Experimentales

ABMZDB — Arquivo Brasileiro de Medicina Veterinaria e Zootecnia

ABN — Anais. Biblioteca Nacional

ABN — Arnold Bennett Newsletter

ABN — Asian Business

ABNG — Amsterdamer Beitraege zur Neueren Germanistik

ABNGAO — Abhandlungen und Berichte. Naturkundemuseums Goerlitz

ABNN — Alberta Native News

ABNRAN — Acta Botanica Neerlandica
ABN Review — ABN [*Algemene Bank Nederland*] Economic Review
ABNUAW — Arquivos Brasileiros de Nutricao
ABO — Anchor Books Original
ABOA — Acta Borealia. B. Humaniora
ABOA — Australian Bibliography of Agriculture
ABOAAB — Acta Borealia. A. Scientia
ABOBAE — Anais. Congresso Nacional. Sociedade Botanica do Brasil
Abo C — Abogado Cristiano
ABOD — Arbeiten zur Bayerisch-Oesterreichischen Dialektgeografie
ABOF — Annales Botanici Fennici
ABOFA — Annales Botanici Fennici
ABOHAW — Acta Botanica. Academiae Scientiarum Hungaricae
ABOHE2 — Acta Botanica Hungarica
A Bohuslaens Hembygds — Arsskrift. Bohuslaens Hembygdsfoerbund
ABOIB — Acta Botanica Indica
A Bologna — Arte a Bologna
ABOPAM — Arquivos de Botanica do Estado de Sao Paulo
ABORI — Annals. Bhandarkar Oriental Research Institute
Aborig Aff Info Paper — Aboriginal Affairs Information Paper
Aborig Child Sch — Aboriginal Child at School
Aborig Hist — Aboriginal History
Aboriginal Hist — Aboriginal History
Aboriginal Q — Aboriginal Quarterly
Aborig LB — Aboriginal Law Bulletin
Abor N — Aboriginal News
Abortion Law Rep — Abortion Law Reporter
ABoT — Ankara Arkeoloji Muzesinde Bulunan Bogazkoy Tableteri
ABourg — Annales de Bourgogne
A Bourgogne — Annales de Bourgogne
About Distance Educ — About Distance Education
ABOVA6 — Acta Botanica Venezuelica
ABP — Annaes de Bibliographia Portugueza
ABP — Arquivo de Bibliografia Portuguesa
ABP — Centraal Planbureau. Bibliotheek. Aanwinsten
ABPBBK — Annual Review of Biophysics and Bioengineering
ABPCA — Abstract Bulletin. Institute of Paper Chemistry
AbPhoto — Abstracts of Photographic Science and Engineering Literature
ABPK — Amtliche Berichte. Preussische Kunstsammlunge
ABPR — African Book Publishing Record
ABPV — Annali del Buon Pastore (Vienna)
ABQ — Erasmusuniversiteit Rotterdam. Universiteitsbibliotheek. Aanwinstenlijst
ABR — Accounting and Business Research
ABr — Altbabylonische Briefe
ABR — American Benedictine Review
ABR — American Book Review
ABr — Annales de Bretagne et des Pays de l'Ouest
ABR — Australian Biblical Review
ABR — Australian Book Review
ABRA — Abracadabra. Association of British Columbia Drama Educators
Abrasive Clean Methods — Abrasive and Cleaning Methods
Abrasive Eng — Abrasive Engineering
Abrasive Eng Soc Mag — Abrasive Engineering Society. Magazine
Abrasiv Eng — Abrasive Engineering
A'B Res Judgm — A'Beckett's Reserved Judgements
ABret — Annales de Bretagne [*Later, Annales de Bretagne et des Pays de l'Ouest*]
Abridg (Brit) Pat — Abridgments of Specification Patents for Inventions (Great Britain)
Abridg Wkly Weath Rep Canb — Abridged Weekly Weather Report for Canberra
AbrIMed — Abridged Index Medicus
Abr Index Med — Abridged Index Medicus
A'B RJ (NSW) — A'Beckett's Reserved and Equity Judgements (New South Wales)
A'B RJPP — A'Beckett's Reserved Judgements (Port Phillip)
Abrn — Abr-nahrain
Abr Read Guide — Abridged Readers' Guide to Periodical Literature
Abr RG — Abridged Reader's Guide to Periodical Literature
A Br Sch Archeol Athens — Annual. British School of Archaeology at Athens
Abr Sci Publ Kodak Res Lab — Abridged Scientific Publications from the Kodak Research Laboratories
Abr Sci Pubs — Abridged Scientific Publications
ABRTDI — Advances in Behaviour Research and Therapy
Abr Trans Philos Soc Roy Londres Pt 8 Matiere Med — Abrege des Transactions Philosophiques. Societe Royale de Londres. Huitieme Partie. Matiere Medicale et Pharmacie
A Brut — Art Brut
Abs — Absalon
ABS — Absatzwirtschaft
ABs — Abside
ABS — Acta Baltico-Slavica
ABS — American Behavioral Scientist
ABS — Annual. British School at Athens
ABS — Australian Building Specification
ABSA — Annual. British School at Athens
Abs Bull Inst Paper Chem — Abstract Bulletin. Institute of Paper Chemistry
ABSCD6 — Annales. Universite de Brazzaville. Serie C. Sciences
Abs Crim Pen — Abstracts on Criminology and Penology
ABSHF — Annuaire-Bulletin. Societe de l'Histoire de France
ABSLAU — Danish Pest Infestation Laboratory. Annual Report
ABSN — American Brahms Society Newsletter
AbSocWk — Abstracts for Social Workers
Absorpt Distrib Transform Excretion Drugs — Absorption, Distribution, Transformation, and Excretion of Drugs
Absorpt Spectra Ultraviolet Visible Reg — Absorption Spectra in the Ultraviolet and Visible Region
ABSP — Arquivos de Biologia (Sao Paulo)

Abs Pap ACS — Abstracts of Papers. American Chemical Society
ABSPDB — Acta Botanica Slovaca. Academiae Scientiarum Slovacae. Series B. Physiologica, Pathophysiologica
Ab Stat Kstmus — Arsbok foer Statens Konstmuseer
Ab Stavanger Mus — Arbok Stavanger Museum
Abst Commun Eur Meet Meat Res Work — Abstracts and Communications Presented. European Meeting of Meat Research Workers
Abst CSICMR — Abstracts. Centre for the Study of Islam and Christian-Muslim Relations
Abstraction Creation A Non Fig — Abstraction, Creation, Art Non-Figuratif
Abstracts Amer Math Soc — Abstracts of Papers Presented to the American Mathematical Society
Abstracts Bulgar Sci Lit Math Phys Sci — Abstracts of Bulgarian Scientific Literature. Mathematical and Physical Sciences
Abstr Air Water Conserv Lit — Abstracts of Air and Water Conservation Literature
Abstrakt Konkr — Abstrakt/Konkret
Abstr Annu Meet Am Soc Microbiol — Abstracts of the Annual Meeting. American Society for Microbiology
Abstr Anthropol — Abstracts in Anthropology
Abstr Appl Anal — Abstract and Applied Analysis
Abstr Bacteriol — Abstracts of Bacteriology
Abstr Bot — Abstracta Botanica
Abstr Bulg Scient Lit — Abstracts of Bulgarian Scientific Literature
Abstr Bulg Sci Lit Agric For Vet Med — Abstracts of Bulgarian Scientific Literature. Agriculture and Forestry, Veterinary Medicine
Abstr Bulg Sci Lit Biol Biochem — Abstracts of Bulgarian Scientific Literature. Biology and Biochemistry
Abstr Bulg Sci Lit Biol Med — Abstracts of Bulgarian Scientific Literature. Biology and Medicine
Abstr Bulg Sci Lit Chem — Abstracts of Bulgarian Scientific Literature. Chemistry
Abstr Bulg Sci Lit Chem Chem Technol — Abstracts of Bulgarian Scientific Literature. Chemistry and Chemical Technology
Abstr Bulg Sci Lit Geol Geogr — Abstracts of Bulgarian Scientific Literature. Geology and Geography
Abstr Bulg Sci Lit Geosci — Abstracts of Bulgarian Scientific Literature. Geosciences
Abstr Bulg Sci Lit Math Phys Astron Geophys Geod — Abstracts of Bulgarian Scientific Literature. Mathematics, Physics, Astronomy, Geophysics, Geodesy
Abstr Bulg Sci Lit Med — Abstracts of Bulgarian Scientific Literature. Medicine
Abstr Bulg Sci Lit Med Phys Cult — Abstracts of Bulgarian Scientific Literature, Medicine, and Physical Culture
Abstr Bulg Sci Lit Ser A Plant Breed For Econ — Abstracts of Bulgarian Scientific Literature. Series A. Plant Breeding and Forest Economy
Abstr Bulg Sci Lit Ser Biol Biochem — Abstracts of Bulgarian Scientific Literature. Series. Biology and Biochemistry
Abstr Bulg Sci Med Lit — Abstracts of Bulgarian Scientific Medical Literature
Abstr Bull — Monthly Abstract Bulletin
Abstr Bull Geol Surv S Aust — Abstracts Bulletin. Geological Survey of South Australia
Abstr Bull Inst Pap Chem — Abstract Bulletin. Institute of Paper Chemistry
Abstr Bull Inst Paper Chem — Abstract Bulletin. Institute of Paper Chemistry
Abstr Collect Eur Neurosci Meet — Abstract Collection. European Neurosciences Meeting
Abstr Comput Lit — Abstracts of Computer Literature
Abstr Conf Pap Trienn Conf Eur Assoc Potato Res — Abstracts of Conference Papers. Triennial Conference. European Association for Potato Research
Abstr Congr Eur Soc Exp Surg — Abstracts. Congress of the European Society for Experimental Surgery
Abstr Congr Heterocycl Chem — Abstracts. Congress of Heterocyclic Chemistry
Abstr Congr Pol Phthisiopneumonol Soc — Abstracts. Congress of the Polish Phthisiopneumonological Society
Abstr Crim & Pen — Abstracts on Criminology and Penology
Abstr Crime Juv Del — Abstracts on Crime and Juvenile Delinquency
Abstr Criminol Penol — Abstracts on Criminology and Penology
Abstr Curr Lit Aerosp Med Assoc — Abstracts of Current Literature. Aerospace Medical Association
Abstr Doct Diss Ohio St Univ — Abstracts of Doctoral Dissertations. Ohio State University
Abstr Engl Stud — Abstracts of English Studies
Abstr Entomol — Abstracts of Entomology
Abstr Eur Soc Surg Res Congr — Abstracts. European Society for Surgical Research. Congress
Abstr Folk Stud — Abstracts of Folklore Studies
Abstr Geochronology Isot Geol — Abstracts of Geochronology and Isotope Geology
Abstr Geol Geogr Pap Publ Jpn — Abstracts of Geological and Geographical Papers Published in Japan
Abstr Geol Soc Am — Abstracts. Geological Society of America
Abstr Health Care Manage Stud — Abstracts of Health Care Management Studies
Abstr Health Eff Environ Pollut — Abstracts on Health Effects of Environmental Pollutants
Abstr Health Environ Pollutants — Abstracts on Health Effects of Environmental Pollutants
Abstr Hospit Manage Stud — Abstracts of Hospital Management Studies
Abstr Hosp Manage Stud — Abstracts of Hospital Management Studies
Abstr Hyg — Abstracts on Hygiene
Abstr Hyg Commun Dis — Abstracts on Hygiene and Communicable Diseases
Abstr Inst Pet — Abstracts. Institute of Petroleum
Abstr Int Congr Gastroenterol — Abstracts. International Congress of Gastroenterology
Abstr Int Congr Virol — Abstracts. International Congress of Virology
Abstr Iran — Abstracta Iranica
Abstr Jap Lit Forest Genet — Abstracts of Japanese Literature in Forest Genetics and Related Fields

Abstr J Chem React Doc Serv — Abstracts Journal. Chemical Reaction Documentation Service

Abstr J Earthq Eng — Abstract Journal in Earthquake Engineering

Abstr J Inf Engl Transl — Abstract Journal. Informatics (English Translation)

Abstr J Inf (Moscow) — Abstract Journal Informations (Moscow)

Abstr Jpn Chem Lit Complete — Abstracts of Japanese Chemical Literature. Complete

Abstr Jpn Med — Abstracts of Japanese Medicine

Abstr J Sci Tech Inf Moscow — Abstract Journal. Scientific and Technical Information (Moscow)

Abstr London Shellac Res Bur — Abstracts. London Shellac Research Bureau

Abstr Meet Weed Soc Am — Abstracts. Meeting of the Weed Society of America

Abstr Mil Bibl — Abstracts of Military Bibliography

Abstr Mil Bibliogr — Abstracts of Military Bibliography

Abstr Mtg ACS — Abstracts of Papers. Meeting of the American Chemical Society

Abstr Mtg Weed Soc Amer — Abstracts. Meeting of the Weed Society of America

Abstr Mycol — Abstracts of Mycology

Abstr N Amer Geol — Abstracts of North American Geology

Abstr Natl Congr Ital Soc Mar Biol — Abstracts. National Congress of the Italian Society of Marine Biology

Abstr New World Archaeol — Abstracts of New World Archaeology

Abstr North Am Geol — Abstracts of North American Geology

Abstr Pap Am Chem Soc — Abstracts of Papers. American Chemical Society

Abstr Pap Aust Workshop Coal Hydrogenation — Australian Workshop on Coal Hydrogenation. Abstract and Papers

Abstr Pap Brighton Sussex Nat Hist Soc — Abstracts of Papers Read. Brighton and Sussex Natural History and PhilosophicalSociety

Abstr Pap Chem Congr North Am Cont — Abstracts of Papers. Chemical Congress. North American Content

Abstr Pap Commun R Soc (London) — Abstracts of the Papers Communicated to the Royal Society (London)

Abstr Pap Congr Heterocycl Chem — Abstracts of Papers. Congress of Heterocyclic Chemistry

Abstr Pap Int Conf At Sptrosc — Abstracts of Papers Accepted for Presentation. International Conference on Atomic Spectroscopy

Abstr Pap Int Conf Phys Chem Asbestos Miner — Abstracts of Papers. International Conference on the Physics and Chemistry of Asbestos Minerals

Abstr Pap Int Conf Phys Electron At Collisions — Abstracts of Papers. International Conference on the Physics of Electronic and Atomic Collisions

Abstr Pap J Jpn Soc Intern Med — Abstracts of Papers. Journal of the Japanese Society of Internal Medicine

Abstr Pap Jt Conf Chem Inst Can Am Chem Soc — Abstracts of Papers. Joint Conference. Chemical Institute of Canada and American Chemical Society

Abstr Pap Lunar Planet Sci Conf — Abstracts of Papers Submitted. Lunar and Planetary Science Conference

Abstr Pap Pac Sci Congr — Abstracts of the Papers. Pacific Science Congress

Abstr Pap Presented Ann Meet Am Soc Range Mange — Abstracts of Papers Presented at the Annual Meeting. American Society of Range Management

Abstr Pap Presented Annu Meet Korean Surg Soc — Abstracts of Papers Presented at the Annual Meeting. Korean Surgical Society

Abstr Pap Printed Philos Trans R Soc (London) — Abstracts of the Papers Printed in the Philosophical Transactions of the Royal Society (London)

Abstr Pap Scand Congr Intern Med — Abstracts of Papers Presented. Scandinavian Congress of Internal Medicine

Abstr Pap Sci Poult Conf — Abstracts of Papers Presented at the Scientific Poultry Conference

Abstr Pap Soc Amer For — Abstracts of Papers. Society of American Foresters Meeting

Abstr Pap Utah Acad Sci — Abstracts of Papers Submitted. Annual Convention. Utah Academy of Sciences

Abstr Pap Work Meet Radiat Interact — Abstracts of Papers. Working Meeting on Radiation Interaction

Abstr Photogr Sci Eng Lit — Abstracts of Photographic Science and Engineering Literature

Abstr Police Sci — Abstracts on Police Science

Abstr Pop Cult — Abstracts of Popular Culture

Abstr Proc Assoc Amer Geol Naturalists — Abstract. Proceedings. Association of American Geologists and Naturalists

Abstr Proc Chem Soc London — Abstracts of the Proceedings. Chemical Society of London

Abstr Proc Cornell Nutr Conf Feed Manuf — Abstracts of Proceedings. Cornell Nutrition Conference for Feed Manufacturers

Abstr Proc Linn Soc NSW — Abstracts of the Proceedings. Linnean Society of New South Wales

Abstr Proc Liverpool Geol Soc — Abstract of the Proceedings. Liverpool Geological Society

Abstr Proc R Soc NSW — Abstract of Proceedings. Royal Society of New South Wales

Abstr Proc Ser CIP — Abstracts and Proceedings Series. CIP

Abstr Proc Soc NSW — Abstracts of Proceedings. Royal Society of New South Wales

Abstr Programs Geol Soc Am — Abstracts with Programs. Geological Society of America

Abstr Publ Pap List Transl CSIRO (Aust) — Abstracts of Published Papers and List of Translations. Commonwealth Scientificand Industrial Research Organisation (Australia)

Abstr Refin Lit — Abstracts of Refining Literature

Abstr Rep Geol Surv West Austr — Abstracts. Reports of the Geological Survey of Western Australia

Abstr Res Pastor Care Couns — Abstracts of Research in Pastoral Care and Counseling

Abstr Res Tob Salt Camphor — Abstracts of Researches. Tobacco, Salt, Camphor

Abstr Rom Sci Tech Lit — Abstracts of Romanian Scientific and Technical Literature

Abstr Rom Tech Lit — Abstracts of Romanian Technical Literature

Abstr Soc Work — Abstracts for Social Workers

Abstr Sov Med — Abstracts of Soviet Medicine

Abstr Sov Med Part A — Abstracts of Soviet Medicine. Part A. Basic Medical Sciences

Abstr Sov Med Part B — Abstracts of Soviet Medicine. Part B. Clinical Medicine

Abstr Symp Nonbenzenoid Aromat Compd Symp Struct Org Chem — Abstracts. Symposium on Nonbenzenoid Aromatic Compounds and Symposium on Structural Organic Chemistry

Abstr Tech Lit Archaeol Fine Arts — Abstracts of the Technical Literature on Archaeology and the Fine Arts

Abstr Tech Pap Water Pollut Control Fed — Abstracts of Technical Papers. Water Pollution Control Federation

Abstr Trop Agri — Abstracts on Tropical Agriculture

Abstr Trop Agric — Abstracts on Tropical Agriculture

Abstr Uppsala Diss Fac Med — Abstracts of Uppsala Dissertations. Faculty of Medicine

Abstr Uppsala Diss Fac Pharm — Abstracts of Uppsala Dissertations. Faculty of Pharmacy

Abstr Uppsala Diss Fac Sci — Abstracts of Uppsala Dissertations. Faculty of Science

Abstr Uppsala Diss Med — Abstracts of Uppsala Dissertations in Medicine

Abstr Uppsala Diss Sci — Abstracts of Uppsala Dissertations in Science

Abstr Wld Med — Abstracts of World Medicine

Abstr World Med — Abstracts of World Medicine

Absts Soc Workers — Abstracts for Social Workers

ABSUD — Amtsblatt. Bayerisches Staatsministerium fuer Landesentwicklung und Umweltfragen

Ab Svensk Stat Kstsaml — Arsbok foer Svenska Statens Konstsamlingen

ABT — Annales de Bibliographie Theologique

Abt Gesteins Erz Kohle Salz Unters Preuss Geol Landesanst Mitt — Abteilung fuer Gesteins-, Erz-, Kohle-, und Salz-Untersuchungen der Preussischen Geologischen Landesanstalt. Mitteilungen

ABTh — Annales de Bibliographie Theologique

ABTIBR — Acta Botanica Islandica

ABTL — Allgemeine Bibliothek der Neuesten Deutschen Theologischen Literatur

Abt Mineral Landesmus Joanneum Mitt — Abteilung fuer Mineralogie am Landesmuseum Joanneum. Mitteilungen

Abt Mineral Landesmus Joanneum Mitteilungsbl — Abteilung fuer Mineralogie am Landesmuseum Joanneum. Mitteilungsblatt

Abtrennung Festst Abwasser Siedlungswasserwirtsch Kolloq — Abtrennung von Feststoffen aus dem Abwasser. Siedlungswasserwirtschaftliches Kolloquium

ABTTAP — Arquivos de Biologia e Tecnologia

Abt Zool Bot Landesmus Joanneum Graz Mitteilungsbl — Abteilung fuer Zoologie und Botanik am Landesmuseum Joanneum (Graz) Mitteilungsblatt

Abt Zool Bot Landesmus Joanneum Graz Mitteilungsh — Abteilung fuer Zoologie und Botanik am Landesmuseum Joanneum, Graz. Mitteilungsheft

ABU — Australian Business Law Review

Ab U Bergen — Arbok for Universitetet i Bergen

ABUC — Archivio Bibliographico. Bibliotheca da Universidade de Coimbra

A Buddhica — Ars Buddhica

ABul — Art Bulletin

ABull — Art Bulletin

A Bull Victoria — Art Bulletin of Victoria

A Bus L Rev — Australian Business Law Review

ABU Tech Rev — ABU [*Asian Broadcasting Union*] Technical Review

ABV — Attic Black-Figure Vase Painters

ABVEAO — Acta Biologica Venezuelica

AbVoc — Abstracts of Research and Related Materials in Vocational and Technical Education

ABVSD — Annales. Association Belge de Radioprotection

ABWADK — Australian Birdwatcher

Abwasser Schlammbehandl Essener Tag — Abwasser- und Schlammbehandlung, Fortschritte und Probleme, Essener Tagung

Abwassertech Abfalltech — Abwassertechnik mit Abfalltechnik

Abwassertech Ver Dok Schriftenr Wiss Prax — Abwassertechnische Vereinigung, Dokumentation, und Schriftenreihe aus Wissenschaft und Praxis

Abwassertech Ver Tech Wiss Schriftenr — Abwassertechnische Vereinigung. Technisch-Wissenschaftliche Schriftenreihe

ABWGA — Abhandlungen. Braunschweigische Wissenschaftliche Gesellschaft

ABWGAZ — Abhandlungen. Braunschweigische Wissenschaftliche Gesellschaft

ABZoMD — Abhandlungen und Berichte des Zoologisch-AntropologischEthnologischen Museums. Dresden

AC — Abinger Chronicle

Ac — Academy

AC — Accent on Worship, Music, and the Arts

AC — Achimoowin. James Smith Reserve

AC — AC [*Asbestos and Cement*]. The Fibrecement Review

AC — Advance California Reports

AC — Albia Christiana

AC — Alma Cubana

AC — American City

AC — Analecta Cisterciensia

AC — Anales Cervantinos

AC — Annales-Conferencia

A C — Annales de Chimie et de Physique, ou Recueil de Memoires Concernant la Chimie et les Arts qui en Dependent

AC — Antike und Christentum

AC — Antiquite Classique

AC — Anuario Colombiano

AC — Applied Christianity

AC — Archaeologia Cambrensis

AC — Archaeologia Classica

AC — Archaeology of Crete

AC — Archivos del Folklore Chileno

AC — Auto-Cite

AcA — Acta Anatomica
ACA — Advance California Appellate Reports
ACA — Amazonia Colombiana Americanista
ACA — American Composers Alliance. Bulletin
ACA — Anuario Centroamericano
A CA — Art of California
ACA — Australian Corporate Affairs Reporter
ACAAB — Annales de Cardiologie et d'Angeiologie
AcAB — Acta Antiqua (Budapest)
ACACA — Anales de Ciencias, Agricultura, Comercio, y Artes
ACACA — Analytica Chimica Acta
ACACB — Acta Crystallographica. Section A. Crystal Physics, Diffraction, Theoretical and General Crystallography
ACACS — Annales. Cercle Archeologique du Canton de Soignies
Acad — [The] Academy
Acad — Academy and Literature
Acad Ag France Comptes Rendus — Academie d'Agriculture de France. Comptes Rendus des Seances
Acad Ag France Compt Rend — Academie d'Agriculture de France. Comptes Rendus des Seances
Acad Agric Fr CR — Academie d'Agriculture de France. Comptes Rendus
Acad Agric Fr CR Seances — Academie d'Agriculture de France. Comptes Rendus des Seances
Acad Agric Tech Olstenensis Acta Agric — Academia Agriculturae ac Technicae Olstenensis. Acta Agricultura
Acad Agric Tech Olstenensis Acta Prot Aquarum Piscatoria — Academia Agriculturae ac Technicae Olstenensis. Acta Protectio Aquarum et Piscatoria
Acad Agric Tech Olstenensis Acta Technol Aliment — Academia Agriculturae ac Technicae Olstenensis. Acta Technologia Alimentorum
Acad Agric Tech Olstenensis Acta Zootech — Academia Agriculturae ac Technicae Olstenensis. Acta Zootechnica
Acad & Annu Archit Rev — Academy and Annual Architectural Review
Acad Anlct Kl Lett — Academiae Analecta. Klasse der Letteren
Acad Anlct Kl S Kst — Academiae Analecta. Klasse der Schoene Kunsten
Acad Anlct Kl Wetsch — Academiae Analecta. Klasse der Wetenschappen
Acad Archit & Archit Rev — Academy Architecture and Architectural Review
Acad Assoc Newsl — Academic Associates Newsletter
Acad B A — Academie des Beaux-Arts
Acad B A Bull Annu — Academie des Beaux-Arts. Bulletin Annuel
Acad B A C R Seances — Academie des Beaux-Arts. Comptes Rendus des Seances
Acad B Lett Caen — Academie des Belles-Lettres de Caen
Acad Boliviana Ciencias Econs R — Academia Boliviana de Ciencias Economicas. Revista
Acad Bookman — Academy Bookman
Acad Brasileira Cienc Anais — Academia Brasileira de Ciencias. Anais
Acad Bul — Academy of Motion Picture Arts and Sciences. Bulletin
Acad Cienc Artes Barc — Academia de Ciencias y Artes de Barcelona. Memorias
Acad Cienc Artes Barcelona Mem — Academia de Ciencias y Artes de Barcelona. Memorias
Acad Cienc Cuba Inf Cient Tec — Academia de Ciencias de Cuba. Informe Cientifico-Tecnico
Acad Cienc Cuba Inst Geol Actas — Academia de Ciencias de Cuba. Instituto de Geologia. Actas
Acad Cienc Cuba Inst Geol Paleontol Publ Espec — Academia de Ciencias de Cuba. Instituto de Geologia y Paleontologia. Publicacion Especial
Acad Cienc Cuba Inst Geol Ser Geol — Academia de Ciencias de Cuba. Instituto de Geologia. Serie Geologica
Acad Cienc Cuba Ser Biol — Academia de Ciencias de Cuba. Serie Biologica
Acad Cienc Estado Sao Paulo Publ — Academia de Ciencias do Estado de Sao Paulo. Publicacao
Acad Cienc Exactas Fis Nat Madrid Mem — Academia de Ciencias Exactas, Fisicas, y Naturales de Madrid. Memorias
Acad Cienc Exactas Fis Nat Madrid Mem Ser Cienc Fis Quim — Academia de Ciencias Exactas, Fisicas, y Naturales de Madrid. Memorias. Serie de Ciencias Fisico-Quimicas
Acad Cienc Exactas Fis Nat Madrid Mem Ser Cienc Natur — Academia de Ciencias Exactas, Fisicas, y Naturales de Madrid. Memorias. Serie de Ciencias Naturales
Acad Cienc Med Cataluna Baleares — Academia de Ciencias Medicas de Cataluna y Baleares
Acad Cienc Med Fis y Naturales Habana Anales — Academia de Ciencias Medicas, Fisicas, y Naturales de la Habana. Anales
Acad d Inscrip Memoires — Academie des Inscriptions et Belles-Lettres. Memoires
Acad d Inscr Mon et Mem — Academie des Inscriptions et Belles-Lettres. Monuments et Memoires
Acad d Inscr (Paris) Mem — Academie des Inscriptions et Belles-Lettres. Memoires (Paris)
Acad d Inscr (Paris) Mon et Mem — Academie des Inscriptions et Belles-Lettres. Monuments et Memoires (Paris)
Acad d Sci d Belgique Mem 4 Cl d Lett — Academie Royale des Sciences, des Lettres, et des Beaux-Arts de Belgique. Memoires 4. Classe des Lettres
Acad d Sci d Belgique Mem 4 Cl d Sci — Academie Royale des Sciences, des Lettres, et des Beaux-Arts de Belgique. Memoires 4. Classe des Sciences
Acad d Sci d Belgique Mem 8 Cl d Lett — Academie Royale des Sciences, des Lettres, et des Beaux-Arts de Belgique. Memoires 8. Classe des Lettres
Acad d Sci d Belgique Mem 8 Cl d Sci — Academie Royale des Sciences, des Lettres, et des Beaux-Arts de Belgique. Memoires 8. Classe des Sciences
Acad D Sci De Cracovie Bul Sci Math Et Nat — Academie des Asbences de Cracovie. Bulletin. Sciences Mathematiques et Naturelles
Acad d Sci Morales Et Pol Compt Rend — Academie des Sciences Morales et Politiques. Paris. Comptes Rendus
Acad d Sci Mor et Pol (Paris) Mem — Academie des Sciences Morales et Politiques (Paris). Memoires
Acad d Sci (Paris) Mem — Academie des Sciences (Paris). Memoires

Acad d Sci (Paris) Mem Div Savants — Academie des Sciences (Paris). Memoires Presentes par Divers Savants
Acad Emerg Med — Academic Emergency Medicine
Academia Bol Real Acad B A San Fernando — Academia. Boletin de la Real Academia de Bellas Artes de San Fernando
Academy of Mgmt Jrnl — Academy of Management. Journal
Academy of Mgmt Review — Academy of Management. Review
Acad Esp Bol — Real Academia Espanola. Boletin
Acad Eur Allergol Immunol Clin CR Reun Annu — Academie Europeenne d'Allergologie et Immunologie Clinique. Comptes Rendus de la Reunion Annuelle
Acad Galega Cienc Bol — Academia Galega de Ciencias. Boletin
Acad Galega Cienc Rev — Academia Galega de Ciencias. Revista
Acad Inscr & B Lett C R Seances — Academie des Inscriptions et Belles-Lettres. Comptes Rendus des Seances
Acad Inscript CR — Academie des Inscriptions et Belles-Lettres. Comptes Rendus
Acad Inscr (Paris) Mem Div Savants — Academie des Inscriptions et Belles-Lettres. Memoires Presentes par Divers Savants (Paris)
Acad Inscr (Paris) Mon et Mem — Institut de France (Paris). Academie des Inscriptions et Belles-Lettres. Monuments et Memoires
Acad Int Law Rec Des Cours — Academy of International Law. Recueil des Cours
Acad J Guangdong Coll Pharm — Academic Journal of Guangdong College of Pharmacy
Acad J Guangdong Med Pharm Coll — Academic Journal of Guangdong Medical and Pharmaceutical College
Acad L Rev — Academy Law Review
Acad Manage J — Academy of Management. Journal
Acad Manage Rev — Academy of Management. Review
Acad Mangt J — Academy of Management. Journal
Acad Marketing Science J — Academy of Marketing Science. Journal
Acad Med — Academic Medicine
Acad Med NJ Bull — Academy of Medicine of New Jersey. Bulletin
Acad Mgt J — Academy of Management. Journal
Acad Mgt R — Academy of Management. Review
Acad Nac Cienc Exactas Fis Nat An Buenos Aires — Academia Nacional de Ciencias Exactas, Fisicas, y Naturales. Annales (Buenos Aires)
Acad Nac Cienc Exactas Fis Nat Monogr — Academia Nacional de Ciencias Exactas, Fisicas, y Naturales. Monografias
Acad Nac Cienc Mem Rev — Academia Nacional de Ciencias. Memorias y Revista
Acad Nac Cienc Misc (Cordoba) — Academia Nacional de Ciencias. Miscelanea (Cordoba)
Acad Nac Med Bol (Braz) — Academia Nacional de Medicina. Boletim (Brazil)
Acad Natl Med Paris Bull — Academie Nationale de Medecine. Paris. Bulletin
Acad Nat Sci Philadelphia Contrib Dep Limnol — Academy of Natural Sciences of Philadelphia. Contributions. Department of Limnology
Acad Nat Sci Philadelphia Not Nat — Academy of Natural Sciences of Philadelphia. Notulae Naturae
Acad Nat Sci Philadelphia Spec Pub — Academy of Natural Sciences of Philadelphia. Special Publication
Acad Nat Sci Phila Mon — Academy of Natural Sciences of Philadelphia Monographs
Acad Nat Sci Phila Monog — Academy of Natural Sciences of Philadelphia Monographs
Acad Natur Sci Phila Proc — Academy of Natural Sciences of Philadelphia. Proceedings
Acad of Nat Sci Jour — Academy of Natural Sciences. Journal
Acad Pap — Academy Papers. American Academy of Physical Education
Acad Pap Am Acad Phys Ed Meet — Academy Papers. American Academy of Physical Education. Meeting
Acad Peru Cir — Academia Peruana de Cirugia
Acad Pol Sci Bull Ser Sci Phys Astron — Academie Polonaise des Sciences. Bulletin. Serie des Sciences Physiques et Astronomiques
Acad Pol Sci Bull Ser Sci Terre — Academie Polonaise des Sciences. Bulletin. Serie des Sciences de la Terre
Acad Pol Sci Bul Ser Sci Tech — Academie Polonaise des Sciences. Bulletin. Serie des Sciences Techniques
Acad Pol Sci Proc — Academy of Political Science. Proceedings
Acad Proc Eng Sci — Academy Proceedings in Engineering Sciences
Acad Radiol — Academic Radiology
Acad R Belg Annu — Academie Royale de Belgique. Annuaire
Acad R Belg Bull Cl Sci — Academie Royale de Belgique. Bulletin. Classe des Sciences
Acad R Belg Cl Sci Collect Octavo Mem — Academie Royale de Belgique. Classe des Sciences. Collection in Octavo. Memoires
Acad R Belg Cl Sci Collect Quarto Mem — Academie Royale de Belgique. Classe des Sciences. Collection in Quarto. Memoires
Acad R Belg Cl Sci Mem — Academie Royale de Belgique. Classe des Sciences. Memoires
Acad R Belg Cl Sci Mem Collect 4 — Academie Royale de Belgique. Classe des Sciences. Memoires. Collection in 4
Acad R Belg Cl Sci Mem Collect 8 — Academie Royale de Belgique. Classe des Sciences. Memoires. Collection in 8
Acad R Belg Mem Cl Sci Collect 8 — Academie Royale de Belgique. Memoires. Classe des Sciences. Collection in 8
Acad R Belg Mem Cl Sci Collect Octavo — Academie Royale de Belgique. Memoires. Classe des Sciences. Collection in Octavo
Acad R Belg Mem Cl Sci Collect Quarto — Academie Royale de Belgique. Memoires. Classe des Sciences. Collection in Quarto
Acad Rep Fac Eng Tokyo Inst Polytech — Academic Reports. Faculty of Engineering. Tokyo Institute of Polytechnics
Acad Repub Pop Rom An Mem Ser B — Academia Republicii Populare Romane. Analele. Memorille. Seria B. Sectiunea de Stiinte Medicale
Acad Repub Pop Rom Bul Stiint A — Academia Republicii Populare Romane. Buletin Stiintific. Seria A. Matematica, Fizica, Chimie, Geologie, Geografie, Biologie: Stiinte Tehnice si Agricole

Acad Repub Pop Rom Bul Stiint A — Academia Republicii Populare Romine. Buletin Stiintific. Seria A

Acad Repub Pop Rom Bul Stiint B — Academia Republicii Populare Romane. Buletin Stiintific. Seria B. Stiinte Medicale

Acad Repub Pop Rom Bul Stiint Sect Biol Stiinte Agric — Academia Republicii Populare Romine. Buletin Stiintific. Sectia de Biologie si Stiinte Agricole

Acad Repub Pop Rom Bul Stiint Sect Biol Stiinte Agric Ser Zool — Academia Republicii Populare Romine. Buletin Stiintific. Sectia de Biologie si Stiinte Agricole. Seria Zoologie

Acad Repub Pop Rom Bul Stiint Sect Geol Geogr — Academia Republicii Populare Romine. Buletin Stiintific. Sectia de Geologie si Geografie

Acad Repub Pop Rom Bul Stiint Sect Stiinte Mat Fiz — Academia Republicii Populare Romine. Buletin Stiintific. Sectia de Stiinte Matematice si Fizice

Acad Repub Pop Rom Bul Stiint Sect Stiinte Med — Academia Republicii Populare Romine. Buletin Stiintific. Sectia de Stiinte Medicale

Acad Repub Pop Rom Bul Stiint Sect Stiinte Teh Chim — Academia Republicii Populare Romine. Buletin Stiintific. Sectiunea de Stiinte Tehnice si Chimice

Acad Repub Pop Rom Bul Stiint Ser Mat Fiz Chim — Academia Republicii Populare Romine. Buletin Stiintific. Seria Matematica, Fizica, Chimie

Acad Repub Pop Rom Bul Stiint Ser Stiinte Med — Academia Republicii Populare Romine. Buletin Stiintific. Seria. Stiinte Medicale

Acad Repub Pop Rom Cen Cercet Metal Stud Cercet Metal — Academia Republicii Populare Romine. Centrul de Cercetari Metalurgice. Studii si Cercetari de Metalurgie

Acad Repub Pop Rom Cent Cercet Metal Stud Cercet Metal — Academia Republicii Populare Romine. Central de Cercetari Metalurgice. Studii si Cercetari de Metalurgie

Acad Repub Pop Rom Fil (Cluj) Stud Cercet Agron — Academia Republicii Populare Romine Filiala (Cluj). Studii si Cercetari de Agronomie

Acad Repub Pop Rom Fil (Cluj) Stud Cercet Biol — Academia Republicii Populare Romine Filiala (Cluj). Studii si Cercetari de Biologie

Acad Repub Pop Rom Fil (Cluj) Stud Cercet Chim — Academia Republicii Populare Romine Filiala (Cluj). Studii si Cercetari de Chimie

Acad Repub Pop Rom Fil (Cluj) Stud Cercet Geol Geogr — Academia Republicii Populare Romine Filiala (Cluj). Studii si Cercetari de Geologie, Geografie

Acad Repub Pop Rom Fil (Cluj) Stud Cercet Mat Fiz — Academia Republicii Populare Romine Filiala (Cluj). Studii si Cercetari de Matematica si Fizica

Acad Repub Pop Rom Fil (Cluj) Stud Cercet Med — Academia Republicii Populare Romine Filiala (Cluj). Studii si Cercetari de Medicina

Acad Repub Pop Rom Fil (Cluj) Stud Cercet Stiint — Academia Republicii Populare Romine Filiala (Cluj). Studii si Cercetari Stiintifice

Acad Repub Pop Rom Fil (Cluj) Stud Cercet Stiint Ser 1 — Academia Republicii Populare Romine Filiala (Cluj). Studii si Cercetari Stiintifice. Seria 1. Stiinte Matematice, Fizice, Chimice, si Tehnice

Acad Repub Pop Rom Fil (Cluj) Stud Cercet Stiint Ser 2 — Academia Republicii Populare Romine Filiala (Cluj). Studii si Cercetari Stiintifice. Seria 2. Stiinte Biologice, Agricole, si Medicale

Acad Repub Pop Rom Fil Iasi Stud Cercet Stiint — Academia Republicii Populare Romine. Filiala Iasi. Studii si Cercetari Stiintifice

Acad Repub Pop Rom Fil (Iasi) Stud Cercet Stiint Chim — Academia Republicii Populare Romine. Filiala (Iasi). Studii si Cercetari Stiintifice. Chimie

Acad Repub Pop Rom Fil (Iasi) Stud Cercet Stiint Med — Academia Republicii Populare Romine. Filiala (Iasi). Studii si Cercetari Stiintifice. Medicina

Acad Repub Pop Rom Fil Iasi Stud Cercet Stiint Ser 1 — Academia Republicii Populare Romine Filiala (Iasi). Studii si Cercetari Stiintifice. Seria 1. Stiinte Matematice, Fizice, Chimice, si Tehnice

Acad Repub Pop Rom Fil (Iasi) Stud Cercet Stiint Ser 2 — Academia Republicii Populare Romine Filiala (Iasi). Studii si Cercetari Stiintifice. Seria 2. Stiinte Biologice, Medicale, si Agricole

Acad Repub Pop Rom Inst Fiz At Rep — Academia Republicii Populare Romine. Institutul de Fizica Atomica Reports

Acad Repub Pop Rom Stud Cercet Biochim — Academia Republicii Populare Romine. Institutul de Biochimie. Studii si Cercetari de Biochimie

Acad Repub Pop Rom Stud Cercet Biol Ser Biol Anim — Academia Republicii Populare Romine. Studii si Cercetari de Biologie. Seria Biologie Animala

Acad Repub Pop Rom Stud Cercet Biol Ser Biol Veg — Academia Republicii Populare Romine. Studii si Cercetari de Biologie. Seria Biologie Vegetala

Acad Repub Pop Rom Stud Cercet Chim — Academia Republicii Populare Romine. Studii si Cercetari de Chimice

Acad Repub Pop Rom Stud Cercet Energ — Academia Republicii Populare Romine. Institutul de Energetica. Studii si Cercetari Energetica

Acad Repub Pop Rom Stud Cercet Energ Ser A — Academia Republicii Populare Romine. Institutul de Energetica. Studii si Cercetari Energetica. Serie A. Energetica Generala si Electroenergetica

Acad Repub Pop Rom Stud Cercet Energ Ser B — Academia Republicii Populare Romine. Institutul de Energetica. Studii si Cercetari Energetica. Serie B. Termoenergetica si Utilizarea Energetica a Combustibililor

Acad Repub Pop Rom Stud Cercet Fiz — Academia Republicii Populare Romine. Institutul de Fizica Atomica si Institutulde Fizica. Studii si Cercetari de Fizica

Acad Repub Pop Rom Stud Cercet Fiziol — Academia Republicii Populare Romine. Institutul de Fiziologie Normala si Patologica Dr. D. Danielolpolu. Studii si Cercetari de Fiziologie

Acad Repub Pop Rom Stud Cercet Geol — Academia Republicii Populare Romine. Studii si Cercetari de Geologie

Acad Repub Pop Rom Stud Cercet Mec Apl — Academia Republicii Populare Romine. Institutul de Energetica. Studii si Cercetari de Mecanica Aplicata

Acad Repub Pop Rom Stud Cercet Med Interna — Academia Republicii Populare Romine. Institutul de Medicina Interna. Studii si Cercetari de Medicina Interna

Acad Repub Pop Rom Stud Cercet Stiint Ser Stiinte Med — Academia Republicii Populare Romine. Studii si Cercetari Stiintifice. Seria Stiinte Medicina

Acad Repub Pop Rom Stud Cercet Stiint Ser Stiint Med — Academia Republicii Populare Romine. Studii si Cercetari Stiintifice. Seria Stiinte Medicina

Acad Repub Soc Rom Inst Fiz At Rep — Academia Republicii Socialiste Romania. Institutul de Fizica Atomica Reports

Acad Repub Soc Rom Mem Sect Stiint — Academia Republicii Socialiste Romania. Memoriile Sectiilor Stiintifice

Acad Rev — Academy Review

Acad Rev Calif Acad Periodontol — Academy Review. California Academy of Periodontology

Acad R Med Belg Bull — Academie Royale de Medecine de Belgique. Bulletin

Acad R Med Belg Bull Mem — Academie Royale de Medecine de Belgique. Bulletin et Memoires

Acad R Med Belg Mem — Academie Royale de Medecine de Belgique. Memoires

Acad Romana Mem Sect Sti — Academia Romana. Memoriile Sectiunei Stiintifice

Acad Roy Belg Bull Cl Sci — Academie Royale de Belgique. Bulletin. Classe des Sciences

Acad Roy Belg Cl Sci Mem Collect 8o — Academie Royale de Belgique. Classe des Sciences. Memoires. Collection in Octavo

Acad Roy Belg Cl Sci Mem Coll in-8 — Academie Royale de Belgique. Classe des Sciences. Memoires. Collection in Octavo

Acad Roy De Med De Belg Bul — Academie Royale de Medecine de Belgique. Bulletin

Acad Roy Sci Bordeaux Seance Publique — Academie Royale des Sciences. Belles-Lettres et Arts de Bordeaux. Seance Publique

Acad Roy Sci Colon Brussels Cl Sci Tech Mem Collect 8 — Academie Royale des Sciences Coloniales (Brussels). Classe des Sciences Techniques. Memoires. Collection in 8

Acad Roy Sci O-Mer B — Academie Royale des Sciences d'Outre-Mer. Bulletin des Seances

Acad Roy Sci Outre-Mer Bul Seances — Academie Royale des Sciences d'Outre-Mer. Bulletin des Seances

Acad Roy Sci Outre Mer Cl Sci Tech Mem 8 Brussels — Academie Royale des Sciences d'Outre-Mer. Classe des Sciences Techniques. Memoires in 8 (Brussels)

Acad R Sci Colon (Brussels) Bull Seances — Academie Royale des Sciences Coloniales (Brussels). Bulletin des Seances

Acad R Sci Colon (Brussels) Cl Sci Nat Med Mem Collect — Academie Royale des Sciences Coloniales (Brussels). Classe des Sciences Naturelles et Medicales. Memoires. Collection in Octavo

Acad R Sci Lett B-Arts Belg Cl Sci Bull — Academie Royale des Sciences, des Lettres, et des Beaux-Arts de Belgique. Classe des Sciences. Bulletin

Acad R Sci Outre-Mer (Brussels) Bull Seances — Academie Royale des Sciences d'Outre-Mer (Brussels). Bulletin des Seances

Acad R Sci Outre-Mer Bull — Academie Royale des Sciences d'Outre-Mer. Bulletin des Seances

Acad Rum Peoples Repub Inst At Phys Rep — Academy. Rumanian People's Republic. Institute of Atomic Physics Report

Acad Sci Agric For Bull (Bucharest) — Academie des Sciences Agricoles et Forestieres. Bulletin (Bucharest)

Acad Sci Artium Slov Cl 3 Math Phys Tech Diss Ser A — Academia Scientiarum et Artium Slovenica. Classis 3. Mathematica, Physica, Technica. Dissertationes. Series A. Mathematica, Physica, Chemica

Acad Sci Belg Bul Cl Beaux-Arts — Academie Royale de Belgique. Bulletin. Classe des Beaux-Arts

Acad Sci Belg Bul Cl Lett — Academie Royale de Belgique. Bulletin. Classe des Lettres et des Sciences Morales et Politiques

Acad Sci Belg Bul Cl Sci — Academie Royale de Belgique. Bulletin. Classe des Sciences

Acad Sci Belg Mem 8 Cl Lett — Academie Royale de Belgique. Memoires. Classe des Lettres et des Sciences Morales et Politiques. Collection in Octavo

Acad Sci Belg Mem 8 Cl Sci — Academie Royale de Belgique. Memoires. Classe des Sciences. Collection in Octavo

Acad Sci B Lett & A Besancon Prog Verbaux & Mem — Academie des Sciences, Belles-Lettres, et Arts de Besancon. Progres-Verbaux et Memoires

Acad Sci Colon CR Seanc — Academie des Sciences Coloniales. Comptes Rendus des Seances

Acad Sci CR Seances Ser 2 — Academie des Sciences. Comptes Rendus des Seances. Serie 2. Mecanique-Physique, Chimie, Sciences de l'Univers, Sciences de la Terre

Acad Sci CR Seances Suppl Ser 123 — Academie des Sciences. Comptes Rendus des Seances. Supplement aux Series 1-2-3

Acad Sci CR Seances Vie Acad — Academie des Sciences. Comptes Rendus des Seances. Vie Academique

Acad Sci CR Ser 2 — Academie des Sciences. Comptes Rendus. Serie 2. Mecanique, Physique, Chimie, Sciences de l'Univers, Sciences de la Terre

Acad Sci CR Ser 3 — Academie des Sciences. Comptes Rendus. Serie 3. Sciences de la Vie

Acad Sci CR Ser Gen Vie Sci — Academie des Sciences. Comptes Rendus. Serie Generale. La Vie des Sciences

Acad Scient Hung Acta Geod Geophys Montan — Academia Scientiarum Hungarica. Acta Geodaetica, Geophysica, et Montanistica

Acad Scient Hung Acta Hist — Academia Scientiarum Hungarica. Acta Historica

Acad Scient Hung Acta Lit — Academia Scientiarum Hungarica. Acta Litteraria

Acad Scient Hung Acta Microbiol — Academia Scientiarum Hungarica. Acta Microbiologica

Acad Scient Hung Act Ant — Academia Scientiarum Hungarica. Acta Antiqua

Acad Scient Hung Acta Oecon — Academia Scientiarum Hungarica. Acta Oeconomica

Acad Sci Hung Act Bot — Academia Scientiarum Hungarica. Acta Botanica

Acad Sci Fenn Ann Ser A-III Geol-Geogr — Academia Scientiarum Fennicae. Annales. Series A-III (Geologica-Geographica)

Acad Sci Inscriptions B L Toulouse Mem — Academie des Sciences. Inscriptions et Belles-Lettres de Toulouse. Memoires

Acad Sci Lith SSR Math Trans — Academy of Sciences of the Lithuanian SSR. Mathematical Transactions

Acad Sci Paris CR — Academie des Sciences. Paris. Comptes Rendus

Acad Sci (Paris) CR Ser B — Academie des Sciences (Paris). Comptes Rendus Hebdomadaires des Seances. Serie B. Sciences Physiques

Acad Sci (Paris) CR Ser C — Academie des Sciences (Paris). Comptes Rendus Hebdomadaires des Seances. Serie C. Sciences Chimiques

Acad Sci (Paris) CR Ser D — Academie des Sciences (Paris). Comptes Rendus Hebdomadaires des Seances. Serie D. Sciences Naturelles

Acad Sci St Louis Trans — Academy of Science of St. Louis. Transactions

Acad Sci Toulouse Mem — Academie des Sciences, Inscriptions, et Belles-Lettres de Toulouse. Memoires

Acad Sci USSR — Academic Science USSR

Acad Sci USSR Dokl Earth Sci Sec — Doklady Academy of Sciences of the USSR. Earth Science Sections

Acad Sci USSR Math Notes — Academy of Sciences of the USSR. Mathematical Notes

Acad Serbe Sci Arts Bull Cl Sci Math Nat Sci Nat — Academie Serbe des Sciences et des Arts. Bulletin. Classe des Sciences Mathematiques et Naturelles. Sciences Naturelles

Acad Serbe Sci Arts Bull Cl Sci Med — Academie Serbe des Sciences et des Arts. Bulletin. Classe des Sciences Medicales

Acad Serbe Sci Arts Cl Sci Med Glas — Academie Serbe des Sciences et des Arts. Classe des Sciences Medicales. Glas

Acad Serbe Sci Arts Cl Sci Nat Math Glas — Academie Serbe des Sciences et des Arts. Classe des Sciences Naturelles et Mathematiques. Glas

Acad Serbe Sci et Arts (Glas) Cl Sci Tech — Academie Serbe des Sciences et des Arts (Glas). Classe des Sciences Techniques

Acad Serb Sci Arts Classe Sci Math Nat (Glas) — Academie Serbe des Sciences et des Arts. Classe des Sciences Mathematiques et Naturelles (Glas)

Acad Sin Inst Bot Annu Rep — Academia Sinica. Institute of Botany. Annual Report

Acad Sin Inst Vertebr Palaeontol Palaeoanthropol Mem — Academia Sinica. Institute of Vertebrate Palaeontology and Palaeoanthropology. Memoir

Acad Sin Inst Zool Monogr Ser — Academia Sinica. Institute of Zoology. Monograph Series

Acad Sin Mem Inst Chem — Academia Sinica. Memoirs. Institute of Chemistry

Acad Sin Mem Natl Res Inst Chem — Academia Sinica. Memoirs. National Research Institute of Chemistry

Acad Sin Nanjing Inst Geol Palaeontol Mem — Academia Sinica. Nanjing Institute of Geology and Palaeontology. Memoirs

Acad Soc Lorraines Sci — Academie et Societe Lorraines des Sciences

Acad Soc Lorraines Sci Bull — Academie and Societe Lorraines des Sciences. Bulletin

Acad Soc Repub Rom Inst At Phys Rep — Academy. Socialist Republic Romania. Institute of Atomic Physics Report

Acad Spectrum — Academie Spectrum. Berliner Journal fuer den Wissenschaftler

Acad Stiinte Agric Silvice Bul Inf — Academia de Stiinte Agricole si Silvice. Buletinul Informativ

Acad (Syr) — Academy (Syracuse)

Acad Tcheque Sci Bull Int Cl Sci Math Nat Med — Academie Tcheque des Sciences. Bulletin International. Classe des Sciences Mathematiques et Naturelles, et de la Medecine

Acad Ther — Academic Therapy

Acad Therapy — Academic Therapy

ACAE — Actes. Congres International des Sciences Anthropologiques et Ethnologiques

ACAE — Annales. Cercle Archeologique d'Enghien

ACAEA — Acta Anaesthesiologica

ACAEAS — Acta Anaesthesiologica

ACAGAY — Acta Agronomica

ACAHA — Acta Chirurgica. Academiae Scientiarum Hungaricae

ACAHE7 — Czechoslovak Academy of Sciences. Institute of Landscape Ecology. Section of Hydrobiology. Annual Report

ACA J Chiropr — American Chiropractic Association. Journal of Chiropractic

ACALAF — Acta Allergologica

ACALDI — Acta Alimentaria

ACAM — Annales. Cercle Archeologique de Mons

A Cambr — Archaeologia Cambrenses

AcAn — Acta Antiqua. Academiae Scientiarum Hungaricae

ACan — Annee Canonique

A Canada — Arts Canada

A C Anal — Annales de Chimie Analytique Appliquee a l'Industrie, a l'Agriculture, a la Pharmacie, et a la Biologie

ACANDO — Acta Anthropogenetica

AC & SJ — Australian Conveyancer and Solicitors' Journal

ACAO — Alaska Construction and Oil

ACAPW — Annales. Cercle Archeologique du Pays de Waes

Ac Ar — Acta Archaeologica

ACAR — Acta Arctica

A Car — Analecta Cartusiana

Ac Arch — Acta Archaeologica

Ac Arch (Ljub) — Acta Archaeologica (Ljubljana)

ACARCZ — Acta Arctica

A Card — Acta Cardiologica

Acarol — Acarologia

Acarol Newsl — Acarology Newsletter

Acarol Proc Int Congr Acarol — Acarology. Proceedings. International Congress of Acarology

Ac As — Acta Asiatica

ACAS — Chinese Art Society of America. Archives

ACASA — Chinese Art Society of America. Archives

ACATA5 — Acta Anatomica

A Catala — Art Catala

A Catedra F Suarez — Anales. Catedra Francisco Suarez

ACB — Accounting and Business Research

AcB — Acta Baltica

ACB — Australian Casemix Bulletin

ACB — Australian Computer Bulletin

ACBCA — Acta Crystallographica. Section B. Structural Crystallography and Crystal Chemistry

Ac Belg B — Academie Royale de Belgique. Bulletin

Ac Bibl — Accademie e Biblioteche d'Italia. Annali. Direzione Generale. Accademie e Biblioteche

ACBLF Bul — Association Canadienne des Bibliothecaires de Langue Francaise. Bulletin

ACBO — Acta Borealia

ACBOBU — Annals of Clinical Biochemistry

ACBPAW — Acta Biologica Paranaense

ACBTDD — Acta Biotechnologica

ACC — Accent

ACC — Accountancy

ACC — Accountant

ACC — Alcuin Club. Collections

ACC — Archiv fuer Urkundenforschung

ACC — Australian Company Law Cases

ACCAA — Acta Cardiologica

Accad Agric Sci Lett Verona Atti Mem — Accademia di Acricoltura Scienze e Lettere di Verona. Atti e Memorie

Accad Agric Torino Ann — Accademia di Agricoltura di Torino. Annali

Accad Bibliot d'Italia — Accademia e Biblioteche d'Italia

Accad Bibl Ital — Accademia e Biblioteche d'Italia

Accad e Bibl Italia — Accademia e Biblioteche d'Italia

Accad Fisiocrit Siena Atti — Accademia dei Fisiocritici in Siena. Atti

Accad Gioenia Sci Nat Catania Atti — Accademia Gioenia di Scienze Naturali in Catania. Atti

Accad Italia Rendi Cl Sci Mor Stor & Filol — Accademia d'Italia, Rendiconti della Classe di Scienze Morali, Storiche e Filologiche

Accad Ital Sci For Ann — Accademia Italiana di Scienze Forestali. Annali

Accad Ital Vite Vino (Siena) Atti — Accademia Italiana della Vite e del Vino (Siena). Atti

Accad Ligure Sci Lett Genoa Atti — Accademia Ligure di Scienze e Lettere. Genoa. Atti

Accad Med — Accademia Medica

Accad Med Chir Di Torino Gior — R. Accademia Medico-Chirurgica di Torino. Giornale

Accad Med Chir Perugia Atti — Accademia Medico-Chirurgica di Perugia. Atti

Accad Med Lomb Atti — Accademia Medica Lombarda. Atti

Accad Naz Agric Ann Italy — Accademia Nazionale di Agricoltura. Annali (Italy)

Accad Naz Ital Entomol Atti Rend — Accademia Nazionale Italiana di Entomologia. Atti. Rendiconti

Accad Naz Lincei Atti Cl Sci Fis Mat e Nat Rend — Atti. Accademia Nazionale dei Lincei. Rendiconti. Classe di Scienze Fisiche, Matematiche, e Naturali

Accad Naz Lincei Atti Cl Sci Fis Mat Nat Rend — Accademia Nazionale dei Lincei. Atti. Classe di Scienze Fisiche, Matematiche, eNaturali. Rendiconti

Accad Naz Lincei Atti Mem Cl Sci Fis Mat Nat Sez 1a — Accademia Nazionale dei Lincei. Atti. Memorie. Classe di Scienze Fisiche, Matematiche, e Naturali. Sezione 1a

Accad Naz Lincei Atti Mem Cl Sci Fis Mat Nat Sez 2a — Accademia Nazionale dei Lincei. Atti. Memorie. Classe di Scienze Fisiche, Matematiche, e Naturali. Sezione 2a

Accad Naz Lincei Atti Mem Cl Sci Fis Mat Nat Sez 3 — Accademia Nazionale dei Lincei. Atti. Memorie. Classe di Scienze Fisiche, Matematiche, e Naturali. Sezione 3

Accad Naz Lincei Cl Sci Fis Mat Nat Atti Rend — Accademia Nazionale dei Lincei. Classe di Scienze Fisiche, Matematiche, e Naturali. Atti. Rendiconti

Accad Naz Lincei Corso Estivo Chim — Accademia Nazionale dei Lincei. Corso Estivo di Chimica

Accad Naz Lincei Quad — Accademia Nazionale dei Lincei. Quaderno

Accad Naz Lincei Rendic Cl Fis Mat Nat — Accademia Nazionale di Lincei. Rendiconti della Classe di Scienze Fisische, Matematiche e Naturali

Accad Naz Sci Lett Arti (Modena) Atti Mem — Accademia Nazionale di Scienze, Lettere, ed Arti (Modena). Atti e Memorie

Accad N Lincei Cl Sci Mor Stor & Filol Rendi — Accademia Nazionale dei Lincei, Classe di Scienze Morali, Storiche e Filologiche. Rendiconti

Accad N Lincei Rendi — Accademie Nazionale dei Lincei. Rendiconti

Accad Pata Sci Lett Arti Collana Accad — Accademia Patavina di Scienze, Lettere, ed Arti. Collana Accademica

Accad Patavina Sci Lett Arti Atti Mem — Accademia Patavina di Scienze, Lettere, ed Arti. Atti e Memorie

Accad Patav Sci Lett Arti Collana Accad — Accademia Patavina di Scienze, Lettere, ed Arti. Collana Accademica

Accad Pontaniana Atti — Accademia Pontaniana. Atti

Accad Pugliese Sci Att Relaz Parte 2 — Accademia Pugliese delle Scienze. Atti e Relazioni. Parte 2. Classe di Scienze Fisiche, Mediche, e Naturali

Accad Sci Fis e Mat Rend — Accademia delle Scienze Fisiche e Matematiche. Rendiconto

Accad Sci Ist Bologna Cl Sci Fis Atti Mem — Accademia delle Scienze. Istituto di Bologna. Classe di Scienze Fisiche. Atti. Memorie

Accad Sci Siena Fisiocrit Atti — Accademia. Scienze di Siena detta de' Fisiocritici. Atti

Accad Sci Torino Atti Cl Sci Fis Mat Nat — Accademia delle Scienze di Torino. Atti. Classe di Scienze Fisiche, Matematiche, e Naturali

Accad Virgiliana Mantova Atti Mem — Accademia Virgiliana di Mantova. Atti e Memorie

Ac Caes Leop N Acta — Nova Acta Physico-Medica Academiae Caes. Leopoldino-Carolinae Naturae Curiosorum

ACCB — Australian Copyright Council. Bulletin

Acc Bus Res — Accounting and Business Research

ACCCA — Acta Cientifica Compostelana

Acc Chem Re — Accounts of Chemical Research

Acc Chem Res — Accounts of Chemical Research

Acc Cient Int — Accion Cientifica International

ACCEL — American College of Cardiology. Extended Learning

Accel Dosim Exper Proc Int Conf Accel Dosim Exper — Accelerator Dosimetry and Experience. Proceedings. International Conference on Accelerator Dosimetry and Experiences

Accel Instrum Annu Workshop — Accelerator Instrumentation. Annual Workshop

Accel Storage Rings — Accelerators and Storage Rings

Acces Hous Bul — Accessible Housing Bulletin

Access Index Little Mag — Access Index to Little Magazines

Access V — Access Video

ACCFC — Ag Chem and Commercial Fertilizer [*Later, Farm Chemicals*]

AccG — Accent Grave

Acc Gar Equip — Accessory and Garage Equipment

Acciaio Inossid — Acciaio Inossidabile

Accid Anal Prev — Accident Analysis and Prevention

Accid Anal Prev (Elmsford NY) — Accident Analysis and Prevention (Elmsford, New York)

Accid Chromosomiques Reprod R Colloq — Accidents Chromosomiques de la Reproduction. Compte-Rendu du Colloque

Accident Anal Prev — Accident Analysis and Prevention

Accident Prevention Bul — Accident Prevention Bulletin

Accid Vasc Cereb Reun Soc Suisse Angiol — Accidents Vasculaires Cerebraux. Diagnostic et Traitement. Reunion de la Societe Suisse d'Angiologie

Ac Cienc Med Habana An — Academia de Ciencias Medicas, Fisicas, y Naturales de la Habana. Annales

Accion Agrar Cuzco — Accion Agraria (Cuzco)

Accion Farm — Accion Farmaceutica

ACCJ Proc Inc Synod Ottawa — Anglican Church of Canada. Journal of Proceedings. Incorporated Synod of the Diocese of Ottawa

Acclim Anim Et Plantes — L'Acclimatation des Animaux et des Plantes

Acc Med (A) — Accion Medica (Argentina)

Acc Med (B) — Accion Medica (Bolivia)

Acc Med (M) — Accion Medica (Mexico)

Acc Naz Linc — Rendiconti. Accademia Nazionale dei Lincei

Acc Naz Linc Mem — Memorie. Accademia Nazionale dei Lincei

Acc Naz Linc Tr — Transunti. Accademia Nazionale dei Lincei

ACCNR — Alaska Climate Center. News and Review

Accomp Oncol — Accomplishments in Oncology

AC Con — Acta Concilii Constanciensis

Accountancy L Rep CCH — Accountancy Law Reports. Commerce Clearing House

Accountants and Secretaries' Educ J — Accountants and Secretaries' Educational Journal

Accountants J — Accountants Journal

Accountants Mag — Accountants Magazine

Account Bus Res — Accounting and Business Research

Account Dig — Accountants Digest

Account Fin — Accounting and Finance

Account Index Suppl — Accountants' Index. Supplement

Accounting and Bus Research — Accounting and Business Research

Accounting R — Accounting Review

Account J — Accountants' Journal

Account Mag — Accountant's Magazine

Account R — Accounting Review

Account Res — Accounting Research

Account Rev — Accounting Review

ACCP — Arquivos. Centro Cultural Portugues

Accredit Qual Assur — Accreditation and Quality Assurance. Journal for Quality, Comparability, and Reliability in Chemical Measurement

Acc Res — Accounting Research

Acc Review — Accounting Review

Acct — Accountants' Journal

Acct & Bus Res — Accounting and Business Research

Acct Chem Res — Accounts of Chemical Research

Acctg Rev — Accounting Review

Accting R — Accounting Review

Acct R — Accounting Review

Accts Sec Educ J — Accountants and Secretaries' Educational Journal

Accumu Vet Index — Accumulative Veterinary Index

ACCV — Anales. Centro de Cultura Valenciana

ACD — Acta Classica. Universitatis Scientiarum Debreceniensis

ACDACX — Australia. Commonwealth Scientific and Industrial Research Organisation. Division of Applied Chemistry. Annual Report

ACDB — Airport Characteristics Data Bank

ACD Bull — ACD [*Association of Canadian Distillers*] Bulletin

ACDF — Annali di Ca'Foscari. Serie Orientale

ACDLAU — Australia. Commonwealth Scientific and Industrial Research Organisation. Division of Land Use Research. Technical Paper

Acdmy Mgt J — Academy of Management. Journal

Acdmy Mgt R — Academy of Management. Review

ACE — Accountancy (England)

ACE — Annales du Commerce Exterieur

ACE — Annals of Public and Cooperative Economy

ACEA Bull — ACEA [*Australian Council for Educational Administration*] Bulletin

Ac Ec — Acta Ecclesiastica

ACEC — Actes. Congres de la Federation International des Associations d'Etudes Classiques

ACEC Rev — ACEC [*Ateliers de Constructions Electriques de Charleroi*] Reviews

ACED — Acta Conciliorum et Epistolae Decretales

ACEELV — Actas do Coloquio de Estudos Etnograficos Dr. Jose Leite de Vasconcelos

ACEF — Acta Entomologica Fennica

ACEHI J/REV ACEDA — Association of Canadian Educators of the Hearing Impaired. Journal/Association Canadienne des Educateurs des Deficients-Auditifs..Revue

ACELB — Actas. Coloquio Internacional de Estudos Luso-Brasileiros

ACENEB — Advances in Clinical Enzymology

Ac Energ — Acero y Energia

ACE News — ACE [*Agricultural Communication in Education*] Newsletter

ACEPC — Preprints of Papers Presented at National Meeting. Division of Environmental Chemistry. American Chemical Society

ACer — Anales Cervantinos

ACER — Annales. Centre d'Etude des Religions

ACERB — Allis-Chalmers Engineering Review

ACER Bull — Australian Council for Educational Research. Bulletin

Acero Energ — Acero y Energia

Acero Energ Numero Espec — Acero y Energia. Numero Especial

ACER Test News — Australian Council for Educational Research. Test News

ACES Bul — ACES [*Association for Comparative Economic Studies*] Bulletin

ACESEQ — Annales de Chirurgie Plastique et Esthetique

ACES Rev — ACES [*Australian Council for Educational Standards*] Review

Acet — Acetylene

AcEt — Acta Ethnographica

Acet J — Acetylene Journal

Acet Light Weld J — Acetylene Lighting and Welding Journal

Acet Weld — Acetylene Welding

Acetylene Gas J — Acetylene-Gas Journal

Acetylene J — Acetylene Journal

Acetylen Wiss Ind — Acetylen in Wissenschaft und Industrie

Acetylen Wiss Ind Beil — Acetylen in Wissenschaft und Industrie. Beilage

Acetylsalicylic Acid New Uses Old Drug Proc Can Conf — Acetylsalicylic Acid. New Uses for an Old Drug. Proceedings. Canadian Conference on Acetylsalicylic Acid. New Uses for an Old Drug

ACF — Accounting and Finance

ACF — Accounting Forum

ACF — Annali di Ca' Foscari

ACF — Annali. Facolta di Lingue e Litterature Straniere di Ca'Foscari

ACF — Annuaire. College de France

ACFA — Anuario. Cuerpo Facultativo de Archiveros, Bibliotecarios, y Arqueologos

ACFAS Assoc Can Fr Av Sci — ACFAS. Association Canadienne Francaise pour l'Avancement des Sciences

ACFBAA — Anales. Academia Nacional de Ciencias Exactas, Fisicas, y Naturales de Buenos Aires

ACFCAD — Annales Universitatis Mariae Curie-Sklodowska. Sectio AA. Physica et Chemia

ACFCBE — Australia. Commonwealth Scientific and Industrial Research Organisation. Division of Fisheries and Oceanography. Circular

ACFF — Annales. Comite Flamand de France

ACFRBP — Australia. Commonwealth Scientific and Industrial Research Organisation. Division of Food Research. Report of Research

ACFS — Anales. Catedra Francisco Suarez

ACFW — Australian Child and Family Welfare

ACFYAB — Acta Fytotechnica

ACGBAF — Acta Horti Gotoburgensis

ACGCBJ — Acta Archaeologica. Academiae Scientiarum Hungaricae

AcGe — Acta Geographica

ACGHAX — Acta Geologica Hispanica

Ac Gioenia Sc Nat Catania B — Accademia Gioenia de Scienze Naturali in Catania. Bollettino delle Sedute

ACGKH — Aichi Gakugei Daigaku Kenkyu Hokoku

ACGLAB — Acta Ginecologica

ACGO Chem Res Commun — ACGO [*Asian Coordinating Group for Chemistry*] Chemical Research Communications

ACGSA — Annales Chirurgiae et Gynaecologiae Fenniae. Supplementum

ACGYA — Annales Chirurgiae et Gynaecologiae Fenniae

A Ch — Annales Chopin

A Ch — Annales de Chimie

A Ch — Antike und Christentum

ACh — Araucaria de Chile

ACHAAH — Acta Haematologica

ACHAD — Documents. American Catholic Historical Association

Achad Leonardi Vinci J Leonardo Stud & Bibliog Vinciana — Achademia Leonardi Vinci. Journal of Leonardo Studies and Bibliography of Vinciana

Achats Entret Mater Ind — Achats et Entretien du Materiel Industriel

Achats et Entretien Mater Ind — Achats et Entretien du Materiel Industriel

ACHCBO — Acta Histochemica et Cytochemica

ACHEMA Jahr — ACHEMA [*Ausstellungs- Tegung fuer Chemisches Apparatewesen*] Jahrbuch

ACHEMA Jahrb — ACHEMA [*Ausstellungetagung fuer Chemisches Apparatewesen. Handbuch*] Jahrbuch

A Chem Scand — Acta Chemica Scandinavica

AcHi — Acta Historica

A Chil — Actes de Chilander

A Chir Belg — Acta Chirurgica Belgica

A Chir It — Acta Chirurgica Italica

A Chir Jug — Acta Chirurgica Jugoslavica

A Chir Plast — Acta Chirurgiae Plasticae

A Chir Scand — Acta Chirurgica Scandinavica

A Ch J — American Chemical Journal

ACHLAG — Acta Historica Leopoldina

ACHMDM — Annales de Chirurgie de la Main

ACH Models Chem — ACH Models in Chemistry

ACHPER Healthy Life J — ACHPER Healthy Lifestyles Journal

ACHR — American Catholic Historical Researches

AchrK — Archiv fuer Christliche Kunst

ACHS — American Catholic Historical Society. Records

ACHS — Anuario Colombiano de Historia Social y de la Cultura

ACHSB — Annales. Cercle Hutois des Sciences et Beaux-Arts

ACHSJ — Australian Catholic Historical Society. Journal

ACHSP — American Catholic Historial Society of Philadelphia. Records

ACHSR — American Catholic Historical Society. Records

Acht Arb Fluess Krist Fluessigkrist Konf Soz Laender — Acht Arbeiten ueber Fluessige Kristalle Fluessigkristall-Konferenz Sozialistischer Laender
ACHVA — Air Conditioning, Heating, and Ventilating
ACI — Advancing the Consumer Interest
ACI — American Council on Consumer Interest. Proceedings
ACi — Analecta Cisterciensia
ACI — Archivio della Cultura Italiana
ACIAC — Actes. Congres International d'Archeologie Chretienne/Atti. Congresso Internaztionale di Archeoogia Cristiana
ACIA CI — Actes du Congresso Internazionale di Archeologia Classica
ACIAm — Actas. Congreso Internacional de Americanistas
ACIAR Proc — ACIAR (Australian Centre for International Agricultural Research) Proceedings
ACIAR Proc Ser — ACIAR (Australian Centre for International Agricultural Research) Proceedings Series
ACIAR Tech Rep — ACIAR (Australian Centre for International Agricultural Research) Technical Reports
ACIBAP — Australia. Commonwealth Scientific and Industrial Research Organisation. Bulletin
ACIC — Atti. Convegno Internazionale per la Pace e la Civita Cristiana
ACIDB — Acta Ciencia Indica
ACIDBW — Acta Ciencia Indica
Acidic Precip Ont Study — Acidic Precipitation in Ontario Study
Acidic Proteins Nucl — Acidic Proteins of the Nucleus
Acidif Res Eval Policy Appl Proc Int Conf M — Acidification Research. Evaluation and Policy Applications. Proceedings. International Conference. Maastricht
Acid Mag — Acid Magazine
Acid Open Hearth Res Assoc Bull — Acid Open Hearth Research Association. Bulletin
Acid Res Neth — Acidification Research in the Netherlands. Final Report. Dutch Priority Programme on Acidification
Acid Sulphate Soils Proc Int Symp — Acid Sulphate Soils. Proceedings. International Symposium on Acid Sulphate Soils
ACIELB — Actas do Coloquio Internacional de Estudos Luso-Brasileiros
Aciers Spec — Aciers Speciaux
Aciers Spec Leurs Emplois — Aciers Speciaux et Leurs Emplois
Aciers Spec Met Alliages — Aciers Speciaux, Metaux, et Alliages
Aciers Spec Monogr Tech — Aciers Speciaux. Monographies Techniques
Aciers Spec Usinabilite Amelior Jour Metall Hisp Fr — Aciers Speciaux a Usinabilite Amelioree. Journees Metallurgiques Hispano-Francaises
ACIFA — Analele Stiintifice ale Universitatii Al. I. Cuza din Iasi. Sectiunea 1. Matematica, Fizica, Chimie
ACIG — Atti. X Congresso Internazionale di Geografia
ACI J — ACI [*American Concrete Institute*] Journal
ACILFR — Actas. Congreso Internacional de Linguistica y Filologia Romanicas
ACI Mater J — ACI (American Concrete Institute) Materials Journal
Ac Imp Lyon Cl Sc Mem — Academie Imperiale des Sciences, Belles-Lettres, et Arts de Lyon. Classe des Sciences. Memoires
ACIN — Actes/Rapports. Congres International de Numismatique
A Cinema — Art Cinematographique
ACIO — Actes. Congres International des Orientalistes
ACI Proc — ACI (American Concrete Institute) Proceedings
ACI Publ — ACI (American Concrete Institute) Publication
Acireale Ac At — Atti e Rendiconti dell' Accademia di Scienze, Lettere, e Arti dei Zelanti. Studio di Acireale
ACISA — Acts. International Congress of Anthropological and Ethnological Sciences
ACISE — Atti. Convegno Internazionale di Studie Etiopici
ACIS Newsletter — American Committee for Irish Studies. Newsletter
ACISR — Atti. Congresso Internazionale di Studi Romanzi
ACIst — Analecta Cisterciensia
ACI Struct J — ACI (American Concrete Institute) Structural Journal
ACIT News/Bu CATP — Associate Committee on Instructional Technology. Newsletter/Bulletin. ComiteAssocie de Technologie Pedagogique
ACJ — Alternative Criminology Journal
ACJ — Amcham Journal (Manila)
ACJ — Australian Commercial Journal
ACJC — Auxilia ad Codicem Juris Canonici
ACJD — Abhandlungen zum Christlich-Juedischen Dialog
ACJ (Mad Pr) — Accident Compensation Journal
ACK — Archiv fuer Christliche Kunst
ACI — Acta Classica
AcL — Acta Linguistica
ACL — Alberta Case Locator
ACL — Ambito Cuaderno Literario
ACL — Amsterdam Classics in Linguistics
ACI — Antiquite Classique
ACL — Australian Chess Lore
ACL — Australian College Libraries
ACL — Australian Current Law
ACLAN — American Comparative Literature Association. Newsletter
AClass — Acta Classica. Verhandelinge van die Klassieke Vereniging van Suid-Afrika
ACL Bull — Australian Current Law Bulletin
ACLC — Australian Company Law Cases
ACLCA9 — Advances in Clinical Chemistry
ACICr — Antichita Classica e Cristiana
ACLD — Australian Current Law Digest
ACLD-A — Architectural Design
AcLg — Acta Linguistica
AcLi — Acta Linguistica
A Cl L — Amsterdam Classics in Linguistics
AcLLB — Academie Royale de Langue et de Litterature Francaise de Belgique. Bulletin
ACL MIT Press Ser Nat Lang Process — ACL-MIT Press Series in Natural Language Processing

ACLPDH — Advances in Clinical Pharmacology
ACLR — Australian Company Law Reports
ACLR — Australian Construction Law Reporter
ACLR — Australian Current Law Review
ACLRBL — Annals of Clinical Research
ACL Rev — Australian Current Law Review
ACLS — American Council of Learned Societies
ACLSC — Annals of Clinical and Laboratory Science
ACLSN — American Council of Learned Societies. Newsletter
ACLS Newsl — ACLS [*American Council of Learned Societies*] Newsletter
ACLSPOL — American Council of Learned Societies. Program in Oriental Languages. Publications
ACLU Leg Act Bull — American Civil Liberties Union. Legislative Action Bulletin
ACLU Leg Action Bull — American Civil Liberties Union. Legislative Action Bulletin
ACLZAA — Anais. Congresso Latino-Americano de Zoologia
ACM — Accountant's Magazine
Ac M — Acta Musicologica
ACM — Annales. Congregation de la Mission
ACM — Annals. Carnegie Museum
ACM — Anuarul Comisiunii Monumentelor Istorice. Sectia pentru Transilvania
ACM (Arq Catarinenses Med) Ed Cult — ACM (Arquivos Catarinenses de Medicina) Edicao Cultural
AcMB — Acta Medica. Magyar Tudomanyos Akademia (Budapest)
ACM Comput Surv — ACM Computing Surveys
ACM Comput Surveys — Association for Computing Machinery Computing Surveys
ACM Disting Diss — ACM Distinguished Dissertations
ACM Doctor Diss Awards — ACM Doctoral Dissertation Awards
Ac Mex Cienc An — Academia Mexicana de Ciencias Exactas, Fisicas, y Naturales. Anuario
ACM Guide Comput Lit — ACM [*Association for Computing Machinery*] Guide to Computing Literature
ACMI — Anuarul Comisiunii Monumentelor Istorice. Sectia Pentru Transilvania
ACMIC — Application of Computer Methods in the Mineral Industry. Proceedings of the International Symposium
ACM Lett Program Lang Syst — ACM Letters on Programming Languages and Systems
ACMMBB — Annals. College of Medicine
ACMODJ — Acta Morphologica
AcMoz — Acta Mozartiana
ACMPD — Annual Conference on Materials for Coal Conversion and Utilization. Proceedings
ACM Proc — ACM [*Association for Computing Machinery*] National Conference Proceedings
ACM Proc Nat Conf — Association for Computing Machinery. Proceedings of National Conference
ACMT — Anuarul Comisiunii Monumentelor Istorice. Sectia Pentru Transilvania
ACMT — Atti. Civici Musei di Storia ed Arte di Trieste
ACMTBW — Museo "Felipe Poey." Academia de Ciencias de Cuba. Trabajos de Divulgacion
ACM T Inf S — ACM [*Association for Computing Machinery*] Transactions on Information Systems
ACM Tr — Anuarul Comisiunii Monumentelor Istorice. Sectia Pentru Transilvania
ACM Trans — ACM [*Association for Computing Machinery*] Transactions
ACM Trans Comp — ACM [*Association for Computing Machinery*] Transactions on Computer Systems
ACM Trans Comput Syst — ACM [*Association for Computing Machinery*] Transactions on Computer Systems
ACM Trans Database Syst — ACM [*Association for Computing Machinery*] Transactions on Database Systems
ACM Trans Database Systems — ACM [*Association for Computing Machinery*] Transactions on Database Systems
ACM Trans Graphics — ACM [*Association for Computing Machinery*] Transactions on Graphics
ACM Trans Inf Syst — ACM Transactions on Information Systems
ACM Trans Math Softw — ACM [*Association for Computing Machinery*] Transactions on Mathematical Software
ACM Trans Math Software — ACM [*Association for Computing Machinery*] Transactions on Mathematical Software
ACM Trans Model Comput Simul — ACM Transactions on Modeling and Computer Simulation
ACM Trans Off Inf Syst — ACM [*Association for Computing Machinery*] Transactions on Office Information Systems
ACM Trans OIS — ACM [*Association for Computing Machinery*] Transactions on Office Information Systems
ACM Trans Program Lang Syst — ACM [*Association for Computing Machinery*] Transactions on Programming Languages and Systems
ACM Trans Software Eng Methodol — ACM Transactions on Software Engineering and Methodology
AcMu — Acta Musicologica
AcMus — Acta Musicologica
ACMVA3 — Acta Medica Venezolana
ACMYAC — Acta Mycologica
ACNAAD — Anales. Academia Chilena de Ciencias Naturales
ACNAC — Atti. Congresso Nazionale di Archeologia Cristiana
Ac Naz Linc A — Atti. Accademia Nazionale dei Lincei
Ac Naz Linc Mem — Memorie. Accademia Nazionale dei Lincei
Ac Naz Linc Ren — Rendiconti. Accademia Nazionale dei Lincei
ACNEAP — Acta Neurovegetativa
ACNI — Acta Naturalia Islandica
ACNLAC — Acta Neurologica
ACNP — Archivos de Criminologia, Neuropsiquiatria, y Disciplinas Conexas
ACNRA — Archivum Chirurgicum Neerlandicum
ACNRCW — Advances in Cyclic Nucleotide Research
ACNREY — Advances in Cyclic Nucleotide and Protein Phosphorylation Research

ACNSA — Activitas Nervosa Superior
Ac N Sc Phila J — Academy of Natural Sciences of Philadelphia. Journal
Ac N Sc Phila Min G Sec Pr — Academy of Natural Sciences of Philadelphia. Mineralogical and Geological Section. Proceedings
Ac N Sc Phila Pr — Academy of Natural Sciences of Philadelphia. Proceedings
Ac Nt C N Acta — Nova Acta Physico-Medica Academiae Caes. Leopoldino-Carolinae Naturae Curiosorum
ACNUA5 — Acta Neurochirurgica
ACo — Acta Comeniana
ACO — Acta Conciliorum Oecumenicorum
ACO — Acta Oeconomica
Ac O — Acta Orientalia. Societatis Orientales. Danica, Finlandica, Norvegica, Suecica
ACO — Actes. Congres International des Orientalistes
Ac OB — Acta Orientalia. Magyar Tudomanyos Akademia
ACOE — Annals of Community-Oriented Education
ACOED — Actualite, Combustibles, Energie
ACOFAR — Agrupacion de Cooperativas Farmaceuticas
ACOG Info — ACOG [*American College of Obstetricians and Gynecologists*] Information
ACOID — Alaska Construction and Oil
A Colombia — Arte en Colombia
ACom — Acta Comeniana
ACOMD — Ars Combinatoria
ACOME — Archivum Combustionis
A Concr — Art Concret
A Concr — Arte Concreta
A Cond Pon Chauss — Annales des Conducteurs des Ponts et Chaussees
A Cons Arts Et Met — Annales du Conservatoire des Arts et Metiers
A Contemp — Art Contemporain
ACOPAT — Acta Ophthalmologica
ACOPD — ASEE [*American Society for Engineering Education*] Annual Conference Proceedings
Acor — Acoreana
AcOr — Acta Orientalia
AcOr(B) — Acta Orientalia. Academiae Scientiarum Hungaricae
Ac Or (H) — Acta Orientalia (Hungary)
AcOr(K) — Acta Orientalia (Copenhagen)
AcOr(L) — Acta Orientalia (Leiden)
ACOSB — Annales Camaldulenses Ordinis Sancti Benedicti
ACOSS Q — ACOSS [*Australian Council of Social Service*] Quarterly
Acoust Abstr — Acoustics Abstracts
Acoust and Noise Control Can — Acoustics and Noise Control in Canada
Acoust Australia — Acoustic Australia
Acoust Bull — Acoustics Bulletin
Acoust Hologr — Acoustical Holography
Acoustical Soc Am — Acoustical Society of America. Journal
Acoustics Abs — Acoustics Abstracts
Acoust Imaging — Acoustical Imaging
Acoust Lett — Acoustics Letters
Acoust Noise Control Can — Acoustics and Noise Control in Canada
Acoust Phys Transl Akust Zh — Acoustical Physics (Translation of Akusticheskii Zhurhal)
Acoust Soc Am J — Acoustical Society of America. Journal
Acoust Soc India J — Acoustical Society of India. Journal
Acoust Ultrason Abstr — Acoustics and Ultrasonics Abstracts
AcP — Acta Poloniae Historica
ACP — Anales Cientificos Paraguayos
ACP — Archiv fuer die Civilistische Praxis
ACP — Australian Company Law and Practice
ACPAP — American Catholic Philosophical Association. Proceedings
ACP Appl Cardiopulm Pathophysiol — ACP. Applied Cardiopulmonary Pathophysiology
ACPBAQ — Advances in Comparative Physiology and Biochemistry
ACPCD — Annual Reports on the Progress of Chemistry. Section C. Physical Chemistry
ACPCDW — Annual Reports on the Progress of Chemistry. Section C. Physical Chemistry
ACPC For — ACPC [*Australian Crime Prevention Council*] Forum
ACPCQJ — Australian Crime Prevention Council. Quarterly Journal
ACPDA — Acta Paedopsychiatrica
AcPe — Action et Pensee
ACPE — Australian Chemical Processing and Engineering
ACPFM — Amitie Charles Peguy. Feuillets Mensuels
A C Phm — Annalen der Chemie und Pharmacie
ACP J Club — ACP [*American College of Physicians*] Journal Club
ACPMA — Actualites Pharmacologiques
ACPR — American Clinical Products Review
AcPs — Acta Psychologica
ACPS/B — Boletin. Academia de Ciencias Politicas y Sociales
ACPTC Proc Comb Cent East West Reg Meet — ACPTC (Association of College Professors of Textiles and Clothing) Proceedings.Combined Central, Eastern, and Western Regional Meetings
ACQ — American Catholic Quarterly
ACQ — American Church Quarterly
Acq Divest — Acquisition/Divestiture Weekly Report
Acq Month — Acquisitions Monthly
ACQR — American Catholic Quarterly Review
Acqua Agric Ig Ind — Acqua nell' Agricoltura, nell' Igiene e nell' Industria
Acqua Campi Abit — Acqua nei Campi e nell' Abitato
Acqua Gas — Acqua e Gas
Acqua Ind — Acqua Industriale
Acqua Ind Inquinamento — Acqua Industriale. Inquinamento
Acque Bonif Costruz — Acque, Bonifiche, Costruzione
Acque Gass — Acque Gassate

Acque Trasp — Acque e Trasporti
Acquired Immune Defic Syndr Res — Acquired Immune Deficiency Syndrome Research
Acquis Chir Infant — Acquisitions en Chirurgie Infantile
Acquis Med Recent — Acquisitions Medicales Recentes
Acquis Tracking Pointing — Acquisition, Tracking, and Pointing
ACR — Accounting Review
Acr — Acropole. Revue du Monde Hellenique
ACR — American Choral Review
ACR — American Classical Review
ACr — Arte Cristiana
ACR — Australasian Catholic Record
ACR — Australian and New Zealand Conveyancing Report
ACR — Australian Coin Review
ACR — Australian Criminal Reports
ACRAAX — Acta Radiologica
Ac R Belg — Memoires. Academie Royale de Belgique
ACRDA — Acta Radiologica. Diagnosis
Acres Aust — Acres Australia
ACRHDN — Acta Rhumatologica
Acrid Abstr — Acridological Abstracts
A Crim R — Australian Criminal Reports
A Crist — Arte Cristiana
A Crit — Art Criticism
ACRL C & RL — ACRL [*Association of College and Research Libraries*] College and ResearchLibraries
ACRL Monogr — Association of College and Research Libraries. Monographs
Acrolein Am Ed — Acrolein (American Edition)
Acrolein Ger Ed — Acrolein (German Edition)
Acros Org Acta — Acros Organics Acta
Across Board (NY) — Across the Board. Conference Board (New York)
Across the Bd — Across the Board
ACRSA — Annales Canonicorum Regularium S. Augustini
Acrylic Fiber Technol Appl — Acrylic Fiber Technology and Applications
ACS — Ancient Culture and Society
ACS — Arab Culture Series
ACS — Asian Cultural Studies
ACSB — Appraisal. Children's Science Books
ACSBA — American Ceramic Society. Bulletin
ACSCC — Australian Consumer Sales and Credit Law Cases
Ac Sc Kansas City Tr — Academy of Science of Kansas City. Transactions
Ac Sc (Paris) C R — Academie des Sciences (Paris). Comptes Rendus
Ac Sc Sioux City Pr — Academy of Science and Letters of Sioux City, Iowa. Proceedings
Ac Sc St L Tr — Academy of Science of St. Louis. Transactions
ACS DGRF — ACS [*American Chemical Society*] Directory of Graduate Research
ACS Div Environ Chem Prepr — American Chemical Society. Division of Environmental Chemistry. Preprints
ACS Div Fuel Chem Prepr — American Chemical Society. Division of Fuel Chemistry. Preprints
ACS Div Pet Chem Prepr — American Chemical Society. Division of Petroleum Chemistry. Preprints
ACS Div Polym Mater Sci Eng Proc — ACS [*American Chemical Society*] Division of Polymeric Materials Science and Engineering. Proceedings
ACSFC — Atti. Convegno di Studi Filosofici Cristiani
ACSMA6 — Archivio Stomatologico
ACS Monogr — ACS [*American Chemical Society*] Monograph
ACS Natl Meet Abstr Pap — American Chemical Society. National Meeting. Abstracts of Papers
ACS Org Coat Appl Polym Sci Proc — ACS (American Chemical Society) Organic Coatings and Applied Polymer Science. Proceedings
ACS Org Coat Plast Chem — ACS (American Chemical Society) Organic Coatings and Plastics Chemistry
ACSPCH — Australia. Commonwealth Scientific and Industrial Research Organisation. ForestProducts Laboratory. Division of Applied Chemistry. Technological Paper
ACSPD — Aciers Speciaux
ACSPDI — Aciers Speciaux
ACSR — American Catholic Sociological Review
ACSS — Analytical Chemistry Symposia Series
ACSS — Congres des Societes de Philosophie de Langue Francaise. Actes. L'Homme et l'Histoire. Societe Strasbourgeoise de Philosophie
ACSSBP — Annales de Chirurgie Thoracique et Cardio-Vasculaire
ACSSCQ — AIChE [*American Institute of Chemical Engineers*] Symposium Series
ACSSDR — Analytical Chemistry Symposia Series
ACS Single Art Announce — ACS [*American Chemical Society*] Single Article Announcement
ACS Symp Kinet Thermodyn Lumping Multicompon Mixtures — ACS Symposium on Kinetic and Thermodynamic Lumping of Multicomponent Mixtures
ACS Symp S — ACS [*American Chemical Society*] Symposium Series
ACS Symp Ser — ACS [*American Chemical Society*] Symposium Series
ACS Symp Ser Am Chem Soc — ACS Symposium Series. American Chemical Society
ACSTBS — Australia. Commonwealth Scientific and Industrial Research Organisation. Soil Mechanics Section. Technical Memorandum
ACSTDU — Advances in Cereal Science and Technology
ACSTN — ACST [*Alaska Council on Science and Technology*] Notes
ACSU — Atti. Colloquio Slavistico di Uppsala
ACSUB — Annals of Clinical Research. Supplement
ACSUC — Atti. Convegno di Studi su Umanesimo e Cristianesimo
ACSVAX — Anales. Casa de Salud Valdecilla
ACT — Accountant
Act — Action
ACT — Actuarial Database

ACT — Advertised Computer Technologies
ACT — Advertising/Communications Times
ACT — Atlantic Canada Teacher
ACT — Societe Historique et Archeologique de Chateau-Thierry. Annales
Acta — Acta Musicologica
Acta A — Acta Archaeologica
ActaA — Acta Asiatica
Acta A Acad Hung — Acta Archaeologica Academiae Scientiarum Hungaricae
Acta A Art Hist — Acta ad Archaeologiam et Artium Historiam Pertinentia
Acta Abo — Acta Academiae Aboensis. Humaniora
Acta Ac Abo — Acta Academiae Aboensis. Humaniora
Acta Acad Aboensis — Acta Academiae Aboensis
Acta Acad Abo Human — Acta Academiae Aboensis. Humaniora
Acta Acad Abo Ser B — Acta Academiae Aboensis. Series B. Mathematica et Physica
Acta Acad Abo Ser B Math Phys Mat Naturvetensk Tek — Acta Academiae Aboensis. Series B. Mathematica et Physica. Matematik Naturvetenskaper Teknik
Acta Acad Agric Tech Olstenensis Agric — Acta Academiae Agriculturae ac Technicae Olstenensis. Agricultura
Acta Acad Agric Tech Olstenensis Prot Aquarum Piscatoria — Acta Academiae Agriculturae ac Technicae Olstenensis. Protectio Aquarum et Piscatoria
Acta Acad Agric Tech Olstenensis Vet — Acta Academiae Agriculturae ac Technicae Olstenensis. Veterinaria
Acta Acad Agric Tech Olstenensis Zootech — Acta Academiae Agriculturae ac Technicae Olstenensis. Zootechnica
Acta Acad Elect Mogunt Sci Util Erfordiae — Acta Academiae Electoralis Moguntinae Scientiarum Utilium Quae Erfordiae Est
Acta Acad Hung — Acta Antique Academiae Scientiarum Hungaricae
Acta Acad Int Hist Med — Acta Academiae Internationalis Historiae Medicinae
Acta Acad Med Hebei — Acta Academiae Medicinae Hebei
Acta Acad Med Nanjing — Acta Academiae Medicinae Nanjing
Acta Acad Med Primae Shanghai — Acta Academiae Medicinae Primae Shanghai
Acta Acad Med Shandong — Acta Academiae Medicinae Shandong
Acta Acad Med Shanghai — Acta Academiae Medicinae Shanghai
Acta Acad Med Sichuan — Acta Academiae Medicinae Sichuan
Acta Acad Med Sinicae — Acta Academiae Medicinae Sinicae
Acta Acad Med Wuhan — Acta Academiae Medicinae Wuhan
Acta Acad Med Wuhan Chin Ed — Acta Academiae Medicinae Wuhan (Chinese Edition)
Acta Acad Med Xian — Acta Academiae Medicinae Xi'an
Acta Acad Paedagog Civitate Pecs Ser 6 Math-Phys-Chem-Tech — Acta Academiae Paedagogicae in Civitate Pecs. Seria 6. Mathematica-Physica-Chemica-Technica
Acta Acad Paedagog Szeged — Acta Academiae Paedagogicae Szegediensis
Acta Acad Polytech Pollack Mihaly Pecs — Acta Academiae Polytechnicae Pollack Mihaly Pecs
Acta Acad Reeks A — Acta Academica. Reeks A
Acta Acad Reeks B — Acta Academica. Reeks B
Acta Acad Reeks C — Acta Academica. Reeks C
Acta Acad Regiae Sci Ups — Acta Academiae Regiae Scientiarum Upsaliensis
Acta Acad Sci Imp Petrop — Acta Academiae Scientiarum Imperialis Petropolitanae
Acta Acad Sci Nat Moravosilesiacae — Acta Academiae Scientiarum Naturalium Moravosilesiacae
Acta Acad Sci Pol — Acta Academiae Scientiarum Polonae
Acta Acad Sci Taurinensis — Acta Academiae Scientiarum Taurinensis
Acta Acad Sci Taurinensis Cl Sci Fis Mat Nat — Acta Academiae Scientiarum Taurinensis. Classe di Scienze Fisiche, Matematiche,e Naturali
Acta A Carp — Acta Archaeologica Carpathica
Acta Acust — Acta Acustica
Acta Adriat — Acta Adriatica
Acta Agral Fenn — Acta Agralia Fennica
Acta Agral Vadens — Acta Agralia Vadensia
Acta Agrar — Acta Agraria
Acta Agrar Silvestria — Acta Agraria et Silvestria
Acta Agrar Silvestria Ser Agrar — Acta Agraria et Silvestria. Series Agraria
Acta Agrar Silvestria Ser Lesna — Acta Agraria et Silvestria. Seria Lesna
Acta Agrar Silvestria Ser Roln — Acta Agraria et Silvestria. Seria Rolnicza
Acta Agrar Silvestria Ser Silvestris — Acta Agraria et Silvestria. Series Silvestris
Acta Agrar Silvestria Ser Zootech — Acta Agraria et Silvestria. Series Zootechnia
Acta Agrar Silv Ser Agrar — Acta Agraria et Silvestria. Series Agraria
Acta Agrar Silv Ser Silv — Acta Agraria et Silvestria. Series Silvestris
Acta Agric Nucleatae Sin — Acta Agriculturae Nucleatae Sinica
Acta Agric Scand — Acta Agriculturae Scandinavica
Acta Agric Scand Sect A — Acta Agriculturae Scandinavica. Section A. Animal Science
Acta Agric Scand Sect B — Acta Agriculturae Scandinavica. Section B. Soil and Plant Science
Acta Agric Scand Suppl — Acta Agriculturae Scandinavica. Supplementum
Acta Agric Sin — Acta Agriculturae Sinica
Acta Agric Suec — Acta Agriculturae Suecana
Acta Agric Suecana — Acta Agriculturae Suecana
Acta Agric Univ Pekinensis — Acta Agriculturae Universitatis Pekinensis
Acta Agrobot — Acta Agrobotanica
Acta Agromech Sin — Acta Agromechanica Sinica
Acta Agron — Acta Agronomica
Acta Agron Acad Sci Hung — Acta Agronomica. Academiae Scientiarum Hungaricae
Acta Agron (Budapest) — Acta Agronomica. Academiae Scientiarum Hungaricae (Budapest)
Acta Agron Hung — Acta Agronomica. Academiae Scientiarum Hungaricae
Acta Agron Hung — Acta Agronomica Hungarica
Acta Agron (Palmira) — Acta Agronomica (Palmira)
Acta Agron Sin — Acta Agronomica Sinica

Acta Agr Scand — Acta Agriculturae Scandinavica
Acta Agr Silv Ser Roln — Acta Agraria et Silvestria. Series Rolnictwo
Acta Agr Sinica — Acta Agriculturae Sinica
Acta Albert — Acta Albertina
Acta Albert Ratisb — Acta Albertina Ratisbonensis
Acta Aliment — Acta Alimentaria
Acta Aliment Acad Sci Hung — Acta Alimentaria. Academiae Scientiarum Hungaricae
Acta Aliment Pol — Acta Alimentaria Polonica
Acta Allerg — Acta Allergologica
Acta Allergol — Acta Allergologica
Acta Allergol Suppl — Acta Allergologica. Supplementum
Acta Am — Acta Americana
Acta Amer — Acta Americana. Inter-American Society of Anthropology and Geography
Acta Anaesth — Acta Anaesthesiologica
Acta Anaesthesiol — Acta Anaesthesiologica
Acta Anaesthesiol Belg — Acta Anaesthesiologica Belgica
Acta Anaesthesiol Hell — Acta Anaesthesiologica Hellenica
Acta Anaesthesiol Ital — Acta Anaesthesiologica Italica
Acta Anaesthesiol (Padova) — Acta Anaesthesiologica (Padova)
Acta Anaesthesiol (Padua) — Acta Anaesthesiologica (Padua)
Acta Anaesthesiol Scand — Acta Anaesthesiologica Scandinavica
Acta Anaesthesiol Scand Suppl — Acta Anaesthesiologica Scandinavica. Supplementum
Acta Anaesthesiol Sin — Acta Anaesthesiologica Sinica
Acta Anaesthes Scand — Acta Anaesthesiologica Scandinavica
Acta Anaesth Scandinav — Acta Anaesthesiologica Scandinavica
Acta Anat — Acta Anatomica
Acta Anat (Basel) — Acta Anatomica (Basel)
Acta Anat Nippon — Acta Anatomica Nipponica
Acta Anat Sin — Acta Anatomica Sinica
Acta Anat Suppl — Acta Anatomica. Supplementum
Acta Anat Suppl Bibl Anat — Acta Anatomica. Supplement. Bibliotheca Anatomica
Acta Ant — Acta Antiqua et Archaeologica
Acta Ant Acad Sci Hung — Acta Antiqua Academiae Scientiarum Hungaricae
Acta Ant Ac Hung — Acta Antique Academiae Scientiarum Hungaricae
Acta Ant Arch — Acta Antiqua et Archaeologica
Acta Ant H — Acta Antiqua. Academiae Scientiarum Hungaricae
Acta Anthr Biol — Acta Anthropobiologica
Acta Anthr (Mex) — Acta Anthropologica (Mexico)
Acta Anthrop Mex — Acta Anthropologica (Mexico City)
Acta Anthropobiol — Acta Anthropobiologica
Acta Anthropog — Acta Anthropogenetica
Acta Anthropogen — Acta Anthropogenetica
Acta Anthropogenet — Acta Anthropogenetica
Acta Anthrop Univ Lodz — Acta Anthropologica Universitatis Lodziensis
Acta Ant Hung — Acta Antique Academiae Scientiarum Hungaricae
Acta Antiq Magyar Tud Akad — Acta Antiqua. Magyar Tudomanyos Akademia
Acta Antropol — Acta Antropologica
Acta Apost Sedis — Acta Apostolicae Sedis
Acta Appl Math — Acta Applicandae Mathematicae
Acta Ar — Acta Archaeologica
Acta Arachnol — Acta Arachnologica
Acta Arachn Tokyo — Acta Arachnologica (Tokyo)
Acta Arch — Acta Archaeologica
Acta Archaeol — Acta Archaeologica
Acta Archaeol Acad Sci Hung — Acta Archaeologica. Academiae Scientiarum Hungaricae
Acta Archaeol & A Historiam Pertinentia — Acta ad Archaeologicam et Artium Historiam Pertinentia
Acta Archaeol (Budapest) — Acta Archaeologica (Budapest)
Acta Archaeol Hung — Acta Archaeologica Academiae Scientiarum Hungaricae
Acta Archaeol (Kobenhavn) — Acta Archaeologica (Kobenhavn)
Acta Archaeol Louvan — Acta Archaeologica Louvaniensia
Acta Archaeol Sin — Acta Archaeologica Sinica
Acta Arch Art Hist Pert — Acta ad Archaeologiam et Artium Historiam Pertinentia
Acta Arch (Bp) — Acta Archaeologica Academiae Scientiarum Hungaricae (Budapest)
Acta Arch Budapest — Acta Archaeologica Academiae Scientiarum Hungaricae (Budapest)
Acta Arch Carp — Acta Archaeologica Carpathica
Acta Arch Carpathica — Acta Archaeologica Carpathica
Acta Arch Kobenhaven — Acta Archaeologica (Kobenhaven)
Acta Arch Lund — Acta Archaeologica Lundensia
Acta Arct — Acta Arctica
Acta Argent Fisiol Fisiopatol — Acta Argentina de Fisiologia y Fisiopatologia
Acta Arith — Acta Arithmetica
Acta As — Acta Asiatica
Acta Asiat — Acta Asiatica
Acta Astr — Acta Astronomica
Acta Astron — Acta Astronomica
Acta Astronaut — Acta Astronautica
Acta Astronom Sinica — Acta Astronomica Sinica
Acta Astron Sin — Acta Astronomica Sinica
Acta Astron Sinica — Acta Astronomica Sinica
Acta Astrophys Sinica — Acta Astrophysica Sinica
Acta Astr Sin — Acta Astronomica Sinica
Acta Athen — Skrifter Utgivna av Svenska Institutet i Athen
Acta Audiol Foniat Hispano-Amer — Acta Audiologica y Foniatrica Hispano-Americana
Acta Automat Sinica — Acta Automatica Sinica
Acta Autom Sin — Acta Automatica Sinica
Acta Baln Pol — Acta Balneologica Polonica
Acta Balt — Acta Baltica

Acta Belg Arte Med Pharm Mil — Acta Belgica de Arte Medicinali et Pharmaceutica Militari
Acta Belg Med Phys — Acta Belgica. Medica Physica
Acta Bib Regiae Stockholm — Acta Bibliothecae Regiae Stockholmiensis
Acta Biochem Biophys Sin — Acta Biochemica et Biophysica Sinica/Sheng Wu Hua Yu Sheng Wu Li Hsueeh Pao
Acta Biochim — Acta Biochimica
Acta Biochim Biophys — Acta Biochimica et Biophysica
Acta Biochim Biophys Acad Sci Hung — Acta Biochimica et Biophysica. Academiae Scientiarum Hungaricae
Acta Biochim Biophys Hung — Acta Biochimica et Biophysica. Academiae Scientiarum Hungaricae
Acta Biochim Biophys Sin — Acta Biochimica et Biophysica Sinica
Acta Biochim Biophys Sinica — Acta Biochimica et Biophysica Sinica
Acta Biochim Iran — Acta Biochimica Iranica
Acta Biochim Pol — Acta Biochimica Polonica
Acta Biochim Polon — Acta Biochimica Polonica
Acta Biochim Pol (Trans) — Acta Biochimica Polonica (Translation)
Acta Biochim Sin — Acta Biochimica Sinica
Acta Biol — Acta Biologica
Acta Biol Acad Sci Hung — Acta Biologica. Academiae Scientiarum Hungaricae
Acta Biol Acad Sci Hung Suppl — Acta Biologica. Academiae Scientiarum Hungaricae. Supplementum
Acta Biol (Budapest) — Acta Biologica. Academiae Scientiarum Hungaricae (Budapest)
Acta Biol Cracov Ser Bot — Acta Biologica Cracoviensia. Series Botanica
Acta Biol Cracov Ser Zool — Acta Biologica Cracoviensia. Series Zoologia
Acta Biol Debrecina — Acta Biologica Debrecina
Acta Biol Exp — Acta Biologiae Experimentalis
Acta Biol Exper Sinica — Acta Biologiae Experimentalis Sinica
Acta Biol Exp Pol Acad Sci — Acta Biologiae Experimentalis. Polish Academy of Sciences
Acta Biol Exp Sin — Acta Biologiae Experimentalis Sinica
Acta Biol Exp (Warsaw) — Acta Biologiae Experimentalis (Warsaw)
Acta Biol Hung — Acta Biologica. Academiae Scientiarum Hungaricae
Acta Biol Hung — Acta Biologica Hungarica
Acta Biol Iugosl Ser A — Acta Biologica Iugoslavica. Serija A
Acta Biol Iugosl Ser B — Acta Biologica Iugoslavica. Serija B
Acta Biol Iugosl Ser B Mikrobiol — Acta Biologica Iugoslavica. Serija B. Mikrobiologija
Acta Biol Iugosl Ser C — Acta Biologica Iugoslavica. Serija C
Acta Biol Iugosl Ser C Iugosl Physiol Pharmacol Acta — Acta Biologica Iugoslavica. Serija C. Iugoslavica Physiologica et Pharmacologica Acta
Acta Biol Iugosl Ser D Eko — Acta Biologica Iugoslavica. Serija D. Ekologija
Acta Biol Iugosl Ser E Ichthyol — Acta Biologica Iugoslavica. Serija E. Ichthyologia
Acta Biol Iugosl Ser F — Acta Biologica Iugoslavica. Serija F. Genetika
Acta Biol Iugosl Ser G Biosistem — Acta Biologica Iugoslavica. Serija G. Biosistematika
Acta Biol Katowice — Acta Biologica Katowice
Acta Biol Latv — Acta Biologica Latvica
Acta Biol Med — Acta Biologica et Medica
Acta Biol Med Exp — Acta Biologiae et Medicinae Experimentalis
Acta Biol Med (Gdansk) — Acta Biologica et Medica (Gdansk)
Acta Biol Med Ger — Acta Biologica et Medica Germanica
Acta Biol Med Ger Suppl — Acta Biologica et Medica Germanica. Supplementband
Acta Biol Parana — Acta Biologica Paranaense
Acta Biol (Szeged) — Acta Biologica (Szeged)
Acta Biol Szeged 1928-37 — Acta Biologica. Acta Litterarum ac Scientiarum. Sectio A (Szeged 1928-37)
Acta Biol (Trent Italy) — Acta Biologica (Trent, Italy)
Acta Biol Turc — Acta Biologica Turcica
Acta Biol Venez — Acta Biologica Venezuelica
Acta Bio-Med Ateneo Parmense — Acta Bio-Medica de l'Ateneo Parmense
Acta Bioquim Clin Latinoam — Acta Bioquimica Clinica Latinoamericana
Acta Biotech — Acta Biotechnologica
Acta Biotechnol — Acta Biotechnologica
Acta Biotheor — Acta Biotheoretica
Acta Biotheor — Acta Biotheoretica [Dordrecht]
Acta Biotheor (Leiden) — Acta Biotheoretica (Leiden)
Acta Borealia A Sci — Acta Borealia. A. Scientia
Acta Bot — Acta Botanica
Acta Bot Acad Sci Hung — Acta Botanica. Academiae Scientiarum Hungaricae
Acta Bot Acad Sci Hungar — Acta Botanica Academiae Scientiarum Hungaricae
Acta Bot Barc — Acta Botanica Barcinonensia
Acta Bot Bohem — Acta Botanica Bohemica
Acta Bot (Budapest) — Acta Botanica. Academiae Scientiarum Hungaricae (Budapest)
Acta Bot Colomb — Acta Botanica Colombiana
Acta Bot Croat — Acta Botanica Croatica
Acta Bot Cubana — Acta Botanica Cubana
Acta Bot Fenn — Acta Botanica Fennica
Acta Bot Horti Bucur — Acta Botanica Horti Bucurestiensis
Acta Bot Hung — Acta Botanica. Academiae Scientiarum Hungaricae
Acta Bot Hung — Acta Botanica Hungarica
Acta Bot Indica — Acta Botanica Indica
Acta Bot Indica (IN) — Acta Botanica Indica (India)
Acta Bot Inst Bot Univ Zagreb — Acta Botanica Instituti Botanici. Universitatis Zagrebensis
Acta Bot Isl — Acta Botanica Islandica
Acta Bot Malacitana — Acta Botanica Malacitana
Acta Bot Neerl — Acta Botanica Neerlandica
Acta Bot Neerland — Acta Botanica Neerlandica
Acta Bot Neerl Suppl — Acta Botanica Neerlandica. Supplement
Acta Bot Sin — Acta Botanica Sinica

Acta Bot Sin (Engl Transl) — Acta Botanica Sinica (English Translation)
Acta Bot Sinica — Acta Botanica Sinica
Acta Bot Slovaca Acad Sci Slovacae Ser B — Acta Botanica Slovaca Academiae Scientiarum Slovacae. Series B. Physiologica, Pathophysiologica
Acta Bot Taiwan — Acta Botanica Taiwanica
Acta Bot Venez — Acta Botanica Venezuelica
Acta Bot Yunnanica — Acta Botanica Yunnanica
Acta Brevia Neerl Physiol Pharmacol Microbiol — Acta Brevia Neerlandica de Physiologia, Pharmacologia, Microbiologia
Acta Brevia Sin — Acta Brevia Sinensia
Acta Brev Neerl Physiol — Acta Brevia Neerlandica de Physiologia, Pharmacologia, Microbiologia
Acta Brev Sin — Acta Brevia Sinensia
Acta Brev Sinensia — Acta Brevia Sinensia
Act Acad Cienc Cordoba — Actas. Academia Nacional de Ciencias de Cordoba
Act Acad Sci Petrop — Acta Academiae Scientiarum Imperialis Petropolitanae
Acta Camp — Acta Campagnologica
Acta Cancerol — Acta Cancerologica
Acta Cardiol — Acta Cardiologica
Acta Cardiol (Brux) — Acta Cardiologica (Bruxelles)
Acta Cardiol Suppl — Acta Cardiologica. Supplementum
Acta Chem — Acta Chemica
Acta Chem Fenn — Acta Chemica Fennica
Acta Chem Mineralog Phys — Acta Chemica, Mineralogica, et Physica
Acta Chem Mineral Phys — Acta Chemica, Mineralogica, et Physica
Acta Chem Phys — Acta Chemica et Physica
Acta Chem Scand — Acta Chemica Scandinavica
Acta Chem Scand (B) — Acta Chemica Scandinavica. Series B. Organic Chemistry and Biochemistry
Acta Chem Scand (DK) — Acta Chemica Scandinavica (Denmark)
Acta Chem Scand Ser A — Acta Chemica Scandinavica. Series A. Physical and Inorganic Chemistry
Acta Chem Scand Ser A Phys Inorg Chem — Acta Chemica Scandinavica. Series A. Physical and Inorganic Chemistry
Acta Chem Scand Ser B — Acta Chemica Scandinavica. Series B. Organic Chemistry and Biochemistry
Acta Chem Scand Ser B Org Chem Biochem — Acta Chemica Scandinavica. Series B. Organic Chemistry and Biochemistry
Acta Chim Acad Sci Hung — Acta Chimica. Academiae Scientiarum Hungaricae
Acta Chim Hung — Acta Chimica Hungarica
Acta Chim Soc Sci Lodz — Acta Chimica. Societatis Scientiarum Lodziensis
Acta Chir Acad Sci Hung — Acta Chirurgica. Academiae Scientiarum Hungaricae
Acta Chir Austriaca — Acta Chirurgica Austriaca
Acta Chir Austriaca Suppl — Acta Chirurgica Austriaca. Supplement
Acta Chir Belg — Acta Chirurgica Belgica
Acta Chir Belg Suppl — Acta Chirurgica Belgica. Supplement
Acta Chir (Budapest) — Acta Chirurgica (Budapest)
Acta Chir Hell — Acta Chirurgica Hellenica
Acta Chir Hung — Acta Chirurgica Hungarica
Acta Chir Ital — Acta Chirurgica Italica
Acta Chir Iugosl — Acta Chirurgica Iugoslavica
Acta Chir Maxillo-Facialis — Acta Chirurgiae Maxillo-Facialis
Acta Chir Orthop Traumatol Cech — Acta Chirurgiae, Orthopaedicae, et Traumatologiae Cechoslovaca
Acta Chir Plast — Acta Chirurgiae Plasticae
Acta Chir Plast (Prague) — Acta Chirurgiae Plasticae (Prague)
Acta Chir Scand — Acta Chirurgica Scandinavica
Acta Chir Scandinav — Acta Chirurgica Scandinavica
Acta Chir Scand Suppl — Acta Chirurgica Scandinavica. Supplementum
Acta Chromatogr — Acta Chromatographica
Acta Ci Compostelana — Acta Cientifica Compostelana
Acta Cienc Indica — Acta Ciencia Indica
Acta Cienc Indica Chem — Acta Ciencia Indica. Series Chemistry
Acta Cienc Indica (IN) — Acta Ciencia Indica (India)
Acta Cienc Indica Math — Acta Ciencia Indica. Mathematics
Acta Cienc Indica Phys — Acta Ciencia Indica. Physics
Acta Cienc Indica Physica — Acta Ciencia Indica. Physica
Acta Cienc Indica Ser Chem — Acta Ciencia Indica. Series Chemistry
Acta Cienc Indica Ser Math — Acta Ciencia Indica. Series Mathematics
Acta Cient — Acta Cientifica
Acta Cient Compostelana — Acta Cientifica Compostelana
Acta Cient Potos — Acta Cientifica Potosina
Acta Cient Potosina — Acta Cientifica Potosina
Acta Cient Venez — Acta Cientifica Venezolana
Acta Cient Venezolana — Acta Cientifica Venezolana. Asociacion Venezolana para el Avance de la Ciencia
Acta Cient Venez Supl — Acta Cientifica Venezolana. Suplemento
Acta Ci Indica — Acta Ciencia Indica
Acta Cir Bras — Acta Cirurgica Brasileira
Acta Ci Venezolana — Acta Cientifica Venezolana. Asociacion Venezolana para el Avance de la Ciencia
Acta Cl — Acta Classica
Acta Class — Acta Classica
Acta Class Debr — Acta Classica. Universitatis Scientiarum Debreceniensis
Acta Class Debrecen — Acta Classica. Universitatis Scientiarum Debreceniensis
Acta Cl Debrecen — Acta Classica. Universitatis Scientiarum Debreceniensis
Acta Clin Belg — Acta Clinica Belgica
Acta Clin Belg Suppl — Acta Clinica Belgica. Supplementum
Acta Odontol — Acta Clinica Odontologica
Acta Commentat Acad Sci Korea — Acta et Commentationes Academiae Scientificae Korea
Acta Commentat Imp Univ Jurjev — Acta et Commentationes Imperialis Universitatis Jurjevensis
Acta Commentat Univ Tartu — Acta et Commentationes Universitatis Tartuensis

Acta Commentat Univ Tartu Dorpat A — Acta et Commentationes Universitatis Tartuensis Dorpatensis A
Acta Commentat Univ Tartu Dorpat C — Acta et Commentationes Universitatis Tartuensis Dorpatensis. C
Acta Comment Univ Dorp — Acta et Commentationes Universitatis Dorpatensis
Acta Congr Int Hist Pharm — Acta Congressus Internationalis Historiae Pharmaciae
Acta Congr Int Ornithol — Acta Congressus Internationalis Ornithologici
Acta Conv Med Intern Hung — Acta Conventus Medicinae Internae Hungarici
Acta Criminol Med Leg Jpn — Acta Criminologiae Medicinae Legalis Japonica
Acta Cryst — Acta Crystallographica
Acta Crystallogr — Acta Crystallographica
Acta Crystallogr A — Acta Crystallographica. Section A
Acta Crystallogr A — Acta Crystallographica. Section A. Foundations of Crystallography
Acta Crystallogr B — Acta Crystallographica. Section B
Acta Crystallogr B — Acta Crystallographica. Section B. Structural Science
Acta Crystallogr C — Acta Crystallographica. Section C. Crystal Structure Communications
Acta Crystallogr Sect A — Acta Crystallographica. Section A. Crystal Physics, Diffraction, Theoretical and General Crystallography
Acta Crystallogr Sect A Cryst Phys — Acta Crystallographica. Section A. Crystal Physics, Diffraction, Theoretical, and General Crystallography
Acta Crystallogr Sect A Found — Acta Crystallographica. Section A. Foundations of Crystallography
Acta Crystallogr Sect A Found Crystallogr — Acta Crystallographica. Section A. Foundations of Crystallography
Acta Crystallogr Sect A Fundam Crystallogr — Acta Crystallographica. Section A. Fundamentals of Crystallography
Acta Crystallogr Sect B — Acta Crystallographica. Section B. Structural Crystallography and Crystal Chemistry
Acta Crystallogr Sect B Struct — Acta Crystallographica. Section B. Structural Science and Crystal Chemistry
Acta Crystallogr Sect B Struct Crystallogr Cryst Chem — Acta Crystallographica. Section B. Structural Crystallography and Crystal Chemistry
Acta Crystallogr Sect B Struct Sci — Acta Crystallographica. Section B. Structural Science
Acta Crystallogr Sect C — Acta Crystallographica. Section C. Crystal Structure Communications
Acta Crystallogr Sect C Cryst — Acta Crystallographica. Section C. Crystal Structure Communications
Acta Crystallogr Sect C Cryst Struct Commun — Acta Crystallographica. Section C. Crystal Structure Communications
Acta Cryst Sect A — Acta Crystallographica. Section A. Crystal Physics, Diffraction, Theoretical and General Crystallography
Acta Cuyana Ing — Acta Cuyana de Ingenieria
Acta Cybernet — Acta Cybernetica
Acta Cytol — Acta Cytologica
Acta Cytol (Baltimore) — Acta Cytologica (Baltimore)
Act Adapt Aging — Activities, Adaptation, and Aging
Acta Davos — Acta Davosiana
Acta Dendrobiol — Acta Dendrobiologica
Acta Derm — Acta Dermatologica/Hifuka Kiyo
Acta Dermatol — Acta Dermatologica
Acta Dermatol (Kyoto) (Engl Ed) — Acta Dermatologica (Kyoto) (English Edition)
Acta Dermatol Kyoto (Jpn Ed) — Acta Dermatologica-Kyoto (Japanese Edition)
Acta Dermato-Venereol — Acta Dermato-Venereologica
Acta Dermato-Venereol Suppl — Acta Dermato-Venereologica. Supplementum
Acta Dermatovenerol Iugosl — Acta Dermatovenerologica Iugoslavica
Acta Dermat Vener — Acta Dermato-Venereologica
Acta Derm-Venereol — Acta Dermato-Venereologica
Acta Derm-Venereol (Stockh) — Acta Dermato-Venereologica (Stockholm)
Acta Derm-Venereol Suppl — Acta Dermato-Venereologica. Supplementum
Acta Derm-Venereol Suppl (Stockh) — Acta Dermato-Venereologica. Supplementum (Stockholm)
Acta Diabetol — Acta Diabetologica
Acta Diabetol Lat — Acta Diabetologica Latina
Acta Eccl — Acta Ecclesiastica
Acta Ecol — Acta Ecologica
Acta Electron — Acta Electronica
Acta Electron Sin — Acta Electronica Sinica
Acta Embryol Exp — Acta Embryologiae Experimentalis
Acta Embryol Exp (Palermo) — Acta Embryologiae Experimentalis [Later, Acta Embryologiae et Morphologiae Experimentalis] (Palermo)
Acta Embryol Morphol Exp — Acta Embryologiae et Morphologiae Experimentalis
Acta Embryol Morphol Exp New Ser — Acta Embryologiae et Morphologiae Experimentalis. New Series
Acta Embryol Morphol Exptl — Acta Embryologiae et Morphologiae Experimentalis
Acta Endocrinol — Acta Endocrinologica
Acta Endocrinol Congr Adv Abstr — Acta Endocrinologica Congress. Advance Abstracts
Acta Endocrinol (Copenh) — Acta Endocrinologica (Copenhagen)
Acta Endocrinol Cubana — Acta Endocrinologica Cubana
Acta Endocrinol Panam — Acta Endocrinologica Panamericana
Acta Endocrinol Suppl — Acta Endocrinologica. Supplementum
Acta Endocrinol Suppl (Copenh) — Acta Endocrinologica. Supplementum (Copenhagen)
Acta Energ Solaris Sin — Acta Energiae Solaris Sinica
Acta Energ Sol Sin — Acta Energiae Solaris Sinica
Acta Ent — Acta Entomologica
Acta Ent Bohemoslov — Acta Entomologica Bohemoslovaca
Acta Ent Fenn — Acta Entomologica Fennica
Acta Ent Jugosl — Acta Entomologica Jugoslavica
Acta Ent Litu — Acta Entomologica Lituanica

Acta Ent Mus Natn (Prague) — Acta Entomologica. Musei Nationalis (Prague)
Acta Ento Bohem — Acta Entomologi a Bohemoslovaca
Acta Entomol Bohemoslov — Acta Entomologica Bohemoslovaca
Acta Entomol Fenn — Acta Entomologica Fennica
Acta Entomol Jugosl — Acta Entomologica Jugoslavica
Acta Entomol Litu — Acta Entomologica Lituanica
Acta Entomol Mus Natl Pragae — Acta Entomologica. Musei Nationalis Pragae
Acta Entomol Sin — Acta Entomologica Sinica
Acta Entomol Sinica — Acta Entomologica Sinica
Acta Ent (Prag) — Acta Entomologica. Musei Nationalis (Prague)
Acta Ent Sin — Acta Entomologica Sinica
Acta Environ Univ Comenianae — Acta Environmentalica Universitatis Comenianae
Acta Erud — Acta Eruditorum
Acta Erudit — Acta Eruditorum
Acta Ethn — Acta Ethnologica
Acta Ethn (Hung) — Acta Ethnographica. Magyar Tudomanyos Akademia (Hungary)
Acta Ethnog Acad Sci Hung — Acta Ethnographica Academiae Scientarum Hungaricae
Acta Ethnog Hung — Acta Ethnographica. Academiae Scientiarum Hungaricae
Acta Ethnogr — Acta Ethnographica
Acta Ethnogr Acad Sci Hung — Acta Ethnographica. Academiae Scientiarum Hungaricae
Acta Ethnogr (Budapest) — Acta Ethnographica (Budapest)
Acta Ethnogr Hung — Acta Ethnographica. Academiae Scientiarum Hungaricae
Acta Ethnol Slov — Acta Ethnologica Slovaca
Acta Eur Fertil — Acta Europaea Fertilitatis
Acta Fac For Zvolen Czech — Acta Facultatis Forestalis. Zvolen. Czechoslovakia
Acta Fac Med Fluminensis — Acta Facultatis Medicae Fluminensis
Acta Fac Med Univ Brun — Acta Facultatis Medicae Universitatis Brunensis
Acta Fac Med Zagreb — Acta Facultatis Medicae Zagrebensis
Acta Fac Paedagog Ostra Ser E — Acta Facultatis Paedagogicae Ostraviensis. Series E
Acta Fac Paedagog Ostrav Ser A Mat Fyz — Acta Facultatis Paedagogicae Ostraviensis. Series A. Matematika, Fyzika
Acta Fac Paedagog Ostrav Ser A Prir Vedy Mat — Acta Facultatis Paedagogicae Ostraviensis. Series A. Prirodni Vedy a Matematika
Acta Fac Paedagog Ostrav Ser E — Acta Facultatis Paedagogicae Ostraviensis. Series E
Acta Fac Pharm Bohemoslov — Acta Facultatis Pharmaceuticae Bohemoslovenicae
Acta Fac Pharm Brun Bratisl — Acta Facultatis Pharmaceuticae Brunensis et Bratislavensis
Acta Fac Pharm Univ Comenianae — Acta Facultatis Pharmaceuticae Universitatis Comenianae
Acta Fac Rer Nat Univ Comen Anthrop — Acta Facultatis Rerum Naturalium Universitatis Comenianae. Anthropologia
Acta Fac Rerum Nat Univ Comenianae Anthropol — Acta Facultatis Rerum Naturalium Universitatis Comenianae. Anthropologica
Acta Fac Rerum Nat Univ Comenianae Astron Geophys — Acta Facultatis Rerum Naturalium Universitatis Comenianae. Astronomia et Geophysica
Acta Fac Rerum Nat Univ Comenianae Bot — Acta Facultatis Rerum Naturalium Universitatis Comenianae. Botanica
Acta Fac Rerum Nat Univ Comenianae Chim — Acta Facultatis Rerum Naturalium Universitatis Comenianae. Chimia
Acta Fac Rerum Nat Univ Comenianae Form Prot Nat — Acta Facultatis Rerum Naturalium Universitatis Comenianae. Formatio et Protectio Naturae
Acta Fac Rerum Nat Univ Comenianae Form Prot Nat (CS) — Acta Facultatis Rerum Naturalium Universitatis Comenianae. Formatio et Protectio Naturae (Czechoslovakia)
Acta Fac Rerum Nat Univ Comenianae Genet — Acta Facultatis Rerum Naturalium Universitatis Comenianae. Genetica
Acta Fac Rerum Nat Univ Comenianae Genet Biol Mol — Acta Facultatis Rerum Naturalium Universitatis Comenianae. Genetica et Biologia Molecularis
Acta Fac Rerum Nat Univ Comenianae Microbiol — Acta Facultatis Rerum Naturalium Universitatis Comenianae. Microbiologia
Acta Fac Rerum Nat Univ Comenianae Phys — Acta Facultatis Rerum Naturalium Universitatis Comenianae. Physica
Acta Fac Rerum Nat Univ Comenianae Physiol Plant — Acta Facultatis Rerum Naturalium Universitatis Comenianae. Physiologia Plantarum
Acta Fac Rerum Nat Univ Comenianae Zool — Acta Facultatis Rerum Naturalium Universitatis Comenianae. Zoologia
Acta Fac Rerum Natur Univ Comenian Math — Acta Facultatis Rerum Naturalium Universitatis Comenianae. Mathematica
Acta Fac Xylol Zvolen — Acta Facultatis Xylologiae Zvolen
Acta Farm Bonaerense — Acta Farmaceutica Bonaerense
Acta Fauna Fl Universali Ser 2 Bot — Acta pro Fauna et Flora Universali. Ser 2. Botanica
Acta Faun Entomol Mus Natl Pragae — Acta Faunistica Entomologica. Musei Nationalis Pragae
Acta Fisioter Iber — Acta Fisioterapica Iberica
Acta Flor Suec — Acta Florae Sueciae
Acta For Fenn — Acta Forestalia Fennica
Acta FRN Univ Comenianae Physiol Plant — Acta F.R.N. Universitatis Comenianae. Physiologia Plantarum
Acta Fytotech — Acta Fytotechnica
Acta Fytotech Univ Agric (Nitra) — Acta Fytotechnica. Universitatis Agriculturae (Nitra)
ActaG — Acta Germanica
Acta Gastro Enter Belg — Acta Gastro-enterologica Belgica
Acta Gastro-Enterol Belg — Acta Gastro-Enterologica Belgica
Acta Gastroenterol Boliv — Acta Gastroenterologica Boliviana
Acta Gastroenterol Latinoam — Acta Gastroenterologica Latinoamericana
Acta Genet Med Gem — Acta Geneticae Medicae et Gemellologiae

Acta Genet Med Gemell — Acta Geneticae Medicae et Gemellologiae
Acta Genet Med Gemellol — Acta Geneticae, Medicae, et Gemellologiae
Acta Genet Sin — Acta Genetica Sinica
Acta Genet Statist Med — Acta Genetica et Statistica Medica
Acta Genet Stat Med — Acta Genetica et Statistica Medica
Acta Geobot Barc — Acta Geobotanica Barcinonensia
Acta Geobot Hung — Acta Geobotanica Hungarica
Acta Geod Cartogr Sin — Acta Geodetica et Cartographica Sinica
Acta Geodet et Cartogr Sinica — Acta Geodetica et Cartographica Sinica
Acta Geod Geophys Montan — Acta Geodaetica, Geophysica, et Montanistica
Acta Geod Geophys Montanistica — Acta Geodaetica, Geophysica, et Montanistica
Acta Geogr — Acta Geographica
Acta Geogr Helsingf — Acta Geographica. Societas Geographica Fenniae. Helsingforsiae
Acta Geogr Lodz — Acta Geographica Lodziensia
Acta Geogr Sin — Acta Geographica Sinica
Acta Geogr Sinica — Acta Geographica Sinica
Acta Geogr Szeged — Acta Geographica. Acta Universitatis Szegediensis
Acta Geogr Univ Lodz — Acta Geographica Universitatis Lodziensis
Acta Geol Acad Sci Hung — Acta Geologica. Academiae Scientiarum Hungaricae
Acta Geol Alp — Acta Geologica Alpina
Acta Geol Budapest — Acta Geologica (Budapest)
Acta Geol Geogr Univ Comenianae Geol — Acta Geologica et Geographica. Universitatis Comenianae. Geologica
Acta Geol Hisp — Acta Geologica Hispanica
Acta Geol Hispan — Acta Geologica Hispanica
Acta Geol Hung — Acta Geologica. Academiae Scientiarum Hungaricae
Acta Geol Leopold — Acta Geologica Leopoldensia
Acta Geol Lilloana — Acta Geologica Lilloana
Acta Geol Pol — Acta Geologica Polonica
Acta Geol Sin — Acta Geologica Sinica
Acta Geol Sin (Engl Transl) — Acta Geologica Sinica (English Translation)
Acta Geol Sinica — Acta Geologica Sinica
Acta Geol Taiwan — Acta Geologica Taiwanica
Acta Geol Taiwanica — Acta Geologica Taiwanica
Acta Geol Trent Italy — Acta Geologica (Trent, Italy)
Acta Geol Univ Comenianae — Acta Geologica Universitatis Comenianae
Acta Geophys Pol — Acta Geophysica Polonica
Acta Geophys Polonica — Acta Geophysica Polonica
Acta Geophys Sin — Acta Geophysica Sinica
Acta Geront — Acta Gerontologica
Acta Gerontol — Acta Gerontologica
Acta Gerontol Belg — Acta Gerontologica Belgica
Acta Gerontol Geriatr Belg — Acta Gerontologica et Geriatrica Belgica
Acta Gerontol Jpn — Acta Gerontologica Japonica
Acta Ginec — Acta Ginecologica
Acta Ginecol — Acta Ginecologica
Acta Ginecol (Madr) — Acta Ginecologica (Madrid)
Act Agron H — Acta Agronomica. Academiae Scientiarum Hungaricae
Acta Gynaecol Obstet Hispano Lusitana — Acta Gynaecologica et Obstetrica Hispano Lusitana
Acta Gynecol Scand — Acta Gynecologica Scandinavica
Acta Gynecol Scand Suppl — Acta Gynecologica Scandinavica. Supplement
Acta HA — Acta Historiae Artium. Magyar Tudomanyos Akademia
Acta Haemat — Acta Haematologica
Acta Haematol — Acta Haematologica
Acta Haematol (Basel) — Acta Haematologica (Basel)
Acta Haematol Jpn — Acta Haematologica Japonica
Acta Haematol Pol — Acta Haematologica Polonica
Acta Helvet — Acta Helvetica Physico-Mathematico-Botanico-Medica
Acta Helv Phys Math — Acta Helvetica, Physico-Mathematico-Anatomico-Botanico-Medica
Acta Hepato-Gastroenterol — Acta Hepato-Gastroenterologica
Acta Hepato-Gastroenterol (Stuttg) — Acta Hepato-Gastroenterologica (Stuttgart/New York)
Acta Hepatol — Acta Hepatologica
Acta Hepatol Jpn — Acta Hepatologica Japonica
Acta Hepatosplen — Acta Hepato-Splenologica
Acta Hepato-Splenol — Acta Hepato-Splenologica
Acta Herbol — Acta Herbologica
Acta Herpetol Jpn — Acta Herpetologica Japonica
Acta Hist — Acta Historica. Societas Academica Dacoromana
Acta Hist A Acad Sci Hung — Acta Historiae Artium Academiae Scientiarum Hungaricae
Acta Hist & Archaeol Med — Acta Historica et Archaeologica Mediaevalia
Acta Hist Art — Magyar Tudomanyos Akademia. Acta Historiae Artium
Acta Hist Art (Hung) — Acta Historiae Artium. Magyar Tudomanyos Akademia (Hungary)
Acta Hist Dac — Acta Historica. Societatis Academica Dacoromana
Acta Hist (Hung) — Acta Historica. Magyar Tudomanyos Akademia (Hungary)
Acta Hist Leopold — Acta Historica Leopoldina
Acta Hist Leopoldina — Acta Historica Leopoldina
Acta Hist Med Pharm Vet — Acta Historica Medicinae Pharmaciae Veterinae
Acta Histochem — Acta Histochemica
Acta Histochem Cytochem — Acta Histochemica et Cytochemica
Acta Histochem (Jena) — Acta Histochemica (Jena)
Acta Histochem Suppl — Acta Histochemica. Supplementband
Acta Histochem Supplementb — Acta Histochemica. Supplementband
Acta Histochem Suppl (Jena) — Acta Histochemica. Supplementband (Jena)
Acta Hist Rerum Natur Nec Non Tech — Acta Historiae Rerum Naturalium Nec Non Technicarum
Acta Hist Rerum Natur Tech — Acta Historiae Rerum Naturalium nec non Technicarum
Acta Hist Sci Nat Med — Acta Historica Scientiarum, Naturalium, et Medicinalium

Acta Hist Sci Nat Med (Odense) — Acta Historica Scientiarum, Naturalium, et Medicinalium (Odense)
Acta Hort — Acta Horticulturae
Acta Hort — Acta Horticulturalia
Acta Hort Gotoburg — Acta Horti Gothoburgensis. Meddelanden fran Goeteborgs Botaniska Traedgard
Acta Horti Beijing — Acta Horticulturalia (Beijing)
Acta Horti Bot Tadshik — Acta Horti Botanici Tadshikistanici
Acta Horti Bot Univ — Acta Horti Botanici Universitatis. Schriften des Botanischen Gartens der Universitaet. Universitates Botaniska Darza Raksti
Acta Horti Bot Univ Lat — Acta Horti Botanici Universitatis Latviensis
Acta Horti Bot Univ Latv — Acta Horti Botanici Universitatis Latviensis
Acta Hortic — Acta Horticulturae
Acta Hortic (Peking) — Acta Horticulturalia (Peking)
Acta Hortic Sin — Acta Horticulturae Sinica
Acta Hortic (The Hague) — Acta Horticulturae (The Hague)
Acta Horti Gothoburg — Acta Horti Gothoburgensis. Meddelanden fran Goeteborgs Botaniska Traedgard
Acta Horti Gotob — Acta Horti Gotoburgensis
Acta Horti Gotoburg — Acta Horti Gotoburgensis
Acta Hort Sin — Acta Horticulturalia Sinica. Chinese Horticultural Society
Acta Hosp — Acta Hospitalia
Acta Humanistica Sci Univ Sangio Kyotiensis — Acta Humanistica et Scientifica. Universitatis Sangio Kyotiensis
Acta Human Sci Univ Sangio Kyotien Natur Sci Ser — Acta Humanistica et Scientifica. Universitatis Sangio Kyotiensis. Natural Science Series
Acta Humboldt — Acta Humboldtiana
Acta Humboldtiana Ser Geog et Ethnograph — Acta Humboldtiana. Series Geographica et Ethnographica
Acta Humboldt Ser Geol Palaeontol — Acta Humboldtiana. Series Geologica et Palaeontologica
Acta Hydrobiol — Acta Hydrobiologica
Acta Hydrobiol Krakow — Acta Hydrobiologica (Krakow)
Acta Hydrobiol Sin — Acta Hydrobiologica Sinica
Acta Hydrobiol Sin Peking — Acta Hydrobiologica Sinica/Shui Sheng Sheng Wu Hsueeh Chi K'an (Peking)
Acta Hydrochim Hydrobiol — Acta Hydrochimica et Hydrobiologica
Acta Hydrol Limnol Protistol — Acta Hydrologica, Limnologica, et Protistologica
Acta Hydrophys — Acta Hydrophysica
Acta Hydrophys (Berl) — Acta Hydrophysica (Deutsche Akademie der Wissenschaften zu Berlin. Zentralinstitut Physik der Erde. Selbstaendige Abteilung Physikalische Hydrographie)
Acta Hyg Epidemiol Microbiol — Acta Hygienica Epidemiologica et Microbiologica
Acta Hymenopt (Tokyo) — Acta Hymenopterologica (Tokyo)
Acta Iber Radiol-Cancerol — Acta Iberica Radiologica-Cancerologica
Acta Ichthyol Piscatoria — Acta Ichthyologica et Piscatoria
Acta IMEKO Proc Int Meas Conf — Acta IMEKO. Proceedings of the International Measurement Conference
Acta Inf — Acta Informatica
Acta Inform — Acta Informatica
Acta Informat — Acta Informatica
Acta Inst Anesthesiol — Acta. Institut d'Anesthesiologie
Acta Inst Bot Acad Sci Slovacae Ser B — Acta Instituti Botanici Academiae Scientiarum Slovacae. Series B. Physiologica,Pathophysiologica
Acta Inst Bot Acad Sci URSS Ser 6 — Acta Instituti Botanici. Academia Scientiarum URSS. Series 6. Introductio Plantarum et Viridaria
Acta Inst For Zvolenensis — Acta Instituti Forestalis Zvolenensis
Acta Inst For Zvolenensis Vysk Ustav Lesn Hospod — Acta Instituti Forestalis Zvolenensis. Vyskumny Ustav Lesneho Hospodarstva
Acta Inst Hort Bot Tartu — Acta Instituti et Horti Botanici Tartuensis
Acta Inst Mus Zool Univ Athen — Acta Instituti et Musei Zoologici Universitatis Atheniensis
Acta Inst Nutr Hum Pragae — Acta Instituti Nutritionis Humanae Pragae
Acta Inst Psychol Univ Zagrabiensis — Acta Instituti Psychologici Universitatis Zagrabiensis
Acta Inst Romani Finland — Acta Instituti Romani Finlandiae
Acta Int Sci Congr Volcano Thera — Acta. International Scientific Congress on the Volcano of Thera
Acta Int Union Cancer — Acta. International Union against Cancer
Acta Int Ver Krebsbekaempf — Acta der Internationalen Vereinigung fuer Krebsbekaempfung
Acta IRF — Acta Instituti Romani Finlandiae
Acta Isot — Acta Isotopica
Acta Jinan Univ Nat Sci Ed — Acta of Jinan University. Natural Sciences Edition
Acta Jpn Med Trop — Acta Japonica Medicinae Tropicalis
Acta Jur Acad Sci Hung — Acta Juridica. Academiae Scientiarum Hungaricae
Acta Jur (Budapest) — Acta Juridica (Budapest)
Acta Jur (Cape Town) — Acta Juridica (Cape Town)
Acta Juridica — Acta Juridica. Academiae Scientiarum Hungaricae
Acta Juridica Acad Sci Hungaricae — Acta Juridica. Academiae Scientiarum Hungaricae
Acta Jutl — Acta Jutlandica
Acta Kirin Med Univ — Acta of Kirin Medical University
Acta Krausi Cuad Inst Nac Microbiol (B Aires) — Acta Krausi. Cuaderno del Instituto Nacional de Microbiologia (Buenos Aires)
Acta Krausi Cuad Inst Nac Microbiol (Buenos Aires) — Acta Krausi. Cuaderno del Instituto Nacional de Microbiologia (Buenos Aires)
ActaL — Acta Latgalica
Acta Lapp — Acta Lapponica
Acta Leiden — Acta Leidensia
Acta Leiden Inst Trop Geneeskd — Acta Leidensia. Instituut voor Tropische Geneeskunde
Acta Leprol — Acta Leprologica
Acta Leprol (Geneve) — Acta Leprologica (Geneve)
Acta Limnol — Acta Limnologica

Acta Limnol Indica — Acta Limnologica Indica
Acta Ling — Acta Linguistica
Acta Ling (Bud) — Acta Linguistica. Magyar Tudomanyos Akademia (Budapest, Hungary)
Acta Linguist — Acta Linguistica
Acta Linguist Hung — Acta Linguistica. Academiae Scientiarum Hungaricae
Acta Lit Et Scient Suec — Acta Literaria et Scientiarum Sueciae
Acta Lit Hung — Acta Litteraria. Academiae Scientiarum Hungaricae
Acta Litt — Acta Litteraria. Magyar Tudomanyos Akademia
Acta Litt Altenburg — Acta Litteraria (Altenburg)
Acta Litt (Hung) — Acta Litteraria. Magyar Tudomanyos Akademia (Budapest, Hungary)
Acta Litt Sci Regiae Univ Hung Francisco Josephinae Sect Med — Acta Litterarum ac Scientiarum Regiae Universitatis Hungaricae Francisco-Josephinae. Sectio Medicorum
Acta Litt Sci Regiae Univ Hung Francisco Josephinae Sect Sci — Acta Litterarum ac Scientiarum Regiae Universitatis Hungaricae Francisco-Josephinae. Sectio Scientiarum Naturalium
Acta Lit Univ Hafn — Acta Literaria Universitatis Hafniensis
Act Allerg — Acta Allergologica
Acta Lund — Acta Universitatis Lundensis
ActaM — Acta Musicologica
ACTA Mag — ACTA [*Art Craft Teachers Association*] Magazine
Acta Manilana A — Acta Manilana. Series A. Natural and Applied Sciences
Acta Manilana Ser A — Acta Manilana. Series A
Acta Manilana Ser A Nat Appl Sci — Acta Manilana. Series A. Natural and Applied Sciences
Acta Marx-Lenin — Acta Marxistica-Leninistica
Acta Mater — Acta Materialia
Acta Mater Compos Sin — Acta Materiae Compositae Sinica
Acta Math — Acta Mathematica
Acta Math Acad Sci Hungar — Acta Mathematica. Academiae Scientiarum Hungaricae
Acta Math Appl Sin — Acta Mathematicae Applicatae Sinica
Acta Math Appl Sinica — Acta Mathematicae Applicatae Sinica
Acta Math Hungar — Acta Mathematica Hungarica
Acta Math Inform Univ Ostraviensis — Acta Mathematica et Informatica Universitatis Ostraviensis
Acta Math Sci — Acta Mathematica Scientia
Acta Math Sin — Acta Mathematica Sinica
Acta Math Sinica — Acta Mathematica Sinica
Acta Math Sinica NS — Acta Mathematica Sinica. New Series
Acta Math Univ Comenian — Acta Mathematica. Universitatis Comenianae
Acta Math Vietnam — Acta Mathematica Vietnamica
Acta Mech — Acta Mechanica
Acta Mech Sin — Acta Mechanica Sinica
Acta Mech Sin (Chin Ed) — Acta Mechanica Sinica (Chinese Edition)
Acta Mech Sinica — Acta Mechanica Sinica
Acta Mech Solida Sin — Acta Mechanica Solida Sinica
Acta Mech Solide Sinica Chinese Soc Theo Appl Mech — Acta Mecanica Solide Sinica. Chinese Society of Theoretical and Applied Mechanics
Acta Med Acad Sci Hung — Acta Medica. Academiae Scientiarum Hungaricae
Acta Med Austriaca — Acta Medica Austriaca
Acta Med Austriaca Suppl — Acta Medica Austriaca. Supplement
Acta Med Auxol (Milan) — Acta Medica Auxologica (Milan)
Acta Med Berol — Acta Medicorum Berolinensium in Incrementum Artis et Scientiarum Collecta et Digesta
Acta Med Biol — Acta Medica et Biologica
Acta Med Biol Niigata — Acta Medica et Biologica (Niigata)
Acta Med Budapest — Acta Medica (Budapest)
Acta Med Bulg — Acta Medica Bulgarica
Acta Med Chir Bras — Acta Medica Chirurgica Brasiliense
Acta Med Colomb — Acta Medica Colombiana
Acta Med Costarric — Acta Medica Costarricense
Acta Med Croatica — Acta Medica Croatica
Acta Med (Fukuoka) — Acta Medica (Fukuoka)
Acta Med Hidalg — Acta Medica Hidalguense
Acta Med Hist Pat — Acta Medicae Historiae Patavina
Acta Med Hist Patav — Acta Medicae Historiae Patavina
Acta Med Hokkaidonensia — Acta Medica Hokkaidonensia
Acta Med Hondur — Acta Medica Hondurena
Acta Med Hung — Acta Medica Hungarica
Acta Med Hyogoensia — Acta Medica Hyogoensia
Acta Medicotech — Acta Medicotechnica
Acta Med Inst Super Med (Sofia) — Acta Medica Instituti Superioris Medici (Sofia)
Acta Med Iran — Acta Medica Iranica
Acta Med Ital Mal Infett Parassit — Acta Medica Italica di Malattie Infettive e Parassitarie
Acta Med Ital Med Trop Subtrop — Acta Medica Italica di Medicina Tropicale e Subtropicale e di Gastroenterologia
Acta Med Ital Med Trop Subtrop Gastroenterol — Acta Medica Italica di Medicina Tropicale e Subtropicale e di Gastroenterologia
Acta Med Iugosl — Acta Medica Iugoslavica
Acta Med Iugosl (Eng Transl) — Acta Medica Iugoslavica (English Translation)
Acta Med Keijo — Acta Medicinalia in Keijo
Acta Med Leg Soc — Acta Medicinae Legalis et Socialis
Acta Med Leg Soc (Liege) — Acta Medicinae Legalis et Socialis (Liege)
Acta Med Medianae — Acta Medica Medianae
Acta Med (Mex) — Acta Medica (Mexico)
Acta Med Mexico City — Acta Medica (Mexico City)
Acta Med Nagasaki — Acta Medica Nagasakiensia
Acta Med Okayama — Acta Medica Okayama
Acta Med Orient — Acta Medica Orientalia
Acta Med Pat — Acta Medica Patavina
Acta Med Pata — Acta Medica Patavina

Acta Med Peru — Acta Medica Peruana
Acta Med Phil Havn — Acta Medica et Philosophica Hafniensia
Acta Med Philipp — Acta Medica Philippina
Acta Med Pol — Acta Medica Polona
Acta Med Port — Acta Medica Portuguesa
Acta Med (Rio De Janeiro) — Acta Medica (Rio De Janeiro)
Acta Med Rom — Acta Medica Romana
Acta Med Roman — Acta Medica Romana
Acta Med Romana — Acta Medica Romana
Acta Med Scand — Acta Medica Scandinavica
Acta Med Scandinav — Acta Medica Scandinavica
Acta Med Scand Suppl — Acta Medica Scandinavica. Supplementum
Acta Med Scand Symp Ser — Acta Medica Scandinavica Symposium Series
Acta Med Suec — Acta Medicorum Suecicorum
Acta Med Tenerife — Acta Medica de Tenerife
Acta Med Turc — Acta Medica Turcica
Acta Med Turc Suppl — Acta Medica Turcica. Supplementum
Acta Med Univ Kagoshima — Acta Medica Universitatis Kagoshimaensis
Acta Med URSS — Acta Medica URSS
Acta Med Venez — Acta Medica Venezolana
Acta Med Vet — Acta Medica Veterinaria
Acta Med Vet (Madr) — Acta Medica Veterinaria (Madrid)
Acta Med Vietnam — Acta Medica Vietnamica
Acta Mem Soc Esp Antr — Acta y Memorias. Sociedad Espanola de Antropologia, Etnografia, y Prehistoria
Acta Metall — Acta Metallurgica
Acta Metall Mater — Acta Metallurgica et Materialia
Acta Metall Sin — Acta Metallurgica Sinica
Acta Metall Sin Chin Ed — Acta Metallurgica Sinica (Chinese Edition)
Acta Metall Sin Engl Lett — Acta Metallurgica Sinica. English Letters
Acta Meteorol Sin — Acta Meteorologica Sinica
Acta Met Sin — Acta Metallurgica Sinica
Acta Mex Cienc y Tecnol — Acta Mexicana de Ciencia y Tecnologia
Acta Mexicana Cienc Tecn — Acta Mexicana de Ciencia y Tecnologia. Instituto Politecnico Nacional
Acta Mexicana Ci Tecn — Acta Mexicana de Ciencia y Tecnologia
Acta Microbiol — Acta Microbiologica
Acta Microbiol Acad Sci Hung — Acta Microbiologica. Academiae Scientiarum Hungaricae
Acta Microbiol Bulg — Acta Microbiologica Bulgarica
Acta Microbiol Hell — Acta Microbiologica Hellenica
Acta Microbiol Hung — Acta Microbiologica Hungarica
Acta Microbiol Immunol Hung — Acta Microbiologica et Immunologica Hungarica
Acta Microbiol Pol — Acta Microbiologica Polonica
Acta Microbiol Polon — Acta Microbiologica Polonica
Acta Microbiol Pol Ser A — Acta Microbiologica Polonica. Series A. Microbiologia Generalis
Acta Microbiol Pol Ser A Microbiol Gen — Acta Microbiologica Polonica. Series A. Microbiologia Generalis
Acta Microbiol Pol Ser B — Acta Microbiologica Polonica. Series B. Microbiologia Applicata
Acta Microbiol Pol Ser B Microbiol Appl — Acta Microbiologica Polonica. Series B. Microbiologia Applicata
Acta Microbiol Sin — Acta Microbiologica Sinica
Acta Microbiol Sin Engl Transl — Acta Microbiologica Sinica (English Translation)
Acta Microbiol Sinica — Acta Microbiologica Sinica
Acta Microbiol Virol Immunol — Acta Microbiologica, Virologica, et Immunologica
Acta Microbiol Virol Immunol (Sofiia) — Acta Microbiologica, Virologica, et Immunologica (Sofiia)
Acta Mineral-Petrogr — Acta Mineralogica-Petrographica
Acta Mineral-Petrogr (Szeged) — Acta Mineralogica-Petrographica (Acta Universitatis Szegediensis)
Acta Mineral Sin — Acta Mineralogica Sinica
Acta Mont — Acta Montana
Acta Mont Ser AB — Acta Montana. Series AB. Geodynamics and Fuel, Carbon, Mineral Processing
Acta Mont Ser B — Acta Montana. Series B. Fuel, Carbon, Mineral Processing
Acta Moravs Muz — Acta Moravske Muzeum
Acta Morphol Acad Sci Hung — Acta Morphologica. Academiae Scientiarum Hungaricae
Acta Morphol Acad Sci Hung Suppl — Acta Morphologica. Academiae Scientiarum Hungaricae. Supplementum
Acta Morphol Hung — Acta Morphologica Hungarica
Acta Morphol Neerl-Scand — Acta Morphologica Neerlando-Scandinavica
Acta Morphol (Sofia) — Acta Morphologica (Sofia)
Acta Mus — Acta Musicologica
Acta Mus Hist Nat — Acta Musei Historiae Naturalis
Acta Mus Hist Nat Acad Pol Litt Sci — Acta Musei Historiae Naturalis. Academia Polona Litterarum et Scientiarum
Acta Mus Horti Bot Bohemiae Borealis Hist Nat — Acta Musei et Horti Botanici Bohemiae Borealis. Historia Naturalis
Acta Music — Acta Musicologica
Acta Musicolog Fenn — Acta Musicologica Fennica
Acta Mus Macedonici Sci Nat — Acta Musei Macedonici. Scientiarum Naturalium
Acta Mus Maced Sci Nat — Acta Musei Macedonici. Scientiarum Naturalium
Acta Mus Morav — Acta Musei Moraviae
Acta Mus Morav Sci Nat — Acta Musei Moraviae. Scientiae Naturales
Acta Mus Morav Sci Natur — Acta Musei Moraviae. Scientiae Naturales
Acta Mus Morav Sci Soc — Acta Musei Moraviae. Scientiae Sociales
Acta Mus Morav Sci Social — Acta Musei Moraviae. Scientiae Sociales
Acta Mus Nap — Acta Musei Napocensis
Acta Mus Napoca — Acta Musei Napocensis
Acta Mus Napocensis — Acta Musei Napocensis
Acta Mus Natl Pragae Ser B — Acta Musei Nationalis Pragae. Series B. Historia Naturalis

Acta Mus Natl Pragae Ser B Hist Nat — Acta Musei Nationalis Pragae. Series B. Historia Naturalis
Acta Mus Pardubic — Acta Musei Pardubicensis
Acta Mus Silesiae Ser A Sci Nat — Acta Musei Silesiae. Series A. Scientiae Naturales
Acta Mycol — Acta Mycologica
Acta Mycol Sin — Acta Mycologica Sinica
Act Anae Sc — Acta Anaesthesiologica Scandinavica
Acta Nat Ateneo Parmense — Acta Naturalia de l'Ateneo Parmense
Acta Nat Isl — Acta Naturalia Islandica
Act Anatom — Acta Anatomica
Acta Neerl Morphol Norm Pathol — Acta Neerlandica Morphologiae Normalis et Pathologicae
Acta Neonatol Jpn — Acta Neonatologica Japonica
Acta Neurobiol Exp — Acta Neurobiologiae Experimentalis
Acta Neurobiol Exp Suppl — Acta Neurobiologiae Experimentalis. Supplementum
Acta Neurobiol Exp (Warsaw) — Acta Neurobiologiae Experimentalis (Warsaw)
Acta Neurobiol Exp (Warsz) — Acta Neurobiologiae Experimentalis (Warszawa)
Acta Neurochir — Acta Neurochirurgica
Acta Neurochir Suppl — Acta Neurochirurgica. Supplementum
Acta Neurochir Suppl (Wien) — Acta Neurochirurgica. Supplementum (Wien)
Acta Neurochir (Wien) — Acta Neurochirurgica (Wien)
Acta Neurol — Acta Neurologica
Acta Neurol Belg — Acta Neurologica Belgica
Acta Neurol Latinoam — Acta Neurologica Latinoamericana
Acta Neurol Latinoamer — Acta Neurologica Latinoamericana
Acta Neurol (Naples) — Acta Neurologica (Naples)
Acta Neurol (Napoli) — Acta Neurologica (Napoli)
Acta Neurol Psychiatr Belg — Acta Neurologica et Psychiatrica Belgica
Acta Neurol Quad — Acta Neurologica. Quaderni
Acta Neurol Scand — Acta Neurologica Scandinavica
Acta Neurol Scand Suppl — Acta Neurologica Scandinavica. Supplementum
Acta Neuropathol — Acta Neuropathologica
Acta Neuropathol (Berl) — Acta Neuropathologica (Berlin)
Acta Neuropathol Suppl — Acta Neuropathologica. Supplementum
Acta Neuropathol Suppl (Berl) — Acta Neuropathologica. Supplementum (Berlin)
Acta Neuropsiquiat Argent — Acta Neuropsiquiatrica Argentina
Acta Neuroveg — Acta Neurovegetativa
Acta Neuroveg Suppl — Acta Neurovegetativa. Supplementum
Acta Nipp Med Trop — Acta Nipponica Medicinae Tropicalis
Acta Nippon Med Trop — Acta Nipponica Medicinae Tropicalis
Act An-Path — Actualites Anatomo-Pathologiques
ActAntHung — Acta Antiqua Hungarica
Act Antiq H — Acta Antiqua. Academiae Scientiarum Hungaricae
Acta Num — Acta Numismatica
Acta Nutr Sin — Acta Nutrimenta Sinica
Acta O — Acta Orientalia
Acta Obstet Ginecol Hisp-Lusit — Acta Obstetrica y Ginecologica Hispano-Lusitana
Acta Obstet Ginecol Hisp-Lusit Supl — Acta Obstetrica y Ginecologica Hispano-Lusitana. Suplemento
Acta Obstet Gynaecol Jpn — Acta Obstetrica et Gynaecologica Japonica
Acta Obstet Gynaecol Jpn (Engl Ed) — Acta Obstetrica et Gynaecologica Japonica (English Edition)
Acta Obstet Gynaecol Jpn (Jpn Ed) — Acta Obstetrica et Gynaecologica Japonica (Japanese Edition)
Acta Obstet Gynecol Scand — Acta Obstetrica et Gynecologica Scandinavica
Acta Obstet Gynecol Scand Suppl — Acta Obstetrica et Gynecologica Scandinavica. Supplement
Acta Obst Gynec Scandinav — Acta Obstetrica et Gynecologica Scandinavica
Acta Oceanogr Taiwan — Acta Oceanographica Taiwanica
Acta Oceanolog Sin — Acta Oceanologica Sinica
Acta Odont — Acta Odontologica
Acta Odont Latinoam — Acta Odontologica Latinoamericana
Acta Odontol Pediatr — Acta Odontologica Pediatrica
Acta Odontol Scand — Acta Odontologica Scandinavica
Acta Odontol Scand Suppl — Acta Odontologica Scandinavica. Supplementum
Acta Odontol Venez — Acta Odontologica Venezolana
Acta Oecol Oecol Appl — Acta Oecologica. Oecologia Applicata
Acta Oecol Oecol Gen — Acta Oecologica. Oecologia Generalis
Acta Oecol Oecol Plant — Acta Oecologica. Oecologia Plantarum
Acta Oecol Ser 1 — Acta Oecologica. Serie 1. Oecologia Generalis
Acta Oecol Ser 2 — Acta Oecologica. Serie 2. Oecologia Applicata
Acta Oecol Ser 3 — Acta Oecologica. Serie 3. Oecologia Plantarum
Acta Oecon — Acta Oeconomica
Acta Oeconomica — Acta Oeconomica. Academiae Scientiarum Hungaricae
Acta Oncol — Acta Oncologica
Acta Oncol Bras — Acta Oncologica Brasileira
Acta Oncol (Madr) — Acta Oncologica (Madrid)
Acta Oper-Oecon — Acta Operativo-Oeconomica
Acta Opht — Acta Ophtalmologica
Acta Ophth — Acta Ophthalmologica
Acta Ophthalmol — Acta Ophthalmologica
Acta Ophthalmol (Copenh) — Acta Ophthalmologica (Copenhagen)
Acta Ophthalmol Iugosl — Acta Ophthalmologica Iugoslavica
Acta Ophthalmol Pol — Acta Ophthalmologica Polonica
Acta Ophthalmol Scand — Acta Ophthalmologica Scandinavica
Acta Ophthalmol Scand Suppl — Acta Ophthalmologica Scandinavica. Supplement
Acta Ophthalmol Suppl — Acta Ophthalmologica. Supplementum
Acta Ophthalmol Suppl (Copenh) — Acta Ophthalmologica. Supplementum (Copenhagen)
Acta Opt Sin — Acta Optica Sinica
Acta Or — Acta Orientalia
Acta Or (B) — Acta Orientalia. Academiae Scientiarum Hungaricae (Budapest)

Acta Organ — Acta Organologica
Acta Orient — Acta Orientalia
Acta Orient Acad Sci Hungar — Acta Orientalia. Academiae Scientiarum Hungaricae
Acta Orientalia Acad Sci Hung — Acta Orientalia Academiae Scientiarum Hungaricae
Acta Orient (Hung) — Acta Orientalia. Magyar Tudomanyos Akademia (Hungary)
Acta ORL Belg — Acta Oto-Rhino-Laryngologica Belgica
Acta ORL Espan — Acta Oto-Rino-Laringologica Espanola
Acta Ornith — Acta Ornithologica
Acta Ornithol (Engl Transl) — Acta Ornithologica (English Translation)
Acta Ornithol (Warsaw) — Acta Ornithologica (Warsaw)
Acta Ornithol (Warsaw) (Engl Transl) — Acta Ornithologica (Warsaw) (English Translation)
Acta Orn Warsz — Acta Ornithologica (Warszawa)
Acta Orthop — Acta Orthopaedica Scandinavica
Acta Orthop Belg — Acta Orthopaedica Belgica
Acta Orthop Ital — Acta Orthopaedica Italica
Acta Orthop Scand — Acta Orthopaedica Scandinavica
Acta Orthop Scandinav — Acta Orthopaedica Scandinavica
Acta Orthop Scand Suppl — Acta Orthopaedica Scandinavica. Supplementum
Acta Ortoped Traum Iber — Acta Ortopedica-Traumatologica Iberica
Acta Oto Lar — Acta Oto-Laryngologica
Acta Oto Lar Orient — Acta Oro-Laryngolocica Orientalia
Acta Oto-Laryng — Acta Oto-Laryngologica
Acta Oto-Laryngol — Acta Oto-Laryngologica
Acta Otolaryngol (Stockh) — Acta Otolaryngologica (Stockholm)
Acta Otolaryngol Suppl — Acta Otolaryngologica. Supplementum
Acta Otolaryngol Suppl (Stockh) — Acta Otolaryngologica. Supplement (Stockholm)
Acta Oto-Rhino-Lar Belg — Acta Oto-Rhino-Laryngologica Belgica
Acta Oto-Rhino-Laryngol Belg — Acta Oto-Rhino-Laryngologica Belgica
Acta Otorhinolaryngol Ital — Acta Otorhinolaryngologica Italica
Acta Otorinolar Esp — Acta Otorinolaringologica Espanola
Acta Oto Rino Lar Ibero Am — Acta Oto-Rino-Laringologica Ibero-Americana
Acta Oto-Rino-Laringo Esp — Acta Oto-Rino-Laringologica Espanola
Acta Oto-Rino-Laringol Ibero-Am — Acta Oto-Rino-Laringologica Ibero-Americana
Acta Otorrinolaringol Esp — Acta Otorrinolaringologica Espanola
Acta Paed Hung — Acta Paediatrica. Academiae Scientiarum Hungaricae
Acta Paediat — Acta Paediatrica
Acta Paediat Belg — Acta Paediatrica Belgica
Acta Paediat Hung — Acta Paediatrica Academiae Scientiarum Hungaricae
Acta Paediat Jap — Acta Paediatrica Japonica
Acta Paediatr — Acta Paediatrica
Acta Paediatr Acad Sci Hung — Acta Paediatrica. Academiae Scientiarum Hungaricae
Acta Paediatr Belg — Acta Paediatrica Belgica
Acta Paediatr (Budapest) — Acta Paediatrica (Budapest)
Acta Paediatr Hung — Acta Paediatrica Hungarica
Acta Paediatr Jpn — Acta Paediatrica Japonica
Acta Paediatr Jpn (Overseas Ed) — Acta Paediatrica Japonica (Overseas Edition)
Acta Paediatr Lat — Acta Paediatrica Latina
Acta Paediatr Scand — Acta Paediatrica Scandinavica
Acta Paediatr Scand Suppl — Acta Paediatrica Scandinavica. Supplementum
Acta Paediatr Sin — Acta Paediatrica Sinica
Acta Paediatr (Stockholm) — Acta Paediatrica (Stockholm)
Acta Paediatr Stockholm Suppl — Acta Paediatrica (Stockholm). Supplement
Acta Paediatr Suppl — Acta Paediatrica. Supplement
Acta Paediat Scandinav — Acta Paediatrica Scandinavica
Acta Paediat Stockh — Acta Paediatrica (Stockholm)
Acta Paediat (Uppsala) — Acta Paediatrica (Uppsala)
Acta Paed Lat — Acta Paediatrica Latina
Acta Paedopsychiat — Acta Paedopsychiatrica
Acta Paedopsychiatr — Acta Paedopsychiatrica
Acta Paedopsychiatr (Basel) — Acta Paedopsychiatrica (Basel)
Acta Paed Scand — Acta Paediatrica Scandinavica
Acta Palaeobot — Acta Palaeobotanica
Acta Palaeontol Pol — Acta Palaeontologica Polonica
Acta Palaeontol Polon — Acta Palaeontologica Polonica
Acta Palaeontol Sin — Acta Palaeontologica Sinica
Acta Palaeont Pol — Acta Palaeontologica Polonica
Acta Palaeont Sin — Acta Palaeontologica Sinica/Ku Sheng Wu Hsueh Pao
Acta Paracels — Acta Paracelsica
Acta Parasit Lith — Acta Parasitologica Lithuanica
Acta Parasitol — Acta Parasitologica
Acta Parasitol Iugosl — Acta Parasitologica Iugoslavica
Acta Parasitol Lith — Acta Parasitologica Lithuanica
Acta Parasitol Litu — Acta Parasitologica Lituanica
Acta Parasitol Pol — Acta Parasitologica Polonica
Acta Parasit Pol — Acta Parasitologica Polonica
Acta Path — Acta Pathologica et Microbiologica Scandinavica
Acta Path Belgr — Acta Pathologica (Belgradiae)
Acta Path Jap — Acta Pathologica Japonica
Acta Path Microbiol Scand — Acta Pathologica et Microbiologica Scandinavica
Acta Path Microbiol Scandinav — Acta Pathologica et Microbiologica Scandinavica
Acta Pathol Jpn — Acta Pathologica Japonica
Acta Pathol Microbiol Immunol Scand — Acta Pathologica, Microbiologica, et Immunologica Scandinavica
Acta Pathol Microbiol Immunol Scand — Acta Pathologica, Microbiologica, et Immunologica Scandinavica. Section A. Pathology
Acta Pathol Microbiol Immunol Scand — Acta Pathologica, Microbiologica, et Immunologica Scandinavica. Section A. Supplement
Acta Pathol Microbiol Immunol Scand — Acta Pathologica, Microbiologica, et Immunologica Scandinavica. Section B. Microbiology

Acta Pathol Microbiol Immunol Scand — Acta Pathologica, Microbiologica, et Immunologica Scandinavica. Section C. Immunology
Acta Pathol Microbiol Immunol Scand Sect A — Acta Pathologica, Microbiologica, et Immunologica Scandinavica. Section A
Acta Pathol Microbiol Immunol Scand Sect A Pathol — Acta Pathologica, Microbiologica, et Immunologica Scandinavica. Section A. Pathology
Acta Pathol Microbiol Immunol Scand Sect A Suppl — Acta Pathologica, Microbiologica, et Immunologica Scandinavica. Section A. Supplement
Acta Pathol Microbiol Immunol Scand Sect B — Acta Pathologica, Microbiologica, et Immunologica Scandinavica. Section B. Microbiology
Acta Pathol Microbiol Immunol Scand Sect B Microbiol — Acta Pathologica, Microbiologica, et Immunologica Scandinavica. Section B. Microbiology
Acta Pathol Microbiol Immunol Scand Sect C — Acta Pathologica, Microbiologica, et Immunologica Scandinavica. Section C. Immunology
Acta Pathol Microbiol Immunol Scand Sect C Immunol — Acta Pathologica, Microbiologica, et Immunologica Scandinavica. Section C. Immunology
Acta Pathol Microbiol Immunol Scand Sect C Immunol Suppl — Acta Pathologica, Microbiologica, et Immunologica Scandinavica. Section C. Immunology. Supplementum
Acta Pathol Microbiol Immunol Scand Sect C Suppl — Acta Pathologica, Microbiologica, et Immunologica Scandinavica. Section C. Supplement
Acta Pathol Microbiol Immunol Scand Suppl — Acta Pathologica, Microbiologica, et Immunologica Scandinavica. Supplement
Acta Pathol Microbiol Scand — Acta Pathologica et Microbiologica Scandinavica
Acta Pathol Microbiol Scand (A) — Acta Pathologica et Microbiologica Scandinavica. Section A
Acta Pathol Microbiol Scand (B) — Acta Pathologica et Microbiologica Scandinavica. Section B
Acta Pathol Microbiol Scand (C) — Acta Pathologica et Microbiologica Scandinavica. Section C
Acta Pathol Microbiol Scand Sect A — Acta Pathologica et Microbiologica Scandinavica. Section A
Acta Pathol Microbiol Scand Sect A Pathol — Acta Pathologica et Microbiologica Scandinavica. Section A. Pathology
Acta Pathol Microbiol Scand Sect A Suppl — Acta Pathologica et Microbiologica Scandinavica. Section A. Supplement
Acta Pathol Microbiol Scand Sect B — Acta Pathologica et Microbiologica Scandinavica. Section B
Acta Pathol Microbiol Scand Sect B Microbiol — Acta Pathologica et Microbiologica Scandinavica. Section B. Microbiology
Acta Pathol Microbiol Scand Sect B Microbiol Immunol — Acta Pathologica et Microbiologica Scandinavica. Section B. Microbiology and Immunology
Acta Pathol Microbiol Scand Sect B Suppl — Acta Pathologica et Microbiologica Scandinavica. Section B. Supplement
Acta Pathol Microbiol Scand Sect C — Acta Pathologica et Microbiologica Scandinavica. Section C
Acta Pathol Microbiol Scand Sect C Immunol — Acta Pathologica et Microbiologica Scandinavica. Section C. Immunology
Acta Pathol Microbiol Scand Sect C Suppl — Acta Pathologica et Microbiologica Scandinavica. Section C. Supplement
Acta Pathol Microbiol Scand Suppl — Acta Pathologica et Microbiologica Scandinavica. Supplementum
Acta Pathol Microbiol Sect A — Acta Pathologica et Microbiologica Scandinavica. Section A. Pathology
Acta Ped Esp — Acta Pediatrica Espanola
Acta Pediat Esp — Acta Pediatrica Espanola
Acta Pediatr Esp — Acta Pediatrica Espanola
Acta Pedol Sin — Acta Pedologica Sinica
Acta Pedol Sinica — Acta Pedologica Sinica
Acta Period Technol — Acta Periodica Technologica
Acta Petrol Mineral — Acta Petrologica et Mineralogica
Acta Petrol Mineral Anal — Acta Petrologica, Mineralogica, et Analytica
Acta Pet Sin — Acta Petrolei Sinica
Acta Pet Sin Pet Process Sect — Acta Petrolei Sinica. Petroleum Processing Section
Acta Phaenol — Acta Phaenologica
Acta Pharm — Acta Pharmaceutica
Acta Pharmaceut Jugoslav — Acta Pharmaceutica Jugoslavica
Acta Pharmacol — Acta Pharmacologica et Toxicologica
Acta Pharmacol Sin — Acta Pharmacologica Sinica
Acta Pharmacol Toxicol — Acta Pharmacologica et Toxicologica
Acta Pharmacol Toxicol (Copenh) — Acta Pharmacologica et Toxicologica (Copenhagen)
Acta Pharmacol Toxicol Suppl — Acta Pharmacologica et Toxicologica. Supplementum
Acta Pharmac Sin — Acta Pharmacologica Sinica
Acta Pharmac Tox — Acta Pharmacologica et Toxicologica
Acta Pharm Fenn — Acta Pharmaceutica Fennica
Acta Pharm Hist — Acta Pharmaciae Historica. Academie Internationale d'Histoire de la Pharmacie
Acta Pharm Hung — Acta Pharmaceutica Hungarica
Acta Pharm Indones — Acta Pharmaceutica Indonesia
Acta Pharm Int — Acta Pharmaceutica Internationalia
Acta Pharm Iugosl — Acta Pharmaceutica Iugoslavica
Acta Pharm Jugosl — Acta Pharmaceutica Jugoslavica
Acta Pharm Nord — Acta Pharmaceutica Nordica
Acta Pharm Sin — Acta Pharmaceutica Sinica
Acta Pharm Sinica — Acta Pharmaceutica Sinica
Acta Pharm Suec — Acta Pharmaceutica Suecica
Acta Pharm Technol — Acta Pharmaceutica Technologica
Acta Pharm Technol Suppl — Acta Pharmaceutica Technologica. Supplement
Acta Pharm Tox — Acta Pharmacologica et Toxicologica
Acta Pharm Turc — Acta Pharmaceutica Turcica
Acta Pharm Zagreb — Acta Pharmaceutica (Zagreb)
Acta Phil — Acta Philologica Scandinavica

Acta Phil Fennica — Acta Philosophica Fennica
Acta Philol — Acta Philologica. Societas Academica Dacoromana
Acta Philol Scand — Acta Philologica Scandinavica
Acta Philos Fenn — Acta Philosophica Fennica
Acta Philos Theol — Acta Philosophica et Theologica. Societas Academica Dacoromana
Acta Phil Soc Dac — Acta Philologica. Societas Academica Dacoromana
Acta Photonica Sin — Acta Photonica Sinica
Acta Phtisiol — Acta Phtisiologica
Acta Phys Acad Sci Hung — Acta Physica. Academiae Scientiarum Hungaricae
Acta Phys Acad Sci Hungar — Acta Physica. Academiae Scientiarum Hungaricae
Acta Phys Acad Sci Hung Suppl — Acta Physica Academiae Scientiarum Hungaricae. Supplement
Acta Phys Austriaca — Acta Physica Austriaca
Acta Phys Austriaca Suppl — Acta Physica Austriaca. Supplementum
Acta Phys Chem — Acta Physica et Chemica
Acta Phys Chem Univ Szeged — Acta Physica et Chemica. Nova Series. Acta Universitatis Szegediensis
Acta Phys Chim (Debrecina) — Acta Physica et Chimica (Debrecina)
Acta Phys Chim Sin — Acta Physico-Chimica Sinica
Acta Phys Hung — Acta Physica Hungarica
Acta Phys Hung New Ser Heavy Ion Phys — Acta Physica Hungarica New Series. Heavy Ion Physics
Acta Physicochim URSS — Acta Physicochimica URSS
Acta Phy Sin Abstr — Acta Physica Sinica. Abstracts
Acta Physiochim — Acta Physiochimica
Acta Physiol Acad Sci Hung — Acta Physiologica. Academiae Scientiarum Hungaricae
Acta Physiol Hung — Acta Physiologica. Academiae Scientiarum Hungaricae
Acta Physiol Hung — Acta Physiologica Hungarica
Acta Physiol Lat Am — Acta Physiologica Latino Americana
Acta Physiol Lat Am (Supl) — Acta Physiologica Latino Americana. Suplemento
Acta Physiol Latinoam — Acta Physiologica Latinoamericana
Acta Physiol Latinoamer — Acta Physiologica Latinoamericana
Acta Physiologica Scandinav — Acta Physiologica Scandinavica
Acta Physiol Pharmac Neerl — Acta Physiologica et Pharmacologica Neerlandica
Acta Physiol Pharmacol Bulg — Acta Physiologica et Pharmacologica Bulgarica
Acta Physiol Pharmacol Latinoam — Acta Physiologica et Pharmacologica Latinoamericana
Acta Physiol Pharmacol Neerl — Acta Physiologica et Pharmacologica Neerlandica
Acta Physiol Pharmacol Ther Latinoam — Acta Physiologica, Pharmacologica, et Therapeutica Latinoamericana
Acta Physiol Plant — Acta Physiologiae Plantarum
Acta Physiol Pol — Acta Physiologica Polonica
Acta Physiol Pol (Engl Transl) — Acta Physiologica Polonica (English Translation)
Acta Physiol Pol Supl — Acta Physiologica Polonica. Suplement
Acta Physiol Pol (Transl) — Acta Physiologica Polonica (Translation)
Acta Physiol Scand — Acta Physiologica Scandinavica
Acta Physiol Scand — Acta Societatis Physiologicae Scandinavicae
Acta Physiol Scand Suppl — Acta Physiologica Scandinavica. Supplementum
Acta Physiol Sin — Acta Physiologica Sinica
Acta Phys Pol — Acta Physica Polonica
Acta Phys Pol A — Acta Physica Polonica. Series A
Acta Phys Pol B — Acta Physica Polonica. Series B
Acta Phys Polon A — Acta Physica Polonica. Series A
Acta Phys Polon B — Acta Physica Polonica. Series B
Acta Phys Pol Ser A — Acta Physica Polonica. Series A
Acta Phys Pol Ser B — Acta Physica Polonica. Series B
Acta Phys Sin — Acta Physica Sinica
Acta Phys Sin Abstr — Acta Physica Sinica Abstracts
Acta Phys Sinica — Acta Physica Sinica
Acta Phys Sin Overseas Ed — Acta Physica Sinica (Overseas Edition)
Acta Phys Slov — Acta Physica Slovaca
Acta Phys Slovaca — Acta Physica Slovaca
Acta Phys Suppl — Acta Physica. Supplement
Acta Phys Temp Humilis Sin — Acta Physica Temperaturae Humilis Sinica
Acta Phys Univ Comenianae — Acta Physica Universitatis Comenianae
Acta Phytochim — Acta Phytochimica
Acta Phytogeogr Suec — Acta Phytogeographica Suecica
Acta Phytomed — Acta Phytomedica
Acta Phytopathol — Acta Phytopathologica
Acta Phytopathol Acad Sci Hung — Acta Phytopathologica. Academiae Scientiarum Hungaricae
Acta Phytopathol (Budapest) — Acta Phytopathologica (Budapest)
Acta Phytopathol Entomol Hung — Acta Phytopathologica et Entomologica Hungarica
Acta Phytopathol Sin — Acta Phytopathologica Sinica
Acta Phytopathol Sinica — Acta Phytopathologica Sinica
Acta Phytopathol Sin Transl Bull — Acta Phytopathologica Sinica Translation Bulletin/Chi Wu Ping Li Hsueeh I P'ao
Acta Phytophylacica Sin — Acta Phytophylacica Sinica
Acta Phytophyl Sinica — Acta Phytophylacica Sinica
Acta Phytophysiologica Sin — Acta Phytophysiologica Sinica
Acta Phytophysiol Sinica — Acta Phytophysiologica Sinica
Acta Phytotax Geobot Kyoto — Acta Phytotaxonomica et Geobotanica/ Shokubutsu Bunrui Chiri (Kyoto)
Acta Phytotaxon Barc — Acta Phytotaxonomica Barcinonensia
Acta Phytotaxon Geobot — Acta Phytotaxonomica et Geobotanica
Acta Phytotaxon Sin — Acta Phytotaxonomica Sinica
Acta Phytother — Acta Phytotherapeutica
Acta Phytotherap — Acta Phytotherapeutica
Acta Pol Hist — Acta Poloniae Historica
Acta Polit — Acta Politica
Acta Politec Mex — Acta Politecnica Mexicana

Acta Polit Helsinki — Acta Politica (Helsinki)
Acta Pol Mar — Acta Poloniae Maritima
Acta Pol Pharm — Acta Poloniae Pharmaceutica
Acta Pol Pharm (Engl Transl) — Acta Poloniae Pharmaceutica (English Translation)
Acta Pol Pharm (Transl) — Acta Poloniae Pharmaceutica (English Translation)
Acta Polym — Acta Polymerica
Acta Polym Sin — Acta Polymerica Sinica
Acta Polytech 1 (Prague) — Acta Polytechnica 1. Stavebni (Prague)
Acta Polytech 2 — Acta Polytechnica 2. Strojni
Acta Polytech 3 — Acta Polytechnica. 3. Elektrotechnicka
Acta Polytech 4 — Acta Polytechnica. 4. Technicko-Teoreticka
Acta Polytech Ceske Vys Uceni Tech v Pr III — Acta Polytechnica. Ceske Vysoke Uceni Technicke v Prace III
Acta Polytech Chem Incl Metall Ser — Acta Polytechnica. Chemistry Including Metallurgy Series
Acta Polytech Civ Eng Build Constr Ser — Acta Polytechnica. Civil Engineering and Building Construction Series
Acta Polytech III — Acta Polytechnica. Series III
Acta Polytech IV (Prague) — Acta Polytechnica. Rada IV. Technicko-Teoreticka (Prague)
Acta Polytech Mech Eng Ser — Acta Polytechnica. Mechanical Engineering Series
Acta Polytech Phys Appl Math — Acta Polytechnica. Physics and Applied Mathematics
Acta Polytech Phys Incl Nucleon Ser — Acta Polytechnica. Physics Including Nucleonics Series
Acta Polytech Prace CVUT — Acta Polytechnica. Prace CVUT v Praze
Acta Polytech Prace CVUT Praze Ser IV Tech Teoret — Acta Polytechnica. Prace CVUT v Praze. Series IV. Technicko-Teoreticka
Acta Polytech Rada 1 Stavebni — Acta Polytechnica. Rada 1. Stavebni
Acta Polytech Rada 2 Strojni — Acta Polytechnica. Rada 2. Strojni
Acta Polytech Rada 3 Prague — Acta Polytechnica. Rada 3. Elektrotechnicka (Prague)
Acta Polytech Rada 4 Prague — Acta Polytechnica. Rada 4. Technicko-Teoreticka (Prague)
Acta Polytech Rada III Elektrotech — Acta Polytechnica. Rada III. Elektrotechnicka
Acta Polytech Rada IV Tech-Teor — Acta Polytechnica. Rada IV. Technicko-Teoreticka
Acta Polytech Scand — Acta Polytechnica Scandinavica
Acta Polytech Scand Appl Phys Ser — Acta Polytechnica Scandinavica. Applied Physics Series
Acta Polytech Scand Chem Incl Metall Ser — Acta Polytechnica Scandinavica. Chemistry Including Metallurgy Series
Acta Polytech Scand Chem Technol Metall Ser — Acta Polytechnica Scandinavica. Chemical Technology and Metallurgy Series
Acta Polytech Scand Chem Technol Ser — Acta Polytechnica Scandinavica. Chemical Technology Series
Acta Polytech Scand Civ Eng Build Constr Ser — Acta Polytechnica Scandinavica. Civil Engineering and Building Construction Series
Acta Polytech Scand Civ Eng Build Constru Ser — Acta Polytechnica Scandinavica. Civil Engineering and Building Construction Series
Acta Polytech Scand Elec Eng Ser — Acta Polytechnica Scandinavica. Electrical Engineering Series
Acta Polytech Scand Electr Eng Ser — Acta Polytechnica Scandinavica. Electrical Engineering Series
Acta Polytech Scand Electr Ser — Acta Polytechnica Scandinavica. Electrical Series
Acta Polytech Scandinavica Chem Incl Met Series — Acta Polytechnica Scandinavica. Chemistry Including Metallurgy Series
Acta Polytech Scand Math and Comput Mach Ser — Acta Polytechnica Scandinavica. Mathematics and Computing Machinery Series
Acta Polytech Scand Math Comput Engrg Ser — Acta Polytechnica Scandinavica. Mathematics Computing and Management in Engineering Series
Acta Polytech Scand Math Comput Mach Ser — Acta Polytechnica Scandinavica. Mathematics and Computing Machinery Series
Acta Polytech Scand Math Comput Sci Ser — Acta Polytechnica Scandinavica. Mathematics and Computer Science Series
Acta Polytech Scand Mech Eng Ser — Acta Polytechnica Scandinavica. Mechanical Engineering Series
Acta Polytech Scand Phys Incl Nucleon Ser — Acta Polytechnica Scandinavica. Physics Including Nucleonics Series
Acta Polytech Scand Phys Incl Nucl Ser — Acta Polytechnica Scandinavica. Physics Including Nucleonics Series
Acta Polytech Scand Phys Nucl Ser — Acta Polytechnica Scandinavica. Physics Including Nucleonics Series
Acta Pontif Acad Sci — Acta Pontificia. Academia Scientiarum
Acta Pont Inst Bibl — Acta Pontificii Instituti Biblici
Acta Praehist — Acta Praehistorica
Acta Praehist Archaeol — Acta Praehistorica et Archaeologica
Acta Praehist et Arch — Acta Praehistorica et Archaeologica
Acta Praehist et Archaeol — Acta Praehistorica et Archaeologica
Acta Pr Hist A — Acta Praehistorica et Archaeologica
Acta Primae Secundae Acad Med Shanghai — Acta Primae et Secundae Academiae Medicinae Shanghai
Acta Prot — Acta Protozoologica
Acta Protozool — Acta Protozoologica
Acta Psiquiatr Psicol Am Lat — Acta Psiquiatrica y Psicologica de America Latina
Acta Psiquiatr Psicol (Argent) — Acta Psiquiatrica y Psicologica (Argentina)
Acta Psych — Acta Psychiatrica et Neurologica
Acta Psychiat Belg — Acta Psychiatrica Belgica
Acta Psychiat Et Neurol — Acta Psychiatrica et Neurologica
Acta Psychiatr Belg — Acta Psychiatrica Belgica
Acta Psychiatr Neurol — Acta Psychiatrica et Neurologica
Acta Psychiatr Neurol Scand — Acta Psychiatrica et Neurologica Scandinavica

Acta Psychiatr Neurol Scand Suppl — Acta Psychiatrica et Neurologica Scandinavica. Supplementum
Acta Psychiatr Scand — Acta Psychiatrica Scandinavica
Acta Psychiatr Scand Suppl — Acta Psychiatrica Scandinavica. Supplementum
Acta Psychiat Scand — Acta Psychiatrica et Neurologica Scandinavica
Acta Psychiat Scand — Acta Psychiatrica Scandinavica
Acta Psychiat Scandinav — Acta Psychiatrica Scandinavica
Acta Psychiat Scand Suppl — Acta Psychiatrica Scandinavica. Supplementum
Acta Psychol — Acta Psychologica
Acta Psychol (Amst) — Acta Psychologica (Amsterdam)
Acta Psychol Fenn — Acta Psychologica Fennica
Acta Psychol Gothoburg — Acta Psychologica Gothoburgensia
Acta Psychol Taiwan — Acta Psychologica Taiwanica
Acta Psychotherap Psychosom Orthopaedagog — Acta Psychotherapeutica, Psychosomatica, et Orthopaedagogica
Acta Psychother Psychosom — Acta Psychotherapeutica et Psychosomatica
Acta Psychother Psychosom Orthopaedagog — Acta Psychotherapeutica, Psychosomatica, et Orthopaedagogica
Acta Psych Scand — Acta Psychiatrica Scandinavica
Acta PT — Acta Psychologica Taiwanica
Acta Radiobotanica Genet Bull Inst Radiat Breed — Acta Radiobotanica et Genetica. Bulletin. Institute of Radiation Breeding
Acta Radiobot Genet — Acta Radiobotanica et Genetica
Acta Radiol — Acta Radiologica
Acta Radiol Diagn — Acta Radiologica. Series One. Diagnosis
Acta Radiol Diagn (Stockh) — Acta Radiologica. Series One. Diagnosis (Stockholm)
Acta Radiol Interam — Acta Radiologica Interamericana
Acta Radiol Oncol — Acta Radiologica. Oncology
Acta Radiol Oncol Radiat Phys Biol — Acta Radiologica. Series Two. Oncology, Radiation, Physics, and Biology
Acta Radiol Oncol Radiat Therapy Phys and Biol — Acta Radiologica. Oncology, Radiation Therapy, Physics, and Biology
Acta Radiol Oncol Radiat Ther Phys Biol — Acta Radiologica. Oncology, Radiation Therapy, Physics, and Biology
Acta Radiol (Stockh) — Acta Radiologica (Stockholm)
Acta Radiol Suppl — Acta Radiologica. Supplementum
Acta Radiol Suppl (Stockh) — Acta Radiologica. Supplementum (Stockholm)
Acta Radiol Ther Phys Biol — Acta Radiologica. Therapy, Physics, Biology [*Later, Acta Radiologica. Series Two. Oncology, Radiation, Physics, and Biology (Stockholm)*]
Acta Radiol Ther (Stockh) — Acta Radiologica. Therapy, Physics, Biology (Stockholm) [*Later, Acta Radiologica. Series Two. Oncology, Radiation, Physics, and Biology (Stockholm)*]
Acta RCF — Acta Rei Cretariae Romanae Fautorum
Act Archaeo — Acta Archaeologica
Act Arch (Copenhagen) — Acta Archaeologica (Copenhagen)
Acta RCRF — Acta Rei Cretariae Romanae Fautorum
Acta Regiae Soc Sci Litt Gothob Zool — Acta Regiae Societatis Scientiarum et Litterarum Gothoburgensis. Zoologica
Acta Regia Soc Physiogr Lund — Acta Regia Societatis Physiographicae Lundensis
Acta Reprod Turc — Acta Reproductiva Turcica
Acta Rerum Nat Dist Silesiae — Acta Rerum Naturalium Districtus Silesiae
Acta Rerum Nat Mus Nat Slov Bratisl — Acta Rerum Naturalium. Musei Nationalis Slovaci Bratislava
Acta Res Nat Est Perscrutandas 1 Ser — Acta ad Res Naturae Estonicae Perscrutandas. 1 Ser. Geologica, Chemica, et Physica
Acta Res Nat Est Perscrutandas 2 Ser — Acta ad Res Naturae Estonicae Perscrutandas. 2 Ser. Biologica
Acta Reumatol — Acta Reumatologica
Acta Rheum — Acta Rheumatica
Acta Rheumatol Scand — Acta Rheumatologica Scandinavica
Acta Rheumatol Scand Suppl — Acta Rheumatologica Scandinavica. Supplementum
Acta Rheumat Scand — Acta Rheumatologica Scandinavica
Acta Rheum Scandinav — Acta Rheumatologica Scandinavica
Acta Rhumatol — Acta Rhumatologica
Acta Rhumatol Belg — Acta Rhumatologica Belgica
Act Arith — Acta Arithmetica
Actas Abr Acad Gen Ci — Actas Abreviadas de Academia General de Ciencias, Bellas-Letras y Nobles Artes
Actas Acad Nac Cienc Cordoba — Actas. Academia Nacional de Ciencias de Cordoba
Actas Acad Nac Cienc Exact Fis Natur Lima — Actas. Academia Nacional de Ciencias Exactas, Fisicas, y Naturales de Lima
Acta Sag — Acta Sagittariana
Acta Salmant Cien — Acta Salmanticensia. Serie de Ciencias
Acta Salmanticensia Ser Cienc — Acta Salmanticensia. Serie de Ciencias
Acta Salmanticensia Ser Filos Letra — Acta Salmanticensia. Serie Filosofia y Letras
Acta Salmanticensia Ser Med — Acta Salmanticensia. Serie de Medicina
Acta Salmant Ser Cienc — Acta Salmanticensia. Serie de Ciencias
Acta Salmant Ser Med — Acta Salmanticensia. Serie de Medicina
Acta Sanct — Acta Sanctorum [*Bollandus*]
Acta Sanctorum — Acta Sanctorum Quotquot Toto Orbe Coluntur, Vel a Catholicis Scriptoribus Celebrantur
Actas & Mem Soc Esp Antropol Etnog & Prehist — Actas y Memorias de la Sociedad Espanol de Antropologia, Etnografia, y Prehistoria
Actas Bioquim — Actas Bioquimicas
Acta Scaenograph — Acta Scaenographica
Acta Sch Med Gifu — Acta Scholae Medicinalis Universitatis in Gifu
Acta Sch Med Univ Gifu — Acta Scholae Medicinalis Universitatis in Gifu
Acta Sch Med Univ Imp (Kioto) — Acta Scholae Medicinalis Universitatis Imperialis (Kioto)

Acta Sch Med Univ Kioto — Acta Scholae Medicinalis Universitatis in Kioto

Acta Sci Circumstantiae — Acta Scientiae Circumstantiae

Acta Sci Litt Schedae Chem Univ Iagellon — Acta Scientiarum Litterarumque. Schedae Chemicae. Universitas Iagellonica

Acta Sci Litt Schedae Phys Univ Iagellon — Acta Scientiarum Litterarumque. Schedae Physicae. Universitas Iagellonica

Acta Sci Math Nat Univ Kolozsvar — Acta Scientiarum Mathematicarum et Naturalium Universitatis Kolozsvar

Acta Sci Math (Szeged) — Acta Scientiarum Mathematicarum (Szeged)

Acta Sci Nat — Acta Scientiarum Naturalium

Acta Sci Nat Acad Sci Bohemoslov (Brno) — Acta Scientiarum Naturalium. Academiae Scientiarum Bohemoslovacae (Brno)

Acta Sci Nat Kirin Univ J Nat Sci — Acta Scientiarum Naturalium. Kirin University Journal. Natural Science

Acta Sci Nat Northeast China Peoples Univ J Nat Sci — Acta Scientiarum Naturalium. Northeastern China People's University Journal. Natural Science

Acta Sci Nat Univ Amoi — Acta Scientiarum Naturalium. Universitatis Amoiensis

Acta Sci Nat Univ Jilin — Acta Scientiarum Naturalium. Universitatis Jilinensis

Acta Sci Nat Univ Norm Hunanensis — Acta Scientiarum Naturalium. Universitatis Normalis Hunanensis

Acta Sci Nat Univ Pekin — Acta Scientiarum Naturalium. Universitatis Pekinensis

Acta Sci Nat Univ Sunyatseni (Zhongshandaxue Xuebao) — Acta Scientiarum Naturalium. Universitatis Sunyatseni (Zhongshandaxue Xuebao)

Acta Sci Nat Univ Szechuan — Acta Scientiarum Naturalium. Universitatis Szechuanensis

Acta Sci Natur Univ Amoien — Acta Scientiarum Naturalium Universitatis Amoiensis

Acta Sci Natur Univ Jilin — Acta Scientiarum Naturalium Universitatis Jilinensis

Acta Sci Natur Univ Norm Hunan — Acta Scientiarum Naturalium Universitatis Normalis Hunanensis

Acta Sci Natur Univ Pekinensis — Acta Scientiarum Naturalium. Universitatis Pekinensis

Acta Sci Natur Univ Sunyatseni — Acta Scientiarum Naturalium Universitatis Sunyatseni

Acta Sci Sin — Acta Scientia Sinica

Acta Sci Soc — Acta Scientiarum Socialium. Societas Academica Dacoromana

Acta Sci Vietnam — Acta Scientiarum Vietnamicarum

Actas Clin Yodice — Actas. Clinica Yodice

Actas Conf Int Util Energ At Fines Pac — Actas. Conferencia Internacional sobre la Utilizacion de la Energia Atomica conFines Pacificos

Actas Cong Geol Argent — Actas. Congreso Geologico Argentino

Actas Congr Int Geoquim Org — Actas del Congreso Internacional de Geoquimica Organica

Actas Congr Int Hist Descobrimentos — Actas. Congreso Internacional de Historia dos Descobrimentos

Actas Congr Mund Contam Aire — Actas. Congreso Mundial sobre Contaminacion del Aire

Actas Congr Mund Psiquiatr — Actas. Congreso Mundial de Psiquiatria

Actas Congr Mund Vet — Actas. Congreso Mundial de Veterinaria

Actas Congr Uniao Fitopatol Mediterr — Actas. Congresso da Uniao Fitopatologica Mediterranea

Acta Scr Metall Conf — Acta-Scripta Metallurgica. Conference

Acta Scr Metall Proc Ser — Acta-Scripta Metallurgica. Proceedings Series

Actas Dermosifiliogr — Actas Dermosifiliograficas

Acta Sedimentol Sin — Acta Sedimentologica Sinica

Acta Seismol Sin — Acta Seismologica Sinica

Actas Encontro Nac Catal Basica Apl Ind Ambiental — Actas do Encontro Nacional de Catalise Basica e Aplicada (Industrial e Ambiental)

Acta Sericol — Acta Sericologica

Acta Sericol Entomol — Acta Sericologica et Entomologica

Actas Guias Excursiones Reun Grupo Esp Trab Cuat — Actas y Guias de Excursiones. Reunion del Grupo Espanol de Trabajo del Cuaternario

Acta Silic Sin — Acta Silicata Sinica

Actas Int Congr Hist Med — Actas. Congreso Internacional de Historia de la Medicina

Actas Jornadas For — Actas Jornadas Forestales

Actas Jornadas Geol Argent — Actas Jornadas Geologicas Argentinas

Actas Jorn Argent Toxicol Anal — Actas. Jornadas Argentinas de Toxicologia Analitica

Actas Luso-Esp Neurol Psiquiatr — Actas Luso-Espanolas de Neurologia, Psiquiatria, y Ciencias Afines

Actas-Luso Esp Neurol Psiquiatr Cienc Afines — Actas Luso-Espanolas de Neurologia, Psiquiatria, y Ciencias Afines

Actas Mem Conf Mund Energ — Actas y Memorias Conferencia Mundial de la Energia

Actas Mem Congr Nat Esp — Actas y Memorias. Congreso de Naturalistas Espanoles

Actas Mem Soc Econ Amigos Pais Prov Segovia — Actas y Memorias. Sociedad Economica de los Amigos del Pais de la Provincia de Segovia

Acta Soc — Acta Sociologica

Acta Soc Bot Pol — Acta Societatis Botanicorum Poloniae

Acta Soc Bot Polon — Acta Societatis Botanicorum Poloniae

Acta Soc Bot Poloniae — Acta Societatis Botanicorum Poloniae. Publications. Societe Botanique de Pologne

Acta Soc Ent Jugosl — Acta Societatis Entomologicae Jugoslavensis

Acta Soc Entomol Cech — Acta Societatis Entomologicae Cechosloveniae

Acta Soc Ent Serbo Cro Slov — Acta Societatis Entomologicae Serbo-Croato-Slovenae

Acta Soc Fauna Flora Fenn — Acta Societatis pro Fauna et Flora Fennica

Acta Sociol — Acta Sociologica

Acta Sociomed Scand — Acta Socio-Medica Scandinavica

Acta Soc Jablonov — Acta Societatis Jablonovianae

Acta Soc Med Fenn Duodecim — Acta Societatis Medicorum Fennicae Duodecim

Acta Soc Med Fenn Duodecim Ser A — Acta Societatis Medicorum Fennicae Duodecim. Serie A

Acta Soc Med Fenn Duodecim Ser B — Acta Societatis Medicorum Fennicae Duodecim. Serie B

Acta Soc Med Ups — Acta Societatis Medicorum Upsaliensis

Acta Soc Med Upsal — Acta Societatis Medicorum Upsaliensis

Acta Soc Med Ups Suppl — Acta Societatis Medicorum Upsaliensis. Supplementum

Acta Soc Ophthalmol Jpn — Acta Societatis Ophthalmologicae Japonicae

Acta Soc Paed Hell — Acta Societatis Paediatricae Hellenicae

Acta Soc Path Jap — Acta Societatis Pathologicae Japonicae

Acta Soc Phil Lips — Acta Societatis Philologae Lipsiensis

Acta Soc Regiae Sci Indo Neerl — Acta Societatis Regiae Scientiarum Indo-Neerlandicae. Verhandelingen der Natuurkundige Vereeniging in Nederlandsch-Indiee

Acta Soc Reg Sci Indo Neerl — Acta Societatis Regiae Scientiarum Indo-Neerlandicae

Acta Soc Scient Fennicae — Acta Societatis Scientiarum Fennicae

Acta Soc Sci Fenn Ser B — Acta Societatis Scientiarum Fennicae. Series B

Acta Soc Sci Natur Moravicae — Acta Societatis Scientiarum Naturalium Moravicae

Acta Soc Zool Bohemoslov — Acta Societatis Zoologicae Bohemoslovenicae

Acta Soc Zool Cechosl — Acta Societatis Zoologicae Cechoslovenicae

Actas Reun Argent Cienc Suelo — Actas. Reunion Argentina de la Ciencia del Suelo

Actas Reun Grupo Trab Cuat — Actas. Reunion del Grupo de Trabajo del Cuaternario

Actas Reun Int Efectos Primarios Radiaciones Quim Biol — Actas. Reunion Internacional sobre los Efectos Primarios de las Radiaciones en Quimica y Biologia

Actas Reun Nac Cuat Medios Semiaridos — Actas. Reunion Nacional el Cuaternario en Medios Semiaridos

Acta SS — Acta Sanctorum

Actas Semin Cienc Mar Rias Galegas — Actas do Seminario de Ciencias do Mar. As Rias Galegas

Actas Simp Iberoam Catal — Actas. Simposio Iberoamericano de Catalise

Acta Stereol — Acta Stereologica

Acta Stomatol Belg — Acta Stomatologica Belgica

Acta Stomatol Croat — Acta Stomatologica Croatica

Acta Stom Pat — Acta Stomatologica Patavina

Act Astron — Acta Astronautica

Acta Sud Am Quim — Acta Sud Americana de Quimica

Acta Supl — Acta Suplemento

Actas Urol Esp — Actas Urologicas Espanolas

Acta Symp Evolut Insect — Acta Symposii de Evolutione Insectorum

Acta Tech Acad Sci Hung — Acta Technica. Academiae Scientiarum Hungaricae

Acta Tech Agric — Acta Technologica Agriculturae [Brno]. A. Facultas Agronomica

Acta Tech (Budap) — Acta Technica (Budapest)

Acta Tech Budapest — Acta Technica (Budapest)

Acta Tech CSAV — Acta Technica. CSAV

Acta Tech Hung — Acta Technica Hungarica

Acta Techn Gedan — Acta Technica Gedanensia

Acta Techn Hung — Acta Technica Hungarica

Acta Tech (Prague) — Acta Technica (Prague)

Acta Tech Univ Ljubljani Teh Fak Ser Chim — Acta Technica. Univerza v Ljubljani. Tehniska Fakulteta. Series Chimica

Acta Teilhard — Acta Teilhardiana

Acta Ther — Acta Therapeutica

Acta Theriol — Acta Theriologica

Acta Theriol Sin — Acta Theriologica Sinica

Acta Toxicol Ther — Acta Toxicologica et Therapeutica

Acta Trop — Acta Tropica

Acta Trop (Basel) — Acta Tropica (Basel)

Acta Trop Suppl — Acta Tropica. Supplementum

Acta Tub — Acta Tuberculosea Scandinavica

Acta Tuberc Belg — Acta Tuberculosea Belgica

Acta Tuberc Jpn — Acta Tuberculosea Japonica

Acta Tuberc Pneumol Belg — Acta Tuberculosea et Pneumologica Belgica

Acta Tuberc Pneumol Scand — Acta Tuberculosea et Pneumologica Scandinavica

Acta Tuberc Pneumol Scand Suppl — Acta Tuberculosea et Pneumologica Scandinavica. Supplementum

Acta Tuberc Scand — Acta Tuberculosea Scandinavica

Acta Tuberc Scand Suppl — Acta Tuberculosea Scandinavica. Supplementum

Acta Umelecko Prumyslove Muz — Acta Umelecko-Prumyslove Muzeum

Acta Unio Int Cancrum — Acta Unio Internationalis Contra Cancrum

Acta Unio Int Contra Cancrum — Acta Unio Internationalis Contra Cancrum

Acta Univ Agr (Brno) — Acta Universitatis Agriculturae (Brno). Facultas Silviculturae. Series C

Acta Univ Agric (Brno) Fac Agron — Acta Universitatis Agriculturae (Brno). Facultas Agronomica

Acta Univ Agric (Brno) Fac Silvic — Acta Universitatis Agriculturae (Brno). Facultas Silviculturae

Acta Univ Agric (Brno) Fac Vet — Acta Universitatis Agriculturae (Brno). Facultas Veterinaria

Acta Univ Agric Fac Agroecon Rada D Spisy Fak Provozne Ekon — Acta Universitatis Agriculturae. Facultas Agroeconomica. Rada D. Spisy Fakulty Provozne Ekonomicke

Acta Univ Agric Fac Agron — Acta Universitatis Agriculturae. Facultas Agronomica

Acta Univ Agric Fac Agron Brno — Acta Universitatis Agriculturae. Facultas Agronomica (Brno)

Acta Univ Agric Fac Silvic — Acta Universitatis Agriculturae. Facultas Silviculturae

Acta Univ Agric Fac Silvic Brno — Acta Universitatis Agriculturae. Facultas Silviculturae (Brno)

Acta Univ Agric Fac Vet — Acta Universitatis Agriculturae. Facultas Veterinaria

Acta Univ Agric Fac Vet Brno — Acta Universitatis Agriculturae. Facultas Veterinaria (Brno)

Acta Univ Agric Fac Vet Rada B — Acta Universitatis Agriculturae. Facultas Veterinaria. Rada B

Acta Univ Agric Ser C (Brno) — Acta Universitatis Agriculturae (Brno). Facultas Silviculturae. Series C

Acta Univ Agric Silvic Brno Rada A — Acta Universitatis Agriculturae et Silviculturae. Brno. Rada A. Spisy Fakulty Agronomicke

Acta Univ Agric Silvic Brno Rada B — Acta Universitatis Agriculturae et Silviculturae. Brno. Rada B. Spisy Veterinarni

Acta Univ Agric Silvic Brno Rada C — Acta Universitatis Agriculturae et Silviculturae. Brno. Rada C. Spisy Fakulty Lesnicke

Acta Univ Agric Silvic Mendelianae Brun — Acta Universitatis Agriculturae et Silviculturae Mendelianae Brunensis

Acta Univ Asiae Mediae — Acta Universitatis Asiae Mediae

Acta Univ Bergen Ser Math Rerumque Nat — Acta Universitatis Bergensis. Series Mathematica. Rerumque Naturalium

Acta Univ Bergen Ser Med — Acta Universitatis Bergensis. Series Medica

Acta Univ Bergen Ser Med Nova Ser — Acta Universitatis Bergensis. Series Medica. Nova Series

Acta Univ Carol Biol — Acta Universitatis Carolinae. Biologica

Acta Univ Carol Geogr — Acta Universitatis Carolinae. Geographica

Acta Univ Carol Geol — Acta Universitatis Carolinae. Geologica

Acta Univ Carol Geol Monogr — Acta Universitatis Carolinae. Geologica. Monographia

Acta Univ Carol Geol Suppl — Acta Universitatis Carolinae. Geologica. Supplementum

Acta Univ Carol Hist — Acta Universitatis Carolinae. Historia

Acta Univ Carolinae Geol — Acta Universitatis Carolinae. Geologica

Acta Univ Carolinae Math et Phys — Acta Universitatis Carolinae. Mathematica et Physica

Acta Univ Carolin Math Phys — Acta Universitatis Carolinae. Mathematica et Physica

Acta Univ Carol Math Phys — Acta Universitatis Carolinae. Mathematica et Physica

Acta Univ Carol Med — Acta Universitatis Carolinae. Medica

Acta Univ Carol Med Monogr — Acta Universitatis Carolinae. Medica. Monographia

Acta Univ Carol Med Monogr (Praha) — Acta Universitatis Carolinae. Medica. Monographia (Praha)

Acta Univ Carol Med (Praha) — Acta Universitatis Carolinae. Medica (Praha)

Acta Univ Carol Med Suppl — Acta Universitatis Carolinae. Medica. Supplementum

Acta Univ Debrec — Acta Universitatis Debreceniensis de Ludovico Kossuth Nominatae. Series Biologica

Acta Univ Debrecen Ludovico Kossuth Nominatae — Acta Universitatis Debreceniensis de Ludovico Kossuth Nominatae

Acta Univ Debrecen Ludovico Kossuth Nominatae Ser 2 — Acta Universitatis Debreceniensis de Ludovico Kossuth Nominatae. Series 2. Biologica

Acta Univ Debrecen Ludovico Kossuth Nominatae Ser Biol — Acta Universitatis Debreceniensis de Ludovico Kossuth Nominatae. Series Biologica

Acta Univ Debrecen Ludovico Kossuth Nominatae Ser Phys Chim — Acta Universitatis Debreceniensis de Ludovico Kossuth Nominatae. Series Physicaet Chimica

Acta Univ Futan Sci Nat — Acta Universitatis Futanensis. Scientiarum Naturalium

Acta Univ Gothoburgensis — Acta Universitatis Gothoburgensis

Acta Univ Latv — Acta Universitatis Latviensis

Acta Univ Latv Agron Ordinis Ser — Acta Universitatis Latviensis. Agronomorum Ordinis Series

Acta Univ Latv Chem Ordinis Ser — Acta Universitatis Latviensis. Chemicorum Ordinis Series

Acta Univ Latviensis — Acta Universitatis Latviensis

Acta Univ Latv Math Phys Ordinis Ser — Acta Universitatis Latviensis. Mathematicorum et Physicorum Ordinis Series

Acta Univ Latv Med Ordinis Ser — Acta Universitatis Latviensis. Medicorum Ordinis Series

Acta Univ Lodz — Acta Universitatis Lodziensis

Acta Univ Lodz Folia Biochim Biophys — Acta Universitatis Lodziensis. Folia Biochimica et Biophysica

Acta Univ Lodz Folia Chim — Acta Universitatis Lodziensis. Folia Chimica

Acta Univ Lodz Folia Math — Acta Universitatis Lodziensis Folia Mathematica

Acta Univ Lodz Folia Philos — Acta Universitatis Lodziensis Folia Philosophica

Acta Univ Lodz Folia Phys — Acta Universitatis Lodziensis. Folia Physica

Acta Univ Lodz Ser 2 — Acta Universitatis Lodziensis. Seria 2. Nauki Matematyczno-Przyrodnicze

Acta Univ Lodz Ser 2 Nauk Mat-Przyr — Acta Universitatis Lodziensis. Seria 2. Nauki Matematyczno-Przyrodnicze

Acta Univ Lund Sect 2 — Acta Universitatis Lundensis. Sectio 2. Medica, Mathematica, Scientiae Rerum Naturalium

Acta Univ Lund Sect II Med Math Sci Rerum Nat — Acta Universitatis Lundensis. Sectio II. Scientiae Rerum Naturalium Medica, Mathematica

Acta Univ Mathaei Belii Nat Sci Ser Ser Math — Matej Bel University. Acta. Natural Science Series. Series Mathematics

Acta Univ Med Secondae Shanghai — Acta Universitatis Medicinalis Secondae Shanghai

Acta Univ Med Tongji (Chin Ed) — Acta Universitatis Medicinae Tongji (Chinese Edition)

Acta Univ Nankin Sci Nat — Acta Universitatis Nankinensis Scientiarum Naturalium

Acta Univ Nicolai Copernici Biol — Acta Universitatis Nicolai Copernici. Biologia

Acta Univ Nicolai Copernici Geogr — Acta Universitatis Nicolai Copernici. Geografia

Acta Univ Nicolai Copernici Nauki Mat Przyr — Acta Universitatis Nicolai Copernici, Nauki Matematyczno-Przyrodnicze

Acta Univ Nicolai Copernici Pr Limnol — Acta Universitatis Nicolai Copernici. Prace Limnologiczne

Acta Univ Ouluensis Ser A — Acta Universitatis Ouluensis. Series A. Scientiae Rerum Naturalium. Geologica

Acta Univ Ouluensis Ser A Sci Rerum Nat Biochem — Acta Universitatis Ouluensis. Series A. Scientiae Rerum Naturalium. Biochemica

Acta Univ Ouluensis Ser A Sci Rerum Nat Biol — Acta Universitatis Ouluensis. Series A. Scientiae Rerum Naturalium. Biologica

Acta Univ Ouluensis Ser C — Acta Universitatis Ouluensis. Series C. Technica

Acta Univ Ouluensis Ser D Med — Acta Universitatis Ouluensis. Series D. Medica

Acta Univ Oulu Ser A Sci Rerum Natur — Acta Universitatis Ouluensis. Series A. Scientiae Rerum Naturalium

Acta Univ Oulu Ser A Sci Rerum Natur Math — Acta Universitatis Ouluensis. Series A. Scientiae Rerum Naturalium. Mathematica

Acta Univ Palack Fac Med — Acta Universitatis Palackianae. Facultatis Medicae

Acta Univ Palacki Olomuc — Acta Universitatis Palackianae Olomucensis

Acta Univ Palacki Olomuc Fac Med — Acta Universitatis Palackianae Olomucensis. Facultatis Medicae

Acta Univ Palacki Olomuc Fac Med Suppl — Acta Universitatis Palackianae Olomucensis. Facultatis Medicae. Supplementum

Acta Univ Palacki Olomuc Fac Rerum Nat — Acta Universitatis Palackianae Olomucensis. Facultas Rerum Naturalium

Acta Univ Palacki Olomuc Fac Rerum Nat Biol — Acta Universitatis Palackianae Olomucensis. Facultas Rerum Naturalium. Biologica

Acta Univ Palacki Olomuc Fac Rerum Nat Chem — Acta Universitatis Palackianae Olomucensis. Facultas Rerum Naturalium. Chemica

Acta Univ Palacki Olomuc Fac Rerum Nat Math — Acta Universitatis Palackianae Olomucensis. Facultas Rerum Naturalium. Mathematica

Acta Univ Palacki Olomuc Fac Rerum Nat Phys — Acta Universitatis Palackianae Olomucensis. Facultas Rerum Naturalium. Physica

Acta Univ Palacki Olomuc Fac Sci — Acta Universitatis Palackianae Olomucensis. Facultas Scientiarum

Acta Univ Palack Olomuc Fac Rerum Nat Ser 2 Biol — Acta Universitatis Palackianae Olomucensis. Facultas Rerum Naturalium. Series 2. Biologica

Acta Univ Palack Olomuc Fac Rerum Natur Math — Acta Universitatis Palackianae Olomucensis. Facultas Rerum Naturalium. Mathematica

Acta Univ Palack Olumuc Fac Rerum Nat Geol — Acta Universitatis Palackianae Olumucensis. Facultas Rerum Naturalium. Geologica

Acta Univ Stockh Stockholm Contrib Geol — Acta Universitatis Stockholmiensis. Stockholm Contributions in Geology

Acta Univ Szeged Acta Biol — Acta Universitatis Szegediensis. Acta Biologica

Acta Univ Szeged Acta Mineral Petrogr — Acta Universitatis Szegediensis. Acta Mineralogica-Petrographica

Acta Univ Szeged Acta Phys et Chem — Acta Universitatis Szegediensis. Acta Physica et Chemica

Acta Univ Szeged Pars Biol Sci Nat Acta Biol — Acta Universitatis Szegediensis. Pars Biologica Scientiarum Naturalium. Acta Biologica

Acta Univ Szeged Pars Phys Chem Sci Nat Acta Phys Chem — Acta Universitatis Szegediensis. Pars Physica et Chemica Scientiarum Naturalium. Acta Physica et Chemica

Acta Univ Szeged Sect Sci Nat Acta Chem Mineral Phys — Acta Universitatis Szegediensis. Sectio Scientiarum Naturalium. Acta Chemica, Mineralogica, et Physica

Acta Univ Szeged Sect Sci Nat Acta Chem Phys — Acta Universitatis Szegediensis. Sectio Scientiarum Naturalium. Acta Chemica etPhysica

Acta Univ Szeged Sect Sci Nat Acta Mineral Petrogr — Acta Universitatis Szegediensis. Sectio Scientiarum Naturalium. Acta Mineralogica, Petrographica

Acta Univ Szeged Sect Sci Nat Pars Bot — Acta Universitatis Szegediensis. Sectio Scientiarum Naturalium. Pars Botanica

Acta Univ Tampere Ser B — Acta Universitatis Tamperensis. Serie B

Acta Univ Tamper Ser A — Acta Universitatis Tamperensis. Series A

Acta Univ Tart Dorpat A — Acta Universitatis Tartuensis (Dorpatensis) A

Acta Univ Tsinghuan — Acta Universitatis Tsinghuanensis

Acta Univ Ups — Acta Universitatis Upsaliensis

Acta Univ Ups Abstr Uppsala Diss Fac Med — Acta Universitatis Upsaliensis. Abstracts of Uppsala Dissertations. Faculty of Medicine

Acta Univ Ups Abstr Uppsala Diss Fac Pharm — Acta Universitatis Upsaliensis. Abstracts of Uppsala Dissertations. Faculty of Pharmacy

Acta Univ Ups Abstr Uppsala Diss Fac Sci — Acta Universitatis Upsaliensis. Abstracts of Uppsala Dissertations. Faculty of Science

Acta Univ Ups Abstr Uppsala Diss Sci — Acta Universitatis Upsaliensis. Abstracts of Uppsala Dissertations in Science

Acta Univ Ups Abstr Upps Diss Med — Acta Universitatis Upsaliensis. Abstracts of Uppsala Dissertations in Medicine

Acta Univ Ups Abstr Upps Diss Sci — Acta Universitatis Upsaliensis. Abstracts of Uppsala Dissertations in Science

Acta Univ Upsal Abstr Uppsala Diss Fac Sci — Acta Universitatis Upsaliensis. Abstracts of Uppsala Dissertations. Faculty of Science

Acta Univ Upsal Abstr Upps Diss Fac Sci — Acta Universitatis Upsaliensis. Abstracts of Uppsala Dissertations. Faculty of Science

Acta Univ Upsaliensis Skr Uppsala Univ C Organ Hist — Acta Universitatis Upsaliensis. Skrifter Roerande Uppsala Universitet. C. Organisation och Historia. Acta Universitatis Upsaliensis

Acta Univ Ups Nova Acta Regiae Soc Sci Up Ser VC — Acta Universitatis Upsaliensis. Nova Acta Regiae Societatis Scientiarum Upsaliensis. Series VC

Acta Univ Ups Nova Acta Regiae Soc Sci Ups Ser VC — Acta Universitatis Upsaliensis. Nova Acta Regiae Societatis Scientiarum Upsaliensis. Series VC

Acta Univ Ups Symb Bot Ups — Acta Universitatis Upsaliensis. Symbolae Botanicae Upsalienses

Acta Univ Voroneg — Acta Universitatis Voronegiensis

Acta Univ Wratislav — Acta Universitatis Wratislaviensis

Acta Univ Wratislaviensis — Acta Universitatis Wratislaviensis

Acta Univ Wratislav Mat Fiz Astron — Acta Universitatis Wratislaviensis. Matematyka, Fizyka, Astronomia

Acta Univ Wratislav Pr Geol Mineral — Acta Universitatis Wratislaviensis. Prace Geologiczno-Mineralogiczne

Acta Univ Wratislav Pr Zool — Acta Universitatis Wratislaviensis. Prace Zoologiczne
Acta Urol Belg — Acta Urologica Belgica
Acta Urol Jpn — Acta Urologica Japonica
Acta U Stockholm — Acta Universitatis Stockholmiensis
Acta U Upsaliensis — Acta Universitatis Upsaliensis
Acta U Upsaliensis Boreas — Acta Universitatis Upsaliensis. Boreas
Acta U Upsaliensis Figura — Acta Universitatis Upsaliensis. Figura
Acta Vel — Acta Academiae Velehradensis
Acta Venez — Acta Venezolana
Acta Vertebr — Acta Vertebratica
Acta Vet Acad Sci Hung — Acta Veterinaria. Academiae Scientiarum Hungaricae
Acta Vet (Belgr) — Acta Veterinaria (Belgrade)
Acta Vet Belgrade — Acta Veterinaria (Belgrade)
Acta Vet (Beogr) — Acta Veterinaria (Beograd)
Acta Vet (Brno) — Acta Veterinaria (Brno)
Acta Vet (Brno) Suppl — Acta Veterinaria (Brno). Supplementum
Acta Vet Budapest — Acta Veterinaria (Budapest)
Acta Vet Hung — Acta Veterinaria Hungarica
Acta Vet Jap — Acta Veterinaria Japonica
Acta Vet Scand — Acta Veterinaria Scandinavica
Acta Vet Scand Suppl — Acta Veterinaria Scandinavica. Supplementum
Acta Vet Zootech Sin — Acta Veterinaria et Zootechnica Sinica
Acta Virol — Acta Virologica
Acta Virol (Engl Ed) — Acta Virologica (English Edition)
Acta Virol (Prague) — Acta Virologica (Prague)
Acta Virol (Prague) (Engl Ed) — Acta Virologica (Prague) (English Edition)
Acta Virol (Praha) — Acta Virologica (Praha)
Acta Vitaminol — Acta Vitaminologica [Later, Acta Vitaminologica et Enzymologica]
Acta Vitaminol Enzymol — Acta Vitaminologica et Enzymologica
Acta Vitaminol Enzymol (Milano) — Acta Vitaminologica et Enzymologica (Milano)
Acta Zoo Hung — Acta Zoologica Hungarica
Acta Zool — Acta Zoologica
Acta Zool Acad Sci Hung — Acta Zoologica. Academiae Scientiarum Hungaricae
Acta Zool Budapest — Acta Zoologica (Budapest)
Acta Zool Bulg — Acta Zoologica Bulgarica
Acta Zool Colomb — Acta Zoologica Colombiana
Acta Zool Cracov — Acta Zoologica Cracoviensia
Acta Zool Cracov (Engl Transl) — Acta Zoologica Cracoviensia (English Translation)
Acta Zool Fenn — Acta Zoologica Fennica
Acta Zool Hung — Acta Zoologica. Academiae Scientiarum Hungaricae
Acta Zool Lilloana — Acta Zoologica Lilloana
Acta Zool Mex — Acta Zoologica Mexicana
Acta Zool Mex Nueva Ser — Acta Zoologica Mexicana. Nueva Serie
Acta Zool Oecol Univ Lodz — Acta Zoologica et Oecologica. Universitatis Lodziensis
Acta Zool Pathol Antverp — Acta Zoologica et Pathologica Antverpiensia
Acta Zool Pathol Antverpiensia — Acta Zoologica et Pathologica Antverpiensia
Acta Zool Sin — Acta Zoologica Sinica
Acta Zool (Stockh) — Acta Zoologica (Stockholm)
Acta Zool Taiw — Acta Zoologica Taiwanica
Acta Zootaxonomica Sin — Acta Zootaxonomica Sinica
Acta Zootech — Acta Zootechnica
Acta Zootech Univ Agric (Nitra) — Acta Zootechnica. Universitatis Agriculturae (Nitra)
Act Bio C B — Acta Biologica Cracoviensia. Series Botanica
Act Bioch H — Acta Biochimica et Biophysica. Academiae Scientiarum Hungaricae
Act Biochim — Actualites Biochimiques
Act Bioch P — Acta Biochimica Polonica
Act Bio C Z — Acta Biologica Cracoviensia. Series Zoologia
Act Bio Ira — Acta Biochimica Iranica
Act Biol H — Acta Biologica. Academiae Scientiarum Hungaricae
Act Bio Med — Acta Biologica et Medica Germanica
Act Bot Bohem — Acta Botanica Bohemica
Act Bot Fenn — Acta Botanica Fennica
Act Bot Nee — Acta Botanica Neerlandica
Act Bot Taiw Rep — Acta Botanica Taiwanica. Science Reports. National Taiwan University. Chih Wu Hsueh Pao
Act Card — Actualites Cardiologiques et Angeiologiques Internationales
Act Cart — Acta Cartographica
Act Chem A — Acta Chemica Scandinavica. Series A. Physical and Inorganic Chemistry
Act Chem B — Acta Chemica Scandinavica. Series B. Organic Chemistry and Biochemistry
Act Chim H — Acta Chimica. Academiae Scientiarum Hungaricae
Act Chir B — Acta Chirurgica Belgica
Act Chir H — Acta Chirurgica. Academiae Scientiarum Hungaricae
Act Chir Sc — Acta Chirurgica Scandinavica
Act Ci — Actas Ciba
Act CIAC — Actes. Congresso Internazionale di Archeologia Classica
Act Cient V — Acta Cientifica Venezolana
Act Clin B — Acta Clinica Belgica
Act Clin Ther — Actualites de Clinique Therapeutique
Act Coll — Actes et Colloques
Act Colloq Int Inst Etud Renaissance Hum — Actes. Colloque International. Institut pour l'Etude de la Renaissance et de l'Humanisme. Universite Libre de Bruxelles
Act Congr Benelux Hist Sci — Actes. Congres Benelux d'Histoire des Sciences
Act Congr Int Etud Byzantines — Actes. Congres International des Etudes Byzantines
Act Congr Int Hist Sci — Actes. Congres International d'Histoire des Sciences
Act Congr Int Phil Sci — Actes. Congres International. Union Internationale de Philosophie des Sciences
Act Cryst A — Acta Crystallographica. Section A

Act Cryst B — Acta Crystallographica. Section B
Act Cult Vet — Actualites et Culture Veterinaires
Act Cytol — Acta Cytologica
Act Dent — Actualite Dentaire
Act Der-Ven — Acta Dermato-Venereologica
Act Develop — Action for Development
Act Diabet — Acta Diabetologica Latina
Act Driven CNS Changes Learn Dev — Activity-Driven CNS Changes in Learning and Development
Act Ec — Actualite Economique
Act Endocr — Acta Endocrinologica
Act Ent Boh — Acta Entomologica Bohemoslovaca
Actes CNS Sav — Actes. Congres National des Societes Savantes. Section de Philologie et d'Historie
Actes Colloq Cent Natl Exploit Oceans Fr — Actes de Colloques. Centre National pour l'Exploitations des Oceans (France)
Actes Colloq IFREMER — Actes de Colloques. IFREMER (Institut Francais de Recherche pour l'Exploitation de la Mer)
Actes Colloq Int — Actes. Colloque International
Actes Colloq Int Soudage Fusion Faisceaux Electrons — Actes. Colloque International. Soudage et Fusion par Faisceaux d'Electrons
Actes Confer Soc Et Juiv — Actes et Conferences. Societe des Etudes Juives
Actes Cong Nat Soc Savant — Actes. Congres National des Societes Savantes
Actes Congr Ceram Int — Actes. Congres Ceramique International
Actes Congr Int Catal — Actes. Congres International de Catalyse
Actes Congr Int Ceram — Actes. Congres International Ceramique
Actes Congr Int Composes Phosphores — Actes. Congres International sur les Composes Phosphores
Actes Congr Int Froid — Actes. Congres International du Froid
Actes Congr Int Geochim Org — Actes. Congres International de Geochimie Organique
Actes Congr Int Hist Sci — Actes. Congres International d'Histoire des Sciences
Actes Congr Int Soc Fr Radioprot — Actes. Congres International. Societe Francaise de Radioprotection
Actes Congr Mond Sci Tab — Actes. Congres Mondial Scientifique du Tabac
Actes Congr Mond Soc Int Etude Corps Gras — Actes. Congres Mondial. Societe Internationale pour l'Etude des Corps Gras
Actes Congr Natl Soc Savantes Sect Sci — Actes. Congres National des Societes Savantes. Section des Sciences
Actes Congr Natl Transfus Sang — Actes. Congres National de Transfusion Sanguine
Actes C R Assoc Colon Sci — Actes et Comptes Rendus de l'Association Colonies-Sciences
Actes Inst Natl Genevois — Actes. Institut National Genevois
Actes Linn Soc Bord — Actes. Societe Linneenne de Bordeaux
Actes Mus Hist Nat — Actes du Museum d'Histoire Naturelle
Actes Rech Sci Soc — Actes de la Recherche en Sciences Sociales
Actes Semin Physiol Comp — Actes. Seminaire de Physiologie Comparee
Actes Soc Helv Sci Nat — Actes. Societe Helvetique des Sciences Naturelles
Actes Soc Helv Sci Nat Parte Sci — Actes. Societe Helvetique des Sciences Naturelles. Parte Scientifique
Actes Soc Linn Bordeaux — Actes. Societe Linneenne de Bordeaux
Actes Soc Linn Bordeaux Ser A — Actes. Societe Linneenne de Bordeaux. Serie A
Actes Soc Linn Bordeaux Ser B — Actes. Societe Linneenne de Bordeaux. Serie B
Actes Soc Med Hop Paris — Actes. Societe Medicale des Hopitaux de Paris
Actes Soc Philol — Actes. Societe Philologique
Actes Symp Int Ombelliferes — Actes. Symposium International sur les Ombelliferes
Actes Xe Congr Internat Et Byzant — Actes du Xe Congres International d'Etudes Byzantines
Actes XIe Congr Internat Sci Hist — XIe Congres International des Sciences Historiques. Actes du Congres
Act Ethn H — Acta Ethnographica. Academiae Scientiarum Hungaricae
Act Ethnogr — Acta Ethnographica
ActF — Action Francaise
Act Faun Fl Un Bot — Acta Pro Fauna et Flora Universali. Serie 2. Botanica
Act For Fenn — Acta Forestalia Fennica
Act Gastr B — Acta Gastro-Enterologica Belgica
Act Genet M — Acta Geneticae, Medicae, et Gemellologiae
Act Geod Geophys et Montan — Acta Geodaetica, Geophysica, et Montanistica
Act Geogr — Acta Geographica
Act Geo S-E — Acta Geologica Sinica-English Edition
Act Gyn — Actualites Gynecologiques
Act Gynaecol Obstet Hisp Lusit — Acta Gynaecologica et Obstetrica Hispano Lusitana
Act Haemat — Acta Haematologica
Act Hem — Actualites Hematologiques
Act Hep-Gas — Acta Hepato-Gastroenterologica
Act Hist Ar — Acta Historiae Artium. Academiae Scientiarum Hungaricae
Act Hist Brux — Acta Historica Bruxellensia
Act Hist Cy — Acta Histochemica et Cytochemica
Act Hist H — Acta Historica. Academiae Scientiarum Hungaricae
Act Histoch — Acta Histochemica
Act Hort Bot Univ Latv — Acta Horti Botanici Universitatis Latviensis
Act Hort Bot Univ Latviensis — Acta Horti Botanici Universitatis Latviensis
ACTH Relat Pept — ACTH Related Peptides
Act Hydrobiol Sin — Acta Hydrobiologica Sinica
ACTIE3 — Anales. Catedra de Tisioneumonologia
Actinides Electron Struct Relat Prop — Actinides. Electronic Structure and Related Properties
Actinides Lanthanides Rev — Actinides and Lanthanides. Reviews
Actinides Rev — Actinides Reviews

Actinometry Atmos Opt Rep Interdep Symp Actinometry Atmos Opt — Actinometry and Atmospheric Optics. Reports. Interdepartmental Symposium on Actinometry and Atmospheric Optics
Actinomycetales Jena Int Symp Taxon — Actinomycetales. Jena International Symposium on Taxonomy
Actinomycetes Relat Org — Actinomycetes and Related Organisms
Action — United Evangelical Action
Action Adap — Action Adaptation
Action Ageing Proc Symp — Action on Ageing. Proceedings of a Symposium
Action Info — Action Information
Action Med — Action Medicale
Action Nat — Action Nationale
Actions Chim Biol Radiat — Actions Chimiques et Biologiques des Radiations
Action Univ — Action Universitaire
Action Use Nat Occurrence Microb Inhib Food Proc — Action, Use, and Natural Occurrence of Microbial Inhibitors in Food Proceedings
Actividad Econ — Actividad Economica
Activity Bul — Activity Bulletin for Teachers in Secondary Schools
Activ Nerv — Activitas Nervosa Superior
Activ Nerv Super — Activitas Nervosa Superior
Activ Petrol — Actividades Petroleras
Activ Port Auto Marseille — Activites. Port Autonome de Marseille
Act Jpn Med Trop — Acta Japonica Medicinae Tropicalis
Act Jur — Actualite Juridique
ActLingH — Acta Linguistica. Academiae Scientiarum Hungaricae
ActLitH — Acta Litteraria. Academiae Scientiarum Hungaricae
Act Litt Sci Regiae Univ Hung Francisco-Josephinae Sect Med — Acta Litterarum Scientiarum Regiae Universitatis Hungaricae Francisco-Josephinae. Sectio Medicorum
Act Macrophages Proc Workshop Conf Hoechst — Activation of Macrophages Proceedings. Workshop Conference Hoechst
Act Math — Acta Mathematica
Act Math H — Acta Mathematica. Academiae Scientiarum Hungaricae
Act Mechan — Acta Mechanica
Act Med — Actualidad Medica
Act Med H — Acta Medica. Academiae Scientiarum Hungaricae
Act Med Oka — Acta Medicinae Okayama
Act Med Per — Actualidad Medica Peruana
Act Med Philos Hafniensia — Acta Medica et Philosophica Hafniensia
Act Med Sc — Acta Medica Scandinavica
Act Metall — Acta Metallurgica
Act Mic P A — Acta Microbiologica Polonica. Series A. Microbiologia Generalis
Act Mic P B — Acta Microbiologica Polonica. Series B. Microbiologia Applicata
Act Microbiol Sin — Acta Microbiologia Sinica
Act Micro H — Acta Microbiologica. Academiae Scientiarum Hungaricae
ACT Monogr Ser — ACT [*American College Testing Program*] Monograph Series
Act Morph H — Acta Morphologica. Academiae Scientiarum Hungaricae
Act Morph N — Acta Morphologica Neerlando-Scandinavica
Act Mozart — Acta Mozartiana
Act Mus Hist Natur Rouen — Actes. Museum d'Histoire Naturelle de Rouen
Act Music — Acta Musicologica
Act Muz — Activitatea Muzeelor
ActN — Action Nationale
Act Nat — Action Nationale
Act Nerv Super — Activitas Nervosa Superior
Act Nerv Super (Praha) — Activitas Nervosa Superior (Praha)
Act Neurob — Acta Neurobiologiae Experimentalis
Act Neuroch — Acta Neurochirurgica
Act Neurop — Acta Neuropathologica
Act Neuro-Phys — Actualites Neurophysiologiques
Act Neur Sc — Acta Neurologica Scandinavica
Act Obst Sc — Acta Obstetrica et Gynecologica Scandinavica
Act Odon Sc — Acta Odontologica Scandinavica
Act Oecon — Acta Oeconomica
Act O-Mer — Actualites d'Outre-Mer
Act Ophth (K) — Acta Ophthalmologica (Kobenhavn)
ActOr — Acta Orientalia
ActOrHung — Acta Orientalia. Academiae Scientiarum Hungaricae
Act Orth Sc — Acta Orthopaedica Scandinavica
Act Oto-Lar — Acta Oto-Laryngologica
ActP — Action Poetique
Act Paed H — Acta Paediatrica. Academiae Scientiarum Hungaricae
Act Paedops — Acta Paedopsychiatrica
Act Paed Sc — Acta Paediatrica Scandinavica
ACT Pap Educ — ACT [*Australian Capital Territory*] Papers on Education
Act Pat Jap — Acta Pathologica Japonica
Act Pat S A — Acta Pathologica et Microbiologica Scandinavica. Section A
Act Pat S B — Acta Pathologica et Microbiologica Scandinavica. Section B
Act Pat S C — Acta Pathologica et Microbiologica Scandinavica. Section C
ACTPCM — Australia. Commonwealth Scientific and Industrial Research Organisation. Division of Food Research. Technical Paper
Act Ped — Actualidad Pediatrica
Act Pedol Sin — Acta Pedologica Sinica
Act Pharm — Action Pharmaceutique
Act Pharm N — Acta Pharmaceutica Nordica
Act Pharm S — Acta Pharmaceutica Suecica
Act Pharm T — Acta Pharmacologica et Toxicologica
Act Phar Si — Acta Pharmacologica Sinica
Act Phy P A — Acta Physica Polonica. Series A
Act Phy P B — Acta Physica Polonica. Series B
Act Phys Au — Acta Physica Austriaca
Act Phys Ch — Acta Physica et Chemica
Act Phys H — Acta Physica. Academiae Scientiarum Hungaricae
Act Physl H — Acta Physiologica. Academiae Scientiarum Hungaricae
Act Physl L — Acta Physiologica Latino Americana

Act Physl P — Acta Physiologica Polonica
Act Physl S — Acta Physiologica Scandinavica
Act Phys Med Acad Nat Cur — Acta Physico-Medica Academiae Caesareae Leopoldino-Franciscanae Naturae Curiosorum Exhibentia Ephemerides Sive Observationes Historias et Experimenta
Act Phys Med Acad Nat Curios — Acta Physico-Medica Academiae Caesareae Leopoldino-Franciscanae Naturae Curiosorum Exhibentia Ephemerides Sive Observationes Historias et Experimenta
Act Phytopath Sin Transl Bull — Acta Phytopathologica Sinica Translation Bulletin/Chi Wu Ping Li Hsueh i P'ao
Act Phytotax Sin — Acta Phytotaxonomica Sinica/Chih Wu Fen Lei Hsueh Pao
Act Pol His — Acta Poloniae Historica
Act Pol Ph — Acta Poloniae Pharmaceutica
Act Poly Ch — Acta Polytechnica Scandinavica. Chemistry Series
Act Poly Ci — Acta Polytechnica Scandinavica. Civil Engineering and Building Construction Series
Act Poly El — Acta Polytechnica Scandinavica. Electrical Engineering Series
Act Poly Ma — Acta Polytechnica Scandinavica. Mathematics and Computing Machinery Series
Act Poly Me — Acta Polytechnica Scandinavica. Mechanical Engineering Series
Act Poly Ph — Acta Polytechnica Scandinavica. Physics Including Nucleonics Series
Act Psiq Ps — Acta Psiquiatrica y Psicologica de America Latina
Act Psychol — Acta Psychologica
Act Psych T — Acta Psychologica Taiwanica
Act Psyc Sc — Acta Psychiatrica Scandinavica
ACTR — Australian Capital Territory. Reports
Act Rad Dgn — Acta Radiologica. Series One. Diagnosis
Act Rad TPB — Acta Radiologica. Therapy, Physics, Biology [*Later, Acta Radiologica. Series Two. Oncology, Radiation, Physics, and Biology (Stockholm)*]
Act Reg — Acta Regia; An Abstract of Rymer's Foedera
Act Rep R & D Assoc — Activities Report. R & D Associates
Act Rep R & D Assoc Res Dev Assoc Mil Food Packag Syst — Activities Report. R & D Associates. Research and Development Associates for Military Food and Packaging Systems
Act Rep React Phys Div — Activity Report of Reactor Physics Division
Act Rep Res Dev Assoc Mil Food Packag Syst — Activities Report. Research and Development Associates for Military Food and Packaging Systems
Act Rep Res Dev Assoc Mil Food Packag Syst Inc — Activities Report. Research and Development Associates for Military Food and Packaging Systems, Incorporated
ACT Res Rep — American College Testing. Research Reports
Acts & Ords Interreg — Acts and Ordinances of the Interregnum
Acts Austl Parl — Acts of the Australian Parliament
Act Sci Mat — Acta Scientiarum Mathematicarum
Act Sci Nat Univ Sunyatseni — Acta Scientiarum Naturalium Universitatis Sunyatseni
Act Sci Nat Univ Wuhan — Acta Scientiarum Naturalium Universitatis Wuhanensis
Act Sci Sin — Acta Scientia Sinica/Chung Kuo K'o Hsueh
Act S Helv — Actes de la Societe Helvetique des Sciences Naturelles
Act Sludge Process Control Ser — Activated Sludge Process Control Series
Act Soc — Acta Sociologica
Act Soc Bot Polon — Acta Societatis Botanicorum Poloniae. Publications. Societe Botanique de Pologne
Act Sociol — Acta Sociologica
Act Soc Linn Bordeaux — Actes. Societe Linneenne de Bordeaux
Act Soc R Sc Indo Neerl — Acta Societatis Regiae Scientiarum Indo-Neerlandicae
Act Soc R Sc Upsal — Acta Societatis Regiae Scientiarum Upsaliensis
ACT Spec Rep Ser — ACT [*American College Testing Program*] Special Report Series
Act Symp Int Sci Phys Math 17 Siecle — Actes. Symposium International des Sciences Physiques et Mathematiques dans la Premiere Moitie du 17e Siecle
Act Syst (GB) — Active Systems (Great Britain)
ACT Teach — ACT [*Australian Capital Territory*] Teachers Federation. Teacher
Act Techn H — Acta Technica. Academiae Scientiarum Hungaricae
ActU — Action Universitaire
Actual Agron — Actualites Agronomiques
Actual Agron Ser B — Actualites Agronomiques. Serie B
Actual Auto — Actualite Automobile
Actual Biochim — Actualites Biochimiques
Actual Biochim Mar — Actualites de Biochimie Marine
Actual Biol — Actualidades Biologicas
Actual Biol Lisbon — Actualidades Biologicas (Lisbon)
Actual Biol Medellin Colomb — Actualidades Biologicas (Medellin, Colombia)
Actual Biol (Paris) — Actualites Biologiques (Paris)
Actual Bot — Actualites Botaniques
Actual Cardiol Int — Actualites Cardiologiques Internationales
Actual Chim — Actualite Chimique
Actual Chim Anal Org Pharm Bromatol — Actualites de Chimie Analytique, Organique, Pharmaceutique, et Bromatologique
Actual Chim Can — Actualite Chimique Canadienne
Actual Chim Contemp — Actualites de Chimie Contemporaine
Actual Chim Ind — Actualite Chimique et Industrielle
Actual Chim Ther — Actualites de Chimie Therapeutique
Actual Chine Popul — Actualite en Chine Populaire
Actual Clin Ther — Actualites de Clinique Therapeutique
Actual Combust Energ — Actualite, Combustibles, Energie
Actual Econ — Actualite Economique
Actual Econ Soc Can Sci Econ — Actualite Economique. Societe Canadienne de Science Economique
Actual Endocrinol — Actualites Endocrinologiques
Actual Endocrinol (Paris) — Actualites Endocrinologiques (Paris)
Actual Formation Perm — Actualite de la Formation Permanente
Actual Gynec — Actualites Gynecologiques

Actual Gynecol — Actualites Gynecologiques
Actual Hemat — Actualites Hematologiques
Actual Hematol — Actualites Hematologiques
Actual Hepato-Gastro-Enterol Hotel-Dieu — Actualites Hepato-Gastro-Enterologiques de l'Hotel-Dieu
Actual Hotel-Dieu — Actualites de l'Hotel-Dieu
Actualid Med Mund B Aires — Actualidades Medicas (Mundial) (Buenos Aires)
Actualid Med Rutherford NJ — Actualidades Medicas (Rutherford, New Jersey)
Actualid Med Sanit — Actualidades Medico-Sanitarias [Rio de Janeiro]
Actual Industr Lorraines — Actualites Industrielles Lorraines
Actual Ing Agron — Actualidades de la Ingenieria Agronomica
Actualite Auto — Actualite Automobile
Actualite Chim Ind — Actualite Chimique et Industrielle
Actualite Econ — Actualite Economique
Actualite Med — Actualite Medicale
Actualite Scient — Actualite Scientifique
Actualites Math — Actualites Mathematiques
Actualites Sci Indust — Actualites Scientifiques et Industrielles
Actualite Ther — Actualite Therapeutique
Actual Jur — Actualite Juridique
Actual Mar — Actualites Marines
Actual Mar Queb — Actualites Marines (Quebec)
Actual Med — Actualidades Medicas
Actual Med — Actualidad Medica
Actual Med — Actualite Medicale
Actual Med Chir — Actualites Medico-Chirurgicales
Actual Med-Chir (Mars) — Actualites Medico-Chirurgicales (Marseille)
Actual Med Chir Marseille — Actualites Medico-Chirurgicales (Marseille)
Actual Nephrol H Necker — Actualites Nephrologiques. Hopital Necker
Actual Nephrol Hop Necker — Actualites Nephrologiques. Hopital Necker
Actual Neurophysiol — Actualites Neurophysiologiques
Actual Neurophysiol (Paris) — Actualites Neurophysiologiques (Paris)
Actual Odontostomat — Actualites Odontostomatologiques
Actual Odontostomatol — Actualites Odontostomatologiques
Actual Odontostomatol (Paris) — Actualites Odonto-Stomatologiques
Actual Pedagog — Actualites Pedagogiques
Actual Pediatr (Granada) — Actualidad Pediatrica (Granada)
Actual Pharm — Actualites Pharmacologiques
Actual Pharmac — Actualites Pharmacologiques
Actual Pharmacol — Actualites Pharmacologiques
Actual Pharmacol (Paris) — Actualites Pharmacologiques (Paris)
Actual Physiol Pathol — Actualites de Physiologie Pathologique
Actual Protozool — Actualites Protozoologiques
Actual Psychiatr — Actualites Psychiatriques
Actual Rel Mo — Actualite Religieuse dans le Monde
Actual Scient — Actualites Scientifiques
Actual Scient Ind — Actualites Scientifiques et Industrielles
Actual Sci Ind — Actualites Scientifiques et Industrielles
Actual Sci Techn — Actualites Scientifiques et Techniques
Actual Specif Eng — Actual Specifying Engineer
Actual Ther — Actualite Therapeutique
Actuar Note — Actuarial Note
ACTU Bul — ACTU [Australian Council of Trade Unions] Bulletin
Actu Econ — Actualite Economique
Actuel Dev — Actuel Developpement
Actuel Develop — Actuel Developpement
Actuel Dr Person — Actuelles des Droits de la Personne
Actuelle Gerontol — Actuelle Gerontologie
Act Univ La Plata — Actos Universitarios. Universidad Nacional de La Plata
Act Un Lund — Acta Universitatis Lundensis. Lunds Universitets Arsskrift. Afdelningen foer Mathematik och Naturvetenskap
Act Upsal — Acta Societatis Regiae Scientiarum Upsaliensis
Act Vet H — Acta Veterinaria. Academiae Scientiarum Hungaricae
Act Vet Sc — Acta Veterinaria Scandinavica
Act Virolog — Acta Virologica
Act Vit Enz — Acta Vitaminologica et Enzymologica
Act Zool H — Acta Zoologica. Academiae Scientiarum Hungaricae
ACUCDN — Acute Care
ACUD — Acta Classica. Universitatis Scientiarum Debreceniensis
A Cuerp Fac — Anuario. Cuerpo Facultativo de Archiveros, Bibliotecarios, y Arqueologos
Ac UG — Acta Universitatis Gothoburgensis / Goeteborgs Universitets Arsskrift
ACUM — Annales. Centre Universitaire Mediterraneen de Nice
ACUN — Annales. Centre Universitaire de Nice
ACUNSOP — Association of Canadian Universities for Northern Studies. Occasional Publications
Acupunct Electro-Ther Res — Acupuncture and Electro-Therapeutics Research
Acupunct Med — Acupuncture in Medicine
ACUR-A — Architectural Record
ACUSA — Acustica
ACUSD — Acta Classica. Universitatis Scientiarum Debreceniensis
Acust — Acustica
Acust Acta Acust — Acustica, United with Acta Acustica
Acustica Akust Beih — Acustica. Akustische Beihefte
Acute Care — Acute Care Journal. International Society on Biotelemetry
Acute Diarrhoea Child Symp — Acute Diarrhoea in Childhood Symposium
Acute Fluid Replacement Ther Shock Pro Conf — Acute Fluid Replacement in the Therapy of Shock. Proceedings. Conference
Acute Leuk — Acute Leukemias. Pharmacokinetics and Management of Relapsed and Refractory Disease
Acute Toxic Data — Acute Toxicity Data
ACUU — Acta Universitatis Upsaliensis. Abstracts of Uppsala Dissertations. Faculty of Science
ACV — Acta Cientifica Venezolana
ACV — Australian and New Zealand Conveyancing Report

ACVIA9 — Acta Vitaminologica [Later, Acta Vitaminologica et Enzymological]
ACVNAO — Atti. Museo Civico di Storia Naturale di Trieste
ACVSA — Acta Cientifica Venezolana. Suplemento
ACVTA — Acta Veterinaria
ACVTB9 — Acta Veterinaria
ACW — Ancient Christian Writers
ACWR — Alaska Cooperative Wildlife Research Unit
ACWS — All-Canada Weekly Summaries
ACYTA — Acta Cytologica
ACZ — PROSI [Public Relations Office of the Sugar Industry] Bulletin Mensuel
ACZBA8 — Centro de Estudos Zoologicos. Universidade do Brasil. Avulso
ACZMN — Arctic Coastal Zone Management. Newsletter
ACZOAD — Acta Zootechnica
AcZS — Acta Zoologica. Internationell Tidskrift for Zoologi (Stockholm)
Ad — Adam. International Review
Ad — Adelphi
AD — After Dark
AD — Amazing Detective Tales
AD — American Documentation
AD — Antike Denkmaeler. Kaiserliches Deutsches Archaeologisches Institut
A D — Appellate Division Reports
AD — Archaiologikon Deltion
AD — Architectural Design
AD — Architectural Digest
AD — Archiv fuer Diplomatik
AD — Army Digest
AD — Art Digest
AD — Assyrian Dictionary
AD — Australian Digest
A D 2d — Appellate Division Reports. Second Series
ADA — Advertising Age
ADA — Alba de America. Revista Literaria
AdA — Amour de l'Art
ADA — Anzeiger fuer Deutsches Altertum und Deutsche Literatur
ADA — Arquivo do Distrito de Aveiro
ADA — Australian Digest
ADA — Azerbaycan Dergisi (Ankara)
ADAB News — Agricultural Development Agencies in Bangladesh News
ADACAT — Advances in Acarology
ADAGA7 — Advances in Agronomy
Ad Age — Advertising Age
Ad Age Eur — Advertising Age Europe
ADAI — Abhandlungen. Deutsches Archaeologisches Institut
ADAJ — Annual. Department of Antiquities of Jordan
Ada Lett — Ada Letters
ADAMAP — Advances in Applied Microbiology
ADAM Int R — ADAM [Arts, Drama, Architecture, Music] International Review
Adam Mickiewicz Univ Inst Chem Ser Chem — Adam Mickiewicz University. Institute of Chemistry. Seria Chemia
Ad & El NS — Adolphus and Ellis' Reports, New Series
Adans — Adansonia
Adansonia NS — Adansonia. New Series
Adapted P Act Q — Adapted Physical Activity Quarterly
Adapt Environ Essays Physiol Mar Anim — Adaptation to Environment. Essays on the Physiology of Marine Animals
Adapt Osob Evol Ptits Plenarnye Dokl Vses Ornitol Konf — Adaptivnye Osobennosti i Evolyutsiya Ptits Plenarnye Doklady Vsesoyuznoi Ornitologicheskoi Konferentsii
Adapt Pingvinov — Adaptatsii Pingvinov
Adapt Sist Avtom Upr — Adaptivnye Sistemy Avtomaticheskogo Upravleniya
Adapt Sistemy Avtomat Upravleniya — Kievski Politekhnicheskii Institut Adaptivnye Sistemy Avtomaticheskogo Upravleniya
ADARA — American Dairy Review
ADASA9 — Advances in the Astronautical Sciences
ADAS Q Rev — ADAS [Agricultural Development and Advisory Service] Quarterly Review
ADAS Q Rev (GB) — ADAS [Agricultural Development and Advisory Service] Quarterly Review (Great Britain)
A Das Sc — Annaes das Sciencias, das Artes, e das Letras por Huma Sociedade de Portuguezes Residentes em Paris
Adate Assoc Dev Audio Vis Tech Ed — Adate. Association pour le Developpement de l'Audio-visuel et de la Technologieen Education
ADAUEJ — Advances in Audiology
ADAW — Abhandlungen. Deutsche Akademie der Wissenschaften zu Berlin. Klasse fuer Sprachen, Literatur, und Kunst
ADAWP — Abhandlungen der Deutschen Akademie der Wissenschaften in Prag
ADAWPPH — Abhandlungen der Deutschen Akademie der Wissenschaften in Prag. Philosophisch-Historische Klasse
ADAYAR — Advances in Activation Analysis
ADB — Academie Delphinale. Bulletin
ADB — Algemeen Dagblad
ADB — Allgemeine Deutsche Biographie
ADB — Australian Dictionary of Biography
ADB — Australian Digest Bulletin
ADBA — Abhandlungen und Vortraege. Deutsches Bibel-Archiv
ADBBBW — Advances in Behavioral Biology
ADBEA6 — Advances in Biochemical Engineering
ADBED9 — Addictive Behaviors
ADBPE9 — Advances in Developmental and Behavioral Pediatrics
ADBRDE — Australia. Commonwealth Scientific and Industrial Research Organisation. Division of Building Research. Annual Report
ADC — Advances in Cell Culture
ADC — Archivo Diocesano de Cuenca
ADCDA8 — Advances in Child Development and Behavior
ADCLDZ — Advances in Cladistics

ADCMAZ — Advances in Chemotherapy
ADCND7 — Advances in Cellular Neurobiology
ADCOEB — Advances in Contraception
Ad Compl — Advertising Compliance Service
Ad Compli S — Advertising Compliance Service. Special Report
Ad Cont — Addison on Contract
ADCOV — Acta et Documenta Concilio Oecumenico Vaticano II Apparando
ADCPAA — Advances in Chemical Physics
ADCSAJ — Advances in Chemistry Series
ADCYA3 — Advances in Chromatography
ADCYB4 — Advances in Cytopharmacology
ADD — American Dialect Dictionary
ADD — Archiv der Deutschen Dominikaner
ADDABASE — Australain Database Development Asssociation
Addict Behav — Addictive Behaviors
Addict Biol — Addiction Biology
Addict Dis — Addictive Diseases
ADDIDV — Addictive Diseases
Addis Ababa Univ Bull Geophys Obs — Addis Ababa University. Bulletin. Geophysical Observatory
Addison-Wesley Ser Comput Sci Inform Process — Addison-Wesley Series in Computer Science and Information Processing
Addison Wesley Stud Nonlinearity — Addison-Wesley Studies in Nonlinearity
Additam Faun Coleopt — Additamenta Faunistica Coleopterorum
Additional Ser Roy Bot — Additional Series. Royal Botanic Gardens
Addit Rubber Plast Pap Meet — Additives for Rubber and Plastics. Papers Presented at the Meeting of the Chemical Marketing Research Association
Addit Schmierst — Additive fuer Schmierstoffe
Addit Ser Kew — Additional Series. Royal Botanical Gardens. Kew
ADDLIS N — ADDLIS [*Alcoholism and Drug Dependence Librarians and Information Services*] News
Address Proc Ontario Soil Crop Impr Ass — Addresses and Proceedings. Ontario Soil and Crop Improvement Association
Address Proc Saskatchewan Univ Farm Home Week — Addresses and Proceedings. Saskatchewan University Farm and Home Week
AdE — Adult Education
ADE — American Demographics
ADE — Archivio di Diritto Ecclesiastico
ADE — Assessor's Data Exchange
ADEB — Association of Departments of English. Bulletin
A Dec — Art Decoratif
A Dec — Arts Decorativa
A Dec Mod — Arte Decorativa Moderna
AdEd — Adult Education
ADEEAL — Annales. Direction des Etudes et de l'Equipement. Service d'Exploitation Industrielle des Tabacs et des Allumettes. Section 1
ADEEBM — Annales. Direction des Etudes et de l'Equipement. Service d'Exploitation Industrielle des Tabacs et des Allumettes. Section 2
ADEGB — Automotive Design Engineering
ADEJB — Arizona Dental Journal
ADEK — Auslanddeutschtum und Evangelische Kirche
Adel — Adelphi
Adel — New Adelphi
Adelaide Children's Hosp Records — Adelaide Children's Hospital. Records
Adelaide Law Rev — Adelaide Law Review
Adelaide LR — Adelaide Law Review
Adelaide L Rev — Adelaide Law Review
Adel Law R — Adelaide Law Review
Adel Law Rev — Adelaide Law Review
Adel LR — Adelaide Law Review
Adel L Rev — Adelaide Law Review
Adelphi P — Adelphi Papers
Adel Stock and Station J — Adelaide Stock and Station Journal
A Delt — Archaiologikon Deltion
Adel Univ Grad Gaz — Adelaide University Graduates Union. Gazette
Adel Univ Grad Union Gaz — Adelaide University Graduates Union. Monthly Newsletter and Gazette
Adel Univ Mag — Adelaide University. Magazine
ADEM — Archivio di Diritto Ecclesiastico. Monografie
Adenine Arabinoside Antiviral Agent Symp — Adenine Arabinoside; an Antiviral Agent. Symposium
Aden LR — Aden Law Reports
Adequacy Dial Pro Conf — Adequacy of Dialysis. Proceedings of a Conference
A Der Hydrog — Annalen der Hydrographie und Maritimen Meteorologie
A Derm — Acta Dermatologica
ADESAT — Anales del Desarrollo
ADETBX — Australia. Commonwealth Scientific and Industrial Research Organisation. Division of Entomology. Annual Report
A Deux Mondes — Art dans les Deux Mondes
ADEVD — Area Development
ADF — Ad Forum
AdF — Arbol de Fuego
ADFA Aud Vis Cat — ADFA [*Alcohol and Drug Foundation, Australia*] Audio Visual Catalogue
ADFCA — Advances in Fluorine Chemistry
ADFCAK — Advances in Fluorine Chemistry
ADFGUW — Ausgrabungen der Deutschen Forschungsgemeinschaft in Uruk-Warka
ADFLB — Association of Departments of Foreign Languages. Bulletin
ADFOAM — Australia. Commonwealth Scientific and Industrial Research Organisation. Division of Fisheries and Oceanography. Report
ADFPBQ — Australia. Commonwealth Scientific and Industrial Research Organisation. Division of Food Preservation. Report of Research
ADFRAV — Alaska. Department of Fisheries. Research Report
ADG — Annales de Geographie
AdG — Archiv der Gegenwart

ADG — Archives Historiques du Departement de la Gironde
ADGB — Archiv fuer Geschichte des Buchwesens
ADGEA — Advances in Genetics
Adgez Rasplavov — Adgeziya Rasplavov
Adgez Rasplavov Paika Mater — Adgeziya Rasplavov i Paika Materialov
ADGMA — Acta et Diplomata Graeca Medii Aevi Sacra et Profana Collecta
ADGOA — Advances in Geophysics
ADGZ — Arbeiten der Deutschen Gesellschaft fuer Zuechtungskunde
ADH — Adherent
Adhaes — Adhaesion
Adhaes Kleben Dichten — Adhaesion. Kleben and Dichten
Adhes Adhes — Adhesion and Adhesives
Adhes Adhes Kyoto — Adhesion and Adhesives (Kyoto)
Adhes Adsorpt Polym — Adhesion and Adsorption of Polymers
Adhes Age — Adhesives Age
Adhesive D — Adhesives Age Directory
Adhesives — Adhesives Age
Adhes Res — Adhesives and Resins
Adhes Resins — Adhesives and Resins
Adhes Sealant Counc J — Adhesive and Sealant Council. Journal
Adhes Sealants — Adhesives and Sealants
Adhes Soc Proc Seventeenth Annu Meet Symp Part Adhes — Adhesion Society. Proceedings of the Seventeenth Annual Meeting and the Symposium on Particle Adhesion
Adhes Tech Ann — Adhesives Technology Annual
ADHGA — Advances in Human Genetics
ADHS — Armidale and District Historical Society. Journal
ADHYA — Advances in Hydroscience
AdI — Annali. Istituto di Corrispondenza Archeologica
ADI — Anuario. Departamento de Ingles
ADIB — Anales de Ingenieria (Bogota)
A Di C — Annali di Chimica
A Di Fm E C — Annali di Farmacoterapia e Chimica
A Dig — Arts Digest
ADIGE — Archivio Dati Italiani di Geologia
A Digest — Art Digest
ADIHDJ — Annual Research Reviews. Anti-Diuretic Hormone
ADIK — Abhandlungen des Deutschen Archaeologischen Instituts. Kairo
ADIM — American Documentation Institute Microfilm
A Dim — Art Dimension
ADIMA — Advances in Immunology
ADIOA — Journal. Audio Engineering Society
A Dion — Actes de Dionysiou
A Dipl — Archiv fuer Diplomatik, Schriftgeschichte, Siegel- und Wappenkunde
Adipose Child Int Symp — Adipose Child Medical and Psychological Aspects. International Symposium
Adipose Tissue Regul Metab Funct — Adipose Tissue. Regulation and Metabolic Functions
Adipositas Kindesalter Symp — Adipositas im Kindesalter Symposium
Adipositas Kreislauf Anorektika Vortr Symp — Adipositas, Kreislauf, Anorektika. Vortraege des Symposions
A Dir — Art Direction
ADIRBD — Australia. Commonwealth Scientific and Industrial Research Organisation. Division of Irrigation Research. Annual Report
A Directors Annu NY — Art Directors' Annual of New York
ADJ — Asian Defense Journal
ADJHDO — Azabu Daigaku Juigakubu Kenkyu Hokoku
Adjuvant Ther Cancer — Adjuvant Therapy of Cancer. Proceedings of the International Conference
Adjuvant Ther Cancer Proc Int Conf — Adjuvant Therapy of Cancer. Proceedings of the International Conference
ADL — Adevarul Literar
AdL — Amor de Libro
AdL — Anuario de Letras
AdL — Arbol de Letras
Ad L 2d(P & F) — Pike and Fischer's Administrative Law Reporter, Second Series
AdlA — Amour de l'Art
ADLA — Anales de Legislacion Argentina
Ad Law Rev — Administrative Law Review
AdLB — Adyar Library Bulletin
AdLBEd — Adult Literacy and Basic Education
ADL Bul — Anti-Defamation League. Bulletin
Ad L Bull — Administrative Law Bulletin
Adler Mus Bull — Adler Museum Bulletin
ADLG — Arbeiten des Deutschen Landwirtschafts-Gesellschaft
ADLI — Album of Dated Latin Inscriptions
ADL-Nachr — ADL-Nachrichten
Ad L R — Adelaide Law Reports
Ad LR — Administrative Law Review
Ad L Rev — Administrative Law Review
ADL Rev — Anti-Defamation League. Review
A d M — Annales du Midi; Revue de la France Meridionale
ADM — Annals of Discrete Mathematics
Ad M — Archives des Missions Scientifiques et Litteraires
ADM — Office Administration and Automation
Adm and Soc — Administration and Society
A/DM & T — PTS [*Predicasts*] Aerospace/Defense Markets and Technology
Adm B — Periodieke Verzameling van Administratieve en Rechterlijke Beslissingen
Adm Bull — Administrators' Bulletin
Adm Change — Administrative Change
ADMDBP — Advances in Metabolic Disorders. Supplement
ADMFAU — Archiv fuer Dermatologische Forschung
ADMIA — Advances in Microwaves
ADMIG Bulletin — Australian Drug and Medical Information Group. Bulletin
Admin — Administration

Admin and Society — Administration and Society
Admin Cent Bal — Administracao Centralizada Balancos
Admin Collect — Administrator's Collection
Admin Desarr Integ — Administracion, Desarrollo, Integracion
Admin Dig — Administrative Digest
Admin Hosp — Administrateur Hospitalier
Admin L 2d P & F — Administrative Law Second. Pike and Fischer
Admin Law — Administrative Law
Admin Man — Administrator. Manitoba Association of Principals
Admin Manage — Administrative Management
Admin Ment Hlth — Administration in Mental Health
Admin Mgmt — Administrative Management
Admin Note — Administrative Notes. Information Dissemination. US Superintendent of Documents. Library Programs Service
Admin pub — Administration Publique
Admin Rev — Administrative Review
Admin Science Q — Administrative Science Quarterly
Admin Sci Q — Administrative Science Quarterly
Admin Sci R — Administrative Science Review
Admin Staff Col India J Man — Administrative Staff College of India. Journal of Management
Admiralty Mar Sci Publ — Admiralty Marine Science Publication
Admixtures Concr Proc Int Symp — Admixtures for Concrete. Improvement of Properties. Proceedings. International Symposium
ADML — Automatic Documentation and Mathematical Linguistics
Adm Law R — Administrative Law Review
ADMLBF — Acta Dermatologica [*Kyoto*]. English Edition
Adm Lex — Administratief Lexicon
Adm Locale — Administration Locale
Adm LR — Administrative Law Review
Adm L Rev — Administrative Law Review
Adm Manage — Administrative Management
Adm Ment He — Administration in Mental Health
Adm Ment Health — Administration in Mental Health
Adm Mgmt — Administrative Management
Adm Mgt — Administrative Management
Adm Notebk — Administrator's Notebook
ADMO — Australian Directory of Music Organisations
ADMOA — Advances in Morphogenesis
ADMPAQ — Australia. Commonwealth Scientific and Industrial Research Organisation. Division of Mathematical Statistics. Technical Paper
Adm Policy Ment Health — Administration and Policy in Mental Health
ADMR — Australian Directory of Music Research
Adm Radiol — Administrative Radiology
ADMRB — Advances in Materials Research
Adm Rep Agric Dep Madras — Administration Report. Agricultural Department. Madras
Adm Rep Dep Agric Mysore — Administration Report. Department of Agriculture. Mysore
Adm Rep Dep Fish Madras — Administration Report of the Department of Fisheries. Madras
Adm Rep Dir Agric Br Guiana — Administration Report of the Director of Agriculture. British Guiana
Adm Rep Dir Agric Trin — Administration Report of the Director of Agriculture. Trinidad and Tobago
Adm Rep Met Allahabad — Administration Report of the Meteorologist at Allahabad
Adm Rep Met Reptr Govt Bengal — Administration Report of the Meteorological Reporter to the Government of Bengal
Adm Rep Met Reptr Govt Unit Prov Agra Oudh — Administration Report of the Meteorological Reporter to the Government. United Provinces of Agra and Oudh
ADM Rev — ADM [*Asociacion Dental Mexicana*] Revista
ADM Rev Asoc Dent Mex — ADM. Revista de la Asociacion Dental Mexicana
ADMSB2 — Advances in Microbiology of the Sea
Adm Sci — Administrative Science Quarterly
Adm Sci Q — Administrative Science Quarterly
Adm Sci Qua — Administrative Science Quarterly
Adm Socie — Administration and Society
Adm Soc Work — Administration in Social Work
Adm Tss — Administrativ Tidsskrift
Adm y Desarr — Administracion y Desarrollo
ADN — Alcohol and Drug News
ADN — Annales de Normandie
ADNDA — Atomic Data and Nuclear Data Tables
ADNEDZ — Advances in Neurochemistry
A d Normandie — Annales de Normandie
ADNRA3 — Advances in Neurology
ADNSA6 — Adansonia
A Dobr — Analele Dobrogei
ADOC — Agora-Documentaire
A Doc — Art Documentation
ADOCA — Advances in Organic Chemistry
A Docs — Art Documents
A D Ocul — Annales d'Oculistique
ADOG — Abhandlungen. Deutsche Orient-Gesellschaft
ADOL — Adolescence
ADOLA — Adolescence
Adoles — Adolescence
Adolesc Med — Adolescent Medicine
Adolesc Med State Arts Rev — Adolescent Medicine State of the Arts Reviews
Adolesc Ment Health Abstr — Adolescent Mental Health Abstracts
Adolesc Psychiatry — Adolescent Psychiatry
Adol Med — Adolescent Medicine
A Dom — Annee Dominicaine
ADORB — Advances in Oto-Rhino-Laryngology

A d P — Almanach der Psychoanalyse
ADP — Archiv fuer Deutsche Postgeschichte
ADP — Archivo de Derecho Publico
ADPA — Accounting and Data Processing Abstracts
ADPADX — Advances in Pathobiology
ADPCA — Advances in Photochemistry
ADPEA — Advances in Pediatrics
ADPh — Arbeiten zur Deutschen Philologie
ADPHDK — Advances in Pharmacotherapy
ADPPB — Advances in Particle Physics
ADPRA — Advances in Parasitology
AD Praem — Acta et Decreta Capitulorum Generalium Ordinis Praemonstratensis
ADPSDJ — Adolescent Psychiatry
AD Publ Am Soc Mech Eng Aerosp Div — AD (Publication) (American Society of Mechanical Engineers, Aerospace Division)
ADPV — Abhandlungen. Deutscher Palaestina-Verein
AdQ — Amis de 1914
ADQ — Australia Newsletter
ADQEA — Advances in Quantum Electronics
A Dr — Annales de Droit
ADR — Journal of Advertising Research
ADRCAC — Annali Italiani di Dermatologia Clinica e Sperimentale
ADREA — American Dyestuff Reporter
ADRED — Archives for Dermatological Research
ADREDL — Archives for Dermatological Research
ADREP — Aircraft Accident/Incident Reporting System
Adriamycin Rev EORTC Int Symp — Adriamycin Review. EORTC (European Organization for Research into Treatment of Cancer) International Symposium
Adriamycin-Symp — Adriamycin-Symposium
Adriat Int Conf Nucl Phys — Adriatic International Conference on Nuclear Physics
Adriat Meet Part Phys — Adriatic Meeting on Particle Physics
A Dr Marit Aer — Annuaire de Droit Maritime et Aerien
ADRPB — Advances in Reproductive Physiology
ADRPBI — Advances in Reproductive Physiology
ADRRAN — Advances in Drug Research
ADRRCP — Australia. Commonwealth Scientific and Industrial Research Organisation. Division of Dairy Research. Annual Report
ADRS — Archivio. Reale Deputazione Romana di Storia Patria
ADRSP — Archivio. Reale Deputazione Romana di Storia Patria
ADS — Administration and Society
ADSAAB — Annali della Sanita Pubblica
ADSCAH — Advancement of Science
Ad Sci — Advancement of Science
ADSCR — Acta et Decreta Sacrorum Conciliorum Recentiorum
Ad Serv Leafl Timb Res Developm Ass — Advisory Service Leaflet. Timber Research and Development Association
AdSL — Advancement of Science (London)
AD Soc Manuf Eng — AD Society of Manufacturing Engineers
Adsorbts Adsorbenty — Adsorbtsiya i Adsorbenty
Adsorbtsiya Poristost Tr Vses Konf Teor Vopr Adsorbtsii — Adsorbtsiya i Poristost Trudy Vsesoyuznoi Konferentsii po Teoreticheskim Voprosam Adsorbtsii
Adsorbts Poristost Tr Vses Konf Teor Vopr Adsorbts — Adsorbtsiya i Poristost. Trudy Vsesoyuznoi Konferentsii po Teoreticheskim Voprosam Adsorbtsii
Adsorpt News — Adsorption News
Adsorpt Sci Technol — Adsorption Science and Technology
ADSP — Annales de Droit et de Sciences Politiques
ADSPA — Annales de Dermatologie et de Syphiligraphie [*Later, Annales de Dermatologie et de Venereologie*]
ADSPE — Atti e Memorie. Deputazione di Storia Patria per le Provincie dell'Emilia
ADSPER — Atti e Memorie. Deputanzione di Storia Patria per l'Emilia e la Romagna
ADSPL — Atti. Deputazione di Storia Patria per la Liguria
ADSPLS — Atti. Deputazione di Storia Patria per la Liguria. Sezione di Savana
ADSPM — Atti e Memorie. Deputazione di Storia Patria per le Antiche Provincie Modenesl
ADSPMa — Atti e Memorie. Deputazione di Storia Patria per le Marche
ADSPR — Atti e Memorie. Deputazione di Storia Patria per le Provincie di Romagna
ADSR — Archives de Sociologie des Religions
AdSR — Archivio della Societa Romana di Storia Patria
ADSUA — Advances in Surgery
ADSV — Antichnaia Drevnost'i Srednie Veka
AD SW — Archiv der Deutschen Seewarte
ADT — Adformatie. Weekblad voor Reclame en Marketing
ADT — Amazing Detective Tales
AdTb — Altdeutsche Textbibliothek
ADTBE — Altdeutsche Textbibliothek. Ergaenzungsreihe
ADTEAS — Advances in Teratology
Ad Techniq — Advertising and Graphic Arts Techniques
AdUA — Annales. Universite d'Abidjan
A d U B — Annales. Universite de Brazzaville
AdUB — Annales. Universite de Brazzaville
ADUL — Annales. Association des Anciens Etudiants. Faculte de Droit.Universite de Louvain
Adult Dis — Adult Diseases
Adult Ed — Adult Education
Adult Ed and Lib — Adult Education and the Library
Adult Ed Bul — Adult Education Bulletin
Adult Ed J — Adult Education Journal
Adult Educ — Adult Education
Adult Educ Q — Adult Education Quarterly
Adult Ed-W — Adult Education-Washington
Adult Lead — Adult Leadership
ADV — Advertising World
Adv — Advocate

Adv — Advocatenblad

ADV — Arbeitsgemeinschaft Deutscher Verfolgten-Organisationen

Adv Abstr Contrib Fish Aquat Sci India — Advance Abstracts of Contributions on Fisheries and Aquatic Sciences in India

Adv Acarol — Advances in Acarology

Adv Act Anal — Advances in Activation Analysis

Adv Adhes Sealants Technol Conf Pap — Advances in Adhesives and Sealants Technology. Conference Papers

Adv Aerobiol Proc Int Conf Aerobiol — Advances in Aerobiology. Proceedings. International Conference on Aerobiology

Adv Aerosol Phys — Advances in Aerosol Physics

Adv Aerosol Phys Engl Transl — Advances in Aerosol Physics (English Translation)

Adv Age — Advertising Age

Adv Agency Mag — Advertising Agency Magazine

Adv Agric Biotech — Advances in Agricultural Biotechnology

Adv Agric Biotechnol — Advances in Agricultural Biotechnology

Adv Agric Technol AAT W US Dep Agric Sci Educ Adm West Reg — Advances in Agricultural Technology. AAT-W. United States Department of Agriculture. Science and Education Administration. Western Region

Adv Agron — Advances in Agronomy

Adv Agron Crop Sci — Advances in Agronomy and Crop Science

Adv Alcohol & Subst Abuse — Advances in Alcohol and Substance Abuse

Adv Alcohol Subst Abuse — Advances in Alcohol and Substance Abuse

Adv Alicyclic Chem — Advances in Alicyclic Chemistry

Adv Allergol Clin Immunol Proc Int Congr Allergol — Advances in Allergology and Clinical Immunology. Proceedings. International Congress of Allergology

Adv Amino Acid Mimetics Peptidomimetics — Advances in Amino Acid Mimetics and Peptidomimetics

Advan Agron — Advances in Agronomy

Adv Anal Chem Instrum — Advances in Analytical Chemistry and Instrumentation

Adv Anal Geochem — Advances in Analytical Geochemistry

Adv Anal Methodol Leaf Smoke Symp Tob Chem Res Conf — Advances in the Analytical Methodology of Leaf and Smoke. Symposium. Tobacco Chemist's Research Conference

Adv Anal Toxicol — Advances in Analytical Toxicology

Advan Appl Mech — Advances in Applied Mechanics

Advan Appl Probab — Advances in Applied Probability

Advan Archaeol Method Theory — Advances in Archaeological Method and Theory

Advan Astronaut Sci — Advances in the Astronautical Sciences

Adv Anat Embryol Cell Biol — Advances in Anatomy, Embryology, and Cell Biology

Adv Anat Pathol — Advances in Anatomic Pathology

Advan Carbohyd Chem — Advances in Carboyhydrate Chemistry

Advan Carbohyd Chem Biochem — Advances in Carboyhydrate Chemistry and Biochemistry

Advance Data — Advance Data from Vital and Health Statistics

Advanced Mgmt Jrnl — Advanced Management Journal

Advanced Mgt — Advanced Management Journal

Advanced Mgt J — Advanced Management Journal

Advanced Mgt-Office Exec — Advanced Management-Office Executive

Advanced Sch Dig — Advanced School Digest. Teachers College. Columbia University

Advanced Textbooks in Econom — Advanced Textbooks in Economics

Advancement Sci — Advancement of Science

Advancem Sci — Advancement of Science. Report. British Association for the Advancement of Science

Advances Agron — Advances in Agronomy

Advances Cancer Res — Advances in Cancer Research

Advances Carbohyd Chem — Advances in Carbohydrate Chemistry [*Later, Advances in Carbohydrate Chemistry and Biochemistry*]

Advances Chemother — Advances in Chemotherapy

Advance Sci — Advancement of Science

Advances Colloid Sci — Advances in Colloid Science

Advances Ecol Res — Advances in Ecological Research

Advances Geophys — Advances in Geophysics

Advances Hydrosci — Advances in Hydroscience

Advances Immun — Advances in Immunology

Advances in Appl Mech — Advances in Applied Mechanics

Advances in Appl Probability — Advances in Applied Probability

Advances in Chem Ser — Advances in Chemistry Series

Advances in Math Suppl Studies — Advances in Mathematics. Supplementary Studies

Advances in Skin & Wound Care — Adv Skin Wound Care

Advances Int Med — Advances in Internal Medicine

Advances Morphogen — Advances in Morphogensis

Advances Pediat — Advances in Pediatrics

Advances Pharmacol — Advances in Pharmacology

Advances Phys Sci — Advances in Physical Sciences

Advances Protein Chem — Advances in Protein Chemistry

Advances Surg — Advances in Surgery

Advanc Front Plant Sci — Advancing Frontiers of Plant Sciences

Advan Chem Eng — Advances in Chemical Engineering

Advan Chem Ser — Advances in Chemistry Series

Advancing Frontiers Plant Sci — Advancing Frontiers of Plant Sciences

Advan Clin Chem — Advances in Clinical Chemistry

Advan Cryog Eng — Advances in Cryogenic Engineering

Adv Androl — Advances in Andrology

Adv & Sell — Advertising and Selling

Advan Electron and Electron Phys — Advances in Electronics and Electron Physics

Advan Front Plant Sci — Advancing Frontiers of Plant Sciences

Advan Genet — Advances in Genetics

Advan Geophys — Advances in Geophysics

Adv Anim Breed — Advanced Animal Breeder

Adv Anim Physiol Anim Nutr — Advances in Animal Physiology and Animal Nutrition

Advan Manage J — Advanced Management Journal

Advan Mol Relaxation Processes — Advances in Molecular Relaxation Processes [*Later, Advances in Molecular Relaxation and Interaction Processes*]

Advan Phys — Advances in Physics

Advan Polymer Sci Fortschr Hochpolym-Forsch — Advances in Polymer Science/Fortschritte der Hochpolymeren-Forschung

Advan Thanatol — Advances in Thanatology

Adv Anthracite Technol Res Proc Conf — Advanced Anthracite Technology and Research. Proceedings of the Conference

Adv Antimicrob Antineoplast Chemother — Advances in Antimicrobial and Antineoplastic Chemotherapy

Advan Virus Res — Advances in Virus Research

Adv Appl Clifford Algebras — Advances in Applied Clifford Algebras

Adv Appl Lipid Res — Advances in Applied Lipid Research

Adv Appl Ma — Advances in Applied Mathematics

Adv Appl Math — Advances in Applied Mathematics

Adv Appl Mech — Advances in Applied Mechanics

Adv Appl Mech Suppl — Advances in Applied Mechanics. Supplement

Adv Appl Microb — Advances in Applied Microbiology

Adv Appl Microbiol — Advances in Applied Microbiology

Adv Appl P — Advances in Applied Probability

Adv Appl Prob — Advances in Applied Probability

Adv Appl Probab — Advances in Applied Probability

Adv Appl Statist — Advances in Applied Statistics

Ap Pr — Advances in Applied Probability

Adv Aquat Microbiol — Advances in Aquatic Microbiology

Adv Archaeol Method Theory — Advances in Archaeological Method and Theory

Adv Artif Hip Knee Jt Technol — Advances in Artificial Hip and Knee Joint Technology

Adv Astron Astrophys — Advances in Astronomy and Astrophysics

Adv Astronaut Sci — Advances in the Astronautical Sciences

Adv Asymmetric Synth — Advances in Asymmetric Synthesis

Adv At Mol Phys — Advances in Atomic and Molecular Physics

Adv At Spectrosc — Advances in Atomic Spectroscopy

Adv Audiol — Advances in Audiology

Adv Autom Anal Technicon Int Congr — Advances in Automated Analysis. Technicon International Congress

Adv Autotrophic Microbiol One Carbon Metab — Advances in Autotrophic Microbiology and One-Carbon Metabolism

Adv Behav Biol — Advances in Behavioral Biology

Adv Behav Pharmacol — Advances in Behavioral Pharmacology

Adv Behav Res Ther — Advances in Behaviour Research and Therapy

Adv Beta-Adrenergic Blocking Ther Sotalol Proc Int Symp — Advances in Beta-Adrenergic Blocking Therapy. Sotalol Proceedings. International Symposium

Adv Bile Acid Res Bile Acid Meet — Advances in Bile Acid Research. Bile Acid Meeting

Adv Biochem Biophys — Advances in Biochemistry and Biophysics

Adv Biochem Eng — Advances in Biochemical Engineering

Adv Biochem Eng/Biotechnol — Advances in Biochemical Engineering/ Biotechnology

Adv Biochem Pharmacol — Advances in Biochemical Pharmacology

Adv Biochem Physiol Plant Lipids Proc Symp — Advances in the Biochemistry and Physiology of Plant Lipids. Proceedings of the Symposium

Adv Biochem Psychopharmacol — Advances in Biochemical Psychopharmacology

Adv Bioeng — Advances in Bioengineering

Adv Bioeng Instrum — Advances in Bioengineering and Instrumentation

Adv Biol & Medic Phys — Advances in Biological and Medical Physics

Adv Biol Berlin — Advances in Biology (Berlin)

Adv Biol Dis — Advances in the Biology of Disease

Adv Biol Med Phys — Advances in Biological and Medical Physics

Adv Biol Psychiatry — Advances in Biological Psychiatry

Adv Biol Skin — Advances in Biology of the Skin

Adv Biol Waste Treat Proc Conf — Advances in Biological Waste Treatment. Proceedings. Conference on Biological Waste Treatment

Adv Biomater — Advances in Biomaterials

Adv Biomed Alcohol Res Congr Int Soc Biomed Res Alcohol — Advances in Biomedical Alcohol Research. Congress. International Society for Biomedical Research on Alcoholism

Adv Biomed Alcohol Res Proc ISBRA RSA Congr — Advances in Biomedical Alcohol Research. Proceedings. ISBRA/RSA Congress

Adv Biomed Eng — Advances in Biomedical Engineering

Adv Biomed Eng Med Phys — Advances in Biomedical Engineering and Medical Physics

Adv Biomol Simul Jt Int Conf IBM Div Chim Phys — Advances in Biomolecular Simulations. Joint International Conference of IBM andDivision de Chimie Physique

Adv Biophys — Advances in Biophysics

Adv Biophys Chem — Advances in Biophysical Chemistry

Adv Biosci — Advances in the Biosciences

Adv Biosci Muzaffarnagar India — Advances in Biosciences (Muzaffarnagar, India)

Adv Biosci (Oxford) — Advances in the Biosciences (Oxford)

Adv Biosens — Advances in Biosensors

Adv Biotechnol Processes — Advances in Biotechnological Processes

Adv Biotechnol Proc Int Ferment Symp — Advances in Biotechnology. Proceedings. International Fermentation Symposium

Adv Biotech Processes — Advances in Biotechnological Processes

Advbl — Advocatenblad

Adv Bl — Advokatbladet

Adv Blood Grouping — Advances in Blood Grouping

Adv Bot Res — Advances in Botanical Research

Adv Bryol — Advances in Bryology

ADVC — Anuario do Distrito de Viana do Castelo

Adv Cancer Chemother — Advances in Cancer Chemotherapy

Adv Cancer Control Proc Annu Meet — Advances in Cancer Control. Innovations and Research. Proceedings. Annual Meeting

Adv Cancer Res — Advances in Cancer Research

Adv Carbene Chem — Advances in Carbene Chemistry

Adv Carbocation Chem — Advances in Carbocation Chemistry

Adv Carbohyd Chem — Advances in Carbohydrate Chemistry and Biochemistry

Adv Carbohydr Anal — Advances in Carbohydrate Analysis

Adv Carbohydr Chem — Advances in Carbohydrate Chemistry [*Later, Advances in Carbohydrate Chemistry and Biochemistry*]

Adv Carbohydr Chem Biochem — Advances in Carbohydrate Chemistry and Biochemistry

Adv Cardiol — Advances in Cardiology

Adv Cardiopulm Dis — Advances in Cardiopulmonary Diseases

Adv Cardiovasc Phys — Advances in Cardiovascular Physics

Adv Card Surg — Advances in Cardiac Surgery

Adv Catal — Advances in Catalysis and Related Subjects

Adv Catal Processes — Advances in Catalytic Processes

Adv Catal Proc Natl Symp Catal — Advances in Catalysis. Science and Technology. Proceedings. National Symposium on Catalysis

Adv Cell Aging Gerontol — Advances in Cell Aging and Gerontology

Adv Cell Biol — Advances in Cell Biology

Adv Cell Cult — Advances in Cell Culture

Adv Cell Mol Biol — Advances in Cell and Molecular Biology

Adv Cell Mol Biol Plants — Advances in Cellular and Molecular Biology of Plants

Adv Cell Neurobiol — Advances in Cellular Neurobiology

Adv Cem Based Mater — Advanced Cement Based Materials

Adv Cem Mater — Advances in Cementitious Materials

Adv Cem Res — Advances in Cement Research

Adv Ceram — Advances in Ceramics

Adv Ceram 3 Meet — Advanced Ceramics 3. Meeting for Advanced Ceramics

Adv Ceram Mat — Advanced Ceramic Materials

Adv Ceram Process Technol — Advanced Ceramic Processing and Technology

Adv Ceram Proc Int Symp — Advanced Ceramics. Proceedings. International Symposium

Adv Cereal Sci Technol — Advances in Cereal Science and Technology

Adv Chem — Advances in Chemistry

Adv Chem Chem Appl (Kyoto) — Advances in Chemistry and Chemical Application (Kyoto)

Adv Chem Diagn Treat Metab Disord — Advances in Chemical Diagnosis and Treatment of Metabolic Disorders

Adv Chem Eng — Advances in Chemical Engineering

Adv Chem Kinet Dyn — Advances in Chemical Kinetics and Dynamics

Adv Chemoreception — Advances in Chemoreception

Adv Chemother — Advances in Chemotherapy

Adv Chem Phys — Advances in Chemical Physics

Adv Chem Se — Advances in Chemistry Series

Adv Chem Ser — Advances in Chemistry Series

Adv Child Dev Behav — Advances in Child Development and Behavior

Adv Chitin Sci — Advances in Chitin Science

Adv Cholesterol Res — Advances in Cholesterol Research

Adv Chromatogr — Advances in Chromatography

Adv Chromatogr Electromigr Methods Biosci — Advanced Chromatographic and Electromigration Methods in Biosciences

Adv Chromatogr (NY) — Advances in Chromatography (New York)

Adv Cladistics — Advances in Cladistics

Adv Classical Trajectory Methods — Advances in Classical Trajectory Methods

Adv Clin Cardiol — Advances in Clinical Cardiology

Adv Clin Chem — Advances in Clinical Chemistry

Adv Clin Enzymol — Advances in Clinical Enzymology

Adv Clin Nutr Proc Int Symp — Advances in Clinical Nutrition. Proceedings. International Symposium

Adv Clin Path — Advances in Clinical Pathology

Adv Clin Pharmacol — Advances in Clinical Pharmacology

Adv CNS Drug Recept Interact — Advances in CNS Drug-Receptor Interactions

Adv Coal Util Technol Symp Pap — Advances in Coal Utilization Technology. Symposium Papers

Adv Coll In — Advances in Colloid and Interface Science

Adv Coll Inter Sci — Advances in Colloid and Interface Science

Adv Colloid and Interface Sci — Advances in Colloid and Interface Science

Adv Colloid Interface Sci — Advances in Colloid and Interface Science

Adv Colloid Sci — Advances in Colloid Science

Adv Colloid Struct — Advances in Colloid Structures

Adv Color Chem Ser — Advances in Color Chemistry Series

Adv Colour Sci Technol — Advances in Colour Science and Technology

Adv Comp — Advances in Computers

Adv Comp Leuk Res Proc Int Symp — Advances in Comparative Leukemia Research. Proceedings. International Symposium on Comparative Research on Leukemia and Related Diseases

Adv Compos Conf — Advanced Composites Conference

Adv Compos Mater — Advanced Composite Materials

Adv Compos Mater II Proc Jpn Fr Semin Compos Mater — Advanced Composite Materials II. Leading Part for the XXIst Century. Proceedings. Japan-France Seminar on Composite Materials

Adv Compos Mater Proc Fr Jpn Semin Compos Mater — Advanced Composite Materials. New Materials, Applications, Processing, Evaluation, and Databases. Proceedings. France-Japan Seminar on Composite Materials

Adv Compos Mater Proc Int Conf — Advances in Composite Materials. Proceedings. International Conferenceon Composite Materials

Adv Comp Physiol Biochem — Advances in Comparative Physiology and Biochemistry

Adv Comp Sec Man — Advances in Computer Security Management

Adv Comput — Advances in Computers

Adv Comput Biol — Advances in Computational Biology

Adv Comput Econom — Advances in Computational Economics

Adv Comput Math — Advances in Computational Mathematics

Adv Comput Methods Bound Inter Layers — Advanced Computational Methods for Boundary and Interior Layers

Adv Contin Process Non-Ferrous Met Ind Ed Proc BNF Int Conf — Advances in Continuous Processing in the Non-Ferrous Metals Industry. Edited Proceedings. BNF [*British Non-Ferrous*] International Conference

Adv Contracept — Advances in Contraception

Adv Contracept Delivery Syst — Advances in Contraceptive Delivery Systems

Adv Contracept Deliv Syst — Advances in Contraceptive Delivery Systems

Adv Control Syst — Advances in Control Systems

Adv Control Systems Signal Process — Advances in Control Systems and Signal Processing

Adv Corros Sci Technol — Advances in Corrosion Science and Technology

Adv Corr Sci Technol — Advances in Corrosion Science and Technology

Adv Course Astrophys — Advanced Course in Astrophysics

Adv Course Ind Toxicol Pap — Advanced Course in Industrial Toxicology. Papers

Adv Course Swiss Soc Astron Astrophys — Advanced Course. Swiss Society of Astronomy and Astrophysics

Adv Cryog — Advanced Cryogenics

Adv Cryog Eng — Advances in Cryogenic Engineering

Adv Crystallogr Cryst Growth Proc Indo Sov Symp Cryst Growth — Advances in Crystallography and Crystal Growth. Proceedings. Indo-Soviet Symposium on Crystal Growth

Adv Cyclic Nucleotide Protein Phosphorylation Res — Advances in Cyclic Nucleotide and Protein Phosphorylation Research

Adv Cyclic Nucleotide Res — Advances in Cyclic Nucleotide Research

Adv Cycloaddit — Advances in Cycloaddition

Adv Cytopharmacol — Advances in Cytopharmacology

Adv Data — Advance Data

Adv Dendritic Macromol — Advances in Dendritic Macromolecules

Adv Dent Res — Advances in Dental Research

Adv Dermatol — Advances in Dermatology

Adv Desalin Proc Nat Symp Desalin — Advances in Desalination. Proceedings. National Symposium on Desalination

Adv Desert Arid Land Technol Dev — Advances in Desert and Arid Land Technology and Development

Adv Detailed React Mech — Advances in Detailed Reaction Mechanisms

Adv Dev Biochem — Advances in Developmental Biochemistry

Adv Dev Biol — Advances in Developmental Biology

Adv Dev Psychol — Advances in Developmental Psychology

Adv Diesel Part Control — Advances in Diesel Particulate Control

Adv Differential Equations — Advances in Differential Equations

Adv Discrete Math Comput Sci — Advances in Discrete Mathematics and Computer Science

Adv Disord Semicond — Advances in Disordered Semiconductors

Adv DNA Sequence Specific Agents — Advances in DNA Sequence Specific Agents

Adv Drug Delivery Rev — Advanced Drug Delivery Reviews

Adv Drug Res — Advances in Drug Research

Adv Drug Ther Ment Illness Proc Symp — Advances in the Drug Therapy of Mental Illness. Based on the Proceedings of a Symposium

Adv Drying — Advances in Drying

Adv Earth and Planet Sci — Advances in Earth and Planetary Sciences

Adv Earth Oriented Appl Space Technol — Advances in Earth-Oriented Applications of Space Technology [*Later, Earth-Oriented Applications of Space Technology*]

Adv Earth Planet Sci — Advances in Earth and Planetary Sciences

Adv Ecol Res — Advances in Ecological Research

Adv Econ Bot — Advances in Economic Botany

Adv Econometrics — Advances in Econometrics

Adv Ed — Advance in Education

ADVED7 — Annales de Dermatologie et de Venereologie

Adv Electrochem Electrochem Eng — Advances in Electrochemistry and Electrochemical Engineering

Adv Electron — Advances in Electronics

Adv Electron Circuit Packag — Advances in Electronic Circuit Packaging

Adv Electron Electron Phys — Advances in Electronics and Electron Physics

Adv Electron Electron Phys Suppl — Advances in Electronics and Electron Physics. Supplement

Adv Electron Transfer Chem — Advances in Electron Transfer Chemistry

Adv Electron Tube Tech — Advances in Electron Tube Techniques

Adv Electrophor — Advances in Electrophoresis

Adv Endocrinol Metab — Advances in Endocrinology and Metabolism

Adv Endog Exog Opioids Proc Int Narc Res Conf — Advances in Endogenous and Exogenous Opioids. Proceedings.International Narcotic Research Conference

Adv Energy Convers — Advanced Energy Conversion

Adv Energy Syst Technol — Advances in Energy Systems and Technology

Adv Eng Ceram — Advanced Engineering with Ceramics

Adv Engng Software — Advances in Engineering Software

Adv Engrg Math — Advanced Engineering Mathematics

Adv Eng Sci Annu Meet Soc Eng Sci — Advances in Engineering Science. Annual Meeting. Society of Engineering Science

Adv Eng Smoke Curing Process Proc Int Sess — Advances in the Engineering of the Smoke Curing Process. Proceedings. International Session

Adv Eng Sof — Advances in Engineering Software

Adv Eng Software — Advances in Engineering Software

Adv Enhanced Heat Transfer Nat Heat Transfer Conf — Advances in Enhanced Heat Transfer. National Heat Transfer Conference

Adventures Exp Phys — Adventures in Experimental Physics

Adv Environ Sci — Advances in Environmental Sciences

Adv Environ Sci Beijing — Advances in Environmental Science (Beijing)

Adv Environ Sci Eng — Advances in Environmental Science and Engineering

Adv Environ Sci Technol — Advances in Environmental Science and Technology

Adv Envir Sci — Advances in Environmental Sciences

Adv Enzym — Advances in Enzymology

Adv Enzyme Regul — Advances in Enzyme Regulation

Adv Enzymol — Advances in Enzymology

Adv Enzymol Relat Areas Mol Biol — Advances in Enzymology and Related Areas of Molecular Biology

Adv Enzymol Relat Subj Biochem — Advances in Enzymology and Related Subjects of Biochemistry [*Later, Advances in Enzymology and Related Areas of Molecular Biology*]

Adv Ephemeroptera Biol Proc Int Conf — Advances in Ephemeroptera Biology. Proceedings. International Conference on Ephemeroptera

Adv Epileptol — Advances in Epileptology

Adv Epitaxy Endotaxy Sel Chem Probl — Advances in Epitaxy and Endotaxy. Selected Chemical Problems

Adverse Drug React Acute Poisoning Rev — Adverse Drug Reactions and Acute Poisoning Reviews

Adverse Drug React Bull — Adverse Drug Reaction Bulletin

Adverse Drug React Toxicol Rev — Adverse Drug Reactions and Toxicological Reviews

Adverse Eff Environ Chem Psychotropic Drugs — Adverse Effects of Environmental Chemicals and Psychotropic Drugs

Adverse Eff Herb Drugs — Adverse Effects of Herbal Drugs

Advert Age — Advertising Age

Advert Bus — Advertising Business

Advert L Anth — Advertising Law Anthology

Advert Q — Advertising Quarterly

Advert World — Advertising World

Adv Ethol — Advances in Ethology

Adv Explor Geophys — Advances in Exploration Geophysics

Adv Exp Med Biol — Advances in Experimental Medicine and Biology

Adv Exp Soc Psychol — Advances in Experimental Social Psychology

Adv Extr Metall Int Symp — Advances in Extractive Metallurgy. International Symposium

Adv Fatigue Lifetime Predict Tech — Advances in Fatigue Lifetime Predictive Techniques

Adv Fertil Control — Advances in Fertility Control

Adv Fertil Res — Advances in Fertility Research

Adv Fert Res — Advances in Fertility Research

Adv Fiber Commun Technol — Advanced Fiber Communications Technologies

Adv Fibrous Reinf Compos — Advanced Fibrous Reinforced Composites

Adv Filtr Sep Technol — Advances in Filtration and Separation Technology

Adv Fire Retardants — Advances in Fire Retardants

Adv Fish Oceanogr — Advances in Fisheries Oceanography

Adv Fluid Mech — Advances in Fluid Mechanics

Adv Fluid Syst — Advances in Fluidized Systems

Adv Fluorine Chem — Advances in Fluorine Chemistry

Adv Fluorine Res Dent Caries Prev — Advances in Fluorine Research and Dental Caries Prevention

Adv Food Nutr Res — Advances in Food and Nutrition Research

Adv Food Res — Advances in Food Research

Adv Food Res Suppl — Advances in Food Research. Supplement

Adv Food Sci — Advances in Food Sciences

Adv Forensic Haemogenet — Advances in Forensic Haemogenetics

Adv Fract Res Proc Int Conf Fract — Advances in Fracture Research. Proceedings. International Conference on Fracture

Adv Free Radical Biol Med — Advances in Free Radical Biology and Medicine

Adv Free Radical Chem — Advances in Free Radical Chemistry

Adv Frontiers Plant Sci — Advancing Frontiers of Plant Sciences

Adv Front Plant Sci — Advancing Frontiers of Plant Sciences

Adv Front Pl Sci — Advancing Frontiers of Plant Sciences

Adv Fusion Glass Proc Int Conf — Advances in the Fusion of Glass. Proceedings. International Conference on Advances in the Fusion of Glass

Adv Fusion Glass Pro Int Conf — Advances in the Fusion of Glass. Proceedings. International Conference

Adv Fuzzy Systems Appl Theory — Advances in Fuzzy Systems. Applications and Theory

Adv Gas Chromatogr — Advances in Gas Chromatography. Proceedings. International Symposium

Adv Gen Cell Pharmacol — Advances in General and Cellular Pharmacology

Adv Genet — Advances in Genetics

Adv Genet Dev Evol Drosophila Proc Eur Drosophila Res Conf — Advances in Genetics, Development, and Evolution of Drosophila. Proceedings. European Drosophila Research Conference

Adv Gene Technol Mol Biol Dev Proc Miami Winter Symp — Advances in Gene Technology. Molecular Biology of Development. Proceedings. Miami Winter Symposium

Adv Gene Technol Mol Biol Endocr Syst Proc Miami Winter Symp — Advances in Gene Technology. Molecular Biology of the Endocrine System. Proceedings. Miami Winter Symposium

Adv Genetic — Advances in Genetics

Adv Genome Biol — Advances in Genome Biology

Adv GeoEcol — Advances in GeoEcology

Adv Geophys — Advances in Geophysics

Adv Gerontol — Advances in Gerontology

Adv Gerontol Res — Advances in Gerontological Research

Advg Front Pl Sci — Advancing Frontiers of Plant Sciences

Advg Fronts Chem — Advancing Fronts in Chemistry

Adv Glass Technol Tech Pap Int Congr Glass — Advances in Glass Technology. Technical Papers. International Congress on Glass

Adv Graphite Furn At Absorpt Spectrom East Anal Symp — Advances in Graphite Furnace Atomic Absorption Spectrometry. Eastern Analytical Symposium

Adv Health Sci Educ Theory Pract — Advances in Health Sciences Education

Adv Heat Pipe Technol Proc Int Heat Pipe Conf — Advances in Heat Pipe Technology. Proceedings. International Heat Pipe Conference

Adv Heat Transfer — Advances in Heat Transfer

Adv Heat Transfer Manuf Process New Mater — Advanced Heat Transfer in Manufacturing and Processing of New Materials

Adv Hematol — Advanced Hematology

Adv Heterocycl Chem — Advances in Heterocyclic Chemistry

Adv Heterocycl Nat Prod Synth — Advances in Heterocyclic Natural Product Synthesis

Adv High Pressure Res — Advances in High Pressure Research

Adv High Temp Chem — Advances in High Temperature Chemistry

Adv Hologr — Advances in Holography

Adv Hortic Sci — Advances in Horticultural Science

Adv Host Def Mech — Advances in Host Defense Mechanisms

Adv Hum Fertil Reprod Endocrinol — Advances in Human Fertility and Reproductive Endocrinology

Adv Hum Gen — Advances in Human Genetics

Adv Hum Genet — Advances in Human Genetics

Adv Hum Nutr — Advances in Human Nutrition

Adv Hum Psychopharmacol — Advances in Human Psychopharmacology

Adv Hydrogen Energy — Advances in Hydrogen Energy

Adv Hydrosci — Advances in Hydroscience

Adv Hydroscience — Advances in Hydroscience

Adv Hydrozoan Biol — Advances in Hydrozoan Biology

Adv Hyperbolic Partial Differential Equations — Advances in Hyperbolic Partial Differential Equations

Adv Image Pickup Disp — Advances in Image Pickup and Display

Adv Imaging Electron Phys — Advances in Imaging and Electron Physics

Adv Immun Cancer Ther — Advances in Immunity and Cancer Therapy

Adv Immunobiol Blood Cell Antigens Bone Marrow Transplant — Advances in Immunobiology. Blood Cell Antigens and Bone Marrow Transplantation. Proceedings. Annual Scientific Symposium

Adv Immunol — Advances in Immunology

Adv in Appl Mech — Advances in Applied Mechanics

Adv Inflammation Res — Advances in Inflammation Research

Adv Infrared Raman Spectrosc — Advances in Infrared and Raman Spectroscopy

Adv Inf Syst Sci — Advances in Information Systems Science

Adv in Hydrodyn — Advances in Hydrodynamics

Adv in Math — Advances in Mathematics

Adv in Math Beijing — Advances in Math (Beijing)

Adv in Math China — Advances in Mathematics (China)

Adv in Mech — Advances in Mechanics

Adv Inorg Biochem — Advances in Inorganic Biochemistry

Adv Inorg Bioinorg Mech — Advances in Inorganic and Bioinorganic Mechanisms

Adv Inorg Chem — Advances in Inorganic Chemistry

Adv Inorg Chem Radiochem — Advances in Inorganic Chemistry and Radiochemistry

Adv in Phys — Advances in Physics

Adv Insect Physiol — Advances in Insect Physiology

Adv Instrum — Advances in Instrumentation

Adv Instrum Control — Advances in Instrumentation and Control

Adv Instrum Control Int Conf Exhib — Advances in Instrumentation and Control. International Conference and Exhibition

Adv Intern Med — Advances in Internal Medicine

Adv Intern Med Pediatr — Advances in Internal Medicine and Pediatrics

Adv Int Mat Child Health — Advances in International Maternal and Child Health

Adv Invertebr Reprod — Advances in Invertebrate Reproduction

Advis Bull Agric Dep Univ Coll Aberyst — Advisory Bulletin. Agricultural Department University College. Wales (Aberystwyth)

Advis Bull War Fd Prod — Advisory Bulletin. War Food Production. Welsh Plant Breeding Station

Advis Circ Rubb Res Inst Ceylon — Advisory Circular. Rubber Research Institute of Ceylon

Advis Circ Rubb Res Scheme Ceylon — Advisory Circular. Rubber Research Scheme. Ceylon

Advis CSIR (Can) Annu Rep — Advisory Council for Scientific and Industrial Research (Canada). Annual Report

Advis Group Aerosp Res Dev — Advisory Group for Aerospace Research and Development

Advis Group Meet Modif Radiosensitivity Biol Syst — Advisory Group Meeting on Modification of Radiosensitivity of Biological Systems

Advis Group Meet Tumour Localization Radioact Agents — Advisory Group Meeting on Tumour Localization with Radioactive Agents

Advis Leafl Bd Agric I O Man — Advisory Leaflet. Board of Agriculture. Isle of Man

Advis Leafl Br Beekprs Ass — Advisory Leaflet. British Beekeepers Association

Advis Leafl Dep Agric Maurit — Advisory Leaflet. Department of Agriculture. Mauritius

Advis Leafl Dep Agric Scotl — Advisory Leaflet. Department of Agriculture. Scotland

Advis Leafl Dep For Queensl — Advisory Leaflet. Queensland Department of Forestry

Advis Leafl Div Pl Ind Qd — Advisory Leaflet. Division of Plant Industry. Department of Agriculture and Stock. Queensland

Advis Leafl Forest Serv Qd — Advisory Leaflet. Forest Service. Queensland

Advis Leafl Qd Dep Agric — Advisory Leaflet. Queensland Department of Agriculture

Advis Leafl R Agric Soc Engl — Advisory Leaflet. Royal Agricultural Society of England

Advis Leafl W Scotl Agric Coll — Advisory Leaflet. West of Scotland Agricultural College

Advis Note Cem Concr Ass — Advisory Note. Cement and Concrete Association

Advis Note Fd Invest Bd — Advisory Note. Food Investigation Board [*London*]

Advis Pamphl Biol Brch Dep Agric Vict — Advisory Pamphlet. Biological Branch. Department of Agriculture. Victoria

Advis Rep Harper Adams Agric Coll — Advisory Report. Harper Adams Agricultural College

Adv Lab Autom Rob — Advances in Laboratory Automation Robotics

Adv Laser Spectros — Advances in Laser Spectroscopy

Adv Leafl Dep For Qd — Advisory Leaflet. Queensland Department of Forestry

Adv Leafl Min Agr Fish Food (Gt Brit) — Advisory Leaflet. Ministry of Agriculture, Fisheries, and Food (Great Britain)

Adv Leafl Queensland Dept Agr Stock Div Plant Ind — Advisory Leaflet. Queensland Department of Agriculture and Stock. Division of Plant Industry

Adv Leafl UPASI Scient Dep — Advisory Leaflet. UPASI (United Planters' Association of Southern India) Scientific Department

Adv Leafl W Scot Agr Coll — Advisory Leaflet. West of Scotland Agricultural College

Adv Lectin Res — Advances in Lectin Research

Adv Lectures Math — Advanced Lectures in Mathematics

Adv Legume Syst — Advances in Legume Systematics

Adv Limnol — Advances in Limnology

Adv Lipid Res — Advances in Lipid Research

Adv Lipobiol — Advances in Lipobiology

Adv Liq Cryst — Advances in Liquid Crystals

Adv Localized Corros Proc Int Conf — Advances in Localized Corrosion. Proceedings. International Conference on Localized Corrosion

Adv Low Temp Biol — Advances in Low-Temperature Biology

Adv Low Temp Plasma Chem Technol Appl — Advances in Low-Temperature Plasma Chemistry, Technology, Applications

Adv Macromol Carbohydr Res — Advances in Macromolecular Carbohydrate Research

Adv Macromol Chem — Advances in Macromolecular Chemistry

Adv Magnesium Res — Advances in Magnesium Research

Adv Magn Opt Reson — Advances in Magnetic and Optical Resonance

Adv Magn Reson — Advances in Magnetic Resonance

Adv Manag — Advanced Management

Adv Manage Cardiovas Dis — Advances in the Management of Cardiovascular Disease

Adv Manage J — Advanced Management Journal

Adv Manage Stud — Advances in Management Studies

Adv Man Clin Heart Dis — Advances in the Management of Clinical Heart Disease

Adv Mar Bio — Advances in Marine Biology

Adv Mar Biol — Advances in Marine Biology

Adv Mass Spectrom — Advances in Mass Spectrometry

Adv Mass Spectrom Biochem Med Proc Int Symp Mass Spectrom — Advances in Mass Spectrometry in Biochemistry and Medicine.Proceedings. International Symposium on Mass Spectrometry in Biochemistry and Medicine

Adv Mater — Advanced Materials

Adv Mater News — Advanced Materials News

Adv Mater Opt Electron — Advanced Materials for Optics and Electronics

Adv Mater Processes — Advanced Materials and Processes

Adv Mater Processes Proc — Advanced Materials and Processes. Proceedings. European Conference on Advanced Materials and Processes

Adv Mater Res — Advances in Materials Research

Adv Mater Res Zug Switz — Advanced Materials Research (Zug, Switzerland)

Adv Mater Sci & Technol — Advances in Materials Science and Technology

Adv Mater Weinh — Advanced Materials (Weinheim)

Adv Math — Advances in Mathematics

Adv Math Sci — Advances in the Mathematical Sciences

Adv Math Sci Appl — Advances in Mathematical Sciences and Applications

ADVMBT — Advances in Microcirculation

Adv Meas Soil Phys Prop Bringing Theory Pract Proc Symp — Advances in Measurement of Soil Physical Properties. Bringing Theory into Practice. Proceedings. Symposium

Adv Meat Res — Advances in Meat Research

Adv Mech Phys Surf — Advances in the Mechanics and Physics of Surfaces

Adv Med — Advanced Medicine

Adv Med Chem — Advances in Medicinal Chemistry

Adv Med Oncol Res Educ Proc Int Cancer Congr — Advances in Medical Oncology. Research and Education. Proceedings.International Cancer Congress

Adv Med Phys Symp Pap Int Conf — Advances in Medical Physics. Symposium Papers. International Conference on Medical Physics

Adv Med Plant Res Plenary Lect Int Congr — Advances in Medicinal Plant Research. Plenary Lectures. InternationalCongress on Medicinal Plant Research

Adv Med Proc Int Congr Intern Med — Advances in Medicine. Proceedings. International Congress of Internal Medicine

Adv Med Symp — Advanced Medicine Symposium

Adv Membr Fluid — Advances in Membrane Fluidity

Adv Membr Technol Better Dairy Prod Abstr Pap IDF Symp — Advances in Membrane Technology for Better Dairy Products. Abstracts of Papers presented at the IDF Symposium

Adv Ment Sci — Advances in Mental Science

Adv Mercury Toxicol Proc Rochester Int Conf Environ Toxic — Advances in Mercury Toxicology. Proceedings. Rochester International Conference on Environmental Toxicity

Adv Metab Disord — Advances in Metabolic Disorders

Adv Metab Disord Suppl — Advances in Metabolic Disorders. Supplement

Adv Methods Protein Sequence Determination — Advanced Methods in Protein Sequence Determination

Adv Met Med — Advances in Metals in Medicine

Adv Met Org Chem — Advances in Metal-Organic Chemistry

Adv Mgmt — Advanced Management

Adv Mgmt J — Advanced Management Journal

Adv Microb Ecol — Advances in Microbial Ecology

Adv Microb Eng Proc Int Symp — Advances in Microbial Engineering. Proceedings. International Symposium

Adv Microbial Physiol — Advances in Microbial Physiology

Adv Microbiol Sea — Advances in Microbiology of the Sea

Adv Microb Physiol — Advances in Microbial Physiology

Adv Microcirc — Advances in Microcirculation

Adv Microelectron — Advancing Microelectronics

Adv Microwaves — Advances in Microwaves

Adv Mod Biol — Advances in Modern Biology

Adv Mod Biol (Moscow) — Advances in Modern Biology (Moscow)

Adv Modell Anal A Gen Math Comput Tools — Advances in Modelling and Analysis. A. General Mathematical and Computer Tools

Adv Modell Anal B Signals Inf Data Patterns — Advances in Modelling and Analysis. B. Signals, Information, Data, Patterns

Adv Modell Anal C — Advances in Modelling and Analysis. C. Systems Analysis, Control, and Design

Adv Mod Environ Toxicol — Advances in Modern Environmental Toxicology

Adv Mod Gen — Advances in Modern Genetics

Adv Mod Nutr — Advances in Modern Nutrition

Adv Mod Toxicol — Advances in Modern Toxicology

Adv Mol Cell Biol — Advances in Molecular and Cell Biology

Adv Mol Cell Endocrinol — Advances in Molecular and Cellular Endocrinology

Adv Mol Cell Immunol — Advances in Molecular and Cellular Immunology

Adv Mol Electron Struct Theory — Advances in Molecular Electronic Structure Theory

Adv Mol Genet — Advances in Molecular Genetics

Adv Mol Genet Plant Microbe Interact Proc Int Symp — Advances in Molecular Genetics of Plant-Microbe Interactions. Proceedings. International Symposium

Adv Mol Model — Advances in Molecular Modeling

Adv Mol Rel — Advances in Molecular Relaxation Processes [*Later, Advances in Molecular Relaxation and Interaction Processes*]

Adv Mol Relaxation and Interaction Processes — Advances in Molecular Relaxation and Interaction Processes

Adv Mol Relaxation Interact Processes — Advances in Molecular Relaxation and Interaction Processes

Adv Mol Relaxation Processes — Advances in Molecular Relaxation Processes [*Later, Advances in Molecular Relaxation and Interaction Processes*]

Adv Mol Relax Interact Processes — Advances in Molecular Relaxation and Interaction Processes

Adv Mol Relax Processes — Advances in Molecular Relaxation Processes [*Later, Advances in Molecular Relaxation and Interaction Processes*]

Adv Mol Similarity — Advances in Molecular Similarity

Adv Mol Spectrosc Proc Int Meet — Advances in Molecular Spectroscopy. Proceedings. International Meetingon Molecular Spectroscopy

Adv Mol Struct Res — Advances in Molecular Structure Research

Adv Molten Salt Chem — Advances in Molten Salt Chemistry

Adv Mol Vib Collision Dyn — Advances in Molecular Vibrations and Collision Dynamics

Adv Morphog — Advances in Morphogenesis

Advmt Sci — Advancement of Science

Advmt Sci (Lond) — Advancement of Science (London)

Adv Multidimens Lumin — Advances in Multidimensional Luminescence

Adv Multi-Photon Processes Spectrosc — Advances in Multi-Photon Processes and Spectroscopy

Adv Mutagen Res — Advances in Mutagenesis Research

Adv Myocardiol — Advances in Myocardiology

Adv N — Advocacy Now

Adv Near Infrared Meas — Advances in Near-Infrared Measurements

Adv Nephrol — Advances in Nephrology

Adv Nephrol Necker Hosp — Advances in Nephrology. Necker Hospital

Adv Neural Sci — Advances in Neural Science

Adv Neuroblastoma Res 3 Proc Symp — Advances in Neuroblastoma Research 3. Proceedings. Symposium on Advances in Neuroblastoma Research

Adv Neurochem — Advances in Neurochemistry

Adv Neurochem Proc All-Union Conf Neurochem — Advances in Neurochemistry. Proceedings. All-Union Conference on Neurochemistry

Adv Neurogerontol — Advances in Neurogerontology

Adv Neuroimmunol — Advances in Neuroimmunology

Adv Neuroimmunology — Advances in Neuroimmunology

Adv Neurol — Advances in Neurology

Adv Neurol Sci — Advances in Neurological Sciences

Adv Neurosci — Advances in Neuroscience

Adv Neurosurg — Advances in Neurosurgery

Adv Next Gener Satell — Advanced and Next-Generation Satellites

Adv Nitrogen Heterocycles — Advances in Nitrogen Heterocycles

Adv Nonlinear Opt — Advances in Nonlinear Optics

Adv Nonradiative Processes Solids — Advances in Nonradiative Processes in Solids

Adv Nucl Phys — Advances in Nuclear Physics

Adv Nucl Quadrupole Reson — Advances in Nuclear Quadrupole Resonance

Adv Nucl Sci Technol — Advances in Nuclear Science and Technology

Adv Numer Anal — Advances in Numerical Analysis

Adv Numer Comput Ser — Advances in Numerical Computation Series

Adv Numer Heat Transfer — Advances in Numerical Heat Transfer

Adv Numer Methods Large Sparse Sets Linear Equations — Advances in Numerical Methods for Large Sparse Sets of Linear Equations

Adv Nurs Sci — Advances in Nursing Science

Adv Nutr Res — Advances in Nutritional Research

Adv Obstet — Advances in Obstetrics and Gynecology

Adv Obstet Gynaecol (Basel) — Advances in Obstetrics and Gynaecology (Basel)

Adv Obstet Gynecol (Baltimore) — Advances in Obstetrics and Gynecology (Baltimore)

Adv Obstet Gynecol (Osaka) — Advances in Obstetrics and Gynecology (Osaka)

Advocates Q — Advocates Quarterly

Advocates Soc J — Advocates Society. Journal

Adv of Science — Advancement of Science

Adv Oncobiol — Advances in Oncobiology

Adv Oper Orthop — Advances in Operative Orthopaedics

Adv Ophthal — Advances in Ophthalmology

Adv Ophthalmic Plast Reconstr Surg — Advances in Ophthalmic, Plastic, and Reconstructive Surgery
Adv Ophthalmol — Advances in Ophthalmology
Adv Opt Electron Microsc — Advances in Optical and Electron Microscopy
Adv Opt Inf Process V — Advances in Optical Information Processing V
Adv Opt Manuf Test — Advanced Optical Manufacturing and Testing
Adv Opt Manuf Test 2 — Advanced Optical Manufacturing and Testing 2
Adv Oral Biol — Advances in Oral Biology
Adv Organ Biol — Advances in Organ Biology
Adv Organobromine Chem — Advances in Organobromine Chemistry
Adv Organometal Chem — Advances in Organometallic Chemistry
Adv Organomet Chem — Advances in Organometallic Chemistry
Adv Organomet Proc Indo Sov Symp Organomet Chem — Advances in Organometallics. Proceedings. Indo-Soviet Symposium on Organometallic Chemistry
Adv Org Chem — Advances in Organic Chemistry. Methods and Results
Adv Org Chem Methods Results — Advances in Organic Chemistry. Methods and Results
Adv Org Coat Sci Technol Ser — Advances in Organic Coatings Science and Technology Series
Adv Org Geochem Proc Int Congr — Advances in Organic Geochemistry. Proceedings. International Congress
Adv Org Geochem Proc Int Meet — Advances in Organic Geochemistry. Proceedings. International Meeting
Adv Oto-Rhino-Laryngol — Advances in Oto-Rhino-Laryngology
Adv Oxygenated Processes — Advances in Oxygenated Processes
ADVPA3 — Advances in Pharmacology [*Later, Advances in Pharmacology and Chemotherapy*]
Adv Packag — Advanced Packaging
Adv Pain Res Ther — Advances in Pain Research and Therapy
Adv Parallel Comput — Advances in Parallel Computing
Adv Parasitol — Advances in Parasitology
Adv Partial Differential Equations — Advances in Partial Differential Equations
Adv Particle Phys — Advances in Particle Physics
Adv Part Phys — Advances in Particle Physics
Adv Pathobiol — Advances in Pathobiology
ADVPB4 — Advances in Planned Parenthood
Adv Pediatr — Advances in Pediatrics
Adv Pediatr Infect Dis — Advances in Pediatric Infectious Diseases
Adv Perform Mater — Advanced Performance Materials
Adv Perinat Med — Advances in Perinatal Medicine
Adv Perinat Thyroidol — Advances in Perinatal Thyroidology
Adv Perit Dial — Advances in Peritoneal Dialysis
Adv Peritoneal Dial — Advances in Peritoneal Dialysis
Adv Pest Control Res — Advances in Pest Control Research
Adv Pet Chem Refin — Advances in Petroleum Chemistry and Refining
Adv Pet Geochem — Advances in Petroleum Geochemistry
Adv Pet Recovery Upgrading Technol Conf — Advances in Petroleum Recovery and Upgrading Technology Conference
Adv Petrol Chem Refin — Advances in Petroleum Chemistry and Refining
Adv Pharmacol — Advances in Pharmacology [*Later, Advances in Pharmacology and Chemotherapy*]
Adv Pharmacol Chemother — Advances in Pharmacology and Chemotherapy
Adv Pharmacol Ther Proc Int Congr — Advances in Pharmacology and Therapeutics. Proceedings. International Congress of Pharmacology
Adv Pharmacother — Advances in Pharmacotherapy
Adv Pharm Sci — Advances in Pharmaceutical Sciences
Adv Pharm Sci (Tokyo) — Advances in Pharmaceutical Sciences (Tokyo)
Adv Photochem — Advances in Photochemistry
Adv Photo Chic — Advertising Photography in Chicago
Adv Photosynth — Advances in Photosynthesis
Adv Photosynth Res Proc Int Congr Photosynth — Advances in Photosynthesis Research. Proceedings. International Congress on Photosynthesis
Adv Phycol Japan — Advance of Phycology in Japan
Adv Phys — Advances in Physics
Adv Phy Sci — Advances in Physical Sciences
Adv Phys Geochem — Advances in Physical Geochemistry
Adv Physics — Advances in Physics
Adv Physiol Educ — Advances in Physiology Education
Adv Physiol Sci Proc Int Congr — Advances in Physiological Sciences. Proceedings. International Congress of Physiological Sciences
Adv Phys Org Chem — Advances in Physical Organic Chemistry
Adv Phys Sci (USSR) — Advances in Physical Sciences (USSR)
Adv Pigm Cell Res Proc Symp Lect Int Pigm Cell Conf — Advances in Pigment Cell Research. Proceedings. Symposia and Lectures. International Pigment Cell Conference
Adv Pineal Res — Advances in Pineal Research
Adv Planned Parent — Advances in Planned Parenthood
Adv Plann Parent — Advances in Planned Parenthood
Adv Plant Cell Biochem Biotechnol — Advances in Plant Cell Biochemistry and Biotechnology
Adv Plant Nutr — Advances in Plant Nutrition
Adv Plant Pathol — Advances in Plant Pathology
Adv Plant Sci Ser — Advances in Plant Sciences Series
Adv Plasma Phys — Advances in Plasma Physics
Adv Plast Reconstr Surg — Advances in Plastic and Reconstructive Surgery
Adv Plast Technol — Advances in Plastics Technology
Adv Pl Morph — Advances in Plant Morphology
Adv Polarogr Proc Int Congr — Advances in Polarography. Proceedings. International Congress
Adv Pollen-Spore Res — Advances in Pollen-Spore Research
Adv Pol Sci — Advances in Political Science
Adv Polyamine Res — Advances in Polyamine Research
Adv Polym Blends Alloys Technol — Advances in Polymer Blends and Alloys Technology

Adv Polymer Sci — Advances in Polymer Science
Adv Polym Sci — Advances in Polymer Science
Adv Polym Technol — Advances in Polymer Technology
Adv Polym Technol Natl Conf — Advances in Polymer Technology. National Conference
Adv Porous Media — Advances in Porous Media
Adv Powder Technol — Advanced Powder Technology
Adv Preconc Dehydr Foods Symp — Advances in Preconcentration and Dehydration of Foods. Symposium
Adv Primatol — Advances in Primatology
Adv Printing Sci — Advances in Printing Science and Technology
Adv Print Sci Technol — Advances in Printing Science and Technology
Adv Probab Related Topics — Advances in Probability and Related Topics
Adv Probab Theory — Advances in Probability Theory
Adv Process Anal Dev For Prod Ind — Advances in Process Analysis and Development in the Forest Products Industry
Adv Process Util For Prod — Advances in Processing and Utilization of Forest Products
Adv Proc Fluid Power Test Symp — Advance Proceedings. Fluid Power Testing Symposium
Adv Prostaglandin Thromboxane Leukot — Advances in Prostaglandin, Thromboxane, and Leukotriene Research
Adv Prostaglandin Thromboxane Leukot Res — Advances in Prostaglandin, Thromboxane, and Leukotriene Research
Adv Prostaglandin Thromboxane Leukotriene Res — Advances in Prostaglandin, Thromboxane, and Leukotriene Research
Adv Prostaglandin Thromboxane Res — Advances in Prostaglandin and Thromboxane Research
Adv Protein Chem — Advances in Protein Chemistry
Adv Protein Phosphatases — Advances in Protein Phosphatases
Adv Protoplast Res Proc Int Protoplast Symp — Advances in Protoplast Research. Proceedings. International ProtoplastSymposium
Adv Protozool Res Proc Int Conf Hung Protozool — Advances in Protozoological Research. Proceedings. International Conference of Hungary on Protozoology
Adv Psych — Advances in Psychology
Adv Psychoanal Theory Res Pract — Advances in Psychoanalysis Theory, Research, and Practice
Adv Psychobiol — Advances in Psychobiology
Adv Psychosom Med — Advances in Psychosomatic Medicine
Adv Psy Med — Advances in Psychosomatic Medicine
Adv Q — Advocates Quarterly
Adv Quant Struct Prop Relat — Advances in Quantitative Structure-Property Relationships
Adv Quant Tech Soc Sci — Advanced Quantitative Techniques in the Social Sciences
Adv Quantum Chem — Advances in Quantum Chemistry
Adv Quantum Electron — Advances in Quantum Electronics
Adv Radia Res Biol Med — Advances in Radiation Research, Biology, and Medicine
Adv Radiat Biol — Advances in Radiation Biology
Adv Radiat Chem — Advances in Radiation Chemistry
Adv Raman Spectrosc — Advances in Raman Spectroscopy
Adv React Phys Des Econ Proc Int Conf — Advanced Reactors. Physics, Design, and Economics. Proceedings. International Conference
Adv Regul Cell Growth — Advances in Regulation of Cell Growth
Adv Rel St — Advanced Religious Studies
Adv Ren Replace Ther — Advances in Renal Replacement Therapy
Adv Reprod — Advances in Reproduction
Adv Reprod Endocrinol — Advances in Reproductive Endocrinology
Adv Reprod Physiol — Advances in Reproductive Physiology
Adv Resist Technol Process — Advances in Resist Technology and Processing
Adv Res Neurodegener — Advances in Research on Neurodegeneration
Adv Res Proj Agency Workshop Needs Dep Def Catal — Advanced Research Projects. Agency Workshop on Needs of the Department of Defense for Catalysis
Adv Res Technol Seeds — Advances in Research and Technology of Seeds
Adv Rob — Advanced Robotics
Adv Robot — Advances in Robotics
Adv R Physl — Advances in Reproductive Physiology
ADVSA — Advances in Veterinary Science [*Later, Advances in Veterinary Science and Comparative Medicine*]
Adv Sci — Advancement of Science
Adv Sci Ann Nat Hist — Advocate of Science and Annals of Natural History
Adv Sci Tech — Advanced Scientific Techniques
Adv Sci Technol Faenza Italy — Advances in Science and Technology (Faenza, Italy)
Adv Sci Tech USSR Math Mech Ser — Advances in Science and Technology in the USSR. Mathematics and Mechanics Series
Adv Sci Tech USSR Phys Ser — Advances in Science and Technology in the USSR. Physics Series
ADVSDF — Advance Data
Adv Seafood Biochem Pap Am Chem Soc Annu Meet — Advances in Seafood Biochemistry. Composition and Quality. Papers. American Chemical Society Annual Meeting
Adv Second Messenger Phosphoprotein Res — Advances in Second Messenger and Phosphoprotein Research
Adv Semicond Epitaxial Growth Processes Lateral Vert Fabr — Advanced Semiconductor Epitaxial Growth Processes and Lateral and Vertical Fabrication
Adv Ser Agric Sci — Advanced Series in Agricultural Sciences
Adv Ser Astrophys Cosmol — Advanced Series in Astrophysics and Cosmology
Adv Ser Ceram — Advanced Series in Ceramics
Adv Ser Circuits Systems — Advanced Series on Circuits and Systems
Adv Ser Complex Systems — Advanced Series on Complex Systems
Adv Ser Dynam Systems — Advanced Series in Dynamical Systems

Adv Ser Electr Comput Engrg — Advanced Series in Electrical and Computer Engineering

Adv Ser Management — Advanced Series in Management

Adv Ser Math Phys — Advanced Series in Mathematical Physics

Adv Ser Nonlinear Dynam — Advanced Series in Nonlinear Dynamics

Adv Ser Phys Chem — Advanced Series in Physical Chemistry

Adv Ser Theoret Phys Sci — Advanced Series on Theoretical Physical Science

Adv Sex Horm Res — Advances in Sex Hormone Research

Adv Shock Res — Advances in Shock Research

Adv Signal Process Algorithms Archit Implementations — Advanced Signal-Processing Algorithms, Architectures, and Implementations

Adv Silicon Chem — Advances in Silicon Chemistry

Adv Sleep Res — Advances in Sleep Research

Adv Small Anim Pract — Advances in Small Animal Practice

Adv Sociodent Res — Advances in Socio-Dental Research

Adv Soil Org Matter Res Impact Agric Environ — Advances in Soil Organic Matter Research. The Impact on Agriculture and the Environment

Adv Soil Sci — Advances in Soil Science

Adv Sol Energy — Advances in Solar Energy

Adv Sol En Tech Newsl — Advanced Solar Energy Technology Newsletter

Adv Solid-State Chem — Advances in Solid-State Chemistry

Adv Solid State Phys — Advances in Solid State Physics

Adv Solid State Technol — Advances in Solid State Technology

Adv Space Biol Med — Advances in Space Biology and Medicine

Adv Space Explor — Advances in Space Exploration

Adv Space Res — Advances in Space Research

Adv Space Res Proc Inter Am Symp Space Res — Advances in Space Research. Proceedings. Inter-American Symposium on Space Research

Adv Space Sci — Advances in Space Science

Adv Space Sci Technol — Advances in Space Science and Technology

Adv Spa Sci — Advances in Space Science and Technology

Adv Spectros — Advances in Spectroscopy

Adv Spectrosc — Advances in Spectroscopy

Adv Spectrosc (Chichester UK) — Advances in Spectroscopy (Chichester, United Kingdom)

Adv Stereoencephalotomy — Advances in Stereoencephalotomy

Adv Steroid Anal 90 Proc Symp Anal Steroids — Advances in Steroid Analysis '90. Proceedings. Symposium on the Analysis of Steroids

Adv Steroid Biochem — Advances in Steroid Biochemistry and Pharmacology

Adv Steroid Biochem Pharmacol — Advances in Steroid Biochemistry and Pharmacology

Adv Strain Org Chem — Advances in Strain in Organic Chemistry

Adv Strawberry Prod — Advances in Strawberry Production

Adv Struct Biol — Advances in Structural Biology

Adv Struct Compos — Advances in Structural Composites

Adv Struct Res Diffr Methods — Advances in Structure Research by Diffraction Methods

Adv Struct Test Anal Des ICSTAD Proc — Advances in Structural Testing, Analysis, and Design. ICSTAD Proceedings

Adv Stud Birth Def — Advances in the Study of Birth Defects

Adv Stud Contemp Math — Advanced Studies in Contemporary Mathematics

Adv Stud Inst Book — Advanced Study Institute Book

Adv Stud Pure Math — Advanced Studies in Pure Mathematics

Adv Stud Theoret Appl Econometrics — Advanced Studies in Theoretical and Applied Econometrics

Adv Study Behav — Advances in the Study of Behavior

Adv Study Birth Defects — Advances in the Study of Birth Defects

Adv Sulfur Chem — Advances in Sulfur Chemistry

Adv Supercond 2 Proc Int Symp Supercond — Advances in Superconductivity 2. Proceedings. International Symposium on Superconductivity</PHR> %

Adv Supercond III Proc Int Symp Supercond — Advances in Superconductivity III. Proceedings. International Symposium on Superconductivity

Adv Supramol Chem — Advances in Supramolecular Chemistry

Adv Surf Coat Technol — Advances in Surface Coating Technology

Adv Surf Eng — Advanced Surface Engineering

Adv Surf Res Proc Surf Phys Symp — Advances in Surface Research. Adsorbate Diffusion, Surface Characterization, and Mobility. Proceedings. Surface Physics Symposium

Adv Surf Thin Film Diffr Symp — Advances in Surface and Thin Film Diffraction. Symposium

Adv Surg — Advances in Surgery

Adv Synth React Solids — Advances in the Synthesis and Reactivity of Solids

Adv Tech Biol Electron Microsc — Advanced Techniques in Biological Electron Microscopy

Adv Tech Chromosome Res — Advanced Techniques in Chromosome Research

Adv Tech Integr Circuit Process — Advanced Techniques for Integrated Circuit Processing

Adv Tech Lib — Advanced Technology Libraries

Adv Tech Mater Invest Fabr — Advanced Techniques for Material Investigation and Fabrication

Adv Technol — Advancing Technologies

Adv Technol Libr — Advanced Technology Libraries

Adv Tech Stand Neurosurg — Advances and Technical Standards in Neurosurgery

Adv Teratol — Advances in Teratology

Adv Test Meas — Advances in Test Measurement

Adv Textbooks Econom — Advanced Textbooks in Economics

Adv Textile Process — Advances in Textile Processing

Adv Texts Econometrics — Advanced Texts in Econometrics

Adv Theor Phys — Advances in Theoretical Physics

Adv Ther — Advanced Therapeutics

Adv Ther — Advances in Therapy

Adv Therm Conduct Pap Int Conf Thermal Conduct — Advances in Thermal Conductivity. Papers. International Conference. Thermal Conductivity

Adv Therm Eng — Advances in Thermal Engineering

Adv Thermodyn — Advances in Thermodynamics

Adv Tomogr Imaging Methods Anal Mater Symp — Advanced Tomographic Imaging Methods for the Analysis of Materials. Symposium

Adv Tracer Methodol — Advances in Tracer Methodology

Adv Transition Met Coord Chem — Advances in Transition Metal Coordination Chemistry

Adv Transp Processes — Advances in Transport Processes

Adv Tuberc Res — Advances in Tuberculosis Research

Adv Tumour Prev Detect Charact — Advances in Tumor Prevention, Detection, and Characterization

Adv Understanding Treat Asthma — Advances in the Understanding and Treatment of Asthma

Adv Urethane Sci Technol — Advances in Urethane Science and Technology

Adv Vasc Biol — Advances in Vascular Biology

Adv Veg Sci — Advances in Vegetation Science

Adv Vehicle News — Advanced Vehicle News

Adv Vet Med (Berl) — Advances in Veterinary Medicine (Berlin)

Adv Vet Sci — Advances in Veterinary Science [*Later, Advances in Veterinary Science and Comparative Medicine*]

Adv Vet Sci Comp Med — Advances in Veterinary Science and Comparative Medicine

Adv Viral Oncol — Advances in Viral Oncology

Adv Virus Res — Advances in Virus Research

Adv Wash State Univ Coll Agric Res Cent — Advance. Washington State University. College of Agriculture Research Center

Adv Waste Treat Res — Advances in Waste Treatment Research

Adv Waste Treat Res Publ — Advanced Waste Treatment Research Publication

Adv Water Resour — Advances in Water Resources

Adv Weld Metall — Advances in Welding Metallurgy

Adv Weld Processes — Advances in Welding Processes. International Conference

Adv Weld Processes Int Conf — Advances in Welding Processes. International Conference

Adv World Archaeol — Advances in World Archaeology

Adv X-Ray Anal — Advances in X-Ray Analysis

Adv X Ray Chem Anal (Jpn) — Advances in X-Ray Chemical Analysis (Japan)

Adv X Ray EUV Radiat Sources Appl — Advanced X-Ray/EUV Radiation Sources and Applications

Adweek E — Adweek/Eastern Edition

Adweek MW — Adweek/Midwest Edition

Adweek MWD — Adweek Directory of Advertising. Midwestern Edition

Adweek NE — Adweek/New England Advertising Week

Adweek Ntl — Adweek/National Marketing Edition

Adweek SAN — Adweek/Southwest Advertising News

Adweek SE — Adweek/Southeast Edition

Adweek SED — Adweek Directory of Advertising. Southeastern Edition

Adweek Spl — Adweek. Special Report

Adweek S W — Adweek/Southwest Edition

Adweek SWD — Adweek Directory of Advertising. Southwestern Edition

Adweek W — Adweek/Western Edition

Adweek WD — Adweek Directory of Advertising. Western Edition

ADWMA — Abhandlungen. Deutsche Akademie der Wissenschaften zu Berlin. Klasse fuer Medizin

Ad World — Advertising World

Ad'yuvanty Vaktsinno Syvorot Dele — Ad'yuvanty v Vaktsinno Syvorotochnom Dele

ADz — Akademiska Dzive

AE — Abside

AE — Acta Ethnographica

AE — Adult Education

Ae — Aegyptus

AE — Aesthetics

Ae — Aevum

AE — Agence Europe

AE — Alaska Economic Report

AE — American Ensemble

AE — Ancient Egypt

AE — Annales de l'Est

AE — Annales d'Ethiopie

AE — Annee Epigraphique

AE — Annuaire Europeen

AE — Arab Economist

AE — Archaiologike Ephemeris

AE — Arheologija un Etnografija

AE — Arkheograficheskii Ezhegodnik

AE — Arte Etrusca

AE — Australian Encyclopaedia

AE — Automotive Engineer

AE — Internationales Archiv fuer Ethnographie

AeA — Aegyptologische Abhandlungen

AEA — Agro-Ecological Atlas of Cereal Growing in Europe

AEA — America. Revista de la Asociacion de Escritores y Artistas Americanos

AEA — Annales d'Ethiopie (Addis Ababa and Paris)

AEA — Anuario de Estudios Americanos

AEA — Anuario de Estudios Atlanticos

AEA — Archivo Espanol de Arqueologia

AEA — Archivo Espanol de Arte

AEAA — Archivo Espanol de Arte y Arqueologia

AEA/AER — American Economic Review. American Economic Association

AeAb — Aegyptologische Abhandlungen

AEACA2 — Aeromedica Acta

AEA Inf Ser LA Agric Exp Stn — AEA Information Series. Louisiana Agricultural Experiment Station

AEAK — Anzeiger fuer Elsaessische Altertumskunde

AEAI — Archives de l'Eglise d'Alsace

AEAIs — Archives de l'Eglise d'Alsace

AEAr — Archivo Espanol de Arqueologia
AEArq — Archivo Espanol de Arqueologia
AEASH — Acta Ethnographica. Academiae Scientiarum Hungaricae
AEB — Analytical and Enumerative Bibliography
AEB — Annual Egyptological Bibliography
Aeb — Archives et Bibliotheques
AEB — Arkheologiia i Etnografiia Bashkirii
AEBOED — Advances in Economic Botany
AeC — Aevum Christianum
AEC — American Economist
AEC — Anuario de Estudios Centroamericanos
AEC — Arab Economist
AEC — Business [*Formerly, Atlanta Economic Review*]
Ae Ch Salz — Aevum Christianum. Salzburger Beitraege zur Religions- und Geistesgeschichte des Abendlandes
AEC Inf — AEC Informations
AE Clemson Agr Exp Sta — AE. Clemson Agricultural Experiment Station
AECL Res & Dev Eng — AECL [*Atomic Energy of Canada Limited*] Research and Development in Engineering
AECN — Annales Ecclesiastici a Christo Nato ad Annum 1198
AEC Newsl — AEC [*National Adult Education Clearinghouse*] Newsletter
AECO — Agora-Economie
AECO — Archivum Europae Centro-Orientalis
AECODH — Agro-Ecosystems
A Econ — Actualite Economique
A Econ (Clermont) — Annales Economiques (Clermont)
A Econ Polit — Annales d'Economie Politique
A Econ Publ Soc Coop — Annales de l'Economie Publique, Sociale, et Cooperative
A Econ Soc Measurement — Annals of Economic and Social Measurement
A Ec R — American Ecclesiastical Review
AEC Symp Ser — AEC [*US Atomic Energy Commission*] Symposium Series
AECTC — Archives of Environmental Contamination and Toxicology
AEC Univ Ky Coop Ext Serv — AEC. University of Kentucky. Cooperative Extension Service
AED — Africa Economic Digest
A Ed — American Education
AEDAAB — Anales de Edafologia y Agrobiologia
AE Del Agr Exp Stat Dept Agr Econ — AE. Delaware Agricultural Experiment Station. Department of Agricultural Economics
AE Dep Agric Econ Rural Social SC Agric Exp Stn Clemson Univ — AE. Department of Agricultural Economics and Rural Sociology. South Carolina Agricultural Experiment Station. Clemson University
AEDS J — AEDS [*Association for Educational Data Systems*] Journal
AEDS Jrnl — AEDS [*Association for Educational Data Systems*] Journal
AEDS Mon — AEDS [*Association for Educational Data Systems*] Monitor
AEDS Monit — AEDS [*Association for Educational Data Systems*] Monitor
AEE — AEI [*American Enterprise Institute*] Economist
AEE — Ancient Egypt and the East
AEECAM — Anales. Estacion Experimental de Aula Dei
AEEEA — Advances in Electrochemistry and Electrochemical Engineering
AEENDO — Agriculture, Ecosystems, and Environment
AEES Univ Ky Coop Ext Serv — AEES. University of Kentucky. Cooperative Extension Service
AeF — Aegyptologische Forschungen
AEF — Agenzia Economica Finanziaria
AEF — Anejos de Estudios Filologicos
AEFDAU — Alabama. Agricultural Experiment Station. Auburn University. Forestry Departmental Series
AEFGP — Alexandrian Erotic Fragments and Other Greek Papyri
AEFVAG — Anales de Edafologia y Fisiologia Vegetal
Aeg — Aegyptus
Aeg — Aegyptus: Rivista Italiana di Egittologia e di Papirologia
AEg — Ancient Egypt
AEG — Annuaire. Association pour l'Encouragement des Etudes Grecques en France
AEG — Australian Estate and Gift Duty Reporter
A Eg B — Annual Egyptological Bibliography
Aeg Christ — Aegyptica Christiana
Aegean Earth Sci — Aegean Earth Sciences
Aeg Forsch — Aegyptologische Forschungen
Aeg Helv — Aegyptiaca Helvetica
AEG Kernreakt — AEG [*Allgemeine Elektrizitaets-Gesellschaft*] Kernreaktoren
AEGL — Assyrian and English Glossary [*Johns Hopkins University*]
AEG Prog — AEG [*Allgemeine Elektrizitaets-Gesellschaft*] Progress
AEGR — Australian Estate and Gift Duty Reporter
AegS — Aegyptus. Serie Scientifica
AEGTCC J — Association of Educators of Gifted, Talented, and Creative Children in British Columbia. Journal
AEG Telefunken Prog — AEG [*Allgemeine Elektrizitaets-Gesellschaft*] - Telefunken Progress
AEG-Telefunken Progr — AEG [*Allgemeine Elektrizitaets-Gesellschaft*] - Telefunken Progress
Aeg U — Aegyptische Urkunden aus den Staatlichen Museen zu Berlin
Aeg UG — Aegyptische Urkunden aus den Staatlichen Museen zu Berlin. Griechische Urkunden
Aegyp Sprache & Altertknd — Aegyptische Sprache und Alterthumskunde
Aegyptol Forschgn — Aegyptologische Forschungen
Aeg Z — Zeitschrift fuer Aegyptische Sprache und Altertumskunde
AEH — Acta Ethnographica. Academiae Scientiarum Hungaricae
AEHEG — Annales. Ecole des Hautes-Etudes de Gand
AEHE IV Sect — Annuaire. Ecole Pratique des Hautes Etudes. IV Section. Sciences Philologiques et Historiques
AEHLA — Archives of Environmental Health
AEHR — Australian Economic History Review

Aehrodin Razrezh Gazov — Aehrodinamika Razrezhennykh Gazov
AEI — Australian Education Index
AEI (Am Enterprise Inst) For Policy and Defense R — AEI (American Enterprise Institute) Foreign Policy and Defense Review
AEICA8 — Contributions. American Entomological Institute
AEI Def R — AEI Defense Review
AEI Econom — AEI [*American Enterprise Institute*] Economist
AEI Eng — AEI [*Associated Electrical Industries*] Engineering
AEI Eng Rev — AEI [*Associated Electrical Industries*] Engineering Review
AEI For Pol Def Rev — AEI [*American Enterprise Institute for Public Policy Research*] Foreign Policy and Defense Review
AEI Forums — American Enterprise Institute for Public Policy Research. AEI Forums
AEI Hoover Pol Stud — AEI [*American Enterprise Institute for Public Policy Research*] Hoover Policy Studies
AE Inform Ser Univ NC State Coll Agr Eng Dept Agr Econ — AE Information Series. University of North Carolina. State College of Agriculture and Engineering. Department of Agricultural Economics
AEISDP — Aerofizicheskie Issledovaniya
AEJ — Adult Education Journal
AEJ — Atlantic Economic Journal
AEJ/JQ — Journalism Quarterly. Association for Education in Journalism
AEJUAX — Aerztliche Jugendkunde
AEKD — Archeion Ekklesiastiku kai Kanoniku Dikaiu
AEKG — Archiv fuer Elsaessische Kirchengeschichte
AEL — Acta Ethnologica et Linguistica
AEL — Atomic Energy Levels and Grotrian Diagrams
AELAAH — Aerztliche Laboratorium
A Electr — Acta Electronica
AeLet — Arts et Lettres
AELK — Allgemeine Evangelisch-Lutherische Kirchenzeitung
AELKZ — Allgemeine Evangelisch-Lutherische Kirchenzeitung
AeLo — Arts et Loisirs
AELR — All England Law Reports
AELRAY — Advances in Ecological Research
AEM — Anuario de Estudios Medievales
AEM — Archaeologisch-Epigraphische Mitteilungen aus Oesterreich
AEM — Archeion Euboikon Meleton
AEMBA — Advances in Experimental Medicine and Biology
AEMBB — Bulletin. Association des Anciens Eleves de l'Ecole Francaise de Meunerie
A Embr Morph Exp — Acta Embryologiae et Morphologiae Experimentalis
AEMEA — Aerospace Medicine
AEMEAY — Aerospace Medicine
AEMED3 — Annals of Emergency Medicine
AEMI — Ancient Egyptian Materials and Industries
AE Mich State Univ Agr Appl Sci Ext Div Agr Econ Dept — AE. Michigan State University of Agriculture and Applied Science. Extension Division. Agricultural Economics Department
A Emilia — Arte in Emilia
AEMMBP — Annales d'Embryologie et de Morphogenese
AEMN — Australian Energy Management News
AEMO — Archaeologisch-Epigraphische Mittheilungen aus Oesterreich-Ungarn
AEMOe — Archaeologisch-Epigraphische Mitteilungen aus Oesterreich
AEMOU — Archaeologisch-Epigraphische Mittheilungen aus Oesterreich-Ungarn
AEMRC7 — Angewandte Elektronik. Mess und Regeltechnik
AEMXA — Acta Embryologiae et Morphologiae Experimentalis
AEN — Annales de l'Est et du Nord
AENA — American Ephemeris and Nautical Almanac
AENBAU — Anales. Escuela Nacional de Ciencias Biologicas
AENDA2 — Annee Endocrinologique
AEN Dep Agric Eng Univ KY — AEN. Department of Agricultural Engineering. University of Kentucky
A End Gyn — Acta Endocrinologica et Gynaecologica Hispanolusitana
A End Ib — Acta Endocrinologica Iberica
A Energy O — Annual Energy Outlook
A Energy R — Annual Energy Review
AENF — Annales Entomologici Fennici
A Enghien — Annales. Cercle Archeologique d'Enghien
AENMP — Acta Entomologica. National Museum (Prague)
AEO — Ancient Egyptian Onomastica
AEOA — Annales de l'Extreme Orient et de l'Afrique
AEODA7 — Anales Espanoles de Odontoestomatologia
AE Okla State Univ Dep Agric Econ — AE. Oklahoma State University. Department of Agricultural Economics
AEOTD — Advances in Earth-Oriented Applications of Space Technology [*Later, Earth-Oriented Applications of Space Technology*]
AeP — Analyse et Prevision
AeP — Anima e Pensiero
A Ep — Annee Epigraphique. Revue des Publications Epigraphiques Relatives a l'Antiquite Romaine
AEP — Australian Economic Papers
AE Pap Okla State Univ Coop Ext Serv — AE Paper. Oklahoma State University. Cooperative Extension Service
AEPHAO — Annales des Epiphyties et de Phytogenetique
AEPHE — Annuaire. Ecole Pratique des Hautes Etudes
AEPHEH — Annuaire. Ecole Pratique des Hautes Etudes. IV Section. Sciences Philologiques et Historiques
AEPHEHP — Annuaire. Ecole Pratique des Hautes Etudes. Section des Sciences Historiques etPhilologiques
AEPHER — Annuaire. Ecole Pratique des Hautes Etudes. Section des Sciences Religieuses
AEPHERV — Annuaire. Ecole Pratique des Hautes Etudes. V Section. Sciences Religieuses
AEPIAR — Annales des Epiphyties

AEpigr — Annee Epigraphique
AEPJ — Association of Educational Psychologists. Journal
AEPP — Southeast / East Asian English Publications in Print
Aeq — Aequatoria
AEQBDE — Anales. Escuela de Quimica y Farmacia y Bioquimica. Universidad de Concepcion
Aequ Math — Aequationes Mathematicae
Aer — Aeronaute
AER — American Ecclesiastical Review
AER — American Economic Review
AeR — Atene e Roma
AER — Atomic Energy Review
AER — Australian Economic Review
AERAA — Advances in Enzymology and Related Areas of Molecular Biology
Aer Arch — Aerial Archaeology
Aere Perennius — Aere Perennius. Verslagen en Mededelinged uit Het Medisch-Encyclopaedisch Instituut van Vrije Universiteit
AERE/RPS — Atomic Energy Research Establishment [*Great Britain*]. Registered Publications Section
AE Res Dep Agric Econ Cornell Univ Agric Exp Stn — AE Research. Department of Agricultural Economics, Cornell University. Agricultural Experiment Station
AE Res NY State Coll Agr Dept Agr Econ — AE Research. New York State College of Agriculture. Department of Agricultural Economics
Aerftliga Aemnesomsaettningsrubbningar Symp — Aerftliga Aemnesomsaettningsrubbningar. Symposium
AERGB — Applied Ergonomics
Aerial Archaeol — Aerial Archaeology
Aerial Forest Surv Res Note Ottawa — Aerial Forest Survey Research Note (Ottawa)
Aerial Leag Bull — Aerial League Bulletin
Aerial Surv Rev — Aerial Survey Review
Aerial Yb — Aerial Year Book
AERit — De Antiquis Ecclesiae Ritibus
Aer J — Aeronautical Journal
AERJ — American Educational Research Journal
AERNA — American Economic Review
Aero Amer — Aerospace America
Aero Bilt — Aero Bilten [*Beograd*]
Aero Club Am Bull — Aero Club of America Bulletin
Aero Def Mark Technol — Aerospace/Defense Markets and Technology
Aero Dig — Aero Digest
Aerodin Razrezh Gazov — Aerodinamika Razrezhennykh Gazov
Aerodyn Note — Aerodynamics Note
Aerodyn Phenom Stellar Atmos Symp Cosmical Gas Dyn — Aerodynamic Phenomena in Stellar Atmospheres. Symposium on Cosmical GasDynamics
Aerodyn Rep (Aust) Aeronaut Res Lab — Aerodynamics Report (Australia). Aeronautics Research Laboratories
Aerodyn Techn Mem — Aerodynamics Technical Memorandum
Aero Eng — Aerospace Engineering
Aero Eng R — Aeronautical Engineering Review
Aero Equip Rev — Aero Equipment Review
Aero F & F — Aerospace Facts and Figures
Aerofiz Issled — Aerofizicheskie Issledovaniya
Aero Fld — Aero Field
Aero Fr — Aero France
Aero J — Aeronautical Journal
Aerol — Aerologist
Aero Mech — Aero Mechanics
Aeromed Acta — Aeromedica Acta
Aeromed Rev — Aeromedical Reviews
Aeromod — Aeromodeller
Aero Mund — Aero Mundial
Aeron — Aeronautica
Aeron — Aeronautique
Aeron Acta A — Aeronomica Acta. A
Aeronaut Astronaut — Aeronautique et l'Astronautique
Aeronaut Astronaut News Lett — Aeronautical and Astronautical News Letter
Aeronaut Eng Rev — Aeronautical Engineering Review
Aeronaut J — Aeronautical Journal
Aeronaut Q — Aeronautical Quarterly
Aeronaut Res Lab Dep Def Aust Rep — Aeronautical Research Laboratories. Department of Defence. Australia. Reports
Aero News Mech — Aero News and Mechanics
Aeron J — Aeronautical Journal
Aeron Q — Aeronautical Quarterly
Aeron Res Rep — Aeronautical Research Report
Aeron Rev — Aeronautic Review
Aeron Wld — Aeronautical World
Aeropl Astron — Aeroplane and Astronautics
Aero Quart — Aeronautical Quarterly
Aero Res Aircr Bull — Aero Research Aircraft Bulletin
Aero Res Tech Notes — Aero Research Technical Notes
Aero Rev — Aero Revue
Aero Rev Suisse — Aero-Revue Suisse
Aero Safe — Aerospace Safety
Aeros Age — Aerosol Age
Aeros Bull — Aerosol Bulletin
Aerosl Age — Aerosol Age
Aeros Ne — Aerosol News
Aerosol 82 — Aerosol Review 1982
Aerosol Cosmet — Aerosol e Cosmeticos
Aerosol Rep — Aerosol Report
Aerosol Sci — Aerosol Science
Aerosol Sci Technol — Aerosol Science and Technology

Aerosol Spray Rep — Aerosol Spray Report
Aerospace Amer — Aerospace America
Aero/Space Eng — Aero/Space Engineering
Aerospace Engrg — Aerospace Engineering
Aerospace Hist — Aerospace Historian
Aerospace Med — Aerospace Medicine
Aerospace Tech — Aerospace Technology
Aerosp and Def Rev — Aerospace and Defence Review
Aerosp Can — Aerospace Canada
Aerosp Corp Rep — Aerospace Corporation Report
Aerosp Dly — Aerospace Daily
Aerosp Eng — Aerospace Engineering
Aerosp Environ Med — Aerospace and Environmental Medicine
Aerosp Intel — Aerospace Intelligence
Aerosp Med — Aerospace Medicine
Aerosp Med Assoc Prepr Annu Sci Meet — Aerospace Medical Association. Preprints. Annual Scientific Meeting
Aerosp Med Biol — Aerospace Medicine and Biology
Aerosp Med Res Lab Tech Rep — Aerospace Medical Research Laboratory. Technical Report
Aerosp Refract Adv Mater Proc Powder Metall Conf Exhib — Aerospace, Refractory, and Advanced Materials. Proceedings. Powder Metallurgy Conference and Exhibition
Aerosp Rep — Aerospace Report
Aerosp Res Lab (US) Rep — Aerospace Research Laboratories (US). Reports
Aerosp Software Eng Collect Concepts — Aerospace Software Engineering. A Collection of Concepts
Aerosp Technol — Aerospace Technology
Aerosp Wash — Aerospace Washington
AERO Sun-T — AERO [*Alternative Energy Resources Organization*] Sun-Times
Aerot — Aerotecnica
Aerotechn — Aerotechnique
Aerotec Missili Spazio — Aerotechnica Missili e Spazio
Aerovox Res Wkr — Aerovox Research Worker
AErS — Acta Eruditorum Anno 1682-1731 Publicata. Supplement. Actorum Eruditorum quae Lipsiae Publicantur
AERS — American Economic Review. Supplement
AE RS PA State Univ Agr Sta Dept Agr Econ Rural Sociol — AE and RS. Pennsylvania State University. Agricultural Experiment Station. Department of Agricultural Economics and Rural Sociology
Aer S Rp — Annual Reports of the Aeronautical Society of Great Britain
AErt — Archaeologiai Ertesito
AERTJ — Association of Education by Radio-Television. Journal
Aerztebl Baden-Wuerttemb — Aerzteblatt fuer Baden-Wuerttemberg
Aerztebl Rheinl Pfalz — Aerzteblatt Rheinland-Pfalz
Aerztebl Sudetenl — Aerzteblatt fuer das Suedetenland
Aerztebl Suedwestdtl — Aerzteblatt fuer Seudwestdeutschland
Aerztebl Wuert — Aerzteblatt fuer Wuerttemberg
Aerztl Forsch — Aerztliche Forschung
Aerztl Fortbildungskurse Zuercher Kanton Liga Tuberk Arosa — Aerztliche Fortbildungskurse der Zuercher Kantonalen Liga Gegen die Tuberkulosein Arosa
Aerztl Fortbildungskurse Zuer Kanton Liga Tuberk Arosa — Aerztliche Fortbildungskurse der Zuercher Kantonalen Liga Gegen die Tuberkulosein Arosa
Aerztl Jb — Aerztliches Jahrbuch
Aerztl Jb Ost — Aerztliches Jahrbuch fuer Oesterreich
Aerztl Jb Ung — Aerztliches Jahrbuch von Ungarn
Aerztl Jugendkd — Aerztliche Jugendkunde
Aerztl Korr — Aerztliche Korrespondenz
Aerztl KorrBl Niedersachsen — Aerztliches Korrespondenzblatt fuer Niedersachsen</PHR> %
Aerztl Kosmetol — Aerztliche Kosmetologie
Aerztl Lab — Aerztliche Laboratorium
Aerztl Mh Berufl Fortbild — Aerztliche Monatshefte fuer Berufliche Fortbildung
Aerztl Mission — Aerztliche Mission
Aerztl Mitt Lpz — Aerztliche Mitteilungen (Leipzig)
Aerztl Mitt Strassb — Aerztliche Mitteilungen (Strasburg)
Aerztl Monats — Aerztliche Monatsschrift. Zeitschrift fuer Soziale Gesetzgebung und Verwaltung und fuer das Gesundheitswesen in Heer, Marine und Polizei
Aerztl Monatsh Berufliche Fortbild — Aerztliche Monatshefte fuer Berufliche Fortbildung
Aerztl Mschr Berl — Aerztliche Monatsschrift (Berlin)
Aerztl Mschr Lpz — Aerztliche Monatsschrift (Leipzig)
Aerztl Nachr — Aerztliche Nachrichten
Aerztl Praktr — Aerztlicher Praktiker
Aerztl Praxis — Aerztliche Praxis
Aerztl Prax Lpz — Aerztliche Praxis (Leipzig)
Aerztl Prax Wien — Aerztliche Praxis (Wien)
Aerztl Psychol — Aerztliche Psychologie
Aerztl Rdsch — Aerztliche Rundschau
Aerztl Reformztg — Aerztliche Reformzeitung
Aerztl Rundsch — Aerztliche Rundschau
Aerztl Sachverst Zeit — Aerztliche Sachverstaendigen-Zeitung
Aerztl SachverstZtg — Aerztliche Sachverstaendigenzeitung
Aerztl Sammelmappe — Aerztliche Sammelmappe
Aerztl S Bl — Aerztliche Sammeblaetter
Aerztl Standesztg — Aerztliche Standeszeitung
Aerztl Stand Ztg — Aerztliche Standeszeitung
Aerztl Taschenb Wien Med Wschr — Aerztliches Taschenbuch der Wiener Medizinischen Wochenschrift
Aerztl Vereinsbl Dtl — Aerztliches Vereinsblatt fuer Deutschland
Aerztl Vierteljrdsch — Aerztliche Vierteljahrsrundschau
Aerztl VjrRdsch — Aerztliche Vierteljahrsrundschau
Aerztl Wochenschr — Aerztliche Wochenschrift

Aerztl Wschr — Aerztliche Wochenschrift
Aerztl ZentAnz — Aerztlicher Zentralanzeiger
Aerztl Zent Ztg — Aerztliche Zentral-Zeitung
Aerztl Ztg — Aerztliche Zeitung
Aerzt Sachverstztg — Aerztliche Sachverstaendigen-Zeitung
AES — Abstracts of English Studies
AeS — Aegyptologische Studien
AES — American Ethnological Society. Bulletin of the Proceedings
AES — American Journal of Economics and Sociology
AES — Archives Europeennes de Sociologie
AESA — Annals of the Entomological Society of America
A Es A — Archivo Espanol de Arte
AESAA — Annals. Entomological Society of America
AES/AE — American Ethnologist. American Ethnological Society
AeSB — Aegyptologische Studien (Berlin)
AESC — Annales: Economies, Societes, Civilisations
AE SC Agric Exp Stn Clemson Univ — AE. South Carolina Agricultural Experiment Station. Clemson University
AESEE — Association Internationale d'Etudes du Sud-Est Europeen. Bulletin
AES Int Pulse Plat Symp Pap — AES [*American Electroplaters' Society*] International Pulse Plating Symposium. Papers
AESIS — Australian Earth Sciences Information System
AESIS Quarterly — Australian Earth Sciences Information System. Quarterly
AESM — American Ethnological Society. Monographs
AESNL — American Ethnological Society. Newsletter
Aesop Inst Newsl — Aesop Institute Newsletter
AESP — American Ethnological Society. Publications
AEsp — Archivo Espanol de Arqueologia
A Esp — Archivo Espanol de Arte y Arqueologia
A Esp — Arte Espanol
A Esp A — Archivo Espanol de Arqueologia
A Esp A — Archivo Espanol de Arte
A Espana — Arte en Espana. Revista Mensual del Arte y de su Historia
A Esp Arqu — Archivo Espanol de Arqueologia
A Esph — Actes d'Esphigmenou
AES Pr — American Ethnological Society. Proceedings
AESQAW — Anais. Escola Superior de Agricultura "Luiz De Queiroz." Universidade de Sao Paulo
AES Res Rep — AES [*American Electroplaters' Society*] Research Report
A Est — Annales de l'Est Nancy
A e St — Arte e Storia
AESTC — Advances in Environmental Science and Technology
AESTD — Atomnye Elektricheskie Stantsii
Aesthetic Plast Surg — Aesthetic Plastic Surgery
Aesthet Med — Aesthetische Medizin
A Est M — Annales de l'Est. Memoires
AESUAB — Agricultural Experiment Station. University of Alaska. Bulletin
AESUATB — Agricultural Experiment Station. University of Alaska. Technical Bulletin
AET — Abhandlungen zur Evangelischen Theologie
A Et — Annales d'Ethiopie
AETEB — Aerospace Technology
AETFA4 — Annales Entomologici Fennici
AETh — Abhandlungen zur Evangelischen Theologie
A Eth — Acta Ethnographica
Aetherische Oele Riechst Parfuem Essenzen Aromen — Aetherische Oele, Riechstoffe, Parfuemerien, Essenzen, und Aromen
Aether Oele — Aetherische Oele, Riechstoffe, Parfuemerien, Essenzen und Aromen
A Ethn (Hung) — Acta Ethnographica. Magyar Tudomanyos Akademia (Hungary)
A Et Int — Annales d'Etudes Internationales
AETJA — Automatic Electric Technical Journal
A Et M — Abhandlungen aus Ethik und Moral
AETODY — Advances in Modern Environmental Toxicology
AETPP — Anuario para o Estudo das Tradicoes Populares Portuguesas
AETQA — Annales. Societe Entomologique du Quebec
AETQA3 — Annals. Entomological Society of Quebec
AEU — Archiv fuer Elektronik und Uebertragungstechnik
AEU — Asia Electronics Union. Journal
AEU-Arch El — AEU-Archiv fuer Elektronik und Uebertragungstechnik
AEU Arch Elektron Uebertrag Electron Commun — AEU. Archiv fuer Elektronik und Uebertragungstechnik. Electronics and Communication
AEU-Arch Elektron Uebertragungstech — AEU-Archiv fuer Elektronik und Uebertragungstechnik
A Eub M — Archeion Euboikon Meleton
AEUMJ — Amalgamated Engineering Union. Monthly Journal
AEU Mon J — Amalgamated Engineering Union. Monthly Journal
AEUNA — AEU. Asia Electronics United
AE Univ Ill Coll Agr Exp Sta Coop Ext Serv — AE. University of Illinois. College of Agriculture. Experiment Station. Cooperative Extension Service
AE Univ Ill Dep Agric Econ — AE. University of Illinois. Department of Agricultural Economics
A Euras — Archivum Eurasiae Medii Aevi
AEU Rep — AEU [*American Ethical Union*] Reports
Aev — Aevum
AEV — Asian Economic Review
A Ev KR — Archiv fuer Evangelisches Kirchenrecht
AEW — American Ethnologist (Washington, D.C.)
AeW — Archiv fuer Exakte Wirtschaftsforschung
AEWK — Allgemeine Enzyklopaedie der Wissenschaften und Kuenste
AEX — American Import/Export Management
AEX — Export
AeZ — Aegyptische Zeitschrift
AeZ — Zeitschrift fuer Aegyptische Sprache und Altertumskunde
AEZRA — Advances in Enzyme Regulation

AF — Aegyptologische Forschungen
Af — Africa [*Italy*]
AF — Allgemeine Forstzeitschrift
AF — American Fabrics
AF — American Forests
AF — Amerique Francaise
AF — Anglistische Forschungen
AF — Arbol de Fuego
AF — Archaeologische Forschungen
AF — Architectural Forum
AF — Archivio di Filosofia
AF — Arte Figurativa
AF — Asiatische Forschungen
AF — Athenaeum Francais
AF — Ausgrabungen und Funde. Nachrichtenblatt fuer Vor- und Fruehgeschichte
AF — L'Asie Francaise
AFA — Acta Fratrum Arvalium
Af A — Afrique et l'Asie [*Later, Afrique et l'Asie Modernes*]
AFA — Archiv fuer Anthropologie
AFA — Archivo de Filologia Aragonesa
AFA — Asociacion Folklorica Argentina. Anales
AFAA Rept — AFA [*Aborigines' Friends' Association*] Annual Report
A Fac Agrar (Bari) — Annali. Facolta di Agraria (Bari)
A Fac Agrar (Milano) — Annali. Facolta di Agraria (Milano)
A Fac Dr Liege — Annales. Faculte de Droit de Liege
A Fac Dr Lyon — Annales. Faculte de Droit de Lyon
A Fac Dr Sci Polit (Clermont) — Annales. Faculte de Droit et de Science Politique (Clermont)
A Fac Econ Com (Palermo) — Annali. Facolta di Economia e Commercio (Palermo)
A Fac Sci Polit (Genova) — Annali. Facolta di Scienze Politica (Genova)
AFAEBG — Acta Faunistica Entomologica. Musei Nationalis Pragae
AfAh — Archiv fuer Augenheilkunde
AFA/JFA — Journal of Field Archaeology. Boston University Association for Field Archaeology
AFAMA5 — Anais. Faculdade de Medicina de Porto Alegre
A Family Stud — Annals of Family Studies
AFAR — Australian Foreign Affairs Record
Afar Cont Oceanic Rifting Proc Int Symp — Afar between Continental and Oceanic Rifting. Proceedings of an International Symposium
AF/AUR — Air University. Review. US Air Force
AfB — Africana Bulletin
AFB — Arbeits- und Forschungsberichte zur Saechsischen Bodenkmalpflege
AFBMAA — Anales. Facultad de Farmacia y Bioquimica. Universidad Nacional Mayor de San Marcos de Lima
AFBODJ — Acta Farmaceutica Bonaerense
AFBRB — American Foundation for the Blind. Research Bulletin
AFB Res Bull — American Foundation for the Blind. Research Bulletin
AFBTAV — Archivos de Farmacia y Bioquimica del Tucuman
AFBTBW — Australia. Commonwealth Scientific and Industrial Research Organisation. ForestProducts Laboratory. Technological Paper
AFBU — Agriculture and Forestry Bulletin. University of Alberta
AFBUD3 — Agriculture and Forestry Bulletin
AFC — Anales de Filologia Clasica
AFC — Archivos del Folklore Chileno
AFC — Archivos del Folklore Cubano
AFC — Armed Forces Comptroller
AFCCDM — Anales. Facultad de Ciencias Quimicas y Farmacologicas. Universidad de Chile
AFCE — Air Force Civil Engineer
AFCMCH — Acta Facultatis Rerum Naturalium Universitatis Comenianae. Microbiologia
AFCPDR — Symposium on Fundamental Cancer Research
AFCU — Archivos del Folklore Chileno. Universidad de Chile
AFD — Anuario. Facultad de Derecho. Universidad de Los Andes
AfD — Archiv fuer Diplomatik
AFDCAO — Advances in Fluorine Research and Dental Caries Prevention
AFDI — Annuaire Francais de Droit International
Afd Inform — Afdeling Informatica
AFDL — Annales. Faculte de Droit de Liege
AFDM — Air Force Driver Magazine
Afd Math Beslisk — Afdeling Mathematische Besliskunde
Afd Math Statist — Afdeling Mathematische Statistiek
Afd Numer Wisk — Afdeling Numerieke Wiskunde
Afd Toegepaste Wisk — Afdeling Toegepaste Wiskunde
Afd Zuiv Wisk — Afdeling Zuivere Wiskunde
AFE — African Trade Review
AfEis — Archiv fuer Eisenbahnwesen
AFEQD — Air Force Engineering and Services Quarterly
AFER — African Ecclesial Review
AFF — Anali Filoloskog Fakulteta
Aff Action Compl Man BNA — Affirmative Action Compliance Manual for Federal Contractors. Bureau ofNational Affairs
Affarsvarld — Affarsvarlden
AFFEC — Anales. Facultad de Filosofia y Educacion. Seccion de Filologia. Universidad de Chile
Aff Est — Affari Esteri
Affinity Tech Enzyme Purif Part B — Affinity Techniques. Enzyme Purification. Part B
Afflecks S Rural Alman — Affleck's Southern Rural Almanac and Plantation and Garden Calendar
AFFPA5 — Anais. Faculdade de Farmacia do Porto
AFFSAE — Anais. Faculdade de Farmacia e Odontologia. Universidade de Sao Paulo
Aff Soc Int — Affari Sociali Internazionali

AFG — Auslandsanfragen. Waren Vertretungen Kooperationen

Afghan Geol Miner Surv Bull — Afghan Geological and Mineral Survey. Bulletin

Afghanistan J — Afghanistan Journal

Afghanistan Q — Afghanistan Quarterly

Afghan Stud — Afghan Studies

AFGIL — Alaska. Department of Fish and Game. Information Leaflet

AFGK — Archiv fuer Frankfurts Geschichte und Kunst

AFGPAA — Annali. Universita di Ferrara. Sezione IX. Scienze Geologiche e Paleontologiche

AFGPRB — Alaska. Department of Fish and Game. Project Progress Reports on Bears

AFGPRC — Alaska. Department of Fish and Game. Project Progress Reports on Caribou

AFGPRD — Alaska. Department of Fish and Game. Project Progress Reports on Deer

AFGPRG — Alaska. Department of Fish and Game. Project Progress Reports on Mountain Goats

AFGPRM — Alaska. Department of Fish and Game. Project Progress Reports on Moose

AFGPRS — Alaska. Department of Fish and Game. Project Progress Reports on Sheep

AFGPRWQ — Alaska. Department of Fish and Game. Project Progress Reports on Wildlife

AFGRR — Alaska. Department of Fish and Game. Research Reports

AFGSDTP — Alaska. Department of Fish and Game. Subsistence Division. Technical Paper

AFGT — Alaska Fish Tales and Game Trails

AFGWTB — Alaska. Department of Fish and Game. Wildlife Technical Bulletin

AfGyn — Archiv fuer Gynaekologie

AFH — Archivum Franciscanum Historicum

Afh Fys Kemi Mineral — Afhandlingar i Fysik, Kemi, och Mineralogi

AFHL — Annuaire. Federation Historique de Lorraine

AFHOAC — Anales de Farmacia Hospitalaria

AFHZAB — Allgemeine Forst- und Holzwirtschaftliche Zeitung

AFI — American Firearms Industry

AFI — Amities France-Israel

AFI Ed News — AFI [*American Film Institute*] Education Newsletter

AFig — Arti Figurative. Rivista d'Arte Antica e Moderna

A Figurativa — Arte Figurativa

A Figurative — Arti Figurative. Rivista d'Arte Antica e Moderna

Afil — Archivio di Filosofia

AFilos — Archivio di Filosofia

AFIPS Conf Proc — AFIPS [*American Federation of Information Processing Societies*] Conference Proceedings

AFIPS Conf Proc Fall Jt Comput Conf — American Federation of Information Processing Societies. Conference Proceedings. Fall Joint Computer Conference

AFIPS Conf Proc Fall Spring Jt Comput Conf — American Federation of Information Processing Societies. Conference Proceedings. Fall and Spring Joint Computer Conferences

AFIPS Conf Proc Spring Jt Comput Conf — American Federation of Information Processing Societies. Conference Proceedings. Spring Joint Computer Conference

AFIPS Nat Comput Conf Expo Conf Proc — AFIPS [*American Federation of Information Processing Societies*] National Computer Conference and Exposition. Conference Proceedings

AFIPS Natl Comp Conf Expo Conf Proc — American Federation of Information Processing Societies. National Computer Conference and Exposition. Conference Proceedings

AFIPS Washington Rep — AFIPS [*American Federation of Information Processing Societies*] Washington Report

AFISAT — Atti. Accademia delle Scienze di Siena. Detta de Fisiocritici

AFJ — Armed Forces Journal

AF JAG L Rev — Air Force JAG [*Judge Advocate General*] Law Review

AFJCE CP — American Federation of Jews from Central Europe. Conference Papers

AFJZ — Allgemeine Forst- und Jagdzeitung

AFJZA — Allgemeine Forst- und Jagdzeitung

AfK — Archiv fuer Keilschriftforschung

AfK — Archiv fuer Kulturgeschichte

AFK — New African

AFKMAL — Ankara Universitesi. Tip Fakultesi. Mecmuasi. Supplementum

AFKo — Archiv fuer Frauenkunde und Konstitutionsforschung

Af L — Afroasiatic Linguistics

AFL — Australian Family Law and Practice

AFLA — Afrique Litteraire et Artistique

AFLA — Annales. Faculte des Lettres d'Aix

AFLA — Annales. Faculte des Lettres et des Sciences Humaines. Universite Aix-Marseilles

A Flam & Holl — Art Flamand et Hollandais

AF Law Rev — Air Force Law Review

AFLB — Annali. Facolta di Lettere e Filosofia. Universita di Bari

AFLB — Australian Family Law Bulletin

AFLB — Faculte des Lettres de Bordeaux. Annales

AFLB Hisp — Annales. Faculte des Lettres de Bordeaux. Bulletin Hispanique

AFLBor — Annales. Faculte des Lettres de Bordeaux. Revue d'Etudes Anciennes

AFLC — Annali. Facolta di Lettere, Filosofia, e Magistero. Universita di Cagliari

AFL Cagl — Annali. Facolta di Lettere. Universita di Cagliari

AFL-CIO Am Fed — AFL-CIO [*American Federation of Labor and Congress of Industrial Organizations*] American Federationist

AFLD — Annales. Faculte des Lettres et Sciences Humaines de l'Universite de Dakar

AFLFB — Annali di Facolta di Lettere e Filosofia. Universita di Bari

AFLFP — Annali. Facolta di Lettere e Filosofia. Universita di Perugia

AFLFUM — Annali. Facolta di Lettere e Filosofia. Universita di Macerata

AFLL — Annali. Facolta di Lettere di Lecce

AFLM — Annali. Facolta di Lettere e Filosofia. Universita di Macerata

AFLN — Annali. Facolta di Lettere e Filosofia. Universita di Napoli

AFLNice — Annales. Faculte des Lettres et Sciences Humaines de Nice

AFLNW — Arbeitsgemeinschaft fuer Forschung des Landes Nordrhein-Westfalen. Geisteswissenschaften

AFLNW/G — Veroeffentlichungen. Arbeitsgemeinschaft fuer Forschung des Landes Nordrhein/Westfalen/Geisteswissenschaften

AFL Pad — Annali. Facolta di Lettere e Filosofia. Universita di Padova

AFLPer — Annali. Facolta di Lettere e Filosofia (Perugia)

AFLQ — Archives de Folklore. Universite Laval (Quebec)

AF L R — Air Force Law Review

AFL Rev — Air Force Law Review

AFLSHA — Annales de la Faculte des Lettres et Sciences Humaines d'Aix

AFLSHN — Annales de la Faculte des Lettres et Sciences Humaines de Nice

AFLSHY — Annales. Faculte des Lettres et Sciences Humaines de Yaounde

AFLT — African Literature Today

AFLT — Annales de la Faculte des Lettres et Sciences Humaines de Toulouse. Litteratures

AFLT — Annales Publiees par la Faculte des Lettres de Toulouse

AFLT Forum — Arizona Foreign Language Teachers Forum

AFLToul — Annales Publiees par la Faculte des Lettres et Sciences Humaines de Toulouse

AFLUB — Annales. Faculte des Lettres. Universite de Bordeaux

AFM — Annales Fonds Maeterlinck

AFM — Archives de la France Monastique

AfM — Archiv fuer Musikwissenschaft

AFM — Aspects de la France et du Monde

AFMAA — Annales Academiae Scientiarum Fennicae. Series A-V (Medica)

AFMAAT — Annales Academiae Scientiarum Fennicae. Series A-V (Medica-Anthropologica)

AFMADW — Armed Forces Medical Journal

AFMAEX — Aquaculture and Fisheries Management

AFMag — Annali. Facolta di Magistero. Universita di Palermo

AFMB — Annali. Facolta di Magistero. Universita di Bari

AFMDA4 — Anais. Faculdade de Medicina. Universidade de Sao Paulo

AFMDBX — Asian Journal of Medicine

AFMEA7 — Anales. Facultad de Medicina. Universidad de la Republica

AFMEB8 — Afrique Medicale

AFMEEB — Agricultural and Forest Meteorology

AfMf — Archiv fuer Musikforschung

AFMIBK — Armed Forces Medical Journal

AFML — Annali. Facolta di Magistero. Universita di Lecce

AFMM — Annales de la Fondation Maurice Maeterlinck

AFMMAV — Anais. Faculdade de Medicina. Universidade Federal de Minas Gerais

AFMMBW — Archivos. Facultad de Medicina de Madrid

Af Mo — African Monthly

AFMP — Annali. Facolta di Magistero. Universita di Palermo

AFMSBG — African Journal of Medical Sciences [*Later, African Journal of Medicine and Medical Sciences*]

AFMUAL — Anales. Facultad de Medicina. Universidad Nacional Mayor de San Marcos de Lima

AFMUB — Annali. Facolta di Magistero. Universita di Bari

Af Mus — African Music

AFMVB — Annali. Facolta di Medicina Veterinaria. Universita di Pisa

AfMw — Archiv fuer Musikwissenschaft

AFN — Asian Finance

AFNABZ — Acta Facultatis Rerum Naturalium Universitatis Comenianae. Anthropologica

AFNBA3 — Acta Facultatis Rerum Naturalium Universitatis Comenianae. Botanica

AFNG — Arbeitsgemeinschaft fuer Forschung des Landes Nordrhein-Westfalen. Geisteswissenschaften

AfNg — Archiv fuer Naturgeschichte

AFNGAI — Acta Facultatis Rerum Naturalium Universitatis Comenianae. Genetica

AfNL — Afghanistan News (London)

AFNN — AFN [*Alaska Federation of Natives*] Newsletter

AFNZA7 — Acta Facultatis Rerum Naturalium Universitatis Comenianae. Zoologia

AFO — AEI [*American Enterprise Institute*] Economist

A Fo — Allgemeine Forstzeitung

AFO — Archiv fuer Orientforschung

AFOAA5 — Agricultural Research Council. Food Research Institute [*Norwich*]. Annual Report

AFOAB6 — Australia. Commonwealth Scientific and Industrial Research Organisation. Division of Fisheries and Oceanography. Annual Report

AFOCEL — Association Foret-Cellulose

AfOF — Archiv fuer Orientforschung

AfOFB — Archiv fuer Orientforschung (Berlin)

A Folk — Archives de Folklore

AFONA — Arizona Forestry Notes

AFONAA — Arizona Forestry Notes

A Fond G Feltrinelli — Annali. Fondazione Giangiacomo Feltrinelli

A Fond L Einaudi — Annali. Fondazione Luigi Einaudi

AFOPAG — Australia. Commonwealth Scientific and Industrial Research Organisation. Division of Fisheries and Oceanography. Technical Paper

AForum — African Forum: A Quarterly Journal of Contemporary Affairs

AFOSAP — Annual Report. Institute for Fermentation (Osaka)

AFP — African Construction, Building, Civil Engineering, Land Development

AfP — Archiv fuer Papyrusforschung

AFP — Archivum Fratrum Praedicatorum

A f Paed — Archiv fuer Paedagogik

AFPAP — Advances in Financial Planning and Forecasting

AfPap — Archiv fuer Papyrusforschung

AFPB — Annales de la Faculte de Philologie de Belgrade

AFPCAG — Acta Facultatis Pharmaceuticae Universitatis Comenianae

AFPE — Agora-English

AFPEAM — Archives Francaises de Pediatrie

A f Ph — Archiv fuer Philosophie
AFPOAI — Anais. Faculdade de Ciencias. Universidade do Porto
AFPPAL — Australia. Commonwealth Scientific and Industrial Research
    Organisation. Division of Forest Products. Technological Paper
AFPPCN — Acta Facultatis Rerum Naturalium Universitatis Comenianae.
    Physiologia Plantarum
AfPsN — Archiv fuer Psychiatrie und Nervenkrankheiten
AFPT — Aftenposten
AFPYA — American Family Physician
AFPYB — American Family Physician
AfQ — Africa Quarterly
AFQ — Alberta Folklore Quarterly
AFQFAU — Anales. Facultad de Quimica y Farmacia. Universidad de Chile
AFQFBV — Anales. Facultad de Quimica y Farmacia. Universidad de Concepcion
AFQSAZ — Anais de Farmacia e Quimica de Sao Paulo
AFQSB2 — Advance Abstracts of Contributions on Fisheries and Aquatic Sciences
    in India
AFR — Africa Confidential
AFR — Africa. Revista Espanola de Colonizacion
Afr — Afrique (Algiers)
AFR — Alaska. Department of Fish and Game. Sport Fish Division. Federal Aid in
    Fish Restoration Studies
A Fr — Alt-Franken
AFR — Anglo-French Review
AfR — Archiv foer Retsvidenskaben og dens Anvendelse
AFR — Archiv fuer Reformationsgeschichte. Texte und Untersuchungen
A Fr — Art Francais
AFR — Australian Financial Review
AFR — Avon Fantasy Reader
AfrA — African Affairs
AfrA — African Arts
AfrAb — African Abstracts
Afr Abstr — African Abstracts
AfrAf — African Affairs
Afr Aff — African Affairs
Afr Affairs — African Affairs
Afr Agric — Afrique Agriculture
Afr Air Rev — African Air Review
Afr Am Chamber Comm News — African-American Chamber of Commerce News
AfrAm S — Afro-American Studies
Afr-Am Stud — Afro-American Studies
A France — Art de France. Revue Annuelle de l'Art Ancien et Moderne
A France — Arts de France
Afr Arch — African Architect
Afr Archaeol Rev — African Archaeological Review
Afr Archit — African Architect
Afr Art — African Arts
Afr Arts — African Arts
Afrasiabskaya Kompleksnaya Arkheol Eksped — Afrasiabskaya Kompleksnaya
    Arkheologicheskaya Ekspeditsiya
Afr Asie — Afrique et l'Asie Modernes
Afr Asie Mod — Afrique et l'Asie Modernes
Afr B — Africana Bulletin
Afr Beekeep — African Beekeeping
Afr Bibl Cent Curr Reading List Ser — African Bibliographic Center Current
    Reading List Series
Afr Bk Publishing Rec — African Book Publishing Record
Afr Bottl Inds — African Bottling Industries
Afr Bull — Africana Bulletin
Afr Bus Chamber Commer Rev — African Business and Chamber of Commerce
    Review
Afr Business — African Business
AFRCA — Acta Facultatis Rerum Naturalium Universitatis Comenianae. Chimia
Afr Ch — Altfraenkische Chronik
Afr Chem Drugg — African Chemist and Druggist
Afr Communist — African Communist
Afr Contemp — Afrique Contemporaine
Afr Contemporaine — Afrique Contemporaine
Afr Contemporary Rec — Africa Contemporary Record
Afr Dev — African Development
Afr Develop — African Development
Afr Dig — Africa Digest
AFRE — African Environment
AFRE — Australian Financial Review
AFREA — Advances in Food Research
Afr Econ H — African Economic History
Afr Econ Hist — African Economic History
Afr Eng — African Engineering
Afr Engng — African Engineering
Afr Environ — African Environment
Afr Environment Suppl — African Environment. Environmental Studies and
    Regional Planning Bulletin. Supplement. Occasional Papers Series
Afr Equat Haut Commis Repub Bull Dir Mines Geol — Afrique Equatoriale. Haut
    Commissariat de la Republique. Bulletin de laDirection des Mines et de la
    Geologie
Afr et As — Afrique et l'Asie [Later, Afrique et l'Asie Modernes]
Afr et Asie Mod — Afrique et l'Asie Modernes
Afr et Asie Modernes — Afrique et l'Asie Modernes
Afr et Langage — Afrique et Langage
AfrF — African Forum
AFRFAZ — Acta Forestalia Fennica
Afr Forum — African Forum
Afr Forum NY — African Forum (New York)
Afr Franc — Afrique Francaise
Afr Fr Chir — Afrique Francaise Chirurgicale

Afr G — Africa Guide
Afr Gandensia — Africana Gandensia
Afr Heute — Afrika Heute
Afr Historian — African Historian
Afr Historian — African Historian. Journal. Historical Society. University of Ife
Afr Historian I — African Historian (Ibadan)
Afr Hist Stud — African Historical Studies
AfrHS — African Historical Studies
AFRIAA — Africana
A Fribourg — Annales Fribourgeoises
Africa — Africa. Fouilles. Monuments et Collections Archeologiques en Tunisie
Africa An Int Business Econ Polit Mon — Africa. An International Business,
    Economic, and Political Monthly
Africa Dev — Africa Development. A Quarterly Journal. Council for the
    Development of Economic and Social Research in Africa
Afric Affairs — African Affairs
Africa IAI — Africa. International African Institute
Africa Inst N Archeol & A — Africa. Institut National d'Archeologie et de l'Art
Africa It — Africa Italiana. Rivista di Storia e d'Arte
Africa Ital — Africa Italiana. Rivista di Storia e d'Arte
Africa Italiana Riv — Africa Italiana. Rivista de Storia e d'Arte
AfricaL — Africa (London)
Africana B — Africana Bulletin
Africana Bull — Africana Bulletin
African Admin Studies — African Administrative Studies
Africana J — Africana Journal
Africana Lib J — Africana Library Journal
Africana Libr J — Africana Library Journal
Africana Marburg — Africana Marburgensia
Africana Res B — Africana Research Bulletin
African Bus — African Business
African Econ Hist — African Economic History
African J Ednl Research — African Journal of Educational Research
African LD — African Law Digest
African LS — African Law Studies
AfricanM — African Music
African R — African Review
African Rev — African Review
African Stud — African Studies
African Stud Bul — African Studies Bulletin
African Studies R — African Studies Review
African Stud R — African Studies Review
Africa R — Africa Report
Africa Rep — Africa Report
Africa Rept — Africa Report
Africa T — Africa Today
Africa Th J — Africa Theological Journal
Afric Bull — Africana Bulletin
Afric Dev — New African Development
Afric Df Jl — African Defence Journal
Afric Lit Today — African Literature Today
Afric Stud — African Studies
Afric Stud R — African Studies Review
Afri Econ — Review of African Political Economy
A Friehedsm Ven — Arsskrift for Frihedsmuseets Venner
Afri I — Africa Italiana. Rivista de Storia e d'Arte
Afri It — Africa Italiana
Afri It Stor Arte — Africa Italiana. Rivista de Storia e d'Arte
Afrika Mat — Afrika Matematika. The First Pan-African Mathematical Journal
Afr Ind — African Industries
Afr Ind Afr Bib Cent Sec — Africa Index. Africa Bibliographic Centre Secretariat
Afr Inds — African Industries
Afr Industrie Infrastructures — Afrique Industrie Infrastructures
Afr Industr Infrastruct — Afrique Industrie Infrastructures
Afr Insight — Africa Insight
Afr Inst B — Africa Institute. Bulletin
Afr Inst Bull — Africa Institute. Bulletin
Afr Insur Rec — African Insurance Record
Afr Int — Africa International
Afrique Contemp — Afrique Contemporaine
Afrique Hist — Afrique Historique
Afrique Lit & A — Afrique Litteraire et Artistique
Afrique Lit et Artistique — Afrique Litteraire et Artistique
AfriS — African Social Research
AfriSt — African Studies Review
AfrIt — Africa Italiana
A Friuli A Trieste — Arte in Friuli, Arte a Trieste
Afr J — Africana Journal
Afr J Agric Sci — African Journal of Agricultural Sciences
Afr J Clin Exp Immunol — African Journal of Clinical and Experimental
    Immunology
Afr J Ecol — African Journal of Ecology
Afr J Int Afr Inst — Africa. Journal of the International African Institute
Afr J Med Med Sci — African Journal of Medicine and Medical Sciences
Afr J Med Sci — African Journal of Medical Sciences [Later, African Journal of
    Medicine and Medical Sciences]
Afr J Mycol Biotechnol — African Journal of Mycology and Biotechnology
Afr J Pharm Pharm Sci — African Journal of Pharmacy and Pharmaceutical
    Sciences
Afr J Psychiatr — African Journal of Psychiatry
Afr J Reprod Health — African Journal of Reproductive Health
Afr J Sci Technol Ser A — African Journal of Science and Technology. Series A.
    Technology
Afr J Sci Technol Ser B — African Journal of Science and Technology. Series B.
    Science

Afr J Trop Hydrobiol Fish — African Journal of Tropical Hydrobiology and Fisheries
Afr J Trop Hydrobiol Fish Spec Issue — African Journal of Tropical Hydrobiology and Fisheries. Special Issue
AfrL — Africana Linguistica
Afr Lab N — African Labour News
Afr Lang & Cult — African Languages and Cultures
Afr Lang Rev — African Language Review
Afr Lang Stud — African Language Studies
Afr Language Rev — African Language Review
Afr Languages — African Languages/Langues Africaines
Afr Language Stud — African Language Studies
Afr Law Stud — African Law Studies
Afr L Digest — African Law Digest
Afr Ling — Africana Linguistica
Afr Lit Ass Newsl — African Literature Association Newsletter
Afr Lit Assoc Bul — African Literature Association. Bulletin
Afr Lit Assoc Newsl — African Literature Association. Newsletter
Afr Litt Artist — Afrique Litteraire et Artistique
Afr Litter et Artist — Afrique Litteraire et Artistique
Afr Lit Tod — African Literature Today
Afr Lit Today — African Literature Today
AfrLJ — Africana Library Journal
AfrLRev — African Language Review
AfrLS — African Language Studies
Afr L Stud — African Law Studies
AfrM — Africana Marburgensia
Afr Man Min — African Manual on Mining
Afr Med — Africa Medica
Afr Med — Afrique Medicale
Afr Mid East Pet Dir — Africa-Middle East Petroleum Directory
Afr Mus — African Music
Afr Music — African Music
Afr Music — African Musicology
AfrN — African Notes
AFRNA — Acta Facultatis Rerum Naturalium Universitatis Comenianae. Physica
Afr Natuurlewe — Afrika Natuurlewe
AfrnB — Africana Bulletin
Afr Ne Lett — African Newsletter
Afr Notes — African Notes
Afr Notes I — African Notes (Ibadan)
Afr Notes News — Africana Notes and News
Afr Now — Africa Now
Afro-Asian and W Aff — Afro-Asian and World Affairs
Afro Asian Econ Rev — Afro-Asian Economic Review
Afro-Asian J Ophtalmol — Afro-Asian Journal of Ophthalmology
Afroasiatic Ling — Afroasiatic Linguistics
A Front — Art Front
Afr Ouest J Pharmacol Rech Drogue — Africaine Ouest Journal de Pharmacologie et Recherche Drogue
AFrP — Athlone French Poets
Afr Perspect — Africa Perspective
Afr Perspectives — African Perspectives
Afr Post — Afrika Post
Afr Pulse — Africa Pulse
Afr Q — Africa Quarterly
AfrqC — Afrique Contemporaine
Afr Quart — Africa Quarterly
Afr R — African Review
AfrR — Africa Report
Afr Religious Res — African Religious Research
Afr Relig Res — African Religious Research
Afr Rep — Africa Report
Afr Report — Africa Report
Afr Res Bull — African Research Bulletin
Afr Res Bull — Africa Research Bulletin Series
Afr Res Bul Ser A Pol — Africa Research Bulletin. Series A. Political
Afr Res Doc — African Research and Documentation
Afr Res Docum — African Research and Documentation
Afr Rpt — Africa Report
Afr Rural Econ Pap — African Rural Economy Paper
AfrS — African Studies
AfrSch — African Scholar
Afr Sem Coll Pap — Africa Seminar. Collected Papers
Afr Social Res — African Social Research
Afr Soc Pretoria Yearb — Africana Society of Pretoria. Yearbook
Afr Soc Res — African Social Research
Afr Soc Security Ser — African Social Security Series
Afr Soc Secur Ser — African Social Security Series
Afr Soils — African Soils
Afr South — Africa South
Afr Sov Stud — Africa in Soviet Studies. Annual
Afr Spectrum — Afrika Spectrum
AfrSR — African Studies Review
Afr St — African Studies
Afr Stud — African Studies
Afr Stud B — African Studies Bulletin
Afr Stud Bull — African Studies Bulletin
Afr Stud [China] — African Studies [China]
Afr Stud Monogr — African Study Monographs
Afr Stud Monogr Suppl — African Study Monographs. Supplementary Issue
Afr Stud Newsl — African Studies Newsletter
Afr Stud R — African Studies Review
Afr Stud Rev — African Studies Review
Afr Stud [S Africa] — African Studies [South Africa]

Afr Stud Ser — African Studies Series
Afr Sug Cott J — African Sugar and Cotton Journal
Afr Sunrise — African Sunrise
Afr-T — Africa-Tervuren
Afr Tervuren — Africa-Tervuren
Afr Th J — Africa Theological Journal
Afr Today — Africa Today
Afr T Rev — African Trade Review
Afr Uebersee — Afrika und Uebersee
Afr und Ueb — Afrika und Uebersee
Afr Urban Notes — African Urban Notes
Afr Urban Q — African Urban Quarterly
Afr Urban Stud — African Urban Studies
Afr u Ubersee — Afrika und Ubersee
Afr Violet — African Violet
Afr Violet Mag — African Violet Magazine
Afr Wildl — African Wildlife
Afr Wild Life — African Wild Life
Afr-Wirtsch — Afrika-Wirtschaft
Afr Wom — Africa Woman
Afr Women — African Women
Afr WS — African Writers Series
AFS — Alaska. Department of Fish and Game. Sport Fish Division. Anadromous Fish Studies
AFS — Armed Forces and Society
AFS — Asian Folklore Studies
AFS Cast Met Res J — AFS [*American Foundrymen's Society*] Cast Metals Research Journal
AF/SD — Air Force and Space Digest
AFS Int Cast Met J — AFS [*American Foundrymen's Society*] International Cast Metals Journal
AFSJ — American Foreign Service Journal
AFS/JAF — Journal of American Folklore. American Folklore Society
AFSM — Air Force Screen Magazine
AFS Res Rep — AFS [*American Foundrymen's Society*] Research Reports
AFSTDH — Animal Feed Science and Technology
AFSWP-TP — Armed Forces Special Weapons Project [*later, DASA*]. Technical Publications
AfT — Africa Today
Aft — Aftonbladet
AFT — Algemeen Fiscaal Tijdschrift
AFT — Australian Federal Tax Reporter
AFTOD7 — Archivos de Farmacologia y Toxicologia
AFTR 2d P-H — American Federal Tax Reports. Second Series. Prentice-Hall
AFTU — Archiv fuer Reformationsgeschichte. Texte und Untersuchungen
AfU — Archiv fuer Urkundenforschung
AFUPBD — Anais. Faculdade de Medicina. Universidade Federal de Pernambuco
AFUW Bul — Australian Federation of University Women. Bulletin
AFV — Archiv fuer Voelkerkunde
AFV — Artesania y Folklore de Venezuela
AFVLA5 — Anales. Facultad de Veterinaria de Leon
AFVUBX — Anales. Facultad de Veterinaria del Uruguay
AFWL — Gesellschaft fuer Foerderung der Westfaelischen Landesuniversitaet. Abhandlungen
AFWLAA — African Wildlife
AFZ — Allgemeine Fischerei-Zeitung
AFZ (Allg Fischwirtschaftsztg) — AFZ. (Allgemeine Fischwirtschaftszeitung)
AFZSA — Allgemeine Forstzeitschrift
AFZTA — Allgemeine Forstzeitung
AG — Acta Geographica
AG — Advance Guard
AG — Agefi
Ag — Agonia
AG — Anales Galdosianos
AG — Ancient Gaza
AG — Andre Gide
AG — Anecdota Graeca
AG — Anecdota Graeca e Codices. Manuscriptis Bibliothecarum Oxoniensium
AG — Anglica Germanica
AG — Annales de Geographie
AG — Annales Geophysicae
AG — Anthologia Graeca
AG — Archivo Giuridico
Ag — Athenian Agora
Ag — August
AG — Australian Geographer
AGA — Aerodrome and Ground Aids
AGA — Agricultural Administration
AGA — American Gas Association. Monthly
AGA 2000 — Gas Energy Supply Outlook, 1980-2000. American Gas Association
Ag Abh — Aegyptologische Abhandlungen
AGA Facts — Gas Facts. American Gas Association
AGAGAS — AGARD [*Advisory Group for Aerospace Research and Development*] Agardograph
AGAH — Hamburg. Universitaet. Abhandlungen aus dem Gebiet der Auslandskunde
AGAHAV — Acta Geologica. Academiae Scientiarum Hungaricae
AGAIHS — Assemblee Generale de Rome, 1954, de l'Association Internationale d'Hydrologie Scientifique
AGAJU — Arbeiten zur Geschichte des Antiken Judentums und des Urchristentums
AGA Lab Res Bull Res Rep — American Gas Association. Laboratories. Research Bulletins, Research Reports
AGald — Anales Galdosianos
Ag Am — Agriculture in the Americas
AGAMA — American Gas Association. Monthly

AGA Mon — American Gas Association. Monthly
Ag & Cr Outlk — Agricultural and Credit Outlook
Ag & Livestock India — Agriculture and Livestock in India
AGA Oper Sec Proc — American Gas Association. Operating Section. Proceedings
AGA Plast Pipe Symp — AGA [American Gas Association] Plastic Pipe Symposium
AGARD Advis Rep — AGARD [Advisory Group for Aerospace Research and Development] Advisory Report
AGARD Adv Rep — AGARD [Advisory Group for Aerospace Research and Development] Advisory Report
AGARD Agardogr — AGARD [Advisory Group for Aerospace Research and Development] Agardograph
AGARD AG Doc — AGARD [Advisory Group for Aeronautical Research and Development] AG Document
AGARD Annu Meet — AGARD [Advisory Group for Aerospace Research and Development] Annual Meeting
AGARD Conf Proc — AGARD [Advisory Group for Aerospace Research and Development] Conference Proceedings
AGARD CP — AGARD [Advisory Group for Aerospace Research and Development] Conference Proceedings
AGARD Lect Ser — AGARD [Advisory Group for Aerospace Research and Development] Lecture Series
AGARD Man — AGARD [Advisory Group for Aerospace Research and Development] Manual
AGARD (NATO) — AGARD [Advisory Group for Aerospace Research and Development] (North Atlantic Treaty Organization)
AGARD Rep — AGARD [Advisory Group for Aerospace Research and Development] Report
AGARD Specif — AGARD [Advisory Group for Aerospace Research and Development] Specification
AGAU — Archief voor de Geschiedenis van het Aartsbisdom Utrecht
A Gb — Alzeyer Geschichtsblaetter
AGB — Anhaltische Geschichtsblaetter
AGB — Archiv fuer Geschichte des Buchwesens
AGB — Association Guillaume Bude. Bulletin
AGBA — Agriculture Bulletin. University of Alberta [Later, Agriculture and Forestry Bulletin]
AGBAAF — Acta Geobotanica Barcinonensia
AgBiotech Bull — AgBiotech Bulletin
Ag Bits Comput Agric Coop Ext Univ Calif — Ag Bits. Computers in Agriculture. Cooperative Extension. University of California
AGBIZ — Agribusiness Information
AGBO — Agroborealis
AGBOBO — Agroborealis
AGC — African Business
AGCACM — Agrichemical Age
AGCCBR — Agrociencia
AGCFAZ — Agriculteurs de France
AGCHA7 — Agricultural Chemicals
Ag Chem — Agricultural Chemicals
Ag Chem Commer Fert — Ag Chem and Commercial Fertilizer [Later, Farm Chemicals]
Ag Chemicals — Agricultural Chemicals
AGCNCR — Agrociencia. Serie A
AGCODV — Agronomia Costarricense
Ag Consult Fieldman — Ag Consultant and Fieldman
AGCPA — AGARD [Advisory Group for Aerospace Research and Development] Conference Proceedings
AGCPAV — AGARD [Advisory Group for Aerospace Research and Development] Conference Proceedings
AGD — Antike Gemmen in Deutschen Sammlungen
AGD — Australian Government Digest
AGDATA — Agricultural Commodities Data Base
AGDBAS — Abhandlungen. Geologischer Dienst
Ag Digest — Agricultural Digest
AGDL — Archiv fuer Geschichte der Dioezese Linz
AGDS — Antike Gemmen in Deutschen Sammlungen
AGDSAB — Aichi-Gakuin Daigaku Shigakkai-Shi
AGE — Agency Sales Magazine
AGE — Asian Geotechnology Engineering Database
Age Ageing Suppl — Age and Ageing. Supplement
Age & Ageing — Age and Ageing Science. Annuals
AGEBAX — Acta Gastro-Enterologica Belgica
Ag Econ Res — Agricultural Economics Research
Ag Ed — Agricultural Education Magazine
Aged Care Serv Rev — Aged Care and Services Review
Age Depend Factors Biokinet Dosim Radionuclides Proc Workshop — Age-Dependent Factors in the Biokinetics and Dosimetry of Radionuclides. Proceedings. Workshop
Aged High Risk Surg Patient Med Surg Anesth Manage — Aged and High Risk Surgical Patient. Medical, Surgical, and Anesthetic Management
AGEFAB — Archiv fuer Gefluegelkunde
AGEFI — Agence Economique et Financiere
Age Indep — Age of Independence
Ageing Fish Proc Int Symp — Ageing of Fish. Proceedings. International Symposium
AGELAT — Acta Geologica Lilloana
Age Lit Supp — Age Literary Supplement
AGENAZ — Agricultural Engineering
Agence Spat Eur Brochure ESA — Agence Spatiale Europeenne. Brochure ESA
Agence Spat Eur Bull — Agence Spatiale Europeenne. Bulletin
Agence Spat Eur ESA STR — Agence Spatiale Europeenne. ESA STR
Agence Spat Eur Rev Sci Tech — Agence Spatiale Europeenne. Revue Scientifique et Technique
A Gen Civ — Annales du Genie Civil

AGEND4 — Agriculture and Environment
Agenda Agric Vigneron — Agenda de l'Agriculteur et du Vigneron
Ag Eng — Agricultural Engineering
Age Nouv — Age Nouveau
A Gen Sc Ps — Annales Generales des Sciences Physiques
Agent Actio — Agents and Actions
Agents Actions Suppl — Agents and Actions. Supplement
Age Nucl — Age Nucleaire
A Geo — Archaeologia Geographica. Beitraege zur Vergleichenden Geographisch-Kartographischen Methode in der Urgeschichtsforschung
A Geogr — Annales de Geographie
A Georgica — Ars Georgica
AGEPA — Annales de Geophysique
AGEPB — Archiv fuer die Gesamte Psychologie
AGER — Agricultural Economics Research
AGERAD — Acta Gerontologica
Ag Europe — Agra Europe
AgExporter US Dep Agric Foreign Agric Serv — AgExporter. United States Department of Agriculture. Foreign Agricultural Service
Agfa Kinetech Mitt — Agfa Kinetechnische Mitteilungen
AGFB — Association de Geographes Francais. Bulletin
AGF/B — Bulletin. Association des Geographes Francais
AGF Mitt — AGF [Arbeitsgemeinschaft der Grossforschungseinrichtungen] Mitteilungen
AgFo — Aegyptologische Forschungen
Ag Food Jl — Agriculture and Food Chemistry. Journal
AGFYA — Arkiv foer Geofysik
AGG — Abhandlungen. Geographische Gesellschaft
AGG — Abhandlungen. Gesellschaft der Wissenschaften zu Goettingen. Philosophisch-Historische Klasse
AGGAA6 — Agricultura y Ganaderia
Ag Gaz NSW — Agricultural Gazette of New South Wales
Ag Gaz of Canada — Agricultural Gazette of Canada
Ag Gaz of New South Wales — Agricultural Gazette of New South Wales
AGGBA9 — Bureau of Mineral Resources, Geology, and Geophysics. Bulletin
AGGBBA — Acta Gerontologica et Geriatrica Belgica
AGGCA — Acta Geologica et Geographica. Universitatis Comenianae. Geologica
AGGEDL — Archives of Gerontology and Geriatrics
AGGHAR — Archiv fuer Gewerbepathologie und Gewerbehygiene
Aggiorn Clinico Ter — Aggiornamenti Clinico Terapeutici
Aggiorn Ematol — Aggiornamenti in Ematologia
Aggiorn Mal Infez — Aggiornamenti sulle Malattie da Infezione
Aggiorn Pediatr — Aggiornamento Pediatrico
Aggiorn Soc — Aggiornamenti Sociali
AGGLA5 — Agronomski Glasnik
Agglom — Agglomeration
Agglom Int Symp — Agglomeration. International Symposium
AGGRAN — Bureau of Mineral Resources, Geology, and Geophysics. Report
AGGRBO — Ahrokhimiia i Hruntoznavstvo Respublikanskii Mizhvidomchyi Tematichnyi Zbirnyk
Aggregate Resour Inventory Pap Ontario Geol Surv — Aggregate Resources Inventory Paper. Ontario Geological Survey
Aggressive Behav — Aggressive Behavior
AGGS — Ausfuehrliche Grammatik der Griechischen Sprache
AGH — Acta Geographica (Helsinki)
Ag H — Agricultural History
AGHA — Archiv fuer Geschichte des Hochstifts Augsburg
AGHCFP — Almeida Garrett. Homenagem do Club Fenianos Portuenses
AGHDAK — International Journal of Aging and Human Development
Ag Hist — Agricultural History
Ag Hist R — Agricultural History Review
AGHJA4 — Agrohemija
AGHPB — Annales de Gastroenterologie et d'Hepatologie
AGHUE7 — Acta Geologica Hungarica
AGHVA6 — Abhandlungen. Gebiet der Hirnforschung und Verhaltensphysiologie
AGHVA6 — Brain and Behavior Research Monograph Series
AGI — Archivio Glottologico Italiano
AGIAA — Associazione Geofisica Italiana. Atti del Convegno Annuale
AGIMBJ — Allergologia et Immunopathologia
AGINEP — Agriculture International
Aging Gametes Proc Int Symp — Aging Gametes, Their Biology and Pathology. Proceedings. International Symposium on Aging Gametes
Aging Hum Dev — Aging and Human Development
Aging Immunol Infect Dis — Aging, Immunology, and Infectious Disease
Aging Leis Living — Aging and Leisure Living
Aging Ment Health — Aging & Mental Health
Aging N — Aging News
Ag Inst R — Agriculture Institute Review
AGIPA — Agricoltura Italiana (Pisa)
AGIPAR — Agricoltura Italiana
AGIS — Attorney General's Information Service
A G It — Archivio Glottologico Italiano
Agitation Ind Chim Symp Int Genie Chim — Agitation dans l'Industrie Chimique. Symposium International de Genie Chimique
AGJOAT — Agronomy Journal
Ag J of British Columbia — Agricultural Journal of British Columbia
Ag J of Egypt — Agricultural Journal of Egypt
Ag J of India — Agricultural Journal of India
AGJU — Arbeiten zur Geschichte des Antiken Judentums und des Urchristentums
AGKBZH — Archiwum Glownej Komisji Badania Zbrodni Hitlerowskich
AGKKN — Archief voor de Geschiedenis van de Katholieke Kerk in Nederland
AGKMW — Antiken Gemmen des Kunsthistorischen Museums in Wien
AGKYAU — Agrokhimiya
AGL — Aglow
Agl — Anglia

AGLAAV — Agricultura (Lisboa)
AGLABW — Agricultural Research Council. Meat Research Institute [Bristol]. Annual Report
AglGr — Anglo-German Review
AGLOA — Angeiologie
AGLPA8 — Acta Geologica Polonica
AGLRA — American Glass Review
AGLTBL — Acta Gastroenterologica Latinoamericana
AGLUAN — Agronomia Lusitana
AGM — Sudhoffs Archiv fuer Geschichte der Medizin und der Naturwissenschaften
A G Mag — Art Gallery. Magazine
AGMA News Bul — Art Galleries and Museums Association of Australia and New Zealand. News Bulletin
AGMANZ News — AGMANZ News. Art Galleries and Museums Association of New Zealand
AGMAzine — American Guild of Musical Artists Magazine
AGMed — Archiv fuer Geschichte der Medezin
AGMGAK — Acta Geneticae, Medicae, et Gemellologiae
AGMMA4 — Annales Geologiques. Service des Mines
AGMOAA — Agronomia
AGMR — Annuaire Geologique et Mineralogique de la Russie
AGMS — American Gem Market System
AGMW — Abhandlungen zur Geschichte der Mathematischen Wissenschaften
AGMYA6 — Agricultural Meteorology
AgN — Age Nouveau
AGN — Anzeiger. Germanisches Nationalmuseum
AGN — Applied Genetics News
AG NC Agric Serv NC State Univ — AG. North Carolina Agricultural Extension Service. North Carolina State University
Agnes Karll Schwest Krankenpfleger — Agnes Karll-Schwester. Der Krankenpfleger
Agni — Agni Review
AGNKA3 — Archiv fuer Genetik
Ag NL — Agricultural Newsletter
AGNM — Anzeiger. Germanisches Nationalmuseum
AGNMBA — Agronomia
AGNNAC — Agricultural Research News Notes
AGNO — Agriculture North
AGNRAO — Advances in Gerontological Research
AGNSAR — Agricultural Gazette of New South Wales
A G NSW Q — Art Gallery of New South Wales Quarterly
AgO — Age d'Or
AGO — American Guild of Organists. Quarterly
AGO — Archiv fuer Geschichte von Oberfranken
AGOHZ — Archief voor de Geschiedenis der Oude Hollandsche Zending
AGORA — Archiwum Gornictwa
Agora Inf Changing World — Agora. Informatics in a Changing World
Agora Math — Agora Mathematica
Ag Outlook — Agricultural Outlook
AGP — Acta Geographica. Comptes Rendus de la Societe de Paris
AGP — Archiv fuer Geschichte der Philosophie
AGP — Arctic Gas Profile
AGP — Australian Government Publications
AGPAAH — Agriculture (Paris)
AGPGAZ — Agricultural Progress
AGPh — Archiv fuer Geschichte der Philosophie
A G Philos — Archiv fuer Geschichte der Philosophie
AGPIC9 — Arbeiten aus dem Geologisch-Palaeontologischen Institut der Universitaet Stuttgart
AGPLAG — Agroplantae
AGPPAS — Archiv fuer die Gesamte Physiologie des Menschen und der Tiere
AGPQAV — Agriculture Pratique
AGPYAL — Agrochemophysica
AGR — AGR. Akten der Gesellschaft fuer Griechische und Hellenistische Rechtsgechichte
AGR — Agrarwirtschaft
Agr — Agricultura
Ag R — Agricultural Review
AGR — American-German Review
AGR — Journal of Agricultural Taxation and Law
AGRA — Agora-General
Agra — Agra High Court Reports
Agr Abroad — Agriculture Abroad
A Graefe's A — Albrecht Von Graefe's Archiv fuer Klinische und Experimentelle Ophthalmologie
Agr Alger — Agriculture Algerienne
Agr Am — Agriculture in the Americas
Agr Amer — Agricultura de las Americas
Agr Ammonia News — Agricultural Ammonia News
Agr Anim Husb — Agriculture and Animal Husbandry
Agrar — Agrarwirtschaft
Agrarpolit Rev — Agrarpolitische Revue
Agrar Rundsch — Agrarische Rundschau
Agrartoert Szle — Agrartoerteneti Szemle
Agrartort Szemle — Agrartoerteneti Szemle
Agrartud — Agrartudomany
Agrartud Egy Agrarkozgazd Kar Kiad — Agrartudomanyi Egyetem Agrarkozgazdasagi Karanak Kiadvanyai
Agrartud Egy Agron Kar Kiad — Agrartudomanyi Egyetem Agronomiai Karanak Kiadvanyai
Agrartud Egy Allattenyesz Karanak Kozl (Godollo) — Agrartudomanyi Egyetem Allattenyesztesi Karanak Koezlemenyei (Goedoelloe)
Agrartud Egyetem Mezoegazdasagtud Kar Koezlem (Goedoelloe) — Agrartudomanyi Egyetem Mezoegazdasagtudomanyi Karanak Koezlemenyei (Goedoelloe)

Agrartud Egyetem Tud Tajekoz (Goedoelloe) — Agrartudomanyi Egyetem Tudomanyos Tajekoztatoja (Goedoelloe)
Agrartud Egyet Kert Szoeloegazdasagtud Karanak Evk — Agrartudomanyi Egyetem Kert- es Szoeloegazdasagtudomanyi Karanak Evkoenyve. Annales Sectionis Horti- et Viticulturae Universitatis Scientiae Agriculturae
Agrartud Egyet Mezoegtud Kar Koezl (Goedoelloe) — Agrartudomanyi Egyetem Mezoegazdasagtudomanyi Karanak Koezlemenyei (Goedoelloe)
Agrartud Egy Kert Szologazdasagtud Karanak Evk — Agrartudomanyi Egyetem Kert-es Szologazdasagtudomanyi Karanak Evkonyve
Agrartud Egy Kert Szologazdasagtud Karanak Kozl — Agrartudomanyi Egyetem Kert-es Szologazdasagtudomanyi Karanak Koezlemenyei
Agrartud Egy Kozl (Godollo) — Agrartudomanyi Egyetem Koezlemenyei (Goedoelloe)
Agrartud Egy Mezogazdasagtud Karanak Kozl — Agrartudomanyi Egyetem Mezoegazdasagtudomanyi Karanak Koezlemenyei
Agrartud Egy Mezogazd Gepeszmern Karanak Kozl — Agrartudomanyi Egyetem Mezoegazdasagi Gepeszmernoki Karanak Koezlemenyei
Agrartud Egy Mezogazd Karanak Evk — Agrartudomanyi Egyetem Mezoegazdasagi Karanak Evkonyve
Agrartud Egy Tud Tajek — Agrartudomanyi Egyetem Tudomanyos Tajekoztatoja
Agrartud Foisk Tud Koezlem (Debrecen) — Agrartudomanyi Foiskola Tudomanyos Koezlemenyei (Debrecen)
Agrartud Foisk Tud Ulesszakanak Eloadasai Debreceni — Agrartudomanyi Foiskola Tudomanyos Ulesszakanak Eloadasai Debreceni
Agrartud Kozl — Agrartudomanyi Koezlemenyek
Agrartud Sz — Agrartudomanyi Szemle
Agrarwirt — Agrarwirtschaft
Agrarwirts — Agrarwirtschaft
Agrarwirt und Agrarsoziol — Agrarwirtschaft und Agrarsoziologie
Agr Asia — Agriculture Asia
Agra Univ Bul — Agra University. Bulletin
Agra Univ Jour Res Sci — Agra University Journal of Research Science
Agra Univ J Res — Agra University. Journal of Research
Agra Univ J Res Sci — Agra University. Journal of Research Science
Agr Aviation — Agricultural Aviation
Agrawirts — Agrarwirtschaft
Agr Banking Finan — Agricultural Banking and Finance
AGRBAU — Agrobiologiya
Agr Biol Ch — Agricultural and Biological Chemistry
Agr Biol Chem — Agricultural and Biological Chemistry
Agr Bresciano — Agricoltore Bresciano
Agr Bull Canterbury Chamber Commer — Agricultural Bulletin. Canterbury Chamber of Commerce
Agr Bull Oreg Dept Agr — Agricultural Bulletin. Oregon Department of Agriculture
Agr Bull Saga Univ — Agricultural Bulletin. Saga University
AGRCAX — Agrochimica
AGRCCZ — Agrociencia. Serie C
Agr Chem — Agricultural Chemicals
AGREA5 — Agricultural Research
Agr Econ Inform Ser Univ MD Coop Ext Serv — Agricultural Economics Information Series. University of Maryland. Cooperative Extension Service
Agr Econ Mimeo Mich State Univ Agr Appl Sci Coop Ext Serv — Agricultural Economics Mimeo. Michigan State University of Agriculture and Applied Science. Cooperative Extension Service
Agr Econ Mimeo Rep Fla Agr Exp Sta — Agricultural Economics Mimeo Report. Florida Agricultural Experiment Station
Agr Econ Pam S Dak Agr Exp Sta — Agricultural Economics Pamphlet. South Dakota Agricultural Experiment Station
Agr Econ Re — Agricultural Economics Research
Agr Econ Rep Kans Agr Exp Sta — Agricultural Economics Report. Kansas Agricultural Experiment Station
Agr Econ Rep Mich State Univ Agr Appl Sci Coop Ext Serv — Agricultural Economics Report. Michigan State University of Agriculture and Applied Science. Cooperative Extension Service
Agr Econ Rep N Dak Agr Exp Sta — Agricultural Economics Report. North Dakota Agricultural Experiment Station
Agr Econ Res — Agricultural Economics Research
AGRED8 — Agricultural Record
Agr Educ Ma — Agricultural Education Magazine
Agregation Plaquettaire Rapp Congr Fr Med — Agregation Plaquettaire. Rapports presentes au Congres Francais de Medecine
Agreg Math — Agregation de Mathematiques
Agr Eng — Agricultural Engineering
Agr Eng Ext Bull NY State Coll Agr Dept Agr Eng — Agricultural Engineering Extension Bulletin. New York State College of Agriculture. Department of Agricultural Engineering
Ag Res — Agricultural Research
Agressolog — Agressologie
Agr Ferrarese — Agricoltore Ferrarese
Agr Ganad — Agricultura y Ganaderia
Agr Gaz NSW — Agricultural Gazette of New South Wales
Agr (Gt Brit) — Agriculture (Great Britain). Ministry of Agriculture, Fisheries, and Food
Agr Hist — Agricultural History
Agr Hist Rev — Agricultural History Review
Agr Hor Gen — Agri Hortique Genetica
Agr Hort — Agriculture and Horticulture
Agri Admin — Agricultural Administration
Agri Afr — Agri-Afrique
AGRIAH — Agricultura (Heverlee)
Agri Bio Chem — Agriculture and Biological Chemistry
Agribus Decis — Agribusiness Decision
Agribus W — Agribusiness Worldwide
Agric — Agriculture
Agric 2000 — Agriculture. Toward 2000

Agric Abroad — Agriculture Abroad
Agric Adm — Agricultural Administration
Agric Adm Ext — Agricultural Administration and Extension
Agric Agroind J — Agriculture and Agro-Industries Journal
Agric Alger — Agriculture Algerienne
Agric Am — Agricultura de las Americas
Agric Am — Agriculture in the Americas
Agric Amer Kansas City — Agricultura de las Americas (Kansas City)
Agric & Biol Chem — Agricultural and Biological Chemistry
Agric Anim Hub — Agriculture and Animal Husbandry
Agric Aomori — Agriculture in Aomori. Aomori Nogyo. Aomori Prefecture Agricultural ImprovementAssociation
Agric Asia — Agriculture Asia
Agric Aviat — Agricultural Aviation
Agric Belge Etranger — L'Agriculteur Belge et Etranger
Agric Biol Chem — Agricultural and Biological Chemistry
Agric Biotechnol News — Agricultural Biotechnology News
Agric Bull — Agriculture Bulletin
Agric Bull Fed Malay States — Agricultural Bulletin. Federated Malay States
Agric Bull Saga Univ — Agricultural Bulletin. Saga University
Agric Bur NSW State Congr — Agricultural Bureau of New South Wales. State Congress
AgricBus News Ky Univ Ky Coop Ext Serv — AgriBusiness News for Kentucky. University of Kentucky. Cooperative Exension Service
Agric Can Annu Rep — Agriculture Canada. Annual Report
Agric Can Monogr — Agriculture Canada. Monograph
Agric Can Rapp Annu — Agriculture Canada. Rapport Annuel
Agric Can Res Branch Rep — Agriculture Canada. Research Branch Report
Agric Can Weed Surv Ser — Agriculture Canada. Weed Survey Series
Agric Chem — Agricultural Chemicals
Agric Chiriqui — Agricultura en Chiriqui
Agric Circ US Dep Agric — Agriculture Circular. United States Department of Agriculture
Agric Colon — Agricoltura Coloniale
Agric Commun Res Rep — Agricultural Communications Research Report
Agric Conspectus Sci — Agriculturae Conspectus Scientificus
Agric Costarricense — Agricultor Costarricense
Agric Econ — Agricultural Economist
Agric Econ B Afr — Agricultural Economics Bulletin for Africa
Agric Econ Bull for Afr — Agricultural Economics Bulletin for Africa
Agric Econ Bull NSW Div Mark Econ Serv — Agricultural Economics Bulletin. New South Wales. Division of Marketing and Economic Services
Agric Econ Ext Ser Univ KY Coop Ext Serv — Agricultural Economics Extension Series. University of Kentucky. Cooperative Extension Service
Agric Econ Fm Mgmt Occ Pap Dep Agric Qd Univ — Agricultural Economics and Farm Management Occasional Paper. Department of Agriculture. University of Queensland
Agric Econ J Int Assoc Agric Econ — Agricultural Economics. Journal. International Association of Agricultural Economics
Agric Econ Rep Dep Agric Econ Mich State Univ — Agricultural Economics Report. Department of Agricultural Economics. Michigan State University
Agric Econ Rep Mich State Univ Dep Agric Econ — Agricultural Economics Report. Michigan State University. Department of Agricultural Economics
Agric Econ Res — Agricultural Economics Research
Agric Econ Research — Agricultural Economics Research
Agric Econ Res Rep Miss Agric For Exp Sta — Agricultural Economics Research Report. Mississippi Agricultural and Forestry Experiment Station
Agric Econ Res US Dep Agric Econ Res Serv — Agricultural Economics Research. United States Department of Agriculture. Economic Research Service
Agric Ecosyst & Environ — Agriculture, Ecosystems, and Environment
Agric Ecosystems Environ — Agriculture, Ecosystems, and Environment
Agric Educ — Agricultural Education
Agric Educ Mag — Agricultural Education Magazine
Agric Electr Inst Rep — Agricultural Electricity Institute. Report
Agric El Salv — Agricultura en El Salvador
Agric El Salvador — Agricultura en El Salvador
Agric-Energy Transp Dig — Agricultural-Energy Transportation Digest
Agric Eng — Agricultural Engineering
Agric Eng (Aust) — Agricultural Engineering (Australia)
Agric Engin — Agricultural Engineering
Agric Eng J — Agricultural Engineering Journal
Agric Eng (Lond) — Agricultural Engineer (London)
Agric Engn — Agricultural Engineer
Agric Engng (Aust) — Agricultural Engineering (Australia)
Agric Eng (S Afr) — Agricultural Engineering (South Africa)
Agric Eng (St Joseph Mich) — Agricultural Engineering (St. Joseph, MI)
Agric Eng Yearb — Agricultural Engineers Yearbook
Agric Enterp Stud Engl Wales Econ Rep — Agricultural Enterprise Studies in England and Wales Economic Report
Agric Environ — Agriculture and Environment
Agric Exp — Agricultura Experimental
Agric Exp Sta Agric Coll Colorado Bull — Agricultural Experiment Station. Agricultural College of Colorado. Bulletin
Agric Exp Sta Arkansas Industr Univ Bull — Agricultural Experiment Station at Arkansas Industrial University. Bulletin
Agric Exp Stn Ala Polytech Inst Prog Rep Ser — Agricultural Experiment Station. Alabama Polytechnic Institute. Progress ReportSeries
Agric Exp Stn Univ VT Bull — Agricultural Experiment Station. University of Vermont. Bulletin
Agric Fact Sh US Dep Agric — Agriculture Fact Sheet. US Department of Agriculture
Agric Fd Chemy — Agricultural and Food Chemistry
Agric Financ Rev — Agricultural Finance Review

Agric Financ Rev US Dep Agric Econ Stat Coop Serv — Agricultural Finance Review. United States Department of Agriculture. Economics, Statistics, and Cooperative Service
Agric Fin Out — Agricultural Finance Outlook
Agric Fin R — Agricultural Finance Review
Agric Fin Rev — Agricultural Finance Review
Agric Food Sci Finl — Agricultural and Food Science in Finland
Agric For Bull — Agriculture and Forestry Bulletin
Agric Forest News — Agriculture and Forestry News/Nung Lin T'ung Hsin
Agric For Meteorol — Agricultural and Forest Meteorology
Agric Fr — Agriculteurs de France
Agric Ganad — Agricultura y Ganaderia
Agric Gaz Can — Agricultural Gazette of Canada
Agric Gaz Canada — Agricultural Gazette of Canada
Agric Gaz NSW — Agricultural Gazette of New South Wales
Agric Gaz Tasm — Agricultural Gazette of Tasmania
Agric Gifu Prefect — Agriculture of Gifu Prefecture/Gifu-ken No Nogyo
Agric Handb US Dep Agric — Agriculture Handbook. United States Department of Agriculture
Agric Handb US Dep Agric Agric Res Serv — Agriculture Handbook. United States Department of Agriculture. Agricultural Research Service
Agric Handb US Dep Agric Comb For Pest Res Dev Program — Agriculture Handbook. United States Department of Agriculture. Combined Forest Pest Research and Development Program
Agrichem Age — Agrichemical Age
Agrichem W — Agrichemical West
Agric Hist — Agricultural History
Agric Hist R — Agricultural History Review
Agric Hist Rev — Agricultural History Review
Agric Hoje — Agricultura de Hoje
Agric Hokkaido — Agriculture in Hokkaido
Agric Hokkaido Hokuno — Agriculture in Hokkaido. Hokuno
Agric Hokkaido Nogyo Hokkaido — Agriculture in Hokkaido/Nogyo Hokkaido
Agric Hort — Agriculture and Horticulture
Agric Hort Engng Abstr — Agricultural and Horticultural Engineering Abstracts
Agric Index — Agricultural Index
Agric Inf Bull US Dep Agric — Agriculture Information Bulletin. United States Department of Agriculture
Agric Inform Bull US Dep Agric — Agriculture Information Bulletin. United States Department of Agriculture
Agric Inst Rev — Agricultural Institute Review
Agric Int — Agriculture International
Agric Intnl — Agriculture International
Agric Ital (Pisa) — Agricoltura Italiana (Pisa)
Agric Ital (Rome) — Agricoltura Italiana (Rome)
Agric J & Mining Rec Maritzburg — Agricultural Journal and Mining Record. Maritzburg
Agric J Barbados — Agricultural Journal. Department of Science and Agriculture (Barbados)
Agric J Br Gui — Agricultural Journal of British Guiana
Agric J Br Guiana — Agricultural Journal of British Guiana
Agric J (Bridgetown Barbados) — Agricultural Journal (Bridgetown, Barbados)
Agric J British Columbia — Agricultural Journal of British Columbia
Agric J Cape GH — Agricultural Journal of the Cape Of Good Hope
Agric J (Cape Town) — Agricultural Journal (Cape Town)
Agric J Dep Agric (Fiji) — Agricultural Journal. Department of Agriculture (Suva, Fiji)
Agric J Dep Agric Fiji Isl — Agricultural Journal. Department of Agriculture. Fiji Islands
Agric J Dept Agric (Victoria BC) — Agricultural Journal. Department of Agriculture (Victoria, British Columbia)
Agric J Egypt — Agricultural Journal of Egypt
Agric J India — Agricultural Journal of India
Agric J Kusunoki Soc — Agricultural Journal. Kusunoki Society. Kusunoki Noho
Agric J S Afr — Agricultural Journal of South Africa
Agric J (Suva Fiji) — Agricultural Journal. Department of Agriculture (Suva, Fiji)
Agric J Union S Afr — Agricultural Journal of the Union of South Africa
Agric Lagunero — El Agricultor Lagunero
Agric Land Our Disappearing Heritage Symp — Agricultural Land. Our Disappearing Heritage. Symposium
Agric Lit Czech — Agricultural Literature of Czechoslovakia
Agric Livestock India — Agriculture and Livestock in India
Agric Mach J — Agricultural Machinery Journal
Agric Mag — Agricultural Magazine. Kuo Li Pei Ching Nung Yeh Chuan Men Hsueeh Hsiao Tsa Chih
Agric Mark (Washington) — Agricultural Marketing (Washington, DC)
Agric Mech Asia — Agricultural Mechanization in Asia
Agric Met — Agricultural Meteorology
Agric Meteorol — Agricultural Meteorology
Agric Mexicano — Agricultor Mexicano y Hogar
Agric Monogr USDA — Agricultural Monographs. US Department of Agriculture
Agric News (Barbados) — Agricultural News (Barbados)
Agric News Lett E I Du Pont De Nemours Co — Agricultural News Letter. E. I. Du Pont De Nemours and Company
Agric Newsl (Manila) — Agricultural Newsletter (Manila)
Agric Nuova — Agricoltura Nuova
Agricoltura Ital (Pisa) — Agricoltura Italiana (Pisa)
Agric OSU Okla State Univ Agric Exp Stn — Agriculture at OSU. Oklahoma State University. Agricultural Experiment Station
Agric Outl — Agricultural Outlook
Agric Outlook — Agricultural Outlook
Agric Outlook AO US Dep Agric Econ Res Serv — Agricultural Outlook AO. US Department of Agriculture. Economic Research Service
Agric Pak — Agriculture Pakistan
Agric Pakistan — Agriculture Pakistan

Agric Prat — Agriculture Pratique

Agric Prat Pays Chauds — Agriculture Pratique des Pays Chauds. Bulletin du Jardin Colonial et des Jardins d'Essai des Colonies Francaises

Agric Prog — Agricultural Progress

Agric Propag — Agriculture Propagation. Gojo Noyu. Miyagi Prefecture Propagation Association

Agric Pugliese — Agricoltura Pugliese

Agric Rec — Agricultural Record

Agric Rec (S Aust) — Agricultural Record (South Australia)

Agric Rec South Aust Dep Agric — Agricultural Record. South Australia Department of Agriculture

Agric Refin Bridge Farm Ind — Agricultural Refineries. A Bridge from Farm to Industry

Agric Res — Agricultural Research

Agric Res Corp (Gezira) Tech Bull — Agricultural Research Corporation (Gezira). Technical Bulletin

Agric Res Counc Food Res Inst (Norwich) Annu Rep — Agricultural Research Council. Food Research Institute (Norwich). Annual Report

Agric Res Counc (GB) Letcombe Lab Annu Rep — Agricultural Research Council (Great Britain). Letcombe Laboratory. Annual Report

Agric Res Counc (GB) Radiobiol Lab — Agricultural Research Council (Great Britain). Radiobiological Laboratory

Agric Res Counc (GB) Radiobiol Lab ARCRL — Agricultural Research Council (Great Britain). Radiobiological Laboratory. ARCRL

Agric Res Counc Meat Res Inst Bien Rep (Bristol) — Agricultural Research Council. Meat Research Institute. Biennial Report (Bristol)

Agric Res Counc Meat Res Inst (Bristol) Annu Rep — Agricultural Research Council. Meat Research Institute (Bristol). Annual Report

Agric Res Counc Meat Res Inst (Bristol) Memo — Agricultural Research Council. Meat Research Institute (Bristol). Memorandum

Agric Res Counc Rep — Agricultural Research Council. Report

Agric Res Counc Soil Surv Tech Monogr — Agricultural Research Council. Soil Survey of England and Wales. Technical Monograph

Agric Res Dev — Agricultural Research for Development

Agric Res Guyana — Agricultural Research Guyana

Agric Res Inst Ukiriguru Prog Rep — Agricultural Research Institute Ukiriguru. Progress Report

Agric Res J Kerala — Agricultural Research Journal of Kerala

Agric Res Kans Kans Agric Exp Stn — Agricultural Research in Kansas. Kansas Agricultural Experiment Station

Agric Res (Kurashiki) — Agricultural Research (Kurashiki)

Agric Res Man US Dep Agric Sci Educ Adm — Agricultural Research Manual. US Department of Agriculture. Science and Education Administration

Agric Res (New Delhi) — Agricultural Research (New Delhi)

Agric Res News Notes (Lima) — Agricultural Research News Notes (Lima)

Agric Res Organ Dep For Ilanot Leaf — Agricultural Research Organization. Department of Forestry. Ilanot Leaflet

Agric Res Organ Div For Ilanot Leafl — Agricultural Research Organization. Division of Forestry. Ilanot Leaflet

Agric Res Organ Pam (Bet-Dagan) — Agricultural Research Organization. Pamphlet (Bet-Dagan)

Agric Res Organ Prelim Rep (Bet-Dagan) — Agricultural Research Organization. Preliminary Report (Bet-Dagan)

Agric Res Organ Volcani Cent Spec Publ — Agricultural Research Organization. Volcani Center. Special Publication

Agric Resour Q — Agriculture and Resources Quarterly

Agric Res Rep (Wageningen) — Agricultural Research Reports (Wageningen)

Agric Res Rep (Wageningen) (Versl Landbouwk Onderz) — Agricultural Research Reports (Wageningen) (Verslagen van Landbouwkundige Onderzoekingen)

Agric Res Rev — Agricultural Research Review

Agric Res Rev (Cairo) — Agricultural Research Review (Cairo)

Agric Res Seoul Natl Univ — Agricultural Research. Seoul National University

Agric Res Taipei — Agricultural Research (Taipei)

Agric Res US Dep Agric Agric Res Serv — Agricultural Research. US Department of Agriculture. Agricultural Research Service

Agric Res US Dep Agric Res Serv — Agricultural Research. United States Department of Agriculture. Research Service

Agric Res (Wash DC) — Agricultural Research (Washington, DC)

Agric Rev — Agriculture Review

Agric Romande — Agriculture Romande

Agric Rural Dev Relat Agencies Appropriations Hearings — Agriculture, Rural Development, and Related Agencies Appropriations for Hearings

Agric Salvadoreno — Agricultor Salvadoreno. Ministerio de Agricultura y Ganaderia

Agric Sao Paulo — Agricultura em Sao Paulo

Agric Sci Bull — Agricultural Science Bulletin

Agric Sci Dig — Agricultural Science Digest

Agric Sci Finl — Agricultural Science in Finland

Agric Sci (Jogjakarta) — Agricultural Science (Jogjakarta)

Agric Sci Peiping — Agricultural Science. National University of Peiping/Nung Hsueeh Yueeh K'an (Peiping)

Agric Sci R — Agricultural Science Review

Agric Sci Rev — Agricultural Science Review

Agric Sci Rev Coop State Res Serv US Dep Agric — Agricultural Science Review. Cooperative State Research Service. US Department of Agriculture

Agric Sci S Afr Agroplantae — Agricultural Science in South Africa. Agroplantae

Agric Sci (Sofia) — Agricultural Science (Sofia)

Agric Serv Bull FAO — Agricultural Services Bulletin. Food and Agriculture Organization of the UnitedNations

Agric Sin — Agricultura Sinica

Agric Situa — Agricultural Situation [*Later, Farmline Magazine*]

Agric Situation India — Agricultural Situation in India

Agric Syst — Agricultural Systems

Agric Technol — Agricultural Technologist

Agric Tec Mex — Agricultura Tecnica en Mexico

Agric Tecn — Agricultura Tecnica. Chile. Direccion General de Agricultura

Agric Tec (Santiago) — Agricultura Tecnica (Santiago)

Agric Trop — Agricultura Tropical

Agricultura Am — Agricultura de las Americas

Agricultura Tec — Agricultura Tecnica

Agricultura Tec Mex — Agricultura Tecnica en Mexico

Agricultura Trop — Agricultura Tropical

Agriculture in Ire — Agriculture in Northern Ireland

Agriculture London — Agriculture. The Journal. Ministry of Agriculture (London)

Agriculture Montreal — Agriculture. Corporation des Agronomes de la Province de Quebec (Montreal)

Agriculture Pakist — Agriculture Pakistan

Agric Univ (Wageningen) Pap — Agricultural University (Wageningen). Papers

Agric Venez — Agricultura Venezolana

Agric Venezie — Agricoltura delle Venezie

Agric Vet Chem — Agricultural and Veterinary Chemicals

Agric Wastes — Agricultural Wastes

Agric Water Manage — Agricultural Water Management

Agric Weather Res Ser — Agricultural Weather Research Series

Agric World — Agricultural World/Nogyo Sekai

Agric Yamaguchi — Agriculture in Yamaguchi/Nogyo Yamaguchi

Agric Y Soc — Agricultura y Sociedad

Agric Zool Rev — Agricultural Zoology Reviews

Agri Dec — Agriculture Decisions

Agrid Net Rev Can Ed — Agridata Network Review. Canadian Edition

Agrid Net Rev Com Ed — Agridata Network Review. Communicator Edition

Agrid Net Rev Dairy Net Ed — Agridata Network Review. Dairy Net Edition

Agrid Net Rev Fin Ed — Agridata Network Review. Financial Edition

Agrid Net Rev Gov Univ Ed — Agridata Network Review. Government/University Edition

Agrid Net Rev Prod Ed — Agridata Network Review. Producer Edition

Agrid Net Rev Telco Ed — Agridata Network Review. Telco Edition

Agrid Net Rev West Livest Ed — Agridata Network Review. Western Livestock Edition

Agrid New Rev Agri Ed Ed — Agridata Network Review. Agricultural Education Edition

Agri Eco Environ — Agriculture Ecosystems and Environment

Agri Hort Genet — Agri Hortique Genetica

Agri Ind — Agriculture Index

Agri Mark — Agricultural Marketing

Agri Mech Asia — Agricultural Mechanization in Asia, Africa, and Latin America

AGRI/MECH Rep Econ Comm Eur — AGRI/MECH Report. Economic Commission for Europe

Agrimed Res Programme Enrich Wine Eur Community — Agrimed Research Programme. The Enrichment of Wine in the Europoean Community

Agri Mktg — Agri Marketing

Agr Inform Bull USDA — Agriculture Information Bulletin. United States Department of Agriculture

Agr Inst Rev — Agricultural Institute Review

Agri Res Seoul Nat Univ — Agricultural Research. Seoul National University

AGRIS — International Information System of the Agricultural Sciences and Technology

Agriscene (Aust) — Agriscene (Australia)

AgriScience — AgriScience

Agr Israel — Agriculture in Israel

Agr Ital — Agricoltura d'Italia

Agri Water Mgmt — Agricultural Water Management

AGRJAK — Agronomia

AGRL — Aspects of Greek and Roman Life

AGRLAQ — Agriculture (London)

Agr Leaders Dig — Agricultural Leaders Digest

Agr (Lisboa) — Agricultura (Lisboa)

Agr Livestock India — Agriculture and Livestock in India

Agr LJ — Agricultural Law Journal

Agr Market (Nagpur) — Agricultural Marketing (Nagpur)

Agr Market (Washington DC) — Agricultural Marketing (Washington, DC)

AGRMBU — Agronomia

Agr Mech — Agricultural Mechanization

Agr Merchant — Agricultural Merchant

Agr Meteor — Agricultural Meteorology

Agr Meteorol — Agricultural Meteorology

Agr Milanese — Agricoltura Milanese

Agr (Montreal) — Agriculture (Montreal)

Agr Napoletana — Agricoltura Napoletana

AGRNAW — Agronomico

AGRNDZ — Agronomie

Agr Newslett — Agricultural Newsletter

Agr N Ireland — Agriculture in Northern Ireland

Agro Al — Agro-Alimentaire

AGROB2 — Agrochemia (Bratislava)

Agrobiol — Agrobiologiya

Agroborealis Alaska Agric Exp Stn (Fairbanks) — Agroborealis. Alaska Agricultural Experiment Station (Fairbanks)

Agroborealis Alaska Agric For Exp Stn Univ Alaska Fairbanks — Agroborealis. Alaska Agricultural and Forestry Experiment Station. University of Alaska. Fairbanks

Agrobot — Agrobotanika

Agrochem — Agrochemia

Agrochem — Agrochemophysica

Agrochem Cour — Agrochem Courier

Agrochem Jpn — Agrochemicals Japan

Agrochim — Agrochimica

Agrochim — Agrochimica. Plsa Universita. Istituto di Chimica Agraria

Agrocienc Ser A — Agrociencia. Serie A

Agrocienc Ser C — Agrociencia. Serie C

Agro-Ecosyst — Agro-Ecosystems
Agro Food Ind Hi Tech — Agro Food Industry Hi-Tech
Agrof Rev — Agroforestry Review
Agrogeol Julk — Agrogeologisia Julkaisuja
Agro Inds — Agro Industries
Agrokem Talajtan — Agrokemia es Talajtan
Agrokem Talajtan Suppl — Agrokemia es Talajtan. Supplement
Agrokhim — Agrokhimiya
Agrokhim Gruntoznst — Agrokhimiya i Gruntoznaustvo
Agrokhim Kharakt Osnovn Tipov Pochv SSSR — Agrokhimicheskaya Kharakteristika Osnovnykh Tipov Pochv SSSR
Agrokhim Kharakt Pochv BSSR — Agrokhimicheskaya Kharakteristika Pochv BSSR
Agrokhim Pochvoved Kharkov — Agrokhimiya i Pochvovedenie (Kharkov)
Agron — Agronomy
Agron Abstr — Agronomy Abstracts
Agron Angol — Agronomia Angolana
Agron Angolana — Agronomia Angolana
Agron Branch Rep (South Aust Dep Agric Fish) — Agronomy Branch Report (South Australia Department of Agriculture and Fisheries)
Agron Colon — Agronomie Coloniale. Bulletin Mensuel. Institut National d'Agronomie de la France d'Outre-Mer
Agron Coop Ext Serv Univ Md — Agronomist. Cooperative Extension Service. University of Maryland
Agron Costarric — Agronomia Costarricense
Agron Data Wash State Univ Coll Agric Res Cent — Agronomic Data. Washington State University. College of Agricultural Research Center
Agron Dept Ser Ohio Agr Exp Sta — Agronomy Department Series. Ohio Agricultural Experiment Station
Agron Food Contrib Challenges Pap Annu Meet Am Soc Agron — Agronomists and Food. Contributions and Challenges. Papers Presented at the Annual Meeting. American Society of Agronomy
Agron Glas — Agronomski Glasnik
Agron Glasn — Agronomski Glasnik
Agron Handb — Agronomy Handbook
Agron Hist Jaarb — Agronomisch-Historisch Jaarboek
Agron J — Agronomy Journal
Agron (Lima) — Agronomia (Lima)
Agron Lusit — Agronomia Lusitana
Agron Lusitana — Agronomia Lusitana
Agron (Manizales) — Agronomia (Manizales)
Agron (Mexico) — Agronomia (Monterrey, Mexico)
Agron Mimeogr Circ N Dak Agr Exp Sta — Agronomy. Mimeograph Circular. North Dakota Agricultural Experiment Station
Agron Mocambicana — Agronomia Mocambicana
Agron Note Univ Ky Coll Agric Coop Ext Serv — Agronomy Notes. University of Kentucky. College of Agriculture. Cooperative Extension Service
Agronomia Angol — Agronomia Angolana
Agronomia Lusit — Agronomia Lusitana
Agronomia Trop — Agronomia Tropical. Revista del Instituto Nacional de Agricultura
Agron Pam S Dak Agr Exp Sta — Agronomy Pamphlet. South Dakota Agricultural Experiment Station
Agron Res Food Pap Annu Meet Am Soc Agron — Agronomic Research for Food. Papers Presented at the Annual Meeting of theAmerican Society of Agronomy
Agron Res Rep AG Agric Exp Stn Univ Fla — Agronomy Research Report AG. Agricultural Experiment Stations. University of Florida
Agron Res Rep LA State Univ Agric Mech Coll Dep Agron — Agronomy Research Report. Louisiana State University and Agricultural and Mechanical College. Department of Agronomy
Agron Soc NZ Spec Publ — Agronomy Society of New Zealand: Special Publication
Agron Soils Res Ser Clemson Agr Exp Sta — Agronomy and Soils Research Series. Clemson Agricultural Experiment Station
Agron Sulriogr — Agronomia Sulriograndense
Agron Sul Rio Grandense — Agronomia Sul Rio Grandense
Agron Sulriograndense — Agronomia Sulriograndense
Agron Trop — Agronomia Tropical
Agron Trop — Agronomie Tropicale
Agron Trop Agron Gen Etude Tech — Agronomie Tropicale. Serie Agronomie Generale. Etudes Techniques
Agron Trop Agron Gen Etud Sci — Agronomie Tropicale. Serie Agronomie Generale. Etudes Scientifiques
Agron Trop Maracaibo — Agronomia Tropical (Maracaibo)
Agron Trop (Maracay) — Agronomia Tropical (Maracay, Venezuela)
Agron Trop (Paris) — Agronomie Tropicale (Paris)
Agron Trop Riz Rizic Cult Vivrieres Trop — Agronomie Tropicale. Serie Riz et Riziculture et Cultures Vivrieres Tropicales
Agron Trop Ser Agron Gen Etud Sci — Agronomie Tropicale. Serie Agronomie Generale. Etudes Scientifiques
Agron Trop Ser Agron Gen Etud Tech — Agronomie Tropicale. Serie Agronomie Generale. Etudes Techniques
Agron Trop Ser Riz Rizic Cult Vivrieres Trop — Agronomie Tropicale. Serie Riz et Riziculture et Cultures Vivrieres Tropicales
Agron Trop Suppl — Agronomie Tropicale. Supplement
Agron Vet — Agronomia y Veterinaria
Agron Views Univ Nebr Coll Agr Home Econ Ext Serv — Agronomy Views. University of Nebraska. College of Agriculture and Home Economics. Extension Service
Agros (Lisb) — Agros (Lisboa)
Agrotec (Madrid) — Agrotecnia (Madrid)
Agrotekh Provid Kul'tur — Agrotekhnika Providnikh Kul'tur
Agrotekh Vozdelyvaniya Ovoshchei Gribov Shampinonov — Agrotekhnika Vozdelyvaniya Ovoshchei i Gribov Shampin'onov

AGRPA4 — Agriculture Pakistan
Agr Pakistan — Agriculture Pakistan
Agr (Paris) — Agriculture (Paris)
Agr Policy Rev — Agricultural Policy Review
Agr Prat — Agriculture Pratique
Agr Prog — Agricultural Progress
Agr Progr — Agricultural Progress
AGRRA — Agricultural Research Review
AGRRAA — Agricultural Research Review
Agr Res — Agricultural Research
Agr Res (India) — Agricultural Research (India)
Agr Res J Kerala — Agricultural Research Journal of Kerala
Agr Res (Pretoria) — Agricultural Research (Pretoria)
Agr Res Rev — Agricultural Research Review
Agr Res (Washington DC) — Agricultural Research (Washington, DC)
Agr Romande — Agriculture Romande
Agr (Santo Domingo) — Agricultura (Santo Domingo)
Agr Sao Paulo — Agricultura em Sao Paulo
Agr Sci Rev — Agricultural Science Review
Agr Sit Ind — Agricultural Situation in India
Agr Situation — Agricultural Situation [*Later, Farmline Magazine*]
Agr Situation India — Agricultural Situation in India
Agr Spezia — Agricoltura della Spezia
Agr Statist N Dak Crop Livestock Rep Serv — Agricultural Statistics. North Dakota Crop and Livestock Reporting Service
Agr Tec — Agricultura Tecnica
Agr Tec Mex — Agricultura Tecnica en Mexico
Agr Trop — Agricultura Tropical
AGR Univ KY Coop Ext Serv — AGR. University of Kentucky. Cooperative Extension Service
Agr Venezie — Agricoltura delle Venezie
Agr Vet Chem — Agricultural and Veterinary Chemicals
Agr Wastes — Agricultural Wastes
AGRYAV — Agronomy
AGS — Agency Sales
AGSA Mz — Abhandlungen der Geistes- und Sozialwissenschaftlichen Klasse. Akademie der Wissenschaften und der Literatur in Mainz
Ag Sci J — Agricultural Science Journal
Ag Sci R — Agricultural Science Review
AGSD — Acta Germanica zur Sprache und Dichtung Deutschlands
AGS/GR — Geographical Review. American Geographical Society
Ag Situation — Agricultural Situation [*Later, Farmline Magazine*]
Ag S J — Journal of the Royal Agricultural Society of England
AGSLAV — Agronomia Sulriograndense
AGSMAY — Acta Genetica et Statistica Medica
AGSMHA — American Geographical Society. Map of Hispanic America. Publications
AGSOA — Agressologie
Ag Sply Ind — Agricultural Supply Industry
AGSSAI — Acta Obstetrica et Gynecologica Scandinavica. Supplement
AGSSP — American Geographical Society Special Publications
Ag Stat — Agricultural Statistics
Ag Stat ND Crop Livest Rep Serv Agric Exp Stn — Ag Statistics. North Dakota Crop and Livestock Reporting Service. Agricultural Experiment Station
AGSU — Arbeiten zur Geschichte des Spaetjudentums und Urchristentums
AGSYD5 — Agricultural Systems
AGT — Australian Grade Teacher
AGTBA6 — Agricultura Tropical
AGTCA9 — Agricultura Tecnica
AGTG — Agenutemagen. Indians of New Brunswick
AGTOAB — Agronomie Tropicale. Serie Agronomie Generale. Etudes Techniques
AGTQA — Annales de Genetique
AGTSAN — Agrokemia es Talajtan. Supplement
Agu — Aguedal
Agua Energ — Agua y Energia
AGUEAK — Annales Guebhard
Agued — Aguedal
AGUSD — Gas + Architecture
AGVEAP — Agricultura Venezolana
AGVIA3 — Archiv fuer die Gesamte Virusforschung
AGVO — Arbeitsgemeinschaft Vorderer Orient
AGW — Abhandlungen. Gesellschaft der Wissenschaften zu Goettingen
AGW — Aging and Work
Agway Coop — Agway Cooperator
AGWD — Australian Government Weekly Digest
AGWG — Abhandlungen. Gesellschaft der Wissenschaften zu Goettingen
AGYRA — Agricultural Research
AGYRAB — Agricultural Research
AGZ — Akta Grodshie i Ziemskie
AgZ — Zeitschrift fuer Aegyptische Sprache und Altertumskunde
AGZPAA — Agrikultura (Nitre)
AH — Aboriginal History
AH — Agricultural History
AH — Algemeen Handelblad
AH — American Heritage
AH — American Historical Review
AH — Analecta Hymnica Medii Aevi
AH — Anjou Historique
AH — Archivium Hibernicum
AH — Archivo Hispalense
AH — Argive Heraeum
AH — Art for Humanity
AHA — Acta Historiae Artium. Magyar Tudomanyos Akademia
AHA — Hitotsubashi Academy. Annals
AHA — Hitotsubashi Journal of Economics

AHAB — Australian Historical Association. Bulletin

AHAG — Annales. Societe d'Histoire et d'Archeologie de Gand

AHA Hosp Tech Alert — AHA [*American Hospital Association*] Hospital Technology Alerts

AHA Hosp Tech Ser — AHA [*American Hospital Association*] Hospital Technology Series

AHAM — Alentejo Historico, Artistico, e Monumental

AHAM — Anales de Historea Antigua y Medieval

AHAM — Association of Home Appliance Manufacturers. Trends and Forecasts

AHAM Facts — Major Appliance Industry Facts Book. Association of Home Appliance Manufacturers

AHA Newsletter — American Historical Association. Newsletter

AHAPAS — Archivos Argentinos de Pediatria

AHA Publ — American Hospital Association. Publications

AHARAY — Archivos Argentinos de Reumatologia

AHA Stat — Hospital Statistics. American Hospital Association

AHAW — Abhandlungen. Heidelberger Akademie der Wissenschaften

AHAWPK — Abhandlungen. Heidelberger Akademie der Wissenschaften. Philosophisch-Historische Klasse

AHB — Annalen der Hydrographie und Maritimen Meteorologie (Berlin)

AHB — Archaeologisch-Historische Bijdragen

AHB — Archives Historiques du Bourbonnais

AHB — [*The*] Australian Hymn Book

AHBAI N — AHBAI [*American Health and Beauty Aids Institute*] News

AHBPAX — Acta Hydrobiologica

AHC — Annuarium Historiae Conciliorum

AHCADU — Aspects of Homogeneous Catalysis

AHCBAU — Acta Hydrochimica et Hydrobiologica

AHCCAX — Aichi Cancer Center Research Institute. Annual Report

AHCE — Asociacion para la Historia de la Ciencia Espanola

AHCI — Arts and Humanities Citation Index

AHCP — Arquivos de Historia de Cultura Portuguesa

AHD — Airport Hotel Directory

AHD — American Heritage Dictionary

AHD — Archives d'Histoire Doctrinale et Litteraire du Moyen Age

AHD — Archives d'Histoire Dominicaine

AHDE — Anuario de la Historia del Derecho Espanol

AHD Esp — Anuario de Historia del Derecho Espanol

AH Dienst — Aussenhandels-Dienst

AHDL — Archives d'Histoire Doctrinale et Litteraire

AHDLMA — Archives d'Histoire Doctrinale et Litteraire du Moyen-Age

AHDO — Archives d'Histoire du Droit Oriental

AHDRA — Archiwum Hydrotechniki

AHE — Annales d'Histoire Economique

AHEAD — Australian Health Education Advisory Digest

AHEB — Analectes pour Servir a l'Histoire Ecclesiastique de la Belgique

AHEMA — Anatomia, Histologia, Embryologia

A Her — Art Heritage

AHES — Annales d'Histoire Economique et Sociale

AHES — Archive for History of Exact Sciences

AHF — Abba Hushi Files

AHF — Archivum Historii, Filozofii, i Mysli Spolecznej

AHF — Australian High Court and Federal Court Practice

AHFPAJ — Allan Hancock Foundation. Publications. Occasional Paper

AHG — Antropologia e Historia de Guatemala

AHG — Archives Historique du Department de la Gironde

AHGA — Archiv fuer Hessische Geschichte und Altertumskunde

AHGAK — Archiv fuer Hessische Geschichte und Altertumskunde

AHGSBY — Acta Hepato-Gastroenterologica

AHHI — Alon Hahevra Hanumismatit le'Israel

AHI — American Hispanist (Indiana)

AHI — American Humanities Index

AHIL Q — Association of Hospital and Institution Libraries. Quarterly

AHISA9 — Acta Histochemica

A Hispal — Arte Hispalense

A Hist — Art History

A HistHung — Acta Historica. Academiae Scientiarum Hungaricae

Ahi Va Golpe — Ahi Va el Golpe

AHJ — American Harp Journal

AHJOA — American Heart Journal

AHJPB6 — Archivum Histologicum Japonicum

AHL — Abstracts of Hungarian Economic Literature

AHL — America: History and Life

AHL — Annuaire d'Histoire Liegeoise

AHLFAJ — Annales d'Hygiene de Langue Francaise. Medecine et Nutrition

AHM — Arquivo Historico da Madeira

AHMA — Archives d'Histoire Doctrinale et Litteraire du Moyen-Age

Ahmadu Bello Univ Abdullahi Bayero Coll Dep Engl Eur Language — Ahmadu Bello University. Kano. Abdullahi Bayero College. Department of English and European Languages. Occasional Papers

AHMC — Anuario Hidrografico de la Marina de Chile

AHME J — Association for Hospital Medical Education. Journal

AHMHAU — Annales Historico-Naturales. Musei Nationalis Hungarici

AHMOAH — American Heart Association. Monograph

AHMS — Abstracts of Hospital Management Studies

AHN — Acta Historiae Neerlandica

AHNMH — Annales Historico-Naturales Musei Nationalis Hungarici. Magyar Nemzeti Muzeum

AHNRH — Annalen des Historischen Vereins fuer den Niederrhein

AHO — Technische Hogeschool Delft. Bibliotheek. Aanwinsten

AHOBAM — Acta Horti Bergiani

AHORA — Acta Horticulturae

AHOSA5 — Anales. Hospital de la Santa Cruz y San Pablo

AHP — Archives Historiques du Poitou

AHP — Archivum Historiae Pontificiae

AHPAA — Annales. Institut Henri Poincare. Section A. Physique Theorique

AHPBA — Annales. Institut Henri Poincare. Section B. Calcul des Probabilites et Statistique

AHPFA5 — Annales Homeopathiques Francaises

AHPLBO — Acta Haematologica Polonica

AHPRB — Advances in High Pressure Research

A H Prov — Annales de Haute-Provence

AHPS — Archiv Fuer Hydrobiologie und Planktonkunde (Stuttgart)

AHQ — Arkansas Historical Quarterly

AHR — Afro-Hispanic Review

AHR — American Historical Review

AHR — Australasian Home Reader

Ahrenlese Georgikons — Ahrenlese des Georgikons

A H Rev — American Historical Review

AHRF — Annales Historiques de la Revolution Francaise

Ahrokhim Hruntozn Resp Mizhvid Temat Zb — Ahrokhimiia i Hruntoznavstvo Respublikanskii Mizhvidomchyi Tematichnyi Zbirnyk

Ahrokhimiia Hruntozn — Ahrokhimiia i Hruntoznavstvo

AHRRBI — Australia. Commonwealth Scientific and Industrial Research Organisation. Division of Horticulture. Research Report

AHRS — Andhra Historical Research Society. Journal

AHRTA — Arhiv za Higijenu Rada i Toksikologiju

AHRTAN — Arhiv za Higijenu Rada i Toksikologiju

AHRW — Alcohol Health and Research World

AHS — African Historical Studies

AHS — Annales d'Histoire Sociale

AHS — Archives Heraldiques Suisses

AHSI — Archivum Historicum Societatis Iesu

AHSJ — Archivum Historicum Societatis Jesu

AHSM — Antiquarian Horological Society. Monograph

AHSMA7 — Acta Historica Scientiarum, Naturalium, et Medicinalium

AHSN — American Handel Society Newsletter

AHSoc — Annales d'Histoire Sociale

AHSSOP — Alberta. Historic Sites Service. Occasional Papers

AHSUA — Acta Histochemica. Supplementband

AHTCB — Advances in High Temperature Chemistry

AHTCBH — Advances in High Temperature Chemistry

AHTJA — Archivum Histologicum Japonicum

AHTRA — Advances in Heat Transfer

AHUBBJ — Annals of Human Biology

A Humor — American Humor

AHUNA — Archivos de Hospitales Universitarios

A Hung — Ars Hungarica

AHUTA — Archiwum Hutnictwa

A Huy — Annales. Cercle Hutois des Sciences et Beaux-Arts. Huy

AHVMF — Archiv des Historischen Vereins von Mainfranken

AHVNR — Annalen des Historischen Vereins fuer den Niederrhein

AHVNRh — Annalen des Historischen Vereins fuer den Niederrhein

AHVsLund — Kungliga Humanistiska Vetenskapssamfundet i Lund. Arsberattelse

AHVsUppsala — Kungliga Humanistiska Vetenskapssamfundet i Uppsala. Arsbok

AHVUA — Archiv des Historischen Vereins von Unterfranken und Aschaffenburg

AHW — Akkadisches Handwoerterbuch

AHW — Altona, Hamburg, Wandsbek

AHYBB5 — Annales d'Hydrobiologie

A Hydrog — Annales Hydrographiques

A Hyg Pbl — Annales d'Hygiene Publique et de Medecine Legale

AHZ — Allgemeine Homoeopathische Zeitung

AI — Acta Iranica

AI — Aerospace Intelligence

AI — Africa Italiana

AI — Afrique Industrie

AI — America Indigena

AI — American Imago

AI — Ancient India

AI — Annals of Iowa

AI — Archives Israelites de France

AI — Ars Islamica

AI — Artificial Intelligence

AI — Art International

AI — Aslib Information

AI — L'Avenir Illustre

Ala — Annals of Iowa

AIA — Archivo Ibero-Americano

AIA — Art in America

AIA/A — Archaeology. Archaeological Institute of America

AIAA ASME ASCE AHS Struct Struct Dyn Mater Conf Collect Tech — AIAA/ASME/ASCE/AHS Structures, Structural Dynamics, and Materials Conference. Collection of Technical Papers

AIAA Bull — AIAA [*American Institute of Aeronautics and Astronautics*] Bulletin

AIAADR — Anales. Instituto Nacional de Investigaciones Agrarias. Serie Agricola

AIAA J — AIAA [*American Institute of Aeronautics and Astronautics*] Journal

AIAA Journal — American Institute of Aeronautics and Astronautics. Journal

AIAA Monogr — AIAA [*American Institute of Aeronautics and Astronautics*] Monographs

AIAA Pap — AIAA [*American Institute of Aeronautics and Astronautics*] Paper

AIAA Stud J — AIAA [*American Institute of Aeronautics and Astronautics*] Student Journal

AIADAX — Annals. Indian Academy of Medical Sciences

AIAEA2 — Archivio Italiano di Anatomia e di Embriologia

AIAHAB — Anales. Instituto Nacional de Antropologia e Historia

AIAIAE — Archivio Italiano di Anatomia e Istologia Patologica

AIA J — AIA [*American Institute of Architects*] Journal

AIA Jnl — AIA [*American Institute of Architects*] Journal

AIAK — Akten des Internationalen Amerikanisten-Kongresses

AIAL — Annales. Institut Archeologique du Luxembourg

AIA Lux — Annales. Institut Archeologique du Luxembourg
AIANAT — Arctic Institute of North America. Annual Report
AIAQA4 — Annales. Institut National Agronomique
AIARA — Archives of Interamerican Rheumatology
AIASAA — Arctic Institute of North America. Special Publication
AIASI — Ancient India
AIAS News — Australian Institute of Aboriginal Studies. Newsletter
AIAS Newslett — AIAS [*Australian Institute of Aboriginal Studies*] Newsletter
AIATAD — Arctic Institute of North America. Technical Paper
AIAW Handbk Dir — AIAW [*Association for Intercollegiate Athletics for Women*] Handbook-Directory
AIB — Academie des Inscriptions et Belles-Lettres. Memoires Presentes par Divers Savants
AIB — Advances in Inorganic Biochemistry
AIB — Arkheologiia i Istoriia Bospora. Sbornik Statei
AIB — Augustana Institute Bulletin
AIB Boll — Associazione Italiana Biblioteche. Bollettino d'Informazioni
AIBDA Bol Espec — AIBDA Boletin Especial. Associacion Interamericana de Bibliotecarios y Documentalistas Agricolas
AIBGAD — Annales. Instituti Biologici [*Tihany*]. Hungaricae Academiae Scientiarum
AIBL — Academie des Inscriptions et Belles-Lettres. Comptes Rendus des Seances
AIBLA — Archives Italiennes de Biologie
AIBLAS — Archives Italiennes de Biologie
AIBLCr — Academie des Inscriptions et Belles-Lettres. Comptes Rendus des Seances
AIBOA3 — Arquivos. Instituto Biologico
AIBPD — Annales. Institut du Petrole (Belgium)
AIBR — Australian Insurance and Banking Record
AIBS — Memoires Presentes par Divers Savants. Academie des Inscriptions et Belles-Lettres. Institut de France
AIBS Bull — AIBS [*American Institute of Biological Sciences*] Bulletin
AIBS Newsl — AIBS [*American Institute of Biological Sciences*] Newsletter
AIBVAO — Arquivos. Instituto de Biologia Vegetal
AIC — Advances in Consumer Research Proceedings
AIC — Aeronautical Information Circular
AICA — Annali. Instituto di Corrispondenza Archeologica
AICA Bull — AICA [*Australasian Institute of Cost Accountants*] Bulletin
AICC — American Indian Crafts and Culture
AICCER — All India Congress Committee. Economic Review
AICHAL — Annali Italiani di Chirurgia
AICHDO — Annals. Institute of Child Health
AIChE Annu Meet Prepr — AIChE [*American Institute of Chemical Engineers*] Annual Meeting. Preprints
AIChE Annu Meet Program Abstr — AIChE [*American Institute of Chemical Engineers*] Annual Meeting. ProgramAbstracts
AIChE Equip Test Proced Evaporators — AIChE (American Institute of Chemical Engineers) Equipment Testing Procedure. Evaporators
AIChEJ — AIChE [*American Institute of Chemical Engineers*] Journal
AIChE Journal — American Institute of Chemical Engineers. Journal
AIChE Monograph Series — American Institute of Chemical Engineers. Monograph Series
AIChE Monogr Ser — AIChE [*American Institute of Chemical Engineers*] Monograph Series
A I Ch E Natl Meet Program Abstr — American Institute of Chemical Engineers. National Meeting. Program Abstracts
AIChE Natl (or Annu) Meet Prepr — AIChE [*American Institute of Chemical Engineers*] National (or Annual) Meeting. Preprints
AIChE Pap — AIChE [*American Institute of Chemical Engineers*] Papers
AIChE Symp Ser — AIChE [*American Institute of Chemical Engineers*] Symposium Series
AIChE Symp Series — American Institute of Chemical Engineers. Symposium Series
AICHE Workshp Ser — AICHE [*American Institute of Chemical Engineers*] Workshop Series
Aichi Cancer Cent Res Inst Annu Rep — Aichi Cancer Center Research Institute. Annual Report
Aichi Gakuin — Aichi-Gakuin Daigaku Shigakkai-Shi
Aichi-Gakuin J Dent Sci — Aichi-Gakuin Journal of Dental Science
Aichi J Exp Med — Aichi Journal of Experimental Medicine
Aichi Univ Educ Res Rep Nat Sci — Aichi University of Education. Research Report. Natural Sciences
AICIA — Archivio Italiano di Chirurgia
AICIAO — Archivio Italiano di Chirurgia
AIC Newsl — AIC [*American Institute of Cooperation*] Newsletter
AICP — Anthropological Index to Current Periodicals in the Library of the Royal Anthropological Institute
AICPA Wash Rep — AICPA [*American Institute of Certified Public Accountants*] Washington Report
AICRA — Advances in Inorganic Chemistry and Radiochemistry
AICS — Anuarul. Institutul de Studii Clasice
AID — Aerospace Information Digest
AID — Australian Industries Development Association. Bulletin
Ai Daig Bung R — Aichi Daigaku Bungaku Ronso
AIDC (Am Ind Development Council) J — AIDC (American Industrial Development Council) Journal
AIDDDH — Analysis and Intervention in Developmental Disabilities
AIdgSp — Anzeiger fuer Indogermanische Sprach- und Altertumskunde
AIDI — Annuaire. Institut de Droit International
AIDP — Advances in Disease Prevention
AIDPA — American Institute of Industrial Engineers. Detroit Chapter. Proceedings of theAnnual Conference
AID Res Dev Abstr — AID [*Agency for International Development*] Research and Development Abstracts
AIDS Anti HIV Agents Ther Vaccines — AIDS. Anti-HIV Agents, Therapies, and Vaccines

AIDS Clin Rev — AIDS Clinical Review
AIDS Educ Prev — AIDS Education and Prevention
AIDS Quart Bibl Per Lit — AIDS [*Acquired Immune Deficiency Syndrome*] Quarterly Bibliography from all Fields of Periodical Literature
AIDS Res — AIDS [*Acquired Immune Deficiency Syndrome*] Research
AIDS Res Hum Retroviruses — AIDS Research and Human Retroviruses
AIDS Res Rev — AIDS Research Reviews
AIDS Res Ther — AIDS [*Acquired Immune Deficiency Syndrome*] Research and Therapy
AIEA — Anales del Instituto de Etnografia Americana
AIEA — Archivos. Instituto de Estudios Africanos
AIEC — Anales. Instituto de Etnografia Americana. Universidad Nacional de Cuyo
AIEC — Anuario. Institut de'Estudios Catalans
AI EDAM — Artificial Intelligence for Engineering Design, Analysis, and Manufacturing
AIEE Proc — American Institute of Electrical Engineers. Proceedings
AIEE Trans — Transactions. American Institute of Electrical Engineers
AIEG — Anales. Instituto de Estudios Gerundenses
AIEM — Anales. Instituto de Estudios Madrilenos
AIEMA — Association Internationale pour l'Etude de la Mosaique Antique. Bulletin d'Information
AIEN — Anales. Instituto Etnico Nacional
AIEO — Annales. Institut d'Etudes Occitanes
AIEO — Annales. Institut d'Etudes Orientales
AIEP — Archivio Internazionale di Etnografia e Preistoria
AIETAX — Annales. Institut Experimental du Tabac de Bergerac
AIF — Annales. Institut Francais de Zagreb
AIF — Anzeiger fuer Indogermanische Sprach- und Altertumskunde
AIFAAF — Anales. Instituto de Farmacologia Espanola
AIFCBM — Annali. Istituto Sperimentale per la Frutticoltura
AIFEA — Archivos. Instituto de Farmacologia Experimental
AIFM Galvanotec Nuove Finiture — AIFM (Associazione Italiana Finiture del Metalli) Galvanotecnica and Nuove Finiture
AIF News — Agricultural, Insecticide, and Fungicide Association. News
A I Fr Zagreb — Annales. Francuski Institut. Zagreb
AIFUA — Annales. Institut Fourier. Universite de Grenoble
AIFZ — Annales. Francuski Institut. Zagreb
AIFZAM — Acta Instituti Forestalis Zvolenensis
AIGC — Annuario. Istituto Giapponese di Cultura in Roma
AIGMA — Anales. Instituto de Geofisica. Universidad Nacional Autonoma de Mexico
AIGPAV — Atti. Istituto Geologico. Universita di Pavia
AIGR — Anuarul. Institutului Geologic al Romaniei
AIH — Aussenhandels-Dienst der Industriekammern und Handelskammern und Wirtschaftsverbande
AIHAA — American Industrial Hygiene Association. Journal
AIHAAP — American Industrial Hygiene Association. Journal
AIHADS — Anales. Instituto Nacional de Investigaciones Agrarias. Serie Higiene y SanidadAnimal
AIHI — Archives Internationales d'Histoire des Idees
AIHM — Archivos Iberoamericanos de Historia de la Medicina
AIHS — Archives Internationales d'Histoire des Sciences
AIHSAB — Archives Internationales d'Histoire des Sciences
AIHT — Archives de l'Institut d'Hessarek Institut Razi (Karaj near Tehran)
AIHTDH — Anais. Instituto de Higiene e Medicina Tropical
AI/I — Interciencia. Asociacion Interciencia
AIIA — Anuarul Institutului de Istorie si Arheologie
AIIAC — Anuarul Institutului de Istorie si Arheologie (Cluj)
AIIAI — Anuarul Institutului de Istorie si Arheologie (Iasi)
AII Ar — Anuarul Institutului de Istorie si Arheologie
AIIBD2 — Anales. Instituto de Investigaciones Marinas de Punta de Betin
AIIC — Anuarul Institutului de Istorie si Arheologie
AIIE — Anales. Instituto de Investigaciones Esteticas
AIIE Ind Engng — American Institute of Industrial Engineers. Industrial Engineering
AIIE Trans — AIIE [*American Institute of Industrial Engineers*] Transactions
AIIE Transactions — American Institute of Industrial Engineers. Transactions
AIIJD — Journal. American Intraocular Implant Society
AIIN — Annali. Istituto Italiano di Numismatica
AIIN — Atti e Memorie. Istituto Italiano di Numismatica
AII Num — Annali. Istituto Italiano di Numismatica
AII Num — Atti e Memorie. Istituto Italiano di Numismatica
AIIS — Aligarh. Institute of Islamic Studies. Bulletin
AIIS — Annali. Istituto Italiano per gli Studi Storici
AIJ — Antike Inschriften aus Jugoslavien
AIJ Man AustAs Life Assur — AIJ [*Australasian Insurance Journal*] Manual of Australasian Life Assurance
AIK — Annaly Instituta Imeni N.P. Kondakova
AIK — Aviacija i Kosmonavtika
AIL — Anales. Instituto de Linguistica. Universidad Nacional de Cuyo
AIL — Australian Industrial Law Review
AILAAB — Archivii Italiani di Laringologia
AILC — Anales. Instituto de Linguistica. Universidad Nacional de Cuyo
AILC — Anales. Instituto de Literaturas Clasicas
A Illus — Arte Illustrata. Rivista d'Arte Antica e Moderna
AILR — Australian Industrial Law Review
AILR — Australian International Law Review
AIM — Aboriginal-Islander-Message
AIM — Abridged Index Medicus
AIM — Abstracts of Instructional Materials in Vocational and Technical Education
AIM — American Inkmaker
AIM — Annali dell'Isturzione Media
AIM — Appraisal Institute. Magazine
AIMAA — Archivio Italiano delle Malattie dell'Apparato Digerente
AIMDAP — Archives of Internal Medicine
AIME — Az Iparmuveszeti Muzeum Evkoenyvei
AIMEA — Annals of Internal Medicine

AIME Proc Annu Miner Symp — American Institute of Mining, Metallurgical, and Petroleum Engineers. Proceedings. Annual Minerals Symposium

AIME Trans — American Institute of Mining, Metallurgical, and Petroleum Engineers. Transactions

AIMHA3 — Annales Immunologiae Hungaricae

AIMJA9 — Ain Shams Medical Journal

AIMK — Akademija Istorii Material'noj Kul'tury

AIMLBG — Annals of Immunology

AIMM Bull — AIMM (Australasian Institute of Mining and Metallurgy) Bulletin

AIMNA — Advances in Internal Medicine

AIMPCT — Annales. Institut Michel Pacha

AIMRAX — Anales. Instituto de Medicina Regional

AIMTA5 — Anais. Instituto de Medicina Tropical

AIM Tech — Association for Integrated Manufacturing Technology [Later, NCS/AIMTECH]

AIN — Atti e Memorie. Istituto Italiano di Numismatica

AIN — Australian and New Zealand Insurance Reporter

AinA — Art in America. An Illustrated Magazine

AINAH — Anales. Instituto Nacional de Antropologia e Historia

AINARP — Arctic Institute of North America. Research Paper

AINCAR — India. Coffee Board. Research Department. Annual Report

AINCBS — Anaesthesia and Intensive Care

AInd — Art Index

AINGA5 — Anales. Instituto Nacional de Investigaciones Agrarias. Serie General

AIN N — AIN [Association of Interpretive Naturalists] News

Ain Shams Med J — Ain Shams Medical Journal

Ain Shams Sci Bull — Ain Shams Science Bulletin

Ain Shams Sci Bull Part A — Ain Shams Science Bulletin. Part A

Ain Shams Univ Fac Agric Bull — Ain Shams University. Faculty of Agriculture. Bulletin

Ain Shams Univ Fac Agric Res Bull — Ain Shams University. Faculty of Agriculture. Research Bulletin

AInst — Annales Institutorum Quae in Urbe Erecta Sunt

A Inst Anat Univ Hels — Acta Instituti Anatomici Universitatis Helsinkiensis

A Inst Anesth — Acta. Institut d'Anesthesiologie

A Inst Chicago Mus Stud — Art Institute of Chicago Museum Studies

A Inst Comp Stud Cult — Annals. Institute of Comparative Studies of Culture

A Inst Et Trav Secur Soc — Annales. Institut d'Etudes du Travail et de la Securite Sociale

A Int — Art International

A Int Criminol — Annales Internationales de Criminologie

AIO — Annales de l'Institut Oceanographique de Monaco

AIOC — All India Oriental Conference. Proceedings and Transactions

AIOK — Akten des Internationalen Orientalisten-Kongresses

AiolikaG — Aiolika Grammata

AION — Annali. Istituto Universitario Orientale (Napoli)

AION-G — Annali. Istituto Universitario Orientale. Sezione Germanica (Napoli)

AION-L — Annali. Istituto Universitario Orientale. Sezione Linguistica (Napoli)

AION Ling — Annali. Istituto Universitario Orientale. Sezione Linguistica

AION-O — Annali. Istituto Universitario Orientale. Sezione Orientale (Napoli)

AION-R — Annali. Istituto Universitario Orientale. Sezione Romanza (Napoli)

AION-S — Annali. Istituto Universitario Orientale. Sezione Slava (Napoli)

AION-SG — Annali. Istituto Universitario Orientale. Sezione Germanica (Napoli)

AION-SL — Annali. Istituto Universitario Orientale. Sezione Linguistica (Napoli)

AION-SO — Annali. Istituto Universitario Orientale. Sezione Orientale (Napoli)

AION-SR — Annali. Istituto Universitario Orientale. Sezione Romanza (Napoli)

AION-SS — Annali. Istituto Universitario Orientale. Sezione Slava (Napoli)

AIOOD3 — Anuario. Instituto de Orientacion y Asistencia Tecnica del Oeste

AIORA — Archivio Italiano di Otologia, Rinologia, e Laringologia

AIOUAlger — Annales. Institut Oriental. Universite d'Alger

AIP — Advances in Psychology

AIP — Aeronautical Information Publication

AIP — Anales de la Instruccion Publica en la Republica de Colombia

AIP — Australian Intellectual Property Cases

AIP — Journal. American Planning Association

AIPAA — Annales. Institut Pasteur

AIPACX — Anales. Instituto Nacional de Investigaciones Agrarias. Serie Produccion Animal

AIPBAY — Archives Internationales de Physiologie et de Biochimie

AIP Conference Proceedings — American Institute of Physics. Conference Proceedings

AIP Conf Proc — AIP [American Institute of Physics] Conference Proceedings

AIP Conf Proc Part Fields Subser — AIP [American Institute of Physics] Conference Proceedings. Particles andFields Subseries

AIPE Facil — AIPE (American Institute of Plant Engineers) Facilities

AIPE Newsl — AIPE [American Institute of Plant Engineers] Newsletter

AIPH — Annales. Institut de Philosophie

A I Ph — Annuaire. Institut de Philologie et d'Histoire Orientales et Slaves

AIPH — Archives. Institut de Paleontologie Humaine

AIPhO — Annuaire. Institut de Philologie et d'Histoire Orientales

A I Ph Or — Annuaire. Institut de Philologie et d'Histoire Orientales et Slaves

AIPhOS — Annuaire. Institut de Philologie et d'Histoire Orientales et Slaves

AIP Inf Progm Newsl — American Institute of Physics. Information Program Newsletter

AIPJA — Journal. American Institute of Planners

AIPLA — Annales. Institut Pasteur de Lille

AIPO — Annuaire. Institut de Philologie et d'Histoire Orientales et Slaves

AIPS — Annuaire. Institut de Philologie et d'Histoire Orientales et Slaves

AIPSCJ — Acta Ichthyologica et Piscatoria

AIPTAK — Archives Internationales de Pharmacodynamie et de Therapie

AIPUA — Archivio Italiano di Patologia e Clinica dei Tumori

AIPUAN — Archivio Italiano di Patologia e Clinica dei Tumori

AIPVAQ — Arquivos. Instituto de Pesquisas Veterinarias "Desiderio Finamor"

AIPVCS — Anales. Instituto Nacional de Investigaciones Agrarias. Serie Produccion Vegetal

AIQ — American Indian Quarterly

AIQSA — Annals of the IQSY

AIR — ADAM [Arts, Drama, Architecture, Music] International Review

AIR — Air et Cosmos. Hebdomadaire de l'Actualite Aerospatiale et des Techniques Avancees

AIR — Air Force Comptroller

AIR — All India Reporter

AIRA — All India Reporter, Allahabad Series

AIR Aj — All India Reporter, Ajmer Series

AIR All — All India Reporter, Allahabad Series

Air Alm — Air Almanac

AIR And — All India Reporter, Andhra Series

AIR Andh — All India Reporter, Andhra Series

AIR Andh Pra — All India Reporter, Andhra Pradesh Series

AIR Arch Interam Rheumatol — AIR. Archives of Interamerican Rheumatology

AIR Asm — All India Reporter, Assam Series

AIR Assam — All India Reporter, Assam Series

Air Assisted Spraying Crop Prot Proc Symp — Air-Assisted Spraying in Crop Protection. Proceedings. Symposium

Air Atmos Chem Air Pollut Semin — Air, Atmospheric Chemistry, and Air Pollution. Seminar

AIRB — All India Reporter, Bombay Series

AIR Bhop — All India Reporter, Bhopal Series

AIR Bilas — All India Reporter, Bilaspur Series

AIR Bom — All India Reporter, Bombay Series

AIRC — All India Reporter, Calcutta Series

AIRCAD — Annales. Institut National de la Recherche Agronomique. Serie C. Annales des Epiphyties

AIR Cal — All India Reporter, Calcutta Series

Air Car Fin Stat — Air Carrier Financial Statistics

Air Carg Mag — Air Cargo Magazine

Airc Engng — Aircraft Engineering

Air CHV — Air Conditioning, Heating, and Ventilating

Air Clas Quart Rev — Air Classics Quarterly Review

Air Classif Solid Wastes — Air Classification of Solid Wastes

Air Clean — Air Cleaning

Air Commerce Bul — Air Commerce Bulletin

Air Cond & Refrig N — Air Conditioning and Refrigeration News

Air Cond Heat & Refrig N — Air Conditioning, Heating, and Refrigeration News

Air Cond Heat & Ven — Air Conditioning, Heating, and Ventilating

Air Cond Heat Refrig News — Air Conditioning, Heating, and Refrigeration News

Air Cond Heat Vent — Air Conditioning, Heating, and Ventilating

Air Cond N — Air Conditioning, Heating, and Refrigeration News

Air Cond Oil Heat — Air Conditioning and Oil Heat

Aircond Refrig Bus — Airconditioning and Refrigeration Business

Air Cos S — Air et Cosmos. Special 1000

Aircraft — Aircraft Engineering

Aircr Eng — Aircraft Engineering

Aircr Missiles — Aircraft and Missiles

Aircr Prod — Aircraft Production

AIRD — Australian Industrial Research Directory

Air D Arty — Air Defense Artillery Magazine

Aird Black — Aird. Blackstone Economised

AIR Dacca — All India Reporter, Dacca Series

AIR East Punjab — All India Reporter, East Punjab Series

AIREEN — AIDS Research

A Ireland — Arts in Ireland

Air Eng — Air Engineering

Air-Espace Tech — Air-Espace Techniques

AIRF — Acta Instituti Romani Finlandiae

AIRFC — All India Reporter, Federal Court Series

Air F Civ Eng — Air Force Civil Engineer

Air F Comp — Air Force Comptroller

Air F J Log — Air Force Journal of Logistics

Air F Mgz — Air Force Magazine

Air Force Civ Eng — Air Force Civil Engineer

Air Force Civil Eng — Air Force Civil Engineer

Air Force Eng Serv Q — Air Force Engineering and Services Quarterly

Air Force Eng Serv Quart — Air Force Engineering and Services Quarterly

Air Force Law R — Air Force Law Review

Air Force Mag — Air Force Magazine

AIR Him Pra — All India Reporter, Himachal Pradesh Series

AIRHP — All India Reporter, Himachal Pradesh Series

AIR Hy — All India Reporter, Hyderabad Series

AIR Hyd — All India Reporter, Hyderabad Series

Air Ind — Air Industriel

AIR Ind Dig — All India Reporter, Indian Digest

Air Int — Air International

AIRJ & K — All India Reporter, Jammu and Kashmir Series

AIR Kerala — All India Reporter, Kerala Series

Air Knife Coat Semin Notes Tech Assoc Pulp Pap Ind — Air Knife Coating. Seminar Notes. Technical Association. Pulp and Paper Industry

AIR Kutch — All India Reporter, Kutch Series

Air L — Air Law

AIR Lahore — All India Reporter, Lahore Series

Air Line Emp — Air Line Employee

Airline Q — Airline Quarterly

Airline Trav Food Serv — Airline and Travel Food Service

Air LR — Air Law Review

Air L Rev — Air Law Review

AIRM — All India Reporter, Madras Series

AIR Mad — All India Reporter, Madras Series

AIR Madh Pra — All India Reporter, Madhya Pradesh Series

AIR Manip — All India Reporter, Manipur Series

AIRMB — All India Reporter, Madhya Bharat Series

AIRMP — All India Reporter, Madhya Pradesh Series
AIR My — All India Reporter, Mysore Series
AIRN — All India Reporter, Nagpur Series
AIR Nag — All India Reporter, Nagpur Series
AIR Oris — All India Reporter, Orissa Series
AIR Oudh — All India Reporter, Oudh Series
AIRP — All India Reporter, Patna Series
Air Pap Symp — Air. Papers Based on Symposia
AIR Pat — All India Reporter, Patna Series
AIRPC — All India Reporter, Privy Council
AIR PEP — All India Reporter, Patiala and East Punjab States Union Series
AIR PEPSU — All India Reporter, Patiala and East Punjab States Union Series
AIR Pesh — All India Reporter, Peshawar Series
AirPolAb — Air Pollution Abstracts
Air Poll Cont Assn J — Air Pollution Control Association. Journal
Air Poll Control Assn J — Air Pollution Control Association. Journal
Air Pollut — Air Pollution
Air Pollut Assoc J — Air Pollution Control Association. Journal
Air Pollut Cancer Man Proc Hanover Int Carcinog Meet — Air Pollution and Cancer in Man. Proceedings of the Hanover International Carcinogenesis Meeting
Air Pollut Control — Air Pollution Control
Air Pollut Control Assoc Annu Meet Pap — Air Pollution Control Association. Annual Meeting. Papers
Air Pollut Control Conf — Air Pollution Control Conference
Air Pollut Control Des Handb — Air Pollution Control and Design Handbook
Air Pollut Control Dist Cty Los Angeles Annu Rep — Air Pollution Control District. County of Los Angeles. Annual Report
Air Pollut Control Ind Energy Prod — Air Pollution Control and Industrial Energy Production
Air Pollut Control Off US Publ AP Ser — Air Pollution Control Office. Publication. AP Series
Air Pollut Control Transp Engines Symp — Air Pollution Control in Transport Engines. Symposium
Air Pollut Ecosyst Proc Int Symp — Air Pollution and Ecosystems. Proceedings. International Symposium
Air Pollut Eff Plant Growth Symp — Air Pollution Effects on Plant Growth. Symposium
Air Pollut Found Rep — Air Pollution Foundation. Report
Air Pollut Model Its Appl — Air Pollution Modeling and Its Application
Air Pollut News — Air Pollution News
Air Pollut Proc Eur Congr — Air Pollution. Proceedings. European Congress on the Influence of Air Pollutionon Plants and Animals
Air Pollut Symp Low Pollut Power Syst Dev — Air Pollution Symposium on Low Pollution Power Systems Development
Air Pollut Tech Rep — Air Pollution Technical Report
Air Pollut Titles — Air Pollution Titles
Airport Adv — Airport Advisory
Airports Int — Airports International
Air Prog Aviat Rev — Air Progress Aviation Rev
AIR Pun — All India Reporter, Punjab Series
Air Qual Cont Dig — Air Quality Control Digest
Air Qual Control Print Ind — Air Quality Control in the Printing Industry
Air Qual Environ Factors — Air Quality and Environmental Factors
Air Qual Instrum — Air Quality Instrumentation
Air Qual Minn — Air Quality in Minnestoa
Air Qual Monogr — Air Quality Monographs
Air Qual Smoke Urban For Fires Proc Int Symp — Air Quality and Smoke from Urban and Forest Fires. Proceedings of the International Symposium
AIRR — Air Reservist
AIRR — All India Reporter, Rajasthan Series
AIR Raj — All India Reporter, Rajasthan Series
Air Reserv — Air Reservist
AIRS — Accident/Incident Reporting System
AIRS — Aerometric Information Retrieval System
Air Saf J — Air Safety Journal
Air Saf Law Technol — Air Safety Law and Technology
Air Sampling Instrum Eval Atmos Contam — Air Sampling Instruments for Evaluation of Atmospheric Contaminants
AIR Sau — All India Reporter, Saurashtra Series
AIRSC — All India Reporter, Supreme Court
AIRSEV — Association for International Cancer Research. Symposia
AIR Simla — All India Reporter, Simla Series
AIR Sind — All India Reporter, Sind Series
AIRTC — All India Reporter, Travancore-Cochin Series
Air Trans Interch — Air Transport Interchange
Air Transp World — Air Transport World
Air Trans W — Air Transport World
AIR Trip — All India Reporter, Tripura Series
Air Univ Libr Index Mil Period — Air University. Library. Index to Military Periodicals
Air Univ R — Air University. Review
Air Univ Rev — Air University. Review
AirUnLibl — Air University. Library. Index to Military Periodicals
Air Un Rev — Air University. Review
AIRVP — All India Reporter, Vindhya Pradesh Series
Air Waste Manage Assoc Annu Meet Proc — Air and Waste Management Association. Annual Meeting. Proceedings
Air/Water Poll Rept — Air/Water Pollution Report
Air Water Pollut — Air and Water Pollution
AISA — Anais. Instituto Superior de Agronomia
AISC — Anuarul Institutului de Studii Classice
AISD — Annali. Istituto di Studi Danteschi
AISFAR — Archivio Italiano di Scienze Farmacologiche
AISHWC — Australian Industrial Safety, Health, and Welfare Cases

AISIN — Alon. Internal Quarterly of the Israel Numismatic Society
AISI Rpt — American Iron and Steel Institute. Annual Statistical Report
AISI Steel Prod Man — American Iron and Steel Institute. Steel Products Manual
AISJB — Journal. American Society for Information Science
A Islam — Ars Islamica
AISLN — Annali. Istituto Superiore di Scienze e Lettere di Santa Chiera (Napoli)
AISMAE — Archivio Italiano di Scienze Mediche Tropicali e di Parassitologia
AISMC — Archivio Italiano di Scienze Mediche Coloniali
AISNC — ASIS [*American Society for Information Science*] Newsletter
AISOBL — Anwendung von Isotopen in der Organischen Chemie und Biochemie
AISP — Annales. Institut Superieur de Philosophie
AISSAW — Annali. Istituto Superiore di Sanita
A I St Cl — Anuarul Institutului de Studii Classice (Cluj)
AISTD4 — Annali. Istituto Sperimentale per il Tabacco
AIS Technical Soc Bul — AIS [*Australian Iron and Steel*] Technical Society. Bulletin
AISZAJ — Annali. Istituto Sperimentale per la Zootecnia
AIT — Adventures in Travel
AIT — AIT. Architektur Innenarchitektur Technischer Ausbau
AITADK — Anales. Instituto Nacional de Investigaciones Agrarias. Serie Tecnologia Agraria
A Italia — Arte in Italia. Rivista Mensile di Belle Arti
AITBA — Annales. Institut Technique du Batiment et des Travaux Publics
A It Dec & Indust — Arte Italiana Decorativa e Industriale
AITEA — Archivum Immunologiae et Therapiae Experimentalis
AITG — Australian Income Tax Guide
AITI — Artikkel-Indeks Tidsskrifter
AITL & P — Australian Income Tax Law and Practice
AITR — Australian and New Zealand Income Tax Reports
AITR — Australian Income Tax Reports
AIUNAR — Archivio Italiano di Urologia e Nefrologia
AIUN SR — Annali. Istituto Universitario. Napoli. Sezione Romanza
AIUO — Annali. Istituto Universitario Orientale. Sezione Germanica
AI(U)ON — Annali. Istituto Universitario Orientale (Napoli)
AIV — Atti. Reale Istituto Veneto di Scienze, Lettere, ed Arti. Classe di ScienzeMorali e Lettere
AIVLAQ — Atti. Istituto Veneto di Scienze, Lettere, ed Arti. Classe di Scienze Matematiche e Naturali
AIVMAT — Anales. Instituto de Investigaciones Veterinarias
AIVMB — Archivos de Investigacion Medica
AIVMBU — Archivos de Investigacion Medica
AIVNDZ — Atti. Istituto Veneto di Scienze, Lettere, ed Arti. Classe di ScienzeFisiche, Matematiche, e Naturali
AIVP — Anais. Instituto do Vinho do Porto
AIVSML — Atti. Reale Istituto Veneto di Scienze, Lettere, ed Arti. Classe di ScienzeMorali e Lettere
AIWHAJ — Animals
AIWR — Arctic International Wildlife Range Society. Newsletter
Aix Mm — Memoires de l'Academie des Sciences, Agriculture, Arts, et Belles-Lettres. Aix
Aix Mm Ac — Memoires de l'Academie des Sciences, Agriculture, Arts, et Belles-Lettres. Aix
AIYS News — American Institute for Yemen Studies Newsletter
AIZ — Arkheologicheskie Izviestiia i Zametki. Moskovskoe Arkheologicheskoe Obshchestvo
AIZAAD — Annali. Istituto Sperimentale per la Zoologia Agraria
AIZLA — Archiwum Inzynierii Ladowej
AIZUN — Annuario dell'Istituto e Museo di Zoologia. Universita di Napoli
AJ — Acta Juridica
AJ — Actualite Juridique
Aj — Ajatus (Helsingfors)
AJ — Alaska Journal of Commerce and Pacific Rim Reporter
AJ — Alkmaars Jaarboekje
AJ — Alliance Journal
Aj — All India Reporter, Ajmer Series
AJ — American Journal of Philology
AJ — Antilliaans Juristenblad
AJ — Antiquaries Journal
AJ — Archaeological Journal
AJ — Architects' Journal
AJ — Art Journal
AJ — Asiatisches Jahrbuch
AJ — Australian Journal
AJ — Australian Journalist
AJA — American Jewish Archives
AJA — American Journal of Agricultural Economics
AJA — American Journal of Archaeology
AJA — Anglo-Jewish Archives
AJADD — Australian Journal of Alcoholism and Drug Dependence
AJAE — American Journal of Agricultural Economics
AJAEB — American Journal of Agricultural Economics
AJAFAC — Agricultural Journal. Department of Agriculture. Fiji Islands
A Jamaica — Arts Jamaica
AJANA — American Journal of Anatomy
AJANA2 — American Journal of Anatomy
AJAPB9 — American Journal of Acupuncture
AJAR — Alexandria Journal of Agricultural Research
AJAr — American Journal of Archaeology
A J Arch — American Journal of Archaeology
AJ Archaeol — American Journal of Archaeology
AJAS — AJAS: Australasian Journal of American Studies
AJAS — Australian Journal of Applied Science
AJATA — American Journal of Art Therapy
AJB — American Journal of Botany
AJB — Antilliaans Juristenblad

AJB — Australian Journal of Botany
AJBA — Australian Journal of Biblical Archaeology
AJBI — Annual. Japanese Biblical Institute
AJBJAT — Arquivos. Jardim Botanico do Rio De Janeiro
AJBOA — American Journal of Botany
AJBOAA — American Journal of Botany
AJBTA — Australian Journal of Botany
AJCBDD — American Journal of Clinical Biofeedback
AJC/C — Commentary. American Jewish Committee
AJCDA — American Journal of Cardiology
AJCDAG — American Journal of Cardiology
AJCHAS — Australian Journal of Chemistry
AJCHDV — Australian Journal of Clinical and Experimental Hypnosis
AJCIDY — African Journal of Clinical and Experimental Immunology
AJCL — American Journal of Comparative Law
AJCMBA — American Journal of Chinese Medicine
AJCNA — American Journal of Clinical Nutrition
AJCNAC — American Journal of Clinical Nutrition
AJCOD — American Journal of Clinical Oncology
AJCODI — American Journal of Clinical Oncology
AJCP — Australian Joint Copying Project
AJCPA — American Journal of Clinical Pathology
AJCPAI — American Journal of Clinical Pathology
AJCPD — American Journal of Physiology. Cell Physiology
AJCS — Australian Journal of Cultural Studies
AJDA — Actualite Juridique. Droit Administratif. Revue Mensuelle
AJDA — American Journal of Alcohol and Drug Abuse
AJDABD — American Journal of Drug and Alcohol Abuse
AJDC — American Journal of Diseases of Children
AJDCA — American Journal of Diseases of Children
AJDCAI — American Journal of Diseases of Children
AJDDA — American Journal of Digestive Diseases [Later, Digestive Diseases and Sciences]
AJDDAL — American Journal of Digestive Diseases [Later, Digestive Diseases and Sciences]
AJDEBP — Australasian Journal of Dermatology
AJDKA8 — Azabu Juika Daigaku Kenkyu Hokoku
AJDTAZ — Australian Journal of Dairy Technology
AJE — American Journal of Economics and Sociology
AJE — American Journal of Education
AJE — Australian Journal of Education
AJEA — Australian Journal of Experimental Agriculture
AJEAEL — Australian Journal of Experimental Agriculture
AJEBAK — Australian Journal of Experimental Biology and Medical Science
AJECDQ — Australian Journal of Ecology
AJEED — Abstract Journal in Earthquake Engineering
AJEPA — American Journal of Epidemiology
AJEPAS — American Journal of Epidemiology
AJER — Alberta Journal of Educational Research
AJES — Aligarh Journal of English Studies
AJES — American Journal of Economics and Sociology
AJESA — American Journal of Economics and Sociology
AJETA6 — American Journal of EEG Technology
AJEV — American Journal of Enology and Viticulture
AJEVAC — American Journal of Enology and Viticulture
AJFE — Alternatives. Journal of the Friends of the Earth
AJFL — Australian Journal of Family Law
AJFS — Australian Journal of Forensic Sciences
AJFS — Australian Journal of French Studies
AJGAA — American Journal of Gastroenterology
AJGAAR — American Journal of Gastroenterology
AJGV — Akademischer Verein fuer Juedische Geschichte und Literatur
AJH — American Jewish History
AJHE — Australian Journal of Higher Education
AJHEA — American Journal of Public Health
AJHEAA — American Journal of Public Health
AJHED — American Journal of Hematology
AJHEDD — American Journal of Hematology
AJHG — American Journal of Human Genetics
AJHGA — American Journal of Human Genetics
AJHGAG — American Journal of Human Genetics
AJHNA3 — American Journal of Clinical Hypnosis
AJHPA — American Journal of Hospital Pharmacy
AJHPA9 — American Journal of Hospital Pharmacy
AJHPER — Australian Journal for Health, Physical Education, and Recreation
AJHQ — American Jewish Historical Quarterly
AJHS — American Jewish Historical Society. Publications
AJHS J — Australian Jewish Historical Society. Journal
AJHYA2 — American Journal of Hygiene
Ajia Keizai — Ajia Keizai. Journal of the Institute of Developing Economics
AJICDC — American Journal of Infection Control
AJIL — American Journal of International Law
A J I Law — American Journal of International Law
AJIMD8 — American Journal of Industrial Medicine
AJINB — American Journal of International Law
AJJ — American Chamber of Commerce in Japan. Journal
AJJR — Annales. Societe Jean-Jacques Rousseau
AJKDD — American Journal of Kidney Diseases
AJKSAX — Archiv der Julius Klaus-Stiftung fuer Vererbungsforschung, Sozialanthropologie,und Rassenhygiene
AJL — Australian Journal of Linguistics
AJLH — American Journal of Legal History
AJLMDN — American Journal of Law and Medicine
A J [London] — Art Journal [London]
AJLS — Australian Journal of Law and Society

AJM — Archivo Jose Marti
AJM — Australian Journal of Management
AJM — Australian Journal of Mining
AJMAA — American Journal of Mathematics
AJMD — American Journal of Mental Deficiency
AJMDA — American Journal of Mental Deficiency
AJMDAW — American Journal of Mental Deficiency
AJME — Australian Journal of Music Education
AJMEA — American Journal of Medicine
AJMEA — Australian Journal of Music Education
AJMEAZ — American Journal of Medicine
AJMFA — Australian Journal of Marine and Freshwater Research
AJMFA4 — Australian Journal of Marine and Freshwater Research
AJMGDA — American Journal of Medical Genetics
AJMMAP — Asian Journal of Modern Medicine
AJMNA — Australian Journal of Mental Retardation
AJMSA — American Journal of the Medical Sciences
AJMSA9 — American Journal of the Medical Sciences
AJMSDC — African Journal of Medicine and Medical Sciences
AJMTA — American Journal of Medical Technology
AJMTAC — American Journal of Medical Technology
AJN — American Journal of Numismatics
AJN — American Journal of Nursing
AJN — Australian Jewish News
AJNAD — Arab Journal of Nuclear Sciences and Applications
AJNED9 — American Journal of Nephrology
A J [New York] — Art Journal [New York]
AJNOD5 — Ajia Nogyo
AJNR — AJNR. American Journal of Neuroradiology
AJNR — American Journal of Neuroradiology
AJNR Am J Neuroradiol — AJNR. American Journal of Neuroradiology
AJNT — Ajurnarmat. Inuit Cultural Institute
AJNUA — American Journal of Nursing
AJNum — American Journal of Numismatics
AJOAAX — American Journal of Optometry and Archives of American Academy of Optometry [Later, American Journal of Optometry and Physiological Optics]
AJOEDE — African Journal of Ecology
AJOGA — American Journal of Obstetrics and Gynecology
AJOGAH — American Journal of Obstetrics and Gynecology
AJOHA — American Journal of Orthodontics
AJOHAK — American Journal of Orthodontics
AJOHBL — Australian Journal of Ophthalmology
AJOHN — Australian Journal of Holistic Nursing
AJOMA — Alabama Journal of Medical Sciences
AJOMAZ — Alabama Journal of Medical Sciences
AJOOA7 — American Journal of Orthodontics and Oral Surgery [Later, American Journal of Orthodontics]
AJOPA — American Journal of Ophthalmology
AJOPAA — American Journal of Ophthalmology
AJOPs — American Journal of Orthopsychiatry
AJORA — American Journal of Orthopsychiatry
AJORAG — American Journal of Orthopsychiatry
AJOT — American Journal of Occupational Therapy
AJOTA — American Journal of Occupational Therapy
AJOTAM — American Journal of Occupational Therapy
AJOTBN — American Journal of Otology
Ajour Ind-Tek — Ajour Industriel-Teknikk
AJOYA — American Journal of Optometry
AJP — American Journal of Pharmacy
AJP — American Journal of Philology
AJP — American Journal of Psychoanalysis
AJP — Annales des Justices de Paix
AJP — Australian Journal of Pharmacy
AJP — Australian Journal of Psychology
AJPA — American Journal of Physical Anthropology
AJPA — Australian Journal of Public Administration
AJPAA — American Journal of Pathology
AJPAA4 — American Journal of Pathology
AJPBA — American Journal of Physical Medicine
AJPBA7 — American Journal of Physical Medicine
AJPCA — American Journal of Psychology
AJPCAA — American Journal of Psychology
AJPDA — American Journal of Pharmaceutical Education
AJPDAD — American Journal of Pharmaceutical Education
AJPEA — American Journal of Public Health and the Nation's Health [Later, American Journal of Public Health]
AJPED — American Journal of Physiology. Endocrinology, Metabolism, and GastrointestinalPhysiology
AJPEEK — American Journal of Perinatology
AJPh — American Journal of Philology
AJPh — American Journal of Philosophy
AJPH — American Journal of Public Health
AJPH — Australian Journal of Politics and History
AJPHA — American Journal of Physiology
AJPHAP — American Journal of Physiology
AJPhil — American Journal of Philology
AJPIA — American Journal of Physics
AJPMEA — American Journal of Preventive Medicine
AJPNA — American Journal of Physical Anthropology
AJPNA9 — American Journal of Physical Anthropology
AJPOA — American Journal of Proctology [Later, American Journal of Proctology, Gastroenterology, and Colon and Rectal Surgery]
AJPOAC — American Journal of Proctology [Later, American Journal of Proctology, Gastroenterology, and Colon and Rectal Surgery]
AJ Pol & Hist — Australian Journal of Politics and History

AJPP — Australasian Journal of Psychology and Philosophy
AJPPCH — Australian Journal of Plant Physiology
AJPPD — American Journal of Physiology. Heart and Circulatory Physiology
AJPRA — American Journal of Pharmacy and the Sciences Supporting Public Health [Later,American Journal of Pharmacy]
AJPRAL — American Journal of Pharmacy and the Sciences Supporting Public Health [Later,American Journal of Pharmacy]
AJPs — American Journal of Psychology
AJPSA — American Journal of Psychiatry
AJPSAO — American Journal of Psychiatry
AJPSBP — Australian Journal of Pharmaceutical Sciences
AJPst — American Journal of Psychotherapy
AJPsy — American Journal of Psychiatry
A J Psy — American Journal of Psychology
AJPsych — American Journal of Psychology
AJ Psychol — American Journal of Psychology
AJPTAR — American Journal of Psychotherapy
AJPTDU — American Journal of Primatology
AJPU — American Journal of Psychiatry (Utica, New York)
AJPXA — Australasian Journal of Pharmacy. Science Supplement
AJPXA5 — Australasian Journal of Pharmacy. Science Supplement
AJPYA8 — American Journal of Psychoanalysis
AJQ — Australian Jazz Quarterly
AJR — AJR. American Journal of Roentgenology
AJR — Australian Journal of Reading
AJR — Australian Jurist Reports
A (Jr A) — Arizoniana (Journal of Arizona History)
AJR Am J Roentgenol — AJR. American Journal of Roentgenology
AJRFD — American Journal of Physiology. Renal, Fluid, and Electrolyte Physiology
AJRI — American Journal of Reproductive Immunology
AJRI Am J Reprod Immunol — AJRI. American Journal of Reproductive Immunology
AJRIM Am J Reprod Immunol Microbiol — AJRIM. American Journal of Reproductive Immunology and Microbiology
AJRMEK — AJRIM. American Journal of Reproductive Immunology and Microbiology
AJR (NC) — Australian Jurist Reports (Notes of Cases)
AJROA — American Journal of Roentgenology
AJROAM — AJR. American Journal of Roentgenology
AJRRA — American Journal of Roentgenology, Radium Therapy, and Nuclear Medicine [Later, American Journal of Roentgenology]
AJRRAV — American Journal of Roentgenology, Radium Therapy, and Nuclear Medicine [Later, American Journal of Roentgenology]
AJRTA — American Journal of Roentgenology and Radium Therapy [Later, American Journal of Roentgenology]
AJS — Actes Juridiques Susiens
AJS — American Journal of Science
AJS — American Journal of Semiotics
AJS — American Journal of Sociology
AJSBD — American Journal of Small Business
AJSC — American Journal of Sociology (Chicago)
AJSCA — American Journal of Science
AJSCAP — American Journal of Science
AJSci — American Journal of Science
AJSemL — American Journal of Semitic Languages and Literatures
AJSI — Australian Journal of Social Issues
AJSIA9 — Australian Journal of Science
AJSL — American Journal of Semitic Languages and Literatures
AJSLL — American Journal of Semitic Languages and Literatures
AJSMD — American Journal of Sports Medicine
AJSN — Association for Jewish Studies. Newsletter
AJSOA — American Journal of Sociology
AJ Soc — American Journal of Sociology
AJ Soc Iss — Australian Journal of Social Issues
AJSPDX — American Journal of Surgical Pathology
AJSR — Australian Journal of Scientific Research
AJSUA — American Journal of Surgery
AJSUAB — American Journal of Surgery
AJSW — Australian Journal of Social Work
AJT — American Journal of Theology
AJTh — American Journal of Theology
AJTHA — American Journal of Tropical Medicine and Hygiene
AJTHAB — American Journal of Tropical Medicine and Hygiene
AJTHBC — African Journal of Tropical Hydrobiology and Fisheries
AJTMH — American Journal of Tropical Medicine and Hygiene
AJTRDA — American Journal of Therapeutics and Clinical Reports
AJTSBB — African Journal of Tropical Hydrobiology and Fisheries. Special Issue
AJu — Archives Juives
A Jug — Archaeologia Jugoslavica
A Jur Rep — Australian Jurist Reports
AJUS — Antarctic Journal of the United States
AJVR — American Journal of Veterinary Research
AJVRA — American Journal of Veterinary Research
AJVRAH — American Journal of Veterinary Research
AJY — American Jewish Yearbook
AJYB — American Jewish Yearbook
AJZOA — Australian Journal of Zoology
AJZOAS — Australian Journal of Zoology
AJZSA6 — Australian Journal of Zoology. Supplementary Title Series
AK — Alaska Music Educator
AK — Al-Kitab
AK — Antike Kunst
AK — Archaeologiai Koezlemenyek
AK — Archiv fuer Kulturgeschichte
AK — Archiv fuer Orientforschung

AK — Arkheologiia
AK — Arkheologiia/Archeologie (Kiev)
AK — Ateneum Kaplanskie
AKABA7 — Arkansas. Agricultural Experiment Station. Bulletin
Akad — Akademos. Revue Mensuelle d'Art Libre et de Critique
Akad Alm — Magyar Tudomanyos Akademia Almanachja
Akad Arkhit — Akademiya Arkhitektury
Akad d Wiss Denksch Philos-Hist Kl — Akademie der Wissenschaften in Wien. Philosophisch-Historische Klasse. Denkschriften
Akad d Wissenschaften in Wien — Akademie der Wissenschaften in Wien
Akad d Wiss Sitzungsb Philos-Hist Kl — Akademie der Wissenschaften in Wien. Philosophisch-Historische Klasse. Sitzungsberichte
Akad Ekon im Oskara Langego Wroclawiu Pr Nauk — Akademia Ekonomiczna imienia Oskara Langego we Wroclawiu. Prace Naukowe
Akad Ekon Poznaniu Zesz Nauk — Akademia Ekonomiczna w Poznaniu Zeszyty Naukowe
Akad Ekon Poznaniu Zesz Nauk Ser 2 — Akademia Ekonomiczna w Poznaniu Zeszyty Naukowe. Seria 2. Prace Habilitacyjne iDoktorskie
Akad Gorniczo-Hutnicza St Staszica Krakow Zesz Nauk Geol — Akademia Gorniczo-Hutnicza Imienia Stanislawa Staszica w Krakowie Zeszyty Naukowe Geologia
Akad Izv — Akademiceskija Izvestija
Akad Landwirtschaftswiss DDR Tagungsber — Akademie der Landwirtschaftswissenschaften der Deutschen Demokratischen Republik. Tagungsbericht
Akad Landwirtschaftswiss Tagungsber — Akademie der Landwirtschaftswissenschaften. Tagungsbericht
Akad Mbll — Akademische Monatsblaetter
Akad Med im Juliana Marchlewskiego Bialymstoku Rocz — Akademia Medyczna imeni Juliana Marchlewskiego w Bialymstoku. Roczniki
Akad Nauka i Umjet Bosne i Hercegov Rad Odjelj Tehn Nauka — Akademija Nauka i Umjetnosti Bosne i Hercegovine. Radovi Odjeljenje Tehnickih Nauka
Akad Nauk Arm Dokl — Akademiya Nauk Armenii. Doklady
Akad Nauk Armenii Dokl — Akademiya Nauk Armenii. Doklady
Akad Nauk Armjan SSR Dokl — Akademija Nauk Armjanskoi SSR. Doklady
Akad Nauk Arm SSR Dokl — Akademiya Nauk Armyanskoy SSR. Doklady
Akad Nauk Armyan SSR Izv Ser Mat — Akademiya Nauk Armyanskoi SSR. Izvestiya. Seriya Matematika
Akad Nauk Armyan SSR Izv Ser Mek — Akademiya Nauk Armyanskoi SSR. Izvestiya. Seriya Mekhanika
Akad Nauka Umjet Bosne Hercegov Rad Odjelj Prirod Mat Nauka — Akademija Nauka i Umjetnosti Bosne i Hercegovine. Radovi Odjeljenje Prirodnih iMatematickih Nauka
Akad Nauka Umjet Bosne Hercegov Rad Odjelj Tehn Nauka — Akademija Nauka i Umjetnosti Bosne i Hercegovine. Radovi Odjeljenje Tehnickih Nauka
Akad Nauk Azerbaidzan SSR Dokl — Akademija Nauk Azerbaidzanskoi SSR. Doklady
Akad Nauk Azerb SSR Dokl — Akademiya Nauk Azerbaydzhanskoy SSR. Doklady
Akad Nauk Azerb SSR Izv Ser Nauk Zemle — Akademiya Nauk Azerbaydzhanskoy SSR. Izvestiya. Seriya Nauk o Zemle
Akad Nauk Belarus SSR Dok — Akademiya Nauk Belarusskoi SSR. Doklady
Akad Nauk BSSR Dokl — Akademiya Nauk BSSR. Doklady
Akad Nauk Gruzin SSR Trudy Tbiliss Mat Inst Razmadze — Akademija Nauk Gruzinskoi SSR. Trudy Tbilisskogo Matematiceskogo Instituta Imeni A. M. Razmadze
Akad Nauk Gruz Izv Ser Biol — Akademiya Nauk Gruzii. Izvestiya. Seriya Biologicheskaya
Akad Nauk Gruz Izv Ser Khim — Akademiya Nauk Gruzii. Izvestiya. Seriya Khimicheskaya
Akad Nauk Gruz Soobshch — Akademiya Nauk Gruzii. Soobshcheniya
Akad Nauk Gruz SSR Geol Inst Tr — Akademiya Nauk Gruzinskoy SSR. Geologicheskiy Institut. Trudy
Akad Nauk Gruz SSR Inst Geofiz Tr — Akademiya Nauk Gruzinskoi SSR. Institut Geofiziki. Trudy
Akad Nauk Gruz SSR Inst Neorg Khim Elektrokhim Sb — Akademiya Nauk Gruzinskoy SSR. Institut Neorganicheskoi Khimii i Elektrokhimii Sbornik
Akad Nauk Gruz SSR Soobshch — Akademiya Nauk Gruzinskoy SSR. Soobshcheniya
Akad Nauk Kazah SSR Trudy Astrofiz Inst — Akademija Nauk Kazahskoi SSR. Trudy Astrofiziceskogo Instituta
Akad Nauk Kazah SSR Trudy Inst Mat i Meh — Akademija Nauk Kazahskoi SSR. Trudy Instituta Matematiki i Mehaniki
Akad Nauk Kazakh SSR Trudy Astrofiz Inst — Akademiya Nauk Kazakhskoy SSR. Trudy Astrofizicheskogo Instituta
Akad Nauk Kazak SSR Izv Ser Fiz Mat — Akademiya Nauk Kazakhskoi SSR. Izvestiya. Seriya Fiziko-Matematicheskaya
Akad Nauk Kaz SSR Inst Geol Nauk Tr — Akademiya Nauk Kazakhskikh Nauk. Institut Geologicheskikh Nauk. Trudy
Akad Nauk Kaz SSR Izv Ser Geol — Akademiya Nauk Kazakhskoy SSR. Izvestiya. Seriya Geologicheskaya
Akad Nauk Latvi SSR Izv Ser Khim — Akademiya Nauk Latviskoi SSR. Izvestiya. Seriya Khimicheskaya
Akad Nauk Respub Kazakhstan Trudy Astrofiz Inst — Akademiya Nauk Respubliki Kazakhstan. Trudy Astrofizicheskogo Instituta
Akad Nauk SSSR Dokl — Akademiya Nauk SSSR. Doklady
Akad Nauk SSSR Doklady Izvestiia Ser Geol — Akademiia Nauk SSSR. Doklady. Izvestiia. Seriia Geologicheskaia
Akad Nauk SSSR Geol Inst Tr — Akademiya Nauk SSSR. Geologicheskiy Institut. Trudy
Akad Nauk SSSR Geol Inst Trudy — Akademiya Nauk SSSR. Geologicheskiy Institut. Trudy
Akad Nauk SSSR Geomorfol Kom Plenum Mater — Akademiya Nauk SSSR. Geomorfologicheskaya Komissiya. Plenum. Materialy
Akad Nauk SSSR Inst Nefti Trud — Akademia Nauk SSSR Institut Nefti Trudy

Akad Nauk SSSR Inst Prikl Mat Preprint — Akademiya Nauk SSSR. Institut Prikladnoi Matematiki. Preprint

Akad Nauk SSSR Izv Ser Fiz — Akademiya Nauk SSSR. Izvestiya. Seriya Fizicheskaya

Akad Nauk SSSR Izv Ser Geogr — Akademiya Nauk SSSR. Izvestiya. Seriya Geograficheskaya

Akad Nauk SSSR Izv Ser Geol — Akademiya Nauk SSSR. Izvestiya. Seriya Geologicheskaya

Akad Nauk SSSR Komi Fil Inst Geol Tr — Akademiya Nauk SSSR. Komi Filial. Institut Geologii. Trudy

Akad Nauk SSSR Kom Izuch Chetvertich Perioda Byull — Akademiya Nauk SSSR. Komissiya po Izucheniyu Chetvertichnogo Perioda. Byulleten

Akad Nauk SSSR Kom Opred Absol Vozrasta Geol Form Tr — Akademiya Nauk SSSR. Kommissiya po Opredeleniyu Absolyutnogo Vozrasta Geologicheskikh Formatsiy. Trudy

Akad Nauk SSSR Metallofizka — Akademiya Nauk SSSR. Metallofizika

Akad Nauk SSSR Mezhduvedomstv Geofiz Kom Geofiz Byull — Akademiya Nauk SSSR Mezhduvedomstvennoyy Geofizicheskiy Komitet pri Presidiume Geofizicheskiy Byulleten

Akad Nauk SSSR Okeanogr Kom Tr — Akademiya Nauk SSSR. Okeanograficheskaya Kommissiya. Trudy

Akad Nauk SSSR Otdel Drevnerus Lit Trudy — Akademiya Nauk SSSR. Otdel Drevnerusskoy Literatury. Trudy

Akad Nauk SSSR Paleontol Inst Tr — Akademiya Nauk SSSR. Paleontologicheskiy Institut Trudy

Akad Nauk SSSR Sibirsk Otdel Vychisl Tsentr Preprint — Akademiya Nauk SSSR. Sibirskoe Otdelenie. Vychislitelnyi Tsentr. Preprint

Akad Nauk SSSR Sibirsk Otdel Vycisl Centr Preprint — Akademija Nauk SSSR. Sibirskoe Otdelenie. Vycislitelnyi Centr. Preprint

Akad Nauk SSSR Sib Otd Inst Geol Geofiz Tr — Akademiya Nauk SSSR. Sibirskoe Otdelenie. Institut Geologii i Geofiziki. Trudy

Akad Nauk SSSR Sib Otd Limnol Inst Tr — Akademiya Nauk SSSR. Sibirskoe Otdelenie. Limnologicheskiy Institut. Trudy Novosibirsk

Akad Nauk SSSR Trudy Jakutsk Filial Ser Fiz — Akademija Nauk SSSR. Trudy Jakutskogo Filiala. Serija Fiziceskaja

Akad Nauk SSSR Ural Fil Tr Inst Khim — Akademiya Nauk SSSR. Ural'skii Filial. Trudy Instituta Khimii

Akad Nauk SSSR Ural Nauchn Tsentr Inst Geol Geokhim Tr — Akademiya Nauk SSSR. Ural'skiy Nauchnyi Tsentr. Institut Geologii i Geokhimii. Trudy

Akad Nauk SSSR Vestn — Akademiya Nauk SSSR. Vestnik

Akad Nauk Tadzh SSR Dokl — Akademiya Nauk Tadzhikskoy SSR. Doklady

Akad Nauk Tadzh SSR Otd Fiz-Mat Geol-Khim Nauk Izv — Akademiya Nauk Tadzhikskoy SSR. Otdeleniye Fiziko-Matematicheskikh i Geologo-Khimicheskikh Nauk. Izvestiya

Akad Nauk Turkm SSR Izv Ser Fiz-Tekh Khim Geol Nauk — Akademiya Nauk Turkmenskoy SSR. Izvestiya. Seriya Fiziko-Tekhnicheskikh. Khimicheskikh i Geologicheskikh Nauk

Akad Nauk Ukrain SSR Inst Mat Preprint — Akademiya Nauk Ukrainskoi SSR. Institut Matematiki. Preprint

Akad Nauk Ukr RSR Dopov Ser B — Akademiya Nauk Ukrainskoy RSR. Dopovidi. Seriya B. Geologiya, Geofizika, Khimiya, ta Biologiya

Akad Nauk Ukr RSR Inst Teploenerg Zb Pr — Akademia Nauk Ukrainskoi RSR. Institut Teploenergetiki. Zbirnik Prats

Akad Nauk Ukr SSR Metallofiz — Akademiya Nauk Ukrainskoi SSR. Metallofizika

Akad Nauk Ukr SSR Ser Metallofiz — Akademiya Nauk Ukrainskoi SSR. Seriya Metallofizika

Akad Roln Szczecinie Rozpr — Akademia Rolnicza w Szczecinie. Rozprawy

Akad Roln Warszawie Zesz Nauk Ogrod — Akademia Rolnicza w Warszawie Zeszyty Naukowe Ogrodnictwo

Akad Roln Warszawie Zesz Nauk Roln — Akademia Rolnicza w Warszawie. Zeszyty Naukowe. Rolnictwo

Akad Roln Warzawe Zesz Nauk Lesn — Akademia Rolnicza w Warszawie. Zeszyty Naukowe. Lesnictwo

Akad Roln Wroclawiu Zesz Nauk Melior — Akademia Rolnicza we Wroclawiu Zeszyty Naukowe Melioracja

Akad Roln Wroclawiu Zesz Nauk Zootech — Akademia Rolnicza we Wroclawiu Zeszyty Naukowe Zootechnika

Akad Rundschau — Akademische Rundschau

Akad Skh Nauk Inst Agropochvoved Tr Leningr Lab — Akademiya Sel'skokhozyaistvennykh Nauk. Institut Agropochvovedeniya. Trudy Leningradskoi Laboratorii

Akad Wiss Abh Math Naturwiss Kl — Akademie der Wissenschaften und der Literatur. Abhandlungen der Mathematisch-Naturwissenschaftlichen Klasse

Akad Wiss Berlin Forschungsber — Akademie der Wissenschaften zu Berlin. Forschungsbericht

Akad Wiss Berlin Sitzungsber — Akademie der Wissenschaften in Berlin. Sitzungsberichte

Akad Wiss DDR Abh Abt Math Naturwiss Tech — Akademie der Wissenschaften der DDR. Abhandlungen. Abteilung Mathematik, Naturwissenschaften, Technik

Akad Wiss DDR Abt Math Naturwiss Tech Abh — Akademie der Wissenschaften der DDR. Abteilung Mathematik, Naturwissenschaften, Technik. Abhandlungen

Akad Wiss DDR Forschungsbereich Geo Kosmoswiss Veroeff — Akademie der Wissenschaften der DDR. Forschungsbereich Geo- und Kosmoswissenschaften. Veroeffentlichungen

Akad Wiss DDR Sitzungsber Math Naturwissen Tech — Akademie der Wissenschaften der DDR. Sitzungsberichte. Mathematik, Naturwissenschaften, Technik

Akad Wiss DDR Zentralinst Isot Strahlenforsch Mitt — Akademie der Wissenschaften der DDR. Zentralinstitut fuer Isotopen- und Strahlenforschung. Mitteilungen

Akad Wiss DDR Zentralinst Phys Erde Veroeff — Akademie der Wissenschaften der DDR. Zentralinstitut fuer Physik der Erde. Veroeffentlichungen

Akad Wiss Goettingen Math Phys Kl Abh Folge 3 — Akademie der Wissenschaften in Goettingen. Mathematisch-Physikalische Klasse. Abhandlungen. Folge 3

Akad Wiss Gottingen Nachr Math-Physikal Kl — Akademie der Wissenschaften in Goettingen. Nachrichten. Mathematisch-Physikalische Klasse

Akad Wiss Lit Abh Math-Naturwiss Kl (Mainz) — Akademie der Wissenschaften und der Literatur in Mainz. Abhandlungen der Mathematisch-Naturwissenschaftlichen Klasse

Akad Wiss Lit Mainz Abh Math-Natur Kl — Akademie der Wissenschaften und der Literatur in Mainz. Abhandlungen der Mathematisch-Naturwissenschaftlichen Klasse

Akad Wiss Lit Mainz Abh Math-Naturwiss Kl — Akademie der Wissenschaften und der Literatur in Mainz. Abhandlungen der Mathematisch-Naturwissenschaftlichen Klasse

Akad Wiss Lit Mainz Jahrb — Akademie der Wissenschaften und der Literatur in Mainz. Jahrbuch (Wiesbaden)

Akad Wiss Lit Mainz Math-Naturwiss Kl Abh — Akademie der Wissenschaften und der Literatur in Mainz. Abhandlungen der Mathematisch-Naturwissenschaftlichen Klasse (Wiesbaden)

Akad Wiss Lit Mainz Math Naturwiss Kl Res Mol Biol — Akademie der Wissenschaften und der Literatur in Mainz. Mathematisch-Naturwissenschaftliche Klasse. Research in Molecular Biology

Akad Wiss Wien — Sitzungsberichte. Akademie der Wissenschaften in Wien

AKAJAV — Journal. American Killifish Association

Ak Alm — Magyar Tudomanyos Akademia Almanachja

AKAM — Ak-Kitab al-Misri

AKAMA6 — Arkansas. Agricultural Experiment Station. Mimeograph Series

AKARAL — Arkansas. Agricultural Experiment Station. Report Series

AKASAO — Arkansas Academy of Science. Proceedings

AKATAR — Aktiebolaget Atomenergi (Stockholm). Rapport AE

AKAW — Abhandlungen. Koenigliche Preussische Akademie der Wissenschaften zu Berlin

AKAW — Anzeiger. Kaiserliche Akademie der Wissenschaften

AKAWB — Abhandlungen der Koeniglichen Akademie der Wissenschaften (Berlin)

AKB — Allatani Kozlemenyek (Budapest)

AKB — Archaeologisches Korrespondenzblatt

AKB — Internationales Afrikaforum

AkBl — Akademische Blaetter

AKBZAG — Archiv fuer Kreislaufforschung

AKCBA — Akita-Kenritsu Chuo Byoin Igaku Zasshi

AKCBAH — Akita-Kenritsu Chuo Byoin Igaku Zasshi

AKCIB5 — Aomori Kenritsu Chuo Byoin Ishi

AKCVA — Archiv fuer Klinische Chirurgie. Langenbecks

AKDDA — Bulletin. Akron Dental Society

AKDEDY — Aktuelle Dermatologie

AKDJA — Arkansas Dental Journal

AKDV — Anzeiger fuer Kunde der Deutschen Vorzeit

AKEDAX — Archiv fuer Klinische und Experimentelle Dermatologie

AKG — Arbeiten zur Kirchengeschichte

AKG — Archiv fuer Kulturgeschichte

AKG — Kerngetallen van Nederlandse Effecten (Amsterdam)

AKGIA — Akusherstvo i Ginekologiya

AKGIAO — Akusherstvo i Ginekologiya

AKGRAH — Aktuelle Gerontologie

Akhboroti Akad Fankhoi RSS Tochikiston Shu-Bai Fankhoi Biol — Akhboroti Akademiyai Fankhoi RSS Tochikiston Shu-Bai Fankhoi Biologi

AKHVL — Arsberaettelse. Kungliga Humanistiska Vetenskapssamfundet i Lund

Akita Cent Hosp Med J — Akita Central Hospital. Medical Journal

Akita J — Akita Journal

AKK — Archiv fuer Katholisches Kirchenrecht

Akkad — Akkadica

AKKR — Archiv fuer Katholisches Kirchenrecht

AKM — Abhandlungen fuer die Kunde des Morgenlandes

AKMDA — Arkhimedes

AKMEA8 — Archiv fuer Klinische Medizin

AK Metro — Auckland Metro

AKML — Abhandlungen zur Kunst, Musik, und Literaturwissenschaft

AKM Ser Theoret Comput Sci — AKM Series in Theoretical Computer Science

AKMTA — Arkiv foer Matematik

AKNHAM — Annals of Kentucky Natural History

AKNKDY — Akita-Kenritsu Nogyo Tanki Daigaku Kenkyu Hokoku

AKNUAR — Aktuelle Neurologie

AKOGAO — Albrecht Von Graefe's Archive for Clinical and Experimental Ophthalmology

AKONA — Archiv fuer Klinische und Experimentelle Ohren-, Nasen-, und Kehlkopfheilkunde

AKONAB — Archiv fuer Klinische und Experimentelle Ohren-, Nasen-, und Kehlkopfheilkunde

A KorrBl — Archaeologisches Korrespondenzblatt

AKPOD — Avtomatizatsiya i Kontrol'no-Izmeritel'nye Pribory v Neftepererabatyvayushchei i Neftekhimicheskoi Promyshlennosti

AkR — Akademische Rundschau

AKR — Aoyama Keizai Ronshu

AKRHDB — Aktuelle Rheumatologie

Akr LR — Akron Law Review

Akron Beaco — Akron Beacon Journal

Akron Bus & Econ R — Akron Business and Economic Review

Akron Bus and Econ Rev — Akron Business and Economic Review

Akron L Rev — Akron Law Review

AKSKBN — Aichi-Ken Shokuhin Shikenshi Nempo

Ak St — Auckland Star

Akt Anal Biol Obektov — Aktivatsionnyi Analiz Biologicheskikh Ob'ektov

Akt Anal Nar Khoz — Aktivatsionnyi Analiz v Narodnom Khozyaistve

Akten Int Leibniz Kongr — Akten des Internationalen Leiniz Kongresses

Akten IX Internat Byzantinistenkongr — Akten des IX. Internationalen Byzantinistenkongresses. Titel Griechisch

Akten XI Internat Byzantinistenkongr — Akten des XI. Internationalen Byzantinistenkongresses

AKTLAU — Agrokemia es Talajtan
Aktoj Int Sci Akad Comenius — Aktoj de Internacia Scienca Akademio Comenius
Akt Pitan Virazko Khvorob — Aktual'ni Pitannya Virazkovoi Khvorobi
Akt Probl Inf Dokum — Aktualne Problemy Informacji i Dokumentacji
AKTRAE — Aktuelle Traumatologie
Aktual Probl Biol Sinezelenykh Vodoroslei — Aktual'nye Problemy Biologii Sinezelenykh Vodoroslei
Aktual Probl Farmakol Farm Vses Nauchn Konf — Aktual'nye Problemy Farmakologii i Farmatsii, Vsesoyuznaya Nauchnaya Konferentsiya
Aktual Probl Inf & Dok — Aktualne Problemy Informacji i Dokumentacji
Aktual Probl Inf Dok — Aktualne Problemy Informacji i Dokumentacji
Aktual Probl Klin Teor Med — Aktual'nye Problemy Klinicheskoi i Teoreticheskoi Meditsiny
Aktual Probl Onkol Med Radiol — Aktual'nye Problemy Onkologii i Meditsinskoi Radiologii
Aktual Probl Prof Patol Resp Mezhved Sb — Aktual'nye Problemy Professional'noi Patologii Respublikanskoi Mezhvedomstvennyi Sbornik
Aktual Probl Razvit Ptitsevod — Aktual'nye Problemy Razvitiya Ptitsevodstva
Aktual Probl Svarki Tsvetn Met Dokl Vses Konf — Aktual'nye Problemy Svarki Tsvetnykh Metallov. Doklady Vsesoyuznoi Konferentsii
Aktual Vopr Biol Pochvoved — Aktual'nye Voprosy Biologii i Pochvovedeniya
Aktual Vopr Dermatol Venerol — Aktual'nye Voprosy Dermatologii i Venerologii
Aktual Vopr Eksp Klin Med — Aktual'nye Voprosy Eksperimental'noi i Klinicheskoi Meditsiny
Aktual Vopr Epidemiol — Aktual'nye Voprosy Epidemiologii
Aktual Vopr Farm — Aktual'nye Voprosy Farmatsii
Aktual Vopr Fiz Tverd Tela — Aktual'nye Voprosy Fiziki Tverdogo Tela
Aktual Vopr Gastroenterol — Aktual'nye Voprosy Gastroenterologii
Aktual Vopr Ginekol — Aktual'nye Voprosy Ginekologii
Aktual Vopr Khimioter Zlokach Opukholei — Aktual'nye Voprosy Khimioterapii Zlokachestvennykh Opukholei
Aktual Vopr Kriobiol Kriomed Mater Simp — Aktual'nye Voprosy Kriobiologii i Kriomeditsiny, Materialy Simpoziuma
Aktual Vopr Oftal — Aktual'nye Voprosy Oftal'mologii
Aktual Vopr Oftal'mol — Aktual'nye Voprosy Oftal'mologii
Aktual Vopr Patol Pecheni — Aktual'nye Voprosy Patologii Pecheni
Aktual Vopr Poluch Fosfora Soedin Ego Osn — Aktual'nye Voprosy Polucheniya Fosfora i Soedinenii na Ego Osnove
Aktual Vopr Sanit Mikrobiol — Aktual'nye Voprosy Sanitarnoi Mikrobiologii
Aktual Vopr Sovrem Biokhim — Aktual'nye Voprosy Sovremennoi Biokhimii
Aktual Vopr Sovrem Onkol — Aktual'nye Voprosy Sovremennoi Onkologii
Aktual Vopr Sovrem Petrogr — Aktual'nye Voprosy Sovremennoi Petrografii
Aktual Vopr Teor Klin Med — Aktual'nye Voprosy Teoreticheskoi i Klinicheskoi Meditsiny
Aktue Aspekte Biotechnol Fortpflanz Wiss Vortragstag — Aktuelle Aspekte der Biotechnologie in der Fortpflanzung. Wissenschaftliche Vortragstagung
Aktuel Dermatol — Aktuelle Dermatologie
Aktuel Fragen Psychiat Neurol — Aktuelle Fragen der Psychiatrie und Neurologie
Aktuel Fragen Psychiatr Neurol — Aktuelle Fragen der Psychiatrie und Neurologie
Aktuel Fragen Psychother — Aktuelle Fragen der Psychotherapie
Aktuel Gerontol — Aktuelle Gerontologie
Aktuelle Gerontol — Aktuelle Gerontologie
Aktuelle Neurol — Aktuelle Neurologie
Aktuelle Probl Chir Orthop — Aktuelle Probleme in Chirurgie und Orthopadie
Aktuelle Radiol — Aktuelle Radiologie
Aktuelle Rheumatol — Aktuelle Rheumatologie
Aktuelle Traumatol — Aktuelle Traumatologie
Aktuelle Urol — Aktuelle Urologie
Aktuell Fot — Aktuell Fotografi
Aktuellt Lantbrukshogs — Aktuellt fran Lantbrukshogskolan
Aktuellt Och Hist — Aktuellt Och Historisk
Aktuel Neurol — Aktuelle Neurologie
Aktuel Onkol — Aktuelle Onkologie
Aktuel Otorhinolaryngol — Aktuelle Otorhinolaryngologie
Aktuel Probl Angiol — Aktuelle Probleme in der Angiologie
Aktuel Probl Chir — Aktuelle Probleme in der Chirurgie [Later, Aktuelle Probleme in Chirurgie und Orthopaedie]
Aktuel Probl Chir Orthop — Aktuelle Probleme in Chirurgie und Orthopaedie
Aktuel Probl Intensivmed — Aktuelle Probleme der Intensivmedizin
Aktuel Probl Klin Biochem — Aktuelle Probleme in der Klinischen Biochemie
Aktuel Probl Landwirtsch Forsch Semin — Aktuelle Probleme der Landwirtschaftlichen Forschung. Seminar ueber Salmonellenin Futtermitteln, Futtermittelbewertung
Aktuel Probl Phoniatr Logop — Aktuelle Probleme der Phoniatrie und Logopaedie
Aktuel Probl Polym-Phys — Aktuelle Probleme der Polymer-Physik
Aktuel Probl Psych Neurol Neurochir — Aktuelle Probleme in der Psychiatrie, Neurologie, Neurochirurgie
Aktuel Rheumatol — Aktuelle Rheumatologie
Aktuel Landbruksdep Opplysningstjeneste (Norw) — Aktuelt Landbruksdepartementet. Opplysningstjeneste (Norway)
Aktuel Traumatol — Aktuelle Traumatologie
Aktuel Urol — Aktuelle Urologie
AKultG — Archiv fuer Kulturgeschichte
Akush Ginekol (Kiev) — Akusherstvo i Ginekologiya (Kiev)
Akush Ginekol (Mosc) — Akusherstvo i Ginekologiya (Moscow)
Akush Ginekol (Moscow) — Akusherstvo i Ginekologiya (Moscow)
Akush Ginekol (Mosk) — Akusherstvo i Ginekologiia (Moskva)
Akush Ginekol (Sofia) — Akusherstvo i Ginekologiya (Sofia)
Akush Ginekol (Sofiia) — Akusherstvo i Ginekologiia (Sofiia)
Akust Beih — Akustische Beihefte
Akust Ul'trazvuk Tekh — Akustika i Ul'trazvukovaya Tekhnika
Akust Z — Akademija Nauk SSSR. Akusticeskii Zurnal
Akust Z — Akusticheskii Zurnal
Akust Z — Akustische Zeitschrift
Akust Zh — Akusticheskii Zhurnal

A Kut — Actes de Kutlumus
Akvariebl — Akvariebladet
Akvar Komnatn Rast — Akvarium i Komnatnye Rastenija
Akvar Terrar — Akvarium es Terrarium
AKVBAA — Arkiv foer Botanik
Ak Waik Hist J — Auckland-Waikato Historical Journal
AKWL — Alaska's Wildlife
Akw Notes — Akwesasne Notes
AKWS — Akwesasne Notes
Akz — Akzente
AKZHA — Akusticheskii Zhurnal
AKZMA — ATOMKI [Atommag Kutato Intezet] Koezlemenyek. Supplement
AL — Acta Linguistica
AL — Acta Universitatis Lundensis
AL — Administratief Lexicon
AL — Ala Breve
AL — Alighieri
AL — Allgemeines Literaturblatt
AL — America Latina
AL — American Libraries
AL — American Literature
AL — American Lutherie
AL — Analytical Letters
AL — Annali Lateranensi
AL — Annee Linguistique
AL — Archivos Leoneses
AL — Art and Letters
ALA — Afrique Litteraire et Artistique
Ala — Alabama Reports
ALA — American Libraries
ALA — Annales. Faculte des Lettres d'Aix-En-Provence
ALA — Annales. Faculte des Lettres et des Sciences Humaines. Universite Aix-Marseilles
ALA — Arts Law Australia
Ala Acad Sci Jour — Alabama Academy of Science. Journal
Ala Acts — Acts of Alabama
Ala Admin Code — Alabama Administrative Code
Ala Ag Exp — Alabama. Agricultural Experiment Station. Publications
Ala Agribus — Alabama Agribusiness
Ala Agribusiness Auburn Univ Ala Coop Ext Serv — Alabama Agribusiness. Auburn University. Alabama Cooperative Extension Service
Ala Agric Exp Stn Ala Polytech Inst Bull — Alabama. Agricultural Experiment Station. Alabama Polytechnic Institute. Bulletin
Ala Agric Exp Stn Annu Rep — Alabama. Agricultural Experiment Station. Annual Report
Ala Agric Exp Stn Auburn Univ Agron Soils Dep Ser — Alabama. Agricultural Experiment Station. Auburn University. Agronomy and SoilsDepartmental Series
Ala Agric Exp Stn Auburn Univ Bull — Alabama. Agricultural Experiment Station. Auburn University. Bulletin
Ala Agric Exp Stn Auburn Univ Dep Agron & Soils Dep Ser — Alabama. Agricultural Experiment Station. Auburn University. Department of Agronomy and Soils. Departmental Series
Ala Agric Exp Stn Auburn Univ For Dep Ser — Alabama. Agricultural Experiment Station. Auburn University. Forestry Departmental Series
Ala Agric Exp Stn Auburn Univ Leafl — Alabama. Agricultural Experiment Station. Auburn University. Leaflet
Ala Agric Exp Stn Auburn Univ Prog Rep — Alabama. Agricultural Experiment Station. Auburn University. Progress Report
Ala Agric Exp Stn Auburn Univ Prog Rep Ser — Alabama. Agricultural Experiment Station. Auburn University. Progress Report Series
Ala Agric Exp Stn Bull — Alabama. Agricultural Experiment Station. Bulletin
Ala Agric Exp Stn Bull (Auburn Univ) — Alabama. Agricultural Experiment Station. Bulletin (Auburn University)
Ala Agric Exp Stn Cir — Alabama. Agricultural Experiment Station. Circular
Ala Agric Exp Stn Leafl — Alabama. Agricultural Experiment Station. Leaflet
Ala Agric Exp Stn Leafl (Auburn Univ) — Alabama. Agricultural Experiment Station. Leaflet (Auburn University)
Ala Agric Exp Stn Prog Rep Ser — Alabama. Agricultural Experiment Station. Progress Report Series
Ala Agric Exp Stn Prog Rep Ser (Auburn Univ) — Alabama. Agricultural Experiment Station. Progress Report Series (Auburn University)
Ala App — Alabama Appellate Court Reports
ALAB — American Lung Association. Bulletin
Alabama Agric Exp Sta Alabama Polytechn Inst Circ — Alabama Agricultural Experiment Station. Alabama Polytechnic Institute. Circular
Alabama Agric Exp Sta Hort Ser — Alabama Agricultural Experiment Station. Horticulture Series
Alabama Geol Soc Bull — Alabama. Geological Society. Bulletin
Alabama Geol Survey Inf Ser — Alabama. Geological Survey. Information Series
Alabama Geol Survey Map — Alabama. Geological Survey. Map
Alabama L Rev — Alabama Law Review
Ala Bar Bull — Alabama Bar Bulletin
ALA Bul — American Library Association. Bulletin
Ala Bus — Alabama Business
Ala Bus and Econ Repts — Alabama Business and Economic Reports
Ala Code — Code of Alabama
Ala Conserv — Alabama Conservation
Ala Corn Variety Rep — Alabama Corn Variety Report
Ala Dept Ind Rel Ann Plan — Alabama Department of Industrial Relations. Annual Planning
ALADI Newsl — ALADI [Asociacion Latinoamericana de Integracion] Newsletter
Alaendsk Odling — Alaendsk Odling. Arsbok
ALAF — Australian Literary Awards and Fellowships
Ala For — Alabama Forests

ALAFO R — ALAFO [*Asociacion Latino Americana de Facultades de Odontologia*] Revista

Ala Geol Surv Atlas Ser — Alabama. Geological Survey. Atlas Series

Ala Geol Surv Bull — Alabama. Geological Survey. Bulletin

Ala Geol Surv Circ — Alabama. Geological Survey. Circular

Ala Geol Surv Cty Rep — Alabama. Geological Survey. County Report

Ala Geol Survey and State Oil and Gas Board Ann Repts — Alabama. Geological Survey and State Oil and Gas Board. Annual Reports

Ala Geol Surv Geo-Petro Notes — Alabama. Geological Survey. Geo-Petro Notes

Ala Geol Surv Inf Ser — Alabama. Geological Survey. Information Series

Ala Geol Surv Map — Alabama. Geological Survey. Map

Ala Geol Surv Spec Rep — Alabama. Geological Survey. Special Report

Ala G S — Alabama. Geological Survey

Ala His S — Alabama Historical Society. Transactions

Ala Hist — Alabama Historian

Ala Hist Q — Alabama Historical Quarterly

ALA Hosp Bk Guide — American Library Association. Association of Hospital and Institution Libraries. Book Guide

AlaHQ — Alabama Historical Quarterly

Ala Ind Sc Soc Pr — Alabama Industrial and Scientific Society. Proceedings

ALA Intellectual Freedom Newsl — American Library Association. Intellectual Freedom Committee. Newsletter

ALAJ — Alaska Journal

Ala J Med Sci — Alabama Journal of Medical Sciences

AlaL — A la Lettre

Ala Law — Alabama Lawyer

Ala Law Jour — Alabama Law Journal

Ala Law R — Alabama Law Review

Ala Libn — Alabama Librarian

ALA Lib Period Round Table Newsl — American Library Association. Library Periodicals Round Table. Newsletter

ALA Lib Serv to Labor News — American Library Association. Adult Services Division. Joint Committee on Library Service to Labor Groups. Library Service to Labor Newsletter

Ala LJ — Alabama Law Journal

Ala LR — Alabama Law Review

Ala L Rev — Alabama Law Review

Ala Mar Res Bull — Alabama Marine Resources Bulletin

Ala Mar Resour Bull — Alabama Marine Resources. Bulletin

Ala Med — Alabama Medicine

Ala Med J — Alabama Medical Journal

Ala Med Surg Age — Alabama Medical and Surgical Age

Al-An — Al-Andalus

ALANBH — Archivos Latinoamericanos de Nutricion

A Lang — Art-Language

Ala Nurse — Alabama Nurse

ALAPDP — Arizona Land and People

Ala Plann Res Checkl — Alabama Planning Resource Checklist

Ala Polytech Inst Eng Exp Stn Eng Bull — Alabama Polytechnic Institute. Engineering Experiment Station. Engineering Bulletin

Ala R — Alabama Review

ALA Ref Serv Div — American Library Association. Reference Services Division. Reference Quarterly

Ala Rev — Alabama Review

ALARM — Australian Library Annual Reports on Microfiche

ALAS — Alaska

ALASA — Allergie und Asthma

ALASAV — Allergie und Asthma

ALASH — Acta Linguistica. Academiae Scientiarum Hungaricae

AlasJ — Alaska Journal

Alaska Admin Code — Alaska Administrative Code

Alaska Admin Jnl — Alaska Administrative Journal

Alaska Ag Exp — Alaska. Agricultural Experiment Station. Publications

Alaska Agric Exp Sta Annual Rep — Alaska Agricultural Experiment Stations. Annual Report

Alaska Agric Exp Stn Bull — Alaska. Agricultural Experiment Station. Bulletin

Alaska Agric Exp Stn Circ — Alaska. Agricultural Experiment Station. Circular

Alaska Bar Br — Alaska Bar Brief

Alaska BB — Alaska Bar Brief

Alaska BJ — Alaska Bar Journal

Alaska Bus and Development — Alaska Business and Development

Alaska Bus Ind — Alaska Business and Industry

Alaska Constr Oil — Alaska Construction and Oil

Alaska Dep Fish Res Rep — Alaska. Department of Fisheries. Research Report

Alaska Dept Fish Game Ann Rep — Alaska Department of Fish and Game. Annual Report

Alaska Dept Fish Game Com Opp — Alaska Department of Fish and Game. Commercial Operators

Alaska Dept Mines Rept Commissioner Mines Bienn — Alaska. Department of Mines. Report of the Commissioner of Mines. Biennium

Alaska Dept Nat Resour Div Mines Miner Rep — Alaska. Department of Natural Resources. Division of Mines and Minerals. Report

Alaska Div Geol Geophys Surv Geochem Rep — Alaska. Division of Geological and Geophysical Surveys. Geochemical Report

Alaska Div Geol Geophys Surv Geol Rep — Alaska. Division of Geological and Geophysical Surveys. Geologic Report

Alaska Div Geol Surv Geochem Rep — Alaska. Division of Geological Survey. Geochemical Report

Alaska Div Mines and Geology Geochem Rept — Alaska. Department of Natural Resources. Division of Mines and Geology. Geochemical Report

Alaska Div Mines and Geology Geol Rept — Alaska. Department of Natural Resources. Division of Mines and Geology. Geologic Report

Alaska Div Mines and Minerals Inf Circ Rept — Alaska. Division of Mines and Minerals. Information Circular. Report

Alaska Div Mines Geol Geochem Rep — Alaska. Division of Mines and Geology. Geochemical Report

Alaska Div Mines Geol Geol Rep — Alaska. Division of Mines and Geology. Geologic Report

Alaska Div Mines Geol Rep — Alaska. Division of Mines and Geology. Report

Alaska Div Mines Miner Rep — Alaska. Division of Mines and Minerals. Report

Alaska Econ Trends — Alaska Economic Trends

Alaska Ind — Alaska Industry

Alaska J — Alaska Journal

Alaska LJ — Alaska Law Journal

Alaska Med — Alaska Medicine

Alaskan Arct Tundra Proc Anniv Celebration Nav Arct Res Lab — Alaskan Arctic Tundra Proceedings. Anniversary Celebration. Naval Arctic Research Laboratory

Alaska Nat N — Alaska Native News

Alaska Oil Gas Conserv Com Stat Rep — Alaska Oil and Gas Conservation Commission. Statistical Report

Alaska Oil Ind N — Alaska Oil and Industry News

Alaska Pet Ind Dir — Alaska Petroleum and Industrial Directory

Alaska Q Rev — Alaska Quarterly Review

Alaska Reg Rep US Dep Agric For Serv — Alaska Region Report. United States Department of Agriculture. Forest Service

Alaska Rev Bus Econ Cond — Alaska Review of Business and Economic Conditions

Alaska R Social and Econ Conditions — Alaska Review of Social and Economic Conditions

Alaska Sci Conf — Alaska Science Conference

Alaska Sci Conf Proc — Alaska Science Conference. Proceedings

Alaska Sess Laws — Alaska Session Laws

Alaska Stat — Alaska Statutes

Alaska Univ Anthrop Pa — Alaska University. Anthropological Papers

Alaska Univ Geophys Inst Rep — Alaska University. Geophysical Institute. Report

Alaska Univ Mineral Industry Research Lab Rept — University of Alaska. Mineral Industry Research Laboratory. Report

Alaska Univ School Mines Pub Bull — Alaska University. School of Mines Publication. Bulletin

Ala Soc Welf — Alabama Social Welfare

Ala State Bar Assn Proc — Alabama State Bar Association. Proceedings

Ala State Highway Dept Bul — Alabama State Highway Department. Bulletin

Ala St B Found Bull — Alabama State Bar Foundation. Bulletin

Ala St Found Bull — Alabama State Foundation Bulletin

ALAT — Alaska Today

ALat — America Latina

Ala Truck — Alabama Trucker

Alauda Rev Int Ornithol — Alauda. Revue Internationale d'Ornithologie

ALA Wash Newsl — American Library Association. Washington Newsletter

ALAZ — ALA [*American Latvian Association*] Zurnals

Al Azhar J Microbiol — Al-Azhar Journal of Microbiology

Al Azhar J Pharm Sci — Al-Azhar Journal of Pharmaceutical Sciences

ALB — Aboriginal Law Bulletin

ALB — Adyar Library Bulletin

Alb — Albania

ALB — Alberta Business

ALB — Allgemeines Literaturblatt

ALB — Almanacco Letterario Bompiani

ALB — Annales. Faculte des Lettres de Besancon

ALB — Anthropological Linguistics (Bloomington)

Albanie Nouv — Albanie Nouvelle

Albany Felt Guide — Albany Felt Guidelines

Albany Inst Pr — Albany Institute. Proceedings

Albany Inst Tr — Albany Institute. Transactions

Albany L R — Albany Law Review

Albany L Rev — Albany Law Review

Albany News Dig — Albany International Weekly News Digest

Alber J Edu — Alberta Journal of Educational Research

Alberta Bs — Alberta Business

Alberta Bus Ind — Alberta Business Index

Alberta Bus J — Alberta Business Journal. Chamber of Resources

Alberta Dep Lands For Annu Rep — Alberta. Department of Lands and Forests. Annual Report

Alberta Dept Mines and Minerals Mines Div Ann Rept — Alberta. Department of Mines and Minerals. Mines Division. Annual Report

Alberta Div — Alberta Diver

Alberta En — Alberta Energy

Alberta Eng N — Alberta English Notes

Alberta Gaz — Alberta Gazette

Alberta Green Nl — Alberta Greenhouse Newsletter

Alberta His — Alberta History

Alberta Hog J — Alberta Hog Journal

Alberta Hort — Alberta Horticulturist. Alberta Horticultural Association

Alberta J Educ Res — Alberta Journal of Educational Research

Alberta Lands For Annu Rep — Alberta Lands and Forests. Annual Report

Alberta L (Can) — Alberta Law Reports (Canada)

Alberta Leg Lib An Rep — Alberta. Legislature Library. Annual Report

Alberta LQ — Alberta Law Quarterly

Alberta L R — Alberta Law Review

Alberta L Rev — Alberta Law Review

Alberta Med Bull — Alberta Medical Bulletin

Alberta M L J — Alberta Modern Language Journal

Alberta Mot — Alberta Motorist

Alberta Oil Sands Technol Res Auth J Res — Alberta Oil Sands Technology and Research Authority. Journal of Research

Alberta Pay Ben — Alberta Pay and Benefits

Alberta Pet Incent Prog — Alberta Petroleum Incentives Program

Alberta Res Annu Rep — Alberta Research. Annual Report

Alberta Res Counc Bull — Alberta Research Council. Bulletin
Alberta Res Counc Inf Ser — Alberta Research Council. Information Series
Alberta Res Counc Rep — Alberta Research Council. Report
Alberta Research Council Bull — Alberta Research Council. Bulletin
Alberta Research Council Inf Ser — Alberta Research Council. Information Series
Alberta Research Council Mem — Alberta Research Council. Memoir
Alberta Research Council Mimeo Circ — Alberta Research Council. Mimeographed Circular
Alberta Research Council Prelim Rept — Alberta Research Council. Preliminary Report
Alberta Research Council Prelim Soil Survey Rept — Alberta Research Council. Preliminary Soil Survey Report
Alberta Research Council Rept — Alberta Research Council. Report
Alberta Res Econ Geol Rep — Alberta Research. Economic Geology Report
Alberta Res Inf Ser — Alberta Research. Information Series
Alberta Res Rep — Alberta Research. Report
Alberta Ser Rep — Alberta Series Report
Alberta Soc Pet Geol Annu Field Conf Guideb — Alberta Society of Petroleum Geologists. Annual Field Conference. Guidebook
Alberta Soc Pet Geol Bull — Alberta Society of Petroleum Geologists. Bulletin
Alberta Soc Petroleum Geologists Jour News Bull — Alberta Society of Petroleum Geologists. Journal. News Bulletin
Alberta Trans — Alberta Transportation
Alberta Univ Dep Chem Div Theor Chem Tech Rep — Alberta. University. Department of Chemistry. Division of Theoretical Chemistry. Technical Report
Alberta Univ Dept Civil Eng Struct Eng Rep — Alberta University. Department of Civil Engineering. Structural Engineering Reports
Alberta West Liv — Alberta's Western Living
Alberta Wild Assoc Nl — Alberta Wilderness Association. Newsletter
Albert Geogr — Albertan Geographer
Albertina Inf — Albertina Informationen
Albertina Stud — Albertina-Studien
AlbH — Alberta Historical Review
ALBI — Alaska Business and Industry
Albiswerk-Ber — Albiswerk-Berichte
Alb I T — Transactions of the Albany Institute
ALBJ — Alberta Business Journal
ALBL — Anti-Locust Bulletin. Anti-Locust Research Centre. British Museum of Natural History (London)
Alb Law J — Albany Law Journal
ALBLB — American Lung Association. Bulletin
Alb LR — Alberta Law Reports
Alb LR — Alberta Law Review
Alb L Rev — Albany Law Review
Alb LS Jour — Albany Law School Journal
ALBN — Alberta Naturalist
ALBO — Analecta Lovaniensia Biblica et Orientalia
Alb R — Alba Regia. Annales Musei Stephani Regis
ALBr — Anuario da Literatura Brasileira
Albrecht Graefes Arch Klin Exp Ophthalmol — Albrecht von Graefes Archiv fuer Klinische und Experimentelle Ophthalmologie
Albrecht Thaer Arch — Albrecht-Thaer-Archiv
Albrecht V Graefe's Arch Ophthal — Albrecht Von Graefe's Archiv fuer Ophthalmologie
Albrecht Von Graefe's Arch Clin Exp Ophthalmol — Albrecht Von Graefe's Archive for Clinical and Experimental Ophthalmology
Albrecht Von Graefe's Arch Klin Exp Ophthalmol — Albrecht Von Graefe's Archiv fuer Klinische und Experimentelle Ophthalmologie
Albrecht Von Graefe's Arch Ophthalmol — Albrecht Von Graefe's Archiv fuer Ophthalmologie
Albright-Knox Gal Notes — Albright-Knox Art Gallery. Notes
Al Brioude — Almanach de Brioude e son Arrondisement
ALBS — Alaskana Book Series
Alb Stud — Albertina Studien
ALBU — Alaska Business Newsletter
Album Figaro — Album du Figaro
Albumin Struct Funct Uses — Albumin Structure, Function, and Uses
Album Natuurmonum Ned Indiee — Album van Natuurmonumenten van Nederlandsch-Indiee
Albums Crocodile — Albums du Crocodile
Album S Kst — Album der Schoone Kunsten
Albuquer JI — Albuquerque Journal
ALBVA — Animal Learning and Behavior
ALBYBL — American Laboratory
Alby LR — Albany Law Review
Alc — Alcantara
ALC — Alcor
Alc & N — Alcock and Napier's Irish King's Bench Reports
Alcan N — Alcan News
ALCC — Acta Literaria (Concepcion, Chile)
ALCDOK — Arbetslivcentrum Dokumentationsenkenten
ALCGP — Annali del Liceo Classico Garibaldi di Palermo
Alcheringa (Assoc Australas Palaeontol) — Alcheringa (Association of Australasian Palaeontologists)
ALCNAQ — Alabama Conservation
ALCO — Alberta Conservationist
ALCOA Res Lab Tech Pap — ALCOA [Aluminum Company of America] Research Laboratories. Technical Paper
Alcoh Alcoh — Alcohol and Alcoholism
Alcoh Health & Res W — Alcohol Health and Research World
Alcoh Hist — Alcohol in History
Alcohol Abnorm Protein Biosynth — Alcohol and Abnormal Protein Biosynthesis
Alcohol Alcohol — Alcohol and Alcoholism
Alcohol Alcohol NY — Alcohol and Alcoholism (New York)
Alcohol Alcohol Oxford — Alcohol and Alcoholism (Oxford)

Alcohol Alcohol Suppl — Alcohol and Alcoholism. Supplement
Alcohol Aldehyde Metab Syst Pap Int Symp — Alcohol and Aldehyde Metabolizing Systems. Papers. International Symposium on Alcohol and Aldehyde Metabolizing Systems
Alcohol Clin Exp Res — Alcoholism Clinical and Experimental Research
Alcohol Clin Update — Alcohol Clinical Update
Alcohol Dig — Alcoholism Digest
Alcohol Drug Res — Alcohol and Drug Research
Alcohol Health Res World — Alcohol Health and Research World
Alcohol Health Res World Natl Inst Alcohol Abuse Alcohol — Alcohol Health and Research World. National Institute on Alcohol Abuse and Alcoholism
Alcohol Intox Withdrawal Pap Symp — Alcohol Intoxication and Withdrawal. Experimental Studies. Papers. Symposium
Alcohol Liver Pathol Proc Int Symp Alcohol Drug Res — Alcoholic Liver Pathology. Proceedings. Liver Pathology Section. International Symposia. Alcohol and Drug Research
Alcohol Res Health — Alcohol Research & Health
AI Commun — AI Communications
Alco Prod Rev — Alco Products Review
ALCR — Alaska Conservation Review
ALCRD7 — Advances in Liquid Crystals
Alc Reg — Alcock's Registry Cases
Al Culukidzis Sahelob Khutnaisi Sahelmc Ped Inst Srom — Al. Culukidzis Sahelobis Khutnaisis Sahelmcipho Pedagogiuri Institutis Sromebi
ALCYAP — Aliphatic Chemistry
ALD — Actualite Legislative Dalloz
ALD — Administrative Law Decisions. Australian
ALD — African Law Digest
ALD — American Library Directory
ALD — Fortschrittliche Betriebsfuehrung und Industrial Engineering
ALDGA — Alloy Digest
ALDJA — Journal. Alabama Dental Association
AI D Nt Ztg — Allgemeine Deutsche Naturhistorische Zeitung
Aldosterone Symp — Aldosterone. A Symposium
ALE — Antitrust Law and Economics Review
A Lead — Adult Leadership
Aleal — Alealoides
ALEC — Anales de la Literatura Espanola Contemporanea
ALED — Alaska Education News
ALELWLE — American Literature, English Literature, and World Literature in English
Alemann Jb — Alemannisches Jahrbuch
ALEN — Alaska Education News
ALEPB9 — Asociacion Latinoamericana de Entomologia. Publicacion
ALES — Alaska Earthlines/Tidelines. Alaska Geographic Society
ALET — Alaska Economic Trends
ALet — Armas y Letras
ALet — Aspetti Letterari
ALetM — Anuario de Letras. M
A Lex — Archiv fuer Lateinische Lexicographie und Grammatik
Alexander Blain Hosp Bull — Alexander Blain Hospital. Bulletin
Alexander Turnbull Libr Bull — Alexander Turnbull Library. Bulletin
Alexandria Eng J — Alexandria Engineering Journal
Alexandria J Agric Res — Alexandria Journal of Agricultural Research
Alexandria J Agr Res — Alexandria Journal of Agricultural Research
Alexandria Med J — Alexandria Medical Journal
Alexandria Univ Bull Fac Sci — Alexandria University. Bulletin of the Faculty of Science
Alexanor Rev Lepid Fr — Alexanor; Revue des Lepidopteristes Francais
Alex Dent J — Alexandria Dental Journal
Alex J Agric Res — Alexandria Journal of Agricultural Research
Alfaatih Univ Bull Fac Eng — Alfaatih University. Bulletin of the Faculty of Engineering
ALFE — Acta Lapponica Fenniae
ALFM — Alaska Farm Magazine
ALFOAA — Alberta Lands and Forests. Annual Report
Alfoeldi Tud Gyuejt — Az Alfoeldi Tudomanyos Gyuejtemeny. Az Alfoeldi Tudomanyos Intezet Evkoenyve. Annales de l'Institut Scientifique de l'Alfoeld
Alfold — Alfoeld: Irodalmi es Muvelodesi Folyoirat
ALFRA — Alta Frequenza
Alfred Benson Symp — Alfred Benson Symposium
Alfred P Sloan Found Rep — Alfred P. Sloan Foundation. Report
Alfred Univ NY State Coll Ceram Mon Rep — Alfred University. New York State. College of Ceramics. Monthly Report
Alfr Hosp Clin Rep — Alfred Hospital. Clinical Reports
ALFZA9 — Allgemeine Fischerei-Zeitung
ALG — Africa. An International Business, Economic, and Political Monthly
ALG — Algol
ALG — Archiv fuer Literaturgeschichte
ALGAB — Alberta Gazette
ALGE — Alaska Geographic
Algebra Anal Vectorial Tensor — Algebra y Analysis, Vectorial, y Tensorial
Algebra Ber — Algebra Berichte
Algebra Colloq — Algebra Colloquium
Algebra Logic Appl — Algebra, Logic, and Applications
Algebras Groups Geom — Algebras, Groups, and Geometries
ALGED — Alaska Geographic
Alger Agric — Algerie Agricole
Algerie Med — Algerie Medicale
Alger Med — Algerie Medicale
Alger Serv Geol Bull — Algeria. Service Geologique. Bulletin
Alg Fisc Tijdsch — Algemeen Fiscaal Tijdschrift
ALGGM — Annuario. Liceo Ginnasio G. Mameli
ALGHJ — Arbeiten zur Literatur und Geschichte des Hellenistischen Judentums

Alg Holl Landbouwbl — Algemeen Hollandsch Landbouwblad. Officieel Orgaan van de Hollandsche Maatschappij van Landbouw
ALGIBW — Allergie et Immunologie
Alg Log — Algebra and Logic
Alg Mag Wetensch — Algemeen Magazijn van Wetenschap, Konst, en Smaak
Algodon Bol Cam Algodonera Peru — Algodon Boletin de la Camara Algodonera del Peru
Algodonero Bol — Algodonero Boletin
Algodon Mex — Algodon Mexicano
Algol Bull — Algol Bulletin
Algol Stud — Algological Studies
Algorithms Chem Comput Symp — Algorithms for Chemical Computations. A Symposium
Algorithms Combin — Algorithms and Combinatorics
Algorithms Combin Study Res Texts — Algorithms and Combinatorics. Study and Research Texts
Algoritmy i Algoritm Jazyki — Algoritmy i Algoritmiceskie Jazyki
Algot Holmbergs Arsb — Algot Holmbergs Arsbok
ALGP — Annali. Liceo Classico G. Garibaldi di Palermo
ALGP — Annuario. Liceo Ginnasio Statale G. Palmieri
Alg Pap-Rund — Allgemeine Papier-Rundschau
Alg Pract Rechtverz — Algemene Practische Rechtverzameling
Alg Proefstn Alg Ver Rubberplant Oostkust Sumatra Vlugschr — Algemeen Proefstation der Algemeene Vereniging van Rubberplanters ter Oostkust van Sumatra. Vlugschrift
Alg Zuivelbl — Algemeen Zuivelblad
Alg Zuivel Melkhyg Weekbl — Algemeen-Zuivel-en Melkhygienisch Weekblad
ALH — Acta Linguistica. Academiae Scientiarum Hungaricae
ALH — Acta Linguistica Hafniensia
ALHa — Acta Linguistica Hafniensia
ALHI — Alaska History Series
ALHisp — Anales de Literatura Hispanoamericana
ALHN — Alaska History News
ALHY — Alaska History
ALI — Alberta Legislation Information
ALI — ALI-ABA [*American Law Institute - American Bar Association*] Course Materials Journal
ALi — Amor de Libro
ALI — Australian Leisure Index
ALI ABA — ALI-ABA [*American Law Institute - American Bar Association*] Course Materials Journal
ALI-ABA Course Mat J — ALI-ABA [*American Law Institute - American Bar Association*] Course Materials Journal
A Lib — American Libraries
A Libre — Art Libre
A Libs J — Art Libraries Journal
ALICE — Archivio Libri Italiani su Calcolatore Electronico
Alicyclic Chem — Alicyclic Chemistry
ALIDA — Alliance Industrielle
ALIE — America Latina Informe Economrnico
Alienist Neurol — Alienist and Neurologist
Aligarh Bull Math — Aligarh Bulletin of Mathematics
Aligarh J Statist — Aligarh Journal of Statistics
Aligarh Muslim Univ Publ Zool Ser — Aligarh Muslim University Publications. Zoological Series
Aligh Ras Bib Dante — Alighieri. Rassegna Bibliografica Dantesca
ALIL — Anuar de Lingvistica si Istorie Literara
ALIM — America Latina Informe de Mercados
ALIMC — Allergie und Immunologie
ALIMCL — Allergie und Immunologie
Aliment Anim — Alimentazione Animale
Aliment Ital — Alimentazione Italiana
Aliment Latinoam — Alimentacion Latinoamericana
Aliment Nutr — Alimentos e Nutricao
Aliment Nutr Anim — Alimentos y Nutricion Animal
Aliment Nutr Metab — Alimentazione Nutrizione Metabolismo
Aliment Pharmacol Ther — Alimentary Pharmacology and Therapeutics
Aliment Quebec — Alimentation au Quebec
Aliments Aliment — Aliments et l'Alimentation
Aliment Trav Symp Int — Alimentation et Travail. Symposium International
Aliment Vie — Alimentation et la Vie
ALIN — Alaska Industry
ALing — Archivum Linguisticum
ALingHung — Acta Linguistica. Academiae Scientiarum Hungaricae
A Links — Art Links
ALIP — Alaska in Perspective
ALIP — America Latina Informe Politico
ALIP — Australian Library and Information Professionals
ALIPC — Art and Letters. India, Pakistan, Ceylon [*London*]
Aliphatic Alicyclic Saturated Heterocycl Chem — Aliphatic, Alicyclic, and Saturated Heterocyclic Chemistry
Aliphatic Chem — Aliphatic Chemistry
Aliphatic Relat Nat Prod Chem — Aliphatic and Related Natural Product Chemistry
ALI Proc — American Law Institute. Proceedings
ALIR — Australian Library and Information Research
ALIS — Automated Library Information System
ALit — Acta Litteraria Academiae Scientiarum Hungaricae
ALit — Annee Litteraire
ALit — Athenaion Literaturwissenschaft
ALitASH — Acta Litteraria. Academiae Scientiarum Hungaricae
ALitH — Acta Litteraria. Academiae Scientiarum Hungaricae
ALJ — Alemannisches Jahrbuch
ALJ — Allahabad Law Journal
ALJ — American Law Journal
ALJ — Australian Law Journal

ALJ — Australian Library Journal
ALJMAO — Antonie Van Leeuwenhoek Journal of Microbiology and Serology [*Later, Antonie Van Leeuwenhoek Journal of Microbiology*]
ALJNS — American Law Journal. New Series
ALJOD — Australian Law Journal
ALJR — Australian Law Journal. Reports
Alkalis Blast Furn Proc Symp — Alkalis in Blast Furnaces. Proceedings. Symposium on "Alkalis in Blast Furnaces. State of the Art"
Alkalmaz Mat Lapok — Alkalmazott Matematikai Lapok
Alkaloidal Clin — Alkaloidal Clinic
Alkaloids Chem Physiol — Alkaloids Chemistry and Physiology
ALKM — Archiv fuer Literatur und Kirchengeschichte des Mittelalters
ALKMA — Archiv fuer Literatur- und Kirchengeschichte des Mittelalters
Alkohol Ind — Alkohol Industrie
Alkohol Ind Wiss Tech Brennereibeil — Alkohol Industrie. Wissenschaftliche Technische Brennereibeilage
AIL — Almanach des Lettres
ALL — Annual LL
ALL — Archiv fuer Lateinische Lexikographie und Grammatik
ALL — Australian Labour Law Reporter
AL/LA — African Languages/Langues Africaines
AllaB — Alla Bottega
Allahabad Fmr — Allahabad Farmer
Allahabad LJ — Allahabad Law Journal
Allahabad Univ Studies — Allahabad University Studies
Alla LJ — Allahabad Law Journal
Allam- es Jogtud — Allam- es Jogtudomany
Allan Hancock Found Occas Pap (New Ser) — Allan Hancock Foundation. Occasional Papers (New Series)
Allan Hancock Found Publ Occas Pap — Allan Hancock Foundation. Publications. Occasional Paper
Allan Hancock Found Pubs Occasional Paper — Allan Hancock Foundation. Publications. Occasional Paper
Allan Hancock Found Tech Rep — Allan Hancock Foundation. Technical Reports
Allan Hancock Monogr Mar Biol — Allan Hancock Monographs in Marine Biology
Allatgyogy Oltoanyagellenorzo Intez Evk — Allatgyogyaszati Oltoanyagellenorzo Intezet Evkonyve
Allat Lapok — Allatorvosi Lapok
Allatorv Koezl — Allatorvosi Koezloeny
Allatorv Lapok — Allatorvosi Lapok
Allattani Kozl — Allattani Kozlemenyek
Allatteny — Allattenyesztestani Tanszek
Allattenyesz Anim Breed — Allattenyesztes/Animal Breeding
Allattenyesz Takarmanyozas — Allattenyesztes es Takarmanyozas
Allatteny Kutatointez Evk — Allattenyesztesi Kutatointezet Evkoenyve
ALLCB — ALLC [*Association for Literary and Linguistic Computing*] Bulletin
ALLC Bull — ALLC [*Association for Literary and Linguistic Computing*] Bulletin
ALLC J — ALLC [*Association for Literary and Linguistic Computing*] Journal
Allegheny Ludlum Horiz — Allegheny Ludlum Horizons
Allem Aujourd — Allemagnes d'Aujourd'hui
All Eng — All England Law Reports
Allen Mem A Mus Bull — Allen Memorial Art Museum Bulletin
All ER — All England Law Reports
Allerg Abstr — Allergy Abstracts
Allerg Asthma — Allergie und Asthma
Allerg Asthmaforsch — Allergie und Asthmaforschung
Allerg Dis Ther — Allergic Disease and Therapy
Allerg Immunol — Allergie und Immunologie
Allerg Immunol (Leipz) — Allergie und Immunologie (Leipzig)
Allerg Immunol (Paris) — Allergie et Immunologie (Paris)
Allergnaed Privileg Anz Saemmtl KK Erblaendern — Allergnaedigst-Privilegirte Anzeigen aus Saemmtlich-Kaiserlich-Koeniglichen Erblaendern
Allergnaed Privileg Realzeitung Wiss — Allergnaedigst Privilegierte Realzeitung der Wissenschaften, Kuenste, und der Commercien
Allergol Immunopathol — Allergologia et Immunopathologia
Allergol Immunopathol (Madr) — Allergologia et Immunopathologia (Madrid)
Allergol Immunopathol Suppl — Allergologia et Immunopathologia. Supplementum
Allergol Int — Allergology International
Allergol Proc Congr Int Assoc Allergol — Allergology. Proceedings. Congress. International Association of Allergology
Allerg Relief Newsl — Allergy Relief Newsletter
Allerg S — Allergy Shot
Allergy 74 Proc Eur Congr Allergol Clin Immunol — Allergy '74. Proceedings of the European Congress of Allergology and Clinical Immunology
Allergy Asthma Proc — Allergy and Asthma Proceedings
Allergy Proc — Allergy Proceedings
Allevamenti Vet — Allevamenti e Veterinaria
Alley Mus — Alley Music
ALLG — Archiv fuer Lateinische Lexikographie und Grammatik
Allg Aerztl Zeitsch F Psychotherap — Allgemeine Aerztliche Zeitschrift fuer Psychotherapie und Psychische Hygiene
Allgaeu Geschfreund — Allgaeuer Geschichtsfreund
Allg & Vergl Archaeol Beitr — Allgemeine und Vergleichende Archaeologie. Beitraege
Allg Anzeiger Bbindereien — Allgemeiner Anzeiger fuer Buchbindereien
Allg Arch Geschkde Preuss Staat — Allgemeines Archiv fuer die Geschichtskunde des Preussischen Staates
All Gazdasag — Allami Gazdasag
Allg Bauztg Abbild — Allgemeine Bauzeitung mit Abbildungen. Oesterreichische Vierteljahresschrift fuer den Oeffentlichen Baudienst
Allg Bot Z — Allgemeine Botanische Zeitschrift
Allg Bot Z Syst — Allgemeine Botanische Zeitschrift fuer Systematik, Floristik, Pflanzengeographie
Allg Bot Ztg Abt B — Allgemeine Botanische Zeitung. Abteilung B. Morphologie und Geobotanik

Allg Brau Hopfenztg — Allgemeine Brauer- und Hopfenzeitung
Allg Deutsche Biblioth — Allgemeine Deutsche Bibliothek
Allg Deutsche Naturhist Zeitung — Allgemeine Deutsche Naturhistorische Zeitung
Allg Deutsche Naturh Ztg — Allgemeine Deutsche Naturhistorische Zeitung
Allg D Heb Ztg — Allgemeine Deutsche Hebammenzeitung
Allg Dt Imkerztg — Allgemeine Deutsche Imkerzeitung
Allg Dtsch Imkerztg — Allgemeine Deutsche Imkerzeitung
Allgem Berg- u Huettenm Ztg — Allgemeine Berg- und Huettenmaennische Zeitung
Allgem Berg Zeitung — Allgemeine Berg- und Huettenmaennische Zeitung
Allgemein Statist Arch — Allgemeines Statistisches Archiv
Allg Fischereiztg — Allgemeine Fischereizeitung
Allg Fischwirtschaftsztg — Allgemeine Fischwirtschaftszeitung
Allg Fisch-Ztg — Allgemeine Fischerei-Zeitung
Allg Forst Holzwirtsch Zeit — Allgemeine Forst- und Holzwirtschaftliche Zeitung
Allg Forst Holzwirtsch Ztg — Allgemeine Forst- und Holzwirtschaftliche Zeitung
Allg Forst Jagd Arch — Allgemeines Forst- und Jagd-Archiv
Allg Forst Jagd Zeitung Vienna — Allgemeine Forst- und Jagd-Zeitung (Vienna)
Allg Forst Jagdztg — Allgemeine Forst- und Jagdzeitung
Allg Forst- u Jagdztg — Allgemeine Forst- und Jagdzeitung
Allg Forstz — Allgemeine Forstzeitschrift
Allg Forstzeitschr — Allgemeine Forstzeitschrift
Allg Forstztg — Allgemeine Forstzeitung
Allg Geogr Ephem — Allgemeine Geographische Ephemeriden
Allg Gerber Ztg — Allgemeine Gerber Zeitung
Allg Hist Reisen — Allgemeine Historie der Reisen zu Wasser und zu Lande oder Sammlung von Reisebeschreibungen
Allg Imkerkal — Allgemeine Imkerkalender
Allg J Chem — Allgemeines Journal der Chemie
Allg Lederind Ztg — Allgemeine Lederindustrie Zeitung
Allg Litt Anz — Allgemeiner Litterarischer Anzeiger, oder Annalen der Gesammten Litteratur fuer die Geschwinde Bekanntmachung Verschiedener Nachrichten aus d Gebiete der Gelehrsamkeit und Kunst
Allg Lit Zeitung — Allgemeine Literatur-Zeitung
Allg Militztg — Allgemeine Militaer-Zeitung
Allg Missions Stud — Allgemeine Missions-Studien
Allg Mus Zeitung — Allgemeine Musikalische Zeitung
ALLG Newsletter — Australian Law Librarians' Group. Newsletter
Allg Nord Ann Chem Freunde Naturkd Arzneiwiss — Allgemeine Nordische Annalen der Chemie fuer die Freunde der Naturkunde und Arzneiwissenschaft
Allg Oecon Forst Mag — Allgemeines Oeconomisches Forst-Magazin
Allg Oel-Fett-Ztg — Allgemeine Oel- und Fett-Zeitung
Allg Oester Gerichtsztg — Allgemeine Oesterreichische Gerichtzeitung
Allg Oesterr Chem Tech-Ztg — Allgemeine Oesterreichische Chemiker und Techniker-Zeitung
Allg Oesterr Z Landwirth — Allgemeine Oesterreichische Zeitschrift fuer den Landwirth, Forstmann, und Gaertner
Allg Papier-Rundschau — Allgemeine Papier-Rundschau
Allg Pap Rundsch — Allgemeine Papier-Rundschau
Allg Photogr Ztg — Allgemeine Photographische Zeitung
Allg Prakt Chem — Allgemeine und Praktische Chemie
Allg Repert Lit — Allgemeines Repertorium der Literatur
Allg Rundsch — Allgemeine Rundschau
Allg Stat Arch — Allgemeines Statistisches Archiv
Allg Statis Arch — Allgemeines Statistisches Archiv
Allg Statist Arch — Allgemeines Statistisches Archiv
Allg Teutsch Gart Mag — Allgemeines Teutsches Garten-Magazin oder Gemeinnuetzige Beitraege fuer alle Theile des Praktischen Gartenwesens
Allg Text Z — Allgemeine Textil-Zeitschrift
Allg Text Z Text Ring — Allgemeine Textil-Zeitschrift und Textil-Ring
Allg Thuering Gartenzeitung — Allgemeine Thueringische Gartenzeitung
Allg Tonind Ztg — Allgemeine Tonindustrie Zeitung
Allg Waermetech — Allgemeine Waermetechnik
Allg Wien Med Ztg — Allgemeine Wiener Medizinische Zeitung
Allg Wien M Ztg — Allgemeine Wiener Medizinische Zeitung
Allg Z Bierbrau Malzfabr — Allgemeine Zeitschrift fuer Bierbrauerei und Malzfabrikation
Allg Zeitsch F Psychiat — Allgemeine Zeitschrift fuer Psychiatrie und Psychischgerichtliche Medizin
Allg Zeits F Psychiat — Allgemeine Zeitschrift fuer Psychiatrie und Psychischgerichtliche Medicin
Allg Zellforsch Mikrosk Anat — Allgemeine Zellforschung und Mikroskopische Anatomie
Allg Z Ent — Allgemeine Zeitschrift fuer Entomologie
Allg Z Psychiat — Allgemeine Zeitschrift fuer Psychiatrie
Allg Z Psychiatr Ihre Grenzgeb — Allgemeine Zeitschrift fuer Psychiatrie und Ihre Grenzgebiete
Allg Ztg — Allgemeine Zeitung
Allg Ztschr Psychiat — Allgemeine Zeitschrift fuer Psychiatrie und Psychisch-Gerichtliche Medizin
All Hawaii — All about Business in Hawaii
ALLI — Alliance/l'Alliance. Voice of Metis and Non-Status Indians of Quebec
ALLIAM — Allionia
Alliance Ind — Alliance Industrielle
Alliance Recd — Alliance Record
Alliance Teach — Alliance Teacher
Allianz Ber Betriebstech Schadenverhuetung — Allianz Berichte fuer Betriebstechnik und Schadenverhuetung
Allied Health & Behav Sci — Allied Health and Behavioral Sciences
Allied Ind Wkr — Allied Industrial Worker
Allied Irish Bank R — Allied Irish Bank Review
Allied Vet — Allied Veterinarian
Allier Bll S Em — Bulletin de la Societe d'Emulation du Departement de l'Allier. Sciences, Arts, et Belles-Lettres

All-India Inst Ment Health Trans — All-India Institute of Mental Health. Transactions
All India Rptr — All India Reporter
All India Symp Radioact Metrol Radionuclides Proc — All India Symposium on Radioactivity and Metrology of Radionuclides. Proceedings
All Ind Rep — All India Reporter
Allis-Chalmers Electr Rev — Allis-Chalmers Electrical Review
Allis-Chalmers Eng Rev — Allis-Chalmers Engineering Review
Allison Res Eng — Allison Research and Engineering
ALLKAS — Allattani Kozlemenyek
Allmaenna J — Allmaenna Journalen
Allmaenna Svenska Utsaedesaktiebol Svaloef — Allmaenna Svenska Utsaedesaktiebolaget Svaloef
Allmaenna Svenska Utsaedesfoeren Tidskr — Allmaenna Svenska Utsaedesfoereningens Tidskrift
Allm Sven Elektr Ab Res — Allmaenna Svenska Elektriska Aktiebolaget. Research
Allm Sven Laekartidn — Allmaenna Svenska Laekartidningen
Alloy Cast Bull — Alloy Casting Bulletin
Alloy Dig — Alloy Digest
Alloy Met Rev — Alloy Metals Review
All Pak Legal Dec — All Pakistan Legal Decisions
All Pak Leg Dec — All Pakistan Legal Decisions
All Pak Sci Conf Proc — All Pakistan Science Conference. Proceedings
ALLR — Alaska Law Review
ALLR — Australian Labour Law Reporter
ALLRDI — Allergologie
All St Sales Tax Rep CCH — All-State Sales Tax Reporter. Commerce Clearing House
All T — Allwedd y Tannau
All the Year — All the Year Round
Allum Nuova Met — Alluminio e Nuova Metallurgia
Allum Nuova Metall — Alluminio e Nuova Metallurgia
All WN — Allahabad Weekly Notes (and Supplement)
ALM — Actual (Merida, Venezuela)
ALM — Al Markazi. Central Bank of Oman
ALM — American Law Magazine
ALM — Archives des Lettres Modernes
ALMA — Archivum Latinitatis Medii Aevi
Alma-Atin Gos Ped Inst Ucen Zap — Alma-Atinskii Gosudarstvennyi Pedagogiceskii Institut Imeni Abaja. Ucenye Zapiski
Al Mag — Al Magazine
Alma Mater Philipp — Alma Mater Philippina
Almanak Agric Brasil — Almanak Agricola Brasileiro
Alman Bibliot Italiani — Almanacco dei Bibliotecari Italiani
Alman Cafetero — Almanaque Cafetero
Alman Carlsbad — Almanach de Carlsbad, ou Melanges Medicaux, Scientifiques et Litteraires, Relatifs a ces Thermes et au Pays
Alman Ci — Almanaque Cientifico
Alman Koenigl Bayer Akad Wiss — Almanach der Koeniglich-Bayerischen Akademie der Wissenschaften
Alman Phys Instruct Amusante — Almanach de la Physique Instructive et Amusante
Alman Utrechtsche Landb Genootsch — Almanak van het Utrechtsche Landbouw-Genootschap
ALMArv — Annales Latini Montium Arvernorum. Bulletin du Groupe d'Etudes Latines. Universite de Clermont
Alm Bat — Almanach du Batiment
Alm Chas Pec — Almanach Chasse et Peche
Alm Cr — Almanach du Crime
ALMD — Alaska Medicine
ALMD — Australian Legal Monthly Digest
ALMDB — Alaska Medicine
ALMF — Annales. Laboratoire de Recherche des Musees de France
Alm Fam Meneghina — Almanacco della Famiglia Meneghina
ALMG — Alaska Mines and Geology
AIMK — Alte und Moderne Kunst
Alm Lit Theo — Almanach fuer Literatur und Theologie
ALMM — Alaska Mining and Minerals
ALMMB6 — Allan Hancock Monographs in Marine Biology
ALMNEC — Alimentaria
Alm NR — Almanak voor Notariaat en Registratie
AlmOAW — Almanach. Oesterreichische Akademie der Wissenschaften
Alm Oesterreich Akad Wiss — Almanach der Oesterreichischen Akademie der Wissenschaften
Alm Oesterr Forsch — Almanach der Oesterreichischen Forschung
AlmP — Almanaque Poetique
Alm Paris — Almanach Parisien
ALMPB — Annals. Medical Section. Polish Academy of Sciences
ALMPBF — Annals. Medical Section. Polish Academy of Sciences
Alm Prov — Almanaque de las Provincias
ALMRB — Memorias. Academia das Ciencias de Lisboa. Classe de Ciencias
Alm Schoone & Goede — Almanak voor het Schoone en Goede
ALMTB — Alimenta
Alm Ved — Almanach des Vedettes
ALN — Administrative Law Decisions. Notes
ALN — Archivos Latinoamericanos de Nutricion
ALN — Australian Law News
ALN — Australian Library News
ALNN — Alaska Native Magazine [Formerly, Alaska Native News]
ALNN — Alaska Native News
ALNO — Alberta North
ALNU — Alaska Nurse
AIO — Alte Orient
ALOF — Alaska Offshore
ALOG — Army Logistician

A Lombarda — Arte Lombarda
ALOR — Alter Orient
ALOS — Annual. Leeds University Oriental Society
A Louviere — Annales. Cercle Archeologique et Folklorique de la Louviere et du Centre
ALP — Administration Laboratory Project File
AIP — A la Page
AIP — Altro Polo
ALP — Revista Portugal. Serie A. A Lingua Portuguesa
ALPD — Australian Legal Profession Digest
ALPDA — Advances in Lipid Research
Alpe Adria Microbiol J — Alpe Adria Microbiology Journal
Alpenlaend Bienenztg — Alpenlaendische Bienenzeitung
Alpes Orient — Alpes Orientales
ALPH — Alaskan Philatelist
Alpha-Fetoprotein Hepatoma Jpn Cancer Assn Symp — Alpha-Fetoprotein and Hepatoma. Japanese Cancer Association. Symposium on Alpha-Fetoprotein and Hepatoma
Alpha-Foeto-Proteine C R Conf Int — Alpha-Foeto-Proteine Compte Rendu. Conference Internationale
Alpha Omega Fr — Alpha Omega France
Alpine J — Alpine Journal
ALPMBL — Asociacion Latinoamericana de Produccion Animal. Memoria
ALPS — Alabama Linguistic and Philological Series
ALPS — Arts, Letters, Printers and Publishers, and Systems
ALPVB — Analyse et Prevision
ALQ — Abraham Lincoln Quarterly
ALQ — Annales du Marche Commun; Revue Bimestrielle pour l'Information et l'Harmonisation du Commerce et de l'Industrie
ALR — Adelaide Law Review
ALR — Administrative Law Review
ALR — Afrika Spectrum
ALR — Alberta Law Reports
AIR — Alger Republicain
ALR — American Literary Realism, 1870-1910
ALR — Argus Law Reports
ALR — Australian Argus Law Reports
ALR — Australian Law Reports
ALR — Australian Left Review
ALRA Bull — ALRA [*American Land Resource Association*] Bulletin
ALRAC — Australian Law Reform Agencies Conference
ALRANL — Abortion Law Reform Association. News Letter
ALRC DP — Australian Law Reform Commission. Discussion Paper
ALR (CN) — Argus Law Reports (Current Notes)
ALRED — Arizona Law Review
AL Rev — American Law Review
ALRIAI — Arid Lands Resource Information Paper
ALRNS — American Law Register, New Series
ALS — African Language Studies
ALS — Australian Literary Studies
ALSAA — Allgemeines Statistisches Archiv
Alsace-Lorraine Serv Carte Geol Mem — Alsace-Lorraine. Service de la Carte Geologique. Memoires
ALSA F — ALSA [*American Legal Studies Association*] Forum
ALSC — Alaska Seas and Coast
ALSIB — Alaska Industry
ALSJ — American Liszt Society Journal
ALSK — Alaskana
ALSPAA — American Littoral Society. Special Publication
ALSSDM — Annual Reviews of Plant Sciences
ALT — African Literature Today
AIT — Alalakh Tablets
ALT — ALT. Alternativ Livsform og Teknologi
Alt — Alternances. Cahiers de Poesie
Alt — Altertum
ALT — Annales. Faculte des Lettres de Toulouse
ALT — Australian Law Times
ALT — Rohstoff-Rundschau; Fachblatt des Gesamten Handels mit Altstoffen und Abfallstoffen, mit Ausfuehrlichen Berichten ueber die Internationalen Rohstoffmarkte und Altstoffmarkte
Alta — Alberta Law Reports
Alta Couns — Alberta Counsellor
Alta Counslttr — Alberta Counselletter
Alta Dir — Alta Direccion
Alta Engl — Alberta English
Alta Freq — Alta Frequenza
Alta Freq Riv Elettron — Alta Frequenza Rivista Di Elettronica
Alta Freq Suppl — Alta Frequenza. Supplemento
Alta Hist — Alberta History
Alta Hist R — Alberta Historical Review
Altajsk Sborn — Altajskij Sbornik
Alta Learn Res J — Alberta Learning Resources Journal
Alta Libr Ass Bull — Alberta Library Association. Bulletin
Alta LR — Alberta Law Reports
Alta LR (2d) — Alberta Law Reports, Second Series
Alta L Rev — Alberta Law Review
Alta Mod Lang J — Alberta Modern Language Journal
Alta Pers — Alberta Perspective
Alta Report — Alberta Reports
Alta Rev Stat — Revised Statutes of Alberta
Alta Sci Ed J — Alberta Science Education Journal
Alta Sci Teach — Alberta Science Teacher
Alta Stat — Statutes of Alberta
Altbayer Monatsschr — Altbayerische Monatsschrift
Altbayer Mschr — Altbayerische Monatsschrift

Alt C I — Alternative Culture and Institutions
Alte & Mod Kst — Alte und Moderne Kunst
Alte & Neue Kst — Alte und Neue Kunst
Alte Mod Kunst — Alte und Moderne Kunst. Oesterreichische Fachzeitschrift des Marktes fuer Antiquitaeten, Bilder, Kunstgegenstaende Alter, und Moderner Kunst
Alt En — Alternative Energy
Alt Energy — Alternative Energy Trends and Forecasts
Alt Energy — Alternative Sources of Energy
Alte Or — Alte Orient
Alte Orient Beih — Alte Orient Beihefte
Alter Med — Alternative Medicine
Altern — Alternate Futures
Alternat — Alternatives
Alternate Energy Mag — Alternate Energy Magazine
Alternatives Lab Anim — Alternatives to Laboratory Animals
Alternatives Lab Anim ATLA — Alternatives to Laboratory Animals. ATLA
Alternative Technol Power Prod — Alternative Technologies for Power Production
Alternat Non-Violentes — Alternatives Non-Violentes
Alternatv — Alternatives
Altern (Chile) — Alternativas (Chile)
Altern Energy Sources — Alternative Energy Sources
Altern Energy Sources Proc Miami Int Conf — Alternative Energy Sources. An International Compendium. Proceedings. Miami International Conference
Altern Fuels Emiss Technol — Alternative Fuels Emissions and Technology
Altern Fut — Alternative Futures
Altern High Ed — Alternative Higher Education
Altern Methods Toxicol — Alternative Methods in Toxicology
Altern Methods Toxicol Life Sci — Alternative Methods in Toxicology and the Life Sciences
Altern Press Index — Alternative Press Index
Alternstheorien Memb Giessener Symp Exp Gerontol — Alternstheorien Zellkern Membranen Giessener Symposion ueber Experimentelle Gerontologie
Altern Sweeteners — Alternative Sweeteners
Altern Ther Health Med — Alternative Therapies in Health and Medicine
Altes Haus-Mod — Altes Haus - Modern
Alt Fors — Altorientalische Forschungen
Alt Frankfurt Vjschr Kst & Gesch — Alt-Frankfurt. Vierteljahresschrift fuer Seine Kunst und Geschichte
Altfranz Bibl — Altfranzoesische Bibliothek
Alt Ftr — Alternative Features
Althaus Mod — Althaus Modernisierung
ALTL — Alaska Tidelines
ALTMEA — Alternative Medicine
Alt Media — Alternative Media
Alt-Neuindische Stud — Alt- und Neuindische Studien
Altnord Sagabibl — Altnordische Saga-Bibliothek
Alt O — Der Alte Orient
Alt Or — Alte Orient
Alt Or F — Altorientalische Forschungen
Altorient Forsch — Altorientalische Forschungen
Alt Press Ind — Alternative Press Index
Altpreuss Forsch — Altpreussische Forschungen
Alt Pr J — Alternative Press, Libraries, Journalism
ALTRD — Alternatives
ALTREU — Allgemeine Treuhandstelle fuer die Juedische Auswanderung
Alt Routes — Alternate Routes
Altschles Bl — Altschlesische Blaetter
Altschul Symp Ser — Altschul Symposia Series
Alt Spr — Alten Sprachen
Alt Thuer — Alt-Thueringen
Alt Wien Kal — Alt-Wiener Kalender
ALTZAB — Allattenyesztes
Alu — Aluta. Muzeul Judetean
ALUB — Besancon. Universite. Annales Litteraires
Alum — Aluminium
ALUMA — Aluminium
Alum Abstr — Aluminum Abstracts
Alum Arch — Aluminum Archiv
Alum Co Am Res Lab Tech Pap — Aluminum Company of America. Research Laboratories. Technical Paper
Alum Finish Soc Kinki J — Aluminum Finishing Society of Kinki. Journal
Alumin Cour — Aluminium Courier
Alumin Wld — Aluminium World
Alum Iron Overload Haemod Int Workshop — Aluminum and Iron Overload in Haemodialysis. An International Workshop
Alum Magnesium — Aluminum and Magnesium
Alum Magnesium Automot Appl Proc Symp — Aluminum and Magnesium for Automotive Applications. Proceedings of a Symposium
Alumnae Assn Womens Med Coll Pa Rpt Proc — Alumnae Association. Women's Medical College of Pennsylvania. Report. Proceedings
Alumnae Mag — Alumnae Magazine
Alumnae Mag (Baltimore) — Alumnae Magazine. Johns Hopkins Hospital. School of Nursing. Alumnae Association (Baltimore)
Alum News Lett — Aluminum News Letter
Alumni Bull — Alumni Bulletin of the Rhode Island School of Design
Alumni Bull Sch Dent Indiana Univ — Alumni Bulletin. School of Dentistry. Indiana University
Alumni Bull Univ Mich Sch Dent — Alumni Bulletin. University of Michigan. School of Dentistry
Alumni Bull Univ Virginia — Alumni Bulletin. University of Virginia
Alumni Gaz Coll William — Alumni Gazette. College of William and Mary
Alumni Mag — Alumni Magazine

Alumni Mag Columbia Univ Presbyt Hosp Sch Nurs — Alumni Magazine. Columbia University - Presbyterian Hospital. School of Nursing. Alumni Association

Alumni Mag (NY) — Alumni Magazine. Columbia University-Presbyterian Hospital. School of NursingAlumni Association (New York)

Alum Non Ferrous Met News — Aluminum and Non-Ferrous Metals News

Alum Non Ferrous Rev — Aluminum and The Non-Ferrous Review

Alum Ranshofen Mitt — Aluminum Ranshofen Mitteilungen

Alum Res Lab Tech Pap — Aluminum Research Laboratories. Technical Paper

Alum Rev — Aluminum Review

Alum Stat — Aluminum Statistical Review

Alum Suisse — Aluminum Suisse

Alum Today — Aluminum Today

Alum Transform Technol Appl Proc Int Symp — Aluminum Transformation Technology and Applications. Proceedings. InternationalSymposium

Alum Wld — Aluminium World

Alum World Brass Copper Ind — Aluminum World and Brass and Copper Industries

ALUOS — Leeds University Oriental Society. Annual

ALUR Rep — Arctic Land Use Research Report

ALV — Archiv fuer Literatur und Volksdichtung

ALW — Archiv fuer Liturgiewissenschaft

ALWG Newsletter — Australian Legal Workers Group. Newsletter

ALWNAO — Abhandlungen. Landesmuseum der Provinz Westfalen. Museum fuer Naturkunde

Alyum Splavy Sb Statei — Alyuminievye Splavy. Sbornik Statei

ALZAAY — ALZA Conference Series

ALZA Conf Ser — ALZA Conference Series

Alzheimer Dis Assoc Disord — Alzheimer Disease and Associated Disorders

Alzheimers Dis — Alzheimer's Disease. New Treatment Strategies

Alzheimers Dis Lessons Cell Biol — Alzheimer's Disease. Lessons from Cell Biology [*monograph*]

Alzheimers Dis Rev — Alzheimer's Disease Review

Alzheimers Res — Alzheimer's Research

AM — Acta Musicologica

A/M — Administrative Management

AM — Alma Mater

AM — Alto Minho

AM — America

Am — Americana

AM — American Machinist

AM — American Mercury

AM — American Motorcyclist

AM — American Music

Am — Americas

AM — [*The*] Americas: A Quarterly Review of Inter-American Cultural History

AM — Annales du Midi; Revue de la France Meridionale

AM — Annali Manzoniani

AM — Annuale Mediaevale

AM — Archiv fuer Molluskenkunde

AM — Archivio Muratoriano

AM — Arheologia Moldovei

AM — Asia Major

AM — Athenische Mitteilungen

AM — Atlantic Monthly

AM — A Travers le Monde, Tour du Monde

AM — Australian Magazine

AM — Australian Monthly

AMA — Academy of Management. Journal

AMA — Agricultural Mechanization in Asia

AMA — Amazing Stories. Annual

AmA — American Annual

AmA — American Anthropologist

AMA — American Antiquity

AmA — American Archivist

AMA — American Magazine of Art

AMA — American Marketing Association. Proceedings

AMA — Antichnyi Mir i Arkheologiia

AMA — Atti e Memorie dell'Arcadia

AMAAA — Atti e Memorie. Accademia di Storia dell'Arte Sanitaria

AMAABJ — INTA [*Instituto Nacional de Tecnologia Agropecuaria*]. Manual Agropecuario

AMA Agric Mech Asia Afr Lat Am — AMA. Agricultural Mechanization in Asia, Africa, and Latin America

AMA Arch Dermatol — AMA [*American Medical Association*] Archives of Dermatology

AMA Arch Dermatol Syphilol — AMA [*American Medical Association*] Archives of Dermatology and Syphilology

AMA Arch Gen Psychiatry — AMA [*American Medical Association*] Archives of General Psychiatry

AMA Arch Ind Health — AMA [*American Medical Association*] Archives of Industrial Health

AMA Arch Ind Hyg Occup Med — AMA [*American Medical Association*] Archives of Industrial Hygiene and Occupational Medicine

AMA Archs Internal Med — AMA [*American Medical Association*] Archives of Internal Medicine

AMAAV — Atti e Memorie. Accademia di Agricoltura, Scienze, e Lettere. Verona

AMAC — Anales del Museo Argentino de Ciencias Naturales Bernardino Rivadavia

Am Acad Actuar Jnl — American Academy of Actuaries. Journal

Am Acad Arts & Sci Mem — American Academy of Arts and Sciences. Memoirs

Am Acad Arts & Sci Proc — American Academy of Arts and Sciences. Proceedings

Am Acad Child Psychiat J — American Academy of Child Psychiatry. Journal

Am Acad Matri Law J — American Academy of Matrimonial Lawyers. Journal

Am Acad Ophthalmol Otolaryngol Trans Sect Ophthalmol — American Academy of Ophthalmology and Otolaryngology. Transactions. Section on Ophthalmology

Am Acad Ophthalmol Otolaryngol Trans Sect Otolaryngol — American Academy of Ophthalmology and Otolaryngology. Transactions. Section on Otolaryngology

Am Acad Opthalmol Otolaryngol Trans — American Academy of Ophthalmology and Otolaryngology. Transactions

Am Acad Optom Ser — American Academy of Optometry Series

Am Acad Orthop Surg Lectures — American Academy of Orthopedic Surgery. Instructional Course Lectures

Am Acad Orthop Surg Symp Osteoarthritis — American Academy of Orthopaedic Surgeons. Symposium on Osteoarthritis

Am Acad Pol & Soc Sci Ann — American Academy of Political and Social Science. Annals

Am Acad Psychoanal J — American Academy of Psychoanalysis. Journal

Am Acad Relig J — American Academy of Religion. Journal

Am Acad Rome Mem — American Academy in Rome. Memoirs

AMACC — Antimicrobial Agents and Chemotherapy

AMACCQ — Antimicrobial Agents and Chemotherapy

Am Ac Mm — Memoirs of the American Academy of Arts and Sciences

Am Ac P — Proceedings of the American Academy of Arts and Sciences

Am Ac Pep Prot — Amino-Acids, Peptides, and Proteins

Am Ac Rome — Album of Dated Latin Inscriptions

AMADBS — Archives Francaises des Maladies de l'Appareil Digestif

A Madi Univl — Arte Madi Universal

A Mag — Art Magazine. A Bi-Monthly Review of the Visual Arts

A Mag — Arts Magazine

AMA Gazette — Australian Medical Association. Gazette

Am Ag Br — American Agent and Broker

AMAHA5 — Acta Microbiologica. Academiae Scientiarum Hungaricae

A Maison — Arts de la Maison

AMAJ — Al-Mujtama al-Jadid

AMAJ — American Alpine Journal

AMA J Dis Child — AMA [*American Medical Association*] Journal of Diseases of Children

Amakusa Mar Biol Lab Contr — Amakusa Marine Biological Laboratory. Contributions

A Mal — Analecta Malacitana

Amal Engr Union MJ — Amalgamated Engineering Union. Monthly Journal

Am Alma — American Almanac

Am Alpine Jour — American Alpine Journal

Am Alpine N — American Alpine News

AMAM — Atti e Memorie. Accademia di Scienze, Lettere, ed Arti di Modena

AMA Mod — Atti e Memorie. Accademia di Scienze, Lettere, ed Arti in Modena

AMan — Accademia di Mantova. Atti e Memorie

Am An — American Anthropologist

Am An Hosp Assoc Bul — American Animal Hospital Association. Bulletin

Am Ann — Americana Annual

Am Annals Deaf — American Annals of the Deaf

Am Annals Educ — American Annals of Education

Am Ann Deaf — American Annals of the Deaf

Am Ant — American Anthropologist

Am Ant — American Antiquity

Am Anth — American Anthropologist

Am Anthro — American Anthropologist

Am Anthro Assoc Newsl — American Anthropological Association. Newsletter

Am Anthrop — American Anthropologist

Am Anthropol — American Anthropologist

Am Antiq — American Antiquarian

Am Antiq — American Antiquity

Am Antiq Soc Proc — American Antiquarian Society. Proceedings

Am Antiques — American Antiques

Am Antiquit — American Antiquity

AMAP — Atti e Memorie. Accademia Patavina di Scienze, Lettere, ed Arti

AMAPe — Atti e Memorie. Accademia Petrarca

Am Arab Affairs — American Arab Affairs

Am Arch — American Architect

Am Arch — American Architect and Building News

Am Archaeol Ser — American Archaeology Series. Pan American Union

Am Archiv — American Archivist

Am Archivis — American Archivist

Am Archivist — American Archivist

Am Arch Rehabil Ther — American Archives of Rehabilitation Therapy

AMart — Anuario Martiano

Am Artist — American Artist

Am Art J — American Art Journal

Am Art Rev — American Art Review

Am As Museums Pr — American Association of Museums. Proceedings

Am As P — Proceedings of the American Association for the Advancement of Science

Am As Petroleum G B — American Association of Petroleum Geologists. Bulletin

Am As Pr Mem — American Association for the Advancement of Science. Proceedings. Memoirs

Am Assn Adv Sci Proc — American Association for the Advancement of Science. Proceedings

Am Assn Coll Reg J — American Association of Collegiate Registrars. Journal

Am Assn Col Teach Educ Yrbk — American Association of Colleges for Teacher Education. Yearbook

Am Assn Ment Deficiency Proc — American Association on Mental Deficiency. Proceedings

Am Assn Pet Geol Bul — American Association of Petroleum Geologists. Bulletin

Am Assn Pet Geologists Bull — American Association of Petroleum Geologists. Bulletin

Am Assn Sch Adm Off Rep — American Association of School Administrators. Official Report

Am Assn Stud Feeblemind Proc — American Association for the Study of the Feebleminded. Proceedings

Am Assn Univ Prof B — American Association of University Professors. Bulletin

Am Assn Univ Women J — American Association of University Women. Journal

Am Assoc Adv Sci Abstr Pap Natl Meet — American Association for the Advancement of Science. Abstracts of Papers. National Meeting

Am Assoc Adv Sci Comm Desert Arid Zones Res Contrib — American Association for the Advancement of Science. Committee on Desert and Arid Zones Research. Contribution

Am Assoc Adv Sci Publ — American Association for the Advancement of Science. Publication

Am Assoc Adv Sci Symp — American Association for the Advancement of Science. Symposium

Am Assoc Cereal Chem Monogr Ser — American Association of Cereal Chemists. Monograph Series

Am Assoc Ind Nurses J — American Association of Industrial Nurses. Journal

Am Assoc Pathol Bacteriol Symp Mono — American Association of Pathologists and Bacteriologists. Symposium Monographs

Am Assoc Pet Geol Bull — American Association of Petroleum Geologists. Bulletin

Am Assoc Pet Geol Mem — American Association of Petroleum Geologists. Memoir

Am Assoc Pet Geol Repr Ser — American Association of Petroleum Geologists. Reprint Series

Am Assoc Pet Geol Study Geol — American Association of Petroleum Geologists. Studies in Geology

Am Assoc Petroleum Geologists Mem — American Association of Petroleum Geologists. Memoir

Am Assoc Petroleum Geologists Pacific Sec Correlation Sec — American Association of Petroleum Geologists. Pacific Section. Correlation Section

Am Assoc Ret Per News Bul — American Association of Retired Persons. News Bulletin

Am Assoc Sm Res Comp N — American Association of Small Research Companies. News

Am Assoc State Local Hist Bull — American Association for State and Local History. Bulletin

Am Assoc Stratigr Palynol Contrib Ser — American Association of Stratigraphic Palynologists. Contribution Series

Am Assoc Text Chem Color Natl Tech Conf Book Pap — American Association of Textile Chemists and Colorists. National Technical Conference. Book of Papers

Am Assoc Univ Prof Bull — American Association of University Professors. Bulletin

Am Assoc Univ Women Jour — American Association of University Women. Journal

Am Assoc Vet Lab Diagn Proc Annu Meet — American Association of Veterinary Laboratory Diagnosticians. Proceedings of Annual Meeting

Am Assoc Zoo Vet Annu Proc — American Association of Zoo Veterinarians. Annual Proceedings

Am Astronaut Soc Publ Sci Technol — American Astronautical Society. Publications. Science and Technology

Am Astronaut Soc Sci Technol Ser — American Astronautical Society. Science and Technology Series

Am Astron Soc Bull — American Astronomical Society. Bulletin

Am Astron Soc Photo Bull — American Astronomical Society. Photo Bulletin

AMAT — Atti e Memorie. Accademia Toscana la Colombaria

AMAT — Atti e Memorie dell'Accademia Toscana di Scienze e Lettere. La Colombaria

Amat Build Man — Amateur Builder's Manual

Amat Cine World — Amateur Cine World

Amat Ent — Amateur Entomologist

Amateur Gard Gard Chron — Amateur Gardener and Gardeners Chronicle

Amateur Gard Springfield — Amateur Gardening, for the Lovers and Cultivators of Flowers and Fruits (Springfield)

Amat Geol — Amateur Geologist

Amatores Herb — Amatores Herbarii/Shokubutsu Shumi

Amat Photogr — Amateur Photographer

Amat Photographer — Amateur Photographer

Amat Phot Prt — Amateur Photographic Print

AMAUBB — Acta Medica Austriaca

Am Auto — American Automobile

Am Auto Dig — American Automobile Digest

Am Aviat — American Aviation

Am Aviation — American Aviation

AMAZAP — Amazoniana

Amazon Col Am — Amazonia Colombiana Americanista

Amaz Per — Amazonia Peruana

AMB — Abstracts of Military Bibliography

AMB — Acta Medica Bulgarica

AMB — AMB. Revista da Associacao Medica Brasileira

AMB — Antarctic Meteorite Bibliography

Am Baby — American Baby

Am Baby — American Baby for Expectant and New Parents

Am Baby Expectant New Parents — American Baby for Expectant and New Parents

AMBAER — Arquivos. Museu Bocage. Serie A

Am Bank — American Banker

Am Bank Assoc Bank Comp — American Bankers Association. Bank Compliance

Am Bank Assoc Bank Jnl — American Bankers Association. Banking Journal

Am Bank Dir US Bank Exec — American Banker Directory of US Banking Executives

Am Bankers Assn J — American Bankers' Association. Journal

Am Bankr L J — American Bankruptcy Law Journal

Am Bankrupt — American Bankruptcy Law Journal

Am Bankruptcy R — American Bankruptcy Review

Am Ban LJ — American Bankruptcy Law Journal

Am Bapt Q — American Baptist Quarterly

Am Bar A J — American Bar Association. Journal

Am Bar Ass J — American Bar Association. Journal

Am Bar Assn J — American Bar Association. Journal

Am Bar Assoc J — American Bar Association. Journal

Am Bar Assoc Jour — American Bar Association Journal

Am Bar Asso Jour — American Bar Association. Journal

Am Bar Found Res J — American Bar Foundation. Research Journal

Am Bar N — American Bar News

Ambas Amer — Ambas Americas. Revista de Educacion, Bibliografia, i Agricultura

Am B Assn Comp L Bur Bul — American Bar Association. Comparative Law Bureau. Bulletin

Am B Assn J — American Bar Association Journal

Am B Assn Rep — American Bar Association. Report

AMBB — Annuaire. Musees Royaux des Beaux-Arts de Belgique

AMBBB — Acta Microbiologica Polonica. Series B. Microbiologia Applicata

Am Bee J — American Bee Journal

Am Beekeep Fed Newsl — American Beekeeping Federation. Newsletter

Am Behavioral Sci — American Behavioral Scientist

Am Behavioral Scientist — American Behavioral Scientist

Am Behav Sci — American Behavioral Scientist

Am Benedictine Rev — American Benedictine Review

AmBenR — American Benedictine Review

Am B Found Res J — American Bar Foundation. Research Journal

AMBG — Annals. Missouri Botanical Garden

AMBGA7 — Annals. Missouri Botanical Garden

AMBHAA — Acta Microbiologica Hellenica

AMBIB — Abhandlungen. Akademie der Wissenschaften in Goettingen. Mathematisch-Physikalische Klasse. Beitraege zum Internationalen Geophysikalischen Jahr

Am Bibliop — American Bibliopolist

Am Bib Repos — American Biblical Repository

AMBIEH — Antibiotics and Medical Biotechnology

AMBIEH — Antibiotiki i Meditsinskaya Biotekhnologiya

Am Biol Tea — American Biology Teacher

Am Biol Teach — American Biology Teacher

Ambio Spec Rep — Ambio. Special Report

Am Biotechnol Lab — American Biotechnology Laboratory

Am Birds — American Birds

Am Bk Collec — American Book Collector

Am Bk Collector — American Book Collector

Am Bld — American Builder

Am Bldg Ass News — American Building Association News

Am Bldr — American Builder and Building Age

AMBNA — Acta Medica et Biologica (Niigata)

AMBNDV — Arquivos. Museu Bocage. Serie B. Notas

Amb Nuova Archit — Ambienti della Nuova Architettura

Am Book Publ Recd — American Book Publishing Record

Am Book Rev — American Book Review

Am Bot — American Botanist

Am Bottl — American Bottler

Am Bottler — American Bottler

Am Boxmkr — American Boxmaker

AMBPBZ — Acta Pathologica et Microbiologica Scandinavica. Section A. Pathology

Am B Q — American Baptist Quarterly

AmBR — American Benedictine Review

Am Breed Mag — American Breeders' Magazine

Am Brew — American Brewer

Am Brew Rev — American Brewer's Review

Am Brit — American in Britain

AMBSDC — Arquivos. Museu Bocage. Serie C. Suplementos

Am Bsns — American Business

Am Bsns Ed — American Business Education

Am Bsns Ed Yrbk — American Business Education Yearbook

AMBT — American Biology Teacher

AMBUDI — Acta Microbiologica Bulgarica

AMBUEJ — American Malacological Bulletin

Ambulance Bull — Ambulance Bulletin

Ambulance J — Ambulance Journal

Am Bur Geog B — American Bureau of Geography. Bulletin

Am Bus Assoc Rep — American Bus Association. Report

Am Business — American Business

Am Bus Law — American Business Law Journal

Am Bus Law J — American Business Law Journal

Am Bus L J — American Business Law Journal

Am Butter Cheese Rev — American Butter and Cheese Review

Am Butter R — American Butter and Cheese Review

AMBYAR — Advances in Marine Biology

AMC — Agricultural Magazine (Cairo)

Am C — American Chemist. A Monthly Journal of Theoretical Chemistry

AMC — American Music Center. Newsletter

Am Cage Bird Mag — American Cage Bird Magazine

Am Camellia Q — American Camellia Quarterly

Am Camellia Soc Yb — American Camellia Society Yearbook

Am Camellia Yearb — American Camellia Yearbook

Am Camellia Yearb (Am Camellia Soc) — American Camellia Yearbook (American Camellia Society)

Am Carbonator — American Carbonator and American Bottler

Am Carbonator Bottler — American Carbonator and Bottler

Am Carp Bldr — American Carpenter and Builder

Am Cath His Rec — American Catholic Historical Society. Records

Am Cath His S — American Catholic Historical Society. Records

Am Cath Hist Soc Rec — American Catholic Historical Society of Philadelphia. Records

AmCathHS — American Catholic Historical Society. Records

Am Cath Q — American Catholic Quarterly Review
Am Cath Sociol Rev — American Catholic Sociological Review
Am Cattle Prod — American Cattle Producer
Am Cattl Prod — American Cattle Producer
Am Ceramic Soc Jour — American Ceramic Society. Journal
Am Ceram S — American Ceramic Society. Bulletin
Am Ceram Soc Bull — American Ceramic Society. Bulletin
Am Ceram Soc Fall Meet Mater Equip Whitewares Div Proc — American Ceramic Society. Fall Meeting. Materials and Equipment. Whitewares Division. Proceedings
Am Cer Soc Bul — American Ceramic Society. Bulletin
Am Cer Soc J — American Ceramic Society. Journal
Am Chamber Commer Japan J — American Chamber of Commerce in Japan. Journal
Am Chem — American Chemist
Am Chem J — American Chemical Journal
Am Chem Soc Dir Grad Res — American Chemical Society Directory of Graduate Research
Am Chem Soc Div Environ Chem Prepr — American Chemical Society. Division of Environmental Chemistry. Preprints
Am Chem Soc Div Fuel Chem Prepr — American Chemical Society. Division of Fuel Chemistry. Preprints
Am Chem Soc Div Fuel Chem Prepr Pap — American Chemical Society. Division of Fuel Chemistry. Preprints of Papers
Am Chem Soc Div Fuel Prepr — American Chemical Society. Division of Fuel Chemistry. Preprints
Am Chem Soc Div Gas Fuel Chem — American Chemical Society. Division of Gas and Fuel Chemistry. Preprints
Am Chem Soc Div Gas Fuel Chem Prepr — American Chemical Society. Division of Gas and Fuel Chemistry. Preprints
Am Chem Soc Div Nucl Chem Technol Symp Exot Nucl Spectrosc — American Chemical Society Division of Nuclear Chemistry and Technology Symposium on Exotic Nuclear Spectroscopy
Am Chem Soc Div Org Coat Plast Chem Pap — American Chemical Society. Division of Organic Coatings and Plastics Chemistry.Papers
Am Chem Soc Div Org Coat Plast Chem Pap Meet — American Chemical Society. Division of Organic Coatings and Plastics Chemistry.Papers Presented at the Meeting
Am Chem Soc Div Pet Chem Gen — American Chemical Society. Division of Petroleum Chemistry. General Papers. Preprints
Am Chem Soc Div Pet Chem Gen Pap Prepr — American Chemical Society. Division of Petroleum Chemistry. General Papers. Preprints
Am Chem Soc Div Pet Chem Prepr — American Chemical Society. Division of Petroleum Chemistry. Preprints
Am Chem Soc Div Pet Chem Symp — American Chemical Society. Division of Petroleum Chemistry. Symposia
Am Chem Soc Div Petr Chem Prepr — American Chemical Society. Division of Petroleum Chemistry. Preprints
Am Chem Soc Div Polym Chem Prepr — American Chemical Society. Division of Polymer Chemistry. Preprints
Am Chem Soc Div Water Air Waste Chem Gen Pap — American Chemical Society. Division of Water, Air, and Waste Chemistry. GeneralPapers
Am Chem Soc J — American Chemical Society. Journal
Am Chem Soc Jt Conf Chem Inst Can Abstr Pap — American Chemical Society. Joint Conference with the Chemical Institute of Canada. Abstracts of Papers
Am Chem Soc Mon — American Chemical Society. Monograph
Am Chem Soc News Edn — American Chemical Society. News Edition
Am Chem Soc Rep Annu Meet Corp Assoc — American Chemical Society. Report. Annual Meeting. Corporation Associates
Am Chem Soc Rubber Div Symp — American Chemical Society. Rubber Division. Symposia
Am Chem Soc Symp — American Chemical Society Symposium
Am Chem Soc Symp Chem Pretreat Nucl Waste Disposal — American Chemical Society Symposium on Chemical Pretreatment of Nuclear Waste for Disposal
Am Chem Soc Symp Ser — American Chemical Society. Symposium Series
Am Child — American Child
Am Childh — American Childhood
Am Child Hlth Ass Publs — American Child Health Association. Publications
Am Chiro — American Chiropractor
Am Choral R — American Choral Review
Am Ch P — Amitie Charles Peguy. Feuillets Mensels
AmChQ — American Church Quarterly
Am Christmas Tree Grow J — American Christmas Tree Growers' Journal
Am Christmas Tree J — American Christmas Tree Journal
Am Church Mo — American Church Monthly
Am Church R — American Church Review
AMCIA — American City
AMCILR — Actas y Memorias. Congreso Internacional de Linguistica Romanica
AMCIM — Actes et Memoires. Congres International de Langue et Litterature du Midi de laFrance
Am Cin — American Cinematographer
Am Cinem — American Cinematographer
Am Cinematgr — American Cinematographer
Am Cinematog — American Cinematographer
AMCISO — Actes et Memoires. Congres International des Sciences Onomastiques
AMCIT — Actes et Memoires. Congres International de Toponymie
Am City — American City
Am City (C ed) — American City (City Edition)
Am City Cty — American City and County
Am City (T & C ed) — American City (Town and Country Edition)
Am Civ LJ — American Civil Law Journal
AMC J — AMC (American Mining Congress) Journal
Am C J — American Chemical Journal
Am Climatol Assn Trans — American Climatological and Clinical Association. Transactions

Am Clin — America Clinica
Am Clin Climatol Assoc Trans — American Clinical and Climatological Association. Transactions
AMCM — Atti e Memorie del Convegno di Studi Storici in Onore di L. A. Muratori
AMCMAU — Annales. Musee Colonial de Marseille
AMCN — American Music Center Newsletter
Am Coal J — American Coal Journal
Am Coll — American Collector
Am Coll Physicians Bull — American College of Physicians. Bulletin
Am Coll Physicians Obs — American College of Physicians. Observer
Am Coll Radio Bull — American College of Radiology Bulletin
Am Col Toxicol J — American College of Toxicology. Journal
Am Concrete Inst J — American Concrete Institute. Journal
Am Concr Inst J — American Concrete Institute. Journal
Am Concr Inst Monogr — American Concrete Institute. Monograph
Am Concr Inst Publ SP — American Concrete Institute. Publication SP
Am Concr Inst SP — American Concrete Institute. Special Publication
Am Cons B — American Consular Bulletin
Am Consul Bul — American Consular Bulletin
Am Contract — American Contractor
Am Coop — American Cooperation
Am Co-Op J — American Co-Operative Journal
Am Correct Ther J — American Corrective Therapy Journal
Am Cosmet Perfum — American Cosmetics and Perfumery
Am Cott Grow — American Cotton Grower
Am Counc Cons Int Proc — American Council on Consumer Interest. Proceedings
Am Counc Jud Issues — American Council for Judaism. Issues
Am County — American County
AMCR — American Choral Review
Am Craft — American Craft
Am Creamery — American Creamery and Poultry Produce Review
Am Cream Poult Prod Rev — American Creamery and Poultry Produce Review
A Mcrgr — Annales de Micrographie, Specialement Consacrees a la Bacteriologie, aux Protophytes et aux Protozoaires
Am Crim Law — American Criminal Law Review
Am Crim L Q — American Criminal Law Quarterly
Am Crim LR — American Criminal Law Review
Am Crim L Rev — American Criminal Law Review
Am Cryst Assoc Trans — American Crystallographic Association. Polycrystal Book Service. Transactions
Am C S J — Journal of the American Chemical Society
AMCSN — Annali. Museo Civico di Storia Naturale
AMCTAH — Antibiotic Medicine and Clinical Therapy
Am Cyanamid Co Miner Dressing Notes — American Cyanamid Company. Mineral Dressing Notes
Am Cyanamid Co Tech Bull — American Cyanamid Company. Technical Bulletin
Am Cy Mag — American City Magazine
AMCZg — Allgemeine Medizinische Zentralzeitung
AMD — American Demographics
AmD — American Dialog
AMD — Scheppend Ambacht. Tweemaandelijks Tijdschrift voor Toegepaste Kunst
Am Daffodil Yearb — American Daffodil Yearbook
Am Dairym — American Dairyman
Am Dairy Prod Mfg Rev — American Dairy Products Manufacturing Review
Am Dairy Prod R — American Dairy Products Review
Am Dairy R — American Dairy Review
Am Dairy Rev — American Dairy Review
AMDEL Bul — AMDEL [*Australian Mineral Development Laboratories*] Bulletin
AMDEL Bull — AMDEL [*Australian Mineral Development Laboratories*] Bulletin
Am Demogr — American Demographics
Am Demographics — American Demographics
Am Dent — American Dentist
Am Dental Assn J — American Dental Association. Journal
Am Dent J — American Dental Journal
Am Dent Surg — American Dental Surgeon
AMDIB — Annales de Medecine Interne
AMDIBO — Annales de Medecine Interne
Am Dietet Assn J — American Dietetic Association. Journal
Am Dietetic Assn J — American Dietetic Association. Journal
AMDM — Atti e Memorie. Deputazione di Storia Patria per le Antiche Provincie Modenesi
AMD Mod — Atti e Memorie. Deputazione di Storia Patria per le Antiche Provincie Modenensi
AMDNA4 — Annali di Medicina Navale
Am Doc — American Documentation
Am Docum — American Documentation
AMDPAA — Acta Medica Polona
Am Drop Forg — American Drop Forger
Am Drop Forger — American Drop Forger
Am Drug — American Druggist
Am Drug Circ Chem Gaz — American Druggists Circular and Chemical Gazette
Am Drugg — American Druggist
Am Druggist — American Druggist
Am Druggist Merch — American Druggist Merchandising
Am Drug Index — American Drug Index
Am Drug Pharm Rec — American Druggist and Pharmaceutical Record
Am Drycleaner — American Drycleaner
AMDS — Agri-Markets Data Service
AMDSPAM — Atti e Memorie. Deputazione di Storia Patria per le Antiche Provincie Modenesi
AMDSPPM — Atti e Memorie. Deputazione di Storia Patria per le Provincie delle Marche
AMD Symp Ser (Am Soc Mech Eng) — AMD Symposia Series (American Society of Mechanical Engineers)
Am Dye Rep — American Dyestuff Reporter

Am Dyest Rep — American Dyestuff Reporter
Am Dyestuf — American Dyestuff Reporter
Am Dyestuff Rep — American Dyestuff Reporter
Am Dyestuff Reptr — American Dyestuff Reporter
AME — American Economist
AME — Automatenmarkt
AMEAB5 — Australia. Commonwealth Scientific and Industrial Research Organisation. Division of Mechanical Engineering. Annual Report
AMEBA — Annales Medicinae Experimentalis et Biologiae Fenniae
Am Eccles Rev — American Ecclesiastical Review
Am Ecl — American Eclectic
Am Econ — American Economist
Am Econ Assn Bul — American Economic Association. Bulletin
Am Econ Assn Publ — American Economic Association. Publications
Am Econ Assoc — American Economic Association. Publications
Am Econ Assoc Publ — American Economic Association. Publications
Am Econ Dev Counc Conf Notes — American Economic Development Council. Conference Notes
Am Economist — American Economist
Am Econ R — American Economic Review
Am Econ Rev — American Economic Review
Am Econ R Pa & Proc — American Economic Review. Papers and Proceedings
Am Ec R — American Economic Review
Am Ec Rev — American Economic Review
AMED — American Education
A Med — Arte Medievale
A Med Biol — Acta Medica et Biologica
A Med Cost — Acta Medica Costarricense
A Med Hist Pat — Acta Medicae Historiae Patavina
A Mediev — Archeologie Medievale
A Med Ir — Acta Medica Iranica
A Medit — Arte Mediterranea
A Med Nag — Acta Medica Nagasakiensia
A Med Ok — Acta Medicinae Okayama
A Med Or — Acta Medica Orientalia
A Med Pat — Acta Medica Patavina
A Med Phil — Acta Medica Philippina
A Med Rep Trudeau Sanat — Annual Medical Report. Trudeau Sanatorium
Am Ed Res J — American Educational Research Journal
A Med Sanit Rep Antigua — Annual Medical and Sanitary Report. Antigua
A Med Sanit Rep Br Solomon Isl — Annual Medical and Sanitary Report. British Solomon Islands
A Med Sanit Rep Colon Gibraltar — Annual Medical and Sanitary Report. Colony of Gibraltar
A Med Sanit Rep Cyprus — Annual Medical and Sanitary Report. Cyprus
A Med Sanit Rep Gambia — Annual Medical and Sanitary Report. Gambia
A Med Sanit Rep Grenada — Annual Medical and Sanitary Report. Grenada
A Med Sanit Rep Leeward Isl — Annual Medical and Sanitary Report. Leeward Islands
A Med Sanit Rep Nigeria — Annual Medical and Sanitary Report. Nigeria
A Med Sanit Rep Nyasaland — Annual Medical and Sanitary Report. Nyasaland Protectorate
A Med Sanit Rep Somaliland — Annual Medical and Sanitary Report. Somaliland Protectorate
A Med Sanit Rep Tanganyika — Annual Medical and Sanitary Report. Tanganyika
A Med Sanit Rep Uganda — Annual Medical and Sanitary Report. Uganda Protectorate
A Med Scand — Acta Medica Scandinavica
A Med Sci Hung — Acta Medica. Academiae Scientiarum Hungaricae
Am Educ — American Education
Am Educ Res — American Educational Research Journal
A Med Univ Kag — Acta Medica Universitatis Kagoshimaensis
A Med Ven — Acta Medica Venezolana
A Med Vietn — Acta Medica Vietnamica
A Meet Ent Soc Am — Annual Meeting. Entomological Society of America
A Meet Kans St Hort Soc — Annual Meeting. Kansas State Horticultural Society
Am Egg & Poultry R — American Egg and Poultry Review
AMELA3 — American Journal of Medical Electronics
A Melbourne — Arts in Melbourne
Am Electrochem Soc Trans — American Electrochemical Society. Transactions
Am Electroplat Soc Ann Tech Conf — American Electroplaters' Society. Annual Technical Conference
Am Electroplat Soc Coat Sol Collect Symp Proc — American Electroplaters' Society. Coatings for Solar CollectorsSymposium. Proceedings
Am Electroplat Soc Contin Strip Plat Symp — American Electroplaters' Society. Continuous Strip Plating Symposium
Am Electroplat Soc Decor Plat Symp — American Electroplaters' Society. Decorative Plating Symposium
Am Electroplat Soc Electroless Plat Symp — American Electroplaters' Society. Electroless Plating Symposium
Am Electroplat Soc Int Pulse Plat Symp Pap — American Electroplaters' Society. International Pulse PlatingSymposium. Papers
Am Electroplat Soc Plat Electron Ind — American Electroplaters' Society. Plating in the Electronics Industry
Am Electroplat Soc Res Rep — American Electroplaters' Society. Research Report
Am Electroplat Surf Finish Soc Annu Tech Conf Proc — American Electroplaters and Surface Finishers Society. Annual Technical Conference. Proceedings
Am Electrother X Ray Era — American Electro-therapeutic and X-Ray Era
AMEMA — Anales de Mecanica y Electricidad
Amenage Territ Droit Foncier — Amenagement du Territoire et Droit Foncier
Amenag et Nature — Amenagement et Nature
Amenag Territ Develop Region — Amenagement du Territoire et Developpement Regional
Am Enameler — American Enameler
Amended Specif (UK) — Amended Specification (United Kingdom)

Am Eng — American Engineer
Am Eng & Railroad J — American Engineer and Railroad Journal
Am Engr Jersey Cy — American Engineer (Jersey City)
Am Ens — American Ensemble
Am Enterp Inst Public Policy Res Natl Energy Study — American Enterprise Institute for Public Policy Research. National Energy Study
Am Entomol Soc Trans — American Entomological Society. Transactions
Am Environ Lab — American Environmental Laboratory
Am Ephem — American Ephemeris and Nautical Almanac
Amer — American
Am ER — American Ecclesiastical Review
Am ER — American Economic Review
Amer A — American Art
Amer A & Ant — American Art and Antiques
Amer A Annu — American Art Annual
Amer Acad Arts & Sci Mem — American Academy of Arts and Sciences. Memoirs
Amer Acad of Arts and Sciences Proc — American Academy of Arts and Sciences. Proceedings
Amer Acad Rome — Memoirs. American Academy in Rome
Amer A Dir — American Art Directory
Amer A J — American Art Journal
Amer Amat Photographer — American Amateur Photographer
Amer A News — American Art News
Amer Ann Phot — American Annual of Photography
Amer Annual Phot — American Annual of Photography
Amer Annu Phot — American Annual of Photography
Amer Ant — American Antiquity. Quarterly Review of American Archaeology
Amer Anthr — American Anthropologist
Amer Anthrop — American Anthropologist
Amer Anthropol — American Anthropologist
Amer Anthropologist — American Anthropologist
Amer Antiq — American Antiquity
Amer Antiq Soc Proc — American Antiquarian Society. Proceedings
Amer Antiq Soc Proc Annual Meeting — American Antiquarian Society. Proceedings. Annual Meeting
Amer Antiqua Soc Proc — American Antiquarian Society Proceedings
Amer Antiquity — American Antiquity
Amer Ant J — American Antiques Journal
Amer A Q — American Art Quarterly
Amer Aquar — American Aquarist
Amer Arch — American Archivist
Amer Archit & Archit Rev — American Architect and the Architectural Review
Amer Archit & Bldg News — American Architect and Building News
Amer Architect — American Architect
Amer Architect & Archit — American Architect and Architecture
Amer Archivist — American Archivist
Amer Arch Rehab Ther — American Archives of Rehabilitation Therapy
Amer A Rev — American Art Review
Amer Artist — American Artist
Amer Art J — American Art Journal
Amerasia J — Amerasia Journal
Amer Assoc Archit Bibliog Pap — American Association of Architectural Bibliographers. Papers
Amer Assoc Pet Geol Bull — American Association of Petroleum Geologists. Bulletin
Amer Avia Hist Soc Jnl — American Aviation Historical Society. Journal
Amer Baker — American Baker
Amer Bar Assoc J — American Bar Association Journal
Amer Bee J — American Bee Journal
Amer Behav Sci — American Behavioral Scientist
Amer Behav Scientist — American Behavioral Scientist
Amer Benedictine Rev — American Benedictine Review
Amer Biol Teacher — American Biology Teacher
Amer Bk Pub Rec — American Book Publishing Record
Amer Bldrs J — American Builder's Journal
Amer Bloodstk Rev — American Bloodstock Review
Amer Book Coll — American Book Collector
Amer Bookman — Bookman
Amer Bot Binghamton — American Botanist Devoted to Economic and Ecological Botany (Binghamton)
Amer Bot San Diego — American Botanist (San Diego)
Amer Breed Assoc Rep — American Breeders Association Report
Amer Brewer — American Brewer
Amer Cath Philos Q — American Catholic Philosophical Quarterly
Amer Cattle Prod — American Cattle Producer
Amer Cer — American Ceramics
Amer Ceram Soc Bull — American Ceramic Society. Bulletin
Amer Cer Circ Bull — American Ceramic Circle Bulletin
Amer Chem Soc Div Fuel Chem Prepr — American Chemical Society. Division of Fuel Chemistry. Preprints
Amer Chem Soc Div Org Coatings Plast Chem Prepr — American Chemical Society. Division of Organic Coatings and Plastics Chemistry.Preprints
Amer Chem Soc Div Petrol Chem Prepr — American Chemical Society. Division of Petroleum Chemistry. Preprints
Amer Chem Soc Div Water Air Waste Chem Gen Pap — American Chemical Society. Division of Water, Air, and Waste Chemistry. GeneralPapers
Amer Chem Soc Int Symp Inorg Met Containing Polym Mater — American Chemical Society International Symposium on Inorganic and Metal-Containing Polymeric Materials
Amer Chem Soc J — Journal. American Chemical Society
Amer Chem Soc Petrol Chem Div Preprints — American Chemical Society. Petroleum Chemistry Division. Preprints
Amer Chem Soc Symp Enzyme Mimetic Relat Polym — American Chemical Society Symposium on Enzyme Mimetic and Related Polymers

Amer Chem Soc Symp Polym Biotechnol — American Chemical Society Symposium on Polymers from Biotechnology
Amer Chem Soc Symp Polym Cosmet Pharm Appl — American Chemical Society Symposium on Polymers for Cosmetic and Pharmaceutical Applications
Amer Chem Soc Symp Prog Biomed Polym — American Chemical Society Symposium on Progress in Biomedical Polymers
Amer Choral R — American Choral Review
Amer Chrysanthemum Annual — American Chrysanthemum Annual
Amer Cinematogr — American Cinematographer
Amer City — American City
Amer Classic Screen — American Classic Screen
Amer Colr — American Collector
Amer Concr Inst Monogr — American Concrete Institute. Monograph
Amer Concr Inst Stand — American Concrete Institute. Standards
Amer Corp — American Corporation
Amer Correct Ther J — American Corrective Therapy Journal
Amer Craft — American Craft
Amer Craft Horiz — American Craft Horizon
Amer Cttee S Asian A Newslett — American Committee for South Asian Art Newsletter
Amer Dairy Rev — American Dairy Review
Amer Demogr — American Demographics
Amer Doc — American Documentation
Amer Drug — American Druggist
Amer Druggist — American Druggist
Amer Dyestuff Rep — American Dyestuff Reporter
Amer Dyestuff Reporter — American Dyestuff Reporter
Amer Econ Assoc Publ — American Economic Association Publications
Amer Economist — American Economist
Amer Econ R — American Economic Review
Amer Econ Rev — American Economic Review
Amer Eng — American Engineer
Amer Entomol — American Entomologist
Amer Ethnol — American Ethnologist
Amer Ethnologist — American Ethnologist
Amer F — American Film
Amer Fabrics — American Fabrics
Amer Feder — American Federationist
Amer Fern J — American Fern Journal
Amer Fish Soc Symp — American Fisheries Society Symposium
Amer Forests — American Forests
Amer Forests Forest Life — American Forests and Forest Life
Amer Fruits — American Fruits
Amer Gard Mag — American Gardener's Magazine and Register of Useful Discoveries and Improvements in Horticulture and Rural Affairs
Amer Gas Ass Mon — American Gas Association. Monthly
Amer Gas Ass Oper Sect Proc — American Gas Association. Operating Section. Proceedings
Amer Gas J — American Gas Journal
Amer Gdnr mag — American Gardener Magazine
Amer Gear Mfr Ass Stand — American Gear Manufacturers Association. Standards
A M Erg H — Mitteilungen des Deutschen Archaeologischen Instituts. Athenische Abteilung
Amer Gladiolus Soc Off Rev — American Gladiolus Society Official Review
AmerH — America. History and Life
Amer Her — American Heritage
Amer Herb Grower — American Herb Grower
Amer Highways — American Highways
Amer Hist Rev — American Historical Review
Amer Homes & Gdns — American Homes and Gardens
Amer Hort Mag — American Horticultural Magazine
Amer Hort Soc Gard Forum — American Horticultural Society Gardeners Forum
Amer Hum — American Humor
Amerl — America Indigena
America Indig — America Indigena
American Assoc Arch Bib — American Association of Architectural Bibliographers. Papers
American Business Law Jrnl — American Business Law Journal
American Church R — American Church Review
American Cl R — American Classical Review
American F — American Film
American Inst Planners Jnl — American Institute of Planners. Journal
American J Ph — American Journal of Philology
American Jrnl of Economics and Sociology — American Journal of Economics and Sociology
American Jrnl of Small Business — American Journal of Small Business
American Planning Assocn Jnl — American Planning Association. Journal
AmericaQ — America. Quito
Amerikastud — Amerikastudien
Amer Imago — American Imago
Amer Imp Exp Bul — American Import Export Bulletin
Amer Imp Exp Man — American Import Export Management
Amer Ind A — American Indian Art
Amer Ind A & Cult — American Indian Arts and Culture
Amer Ind Bask — American Indian Basketry
Amerind Cosmol — Amerindian Cosmology
Amer Ind Cult & Res J — American Indian Culture and Research Journal
Amer Ind Hyg Assoc J — American Industrial Hygiene Association Journal
Amer Indian Art — American Indian Art Magazine
Amer Indian Bask Mag — American Indian Basketry Magazine
Amer Indian Q — American Indian Quarterly
Amer Indian Rock Art — American Indian Rock Art
Amer Indig — America Indigena
Amer Ind J — American Indian Journal

Amer Ind Trad — American Indian Tradition
Amer Industr Hyg Assoc J — American Industrial Hygiene Association. Journal
Amer Inkmaker — American Inkmaker
Amer Inst Phys Transl Ser — American Institute of Physics Translation Series
Amer Iron Steel Inst Contrib Met Steel — American Iron and Steel Institute. Contributions to the Metallurgy of Steel
Amer Iron Steel Inst Reg Tech Meetings Addresses — American Iron and Steel Institute. Regional Technical Meetings. Addresses
Amer Iron Steel Steel Res Constr Bull — American Iron and Steel Institute. Steel Research for Construction. Bulletin
Amer J Agr Econ — American Journal of Agricultural Economics
Amer J Agric Econ — American Journal of Agricultural Economics
Amer J Anc Hist — American Journal of Ancient History
Amer J Archaeol — American Journal of Archaeology
Amer J Art Ther — American Journal of Art Therapy
Amer J Bot — American Journal of Botany
Amer J Cardiol — American Journal of Cardiology
Amer J Chinese Medicine — American Journal of Chinese Medicine
Amer J Clin Hypnosis — American Journal of Clinical Hypnosis
Amer J Clin Nutr — American Journal of Clinical Nutrition
Amer J Clin Pathol — American Journal of Clinical Pathology
Amer J Comp L — American Journal of Comparative Law
Amer J Comp Law — American Journal of Comparative Law
Amer J Dermatol Genito Urin Dis — American Journal of Dermatology and Genito-Urinary Diseases
Amer J Digest Dis — American Journal of Digestive Diseases [*Later, Digestive Diseases and Sciences*]
Amer J Digestive Dis Nutr — American Journal of Digestive Diseases and Nutrition
Amer J Dis Child — American Journal of Diseases of Children
Amer J Econ & Soc — American Journal of Economics and Sociology
Amer J Econ Sociol — American Journal of Economics and Sociology
Amer Jew Hist Quart — American Jewish Historical Quarterly
Amer Jew Yearb — American Jewish Yearbook
Amer J Hort Florists Companion — American Journal of Horticulture and Florist's Companion
Amer J Hosp Pharm — American Journal of Hospital Pharmacy
Amer J Hum Biol — American Journal of Human Biology
Amer J Hum Genet — American Journal of Human Genetics
Amer J Hum Genetics — American Journal of Human Genetics
Amer J Hyg — American Journal of Hygiene
Amer J Internat Law — American Journal of International Law
Amer J Int Law — American Journal of International Law
Amer J Int'l L — American Journal of International Law
Amer J Juris — American Journal of Jurisprudence
Amer J Leg Hist — American Journal of Legal History
Amer J Math — American Journal of Mathematics
Amer J Math Management Sci — American Journal of Mathematical and Management Sciences
Amer J Med Genet — American Journal of Medical Genetics
Amer J Med Sci — American Journal of the Medical Sciences
Amer J Ment Defic — American Journal of Mental Deficiency
Amer J Mining — American Journal of Mining
Amer Jnl Reprod Immun — American Journal of Reproductive Immunology
Amer Jnl Rural Health — American Journal of Rural Health
Amer J Nursing — American Journal of Nursing
Amer J Obstet Gyn — American Journal of Obstetrics and Gynecology
Amer J of Phys — American Journal of Physics
Amer J Ophthalmol — American Journal of Ophthalmology
Amer J Optom and Arch Amer Acad Optom — American Journal of Optometry and Archives of American Academy of Optometry [*Later, American Journal of Optometry and Physiological Optics*]
Amer J Optom Physiol Opt — American Journal of Optometry and Physiological Optics
Amer J Orthopsychiat — American Journal of Orthopsychiatry
Amer Journ Arch — American Journal of Archaeology
Amer Journ Intern Law — American Journal of International Law
Amer Journ Philol — American Journal of Philology
Amer Journ Sem Lang — American Journal of Semitic Languages and Literature
Amer Jour Psych — American Journal of Psychology
Amer J Pathol — American Journal of Pathology
Amer J Pharm — American Journal of Pharmacy
Amer J Philo — American Journal of Philology
Amer J Philol — American Journal of Philology
Amer J Phot & Allied A & Serv — American Journal of Photography and the Allied Arts and Services
Amer J Phys — American Journal of Physics
Amer J Phys Anthrop — American Journal of Physical Anthropology
Amer J Phys Anthropol — American Journal of Physical Anthropology
Amer J Physiol — American Journal of Physiology
Amer J Phys Med — American Journal of Physical Medicine
Amer J Polit Sci — American Journal of Political Science
Amer J Psych — American Journal of Psychiatry
Amer J Psychiat — American Journal of Psychiatry
Amer J Psychiatry — American Journal of Psychiatry
Amer J Psychoanal — American Journal of Psychoanalysis
Amer J Psychol — American Journal of Psychology
Amer J Psychother — American Journal of Psychotherapy
Amer J Psychotherap — American Journal of Psychotherapy
Amer J Roentg — American Journal of Roentgenology
Amer J Roentgenol — American Journal of Roentgenology
Amer J Sci — American Journal of Science
Amer J Sci Arts — American Journal of Science and Arts
Amer J Sci Radiocarbon Suppl — American Journal of Science. Radiocarbon Supplement

Amer J Semitic Lang — American Journal of Semitic Languages

Amer J Semit Lang & Lit — American Journal of Semitic Languages and Literatures

Amer J Sociol — American Journal of Sociology

Amer J Surg — American Journal of Surgery and Gynecology

Amer J Theol Phil — American Journal of Theology and Philosophy

Amer J Trop Dis Prev Med — American Journal of Tropical Diseases and Preventive Medicine

Amer J Trop Med Hyg — American Journal of Tropical Medicine and Hygiene

Amer J Vet Res — American Journal of Veterinary Research

Amer Kenkyu — America Kenkyu

Amer Landscape Architect — American Landscape Architect

Amer Lat — America Latina

Amer Lat Un Sov — America Latina Union Sovietica

Amer Law — American Lawyer

Amer Law Rev — American Law Review

Amer Lawy — American Lawyer

Amer Liszt Soc J — American Liszt Society. Journal

Amer Lit — American Literature

AmerLitAb — American Literature Abstracts

Amer Livestock J — American Livestock Journal

Amer Mach — American Machinist

Amer Mag A — American Magazine of Art

Amer Manage Ass Res Stud — American Management Associations. Research Study

Amer Math Mon — American Mathematical Monthly

Amer Math Monthly — American Mathematical Monthly

Amer Math Mthly — American Mathematical Monthly

Amer Math Soc Colloq Publ — American Mathematical Society. Colloquium Publications

Amer Math Soc Transl — American Mathematical Society. Translations

Amer Mech Mag — American Mechanic's Magazine

Amer Med — American Medicine

Amer Midl Nat — American Midland Naturalist

Amer Midl Naturalist — American Midland Naturalist. Devoted to Natural History. Primarily that of the Prairie States

Amer Miller Process — American Miller and Processor

Amer Mineral — American Mineralogist

Amer M Instrument Soc J — American Musical Instrument Society. Journal

Amer Mus J — American Museum Journal

Amer Mus Nat Hist Bull — American Museum of Natural History Bulletin

Amer Nat — American Naturalist

Amer Natur — American Naturalist

Amer Naturalist — American Naturalist. A Popular Illustrated Magazine of Natural History

Amer Neptune — American Neptune

Amer Notes Quer — American Notes and Queries

Amer Numi Soc Mus Notes — American Numismatic Society Museum Notes

Amer Num Soc N Mon — Numismatic Notes and Monographs. American Numismatic Society

Amer Nurserym — American Nurseryman

Amer O — American Opinion

Amer Oil Gas Reporter — American Oil and Gas Reporter

Amer Oriental Soc Jour — American Oriental Society. Journal

Amer Orient Ser — American Oriental Series

Amer Orient Soc J — Journal. American Oriental Society

Amer Palest Explor Soc — American Palestine Exploration Society

Amer Pap Ind — American Paper Industry

Amer Pecan J — American Pecan Journal

Amer Peony Soc Bull — American Peony Society Bulletin

Amer Petrol Inst Div Prod Drilling Prod Pract Pap — American Petroleum Institute. Division of Production, Drilling, and Production Practice. Papers

Amer Petrol Inst Stand — American Petroleum Institute. Standards

Amer Philos Q — American Philosophical Quarterly

Amer Philos Quart Monograph Ser — American Philosophical Quarterly. Monograph Series

Amer Philos Soc Proc — American Philosophical Society. Proceedings

Amer Philos Soc Trans — American Philosophical Society. Transactions

Amer Phil Quart — American Philosophical Quarterly

Amer Phot — American Photography

Amer Photogr — American Photographer

Amer Photographer — American Photographer

Amer Phys Teacher — American Physics Teacher

Amer Poinsettia Soc Newslett — American Poinsettia Society Newsletter

Amer Polit Quart — American Politics Quarterly

Amer Polit Sci R — American Political Science Review

Amer Polit Sci Rev — American Political Science Review

Amer Pomol Ames — American Pomology (Ames)

Amer Po R — American Poetry Review

Amer Prem — American Premiere

Amer Psychol — American Psychologist

Amer Q — American Quarterly

Amer Quart — American Quarterly

Amer Quart J Agric Sci — American Quarterly Journal of Agriculture and Science

Amer R — American Review

Amer Recorder — American Recorder

Amer Rehab — American Rehabilitation

Amer Repert Arts Sci Manufactures — American Repertory of Arts, Sciences, and Manufactures

Amer Res Cent Egypt Newslett — American Research Center in Egypt Newsletter

Amer Res Center Egypt Cat — American Research Center in Egypt/Catalogs

Amer Rev Sci — American Review of Science, Art, Inventions

Amer Rev Tuberc — American Review of Tuberculosis

Amer Rose Annual — American Rose Annual

Amer Rose Quart — American Rose Quarterly

AmerS — American Studies

Amer Scand Rev — American Scandinavian Review

Amer Sch — American Scholar

Amer Scholar — American Scholar

Amer Sch Prehist Res Bull — American School of Prehistoric Research Bulletin

Amer Sci — American Scientist

Amer Scient — American Scientist

Amer Scientist — American Scientist

Amer Sci Press Ser Math Management Sci — American Sciences Press Series in Mathematical and Management Sciences

Amer Silk Grower Agric — American Silk Grower and Agriculturist

Amer Silk Grower Farmers Manual — American Silk Grower and Farmer's Manual

Amer Slav East Eur Rev — American Slavic and East European Review

Amer Slavic East Europe Rev — American Slavic and East European Review

Amer Soc Abrasive Method Nat Tech Conf Proc — American Society for Abrasive Methods. National Technical Conference. Proceedings

Amer Soc Excav Sardis — American Society for the Excavation of Sardis

Amer Soc Hypertens Symp Ser — American Society of Hypertension Symposium Series

Amer Sociol — American Sociologist

Amer Sociologist — American Sociologist

Amer Sociol R — American Sociological Review

Amer Sociol Rev — American Sociological Review

Amer Soc Mech Eng Intern Combust Engine Div Publ ICE — American Society of Mechanical Engineers. Internal Combustion Engine Division. Publication. ICE

Amer Soc Quality Contr Tech Conf Trans — American Society for Quality Control. Annual Technical Conference. Transactions

Amer Soc Testing & Mat Proc — American Society for Testing and Materials Proceedings

Amer Sp — American Speech

Amer Stat — American Statistician

Amer Stat Ind — American Statistics Index

Amer Statist — American Statistician

Amer Stud — American Studies

Amer Univ Fieldstaff Rep Africa Cent Sth Afr Ser — American Universities Field Staff Reports. Africa. Central and Southern Africa Series

Amer Univ Fieldstaff Rep Africa W Afr Ser — American Universities Field Staff Reports. Africa. West Africa Series

Amer Univ L Rev — American University Law Review

Amer Univ Stud Ser V Philos — American University Studies. Series V. Philosophy

Amer Veg Grower — American Vegetable Grower

Amer Welding Soc Stand — American Welding Society. Standards

Amer West — American West

Amer Woods US For Serv — American Woods. United States Forest Service

Amer Zool — American Zoologist

AMESA — Archiwum Mechaniki Stosowanej

Ames Lab Bull Ser — Ames Laboratory. Bulletin Series

AMET — Advances in Modern Environmental Toxicology

A Met — Annalen der Meteorologie

A Metal — Art du Metal

A Met Bull Bangkok — Annual Meteorological Bulletin. Bangkok

A Met Data Bangkok — Annual Meteorological Data. Bangkok

Am Ethnol — American Ethnologist

Am Ethnol Soc Monogr — American Ethnological Society Monographs

A Meth Th — Advances in Archaeological Method and Theory

A Met Rep Falkl Isl — Annual Meteorological Report Falkland Islands Dependencies Bases

A Met Rep Fiji — Annual Meteorological Report. Fiji

A Met Rep Gambia — Annual Meteorological Report. Gambia

A Met Rep Isthmian Canal Commn — Annual Meteorological Report. Isthmian Canal Commission

A Met Rep Nanking — Annual Meteorological Report (Nanking)

A Met Rep Straits Settl — Annual Meteorological Report. Straits Settlements

A Met Ret Bermuda — Annual Meteorological Return. Bermuda

A Met Sin — Acta Meteorologica Sinica

A Met Summ Edmonton etc — Annual Meteorological Summary. Edmonton, Calgary, Halifax N.S., Winnipeg, Regina, Vancouver Airport and City

A Met Summ Fiji — Annual Meteorological Summary. Fiji

A Met Summ Toronto — Annual Meteorological Summary of Toronto

A Met Summ US — Annual Meteorological Summary with Comparative Data. U.S. Weather Bureau

A Met Tables Falkl Isl — Annual Meteorological Tables. Falkland Islands and Dependencies Meteorological Service

Am Ex — American Examiner

AMEX — AMEX-Canada

A Mexico — Artes de Mexico

Am Exp Mark — American Export Marketer

Am Exporter — American Exporter

AMEZAB — Annali di Microbiologia ed Enzimologia

AME Zion QR — AME [*African Methodist Episcopal*] Zion Quarterly Review

A Mezzogiorno — Annali del Mezzogiorno

AmF — [*The*] Americas: A Quarterly Review of Inter-American Cultural History

AmF — Amerique Francaise

AMF — A. Merritt's Fantasy Magazine

AMF — Anais do Municipio de Faro

A Mf — Archiv fuer Musikforschung

Am Fabric Fashion — American Fabrics and Fashions

Am Fabrics — American Fabrics

Am Fam — American Family

Am Fam Phys — American Family Physician

Am Fam Physician — American Family Physician

Am Fam Physician GP — American Family Physician - GP

Am Farm Bur Feder W News Letter — American Farm Bureau Federation. Weekly News Letter

Am Farm Bur N L — American Farm Bureau Federation. Weekly News Letter
Am Farriers J — American Farriers' Journal
Am Fed — American Federationist
Am Federationist — American Federationist
Am Fed Teach Conv Proc — American Federation of Teachers. Convention Proceedings
Am Feed Manuf Assoc Nutr Counc Proc — American Feed Manufacturers Association. Nutrition Council. Proceedings
Am Feed Manuf Assoc Proc Meet Nutr Counc — American Feed Manufacturers Association. Proceedings. Meeting of the Nutrition Council
Am Fencing — American Fencing
Am Fern J — American Fern Journal
Am Fert — American Fertilizer and Allied Chemicals
Am Fert Allied Chem — American Fertilizer and Allied Chemicals
AMFGAR — American Fruit Grower
Am Film — American Film
Am Fisheries Soc Trans — American Fisheries Society. Transactions
Am Fish Soc Fish Cult Sect Publ — American Fisheries Society. Fish Culture Section. Publication
Am Fish Soc Monogr — American Fisheries Society. Monograph
Am Fish Soc Spec Publ — American Fisheries Society. Special Publication
Am Fish Soc Trans — American Fisheries Society. Transactions
AM Fit — American Fitness
Am Flint — American Flint
Am Flor — American Florist
AMFNAE — Annales Medicinae Internae Fenniae
AMFO — American Forests
AMFOA — American Forests
Am Folk Newsl — American Folklore Newsletter
Am Folk Soc Newsl — American Folklore Society. Newsletter
Am For — American Forests
Am Forests — American Forests
Am For Serv Jour — American Foreign Service Journal
Am Found Blind Res Bull — American Foundation for the Blind. Research Bulletin
Am Found Blind Res Ser — American Foundation for the Blind. Research Series
Am Foundryman — American Foundryman
Am Foundrymens Soc Res Rep — American Foundrymen's Society. Research Reports
Am Found Study Man Publ — American Foundation for the Study of Man. Publications
Am Fox and Fur Farmer — American Fox and Fur Farmer
Am Fruit Grow — American Fruit Grower
Am Fruit Grower — American Fruit Grower
Am Fruit Grow Mag — American Fruit Grower Magazine
Am G — American Geologist
AMG — Annales. Musee Guimet
AMG — Association Management
Am Game Bull Am Game Protect Ass — American Game Bulletin. American Game Protective Association
Am Gas — American Gas
Am Gas As M — American Gas Association. Monthly
Am Gas Ass Mon — American Gas Association. Monthly
Am Gas Assoc Abstr — American Gas Association. Abstracts
Am Gas Assoc Annu Rep — American Gas Association. Annual Report
Am Gas Assoc Bull Abstr — American Gas Association. Bulletin of Abstracts
Am Gas Assoc Mon — American Gas Association. Monthly
Am Gas Assoc Oper Sect Proc — American Gas Association. Operating Section. Proceedings
Am Gas Assoc Prepr — American Gas Association. Preprints
Am Gas Assoc Proc — American Gas Association. Proceedings
Am G As B — American Geological Association. Bulletin
Am Gas Eng J — American Gas Engineering Journal
Am Gas Inst Abstr — American Gas Institute. Abstracts
Am Gas Inst Bull Abstr — American Gas Institute. Bulletin of Abstracts
Am Gas J — American Gas Journal
Am Gas Jrl — American Gas Journal
Am Gas Light J — American Gas Light Journal
AMGBA — Archiv fuer Meteorologie, Geophysik, und Bioklimatologie. Serie B
AMGBCJ — Argentina. Servicio Nacional Minero Geologico. Boletin
AMGDAN — Annali. Museo Civico di Storia Naturale "Giacomo Doria"
Am Geneal — American Genealogist
Am Geog Soc B J — American Geographical Society. Bulletin. Journal
Am Geog Soc Bul — American Geographical Society. Bulletin
Am Geog Soc Jour — American Geographical Society. Journal
Am Geog Soc Special Pub — American Geographical Society. Special Publication
Am Geog Stat Soc J — American Geographical and Statistical Society. Journal
Am Geol — American Geologist
Am Geol Inst Repr Ser — American Geological Institute. Reprint Series
Am Geol Inst Rept — American Geological Institute. Report
Am Geophys Union Antarct Res Ser — American Geophysical Union. Antarctic Research Series
Am Geophys Union Trans — American Geophysical Union. Transactions
AMGGA — Archiv fuer Meteorologie, Geophysik, und Bioklimatologie. Serie A
AMGHB2 — Ameghiniana
Am Glass Rev — American Glass Review
AMGLS — American Museum of Natural History. Guide Leaflet Series
Am Group Psychother Assoc Monogr Ser — American Group Psychotherapy Association. Monograph Series
AMGYAI — Anales. Sociedad Medico-Quirurgica del Guayas
Am Gynecol Soc Trans — American Gynecological Society. Transactions
AmH — American Heritage
AMH — Annals of Medical History
Am Harp J — American Harp Journal
AMHCB — Applied Mathematics and Computation
AMHC Forum — Association of Mental Health Chaplains. Forum

AMHE — American Health
Am Health — American Health
Am Health Care Assoc J — American Health Care Association. Journal
Am Heart Assoc Monogr — American Heart Association. Monograph
Am Heart J — American Heart Journal
Am Heb — American Hebrew
Am Her — American Heritage
Am Herit — American Heritage
Am Heritage — American Heritage
AMHGD6 — Arquivos. Museu de Historia Natural. Universidade Federal de Minas Gerais
Am Highw — American Highways
Am His R — American Historical Review
Am Hist Assn Ann Rep — American Historical Association. Annual Report
Am Hist Assn Ann Rpt — American Historical Association. Annual Report
Am Hist Assn Rept — American Historical Association. Reports
Am Hist Assoc Rep — American Historical Association. Annual Report
Am Hist Ill — American History Illustrated
Am Hist Illus — American History Illustrated
Am Hist Life — America. History and Life
Am Hist Life Part A — America. History and Life. Part A. Article Abstracts and Citations
Am Hist Life Part B — America. History and Life. Part B. Index to Book Reviews
Am Hist Life Part C — America. History and Life. Part C. American History Bibliography, Books, Articles, and Dissertations
Am Hist Life Part D — America. History and Life. Part D. Annual Index
Am Hist Life Suppl — America. History and Life. Supplement
Am Hist M — American Historical Magazine
Am Hist R — American Historical Review
Am Hist Rec — American Historical Record
Am Hist Reg — American Historical Register
Am Hist Rev — American Historical Review
AMHN — Anais do Museu Historico Nacional [*Rio de Janeiro*]
AMHNAO — Anales. Museo Nacional de Historia Natural de Montevideo
AMHNL — Archives du Museum d'Histoire Naturelle de Lyon
AMHNP — Archives. Museum National d'Histoire Naturelle
Am Home — American Home
Am Homes — American Homes and Gardens
Am Horo Jewel — American Horologist and Jeweler
Am Horol Jeweler — American Horologist and Jeweler
Am Hort — American Horticulturist
Am Hortic — American Horticulturist
Am Hort Mag — American Horticultural Magazine
Am Hosta Soc Newsl — American Hosta Society. Newsletter
AMHR — American Historical Review
AMHR — Annuaire. Musee d'Histoire de la Religion et de l'Atheisme
AMHSJ — AMHS [*American Material Handling Society*] Journal
AMHSJ — Australasian Methodist Historical Society. Journal and Proceedings
AMHUDE — Acta Morphologica Hungarica
AMHUEF — Acta Microbiologica Hungarica
Am Humanit Index — American Humanities Index
AmHy — American History Illustrated
AMI — Advertising and Marketing Intelligence
Ami — Amicus
AMI — Archaeologische Mitteilungen aus Iran
AMI — Journal of American Insurance
AMIAA — American Imago
AMIB — American Indian Basketry Magazine
AMI Ber — AMI [*Institute fuer Arzneimittel*]-Berichte
Amic A — Amic des Arts
AMICD — Annual Meeting. International Water Conference
Ami Champs — Ami des Champs. Societe Philomathique de Bordeaux
Amici G Tosc — Giornale Toscano di Scienze Mediche, Fisiche, e Naturali. Amici, Bufalini
Amicis Jb Oesterreich Gal — Amicis. Jahrbuch der Oesterreichischen Galerie
A Micr Acad Sci Hung — Acta Microbiologica. Academiae Scientiarum Hungaricae
AMid — Annales du Midi; Revue de la France Meridionale
AMIED5 — Advances in Microbial Ecology
Amiens Ac Mm — Memoires de l'Academie des Sciences, Agriculture, Commerce, Belles-Lettres, et Arts du Departement de la Somme. Amiens
Amiens Mm — Memoires de l'Academie des Sciences, Agriculture, Commerce, Belles-Lettres, et Arts du Departement de la Somme. Amiens
Amiens Mm Ac — Memoires de l'Academie des Sciences, Agriculture, Commerce, Belles-Lettres, et Arts du Departement de la Somme. Amiens
Amiens Mm Ac Sc — Memoires de l'Academie des Sciences, Agriculture, Commerce, Belles-Lettres, et Arts du Departement de la Somme. Amiens
AMIGB — Acta Microbiologica Polonica. Series A. Microbiologia Generalis
AMIHA — AMA [*American Medical Association*] Archives of Industrial Health
AMIIN — Atti e Memorie. Istituto Italiano di Numismatica
AMIJAH — JAAMI. Journal. Association for the Advancement of Medical Instrumentation
Ami Jard — Ami des Jardins
AMIKA — American Inkmaker
AMILAN — Annales de Medecine Legale
Am Ill — Americana Illustrated
Am Im — American Imago
Am Imago — American Imago
Am I M Eng Tr B — American Institute of Mining Engineers. Transactions. Bulletin
Am I Mn E T — Transactions of the American Institute of Mining Engineers
Am Import Export Bul — American Import/Export Bulletin
Am Import/Export Bull — American Import/Export Bulletin
Am Import/Export Manage — American Import/Export Management
Am Import/Export Mgt — American Import/Export Management
AMIN — Amerindian
AMINCO Lab News — AMINCO [*American Instrument Company*] Laboratory News

Am Ind — America Indigena
Am Ind — American Industries
Am Ind Bas Mag — American Indian Basketry Magazine
Am Ind Hyg — American Industrial Hygiene Association. Journal
Am Ind Hyg Ass J — American Industrial Hygiene Association. Journal
Am Ind Hyg Assn J — American Industrial Hygiene Association. Journal
Am Ind Hyg Assoc J — American Industrial Hygiene Association. Journal
Am Ind Hyg Assoc Q — American Industrial Hygiene Association. Quarterly
Am Ind Hygiene Assn J — American Industrial Hygiene Association. Journal
Am Indian Alsk Native Ment Health Res — American Indian and Alaska Native Mental Health Research
Am Indian Alsk Native Ment Health Res Monogr Ser — American Indian and Alaska Native Mental Health Research Monograph Series
Am Indian Alsk Native Ment Health Res Online — American Indian and Alaska Native Mental Health Research (Online)
Am Indian Art Mag — American Indian Art Magazine
Am Indian Index — American Indian Index
Am Indian J — American Indian Journal
Am Indian L Rev — American Indian Law Review
Am Indigena — America Indigena
Am Ind LR — American Indian Law Review
Am Indust Hyg A J — American Industrial Hygiene Association. Journal
Am Indust Hyg A Quart — American Industrial Hygiene Association. Quarterly
Amine Fluores Histochem Scand Jpn Seminar — Amine Fluorescence Histochemistry. Scandinavia-Japan Seminar
A Mines — Annales des Mines, ou Recueil des Memoires sur l'Exploitation des Mines, et sur les Sciences et les Arts qui s'y Rapportent
A Mines Belg — Annales des Mines de Belgique
Am Ink — American Inkmaker
Am Inkmaker — American Inkmaker
Amino Acids Anim Husb Int Symp Rep — Amino Acids in Animal Husbandry. International Symposium. Reports
Amino Acids Chem Biol Med Pap Int Congr Amino Acid Res — Amino Acids. Chemistry, Biology, and Medicine. Papers. International Congress on Amino Acid Research
Amino Acids Pept — Amino Acids and Peptides
Amino Acids Pept Prot Abstr — Amino Acids, Peptide, and Protein Abstracts
Amino Acids Pept Proteins — Amino Acids, Peptides, and Proteins
Amino Acid Transp Uric Acid Transp Symp — Amino Acid Transport and Uric Acid Transport Symposium
Aminokisloty Zhivotnovod Mezhdunar Simp Dokl — Aminokisloty v Zhivotnovodstve Mezhdunarodnyi Simpozium. Doklady
Aminosaeuren Tierz Int Symp Vortr — Aminosaeuren in Tierzucht. Internationales Symposium. Vortraege
Am Inst Aeronaut Astronaut Monogr — American Institute of Aeronautics and Astronautics. Monographs
Am Inst Aeronaut Astronaut Pap — American Institute of Aeronautics and Astronautics. Paper
Am Inst Arch Int Dir — American Institute of Architects. International Directory
Am Inst Archit J — American Institute of Architects. Journal
Am Inst Archit Q Bull — American Institute of Architects. Quarterly Bulletin
Am Inst Arch J — American Institute of Architects. Journal
Am Inst Bank Bul — American Institute of Banking. Bulletin
Am Inst Biol Sci — American Institute of Biological Sciences
Am Inst Biol Sci Bull — American Institute of Biological Sciences. Bulletin
Am Inst Biol Sci Publ — American Institute of Biological Sciences. Publications
Am Inst Biol Sci Symp — American Institute of Biological Sciences. Symposia
Am Inst Chem Eng Natl Heat Transfer Conf Prepr AIChE Pap — American Institute of Chemical Engineers. National Heat Transfer Conference. Preprints. AIChE Paper
Am Inst Chem Eng Pap — American Institute of Chemical Engineers. Paper
Am Inst Chem Eng Symp Ser — American Institute of Chemical Engineers. Symposium Series
Am Inst Conserv J — American Institute for Conservation. Journal
Am Inst Dent Med Annu Meet — American Institute of Dental Medicine. Annual Meeting
Am Inst Hist Pharm Publ — American Institute of the History of Pharmacy. Publication
Am Inst Homeop J — American Institute of Homeopathy. Journal
Am Inst Ind Eng Detroit Chapter Proc Annu Conf — American Institute of Industrial Engineers. Detroit Chapter. Proceedings of the Annual Conference
Am Instit Crim Law and Criminol Jour — American Institute of Criminal Law and Criminology. Journal
Am Inst Met J — American Institute of Metals. Journal
Am Inst Met Trans — American Institute of Metals. Transactions
Am Inst Min Metall Eng Contrib — American Institute of Mining and Metallurgical Engineers. Contributions
Am Inst Min Metall Eng Inst Met Div Spec Rep Ser — American Institute of Mining and Metallurgical Engineers. Institute of Metals Division. Special Report Series
Am Inst Min Metall Eng Tech Publ — American Institute of Mining and Metallurgical Engineers. Technical Publications
Am Inst Min Metall Pet Eng Annu Meet Proc Sess — American Institute of Mining, Metallurgical, and Petroleum Engineers. Annual Meeting. Proceedings of Sessions
Am Inst Min Metall Pet Eng Annu Meet Proc Sess Light Met — American Institute of Mining, Metallurgical, and Petroleum Engineers. Annual Meeting. Proceedings of Sessions. Light Metals
Am Inst Min Metall Pet Eng Minn Sect Annu Meet — American Institute of Mining, Metallurgical, and Petroleum Engineers. Minnesota Section. Annual Meeting
Am Inst Min Metall Pet Eng Minn Sect Proc Annu Meet — American Institute of Mining, Metallurgical, and Petroleum Engineers. Minnesota Section. Proceedings. Annual Meeting

Am Inst Min Metall Pet Eng Soc Min Eng AIME Trans — American Institute of Mining, Metallurgical, and Petroleum Engineers. Society of Mining Engineers of AIME. Transactions
Am Inst Min Metall Pet Eng Trans — American Institute of Mining, Metallurgical, and Petroleum Engineers. Transactions
Am Inst Min Metall Petr Eng Inst Met Div Spec Rep Ser — American Institute of Mining, Metallurgical, and Petroleum Engineers. Institute of Metals Division. Special Report Series
Am Inst Min Metal Pet Eng Pet Trans — Petroleum Transactions. AIME (American Institute of Mining, Metallurgy, and Petroleum Engineering)
Am Inst of Instruc — American Institute of Instruction
Am Inst Oral Biol Annu Meet — American Institute of Oral Biology. Annual Meeting
Am Inst Phys Conf Proc — American Institute of Physics. Conference Proceedings
Am Inst Plan — American Institute of Planners. Journal
Am Inst Plan J — American Institute of Planners. Journal
Am Inst Planners J — American Institute of Planners. Journal
Am Inst Plann J — American Institute of Planners. Journal
Am Inst Plann Pap — American Institute of Planners. Papers
Am Inst Plant Eng J — American Institute of Plant Engineers. Journal
Am Inst Prof Geol Calif Sect Annu Meet Proc — American Institute of Professional Geologists. California Section. Annual Meeting. Proceedings
Am Inst Real Estate Appraisers J — American Institute of Real Estate Appraisers. Journal
Am Inst Refrig Proc — American Institute of Refrigeration. Proceedings
Am Int J — American Intelligence Journal
Am Intra Ocul Implant Soc J — American Intra-Ocular Implant Society. Journal
AmiP — Ami du Peuple
AMIPAZ — Anais. Faculdade de Medicina. Universidade do Parana
AMIran — Archaeologische Mitteilungen aus Iran
Am Irish His S J — American Irish Historical Society. Journal
Am Irish Hist Soc Jour — American Irish Historical Society. Journal
AMIS — Amis du Film et de la Television
AMIS — Australian Municipal Information
AMISEE — Israel. Geological Society. Annual Meeting
AMIS J — American Musical Instrument Society. Journal
Amis Mnmts & A — Amis des Monuments et des Arts
Amis Mus Lille Bull Trimest — Amis des Musees de Lille. Bulletin Trimestriel
AMIS N — American Musical Instrument Society. Newsletter
Am I T — Reports and Transactions of the American Institute of the City of New York
AMIUA — Acta Medica Iugoslavica
AMIV — Atti e Memoire. Istituto Veneto
AMJ — Academy of Management. Journal
AMJ — Advanced Management Journal
AMJ — Alexandria Medical Journal
Am J — American Journal of Archaeology
AMJ — American Museum Journal
AmJA — American Jewish Archives
Am J Acupunct — American Journal of Acupuncture
Am J Addict — American Journal on Addictions
Am J Ag Econ — American Journal of Agricultural Economics
Am J Agr — American Journal of Agriculture and Science
Am J Agr Ec — American Journal of Agricultural Economics
Am J Agr Econ — American Journal of Agricultural Economics
Am J Agric Econ — American Journal of Agricultural Economics
Am J Alternative Agric — American Journal of Alternative Agriculture
Am J Alzheimers Dis Other Demen — American Journal of Alzheimer's Disease and Other Dementias
Am J Anat — American Journal of Anatomy
Am J Anc Hist — American Journal of Ancient History
Am J Arab St — American Journal of Arabic Studies
Am J Archae — American Journal of Archaeology
Am J Archaeol — American Journal of Archaeology
Am J Art Th — American Journal of Art Therapy
Am J Art Ther — American Journal of Art Therapy
Am J Audiol — American Journal of Audiology
Am J Bot — American Journal of Botany
Am J Canc — American Journal of Cancer
Am J Cancer — American Journal of Cancer
Am J Card — American Journal of Cardiology
Am J Card Imaging — American Journal of Cardiac Imaging
Am J Cardiol — American Journal of Cardiology
Am J Cardiovasc Pathol — American Journal of Cardiovascular Pathology
Am J Ch — American Jewish Chronicle
Am J Chinese Med — American Journal of Chinese Medicine
Am J Chin Med — American Journal of Chinese Medicine
Am J Clin Assess — American Journal of Clinical Assessment
Am J Clin Biofeedback — American Journal of Clinical Biofeedback
Am J Clin Hypn — American Journal of Clinical Hypnosis
Am J Clin Hypnosis — American Journal of Clinical Hypnosis
Am J Clin Med — American Journal of Clinical Medicine
Am J Clin N — American Journal of Clinical Nutrition
AmiP Clin Nutr — American Journal of Clinical Nutrition
Am J Clin Nutrition — American Journal of Clinical Nutrition
Am J Clin Oncol — American Journal of Clinical Oncology
Am J Clin P — American Journal of Clinical Pathology
Am J Clin Path — American Journal of Clinical Pathology
Am J Clin Pathol — American Journal of Clinical Pathology
Am J Community Psychol — American Journal of Community Psychology
Am J Comparative Law — American Journal of Comparative Law
Am J Compar Law — American Journal of Comparative Law
Am J Comp L — American Journal of Comparative Law
Am J Comp Law — American Journal of Comparative Law
Am J Comput Ling — American Journal of Computational Linguistics

Am J Conch — American Journal of Conchology
Am J Contact Dermat — American Journal of Contact Dermatitis
Am J Corr — American Journal of Correction
Am J Correction — American Journal of Correction
Am J Crim L — American Journal of Criminal Law
Am J Crit Care — American Journal of Critical Care
Am J Dent Sci — American Journal of Dental Science
Am J Dermat Gen Urin Dis — American Journal of Dermatology and Genito-Urinary Diseases
Am J Dermatopathol — American Journal of Dermatopathology
Am J Dig Di — American Journal of Digestive Diseases [*Later, Digestive Diseases and Sciences*]
Am J Dig Dis — American Journal of Digestive Diseases [*Later, Digestive Diseases and Sciences*]
Am J Dig Dis Nutr — American Journal of Digestive Diseases and Nutrition
Am J Digest Dis — American Journal of Digestive Diseases
Am J Dis Ch — American Journal of Diseases of Children
Am J Dis Child — American Journal of Diseases of Children
Am J Drug Alcohol Abuse — American Journal of Drug and Alcohol Abuse
Am J Econ — American Journal of Economics and Sociology
Am J Econ S — American Journal of Economics and Sociology
Am J Econ Soc — American Journal of Economics and Sociology
Am J Econ Sociol — American Journal of Economics and Sociology
Am J Econ Sociol (New York) — American Journal of Economics and Sociology (New York)
Am J Educ — American Journal of Education
Am J EEG Technol — American Journal of EEG Technology
Am J Emerg Med — American Journal of Emergency Medicine
Am J Enol — American Journal of Enology
Am J Enol V — American Journal of Enology and Viticulture
Am J Enol Viti — American Journal of Enology and Viticulture
Am J Enol Vitic — American Journal of Enology and Viticulture
Am J Epid — American Journal of Epidemiology
Am J Epidem — American Journal of Epidemiology
Am J Epidemiol — American Journal of Epidemiology
Am Jew Arch — American Jewish Archives
Am Jew Archs — American Jewish Archives
Am Jew Congr News — American Jewish Congress. News
Am Jew H — American Jewish History
Am Jew His — American Jewish Historical Society. Publications
Am Jew Hist — American Jewish History
Am Jew Hist Q — American Jewish Historical Quarterly
Am Jew Hist Soc Publ — American Jewish Historical Society. Publications
Am Jewish A — American Jewish Archives
Am Jewish H — American Jewish Historical Quarterly
Am Jew Yb — American Jewish Yearbook
Am Jew Yr Bk — American Jewish Yearbook
Am J Forensic Med Pathol — American Journal of Forensic Medicine and Pathology
Am J Gastro — American Journal of Gastroenterology
Am J Gastroenterol — American Journal of Gastroenterology
Am J Geriatr Cardiol — American Journal of Geriatric Cardiology
Am J Geriatr Psychiatry — American Journal of Geriatric Psychiatry
AmJH — American Jewish Historical Quarterly
AM J Health Beh — American Journal of Health Behavior, Education, & Promotion
Am J Health Behav — American Journal of Health Behavior
Am J Health Plann — American Journal of Health Planning
AM J Health Promotion — American Journal of Health Promotion
Am J Health Syst Pharm — American Journal of Health-System Pharmacy
Am J Hematol — American Journal of Hematology
Am J His — American Jewish History
Am J Hosp Care — American Journal of Hospice Care
Am J Hosp P — American Journal of Hospital Pharmacy
Am J Hosp Pharm — American Journal of Hospital Pharmacy
Am J Hu Gen — American Journal of Human Genetics
Am J Human Biol — American Journal of Human Biology
Am J Human Genet — American Journal of Human Genetics
Am J Hum Biol — American Journal of Human Biology
Am J Hum Genet — American Journal of Human Genetics
Am J Hum Gntcs — American Journal of Human Genetics
Am J Hyg — American Journal of Hygiene
Am J Hyg Monogr Ser — American Journal of Hygiene. Monographic Series
Am J Hypertens — American Journal of Hypertension
Am J Ind Med — American Journal of Industrial Medicine
Am J Ind Psych — American Journal of Individual Psychology
Am J Inf Con — American Journal of Infection Control
Am J Infect Control — American Journal of Infection Control
Am J Insan — American Journal of Insanity
Am J Internat Law — American Journal of International Law
Am J Int L — American Journal of International Law
Am J Int Law — American Journal of International Law
Am J Int Law Proc — American Journal of International Law. Proceedings
Am J Int'l L — American Journal of International Law
Am J Int L Supp — American Journal of International Law. Supplement
Am J IV Clin Nutr — American Journal of Intravenous Therapy and Clinical Nutrition
Am J IV Ther — American Journal of Intravenous Therapy [*Later, American Journal of Intravenous Therapy and Clinical Nutrition*]
Am J IV Therapy — American Journal of Intravenous Therapy [*Later, American Journal of Intravenous Therapy and Clinical Nutrition*]
Am J IV Ther Clin Nutr — American Journal of Intravenous Therapy and Clinical Nutrition
Am J Jur — American Journal of Jurisprudence
Am J Juris — American Journal of Jurisprudence
Am J Jurispr — American Journal of Jurisprudence

Am J Jurisprud — American Journal of Jurisprudence
Am J Kidney — American Journal of Kidney Diseases
Am J Kidney Dis — American Journal of Kidney Diseases
Am J Knee Surg — American Journal of Knee Surgery
AmJL — American Journal of Legal History
Am JL and M — American Journal of Law and Medicine
Am JL & Med — American Journal of Law and Medicine
Am J Law Med — American Journal of Law and Medicine
Am J Legal Hist — American Journal of Legal History
Am J Leg Hist — American Journal of Legal History
Am JLH — American Journal of Legal History
Am Jl Ph — American Journal of Pharmacy
Am J Math — American Journal of Mathematics
Am J Math Manage Sci — American Journal of Mathematical and Management Sciences
Am J Md Sc — American Journal of the Medical Sciences
Am J Med — American Journal of Medicine
Am J Med Electron — American Journal of Medical Electronics
Am J Med Genet — American Journal of Medical Genetics
Am J Med Genet Suppl — American Journal of Medical Genetics. Supplement
Am J Med Jurispr — American Journal of Medical Jurisprudence
Am J Med Qual — American Journal of Medical Quality
Am J Med Sc — American Journal of the Medical Sciences
Am J Med Sci — American Journal of the Medical Sciences
Am J Med Te — American Journal of Medical Technology
Am J Med Technol — American Journal of Medical Technology
Am J Men Deficiency — American Journal of Mental Deficiency
Am J Mental Deficiency — American Journal of Mental Deficiency
Am J Ment D — American Journal of Mental Deficiency
Am J Ment Defic — American Journal of Mental Deficiency
Am J Ment Deficiency — American Journal of Mental Deficiency
Am J Ment Dis — American Journal of Mental Diseases
Am J Ment Retard — American Journal of Mental Retardation
Am J Micr (NY) — American Journal of Microscopy and Popular Science (New York)
Am JM Sc — American Journal of the Medical Sciences
Am J M Sci — American Journal of the Medical Sciences
Am J Mth — American Journal of Mathematics
AMJN — American Journal of Nursing
Am J Nephr — American Journal of Nephrology
Am J Nephrol — American Journal of Nephrology
Am J Neurop — American Journal of Neuropathy
Am J Neuropathy — American Journal of Neuropathy
Am Jnl Archae — American Journal of Archaeology
Am Jnl Econ & Soc — American Journal of Economics and Sociology
Am Jnl International Law — American Journal of International Law
Am Jnl Numis — American Journal of Numismatics
Am Jnl Philol — American Journal of Philology
Am Jnl Psych — American Journal of Psychiatry
Am Jnl Psychotherapy — American Journal of Psychotherapy
Am Jnl Soc — American Journal of Sociology
Am J Nurs — American Journal of Nursing
Am J Nursing — American Journal of Nursing
Am J Ob Gyn — American Journal of Obstetrics and Gynecology
Am J Obst — American Journal of Obstetrics and Diseases of Woman and Children
Am J Obstet Gynecol — American Journal of Obstetrics and Gynecology
Am J Obst G — American Journal of Obstetrics and Gynecology
Am J Obst Gynec — American Journal of Obstetrics and Gynecology
Am J Obst NY — American Journal of Obstetrics and Diseases of Women and Children (New York)
Am J Occup Ther — American Journal of Occupational Therapy
Am J Occup Therapy — American Journal of Occupational Therapy
Am J Occu T — American Journal of Occupational Therapy
Am J Occu Ther — American Journal of Occupational Therapy
Am J of Arch — American Journal of Archaeology
Am J Ophth — American Journal of Ophthalmology
Am J Ophthal — American Journal of Ophthalmology
Am J Ophthalmol — American Journal of Ophthalmology
Am J Optom — American Journal of Optometry and Physiological Optics
Am J Optom and Arch Am Acad Optom — American Journal of Optometry and Archives of American Academy of Optometry [*Later, American Journal of Optometry and Physiological Optics*]
Am J Optom Arch Am Acad Optom — American Journal of Optometry and Archives of American Academy of Optometry [*Later, American Journal of Optometry and Physiological Optics*]
Am J Optom Physiol Opt — American Journal of Optometry and Physiological Optics
Am J Orth — American Journal of Orthopedics
Am J Orthod — American Journal of Orthodontics
Am J Orthod Dentofacial Orthop — American Journal of Orthodontics and Dentofacial Orthopedics
Am J Orthod Oral Surg — American Journal of Orthodontics and Oral Surgery [*Later, American Journal of Orthodontics*]
Am J Orthod Oral Surg Oral Surg — American Journal of Orthodontics and Oral Surgery [*Later, American Journal of Orthodontics*]. Oral Surgery
Am J Orthop — American Journal of Orthopedics
Am J Orthop — American Journal of Orthopsychiatry
Am J Orthopsych — American Journal of Orthopsychiatry
Am J Orthopsychiat — American Journal of Orthopsychiatry
Am J Orthopsychiatr — American Journal of Orthopsychiatry
Am J Orthopsychiatry — American Journal of Orthopsychiatry
Am J Orth Psych — American Journal of Orthopsychiatry
Am J Orth Surg — American Journal of Orthopedic Surgery
Am J Otol — American Journal of Otology
Am J Otolaryngol — American Journal of Otolaryngology

Am Jour Econ Sociol — American Journal of Economics and Sociology
Am Jour Internat Law — American Journal of International Law
Am Jour Internatl Law — American Journal of International Law
Am Jour Legal Hist — American Journal of Legal History
Am Journal Arch — American Journal of Archaeology
Am Journ Arch — American Journal of Archaeology
Am Journ Archaeol — American Journal of Archaeology
Am Journ Num — American Journal of Numismatics
Am Journ of Ph — American Journal of Philology
Am Journ Phil — American Journal of Philology
Am Journ Sem Lang — American Journal of Semitic Languages and Literatures
Am Jour Phys Anthropol — American Journal of Physical Anthropology
Am Jour Pol — American Journal of Politics
Am Jour Psychiatry — American Journal of Psychiatry
Am Jour Sci — American Journal of Science
Am Jour Sociol — American Journal of Sociology
Am Jour Trop Med Baltimore — American Journal of Tropical Medicine (Baltimore)
Am JPA — American Journal of Physical Anthropology
Am J P Anth — American Journal of Physical Anthropology
Am J Path — American Journal of Pathology
Am J Pathol — American Journal of Pathology
Am J Pediatr Hematol Oncol — American Journal of Pediatric Hematology/Oncology
Am J Perinatol — American Journal of Perinatology
AmJPh — American Journal of Philology
Am J Phar E — American Journal of Pharmaceutical Education
Am J Pharm — American Journal of Pharmacy
Am J Pharm — American Journal of Pharmacy and the Sciences Supporting Public Health [Later, American Journal of Pharmacy]
Am J Pharm Educ — American Journal of Pharmaceutical Education
Am J Pharm Sci Supporting Public Health — American Journal of Pharmacy and the Sciences Supporting Public Health [Later, American Journal of Pharmacy]
Am J Phil — American Journal of Philology
Am J Philol — American Journal of Philology
Am J Photogr — American Journal of Photography
Am J Phys — American Journal of Physics
Am J Phys Anthr — American Journal of Physical Anthropology
Am J Phys Anthro — American Journal of Physical Anthropology
Am J Phys Anthrop — American Journal of Physical Anthropology
Am J Phys Anthrop ns — American Journal of Physical Anthropology. New Series
Am J Phys Anthropol — American Journal of Physical Anthropology
Am J Physics — American Journal of Physics
Am J Physiol — American Journal of Physiology
Am J Physiol Cell Physiol — American Journal of Physiology. Cell Physiology
Am J Physiol Endocrinol Metab — American Journal of Physiology. Endocrinology and Metabolism
Am J Physiol Endocrinol Metab Gastrointest Physiol — American Journal of Physiology. Endocrinology, Metabolism, and GastrointestinalPhysiology
Am J Physiol Gastrointest Liver Physiol — American Journal of Physiology. Gastrointestinal and Liver Physiology
Am J Physiol Heart Circ Physiol — American Journal of Physiology. Heart and Circulatory Physiology
Am J Physiol Imag — American Journal of Physiologic Imaging
Am J Physiol Imaging — American Journal of Physiologic Imaging
Am J Physiol Lung Cell Mol Physiol — American Journal of Physiology. Lung Cellular and Molecular Physiology
Am J Physiol Regul Integr Comp Physiol — American Journal of Physiology. Regulatory, Integrative, and Comparative Physiology
Am J Physiol Renal Fluid Electrolyte Physiol — American Journal of Physiology. Renal, Fluid, and Electrolyte Physiology
Am J Physiol Renal Physiol — American Journal of Physiology. Renal Physiology
Am J Physl — American Journal of Physiology
Am J Phys M — American Journal of Physical Medicine
Am J Phys Med — American Journal of Physical Medicine
Am J Phys Med Rehabil — American Journal of Physical Medicine and Rehabilitation
Am J Pol — American Journal of Politics
Am J Police Sci — American Journal of Police Science
Am J Pol Sc — American Journal of Political Science
Am J Pol Sci — American Journal of Political Science
Am J Potato Res — American Journal of Potato Research
Am J Pract Nurs — American Journal of Practical Nursing
Am J Prev Med — American Journal of Preventive Medicine
Am J Primatol — American Journal of Primatology
Am J Proct — American Journal of Proctology [Later, American Journal of Proctology, Gastroenterology, and Colon and Rectal Surgery]
Am J Proctol — American Journal of Proctology [Later, American Journal of Proctology, Gastroenterology, and Colon and Rectal Surgery]
Am J Proctol Gastroenterol Colon Rectal Surg — American Journal of Proctology, Gastroenterology, and Colon and Rectal Surgery
Am J Proctol Gastroenterol Colon Rectal Surg (Georgetown) — American Journal of Proctology, Gastroenterology, and Colon and Rectal Surgery (Georgetown)
Am J Progr Ther — American Journal of Progressive Therapeutics
Am J Psych — American Journal of Psychiatry
Am J Psycha — American Journal of Psychoanalysis
Am J Psychi — American Journal of Psychiatry
Am J Psychiat — American Journal of Psychiatry
Am J Psychiatr — American Journal of Psychiatry
Am J Psychiatry — American Journal of Psychiatry
Am J Psycho — American Journal of Psychology
Am J Psychoanal — American Journal of Psychoanalysis
Am J Psychol — American Journal of Psychology
Am J Psychoth — American Journal of Psychotherapy
Am J Psychother — American Journal of Psychotherapy

Am J Psycht — American Journal of Psychotherapy
Am J Pub He — American Journal of Public Health
Am J Pub Health — American Journal of Public Health
Am J Pub Health — American Journal of Public Health and the Nation's Health [Later, American Journal of Public Health]
Am J Publ Heal — American Journal of Public Health
Am J Public Health — American Journal of Public Health
Am J Public Health Nation's Health — American Journal of Public Health and the Nation's Health [Later, American Journal of Public Health]
Am J Public Health Suppl — American Journal of Public Health. Supplement
Am J Reprod Im — American Journal of Reproductive Immunology
Am J Reprod Immunol — American Journal of Reproductive Immunology
Am J Reprod Immunol Microbiol — American Journal of Reproductive Immunology and Microbiology
Am J Respir Cell Mol Biol — American Journal of Respiratory Cell and Molecular Biology
Am J Respir Crit Care Med — American Journal of Respiratory and Critical Care Medicine
Am J Rhinol — American Journal of Rhinology
Am J Roentg — American Journal of Roentgenology
Am J Roentgen — American Journal of Roentgenology
Am J Roentgenol — American Journal of Roentgenology
Am J Roentgenol — American Journal of Roentgenology, Radium Therapy, and Nuclear Medicine [Later, American Journal of Roentgenology]
Am J Roentgenol Radium Ther — American Journal of Roentgenology and Radium Therapy [Later, American Journalof Roentgenology]
Am J Roentgenol Radium Ther Nucl Med — American Journal of Roentgenology, Radium Therapy, and Nuclear Medicine [Later, American Journal of Roentgenology]
Am JS — American Journal of Sociology
Am J Sc — American Journal of Science and Arts
Am J Sc and Arts — American Journal of Science and Arts
Am J School Hygiene — American Journal of School Hygiene
Am J Sci — American Journal of Science
Am J Sci Arts — American Journal of Science and Arts
Am J Sci Radiocarbon Suppl — American Journal of Science. Radiocarbon Supplement
Am J Sem Lang — American Journal of Semitic Languages and Literatures
Am J Small Bus — American Journal of Small Business
Am J Soc — American Journal of Sociology
Am J Socio — American Journal of Sociology
Am J Sociol — American Journal of Sociology
Am J Soc Psychiatr — American Journal of Social Psychiatry
Am J Soc Sci — American Journal of Social Science
Am J Sports Med — American Journal of Sports Medicine
Am J Stomat — American Journal of Stomatology
Am J Surg — American Journal of Surgery
Am J Surgery — American Journal of Surgery
Am J Surg Pathol — American Journal of Surgical Pathology
Am J Syph — American Journal of Syphilis
Am J Syph Gonorrhea Vener Dis — American Journal of Syphilis, Gonorrhea, and Venereal Diseases
Am J Syph Neurol — American Journal of Syphilis and Neurology
AmJTh — American Journal of Theology
Am J Theol — American Journal of Theology
Am J Ther — American Journal of Therapeutics
Am J Ther Clin Rep — American Journal of Therapeutics and Clinical Reports
Am J Th Ph — American Journal of Theology and Philosophy
Am J Times — American Jewish Times
Am J Trial Ad — American Journal of Trial Advocacy
Am J Trial Advocacy — American Journal of Trial Advocacy
Am J Trop Dis (New Orleans) — American Journal of Tropical Diseases and Preventive Medicine (New Orleans)
Am J Trop M — American Journal of Tropical Medicine and Hygiene
Am J Trop Med — American Journal of Tropical Medicine [Later, American Journal of Tropical Medicine and Hygiene]
Am J Trop Med Hyg — American Journal of Tropical Medicine and Hygiene
Am Jud Soc — American Judicature Society. Journal
Am Jud Soc J — American Judicature Society. Journal
Am Jud Soc'y — Journal. American Judicature Society
Am Jurist — American Jurist and Law Magazine
Am J Vet Med — American Journal of Veterinary Medicine
Am J Vet Re — American Journal of Veterinary Research
Am J Vet Res — American Journal of Veterinary Research
Am J Vet Sci — American Journal of Veterinary Science
AMK — Academy of Marketing Science. Journal
AmL — Amor de Libro
Am Lab — American Laboratory
Am Lab (Boston) — American Laboratory (Boston)
Am Lab (Fairfield Conn) — American Laboratory (Fairfield, Connecticut)
Am Lab Leg R — American Labor Legislation Review
Am Lab Leg Rev — American Labor Legislation Review
Am Labor Legis Rev — American Labor Legislation Review
Am Labor Leg R — American Labor Legislation Review
Am Land — American Land
Am Landrace — American Landrace
Am Lat — America Latina
Am Laund Dig — American Laundry Digest
Am Laundry Dig — American Laundry Digest
Am Law — American Lawyer
Am Law J — American Law Journal
Am Law J NS — American Law Journal. New Series
Am Law Mag — American Law Magazine
Am Law R — American Law Review
Am Law Reg R — American Law Register and Review

Am Law Rev — American Law Review
Am Lawy — American Lawyer
Am Lawyer — American Lawyer
AMLB — Advertising and Marketing Law Bulletin
Am Leather Chem Assoc J — American Leather Chemists Association. Journal
Am Lect Ser — American Lecture Series
Am Legion M — American Legion Magazine
Am Leg Mag — American Legion Magazine
Am Li — Amor de Libro
Am Lib — American Libraries
Am Lib Assn Bul — American Library Association. Bulletin
Am Lib Assn Proc — American Library Association. Proceedings Issued in Bulletin
Am Libr — American Libraries
Am Libr (Chicago) — American Libraries (Chicago)
Am Libs — American Libraries
AMLICP — [A] Monthly Lesson in Criminal Politics
Am L Inst Proc — American Law Institute. Proceedings
AmLit — American Literature
Am Literature — American Literature. Duke University Press
Am Lit M — American Literary Magazine
Am Lit Real — American Literary Realism, 1870-1910
Am Lit Realism — American Literary Realism, 1870-1910
Am Littoral Soc Spec Publ — American Littoral Society. Special Publication
Am Livestock J — American Livestock Journal
Am LJ — American Law Journal
Am LJNS — American Law Journal. New Series
Am LJ (O) — American Law Journal (Ohio)
Am LJ OS — American Law Journal. Old Series
Am LM — American Law Magazine
Am Logger Lumberman — American Logger and Lumberman
Am Log Lumber — American Logger and Lumberman
AMLP — Anales del Museo de La Plata
AMLPAG — Arquivos Mineiros de Leprologia
Am L R — American Law Review
Am L Rev — American Law Review
Am L S — American Library Scholarship
AMLSBQ — American Lecture Series
Am L Sch R — American Law School Review
Am Lumberman — American Lumberman
Am Lung Assoc Bull — American Lung Association. Bulletin
Am Luth — American Lutheran
Am Lutherie — American Lutherie
Am M — American Magazine
AMM — American Mathematical Monthly
AmM — American Mercury
AMM — Annuaire du Monde Musulman
AMM — Asian Marketing Monitor
Am Mach — American Machinist
Am Machin — American Machinist
Am Machinist — American Machinist
Am Mach/Metalwork Manuf — American Machinist/Metalworking Manufacturing
Am Mag — American Magazine
Am Mag Art — American Magazine of Art
Am Malacol Bull — American Malacological Bulletin
Am Malacolog Union Ann Rept — American Malacological Union. Annual Report
Am Malacol Union Bull — American Malacological Union. Bulletin [Later, American Malacological Bulletin]
Am Malacol Union Inc Annu Rep — American Malacological Union, Incorporated. Annual Report
Am Malacol Union Inc Bull — American Malacological Union, Incorporated. Bulletin [Later, American Malacological Bulletin]
Am Management Assn Survey Rpt — American Management Association. Survey Report
Am Management R — American Management Review
Am Manuf — American Manufacturer
Am Mar Cas — American Maritime Cases
Am Marche — Atti e Memorie. Deputazione di Storia Patria per le Provincie delle Marche
Am Marine Engineer — American Marine Engineer
Am M Art — American Magazine of Art
Am M Assn Bul — American Medical Association. Bulletin
Am M Assn J — American Medical Association. Journal
Am Math M — American Mathematical Monthly
Am Math Mo — American Mathematical Monthly
Am Math Mon — American Mathematical Monthly
Am Math Soc Bul — American Mathematical Society. Bulletin
Am Math Soc Mem — American Mathematical Society. Memoirs
Am Math Soc Memoirs — American Mathematical Society. Memoirs
AMMBAD — Argentina. Direccion Nacional de Geologia y Mineria. Boletin
Am M Civics — American Magazine of Civics
Am M Cong — American Mining Congress. Journal
Am Mcr J — American Monthly Microscopical Journal
Am Mcr S P — Proceedings of the American Microscopical Society
Am Mcr S T — Transactions of the American Microscopical Society
Am Md Ph Reg — American Medical and Philosophical Register or Annals of Medicine, Natural History, Agriculture, and the Arts
Am Meat Inst Found Bull — American Meat Institute. Foundation Bulletin
Am Meat Inst Found Circ — American Meat Institute. Foundation Circular
Am Med — American Medicine
Am Med Assn J — American Medical Association. Journal
Am Med Assn Trans — American Medical Association. Transactions
Am Med Assoc Congr Environ Health — American Medical Association. Congress on Environmental Health
Am Med Assoc Cost Effect Pl — American Medical Association's Cost Effectiveness Plan

Am Med News — American Medical News
Am Med News Impact — American Medical News Impact
Am Med Psychol Assn Proc — American Medico-Psychological Association. Proceedings
Am Med W — American Medical Weekly
Am Mer — American Mercury
AmMerc — American Mercury
Am Mercury — American Mercury
Am Mess Jew — American Messianic Jew
Am Meteorological J — American Meteorological Journal
Am Meteorol Soc Bull — American Meteorological Society. Bulletin
Am Meth M — American Methodist Magazine
Am Met J — American Meteorological Journal
Am Met Mark — American Metal Market
Am Met Mark Metalwork News Ed — American Metal Market. Metalworking News Edition
Am Met Soc Bull — American Meteorological Society. Bulletin
AMMIA — American Mineralogist
Am Micro Soc Pr — American Microscopical Society. Proceedings
Am Micros Soc Trans — American Microscopical Society. Transactions
Am Midland Natural — American Midland Naturalist
Am Midl Nat — American Midland Naturalist
Am Midl Natur — American Midland Naturalist
Am Milk R — American Milk Review
Am Milk Rev — American Milk Review
Am Milk Rev Milk Plant Mon — American Milk Review and Milk Plant Monthly
Am Miller — American Miller
Am Miller Process — American Miller and Processor
Am Min — American Mineralogist
Ammin & Politica — Amministrazione e Politica
Am Min Congr J — American Mining Congress. Journal
Am Min Congr Proc — American Mining Congress. Proceedings
Am Min Congr Sess Pap — American Mining Congress. Session Papers
Am Miner — American Mineralogist
Am Mineral — American Mineralogist
Am Mineral J — American Mineralogical Journal
Am Mineralogist — American Mineralogist
Am Miner J — American Mineralogical Journal
AMMKA — American Metal Market
AMMO — Australian Mining, Minerals, and Oil
AMMOHOUSE Bull — AMMOHOUSE [Ammunition House] Bulletin
Am Mo M — American Monthly Magazine
Ammonia Plant Saf — Ammonia Plant Safety and Related Facilities
Am Mo R — American Monthly Review
Am Mosq Control Assoc — American Mosquito Control Association. Journal
Am Mosq Control Assoc Bull — American Mosquito Control Association. Bulletin
AMMSBV — Acta Musei Macedonici. Scientiarum Naturalium
Am Ms Mag — American Ms Magazine
Am Mtl Mkt — American Metal Market
Am Munic — American Municipalities
Am Mus — American Music
Am Mus Dgt — American Musical Digest
Am Museum J — American Museum Journal
Am Mus Exp Buy G — American Music Export Buyers Guide
Am Musicol Soc J — American Musicological Society. Journal
Am Mus J — American Museum Journal
Am Mus Nat Hist Anthrop Pap — American Museum of Natural History. Anthropological Papers
Am Mus Nat History Bull — American Museum of Natural History. Bulletin
Am Mus Nat History Bull Sci Guide Special Pub — American Museum of Natural History. Bulletin. Science Guide. Special Publication
Am Mus N H B Mem — American Museum of Natural History. Bulletin. Memoirs
Am Mus Novit — American Museum Novitates
Am Mus Novitates — American Museum Novitates
Am Mus Res — American Music Research Center Journal
Am Mus Tcr — American Music Teacher
Am Mus Teach — American Music Teacher
AMMYA — American Mathematical Monthly
AMMYAE — American Mathematical Monthly
AMN — Acta Musei Napocensis
AMN — Amazing Stories. Science Fiction Novels
AMN — American Salesman
AMN — Analecta Mediaevalia Namurcensia
AMN — Arizona Music News
AMN — Arquivos do Museu Nacional [Rio de Janeiro]
AMN — SAM [Society for Advancement of Management] Advanced Management Journal
AMNAA — American Midland Naturalist
AMNAAF — American Midland Naturalist
AMNADI — Annales Medicales de Nancy et de l'Est
Am N & Q — American Notes and Queries
Am Nat — American Naturalist
Am Natl Red Cross Annu Sci Symp — American National Red Cross. Annual Scientific Symposium
Am Natl Red Cross Annu Symp — American National Red Cross. Annual Symposium
Am Natl Stand Inst Stand — American National Standards Institute. Standards
Am Nat Pr — American Native Press
Am Natural — American Naturalist
Am Naturalist — American Naturalist
AmNB — American Naturalist (Boston)
AMNBA — Anales del Museo Nacional de Buenos Aires
AMNDS — Annales de la Mission de N.-D. de Sion en Terre Sainte (1877-1912)
Am Nep — American Neptune
Am Neptune — American Neptune

AMNG — Antiken Muenzen Nord-Griechenlands
AMNGA — Arkiv foer Mineralogi och Geologi
AMNGAX — Arkiv foer Mineralogi och Geologi
AMNH — American Museum of Natural History
AMNHA2 — Annals and Magazine of Natural History
AMNHN — Anales del Museo Nacional de Historia Natural Bernardino Rivadavia [*Buenos Aires*]
AMNH/NH — Natural History. American Museum of Natural History
AMNIB — Acta Manilana. Series A. Natural and Applied Sciences
AMNJA8 — Arquivos. Museu Nacional do Rio De Janeiro
AMNM — Anales del Museo Nacional de Montevideo
A Mnmts & Mem — Arts. Monuments et Memoires
AMNND — American Midland Naturalist. Notre Dame University
A M Nordwest D — Archaeologische Mitteilungen aus Nordwestdeutschland
Am Note Que — American Notes and Queries
Am Notes & Queries — American Notes and Queries
AMNP — Annuaire. Musee National Archeologique (Plovdiv)
AMNP — Archives de Medecine Navale
AMNSAZ — Acta Morphologica Neerlando-Scandinavica
Am Nt — American Naturalist
AMNTA — American Naturalist
AMNTA4 — American Naturalist
Am Ntlist — American Naturalist
Am Nucl Soc Conf At Nucl Methods Fossil Fuel Energy Res — American Nuclear Society. Conference on Atomic and Nuclear Methods inFossil Fuel Energy Research
Am Nucl Soc Eur Nucl Soc Top Meet Therm React Saf — American Nuclear Society/European Nuclear Society Topical Meeting.Thermal Reactor Safety
Am Nucl Soc Int Top Meet — American Nuclear Society. International Topical Meeting
Am Nucl Soc Natl Meet Pap — American Nuclear Society. National Meeting Papers
Am Nucl Soc Natl Top Meet — American Nuclear Society. National Topical Meeting
Am Nucl Soc Proc Pac Basin Conf Nucl Power Dev Fuel Cycle — American Nuclear Society. Proceedings. Pacific Basin Conference on Nuclear Power Development and the Fuel Cycle
Am Nucl Soc Top Meet Adv React Phys Proc — American Nuclear Society. National Topical Meeting on Advances inReactor Physics. Proceedings
Am Nucl Soc Top Meet Gas-Cooled React HTGR GCFBR — American Nuclear Society Topical Meeting on Gas-Cooled Reactors. HTGR and GCFBR
Am Nucl Soc Top Meet Irradiat Exp Fast React — American Nuclear Society Topical Meeting. Irradiation Experimentation in Fast Reactors
Am Nucl Soc Top Meet Light Water React Fuel Perform — American Nuclear Society. Topical Meeting on Light Water Reactor FuelPerformance
Am Nucl Soc Trans — American Nuclear Society. Transactions
AMNUDA — Advances in Modern Nutrition
Am Num Soc Mus Notes — American Numismatic Society. Museum Notes
Am Nurse — American Nurse
Am Nurseryman — American Nurseryman
Am Nurseryman Natl Nurseryman — American Nurseryman and the National Nurseryman
Am Nut J — American Nut Journal
AMNYAJ — Annales Medicales de Nancy
AMO — Acta Medica Orientalia
AMO — Applied Methods in Oncology
AMo — Atlantic Monthly
Am OAS — Americas. Organization of American States
AMOBAN — AMMOHOUSE [*Ammunition House*] Bulletin
AMOCBR — Agronomia Mocambicana
A Mod — Arte Moderna
A Mod [*Brussels*] — Art Moderne [*Brussels*]
Am OEA Span Wash — Americas. Organizacion de los Estados Americanos (Washington, DC)
AMOF — Matter of Fact
Am Oil Chemists Soc J — American Oil Chemists' Society. Journal
Am Oil Chem Soc J — American Oil Chemists' Society. Journal
Am Oil Chem Soc Monogr — American Oil Chemists' Society. Monograph
AMOJ — Acta Medica Orientalia (Jerusalem and Tel Aviv)
A Mold — Arheologia Moldovei
AMollK — Archiv fuer Molluskenkunde
AMOMB — Applied Mathematics and Optimization
AMon — Analecta Monastica
AMon — Atlantic Monthly
A Mons — Annales. Cercle Archeologique de Mons
AMontserr — Analecta Montserratensia
Am Oph S T — Transactions of the American Ophthalmological Society
Am Ophthal Soc J — American Opthalmological Society. Journal
Am Ophthal Soc Trans — American Ophthalmological Society. Transactions
Am Opinion — American Opinion
Am Optom Assoc J — American Optometric Association. Journal
Am Optomet Assoc J — American Optometric Association. Journal
Am Orchid Soc Bull — American Orchid Society. Bulletin
Am Orch Soc B — American Orchid Society. Bulletin
Am Orch Soc Yb — American Orchid Society. Yearbook
Am Org — American Organist
Am Oriental Soc J — American Oriental Society. Journal
Am Orient Soc J — American Oriental Society. Journal
Am Orn — American Ornithology
Amorphous Liq Mater — Amorphous and Liquid Materials
Amorphous Liq Semicond — Amorphous and Liquid Semiconductors
Amorphous Liq Semicond Proc Int Conf — Amorphous and Liquid Semiconductors. Proceedings. International Conference
Amorphous Magn Proc Int Symp — Amorphous Magnetism. Proceedings. International Symposium onAmorphous Magnetism

Amorphous Mater Model Struct Prop Proc Symp — Amorphous Materials. Modeling of Structure and Properties. Proceedings.Symposium
Amorphous Mater Pap Int Conf Phys Non Cryst Solids — Amorphous Materials. Papers Presented. International Conference on the Physics of Non-Crystalline Solids
Amorphous Met Semicond Proc Int Workshop — Amorphous Metals and Semiconductors. Proceedings. InternationalWorkshop
Amorphous Semicond — Amorphous Semiconductors
Amorphous Semicond Proc Int Conf — Amorphous Semiconductors. Proceedings. International Conference
Am Orth J — American Orthoptic Journal
Am Orthopsych Assoc Pap — American Orthopsychiatric Association. Papers Presented. Annual Convention
Am Orthopt J — American Orthoptic Journal
Am Osteopath Assoc J — American Osteopathic Association. Journal
AMOTA9 — Anales. Sociedad Mexicana de Otorrinolaringologia
Amour A — Amour de l'Art
AmOx — American Oxonian
Amoxycillin (BRL 2333) Pap Int Symp — Amoxycillin (BRL 2333) Papers. International Symposium
AMP — Academie des Sciences Morales et Politiques. Seances et Travaux. Comptes Rendus
AMP — Acta Medica Polona
Am P — American Psychologist
Amp — Ampurias
AMP — Anais do Museu Paulista [*Sao Paulo*]
AMP — Annales Medico-Psychologiques
AMP — Arquivo de Medicina Popular
AMP — Audiovisual Market Place
Am P Advocate — American Poultry Advocate
Am Paint — American Paint and Coatings Journal
Am Paint Coat J — American Paint and Coatings Journal
Am Paint Contract — American Painting Contractor
Am Painter Decor — American Painter and Decorator
Am Paint J — American Paint Journal [*Later, American Paint and Coatings Journal*]
Am Paint Varn Mmanuf Assoc Sci Sect Circ — American Paint and Varnish Manufacturers' Association. Scientific Section. Circulars
Am Pap Converter — American Paper Converter
Am Paper Ind — American Paper Industry
Am Paper Merch — American Paper Merchant
Am Pap Ind — American Paper Industry
Am Pap Merchant — American Paper Merchant
Am Pat L Assoc Bull — American Patent Law Association. Bulletin
Am Pat LQJ — APLA (American Patent Law Association). Quarterly Journal
AMPBAS — Anais. Sociedade de Medicina de Pernambuco
AMPC — Arquivos do Museu Paranaense (Curitiba)
AMPCA — Archivio "E. Maragliano" di Patologia e Clinica
AMPCAV — Archivio e Maragliano di Patologia e Clinica
AMPCB — American Psychological Association. Proceedings of the Annual Convention
AMPDA — Australian Machinery and Production Engineering
AMPEA3 — American Miller and Processor
Am Peace Dir — American Peace Directory
Am Peanut Res Educ Assoc J — American Peanut Research and Education Association. Journal
Am Peanut Res Educ Assoc Proc — American Peanut Research and Education Association. Proceedings
Am Peanut Res Educ Soc Proc — American Peanut Research and Education Society. Proceedings
Am Pediat Soc Trans — American Pediatric Society. Transactions
Am Pept Symp — American Peptide Symposium
Ampere Int Summer Sch Magn Reson Chem Biol — Ampere International Summer School on Magnetic Resonance in Chemistry and Biology
Ampere Int Summer Sch Proc — Ampere International Summer School. Proceedings
Am Perfum — American Perfumer
Am Perfum Aromat — American Perfumer and Aromatics
Am Perfum Cosmet — American Perfumer and Cosmetics
Am Perfum Cosmet Toilet Prep — American Perfumer, Cosmetics, Toilet Preparations
Am Perfume — American Cosmetics and Perfumery
Am Perfumer — American Perfumer and Cosmetics
Am Perfumer & Aromatics — American Perfumer and Aromatics
Am Perfumer Arom — American Perfumer and Aromatics
Am Perfumer Ess Oil Rev — American Perfumer and Essential Oil Review
Am Perfum Essent Oil Rev — American Perfumer and Essential Oil Review
Am Perfum Esst Oil Rev — American Perfumer and Essential Oil Review
Ampersand Ent Gd — Amersand's Entertainment Guide
Am Perspect — American Perspective
Am Pet Inst Abstr Refin Lit — American Petroleum Institute. Abstracts of Refining Literature
Am Pet Inst Bul — American Petroleum Institute. Bulletin
Am Pet Inst Div Refin Proc — American Petroleum Institute. Division of Refining. Proceedings
Am Pet Inst Proc — American Petroleum Institute. Proceedings
Am Pet Inst Publ — American Petroleum Institute. Publication
Am Pet Inst Q — American Petroleum Institute. Quarterly
Am Pet Inst Refin Dep Proc — American Petroleum Institute. Refining Department. Proceedings
Am Pet Inst Refin Dept Proc — American Petroleum Institute. Refining Department. Proceedings
Am Pet Inst Stat Bull — American Petroleum Institute. Statistical Bulletin
Am Pet Inst Tech Abstr — American Petroleum Institute. Technical Abstracts
Am Petr Inst Quart — American Petroleum Institute. Quarterly

Am Petr Inst Wkly Stat Bull — American Petroleum Institute. Weekly Statistical Bulletin
Am Petroleum Inst Drilling and Production Practice — American Petroleum Institute. Drilling and Production Practice
AMPH — American Pharmacy
Am Pharm — American Pharmacy
Am Pharm Assoc J — American Pharmaceutical Association. Journal
AMPHDF — American Pharmacy
Amphib Reptilia — Amphibia-Reptilia
Am Phil — Americam Philatelist
Am Philos Q — American Philosophical Quarterly
Am Philos Soc Lib Bull — American Philosophical Society. Library Bulletin
Am Philos Soc Mem — American Philosophical Society. Memoirs
Am Philos Soc Proc — American Philosophical Society. Proceedings
Am Philos Soc Trans — American Philosophical Society. Transactions
Am Philos Soc YB — American Philosophical Society. Yearbook
Am Philos Soc Yearbook — American Philosophical Society. Yearbook
Am Phil Soc Proc — American Philosophical Society. Proceedings
Am Phm As P — Proceedings of the American Pharmaceutical Association
Am Phot — American Photography
Am Photo Engraver — American Photo Engraver
Am Photog — American Photography
Am Photogr — American Photography
Am Ph S P — Proceedings of the American Philosophical Society
Am Ph S T — Transactions of the American Philosophical Society
Am Phys Ed Assn Res Q — American Physical Education Association. Research Quarterly
Am Phys Educ R — American Physical Education Review
Am Phys Educ Rev — American Physical Education Review
Am Physiol Soc Methods Physiol Ser — American Physiological Society. Methods in Physiology Series
Am Physn Philad — American Physician (Philadelphia)
Am Physn Rahway — American Physician (Rahway, N.J.)
Am Phys Soc Bull — American Physical Society. Bulletin
Am Phys Soc Div Part Fields Annu Meet — American Physical Society. Division of Particles and Fields. AnnualMeeting
Am Phys Soc Top Conf Shock Waves Condens Matter — American Physical Society. Topical Conference on Shock Waves inCondensed Matter
Am Phys Teach — American Physics Teacher
Am Phytopathol Soc Monogr — American Phytopathological Society. Monograph
Am Phytopathol Soc Proc — American Phytopathological Society. Proceedings
AMPIAF — Acta Medica Philippina
AMPI (Assoc Med Phys India) Med Phys Bull — AMPI (Association of Medical Physicists of India) Medical Physics Bulletin
AMPIB — Advances in Microbial Physiology
AMPIE — American Psycho/Info Exchange
Am Pilot AircrMan — American Pilot and Aircraftsman
Am P J — American Poultry Journal
AMPL — Antiguo Mercurio Peruano (Lima)
Am Plan Assn J — American Planning Association. Journal
Am Plann Assoc J — American Planning Association. Journal
Am Planning — American Planning and Civic Planning
AMPLJ — Australian Mining and Petroleum Law Journal
Am Pls — American Plants
AMPM — Academie des Sciences Morales et Politiques. Memoires
AMPM — Institut de France. Academie des Sciences Morales et Politiques. Memoires
AMPMA — Archives des Maladies Professionnelles de Medecine du Travail et de Securite Sociale
AMP News — AMP [*Australian Mutual Provident Society*] News and Views
AMPOAX — Acta Microbiologica Polonica
Am Poet Rev — American Poetry Review
Am Poetry — American Poetry Review
Am Poli Sci — American Political Science Review
Am Politics Q — American Politics Quarterly
Am Polit Q — American Politics Quarterly
Am Polit Sci R — American Political Science Review
Am Pol J — American Polytechnic Journal
Am Pol Q — American Politics Quarterly
Am Pol Sci — American Political Science Review
Am Pol Sci Assn Proc — American Political Science Association. Proceedings
Am Pol Science R — American Political Science Review
Am Pol Science Rev — American Political Science Review
Am Pol Sci R — American Political Science Review
Am Pol Sci Rev — American Political Science Review
Am Pol Sc Rev — American Political Science Review
Am Pomol — American Pomology
Am Pom Soc Pro — American Pomological Society. Proceedings
Am Postal Wkr — American Postal Worker
Am Potato J — American Potato Journal
Am Potato Yb — American Potato Yearbook
Am Pot J — American Potato Journal
Am Poult J — American Poultry Journal
Am Poultry J — American Poultry Journal
Am Power Conf Proc — American Power Conference. Proceedings
AMPR — Academie des Sciences Morales et Politiques. Revue des Travaux
Am Pract — American Practitioner
Am Pract Digest Treat — American Practitioner and Digest of Treatment
Am Pract Dig Treat — American Practitioner and Digest of Treatment
Am Practitioner — American Practitioner
Am Practnr Dig Treat — American Practitioner and Digest of Treatment
Am Practnr Louisville — American Practitioner (Louisville)
Am Practnr Philad — American Practitioner (Philadelphia)
AMPRB9 — Annales de Medecine et de Pharmacie de Reims
Am Prefs — American Prefaces

Am Presb R — American Presbyterian Review
Am Pressman — American Pressman
Am Pressman Rept — American Pressman Reports
Am Print — American Printer
Am Printer — American Printer
Am Printer Lithogr — American Printer and Lithographer [*Later, American Printer*]
Am Pris Assn Proc — American Prison Association. Proceedings
Am Prison Assn Proc — American Prison Association. Proceedings
Am Prnt Lith — American Printer and Lithographer [*Later, American Printer*]
Am Prod Grow — American Produce Grower
Am Prod R — American Produce Review
Am Prod Rev — American Produce Review
Am Prof Pharm — American Professional Pharmacist
Am Proj Ser — American Project Series
AMPS — Academie des Sciences Morales et Politiques. Seances et Travaux
AM-Ps — Annales Medico-Psychologiques
AMPSA — American Psychologist
AMPSAB — American Psychologist
Am Psychiatr Assoc Ment Hosp Serv Monogr Ser — American Psychiatric Association. Mental Hospital Service. Monograph Series
Am Psychoana Assn J — American Psychoanalytic Association. Journal
Am Psychoanal Assn J — American Psychoanalytic Association. Journal
Am Psychoanal Assoc J Monogr Ser — American Psychoanalytic Association. Journal. Monograph Series
Am Psychol — American Psychologist
Am Psychol Assn Proc — American Psychological Association. Proceedings
Am Psychologist — American Psychologist
Am Psychopathol Assoc Proc Annu Meet — American Psychopathological Association. Proceedings. Annual Meeting
Am Ptr & Lith — American Printer and Lithographer [*Later, American Printer*]
Am Pub Health Ass Rep — American Public Health Association. Reports
Am Public Health Assoc Yearb — American Public Health Association. Yearbook
Am Public Works Assoc Yearb — American Public Works Association. Yearbook
AMPYA — Annales Medico-Psychologiques
AMPYAT — Annales Medico-Psychologiques
AMQ — Amazing Stories. Quarterly
Am Q — American Quarterly
Am Q — American Quarterly Review
Am Q J Agr — American Quarterly Journal of Agriculture and Science
Am Q Micro J — American Quarterly Microscopical Journal
Am Q Obs — American Quarterly Observer
Am Q Reg — American Quarterly Register
Am Q Roentg — American Quarterly of Roentgenology
Am Q Roentgenol — American Quarterly of Roentgenology
Am Q Sov Union — American Quarterly on the Soviet Union
Am Quar — American Quarterly
Am Quart — American Quarterly
Am (Quito) — America (Quito)
AMR — Academy of Management. Review
AMR — Amazing Stories. Quarterly Reissue
AMR — Ambtenaar
AMR — American Book Review
Am R — American Review [*Formerly, New American Review*]
Am R — American Review of Reviews
AMR — Applied Mechanics Reviews
AMR — Arctic Medical Research Report. Nordic Council
AMR — Australian Marketing Researcher
Am Rabbit J — American Rabbit Journal
AMRAC — Annales. Musee Royal de l'Afrique Centrale
Am Railw Eng Assoc Bull — American Railway Engineering Association. Bulletin
Am Railw Eng Assoc Proc — American Railway Engineering Association. Proceedings
Am Railw Eng Assoc Tech Conf Proc — American Railway Engineering Association. Technical ConferenceProceedings
Am Railw Eng Maint Way Assoc Proc Annu Conv — American Railway Engineering and Maintenance-of-Way Association. Proceedings. Annual Convention
AM + R Angew Elektron Mess Regeltech — AM + R. Angewandte Elektronik. Mess und Regeltechnik
AM + R Angew Mess Regeltech — AM + R. Angewandte Mess- und Regeltechnik
AMRB — Annuaire. Musees Royaux des Beaux-Arts de Belgique
AMRBB5 — Alabama Marine Resources. Bulletin
AMRCJ — American Music Research Center Journal
AMRC Rev — AMRC [*Australian Meat Research Committee*] Review
AMRC Rev Aust Meat Res Comm — AMRC Review (Australian Meat Research Committee)
Am Rd Bldr — American Road Builder
Am Rd Builders Assn Proc — American Road Builders Association. Summary Proceedings
Am Real Estate & Urb Econ Assn J — American Real Estate and Urban Economics Association. Journal
Am Rec G — American Record Guide
Am Rec Guide — American Record Guide
Am Recorder — American Recorder
Am Record Gd — American Record Guide
Am Red Angus — American Red Angus
Am Red Cross Sci Symp Impact Recomb Technol Hemostasis Thromb — American Red Cross Scientific Symposium. Impact of Recombinant Technology in Hemostasis and Thrombosis
AMREEH — Amphibia-Reptilia
Am Ref Bk Ann — American Reference Books Annual
Am Refract Inst Inf Circ — American Refractories Institute. Information Circular
Am Refract Inst Tech Bull — American Refractories Institute. Technical Bulletin
Am Rehabil — American Rehabilitation
Am Rev — American Review [*Formerly, New American Review*]

Am Rev Resp Dis — American Review of Respiratory Disease
Am Rev Respir Dis — American Review of Respiratory Disease
Am Rev Respir Dis — American Review of Respiratory Diseases
Am Rev Sov Med — American Review of Soviet Medicine
Am Rev Sov Union — American Review on the Soviet Union
Am Rev SU — American Review of the Soviet Union
Am Rev Trop Agric — American Review of Tropical Agriculture
Am Rev Tub — American Review of Tuberculosis and Pulmonary Diseases
Am Rev Tuberc — American Review of Tuberculosis
Am Rev Tuberc Pulm Dis — American Review of Tuberculosis and Pulmonary Diseases
AMrhKG — Archiv fuer Mittelrheinische Kirchengeschichte
Am Rhodod Soc Yb — American Rhododendron Society Yearbook
AMRIA — Americas
AMRIB — America
AMRM — Australasian Model Railroad Magazine
AMRMC5 — Agricultural Research Council. Meat Research Institute [Bristol]. Memorandum
AMROBA — Acta Medica Romana
Am Rocket Soc Pap — American Rocket Society. Paper
AM Rom — Atti e Memorie. Deputazione di Storia Patria. Provincie di Romagna
Am Rose Annu — American Rose Annual
AMRPDF — Advances in Molecular Relaxation and Interaction Processes
Am R Public Admin — American Review of Public Administration
AMRR — Arctic Medical Research Report. Nordic Council
Am R Resp D — American Review of Respiratory Disease
Am R Tuberc — American Review of Tuberculosis
AMRWA — Anglo-German Medical Review
AMS — Academy of Marketing Science. Journal
AMS — Acta Martyrum et Sanctorum
AMS — Advances in Management Studies
AMS — American Magazine (Springfield, Ohio)
AMS — American Musicological Society. Journal
AMS — American Salesman
AmS — American Scholar
AmS — American Speech
AmS — American Studies
AMS — [The] Americas: A Quarterly Review of Inter-American Cultural History
AMS — Arthritis and Musculoskeletal and Skin Diseases Database
AMS — Australian Minesweeper
AMS — Joseph Quincy Adams Memorial Studies
AMSAC — AMSAC [American Society of African Culture] Newsletter
Am Samoa — American Samoa Reports
Am Samoa Admin Code — American Samoa Administrative Code
Am Samoa Code Ann — American Samoa Code Annotated
AMSAPM — Atti e Memorie. Deputazione di Storia Patria per le Antiche Provincie Modenesi
AMSC — Advances in Molten Salt Chemistry
AmSc — American Scientist
AMSCA — American Scientist
AMSCAC — American Scientist
Am Scandinavian Rev — American Scandinavian Review
Am Scand R — American-Scandinavian Review
Am Scand Rev — American Scandinavian Review
Am Sca R — Americn Scandinavian Review
AMSCC — Advances in Molten Salt Chemistry
Am Scenic and Historic Preservation Soc An Rp — American Scenic and Historic Preservation Society. Annual Report
Am Sch — American Scholar
Am Sch & Univ — American School and University
Am Sch Bd J — American School Board Journal
Am Sch Board J — American School Board Journal
Am Sch Brd J — American School Board Journal
Am Schol — American Scholar
Am Scholar — American Scholar
Am School Bd J — American School Board Journal
Am Sch Orient Res Bul — American Schools of Oriental Research. Bulletin
Am Sci — American Scientist
Am Scient — American Scientist
Am Scientist — American Scientist
AMSDSP — Atti e Memorie. Società Dalmata di Storia
AMSE — Americas (Espanol)
AMSEAEP — Actas y Memorias. Sociedad Espanola de Antropologia, Etnografia, y Prehistoria
AMSE Antr — Acta y Memorias. Sociedad Espanola de Antropologia, Etnografia, y Prehistoria
AMSEAP — Acta y Memorias. Sociedad Espanola de Antropologia, Etnografia, y Prehistoria.
Am Sec Educ — American Secondary Education
Am Sect Int Sol Energy Soc Proc Annu Meet — American Section. International Solar Energy Society. Proceedings. Annual Meeting
Am Seph — American Sephardi
AMSER — Atti e Memorie. Reale Deputazione di Storia Patria per l'Emilia et la Romagna
AmSF — Amis de Saint Francois
AMSHAR — Acta Morphologica. Academiae Scientiarum Hungaricae
Am Sheep B & W — American Sheep Breeder and Wool Grower
Am Shipp — American Shipper
Am Show — American Showcase
AMSI — Atti e Memorie. Societa Istriana di Archeologia e Storia Patria
AMSIA — Atti e Memorie. Societa Istriana di Archeologia e Storia Patria
Am Silk J — American Silk Journal
Am Silk Rayon J — American Silk Rayon Journal
AMSIstriana — Atti e Memorie. Societa Istriana di Archeologia e Storia Patria
AMSJ — American Musicological Society. Journal

AMSJAX — Journal. Aero Medical Society of India
AMS JI — American Musicological Society. Journal
Am SI — American Slavic and East European Review
AMSL — Archives des Missions Scientifiques et Litteraires
Am Slavic EER — American Slavic and East European Review
Am Slavic R — American Slavic and East European Review
AMSM — Atti e Memorie. Reale Deputazione di Storia Patria per le Marche
AMSN — American Musicological Society Newsletter
Am Soc — American Sociologist
Am Soc Abrasive Methods Natl Tech Conf Proc — American Society for Abrasive Methods. National Technical Conference. Proceedings
Am Soc Ag Eng — American Society of Agricultural Engineers. Transactions
Am Soc Agric Eng Microfiche Collect — American Society of Agricultural Engineers. Microfiche Collection
Am Soc Agric Eng Pap — American Society of Agricultural Engineers. Paper
Am Soc Agric Eng Publ — American Society of Agricultural Engineers. Publication
Am Soc Agron J — American Society of Agronomy. Journal
Am Soc Agron Spec Publ — American Society of Agronomy. Special Publication
Am Soc Anim Prod Rec Proc Annu Meet — American Society of Animal Production. Record of Proceedings. Annual Meeting
Am Soc Anim Sci West Sect Proc — American Society of Animal Science. Western Section. Proceedings
Am Soc Anim Sci West Sect Proc Annu Meet — American Society of Animal Science. Western Section. Proceedings.Annual Meeting
Am Soc Artif Intern Organs J — American Society of Artificial Internal Organs. Journal
Am Soc Artif Intern Organs Trans — American Society of Artificial Internal Organs. Transactions
Am Soc Brew Chem Proc — American Society of Brewing Chemists. Proceedings
Am Soc C E Proc — American Society of Civil Engineers. Proceedings
Am Soc Church Hist Pap — American Society of Church History. Papers
Am Soc Church Hist Papers — American Society of Church History. Papers
Am Soc Civ E J Struct Div — American Society of Civil Engineers. Journal. Structural Division
Am Soc Civ E J Waterway Port Div — American Society of Civil Engineers. Waterway, Port, Coastal, and Ocean Division
Am Soc Civ Eng City Plann Div J — American Society of Civil Engineers. City Planning Division. Journal
Am Soc Civ Eng Environ Eng Div J — American Society of Civil Engineers. Environmental EngineeringDivision. Journal
Am Soc Civ Eng Hydraul Div Annu Spec Conf Proc — American Society of Civil Engineers. Hydraulics Division. Annual Specialty Conference. Proceedings
Am Soc Civ Eng J Energy Div — American Society of Civil Engineers. Journal. Energy Division
Am Soc Civ Eng Proc Eng Issues J Prof Act — American Society of Civil Engineers. Proceedings. Engineering Issues. Journal of Professional Activities
Am Soc Civ Eng Proc J Hydraul Div — American Society of Civil Engineers. Proceedings. Journal. Hydraulics Division
Am Soc Civ Eng Proc J Irrig Drain Div — American Society of Civil Engineers. Proceedings. Journal. Irrigation and Drainage Division
Am Soc Civ Eng Proc Transp Eng J — American Society of Civil Engineers. Proceedings. Transportation Engineering Journal
Am Soc Civ Eng Trans — American Society of Civil Engineers. Transactions
Am Soc Civ E Transp Eng J — American Society of Civil Engineers. Transportation Engineering Journal
Am Soc Civil Engineers Proc Jour Hydraulics Div — American Society of Civil Engineers. Proceedings. Journal. Hydraulics Division
Am Soc Civil Engineers Proc Jour Sanitary Eng Div — American Society of Civil Engineers. Proceedings. Journal. Sanitary Engineering Division
Am Soc Civil Engineers Proc Jour Structural Div — American Society of Civil Engineers. Proceedings. Journal. Structural Division
Am Soc Civil Engineers Proc Jour Surveying and Mapping Div — American Society of Civil Engineers. Proceedings. Journal. Surveying and Mapping Division
Am Soc Civil Engineers Trans — American Society of Civil Engineers. Transactions
Am Soc Civil Eng Proc — American Society of Civil Engineers. Proceedings
Am Soc Civil Eng Proc J Geotech Eng Div — American Society of Civil Engineers. Proceedings. Journal. Geotechnical Engineering Division
Am Soc Civil Engrs Constr — American Society of Civil Engineers. Proceedings. Journal. Construction Division
Am Soc Civil Engrs Geotech — American Society of Civil Engineers. Proceedings. Journal. Geotechnical Division
Am Soc Civil Engrs Struct — American Society of Civil Engineers. Proceedings. Journal. Structural Division
Am Soc Civil Engrs Transpn — American Society of Civil Engineers. Proceedings. Journal of Transportation Engineering
Am Soc Civil Engrs Urb Plann — American Society of Civil Engineers. Journal of Urban Planning
Am Soc Clin Pathol Sum Rep — American Society of Clinical Pathologists. Summary Report
Am Soc Compos Tech Conf Proc — American Society for Composites. Technical Conference. Proceedings
Am Soc Eng Educ COED Trans — American Society for Engineering Education. Computers in Education Division. Transactions
Am Soc Eng Educ Comput Educ Div Trans — American Society for Engineering Education. Computers in Education Division. Transactions
Am Soc Heat Refrig Air Cond Eng ASHRAE Handb Prod Dir — American Society of Heating, Refrigerating, and Air-Conditioning Engineers. ASHRAE Handbook and Product Directory
Am Soc Heat Refrig Air Cond Eng J — American Society of Heating, Refrigerating, and Air-ConditioningEngineers. Journal
Am Soc Heat Refrig Air Cond Eng Trans — American Society of Heating, Refrigerating, and Air-ConditioningEngineers. Transactions

Am Soc Heat Vent Eng Guide — American Society of Heating and Ventilating Engineers. Guide
Am Soc Hortic Sci Trop Reg Proc — American Society for Horticultural Science. Tropical Region. Proceedings
Am Soc Hort Sci J — American Society for Horticultural Science. Journal
Am Soc Info Science Bul — Bulletin. American Society for Information Science
Am Soc Info Science J — Journal. American Society for Information Science
Am Soc Inf Sci J — American Society for Information Science. Journal
Am Soc Inf Sci Proc — American Society for Information Science. Proceedings
Am Soc Inf Sci Proc Annu Meet — American Society for Information Science. Proceedings. Annual Meeting
Am Soc Inf Sci Proc ASIS Annu Meet — American Society for Information Science. Proceedings of the ASIS Annual Meeting
Am Soc Int Law Proc — American Society of International Law. Proceedings
Am Soc Int'l L Proc — American Society of International Law. Proceedings
Am Soc Int L Proc — American Society of International Law. Proceedings
Am Sociol — American Sociologist
Am Sociological R — American Sociological Review
Am Sociologist — American Sociologist
Am Sociol R — American Sociological Review
Am Sociol Rev — American Sociological Review
Am Sociol S — American Sociological Society. Publications
Am Sociol Soc Pap Proc — American Sociological Society. Papers and Proceedings
Am Sociol Soc Proc — American Sociological Society. Papers and Proceedings
Am Socio Rev — American Sociological Review
Am Soc Limnol Oceangr Spec Symp — American Society of Limnology and Oceanography. Special Symposium
Am Soc Limnol Oceanogr Spec Symp — American Society of Limnology and Oceanography. Special Symposium
Am Soc Lubr Eng Spec Publ — American Society of Lubrication Engineers. Special Publication
Am Soc Lubr Eng Tech Prepr — American Society of Lubrication Engineers. Technical Preprints
Am Soc Lubr Eng Trans — American Society of Lubrication Engineers. Transactions
Am Soc Mechanical Engineers Trans — American Society of Mechanical Engineers. Transactions
Am Soc Mech Eng Aerosp Div Publ AD — American Society of Mechanical Engineers. Aerospace Division. Publication AD
Am Soc Mech Eng Appl Mech Div (AMD) — American Society of Mechanical Engineers. Applied Mechanics Division (AMD)
Am Soc Mech Eng Appl Mech Div Appl Mech Symp Ser — American Society of Mechanical Engineers. Applied Mechanics Division. Applied Mechanics Symposia Series
Am Soc Mech Eng Cavitation Polyphase Flow Forum — American Society of Mechanical Engineers. Cavitation and Polyphase FlowForum
Am Soc Mech Eng Fla Sect Citrus Eng Conf Trans — American Society of Mechanical Engineers. Florida Section. CitrusEngineering Conference. Transactions
Am Soc Mech Eng Fluids Eng Div Publ FED — American Society of Mechanical Engineers. Fluids Engineering Division.Publication FED
Am Soc Mech Eng Fuels Combust Technol Div Publ FACT — Americal Society of Mechanical Engineers. Fuels and Combustion Technologies Division. Publication. FACT
Am Soc Mech Eng Heat Transfer Div Publ HTD — American Society of Mechanical Engineers. Heat Transfer Division. Publication HTD
Am Soc Mech Eng Jpn Soc Mech Eng Therm Eng Jt Conf Proc — American Society of Mechanical Engineers. Japan Society of Mechanical Engineers. Thermal Engineering Joint Conference. Proceedings
Am Soc Mech Eng Met Prop Counc Publ MPC — American Society of Mechanical Engineers and Metal Properties Council. Publication MPC
Am Soc Mech Eng NM Sect Proc Annu ASME Symp — American Society of Mechanical Engineers. New Mexico Section.Proceedings. Annual ASME Symposium
Am Soc Mech Eng Pap — American Society of Mechanical Engineers. Papers
Am Soc Mech Eng Pressure Vessels — American Society of Mechanical Engineers. Pressure Vessels and Piping Division.Technical Report. PVP
Am Soc Mech Eng Pressure Vessels Piping Div Publ PVP — American Society of Mechanical Engineers. Pressure Vessels and Piping Division.Publication PVP
Am Soc Mech Eng Pressure Vessels Piping Div Publ PVP-PB — American Society of Mechanical Engineers. Pressure Vessels and PipingDivision. Publication PVP-PB
Am Soc Mech Eng Pressure Vessels Piping Div PVP — American Society of Mechanical Engineers. Pressure Vessels and Piping Division.Publication PVP
Am Soc Mech Eng Prod Eng Div Publ PED — American Society of Mechanical Engineers. Production EngineeringDivision. Publication PED
Am Soc Mech Eng Rail Transp Div Publ RTD — American Society of Mechanical Engineers. Rail Transportation Division. Publication RTD
Am Soc Mech Eng Winter Annu Meet — American Society of Mechanical Engineers. Winter Annual Meeting
Am Soc Met Mater Metalwork Technol Ser — American Society for Metals. Materials/Metalworking. Technology Series
Am Soc Met Tech Rep Syst — American Society for Metals. Technical Report System
Am Soc Met Trans Q — American Society for Metals. Transactions Quarterly
Am Soc Microbiol East Pa Branch Annu Symp Proc — American Society for Microbiology. Eastern Pennsylvania Branch. AnnualSymposium. Proceedings
Am Soc Microbiol East Penn Br Symp — American Society for Microbiology. Eastern Pennsylvania Branch. Symposia
Am Soc Munic Eng Int Assoc Public Works Off Yearb — American Society of Municipal Engineers. International Association ofPublic Works Officials. Yearbook
Am Soc Munic Eng Off Proc — American Society of Municipal Engineers. Official Proceedings

Am Soc Munic Imp — American Society for Municipal Improvements. Proceedings
Am Soc Munic Improv Proc — American Society for Municipal Improvements. Proceedings
Am Soc Naval Eng J — American Society of Naval Engineers. Journal
Am Soc Nondestr Test Natl Fall Conf — American Society for Nondestructive Testing. National Fall Conference
Am Soc Photogramm Annu Meet Proc — American Society of Photogrammetry. Annual Meeting. Proceedings
Am Soc Photogramm Fall Conv Proc — American Society of Photogrammetry. Fall Convention. Proceedings
Am Soc Plast Reconstr Surg Educ Found Proc Symp — American Society of Plastic and Reconstructive Surgeons. Educational Foundation. Proceedings of the Symposium
Am Soc Psychical Res J — American Society for Psychical Research. Journal
Am Soc Psych Res J — American Society for Psychical Research. Journal
Am Soc Qual Control Chem Div Trans — American Society for Quality Control. Chemical Division. Transactions
Am Soc R — American Sociological Review
Am Soc Refrig Eng J — American Society of Refrigerating Engineers. Journal
Am Soc Rev — American Sociological Review
Am Soc Safety Eng J — American Society of Safety Engineers. Journal
Am Soc Sci J — American Journal of Social Science
Am Soc Testing and Materials Spec Tech Pub — American Society for Testing and Materials. Special Technical Publication
Am Soc Testing Materials Special Tech Pub — American Society for Testing and Materials. Special Technical Publication
Am Soc Test Mater Annu Book ASTM Stand — American Society for Testing and Materials. Annual Book of ASTM Standards
Am Soc Test Mater ASTM Stand — American Society for Testing and Materials. Book of ASTM Standards
Am Soc Test Mater Book ASTM Stand — American Society for Testing and Materials. Book of ASTM Standards
Am Soc Test Mater Book ASTM Stand Relat Mater — American Society for Testing and Materials. Book of ASTM Standards withRelated Material
Am Soc Test Mater Book ASTM Tentative Stand — American Society for Testing and Materials. Book of ASTM Tentative Standards
Am Soc Test Mater Data Ser — American Society for Testing and Materials. Data Series
Am Soc Test Mater Proc — American Society for Testing and Materials. Proceedings
Am Soc Test Mater Spec Tech Publ — American Society for Testing and Materials. Special Technical Publication
Am Soc Test Mater Symp Consistency — American Society for Testing and Materials. Symposium on Consistency
Am Soc Test Mater Symp Plast — American Society for Testing and Materials. Symposium on Plastics
Am Soc Trop Med Papers — American Society of Tropical Medicine. Papers
Am Soc Vet Clin Pathol Bull — American Society of Veterinary Clinical Pathologists. Bulletin
Am Soc Zool Proc — American Society of Zoologists. Proceedings
Am Sov Sci Soc Sci Bull — American-Soviet Science Society. Science Bulletin
Am Sp — American Speech
AMSPA — Advances in Mass Spectrometry
Am Spect — American Spectator
Am Spectator — American Spectator
Am Speech — American Speech
AMSPR — Atti e Memorie. Deputazione di Storia Patria per le Provincie di Romagna
AMSR — Amer-Scandinavian Review
AMSSAQ — Acta Medica Scandinavica. Supplementum
AmSt — American Studies
Amst — Amerikastudien
AMST — Atti e Memorie. Societa Tiburtina di Storia e d'Arte. Tivoli
Amst Ak Jb — Jaarboek van de Koninklijke Akademie van Wetenschappen Gevestigd te Amsterdam
Amst Ak P — Koninklijke Akademie van Wetenschappen te Amsterdam. Proceedings of the Section of Sciences
Amst Ak Vh — Verhandelingen der Koninklijke Akademie van Wetenschappen (Amsterdam)
Amst Ak Vs M — Verslagen en Mededeelingen der Koninklijke Akademie van Wetenschappen. Afdeeling Natuurkunde (Amsterdam)
Amst Ak Wet P — Processen-Verbaal van de Gewone Vergaderingen der Koninklijke Akademie van Wetenschappen. Afdeeling Natuurkunde (Amsterdam)
Am Stat — American Statistician
Am Stat Assn J — American Statistical Association. Journal
Am Stat Assoc Quar Publ — American Statistical Association. Quarterly Publications
Am Stat Index — American Statistics Index
Am Statis Assn — American Statistical Association. Quarterly Publications
Am Statist Assn J — American Statistical Association. Journal
Am Statist Assn Publ — American Statistical Association. Publications
Am Statistician — American Statistician
Am Statistn — American Statistician
Amstel — Amstelodamum
Amsterdams Sociol Tijds — Amsterdams Sociologisch Tijdschrift
Amst I — Het Instituut (Amsterdam)
Amst Jb — Jaarboek van de Koninklijke Akademie van Wetenschappen Gevestigd te Amsterdam
Amst Jb Ak — Jaarboek van de Koninklijke Akademie van Wetenschappen Gevestigd te Amsterdam
Amst N Vh — Nieuwe Verhandelingen der Eerste Klasse van het Koninklijk Nederlandsche Instituut van Wetenschappen, Letterkunde, en Schoone Kunsten te Amsterdam
Am Stock Ex Guide CCH — American Stock Exchange Guide. Commerce Clearing House

Am Stockman — American Stockman
Am Stomat — American Stomatologist
Am St P — American Studies in Papyrology
Amst St IV — Amsterdam Studies in the Theory and History of Linguistic Science. Series IV. Current Issues in Linguistic Theory
Amst Ts Nt Wet — Tijdschrift voor Natuurkundige Wetenschappen en Kunsten (Amsterdam)
Amst Ts Ws Nt Wet — Tijdschrift voor de Wis- en Natuurkundige Wetenschappen, Letterkunde, en Schoone Kunsten te Amsterdam
Am Stud — American Studies
Am Stud Int — American Studies International
Am Stud Sc — American Studies in Scandinavia
Amst Vh — Verhandelingen der Eerste Klasse van het Koninklijk Nederlandsche Instituut van Wetenschappen, Letterkunde, en Schoone Kunsten te Amsterdam
Amst Vh Ak — Verhandelingen der Eerste Klasse van het Koninklijk Nederlandsche Instituut van Wetenschappen, Letterkunde, en Schoone Kunsten te Amsterdam
Amst Vs Ak — Verslagen en Mededeelingen der Koninklijke Akademie van Wetenschappen. Afdeeling Natuurkunde (Amsterdam)
AMSUA — American Surgeon
AMSUAW — American Surgeon
AMSUBX — Acta Medica Turcica. Supplementum
Am Sugar Ind — American Sugar Industry
Am Surg — American Surgeon
Am Surg Assn Trans — American Surgical Association. Transactions
Am Surgeon — American Surgeon
Am Suzuki J — American Suzuki Journal
AMSVAZ — Acta Medica Scandinavica
Ams Wash — Americas (Washington, DC)
AM Swim — American Swimming
AMT — Advanced Manufacturing Technology
AMT — American Music Teacher Magazine
AMt — Analecta Montserratensia
A Mt — Annali di Matematica pura ed Applicata
AMT — El-Amarna Tafeln. Vorderasiatische Bibliothek
Am Taxp Q — American Taxpayers' Quarterly
Am Tcr — American Teacher
AMTDA — Advances in Metabolic Disorders
Am Teach — American Teacher
Am Teleph J — American Telephone Journal
Am Text — America's Textiles
Am Textil — America's Textiles
Am Textil Knit Ap Ed — America's Textiles. Knitter/Apparel Edition
Am Text Int — America's Textiles International
Am Text Rep — America's Textiles Reporter
Am Text Rep Bull Ed — America's Textiles Reporter/Bulletin Edition
AMTFAQ — Acta Medica de Tenerife
A Mtg Am Ass Orthod — Annual Meeting. American Association of Orthodontists
A Mtg Am Soc Orthod — Annual Meeting. American Society of Orthodontists
A Mtg Cent Coun Distr Nurs — Annual Meeting. Central Council for District Nursing
A Mtg Inter Soc Cytol Coun — Annual Meeting. Inter-Society Cytology Council
A Mtg Natn Anti Vacc Leag — Annual Meeting. National Anti-Vaccination League
A Mth — Annals of Mathematics
Am Themis — American Themis
Am Theol Lib Assn Newsl — American Theological Library Association. Newsletter
A Mthly — Art Monthly
A Mthly [Australia] — Art Monthly [Australia]
A Mthly Rev & Phot Port — Art Monthly Review and Photographic Portfolio
Am Thresherman — American Thresherman
AMTIC — Archivio Monaldi per la Tisiologia e le Malattie dell'Apparato Respiratorio
Amtl Ber — Amtliche Berichte. Koenigliche Kunstsammlungen
Amtl Ber Kgl Kunsts — Amtliche Berichte aus den Koeniglichen Kunstsammlungen
Amtl Ber Koen Kstsamml — Amtliche Berichte aus den Koeniglichen Kunstsammlungen
Amtl Ber Versamml Deutsch Naturf Aerzte — Amtlicher Bericht ueber die Versammlung Deutscher Naturforscher und Aerzte
Amtl Ber Versamml Dtsch Naturforsch Aerzte — Amtlicher Bericht der Versammlung Deutscher Naturforscher und Aerzte
Amtl Ber Verw Smlgg Westpr Prov Mus — Amtlicher Bericht ueber die Verwaltung der Sammlungen des Westpreussischen Provinzialmuseums
Amtl Nachr Reichsversichgsamt — Amtliche Nachrichten des Reichsversicherungsamts
Amtl Ztg Deutsch Fleischer-Verbandes — Amtliche Zeitung. Deutscher Fleischer-Verband
AMTODM — Advances in Modern Toxicology
AMTOEN — Alternative Methods in Toxicology
Am Tom Yb — American Tomato Yearbook
Am Toy Mfr — American Toy Manufacturer
AMTPBN — Annales. Belgische Vereinigingen voor Tropische Geneeskunde voor Parasitologie en voor Menselijke en Dierlijke Mycologie
AmTQ — American Transcendental Quarterly
Am Transcen — American Transcendental Quarterly
Am Trav — American Traveler
Am Trial Law J — American Trial Lawyers Journal
Am Trop Med — American Journal of Tropical Medicine and Hygiene
Am Trust Rev Pacific — American Trust Review of the Pacific
Amts & Intellbl Ksr Koen Ztg — Amts- und Intelligenzblatt zur Kaiserlichen Koeniglichen Zeitung
Amtsbl Bayer Staatsminist Landesentwickl Umweltfragen — Amtsblatt. Bayerisches Staatsministerium fuer Landesentwicklung und Umweltfragen
Amtsbl Eur Gem — Amtsblatt. Europaeische Gemeinschaften
Amtsbl Wien — Amstblatt der Stadt Wien
Amts Mitteilungsbl Bundesanst Materialforsch Pruef — Amts- und Mitteilungsblatt der Bundesanstalt fuer Materialforschung und -Pruefung

Amts- Mitteilungsbl Bundesanst Materialpruef — Amts- und Mitteilungsblatt. Bundesanstalt fuer Materialpruefung
Amts Mitteilungsbl Bundesanst Materialpruef (Berlin) — Amts- und Mitteilungsblatt. Bundesanstalt fuer Materialpruefung (Berlin)
AMTUA3 — Acta Medica Turcica
Am Tung News — American Tung News
Am Tung Oil Top — American Tung Oil Topics
Amt Vet Nachr — Amtliche Veterinaernachrichten
AMu — Annales Musicologiques
AMUBBK — American Malacological Union, Incorporated. Bulletin [Later, American Malacological Bulletin]
AMUGAY — Annales Musei Goulandris
AMUGS — Antike Muenzen und Geschnittene Steine
AMUKAC — Acta Medica Universitatis Kagoshimaensis
Am ULR — American University Law Review
Am U L Rev — American University Law Review
AMUNAL — American Museum Novitates
Am Univ Beirut Fac Agric Sci Publ — American University of Beirut. Faculty of Agricultural Sciences. Publication
Am Univ Field Staff Rep Asia — American Universities Field Staff. Reports. Asia
Am Univ Field Staff Rep North Am — American Universities Field Staff. Reports. North America
Am Univ Field Staff Rep South Am — American Universities Field Staff. Reports. South America
Am Univ L Rev — American University Law Review
AMur — Archivio Muratoriano
AMURAX — Anais. Faculdade de Medicina. Universidade do Recife
Amur Sb — Amurskii Sbornik
A Mus — Acta Musicologica
AMus — Asian Music
A Mus Napocensis — Acta Musei Napocensis
A Mus Plovdiv — Godishnik na Narodniia Arkheologicheski Muzei. Plovdiv
A Mus Porol — Acta Musei Porolissensis
AMUTA — American Music Teacher
AMV — Archiv fuer Mathematische Versicherungswissenschaft
AMVEAX — Acta Medica Veterinaria
Am Veg Grow — American Vegetable Grower
Am Veg Grower — American Vegetable Grower
Am Veg Grow Greenhouse Grow — American Vegetable Grower and Greenhouse Grower
Am Vet Med Assn J — American Veterinary Medical Association. Journal
Am Vet Med Assn Proc — American Veterinary Medical Association. Proceedings
Am Vet Med Assoc Sci Proc Annu Meet — American Veterinary Medical Association. Scientific Proceedings of the Annual Meeting
Am Vet Rev — American Veterinary Review
AMVIAB — Acta Medica Vietnamica
AMVIDE — Acta Microbiologica, Virologica, et Immunologica
Am Vinegar Ind — American Vinegar Industry
Am Vinegar Ind Fruit Prod J — American Vinegar Industry and Fruit Products Journal
AMVM — Atti e Memorie. Accademia Vergiliana di Scienze, Lettere, ed Arte di Mantova
Am Voc J — American Vocational Journal
AMVRA — Annales de Medecine Veterinaire
AMVRA4 — Annales de Medecine Veterinaire
AMVTA — Annali. Facolta di Medicina Veterinaria di Torino
AMW — Archiv fuer Musikwissenschaft
Am Water Resour Assoc Proc Ser — American Water Resources Association. Proceedings Series
Am Water Resour Assoc Symp Proc — American Water Resources Association. Symposium. Proceedings
Am Water Resour Assoc Tech Publ Ser TPS-85-1 — American Water Resources Association. Technical Publication Series.TPS-85-1
Am Water Resour Assoc Tech Publ Ser TPS-85-2 — American Water Resources Association. Technical Publication Series. TPS-85-2
Am Water Works Assn J — American Water Works Association. Journal
Am Water Works Assoc Annu Conf Proc — American Water Works Association. Annual Conference. Proceedings
Am Water Works Assoc Disinfect Semin Proc — American Water Works Association. Disinfection Seminar. Proceedings
Am Water Works Assoc J — American Water Works Association. Journal
Am Water Works Assoc Jour Southeastern Sec — American Water Works Association. Journal. Southeastern Section
Am Water Works Assoc Ont Sect Proc Annu Conf — American Water Works Association. Ontario Section. Proceedings.Annual Conference
Am Water Works Assoc Semin Water Treat Waste Disposal Proc — American Water Works Association. Seminar on Water Treatment Waste Disposal. Proceedings
Am Water Works Assoc Technol Conf Proc — American Water Works Association. Technology Conference Proceedings
Am Weld Soc J — American Welding Society. Journal
Am Weld Soc Publ — American Welding Society. Publication
Am Weld Soc Publ AWS A58-76 — American Welding Society. Publication AWS A.58-76
Am West — American West
Am Whig R — American Whig Review
Am Wine Liquor J — American Wine and Liquor Journal
Am Wine Soc J — American Wine Society. Journal
Am Wood — An American Wood
Am Wood Preserv Assoc Proc Annu Meet — American Wood-Preservers' Association. Proceedings. Annual Meeting
Am Wool Cotton Financ Rep — American Wool, Cotton, and Financial Reporter
Am Wool Cotton Rep — American Wool and Cotton Reporter
AMWS — American Men and Women of Science
AMXCB — Acta Mexicana de Ciencia y Tecnologia

Amyloid Amyloidosis Int Symp Amyloidoisis — Amyloid and Amyloidosis. International Symposium on Amyloidosis

Amyloid Amyloidosis Proc Int Symp — Amyloid and Amyloidosis. Proceedings. International Symposium onAmyloidosis

Amyloidosis EARS Proc Eur Amyloidosis Res Symp — Amyloidosis. EARS [*European Amyloidosis Research Symposium*]. Proceedings. European Amyloidosis Research Symposium

Amyloidosis Proc Int Symp Amyloidosis Dis Complex — Amyloidosis. Proceedings. International Symposium on Amyloidosis.The Disease Complex

Amyloidosis Proc Sigrid Juselius Found Symp — Amyloidosis. Proceedings of the Sigrid Juselius Foundation Symposium

Amyotrophic Lateral Scler Conf — Amyotrophic Lateral Sclerosis Recent Research Trends. Conference on Research Trends in Amyotrophic Lateral Sclerosis

Amyotroph Lateral Scler Other Motor Neuron Disord — Amyotrophic Lateral Sclerosis and Other Motor Neuron Disorders

AMZ — Allgemeine Missionszeitschrift

AMZ — Allgemeine Musikalische Zeitung

AMz — Allgemeine Musikzeitung

AMZ — Amazing Stories

AMZAC — Annales du Musee Zoologique de l'Academie Imperiale des Sciences de St. Petersbourg

Am Zinc Inst J — American Zinc Institute. Journal

Am Zion Fed News Views — American Zionist Federation. News and Views

Am Zionist — American Zionist

AMZOA — American Zoologist

AMZOAF — American Zoologist

Am Zool — American Zoologist

Am Zoolog — American Zoologist

Am Zoologist — American Zoologist

AMZZg — Allgemeine Medizinische Zentralzeitung

AN — Acta Neophilologica

AN — Advertising News

AN — Afrique Nouvelle

AN — Age Nouveau

AN — Americana Norvegica

AN — American Naturalist

An — Anais

An — Annales Politiques et Litteraires

An — Annales. Revue Mensuelle de Lettres Francaises

An — Anthropos

AN — Antilliaanse Nieuwsbrief

An — Antonianum

AN — Aquileia Nostra

A N — Art National

AN — Art News

AN — Australia's Neighbours

ANA — Akademiia Nauk Armianskoi SSR

ANA — American Archivist

An A — Anatomischer Anzeiger

AnAA — Annals of American Academy

AnAB — Annales. Societe d'Archeologie de Bruxelles

ANABA — Asociacion Nacional de Bibliotecarios, Arquiveros, y Arqueologos

Anac — Analecta Calsanctiana

ANACAD4 — Analytical Calorimetry

An Acad Arg Geogr BA — Anales. Academia Argentina de Geografia (Buenos Aires)

An Acad Biol Univ Catol Chile — Anales. Academia de Biologia. Universidad Catolica de Chile

An Acad Bras Cienc — Anais. Academia Brasileira de Ciencias

An Acad Bras Cien Rio — Anais da Academia Brasileira da Ciencias (Rio de Janeiro)

An Acad Brasil Ci — Anais. Academia Brasileira de Ciencias

An Acad Brasil Cienc — Anais. Academia Brasileira de Ciencias

An Acad Chil Cienc Nat — Anales. Academia Chilena de'Ciencias Naturales

An Acad Cienc Med Fis Nat Habana — Anales. Academia de Ciencias Medicas, Fisicas, y Naturales de La Habana

An Acad Cien Med Fis Nat Hav — Anales. Academia de Ciencias Medicas, Fisicas, y Naturales (Habana)

An Acad Farm (Madrid) — Anales. Real Academia de Farmacia (Madrid)

An Acad Fr — Annales de l'Academie Francaise

An Acad Geog & Hist Guatemala — Anales de la Academia de Geografia e Historia de Guatemala

An Acad Hist Cuba Hav — Anales. Academia de la Historia de Cuba (Habana)

An Acad N A & Let — Anales de la Academia Nacional de Artes y Letras

An Acad Nac Cienc Exactas Fis Nat — Anales. Academia Nacional de Ciencias Exactas, Fisicas, y Naturales

An Acad Nac Cienc Exactas Fis Nat B Aires — Anales. Academia Nacional de Ciencias Exactas, Fisicas, y Naturales de Buenos Aires

An Acad Nac Cienc Exactas Fis Nat Buenos Aires — Anales. Academia Nacional de Ciencias Exactas, Fisicas, y Naturales de Buenos Aires

An Acad Nac Farm — Anales. Academia Nacional de Farmacia

An Acad Port Hist — Anais. Academia Portuguesa da Historia

An Acad Repub Pop Rom — Analele Academiei Republicii Populare Romine

An Acad Repub Pop Rom Mem Ser B — Analele Academiei Republicii Populare Romine. Memoriile. Seria B.Sectiunea de Stiinte Medicale

An Acad Repub Soc Rom — Analele. Academiei Republicii Socialiste Romania

An Acad Rom — Analele. Academiei Romane

An Acad Romane — Analele Academiei Romane

An Acad Royale Archeol Belgique — Annales de l'Academie Royale d'Archeologie de Belgique

An Ac Brasi — Anais. Academia Brasileira de Ciencias

A Nachr Bad — Archaeologische Nachrichten aus Baden

ANA Clin Conf — ANA [*American Nurses' Association*] Clinical Conferences

ANA Clin Sess — ANA [*American Nurses' Association*] Clinical Session

An Ac R — Analele. Academiei Romane

An Ac Rov — Memoriile Sectiunii Istorice. Academia Romana

An Ad — Annuaire Administratif et Judiciaire de Belgique

An Adm Nac Bosques Minist Agric Ganad (Repub Argent) — Anales. Administracion Nacional de Bosques. Ministerio de Agricultura y Ganaderia (Republica Argentina)

Anadolu Aras — Anadolu Arastirmalari

Anadolu Aras Jahrb Klein Forsch — Anadolu Arastirmalari. Jahrbuch fuer Kleinasiatische Forschung

Anae — Anales. Instituto de Estudios Madrilenos

ANAEA3 — Annals of Allergy

AnAeg — Analecta Aegyptiaca

Anaerobes Anaerobic Infect Symp Int Congr Microbiol — Anaerobes and Anaerobic Infections. Symposia. International Congress of Microbiology

Anaerobic Bact Role Dis Int Conf — Anaerobic Bacteria. Role in Disease. International Conference on Anaerobic Bacteria

Anaerobic Dig Proc Int Symp — Anaerobic Digestion. Proceedings. International Symposium onAnaerobic Digestion

Anaesth — Anaesthesia

Anaesth — Anaesthesist

Anaesth Alter Ber Symp — Anaesthesie im Alter. Bericht. Symposium. Anaesthesie und Intensivtherapie

Anaesthesiol Inf — Anaesthesiologische Informationen

Anaesthesiol Intensive Care Med — Anaesthesiology and Intensive Care Medicine

Anaesthesiol Intensivmed — Anaesthesiologie und Intensivmedizin

Anaesthesiol Intensivmed (Berlin) — Anaesthesiologie und Intensivmedizin (Berlin)

Anaesthesiol Intensivmed (Erlangen Fed Repub Ger) — Anaesthesiologie und Intensivmedizin (Erlangen, Federal Republic ofGermany)

Anaesthesiol Intensivmed Prax — Anaesthesiologische und Intensivmedizinische Praxis

Anaesthesiol Intenzv Ther — Anaesthesiologia es Intenziv Therapia

Anaesthesiolo Sin — Anaesthesiologica Sinica

Anaesthesiol Proc World Congr — Anaesthesiology. Proceedings of the World Congress of Anaesthesiology

Anaesthesiol Proc World Congr Anaesthesiol — Anaesthesiology. Proceedings of the World Congress ofAnaesthesiologists

Anaesthesiol Reanim — Anaesthesiologie und Reanimation. Zeitschrift fuer Anaesthesie,Intensivtherapie, und Dringliche Medizinische Hilfe

Anaesthesiol Resusc — Anaesthesiology and Resuscitation

Anaesthesiol Resuscitation — Anaesthesiology and Resuscitation

Anaesthesiol Sin — Anaesthesiologica Sinica

Anaesthesiol Wiederbeleb — Anaesthesiologie und Wiederbelebung

Anaesthesiol Wiederbelebung — Anaesthesiologie und Wiederbelebung

Anaesth Intensive Care — Anaesthesia and Intensive Care

Anaesth Intensivther Notfallmed — Anaesthesie, Intensivtherapie, Notfallmedizin

Anaesth Pharmacol Rev — Anaesthetic Pharmacology Review

Anaesth Pharmacol Spec Sect Prof Hazards — Anaesthesia and Pharmacology, with a Special Section on Professional Hazards

Anaesth Proc World Congr Anaesthesiol — Anaesthesia Safety for All. Proceedings. World Congress ofAnaesthesiologists

Anaesth Resusc Intensive Ther — Anaesthesia, Resuscitation, and Intensive Therapy

ANAFA6 — Annales Agriculturae Fenniae

ANAFJ — Army-Navy-Air Force Journal

ANAFTA — Army-Navy-Air Force Times Alliance

ANAGA — Annales Agronomiques

An Agron — Anales Agronomicos

Anah — Annalen der Historischen Verein fuer den Niederrhein

AnAI — Annuaire des Archives Israelites

ANAIA — Annales de la Nutrition et de l'Alimentation

ANAIDI — Annals. National Academy of Medical Sciences

Anais Acad Bras Cienc — Anais. Academia Brasileira de Ciencias

Anais Brasil Ginecol — Anais Brasileiros de Ginecologia. Sociedade Brasileira de Ginecologia

Anais Esc Sup Agric "Luiz Queiroz" — Anais. Escola Superior de Agricultura "Luiz De Queiroz"

Anais Fac Cienc Porto — Anais. Faculdade de Ciencias. Universidade do Porto

Anais Fac Med — Anais. Faculdade de Medicina e Cirurgia

Anais Fac Sci Porto — Anais. Faculdade de Sciencias do Porto

Anais II Congr Latin-Amer Zool — Anais. II Congresso Latino-Americano de Zoologia

Anais Inst Sup Agron Lisboa — Anais. Instituto Superior de Agronomia. Universidade Tecnica de Lisboa

Anais Inst Sup Agron Univ Tec Lisb — Anais. Instituto Superior de Agronomia. Universidade Tecnica de Lisboa

Anais Soc Biol Pernambuco — Anais da Sociedade de Biologia de Pernambuco

Anais Soc Ent Brasil — Anais. Sociedade Entomologica do Brasil

Anaisthesiol — Ellenike Anaisthesiologia

Anal — Analyst

ANALA — Analyst (London)

Analabs Res Notes — Analabs, Incorporated. Research Notes

Anal Abstr — Analytical Abstracts

Anal Acad Nac Cienc Exactas Fis Nat — Anales. Academia Nacional de Ciencias Exactas, Fisicas, y Naturales

Anal Acad Rom — Analele. Academiei Romane

Anal Ac Rom — Memoriile Sectiunii Istorice. Academia Romana

Anal Adv — Analytical Advances

Anal Appl Rare Earth Mater NATO Adv Study Inst — Analysis and Application of Rare Earth Materials. NATO [*North Atlantic Treaty Organization*] Advanced Study Institute

Anal Appl Spectrosc 2 Proc Int Conf Spectrosc Spectrum — Analytical Applications of Spectroscopy 2. Proceedings. International Conference on Spectroscopy across the Spectrum

Anal Aspects Drug Test — Analytical Aspects of Drug Testing

Anal Aspects Environ Chem — Analytical Aspects of Environmental Chemistry

Anal At Spectrosc — Analytical Atomic Spectroscopy

Anal Aug — Analecta Augustiniana

ANALB — Analytical Letters

Anal Ber Gesellschaftswiss — Analysen und Berichte aus Gesellschaftswissenschaften

Anal Biochem — Analytical Biochemistry

Anal Biochem Insects — Analytical Biochemistry of Insects

Anal Boll — Analecta Bollandiana

Anal Bolland — Analecta Bollandiana

Anal Calorim — Analytical Calorimetry

Anal Calorimetry — Analytical Calorimetry

Anal Cell Pathol — Analytical Cellular Pathology

Anal Charact Oils Fats Fat Prod — Analysis and Characterization of Oils, Fats, and Fat Products

Anal Chem — Analytical Chemistry

Anal Chem (Changchung People's Repub China) — Analytical Chemistry (Changchung, People's Republic of China)

Anal Chem Instrum Proc Conf Anal Chem Energy Technol — Analytical Chemistry Instrumentation. Proceedings. Conference onAnalytical Chemistry in Energy Technology

Anal Chem Nitrogen Its Compd — Analytical Chemistry of Nitrogen and Its Compounds

Anal Chem Nucl Fuel Reprocess Proc ORNL Conf — Analytical Chemistry in Nuclear Fuel Reprocessing. Proceedings.ORNL [*Oak Ridge National Laboratory*] Conference on Analytical Chemistry in Energy Technology

Anal Chem Nucl Fuels Proc Panel — Analytical Chemistry of Nuclear Fuels. Proceedings of the Panel

Anal Chem Nucl Technol Proc Conf Anal Chem Energy Technol — Analytical Chemistry in Nuclear Technology. Proceedings. Conference on Analytical Chemistry in Energy Technology

Anal Chem Phosphorus Compd — Analytical Chemistry of Phosphorus Compounds

Anal Chem Sulfur Its Compd — Analytical Chemistry of Sulfur and Its Compounds

Anal Chem Symp Ser — Analytical Chemistry Symposia Series

Anal Chem Synth Dyes — Analytical Chemistry of Synthetic Dyes

Anal Chim Ac — Analytica Chimica Acta

Anal Chim Acta — Analytica Chimica Acta

Anal Chimica Acta — Analytica Chimica Acta

Anal Cienc Hum — Anales de Ciencias Humanas

Anal Cist — Analecta Cisterciensia

Anal Clin Specimen — Analysis of Clinical Specimens

Anal Commun — Analytical Communications

Anal Div — Analysis Division. Proceedings. Annual ISA Analysis DivisionSymposium

Anal Drugs Metab Gas Chromatogr Mass Spectrom — Analysis of Drugs and Metabolites by Gas Chromatography. Mass Spectrometry

Analecta Boer — Analecta Boerhaaviana

Analecta Farm Gerund — Analecta Farmacia Gerundense

Analecta Geol — Analecta Geologica

Analecta Ord S Bas Magni — Analecta Ordinis Sancti Basilii Magni

Analecta Vet — Analecta Veterinaria

Analecten Belust — Analecten zur Belustigung, Belehrung, und Unterhaltung fuer Leser aus Allen Staenden

Analectes Hist Eccl Belg — Analectes pour Servir a l'Histoire Ecclesiatique de la Belgique

Analectic M — Analectic Magazine

Analele Acad Republ Populare Romane — Analele Academiei Republicii Populare Romane

Analele Acad Rom — Memoriile Sectiunii Istorice. Academia Romana

Analele Inst Cercet Exp Forest — Analele Institutului de Cercetari si Experimentatie Forestiera

Anal Enum Bibliog — Analytical and Enumerative Bibliography

Anales Acad Chilena Ci Nat — Anales. Academia Chilena de Ciencias Naturales

Anales Acad Nac Ci Exact Buenos Aires — Anales. Academia Nacional de Ciencias Exactas, Fisicas, y Naturales de Buenos Aires

Anales Asoc Esp Progr Ci — Anales. Asociacion Espanola Para el Progreso de la Ciencias

Anales Ci Nat — Anales de Ciencias Naturales

Anales Ci Nat Inst Jose De Acosta — Anales de Ciencias Naturales. Instituto Jose de Acosta

Anales Estac Exp Aula Dei — Anales. Estacion Experimental de Aula Dei

Anales Fac Ci Nat Mus Univ Nac La Plata Secc Bot — Anales. Facultad de Ciencias Naturales y Museo. Universidad Nacional. La Plata.Seccion Botanica

Anales Inst Biol UNAM Ser Bot — Anales. Instituto de Biologia. Universidad Nacional Autonoma de Mexico.Serie Botanica

Anales Inst Biol UNAM Ser Zool — Anales. Instituto de Biologia. Universidad Nacional Autonoma de Mexico.Serie Zoologia

Anales Inst Biol Univ Nac Mexico — Anales. Instituto de Biologia. Universidad Nacional de Mexico

Anales Inst Edafol — Anales. Instituto de Edafologia, Ecologia, y Fisiologia Vegetal

Anales Inst Fitotecn Santa Catalina — Anales. Instituto Fitotecnico de Santa Catalina

Anales Inst Invest Ci — Anales. Instituto de Investigaciones Cientificas

Anales Inst Nac Antropol — Anales. Instituto Nacional de Antropologia e Historia

Anales Jard Bot Madrid — Anales. Jardin Botanico de Madrid

Anales Jur — Anales de Jurisprudencia

Anales Mex Ci — Anales Mexicanos de Ciencias, Literatura, Mineria, Agricultura, Artes, Industria y Comercio en la Republica Mexicana

Anales Mus Nac Montevideo — Anales. Museo Nacional de Montevideo

Anales Mus Nahuel Huapi — Anales. Museo Nahuel Huapi. Ministerio de Obras Publicas de la Nacion. Administracion General de Parques Nacionales y Turismo

Anales Soc Ci Argent — Anales de Sociedad Cientifica Argentina

Anales Soc Humboldt — Anales. Sociedad Humboldt

Anale Stat Cent Apic Seri — Anale. Statiunea Centrala de Apicultura si Sericultura

Anales Univ Centr Ecuador — Anales. Universidad Central del Ecuador

Anales Univ Nac — Anales. Universidad Nacional

Anales Univ Nac La Plata Secc B Paleobot — Anales. Universidad Nacional de La Plata. Instituto del Museo. Seccion B. Paleobotanica

Anal et Previs — Analyse et Prevision

Anal Financ — Analyse Financiere

Anal Fran — Analecta Franciscana

Anal Franc — Analecta Franciscana

Anal Francisc — Analecta Franciscana

Anal Gas Chromatogr Biochem — Analysis by Gas Chromatography of Biochemicals

Anal Greg — Analecta Gregoriana

Anal Hazard Subst Biol Mater — Analyses of Hazardous Substances in Biological Materials

Anal Hib — Analecta Hibernica

Anal Hus Yb — Analecta Husserliana. Yearbook of Phenomenological Research

Anali Accad Agric (Torino) — Annali. Accademia di Agricoltura (Torino)

AnaliFF — Anali Filoloskog Fakulteta Beogradskog Univerziteta

Anal Inst Cent Cerc Agric Sect Pedol — Anale. Institutul Central de Cercetari Agricole. Sectiei de Pedologie

Anal Inst Cerc Agron — Analele. Institutului de Cercetari Agronomice. Academia Republicii Populare Romine

Anal Inst Cerc pentru Cereale Pl Tehn-Fundulea — Analele. Institutului de Cercetari pentru Cereale si Plante Tehnice-Fundulea

Anal Inst Cerc Prot Plantelor — Analele. Institutului de Cercetari pentru Protectia Plantelor

Anal Inst Cerc Zooteh — Analele. Institutului de Cercetari. Zootehnice

Anal Instrum — Analysis Instrumentation

Anal Instrum Comput — Analytical Instruments and Computers

Anal Instrum (NY) — Analytical Instrumentation (New York)

Anal Instrum (Research Triangle Park NC) — Analysis Instrumentation (Research Triangle Park, North Carolina)

Anal Instrum (Tokyo) — Analytical Instruments (Tokyo)

Anal Intervention Dev Disabil — Analysis and Intervention in Developmental Disabilities

Anal Intrauterine Contracept Proc Int Conf — Analysis of Intrauterine Contraception. Proceedings.International Conference on Intrauterine Contraception

Analise Conjuntural Econ Nordestina — Analise Conjuntural da Economia Nordestina

Anal Khim Neorg Soedin — Analiticheskaya Khimiya Neorganicheskikh Soedinenij

Anal Kontrol Proizvod Azotn Promsti — Analiticheskii Kontrol Proizvodstva v Azotnoi Promyshlennosti

Anal Kosmet DGK Symp — Analytik in der Kosmetik. Moeglichkeiten, Grenzen, Bewertung, DGK-Symposium

Anal Lab — Analytical Laboratory

Anal Laser Spectrosc — Analytical Laser Spectroscopy

Anal Lett — Analytical Letters

Anal Letter — Analytical Letters

Anal Letters — Analytical Letters

Anal Lett Part A — Analytical Letters. Part A. Chemical Analysis

Anal Ling — Analecta Linguistica

Anal M — Analectic Magazine

Anal Math — Analysis Mathematica

Anal Methods Appl Air Pollut Meas — Analytical Methods Applied to Air Pollution Measurements

Anal Methods Instrum — Analytical Methods and Instrumentation

Anal Methods Pestic Plant Growth Regul — Analytical Methods for Pesticides and Plant Growth Regulators

Anal Methods Pestic Plant Growth Regul Food Addit — Analytical Methods for Pesticides, Plant Growth Regulators, and Food Additives

Anal Metody Geokhim Issled Mater Geokhim Konf — Analiticheskie Metody pri Geokhimicheskikh Issledovaniyakh. MaterialyGeokhimicheskoi Konferentsii

Anal Microbiol Methods — Analytical Microbiology Methods. Chromatography and Mass Spectrometry

Anal Modern Apl — Analiza Moderna si Aplicatii

Anal Mon — Analecta Monastica

Anal Mont — Analecta Montserratensia

Anal News Perkin Elmer Ltd — Analytical News. Perkin-Elmer Limited

Anal Numer Theor Approx — L'Analyse Numerique et la Theorie de l'Approximation

Anal O — Analecta Orientalia

Analog Integr Circuits Signal Process — Analog Integrated Circuits and Signal Processing

Analogovaya Analogo-Tsifrovaya Vychisl Tekh — Analogovaya i Analogo-Tsifrovaya Vychislitel'naya Tekhnika

Anal Or — Analecta Orientalia

Anal Org Mater — Analysis of Organic Materials

Anal Org Micropollut Water Proc Eur Symp — Analysis of Organic Micropollutants in Water. Proceedings.European Symposium

Anal Pet Trace Met Symp — Analysis of Petroleum for Trace Metals. A Symposium

Anal Plant Probl Engrais Miner Colloq — Analyse des Plantes et Problemes des Engrais Mineraux. Colloque

Anal Praem — Analecta Praemonstratensia

Anal Prep Isotachophoresis Proc Int Symp Isotachophoresis — Analytical and Preparative Isotachophoresis. Proceedings. InternationalSymposium on Isotachophoresis

Anal Previs — Analyse et Prevision

Anal Prevision — Analyse et Prevision

Anal Prichin Avarii Povrezhdenii Stroit Konstr — Analiz Prichin Avarii i Povrezhdenii Stroitel'nykh Konstruktsii

Anal Prichin Avarii Stroit Konstr — Analiz Prichin Avarii Stroitel'nykh Konstruktsii

Anal Proc — Analytical Proceedings

Anal Proc (London) — Analytical Proceedings (London)

Anal Proc R Soc Chem — Analytical Proceedings. Royal Society of Chemistry

Anal Profiles Drug Subst — Analytical Profiles of Drug Substances

Anal Progn — Analysen und Prognosen ueber die Welt von Morgen

Anal Progn Welt Morgen — Analysen und Prognosen ueber die Welt von Morgen

Anal Propellants Explos Chem Phys Methods Int Annu Conf ICT — Analysis of Propellants and Explosives. Chemical and Physical Methods. International Annual Conference of ICT

Anal Psychol — Analytische Psychologie

Anal Pyrolysis — Analytical Pyrolysis

Anal Pyrolysis Proc Int Symp — Analytical Pyrolysis. Proceedings of the International Symposium on Analytical Pyrolysis

Anal Quant Cytol — Analytical and Quantitative Cytology

Anal Quant Cytol Histol — Analytical and Quantitative Cytology and Histology

Anal Quant Methods Microsc — Analytical and Quantitative Methods in Microscopy

Anal Raman Spectrosc — Analytical Raman Spectroscopy

Anal Res (Tokyo) — Analysis and Research (Tokyo)

Anal Rev Tech Merlin Gerin — Analyses. Revue Technique Merlin Gerin

Anal Rom — Analecta Romana Instituti Danici

Anal Rud Tsvetn Met Prod Ikh Pererab — Analiz Rud Tsvetnykh Metallov i Produktov Ikh Pererabotki

Anal Sacra Tarraconensia — Analecta Sacra Tarraconensia. Annuari de la Biblioteca Balmes

Anal Sacr Tarrac — Analecta Sacra Tarraconensia. Revista de Ciencias Historico-Eclesiasticas

Anal Schnellverfahren Betr Vortr Metall Semin — Analytische Schnellverfahren im Betrieb. Vortraege beim Metallurgischen Seminar

Anal Sci — Analytical Sciences

Anal Sci Monogr — Analytical Sciences Monographs

Anal Sci Technol — Analytical Science and Technology

Anal SEDEIS (Societe d'Etudes et de Documentation Economiques Industrielles et Sociales) — Analyses de la SEDEIS

Anal Simul Biochem Syst — Analysis and Simulation of Biochemical Systems

Anal Soc — Analise Social

Anal Spectrosc Libr — Analytical Spectroscopy Library

Anal Spectrosc Proc Conf Anal Chem Energy Technol — Analytical Spectroscopy. Proceedings. Conference on AnalyticalChemistry in Energy Technology

Anal Spectrosc Ser — Analytical Spectroscopy Series

Anal Stiint Univ Cuza Iasi Chim — Analele Stiintifice ale Universitatii Al. I. Cuza din Iasi. Sectiunea 1c. Chimie

Anal Struct Amplitudes Collision Les Houches June Inst — Analyse Structurale des Amplitudes de Collision Les Houches. June Institute

Anal Struct Compos Mater — Analysis of Structural Composite Materials

Anal Syst Zastos — Analiza Systemowa i jej Zastosowania

Anal Taschenb — Analytiker-Taschenbuch

Anal Tech — Analytical Techniques

Anal Tech Determ Air Pollut Symp — Analytical Techniques in the Determination of Air Pollutants.Symposium

Anal Tech Environ Chem Proc Int Congr — Analytical Techniques in Environmental Chemistry. Proceedings. International Congress

Anal Tekhnol Blagorodn Met Tr Soveshch — Analiz i Tekhnologiya Blagorodnykh Metallov. Trudy Soveshchaniya poKhimii, Analizu, i Tekhnologii Blagorodnykh Metallov

Anal Temperate For Ecosyst — Analysis of Temperate Forest Ecosystems

Anal Univ Buc Biol Anim — Analele. Universitatii Bucuresti. Biologie Animala

Anal Univ Buc Ser Stiint Nat Biol — Analele. Universitatii Bucuresti. Seria Stiintele Naturii. Biologie

Anal Univ Bucuresti — Analele. Universitatii Bucuresti. Stiinte Sociale. Seria Istorie

Anal Univ C I Parhon — Analele. Universitatii C. I. Parhon

Anal Univ Craiova — Analele. Universitatii din Craiova. Seria Istorie, Geografie, Filologie

Anal Univ Hisp Ser Vet — Anales. Universidad Hispalense. Serie Veterinaria

Analysts J — Analysts Journal

Analyt Abs — Analytical Abstracts

Analyt Abstr — Analytical Abstracts

Analyt Bioc — Analytical Biochemistry

Analyt Biochem — Analytical Biochemistry

Analyt Chem — Analytical Chemistry

Analyt Chim — Analytica Chimica Acta

Analytical Biochem — Analytical Biochemistry

Analytical Chem — Analytical Chemistry in Memory of Professor Anders Ringbom

Analytical Rev — Analytical Review. Or History of Literature, Domestic and Foreign, on an Enlarged Plan

Analytic Instrum Comput — Analytical Instruments and Computers

Analyt Lett — Analytical Letters

Analyt Proc — Analytical Proceedings

Analyt Tables For Trade Sect D — Analytical Tables of Foreign Trade. Section D

An Am Acad Pol Soc Sci — Annals. American Academy of Political and Social Science

An Am Acad Pol Soc Sc Phila — Annals. American Academy of Political and Social Science (Philadelphia)

ANAMD — Archiwum Nauki o Materialach

An Amer Sch Orient Res — Annals of the American Schools of Oriental Research

An-Am LR — Anglo-American Law Review

A Namur — Annales. Societe Archeologique de Namur

ANANA — Anatomischer Anzeiger; Zentralblatt fuer die Gesamte Wissenschaftliche Anatomie

An Anat — Anales de Anatomia

An & Bol de la Real Academia S Fernando — Anales y Boletin de la Real Academia de S Fernando

An & Bol Mus A Barcelona — Anales y Boletin de los Museos de Arte de Barcelona

An Antrop — Anales de Antropologia

An Antrop Hist — Anales de Antropologia e Historia

An Antrop Mex — Anales de Antropologia. Instituto de Investigaciones Historicas. Universidad Nacional Autonoma (Mexico)

An Antropol — Anales de Antropologia

ANA Nurs Res Conf — American Nurses' Association. Nursing Research Conferences

ANAPA — Annales d'Anatomie Pathologique

ANAPC4 — Analytische Psychologie

ANA Publ — American Nurses' Association. Publications

Anaquel S Salvador — Anaqueles (San Salvador)

AnAr — Anadolu Arastirmalari

ANAR — An-Nahar Arab Report

Anarch — Anarchism

An Archaeol & Anthropol — Annals of Archaeology and Anthropology

An Archeol — Annales Archeologiques

An Archeol Arabes Syr — Annales Archeologiques Arabes Syriennes. Revue d'Archeologie et d'Histoire

An Archeol Syrie — Annales Archeologiques de Syrie. Revue d'Archeologie et d'Histoire Syriennes

An Archit Cent — Annali di Architettura del Centro Internazionale di Studi di Architettura Andrea Palladio

AnArchSyr — Annales Archeologiques de Syrie

ANARE (Aust Natl Antarct Res Exped) Res Notes — ANARE (Australian National Antarctic Research Expeditions) Research Notes

ANARE Data Rep — ANARE [*Australian National Antarctic Research Expeditions*] Data Reports

ANARE Data Rep Ser B — ANARE [*Australian National Antarctic Research Expeditions*] Data Reports. Series B

ANARE Data Rep Ser C — ANARE [*Australian National Antarctic Research Expeditions*] Data Reports. Series C

ANARE Interim Rep — ANARE [*Australian National Antarctic Research Expeditions*] Interim Reports

ANARE Interim Rep Ser A — ANARE [*Australian National Antarctic Research Expeditions*] Interim Reports. Series A

ANAREN — ANARE [*Australian National Antarctic Research Expeditions*] News

ANARE Rep — ANARE [*Australian National Antarctic Research Expeditions*] Report

ANARE Rep Ser B — ANARE [*Australian National Antarctic Research Expeditions*] Report. SeriesB

ANARE Rep Ser C — ANARE [*Australian National Antarctic Research Expeditions*] Report. SeriesC

ANARE Sci Rep — ANARE [*Australian National Antarctic Research Expeditions*] Scientific Reports

ANARE Sci Rep Ser A IV Publ — ANARE [*Australian National Antarctic Research Expeditions*] Scientific Reports. Series A-IV. Publications

ANARE Sci Rep Ser B IV Med Sci — ANARE [*Australian National Antarctic Research Expeditions*] Scientific Reports. Series B-IV. Medical Science

ANARE Sci Rep Ser B I Zool — ANARE [*Australian National Antarctic Research Expeditions*] Scientific Reports. Series B-I. Zoology

An (Argent) Dir Nac Geol Min — Anales (Argentina). Direccion Nacional de Geologia y Mineria

An Arqueol & Etnog — Anales de Arqueologia y Etnografia

An Arqueol Etnol — Anales de Arqueologia y Etnologia

An Arquit — Anales de Arquitectura

An Ars Med — Anales de Ars Medici

ANASA — Anaesthesia

An Asoc Esp Prog Cienc — Anales. Asociacion Espanola para el Progreso de las Ciencias

An Asoc Quim Arg BA — Anales. Asociacion Quimica Argentina (Buenos Aires)

An Asoc Quim (Argent) — Anales. Asociacion Quimica (Argentina)

An Asoc Quim Farm Urug — Anales. Asociacion de Quimica y Farmacia del Uruguay

An As Quim — Anales. Asociacion Quimica

An As Quim Farm Urug — Anales. Asociacion de Quimica y Farmacia del Uruguay

An Assoc Amer Geog — Annals of the Association of American Geographers

An Assoc Bras Quim — Anais. Associacao Brasileira de Quimica

An Assoc Quim Bras — Anais. Associacao Quimica do Brasil

Anasthesiol Intensivmed Notfallmed Schmerzther — Anasthesiologie, Intensivmedizin, Notfallmedizin, Schmerztherapie

Anasthesiol Intensivmed Prax — Anaesthesiologische und Intensivmedizinische Praxis

Anasth Intensivther Notfallmed — Anaesthesie, Intensivtherapie, Notfallmedizin

ANATA — Der Anaesthesist

ANATAE — Anaesthesist

Anat Anthropol Embryol Histol — Anatomy, Anthropology, Embryology, and Histology

Anat Anz — Anatomischer Anzeiger; Zentralblatt fuer die Gesamte Wissenschaftliche Anatomie

Anat Anz Ergaenzungsh — Anatomischer Anzeiger. Ergaenzungsheft

Anat Chir — Anatomia e Chirurgia

Anat Clin — Anatomia Clinica

Anat Embryo — Anatomy and Embryology

Anat Embryol — Anatomy and Embryology

Anat Embryol (Berl) — Anatomy and Embryology (Berlin)

An Ateneo Clin Quir — Anales. Ateneo de Clinica Quirurgica

Anat Entw Gesch Monogr — Anatomische und Entwicklungsgeschichtliche Monographien

Anat Gesell Jena Verhandl — Anatomische Gesellschaft. Jena. Verhandlungen

Anat Ges Verh — Anatomische Gesellschaft. Verhandlungen

Anat H — Anatomische Hefte

Anat Hefte Abt 2 — Anatomische Hefte. Abteilung 2

Anat His Em — Anatomia, Histologia, Embryologia. Zentralblatt fuer Veterinaermedizin. Reihe C

Anat Histol Embryol — Anatomia, Histologia, Embryologia

Anatolian Stud — Anatolian Studies

Anatol Stud — Anatolian Studies. Journal of the British Institute at Ankara

Anat Rec — Anatomical Record
Anat Rec Suppl — Anatomical Record. Supplement
AnatS — Anatolian Studies
Anat Skr — Anatomiske Skrifter
AnatSt — Anatolian Studies
Anat Stud — Anatolian Studies
A Natur Wiss — Archaeologie und Naturwissenschaften
An Avignon — Annales d'Avignon
ANAz — Akademiia Nauk Azerbaidzhanskoi SSR
ANAZAW — Anais Azevedos
ANAZBX — Annals of Arid Zone
An Azevedos — Anais Azevedos
ANAzIG — Akademiia Nauk Azerbaidzhanskoi SSR. Institut Geologii
An B — Analecta Bollandiana
ANB — Andover Newton Bulletin
AnB — Animal Behaviour
AnB — Annales de Bourgogne
ANB — Antitrust Bulletin
ANB — Arab News Bulletin
ANB — Archaeologische Nachrichten aus Baden
ANB — Australian National Bibliography
Anbar Abs (Account Data) — Anbar Abstracts (Accounting and Data)
Anbar Abs (Mktng Distr) — Anbar Abstracts (Marketing and Distribution)
Anbar Abs (Personn Trng) — Anbar Abstracts (Personnel and Training)
Anbar Abs (Top Mgmt) — Anbar Abstracts (Top Management)
Anbar Abs (Wk Study) — Anbar Abstracts (Work Study)
Anbar Mgmt Serv — Anbar Management Services Joint Index
AnBC — Anuario Bibliografico Cubano
ANBCA — Analytical Biochemistry
ANBEA — Animal Behaviour
An Bekk — Anecdota Graeca
An Belg — Annales de Belgique
An Bhandarkar Orient Res Inst — Annals of the Bhandarkar Oriental Research Institute
An Bhand Or Res Inst — Annals. Bhandarkar Oriental Research Institute
An Bi — Analecta Biblica
ANBI — Annales Biologiques
An Bib — Analecta Biblica
An Bibl — Analecta Biblica
An Bib Stat & Lib Civ Cremona — Annali della Biblioteca Statale e Libreria Civica di Cremona
ANBKAQ — Antibiotiki Respublikanskii Mezhvedomstvennyi Sbornik
ANBLAT — Annee Biologique
ANBMAW — Animal Behavior Monographs
ANBOA — Annals of Botany
AnBol — Analecta Bollandiana
AnBoll — Analecta Bollandiana
An Bot Herb "Barbosa Rodrigues" — Anais Botanicos. Herbario "Barbosa Rodrigues"
An Bourgogne — Annales de Bourgogne
ANBPA7 — Anais. Sociedade de Biologia de Pernambuco
AnBr — Annales de Bretagne [*Later, Annales de Bretagne et des Pays de l'Ouest*]
ANBRAD — Anales de Bromatologia
An Bras Dermatol — Anais Brasileiros de Dermatologia
An Bras Dermatol Sifilogr — Anais Brasileiros de Dermatologia e Sifilografia
An Bras Gin — Anais Brasileiros de Ginecologia
An Bras Ginecol — Anais Brasileiros de Ginecologia
AnBret — Annales de Bretagne [*Later, Annales de Bretagne et des Pays de l'Ouest*]
An Bretagne — Annales de Bretagne
An Brom — Annales de Bromatologia
An Bromat — Anales de Bromatologia
An Bromatol — Anales de Bromatologia
ANBW — Arab News Bulletin (Washington)
ANC — Asia Research Bulletin
ANC — New South Wales Conveyancing Law and Practice
An Cap Prov Mus — Annals of the Cape Provincial Museums
An Carnegie Mus — Annals of the Carnegie Museum
An Casa Salud Valdecilla — Anales. Casa de Salud Valdecilla
An Casa Salud Valdecilla (Santander) — Anales. Casa de Salud Valdecilla (Santander)
An Catedra de Patol Clin Tuberc Univ B Aires — Anales. Catedra de Patologia y Clinica de la Tuberculosis. Universidad de Buenos Aires
An Catedra Tisioneumonol — Anales. Catedra de Tisioneumonologia
An Cated Suarez — Anales. Catedra Francisco Suarez
Anc Ceylon — Ancient Ceylon
AncEg — Ancient Egypt
An Cent Cult Valenc — Anales del Centro de Cultura Valenciana
An Cent Invest Desarrollo Tecnol Pint — Anales. Centro de Investigacion y Desarrollo en Tecnologia de Pinturas
An Cent Invest Tisiol — Anales. Centro de Investigaciones Tisiologicas
AnCEtRel — Annales. Centre d'Etude des Religions
AnCF — Annuaire du College de France
Anc Flandre — Arts Anciens de Flandre
ANCHA — Analytical Chemistry
ANCHB — Annales de Chirurgie
An Chem — Analytical Chemistry
An Chilenos Hist Med — Anales Chilenos de Historia de la Medicina
An Chim & Phys — Annales de Chimie et de Physique
An Chopin — Annales Chopin
Anchorag DN — Anchorage Daily News
Anchor Rev — Anchor Review
ANCIAP — Anales de Cirugia
An CIDEPINT — Anales. CIDEPINT
An Cienc — Anales de Ciencias

An Cienc Natur — Anales de Ciencias Naturales
An Cient — Anales Cientificos
Ancient Biomol — Ancient Biomolecules
An Cient (La Molina) — Anales Cientificos (La Molina)
An Cient (Lima) — Anales Cientificos (Lima)
Ancient Mesoamer — Ancient Mesoamerica
Ancient Monuments Soc Trans — Ancient Monuments Society. Transactions
Ancient Phil — Ancient Philosophy
Ancient Technol Mod Sci — Ancient Technology to Modern Science
An Cient UNA (Univ Nac Agrar) — Anales Cientificos. UNA (Universidad Nacional Agraria)
Anc Ind — Ancient India
Anc India — Ancient India
An Circ Med Argent — Anales. Circa Medico Argentino
An Cir (Rosario) — Anales de Cirugia (Rosario)
An Cist — Analecta Cisterciensia
An Cl — Antiquite Classique
ANCLAY — Australian National Clay
An Clim — Anales Climatologicos. Servicio Meteorologico Nacional
An Clim Port — Anuario Climatologico de Portugal
Anc Mesoamerica — Ancient Mesoamerica
Anc Nepal — Ancient Nepal
ANCOLD Bull — ANCOLD [*Australian National Committee on Large Dams*] Bulletin
An Colmar — Annuaire. Societe Historique et Literaire de Colmar
An Col Nac Med Mil (Mexico City) — Anales. Colegio Nacional del Medicos Militares (Mexico City)
An Com — Annales des Sciences Commerciales et Economiques
An Com Ext Mex Banco Nac Com Ext — Anuario de Comercio Exterior de Mexico. Banco Nacional de ComercioExterior
An Com Invest Cient Prov Buenos Aires — Anales. Comision de Investigaciones Cientificas. Provincia de Buenos Aires
An Com Mon Trans — Anuarul Comisiunii Monumentelor Istorice. Sectia Pentru Transilvania
An Conf Fis Quim Org — Anais. Conferencia de Fisico-Quimica Organica
An Cong Lat-Am Zool — Anais. Congresso Latino-Americano de Zoologia
An Cong Nac Soc Bot Bras — Anais. Congresso Nacional. Sociedade Botanica do Brasil
An Congr Bras Ceram — Anais. Congresso Brasileiro de Ceramica
An Congr Bras Ceram III Iberoam Ceram Vidrios Refract — Anais. Congresso Brasileiro de Ceramica e III Iberoamericano de Ceramica, Vidrios, y Refractarios
An Congr Estadual Quim Technol — Anais. Congresso Estadual de Quimica Technologica
An Congr Lat Am Eng Equip Ind Pet Petroquim — Anais. Congresso Latino-Americano de Engenharia e Equipamentos para asIndustrias de Petroleo e Petroquimica
An Congr Nac Med Vet Zootec — Anales. Congreso Nacional de Medicina Veterinaria y Zootecnia
An Congr Nac Metal — Anales. Congreso Nacional de Metalurgia
An Congr Panam Eng Minas Geol — Anais. Congresso Panamericano de Engenharia de Minas e Geologia
An Congr Panam Ing Minas Geol — Anales. Congreso Panamericano di Ingenieria de Minas y Geologia
ANCPA — Annales de Chimie (Paris)
Anc Pakistan — Ancient Pakistan
ANCPDF — AAZPA [*American Association of Zoological Parks and Aquariums*] National Conference
AnCracov — Analecta Cracoviana
ANCS — ANCSA News. Alaska Native Claims Settlement Act. Bureau of Land Management
ANCSBM — Acta Neurochirurgica. Supplementum
Anc Soc — Ancient Society
An Cte Flam France — Annales du Comite Flamand de France
AnCUM — Annales du Centre Universitaire Mediterraneen
Anc W — Ancient World
Anc World — Ancient World
And — Al-Andalus
An D — Analele Dobrogei
And — Anderseniana
AND — Australian News Digest
Andb — Andelsbladet
Andean Quart Santiago — Andean Quarterly (Santiago)
Andean Rpt — Andean Report
An Demog Hist — Annales de Demographie Historique
Anders — Anderseniana
Anderson Localization Proc Taniguchi Int Symp — Anderson Localization. Proceedings. Taniguchi InternationalSymposium
An Desarrollo — Anales del Desarrollo
An Desarrollo (Granada Spain) — Anales del Desarrollo (Granada, Spain)
An De Univ De Chile — Anales de la Universidad de Chile
ANDFA — American Annals of the Deaf
ANDGAO — Anales. Museo Nacional David J. Guzman
Andhra Agric J — Andhra Agricultural Journal
Andhra Agr J — Andhra Agricultural Journal
Andhra Pradesh Ground Water Dep Dist Ser — Andhra Pradesh Ground Water Department. District Series
Andhra Pradesh Ground Water Dep Res Ser — Andhra Pradesh Ground Water Department. Research Series
Andhra WR — Andhra Weekly Reporter
Andh WR — Andhra Weekly Reporter
An Dir Gen Of Quim Nac (Argent) — Anales. Direccion General de Oficinas Quimica Nacionales(Argentina)
An Dir Gen Of Quim Nac (Argentina) — Anales. Direccion General de Oficinas Quimica Nacionales (Argentina)
An Dir Nac Quim (Argent) — Anales. Direccion Nacional de Quimica (Argentina)

An Dir Nac Quim (Argentina) — Anales. Direccion Nacional de Quimica (Argentina)

An Dispensario Publico Nac Enferm Apar Dig (Argent) — Anales. Dispensario Publico Nacional para Enfermedades del AparatoDigestivo (Argentina)

An Dispensario Publico Nac Enferm Apar Dig (Argentina) — Anales. Dispensario Publico Nacional para Enfermedades del Aparato Digestivo (Argentina)

ANDLA — Andrologie

AndNewQ — Andover Newton Quarterly

AndNewtQ — Andover Newton Quarterly

An Dobr — Analele Dobrogei

Andover R — Andover Review

And Past — Andean Past

And R — Andover Review

Androgens Antiandrogens Pap Int Symp — Androgens and Antiandrogens. Papers Presented at the International Symposium onAndrogens and Antiandrogens

Androgens Norm Pathol Cond Proc Symp Steroid Horm — Androgens in Normal and Pathological Conditions. Proceedings. Symposium on Steroid Hormones

AndrUnSS — Andrews University. Seminary Studies

An D S P — Annales de Droit et de Sciences Politiques

An Dubrovnik — Anali Historijskog Instituta u Dubrovniku

And WR — Andhra Weekly Reporter

ANE — Ancient Near East

An E — Annales de l'Est

AnE — Annales de l'Est et du Nord

AnE — Annales d'Esthetique. Chronika Aisthetikes

ANE — Annales du Notariat et de l'Enregistrement

AnE — Annales Encyclopediques

Ane — Anthropologie

ANE — Atomics and Nuclear Energy

Anecd Graec — Anecdota Graeca

Anecd Graec Oxon — Anecdota Graeca e Codices. Manuscriptis Bibliothecarum Oxoniensium

Anecd Med Graec — Anecdota Medica Graeca

Anecd Ox — Anecdota Graeca e Codices. Manuscriptis Bibliothecarum Oxoniensium

Anecd Stud — Anecdota Varia Graeca et Latina

Anec Gr Paris — Anecdota Graeca e Codices. Manuscriptis Bibliothecae Regiae Parisienses

An Econ Estad Bogota — Anales de Economia y Estadistica (Bogota)

An Econ Mex Mex Econ — Anuario de la Economica Mexicana/Mexican Economy Annual

An Econ Soc Civilis — Annales, Economies, Societes, Civilisations

An Edafol Agrobiol — Anales de Edafologia y Agrobiologia

An Edafol Fisiol Veg — Anales de Edafologia y Fisiologia Vegetal

AnEgB — Annual Egyptological Bibliography

ANEMD — Anatomy and Embryology

ANEMDG — Anatomy and Embryology

AnEN — Annales de l'Est et du Nord

ANENAG — Annales d'Endocrinologie

An Encontro Nac Fis Reatores Termoidraulica — Anais. Encontro Nacional de Fisica de Reatores e Termoidraulica

ANENDJ — Annals of Nuclear Energy

ANEP — Ancient Near East in Pictures Relating to the Old Testament

An Ep — Annee Epigraphique. Revue des Publications Epigraphiques Relatives a l'Antiquite Romaine

ANESA — Anesthesiology

AnESC — Annales. Economies, Societes, Civilisations

An Esc Agron Vet Univ Fed Goias — Anais. Escola de Agronomia e Veterinaria. Universidade Federal deGoias

An Esc Farm Fac Cienc Med Univ Nac Mayor San Marcos — Anales. Escuela de Farmacia. Facultad de Ciencias Medicas. Universidad NacionalMayor de San Marcos

An Esc Farm Univ S Marcos — Anales. Escuela de Farmacia. Universidad Nacional Mayor de San Marcos

An Esc Nac Cienc Biol (Mex) — Anales. Escuela Nacional de Ciencias Biologicas (Mexico)

An Esc Nac Cienc Biol (Mexico City) — Anales. Escuela Nacional de Ciencias Biologicas (Mexico City)

An Esc Nac Saude Publica Med Trop — Anais. Escola Nacional de Saude Publica e de Medicina Tropical

An Esc Nac Saude Publica Med Trop (Lisbon) — Anais. Escola Nacional de Saude Publica e de Medicina Tropical(Lisbon)

An Esc Perit Agric Barcelona — Anales de la Escuela de Peritos Agricolas y Superior de Agricultura (Barcelona)

An Esc Quim Farm Bioquim Univ Concepcion — Anales. Escuela de Quimica y Farmacia y Bioquimica. Universidad de Concepcion

An Esc Super Agric Luiz de Queiroz — Anais. Escola Superior de Agricultura Luiz de Queiroz

An Esc Super Agric "Luiz De Queiroz" Univ Sao Paulo — Anais. Escola Superior de Agricultura "Luiz de Queiroz." Universidade de SaoPaulo

An Esc Super Agr "Luiz De Queiroz" — Anais. Escola Superior de Agricultura "Luiz De Queiroz"

An Esc Super Med Vet (Lisb) — Anais. Escola Superior de Medicina Veterinaria (Lisbon)

An Esc Super Quim Univ Recife — Anais. Escola Superior de Quimica. Universidade do Recife

An Esc Sup Vet Madr — Anales de la Escuela Superior de Veterinaria de Madrid

An Escuela Nac Cien Biol Mex — Anales. Escuela Nacional de Ciencias Biologicas (Mexico)

An Escuela Nac Cienc Biol — Anales. Escuela Nacional de Ciencias Biologicas

An Esc Vet Urug — Anales de la Escuela de Veterinaria del Uruguay

An Esp Odontoestomat — Anales Espanoles de Odontoestomatologia

An Esp Odontoestomatol — Anales Espanoles de Odontoestomatologia

An Esp Pediatr — Anales Espanoles de Pediatria

An Est — Annales de l'Est

An Estac Exp Aula Dei — Anales. Estacion Experimental de Aula Dei

An Estac Exp Aula Dei Cons Super Invest Cient — Anales. Estacion Experimental de Aula Dei. Consejo Superior de Investigaciones Cientificas

An Estac Exp Aula Dei (Zaragoza) — Anales. Estacion Experimental de Aula Dei (Zaragoza)

An Estad Andes Venez — Anuario Estadistico de Los Andes. Venezuela

An Estat Parana — Anuario Estatistico Parana

Anesteziol Reanimatol — Anesteziologiya i Reanimatologiya

Anestezjol Intensywna Ter — Anestezjologia, Intensywna Terapia

Anesth Abstr — Anesthesia Abstracts

Anesth Anal — Anesthesia and Analgesia

Anesth Analg — Anesthesia and Analgesia

Anesth Analg — Current Researches in Anesthesia and Analgesia

Anesth Analg (Cleve) — Anesthesia and Analgesia (Cleveland)

Anesth Analg (NY) — Anesthesia and Analgesia (New York)

Anesth Analg (Paris) — Anesthesie, Analgesie, Reanimation (Paris)

Anesth Analg Reanim — Anesthesie, Analgesie, Reanimation

Anesth An R — Anesthesie, Analgesie, Reanimation

Anesthesiol — Anesthesiology

Anesthesiol Clin — International Anesthesiology Clinics

Anesthesiol Clin North Am — Anesthesiology Clinics of North America

Anesthesiol Reanim — Anesthesiologie et Reanimation

Anesth Intensive Care — Anaesthesia and Intensive Care

Anesth Neurosurg — Anesthesia and Neurosurgery

Anesth Pharmacol & Physiol Rev — Anesthetic Pharmacology and Physiology Review

Anesth Pharmacol Rev — Ahesthetic Pharmacology Review

Anesth Prog — Anesthesia Progress

Anesth Prog Dent — Anesthesia Progress in Dentistry

Anesth Reanim Perinat Journ Inf Post Univ — Anesthesie-Reanimation et Perinatologie. Journees d'Information Post-Universitaire

Anest Reanim — Anestezja i Reanimacja

Anest Reanim Intensywna Ter — Anestezja i Reanimacja. Intensywna Terapia

ANET — Ancient Near Eastern Texts Relating to the Old Testament

AnEth — Annales d'Ethiopie

An Ethiopie — Annales d'Ethiopie

An Etud Int — Annales d'Etudes Internationales

A News — Archaeological News

A Newspaper — Art Newspaper

ANEXA — Acta Neurobiologiae Experimentalis

ANEXAC — Acta Neurobiologiae Experimentalis

ANEXBD — Acta Neurobiologiae Experimentalis. Supplementum

ANF — Arkiv foer Nordisk Filologi

An Fabbrica Duomo — Annali della Fabbrica del Duomo

An Fac Biol Cienc Med Santiago — Anales de la Facultad de Biologia y Ciencias Medicas (Santiago de Chile)

An Fac Cienc Fis Mat Univ Concepcion — Anales. Facultad de Ciencias Fisicas y Matematicas. Universidad de Concepcion

An Fac Cienc Med Univ Nac La Plata — Anales de la Facultad de Ciencias Medicas. Universidad Nacional de La Plata

An Fac Cienc Med Univ Nac Parag — Anales de la Facultad de Ciencias Medicas. Universidad Nacional del Paraguay

An Fac Cienc Univ Porto — Anais. Faculdade de Ciencias. Universidade do Porto

An Fac Cienc Univ S Marcos — Anales de la Facultad de Ciencias. Universidad Mayor de San Marcos

An Fac Cienc Zaragoza — Anales de la Facultad de Ciencias de Zaragoza

An Fac Cien Jur Soc La Plata — Anales. Facultad de Ciencias Juridicas y Sociales. Universidad de La Plata

An Fac Cien Med Asuncion — Anales. Facultad de Ciencias Medicas (Asuncion)

An Fac Ci Univ Porto — Anais. Faculdade de Ciencias. Universidade do Porto

An Fac Farm Bioquim Univ Nac Mayor San Marcos — Anales. Facultad de Farmacia y Bioquimica. Universidad Nacional Mayor de San Marcos

An Fac Farm Bioquim Univ Nac Mayor San Marcos Lima — Anales. Facultad de Farmacia y Bioquimica. Universidad Nacional Mayor de San Marcos de Lima

An Fac Farm Odontol Univ Sao Paulo — Anais. Faculdade de Farmacia e Odontologia. Universidade de Sao Paulo

An Fac Farm Porto — Anais. Faculdade de Farmacia do Porto

An Fac Farm Univ Fed Pernambuco — Anais. Faculdade de Farmacia. Universidade Federal de Pernambuco

An Fac Farm Univ Recife — Anais. Faculdade de Farmacia. Universidade do Recife

An Fac Filos & Lett U Milano — Annali della Facolta di Filosofia e Lettere dell'Universita di Milano

An Fac Ing Univ Concepcion — Anales. Facultad de Ingenieria. Universidad de Concepcion

An Fac Lett Aix en Provence — Annales de la Faculte des Lettres d'Aix-en-Provence

An Fac Lett & Filos U Napoli — Annali della Facolta di Lettere e Filosofia dell'Universita di Napoli

An Fac Lett & Filos U Stud [Perugia] — Annali della Facolta di Lettere e Filosofia dell'Universita degli Studi [Perugia]

An Fac Ling & Lett Stran Ca Foscari — Annali della Facolta di Lingue e Lettere Straniere di Ca' Foscari

An Fac Magistero U Cagliari — Annali della Facolta di Magistero dell'Universita di Cagliari

An Fac Med Bahia Univ Bahia — Anais. Faculdade de Medicina. Bahia. Universidade da Bahia

An Fac Med Farm Habana — Anales de la Facultad de Medicina y Farmacia (La Habana)

An Fac Med Lima — Anales. Facultad de Medicina. Universidad Nacional Mayor de San Marcos de Lima

An Fac Med (Montevideo) — Anales. Facultad de Medicina. Universidad de la Republica (Montevideo)

An Fac Med Porto Alegre — Anais. Faculdade de Medicina de Porto Alegre
An Fac Med Univ Fed Minas Gerais (Belo Horizonte) — Anais. Faculdade de Medicina. Universidade Federal de Minas Gerais (Belo Horizonte)
An Fac Med Univ Fed Pernambuco — Anais. Faculdade de Medicina. Universidade Federal de Pernambuco
An Fac Med Univ Montevideo — Anales de la Facultad de Medicina. Universidad de Montevideo
An Fac Med Univ Nac Mayor San Marcos Lima — Anales. Facultad de Medicina. Universidad Nacional Mayor de San Marcos de Lima
An Fac Med Univ Nac Mayor San Marcos Lima (Peru) — Anales. Facultad de Medicina. Universidad Nacional Mayor de San Marcos de Lima(Peru)
An Fac Med Univ Parana (Curitiba) — Anais. Faculdade de Medicina. Universidade do Parana (Curitiba)
An Fac Med Univ Recife — Anais. Faculdade de Medicina. Universidade do Recife
An Fac Med Univ Repub (Montev) — Anales. Facultad de Medicina. Universidad de la Republica (Montevideo)
An Fac Med Univ Repub Montevideo — Anales. Facultad de Medicina. Universidad de la Republica. Montevideo
An Fac Med Univ Repub Orient Urug — Anales. Facultad de Medicina. Universidad de la Republica Oriental del Uruguay
An Fac Med Univ Sao Paulo — Anais. Faculdade de Medicina. Universidade de Sao Paulo
An Fac Med Univ S Marcos — Anales de la Facultad de Medicina. Universidad Nacional Mayor de San Marcos de Lima
An Fac Med Univ Zaragoza — Anales de la Facultad de Medicina. Universidad de Zaragoza
An Fac Odontol — Anales de la Facultad de Odontologia (Uruguay)
An Fac Odontol Univ Fed Pernambuco — Anais. Faculdade de Odontologia. Universidade Federal de Pernambuco
An Fac Odontol Univ Fed Rio De J — Anais. Faculdade de Odontologia. Universidade Federal do Rio De Janeiro
An Fac Odontol Univ Repub Urug — Anales. Facultad de Odontologia. Universidad de la Republica
An Fac Odont Univ Urug — Anales de la Facultad de Odontologia. Universidad de la Republica Oriental del Uruguay
An Fac Quim Farm (Santiago) — Anales. Facultad de Quimica y Farmacia. Universidad de Chile (Santiago)
An Fac Quim Farm Univ Chile — Anales. Facultad de Quimica y Farmacia. Universidad de Chile
An Fac Quim Farm Univ Concepcion — Anales. Facultad de Quimica y Farmacia. Universidad de Concepcion
An Fac Quim Farm Univ Repub Orient Urug — Anales. Facultad de Quimica y Farmacia. Universidad de la Republica Oriental del Uruguay
An Fac Quim Farm Univ Urug — Anales de la Facultad de Quimica y Farmacia. Universidad de Uruguay
An Fac Quim Univ Repub Orient Urug — Anales. Facultad de Quimica. Universidad de la Republica Oriental del Uruguay
An Fac Quim Univ Repub Urug — Anales de la Facultad de Quimica. Universidad de la Republica del Uruguay
An Fac Quim Univ Urug — Anales. Facultad de Quimica. Universidad de la Uruguay
An Fac Vet Inst Invest Vet Madrid — Anales. Facultad de Veterinaria. Instituto de Investigaciones Veterinaria de Madrid
An Fac Vet Leon — Anales. Facultad de Veterinaria de Leon
An Fac Vet Univ Madr — Anales de la Facultad de Veterinaria de la Universidad de Madrid
An Fac Vet Univ Madrid Inst Invest Vet — Anales. Facultad de Veterinaria. Universidad de Madrid. Instituto de Investigaciones Veterinarias
An Fac Vet Univ Zaragoza — Anales. Facultad de Veterinaria. Universidad de Zaragoza
An Fac Vet Urug — Anales. Facultad de Veterinaria del Uruguay
An Farm Bioquim Bogota — Anales de Farmacia y Bioquimica (Bogota)
An Farm Bioquim (Buenos Aires) — Anales de Farmacia y Bioquimica (Buenos Aires)
An Farm Hosp — Anales de Farmacia Hospitalaria
An Farm Quim — Anais de Farmacia e Quimica
An Farm Quim Sao Paulo — Anais de Farmacia e Quimica de Sao Paulo
ANFEBT — Annali. Universita di Ferrara. Sezione I. Ecologia
An Fed Archeol & Hist Belgique — Annales de la Federation Archeologique et Historique de Belgique
An Fis — Anales de Fisica
An Fisica — Anales de Fisica
An Fis Monogr — Anales de Fisica. Monografias
An Fis Quim — Anales de Fisica y Quimica
An Fis Ser A — Anales de Fisica. Serie A
An Fis Ser B — Anales de Fisica. Serie B
AnFP — Analecta Sacri Ordinis Fratrum Praedicatorum
ANFRIDI — Annuaire Francais de Droit International
ANG — Acta Nuntiaturae Gallicae
ANG — Akademiia Nauk Gruzinskoi SSR
Ang — Angelicum
Ang — Anglia
Ang Bbl — Anglia Beiblatt
Ang Bot — Angewandte Botanik
ANGE — Los Angeles Times
ANGE-A — Annales de Geographie
ANGED — Annales Geophysicae
An Geog — Annales de Geographie
Angers Ac Sc Mm — Memoires de l'Academie des Sciences et Belles-Lettres d'Angers
Angers S Sc Bll — Bulletin de la Societe d'Etudes Scientifiques d'Angers
Angest Versich — Angestellten-Versicherung
Angew Bot — Angewandte Botanik
Angew Chem — Angewandte Chemie
Angew Chem Ausg A — Angewandte Chemie. Ausgabe A. Wissenschaftlicher Teil

Angew Chem Ausg B — Angewandte Chemie. Ausgabe B. Technisch-Wirtschaftlicher-Teil
Angew Chem Beil — Angewandte Chemie. Beilage
Angew Chem Int Ed — Angewandte Chemie. International Edition
Angew Chem Int Ed Engl — Angewandte Chemie. International Edition in English
Angew Chem Int Ed Engl Suppl — Angewandte Chemie. International Edition in English. Supplement
Angew Chem Intern Ed — Angewandte Chemie. International Edition in English
Angew Chromatogr — Angewandte Chromatographie
Angew Elektrochem Tagungsband Ulmer Elektrochem Tage — Angewandte Elektrochemie. Tagungsband. Ulmer Elektrochemische Tage
Angew Elektron — Angewandte Elektronik
Angew Elektron Mess & Regeltech — Angewandte Elektronik. Mess und Regeltechnik
Angew Geogr — Angewandte Geographie
Angew Inf — Angewandte Informatik/Applied Informatics
Angew Inf Appl Inf — Angewandte Informatik/Applied Informatics
Angew Infor — Angewandte Informatik/Applied Informatics
Angew Kosmet — Angewandte Kosmetik
Angew Makro — Angewandte Makromolekulare Chemie
Angew Makromol Chem — Angewandte Makromolekulare Chemie
Angew Math — Angewandte Mathematik
Angew Mess Regeltech — Angewandte Mess- + Regeltechnik
Angew Met — Angewandte Meteorologie
Angew Meteorol — Angewandte Meteorologie
Angew Ornithol — Angewandte Ornithologie
Angew Parasit — Angewandte Parasitologie
Angew Parasitol — Angewandte Parasitologie
Angew Pflanzensoziol — Angewandte Pflanzensoziologie
Angew PflSoziol — Angewandte Pflanzensoziologie
Angew Statist Oekon — Angewandte Statistik und Oekonometrie
Angew Statist Okonometrie — Angewandte Statistik und Okonometrie
Angew Systemanal — Angewandte Systemanalyse
Angew Systemanal — Angewandte Systemanalyse. Theorie und Praxis
Angew UV Spektrosk — Angewandte UV-Spektroskopie
ANGIA — Angiology
Angiol — Angiologia
Angiol Symp — Angiologisches Symposion
Angiol Symp (Kitzbuehel) — Angiologisches Symposion (Kitzbuehel)
Angiopatias Rio de Janiero — Angiopatias (Rio de Janiero). Revista Brasiliera de Angiologia
ANGK — Sammlung Zwangloser Abhandlungen aus dem Gebiete der Nerven- und Geisteskrankheiten
Ang L — Angela Luisa
Angl — Anglia. Zeitschrift fuer Englische Philologie
ANGL — Annals of Glaciology
ANGLA — Angiologica
AnglB — Anglia Beiblatt
Angl Bei — Anglia Beiblatt
Angle Orthod — Angle Orthodontist
Anglesey Hist Soc Trans — Anglesey Historical Society Transactions
Angl F — Anglistische Forschungen
Anglican R — Anglican Review
Angl Malaya — Angling in Malaya
Anglo Amer Mag — Anglo-American Magazine
Anglo-Am Law Rev — Anglo-American Law Review
Anglo-Am LR — Anglo-American Law Review
Anglo-Am L Rev — Anglo-American Law Review
Anglo Am M — Anglo-American Magazine
Anglo Bat Soc Proc — Anglo Batarian Society. Proceedings
Anglo-Ger Med Rev — Anglo-German Medical Review
Anglo Irish Stud — Anglo-Irish Studies
Anglo Ir Stud — Anglo Irish Studies
Anglo Norman Stud — Anglo-Norman Studies
Anglo Norman Text Soc — Anglo-Norman Text Society
Angl Orthod — Angle Orthodontist
Anglosax En — Anglosaxon England
Anglo-Saxon Engl — Anglo-Saxon England
Anglo Saxon Stud Archaeol & Hist — Anglo-Saxon Studies in Archaeology and History
Anglo-Sp Q Rev — Anglo-Spanish Quarterly Review
Anglo-Welsh — Anglo-Welsh Review
Angl Th R — Anglican Theological Review
AnglTR — Anglican Theological Review
ANGM — Anglican Messenger
ANGNDT — Abhandlung. Naturhistorische Gesellschaft Nuernberg
ANGOA — Angiologia
Angola Serv Geol Minas Bol — Angola. Servicos de Geologia e Minas. Boletim
Angora Goat Mohair J — Angora Goat and Mohair Journal
Ango Wels Rev — Angelo-Welsh Review
An G Paleont — Annales de Geologie et de Paleontologie
Ang Paras — Angewandte Parasitologie
An Gr — Anecdota Graeca
An Graf — Anales Graficos
An Graf BA — Anales Graficos (Buenos Aires)
Ang Theol Rev — Anglican Theological Review
Angus Wildl Rev — Angus Wildlife Review
ANGYBQ — Advances in Nephrology
An H — Anatomische Hefte
Anh — Anhembi
A NH — Annals of Natural History, or Magazine of Zoology, Botany, and Geology
Anhalt Gartenbau Zeitung — Anhaltische Gartenbau-Zeitung. Mit Beruecksichtigung der Landwirthschaft
Anhalt Vh Nt Vr — Verhandlungen des Naturhistorischen Vereins fuer Anhalt in Dessau

Anharmonic Lattices Struct Transitions Melting — Anharmonic Lattices, Structural Transitions, and Melting
ANH/B — Boletin. Academia Nacional de la Historia
ANHEA4 — Animal Health
An HE Sc Rel — Annuaire. Ecole Pratique des Hautes Etudes. V Section. Sciences Religeuses
ANHGAA — Annals of Human Genetics
ANHIAG — Annales d'Histochimie
ANHIDJ — Archives of Natural History
An Hidrogr B Aires — Anales Hidrograficos (Buenos Aires)
An Hidrol B Aires — Anales Hidrologicos. Servicio Meteorologico Nacional (Buenos Aires)
An Hisp — Anales. Universidad Hispalense
An Hisp Am Hidrol Med — Anales Hispano-Americanos de Hidrologia Medica y Climatologia (Madrid)
An Hist — Anais de Historia
An Hist A — Anales de Historia del Arte
An Hist A & Archeol — Annales d'Histoire de l'Art et d'Archeologie
An Hist Compiegnoises — Annales Historiques Compiegnoises
An Hist Der — Anuario de la Historia del Derecho Espanol
An Hist Inst Dubrovniku — Anali Historijskog Instituta u Dubrovniku
An Hist Inst JAZU Dubrovnik — Anali Historijskogo Instituta JAZU [*Jugoslavenska Akademija Znanosti i Umjetnosti*] u Dubrovniku
An Hist Ver Niederrhein Alte Erzbistum Koeln — Annalen des Historischen Vereins fuer den Niederrhein, Insbesondere das Alte Erzbistum Koeln
ANHNAV — Annuaire. Museum National d'Histoire Naturelle
An Hosp Mil Cent Lima — Anales. Hospital Militar Central. Lima
An Hosp Mil Cent (Lima Peru) — Anales. Hospital Militar Central (Lima, Peru)
An Hosp Ninos B Aires — Anales del Hospital de Ninos (Buenos Aires)
An Hosp Ninos Rosario — Anales del Hospital de Ninos e Instituto de Puericultura de Rosario
An Hosp S Jose Madr — Anales del Hospital de San Jose y Santa Adela (Madrid)
An Hosp St Cruz San Pablo — Anales. Hospital de la Santa Cruz y San Pablo
AnHP — Annales de la Haute Provence
AnHRF — Annales Historiques de la Revolution Francaise
ANHW — Annalen des Naturhistorischen Hofmuseums. Vienna
An ICCS Sfecla Zahar — Analele ICCS. Sfecla de Zahar
ANICD6 — Annals. ICRP
A (Nice) — Annales. Societe des Lettres, Sciences, et Arts des Alpes-Maritimes (Nice)
ANIEK — Akademiia Nauk SSSR. Institut Etnografii. Kratkie Soobshcheniia
ANIET — Akademiia Nauk SSSR. Institut Etnografii. Trudy
AniF — Annali Fondazione Italiana per Storia Amministrativa
ANIFA — Annales de Chirurgie Infantile
ANIGDI — Anales. Instituto Nacional de Investigaciones Agrarias. Serie Ganadera
Anilinfarben Ind — Anilinfarben-Industrie
Anilinokras Promst — Anilinokrasochnaya Promyshlennost
An Ilus Col Of Med Prov Lerida — Anales Ilustrados. Colegio Oficial de Medicina. Provincia de Lerida
Animadv Syst Herb Univ Tomsk — Animadversiones Systematicae ex Herbario Universitatis Tomskensis
Animadv Syst Mus Zool Univ Tomsk — Animadversiones Systematicae ex Museo Zoologico Instituti Biologici Universitatis Tomskensis
Anim Ailm — Animal Ailments
Animal Behav — Animal Behaviour
Animal Prod — Animal Production
Animal Sci P Poult Purdue Univ Coop Ext Serv — Animal Sciences P. Poultry. Purdue University. Cooperative Extension Service
Anim Appl Res Mamm Dev — Animal Applications of Research in Mammalian Development
Anim Behav — Animal Behavior
Anim Behav Abstr — Animal Behavior Abstracts
Anim Behav Monogr — Animal Behavior Monographs
Anim Blood Groups Biochem Genet — Animal Blood Groups and Biochemical Genetics
Anim Blood Groups Biochem Genet (Suppl) — Animal Blood Groups and Biochemical Genetics (Supplement)
Anim Breed — Animal Breeding
Anim Breed Abstr — Animal Breeding Abstracts
Anim Breed Feed — Animal Breeding and Feeding
ANIMC — Annales d'Immunologie
Anim Can — Animals Canada
Anim Cell Biotechnol — Animal Cell Biotechnology
Anim Compagnie — Animal de Compagnie
ANIMD2 — Anaesthesiologie und Intensivmedizin
ANIMD2 — Anaesthesiology and Intensive Care Medicine
Anim Damage Control ADC Purdue Univ Coop Ext Serv — Animal Damage Control ADC. Purdue University Cooperative Extension Service
Anim Def Anti-Viv — Animals Defender and Anti-Vivisectionist
Anim Feed S — Animal Feed Science and Technology
Anim Feed Sci Technol — Animal Feed Science and Technology
Anim Genet — Animal Genetics
Anim Genet Evol Sel Pap Int Congr Gen — Animal Genetics and Evolution. Selected Papers. International Congress of Genetics.
Anim Health — Animal Health
Anim Health VY Purdue Univ Coop Ext Serv — Animal Health VY. Purdue University Cooperative Extension Service
Anim Hlth — Animal Health
Anim Hlth For Publs — Animal Health and Forestry Publications. Colonial Advisory Council of Agriculture
Anim Hlth Int — Animal Health International
Anim Hlth Int Dir — Animal Health International Directory
Anim Hlth Leafl — Animal Health Leaflet. Ministry of Agriculture, Fisheries, and Food
Anim Hlth Rev Ser — Animal Health Review Series. Imperial Agricultural Bureaux

Anim Hlth Yb — Animal Health Yearbook
Anim Hum Health — Animal and Human Health
Anim Husb — Animal Husbandry
Anim Husb Agric J — Animal Husbandry and Agricultural Journal
Anim Husb Circ Sask — Animal Husbandry Circular. Department of Agriculture (Saskatchewan)
Anim Husb Mimeogr Ser Fla Agr Exp Sta — Animal Husbandry Mimeograph Series. Florida Agricultural Experiment Station
Anim Husb (Tokyo) — Animal Husbandry (Tokyo)
Anim Husb Vet Med — Animal Husbandry and Veterinary Medicine
Anim Ind Ser Taipei — Animal Industry Series (Taipei)
Anim Ind Today — Animal Industry Today
Anim Ind Tokyo — Animal Industry (Tokyo)
Anim Int World Soc Prot Anim — Animal International. World Society for the Protection of Animals
Anim Kingd — Animal Kingdom
Anim Kingdom — Animal Kingdom
Anim Lear B — Animal Learning and Behavior
Anim Learn Behav — Animal Learning and Behavior
Anim Models Hum Dis — Animal Models of Human Disease
Anim Models Thromb Hemorrhagic Dis — Animal Models of Thrombosis and Hemorrhagic Diseases
Anim Nutr Health — Animal Nutrition and Health
Anim Nutr Res Counc Proc Annu Meet — Animal Nutrition Research Council. Proceedings of the Annual Meeting
Anim Plant Microb Toxins Proc Int Symp M — Animal, Plant, and Microbial Toxins. Proceedings of the International Symposium on Animal, Plant, and Microbial Toxins
Anim Prod — Animal Production
Anim Produc — Animal Production
Anim Quar — Animal Quarantine
Anim Regul Stud — Animal Regulation Studies
Anim Reprod Sci — Animal Reproduction Science
Anim Res Lab Tech Pap Aust CSIRO — Animal Research Laboratories Technical Paper. Australia Commonwealth Scientificand Industrial Research Organisation
Anim Rights L Rep — Animal Rights Law Reporter
Anims Advoc — Animals' Advocate
Anims Ailm — Animals and their Ailments
Anim Sci — Animal Science
Anim Sci J Pak — Animal Science Journal of Pakistan
Anim Sci Mimeogr Rep Fla Agr Exp Sta — Animal Science Mimeograph Report. Florida Agricultural Experiment Station
Anim Sci Mimeogr Ser Ohio State Agr Exp Sta — Animal Science Mimeograph Series. Ohio State Agricultural Experiment Station
Anim Sci Pap Rep — Animal Science Papers and Reports
Anim Sci (Pretoria) — Animal Sciences (Pretoria)
Anim Sci Res Rep — Animal Science Research Report
Anim Sci (Sofia) — Animal Science (Sofia)
Anim Sci Technol — Animal Science and Technology
Anims Def Anti Vivisect — Animals Defender and Anti-Vivisectionist
Anims Def Zoophil — Animals Defender and Zoophilist
Anims Friend — Animals' Friend
Anims Guard — Animals' Guardian
Anim Technol — Animal Technology
Anim Technol J Inst Anim Technol — Animal Technology. Journal. Institute of Animal Technology
Anim Toxins Collect Pap Int Symp — Animal Toxins. A Collection of Papers Presented at the International Symposium on Animal Toxins
Anim Virol — Animal Virology
Anim Welfare Inst Q — Animal Welfare Institute Quarterly
Anim Wld — Animal World
Anim Yb — Animal Year Book
Anim Zoo Mag — Animal and Zoo Magazine
AnINA — Anales. Instituto Nacional de Antropologia e Historia
ANINE6 — Analytical Instrumentation
An Ing — Anales de Ingenieria
An INIA Ser Agric Spain — Anales. INIA [*Instituto Nacional de Investigaciones Agrarias*]. Serie. Agricola (Spain)
An INIA Ser Gen (Spain) — Anales. INIA [*Instituto Nacional de Investigaciones Agrarias*]. Serie. General (Spain)
An INIA Ser Prod Anim — Anales del INIA [*Instituto Nacional de Investigaciones Agrarias*]. Serie. Produccion Animal (Spain)
An INIA Ser Prod Veg — Anales. INIA [*Instituto Nacional de Investigaciones Agrarias*]. Serie. Produccion Vegetal
An INIA Ser Prot Veg — Anales. INIA (Instituto Nacional de Investigaciones Agrarias). Serie. Proteccion Vegetal (Spain)
An INIA Ser Recur Nat — Anales. INIA [*Instituto Nacional de Investigaciones Agrarias*]. Serie. Recursos Naturales
An INIA Ser Techol Agrar — Anales del INIA (Instituto Nacional de Investigaciones Agrarias). Serie. Techologia Agraria (Spain)
An Inst A Amer & Invest Estet — Anales del Instituto de Arte Americano e Investigaciones Esteticas
An Inst Agron (Lisboa) — Anais. Instituto Superior de Agronomia (Lisboa)
An Inst Antrop Hist — Anales. Instituto Nacional de Antropologia e Historia
An Inst Art Am Invest Estet BA — Anales. Instituto de Arte Americano e Investigaciones Esteticas (Buenos Aires)
An Inst Biol Mex — Anales. Instituto de Biologia (Mexico)
An Inst Biol (Mexico) — Anales. Instituto de Biologia. Universidad Nacional Autonoma de Mexico
An Inst Biol Univ Mex — Anales. Instituto de Biologia. Universidad Nacional Autonoma de Mexico
An Inst Biol Univ Nac Auton Mex — Anales. Instituto de Biologia. Universidad Nacional Autonoma de Mexico
An Inst Biol Univ Nac Auton Mex Ser Biol Exp — Anales. Instituto de Biologia. Universidad Nacional Autonoma de Mexico. Serie Biologia Experimental

An Inst Biol Univ Nac Auton Mex Ser Bot — Anales. Instituto de Biologia. Universidad Nacional Autonoma de Mexico. Serie Botanica

An Inst Biol Univ Nac Auton Mex Ser Cienc Mar Limnol — Anales. Instituto de Biologia. Universidad Nacional Autonoma de Mexico. Serie Ciencias del Mar y Limnologia

An Inst Biol Univ Nac Auton Mex Ser Zool — Anales. Instituto de Biologia. Universidad Nacional Autonoma de Mexico. Serie Zoologia

An Inst Bot A J Cavanilles — Anales. Instituto Botanico A. J. Cavanilles

An Inst Bot A J Cavanilles (Madrid) — Anales. Instituto Botanico A. J. Cavanilles (Madrid)

An Inst Cent Cercet Agric Sect Pedol — Analele. Institutul Central de Cercetari Agricole. Sectiei de Pedologie

An Inst Cent Cercet Agric Sect Prot Plant — Analele. Institutul Central de Cercetari Agricole. Sectiei de Protectia Plantelor

An Inst Cent Cercet Agric Ser A — Anale. Institutul Central de Cercetari Agricole. Seria A. Pedologie, Agrochimie, si Imbunatatiri Funciare

An Inst Cent Cercet Agric Ser B — Anale. Institutul Central de Cercetari Agricole. Seria B. Porumbul Dublu Hibrid

An Inst Cent Cercet Agr Sect Econ Agr (Bucharest) — Anale. Institutul Central de Cercetari Agricole. Sectiei de Economice Agricole (Bucharest)

An Inst Cent Cercet Agr Sect Prot Plant — Anale. Institutul Central de Cercetari Agricole. Sectiei de Protectia Plantelor

An Inst Cent Cercet Agr Ser A (Bucharest) — Anale. Institutul Central de Cercetari Agricole. Series A (Bucharest)

An Inst Cent Cercet Agr Ser B (Bucharest) — Anale. Institutul Central de Cercetari Agricole. Series B (Bucharest)

An Inst Cent Cercet Agr Ser C (Bucharest) — Anale. Institutul Central de Cercetari Agricole. Series C (Bucharest)

An Inst Cercet Agron — Analele Institutului de Cercetari Agronomice

An Inst Cercet Agron Rom — Analele Institutului de Cercetari Agronomice al Romaniei

An Inst Cercet Agron Ser A — Analele Institutului de Cercetari Agronomice. Seria A. Agroclimatologie, Pedologie, Agrochimie si Imbunatatiri Funciare

An Inst Cercet Agron Ser B — Analele Institutului de Cercetari Agronomice. Seria B. Agrotehnica, Pasuni si Finete, Economie, si Organizarea Agriculturii Socialiste

An Inst Cercet Agron Ser C — Analele Institutului de Cercetari Agronomice. Seria C. Fiziolgie, Genetica, Ameliorare, Protectia Plantelor si Tehnologie Agricola

An Inst Cercet Cereale Plante Teh-Fundulea — Analele. Institutului de Cercetari pentru Cereale si Plante Tehnice-Fundulea

An Inst Cercet Cul Cartofului Sfeclei Zahar (Brasov) Cartofu — Anale. Institutul de Cercetari pentru Cultura Cartofului si Sfeclei de Zahar (Brasov). Cartoful

An Inst Cercet Imbunatatiri Funciare Pedol Ser Hidroteh — Analele. Institutului de Cercetari pentru Imbunatatiri Funciare si Pedologie. Seria Hidrotehnica

An Inst Cercet Imbunatatiri Funciare Pedol Ser Pedol — Analele. Institutului de Cercetari pentru Imbunatatiri Funciare si Pedologie. Seria Pedologie

An Inst Cercet Pedol Agrochim — Analele. Institutului de Cercetari pentru Pedologie si Agrochimie

An Inst Cercet Pedol Agrochim Acad Stiinte Agric Silvice — Analele Institutului de Cercetari pentru Pedologie si Agrochimie. Academia de Stiinte Agricole si Silvice

An Inst Cercet pentru Cereale Plante Teh-Fundulea — Analele. Institutului de Cercetari pentru Cereale si Plante Tehnice-Fundulea

An Inst Cercet pentru Cereale Plante Teh-Fundulea Ser A — Analele. Institutului de Cercetari pentru Cereale si Plante Tehnice-Fundulea. Seria A

An Inst Cercet pentru Cereale Plante Teh-Fundulea Ser B — Analele. Institutului de Cercetari pentru Cereale si Plante Tehnice-Fundulea. Seria B

An Inst Cercet pentru Cereale Plante Teh-Fundulea Ser C — Analele. Institutului de Cercetari pentru Cereale si Plante Tehnice-Fundulea. Seria C

An Inst Cercet Prot Plant — Analele. Institutului de Cercetari pentru Protectia Plantelor

An Inst Cercet Prot Plant Acad Stiinte Agric Silvice — Analele. Institutului de Cercetari pentru Protectia Plantelor. Academia de Stiinte. Agricole si Silvice

An Inst Cercet Prot Plant Inst Cent Cercet Agric (Bucharest) — Analele. Institutului de Cercetari pentru Protectia Plantelor. Institutul Central de Cercetari Agricole (Bucharest)

An Inst Cercet Zooteh (Bucharest) — Analele. Institutului de Cercetari. Zootehnice (Bucharest)

An Inst (Cluj) — Anuarul. Institutului de Istorie si Arheologie (Cluj-Napoca)

An Inst Cluj — Anuarul Institutului de Studii Classice (Cluj)

An Inst Corachan — Anales. Instituto Corachan

An Inst Edafol Ecol Fisiol Veg — Anales del Instituto de Edafologia. Ecologia y Fisiologia Vegetal

An Inst Esp Edafol Ecol Fisiol Veg — Anales. Instituto Espanol de Edafologia, Ecologia, y Fisiologia Vegetal

An Inst Estud Gerund — Anales del Instituto de Estudios Gerundenses

An Inst Estud Gironins — Annales de l'Institut Estudis Gironins

An Inst Estud Madril — Anales del Instituto de Estudios Madrilenos

An Inst Estud Madrilenos — Anales. Instituto de Estudios Madrilenos

An Inst Etud Orient U Alger — Annales de l'Institut d'Etudes Orientales de l'Universite d'Alger

An Inst Farmac Esp — Anales. Instituto de Farmacologia Espanola

An Inst Farmacol Esp — Anales. Instituto de Farmacologia Espanola

An Inst For Invest Exper (Madr) — Anales. Instituto Forestal de Investigaciones y Experiencias (Madrid)

An Inst Geofis UNAM — Anales. Instituto de Geofisica. Universidad Nacional Autonoma de Mexico

An Inst Geofis Univ Nac Auton Mex — Anales. Instituto de Geofisica. Universidad Nacional Autonoma de Mexico

An Inst Geol Mex — Anales. Instituto Geologico de Mexico

An Inst Geol Univ Nac Auton Mex — Anales. Instituto de Geologia. Universidad Nacional Autonoma de Mexico

An Inst Hig Med Trop — Anais. Instituto de Higiene e Medicina Tropical

An Inst Hig Med Trop (Lisb) — Anais. Instituto de Higiene e Medicina Tropical (Lisbon)

An Inst Hort Fromont — Annales de l'Institut Horticole de Fromont

An Inst (Iasi) — Anuarul Institutului de Istorie si Arheologie (Iasi)

An Insti Nac Invest Agrar (Spain) Ser Prot Veg — Anales. Instituto Nacional de Investigaciones Agrarias (Spain). Serie Proteccion Vegetal

An Inst Invest Cientif Monterrey — Anales de Investigaciones Cientificas (Monterrey)

An Inst Invest Cient Tecnol Univ Nac Litoral — Anales. Instituto de Investigaciones Cientificas y Tecnologicas. Universidad Nacional del Litoral

An Inst Invest Cient Univ Nuevo Leon — Anales. Instituto de Investigaciones Cientificas. Universidad de Nuevo Leon

An Inst Invest Estet — Anales del Instituto de Investigaciones Esteticas

An Inst Invest Estet Mex — Anales de Investigaciones Esteticas (Mexico)

An Inst Invest Mar Punta Betin — Anales. Instituto de Investigaciones Marinas de Punta de Betin

An Inst Invest Odontol (Maracaibo) — Anales. Instituto de Investigaciones Odontologicas. Universidad del Zulia (Maracaibo)

An Inst Invest Vet — Anales. Instituto de Investigaciones Veterinarias

An Inst Invest Vet (Madrid) — Anales. Instituto de Investigaciones Veterinarias (Madrid)

An Inst Ist Arh (Cluj) — Anuarul. Institutului de Istorie si Arheologie (Cluj-Napoca)

An In St Ma — Annals. Institute of Statistical Mathematics

An Inst Mat Univ Nac Autonoma Mexico — Anales. Instituto de Matematicas. Universidad Nacional Autonoma de Mexico

An Inst Med Exp Angel H Roffo — Anales. Instituto de Medicina Experimental Angel H. Roffo

An Inst Med Exp Estud Trat Cancer — Anales del Instituto de Medicina Experimental para el Estudio y Tratamiento del Cancer

An Inst Med Exp Valencia — Anales. Instituto de Medicina Experimental de Valencia

An Inst Med Nac — Anales del Instituto Medico Nacional

An Inst Med Nac (Mexico) — Anales. Instituto Medico Nacional (Mexico)

An Inst Med Reg — Anales. Instituto de Medicina Regional

An Inst Med Trop — Anais. Instituto de Medicina Tropical

An Inst Med Trop (Lisb) — Anais. Instituto de Medicina Tropical (Lisbon)

An Inst Med Trop Lisbon — Anais. Instituto de Medicina Tropical. Lisbon

An Inst Med Trop Lisbon Supl — Anais do Instituto de Medicina Tropical. Lisbon. Suplemento

An Inst Mun Hig Zaragoza — Anales. Instituto Municipal de Higiene de Zaragoza

An Inst Munic Hig Z — Anales. Instituto Municipal de Higiene de Zaragoza

An Inst Munic Hig Zaragoza — Anales. Instituto Municipal de Higiene de Zaragoza

An Inst Nac Antrop Hist Mex — Anales. Instituto Nacional de Antropologia e Historia (Mexico)

An Inst Nac Antropol Hist — Anales. Instituto Nacional de Antropologia e Historia

An Inst Nac Invest Agrar Ser Agric — Anales. Instituto Nacional de Investigaciones Agrarias. Serie Agricola

An Inst Nac Invest Agrar Ser Ganad — Anales. Instituto Nacional de Investigaciones Agrarias. Serie Ganadera

An Inst Nac Invest Agrar Ser Gen — Anales. Instituto Nacional de Investigaciones Agrarias. Serie General

An Inst Nac Invest Agrar Ser Gen Spain — Anales. Instituto Nacional de Investigaciones Agrarias. Serie. General (Spain)

An Inst Nac Invest Agrar Ser Hig Sanid Anim — Anales. Instituto Nacional de Investigaciones Agrarias. Serie Higiene y SanidadAnimal

An Inst Nac Invest Agrar Ser Prod Anim — Anales. Instituto Nacional de Investigaciones Agrarias. Serie Produccion Animal

An Inst Nac Invest Agrar Ser Prod Anim (Spain) — Anales. Instituto Nacional de Investigaciones Agrarias. Serie. Produccion Animal (Spain)

An Inst Nac Invest Agrar Ser Prod Veg — Anales. Instituto Nacional de Investigaciones Agrarias. Serie Produccion Vegetal

An Inst Nac Invest Agrar Ser Prot Veg — Anales. Instituto Nacional de Investigaciones Agrarias. Serie Proteccion Vegetal

An Inst Nac Invest Agrar Ser Prot Veg Spain — Anales del Instituto Nacional de Investigaciones Agrarias. Serie. Proteccion Vegetal (Spain)

An Inst Nac Invest Agrar Ser Recur Nat — Anales. Instituto Nacional de Investigaciones Agrarias. Serie Recursos Naturales

An Inst Nac Invest Agrar Ser Technol Agrar Spain — Anales. Instituto Nacional de Investigaciones Agrarias. Serie. Tecnologia Agraria (Spain)

An Inst Nac Invest Agrar Ser Tecnol Agrar — Anales. Instituto Nacional de Investigaciones Agrarias. Serie Tecnologia Agraria

An Inst Nac Invest Agrar (Spain) Ser Prod Anim — Anales. Instituto Nacional de Investigaciones Agrarias (Spain). Serie Produccion Animal

An Inst Nac Invest Agrar (Spain) Ser Prod Veg — Anales. Instituto Nacional de Investigaciones Agrarias (Spain). Serie Produccion Vegetal

An Inst Nac Invest Agrar (Spain) Ser Recur Nat — Anales. Instituto Nacional de Investigaciones Agrarias (Spain). Serie RecursosNaturales

An Inst Nac Invest Agron (Madr) — Anales. Instituto Nacional de Investigaciones Agronomicas (Madrid)

An Inst Nac Invest Agron (Spain) — Anales. Instituto Nacional de Investigaciones Agronomicas (Spain)

An Inst Nac Microbiol (B Aires) — Anales. Instituto Nacional de Microbiologia (Buenos Aires)

An Inst N Antropol & Hist — Anales del Instituto Nacional de Antropologia e Historia

An Inst Natl Zooteh Rom — Analele Institutului National Zootehnic al Romaniei

An Inst Oncol Angel H Roffo — Anales. Instituto de Oncologia "Angel H. Roffo"

An Inst Oncol Angel H Roffo (B Aires) — Anales. Instituto de Oncologia "Angel H. Roffo" (Buenos Aires)

An Inst Patagonia — Anales. Instituto de la Patagonia

An Inst Pinheiros — Anales. Instituto Pinheiros

An Inst Psicol — Anales. Instituto de Psicologia

An Inst Radio Quir Guipuzcoa — Anales. Instituto Radio Quirurgico de Guipuzcoa

An Instr Prim Monte — Anales de la Instruccion Primaria. Consejo Nacional de Ensenanza Primaria y Normal (Montevideo)

An Inst Stud Cercet Pedol — Analele. Institutului de Studii si Cercetari Pedologice

An Inst Stud Cercet Pedol Acad Stiinte Agric Silvice — Analele Institutului de Studii si Cercetari Pedologice. Academia de Stiinte Agricole si Silvice

An Inst Super Agron (Lisboa) — Anais. Instituto Superior de Agronomia (Lisboa)

An Inst Super Agron Univ Tec Lisb — Anais. Instituto Superior de Agronomia. Universidade Tecnica de Lisboa

An Inst Super Agron Univ Tec Lisboa — Anais do Instituto Superior de Agronomia. Universidade Tecnica de Lisboa

An Inst Vinho Porto — Anais. Instituto do Vinho do Porto

An Invest Agron — Anales de Investigaciones Agronomicas

An Invest Text — Anales de Investigacion Textil

Anionic Surfactants Chem Anal — Anionic Surfactants Chemical Analysis

AnIowa — Annals of Iowa

AnIP — Annales de l'Institut de Philosophie

ANIPA — Animal Production

ANIRAE — Acta Naturalia Islandica

Ani Sci — Animal Science

An Isl — Annales Islamologiques

An Islam — Annales Islamologiques

Anisotropy Eff Supercond Proc Int Discuss Meet — Anisotropy Effects in Superconductors. Proceedings of an International Discussion Meeting. Atominstitut der Oesterreichischen Universitaeten

An Ist & Mus Stor Sci Firenze — Annali dell'Istituto e Museo di Storia della Scienza di Firenze

An Ist Corr Archeol — Annali dell'Istituto di Corrispondenza Archeologica

An Ist It Num — Annali dell'Istituto Italiano di Numismatica

An Ist Stor It Ger Trento — Annali dell'Istituto Storico Italo-Germanico in Trento

An Ist Sup Sci & Lett S Chiara — Annali dell'Istituto Superiore di Scienza e Lettere 'S Chara'

A Nivelles — Annales. Societe d'Archeologie d'Histoire et de Folklore de Nivelles et du Brabant Wallon

A Nivernais — Annales des Pays Nivernais

ANIVK — Akademiia Nauk SSSR. Institut Vostokovedeniia. Kratkie Soobshcheniia

AnIW — Arbeiten aus dem Neurologischen Institut der Universitaet Wien

ANJ — Australian Numismatic Journal

An Jard Bot Madrid — Anales. Jardin Botanico de Madrid

ANJO — Anglican Journal

An Jorn Geol Argent — Anales Jornadas Geologicas Argentinas

An Junta Invest Ultramar — Anais. Junta de Investigacoes do Ultramar

An Junta Invest Ultramar (Port) — Anais. Junta de Investigacoes do Ultramar (Portugal)

An Junta Missoes Geogr Invest Ultramar Port — Anais. Junta das Missoes Geograficas e de Investigacoes do Ultramar (Portugal)

An Jur Soc Santiago — Anales Juridico-Sociales (Santiago)

ANK — Akademiia Nauk Kazakhskoi SSR

ANK — Consommation

Ankara Nucl Res Cent Tech J — Ankara Nuclear Research Center. Technical Journal

Ankara Nucl Res Train Cent Tech J — Ankara Nuclear Research and Training Center. Technical Journal

Ankara U Arastirmalari Derg — Ankara Universitesi dil ve Tarih Arastirmalari Dergisi

Ankara U Dil Tarih Corafya Fak Derg — Ankara Universitesi dil ve Tarih-Co'rafya Fakultesi Dergisi

Ankara U Lahiyat Fak Yillik Arastirmalari Derg — Ankara Universitesi Ilahiyat Fakultesi Yillik Arastirmalari Dergisi

Ankara Univ Eczacilik Fak Mecm — Ankara Universitesi Eczacilik Fakultesi Mecmuasi

Ankara Univ Fac Agric Publ — Ankara University. Faculty of Agriculture. Publications

Ankara Univ Hekim Fak Derg — Ankara Universitesi dis Hekimligi Fakultesi Dergisi

Ankara Univ Tip Fak Mecm — Ankara Universitesi. Tip Fakultesi. Mecmuasi

Ankara Univ Tip Fak Mecm Suppl — Ankara Universitesi. Tip Fakultesi. Mecmuasi. Supplementum

Ankara Univ Vet Fak Derg — Ankara Universitesi. Veteriner Fakultesi. Dergisi

Ankara Univ Ziraat Fak Yayin — Ankara Universitesi. Ziraat Fakultesi. Yayinlari

Ankara Univ Ziraat Fak Yilligi — Ankara Universitesi Ziraat Fakultesi Yilligi

ANKi — Akademiia Nauk Kirghizskoi SSR

ANKIAV — Animal Kingdom

ANKIDY — Annales de Kinesitherapie

An Klin Boln Dr M Stojanovic — Anali Klinicke Bolnice Dr. M. Stojanovic

An Klin Boln Dr M Stojanovic Supl — Anali Klinicke Bolnice Dr. M. Stojanovic. Suplement

AnKu — Antike Kunst

AnkUDerg — Ankara Universitesi Dil ve Tarih-Cografya Fakultesi. Dergisi

ANL — Accademia Nazionale dei Lincei

ANL — Altnuernberger Landschaft. Mitteilungen

AnL — Anthropological Linguistics

ANL — Archaeological News Letter

ANL — Atti. Reale Accademia Nazionale dei Lincei. Classe di Scienze Morali, Storiche,e Filologiche

ANLA — Atti. Reale Accademia Nazionale dei Lincei. Classe di Scienze Morali, Storiche,e Filologiche

ANLAAC — Acta Neurologica Latinoamericana

An Lab Ensayo Mater Invest Tecnol Prov Buenos Aires — Anales. Laboratorio de Ensayo de Materiales e Investigaciones Tecnologicas. Provinca de Buenos Aires

An Lab Rech Mus France — Annales du Laboratoire de Recherche des Musees de France

An Lactol Quim Agric (Zaragoza) — Anales de Lactologia y Quimica Agricola (Zaragoza)

ANLADF — Auris Nasus Larynx

An Lateranensi — Annali Lateranensi

ANLBA — Bulletin. Australian Mathematical Society

AnIct Bolland — Analecta Bollandiana

AnIct Calasanct — Analecta Calasanctiana

AnIct Cartusiana — Analecta Cartusiana

AnIct Cisterc — Analecta Cisterciensia

AnIct Mag — Analectic Magazine

AnIct Orient — Analecta Orientalia

AnIct Praemonstratensia — Analecta Praemonstratensia

AnIct Romana Inst Dan — Analecta Romana Instituti Danici

AnIct Soc Ordinis Cisterc — Analecta Societatis Ordinis Cisterciensis

An Leab — An Leabharlann

An Leab Ir — An Leabharlann. Library Association of Ireland

ANLEDR — Antonie Van Leeuwenhoek Journal of Microbiology

AnLeeds — Annual. Leeds University Oriental Society

An Leeds UOS — Annual. Leeds University Oriental Society

ANL EES TM Argonne Natl Lab Energy Environ Syst Div — ANL EES (Argonne National Laboratory. Energy and Environmental Systems Division) TM

Anleit Bienenzuechter — Anleitungen Bienenzuechter

ANL FPP Tech Mem — ANL FPP [*Argonne National Laboratory. Fusion Power Program*] Technical Memorandum

ANL HEP CP — ANL HEP [*Argonne National Laboratory. High Energy Physics*] CP

ANLIA2 — Annali. Accademia Italiana di Scienze Forestali

ANLIB — Annales de Limnologie

An Liceo Class G Garibaldi Palermo — Annali del Liceo Classico 'G. Garibaldi' di Palermo

ANLKB — Archiv fuer die Naturkunde Liv-, Est-, und Kurlands

ANLL — Archaeological News Letter. University of London

ANLM — Accademia Nazionale dei Lincei. Memorie

ANLMSF — Accademia Nazionale dei Lincei. Rendiconti. Classe di Scienze Morali, Storiche,e Filologiche

An Lorraine — Annuaire. Societe d'Histoire et d'Archeologie de la Lorraine

AnLov — Analecta Lovanensia

ANL/PHY Rep — Argonne National Laboratory. Physics Division. Report

ANLRAT — Annales de Radiologie

ANLSBX — Acta Neuropathologica. Supplementum

ANLSCY — Analusis

ANLSD — Argonne National Laboratory. Energy and Environmental Systems Division. Report ANL/CNSV

AnIs Prob — Annals of Probability

AnIs Stat — Annals of Statistics

AnLUB — Annales Litteraires de l'Universite de Besancon

ANL US Argonne Natl Lab Rep — ANL. United States Argonne National Laboratory. Report

AnM — Annales du Midi; Revue de la France Meridionale

AnM — Annales Malgaches. Serie Lettres et Sciences Humaines

AnM — Annuale Mediaevale

An M — Anuario Musical

ANMAE — Akademiia Nauk SSSR. Muzei Antropologii i Etnografii. Sbornik

An Mag N H — Annals and Magazine of Natural History

An Malgaches — Annales Malgaches

An Mat Fiz Chim Electroteh Univ Craiova — Anale. Universitatea din Craiova. Seria Matematica, Fizica, Chimie, Electrotehnica

ANMBC — Annales de Microbiologie

ANMBCM — Annales de Microbiologie

An M Belgique — Annales des Mines de Belgique

ANMCAN — Annali di Microbiologia

ANMCB — Angewandte Makromolekulare Chemie

ANMDAQ — Antioquia Medica

An Mec Elect — Anales de Mecanica y Electricidad

An Mec Electr — Anales de Mecanica y Electricidad

An Med — Anales de Medicina

An Med Acad Cienc Med Cataluna Baleares — Anales de Medicina. Academia de Ciencias Medicas de Cataluna y Baleares

An Med Assoc Med Hosp Am Br Cowdray — Anales Medicos. Asociacion Medica. Hospital Americano-Britanico Cowdray

An Med Cir — Anales de Medicina. Cirugia

An Med Espec — Anales de Medicina. Especialidades

An Med Interna — Anales de Medicina Interna

An Med (Lima) — Anales de Medicina (Lima)

An Med Med — Anales de Medicina. Medicina

An Med Publ — Anales de Medicina Publica

An Med Quir — Anales Medicoquirurgicos

An Med Sec Med — Anales de Medicina. Seccion de Medicina

An Med (Sevilla) — Anales de Medicina (Sevilla)

ANMEDW — Annals. Medicina Academia de Ciencies Mediques de Catalunya i de Balears

Anmeld Paedagog Tidsskr — Anmeldelser i Paedagogiske Tidsskrifter

An Met Fr — Annuaire Meteorologique de la France

An Mex Cienc — Anales Mexicanos de Ciencias

An Micr — Anais de Microbiologia

An Microbiol — Anais de Microbiologia

An Microbiol (Rio De J) — Anais de Microbiologia (Rio De Janeiro)

An Midi — Annales du Midi. Revue Archeologique, Historique, et Philologique de la France Meridionale

An Minelor Rom — Analele Minelor din Romania

An Mines — Annales des Mines

An Minist Ultramar Junta Invest Ultramar Port — Anais. Ministerio do Ultramar. Junta de Investigacoes do Ultramar (Portugal)

AnMNH — Annals and Magazine of Natural History

An Moneg — Annales Monegasques

AN Morph — Acta Neerlandica Morphologiae Normalis et Pathologicae

ANMR — Alaska Native Management Report

ANMRC2 — Annales de Medecine de Reims

ANMSC — Anales del Museo Nacional. Etnologia (Santiago de Chile)

ANMUA9 — Annale. Natalse Museum

An Mun Faro — Anais. Municipio de Faro

An Munster — Annuaire. Societe d'Histoire du Val et de la Ville de Munster

An Mun Tomar — Anais do Municipio de Tomar

An Mus Argent Cienc Nat Bernardino Rivadavia — Anales. Museo Argentino de Ciencias Naturales Bernardino Rivadavia

An Mus Civ La Spezia — Annali del Museo Civico di La Spezia

An Mus Congo Belge Anthropol & Ethnog — Annales du Musee du Congo Belge. Anthropologie et Ethnographie

An Mus Guimet — Annales du Musee Guimet

An Mus Hist Nat Valparaiso — Anales. Museo de Historia Natural de Valparaiso

An Mus Michoacano — Anales del Museo Michoacano

An Mus Nac Arqueol Hist Etnogr Mex — Anales. Museo Nacional de Historia y Etnografia (Mexico)

An Mus Nac David J Guzman — Anales. Museo Nacional David J. Guzman

An Mus Nac Guzman S Salvador — Anales. Museo Nacional David J. Gusman (San Salvador)

An Mus Nac Hist Nat Montev — Anales. Museo Nacional de Historia Natural de Montevideo

An Mus Nac Repub Salvador — Anales del Museo Nacional. Republica de El Salvador

An Mus Nahuel Huapi — Anales. Museo de Nahuel Huapi

An Mus N Arqueol Hist & Etnog — Anales del Museo Nacional de Arqueologia, Historia, y Etnografia

An Mus Puebl Esp — Anales del Museo del Pueblo Espanol

An Mus Royal Afrique Cent — Annales du Musee Royal de l'Afrique Centrale

ANMWAF — Annalen des Naturhistorischen Museums in Wien

Ann — Annalen der Chemie. Justus Liebigs

Ann — Annales

AnN — Annales de Normandie

ANNAAM — Annales de l'Abeille

Ann AAS — Annales Archeologiques Arabes Syriennes

AnnAB — Annuaire. Academie Royale de Belgique

Ann Abeille — Annales de l'Abeille

Ann Acad Bras Cienc — Annaes. Academia Brasileira de Ciencias

Ann Acad Brasil Sci — Annaes. Academia Brasileira de Sciencias

Ann Acad Horti Vitic — Annales Academiae Horti- et Viticulturae

Ann Acad Jenensis — Annales Academiae Jenensis

Ann Acad Lugduno Batavae — Annales Academiae Lugduno-Batavae

Ann Acad Med Bialostoc — Annales Academiae Medicae Bialostocensis

Ann Acad Med Bialostoc Suppl — Annales Academiae Medicae Bialostocensis. Supplementum

Ann Acad Med Gedanensis — Annales Academiae Medicae Gedanensis

Ann Acad Med Lodz — Annales Academiae Medicae Lodzensis

Ann Acad Med Lodz Supl — Annales Academiae Medicae Lodzensis. Suplement

Ann Acad Med (Singapore) — Annals. Academy of Medicine (Singapore)

Ann Acad Med Stetin — Annales Academiae Medicae Stetinensis

Ann Acad Med Stetin Supl — Annales Academiae Medicae Stetinensis. Suplement

Ann Acad Nac Med Rio De Janeiro — Annaes. Academia Nacional de Medicina do Rio de Janeiro

Ann Acad R Agric Suede — Annales. Academie Royale d'Agriculture de Suede

Ann Acad R Agric Sylvic Suede — Annales. Academie Royale d'Agriculture et de Sylviculture de Suede

Ann Acad R Agric Sylvic Suede Suppl — Annales. Academie Royale d'Agriculture et de Sylviculture de Suede. Supplement

Ann Acad Regiae Sci Ups — Annales Academiae Regiae Scientiarum Upsaliensis

Ann Acad Reg Sci Upsal — Annales Academiae Regiae Scientiarum Upsaliensis

Ann Acad Sci Colon — Annales. Academie des Sciences Coloniales

Ann Acad Sci Fen — Annales Academiae Scientiarum Fennicae

Ann Acad Sci Fenn A I — Annales Academiae Scientiarum Fennicae. Series A-I (Mathematica)

Ann Acad Sci Fenn A II — Annales Academiae Scientiarum Fennicae. Series A-II (Chemica)

Ann Acad Sci Fenn A VI — Annales Academiae Scientiarum Fennicae. Series A-VI (Physica)

Ann Acad Sci Fenn (Biol) — Annales Academiae Scientiarum Fennicae. Series A-IV (Biologica)

Ann Acad Sci Fennicae — Annales Academiae Scientiarum Fennicae. Serie B

Ann Acad Sci Fenn Math — Academiae Scientiarum Fennicae. Annales. Mathematica

Ann Acad Sci Fenn Math Diss — Academiae Scientiarum Fennicae. Annales. Mathematica. Dissertationes

Ann Acad Sci Fenn (Med) — Annales Academiae Scientiarum Fennicae. Series A-V (Medica)

Ann Acad Sci Fenn Ser A — Annales Academiae Scientarum Fennicae. Series A

Ann Acad Sci Fenn Ser A — Annales. Academie Scientiarum Fennicae. Serie A. Suomalaisen Tiedeakatemian Toimtuksia

Ann Acad Sci Fenn Ser A 3 Geol — Annales. Academiae Scientiarum Fennicae. Series A 3. Geologica-Geographica

Ann Acad Sci Fenn Ser A 5 Medica — Annales. Academiae Scientiarum Fennicae. Series A 5. Medica

Ann Acad Sci Fenn Ser A I — Annales Academiae Scientiarum Fennicae. Series A-I (Mathematica)

Ann Acad Sci Fenn Ser A II — Annales Academiae Scientiarum Fennicae. Series A-II (Chemica)

Ann Acad Sci Fenn Ser A II (Chem) — Annales Academiae Scientiarum Fennicae. Series A-II (Chemica)

Ann Acad Sci Fenn Ser A III — Annales Academiae Scientiarum Fennicae. Series A-III (Geologica-Geographica)

Ann Acad Sci Fenn Ser A III (Geol Geogr) — Annales Academiae Scientiarum Fennicae. Series A-III (Geologica-Geographica)

Ann Acad Sci Fenn Ser A I (Math) — Annales Academiae Scientiarum Fennicae. Series A-I (Mathematica)

Ann Acad Sci Fenn Ser AI (Math) Dissertationes — Annales Academiae Scientiarum Fennicae. Series A-I (Mathematica). Dissertationes

Ann Acad Sci Fenn Ser AI (Math Phy) — Annales Academiae Scientiarum Fennicae. Series A-I (Mathematica-Physica)

Ann Acad Sci Fenn Ser A IV — Annales Academiae Scientiarum Fennicae. Series A-IV (Biologica)

Ann Acad Sci Fenn Ser A IV (Biol) — Annales Academiae Scientiarum Fennicae. Series A-IV (Biologica)

Ann Acad Sci Fenn Ser A V — Annales Academiae Scientiarum Fennicae. Series A-V (Medica)

Ann Acad Sci Fenn Ser A VI — Annales Academiae Scientiarum Fennicae. Series A-VI (Physica)

Ann Acad Sci Fenn Ser A VI (Phys) — Annales Academiae Scientiarum Fennicae. Series A-VI (Physica)

Ann Acad Sci Fenn Ser A V (Med) — Annales Academiae Scientiarum Fennicae. Series A-V (Medica)

Ann Acad Sci Fenn Ser A V (Med-Anthropol) — Annales Academiae Scientiarum Fennicae. Series A-V (Medica-Anthropologica)

Ann Acad Sci Tech Varsovie — Annales. Academie des Sciences Techniques a Varsovie

Ann Acad The Hague Leiden — Annales Academici (The Hague and Leiden)

Ann Accad Agric (Torino) — Annali. Accademia di Agricoltura (Torino)

Ann Accad Ital Sci For — Annali. Accademia Italiana di Scienze Forestali

Ann Ac Etr — Annuario. Accademia Etrusca di Cortona

Ann ACFAS — Annales. ACFAS

Ann Ac Fenn — Annales Academiae Scientiarum Fennicae

Ann Ac Torino — Annuario. Accademia delle Scienze di Torino

Ann Adv Ed Art Des — Annual of Advertising, Editorial Art, and Design

Ann Aequator — Annales Aequatoria

Annaes Soc Lit Port — Annaes da Sociedade Literaria Portuense

Ann Agr Fenn — Annales Agriculturae Fenniae

Ann Agric Environ Med — Annals of Agricultural and Environmental Medicine

Ann Agric Exp Sta Gov Gen Chosen — Annals. Anricultural Experiment Station. Government General of Chosen/Noji Shikenjo Iho

Ann Agric Exp Stn Gov Gen Chosen — Annals. Agricultural Experiment Station. Government General of Chosen

Ann Agric Fenn — Annales Agriculturae Fenniae

Ann Agric Fenniae — Annales Agriculturae Fenniae. Maatalouden Tutkimuskeskuksen Aikakauskirja/Journal. Agricultural Research Centre

Ann Agric Fenn Ser Agrogeol -Chim -Phys — Annales Agriculturae Fenniae. Seria Agrogeologia, -Chimica, et -Physica

Ann Agric Fenn Suppl — Annales Agriculturae Fenniae. Supplementum

Ann Agric Rome — Annali di Agricoltura. Italy. Ministerio d'Agricoltura, Industria e Commercio (Rome)

Ann Agric Sci (Cairo) — Annals of Agricultural Science (Cairo)

Ann Agric Sci (Moshtohor) — Annals of Agricultural Science (Moshtohor)

Ann Agric Sci Ser E — Annals of Agricultural Sciences. Series E. Plant Protection

Ann Agric Sci Univ A'in Shams — Annals of Agricultural Science. University of A'in Shams

Ann Agron — Annales Agronomiques

Ann Agron Hors-Ser — Annales Agronomiques. Hors-Serie

Ann Agron Minist Agric — Annales Agronomiques. Ministere de l'Agriculture

Ann Agron (Paris) — Annales Agronomiques (Paris)

An-Nahar Arab Rept and Memo — An-Nahar Arab Report and Memo

Ann Aid Rev — Annual Aid Review

AnnAIF — Annuaire des Archives Israelites (de France)

ANNA J — ANNA [*American Nephrology Nurses Association*] Journal

Annales — Annales. Service des Antiquites de l'Egypt

Annales Acad Scient Fenn — Suomalaisen Tiedeakatemian Toimituksia. Annales Academiae Scientiarum Fennicae

Annales Afr — Annales Africaines

Annales Arch Syrie — Annales Archeologiques Arabes Syriennes

Annales Bull Soc Sc Med Nat — Annales et Bulletin. Societe Royale des Sciences Medicales et Naturelles de Bruxelles

Annales De Geog — Annales de Geographie

Annales del'Inst Arch — Annali. Instituto di Corrispondenza Archeologica

Annales D Hyg Et De Med Col — Annales d'Hygiene et de Medecine Coloniales

Annales Econ — Annales. Economies, Societes, Civilisations

Annales-ESC — Annales: Economies, Societes, Civilisations

Annales INSEE — Annales de l'INSEE

Annales Institutorum — Annales Institutorum Quae Provehendis Humanioribus Disciplinis Artibusque Colendis a Variis in Urbe Erecta Sunt Nationibus

Annales Int'l de Crimin — Annales Internationales de Criminologie

Annales J J Rousseau — Annales. Societe Jean-Jacques Rousseau

Annales Med Physiol — Annales de la Medicine Physiologique

Annales Med Psychol — Annales Medico-Psychologiques

Annales Polit Et Litt — Annales Politiques et Litteraires

Annales Service Antiqu — Annales du Service des Antiquites

Annales Univ Budapest — Annales. Universitatis Scientiarum Budapestinenses de Rolando Eoetvoes Nominatae

Ann Alger Chir — Annales Algeriennes de Chirurgie

Ann Algeriennes Geogr — Annales Algeriennes de Geographie

Annali Accad Naz Agric (Bologna) — Annali. Accademia Nazionale di Agricoltura (Bologna)

Annali Chim Appl — Annali di Chimica Applicata

Annali dell'Inst Arch — Annali. Instituto di Corrispondenza Archeologica

Annali d Univ Toscane — Annali delle Universita Toscane

Annali Fac Agr Portici — Annali. Facolta di Agraria di Portici. Reale Universita di Napoli

Annali Fac Agr Univ Bari — Annali. Facolta di Agraria. Universita di Bari

Annali Fac Agr Univ Milano — Annali. Facolta di Agraria. Universita di Milano

Annali Fac Agr Univ Perugia — Annali. Facolta di Agraria. Universita degli Studi di Perugia

Annali Fac Sci Agr Univ Napoli — Annali. Facolta di Scienze Agrarie. Universita degli Studi di Napoli

Annali Fac Sci Agr Univ Torino — Annali. Facolta di Scienze Agrarie. Universita degli Studi di Torino

Annali Geofisica — Annali di Geofisica

Annali Idrol — Annali Idrologici

Annali Ig Sper — Annali d'Igiene. Sperimentali

Annali Ist Carlo Forlanini — Annali. Istituto Carlo Forlanini

Annali Ist Sper Zool Agr — Annali. Istituto Sperimentale per la Zoologia Agraria
Annali Microbiol — Annali di Microbiologia ed Enzimologia
Annali Mus Civ Stor Nat Giacomo Doria — Annali. Museo Civico di Storia Naturale "Giacomo Doria"
Annali Sper Agr — Annali della Sperimentazione Agraria
Annali Staz Chim-Agr Sper Roma — Annali. Reale Stazione Chimico-Agraria Sperimentale di Roma
Annali Staz Sper Risicolt Vercelli — Annali. Stazione Sperimentale di Risicoltura e delle Colture Irrigue. Vercelli
Annali Univ Tosc — Annali. Universita Toscane
Ann Allergy — Annals of Allergy
Ann Allergy Asthma Immunol — Annals of Allergy, Asthma, and Immunology
Annal Mid — Annales du Midi. Revue de la France Meridionale
Annals — Annals. American Academy of Political and Social Science
Annals Air and Space — Annals of Air and Space Law
Annals Air and Space L — Annals of Air and Space Law
Annals Am Acad — Annals. American Academy of Political and Social Science
Annals and Mag Nat History — Annals and Magazine of Natural History
Annal Sclavo Monogr — Annali Sclavo Monograph
Annals General Prac — Annals of General Practice
Annals Gen Pract — Annals of General Practice
Annals Internat Studies — Annals of International Studies
Annals KY Nat History — Annals of Kentucky Natural History
Annals Lib Sci — Annals of Library Science
Annals Math Log — Annals of Mathematical Logic
Annals Occup Hyg — Annals of Occupational Hygiene
Annals of A A — Annals of Archaeology and Anthropology
Annals of Gen Prac — Annals of General Practice
Annals Ophthal Otol — Annals of Ophthalmology and Otology
Annals Otol Rhinol Laryngol — Annals of Otology, Rhinology, and Laryngology
Annals Phys Orlando Fl — Annals of Physics (Orlando, Florida)
Annals Public and Coop Economy — Annals of Public and Cooperative Economy
Annal Stud Giurid Socio Econ Serv Sanit Naz Reg — Annali di Studi Giuridici e Socio-Economici sui Servizii Sanitari Nazionale e Regionale
Annaly Biol — Annaly Biologii
Annaly Mechnik Inst Kharkiv — Annaly. Mechnikovskii Institu (Kharkiv)
Ann Am Acad — Annals. American Academy of Political and Social Science
Ann Am Acad Poli Soc Sci — Annals. American Academy of Political and Social Science
Ann Am Acad Polit Social Sci — Annals. American Academy of Political and Social Sciences
Ann Am Acad Pol Sci — Annals. American Academy of Political and Social Science
Ann Am Acad Pol Soc Sci (Philadelphia) — Annals. American Academy of Political and Social Science (Philadelphia)
Annamalai Univ Agric Res Annu — Annamalai University. Agricultural Research Annual
Ann Am Conf Gov Ind Hyg — Annals. American Conference of Governmental Industrial Hygienists
Ann Amelior Pl — Annales. Amelioration des Plantes. Institut National de la Recherche Agronomique
Ann Amelior Plantes — Annales de l'Amelioration des Plantes
Ann Amelior Plantes Inst Nat Rech Agron Ser B — Annales de l'Amelioration des Plantes. Institut National de la Recherche Agronomique. Serie B
Ann Amelior Plant (Paris) — Annales de l'Amelioration des Plantes (Paris)
Ann Amer Acad Polit Soc Sci — Annals. American Academy of Political and Social Science
Ann Am Poli — Annals. American Academy of Political and Social Science
Ann Anat — Annals of Anatomy
Ann Anat Pathol — Annales d'Anatomie Pathologique
Ann Anat Pathol Anat Norm Med Chir — Annales d'Anatomie Pathologique et d'Anatomie Normale. Medico Chirurgicale
Ann Anat Pathol (Paris) — Annales d'Anatomie Pathologique (Paris)
Ann and Mag Nat Hist — Annals and Magazine of Natural History
Ann Anesthesiol Fr — Annales de l'Anesthesiologie Francaise
Ann Anim Ps — Annales of Animal Psychology
Ann Ant Jord — Annual. Department of Antiquities of Jordon
Ann Ap Biol — Annals of Applied Biology
Ann A Plant — Annales de l'Amelioration des Plantes
Ann App Biol — Annals of Applied Biology
Ann Appl Biol — Annals of Applied Biology
Ann Appl Biol Suppl — Annals of Applied Biology. Supplement
Ann Appl Nematol — Annals of Applied Nematology
Ann Appl Probab — Annals of Applied Probability
An Naprstek Mus — Annals of the Naprstek Museum
Ann Arbor Obs — Ann Arbor Observer
Ann Arch — Annales Archeologiques
Ann Arch Anthr Liverpool — Annals of Archaeology and Anthropology (Liverpool)
Ann Arch Brux — Annales. Societe Royale d'Archeologie de Bruxelles
Ann Archeol Syrie — Annales Archeologiques de Syrie
Ann Arch Syr — Annales Archeologiques Syrie
Ann Arid Zone — Annals of Arid Zone
Ann As Am G — Annals. Association of American Geographers
Ann Ass Amer Geogr — Annals. Association of American Geographers
Ann Ass Am Geogr — Annals. Association of American Geographers
Ann Ass Int Calcul Analogique — Annales. Association Internationale pour le Calcul Analogique
Ann Assn Am Geog — Annals. Association of American Geographers
Ann Assoc Amer Geogr — Annals. Association of American Geographers
Ann Assoc Am Geogr — Annals. Association of American Geographers
Ann Assoc Belge Radioprot — Annales. Association Belge de Radioprotection
Ann Assoc Can Fr Av Sci — Annals. Association Canadienne-Francaise pour l'Avancement des Sciences

Ann Assoc Int Calcul Analogique — Annales. Association Internationale pour le Calcul Analogique
Ann Assoc Philom Vogeso Rhenane — Annales. Association Philomatique Vogeso-Rhenane, Faisant Suite a la Flore d'Alsace de F. Kirschleger
Ann Assur Sci Proc Reliab Maint Conf — Annals of Assurance Sciences. Proceedings of Reliability and Maintainability Conference
Ann A Stor Ant — Annali. Seminario di Studi del Mondo Classico. Sezione di Archeologia e Storia Antica
Ann Astrophys — Annales d'Astrophysique
Ann Astrophys Suppl — Annales d'Astrophysique. Supplement
Ann A Syr — Annales Archeologiques Arabes Syriennes
An Natal Mus — Annals of the Natal Museum
An Natphilos — Annalen der Naturphilosophie
Ann Aust Coll Dent Surg — Annals. Australian College of Dental Surgeons
Ann Bad Gerichte — Annalen der Badischen Gerichte
Ann Bari — Annali. Facolta di Lettere e Filosofia. Universita di Bari
Ann Bar-Il — Annual. Bar-Ilan University Studies in Judaica and Humanities
Ann Behav Med — Annals of Behavioral Medicine
Ann Belg Med Mil — Annales Belges de Medecine Militaire
Ann Belg Ver Hosp — Annalen Belg Vereniging voor Hospitaalgeschiedenis
Ann Belg Ver Stralingsbescherming — Annalen van de Belgische Vereniging voor Stralingsbescherming
Ann Belg Ver Trop Geneeskd — Annales. Belgische Vereniging voor Tropische Geneeskunde
Ann Belg Ver Trop Geneeskd Parasitol Mensel Dierl Mycol — Annales. Belgische Verenigingen voor Tropische Geneeskunde voor Parasitologie en voor Menselijke en Dierlijke Mycologie
Ann Benac — Annali Benacensi
Ann Bhandarkar Orient Res Inst — Annals of the Bhandarkar Oriental Research Institute
AnnBhl — Annals. Bhandarkar Oriental Research Institute
Ann Biochem Exp Med — Annals of Biochemistry and Experimental Medicine
Ann Biochem Exp Med (Calcutta) — Annals of Biochemistry and Experimental Medicine (Calcutta and New Delhi)
Ann Biochim Clin Que — Annales de Biochimie Clinique du Quebec
Ann Biol — Annales Biologiques
Ann Biol An — Annales de Biologie Animale, Biochimie, et Biophysique
Ann Biol Anim Biochim Biophys — Annales de Biologie Animale, Biochimie, et Biophysique
Ann Biol Cl — Annales de Biologie Clinique
Ann Biol Clin (Paris) — Annales de Biologie Clinique (Paris)
Ann Biol Cons Perm Int Explor Mer — Annales Biologiques. Conseil Permanent International pour l'Exploration de la Mer
Ann Biol (Copenhagen) — Annales Biologiques (Copenhagen)
Ann Biol Lacustre — Annales de Biologie Lacustre
Ann Biol (Ludhiana) — Annals of Biology (Ludhiana)
Ann Biol Moscow — Annaly Biologii. Moskovskoe Obscestvo Ispytatelej Prirody. Sekcijo Istorii Estestvoznanija (Moscow)
Ann Biol Norm Pathol — Annali Biologia Normale e Pathologica
Ann Biol Univ Hungariae — Annales Biologicae Universitatum Hungariae. A Magyar Tudomanyegyejetenek Biologiai Intezeteinek Evkoenyve
Ann Biomed — Annals of Biomedical Engineering
Ann Biomed Eng — Annals of Biomedical Engineering
Ann Blumisterei Gartenbesitz — Annalen der Blumisterei fuer Gartenbesitzer, Kunstgaertner, Samenhaendler, und Blumenfreunde
Ann Bogor — Annales Bogoriensis
Ann Bot — Annals of Botany
Ann Bot Fenn — Annales Botanici Fennici
Ann Bot Genoa — Annali di Botanica (Genoa)
Ann Bot (London) — Annals of Botany (London)
Ann Bot (Rome) — Annali di Botanica (Rome)
Ann Bot Soc Canada — Annals. Botanical Society of Canada
Ann Bot Soc Zool Bot Fenn "Vanamo" — Annales Botanici Societatis Zoologicae Botanicae Fennicae "Vanamo"
Ann Bot Syst — Annales Botanicae Systematicae
AnnBourg — Annales de Bourgogne
Ann Bourgogne — Annales de Bourgogne
Ann Bras Gynecol — Annaes Brasileiros de Gynecologia
Ann Brass Distill — Annales de la Brasserie et de la Distillerie
Ann Bret — Annales de Bretagne [Later, Annales de Bretagne et des Pays de l'Ouest]
Ann Bretagne — Annales de Bretagne et des Pays de l'Ouest
Ann Bretagne Pays Ouest — Annales de Bretagne et des Pays de l'Ouest
Ann Br Sch Ath — Annual. British School at Athens
Ann Br Sch Athens — Annual. British School at Athens
Ann Brux 1 — Annales. Societe Scientifique de Bruxelles. Serie 1
Ann Bryol — Annales Bryologici. A Yearbook Devoted to the Study of Mosses and Hepatics
Ann B S Arch Ath — Annual. British School of Archaeology at Athens
Ann Bul Hist Lit — Annual Bulletin of Historical Literature. Historical Association
Ann Bull Soc Med Anvers — Annales et Bulletin. Societe de Medecine d'Anvers
Ann Bull Soc Med Gand — Annales et Bulletin. Societe de Medecine de Gand
Ann Bull Soc R Med Gand — Annales et Bulletin. Societe Royale de Medecine de Gand
Ann Bull Soc R Sci Med Nat Bruxelles — Annales et Bulletin. Societe Royale des Sciences Medicales et Naturelles de Bruxelles
Ann Bus Surv Mens Store Op Exp — Annual Business Survey. Men's Store Operating Experiences
Ann Byz Conf — Annual Byzantine Studies Conference. Abstracts of Papers
Ann Cagliari — Annali. Facolta di Lettere, Filosofia, e Magistero. Universita di Cagliari
Ann Cape Prov Mus — Annals. Cape Provincial Museums
Ann Cape Prov Mus Hum Sci — Annals. Cape Provincial Museums. Human Sciences

Ann Cape Prov Mus Nat Hist — Annals. Cape Provincial Museums. Natural History

Ann Card An — Annales de Cardiologie et d'Angeiologie

Ann Cardiol Angeiol — Annales de Cardiologie et d'Angeiologie

Ann Carnegie Mus — Annals. Carnegie Museum

Ann Cattedra Petrarchesca — Annali. Cattedra Petrarchesca. Reale Accademia Petrarca di Lettere, Arti, e Scienze. Arezzo

Ann Cent Enseignement Sup Brazzaville — Annales du Centre d'Enseignement Superieur de Brazzaville

Ann Cent Enseign Super Brazzaville — Annales. Centre d'Enseignement Superieur de Brazzaville

Ann Cent Rech Agron Bambey Senegal — Annales. Centre de Recherches Agronomiques de Bambey au Senegal

Ann Centre Etude Evol HommeNat — Annales. Centre d'Etude sur l'Evolution de l'Homme et de la Nature

Ann Cerc Archeol Canton Soignies — Annales. Cercle Archeologique du Canton de Soignies

Ann Cerc Archeol Enghien — Annales. Cercle Archeologique d'Enghien

Ann Cerc Archeol Mons — Annales. Cercle Archeologique de Mons

Ann Cercle Archeol Enghien — Annales. Cercle Archeologique d'Enghien

Ann Chambre Cent Poids Mes — Annales. Chambre Centrale des Poids et Mesures

Ann Chem — Annalen der Chemie

Ann Chem — Liebigs Annalen der Chemie

Ann Chem (Justus Liebigs) — Annalen der Chemie (Justus Liebigs)

Ann Chem Pharm — Annalen der Chemie und Pharmacie

Ann Chim — Annali di Chimica

Ann Chim Anal — Annales de Chimie Analytique

Ann Chim Anal Chim Appl — Annales de Chimie Analytique et de Chimie Applique et Revue de Chimie Analytique Reunies

Ann Chim Anal Rev Chim Anal Reunies — Annales de Chimie Analytique et Revue de Chimie Analytique Reunies

Ann Chim Appl — Annali di Chimica Applicata

Ann Chim Appl Farm — Annali di Chimica Applicata alla Farmacia ed alla Medicina

Ann Chim Appl Med — Annali di Chimica Applicata alla Medicina Cioe alla Farmacia

Ann Chim Athens A — Annales Chimiques (Athens). Section A

Ann Chim Athens B — Annales Chimiques (Athens). Section B

Ann Chim Farm — Annali di Chimica Farmaceutica

Ann Chim (Fr) — Annales de Chimie (Paris, France)

Ann Chim (Istanbul) — Annales de Chimie (Istanbul)

Ann Chim (Paris) — Annales de Chimie (Paris, France)

Ann Chim Phys — Annales de Chimie et de Physique

Ann Chim (Rome) — Annali di Chimica (Rome)

Ann Chir — Annales de Chirurgie

Ann Chir Gy — Annales Chirurgiae et Gynaecologiae Fenniae

Ann Chir Gynaecol — Annales Chirurgiae et Gynaecologiae

Ann Chir Gynaecol — Annales Chirurgiae et Gynaecologiae Fenniae

Ann Chir Gynaecol Fenn — Annales Chirurgiae et Gynaecologiae Fonniae

Ann Chir Gynaecol Fenn Suppl — Annales Chirurgiae et Gynaecologiae Fenniae. Supplementum

Ann Chir Gynaecol Suppl — Annales Chirurgiae et Gynaecologiae Fenniae. Supplementum

Ann Chir Gynaecol Suppl — Annales Chirurgiae et Gynaecologiae. Supplementum

Ann Chir In — Annales de Chirurgie Infantile

Ann Chir Infant — Annales de Chirurgie Infantile

Ann Chir Main — Annales de Chirurgie de la Main

Ann Chir Main Memb Super — Annales de Chirurgie de la Main et du Membre Superieur

Ann Chir (Paris) — Annales de Chirurgie (Paris)

Ann Chir Pl — Annales de Chirurgie Plastique

Ann Chir Plast — Annales de Chirurgie Plastique

Ann Chir Plast Esthet — Annales de Chirurgie Plastique et Esthetique

Ann Chir Plast Esthetique — Annales de Chirurgie Plastique et Esthetique

Ann Chir Sem Hop — Annales de Chirurgie. Semaine des Hopitaux

Ann Chir Thorac Cardio-Vasc — Annales de Chirurgie Thoracique et Cardio-Vasculaire

Ann CIRP — Annals of the CIRP

Ann Cisalp Hist Soc — Annales Cisalpines d'Histoire Sociale

Ann Civili Regno Due Sicilie — Annali Civili del Regno Delle Due Sicilie

Ann Clin Biochem — Annals of Clinical Biochemistry

Ann Clin Lab Sci — Annals of Clinical and Laboratory Science

Ann Clin Med — Annals of Clinical Medicine

Ann Clin Med Med Sper — Annali di Clinica Medica e di Medicina Sperimentale

Ann Clin Psychiatry — Annals of Clinical Psychiatry

Ann Clin R — Annals of Clinical Research

Ann Clin Res — Annals of Clinical Research

Ann Clin Res Suppl — Annals of Clinical Research. Supplement

Ann Coll — Annuaire. College de France

Ann Coll Int Etude Sci Tech Prod Mec — Annales. College International pour l'Etude Scientifique des Techniques de Production Mecanique

Ann Coll Med Antwerp — Annales Collegii Medici Antwerpiensis

Ann Coll Med (Mosul) — Annals. College of Medicine (Mosul)

Ann Coll R Med Chir Can — Annales. College Royal des Medecins et Chirurgiens du Canada

Ann Comm Orient Educ — Annals of Community-Oriented Education

Ann Compos — Annales des Composites

Ann Conf Health Inspectors NSW — Annual Conference of Health Inspectors of New South Wales

Ann Conf Proc Am Prod Inv Cont Soc — Annual Conference Proceedings. American Production and Inventory Control Society

Ann Conf Proc Theme Ses Road Transp Assoc Can — Annual Conference Proceedings. Theme Sessions. Roads and Transportation Association of Canada

Ann Conf Proc Trav Res Assoc — Annual Conference Proceedings. Travel Research Association

Ann Conf Res Med Ed — Annual Conference on Research in Medical Education

Ann Congr Federation Archeol Hist Belg — Annales. Congres de la Federation Archeologique et Historique de Belgique

Ann Corp Prof Comp Gen Lic Quebec — Annuaire. Corporation Professionnelle des Comptables Generaux Licenciesdu Quebec

Ann Cryptogam Exot — Annales de Cryptogamie Exotique

Ann Cryptogam Phytopathol — Annales Cryptogamici et Phytopathologici

Ann Cryptog Exot — Annales de Cryptogamie Exotique

Ann Czech Acad Agric — Annals. Czechoslovak Academy of Agriculture

Ann D A (J) — Annual. Department of Antiquities (Jordan)

Ann Dakar Univ Fac Sci — Annales. Dakar Universite. Faculte des Sciences

Ann de Bourgogne — Annales de Bourgogne

Ann de Bret — Annales de Bretagne [Later, Annales de Bretagne et des Pays de l'Ouest]

Ann de Droit — Annales de Droit. Revue Trimestrielle de Droit Belge

Ann de Droit Internat Med — Annales de Droit International Medical

Ann de la Fac de Droit de Liege — Annales. Faculte de Droit de Liege

Ann de la Fac de Droit d'Istanbul — Annales. Faculte de Droit d'Istanbul

Ann de la Fac de Droit et des Sci Econ (Beyrouth) — Annales. Faculte de Droit et des Sciences Economiques

Ann de la Fac de Droit et des Sci Econ de Lille — Annales. Faculte de Droit et des Sciences Economiques de Lille, France

Ann Della Univ Bari — Annali del Seminario Giuridico-Economico della Reale Universita di Bari

Ann Della Univ Palermo — Annali del Seminario Giuridico della Reale Universita di Palermo

Ann Delle Univ Toscane — Annali delle Universita Toscane

Ann Dell Osped Psichiat Di Messina — Annali dell'Ospedale Psichiatrico di Messina

Ann Dell Osped Psichiat Di Perugia — Annali dell'Ospedale Psichiatrico di Perugia

Ann de Med Belge — Annales de Medecine Belge et Etrangere

Ann De Med Leg — Annales de Medecine Legale, de Criminologie, et de Police Scientifique

Ann Dem Hist — Annales de Demographie Historique

Ann Demogr Hist — Annales de Demographie Historique

Ann Dent — Annals of Dentistry

Ann Dermatol Syphiligr — Annales de Dermatologie et de Syphiligraphie [Later, Annales de Dermatologie et de Venereologie]

Ann Dermatol Venereol — Annales de Dermatologie et de Venereologie

Ann Der Syp — Annales de Dermatologie et de Syphiligraphie [Later, Annales de Dermatologie et de Venereologie]

Ann Des Falsif Et Des Fraudes — Annales des Falsifications et des Fraudes

Ann Des Mal Ven — Annales des Maladies Veneriennes

Ann Dev — Annals of Development

AnnDG — Richters Annalen der Deutschen Geschichte

Ann Diagn Pathol — Annals of Diagnostic Pathology

Ann Di Clin Med — Annali di Clinica Medica

Ann Differential Equations — Annals of Differential Equations

Ann Di Neurol — Annali di Neurologia

Ann d Inst — Annali. Instituto di Corrispondenza Archeologica

Ann Dir Comp — Annuario di Diritto Comparato e di Studi Legislativi

Ann Dir Etud Equip Ser Exploit Ind Tab Allumettes Sec 1 — Annales. Direction des Etudes et de l'Equipement. Service d'Exploitation Industrielle des Tabacs et des Allumettes. Section 1

Ann Dir Etud Equip Serv Exploit Ind Tab Allumettes Sec 2 — Annales. Direction des Etudes et de l'Equipement. Service d'Exploitation Industrielle des Tabacs et des Allumettes. Section 2

Ann Dir Int — Annali di Diritto Internazionale

Ann Discrete Math — Annals of Discrete Mathematics

Ann Dog Watch — Annual Dog Watch

Ann Dr — Annales de Droit

Ann Dr Com Fr Etr Int — Annales de Droit Commercial Francais, Etranger, et International

Ann Dr Com Ind Fr Etr — Annales de Droit Commercial et Industriel Francais, Etranger, et International

Ann Dr et Sc Polit — Annales de Droit et de Sciences Politiques

Ann Dr Liege — Annales. Faculte de Droit de Liege

Ann Droit Int Med — Annales de Droit International Medical

Ann Dr Sc Pol — Annales de Droit et de Sciences Politiques. Revue Trimestrielle

Ann Dr Sc Polit — Annales de Droit et de Sciences Politiques

Ann d R Scuol Arch Aten Miss Ital Oriente — Annuario. Scuola Archeologica di Atene e delle Missioni Italiani in Oriente

Ann Dt Reich — Annalen des Deutschen Reiches

Ann Durban Mus — Annales. Durban Museum

Ann du Serv — Annales. Service des Antiquites de l'Egypt

Ann du Service des Ant — Annales. Service des Antiquites de l'Egypt

Ann Ec Fr Dr Beyrouth — Annales. Faculte de Droit. Ecole Francaise de Droit de Beyrouth

Ann Ec Natl Agric Alger — Annales. Ecole Nationale d'Agriculture d'Alger

Ann Ec Natl Agric Montpellier — Annales. Ecole Nationale d'Agriculture de Montpellier

Ann Ec Natl Eaux For Stn Rech Exper For — Annales. Ecole Nationale des Eaux et Forets et de la Station de Recherches et Experiences Forestieres

Ann Ec Natl Super Agron (Montpellier) — Annales. Ecole Nationale Superieure Agronomique (Montpellier)

Ann Ec Natl Super Geol Appl Prospect Min Univ Nancy — Annales. Ecole Nationale Superieure de Geologie Appliquee et de Prospection Miniere. Universite de Nancy

Ann Ecole Nat Agr Alger — Annales. Ecole Nationale d'Agriculture d'Alger

Ann Ecole Natl Agric Rennes — Annales. Ecole Nationale d'Agriculture de Rennes

Ann Ecole Natl Super Agron Toulouse — Annales. Ecole Nationale Superieure Agronomique de Toulouse

Ann Ecole Nat Super Agron — Annales. Ecole Nationale Superieure Agronomique
Ann Ecole Nat Sup Mec (Nantes) — Annales. Ecole Nationale Superieure de Mecanique (Nantes)
Ann Econ — Annales de Droit Economique
Ann Econ — Annales Economiques
Ann Econom Coll — Annales d'Economie Collective
Ann Econom Statist — Annales d'Economie et de Statistique
Ann Econ Rep Nebraska — Annual Economic Report. Nebraska
Ann Econ Sm — Annals of Economic and Social Measurement
Ann Econ So — Annales d'Economie et de Sociologie Rurales
Ann Econ Soc Civ — Annales: Economies, Societes, Civilisations
Ann Econ Soc Civiliations — Annales. Economies, Societes, Civillizations
Ann Econ Soc Civilis — Annales: Economies, Societes, Civilisations
Ann Ec Polytech Budapest — Annales. Ecole Polytechnique. Budapest
Ann Ec Pr — Annuaire. Ecole Pratique des Hautes Etudes
Ann Ec Pr — Annuaire. Ecole Pratique des Hautes Etudes. V Section. Sciences Religieuses
Ann Ec Prat HEt — Annuaire. Ecole Pratique des Hautes Etudes, IVeme Section
Ann Ec R Super Agric Suede — Annales. Ecole Royale Superieure d'Agriculture de la Suede
Ann Ec Sci Univ Abidjan — Annales. Ecole des Sciences. Universite d'Abidjan
Ann Ec Super Agric Suede — Annales. Ecole Superieure d'Agriculture de la Suede
Ann Ec Super Mines Oural Ekatherinebourg — Annales. Ecole Superieure des Mines de l'Oural a Ekatherinebourg
Ann Ec Super Sci Inst Hautes Etud (Dakar) — Annales. Ecole Superieure des Sciences. Institut des Hautes Etudes (Dakar)
Ann Ed Read Anthro — Annual Editions. Readings in Anthropology
Ann Ed Read Educ — Annual Editions. Readings in Education
Ann Ed Read H — Annual Editions. Readings in Health
Ann Ed Read Mar Fam — Annual Editions. Readings in Marriage and Family
Ann Ed Read Soc — Annual Editions. Readings in Sociology
Annee Aeronaut — Annee Aeronautique
Annee Afr — Annee Africaine
Annee Agr — Annee Agricole
Annee Biol — Annee Biologique
Annee Biol (Paris) — Annee Biologique (Paris)
Annee Cardiol Int — Annee Cardiologique Internationale
Annee Cartogr — Annee Cartographique
Annee Clin — Annee Clinique
Annee Elect Electrother Radiogr — Annee Electrique, Electrotherapique, et Radiographique
Annee Electroradiol — Annee Electro-Radiologique
Annee Endocr — Annee Endocrinologique
Annee Endocrinol — Annee Endocrinologique
Annee Ep — Annee Epigraphique
Annee Epig — Annee Epigraphique. Revue des Publications Epigraphiques Relatives a l'Antiquite Romaine
Annee Epigr — Annee Epigraphique. Revue des Publications Epigraphiques Relatives a l'Antiquite Romaine
Annee Ferrov — Annee Ferroviaire
Annee For — Annee Forestiere
Annee Geophys Int — Annee Geophysique Internationale
Annee Med — Annee Medicale
Annee Med Chir — Annee Medico-Chirurgicale
Annee Obstet — Annee Obstetricale
Annee Odonto Stomat Maxillo Fac — Annee Odonto-Stomatologique et Maxillo-Faciale
Annee Pedagog — Annee Pedagogique
Annee Pediat — Annee Pediatrique
Annee Pharm — Annee Pharmaceutique
Annee Phil — Annee Philosophique
Annee Polit Econ — Annee Politique et Economique
Annee Psychol — Annee Psychologique
Annees Acad Sci Besancon — Annees. Academie des Sciences, Belles-Lettres, et Arts de Besancon
Annee Scient Ind — Annee Scientifique et Industrielle
Annee Sociol — Annee Sociologique
Annee Tech — Annee Technique
Annee Ther — Annee Therapeutique
Annee Ther Clin Ophtalmol — Annee Therapeutique et Clinique en Ophtalmologie
Ann Eg Bibl — Annual Egyptological Bibliography
Ann Egypt Bib — Annual Egyptological Bibliography
Ann Embryol Morphog — Annales d'Embryologie et de Morphogenese
Ann Emerg Med — Annals of Emergency Medicine
Ann Endocr — Annales d'Endocrinologie
Ann Endocrinol — Annales d'Endocrinologie
Ann Endocrinol (Paris) — Annales d'Endocrinologie (Paris)
Ann Ent Fenn — Annales Entomologici Fennici
Ann Entomol Fenn — Annales Entomologici Fennici
Ann Entomol Soc Am — Annals. Entomological Society of America
Ann Entomol Soc Que — Annals. Entomological Society of Quebec
Ann Entom Soc Am — Annals. Entomological Society of America
Ann Ent S A — Annals. Entomological Society of America
Ann Ent Soc Am — Annals. Entomological Society of America
Ann Ent Soc Queb — Annals. Entomological Society of Quebec
Ann Eoetvoes — Annales. Universitatis Scientiarum Budapestinensis de Rolando Eoetvoes Nominatae
AnnEp — L'Annee Epigraphique
Ann EPH Et — Annuaire. Ecole Pratique des Hautes Etudes. IV Section. Sciences Philologiques et Historiques
Ann Epidemiol — Annals of Epidemiology
Ann Epigr — Annee Epigraphique
Ann Epiphyt — Annales des Epiphyties
Ann Epiphyt (Paris) — Annales des Epiphyties (Paris)

Ann Epiphyt Phytogenet — Annales des Epiphyties et de Phytogenetique
Ann Erd Voelker Staatenk — Annalen der Erd-, Voelker- und Staatenkunde
Ann ESC — Annales. Economies, Societes, Civilisations
Ann Est — Annales de l'Est
Ann Esth — Annales d'Esthetique
AnnEth — Annales d'Ethiopie
Ann Ethiopie — Annales d'Ethiopie
Ann Eugen — Annals of Eugenics
Ann Eur — Annuaire Europeen
An Neurocirug — Anales de Neurocirugia
An Neuropsiquiat — Anales Neuropsiquatricos
Ann Eur Phys Veg Econ Publique — Annales Europeennes de Physique Vegetale et d'Economie Publique
Annexe Bull Inst Int Froid — Annexe au Bulletin. Institut International de Froid
Ann Exp For — Annales pro Experimentis Foresticis
Ann FA Belg — Annales. Federation Archeologique et Historique de Belgique
Ann Fac Agrar Portici Regia Univ Napoli — Annali. Facolta di Agraria di Portici. Regia Universita di Napoli
Ann Fac Agrar Regia Univ Pisa — Annali. Facolta di Agraria. Regia Universita di Pisa
Ann Fac Agrar Univ Bari — Annali. Facolta di Agraria. Universita di Bari
Ann Fac Agrar Univ Catt Sacro Cuore — Annali. Facolta di Agraria. Universita Cattolica del Sacro Cuore
Ann Fac Agrar Univ Pisa — Annali. Facolta di Agraria. Universita di Pisa
Ann Fac Agrar Univ Studi Milano — Annali. Facolta di Agraria. Universita degli Studi di Milano
Ann Fac Agrar Univ Stud Perugia — Annali. Facolta di Agraria. Universita degli Studi di Perugia
Ann Fac Agron Univ Sci Agric — Annales Facultatis Agronomicae Universitatis Scientiae Agriculturae
Ann Fac Agr (Perugia) — Annali. Facolta di Agraria (Perugia)
Ann Fac Agr Univ Cattol Sacro Cuore (Milan) — Annali. Facolta di Agraria. Universita Cattolica del Sacro Cuore (Milan)
Ann Fac Agr Univ Pisa — Annali. Facolta di Agraria. Universita di Pisa
Ann Fac Agr Univ Studii Perugia — Annali. Facolta di Agraria. Universita degli Studi di Perugia
Ann Fac Bari — Annali. Facolta di Giurisprudenza. Universita di Bari
Ann Fac Beyrouth — Annales. Faculte de Droit et des Sciences Economiques de Beyrouth. Faculte de Droit
Ann Fac De Med De Sao Paulo — Annales de Faculdade de Medicina de Sao Paulo
Ann Fac Dr L — Annales. Faculte de Droit de Liege
Ann Fac Droit Univ Natn Zaire — Annales. Faculte de Droit. Universite Nationale du Zaire
Ann Fac Econ Commer Univ Bari — Annali. Facolta di Economia e Commercio. Universita di Bari
Ann Fac Econ Commer Univ Studi Mesina — Annali. Facolta di Economia e Commercio. Universita degli Studi di Messina
Ann Fac For Univ Belgrade — Annales. Faculte Forestiere. Universite de Belgrade
Ann Fac Istanbul — Annales. Faculte de Droit d'Istanbul
Ann Fac Lettere Univ Cagliari — Annali. Facolta di Lettere, Filosofia, e Magistero. Universita di Cagliari
Ann Fac Lett et Sci Hum — Annales. Faculte des Lettres et Sciences Humaines de Yaounde
Ann Fac Lett Fil Magist Univ Cagliari — Annali. Facolta di Letter Filosofia e Magistero. Universita di Cagliari
Ann Fac Lett Filosof — Annali. Facolta di Lettere e Filosofia
Ann Fac Lett Filos Univ Padova — Annali. Facolta di Lettere e Filosofia. Universita di Padova
Ann Fac Lett Fil Univ Napoli — Annali. Facolta di Lettere Filosofia. Universita di Napoli
Ann Fac Lettres et Sci Hum Univ Dakar — Annales. Faculte des Lettres et Sciences Humaines. Universite de Dakar
Ann Fac Lett Sci Humaines Aix — Annales. Faculte des Lettres et Sciences Humaines d'Aix
Ann Fac Liege — Annales. Faculte de Droit de Liege
Ann Fac Lyon — Annales. Faculte de Droit et des Sciences Economiques de Lyon
Ann Fac Med Chir Univ Studi Perugia Atti Accad Anat Chir — Annali. Facolta di Medicina e Chirurgia. Universita degli Studi di Perugia che Pubblicano gli Atti della Accademia Anatomico-Chirurgica
Ann Fac Med Chirurg — Annali. Facolta di Medicina e Chirurgia
Ann Fac Med Pharm Univ Natl Zaire — Annales. Faculte de Medecine et de Pharmacie. Universite Nationale du Zaire
Ann Fac Med S Paulo — Annales. Faculdade de Medicina de Sao Paulo
Ann Fac Med Univ Sao Paulo — Annaes. Faculdade de Medicina. Universidade de Sao Paulo
Ann Fac Med Vet Pisa Univ Studi Pisa — Annali. Facolta di Medicina Veterinaria di Pisa. Universita degli Studi di Pisa
Ann Fac Med Vet Torino — Annali. Facolta di Medicina Veterinaria di Torino
Ann Fac Med Vet Univ Pisa — Annali. Facolta di Medicina Veterinaria. Universita di Pisa
Ann Fac Med Vet Univ Studi Pisa — Annali. Facolta di Medicina Veterinaria. Universita degli Studi di Pisa
Ann Fac Med Vet Univ Torino — Annali. Facolta di Medicina Veterinaria. Universita di Torino
Ann Fac Sci Agrar Napoli (Portici) — Annali. Facolta di Scienze Agrarie. Universita degli Studi di Napoli (Portici)
Ann Fac Sci Agrar Univ Palermo — Annali. Facolta di Scienze Agrarie. Universita di Palermo
Ann Fac Sci Agrar Univ Studi Napoli (Portici) — Annali. Facolta di Scienze Agrarie. Universita degli Studi di Napoli (Portici)
Ann Fac Sci Agrar Univ Studi Torino — Annali. Facolta di Scienze Agrarie. Universita degli Studi di Torino
Ann Fac Sci Agr Univ Napoli Ser 3 — Annali. Facolta di Scienze Agrarie. Universita di Napoli. Serie 3

Ann Fac Sci Agr Univ Stud Napoli (Portici) — Annali. Facolta di Scienze Agrarie. Universita degli Studi di Napoli (Portici)

Ann Fac Sci Agr Univ Torino — Annali. Facolta di Scienze Agrarie. Universita di Torino

Ann Fac Sci Cameroun — Annales. Faculte des Sciences du Cameroun

Ann Fac Sci Mars — Annales. Faculte des Sciences de Marseille

Ann Fac Sci Marseille — Annales. Faculte des Sciences de Marseille

Ann Fac Sci Polit Univ Studi Perugia NS — Annali. Facolta di Scienze Poltiche ed Economia e Commercio. Universita degli Studi di Perugia. NS

Ann Fac Sci Sect Biol Chim Sci Terre Univ Kinshasa — Annales. Faculte des Sciences. Section Biologie. Chimie et Sciences de la Terre. Universite de Kinshasa

Ann Fac Sci Sect Biol Chim Sci Terre (Univ Natl Zaire) — Annales. Faculte des Sciences. Section Biologie, Chimie, et Sciences de la Terre (Universite Nationale du Zaire)

Ann Fac Sci Toulouse Math — Annales. Faculte des Sciences de Toulouse. Mathematiques

Ann Fac Sci Toulouse Math 6 — Toulouse Faculte des Sciences. Annales. Mathematiques. Serie 6

Ann Fac Sci Toulouse Math Ser 5 — Toulouse. Faculte des Sciences. Annales Mathematiques. Serie 5

Ann Fac Sci Univ Abidjan — Annales. Faculte des Sciences. Universite d'Abidjan

Ann Fac Sci Univ Clermont — Annales. Faculte des Sciences. Universite de Clermont

Ann Fac Sci Univ Clermont Ser Biol Anim — Annales. Faculte des Sciences. Universite de Clermont. Serie Biologie Animale

Ann Fac Sci Univ Dakar — Annales. Faculte des Sciences. Universite de Dakar

Ann Fac Sci Univ Nat Zaire (Kinshasa) Sect Math-Phys — Annales. Faculte des Sciences. Universite Nationale du Zaire (Kinshasa). Section Mathematique-Physique

Ann Fac Sci Univ Saigon — Annales. Faculte des Sciences. Universite de Saigon

Ann Fac Sci Univ Toulouse — Annales. Faculte des Sciences. Universite de Toulouse

Ann Fac Sci Univ Toulouse Sci Math Sci Phys — Annales. Faculte des Sciences. Universite de Toulouse pour les Sciences Mathematiques et les Sciences Physiques

Ann Fac Sci Univ Yaounde Ser 3 — Annales. Faculte des Sciences. Universite de Yaounde. Serie 3. Biologie-Biochimie

Ann Fac Sci Yaounde — Annales. Faculte des Sciences. Universite de Yaounde

Ann Fals Expert Chim — Annales des Falsifications et de l'Expertise Chimique

Ann Falsif — Annales des Falsifications

Ann Falsif Expert Chim — Annales des Falsifications et de l'Expertise Chimique [*Later, Annales des Falsifications et de l'Expertise Chimique et Toxicologique*]

Ann Falsif Expert Chim Toxicol — Annales des Falsifications et de l'Expertise Chimique et Toxicologique

Ann Falsif Expertise Chim — Annales des Falsifications et de l'Expertise Chimique [*Later, Annales des Falsifications et de l'Expertise Chimique et Toxicologique*]

Ann Falsif Fraudes — Annales des Falsifications et des Fraudes [*Later, Annales des Falsifications et de l'Expertise Chimique*]

Ann Farmacot Chim — Annali di Farmacoterapia c Chimica

Ann Ferment — Annales des Fermentations

Ann Finan Rep Michigan — Annual Financial Report. State of Michigan

Ann Finan Rep Oregon — Annual Financial Report. State of Oregon

Ann Finan Rep Rep Op Pub Emp Ret Sys Calif — Annual Financial Report and Report of Operations. Public Employees' Retirement System. California

Ann Fin Rep Baltimore — Annual Financial Report. City of Baltimore, Maryland

Ann Fis — Annali di Fisica

Ann Fitopatol — Annali di Fitopatologia

Ann Fogg — Annual Report. Fogg Art Museum

Ann Fond Louis Broglie — Annales. Fondation Louis de Broglie

Ann Fond Louis de Broglie — Annales. Fondation Louis de Broglie

Ann Fond Luigi Einaudi — Annali della Fondazione Luigi Einaudi

Ann Fond Oceanogr Ricard Vie Mar — Annales. Fondation Oceanographique Ricard. Vie Marine

Ann Food Technol Chem — Annals. Food Technology and Chemistry

Ann Forst Jagd Wiss — Annalen der Forst- und Jagd-Wissenschaft

Ann For (Zagreb) — Annales Forestales (Zagreb)

Ann Fr Anesth Reanim — Annales Francaises d'Anesthesie et de Reanimation

Ann Fr Chronom — Annales Francaises de Chronometrie

Ann Fr Chronom Micromec — Annales Francaises de Chronometrie et de Micromecanique [*Later, Annales Francaises des Microtechniques et de Chronolmetrie*]

Ann Fr Microtech et Chronom — Annales Francaises des Microtechniques et de Chronometrie

Ann Gaertnerey — Annalen der Gaertnerey. Nebst Einem Allgemeinen Intelligenzblatt fuer Garten- und Blumen-Freunde

Ann Gand — Handelingen der Maatschappij voor Geschied- en Oudheidkunde te Gent

Ann Gastro — Annales de Gastroenterologie et d'Hepatologie

Ann Gastroenterol Hepatol — Annales de Gastroenterologie et d'Hepatologie

Ann Gembloux — Annales de Gembloux

Ann Genet — Annales de Genetique

Ann Genet — Annales de Genetique. Museum National d'Histoire Naturelle

Ann Genet Sel Anim — Annales de Genetique et de Selection Animale

Ann Genie Chim — Annales du Genie Chimique

Ann Genie Chimie — Annales du Genie Chimique

Ann Gen Pract — Annals of General Practice

Ann Geofis — Annali di Geofisica

Ann Geog — Annales de Geographie

Ann Geogr — Annales de Geographie

Ann Geol Madagascar — Annales Geologiques de Madagascar

Ann Geol Opname Repub S Afr — Annale van Geologiese Opname. Republiek van Suid-Afrika

Ann Geol Opname (S Afr) — Annale van die Geologiese Opname (South Africa)

Ann Geol Pays Hell — Annales Geologiques des Pays Helleniques

Ann Geol Peninsule Balk — Annales Geologiques de la Peninsule Balkanique

Ann Geol Serv Mines (Madagascar) — Annales Geologiques. Service des Mines (Madagascar)

Ann Geol Surv — Annals. Geological Survey

Ann Geol Surv Egypt — Annals. Geological Survey of Egypt

Ann Geol Surv S Afr — Annals. Geological Survey of South Africa

Ann Geomorphol — Annals of Geomorphology

Ann Geophy — Annales de Geophysique

Ann Geophys — Annales de Geophysique

Ann Geophys CNRS — Annales de Geophysique. Centre National de la Recherche Scientifique

Ann Geophys Gauthier Villars — Annales Geophysicae (Gauthier-Villars)

Ann Geophys Ser A — Annales Geophysicae. Series A. Upper Atmosphere and Space Sciences

Ann Geophys Ser B — Annales Geophysicae. Series B. Terrestrial and Planetary Physics

Ann Gesammten Litt — Annalen der Gesammten Litteratur

Ann Gesammten Med — Annalen der Gesammten Medicin als Wissenschaft und als Kunst, zur Beurtheilung ihrer Neuesten Erfindungen, Theorien, Systeme und Heilmethoden

Ann Ges Hebammw — Annalen fuer das Gesamte Hebammenwesen

Ann Gifu College Ed — Gifu College of Education. Annals

Ann Glaciol — Annals of Glaciology

Ann Global Anal Geom — Annals of Global Analysis and Geometry

ANNGS — Ad Novas. Norwegian Geographical Studies

Ann Guebhard — Annales Guebhard

Ann Guebhard Severine — Annales Guebhard Severine

Ann Gynaec Pediat — Annals of Gynaecology and Pediatry

Ann Hebert Haug — Annales. Hebert et Haug

Ann Heb Union Coll — Annals. Hebrew Union College

Ann Hematol — Annals of Hematology

Ann HES — Annales d'Histoire Economique et Sociale

Ann High Perform Pap Soc Jpn — Annals. High Performance Paper Society. Japan

Ann Hist A Lor — Annuaire. Societe d'Histoire et d'Archeologie de la Lorraine

Ann Hist Comput — Annals of the History of Computing

Ann Hist-Nat Mus Natl Hung — Annales Historico-Naturales. Musei Nationalis Hungarici

Ann Hist Nat Mus Natl Hung Termeszettud Muz Evk — Annales Historico-Naturales Musei Nationalis Hungarici/ Termeszettudomanyi Muzeum Evkonyve

Ann Hist Natur Mus Nat Hung Pars Zool — Annales Historico-Naturales. Musei Nationalis Hungarici. Pars Zoologica

Ann Histoch — Annales d'Histochimie

Ann Histochim — Annales d'Histochimie

Ann Hist R — Annales Historiques de la Revolution Francaise

Ann Hist Revol Franc — Annales Historiques de la Revolution Francaise

Ann Hitotsubashi Acad — Annals. Hitotsubashi Academy

AnnHL — Annuaire d'Histoire Liegeoise

Ann Homeopath Fr — Annales Homeopathiques Francaises

Ann Hort Belgique — Annales de l'Horticulture in Belgique

Ann Hort Bot — Annales d'Horticulture et de Botanique ou Flore des Jardins du Royaume des Pays-Bas

Ann Hosp Gen Catalunya — Annales. Hospital General de Catalunya

Ann Hosp St Cruz San Pablo — Annales. Hospital de la Santa Cruz y San Pablo

Ann Human Genetics — Annals of Human Genetics

Ann Hum Bio — Annals of Human Biology

Ann Hum Biol — Annals of Human Biology

Ann Hum Gen — Annals of Human Genetics

Ann Hum Genet — Annals of Human Genetics

Ann Hung Geol Inst — Annals. Hungarian Geological Institute

Ann Hydrob — Annales d'Hydrobiologie

Ann Hydrobiol — Annales d'Hydrobiologie

Ann Hydrogr — Annalen der Hydrographie und Maritimen Meteorologie

Ann Hydrogr — Annales Hydrographiques

Ann Hydrogr Marit Meteorol — Annales. Hydrographie und Maritimen Mcteorologie

Ann Hyg et Med Colon — Annales d'Hygiene et de Medecine Coloniales

Ann Hyg Lang Fr Med Nutr — Annales d'Hygiene de Langue Francaise. Medecine et Nutrition

Ann Hyg Pub et Med Legale — Annales d'Hygiene Publique et de Medecine Legale

Ann Hyg Publique Ind Soc — Annales d'Hygiene Publique. Industrielle et Sociale

Ann Hyg Publique Med Leg — Annales d'Hygiene Publique et de Medecine Legale

Ann Hyg Publique Tokyo — Annales d'Hygiene Publique (Tokyo)

AnnI — Annals of Iowa

Ann IA — Annals of Iowa

Ann ICRP — Annals. ICRP

Ann Idrogr — Annali Idrografici. Institute Idrografica della Regia Marina

Ann Idrol — Annali Idrologici

AnnIEO — Annales. Institut d'Etudes Orientales. Faculte des Lettres d'Alger

AnnIEOc — Annales. Institut d'Etudes Occidentes

Ann I Four — Annales. Institut Fourier

Ann Ifr Z — Annales. Institut Francais de Zagreb

Ann Ig — Annali d'Igiene

Ann Ig Microbiol — Annali d'Igiene e Microbiologia

Ann Ig Sper — Annali d'Igiene. Sperimentali

Ann I Hen A — Annales. Institut Henri Poincare. Section A. Physique Theorique

Ann I Hen B — Annales. Institut Henri Poincare. Section B. Calcul des Probabilites et Statistique

Ann IHP Phys Theor — Annales. IHP Physique Theorique

Ann Immunol — Annales d'Immunologie

Ann Immunol Hung — Annales Immunologiae Hungaricae

Ann Immunol (Paris) — Annales d'Immunologie (Paris)

Ann Indian Acad Med Sci — Annals. Indian Academy of Medical Sciences

Ann Ind Prop L — Annual of Industrial Property Law

Ann Indus Prop L — Annual of Industrial Property Law
Ann INSEE — Annales. INSEE
Ann Inst — Annales Institutorum
Ann Inst — Annali. Istituto di Corrispondenza Archeologica
Ann Inst Agric Serv Rech Exp Agric Alger — Annales. Institut Agricole et Services de Recherche et d'Experimentation Agricoles de l'Algerie
Ann Inst Agron Cent Exp — Annales Instituti Agronomici Centralis Experimentalis
Ann Inst Agron Moscow — Annales. Institut Agronomique de Moscow
Ann Inst Anal Phys Chim Leningrad — Annales. Institut d'Analyse Physico-Chemique (Leningrad)
Ann Inst Archeol Luxemb — Annales. Institut Archeologique du Luxembourg
Ann Inst Archit Genie Civil Sofia Fasc II Math — Institute d'Architecture et de Genie Civil Sofia. Annuaire. Fascicule II. Mathematiques
Ann Inst Arch Luxembourg — Annales. Institut Archeologique du Luxembourg
Ann Inst Belge Pet — Annales. Institut Belge du Petrole
Ann Inst Belge Petrol — Annales. Institut Belge du Petrole
Ann Inst Biol Pervestigandae Hung — Annales. Instituti Biologici Pervestigandae Hungarici
Ann Inst Biol (Tihany) Hung — Annales. Instituti Biologici (Tihany). Hungaricae Academiae Scientiarum
Ann Inst Biol (Tihany) Hung Acad Sci — Annales. Instituti Biologici (Tihany). Hungaricae Academiae Scientiarum
Ann Inst Bot Geol Colon Marseille — Annales. Institut Botanico-Geologique Colonial de Marseille
Ann Inst Cent Ampelol R Hong — Annales. Institut Central Ampelologique Royal Hongrois
Ann Inst Child Health (Calcutta) — Annals. Institute of Child Health (Calcutta)
Ann Inst Dr Int — Annuaire. Institut de Droit International
Ann Inst Et Orient — Annales. Institut d'Etudes Orientales. Faculte des Lettres. Universite d'Alger
Ann Inst Etud Orient Univ Alger — Annales. Institut d'Etudes Orientales. Universite d'Alger
Ann Inst Exp Tabac Bergerac — Annales. Institut Experimental du Tabac de Bergerac
Ann Inst Fourier — Annales. Institut Fourier
Ann Inst Fourier (Grenoble) — Annales. Institut Fourier (Grenoble)
Ann Inst Fourier Univ Grenoble — Annales. Institut Fourier. Universite de Grenoble
Ann Inst Franc Zagreb — Annales. Institut Francais de Zagreb
Ann Inst Geol Hong — Annales. Institut Geologique de Hongrie
Ann Inst Geol Publ Hung — Annales. Instituti Geologici Publici Hungarici
Ann Inst Geol Publici Hung — Annales Instituti Geologici Publici Hungarici
Ann Inst Henri Poincare — Annales. Institut Henri Poincare
Ann Inst Henri Poincare A — Annales. Institut Henri Poincare. Section A. Physique Theorique
Ann Inst Henri Poincare B — Annales. Institut Henri Poincare. Section B. Calcul des Probabilites et Statistique
Ann Inst Henri Poincare Phys Theor — Annales. Institut Henri Poincare. Physique Theorique
Ann Inst Henri Poincare Sect A — Annales. Institut Henri Poincare. Section A. Physique Theorique
Ann Inst Henri Poincare Sect B — Annales. Institut Henri Poincare. Section B. Calcul des Probabilites et Statistique
Ann Inst H Poincare Anal Non Lineaire — Annales de l'Institut Henri Poincare. Analyse Non Lineaire
Ann Inst H Poincare Phys Theor — Annales de l'Institut Henri Poincare. Physique Theorique
Ann Inst H Poincare Probab Statist — Annales de l'Institut Henri Poincare. Probabilites et Statistique
Ann Inst H Poincare Sect A — Annales. Institut Henri Poincare. Section A
Ann Inst H Poincare Sect A NS — Annales. Institut Henri Poincare. Section A. Physique Theorique. Nouvelle Serie
Ann Inst H Poincare Sect B — Annales. Institut Henri Poincare. Section B
Ann Inst H Poincare Sect B NS — Annales. Institut Henri Poincare. Section B. Nouvelle Serie
Ann Inst Hydrol Climatol — Annales. Institut d'Hydrologie et de Climatologie
Ann Inst Kond — Annali Instituta Imeni N. P. Kondakova
Ann Inst Kondakov — Annales. Institut Kondakov/Seminarium Kondakovianum
Ann Inst Med Exp Univ Nac Buenos Aires — Annales. Instituto de Medicina Experimental. Universidad Nacional de Buenos Aires
Ann Inst Michel Pacha — Annales. Institut Michel Pacha
Ann Inst Mines Leningrade — Annales. Institut des Mines a Leningrade
Ann Inst Nat Agron — Annales. Institut National Agronomique
Ann Inst Natl Agron — Annales. Institut National Agronomique
Ann Inst Natl Rech A — Annales. Institut National de la Recherche Agronomique de Tunisie
Ann Inst Natl Rech Agron Ser A — Annales. Institut National de la Recherche Agronomique. Serie A. Annales Agronomiques
Ann Inst Natl Rech Agron Ser A Bis Ann Physiol Veg — Annales. Institut National de la Recherche Agronomique. Serie A Bis. Annales dePhysiologie Vegetale
Ann Inst Natl Rech Agron Ser B — Annales. Institut National de la Recherche Agronomique. Serie B. Annales de l'Amelioration des Plantes
Ann Inst Natl Rech Agron Ser C — Annales. Institut National de la Recherche Agronomique. Serie C. Annales des Epiphyties
Ann Inst Natl Rech Agron Ser C Ann Epiphyt — Annales. Institut National de la Recherche Agronomique. Serie C. Annales des Epiphyties
Ann Inst Natl Rech Agron Ser C Bis — Annales. Institut National de la Recherche Agronomique. Serie C. Bis
Ann Inst Natl Rech Agron Ser C Bis Ann Abeille — Annales. Institut National de la Recherche Agronomique. Serie C Bis. Annales de l'Abeille
Ann Inst Natl Rech Agron Ser D — Annales. Institut National de la Recherche Agronomique. Serie D. Annales de Zootechnie
Ann Inst Natl Rech Agron Ser D Ann Zootech — Annales. Institut National de la Recherche Agronomique. Serie D. Annales de Zootechnie

Ann Inst Natl Rech Agron Ser E — Annales. Institut National de la Recherche Agronomique. Serie E. Annales de Technologie Agricole
Ann Inst Natl Rech Agron Ser E Ann Technol Agric — Annales. Institut National de la Recherche Agronomique. Serie E. Annales de Technologie Agricole
Ann Inst Natl Rech Agron Tunis — Annales. Institut National de la Recherche Agronomique de Tunisie
Ann Inst Natl Zootech Roum — Annales. Institut National Zootechnique de Roumanie
Ann Inst Nat Rech For Tunis — Annales. Institut National de Recherches Forestieres de Tunisie
Ann Inst Oceanogr — Annales. Institut Oceanographique
Ann Inst Oceanogr (Paris) — Annales. Institut Oceanographique (Paris)
Ann Inst Pasteur — Annales. Institut Pasteur
Ann Inst Pasteur Immun — Annales. Institut Pasteur. Immunologie
Ann Inst Pasteur Immunol — Annales. Institut Pasteur. Immunologie
Ann Inst Pasteur Lille — Annales. Institut Pasteur de Lille
Ann Inst Pasteur Microb — Annales. Institut Pasteur. Microbiologie
Ann Inst Pasteur Microbiol — Annales. Institut Pasteur. Microbiologie
Ann Inst Pasteur (Paris) — Annales. Institut Pasteur (Paris)
Ann Inst Pasteur Virol — Annales. Institut Pasteur. Virologie
Ann Inst Phil Hist Orient — Annuaire. Institut de Philologie et d'Histoire Orientales et Slaves
Ann Inst Phys Globe Univ Paris Bur Cent Magn Terr — Annales. Institut de Physique du Globe. Universite de Paris et BureauCentral de Magnetisme Terrestre
Ann Inst Phytopathol Benaki — Annales. Institut Phytopathologique Benaki
Ann Inst Poincare Sect A — Annales. Institut Henri Poincare. Section A. Physique Theorique
Ann Inst Poincare Sect B — Annales. Institut Henri Poincare. Section B. Calcul des Probabilites et Statistique
Ann Inst Polytech Oural — Annales. Institut Polytechnique de l'Oural
Ann Inst Prot Plant Hung — Annales Instituti Protectionis Plantarum Hungarici
Ann Inst Rech Agron Trop Cult Vivrieres Senegal — Annales. Institut de Recherches Agronomiques Tropicales et des Cultures Vivrieres au Senegal
Ann Inst Rech Amelior Foncieres Sci Sol Ser Amelior Fonciere — Annales. Institut de Recherches d'Ameliorations Foncieres et de la Science du Sol. Serie Ameliorations Foncieres
Ann Inst Rech Amelior Foncieres Sci Sol Ser Hydrotech — Annales. Institut de Recherches d'Ameliorations Foncieres et de la Science du Sol. Serie Hydrotechnique
Ann Inst Rech Amelior Foncieres Sci Sol Ser Sci Sol — Annales. Institut de Recherches d'Ameliorations Foncieres et de la Science du Sol. Serie Science du Sol
Ann Inst Rech Zootech Roum — Annales. Institut de Recherches Zootechniques de Roumanie
Ann Inst Sec Law Reg Proc — Annual Institute on Securities Law and Regulations. Proceedings
Ann Inst Statist Math — Annals. Institute of Statistical Mathematics
Ann Inst Super Phil Univ Cath Louvain — Annales. Institut Superieur de Philosophie. Universite Catholique de Louvain
Ann Inst Tech Batim Trav Publics — Annales. Institut Technique du Batiment et des Travaux Publics
Ann Inter Comm Radiol Prot — Annals. International Commission of Radiological Protection
Ann Internat Criminologie — Annales Internationales de Criminologie
Ann Internat Soc Dynam Games — Annals of the International Society of Dynamic Games
Ann Intern Med — Annals of Internal Medicine
Ann Int Geophys Year — Annals of the International Geophysical Year
Ann Int Inst Prod Eng Res — Annals. International Institution for Production Engineering Research
Ann Int Med — Annals of Internal Medicine
Ann I Ocean — Annales. Institut Oceanographique
AnnION — Annali. Istituto Universitario Orientale (Napoli)
Ann Iowa — Annals of Iowa
Ann Iowa Manpower Pl Rep — Annual Iowa Manpower Planning Report
Ann IQSY — Annals of the IQSY
Ann Isnardi — Annali Isnardi
Ann Isnardi Auxol Norm Patol — Annali Isnardi di Auxologia Normale e Patologica
Ann Israel Phys Soc — Annals. Israel Physical Society
Ann Isr Phys Soc — Annals. Israel Physical Society
Ann I Stat — Annals. Institute of Statistical Mathematics
Ann Ist Carlo Forlanini — Annali. Istituto Carlo Forlanini
Ann Ist Feltrinelli — Istituto Giangiacomo Feltrinelli. Annali
Ann Ist It Num — Annali. Istituto Italiano di Numismatica
Ann Ist Mus Stor — Annali. Istituto e Museo di Storia della Scienza di Firenze
Ann Ist Mus Stor Sci Firenze — Annali. Istituto e Museo di Storia della Scienze di Firenze
Ann Ist Num — Annali. Istituto Italiano di Numismatica
Ann Ist Orient Napoli — Annali. Istituto Orientale di Napoli
Ann Ist Sper Agron — Annali. Istituto Sperimentale Agronomico
Ann Ist Sper Agrumic — Annali. Istituto Sperimentale per l'Agrumicoltura
Ann Ist Sper Asses For Alpic — Annali. Istituto Sperimentale per l'Assestamento Forestale e per l'Alpicoltura
Ann Ist Sper Assestamento For Apic — Annali. Istituto Sperimentale per l'Assestamento Forestale e per l'Apicoltura
Ann Ist Sper Cereal — Annali. Istituto Sperimentale per la Cerealicoltura
Ann Ist Sper Cerealic — Annali. Istituto Sperimentale per la Cerealicoltura
Ann Ist Sper Colt Foraggere — Annali. Istituto Sperimentale per le Colture Foraggere
Ann Ist Sper Colt Ind — Annali. Istituto Sperimentale per le Colture Industriali
Ann Ist Sper Elaiotec — Annali dell'Istituto Sperimentale per la Elaiotecnica
Ann Ist Sper Enol (Asti) — Annali. Istituto Sperimentale per l'Enologia (Asti)
Ann Ist Sper Flori — Annali. Istituto Sperimentale per la Floricoltura
Ann Ist Sper Floric — Annali. Istituto Sperimentale per la Floricoltura

Ann Ist Sper Floricolt — Annali. Istituto Sperimentale per la Floricoltura
Ann Ist Sper Fruittic Rome — Annali dell'Istituto Sperimentale per la Frutticoltura (Rome)
Ann Ist Sper Fruttic — Annali. Istituto Sperimentale per la Frutticoltura
Ann Ist Sper Frutticolt — Annali. Istituto Sperimentale per la Frutticoltura
Ann Ist Sper Nutr Piante — Annali. Istituto Sperimentale per la Nutrizione delle Piante
Ann Ist Sper Olivic Numero Spec — Annali delle'Istituto Sperimentale per l'Olivicoltura. Numero Speciale
Ann Ist Sper Selvi — Annali. Istituto Sperimentale per la Selvicoltura
Ann Ist Sper Selvic — Annali. Istituto Sperimentale per la Selvicoltura
Ann Ist Sper Stud Dif Suolo — Annali. Istituto Sperimentale per lo Studio e la Difesa del Suolo
Ann Ist Sper Tab — Annali. Istituto Sperimentale per il Tabacco
Ann Ist Sper Valorizzazione Tecnol (Milan) — Annali. Istituto Sperimentale per la Valorizzazione Tecnologica (Milan)
Ann Ist Sper Vitic (Conegliano Italy) — Annali. Istituto Sperimentale per la Viticoltura (Conegliano, Italy)
Ann Ist Sper Zool Agrar — Annali. Istituto Sperimentale per la Zoologia Agraria
Ann Ist Sper Zootec — Annali. Istituto Sperimentale per la Zootecnia
Ann Ist Sper Zootec Roma — Annali. Istituto Sperimentale Zootecnico di Roma
Ann Ist Stor Italo Germ Trento — Annali. Istituto Storico Italo-Germanico in Trento
Ann Ist Stud Eur Alc Gasp — Annali. Istituto di Studi Europei Alcide de Gasperi
Ann Ist Super Sanita — Annali. Istituto Superiore di Sanita
Ann Ital Chir — Annali Italiani di Chirurgia
Ann Ital Dermatol Clin Sper — Annali Italiani di Dermatologia Clinica e Sperimentale
Ann Ital Dermatol Sifilol — Annali Italiani di Dermatologia e Sifilologia
Ann Ital Med Int — Annali Italiani di Medicina Interna
Ann Ital Pediatr — Annali Italiani di Pediatria
Anniv Bull Chuo Univ — Anniversary Bulletin. Chuo University
Ann Japan Assoc Philos Sci — Annals. Japan Association for Philosophy of Science
Ann J Kerou — Annals. Jack Kerouac School of Disembodied Poetics
Ann JP — Annales des Justices de Paix
Ann Jpn Assoc Philos Sci — Annals. Japan Association for Philosophy of Science
Ann Kinesither — Annales de Kinesitherapie
Ann K Landwirtsch Hochsch Schwed — Annalen der Koeniglichen Landwirtschaftlichen Hochschule Schwedens
Ann K Mus Belg Congo Reeks 8 Geol Wet — Annalen van het Koninklijk Museum van Belgisch Congo. Reeks in 8 Geologische Wetenschappen
Ann Kurashiki Cent Hosp — Annals. Kurashiki Central Hospital
Ann KY Nat Hist — Annals of Kentucky Natural History
Ann Landwirtsch Hochsch Schwed — Annalen Landwirtschaftlichen Hochschule Schwedens
Ann Landw Landw Recht — Annalen fuer die Landwirtschaft und das Landwirthschafts-Recht
Ann Laringol — Annali di Laringologia, Otologia, Rinologia, Laringologia
Ann Laringol Otol Rinol Faringol — Annali di Laringologia, Otologia, Rinologia, Faringologia
Ann Laringol Otol Rinol Laringol — Annali di Laringologia, Otologia, Rinologia, Laringologia
AnnLat — Annali Lateranensi
Ann Lav Pubblici — Annali dei Lavori Pubblici
Ann Law Dig — Annual Law Digest
Ann Law Reg — Annual Law Register of the United States
Ann Lecce — Annali. Universita di Lecce. Facolta di Lettere e Filosofia e di Magistero
Ann Lecce Mag — Annali. Facolta di Magistero. Universita di Lecce
Ann Leeds Un Or Soc — Annual. Leeds University Oriental Society
Ann Leg Bib Harvard — Annual Legal Bibliography. Harvard University. Law School Library
Ann Leg Forms Mag — Annotated Legal Forms Magazine
Ann Leg Fr — Annuaire de Legislation Francaise
Ann Leg Fr Etr — Annuaire de Legislation Francaise et Etrangere
Ann Libr Sci — Annals of Library Science and Documentation
Ann Libr Sci Docum — Annals of Library Science and Documentation
Ann Lib Sci Doc — Annals of Library Science and Documentation
Ann Life Ins Med — Annals of Life Insurance Medicine
Annli Ist Numismatica — Annali. Istituto Italiano di Numismatica
Ann Limnol — Annales de Limnologie
Ann Liv — Annals of Archaeology and Anthropology (Liverpool)
Annln Naturh Mus Wien — Annalen des Naturhistorischen Museums in Wien
Ann Loisir Est Quebec — Annuaire du Loisir de l'Est du Quebec
Annls Abeille — Annales de l'Abeille
Annls Agric Fenn — Annales Agriculturae Fenniae
Annls Agric Fenniae — Annales Agriculturae Fenniae
Annls Agron — Annales Agronomiques
Annls Amel Pl — Annales de l'Amelioration des Plantes
Annls Biol — Annales de Biologie
Annls Biol Anim Biochim Biophys — Annales de Biologie Animale, Biochimie, et Biophysique
Annls Biol Clin — Annales de Biologie Clinique
Annls Biol Copenh — Annales Biologiques. Conseil Permanent International pour l'Exploration de la Mer (Copenhague)
Annls Biol Lacustre — Annales de Biologie Lacustre
Annls Brass Distill — Annales de la Brasserie et de la Distillerie
Annls Bryol — Annales Bryologici
Annls Bur Cent Met Fr — Annales du Bureau Central Meteorologique de France
Annls Bur Longit — Annales du Bureau des Longitudes et de l'Observatoire Astronomique de Montsouris
Annls Cent Etud Docum Paleont — Annales du Centre d'Etudes et de Documentation Paleontologiques
Annls Cent Rech Agron Bambey — Annales. Centre de Recherches Agronomiques de Bambey au Senegal

Annls Chim — Annales de Chimie
Annls Chim Analyt — Annales de Chimie Analytique
Annls Chim Phys — Annales de Chimie et de Physique
Annls Chir Gynaec Fenn — Annales Chirurgiae et Gynaecologiae Fenniae
Annls Chir Infant — Annales de Chirurgie Infantile
Annls Chir Plast — Annales de Chirurgie Plastique
Annls Climat Obs Ksara — Annales Climatologiques de l'Observatoire de Ksara
Annls Climat Serv Met Cameroun — Annales Climatologiques. Service Meteorologique du Cameroun sous Tutelle Francaise
Annls Clin Chir Delbet — Annales de la Clinique Chirurgicale du Prof. Pierre Delbet
Annls Clin Radiodiagn — Annales de Clinique et Radiodiagnostique
Annls Coll Int Etude Scient Tech Prod Mec — Annales. College Internationale pour l'Etude Scientifique des Techniques de Production Mecanique
Annls Commn Etud Raz Maree — Annales de la Commission pour l'Etude des Raz de Maree. Union Geodesique et Geophysique Internationale
Annls Commn Int Agric — Annales de la Commission Internationale d'Agriculture
Annls Cryptog Exot — Annales de Cryptogamie Exotique
Annls Cryptog Phytopath — Annales Cryptogamici et Phytopathologici
Annls Derm Syph — Annales de Dermatologie et de Syphiligraphie
Annls Endocr — Annales d'Endocrinologie
Annls Epiphyt — Annales des Epiphyties et de Phytogenetique
Annls Fac Sci Marseille — Annales. Faculte des Sciences de Marseille
Annls Falsif Expert Chim — Annales des Falsifications et de l'Expertise Chimique [*Later, Annales des Falsifications et de l'Expertise Chimique et Toxicologique*]
Annls Gembloux — Annales de Gembloux
Annls Hist-Nat Mus Natn Hung — Annalis. Historico-Naturales Musei Nationalis Hungarici
Annls Histochim — Annales d'Histochimie
Annls Inst Agorum Cult Exp Debrecen — Annales Instituti Agrorum Culturae Experiendae, Debrecen
Annls Inst Agric Alger — Annales. Institut Agricole et Services de Recherche et d'Experimentation Agricoles de l'Algerie
Annls Inst Biol Pervest Hung — Annales Instituti Biologiae Pervestigandae Hungarici
Annls Inst Biol Tihany — Annales Instituti Biologici, Tihany, Hungaricae Academiae Scientiarum
Annls Inst Geol Publ Hung — Annales Instituti Geologici Publici Hungarici
Annls Inst Hydrol Clim Paris — Annales de l'Institut d'Hydrologie et de Climatologie (Paris)
Annls Inst Med Leg Univ Lyon — Annales de l'Institut de Medecine Legale de l'Universite de Lyon
Annls Inst Natn Agron (Paris) — Annales. Institut National Agronomique (Paris)
Annls Inst Natn Rech Agron Ser C Paris — Annales de l'Institut National de la Recherche Agronomique. Ser. C. Annales des Epiphyties (Paris)
Annls Inst Natn Rech Agron Ser D Paris — Annales de l'Institut National de la Recherche Agronomique. Ser. D. Annales de Zootechnie (Paris)
Annls Inst Natn Rech Agron Ser E Bis Paris — Annales de l'Institut National de la Recherche Agronomique. Ser. E bis. Annales de Biologie Animale, Biochemie, et Biophysique (Paris)
Annls Inst Natn Rech Agron Ser E Paris — Annales de l'Institut National de la Recherche Agronomique. Ser. E. Annales de Technologie Agricole (Paris)
Annls Inst Natn Rech Agron Tunisie — Annales. Institut National de la Recherche Agronomique de Tunisie
Annls Inst Oceanogr Monaco — Annales de l'Institut Oceanographique (Monaco)
Annls Inst Past — Annales. Institut Pasteur
Annls Inst Pasteur Lille — Annales de l'Institut Pasteur de Lille
Annls Inst Pasteur (Paris) — Annales. Institut Pasteur (Paris)
Annls Inst Phys Globe Univ Paris — Annales de l'Institut de Physique du Globe de l'Universite de Paris
Annls Inst Phys Globe Univ Strasb 1 — Annales de l'Institut de Physique du Globe de l'Universite de Strasbourg. 1. Meteorologie
Annls Inst Phys Globe Univ Strasb 2 — Annales de l'Institut de Physique du Globe de l'Universite de Strasbourg. 2. Seismologie
Annls Inst Phys Globe Univ Strasb 3 — Annales de l'Institut de Physique du Globe de l'Universito de Strasbourg. 3. Geophysique
Annls Inst Phytopath Benaki — Annales. Institut Phytopathologique Benaki
Annls Inst Polytech Grenoble — Annales de l'Institut Polytechnique de Grenoble
Annls Inst Scient Cherif — Annales de l'Institut Scientifique Cherifien
Annls Inst Tech Batim — Annales de l'Institut Technique du Batiment et des Travaux Publics
Annls Med Pharm Colon — Annales de Medecine et de Pharmacie Coloniales
Annls Med Vet — Annales de Medecine Veterinaire
Annls Mines Belg — Annales des Mines de Belgique
Annls Mines (Paris) — Annales des Mines (Paris)
Annls Mus R Afr Cent Ser 8vo — Annales. Musee Royal de l'Afrique Centrale. Serie in Octavo
Annls Nutr Aliment — Annales de la Nutrition et de l'Alimentation
Annls Pharm Fr — Annales Pharmaceutiques Francaises
Annls Physiol Veg (Brux) — Annales de Physiologie Vegetale (Bruxelles)
Annls Physiol Veg (Paris) — Annales de Physiologie Vegetale (Paris)
Annls Scient Univ Jassy — Annales Scientifiques. Universite de Jassy
Annls Sci Nat A Bot — Annales des Sciences Naturelles. A. Botanique
Annls SEITA — Annales Direction des Etudes et de l'Equipement. Service d'Exploitation Industrielle des Tabacs et des Allumettes
Annls Soc Belge Med Trop — Annales. Societe Belge de Medecine Tropicale
Annls Soc Ent Fr — Annales. Societe Entomologique de France
Annls Soc Lit Eston Am — Annales Societatis Litterarum Estonicae in America
Annls Soc R Zool Belg — Annales. Societe Royale Zoologique de Belgique
Annls Soc Tartu — Annales Societatis Tartu
Annls Univ Mariae Curie-Sklodowska — Annales Universitatis Mariae Curie-Sklodowska
Annls Zool Ecol Anim — Annales de Zoologie - Ecologie Animale
Annls Zool Fennici — Annales Zoologici Fennici
Annls Zootech — Annales de Zootechnie

Ann Lux — Annales. Institut Archeologique du Luxembourg
Ann Lyceum Nat Hist (NY) — Annals. Lyceum of Natural History (New York)
AnnM — Annalen der Mathematik
Ann M — Annales Musicologiques
AnnMAfrC — Annales. Musee Royal de l'Afrique Centrale
Ann Mag Nat Hist — Annals and Magazine of Natural History
Ann Mag Natur Hist — Annals and Magazine of Natural History
Ann Malg — Annales Malgaches
Ann Malg — Annales. Universite de Madagascar
Ann Marit Colon — Annales Maritimes et Coloniales
Ann Marocaines de Sociologie — Annales Marocaines de Sociologie
Ann Math — Annals of Mathematics
Ann Math Artificial Intelligence — Annals of Mathematics and Artificial Intelligence
Ann Math Blaise Pascal — Annales Mathematiques Blaise Pascal
Ann Math Logic — Annals of Mathematical Logic
Ann Math Sil — Annales Mathematicae Silesianae
Ann Math Stat — Annals of Mathematical Statistics
Ann Mat Pura Appl — Annali di Matematica Pura ed Applicata
AnnMCB-L — Annales. Musee Royal du Congo Belge. Linguistique
Ann Mecklenburg Landwirthschaftsges — Annalen der Mecklenburgischen Landwirthschaftsgesellschaft
Ann Med — Annals of Medicine
Ann Med — Annuale Mediaevale
Ann Med Acad Cienc Med Catalunya Balears — Annals. Medicina Academia de Ciencias Mediques de Catalunya i de Balears
Ann Med Belges — Annales Medicales Belges
Ann Med Chir Hainaut — Annales Medico-Chirurgicales du Hainaut
Ann Med et Chir Inf — Annales de Medecine et Chirurgie Infantiles
Ann Med et Pharm Colon — Annales de Medecine et de Pharmacie Coloniales
Ann Med Exp Biol Fenn — Annales Medicinae Experimentalis et Biologiae Fenniae
Ann Med Exp Biol Fenn Suppl — Annales Medicinae Experimentalis et Biologiae Fenniae. Supplementum
Ann Med (Hagerstown Maryland) — Annals of Medicine (Hagerstown, Maryland)
Ann Med Helsinki — Annals of Medicine (Helsinki)
Ann Med Hist — Annals of Medical History
Ann Mediaev — Annuale Mediaevale
Ann Med In — Annales de Medecine Interne
Ann Med Intern — Annales de Medecine Interne
Ann Med Interne — Annales de Medecine Interne
Ann Med Intern Fenn — Annales Medicinae Internae Fenniae
Ann Med Intern Fenn Suppl — Annales Medicinae Internae Fenniae. Supplementum
Ann Med Leg — Annales de Medecine Legale
Ann Med Leg Criminol — Annales de Medecine Legale et de Criminologie
Ann Med Leg Criminol Police Sci Med Soc Toxicol — Annales de Medecine Legale de Criminologie, Police Scientifique, Medecine Sociale, et Toxicologie
Ann Med Leg Criminol Police Toxicol — Annales de Medecine Legale, Criminologie, Police Scientifique, et Toxicologie
Ann Med Leg Crimin Police Sci — Annales de Medecine Legale de Criminologie et de Police Scientifique
Ann Med (Milan) — Annali Medici (Milan)
Ann Med Mil Fenn — Annales Medicinae Militaris Fenniae
Ann Med Nancy — Annales Medicales de Nancy
Ann Med Nancy Est — Annales Medicales de Nancy et de l'Est
Ann Med Nav — Annali di Medicina Navale
Ann Med Nav e Colon — Annali di Medicina Navale e Coloniale
Ann Med Nav Trop — Annali di Medicina Navale e Tropicale
Ann Med (Paris) — Annales de Medecine (Paris)
AnnM Pharm Reims — Annales de Medecine et de Pharmacie de Reims
Ann Med-Psy — Annales Medico-Psychologiques
Ann Med-Psychol — Annales Medico-Psychologiques
Ann Med Reims — Annales de Medecine de Reims
Ann Med Reims-Champagne-Ardennes — Annales de Medecine de Reims-Champagne-Ardennes
Ann Med Sect Pol Acad Sci — Annals. Medical Section. Polish Academy of Sciences
Ann Med Sondalo — Annali Medici di Sondalo
Ann Med Straniera — Annali di Medicina Straniera
Ann Med Univ Bialystok Pol — Annals of the Medical University. Bialystok, Poland
Ann Med Univ Bialyst Pol — Annals. Medical University. Bialystok, Poland
Ann Med Vet — Annales de Medecine Veterinaire
Ann Med Veterin — Annales de Medecine Veterinaire
Ann Meet Minn Sect SME Proc — Annual Meeting of the Minnesota Section. SME. Proceedings
Ann Mem Assoc Int Pedagog Univ — Annuaire des Membres. Association Internationale de PedagogieUniversitaire
Ann Merceol Sicil — Annali di Merceol Siciliana
Ann Meteorol — Annales der Meteorologie
Ann Microb — Annales de Microbiologie
Ann Microbiol — Annali di Microbiologia
Ann Microbiol Enzimol — Annali di Microbiologia ed Enzimologia
Ann Microbiol (Milan) — Annali di Microbiologia (Milan)
Ann Microbiol (Paris) — Annales de Microbiologie (Paris)
Ann Midi — Annales du Midi; Revue de la France Meridionale
Ann Mijnen Belg — Annalen der Mijnen van Belgie
Ann Min — Annales des Mines
Ann Mines — Annales des Mines
Ann Mines Belg — Annales des Mines de Belgique
Ann Mines Carbur Doc — Annales des Mines et des Carburants. Documentation
Ann Mines Carbur Mem — Annales des Mines et des Carburants. Memoires
Ann Mines Carbur Partie Tech — Annales des Mines et des Carburants. Partie Technique
Ann Mines Doc — Annales des Mines. Documentation
Ann Mines Geol Tunis — Annales des Mines et de la Geologie. Tunisia
Ann Mines Geol (Tunisia) — Annales des Mines et de la Geologie (Tunisia)

Ann Mines Geol Tunis Ser 1 — Annales des Mines et de la Geologie. Tunisia. Serie 1. Geologie Generale et Etudes Reginales
Ann Mines Geol Tunis Ser 3 — Annales des Mines et de la Geologie. Tunisia. Serie 3. Hydrogeologie
Ann Mines Mem — Annales des Mines. Memoires
Ann Mines Partie Adm — Annales des Mines. Partie Administrative
Ann Mines Roum — Annales des Mines de Roumanie
Ann Missouri Hist Soc — Annals. Missouri Historical and Philosophical Society
Ann MO Bot — Annals. Missouri Botanical Garden
Ann MO Bot Gard — Annals. Missouri Botanical Garden
Ann MO Bot Gdn — Annals. Missouri Botanical Garden
Ann Mus Alex — Annuaire. Musee Greco-Romain d'Alexandrie
Ann Mus Civ Stor Nat Genova — Annali. Museo Civico di Storia Naturale Genova
Ann Mus Civ Stor Nat "Giacomo Doria" — Annali. Museo Civico di Storia Naturale "Giacomo Doria"
Ann Mus Civ Stor Nat Giacomo Doria Suppl — Annali. Museo Civico di Storia Naturali Giacomo Doria. Supplemento
Ann Mus Colon Mars — Annales. Musee Colonial de Marseille
Ann Mus Colon Marseille — Annales du Musee Colonial de Marseille
Ann Mus Francisc — Annales. Museum Francisceum
Ann Mus Goulandris — Annales Musei Goulandris
Ann Mus Gr Rd Alex — Annuaire. Musee Greco-Romain d'Alexandrie
Ann Mus Guimet — Annales. Musee Guimet
Ann Mus Guimet Bibl Etud — Annales. Musee Guimet. Bibliotheque d'Etudes
Ann Mus Hist Nat Nice — Annales. Museum d'Histoire Naturelle de Nice
Ann Mus Nat Arch (Plovdiv) — Annuaire. Musee National Archeologique (Plovdiv)
Ann Mus Natl Hist Nat — Annales du Museum National d'Histoire Naturelle
Ann Mus R Afr Cent Ser 8 Sci Geol — Annales. Musee Royal de l'Afrique Centrale. Serie in Octavo. Sciences Geologiques
Ann Mus R Afr Cent Ser Quarto Zool — Annales. Musee Royal de l'Afrique Centrale. Serie in Quarto. Zoologie
Ann Mus R Congo Belge Ser 8o Sci Geol — Annales. Musee Royal du Congo Belge. Serie in Octavo. Sciences Geologiques
Ann Mycol — Annales Mycologici. Editi in Notitiam Scientiae Mycologicae Universalis
Ann Nap — Annali. Facolta di Lettere e Magistero. Universita di Napoli
Ann Nap Filos — Annali. Facolta di Lettere e Filosofia. Universita di Napoli
Ann Naprstek Mus — Annals of the Naprstek Museum
Ann Natal Mus — Annale. Natalse Museum
Ann Natal Mus — Annals. Natal Museum
Ann Natl Acad Med Sci — Annals. National Academy of Medical Sciences
Ann Natl Acad Med Sci (India) — Annals. National Academy of Medical Sciences (India)
Ann Natphilos — Annalen der Naturphilosophie
Ann Naturgesch — Annalen der Naturgeschichte
Ann Naturhist Hofmus — Annalen des Naturhistorischen Hofmuseums
Ann Naturhist Mus Wien — Annalen des Naturhistorischen Museums in Wien
Ann Naturhist Mus Wien Ser A — Annalen des Naturhistorischen Museums in Wien. Serie A. fuer Mineralogie und Petrographie, Geologie und Palaentologie, Anthropologie und Praehistorie
Ann Naturhist Mus Wien Ser B Bot Zool — Annalen des Naturhistorischen Museums in Wien. Serie B. Botanik und Zoologie
Ann Naturhist Mus Wien Ser C Jahresber — Annalen des Naturhistorischen Museums in Wien. Serie C. Jahresberichte
Ann Natur Kulturphil — Annalen der Natur- und Kulturphilosophie
Ann Naturphil — Annalen der Naturphilosophie
Ann Nauchno Issled Inst Melior Pochvoved Ser Gidrotekh — Annaly Nauchno-Issledovatel'skogo Instituta Melioratsii i Pochvovedeniya. Seriya Gidrotekhnika
Ann Nauchno Issled Inst Melior Pochvoved Ser Melior — Annaly Nauchno-Issledovatel'skogo Instituta Melioratsii i Pochvovedeniya. Seriya Melioratsiya
Ann Nauchno Issled Inst Melior Pochvoved Ser Pochvoved — Annaly Nauchno-Issledovatel'skogo Instituta Melioratsii i Pochvovedeniya. Seriya Pochvovedenie
Ann Nestle (Fr) — Annales Nestle (France)
Ann Neur — Annali di Neurologia
Ann Neurol — Annals of Neurology
Ann Neuropsichiatr Psicoanal — Annali di Neuropsichiatria e Psicoanalisi
Ann Neur Psich Psic — Annali di Neuropsichiatria e Psicoanalisi
Ann Nevrol — Annali di Nevrologia
Ann New York Acad Sc — Annals. New York Academy of Sciences
Ann New York Acad Sci — Annals. New York Academy of Sciences
Ann Noninvasive Electrocardiol — Annals of Noninvasive Electrocardiology
AnnNorm — Annales de Normandie
Ann Normandie — Annales de Normandie
Ann Not — Annales du Notariat et de l'Enregistrement
Ann Not Enr — Annales du Notariat et de l'Enregistrement
Ann Notre Dame Est Plan Inst — Annual. Notre Dame Estate Planning Institute
Ann N Ph — Annalen der Naturphilosophie
Ann Nuc Eng — Annals of Nuclear Energy
Ann Nucl Energy — Annals of Nuclear Energy
Ann Nucl Med — Annals of Nuclear Medicine
Ann Nucl Sci and Eng — Annals of Nuclear Science and Engineering
Ann Nucl Sci Eng — Annals of Nuclear Science and Engineering
Ann Nucl Sci Engng — Annals of Nuclear Science and Engineering
Ann Numer Math — Annals of Numerical Mathematics
Ann Nutr Al — Annales de la Nutrition et de l'Alimentation
Ann Nutr Aliment — Annales de la Nutrition et de l'Alimentation
Ann Nutr Aliment Ann Nutr Food — Annales de la Nutrition et de l'Alimentation/Annals of Nutrition and Food
Ann Nutr Metab — Annals of Nutrition and Metabolism
Ann NY Acad — Annals. New York Academy of Sciences
Ann NY Acad Sci — Annals. New York Academy of Sciences
Ann NY Ac Sci — Annals. New York Academy of Sciences
Ann O — Annals of Otology, Rhinology, and Laryngology
Ann Obs Besancon — Annales. Observatoire de Besancon
Ann Obs Nat — Annales. Observatoire National d'Athenes

Ann Obstet — Annee Obstetricale
Ann Occup Hyg — Annals of Occupational Hygiene
Ann Ocul — Annales d'Oculistique
Ann Oculist — Annales d'Oculistique
Ann Ocul (Paris) — Annales d'Oculistique (Paris)
Ann Odonto-Stomatol — Annales Odonto-Stomatologiques
Ann Off Acad Med Vet Quebec — Annuaire Officiel. Academie de Medecine Veterinaire du Quebec
Ann Off Natl Combust Liq (France) — Annales. Office National des Combustibles Liquides (France)
Ann Off Sal Dir — Annual Office Salaries Directory
Ann of Math (2) — Annals of Mathematics. Second Series
Ann of Math Stud — Annals of Mathematics. Studies
Ann of Math Studies — Annals of Mathematics. Studies
Ann of Sci — Annals of Science
Ann Oftalmol Clin Ocul — Annali di Oftalmologia e Clinica Oculistica
Ann Oil Gas Stat — Annual Oil and Gas Statistics
Ann Okla Acad Sci — Annals. Oklahoma Academy of Science
Ann Oncol — Annals of Oncology
Ann Ophth — Annals of Ophthalmology
Ann Ophthal — Annals of Ophthalmology
Ann Ophthalmol — Annals of Ophthalmology
Ann Ophthalmol Otol — Annals of Ophthalmology and Otology
Ann Ophth Otol — Annals of Ophthalmology and Otology
Ann OR — Annals of Oriental Research. University of Madras
An Nord Oldknd — Annaler for Nordisk Oldkyndighed
Ann Or (Napoli) — Annali. Istituto Universitario Orientale (Napoli)
Ann OSBM — Analecta Ordinis Sancti Basilii Magni
Ann Osp Maria Vittoria Torino — Annali. Ospedale Maria Vittoria di Torino
Ann Osserv Astron Torino — Annali. Osservatorio Astronomico. Universita di Torino
Ann Oss Vesuviano — Annali. Osservatorio Vesuviano
Ann Ostet Ginecol — Annali di Ostetricia e Ginecologia
Ann Ostet Ginecol Med Perinat — Annali di Ostetricia, Ginecologia, Medicina Perinatale
Ann Ot — Annals of Otology, Rhinology, and Laryngology
Annot Acct Fungi Imp Bur Mycol — Annotated Account of Fungi Received at the Imperial Bureau of Mycology
Annot Bibliogr Anim/Hum Ser Commonw Bur Anim Health — Annotated Bibliography. Animal/Human Series. Commonwealth Bureau of Animal Health
Annot Bibliography of Econ Geology — Annotated Bibliography of Economic Geology
Annot Bibliogr Commonw Bur Nutr — Annotated Bibliography. Commonwealth Bureau of Nutrition
Annot Bibliogr Commonw Bur Pastures Field Crops — Annotated Bibliography. Commonwealth Bureau of Pastures and Field Crops
Annot Bibliogr Commonw Bur Soils — Annotated Bibliography. Commonwealth Bureau of Soils
Annot Bibliogr Econ Geol — Annotated Bibliography of Economic Geology
Annot Bibliogr Med Myc — Annotated Bibliography of Medical Mycology
Annot Bibliogr Occurrence Biol Eff Fluorine Compd Suppl — Annotated Bibliography. The Occurrence and Biological Effects of Fluorine Compounds. Supplement
Annot Biblphy Cortisone — Annotated Bibliography of Cortisone, A.C.T.H. and Related Hormonal Substances
Annot Biblphy Econ Geol — Annotated Bibligraphy of Economic Geology
Annot Biblphy Hydrol Sediment US & Can — Annotated Bibliography on Hydrology and Sedimentation. United States and Canada
Annot Biblphy Hydrol US & Can — Annotated Bibliography on Hydrology. United States and Canada
Annot Biblphy Med Mycol — Annotated Bibliography of Medical Mycology
Annot Dokl Semin Inst Prikl Mat Tbilis Univ — Annotatsii Dokladov. Seminar Instituta Prikladnoj Matematiki. Tbilisskij Universitet
Annot Dokl Soveshch Yad Spektrosk Teor Yadra — Annotatsii Dokladov. Soveshchanie po Yadernoi Spektroskaopii i Teorii Yadra
Annotness Zool Bot (Bratislava) — Annotationes Zoologicae et Botanicae (Bratislava)
Annotness Zool Jap — Annotationes Zoologicae Japonenses
Ann Oto-Lar — Annales d'Oto-Laryngologie et de Chirurgie Cervico-Faciale
Ann Otolaryng — Annales d'Oto-Laryngologie et de Chirurgie Cervico-Faciale
Ann Oto-Laryngol — Annales d'Oto-Laryngologie [Later, Annales d'Oto-Laryngologie et de Chirurgie Cervico-Faciale]
Ann Oto-Laryngol Chir Cervico-Fac — Annales d'Oto-Laryngologie et de Chirurgie Cervico-Faciale
Ann Otol Rh — Annals of Otology, Rhinology, and Laryngology
Ann Otol Rhin Laryng — Annals of Otology, Rhinology, and Laryngology
Ann Otol Rhinol Laryngol — Annals of Otology, Rhinology, and Laryngology
Ann Otol Rhinol Laryngol Suppl — Annals of Otology, Rhinology, and Laryngology. Supplement
Ann Oto Rhinol Laryngol — Annals of Otology, Rhinology, and Laryngology
Ann Ottalmol — Annali di Ottalmologia
Ann Ottalmol Clin Ocul — Annali di Ottalmologia e Clinica Oculistica
Ann Ottalmol Clin Oculist — Annali di Ottalmologia e Clinica Oculistica
Annot Zool Bot — Annotationes Zoologicae et Botanicae
Annot Zool Jap — Annotationes Zoologicae Japonenses
Annot Zool Japon — Annotationes Zoologicae Japonenses
Annot Zool Jpn — Annotationes Zoologicae Japonenses
Ann Oudheid Kring Land Waas — Annalen van de Oudheidkundige Kring van het Land van Waas
Ann Paediat Jpn — Annales Paediatrici Japonici
Ann Paediatr — Annales Paediatrici
Ann Paediatr Fenn — Annales Paediatriae Fenniae
Ann Paediatr Fenn Suppl — Annales Paediatriae Fenniae. Supplementum
Ann Paediatr Int Rev Pediatr — Annales Paediatrici. International Review of Pediatrics

Ann Paediatr Suppl — Annales Paediatrica. Supplementum
Ann Paed Jap — Annales Paediatrici Japonici
Ann Pal — Annali. Facolta di Magistero. Universita di Palermo
Ann Paleontol — Annales de Paleontologie
Ann Paleontol Invertebr — Annales de Paleontologie Invertebre
Ann Paleontol Invertebre — Annales de Paleontologie Invertebre
Ann Paleontol Vertebr — Annales de Paleontologie Vertebre
Ann Paleontol Vertebr Invertebr — Annales de Paleontologie Vertebres-Invertebres
Ann Parasit — Annales de Parasitologie Humaine et Comparee
Ann Parasitol — Annales de Parasitologie Humaine et Comparee
Ann Parasitol Hum Comp — Annales de Parasitologie Humaine et Comparee
Ann Paris — Annales. Universite de Paris
Ann Parl — Annales Parlementaires
Ann Pathol — Annales de Pathologie
Ann Paulist Med e Cirurg — Annales Paulistas de Medicina e Cirurgia
Ann Paul Med Cir — Annaes Paulistas de Medicina e Cirurgia
Ann P C — Annales Parlementaires. Chambre de Representants
Ann Ped — Annee Pediatrique
Ann Pediatr — Annales de Pediatrie
Ann Pediatr Jpn Kioto Univ — Annales Paediatrici Japonici. Kioto Universitatis
Ann Pediatr (Paris) — Annales de Pediatrie (Paris)
Ann Perugia — Annali. Facolta di Lettere e Filosofia. Universita degli Studi di Perugia
Ann Pharmacother — Annals of Pharmacotherapy
Ann Pharm Belg — Annales Pharmaceutiques Belges
Ann Pharm F — Annales Pharmaceutiques Francaises
Ann Pharm Fr — Annales Pharmaceutiques Francaises
Ann Pharm (Lemgo Germany) — Annalen der Pharmacie (Lemgo, Germany)
Ann Pharm (Poznan) — Annales Pharmaceutici (Poznan)
Ann Pharm Pract Chem — Annals of Pharmacy and Practical Chemistry
Ann Phil — Annals of Philosophy
Ann Phil Hist — Annuaire. Institut de Philologie et d'Histoire Orientales et Slaves
Ann Phil Hist — Brussels. Universite Libre. Institut de Philologie et d'Histoire. Annuaire
Ann Phil Hist Orient — Annuaire. Institut de Philologie et d'Histoire Orientales et Slaves
Ann Philos — Annals of Philosophy
Ann Philos Nat Hist — Annals of Philosophy, Natural History, Chemistry, Literature, Agriculture, and the Mechanical and Fine Arts
Ann Phys — Annales de Physique
Ann Phys — Annals of Physics
Ann Phys Bi — Annales de Physique Biologique et Medicale
Ann Phys Biol Med — Annales de Physique Biologique et Medicale
Ann Phys Chem — Annalen der Physik und Chemie
Ann Phys (Germ) — Annalen der Physik (Germany)
Ann Physics — Annals of Physics
Ann Physik — Annalen der Physik
Ann Physik (7) — Annales der Physik. 7 Folge
Ann Physiol Anthropol — Annals of Physiological Anthropology
Ann Physiol Physicochim Biol — Annales de Physiologie et de Physicochimie Biologique
Ann Physiol Veg — Annales de Physiologie Vegetale
Ann Physiol Veg (Paris) — Annales de Physiologie Vegetale (Paris)
Ann Physiol Veg Univ Brux — Annales de Physiologie Vegetale. Universite de Bruxelles
Ann Physiol Veg Univ Bruxelles — Annales de Physiologie Vegetale. Universite de Bruxelles
Ann Physiq — Annales de Physique
Ann Phys (Leipzig) — Annalen der Physik (Leipzig)
Ann Phys Les Ulis — Annales de Physique (Les Ulis)
Ann Phys Les Ulis Colloq — Annales de Physique (Les Ulis). Colloque
Ann Phys Med — Annals of Physical Medicine
Ann Phys (New York) — Annals of Physics (New York)
Ann Phys NY — Annals of Physics (New York)
Ann Phys (Paris) — Annales de Physique (Paris)
Ann Phys Phys Chem — Annalen der Physik und Physikalischen Chemie
Ann Phys Phys Chim — Annales de Physiologie et de Physicochimie Biologique
Ann Phytopath — Annales de Phytopathologie
Ann Phytopathol — Annales de Phytopathologie
Ann Phytopathol Soc Jap — Annals. Phytopathological Society of Japan
Ann Phytopathol Soc Jpn — Annals. Phytopathological Society of Japan
Ann Pisa — Annali. Scuola Normale Superiore di Pisa
Ann Pisa Univ Fac Agrar — Annali. Pisa Universita. Facolta di Agraria
Ann Plan Info Anniston SMSA — Annual Planning Information. Anniston SMSA
Ann Plan Info Connecticut — Annual Planning Information for Connecticut
Ann Plan Info Hawaii SMSA — Annual Planning Information. State of Hawaii and Honolulu SMSA
Ann Plan Info Iowa — Annual Planning Information. State of Iowa
Ann Plan Info Macon Georgia SMSA — Annual Planning Information. Macon, Georgia SMSA (Standard Metropolitan Statistical Area)
Ann Plan Info Modesto SMSA — Annual Planning Information. Modesto SMSA (Standard Metropolitan Statistical Area)
Ann Plan Info Rep Daytona Beach SMSA — Annual Planning Information Report. Daytona Beach SMSA (Standard Metropolitan Statistical Area)
Ann Plan Info Salinas Seaside Monterey SMSA — Annual Planning Information. Salinas-Seaside-Monterey SMSA (Standard Metropolitan Statistical Area)
Ann Plan Info SMSA New York — Annual Planning Information for Manpower Planners. New York SMSA (Standard Metropolitan Statistical Area)
Ann Plan Info SMSA Syracuse — Annual Planning Information for Manpower Planners. Syracuse SMSA (Standard Metropolitan Statistical Area)
Ann Plan Rep DC — Annual Planning Report. District of Columbia
Ann Plan Rep Lexington SMSA — Annual Planning Report. Lexington SMSA (Standard Metropolitan Statistical Area)

Ann Plan Rep Spokane SMSA — Annual Planning Report. Spokane SMSA (Standard Metropolitan Statistical Area) Washington

Ann Plast Surg — Annals of Plastic Surgery

Ann Plovdiv — Godishnik na Plovdivskata Narodna Biblioteka i Muzei v Plovdiv

Ann Pol et Econ — Annee Politique et Economique

Ann Pol et Litt — Annales Politiques et Litteraires

Ann Polit Econ Coop — Annee Politique, Economique, et Cooperative

Ann Polit Litt — Annales Politiques et Litteraires

Ann Pol Math — Annales Polonici Mathematici

Ann Polon Math — Annales Polonici Mathematici

Ann Pol Rom Cath Church Union — Annals. Polish Roman Catholic Church Union Archives and Museum

Ann Pontificio Mus Mission Etnol — Annali. Pontificio Museo Missionario Etnologico

Ann Pontif Mus Miss Etnol (Vatican) — Annali. Pontificio Museo Missionario Etnologico (Vatican)

Ann Ponts Chaussees — Annales des Ponts et Chaussees

Ann Poul Mark Rev — Annual Poultry Market Review

Ann Poznan Agric Univ — Annals of Poznan Agricultural University

Ann Probab — Annals of Probability

Ann Probability — Annals of Probability

Ann Proc Fed Assis Rep — Annual Procurement and Federal Assistance Report

Ann Proc Nat Asso R Coms — Annual Proceedings. National Association of Railway Commissions

Ann Prog Rep Geol Surv West Austr — Annual Progress Report. Geological Survey. Western Australia

Ann Prog Rep Nat Found Cancer Res — Annual Progress Report. National Foundation for Cancer Research

Ann Prog Rep Pak For Inst Pesh — Annual Progress Report. Pakistan Forest Institute. Peshawar

Ann Prop Ind — Annales de la Propriete Industrielle, Artistique, et Litteraire

Ann Propr Ind — Annales de la Propriete Industrielle, Artistique, et Litteraire

Ann Protist — Annales de Protistologie

Ann P S — Annales Parlementaires. Senat

AnnPsych — Annee Psychologique

Ann Psychol — Annee Psychologique

Ann Public and Coop Econ — Annals of Public and Cooperative Economy [Formerly, Annals of Collective Economy]

Ann Pur App — Annals of Pure and Applied Logic

Ann Purdue Air Qual Conf Proc — Annual Purdue Air Quality Conference. Proceedings

Ann Pure Appl Logic — Annals of Pure and Applied Logic

Ann R Accad Agric Torino — Annali. Reale Accademia d'Agricoltura di Torino

Ann Rad Diagn — Annali di Radiologia Diagnostica

Ann Radioelectr — Annales de Radioelectricite

Ann Radiol — Annales de Radiologie

Ann Radiol Diagn — Annali di Radiologia Diagnostica

Ann Radiol Fis Med — Annali di Radiologia e Fisica Medica

Ann Radiol Med Nucl — Annales de Radiologie. Medecine Nucleaire

Ann Radiol Med Nucl Rev Imag Med — Annales de Radiologie Medecine Nucleaire-Revue d'Imagerie Medicale

Ann Radiopro — Annali di Radioprotezione

Ann R Agric Coll Swed — Annals. Royal Agricultural College of Sweden

Ann Rainf Aust — Annual Rainfall, Australia

Ann R Anthr — Annual Review of Anthropology

Ann R Astro — Annual Review of Astronomy and Astrophysics

Ann R Australas Coll Dent Surg — Annals. Royal Australasian College of Dental Surgeons

Ann R Bioch — Annual Review of Biochemistry

Ann R Bioph — Annual Review of Biophysics and Bioengineering

Ann R Coll Physicians Surg Can — Annals. Royal College of Physicians and Surgeons of Canada

Ann R Coll Surg Eng — Annals. Royal College of Surgeons of England

Ann R Coll Surg Engl — Annals. Royal College of Surgeons of England

Ann RC Surg — Annals. Royal College of Surgeons of England

Ann Readaptation Med Phys — Annales de Readaptation et de Medecine Physique

Ann Readapt Med Phys — Annales de Readaptation et de Medecine Physique

Ann Reale Scuola Super Agric Portici — Annali. Reale Scuola Superiore di Agricoltura di Portici

Ann R Earth — Annual Review of Earth and Planetary Sciences

Ann Rech For Maroc — Annales de la Recherche Forestiere au Maroc

Ann Rech Med Paris — Annales de la Recherche Medicale (Paris)

Ann Rech Vet — Annales de Recherches Veterinaires

Ann Rech Vet Ann Vet Res — Annales de Recherches Veterinaires/Annals of Veterinary Research

Ann R Ecol — Annual Review of Ecology and Systematics

Ann Reg — American Annual Register

Ann Reg Assoc Can Vol Ball — Annuaire et Regles de Jeu. Association Canadienne de Volley-Ball

Ann Regia Sc Super Agric Portici — Annali. Regia Scuola Superiore di Agricoltura in Portici

Ann Regia Super Agric (Portici) — Annali. Regia Scuola Superiore di Agricoltura (Portici)

Ann Regio Ist Super Agrar Portici — Annali. Regio Istituto Superiore Agrario di Portici

Ann R Entom — Annual Review of Entomology

Ann Rep Acc India Man Assoc — Annual Report and Accounts. All India Management Association

Ann Rep Acc Lond Transp Ex — Annual Report and Accounts. London Transport Executive

Ann Rep Adm Off Court Georgia — Annual Report. Administrative Office. Courts of Georgia

Ann Rep Alberta Dis Serv — Annual Report. Alberta Disaster Services

Ann Rep Alberta Health Occ Bd — Annual Report. Alberta Health Occupations Board

Ann Rep Alberta Home Mort Corp — Annual Report. Alberta Home Mortgage Corporation

Ann Rep Alberta Hous Corp — Annual Report. Alberta Housing Corp.

Ann Rep Am Jud Soc — Annual Report. American Judicature Society

Ann Rep Anti Dump Trib — Annual Report. Anti-dumping Tribunal

Ann Rep Argonne Nat Lab Div Bio Med Res — Annual Report. Argonne National Laboratory. Division of Biological and Medical Research

Ann Rep Arkansas Hous Dev Agen — Annual Report. Arkansas Housing Development Agency

Ann Rep Atlanta Reg Com — Annual Report. Atlanta Regional Commission

Ann Rep Bal Sh B Markazi Iran — Annual Report and Balance Sheet. Bank Markazi. Iran

Ann Rep Bank Ceylon — Annual Report. Bank of Ceylon

Ann Rep Brooklyn — Annual Report. Brooklyn Museum

Ann Rep Calif Adm Law — Annual Report. California. Office of Administrative Law

Ann Rep Calif Pub Broadc Com — Annual Report. California Public Broadcasting Commission

Ann Rep Can Dept Fish Oceans Newfoundland Reg — Annual Report. Canada Department of Fisheries and Oceans. Newfoundland Region

Ann Rep Cent Adult Dis (Osaka) — Annual Report. Center for Adult Diseases (Osaka)

Ann Rep Civ Serv Com Toronto — Annual Report. Civil Service Commission. Toronto

Ann Rep Cocoa Res Inst (Tafo Ghana) — Annual Report. Cocoa Research Institute (Tafo, Ghana)

Ann Rep Com Corp — Annual Report. Committee on Corporations

Ann Rep Com Sci Fr Resp — Annual Report. Committee on Scientific Freedom and Responsibility

Ann Rep Cult Soc Cent Asian Pac Reg — Annual Report. Cultural and Social Centre for the Asian and Pacific Region

Ann Rep Cypr — Annual Report. Director. Department of Antiquiities. Cyprus

Ann Rep Dep Hlth NZ — Annual Report. Department of Health

Ann Rep Dept Com Wel West Aust — Annual Report. Department for Community Welfare. Western Australia

Ann Rep Dept Emp Lab Rel Queensland — Annual Report. Department of Employment and Labour Relations. Queensland

Ann Rep Dept Env (India) — Annual Report. Department of Environment (India)

Ann Rep Dept Fish Pr Ed Isl — Annual Report. Department of Fisheries. Prince Edward Island

Ann Rep Dept Lab Ind (West Aust) — Annual Report. Department of Labour and Industry (Western Australia)

Ann Rep Dept Pub Wk Nova Scotia — Annual Report. Department of Public Works. Nova Scotia

Ann Rep Dept Soc Serv Charlottetown — Annual Report. Department of Social Services. Charlottetown

Ann Rep Dir Civ Cons Corp (US) — Annual Report. Director of the Civilian Conservation Corps (US)

Ann Rep Dir Oklahoma Lib — Annual Report and Directory of Oklahoma Libraries

Ann Rep Dir Sea Fish (S Africa) — Annual Report. Director of Sea Fisheries (South Africa)

Ann Rep DS — Annual Report. Dante Society

Ann Rep East Afr Rail Corp — Annual Report. East African Railways Corp.

Ann Rep Emp Sec Com New Mexico — Annual Report. Employment Security Commission of New Mexico

Ann Rep Farm Facts — Annual Report and Farm Facts

Ann Rep Fed En Adm — Annual Report. Federal Energy Administration

Ann Rep Ferm Proc — Annual Reports on Fermentation Processes

Ann Rep Fogg Art Mus — Annual Report. Fogg Art Museum

Ann Rep Hal Inf — Annual Report. Halifax Infirmary

Ann Rep Hawaii Bicent Com — Annual Report. Hawaii Bicentennial Commission

Ann Rep Henry Luce Found — Annual Report. Henry Luce Foundation

Ann Rep High Tech Mat — Annual Report on High-Tech Materials

Ann Rep Hlth Med Serv — Annual Report. Health and Medical Services of the State of Queensland

Ann Rep Ind Robots — Annual Report on Industrial Robots

Ann Rep Inorg Gen Synth — Annual Reports in Inorganic and General Syntheses

Ann Rep Inst Geol Sci — Annual Report. Institute of Geological Sciences

Ann Rep Inst Med Vet Sci — Annual Report. Institute of Medical and Veterinary Science

Ann Rep Inst Vir Res — Annual Report. Institute for Virus Research

Ann Rep Int Telecom Sat Org — Annual Report. International Telecommunications Satellite Organization

Ann Rep Iowa En Pol Counc — Annual Report. Iowa Energy Policy Council

Ann Rep Iowa Env Qual Com — Annual Report. Iowa Environmental Quality Commission

Ann Rep Maine Adv Counc Voc Ed — Annual Report. Maine Advisory Council on Vocational Education

Ann Rep Maine St Bd Reg Prof Eng — Annual Report. Maine State Board of Registration for Professional Engineers

Ann Rep Manag Adel Hosp — Annual Report. Board of Management. Royal Adelaide Hospital

Ann Rep Manitoba Dept Econ Dev Tour — Annual Report. Manitoba Department of Economic Development and Tourism

Ann Rep Manitoba Lot Com — Annual Report. Manitoba Lotteries Commission

Ann Rep Mass Tran Div Dept Transp Oregon — Annual Report. Mass Transit Division. Department of Transportation. State of Oregon

Ann Rep Med Chem — Annual Reports in Medicinal Chemistry

Ann Rep Med Res Counc Nigeria — Annual Report. Medical Research Council of Nigeria

Ann Rep MFA — Annales. Cercle Archeologique et Folklorique de la Louviere et du Centre

Ann Rep Milk Cont Bd Manitoba — Annual Report. Milk Control Board of Manitoba

Ann Rep Minnestoa Mississippi Head Bd — Annual Report. Minnesota Mississippi Headwaters Board

Ann Rep Min Res Div (Fiji) — Annual Report. Mineral Resources Division (Fiji)

Ann Rep Mississippi Medicaid Com — Annual Report. Mississippi Medicaid Commission

Ann Rep Missouri Riv Basin Com — Annual Report. Missouri River Basin Commission

Ann Rep NACA — Annual Report. United States National Advisory Committee for Aeronautics

Ann Rep Nat Arc Rec Cent Singapore — Annual Report. National Archives and Records Centre. Singapore

Ann Rep Nat Res Counc Can — Annual Report. National Research Council of Canada

Ann Rep New Jersey Dept Lab Ind — Annual Report. New Jersey Department of Labor and Industry

Ann Rep New Jersey Dept Transp — Annual Report. New Jersey Department of Transportation

Ann Rep Nova Scotia Dept Lab — Annual Report. Nova Scotia Department of Labour

Ann Rep Past Ins SI — Annual Report. Pasteur Institute of Southern India

Ann Rep Pr Ed Isl Dept Ind Com — Annual Report. Government of the Provinces of Prince Edward Island. Department of Industry and Commerce

Ann Rep Prog Chem Sect C Phys Chem — Annual Reports on the Progress of Chemistry. Section C. Physical Chemistry

Ann Rep Prog Georgia Dept MMG — Annual Report of Progress. Georgia Department of Mines, Mining, and Geology

Ann Rep Rev Op (Port Melbourne) — Annual Report and Review of Operations (Port of Melbourne)

Ann Rep S Afr Inst Med Res — Annual Report. South African Institute for Medical Research

Ann Rep Smith Inst — Annual Report. Smithsonian Institution

Ann Rep Soc Libyan Stud — Annual Report. Society for Libyan Studies

Ann Rep Stat Acc NZ Milk B — Annual Report and Statement of Accounts. New Zealand Milk Board

Ann Rept Fogg — Annual Report. Fogg Art Museum

Ann Rept Progr Chem — Annual Reports on the Progress of Chemistry

Ann Rept Tokyo Univ Agr Technol — Annual Report. Tokyo University of Agriculture and Technology

Ann Rep United Fruit Co Med Dept — Annual Report. United Fruit Company. Medical Department

Ann Rep Yearb Adv Res Found — Annual Report and Yearbook. Advertising Research Foundation

Ann Rep Yorkshire Phil Soc — Annual Report. Yorkshire Philosophical Society

Ann Res Inst Environ Med Nagoya Univ — Annals. Research Institute of Environmental Medicine. Nagoya University

Ann Res Inst Epidemiol Microbiol — Annals. Research Institute of Epidemiology and Microbiology

Ann Res Inst Land Reclam Soil Sci Hydrotech Ser — Annals. Research Institute for Land Reclamation and Soil Science. HydrotechnicsSeries

Ann Res Inst Land Reclam Soil Sci Land Reclam Ser — Annals. Research Institute for Land Reclamation and Soil Science. Land Reclamation Series

Ann Res Inst Land Reclam Soil Sci Soil Sci Ser — Annals. Research Institute for Land Reclamation and Soil Science. Soil Science Series

Ann Res Inst Micr Dis — Annals. Research Institute for Microbial Diseases

Ann Res Inst Plant Prot Cent Res Inst Agric Bucharest — Annals. Research Institute for Plant Protection. Central Research Institute forAgriculture. Bucharest

Ann Res Rep Red River Valley Agric Exp Stn — Annual Research Report. Red River Valley Agricultural Experiment Station

Ann Res Rep Univ Br Col Agri Sci — Annual and Research Report. University of British Columbia. Faculty of Agricultural Sciences

Ann Rev Acad Nat Sci Philad — Annual Review. Academy of Natural Sciences of Philadelphia

Ann Rev Analyt Chem — Annual Review of Analytical Chemistry

Ann Rev Austr Min Ind — Annual Review. Australian Mineral Industry

Ann Rev Biochem — Annual Review of Biochemistry

Ann Rev Ecol — Annual Review of Ecology and Systematics

Ann Rev Ecol Sys — Annual Review of Ecology and Systematics

Ann Rev Ent — Annual Review of Entomology

Ann Rev Entomol — Annual Review of Entomology

Ann Rev Gen — Annual Review of Genetics

Ann Rev Jazz Studies — Annual Review of Jazz Studies

Ann Rev Med — Annual Review of Medicine

Ann Rev Microbiol — Annual Review of Microbiology

Ann Rev Nuclear Sci — Annual Review of Nuclear Science [*Later, Annual Review of Nuclear and ParticleScience*]

Ann Rev Nucl Sci — Annual Review of Nuclear Science [*Later, Annual Review of Nuclear and ParticleScience*]

Ann Rev Pharm — Annual Review of Pharmacology [*Later, Annual Review of Pharmacology and Toxicology*]

Ann Rev Pharmacol — Annual Review of Pharmacology [*Later, Annual Review of Pharmacology and Toxicology*]

Ann Rev Phys Chem — Annual Review of Physical Chemistry

Ann Rev Physiol — Annual Review of Physiology

Ann Rev Phytopath — Annual Review of Phytopathology

Ann Rev Plant Physiol — Annual Review of Plant Physiology

Ann R Fluid — Annual Review of Fluid Mechanics

Ann R Genet — Annual Review of Genetics

Ann Rheumat Dis — Annals of the Rheumatic Diseases

Ann Rheum D — Annals of the Rheumatic Diseases

Ann Rheum Dis — Annals of the Rheumatic Diseases

Ann R Infor — Annual Review of Information Science and Technology

Ann R Mater — Annual Review of Materials Science

Ann R Med — Annual Review of Medicine

Ann R Micro — Annual Review of Microbiology

Ann R Nucl — Annual Review of Nuclear Science [*Later, Annual Review of Nuclear and ParticleScience*]

Ann Roentg — Annals of Roentgenology

Ann Roentgenol Radiol — Annales de Roentgenologie et de Radiologie

Ann R Oss Meteorol — Annali del Reale Osservatorio Meteorologico Vesuviano

Ann R Oss Vesuviano — Annali. Reale Osservatorio Vesuviano

Ann Roy Bot Gard Calcutta — Annals. Royal Botanic Garden (Calcutta)

Ann Roy Bot Gard Peradeniya — Annals. Royal Botanic Garden (Peradeniya)

Ann Roy Coll Surg — Annals. Royal College of Surgeons of England

Ann Rp Ch A — Annual Reports on the Progress of Chemistry. Section A. General, Physical, and Inorganic Chemistry

Ann Rp Ch B — Annual Reports on the Progress of Chemistry. Section B. Organic Chemistry

Ann R Pharm — Annual Review of Pharmacology [*Later, Annual Review of Pharmacology and Toxicology*]

Ann R Ph Ch — Annual Review of Physical Chemistry

Ann R Physl — Annual Review of Physiology

Ann R Phyto — Annual Review of Phytopathology

Ann R Plant — Annual Review of Plant Physiology

Ann R Psych — Annual Review of Psychology

Ann R Scu Norm Sup Pisa — Annali. Scuola Normale Superiore di Pisa. Classe di Lettere e Filosofia

Ann R Sociol — Annual Review of Sociology

AnnS — Annales Silesiae

AnnS — Annals of Science

ANNSA8 — Annals of Science

Ann SAE — Annales. Service des Antiquites de l'Egypte

Ann SA Eg — Annales. Service des Antiquites de l'Egypt

Ann S Afr Mus — Annals. South Africa Museum

Ann Sanita Pubblica — Annali della Sanita Pubblica

Ann Sanita Pubblica Suppl — Annali della Sanita Pubblica. Supplemento

Ann Sanit Int — Annuaire Sanitaire International

Ann San Rep Prov Assam — Annual Sanitary Report of the Province of Assam

Ann Saudi Med — Annals of Saudi Medicine

Ann Sc At — Annuario. Scuola Archeologica di Atene e delle Missioni Italiani in Oriente

Ann Sc At — Annuario. Scuola Archeologica di Atene e Missioni Italiani in Oriente

Ann Sc Econ Appliq — Annales des Sciences Economiques Appliquees

Ann Schiapparelli — Annali Schiapparelli

Ann Sci — Annals of Science

Ann Sci Agron — Annales de la Science Agronomique

Ann Sci Agron Fr — Annales de la Science Agronomique Francaise et Etrangere

Ann Sci Agron Franc Etrangere — Annales. Science Agronomique Francaise et Etrangere

Ann Sci Agron Fr Etrang — Annales de la Science Agronomique Francaise et Etrangere

Ann Sci Auvergne — Annales Scientifiques, Litteraires, et Industrielles de l'Auvergne

Ann Sci Ec — Annales Scientifiques. Ecole Normale Superieure

Ann Sci Ecole Norm Sup — Annales Scientifiques. Ecole Normale Superieure

Ann Sci Econ Appl — Annales des Sciences Economiques Appliquees

Ann Sciences Econs Appliquees — Annales des Sciences Economiques Appliquees

Ann Sci For — Annales des Sciences Forestieres

Ann Sci For (Paris) — Annales des Sciences Forestieres (Paris)

Ann Sci Franche Comte — Annales Scientifiques de Franche Comte

Ann Sci Hom — Annuaire Sciences de l'Homme

Ann Sci Kanazawa Univ — Annals of Science. Kanazawa University

Ann Sci Kanazawa Univ Part 2 Biol-Geol — Annals of Science. Kanazawa University. Part 2. Biology-Geology

Ann Sci Lett — Annali di Scienze e Lettere

Ann Sci (Lond) — Annals of Science (London)

Ann Sci Math Quebec — Annales des Sciences Mathematiques du Quebec

Ann Sci Nat — Annaes de Sciencias Naturaes

Ann Sci Nat Bot — Annales des Sciences Naturelles. A. Botanique

Ann Sci Nat Bot Biol Veg — Annales des Sciences Naturelles. Botanique et Biologie Vegetale

Ann Sci Nat Oporto — Annaes de Sciencias Naturaes (Oporto)

Ann Sci Natur Bot Biol Veg — Annales des Sciences Naturelles. Botanique et Biologie Vegetale

Ann Sci Nat Zool — Annales des Sciences Naturelles. B. Zoologie

Ann Sci Nat Zool Biol Anim — Annales des Sciences Naturelles. Zoologie et Biologie Animale

Ann Sci Soc Portug Paris — Annaes das Sciencias, das Artes, e das Letras. Por Huma Sociedade de Portuguezes Residentes em Paris

Ann Sci Text Belg — Annales Scientifiques Textiles Belges

Ann Sci Univ Bes — Annales Scientifiques. Universite de Besancon

Ann Sci Univ Besancon — Annales Scientifiques. Universite de Besancon

Ann Sci Univ Besancon Biol Anim — Annales Scientifiques. Universite de Besancon. Biologie Animale

Ann Sci Univ Besancon Biol Veg — Annales Scientifiques. Universite de Besancon. Biologie Vegetale

Ann Sci Univ Besancon Bot — Annales Scientifiques. Universite de Besancon. Botanique

Ann Sci Univ Besancon Chim — Annales Scientifiques. Universite de Besancon. Chimie

Ann Sci Univ Besancon Climatol — Annales Scientifiques. Universite de Besancon. Climatologie

Ann Sci Univ Besancon Geol — Annales Scientifiques. Universite de Besancon. Geologie

Ann Sci Univ Besancon Hydrogr — Annales Scientifiques. Universite de Besancon. Hydrographie

Ann Sci Univ Besancon Math — Annales Scientifiques. Universite de Besancon. Mathematiques

Ann Sci Univ Besancon Math 3 — Annales Scientifiques. Universite de Besancon. Mathematiques. 3e Serie

Ann Sci Univ Besancon Mec Phys Theor — Annales Scientifiques. Universite de Besancon. Mecanique et Physique Theorique

Ann Sci Univ Besancon Med — Annales Scientifiques. Universite de Besancon. Medecine

Ann Sci Univ Besancon Meteorol — Annales Scientifiques. Universite de Besancon. Meteorologie

Ann Sci Univ Besancon Phys — Annales Scientifiques. Universite de Besancon. Physique

Ann Sci Univ Besancon Physiol Biol Anim — Annales Scientifiques. Universite de Besancon. Physiologie et Biologie Animale

Ann Sci Univ Besancon Zool — Annales Scientifiques. Universite de Besancon. Zoologie

Ann Sci Univ Besancon Zool Physiol — Annales Scientifiques. Universite de Besancon. Zoologie et Physiologie

Ann Sci Univ Besancon Zool Physiol Biol Anim — Annales Scientifiques. Universite de Besancon. Zoologie, Physiologie, et Biologie Animale

Ann Sci Univ Clermont — Annales Scientifiques. Universite de Clermont

Ann Sci Univ Clermont Ferrand 2 — Annales Scientifiques. Universite de Clermont-Ferrand 2

Ann Sci Univ Clermont-Ferrand II Math — Annales Scientifiques. Universite de Clermont-Ferrand. II. Mathematiques

Ann Sci Univ Clermont Ferrand II Probab Appl — Annales Scientifiques de l'Universite de Clermont-Ferrand II. Probabilites et Applications

Ann Sci Univ Clermont Math — Annales Scientifiques. Universite de Clermont. Serie Mathematique

Ann Sci Univ Franche Comte Besancon Math 4 — Annales Scientifiques de l'Universite de Franche-Comte Besancon. Mathematiques.4eme Serie

Ann Sci Univ Franche Comte Besancon Med Pharm — Annales Scientifiques. Universite de Franche-Comte-Besancon. Medecine et Pharmacie

Ann Sci Univ Jass Sect 1 — Annales Scientifiques. Universite de Jassy. Section 1. Mathematiques, Physique,Chimie

Ann Sci Univ Jassy — Annales Scientifiques. Universite de Jassy

Ann Sci Univ Jassy Sect 1 — Annales Scientifiques. Universite de Jassy. Section 1. Mathematiques, Physique,Chimie

Ann Sci Univ Jassy Sect 2 — Annales Scientifiques. Universite de Jassy. Section 2. Sciences Naturelles

Ann Sci Univ Reims ARERS — Annales Scientifiques. Universite de Reims et ARERS

Ann Sci Univ Reims ARERS (Assoc Reg Etude Rech Sci) — Annales Scientifiques. Universite de Reims et ARERS (Association Regionale pourl'Etude et la Recherche Scientifiques)

Ann Sclavo — Annali Sclavo

Ann Sc Nat — Annales des Sciences Naturelles

Ann Sc Nat Zool — Annales des Sciences Naturelles. Zoologie

Ann Sc Norm Super Pisa — Annali. Scuola Normale Superiore di Pisa

Ann Sc Norm Super Pisa Sci Fis Mat — Annali. Scuola Normale Superiore di Pisa. Scienze, Fisiche, e Matematiche

Ann Sc Pisa — Annali. Scuola Normale Superiore di Pisa. Classe di Lettere e Filosofia

Ann Scu Archeol Atene — Annuario. Scuola Archeologica di Atene e Missioni Italiane in Oriente

Ann Scu Norm Sup — Annali. Scuola Normale Superiore

Ann Scu Norm Super Pisa — Annali. Scuola Normale Superiore di Pisa

Ann Scuola Norm Sup Pisa Cl Sci — Annali. Scuola Normale Superiore di Pisa. Classe di Scienze

Ann Scuola Norm Sup Pisa Cl Sci 4 — Annali. Scuola Normale Superiore di Pisa. Classe di Scienze. Serie IV

Ann Scuola Norm Sup Pisa Sci Fis Mat — Annali. Scuola Normale Superiore di Pisa. Scienze, Fisiche, e Matematiche

Ann Scuola Pisa — Annali. Scuola Normale Superiore di Pisa. Classe di Lettere e Filosofia

Ann Sect Dendrol Soc Bot Pol — Annales. Section Dendrologique. Societe Botanique de Pologne

Ann Sect Horti Vitic Univ Sci Agric — Annales Sectionis Horti et Viticulturae Universitatis Scientiae Agriculturae

Ann Sect Platine Autres Met Precieux Inst Chim Gen — Annales du Secteur du Platine et des Autres Metaux Precieux. Institut de ChimieGenerale

Ann Seism — Annuaire Seismique

Ann Sem Giur — Annali. Seminario Giuridico. Universita di Palermo

Ann Sem Giur Catania — Annali. Seminario Giuridico. Universita Catania

Ann Seminar Metaf — Annales. Seminario de Metafisica

Ann Sem Stud Eur Orient Sez Ling Filol Ist Univ Orient — Annali. Seminario di Studi dell'Europa Orientale. Sezione Linguistico-Filogica.Istituto Universitario Orientale

Ann Serv — Annales. Service des Antiquites de l'Egypte

Ann Serv Ant — Annales. Service des Antiquites de l'Egypte

Ann Serv Ant Eg — Annales. Service des Antiquites de l'Egypt

Ann Serv Antiq Egypte — Annales du Service des Antiquites de l'Egypte

Ann Serv Antiqu — Annales. Service des Antiquites de l'Egypte

Ann Serv Bot Agron Dir Aff Econ Tunis — Annales. Service Botanique et Agronomique. Direction des Affaires Economique de Tunisie

Ann Serv Bot Agron Dir Gen Agric Tunis — Annales. Service Botanique et Agronomique. Direction Generale de l'Agriculture de Tunisie

Ann Serv Bot Agron Tunis — Annales. Service Botanique et Agronomique de Tunisie

Ann Serv Bot Direct Gen Agric — Annales du Service Botanique et Agronomique. Direction Generale de l'Agriculture

Ann Serv Bot Tunis — Annales. Service Botanique de Tunisie

Ann Serv Bot Tunisie — Annales. Service Botanique et Agronomique. Direction Generale de l'Agriculture Tunisie

Ann Service des Ant — Annales. Service des Antiquites de l'Egypte

Ann Serv Mines Com Spec Katanga — Annales. Service des Mines. Comite Special du Katanga

Ann Serv Suppl — Annales. Service des Antiquites de l'Egypt. Supplement

Ann Sez Ling — Annali. Sezione Linguistica. Istituto Universitario Orientale

Ann Skh Nauk — Annaly Sel'skokhozyaistvennykh Nauk

Ann Skh Nauk Ser C — Annaly Sel'skokhozyaistvennykh Nauk. Seriya C. Sel'skokhozyaistvennaya Tekhnika

Ann Skh Nauk Ser E — Annaly Sel'skokhozyaistvennykh Nauk. Seriya E. Zashchita Rastenii

Ann Skopje — Godisen Zbornik. Filozofski Fakultet na Univerzitetot Skopje

Ann Soc Arch Namur — Annales. Societe Archeologique de Namur

Ann Soc BCG Immunother — Annals. Society of BCG (Bacillus Calmette-Guerin) Immunotherapy

Ann Soc Belge Astr — Annuaire. Societe Belge d'Astronomie

Ann Soc Belge Etude Pet Ses Deriv Succedanes — Annales. Societe Belge pour l'Etude du Petrole, de Ses Derives, et Succedanes

Ann Soc Belge Med Trop — Annales. Societe Belge de Medecine Tropicale

Ann Soc Belge Neurol — Annales. Societe Belge de Neurologie

Ann Soc Belg Hist Hop — Annales. Societe Belge d'Histoire des Hopitaux

Ann Soc Belg Med Trop — Annales. Societe Belge de Medecine Tropicale

Ann Soc Belg Med Trop Parasitol Mycol — Annales. Societes Belges de Medecine Tropicale, de Parasitologie, et de Mycologie

Ann Soc Belg Pharm — Annales. Societatis Belgicae Pharmaceuticae

Ann Soc Biol Pernambuco — Annaes. Sociedade de Biologia de Pernambuco

Ann Soc Brass Enseign Prof — Annales. Societe des Brasseurs pour l'Enseignement Professionel

Ann Soc Chim Fr — Annuaire. Societe Chimique de France

Ann Soc Chim Pol — Annales Societatis Chimicae Polonorum

Ann Soc Doctrinae Stud Acad Med Silesiensis — Annales Societatis Doctrinae Studentium Academiae Medicae Silesiensis

Ann Soc Emul Ain — Annales. Societe d'Emulation, Agriculture, Sciences, Lettres, et Arts de l'Ain

Ann Soc Emulation Bruges — Annales. Societe d'Emulation de Bruges

Ann Soc Ent — Annales. Societe Entomologique de France

Ann Soc Entomol Fr — Annales. Societe Entomologique de France

Ann Soc Entomol Que — Annales. Societe Entomologique du Quebec

Ann Soc Fr Econ Alp — Annuaire. Societe Francaise d'Economie Alpestre

Ann Soc Geol Belg — Annales. Societe Geologique de Belgique

Ann Soc Geol Belg Bull — Annales. Societe Geologique de Belgique. Bulletin

Ann Soc Geol Belg Bull Suppl — Annales. Societe Geologique de Belgique. Bulletin. Supplement

Ann Soc Geol Belgique — Annales. Societe Geologique de Belgique

Ann Soc Geol Belg Mem — Annales. Societe Geologique de Belgique. Memoires

Ann Soc Geol Nord — Annales. Societe Geologique du Nord

Ann Soc Geol Pol — Annales Societatis Geologorum Poloniae

Ann Soc Geol Pol — Annales. Societe Geologique de Pologne

Ann Soc Hist Archeol Arrondissement Saint Malo — Annales. Societe Historique et Archeologique de l'Arrondissement de Saint-Malo

Ann Soc Hort Haute Garonne — Annales. Societe d'Horticulture de la Haute-Garonne

Ann Soc Hydr Med — Annales. Societe d'Hydrologie Medicale de Paris

Ann Soc Ingeg — Annali. Societa degli Ingegneri e degli Architetti Italiani

Ann Sociol — Annee Sociologique

Ann Soc Lin Lyon — Annales. Societe Lineenne de Lyon

Ann Soc Linn Dep Maine et Loire — Annales. Societe Linneenne du Departement de Maine-et-Loire

Ann Soc Linn Lyon — Annales. Societe Linneenne de Lyon

Ann Soc Litt Estonicae — Annales Societatis Litterarum Estonicae in Svecia

Ann Soc Math Pol Ser IV Fundam Inf — Annales Societatis Mathematicae Polonae. Series IV. Fundamenta Informaticae

Ann Soc Med Anvers — Annales. Societe de Medecine d'Anvers

Ann Soc Med-Chir Bruges — Annales. Societe Medico-Chirurgicale de Bruges

Ann Soc Med Leg Belg — Annales. Societe de Medecine Legale de Belgique

Ann Soc Nat Hort Fr — Annales. Societe Nationale de l'Horticulture de France

Ann Soc Pharm Chim Sao Paulo — Annaes. Sociedade de Pharmacia e Chimica de Sao Paulo

Ann Soc Pharm Quim Sao Paulo — Annaes. Sociedade de Pharmacia e Quimica de Sao Paulo

Ann Soc Pol Math — Annales. Societe Polonaise de Mathematique

Ann Soc Rebus Nat Invest Univ Tartu Const — Annales Societatis Rebus Naturae Investigandis in Universitate Tartuensi Constituta

Ann Soc Roy Arch Bruxelles — Annales. Societe Royale d'Archeologie de Bruxelles

Ann Soc Roy Sci Med — Annales. Societe Royale des Sciences Medicales et Naturelles de Bruxelles

Ann Soc R Sci Med Nat Bruxelles — Annales. Societe Royale des Sciences Medicales et Naturelles de Bruxelles

Ann Soc R Zool Belg — Annales. Societe Royale Zoologique de Belgique

Ann Soc Sci Bruxelles — Annales. Societe Scientifique de Bruxelles

Ann Soc Sci Bruxelles Ser 1 — Annales. Societe Scientifique de Bruxelles. Serie 1

Ann Soc Sci Bruxelles Ser 2 — Annales. Societe Scientifique de Bruxelles. Serie 2. Sciences Naturelles et Medicales

Ann Soc Sci Bruxelles Ser 3 — Annales. Societe Scientifique de Bruxelles. Serie 3. Sciences Economiques

Ann Soc Sci Bruxelles Ser A — Annales. Societe Scientifique de Bruxelles. Serie A. Sciences Mathematiques

Ann Soc Sci Brux Ser 1 — Annales. Societe Scientifique de Bruxelles. Serie 1

Ann Soc Scient Bruxelles S B Sc Phys Nat — Annales. Societe Scientifique de Bruxelles. Serie B. Sciences Physiques et Naturelles

Ann Soc Scient Bruxelles S C Sci Med — Annales. Societe Scientifique de Bruxelles. Serie C. Sciences Medicales

Ann Soc Sci Faeroe — Annales Societatis Scientiarum Faeroensis

Ann Soc Sci Faeroe Suppl — Annales Societatis Scientiarum Faeroensis. Supplementum

Ann Soc Sci Litt Cannes — Annales. Societe de Science et Litterature de Cannes

Ann Soc Sci Med Bruxelles — Annales. Societe des Sciences Medicales et Naturelles de Bruxelles

Ann Soc Sci Med Nat Bruges — Annales. Societe de Sciences Naturelles de Bruges

Ann Soc Sci Nat Charente-Marit — Annales. Societe des Sciences Naturelles de la Charente-Maritime

Ann Soc Suisse Zool Mus Hist Nat Geneve — Annales. Societe Suisse de Zoologie et du Museum d'Histoire Naturelle de Geneve

Ann Soc Zool Belg — Annales. Societe Royale Zoologique de Belgique

Ann (Sofia) — Godishnik na Narodniia Arkheologicheski Muzei (Sofia)

Ann Soz P — Annalen fuer Soziale Politik und Gesetzgebung

Ann Speleol — Annales de Speleologie

Ann Sper Agr — Annali della Sperimentazione Agraria

Ann Sper Agrar — Annali della Sperimentazione Agraria

Ann Sports Med — Annals of Sports Medicine

AnnSR — Annales. Societa Retorumantscha

Ann SRA Brux — Annales. Societe Royale d'Archeologie de Bruxelles

Ann Sta Chim-Agr Sper Roma Ser 3 — Annali. Stazione Chimico-Agraria Sperimentale di Roma. Serie 3

Ann Staedt Allg Krankenhaeuser Muenchen — Annalen. Staedtische Allgemeine Krankenhaeuser zu Muenchen

Ann Sta Sperim Agrumicoltura — Annali. Reale Stazione Sperimentale di Agrumicoltura e Frutticoltura in Acireale

Ann Stat Belg — Annuaire Statistique de la Belgique

Ann Stat Centr Hydrobiol Appl — Annales. Station Centrale d'Hydrobiologie Appliquee

Ann Stat Guid — Annuario di Statistiche Guidiziarie

Ann Statist — Annals of Statistics

Ann Statist Tun — Annuaire Statistique de la Tunisie

Ann Stat Oceanogr Salammbo — Annales. Station Oceanographique de Salammbo

Ann Stat Sec Soc — Annuaire Statistique de la Securite Sociale

Ann Stat Tunisie — Annuaire Statistique de la Tunisie

Ann St Dir — Annali di Storia del Diritto

Ann Stn Biol Besse-En-Chandesse — Annales. Station Biologique de Besse-En-Chandesse

Ann Stn Cent Hydrobiol Appl — Annales. Station Centrale d'Hydrobiologie Appliquee

Ann Stn Chim Agrar Sper Roma — Annali. Stazione Chimico-Agraria Sperimentale di Roma

Ann Stn Chim-Agrar Sper Roma Ser 3 Pubbl — Annali. Stazione Chimico-Agraria Sperimentale di Roma. Serie 3. Pubblicazione

Ann Stn Fed Rech For Zurich — Annales. Station Federale de Recherches Forestieres. Zurich

Ann Stom — Annali di Stomatologia

Ann Stomatol — Annali di Stomatologia

Ann Stomatol Clin Odontoiatr — Annali di Stomatologia e Clinica Odontoiatrica

Ann Stomatol Ist Super Odontoiatr G Eastman — Annali di Stomatologia. Istituto Superiore di Odontoiatria G. Eastman

Ann Stomatol (Roma) — Annali di Stomatologia (Roma)

Ann Storia Nat — Annali di Storia Naturale

Ann Sulsses Sci Appl Tech — Annales Suisses des Sciences Appliquees et de la Technique

Ann Surg — Annals of Surgery

Ann Surg Oncol — Annals of Surgical Oncology

Ann Surv Am L — Annual Survey of American Law

Ann Surv Comm L — Annual Survey of Commonwealth Law

Ann Surv Commonw L — Annual Survey of Commonwealth Law

Ann Survey Am L — Annual Survey of American Law

Ann Surv Law — Annual Survey of Law

Ann Surv Mass L — Annual Survey of Massachusetts Law

Ann Surv Mass Law — Annual Survey of Massachusetts Law

Ann Surv of Law — Annual Survey of Law

Ann Surv SAL — Annual Survey of South African Law

Ann Sys Process Sal Rep — Annual Systems and Processing Salaries Report

Ann Systems Res — Annals of Systems Research

Ann Syst Res — Annals of Systems Research

Annt — Annals. American Academy of Political and Social Sciences

Ann Tab Sec 1 — Annales du Tabac. Section 1

Ann Tab Sect 2 — Annales du Tabac. Section 2

Ann Tadzh Astron Obs Dushanbe USSR — Annals. Tadzhik Astronomical Observatory (Dushanbe, USSR)

Ann Tec Agr — Annales de Technologie Agricole

Ann Tech Agric — Annales de Technologie Agricole

Ann Tech Assoc Man Made Fiber Paper Jpn — Annals. Technical Association of Man-Made Fiber Paper. Japan

Ann Technol Agr — Annales de Technologie Agricole

Ann Technol Agric (Paris) — Annales de Technologie Agricole (Paris)

Ann Telecom — Annales des Telecommunications

Ann Telecomm — Annales des Telecommunications

Ann Telecommun — Annales des Telecommunications

Ann Tenn Air Qual Rep St Loc — Annual Tennessee Air Quality Report. State and Local

Ann Theol — Annee Theologique Augustinienne

Ann Ther — Annee Therapeutique

AnnThijm — Annalen van het Thijmgenootschap

Ann Thijmgenoot — Annales Thijmgenootschap

Ann Thorac — Annals of Thoracic Surgery

Ann Thoracic Surg — Annals of Thoracic Surgery

Ann Thorac Surg — Annals of Thoracic Surgery

Ann Thor Surg — Annals of Thoracic Surgery

Ann Tokyo Astr Obs — Annals of the Tokyo Astronomical Observatory

Ann Tokyo Astron Obs — Annals. Tokyo Astronomical Observatory

Ann Transplant — Annals of Transplantation

Ann Transvaal Mus — Annals. Transvaal Museum

Ann Transv Mus — Annals. Transvaal Museum

Ann Trav Agr Sci — Annales des Travaux Agricoles Scientifiques

Ann Trav Publics Belg — Annales des Travaux Publics de Belgique

AnnTriest — Annali Triestini

Ann Triest Cura Univ Trieste Sez II — Annali Triestini a Cura. Universita di Trieste. Sezione II. Scienze ed Ingegneria

Ann Trop M — Annals of Tropical Medicine and Parasitology

Ann Trop Med — Annals of Tropical Medicine and Parasitology

Ann Trop Med Paras — Annals of Tropical Medicine and Parasitology

Ann Trop Med Parasit — Annals of Tropical Medicine and Parasitology

Ann Trop Med Parasitol — Annals of Tropical Medicine and Parasitology

Ann Trop Paediatr — Annals of Tropical Paediatrics

Ann Trop Res — Annals of Tropical Research

Ann Tschech Akad Landwirtsch — Annalen der Tschechoslowakischen Akademie der Landwirtschaft

Ann Tuberc — Annals of Tuberculosis

Ann Tuberc Tenri — Annals of Tuberculosis (Tenri, Nara)

Ann Tvl Mus — Annals. Transvaal Museum

Annu 30s Soc London — Annual of the 30s Society, London

AnnUA — Annals. Ukrainian Academy of Arts and Sciences in the US

Annu A A A — Annuaire des Auditeurs et Anciens Auditeurs. Academie de Droit International de la Haye

Annu Acad Med Valko Tchervenkov — Annuaire. Academie de Medecine Valko Tchervenkov

Annu Acad Royale Belgique Jb Kon Acad Belgie — Annuaire de l'Academie Royale de Belgique/Jaarboek van de Koninklijke Academie van Belgie

Annu Acad Royale Sci & B Lett Bruxelles — Annuaire de l'Academie Royale des Sciences et Belles-Lettres de Bruxelles

Annu Acad Royale Sci Lett & B A Belgique — Annuaire de l'Academie Royale des Sciences, des Lettres, et des Beaux Arts de Belgique

Annu Acad Roy Belg — Annuaire. Academie Royale de Belgique

Annu Acad R Sci Outre Mer — Annuaire. Academie Royale des Sciences d'Outre Mer

Annu Acad R Sci Outre Mer Brussels — Annuaire. Academie Royale des Sciences d'Outre-Mer (Brussels)

Annu Acad Rurale Sofia Fac Agron — Annuaire. Academie Rurale. Sofia. Faculte d'Agronomie

Annu Acad Rurale Sofia Fac For — Annuaire. Academie Rurale. Sofia. Faculte Forestiere

Annu Accad Etrus Cortona — Annuario dell'Accademia Etrusca di Cortona

Annu Accad Ital — Annuario. Reale Accademia d'Italia

Annu Accad Univ Stud — Annuario Accademico. Regia Universita degli Studi de Siena

Annu Admin Statistique & Commerc Aube — Annuaire Administratif Statistique et Commercial de l'Aube

Annu Afr Moyen Orient — Annuaire de l'Afrique et du Moyen Orient

Annu Afr N — Annuaire de l'Afrique du Nord

Annu Afr Nord — Annuaire de l'Afrique du Nord

Annu Agric Suisse — Annuaire Agricole de la Suisse

Annuaire Acad Roy Sci Bruxelles — Annuaire. Academie Royale des Sciences et Belles-Lettres de Bruxelles

Annuaire Agrumes — Annuaire des Agrumes. Annuaire de l'Arboriculture Fruitiere

Annuaire Bull Soc Hist Fr — Annuaire-Bulletin. Societe de l'Histoire de France

Annuaire Conserv Jard Bot Geneve — Annuaire. Conservatoire du Jardin Botaniques de Geneve

Annuaire Francais Droit Int — Annuaire Francais de Droit International

Annuaire Hort Belge — Annuaire de l'Horticulture Belge

Annuaire Sci Hist — Annuaire des Sciences Historiques

Annuaire Soc Franc Numism — Annuaire. Societe Francaise de Numismatique et d'Archeologie

Annuaire Soc Roy Belge Dahlia — Annuaire. Societe Royale Belge du Dahlia

Annuaire Univ Sofia Fac — Annuaire. Universite de Sofia. Faculte de Mathematiques

Annuaire Univ Sofia Fac Math Inform — Annuaire de l'Universite de Sofia St. Kliment Ohridski. Faculte de Mathematiques

Annuaire Univ Sofia Fac Math Mec — Annuaire. Universite de Sofia. Faculte de Mathematiques et Mecanique

Annuaire Univ Sofia Fac Phys — Annuaire. Universite de Sofia. Faculte de Physique

Annu Airlines Plat Forum Proc — Annual Airlines Plating Forum. Proceedings

Annu Air Pollut Control Conf — Annual Air Pollution Control Conference

Annual Br Sc Athens — Annual. British School at Athens

Annual Bull Hort Technol Soc — Annual Bulletin of Horticultural Technological Society/Engei Gijutsu Kondankai Nenpo

Annual Dep Jordan — Annual. Department of Antiquities of Jordan

Annual Law R — Annual Law Review

Annual Peking Biol Sci Assoc — Annual. Peking Biological Science Association/Pe Ching Sheng Wu K'o Hsueeh Hsueeh Hui Nien Pao

Annual Rep Acclim Soc Victoria — Annual Report. Acclimatisation Society of Victoria

Annual Rep Arkansas Agric Exp Sta Arkansas Industr Univ — Annual Report. Arkansas Agricultural Experiment Station at Arkansas Industrial University

Annual Rep Asahikawa Med College — Annual Report of Asahikawa Medical College

Annual Rep Assoc Int Bot Jena — Annual Report. Association Internationale des Botanistes. (Jena)

Annual Rep Birmingham Nat Hist Microscop Soc — Annual Report. Birmingham Natural History and Microscopical Society

Annual Rep Birmingham Nat Hist Philos Soc — Annual Report. Birmingham Natural History and Philosophical Society

Annual Rep Calif Avocado Assoc — Annual Report. California Avocado Assocation

Annual Rep Calif Inst Technol — Annual Report. California Institute of Technology

Annual Rep Centr Hyg Exp Sta — Annual Report. Central Hygiene Experiment Station/Chung-Yang Wei-Shong Shih-YenSo Nein Pao

Annual Rep Coffee Res Sta Lyamungu — Annual Report. Coffee Research Station. Lyamungu

Annual Rep Council Roy Inst S Wales — Annual Report. Council. Royal Institution of South Wales with Appendix of Original Papers on Scientific Subjects

Annual Rep Dept Agric — Annual Report. Department of Agriculture for the Fiscal Year Ended June 30

Annual Rep Econ Poisons Agric Exp Sta Univ Arizona Spec Bull — Annual Report. Economic Poisons. Agricultural Experiment Station. University ofArizona. Special Bulletin

Annual Rep Fac Ed Univ Iwate — Annual Report. Faculty of Education. University of Iwate

Annual Rep Fruit Growers Assoc Ontario — Annual Report. Fruit Growers' Association of Ontario

Annual Rep Gakugei Fac Iwate Univ — Annual Report. Gakugei Faculty. Iwate University/Iwate Daigaku. Gakugeigakubu Kenkyu Nempo

Annual Rep Hydrogr Observ — Annual Report of Hydrographical Observations. Fusan Fishery Experiment Station

Annual Rep Illinois Agric Exp Sta — Annual Report. Illinois Agricultural Experiment Station

Annual Rep Insects Missouri — Annual Report on the Noxious, Beneficial, and Other Insects of the State of Missouri

Annual Rep Inst Microbiol Rutgers Univ — Annual Report. Institute of Microbiology. Rutgers University

Annual Rep Laguna Mar Lab — Annual Report. Laguna Marine Laboratory

Annual Rep Liverpool Mar Biol Sta Puffin Island — Annual Report. Liverpool Marine Biological Station on Puffin Island

Annual Rep Michigan Acad Sci — Annual Report. Michigan Academy of Science, Arts, and Letters

Annual Rep Michigan State Hort Soc — Annual Report. Michigan State Horticultural Society

Annual Rep Minnesota State Hort Soc — Annual Report. Minnesota State Horticultural Society

Annual Rep Montreal Hort Soc — Annual Report. Montreal Horticultural Society and Fruit Growers Association. Province of Quebec

Annual Rep Nagoya Fertilizer Inspect Sta Fertilizer Sect — Annual Report. Nagoya Fertilizer and Feed Inspection Station. Fertilizer Section/Nagoya Hishiryo Kensajo Jigyo Hokoku Hiryo No Bu

Annual Rep Nat Hist Soc New Brunswick — Annual Report. Natural History Society of New Brunswick

Annual Rep Natl Inst Genet — Annual Report. National Institute of Genetics

Annual Rep Natl Sci Found — Annual Report. National Science Foundation

Annual Rep Noto Mar Lab — Annual Report. Noto Marine Laboratory. Faculty of Science. University of Kanazawa

Annual Rep Ohio State Forest Bur — Annual Report. Ohio State Forestry Bureau

Annual Rep Oil Palm Res Sta — Annual Report. Oil Palm Research Station

Annual Rep Papua — Annual Reports of Papua

Annual Rep Proc Barrow Naturalists Field Club — Annual Reports. Proceedings. Barrow Naturalists' Field Club and Literary and Scientific Association

Annual Rep Proc Belfast Naturalists Field Club — Annual Report and Proceedings. Belfast Naturalists' Field Club

Annual Rep Quebec Soc Protect Pl — Annual Report. Quebec Society for the Protection of Plants

Annual Rep Roy Soc South Australia — Annual Report. Royal Society of South Australia

Annual Rep Santa Barbara Bot Gard — Annual Report. Santa Barbara Botanic Garden

Annual Rep Scott Pl Breed Sta — Annual Report. Scottish Plant Breeding Station

Annual Rep Seed Test Lab — Annual Report. Seed Testing Laboratory/Shubyo Kensa Nenpo

Annual Rep Shropshire Nat Hist Soc — Annual Report. Shropshire and North Wales Natural History and Antiquarian Society

Annual Rep State Agric Exp Sta — Annual Report. State Agricultural Experiment Station

Annual Rep Storrs School Agric Exp Sta — Annual Report. Storrs School Agricultural Experiment Station

Annual Rep Trans Worcester Agric Soc — Annual Report and Transactions. Worcester (Massachusetts) Agricultural Society

Annual Rep US Regional Pasture Res Lab — Annual Report. US Regional Pasture Research Laboratory

Annual Rep Veg Fl Res Works Japan — Annual Report of Vegetables and Flowers Research Works in Japan/Sosai Kaki Shiken Kenkyu Nenpo

Annual Rep Warwickshire Nat Hist Soc — Annual Report. Warwickshire Natural History and Archaeological Society

Annual Rep Worcester Nat Hist Soc — Annual Reports. Worcester Natural History Society

Annual Rep Wrapper Hookah Tobacco Res Sta — Annual Report. Wrapper and Hookah Tobacco Research Station

Annual Rev Comput Phys — Annual Reviews of Computational Physics

Annual Rev Hist Lit — Annual Review and History of Literature

Annual Rev Pharmacol — Annual Review of Pharmacology

Annual Rev Physiol — Annual Review of Physiology

Annual Rev Phytopathol — Annual Review of Phytopathology

Annual R Residential Care Assoc — Annual Review. Residential Care Association

Annual Surv Res Pharm — Annual Survey of Research in Pharmacy

Annu Amer Inst Coop — Annual. American Institute of Cooperation

Annu Amer Sch Orient Res — Annual of the American Schools of Oriental Research

Annu Amer Sch Orient Res Jerusalem — Annual of the American School of Oriental Research in Jerusalem

Annu Anim Psychol — Annual of Animal Psychology

Annuar Fr Dr Int — Annuaire Francais de Droit International

Annuario Acc Etr Cortona — Annuario. Accademia Etrusca di Cortona

Annuario Ac Etr — Annuario. Accademia Etrusca di Cortona

Annuario At — Annuario. Scuola Archeologica di Atene e Missioni Italiani in Oriente

Annuario Chim Ital — Annuario Chimico Italiano

Annuario Reale Scuola Super Agric Portici — Annuario. Reale Scuola Superiore di Agricoltura di Portici

Annuario Sc Archeol Atene — Annuario. Scuola Archeologica di Atene e delle Missioni Italiani in Oriente

Annuario Soc Alpin Trident — Societa degli Alpinisti Tridentini. Annuario

Annuar Arkansas Water Works Pollut Control Conf Short Sch Proc — Annual Arkansas Water Works and Pollution Control Conference and Short School. Proceedings

Annuar Scuola Arch Atene — Annuario. Scuola Archeologica di Atene e delle Missioni Italiani in Oriente

Annu ASME Symp NM Sect Am Soc Mech Eng — Annual ASME (American Society of Mechanical Engineers) Symposium. New Mexico Section. American Society of Mechanical Engineers

Annu Ass Ott Ital — Annuario. Associazione Ottica Italiana

Annu Astron Osserv — Annuario Astronomico. Osservatorio Astronomico. Universita di Torino

Annu Battery Conf Appl Adv — Annual Battery Conference on Applications and Advances

Annu Bibliog Ind Archaeol — Annual Bibliography of Indian Archaeology

Annu Bibliogr Engl Lang Lit — Annual Bibliography of English Language and Literature

Annu Bibliogr Mod Humanit Res Assoc — Annual Bibliography. Modern Humanities Research Association

Annu Bibliog Stor A — Annuario Bibliografico di Storia dell'Arte

Annu Biochem Eng Symp Proc — Annual Biochemical Engineering Symposium. Proceedings

Annu Biol Colloq — Annual Biology Colloquium

Annu Biol Div Res Conf — Annual Biology Division Research Conference

Annu Biol Fac Sci Nat Univ Kiril Metodij (Skopje) — Annuaire. Biologie. Faculte des Sciences Naturelles. Universite Kiril. Metodij (Skopje)

Annu Birth Defects Inst Symp — Annual Birth Defects Institute Symposium

Annu Book ASTM Stand — Annual Book of ASTM [*American Society for Testing and Materials*] Standards

Annu Brew Assoc Jpn — Annual. Brewers Association Japan

Annu Brit Sch Athens — Annual. British School at Athens

Annu Brit School Athens — Annual. British School at Athens

Annu Bull Dep Agric North Rhod — Annual Bulletin. Department of Agriculture. Northern Rhodesia

Annu Bull Dep Sci Living Kyoritsu Womens Jr Coll — Annual Bulletin. Department of the Science of Living. Kyoritsu Women's Junior College

Annu Bull Int Dairy Fed — Annual Bulletin. International Dairy Federation

Annu Bull N Gal Victoria — Annual Bulletin of the National Gallery of Victoria

Annu Bull N Mus W A — Annual Bulletin of the National Museum of Western Art

Annu Bull Soc Hist France — Annuaire-Bulletin. Societe d'Histoire de France

Annu Bull Soc Jersiaise — Annual Bulletin. Societe Jersiaise

Annu Bur Longitudes (Paris) — Annuaire. Bureau de Longitudes (Paris)

Annu Chim — Annuaire de Chimie

Annu Clin Conf Cancer — Annual Clinical Conference on Cancer

Annu Clin Congr Am Coll Surg — Annual Clinical Congress. American College of Surgeons

Annu Clin Symp — Annual Clinical Symposium

Annu Coll France Resume Cours & Trav — Annuaire du College de France. Resume des Cours et Travaux

Annu Colmar — Annuaire de Colmar

Annu Combust Fuels Technol Program Contract Rev Meet Rep — Annual Combustion and Fuels Technology Program Contractor Review Meeting. Report

Annu Com Etat Geol (Rom) — Annuaire. Comite d'Etat pour la Geologie (Romania)

Annu Com Geol Rom — Annuaire. Comite Geologique (Romania)

Annu Comput Neurosci Conf — Annual Computational Neuroscience Conference

Annu Comput Secur Appl Conf — Annual Computer Security Applications Conference

Annu Conf Adhes Adhes — Annual Conference on Adhesion and Adhesives

Annu Conf Alcohol — Annual Conference of Alcoholism

Annu Conf Aust Inst Met — Annual Conference. Australian Institute of Metals [*Later, Annual Conference. Australasian Institute of Metals*]

Annu Conf Australas Corros Assoc — Annual Conference. Australasian Corrosion Association

Annu Conf Australas Corros Assoc Prepr Pap — Annual Conference. Australasian Corrosion Association. Preprinted Papers

Annu Conf Australas Inst Met — Annual Conference. Australasian Institute of Metals

Annu Conf Australas Inst Min Metall Prepr Pap — Annual Conference. Australasian Institute of Mining and Metallurgy. Preprint ofPapers

Annu Conf Aviat Astronaut — Annual Conference. Aviation and Astronautics

Annu Conf B C Water Waste Assoc Proc — Annual Conference. British Columbia Water and Waste Association. Proceedings

Annu Conf Calif Mosq Vector Control Assoc Proc Pap — Annual Conference. California Mosquito and Vector Control Association. Proceedings and Papers

Annu Conf Can Nucl Soc — Annual Conference. Canadian Nuclear Society

Annu Conf Cell Plast Div Soc Plast Ind — Annual Conference. Cellular Plastics Division. Society. Plastics Industry

Annu Conf Environ Toxicol — Annual Conference on Environmental Toxicology

Annu Conf Eur Phys Soc Condens Matter Div — Annual Conference. European Physical Society. Condensed Matter Division

Annu Conf Fossil Energy Mater — Annual Conference on Fossil Energy Materials

Annu Conf Glass Prob — Annual Conference on Glass Problems

Annu Conf Glass Prob Collect Pap — Annual Conference on Glass Problems. Collected Papers

Annu Conf Hung Physiol Soc — Annual Conference. Hungarian Physiological Society

Annu Conf Int Dist Heat Assoc Off Proc — Annual Conference. International District Heating Association. Official Proceedings

Annu Conf Int Iron Steel Inst Rep Proc — Annual Conference. International Iron and Steel Institute. Report of Proceedings

Annu Conf Int Nucl Target Dev Soc Proc — Annual Conference. International Nuclear Target Development Society. Proceedings

Annu Conf Kidney — Annual Conference on the Kidney

Annu Conf Manit Agron — Annual Conference. Manitoba Agronomists

Annu Conf Mar Technol Soc — Annual Conference. Marine Technology Society

Annu Conf Mater Coal Convers Utiliz Proc — Annual Conference on Materials for Coal Conversion and Utilization. Proceedings

Annu Conf Metall CIM — Annual Conference of Metallurgists of CIM

Annu Conf Metall Proc — Annual Conference of Metallurgists. Proceedings

Annu Conf Microbeam Anal Soc Proc — Annual Conference. Microbeam Analysis Society. Proceedings

Annu Conf Natl Soc Clean Air — Annual Conference. National Society for Clean Air

Annu Conf Natl Water Supply Improv Assoc Tech Proc — Annual Conference. National Water Supply Improvement Association. Technical Proceedings

Annu Conf Ont Pet Inst Proc — Annual Conference. Ontario Petroleum Institute. Proceedings

Annu Conf Phys Electron Top Conf Am Phys Soc — Annual Conference on Physical Electronics. Topical Conference. American Physical Society

Annu Conf Proc Am Water Works Associ — Annual Conference Proceedings. American Water Works Association

Annu Conf Proc Can Nucl Soc — Annual Conference Proceedings. Canadian Nuclear Society

Annu Conf Protein Metab Proc — Annual Conference on Protein Metabolism. Proceedings

Annu Conf Res Med Educ — Annual Conference on Research in Medical Education

Annu Conf Restor Coastal Veg Fla Proc — Annual Conference on the Restoration of Coastal Vegetation in Florida. Proceedings

Annu Conf Semin Qual Control Soc Photogr Sci Eng Summ Pap — Annual Conference and Seminar on Quality Control. Society of Photographic Scientists and Engineers. Summaries of Papers

Annu Conf Soil Mech Found Eng — Annual Conference. Soil Mechanics and Foundation Engineering

Annu Conf SPI Reinf Plast Compos Inst Proc — Annual Conference. SPI Reinforced Plastics/Composites Institute. Proceedings

Annu Conf Steel Cast Res Trade Assoc Discuss — Annual Conference. Steel Castings Research and Trade Association. Discussion

Annu Conf Steel Cast Res Trade Assoc Pap — Annual Conference. Steel Castings Research and Trade Association. Papers

Annu Conf Steel Foundry Pract Discuss — Annual Conference. Steel Foundry Practice. Discussion

Annu Conf Steel Foundry Pract Pap — Annual Conference. Steel Foundry Practice. Papers

Annu Conf Supercond Appl — Annual Conference on Superconductivity and Applications

Annu Conf Text Inst (Manchester Engl) — Annual Conference. Textile Institute (Manchester, England)

Annu Conf Wastes Eng Univ Minn Cent Contin Study — Annual Conference in Wastes Engineering. University of Minnesota. Center for Continuation Study

Annu Congr Am Soc Hortic Sci Trop Reg — Annual Congress. American Society for Horticultural Science. Tropical Region

Annu Connector Interconnect Technol Symp Proc — Annual Connectors and Interconnection Technology Symposium Proceedings

Annu Connector Symp Proc — Annual Connector Symposium. Proceedings

Annu Conv Proc Wash Ass Wheat Growers — Annual Convention Proceedings. Washington Association of Wheat Growers

Annu de la Fac de Droit de Skopje — Annuaire. Faculte de Droit de Skopje

Annu de l'Inst de Droit Internat — Annuaire. Institut de Droit International

Annu Dep Semin Univ Singapore Dep Chem — Annual Department Seminar. University of Singapore. Department of Chemistry

Annu Dept Ant Jordan — Annual of the Department of Antiquities of Jordan

Annu Diagn Paediatr Pathol — Annuals of Diagnostic Paediatric Pathology

Annu Dr Marit Aer — Annuaire de Droit Maritime et Aerien

Annu Dry Bean Conf Proc — Annual Dry Bean Conference. Proceedings

Annu Ecole Pratique Hautes Etud — Annuaire. Ecole Pratique des Hautes Etudes

Annu Ecole Pratique Hautes Etud Ve Sect Sci Relig — Annuaire de l'Ecole Pratique des Hautes Etudes. Ve Section. Sciences Religieuses

Annu Ec Polytech Etat Sofia — Annuaire. Ecole Polytechnique d'Etat. Sofia

Annu Ec Super Chim Technol Sofia — Annuaire. Ecole Superieure de Chimie Technologique. Sofia

Annu Ec Super Mech Tech — Annuaire. Ecoles Superieures. Mechanique Technique

Annu Ec Super Mines Geol Sofia — Annuaire. Ecole Superieure des Mines et de Geologie. Sofia

Annu Ec Tech Super Mech Appl — Annuaire. Ecoles Techniques Superieures. Mechanique Appliquee

Annu Ec Tech Super Phys — Annuaire. Ecoles Techniques Superieures. Physique

Annu Electron Micros Colloq Proc — Annual Electron Microscopy Colloquium. Proceedings

Annu Eng Conf Conf Pap — Annual Engineering Conference. Conference Papers

Annu Eng Conf Inst Eng Aust Pap — Annual Engineering Conference. Institution of Engineers of Australia. Papers

Annu Environ Eng Sci Conf Proc — Annual Environmental Engineering and Science Conference. Proceedings

Annu Europ — Annuaire Europeen

Annu Fac Agric Sylvic Univ Skopje Agric — Annuaire. Faculte d' Agriculture et de Sylviculture. Universite de Skopje. Agriculture

Annu Fac Agric Sylvic Univ Skopje Sylvic — Annuaire. Faculte d'Agriculture et de Sylviculture. Universite de Skopje. Sylviculture

Annu Fac Agric Sylvi Univ Skopje Pomol — Annuaire. Faculte d'Agriculture et de Sylviculture. Universite de Skopje. Pomologie

Annu Fac Agric Sylvi Univ Skopje Viti — Annuaire. Faculte d'Agriculture et de Sylviculture. Universite de Skopje. Viticulture

Annu Fac Agric Sylvi Univ Skopje Zootech — Annuaire. Faculte d'Agriculture et de Sylviculture. Universite de Skopje. Zootechnie

Annu Fac Agric Univ Skopje — Annuaire. Faculte d'Agriculture et de Sylviculture. Universite de Skopje

Annu Fac Agric Univ Skopje — Annuaire. Faculte d'Agriculture. Universite de Skopje

Annu Fac Biol Univ Kiril Metodij Skopje — Annuaire. Faculte de Biologie. Universite Kiril et Metodij-Skopje

Annu Fac Educ Gunma Univ Art Technol Ser — Annual Report. Faculty of Education. Gunma University. Art and Technology Series

Annu Fac Philos Univ Skopje Sect Sci Nat — Annuaire. Faculte de Philosophie. Universite de Skopje. Section des Sciences Naturelles

Annu Fac Sci Nat Univ Kiril Metodij (Skopje) Biol — Annuaire. Faculte des Sciences Naturelles. Universite Kiril et Metodij (Skopje). Biologie

Annu Fac Sci Nat Univ Kiril Metodij (Skopje) Math Phys Chim — Annuaire. Faculte des Sciences Naturelles. Universite Kiril et Metodij (Skopje). Mathematique, Physique, et Chimie

Annu Fac Sylvic Univ Skopje — Annuaire. Faculte de Sylviculture. Universite de Skopje

Annu Field Conf Intermt Assoc Geol Guideb — Annual Field Conference. Intermountain Association of Geologists. Guidebook

Annu For Symp — Annual Forestry Symposium

Annu Forum Proc Am Helicopter Soc — Annual Forum Proceedings. American Helicopter Society

Annu Franc de Droit Internat — Annuaire Francais de Droit International

Annu Franc Dr Homme — Annuaire Francais des Droits de l'Homme

Annu Franc Dr Int — Annuaire Francais de Droit International

Annu Freq Control Symp — Annual Frequency Control Symposium

Annu Freq Control Symp Proc — Annual Frequency Control Symposium. Proceedings

Annu Gas Compressor Inst — Annual. Gas Compressor Institute

Annu Gas Meas Inst — Annual. Gas Measurement Institute

Annu Geol Mineral Russ — Annuaire Geologique et Mineralogique de la Russie

Annu Hebrew Union Coll — Annual. Hebrew Union College

Annu Higher Inst Min Geol (Sofia) — Annual. Higher Institute of Mining and Geology (Sofia)

Annu Highway Geol Symp Proc — Annual Highway Geology Symposium. Proceedings

Annu Houston Neurol Sci Symp — Annual Houston Neurological Scientific Symposium

Annu IEEE Semicond Therm Meas Manage Symp — Annual IEEE Semiconductor Thermal Measurement and Management Symposium

Annu Ind Air Pollut Contam Control Semin Book Proc — Annual Industrial Air Pollution/Contamination Control Seminar. Book of Proceedings

Annu Ind Air Pollut Control Conf Proc — Annual Industrial Air Pollution Control Conference. Proceedings

Annu Ind Air Pollut Control Semin Book Proc — Annual Industrial Air Pollution Control Seminar. Book of Proceedings

Annu Ind Air Water Pollut Contam Control Semin Book Proc — Annual Industrial Air and Water Pollution/Contamination Control Seminar. Book of Proceedings

Annu Ind Chim — Annuaire de l'Industrie Chimique

Annu Index Pop Music Rec Rev — Annual Index to Popular Music Record Reviews

Annu Ind Water Waste Conf Pre Printed Pap — Annual Industrial Water and Waste Conference. Pre-Printed Papers

Annu Inf Meet Heavy Sect Steel Technol Program — Annual Information Meeting. Heavy Section Steel Technology Program

Annu Inst Archit Genie Civ Sofia — Annuaire. Institut d'Architecture et de Genie Civil-Sofia

Annu Inst Europ Secur Soc — Annuaire. Institut Europeen de Securite Sociale

Annu Inst Genie Civ Sofia — Annuaire. Institut du Genie Civil. Sofia

Annu Inst Geol Geophys (Rom) — Annuaire. Institut de Geologie et de Geophysique (Romania)

Annu Inst Geol Roum — Annuaire. Institut Geologique de Roumanie

Annu Inst Mec Appl Electrotech — Annuaire. Institut de Mecanique Appliquee et d'Electrotechnique

Annu Inst Mec Appl Electrotech Sofia — Annuaire. Institut de Mecanique Appliquee et d'Electrotechnique. Sofia

Annu Inst Min Geol Sofia — Annuaire. Institut Minier et Geologique. Sofia

Annu Inst Philol Hist Orient — Annuaire. Institut de Philologie et d'Histoire Orientales et Slaves. UniversiteLibre de Bruxelles

Annu Inst Philol Hist Orient Slav — Annuaire. Institut de Philologie et d'Histoire Orientales et Slaves

Annu Inst Super Genie Civ Sofia — Annuaire. Institut Superieure de Genie Civil. Sofia

Annu Inst Super Pedagog Choumen — Annuaire. Institut Superieur Pedagogique a Choumen

Annu Int Bulk Solids Conf Pap Discuss — Annual International Bulk Solids Conference. Papers and Discussions

Annu Int Conf Can Nucl Assoc — Annual International Conference. Canadian Nuclear Association

Annu Int Conf Can Nucl Assoc Proc — Annual International Conference. Canadian Nuclear Association. Proceedings

Annu Int Conf Proc Am Prod Inventory Control Soc — Annual International Conference Proceedings. American Production and Inventory Control Society

Annu Int Electron Packag Conf — Annual International Electronics Packaging Conference

Annu Int Fonction Publ — Annuaire International de la Fonction Publique

Annu ISA Conf Proc — Annual ISA (Instrument Society of America) Conference Proceedings

Annu Ist Giappon Cult Roma — Annuario dell'Istituto Giapponese di Cultura in Roma

Annu Ist Sper Chim Agrar Torino — Annuario. Istituto di Sperimentazione per la Chimica Agraria in Torino

Annu Ist Stor A [Rome] — Annuario dell'Istituto di Storia dell'Arte [Rome]

Annu Ist Tec Stat Geom Carlo d Arco — Annuario dell'Istituto Tecnico Statale per Geometri 'Carlo d'Arco'

Annu Ist Ung Stor A — Annuario dell'Istituto Ungherese di Storia dell'Arte

Annu J Diet Software — Annual Journal of Dietetic Software

Annu J Inst Eng — Annual Journal. Institution of Engineers

Annu Jt AIEE IRE Conf Electron Nucleon Med Pap — Annual Joint AIEE-IRE Conference on Electronics in Nucleonics and Medicine. Papers

Annu Karcher Symp — Annual Karcher Symposium

Ann Ukr Acad Arts Sci US — Annals. Ukrainian Academy of Arts and Sciences in the US

Ann Ukrain Acad US — Annals. Ukrainian Academy of Arts and Sciences in the United States

Annu Landfill Gas Symp — Annual Landfill Gas Symposium

Annu Landfill Symp — Annual Landfill Symposium

Annu Leg Bibliogr — Annual Legal Bibliography

Annu Liceo Gin Stat Osimo — Annuario del Liceo Ginnasio Statale d'Osimo

Annu Lightwood Res Conf Proc — Annual Lightwood Research Conference. Proocodings

Annu Madison Conf Appl Res Pract Munic Ind Waste — Annual Madison Conference of Applied Research and Practice on Municipal and Industrial Waste

Annu Mar Coat Conf Proc — Annual Marine Coatings Conference. Proceedings

Ann UMCS — Annales Universitatis Mariae Curie-Sklodowska

Annu Meat Sci Inst Proc — Annual Meat Science Institute. Proceedings

Annu Med Chem Symp — Annual Medicinal Chemistry Symposium

Annu Med Egypt — Annuaire Medical Egyptien

Annu Med Pharm Fr — Annuaire Medical et Pharmaceutique de la France

Annu Med Sci Conf Natl Alcohol Forum — Annual Medical-Scientific Conference. National Alcoholism Forum

Annu Med Suisse — Annuaire Medical Suisse

Annu Meet Am Coll Nutr — Annual Meeting. American College of Nutrition

Annu Meet Am Inst Dent Med — Annual Meeting. American Institute of Dental Medicine

Annu Meet Am Inst Min Metall Pet Eng — Annual Meeting. American Institute of Mining, Metallurgical, and Petroleum Engineeers

Annu Meet Am Inst Oral Biol — Annual Meeting. American Institute of Oral Biology

Annu Meet Am Mosq Control Assoc — Annual Meeting. American Mosquito Control Association

Annu Meet Am Psychopathol Assoc — Annual Meeting. American Psychopathological Association

Annu Meet Biomass Energy Inst — Annual Meeting. Biomass Energy Institute

Annu Meet Br Assoc Adv Sci — Annual Meeting. British Association for the Advancement of Science

Annu Meet Can Coll Neuropsychopharmacol — Annual Meeting. Canadian College of Neuropsychopharmacology

Annu Meet Corp Assoc Am Chem Soc — Annual Meeting. Corporation Associates. American Chemical Society

Annu Meet Electron Microsc Soc Am — Annual Meeting. Electron Microscopy Society of America

Annu Meet Eur Bone Marrow Transplant Group — Annual Meeting. European Bone Marrow Transplantation Group

Annu Meet Eur Environ Mutagen Soc — Annual Meeting. European Environmental Mutagen Society

Annu Meet Eur Soc Radiobiol — Annual Meeting. European Society for Radiobiology

Annu Meet Exhib Air Waste Manage Assoc — Annual Meeting and Exhibition. Air and Waste Management Association

Annu Meet Fed Am Soc Environ Biol — Annual Meeting. Federation of American Societies for Environmental Biology

Annu Meet Fed Anal Chem Spectrosc Soc Pap — Annual Meeting. Federation of Analytical Chemistry and Spectroscopy Societies. Papers

Annu Meet Inf Counc Fabr Flammability Proc — Annual Meeting. Information Council on Fabric Flammability. Proceedings

Annu Meet Inter Soc Cytol Counc Trans — Annual Meeting. Inter-Society Cytology Council. Transactions

Annu Meet Int Found Biochem Endocrinol — Annual Meeting. International Foundation for Biochemical Endocrinology

Annu Meet Int Inst Synth Rubber Prod — Annual Meeting. International Institute of Synthetic Rubber Producers

Annu Meet Int Soc Blood Purif — Annual Meeting of the International Society of Blood Purification

Annu Meet Int Soc Exp Hematol — Annual Meeting. International Society for Experimental Hematology

Annu Meet Int Soc Heart Res — Annual Meeting. International Society for Heart Research

Annu Meet Int Water Conf — Annual Meeting. International Water Conference

Annu Meet Jpn Assoc Anim Cell Technol — Annual Meeting. Japanese Association for Animal Cell Technology

Annu Meet Mar Technol Soc — Annual Meeting. Marine Technology Society

Annu Meet Meteorit Soc — Annual Meeting. Meteoritical Society

Annu Meet Microbeam Anal Soc — Annual Meeting. Microbeam Analysis Society

Annu Meet Minn Sect AIME Proc — Annual Meeting. Minnesota Section. AIME [*American Institute of Mining, Metallurgical, and Petroleum Engineers*]. Proceedings

Annu Meet Miss River Res Consortium — Annual Meeting. Mississippi River Research Consortium

Annu Meet Mod Approaches New Vaccines — Annual Meeting on Modern Approaches to New Vaccines

Annu Meet Natl Counc Radiat Prot Meas — Annual Meeting. National Council on Radiation Protection and Measurements

Annu Meet Natl Mastitis Counc — Annual Meeting. National Mastitis Council

Annu Meet Natl Mastitis Counc Inc — Annual Meeting. National Mastitis Council, Inc.

Annu Meet NJ Mosq Control Assoc Proc — Annual Meeting. New Jersey Mosquito Control Association. Proceedings

Annu Meet Pan Am Biodeterior Soc — Annual Meeting. Pan American Biodeterioration Society

Annu Meet Perinat Biochem Group Span Biochem Soc — Annual Meeting. Perinatal Biochemical Group. Spanish Biochemical Society

Annu Meet Prepr Tech Assoc Pulp Pap Ind — Annual Meeting Preprint. Technical Association. Pulp and Paper Industry

Annu Meet Proc Am Soc Photogramm — Annual Meeting-Proceedings. American Society of Photogrammetry

Annu Meet Proc Int Inst Synth Rubber Prod — Annual Meeting Proceedings. International Institute of Synthetic Rubber Producers

Annu Meet Proc Tech Assoc Pulp Pap Ind — Annual Meeting Proceedings. Technical Association. Pulp and Paper Industry

Annu Meet Scand Soc Immunol Abstr Pap — Annual Meeting. Scandinavian Society for Immunology. Abstracts of Papers

Annu Meet Soc Eng Sci Proc — Annual Meeting. Society of Engineering Science. Proceedings

Annu Meet Tech Assoc Pulp Pap Ind — Annual Meeting. Technical Association. Pulp and Paper Industry

Annu Meet Tech Sect Can Pulp Pap Assoc Prepr Pap — Annual Meeting. Technical Section. Canadian Pulp and Paper Association. Preprints of Papers

Annu Mem Com Etud Hist Scient Afr Occ — Annuaire et Memoires du Comite d'Etudes Historiques et Scientifiques de l'Afrique Occidentale

Annu Metall — Annuaire de Metallurgie

Annu Met Geophys Alger — Annuaire Meteorologique et Geophysique. Algerie du Nord

Annu Met Geophys Sahara — Annuaire Meteorologique et Geophysique. Sahara

Annu Met Hydrogr Luxemb — Annuaire Meteorologique et Hydrographique (Luxembourg)

Annu Met Isl — Annuaire Meteorologique d'Islande

Annu Met Stn Geogr Math Gand — Annuaire Meteorologique de la Station de Geographie Mathematique (Gand)

Annu Microseism Macroseism Beogr — Annuaire Microseismique et Macroseismique (Beograd)

Annu Miner Symp Proc — Annual Minerals Symposium Proceedings

Annu Min Symp — Annual Mining Symposium

Annu Min Symp Proc — Annual Mining Symposium. Proceedings

Annu Mus Gr Romain Alexandrie — Annuaire du Musee Greco-Romain a Alexandrie

Annu Mus Gr Romano Alessandria — Annuario del Museo Greco-Romano di Alessandria

Annu Mus Natl Hist Nat — Annuaire. Museum National d'Histoire Naturelle

Annu Mus Royaux B A Belgique Jb Kon Mus S Kst Belgie — Annuaire des Musees Royaux des Beaux-Arts de Belgique/Jaarboek der Koninklijke Musea voor Schone Kunsten van Belgie

Annu Natl Conf Natl Organ Black Chem Chem Eng — Annual National Conference. National Organization for Black Chemists and Chemical Engineers

Annu Natl Conf Plast Rubber Inst — Annual National Conference. Plastics and Rubber Institute

Annu Natl Conf PRI — Annual National Conference. PRI

Annu Natl Conf Radiat Control — Annual National Conference on Radiation Control

Annu Natl Inf Retr Colloq — Annual National Information Retrieval Colloquium

Ann Un Bud — Annales Universitatis Scientiarum Budapestensis de Rolando Eoetvoes Nominatae. Sectio Classica

Annu NC Cattlemens Conf — Annual North Carolina Cattlemen's Conference

Annu N Engl (Northeast) Bioeng Conf Proc — Annual New England (Northeast) Bioengineering Conference. Proceedings

Annu Newslett Scand Inst Asian Stud — Annual Newsletter of the Scandinavian Institute of Asian Studies

Ann Univ Abidjan — Annales. Universite d'Abidjan

Ann Univ Abidjan Med — Annales. Universite d'Abidjan. Medecine

Ann Univ Abidjan Ser B Med — Annales. Universite d'Abidjan. Serie B. Medecine

Ann Univ Abidjan Ser C — Annales. Universite d'Abidjan. Serie C. Sciences

Ann Univ Abidjan Ser C Sci — Annales. Universite d'Abidjan. Serie C. Sciences

Ann Univ Abidjan Ser E Ecol — Annales. Universite d'Abidjan. Serie E. Ecologie

Ann Univ Abidjan Ser G — Annales. Universite d'Abidjan. Serie G. Geographie

Ann Univ Ankara — Annales. Universite d'Ankara

Ann Univ ARERS — Annales. Universite et ARERS

Ann Univ Assoc Reg Etude Rech Sci — Annales. Universite et de l'Association Regionale pour l'Etude et la Recherche Scientifiques

Ann Univ Belgique — Annales. Universites de Belgique

Ann Univ Besancon — Annales Litteraires. Universite de Besancon

Ann Univ Bp — Annales Universitatis Scientiarum Budapestensis

Ann Univ Brazzaville — Annales. Universite de Brazzaville

Ann Univ Brazzaville Ser C — Annales. Universite de Brazzaville. Serie C. Sciences

Ann Univ Brazzaville Ser C Sci — Annales. Universite de Brazzaville. Serie C. Sciences

Ann Univ Budapest — Annales Universitatis Scientiarum Budapestinenses

Ann Univ Craiova Chem Ser — Annals of the University of Craiova. Chemistry Series

Ann Univ Craiova Ser Biol Med Agric Sci — Annals. University of Craiova. Series. Biology, Medicine, Agricultural Science

Ann Univ Craiova Ser Mat Fiz Chim Electroteh — Annals. University of Craiova. Seria. Matematica, Fizica, Chimie, Electrotehnica

Ann Univ Fenn Abo — Annales Universitatis Fennicae Aboensis

Ann Univ Ferrara — Annali. Universita di Forrara

Ann Univ Ferrara Nuova Ser Sez XX Biol — Annali. Universita di Ferrara. Nuova Serie. Sezione XX. Biologia

Ann Univ Ferrara Sez 5 — Annali. Universita di Ferrara. Sezione 5. Chimica Pura ed Applicata

Ann Univ Ferrara Sez 6 — Annali. Universita di Ferrara. Sezione 6. Fisiologia e Chimica Biologica

Ann Univ Ferrara Sez 9 Sci Geol Mineral — Annali. Universita di Ferrara. Sezione 9. Scienze Geologiche e Mineralogiche

Ann Univ Ferrara Sez 11 — Annali. Universita di Ferrara. Sezione 11. Farmacologia e Terapia

Ann Univ Ferrara Sez 17 — Annali. Universita di Ferrara. Sezione 17. Scienze Mineralogiche e Petrografiche

Ann Univ Ferrara Sez I Ecol — Annali. Universita di Ferrara. Sezione I. Ecologia

Ann Univ Ferrara Sez III Biol Anim — Annali. Universita di Ferrara. Sezione III. Biologia Animale

Ann Univ Ferrara Sez IV — Annali. Universita di Ferrara. Sezione IV. Fisiologia e Chimica Biologica

Ann Univ Ferrara Sez IV Bot — Annali. Universita di Ferrara. Sezione IV. Botanica

Ann Univ Ferrara Sez IX — Annali. Universita di Ferrara. Nuovo Serie. Sezione IX. Scienze Geologiche e Paleontologiche

Ann Univ Ferrara Sez IX Sci Geol Mineral — Annali. Universita di Ferrara. Sezione IX. Scienze Geologiche e Mineralogiche

Ann Univ Ferrara Sez IX Sci Geol Paleontol — Annali. Universita di Ferrara. Sezione IX. Scienze Geologiche e Paleontologiche

Ann Univ Ferrara Sez V — Annali. Universita di Ferrara. Sezione V. Chimica Pura ed Applicata

Ann Univ Ferrara Sez VI Fisiol Chim Biol — Annali. Universita di Ferrara. Sezione VI. Fisiologia e Chimica Biologica

Ann Univ Ferrara Sez VII — Annali. Universita di Ferrara. Nuovo Serie. Sezione VII. Scienze Matematiche

Ann Univ Ferrara Sez VII NS — Annali. Universita di Ferrara. Nuovo Serie. Sezione VII

Ann Univ Ferrara Sez V Suppl — Annali. Universita di Ferrara. Sezione V. Chimica Pura ed Applicata. Supplemento

Ann Univ Ferrara Sez XI — Annali. Universita di Ferrara. Sezione XI. Farmacologia e Terapia

Ann Univ Ferrara Sez XI Farmacol Ter — Annali. Universita di Ferrara. Sezione XI. Farmacologia e Terapia

Ann Univ Ferrara Sez XIII Anat Comp — Annali. Universita di Ferrara. Sezione XIII. Anatomia Comparata

Ann Univ Genova — Annali. Reale Universita di Genova

Ann Univ Grenoble — Annales. Universite de Grenoble

Ann Univ Lyon 3e Ser Lett — Annales. Universite de Lyon. 3e Serie. Lettres

Ann Univ Lyon Fasc Spec — Annales. Universite de Lyon. Fascicule Special

Ann Univ Lyon Nouv Ser 2 — Annales. Universite de Lyon. Nouvelle Serie 2. Droit. Lettres

Ann Univ Lyon Sci Med — Annales. Universite de Lyon. Sciences. Medecine

Ann Univ Lyon Sci Sect A — Annales. Universite de Lyon. Sciences. Section A. Sciences Mathematiques et Astronomie

Ann Univ Lyon Sci Sect B — Annales. Universite de Lyon. Sciences. Section B. Sciences Physiques et Chimiques

Ann Univ Lyon Sci Sect C — Annales. Universite de Lyon. Sciences. Section C. Sciences Naturelles

Ann Univ Madag — Annales. Universite de Madagascar

Ann Univ Madagascar Fac Droit et Sci Econ — Annales. Universite de Madagascar. Faculte de Droit et des Sciences Economiques

Ann Univ Madagascar Ser Lett et Sci Hum — Annales. Universite de Madagascar. Serie Lettres et Sciences Humaines

Ann Univ Madagascar Ser Sci Nat Math — Annales. Universite de Madagascar. Serie Sciences de la Nature et Mathematiques

Ann Univ Madagascar Ser Sci Nature Math — Annales. Universite de Madagascar. Serie Sciences de la Nature et Mathematiques

Ann Univ Mariae Curie Sect C — Annales Universitatis Mariae Curie-Sklodowska. Sectio C

Ann Univ Mariae Curie Sect F — Annales Universitatis Mariae Curie-Sklodowska. Sectio F

Ann Univ Mariae Curie-Sklodowska — Annales. Universitatis Mariae Curie-Sklodowska. Sectio AAA. Physica

Ann Univ Mariae Curie-Sklodowska — Annales. Universitatis Mariae Curie-Sklodowska. Sectio AA. Chemia

Ann Univ Mariae Curie-Sklodowska — Annales. Universitatis Mariae Curie-Sklodowska. Sectio AA. Physics and Chemistry

Ann Univ Mariae Curie-Sklodowska Med — Annales Universitatis Mariae Curie-Sklodowska. Sectio D. Medicina

Ann Univ Mariae Curie Sklodowska Sect 3 Biol — Annales Universitatis Mariae Curie-Sklodowska. Roczniki Universytetu Marii Curie-Sklodowskiej. Sect 3. Biologia

Ann Univ Mariae Curie-Sklodowska Sect A — Annales Universitatis Mariae Curie-Sklodowska. Sectio A. Mathematica

Ann Univ Mariae Curie-Sklodowska Sect AA — Annales Universitatis Mariae Curie-Sklodowska. Sectio AA. Physica et Chemia

Ann Univ Mariae Curie-Sklodowska Sect AAA — Annales Universitatis Mariae Curie-Sklodowska. Sectio AAA (Physica)

Ann Univ Mariae Curie Sklodowska Sect AAA Phys — Annales Universitatis Mariae Curie-Sklodowska. Sectio AAA. Physica

Ann Univ Mariae Curie Sklodowska Sect AA Chem — Annales Universitatis Mariae Curie-Sklodowska. Sectio AA. Chemia

Ann Univ Mariae Curie Sklodowska Sect AA Phys Chem — Annales. Universitatis Mariae Curie-Sklodowska. Sectio AA. Physica et Chemia

Ann Univ Mariae Curie-Sklodowska Sect B — Annales Universitatis Mariae Curie-Sklodowska. Sectio B. Geographia, Geologia, Mineralogia, et Petrographia

Ann Univ Mariae Curie-Sklodowska Sect C — Annales Universitatis Mariae Curie-Sklodowska. Sectio C. Biologia

Ann Univ Mariae Curie-Sklodowska Sect C Biol — Annales Universitatis Mariae Curie-Sklodowska. Sectio C. Biologia

Ann Univ Mariae Curie-Sklodowska Sect C Suppl — Annales Universitatis Mariae Curie-Sklodowska. Sectio C. Biologia. Supplementum

Ann Univ Mariae Curie-Sklodowska Sect D — Annales Universitatis Mariae Curie-Sklodowska. Sectio D. Medicina

Ann Univ Mariae Curie-Sklodowska Sect DD — Annales Universitatis Mariae Curie-Sklodowska. Sectio DD. Medicina Veterinaria

Ann Univ Mariae Curie-Sklodowska Sect DD Med Vet — Annales Universitatis Mariae Curie-Sklodowska. Sectio DD. Medicina Veterinaria

Ann Univ Mariae Curie-Sklodowska Sect D Med — Annales Universitatis Mariae Curie-Sklodowska. Sectio D. Medicina

Ann Univ Mariae Curie-Sklodowska Sect E — Annales Universitatis Mariae Curie-Sklodowska. Sectio E. Agricultura

Ann Univ Mariae Curie-Sklodowska Sect E Agric — Annales Universitatis Mariae Curie-Sklodowska. Sectio E. Agricultura

Ann Univ Mariae Curie-Sklodowska Sect EE — Annales Universitatis Mariae Curie-Sklodowska. Sectio EE. Agraria

Ann Univ Mariae Curie-Sklodowska Sect E Suppl — Annales Universitatis Mariae Curie-Sklodowska. Sectio E. Agricultura. Supplementum

Ann Univ M Curie-Sklodowska Sect AA — Annales Universitatis Mariae Curie-Sklodowska. Sectio AA. Physica et Chemia

Ann Univ M Curie-Sklodowska Sect AAA (Phys) — Annales Universitatis Mariae Curie-Sklodowska. Sectio AAA (Physica)

Ann Univ M Curie-Sklodowska Sect C — Annales Universitatis Mariae Curie-Sklodowska. Sectio C. Biologia

Ann Univ M Curie-Sklodowska Sect D — Annales Universitatis Mariae Curie-Sklodowska. Sectio D. Medicina

Ann Univ Montp Suppl Sci Ser Bot — Annales. Universite de Montpellier. Supplement Scientifique. Serie Botanique

Ann Univ Padova — Annale. Universita di Padova. Facolta di Economia e Commercio in Verona

Ann Univ Paris — Annales. Universite de Paris

Ann Univ Provence Geol Mediterr — Annales. Universite de Provence. Geologie Mediterraneenne

Ann Univ Sara Math Naturwiss Fak — Annales Universitatis Saraviensis (Reihe). Mathematisch-Naturwissenschaftliche Fakultaet

Ann Univ Sara Naturwiss — Annales Universitatis Saraviensis. Naturwissenschaften

Ann Univ Sara Sci — Annales Universitatis Saraviensis. Scientia

Ann Univ Saraviensis Med — Annales Universitatis Saraviensis. Medizin

Ann Univ Saraviensis Naturwiss — Annales Universitatis Saraviensis. Naturwissenschaften

Ann Univ Saraviensis Phil — Annales Universitatis Saraviensis. Philosophie

Ann Univ Saraviensis Sci — Annales Universitatis Saraviensis. Scientia

Ann Univ Saraviensis Wiss — Annales Universitatis Saraviensis. Wissenschaften

Ann Univ Sarav Math-Natur Fak — Annales Universitatis Saraviensis. Mathematisch-Naturwissenschaftliche Fakultaet

Ann Univ Sarav Med — Annales Universitatis Saraviensis. Medizin

Ann Univ Sarav Naturwiss — Annales Universitatis Saraviensis. Naturwissenschaften

Ann Univ Sarav (Reihe) Math-Naturwiss Fak — Annales Universitatis Saraviensis (Reihe). Mathematisch-NaturwissenschaftlicheFakultaet

Ann Univ Sarav Sci — Annales. Universitatis Saraviensis. Scientia

Ann Univ Sarav Ser Math — Annales Universitatis Saraviensis. Series Mathematicae

Ann Univ Sarav Wiss Sci — Annales Universitatis Saraviensis. Wissenschaften/Sciences

Ann Univ Sci Budapest Eotvos Sect Math — Annales Universitatis Scientiarum Budapestensis de Rolando Eoetvoes Nominatae. Sectio Mathematica

Ann Univ Sci Budapest Rolando Eotvoes Sect Biol — Annales Universitatis Scientiarum Budapestinensis de Rolando Eotvoes Nominatae.Sectio Biologica

Ann Univ Sci Budapest Rolando Eotvos Nominatae Sect Chim — Annales Universitatis Scientiarum Budapestensis de Rolando Eoetvoes Nominatae. Sectio Chimica

Ann Univ Sci Budapest Sect Comput — Annales Universitatis Scientiarum Budapestensis de Rolando Eoetvoes Nominatae. Sectio Computatorica

Ann Univ Sci Budap Rolando Eotvos Nominatae Sect Biol — Annales Universitatis Scientiarum Budapestensis de Rolando Eoetvoes Nominatae. Sectio Biologica

Ann Univ Sci Budap Rolando Eotvos Nominatae Sect Chim — Annales Universitatis Scientiarum Budapestensis de Rolando Eoetvoes Nominatae. Sectio Chimica

Ann Univ Sci Budap Rolando Eotvos Nominatae Sect Geol — Annales Universitatis Scientiarum Budapestensis de Rolando Eoetvoes Nominatae. Sectio Geologica

Ann Univ Stellenbosch Reeks B — Annale. Universiteit van Stellenbosch. Reeks B

Ann Univ Stellenbosch Ser A — Annale. Universiteit van Stellenbosch. Serie A

Ann Univ Stellenbosch Ser A1 — Annale. Universiteit van Stellenbosch. Serie A1. Geologie

Ann Univ Stellenbosch Ser A2 — Annale. Universiteit van Stellenbosch. Serie A2. Soologie

Ann Univ Stellenbosch Ser A 3 Landbouwet — Annale. Universiteit van Stellenbosch. Serie A-3. Landbouwetenskappe

Ann Univ Stellenbosch Ser A4 — Annale. Universiteit van Stellenbosch. Serie A4. Bosbou

Ann Univ Stellenbosch Ser A III Landbou — Annale. Universiteit van Stellenbosch. Serie A-III. Landbouwetenskappe

Ann Univ Stellenbosch Ser A II Sool — Annale. Universiteit van Stellenbosch. Serie A-II. Soologie

Ann Univ Stellenbosch Ser B — Annale. Universiteit van Stellenbosch. Serie B

Ann Univ Sternw Wien — Annalen der Universitaets-Sternwarte Wien

Ann Univ Toscane — Annali. Universita Toscane

Ann Univ Turk Ser A II Biol-Geogr — Annales Universitatis Turkuensis. Series A-II. Biologica-Geographica

Ann Univ Turk Ser A II Biol-Geogr-Geol — Annales Universitatis Turkuensis. Series A-II. Biologica-Geographica-Geologica

Ann Univ Turku Ser A — Annales Universitatis Turkuensis. Series A

Ann Univ Turku Ser A I — Annales Universitatis Turkuensis. Series A-I. Astronomica-Chemica-Physica-Mathematica

Ann Univ Turku Ser A II — Annales Universitatis Turkuensis. Series A-II. Biologica-Geographica

Ann Univ Turku Ser D — Annales Universitatis Turkuensis. Series D. Medica-Odontologica

Ann Uniw Marii Curie-Sklodowskiej Sect C Biol — Annales. Uniwersytet Marii Curie-Sklodowskiej. Sectio C. Biologia

Ann Uniw Marii Curie Sklodowskiej Sect E Agric — Annales. Uniwersytet Marii Curie-Sklodowskiej. Sectio E. Agricultura

Annu North Am Weld Res Conf Adv Weld Technol Proc — Annual North American Welding Research Conference. Advances in Welding Technology. Proceedings

Annu Northeast Bioeng Conf Proc — Annual Northeast Bioengineering Conference. Proceedings

Annu Northeast Reg Antipollu Conf — Annual Northeastern Regional Antipollution Conference

Annu NSF Trace Contam Conf — Annual NSF [*National Science Foundation*] Trace Contaminants Conference

Annu Nucl Med Semin — Annual Nuclear Medicine Seminar

Annu Number Natl Acad Sci India — Annual Number. National Academy of Sciences. India

Annu Oak Ridge Natl Lab Life Sci Symp — Annual Oak Ridge National Laboratory Life Science Symposium

Annu Observ Belg Annu Meteorol — Annuaire. Observatoire Royale de Belgique. Deuxieme Serie. Annuaire Meteorologique

Annu Obs Mun Paris — Annuaire de l'Observatoire Municipal de Paris, dit Observatoire de Montsouris

Annu Obsns Met Obs Lomnicky Stit — Annuaire des Observations Meteorologiques de l'Observatoire au Lomnicky Stit

Annu Obsns Met Obs Met Geophys Stara Dala — Annuaire des Observations Meteorologiques de l'Observatoire Meteorologique et Geophysique d'Etat de Stara Dala

Annu Obs r Belg — Annuaire de l'Observatoire Royale de Belgique

Annu Offshore Technol Conf Prepr — Annual Offshore Technology Conference. Preprints

Annu Offshore Technol Conf Proc — Annual Offshore Technology Conference. Proceedings

Annu Ordre Souverain Mil Malte — Annuaire. Ordre Souverain Militaire de Malte

AnnUP — Annales. Universite de Paris

Annu Pac Tech Conf Tech Pap Soc Plast Eng — Annual Pacific Technical Conference. Technical Papers. Society of Plastics Engineers

Annu Pays Ocean Indien — Annuaire des Pays de l'Ocean Indien

Annu Pfizer Res Conf Proc — Annual Pfizer Research Conference. Proceedings

Annu Pipeline Oper Maint Inst — Annual Pipeline Operation and Maintenance Institute

Annu Pittsburgh Conf Model Simul — Annual Pittsburgh Conference on Modeling and Simulation

Annu Plant Biochem Physiol Symp — Annual Plant Biochemistry and Physiology Symposium

Annu Plant Rev — Annual Plant Reviews

Annu Polit Int — Annuario di Politica Internazionale

Annu Pollut Control Conf Water Wastewater Equip Manuf Assoc — Annual Pollution Control Conference. Water and Wastewater Equipment Manufacturers Association

Annu Pontif Accad Sci — Annuario. Pontificia Accademia delle Scienze

Annu Precise Time Time Interval PTTI Appl Plann Meet — Annual Precise Time and Time Interval (PTTI) Applications and Planning Meeting

Annu Priestley Lect — Annual Priestley Lectures

Annu Proc Am Assoc Zoo Vet — Annual Proceedings. American Association of Zoo Veterinarians

Annu Proc Am Tung Oil Assoc — Annual Proceedings. American Tung Oil Association

Annu Proc Ariz Water Symp — Annual Proceedings. Arizona Water Symposium

Annu Proc Assoc Sci & Tech Soc S Afr — Annual Proceedings. Associated Scientific and Technical Societies of South Africa

Annu Proc Gifu Coll Pharm — Annual Proceedings. Gifu College of Pharmacy

Annu Proc Gifu Pharm Univ — Annual Proceedings. Gifu Pharmaceutical University

Annu Proc Phytochem Soc — Annual Proceedings. Phytochemical Society

Annu Proc Phytochem Soc Eur — Annual Proceedings. Phytochemical Society of Europe

Annu Proc Reliab Phys (Symp) — Annual Proceedings. Reliability Physics (Symposium)

Annu Proc Tech Sess Am Electroplat Soc — Annual Proceedings. Technical Sessions. American Electroplaters' Society

Annu Prod Chim Drog — Annuaire des Produits Chimiques et de la Droguerie

Annu Prof Day Chem Teach — Annual Professional Day for Chemistry Teachers

Annu Prog Child Psychiatry Chil Dev — Annual Progress in Child Psychiatry and Child Development

Annu Prog Rep Geol Surv West Aust — Annual Progress Report. Geological Survey of Western Australia

Annu Prog Rep La Agric Exp Stn — Annual Progress Report. Louisiana Agricultural Experiment Station

Annu Prog Rep Oak Ridge Natl Lab Phys Div — Annual Progress Report. Oak Ridge National Laboratory. Physics Division

Annu Prog Rep Res Cent Supercond Mater Electron Osaka Univ — Annual Progress Report of Research Center for Superconducting Materials and Electronics. Osaka University

Annu Prog Rep SEATO Med Res Lab — Annual Progress Report. SEATO [*Southeast Asia Treaty Organization*] Medical Research Laboratories

Annu Prog Rep Southeast Res Stn La Agric Exp Stn — Annual Progress Report. Southeast Research Station. Louisiana Agricultural Experiment Station

Annu Prog Rep Southeast SD Agric Exp Stn SD State Univ — Annual Progress Report. Southeast South Dakota Agricultural Experiment Station.South Dakota State University

Annu Prog Rep Tokai Works — Annual Progress Report. Tokai Works

Annu Psychoanal — Annual of Psychoanalysis

Annu Public Water Supply Eng Conf Proc — Annual Public Water Supply Engineers' Conference. Proceedings

Annu Purdue Air Qual Conf Proc — Annual Purdue Air Quality Conference. Proceedings

Annu Qual Congr Trans — Annual Quality Congress Transactions

Annu R Accad Ital — Annuario. Reale Accademia d'Italia

Annu Reale Accad Italia — Annuario della Reale Accademia d'Italia

Annu Reale Accad S Luca — Annuario della Reale Accademia di San Luca

Annu Reale Ist Tec & Naut Bari — Annuario del Reale Istituto Tecnico e Nautico di Bari

Annu Regia Stn Chim Agrar Torino — Annuario. Regia Stazione Chimico-Agraria di Torino

Annu Reliab Phys Symp Proc — Annual Reliability Physics Symposium. Proceedings

Annu Remote Sens Earth Resour Conf Tech Pap — Annual Remote Sensing of Earth Resources Conference. Technical Papers

Annu Rep Acc Cornish Chamber Mines — Annual Report and Accounts. Cornish Chamber of Mines

Annu Rep Agric Chem Insp Stn Jpn — Annual Report. Agricultural Chemical Inspection Station (Japan)

Annu Rep Agric Exp Stn Ala Polytech Inst Ala — Annual Report. Agricultural Experiment Station. Alabama Polytechnic Institute (Alabama)

Annu Rep Agric Exp Stn (Nebr) — Annual Report. Agricultural Experiment Station (Nebraska)

Annu Rep Agric Exp Stn Univ MD — Annual Report. Agricultural Experiment Station. University of Maryland

Annu Rep Agric Hortic Res Stn Long Ashton Bristol — Annual Report. Agricultural and Horticultural Research Station. Long Ashton, Bristol

Annu Rep Agric Res Counc Letcombe Lab — Annual Report. Agricultural Research Council. Letcombe Laboratory

Annu Rep Agric Res Inst North Irel — Annual Report. Agricultural Research Institute of Northern Ireland

Annu Rep Aichi Agric Exp Stn — Annual Report. Aichi Agricultural Experiment Station

Annu Rep Air Pollut Control Dist Cty Los Angeles — Annual Report. Air Pollution Control District. County of Los Angeles

Annu Rep Air Resour Atmos Turbul Diffus Lab — Annual Report. Air Resources Atmospheric Turbulence and Diffusion Laboratory

Annu Rep Akita Prefect Inst Public Health — Annual Report. Akita Prefectural Institute of Public Health

Annu Rep Ala Agr Exp Sta — Annual Report. Alabama Agricultural Experiment Station

Annu Rep AMDEL — Annual Report AMDEL

Annu Rep Amer Hist Ass — Annual Report. American Historical Association

Annu Rep Am Gas Assoc — Annual Report. American Gas Association

Annu Rep Am Inst Phys — Annual Report. American Institute of Physics

Annu Rep Anal At Spectrosc — Annual Reports on Analytical Atomic Spectroscopy

Annu Rep & Bull Walker A G Liverpool — Annual Report and Bulletin. Walker Art Gallery (Liverpool)

Annu Rep Anim Nutr Allied Sci Rowett Res Inst — Annual Report on Animal Nutrition and Allied Sciences. Rowett Research Institute

Annu Rep Archaeol Dept Nizams Dominions — Annual Report of the Archaeological Department of His Exalted Highness the Nizam's Dominions

Annu Rep Archaeol Surv Ceylon — Annual Report of the Archaeological Survey of Ceylon

Annu Rep Archaeol Surv India — Annual Report. Archaeological Survey of India

Annu Rep Armour Res Found — Annual Report. Armour Research Foundation

Annu Rep Asahi Glass Found Contrib Ind Technol — Annual Report. Asahi Glass Foundation for Contributions to Industrial Technology

Annu Rep Aust At Energy Comm — Annual Report. Australian Atomic Energy Commission

Annu Rep BC Minist Mines Pet Resour — Annual Report. British Columbia. Minister of Mines and Petroleum Resources

Annu Rep Bean Improv Coop — Annual Report. Bean Improvement Cooperative

Annu Rep Biol Works Fac Sci Osaka Univ — Annual Report of Biological Works. Faculty of Science. Osaka University

Annu Rep Board Greenkeeping Res — Annual Report. Board of Greenkeeping Research

Annu Rep Brit Sch Archaeol Athens — Annual Report of the British School of Archaeology at Athens

Annu Rep Br Non Ferrous Met Res Assoc — Annual Report. British Non Ferrous Metals Research Association

Annu Rep Bureau Amer Ethnol Secretary Smithsonian Inst — Annual Report of the Bureau of American Ethnology to the Secretary of the Smithsonian Institution

Annu Rep Bur Mines (Philipp) — Annual Report. Bureau of Mines and Geo-Sciences (Philippines)

Annu Rep Bur Rec Geol Min — Annual Report. Bureau de Recherches Geologiques et Minieres

Annu Rep Cacao Res Imp Coll Trop Agric St Augustine Trinidad — Annual Report on Cacao Research. Imperial College of Tropical Agriculture. St. Augustine. Trinidad

Annu Rep Cacao Res Univ West Indies — Annual Report on Cacao Research. University of the West Indies

Annu Rep Calif Water Resour Cent — Annual Report. California Water Resources Center

Annu Rep Can Board Grain Comm Grain Res lab — Annual Report. Canada. Board of Grain Commissioners. Grain Research Laboratory

Annu Rep Cancer Res Campaign — Annual Report. Cancer Research Campaign

Annu Rep Cancer Res Inst Kanazawa Univ — Annual Report. Cancer Research Institute. Kanazawa University

Annu Rep Can Seed Growers Ass — Annual Report. Canadian Seed Growers Association

Annu Rep Carnegie Inst Wash Dep Plant Biol — Annual Report. Carnegie Institution of Washington. Department of Plant Biology

Annu Rep Cent Adult Dis (Osaka) — Annual Report. Center for Adult Diseases (Osaka)

Annu Rep Cent Reg Arecanut Res Stn — Annual Report. Central and Regional Arecanut Research Stations

Annu Rep Centre Resour Stud — Annual Report. Centre for Resource Studies

Annu Rep Ceram Eng Res Lab Nagoya Inst Technol — Annual Report. Ceramic Engineering Research Laboratory. Nagoya Institute of Technology

Annu Rep Ceram Res Lab Nagoya Inst Technol — Annual Report. Ceramics Research Laboratory. Nagoya Institute of Technology

Annu Rep Chamber Mines Precambrian Res Unit — Annual Report. Chamber of Mines Precambrian Research Unit. University of Cape Town

Annu Rep Chem Lab Am Med Assoc — Annual Reports. Chemical Laboratory. American Medical Association

Annu Rep Chem Soc Sect A Phys Inorg Chem — Annual Reports. Chemical Society. Section A. Physical and Inorganic Chemistry

Annu Rep Chiba Prefect Lab Water Pollut — Annual Report. Chiba Prefectural Laboratory of Water Pollution

Annu Rep Clemson Agr Exp Sta — Annual Report. Clemson Agricultural Experiment Station

Annu Rep Coastal Water Res Proj South Calif — Annual Report. Coastal Water Research Project (Southern California)

Annu Rep Cocoa Res Inst Tafo Ghana — Annual Report. Cocoa Research Institute (Tafo, Ghana)

Annu Rep Colo Agric Exp Stn — Annual Report. Colorado Agricultural Experiment Station

Annu Rep Comb Chem Mol Diversity — Annual Reports in Combinatorial Chemistry and Molecular Diversity

Annu Rep Conf Electr Insul — Annual Reports. Conference on Electrical Insulation

Annu Rep Conf Electr Insul Dielectr Phenom — Annual Report. Conference on Electrical Insulation and Dielectric Phenomena

Annu Rep Cornish Min Dev Ass — Annual Report. Cornish Mining Development Association

Annu Rep Counc Miner Technol — Annual Report. Council for Mineral Technology

Annu Rep CSIR — Annual Report. CSIR

Annu Rep CSIRO Aust — Annual Report. Commonwealth Scientific and Industrial Research Organization (Australia)

Annu Rep CSIRO Mar Biochem Unit — Annual Report. Commonwealth Scientific and Industrial Research Organisation. Marine Biochemistry Unit

Annu Rep CSIRO Plant Ind — Annual Report. Commonwealth Scientific and Industrial Research Organisation. Plant Industry

Annu Rep Daiichi Coll Pharm Sci — Annual Report. Daiichi College of Pharmaceutical Sciences

Annu Rep Dairy Res Inst Vidin Bulg — Annual Reports. Dairy Research Institute. Vidin, Bulgaria

Annu Rep Dante Soc — Annual Report. Dante Society

Annu Rep Dep Agric Stock Queensl — Annual Report. Department of Agriculture and Stock. Queensland

Annu Rep Dep Agr NSW — Annual Report. Department of Agriculture. New South Wales

Annu Rep Dep At Energy Gov India — Annual Report. Department of Atomic Energy. Government of India

Annu Rep Dep Miner Energy (Victoria) — Annual Report. Department of Minerals and Energy (Victoria)

Annu Rep Dep Miner Resour (NSW) — Annual Report. Department of Mineral Resources (New South Wales)

Annu Rep Dep Mines Energy (South Aust) — Annual Report. Department of Mines and Energy (South Australia)

Annu Rep Dep Mines (West Aust) — Annual Report. Department of Mines (Western Australia)

Annu Rep Dep Sci Agric Barbados — Annual Report. Department of Science and Agriculture (Barbados)

Annu Rep Dir Dep Terr Magn Carnegie Inst — Annual Report of the Director. Department of Terrestrial Magnetism. Carnegie Institution

Annu Rep Dir Res Philipp Sugar Assoc — Annual Report. Director of Research. Philippine Sugar Association

Annu Rep E Afr Agr Forest Res Organ — Annual Report. East African Agriculture and Forestry Research Organization

Annu Rep East Malling Res Stn (Kent) — Annual Report. East Malling Research Station (Kent)

Annu Rep Energy Mines Resour (Can) — Annual Report. Energy, Mines, and Resources (Canada)

Annu Rep Eng Res Inst Fac Eng Univ Tokyo — Annual Report. Engineering Research Institute. Faculty of Engineering. University of Tokyo

Annu Rep Eng Res Inst Tokyo Univ — Annual Report. Engineering Research Institute. Tokyo University

Annu Rep Eng Res Inst Univ Tokyo — Annual Report. Engineering Research Institute. University of Tokyo

Annu Rep Entomol Soc Ont — Annual Report. Entomological Society of Ontario

Annu Rep Environ Pollut Res Cent Fukui Prefect — Annual Report. Environmental Pollution Research Center. Fukui Prefecture

Annu Rep Environ Pollut Res Cent Ibaraki-Ken — Annual Report. Environmental Pollution Research Center of Ibaraki-Ken

Annu Rep Environ Radioact Res Inst Miyagi — Annual Report. Environmental Radioactivity Research Institute of Miyagi

Annu Rep Environ Sci Lab Ube Jr Coll — Annual Report. Environmental Science Laboratory. Ube Junior College

Annu Rep Fac Educ Gunma Univ — Annual Report. Faculty of Education. Gunma University

Annu Rep Fac Educ Gunma Univ Art Technol Ser — Annual Report. Faculty of Education. Gunma University. Art and Technology Series

Annu Rep Fac Educ Iwate Univ — Annual Report. Faculty of Education. Iwate University

Annu Rep Fac Educ Univ Iwate — Annual Report. Faculty of Education. University of Iwate

Annu Rep Fac Pharm Kanazawa Univ — Annual Report. Faculty of Pharmacy. Kanazawa University

Annu Rep Fac Pharm Pharm Sci Fukuyama Univ — Annual Report. Faculty of Pharmacy and Pharmaceutical Sciences. Fukuyama University

Annu Rep Fac Pharm Sci Nagoya City Univ — Annual Report. Faculty of Pharmaceutical Sciences. Nagoya City University

Annu Rep Fac Pharm Sci Tokushima Univ — Annual Reports. Faculty of Pharmaceutical Sciences. Tokushima University

Annu Rep Farmers Union Grain Terminal Ass — Annual Report. Farmers Union Grain Terminal Association

Annu Rep Ferment Process — Annual Reports on Fermentation Processes

Annu Rep Ferment Processes — Annual Reports on Fermentation Processes

Annu Rep Finan Statements Inst Corn Agr Merchants — Annual Report and Financial Statements. Institute of Corn and Agricultural Merchants

Annu Rep Fla Coop Ext Serv — Annual Report. Florida Cooperative Extension Service

Annu Rep Fla Univ Agr Exp Sta — Annual Report. Florida University. Agricultural Experiment Station

Annu Rep Fogg A Mus Harvard U — Annual Report. Fogg Art Museum. Harvard University

Annu Rep Food Res Inst Aichi Prefect — Annual Report. Food Research Institute. Aichi Prefecture

Annu Rep Freshwater Biol Assoc — Annual Report. Freshwater Biological Association

Annu Rep Fukuoka City Hyg Lab — Annual Report. Fukuoka City Hygienic Laboratory

Annu Rep Fukuoka City Inst Public Health — Annual Report. Fukuoka City Institute of Public Health

Annu Rep Geol Surv Borneo Reg Malays — Annual Report. Geological Survey. Borneo Region. Malaysia

Annu Rep Geol Surv Dep Br Territ Borneo — Annual Report. Geological Survey Department. British Territories in Borneo

Annu Rep Geol Surv Dep (Cyprus) — Annual Report. Geological Survey Department (Cyprus)

Annu Rep Geol Surv Dep (Malawi) — Annual Report. Geological Survey Department (Malawi)

Annu Rep Geol Surv Div (Niger) — Annual Report. Geological Survey Division (Nigeria)

Annu Rep Geol Surv Fed Niger — Annual Report. Geological Survey. Federation of Nigeria

Annu Rep Geol Surv Iowa — Annual Report. Geological Survey (Iowa)

Annu Rep Geol Surv Malays — Annual Report. Geological Survey of Malaysia

Annu Rep Geol Surv Malaysia — Annual Report. Geological Survey of Malaysia

Annu Rep Geol Surv Mines Dep (Swaziland) — Annual Report. Geological Survey and Mines Department (Swaziland)

Annu Rep Geol Surv (New Hebrides) — Annual Report. Geological Survey (New Hebrides)

Annu Rep Geol Surv West Aust — Annual Report. Geological Survey. Western Australia

Annu Rep Geophys Comm (Norw) — Annual Report. Geophysical Commission (Norway)

Annu Rep Geophys Res Norw — Annual Report on Geophysical Research in Norway

Annu Rep Gohei Tanabe Co — Annual Report. Gohei Tanabe Co.

Annu Rep Gov Chem Lab West Aust — Annual Report. Government Chemical Laboratories. Western Australia

Annu Rep Governor Kans Wheat Comm — Annual Report to the Governor. Kansas Wheat Commission

Annu Rep Gunma Inst Public Health — Annual Report. Gunma Institute of Public Health

Annu Rep Gunma Inst Public Health Gunma Res Cent Environ Sci — Annual Report. Gunma Institute of Public Health and Gunma Research Center for Environmental Science

Annu Rep Gunmaken Ind Res Lab — Annual Report. Gunmaken Industrial Research Laboratory

Annu Rep Gunma Prefect Ind Technol Res Lab — Annual Report of Gunma Prefectural Industrial Technology Research Laboratory

Annu Rep Gunma Prefect Inst Public Health Environ Sci — Annual Report. Gunma Prefectural Institute of Public Health and Environmental Sciences

Annu Rep Guyana Geol Surv Dep — Annual Report. Guyana. Geological Survey Department

Annu Rep Hiroshima City Inst Public Health — Annual Report. Hiroshima City Institute of Public Health

Annu Rep Hiroshima Fish Exp Stn — Annual Report. Hiroshima Fisheries Experimental Station

Annu Rep Hokkaido Branch For For Prod Res Inst — Annual Report. Hokkaido Branch. Forestry and Forest Products Research Institute

Annu Rep Hokkaido Branch Gov For Exp Stn — Annual Report. Hokkaido Branch. Government Forest Experiment Station

Annu Rep Hokusei Gakuin Jr Coll — Annual Report. Hokusei Gakuin Junior College

Annu Rep Hormel Inst Univ Minn — Annual Report. Hormel Institute. University of Minnesota

Annu Rep Hoshi Coll Pharm — Annual Report. Hoshi College of Pharmacy

Annu Rep Hung Geol Inst — Annual Report. Hungarian Geological Institute

Annu Rep Hydrogen Isot Res Cent Toyama Univ — Annual Report of Hydrogen Isotope Research Center. Toyama University

Annu Rep Hydrosci Geotechnol Lab Fac Eng Saitama Univ — Annual Report. Hydroscience and Geotechnology Laboratory. Faculty of Engineering. Saitama University

Annu Rep Hyg Lab Okayama Prefect — Annual Report. Hygienic Laboratory of Okayama Prefecture

Annu Rep Ill Soc Eng — Annual Report. Illinois Society of Engineers

Annu Rep Ind Agric Exp Stn — Annual Report. Indiana Agricultural Experiment Station

Annu Rep Ind Epig — Annual Report on Indian Epigraphy

Annu Rep Indian Tea Assoc Tocklai Exp Stn — Annual Report. Indian Tea Association. Tocklai Experimental Station

Annu Rep Inorg Gen Synth — Annual Reports in Inorganic and General Syntheses

Annu Rep Inst Bodemvruchtbaarheid — Annual Report. Instituut voor Bodemvruchtbaarheid

Annu Rep Inst Endocrinol Gunma Univ — Annual Report. Institute of Endocrinology. Gunma University

Annu Rep Inst Environ Pollut Public Health Oita Pref — Annual Report. Institute of Environmental Pollution and Public Health. Oita Prefecture

Annu Rep Inst Environ Pollut Public Health Oita Prefect — Annual Report of Institute of Environmental Pollution and Public Health. Oita Prefecture

Annu Rep Inst Ferment (Osaka) — Annual Report. Institute for Fermentation (Osaka)

Annu Rep Inst Food Microbiol Chiba Univ — Annual Report. Institute of Food Microbiology. Chiba University

Annu Rep Inst Geosci Univ Tsukuba — Annual Report. Institute of Geoscience. University of Tsukuba

Annu Rep Inst Mar Eng — Annual Report. Institute of Marine Engineers

Annu Rep Inst Nucl Stud Univ Tokyo — Annual Report. Institute for Nuclear Study. University of Tokyo

Annu Rep Inst Phys Acad Sin — Annual Report. Institute of Physics. Academia Sinica

Annu Rep Inst Popul Probl — Annual Reports. Institute of Population Problems

Annu Rep Inst Sci Technol Meiji Univ — Annual Report. Institute of Sciences and Technology. Meiji University

Annu Rep Inst Sociol — Annual Report. Institute of Sociology

Annu Rep Inst Virus Res Kyoto Univ — Annual Report. Institute for Virus Research. Kyoto University

Annu Rep Int Assoc Milk Sanit — Annual Report. International Association of Milk Sanitarians

Annu Rep Int Cent Med Res — Annual Reports. International Center for Medical Research

Annu Rep Int Crop Impr Ass — Annual Report. International Crop Improvement Association

Annu Rep Interdiscip Res Inst Environ Sci — Annual Report. Interdisciplinary Research Institute of Environmental Sciences

Annu Rep Int Tin Res Counc — Annual Report. International Tin Research Council

Annu Rep Iowa Agric Home Econ Exp Stn — Annual Report. Iowa Agriculture and Home Economics Experiment Station

Annu Rep Iowa Eng Soc — Annual Report. Iowa Engineering Society

Annu Rep Iowa Geol Surv — Annual Report. Iowa Geological Survey

Annu Rep Itsuu Lab — Annual Report. Itsuu Laboratory

Annu Rep Iwate Med Univ Sch Lib Arts Sci — Annual Report. Iwate Medical University School of Liberal Arts and Sciences

Annu Rep Iwate Prefect Inst Public Health — Annual Report. Iwate Prefectural Institute of Public Health

Annu Rep John Innes Hortic Inst — Annual Report. John Innes Horticultural Institution

Annu Rep Jpn Assoc Radiat Res Polym — Annual Report. Japanese Association for Radiation Research on Polymers

Annu Rep Jpn Assoc Tuberc — Annual Report. Japanese Association for Tuberculosis

Annu Rep Jpn Res Soc Synth Deterg — Annual Report. Japanese Research Society for Synthetic Detergents

Annu Rep Jpn Soc Tuber — Annual Report. Japanese Society for Tuberculosis

Annu Rep Kagawa Prefect Environ Res Cent — Annual Report of Kagawa Prefecture Environmental Research Center

Annu Rep Kagawa Prefect Ferment Food Exp Stn — Annual Report. Kagawa Prefectural Fermentation and Food Experimental Station

Annu Rep Kagoshima Prefect Inst Environ Sci — Annual Reports. Kagoshima Prefectural Institute of Environmental Science

Annu Rep Kanazawa Prefect Public Health Lab — Annual Report. Kanazawa Prefecture Public Health Laboratory

Annu Rep Kawasaki Res Inst Environ Prot — Annual Report. Kawasaki Research Institute for Environmental Protection

Annu Rep Kinki Univ At Energy Res Inst — Annual Reports. Kinki University Atomic Energy Research Institute

Annu Rep Kumamoto Livest Exp Stn — Annual Report. Kumamoto Livestock Experiment Station

Annu Rep Kurashiki Cent Hosp — Annual Reports. Kurashiki Central Hospital

Annu Rep Ky Agric Exp Stn — Annual Report. Kentucky. Agricultural Experiment Station

Annu Rep Kyoritsu Coll Pharm — Annual Report. Kyoritsu College of Pharmacy

Annu Rep Kyoto City Environ Monit Res Cent — Annual Report. Kyoto City Environmental Monitoring and Research Center

Annu Rep Kyoto Prefect Inst Hyg Environ Sci — Annual Report. Kyoto Prefectural Institute of Hygienic and Environmental Sciences

Annu Rep Kyushu Agric Exp Stn — Annual Report. Kyushu Agricultural Experiment Station

Annu Rep Lab Algol (Trebon) — Annual Report. Laboratory of Algology (Trebon)

Annu Rep Lab Exp Algol Dep Appl Algol (Trebon) — Annual Report. Laboratory of Experimental Algology and Department of Applied Algology (Trebon)

Annu Rep Lab Kyoto Prefect Pharm Assoc — Annual Report. Laboratory. Kyoto Prefectural Pharmaceutical Association

Annu Rep Lab Public Health Hiroshima Prefect — Annual Report. Laboratory of Public Health. Hiroshima Prefecture

Annu Rep LA Plan Comm — Annual Report of the Los Angeles Planning Commission

Annu Rep Libr Counc Phila — Annual Report. Library Council of Philadelphia

Annu Rep Macaulay Inst Soil Res — Annual Report. Macaulay Institute for Soil Research

Annu Rep MAFES Miss Agric For Exp St — Annual Report. MAFES. Mississippi Agricultural and Forestry Experiment Station

Annu Rep Mauritius Sugar Ind Res Inst — Annual Report. Mauritius Sugar Industry Research Institute

Annu Rep Md Agric Exp Stn — Annual Report. Maryland Agricultural Experiment Station

Annu Rep Med Chem — Annual Reports in Medicinal Chemistry

Annu Rep Med Res Inst Tokyo Med Dent Univ — Annual Report. Medical Research Institute. Tokyo Medical and Dental University

Annu Rep Med Res Soc Min Smelting Ind — Annual Report. Medical Research Society for Mining and Smelting Industries

Annu Rep Meiji Seika Co — Annual Report. Meiji Seika Company

Annu Rep Mich State Hortic Soc — Annual Report. Michigan State Horticultural Society

Annu Rep Mie Prefect Inst Public Health — Annual Report. Mie Prefectural Institute of Public Health

Annu Rep Miner Resour Dep (Fiji) — Annual Report. Mineral Resources Department (Fiji)

Annu Rep Miner Resour Div (Manitoba) — Annual Report. Mineral Resources Division (Manitoba)

Annu Rep Mines Dep Mines NS — Annual Report on Mines. Department of Mines. Nova Scotia

Annu Rep Mines NS Dep Mines — Annual Report on Mines. Nova Scotia Department of Mines

Annu Rep Mines Serv (Cyprus) — Annual Report. Mines Service (Cyprus)

Annu Rep Minist Mines Pet Resour BC — Annual Report. Minister of Mines and Petroleum Resources. British Columbia

Annu Rep Minn State Hortic Soc — Annual Report. Minnesota State Horticultural Society

Annu Rep Miss Agric For Exp Stn — Annual Report. Mississippi Agricultural and Forestry Experiment Station

Annu Rep Miss State Univ Agr Exp Sta — Annual Report. Mississippi State University. Agricultural Experiment Station

Annu Rep Miyagi Prefect Inst Public Health Environ — Annual Report. Miyagi Prefectural Institute of Public Health and Environment

Annu Rep Miyazaki Prefect Inst Public Health Environ — Annual Report. Miyazaki Prefectural Institute for Public Health and Environment

Annu Rep Mo Water Sewerage Conf — Annual Report. Missouri Water and Sewerage Conference

Annu Rep Mus Anthropol U MO — Annual Report of the Museum of Anthropology. University of Missouri

Annu Rep Mysore Archaeol Dept — Annual Report of the Mysore Archaeological Department

Annu Rep Nagasaki Prefect Inst Public Health Environ Sci — Annual Report. Nagasaki Prefectural Institute of Public Health and Environmental Sciences

Annu Rep Nagoya City Health Res Inst — Annual Report. Nagoya City Health Research Institute

Annu Rep Nat Inst Genet (Jap) — Annual Report. National Institute of Genetics (Japan)

Annu Rep Natl Bur Stand US — Annual Report. National Bureau of Standards (US)

Annu Rep Natl Ind Res Inst — Annual Report. National Industrial Research Institute

Annu Rep Natl Inst Genet — Annual Report. National Institute of Genetics

Annu Rep Natl Inst Nutr — Annual Report. National Institute of Nutrition

Annu Rep Natl Inst Nutr (Jpn) — Annual Report. National Institute of Nutrition (Japan)

Annu Rep Natl Inst Nutr (Tokyo) — Annual Report. National Institute of Nutrition (Tokyo)

Annu Rep Natl Res Inst Chin Med Taiwan — Annual Reports. National Research Institute of Chinese Medicine (Taiwan)

Annu Rep Natl Veg Res Stn Wellesbourne Engl — Annual Report. National Vegetable Research Station. Wellesbourne, England

Annu Rep Natl Vet Assay Lab — Annual Report. National Veterinary Assay Laboratory

Annu Rep Natl Vet Assay Lab (Jpn) — Annual Report. National Veterinary Assay Laboratory (Japan)

Annu Rep Nat Prod Res Inst Seoul Natl Univ — Annual Reports. Natural Products Research Institute. Seoul National University

Annu Rep Natur Sci Home Econ Kinjo Gakuin Coll — Annual Report of Natural Science and Home Economics. Kinjo Gakuin College

Annu Rep Nat Veg Res Stn (Wellesbourne Eng) — Annual Report. National Vegetable Research Station (Wellesbourne, England)

Annu Rep Nebr Grain Impr Ass — Annual Report. Nebraska Grain Improvement Association

Annu Rep Nebr Wheat Comm — Annual Report. Nebraska Wheat Commission

Annu Rep Neth Inst Sea Res — Annual Report. Netherlands Institute for Sea Research

Annu Rep Nigeria Cocoa Res Inst — Annual Report. Nigeria Cocoa Research Institute

Annu Rep Nigerian Inst Oceanogr Mar Res (Lagos) — Annual Report. Nigerian Institute for Oceanography and Marine Research (Lagos)

Annu Rep N Mex Agr Exp Sta — Annual Report. New Mexico Agricultural Experiment Station

Annu Rep NMR Spectrosc — Annual Reports on NMR Spectroscopy

Annu Rep North Nut Grow Assoc — Annual Report. Northern Nut Growers Association

Annu Rep Noto Mar Lab — Annual Report. Noto Marine Laboratory

Annu Rep NS Fruit Grow Assoc — Annual Report. Nova Scotia Fruit Growers' Association

Annu Rep NY State Agric Exp Stn — Annual Report. New York State Agricultural Experiment Station

Annu Rep NY State Assoc Dairy Milk Insp — Annual Report. New York State Association of Dairy and Milk Inspectors

Annu Rep NY State Assoc Milk Food Sanit — Annual Report. New York State Association of Milk and Food Sanitarians

Annu Rep Ohio Conf Water Purif — Annual Report. Ohio Conference on Water Purification

Annu Rep Ohio State Hortic — Annual Report. Ohio State Horticultural Society

Annu Rep Ohio State Hortic Soc — Annual Report. Ohio State Horticultural Society

Annu Rep Oita Prefect Inst Health Environ — Annual Report. Oita Prefectural Institute of Health and Environment

Annu Rep Okayama Prefect Inst Environ Sci Public Health — Annual Report. Okayama Prefectural Institute for Environmental Science and Public Health

Annu Rep Okayama Prefect Res Cent Environ Public Health — Annual Report. Okayama Prefectural Research Center of Environment and Public Health

Annu Rep Okinawa Prefect Inst Public Health — Annual Report. Okinawa Prefectural Institute of Public Health

Annu Rep Okla Agric Exp Stn — Annual Report. Oklahoma Agricultural Experiment Station

Annu Rep Ont Dep Mines — Annual Report. Ontario Department of Mines

Annu Rep Oreg Hortic Soc — Annual Report. Oregon Horticultural Society

Annu Rep Oreg State Hort Soc — Annual Report. Oregon State Horticultural Society

Annu Rep Orient Hosp — Annual Report. Orient Hospital

Annu Rep Orient Hosp (Beirut) — Annual Report. Orient Hospital (Beirut)

Annu Rep Osaka City Inst Public Health Environ Sci — Annual Report. Osaka City Institute of Public Health and Environmental Sciences

Annu Rep Osaka Prefect Radiat Res — Annual Report. Osaka Prefectural Radiation Research Institute

Annu Rep Osaka Prefect Radiat Res Inst — Annual Report. Osaka Prefectural Radiation Research Institute

Annu Rep Pak Cent Jute Comm — Annual Report. Pakistan Central Jute Committee

Annu Rep Peanut Collab Res Support Program CRSP — Annual Report. Peanut Collaborative Research Support Program. CRSP

Annu Rep Peterborough Natur Hist Sci Archaeol Soc — Annual Report. Peterborough Natural History, Scientific, and Archaeological Society

Annu Rep PETROBRAS — Annual Report PETROBRAS

Annu Rep Philipp Sugar Assoc — Annual Report. Philippine Sugar Association

Annu Rep Prefect Univ Mie Sect 2 — Annual Report. Prefectural University of Mie. Section 2. Natural Science

Annu Rep Prod Ammonia Using Coal Source Hydrogen — Annual Report. Production of Ammonia Using Coal as a Source of Hydrogen

Annu Rep Prog Chem — Annual Reports on the Progress of Chemistry

Annu Rep Prog Chem Sect A — Annual Reports on the Progress of Chemistry. Section A. General, Physical, and Inorganic Chemistry

Annu Rep Prog Chem Sect A Gen Phys Inorg Chem — Annual Reports on the Progress of Chemistry. Section A. General, Physical, and Inorganic Chemistry

Annu Rep Prog Chem Sect A Inorg Chem — Annual Reports on the Progress of Chemistry. Section A. Inorganic Chemistry

Annu Rep Prog Chem Sect B — Annual Reports on the Progress of Chemistry. Section B. Organic Chemistry

Annu Rep Prog Chem Sect B Org Chem — Annual Reports on the Progress of Chemistry. Section B. Organic Chemistry

Annu Rep Prog Chem Sect C — Annual Reports on the Progress of Chemistry. Section C. Physical Chemistry

Annu Rep Prog Chem Sect C Phys Chem — Annual Reports on the Progress of Chemistry. Section C. Physical Chemistry

Annu Rep Prog Rubber Technol — Annual Report on the Progress of Rubber Technology

Annu Rep Public Health Div Pharm Soc Jpn — Annual Report. Public Health Division. Pharmaceutical Society of Japan

Annu Rep Punjab Irrig Res Inst — Annual Report. Punjab Irrigation Research Institute

Annu Rep Queens Dep Agric Stock — Annual Report. Queensland Department of Agriculture and Stock

Annu Rep Queensland Dep Mines — Annual Report. Queensland Department of Mines

Annu Rep Que Soc Prot Plants — Annual Report. Quebec Society for the Protection of Plants

Annu Rep Radiat Cent Osaka Prefect — Annual Report. Radiation Center of Osaka Prefecture

Annu Rep Res Act IPCR — Annual Report. Research Activities. IPCR

Annu Rep Res Cent Assoc Am Railroads — Annual Report. Research Center. Association of American Railroads

Annu Rep Res Dep Coffee Board India — Annual Report. Research Department. Coffee Board (India)

Annu Rep Res Div Sudan Minist Agric — Annual Report. Research Division. Sudan. Ministry of Agriculture

Annu Rep Res Inst Chem Fibers Jpn — Annual Report. Research Institute for Chemical Fibers. Japan

Annu Rep Res Inst Chemobiodyn Chiba Univ — Annual Report. Research Institute for Chemobiodynamics. Chiba University

Annu Rep Res Inst Environ Med Nagoya Univ — Annual Report. Research Institute of Environmental Medicine. Nagoya University

Annu Rep Res Inst Environ Med Nagoya Univ (Engl Ed) — Annual Report. Research Institute of Environmental Medicine. Nagoya University (English Edition)

Annu Rep Res Inst Environ Med Nagoya Univ Jpn Ed — Annual Report. Research Institute of Environmental Medicine. Nagoya University (Japanese Edition)

Annu Rep Res Inst Ind Med Yamaguchi Med Sch — Annual Report. Research Institute of Industrial Medicine. Yamaguchi Medical School

Annu Rep Res Inst Org Synth Chem — Annual Report. Research Institute for Organic Synthetic Chemistry

Annu Rep Res Inst Phys Swed — Annual Report. Research Institute of Physics (Sweden)

Annu Rep Res Inst Tuberc Kanazawa Univ — Annual Report. Research Institute of Tuberculosis. Kanazawa University

Annu Rep Res Inst Wakan-Yaku Toyama Med Pharm Univ — Annual Report. Research Institute for Wakan-Yaku Toyama Medical and Pharmaceutical University

Annu Rep Res Lab Ground Failure Niigata Univ Fac Sci — Annual Report. Research Laboratory of Ground Failure. Niigata University. Faculty of Science

Annu Rep Res Mishima Coll Human Sci Nihon Univ — Annual Report of the Researches. Mishima College of Humanities and Sciences. Nihon University

Annu Rep Res Mishima Coll Human Sci Nihon Univ Nat Sci — Annual Report of the Researches. Mishima College of Humanities and Sciences. Nihon University. Natural Sciences

Annu Rep Res React Inst Kyoto Univ — Annual Reports. Research Reactor Institute. Kyoto University

Annu Rep Res Reactor Inst Kyoto Univ — Annual Reports. Research Reactor Institute. Kyoto University

Annu Rep Res Tech Work Dep Agric North Irel — Annual Report on Research and Technical Work. Department of Agriculture for Northern Ireland

Annu Rep R Soc Chem Sect B — Annual Reports. Royal Society of Chemistry. Section B. Inorganic Chemistry

Annu Rep R Soc Chem Sect C — Annual Reports. Royal Society of Chemistry. Section C. Physical Chemistry

Annu Rep Rubber Res Inst Malaya — Annual Report. Rubber Research Institute of Malaya

Annu Rep Sado Mar Biol Stn Niigata Univ — Annual Report. Sado Marine Biological Station. Niigata University

Annu Rep S Afr Wool Text Res Inst — Annual Report. South African Wool and Textile Research Institute

Annu Rep Sankyo Res Lab — Annual Report. Sankyo Research Laboratories

Annu Rep Saranac Lab Stud Tuberc — Annual Report. Saranac Laboratory for the Study of Tuberculosis

Annu Rep Saskatchewan Energy Mines — Annual Report. Saskatchewan Energy and Mines

Annu Rep Sci Living Osaka City Univ — Annual Report of the Science of Living. Osaka City University

Annu Rep Sci Res Counc Jamaica — Annual Report. Scientific Research Council of Jamaica

Annu Rep Sci Works Fac Sci Osaka Univ — Annual Report of Scientific Works. Faculty of Science. Osaka University

Annu Rep SEAFDEC Aquacult Dep — Annual Report. SEAFDEC Aquaculture Department

Annu Rep Secr State Hortic Soc Mich — Annual Report. Secretary of the State Horticultural Society of Michigan

Annu Rep Secr State Pomol Soc Mich — Annual Report. Secretary. State Pomological Society of Michigan

Annu Rep Shionogi Res Lab — Annual Report. Shionogi Research Laboratory

Annu Rep Shizuoka Public Health Lab — Annual Report. Shizuoka Public Health Laboratory

Annu Rep Showa Coll Pharm Sci — Annual Report. Showa College of Pharmaceutical Sciences

Annu Rep Smiths Inst — Annual Report. Smithsonian Institution

Annu Rep Soc Chem Ind Prog Appl Chem — Annual Reports. Society of Chemical Industry on the Progress of Applied Chemistry

Annu Rep Soc Libyan Stud — Annual Report. Society for Libyan Studies

Annu Rep Soc Plant Prot N Jap — Annual Report. Society of Plant Protection of North Japan

Annu Rep Soc Plant Prot North Jpn — Annual Report. Society of Plant Protection of North Japan

Annu Rep Soc Promot Constr Eng — Annual Report. Society for the Promotion of Construction Engineering

Annu Rep Soc Yamaguchi Ind Health — Annual Report. Society of Yamaguchi Industrial Health

Annu Rep South Calif Coastal Water Res Proj — Annual Report. Southern California Coastal Water Research Project

Annu Rep Steril Res Inst R Vet Agric Univ — Annual Report. Sterility Research Institute. Royal Veterinary and Agricultural University

Annu Rep Stress — Annual Report on Stress

Annu Rep Stud Anim Nutr Allied Sci Rowett Res Inst — Annual Report of Studies in Animal Nutrition and Allied Sciences. Rowett Research Institute

Annu Rep Stud Doshisha Women's Coll Lib Arts — Annual Report of Studies. Doshisha Women's College of Liberal Arts

Annu Rep Stud Jissen Womens Univ Nat Domest Sci — Annual Report of Studies. Jissen Women's University. Natural and Domestic Sciences

Annu Rep Sudan Minist Agric — Annual Report. Sudan. Ministry of Agriculture

Annu Rep Sudan Minist Agric Agric Res Div — Annual Report. Sudan. Ministry of Agriculture. Agricultural Research Division

Annu Rep Surv Res Air Pollut Kanagawa Prefect Jpn — Annual Report. Survey and Research of Air Pollution in Kanagawa Prefecture. Japan

Annu Rep Takamatsu Tech Coll — Annual Reports. Takamatsu Technical College

Annu Rep Takamine Lab — Annual Report of Takamine Laboratory

Annu Rep Takeda Res Lab — Annual Report. Takeda Research Laboratories

Annu Rep Tanabe Seiyaku Co Ltd — Annual Report. Tanabe Seiyaku Company Limited

Annu Rep Tech Div Natl Inst Physiol Sci — Annual Report. Technical Division. National Institute for Physiological Sciences

Annu Rep Tob Inst PR — Annual Report. Tobacco Institute of Puerto Rico

Annu Rep Tob Res Inst — Annual Report. Tobacco Research Institute

Annu Rep Tob Res Inst Taiwan Tob & Wine Monop Bur — Annual Report. Tobacco Research Institute. Taiwan Tobacco and Wine Monopoly Bureau

Annu Rep Tohoku Coll Pharm — Annual Report. Tohoku College of Pharmacy

Annu Rep Tokushima Prefect Inst Public Health Environ Sci — Annual Report. Tokushima Prefectural Institute of Public Health and Environmental Sciences

Annu Rep Tokyo Coll Pharm — Annual Report. Tokyo College of Pharmacy

Annu Rep Tokyo Metrop Labs Med Sci — Annual Report. Tokyo Metropolitan Laboratories for Medical Sciences

Annu Rep Tokyo Metrop Res Inst Environ Prot — Annual Report. Tokyo Metropolitan Research Institute for Environmental Protection

Annu Rep Tokyo Metrop Res Inst Environ Prot Engl Transl — Annual Report. Tokyo Metropolitan Research Institute for Environmental Protection. English Translation

Annu Rep Tokyo Metrop Res Inst Environ Prot Jpn Ed — Annual Report. Tokyo Metropolitan Research Institute for Environmental Protection. Japanese Edition

Annu Rep Tokyo Metrop Res Lab Public Health — Annual Report. Tokyo Metropolitan Research Laboratory of Public Health

Annu Rep Tokyo to Lab Med Sci — Annual Report. Tokyo-to Laboratories for Medical Science

Annu Rep Tokyo Univ Agric Technol — Annual Report. Tokyo University of Agriculture and Technology

Annu Rep Torry Res Stn (Aberdeen UK) — Annual Report. Torry Research Station (Aberdeen, UK)

Annu Rep Toyama Inst Health — Annual Report. Toyama Institute of Health

Annu Rep Tritium Res Cent Toyama Univ — Annual Report. Tritium Research Center. Toyama University

Annu Rep United Dent Hosp Sydney Inst Dent Res — Annual Report. United Dental Hospital of Sydney. Institute of Dental Research

Annu Rep Univ Del Coll Agric Sci Agric Exp Stn Coop Ext Serv — Annual Report. University of Delaware. College of Agricultural Sciences. Agricultural Experiment Station and Cooperative Extension Service

Annu Rep Univ GA Coll Agr Exp Sta — Annual Report. University of Georgia. College of Agriculture. Experiment Stations

Annu Rep Univ Leeds Res Inst Afr Geol Dep Earth Sci — Annual Report. University of Leeds. Research Institute of African Geology and Department of Earth Sciences

Annu Rep Univ Minn Hormel Inst — Annual Report. University of Minnesota. Hormel Institute

Annu Rep US Crude Oil Nat Gas Reserves — Annual Report. US Crude Oil and Natural Gas Reserves

Annu Rep Veg Growers Ass Amer — Annual Report. Vegetable Growers Association of America

Annu Rep Veg Growers Assoc Am — Annual Report. Vegetable Growers Association of America

Annu Rep Wakayama Prefect Inst Public Health — Annual Report. Wakayama Prefectural Institute of Public Health

Annu Rep Wakayama Prefect Res Cent Environ Public Health — Annual Report. Wakayama Prefectural Research Center of Environment and Public Health

Annu Rep Welsh Plant Breed Stn (Aberystwyth Wales) — Annnual Report. Welsh Plant Breeding Station (Aberystwyth, Wales)

Annu Rep Welsh Plant Breed Stn Univ Coll Wales (Aberystwyth) — Annual Report. Welsh Plant Breeding Station. University College of Wales (Aberystwyth)

Annu Rep West Aust Dep Mines — Annual Report. Western Australia. Department of Mines

Annu Rep Wye Coll Univ London Dep Hop Res — Annual Report. Wye College. University of London. Department of Hop Research

Annu Rep Yakult Inst Microbiol Res — Annual Report. Yakult Institute for Microbiological Research

Annu Rep Yamaguchi Prefect Environ Pollut Res Cent — Annual Report. Yamaguchi Prefectural Environmental Pollution Research Center

Annu Rep Yamanashi Inst Public Health — Annual Report. Yamanashi Institute for Public Health

Annu Rep Yokohama City Inst Health — Annual Report. Yokohama City Institute of Health

Annu Res Conf Bur Biol Res Rutgers Univ — Annual Research Conference. Bureau of Biological Research. Rutgers University

Annu Res Inst Environ Med Nagoya Univ — Annuals. Research Institute of Environmental Medicine. Nagoya University

Annu Res Rep Kuwait Inst Sci Res — Annual Research Report. Kuwait Institute for Scientific Research

Annu Res Rep Red River Valley Agric Exp Stn — Annual Research Report. Red River Valley Agricultural Experiment Station

Annu Res Rev Angina Pectoris — Annual Research Reviews. Angina Pectoris

Annu Res Rev Anti-Diuretic Horm — Annual Research Reviews. Anti-Diuretic Hormone

Annu Res Rev Biofeedback — Annual Research Reviews. Biofeedback

Annu Res Rev Duodenal Ulcer — Annual Research Reviews. Duodenal Ulcer

Annu Res Rev Eff Psychother — Annual Research Reviews. Effects of Psychotherapy

Annu Res Rev Hodgkin's Dis Lymphomas — Annual Research Reviews. Hodgkin's Disease and the Lymphomas

Annu Res Rev Horm & Aggression — Annual Research Reviews. Hormones and Aggression

Annu Res Rev Hypothal Releasing Factors — Annual Research Reviews. Hypothalamic Releasing Factors

Annu Res Rev Intrauterine Contracept — Annual Research Reviews. Intrauterine Contraception

Annu Res Rev Oral Contracept — Annual Research Reviews. Oral Contraceptives

Annu Res Rev Peripher Metab Action Thyroid Horm — Annual Research Reviews. Peripheral Metabolism and Action of Thyroid Hormones

Annu Res Rev Physiol Pathol Aspects Prolactin Secretion — Annual Research Reviews. Physiological and Pathological Aspects of Prolactin Secretion

Annu Res Rev Pineal — Annual Research Reviews. Pineal

Annu Res Rev Prolactin — Annual Research Reviews. Prolactin

Annu Res Rev Prostaglandins Gut — Annual Research Reviews. Prostaglandins and the Gut

Annu Res Rev Proteins Anim Cell Plasma Membr — Annual Research Reviews. Proteins of Animal Cell Plasma Membranes

Annu Res Rev Regul Growth Horm Secretion — Annual Research Reviews. Regulation of Growth Hormone Secretion

Annu Res Rev Renal Prostaglandins — Annual Research Reviews. Renal Prostaglandins

Annu Res Rev Renin — Annual Research Reviews. Renin

Annu Res Rev Rheum Arthritis Relat Cond — Annual Research Reviews. Rheumatoid Arthritis and Related Conditions

Annu Res Rev Somatostatin — Annual Research Reviews. Somatostatin

Annu Res Rev Sphingolipidoses Allied Disord — Annual Research Reviews. Sphingolipidoses and Allied Disorders

Annu Res Rev Subst P — Annual Research Reviews. Substance P

Annu Res Rev Ultrastruct Pathol Hum Tumors — Annual Research Reviews. Ultrastructural Pathology of Human Tumors

Annu Res Rev Vitam Trace Miner Protein Interact — Annual Research Reviews. Vitamin-Trace Mineral-Protein Interactions

Annu Rev Anthrop — Annual Review of Anthropology

Annu Rev Anthropol — Annual Review of Anthropology

Annu Rev Astron Astrophys — Annual Review of Astronomy and Astrophysics

Annu Rev Autom Program — Annual Review in Automatic Programming

Annu Rev Behav Ther Theory Pract — Annual Review of Behavior Therapy Theory and Practice

Annu Rev Biochem — Annual Review of Biochemistry

Annu Rev Biochem Allied Res India — Annual Review of Biochemical and Allied Research in India

Annu Rev Biophys Bioeng — Annual Review of Biophysics and Bioengineering

Annu Rev Biophys Biomol Struct — Annual Review of Biophysics and Biomolecular Structure

Annu Rev Biophys Biophys Chem — Annual Review of Biophysics and Biophysical Chemistry

Annu Rev Cell Biol — Annual Review of Cell Biology

Annu Rev Cell Dev Biol — Annual Review of Cell and Developmental Biology

Annu Rev Chemother Physiatr Cancer — Annual Review of Chemotherapy and Physiatrics of Cancer

Annu Rev Chronopharmacol — Annual Review of Chronopharmacology

Annu Rev Clin Biochem — Annual Review of Clinical Biochemistry

Annu Rev Comput Phys — Annual Reviews of Computational Physics

Annu Rev Earth Planet Sci — Annual Review of Earth and Planetary Sciences

Annu Rev Ecol Syst — Annual Review of Ecology and Systematics

Annu Rev Energy — Annual Review of Energy

Annu Rev Entomol — Annual Review of Entomology

Annu Rev Fluid Mech — Annual Review of Fluid Mechanics

Annu Rev Food Technol — Annual Review of Food Technology

Annu Rev Food Technol (Mysore) — Annual Review of Food Technology (Mysore)

Annu Rev Genet — Annual Review of Genetics

Annu Rev Heat Transfer — Annual Review of Heat Transfer

Annu Rev Immunol — Annual Review of Immunology

Annu Rev Ind Eng Chem — Annual Reviews of Industrial and Engineering Chemistry

Annu Rev Inf Sci Technol — Annual Review of Information Science and Technology

Annu Rev Inst Plasma Phys Nagoya — Annual Review. Institute of Plasma Physics. Nagoya University

Annu Rev Inst Plasma Phys Nagoya Univ — Annual Review. Institute of Plasma Physics. Nagoya University

Annu Rev Mater Sci — Annual Review of Materials Science

Annu Rev Med — Annual Review of Medicine

Annu Rev Microbiol — Annual Review of Microbiology

Annu Rev Neurosci — Annual Review of Neuroscience

Annu Rev NMR Spectrosc — Annual Review of NMR Spectroscopy

Annu Rev Nucl Part Sci — Annual Review of Nuclear and Particle Science

Annu Rev Nucl Sci — Annual Review of Nuclear Science [*Later, Annual Review of Nuclear and ParticleScience*]

Annu Rev Numer Fluid Mech Heat Transfer — Annual Review of Numerical Fluid Mechanics and Heat Transfer

Annu Rev Nurs Res — Annual Review of Nursing Research

Annu Rev Nutr — Annual Review of Nutrition

Annu Rev Pet Technol (London) — Annual Review of Petroleum Technology (London)

Annu Rev Pharmacol — Annual Review of Pharmacology [*Later, Annual Review of Pharmacology and Toxicology*]

Annu Rev Pharmacol Toxicol — Annual Review of Pharmacology and Toxicology

Annu Rev Pharm Tox — Annual Review of Pharmacology and Toxicology

Annu Rev Photochem — Annual Review of Photochemistry

Annu Rev Phys Chem — Annual Review of Physical Chemistry

Annu Rev Physiol — Annual Review of Physiology

Annu Rev Phytopathol — Annual Review of Phytopathology

Annu Rev Plant Physiol — Annual Review of Plant Physiology

Annu Rev Plant Physiol Plant Mol Biol — Annual Review of Plant Physiology and Plant Molecular Biology

Annu Rev Plant Sci — Annual Reviews of Plant Sciences

Annu Rev Prog Appl Comput Electromagn — Annual Review of Progress in Applied Computational Electromagnetics

Annu Rev Psychol — Annual Review of Psychology

Annu Rev Public Health — Annual Review of Public Health

Annu Rev Rehabil — Annual Review of Rehabilitation

Annu Rev Rubber Res Inst Sri Lanka — Annual Review. Rubber Research Institute of Sri Lanka

Annu Rev Schizophr Syndr — Annual Review of the Schizophrenic Syndrome

Annu Rev Sex Res — Annual Review of Sex Research

Annu Rev Sociol — Annual Review of Sociology

Annu Rev Tel Aviv Mus — Annual Review. Tel Aviv Museum

Annu R Hung Cent Exp Stn Vine Wine Cult Ampelol Inst — Annual. Royal Hungarian Central Experiment Station for Vine and Wine Culture. Ampelological Institute

Ann Urol — Annales d'Urologie

Annu Romant Bibliogr — Annual Romantic Bibliography

Annu Roum Anthrop — Annuaire Roumain d'Anthropologie

Annu Roum Anthropol — Annuaire Roumain d'Anthropologie

AnnUS — Annales Universitatis Saraviensis. Philosophie- Lettres

Annu Sanit Int — Annuaire Sanitaire International

Annu Sante Anim — Annuaire de la Sante Animale

Annu Sci Conf Proc Belfer Grad Sch Sci — Annual Science Conference Proceedings. Belfer Graduate School of Science

Annu Sci Meet Aerosp Med Assoc — Annual Scientific Meeting. Aerospace Medical Association

Annu Sci Pap Higher Med Inst Varna — Annual Scientific Papers. Higher Medical Institute. Varna

Annu Sci Pap Med Acad Fac Med Varna — Annual Scientific Papers. Medical Academy. Faculty of Medicine. Varna

Annu Scu Archeol Atene & Miss It Oriente — Annuario della Scuola Archeologica di Atene e delle Missioni Italiane in Oriente

Annu Seism Beogr — Annuaire Seismique (Beograd)

Annu Semin Theor Phys Proc — Annual Seminar on Theoretical Physics. Proceedings

Annu Serv Met Afr Occid Fr 1 — Annuaire du Service Meteorologique de l'Afrique Occidentale Francaise. 1. Frequences

Annu Serv Met Afr Occid Fr 2 — Annuaire du Service Meteorologique de l'Afrique Occidentale Franciase. 2. Bulletin Seismique

Annu Simul Symp (Rec Proc) — Annual Simulation Symposium (Record of Proceedings)

Annu Skira — Annuel Skira

Annu Soc Amis Vieux Strasbourg — Annuaire de la Societe des Amis du Vieux Strasbourg

Annu Soc Arch Bruxelles — Annuaire. Societe Royal d'Archeologie de Bruxelles

Annu Soc Belge Astr — Annuaire de la Societe Belge d'Astronomie

Annu Soc Chim Fr — Annuaire de la Societe Chimique de France

Annu Soc Chim Phys — Annuaire. Societe de Chimie Physique

Annu Soc Fr Econ Alp — Annuaire de la Societe Francaise d'Economie Alpestre

Annu Soc Fr Ingrs Techns Vide — Annuaire de la Societe Francaise des Ingenieurs Techniciens du Vide

Annu Soc Fr Phys — Annuaire de la Societe Francaise de Physique

Annu Soc Helv Sci Nat Partie Sci — Annuaire. Societe Helvetique des Sciences Naturelles. Partie Scientifique

Annu Soc Hist Sundgovienne — Annuaire. Societe de l'Histoire de Sundgovienne

Annu Soc Hist Val et Ville Munster — Annuaire. Societe d'Histoire du Val et de la Ville de Munster

Annu Soc Ind Miner — Annuaire. Societe de l'Industrie Minerale

Annu Soc Ingrs Civ Fr — Annuaire de la Societe des Ingenieurs Civils de France

Annu Soc Int Electns — Annuaire de la Societe Internationale des Electriciens

Annu Soc Med Paris — Annuaire de la Societe de Medecine de Paris

Annu Soc Meteorol Fr — Annuaire. Societe Meteorologique de France

Annu Soc Met Fr — Annuaire de la Societe Meteorologique de France

Annu Southwest IEEE Conf Exhib Rec — Annual Southwestern IEEE [*Institute of Electrical and Electronics Engineering*] Conference and Exhibition. Record

Annu Sta Chim-Agr Sper Torino — Annuario. Stazione Chimico-Agraria Sperimentale di Torino

Annu Stat Summ Mich Geol Surv Div — Annual Statistical Summary. Michigan. Geological Survey Division

Annu Stn Sper Agrar Torino — Annuario. Stazione Sperimentale Agraria di Torino

Annu Stn Sper Viti Enol Conegliano Italy — Annuario. Stazione Sperimentale di Viticoltura e Enologia. Conegliano, Italy

Annu Study Rep Brain Sci Found — Annual Study Report. Brain Science Foundation

Annu Suisse Sci Polit — Annuaire Suisse de Science Politique

Annu Surv Am Chem Nat Res Counc — Annual Survey of American Chemistry. National Research Council

Annu Surv of Afr L — Annual Survey of African Law

Annu Surv of Amer L — Annual Survey of American Law

Annu Surv of Indian L — Annual Survey of Indian Law

Annu Surv of South Afr L — Annual Survey of South African Law

Annu Surv Organomet Chem — Annual Survey of Organometallic Chemistry

Annu Surv Photochem — Annual Survey of Photochemistry

Annu Symp Am Coll Cardiol — Annual Symposium. American College of Cardiology

Annu Symp Biomath Comput Sci Life Sci Abstr — Annual Symposium on Biomathematics and Computer Science in the Life Sciences. Abstracts

Annu Symp Bot — Annual Symposium in Botany

Annu Symp East Afr Acad Proc — Annual Symposium. East African Academy. Proceedings

Annu Symp East PA Branch Am Soc Microbiol Proc — Annual Symposium. Eastern Pennsylvania Branch, American Society for Microbiology. Proceedings

Annu Symp Found Comput Sci (Proc) — Annual Symposium on Foundations of Computer Science (Proceedings)

Annu Symp Fundam Cancer Res Proc — Annual Symposium on Fundamental Cancer Research. Proceedings

Annu Symp Gynecol Endocrinol — Annual Symposium on Gynecologic Endocrinology

Annu Symp Instrum Process Ind Proc — Annual Symposium on Instrumentation for the Process Industries. Proceedings

Annu Symp Int Coll Appl Nutr — Annual Symposium. International College of Applied Nutrition

Annu Symp Marie Curie Meml Found Cancer Proc — Annual Symposium. Marie Curie Memorial Foundation on Cancer. Proceedings

Annu Symp Microlithogr — Annual Symposium on Microlithography

Annu Symp Nurs Fac Pract — Annual Symposium on Nursing Faculty Practice

Annu Symp Photomask Technol — Annual Symposium on Photomask Technology

Annu Symp Photomask Technol Manage — Annual Symposium on Photomask Technology and Management

Annu Symp Plant Physiol — Annual Symposium in Plant Physiology

Annu Symp Radio Space Sci Invited Spec Artic — Annual Symposium on Radio and Space Sciences. Invited Special Articles

Annu Symp Safeguards Nucl Mater Manage — Annual Symposium on Safeguards and Nuclear Material Management

Annu Symp Sci Basis Med — Annual Symposium on the Scientific Basis of Medicine

Annu Symp SSIEM — Annual Symposium. SSIEM (Society for the Study of Inborn Errors of Metabolism)

Annu Symp Uranium Precious Met — Annual Symposium on Uranium and Precious Metals

Annu Tech Conf Am Electroplat Soc — Annual Technical Conference. American Electroplaters' Society

Annu Tech Conf ANTEC Conf Proc — Annual Technical Conference. ANTEC. Conference Proceedings

Annu Tech Conf Proc Irrig Assoc — Annual Technical Conference Proceedings. Irrigation Association

Annu Tech Conf Proc Soc Vac Coaters — Annual Technical Conference Proceedings. Society of Vacuum Coaters

Annu Tech Conf Proc Sprinkler Irrig Assoc — Annual Technical Conference Proceedings. Sprinkler Irrigation Association

Annu Tech Conf Soc Plast Eng — Annual Technical Conference. Society of Plastics Engineers

Annu Tech Conf SPI Reinf Plast Compos Div Proc — Annual Technical Conference. SPI Reinforced Plastics/Composites Division. Proceedings

Annu Tech Conf Trans Am Soc Qual Control — Annual Technical Conference Transactions. American Society for Quality Control

Annu Tech Manage Conf Reinf Plast Div Soc Plast Ind — Annual Technical and Management Conference. Reinforced Plastics Division. Society of the Plastics Industry

Annu Tech Meet Pet Soc CIM Prepr — Annual Technical Meeting. Petroleum Society of CIM. Preprints

Annu Tech Proc Am Electroplat Soc — Annual Technical Proceedings. American Electroplaters Society

Annu Tech Symp SPIE Proc — Annual Technical Symposium. SPIE. (Society of Photo-Optical Instrumentation Engineers) Proceedings

Annu Testis Workshop — Annual Testis Workshop

Annu Tex Conf Util At Energy — Annual Texas Conference. Utilization of Atomic Energy

Annu Tiers-Monde — Annuaire du Tiers-Monde

Annu Transactions Nord Rheol Soc — Annual Transactions of the Nordic Rheology Society

Annu UMR-DNR Conf Energy Proc — Annual UMR-DNR [*University of Missouri, Rolla - Department of Natural Resources*] Conference on Energy. Proceedings

Annu UMR-MEC Conf Energy Proc — Annual UMR-MEC [*University of Missouri, Rolla-Missouri Energy Council*] Conference on Energy. Proceedings

Annu Underground Coal Convers Symp Proc — Annual Underground Coal Conversion Symposium. Proceedings

Annu Univ Modena — Annuario. Reale Universita di Modena

Annu Univ R Vet Agron Copenhagen — Annuaire. Universite Royale Veterinaire et Agronomique (Copenhagen)

Annu Univ Sofia Fac Agron — Annuaire. Universite de Sofia. Faculte d'Agronomie

Annu Univ Sofia Fac Agron Sylvic — Annuaire. Universite de Sofia. Faculte d'Agronomie et de Sylviculture

Annu Univ Sofia Fac Biol — Annuaire. Universite de Sofia. Faculte de Biologie

Annu Univ Sofia Fac Biol Geol Geogr — Annuaire. Universite de Sofia. Faculte de Biologie, Geologie, et Geographie

Annu Univ Sofia Fac Geol Geogr — Annuaire. Universite de Sofia. Faculte de Geologie et Geographie

Annu Univ Sofia Fac Phys — Annuaire. Universite de Sofia. Faculte de Physique

Annu Univ Sofia Fac Phys Math — Annuaire. Universite de Sofia. Faculte Physico-Mathematique

Annu Univ Sofia Fac Sci — Annuaire. Universite de Sofia. Faculte des Sciences

Annu Univ Sofia Fac Sci Phys Math — Annuaire. Universite de Sofia. Faculte des Sciences Physiques et Mathematiques

Annu Univ Sofia Fac Sylvic — Annuaire. Universite de Sofia. Faculte de Sylviculture

Annu Univ Sofia Kliment Ochridski-Fac Biol — Annuaire. Universite de Sofia. Kliment Ochridski-Faculte de Biologie

Annu Univ Sofia Kliment Ohridski Fac Chim — Annuaire. Universite de Sofia Kliment Ohridski. Faculte de Chimie

Annu Univ Sofia Kliment Ohridski Fac Geol Geogr — Annuaire. Universite de Sofia Kliment Ohridski. Faculte de Geologie et Geographie

Annu Univ Sofia Kliment Ohridski Fac Math Mec — Annuaire. Universite de Sofia Kliment Ohridski. Faculte de Mathematiques et Mecanique

Annu Univ Sofia Kliment Ohridski Fac Phys — Annuaire. Universite de Sofia Kliment Ohridski. Faculte de Physique

Annu Univ Sofia Kliment Ohridski Phys Technol Semicond — Annuaire. Universite de Sofia Kliment Ohridski. Physique et Technologie des Semiconducteurs

Annu Uranium Semin Proc — Annual Uranium Seminar. Proceedings

Annu URSS — Annuaire de l'URSS et des Pays Socialistes Europeens

Annu Visit Lect Ser Coll Pharm Univ Tex — Annual Visiting Lecture Series. College of Pharmacy. University of Texas

Annu Vol Inst Mar Eng — Annual Volume. Institute of Marine Engineers

Annu West Plast Tool Conf — Annual Western Plastics for Tooling Conference

Annu Winter Conf Brain Res — Annual Winter Conference on Brain Research

Annu Workshop Chem Biochem Herbic — Annual Workshop. Chemistry and Biochemistry of Herbicides

Annu Workshop Pestic Residue Anal (West Can) — Annual Workshop for Pesticide Residue Analysts (Western Canada)

Annu World Conf Magnesium Proc — Annual World Conference on Magnesium. Proceedings

Annu Yonne — Annuaire de l'Yonne

Ann Vasc Surg — Annals of Vascular Surgery

Ann Verh Arbeiten Oecon Patriot Soc Fuerstenth Schweidnitz — Annalen aller Verhandlungen und Arbeiten der Oeconomisch-Patriotischen Societaet des Fuerstenthumes Schweidnitz

Ann Vet Res — Annals of Veterinary Research

Ann Villaggio Sanat Sondalo — Annali. Villaggio Sanatoriale di Sondalo

Ann Virol — Annales de Virologie
Ann Virol (Paris) — Annales de Virologie (Paris)
Ann Voyages — Annales des Voyages, de la Geographie, et de l'Histoire
Ann War — Annals of War
Ann Warsaw Agric Univ Agric — Annals of Warsaw Agricultural University. Agriculture
Ann Warsaw Agric Univ SGGW-AR Anim Sci — Annals. Warsaw Agricultural University. SGGW-AR [*Szkola Glowna Gospodarstwa Wiejskiego - Akademia Rolnicza*]. Animal Science
Ann Warsaw Agric Univ SGGW AR For Wood Technol — Annals. Warsaw Agricultural University SGGW-AR [*Szkola Glowna Gospodarstwa Weijskiego-Akademia Rolnicza*]. Forestry and Wood Technology
Ann Warsaw Agric Univ SGGW AR Hortic — Annals. Warsaw Agricultural University SGGW-AR (Szkola Glowna Gospodarstwa Weijskiego-Akademia Rolnicza). Horticulture
Ann Warsaw Agric Univ SGGW AR Land Reclam — Annals. Warsaw Agricultural University SGGW-AR (Szkola Glowna Gospodarstwa Weijskiego-Akademia Rolnicza). Land Reclamation
Ann Warsaw Agric Univ SGGW AR Vet Med — Annals. Warsaw Agricultural University SGGW-AR [*Szkola Glowna Gospodarstwa Weijskiego-Akademia Rolnicza*]. Veterinary Medicine
Ann Weissruss Staatl Akad Land Forstwirtsch Gory Gorki — Annalen der Weissrussischen Staatlichen Akademie fuer Land- und Forstwirtschaft in Gory-Gorki
Ann Western Med Surg — Annals of Western Medicine and Surgery. Los Angeles County Medical Association
Ann West Med Surg — Annals of Western Medicine and Surgery
Ann West Univ Timisoara Ser Chem — Annals of West University of Timisoara. Series of Chemistry
Ann White Russ Agric Inst — Annals. White Russian Agricultural Institute
Ann Worc Art Mus — Annual Report. Worcester Art Museum
Ann Wyo — Annals of Wyoming
Ann Wyoming — Annals of Wyoming. State Dept. of History
Anny — Advertising News of New York [*Later, Adweek*]
An NY Acad Sci — Annals of the New York Academy of Sciences
Ann Zimbabwe Geol Surv — Annals. Zimbabwe Geological Survey
Ann Zool — Annals of Zoology
Ann Zool (Agra) — Annals of Zoology (Agra)
Ann Zool Agra India — Annals of Zoology (Agra, India)
Ann Zool Ecol Anim — Annales de Zoologie - Ecologie Animale
Ann Zool Fenn — Annales Zoologici Fennici
Ann Zool Soc Zool-Bot Fenn "Vanamo" — Annales Zoologici. Societatis Zoologicae-Botanicae Fennicae "Vanamo"
Ann Zool (Warsaw) — Annales Zoologici (Warsaw)
Ann Zootech — Annales de Zootechnie
Ann Zootech Inst Nat Rech Agron — Annales de Zootechnie. Institut National de la Recherche Agronomique
Ann Zootech (Paris) — Annales de Zootechnie (Paris)
Ann Zymol — Annales de Zymologie
ANO — Air Navigation Order
AnO — Anneau d'Or
ANOAAR — Antropologicky Archiv
An Obs Astr Met — Analele Observatorului Astronomic si Meteorologic
An Obs Astr Met S Salvador — Anales del Observatorio Astronomico y Meteorologico de San Salvador
An Obs Buc — Anuarul. Observatorului din Bucuresti
An Obs Col Nuestra Senora de Montserrat Habana — Anales del Observatorio. Colegio Nuestra Senora de Montserrat (Habana)
An Obs Met Nac Ciud Univ — Anales del Observatorio Meteorologico Nacional Ciudad Universitaria [*Bogota*]
An Obs Nac Met La Aurora — Anales del Observatorio Nacional Meteorologico de La Aurora [*Guatemala*]
An Obs Nac Met S Salv — Anales. Observatorio Nacional Meteorologico de San Salvador
An Obs Nac S Bartolome — Anales. Observatorio Nacional de San Bartolome
An OCD — Analecta Ordinis Carmelitarum Discalceatorum
An O Cist — Analecta Sacri Ordinis Cisterciensis
Ano Cult Esp — Ano Cultural Espanol
Anodes Electrowinning Proc Sess AIME Annu Meet — Anodes for Electrowinning. Proceedings. Sessions held at the AIME Annual Meeting
Anodic Behav Met Semicond Ser — Anodic Behavior of Metals and Semiconductors Series
Anodnaya Zashch Met Dokl Mezhvuz Konf — Anodnaya Zashchita Metallov. Doklady Mezhvuzovskoi Konferentsii
An Of Met Argent — Anales de la Oficina Meteorologica Argentina
An Of Met Prov B Aires — Anales. Oficina Meteorologica de la Provincia de Buenos Aires
An Of Quim Prov B Aires — Anales de la Oficina Quimica de la Provincia de Buenos Aires
An Oftal — Anales de Oftalmologia
An Oftal Oto Rino Lar Parag — Anales de Oftalmologia y Oto-Rino-Laringologia del Paraguay
ANOH — Aarboeger foer Nordisk Oldkyndighed og Historie
ANOMA — Alluminio e Nuova Metallurgia
Anomalous Nucl Eff Deuterium Solid Syst — Anomalous Nuclear Effects in Deuterium/Solid Systems
AnOr — Analecta Orientalia. Commentationes Scientificae de Rebus Orientis Antiqui. Pontificium Institutum Biblicum
An Or — Anneau d'Or. Cahiers de Spiritualite Familiale
ANORA — Angle Orthodontist
ANORBB — Applied Ornithology
An Ordre Souverain Mil Malte — Annales de L'Ordre Souverain Militaire de Malte
Anorexia Nerv Multidisciplinary Conf — Anorexia Nervosa. Multidisciplinary Conference of Anorexia Nervosa

Anorg Allg Chem Einzel — Anorganische und Allgemeine Chemie in Einzeldarstellungen
An ORL Ibero-Amer — Anales Otorrinolaringologicos Ibero-Americanos
A Norm — Annales de Normandie
A Normandie — Annales de Normandie; Revue Trimestrielle d'Etudes Regionales
An Or Res — Annals of Oriental Research
An Ortop Traum Mex — Anales de Ortopedia y Traumatologia (Mexico)
An Oto Rino Lar Urug — Anales de Oto-Rino-Laringologia del Uruguay
An Otorrinolaringol Ibero Am — Anales Otorrinolaringologicos Iberoamericanos
An Otorrinolaringol Iber-Am — Anales Otorrinolaringologicos Ibero-Americanos
Anot Pediatr — Anotaciones Pediatricas
An Oudhdknd Kring Land van Waas An Cerc Archeol Pays de Waes — Annalen van de Oudheidkundige Kring van het Land van Waas/Annales du Cercle Archeologique du Pays de Waes
An Oviedo Univ Fac Vet (Leon) — Anales. Oviedo Universidad. Facultad de Veterinaria (Leon)
A Now — Art Now
ANP — Acta Neurologica et Psychiatrica Belgica
ANP — Algemeen Nederlandsch Politieweekblad
ANP — Anales de la Narrativa Espanola Contemporanea
AnP — Annee Philosophique
AnP — Annee Propedeutique
An Paleont — Annales de Paleontologie
An Par — Anecdota Graeca e Codices. Manuscriptis Bibliothecae Regiae Parisienses
An Parana Tuber Doencas Torac — Anais Paranaenses de Tuberculose e Doencas Toracicas
ANPA/RI Bull — ANPA/RI [*American Newspaper Publishers Association. Research Institute*] Bulletin
An Parq Nac B Aires — Anales de Parques Nacionales (Buenos Aires)
An Parques Nac (B Aires) — Anales de Parques Nacionales (Buenos Aires)
ANPA Stat — American Newspaper Publishers Association. Newsprint Statistics
An Paul Med Cir — Anais Paulistas de Medicina e Cirurgia
An Paul Med Cir Supl — Anais Paulistas de Medicina e Cirurgia. Suplemento
ANPBA — Acta Neurologica et Psychiatrica Belgica
ANPBAZ — Acta Neurologica et Psychiatrica Belgica
AnPC — Annales de la Philosophie Chretienne
ANPCD7 — Specialist Periodical Reports. Aliphatic and Related Natural Product Chemistry
ANPEDD — Annual Research Reviews. Angina Pectoris
An Pediat — Anales de Pediatria
AnPh — L'Annee Philologique
ANPHA — Annales de Physique
ANPHCL — Applied Neurophysiology
An Phil Chin Hist Asso — Annals. Philippine Chinese Historical Association
ANPHI Pap — ANPHI [*Academy of Nursing of the Philippines*] Papers
An Physik — Annalen der Physik und Chemie
ANPIA — Arquivos de Neuro-Psiquiatria
ANPI Dossier Tech — ANPI. Dossier Technique
ANPMD3 — Acta Naturalia de l'Ateneo Parmense
An Policlin Enferm Infecc Prof Videla — Anales. Policlinica de Enfermedades Infecciosas del Profesor Adjunto Dr. Carlos Alberto Videla
An Ponts & Chaussees — Annales des Ponts et Chaussees
ANPQA — Annee Psychologique
AnPraem — Analecta Praemonstratensia
ANPRDI — Analytical Proceedings
An Programa Acad Med Univ Nac Mayor San Marcos (Lima) — Anales. Programa Academico de Medicina. Universidad Nacional Mayor de San Marcos (Lima)
An Provence — Annales de Provence
An Prov Francis S Evan Mex — Anales. Provincia Franciscana del Santo Evangelio de Mexico
ANPSAI — Archives of Neurology and Psychiatry
An Psicol — Anales de Psicologia
An Psicotec — Anales de Psicotecnia
ANPTAL — Acta Neuropathologica
ANPTBM — Annales de Phytopathologie
ANPYA — Annalen der Physik
ANQ — American Notes and Queries
ANQ — Andover Newton Quarterly
AnQu — Anthropological Quarterly
ANQU-A — Anthropological Quarterly
ANQUBU — Anales de Quimica
An Quim — Anales de Quimica
An Quim A-Fis Tec — Anales de Quimica. Serie A. Quimica Fisica y Quimica Tecnica
An Quim B Inorg Anal — Anales de Quimica. Serie B. Quimica Inorganica y Quimica Analitica
An Quim C Org Bioquim — Anales de Quimica. Serie C. Quimica Organica y Bioquimica
An Quim Farm — Anales de Quimica y Farmacia
An Quimica — Anales de Quimica
An Quim Int Ed — Anales de Quimica International Edition
An Quim Ser B — Anales de Quimica. Serie B. Quimica Inorganica y Quimica Analitica
An Quim Ser C — Anales de Quimica. Serie C. Quimica Organica y Bioquimica
An Quim Ser C Quim Org Bioquim — Anales de Quimica. Serie C. Quimica Organica y Bioquimica
AnR — Anatomical Record
AnR — Antigonish Review
AnR — Antioch Review
An R Acad Cienc Med Fis Nat Habana — Anales. Real Academia de Ciencias Medicas, Fisicas, y Naturales de la Habana
An R Acad Farm — Anales. Real Academia de Farmacia
An R Acad Med — Anales. Reale Academia de Medicina

An R Acad Med Cir Valladolid — Anales. Real Academia de Medicina y Cirugia de Valladolid

An R Acad Nacl Med (Madr) — Anales. Real Academia Nacional de Medicina (Madrid)

An R Acad Nac Med (Madr) — Anales. Real Academia Nacional de Medicina (Madrid)

An R Acad Nac Med Spain — Anales. Real Academia Nacional de Medicina (Spain)

An Radiol — Anales de Radiologia

ANRCEI — Annual Review of Chronopharmacology

ANREA — Anatomical Record

An Real Acad B A Cadiz — Anales de la Real Academia de Bellas Artes de Cadiz

An Real Acad Farm — Anales. Real Academia de Farmacia. Instituto de Espana

An Rehabil — Anales de Rahabilitacion

An Rep Econ Fac Tohoku Univ Sendai — Annual Report. Economic Faculty. Tohoku University. Sendai

An Rep Econ Keio Gijuku Univ — Keio Gijuku University [Tokyo]. Annual Report. Economics

An Reun Fitossanit Bras — Anais. Reuniao de Fitossanitarisatas do Brasil

An Reuniao Fitossanit Brasil — Anais. Reuniao de Fitossanitarisatas do Brasil

An Rev Mens Med Cirug — Anales y Revista Mensual de Medicina, Cirugia y Especialidades

ANRGGSIC — Alaska. Department of Natural Resources. Division of Geological and GeophysicalSurveys. Information Circular

ANRGGSSR — Alaska. Department of Natural Resources. Division of Geological and GeophysicalSurveys. Special Report

Anritsu Tech Bull — Anritsu Technical Bulletin

ANRM — Alaska. Department of Natural Resources. Division of Mines and Geology

ANRMI — Alma Nova. Revista Mensal Ilustrada

An Rom — Analecta Romana Instituti Danici

An Roma — Analecta Romana Instituti Danici

An Rom Sov — Analele Romino-Sovietice

ANRPEN — ANARE [Australian National Antarctic Research Expeditions] Report

AnRS — Annual Reports of Studies

ANRSAS — Acta Neurologica Scandinavica

An R Soc Esp Fis Quim — Anales. Real Sociedad Espanola de Fisica y Quimica

An R Soc Esp Fis Quim Ser A — Anales. Real Sociedad Espanola de Fisica y Quimica. Serie A. Fisica

An R Soc Esp Fis Quim Ser B — Anales. Real Sociedad Espanola de Fisica y Quimica. Serie B. Quimica

An R Soc Esp Fis Quim Ser B Quim — Anales. Real Sociedad Espanola de Fisica y Quimica. Serie B. Quimica

An R Soc Esp Fis y Quim A — Anales. Real Sociedad Espanola de Fisica y Quimica. Serie A

ANRTB — ANSI [American National Standards Institute] Reporter

ANRVA — Argonne National Laboratory. Reviews

ANRW — Aufstieg und Niedergang der Roemischen Welt

ANS — Advances in Nursing Science

ANS — Antarctic Science

ANS — Archiv fuer das Studlum der Neueren Sprachen

ANSA — Automatic New Structure Alert

ANS Adv Nurs Sci — ANS. Advances in Nursing Science

ANSAE — Annales. Service des Antiquites de l'Egypte

An S Afr Mus — Annals of the South African Museum

An Sala VIII Hosp F J Muniz — Anales de la Sala VIII. Hospital F. J. Muniz [Buenos Aires]

An Sanat Pedralbes — Anales del Sanatorio Pedralbes

An Sanat Valdes — Anales del Sanatorio Valdes

An Sanid Milit — Anales de Sanidad Militar

AnSATarrac — Analecta Sacra Tarraconensia

ANSA Tip Bul — ANSA (Antibiotik Ve Ilac Hammaddeleri Sanayii AS) Tip Bulteni

AnSB — Anthropological Society of Bombay. Journal

AnSc — Annals of Science

ANSC — Antarctic Science

An Sc (Cleveland) — Annals of Science (Cleveland)

ANS Cent — American Numismatic Society. Centennial Publication

ANS Cent Pub — American Numismatic Society. Centenial Publication

An Sc Geol — Annales des Sciences Geologiques

An Sci — Annals of Science

An Sci Phys & Nat Agric & Indust — Annales des Sciences Physiques et Naturelles, d'Agriculture, et d'Industrie

An Sc Nat Zool — Annales des Sciences Naturelles. Zoologie

ANSCP — American Numismatic Society. Centennial Publication

An Scu Norm Sup Pisa — Annali della Scuola Normale Superiore di Pisa

An Scu Norm Sup Pisa Lett Stor & Filos — Annali della Scuola Normale Superiore di Pisa, Lettere, Storia, e Filosofia

ANSDB — ANSI [American National Standards Institute] Standards Action

ANSDL — Australisch-Neuseelaendische Studien zur Deutschen Sprache und Literatur

ANSDSL — Australisch-Neuseelaendische Studien zur Deutschen Sprache und Literatur

An Secc Cienc Col Univ Gerona Univ Auton Barcelona — Anales. Seccion de Ciencias. Colegio Universitario de Gerona. Universidad Autonoma de Barcelona

An Secc Orient Prof Esc Trab Barcelona — Anales de la Seccion de Orientacion Profesional, Escuela del Trabajo (Barcelona)

An Secr Comun Obr Publ Mex — Anales de la Secretaria de Comunicaciones y Obras Publicas (Mexico)

An Sect Pedol Inst Cent Cercet Agric — Analele. Sectiei de Pedologie. Institutul Central de Cercetari Agricole

An Sect Prot Plant Inst Cent Cercet Agric (Bucharest) — Analele. Sectiei de Protectia Plantelor. Institutul Central de Cercetari Agricole (Bucharest)

An Seguntinos — Anales Seguntinos

An Selestat — Annuaire. Societe des Amis. Bibliotheque de Selestat

An Seminar Brasil Herbic Ervas Danin — Anais. Seminario Brasileiro de Herbicidas e Ervas Daninhas

An Semin Nac Pesquis Soja — Anais. Seminario Nacional de Pesquisa de Soja

An Ser Prod Anim Inst Nac Invest Agrar — Anales. Serie Produccion Animal. Instituto Nacional de Investigaciones Agrarias

An Serv Geol Nac El Salvador Bol — Anales. Servicio Geologico Nacional de El Salvador. Boletin

An Serv Geol Nac Salvador Bol — Anales. Servico Geologico Nacional de El Salvador. Boletin

An Service Ant Egypte — Annales du Service des Antiquites de l'Egypte

An Serv Traum Cirug Ortoped Hosp Prov Valencia — Anales del Servicio de Traumatologia, Cirugia Ortopedica y Accidentes del Trabajo del Hospital Provincial de Valencia

An Serv Traum Lopez Trigo — Anales. Servicio de Traumatologia del Dr. Lopez-Trigo

An SEV — Annuaire. Societe d'Emulation de la Vendee

ANSFAS — Annales des Sciences Forestieres

ANSI/ASCE Stand Eng Prac Data — ANSI/ASCE Standards, Engineering Practices, and Data

An Simp Anu ACIESP — Anais. Simposio Anual da ACIESP (Academia de Ciencias do Estado de Sao Paulo)

An Simp Bras Eletroquim Eletroanal — Anais. Simposio Brasileiro de Eletroquimica e Eletroanalitica

An Simp Cult Celulas — Anais. Simposio sobre Culturas de Celulas

An Simp Int Tecnol Alcoois Combust — Anais. Simposio Internacional sobre Tecnologia dos Alcoois como Combustivel

An Simp Quim Vale Rio Doce — Anais. Simposio de Quimica do Vale do Rio Doce

ANSI Reptr — ANSI [American National Standards Institute] Reporter

An Sism B Aires — Anales Sismologicos. Servicio Meteorologico Nacional (Buenos Aires)

ANSI Stand — ANSI [American National Standards Institute] Standards

ANSI Std Action — ANSI [American National Standards Institute] Standards Action

AnSJJR — Annales de la Societe Jean-Jacques Rousseau

AnSL — Annals of Science. Quarterly Review of the History of Science Since the Renaissance (London)

ANSLA — Acta Neurologica Scandinavica. Supplementum

ANSM — American Numismatic Society. Notes and Monographs

ANSMN — American Numismatic Society. Museum Notes

ANSMusN — American Numismatic Society. Museum Notes

ANSN — American Numismatic Society. Museum Notes

ANSNNM — American Numismatic Society. Numismatic Notes and Monographs

ANSNS — American Numismatic Society. Numismatic Studies

AnSoc — Ancient Society

An Soc Agron Santiago — Anales de la Sociedad Agronomica de Santiago

An Soc Biol Bogota — Anales. Sociedad de Biologia de Bogota

An Soc Biol Pernambuco — Anais. Sociedade de Biologia de Pernambuco

An Soc Bot Bras — Anais. Sociedade Botanica do Brasil

An Soc Bras Filos Rio — Anais da Sociedade Brasileira de Filosofia (Rio de Janeiro)

An Soc Cient Argent — Anales. Sociedad Cientifica Argentina

An Soc Cient Argent Secc St Fe — Anales. Sociedad Cientifica Argentina. Seccion Santa Fe

An Soc Cient Argent Sec S Fe — Anales. Sociedad Cientifica Argentina. Seccion Santa Fe

An Soc Cientif Arg BA — Anales. Sociedad Cientifica Argentina (Buenos Aires)

An Soc Cient S Fe — Anales. Sociedad Cientifica de Santa Fe

An Soc Cient St Fe — Anales. Sociedad Cientifica de Santa Fe

An Soc Entomol Bras — Anais. Sociedade Entomologica do Brasil

An Soc Espan Fis Quim — Anales. Sociedad Espanola de Fisica y Quimica

An Soc Esp Fis Quim — Anales. Sociedad Espanola de Fisica y Quimica

An Soc Esp Hidrol Med — Anales. Sociedad Espanola de Hidrologia Medica

An Soc Geog & Hist Guatemala — Anales de la Sociedad de Geografia y Historia de Guatemala

An Soc Geog Commerc — Annales de la Societe Geographique Commerciale

An Soc Geogr Hist — Anales. Sociedad de Geografia e Historia

An Soc Geogr Hist Guat — Anales. Sociedad de Geografia e Historia de Guatemala

An Soc Geogr Hist Guatem — Anales. Sociedad de Geografia e Historia de Guatemala

An Soc Hist & Archeol Gatinais — Annales de la Societe Historique et Archeologique du Gatinais

An Soc Hist & Archeol Tournai — Annales de la Societe Historique et Archeologique de Tournai

An Soc Libre B A — Annales de la Societe Libre des Beaux-Arts

An Soc Med Pern — Anais. Sociedade de Medicina de Pernambuco

An Soc Med Pernambuco — Anais. Sociedade de Medicina de Pernambuco

An Soc Med-Quir Guayas — Anales. Sociedad Medico-Quirurgica del Guayas

An Soc Mex Hist Cienc Tecn — Anales. Sociedad Mexicana de Historia de la Ciencia y de la Tecnologia

An Soc Mex Hist Cienc Tecnol — Anales. Sociedad Mexicana de Historia de la Ciencia de la Tecnologia

An Soc Mex Oftalmol — Anales. Sociedad Mexicana de Oftalmologia

An Soc Mex Otorrinolaringol — Anales. Sociedad Mexicana de Otorrinolaringologia

An Soc Mex Otorrinolaringol Broncoesofagol — Anales. Sociedad Mexicana de Otorrinolaringologia y Broncoesofagologia

An Soc Peruana Hist Med — Anales. Sociedad Peruana de Historia de la Medicina

An Soc Pharm Quim Sao Paulo — Anais. Sociedade de Pharmacia e Quimica de Sao Paulo

An Soc Quim Argent — Anales. Sociedad Quimica Argentina

An Soc Royale Archeol Bruxelles — Annales de la Societe Royale d'Archeologie de Bruxelles

An Soc R Sci Med Nat Bruxelles — Annales. Societe Royale des Sciences Medicales et Naturelles de Bruxelles

An Soc Rural Argent — Anales. Sociedad Rural Argentina

An Soc Rur Argent — Anales. Sociedad Rural Argentina

An Soc Sci Orleans — Annales. Societe des Sciences, Belles-Lettres, et Arts d'Orleans

An Soc Vet Zootec — Anales. Sociedad Veterinaria de Zootecnia

ANSP — Annali. Scuola Normale Superiore di Pisa. Classe di Lettere e Filosofia

ANSPAO — Australia. Commonwealth Scientific and Industrial Research Organisation. National Standards Laboratory. Technical Paper

ANSSSR — Akademija Nauk SSSR

AnST — Analecta Sacra Tarraconensia

AnSt — Anatolian Studies. Journal of the British Institute of Archaeology at Ankara

AnSTar — Analecta Sacra Tarraconensia

An Staz Sper Agr M — Annali. Stazione Sperimentale Agrario di Modena

An St Casa Santos — Anais. Santa Casa de Santos

AnStEbr — Annuario di Studi Ebraici. Collegio Rabbinico Italiano

An Stiint Univ Al I Cuza Iasi Mat — Analele Stiintifice ale Universitatii Al. I Cuza din Iasi. Matematica

An Stiint Univ Al I Cuza Iasi Sect 1 — Analele Stiintifice ale Universitatii Al. I. Cuza din Iasi. Sectiunea 1. Matematica, Fizica, Chimie

An Stiint Univ Al I Cuza Iasi Sect 1a — Analele Stiintifice ale Universitatii Al. I. Cuza din Iasi. Sectiunea 1a. Matematica

An Stiint Univ Al I Cuza Iasi Sect 1a Mat — Analele Stiintifice ale Universitatii Al. I. Cuza din Iasi. Seria Noua. Sectiunea 1a. Matematica

An Stiint Univ Al I Cuza Iasi Sect 1a Mat NS — Analele Stiintifice ale Universitatii Al. I. Cuza din Iasi. Seria Noua. Sectiunea 1a. Matematica

An Stiint Univ Al I Cuza Iasi Sect 1b — Analele Stiintifice ale Universitatii Al. I. Cuza din Iasi. Sectiunea 1b. Fizica

An Stiint Univ Al I Cuza Iasi Sect 1b Fiz N S — Analele Stiintifice ale Universitatii Al. I. Cuza din Iasi. Sectiunea 1b. Fizica. Seria Noua

An Stiint Univ Al I Cuza Iasi Sect 1 Biol Anim — Analele Stiintifice ale Universitatii Al. I Cuza din Iasi. Sectiunea 1. Biologie Animala

An Stiint Univ Al I Cuza Iasi Sect 1c — Analele Stiintifice ale Universitatii Al. I. Cuza din Iasi. Sectiunea 1c. Chimie

An Stiint Univ Al I Cuza Iasi Sect 2 — Analele Stiintifice ale Universitatii Al. I. Cuza din Iasi. Sectiunea 2. Stiinte Naturale

An Stiint Univ Al I Cuza Iasi Sect 2a — Analele Stiintifice ale Universitatii Al. I. Cuza din Iasi. Sectiunea 2a. Biologie

An Stiint Univ Al I Cuza Iasi Sect 2a Biol — Analele Stiintifice ale Universitatii Al. I. Cuza din Iasi. Sectiunea 2a. Biologie

An Stiint Univ Al I Cuza Iasi Sect 2b — Analele Stiintifice ale Universitatii Al. I. Cuza din Iasi. Sectiunea 2b. Geologie

An Stiint Univ Al I Cuza Iasi Sect 2 Biol Geol Geogr — Analele Stiintifice ale Universitatii Al. I. Cuza din Iasi. Sectiunea 2. Biologie, Geologie, Geografie

An Stiint Univ Al I Cuza Iasi Sect 2c — Analele Stiintifice ale Universitatii Al. I. Cuza din Iasi. Sectiunea 2c. Geografie

An Stiint Univ Al I Cuza Iasi Sect 2 Stiinte Nat — Analele Stiintifice ale Universitatii Al I Cuza din Iasi. Sectiunea 2. Stiinte Naturale

An Stiint Univ Al I Cuza Iasi Stiinte Nat Biol — Analele Stiintifice ale Universitatii Al. I. Cuza din Iasi. Stiinte Naturale. Biologia

An Stiint Univ Ovidius Constanta Ser Mat — Analele Stiintifice. Universitatii Ovidius Constanta

An Sti Univ Al I Cuza Iasi Sect 1b Fiz — Analele Stiintifice ale Universitatii Al. I. Cuza din Iasi. Sectiunea 1b. Fizica. Seria Noua

An Sti Univ Al I Cuza Iasi Sect 1 Mat — Analele Stiintifice ale Universitatii Al. I. Cuza din Iasi. Seria Noua. Sectiunea 1. Matematica

ANS Top Meet Gas Cooled React HTGR GCFBR — ANS Topical Meeting. Gas-Cooled Reactors. HTGR (High-Temperature Gas-Cooled Reactor) and GCFBR (Gas-Cooled Fast Breeder Reactor)

AnStud — Anatolian Studies. Journal of the British Institute of Archaeology at Ankara

AnSu — Antiquity and Survival

ANSUA5 — Annals of Surgery

An Sumar (Zagreb) — Anali za Sumarstvo (Zagreb)

AnSur — Antiquity and Survival

An Sur Am L — Annual Survey of American Law

ANT — Altalanos Nyelveszeti Tanulmanyok

ANT — Anglo-Norman Texts

AnT — Annales Publiees Trimestriellement par l'Universite de Toulouse-Le Mirail. Litteratures

Ant — Antaios

Ant — Antares. Franzoesische Hefte fuer Kunst, Literatur, und Wissenschaft

Ant — Anthropos

Ant — Antichthon. Journal of the Australian Society for Classical Studies

Ant — Antike

ANT — Antilliaanse Nieuwsbrief. Tweewekelijkse Uitgave van het Kabinet van de Gevolmachtigde Minister van de Nederlandse Antillen

Ant — Antiquary

Ant — Antiquity

Ant — Antonianum

ANTa — Akademiia Nauk Tadzhikskoi SSR

AnTA — Annee Theologique Augustinienne

ANTA — Antarctic

Ant Ab — Antike und Abendland

Ant Afr — Antiquites Africaines

Ant Altoadriat — Antichita Altoadriatiche

An Tan — Antik Tanalmanyok

Antananarivo Annu — Antananarivo Annual

Ant & Abenland — Antike und Abendland

Ant & F A — Antiques and Fine Art

Ant & Survival — Antiquity and Survival. An International Review of Traditional Art and Culture

ANTAR — Antarctic Record

Antarc J US — Antarctic Journal. United States

Antarct Earth Sci Pap Int Symp — Antarctic Earth Science. Papers. International Symposium on Antarctic Earth Sciences

Antarct Geol Map Ser — Antarctic Geological Map Series

Antarct Geol Proc Int Symp — Antarctic Geology. Proceedings. International Symposium on Antarctic Geology

Antarct Geosci Symp Antarct Geol Geophys — Antarctic Geoscience. Symposium on Antarctic Geology and Geophysics

Antarctic J — Antarctic Journal of the United States

Antarct J US — Antarctic Journal of the United States

Antarct Meteorite Res — Antarctic Meteorite Research

Antarct Nutr Cycles Food Webs SCAR Symp Antarct Biol — Antarctic Nutrient Cycles and Food Webs. SCAR (Scientific Committee on Antarctic Research) Symposium on Antarctic Biology

Antarct Rec — Antarctic Record

Antarct Rec (Tokyo) — Antarctic Record (Tokyo)

Antarct Res Ser — Antarctic Research Series

Antar Jour US — Antarctic Journal of the United States

Antarktika Doklady Kom — Antarktika Doklady Komissii

AntAS — Antike, Alte Sprachen und Deutsche Bildung

Ant Ath — Antiquities of Athens

ANTBAL — Antibiotiki

ANTBDO — Antibiotics

Ant Bk — Antiquarian Bookman

AntC — Antiquite Classique

Ant Chr — Antike und Christentum

Ant Cl — Antiquite Classique

Ant Class — Antiquite Classique

Ant Coll — Australasian Antique Collector

Ant Collct — Antique Collecting

Ant Colr — Antique Collector

Ant Dealer & Colrs Guide — Antique Dealer and Collector's Guide

Ant Denk — Antike Denkmaeler

Ant Denkm — Antike Denkmaeler. Kaiserliches Deutsches Archaeologisches Institut

Ant Dkml — Antike Demkmaeler

ANTEDX — Animal Technology

Antek Appl News — Antek. Application News

Antennas Propag Soc Int Symp — Antennas and Propagation Society. International Symposium

Ant F — Anthropological Forum

ANTF — Arbeiten zur NT Textforschung

AnTh — Annee Theologique

ANTH — Anthropologica

Ant H — Antiquitas Hungarica

An Thann — Annuaire. Societe d'Histoire des Regions de Thann-Guebwiller

Anth Graec — Anthologia Graeca

Anth (Hung) — Anthropologiai Koezlemenyek (Hungary)

AnThijm — Annalen van het Thijmgenootschap

AnThj — Annalen van het Thjmgenootschap

AnthL — Anthropological Linguistics

Anth Lyr — Anthologia Lyrica Graeca

Anth Lyr Graec — Anthologia Lyrica Graeca

Anth Lyr Graeca — Anthologia Lyrica Graeca

Anthol Annua — Anthologica Annua. Publicaciones. Instituto Espanol de Estudios Eclesiasticos

Anthol Arch Sint Dermatol — Anthologica. Archivio di Sintesi Dermatologica

Anthol Hib — Anthologia Hibernica

Anthol Med Dermatol — Anthologica Medica Dermatologica

Anthol Med Santoriana — Anthologica Medica Santoriana

Anthol Palatina — Anthologia Palatina

Anthonys Phot Bull — Anthony's Photographic Bulletin

AnthQ — Anthropological Quarterly

Anth Quart — Anthropological Quarterly

Anthr — Anthropos

Anthracite Conf Lehigh Univ — Anthracite Conference of Lehigh University

Anthr H — Anthropologia Hungarica

Anthr Hung — Anthropologia Hungarica

Anthr J Can — Anthropological Journal of Canada

Anthr K — Anthropologiai Koezlemenyek

Anthr Kozl — Anthropologiai Koezlemenyek

Anthr Ling — Anthropological Linguistics

Anthro Anz — Anthropologischer Anzeiger

Anthro Forum — Anthropological Forum

Anthro I — Anthropological Index

Anthro Ling — Anthropological Linguistics

Anthrop Action — Anthropology in Action

Anthrop Anz — Anthropologischer Anzeiger

Anthrop Educ Q — Anthropology and Education Quarterly

Anthrop Forum — Anthropological Forum

Anthrop Gesells Wien Mitteil — Mitteilungen der Anthropologischen Gesellschaft in Wien

Anthrop Gesell Wien Mitt — Anthropologische Gesellschaft in Wien. Mitteilungen

Anthrop Hung — Anthropologia Hungarica

Anthrop J — Anthropological Institute. Journal

Anthrop J Eur Cult — Anthropological Journal on European Cultures

Anthrop Kizl — Anthropologiai Kizlemenyek

Anthrop Ling — Anthropological Linguistics

Anthrop Linguistics — Anthropological Linguistics

Anthropol Anz — Anthropologischer Anzeiger

Anthropol BC — Anthropology in British Columbia

Anthropol(Brno) — Anthropologie. Marovske Muzeum (Brno)

Anthropol Forum — Anthropological Forum

Anthropol Gesell In Wien Mitt — Anthropologische Gesellschaft in Wien. Mitteilungen

Anthropol Gesell In Wien Sitzungsb — Anthropologische Gesellschaft in Wien. Sitzungsberichte

Anthropol (H) — Anthropologie (Hamburg)

Anthropol Index — Anthropological Index

Anthropol Koezlem — Anthropologiai Koezlemenyek

Anthropol Kozl — Anthropologiai Koezlemenyek
Anthropol Ling — Anthropological Linguistics
Anthropol Lit — Anthropological Literature
Anthropol Mem Field Mus Nat Hist — Anthropological Memoires of the Field Museum of Natural History
Anthropol MM — Anthropologie Marovske Muzeum
Anthropology Br Columb — Anthropology in British Columbia
Anthropology Br Columb Mem — Anthropology in British Columbia. Memoir
Anthropology Design Ser — Anthropology Design Series
Anthropology Rep Papua — Anthropology Reports. Papua
Anthropol (P) — Anthropologie (Paris)
Anthropol Pap Amer Mus Nat Hist — Anthropological Papers. American Museum of Natural History
Anthropol Pap Am Mus Nat Hist — Anthropological Papers. American Museum of Natural History
Anthropol Pap Mus Anthropol Univ Mich — Anthropological Papers. Museum of Anthropology. University of Michigan
Anthropol(Paris) — Anthropologie (Paris)
Anthropol (Pr) — Anthropologie. Casopis Venovany Fysicke Anthropologii (Prague)
Anthropol Quart — Anthropological Quarterly
Anthropol R — Anthropological Review
Anthropol Rec Univ Calif — Anthropological Records. University of California
Anthropol Soc Lond Mem — Anthropological Society of London. Memoirs
Anthropos — Anthropos Internationale Zeitschrift fuer Voelker- und Sprachenkunde
Anthropos Bib — Anthropos-Bibliothek
Anthropos Ethnol Biblthk — Anthropos-Ethnologische Bibliothek
Anthrop Pap Alaska — Anthropological Papers [*Alaska*]
Anthrop Prehist — Anthropologie et Prehistoire
Anthrop Q — Anthropological Quarterly
Anthrop R — Anthropological Review
Anthrop Soc — Anthropologie et Societes. U
Anthrop Today — Anthropology Today
Anthr Pap — Anthropological Papers. American Museum of Natural History
Anthrplgica — Anthropologica
Anthr P Mic — Anthropological Papers. Museum of Anthropology. University of Michigan
Anthr Q — Anthropological Quarterly
Anthr Quart — Anthropological Quarterly
Anthr Rep Pap — Anthropological Report of Papua
Anthr-UCLA — Anthropology-UCLA
AntHung — Antiquitas Hungarica
ANTIB — Antincendio
Antibakt Chemother Urol Norddtsch Therapiegespraeche — Antibakterielle Chemotherapie in der Urologie. Norddeutsche Therapiegespraeche
Antibio Med Clin Ther — Antibiotic Medicine and Clinical Therapy
Antibiot — Antibiotiki
Antibiot and Chemother — Antibiotics and Chemotherapy
Antibiot Annu — Antibiotics Annual
Antibiot Annual — Antibiotics Annual
Antibiot Chemother — Antibiotica et Chemotherapia
Antibiot Chemother Basel — Antibiotica et Chemotherapia (Basel)
Antibiot Chemother (Basel) — Antibiotics and Chemotherapy (Basel)
Antibiot Chemother (Moscow) — Antibiotics and Chemotherapy (Moscow)
Antibiot Chemother Osaka — Antibiotics and Chemotherapy (Osaka)
Antibiot Chemother (Wash DC) — Antibiotics and Chemotherapy (Washington, DC)
Antibiotica Chemother — Antibiotica et Chemotherapia
Antibiotic Med Clin Therapy — Antibiotic Medicine and Clinical Therapy
Antibiotic Med Clin Ther Br Edit — Antibiotic Medicine and Clinical Therapy. British Edition
Antibiotics A — Antibiotics Annual
Antibiotics Chemother — Antibiotics and Chemotherapy
Antibiot Khimioter — Antibiotiki i Khimioterapiya
Antibiot Med — Antibiotic Medicine
Antibiot Med Biotechnol — Antibiotics and Medical Biotechnology
Antibiot Med Biotekhnol — Antibiotiki i Meditsinskaya Biotekhnologiya
Antibiot Med Clin Ther (London) — Antibiotic Medicine and Clinical Therapy (London)
Antibiot Med Clin Ther (NY) — Antibiotic Medicine and Clinical Therapy (New York)
Antibiot Monogr — Antibiotics Monographs
Antibiot Other Second Metab Biosynth Prod — Antibiotics and Other Secondary Metabolites. Biosynthesis and Production
Antibiot Resp Mezhved Sb — Antibiotiki Respublikanskii Mezhvedomstvennyi Sbornik
Antibiot Vitam Horm — Antibiotics, Vitamins, and Hormones
Antib Khim — Antibiotiki i Khimioterapiya
Antibodies Hum Diagn Ther — Antibodies in Human Diagnosis and Therapy
Antibody Immunoconjugates Radiopharm — Antibody, Immunoconjugates, and Radiopharmaceuticals
Anti-Cancer Drug Des — Anti-Cancer Drug Design
Anti Cancer J — Anti-Cancer Journal
Anticancer Res — Anticancer Research
Anticarcinog Radiat Prot 2 Proc Int Conf — Anticarcinogenesis and Radiation Protection 2. Proceedings. International Conference on Anticarcinogenesis and Radiation Protection. Strategies in Protection against Radiation and Cancer
Anti-Corr Meth Mat — Anti-Corrosion Methods and Materials
Anti-Corros — Anti-Corrosion Methods and Materials
Anti-Corrosion — Anti-Corrosion Methods and Materials
Anti-Corrosion Meth & Mat — Anti-Corrosion Methods and Materials
Anti-Corrosion Methods Mats — Anti-Corrosion Methods and Materials
Anti Corros Man — Anti-Corrosion Manual
Anti-Corros Methods Mater — Anti-Corrosion Methods and Materials
Antidepressant Drugs Proc Int Symp — Antidepressant Drugs. Proceedings. International Symposium

Antifungal Compd — Antifungal Compounds
Antigon Rev — Antigonish Review
AntigR — Antigonish Review
Antiinflammatory Agents Chem Pharmacol — Antiinflammatory Agents. Chemistry and Pharmacology
Antike Aben — Antike und Abendland
Antike Abendl — Antike und Abendland
Antike Mus Ges St — Antike Muenzen und Geschnittene Steine
Antikva Arkv — Antikvariskt Arkiv
Antikva Stud — Antikvarisker Studier
Antikv Tidskr Sverige — Antikvarisk Tidskrift foer Sverige
Anti-Locust Bull — Anti-Locust Bulletin
Anti-Locust Mem — Anti-Locust Memoir
Anti-Locust Res Cent Rep — Anti-Locust Research Centre [*Later, Centre for Overseas Pest Research*] Report
Antim Ag Ch — Antimicrobial Agents and Chemotherapy
Anti Microb Ag A — Antimicrobial Agents Annual
Antimicrob Agents Annu — Antimicrobial Agents Annual
Antimicrob Agents Chemother — Antimicrobial Agents and Chemotherapy
Antimicrob Newsl — Antimicrobic Newsletter
Antineoplast Chemother — Antineoplastische Chemotherapie
Antineoplast Immunosuppr Agents — Antineoplastic and Immunosuppressive Agents
Anti Nk — Anti Nuclear
Antioch R — Antioch Review
Antioch Rev — Antioch Review
Antioquia Med — Antioquia Medica
Antioxid Health Dis — Antioxidants in Health and Disease
Antioxid Redox Signal — Antioxidants & Redox Signalling
Antioxid Ther Prev Med — Antioxidants in Therapy and Preventive Medicine
Antiproton Nucleon Antiproton Nucl Interact — Antiproton-Nucleon and Antiproton-Nucleus Interactions
Antiq — Antiques
Antiq — Antiquity
Antiq Afr — Antiquites Africaines
Antiq Bkman — Antiquarian Bookman
Antiq Cl — Antiquite Classique
Antiq Class — Antiquite Classique
Antiq Gesell in Zuerich Mitt — Antiquarische Gesellschaft in Zuerich. Mitteilungen
Antiq Horol — Antiquarian Horology
Antiq Horology — Antiquarian Horology
Antiq Horology — Antiquarian Horology and the Proceedings of the Antiquarian Horological Society
Antiq J — Antiquaries Journal
Antiq Jnl — Antiquaries Journal
Antiq Journ — Antiquaries Journal
Antiq Nat — Antiquites Nationales
Antiq (n s) — Antiquary (New Series)
Antiq Rund — Antiquitaeten Rundschau
Antiq S Afr — Antiques in South Africa
Antiq Sunderland — Antiquities of Sunderland
Antiqu Africaines — Antiquites Africaines
Antiqua Horology — Antiquarian Horology
Antiqua J — Antiquaries Journal
Antiquaries J — Antiquaries Journal
Antiquaries Jnl — Antiquaries Journal
Antiquar J — Antiquaries Journal
Antiquary — Antiquary, Jewitt's
Antiqu Class — Antiquite Classique
Antique Eng — Antique Engines
Antiques J — Antiques Journal
Antiqu Hung — Antiquitas Hungarica
Antiquite Cl — Antiquite Classique
Antiquites Afr — Antiquites Africaines
Antiquit Rundsch — Antiquitaten Rundschau
Antiqu Journal — Antiquaries Journal
Antiqu Nationales — Antiquites Nationales
AntiR — Antigonish Review
Antisense Nucleic Acid Drug Dev — Antisense and Nucleic Acid Drug Development
Antisense Res Dev — Antisense Research and Development
Anti Slav Rep Abor Friend — Anti-Slavery Reporter and Aborigines' Friend
Anti Slav Reptr — Anti-Slavery Reporter
Antitr L and Ec R — Antitrust Law and Economics Review
Antitr Law Symp — Antitrust Law Symposium
Antitr LJ — Antitrust Law Journal
Antitrust & Trade Reg Rep — Antitrust and Trade Regulation Report
Antitrust & Trade Reg Rep BNA — Antitrust and Trade Regulation Report. Bureau of National Affairs
Antitrust B — Antitrust Bulletin
Antitrust Bull — Antitrust Bulletin
Antitrust L & Econ Rev — Antitrust Law and Economics Review
Antitrust L & Trade Reg Rep — Antitrust Law and Trade Regulations Report
Antitrust Law and Econ R — Antitrust Law and Economics Review
Antitrust Law Econ Rev — Antitrust Law and Economics Review
Antitrust LJ — Antitrust Law Journal
Antitrust L Sym — Antitrust Law Symposium
Antitrust Newsl — Antitrust Newsletter
Anti Tuberc Bull — Anti-Tuberculosis Bulletin
Antitumor Stud Nitrocaphane (AT-1258) — Antitumor Studies on Nitrocaphane (AT-1258)
Antiviral Res — Antiviral Research
Antiviral Ther — Antiviral Therapy
Antivir Chem Chemother — Antiviral Chemistry & Chemotherapy
Antivir Ther — Antiviral Therapy

Anti Vivis News — Anti-Vivisection News
AntJ — Antiquaries Journal
Ant J — Antiques Journal
Ant Journ — Antiquaries Journal. Society of Antiquaries of London
AntK — Antike Kunst
Ant Kst — Antike Kunst
Ant Kunst — Antike Kunst
Ant N — Antiquites Nationales
Ant Nat — Antiquites Nationales
Antol B A — Antologia di Belle Arti
An Toled — Anales Toledanos
Anton — Antonianum
Antonianum — Antonianum Periodicum Trimetre Editumcura Professorum Pontificii Athenaei Antoniani de Urbe
Antonie Leeuwenhoek J Microbiol — Antonie van Leeuwenhoek Journal of Microbiology
Antonie Van Leeuwenhoek Ned Tijdschr Hyg — Antonie van Leeuwenhoek Nederlandsch Tijdschrift voor Hygiene, Microbiologie, en Serologie. Netherlands Society of Microbiology
Antonie Van Leeuwenhoek J Microbiol Serol — Antonie Van Leeuwenhoek Journal of Microbiology and Serology [Later, Antonie Van Leeuwenhoek Journal of Microbiology]
AntP — Antike Plastik
Ant Pis — Antichita Pisane
Ant Pl — Antike Plastik
Ant Plast — Antike Plastik
ANTR — Antarctic Record
Ant R — Antioch Review
An Trav Pub Belgique — Annales des Travaux Publics de Belgique
ANTRD — Anticancer Research
ANTRD4 — Anticancer Research
Antrol — Anthropological Index
Antrop Caracas — Antropologica La Salle (Caracas)
Antrop Hist — Antropoligia e Historia
Antrop Hist Guat — Antropologia e Historia de Guatemala
Antropol & Hist Guatemala — Antropologia e Historia de Guatemala
Antropol Arch — Antropologicky Archiv
Antropologi — Antropologica
Antropologja Etnol — Antropologja i Etnologja
Antrop Port — Antropologia Portuguesa
Antrop Santiago — Antropologia (Santiago)
Antrop Y Etnol — Antropologia y Etnologia. CSIC (Consejo Superior de Investigaciones Cientificas)
ANTRS — Antarctic Research Series
Ant St — Anatolian Studies
AntSurv — Antiquity and Survival
ANTsW — Algemeen Nederlands Tijdschrift voor Wijsbegeerte en Psychologie
Ant Tardive — Antiquite Tardive. Revue Internationale d'Histoire et d'Archeologie
Ant Tidskr — Antikvarisk Tidskrift foer Sverige
ANTu — Akademiia Nauk Turkmenskoi SSR
Ant Viva — Antichita Viva. Rassegna d'Arte
ANTW — Algemeen Nederlands Tijdschrift voor Wijsbegeerte
Antw — Antwerpiensia
AntWelt — Antike Welt
Antwerp Archvbl — Antwerpsch Archievenblad
Antwerpen Tijdschr — Antwerpen; Tijdschrift der Stad Antwerpen
ANTWP — Algemeen Nederlands Tijdschrift voor Wijsbegeerte en Psychologie
Antybiot Badaniu Procesow Biochem — Antybiotyki w Badaniu Procesow Biochemicznych
ANU — Akademiia Nauk Uzbekskoi SSR
AnU — Anales de la Universidad
An U Abidjan — Annales de l'Universite d'Abidjan
Anuar Aerol — Anuar Aerologic
Anuar Bibliotec Archivon Mex — Anuario de Biblioteconomia y Archivonomia (Mexico)
Anuar Col Hist Soc Cult Bogota — Anuario Colombiano de Historia Social y de la Cultura (Bogota)
Anuar Escuela Bibl Arch Caracas — Anuario. Escuela de Biblioteconomia y Archivos (Caracas)
Anuar Estud Am Sevilla — Anuario de Estudios Americanos (Sevilla)
Anuar Fac Sti Agric Chisinau — Anuar Facultatii de Stiinte Agricole Chisinau
Anuar Filol Maracaibo — Anuario de Filologia. Facultad de Humanidades y Educacion (Maracaibo)
Anuar Geogr Mex — Anuario de Geografia (Mexico)
Anuar Hist Mex — Anuario de Historia (Mexico)
Anuari Inst — Anuari. Institut d'Estudis Catalans. Seccio Historico-Arqueologica
Anuari Inst Cat — Anuari. Institut d'Estudis Catalans. Seccio Historico-Arqueologica
Anuar Indig Mex — Anuario Indigenista (Mexico)
Anuar Inst Antrop Hist Caracas — Anuario. Instituto de Antropologia e Historia (Caracas)
Anuar Inter Am Inst Music Res New Orleans — Anuario. Inter-American Instituto for Musical Research (New Orleans)
Anuario Acad Mex Ci Exact — Anuario. Academia Mexicana de Ciencias Exactas, Fisicas, y Naturales
Anuario Brasil Econ Florest — Anuario Brasileiro de Economia Florestal
Anuario Comis Impuls Invest Ci — Anuario. Comision Impulsora y Coordinadora de la Investigacion Cientifica
Anuario Estud Centroam — Anuario de Estudios Centroamericanos
AnuarioF — Anuario de Filologia
Anuario Hidrol — Anuario Hidrologico. Servicio Nacional de Meteorologia e Hidrologia
Anuario Prov Caracas Soc Econ Amigos Pais — Anuario. Provincia de Caracas. Sociedad Economica de Amigos del Pais
Anuar Letr Mex — Anuario de Letras (Mexico)
Anuar Psicol Guat — Anuario de Psicologia (Guatemala)

Anu Asoc Arquitectos — Anuario para la Asociacion de Arquitectos
Anu Asoc Francisco de Vitoria — Anuario. Asociacion Francisco de Vitoria
Anu Bago Invest Cient — Anuario Bago de Investigaciones Cientificas
ANUBBR — Acta Neurologica Belgica
AnUBLG — Analele. Universitatii Bucuresti. Limbi Germanice
AnUBLUC — Analele. Universitatii Bucuresti. Literatura Universala Comparata
Anu Bras Econ Florestal — Anuario Brasileiro de Economia Florestal
Anu Bras Econ Flor Inst Nac Pinho — Anuario Brasileiro de Economia Florestal. Instituto Nacional de Pinho
Anu Bras Odontol — Anuario Brasileiro de Odontologia
Anu Cent Edafol Biol Apl CSIC — Anuario. Centro de Edafologia y Biologia Aplicada del CSIC (Centro de Edafologia y Biologia Aplicada)
Anu Cent Edafol Biol Apl Salamanca — Anuario. Centro de Edafologia y Biologia Aplicada de Salamanca
Anu Com Geol Rom — Anuarul Comitetului Geologic (Romania)
Anu Com Stat Geol Repub Soc Rom — Anuarul. Comitetului de Stat al Geologiei. Republica Socialista Romania
Anu Com Stat Geol (Rom) — Anuarul Comitetului de Stat al Geologiei (Romania)
Anu Cuerpo Fac Archv Bib & Arqueol — Anuario del Cuerpo Facultativo de Archiveros, Bibliotecarios, y Arqueologos
Anu de Filos del Derecho — Anuario de Filosofia del Derecho
Anu Dept Hist & Teor A — Anuario del Departamento de Historia y Teoria del Arte
Anu Derecho Penal Ci Penales — Anuario de Derecho Penal y Ciencias Penales. Instituto Nacional de Estudios Juridicos
Anu Der Univ Panama — Anuario de Derecho. Universidad de Panama
Anu Divulg Cient — Anuario de Divulgacao Cientifica
AnuE — Anuario de Estudios Americanos
Anu Ecuator Der Int — Anuario Ecuatoriano de Derecho Internacional
Anu Estad Min Mex — Anuario Estadistico de la Mineria Mexicana
Anu Est Am — Anuario de Estudios Americanos. Escuela de Estudios Hispanoamericanos
Anu Estud Amer — Anuario de Estudios Americanos
Anu Estud Atl — Anuario de Estudios Atlanticos
Anu Estud Med — Anuario de Estudios Medievales
Anu Eusko Folkl — Anuario de Eusko-Folklore
Anu Fac Der — Anuario. Facultad de Derecho
Anu Filosof — Anuario Filosofico
AnUG — Annales. Universite de Grenoble
ANUHAA — Animal Nutrition and Health
An U Hispal — Anales de la Universidad Hispalense
Anu Hist Derecho Espan — Anuario de Historia de Derecho Espanol. Instituto Nacional de Estudios Juridicos. Ministerio de Justicia y CSIC (Consejo Superior de Investigaciones Cientificas)
Anu Hist J — Annual History Journal
ANU Hist J — ANU [Australian National University] Historical Journal
ANU Hist Jnl — ANU [Australian National University] Historical Journal
ANUHJ — Australian National University. Historical Journal
Anul — Anuarul Institutului de Istorie si Arheologie
AnUILingv — Analele Stiintifice ale Universitatii Al. I. Cuza din Iasi. Seria Noua. Sectiunea 3e (Stiinte Sociale). Lingvistica
AnUILit — Analele Stiintifice ale Universitatii Al. I. Cuza din Iasi. Serie Noua. Sectiunea 3f. Literatura
Anu Indig — Anuario Indigenista
Anu Indig Mex — Anuario Indigenista [Mexico]
Anu Inst Cienc Pen Criminol — Anuario. Instituto de Ciencias Penales y Criminologicas
Anu Inst Est Catalans — Anuari. Institut d'Estudis Catalans
Anu Inst Estud Cat — Anuari de l'Institut d'Estudis Catalans
Anu Inst Geol (Rom) — Anuarul. Institutului Geologic (Romania)
Anu Inst Istor Arheologie — Anuarul. Institutului de Istorie si Arheologie
Anu Inst Orientac Asist Tec Oeste — Anuario. Instituto de Orientacion y Asistencia Tecnica del Oeste
Anu Inst Orientac Asist Tec Oeste Cent Edafol Biol Apl CSIC — Anuario. Instituto de Orientacion y Asistencia Tecnica del Oeste. Centro de Edafologia y Biologia Aplicada del CSIC
Anu Inst Patol Ig Anim — Anuarul. Institutului de Patologie si Igiena Animala
Anu Inst Patol Ig Anim (Bucur) — Anuarul. Institutului de Patologie si Igiena Animala (Bucuresti)
Anu Inst Seruri Vaccinuri Pasteur Bucuresti — Anuarul Institutului de Seruri si Vaccinuri Pasteur. Bucuresti
Anu Inst Stud Cl — Anuarul. Institutul de Studii Clasice. Universitate din Cluj
AnUL — Annales. Universite de Lyon
An U Lecce — Annali dell'Universita di Lecce
Anu Lucr Stiint Inst Agron Dr Petru Coroza — Anuar Lucrarilor Stiintifice. Institutul Agronomic Dr. Petru Coroza
ANum — Acta Numismatica
AnUMC — Annales Universitatis Mariae Curie-Sklodowska
Anu Miner Bras — Anuario Mineral Brasileiro
Anu Miner Brasil — Anuario Mineral Brasileiro
Anu Mus — Anuario Musical
Anu Music — Anuario Musical. Instituto Espanol de Musicologia. CSIC (Consejo Superior de Investigaciones Cientificas)
ANU News — Australian National University. News
An Univ Barcelona — Anales. Universidad de Barcelona
An Univ Bras Rio — Anais da Universidade do Brasil (Rio de Janeiro)
An Univ Bucur Biol — Analele. Universitatii Bucuresti. Biologie Animala
An Univ Bucur Biol Anim — Analele. Universitatii Bucuresti. Biologie Animala
An Univ Bucur Biol Veg — Analele. Universitatii Bucuresti. Biologie Vegetala
An Univ Bucur Chim — Analele. Universitatii Bucuresti. Chimie
An Univ Bucuresti Biol — Analele Universitatii Bucuresti. Seria. Biologie
An Univ Bucuresti Biol Anim — Analele Universitatii Bucuresti. Biologie Animala
An Univ Bucuresti Biol Veg — Analele Universitatii Bucuresti. Biologie Vegetala
An Univ Bucuresti Fiz — Analele Universitatii Bucuresti. Fizica
An Univ Bucuresti Geogr — Analele. Universitatii Bucuresti. Geografie
An Univ Bucuresti Geol — Analele. Universitatii Bucuresti. Geologie

An Univ Bucuresti Mat — Analele. Universitatii Bucuresti. Matematica
An Univ Bucuresti Mat Mec — Analele. Universitatii Bucuresti. Matematica-Mecanica
An Univ Bucuresti Seria Stiint Nat Mat Mec — Analele. Universitatii Bucuresti. Seria Stiintele Naturii. Matematica-Mecanica
An Univ Bucuresti Ser Mat — Analele. Universitatii Bucuresti. Seria Matematica
An Univ Bucuresti Ser Stiint Nat — Analele. Universitatii Bucuresti. Seria Stiintele Naturii
An Univ Bucuresti Ser Stiint Nat Biol — Analele. Universitatii Bucuresti. Seria Stiintele Naturii. Biologie
An Univ Bucuresti Ser Stiint Nat Chim — Analele. Universitatii Bucuresti. Seria Stiintele Naturii. Chimie
An Univ Bucuresti Ser Stiint Nat Fiz — Analele. Universitatii Bucuresti. Seria Stiintele Naturii. Fizica
An Univ Bucuresti Ser Stiint Nat Geol Geogr — Analele. Universitatii Bucuresti. Seria Stiintele Naturii. Geologie, Geografie
An Univ Bucuresti Ser Stiint Nat Mat Mec — Analele Universitatii Bucuresti. Seria Stiintele Naturii. Matematica-Mecanica
An Univ Bucuresti Stiint Nat — Analele. Universitatii Bucuresti. Stiintele Naturii
An Univ Bucuresti Sti Natur — Analele. Universitatii Bucuresti. Stiintele Naturii
An Univ Bucur Fiz — Analele. Universitatii Bucuresti. Fizica
An Univ Bucur Geol — Analele. Universitatii Bucuresti. Geologie
An Univ Bucur Mat Mec — Analele. Universitatii Bucuresti. Matematica-Mecanica
An Univ Bucur Ser Stiint Nat Chim — Analele. Universitatii Bucuresti. Seria Stiintele Naturii. Chimie
An Univ Bucur Stiint Nat — Analele. Universitatii Bucuresti. Stiintele Naturii
An Univ Catol Valparaiso — Anales. Universidad Catolica de Valparaiso
An Univ Cent Caracas — Anales. Universidad Central de Venezuela (Caracas)
An Univ Cent Ecuador — Anales. Universidad Central del Ecuador
An Univ Cent Quito — Anales. Universidad Central del Ecuador (Quito)
An Univ Chile — Anales. Universidad de Chile
An Univ Chile Santiago — Anales. Universidad de Chile (Santiago)
An Univ CI Parhon Bucuresti Ser Stiint Nat — Analele Universitatii C.I. Parhon Bucuresti. Seria Stiintelor Naturii
An Univ C I Parhon Ser Stiint Nat — Analele. Universitatii C. I. Parhon. Seria Stiintele Naturii
An Univ Craiova Biol Agron Hortic — Analele Universitatii din Craiova. Biologie, Agronomie, Horticultura
An Univ Craiova Biol Stiinte Agric Ser A 3a — Analele. Universitatii din Craiova. Biologie Stiinte. Agricole. Seria A 3a
An Univ Craiova Mat Fiz-Chim — Analele. Universitatii din Craiova. Matematica. Fizica-Chimie
An Univ Craiova Ser 3 — Analele. Universitatii din Craiova. Seria 3a. Stiinte Agricole
An Univ Craiova Ser Biol Med Stiinte Agr — Analele. Universitatii din Craiova. Seria Biologie Medicina Stiinte Agricole
An Univ Craiova Ser Biol Med Stiinte Agric — Analele Universitatii din Craiova. Seria. Biologie, Medicina, Stiinte Agricole
An Univ Craiova Ser Chim — Analele Universitatii din Craiova. Seria Chimie
An Univ Craiova Ser Mat Fiz Chim — Analele Universitatii din Craiova. Seria. Matematica Fizica-Chimie
An Univ Craiova Ser Mat Fiz Chim Electroteh — Anale. Universitatea din Craiova. Seria Matematica, Fizica, Chimie, Electrotehnica
An Univ Cuenca — Anales. Universidad de Cuenca
An Univ Galati Fasc 6 — Analele. Universitatii din Galati. Fascicula 6. Tehnologia si ChimiaProduselor Alimentare
An Univ Galati Fasc 9 — Analele. Universitatii din Galati. Fascicula 9. Metalurgie siCocsochimie
An Univ Galati Metal — Analele Universitatii din Galati. Metalurgie
An Univ Hisp — Anales. Universidad Hispalense
An Univ Hispalense — Anales. Universidad Hispalense
An Univ Hispalense Ser Cienc — Anales. Universidad Hispalense. Serie de Ciencias
An Univ Hisp Ser Cienc — Anales. Universidad Hispalense. Serie de Ciencias
An Univ Hisp Ser Med — Anales. Universidad Hispalense. Serie Medicina
An Univ Hisp Ser Vet — Anales. Universidad Hispalense. Serie Veterinaria
An Univ Madrid — Anales. Universidad de Madrid
An Univ Murcia — Anales. Universidad de Murcia
An Univ Murcia Cienc — Anales. Universidad de Murcia. Ciencias
An Univ Narino Pasto — Anales. Universidad de Narino (Pasto, Colombia)
An Univ Norte Antofagasta — Anales. Universidad del Norte (Antofagasta)
An Univ Norte (Chile) — Anales. Universidad del Norte (Chile)
An Univ Ovidius Constanta Ser Mat — Analele. Universitatii Ovidius Constanta. Seria Matematica
An Univ Patagonia San Juan Bosco Cienc Geol — Anales. Universidad de la Patagonia San Juan Bosco. Ciencias Geologicas
An Univ S Dom C Trujillo S Domingo — Anales. Universidad de Santo Domingo (Santo Domingo)
An Univ S Marcos Lima — Anales. Universidad Mayor de San Marcos (Lima)
An Univ St Domingo — Anales. Universidad de Santo Domingo
An Univ Timisoara Ser Mat Inform — Universitatii din Timisoara. Analele. Seria Matematica-Informatica
An Univ Timisoara Ser Sti Fiz-Chim — Analele. Universitatii din Timisoara. Seria Stiinte Fizice-Chimice
An Univ Timisoara Ser Stiinte Fiz Chim — Analele. Universitatii din Timisoara. Seria Stiinte Fizice-Chimice
An Univ Timisoara Ser Stiinte Mat-Fiz — Analele. Universitatii din Timisoara. Seria Stiinte Matematice-Fizice
An Univ Timisoara Ser Stiint Fiz — Analele Universitatii din Timisoara. Seria Stiinte Fizice
An Univ Timisoara Ser Stiint Fiz-Chim — Analele. Universitatii din Timisoara. Seria Stiinte Fizice-Chimice
An Univ Timisoara Ser Stiint Mat — Analele. Universitatii din Timisoara. Seria Stiinte Matematice

An Univ Timisoara Ser Sti Mat — Analele. Universitatii din Timisoara. Seria Stiinte Matematice
An Univ Timisoara Stiinte Fiz — Analele Universitatii din Timisoara. Stiinte Fizice
An Univ Timisoara Stiinte Fiz Chim — Analele. Universitatii din Timisoara. Seria Stiinte Fizice-Chimice
ANUOA — Actualites Neurophysiologiques
ANUPB — Advances in Nuclear Physics
ANURD9 — Advances in Nutritional Research
AnUS — Annual of Urdu Studies
An U Sarav Philos — Annales Universitatis Saraviensis. Philosophiae
ANUSDC — Annual Review of Nuclear and Particle Science
Anu Soc Broteriana — Anuario. Sociedade Broteriana
An U S S — Andrews University. Seminary Studies
ANUSSM — Australian National University. Social Science Monograph
ANUTA — Advances in Nuclear Science and Technology
Anu Tec Inst Pesqui Zootec "Francisco Osorio" — Anuario Tecnico. Instituto de Pesquisas Zootecnicas "Francisco Osorio"
AnUTFil — Analele. Universitatii din Timisoara. Seria Stiinte Filologice
An U Valencia — Anales de la Universidad de Valencia
ANV — Australian and New Zealand Environmental Report
ANVA — Afhandlinger. Norske Videnskaps-Akademi i Oslo
ANVA — Avhandlinger Utgitt av Norsk Videnskaps-Akademi I Oslo
ANVAO — Avhandlinger Utgitt av Norsk Videnskaps-Akademi I Oslo. II
ANVBAV — Abhandlungen. Naturwissenschaftlicher Verein zu Bremen
An Ver Gesch Belg Protestantisme — Annalen van der Vereniging voor de Geschiedenis van het Belgsch Protestantisme
Anvers A S Md — Annales de la Societe de Medecine d'Anvers
Anvers J Phm — Journal de Pharmacie. Publie par la Societe de Pharmacie d'Anvers
ANVHEJ — Abhandlungen. Naturwissenschaftlicher Verein in Hamburg
ANVIDL — Annales de Virologie
ANVTAH — Analecta Veterinaria
Anwend Isot Org Chem Biochem — Anwendung von Isotopen in der Organischen Chemie und Biochemie
ANWG — Arbeitsgemeinschaft fuer Forschung des Landes Nordrhein-Westfalen Geisteswissenschaften
ANWIAN — Anaesthesiologie und Wiederbelebung
An WR — Andhra Weekly Reporter
ANX — Annalen der Gemeinwirtschaft
ANY — Architecture New York
ANY — Areito (New York)
ANYAA — Annals. New York Academy of Sciences
ANYAA9 — Annals. New York Academy of Sciences
ANYAS — Annals. New York Academy of Sciences
A NZ — Art New Zealand
ANZAAS Congress — Australian and New Zealand Association for the Advancement of Science. Congress
ANZAAS Papers — Australian and New Zealand Association for the Advancement of Science. Papers
Anz Akad (Wien) — Anzeiger der Oesterreichischen Akademie der Wissenschaften. Philosophisch-Historische Klasse (Wien)
Anz Akad Wiss Krakow — Anzeiger der Akademie der Wissenschaften. Krakow
Anz Akad Wiss Wien — Anzeiger der Akademie der Wissenschaften Wien
Anz Akad Wiss Wien Math Naturwis Kl — Anzeiger. Akademie der Wissenschaften in Wien. Mathematisch-Naturwissenschaftliche Klasse
Anz Ak (Wien) — Anzeiger der Oesterreichischen Akademie der Wissenschaften. Philosophisch-Historische Klasse (Wien)
Anz Alt — Anzeiger fuer die Altertumswissenschaft
Anz Altertumsw — Anzeiger fuer die Altertumswissenschaft
Anz Altertumswiss — Anzeiger fuer die Altertumswissenschaft
AnzAltW — Anzeiger fuer die Altertumswissenschaft
ANZATVH Newsl — ANZATVH [*Australian and New Zealand Association of Teachers of the Visually Handicapped*] Newsletter
AnzAW — Anzeiger fuer die Altertumswissenschaft
ANZ Bank — Australia and New Zealand Bank. Quarterly Survey
ANZ Bank Q — ANZ [*Australia and New Zealand*] Bank. Quarterly
ANZC Hals — Australian and New Zealand Commentary on Halsbury's Laws of England
Anz Churfuerstl Saechs Leipziger Oekon Soc — Anzeigen der Churfuerstlichen Saechsischen Leipziger Oekonomischen Societaet
ANZ Conv R — Australian and New Zealand Conveyancing Report
ANZDDQ — Australian and New Zealand Journal of Developmental Disabilities
Anz Dt Altert — Anzeiger fuer Deutsches Altertum
Anzeig d Bayer Akd Wiss — Gelehrte Anzeiger der Bayerischen Akademie der Wissenschaften
Anzeiger Berlin — Archaeologischer Anzeiger (Berlin)
Anzeiger (Wien) — Anzeiger der Oesterreichischen Akademie der Wissenschaften. Philosophisch-Historische Klasse (Wien)
Anz f D Altert — Anzeiger fuer Deutsches Altertum
Anz f Schw AK — Anzeiger fuer Schweizerische Altertumskunde
Anz Germ Nationalmus — Anzeiger des Germanischen Nationalmuseums
Anz Germ Nat Mus — Anzeiger. Germanisches Nationalmuseum
Anz Ger Nazionalmus — Anzeiger. Germanisches Nationalmuseum
Anz Ger Nmus — Anzeiger des Germanischen Nationalmuseums
ANZHESJ — ANZHES [*Australian and New Zealand History of Education Society*] Journal
ANZ Ind — Australia and New Zealand Bank. Business Indicators
Anz Ing Tech — Anzeiger fuer Ingenieure und Techniker
ANZ Insp Sch J — Australian and New Zealand Association of Inspectors of Schools. Journal
ANZ Insurance Cases — Australian and New Zealand Insurance Cases
ANZJC — Australian and New Zealand Journal of Criminology
ANZJ Crim — Australian and New Zealand Journal of Criminology
ANZJ of Crim — Australian and New Zealand Journal of Criminology
ANZJOS — Australian and New Zealand Journal of Sociology

ANZJS — Australian and New Zealand Journal of Sociology
Anz J Surg — Anz Journal of Surgery
Anz Kais Akad Wiss Wien Math Naturwiss Kl — Anzeiger der Kaiserlichen Akademie der Wissenschaften in Wien. Mathematisch-Naturwissenschaftliche Klasse
Anz Kde Dt Vorzeit — Anzeiger fuer Kunde der Deutschen Vorzeit
Anz Knd Dt Vorzt — Anzeiger fuer Kunde der Deutschen Vorzeit
Anz Koenigl Saechs Leipziger Oekon Soc — Anzeigen der Koeniglich-Saechsischen Leipziger Oekonomischen Societaet
Anz Kurfuerstl Saechs Oberlausiz Ges Wiss — Anzeigen der Kurfuerstlich Saechsischen Oberlausizischen Gesellschaft der Wissenschaften
Anz Maschinenwes — Anzeiger fuer Maschinenwesen
ANZOAM — Archives Neerlandaises de Zoologie
Anz OAW — Anzeiger der Oesterreichischen Akademie der Wissenschaften. Philosophisch-Historische Klasse
Anz Oberlausitz Ges Wiss Goerlitz — Anzeigen der Oberlausitzischen Gesellschaft der Wissenschaften zu Goerlitz
Anz Oe Ak — Anzeiger der Oesterreichischen Akademie der Wissenschaften. Philosophisch-Historische Klasse
ANZOEQ — Australian and New Zealand Journal of Ophthalmology
Anz Oester Akad Wiss Phil Hist Kl — Anzeiger der Oesterreichischen Akademie der Wissenschaften. Philosophisch-Historische Klasse
Anz Oesterr Akad Wiss — Anzeiger der Oesterreichischen Akademie der Wissenschaften
Anz Oesterr Akad Wiss Math Naturwiss Kl — Anzeiger. Oesterreichische Akademie der Wissenschaften [*Wien*]. Mathematisch-Naturwissenschaftliche Klasse
Anz Oesterr Akad Wiss Phil Hist Klasse — Anzeiger der Oesterreichischen Akademie der Wissenschaften. Philosophisch-Historische Klasse
Anz Oesterreich Akad Wiss Philos Hist Kl — Anzeiger der Oesterreichischen Akademie der Wissenschaften. Philosophisch-Historische Klasse
Anz Orn Ges Bayern — Anzeiger. Ornithologische Gesellschaft in Bayern
Anz Ornithol Ges Bayern — Anzeiger. Ornithologische Gesellschaft in Bayern
Anz Osterr Akad Wiss Math-Naturwiss Kl — Anzeiger. Oesterreichische Akademie der Wissenschaften. Mathematisch-Naturwissenschaftliche Klasse
ANZQ — ANZ [*Australia and New Zealand*] Bank. Quarterly Survey
ANZQ Survey — ANZ [*Australia and New Zealand*] Bank. Quarterly Survey
ANZ Quart Surv — ANZ [*Australia and New Zealand*] Bank. Quarterly Survey
Anz Saml Privatges Oberlausiz — Anzeige von den Samlungen einer Privatgesellschaft in der Oberlausiz
Anz Schaedlingskd — Anzeiger fuer Schaedlingskunde
Anz Schaedlingskd Pflanz — Anzeiger fuer Schaedlingskunde, Pflanzenschutz, Umweltschutz
Anz Schaedlingskd Pflanzenschutz — Anzeiger fuer Schaedlingskunde und Pflanzenschutz [*Later, Anzeiger fuer Schaedlingskunde, Pflanzenschutz, Umweltschutz*]
Anz Schaedlingskd Pflanzenschutz Umweltschutz — Anzeiger fuer Schaedlingskunde, Pflanzenschutz, Umweltschutz
Anz Schaedlingskd Pflanzen- und Umweltschutz — Anzeiger fuer Schaedlingskunde, Pflanzen- und Umweltschutz
Anz Schaedlingskd Pflanz- Umweltschutz — Anzeiger fuer Schaedlingskunde, Pflanzen- und Umweltschutz
Anz Schles Landesmus Troppau — Anzeiger des Schlesischen Landesmuseums in Troppau
Anz Schw Alt — Anzeiger fuer Schweizerische Altertumskunde
Anz Schweiz — Anzeiger fuer Schweizerische Altertumskunde
Anz Schweiz AK — Anzeiger fuer Schweizerische Altertumskunde
Anz Schweiz Alt — Anzeiger fuer Schweizerische Altertumskunde
Anz Schweiz Altertknd — Anzeiger fuer Schweizerische Altertumskunde
Anz Schweiz Altkde — Anzeiger fuer Schweizerische Altertumskunde
Anz Schweiz Gesch — Anzeiger fuer Schweizerische Geschichte
Anz Slav Philol — Anzeiger fuer Slavische Philologie
ANZ Sur — ANZ [*Australia and New Zealand*] Bank. Quarterly Survey
Anz (Wien) — Anzeiger. Akademie der Wissenschaften (Wien)
Anz (Wien) — Anzeiger der Oesterreichischen Akademie der Wissenschaften. Philosophisch-Historische Klasse (Wien)
Anz (Wien) — Anzeiger. Oesterreichische Akademie der Wissenschaften (Wien)
AO — Acta Orientalia
AO — Alandsk Odling: Arsbok
AO — Almanaque d'Ovar
AO — Alte Orient
AO — American Organist
AO — American Oxonian
AO — Anecdota Graeca e Codices. Manuscriptis Bibliothecarum Oxoniensium
AO — Archiv Orientalni
AO — Arco
AO — Arhivele Olteniei
AO — Australian Outlook
AO — Der Alte Orient. Gemeinverstaendliche Darstellungen
AOAPA9 — Australia. Commonwealth Scientific and Industrial Research Organisation. AnimalResearch Laboratories. Technical Paper
AOASH — Acta Orientalia. Academiae Scientiarum Hungaricae
AOAT — Alter Orient und Altes Testament
AOATS — Alter Orient und Altes Testament. Sonderreihe
AOAW — Anzeiger. Oesterreichische Akademie der Wissenschaften [*Wien*]. Philosophisch-Historische Klasse
AOB — Acta Orientalia
AOB — Acta Orientalia Academiae Scientiarum Hungaricae (Budapest)
AOB — Altorientalische Bibliothek
AOB — Altorientalische Texte und Bilder zum Alten Testament
AOBAA3 — Archivos de Oftalmologia de Buenos Aires
AOBEAF — Acta Orthopaedica Belgica
AOBIAR — Archives of Oral Biology
AOBRDN — Acta Oncologica Brasileira
AOC — Archives de l'Orient Chretien

AOCCA — Annales d'Oto-Laryngologie et de Chirurgie Cervico-Faciale
AOCEDN — Archaeology in Oceania
AO Chr — Archives de l'Orient Chretien
AOC Newsl — Administrative Office of the Courts. Newsletter
AOCSSSR — Alaska Outer Continental Shelf Socioeconomic Studies Program. Special Reports
AOCSSTR — Alaska Outer Continental Shelf Socioeconomic Studies Program. Technical Reports
AOD — Altorientalische Denkmaeler im Vorderasiatischen Museum zu Berlin
AODNS — Acta Orientalia
AOe — Archiv fuer Oesterreichische Geschichte
AOE — Arv og Eje
AOEG — Archiv fuer Oesterreichische Geschichte
AOEMAK — Advances in Optical and Electron Microscopy
AOF — Altorientalische Forschungen
AOF — Archiv fuer Orientforschung
AOFFA4 — Analysis and Characterization of Oils, Fats, and Fat Products
AOFPAY — Australia. Commonwealth Scientific and Industrial Research Organisation. Division of Food Preservation. Technical Paper
AOFSA4 — Australia. Commonwealth Scientific and Industrial Research Organisation. Division of Fisheries and Oceanography. Fisheries Synopsis
AOG — Archiv fuer Oesterreichische Geschichte
AOGB — Anzeiger der Ornithologischen Gesellschaft in Bayern
AOGBAV — Anzeiger. Ornithologische Gesellschaft in Bayern
AOGJAL — Australasian Oil and Gas Journal
AOGLAR — Acta Obstetrica et Gynaecologica Japonica
AOGMA — Annali di Ostetricia, Ginecologia, Medicina Perinatale
AOGN — Alaska Oil and Gas News
AOGNAX — Archivio di Ostetricia e Ginecologia
AOGRDE — Australasian Oil and Gas Review
AOGSAE — Acta Obstetrica et Gynecologica Scandinavica
AOGYA — Advances in Obstetrics and Gynecology
AOH — Acta Orientalia. Academiae Scientiarum Hungaricae
AOH — Acta Orientalia (Hauniae)
AOHSA — Annals of Occupational Hygiene. Supplement
AOHYA — Annals of Occupational Hygiene
AOI — Accent on Information
AOI — Airways Operations Instructions
AOIAA — Annals of Oto-Rino-Laryngologica Ibero-Americana
AOIAA4 — Anales Otorrinolaringologicos Ibero-Americanos
AOIAC — Atlantida. Orgao do Instituto Acoriano de Cultura
AOIRAL — Australia. Commonwealth Scientific and Industrial Research Organisation. Division of Plant Industry. Field Station Record
AOJP — Australian Official Journal of Patents, Trade Marks, and Designs
AOJPTMD — Australian Official Journal of Patents, Trade Marks, and Designs
AOJTAW — American Orthoptic Journal
AOKAT — Altorientalischer Kommentar zum Alten Testament
AOKW — Annalen van de Oudheidkundige Kring van het Land van Waas
AOL — Archives de l'Orient Latin
AOLAA — Acta Oto-Laryngologica
AOLAEN — Acta Odontologica Latinoamericana
AOLPAU — Australia. Commonwealth Scientific and Industrial Research Organisation. Division of Land Research and Regional Survey. Technical Paper
AOLSA5 — Acta Oto-Laryngologica. Supplementum
AOLVA — Archivio di Oceanografia e Limnologia
AOLVAE — Archivio di Oceanografia e Limnologia
AOMCA — Advances in Organometallic Chemistry
AOMOD — AOCS Monograph
Aomori J Med — Aomori Journal of Medicine
AOMPAU — Australia. Commonwealth Scientific and Industrial Research Organisation. Division of Meteorological Physics. Technical Paper
AON — Acta Orientalia Neerlandica
AONCAZ — Acta Oncologica
AONGAD — Archives. Office du Niger
AONK — Archiv fuer Ohren-, Nasen-, und Kehlkopfheilkunde
AONSEJ — Archives of Otolaryngology and Head and Neck Surgery
Aontas Rev — Aontas Review
A Ontem & Hoje — Arte de Ontem e de Hoje
AOP — Analectes. Ordre de Premontre
AOP — Analyser og Problemer
AOP — Annals of Probability
AOP — Archiv Orientalni. Journal of the Czechoslovak Oriental Institute (Prague)
AOP — Archivum Orientale Pragense
AOPA Gen Aviat Natl Rep — AOPA [*Aircraft Owners and Pilots Association*] General Aviation National Report
AOPA Mo Mag — AOPA [*Aircraft Owners' and Pilots' Association*] MonthlyMagazine
AOPCD — Annual Report. Organization of the Petroleum Exporting Countries
AOPIBU — Acta Ophthalmologica Iugoslavica
AOPOCF — American Journal of Optometry and Physiological Optics
AOPRAM — Australia. Commonwealth Scientific and Industrial Research Organisation. Division of Plant Industry. Annual Report
AOPSAP — Acta Ophthalmologica. Supplementum
AOR — Analecta Orientalia
AOR — Annals of Oriental Research
AOR — Anuari. Oficina Romanica
AOR — Archiv Orientalni
AOr — Ars Orientalis. The Arts of Islam and the East
AORBA — Advances in Oral Biology
AORBAI — Advances in Oral Biology
AOREDU — Archivio di Ortopedia e Reumatologia
AORHA — Annals of Otology, Rhinology, and Laryngology
AORIA — Acta Oto-Rino-Laringologica Ibero-Americana
A Orient — Ars Orientalis
AOrientHung — Acta Orientalia. Academiae Scientiarum Hungaricae

AORLA — Acta Oto-Rhino-Laryngologica Belgica
AORLCG — Archives of Oto-Rhino-Laryngology
AORM — Annals of Oriental Research (Madras)
AORNAK — Acta Ornithologica
AORNBD — Acta Ornithologica
AORN J — Association of Operating Room Nurses. Journal
AORP — Aguia. Orgao da Renascenca Portuguesa
AOS — Accounting, Organizations, and Society
AOS — American Oriental Series
AOS — American Oriental Society. Journal
AOS — Annals of Statistics
AOSAAK — Acta Orthopaedica Scandinavica
AOSADN — Acta Oecologica. Oecologia Applicata
AOSBAN — American Orchid Society. Bulletin
AOSBM — Analecta Ordinis Sancti Basilii Magni
AOSCA — Acta Odontologica Scandinavica
AOSERP — Alberta Oil Sands Environmental Research Program
AOSG — Arbeiten aus dem Orientalischen Seminar der Universitaet Giessen
AOSGA4 — Attualita di Ostetricia e Ginecologia
AOSGD7 — Acta Oecologica. Oecologia Generalis
AOSI — Alberta Oil Sands Index
AOSLAJ — Australia. Commonwealth Scientific and Industrial Research Organisation. Soils and Land Use Series
AOSMAM — Archivio. Ospedale al Mare
AOSPDY — Acta Oecologica. Oecologia Plantarum
AOSRB4 — Ambio. Special Report
AOSRD6 — Archiwum Ochrony Srodowiska
AOSTRA J Res — AOSTRA (Alberta Oil Sands Technology and Research Authority) Journal of Research
AOSUAC — Acta Orthopaedica Scandinavica. Supplementum
AOT — Altorientalische Texte zum Alten Testament
AOTADS — Acta Oceanographica Taiwanica
AOTSDE — Archives of Orthopaedic and Traumatic Surgery
AOTU — Altorientalische Texte und Untersuchungen
A Ouest — Arts de l'Ouest
AOUNAZ — Archiv fuer Orthopaedische und Unfall-Chirurgie
AOVEBE — Acta Odontologica Venezolana
A Ox — Anecdota Oxonensia
Aoyama J Gen Educ — Aoyama Journal of General Education
AP — Acta Praehistorica
AP — Algemeen Politieblad van het Koninkrijk der Nederlanden
AP — American Psychologist
AP — Analecta Praemonstratensia
AP — Anecdota Graeca e Codices. Manuscriptis Bibliothecae Regiae Parisienses
AP — Annalen der Philosophie und Philosophischen Kritik
AP — Annals of Philosophy
AP — Annee Philologique
AP — Anthropological Papers
Ap — Approach
Ap — April
AP — Archaeologia Polona
AP — Archeion Pontou
AP — Archeologia Polski
AP — Archives de Philosophie
AP — Archiv fuer Papyrusforschung und Verwandte Gebiete
AP — Archiv Patologii
AP — Arheoloski Pregled
AP — Arkheologichni Pamiatky Ursr
AP — Arqueologo Portugues
AP — Ars Poetica
AP — Aryan Path
AP — Asian Perspectives
AP — Aurea Parma
APA — Abhandlungen. Akademie der Wissenschaften in Prag
APA — Acta Praehistorica et Archaeologica
APA — Australian Planning Appeal Decisions
APA — Philological Monographs. American Philological Association
APAA — Atti. Pontificia Accademia Romana di Archeologia
APACAB — Acta Physiologica. Academiae Scientiarum Hungaricae
APACB — American Painting Contractor
APad — Annales Paderewski
APAD — Australian Planning Appeal Decisions
A Paed — Acta Paediatrica
A Paed Belg — Acta Paediatrica Belgica
A Paed Lat — Acta Paediatrica Latina
APAIS — Australian Public Affairs Information Service
APAIS Aust Public Affairs Inf Serv — APAIS. Australian Public Affairs Information Service
APAJ — Alaska Public Affairs Journal
APALA4 — Arquivo de Patologia
APA Legisl Bull — American Pulpwood Association. Legislative Bulletin
APAM — Anthropological Papers. American Museum of Natural History
APAMNH — Anthropological Papers. American Museum of Natural History
APANDD — Avances en Produccion Animal
APANEE — Annals of Physiological Anthropology
A Pant — Actes du Pantocrator
APAO — Archaeology and Physical Anthropology in Oceania
APAOBE — Archaeology and Physical Anthropology in Oceania [Later, Archaeology in Oceania]
APA-PSIEP Rep — APA-PSIEP [American Psychological Association-Project on Scientific Information Exchange in Psychology] Report
APA Pulpwood Highl — American Pulpwood Association. Pulpwood Highlights
APA Pulpwood Statist — American Pulpwood Association. Pulpwood Statistics
APA Pulpwood Sum — American Pulpwood Association. Monthly Pulpwood Summary

APar — Aurea Parma
APARA — Atti. Pontificia Accademia Romana di Archeologia
APARAR — Atti. Pontificia Accademia Romana di Archeologia. Rendiconti
Apar Nauk Dydakt — Aparatura Naukowa i Dydaktyczna
A Par Pol — Acta Parasitologica Polonica
Apar Respir Tuberc — Aparato Respiratorio y Tuberculosis
Apar Resp Tuberc La Paz — Aparato Respiratorio y Tuberculosis (La Paz)
Apar Resp Tuberc Santiago — Aparato Respiratorio y Tuberculosis (Santiago)
APA Safety Alert — American Pulpwood Association. Safety Alert
APAT — American Philological Association. Transactions
APATB — Applied Atomics
APA Tech Papers — American Pulpwood Association. Technical Papers
APA Tech Release — American Pulpwood Association. Technical Release
A Path Jap — Acta Pathologica Japonica
Apatitovye Proyavleniya Sev Kavk — Apatitovye Proyavleniya Severnogo Kavkaza
APAVE — APAVE. Revue Technique du Groupement des Associations de Proprietaires d'Appareils a Vapeur et Electriques
APA VIC News — Australian Pre-School Association. Victorian Branch. Newsletter
APAW — Abhandlungen. Preussische Akademie der Wissenschaften
APB — Algemeen Politieblad van het Koninkrijk der Nederlanden
APB — Appalachian Business Review
APBDAJ — Archiv der Pharmazie und Berichte der Deutschen Pharmazeutischen Gesellschaft
Ap Bl — Apologetische Blaetter
APBMBD — Annales de Physique Biologique et Medicale
APBMDF — Acta Pathologica et Microbiologica Scandinavica. Section B. Microbiology
APC — Airport Forum News Services
APC — Annales de la Philosophie Chretienne
APC — Archives Paul Claudel
APC — Australian Personal Computer
APCA Abstr — APCA [Air Pollution Control Association] Abstracts
APCA Annu Meet Proc — APCA [Air Pollution Control Association] Annual Meeting. Proceedings
APCAD — Applied Catalysis
APCA J — APCA [Air Pollution Control Association] Journal
APCCBM — Annual Progress in Child Psychiatry and Child Development
APCCDO — Annual Reports on the Progress of Chemistry. Section A. Inorganic Chemistry
APCE — Annals of Public and Cooperative Economy [Formerly, Annals of Collective Economy]
APCEAR — Archiv foer Pharmaci og Chemi
APCHA — Advances in Protein Chemistry
APCMA — Archivio di Patologia e Clinica Medica
APCMAH — Archivio di Patologia e Clinica Medica
APCOB — Archivio Putti di Chirurgia degli Organi di Movimento
APCOD — Applied Physics Communications
APCOM — Application of Computers and Mathematics in the Mineral Industry
APCOM 77 Pap Int Symp Appl Comput Oper Res Miner Ind — APCOM 77. Papers Presented at the International Symposium on the Application ofComputers and Operations Research in the Mineral Industries
APCPCS — American Institute of Physics. Conference Proceedings
APCRAW — Advances in Pest Control Research
APC Review — APC Review. Australian Parents Council
APCSD4 — Annals of Plastic Surgery
APD — Archives de Philosophie du Droit
APD — Aslib Proceedings
APDBA — Acta Physica et Chimica (Debrecina)
APDEAW — Aptechnoe Delo
APDEB — Current Problems in Dermatology
APDIAO — Annals of the Rheumatic Diseases
APDKA — Aktualne Problemy Informacji i Dokumentacji
APDPD — Annual Power Distribution Conference. Proceedings
APDTA9 — American Practitioner and Digest of Treatment
APE — Applied Economics
APEA J — APEA [Australian Petroleum Exploration Association] Journal
APE Eng — APE [Amalgamated Power Engineering Ltd.] Engineering
APE Engng — APE [Amalgamated Power Engineering Ltd.] Engineering
APEF — Annual. Palestine Exploration Fund
Apeir — Apeiron Journal for Ancient Philosophy and Science
APEMAR — Archives Roumaines de Pathologie Experimentale et de Microbiologie
APen — Anima e Pensiero
APEND — Applied Energy
Apercus Econ Tchecosl — Apercus sur l'Economie Tchecoslovaque
A Period F A — Artes. Periodical·of the Fine Arts
A Petrol Nat Gas Statist Yb Sask — Annual Petroleum and Natural Gas Statistical Yearbook (Saskatchewan)
APF — Acta Philosophica Fennica
APF — Annales de la Propagation de la Foi
APF — Archiv fuer Papyrusforschung und Verwandte Gebiete
APF — Archivos Peruanos de Folklore
AP Faith — Annals of the Propagation of the Faith
APFL — Annales de la Propagation de la Foi (Lyons)
APFNC3 — Department of Primary Industries. Brisbane Fisheries Branch. Fisheries Notes
APFRAD — Annales Pharmaceutiques Francaises
APG — Acta Phytotaxonomica et Geobotanica
APG — Archiv fuer Politik und Geschichte
APGAAZ — Arquivos de Patologia Geral e Anatomia Patologica. Universidade de Coimbra
A Pg B — Archiv fuer Postgeschichte in Bayern
APGE — Abhandlungen zur Philosophie und ihrer Geschichte (Erdmanns)
APGF — Abhandlungen zur Philosophie und ihrer Geschichte (Falckenbergs)
APh — Acta Philologica. Societa Accademica Romena

APh — Acta Philologica. Societas Academica Dacoromana
APH — Acta Poloniae Historica
APH — Air Power History
APH — Animal Pharm World Animal Health News
APh — Annee Philologique
Aph — Archives de Philosophie [*Paris*]
A Ph — Archiv fuer Philosophie
APHA — American Public Health Association. Public Health Education. Section Newsletter
APhAP — Archives de Philologie. Academie Polonaise des Sciences et des Lettres
A Pharm — Archiv der Pharmazie
A Pharm Hung — Acta Pharmaceutica Hungarica
A Pharm Int — Acta Pharmaceutica Internationalia
APHC — Annales de Parasitologie Humaine et Comparee
APHCA — Annales de Parasitologie Humaine et Comparee
APH-CARL — American Printing House for the Blind - Central Automated Resource List
A Ph Ch — Archiv for Pharmaci og Chemi
APhD — Acta Philologica. Societas Academica Dacoromana
APHGAO — Acta Pharmaceutica Hungarica
APHHDU — Acta Physiologica Hungarica
A Phil — Actes de Philothee
APhilos — Archives de Philosophie
APHIS 81 US Dep Agric Anim Plant Health Inspect — APHIS 81. US Department of Agriculture. Animal and Plant Health Inspection Service
APHIS 91 US Dep Agric Anim Plant Health Inspect — APHIS 91. US Department of Agriculture. Animal and Plant Health Inspection Service
APHL — Archivo de Prehistoria Levantina
APHMA8 — Advances in Pharmaceutical Sciences
APhMGW — Abhandlungen und Sitzungsberichte der Physikalisch-Medizinischen Gesellschaft. Wuerzburg
A Ph Ph K — Annalen der Philosophie und Philosophischen Kritik
APHRA — Ars Pharmaceutica
APHRDQ — Archives of Pharmacal Research
APhS — Acta Philologica Scandinavica. Tidsskrift foer Nordisk Sprogforskning
AphS — Archives de Philosophie [*Paris*]. Supplement Bibliographique
A Ph S — Asian Philosophical Studies
A Ph Sc — Acta Philologica Scandinavica
APHYC — Applied Physics
A Phys Pol — Acta Physica Polonica
A Phys Pol — Acta Physiologica Polonica
A Phys Scand — Acta Physiologica Scandinavica
A Phytother — Acta Phytotherapeutica
API — Alternative Press Index
API — Annali della Pubblica Istruzione
API — Australian Periodicals Index
API Abstr Refin Lit — API (American Petroleum Institute) Abstracts of Refining Literature
Apiary Circ BC Dep Agric — Apiary Circular. British Columbia Department of Agriculture
Apiary Circ (Victoria) — Apiary Circular (Victoria)
Apic Abstr — Apicultural Abstracts
Apic Am — Apicultor Americano
Apic Argent — Apicultura Argentina
Apic Belge — Apiculture Belge
Apic Fr — Apiculture Francaise
Apic Ital — Apicoltore d'Italia
Apic Mod — Apicoltore Moderno
Apic Newsl Pl Ind Div Alberta Dep Agric — Apiculture Newsletter. Plant Industry Division. Alberta Department of Agriculture
Apic Nouv — Apiculture Nouvelle
Apicolt Ital — Apicoltore d'Italia
Apicolt Mod — Apicoltore Moderno
Apic Ration — Apiculture Rationelle
Apic Razion — Apicoltura Razionale
Apic Rom — Apicultura in Romania
APIC Stud Data Processing — APIC Studies in Data Processing
Apicult Abstr — Apicultural Abstracts
Apicult Alger — Apiculteur Algerien
Apicult Als-Lorr — Apiculteur d'Alsace et de Lorraine
Apicult Am — Apicultor Americano
Apicult Belge — Apiculteur Belge
Apicult Chil — Apicultor Chileno
Apicult Lunar — Apicultorul Lunar
Apicult Nord-Afr — Apiculteur Nord-Africain
Apicult Pratn — Apiculteur Praticien
Apic Venezol — Apicultura Venezolana
Apic W Aust — Apiculture in Western Australia
API Food Add Ref — American Paper Institute. Food Additives Reference Manual
APIGAT — Anuarul. Institutului de Patologie si Igiena Animala
APIJ — APIJ. Australian Planning Institute. Journal
Ap I J — Journal of the Anthropological Institute of Great Britain and Ireland
API Journal — Australian Planning Institute. Journal
API Med Res Publ — American Petroleum Institute. Medical Research Publications
API Monogr Ser — API (American Petroleum Institute) Monograph Series
API Newsprint Bull — American Paper Institute. Newsprint Division. Bulletin
AP Inf B — Agerpres Information Bulletin
APIOS Rep — APIOS Report
APIP — Associations' Publications in Print
APIPAM — Australia. Commonwealth Scientific and Industrial Research Organisation. Division of Plant Industry. Technical Paper
API Publ — American Petroleum Institute. Publication
API Refining Dep Midyear Meet Prepr — American Petroleum Institute. Refining Department. Midyear Meeting. Preprints
API Statist Sum — American Paper Institute. Monthly Statistical Summary

API Tech Abstr — API (American Petroleum Institute) Technical Abstracts
API Wood Pulp Statist — American Paper Institute. Wood Pulp Statistics
APJ — Aberdeen Press and Journal
APJ — American Paint and Coatings Journal
Ap J — Appenzellische Jahrbuecher
APJ — Appraisal Journal
Ap Jahr — Appenzellische Jahrbuecher
APJL — Alpine Journal
APJSA — Astrophysical Journal. Supplement Series
APJUA8 — Acta Pharmaceutica Jugoslavica
APK — Agricultural Pakistan (Karachi)
APK — Aufsaetze zur Portugiesischen Kulturgeschichte
APKCA — Allgemeine und Praktische Chemie
APKTAA — Archeia tes Pharmakeutikes (Athens)
APL — Ancien Pays de Looz
APL — Annales Politiques et Litteraires
APL — Annales. Prince de Ligne
ApL — Approdo Letterario
APL — Archives de l'Orient Chretien
APL — Archivo de Prehistoria Levantina
APLA Bull — Atlantic Provinces Library Association. Bulletin
APLA Bull — Bulletin. American Patent Law Association
Ap Laic — Apostolado Laico
APLA Newsl — APLA Newsletter
APLA Occ Pap — APLA Occasional Paper
APLA QJ — APLA [*American Patent Law Association*] Quarterly Journal
A Plast — Arta Plastica
A Plast — Arts Plastiques
AP Lev — Archivo de Prehistoria Levantina
Aplik Mat — Aplikace Matematiky
ApLit — Apocalyptic Literature
APL JHU SR — Applied Physics Laboratory. Johns Hopkins University. Special Report
APLMAS — Archives of Pathology and Laboratory Medicine
Apl Mat — Aplikace Matematiky
APLPB — Advances in Plasma Physics
APLRDC — Advances in Polyamine Research
APLSA — Annales de Chirurgie Plastique
APLSDF — Aspects of Plant Sciences
APLTAF — Acta Physiologica Latinoamericana
APL Tech Dig — APL [*Applied Physics Laboratory*] Technical Digest
APLTR — Asian Pacific Law and Tax Review
APM — Anuario de Prehistoria Madrilena
APM — Australian Personnel Management
APMA — Anthropological Papers of the Museum of Anthropology of the University of Michigan
APMA — MMS Asia/Pacific Market Analysis
APMBAY — Applied Microbiology [*Later, Applied & Environmental Microbiology*]
APMCA3 — Anais Paulistas de Medicina e Cirurgia
APMCB4 — Annales Pharmaceutici
APMCC5 — Applied Mathematics and Computation
APMDA6 — Annals of Physical Medicine
ApMec — Applied Mechanics Reviews
APMEDC — Applied Psychological Measurement
APMHAI — Archives of Physical Medicine and Rehabilitation
APMIAL — Acta Pathologica et Microbiologica Scandinavica
APMIBM — Acta Pathologica et Microbiologica Scandinavica. Section B. Microbiology and Immunology
ApMicrobiol — Applied Microbiology [*Later, Applied and Environmental Microbiology*]
APMIS — Acta Pathologica, Microbiologica, et Immunologica Scandinavica
APMIS — APMIS. Acta Pathologica, Microbiologica, et Immunologica Scandinavica
APMIS Acta Pathol Microbiol Immunol Scand — APMIS. Acta Pathologica, Microbiologica, et Immunologica Scandinavica
APMIS Suppl — APMIS [*Acta Pathologica, Microbiologica, et Immunologica Scandinavica*] Supplement
APMNHOP — Alberta Provincial Museum. Natural History. Occasional Paper
APMR — Archives of Physical Medicine and Rehabilitation
APMS — Altpreussische Monatsschrift
APMSDK — Archives of Podiatric Medicine and Foot Surgery
APMUAN — Acta Pathologica et Microbiologica Scandinavica. Supplementum
APN — Annales des Pays Nivernais
APNAA — Arhiv za Poljoprivredne Nauke
APNAA2 — Arhiv za Poljoprivredne Nauke
APNDAB — Anales de Parques Nacionales
APNPA — Archivio di Psicologia, Neurologia, e Psichiatria
APNPAD — Archivio di Psicologia, Neurologia, e Psichiatria
APNTAP — Arhiv za Poljoprivredne Nauke i Tehniku
APNVAV — Archiv fuer Psychiatrie und Nervenkrankheiten
Apo — Apollo
APO — APO. The Australian Post Office Magazine
APOA — APOA [*Arctic Petroleum Operators Association*] Review
APOA — Arctic Petroleum Review
APOAR — APOA [*Arctic Petroleum Operators Association*] Reports
APOCA — Acta Polytechnica. Chemistry Including Metallurgy Series
APOD — Australian Pocket Oxford Dictionary
APOJA — American Potato Journal
APOJAY — American Potato Journal
A Pol — Archaeologia Polona
A Pol — Archeologia Polski
APOL — Australian Political Register
A Pol Econ — Annee Politique et Economique
A Pol J — Australian Police Journal
Apollo Annu — Apollo Annual
A Polona — Archaeologia Polona

A Polski — Archeologia Polski
A Polytechn — Acta Polytechnica
A Pon Chauss — Annales des Ponts et Chausses. Memoires et Document Relatifs a l'Art des Constructions et au Service de l'Ingenieur
A Pontif Mus Miss Etnol — Annali. Pontifico Museo Missionario Ethnologico gia Lateranensi
Apool Lett — Artpool Letter
Ap Optics — Applied Optics
Apoptosis Immunol — Apoptosis in Immunology
APORA — Advances in Physical Organic Chemistry
A Port — Arte Portuguesa
A Port — O Arqueologo Portugues
Aportaciones Mat — Aportaciones Matematicas
Aportaciones Mat Comun — Aportaciones Matematicas. Comunicaciones
Aportaciones Mat Notas Investigacion — Aportaciones Matematicas. Notas de Investigacion
Aportaciones Mat Textos — Aportaciones Matematicas. Textos
Apothekar Ztg — Apothekar-Zeitung
Apothekerprakt Pharm Tech Assist — Apothekerpraktikant und Pharmazeutisch-Technischer Assistent
Apothekerzeitung Berl — Apothekerzeitung (Berlin)
Apoth Ztg — Apotheker-Zeitung
Apoth Ztg (Hanslian Ed) — Apotheker-Zeitung (Hanslian Edition)
Apot Vjesn — Apotekarski Vjesnik
APP — Alternative Pink Pages. Australasian Plant Pathology
APP — Ancient Peoples and Places
APP — Approach
APP — Arte Popular em Portugal
APP — Australian Psychologists Press
Appalachia Mag — Appalachia Magazine
Appalachian Geol Soc Bull — Appalachian Geological Society. Bulletin
Appalach J — Appalachian Journal
Appal J — Appalachian Journal
Appaloosa N — Appaloosa News
App Anal — Applicable Analysis
App Anth — Epigrammatum Anthologia Palatina cum Planudeis
Apparecch Idraul Pneum — Apparecchiature Idrauliche e Pneumatiche
Apparel Int — Apparel International
Appar Mash Kislorodn Kriog Ustanovok — Apparaty i Mashiny Kislorodnykh i Kriogennykh Ustanovok
Appar Metody Rentgenovskogo Anal — Apparatura i Metody Rentgenovskogo Analiza
Appar Places Fund Stars — Apparent Places of Fundamental Stars
APP Australas Plant Pathol — APP. Australasian Plant Pathology
APPBD — Acta Physiologica et Pharmacologica
APPBDI — Acta Physiologica et Pharmacologica Bulgarica
APPC — Associacao Portuguesa para o Progresso das Ciencias
APPCD — Applied Physics. Part B. Photophysics and Laser Chemistry
App Court Ad Rev — Appellate Court Administration Review
AP Pd — Abhandlungen zur Philosophie und Paedagogik
App DC — Appeal Cases. District of Columbia
APPEA J — APPEA [*Australian Petroleum Production and Exploration Association*] Journal
App Econ — Applied Economics
Appel Med — Appel Medical
Append Provis Nomencl Symb Terminol Conv IUPAC — Appendices on Provisional Nomenclature Symbols, Terminology, and Conventions. International Union of Pure and Applied Chemistry
App Environ Microbiol — Applied and Environmental Microbiology
Appenzell Jb — Appenzellische Jahrbuecher
App et Soc — Apprentissage et Socialisation
App Geomech — Applied Geomechanics
APPHCZ — Annual Proceedings. Phytochemical Society
APPIB — American Paper Industry
APPITA — APPITA. Journal of the Australian and New Zealand Pulp and Paper Industry Technical Association
Appita J — Appita Journal
APPITA Proc — Australian Pulp and Paper Industry Technical Association. Proceedings
Appl Acoust — Applied Acoustics
Appl Admixtures Concr — Application of Admixtures in Concrete
Appl Agric Res — Applied Agricultural Research
Appl Algebra Engrg Comm Comput — Applicable Algebra in Engineering, Communication, and Computing
Appl Anal — Applicable Analysis
Appl Anim Behav Sci — Applied Animal Behaviour Science
Appl Anim Ethol — Applied Animal Ethology
Appl Anim Ethology — Applied Animal Ethology
Appl Anthrop — Applied Anthropology
Appl Anthrop Newsl — Applied Anthropology Newsletter
Appl Artif Intell — Applications of Artificial Intelligence
Appl Artif Intell 10 Knowl Based Syst — Applications of Artificial Intelligence 10. Knowledge-Based Systems
Appl At — Applied Atomics
Appl At Collision Phys — Applied Atomic Collision Physics
Appl At Energy Agric — Application of Atomic Energy in Agriculture
Appl At Spectrosc — Applied Atomic Spectroscopy
Appl Autom Technol Fatigue Fract Test — Applications of Automation Technology to Fatigue and Fracture Testing
Appl Biocatal — Applied Biocatalysis
Appl Biochem Bioeng — Applied Biochemistry and Bioengineering
Appl Biochem Biotechnol — Applied Biochemistry and Biotechnology
Appl Biochem Micr — Applied Biochemistry and Microbiology
Appl Biochem Microbiol — Applied Biochemistry and Microbiology

Appl Biochem Microbiol (Engl Transl Prikl Biokhim Mikrobiol) — Applied Biochemistry and Microbiology (English Translation of Prikladnaya Biokhimiya i Mikrobiologiya)
Appl Biochem Microbiol Moscow — Applied Biochemistry and Microbiology (Moscow)
Appl Biochem Syst Org Chem — Applications of Biochemical Systems in Organic Chemistry
Appl Biol — Applied Biology
Appl Biol Sci — Applied Biological Science
Appl Bot — Applied Botany
Appl Cardiol — Applied Cardiology
Appl Cardiopulm Pathophysiol — Applied Cardiopulmonary Pathophysiology
Appl Catal — Applied Catalysis
Appl Catal A — Applied Catalysis. A. General
Appl Catal B — Applied Catalysis. B. Environmental
Appl Catal B Environ — Applied Catalysis B. Environmental
Appl Categ Structures — Applied Categorical Structures
Appl Charge Density Res Chem Drug Des — Application of Charge Density Research to Chemistry and Drug Design
Appl Chem Eng Treat Sewage Ind Liq Effluents Symp — Application of Chemical Engineering to the Treatment of Sewage and Industrial Liquid Effluents. Symposium
Appl Chem Mfr Arts — Applied Chemistry in Manufacturer Arts
Appl Chem Protein Interfaces Symp — Applied Chemistry at Protein Interfaces. Symposium
Appl Chromatogr — Applied Chromatography
Appl Clay Sci — Applied Clay Science
Appl Commer Oxygen Water Wastewater Syst — Applications of Commercial Oxygen to Water and Wastewater Systems
Appl Commun Theory — Applications of Communications Theory
Appl Compos Mater — Applied Composite Materials
Appl Comput Harmon Anal — Applied and Computational Harmonic Analysis. Time-Frequency and Time-Scale Analysis. Wavelets, Numerical Algorithms, and Applications
Appl Cryog Technol — Applications of Cryogenic Technology
Appl Digital Image Process — Applications of Digital Image Processing
Appl Discrete Math Theoret Comput Sci — Applied Discrete Mathematics and Theoretical Computer Science
Appld Sci Res — Applied Scientific Research
Appl Earth Sci — Applied Earth Science
Appl Econ — Applied Economics
Apple Educ Newsl — Apple Educators' Newsletter
APPLEF — Acta Physiologica et Pharmacologica Latinoamericana
Appl El Ann — Applied Electronics Annual
Appl Electron A — Applied Electronics Annual
Appl Electron Struct Theory — Applications of Electronic Structure Theory
Appl Electr Phenom — Applied Electrical Phenomena
Appl Electr Phenom (Engl Transl) — Applied Electrical Phenomena (English Translation)
Appl Energy — Applied Energy
Appl Engrg Math Ser — Applied and Engineering Mathematics Series
Appl Entomol Zool — Applied Entomology and Zoology
Appl Ent Zool — Applied Entomology and Zoology
Appl Envir Microbiol — Applied and Environmental Microbiology
Appl Environ Microbiol — Applied and Environmental Microbiology
Appl Enzyme Biotechnol Proc Tex AM Univ IUCCP Symp — Applications of Enzyme Biotechnology. Proceedings. Texas A&M University. IUCCP Symposium on Applications of Enzyme Biotechnology
Apple Res Dig — Apple Research Digest
Apple Res Digest — Apple Research Digest. Washington Department of Agriculture
Appl Ergon — Applied Ergonomics
Appl Ergonomics — Applied Ergonomics
Applesauc — Applesauce
Appleton — Appleton's Journal
Appleton M — Appleton's Magazine
Appletons J — Appleton's Journal
Appl Fluoresc Technol — Applied Fluorescence Technology
Appl Fundam Aspects Plant Cell Tissue Organ Cult — Applied and Fundamental Aspects of Plant Cell Tissue and Organ Culture
Appl Geochem — Applied Geochemistry
Appl Geochem Suppl — Applied Geochemistry. Supplement
Appl Herbic Oil Crops Plant — Application of Herbicides in Oil Crops Plantings
Appl High Mag Fields Semicond Phys Lect Int Conf — Application of High Magnetic Fields in Semiconductor Physics. Lectures Presented at the International Conference
Appl Human Sci — Applied Human Science
Appl Hydraul — Applied Hydraulics
Appliance Manuf — Appliance Manufacturer
Applicable Anal — Applicable Analysis
Applic Anal — Applicable Analysis
Applic Artif Intell Eng — Applications of Artificial Intelligence in Engineering
Applications Math — Applications of Mathematics
Applic Rep Radio Div Siemens Edison Swan — Application Report. Radio Division. Siemens Edison Swan
Applics Elect Rlys — Applications of Electricity to Railways. Bibliography of Periodical Articles. Association of American Railroads
Applic Sh Heenan Froude — Application Sheets. Heenan and Froude
Applics Ind — Applications and Industry
Applics Nickel Paris — Applications du Nickel (Paris)
Applics Therm Elect — Applications Thermiques de l'Electricite
Applied Econ — Applied Economics
Applied Phil — Applied Philosophy
Applied Radiol — Applied Radiology
Applied Sc — Applied Science
Appl Immunohistochem — Applied Immunohistochemistry

Appl Immunohistochem Molecul Morphol — Applied Immunohistochemistry & Molecular Morphology
Appl Ind — Applications and Industry
Appl Ind Hyg — Applied Industrial Hygiene
Appl Inform Tech — Applied Information Technology
Appl Intell — Applied Intelligence
Appl Isot Tech Hydrol Hydraul — Application of Isotope Techniques in Hydrology and Hydraulics
Appl Lang Stud — Applied Language Studies
Appl Laser Spectrosc — Applied Laser Spectroscopy
Appl Macromol Chem Phys — Applied Macromolecular Chemistry and Physics
Appl Magn Reson — Applied Magnetic Resonance
Appl Mater Res — Applied Materials Research
Appl Math — Applications of Mathematics
Appl Math and Comput — Applied Mathematics and Computation
Appl Math and Mech — Applied Mathematics and Mechanics
Appl Math and Optimiz — Applied Mathematics and Optimization
Appl Math Comput — Applied Mathematics and Computation
Appl Math Comput (New York) — Applied Mathematics and Computation (New York)
Appl Math Comput Sci — Applied Mathematics and Computer Science
Appl Math Engrg Sci Texts — Applied Mathematics and Engineering Science Texts
Appl Math J Chinese Univ Ser B — Applied Mathematics. A Journal of Chinese Universities. Series B
Appl Math Lett — Applied Mathematics Letters
Appl Math Math Comput — Applied Mathematics and Mathematical Computation
Appl Math Mech — Applied Mathematics and Mechanics
Appl Math Mech (English Ed) — Applied Mathematics and Mechanics (English Edition)
Appl Math Model — Applied Mathematical Modelling
Appl Math Modelling — Applied Mathematical Modelling
Appl Math Notes — Applied Mathematics Notes
Appl Math O — Applied Mathematics and Optimization
Appl Math Optim — Applied Mathematics and Optimization
Appl Math Sci — Applied Mathematical Sciences
Appl Math Ser — Applicable Mathematics Series
Appl Math Warsaw — Applicationes Mathematicae (Warsaw)
Appl Mech — Applied Mechanics
Appl Mech Div Symp Ser (Am Soc Mech Eng) — Applied Mechanics Division. Symposia Series (American Society of Mechanical Engineers)
Appl Mech Eng — Applied Mechanics and Engineering
Appl Mech Proc Int Congr — Applied Mechanics. Proceedings. International Congress of Applied Mechanics
Appl Mech Rev — Applied Mechanics Reviews
Appl Mech Symp Ser — Applied Mechanics Symposia Series
Appl Methods Oncol — Applied Methods in Oncology
Appl Metrol Laser Methods Mach Syst — Application of Metrological Laser Methods in Machines and Systems
Appl Mfr — Appliance Manufacturer
Appl Microb — Applied Microbiology [*Later, Applied and Environmental Microbiology*]
Appl Microbiol — Applied Microbiology [*Later, Applied and Environmental Microbiology*]
Appl Microbiol Biotechnol — Applied Microbiology and Biotechnology
Appl Microbiol Sofia — Applied Microbiology (Sofia)
Appl Microwave Wireless — Applied Microwave and Wireless
Appl Mineral — Applied Mineralogy. Technische Mineralogie
Appl Mineral Proc Int Congr Appl Mineral Miner Ind — Applied Mineralogy. Proceedings. International Congress on Applied Mineralogy in the Minerals Industry
Appl Modern Tech Business — Applications of Modern Technology in Business
Appl Mod Phys Earth Planet Inter Conf — Application of Modern Physics to the Earth and Planetary Interiors. Conference
Appl Moessbauer Spectrosc — Applications of Moessbauer Spectroscopy
Appl Neurop — Applied Neurophysiology
Appl Neurophysiol — Applied Neurophysiology
Appl Newer Tech Anal — Applications of the Newer Techniques of Analysis
Appl New Mass Spectrom Tech Pestic Chem — Applications of New Mass Spectrometry Techniques in Pesticide Chemistry
Appl News — Appalachian News Service
Appl Notes JASCO — Application Notes. JASCO
Appl Nucl Radiochem — Applied Nuclear Radiochemistry
Appl Numer Math — Applied Numerical Mathematics
Appl Num M — Applied Numerical Mathematics
Appl Nurs Res — Applied Nursing Research
Appl Nutr — Applied Nutrition
Appl Occup Environ Hyg — Applied Occuational and Environmental Hygiene
Appl Ocean Res — Applied Ocean Research
Appl Opt — Applied Optics
Appl Opt Hologr Int Conf — Applications of Optical Holography. International Conference
Appl Optics — Applied Optics
Appl Optim — Applied Optimization
Appl Opt Instrum Med — Application of Optical Instrumentation in Medicine
Appl Opt Metrol Tech Meas — Application of Optical Metrology. Techniques and Measurements
Appl Opt Suppl — Applied Optics. Supplement
Appl Organomet Chem — Applied Organometallic Chemistry
Appl Ornithol — Applied Ornithology
Appl Parasitol — Applied Parasitology
Appl Pathol — Applied Pathology
Appl Pat Int Arrange S Afr — Application for a Patent under International Arrangements (South Africa)
Appl Pat Isr — Application for Patent (Israel)

Appl Pat S Afr — Application for a Patent (South Africa)
Appl Pharmacokinet — Applied Pharmacokinetics
Appl Photochem Probing Biol Targets — Applications of Photochemistry in Probing Biological Targets
Appl Phys — Applied Physics
Appl Phys A — Applied Physics. Part A. Solids and Surfaces
Appl Phys A Mater Sci Process — Applied Physics A. Materials Science and Processing
Appl Phys A Solids Surf — Applied Physics A. Solids and Surfaces
Appl Phys A Solids Surfaces — Applied Physics. A. Solids and Surfaces
Appl Phys B — Applied Physics. Part B. Photophysics and Laser Chemistry
Appl Phys B Lasers Opt — Applied Physics B. Lasers and Optics
Appl Phys B Photophys Laser Chem — Applied Physics. B. Photophysics amd Laser Chemistry
Appl Phys Chem Methods Chem Anal Proc Conf — Application of Physico-Chemical Methods in the Chemical Analysis. Proceedings. Conference
Appl Phys Comm — Applied Physics Communications
Appl Phys Commun — Applied Physics Communications
Appl Phys Eng — Applied Physics and Engineering
Appl Phys Jpn — Applied Physics. Japan
Appl Phys L — Applied Physics Letters
Appl Phys Lett — Applied Physics Letters
Appl Phys (London) — Applied Physics (London)
Appl Phys Med Biol Proc Int Conf — Applications of Physics to Medicine and Biology. Proceedings. International Conference
Appl Phys NY — Applied Physics (New York)
Appl Phys Part A — Applied Physics. Part A. Solids and Surfaces
Appl Phys Part B — Applied Physics. Part B. Photophysics and Laser Chemistry
Appl Phys Q — Applied Physics Quarterly
Appl Phys Sci Food Res Process Preserv Proc Conf — Application of Physical Sciences to Food Research, Processing, Preservation. Proceedings. Conference
Appl Plant Sci Toegepaste Plantwetenskap — Applied Plant Science/Toegepaste Plantwetenskap
Appl Plasma Source Mass Spectrom Sel Pap Int Conf — Application of Plasma Source Mass Spectrometry. Selected Papers. International Conference on Plasma Source Mass Spectrometry
Appl Plast — Applied Plastics
Appl Plast Reinf Plast Rev — Applied Plastics and Reinforced Plastics Review
Appl Polym Concr — Applications of Polymer Concrete
Appl Polym Emulsions — Applications of Polymer Emulsions
Appl Polym Proc Am Chem Soc Symp O A Battista Appl Polym Sci — Applications of Polymers. Proceedings. American Chemical Society Symposium Honoring O.A. Battista on Applied Polymer Science
Appl Polym Sci — Applied Polymer Science [*monograph*]
Appl Polym Spectrosc — Applications of Polymer Spectroscopy [*monograph*]
Appl Polym Symp — Applied Polymer Symposia
Appl Probab Index — Applied Probability. Complete Author and Subject Index. Journal of Applied Probability and Advances in Applied Probability
Appl Probab Ser Appl Probab Trust — Applied Probability. Series of the Applied Probability Trust
Appl Protein Chem — Applied Protein Chemistry
Appl Psych Monogr — Applied Psychology Monographs
Appl Psycholinguist — Applied Psycholinguistics
Appl Psychol Meas — Applied Psychological Measurement
Appl Radiat Isot — Applied Radiation and Isotopes
Appl Radio Freq Power Plasmas Top Conf — Applications of Radio-Frequency Power to Plasmas. Topical Conference
Appl Radiol — Applied Radiology
Appl Radiol Nucl Med — Applied Radiology and Nuclear Medicine [*Later, Applied Radiology*]
Appl Res Ment Retard — Applied Research in Mental Retardation
Appl Res Pract Munic Ind Waste — Applied Research and Practice on Municipal and Industrial Waste
Appl Res Tech Rep Beckman Instrum Inc — Applications Research Technical Report. Beckman Instruments, Inc.
Appl Retention Refin Technol Proc Midwest Reg Conf — Application of Retention and Refining Technology. Proceedings. Midwest Regional Conference
Appl Rheol — Applied Rheology
Appl Sci Cast Met — Applied Science in the Casting of Metals
Appl Sci Dev — Applied Sciences and Development
Appl Sci Med Sport Pap Annu Meet Can Assoc Sports Sci — Application of Science and Medicine to Sport. Papers Presented. Annual Meeting.Canadian Association of Sports Sciences
Appl Sci Re — Applied Scientific Research
Appl Sci Res — Applied Scientific Research
Appl Sci Res Corp Thailand Misc Invest — Applied Scientific Research Corporation of Thailand. Miscellaneous Investigation
Appl Sci Res Corp Thail Annu Rep — Applied Scientific Research Corporation of Thailand. Annual Report
Appl Sci Res Sect A — Applied Scientific Research. Section A. Mechanics, Heat, Chemical Engineering, Mathematical Methods
Appl Sci Res Sect B — Applied Scientific Research. Section B. Electrophysics, Acoustics, Optics, Mathematical Methods
Appl Sci Res (The Hague) — Applied Scientific Research (The Hague)
Appl Sci Technol Index — Applied Science and Technology Index
Appl Soil Trace Elem — Applied Soil Trace Elements [*monograph*]
Appl Solar Energy (Engl Transl) — Applied Solar Energy (English Translation)
Appl Sol Energ Proc Southeast Conf 1st — Application of Solar Energy. Proceedings of the Southeastern Conference on Application of Solar Energy. 1st
Appl Sol Energy — Applied Solar Energy
Appl Solid State Sci — Applied Solid State Science
Appl Solid State Sci Suppl — Applied Solid State Science. Supplement
Appl Spect — Applied Spectroscopy

Appl Spectr — Applied Spectroscopy
Appl Spectrosc — Applied Spectroscopy
Appl Spectrosc Rev — Applied Spectroscopy Reviews
Appl Spectry — Applied Spectroscopy
Appl Sp Rev — Applied Spectroscopy Reviews
Appl Stat — Applied Statistics
Appl Stat Field Theory Methods Condens Matter — Applications of Statistical and Field Theory Methods in Condensed Matter
Appl Stats — Applied Statistics
Appl Stochastic Models Data Anal — Applied Stochastic Models and Data Analysis
Appl Supercond — Applied Superconductivity
Appl Supercond Conf — Applied Superconductivity Conference
Appl Surf Chem Tainan Taiwan — Applied Surface Chemistry (Tainan, Taiwan)
Appl Surf Sci — Applications of Surface Science
Appl Synchrotron Radiat — Applications of Synchrotron Radiation
Appl Theor Electrophor — Applied and Theoretical Electrophoresis
Appl Ther — Applied Therapeutics
Appl Ther Drug Monit — Applied Therapeutic Drug Monitoring [*monograph*]
Appl Therm Eng — Applied Thermal Engineering. Design, Processes, Equipment, Economics
Appl Thermodyn Metall Processes Short Course — Applications of Thermodynamics to Metallurgical Processes. [A] Short Course.
Appl Thin Film Multilayered Struct Figured X Ray Opt — Applications of Thin-Film Multilayered Structures to Figured X-Ray Optics
Appl Toxicol Pet Hydrocarbons — Applied Toxicology of Petroleum Hydrocarbons
Appl Tumor Immunol Proc Int Symp — Applied Tumor Immunology. Proceedings. International Symposium
Appl UV Spectrosc — Applied UV Spectroscopy
Appl X Ray Topogr Methods Mater Sci Proc Fr USA Semin — Applications of X-Ray Topographic Methods to Materials Science. Proceedings. France-USA Seminar
App Math & Mech — Applied Mathematics and Mechanics
App Math Ser — Applied Mathematics Series
App Metody Rentgenovskogo Anal — Apparatura i Metody Rentgenovskogo Analiza
App Microbiol — Applied Microbiology [*Later, Applied and Environmental Microbiology*]
App Op — Applied Optics
App Opt — Applied Optics
App Optics — Applied Optics
Apports Sci Dev Ind Text Conf Conjointe — Apports de la Science au Developpement de l'Industrie Textile. Conference Conjointe
APPP — Abhandlungen zur Philosophie, Psychologie, und Paedagogik
App Phys — Applied Physics
Appraisal Halogenated Fire Extinguishing Agents Proc Symp — Appraisal of Halogenated Fire Extinguishing Agents. Proceedings. Symposium
Appraisal J — Appraisal Journal
Appraisal Jrnl — Appraisal Journal
Apprent Social — Apprentissage et Socialisation
App Ret — Appliance Retailing
Appretur Ztg — Appretur Zeitung
App Rev J — Appraisal Review Journal
Approach Dis Immunol Hematol Cancer Proc Fukuoka Int Symp Med Sci — Approach to Diseases. Immunology, Hematology, Cancer. Proceedings of the Fukuoka International Symposium on Medical Science
Approaches Automot Emiss Control Symp — Approaches to Automotive Emissions Control. Symposium
Approaches Cell Biol Neurons — Approaches to the Cell Biology of Neurons
Approaches Genet Anal Mamm Cells Mich Conf Genet — Approaches to the Genetic Analysis of Mammalian Cells. Michigan Conference on Genetics
Approaches Plann Des Health Care Facil Dev Areas — Approaches to Planning and Design of Health Care Facilities in Developing Areas
Approaches Pract Solutions — Approaches to Practical Solutions
Approach Phys Sci Summer Sch — Approach to Physical Sciences. Summer School. University of New South Wales
Appropriate Technol — Appropriate Technology
Approp Technol — Appropriate Technology
Approx Optim — Approximation and Optimization
Approx Theory Appl — Approximation Theory and its Applications
App Rx Dr Prod — Approved Rx Drug Products
APPSDZ — Applied Psycholinguistics
App World — Apparel World
APPYA — Annual Review of Phytopathology
APPYAG — Annual Review of Phytopathology
APQ — American Philosophical Quarterly
APQ — Asian Pacific Quarterly of Cultural and Social Affairs
APQAAH — Arquivos. Instituto de Pesquisas Agronomicas
APQPA — Acta Psiquiatrica y Psicologica de America Latina
APR — Algemene Practische Rechtverzameling
APR — American Poetry Review
APr — Analecta Praemonstratensia
APr — Annee Propedeutique
APR — Asoma (Puerto Rico)
APR — Atlantic Province Reports
APR — Atlantic Provinces Reports
APR — Australasian Photo Review
A Praehist — Ars Praehistorica
APraem — Analecta Praemonstratensia
APRAJ — Australasian Performing Right Association. Journal
APR Allg Pap Rundsch — APR. Allgemeine Papier-Rundschau
A Pregl — Arheoloski Pregled Arheolosko Drustvo Jugoslavije
A Press — Art Press
APrF — Altpreussische Forschungen

APRG S Afr CSIR — APRG [*Air Pollution Research Group*] (South Africa. Council for Scientificand Industrial Research)
APRKAI — Archiv fuer Protistenkunde
APrM — Altpreussische Monatsschrift
A Prob — Adult Probation
APRO Bull — APRO [*Aerial Phenomena Research Organization*] Bulletin
A Proc Ass Tech Socs S Afr — Annual Proceedings. Associated and Technical Societies of South Africa
A Proc Electron Microsc Soc Am — Annual Proceedings. Electron Microscopy Society of America
A Proc Gifu Coll Pharm — Annual Proceedings. Gifu College of Pharmacy
A Proc Inst Aust Foundrymen — Annual Proceedings. Institute of Australian Foundrymen
A Prod — Archives de Saint Jean-Prodrome sur le Mont Menecee
A Prot — Actes du Protaton
APRSCA — Annual Progress Report. SEATO [*Southeast Asia Treaty Organization*] Medical Research Laboratories
APRSEC — Advances in Plastic and Reconstructive Surgery
APRV — Algemene Practische Rechtverzameling
APS — Acta Philologica Scandinavica
APS — Acta Psychologica Sinica
APS — American Philosophical Society. Proceedings
APs — American Psychologist
APS — Anatolische Personennamensippen
A Ps — Annalen der Physik. Drude
APS — Annals. American Academy of Political and Social Science
APSACT — Annual of Psychoanalysis
APSA/R — American Political Science Review. American Political Science Association
APSBAU — Archives Portugaises des Sciences Biologigues
A Ps C — Annalen der Physik und Chemie. Poggendorff, Wiedemann
APSCA — Acta Physiologica Scandinavica
A Ps C Beibl — Beiblaetter zu den Annalen
APSCD2 — Acta Pathologica et Microbiologica Scandinavica. Section C. Immunology
APSE — Alternatives. Perspectives on Society and Environment
APSHA — Annales de Pediatrie
APSHDH — American Journal of Pharmacy and the Sciences Supporting Public Health [*Later,American Journal of Pharmacy*]
APSID — Advances in Polymer Science
APS Int Symp Dig — AP-S International Symposium (Digest) (IEEE Antennas and Propagation Society)
APSL — Amsterdamer Publikationen zur Sprache und Literatur
APSOA — Acta Psychologica (Amsterdam)
APS/P — Proceedings. American Philosophical Society
APSPA4 — Applied Spectroscopy
APSR — American Political Science Review
APSRDD — Advances in Pollen-Spore Research
APSS — American Academy of Political and Social Science. Annals
APSTA — Applied Statistics
APSTCI — Acta Psychologica Taiwanica
APSVC — Acta Physica Slovaca
APSXAS — Acta Pharmaceutica Suecica
A Psy — American Psychologist
APSYB — American Philosophical Society Year Book
APsyc — Archiv fuer die Gesamte Psychologie
APsych — Acta Psychologica
APT — Acta Psychologica Taiwanica
Aptechn Delo — Aptechnoe Delo
APTEDD — Acta Pharmaceutica Technologica
APTGAG — Anales. Catedra de Patologia y Clinica de la Tuberculosis. Universidad de Buenos Aires
APTHDM — Applied Pathology
APTIC — Air Pollution Technical Information Center File
APTKAS — Archiv fuer Physikalische Therapie
APTOA6 — Acta Pharmacologica et Toxicologica
APTPED — Advances in Psychoanalysis Theory, Research, and Practice
APTRDI — Advances in Prostaglandin and Thromboxane Research
APTSAI — Acta Pharmacologica et Toxicologica. Supplementum
APTUA — Archives. Institut Pasteur de Tunis
APTVAR — Anales. Instituto Nacional de Investigaciones Agrarias. Serie Proteccion Vegetal
APUA — Anthropological Papers. University of Alaska
A Pubbl Istr — Annali della Pubblica Istruzione
APUL — Aus der Papyrussammlung der Universitaetsbibliothek in Lund
Apulum — Apulum. Acta Musei Apulensis
APUM — Anthropological Publications of the University Museum [*Philadelphia*]
Apuntes Forest Trop — Apuntes Forestales Tropicales. Instituto de Dasonomia Tropical
APURAK — Archivos de Pediatria del Uruguay
APV — A Povoa de Varzim
APVBAB — Annales de Physiologie Vegetale. Universite de Bruxelles
APVGAQ — Annales de Physiologie Vegetale
APW — American Perspective (Washington, DC)
APWA Am Public Works Assoc Yearb — APWA (American Public Works Association) Yearbook
APY — Australian Pay-Roll Tax Manual
APYMAP — American Phytopathological Society. Monograph
APYSA9 — Acta Psychiatrica Scandinavica
APYTA — Acta Psychotherapeutica et Psychosomatica
ApZg — Apothekerzeitung
AQ — Africa Quarterly
AQ — Amazing Stories. Quarterly
AQ — American Quarterly
AQ — Anthropological Quarterly

AQ — Arizona Quarterly
AQ — Art Quarterly
AQ — Asian Quarterly
AQ — Asiatic Quarterly
AQ — Atlantic Quarterly
AQ — Australian Quarterly
AQARD — Acqua Aria
AQBOAP — Arquivos Brasileiros de Oftalmologia
AQBODS — Aquatic Botany
AQBPA — Arquivos Brasileiros de Psicotecnica
A Q C — Analytical and Quantitative Cytology
AQCHED — Analytical and Quantitative Cytology and Histology
AQCLAL — Aquaculture
AQCYDT — Analytical and Quantitative Cytology
AQ [Detroit] — Art Quarterly [Detroit]
AQEIC Bol Tec — AQEIC (Asociacion Quimica Espanola de la Industria del Cuero) Boletin Tecnico
AQFEDI — Aqua Fennica
AQIND — Aquatic Insects
AQINDQ — Aquatic Insects
AQJOAV — Aquarium Journal
AQ [London] — Art Quarterly [London]
AQMAA4 — Aquarien Magazin
AQMAD7 — Aquatic Mammals
AQMPAF — Arquivos. Museu Paranaense
AQPTA — Arquivos de Patologia
AQR — Asiatic Quarterly Review
AQRMAV — Aquarium
AQSBD6 — Anales de Quimica. Serie C. Quimica Organica y Bioquimica
AQSZ — Aquilo Serie Zoologica
AQTEAH — Aqua Terra
AQTEBI — Aquarien Terrarien
AQTOD — Aquatic Toxicology
AQTSA — Arquivos de Tisiologia
Aqua Biol Ab — Aquatic Biology Abstracts
Aquacult Dep Southeast Asian Fish Dev Cent Q Res Rep — Aquaculture Department. Southeast Asian Fisheries Development Center. QuarterlyResearch Report
Aquacult Eng — Aquaculture Engineering
Aquacult Fish Manage — Aquaculture and Fisheries Management
Aquacult Hung — Aquacultura Hungarica
Aquacult Nutr — Aquaculture Nutrition
Aquaculture Mag — Aquaculture Magazine
Aqua Fenn — Aqua Fennica
Aqualine Abstr — Aqualine Abstracts
Aquarien Mag — Aquarien Magazin
Aquarien Terrar Z — Aquarien- und Terrarien-Zeitschrift
Aquarium J — Aquarium Journal
Aquarium Sci Conserv — Aquarium Sciences and Conservation
Aquarium Syst — Aquarium Systems
Aquar J — Aquarium Journal
Aquar News Brooklyn — Aquarium News (Brooklyn)
Aquar Newslett — Aquarium Newsletter
Aquar Rev — Aquarium Review. British Aquarists' Association
A Quart — Australian Quarterly
Aqua Sci & Fish Abstr — Aquatic Sciences and Fisheries Abstracts
Aqua Sci Tech Rev — Aqua Scientific and Technical Review
Aquat Bot — Aquatic Botany
Aquat Ecol — Aquatic Ecology
Aquat Ecol Chem — Aquatic Ecological Chemistry
Aquat Geochem — Aquatic Geochemistry
Aquat Insec — Aquatic Insects
Aquat Insects — Aquatic Insects
Aquat Mamm — Aquatic Mammals
Aquat Microbiol — Aquatic Microbiology
Aquat Microbiol Ecol Proc — Aquatic Microbial Ecology. Proceedings of the Conference
Aquat Oligochaete Biol Proc Int Symp — Aquatic Oligochaete Biology. Proceedings. International Symposium
Aquat Pollut Transform Biol Eff Proc Int Symp — Aquatic Pollutants. Transformation and Biological Effects. Proceedings. International Symposium on Aquatic Pollutants
Aquat Sci — Aquatic Sciences
Aquat Sci Fish Abst Part I — Aquatic Sciences and Fisheries Abstracts. Part I. Biological Sciencesand Living Resources
Aquat Sci Fish Abst Part II — Aquatic Sciences and Fisheries Abstracts. Part II. Ocean Technology,Policy, and Non-Living Resources
Aquat Toxicol — Aquatic Toxicology
Aquat Toxicol (Amst) — Aquatic Toxicology (Amsterdam)
Aquat Toxicol Environ Fate 9th Vol Symp — Aquatic Toxicology and Environmental Fate. 9th Volume. Symposium
Aquat Toxicol Hazard Assess Proc Annu Symp Aquat Toxicol — Aquatic Toxicology and Hazard Assessment. Proceedings. Annual Symposium on Aquatic Toxicology
Aquat Toxicol Hazard Eval Proc Annu Symp Aquat Toxicol — Aquatic Toxicology and Hazard Evaluation. Proceedings. Annual Symposium on Aquatic Toxicology
Aquat Toxicol (NY) — Aquatic Toxicology (New York)
A Quatuor Coronatorum — Ars Quatuor Coronatorum
Aquat Weed Control Soc Proc — Aquatic Weed Control Society. Proceedings
Aquat Weeds South East Asia Proc Reg Semin Noxious Aquat Veg — Aquatic Weeds in South East Asia. Proceedings of a Regional Seminar on Noxious Aquatic Vegetation

Aqueous Biphasic Sep Proc Am Chem Soc Symp — Aqueous Biphasic Separations. Biomolecules to Metal Ions. Proceedings of an American Chemical Society Symposium on Aqueous Biphasic Separations
Aqueous Environ Chem Met — Aqueous-Environmental Chemistry of Metals
Aqueous Polym Coat Pharm Dosage Forms — Aqueous Polymeric Coatings for Pharmaceutical Dosage Forms
Aqueous Powder Coat Powder Electropaints — Aqueous Powder Coatings and Powder Electropaints
Aqueous Reprocess Chem Irradiat Fuels Symp — Aqueous Reprocessing Chemistry for Irradiated Fuels. Symposium
Aqui Ahora Juv — Aqui y Ahora la Juventud
Aquifer Restor Ground Water Rehab — Aquifer Restoration and Ground Water Rehabilitation
Aquil Nost — Aquileia Nostra
Aquil Ser Bot — Aquilo Serie Botanica
Aquilo Ser Zool — Aquilo Serie Zoologica
Aqui N — Aquileia Nostra. Bollettino. Associazione Nazionale per Aquileia
A Quin — Arte Quincenal
AQUIRE — Aquatic Information Retrieval
Aqu Law J — Aquinas Law Journal
AQW — Anthropological Quarterly (Washington, D.C.)
AR — A and R. Analysis and Research
AR — Accao Regional
AR — Accounting Review
AR — Africa Report
AR — Alabama Review
AR — Alberta Reports
AR — Alliance Review
AR — American Recorder
AR — American Record Guide
AR — American Review [Formerly, New American Review]
AR — Anthropological Review
AR — Antioch Review
AR — Antiquitaeten-Rundschau
AR — Antiviral Research
AR — Arbor
Ar — Archaeologia
AR — Archaeological Reports
AR — Archaeological Review
Ar — Arche
Ar — Archeologia
Ar — Archeologie. Centre National de Recherches Archeologiques en Belgique
AR — Archeologike Rozhledy
AR — Architectural Review
Ar — Archive
AR — Archiv fuer Reformationsgeschichte
Ar — Archivio
AR — Archivum Romanicum
AR — Areito
Ar — Arena
AR — Arizona Review
AR — Asian Review
AR — Asiatic Review
AR — Atene e Roma
AR — Industrial Arbitration Reports
ARA — Ancient Records of Assyria and Babylonia
ARA — ARAMCO [Arabian American Oil Company] World Magazine
ARA — Araucaria
ArA — Archaeologia Aeliana
ArA — Arts Asiatiques
ARA — PTS [Predicasts] Annual Reports Abstracts
ARAA — Annual Review of Astronomy and Astrophysics
Ar A A — Arbeiten aus Anglistik und Amerikanistik
ARAA — Archivio per l'Alto Adige
ARAAA — Annual Review of Astronomy and Astrophysics
ARAAS — Annual Reports on Analytical Atomic Spectroscopy [Later, JAAS]
ArAAS — Artibus Asiae (Ascona, Switzerland)
Arab — Arabica Revue de Etudes Arabes
ARABAn — Academie Royale d'Archeologie de Belgique. Annales
Arab Archaeol & Epig — Arabian Archaeology and Epigraphy
ARABBull — Academie Royale d'Archeologie de Belgique. Bulletin
Arab Com Cent N — Arab Community Centre News
Arab Com Law Rev — Arab Commercial Law Review
Arab Enrgy — Arab Energy. Prospects to 2000
Arab F & TV — Arab Film and Television Center News
Arab Gulf J — Arab Gulf Journal
Arab Gulf J Sci Res — Arab Gulf Journal of Scientific Research
Arab Gulf J Sci Res A Math Phys Sci — Arab Gulf Journal of Scientific Research. A. Mathematical and Physical Sciences
Arabian J Sci and Eng — Arabian Journal for Science and Engineering
Arabian J Sci Eng — Arabian Journal for Science and Engineering
Arabian J Sci Engrg — Arabian Journal for Science and Engineering
Arabian J Sci Eng Sect A — Arabian Journal for Science and Engineering. Section A. Sciences
Arabian J Sci Eng Sect B — Arabian Journal for Science and Engineering. Section B. Engineering
Arabic Sci Philos — Arabic Sciences and Philosophy
Arabidopsis Inf Serv — Arabidopsis Information Service
Arab Int Lubr Oil Ind Arab Lubr Oils Semin — Arab and International Lubricating Oil Industry. Arab Lubricating Oils Seminar
Arab J Math — [The] Arab Journal of Mathematics
Arab J Math Sci — Arab Journal of Mathematical Sciences
Arab J Nucl Sci Appl — Arab Journal of Nuclear Sciences and Applications
Arab Metall News — Arab Metallurgical News
Arab Min J — Arab Mining Journal

Arab Pet Congr Collect Pap — Arab Petroleum Congress. Collection of Papers
Arab Press Bull — Arab Press Bulletin
Arab Reg Conf Sulphur Its Usages Arab World — Arab Regional Conference on Sulphur and Its Usages in the Arab World
Arab Sci Congr Pap — Arab Science Congress. Papers
Arab Stud — Arabian Studies
Arab Studies Q — Arab Studies Quarterly
Arab Stud Quart — Arab Studies Quarterly
Arab Trans — Arabian Transport
Arab Vet Med Assoc J — Arab Veterinary Medical Association. Journal
ArabW — Arab World
ARAC — Art and Architecture
ARac — Autour de Racine
ARACC — Archives of Acoustics
Arachidonic Acid Metab Nerv Syst — Arachidonic Acid Metabolism in the Nervous System. Physiological and Pathological Significance
Arachidonic Acid Metab Tumor Initiation — Arachidonic Acid Metabolism and Tumor Initiation [*monograph*]
Arachidonic Acid Metab Tumor Promot — Arachidonic Acid Metabolism and Tumor Promotion
Arachn Entomol Lek — Arachno Entomologia Lekarska
ARADAS — Annual Report. Center for Adult Diseases
ARADI — Annual Report. Archaeological Department of India
A Rad Raspr — Arheoloski Radovi i Rasprave
ARAFAY — Anales. Real Academia de Farmacia
ARAI — Annuario. Reale Accademia d'Italia
ARAL — Annual Review of Applied Linguistics
ARAL — Atti della Reale Accademia del Lincei, Memorie, Classe di Scienze Morali, Storiche e Filologiche
ARALNS — Atti. Reale Accademia dei Lincei. Notizie degli Scavi
ArAm — Art in America
ARAMCO W — ARAMCO [*Arabian American Oil Company*] World Magazine
ARAMCO World M — ARAMCO [*Arabian American Oil Company*] World Magazine
ARAMIS — Agencement en Rames Automatisees de Modules Independants dans les Stations
ARAMIS — American Rheumatism Association Medical Information System
ARANA — Anales. Real Academia Nacional de Medicina
ARANAO — Anales. Real Academia Nacional de Medicina
ARANBP — Arctic Anthropology
ARANDR — Archives of Andrology
Araneta J Agric — Araneta Journal of Agriculture
Araneta Res J — Araneta Research Journal
ARANS — Atti. Reale Accademia dei Lincei. Notizie degli Scavi
ARAOAR — Agronomia Angolana
ArAP — Arts Asiatiques. Annales du Musee Guimet et du Musee Cernuschi (Paris)
ARAPCW — Annual Review of Anthropology
ARAR — Algemeen Rijksambtenaren Reglement
ARAR — Arctic and Alpine Research
Ar As — Arts Asiatiques
ARASA5 — Acta Radiologica. Supplementum
ARASC7 — Annual Reports on Analytical Atomic Spectroscopy
ARAST — Atti. Reale Accademia delle Scienze di Torino
Ar Au — Archaeologie Austriaca
Araucariana Ser Bot — Araucariana. Serie Botanica
Araucariana Ser Geocienc — Araucariana. Serie Geociencias
Araucariana Ser Zool — Araucariana. Serie Zoologia
AR Austrl — Industrial Arbitration Reports, New South Wales (Australia)
ARAWDK — Abhandlungen. Rheinisch-Westfaelische Akademie der Wissenschaften
ARB — Academie Royale de Belgique. Bulletin. Classe des Lettres et des Sciences Morales et Politiques
ARB — Africana Research Bulletin
Arb — Arbeidsblad
ARB — Arbitration Journal
ARB — Arbitron Radio Summary Data
Arb — Arbor
Arb — Arbor Ciencia, Pensamiento y Cultura
ARB — Armenian Review (Boston)
ARB — Asiatic Research Bulletin
ARB — Australian Ranger Bulletin
ARB — Periodieke Verzameling van Administratieve en Rechterlijke BeslissingenBetreffende het Openbaar Bestuur in Nederland met Register Volgens Kaartsys
ARBA — American Reference Books Annual
ARBA — Anais da Reuniao Brasileira de Antropologia
ARBAE — Annual Report of the Bureau of American Ethnology
Arb Allruss Inst Exp Med — Arbeiten des Allrussischen Instituts fuer Experimentelle Medizin
Arb Allruss Inst Zells Papierkd — Arbeiten des Allrussischen Instituts fuer Zellstoff- und Papierkunde
Arb Allruss Mendelejew Kongr Theor Angew Chem — Arbeiten des Allrussischen Mendelejew-Kongresses fuer Theoretische und Angewandte Chemie
Arb Allruss Zent Wiss Fett Forschungsinst — Arbeiten des Allrussischen Zentralen Wissenschaftlichen Fett-Forschungsinstituts
Arb Anat Inst — Arbeiten. Anatomisches Institut
Arb Anat Inst Kais Jpn Univ Sendai — Arbeiten. Anatomisches Institut. Kaiserlich Japanischen Universitaet zu Sendai
Arb Arb Hist — Arbog for Arbejderbevaegelsens Historie
Arb Archang Wiss Forschungsinst Algen — Arbeiten des Archangelsk'schen Wissenschaftlichen Forschungsinstitut fuer Algen
ARBBCL — Academie Royale de Belgique. Bulletin. Classe des Lettres et des Sciences Morales et Politiques
Arb Ber Sueddtsch Ver Forschungsanst Milchwirtsch — Arbeiten und Berichte. Sueddeutsche Versuchs- und Forschungsanstalt fuer Milchwirtschaft

Arb Biol Meeresstation Schwarzen Meer Varna — Arbeiten aus der Biologischen Meeresstation am Schwarzen Meer in Varna
Arb Biol Meeresstation Stalin — Arbeiten aus der Biologischen Meeresstation in Stalin
Arb Biol Reichanst Land Forstw (Berlin) — Arbeiten. Biologischen Reichsanstalt fuer Land- und Forstwirtschaft (Berlin)
Arb Biol Reichsanst — Arbeiten aus der Biologischen Reichsanstalt
Arb Biol Reichsanst Land Forstwirtsch Berlin Dahlem — Arbeiten aus der Biologischen Reichsanstalt fuer Land- und Forstwirtschaft. Berlin-Dahlem
Arb Bl Rest — Arbeitsblaetter fuer Restauratoren
Arb Bot Inst Wurz — Arbeiten. Botanischen Instituts in Wurzburg
ARBBull — Academie Royale de Belgique. Bulletin. Classe des Lettres et des Sciences Morales et Politiques et Classe des Beaux-Arts
ARBCEY — Annual Review of Biophysics and Biophysical Chemistry
ARBDD — Arbeidervern
Arb Deut Landwirt Ges — Arbeiten. Deutsche Landwirtschafts-Gesellschaft
Arb DPT — Arbog for Det Danske Post- og Telegrafvaesen
Arb Dritten Abt Anat Inst Kais Univ Kyoto Ser A — Arbeiten. Dritte Abteilung des Anatomischen Institutes der Kaiserlichen Universitaet Kyoto. Serie A. Untersuchungen ueber das Periphere Nervensystem
Arb Dritten Abt Anat Inst Kais Univ Kyoto Ser C — Arbeiten. Dritte Abteilung des Anatomischen Institutes der Kaiserlichen Universitaet Kyoto. Serie C. Experimentelle Tuberkuloseforschung
Arb Dritten Abt Anat Inst Kais Univ Kyoto Ser D — Arbeiten. Dritte Abteilung des Anatomischen Institutes der Kaiserlichen Universitaet Kyoto. Serie D. Lymphatologie
Arb D Skol — Arbog for Dansk Skolehistorie
Arb Dtsch Landwirtsch Ges Berlin — Arbeiten der Deutschen Landwirtschafts-Gesellschaft. Berlin
ArBegriffsg — Archiv fuer Begriffsgeschichte
Arbeitbl Restauratoren — Arbeitsblaetter fuer Restauratoren
Arbeiten Angew Statist — Arbeiten zur Angewandten Statistik
Arbeiten Bot Inst Wuerzburg — Arbeiten des Botanischen Instituts in Wuerzburg
Arbeiten Deutsch Landw Ges — Arbeiten der Deutschen Landwirtschafts-Gesellschaft
Arbeiten Exp Biol — Arbeiten aus dem Gebiet der Experimentellen Biologie
Arbeiten Inst Allg Bot Univ Zuerich — Arbeiten aus dem Institut fuer Allgemeine Botanik der Universitaet Zuerich
Arbeiten Inst Palaeobot — Arbeiten aus dem Institut fuer Palaeobotanik und Petrographie der Brennsteine
Arbeiten Koenigl Bot Gart Breslau — Arbeiten aus dem Koeniglichen Botanischen Garten zu Breslau
Arbeiten Niedersaechs Staats- u Universitaetsbibl — Arbeiten aus der Niedersaechsischen Staats- und Universitaetsbibliothek
Arbeiten Vereinigten Ges Oberlausitz — Arbeiten einer Vereinigten Gesellschaft in der Oberlausitz zu den Geschichten und der Gelahrtheit Ueberhaupt Gehoerende
Arbeit Illus Ztg — Arbeiter Illustrierte Zeitung
Arbeitneh Aus — Arbeitnehmerverdienste im Ausland
Arbeitsber Inst Math Masch Datenverarb Band 14 — Arbeitsberichte. Instituts fuer Mathematische Maschinen und Datenverarbeitung. Band 14
Arbeitsber Inst Math Masch Datenverarb Band 15 — Arbeitsberichte. Instituts fuer Mathematische Maschinen und Datenverarbeitung. Band 15
Arbeitsber Inst Math Masch Datenverarb Inform — Arbeitsberichte des Instituts fuer Mathematische Maschinen und Datenverarbeitung (Informatik)
Arbeitsber Oekol Umwelttech — Arbeitsberichte Oekologie/Umwelttechnik
Arbeitsber Psych Methoden — Arbeitsberichte Psychologische Methoden
Arbeitsber Rechenzentrum — Arbeitsberichte des Rechenzentrums
Arbeitsbl Restauraturen — Arbeitsblaetter fuer Restauratoren
Arbeitsgem-Forsch Landes Nordrh-Westfalen — Arbeitsgemeinschaft fuer Forschung des Landes Nordrhein-Westfalen
Arbeitsgem Getreideforsch Veroeff — Arbeitsgemeinschaft Getreideforschung. Veroeffentlichungen
Arbeitsgem Kartoffelforsch Veroeff — Arbeitsgemeinschaft Kartoffelforschung. Veroeffentlichungen
Arbeitsgem Pharm Verfahrenstech Paperback APV — Arbeitsgemeinschaft fuer Pharmazeutische Verfahrenstechnik. Paperback APV
Arbeitsgem Rheinwasserwerke Ber — Arbeitsgemeinschaft Rheinwasserwerke. Bericht
Arbeitsgem Verstaerkte Kunstst Oeff Jahrestag Vorabdruck — Arbeitsgemeinschaft Verstaerkte Kunststoffe. Oeffentliche Jahrestagung. Vorabdruck
Arbeitsmed Kolloq Ber Jahrestag Dtsh Ges Arbeitsmed — Arbeitsmedizinisches Kolloquium Bericht ueber die Jahrestagung der Deutschen Gesellschaft fuer Arbeitsmedizin
Arbeitsmed Probl Dienstleistungsgewerbes — Arbeitsmedizinische Probleme des Dienstleistungsgewerbes
Arbeitsmed Sozialmed Arbeitshyg — Arbeitsmedizin, Sozialmedizin, Arbeitshygiene [*Later, Arbeitsmedizin, Sozialmedizin, Praeventivmedizin*]
Arbeitsmed Sozialmed Praeventivmed — Arbeitsmedizin, Sozialmedizin, Praeventivmedizin
Arbeitspapiere Pol Soziol — Arbeitspapiere zur Politischen Soziologie
Arbeitsschutz Anwend Chem Technol — Arbeitsschutz bei der Anwendung Chemischer Technologien
Arbeitstag Exp Klin Hepatol — Arbeitstagung Experimentelle und Klinische Hepatologie
Arbeitstag Extraterr Biophys Biol Raumfahrtmed Tagungsber — Arbeitstagung ueber Extraterrestrische Biophysik und Biologie und Raumfahrtmedizin. Tagungsbericht
Arbeitstag Mengen Spurenelem — Arbeitstagung Mengen- und Spurenelemente
Arbeitstag Physiol Pathophysiol Prostata — Arbeitstagung ueber Physiologie und Pathophysiologie der Prostata
Arbeitstech Pharm Ind — Arbeitstechniken der Pharmazeutischen Industrie
Arbeits u Forschber Sachsen — Arbeits- und Forschungsberichte zur Saechsischen Bodenkmalpflege

Arbeit U Beruf — Arbeit und Beruf
Arbeit und Sozialpol — Arbeit und Sozialpolitik
Arbeit und Wirt — Arbeit und Wirtschaft
Arbeit U Recht — Arbeit und Recht
Arbeit Ztg — Arbeiter Zeitung
Arbejder Univ Bot Have — Arbejder. Universitet. Botanisk Have
Arbejdsmark (Kob) — Nationalmuseets Arbejdsmark (Kobenhavn)
Ar Berne — Archiv des Historischen Vereins des Kantons Bern
Arb F Ber Saechs — Arbeits- und Forschungsberichte zur Saechsischen Bodendenkmalpflege
Arb ForschBer Saechs BodDenkmPfl — Arbeits- und Forschungsberichte zur Saechsischen Bodendenkmalspflege. Landesmuseum fuer Vorgeschichte mit Archaeologischem Landesamt
Arb Futterbau — Arbeiten aus dem Gebiete des Futterbaues
Arbg — Arbejdsgiveren
ARBGB9 — Acta Radiobotanica et Genetica
Arb Gebiete Futterbaues — Arbeiten aus dem Gebiete des Futterbaues
Arb Gelehrten Ges Erforsch Weissruthen — Arbeiten der Gelehrten Gesellschaft zur Erforschung Weissrutheniens
Arb Geol Palaeontol Inst Univ Stuttgart — Arbeiten aus dem Geologisch-Palaeontologischen Institut der Universitaet Stuttgart
ArbGeschAntJudUrchr — Arbeiten zur Geschichte des Antiken Judentums und des Urchristentums
Arb Gesund — Arbeit und Gesundheit
Arb Gory Goretzkschen Gelehrten Ges — Arbeiten der Gory-Goretzkschen Gelehrten Gesellschaft
Arbh — Arbejderhojskolen
ARBIDH — Basel Institute for Immunology. Annual Report
ArbleTh — Arbeiten aus dem Institut fuer Experimentelle Therapie
Arb Inst Exp Therap — Arbeiten aus dem Institut fuer Experimentelle Therapie
Arb Inst Exp Ther Frankfurt am Main — Arbeiten aus dem Institut fuer Experimentelle Therapie zu Frankfurt am Main
Arb Inst Geol Palaeontol Univ Stuttgart — Arbeiten aus dem Institut fuer Geologie und Palaeontologie an der Universitaet Stuttgart
Arb Inst Gesch Med Univ Leipzig — Arbeiten des Instituts fuer Geschichte der Medizin an der Universitaet Leipzig
Arb Inst Reine Chem Reagenzien — Arbeiten des Institutes fuer Reine Chemische Reagenzien
Arbit J — Arbitration Journal
Arbitration J — Arbitration Journal
Arbitration Jrnl — Arbitration Journal
Arbitrat J — Arbitration Journal
Arbitr J — Arbitration Journal
Arb J — Arbitration Journal
ARBJAH — American Rabbit Journal
Arb J (NS) — Arbitration Journal (New Series)
Arb J of the Inst of Arbitrators — Arbitration Journal. Institute of Arbitrators
Arb J (OS) — Arbitration Journal (Old Series)
Arb Kais Biol Anst Land Forstwirtsch — Arbeiten der Kaiserlichen Biologischen Anstalt fuer Land und Forstwirtschaft
ARBKAK — Archiv fuer Bienenkunde
Arb Lab Unters Eiweiss Eiweissstoffwechsels Org — Arbeiten des Laboratoriums zur Untersuchung von Eiweiss und des Eiweissstoffwechsels im Organismus
ARBLAN — Arquivos de Biologia
Arb Leist — Arbeit und Leistung
Arb Leningr Inst Gewerbehyg Sicherheitstech — Arbeiten des Leningrader Instituts fuer Gewerbehygiene und Sicherheitstechnik
Arb Leningr Inst Gewerbehyg Unfallverhuet — Arbeiten des Leningrader Instituts fuer Gewerbehygiene und Unfallverhuetung
ARBMA — Arbok fuer Universitetet i Bergen. Matematisk-Naturvitenskapelig Serie
Arb Med Fak Okayama — Arbeiten aus der Medizinischen Fakultaet Okayama
Arb Med Univ Okayama — Arbeiten aus der Medizinischen Universitaet Okayama
Arbm F — Arbejdsmaendenes Fagblad
Arb Milchwirtsch Inst Wologda — Arbeiten des Milchwirtschaftlichen Instituts zu Wologda
ARBOA — Annual Review of Biochemistry
ARBOAW — Annual Review of Biochemistry
Arbog Dan Geol Unders — Arbog-Danmarks Geologiske Undersoegelse
Arbog Dan Skokehist — Arbog foer Dansk Skolehistorie
Arbok Norske Vidensk Akad Oslo — Arbok. Norske Videnskaps-Akademi i Oslo
Arbok Univ Bergen Mat-Natur Ser — Arbok fuer Universitetet i Bergen. Matematisk-Naturvitenskapelig Serie
Arbok Univ Bergen Mat-Naturvitensk Ser — Arbok fuer Universitetet i Bergen. Matematisk-Naturvitenskapelig Serie
Arbok Univ Bergen Med Ser — Arbok fuer Universitetet i Bergen. Medisinsk Serie
Arbok Univ Bergen Naturvitensk Rekke — Arbok Universitetet i Bergen. Naturvitenskapelig Rekke
Arbor Ass J — Arboricultural Association. Journal
Arbor Bull Arbor Found (Seattle) Univ Wash — Arboretum Bulletin. Arboretum Foundation (Seattle). University of Washington
Arbor Bull Assoc — Arboretum Bulletin. Associates. Morris Arboretum
Arbor Bull Assoc Morris Arbor — Arboretum Bulletin. Associates of the Morris Arboretum
Arboric Fruit — Arboriculture Fruitiere
Arboric J — Arboricultural Journal
Arboric Soc South Africa — Arboricultural Society of South Africa
Arboricult Fruit — Arboriculture Fruitiere
Arbor Kornickie — Arboretum Kornickie
Arbor Leaves — Arboretum Leaves
Arbor Scientiarum Beitraege Wissenschaftsgeschichte Reihe C — Arbor Scientiarum. Beitraege Wissenschaftsgeschichte. Reihe C. Bibliographien
Arbor Soc Bull — Arboretum Society Bulletin
Arbor Sun — Ann Arbor Sun

Arborviruses Mediterr Countries FEMS Symp — Arborviruses in the Mediterranean Countries. FEMS Symposium
Arb Ost Sib Staats Univ — Arbeiten der Ost-Sibirischen Staats-Universitaet
Arbovirus Res Aust Proc Symp — Arbovirus Research in Australia. Proceedings. Symposium
Arb Paul-Ehrlich-Inst — Arbeiten. Paul-Ehrlich-Institut
Arb Paul Ehrlich Inst Bundesamt Sera Impfst Langen — Arbeiten aus dem Paul-Ehrlich-Institut. Bundesamt fuer Sera und Impfstoffe. Langen
Arb Paul Ehrlich Inst Bundesamt Sera Impfstoffe Frankf AM — Arbeiten aus dem Paul-Ehrlich-Institut. Bundesamt fuer Sera und Impfstoffe zu Frankfurt am Main
Arb Paul Ehrlich Inst Georg Speyer Haus Ferdinand Blum Inst — Arbeiten. Paul-Ehrlich-Institut, Georg-Speyer-Haus, und Ferdinand-Blum-Institut
ARBPD4 — Annual Review of Behavior Therapy Theory and Practice
Arb Physiol Angew Entomol Berlin Dahlem — Arbeiten ueber Physiologische und Angewandte Entomologie aus Berlin Dahlem
Arb Pr A — Historisk Samfund for Praesto Amt. Arbog
ARBQA4 — Koninklijk Academie van Belgie. Jaarboek
ARBRA7 — Annual Review of Biochemical and Allied Research in India
Arb Reichsgesdhtsamt — Arbeiten aus dem Reichsgesundheitsamt
Arb Reinische Landeskunde — Arbeiten zur Reinischen Landeskunde
ARBRSI — Annual Report. Board of Regents of the Smithsonian Institution
ARBS — Annual Report. American Bible Society
Arb So A — Arbog for Historisk Samfund for Soro Amt
Arb Staatl Inst Exp Ther Georg Speyer Haus Frankfurt am Main — Arbeiten aus dem Staatlichen Institut fuer Experimentelle Therapie und dem Georg-Speyer-Haus zu Frankfurt am Main
Arb Staatl Wiss Forschungsinst Flugzeugwerkstoffe Moscow — Arbeiten des Staatlichen Wissenschaftlichen Forschungsinstituts fuer Flugzeugwerkstoffe. Moscow
Arb Staatsinst Exp Ther Georg Speyer Haus Frankfurt am Main — Arbeiten aus dem Staatsinstitut fuer Experimentelle Therapie und dem Georg-Speyer-Hans zu Frankfurt am Main
ArbT — Arbeiten zur Theologie
Arb Tech Hochsch Brno — Arbeiten der Technischen Hochschule in Brno
ARBTM — Arab Times
ARBU — Arctic Bulletin
Arb U B Mat — Arbok fuer Universitetet i Bergen. Matematisk-Naturvitenskapelig Serie
ARBUD — Arctic Bulletin
ARBUDJ — Arctic Bulletin
Arb Ung Biol Forschungsinst — Arbeiten des Ungarischen Biologischen Forschungsinstitutes
Arb Univ Hohenheim (Landwirtsch Hochsch) — Arbeiten. Universitaet Hohenheim (Landwirtschaftliche Hochschule)
ARBWAM — Annual Report of Biological Works. Faculty of Science. Osaka University
Arb Wiss Forsch Sekt Leningr Gouv Abt Arbeitsschutzes — Arbeiten der Wissenschaftlichen Forschungs-Sektion der Leningrader Gouvernements Abteilung des Arbeitsschutzes
Arb Wiss Samoilow Inst Duengem Insektofungic Moscow — Arbeiten des Wissenschaftlichen Samoilow-Institut fuer Duengemittel und Insektofungicide. Moscow
Arb W W Kujbyschews Staats Univ Tomsk — Arbeiten der W. W. Kujbyschews Staats Universitaet in Tomsk
Arb Zent Forschungsinst Zuckerind — Arbeiten des Zentralen Forschungsinstituts fuer Zuckerindustrie
Arb Zent Staatl Wiss Forschungsinst Nichteisenmet — Arbeiten des Zentralen Staatlichen Wissenschaftlichen Forschungsinstituts fuer Nichteisenmetalle
Arb z Roman Philol — Arbeiten zur Romanische Philologie
Arc — Arcadia
Arc — Arcadie
ARC — Architectural Review (Chearn, England)
Arc — Arctos. Acta Philologica Fennica
Arca — Arcadia
Arcad — Arcadia Zeitschrift fuer Vergleichende Literaturwissenschaft
ARCAEX — Archives of Research on Industrial Carcinogenesis
Arca Lovan — Arca Lovaniensis
Arcana Sci Art — Arcana of Science and Art
ARCBE2 — Annual Review of Cell Biology
ARCC — Arctic Circle
ARCCD4 — Australia. Commonwealth Scientific and Industrial Research Organisation. Division of Protein Chemistry. Annual Report
ArCCP — Arquivos. Centro Cultural Portugues
ARCE News — American Research Center in Egypt Newsletter
Arc Furn Meet Pap — Arc Furnace Meeting. Papers
ARCGDG — Archives of Gynecology
ARCH — Archaeologia
Arch — Archaeology
Arch — Architecture in Australia [*Later, Architecture Australia*]
Arch — Architekt
Arch — Archivio
ARCH — Archivist. Public Archives of Canada
Arch — Archivum
Arch A — Archaeologie Austriaca
Arch A Ad — Archivio per l'Alto Adige
Arch Acad Ecuat Med — Archivos. Academia Ecuatoriana de Medicina
Arch Acker-Pflanzenbau Bodenkd — Archiv fuer Acker- und Pflanzenbau und Bodenkunde
Arch Acoust — Archives of Acoustics
Archaean Geochem — Archaean Geochemistry
Arch Aeg Arch — Archiv fuer Aegyptische Archaeologie
Arch Ael — Archaeologia Aeliana
Arch Aeliana — Archaeologica Aeliana

Archaeoastron — Archaeoastronomy Supplement. Journal for the History of Astronomy

Archaeoastronomy Bull Cent Archaeoastron — Archaeoastronomy. Bulletin. Center for Archaeoastronomy

Archaeoastronomy J Cent Archaeoastron — Archaeoastronomy. Journal. Center for Archaeoastronomy

Archaeographie — Archaeographie. Archaeologie und Elektronische Datenverarbeitung

Archaeol — Archaeologia

Archaeol Aeliana — Archaeologia Aeliana

Archaeol Aeliana 5 Ser — Archaeologia Aeliana. Series 5

Archaeol Amer — Archaeologia Americana. Transactions and Collections of the American Antiquarian Society

Archaeol & It Soc — Archaeology and Italian Society

Archaeol Anz — Archaeologischer Anzeiger

Archaeol Austr — Archaeologia Austriaca

Archaeol Austriaca — Archaeologia Austriaca

Archaeol Belgica — Archaeologia Belgica

Archaeol Ber Yemen — Archaeologische Berichte aus dem Yemen

Archaeol Biblio — Archaeologische Bibliographie

Archaeol Brit — Archaeology in Britain

Archaeol Camb — Archaeologia Cambrensis

Archaeol Cambr — Archaeologia Cambrensis. Journal. Cambrian Archaeological Association

Archaeol Cambrensis — Archaeologia Cambrensis

Archaeol Cantiana — Archaeologia Cantiana

Archaeol Chem Symp — Archaeological Chemistry. [A] Symposium

Archaeol East N Amer — Archaeology of Eastern North America

Archaeol Epigr Mitt — Archaeologisch-Epigraphische Mitteilungen aus Oesterreich-Ungarn

Archaeol Ert — Archaeologiai Ertesito

Archaeol Geol — Archaeological Geology

Archaeol Hist — Archaeologia Historica

Archaeol Interreg — Archaeologia Interregionalis

Archaeol J — Archaeological Journal

Archaeol Jamaica — Archaeology Jamaica

Archaeol J (London) — Archaeological Journal (London)

Archaeol Korrbl — Archaeologisches Korrespondenzblatt

Archaeol Korrespbl — Archaeologisches Korrespondenzblatt

Archaeol Lund — Archaeologica Lundensia. Investigationes de Antiquitibus urbis Lundae

Archaeol Meth Theory — Archaeological Method and Theory

Archaeol Mitt Iran — Archaeologische Mitteilungen aus Iran

Archaeol News — Archaeological News

Archaeol Newsl R Ont Mus — Archaeological Newsletter. Royal Ontario Museum

Archaeol NZ — Archaeology in New Zealand

Archaeol Oceania — Archaeology in Oceania

Archaeologia [Soc Antiqua London] — Archaeologia [Society of Antiquaries of London]

Archaeological Jnl — Archaeological Journal

Archaeolog Zeitung — Archaeologische Zeitung

Archaeol Phy Anthrop Oceania — Archaeology and Physical Anthropology in Oceania [Later, Archaeology in Oceania]

Archaeol Phys Anthropol Oceania — Archaeology and Physical Anthropology in Oceania [Later, Archaeology in Oceania]

Archaeol Pol — Archaeologia Polona

Archaeol Polona — Archaeologia Polona

Archaeol Rep — Archaeological Reports

Archaeol Rep Council Soc Promotion Hell Stud & Managing Ctte — Archaeological Reports. Council of the Society for the Promotion of Hellenic Studies and the Managing Committee of the British School of Archaeology at Athens

Archaeol Rep Soc Promot Hell Stud — Archaeological Reports of the Society for the Promotion of Hellenic Studies

Archaeol Rev — Archaeological Review

Archaeol Rev Camb — Archaeological Review from Cambridge

Archaeol Samml U Zuerich — Archaeologische Sammlung der Universitaet Zuerich

Archaeol Surv Alberta Occas Pap — Archaeological Survey of Alberta. Occasional Papers

Archaeol Surv Ceylon Annu Rep — Archaeological Survey of Ceylon. Annual Report

Archaeol Surv India — Archaeological Survey of India

Archaeol Surv India Annu Rep — Archaeological Survey of India Annual Reports

Archaeol Surv India Frontier Circ — Archaeological Survey of India. Frontier Circle

Archaeol Surv India Prog Rep W Circ — Archaeological Survey of India. Progress Reports. Western Circle

Archaeol Surv Temples — Archaeological Survey of Temples

Archaeol Transatlant — Archaeologia Transatlantica

Archaeol Viva — Archaeologia Viva

Archaeol Zeitung — Archaeologische Zeitung

Archaeol Ztg — Archaeologische Zeitung

Archaeometr — Archaeometry

Arch Agriculturchem Denkende Landwirthe — Archiv der Agriculturchemie fuer Denkende Landwirthe

Arch Agron Soil Sci — Archives of Agronomy and Soil Science

Arch Agustin — Archivo Agustiniano. Revista do Investigacion Historica de los P.P. Agustinos Espanoles

Arch Agustiniano — Archivo Agustiniano

Arch Aids Res — Archives of AIDS Research

Archaiol Anlkt Athinon — Archaiologika Analekta ex Athinon

Archaiol Chron — Archaiologiki Chronika

Archaiol Deltion — Archaiologikon Deltion

Archaiol Ephem — Archaiologike Ephemeris

Archaiol Ephemeris — Archaiologiki Ephemeris

Arch Akust — Archiwum Akustyki

Arch Aller Buergerl Wiss — Archiv aller Buergerlichen Wissenschaften zum Nutzen und Vergnuegen wie auch zum Selbstunterricht in Reiferen Jahren

Arch Allg Fragen Lebensforsch — Archiv fuer die Allgemeinen Fragen der Lebensforschung

Arch Alum — Architectural Aluminum Industry. Annual Statistical Review

Arch Am Art — Archives of American Art. Journal

Arch Analekta — Archaiologika Analekta ex Athenon

Arch Anat Cytol Pathol — Archives d'Anatomie et de Cytologie Pathologiques

Arch An Ath — Archaiologika Analekta ex Athenon

Arch Anat Histol Embryol — Archives d'Anatomie, d'Histologie, et d'Embryologie

Arch Anat Histol Embryol Norm Exp — Archives d'Anatomie, d'Histologie, et d'Embryologie; Normales et Experimentales

Arch Anat Histol Embryol (Strasb) — Archives d'Anatomie, d'Histologie, et d'Embryologie (Strasbourg)

Arch Anat M — Archives d'Anatomie Microscopique et de Morphologie Experimentale

Arch Anat Microsc Morphol Exp — Archives d'Anatomie Microscopique et de Morphologie Experimentale

Arch Anat Microscop Morphol Exp — Archives d'Anatomie Microscopique et de Morphologie Experimentale

Arch Anat Pathol (Paris) — Archives d'Anatomie Pathologique (Paris)

Arch Anat Pathol Sem Hop — Archives d'Anatomie Pathologique. Semaine des Hopitaux

Arch Anat Physiol — Archiv fuer Anatomie, Physiologie, und Wissenschaftliche Medizin

Arch Anat Physiol Anat Abt — Archiv fuer Anatomie und Physiologie. Anatomische Abteilung

Arch Anat Physiol Physiol Abt — Archiv fuer Anatomie und Physiologie. Physiologische Abteilung

Arch Anat Physiol Wiss Med — Archiv fuer Anatomie, Physiologie, und Wissenschaftliche Medicin

Arch Anat Phys Wiss Med — Archiv fuer Anatomie, Physiologie, und Wissenschaftliche Medizin

Arch & Arts — Architecture and Arts

Arch & B — Architecture and Building

Arch & Bldg — Architecture and Building

Arch & BM — Architects' and Builders' Magazine

Arch & Eng — Architect and Engineer

Arch & Manus — Archives and Manuscripts

Arch and Manuscripts — Archives and Manuscripts

Arch Androl (New York) — Archives of Andrology (New York)

Arch Anim Nutr — Archives of Animal Nutrition

Arch An Mcr — Archives d'Anatomie Microscopique

Arch An Pl — Archiv fuer Anatomie, Physiologie, und Wissenschaftliche Medicin

Arch An Pl An Abh — Archiv fuer Anatomie und Physiologie. Anatomische Abteilung. Archiv fuer Anatomie und Entwickelungsgeschichte

Arch An Pl Pl Ab — Archiv fuer Anatomie und Physiologie. Physiologische Abteilung. Archiv fuer Physiologie

Arch Anthrop — Archiv fuer Anthropologie

Arch Anthropol Criminelle — Archives d'Anthropologie Criminelle, de Medecine Legale, et de Psychologie Normale et Pathologique

Arch Antibiot — Archives of Antibiotics

Arch Antr Etn — Archivio per l'Antropologia e l'Etnologia

Arch Antrop e Etnol — Archivio per l'Antropologia e la Etnologia

Arch Antropol Crim Psichiatr Med Leg — Archivio di Antropologia Criminale, Psichiatria, e Medicina Legale

Arch Antropol Etnol — Archivio per l'Antropologia e la Etnologia

ArchAnz — Archaeologischer Anzeiger

Arch Apoth Ver Noerd Deutschl — Archiv des Apotheker Vereins im Noerdlichen Deutschland

Arch Appl Mech — Archive of Applied Mechanics

Arch Argent Dermatol — Archivos Argentinos de Dermatologia

Arch Argent Neurol — Archivos Argentinos de Neurologia

Arch Argent Pediatr — Archivos Argentinos de Pediatria

Arch Argent Reumatol — Archivos Argentinos de Reumatologia

Arch Argent Tisiol Neumonol — Archivos Argentinos de Tisiologia y Neumonologia

ArchArm — Archeologie Armoricaine

Arch Arti Dec — Architettura e Arti Decorative. Rivista d'Arte e di Storia

Arch Arzneither — Archiv fuer Arzneitherapie

Arch Asoc Peruana Progr Ci — Archivos. Asociacion Peruana para el Progreso de la Ciencia

Arch Atlas Norm Pathol Anat Roentgenbild — Archiv und Atlas der Normalen und Pathologischen Anatomie in Typischen Roentgenbildern

Arch Atti Soc Med Chir Messina — Archivio ed Atti. Societa Medico-Chirurgica di Messina

Arch Augen — Archiv fuer Augenheilkunde

Arch Augenh — Archiv fuer Augenheilkunde

Arch Augenheilk — Archiv fuer Augenheilkunde

Arch Augenheilkd — Archiv fuer Augenheilkunde

Arch Aughlkde — Archiv fuer Augenheilkunde

Arch Aujourd'hui — Architecture d'Aujourd'hui

Arch Austr — Archaeologia Austriaca

Arch Austriaca — Archaeologie Austriaca

Arch Automat i Telemech — Archiwum Automatyki i Telemechaniki

Arch Automat Telemech — Archiwum Automatyki i Telemechaniki

Arch Autom Telemech — Archiwum Automatyki i Telemechaniki

Arch Badewes — Archiv des Badewesens

Arch Balaton — Archivum Balatonicum

Arch Balatonicum — Archivum Balatonicum

Arch Balkaniques Med Chir Spec — Archives Balkaniques de Medecine. Chirurgie et Leurs Specialites

Arch-Bat-Constr — Architecture-Batiment-Construction

Arch Begriff — Archiv fuer Begriffsgeschichte
Arch Begriffs Gesch — Archiv fuer Begriffs-Geschichte
Arch Belg — Archaeologia Belgica
Arch Belg — Archeologie. Centre National de Recherches Archeologiques en Belgique
Arch Belg — Archives Belges. Medecine Sociale, Hygiene, Medecine du Travail, Medecine Legale
Arch Belg Dermatol — Archives Belges de Dermatologie
Arch Belg Dermatol Syphiligr — Archives Belges de Dermatologie et de Syphiligraphie
Arch Belges Dermatol Syphiligr — Archives Belges de Dermatologie et de Syphiligraphie
Arch Belges Med Soc Hyg Med Trav Med Leg (Belgium) — Archives Belges de Medecine Sociale, Hygiene, Medecine du Travail, et Medecine Legale (Belgium)
Arch Belg Med Soc — Archives Belges de Medecine Sociale, Hygiene, Medecine du Travail, et Medecine Legale
Arch Belg Med Soc Hyg Med Trav Med Leg — Archives Belges de Medecine Sociale, Hygiene, Medecine du Travail, et Medecine Legale
Arch Belg Med Soc Hyg Rev Pathol Physiol Trav — Archives Belges de Medecine Sociale et d'Hygiene et Revue de Pathologie et de Physiologie du Travail
Arch Belg Serv Sante Armee — Archives Belges du Service de Sante de l'Armee
Arch Bergbau — Archiv fuer Bergbau und Huettenwesen
ArchBg — Archaeologische Bibliographie
Arch Bib G Brit — Archaeological Bibliography for Great Britain and Ireland
Arch Bibl — Archives et Bibliotheques de Belgique
Arch Bibl et Mus — Archives, Bibliotheques, et Musees de Belgique [*Later, Archives et Bibliotheques de Belgique*]
Arch Bienenk — Archiv fuer Bienenkunde
Arch Bienenkd — Archiv fuer Bienenkunde
Arch Bioch — Archives of Biochemistry and Biophysics
Arch Biochem — Archives of Biochemistry
Arch Biochem — Archives of Biochemistry and Biophysics
Arch Biochem Biophys — Archives of Biochemistry and Biophysics
Arch Biochem Biophys Suppl — Archives of Biochemistry and Biophysics. Supplement
Arch Biochim Cosmetol — Archives de Biochimie et Cosmetologie
Arch Biogr Contemp — Archives Biographiques Contemporaines
Arch Biol — Archives de Biologie
Arch Biol — Archives of Biology
Arch Biol Andina — Archivos de Biologia Andina
Arch Biol Hung — Archiva Biologia Hungarica
Arch Biol M — Archivos de Biologia y Medicina Experimentales
Arch Biol Med Exp — Archivos de Biologia y Medicina Experimentales
Arch Biol Med Exp Supl — Archivos de Biologia y Medicina Experimentales. Suplemento
Arch Biol Paris — Archives de Biologie (Paris)
Arch Biol Sao Paolo — Archivos de Biologia (Sao Paolo)
Arch Biol Sci — Archives of Biological Sciences
Arch Biol Sci (Belgrade) — Archives of Biological Sciences (Belgrade)
Arch Biol Sci (Engl Transl) — Archives of Biological Sciences (English Translation of Arhiv Bioloskih Nauka)
Arch Biol Sci (Engl Transl Arh Biol Nauka) — Archives of Biological Sciences (English Translation of Arhiv Bioloskih Nauka)
Arch Biol Veg Teor Aplicada — Archivo de Biologia Vegetal Teorica y Aplicada
Arch Bioquim — Archivos de Bioquimica, Quimica, y Farmacia. Universidad Nacional de Tucuman
Arch Bioquim Quim Farm — Archivos de Bioquimica, Quimica, y Farmacia
Arch Bioquim Quim Farm (Tucuman) — Archivos de Bioquimica, Quimica, y Farmacia (Tucuman)
Arch B M — Archeion ton Byzantinon Mnemeion tes Hellados
Arch Bodenfruchtbarkeit Pflanzenprod — Archiv fuer Bodenfruchtbarkeit und Pflanzenproduktion
Arch Bot — Archivio Botanico
Arch Bot Biogeogr Ital — Archivio Botanico e Biogeografico Italiano
Arch Bot Bull Mens — Archives de Botanique. Bulletin Mensuel
Arch Bot Forli — Archivio Botanico (Forli)
Arch Bot Mem — Archives de Botanique. Memoires
Arch Bot Paris — Archives de Botanique (Paris)
Arch Bot Sist — Archivio Botanico per la Sistematica, Fitogeografic, e Genetica. Storia e Sperimentale. Bulletino. Istituto Botanico. Reale Universita di Modena
Arch Brasilerios — Archivos Brasileiros
Arch Brasil Med — Archivos Brasileiros de Medicina
Arch Bronconeumol — Archivos de Bronconeumologia
Arch Buchgew — Archiv fuer Buchgewerbe und Gebrauchsgraphik
Arch Budowy Masz — Archiwum Budowy Maszyn
Arch Budowy Maszyn — Archiwum Budowy Maszyn
Arch Build Eng — Architecture, Building, Structural Engineering
Arch Byz Mnem — Archeion ton Byzantinon Mnemeion tes Hellados
Arch Cal Chiro — Archives. California Chiropractic Association
Arch Cam — Archaeologia Cambrenses
Arch Camb — Archaeologia Cambrensis
Arch Cambrensis — Archaeologia Cambrensis
Arch Can — Architecture Canada
Arch Cant — Archaeologia Cantiana
Arch Cantiana — Archaeologia Cantiana. Transactions of the Kent Archaeological Society
Arch Cardio y Hematol — Archivos de Cardiologia y Hematologia
Arch Cas — Archivni Casopis
Arch Celt Lexikogr — Archiv fuer Celtische Lexikographie
Arch Chem Farm — Archiwum Chemji i Farmacji
Arch Chem Meteorol — Archiv fuer Chemie und Meteorologie
Arch Chem Mikrosk — Archiv fuer Chemie und Mikroskopie
Arch Child Health — Archives of Child Health
Arch Chim Pharm Warsaw — Archives de Chimie et de Pharmacie (Warsaw)

Arch Chim Pharm (Zagreb) — Archives de Chimie et de Pharmacie (Zagreb)
Arch Chim Technol — Archives de Chimie et de Technologie
Arch Chir Neerl — Archivum Chirurgicum Neerlandicum
Arch Chir Ortop Med — Archivio di Chirurgia Ortopedica e di Medicina
Arch Chir Torac Cardiovasc — Archivio di Chirurgia Toracica e Cardiovascolare
Arch Chir Torace — Archivio di Chirurgia del Torace
Arch Cl — Archeologia Classica
ArchClass — Archeologia Classica
Arch Classica — Archeologia Classica
Arch Clin Bordeaux — Archives Cliniques de Bordeaux
Arch Clin Inst Endocrinol (Montevideo) — Archivos. Clinica e Instituto de Endocrinologia (Montevideo)
Arch Col Med El Salv — Archivos. Colegio Medico de El Salvador
Arch Col Med El Salvador — Archivos. Colegio Medico de El Salvador
Arch Combust — Archivum Combustionis
Arch Combust Processes — Archives of Combustion Processes
Arch Comp Med Surg — Archives of Comparative Medicine and Surgery
Arch Comput Methods Engrg — Archives of Computational Methods in Engineering. State of the Art Reviews
Arch Concept — Architecture Concept
Arch Conf Med Hosp Ramos Mejia — Archivos. Conferencia de Medicos del Hospital Ramos-Mejia
Arch Control Sci — Archives of Control Sciences
Arch Corrisp Sci Italiani — Archivio della Corrispondenza degli Scienziati Italiani
Arch Criminol Neuro Psiquiatr Discip Conexas — Archivos de Criminologia Neuro-Psiquiatria y Disciplinas Conexas
Arch Cubanos Cancerol — Archivos Cubanos de Cancerologia
ArchD — Architectural Design
Arch d'Aujourd'hui — Architecture d'Aujourd'hui
Arch De L Electr — Archives de l'Electricite
Arch Delt — Archaiologikon Deltion
Arch Deltion — Archaiologikon Deltion
Arch De Med Cir Y Espec — Archivos de Medicina, Cirugia, y Especialidades
Arch De Med Des Enf — Archives de Medecine des Enfants
Arch De Med Leg — Archivo de Medicina Legal
Arch De Philos Du Dr — Archives de Philosophie du Droit et de Sociologie Juridique
Arch Dep Rom — Archivio. Deputazione Romana di Storia Patria
Arch Deputazione Romana Stor Patria — Archivio. Reale Deputazione Romana di Storia Patria
Arch Derecho Publico — Archivo de Derecho Publico. Universidad de Granada
Arch Dermat — Archives of Dermatology
Arch Dermat and Syph (Chicago) — Archives of Dermatology and Syphilology (Chicago)
Arch Dermatol — Archives of Dermatology
Arch Dermatol Exp Funct — Archivum de Dermatologia Experimentale et Functionale
Arch Dermatol Forsch — Archiv fuer Dermatologische Forschung
Arch Dermatol Res — Archives for Dermatological Research
Arch Dermatol Sper — Archivii di Dermatologia Sperimentale
Arch Dermatol Syphiligr Sao Paulo — Archivos de Dermatologia e Syphiligraphia de Sao Paulo
Arch Dermatol Syphilol — Archives of Dermatology and Syphilology
Arch Dermatol Syphiligr Clin Hop Saint Louis — Archives Dermato-Syphiligraphiques. Clinique de l'Hopital Saint Louis
Arch Dermat u Syph — Archiv fuer Dermatologie und Syphilis
Arch Derm F — Archiv fuer Dermatologische Forschung
Arch Derm R — Archives for Dermatological Research
Arch Des — Architectural Design
Arch De Vecchi Anat Patol — Archivio "De Vecchi" per l'Anatomia Patologica e la Medicina Clinica
Arch De Vecchi Anat Patol Med Clin — Archivio "De Vecchi" per l'Anatomia Patologica e la Medicina Clinica
Arch Diagn — Archives of Diagnosis
Arch di Fisiol — Archivio di Fisiologia
Arch Diplomatik — Archiv fuer Diplomatik
Arch Dis Ch — Archives of Disease in Childhood
Arch Dis Child — Archives of Disease in Childhood
Arch Dis Child Fetal Neonatal Ed — Archives of Disease in Childhood. Fetal and Neonatal Edition
Arch Dis Childhood — Archives of Disease in Childhood
Arch DRSP — Archivio. Deputazione Romana di Storia Patria
Arch Druck Pap — Archiv fuer Druck und Papier
Arch Ed — Architectural Education
Arch ed Atti Soc Ital Chir — Archivio ed Atti. Societa Italiana di Chirurgia
Archeion Byz Mnimeion Ellados — Archeion ton Byzantinon Mnimeion tis Ellados
Arch Eisenbahntech — Archiv fuer Eisenbahntechnik
Arch Eisenh — Archiv fuer das Eisenhuettenwesen
Arch Eisenhuettenwes — Archiv fuer das Eisenhuettenwesen
Arch Eisenhuttenwesen — Archiv fuer das Eisenhuettenwesen
Arch Ekkl Hist — Archeion Ekklesiastikes Historias
Arch Elektr — Archiv fuer Elektrotechnik
Arch Elektron Uebertragungstech — Archiv fuer Elektronik und Uebertragungstechnik
Arch Elektron und Uebertragungstech — Archiv fuer Elektronik und Uebertragungstechnik
Arch Elektrotech — Archiwum Elektrotechniki
Arch Elektrotech (Berlin) — Archiv fuer Elektrotechnik (Berlin)
Arch Elektr Uebertrag — Archiv der Elektrischen Uebertragung
Arch Elek Ubertr — Archiv fuer Elektronik und Uebertragungstechnik
Arch Elek Uebertragung — Archiv der Elektrischen Uebertragung
Arch "E Maragliano" Patol Clin — Archivio "E. Maragliano" di Patologia e Clinica
Arch Energ — Archiwum Energetyki
Arch Energiewirtsch — Archiv fuer Energiewirtschaft

Arch Eng Calif Pac Coast — Architect and Engineer of California and the Pacific Coast

Arch Entsch Oberst Gerichte — Seufferts Archiv fuer Entscheidungen der Obersten Gerichte in den Deutschen Staaten

Arch Entwicklungsmech Org — Archiv fuer Entwicklungsmechanik der Organismen

Arch Entwicklungsmech Org (Wilhelm Roux) — Archiv fuer Entwicklungsmechanik der Organismen (Wilhelm Roux)

Arch Entwmech Org — Archiv fuer Entwicklungsmechanik der Organismen

Arch Env He — Archives of Environmental Health

Arch Envir Health — Archives of Environmental Health

Arch Environ Contam Toxicol — Archives of Environmental Contamination and Toxicology

Arch Environ Health — Archives of Environmental Health

Arch Environ Hlth — Archives of Environmental Health

Arch Environ Prot — Archives of Environmental Protection

Archeocivil — Archeocivilisation

Archeogr Triest — Archeolgrafo Triestino

Archeol Bulg — Archeologija Bulgarska

Archeol Chem Symp — Archeological Chemistry. A Symposium

Archeol Class — Archeologia Classica

Archeol Geog — Archeologia Goegraphica

Archeol Homerica — Archeologia Homerica

Archeol Laziale — Archeologia Laziale

Archeol Med — Archeologia Medievale. Cultura Materiale, Insediamenti, Territorio

Archeol Med — Archeologie Medievale

Archeologia (Paris) — Archeologia. Tresors des Ages (Paris)

Archeologia (Warzawa) — Archeologia. Rocznik Instytutu Historii Kultury Materialnej Polskiej Akademii Nauk (Warszawa)

Archeologija (Kiev) — Archeologija. Akademija Nauk Ukrains'koi RSR. Institut Archeologii (Kiev)

Archeologija (Sof) — Archeologija. Organ na Archeologiceskija Institut i Muzej pri B'lgarskata Akademija na Naukite (Sofia)

Archeologo Port — Archeologo Portugues

Archeol Pap Amer Anthrop Ass — Archeological Papers. American Anthropological Association

Archeol Pol — Archeologia Polski

Archeol Polski — Archeologia Polski

Archeol Prag — Archeologica Pragensia

Archeol Rozhl — Archeologicke Rozhledy

Archeol Transatlant — Archeologia Transatlantica

Arch Eph — Archaiologike Ephemeris

Arch Ephem — Archaiologike Ephemeris

Arch Ephemeris — Archaiologike Ephemeris

Archepigr Mitt — Archaeologisch-Epigraphische Mittheilungen aus Oesterreich-Ungarn

Arch Epigr Mitt Oesterreich — Archaeologisch-Epigraphische Mittheilungen aus Oesterreich-Ungarn

Arch Ep Mitt — Archaeologisch-Epigraphische Mittheilungen aus Oesterreich-Ungarn

Arch Erbergbau Erzaufbereit Metallhuettenwes — Archiv fuer Erzbergbau, Erzaufbereitung, Metallhuettenwesen

Arch Ert — Archaeologiai Ertesito

Arch Ertes — Archaeologiai Ertesitoe

Arch Ertesitoe — Archaeologiai Ertesitoe

Archery Wld — Archery World

Arch Esp — Archivo Espanol de Arte y Arqueologia

Arch Esp A — Archivo Espanol de Arqueologia

Arch Esp A — Archivo Espanol de Arte

Arch Espan Arqueol — Archivo Espanol de Arqueologia. CSIC (Consejo Superior de Investigaciones Cientificas)

Arch Espan Arte — Archivo Espanol de Arte. CSIC (Consejo Superior de Investigaciones Cientificas)

Arch Esp Ar — Archivo Espanol de Arte

Arch Esp Arch — Archivo Espanol de Arqueologia

Arch Esp Arq — Archivo Espanol de Arqueologia

Arch Esp Art — Archivo Espanol de Arte

Arch Esp Farmacol Exp — Archivos Espanoles de Farmacologia Experimental

Arch Esp Morfol — Archivo Espanol de Morfologia

Arch Esp Urol — Archivos Espanoles de Urologia

Arch Estud Med Aragon — Archivos de Estudios Medicos Aragoneses

Arch Ethnogr — Archiv fuer Ethnographie

Arch Eur Centro Orient — Archivum Europae Centro-Orientalis

ArchEurCO — Archivum Europae Centro-Orientalis

Arch Eur So — Archives Europeennes de Sociologie

Arch Eur Sociol — Archives Europeennes de Sociologie

Arch Exp Pathol — Archiv fuer Experimentelle Pathologie und Pharmakologie

Arch Exp Pathol Pharmakol — Archiv fuer Experimentelle Pathologie und Pharmakologie

Arch Exp Path Pharmak — Archiv fuer Experimentelle Pathologie und Pharmakologie

Arch Exp Ve — Archiv fuer Experimentelle Veterinaermedizin

Arch Exp Veterinaermed — Archiv fuer Experimentelle Veterinaermedizin

Arch Exp Vetmed — Archiv fuer Experimentelle Veterinaermedizin

Arch Exp Zellforsch Besonders Gewebezuecht — Archiv fuer Experimentelle Zellforschung Besonders Gewebezuechtung

Arch Facial Plast Surg — Archives of Facial Plastic Surgery

Arch Fac Med Madr — Archivos. Facultad de Medicina de Madrid

Arch Fac Med Madrid — Archivos. Facultad de Medicina de Madrid

Arch Fac Med Zaragoza — Archivos. Facultad de Medicina de Zaragoza

Arch Fac Med Zaragoza Supl — Archivos. Facultad de Medicina de Zaragoza. Suplemento

Arch Fam Med — Archives of Family Medicine

Archf & Bibwzn Belgie — Archief- en Bibliotheekwezen in Belgie

Arch f Anthr — Archiv fuer Anthropologie, Voelkerforschung, und Kolonialen Kulturwandel

ArchFAr — Archivo de Filologia Aragonesa

Arch Farmacol Sper Sci Affini — Archivio di Farmacologia Sperimentale e Scienze Affini

Arch Farmacol Toxicol — Archivos de Farmacologia y Toxicologia

Arch Farm (Bago) — Archivos Farmaceuticos (Bago)

Arch Farm Bioquim Tucuman — Archivos de Farmacia y Bioquimica del Tucuman

Arch Farmcol Sperim Sci Affini — Archivio di Farmacologia Sperimentale e Scienze Affini

Arch FA Waff — Archiv fuer Offiziere aller Waffen [*Muenchen*]

Arch f Begriffsgeschichte — Archiv fuer Begriffsgeschichte

Arch f d Stud d Neur Spr u Lit — Archiv fuer der Studium der Neuren Sprachen und Literaturen

Arch f d Studium d Neur Spr u Lit — Archiv fuer der Studium der Neuren Sprachen und Literaturen

Arch f G d Philos — Archiv fuer Geschichte der Philosophie

Arch f Gesch der Philos — Archiv fuer Geschichte der Philosophie

Arch f Gesch d Philos — Archiv fuer Geschichte der Philosophie

Arch f G Philos — Archiv fuer Geschichte der Philosophie

Arch Filol Aragonesa — Archivo de Filologia Aragonesa. Institucion Fernando el Catolico de la Excma. Diputacion Provincial

Arch Filosof — Archivio di Filosofia

Arch Fisch — Archiv fuer Fischereiwissenschaft

Arch Fischereiwiss — Archiv fuer Fischereiwissenschaft

Arch Fischereiwiss Beih — Archiv fuer Fischereiwissenschaft. Beiheft

Arch Fisiol — Archivio di Fisiologia

Arch f Lat Lex — Archiv fuer Lateinische Lexicographie und Grammatik

Arch Fl France Allemagne — Archives de la Flore de France et d'Allemagne

Archf Ned Kstgesch — Archief voor Nederlandsche Kunstgeschiedenis

Arch Folk — Archives de Folklore

Arch Folk Chil Santiago — Archivos del Folklore Chileno (Santiago)

Arch f Orientfors — Archiv fuer Orientforschung

Arch Forstw — Archiv fuer Forstwesen

Arch Forstwes — Archiv fuer Forstwesen

Arch Forstwesen — Archiv fuer Forstwesen

Arch Forum — Architectural Forum

Arch f Pap — Archiv fuer Papyrusforschung und Verwandte Gebiete

Arch f Prot — Archiv fuer Protistenkunde

Arch F Psychiat — Archiv fuer Psychiatrie und Nervenkrankheiten

Arch Franciscanum Hist — Archivum Franciscanum Historicum

Arch F Rassen U Gesell Biol — Archiv fuer Rassen- und Gesellschafts-Biologie, Einschleisslich Rassen- und Gesellschafts-Hygiene

Arch Fratrum Praedicatorum — Archivum Fratrum Praedicatorum

Arch Frauenkde Konstitutforsch — Archiv fuer Frauenkunde und Konstitutionsforschung

Arch F Rechtspfl In Sachsen Thuer U Anhalt — Archiv fuer Rechtspflege in Sachsen, Thueringen, und Anhalt

Arch F Rechts U Wirtschaftsphilos — Archiv fuer Rechts- und Wirtschafts-Philosophie mit Besonderer Beruecksichtigung der Gesetzgebungsfragen

Arch Freunde Naturgesch Mecklenburg — Archiv. Freunde der Naturgeschichte in Mecklenburg

Arch Fr Mal — Archives Francaises des Maladies de l'Appareil Digestif

Arch Fr Mal Appar Dig — Archives Francaises des Maladies de l'Appareil Digestif

Arch Fr Mal Appar Dig Suppl — Archives Francaises des Maladies de l'Appareil Digestif. Supplement

Arch Fr Mal App Dig — Archives Francaises des Maladies de l'Appareil Digestif

Arch Fr Ped — Archives Francaises de Pediatrie

Arch Fr Pediatr — Archives Francaises de Pediatrie

Arch f Rw — Archiv fuer Religionswissenschaft

Arch F Soz Hyg U Demog — Archiv fuer Soziale Hygiene und Demographie

Arch F Sozialwiss U Sozialpol — Archiv fuer Sozialwissenschaft und Sozialpolitik

Arch F Strafr U Strafproz — Archiv fuer Strafrecht und Strafprozess

Arch fuer Pap — Archiv fuer Papyrusforschung und Verwandte Gebiete

Arch Fund Roux-Ocefa — Archivos. Fundacion Roux-Ocefa

Arch Gartenb — Archiv fuer Gartenbau

Arch Gartenbau — Archiv fuer Gartenbau

Arch Garten Blumenbau Vereins Hamburg — Archiv des Garten- und Blumenbau-Vereins fuer Hamburg, Altona, und deren Umgegenden

Arch Gastroenterol — Archives of Gastroenterology

Arch Gefluegelk — Archiv fuer Gefluegelkunde

Arch Gefluegelkd — Archiv fuer Gefluegelkunde

Arch Gefluegelz Kleintierk — Archiv fuer Gefluegelzucht und Kleintierkunde

Arch Gefluegelzucht Kleintierk — Archiv fuer Gefluegelzucht und Kleintierkunde

Arch Geflugelkd Eur Poult Sci Rev Sci Avicole Eur — Archiv fuer Gefluegelkunde/European Poultry Science/Revue de Science Avicole Europeenne

Arch Gemeinnuetz Phys Med Kenntn — Archiv Gemeinnuetziger Physischer und Medizinischer Kenntnisse

Arch Gen Di Neurol Psichiat E Psicoanal — Archivio Generale di Neurologia, Psichiatria, e Psicoanalisi

Arch Geneal Herald — Archivo de Genealogia y Heraldica

Arch Genet — Archiv fuer Genetik

Arch Gen Md — Archives Generales de Medecine

Arch Gen Med — Archives Generales de Medecine

Arch Gen Psychiat — Archives of General Psychiatry

Arch Gen Psychiatr — Archives of General Psychiatry

Arch Gen Psychiatry — Archives of General Psychiatry

Arch Geogr — Archaeologia Geographica

Arch Geogr — Archiv fuer Geographie, Historie, Staats- und Kriegskunst

Arch Geol Vietnam — Archives Geologiques du Vietnam

Arch Gerichtl Med Kriminol — Archiv fuer Gerichtliche Medizin und Kriminologie

Arch Gerontol Geriatr — Archives of Gerontology and Geriatrics

Arch Gerontol Geriatr Suppl — Archives of Gerontology and Geriatrics. Supplement

Arch Gesamte Naturl — Archiv fuer die Gesamte Naturlehre
Arch Gesamte Physiol Mens Tiere (Pfluegers) — Archiv fuer die Gesamte Physiologie des Menschen und der Tiere (Pfluegers)
Arch Gesamte Virusforsch — Archiv fuer die Gesamte Virusforschung
Arch Gesamte Waermetech — Archiv fuer die Gesamte Waermetechnik
Arch Gesch — Archiv fuer Geschichte der Philosophie
Arch Gesch — Archiv fuer Geschichte, Statistik, Literatur, und Kunst
Arch Gesch Dioez Linz — Archiv fuer Geschichte der Dioezese Linz
Arch Geschichte Sozial — Archiv fuer die Geschichte des Sozialismus und der Arbeiterbewegung
Arch Gesch Math — Archiv fuer die Geschichte der Mathematik, der Naturwissenschaften und der Technik
Arch Gesch Math Naturwiss Techn — Archiv fuer Geschichte der Mathematik, der Naturwissenschaften, und der Technik
Arch Gesch Med — Archiv fuer Geschichte der Medizin
Arch Gesch Med Naturwiss Sudhoffs — Archiv fuer Geschichte der Medizin und der Naturwissenschafter. Sudhoff's
Arch Gesch Naturwiss Tech — Archiv fuer dle Geschichte der Naturwissenschaften und der Technik. Berliner Gesellschaft fuer Geschichte der Naturwissenschaften und Medizin
Arch Gesch Natwiss — Archiv fuer Geschichte der Naturwissenschaften und Technik
Arch Gesch Oberfranken — Archiv fuer Geschichte von Oberfranken
Arch Gesch Phil — Archiv fuer Geschichte der Philosophie
Arch Geschw — Archiv fuer Geschwulstforschung
Arch Geschwulstforsch — Archiv fuer Geschwulstforschung
Arch Ges Physiol — Pfluegers Archiv fuer die Gesamte Physiologie
Arch Gewerbepathol Gewerbehyg — Archiv fuer Gewerbepathologie und Gewerbehygiene
Arch Gewerbl Rechtspflege — Archiv fuer Gewerbliche Rechtspflege
Arch Giur — Archivio Giuridico
Arch Gl It — Archivio Glottologico Italiano
Arch Glot Ital — Archivio Glottologico Italiano
Arch Glotl It — Archivio Glottologico Italiano
Arch Gorn — Archiwum Gornictwa
Arch Gorn Hutn — Archiwum Gornictwa i Hutnictwa
Arch G Psyc — Archives of General Psychiatry
Arch G Utrecht — Archief voor de Geschiedenis van het Aartsbisdom Utrecht
Arch Gyn — Archiv fuer Gynaekologie. Deutsche Gesellschaft fuer Gynaekologie
Arch Gynaekol — Archiv fuer Gynaekologie
Arch Gynecol — Archives of Gynecology
Arch Gynecol Obstet — Archives of Gynecology and Obstetrics
Arch Helv — Archaeologia Helvetica
Arch Herald — Archivum Heraldicum
Arch Herald Suisses — Archives Heraldiques Suisses. Annuaire
Arch Hess Gesch Altertumskde — Archiv fuer Hessische Geschichte und Altertumskunde
Arch Hib — Archivium Hibernicum
Arch Hisp — Archivo Hispalense
Arch Hist Carm — Archivum Historicum Carmelitanum
Arch Hist D O — Archives d'Histoire du Droit Oriental
Arch Hist Doctrinale Litt Moyen Age — Archives d'Histoire Doctrinale et Litteraire du Moyen-Age
Arch Hist Dom — Archives d'Histoire Dominicaine
Arch Hist Droit Oriental — Archives d'Histoire du Droit Oriental
Arch Hist E — Archive for History of Exact Sciences
Arch Hist Exact Sci — Archive for History of Exact Sciences
Arch Hist J — Archivum Histologicum Japonicum
Arch Hist Jap — Archivum Histologicum Japonicum
Arch Hist Lang Geogr Ethnogr Arts Asie Orient — Archives Concernant l'Histoire, les Langues, la Geographie, l'Ethnographie, etles Arts de l'Asie Orientale
Arch Hist Lev — Archivo de Prehistoria Levantina
Arch Hist Med — Archiwum Historii Medycyny
Arch Hist Med Argent — Archivos de Historia de la Medicina Argentina
Arch Hist Med Venezuela — Archivos de Historia Medica de Venezuela
Arch Hist Med (Warsz) — Archiwum Historii Medycyny (Warszawa)
Arch Hist Nat — Archives d'Histoire Naturelle
Arch Histol — Archivum Histologicum
Arch Histol Cytol — Archives of Histology and Cytology
Arch Histol Jpn — Archivum Histologicum Japonicum
Arch Histol Norm Patol — Archivos de Histologia Normal y Patologica
Arch History Exact Sci — Archive for History of Exact Sciences
Arch Hist Sci — Archives de l'Histoire des Sciences
Arch Hist Soc Iesu — Archivum Historicum Societatis Iesu
Arch Hist Soc Jesu — Archivum Historicum Societatis Jesu
Arch Hist Ver Unterfranken — Archiv des Historischen Vereins von Unterfranken und Aschaffenburg
Arch Hom — Archaeologia Homerica
Arch Hosp — Archives Hospitalieres
Arch Hosp Cruz Roja — Archivos. Hospital de la Cruz Roja de Barcelona
Arch Hosp Rosales — Archivos. Hospital Rosales
Arch Hosp Univ Gen Calixto Garcia — Archivos. Hospital Universitario General Calixto Garcia
Arch Hosp Univ (Havana) — Archivos de Hospitales Universitarios (Havana)
Arch Hosp Vargas — Archivos. Hospital Vargas
Arch Hosp Vargas (Caracas) — Archivos. Hospital Vargas (Caracas)
Arch Hung — Archaeologia Hungarica
Arch Hutn — Archiwum Hutnictwa
Arch Hydrob — Archiv fuer Hydrobiologie
Arch Hydrobiol — Archiv fuer Hydrobiologie
Arch Hydrobiol Beih — Archiv fuer Hydrobiologie. Beiheft
Arch Hydrobiol Beih Ergeb Limnol — Archiv fuer Hydrobiologie. Beiheft. Ergebnisse der Limnologie
Arch Hydrobiol Planktonk — Archiv fuer Hydrobiologie und Planktonkunde

Arch Hydrobiol Rybactwa — Archivum Hydrobiologii i Rybactwa
Arch Hydrobiol Suppl — Archiv fuer Hydrobiologie. Supplementband
Arch Hydrobiol Supplementb — Archiv fuer Hydrobiologie. Supplementband
Arch Hydrobiol u Planktonkunde — Archiv fuer Hydrobiologie und Planktonkunde
Arch Hydrotech — Archiwum Hydrotechniki
Arch Hyg — Archiv fuer Hygiene
Arch Hyg (Athens) — Archives of Hygiene (Athens)
Arch Hyg Bakt — Archiv fuer Hygiene und Bakteriologie
Arch Hyg Bakteriol — Archiv fuer Hygiene und Bakteriologie
ArchIA — Archivo Ibero-Americano
Archi & Manu — Archives and Manuscripts
Arch Iatr Epistem — Archeion Iatrikon Epistemon
Arch Ib Am Hist Med — Archivo Iberoamericano de Historia de la Medicina y de Antropologia Medica
Arch Ibero Am — Archivo Ibero-Americano
Arch Ibero Am — Revista de Estudios Historicos de los P.P. Franciscanos Espanoles
Arch Iberoamer Hist Med — Archivos Iberoamericanos de Historia de la Medicina y Antropologia Medica
Arch Ibero Am Hist Medicina — Archivos Iberoamericanos de Historia de la Medicina. CSIC (Consejo Superior de Investigaciones Cientificas)
Arch Ibero Am Madrid — Archivo Ibero-Americano (Madrid)
Arch I Card — Archivos. Instituto de Cardiologia de Mexico
Arch IE Afr — Archivos. Instituto de Estudios Africanos
Archief Nederld Kerkgesch — Archief voor Nederlandsch Kerkgeschiedenis
Archig — Archiginnasio
Archi Hosp Rev Sci Sante Reunies — Archives Hospitalieres et Revue de Science et Sante Reunies
Archimedes Workshop Mol Solids Pressure — Archimedes Workshop on Molecular Solids under Pressure
Arch Immunol Ter Dosw — Archiwum Immunologii i Terapii Doswiadczalnej
Arch Immunol Ther Exp — Archivum Immunologiae et Therapiae Experimentalis
Arch Immunol Ther Exp Engl Transl — Archivum Immunologiae et Therapiae Experimentalis (English Translation)
Arch Immunol Ther Exp (Warsz) — Archivum Immunologiae et Therapiae Experimentalis (Warszawa)
Arch in Aust — Architecture in Australia [*Later, Architecture Australia*]
Arch Ind Hlth — Archives of Industrial Health
Arch Ind Hyg Occup Med — Archives of Industrial Hygiene and Occupational Medicine
Arch Ind Hyg Toxicol — Archives of Industrial Hygiene and Toxicology
Arch Indust Health — Archives of Industrial Health
Arch Industr Hlth — Archives of Industrial Health
Arch Inf — Archaeologische Informationen
Arch In Med — Archives of Internal Medicine
Arch Inn Kolonis — Archiv fuer Innere Kolonisation
Arch Inn Med — Archiv fuer Innere Medizin
Arch Insect Biochem Physiol — Archives of Insect Biochemistry and Physiology
Arch Inst Aclim (Almeria Esp) — Archivos. Instituto de Aclimatacion (Almeria, Espana)
Arch Inst Aclim Cons Super Invest Ci — Archivos. Instituto de Aclimatacion. Consejo Superior de Investigaciones Cientificas
Arch Inst Biol — Archivos. Instituto Biologico
Arch Inst Biol Andina (Lima) — Archivos. Instituto de Biologia Andina (Lima)
Arch Inst Biol Sao Paulo — Archivos do Instituto Biologico (Sao Paulo)
Arch Inst Bot Univ Liege — Archives. Institut de Botanique. Universite de Liege
Arch Inst Cardiol Mex — Archivos. Instituto de Cardiologia de Mexico
Arch Inst Est Afr — Archivos. Instituto de Estudios Africanos
Arch Inst Est Africanos — Archivos. Instituto de Estudios Africanos. CSIC (Consejo Superior de Investigaciones Cientificas)
Arch Inst Estud Afr — Archivos. Instituto de Estudios Africanos
Arch Inst Farmacol Exp (Madrid) — Archivos. Instituto de Farmacologia Experimental (Madrid)
Arch Inst Farmacol Exp (Med) — Archivos. Instituto de Farmacologia Experimental (Medicina)
Arch Inst Farm Exp — Archivos. Instituto de Farmacologia Experimental
Arch Inst Grand-Ducal Luxemb Sect Sci — Archives. Institut Grand-Ducal de Luxembourg. Section des Sciences Naturelles, Physiques, et Mathematiques
Arch Inst Grand Ducal Luxemb Sect Sci Nat Phys Math — Archives. Institut Grand-Ducal de Luxembourg. Section des Sciences Naturelles, Physiques, et Mathematiques
Arch Inst Hessarek — Archives. Institut d'Hessarek
Arch Inst Hessarek (Inst Razi) — Archives. Institut d'Hessarek (Institut Razi)
Arch Inst Med Leg Lisboa Ser B — Archivos. Instituto de Medicina Legal de Lisboa. Serie B
Arch Inst Past Alg — Archives. Institut Pasteur d'Algerie
Arch Inst Pasteur Afrique N — Archives. Instituts Pasteur de l'Afrique du Nord
Arch Inst Pasteur Afrique Nord — Archives. Instituts Pasteur de l'Afrique du Nord
Arch Inst Pasteur Alger — Archives. Institut Pasteur d'Algerie
Arch Inst Pasteur Algerie — Archives. Institut Pasteur d'Algerie
Arch Inst Pasteur Hell — Archives. Institut Pasteur Hellenique
Arch Inst Pasteur Indochine — Archives. Instituts Pasteur d'Indochine
Arch Inst Pasteur Madagascar — Archives. Institut Pasteur de Madagascar
Arch Inst Pasteur Tananarive — Archives. Institut Pasteur de Tananarive
Arch Inst Pasteur Tunis — Archives. Institut Pasteur de Tunis
Arch Inst Past Tunis — Archives. Institut Pasteur de Tunis
Arch Inst Prophyl — Archives. Institut Prophylactique
Arch Inst Radium Univ Paris Fond Curie Radiophysiol Radiothe — Archives. Institut du Radium. Universite de Paris et de la Fondation Curie. Radiophysiologie et Radiotherapie
Arch Inst Razi — Archives. Institut Razi
Arch Inst R Bacteriol Camara Pestana — Archives. Institut Royal de Bacteriologie Camara Pestana
Arch Int Chir — Archives Internationales de Chirurgie
Arch Int Claude Bernard — Archives Internationales Claude Bernard

Arch Intelligenzblatt — Archaeologisches Intelligenzblatt zur Allgemeinen Literatur Zeitung
Arch Interamerican Rheumatol — AIR. Archives of Interamerican Rheumatology
Arch Interam Rheumatol — Archives of Interamerican Rheumatology
Arch Internat Histoire Sci — Archives Internationales d'Histoire des Sciences
Arch Internat Hist Sci — Archives Internationales d'Histoire des Sciences
Arch Intern Med — Archives of Internal Medicine
Arch Intern Med Moscow — Archives of Internal Medicine (Moscow)
Arch Int Etnogr Preist — Archivio Internazionale di Etnografia e Preistoria
Arch Int Hidatidosis — Archivos Internacionales de la Hidatidosis
Arch Int Hist Sci — Archives Internationales d'Histoire des Sciences
Arch Int Laryngol — Archives Internationales de Laryngologie, d'Otologie, de Rhinologie et de Bronchooesophagoscopie
Arch Int Med — Archives of Internal Medicine
Arch Int Med Exp — Archives Internationales de Medecine Experimentale
Arch Int Neur — Archives Internationales de Neurologie
Arch Int Neurol — Archives Internationales de Neurologie
Arch Int Pharmacodyn Ther — Archives Internationales de Pharmacodynamie et de Therapie
Arch Int Physiol — Archives Internationales de Physiologie
Arch Int Physiol Biochim — Archives Internationales de Physiologie et de Biochimie
Arch Int Physiol Biochim Biophys — Archives Internationales de Physiologie, de Biochimie, et de Biophysique
Arch Int Sociol Coop — Archives Internationales de Sciologie de la Cooperation
Arch Invest Med — Archivos de Investigacion Medica
Arch Inv M — Archivos de Investigacion Medica
Arch Inz Ladowej — Archiwum Inzynierii Ladowej
Arch I Phar — Archives Internationales de Pharmacodynamie et de Therapie
Arch I Phys — Archives Internationales de Physiologie et de Biochimie
Arch Ist Biochim Ital — Archivio. Istituto Biochimico Italiano
Arch Ist Osp St Corona — Archivio. Istituti Ospedalieri Santa Corona
Archit — Architecture in Australia [*Later, Architecture Australia*]
Arch Ital Anat Embriol — Archivio Italiano di Anatomia e di Embriologia
Arch Ital Anat Istol Patol — Archivio Italiano di Istologia Patologica
Arch Ital Biol — Archives Italiennes de Biologie
Archit Album — Architektonisches Album
Arch Ital Chir — Archivio Italiano di Chirurgia
Arch Ital Clin Med — Archivio Italiano di Clinica Medica
Arch Ital Dermatol Sifilogr Venereol — Archivio Italiano di Dermatologia, Sifilografia, e Venereologia
Arch Ital Dermatol Venereol Sessuol — Archivio Italiano di Dermatologia, Venereologia, e Sessuologia
Arch Ital Di Psicol — Archivio Italiano di Psicologia
Archit Algorithms Digital Image Process — Architectures and Algorithms for Digital Image Processing
Arch Ital Laringol — Archivii Italiani di Laringologia
Arch Ital Mal Appar Dig — Archivio Italiano delle Malattie dell'Apparato Digerente
Arch Ital Malatt Nerv — Archivio Italiano per le Malattie Nervose
Arch Ital Mal Nerv Ment — Archivio Italiano per le Malattie Nervose e Mentali
Arch Ital Med Sper — Archivio Italiano di Medicina Sperimentale
Arch Ital Otol Rinol Laringol — Archivio Italiano di Otologia, Rinologia, e Laringologia
Arch Ital Otol Rinol-Laringol Patol Cervico-Facciale — Archivio Italiano di Otologia, Rinologia-Laringologia, e Patologia Cervico-Facciale
Arch Ital Patol Clin Tumori — Archivio Italiano di Patologia e Clinica dei Tumori
Arch Ital Pediatr Pueri — Archivio Italiano di Pediatria e Puericoltura
Arch Ital Sci Colon Parassitol — Archivio Italiano di Scienze Coloniati e di Parassitologia
Arch Ital Sci Farmacol — Archivio Italiano di Scienze Farmacologiche
Arch Ital Sci Med Trop Parassitol — Archivio Italiano di Scienze Mediche Tropicali e di Parassitologia
Arch Ital Sc Med Colon — Archivio Italiano di Scienze Mediche Coloniali
Arch Ital Urol — Archivio Italiano di Urologia
Arch Ital Urol Androl — Archivio Italiano di Urologia, Andrologia
Arch Ital Urol Nefrol — Archivio Italiano di Urologia e Nefrologia
Archit & A — Architecture and Arts
Archit & A Dec — Architettura e le Arti Decorative
Archit & Archaeol Soc Durham & Northumb Trans — Architectural and Archaeological Society of Durham and Northumberland. Transactions
Archit & Bldg — Architecture and Building
Archit & Budownictwo — Architektura i Budownictwo
Archit & Wohnen — Architektur und Wohnen
Archit & Wohnform — Architektur und Wohnform
Archit Archaeol & Hist Soc Co City & Neighbourhood Chester J — Architectural, Archaeological, and Historical Society for the County, City, and Neighbourhood of Chester. Journal
Archit Archaeol Soc Durham Northumberl Trans — Architectural and Archaeological Society of Durham and Northumberland. Transactions
Archit Archv — Architettura. Archivi
Archit Arkithist Aaskr — Architectura. Arkitekturhistorisk Aarsskrift
Archit Assoc J — Architectural Association Journal
Archit Assoc Q — Architectural Association. Quarterly
Archit Auj — Architecture d'Aujourd'hui
Archit Aujourd — Architecture d'Aujourd'hui
Archit Aust — Architecture Australia
Archit Australia — Architecture in Australia
Arch It Bio — Archives Italiennes de Biologie
Archit Build — Architect and Builder
Archit Bull — Architectural Bulletin
Archit Canada — Architecture Canada
Archit Concept — Architecture Concept
Archit Cronache Storia — Architettura Cronache e Storia
Archit Cron & Stor — Architettura. Cronache e Storia
Archit CSR — Architektura CSR

Archit d'Aujourd'hui — Architecture d'Aujourd'hui
Archit DDR — Architektur der DDR
Archit Des — Architectural Design
Archit Dig — Architectural Digest
Architect & Bldg News — Architect and Building News
Architect & Bldr — Architect and Builder
Architect & Engin — Architect and Engineer
Architect & Engin CA — Architect and Engineer of California
Architect Bldr & Engin — Architect, Builder, and Engineer
Architect Hist — Architectural History
Architect J Jap Architects Assoc — Architect. Journal of the Japanese Architects' Association
Architect Rev — Architectural Review
Architects J — Architects' Journal
Architects Yb — Architect's Year-book
Architecture & Comportement/Archre & Behavior — Architecture et Comportement/Architecture and Behavior
Archit Eng — Architect and Engineer
Archit Formes & Fonct — Architecture. Formes et Fonctions
Archit Forum — Architectural Forum
Archit Fr — Architecture Francaise
Archit Her — Architectural Heritage
Archit Hisp — Architectura Hispalense
Archit Hist — Architectural History
Archit in Aust — Architecture in Australia [*Later, Architecture Australia*]
Archit Innenarchit Tech Ausbau — Architektur, Innenarchitektur, Technischer Ausbau. AIT
Archit Interieure Creee — Architecture Interieure Creee
Archit Israel — Architecture of Israel
Archit J — Architects' Journal
Archit J — Architectural Journal
Archit Mag — Architectural Magazine
Archit Medit — Architecture Mediterraneenne
Archit Met — Architectural Metals
Archit MN — Architecture Minnesota
Archit Mono — Architectural Monographs
Archit Movt Cont — Architecture, Mouvement, Continuite
Archit [*New York*] — Architecture [*New York*]
Archit Obzor — Architektonicky Obzor
Archit Per Ind — Architectural Periodicals Index
Archit Period Index — Architectural Periodicals Index
Archit Plus — Architecture Plus
Archit R — Architectural Review
Archit Rec — Architectural Record
Archit Rev — Architectural Review
Archit Rev & Amer Bldrs J — Architectural Review and American Builders Journal
Archit Rev [*Boston*] — Architectural Review [*Boston*]
Archit Rev [*London*] — Architectural Review [*London*]
Archit Riv Sind N Fasc Architetti — Architettura. Rivista del Sindicato Nazionale Fascista degli Architetti
Archit Rundschau — Architektonische Rundschau
Archit SA — Architecture SA
Archit S Africa — Architecture in South Africa
Archit Sci Rev — Architectural Science Review
Archit Show — Architecture Show
Archits News — Architects News
Archit Stor & Doc — Architettura. Storia e Documenti
Archit Surv — Architect and Surveyor
Archit Themata Archit Greece — Architectural Themes/Architecture in Greece
Archit Today — Architecture Today
Archit Viv — Architecture Vivante
Archit W Midlands — Architecture West Midlands
Archit Wohnwelt — Architektur und Wohnwelt
Archit Z Gesch & Aesth Baukst — Architectura. Zeitschrift fuer Geschichte und Aesthetik der Baukunst
Arohit Z Geoch Archit — Architectura. Zeitschrift fuer Geschichte der Architektur
Archit Z Gesch Baukst — Architectura. Zeitschrift fuer Geschichte der Baukunst
Archlug — Archaeologia Iugoslavica
Archiv — Archiv fuer das Studium der Neueren Sprachen und Literaturen
Archiv — Archiv fuer Reformationsgeschichte
Archival Z — Archivalische Zeitschrift
Archiv Anthrop — Archiv fuer Anthropologie und Voelkerforschung
Archiv Antropol Etnol — Archivio per l'Antropologia e la Etnologia
Archiv As Art — Archives of Asian Art
Archiv Chim — Archives de Chimie
Archiv Diplom Consul — Archives Diplomatiques et Consulaires
ArchiveP — [*The*] Archive (Philippines)
Archives & Bibl — Archives et Bibliotheques de Belgique
Archives and Mss — Archives and Manuscripts
Archives De Med Nav — Archives de Medecine Navale
Archives Dermat Syph — Archives of Dermatology and Syphilology
Archives D Mal Du Coeur — Archives des Maladies du Coeur, des Vaisseaux, et du Sang
Archives Environ Health — Archives of Environmental Health
Archives Environ Hlth — Archives of Environmental Health
Archives Eur Sociol — Archives Europeennes de Sociologie
Archives Gen Psychiat — Archives of General Psychiatry
Archives Ind Hyg & Occup Med — Archives of Industrial Hygiene and Occupational Medicine
Archives Ital De Biol — Archives Italiennes de Biologie
Archives Missions Scientif — Archives des Missions Scientifiques et Litteraires
Archives Neurol — Archives of Neurology
Archives of Science Orleans Co Soc N Sc Tr — Archives of Science. Orleans County Society of Natural Sciences. Transactions
Archives Ophthal — Archives of Ophthalmology

Archiv Espan Arq — Archivo Espanol de Arqueologia
Archiv Espan Arte — Archivo Espanol de Arte
Archives Pediat — Archives of Pediatrics
Archives Philos — Archives de Philosophie
Archives Psychol — Archives of Psychology
Archives Sci — Archives des Sciences
Archives Sci Sociales Relig — Archives de Sciences Sociales des Religions
Archives Sociol Relig — Archives de Sociologie des Religions
Archives Suisses Anthrop Gen — Archives Suisses d'Anthropologie Generale
Archiv Europ Sociol — Archives Europeennes de Sociologie
Archiv Eur Sociol — Archives Europeennes de Sociologie
Archiv Exp Zellforsch Besonders Gewebezuecht — Archiv fuer Experimentelle Zellforschung Besonders Gewebezuechtung
Archiv F Anthropol — Archiv fuer Anthropologie
Archiv F Dermat U Syph — Archiv fuer Dermatologie und Syphilis
Archiv F D Stud D Kolonialsp — Archiv fuer das Studium Deutscher Kolonialsprachen
Archiv F Kriminalanthropol — Archiv fuer Kriminalanthropologie und Kriminalistik
Archiv f Lat Lex — Archiv fuer Lateinische Lexicographie und Grammatik
Archiv f Oesterr Geschichte — Archiv fuer Oesterreichische Geschichte
Archiv F Pathol Anat — Archiv fuer Pathologische Anatomie und Physiologie und Klinische Medizin
Archiv F Religionswis — Archiv fuer Religionswissenschaft
Archiv F Schiffs U Tropen Hyg — Archiv fuer Schiffs- und Tropen-Hygiene
Archiv f Stud — Archiv fuer das Studium der Neueren Sprachen und Literaturen
Archiv fuer Latein Lexik — Archiv fuer Lateinische Lexicographie und Grammatik
Archiv fuer Mus — Archiv fuer Musikwissenschaft
Archiv Gesch Buchw — Archiv fuer Geschichte des Buchwesens
Archiv Gesch Buchwes — Archiv fuer Geschichte des Buchwesens
Archiv Hist Dr Or — Archives d'Histoire du Droit Oriental
Archiv Hist Dr Orient — Archives d'Histoire du Droit Oriental
Archiv Ibero — Archivo Ibero-Americano
Archiv Inst Paleont Hum Mem — Archives. Institut de Paleontologie Humaine
Archiv Int Sociol Coop Develop — Archives Internationales de Sociologie de la Cooperation et du Developpement
Archivio Antropol Etnol — Archivio per l'Antropologia e l'Etnologia
Archivio Di Psichiat — Archivio di Psichiatria
Archivio Glottol — Archivio Glottologico Italiano
Archivio Internaz Etnogr Preist — Archivio Internazionale di Etnografia e Preistoria
Archivio Per L Antropol E L Etnol — Archivio per l'Antropologia e l'Etnologia
Archivio Stor Lomb — Archivio Storico Lombardo
Archivio Zool Anat — Archivio per la Zoologia, l'Anatomia, e la Fisiologia
Archivists Newslett — Archivists' Newsletter
Archiv Kommunalwiss — Archiv fuer Kommunalwissenschaften
Archiv Ling — Archivum Linguisticum
Archiv Meteorologie Geophysik u Bioklimatolgie Ser A — Archiv fuer Meteorologie, Geophysik, und Bioklimatologie. Serie A. Meteorologieund Geophysik
Archiv Mis — Archives des Missions Scientifiques et Litteraires
Archiv Miss — Archives. Missions Scientifiques et Litteraires
Archivo Anat Anthrop — Archivo de Anatomia e Anthropologia
Archivo Biol Veg Teor Apl — Archivo de Biologia Vegetal Teorica y Aplicada
Archivo Cienc Biol Nat Teor Apl — Archivo de Ciencias Biologicas y Naturales Teoricas y Aplicades
Archivo Colon Lisb — Archivo das Colonias (Lisboa)
Archivo Espanol Arqu — Archivo Espanol de Arqueologia
Archivo Esp Arq — Archivo Espanol de Arqueologia
Archivo Esp Arte — Archivo Espanol de Arte
Archiv Oesterr Gesch — Archiv fuer Oesterreichische Geschichte
Archiv Off Rechts — Archiv des Oeffentlichen Rechts
Archivo Fitotec Urug — Archivo Fitotecnico del Uruguay
Archivo Geogr Penins Iber — Archivo Geografico de la Peninsula Iberica
Archivo Med Leg — Archivo de Medicina Legal
Archivo Med Porto — Archivo de Medicina (Porto)
Archivo Patol — Archivo de Patologia
Archivo Prehist Levantina — Archivo de Prehistoria Levantina
Archiv Or — Archiv Orientalni
Archivo Repart Antrop Crim Porto — Archivo da Reparticao de Antropologia Criminal, Psicologia Experimental e Identificacao Civil do Porto
Archivo Revta Hosp Habana — Archivo y Revista de Hospitales (Habana)
Archiv Orientforsch — Archiv fuer Orientforschung
Archivos Psiquiat Y Criminol — Archivos de Psiquiatria y Criminologia. Medicina Legal
Archivo St Siciliano — Archivio Storico Siciliano
Archivo Trav Fac Med Porto — Archivo de Trabalhos da Faculdade de Medicina do Porto
Archiv Pap — Archiv fuer Papyrusforschung und Verwandte Gebiete
Archiv Philos — Archiv fuer Geschichte der Philosophie
ArchivPhilos — Archiv fuer Philosophie
Archiv Philos Dr — Archives de Philosophie du Droit
Archiv Post U Fernmeldewesen — Archiv fuer das Post- und Fernmeldewesen
Archiv Rechts u Soz-Philos — Archiv fuer Rechts- und Sozialphilosophie
Archiv Rel — Archiv fuer Religionswissenschaft
Archiv Rom — Archivum Romanicum
Archiv Sci Soc Rel — Archives de Sciences Sociales des Religions
Archiv Sci Soc Relig — Archives de Sciences Sociales des Religions
Archiv Sex Behav — Archives of Sexual Behavior
Archiv Soc Rel — Archives de Sociologie des Religions
Archiv Soz Gesch — Archiv fuer Sozialgeschichte
Archiv Stor — Archivio Storico
Archiv Suisses Anthropol Gen — Archives Suisses d'Anthropologie Generale
Archivum Hist Soc Iesu — Archivum Historicum Societatis Iesu
Archiv Urk — Archiv fuer Urkundenforschung
Archiv Voelkerk — Archiv fuer Voelkerkunde

Archiv Volkerrechts — Archiv des Voelkerrechts
Archiwm Nauk — Archiwum Naukowe
Arch J — Archaeological Journal
Arch J — Architects' Journal
Arch Jahrb — Jahrbuch des Deutschen Archaeologischen Instituts
Arch Java Suikerindustr — Archief voor de Java Suikerindustrie
Arch J Marti Hav — Archivo Jose Marti (Habana)
Arch Journ — Archaeological Journal
Arch Jpn Chir — Archiv fuer Japanische Chirurgie
Arch Jug — Archaeologia Jugoslavica
Arch Jugoslavica — Archaeologia Jugoslavica
Arch Jugo Zapad Ross — Archiv Jugozapadnoj Rossii
Arch Juives — Archives Juives. Cahiers de la Commission des Archives Juives
Arch Julius Klaus Stiftung Vererbungsf — Archiv der Julius Klaus-Stiftung fuer Vererbungsforschung, Sozialanthropologie,und Rassenhygiene
Arch Julius Klaus-Stift Vererbforsch — Archiv der Julius Klaus-Stiftung fuer Vererbungsforschung, Sozialanthropologie,und Rassenhygiene
Arch K — Archaeologiai Koezlemenyek
ArchK — Archiv fuer Kulturgeschichte
Arch Keilschrforsch — Archiv fuer Keilschriftforschung
Arch Kinderh — Archiv fuer Kinderheilkunde
Arch Kinderheilkd — Archiv fuer Kinderheilkunde
Arch Kinderheilkd Beih — Archiv fuer Kinderheilkunde. Beihefte
Arch Klaerung Wuenschelrutenfrage — Archiv zur Klaerung der Wuenschelrutenfrage
Arch Klin Chir — Archiv fuer Klinische Chirurgie
Arch Klin Chir Langenbecks — Archiv fuer Klinische Chirurgie. Langenbecks
Arch Klin Exp Dermatol — Archiv fuer Klinische und Experimentelle Dermatologie
Arch Klin Exp Ohren- Nasen- Kehlkopfheilkd — Archiv fuer Klinische und Experimentelle Ohren-, Nasen-, und Kehlkopfheilkunde
Arch Klin Exp Ophtalmol — Archiv fuer Klinische und Experimentelle Ophtalmologie
Arch Klin Med — Archiv fuer Klinische Medizin
Arch Koezl — Archaeologiai Koezlemenyek
Arch Koezlemenyek — Archaeologiai Koezlemenyek
Arch Koffiecult Indones — Archief voor de Koffiecultuur in Indonesie
Arch Koffiecult Ned Indie — Archief voor de Koffiecultuur in Nederlandsch-Indie
Arch Kohno Clin Med Res Inst — Archives. Kohno Clinical Medicine Research Institute
Arch Kommunalwiss — Archiv fuer Kommunalwissenschaften
Arch Korr — Archaeologisches Korrespondenzblatt
Arch Korrbl — Archaeologisches Korrespondenzblatt
Arch Korrespondenzbl — Archaeologisches Korrespondenzblatt
Arch Kreislaufforsch — Archiv fuer Kreislaufforschung
Arch Krim Anthr — Archiv fuer Kriminalanthropolgie und Kriminalistik
Arch Kriminol — Archiv fuer Kriminologie
Arch Kulturgesch — Archiv fuer Kulturgeschichte
Arch Kunstgesch — Archiv fuer Kunstgeschichte
ArchL — Archivum Linguisticum
Arch Lagerstaettenforsch — Archiv fuer Lagerstaettenforschung
Arch Lagerstaettenforsch Ostalpen — Archiv fuer Lagerstaettenforschung in den Ostalpen
Arch Lagerstattenforsch Geol Bundesanst — Archiv fuer Lagerstaettenforschung der Geologischen Bundesanstalt
Arch Landb Bergstreken Ned Indie — Archief voor den Landbouw der Bergstreken in Nederlandsch-Indie
Arch Landtech — Archiv fuer Landtechnik
Arch Laryngol — Archives of Laryngology
Arch Laryngol — Archiv fuer Laryngologie
Archl Assocn Annual Review — Architectural Association. Annual Review
Arch Latinoamer Nutr — Archivos Latinoamericanos de Nutricion
Arch Latinoam Nutr — Archivos Latinoamericanos de Nutricion
Arch Lat Lex — Archiv fuer Lateinische Lexicographie und Grammatik
Arch Latr Epistem — Archeion Latrikon Epistemon
Arch Lebensm Hyg — Archiv fuer Lebensmittel-Hygiene
Arch Lebensmittelhyg — Archiv fuer Lebensmittelhygiene
Arch Leoneses — Archivos Leoneses. CSIC (Consejo Superior de Investigaciones Cientificas)
Arch Ling — Archivum Linguisticum
Arch Linguist — Archivum Linguisticum
Arch Linguisticum — Archivum Linguisticum
ArchLit — Archiv fuer Literatur und Volksdichtung
ArchLitg — Archiv fuer Liturgiewissenschaft
Arch Litgesch — Archiv fuer Literaturgeschichte
Arch Liturg — Archiv fuer Liturgiewissenschaft
Arch LMA — Bulletin du Cange. Archivum Latinitatis Medii Aevi
Arch Logica Filos Mat — Archivio di Logica e Filosofia della Matematica
Arch Mal Appar Dig Mal Nutr — Archives des Maladies de l'Appareil Digestif et des Maladies de la Nutrition
Arch Mal C — Archives des Maladies du Coeur et des Vaisseaux
Arch Mal Coeur — Archives des Maladies du Coeur et des Vaisseaux
Arch Mal Coeur Vaiss — Archives des Maladies du Coeur et des Vaisseaux
Arch Mal Coeur Vaiss Sang — Archives des Maladies du Coeur, des Vaisseaux, et du Sang
Arch Mal Coeur Vaiss Suppl — Archives des Maladies du Coeur et des Vaisseaux. Supplement
Arch Mal Pr — Archives des Maladies Professionnelles de Medecine du Travail et de Securite Sociale
Arch Mal Prof — Archives des Maladies Professionnelles de Medecine du Travail et de Securite Sociale
Arch Mal Prof Hyg Toxicol Ind — Archives des Maladies Professionnelles, Hygiene, et Toxicologie Industrielles
Arch Mal Prof Med Trav Secur Soc — Archives des Maladies Professionnelles de Medecine du Travail et de Securite Sociale
Arch Manuscr — Archives and Manuscripts

Arch Maragliano Patol Clin — Archivio e Maragliano di Patologia e Clinica
Arch Maryland — Archives of Maryland
Arch Mass Spectral Data — Archives of Mass Spectral Data
Arch Math — Archiv der Mathematik
Arch Math (Basel) — Archiv der Mathematik (Basel)
Arch Math (Brno) — Archivum Mathematicum (Brno)
Arch Math Log — Archiv fuer Mathematische Logik und Grundlagenforschung
Arch Math Logic — Archive for Mathematical Logic
Arch Math Logik Grundlag — Archiv fuer Mathematische Logik und Grundlagenforschung
Arch Math Logik Grundlagenforsch — Archiv fuer Mathematische Logik und Grundlagenforschung
Arch Math Logik und Grundlagenforsch — Archiv fuer Mathematische Logik und Grundlagenforschung
Arch Mat Naturvidensk — Archiv foer Matematik og Naturvidenskab
Arch Md Exp — Archives de Medecine Experimentale et d'Anatomie Pathologique
Arch Md Nv — Archives de Medecine Navale
Arch Md Phm Mil — Archives de Medecine et de Pharmacie Militaires
Arch Meat Fish Dairy Sci — Archives of Meat, Fish, and Dairy Science
Arch Mec Appl — Archives de Macanique Appliquee
Arch Mech — Archives of Mechanics
Arch Mech (Arch Mech Stosow) — Archives of Mechanics (Archiwum Mechaniki Stosowanej)
Arch Mech Stosow — Archiwum Mechaniki Stosowanej
Arch Mech Stosowanej — Archiwum Mechaniki Stosowanej
Arch Mecklenburg Naturf — Archiv Mecklenburgischer Naturforscher
Arch Med — Archives Medicales
Arch Med Angers — Archives Medicales d'Angers
Arch Med Belg — Archiva Medica Belgica
Arch Med Chir Appareil Resp — Archives Medico-Chirurgicales de l'Appareil Respiratoire
Arch Med Chir Appar Respir — Archives Medico-Chirurgicales de l'Appareil Respiratoire
Arch Med Cuba — Archivos Medicos de Cuba
Arch Med Enf — Archives de Medecine des Enfants
Arch Med Enfants — Archives de Medecine des Enfants
Arch Med Exp — Archivos de Medicina Experimental
Arch Med Exper et Anat Path — Archives de Medecine Experimentale et d'Anatomie Pathologique
Arch Med Gen Trop — Archives de Medecine Generale et Tropicale
Arch Med Hydrol — Archives of Medical Hydrology
Arch Med Interna — Archivio di Medicina Interna
Arch Med Leg — Archives Belges de Medecine Legale
Arch Med Leg — Archivo de Medicina Legal
Arch Med (Lisbon) — Archivos de Medicina (Lisbon)
Arch Med Mex — Archivos Medicos Mexicanos
Arch Med (Mexico City) — Archivos Medicos (Mexico City)
Arch Med Nav — Archives de Medecine Navale
Arch Med Navale — Archives de Medecine Navale
Arch Med Normandie — Archives Medicales de Normandie
Arch Med Panameno — Archivos Medicos Panamenos
Arch Med Pharm Nav — Archives de Medecine et Pharmacie Navales
Arch Med Res — Archives of Medical Research
Arch Med Sadowej Kryminol — Archiwum Medycyny Sadowej i Kryminologii
Arch Med San Lorenzo — Archivos Medicos de San Lorenzo
Arch Med (Sarajevo) — Archives de Medecine (Sarajevo)
Arch Med Soc Hyg Rev Pathol Physiol Trav — Archives de Medecine Sociale et d'Hygiene et Revue de Pathologie et de Physiologie du Travail
Arch Med Vet — Archivos de Medicina Veterinaria
Arch Med Vet (Valdivia) — Archivos de Medicina Veterinaria (Valdivia)
Arch Melit — Archivum Melitense. Malta Historical and Scientific Society/Societa Storico-Scientifica Matenese
Arch Menschen Buerger — Archiv fuer den Menschen und Buerger in Allen Verhaeltnissen
Arch Metall — Archives of Metallurgy
Arch Metallkd — Archiv fuer Metallkunde
Arch Meteorol Geophys Bioclimatol Ser B Theor Appl Climatol — Archives for Meteorology, Geophysics, and Bioclimatology. Series B. Theoreticaland Applied Climatology
Arch Meteorol Geophys Bioklimatol Ser A — Archiv fuer Meteorologie, Geophysik, und Bioklimatologie. Serie A
Arch Meteorol Geophys Bioklimatol Ser B — Archiv fuer Meteorologie, Geophysik, und Bioklimatologie. Serie B
Arch Met Geophys Bioklimatologie Ser B — Archiv fuer Meteorologie, Geophysik, und Bioklimatologie. Serie B
Arch Met Geophys Bioklim Ser A Meteorologie und Geophysik — Archiv fuer Meteorologie, Geophysik, und Bioklimatologie. Serie A. Meteorologieund Geophysik
Arch Mex Anat — Archivos Mexicanos de Anatomia
Arch Mex Neurol Psiquiatr — Archivos Mexicanos de Neurologia y Psiquiatria
Arch Mex Venereol Dermatol — Archivos Mexicanos de Venereologia y Dermatologia
Arch Mex Venereo Sifilis Dermatol — Archivos Mexicanos de Venereo-Sifilis y Dermatologia
Arch MGB A — Archiv fuer Meteorologie, Geophysik, und Bioklimatologie. Serie A
Arch MGB B — Archiv fuer Meteorologie, Geophysik, und Bioklimatologie. Serie B
Arch Microb — Archives of Microbiology
Arch Microbiol — Archives of Microbiology
Arch Mikr Anat — Archiv fuer Mikroskopische Anatomie
Arch Mikrobiol — Archiv fuer Mikrobiologie
Arch Mikrosk Anat Entwicklungsmech — Archiv fuer Mikroskopische Anatomie und Entwicklungsmechanik
Arch Mikrosk Anat Entwmech — Archiv fuer Mikroskopische Anatomie und Entwicklungsmechanik
Arch Mineir Dermato Syphiligr — Archivos Mineiros de Dermato-Syphiligraphia

Arch Miner — Archiv fuer Mineralogie, Geognosie, Bergbau, und Huettenkunde
Arch Mineral — Archiwum Mineralogiczne
Arch Mineral Soc Sci Varsovie — Archives de Mineralogie. Societe des Sciences et des Lettres de Varsovie
Arch Mineral Tow Nauk Warsz — Archiwum Mineralogiczne Towarzystwa Naukowego Warszawskiego
Arch Min Sci — Archives of Mining Sciences
ArchMIran — Archaeologische Mitteilungen aus Iran. Neue Folge
Arch Miss — Archives des Missions Scientifiques et Litteraires
Arch Missions Sci Litt — Archives des Missions Scientifiques et Litteraires
Arch Mitt Iran — Archaeologische Mitteilungen aus Iran
Arch Mkr An — Archiv fuer Mikroskopische Anatomie
Arch Molluskenkd — Archiv fuer Molluskenkunde
Arch Monaldi — Archivio Monaldi
Arch Monaldi Tisiol Mal Appar Respir — Archivio Monaldi per la Tisiologia e le Malattie dell'Apparato Respiratorio
Arch Mth Ntvd — Archiv for Mathematik og Naturvidenskab
Arch Mth Ps — Archiv der Mathematik und Physik. Grunert
Arch Mus — Archiv fuer Musikwissenschaft
Arch Mus Hist Nat — Archives du Museum d'Histoire Naturelle
Arch Mus Hist Nat Lyon — Archives. Museum d'Histoire Naturelle de Lyon
Arch Musik — Archiv fuer Musikwissenschaft
Arch Musikw — Archiv fuer Musikwissenschaft
Arch Mus Natl Hist Nat (Paris) — Archives. Museum National d'Histoire Naturelle (Paris)
Arch Mus Teyler — Archives. Musee Teyler
Arch N — Archaeological News
Arch Nachr Baden — Archaeologische Nachrichten aus Baden
Arch Nat Hist — Archives of Natural History
Arch NatSchutz — Archiv fuer Naturschutz
Arch NatSchutz LandschForsch — Archiv fuer Naturschutz und Landschaftsforschung
Arch Naturg — Archiv fuer Naturgeschichte
Arch Naturg (Berlin) — Archiv fuer Naturgeschichte (Berlin)
Arch Naturgesch — Archiv fuer Naturgeschichte
Arch Natur Hist — Archives of Natural History
Arch Naturkd Estlands 1 Ser — Archiv fuer die Naturkunde Estlands. 1 Serie Geologica, Chemica, et Physics
Arch Naturkd Liv Ehst Kurlands 2 Ser — Archiv fuer die Naturkunde Liv-, Ehst- und Kurlands. 1 Serie. Biologische Naturkunde
Arch Naturkd Liv- Est- Kurlands — Archiv fuer die Naturkunde Liv-, Est-, und Kurlands
Arch Naturkd Ostbaltikums 2 Ser — Archiv fuer die Naturkunde Ostbaltikums. 2 Serie. Biologische Naturkunde
Arch Naturk Liv Ehst Kurlands Ser 2 Biol Naturk — Archiv fuer die Naturkunde Liv-, Ehst- und Kurlands. Serie 2. Biologische Naturkunde
Arch Naturschutz Landschaftsf — Archiv fuer Naturschutz und Landschaftsforschung. Deutsche Akademie der Landwirtschaftswissenschaften zu Berlin
Arch Naturschutz Landschaftsforsch — Archiv fuer Naturschutz und Landschaftsforschung
Arch Naturw — Archaeologie und Naturwissenschaften
Arch Naturwiss Landesdurchf Boehmen — Archiv fuer die Naturwissenschaftliche Landesdurchforschung von Boehmen
Arch Natw Ldsdurchforsch Boehmen — Archiv der Naturwissenschaftlichen Landesdurchforschung von Boehmen
Arch Nauki Mater — Archiwum Nauki o Materialach
Arch Neerl — Archives Neerlandaises des Sciences Exactes et Naturelles
Arch Neerl Phon Exp — Archives Neerlandaises de Phonetique Experimentale
Arch Neerl Physiol — Archives Neerlandaises de Physiologie
Arch Neerl Sci Exactes Nat — Archives Neerlandaises des Sciences Exactes et Naturelles
Arch Neerl Sci Exactes Nat Ser 3A — Archives Neerlandaises des Sciences Exactes et Naturelles. Serie 3A. Sciences Exactes
Arch Neerl Sci Exactes Nat Ser 3B — Archives Neerlandaises des Sciences Exactes et Naturelles. Serie 3B. Sciences Naturelles
Arch Neerl Sci Exactes Nat Ser 3C — Archives Neerlandaises des Sciences Exactes et Naturelles. Serie 3C. Archives Neerlandaises de Physiologie
Arch Neerl Sci Exactes Nat Ser 4A — Archives Neerlandaises des Sciences Exactes et Naturelles. Serie 4A. Physica
Arch Neerl Sci Exactes Nat Ser 4B — Archives Neerlandaises des Sciences Exactes et Naturelles. Serie 4B. Archives Neerlandaises de Zoologie
Arch Neerl Sci Exactes Nat Ser 4C — Archives Neerlandaises des Sciences Exactes et Naturelles. Serie 4C. Acta Physiologica et Pharmacologica Neerlandica
Arch Neerl Sci Exact Nat — Archives Neerlandaises des Sciences Exactes et Naturelles
Arch Neerl Zool — Archives Neerlandaises de Zoologie
Arch Neuesten Entdeck Urwelt — Archiv fuer die Neuesten Entdeckungen aus der Urwelt
Arch Neurobiol — Archivos de Neurobiologia
Arch Neurocienc — Archivos de Neurociencias
Arch Neurol — Archives of Neurology
Arch Neurol (Chicago) — Archives of Neurology (Chicago)
Arch Neurol Psychiat — Archives of Neurology and Psychiatry
Arch Neurol Psychiatry — Archives of Neurology and Psychiatry
Arch Neurol Psychopathol — Archives of Neurology and Psychopathology
Arch News — Archaeological News
Arch NL — Archaeological News Letter
ArchNPhonExp — Archives Neerlandaises de Phonetique Experimentale
Arch Oceanogr Limnol — Archivio di Oceanografia e Limnologia
Arch Ochr Srodowiska — Archiwum Ochrony Srodowiska
Arch Odontoestomatol — Archivos de Odontoestomatologia
Arch Oeff Gesundh Pflege Els Lothr — Archiv fuer Oeffentliche Gesundheitspflege in Elsass-Lothringen

Arch Oeff Recht — Archiv des Oeffentlichen Rechts
Arch Oeff Rechts — Archiv des Oeffentlichen Rechts
Arch Oesterr Gesch — Archiv fuer Oesterreichische Geschichte
ArchOF — Archiv fuer Orientforschung
Arch Off Niger — Archives. Office du Niger
Arch Off R — Archiv des Oeffentlichen Rechts
Arch of Ped — Archives of Pediatrics
Arch Oftal Hispano-Am — Archivos de Oftalmologia Hispano-Americanos
Arch Oftalmol B Aires — Archivos de Oftalmologia de Buenos Aires
Arch Oftalmol Hisp-Am — Archivos de Oftalmologia Hispano-Americanos
Arch Ohrenh — Archiv fuer Ohrenheilkunde
Arch Ohrenheilk — Archiv fuer Ohrenheilkunde
Arch Ohren- Nasen- Kehlkopfheilkd — Archiv fuer Ohren-, Nasen-, und Kehlkopfheilkunde
Arch Ohrh — Archiv fuer Ohrenheilkunde
Arch Ohr-Nas Kehlkopfheilk — Archiv fuer Ohren-, Nasen-, und Kehlkopfheilkunde
Archo Med Chir — Archivio di Medicina e Chirurgia
Archo Med Interna — Archivio di Medicina Interna
Archo Neurochir — Archivio di Neurochirurgia
Archo Neurol — Archivio di Neurologia
Archo Oceanogr Limnol — Archivio di Oceanografia e Limnologia
Archo Oftal — Archivio di Oftalmoiatria
Archo Ortop — Archivio di Ortopedia
Archo Osp Mare — Archivio dell'Ospedale al Mare
Archo Ostet Ginec — Archivio di Ostetricia e Ginecologia
Archo Ottal — Archivio di Ottalmologia
Archo Patol Clin Infant — Archivio di Patologia e Clinica Infantile
Archo Patol Clin Med — Archivio di Patologia e Clinica Medica
Arch Oph — Archives of Ophthalmology
Arch Oph Ot — Archives of Ophthalmology and Otology
Arch Ophtal — Archives d'Ophtalmologie
Arch Ophtalmol — Archives d'Ophtalmologie
Arch Ophtalmol (Paris) — Archives d'Ophtalmologie et Revue Generale d'Ophtalmologie (Paris)
Arch Ophtalmol Rev Gen Ophtalmol — Archives d'Ophtalmologie et Revue Generale d'Ophtalmologie
Arch Ophth — Archives of Ophthalmology
Arch Ophthalm — Graefes Archiv fuer Ophthalmologie
Arch Ophthalmol — Archives of Ophthalmology
Arch Ophthalmol Albrecht von Graefes — Archiv fuer Ophthalmologie. Albrecht von Graefes
Arch Ophthalmol Chicago — Archives of Ophthalmology (Chicago)
Arch Opht (Paris) — Archives d'Ophtalmologie (Paris)
Archo Psichiat Antrop Crim — Archivio di Psichiatria, Antropologia Criminale
Archo Psicol Collett — Archivio di Psicologia Collettiva e Scienze Affini
Archo Psicol Neurol Psichiat — Archivio di Psicologia, Neurologia e Psichiatria
Arch Opt — Archiv fuer Optik
Arch Optik — Archiv fuer Optik
Archo Putti — Archivio Putti di Chirurgia degli Organi di Movimento
ArchOr — Archiv Orientalni
Archo Radiol — Archivio di Radiologia
Arch Oral B — Archives of Oral Biology
Arch Oral Biol — Archives of Oral Biology
Arch Orient — Archiv fuer Orientforschung
ArchOrient — Archiv Orientalni
Arch Orientforsch — Archiv fuer Orientforschung
Arch Orient Med Chir — Archives Orientales de Medecine et de Chirurgie
Arch Or Lat — Archives de l'Orient Latin
Arch Orthop — Archiv fuer Orthopaedische und Unfall-Chirurgie
Arch Orthop Mechanother Unfallchir — Archiv fuer Orthopaedie, Mechanotherapie, und Unfallchirurgie
Arch Orthop Trauma Surg — Archives of Orthopaedic and Traumatic Surgery
Arch Orthop Unfall-Chir — Archiv fuer Orthopaedische und Unfall-Chirurgie
Arch Ortop — Archivio di Ortopedia
Arch Ortop Reumatol — Archivio di Ortopedia e Reumatologia
Archos Am Med — Archivos Americanos de Medicina
Archos Anat Patol Coimbra — Archivos de Anatomia Patologica, Patologia Correlativa e Neuro-Ergenologia (Coimbra)
Archos Anat Santiago — Archivos de Anatomia (Santiago de Compostela)
Archos Argent Derm — Archivos Argentinos de Dermatologia
Archos Argent Enferm Apar Dig — Archivos Argentinos de Enfermedades del Aparato Digestivo y de la Nutricion
Archos Bioquim Quim Farmac (Tucuman) — Archivos de Bioquimica, Quimica, y Farmacia (Tucuman)
Archos Bromat — Archivos de Bromatologia
Archo Sci Biol — Archivio di Scienze Biologiche
Archo Sci Cerebraz — Archivio di Scienze della Cerebrazione e dei Psichismi
Archo Scient Med Vet — Archivio Scientifico di Medicina Veterinaria
Archo Sci Med — Archivio per le Scienze Mediche
Archo Sci Osped — Archivio di Scienza Ospedaliera
Archos Hosps B Aires — Archivos de los Hospitales (Buenos Aires)
Archos Hosps S Casa S Paulo — Archivos dos Hospitals da Santa Casa de Sao Paulo
Archos Hyg Patol Exot Lisb — Archivos de Hygiene e Patologia Exoticas (Lisboa)
Archos Iberoam Hist Med — Archivos Iberoamericanos de Historia de la Medicina y de Antropologia Medica
Archos Ibit — Archivos do Ibit
Archos Indo Port Med Hist Nat — Archivos Indo-Portugueses de Medicina e Historia Natural
Archos Inst Aclim (Almeria) — Archivos. Instituto de Aclimatacion (Almeria, Espana)
Archos Inst Antrop (Natal) — Archivos. Instituto Antropologia (Natal)
Archos Inst Biol Def Agric Anim S Paulo — Archivos do Instituto Biologico de Defesa Agricola e Animal (Sao Paulo)

Archos Inst Biol Exerc Madr — Archivos del Instituto de Biologia do Exercito (Madrid)
Archos Inst Biol Exerc Rio de J — Archivos do Instituto de Biologia do Exercito (Rio de Janeiro)
Archos Inst Biol (S Paulo) — Archivos. Instituto Biologico (Sao Paulo)
Archos Inst Biol Veg Rio de J — Archivos do Instituto de Biologia Vegetal (Rio de Janeiro)
Archos Inst Bras Invest Tuberc — Archivos do Instituto Brasileiro para Investigacao da Tuberculose
Archos Inst Cardiol Mex — Archivos del Instituto de Cardiologia de Mexico
Archos Inst Cirug Prov B Aires — Archivos del Instituto de Cirugia de la Provincia de Buenos Aires Prof. Dr. Luis Guemes
Archos Inst Estud Afr — Archivos Instituto de Estudios Africanos
Archos Inst Farmac Exp Madr — Archivos del Instituto de Farmacologia Experimental (Madrid)
Archos Inst Farmac Univ Coimbra — Archivos do Instituto de Farmacologia e Terapeutica Experimental (Universidade de Coimbra)
Archos Inst Med Le Gal Lisb — Archivos do Instituto de Medicina Le Gal de Lisboa
Archos Inst Med Leg Rio de J — Archivos do Instituto Medico-Legal (Rio de Janeiro)
Archos Inst Med Pract — Archivos del Instituto de Medicina Practica
Archos Inst Nac Hidrol Clim Med Habana — Archivos del Instituto Nacional de Hidrologia y Climatologia Medicas (Habana)
Archos Inst Nac Hig Alfonso XIII — Archivos del Instituto Nacional de Higiene de Alfonso XIII
Archos Inst Patol Ger Univ Coimbra — Archivos do Instituto de Patologia Geral da Universidade de Coimbra
Archos Inst Pesq Agron Pernambuco — Archivos do Instituto de Pesquisas Agronomicas (Pernambuco)
Archos Inst Pesq Vet Desiderio Finamor — Archivos do Instituto de Pesquisas Veterinarias Desiderio Finamor
Archos Inst Quim Biol Minas Gerais — Archivos do Instituto Quimico-Biologico do Estado de Minas Gerais
Archos Inst Vital Brazil — Archivos do Instituto Vital Brazil
Archos Int Hidatid — Archivos Internacionales de la Hidatidosis
Archos Jard Bot Rio de J — Archivos do Jardim Botanico (Rio de Janeiro)
Archos Lat Am Cardiol Hemat — Archivos Latino-Americanos de Cardiologia y Hematologia
Archos Lat Am Neurol Psiquiat Med Leg — Archivos Latino-Americanos de Neurologia, Psiquiatria, Medicina Legal
Archos Lat Am Pediat — Archivos Latino-Americanos de Pediatria
Archos Lat Med Biol — Archivos Latinos de Medicina y de Biologia
Archos Lat Rinol Lar Otol — Archivos Latinos de Rinologia, Laringologia, Otologia
Archos Lepra Bogota — Archivos de Lepra (Bogota)
Archos Manicom Judic Heitor Carrilho — Archivos do Manicomio Judiciario Heitor Carrilho
Archos Med Cirug Espec — Archivos de Medicina, Cirugia y Especialidades
Archos Mus Paranaie — Archivos. Museu Paranaie
Arch Osp Mare — Archivio. Ospedale al Mare
Archos Soc Biol Montev — Archivos. Sociedad de Biologia de Montevideo
Arch Ostet Ginecol — Archivio di Ostetricia e Ginecologia
Archo Stor Sci — Archivio di Storia della Scienza
Archo Stud Fisiopatol Clin Ricam — Archivio per lo Studio della Fisiopatologia e Clinica del Ricambio
Archos Venez Nutr — Archivos Venezolanos de Nutricion
Archos Venez Puericult Pediat — Archivos Venezolanos de Puericultura y Pediatria
Archos Venez Soc Oto Rino Lar — Archivos Venezolanos de la Sociedad de Oto-rino-laringologia, Oftalmologia, Neurologia
Archos Vet Pract La Coruna — Archivos de Veterinaria Practica (La Coruna)
Archos Zool Est S Paulo — Archivos de Zoologia do Estado de Sao Paulo
Archos Zootecnia — Archivos de Zootecnia
Arch Ot — Archives of Otology
Archo Tisiol — Archivio di Tisiologia e delle Malattie dell'Aparato Respiratorio
Arch Otol — Archives of Otology
Arch Otolar — Archives of Otolaryngology
Arch Otolaryng — Archives of Otolaryngology
Arch Otolaryngol — Archives of Otolaryngology
Arch Otolaryngol Head and Neck Surg — Archives of Otolaryngology and Head and Neck Surgery
Arch Otolaryngol Head Neck Surg — Archives of Otolaryngology and Head and Neck Surgery
Arch Oto-R — Archives of Oto-Rhino-Laryngology
Arch Oto-Rhino-Laryngol — Archives of Oto-Rhino-Laryngology
Arch Otorhinolaryngol Suppl — Archives of Oto-Rhino-Laryngology. Supplement
Arch Ottalmol — Archivio di Ottalmologia
Archo Vet Ital — Archivio Veterinario Italiano
Arch Oxon — Archaeologia Oxoniensis
Archo Zool Ital — Archivio Zoologico Italiano
Arch (P) — Archeologia (Paris)
Arch P — Archiv fuer Papyrusforschung
Arch Pamjatki URSR — Arkheologichni Pamiatky URSR
Arch Pap — Archiv fuer Papyrusforschung
Arch Papyrusf — Archiv fuer Papyrusforschung und Verwandte Gebiete
Arch Parasitol — Archives de Parasitologia
Arch Parasitol (Paris) — Archives de Parasitologie (Paris)
Arch (Paris) — Archeologia (Paris)
Arch Path — Archives of Pathology [*Later, Archives of Pathology and Laboratory Medicine*]
Arch Path Anat — Archiv fuer Pathologische Anatomie und Physiologie und fuer Klinische Medizin
Arch Path and Lab Med — Archives of Pathology and Laboratory Medicine
Arch Pathol — Archives of Pathology [*Later, Archives of Pathology and Laboratory Medicine*]

Arch Pathol Anat — Virchows Archiv fuer Pathologische Anatomie und Physiologie
Arch Pathol Lab Med — Archives of Pathology and Laboratory Medicine
Arch Patol Clin Med — Archivio di Patologia e Clinica Medica
Arch Patol e Clin Med — Archivio di Patologia e Clinica Medica
Arch Pediat — Archives of Pediatrics
Arch Pediatr — Archives de Pediatrie
Arch Pediatr — Archives of Pediatrics
Arch Pediatr Adolesc Med — Archives of Pediatrics and Adolescent Medicine
Arch Pediatr Urug — Archivos de Pediatria del Uruguay
Arch Pelzk — Archiv fuer Pelzkunde
Arch per l Ante l Etn — Archivio per l'Antropologia e l'Etnologia
Arch Peru Patol Clin — Archivos Peruanos de Patologia y Clinica
Arch Peru Patol Clin (Lima) — Archivos Peruanos de Patologia e Clinica (Lima)
Arch PF — Archiv fuer Papyrusforschung und Verwandte Gebiete
Arch Pflanzenbau — Archiv fuer Pflanzenbau
Arch Pflanzenbau Abt A Wiss Arch Landwirtsch — Archiv fuer Pflanzenbau. Abt. A der Wissenschaftliches Archiv fuer Landwirtschaft
Arch Pflanzenschutz — Archiv fuer Pflanzenschutz
Arch PflBau — Archiv fuer Pflanzenbau
Arch Pflsch — Archiv fuer Pflanzenschutz
Arch Pflschutz — Archiv fuer Pflanzenschutz
Arch Pharm — Archiv der Pharmazie
Arch Pharmacal Res — Archives of Pharmacal Research
Arch Pharmacal Res (Seoul) — Archives of Pharmacal Research (Seoul)
Arch Pharmacol — Archives of Pharmacology
Arch Pharm Aerztl Naturk — Archiv fuer die Pharmacie und Aerztliche Naturkunde
Arch Pharmakol Exp Pathol — Archiv fuer Pharmakologie und Experimentelle Pathologie. Naunyn-Schmiedebergs
Arch Pharmakol Naunyn-Schmiedebergs — Archiv fuer Pharmakologie. Naunyn-Schmiedebergs
Arch Pharm Apotheker Vereins Noerdl Teutschl — Archiv der Pharmacie des Apotheker-Vereins im Noerdlichen Teutschland
Arch Pharm (Athens) — Archeia tes Pharmakeutikes (Athens)
Arch Pharm Ber Dtsch Pharm Ges — Archiv der Pharmazie und Berichte der Deutschen Pharmazeutischen Gesellschaft
Arch Pharm (Berl) — Archiv der Pharmazie und Berichte der Deutschen Pharmazeutischen Gesellschaft (Berlin)
Arch Pharm Berlin — Archiv der Pharmacie. Eine Zeitschrift des Apotheker-Vereins im Noerdlichen Teutschland (Berlin)
Arch Pharm Chem — Archiv foer Pharmaci og Chemi
Arch Pharm Chem Sci Ed — Archiv foer Pharmaci og Chemi. Scientific Edition
Arch Pharm (Paris) — Archives de Pharmacie (Paris)
Arch Pharm Res — Archives of Pharmacal Research
Arch Pharm (Weinheim) — Archiv der Pharmazie (Weinheim)
Arch Pharm (Weinheim Ger) — Archiv der Pharmazie (Weinheim, Germany)
Arch Pharm Weinheim Ger Beil — Archiv der Pharmazie und Berichte der Deutschen Pharmazeutischen Gesellschaft (Weinheim, Germany)
Arch Phil — Archives de Philosophie
Arch Phil Dr — Archives de Philosophie du Droit
Arch Philos — Archives de Philosophie
Arch Phil Paris — Archives de Philosophie (Paris)
Arch Phm — Archiv des Apothekervereins im Nordlichen Teutschland. Archiv der Pharmacie
Arch Phys Biol — Archives de Physique Biologique
Arch Phys Biol Chim Phys Corps Organ — Archives de Physique Biologique et de Chimie Physique des Corps Organises
Arch Phys Diaetet Ther — Archiv fuer Physikalisch-Diaetetische Therapie in der Aerztlichen Praxis
Arch Physiol — Archiv fuer die Physiologie
Arch Physiol — Archiv fuer Physiologie
Arch Physiol Biochem — Archives of Physiology and Biochemistry
Arch Phys M — Archives of Physical Medicine and Rehabilitation
Arch Phys Med — Archives of Physical Medicine
Arch Phys Med — Archives of Physical Medicine and Rehabilitation
Arch Phys Med Med Tech — Archiv fuer Physikalische Medizin und Medizinische Technik
Arch Phys Med Rehab — Archives of Physical Medicine and Rehabilitation
Arch Phys Med Rehabil — Archives of Physical Medicine and Rehabilitation
Arch Phys Ther — Archiv fuer Physikalische Therapie
Arch Phys Ther Baln Klim — Archiv fuer Physikalische Therapie, Balneologie, und Klimatologie
Arch Phys Ther X Ray Radium — Archives of Physical Therapy, X-Ray, Radium
Arch Phytopathol Pflanzenschutz — Archiv fuer Phytopathologie und Pflanzenschutz
Arch Phytopathol Plant Prot — Archives of Phytopathology and Plant Protection
Arch Phytopath Pflschutz — Archiv fuer Phytopathologie und Pflanzenschutz
Arch Plasmol Gen — Archives de Plasmologie Generale
Arch Podiatr Med Foot Surg — Archives of Podiatric Medicine and Foot Surgery
Arch Pol — Archeologia Polski
Arch Pol Criminelle — Archives de Politique Criminelle
Arch Polon — Archaeologia Polona
Arch Polona — Archaeologia Polona
Arch Polski — Archeologia Polski
Arch Pont — Archeion Pontou
Arch Pontou — Archeion Pontou
Arch Port Sci Biol — Archives Portugaises des Sciences Biologiques
Arch Portugues — Arqueologo Portugues
Arch Post Telegr — Archiv fuer Post und Telegraphie
Arch Post u Fernmeldew — Archiv fuer das Post- und Fernmeldewesen
Arch Post und Fernmeldewes — Archiv fuer das Post- und Fernmeldewesen
Arch Poult Sci — Archives of Poultry Science
Arch Pract Pharm — Archives of Practical Pharmacy
Arch Prehist Levantina — Archivo de Prehistoria Levantina. CSIC (Consejo Superior de Investigaciones Cientificas)
Arch Pr Hist Lev — Archivo de Prehistoria Levantina

Arch Prirodov Prozk Moravy Odd Bot — Archiv na Prirodovedecke Prozkoumani Moravy Oddel Botanicky</PHR> %
Arch Prirodov Vyzk Cech — Archiv pro Prirodovedecky Vyzkum Cech
Arch Prirod Vyzk Cech Prag — Archiv pro Prirodovedecky Vyzkum Cech (Praha)
Arch Prir Vyzk Cech — Archiv pro Prirodovedecky Vyzkum Cech
Arch Pr Lev — Archivo de Prehistoria Levantina
Arch Procesow Spalania — Archiwum Procesow Spalania
Arch Protistenk — Archiv fuer Protistenkunde
Arch Protistenkd — Archiv fuer Protistenkunde. Protozoen-Algen-Pilze
Arch Prov Chir — Archives Provinciales de Chirurgie
Arch Psichiatr — Archivio di Psichiatria
Arch Psicol Neurol Psichiatr — Archivio di Psicologia, Neurologia, e Psichiatria
Arch Psych — Archiv fuer Psychologie
Arch Psychi — Archiv fuer Psychiatrie und Nervenkrankheiten
Arch Psychiat Nervenkr — Archiv fuer Psychiatrie und Nervenkrankheiten
Arch Psychiat NervKrankh — Archiv fuer Psychiatrie und Nervenkrankheiten
Arch Psychiatr — Archiv fuer Psychiatrie und Nervenheilkunde
Arch Psychiatr Nervenkr — Archiv fuer Psychiatrie und Nervenkrankheiten
Arch Psychiatr Nervenkrankh — Archiv fuer Psychiatrie und Nervenkrankheiten
Arch Psychiatr Nurs — Archives of Psychiatric Nursing
Arch Psychiatry Neurol Sci — Archives of Psychiatry and Neurological Sciences
Arch Psychol — Archives of Psychology [*New York*]
Arch Psychol (Frankf) — Archiv fuer Psychologie (Frankfurt Am Main)
Arch Putti Chir Organi Mov — Archivio Putti di Chirurgia degli Organi di Movimento
Arch Quebec — Archeologie Quebec
Arch R — Archeologia (Rome)
Arch R — Architectural Review
Arch Radiol — Archivio di Radiologia
Arch Radiol (Napoli) — Archivio di Radiologia (Napoli)
Arch Rass Ital Ottalmol — Archivio e Rassegna Italiana di Ottalmologia
Arch Rass- u Ges Biol — Archiv fuer Rassen- und Gesellschafts-Biologie Einschliessend Rassen- und Gesellschaftshygiene
Arch Rational Mech Anal — Archive for Rational Mechanics and Analysis
Arch Ration Mech Anal — Archive for Rational Mechanics and Analysis
Arch Ration Mech and Anal — Archive for Rational Mechanics and Analysis
Arch Ration Ther — Archiv fuer Rationelle Therapie
Archre Australia — Architecture Australia
Arch Rec — Architectural Record
Arch Rech Agron Pastorales Vietnam — Archives des Recherches Agronomiques et Pastorales au Vietnam
Arch Rechtspfl Sachs — Archiv fuer Rechtspflege in Sachsen. Thueringen und Anhalt
Arch Rechts Soz — Archiv fuer Rechts- und Sozialphilosophie
Arch Rechts Sozialphil — Archiv fuer Rechts- und Sozialphilosophie
Archre East Midlands — Architecture East Midlands
Arch Reformation Hist — Archive for Reformation History
Arch Reformationsgesch — Archiv fuer Reformationsgeschichte
Archre from Scandinavia — Architecture from Scandinavia
Archre in Australia — Architecture in Australia [*Later, Architecture Australia*]
Archre in Greece — Architecture in Greece
Archre in Ireland — Architecture in Ireland
Archre in Israel — Architecture in Israel
Arch Relig — Archiv fuer Religionswissenschaft
Arch Religionsw — Archiv fuer Religionswissenschaft
Arch Rel Wiss — Archiv fuer Religionswissenschaft
Archre Nebr — Architecture Nebraska
Arch Rep — Archaeological Reports
Arch Reports — Archaeological Reports
Archre SA — Architecture South Africa
Arch Res Ind Carcinog — Archives of Research on Industrial Carcinogenesis
Arch Rettungsw — Archiv fuer Rettungswesen und Erste Aerztliche Hilfe
Arch Rev — Architectural Review
Arch Revista Ci Hist — Archivo. Revista de Ciencias Historicas
Archre West Midlands — Architecture West Midlands
Arch Ricam — Archivio del Ricambio
Arch R Inst Bacteriol Camara Pestana — Archivos. Real Instituto Bacteriologico Camara Pestana
Arch R Mech — Archive for Rational Mechanics and Analysis
Arch Rom — Archivum Romanicum
Arch Roman — Archivum Romanicum
Arch Roum Pathol Exp Microbiol — Archives Roumaines de Pathologie Experimentale et de Microbiologie
Arch Roz — Archeologike Rozhledy
Arch Rozhl — Archeologike Rozhledy
Arch Rozhledy — Archeologicke Rozhledy
Arch R Soz Phil — Archiv fuer Rechts und Sozialphilosophie
Arch Rubbercult — Archief voor de Rubbercultuur
Arch Rubber Cultiv — Archives of Rubber Cultivation
Arch Rubber Cultivation — Archives of Rubber Cultivation
Arch Rubber Cultiv (Bogor) — Archives of Rubber Cultivation (Bogor)
Arch Rubbercult Ned Indie — Archief voor de Rubbercultuur in Nederlandsch-Indie
ArchRW — Archiv fuer Religionswissenschaft
Arch S — Archaeologie des Schweiz
Archs Anat Microsc — Archives d'Anatomie Microscopique
Archs Anat Microsc Morph Exp — Archives d'Anatomie Microscopique et de Morphologie Experimentale
Arch S A Of — Archivos. Sociedad Americana de Oftalmologia y Optometria
Archs Biochem — Archives of Biochemistry
Archs Biochem Biophys — Archives of Biochemistry and Biophysics
Archs Biol (Liege) — Archives de Biologie (Liege)
Arch Sc — Archives of Science and Transactions of the Orleans County Society of Natural Sciences
Arch Schiffb Schiff — Archiv fuer Schiffbau und Schiffahrt
Arch Schiffs-u Tropen-Hyg — Archiv fuer Schiffs-und Tropen-Hygiene

Arch Schlesische Kirchengesch — Archiv fuer Schlesische Kirchengeschichte
Arch Schreib u Buchw — Archiv fuer Schreib- und Buchwesen
Arch Schriftkde — Archiv fuer Schriftkunde
Arch Sci — Archives des Sciences
Arch Sci Avic — Archives de Science Avicole
Arch Sci Avicole — Archives de Science Avicole
Arch Sci Biol — Archivio di Scienze Biologiche
Arch Sci Biol (Belgrade) — Archives des Sciences Biologiques (Belgrade)
Arch Sci Biol Fr Ed — Archives des Sciences Biologiques (French Edition)
Arch Sci Biol Naples — Archivio di Scienze Biologiche (Naples)
Arch Sci Biol (USSR) — Archives des Sciences Biologiques (USSR)
Arch Sci C R Seances Soc — Archives des Sciences et Compte Rendu Seances de la Societe
Arch Science R — Architectural Science Review
Arch Sci (Geneva) — Archives des Sciences (Geneva)
Arch Sci Lav — Archivio di Scienze del Lavoro
Arch Sci Med — Archivio per le Scienze Mediche
Arch Sci Ph — Archives des Sciences Physiologiques
Arch Sci Physiol — Archives des Sciences Physiologiques
Arch Sci Phys Nat — Archives des Sciences Physiques et Naturelles. Supplement a la Bibliotheque Universelle
Arch Sci Rev — Architectural Science Review
Arch Sci Soc Coop Dev — Archives de Sciences Sociales de la Cooperation et du Developpement
Arch Sci Social Relig — Archives de Sciences Sociales des Religions
Arch Sci Soc Phys Hist Nat Geneve — Archives des Sciences. Societe de Physique et d'Histoire Naturelle de Geneve
Arch Sci Soc Relig — Archives de Sciences Sociales des Relgions
Arch Sci Suppl — Archives des Sciences. Supplement
Arch Sci Trans Orleans County Soc Nat Sci — Archives of Science and Transactions. Orleans County Society of Natural Sciences
Arch Sc Med (Torino) — Archivio per le Scienze Mediche (Torino)
Arch Scot — Archaeologia Scotia
Arch Sc Phys Nat — Archives des Sciences Physiques et Naturelles
Arch Sc Ps Nt — Bibliotheque Universelle. Archives des Sciences Physiques et Naturelles
Archs Derm — Archives of Dermatology
Arch Sect Sci Nat Phys Math Inst Grand Ducal Luxem — Archives. Section des Sciences Naturelles, Physiques, et Mathematiques. Institut Grand-Ducal de Luxembourg
Archs Envir Contam Toxic — Archives of Environmental Contamination and Toxicology
Archs Envir Hlth — Archives of Environmental Health
Arch Serbes Med Gen — Archives Serbes de Medecine Generale
Arch Serv Sante Armee Belge — Archives. Service de Sante de l'Armee Belge
Archs et Biblioths Belgique — Archives et Bibliotheques de Belgique
Archs Eur Sociologie — Archives Europeennes de Sociologie
Arch Sex Be — Archives of Sexual Behavior
Arch Sex Behav — Archives of Sexual Behavior
Arch SexForsch — Archiv fuer Sexualforschung
Archs Hist Exact Sci — Archives for History of Exact Sciences
Archs Horlog — Archives de l'Horlogerie
Archs Hosp — Archives Hospitalieres
Archs Ind Hyg — Archives of Industrial Hygiene and Occupational Medicine
Archs Ingr Cons — Archives de l'Ingenieur-Conseil
Archs Ins Prophyl — Archives de l'Institut Prophylactique
Archs Inst Bot Univ Liege — Archives de l'Institut Botanique de l'Universite de Liege
Archs Inst Gr-Duc Luxemb — Archives. Institut Grand-Ducal de Luxembourg
Archs Inst Hessarek — Archives de l'Institut d'Hessarek
Archs Inst Med Leg Lille — Archives de l'Institut de Medecine Legale et de Medecine Sociale de Lille
Archs Inst Paleont Hum — Archives de l'Institut de Paleontologie Humaine. Memoires
Archs Inst Pasteur Alger — Archives de l'Institut Pasteur d'Algerie
Archs Inst Pasteur Guyana Terr Inini — Archives de l'Institut Pasteur de la Guyana et du Territoire de l'Inini
Archs Inst Pasteur Guyane Fr — Archives de l'Institut Pasteur de la Guyane Francaise
Archs Inst Pasteur Hellen — Archives de l'Institut Pasteur Hellenique
Archs Inst Pasteur Iran — Archives de l'Institut Pasteur de l'Iran
Archs Inst Pasteur Maroc — Archives de l'Institut Pasteur du Maroc
Archs Inst Pasteur Martinique — Archives de l'Institut Pasteur de la Martinique
Archs Inst Pasteur Tananarive — Archives de l'Institut Pasteur de Tananarive
Archs Inst Past Guy — Archives. Institut Pasteur de la Guyane et du Territoire de l'Inini
Archs Inst Past Guy Ter L In — Archives. Institut Pasteur de la Guyane Francaise et du Territoire de l'Inini
Archs Inst Past Mart — Archives. Institut Pasteur de la Martinique
Archs Insts Pasteur Afr N — Archives. Instituts Pasteur de l'Afrique du Nord
Archs Intern Med — Archives of Internal Medicine
Archs Int Pharmacodyn Ther — Archives Internationales de Pharmacodynamie et de Therapie
Archs Int Physiol — Archives Internationales de Physiologie
Archs Int Physiol Biochim — Archives Internationales de Physiologie et de Biochimie
Arch Sippenforsch — Archiv fuer Sippenforschung und alle Verwandten Gebiete
Arch Skand Beitr Naturgesch — Archiv Skandinavischer Beitraege zur Naturgeschichte
Arch Slaves Biol — Archives Slaves de Biologie
Archs Med-Chir Normandie — Archives Medico-Chirurgicales de Normandie
Archs Neerl Zool — Archives Neerlandaises de Zoologie
Arch Soc Am Oftalmol Optom — Archivos. Sociedad Americana de Oftalmologia y Optometria
Arch Soc Biol Montev — Archivos. Sociedad de Biologia de Montevideo

Arch Soc Biol Montevideo Supl — Archivos. Sociedad de Biologia de Montevideo. Suplemento
Arch Soc Canaria Oftalmol — Archivos. Sociedad Canaria de Oftalmologia
Arch Soc Esp Oftalmol — Archivos. Sociedad Espanola de Oftalmologia
Arch Soc Estud Clin Habana — Archivos. Sociedad de Estudios Clinicos de la Habana
Arch Soc Fr Biol Med — Archives. Societe Francaise de Biologie Medicale
Arch Soc Fr Chir Plast Reconstr — Archives. Societe Francaise de Chirurgie Plastique et Reconstructive
Arch Soc Geneeskd Hyg Tijdschr Pathol Physiol Arb — Archief van Sociale Geneeskunde en Hygiene en Tijdschrift voor Pathologie en Physiologie van den Arbeid
Arch Sociol Relig — Archives de Sociologie des Religions
Arch Soc Oftalmol Hisp-Am — Archivos. Sociedad Oftalmologica Hispano-Americana
Arch Soc Rom — Archivio. Deputazione Romana di Storia Patria
Arch Soc Zool-Bot Fenn "Vanamo" — Archivum Societatis Zoologicae-Botanicae Fennicae "Vanamo"
Arch (Sofia) — Archeologie (Sofia)
Archs Orient Med Chir — Archives Orientales de Medecine et de Chirurgie
Archs Orthod — Archives of Orthodontics
Archs Otol — Archives of Otology
Archs Otolar — Archives of Otolaryngology
Arch Sozialgesch — Archiv fuer Sozialgeschichte
Archs Parasit — Archives de Parasitologie
Archs Path — Archives of Pathology
Archs Path Inst Lond — Archives of the Pathological Institute. London Hospital
Archs Pediat — Archives of Pediatrics
Archs Phil Psychol Scient Meth — Archives of Philosophy, Psychology, and Scientific Methods
Archs Phys Biol — Archives de Physique Biologique
Archs Physiol Ther — Archives of Physiological Therapy
Archs Phys Med — Archives of Physical Medicine
Archs Phys Med Rehabil — Archives of Physical Medicine and Rehabilitation
Archs Phys Ther — Archives of Physical Therapy (X-ray, Radium)
Archs Plasmol Gen — Archives de Plasmologie Generale
Archs Pop Ass Japan — Archives of the Population Association of Japan
Archs Port Sci Biol — Archives Portugaises des Sciences Biologiques
Archs Prov Chir — Archives Provinciales de Chirurgie
Archs Psychoanal — Archives of Psychoanalysis
Archs Psychol Geneve — Archives de Psychologie (Geneve)
Archs Psychol NY — Archives of Psychology (New York)
Archs Psychol Suisse Romande — Archives de Psychologie de la Suisse Romande
Archs Publ Hlth Lab Univ Manchr — Archives of the Public Health Laboratory of the University of Manchester
Archs Radiol Electrother — Archives of Radiology and Electrotherapy
Archs Ration Mech Analysis — Archive for Rational Mechanics and Analysis
Archs Rech Agron Cambodge Laos Vietnam — Archives des Recherches Agronomiques au Cambodge, au Laos, et au Vietnam
Archs Rech Agron Past Viet Nam — Archives des Recherches Agronomiques et Pastorales au Viet Nam
Archs Rhum — Archives de Rhumatologie
Archs Roentg Ray — Archives of the Roentgen Ray
ArchSS — Archivio Storico Siciliano
Arch S Sardo — Archivio Storico Sardo
Archs Sci Physiol — Archives des Sciences Physiologiques
Archs Sci Soc Religions — Archives de Sciences Sociales des Religions
Arch S Sic — Archivio Storico Siciliano
Arch SS Rel — Archives de Sciences Sociales des Religions
Archs Suisses Anthrop Gen — Archives Suisses d'Anthropologie Generale
Arch Stomatol — Archivio Stomatologico
Arch Stor — Archivio Storico Italiano
Arch Stor Cal — Archivio Storico della Calabria
Arch Stor Calabria — Archivio Storico per la Calabria e la Lucania
Arch Stor Cal Luc — Archivio Storico per la Calabria e la Lucania
Arch Stor Cla — Archivio Storico per la Calabria e la Lucania
Arch Stor Dalmazia — Archivio Storico per la Dalmazia
Arch Stor I — Archivio Storico Italiano
Arch Storia Sci — Archivio di Storia della Scienza
Arch Storico per Prov Nap — Archivio Storico per la Provincie Napoletane
Arch Stor Ital — Archivio Storico Italiano
Arch Stor Lodigiano — Archivo Storico Lodigiano
Arch Stor Lomb — Archivio Storico Lombardo
Arch Stor Patria — Archivio. Societa Romana di Storia Patria
Arch Stor Prov Nap — Archivio Storico per la Provincie Napoletane
Arch Stor Prov Parmensi — Archivio Storico per le Provincie Parmensi
Arch Stor Publiese — Archivio Storico Pugliese
Arch Stor Pugl — Archivio Storico Pugliese
Arch Stor Sardo — Archivio Storico Sardo
Arch Stor Sic — Archivio Storico per la Sicilia Orientale
Arch Stor Sicil — Archivio Storico Siciliano
Arch Stor Sicilia — Archivio Storico per la Sicilia Orientale
Arch Stor Sicilia Orient — Archivio Storico per la Sicilia Orientale
Arch Stor Sicil Ser 3 — Archivio Storico Siciliano. Serie 3
Arch Stor Sic Or — Archivio Storico per la Sicilia Orientale
Arch Stud Fisiopatol Clin Ricamb — Archivio per lo Studio della Fisiopatologia e Clinica del Ricambio
Arch Suikerind Ned Indie — Archief voor de Suikerindustrie in Nederlandsch-Indie
Arch Suikerind Ned Ned Indie — Archief voor de Suikerindustrie in Nederland en Nederlandsch-Indie
Arch Suikerindustr Ned Ned Indie — Archief voor de Suikerindustrie in Nederland en Nederlandsch-Indie
Arch Suisses Anthrop — Archives Suisses d'Anthropologie Generale
Arch Suisses Anthropol Gen — Archives Suisses d'Anthropologie Generale

Arch Suisses Neurol Neurochir Psychiatr — Archives Suisses de Neurologie, Neurochirurgie, et de Psychiatrie

Archs Un Med Balkan — Archives. Union Medicale Balkanique

Arch Surg — Archives of Surgery

Arch Surg Chicago — Archives of Surgery (Chicago)

Archs Virol — Archives of Virology

Arch Svizz Neurol Neurochir Psichiatr — Archivio Svizzero di Neurologia, Neurochirurgia, e Psichiatria

Arch Svizz Neurol Psichiatr — Archivio Svizzero di Neurologia e Psichiatria

Archs Zool Exp Gen — Archives de Zoologie Experimentale et Generale

ArchT — Archeion Thrakes

Arch (T) — Archeologia (Torun)

Archt & Bldr — Architect and Builder

Archt & Surveyor — Architect and Surveyor

Arch Tea Cultiv — Archives of Tea Cultivation

Arch Tech — Architectural Technology

Arch Tech Mess — Archiv fuer Technisches Messen

Arch Tech Mess Ind Messtech — Archiv fuer Technisches Messen und Industrielle Messtechnik

Arch Tech Mess Messtech Prax — Archiv fuer Technisches Messen und Messtechnische Praxis

Arch Tech Mess und Ind Messtech — Archiv fuer Technisches Messen und Industrielle Messtechnik

Arch Tech Mess und Messtech Prax — Archiv fuer Technisches Messen und Messtechnische Praxis

Arch Termodyn — Archiwum Termodynamiki

Arch Termodyn Spal — Archiwum Termodynamiki i Spalania

Arch Termodyn Spalania — Archiwum Termodynamiki i Spalania

Arch Tess — Archeion Thessalikon Meleton

Arch Teutsch Landw — Archiv der Teutschen Landwirthschaft

Arch Theecult — Archief voor de Theecultuur

Arch Theecult Ned Indie — Archief voor de Theecultuur in Nederlandsch-Indie

Arch Thermodyn — Archives of Thermodynamics

Arch Thermodyn Combust — Archives of Thermodynamics and Combustion

Arch Thess Mel — Archeion Thessalikon Meleton

Arch Tieraerztl Fortbild — Archiv fuer Tieraerztliche Fortbildung

Arch Tierernaehr — Archiv fuer Tierernaehrung

Arch Tierernaehr Tierz Abt B Wiss Arch Landwirtsch — Archiv fuer Tierernaehrung und Tierzucht. Abteilung B der Wissenschaftliches Archiv fuer Landwirtschaft

Arch Tierernahr Arch Anim Nutr — Archiv fuer Tierernaehrung/Archives of Animal Nutrition

Arch Tierz — Archiv fuer Tierzucht

Arch Tisiol Mal Appar Respir — Archivio di Tisiologia e delle Malattie dell'Apparato Respiratorio

Arch Tisiol Mal App Resp — Archivio di Tisiologia e delle Malattie dell'Apparato Respiratorio

Archtl Bull — Architectural Bulletin

Archtl Design — Architectural Design

Archtl Forum (Dublin) — Architectural Forum (Dublin)

Archtl History — Architectural History

Archtl Jnl — Architectural Journal

Archtl Magazine Egyptian Assocn of Archts — Architectural Magazine. Egyptian Association of Architects

Archtl Monographs — Architectural Monographs

Archtl Preservation — Architectural Preservation

Archtl Psychology Newsletter — Architectural Psychology Newsletter

Archtl Record — Architectural Record

Archtl Review — Architectural Review

Archtl Science Review — Architectural Science Review

Arch Today — Architecture Today

Arch Towarz Nauk We Lwowie Dzial 3 Mat Przyr — Archiwum Towarzystwa Naukowego we Lwowie. Dzial 3. Matematyczno-Przyrodniczy

Arch Toxic — Archives of Toxicology

Arch Toxicol — Archives of Toxicology

Arch Toxicol (Berl) — Archives of Toxicology (Berlin)

Arch Toxicol Suppl — Archives of Toxicology. Supplement

Arch Toxikol — Archiv fuer Toxikologie [Later, Archives of Toxicology]

Arch Toxikol Suppl — Archiv fuer Toxikologie. Supplement

Arch Triennale Lab Bot Crittog — Archivio Triennale. Laboratorio di Botanica Crittogamica

Arch Triest — Archeolgrafo Triestino

Archt Sci Rev — Architectural Science Review

Archts Forum — Architects Forum

Archts Jnl — Architects' Journal

Archts News — Architects News

Archts Trade Jnl — Architects' Trade Journal

Arch Turk Acad Med — Archives. Turkish Academy of Medicine

Arch Union Med Balk — Archives. Union Medicale Balkanique

Arch Union Med Balk Bull Union Med Balk — Archives. Union Medicale Balkanique. Bulletin. Union Medicale Balkanique

Arch Urkdforsch — Archiv fuer Urkundenforschung

Arch Urkundenforsch — Archiv fuer Urkundenforschung

Arch Urug Med Cir Espec — Archivos Uruguayos de Medicina, Cirujia, y Especialidades

Arch Uruguayos Med — Archivos Uruguayos de Medicina, Cirugia y Especialidades

ArchV — Archiv fuer Voelkerkunde

Archv A Lovan — Archivum Artis Lovaniense

Archv & Forsch — Archiv und Forschungen

Archv Anthropol — Archiv fuer Anthropologie

Archv Anthropol & Vlkforsch — Archiv fuer Anthropologie und Voelkerforschung

Archv Antropol & Etnol — Archivio per l'Antropologia e l'Etnologia

Archv A Valenc — Archivo de Arte Valenciano

Archv Begriffsgesch — Archiv fuer Begriffsgeschichte

Archv Bild Kst Ger Nmus Nuremberg — Archiv fuer Bildende Kunst. Germanisches Nationalmuseum. Nuremberg

Archv Cesky — Archiv Cesky

Archv Christ Kst — Archiv fuer Christliche Kunst

Archv Dominicano — Archivo Dominicano

Archv Elsaess Kstgesch — Archiv fuer Elsaessische Kunstgeschichte

Arch Veneto — Archivio Veneto

Arch Veneto Ser 5 — Archivio Veneto. Serie 5

Arch Venez Folk Caracas — Archivos Venezolanos de Folklore (Caracas)

Arch Venez Med Trop Parasitol Med — Archivos Venezolanos de Medicina Tropical y Parasitologia Medica

Arch Venez Nutr — Archivos Venezolanos de Nutricion

Arch Venez Patol Trop Parasitol Med — Archivos Venezolanos de Patologia Tropical y Parasitologia Medica

Arch Venez Pueric Pediatr — Archivos Venezolanos de Puericultura y Pediatria

Arch Verdau Kr — Archiv fuer Verdauungs-Krankheiten

Arch Verdau Krankh — Archiv fuer Verdauungs-Krankheiten

Arch Verdau Krankh Stoffwechselpathol Diaet — Archiv fuer Verdauungs-Krankheiten Stoffwechselpathologie und Diaetetik

Arch Verdau Kr Stoffwechselpathol Diaet — Archiv fuer Verdauungs-Krankheiten mit Einschluss der Stoffwechselpathologie und der Diaetetik

Arch Verdauungskr — Archiv fuer Verdauungs-Krankheiten mit Einschluss der Stoffwechselpathologie und der Diaetetik

Arch Vereins Siebenbuerg Landesk — Archiv des Vereins fuer Siebenbuergische Landeskunde

Arch Vergl Phonetik — Archiv fuer Vergleichende Phonetik

Archv Esp A — Archivo Espanol de Arte

Archv Esp A & Arqueol — Archivo Espanol de Arte y Arqueologia

Archv Esp Arqueol — Archivo Espanol de Arqueologia

Arch Vestnik — Arheoloski Vestnik

Arch Vet — Archiva Veterinaria

Arch Vet (Buchar) — Archiva Veterinaria (Bucharest)

Arch Vet Ital — Archivio Veterinario Italiano

Arch Vet Ital Suppl — Archivio Veterinario Italiano. Supplemento

Arch Vet Pol — Archivum Veterinarium Polonicum

Archv Franciscanum Hist — Archivum Franciscanum Historicum

Archv Frankfurt Gesch & Kst — Archiv fuer Frankfurts Geschichte und Kunst

Archv Fratrum Praedicatorum — Archivum Fratrum Praedicatorum

Archv Gesch Bwsn — Archiv fuer Geschichte des Buchwesens

Archv Gesch Dt Bhand — Archiv fuer Geschichte des Deutschen Buchhandels

Archv Gesch Oberfranken — Archiv fuer Geschichte von Oberfranken

Archv Gtnbau — Archiv fuer Gartenbau

Archv Herald — Archiv Heraldy

Archv Herald — Archivum Heraldicum

Archv Hispal — Archivo Hispalense

Archv Hist Pont — Archivum Historiae Pontificiae

Archv Hist Soc Iesu — Archivum Historicum Societatis Iesu

Arch Virol — Archives of Virology

Arch Virol Suppl — Archives of Virology. Supplementum

Archv Italia & Rass Int Archv — Archivi d'Italia e Rassegna Internazionale degli Archivi

Archv It Stor Pieta — Archivio Italiano per la Storia della Pieta

Arch Viva — Archaeologia Viva

Archv Knd Oesterreich Gesch Quellen — Archiv fuer Kunde Oesterreichischer Geschichts-Quellen

Archv Kstgesch — Archiv fuer Kunstgeschichte

Archv Kultgesch — Archiv fuer Kulturgeschichte

Archv Lecco — Archivi di Lecco

Archvm Balaton Bpest — Archivum Balatonicum (Budapest)

Archvm Chir Bpest — Archivum Chirurgicum (Budapest)

Archvm Chir Neerl — Archivum Chirurgicum Neerlandicum

Archvm Chir Oris Bologna — Archivum Chirurgiae Oris (Bologna)

Archv Medaillen & Plakettenknd — Archiv fuer Medaillen- und Plakettenkunde

Archv Melitense — Archivum Melitense

Archvm Histol Jap — Archivum Histologicum Japonicum

Archv Mittelrhein Kirchgesch — Archiv fuer Mittelrheinische Kirchengeschichte

Archvm Melit — Archivum Melitense

Archvm Stomat Bpest — Archivum Stomatologiae (Budapestini)

Archvm Zool Bpest — Archivum Zoologicum (Budapestini)

Archv Nat Hist — Archive of Natural History

Archv News — Archive News

Arch Voelkerechts — Archiv des Voelkerrechts

Arch Voelkerk — Archiv fuer Voelkerkunde

Arch Voelkerkunde — Archiv fuer Voelkerkunde

Archv Oesterreich Gesch — Archiv fuer Oesterreichische Geschichte

Arch Volkswohlfahrt — Archiv fuer Volkswohlfahrt

Archv Orient — Archiv Orientalni

Archv Orientforsch — Archiv fuer Orientforschung

Archv Ott — Archivum Ottomanicum

Archv Prehist Levant — Archivio de Preistoria Levantina

Archv Saechs Gesch — Archiv fuer die Saechsische Geschichte

Archvs A Fr — Archives de l'Art Francais

Archvs Alsac Hist A — Archives Alsaciennes d'Histoire de l'Art

Archvs Amer A J — Archives of American Art Journal

Archvs & Mus Inf — Archives and Museum Informatics

Archvs Archit Mod — Archives de l'Architecture Moderne

Archvs Asian A — Archives of Asian Art

Archvs Bib & Mus Belgique — Archives, Bibliotheques, et Musees de Belgique

Archvs Cent Cult Port — Archives du Centre Culturel Portugais

Archvs Chin A Soc America — Archives of the Chinese Art Society of America

Archv Schles Kirchgesch — Archiv fuer Schlesische Kirchengeschichte

Archvs Eglise Alsace — Archives de l'Eglise d'Alsace

Archvs Ethnos — Archivos Ethnos

Archvs Etud Orient — Archives d'Etudes Orientales

Archvs Herald Suisses — Archives Heraldiques Suisses

Archvs Hist A & Litt — Archives Historiques, Artistiques, et Litteraires

Archvs Hist Doctr & Litt Moyen Age — Archives d'Histoire Doctrinale et Litteraire du Moyen Age

Archvs Hist N France & Midi Belgique — Archives Historiques du Nord de la France et du Midi de la Belgique

Archvs Inst Palaeontol Humaine — Archives de l'Institut de Paleontologie Humaine

Archvs Int Hist Sci — Archives Internationales d'Histoire des Sciences

Archv Sippenforsch & Verw Geb — Archiv fuer Sippenforschung und alle Verwandten Gebiete

Archvs Leoneses — Archivos Leoneses

Archv Soc Romana Stor Patria — Archivio della Societa Romana di Storia Patria

Archvs Psychol — Archives de Psychologie

Archv Stor A — Archivio Storico dell'Arte

Archv Stor Belluno Feltre & Cadore — Archivio Storico di Belluno, Feltre, e Cadore

Archv Stor Bergam — Archivio Storico Bergamasco

Archv Stor Dalmazia — Archivio Storico per la Dalmazia

Archv Stor It — Archivio Storico Italiano

Archv Stor Lodi — Archivio Storico Lodigiano

Archv Stor Lombardo — Archivio Storico Lombardo

Archv Stor Marche & Umbria — Archivio Storico per le Marche e per l'Umbria

Archv Stor Messin — Archivio Storico Messinese

Archv Stor Prat — Archivio Storico Pratese

Archv Stor Prov Napolet — Archivio Storico per le Province Napoletane

Archv Stor Prov Parm — Archivio Storico per le Province Parmensi

Archv Stor Pugl — Archivio Storico Pugliese

Archv Stor Sicilia Orient — Archivio Storico per la Sicilia Orientale

Archv Stor Siracus — Archivio Storico Siracusano

Archv Tec Mnmts Prehisp — Archivo Tecnico de Monumentos Prehispanicos

Archv Trent — Archivio Trentino

Archv Vaterlaend Gesch & Top — Archiv fuer Vaterlaendische Geschichte und Topographie

Archv Ven — Archivio Veneto

Archv Ven Trident — Archivio Veneto-Tridentino

Archv Vlkerknd — Archiv fuer Voelkerkunde

Archv Zeich Kst — Archiv fuer die Zeichnenden Kuenste

Arch Waermewirtsch — Archiv fuer Waermewirtschaft

Arch Waermewirtsch Dampfkesselwes — Archiv fuer Waermewirtschaft und Dampfkesselwesen

Arch Wanderungswesen — Archiv fuer Wanderungswesen

Arch Welt Erd Staatenk — Archiv fuer Welt-, Erd- und Staatenkunde und Ihre Hilfswissenschaften und Litteratur

Arch Wiss Bot — Archiv fuer Wissenschaftliche Botanik

Arch Wissensch u Prakt Tierh — Archiv fuer Wissenschaftliche und Praktische Tierheilkunde

Arch Wiss Kde Russland — Archiv fuer Wissenschaftliche Kunde von Russland

Arch Wiss Kunde Russland — Archiv fuer Wissenschaftliche Kunde von Russland

Arch Wiss Phot — Archiv fuer Wissenschaftliche Photographie

Arch Wiss Prakt Tierheilkd — Archiv fuer Wissenschaftliche und Praktische Tierheilkunde

Archwm Automat Telemech — Archiwum Automatyki i Telemechaniki

Archwm Budowy Masz — Archiwum Budowy Maszyn

Archwm Chem Farm — Archiwum Chemji i Farmacji

Archwm Elektrotech — Archiwum Elektrotechniki

Archwm Etnogr — Archiwum Etnograficzne

Archwm Etnol — Archiwum Etnologiczne

Archwm Gorn — Archiwum Gornictwa

Archwm Gorn Hutn — Archiwum Gornictwa i Hutnictwa

Archwm Hig — Archiwum Higjeny

Archwm Hist Filoz Med — Archiwum Historji i Filozofji Medycyny

Archwm Hist Med — Archiwum Historji Medycyny

Archwm Hutn — Archiwum Hutnictwa

Archwm Hydrobiol Ryb — Archiwum Hydrobiologji i Rybactwa

Archwm Hydrotech — Archiwum Hydrotechniki

Archwm Hyg — Archiwum Hygieny

Archwm Immun Terap — Archiwum Immunologii i Terapii Doswiadczalnej

Archwm Inzyn Ladow — Archiwum Inzynierii Ladowej

Archwm Mech Stosow — Archiwum Mechaniki Stosowanej

Archwm Miner — Archiwum Mineralogiczne

Archwm Nauk Antrop — Archiwum Nauk Antropologicznych

Archwm Nauk Biol — Archiwum Nauk Biologicznych

Archwm Ryb Pol — Archiwum Rybactwa Polskiego

Archwm Tow Nauk Lwow — Archiwum Towarzystwa Naukowego we Lwowie

Arch Yearb S Afr Hist — Archives Yearbook for South African History

Arch Yr — Architect's Yearbook

Arch Yrbk — Architect's Yearbook

Arch Zeit — Archaeologische Zeitung

Arch Zellforsch — Archiv fuer Zellforschung

Arch Z Exp — Archives de Zoologie Experimentale et Generale

Arch Z Ges — Architectura. Zeitschrift fuer Geschichte der Baukunst

Arch Ziv Pr — Archiv fuer die Zivilistische Praxis

Arch Ziv Prax — Archiv fuer Zivilistische Praxis

Arch Zool Exper et Gen — Archives de Zoologie Experimentale et Generale

Arch Zool Exp Gen — Archives de Zoologie Experimentale et Generale

Arch Zool Exp Gen Notes Rev — Archives de Zoologie Experimentale et Generale. Notes et Revue

Arch Zool Ital — Archivio Zoologico Italiano

Arch Zool Mus Moscow State Univ — Archives of Zoological Museum. Moscow State University

Arch Zootec — Archivos de Zootecnia

ArchZtg — Archaeologische Zeitung

Arch Zuechtungsforsch — Archiv fuer Zuechtungsforschung

ARCI — Arctic Circular

Arcisp S Anna di Ferrara — Arcispedale S. Anna di Ferrara

ArcL — Arc. Cahiers Mediterraneens

ARCLEW — Czechoslovak Academy of Sciences. Institute of Landscape Ecology. Hydrobiological Laboratory. Annual Report

Arclight Rev — Arclight Review

Arco di Ulisso — Arco di Ulisso. Collana di Testi e Documenti nelle Lingue Originali

Arcos Tech Bull — Arcos Technical Bulletin

ArcP — Archeion Pontou

ARCPEA — Australia Commonwealth Scientific and Industrial Research Organisation. Tropical Crops and Pastures. Annual Report

ArcR — Archivum Romanicum. Nuova Rivista di Filologia Romanza

ARCRBD — Annual Report on Cacao Research. University of the West Indies

ARCRDF — Australia. Commonwealth Scientific and Industrial Research Organisation. Division of Forest Research. Annual Report

ARC Res Rev (UK) — ARC [*Agricultural Research Council*] Research Review (United Kingdom)

ARCRL Rep — Agricultural Research Council. Radiobiology Laboratory Report

ARCSA — Annals. Royal College of Surgeons of England

ARCSB — Archivio Stomatologico

ARCT — Arctic

Arct Aeromed Lab (US) Tech Doc Rep — Arctic Aeromedical Laboratory (United States). Technical Documentary Report

Arct Aeromed Lab (US) Tech Note — Arctic Aeromedical Laboratory (United States). Technical Note

Arct Aeromed Lab (US) Tech Rep — Arctic Aeromedical Laboratory (United States). Technical Report

Arct Alp Res — Arctic and Alpine Research

Arct Alp Res (Boulder Colo) — Arctic and Alpine Research (Boulder, Colorado)

Arct Anthrop — Arctic Anthropology

Arct Anthropol — Arctic Anthropology

Arct Bibl — Arctic Bibliography

Arct Bibliogr — Arctic Bibliography

Arct Biblphy — Arctic Bibliography

Arct Bull — Arctic Bulletin

Arct Circ — Arctic Circular

Arctic Alp Res — Arctic and Alpine Research

Arctic Anthropol — Arctic Anthropology

Arctic Bibliogr — Arctic Bibliography. US Department of Defense

Arctic Bul — Arctic Bulletin

Arctic Inst North America Research Paper — Arctic Institute of North America. Research Paper

Arctic Inst North America Special Pub — Arctic Institute of North America. Special Publication

Arctic Inst North America Tech Paper — Arctic Institute of North America. Technical Paper

Arctic Med Res — Arctic Medical Research

Arct Inst N Am Annu Rep — Arctic Institute of North America. Annual Report

Arct Inst N Am Spec Publ — Arctic Institute of North America. Special Publication

Arct Inst N Am Tech Pap — Arctic Institute of North America. Technical Paper

Arct Inst North Am Annu Rep — Arctic Institute of North America. Annual Report

Arct Inst North America Tech Pap — Arctic Institute of North America. Technical Paper

Arct Land Use Res Program Rep ALUR (Can) — Arctic Land Use Research Program Report. ALUR (Canada)

Arct News — Arctic News

Arct News Lett — Arctic News Letter

Arct Serv News Du Pont de Nemours — Arctic Service News. R. and H. Chemicals Dept. E.I. Du Pont de Nemours and Co.

ARCU — Architektura a Urbanizmus

ARCU — Arcturus. Department of Education. Northwest Territories

Arcueil Mm — Memoires de Physique et de Chimie de la Societe d'Arcueil

Arcueil Mm Ps — Memoires de Physique et de Chimie de la Societe d'Arcueil

ARCVBP — Annales de Recherches Veterinaires

ARCWD — Architektur und Wohnwelt

ARD — Ahora (Dominican Republic)

ARD — Architectural Record

ARD — Army Research and Development [*Later, R, D & A*]

ARDAAY — Annali di Radiologia Diagnostica

ARDAD — Army R D and A

ARDBA — Advances in Radiation Biology

ARDC — Annual Report. Director. Department of Antiquiities. Cyprus

ARDCB — Advances in Radiation Chemistry

AR de M — Archives Royales de Mari

Arden's Sydney Mag — Arden's Sydney Magazine

ARDH-A — Architecture d'Aujourd'hui

Ardn — Arnoldian

ARDRA — Australian Road Research

ARDRSP — Archivio. Reale Deputazione Romana di Storia Patria

ARDS — Annual Report. Dante Society

ARDSB — American Review of Respiratory Disease

ARDSBL — American Review of Respiratory Disease

ARDSDN — Zimbabwe. Division of Livestock and Pastures. Annual Report

ARDVA — Army Research and Development

ARDYA4 — Applied Radiology

ARE — Ancient Records of Egypt

ARE — Annual Review of Entomology</PHR> %

A Re — Archiv fuer Religionswissenschaft

AREA — Association for Religious Education Aspects of Education. Bulletin

Area Dev — Area Development

AREAER — Annual Report on Exchange Arrangements and Exchange Restrictions

ArEB — Arizona English Bulletin

AREBA8 — Bulletin. ARERS

ARECB — Annual Review of Ecology and Systematics

ARECBC — Annual Review of Ecology and Systematics

Arecos Quart Ind Per Lit Aging — Areco's Quarterly Index to Periodical Literature on Aging
AREDD — Annual Report on Energy Research, Development, and Demonstration. InternationalEnergy Agency
AREGB — Archiwum Energetyki
AREHDT — Annual Review of Public Health
A Rel — Archiv fuer Religionswissenschaft
ARELA — Archiwum Elektrotechniki
ARENA — Annual Review of Entomology
ARENAA — Annual Review of Entomology
Arena Rev — Arena Review
Arena Teks — Arena Tekstil
AREND — Annual Review of Energy
A Rep (London) — Archaeological Report (London)
A Rep Natn Inst Anim Ind (Japan) — Annual Report. National Institute for Animal Industry. Ministry of Agriculture and Forestry (Japan)
A Rep Rec Res — Annual Report. Record Research. East African Agriculture and Forestry Research Organisation
A Rep Res Tech Wk Minist Agric Nth Ire — Annual Report on Research and Technical Work. Ministry of Agriculture for Northern Ireland
A Rep Tokyo Metropol Res Lab Publ Hlth — Annual Report. Tokyo Metropolitan Research Laboratory of Public Health
ARERAM — Arerugi
ARERI — Australian Renewable Energy Resources Index
ARES — Agricultural Research
ArES — Archives Europeennes de Sociologie
ARESDS — Animal Regulation Studies
A Res Nerv Ment Dis Proc — Association for Research in Nervous and Mental Disease. Proceedings
ArEspArq — Archivo Espanol de Arqueologia
Areth — Arethusa
AREUEA Jrnl Amer Real Estate and Urban Economics Assn — AREUEA Journal. American Real Estate and Urban Economics Association
A Rev — Arts Review
A Rev Biochem — Annual Review of Biochemistry
A Rev Ecol Syst — Annual Review of Ecology and Systematics
A Rev Ent — Annual Review of Entomology
A Rev Genet — Annual Review of Genetics
A Rev Microbiol — Annual Review of Microbiology
A Rev Pharmac Toxic — Annual Review of Pharmacology and Toxicology
A Rev Phytopath — Annual Review of Phytopathology
A Rev Pl Physiol — Annual Review of Plant Physiology
A Rev Psychol — Annual Review of Psychology
AREX — Arctic Explorer. Travel Arctic. Northwest Territories
ArF — Archivio di Filosofia
ARF — Area Resource File
ARFAA — Academia Republicii Populare Romine. Institutul de Fizica Atomica si Institutulde Fizica. Studii si Cercetari de Fizica
ARFHA — Australian Refrigeration, Air Conditioning, and Heating
Ar Fi — Archivio di Filosofia
ARFIA — Archivio di Fisiologia
ARFIAY — Archivio di Fisiologia
Ar Fil — Archivio di Filosofia
ArfK — Archiv fuer Kulturgeschichte
ARFLBA — Agricultural Research Organization. Division of Forestry. Ilanot Leaflet
ARFMA — Arhiv za Farmaciju
ARFMAC — Arhiv za Farmaciju
ARFMBS — Altitute. Revista da Federacao dos Municipios da Beira-Serra
ArfR — Archiv fuer Reformationsgeschichte
Ar F Schweiz — Archaeologische Fuehrer der Schweiz
ARFTAX — Annual Review of Food Technology
ARFVP — Attic Red-Figure Vase Painters
ARG — Abridged Reader's Guide to Periodical Literature
ARG — American Record Guide
ARG — Archiv fuer Reformationsgeschichte
Arg — Argensola
Arg — Arguments
ARGA — Arbeiten aus dem Reichsgesundheitsamt
ARGAP — Research Guide to Australian Politics
Arg Austral BA — Argentina Austral (Buenos Aires)
ARGEAR — Archiv fuer Geschwulstforschung
Argent Com Nac Energ At CNEA NT — Argentina. Comision Nacional de Energia Atomica. CNEA NT
Argent Com Nac Energ At Dep Radiobiol Prog Rep — Argentina. Comision Nacional de Energia Atomica. Department of Radiobiology. Progress Report
Argent Com Nac Energ At Inf — Argentina. Comision Nacional de Energia Atomica. Informe
Argent Com Nac Energ At Publ Ser Inf — Argentina. Comision Nacional de Energia Atomica. Publicaciones. SerieInforme
Argent Dir Gen Ind Min An — Argentina. Direccion General de Industria Minera. Anales
Argent Dir Gen Ind Minera Bol — Argentina. Direccion General de Industria Minera. Boletin
Argent Dir Gen Ind Min Publ — Argentina. Direccion General de Industria Minera. Publicacion
Argent Dir Gen Minas Geol Bol — Argentina. Direccion General de Minas y Geologia. Boletin
Argent Dir Gen Minas Geol Publ — Argentina. Direccion General de Minas y Geologia. Publicacion
Argent Dir Minas Geol An — Argentina. Direccion de Minas y Geologia. Anales
Argent Dir Minas Geol Bol — Argentina. Direccion de Minas y Geologia. Boletin
Argent Dir Minas Geol Hidrol Bol — Argentina. Direccion de Minas, Geologia, e Hidrologia. Boletin
Argent Dir Minas Geol Publ — Argentina. Direccion de Minas y Geologia. Publicacion

Argent Dir Nac Geol Min An — Argentina. Direccion Nacional de Geologia y Mineria. Anales
Argent Dir Nac Geol Min Bol — Argentina. Direccion Nacional de Geologia y Mineria. Boletin
Argent Dir Nac Geol Min Inf Tec — Argentina. Direccion Nacional de Geologia y Mineria. Informe Tecnico
Argent Dir Nac Geol Min Publ — Argentina. Direccion Nacional de Geologia y Mineria. Publicacion
Argent Dir Nac Min Bol — Argentina. Direccion Nacional de Mineria. Boletin
Argent Dir Nac Quim Bol Inf — Argentina. Direccion Nacional de Quimica. Boletin Informativo
Argent Eco — Economic Report. Summary (Argentina)
Argent Electroenerg — Argentina Electroenergetica
Argenteuil Symp — Argenteuil Symposium
Argent Inst Nac Geol Min An — Argentina. Instituto Nacional de Geologia y Mineria. Anales
Argent Inst Nac Geol Min Bol — Argentina. Instituto Nacional de Geologia y Mineria. Boletin
Argent Inst Nac Tecnol Agropecu Man Agropecu — Argentina. Instituto Nacional de Tecnologia Agropecuaria. Manual Agropecuario
Argent Inst Nac Tecnol Ind Bol Tec — Argentina. Instituto Nacional de Tecnologia Industrial. Boletin Tecnico
Argent Repub Com Nac Energ At CNEA — Argentina. Republica. Comision Nacional de Energia Atomica. Report CNEA
Argent Repub Com Nac Energ At Publ Ser Quim — Argentina. Republica. Comision Nacional de Energia Atomica.Publicaciones. Serie Quimica
Argent Repub Dir Nac Geol Min An — Argentina. Republica. Direccion Nacional de Geologia y Mineria. Anales
Argent Repub Dir Nac Geol Min Bol — Argentina. Republica. Direccion Nacional de Geologia y Mineria.Boletin
Argent Repub Dir Nac Geol Min Inf Tec — Argentina. Republica. Direccion Nacional de Geologia y Mineria.Informe Tecnico
Argent Repub Dir Nac Geol Min Publ — Argentina. Republica. Direccion Nacional de Geologia y Mineria.Publicacion
Argent Repub Estud Geol Min Econ — Argentina. Republica. Estudios de Geologia y Mineria Economica. SerieArgentina
Argent Repub Inst Nac Geol Min Bol — Argentina. Republica. Instituto Nacional de Geologia y Mineria. Boletin
Argent Repub Inst Nac Geol Min Rev — Argentina. Republica. Instituto Nacional de Geologia y Mineria. Revista
Argent Repub Minist Agric Dir Inf Publ Misc — Argentina. Republica. Ministerio de Agricultura. Direccion deInformaciones. Publicacion Miscelanea
Argent Repub Minist Agric Ganad Publ — Republica de Argentina. Ministerio de Agricultura y Ganaderia. Publicacion Miscelanea
Argent Repub Minist Agric Ganad Publ Tec — Republica de Argentina. Ministerio de Agricultura y Ganaderia. Publicacion Tecnia
Argent Repub Minist Econ Nac Dir Nac Geol Min An — Argentina. Republica. Ministerio de Economia de la Nacion. DireccionNacional de Geologia y Mineria. Anales
Argent Repub Minist Econ Nac Dir Nac Geol Min Publ — Argentina. Republica. Ministerio de Economia de la Nacion. DireccionNacional de Geologia y Mineria. Publicacion
Argent Repub Minist Ind Comer Nac Dir Nac Min An — Argentina. Republica. Ministerio de Industria y Comercio de la Nacion.Direccion Nacional de Mineria. Anales
Argent Repub Minist Ind Comer Nac Dir Nac Min Bol — Argentina Republica. Ministerio de Industria y Comercio de la Nacion. DireccionNacional de Mineria. Boletin
Argent Repub Minist Ind Comer Nac Dir Nac Min Publ — Argentina. Republica. Ministerio de Industria y Comercio de la Nacion.Direccion Nacional de Mineria. Publicacion
Argent Repub Secr Agric Ganad Dir Inf Publ Misc — Argentina. Republica. Secretaria de Agricultura Ganaderia. Direccion deInformaciones. Publicacion Miscelanea
Argent Repub Subsecr Min Estud Geol Min Econ Ser Argent — Argentina. Republica. Subsecretaria de Mineria. Estudios de Geologia yMineria Economica. Serie Argentina
Argent Repub Subsecr Min Ser Argent — Republica de Argentina. Subsecretaria de Mineria. Serie Argentina
Argent Secr Ind Comer Bol — Argentina. Secretaria de Industria y Comercio. Boletin
Argent Serv Geol Nac Bol — Argentina. Servicio Geologico Nacional. Boletin
Argent Serv Hidrogr Naval Bol — Argentina Servicio de Hidrografia Naval. Boletin
Argent Serv Nac Min Geol Bol — Argentina. Servicio Nacional Minero Geologico. Boletin
Argent Serv Nac Min Geol Rev — Argentina. Servicio Nacional Minero Geologica. Revista
Argent Text — Argentina Textil
ARGG — Annual Review of Gerontology and Geriatrics
Arg Inform — Informe Economico (Argentina)
ArGlottIt — Archivio Glottologico Italiano
Arg LR — Argus Law Reports
ARGOA — Argosy
Argomenti Farmacoter — Argomenti de Farmacoterapia
Argomenti Stor A — Argomenti di Storia dell'Arte
Argonne Natl Lab Energy Envirn Syst Div Tech Rep — Argonne National Laboratory. Energy and Environmental Systems Division.Technical Report
Argonne Natl Lab Fusion Power Program ANL/FPP Tech Mem — Argonne National Laboratory. Fusion Power Program. ANL/FPP TechnicalMemorandum
Argonne Natl Lab High Energy Phys Div Rep — Argonne National Laboratory. High Energy Physics Division. Report
Argonne Natl Lab News Bull — Argonne National Laboratory. News Bulletin
Argonne Natl Lab Off Electrochem Proj Manage Rep ANL/OEPM — Argonne National Laboratory. Office of Electrochemical ProjectManagement. Report ANL/OEPM

Argonne Natl Lab Phys Div Rep — Argonne National Laboratory. Physics Division. Report
Argonne Natl Lab Rep — Argonne National Laboratory. Report
Argonne Natl Lab Rep ANL — Argonne National Laboratory. Report ANL
Argonne Natl Lab Rep ANL-CT — Argonne National Laboratory. Report ANL-CT
Argonne Natl Lab Rep ANL/OTEC — Argonne National Laboratory. Report ANL/OTEC
Argonne Natl Lab Rev — Argonne National Laboratory. Reviews
Argonne Natl Lab Tech Rep ANL/CNSV-TM — Argonne National Laboratory. Technical Report ANL/CNSV-TM
Argonne Natl Lab Tech Rep ANL/EES-TM — Argonne National Laboratory. Technical Report ANL/EES-TM
Argonne Natl Lab Water Resour Res Program (Rep) ANL/WR — Argonne National Laboratory. Water Resources Research Program (Report) ANL/WR
Argonne Rev — Argonne Reviews
ArGP — Archiv fuer Geschichte der Philosophie
ARGPA — Archives of General Psychiatry
ARGPAQ — Archives of General Psychiatry
Arg Rep — Argus Law Reports
Arg S Ci A — Anales de la Sociedad Cientifica Argentina
ARGTU — Archiv fuer Reformationsgeschichte. Texte und Untersuchungen
ARGUC9 — Agricultural Research Guyana
Argus Arab Bus — Argus of Arab Business
Argus J — Argus Journal
Argus LR — Argus Law Reports
Argus LR (CN) — Argus Law Reports (Current Notes)
Argus L Rep — Argus Law Reports
Argus (Newspr) (VIC) — Argus Reports (Newspaper) (Victoria)
ARGYAJ — Archiv fuer Gynaekologie
Arh — Archives
ArH — Archivo Hispalense
Arh Biol Nauk — Arhiv Biologiceskih Nauk/Archives des Sciences Biologiques
Arh Biol Nauka — Arhiv Bioloskih Nauka
ARHEA — Arthritis and Rheumatism
Arheol Moldovei — Arheologia Moldovei
Arheoloski Vest (L) — Arheoloski Vestnik (Ljubljana)
Arheol Rad Raspr — Arheoloski Radovi i Rasprave
Arheol Vestn — Arheoloski Vestnik
Arheol Vestnik — Arheoloski Vestnik
Arh Farm — Arhiv za Farmaciju
Arh Farm (Belgr) — Arhiv za Farmaciju (Belgrade)
Arh Hem Farm — Arhiv za Hemiju i Farmaciju
Arh Hig Rada — Arhiv za Higijenu Rada
Arh Hig Rada Toksikol — Arhiv za Higijenu Rada i Toksikologiju
Arh Hig Rad Toksikol — Arhiv za Higijenu Rada i Toksikologiju
Ar Hisp — Archivo Hispalense. Revista Historica, Litteraria, y Artistica
Arhitekt SSSR — Arhitektura SSSR
Arhit Hrvatskoj 1945-85 — Arhitektura u Hrvatskoj 1945-85
Arhit Urb — Arhitektura Urbanizam
Arh Kem — Arhiv za Kemiju
Arh Kem Tehnol — Arhiv za Kemiju i Tehnologiju
ARHMB — Archiwum Historii Medycyny
ARHMBN — Archiwum Historii Medycyny
Arh Minist Poljopr (Yugoslavia) — Arhiv Ministarstva Poljoprivrede (Yugoslavia)
Arh Mol — Arheologia Moldovei
Arh Mold — Arheologia Moldovei
Arh Moldovei — Arheologia Moldovei
Arh Olt — Arhivele Olteniei
Arh Pam URSR — Arkheologichni Pamiatky URSR
Arh Poljopriv Nauke — Arhiv za Poljoprivredne Nauke
Arh Poljopr Nauke — Arhiv za Poljoprivredne Nauke
Arh Poljopr Nauke Teh — Arhiv za Poljoprivredne Nauke i Tehniku
ArHPont — Archivum Historiae Pontificiae
Arh Pr — Arheoloski Pregled
Arh Preg — Arheoloski Pregled
Arh Pregl — Arheoloski Pregled
Arh Pregled — Arheoloski Pregled
ArHQ — Arkansas Historical Quarterly
Arh Rud Tehnol — Arhiv za Rudarstvo i Tehnologiju
Arh Russk Protistol Obsc — Arhiv Russkogo Protistologiceskogo Obscestva/Archives. Societe Russe de Protistologie
Arh Sb — Arkheologicheskii Sbornik
ARHS Bull — Australian Railway Historical Society. Bulletin
Arh St Arb — Arhus Stifts Arboger
Arh Tehnol — Arhiv za Tehnologiju
Arhun Etn — Arheologija un Etnografija
ArhV — Arheoloski Vestnik
Arhv Arbanasku Starinu Jezik & Etnol — Arhiv za Arbanasku Starinu, Jezik, i Etnologiju
Arh Vest — Arheoloski Vestnik
Arh Vestnik — Arheoloski Vestnik
Arl — Archivo Ibero-Americano
ARI — Ariadne
Arl — Ars Islamica
ARIA — Annual Report. Institute of Archaeology
ARIADS — Industrial Environmental Research Laboratory [*Research Triangle Park*]. Annual Report
ARIC — Arctic in Colour
ARID — Analecta Romana Instituti Danici
Ari D — Arion's Dolphin
Arid Lands Newsl — Arid Lands Newsletter
Arid Lands Newslett — Arid Lands Newsletter
Arid Lands Resour Inf Pap — Arid Lands Resource Information Paper
Aridnye Pochvy Ikh Genezis Geokhim Ispol — Aridnye Pochvy Ikh Genezis Geokhimiya Ispol'zovanie

Arid Soils Their Genesis Geochem Util — Arid Soils. Their Genesis, Geochemistry, Utilization
Arid Zone Newsl Div Land Res CSIRO — Arid Zone Newsletter. Division of Land Research. Commonwealth Scientific and Industrial Research Organisation
Arid Zone Res — Arid Zone Research
Arid Zone Res UNESCO — Arid Zone Research. United Nations Educational, Scientific, and Cultural Organization
Ariel E — Ariel: a Review of International English Literature
ARIFD9 — International Commission for the Northwest Atlantic Fisheries. Annual Report
ARIMDU — Annual Review of Immunology
ARINAU — Annual Report. Research Institute of Environmental Medicine. Nagoya University
ARIPUC — Annual Report. Institute of Phonetics. University of Copenhagen
ARIQD8 — Annual Report. Nigerian Institute for Oceanography and Marine Research
ARIS — Alabama Resources Information System
ARISBC — Annual Review of Information Science and Technology
ARISDE — Institute of Oceanographic Sciences. Annual Report
Aris Phil C — Aris and Phillips Central Asian Studies
Aris Soc — Aristotelian Society. Supplementary Volume
Aristot Panepist Thessalonikis Epet Geopon Dasolog Skol — Aristoteleion Panepistemion Thessalonikis Epetiris tis Geoponikis kai Dasologikis Skolis
Arith Teach — Arithmetic Teacher
ARIVAK — Annual Report. Institute for Virus Research. Kyoto University
AriW — Arizona and the West
Ariz — Arizona Reports
Ariz — Arizona Supreme Court Reports
Ariz Acad Sci J — Arizona Academy of Science. Journal
Ariz Admin Dig — Arizona Administrative Digest
Ariz Ag Exp — Arizona. Agricultural Experiment Station. Publications
Ariz Agric Exp Stn Bull — Arizona. Agricultural Experiment Station. Bulletin
Ariz Agric Exp Stn Mimeogr Rep — Arizona. Agricultural Experiment Station. Mimeographed Report
Ariz Agric Exp Stn Rep — Arizona. Agricultural Experiment Station. Report
Ariz Agric Exp Stn Res Rep — Arizona. Agricultural Experiment Station. Research Report
Ariz Agric Exp Stn Tech Bull — Arizona. Agricultural Experiment Station. Technical Bulletin
Ariz and West — Arizona and the West
Ariz App — Arizona Appeals Reports
Ariz Bar Briefs — Arizona Bar Briefs
Ariz BJ — Arizona Bar Journal
Ariz Bsn G — Arizona Business Gazette
Ariz Bur Mines Bull — Arizona. Bureau of Mines. Bulletin
Ariz Bur Mines Bull Geol Ser — Arizona. Bureau of Mines. Bulletin. Geological Series
Ariz Bur Mines Bull Mineral Technology Ser — Arizona. Bureau of Mines. Bulletin. Mineral Technology Series
Ariz Bur Mines Circ — Arizona. Bureau of Mines. Circular
Ariz Bur Mines Field Notes — Arizona. Bureau of Mines. Field Notes
Ariz Bus — Arizona Business
Ariz Comm Agric Hortic Annu Rep — Arizona. Commission of Agriculture and Horticulture. Annual Report
Ariz Comp Admin R & Regs — Arizona Official Compilation of Administrative Rules and Regulations
Ariz Dairy Newsl Univ Ariz Coop Ext Serv — Arizona Dairy Newsletter. University of Arizona. Cooperative Extension Service
Ariz Dent J — Arizona Dental Journal
Ariz Dept Mineral Res Ann Rept — Arizona. Department of Mineral Resources. Annual Report
Ariz Farmer Stockman — Arizona Farmer-Stockman
Ariz For Notes — Arizona Forestry Notes
Ariz For Note Sch For Nth Ariz Univ — Arizona Forestry Notes. School of Forestry. Northern Arizona University
Ariz Game Fish Dep Wildl Bull — Arizona. Game and Fish Department. Wildlife Bulletin
Ariz Geol Soc Dig — Arizona Geological Society Digest
Ariz Geol Soc Digest Ann — Arizona Geological Society. Digest. Annual
Ariz Geol Soc South Ariz Guideb — Arizona Geological Society. Southern Arizona Guidebook
Ariz H — Arizona Highways
Ariz His R — Arizona Historical Review
Ariz Hist Rev — Arizona Historical Review
Ariz Land & People — Arizona Land and People
Ariz Law R — Arizona Law Review
Ariz Legis Serv — Arizona Legislative Service
Ariz Legis Serv (West) — Arizona Legislative Service (West)
Ariz Libn — Arizona Librarian
Ariz Librn — Arizona Librarian
Ariz LR — Arizona Law Review
Ariz L Rev — Arizona Law Review
Ariz M — Arizona Monthly
Ariz Med — Arizona Medicine
Ariz Min J — Arizona Mining Journal
Ariz Nev Acad Sci J — Arizona-Nevada Academy of Science. Journal
Ariz Nurse — Arizona Nurse
Arizona Acad Sci Jour — Arizona Academy of Science. Journal
Arizona Agric Exp Sta Bull — Arizona Agricultural Experiment Station. Bulletin
Arizona & W — Arizona and the West
Arizona Bur Mines Bull — Arizona. Bureau of Mines. Bulletin
Arizona Med — Arizona Medicine
Arizona Q — Arizona Quarterly
Arizona R — Arizona Review
Arizona State LJ — Arizona State Law Journal

Ariz Q — Arizona Quarterly
Ariz Quart Tucson — Arizona Quarterly (Tucson)
Ariz R — Arizona Review
Ariz REP — Arizona Real Estate Press
Ariz Repub — Arizona Republic
Ariz Rev AR — Arizona Review. AR
Ariz Rev Stat Ann — Arizona Revised Statutes Annotated
Ariz Sess Laws — Session Laws. Arizona
Ariz State Land Dept Water Res Rept — Arizona State Land Department. Water Resources Report
Ariz State Land Dep Water Resour Rep — Arizona State Land Department. Water Resources Report
Ariz State Law J — Arizona State Law Journal
Ariz St Bur Mines B — Arizona State Bureau of Mines. Bulletin
Ariz St LF — Arizona State Law Forum
Ariz St L J — Arizona State Law Journal
Ariz SU Ant — Arizona State University. Anthropological Research Papers
Ariz Teach — Arizona Teacher
Ariz Univ Agr Expt Bull — Arizona University. Agricultural Experiment Station. Bulletin
Ariz Univ Agr Expt Bull Phys Sci Bull — Arizona University. Agricultural Experiment Station. Bulletin. Physical ScienceBulletin
Ariz Univ Agric Exp Stn Rep — Arizona. University. Agricultural Experiment Station. Report
Ariz Univ Agric Exp Stn Tech Bull — Arizona University. Agricultural Experiment Station. TechnicalBulletin
Ariz Univ Lab Tree-Ring Res Pap — Arizona University. Laboratory of Tree-Ring Research. Papers
Ariz Univ Lunar Planet Lab Commun — Arizona University. Lunar and Planetary Laboratory. Communications
ArizW — Arizona and the West
Ariz Water Comm Bull — Arizona. Water Commission. Bulletin
Ariz West — Arizona and the West
Ar J — Arbitration Journal
ARJID — Japan. Atomic Energy Research Institute. Annual Report and Account
ARJKAQ — Agricultural Research Journal of Kerala
ARJSAG — Japanese Society for Tuberculosis. Annual Report
ARJU — Arjungnagimmat. Inuit Cultural Institute
ARK — Arkansas Business and Economic Review
Ark — Arkansas Reports
Ark — Arkitekten
Ark Acad Sci Proc — Arkansas Academy of Science. Proceedings
Ark Acts — General Acts of Arkansas
Ark Ag Exp — Arkansas. Agricultural Experiment Station. Publications
Arkansas Acad Sci Proc — Arkansas Academy of Science. Proceedings
Arkansas Agric Exp Stn Bull — Arkansas. Agricultural Experiment Station. Bulletin
Arkansas Agric Exp Stn Mimeogr Ser — Arkansas. Agricultural Experiment Station. Mimeograph Series
Arkansas Agric Exp Stn Rep Ser — Arkansas. Agricultural Experiment Station. Report Series
Arkansas Agric Exp Stn Res Ser — Arkansas. Agricultural Experiment Station. Research Series
Arkansas Agric Exp Stn Spec Rep — Arkansas. Agricultural Experiment Station. Special Report
Arkansas Anim Morb Rep — Arkansas Animal Morbidity Report
Arkansas B — Arkansas Business
Arkansas Cattle Bus — Arkansas Cattle Business
Arkansas Dent J — Arkansas Dental Journal
Arkansas Div Geol Bull — Arkansas. Division of Geology. Bulletin
Arkansas Eng Exper Stn Bull — Arkansas. Engineering Experiment Station. Bulletin
Arkansas Farm Res — Arkansas Farm Research
Arkansas Farm Res Arkansas Agric Exp Stn — Arkansas Farm Research. Arkansas Agricultural Experiment Station
Arkansas Farm Res Rep Ser — Arkansas Farm Research. Report Series. University of Arkansas Agricultural Experiment Station
Arkansas Geol Comm Bull — Arkansas. Geological Commission. Bulletin
Arkansas Geol Comm Inform Circ — Arkansas. Geological and Conservation Commission. Information Circular
Arkansas Geol Comm Water Resour Circ — Arkansas. Geological Commission. Water Resources Circular
Arkansas Geol Comm Water Resour Summ — Arkansas. Geological Commission. Water Resources Summary
Arkansas Geol Conserv Comm Bull — Arkansas. Geological and Conservation Commission. Bulletin
Arkansas Geol Conserv Comm Inf Circ — Arkansas. Geological and Conservation Commission. Information Circular
Arkansas Geol Conserv Comm Water Resour Circ — Arkansas. Geological and Conservation Commission. Water Resources Circular
Arkansas Geol Conserv Comm Water Resour Summ — Arkansas. Geological and Conservation Commission. Water ResourcesSummary
Arkansas Geol Surv Bull — Arkansas. Geological Survey. Bulletin
Arkansas Hist Q — Arkansas Historical Quarterly
Arkansas Industr Univ Agric Exp Sta Bull — Arkansas Industrial University. Agricultural Experiment Station. Bulletin
Arkansas Lib — Arkansas Libraries
Arkansas L Rev — Arkansas Law Review
Arkansas Med Soc J — Arkansas Medical Society. Journal
Arkansas Nutr Conf Proc — Arkansas Nutrition Conference. Proceedings
Arkansas Resour Dev Comm Div Geol Bull — Arkansas. Resources and Development Commission. Division of Geology.Bulletin
Arkansas Univ Eng Exp Sta Res Rep — Arkansas University. Engineering Experiment Station. Research Report
Arkansas Univ Eng Exp Stn Res Rep Ser — Arkansas University. Engineering Experiment Station. Research Report Series

Arkansas Univ (Fayetteville) Agric Exp Stn Bull — Arkansas University (Fayetteville). Agricultural Experiment Station.Bulletin
Arkansas Univ Fayetteville Agric Exp Stn Mimeogr Ser — Arkansas. University. Fayetteville. Agricultural Experiment Station. MimeographSeries
Arkansas Univ (Fayetteville) Agric Exp Stn Rep Ser — Arkansas University (Fayetteville). Agricultural Experiment Station.Report Series
Arkansas Univ Fayetteville Agric Exp Stn Spec Rep — Arkansas. University. Fayetteville. Agricultural Experiment Station. Special Report
Arkansas Univ Seismol Bull — Arkansas University. Seismological Bulletin
Arkansas Water Sewage Conf Short Course Proc — Arkansas Water and Sewage Conference and Short Course. Proceedings
Arkansas Water Works Pollut Control Conf Short Sch Proc — Arkansas Water Works and Pollution Control Conference and Short School.Proceedings
Arkans Fm Res — Arkansas Farm Research
Ark Antarkt Nauchno Issled Inst Tr — Arkticheskii i Antarkticheskii Nauchno-Issledovatel'skii Institut.Trudy
Ark Astron — Arkiv foer Astronomi
Ark B Assn Proc — Arkansas Bar Association. Proceedings
Ark Bot — Arkiv foer Botanik
Ark Bus and Econ R — Arkansas Business and Economic Review
ARKCDA — Kenya Tuberculosis Investigation Centre. Annual Report
ARKCEB — Kenya Tuberculosis and Respiratory Diseases Research Centre. Annual Report
Ark Dent — Arkansas Dentistry
Ark Derg — Tuerk Tarih Arkeologya ve Etnografya Dergisi
ARKEAD — Arkiv foer Kemi
ArKF — Archiv fuer Keilschriftforschung
Ark Farm Res — Arkansas Farm Research
Ark Fys — Arkiv foer Fysik
Ark Fys Semin Trondheim — Arkiv foer det Fysiske Seminar i Trondheim
Ark Gazet — Arkansas Gazette
Ark Geofys — Arkiv foer Geofysik
Ark G S — Arkansas. Geological Survey
ArkH — Arkansas Historical Quarterly
Arkh — Arkheologiia
Arkh Anat Gistol Embriol — Arkhiv Anatomii, Gistologii, i Embriologii
Arkhang Lesotekh Inst Tr — Arkhangel'skii Lesotekhnicheskii Institut. Trudy
Arkh Biol Nauk — Arkhiv Biologicheskikh Nauk
Arkheologiia — Arkheologiia Organ na Arkheologicheskiia Institut i Muzei pri B'lgarskata Akademiia na Naukite
Arkheol Pam Feodal Gruz — Arkheologicheskiya Pamyatniki Feodal'noy Gruzii
Arkheol Raboty Tadzhikistane — Arkheologicheskiye Raboty v Tadzhikstane
Arkh Ez — Arkheografecheskii Ezhogodnik
Arkh Etn — Arkheologiia i Etnografiia Bashkirii
Ark His As — Arkansas Historical Association. Publications
Arkh Issl — Arkheologicheskie Issledovaniia na Ukraine
Ark Hist Assn Rpt — Arkansas Historial Association. Report
Ark Hist Assoc Publ — Arkansas Historical Association. Publications
Ark Hist Q — Arkansas Historical Quarterly
Ark Hist Quar — Arkansas Historical Quarterly
Arkhit & Stroitelstvo Moskvy — Arkhitektura i Stroitel'stvo Moskvy
Arkhit Leningrada — Arkhitektura Leningrada
Arkhit Moskva — Arkhitekturnaya Moskva
Arkhit Nasledstvo — Arkhitekturnoye Nasledstvo
Arkhit Radyanskoi Ukraini — Arkhitektura Radyans'koi Ukraini
Arkhit SSSR — Arkhitektura SSSR
Arkhit Stroit Leningrada — Arkhitektura i Stroitelstvo Leningrada
Arkhit Ukrainy — Arkhitektura Ukrainy
Arkhivi Ukr — Arkhivi Ukraini. Naukovo Informatsiinii Biuleten' Arkhivnogo Upravliniia pri Radi Ministriv URSR
Arkh Klin i Ekspi Med (Moskva) — Arkhiv Klinicheskoi i Eksperimental'noi Meditsiny (Moskva)
Arkh Med Nauk — Arkhiv Meditsinskikh Nauk
Arkh Pam — Arkheologichni Pamiatky Ursr
Arkh Patol — Arkhiv Patologii
ArkHQ — Arkansas Historical Quarterly
Arkh Rask — Arkheologicheskie Raskopi v Armenii
Arkh Russk Protist Obsh — Arkhiv Russkogo Protistologicheskogo Obshchestva
Arkh Sbor — Arkheologicheskii Sbornik
Arkh Sbornik — Arkheologicheskii Sbornik
ARKIAP — Archiv fuer Kinderheilkunde
Ar (Kiev) — Arkheologiya (Kiev)
Ark Inre Med — Arkiv foer Inre Medicine
Ark Issl Gruz — Arkheologicheskie Issledovaniia v Gruzii
Arkiv — Arkiv foer Nordisk Filologi
Arkiv f Nord Filologi — Arkiv foer Nordisk Filologi
Arkiv Nord Filol — Arkiv foer Nordisk Filologi
ARKK-A — Arkkitehti
Ark Kemi — Arkiv foer Kemi
Ark Kemi Mineral Geol — Arkiv foer Kemi, Mineralogi, och Geologi
Ark Kemi Miner Geol — Arkiv foer Kemi, Mineralogi, och Geologi
Ark (Kiev) — Arkheologiia (Kiev)
Ark Landtm Traeg Odlare — Arkif foer Landtmaen och Traegards-Odlare
Ark Law — Arkansas Lawyer
Ark Law R — Arkansas Law Review
ARKLAY — Arkheologiya (Kiev)
Ark Lib — Arkansas Libraries
Ark Light Newsl — Ark-Light Newsletter
Ark LR — Arkansas Law Review
Ark L Rev — Arkansas Law Review
Ark Mat — Arkiv foer Matematik
Ark Mat Astron Fys — Arkiv foer Matematik, Astronomi, och Fysik
Ark Matemat — Arkiv foer Matematik
Ark Med Soc J — Arkansas Medical Society. Journal
Ark Mineral Geol — Arkiv foer Mineralogi och Geologi

Ark M Soc J — Arkansas Medical Society. Journal
Ark Muez Yayim — Arkeoloj Muezeleri Yayinlari
Ark Munic — Arkansas Municipalities
Ark Nurse — Arkansas Nurse
Ark Otkr — Arkheologicheskie Otkrytiia
Ark Pam URSR — Arkheologichi Pamiatniki URSR
ARKRAI — Archiv fuer Kriminologie
Ark Reg — Arkansas Register
Ark Res Devel Comm Div Geology Bull Inf Circ — Arkansas. Resources and Development Commission. Division of Geology. Bulletin. Information Circular
Ark Riv — Ark River Review
ARKSN — Annuarium des Roomsch-Katholieke Studenten in Nederland
Ark Stat Ann — Arkansas Statutes Annotated
Ark State Nurses Assoc Newsl — Arkansas State Nurses' Association. Newsletter
ARKT-B — Architektura
ArkUkr — Arkheologija. Publies par l'Academie des Sciences d'Ukraine
ArKulturg — Archiv fuer Kulturgeschichte
Ark Univ Inst Sci and Technology Research Ser — Arkansas University. Institute of Science and Technology. Research Series
Ark Zool — Arkiv foer Zoologi
Ark Zool (Stockholm) — Arkiv foer Zoologi (Stockholm)
ArL — Archivum Linguisticum
ARL — Army Review (London)
ARL — Asian Review (London)
ARLAB — Archiv fuer Landtechnik
Ar Leon — Archivos Leoneses
AR Libyan Studies — Annual Report. Society for Libyan Studies
ARLIS Newsl — ARLIS [*Art Libraries Society/North America*] Newsletter
ARLIS Newslett — Art Libraries Society Newsletter
ARL Mech Eng Rep Aust Aeronaut Res Lab — ARL Mechanical Engineering Report. Australia Aeronautical Research Laboratories
ARL Mins — Association of Research Libraries. Minutes
ArLP — Arts et Livres de Provence
ArlQ — Arlington Quarterly
ARL/TR — Australian Radiation Laboratory. Technical Report
Ar Lw — Archiv fuer Liturgiewissenschaft
ARM — Abstracts of Research and Related Materials in Vocational and Technical Education
ARM — Archives Royales de Mari
ArM — Arte (Milan)
Arma Int — Armada International
ARMC — Architecture, Mouvement, Continuite
ArmC — Arms Control and Disarmament
ARMCA — Annual Review of Medicine
ARMCAH — Annual Review of Medicine
ARMCBI — Annual Reports in Medicinal Chemistry
Armchair Det — [*The*] Armchair Detective
Arm D — [*The*] Armchair Detective
Armdale & Dist Hist Soc J & Proc — Armidale and District Historical Society. Journal and Proceedings
ARMEA — Arizona Medicine
ARMEAN — Arizona Medicine
Arme Ant — Arme Antiche
ARMED — Armement
Armed Forces Chem J — Armed Forces Chemical Journal
Armed Forces Med J — Armed Forces Medical Journal
Armed Forces Med J (Arab Repub Egypt) — Armed Forces Medical Journal (Arab Republic of Egypt)
Armed Forces Med J (India) — Armed Forces Medical Journal (India)
Armed Forces Soc — Armed Forces and Society
Armees Aujourd — Armees d'Aujourd'hui
Armeeztg — Armeezeitung
Armement Bull Inf Liaison — Armement. Bulletin d'Information et de Liaison
Armenian N J — Armenian Numismatic Journal
Armen Q — Armenian Quarterly
Armen Rev — Armenian Review
Arm FJ Int — Armed Forces Journal International
Arm Frc — Armed Forces
Arm Hist Soc J — Armidale Historical Society. Journal
ARMIA — Annual Review of Microbiology
ARMIAZ — Annual Review of Microbiology
Armidale Dist Hist Soc J — Armidale and District Historical Society. Journal
Armidale Hist Soc J — Armidale and District Historical Society. Journal
Armidale New Engl Univ Explor Soc Rep — Armidale. University of New England. Exploration Society. Report
Armidale Teach Coll Bull — Armidale Teachers' College. Bulletin
Armid Teach Coll Bul — Armidale Teachers' College. Bulletin
Armitano A — Armitano Arte
Armjan Gos Ped Inst Sb Naucn Trud Ser Fiz-Mat — Armjanskii Gosudarstvennyi Pedagogiceskii Institut Imeni H. Abovjana. Sbornik Naucnyh Trudov. Serija Fiziko-Matematiceskaja
Arm Khim Zh — Armyanskii Khimicheskii Zhurnal
Arm Nauchno-Issled Inst Stroit Mater Sooruzh Nauchn Soobshch — Armyanskii Nauchno-Issledovatel'skii Institut Stroitel'nykh Materialov i Sooruzhenii Nauchnye Soobshcheniya
Arm Nauchno Issled Inst Vinograd Vinodel Plodovod Tr — Armyanskii Nauchno-Issledovatel'skii Institut Vinogradarstva,Vinodeliya, i Plodovodstva. Trudy
Arm Nauchno Issled Inst Zhivotnovod Vet Nauchn Tr — Armyanskii Nauchno-Issledovatel'skii Institut Zhivotnovodstva iVeterinarii. Nauchnye Trudy
ARMND — Annales de Radiologie. Medecine Nucleaire
ArMo — Art Moderne. Revue Critique des Arts et de la Litterature
Armored Cavalry J — Armored Cavalry Journal
Armotsem Konstr — Armotsementnye Konstruktsii
Armour Res Found Rep — Armour Research Foundation. Report
ARMPEQ — Annales de Readaptation et de Medecine Physique

Arm Rev — Armenian Review
ARMREW — Applied Research in Mental Retardation
Arms Con T — Arms Control Today
Arms Explos — Arms and Explosives
Arm Skh Inst Sb Nauchn Tr — Armyanskii Sel'skokhozyaistvennyi Institut. Sbornik Nauchnykh Trudov
Armstrong Aerosp Med Res Lab Tech Rep AAMRL TR (US) — Armstrong Aerospace Medical Research Laboratory. Technical ReportAAMRL-TR (US)
ARMT — Archives Royales de Mari. Textes Administratives
ARMT — Archives Royales de Mari. Transcriptions et Traductions
ARMUA3 — American Malacological Union, Incorporated. Annual Report
ARMUB — Arts et Manufactures
Army — Australian Army
Army Adm — Army Administrator
Armyanskii Khim Zh — Armyanskii Khimicheskii Zhurnal
Army Av D — US Army. Aviation Digest
Army Comm — Army Communicator
Army Law — Army Lawyer
Army Lawy — Army Lawyer
Army Log — Army Logistician
Army Logis — Army Logistician
Army Mater Mech Res Cent Rep AMMRC MS (US) — Army Materials and Mechanics Research Center. Report AMMRC MS (US)
Army Mater Technol Conf Ser — Army Materials Technology Conference Series
Army Med Bull — Army Medical Bulletin
Army Med Dept Rep (London) — Army Medical Department. Reports (London)
Army Med Res Dev Command Biomed Lab Tech Rep (US) — Army Medical Research and Development Command. Biomedical LaboratoryTechnical Report (US)
Army Q Def J — Army Quarterly and Defence Journal
Army Quart Defence J — Army Quarterly and Defence Journal
Army Res & Devel — Army Research and Development [*Later, R, D & A*]
Army Reserv — Army Reserve Magazine
ARNAAG — Annuaire Roumain d'Anthropologie
ARNBB — Archivos de Neurobiologica
ARNBBK — Archivos de Neurobiologia
ARNCAM — Agronomia
ARND — Arctic and Northern Development Digest
ARNE — Arctic News
ArNe — Art News
ARNEA — Archives of Neurology
ARNEAS — Archives of Neurology
ARN J — American Rehabilitation Nursing Journal
ARN J — ARN [*Association of Rehabilitation Nurses*] Journal
ARNLBG — Archiv fuer Naturschutz und Landschaftsforschung
ARNMDL — Applied Radiology and Nuclear Medicine [*Later, Applied Radiology*]
ARNNA — Annual Report. National Institute of Nutrition
ARNOAO — Arnoldia
Arnold Arboretum J — Arnold Arboretum. Journal
Arnold Arbor Harv Univ J — Arnold Arboretum. Harvard University. Journal
Arnold Arbor J — Harvard University. Arnold Arboretum Journal
Arnold O Beckman Conf Clin Chem Proc — Arnold O. Beckman Conference in Clinical Chemistry. Proceedings
Arnold (Zim) — Arnoldia (Zimbabwe)
ARNPBS — Arnoldia Rhodesia
ARNSD5 — Annual Review of Neuroscience
AR(NSW) — Industrial Arbitration Reports (New South Wales)
ARNTD8 — Annual Review of Nutrition
ARNUA — Annual Review of Nuclear Science [*Later, Annual Review of Nuclear and ParticleScience*]
ARNUA8 — Annual Review of Nuclear Science [*Later, Annual Review of Nuclear and ParticleScience*]
ArNVA — Arbok det Norske Videnskapsakademi
ARNYA — Annual Report. Natural Science Research Institute. Yonsei University
ARO — Anciennes Religions Orientales
ArO — Archiv Orientalni
AROABM — Agroanimalia
AROBDR — Acta Radiologica. Oncology
AROF — Arctic Offshore. Publication of the Alaska Oil and Gas Association
AROHA8 — Archives d'Ophtalmologie et Revue Generale d'Ophtalmologie
ARom — Archivum Romanicum
Aroma Res Proc Int Symp A — Aroma Research. Proceedings of the International Symposium on Aroma Research. Central Institute for Nutrition and Food Research
Aromat Amino Acids Brain Symp — Aromatic Amino Acids in the Brain. Symposium
Aromat Heteroaromat Chem — Aromatic and Heteroaromatic Chemistry
ARONDT — Acta Radiologica. Oncology, Radiation Therapy, Physics, and Biology
A Ronse — Annalen van de Geschied- en Oud-Heidkundige Kring van Ronse
AROPAW — Archives of Ophthalmology
AROPDZ — Archives d'Ophtalmologie
Ar Or — Archiv fuer Orientforschung
Ar Or — Archiv Orientalni
ARORA — Archivio di Ortopedia [*Later, Archivio di Ortopedia e Reumatologia*]
ARO Rep — ARO (US Army Research Office) Report
AROTA — Archives of Otolaryngology
AROTAA — Archives of Otolaryngology
ArOtt — Archivum Ottomanicum
A Rozhl — Archeologicke Rozhledy
ARP — Arbeiten zur Romanischen Philologie
ARp — Archaeological Report Comprising the Recent Work of the Egypt Exploration Fund and the Progress of Egyptology
Ar (P) — Archeologia (Paris)
ArP — Aryan Path

ARPAAQ — Archives of Pathology [*Later, Archives of Pathology and Laboratory Medicine*]

Ar Pap — Archiv fuer Papyrusforschung und Verwandte Gebiete

ArPapF — Archiv fuer Papyrusforschung

ARPEA4 — Archives of Pediatrics

Ar Pf — Archiv fuer Papyrusforschung

ARPH — Annual Review of Public Health

Ar Ph — Archives de Philosophie

ArPh — Archives of Philosophy

ARPh — Archiv fuer Rechts- und Wirtschaftsphilosophie

ARPHA — Annual Review of Physiology

ARPHAD — Annual Review of Physiology

ARPLA — Annual Review of Physical Chemistry

ARPMAS — Archiv der Pharmazie

ARPPA — Annual Review of Plant Physiology

ARPPA3 — Annual Review of Plant Physiology

ARPR — Arctic Policy Review

ARPRD — Arbitrazni Praxe

Ar Preg — Arheoloski Pregled

ARPs — Archiv fuer Religionspsychologie

ARPSA — Annual Review of Psychology

ARPSAC — Annual Review of Psychology

ARPSD — Annual Review of Nuclear and Particle Science

ARPTA — Arkhiv Patologii

ARPTAF — Arkhiv Patologii

ARPTD — Annual Review of Pharmacology and Toxicology

ARPTDI — Annual Review of Pharmacology and Toxicology

ArQ — Arizona Quarterly

ArQ — Army Quarterly

ARQ — Australian Resources Quarterly

Arq Anat Antrop — Arquivo de Anatomia e Antropologia

Arq Anat Antropol — Arquivo de Anatomia e Antropologia

Arq Beja — Arquivo de Beja

Arq Biol (Sao Paulo) — Arquivos de Biologia (Sao Paulo)

Arq Biol Tecnol — Arquivos de Biologia e Tecnologia

Arq Biol Tecnol (Curitiba) — Arquivos de Biologia e Tecnologia (Curitiba)

Arq Bot Estado Sao Paulo — Arquivos de Botanica do Estado de Sao Paulo

Arq Bras Cardiol — Arquivos Brasileiros de Cardiologia

Arq Bras Endocrinol — Arquivos Brasileiros de Endocrinologia

Arq Bras Endocrinol Metabol — Arquivos Brasileiros de Endocrinologia e Metabologia

Arq Brasil Cardiol — Arquivos Brasileiros de Cardiologia

Arq Bras Med — Arquivos Brasileiros de Medicina

Arq Bras Med Nav — Arquivos Brasileiros de Medicina Naval

Arq Bras Med Vet Zootec — Arquivo Brasileiro de Medicina Veterinaria e Zootecnia

Arq Bras Nutr — Arquivos Brasileiros de Nutricao

Arq Bras Oftal — Arquivos Brasileiros de Oftalmologia

Arq Bras Oftalmol — Arquivos Brasileiros de Oftalmologia

Arq Bras Ps — Arquivos Brasileiros de Psicologia Aplicada

Arq Bras Tuberc Doencas Torax — Arquivos Brasileiros de Tuberculose e Doencas do Torax

Arq Bromatol — Arquivos de Bromatologia

Arq Catarinenses Med — Arquivos Catarinenses de Medicina

Arq Cent Estud Curso Odontol Univ Fed Minas Gerais — Arquivos. Centro de Estudos do Curso de Odontologia. Universidade Federal de Minas Gerais

Arq Cent Estud Fac Odontol Univ Fed Minas Gerais — Arquivos. Centro de Estudos da Faculdade de Odontologia. Universidade Federal de Minas Gerais

Arq Cent Estud Fac Odontol Univ Minas Gerais (Belo Horiz) — Arquivos. Centro de Estudos da Faculdade de Odontologia. Universidade de Minas Gerais (Belo Horizonte)

Arq Centro Cult Port — Arquivos. Centro Cultural Portugues

Arq Cienc Mar — Arquivos de Ciencias do Mar

Arq Cir Clin Exp (Sao Paulo) — Arquivos de Cirurgia Clinica e Experimental (Sao Paulo)

Arq Congr Int Microbiol — Arquivos. Congresso Internacional de Microbiologia

Arq Dep Assist Psicop S Paulo — Arquivos. Departamento de Assistencia a Psicopates. Estado de Sao Paulo

Arq Dermatol Sifiligr Sao Paulo — Arquivos de Dermatologia e Sifiligrafia de Sao Paulo

Arq Entomol Ser A — Arquivos de Entomologia. Serie A

Arq Entomol Ser B — Arquivos de Entomologia. Serie B

Arq Esc Super Vet Univ Estado Minas Gerais — Arquivos. Escola Superior de Veterinaria. Universidade do Estado deMinas Gerais

Arq Esc Super Vet Univ Rur Estado Minas Gerais — Arquivos. Escola Superior de Veterinaria. Universidade Rural. Estado de Minas Gerais

Arq Esc Vet Univ Fed Minas Gerais — Arquivos. Escola de Veterinaria. Universidade Federal de Minas Gerais

Arq Esc Vet Univ Minas Gerais — Arquivos. Escola de Veterinaria. Universidade Federal de Minas Gerais

Arq Estac Biol Mar Univ Ceara — Arquivos. Estacao de Biologia Marinha da Universidade do Ceara

Arq Estac Biol Mar Univ Fed Ceara — Arquivos. Estacao de Biologia Marinha da Universidade Federal do Ceara

Arq Fac Hig Saude Publica Univ Sao Paulo — Arquivos. Faculdade de Higiene e Saude Publica. Universidade de Sao Paulo

Arq Fac Hig S Paul — Arquivos. Faculdade de Higiene e Saude Publica. Universidade de Sao Paulo

Arq Fac Nac Med — Arquivos. Faculdade Nacional de Medicina

Arq Fac Nac Med (Rio De Janeiro) — Arquivos. Faculdade Nacional de Medicina (Rio De Janeiro)

ARQGAF — Archives of Gastroenterology

Arq Gastroenterol — Arquivos de Gastroenterologia

Arq Geol — Arquivos de Geologia

Arq Geol Univ Recife Curso Geol — Arquivos de Geologia. Universidade do Recife. Curso de Geologia

Arq Geol Univ Recife Esc Geol Pernambuco — Arquivos de Geologia. Universidade do Recife. Escola de Geologia dePernambuco

Arq Hig (Rio De J) — Arquivos de Higiene (Rio De Janeiro)

Arq Hig Saude Publica (Sao Paulo) — Arquivos de Higiene e Saude Publica (Sao Paulo)

Arq Hyg Saude Publica — Arquivos de Higiene e Saude Publica

Arq IBIT — Arquivos. IBIT

Arq Inst Anat Univ Fed Rio Grande Sul — Arquivos. Instituto de Anatomia. Universidade Federal do Rio GrandeDo Sul

Arq Inst Anat Univ Rio Grande Do Sul — Arquivos. Instituto de Anatomia. Universidade do Rio Grande Do Sul

Arq Inst Bacteriol Camara Pestana — Arquivos. Instituto Bacteriologico. Camara Pestana

Arq Inst Bacteriol Camara Pestana (Lisbon) — Arquivos. Instituto Bacteriologico Camara Pestana (Lisbon)

Arq Inst Bacteriol Cam Pestana — Arquivos. Instituto Bacteriologico. Camara Pestana

Arq Inst Biol — Arquivos. Instituto Biologico

Arq Inst Biol Anim (Rio De J) — Arquivos. Instituto de Biologia Animal (Rio De Janeiro)

Arq Inst Biol Exerc — Arquivos. Instituto de Biologia do Exercito

Arq Inst Biol Exerc (Rio De Janeiro) — Arquivos. Instituto de Biologia do Exercito (Rio De Janeiro)

Arq Inst Biol (Sao Paulo) — Arquivos. Instituto Biologico (Sao Paulo)

Arq Inst Biol (Sao Paulo) Supl — Arquivos. Instituto Biologico (Sao Paulo). Suplemento

Arq Inst Biol Veg — Arquivos. Instituto de Biologia Vegetal

Arq Inst Biol Veg (Rio De J) — Arquivos. Instituto de Biologia Vegetal (Rio De Janeiro)

Arq Inst Mil Biol (Rio De Janeiro) — Arquivos. Instituto Militar de Biologia (Rio De Janeiro)

Arq Inst Pesqui Agron — Arquivos. Instituto de Pesquisas Agronomicas

Arq Inst Pesqui Agron (Recife) — Arquivos. Instituto de Pesquisas Agronomicas (Recife)

Arq Inst Pesqui Vet Desiderio Finamor — Arquivos. Instituto de Pesquisas Veterinarias "Desiderio Finamor"

Arq Interam Reumatol — Arquivos Interamericanos de Reumatologia

Arq Jard Bot Rio De J — Arquivos. Jardim Botanico do Rio De Janeiro

Arq Jard Bot Rio De Janeiro — Arquivos. Jardim Botanico do Rio De Janeiro

Arq Med Leg — Arquivo de Medicina Legal

Arq Min Leprol — Arquivos Mineiros de Leprologia

Arq Mus Bocage — Arquivos. Museu Bocage

Arq Mus Bocage Ser A — Arquivos. Museu Bocage. Serie A

Arq Mus Bocage Ser B Notas — Arquivos. Museu Bocage. Serie B. Notas

Arq Mus Bocage Ser C Supl — Arquivos. Museu Bocage. Serie C. Suplementos

Arq Mus Boc Nota Sup — Arquivos. Museu Bocage. Notas e Suplementos

Arq Mus Hist Nat Univ Fed Minas Gerais — Arquivos. Museu de Historia Natural. Universidade Federal de Minas Gerais

Arq Mus Nac Rio De J — Arquivos. Museu Nacional do Rio De Janeiro

Arq Mus Nac Rio De Janeiro — Arquivos. Museu Nacional do Rio de Janeiro

Arq Mus Parana — Arquivos. Museu Paranaense

Arq Neuro-Psiquiatr — Arquivos de Neuro-Psiquiatria

ARQOA5 — Arquivos de Oncologia

Arq Oncol — Arquivos de Oncologia

Arq Oncol (Salvador Braz) — Arquivos de Oncologia (Salvador, Brazil)

Arq Patol — Arquivo de Patologia

Arq Patol Geral Anat Patol — Arquivos de Patologia Geral e Anatomia Patologica

Arq Patol Geral Anat Patol Univ Coimbra — Arquivos de Patologia Geral e Anatomia Patologica. Universidade de Coimbra

Arq Patol (Lisbon) — Arquivos de Patologia (Lisbon)

Arq Pediat — Arquivos de Pediatria

Arq Port — Arqueologo Portugues

Arq Port Bioquim — Arquivos Portugueses de Bioquimica

Arq Portugues — Arqueologo Portugues

Arq Rio Grandenses Med — Arquivos Rio-Grandenses de Medicina. Sociedade de Medicina de Porto Alegre

Arq Semin Estud Galegos — Arquivos. Seminario de Estudos Galegos

Arq Serv Florest — Arquivos do Servico Florestal

Arq Serv Florestal (Rio De J) — Arquivos. Servico Florestal (Rio De Janeiro)

ARQT — Arquitectura

Arq Tisiol — Arquivos de Tisiologia

Arqu Bol — Arqueologia Boliviana

Arque Hist — Arqueologia e Historia

Arqueol Hist — Arqueologia e Historia

Arqueol Port — Arqueologo Portugues

Arquit & Soc — Arquitectura y Sociedad

Arquit & Urb — Arquitectura y Urbanismo

Arquit & Urb Sao Paulo — Arquitetura e Urbanismo de Sao Paulo

Arquit & Viv — Arquitectura y Vivienda

Arquit Bis — Arquitecturas Bis

Arquit Brasil — Arquitectura do Brasil

Arquitec Bis — Arquitecturas Bis

Arquitec Hav — Arquitectura (Habana)

Arquitecto Peru — Arquitecto Peruano

Arquitet Rio — Arquitetura (Rio de Janeiro)

Arquit Mexico — Arquitectura de Mexico

Arquit Peru — Arquitectura Peruana

Arquiv Beja — Arquivo de Beja

Arquiv Bras Psicotec Rio — Arquivos Brasileiros de Psicotecnica (Rio de Janeiro)

Arquiv Coimbrao — Arquivo Coimbrao

Arquiv Distr Aveiro — Arquivo do Distrito de Aveiro

Arquiv Econ Brasilia — Arquivos Economicos (Brasilia)

Arquiv Inst Antrop Univ R Grande Norte Natal — Arquivos do Instituto de Antropologia. Universidade do Rio Grande do Norte (Natal, Brazil)
Arquiv Inst Direit Soc S Paulo — Arquivos do Instituto de Direito Social (Sao Paulo)
Arquiv Inst Gulbenkian Ci A Estud Mat Fis-Mat — Arquivo. Instituto Gulbenkian de Ciencia. A. Estudos Matematicos e Fisico-Matematicos
Arquivos Brasil Psicol Ap — Arquivos Brasileiros de Psicologia Aplicada
Arquiv Rio — Arquivos. Revista Bimestral. Ministerio da Educacao e Saude (Rio de Janeiro)
Arquivs Angola — Arquivos de Angola
Arquivs Cent Cult Port — Arquivos do Centro Cultural Portugues
Arquiv Univ Bahia Salvador — Arquivos da Universidade da Bahia (Salvador, Brazil)
Arqu Mus Nac — Arquivos. Museu Nacional do Rio De Janeiro
Arq Univ Bahia Fac Med — Arquivos. Universidade de Bahia. Faculdade de Medicina
Arq Univ Fed Rural Rio De Janeiro — Arquivos. Universidade Federal Rural do Rio De Janeiro
Arq Univ Recife Inst Terra Div Ci Geogr — Arquivos. Universidade do Recife. Instituto da Terra. Divisao de Ciencias Geograficas
Arqu Port — Arqueologo Portugues
ARQZA4 — Arquivos de Zoologia
Arq Zool — Arquivos de Zoologia
Arq Zool Estado Sao Paulo — Arquivos de Zoologia do Estado de Sao Paulo
Arq Zool (Sao Paulo) — Arquivos de Zoologia (Sao Paulo)
ARR — American Review of Reviews
ARR — Andean Group Regional Report
ArR — Archivi (Rome)
ARR — Arheoloski Radovi i Rasprave
Arran Nat — Arran Naturalist
ARRDA — American Review of Respiratory Disease
ARREEI — Annual Review of Rehabilitation
ArRefg — Archiv fuer Reformationsgeschichte
Ar Rep — Argus Reports
Arr et Av Cons Etat — Arrets et Avis du Conseil d'Etat
ARRIP — Australian Road Research in Progress
ARROAA — Annual Report. Radiation Center of Osaka Prefecture
Ar Roz — Archeologike Rozhledy
ARR Rep Aust Road Res Board — ARR Report. Australian Road Research Board
ArRS — Archiv fuer Rechts- und Soziaphilosophie
ArRW — Archiv fuer Religionswissenschaft
ARRWB — Argonne Reviews
ARS — Advanced Religious Studies
ARS — Analele Romano-Sovietice
ARS — Ancient Roman Statutes
Ars As — Ars Asiatica
ARSB — Arctic Seas Bulletin. Canadian Arctic Resources Committee
Arsberaettelse Lund — Arsberaettelse. Kungliga Humanistiska Vetenskapssamfundet i Lund
Arsber Danm Fisk Havund — Arsberetning fra Danmarks Fiskeri og Havundersogelser
Arsberet Nor Fisk — Arsberetning Norges Fiskerier
Arsberet Statens Forsoegsmejeri — Arsberetning. Statens Forsoegsmejeri
Arsberet Vedkomm Nor Fisk — Arsberetning Vedkommende Norges Fiskerier
Arsber Sver Geol Unders — Arsberaettelse. Sverings Geologiska Undersoekning
Arsb Finska Vetensk Soc — Arsbok. Finska Vetenskaps Societeten
Arsb Foren Skogstradsfor — Arsbok. Foreningen Skogstradsforadling
Arsb Kungl Humanist Vet Samf — Kungliga Humanistika Vetenskaps-Samfundets Arsbok
Arsb Sodermanlands Lans Hushallningssallsk — Arsbok. Sodermanlands Lans Hushallningssallskaps
Arsb Sver Met Hydrol Inst — Arsbok. Sveriges Meteorologisk och Hydrologiska Institut
Arsb Vet Soc Lund — Arsbok. Vetenskaps-Societetn i Lund
ARSC — Annals of Regional Science
ARSC — Association for Recorded Sound Collections. Journal
ARSC — Association for Recorded Sound Collections. Newsletter
ARSCAD — Acta Rheumatologica Scandinavica
ARsch — Allgemeine Rundschau
ARSCJ — Association for Recorded Sound Collections. Journal
Ars Comb — Ars Combinatoria
Ars Combin — Ars Combinatoria
Ars Curandi Odontol — Ars Curandi em Odontologia
Arsenical Pestic Symp — Arsenical Pesticides. Symposium
ARSFA — Anales. Real Sociedad Espanola de Fisica y Quimica. Serie A. Fisica
Ars H — Ars Hungarica
Ars Hisp — Ars Hispaniae
ARSI — Annual Reports of the Board of Regents of the Smithsonian Institution
ARSIA — Annuario. Regia Scuola Archeologica Italiana di Atene
Ars Isl — Ars Islamica
Ars Islam — Ars Islamica
ARSJ — American Rocket Society. Journal
Ars J — Ars Journal
ARS Jnl — ARS [*American Rocket Society*] Journal
ArSK — Archiv fuer Schriftkunde
ARSMBA — Ars Medici
Ars Med Drug Ser — Ars Medici Drug Series
Ars Med (Ed Fr) — Ars Medici (Edition Francaise)
Arsmelding St Smabrlaerarsk — Arsmelding Statens Smabrukslaerarskole
Ars Mus Den — Ars Musica Denver
ARS NE US Agric Res Serv Northeast Reg — ARS NE. United States Agricultural Research Service. Northeastern Region
ARSNSP — Atti. Reale Scuola Normale Superiore di Pisa
ARSOB — Arts in Society
ArSocRel — Archives de Sociologie des Religions

A R Soc Sci Rel — Annual Review of the Social Sciences of Religion
Arson Anal Newsl — Arson Analysis Newsletter
ArsOr — Ars Orientalis
Ars Orient — Ars Orientalis
ARSP — Archiv fuer Rechts- und Sozialphilosophie
Ars Pharm — Ars Pharmaceutica
Ars Pharm — Ars Pharmaceutica. Revista. Facultad de Farmacia. Universite de Granada
ARSQA — Anales. Real Sociedad Espanola de Fisica y Quimica. Serie B. Quimica
ARSQAL — Anales. Real Sociedad Espanola de Fisica y Quimica. Serie B. Quimica
Ar SR — Archives de Sociologie des Religions
ARSRDR — Antiviral Research
ARSR Mem Sect Stiint Ist — Academia Republicii Socialiste Romania. Memoriile. Sectei de Stiinte Istorice
Ars S — Ars Semiotica
ARSSAR — Acta Rheumatologica Scandinavica. Supplementum
Ars Semiot — Ars Semiotica
Arsskr Alnarps Lantbruks Mejeri Traedgardsinstitut — Arsskrift fran Alnarps Lantbruks-, Mejeri, och Traedgardsinstitut
Arsskr f Modersmalslararnas Foren — Arsskrift foer Modersmalslararnas Forening
Arsskr K Vet Landbohoejsk — Arsskrift den Kongelige Veterinaer og Landbohoejskole
Arsskr Nor Skogplanteskoler — Arsskrift foer Norske Skogplanteskoler
Arsskr Univ — Arsskrift Universitet
ARS S US Agric Res Serv South Reg — ARS S. United States Agricultural Research Service. Southern Region
ARSUAX — Archives of Surgery
ARS US Dep Agric Agric Res Serv — ARS. US Department of Agriculture. Agricultural Research Service
Ars Vet — Ars Veterinaria
ARSZAE — Acta Regiae Societatis Scientiarum et Litterarum Gothoburgensis. Zoologica
ART — Americas Review (Texas)
Art — Art/Film/Criticism
ART — Arts in Society
Art Am — Art in America
Art & Arch — Art and Archaeology
Art & Archre — Art et Architecture
Art and Aust — Art and Australia
Art & Dec — Art and Decoration
Art & Ind — Art and Industry
Art & L — Art and the Law
ArtArch — Art and Archaeology. Technical Abstracts
Art Archaeol Res Papers — Art and Archaeology. Research Papers
Art Archaeol Tech Abstr — Art and Archaeology. Technical Abstracts
Art As — Artibus Asiae
Art Asia — Arts of Asia
Art Asiae — Artibus Asiae
ArtB — Art Bulletin
ARTBCH — Agricultural Research Corporation [*Gezira*]. Technical Bulletin
ARTbibliogr Curr Titles — ARTbibliographies. Current Titles
ARTbibliogr Mod — ARTbibliographies Modern
Art Bul — Art Bulletin
Art Bull — Art Bulletin
Art Crit — Art Criticism
ArtD — Art Digest
ARTDA — Art Direction
Art Des Photo — Art, Design, Photo
Art Dir — Art Direction
Art Direct — Art Direction
ARTE — Obras Espuestas en Museos Espanoles
Artech House Commun Electron Def Lib — Artech House Communication and Electronic Defense Library
Artech House Telecom Lib — Artech House Telecom Library
Arte Dan — Arte do Dancar
Arte Doc — Arte Documento
Art Educ — Art Education
Arte e Stor — Arte e Storia
ARTEF — Arbeiter Teater Farband
Arte Info — Arte Informa
Arte Lomb — Arte Lombarda
Arte Mus — Arte Musical
ArteP — Arte e Poesia
Arterioscler Thromb — Arteriosclerosis and Thrombosis
Arterioscler Thromb — Arterioscleros Thrombos
Arterioscler Thromb Vasc Biol — Arteriosclerosis, Thrombosis, and Vascular Biology
Arter Throm — Arteriosclerosis and Thrombosis
Artesan Amer — Artesanias de America
Artes Graf BA — Artes Graficas (Buenos Aires)
Artes Mex — Artes de Mexico
Art Espanol — Arte Espanol. Revista. Sociedad Espanola de Amigos del Arte
Artes Pop — Artes Populares
Arte Ven — Arte Veneta
Arte y Var — Arte y Variedades
Artf — Artforum
Art Gall NSW Q — Art Gallery of New South Wales. Quarterly
ArTGran — Archivo Teologico Granadino
Arth — Arthaniti
Artha Vij — Artha Vijnana
Artha Vijnana J Gokhale Inst Polit Econ — Artha Vijnana. Journal of the Gokhale Institute of Politics and Economics
Artha Vik — Artha Vikas
Art Hist — Art History
Arth Rheum — Arthritis and Rheumatism

Arthritis Res — Arthritis Research
Arthritis Rheum — Arthritis and Rheumatism
Arthropods Fla Neighboring Land Areas — Arthropods of Florida and Neighboring Land Areas
Arthurian Lit — Arthurian Literature
Artl — Art Index
Artl — Art International
ARTIA2 — Archiv fuer Tierernaehrung
Artibus A — Artibus Asiae
Artibus & Hist — Artibus et Historiae
Artibus As — Artibus Asiae
Artibus Orient — Artibus Orientalis
Artic Anth — Arctic Anthropology
Artic Cl J Exam — Articled Clerks' Journal and Examiner
ARTID5 — Annual Report on Research and Technical Work. Department of Agriculture for Northern Ireland
Artif Cells Blood Substit Immobil Biotechnol — Artificial Cells, Blood Substitutes, and Immobilization Biotechnology
Artif Cells Blood Substitutes Immobilization Biotechnol — Artificial Cells, Blood Substitutes, and Immobilization Biotechnology
Artif Earth Satell (USSR) — Artificial Earth Satellites (USSR)
Artif Fiber — Artificial Fiber
Arti Fig — Arti Figurative. Rivista d'Arte Antica e Moderna
Artif Intel — Artificial Intelligence
Artif Intell — Artificial Intelligence
Artif Intell Abstr — Artificial Intelligence Abstracts
Artif Intell Eng — Artificial Intelligence in Engineering
Artif Intell Med — Artificial Intelligence in Medicine
Artif Intell Rev — Artificial Intelligence Review
Artif Life — Artificial Life
Artif Lungs Acute Respir Failure Pap Int Conf — Artificial Lungs for Acute Respiratory Failure. Theory and Practice. Papers Presented at the International Conference on Membrane Lung Technology and ProlongedExtracorporeal Perfusion
Artif Organs — Artificial Organs
Artif Organs Today — Artificial Organs Today
Artif Rainf Newsl — Artificial Rainfall Newsletter
Artif Satell — Artificial Satellites
Artif Silk Staple Fibre J Jpn — Artificial Silk and Staple Fibre Journal of Japan
Artif Silk World — Artificial Silk World
Artig Wash Monte — Artigas-Washington (Montevideo)
Arti M — Arti Musices
Arti Mens Inf A — Arti. Mensile di Informazione Artistica
Arti Mus — Arti Musices
Art in Am — Art in America
Art in Amer — Art in America
Art Ind — Art Index
Art Inst of Chicago Bull — Art Institute of Chicago. Bulletin
Art Int — Art International
Arti Rass Bimest A Ant & Mod — Arti. Rassegna Bimestrale dell'Arte Antica e Moderna
Artisan Lithurg — Artisan Lithurgique
Artist & J Home Cult — Artist and Journal of Home Culture
Artists Int Assoc Bull — Artists International Association Bulletin
Artists Int Assoc Newslett — Artists International Association Newsletter
Artists Int Bull — Artists International Bulletin
Artists Repository & Drg Mag — Artists Repository and Drawing Magazine
Art J — Art Journal
Art Jnl — Art Journal
Art Jour — Art Journal
Art J P E — Art Journal. Paris Edition
Art Lib J — Art Libraries Journal
Art Libraries Jnl — Art Libraries Journal
Art Lomb — Arte Lombarda
ArtM — Art Magazine
Art Mag — Arts Magazine
Art Mthly — Art Monthly
Art N — Art News
ArtNA — Art News Annual
ARTNB — Art News
ARTnews Annu — ARTnews Annual
Art NZ — Art New Zealand
ARTODN — Archives of Toxicology/Archiv fuer Toxikologie
ARTPA — American Review of Tuberculosis and Pulmonary Diseases
ARTPAN — American Review of Tuberculosis and Pulmonary Diseases
Art Plast Hav — Artes Plasticas (Habana)
Art Psychot — Art Psychotherapy
ArtQ — Art Quarterly
Art Quart — Art Quarterly
ARTRD — Arteriosclerosis (Dallas)
Art Rep Tenn Art Com — Arts Report. Tennessee Arts Commission
Arts — Arts Magazine
Art S — Art Studies. Medieval, Renaissance, and Modern
ArtsA — Arts
Arts Act — Arts Action
Arts Afr Noire — Arts d'Afrique Noire
Arts & Arch — Arts and Architecture
Arts & Archre — Arts and Architecture
Arts & D — Arts and Decoration
Arts and Dec — Arts and Decoration
Arts & Hum Cit Ind — Arts and Humanities Citation Index
Arts As — Arts of Asia
Arts Asiat — Arts Asiatiques
Artscan — Artscanada

Art Script — Artium Scriptores. Oesterreichische Akademie der Wissenschaften. Philosophisch-Historische Klasse. Sitzungsberichte
Arts d Afr Noire — Arts d'Afrique Noire
ARTSDOC — Arts Documentation Service
Arts Doc Mthly — Arts Documentation Monthly
Arts Humanit Citation Index — Arts and Humanities Citation Index
Arts in Soc — Arts in Society
Arts Int — Arts International
Arts Ir — Arts in Ireland
Arts Let Quebec — Arts et Lettres du Quebec
Arts Mag — Arts Magazine
Arts Man — Arts Manitoba
Arts Manuf — Arts et Manufactures
Arts Metiers — Arts et Metiers
Arts Psychother — Arts in Psychotherapy
Arts Reptg Ser — Arts Reporting Service
Arts Rev — Arts Review
Arts Rev Yearb Dir — Arts Review Yearbook and Directory
ArtsS — Arts in Society
ArtSt — Arte Stampa
Art St — Art Stamps
Art Teach — Art Teacher
Art Technol Health Phys Educ Sci Hum Living Ser — Art, Technology, Health, Physical Education, and Science of Human Living Series
ARTU — Archiv fuer Reformationsgeschichte. Texte und Untersuchungen
ARTUD7 — Acta Reproductiva Turcica
ArtV — Arts de la Vie
Art Ven — Arte Veneta
Art Vict — Arts Victoria
Artwork N — Artworkers News
ARU — Assyrische Rechtsurkunden
ARUCAN — Archives of Rubber Cultivation
ARUMD — Argumente
ARUPAS — Annales Academiae Regiae Scientiarum Upsaliensis
Arup J — Arup Journal
Arup Jnl — Arup Journal
ARUS — Arctic Research in the United States
ARUSE7 — University of Maine at Orono. Maine Agricultural Experiment Station. Annual Report
ARV — Allgemeiner Rabbiner-Verband
ArV — Art Vivant
ARV — Attic Red-Figure Vase Painters
ARVEBZ — Archiva Veterinaria
Ar Ven — Archivio Veneto
ARVFA — Annual Review of Fluid Mechanics
ARVFA3 — Annual Review of Fluid Mechanics
ARVGB — Annual Review of Genetics
ARVGB7 — Annual Review of Genetics
ARVID — Archives of Virology
ARVIDF — Archives of Virology
Ar Vk — Archiv fuer Voelkerkunde
ARVP — Attic Red-Figure Vase Painters
ARVPA — Annual Review of Pharmacology [*Later, Annual Review of Pharmacology and Toxicology*]
ARVPAX — Annual Review of Pharmacology [*Later, Annual Review of Pharmacology and Toxicology*]
ARVSDB — Annual Review of Sociology
ARW — Archiv fuer Religionswissenschaft
ARWBA — American Railway Engineering Association. Bulletin
ARWMA — Archiwum Mineralogiczne
ARWP — Archiv fuer Rechts- und Wirtschaftsphilosophie
ARWSDG — US Department of Agriculture. Science and Education Administration. Agricultural Research Results. ARR-W
ARX — Soviet and Eastern European Foreign Trade. A Journal of Translations
Arxivs Secc Ci Inst Estud Catalans — Arxivs. Seccio de Ciencies. Institut d'Estudis Catalans
Arx Sec Cien — Arxius de la Seccio de Ciences
Aryan Path — Aryan Pathology [*Bombay*]
AryP — Aryan Path
ARZ — Arizona Business
ARZMAA — Aerztliche Monatshefte fuer Berufliche Fortbildung
ARZNA — Arzneimittel-Forschung
ARZNAD — Drug Research
Arzneib DDR Komment — Arzneibuch der Deutschen Demokratischen Republik. Kommentare
Arzneib Komment DDR — Arzneibuch Kommentare. Deutsche Demokratische Republik
Arznei-For — Arzneimittel-Forschung
Arzneim-Forsch — Arzneimittel-Forschung
Arzneim Forsch Beih — Arzneimittel-Forschung. Beiheft
Arzneim Forsch Drug Res — Arzneimittel-Forschung/Drug Research
Arzneimittelallerg Kongr Dtsch Ges Allerg Immunitaetsforsch — Arzneimittelallergie. Kongress der Deutschen Gesellschaft fuer Allergie- und Immunitaetsforschung
Arzneimittel-Forsch — Arzneimittel-Forschung
Arzneyk Ann — Arzneykundige Annalen
ARZOA — Arkiv foer Zoologi
ARZOAG — Arkiv foer Zoologi
Arzt Apoth Krankenhaus — Arzt, Apotheker, Krankenhaus
Arzt Krankenh — Arzt im Krankenhaus
ARZWA6 — Aerztliche Wochenschrift
AS — Aarbog for Aarhusstift
AS — Alten Sprachen
AS — Alternativas (Santiago)
AS — American Scholar

AS — American Speech
AS — American String Teacher
AS — Amtliche Sammlung der Bundesgesetze und Verordnungen derSchweizerischen Eidgenoessenschaft
AS — Anatolian Studies
AS — Anglistisches Seminar
AS — Annales. Service des Antiquites de l'Egypt
AS — Annals of Science
AS — Antiquity and Survival
AS — Apostolado Sacerdotal
AS — Applied Statistics
AS — Archaeologie des Schweiz
AS — Arkhiv Samizdata. Sobranie Documentov Samizdata
AS — Art Scholar
AS — Arts in Society
AS — Asbury Seminarian
As — Asia
AS — Asian Survey
AS — Asiatische Studien
As — Asomante
AS — Assyriological Studies. Oriental Institute. University of Chicago
As — Astronomie. Revue d'Astronomie Populaire, de Meteorologie et de Physique du Globe
AS — Australasian Sketcher
ASA — Anatolian Studies (Ankara)
ASA — Annales. Service des Antiquites de l'Egypt
ASA — Annuario. Scuola Archeologica di Atene e delle Missioni Italiani in Oriente
ASA — Anzeiger fuer Schweizerische Altertumskunde
As A — Asie et l'Afrique
ASA — Societe d'Emulation, Agriculture, Sciences, Lettres, et Arts de l'Ain. Annales
ASA — (Specification) Standards Association of Australia
ASAA — Annuario. Reale Scuola Archeologica di Atene
ASAAN — Annales. Societe Archeologique de l'Arrondissement de Nivelles
ASA/ASR — American Sociological Review. American Sociological Association
ASAB — Annales. Societe d'Archeologie de Bruxelles
ASA Bull — ASA [*Australian Society of Accountants*] Bulletin
Asac — Art Sacre
ASAE — Anales de la Sociedad Argentina de Estudios Geograficos
ASAE — Annales. Service des Antiquites de l'Egypte
ASAE Publ — ASAE [*American Society of Agricultural Engineers*] Publication
ASAE Tech Pap — ASAE [*American Society of Agricultural Engineers*] Technical Paper
ASAE Trans — American Society of Agricultural Engineers. Transactions
ASAF — Archives de la Societe Americaine de France
As Aff (L) — Asian Affairs (London)
As Aff (NY) — Asian Affairs (New York)
As Afr Stud (B) — Asian and African Studies (Bratislava)
ASAG — Archives Suisses d'Anthropologie Generale
Asa Gray Bull — Asa Gray Bulletin. A Botanical Quarterly Published in the Interests of the GrayMemorial Botanical Association. The Botanical Gardeners Association. Universityof Michigan Botanical Club
Asahi Cam — Asahi Camera
ASAI — Annales. Service Archeologique de l'Iran
ASAIHL Bul — ASAIHL (Association of Southeast Asian Institutions of Higher Learning) Bulletin
ASAIO — Annuario. Scuola Archeologica di Atene e delle Missioni Italiani in Oriente
ASAIO J — ASAIO [*American Society for Artificial Internal Organs*] Journal
ASAIO Trans — Transactions. American Society for Artificial Internal Organs
ASAK — Anzeiger fuer Schweizerische Altertumskunde
ASal — Acta Salmanticensia
ASAL — Annuaire. Societe d'Histoire et d'Archeologie de la Lorraine
ASAL — Annual Survey of African Law
ASAL — Annual Survey of American Law
ASALAP — Acta Salmanticensia. Serie de Ciencias
ASAMAS — Annals. South African Museum
Asamblea Latinoam Fitoparasitol — Asamblea Latinoamericana de Fitoparasitologia
As Am Geog — Association of American Geographers. Annals
As Am G Rp — Association of American Geologists and Naturalists. Reports
ASAN — Annales. Societe Archeologique de Namur
As & Asps — Astronomy and Astrophysics
A S & T Ind — Applied Science and Technology Index
ASA Newsl — ASA [*American Society of Agronomy*] Newsletter
ASA Newsl — Association for the Study of Abortion. Newsletter
ASA Newsletter — American Society of Anesthesiologists. Newsletter
ASAOP — Archaeological Survey of Alberta. Occasional Papers
ASAPA3 — Archives Suisses d'Anthropologie Generale
ASA Pro Bu Ec — American Statistical Association. Proceedings of Business and Economic Statistics Section
ASA Pro So St — American Statistical Association. Proceedings of Social Statistics Section
ASA Pro St Cp — American Statistical Association. Proceedings of Statistical Computing Section
ASA Publ — ASA [*American Society of Agronomy*] Publication
ASA Rev Bks — ASA (African Studies Association) Review of Books
ASASDF — Advanced Series in Agricultural Sciences
ASA Spec Publ — ASA [*American Society of Agronomy*] Special Publication
ASA Spec Publ Am Soc Agron — ASA Special Publication. American Society of Agronomy
ASA Tech Bul — ASA [*Australian Society of Accountants*] Technical Bulletin
A S Atene — Annuario. Scuola Archeologica di Atene e Missioni Italiane in Oriente
ASAW — Abhandlungen. Saechsische Akademie der Wissenschaften zu Leipzig. Philosophisch-Historische Klasse
ASAWL — Abhandlungen. Saechsische Akademie der Wissenschaften zu Leipzig

ASAWL PHK — Abhandlungen. Saechsische Akademie der Wissenschaften zu Leipzig. Philosophisch-Historische Klasse
ASB — Accademia delle Scienze di Bologna. Memorie
ASB — African Studies Bulletin
ASB — American Journal of Small Business
ASB — Annales. Societe Scientifique de Bruxelles. Section SciencesEconomiques
ASB — Anzeiger fuer Schaedlingskunde (Berlin)
ASB — Asia Letter. An Authoritative Analysis of Asian Affairs
ASB — Asiatic Society of Bengal. Journal
AsB — Asien (Berlin)
ASB — Australian Stud Book
ASBA — Atas. Simposio Sobre a Biota Amazonica
ASB Bull — ASB [*Association of Southeastern Biologists*] Bulletin
ASBEA9 — Annales Scientifiques. Universite de Besancon. Medecine
ASBEB — Acta Stomatologica Belgica
ASBFC — Archivio Storico per Belluno, Feltre, e Cadore
ASBGAF — Annales Scientifiques. Universite de Besancon. Geologie
ASBIA — Archivio di Scienze Biologiche
ASBIAL — Archivio di Scienze Biologiche
ASBJ — Journal. Asiatic Society of Bangladesh
As Bk Tr Dir — Asian Book Trade Directory
ASBLAU — Archivos. Sociedad de Biologia de Montevideo
ASBMAX — Annales. Belgische Vereniging voor Tropische Geneeskunde
ASBOA5 — Annales Scientifiques. Universite de Besancon. Botanique
A S Boll — Acta Sanctorum
A Sbor — Archeologiceskij Sbornik Gosudarstvennyj Ordena Lenina Ermitaz
A Sbor — Arkheologicheskii Sbornik
ASBP — Asiatic Society of Bengal. Proceedings
ASBRAE — Anuario. Sociedade Broteriana
AsbSem — Asbury Seminarian
ASBYP — Appraisal. Science Books for Young People
ASBZA4 — Annales Scientifiques. Universite de Besancon. Zoologie et Physiologie
ASc — American Scholar
ASC — Annales des Sciences Commerciales et Economiques
ASc — Annales Scientifiques
ASc — Annals of Science
ASC — Annual Survey of Colleges
ASC — Archivio Storico di Corsica
ASC — ASCI [*Administrative Staff College of India*] Journal of Management
ASC — Atlas World Press Review
ASC — Australian Consumer Sales and Credit Law Reporter
ASCA — Anales de la Sociedad Cientifica de Argentina
ASCA — Automatic Subject Citation Alert
ASCAA — Anales. Sociedad Cientifica Argentina
ASCAP — ASCAP [*American Society of Composers, Authors, and Publishers*] in Action
ASCAP — ASCAP [*American Society of Composers, Authors, and Publishers*] Today
ASCAP Cop L Symp — Copyright Law Symposium. American Society of Composers, Authors, and Publishers
ASCAP Copyright L Sym — ASCAP [*American Society of Composers, Authors, and Publishers*] Copyright Law Symposium
ASCAP Copyright L Symp — Copyright Law Symposium. American Society of Composers, Authors, and Publishers
ASCBull — Academie des Sciences de Cracovie. Bulletin International
ASC Commun — ASC [*American Society for Cybernetics*] Communications
ASCE Annu Comb Index — ASCE [*American Society of Civil Engineers*] Annual Combined Index
ASCE Combined Sewer Separation Proj Tech Memo — ASCE [*American Society of Civil Engineers*] Combined Sewer Separation Project. Technical Memorandum
ASCE Eng Issues — ASCE [*American Society of Civil Engineers*] Engineering Issues
ASCE Eng Issues J Prof Activ — ASCE [*American Society of Civil Engineers*] Engineering Issues. Journal of Professional Activities
ASCE J Constr Div — ASCE [*American Society of Civil Engineers*] Journal of the Construction Division
ASCE J Eng Mech Div — ASCE [*American Society of Civil Engineers*] Journal of the Engineering Mechanics Division
ASCE J Environ Eng Div — ASCE [*American Society of Civil Engineers*] Journal of the Environmental Engineering Division
ASCE J Geotech Eng Div — ASCE [*American Society of Civil Engineers*] Journal of the Geotechnical Engineering Division
ASCE J Hydraul Div — ASCE [*American Society of Civil Engineers*] Journal of the Hydraulics Division
ASCE J Irrig Drain Div — ASCE [*American Society of Civil Engineers*] Journal of the Irrigation and Drainage Division
ASCE J Power Div — ASCE [*American Society of Civil Engineers*] Journal of the Power Division
ASCE J Prof Activ — ASCE [*American Society of Civil Engineers*] Journal of Professional Activities
ASCE J Sanit Eng Div — ASCE [*American Society of Civil Engineers*] Journal of the Sanitary Engineering Division
ASCE J Soil Mech Found Div — ASCE [*American Society of Civil Engineers*] Journal of the Soil Mechanicsand Foundations Division
ASCE J Struct Div — ASCE [*American Society of Civil Engineers*] Journal of the Structural Division
ASCE J Surv Mapp Div — ASCE [*American Society of Civil Engineers*] Journal of the Surveying and Mapping Division
ASCE J Urban Plann Dev Div — ASCE [*American Society of Civil Engineers*] Journal of the Urban Planning and Development Division
ASCE Waterw Harbors Coastal Eng Div — ASCE [*American Society of Civil Engineers*] Journal of the Waterways, Harbors, and Coastal Engineering Division

ASCE Man Rep Eng Pract — ASCE [*American Society of Civil Engineers*] Manuals and Reports on Engineering Practice

ASCE Proc — American Society of Civil Engineers. Proceedings

ASCE Proc Transp Eng J — American Society of Civil Engineers. Proceedings. Transportation Engineering Journal

ASCE Publ Abstr — ASCE [*American Society of Civil Engineers*] Publications Abstracts

ASCE Publ Inf — ASCE [*American Society of Civil Engineers*] Publications Information

ASCE Transp Eng J — ASCE [*American Society of Civil Engineers*] Transportation Engineering Journal

ASCE Urban Water Resour Res Program Tech Mem — ASCE [*American Society of Civil Engineers*] Urban Water Resources ResearchProgram. Technical Memorandum

ASCE Urban Water Resour Res Program Tech Memo IHP — ASCE [*American Society of Civil Engineers*] Urban Water Resources Research Program. Technical Memorandum IHP

ASCG — Annnales. Societe Scientifique et Litteraire de Cannes et de l'Arrondissement de Grasse

ASCGD — Anales. Seccion de Ciencias. Colegio Universitario de Gerona. Universidad Autonoma de Barcelona

Asch — Altschlesien

ASch — American Scholar

Aschaffenb MF Kr Ps — Aschaffenburgs Monatsschrift fuer Kriminalpsychologie

Aschaffenburger Jb — Aschaffenburger Jahrbuch

ASCH/CH — Church History. American Society of Church History. University of Chicago

ASCHDQ — Assignment Children

Aschener Bl Aufbereit Verkoken Briket — Aschener Blaetter fuer Aufbereiten Verkoken Brikettieren

A Schw — Archaeologie der Schweiz. Mitteilungsblatt der Schweizerischen Gesellschaft fuer Ur- und Fruehgeschichte

Asci — Actualites Scientifiques et Industrielles

ASci — American Scientist

ASCI (Admin Staff Col India) J Mgt — ASCI (Administrative Staff College of India) Journal of Management

A Sci Econ Appl — Annales des Sciences Economiques Appliquees

ASCL — Annual Survey of Commonwealth Law

ASCL — Archivio Storico per la Calabria e la Lucania

A Sc Lomb Ven — Annali delle Scienze del Regno Lombardo-Veneto

A Sc Nt — Annales des Sciences Naturelles, Comprenant la Physiologie Animale et Vegetale, l'Anatomie Comparee des deux Regnes, la Zoologie, la Botanique, la Mineralogie, et la Geologie

ASCOA — American Scholar

Ascom Tech Rev — Ascom Technical Review

AS Coop Ext Serv Purdue Univ — AS. Cooperative Extension Service. Purdue University

AScPhN — Archives des Sciences Physiques et Naturelles [*Genf*]

As Cult Q — Asian Culture Quarterly

ASC Univ Ky Coop Ext Serv — ASC University of Kentucky. Cooperative Extension Service

A Scuol Pisa — Annali. Scuola Normale Superiore di Pisa. Classe di Lettere e Filosofia

ASD — Annali di Storia del Diritto

ASD — Archivio Storico per la Dalmazia

ASD — Aviation Safety Digest

ASD — Memoires. Academie des Sciences, Arts, et Belles Lettres de Dijon

ASDA News — American Student Dental Association. News

ASDC J Dent Child — ASDC [*American Society of Dentistry for Children*]Journal of Dentistryfor Children

As Def J — Asian Defence Journal

ASDIDY — Agricultural Science Digest

ASDMA — Advances in Structure Research by Diffraction Methods

ASDSAR — Annali. Istituto Sperimentale per lo Studio e la Difesa del Suolo

ASE — Anglo-Saxon England

ASE — Annales des Sciences Economriques Appliquees

ASE — Annuario di Studi Ebraici

ASE — Archaeological Survey of Egypt

ASE — Memoirs. Archaeological Survey of Egypt

ASEA — Asiatische Studien/Etudes Asiatiques

ASEA Bul — Australian Society for Education through the Arts. Bulletin

ASEA Bull — Australian Society for Education through the Arts. Bulletin

ASEA J — ASEA [*Allmaenna Svenska Elektriska Aktiebolaget*] Journal

ASEAN (Assn South East Asian Nations) Bus Q — ASEAN (Association of South East Asian Nations) Business Quarterly

ASEAN Bus — ASEAN [*Association of South East Asian Nations*] Business Quarterly

ASEAN Food J — ASEAN [*Association of South East Asian Nations*] Food Journal

ASEAN Food Jnl — ASEAN Food Journal

ASEAN J Clin Sci — ASEAN [*Association of South East Asian Nations*] Journal of Clinical Sciences

ASEA Res — ASEA [*Allmaenna Svenska Elektriska Aktiebolaget*] Research

ASEA Tidn — ASEA [*Allmaenna Svenska Elektriska Aktiebolaget*] Tidning

ASEA Z — ASEA [*Allmaenna Svenska Elektriska Aktiebolaget*] Zeitschrift

ASEB — Acta Societatis Entomologicae Bohemiae

ASEB — Annales. Societe d'Emulation de Bruges

As Econ — Asian Economies

ASE/E — Ethnohistory. Journal of the American Society for Ethnohistory

ASEER — American Slavic and East European Review

ASEF — Annales. Societe d'Emulation pour l'Etude de l'Histoire et des Antiquites de Flandre

ASEG — Arquivos. Seminario d'Estudos Galegos

ASEGB — Australian Society of Exploration Geophysicists. Bulletin

ASEJ — Annuaire. Societe des Etudes Juives

A S e L — Acta Semiotica et Linguistica

ASEL — Annual Survey of English Law

ASEMC — Aviation, Space, and Environmental Medicine

ASEMCG — Aviation, Space, and Environmental Medicine

ASEMI — Asie du Sud-est et Monde Insulinden

ASENBI — Anais. Sociedade Entomologica do Brasil

As Eng Soc J — Association of Engineering Societies. Journal

ASEOAK — Archivos. Sociedad Espanola de Oftalmologia

ASEPAN — Australia. Commonwealth Scientific and Industrial Research Organisation. Division of Entomology. Technical Paper

Asepelt S — Asepelt Series

ASET Yearb — Australian Society of Educational Technology. Yearbook

ASEU — Archivo per la Storia Ecclesiastica dell'Umbria

ASEV — Societe d'Emulation de la Vendee. Annuaire Departemental

ASF — Analog Science Fiction

ASF — Archivio di Storia della Filosofia

AsF — Asie Francaise

ASF — Astounding Science Fiction

ASFA — Aquatic Sciences and Fisheries Abstracts

Asfar Publ Documentatiebureau Islam-Chris Rijksuniv Leiden — Asfar. Publikaties van het Documentatiebureau Islam-Christendom van de Rijksuniversiteit te Leiden

ASFF — Acta Societatis pro Fauna et Flora

ASFI — Archivio di Storia della Filosofia Italiana

ASFJAA — Arquivos. Servico Florestal

ASFM — Anuario. Sociedad Folklorico de Mexico

ASFN — Annuaire. Societe Francaise de Numismatique

As Folk Stud — Asian Folklore Studies

As For — Asiatischer Forschungen

ASFPAS — Australia. Commonwealth Scientific and Industrial Research Organisation. Division of Food Preservation and Transport. Technical Paper

ASFR — Australian Science Fiction Review

ASFR — Avon Science Fiction Reader

As Franc C R — Association Francaise pour l'Avancement des Sciences. Comptes-Rendus

As Fr C R — Association Francaise pour l'Avancement des Sciences. Compte Rendu

ASFZA — Analele. Universitatii Bucuresti. Seria Stiintele Naturii. Fizica

ASG — Abhandlungen. Koenigliche Saechsische Gesellschaft der Wissenschaften

ASG — Abhandlungen. Philosophisch-Historische Klasse der Saechsischen Gesellschaft

ASGA — Neues Archiv fuer Saechsische Geschichte und Altertumskunde

ASGH — Anales. Sociedad de Geografia e Historia

ASGHA9 — Anales. Sociedad de Geografia e Historia

ASGHG — Anales. Sociedad de Geografia e Historia de Guatemala

ASGIDF — Woods Hole Oceanographic Institution. Annual Sea Grant Report

ASGJA — American Society for Geriatric Dentistry. Journal

ASGLM — Atti. Sodalizio Glottologico Milanese

ASGM — Atti. Sodalizio Glottologico Milanese

ASGP — Annali. Seminario Giuridico di Palermo

ASGS — Archiv fuer Soziale Gesetzgebung und Statistik

ASGVAH — Archives des Sciences (Geneva)

ASGW — Abhandlungen. Philologisch-Historische Klasse. Koenigliche Saechsische Gesellschaft der Wissenschaften

Ash — Astonishing Stories

ASH — Australian Industrial Safety, Health, and Welfare

ASHA — ASHA. Journal of the American Speech and Hearing Association

ASHAG — Annales. Societe d'Histoire et d'Archeologie de Gand

ASHA J Am Speech Hear Assoc — ASHA. Journal of the American Speech and Hearing Association

ASHAL — Annuaire. Societe d'Histoire et d'Archeologie de la Lorraine

ASHA Monogr — ASHA [*American Speech and Hearing Association*] Monographs

ASHA Rep — ASHA [*American Speech and Hearing Association*] Reports

ASHA Suppl — ASHA [*American Speech and hearing Association*] Supplement

ASHAT — Annales. Societe Historique et Archeologique de Tournai

Ashers Guide Bot Period — Asher's Guide to Botanical Periodicals

ASHFY — American Swedish Historical Foundation. Yearbook

Ash G Bot Per — Asher's Guide to Botanical Periodicals

Ashikaga Inst Technol Res Rep — Ashikaga Institute of Technology. Research Reports

Ash M — Ashmolean Museum

Ashmol S P — Abstracts of the Proceedings of the Ashmolean Society

Ashmol S T — Transactions of the Ashmolean Society

ASHRAE B — American Society of Heating, Refrigerating, and Air-Conditioning Engineers. Bulletin

ASHRAE Handb Fundam — American Society of Heating, Refrigerating, and Air-Conditioning Engineers. Handbook of Fundamentals

ASHRAE Handb Prod Dir — ASHRAE [*American Society of Heating, Refrigerating, and Air-Conditioning Engineers*] Handbook and Product Directory

ASHRAE J — American Society of Heating, Refrigerating, and Air-Conditioning Engineers. Journal

ASHRAE Jol — American Society of Heating, Refrigerating, and Air-Conditioning Engineers. Journal

ASHRAE Trans — American Society of Heating, Refrigerating, and Air-Conditioning Engineers. Transactions

ASHS — Annuaire. Societe d'Histoire Sundgovienne

ASHY — American Swedish Historical Foundation. Yearbook

ASI — American Statistics Index

ASI — Archivio Storico Italiano

ASI — Atti della Societa Italiana di Scienze Naturali, e del Museo Civile di Storia Naturale

ASI — Australian Science Index

Asia — Asia and the Americas

ASIA — Asia Pacific Business

ASIA — Atti e Memorie. Societa Istriana di Archeologia e Storia Patria

Asia Afr R — Asia and Africa Review

Asia Afr Rev — Asia and Africa Review
Asia & Oceania Cong Endocrinol — Asia and Oceania Congress of Endocrinology
Asia Comp Yearbk — Asian Computer Yearbook
Asia Folkl Stud — Asian Folklore Studies
Asia Found News — Asia Foundation News
Asia J Econ — Asian Journal of Economics
ASIAM — [*The*] Asian American Magazine
Asia Mes — Asian Messenger
Asia Min — Asia Mining
Asia Mon — Asia Monitor
Asian A — Asian Art
Asian Aff — Asian Affairs
Asian Aff (London) — Asian Affairs. Journal of the Royal Central Asian Society (London)
Asian Aff (New York) — Asian Affairs (New York)
Asian Afr Stud — Asian and African Studies. Journal. Israeli Oriental Society
Asian Am Pac Isl J Health — Asian American and Pacific Islander Journal of Health
Asian & African Stud (Bratislava) — Asian and African Studies (Bratislava)
Asian Arch Anaesthesiol Resusc — Asian Archives of Anaesthesiology and Resuscitation
Asian Australasian J Anim Sci — Asian-Australasian Journal of Animal Sciences
Asian Australas J Anim Sci — Asian-Australasian Journal of Animal Sciences
A'sian Baker — Australasian Baker and Millers' Journal
Asian Bldg & Construction — Asian Building and Construction
A'sian Boating — Australasian Boating
Asian Bus — Asian Business and Industry [*Later, Asian Business*]
Asian Bus and Industry — Asian Business and Industry [*Later, Asian Business*]
A'sian Bus Cond Bul — Australasian Business Conditions Bulletin
Asian Cancer Conf — Asian Cancer Conference
A'sian Catholic R — Australasian Catholic Record
A'sian Catholic Rec — Australasian Catholic Record
Asian Chem Lett — Asian Chemistry Letters
Asian Chem News — Asian Chemical News
A'sian Confectioner — Australasian Confectioner and Restaurant Journal
Asian Congr Obstet Gynaecol Proc — Asian Congress of Obstetrics and Gynaecology. Proceedings
Asian Cult — Asian Culture
Asian Cult UNESCO Bhutan — Asian Culture for UNESCO Bhutan
Asian Dev — Asian Development. Quarterly Newsletter
Asian Econ — Asian Economics
Asian Econ R — Asian Economic Review
Asian Econ Rev — Asian Economic Review. Journal. Indian Institute of Economics
A'sian Eng — Australasian Engineering
A'sian Engineer — Australasian Engineer
Asian Environ — Asian Environment
Asian Exec Rep — Asian Executive Report
A'sian Exhibitor — Australasian Exhibitor
Asian Fin — Asian Finance
Asian Folk — Asian Folklore Studies
Asian Folkl Stud — Asian Folklore Studies
A'sian Grocer — Australasian Grocer
A'sian Inst Min & Metallurgy Proc — Australasian Institute of Mining and Metallurgy. Proceedings
Asian Inst Tech Newsl — Asian Institute of Technology. Newsletter
Asian Inst Tech Rev — Asian Institute of Technology. Review
A'sian Insurance & Banking Rec — Australasian Insurance and Banking Record
A'sian Insurance J — Australasian Insurance Journal
A'sian Irrigator — Australasian Irrigator
Asian J Aesthet Dent — Asian Journal of Aesthetic Dentistry
Asian J Androl — Asian Journal of Andrology
Asian J Chem — Asian Journal of Chemistry
Asian J Chem Rev — Asian Journal of Chemistry Reviews
Asian J Dairy Res — Asian Journal of Dairy Research
Asian J Infect Dis — Asian Journal of Infectious Diseases
Asian J Med — Asian Journal of Medicine
Asian J Mod Med — Asian Journal of Modern Medicine
Asian J Pharm — Asian Journal of Pharmacy
A'sian J Pharmacy — Australasian Journal of Pharmacy
Asian J Pharm Sci — Asian Journal of Pharmaceutical Sciences
A'sian J Phil — Australasian Journal of Philosophy
Asian J Phys — Asian Journal of Physics
Asian J Plant Sci — Asian Journal of Plant Science
Asian J Spectrosc — Asian Journal of Spectroscopy
A'sian Leather and Footwear R — Australasian Leather and Footwear Review
A'sian Leather Trades R — Australasian Leather Trades Review
Asian M — Asian Music
A'sian Manuf — Australasian Manufacturer
A'sian Manufacturer — Australasian Manufacturer
A'sian Manuf Ind Ann — Australasian Manufacturer. Industrial Annual
Asian Med J — Asian Medical Journal
Asian Med Jnl — Asian Medical Journal
A'sian Meth Hist Soc J & Proc — Australasian Methodist Historical Society. Journal and Proceedings
Asian Mus — Asian Music
A'sian Oil & Gas J — Australasian Oil and Gas Journal
Asian Pac Cens Forum — Asian and Pacific Census Forum
Asian Pac Congr Cardiol Proc — Asian-Pacific Congress of Cardiology. Proceedings
Asian Pac Congr Clin Biochem — Asian-Pacific Congress of Clinical Biochemistry
Asian Pac Corros Control Conf — Asian-Pacific Corrosion Control Conference
Asian Pac Counc Food Fert Technol Cent Book Ser — Asian and Pacific Council. Food and Fertilizer Technology Center. Book Series
Asian Pac Counc Food Fert Technol Cent Ext Bull — Asian and Pacific Council. Food and Fertilizer Technology Center. Extension Bulletin

Asian Pac Counc Food Fert Technol Cent Newsl — Asian and Pacific Council. Food and Fertilizer Technology Center. Newsletter
Asian Pac Counc Food Fert Technol Cent Tech Bull — Asian and Pacific Council. Food and Fertilizer Technology Center.Technical Bulletin
Asian Pacific Cult — Asian Pacific Culture
Asian Pacif Quart Cult Soc Aff — Asian Pacific Quarterly of Cultural and Social Affairs
Asian Pac J Allergy Immunol — Asian Pacific Journal of Allergy and Immunology
Asian Pac Popul Programme News — Asian and Pacific Population Programme News
Asian Pac Rev — Asian Pacific Review
Asian Pac Weed Sci Soc Conf — Asian-Pacific Weed Science Society Conference
Asian Persp — Asian Perspectives
Asian Perspect — Asian Perspectives
A'sian Post — Australasian Post
A'sian Pr — Australasian Printer
A'sian Printer — Australasian Printer
Asian R — Asian Review
Asian Res Trend — Asian Research Trends
Asian Rev — Asian Review
A'sian R'way & Locomotive Hist Soc Bul — Australasian Railway and Locomotive Historical Society. Bulletin
Asian S — Asian Survey
Asian Sch — Bulletin of Concerned Asian Scholars
Asian Soc Sci Bibliogr Annot Abstr — Asian Social Science Bibliography with Annotations and Abstracts
Asian Stud — Asian Studies
Asian Stud Prof R — Asian Studies. Professional Review
Asian Surv — Asian Survey
Asian Symp Med Plants Spices — Asian Symposium on Medicinal Plants and Spices
A'sian Univ Mod Lang Assoc Congress Proc — Australasian Universities Modern Language Association. Proceedings of Congress
Asian Wall St J — Asian Wall Street Journal
Asian WSJ — Asian Wall Street Journal
Asia Oceania Congr Perinatol — Asia Oceania Congress of Perinatology
Asia Oceania J Obstet Gynaecol — Asia Oceania Journal of Obstetrics and Gynaecology
Asia Pac — Asia and Pacific
Asia Pac Chem — Asia-Pacific Chemicals
Asia Pac Com — Asia Pacific Community
Asia Pac Commun Biochem — Asia Pacific Communications in Biochemistry
Asia Pacific J Oper Res — Asia-Pacific Journal of Operational Research
Asia Pac Int Jnl Manage Dev — Asia Pacific International Journal of Management Development
Asia Pac J Clin Nutr — Asian Pacific Journal of Clinical Nutrition
Asia Pac J Pharmacol — Asia Pacific Journal of Pharmacology
Asia Pac J Public Health — Asia-Pacific Journal of Public Health
Asia Pac Pet Dir — Asia-Pacific Petroleum Directory
Asia Pac Q — Quarterly Bulletin of Statistics for Asia and the Pacific
Asia Pac Top Manage Dig — Asia Pacific Top Management Digest
Asia Q — Asia Quarterly
Asia Quart — Asia Quarterly
Asia R — Asiatic Review
Asia Res Bul — Asia Research Bulletin
Asia Ship — Asia Pacific Shipping
Asiatic R — Asiatic Review
Asiatic R ns — Asiatic Review. New Series
Asiatic Soc Japan Trans — Asiatic Society of Japan. Transactions
Asiatische Stud — Asiatische Studien
Asiat Res — Asiatic Researches
Asiat Rev — Asiatic Review
Asiat Soc J — Asiatic Society Journal
Asiat Stud — Asiatische Studien
ASIDIC News — ASIDIC [*Association of Information and Dissemination Centers*] Newsletter
Asien Afr Lateinam — Asien, Afrika, Lateinamerika
Asie Nouv — Asie Nouvelle
Asie SE & Monde Insulind — Asie du Sud-Est et Monde Insulindien
Asie SE Monde Insul — Asie du Sud-Est Monde Insulindien
Asie Sud-Est Monde Insulind — Asie du Sud-Est et Monde Insulindien
ASIL — Annual Survey of Indian Law
ASILO — Adalbert Stifter Institut des Landes Oberoesterreich. Vierteljahresschrift
ASIL Proc — Proceedings. American Society of International Law
ASILS Intl LJ — ASILS [*Association of Student International Law Societies*] International Law Journal
ASIMAY — Atti. Societa Italiana di Scienze Naturali. Museo Civico di Storia Naturale di Milano
ASIN — Arts in Alaska. Newsletter. Alaska State Council on the Arts
ASInt — American Studies International
ASIP — Australian Serials in Print
ASIRAF — Australia. Commonwealth Scientific and Industrial Research Organisation. AnnualReport
ASIS — Atti. Societa Italiana di Statistica
ASISAI — Atti. Societa Italiana delle Scienze Veterinarie
ASIS Newsl — ASIS [*American Society for Information Science*] Newsletter
ASIST — Alberta Statistical Information System
Asi St/Et As — Asiatische Studien/Etudes Asiatiques
ASJ — American Suzuki Journal
As J — Astronomical Journal
ASJE — Actes. Societe Jurassienne d'Emulation
ASJPA — Australian Journal of Psychology
ASJPAE — Australian Journal of Psychology
ASKG — Archiv fuer Schlesische Kirchengeschichte
ASL — Annual Survey of Law

ASL — Archivio Storico Lombardo

ASL — Arsbok Utgiven av Seminarierna i Slaviska Sprak. Jaemfoerande Sprakforskning. Finsk-Ugriska Sprak och Oestasiatika Sprak vid Lunds Universitet

As Lab — Asian Labour

ASLA Pres Newsl — Association of State Library Agencies. President's Newsletter

ASLC — Australian Securities Law Cases

ASLE (Am Soc Lubr Eng) Annu Meet Prepr — ASLE (American Society of Lubrication Engineers) Annual Meeting. Preprints

ASLE Annu Meet Prepr — ASLE [American Society of Lubrication Engineers] Annual Meeting. Preprints

ASLE Pap — ASLE [American Society of Lubrication Engineers] Papers

ASLE Prepr — ASLE [American Society of Lubrication Engineers] Preprints

ASLE Proc Int Conf Solid Lubr — ASLE [American Society of Lubrication Engineers] Proceedings. International Conference on Solid Lubrication

ASLE Spec Publ — ASLE [American Society of Lubrication Engineers] Special Publication

ASLE Trans — ASLE [American Society of Lubrication Engineers] Transactions

ASLF — Annales de Saint-Louis des Francais

ASLG — Atti. Societa Linguistica di Scienze e Lettere di Genova

ASLH — American Society of the Legion of Honor. Magazine

ASLHM — American Society of the Legion of Honor. Magazine

Aslib Inf — Aslib Information

Aslib Info — Aslib Information

Aslib Occas Publ — Aslib Occassional Publications

Aslib Proc — Aslib Proceedings

AS Lig — Atti. Deputazione di Storia Patria per la Liguria

ASLig — Atti. Societa Ligure di Storia Patria

ASLJD — Arizona State Law Journal

ASLL — Acta Societatis Humaniorum Litterarum Lundensis

ASLN — Australian Special Libraries News

ASLOBM — American Society of Limnology and Oceanography. Special Symposium

ASLod — Archivio Storico Lodigiano

ASLO (London) Rep — Australian Scientific Liaison Office (London). Report

AsIP — Aslib. Proceedings

ASLP Bul — Association of Special Libraries of the Philippines. Bulletin

ASLP Bull — Association of Special Libraries of the Philippines. Bulletin

ASLP Bulletin — Australian Society of Legal Philosophy. Bulletin

ASLP Proceedings — Australian Society of Legal Philosophy. Proceedings

ASLR — Australian Securities Law Reporter

ASLRAU — Australia. Commonwealth Scientific and Industrial Research Organisation. Land Research Series

ASL Res Rep — ASL [American Scientific Laboratories] Research Report

ASLSP — Atti. Societa Ligure di Storia Patria

ASLU — Acta Societatis Linguisticae Upsaliensis

ASLund — Arsbok Utgiven av Seminarierna i Slaviska Sprak, Jamforande Sprakforskning, Finsk-Ugriska Sprak och Ostasiatika Sprak Vid Lunds Universitet

ASLVA8 — Agricultura en El Salvador

ASM — Agency Sales Magazine

ASM — American Swedish Monthly

ASM — Annual Survey of Manufactures

ASM — Archeologicke Studijni Materialy

ASM — Archivio Storico Messinese

AsM — Asia Major

ASM — Asian Music

ASM — Asiatic Society Monographs

ASM — Association and Society Manager

ASM — Association Management

ASM-1 — Annual Survey of Manufacturers. AS-1. General Statistics for Industry Groups and Industries

ASM-2 — Annual Survey of Manufacturers. AS-2. Value of Product Shipments

As Ma — Asia Major

ASMA — Journal. Australian Stipendiary Magistrates' Association

Asmat Sketch Bk — Asmat Sketch Book

ASMEA — Archivio per le Scienze Mediche

ASME Adv Energy Syst Div Publ AES — American Society of Mechanical Engineers. Advanced Energy Systems Division. Publication AES

ASME Aerosp Div Publ AD — American Society of Mechanical Engineers. Aerospace Division. Publication AD

ASME Air Pollut Control Div Nat Symp — ASME [American Society of Mechanical Engineers] Air Pollution Control Division. National Symposium

ASME Air Pollut Control Div Reg Meet — ASME [American Society of Mechanical Engineers] Air Pollution Control Division. Regional Meeting

ASME ANS Int Conf Adv Nucl Energy Syst Pap — ASME-ANS [American Society of Mechanical Engineers Advanced Nuclear Systems] International Conference on Advanced Nuclear Energy Systems. Papers

ASMEAU — Archivio per le Scienze Mediche

ASME Bioeng Div Publ BED — American Society of Mechanical Engineers. Bioengineering Division. Publication BED

ASME Boiler Pressure Vessel Code — American Society of Mechanical Engineers. Boiler and Pressure Vessel Code

ASME Cent Res Technol Publ CRTD — American Society of Mechanical Engineers. Center for Research and Technology Development. Publication CRTD

ASME Comput Eng Div CED — American Society of Mechanical Engineers. Computer Engineering Division. CED

ASME Des Eng Div Publ DE — American Society of Mechanical Abngineers. Design Engineering Division. Publication DE

ASME Dyn Syst Control Div Publ DSC — American Society of Mechanical Engineers. Dynamic Systems and Control Division. Publication DSC

ASME EEP — American Society of Mechanical Engineers. EEP

ASME Environ Control Div Publ EC — American Society of Mechanical Engineers. Environmental Control Division. Publication EC

ASME Fluids Eng Div Publ FED — American Society of Mechanical Engineers. Fluids Engineering Division. Publication FED

ASME Fuels Combust Technol Div Publ FACT — American Society of Mechanical Engineers. Fuels and Combustion Technologies Division. Publication FACT

ASME Heat Transfer Div Publ HTD — American Society of Mechanical Engineers. Heat Transfer Division. Publication HTD

ASME Intern Combust Engine Div Publ ICE — American Society of Mechanical Engineers. Internal Combustion Engine Division. Publication ICE

ASME Int Gas Turbine Inst Publ IGTI — American Society of Mechanical Engineers. International Gas Turbine Institute. Publication IGTI

ASME JSES JSME Int Sol Energ Conf — ASME-JSES-JSME International Solar Energy Conference

ASME Mater Div Publ MD — American Society of Mechanical Engineers. Materials Division. Publication MD

ASME Mater Handl Div Publ MH — American Society of Mechanical Engineers. Material Handling Division. MH

ASME Mater Prop Counc MPC — American Society of Mechanical Engineers. Materials Properties Council. MPC

ASME Nat Waste Process Conf Proc — ASME [American Society of Mechanical Engineers] National Waste Processing Conference. Proceedings

ASME Noise Control Acoust Div Publ NCA — American Society of Mechanical Engineers. Noise Control and Acoustics Division. Publication NCA

ASME Nucl Eng Div Publ NE — American Society of Mechanical Engineers. Nuclear Engineering Division. Publication NE

ASME Pap — American Society of Mechanical Engineers. Papers

ASME Paper — American Society of Mechanical Engineers. Papers

ASME Perform Test Codes — American Society of Mechanical Engineers. Performance Test Codes

ASME Pet Div Publ PD — American Society of Mechanical Engineers. Petroleum Division. Publication PD

ASME Power Div Publ PWR — American Society of Mechanical Engineers. Power Division. Publication PWR

ASME Pressure Vessels Piping Div Publ PVP — American Society of Mechanical Engineers. Pressure Vessels and Piping Division. Publication PVP

ASME Prod Eng Div Publ PED — American Society of Mechanical Engineers. Production Engineering Division. Publication PED

ASME Publ NDE — American Society of Mechanical Engineers. Publication NDE

ASME Sol Energy Div Publ SED — American Society of Mechanical Engineers. Solar Energy Division. Publication SED

ASME Tech Soc Publ TS — American Society of Mechanical Engineers. Technology and Society Division. Publication TS

ASME Trans — American Society of Mechanical Engineers. Transactions

ASME Trans Ser F — American Society of Mechanical Engineers. Transactions. Series F

ASME Trans Ser I — American Society of Mechanical Engineers. Transactions. Series I.

ASMG — Atti e Memorie. Societa Magna Grecia

ASMIEC — Aspects of Microbiology

AS Mimeogr Circ LA State Univ Agr Exp Sta — Animal Science Mimeograph Circular. Louisiana State University. Agricultural Experiment Station

ASML — Annual Survey of Massachusetts Law

AsML — Asia Major (London and Leipzig)

ASM M81AS-4 — Annual Survey of Manufacturers. M81AS-4. Expenditures for Plant and Equipment

ASM M81AS-5 — Annual Survey of Manufacturers. M81AS-5. Orgin of Exports of Manufactured Products

ASMMA — Atti. Seminario Matematico e Fisico. Universita di Modena

ASM News — American Society for Microbiology. News

ASMOAQ — Anales. Sociedad Mexicana de Oftalmologia

ASMODT — Analytical Sciences Monographs

ASMTQ — ASM [American Society for Metals] Transactions Quarterly

ASM Trans Q — ASM [American Society for Metals] Transactions Quarterly

ASM Trans Quart — ASM [American Society for Metals] Transactions Quarterly

ASMUAA — Acta Scholae Medicinalis Universitatis in Kioto

As Music — Asian Music

ASMVAD — Anais. Escola Superior de Medicina Veterinaria

ASN — Annali. Scuola Normale Superiore di Pisa

ASN — Archivio Storico per le Provincie Napoletane

ASNA Reporter — ASNA [Alabama State Nurses' Association] Reporter

ASNBAQ — Annales des Sciences Naturelles. Zoologie et Biologie Animale

ASNED — ASIS [American Society for Information Science] News

ASNEE5 — Society for Neuroscience. Abstracts

ASNGA7 — Abhandlungen. Senckenbergische Naturforschende Gesellschaft

ASNMAP — Atti. Societa dei Naturalisti e Matematici di Modena

ASNOA — Astrophysica Norvegica

ASNP — Annales des Sciences Naturelles (Paris)

ASNP — Annali. Scuola Normale Superiore di Pisa

ASNPBZ — Annali. Istituto Sperimentale per la Nutrizione delle Piante

As Nr — Astronomische Nachrichten. Schumacher

ASNS — Archiv fuer das Studium der Neueren Sprachen und Literaturen

ASNSL — Archiv fuer das Studium der Neueren Sprachen und Literaturen

ASNSP — Annali. Scuola Normale Superiore di Pisa

ASNU — Acta Seminarii Neotestamentici Upsaliensis

ASNVAI — Annales des Sciences Naturelles. Botanique et Biologie Vegetale

ASO — American Journal of Economics and Sociology

AsO — Asian Outlook

Aso — Asomante

ASOC — Analecta Sacri Ordinis Cisterciensis

ASoc — Annales Sociologiques

ASoc — Annee Sociologique

ASoc — Arts in Society

Asoc A Concr Inven — Asociacion Arte Concreto Invencion

A Soc Arch Namur — Annales. Societe Archeologique de Namur

Asoc Argent Farm Bioquim Ind — Asociacion Argentina de Farmacia y Bioquimica Industrial

Asoc Argent Microbiol Rev — Asociacion Argentina de Microbiologia. Revista

Asoc Argent Mineral Petrol Sediment Rev — Asociacion Argentina de Mineralogia, Petrologia, y Sedimentologia. Revista

ASOCAY — Atti. Societa Italiana di Cardiologia

Asoc Colombiana Bibl Bol — Asociacion Colombiana de Bibliotecarios. Boletin

Asoc Cuba Bibl Bol — Asociacion Cubana de Bibliotecarios. Boletin

Asoc Dent Mex Rev — Asociacion Dental Mexicana. Revista

Asoc Esp Farm Hosp Rev — Asociacion Espanola de Farmaceuticos de Hospitales. Revista

Asoc Esp Prog Cienc An — Asociacion Espanola para el Progreso de las Ciencias. Anales

Asoc Farm Mex Rev — Asociacion Farmaceutica Mexicana. Revista

Asoc Geol Argent Monogr — Asociacion Geologica Argentina. Monografia

Asoc Geol Argent Rev — Asociacion Geologica Argentina. Revista

Asoc Ing Agron Rev — Asociacion de Ingenieros Agronomos. Revista

Asoc Ing Uruguay Rev Ingenieria — Asociacion de Ingenieros del Uruguay. Revista de Ingenieria

Asoc Invest Tec Ind Papelera Esp Jorn Tec Papeleras — Asociacion de Investigacion Tecnica de la Industria Papelera Espanola.Jornadas Tecnicas Papeleras

A Sociol (Milano) — Annali di Sociologia (Milano)

Asoc Latinoam Entomol Publ — Asociacion Latinoamericana de Entomologia. Publicacion

Asoc Latinoam Prod Anim Mem — Asociacion Latinoamericana de Produccion Animal. Memoria

Asoc Mat Espanola — Asociacion Matematica Espanola

Asoc Med Argent Rev — Asociacion Medica Argentina. Revista

Asoc Med Ferrocarriles Nac Mex Rev Med — Asociacion Medica de los Ferrocarriles Nacionales de Mexico. RevistaMedica

Asoc Med PR — Asociacion Medica de Puerto Rico

Asoc Mex Geol Pet Bol — Asociacion Mexicana de Geologos Petroleros. Boletin

Asoc Mexicana Geofisicos Explor Bol — Asociacion Mexicana de Geofisicos de Exploracion. Boletin

Asoc Mex Tec Ind Celul Pap Bol — Asociacion Mexicana de Tecnicos de las Industrias de la Celulosa y del Papel. Boletin

Asoc Nac Ing Agron Bol — Asociacion Nacional de Ingenieros Agronomos. Boletin

Asoc Odontol Argent Rev — Asociacion Odontologica Argentina. Revista

Asoc Quim Esp Ind Cuero Bol Tec — Asociacion Quimica Espanola de la Industria del Cuero. Boletin Tecnico

A Soc R — American Sociological Review

A Soc Sci Litt Cannes — Annales. Societe Scientifique Litteraire de Cannes et de l'Arrondissement de Grasse

Asoc Tec Azucar Cuba ATAC — Asociacion de Tecnicos Azucareros de Cuba. ATAC

Asoc Tec Azucar Cuba Bol Of — Asociacion de Tecnicos Azucareros de Cuba. Boletin Oficial

Asoc Venez Geol Min Pet Bol — Asociacion Venezolana de Geologia Mineria y Petroleo. Boletin

ASOFDC — Archivos. Sociedad Canaria de Oftalmologia

ASOHAF — Archivos. Sociedad Oftalmologica Hispano-Americana

A Soignies — Annales. Cercle Archeologique du Canton de Soignies

ASOL — American Symphony Orchestra League. Newsletter

ASOM — Academie des Sciences d'Outre-Mer

Asom — Asomante

ASOR — American Schools of Oriental Research. Newsletter

ASORA — Australian Journal of Soil Research

ASORAB — Australian Journal of Soil Research

ASORBA — American Schools of Oriental Research. Biblical Archaeologist

ASOR Bul — American Schools of Oriental Research. Bulletin

ASOR PJSA — American Schools of Oriental Research. Publications of the Jerusalem School. Archaeology

ASOTBI — Australia. Commonwealth Scientific and Industrial Research Organisation. Division of Soil Mechanics. Technical Paper

As Outlook — Asian Outlook

ASozHy — Archiv fuer Soziale Hygiene

ASP — Advertising and Sales Promotion

ASP — American Studies in Papyrology

ASP — Annales Sociologiques (Paris)

ASP — Apuntes (Peru)

ASP — Archiv fuer Slavische Philologie

ASP — Archivio Storico Pratese

ASP — Archivio Storico Pugliese

AsP — Asian Profile

ASP — Asiatic Society of Pakistan. Journal

ASP — Australian Superannuation and Employee Benefits Guide

ASP — Australian Superannuation Practice

ASPA — Atti. Societa Piemontese di Archeologia e Belle Arti

ASPABA — Atti. Societa Piemontese di Archeologia e Belle Arti

ASPAC Q Cul & Soc Aff — ASPAC Quarterly of Cultural and Social Affairs

ASPap — American Studies in Papyrology

AS Parm — Archivio Storico per la Provincie Napoletane

ASPBB3 — Annales Scientifiques. Universite de Besancon. Physiologie et Biologie Animale

ASPCD8 — Auspicium

ASP Ctrattack — ASP Counterattack

ASPEA — Advances in Spectroscopy

Aspects Actuels Mycoses Journ Int Biol — Aspects Actuels des Mycoses. Journees Internationales de Biologie

Aspects Adhes — Aspects of Adhesion

Aspects Allergy Appl Immunol — Aspects of Allergy and Applied Immunology

Aspects Appl Biol — Aspects of Applied Biology

Aspects Ed — Aspects of Education

Aspects Energy Convers Proc Summer Sch — Aspects of Energy Conversion. Proceedings of a Summer School

Aspects Fish Parasitol Symp Br Soc Parasitol — Aspects of Fish Parasitology. Symposium of the British Society for Parasitology

Aspects Homogeneous Catal — Aspects of Homogeneous Catalysis

Aspects Maison Monde — Aspects de la Maison dans le Monde

Aspects Microbiol — Aspects of Microbiology

Aspects Nucl Struct Funct — Aspects of Nuclear Structure and Function

Aspects of Ed — Aspects of Education

Aspects of Math — Aspects of Mathematics

Aspects of Math E — Aspects of Mathematics. E

Aspects Plant Sci — Aspects of Plant Sciences

Aspects Pl Sci — Aspects of Plant Sciences

Aspects Statist Region Paris — Aspects Statistiques de la Region Parisienne

Aspects Teratol — Aspects of Teratology

Asp Educ Technol — Aspects of Educational Technology

Aspen — Aspen Anthology

Aspen A — Aspen Anthology

Aspen J — Aspen Journal of the Arts

Aspen J Art — Aspen Journal for the Arts

As Perspect (H) — Asian Perspectives (Honolulu)

As Perspect (S) — Asian Perspectives (Seoul)

AspF — Aspects de la France et l'Independance Francaise

Asp Fr — Aspects de la France et du Monde

ASPG J — Alberta Society of Petroleum Geologists. Journal

ASPh — Archiv fuer Systematische Philosophie

ASPHAK — Archives des Sciences Physiologiques

Asphalt Inst Constr Ser — Asphalt Institute. Construction Series

Asphalt Inst Inf Ser — Asphalt Institute. Information Series

Asphalt Inst Q — Asphalt Institute. Quarterly

Asphalt Inst Res Ser — Asphalt Institute. Research Series

Asphalt Paving Technol — Asphalt Paving Technology

Asphalt Teerind Ztg — Asphalt Teerindustrie. Zeitung

Asphalt Teer Strassenbautech — Asphalt und Teer. Strassenbautechnik

Aspirin 2000 Proc Int Meet — Aspirin. Towards 2000. Proceedings. International Meeting

Aspirin Relat Drugs Their Actions Uses Proc Symp — Aspirin and Related Drugs. Their Actions and Uses. Proceedings of the Symposium

Aspir Rab Nauchno Issled Inst Udobr Insektofungits (Moscow) — Aspirantskie Raboty Nauchno Issledovatel'skii Institut po Udobrenii i Insektofungitsidam (Moscow)

ASPJ — Asiatic Society of Pakistan. Journal

Asp Komplexer Systeme — Aspekte Komplexer Systeme

AspL — Aspetti Letterari

ASPM — Advanced Studies in Pure Mathematics

ASPN — Archives des Sciences Physiques et Naturelles

ASPN — Archivio Storico per le Provincie Napolitane

ASPND7 — Ata Reumatologica Brasileira

ASPO — Agora-Sports

ASPP — Archivio Storico per le Provincie Parmensi

ASPP — Asiatic Society of Pakistan. Publication

A Spr — Alten Sprachen

ASPR — Anglo-Saxon Poetic Records

ASPR — Annuaire de la Societe Paleontologique de Russie

ASPR — Australasian Small Press Review

A S Prat — Archivio Storico Pratese

As Profile — Asian Profile

ASPS — Atti. Societa Italiana per il Progresso delle Scienze

ASPSA — Atti. Societa Peloritana di Scienze Fisiche, Matematiche, e Naturali

ASPSAJ — Atti. Societa Peloritana di Scienze Fisiche, Matematiche, e Naturali

Asps J — Astrophysical Journal

ASPUD — ASAE [*American Society of Agricultural Engineers*] Publication

ASPZA — Avtomatizatsiya Staleplavil'nogo Proizvodstva

ASQ — Administrative Science Quarterly

As Q — Asia Quarterly

ASQBA7 — Association Senegalaise pour l'Etude du Quaternaire de l'Ouest Africain. Bulletin de Liaison

ASR — American Iron and Steel Institute. Statistical Report

ASR — American-Scandinavian Review

ASR — American Slavic Review

ASR — American Sociological Review

ASR — Annales. Societa Retorumantscha

ASR — Annales. Societe J.J. Rousseau

ASR — Antiken Sarkophagreliefs

ASR — Archives de Sociologie des Religions

AsR — Asiatic Researches

ASR — Australasian Software Report

ASR — Australian Securities Law Reporter

ASR — Automotive Service Reports

ASR — Avon Science Fiction Reader

ASRA — Atti della Societa Romana di Antropologia

ASRAB — Annales. Societe Royale d'Archeologie de Bruxelles

ASR Bull INORGA — ASR [*Automatizovane Systemy Rizeni*] Bulletin INORGA

ASRE J — ASRE [*American Society of Refrigerating Engineers*] Journal

As Researches — Asiatick Researches. Or Transactions of the Society, Instituted in Bengal, for inquiring into the History and Antiquities, Arts, Sciences, and Literature of Asia

ASRHAT — Annales. Societe Royale d'Histoire et d'Archeologie de Tournai

ASRNDH — Anales. Instituto Nacional de Investigaciones Agrarias. Serie Recursos Naturales

ASRPCM — Australia. Commonwealth Scientific and Industrial Research Organisation. Division of Soils. Report on Progress

ASRRAQ — ASL [*American Scientific Laboratories*] Research Report

ASRS — Archivio. Societa Romana di Storia Patria

ASRSD — Advances in Space Research

ASRSP — Archivio. Societa Romana di Storia Patria

ASRU — Archivio Storico del Risorgimento Umbrio

ASRWA7 — Agricultural Science Review. Cooperative State Research Service. US Department of Agriculture

ASS — Acta Sanctae Sedis

ASS — Amazing Science Stories

ASS — American Studies

ASS — Archivio Storico Siciliano

ASS — Argenteuil Symposia Series

AsS — Asian Survey

AsS — Asiatische Studien

ASSAL — Annual Survey of South African Law

Assam Agric Univ J Res — Assam Agricultural University. Journal of Research

Assam Dept Agric Fruit Ser — Assam Department of Agriculture. Fruit Series

Assam Rev Tea News — Assam Review and Tea News

Assam Sci Soc J — Assam Science Society. Journal

ASSar — Archivio Storico Sardo

AS Sard — Archivio Storico Sardo

AS Sardo — Archivio Storico Sardo

Assaults Fed Off — Assaults on Federal Officers

Ass Bibliot Fr Bull Inf — Association des Bibliothecaires Francais. Bulletin d'Informations

ASSC — Actes de la Societe Scientifique du Chili

ASSc — Archivio di Storia della Scienza

Assd — Assurandoren

ASSE J — ASSE Journal

Assem Autom — Assembly Automation

Assembly Eng — Assembly Engineering

Assem Eng — Assembly Engineering

Assem Eur Fed Chem Eng — Assembly. European Federation of Chemical Engineering

Assem Fastener Eng — Assembly and Fastener Engineering

Assem Gen Comm Int Tech Sucr — Assemblee Generale. Commission Internationale Technique de Sucrerie

As SE Monde Insul — Asie du Sud-Est et Monde Insulindien

Assess & Eval in Higher Educ — Assessment and Evaluation in Higher Education

Assess Arct Mar Environ Sel Top Symp — Assessment of the Arctic Marine Environment. Selected Topics. Based on a Symposium Held in Conjunction with Third International Conference on Port and Ocean Engineering under Arctic Conditions

Assess Environ Pollut Proc Natl Symp — Assessment of Environmental Pollution. Proceedings. National Symposium

Assess J — Assessors Journal

Assessment in Higher Ed — Assessment in Higher Education

Assessors J — Assessors Journal

Assess Pharmacodyn Eff Hum Pharmacol Symp — Assessment of Pharmacodynamic Effects in Human Pharmacology. Symposium

Assess Radioact Contam Man Proc Symp — Assessment of Radioactive Contamination in Man. Proceedings. Symposium on Assessment of Radioactive Organ and Body Burdens

ASSET — Abstracts of Selected Solar Energy Technology

ASSF — Acta Societatis Scientiarum Fennicae

Ass Franc Avance Sc C R — Association Francaise pour l'Avancement des Sciences. Comptes-Rendus.

ASSIA — Applied Social Sciences Index and Abstracts

AS Sic — Archivio Storico Siciliano

AS Sic O — Archivio Storico per la Sicilia Orientale

Assicurazioni Soc — Assicurazioni Sociali

Assiette Beurre — Assiette au Beurre

Assignment Chil — Assignment Children

Assignment Child — Assignment Children

AS Sir — Archivio Storico Siracusano

Assises Annu Assoc Que Tech Eau — Assises Annuelles. Association Quebecoise des Techniques de l'Eau

Assises Fr Gynecol Rapp — Assises Francaises de Gynecologie. Rapports

Assistant Librn — Assistant Librarian

Assisted Reprod Technol Androl — Assisted Reproductive Technology/Andrology

Assistenza Infermieristica E Ricerca — Assist Inferm Ric

Assistenza Soc — Assistenza Sociale

Assist Inf — Assistance Informations

Assist Libn — Assistant Librarian

Assist Soc — Assistenza Sociale

Assiut J Agric Sci — Assiut Journal of Agricultural Sciences

Assiut Univ Fac Eng Bull — Assiut University. Faculty of Engineering. Bulletin

Assiut Univ Fac Sci Bull — Assiut University. Faculty of Science. Bulletin

ASSL — Archiv fuer das Studium der Neuren Sprachen und Literaturen

ASSLAD — Astrophysics and Space Science Library

ASSMBH — Acta Salmanticensia. Serie de Medicina

As S Mm — Memoirs of the Royal Astronomical Society of London

As S M Not — Monthly Notices of the Royal Astronomical Society of London

Assn Am Ag Coll & Exp Pro — Association of American Agricultural Colleges and Experiment Stations. Proceedings

Assn Am Anat Proc — Association of American Anatomists. Proceedings

Assn Am Col Bul — Association of American Colleges. Bulletin

Assn Am Geog Ann — Association of American Geographers. Annals

Assn Am M Col J — Association of American Medical Colleges. Journal

Assn Asian Stud Newsletter — Association for Asian Studies. Newsletter

Ass Naz Ing Architetti Ital Quad — Associazione Nazionale degli Ingegneri ed Architetti Italiani. Quaderni

Assn Bar City NY Rec — Association of the Bar of the City of New York. Record

Assn Bibl Francais Bull Inf — Association des Bibliothecaires Francais. Bulletin d'Informations

Assn Canadienne Bibl Langue Francaise Bul — Association Canadienne des Bibliothecaires de Langue Francaise. Bulletin

Assn Comp Mach J — Association for Computing Machinery. Journal

Assn D Licen Univ Liege Bul — Association des Licencies de l'Universite de Liege. Bulletin

Assn Ed Radio J — Association for Education by Radio. Journal

Assn for Sup & Curric Develop Yearbook — Association for Supervision and Curriculum Development. Yearbook

Assn Italiana Bibl Boll Inf — Associazione Italiana Biblioteche. Bollettino d'Informazioni

Assn Life Insur Pres Proc — Association of Life Insurance Presidents. Proceedings

Assn Men — Association Men (Rural Manhood)

Assn Mgt — Association Management

Assn Of Dir Poor & Char & Correc Proc — Association of the Directors of the Poor and Charities and Correction of the State of Pennsylvania. Proceedings

Assn Offic Ag Chem J — Association of Official Agricultural Chemists. Journal

Assn of Gov Bds of State Univ & Allied Insts Proc — Association of Governing Boards of State Universities and Allied Institutions. Proceedings

Assn Res Nerv & Ment Dis Proc — Association for Research in Nervous and Mental Diseases. Proceedings

Assn Sch Bsns Officials US & Canada Proc — Association of School Business Officials of the United States and Canada. Proceedings

Assn Stud Teach Yrbk — Association for Student Teaching. Yearbook

Assn Sup & Curric Devel Yrbk — Association for Supervision and Curriculum Development. Yearbook

ASSO — Archivio Storico per la Sicilia Orientale

Assoc Adv Agric Sci Afr J — Association for the Advancement of Agricultural Sciences in Africa.Journal

Assoc Adv Med Instrum Technol Anal Rev — Association for the Advancement of Medical Instrumentation Technology Analysis and Review

Assoc Adv Med Instrum Technol Assess Rep — Association for the Advancement of Medical Instrumentation Technology.Assessment Report

Assoc Adv Pol Stud Bul — Association for the Advancement of Polish Studies. Bulletin

Assoc Afr Stud Nagoya Univ Prelim Rep Afr Stud — Association for African Studies. Nagoya University. Preliminary Report of African Studies

Assoc Am Fert Control Off Off Publ — Association of American Fertilizer Control Officials. Official Publication

Assoc Am Geog Ann — Association of American Geographers. Annals

Assoc Am Geographers Annals — Association of American Geographers. Annals

Assoc Am Geographers Comm Coll Geography Resource Paper — Association of American Geographers. Commission on College Geography. Resource Paper

Assoc Am Geogr Comm Coll Geogr Publ — Association of American Geographers. Commission on College Geography. Publication

Assoc Am Physicians Trans — Association of American Physicians. Transactions

Assoc Am Plant Food Control Off Off Publ — Association of American Plant Food Control Official. Official Publication

Assoc Archit Soc Rep & Pap — Associated Architectural Societies Reports and Papers

Assoc Asphalt Paving Technol — Association of Asphalt Paving Technologists. Conference

Assoc Asphalt Paving Technol Proc Tech Sess — Association of Asphalt Paving Technologists. Proceedings. TechnicalSessions

Assoc Belge Dev Pac Energ At Bull Inf — Association Belge pour le Developpement Pacifique de l'Energie Atomique. Bulletin d'Information

Assoc Belge Photogr Cinematogr Bull — Association Belge de Photographie et de Cinematographie. Bulletin

Assoc Belge Radioprot Ann — Association Belge de Radioprotection. Annales

Assoc Belge Technol Lab Rev — Association Belge des Technologues de Laboratoire. Revue

Assoc Belgo Neerl Etude Cereales CR — Association Belgo-Neerlandaise pour l'Etude des Cereales. Comptes Rendus

Assoc Bibl Francais Bul — Association des Bibliothecaires Francais. Bulletin d'Informations

Assoc Bibl Fr Ann — Association des Bibliothecaires Francais. Annuaire

Assoc Biochim Hop Que Bull — Association des Biochimistes des Hopitaux du Quebec. Bulletin

Assoc Bras Ind Aliment Rcv — Associacao Brasileira das Industrias da Alimentacao. Revista

Assoc Bras Ind Aliment Setor Aliment Calorico Proteicos Rev — Associacao Brasileira das Industrias da Alimentacao. Setor de Alimentos Calorico Proteicos. Revista

Assoc Bras Met Bol — Associacao Brasileira de Metais. Boletim

Assoc Bras Met Congr Anu — Associacao Brasileira de Metais. Congresso Anual

Assoc Bras Met Not — Associacao Brasileira de Metais. Noticiario

Assoc Bras Pesqui Plant Aromat Oleos Essen Bol — Associacao Brasileira de Pesquisas sobre Plantas Aromaticas e Oleos Essenciais.Boletim

Assoc Bras Quim Secc Reg Sao Paulo Simp Ferment — Associacao Brasileira de Quimica. Seccao Regional de Sao Paulo.Simposio de Fermentacao

Assoc Bret C R Proces Verbaux — Association Bretonne. Comptes-Rendus. Proces-Verbaux

Assoc Bull Int Assoc Milk Dealers — Association Bulletin. International Association of Milk Dealers

Assoc Cadres Dir Industr B — Association de Cadres Dirigeants de l'Industrie pour le Progres Social et Economique. Bulletin

Assoc Canadienne-Francaise Av Sci Annales — Association Canadienne-Francaise pour l'Avancement des Sciences. Annales

Assoc Can Bibl Lang Fr Bull — Association Canadienne des Bibliothecaires de Langue Francaise. Bulletin

Assoc Can Diet J — Association Canadienne des Dietetistes. Journal

Assoc Can Fr Av Sci Ann — Association Canadienne-Francaise pour l'Avancement des Sciences. Annales

Assoc Clin Pathol Symp — Association of Clinical Pathologists Symposia

Assoc Comm Agric South States Proc — Association. Commissioners of Agriculture of Southern States. Proceedings

Assoc Comput Mach Commun — Association for Computing Machinery. Communications

Assoc Comput Mach Proc Annu Conf — Association for Computing Machinery. Proceedings. Annual Conference

Assoc Cons Eng Dir — Association of Consulting Engineers Directory

Assoc Demographes Quebec Bul — Bulletin. Association de Demographes du Quebec

Assoc Econ Biol Coimbatore Proc — Association of Economic Biologists. Coimbatore. Proceedings

Assoc Electr Ind Eng — Associated Electrical Industries Engineering

Assoc Electr Ind Eng Rev — Associated Electrical Industries Engineering Review

Assoc Elettrotec Elettron Ital Rend Riun Annu — Associazione Elettrotecnica ed Elettronica Italiana. Rendiconti della Riunione Annuale

Assoc Elettrotec Ital Rend Riun Annu — Associazione Elettrotecnica Italiana. Rendiconti della Riunione Annuale

Assoc Eng Geol Ann Meet Program Abstr — Association of Engineering Geologists. Annual Meeting. Program and Abstracts

Assoc Eng Geol Annu Mtg Guideb — Association of Engineering Geologists. Annual Meeting. Guidebook

Assoc Eng Geol Annu Mtg Guide Field Trips — Association of Engineering Geologists. Annual Meeting. Guide to Field Trips

Assoc Eng Geol Bull — Association of Engineering Geologists. Bulletin

Assoc Exec Buy Gui Meet Plan — Association Executives Buyers' Guide and Meeting Planner

Assoc Food and Drug Off Q Bull — Association of Food and Drug Officials. Quarterly Bulletin

Assoc Food Drug Off US Q Bull — Association of Food and Drug Officials of the United States. QuarterlyBulletin

Assoc Franc Avancem Sci Conf — Association Francaise pour l'Avancement des Sciences. Conferences Faites En

Assoc Fr Chim Ind Cuir Conf — Association Francaise des Chimistes des Industries du Cuir. Conference

Assoc Fr Cybern Econ Tech Annu — Association Francaise pour la Cybernetique Economique et Technique. Annuaire

Assoc Fr Etude Quat Bull — Association Francaise pour l'Etude du Quaternaire. Bulletin

Assoc Fr Etude Sol Bull — Association Francaise pour l'Etude du Sol. Bulletin

Assoc Fr Gemmol Bull — Association Francaise de Gemmologie. Bulletin

Assoc Fr Tech Pet Rev — Association Francaise des Techniciens du Petrole. Revue

Assoc Geofis Ital Atti Conv Annu — Associazione Geofisica Italiana. Atti del Convegno Annuale

Assoc Geographes Francais Bull — Association de Geographes Francais. Bulletin

Assoc Geogr Fr Bull — Association de Geographes Francais. Bulletin

Assoc Geog Teach Ir J — Assocation of Geography Teachers of Ireland. Journal

Assoc Geol Bassin Paris Bull — Association des Geologues du Bassin de Paris. Bulletin

Assoc Geol Bassin Paris Bull Inf — Association des Geologues du Bassin de Paris. Bulletin d'Information

Assoc Green Crop Driers Yearb — Association of Green Crop Driers. Yearbook

Assoc Ind Angola Bol — Associacao Industrial de Angola. Boletim

Assoc Ind Med Off Trans — Association of Industrial Medical Officers. Transactions

Assoc Ind Metall Mecc Affini Not Tec AMMA — Associazione Industriali Metallurgici Meccanici Affini. NotiziarioTecnico AMMA

Assoc Ind NY Bull — Associated Industries of New York State. Bulletin

Assoc Ing Electr Sortis Inst Electrotech Montefiore Bull — Association des Ingenieurs Electriciens Sortis de l'Institut Electrotechnique Montefiore. Bulletin

Assoc Ing Sortis Univ Libre Bruxelles Bull Tech — Association des Ingenieurs Sortis de l'Universite Libre de Bruxelles. Bulletin Technique

Assoc Int Cancer Res Symp — Association for International Cancer Research. Symposia

Assoc Int Distrib Eau Congr — Association Internationale des Distributions d'Eau. Congres

Assoc Int Doc Tech Inf Bull — Association Internationale des Documentalistes et Techniciens de l'Information. Bulletin

Assoc Int Etude Argiles — Association Internationale pour l'Etude des Argiles

Assoc Int Geol Ing Bull — Association Internationale de Geologie de l'Ingenieur. Bulletin

Assoc Int Limnol Theor Appl Commun — Association Internationale de Limnologie Theoretique et Appliquee.Communications

Assoc Int Limnol Theor Appl Trav — Association Internationale de Limnologie Theoretique et Appliquee. Travaux

Assoc Int Odonto Stomatol Infant J — Association Internationale d'Odonto Stomatologie Infantile. Journal

Assoc Int Sci Hydrol Publ — Association Internationale des Sciences Hydrologiques. Publication

Assoc Iron Steel Electr Eng Proc — Association of Iron and Steel Electrical Engineers. Proceedings

Assoc Ital Bibl Quad Bol Inf — Associazione Italiana Biblioteche. Quaderni del Bollettino d'Informazioni

Assoc Ital Fis Sanit Prot Radiaz Atti Congr Naz — Associazione Italiana di Fisica Sanitaria e di Protezione contro leRadiazioni. Atti del Congresso Nazionale

Assoc Ital Ind Prod Aliment Bol — Associazione Italiana Industriali Prodotti Alimentari. Bollettino

Assoc Ital Metall Atti Not — Associazione Italiana di Metallurgia. Atti Notizie

Assoc Ital Tec Ind Vernici Affini Boll — Associazione Italiana Tecnici Industrie Vernici Affini. Bollettino

Assoc Jewish Stud Newsl — Association for Jewish Studies Newsletter

Assoc Jpn Portland Cem Eng Rev Gen Meet — Association of Japanese Portland Cement Engineers. Review of General Meeting

Assoc Kinet India Bull — Association of Kineticists of India. Bulletin

Assoc Latinoam Entomol Publ — Associacion Latinoamericana de Entomologia. Publicacion

Assoc Manage — Association Management

Assoc Med Bras Rev — Associacao Medica Brasileira. Revista

Assoc Med Minas Gerais Rev AMMG — Associacao Medica de Minas Gerais. Revista da AMMG

Assoc Metall Mecc Affini Not Tec AMMA — Associazione Metallurgici Meccanici Affini. Notiziario Tecnico AMMA

Assoc Met Sprayers Pap Symp Eng Appl Met Spraying — Association of Metal Sprayers. Papers. Symposium on Engineering Applications ofMetal Spraying

Assoc Mine Mangr S Afr Circ — Association of Mine Managers of South Africa. Circulars

Assoc Mine Mangr S Afr Pap Discuss — Association of Mine Managers of South Africa. Papers and Discussions

Assoc Nat Enseign Agric Public Bull Trimest — Association des Naturalistes de l'Enseignement Agricole Public. Bulletin Trimestriel

Assoc Natl Prot Incendie Dossier Tech — Association Nationale pour la Protection contre l'Incendie. Dossier Technique

Assoc Natl Serv Eau (Belg) Bull Inf — Association Nationale des Services d'Eau (Belgium). Bulletin d'Information

Assoc News — Associate News

Assoc Nucl Can Congr Int Ann — Association Nucleaire Canadienne. Congres International Annuel

Assoc Off Anal Chem J — Association of Official Analytical Chemists. Journal

Assoc Off Analyt Chemists J — Association of Official Analytical Chemists. Journal

Assoc Official Agr Chemists Jour — Association of Official Agricultural Chemists. Journal

Assoc Off Seed Anal Proc — Association of Official Seed Analysts. Proceedings

Assoc Pacific Coast Geographers Yearbook — Association of Pacific Coast Geographers. Yearbook

Assoc Paul Cir Dent Rev — Associacao Paulista de Cirurgioes Dentistas. Revista

Assoc Preserv Technol Suppl Communique — Association for Preservation Technology Supplement Communique

Assoc Public Analysts J — Association of Public Analysts. Journal

Assoc Que Tech Eau Assises Annu — Association Quebecoise des Techniques de l'Eau. Assises Annuelles

Assoc Que Tech Eau Congr AQTE — Association Quebecoise des Techniques de l'Eau. Congres AQTE

Assoc R Anc Etud Brass Univ Louvain Bull — Association Royale des Anciens Etudiants en Brasserie. Universite deLouvain. Bulletin

Assoc Rech Tech Exploit Pet CR Colloque ARTEP — Association de Recherche sur les Techniques d'Exploitation du Petrole. Comptes Rendus du Colloque de l'ARTEP

Assoc Rech Tech Forage Prod CR Colloq — Association de Recherche sur les Techniques de Forage et de Production.Comptes Rendus du Colloque

Assoc Recor — Association for Recorded Sound Collections. Journal

Assoc Reg Etude Rech Sci Bull — Association Regionale pour l'Etude et la Recherche Scientifiques. Bulletin

Assoc Reg Etude Sci Bull — Association Regionale pour l'Etude et la Recherche Scientifiques. Bulletin

Assoc Res Nerv Ment Dis Res Publ — Association for Research in Nervous and Mental Disease. Research Publications

Assoc Res Nerv Ment Dis Ser Res Publ — Association for Research in Nervous and Mental Disease. Series of Research Publications

Assoc Sci Int Cafe Colloq — Association Scientifique Internationale du Cafe. Colloque

Assoc Sci Prod Anim Congr Naz — Associazione Scientifica di Produzione Animale. Congresso Nazionale

Assoc Sci Tech Soc S Afr Annu Proc — Associated Scientific and Technical Societies of South Africa. Annual Proceedings

Assoc Senegal Etude Quat Afr Bull Liaison — Association Senegalaise pour l'Etude du Quaternaire de l'Ouest Africain. Bulletin de Liaison

Assoc Senegal Etud Quat Ouest Afr Bull Liaison — Association Senegalaise pour l'Etude du Quaternaire de l'Ouest Africain. Bulletin de Liaison

Assoc Soc Manager — Association and Society Manager

Assoc South Agric Work Proc — Association of Southern Agricultural Workers. Proceedings

Assoc South East Asian Nations Food J — Association of South East Asian Nations. Food Journal

Assoc Suisse Chim Tech Ind Vernis Couleurs Bull — Association Suisse des Chimistes et Techniciens de l'Industrie des Vernis et Couleurs. Bulletin

Assoc Tec Bras Celul Pap Bol — Associacao Tecnica Brasileira de Celulose e Papel. Boletim

Assoc Tech Energ Nucl Bull Inf — Association Technique pour l'Energie Nucleaire. Bulletin d'Information

Assoc Tech Ind Gaz — Association Technique de l'Industrie du Gaz en France. Proceedings

Assoc Tech Ind Papet Bull — Association Technique de l'Industrie Papetiere. Bulletin

Assoc Trop Biol Bull — Association for Tropical Biology Bulletin

Assoc Univ Programs Health Admin Program Notes — Association of University Programs in Health Administration. Program Notes

Assoc Vet Anaesth GB Irel J — Association of Veterinary Anaesthetists of Great Britain and Ireland. Journal

Assortiment Oeuvres Spec Sci Ec Polytech Brno A — Assortiment des Oeuvres Specialises et Scientifiques. EcolePolytechniques a Brno. A

Assortiment Oeuvres Spec Sci Ec Polytech Brno B — Assortiment des Oeuvres Specialises et Scientifiques. EcolePolytechniques a Brno. B

As S Pac Pb — Publications of the Astronomical Society of the Pacific

ASSPAP — Australia. Commonwealth Scientific and Industrial Research Organisation. Soil Publication

ASS Ph — Annales. Cercle Archeologique du Canton de Soignies

ASSPh — Annales. Societe Suisse de Philosophie

ASSR — Archives de Sciences Sociales des Religions

ASSRFM — Alaska Series Special Reports for Management

AssSeign — Assemblees du Seigneur

ASS Short-Circuit Test Auth Publ — Association of Short-Circuit Testing Authorities. Publication

AsSt — Asian Student
As St — Asiatische Studien
ASSTA — Acier-Stahl-Steel
Asst Libn — Assistant Librarian
ASSUA6 — Acta Psychiatrica Scandinavica. Supplementum
ASSUD9 — US Department of Agriculture. Science and Education Administration. Agricultural Research Results. ARR-S
Assuntos Eur — Assuntos Europeus
Assuring Radiat Prot Annu Natl Conf Radiat Control — Assuring Radiation Protection. Annual National Conference on Radiation Control
Assur Mg — Assurance Magazine and Journal of the Institute of Actuaries
As Surv — Asian Survey
ASSVB — Annali. Istituto Sperimentale per la Selvicoltura
Assy Misc — Assyriological Miscellanies
Assyr Engl Glossary — Assyrian and English Glossary
Assyriol Stud — Assyriologische Studien
Assyriol Studies — Assyriological Studies
Assyr S — Assyriological Studies
Assyr S — Assyriologische Studien
AssyrSt — Assyriological Studies
A St — Aberystwyth Studies
AST — American Statistician
AST — American String Teacher
AST — Analecta Sacra Tarraconensia
A St — Anatolian Studies
AST — Applied Science and Technology Index
ASt — Asian Studies
ASt — Asiatische Studien
AST — Astonishing Stories
AST — Atti e Memorie. Societa Tiburtina di Storia e d'Arte
Ast & AstroAb — Astronomy and Astrophysics. Abstracts
A S Tarr — Analecta Sacra Tarraconensia
ASTC — Australian Sales Tax Cases
A St Dal — Archivio Storico per la Dalmazia
Asthet Med (Berl) — Asthetische Medizin (Berlin)
Asthma Bronchial Hyperreact Congr Eur Soc Pneumol — Asthma and Bronchial Hyperreactivity. Congress. European Society of Pneumology
As Thought Soc — Asian Thought and Society
ASTI — Annual. Swedish Theological Institute
ASTI — Applied Science and Technology Index
ASTIB — Army Scientific and Technical Intelligence Bulletin
ASTic — Archivio Storico Ticinese
Astin Bull — Astin Bulletin
ASTIS — Arctic Science and Technology Information System
A St It — Archivio Storico Italiano
ASTL — Archivio Storico di Terra di Lavoro
A St Lomb — Archivio Storico Lombardo
A St Malo — Annales. Societe d'Histoire et d'Archeologie de l'Arrondisement de Saint-Malo
ASTM (Am Soc Test Mater) Data Ser — ASTM (American Society for Testing and Materials) Data Series
ASTM Book ASTM Stand — American Society for Testing and Materials. Book of ASTM Standards
ASTM Bul — American Society for Testing and Materials. Bulletin
ASTM Cem Concr Aggregates — ASTM [*American Society for Testing and Materials*] Cement, Concrete, and Aggregates
ASTM Data Ser — ASTM [*American Society for Testing and Materials*] Data Series
ASTME/ASM West Metal Tool Conf — American Society of Tool and Manufacturing Engineers. ASTME/ASM Western Metal and Tool Conference
ASTME Collect Papers — American Society of Tool and Manufacturing Engineers. ASTME Collected Papers
ASTME Creative Mfg Semin Tech Papers — American Society of Tool and Manufacturing Engineers. Creative Manufacturing Seminars. Technical Papers
ASTM Geotechnical Testing Journal — American Society for Testing and Materials. Geotechnical Testing Journal
ASTM Geotech Test J — ASTM [*American Society for Testing and Materials*] Geotechnical Testing Journal
ASTM J Testing Evaln — ASTM [*American Society for Testing and Materials*] Journal of Testing and Evaluation
ASTM Meet Prepr — American Society for Testing and Materials. Meeting. Preprints
ASTM Proc — ASTM [*American Society for Testing and Materials*] Proceedings
ASTM SP — ASTM [*American Society for Testing and Materials*] Special Technical Publication
ASTM Special Technical Publication — American Society for Testing and Materials. Special Technical Publication
ASTM Spec Tech Publ — ASTM [*American Society for Testing and Materials*] Special Technical Publication
ASTM Stand — ASTM [*American Society for Testing and Materials*] Standards
ASTM Stand N — ASTM [*American Society for Testing and Materials*] Standardization News
ASTM Stand News — ASTM [*American Society for Testing and Materials*] Standardization News
ASTM Std — ASTM [*American Society for Testing and Materials*] Standards
ASTM Stdn News — ASTM [*American Society for Testing and Materials*] Standardization News
ASTM Tentative Stand — ASTM [*American Society for Testing and Materials*] Tentative Standards
Ast Nap — Archivio Storico per la Provincie Napoletane
ASTOAR — Annali di Stomatologia
ASTP — Archives Suisses des Traditions Populaires
ASTPCW — Australia. Commonwealth Scientific and Industrial Research Organisation. Division of Soil Research. Technical Paper
A St Pugl — Archivio Storico Pugliese
Astr Ast SS — Astronomy and Astrophysics Supplement Series

Astro Aeron — Astronautics and Aeronautics
Astro Ephem — Astronomical Ephemeris
Astrofiz — Astrofizika
Astrofiz Issled — Astrofizicheskie Issledovaniya
Astrofiz Issled Izv Spets Astrofiz Obs — Astrofizicheskie Issledovaniya. Izvestiya Spetsial'noi Astrofizicheskoi Observatorii
Astrofiz Issled (Leningrad) — Astrofizicheskie Issledovaniya (Leningrad)
Astrofiz Issled (Sofia) — Astrofizicheskie Issledovaniya (Sofia)
Astrol 77 — Astrology '77
Astrol 78 — Astrology '78
Astrol Now — Astrology Now
Astrom Astrofiz — Astrometriya i Astrofizika
Astrometriya & Astrofiz — Astrometriya i Astrofizika
Astron — Astronomy and Astrophysics
Astron Abhandl Ergaenzungshefte Astron Nachr — Astronomische Abhandlungen als Ergaenzungshefte zu den Astronomischen Nachrichten
Astron & Geophys — Astronomy and Geophysics
Astron & Space — Astronomy and Space
Astron Astr — Astronomy and Astrophysics
Astron Astrophys — Astronomy and Astrophysics
Astron Astrophys Abstr — Astronomy and Astrophysics. Abstracts
Astron Astrophys Suppl Ser — Astronomy and Astrophysics. Supplement Series
Astron Astrophys Trans — Astronomical and Astrophysical Transactions
Astronaut Acta — Astronautica Acta
Astronaut Aeronaut — Astronautics and Aeronautics
Astronaut Aerosp Eng — Astronautics and Aerospace Engineering
Astronaut Forschungsber Dtsch Raketen Ges eV — Astronautische Forschungsberichte. Deutsche Rakete Gesellschaft eV
Astronaut Forschungsber Hermann Oberth Ges — Astronautische Forschungsberichte. Hermann Oberth Gesellschaft
Astronautics Aerospace Eng — Astronautics and Aerospace Engineering
Astronaut Sci Rev — Astronautical Sciences Review
Astron Circ Acad Sin — Astronomical Circulars. Academia Sinica
Astron Ex — Astronomy Express
Astron Geod Arb Schweiz — Astronomisch-Geodaetische Arbeiten in der Schweiz
Astron Her — Astronomical Herald
Astron J — Astronomical Journal
Astron Jahresber — Astronomischer Jahresbericht
Astron Kal (Moscow) — Astronomicheskii Kalendar (Moscow)
Astron Lett Transl of Pisma Astron Zh — Astronomy Letters (Translation of Pis'ma v Astronomicheskii Zhurnal)
Astron (Milwaukee) — Astronomy (Milwaukee)
Astron Nach — Astronomische Nachrichten
Astron Nachr — Astronomische Nachrichten
Astronom and Astrophys — Astronomy and Astrophysics
Astronom Astrophys Lib — Astronomy and Astrophysics Library
Astronom Astrophys Ser — Astronomy and Astrophysics. Supplement Series
Astronomiya Itogi Nauki Tekh — Astronomiya Itogi Nauki i Tekhniki
Astronom J — Astronomical Journal
Astronom Nachr — Astronomische Nachrichten
Astronom Z — Akademija Nauk SSSR. Astronomiceskii Zurnal
Astronom Zh — Astronomicheskii Zhurnal
Astron-Opt Inst Univ Turku Inf — Astronomia-Optika Institucio. Universitato de Turku. Informo
Astron (Paris) — Astronomie (Paris)
Astron (Paris) Suppl — Astronomie (Paris). Supplement
Astron Q — Astronomy Quarterly
Astron Raumfahrt — Astronomie und Raumfahrt
Astron Rep Transl of Astron Zh — Astronomy Reports (Translation of Astronomicheskii Zhurnal)
Astron Saellsk — Astronomiska Saellskapet
Astron Soc Aust Proc — Astronomical Society of Australia. Proceedings
Astron Soc Aust Publ — Astronomical Society of Australia. Publications
Astron Soc India Bull — Astronomical Society of India. Bulletin
Astron Soc Jpn Publ — Astronomical Society of Japan. Publications
Astron Soc Pac Conf Ser — Astronomical Society of the Pacific Conference Series
Astron Soc Pacific Pubs — Astronomical Society of the Pacific. Publications
Astron Soc Pac Leafl — Astronomical Society of the Pacific. Leaflet
Astron Tidsskr — Astronomisk Tidsskrift
Astron Tsirk — Astronomicheskii Tsirkulyar
Astron Vestn — Astronomicheskii Vestnik
Astron Zh — Astronomicheskii Zhurnal
Astron Zs — Astronomische Zeitschrift
Astroph J S — Astrophysical Journal. Supplement Series
Astrophys — Astrophysics
Astrophys Gravitation Proc Solvay Conf Phys — Astrophysics and Gravitation. Proceedings of the Solvay Conference on Physics
Astrophysics (Engl Transl) — Astrophysics (English Translation)
Astrophys J — Astrophysical Journal
Astrophys J Lett Ed — Astrophysical Journal. Letters to the Editor
Astrophys J Suppl — Astrophysical Journal. Supplement
Astrophys J Suppl Ser — Astrophysical Journal. Supplement Series
Astrophys L — Astrophysical Letters
Astrophys Lett — Astrophysical Letters
Astrophys Norv — Astrophysica Norvegica
Astrophys Space Phys Rev — Astrophysics and Space Physics Reviews
Astrophys Space Sci — Astrophysics and Space Science
Astrophys Space Sci Lib — Astrophysics and Space Science Library
Astrophys Space Sci Libr — Astrophysics and Space Science Library
Astro Sp Sc — Astrophysics and Space Science
Astr T — Astronomisk Tidsskrift
ASTSC — Annals of Statistics
A St Sic Or — Archivio Storico per la Sicilia Orientale
ASTT — Astarte. Journal of Arctic Biology

ASTTA8 — ASTM [*American Society for Testing and Materials*] Special Technical Publication
ASTTB9 — Astarte
A Stud — Art Studies
A Stud Med Ren & Mod — Art Studies, Medieval, Renaissance, and Modern
ASTYD — Aerosol Science and Technology
ASTZA5 — Atti. Simposio Internazionale di Zootecnia
ASU — American School and University
ASu — Anthroponymica Suecana
As U A — Annales. Universite d'Abidjan
ASU Bus Tchr — Arizona State University. Business Teacher
ASUC — American Society of University Composers. Proceedings
ASUHA — Asufaruto
ASUI — Analele Stiintifice ale Universitatii (Iasi)
ASUJ — Annales Scientifiques de l'Universite de Jassy
ASULAN — Agrisul
ASUNB — American School and University
Asuntos Agr — Asuntos Agrarios
A Suom Taide — Ars Suomen Taide
Asutustoiminnan Aikak — Asutustoiminnan Aikakauskirja
ASUVDM — Annales Scientifiques. Universite de Besancon. Biologie Vegetale
ASV — Archivio di Stato di Venezia
ASW — Abstracts for Social Workers
ASW — Administration in Social Work
ASW — American Scholar (Washington, D.C.)
ASW — Anthropological Society of Washington. Division of Archaeology. US National Museum (Washington, D.C.)
ASW — Australian Social Welfare
ASWG — Abhandlungen der Philologisch-Historische Klasse der Saechsischen Akademie der Wissenschaften
ASXBA8 — Archives of Sexual Behavior
ASY — Agriculture Statistical Yearbook and Agriculture Sample
ASY — Aslib Information
ASY — Association and Society Manager
ASY — Astounding Stories Yearbook
Asymmetric Org Synth Proc Nobel Symp — Asymmetric Organic Synthesis. Proceedings. Nobel Symposium
Asymptotic Anal — Asymptotic Analysis
ASZ — Allgemeine Sport-Zeitung
ASZ — Assistenz
ASZBAI — Archivum Societatis Zoologicae-Botanicae Fennicae "Vanamo"
A Szekely Nemz Muz — A Szekely Nemzeti Muzeum Ertesitoeje
A Szekely Nemz Muz Ertes — A Szekely Nemzeti Muzeum Ertesitoeje
AS Zg — Aerztliche Sachverstaendigen-Zeitung
ASZOAN — Annales Scientifiques. Universite de Besancon. Zoologie
AT — Acta Tropica
AT — Africa Today
AT — Alalakh Tablets
AT — Analecta Sacra Tarraconensia. Revista de Ciencias Historico-Eclesiasticas
AT — Analecta Tarraconensia
AT — Anthropology Tomorrow
AT — Antik Tanulmanyok
AT — Archeolgrafo Triestino
AT — Arquivo Transtagano
AT — ASCAP [*American Society of Composers, Authors, and Publishers*] in Action
At — Atenea
At — Atlantida
AT — Atlantis
AT — Atlin News Miner
AT — Aufbereitungs-Technik
AT — Autumn
ATA — Abstracts on Tropical Agriculture
ATA — Alttestamentliche Abhandlungen
ATA — Annee Theologique Augustinienne
AT/A — Antiquity. A Quarterly Review of Archaeology. Antiquity Trust
Ata — Antropologica
At Absorpt Newsl — Atomic Absorption Newsletter
At Acad Med S Paulo — Atos. Academia de Medicina de Sao Paulo
ATAC (Asoc Tec Azucar Cuba) — ATAC (Asociacion de Tecnicos Azucareros de Cuba)
ATACC7 — ATAC (Asociacion de Tecnicos Azucareros de Cuba)
ATACC J — ATACC [*Alberta Teachers' Association, Computer Council*] Journal
At Acc Nap — Atti. Accademia Nazionale di Scienze Morali e Politiche. Napoli
At Acc Napoli — Atti. Accademia Pontaniana (Napoli)
At Acc Sc Pa — Atti. Accademia di Scienze, Lettere, e Arti di Palermo
ATAC Rev Bimest Asoc Tec Azucar Cuba — ATAC. Revista Bimestral. Asociacion de Tecnicos Azucareros de Cuba
ATAEBC — Agronomie Tropicale. Serie Agronomie Generale. Etudes Scientifiques
ATAGDK — Atualidades Agronomicas
ATAKDW — Allattenyesztes es Takarmanyozas
Atalanta Norv — Atalanta Norvegica
ATA Mag — ATA [*Alberta Teachers Association*] Magazine
AT & T Co Com L — American Telephone & Telegraph Co. Commission. Leaflets
AT&T Tech J — AT&T Technical Journal
AT&T Technol — AT&T Technology
ATA Newsletter — Alberta Teachers Association. Newsletter
ATANT — Abhandlungen zur Theologie des Alten und Neuen Testaments
ATAPAA — Annales de Technologie Agricole
Ata Reumatol Bras — Ata Reumatologica Brasileira
Atas Inst Micol Univ Fed Pernambuco — Atas. Instituto de Micologia da Universidade Federal de Pernambuco
Atas Simp Reg Geol — Atas. Simposio Regional de Geologia
Atas Soc Biol Rio De J — Atas. Sociedade de Biologia do Rio De Janeiro
Atas Soc Biol Rio De Janeiro — Atas. Sociedade de Biologia do Rio De Janeiro
At At Eng — Atomics and Atomic Engineering

At At Technol — Atomics and Atomic Technology
Ataturk Univ Fen Bilimleri Derg — Ataturk Universitesi Fen Bilimleri Dergisi
Ataturk Univ Fen Fak Derg — Ataturk Universitesi Fen Fakultesi Dergisi
Ataturk Univ J Sci — Ataturk University Journal of Sciences
ATAVJ — Art Teachers Association of Victoria. Journal
ATAV News — Art Teachers Association of Victoria. News Sheet
ATAV News Sheet — Art Teachers Association of Victoria. News Sheet
ATB — Altdeutsche Textbibliothek
ATB Metall — ATB [*Acta Technica Belgica*] Metallurgie
AtC — Atenea. Revista Mensual de Ciencias, Letras, y Artes Publicada por la Universidade de Concepcion
ATC — Australian Tax Cases
ATCAA — Automatica
ATCCBG — Acta Cancerologica
ATCCEJ — Adjuvant Therapy of Cancer
ATCL — Atlin Claim
ATCP — ATCP
ATCSD — Annual Technical Conference. American Electroplaters' Society
ATCYA — Appropriate Technology
ATD — Acta Theologica Danica
ATD — Australasian Tax Decisions
ATD — Australian Tax Decisions
ATD — Australian Teacher of the Deaf
At Data — Atomic Data [*Later, Atomic Data and Nuclear Data Tables*]
At Data Nucl Data Tables — Atomic Data and Nuclear Data Tables
At Data Workshop — Atomic Data Workshop
At Diffus Semicond — Atomic Diffusion in Semiconductors
ATDSAY — ASTM [*American Society for Testing and Materials*] Data Series
ATE — Advanced Textbooks in Economics
Ate — Atenea
ATE — Bedrijfsvoering; Tijdschrift voor Organisatiekunde en Arbeidskunde, Produktie, Onderhoud, Inkoop, en Logistiek
ATEHA6 — Agrotecnia
A Tel — Annales Telegraphiques, Publiees sous le Patronage du Directeur General des Lignes Telegraphiques
A Telecom — Annales des Telecommunications
At Elektr Stn — Atomnye Elektricheskie Stantsii
Atelier — Atelier des Photographen
Atelier Photogr Allg Photographztg — Atelier des Photographen und Allgemeine Photographenzeitung
Atelier Photogr Dtsch Photogr Kunst — Atelier des Photographen und Deutsche Photographische Kunst
Ateliers A Graph — Ateliers d'Art Graphique
Atemwegs- Lungenkr — Atemwegs- und Lungenkrankheiten
Atemwegs Lungenkrankh — Atemwegs- und Lungenkrankheiten
ATEN — Atenea
ATEN — Atmospheric Environment
At En — Atomnaya Energiya
ATENEA PR — Atenea. Facultad de Artes y Ciencias (Puerto Rico)
Ateneo Ci — Ateneo Cientifico. Memoria Leida en la Junta General
Ateneo Parmense Acta Bio-Med — Ateneo Parmense. Acta Bio-Medica
Ateneo Parmense Acta Nat — Ateneo Parmense. Acta Naturalia
Ateneo Parmense Sez 1 — Ateneo Parmense. Sezione 1. Acta Bio-Medica
Ateneo Parmense Sez 2 — Ateneo Parmense. Sezione 2. Acta Naturalia
Ateneo Ven — Ateneo Veneto
At Energ — Atomnaya Energiya
At Energ Itogi Nauki Tekh — Atomnaya Energetika Itogi Nauki i Tekhniki
At Energiya (USSR) — Atomnaya Energiya (USSR)
At Energ Prilozh — Atomnaya Energiya Prilozhenie
At Energy Aust — Atomic Energy in Australia
At Energy Board Rep PEL (S Afr) — Atomic Energy Board. Report PEL (South Africa)
At Energy Board Rep PER — Atomic Energy Board. Report PER
At Energy Board (Repub S Afr) Rep — Atomic Energy Board (Republic of South Africa). Report
At Energy Bull — Atomic Energy Bulletin
At Energy Can Ltd AECL (Rep) — Atomic Energy of Canada Limited. AECL (Report)
At Energy Can Ltd Mat Res AECL — Atomic Energy of Canada Limited. Materials Research in AECL
At Energy Cent Dacca AECD Rep — Atomic Energy Centre. Dacca. AECD Report
At Energy Cent Rep PAECL Pak — Atomic Energy Centre. Report PAECL
At Energy Control Board Res Rep — Atomic Energy Control Board. Research Report
At Energy Establ (Trombay India) Rep — Atomic Energy Establishment (Trombay, India). Reports
At Energy Establ Winfrith Memo — Atomic Energy Establishment Winfrith. Memorandum
At Energy Establ Winfrith Rep — Atomic Energy Establishment Winfrith. Report
At Energy Law J — Atomic Energy Law Journal
At Energy Law Rep — Atomic Energy Law Reports
At Energy Miner Cent (Pak) Rep — Atomic Energy Minerals Centre (Pakistan). Report
At Energy Miner Cent Rep AEMC (Pak) — Atomic Energy Minerals Centre. Report AEMC (Pakistan)
At Energy NY — Atomic Energy (New York)
At Energy Organ Iran Sci Bull — Atomic Energy Organization of Iran. Scientific Bulletin
At Energy Organ Iran Tech Bull — Atomic Energy Organization of Iran. Technical Bulletin
At Energy (Peking) — Atomic Energy (Peking)
At Energy Res Establ GB Anal Method — Atomic Energy Research Establishment, Great Britain. Analytical Method
At Energy Res Establ (GB) Bibliogr — Atomic Energy Research Establishment (Great Britain). Bibliography

At Energy Res Establ GB Lect — Atomic Energy Research Establishment, Great Britain. Lectures
At Energy Res Establ (GB) Mem — Atomic Energy Research Establishment (Great Britain). Memorandum
At Energy Res Establ (GB) Memo — Atomic Energy Research Establishment (Great Britain). Memorandum
At Energy Res Establ (GB) Rep — Atomic Energy Research Establishment (Great Britain). Report
At Energy Res Establ (GB) Transl — Atomic Energy Research Establishment (Great Britain). Translation
At Energy Res Establ Rep AERE G (UK) — Atomic Energy Research Establishment. Report AERE-G (United Kingdom)
At Energy Res Q Rep — Atomic Energy Research. Quarterly Report
At Energy Rev — Atomic Energy Review
At Energy Rev Spec Issue — Atomic Energy Review. Special Issue
At Energy Sci Technol — Atomic Energy Science and Technology
At Energy (Sydney) — Atomic Energy (Sydney)
At Enerj Kom Gen Sekr Seri B (Turk) — Atom Enerjisi Komisyonu. Genel Sekreterligi. Seri B (Turkey)
At Enerj Kom (Turkey) Bilimsel Yayin Seri — Atom Enerjisi Komisyonu (Turkey) Bilimsel Yayinlar Seri
At Enerj Kom (Turk) K — Atom Enerjisi Komisyonu (Turkey). Report K
Atene Rom — Atene e Roma
At Eng — Atomic Energy in Australia
At Eng Tech — Atomics. Engineering and Technology
At Eng Technol — Atomic Engineering Technology
Aten It — Ateneo Italiano
Aten Med — Atencion Medica
At En Newsl — Atomic Energy Newsletter
Aten Primaria — Atencion Primaria
At En Rev — Atomic Energy Review
At En Yb — Atomic Energy Yearbook
Ate R — Atene e Roma
ATERD — Archiwum Termodynamiki
ATESD8 — Aristoteleion Panepistemion Thessalonikis Epistimoniki Epetiris Geoponikis kai Dasologikis Skolis
ATES Newsl — ATES [*Aquifer Thermal Energy Storage*] Newsletter
A Textiles — Artes Textiles
A Textrina — Ars Textrina
ATF — Accounting and Finance
ATFCC — ATF Colada
ATF Rep — Australian Teachers' Federation. Report
ATG — Archivo Teologico Granadino
ATG — Australian Income Tax Guide
ATGAAT — Antropologica
A Th — Annee Theologique Augustinienne
ATh — Arbeiten zur Theologie
Ath — Athenaeum
Ath — Athenee. Bulletin de la Federation de l'Enseignement Moyen Officiel du Degre Superieur de Belgique
Ath — Athene. The American Magazine of Hellenic Thought
ATHAA — Albrecht-Thaer-Archiv
ATHABZ — Applied Scientific Research Corporation of Thailand. Annual Report
Ath Adm — Athletic Administration
AThANT — Abhandlungen zur Theologie des Alten und Neuen Testaments
AThAug — Annee Theologique Augustinienne
ATHBA — Acta Radiologica. Therapy, Physics, Biology [*Later, Acta Radiologica. Series Two. Oncology, Radiation, Physics, and Biology*]
ATHBA3 — Acta Radiologica. Therapy, Physics, Biology [*Later, Acta Radiologica. Series Two. Oncology, Radiation, Physics, and Biology*]
Ath Bus — Athletic Business
Ath Coach — Athletics Coach
ATHCOM — Australasian Tertiary Handbook Collection on Microfiche
AThD — Acta Theologica Danica
Athen — Athena. Syngramma Periodikon tes en Athenais Epistemonikes Hetaireias
Athenae — Athenaeum. Studi Periodici di Letteratura e Storia dell'Antichita. Universita di Pavia
Athenaeum Pavia — Athenaeum. Studi Periodici di Letteratura e Storia dell'Antichita. Universita di Pavia
Athenaeum Wiss — Athenaeum fuer Wissenschaft, Kunst, und Leben
Athenee Orient — Athenee Oriental. Memoires
Athenes Obs Nat A — Annales de l'Observatoire National d'Athenes
Athens An Archaeol — Athens Annals of Archaeology
Athens Ann Arch — Archaiologika Analekta ex Athenon
Atherogenesis Proc Int Symp — Atherogenesis. Proceedings of the International Symposium
Atheroscler — Atherosclerosis
Atheroscler Coron Heart Dis Hahnemann Symp — Atherosclerosis and Coronary Heart Disease. Hahnemann Symposium
Atheroscler Drug Discovery — Atherosclerosis Drug Discovery
Atheroscler Proc Int Symp — Atherosclerosis. Proceedings. International Symposium on Atherosclerosis
Atheroscler Rev — Atherosclerosis Reviews
Atheroscler Suppl — Atherosclerosis. Supplements
AThG — Archiv fuer Theatergeschichte
ATHHA Newsl — ATHA [*Association for Traditional Hooking Artists*] Newsletter
AThijmG — Annalen van het Thijmgenootschap
Athiop Forsch — Athiopistische Forschungen
Ath J — Athletic Journal
Athl Adm — Athletic Administration
Athl Coach — Athletics Coach
Athl Educ Rep — Athletic Educator's Report
Athletic J — Athletic Journal
Athl J — Athletic Journal
Athl Train — Athletic Training

A Th M — Archeion Thessalikon Meleton
Ath Management — Athletic Management
Ath Mitt — Mitteilungen. Deutsches Archaeologische Institut. Abteilung Athens
Ath Mitt-BH — Athenische Mitteilungen. Beiheft
ATHPB — Advances in Theoretical Physics
Ath Pur and Fac — Athletic Purchasing and Facilities
AThR — Anglican Theological Review
Athr — Anthropos
ATHSAK — Annals of Thoracic Surgery
Ath Train — Athletic Training
ATI — Atomwirtschaft Atomtechnik
ATI — Australian Transport Index
ATIAA5 — Acta. Institut d'Anesthesiologie
ATIAD8 — Anuario Tecnico. Instituto de Pesquisas Zootecnicas "Francisco Osorio"
ATIBA8 — Antibiotica
ATIC — Atlantic Business
ATID — Australian Transport Information Directory
At Ind — Atom Industry
A T Index — Alternative/Appropriate Technology Index
At Indones — Atom Indonesia
At-Inf — Atom-Informationen
At Inn Shell Processes — Atomic Inner-Shell Processes
ATIR — Atlantica and Iceland Review
ATIRA Tech Dig — ATIRA [*Ahmedabad Textile Industry's Research Association*] Technical Digest
ATJ — Australasian Typographical Journal
At Jpn — Atoms in Japan
ATJSA — Atoms in Japan. Supplement
AtKap — Ateneum Kaplanskie
Atkinsons Saturday Eve Post — Atkinson's Saturday Evening Post
ATL — Athenian Tribute Lists
Atl — Atlantic Monthly
Atl — Atlantico
Atl — Atlantic Reporter
Atl — Atlantida
Atl — Atlantis
ATL — Atlantisch Perspektief
ATLA — Alternatives to Laboratory Animals
Atla — Atlantis
ATLA-Alt L — ATLA-Alternatives to Laboratory Animals
ATLA Alt Lab Anim — ATLA. Alternatives to Laboratory Animals
ATLABL — Atalanta Norvegica
Atl Adv — Atlantic Advocate
Atlan — Atlantic Monthly
Atlan Adv — Atlantic Advocate
Atlan Bs C — Atlanta Business Chronicle
Atlan Com Dir — Atlantic Communication Arts Directory
Atlan Com Q — Atlantic Community Quarterly
Atlan Cons — Atlanta Constitution
Atlan Insight — Atlantic Insight
Atlan M — Atlantic Monthly
Atlan Mo — Atlantic Monthly
Atlan Mon — Atlantic Monthly
Atlanta Econ R — Atlanta Economic Review
Atlanta ER — Atlanta Economic Review
Atlanta Hist J — Atlanta Historical Journal
Atlanta Jou — Atlanta Journal/Atlanta Constitution Weekend
Atlanta M — Atlanta Magazine
Atlanta Med — Atlanta Medicine
Atlante Bresc — Atlante Bresciano
Atlantic — Atlantic Monthly
Atlantic & Ice Rev — Atlantic and Icelandic Review
Atlantic Community Q — Atlantic Community Quarterly
Atlantic Econ J — Atlantic Economic Journal
Atlantic Mthly — Atlantic Monthly. Devoted to Literature, Art, and Politics
Atlantic Pap — Atlantic Papers
Atlan Tr Tran Rev — Atlantic Truck Transport Review
ATLA Pro — American Theological Library Association. Proceedings
Atlas Bin Alloy Period Index — Atlas of Binary Alloys. A Periodic Index
Atlas Div Fish Oceanogr CSIRO — Atlas. Division of Fisheries and Oceanography. Commonwealth Scientific and Industrial Organisation
Atlas Fiz Svoistv Miner Porod Khibinskikh Mestorozhd — Atlas Fizicheskikh Svoistv Mineralov i Porod Khibinskikh Mestorozhdenii
Atlas Jap Fossils — Atlas of Japanese Fossils
Atlas Newsl — Atlas Newsletter
Atlas of Aust Resources — Atlas of Australian Resources
Atlas Pa Bur Topogr Geol Surv — Atlas. Pennsylvania. Bureau of Topographic and Geologic Survey
Atlas Protein Sequence Struct — Atlas of Protein Sequence and Structure
Atlas Radiol Clin — Atlas de Radiologie Clinique
Atlas Radiol Clin Presse Med — Atlas de Radiologie Clinique. Presse Medicale
Atlas Visualization — Atlas of Visualization
Atlas W P Rev — Atlas World Press Review
Atl Community Quar — Atlantic Community Quarterly
Atl Com Q — Atlantic Community Quarterly
Atl Econ R — Atlanta Economic Review
Atl Fisherman — Atlantic Fisherman
ATLGT — Archeion tou Thrakikou Laographikou kai Glossikou Thesaurou
ATLIS — Australian Transport Literature Information System
ATI L J — American Trial Lawyers Journal
Atl M — Atlantic Monthly
Atl Med J — Atlantic Medical Journal
Atl Mo — Atlantic Monthly
Atl Nat — Atlantic Naturalist
ATLNDS — Atalanta

ATLPA — Arctic and Alpine Research
ATLPAV — Arctic and Alpine Research
Atl Pro Bk R — Atlantic Provinces Book Review
Atl Prof — Atlanta Professional
ATLRD6 — Advances in Prostaglandin, Thromboxane, and Leukotriene Research
Atl Rep — Atlantide Report
Atl Rep (Ottawa) — Atlantic Report (Ottawa)
Atl Salmon J — Atlantic Salmon Journal
Atl Salmon Ref — Atlantic Salmon References
Atl Workshop — Atlantic Workshop
Atl Workshop Proc — Atlantic Workshop. Proceedings
ATM — Advances in Tracer Methodology
AtM — Atlantic Monthly
ATMAAP — Atti. Societa Toscana di Scienze Naturali Residente in Pisa. Memorie. Serie A
ATM Arch Tech Mess Ind Messtech — ATM. Archiv fuer Technisches Messen und Industrielle Messtechnik
ATM Arch Tech Mess Messtech Prax — ATM. Archiv fuer Technisches Messen und Messtechnische Praxis
At Masses Fundam Constants — Atomic Masses and Fundamental Constants
At Masses Fundam Constants Proc Int Conf M — Atomic Masses and Fundamental Constants. Proceedings of the International Conference on Atomic Masses and Fundamental Constants
ATMED6 — Atualidades Medicas
ATM Mess Pr — ATM. Archiv fuer Technisches Messen und Messtechnische Praxis
ATM Messtech Prax — ATM. Archiv fuer Technisches Messen und Messtechnische Praxis
ATMNA — Automation
AtMo — Atlantic Monthly
ATMO — Atmosphere
At Mol Beam Methods — Atomic and Molecular Beam Methods
At Mol Phy — Atomic and Molecular Physics
At Mol Phys Proc Natl Workshop — Atomic and Molecular Physics. Proceedings. National Workshop
At Mol Phys US Mex Symp — Atomic and Molecular Physics. US/Mexico Symposium
Atmos Apsauga Uztersimu — Atmosferos Apsauga nuo Uztersimu
Atmos Chem Air Pollut Semin — Atmospheric Chemistry and Air Pollution. Seminar
Atmos Chem Probl Scope — Atmospheric Chemistry Problems and Scope
Atmos Corros — Atmospheric Corrosion
Atmos Early Type Stars Proc Workshop — Atmospheres of Early-Type Stars. Proceedings. Workshop
Atmos Elektr Tr Vses Simp — Atmosfernoe Elektrichestvo Trudy Vsesoyuznogo Simpoziuma po Atmosfernomu Elektrichestvu
Atmos Env — Atmospheric Environment
Atmos Envir — Atmospheric Environment
Atmos Environ — Atmospheric Environment
Atmos Environ Part A — Atmospheric Environment. Part A. General Topics
Atmos Environ Part B — Atmospheric Environment. Part B. Urban Atmosphere
Atmos Fiz — Atmosferos Fizika
Atmos-Ocean — Atmosphere-Ocean
Atmos Oceanic Phys — Atmospheric and Oceanic Physics
Atmos Oceanic Phys (Engl Ed) — Atmospheric and Oceanic Physics (English Edition)
Atmos Ozon — Atmosfernyi Ozon
Atmos Ozone Opt Atmos Sol Radiat (Belsk) — Atmospheric Ozone Optics of Atmosphere Solar Radiation (Belsk)
Atmos Ozon Mater Mezhduved Soveshch — Atmosfernyi Ozon. Materialy Mezhduvedomstvennogo Soveshchaniya poAtmosfernomu Ozonu
Atmos Phys — Atmospheric Physics
Atmos Pollut Proc Int Colloq — Atmospheric Pollution. Proceedings of the International Colloquium
Atmos Propag Remote Sens — Atmospheric Propagation and Remote Sensing
Atmos Qual Improv Tech Bull — Atmospheric Quality Improvement. Technical Bulletin
Atmos Res — Atmospheric Research
Atmos Sci Rep Alberta Res Counc — Atmospheric Sciences Report. Alberta Research Council
Atmos Technol — Atmospheric Technology
ATMP — Annals of Tropical Medicine and Parasitology
ATMPA2 — Annals of Tropical Medicine and Parasitology
Atm Poll Bull — Atmosphere Pollution Bulletin
ATMSAB — Atualidades Medico Sanitarias
ATMTas — Adabietsunaslik va Tilsunaslik Masalalari/Voprosy Literaturovedenija i Jazykoznanija (Taskent)
ATMVAK — Agronomia Tropical (Maracay, Venezuela)
ATMXAQ — Agricultura Tecnica en Mexico
ATNBAX — Atti. Societa Toscana di Scienze Naturali. Processi Verbali e Memorie. Serie B
ATNED — ATES [Aquifer Thermal Energy Storage] Newsletter
ATNM — Alcoholism. The National Magazine
ATNMAW — Agronomie Tropicale. Serie Riz et Riziculture et Cultures Vivrieres Tropicales
At Nucl — Atoms and Nuclei
At Nucl En — Atomics and Nuclear Energy
At Nucl Energy — Atomics and Nuclear Energy
ATOIA — Automobil-Industrie
Atoll Res Bull — Atoll Research Bulletin
Atom — Atomics
Atom Absorpt Newsl — Atomic Absorption Newsletter
Atomedia Philipp — Atomedia Philippines
Atom Ener A — Atomic Energy in Australia
Atom Ener R — Atomic Energy Review
Atomic Data — Atomic Data and Nuclear Data Tables

Atomic Energy in Aust — Atomic Energy in Australia
Atomic Energy Law J — Atomic Energy Law Journal
Atomic Energy L J — Atomic Energy Law Journal
Atomic Eng LJ — Atomic Energy Law Journal
Atomic Sci — Bulletin of the Atomic Scientists
Atom Indones — Atom Indonesia
Atomisation Spray Technol — Atomisation and Spray Technology
Atomkernene — Atomkernenergie
Atomkernenerg Kerntech — Atomkernenergie Kerntechnik
ATOMKI Kozl — ATOMKI [Atommag Kutato Intezet] Koezlemenyek
Atomnaya En — Atomnaya Energiya
Atomn Energ — Atomnaya Energiya
Atomo Petrol Elet — Atomo, Petrol, Elettricita
Atomprax — Atompraxis
Atoms Peace Dig — Atoms for Peace Digest
Atomtech Tajek — Atomtechnikai Tajekoztato
Atom U Strom — Atom und Strom
Atomwirtsch — Atomwirtschaft Atomtechnik
Atomwirtsch Atomtech — Atomwirtschaft Atomtechnik
Atoomenerg Haar Toepass — Atoomenergie en Haar Toepassingen
Atoomenerg Toepass — Atoomenergie en Haar Toepassingen
ATopPir — Actas. Primera Reunion de Toponimia Pirenaica
A Tor — Atti. Accademia delle Scienze di Torino
ATOR — Australian Torts Reporter
A Toulon — Annales. Societe des Sciences Naturelles et d'Archeologie de Toulon et du Var
ATP — Archivio per lo Studio delle Tradizioni Populari
ATP — Arts et Traditions Populaires
AtP — Ateneo Puertorriqueno
ATP — A Terra Portuguesa
ATP — Australian Trade Practices Report
ATPAD6 — Annals of Tropical Paediatrics
At Par Col Monogr — Ateneo Parmense. Collana di Monografie
At Parm — Ateneo Parmense
ATPDC — Advances in Tumor Prevention, Detection, and Characterization
At Phys — Atomic Physics
At Phys Int Conf At Phys — Atomic Physics. International Conference on Atomic Physics
ATPLH — Antonio Tomas Pires. Livro de Homenagem
At Power — Atomic Power
At Pow R — Atomic Power Review
ATPR — Australian Trade Practices Reporter
ATPR (Com) — Australian Trade Practices Reporter. Commission Decisions
ATPR (Digest) — Australian Trade Practices Reporter. Cases and Decisions Digest
At Processes Appl — Atomic Processes and Applications
At Processes Plasmas — Atomic Processes in Plasmas
ATPSD — ACM [Association for Computing Machinery] Transactions on Programming Languages and Systems
ATQ — American Transcendental Quarterly
ATQK — Atuaqunik. Newsletter of Northern Quebec
At Quart — Art Quarterly
Atqy — Antiquity
ATR — African Trade Review
ATR — Anglican Theological Review
At R — Atene e Roma
ATR — Australasian Tax Reports
ATR — Australian Telecommunication Research
At Radiat — Atomes et Radiations
ATR Aust Telecommun Res — ATR: Australian Telecommunication Research
Atrazine Inform Sheet Geigy Agr Chem Atrazine Herbic — Atrazine Information Sheet. Geigy Agricultural Chemicals. Atrazine Herbicides
ATRCA — Atlas de Radiologie Clinique
ATREDV — Annals of Tropical Research
ATren — Archivio Trentino
At Res B — Atoll Research Bulletin
AT Rev — Australian Tax Review
A Trial Law Am LJ — Association of Trial Lawyers of America. Law Journal
A Tribal — Art Tribal/Tribal Art
ATriest — Archeolgrafo Triestino
ATRIP — Australian Transport Research in Progress
ATRIS — Air Transportation Research Information Service
ATRJ — Association of Teachers of Russian. Journal
ATRMA — Advances in Tracer Methodology
At Roma — Atene e Roma
A Trop — Acta Tropica
ATRR — Antitrust and Trade Regulation Report
ATS — Arabic Translation Series
ATS — Arbeiten und Texte zur Slavistik
ATS — Australian Treaty Series
ATSAAL — Associated Scientific and Technical Societies of South Africa. Annual Proceedings
At Sci J — Atomic Scientists Journal
At Sci News — Atomic Scientists News
At Sc It — Riunione degli Scienziati Italiani
ATSED2 — Annales du Tabac. Section 2
At S Elvet — Atti della Societa Elvetica delle Scienze Naturali
Atsk Bio Ent Sta Darb — Atskats uf Bio-entomologiskas Stazijas Darbibu
ATS List Transl — Associated Technical Services, Inc. List of Translations
At Spectra Oscillator Strengths Astrophys Fusion Res — Atomic Spectra and Oscillator Strengths for Astrophysics and Fusion Research
At Spectrosc — Atomic Spectroscopy
At Spektrosk Spekr Anal Mater Resp Soveshch — Atomnaya Spektroskopiya i Spektral'nyi Analiz. Materialy Respublikanskogo Soveshchaniya
At Stolknoveniya — Atomnye Stolknoveniya
ATS Trans — Danish Academy of Technical Sciences. Transactions

At Strom — Atom und Strom

At Strong Fields — Atoms in Strong Fields

At Struct Mech Prop Met — Atomic Structure and Mechanical Properties of Metals

ATSUDG — Archives of Toxicology. Supplement

ATSVA — Avtomatika, Telemekhanika, i Svyaz

ATSZA — Automazione e Strumentazione

Att ANL R F — Atti. Accademia Nazionale dei Lincei. Rendiconti. Classe di Scienze Fisiche, Matematiche, e Naturali

Att Ass Gen — Atti. Associazione Genetica Italiana

At Tekh Rubezhom — Atomnaya Tekhnika za Rubezhom

Attempt Sedimentol Charact Carbonate Deposits — Attempt at Sedimentological Characterization of Carbonate Deposits

Atti — Atti. Congresso Internazionale di Estetica

Atti Acad Lig Sci Lettere Genova — Atti. Accademia Ligure di Scienze e Lettere di Genova

Atti Accad Agric Sci & Lett Verona — Atti dell'Accademia d'Agricoltura, Scienze, e Lettere di Verona

Atti Accad Anat Chir (Perugia) — Atti. Accademia Anatomico-Chirurgica (Perugia)

Atti Accad Archeol Lett & B A — Atti dell'Accademia di Archeologia, Lettere, e Belle Arti

Atti Accad B A Venezia — Atti dell'Accademia di Belle Arti. Venezia

Atti Accad Crusca — Atti. Reale Accademia della Crusca

Atti Accad Econ Agrar Geografili Firenze — Atti. Reale Accademia Economico-Agraria dei Geografoli di Firenze

Atti Accad Fisiocrit Siena — Atti. Accademia dei Fisiocritici in Siena

Atti Accad Fisiocrit Siena Sez Agrar — Atti. Accademia dei Fisiocritici in Siena. Sezione Agraria

Atti Accad Fisiocrit Siena Sez Med-Fis — Atti. Accademia dei Fisiocritici in Siena. Sezione Medico-Fisica

Atti Accad Fis-Med-Statist Milano — Atti. Accademia Fisio-Medico-Statistica di Milano

Atti Accad Geogrof — Atti. Accademia de' Geografili

Atti Accad Geografili — Atti. Reale Accademia dei Geografili di Firenze

Atti Accad Georgof Firenze — Atti dell'Accademia dei Georgofili di Firenze

Atti Accad Gioenia Sci Nat — Atti dell'Accademia Gioenia di Scienze Naturali

Atti Accad Gioenia Sci Nat Catania — Atti. Accademia Gioenia di Scienze Naturali in Catania

Atti Accad Ital Mem Cl Sci Fis Mat Natur — Atti. Reale Accademia d'Italia. Memorie. Classe di Scienze Fisiche, Matematiche, e Naturali

Atti Accad Ital Mem Cl Sci Morali Stor Filol — Atti. Reale Accademia d'Italia. Memorie. Classe di Scienze Morali, Storiche, e Filologiche

Atti Accad Ital Rendic Cl Sci Fis Mat Natur — Atti. Reale Accademia d'Italia. Rendiconti. Classe di Scienze Fisiche, Matematiche, e Naturali

Atti Accad Ital Rendic Cl Sci Morali Stor Filol — Atti. Reale Accademia d'Italia. Rendiconti. Classe di Scienze Morali, Storiche,e Filologiche

Atti Accad Ital Vite Vino (Siena) — Atti. Accademia Italiana della Vite e del Vino (Siena)

Atti Accad Ligure — Atti dell'Accademia Ligure di Scienze e Lettere

Atti Accad Ligure Sci Lett — Atti. Accademia Ligure di Scienze e Lettere

Atti Accad Ligure Sci Lett (Genoa) — Atti. Accademia Ligure di Scienze e Lettere (Genoa)

Atti Accad Lincei — Atti. Reale Accademia Nazionale dei Lincei

Atti Accad Lincei Mem Cl Sci Fis Mat Natur — Atti. Reale Accademia dei Lincei. Memorie. Classe di Scienze Fisiche, Matematiche, e Naturali

Atti Accad Lincei Mem Cl Sci Morali Stor Filol — Atti. Reale Accademia dei Lincei. Memorie. Classe di Scienze Morali, Storiche, e Filologiche

Atti Accad Lincei Rendic Cl Sci Fis Mat Natur — Atti. Reale Accademia dei Lincei. Rendiconti. Classe di Scienze Fisiche, Matematiche, e Naturali

Atti Accad Lincei Rendic Cl Sci Morali Stor Filol — Atti. Reale Accademia dei Lincei. Rendiconti. Classe di Scienze Morali, Storiche, e Filologiche

Atti Accad Lincei Rendic Sedute Solenni — Atti. Reale Accademia dei Lincei. Rendiconti delle Sedute Solenni

Atti Accad Linc Mem — Atti. Reale Accademia dei Lincei. Memorie

Atti Accad Lucchese — Atti dell'Accademia Lucchese di Scienze, Lettere, ed Arti

Atti Accad Med Chir (Napoli) — Atti. Reale Accademia Medico-Chirurgica (Napoli)

Atti Accad Med Chir Perugia — Atti dell'Accademia Medico-Chirurgica di Perugia

Atti Accad Med Lomb — Atti. Accademia Medica Lombarda

Atti Accad Med Lombarda — Atti. Accademia Medica Lombarda

Atti Accad Med Torino — Atti. Accademia di Medicina de Torino

Atti Accad Naz Ital Entomol Rend — Atti. Accademia Nazionale Italiana di Entomologia. Rendiconti

Atti Accad Naz Lincei — Atti. Accademia Nazionale dei Lincei

Atti Accad Naz Lincei Cl Sci Fis Mat Nat Rend — Atti. Accademia Nazionale dei Lincei. Classe di Scienze Fisiche, Matematiche, eNaturali. Rendiconti

Atti Accad Naz Lincei Mem Cl Sci Fis Mat Nat — Atti. Accademia Nazionale dei Lincei. Memorie. Classe di Scienze Fisiche, Matematiche, e Naturali

Atti Accad Naz Lincei Mem Cl Sci Fis Mat Nat Sez 1a — Atti. Accademia Nazionale dei Lincei. Memorie. Classe di ScienzeFisiche, Matematiche, e Naturali. Sezione 1a. Matematica, Meccanica, Astronomia, Geodesia, e Geofisica

Atti Accad Naz Lincei Mem Cl Sci Fis Mat Nat Sez 2a — Atti. Accademia Nazionale dei Lincei. Memorie. Classe di Scienze Fisiche, Matematiche, e Naturali. Sezione 2a. Fisica, Chimica, Geologia, Paleontologia, e Mineralogia

Atti Accad Naz Lincei Mem Cl Sci Fis Mat Nat Sez 3a — Atti. Accademia Nazionale dei Lincei. Memorie. Classe di Scienze Fisiche, Matematiche, e Naturali. Sezione 3a. Botanica, Zoologia, Fisiologia, Patologia

Atti Accad Naz Lincei Mem Cl Sci Fis Mat Natur — Atti. Reale Accademia Nazionale dei Lincei. Memorie. Classe di Scienze Fisiche,Matematiche, e Naturali

Atti Accad Naz Lincei Mem Cl Sci Fis Mat Natur Sez 1a — Atti. Accademia Nazionale dei Lincei. Memorie. Classe di Scienze Fisiche, Matematiche, e Naturali. Sezione 1a. Matematica, Meccanica, Astronomia, Geodesia, e Geofisica

Atti Accad Naz Lincei Mem Cl Sci Mor Stor Filol — Atti. Accademia Nazionale dei Lincei. Memorie Classe di Scienze Morale, Storiche, e Filologiche

Atti Accad Naz Lincei Memorie — Atti dell'Accademia Nazionale dei Lincei. Memorie

Atti Accad Naz Lincei Rc — Atti dell'Accademia Nazionale dei Lincei. Rendiconti

Atti Accad Naz Lincei Rc Sed Solen — Atti dell'Accademia Nazionale dei Lincei. Rendiconti delle Sedute Solenni

Atti Accad Naz Lincei Rend Cl Sci Fis Mat & Nat — Atti. Accademia Nazionale dei Lincei. Rendiconti. Classe di Scienze Fisiche, Matematiche, e Naturali

Atti Accad Naz Lincei Rend Cl Sci Fis Mat Natur — Atti. Accademia Nazionale dei Lincei. Rendiconti. Classe di Scienze Fisiche, Matematiche, e Naturali

Atti Accad Naz Lincei Rend Cl Sci Fis Mat Natur (8) — Atti. Accademia Nazionale dei Lincei. Rendiconti. Classe di Scienze Fisiche, Matematiche, e Naturali (Serie 8)

Atti Accad Naz Lincei Rendic Cl Sci Fis Mat Natur — Atti. Reale Accademia Nazionale dei Lincei. Rendiconti. Classe di Scienze Fisiche, Matematiche, e Naturali

Atti Accad Naz Lincei Rendic Cl Sci Morali Stor Filol — Atti. Reale Accademia Nazionale dei Lincei. Rendiconti. Classe di Scienze Morali, Storiche, e Filologiche

Atti Accad Naz Lincei Rendic Sedute Solenni — Atti. Reale Accademia Nazionale dei Lincei. Rendiconti delle Sedute Solenni

Atti Accad Naz Lincei (Serie Ottava) — Atti. Accademia Nazionale dei Lincei (Serie Ottava)

Atti Accad N Lincei — Atti dell'Accademia Nazionale dei Lincei

Atti Accad N Lincei Mem Cl Sci Morali Stor & Filol — Atti dell'Accademia Nazionale dei Lincei. Memorie della Classe di Scienze, Morali, Storiche, e Filologiche

Atti Accad Olimp — Atti dell'Accademia Olimpica

Atti Accad Palermo — Atti. Accademia di Scienze, Lettere, e Arti di Palermo

Atti Accad Peloritana — Atti dell'Accademia Peloritana

Atti Accad Peloritana — Atti. Reale Accademia Peloritana

Atti Accad Peloritana Cl Sci Fis Mat Biol — Atti. Reale Accademia Peloritana. Classe di Scienze Fisiche, Matematiche, e Biologiche PB

Atti Accad Peloritana Cl Sci Med Biol — Atti. Accademia Peloritana. Classe di Scienze Medico-Biologiche

Atti Accad Peloritana Pericolanti Cl Sci Fis Mat Nat — Atti. Accademia Peloritana dei Pericolanti. Classe di Scienze Fisiche, Matematiche, e Naturali

Atti Accad Peloritana Pericolanti Cl Sci Fis Mat Natur — Atti. Accademia Peloritana dei Pericolanti. Classe di Scienze Fisiche, Matematiche, e Naturali

Atti Accad Peloritana Pericolanti Cl Sci Med Biol — Atti. Accademia Peloritana dei Pericolanti. Classe di Scienze Medico-Biologiche

Atti Accad Pontan — Atti. Accademia Pontaniana

Atti Accad Pontaniana — Atti. Accademia Pontaniana

Atti Accad Pontaniana NS — Atti della Accademia Pontaniana. Nuova Serie

Atti Accad Pontif Nuovi Lincei — Atti dell'Accademia Pontificia dei Nuovi Lincei

Atti Accad Properz Subas Assisi — Atti dell'Accademia Properziana del Subasio in Assisi

Atti Accad Properz Subasio Assisi — Atti della Accademia Properziana del Subasio-Assisi

Atti Accad Roveretana Agiati — Atti. Accademia Roveretana degli Agiati

Atti Accad Scient Veneto Trent Istriana — Atti dell'Accademia Scientifica Veneto-Trentino-Istriana

Atti Accad Scienze di Torino — Atti. Accademia delle Scienze di Torino

Atti Accad Sci Ferrara — Atti. Accademia delle Scienze di Ferrara

Atti Accad Sci Fis — Atti. Accademia delle Scienze Fisiche e Matematiche

Atti Accad Sci Fis Mat Napoli — Atti. Accademia delle Scienze Fisiche e Matematiche di Napoli

Atti Accad Sci Ist Bologna Cl Sci Fis Mem — Atti. Accademia delle Scienze. Istituto di Bologna. Classe di Scienze Fisiche. Memorie

Atti Accad Sci Ist Bologna Cl Sci Fis Mem Ser IV — Atti. Accademia delle Scienze. Istituto di Bologna. Classe di Scienze Fisiche. Memorie. Serie IV

Atti Accad Sci Ist Bologna Cl Sci Fis Rend — Atti. Accademia delle Scienze. Istituto di Bologna. Classe di Scienze Fisiche. Rendiconti

Atti Accad Sci Ist Bologna Cl Sci Fis Rend Ser XIII — Atti. Accademia delle Scienze. Istituto di Bologna. Classe di Scienze Fisiche. Rendiconti. Serie XIII

Atti Accad Sci Ist Bologna Memorie — Atti dell'Accademia delle Scienze dell'Istituto di Bologna. Memorie

Atti Accad Sci Ist Bologna Rc — Atti dell'Accademia delle Scienze dell'Istituto di Bologna. Rendiconti

Atti Accad Sci Ist Bologna Ren — Atti. Accademia delle Scienze. Istituto di Bologna. Rendiconti

Atti Accad Sci Istit Bologna Cl Sci Fis Rend 14 — Atti della Accademia delle Scienze dell'Istituto di Bologna. Classe di Scienze Fisiche. Rendiconti. Serie XIV

Atti Accad Sci Istit Bologna Cl Sci Fis Rend XIII — Atti. Accademia delle Scienze. Istituto di Bologna. Classe di Scienze Fisiche. Rendiconti. Serie XIII

Atti Accad Sci Lett & A Udine — Atti dell'Accademia di Scienze, Lettere, e Arti di Udine

Atti Accad Sci Lett Arti Agiati Rovereto — Atti. Accademia di Scienze, Lettere, ed Arti. Agiati in Rovereto

Atti Accad Sci Lett Arti di Palermo Parte I — Atti. Accademia di Scienze, Lettere, ed Arti di Palermo. Parte Prima. Scienze

Atti Accad Sci Lett Arti Palermo — Atti. Accademia di Scienze, Lettere, ed Arti di Palermo

Atti Accad Sci Lett Arti Palermo Parte I — Atti. Accademia di Scienze, Lettere, ed Arti di Palermo. Parte Prima. Scienze

Atti Accad Sci Lett Arti Palermo Parte I 4 — Atti. Accademia di Scienze, Lettere, ed Arti di Palermo. Parte Prima. Scienze. Serie Quarta

Atti Accad Sci Lett Arti Palermo Parte Prima Sci — Atti. Accademia di Scienze, Lettere, ed Arti di Palermo. Parte Prima. Scienze

Atti Accad Sci Lett Arti Palermo Ser 5 — Atti della Accademia di Scienze Lettere e Arti di Palermo. Serie V

Atti Accad Sci Lett Arti Palermo Ser Quarta Sci — Atti. Accademia di Scienze, Lettere, ed Arti di Palermo. Serie Quarta. Scienze

Atti Accad Sci Lett Palermo — Atti dell'Accademia di Scienze, Lettere, ed Arti (Palermo)

Atti Accad Sci Med Chir (Napoli) — Atti. Reale Accademia delle Scienze Medico-Chirurgiche (Napoli)

Atti Accad Sci Med Nat Ferrara — Atti dell'Accademia delle Scienze Mediche e Naturali in Ferrara

Atti Accad Sci Siena — Atti. Accademia delle Scienze di Siena detta de' Fisiocritici

Atti Accad Sci Siena Fisiocrit — Atti. Accademia delle Scienze di Siena. Detta de Fisiocritici

Atti Accad Sci Torino — Atti. Accademia delle Scienze di Torino

Atti Accad Sci Torino Cl Sci Fis Mat Nat — Atti. Accademia delle Scienze di Torino. Classe di Scienze Fisiche, Matematiche, e Naturali

Atti Accad Sci Torino Cl Sci Fis Mat Natur — Atti. Accademia delle Scienze di Torino. Classe di Scienze Fisiche, Matematiche, e Naturali

Atti Accad Sci Torino Cl Sci Morali Stor Filol — Atti. Reale Accademia delle Scienze di Torino. Classe di Scienze Morali, Storiche, e Filologiche

Atti Accad Sci Torino Cl Sci Mor Stor Filol — Atti. Accademia delle Scienza di Torino. Classe di Scienze Morali, Storiche, e Filologiche

Atti Accad Sci Torino I — Atti. Accademia delle Scienze di Torino. I

Atti Accad Sci Torino I Cl Sci Fis Mat Nat — Atti. Accademia delle Scienze di Torino. I. Classe di Scienze Fisiche, Matematiche, e Naturali

Atti Accad Sci Veneto-Trentino-Istriana — Atti. Accademia Scientifica Veneto-Trentino-Istriana

Atti Accad Toscana Sci & Lett La Colombaria — Atti dell'Accademia Toscana di Scienze e Lettere La Colombaria

Atti Acc Arch N — Atti. Reale Accademia di Archeologia, Lettere, e Belle Arti di Napoli

Atti Acc Arch Napoli — Atti. Reale Accademia di Archeologia, Lettere, e Belle Arti di Napoli

Atti Acc Lig — Atti. Accademia Ligure di Scienze e Lettere

Atti Acc Linc — Atti. Reale Accademia dei Lincei

Atti Acc Med Lomb — Atti. Accademia Medica Lombarda

Atti Acc (Nap) — Atti. Accademia Nazionale di Scienze Morali e Politiche (Napoli)

Atti Acc Nap — Rendiconti. Accademia di Archeologia, Lettere, e Belle Arti di Napoli

Atti Acc Napoli — Rendiconti. Accademia di Archeologia, Lettere, e Belle Arti di Napoli

Atti Acc Naz Linc — Atti. Accademia Nazionale dei Lincei

Atti Acc Olimp — Atti. Accademia Olimpica

Atti Ac Cos — Atti. Accademia Cosentina

Atti Acc Pel — Atti. Accademia Peloritana

Atti Acc Pont — Atti. Pontificia Accademia Romana di Archeologia

Atti Acc Scienze Torino — Atti. Accademia delle Scienze di Torino

Atti Acc Sci Torino — Atti. Accademia delle Scienze di Torino

Atti Acc Stor Arte San — Atti e Memorie. Accademia di Storia dell'Arte Sanitaria

Atti Acc Tosc — Atti e Memorie. Accademia Toscana di Scienze e Lettere La Colombaria

Atti Ac Pont — Atti. Accademia Pontaniana

Atti Ac Torino — Atti. Accademia delle Scienze di Torino

Atti Ac Udine — Atti. Accademia di Scienze, Lettere, ed Arti di Udine

Atti & Mem Accad Clementina Bologna — Atti e Memorie dell'Accademia Clementina di Bologna

Atti & Mem Accad Fiorent Sci Morali La Colombaria — Atti e Memorie dell'Accademia Fiorentina di Scienze Morali La Colombaria

Atti & Mem Accad N Lincei Atti Cl Sci Morali — Atti e Memorie dell'Accademia Nazionale dei Lincei. Atti della Classe di Scienze Morali

Atti & Mem Accad N Virgil Mantova — Atti e Memorie dell'Accademia Nazionale Virgiliana di Mantova

Atti & Mem Accad Patavina Sci Lett & A — Atti e Memorie dell'Accademia Patavina di Scienze, Lettere, ed Arti

Atti & Mem Accad Petrarca Lett A & Sci — Atti e Memorie dell'Accademia Petrarca di Lettere, Arte, e Scienze

Atti & Mem Deput Stor Patria Marche — Atti e Memorie della Deputazione di Storia Patria per le Marche

Atti & Mem Deput Stor Patria Prov Romagna — Atti e Memorie della Deputazione di Storia Patria per le Province di Romagna

Atti & Mem Reale Accad Archeol Lett & B A Napoli — Atti e Memorie della Reale Accademia di Archeologia, Lettere, e Belle Arti di Napoli

Atti & Mem Reale Accad Sci Lett & A Padova — Atti e Memorie della Reale Accademia di Scienze, Lettere, ed Arti in Padova

Atti & Mem Reale Accad S Luca Annuario — Atti e Memorie della Reale Accademia di San Luca. Annuario

Atti & Mem Reale Deput Stor Patria Emilia & Romagna — Atti e Memorie della Reale Deputazione di Storia Patria per l'Emilia e la Romagna

Atti & Mem Reale Deput Stor Patria Marche — Atti e Memorie della Reale Deputazione di Storia Patria per le Marche

Atti & Mem Reale Deput Stor Patria Prov Moden — Atti e Memorie della Reale Deputazione di Storia Patria per le Province Modenesi

Atti & Mem Regia Deput Stor Patria Prov Romagna — Atti e Memorie della Regia Deputazione di Storia Patria per le Province della Romagna

Atti & Mem RR Deput Stor Patria Prov Emilia — Atti e Memorie delle RR. Reali Deputazioni di Storia Patria per le Province dell'Emilia

Atti & Mem RR Deput Stor Patria Prov Moden & Parm — Atti e Memorie delle RR. Reali Deputazioni di Storia Patria per le Province Modenesi e Parmensi

Atti & Mem Soc Savon Stor Patria — Atti e Memorie della Società Savonese di Storia Patria

Atti & Mem Soc Tiburtina Stor & A — Atti e Memorie della Società Tiburtina di Storia e d'Arte

Atti & Mem Stor Patria Prov Romagna — Atti e Memorie della Storia Patria per la Provincia Romagna

Atti Ass Elettrotec Ital — Atti dell'Associazione Elettrotecnica Italiana

Atti Ass Genet Ital — Atti. Associazione Genetica Italiana

Atti Ass Ital Aerotec — Atti. Associazione Italiana di Aerotecnica

Atti Assoc Genet Ital — Atti. Associazione Genetica Italiana

Atti Ateneo Sci Lett & A — Atti dell'Ateneo di Scienze, Lettere, e Arti

Atti C Ant Cl — Atti. Centro Ricerche e Documentazione sull'Antichita Classica

Atti C Cos — Atti. Accademia Cosentina

Atti Cent Naz Mecc Agr — Atti. Centro Nazionale Meccanico Agricolo

Atti Cent Ric & Doc Ant Class — Atti del Centro di Ricerca e Documentazione dell'Antichita Classica

Atti Cent Stud & Doc Italia Romana — Atti del Centro di Studi e Documentazione sull'Italia Romana

Atti Ce SDIR — Atti. Centro Richerche Documentazione sull'Antichita Classica

Atti C It Rom — Atti. Centro Studi e Documentazione sull'Italia Romana

Atti Civ Mus Stor & A Trieste — Atti dei Civici Musei di Storia ed Arti di Trieste

Atti Clin Odont — Atti. Clinica Odontoiatrica e Società Napolitana di Stomatologia

Atti Clin Odontoi Soc Napolitana Stomatol — Atti. Clinica Odontoiatrica e Società Napolitana di Stomatologia

Atti Clin Oto-Rino-Laringoiatr Univ Palermo — Atti. Clinica Oto-Rino-Laringoiatrica. Universita di Palermo

Atti Clin Otorinolaringol Reale Univ Napoli — Atti. Clinica Otorinolaringologica. Reale Universita di Napoli

Atti C N St R — Atti. Congresso Nazionale di Studi Romani

Atti Coll Architetti & Ingeg — Atti del Collegio degli Architetti ed Ingegneri

Atti Coll Ingeg & Architetti Milano — Atti del Collegio degli Ingegneri ed Architetti di Milano

Atti Coll Ing Milano — Atti. Collegio deglie Ingegneri di Milano

Atti Colloq Ovulo Seme — Atti. Colloquio. Ovulo al Seme

Atti Com Cons Mon Prov Ter Lavoro — Atti. Commissione Conservatrice dei Monumenti e Belle Arti. Provincia di Terra di Lavoro

Atti Conf Avic Eur — Atti Conferenza Avicola Europea

Atti Conf Soc Ital Fis — Atti di Conference. Società Italiana di Fisica

Atti Cong Nat Ital — Atti. Congresso del Naturalis i Italiani

Atti Cong Or — Actes du Congres International des Orientalistes

Atti Congr Geogr Ital — Atti. Congresso Geografico Italiano

Atti Congr Int Amer — Atti. Congresso Internazionale degli Americanisti

Atti Congr Int Ceram — Atti. Congresso Internazionale della Ceramica

Atti Congr Int Elettron — Atti. Congresso Internazionale per l'Elettronica

Atti Congr Int Fil — Atti. Congresso Internazionale di Filosofia

Atti Congr Int Genet — Atti. Congresso Internazionale di Genetica

Atti Congr Int Mat — Atti. Congresso Internazionale dei Matematici

Atti Congr Int Mater Plast — Atti. Congresso Internazionale delle Materie Plastiche

Atti Congr Int Mater Plast Elastomeriche — Atti. Congresso Internazionale delle Materie Plastiche ed Elastomeriche

Atti Congr Int Microbiol — Atti. Congresso Internazionale di Microbiologia

Atti Congr Int Panif — Atti. Congresso Internazionale di Panificazione

Atti Congr Int Stand Immunomicrobiol — Atti. Congresso Internazionale di Standardizzazione Immunomicrobiologica

Atti Congr Int Stor Med — Atti. Congresso Internazionale di Storia della Medicina

Atti Congr Int Stud Bizantini — Atti. Congresso Internazionale degli Studi Bizantini

Atti Congr Int Vetro — Atti. Congresso Internazionale del Vetro

Atti Congr Lega Int Reum — Atti. Congresso della Lega Internazionale Contro il Reumatismo

Atti Congr Naz Apic Ital — Atti. Congresso Nazionale della Sezione Apicultori Italiani

Atti Congr Naz Assoc Ital Fis Sanit Prot Radiaz — Atti. Congresso Nazionale. Associazione Italiana di Fisica Sanitaria e di Protezione contro le Radiazioni

Atti Congr Naz Assoc Sci Prod Anim — Atti. Congresso Nazionale. Associazione Scientifica di Produzione Animale

Atti Congr Naz Chim Ind — Atti. Congresso Nazionale di Chimica Industriale

Atti Congr Naz Chim Pura Appl — Atti. Congresso Nazionale di Chimica Pura ed Applicata

Atti Congr Naz Ig — Atti. Congresso Nazionale d'Igiene

Atti Congr Naz Ital Entomol — Atti. Congresso Nazionale Italiano di Entomologia

Atti Congr Naz Risorg — Atti e Memorie del Congresso Nazionale del Risorgimento

Atti Congr Naz Soc Ital Biol Mar Riass — Atti. Congresso Nazionale della Società Italiana di Biologia Marina Riassunti

Atti Congr Qual — Atti. Congresso della Qualita

Atti Congr Sci Rass Int Elettron Nucl — Atti. Congresso Scientifico. Rassegna Internazionale Elettronica e Nucleare

Atti Congr Soc Ital Ortod — Atti del Congresso. Società Italiana di Ortodonzia

Atti Congr Stor Risorg Ital — Atti del Congresso di Storia del Risorgimento Italiano

Atti Congr Unione Mat Ital — Atti. Congresso dell'Unione Matematica Italiana

Atti Conv Diabete Second — Atti. Convegno sul Diabete Secondario

Atti Convegi Lincei — Atti. Convegni Lincei

Atti Conv Eutrofizziazione Ital — Atti. Convegno sulla Eutrofizzazione in Italia

Atti Conv Int Grano Duro — Atti. Convegno Internazionale del Grano Duro

Atti Conv Int Lipidi Aliment Simp Genuinita Oli Aliment — Atti. Convegno Internazionale dei Lipidi Alimentari e del Simposio sulla Genuinita degli Oli per l'Alimentazione

Atti Conv Int Mater Plast Confezionamento Prod Farm — Atti. Convegno Internazionale sulle Materie Plastiche nel Confezionamento dei Prodotti Farmaceutici

Atti Conv Naz Apic — Atti. Convegno Nazionale della Apicultori

Atti Conv Naz Olii Essenz Sui Deriv Agrum — Atti. Convegno Nazionale sugli Olii Essenziali e Sui Derivati Agrumari

Atti Conv Naz Qual — Atti. Convegno Nazionale della Qualita

Atti Conv Naz Tec Nav — Atti. Convegno Nazionale di Tecnica Navale

Atti Conv Prev Soc — Atti. Convegno "Fiscalizzazione Oneri Sociala e Riforma della Previdenza Sociale"

Atti Conv Qual — Atti. Convegno sulla Qualita

Atti Conv Reg Aliment — Atti. Convegno Regionale dell'Alimentazione

Atti Conv Salute — Atti. VI Convegno della Salute

Atti Conv Sc Fondam Transform Mater Polim Polym Process — Atti. Convegno-Scuola su Fondamenti della Transformazione dei Materiali Polimerici Polymer Processing

Atti Conv Sc Sint Polim — Atti. Convegno-Scuola su Sintesi di Polimeri

Atti C St R — Atti. Congresso Nazionale di Studi Romani

ATTID — AT Times

Atti del Congr Intern di Sc Storiche — Atti del Congresso Internazionale di Scienze Storiche

Atti D Real Acad D Sci Morali E Pol — Atti del Accademia di Scienze Morali e Politiche della Societa Reale di Napoli

Atti D Real Ist Veneto Di Sci Lett Ed Arti — Atti del Reale Istituto Veneto di Scienze, Lettere, ed Arti

Atti e Mem Deput Ferrar Stor Patria — Atti e Memorie della Deputazione Ferrarese di Storia Patria

Atti e Mem Ist Ital Num — Atti e Memorie. Istituto Italiano di Numismatica

Atti e Mem Ital Num — Atti e Memorie. Istituto Italiano di Numismatica

Atti e Mem Mantova — Atti e Memorie. Reale Accademia di Mantova

Atti Fac Ing Univ Bologna — Atti. Facolta d'Ingegneria. Universita di Bologna

Atti Fond Giorgio Ronchi — Atti. Fondazione Giorgio Ronchi

Atti Fond Giorgio Ronchi & Contrib Ist Naz Ottica — Atti. Fondazione Giorgio Ronchi e Contributi dell'Istituto Nazionale di Ottica

Atti Fond Ronchi — Atti. Fondazione Giorgio Ronchi

Atti Fond Ronchi — Atti. Fondazion Giorgio Ronchi e Contributi. Istituto Nazionale de Ottica

Atti Genoa — Atti. Accademia Ligure di Scienze e Lettere di Genova

Atti Georgofili — Atti dei Georgofili

Atti Giornate Energ Nucl — Atti. Giornate dell'Energia Nucleare

Atti Giornate Fitopatol — Atti della Giornate Fitopatologiche

Atti Imp Accad Pistojese Sci — Atti. Imperiale Accademia Pistojese di Scienze e Lettere

Atti Imp & Reale Accad Georgofili — Atti della Imperiale e Reale Accademia dei Georgofili

Atti Imp Regia Accad Rovereto — Atti. Imperiale Regia Accademia di Scienze, Lettere, ed Arti Degli Agiati di Rovereto

Atti Imp Regia Accad Sci Lett & A Agiati Rovero — Atti della Imperiale Regia Accademia di Scienze, Lettere, ed Arti degli Agiati in Rovero

Atti IR Accad Sci Lett Arti Agiati Rovereto — Atti. IR Accademia di Scienze. Lettere ed Arti degli Agiati in Rovereto

Atti Ist Bot Giovanni Briosi — Atti. Istituto Botanico Giovanni Briosi e Laboratorio Crittogamica Italiano. Reale Universita di Pavia

Atti Ist Bot Giovanni Briosi Lab Crittogam Univ Pavia — Atti. Istituto Botanico Giovanni Briosi. Laboratorio Crittogamico. Universita di Pavia

Atti Ist Bot Lab Crittogam Univ Pavia — Atti. Istituto Botanico e Laboratorio Crittogamico. Universita di Pavia

Atti Ist Bot Labor Crittog Univ Pavia — Atti. Istituto Botanico e Laboratorio Crittogamico. Universita di Pavia

Atti Ist Bot Univ Lab Crittogam Pavia — Atti. Istituto Botanico. Universita. Laboratorio Crittogamico. Pavia

Atti Ist Bot Univ Pavia — Atti. Istituto Botanico. Universita di Pavia

Atti Ist Geol Univ Genova — Atti. Istituto di Geologia. Universita di Genova

Atti Ist Geol Univ Pavia — Atti. Istituto Geologico. Universita di Pavia

Atti Istr — Atti e Memorie. Societa Istriana di Archeologia e Storia Patria

Atti Ist Veneto — Atti. Istituto Veneto di Scienze, Lettere, ed Arti

Atti Ist Veneto Sci Lett Arti — Atti. Istituto Veneto di Scienze, Lettere, ed Arti

Atti Ist Veneto Sci Lett Arti Cl Sci Mat Nat — Atti. Istituto Veneto di Scienze, Lettere, ed Arti. Classe di Scienze Matematiche e Naturali

Atti Ist Veneto Sci Lett Arti (Venezia) Cl Sci Fis Mat Nat — Atti. Istituto Veneto di Scienze, Lettere, ed Arti (Venezia). Classe di ScienzeFisiche, Matematiche, e Naturali

Atti Ist Ven Sci Lett & A — Atti dell'Istituto Veneto di Scienze, Lettere, ed Arti

Atti Linc — Atti. Accademia Nazionale dei Lincei

Atti Mem Accad Agric Commer Arti Verona — Atti e Memorie. Accademia di Agricoltura, Commercio, ed Arti di Verona

Atti Mem Accad Agric Sci Lett Arti Commer Verona — Atti e Memorie. Accademia di Agricoltura, Scienze Lettere, Arti, e Commercio di Verona

Atti Mem Accad Agric Sci Lett (Verona) — Atti e Memorie. Accademia di Agricoltura, Scienze, e Lettere (Verona)

Atti Mem Accad Mod — Atti e Memorie. Accademia di Scienze, Lettere, ed Arti in Modena

Atti Mem Accad Naz Sci Lett Arti (Modena) — Atti e Memorie. Accademia Nazionale di Scienze, Lettere, ed Arti (Modena)

Atti Mem Accad Patavina — Atti e Memorie dell'Accademia Patavina di Scienze, Lettere ed Arti. Classe di Scienze Morali

Atti Mem Accad Patavina Sci Lett Arti — Atti e Memorie. Accademia Patavina di Scienze, Lettere, ed Arti

Atti Mem Accad Patavina Sci Lett Arti Cl Sci Mor Lett Arti — Atti e Memorie. Accademia Patavina di Scienze, Lettere ed Arti. Classe di Scienze Morali, Lettere, ed Arti

Atti Mem Accad Patav Sci Lett Arti — Atti e Memorie. Accademia Patavina di Scienze, Lettere, ed Arti

Atti Mem Accad Petrarca Lett Arti Sci — Atti e Memorie. Reale Accademia Petrarca di Lettere, Arti, e Scienze

Atti Mem Accad Sci Lett Arti Modena — Atti e Memorie. Accademia di Scienze, Lettere, ed Arti de Modena

Atti Mem Accad Sci Lett Arti Padova — Atti e Memorie. Reale Accademia di Scienze, Lettere, ed Arti in Padova

Atti Mem Accad Stor Arte Sanit — Atti e Memorie. Accademia di Storia dell'Arte Sanitaria

Atti Mem Accad Tosc Sci Lettere La Colombaria — Atti e Memorie dell'Accademia Toscana di Scienze e Lettere La Colombaria

Atti Mem Accad Virgiliana Mantova — Atti e Memorie. Accademia Virgiliana di Mantova

Atti Mem Acc Virg — Atti e Memorie. Reale Accademia Virgiliana

Atti Mem Bologna — Memorie. Accademia delle Scienze. Istituto di Bologna

Atti Mem Deputazione Stor Antiche Prov Modenesi — Atti e Memorie. Deputazione di Storia Patria per le Antiche Provincie Modenesi

Atti Mem Deputazione Stor Emilia Romagna — Atti e Memorie. Reale Deputazione di Storia Patria per l'Emilia e la Romagna

Atti Mem Deputazione Stor Modenesi — Atti e Memorie. Reale Deputazione di Storia Patria per le Provincie Modenesi

Atti Mem Deputazione Stor Modenesi Parmensi — Atti e Memorie. Reale Deputazione di Storia Patria per le Provincie Modenesi e Parmensi

Atti Mem Deputazione Stor Patria Antiche Prov Modenesi — Atti e Memorie. Deputazione di Storia Patria per le Antiche Provincie Modenesi

Atti Mem Deputazione Stor Romagna — Atti e Memorie. Reale Deputazione di Storia Patria per le Provincie di Romagna

Atti Mem Istriana — Atti e Memorie. Societa Istriana di Archeologia e Storia Patria

Atti Mem Ist Veneto — Atti e Memoire. Istituto Veneto

Atti Mem M — Atti e Memorie. Reale Accademia di Mantova

Atti Mem Modena — Atti e Memorie. Deputazione di Storia Patria per le Antiche Provincie Modenesi

Atti Memo Acad Agric Sci Lett (Verona) — Atti e Memorie. Accademia di Agricoltura, Scienze, e Lettere (Verona)

Atti Mem R Accad Sci Lett Arti Modena — Atti e Memorie. Reale Accademia di Scienze, Lettere, ed Arti in Modena

Atti Mem R Accad Virgiliana — Atti e Memorie. Reale Accademia Virgiliana

Atti Mem Regia Accad Sci Lett Arti Padova — Atti e Memorie. Regia Accademia di Scienze, Lettere, ed Arti in Padova

Atti Mem Romagna — Atti e Memorie. Deputazione di Storia Patria. Provincie di Romagna

Atti Mem Soc Istriana — Atti e Memorie. Societa Istriana di Archeologia e Storia Patria

Atti Mem Soc Mag Gr — Atti e Memorie. Societa Magna Grecia

Atti Mem Soc Magna Grecia — Atti e Memorie. Societa Magna Grecia

Atti Mem Soc Tiburtina — Atti e Memorie. Societa Tiburtina di Storia e d'Arte

Atti Mem Stor Patria Prov Modenesi — Atti e Memorie della Regia Deputazione di Storia Patria per le Province Modenesi

Atti M Gr — Atti e Memorie. Societa Magna Grecia

Atti M Grecia — Atti e Memorie. Societa Magna Grecia

Atti Mod — Atti e Memorie. Reale Accademia di Scienze, Lettere, ed Arti de Modena

Atti Mus Civico Storia Nat Trieste — Atti. Museo Civico di Storia Naturale di Trieste

Atti Mus Civ Stor Nat Triesti — Atti. Museo Civico di Storia Naturale di Triesti

Atti Mus Trieste — Atti. Civici Musei di Storia ed Arte di Trieste

Atti Nap — Atti. Accademia Nazionale di Scienze Morali e Politiche (Napoli)

Atti Napoli — Atti. Societa Pontaniana. Napoli

Atti Not Assoc Ital Metall — Atti Notizie. Associazione Italiana di Metallurgia

Atti Ortop Traum — Atti di Ortopedia e Traumatologia

Atti Pal — Atti. Accademia di Scienze, Lettere, e Arti di Palermo

Atti Palermo — Atti. Accademia di Scienze, Lettere, ed Arti di Palermo

Atti PARA — Atti. Pontificia Accademia Romana di Archeologia

Atti Pont — Atti. Societa Pontaniana (Napoli)

Atti Pont Acc — Atti. Pontificia Accademia Romana di Archeologia

Atti Pont Accad Romana Archeol — Atti della Pontificia Accademia Romana di Archeologia

Atti Pontif Accad Romana Nuovi Lincei — Atti. Pontificia Accademia Romana dei Nuovi Lincei

Atti Pontif Accad Sci — Atti. Pontificia Accademia delle Scienze

Atti Pontif Accad Sci Nuovi Lincei — Atti. Pontificia Accademia delle Scienze. Nuovi Lincei

Atti R Accad Fisiocrit Siena — Atti. Regla Accademia dei Fisiocritici in Siena

Atti R Accad Geografili — Atti. Reale Accademia dei Geografili

Atti R Accad Ital Mem Cl Sci Fis Mat Nat — Atti. Reale Accademia d'Italia. Memorie. Classe di Scienze Fisiche, Matematiche, e Naturali

Atti R Accad Ital Rend Cl Sci Fis Mat Nat — Atti. Reale Accademia d'Italia. Rendiconti. Classe di Scienze Fisiche, Matematiche, e Naturali

Atti R Accad Lincei — Atti. Reale Accademia dei Lincei

Atti R Accad Lincei Mem Cl Sc Fis Mat e Nat — Atti. Reale Accademia dei Lincei. Memorie. Classe di Scienze Fisiche, Matematiche, e Naturali

Atti R Accad Lincei Rendic Cl Sc Fis Mat e Nat — Atti. Reale Accademia dei Lincei. Rendiconti. Classe di Scienze Fisiche, Matematiche, e Naturali

Atti R Accad Lincei (Roma) Mem Cl Sc Fis Mat e Nat — Atti. Reale Accademia dei Lincei (Roma). Memorie. Classe di Scienze Fisiche, Matematiche, e Naturali

Atti R Accad Lincei (Roma) Rendic Cl Sc Fis Mat e Nat — Atti. Reale Accademia dei Lincei (Roma). Rendiconti. Classe di Scienze Fisiche,Matematiche, e Naturali

Atti R Accad Naz Lincei Mem Cl Sci Fis Mat Nat — Atti. Reale Accademia Nazionale dei Lincei. Memorie. Classe di Scienze Fisiche,Matematiche, e Naturali

Atti R Accad Naz Lincei Rend Cl Sci Fis Mat Nat — Atti. Reale Accademia Nazionale dei Lincei. Rendiconti. Classe di Scienze Fisiche, Matematiche, e Naturali

Atti R Accad Naz Lincei (Roma) — Atti. Reale Accademia Nazionale dei Lincei (Roma)

Atti R Accad Peloritana — Atti. Reale Accademia Peloritana

Atti R Accad Peloritana Cl Sci Fis Mat Biol — Atti. Reale Accademia Peloritana. Classe di Scienze Fisiche, Matematiche, e Biologiche

Atti R Accad Sci Lett Arti Palermo — Atti. Reale Accademia di Scienze, Lettere, e Arti di Palermo

Atti R Accad Sci Lett Belle Arti Palermo — Atti. Reale Accademia di Scienze, Lettere, e Belle Arti di Palermo

Atti R Accad Sci Torino Cl Sci Fis Mat Nat — Atti. Reale Accademia delle Scienze di Torino. Classe di Scienze Fisiche, Matematiche, e Naturali

Atti Rass Tec Soc Ing Archit Torino — Atti e Rassegna Tecnica. Societa degli Ingegneri e degli Architetti in Torino

Atti Reale Accad Econ Agrar Geograf Firenze — Atti. Reale Accademia Economico-Agraria dei Geografili di Firenze

Atti Reale Accad Geograf Firenze — Atti. Reale Accademia dei Geografili di Firenze

Atti Reale Accad It Rendi Sci Fisiche — Atti della Reale Accademia Italiana. Rendiconti di Scienze Fisiche

Atti Reale Accad Lincei — Atti. Reale Accademia dei Lincei

Atti Reale Accad Lincei Rendiconti Cl Sci Fis — Atti. Reale Accademia dei Lincei. Rendiconti. Classe di Scienze Fisiche, Matematiche, e Naturale

Atti Reale Accad Lucchese Sci — Atti. Reale Accademia Lucchese di Scienze, Lettere, ed Arti

Atti Reale Accad Naz Lincei Mem Cl Sci Fis — Atti. Reale Accademia Nazionale dei Lincei. Memorie. Classe di Scienze Fisiche,Matematiche, e Naturale

Atti Reale Accad Naz Lincei Rendiconti Cl Sci Fis — Atti. Reale Accademia Nazionale dei Lincei. Rendiconti. Classe di Scienze Fisiche, Matematiche, e Naturale

Atti Reale Accad Sci Napoli — Atti. Reale Accademia delle Scienze e Belle-Lettere di Napoli

Atti Reale Accad Sci Torino — Atti della Reale Accademia delle Scienze di Torino

Atti Reale Ist Ven Sci Lett & A — Atti del Reale Istituto Veneto di Scienze, Lettere, ed Arti

Atti Real Ist Incoragg Sci Nat Napoli — Atti. Real Istituto d'Incoraggiamento alle Scienze Naturali di Napoli

Atti Regia Accad Fisiocrit Siena — Atti. Regia Accademia dei Fisiocritici in Siena

Atti Regia Accad Fisiocrit Siena Sez Med Fis — Atti. Regia Accademia dei Fisiocritici in Siena. Sezione Medico-Fisica

Atti Relaz Accad Pugliese Sci Parte 2 — Atti e Relazioni. Accademia Pugliese delle Scienze. Parte 2. Classe di Scienze Fisiche, Mediche, e Naturali

Atti Rend Accad Naz Lincei Cl Sci Fis Mat Natur — Atti. Rendiconti. Accademia Nazionale dei Lincei. Classe di Scienze Fisiche, Matematiche, e Naturali

Atti R Ist Incoraggiamento Napoli — Atti. Reale Istituto d'Incoraggiamento di Napoli

Atti R Ist Ven — Atti. Istituto Veneto di Scienze, Lettere, ed Arti

Atti Riunione Sci Ital — Atti. Riuione degli Scienziati Italiani

Atti Riun Sci Ist It Preist & Protostor — Atti della Riunione Scientifica. Istituto Italiano di Preistoria e Protostoria

Atti Roveretana — Atti. Accademia Roveretana degli Agiati

Atti R Univ Genova — Atti. Reale Universita di Genova

Atti Sci Sci Nat — Atti Scientifici. Societa Elvetica di Scienze Naturali

Atti Semin Mat & Fis Univ Modena — Atti. Seminario Matematico e Fisico. Universita di Modena

Atti Sem Mat Fis Univ Modena — Atti. Seminario Matematico e Fisico. Universita di Modena

Atti Simp Conferme Prospettive Uso Calcitonina — Atti. Simposio Conferme e Prospettive nell'Uso della Calcitonina

Atti Simp Detersivi — Atti. Simposio sui Detersivi

Atti Simp Int Agrochim — Atti. Simposio Internazionale di Agrochimica

Atti Simp Int Zootec — Atti. Simposio Internazionale di Zootecnia

Atti Simp Naz C3 — Atti. Simposio Nazionale sul C3

Atti Sind Ing Lombardia — Atti. Sindacati Ingegneri di Lombardia

Atti Sind Prov Fasc Ingeg Lombardia — Atti del Sindacato Provinciale Fascista degli Ingegneti di Lombardia

Atti SMG — Atti e Memorie. Societa Magna Grecia

Atti S M Graecia — Atti e Memorie. Societa Magna Grecia

Atti Soc Archeol & B A Prov Torino — Atti della Societa di Archeologia e Belle Arti per la Provincia di Torino

Atti Soc Astron Ital — Atti. Societa Astronomica Italiana

Atti Soc Cultori Sc Med e Nat Cagliari — Atti. Societa fra i Cultori delle Scienze Mediche e Naturali in Cagliari

Atti Soc Derm Sif Bologna — Atti della Societa di Dermatologia e Sifilografia e delle Sezione Interprovinciali (Bologna)

Atti Soc Econ Firenze Ossia Georgofili — Atti. Societa Economica di Firenze Ossia dei Georgofili

Atti Soc Elvet Sci Nat — Atti. Societa Elvetica delle Scienze Naturali

Atti Soc Elv Sci Nat — Atti. Societa Elvetica di Scienze Naturali

Atti Soc Elv Sci Nat Parte Sci — Atti. Societa Elvetica di Scienze Naturali. Parte Scientifica

Atti Soc Freniat Ital — Atti della Societa Freniatrica Italiana

Atti Soc Friuli — Atti. Societa per la Preistoria e Protostoria della Regione Friuli-Venezia Giulia

Atti Soc Ing Archit Trieste — Atti della Societa degli Ingegneri e degli Architetti di Trieste

Atti Soc Istr — Atti e Memorie. Societa Istriana di Archeologia e Storia Patria

Atti Soc Ital Anat — Atti. Societa Italiana di Anatomia

Atti Soc Ital Buiatria — Atti. Societa Italiana di Buiatria

Atti Soc Ital Cancer — Atti della Societa Italiana di Cancerologia

Atti Soc Ital Cancerol Congr Naz — Atti. Societa Italiana di Cancerologia. Congresso Nazionale

Atti Soc Ital Cardiol — Atti. Societa Italiana di Cardiologia

Atti Soc Ital Genet Eugen — Atti della Societa Italiana di Genetica ed Eugenica

Atti Soc Ital Oftal — Atti. Societa Italiana di Oftalmologia

Atti Soc Ital Ostet Ginec — Atti della Societa Italiana di Ostetricia e Ginecologia

Atti Soc Ital Patol — Atti della Societa Italiana di Patologia

Atti Soc Ital Progr Sci — Atti. Societa Italiana per il Progresso delle Scienze

Atti Soc Ital Prog Sci — Atti. Societa Italiana per il Progresso delle Scienze

Atti Soc Ital Sci Nat — Atti. Societa Italiana di Scienze Naturali. Museo Civile di Storia Naturale

Atti Soc Ital Sci Nat Mus Civ Stor Nat Milano — Atti. Societa Italiana di Scienze Naturali. Museo Civico di Storia Naturale di Milano

Atti Soc Ital Sci Vet — Atti. Societa Italiana delle Scienze Veterinarie

Atti Soc Ital Sc Nat (Milano) — Atti. Societa Italiana di Scienze Naturali (Milano)

Atti Soc Ital Stor Crit Sci Med Nat — Atti della Societa Italiana di Storia Critica delle Scienze Mediche e Naturali

Atti Soc Ital Stor Crit Sci Med Natur — Atti della Societa Italiana di Storia Critica delle Scienze Mediche e Naturali

Atti Soc Ital Urol — Atti della Societa Italiana di Urologia

Atti Soc Lig Stor Patria — Atti. Societa Ligure di Storia Patria

Atti Soc Ligure Stor Patria — Atti della Societa Ligure di Storia Patria

Atti Soc Ligust Sc Nat e Geogr — Atti. Societa Ligustica di Scienze Naturali e Geografiche

Atti Soc Lomb Sci Med Biol — Atti. Societa Lombarda di Scienze Mediche e Biologiche

Atti Soc Med Biol Milano — Atti della Societa Medico-Biologica di Milano

Atti Soc Med Bolzano — Atti della Societa Medica di Bolzano

Atti Soc Med Chir Bolzano — Atti della Societa Medico-Chirurgica di Bolzano

Atti Soc Med Chir Padova — Atti della Societa Medico-Chirurgica di Padova

Atti Soc Med-Chir Padova Fac Med Chir Univ Padova — Atti. Societa Medico-Chirurgica di Padova e Facolta di Medicina e Chirurgia della Universita di Padova

Atti Soc Med Leg Roma — Atti della Societa di Medicina Legale in Roma</PHR> %

Atti Soc Med Novarese — Atti della Societa di Cultura Medica Novarese

Atti Soc Napol Chir — Atti. Societa Napoletana di Chirurgia

Atti Soc Nat Mat — Atti della Societa dei Naturalisti e Matematici

Atti Soc Nat Mat Modena — Atti. Societa dei Naturalisti e Matematici di Modena

Atti Soc Naturalisti Mat Modena — Atti. Societa dei Naturalisti e Matematici di Modena

Atti Soc Naturalisti Modena — Atti. Societa dei Naturalisti di Modena

Atti Soc Oftal Ital — Atti della Societa Oftalmologica Italiana

Atti Soc Oftal Lomb — Atti della Societa Oftalmologica Lombarda

Atti Soc Oftalmol Lomb — Atti. Societa Oftalmologica Lombarda

Atti Soc Peloritana Sci Fis Mat e Nat — Atti. Societa Peloritana di Scienze Fisiche, Matematiche, e Naturali

Atti Soc Peloritana Sci Fis Mat Nat — Atti. Societa Peloritana di Scienze Fisiche, Matematiche, e Naturali

Atti Soc Peloritana Sci Fis Mat Natur — Atti. Societa Peloritana di Scienze Fisiche, Matematiche, e Naturali

Atti Soc Peloritana Sci NS — Atti della Societa Peloritana di Scienze. Nuova Serie

Atti Soc Peloritan Sci Fis Mat e Nat — Atti. Societa Peloritana di Scienze Fisiche, Matematiche, e Naturali

Atti Soc Pelorit Sci Fis Mat Nat — Atti. Societa Peloritana di Scienze Fisiche, Matematiche, e Naturali

Atti Soc Piemont Archeol & B A — Atti della Societa Piemontese di Archeologia e Belle Arti

Atti Soc Reg Ostet Ginec — Atti della Societa Regionali di Ostetricia e di Ginecologia

Atti Soc Romana Antrop — Atti della Societa Romana di Antropologia

Atti Soc Salernitana Med Chir — Atti. Societa Salernitana di Medicina e Chirurgia

Atti Soc Savon Stor Patria — Atti della Societa Savonese di Storia Patria

Atti Soc Sci Lett Genova — Atti della Societa di Scienze e Lettere di Genova

Atti Soc Sci Nat Toscana Pisa Mem — Atti. Societa di Scienze Naturali Toscana Residente in Pisa. Memorie

Atti Soc Studi Malar — Atti della Societa per gli Studi della Malaria

Atti Soc Tib — Atti e Memorie. Societa Tiburtina di Storia e d'Arte

Atti Soc Tiburtina — Atti e Memorie. Societa Tiburtina di Storia e d'Arte

Atti Soc Toscana Sci Nat Pisa — Atti. Societa Toscana di Scienze Naturali Residente in Pisa

Atti Soc Toscana Sci Nat Pisa Mem — Atti. Societa Toscana di Scienze Naturali Residente in Pisa. Memorie

Atti Soc Toscana Sci Nat Pisa Mem Ser A — Atti. Societa Toscana di Scienze Naturali Residente in Pisa. Memorie. Serie A

Atti Soc Toscana Sci Nat Pisa Mem Ser B — Atti. Societa Toscana di Scienze Naturali Residente in Pisa. Memorie. Serie B

Atti Soc Toscana Sci Nat Pisa P V — Atti. Societa Toscana di Scienze Naturali Residente in Pisa. Processi Verbali

Atti Soc Toscana Sci Nat Pisa P V Mem Ser A — Atti. Societa Toscana di Scienze Naturali Residente in Pisa. Processi Verbali e Memorie. Serie A

Atti Soc Toscana Sci Nat P V Mem Ser B — Atti. Societa Toscana di Scienze Naturali. Processi Verbali e Memorie. Serie B

Atti Soc Toscana Sci Nat Resid Pisa Mem Ser A — Atti. Societa Toscana di Scienze Naturali Residente in Pisa. Memorie. Serie A

Atti Soc Tosc Sci Nat Pisa Mem — Atti. Societa Toscana di Scienze Naturali di Pisa. Memorie

Atti Solenne Distrib Premi Agric Industr — Atti. Solenne Distribuzione di Premi d'Agricoltura e d'Industria

Atti Symp Int Estere Cori Glucidi Fosforilati — Atti. Symposium Internazionale sull'Estere di Cori e sui Glucidi Fosforilati

Atti Tor — Atti. Reale Accademia della Scienze di Torino

Atti Torino — Atti. Accademia delle Scienze di Torino

Atti Uff Congr Naz Vitic Enol Ital — Atti Ufficiali del Congresso Nazionale dei Viticoltori ed Enologi Italiani

Atti Uff Conv Int Comun — Atti Ufficiali del Convegno Internazionale delle Comunicazioni

Atti Uffic Congr Int Energ Nucl — Atti Ufficiali. Congresso Internazionale per l'Energia Nucleare

Atti Univ Genova — Atti della Universita di Genova

Atti Ven — Atti. Istituto Veneto di Scienze, Lettere, ed Arti

Atti Venezia — Atti. Istituto Veneto di Scienze, Lettere, ed Arti

Atti VI Congr Internaz Sci Preistor Protoistor — Atti del IV Congresso Internazionale delle Scienze Preistoriche e Protoistoriche

Atti VIII Congr Internaz Studi Bizant — Atti dello VIII Congresso Internazionale di Studi Bizantini

Attiv Med Ital — Attivita Medica Italiana

Atti V Simp Int Agrochim "Zolfo in Agricoltura" — Atti. V Simposio Internazionale di Agrochimica su "Lo Zolfo in Agricoltura"

Attiv Sole — Attivita del Sole

Attiv Tec Off — Attivita Tecnica di Officina

Att Mem Soc Magna Grecia — Atti e Memorie. Societa Magna Grecia

Attual Chemioter — Attualita di Chemioterapia

Attual Dent — Attualita Dentale

Attual Lab — Attualita di Laboratorio

Attual Med — Attualita Medica

Attual Med Firenze — Attualita Mediche (Firenze)

Attual Med Milano — Attualita Medica (Milano)

Attual Med Roma — Attualita Medica (Roma)

Attual Ostet Ginecol — Attualita di Ostetricia e Ginecologia

Attual Zool — Attualita Zoologiche

ATTUD — Advances in Tunnelling Technology and Subsurface Use

ATU — Altorientalische Texte und Untersuchungen

Atual Agron — Atualidades Agronomicas

Atual Agron (Sao Paulo) — Atualidades Agronomicas (Sao Paulo)

Atual Agropecu — Atualidades Agropecuarias
Atual Agrovet — Atualidades Agroveterinarias
Atual Fis Quim Org — Atualidades de Fisico-Quimica Organica
Atual Med — Atualidades Medicas
Atual Med Sanit — Atualidades Medico Sanitarias
Atual Vet — Atualidades Veterinarias
Atual Vet (Sao Paulo) — Atualidades Veterinarias (Sao Paulo)
At und Strom — Atom und Strom
At Unusual Situat — Atoms in Unusual Situations
ATV — Agronomia Tropical (Venezuela)
AtV — Ateneo Veneto
ATVED — Atualidades Veterinarias
ATVEDH — Atualidades Veterinarias
At Ven — Ateneo Veneto. Rivista di Scienze, Lettere, ed Arti
ATV Landesgruppen Tag — ATV-Landesgruppen-Tagungen
ATVMA4 — Annals. Transvaal Museum
At-Vodorodnaya Energ Tekhnol — Atomno-Vodorodnaya Energetika i Tekhnologiya
ATV Schrift — ATV-Schriftenreihe
ATW — Air Transport World
ATW Atomwirtsch Atomtech — ATW. Atomwirtschaft, Atomtechnik
At Weapons Res Establ (UK) Rep O — Atomic Weapons Research Establishment (United Kingdom). Report. Series O
ATW Int Z Kernenerg — ATW. Internationale Zeitschrift fuer Kernenergie
At World — Atomic World
ATX — Australian Sales Tax Guide
ATX — Business. The Magazine of Managerial Thought and Action
ATY — Automatie, Maandblad voor Meettechniek en Regeltechniek, Mechanisering, en Automatisering
ATYBAK — Annales. Universitatis Turkuensis. Series A-II. Biologica-Geographica-Geologica
Atyp Mycobacteria Proc Symp — Atypical Mycobacteria. Proceedings. Symposium
A Typograph — Ars Typographica
ATZ — Akademische Turn-Zeitung
ATZ Automobiltech Z — ATZ. Automobiltechnische Zeitschrift
ATZOAU — Attualia Zoologiche
ATZS — Aquarien- und Terrarien-Zeitschrift (Stuttgart)
AU — Afrika und Uebersee
AU — Altsprachliche Unterricht
AU — Amaru (Revista Literaria)
AU — Annals of the University
Au — Audio
Au — Augustiniana
Au — Ausland
Au — Ausonia
AU — Der Altsprachliche Unterricht
AuA — Anglistik und Amerikanistik
AUA — Annals. Ukrainian Academy of Arts and Sciences in the US
Au A — Antike und Abendland
AUA — Anuario Universidad de Los Andes
AUAA J — AUAA [*American Urological Association Allied*] Journal
AUAEAI — Annales. Universite d'Abidjan. Serie E. Ecologie
AUAFA — Acta Universitatis Agriculturae. Facultas Silviculturae. Series C
AUAM — Acta Universitatis Asiae Mediae
AUAMCA — Annales. Universite d'Abidjan. Serie B. Medecine
AUA Newsl — AUA [*Association of University Architects*] Newsletter
AUARAN — Arkansas. Agricultural Experiment Station. Special Report
AUARBO — Australia. Commonwealth Scientific and Industrial Research Organisation. Division of Animal Physiology. Annual Report
AUASAQ — Annals. Ukrainian Academy of Arts and Sciences in the US
AUB — Al-Urwa (Bombay)
AUB — American University of Beirut
AUB — Analele. Universitatii Bucuresti
AUB — Annales Universitatis Scientiarum Budapestensis de Rolando Eoetvoes Nominatae
AUB — Annales. Universitatis Scientiarum Budapestinenses de Rolando Eoetvoes Nominatae
AUB — Annales. Universite de Besancon
AuB — Autour de la Bible
AUB — Bruxelles. Universite. Annales
AUBADE — Annales Scientifiques. Universite de Besancon. Biologie Animale
AUBCB — Analele. Universitatii Bucuresti. Chimie
AUBCBI — Analele. Universitatii Bucuresti. Chimie
AUBEAN — Acta Urologica Belgica
Aube Mm S Ac — Memoires de la Societe Academique d'Agriculture, des Sciences, et des Lettres du Departement de l'Aube
Aube Mm S Ag — Memoires de la Societe Academique d'Agriculture, des Sciences, et des Lettres du Departement de l'Aube
AUBFF — Arquivos. Universidade de Bahia. Faculdade de Filosofia
AUBG — Acta Universitatis Upsaliensis
AuBiR — Australian Biblical Review
AUB Ist — Analele Universitatii Bucuresti. Stiinte Sociale. Istorie
AUBKA7 — Archives. Union Medicale Balkanique
AUB-LCO — Analele. Universitatii Bucuresti. Limbi Clasice si Orientale
AUB-LG — Analele. Universitatii Bucuresti. Limbi Germanice
AUBLL — Analele. Universitatii Bucuresti. Limba si Literatura Romana
AUB-LLR — Analele. Universitatii Bucuresti. Limba Literara
AUBLR — Analele. Universitatii Bucuresti. Limbi Romanice
AUB-LUC — Analele. Universitatii Bucuresti. Literatura Universala Comparata
AUBSSS — American University of Beirut. Social Science Series
AUBSSSF — Analele Universitatii Bucuresti Seria Stinte Sociale. Filologie
AUBud — Annales Universitatis Scientiarum Budapestensis de Rolando Eoetvoes Nominatae.Sectio Philologica
Auburn Univ Agric Exp Stn Bull — Auburn University. Agricultural Experiment Station. Bulletin

Auburn Univ Agric Exp Stn Circ — Auburn University. Agricultural Experiment Station. Circular
Auburn Univ Agric Exp Stn Leafl — Auburn University. Agricultural Experiment Station. Leaflet
Auburn Univ Agric Exp Stn Prog Rep Ser — Auburn University. Agricultural Experiment Station. Progress Report Series
Auburn Univ Eng Exp Stn Bull — Auburn University. Engineering Experiment Station. Bulletin
Auburn Univ Water Resour Res Inst WRRI Bull — Auburn University. Water Resources Research Institute. WRRI Bulletin
AUC — Acta Universitatis Carolinae
AUC — Anales. Universidad de Chile
Au C — Antike und Christentum
AUC — Anuarul. Universitatea Cluj
AUC — Au Courant
AUC — Auteursrecht
AUCal — Annali. Facolta di Lettere, Filosofia, e Magistero. Universita di Cagliari
AuCaRec — Australasian Catholic Record
AUCC — Annuario. Universita Cattolica del Sacro Cuore
AUCE — Anales. Universidad Central del Ecuador
AUCG-B — Acta Universitatis Carolinae. Geographica
AuChr — Antike und Christentum
AUCII — Archivio Unione Comunita Israelitiche Italiane
Auckland U Coll Bull — Auckland University College Bulletin
Auckland U L Rev — Auckland University. Law Review
Auckland Univ L Rev — Auckland University. Law Review
Auckland Waikato Hist J — Auckland/Waikato Historical Journal
Auck ULR — Auckland University. Law Review
Auck UL Rev — Auckland University. Law Review
AUCMB — Acta Universitatis Carolinae. Medica. Monographia
AUCP — Acta Universitatis Carolinae Pragensis
AUCPD — Annual UMR-DNR [*University of Missouri, Rolla - Department of Natural Resources*] Conference on Energy. Proceedings
AUC Ph — Acta Universitatis Carolinae. Philologica
AUCQ — Anales de la Universidad Central (Quito)
Auctar — Auctarium Bibliothecae Hagiographicae Graecae
AUD — Acta et Commentationes Universitatis Dorpatensis
Aud — Audace. Recueil Litteraire Trimestriel
Aud — Audience
Aud — Audubon
AUDBAO — Australia. Commonwealth Scientific and Industrial Research Organisation. Division of Building Research. Technical Paper
Aud Biochem — Auditory Biochemistry
Audenaerde — Annales. Cercle Archeologique et Historique d'Audenaerde
Aud Freq Sel — Auditory Frequency Selectivity
Audi — Audience
Audio Engg — Audio Engineering
Audio Eng Soc J — Audio Engineering Society. Journal
Audio Eng Soc Prepr — Audio Engineering Society. Preprint
Audiol — Audiology
Audiol Akust — Audiologische Akustik
Audiol (Jap) — Audiology (Japan)
Audiol Neuro Otol — Audiology and Neuro-Otology
Audiol Neurootol — Audiology and Neuro-Otology (Basel)
Audio Scene Can — Audio Scene Canada
Audiov Commun — Audiovisual Communications
Audio Video Can — Audio Video Canada
Audiov Instr — Audiovisual Instruction
Audiovis Instr — Audiovisual Instruction
Audio Visual Communic Rev — Audio-Visual Communications Review
Audio Visual G — Audio Visual Guide
Audio-Visual Language J — Audio-Visual Language Journal
Audio Visual Lib — Audio Visual Librarian
Audiov Libr — Audiovisual Librarian
Auditor — Internal Auditor
AUDJDK — Audiology
AUDLA — Audiology
AUDLAK — Audiology
Aud Mark — Audio Marketnews
Audn — Audience
Aud Neurosci — Auditory Neuroscience
Aud Physiol Percept Proc Int Symp Hear — Auditory Physiology and Perception. Proceedings. International Symposium on Hearing
Aud Syst — Auditory System
AUDTCF — Ankara Universitesi Dil ve Tarih-Cografya Fakultesi. Dergisi
AUDTCFY — Ankara Universitesi Dil ve Tarih-Cografya Fakultesi. Yayinlari
AUDUA — Audio
AUDUAD — Audubon
Audubon Mag — Audubon Magazine
Audubon Soc RI Bull — Audubon Society of Rhode Island. Bulletin
AuE — Arheologija un Etnografija
AUELA — Automatica si Electronica
AUENA — Automobile Engineer
Auerbach Data Base Manage — Auerbach Data Base Management
Auerbach Rep — Auerbach Reporter
AUF — Archiv fuer Urkundenforschung
AUFB-A — Aufbau
AUFBE4 — Annali. Universita di Ferrara. Nuova Serie. Sezione XX. Biologia
Aufbereit — Aufbereitungs-Technik
Aufbereit PVC — Aufbereiten von PVC
Aufbereit-Tech — Aufbereitungs-Technik
Aufbereitungs-Tech — Aufbereitungs-Technik
Aufbereitungstech Huettenwerken Vortr Metall Semin — Aufbereitungstechnik in Huettenwerken. Vortraege beim Metallurgischen Seminar
AUFNA2 — Audubon Field Notes

AUFS — American Universities Field Staff. Reports Service. West Coast South America Series

Aufschluss Sonderh — Aufschluss Sonderheft

AUFS EA — American Universities Field Staff. Reports. East Asia Series

AUFSRS — American Universities Field Staff. Reports Series

AUFS SA — American Universities Field Staff. Reports. South Asia Series

AUFS SEA — American Universities Field Staff. Reports. Southeast Asia Series

Aufstieg & Niedergang Roem Welt — Aufstieg und Niedergang der Roemischen Welt

Au Fu — Ausgrabungen und Funde

AUG — Acta Universitatis Gothoburgensis/Goeteborgs Universitets Arsskrift

AUG — Anales. Universidad de Guayaquil

AUG — Annales. Universite de Grenoble

Aug — Augustiniana

AugLv — Augustiniana (Louvain)

AugMad — Augustinus (Madrid)

AugRom — Augustinianum (Rome)

Augsbg Math Naturwiss Schrift — Augsburger Mathematisch-Naturwissenschaftliche Schriften

Augsb Nt Vr B — Bericht des Naturhistorischen Naturwissenschaftlichen Vereins in Augsburg

Augsburg Allg Ztg — Augsburger Allgemeine Zeitung

Augsburg Mtl Kstbl — Augsburgisches Monatliches Kunstblatt

Augst Mushft — Augster Museumshefte

Aug Stud — Augustinian Studies

Augustana Libr Pub — Augustana Library Publications

Augusteum Jschr — Augusteum Jahresschrift

Augustin Stud — Augustinian Studies

AUH — Anales. Universidad Hispalense

AUHisp — Anales. Universidad Hispalense

AUHJ — Australian Journal for Health, Physical Education, and Recreation

AUHPAI — Australian Journal of Hospital Pharmacy

AUI — Analele. Universitatii Al. I. Cuza (Iasi)

AUIBA — Analele Stiintifice ale Universitatii Al. I. Cuza din Iasi. Sectiunea 2a. Biologie

AUINA — Automotive Industries

AUIRAT — Australia. Commonwealth Scientific and Industrial Research Organisation. Irrigation Research Stations. Technical Paper

AUJ — Aberdeen University. Journal

Auj — Aujourd'hui

Au JBA — Australian Journal of Biblical Archaeology

AUJDDT — Australian Journal of Developmental Disabilities

Aujourd'hui — Aujourd'hui: Art et Architecture

AUJR — Agra University. Journal of Research

AUJRL — Agra University Journal of Research. Letters

AUJRS — Agra University. Journal of Research. Science

AUJSA — Australian Journal of Statistics

AUL — Acta Universitatis Latviensis

AUL — Acta Universitatis Lundensis

AUL — Annales. Universite de Lyon

AUL — Annali. Universita di Lecce

AUL — Bulletin. Association des Amis de l'Universite de Liege

AULA — Revista General. Universidad Nacional Pedro Henriquez Urena

Aula Prat Quim Org 1 Prat Basica Quim Org Prep 27 Exper — Aula Pratica de Quimica Organica 1. Pratica Basica da Quimica Organica. Preparacoes. 27 Experiencias

AULJA — Australian Library Journal

AULR — American University Law Review

AUM — Adelaide University. Magazine

AUM — Anales. Universidad de Murcia

AUM — Andrews University. Monographs

AUMACY — Australian Mammalogy

AUMCA4 — Archivos Uruguayos de Medicina, Cirujia, y Especialidades

AUMCS — Annales Universitatis Mariae Curie-Sklodowska. Sectio F. Nauki Filozoficzne i Humanistyczne

AUMDC — Automedica

AUMGAG — Audubon Magazine

AUMIA — Australian Mineral Industry

AUMID — Australian Miner

AUMKA — Annales Universitatis Mariae Curie-Sklodowska. Sectio D. Medicina

AUMLA — Australasian Universities Modern Language Association. Journal

AUMLA — Journal of the Australasian Universities Language and Literature Association

AUMMAY — Australian Museum. Magazine

AUMNA — Australian Mining

AUMTA — Automatisme

AUN — Annali. Facolta di Lettere e Filosofia. Universita di Napoli

Au N — Aufstieg und Niedergang der Roemischen Welt

A Una — Ars Una

AUNAB4 — Annales. Universite et ARERS

AUNC — Anales de la Universidad Nacional de los Estados Unidos de Colombia

A und E — Anglistik und Englischunterricht

AUNED — Australian Uranium News

AUNHA — Australian Natural History

A Univ Abidjan Ethnosociologie — Annales. Universite d'Abidjan. Ethnosociologie

A Univ Abidjan Histoire — Annales. Universite d'Abidjan. Histoire

A Univ Abidjan Lettres — Annales. Universite d'Abidjan. Lettres

A Univ Abidjan Linguist — Annales. Universite d'Abidjan. Linguistique

A Univ Abidjan Ser A Dr — Annales. Universite d'Abidjan. Serie A. Droit

A Univ Madagascar Ser Dr Sci Econ — Annales. Universite de Madagascar. Serie de Droit et des Sciences Economiques

A Univ M Curie-Sklodowska — Annales Universitatis Mariae Curie-Sklodowska

A Univ M Curie-Sklodowska Oecon — Annales Universitatis Mariae Curie-Sklodowska. Sectio Oeconomica

A Univ Sci Budapest Sect Geogr — Annales Universitatis Scientiarum Budapestensis de Rolando Eoetvoes Nominatae. Sectio Geographica

A Univ Sci Soc Toulouse — Annales. Universite des Sciences Sociales de Toulouse

AUNMA5 — Australian Museum [Sydney]. Memoirs

AUNP — Anales de la Universidad de Narino (Pasto)

AUNS — Al'manakh Ukraiens'koho Narodnoho Soiuzu

AUNVAW — Avhandlinger Utgitt av Norsk Videnskaps-Akademi I Oslo. Matematisk-Naturvidenskapelig Klasse

AUO — Arbok Universitetets Oldsaksamling

AuO — Australian Outlook

AUOASRN — Acta Universitatis Ouluensis. Series A. Scientiae Rerum Naturalium

AUONAD — Collected Reports. Natural Science Faculty. Palacky University

AUO-Ph — Acta Universitatis Palackianae Olomucensis. Facultas Philosophica. Philologica

AUP — Annales. Universite de Paris

AU/P — Phylon. Atlanta University

AUPHAY — Australasian Journal of Pharmacy

AUPHB — Australian Physicist

AUPJB — Australian Paediatric Journal

AUPMDI — Australasian Physical and Engineering Sciences in Medicine

AUPO — Acta Universitatis Palackianae Olomucensis

AUPO — Acta Universitatis Palackianae Olomucensis Historica

AUPRD — AUTOTESTCON [Automatic Testing Conference] Proceedings

AuQ — Australian Quarterly

AUR — Aberdeen University. Review

Aur — Aurora

Aur — Aurore

AUR — Automatisering Gids

AURCA — Automation and Remote Control

AURDAW — Australasian Radiology

AUROAV — Annales d'Urologie

Aurora Eichendorff Alm — Aurora. Eichendorff Almanach

AUS — Annales Universitatis Saraviensis

AUS — Annuaire. Universite de Sofia. Faculte des Lettres

Aus — Ausonia

Aus — [The] Australian

AUS — Australian Coal Report

AUSAEW — Annale. Universiteit van Stellenbosch. Serie A-3. Landbouwetenskappe

AUS AG & R — Acta Universitatis Szegediensis. Acta Germanica et Romanica

AUS AHLH — Acta Universitatis Szegediensis de Attila Jozsef Nominatae. Sectio: Acta Historiae Litterarum Hungaricarum

AUSB — Australian Business

AUSBDY — Annale. Universiteit van Stellenbosch. Serie A-4. Bosbou

Ausbild Fortbild Gesundheitsoekon — Ausbildung und Fortbildung in Gesundheitsoekonomie

AusBiR — Australian Biblical Review

Aus BR — Australian Biblical Review

Ausbreitungsrechn Messverfahren Luftueberwach — Ausbreitungsrechnung und Messverfahren zur Luftueberwachung

Aus Comp Bul — Australian Computer Bulletin

Aus Comp J — Australian Computer Journal

AusCR — Australian Catholic Record

Aus C Rec — Australasian Catholic Record

AusCRec — Australian Catholic Record

Aus d Heimat — Aus der Heimat. Blaetter des Vereins fuer Gothaische Geschichte

AUS E & L — Acta Universitatis Szegediensis de Attila Jozsef Nominatae. Sectio: Ethnographica et Linguistica

Aus Educ Ind — Australian Education Index

AUSem St — Andrews University. Seminary Studies

Auserlesene Bibilioth Neuesten Deutsch Lit — Auserlesene Bibliothek der Neuesten Deutschen Literatur

Ausgewaehlte Phys Methoden Org Chem — Ausgewaehlte Physikalische Methoden der Organischen Chemie

Ausgrab Fun — Ausgrabungen und Funde

Ausgrab Fund — Ausgrabungen und Funde. Akademie Verlag fuer Zentralinstitut fuer Alte Geschichte und Archaeologie

Ausgr Berlin — Ausgrabungen in Berlin

Ausgr Fu — Ausgrabungen und Funde. Nachrichtenblatt fuer Vor- und Fruehgeschichte

Ausgr Funde — Ausgrabungen und Funde. Nachrichtenblatt fuer Vor- und Fruehgeschichte

Ausg u Abhand — Ausgaben und Abhandlungen aus dem Gebiete der Romanischen Philologie

AUSHAF — Acta Physica et Chemica

Aus Hamburgs Verwaltung U Wirtschaft — Aus Hamburgs Verwaltung und Wirtschaft Monatsschrift des Statistischen Landesamts

Aushandel — Nachrichten fuer Aussenhandel

AusIMM Annu Conf — AusIMM Annual Conference

AusIMM Bull Proc — AusIMM (Australasian Institute of Mining and Metallurgy) Bulletin and Proceedings

AusIMM Extr Metall Conf — AusIMM Extractive Metallurgy Conference

AusIMM Spectrum Ser — AusIMM Spectrum Series

AusJBibArch — Australian Journal of Biblical Archaeology

AUS J HPER — Australian Journal for Health, Physical Education, and Recreation

AusJP — Australian Journal of Politics and History

AUS J Sci & Med — Australian Journal of Science & Medicine in Sport

Aus J Screen Theory — Australian Journal of Screen Theory

Aus J Sport Sci — Australian Journal of Sport Sciences

Aus J Sports Med — Australian Journal of Sports Medicine

AusL — Ausland

AusL — Australian Letters

Auslandsdeutschtum Evang Kirche — Auslandsdeutschtum und Evangelische Kirche

Auslegeschrift Fed Repub Ger — Auslegeschrift (Federal Republic of Germany)

Auslegeschrift (Switz) — Auslegeschrift (Switzerland)
Aus Leg Mon Dig — Australian Legal Monthly Digest
AUSLOAN — AUSLOAN: Australian Inter-Library Loans Manual
AUSMBV — Australia. Commonwealth Scientific and Industrial Research Organisation. Soil Mechanics Section. Technical Paper
Aus Mo Motor Manual — Australian Monthly Motor Manual
Aus Nat — Aus der Natur
Aus Nat Mus — Aus Natur und Museum
Aus Natur Mus — Aus Natur und Museum
Aus PAIS — Australian Public Affairs Information Service
AUS-PEAS — Acta Universitatis Szegediensis de Attila Jozsef Nominatae. Papers in English and American Studies
Aus Polit U Zeitgesch — Aus Politik und Zeitgeschichte
AusQ — Australian Quarterly
AUSQA — Australian Quarterly
Aus Quart — Australian Quarterly
AUSRA — Records. Australian Academy of Science
AUSS — Andrews University. Seminary Studies
Ausschuss Wirtsch Fertigung Mitt — Ausschuss fuer Wirtschaftliche Fertigung Mitteilungen
Aus Sci Ind — Australian Science Index
Aussenpol — Aussenpolitik
Aussenpoli — Aussenpolitik
Aussenwirt — Aussenwirtschaft
Aus Speleo Abstr — Australian Speleo Abstracts
Aust — [The] Australian
Aust Aborig — Australian Aborigines Annual Bibliography
Aust Aborig Stud — Australian Aboriginal Studies
Aust Acacias — Australian Acacias
Aust Acad and Res Lib — Australian Academic and Research Libraries
Aust Acad H — Australian Academy of the Humanities. Proceedings
Aust Acad Res Libr — Australian Academic and Research Libraries
Aust Acad Sci Rep — Australian Academy of Science. Reports
Aust Acad Sci Sci Ind Forum Forum Rep — Australian Academy of Science. Science and Industry Forum. Forum Report
Aust Acad Sci Silver Jubilee Symp — Australian Academy of Science. Silver Jubilee Symposium
Aust Acc — Australian Accountant
Aust Accnt — Australian Accountant
Aust Accountancy Progress — Australian Accountancy Progress
Aust Accountancy Student — Australian Accountancy Student
Aust Accountant — Australian Accountant
Aust Acct — Australian Accountant
Aust Acctnt — Australian Accountant
Aust Acct Stud — Australian Accountancy Student
Aust Adv Vet Sci — Australian Advances in Veterinary Science
Aust AEC AAEC/E Rep — Australian Atomic Energy Commission. AAEC/E. Report
Aust AEC AAEC/TM Rep — Australian Atomic Energy Commission. AAEC/TM. Report
Aust AEC Inf Pap — Australian Atomic Energy Commission. Information Paper
Aust AEC Res Establ AAEC/E — Australian Atomic Energy Commission Research Establishment. AAEC/E
Aust AEC Res Establ Rep — Australian Atomic Energy Commission. Research Establishment. Report
Aust AEC Res Establ Rep AAEC/S — Australian Atomic Energy Commission. Research Establishment. Report AAEC/S
Aust AEC TRG Rep — Australian Atomic Energy Commission. TRG Report
Aust Aeronaut Comm Rep ACA — Australian Aeronautical Research Committee. Report ACA
Aust Aeronaut Res Comm Rep — Australian Aeronautical Research Committee. Report
Aust Aeronaut Res Comm Rep ACA — Australian Aeronautical Research Committee. Report ACA
Aust Aeronaut Res Lab Aerodyn Rep — Australia. Aeronautical Research Laboratories. Aerodynamics Report
Aust Aeronaut Res Lab Guided Weapons Note — Australia. Aeronautical Research Laboratories. Guided Weapons Note
Aust Aeronaut Res Lab Mater Note — Australia. Aeronautical Research Laboratories. Materials Note
Aust Aeronaut Res Lab Mater Rep — Australia. Aeronautical Research Laboratories. Materials Report
Aust Aeronaut Res Lab Mech Eng Note — Australia. Aeronautical Research Laboratories. Mechanical Engineering Note
Aust Aeronaut Res Lab Mech Eng Rep — Australia. Aeronautical Research Laboratories. Mechanical Engineering Report
Aust Aeronaut Res Lab Metall Note — Australia. Aeronautical Research Laboratories. Metallurgy Note
Aust Aeronaut Res Lab Metall Rep — Australia. Aeronautical Research Laboratories. Metallurgy Report
Aust Aeronaut Res Lab Metall Tech Mem — Australia. Aeronautical Research Laboratories. Metallurgy Technical Memorandum
Aust Aeronaut Res Lab Rep MET — Australia. Aeronautical Research Laboratories. Report MET (Metallurgy)
Aust Aeronaut Res Lab Struct — Australia. Aeronautical Research Laboratories. Structures and Materials Note
Aust Aeronaut Res Lab Struct Mater Note — Australia. Aeronautical Research Laboratories. Structures and Materials Note
Aust Aeronaut Res Lab Struct Mater Rep — Australia. Aeronautical Research Laboratories. Structures and Materials Report
Aust Aeronaut Res Lab Struct Note — Australia. Aeronautical Research Laboratories. Structures Note
Aust Aeronaut Res Lab Struct Rep — Australia. Aeronautical Research Laboratories. Structures Report
Aust Agric News — Australian Agricultural Newsletter
Aust Amateur Mineral — Australian Amateur Mineralogist

Aust Amateur Mineralogist — Australian Amateur Mineralogist
Aust Amat Miner — Australian Amateur Mineralogist
Aust-American Assn Canb News Bul — Australian-American Association in Canberra. News Bulletin
Aust-American J — Australian-American Journal
Aust & NZ Environ Rep — Australian and New Zealand Environmental Report
Aust & NZ General Practitioner — Australian and New Zealand General Practitioner
Aust & NZJ Crim — Australian and New Zealand Journal of Criminology
Aust & NZ J Criminol — Australian and New Zealand Journal of Criminology
Aust & NZ J Surgery — Australian and New Zealand Journal of Surgery
Aust & NZ W — Australia and New Zealand Weekly
Aust & Pac Book Prices Curr — Australian and Pacific Book Prices Current
Aust Ann Med — Australasian Annals of Medicine
Aust Ann of Med — Australasian Annals of Medicine
Aust Arab Horse News — Australian Arabian Horse News
Aust Archaeol — Australian Archaeology
Aust Argus L Rep — Australian Argus Law Reports
Aust Army J — Australian Army Journal
Aust Aronaut Lab Struct Mater Rep — Australia. Aeronautical Research Laboratories. Structures and Materials Report
Aust Aronaut Res Lab Metall Tech Memo — Australia. Aeronautical Research Laboratories. Metallurgy Technical Memorandum
Aust As Rp — Report of the Meeting of the Australasian Association for the Advancement of Science
Aust Assoc Neurol Proc — Australian Association of Neurologists. Proceedings
Aust At Energy Symp Proc — Australian Atomic Energy Symposium. Proceedings of a Symposium on the Peaceful Uses of Atomic Energy. University of Sydney, June 2-6, 1958
Austauschbarkeit Gasen Vortr Semin — Austauschbarkeit von Gasen. Vortraege zum Seminar
Aust Auth — Australian Author
Aust Automobile Trade J — Australian Automobile Trade Journal
Aust Automot Eng & Equip — Australian Automotive Engineering and Equipment
Aust Aviation Newsletter — Australian Aviation Newsletter
Aust Aviat Newsl — Australian Aviation Newsletter
Aust Aviat Yb — Australian Aviation Yearbook
Aust Avicult — Australian Aviculture
Aust Baker — Australian Baker and Millers' Journal
Aust Bank — Australian Banker
Aust Bankr Cas — Australian Bankruptcy Cases
Aust Baptist — Australian Baptist
Aust Bar Gaz — Australian Bar Gazette
Aust Bar Rev — Australian Bar Review
Aust Bee J — Australian Bee Journal
Aust Bib R — Australian Biblical Review
Aust Biochem Soc Proc — Australian Biochemical Society. Proceedings
Aust Bird Bander — Australian Bird Bander
Aust Birdwatcher — Australian Birdwatcher
Aust BL — Australian Bulletin of Labour
Aust Bldg Forum — Australia Building Forum
Aust Bldr — Australian Builder
Aust Boat Ind — Australian Boating Industry
Aust Boating — Australian Boating
Aust Book Auction Rec — Australian Book Auction Records
Aust Book R — Australian Book Review
Aust Book Rev — Australian Book Review
Aust Book Rev Children's Book & Ed Suppl — Australian Book Review. Children's Books and Educational Supplement
Aust Brewing Wine J — Australian Brewing and Wine Journal
Aust Brit Bus Dir — Australian British Business Directory
Aust Build — Australian Builder
Aust Builder — Australian Builder
Aust Build Forum — Australian Building Forum
Aust Build Sci Technol — Australian Building Science and Technology
Aust Build Technol — Australian Building Technology
Aust Bull Labour — Australian Bulletin of Labour
Aust Bur Miner Resour Geol Geophys BMR J Aust Geol Geophys — Australia. Bureau of Mineral Resources. Geology and Geophysics. BMR Journal of Australian Geology and Geophysics
Aust Bur Miner Resour Geol Geophys Bull — Australia. Bureau of Mineral Resources. Geology and Geophysics. Bulletin
Aust Bur Miner Resour Geol Geophys Pam — Australia. Bureau of Mineral Resources. Geology and Geophysics. Pamphlet
Aust Bur Miner Resour Geol Geophys Rep — Australia. Bureau of Mineral Resources. Geology and Geophysics. Report
Aust Bur Stat Adopt — Australia. Bureau of Statistics. Adoptions
Aust Bur Stat Bank Aust — Australia. Bureau of Statistics. Banking Australia
Aust Bur Stat Fin Co Aust — Australia. Bureau of Statistics. Finance Companies, Australia
Aust Bur Stat Rural Ind Bul — Australia. Bureau of Statistics. Rural Industries Bulletin
Aust Bur Stat Tech Pap — Australia. Bureau of Statisticss. Technical Papers
Aust Bus — Australian Business
Aust Bus Cond Bull — Australasian Business Conditions Bulletin
Aust Bush Nursing J — Australian Bush Nursing Journal
Aust Business L Rev — Australian Business Law Review
Aust Bus Law R — Australian Business Law Review
Aust Bus L Rev — Australian Business Law Review
Aust Bus Rev — Australian Business Law Review
Aust Camera — Australian Camera and Cine
Aust Canegrow — Australian Canegrower
Aust Canning Convention — Australian Canning Convention. Proceedings
Aust Canning Convention Procs — Australian Canning Convention. Proceedings
Aust Cath Hist Soc J — Australian Catholic Historical Society. Journal

Aust Catholic D — Australian Catholic Digest
Aust Catholic Truth Soc Rec — Australian Catholic Truth Society. Record
Aust Cent Int Agric Res Proc — Australian Centre for International Agricultural Research Proceedings
Aust Cent Int Agric Res Tech Rep — Australian Centre for International Agricultural Research Technical Reports
Aust Ceram Conf Proc — Australian Ceramic Conference. Proceedings
Aust Chem Abstr — Australian Chemical Abstracts
Aust Chem Eng — Australian Chemical Engineering
Aust Chem Eng Conf — Australian Chemical Engineering. Conference
Aust Chem Engineering — Australian Chemical Engineering
Aust Chem Engng — Australian Chemical Engineering
Aust Chem Inst J Proc — Australian Chemical Institute. Journal and Proceedings
Aust Chem Inst J Proc Suppl — Australian Chemical Institute Journal and Proceedings. Supplement
Aust Chem Proc — Australian Chemical Processing
Aust Chem Process — Australian Chemical Processing
Aust Chem Process Eng — Australian Chemical Processing and Engineering
Aust Chem Process Engng — Australian Chemical Processing and Engineering
Aust Chem Processing — Australian Chemical Processing
Aust Child Fam Welfare — Australian Child and Family Welfare
Aust Child Limited — Australian Children Limited
Aust Child Ltd — Australian Children Limited
Aust Children Ltd — Australian Children Limited
Aust Christian — Australian Christian
Aust Church Q — Australian Church Quarterly
Aust Church Rec — Australian Church Record
Aust Citizen Ltd — Australian Citizen Limited
Aust Citrus News — Australian Citrus News
Aust Civ Eng — Australian Civil Engineering
Aust Civ Engng — Australian Civil Engineering
Aust Civ Engng Constr — Australian Civil Engineering and Construction
Aust Civil Eng Construc — Australian Civil Engineering and Construction
Aust Climatol Summ — Australian Climatological Summary
Aust Clin Rev — Australian Clinical Review
Aust CL Rev — Australian Current Law Review
Aust Coal & Harbour — Australian Coal, Shipping, Steel, and the Harbour
Aust Coal Ass (Res) Rep — Australian Coal Association (Research) Limited. Report
Aust Coal Ind Res Lab Publ Rep PR — Australian Coal Industry Research Laboratories. Published Report. PR
Aust Coalmining — Australian Coalmining and Mine Mechanisation
Aust Coal Prep Conf — Australian Coal Preparation Conference
Aust Coin — Australian Coin Review
Aust Coll Educ Vic Chapter Newsl — Australian College of Education. Victorian Chapter. Newsletter
Aust Coll Speech Ther J — Australian College of Speech Therapists. Journal
Aust Commonw Advis Counc Sci Ind Bull — Australia. Commonwealth Advisory Council of Science and Industry. Bulletin
Aust Commonw Advis Counc Sci Ind Pam — Australia. Commonwealth Advisory Council of Science and Industry. Pamphlet
Aust Commonw Counc Sci Ind Res Bull — Australia. Commonwealth Council for Scientific and Industrial Research. Bulletin
Aust Commonw Counc Sci Ind Res Pam — Australia. Commonwealth Council for Scientific and Industrial Research. Pamphlet
Aust Commonw CSIR Bull — Australia. Commonwealth. Council for Scientific and Industrial Research. Bulletin
Aust Commonw CSIR Pam — Australia. Commonwealth. Council for Scientific and Industrial Research. Pamphlet
Aust Commonw Dep Supply Aeronaut Res Comm Rep ACA — Australia. Commonwealth Department of Supply. Aeronautical Research Committee. Report ACA
Aust Commonw Dep Supply Aeronaut Res Consult Comm Rep ACA — Australia. Commonwealth Department of Supply. Aeronautical Research Consultative Committee. Report ACA
Aust Commonw Dep Supply Aeronaut Res Guided Weapons Note — Australia. Commonwealth Department of Supply. Aeronautical Research Laboratories. Guided Weapons Note
Aust Commonw Dep Supply Aeronaut Res Lab Guided Weapons Note — Australia. Commonwealth. Department of Supply. Aeronautical Research Laboratories. Guided Weapons Note
Aust Commonw Dep Supply Aeronaut Res Lab Metall Note — Australia. Commonwealth Department of Supply. Aeronautical Research Laboratories. Metallurgy Note
Aust Commonw Dep Supply Aeronaut Res Lab Metall Tech Memo — Australia. Commonwealth Department of Supply. Aeronautical Research Laboratories. Metallurgy Technical Memorandum
Aust Commonw Dep Supply Aeronaut Res Lab Rep MET — Australia. Commonwealth Department of Supply. Aeronautical Research Laboratories. Report MET (Metallurgy)
Aust Commonw Dep Supply Aeronaut Res Lab Rep SM — Australia. Commonwealth Department of Supply. Aeronautical Research Laboratories. Report SM
Aust Commonw Dep Supply Def Res Lab Rep — Australia. Commonwealth Department of Supply. Defence Research Laboratories. Report
Aust Commonw Dep Supply Def Res Lab Report — Australia. Commonwealth Department of Supply. Defence Research Laboratories. Report
Aust Commonw Dep Supply Def Res Lab Tech Note — Australia. Commonwealth Department of Supply. Defence Research Aboratories. Technical Note
Aust Commonw Dep Supply Def Stand Lab Rep — Australia. Commonwealth Department of Supply. Defence Standards Laboratories. Report
Aust Commonw Dep Supply Def Stand Lab Tech Note — Australia. Commonwealth Department of Supply. Defence Standards Laboratories. Technical Note

Aust Commonw Dep Supply Res Lab Tech Note — Australia. Commonwealth Department of Supply. Defence Research Laboratories. Technical Note
Aust Commonw Dept Supply Aeronaut Res Comm Rep — Australia. Commonwealth Department of Supply. Aeronautical Research Committee. Report
Aust Commonw Inst Sci Ind Bull — Australia. Commonwealth Institute of Science and Industry. Bulletin
Aust Commonw Inst Sci Ind Pam — Australia. Commonwealth Institute of Science and Industry. Pamphlet
Aust Commonw Sci Ind Res Organ Div Metrol Tech Pap — Australia. Commonwealth Scientific and Industrial Research Organisation. Division of Metrology. Technical Paper
Aust Comp Law Cases — Australian Company Law Cases
Aust Comput Bull — Australian Computer Bulletin
Aust Comput J — Australian Computer Journal
Aust Comput Sci Commun — Australian Computer Science Communications
Aust Conf Chem Eng — Australian Conference on Chemical Engineering
Aust Conf Eng Mater Proc — Australian Conference on Engineering Materials. Proceedings
Aust Conf Nucl Tech Anal Proc — Australian Conference on Nuclear Techniques of Analysis. Proceedings
Aust Conf Nucl Tech Anal Summ Proc — Australian Conference on Nuclear Techniques of Analysis. Summary of Proceedings
Aust Con LR — Australian Construction Law Reporter
Aust Conserv Found Newsl — Australian Conservation Foundation. Newsletter
Aust Conv — Australian Conveyancer and Solicitors' Journal
Aust Conveyancer — Australian Conveyancer and Solicitors' Journal
Aust Conv Sol J — Australian Conveyancer and Solicitors' Journal
Aust Cordial Maker — Australian Cordial Maker, Brewer, and Bottler's Gazette
Aust Corr Eng — Australian Corrosion Engineering
Aust Corros Eng — Australian Corrosion Engineering
Aust Corros Engng — Australian Corrosion Engineering
Aust Corrosion Eng — Australian Corrosion Engineering
Aust Cott Grow — Australian Cotton Grower
Aust Cott Grow Fmr Dairym — Australian Cotton Grower, Farmer, and Dairyman
Aust Counc Aeronaut Rep ACA — Australian Council for Aeronautics. Report ACA
Aust Counc Educ Admin — Australian Council for Educational Administration. Bulletin
Aust Country — Australian Country Magazine
Aust Country Mag — Australian Country Magazine
Aust CSIRO Abstr Publ Pap List Transl — Australia. Commonwealth Scientific and Industrial Research Organisation. Abstracts of Published Papers and List of Translations
Aust CSIRO Anim Res Lab Tech Pap — Australia. Commonwealth Scientific and Industrial Research Organisation. AnimalResearch Laboratories. Technical Paper
Aust CSIRO Annu Rep — Australia. Commonwealth Scientific and Industrial Research Organisation. AnnualReport
Aust CSIRO Bull — Australia. Commonwealth Scientific and Industrial Research Organisation. Bulletin
Aust CSIRO Chem Res Lab Tech Pap — Australia. Commonwealth Scientific and Industrial Research Organisation. Chemical Research Laboratories. Technical Paper
Aust CSIRO Coal Res Div Locat Rep — Australia. Commonwealth Scientific and Industrial Research Organisation. Coal Research Division. Location Report
Aust CSIRO Coal Res Div Misc Rep — Australia. Commonwealth Scientific and Industrial Research Organisation. Coal Research Division. Miscellaneous Report
Aust CSIRO Coal Res Div Tech Commun — Australia. Commonwealth Scientific and Industrial Research Organisation. Coal Research Division. Technical Communication
Aust CSIRO Coal Res Lab Locat Rep — Australia. Commonwealth Scientific and Industrial Research Organization. Coal Research Laboratory Location Report
Aust CSIRO CSIRO Wildl Res — Australia. Commonwealth Scientific and Industrial Research Organisation. CSIRO Wildlife Research
Aust CSIRO Div Anim Genet Res Rep — Australia. Commonwealth Scientific and Industrial Research Organisation. Division of Animal Genetics. Research Report
Aust CSIRO Div Anim Health Annu Rep — Australia. Commonwealth Scientific and Industrial Research Organisation. Division of Animal Health. Annual Report
Aust CSIRO Div Anim Health Prod Tech Pap — Australia. Commonwealth Scientific and Industrial Research Organisation. Division of Animal Health and Production. Technical Paper
Aust CSIRO Div Anim Physiol Annu Rep — Australia. Commonwealth Scientific and Industrial Research Organisation. Division of Animal Physiology. Annual Report
Aust CSIRO Div Appl Chem Annu Rep — Australia. Commonwealth Scientific and Industrial Research Organisation. Division of Applied Chemistry. Annual Report
Aust CSIRO Div Appl Chem Tech Pap — Australia. Commonwealth Scientific and Industrial Research Organisation. Division of Applied Chemistry. Technical Paper
Aust CSIRO Div Appl Geomech Tech Memo — Australia. Commonwealth Scientific and Industrial Research Organisation. Division of Applied Geomechanics. Technical Memorandum
Aust CSIRO Div Appl Geomech Tech Pap — Australia. Commonwealth Scientific and Industrial Research Organisation. Division of Applied Geomechanics. Technical Paper
Aust CSIRO Div Appl Geomech Tech Rep — Australia. Commonwealth Scientific and Industrial Research Organisation. Division of Applied Geomechanics. Technical Report
Aust CSIRO Div Appl Org Chem Res Rep — Australia. Commonwealth Scientific and Industrial Research Organisation. Division of Applied Organic Chemistry. Research Report
Aust CSIRO Div Appl Org Chem Tech Pap — Australia. Commonwealth Scientific and Industrial Research Organisation. Division of Applied Organic Chemistry. Technical Paper

Aust CSIRO Div Atmos Phys Tech Pap — Australia. Commonwealth Scientific and Industrial Research Organisation. Division of Atmospheric Physics. Technical Paper

Aust CSIRO Div Build Res Annu Rep — Australia. Commonwealth Scientific and Industrial Research Organisation. Division of Building Research. Annual Report

Aust CSIRO Div Build Res Tech Pap — Australia. Commonwealth Scientific and Industrial Research Organisation. Division of Building Research. Technical Paper

Aust CSIRO Div Chem Eng Rep — Australia. Commonwealth Scientific and Industrial Research Organisation. Division of Chemical Engineering. Report

Aust CSIRO Div Chem Phys Annu Rep — Australia. Commonwealth Scientific and Industrial Research Organisation. Division of Chemical Physics. Annual Report

Aust CSIRO Div Chem Technol Res Rev — Australia. Commonwealth Scientific and Industrial Research Organisation. Division of Chemical Technology. Research Review

Aust CSIRO Div Chem Technol Tech Pap — Australia. Commonwealth Scientific and Industrial Research Organisation. Division of Chemical Technology. Technical Paper

Aust CSIRO Div Coal Res Locat Rep — Australia. Commonwealth Scientific and Industrial Research Organisation. Division of Coal Research. Location Report

Aust CSIRO Div Coal Res Misc Rep — Australia. Commonwealth Scientific and Industrial Research Organisation. Division of Coal Research. Miscellaneous Report

Aust CSIRO Div Coal Res Ref LR — Australia. Commonwealth Scientific and Industrial Research Organisation. Division of Coal Research. Reference LR

Aust CSIRO Div Coal Res Tech Commun — Australia. Commonwealth Scientific and Industrial Research Organisation. Division of Coal Research. Technical Communication

Aust CSIRO Div Dairy Res Annu Rep — Australia. Commonwealth Scientific and Industrial Research Organisation. Division of Dairy Research. Annual Report

Aust CSIRO Div Entomol Annu Rep — Australia. Commonwealth Scientific and Industrial Research Organisation. Division of Entomology. Annual Report

Aust CSIRO Div Entomol Tech Pap — Australia. Commonwealth Scientific and Industrial Research Organisation. Division of Entomology. Technical Paper

Aust CSIRO Div Fish Oceanogr Annu Rep — Australia. Commonwealth Scientific and Industrial Research Organisation. Division of Fisheries and Oceanography. Annual Report

Aust CSIRO Div Fish Oceanogr Circ — Australia. Commonwealth Scientific and Industrial Research Organisation. Division of Fisheries and Oceanography. Circular

Aust CSIRO Div Fish Oceanogr Rep — Australia. Commonwealth Scientific and Industrial Research Organisation. Division of Fisheries and Oceanography. Report

Aust CSIRO Div Fish Oceanogr Tech Pap — Australia. Commonwealth Scientific and Industrial Research Organisation. Division of Fisheries and Oceanography. Technical Paper

Aust CSIRO Div Fish Tech Pap — Australia. Commonwealth Scientific and Industrial Research Organisation. Division of Fisheries. Technical Paper

Aust CSIRO Div Food Preserv Rep Res — Australia. Commonwealth Scientific and Industrial Research Organisation. Division of Food Preservation. Report of Research

Aust CSIRO Div Food Preserv Tech Pap — Australia. Commonwealth Scientific and Industrial Research Organisation. Division of Food Preservation. Technical Paper

Aust CSIRO Div Food Preserv Transp Tech Pap — Australia. Commonwealth Scientific and Industrial Research Organisation. Division of Food Preservation and Transport. Technical Paper

Aust CSIRO Div Food Res Rep Res — Australia. Commonwealth Scientific and Industrial Research Organisation. Division of Food Research. Report of Research

Aust CSIRO Div Food Res Tech Pap — Australia. Commonwealth Scientific and Industrial Research Organisation. Division of Food Research. Technical Paper

Aust CSIRO Div For Prod For Prod Newsl — Australia. Commonwealth Scientific and Industrial Research Organisation. Division of Forest Products. Forest Products Newsletter

Aust CSIRO Div For Prod Technol Pap — Australia. Commonwealth Scientific and Industrial Research Organisation. Division of Forest Products. Technological Paper

Aust CSIRO Div For Res Annu Rep — Australia. Commonwealth Scientific and Industrial Research Organisation. Division of Forest Research. Annual Report

Aust CSIRO Div Hortic Res Rep — Australia. Commonwealth Scientific and Industrial Research Organisation. Division of Horticulture. Research Report

Aust CSIRO Div Ind Chem Tech Pap — Australia. Commonwealth Scientific and Industrial Research Organisation. Division of Industrial Chemistry. Technical Paper

Aust CSIRO Div Irrig Res Annu Rep — Australia. Commonwealth Scientific and Industrial Research Organisation. Division of Irrigation Research. Annual Report

Aust CSIRO Div Irrig Res Rep — Australia. Commonwealth Scientific and Industrial Research Organisation. Division of Irrigation. Research Report

Aust CSIRO Div Land Resour Manage Tech Pap — Australia. Commonwealth Scientific and Industrial Research Organisation. Division of Land Resources Management. Technical Paper

Aust CSIRO Div Land Res Reg Surv Tech Pap — Australia. Commonwealth Scientific and Industrial Research Organisation. Division of Land Research and Regional Survey. Technical Paper

Aust CSIRO Div Land Res Tech Pap — Australia. Commonwealth Scientific and Industrial Research Organisation. Division of Land Research. Technical Paper

Aust CSIRO Div Land Use Res Tech Pap — Australia. Commonwealth Scientific and Industrial Research Organisation. Division of Land Use Research. Technical Paper

Aust CSIRO Div Math Stat Tech Pap — Australia. Commonwealth Scientific and Industrial Research Organisation. Division of Mathematical Statistics. Technical Paper

Aust CSIRO Div Mech Eng Annu Rep — Australia. Commonwealth Scientific and Industrial Research Organisation. Division of Mechanical Engineering. Annual Report

Aust CSIRO Div Meteorol Phys Tech Pap — Australia. Commonwealth Scientific and Industrial Research Organisation. Division of Meteorological Physics. Technical Paper

Aust CSIRO Div Metrol Tech Pap — Australia. Commonwealth Scientific and Industrial Research Organisation. Division of Metrology. Technical Paper

Aust CSIRO Div Mineral Tech Commun — Australia. Commonwealth Scientific and Industrial Research Organisation. Division of Mineralogy. Technical Communication

Aust CSIRO Div Miner Chem Invest Rep — Australia. Commonwealth Scientific and Industrial Research Organisation. Division of Mineral Chemistry. Investigation Report

Aust CSIRO Div Miner Chem Locat Rep — Australia. Commonwealth Scientific and Industrial Research Organisation. Division of Mineral Chemistry. Location Report

Aust CSIRO Div Miner Chem Tech Commun — Australia. Commonwealth Scientific and Industrial Research Organisation. Division of Mineral Chemistry. Technical Communication

Aust CSIRO Div Nutr Biochem Res Rep — Australia. Commonwealth Scientific and Industrial Research Organisation. Division of Nutritional Biochemistry. Research Report

Aust CSIRO Div Plant Ind Annu Rep — Australia. Commonwealth Scientific and Industrial Research Organisation. Division of Plant Industry. Annual Report

Aust CSIRO Div Plant Ind Field Stn Rec — Australia. Commonwealth Scientific and Industrial Research Organisation. Division of Plant Industry. Field Station Record

Aust CSIRO Div Plant Ind Tech Pap — Australia. Commonwealth Scientific and Industrial Research Organisation. Division of Plant Industry. Technical Paper

Aust CSIRO Div Soil Mech Tech Pap — Australia. Commonwealth Scientific and Industrial Research Organisation. Division of Soil Mechanics. Technical Paper

Aust CSIRO Div Soil Res Tech Pap — Australia. Commonwealth Scientific and Industrial Research Organisation. Division of Soil Research. Technical Paper

Aust CSIRO Div Soils Div Rep — Australia. Commonwealth Scientific and Industrial Research Organisation. Division of Soils. Divisional Report

Aust CSIRO Div Soils Notes Soil Tech — Australia. Commonwealth Scientific and Industrial Research Organisation. Division of Soils. Notes on Soil Techniques

Aust CSIRO Div Soils Rep Prog — Australia. Commonwealth Scientific and Industrial Research Organisation. Division of Soils. Report on Progress

Aust CSIRO Div Soils Soils Land Use Ser — Australia. Commonwealth Scientific and Industrial Research Organisation. Division of Soils. Soils and Land Use Series

Aust CSIRO Div Soils Tech Pap — Australia. Commonwealth Scientific and Industrial Research Organisation. Division of Soils. Technical Paper

Aust CSIRO Div Text Ind Rep — Australia. Commonwealth Scientific and Industrial Research Organisation. Division of Textile Industry. Report

Aust CSIRO Div Trop Agron Annu Rep — Australia. Commonwealth Scientific and Industrial Research Organisation. Division of Tropical Agronomy. Annual Report

Aust CSIRO Div Trop Agron Tech Pap — Australia. Commonwealth Scientific and Industrial Research Organisation. Division of Tropical Agronomy. Technical Paper

Aust CSIRO Div Trop Crops Pastures Tech Pap — Australia. Commonwealth Scientific and Industrial Research Organisation. Division of Tropical Crops and Pastures. Technical Paper

Aust CSIRO Div Trop Crops Pastures Trop Agron Tech Memo — Australia. Commonwealth Scientific and Industrial Research Organisation. Division of Tropical Crops and Pastures. Tropical Agronomy. Technical Memorandum

Aust CSIRO Div Trop Pastures Annu Rep — Australia. Commonwealth Scientific and Industrial Research Organisation. Division of Tropical Pastures. Annual Report

Aust CSIRO Div Trop Pastures Tech Pap — Australia. Commonwealth Scientific and Industrial Research Organisation. Division of Tropical Pastures. Technical Paper

Aust CSIRO Div Water Land Resour Div Rep — Australia. Commonwealth Scientific and Industrial Research Organisation. Division of Water and Land Resources. Divisional Report

Aust CSIRO Div Water Land Resour Nat Resour Ser — Australia. Commonwealth Scientific and Industrial Research Organisation. Division of Water and Land Resources. Natural Resources Series

Aust CSIRO Div Water Resour Div Rep — Australia. Commonwealth Scientific and Industrial Research Organisation. Division of Water Resources. Divisional Report

Aust CSIRO Div Wildl Rangelands Res Tech Pap — Australia. Commonwealth Scientific and Industrial Research Organisation. Division of Wildlife and Rangelands Research. Technical Paper

Aust CSIRO Div Wildl Res Rep — Australia. Commonwealth Scientific and Industrial Research Organisation. Division of Wildlife Research. Report

Aust CSIRO Div Wildl Res Tech Pap — Australia. Commonwealth Scientific and Industrial Research Organisation. Division of Wildlife Research. Technical Paper

Aust CSIRO Food Preserv Q — Australia. Commonwealth Scientific and Industrial Research Organisation. Food Preservation Quarterly

Aust CSIRO Food Res Q — Australia. Commonwealth Scientific and Industrial Research Organisation. Food Research Quarterly

Aust CSIRO For Prod Lab Div Appl Chem Technol Pap — Australia. Commonwealth Scientific and Industrial Research Organisation. ForestProducts Laboratory. Division of Applied Chemistry. Technological Paper

Aust CSIRO For Prod Lab Div Build Res Technol Pap — Australia. Commonwealth Scientific and Industrial Research Organisation. ForestProducts Laboratory. Division of Building Research. Technological Paper

Aust CSIRO For Prod Lab Technol Pap — Australia. Commonwealth Scientific and Industrial Research Organisation. ForestProducts Laboratory. Technological Paper

Aust CSIRO Inst Biol Resour Div Water Land Resour Tech Memo — Australia. Commonwealth Scientific and Industrial Research Organisation.Institute of Biological Resources. Division of Water and Land Resources.Technical Memorandum

Aust CSIRO Inst Nat Resour Environ Div Water Resour Tech Mem — Australia. Commonwealth Scientific and Industrial Research Organisation.Institute of Natural Resources and Environment. Division of Water Resources.Technical Memorandum

Aust CSIRO Irrig Res Stn Techn Pap — Australia. Commonwealth Scientific and Industrial Research Organisation. Irrigation Research Stations. Technical Paper

Aust CSIRO Irrig Res Stn Tech Pap — Australia. Commonwealth Scientific and Industrial Research Organisation. Irrigation Research Stations. Technical Paper

Aust CSIRO Land Resour Lab Div Soils Bienn Rep — Australia. Commonwealth Scientific and Industrial Research Organisation. Land Resources Laboratories. Division of Soils. Biennial Report

Aust CSIRO Land Resour Manage Tech Pap — Australia. Commonwealth Scientific and Industrial Research Organisation. Land Resources Management Technical Paper

Aust CSIRO Land Res Ser — Australia. Commonwealth Scientific and Industrial Research Organisation. Land Research Series

Aust CSIRO Mar Biochem Unit Annu Rep — Australia. Commonwealth Scientific and Industrial Research Organisation. MarineBiochemistry Unit. Annual Report

Aust CSIRO Mar Lab Rep — Australia. Commonwealth Scientific and Industrial Research Organisation. MarineLaboratories Report

Aust CSIRO Min Dep Univ Melbourne Ore Dressing Invest Rep — Australia. Commonwealth Scientific and Industrial Research Organisation. MiningDepartment. University of Melbourne. Ore Dressing Investigations. Report

Aust CSIRO Mineragraphic Invest Tech Pap — Australia. Commonwealth Scientific and Industrial Research Organisation. Mineragraphic Investigations. Technical Paper

Aust CSIRO Miner Res Lab Annu Rep — Australia. Commonwealth Scientific and Industrial Research Organisation. Minerals Research Laboratories. Annual Report

Aust CSIRO Miner Res Lab Invest Rep — Australia. Commonwealth Scientific and Industrial Research Organisation. Minerals Research Laboratories. Investigation Report

Aust CSIRO Natl Meas Lab Bienn Rep — Australia. Commonwealth Scientific and Industrial Research Organisation. National Measurement Laboratory. Biennial Report

Aust CSIRO Natl Meas Lab Tech Pap — Australia. Commonwealth Scientific and Industrial Research Organisation. National Measurement Laboratory. Technical Paper

Aust CSIRO Natl Stand Lab Bienn Rep — Australia. Commonwealth Scientific and Industrial Research Organisation. National Standards Laboratory. Biennial Report

Aust CSIRO Natl Stand Lab Tech Pap — Australia. Commonwealth Scientific and Industrial Research Organisation. National Standards Laboratory. Technical Paper

Aust CSIRO Nat Stand Lab Tech Pap — Australia. Commonwealth Scientific and Industrial Research Organisation. National Standards Laboratory. Technical Paper

Aust CSIRO Sch Mines West Aust Kalgoorlie Ore Dressing Inves — Australia. Commonwealth Scientific and Industrial Research Organization and theSchool of Mines of Western Australia. Kalgoorlie. Ore Dressing Investigations

Aust CSIRO Soil Mech Sect Tech Memo — Australia. Commonwealth Scientific and Industrial Research Organisation. Soil Mechanics Section. Technical Memorandum

Aust CSIRO Soil Mech Sect Tech Pap — Australia. Commonwealth Scientific and Industrial Research Organisation. Soil Mechanics Section. Technical Paper

Aust CSIRO Soil Publ — Australia. Commonwealth Scientific and Industrial Research Organisation. Soil Publication

Aust CSIRO Soils Land Use Ser — Australia. Commonwealth Scientific and Industrial Research Organisation. Soils and Land Use Series

Aust CSIRO Trop Crops & Pastures Div Rep — Australia. Commonwealth Scientific and Industrial Research Organisation. Tropical Crops and Pastures. Divisional Report

Aust CSIRO Trop Crops Pastures Ann Rep — Australia. Commonwealth Scientific and Industrial Research Organisation. Tropical Crops and Pastures. Annual Report

Aust CSIRO Wheat Res Unit Annu Rep — Australia. Commonwealth Scientific and Industrial Research Organisation. Wheat Research Unit. Annual Report

Aust CSIRO Wildl Res — Australia. Commonwealth Scientific and Industrial Research Organisation. Wildlife Research

Aust CSIRO Wildl Surv Sect Tech Pap — Australia. Commonwealth Scientific and Industrial Research Organisation. Wildlife Survey Section. Technical Paper

Aust Ctry Mag — Australian Country Magazine

Aust Culturist — Australian Culturist

Aust Curr Law Rev — Australian Current Law Review

Aust Curr L Rev — Australian Current Law Review

Aust Dairy R — Australian Dairy Review

Aust Dairy Rev — Australian Dairy Review

Aust Def Res Lab Paint Notes — Australia. Defence Research Laboratories. Paint Notes

Aust Def Res Lab Plat Notes — Australia. Defence Research Laboratories. Plating Notes

Aust Def Sci Serv Mater Res Lab Tech Note — Australian Defence Scientific Service. Materials Research Laboratory. TechnicalNote

Aust Def Sci Serv Weapons Res Est Tech Note — Australian Defence Scientific Service. Weapons Research Establishment. Technical Note

Aust Def Sc Serv ARL Report — Australian Defence Scientific Service. Aeronautical Research Laboratories. Report

Aust Def Stand Lab Rep — Australia. Defence Standards Laboratories. Report

Aust Def Stand Lab Tech Mem — Australia. Defence Standards Laboratories. Technical Memorandum

Aust Def Stand Lab Tech Memo — Australia. Defence Standards Laboratories. Technical Memorandum

Aust Def Stand Lab Tech Note — Australia. Defence Standards Laboratories. Technical Note

Aust Demographic R — Australian Demographic Review

Aust Dental J — Australian Dental Journal

Aust Dent J — Australian Dental Journal

Aust Dent Mirr — Australian Dental Mirror

Aust Dent Summ — Australian Dental Summary

Aust Dep Agric Biol Branch Tech Pap — Australia. Department of Agriculture. Biology Branch. Technical Paper

Aust Dep Def Mater Res Lab Rep — Australia. Department of Defence. Materials Research Laboratories. Report

Aust Dep Def Mater Res Lab Tech Note — Australia. Department of Defence. Materials Research Laboratories. Technical Note

Aust Dep Def Weapons Res Establ Tech Rep — Australia. Department of Defence. Weapons Research Establishment. Technical Report

Aust Dep Health Aust Radiat Lab Tech Rep ARL/TR — Australia. Department of Health. Australian Radiation Laboratory. Technical Report Series ARL/TR

Aust Dep Health Aust Radiat Lab Tech Rep Ser ARL/TR — Australia. Department of Health. Australian Radiation Laboratory. Technical Report Series ARL/TR

Aust Dep Munitions Paint Notes — Australia. Department of Munitions. Paint Notes

Aust Dep Supply Aeronaut Res Lab Mech Eng Note — Australia. Department of Supply. Aeronautical Research Laboratories. MechanicalEngineering Note

Aust Dep Supply Aeronaut Res Lab Struct Mater Note — Australia. Department of Supply. Aeronautical Research Laboratories. Structuresand Materials Note

Aust Dep Supply Def Res Lab Paint Notes — Australia. Department of Supply. Defence Research Laboratories. Paint Notes

Aust Dep Supply Def Res Lab Plat Notes — Australia. Department of Supply. Defence Research Laboratories. Plating Notes

Aust DFA Treaty Series — Australia. Department of Foreign Affairs. International Treaties and Conventions

Aust Digest — Australian Digest

Aust Dir — Australian Director

Aust Director — Australian Director

Aust Dirt Bike — Australasian Dirt Bike

AUSTDK — Austrobaileya

Aust Draftsmen — Australian Draftsmen

Aust Dried Fruit News — Australian Dried Fruit News

Aust Dr Wkly — Australian Doctor Weekly

Aust Early Child Resource Booklets — Australian Early Childhood Resource Booklets

Aust Econ — Australian Economic Papers

Aust Econ H — Australian Economic History Review

Aust Econ Hist R — Australian Economic History Review

Aust Econ Hist Rev — Australian Economic History Review

Aust Econ News Dig — Australian Economic News Digest

Aust Econ P — Australian Economic Papers

Aust Econ Pap — Australian Economic Papers

Aust Econ R — Australian Economic Review

Aust Econ Rev — Australian Economic Review

Aust Educ Index — Australian Education Index

Aust Educ R — Australian Education Review

Aust Educ Res — Australian Education Researcher

Aust Educ Res Dev Com Ann Rep — Australia. Education Research and Development Committee. Annual Report

Aust Educ Rev — Australian Education Review

Aust Electrochem Conf — Australian Electrochemistry Conference

Aust Electron Bull — Australian Electronics Bulletin

Aust Electron Eng — Australian Electronics Engineering

Aust Electron Engng — Australian Electronics Engineering

Aust Electron M — Australian Electronics Monthly

Aust Electr World — Australian Electrical World

Aust Elect Wld — Australian Electrical World

Aust Elec World — Australian Electrical World

Aust Encycl — Australian Encyclopaedia

Aust Endeavourer — Australian Endeavourer

Aust Engineer — Australasian Engineer

Aust Engr — Australasian Engineer

Aust Ent Mag — Australian Entomological Magazine

Aust Entomol Mag — Australian Entomological Magazine

Aust Entomol Soc J — Australian Entomological Society. Journal

Aust Entomol Soc Misc Publ — Australian Entomological Society. Miscellaneous Publication

Aust Eval Newsl — Australian Evaluation Newsletter

Aust Exporter — Australian Exporter

Aust External Terr — Australian External Territories

Aust Ext Terr — Australian External Territories

Aust Fact — Australian Factory

Aust Factory — Australian Factory

Aust Fam Physician — Australian Family Physician

Aust Fam Safe — Australian Family Safety

Aust Fashion News — Australian Fashion News

Aust Fd Manuf — Australian Food Manufacturer and Distributor

Aust Fd Mf — Australian Food Manufacturer and Distributor

Aust Fd Mfr — Australian Food Manufacturer and Distributor

Aust Financial R — Australian Financial Review

Aust Financial Rev — Australian Financial Review

Aust Financial Times — Australian Financial Times

Aust Financ Rev — Australian Financial Review

Aust Finish — Australian Finishing

Aust Finish Rev — Australian Finishing Review

Aust Fin Rev — Australian Financial Review

Aust Fish — Australian Fisheries
Aust Fish Dept Fish Inf Publ — Australia. Fisheries Department. Fisheries Information Publication
Aust Fish Educ Leafl — Australian Fisheries Education Leaflet
Aust Fish Newsl — Australian Fisheries Newsletter
Aust Fish Pap — Australian Fisheries Paper
Aust Fm Mgmt J — Australian Farm Management Journal
Aust Food Manuf — Australian Food Manufacturer and Distributor
Aust Food Manuf Distrib — Australian Food Manufacturer and Distributor
Aust Food Mfr Distrib — Australian Food Manufacturer and Distributor
Aust For — Australian Forestry
Aust For Aff R — Australian Foreign Affairs Record
Aust Foreign Aff Rec — Australian Foreign Affairs Record
Aust Foreign Aff Trade — Australian Foreign Affairs and Trade
Aust Forest — Australian Forest Research
Aust Forester — Australian Forester
Aust Forest Inds J — Australian Forest Industries Journal
Aust Forest Res — Australian Forest Research
Aust Forestry — Australian Forestry
Aust For Grow — Australian Forest Grower
Aust For Ind J — Australian Forest Industries Journal
Aust For Ind J Aust Log — Australian Forest Industries Journal and Australian Logger
Aust For J — Australian Forest Journal
Aust For (Perth) — Australian Forestry (Perth)
Aust For Res — Australian Forest Research
Aust For Resour — Australian Forest Resources
Aust For Tree Nutr Conf Contrib Pap — Australian Forest Tree Nutrition Conference. Contributed Papers
Aust Foundry Trade J — Australian Foundry Trade Journal
Aust Found Trade J — Australian Foundry Trade Journal
Aust Fract Group Conf Proc — Australian Fracture Group Conference. Proceedings
Aust Furn Trade J — Australian Furnishing Trade Journal
Aust Gas Bull — Australian Gas Bulletin
Aust Gas J — Australian Gas Journal
Aust Gem — Australian Gem and Treasure Hunter
Aust Gemmol — Australian Gemmologist
Aust Gemmologist — Australian Gemmologist
Aust Gems — Australian Gems and Crafts
Aust Geneal — Australian Genealogist
Aust Genealogist — Australian Genealogist
Aust Geog — Australian Geographer
Aust Geogr — Australian Geographer
Aust Geographer — Australian Geographer
Aust Geog Rec — Australian Geographical Record
Aust Geog Record — Australian Geographical Record
Aust Geogr Rec — Australian Geographical Record
Aust Geogr Stud — Australian Geographical Studies
Aust Geogr Studies — Australian Geographical Studies
Aust Geog S — Australian Geographical Studies
Aust Geog Stud — Australian Geographical Studies
Aust Geog Studies — Australian Geographical Studies
Aust Geol — Australian Geologist
Aust Geomechanics J — Australian Geomechanics Journal
Aust Geomech J — Australian Geomechanics Journal
Aust Gliding — Australian Gliding
Aust Goat World — Australian Goat World
Aust Gourmet — Australian Gourmet
Aust Gov Anal Lab Rep Invest — Australian Government Analytical Laboratories. Report of Investigations
Aust Gov Publ — Australian Government Publications
Aust Grade Teach — Australian Grade Teacher
Aust Grapegr — Australian Grapegrower [*Later, Australian Grapegrower and Winemaker*]
Aust Grapegrow — Australian Grapegrower and Winemaker
Aust Hand Weaver — Australian Hand Weaver and Spinner
Aust Hardware J — Australian Hardware Journal
Aust Her — Australia's Heritage
Aust Hereford A — Australian Hereford Annual
Aust Hereford Ann — Australian Hereford Annual
Aust Hereford Annu — Australian Hereford Annual
Aust Hereford J — Australian Hereford Journal
Aust Hereford Soc Q — Hereford Quarterly. Australian Hereford Society
Aust Hi-Fi — Australian Hi-Fi
Aust Highway — Australian Highway
Aust Hist Teach — Australian History Teacher
Aust Home Beaut — Australian Home Beautiful
Aust Home J — Australian Home Journal
Aust Homemaker — Australian Homemaker
Aust Hosp — Australian Hospital
Aust Hospital — Australian Hospital
Aust House and Garden — Australian House and Garden
Aust House Gard — Australian House and Garden
Aust Housing — Australian Housing
Aust Human Res Cncl A Rept — Australian Humanities Research Council. Annual Report
Aust Hwy — Australian Highway
Aust Immigr Consol Stat — Australian Immigration: Consolidated Statistics
Austin BJ — Austin Business Journal
Aust Ind Assist Com Ann Rep — Australia. Industries Assistance Commission. Annual Report
Aust Ind Dev Assoc Dir Repts — Australian Industries Development Association. Director Reports

Aust Ind Development Assn Director Report — Australian Industries Development Association. Director Reports
Aust Ind LR — Australian Industrial Law Review
Aust Ind Min Stand — Australian Industrial and Mining Standard
Austin Sem Bul — Austin Seminary Bulletin. Faculty Edition
Aust Inst Energy Natl Conf Pap — Australian Institute of Energy National Conference. Papers
Aust Inst Energy News J — Australian Institute of Energy News Journal
Aust Inst Fam Stud Work Pap — Australian Institute of Family Studies. Working Paper
Aust Inst Internat Aff NSW Br — Australian Institute of International Affairs. New South Wales Branch
Aust Inst Mar Sci Monogr Ser — Australian Institute of Marine Science. Monograph Series
Aust Inst Pet South Aust Branch Annu Semin — Australian Institute of Petroleum. South Australian Branch. Annual Seminar
Aust Intercollegian — Australian Intercollegian
Aust Irrig — Australasian Irrigator and Pasture Improver
Aust Irrig Past Improver — Australasian Irrigator and Pasture Improver
Aust J — Australian Journal
Aust J Adult Ed — Australian Journal of Adult Education
Aust J Adult Educ — Australian Journal of Adult Education
Aust J Adv Nurs — Australian Journal of Advanced Nursing
Aust J Ag E — Australian Journal of Agricultural Economics
Aust J Ag Econ — Australian Journal of Agricultural Economics
Aust J Ag R — Australian Journal of Agricultural Research
Aust J Agr — Australian Journal of Agricultural Research
Aust J Agr Econ — Australian Journal of Agricultural Economics
Aust J Ag Res — Australian Journal of Agricultural Research
Aust J Agric Econ — Australian Journal of Agricultural Economics
Aust J Agric Res — Australian Journal of Agricultural Research
Aust J Agr Res — Australian Journal of Agricultural Research
Aust J Alcohol & Drug Depend — Australian Journal of Alcoholism and Drug Dependence
Aust J Anthrop — Australian Journal of Anthropology
Aust J Appl Sci — Australian Journal of Applied Science
Aust J Arch & Arts — Australian Journal of Architecture and Arts
Aust J Biblical Archaeol — Australian Journal of Biblical Archaeology
Aust J Biol — Australian Journal of Biological Sciences
Aust J Biol Sci — Australian Journal of Biological Sciences
Aust J Biotechnol — Australian Journal of Biotechnology
Aust J Bot — Australian Journal of Botany
Aust J Botany — Australian Journal of Botany
Aust J Bot Supplry Ser Suppl — Australian Journal of Botany. Supplementary Series. Supplement
Aust J Bot Suppl Ser — Australian Journal of Botany. Supplementary Series
Aust J Bot Suppl Ser Suppl — Australian Journal of Botany. Supplementary Series. Supplement
Aust J Chem — Australian Journal of Chemistry
Aust J Chem Eng — Australian Journal of Chemical Engineers
Aust J Clin Exp Hypn — Australian Journal of Clinical and Experimental Hypnosis
Aust J Coal Min Technol Res — Australian Journal of Coal Mining Technology and Research
Aust J Dair — Australian Journal of Dairy Technology
Aust J Dairy Tech — Australian Journal of Dairy Technology
Aust J Dairy Technol — Australian Journal of Dairy Technology
Aust J Dairy Technology — Australian Journal of Dairy Technology
Aust J Dairy Technol Suppl — Australian Journal of Dairy Technology. Supplement
Aust J Dent — Australian Journal of Dentistry
Aust J Dentistry — Australian Journal of Dentistry
Aust J Derm — Australasian Journal of Dermatology
Aust J Derm — Australian [*later, Australasian*] Journal of Dermatology
Aust J Dermatol — Australasian Journal of Dermatology
Aust J Dermatol — Australian [*later, Australasian*] Journal of Dermatology
Aust J Dev Disabil — Australian Journal of Developmental Disabilities
Aust J Dev Disabilities — Australian Journal of Developmental Disabilities
Aust J Early Child — Australian Journal of Early Childhood
Aust J Earth Sci — Australian Journal of Earth Sciences
Aust J Ecol — Australian Journal of Ecology
Aust J Ed — Australian Journal of Education
Aust J Educ — Australian Journal of Education
Aust Jewish Herald — Australian Jewish Herald
Aust Jewish Hist Soc J Proc — Australian Jewish Historical Society. Journal and Proceedings
Aust Jewish News — Australian Jewish News
Aust Jewish Outlook — Australian Jewish Outlook
Aust J Ex A — Australian Journal of Experimental Agriculture and Animal Husbandry
Aust J Ex B — Australian Journal of Experimental Biology and Medical Science
Aust J Exp Agr Anim Husb — Australian Journal of Experimental Agriculture and Animal Husbandry
Aust J Exp Agric — Australian Journal of Experimental Agriculture
Aust J Exp Agric An Husb — Australian Journal of Experimental Agriculture and Animal Husbandry
Aust J Exp Agric Anim Husb — Australian Journal of Experimental Agriculture and Animal Husbandry
Aust J Exp B — Australian Journal of Experimental Biology and Medical Science
Aust J Exp Biol — Australian Journal of Experimental Biology and Medical Science
Aust J Exp Biol Med Sci — Australian Journal of Experimental Biology and Medical Science
Aust J Exper Agric — Australian Journal of Experimental Agriculture
Aust J Exper Agric — Australian Journal of Experimental Agriculture and Animal Husbandry

Aust J Expl Biol Med Sci — Australian Journal of Experimental Biology and Medical Science
Aust J Fam Ther — Australian Journal of Family Therapy
Aust J Forensic Sci — Australian Journal of Forensic Sciences
Aust J For Sci — Australian Journal of Forensic Sciences
Aust J French Stud — Australian Journal of French Studies
Aust J Fr S — Australian Journal of French Studies
Aust J Fr Stud — Australian Journal of French Studies
Aust J Geod Photogramm and Surv — Australian Journal of Geodesy, Photogrammetry, and Surveying
Aust J Grape Wine Res — Australian Journal of Grape and Wine Research
Aust J Health Phys Educ Recreation — Australian Journal for Health, Physical Education, and Recreation
Aust J Health Phys Edu Recreation — Australian Journal for Health, Physical Education, and Recreation
Aust J Higher Ed — Australian Journal of Higher Education
Aust J Higher Educ — Australian Journal of Higher Education
Aust J Hosp Pharm — Australian Journal of Hospital Pharmacy
Aust J Inst — Australian Journal of Instrumentation and Control
Aust J Instrum Control — Australian Journal of Instrumentation and Control
Aust J Instrument Tech — Australian Journal of Instrument Technology
Aust J Instrument Technology — Australian Journal of Instrument Technology
Aust J Instrum Tech — Australian Journal of Instrument Technology
Aust J Instrum Technol — Australian Journal of Instrument Technology
Aust J Inst Trans — Australian Journal. Institute of Transport
Aust JL & Soc — Australian Journal of Law and Society
Aust JLS — Australian Journal of Law and Society
Aust JM — Australian Journal of Management
Aust J Manage — Australian Journal of Management
Aust J Mar — Australian Journal of Marine and Freshwater Research
Aust J Mar Freshwater Res — Australian Journal of Marine and Freshwater Research
Aust J Mar Freshwat Res — Australian Journal of Marine and Freshwater Research
Aust J Mar Freshw Res — Australian Journal of Marine and Freshwater Research
Aust J Med Lab Sci — Australian Journal of Medical Laboratory Science
Aust J Med Technol — Australian Journal of Medical Technology
Aust J Ment Retard — Australian Journal of Mental Retardation
Aust J Music Ed — Australian Journal of Music Education
Aust J Music Educ — Australian Journal of Music Education
Aust Jnl of Forensic Sciences — Australian Journal of Forensic Sciences
Aust Jnl of Social Issues — Australian Journal of Social Issues
Aust J of Screen Th — Australian Journal of Screen Theory
Aust J Ophthalmol — Australian Journal of Ophthalmology
Aust J Optom — Australian Journal of Optometry
Aust J Optometry — Australian Journal of Optometry
Aust J Pharm — Australian Journal of Pharmacy
Aust J Pharmacy — Australian Journal of Pharmacy
Aust J Pharm Sci — Australian Journal of Pharmaceutical Sciences
Aust J Pharm Suppl — Australian Journal of Pharmacy. Supplement
Aust J Phil — Australasian Journal of Philosophy
Aust J Phys — Australian Journal of Physics
Aust J Phys Astrophys Suppl — Australian Journal of Physics. Astrophysical Supplement
Aust J Phys Ed — Australian Journal of Physical Education
Aust J Phys Educ — Australian Journal of Physical Education
Aust J Physical Educ — Australian Journal of Physical Education
Aust J Physiother — Australian Journal of Physiotherapy
Aust J Physiotherapy — Australian Journal of Physiotherapy
Aust J Plan — Australian Journal of Plant Physiology
Aust J Plant Physiol — Australian Journal of Plant Physiology
Aust J Pl Physiol — Australian Journal of Plant Physiology
Aust Jpn Workshop Gaseous Electron Its Appl — Australia-Japan Workshop on Gaseous Electronics and Its Applications
Aust J Pol and Hist — Australian Journal of Politics and History
Aust J Pol Hist — Australian Journal of Politics and History
Aust J Poli — Australian Journal of Politics and History
Aust J Poli & Hist — Australian Journal of Politics and History
Aust J Polit Hist — Australian Journal of Politics and History
Aust J Politics & History — Australian Journal of Politics and History
Aust J Politics Hist — Australian Journal of Politics and History
Aust J Ps Phil — Australasian Journal of Psychology and Philosophy
Aust J Psyc — Australian Journal of Psychology
Aust J Psych — Australian Journal of Psychology
Aust J Psychol — Australian Journal of Psychology
Aust J Psychological Research — Australian Journal of Psychological Research
Aust J Psychology — Australian Journal of Psychology
Aust J Psych Res — Australian Journal of Psychological Research
Aust J Pub Admin — Australian Journal of Public Administration
Aust J Publ — Australian Journal of Public Administration
Aust J Public Health — Australian Journal of Public Health
Aust Jr — Australian Jurist
Aust J Reading — Australian Journal of Reading
Aust J Rem Educ — Australian Journal of Remedial Education
Aust Jr R — Australian Jurist Reports
Aust J Sci — Australian Journal of Science
Aust J Science — Australian Journal of Science
Aust J Scientific Research — Australian Journal of Scientific Research
Aust J Scient Res — Australian Journal of Scientific Research
Aust J Sci Med Sport — Australian Journal of Science and Medicine in Sport
Aust J Sci Res B — Australian Journal of Scientific Research. Series B. Biological Sciences
Aust J Sci Res Ser A — Australian Journal of Scientific Research. Series A. Physical Sciences
Aust J Sci Res Ser B — Australian Journal of Scientific Research. Series B. Biological Sciences
Aust J Soc — Australian Journal of Social Issues
Aust J Social Iss — Australian Journal of Social Issues
Aust J Social Issues — Australian Journal of Social Issues
Aust J Social Work — Australian Journal of Social Work
Aust J Soc Is — Australian Journal of Social Issues
Aust J Soc Issues — Australian Journal of Social Issues
Aust J Soc Work — Australian Journal of Social Work
Aust J Soil — Australian Journal of Soil Research
Aust J Soil Res — Australian Journal of Soil Research
Aust J Soil Water Conserv — Australian Journal of Soil and Water Conservation
Aust J Sp Med Ex Sci — Australian Journal of Sports Medicine and Exercise Sciences
Aust J Stat — Australian Journal of Statistics
Aust J Statist — Australian Journal of Statistics
Aust J Stats — Australian Journal of Statistics
Aust J Teach Educ — Australian Journal of Teacher Education
Aust J Teach Pract — Australian Journal of Teaching Practice
Aust Junior Farmer — Australian Junior Farmer
Aust Jur — Australian Jurist
Aust Jur — Australian Jurist Reports
Aust Jur R — Australian Jurist Reports
Aust Jur Rep — Australian Jurist Reports
Aust J Zool — Australian Journal of Zoology
Aust J Zool Supplry Ser — Australian Journal of Zoology. Supplementary Series
Aust J Zool Supplry Ser Suppl — Australian Journal of Zoology. Supplementary Series. Supplement
Aust J Zool Suppl Ser — Australian Journal of Zoology. Supplementary Series
Austl and NZJ Criminology — Australian and New Zealand Journal of Criminology
Aust Lapidary — Australian Lapidary Magazine
Austl Argus LR — Australian Argus Law Reports
Aust Law — Australian Lawyer
Aust Law J — Australian Law Journal
Aust Law News — Australian Law News
Aust Law Rev — Australian Law Review
Aust Lawyer — Australian Lawyer
Austl Bankr Cas — Australian Bankruptcy Cases
Austl Bus L Rev — Australian Business Law Review
Austl Com J — Australian Commercial Journal
Aust Leather J — Australian Leather Journal. Boot and Shoe Recorder
Aust Leath Footwear Rev — Australasian Leather and Footwear Review
Aust Leath J — Australian Leather Journal. Boot and Shoe Recorder
Aust Leath Tr Rev — Australian Leather Trades Review
Aust Left R — Australian Left Review
Aust Leg Mon Dig — Australian Legal Monthly Digest
Aust Lett — Australian Letters
Aust Liberal — Australian Liberal
Aust Lib J — Australian Library Journal
Aust Libr J — Australian Library Journal
Aust Libr J Suppl — Australian Library Journal. Supplement
Aust Literary Letter — Australian Literary Letter
Aust Lit S — Australian Literary Studies
Aust Lit St — Australian Literary Studies
Aust Lit Stud — Australian Literary Studies
Aust L J — Australian Law Journal
Austl J For Sci — Australian Journal of Forensic Sciences
Austl J Phil — Australasian Journal of Philosophy
Austl LJ Rep — Australian Law Journal. Reports
Austl Jur R — Australian Jurist Reports
Austl LJ — Australian Law Journal
Austl LJ Rep — Australian Law Journal. Reports
Aust LN — Australian Law News
Aust L Rep — Australian Law Reports
Aust LT — Australian Law Times
Austl Tax — Australian Tax Decisions
Austl Tax Rev — Australian Tax Review
Austl YB Int'l L — Australian Yearbook of International Law
Aust Machinery & Prod Eng — Australian Machinery and Production Engineering
Aust Mach Prod Eng — Australian Machinery and Production Engineering
Aust Mach Prod Engng — Australian Machinery and Production Engineering
Aust Mag — Australian Magazine
Aust Mammal — Australian Mammalogy
Aust Man — Australian Manager
Aust Manager — Australian Manager
Aust Manag R — Australian Management Review
Aust Manuf — Australasian Manufacturer
Aust Mar Sci Bull — Australian Marine Science Bulletin
Aust Mar Sci Newsl — Australian Marine Sciences Newsletter
Aust Marxist Rev — Australian Marxist Review
Aust Mater Res Lab Rep — Australia. Materials Research Laboratories. Report
Aust Mater Res Lab Tech Note — Australia. Materials Research Laboratories. Technical Note
Aust Math Soc Bul — Australian Mathematical Society. Bulletin
Aust Math Soc Bull — Australian Mathematical Society. Bulletin
Aust Math Soc J — Australian Mathematical Society. Journal
Aust Math Soc J Ser A — Australian Mathematical Society. Journal. Series A
Aust Maths Teach — Australian Mathematics Teacher
Aust Math Teach — Australian Mathematics Teacher
Aust Mech Eng — Australian Mechanical Engineering
Aust Mech Engng — Australian Mechanical Engineering
Aust Mech Engr — Australian Mechanical Engineering
Aust Med J — Australian Medical Journal
Aust Merino Wool Campaign — Australian Merino Wool Campaign
Aust Meteorol Mag — Australian Meteorological Magazine

Aust Methodist Hist Soc J Proc — Australasian Methodist Historical Society. Journal and Proceedings
Aust Methods Eng — Australian Methods Engineer
Aust Met Mag — Australian Meteorological Magazine
Aust Mgr — Australian Manager
Aust Milk Dairy Prod J — Australian Milk and Dairy Products Journal
Aust Min — Australian Mining
Aust Min Counc Newsl — Australian Mining Council. Newsletter
Aust Min Dev Lab Bull — Australian Mineral Development Laboratories [AMDEL]. Bulletin
Aust Min Dev Labs Bull — Australian Mineral Development Laboratories [AMDEL]. Bulletin
Aust Min Engng Rev — Australian Mining and Engineering Review
Aust Min Eng Rev — Australian Mining and Engineering Review
Aust Mineral — Australian Mineralogist
Aust Miner Dev Lab Bull — Australian Mineral Development Laboratories [AMDEL]. Bulletin
Aust Miner Dev Lab Rep — Australian Mineral Development Laboratories [AMDEL]. Report
Aust Miner Ind — Australian Mineral Industry
Aust Miner Ind Annu Rev — Australian Mineral Industry. Annual Review
Aust Miner Ind Q — Australian Mineral Industry. Quarterly
Aust Miner Ind Rev — Australian Mineral Industry. Review
Aust Miner Ind Stat — Australian Mineral Industry. Statistics
Aust Min Ind — Australian Mineral Industry
Aust Min Ind Stat — Australian Mineral Industry. Statistics
Aust Mining — Australian Mining
Aust Min Mon — Australia's Mining Monthly
Aust Min Pet Law J — Australian Mining and Petroleum Law Journal
Aust Min Stand — Australian Mining Standard
Aust Min Year Book — Australian Mining Year Book
Aust Mod Rail — Australian Model Railway Magazine
Aust Mon Weath Rep — Australian Monthly Weather Report and Meteorological Abstract
Aust Mot Cycle News — Australian Motor Cycle News
Aust Motorist — Australian Motorist
Aust Motor Sports — Australian Motor Sports
Aust Munic J — Australian Municipal Journal
Aust Mus Dir — Australian Music Directory
Aust Museum Mag — Australian Museum. Magazine
Aust Musical News & D — Australian Musical News and Musical Digest
Aust Mus Mag — Australian Museum. Magazine
Aust Mus Rec — Australian Museum. Records
Aust Mus (Syd) Mem — Australian Museum (Sydney). Memoirs
Aust Mus (Sydney) Mem — Australian Museum (Sydney). Memoirs
Austn Amer — Austin American-Statesman
Aust Nat — Australian Naturalist
Aust Nat Bibliogr — Australian National Bibliography
Aust Nat Clay — Australian National Clay
Aust Nat H — Australian Natural History
Aust Nat Hist — Australian Natural History
Aust Natl Meas Lab Tech Pap — Australia. National Measurement Laboratory. Technical Paper
Aust Natl Univ Dep Eng Phys Energy Convers Tech Rep — Australian National University. Department of Engineering Physics. Energy Conversion Technical Report
Aust Natl Univ Res Sch Phys Sci Dep Eng Phys Publ — Australian National University. Research School of Physical Sciences. Department of Engineering Physics. Publication
Aust Natn Clay — Australian National Clay
Aust Nat Univ News — Australian National University. News
Aust Nat Univ Res Sch Pacif Stud Geog Pub — Australian National University. Research School of Pacific Studies. Department of Geography. Publication
Aust Natural History — Australian Natural History
Aust Natur His — Australian Natural History
Aust Natur Hist — Australian Natural History
Aust Neigh — Australia's Neighbours
Aust Neighb — Australia's Neighbours
Aust Neighbours — Australia's Neighbours
Aust News — Austral News
Aust News (Johannesburg) — Austral News (Johannesburg)
Aust News (Montreal) — Austral News (Montreal)
Aust News R — Austral News Review
Aust News (Singapore) — Austral News (Singapore)
Aust News (Wellington) — Austral News (Wellington)
Aust New Zeal Environ Rep — Australian and New Zealand Environmental Report
Aust Now — Australia Now
Aust Nucl Sci Technol Organ Rep — Australian Nuclear Science and Technology Organisation. Report
Aust Nucl Sci Technol Organ Rep ANSTO E — Australian Nuclear Science and Technology Organisation. Report. ANSTO/E
Aust Numismatic J — Australian Numismatic Journal
Aust Numismatic Soc Rep — Australian Numismatic Society. Report
Aust Num J — Australian Numismatic Journal
Aust Num Meteor Res Centr (Melb) Ann Rep — Australian Numerical Meteorology Research Centre (Melbourne). Annual Report
Aust Num Soc Rept — Australian Numismatic Society. Report
Aust Nurses J — Australian Nurses' Journal
Aust Nurses J (Melbourne) — Australian Nurses' Journal (Melbourne)
Aust NZ Assoc Adv Sci Congr Pap — Australian and New Zealand Association for the Advancement of Science. Congress. Papers
Aust NZ Conf Geomech Proc — Australian-New Zealand Conference on Geomechanics. Proceedings
Aust NZ Conf Pain — Australia. New Zealand Conference on Pain
Aust NZ Gen Practnr — Australian and New Zealand General Practitioner

Aust NZ J C — Australian and New Zealand Journal of Criminology
Aust NZ J Dev Disabil — Australian and New Zealand Journal of Developmental Disabilities
Aust NZ J M — Australian and New Zealand Journal of Medicine
Aust NZ J Med — Australian and New Zealand Journal of Medicine
Aust NZ J Med Suppl — Australian and New Zealand Journal of Medicine. Supplement
Aust NZ J O — Australian and New Zealand Journal of Obstetrics and Gynaecology
Aust NZ J Obstet Gynaec — Australian and New Zealand Journal of Obstetrics and Gynaecology
Aust NZ J Obstet Gynaecol — Australian and New Zealand Journal of Obstetrics and Gynaecology
Aust NZ J Obstet Gynaecol (Suppl) — Australian and New Zealand Journal of Obstetrics and Gynaecology (Supplement)
Aust NZ J Ophthalmol — Australian and New Zealand Journal of Ophthalmology
Aust NZ J P — Australian and New Zealand Journal of Psychiatry
Aust NZ J Psychiat — Australian and New Zealand Journal of Psychiatry
Aust NZ J Psychiatry — Australian and New Zealand Journal of Psychiatry
Aust NZ J S — Australian and New Zealand Journal of Surgery
Aust NZ J Soc — Australian and New Zealand Journal of Sociology
Aust NZ J Sociol — Australian and New Zealand Journal of Sociology
Aust NZ J Surg — Australian and New Zealand Journal of Surgery
Aust NZ Rose A — Australian and New Zealand Rose Annual
Aust NZ Soc — Australian and New Zealand Journal of Sociology
Aust NZ Symp Microcirc — Australian and New Zealand Symposium on the Microcirculation
Aust NZ W — Australian and New Zealand Weekly
Aust OCCA Proc News — Australian OCCA [Oil and Colour Chemists Association] Proceedings and News
Aust Occupational Ther J — Australian Occupational Therapy Journal
Aust Occup Ther J — Australian Occupational Therapy Journal
Aust Off J Pat — Australian Official Journal of Patents
Aust Off J Pat — Australian Official Journal of Patents, Trade Marks, and Designs
Aust Off J Pat Trade Marks Des — Australian Official Journal of Patents, Trade Marks, and Designs
Aust Off J Pat Trade Marks Des Pat Abr Suppl — Australian Official Journal of Patents, Trade Marks, and Designs. Patent Abridgments Supplement
Aust Oil Colour Chem Assoc Proc News — Australian Oil and Colour Chemists Association. Proceedings and News
Aust Oil Gas J — Australasian Oil and Gas Journal
Aust Oil Seed Gr — Australian Oil Seed Grower
Aust Orchid Rev — Australian Orchid Review
Aust Orthod J — Australian Orthodontic Journal
Aust Out — Australian Outlook
Aust Outdoors — Australian Outdoors
Aust Outl — Australian Outlook
Aust Outloo — Australian Outlook
Aust Outlook — Australian Outlook
Aust Packaging — Australian Packaging
Aust Paedia — Australian Paediatric Journal
Aust Paediat J — Australian Paediatric Journal
Aust Paediatric J — Australian Paediatric Journal
Aust Paediatr J — Australian Paediatric Journal
Aust Paint J — Australian Paint Journal
Aust Paint J Aust Finish Rev — Australian Paint Journal. Incorporating the Australian Finishing Review
Aust Paint J Suppl — Australian Paint Journal. Supplement
Aust Parks — Australian Parks [Later, Australian Parks and Recreation]
Aust Parks — Australian Parks and Recreation
Aust Parks Recreat — Australian Parks and Recreation
Aust Parl Deb House Rep — Australia. House of Representatives. Parliamentary Debates
Aust Parl Deb Senate — Australia. Parliament. Senate. Parliamentary Debates
Aust Parl H of R Parl Deb — Australia. Parliament. House of Representatives. Parliamentary Debates
Aust Parl Paper — Australian Parliamentary Paper
Aust Parl Sen Parl Deb — Australia. Parliament. Senate. Parliamentary Debates
Aust Past — Australian Pastoralist
Aust Pat Doc — Australian (Patent Document)
Aust Pat Off Aust Off J Pat — Australia. Patent Office. Australian Official Journal of Patents
Aust Pat Off Aust Off J Pat Trade Marks Des — Australia. Patent Office. Australian Official Journal of Patents, Trade Marks, and Designs
Aust Pat Specif (Petty) — Australia. Patent Specification (Petty)
Aust Pet Explor Assoc J — Australian Petroleum Exploration Association. Journal
Aust Phot — Australian Photography
Aust Photogr J — Australian Photographic Journal
Aust Phys — Australian Physicist
Aust Physicist — Australian Physicist
Aust Physiol Pharmacol Soc Proc — Australian Physiological and Pharmacological Society. Proceedings
Aust Pl — Australian Plants
Aust Plan Inst J — Australian Planning Institute. Journal
Aust Plann Inst J — Australian Planning Institute. Journal
Aust Plant Dis Rec — Australian Plant Disease Recorder
Aust Plant Introd Rev — Australian Plant Introduction Review
Aust Plant Pathol Soc Newsl — Australian Plant Pathology Society. Newsletter
Aust Plants — Australian Plants
Aust Plas Rubb J — Australian Plastics and Rubber Journal
Aust Plast — Australian Plastics
Aust Plast All Trades Rev — Australian Plastics and Allied Trades Review
Aust Plast & Rubber Buy Guide — Australian Plastics and Rubber Buyers Guide
Aust Plastics & Rubber J — Australian Plastics and Rubber Journal
Aust Plastics J — Australian Plastics Journal
Aust Plastics Yrbk — Australian Plastics Year Book

Aust Plast J — Australian Plastics Journal
Aust Plast Rubb — Australian Plastics and Rubber
Aust Plast Rubber — Australian Plastics and Rubber
Aust Plast Rubber J — Australian Plastics and Rubber Journal
Aust Plast Yb — Australian Plastics Year Book
Aust Pl Dis Rec — Australian Plant Disease Recorder
Aust Police J — Australian Police Journal
Aust Pol J — Australian Police Journal
Aust Pop Phot — Australian Popular Photography
Aust Post Office Res Lab Rep — Australian Post Office Research Laboratories. Report
Aust Power Eng — Australian Power Engineering
Aust Pr — Australian Printer
Aust Pre-School Assn Biennial Conf — Australian Pre-School Association. Biennial Conference
Aust Pre-School Q — Australian Pre-School Quarterly
Aust Pre-School Quart — Australian Pre-School Quarterly
Aust Pre-Sch Quart — Australian Pre-School Quarterly
Aust Press Statement — Australia. Government Public Relations Office. Ministerial Press Statements
Aust Printer — Australasian Printer
Aust Process Eng — Australian Process Engineering
Aust Processs Engng — Australian Process Engineering
Aust Prod — Australia. Commonwealth Bureau of Census and Statistics. Monthly Bulletin of Production Statistics
Aust Psych — Australian Psychologist
Aust Psychl — Australian Psychologist
Aust Psychol — Australian Psychologist
Aust Public Aff Inf Serv — Australian Public Affairs Information Service
Aust Pulp Pap Ind Tech Assoc Proc — Australian Pulp and Paper Industry Technical Association. Proceedings
Aust Pump J — Australian Pump Journal
Aust Pwr Engng — Australian Power Engineering
Aust Q — Australian Quarterly
Aust Qly — Australian Quarterly
Aust Quart — Australian Quarterly
Aust R — Australian Review
Aus Trade — Austrian Trade News
Aust Radiat Lab Tech Rep ARL/TR — Australian Radiation Laboratory. Technical Report ARL/TR
Aust Radiat Lab Tech Rep Ser ARL/TR — Australian Radiation Laboratory. Technical Report Series ARL/TR
Aust Radiat Rec — Australian Radiation Records
Aust Radio — Australasian Radiology
Aust Radiol — Australasian Radiology
Aust Railway Hist Soc Bul — Australian Railway Historical Society. Bulletin
Austral A — Australian Art
Austral Aboriginal Stud — Australian Aboriginal Studies
Austral A Educ — Australasian Art Education
Austral & NZ Soc Int L Proc — Australian and New Zealand Society of International Law. Proceedings
Austral Ant Colr — Australian Antique Collector
Australas Ann Med — Australasian Annals of Medicine
Australas Baker — Australasian Baker and Millers' Journal
Australas Baker Millers J — Australasian Baker and Millers' Journal
Australas Beekpr — Australasian Beekeeper
Australas Biotechnol — Australasian Biotechnology
Australas Bull Med Phys Biophy — Australasian Bulletin of Medical Physics and Biophysics
Australas Bull Med Phys Biophys — Australasian Bulletin of Medical Physics and Biophysics
Australas Chem Eng Conf — Australasian Chemical Engineering Conference
Australas Chem Metall — Australasian Chemist and Metallurgist
Australas Conf Grassl Invertebr Ecol — Australasian Conference on Grassland Invertebrate Ecology
Australas Conf Heat Mass Transfer Proc — Australasian Conference on Heat and Mass Transfer. Proceedings
Australas Corros — Australasian Corrosion Engineering
Australas Corros Assoc Conf — Australasian Corrosion Association. Conference
Australas Corros Assoc Prepr Pap Annu Conf — Australasian Corrosion Association. Preprinted Papers of the Annual Conference
Australas Corros Assoc Tech Pap Annual Conf — Australasian Corrosion Association. Technical Paper of the Annual Conference
Australas Corros Eng — Australasian Corrosion Engineering
Australas Corros Engng — Australasian Corrosion Engineering
Australas Eng — Australasian Engineer
Australas Engng Mach — Australasian Engineering and Machinery
Australas Engr — Australasian Engineer
Australas Environ — Australasian Environment
Australas Hardware Machinery — Australasian Hardware and Machinery
Australas Herb News — Australasian Herbarium News
Australasian Ann Med — Australasian Annals of Medicine
Australasian As Rp — Australasian Association for the Advancement of Science. Reports
Australasian Bk News — Australasian Book News and Library Journal
Australasian J Psychol — Australasian Journal of Psychology and Philosophy
Australas IMM Conf — Australasian Institute of Mining and Metallurgy. Conference
Australas Inst Met Annu Conf — Australasian Institute of Metals. Annual Conference
Australas Inst Met Annu Conf Proc — Australasian Institute of Metals. Annual Conference. Proceedings
Australas Inst Met J — Australasian Institute of Metals. Journal
Australas Inst Met Met Congr — Australasian Institute of Metals. Metals Congress
Australas Inst Mining Met Proc — Australasian Institute of Mining and Metallurgy. Proceedings

Australas Inst Min Metall Bull — Australasian Institute of Mining and Metallurgy. Bulletin
Australas Inst Min Metall Bull Proc — Australasian Institute of Mining and Metallurgy. Bulletin and Proceedings
Australas Inst Min Metall Conf — Australasian Institute of Mining and Metallurgy. Conference
Australas Inst Min Metall Conf Ser — Australasian Institute of Mining and Metallurgy. Conference Series
Australas Inst Min Metall Monogr Ser — Australasian Institute of Mining and Metallurgy. Monograph Series
Australas Inst Min Metall Proc — Australasian Institute of Mining and Metallurgy. Proceedings
Australas Inst Min Metall Publ Ser — Australasian Institute of Mining and Metallurgy Publication Series
Australas Inst Min Metall Spectrum Ser — Australasian Institute of Mining and Metallurgy Spectrum Series
Australas Inst Min Metall Symp Ser — Australasian Institute of Mining and Metallurgy. Symposia Series
Australas Irrig — Australasian Irrigator and Pasture Improver
Australas J Combin — Australasian Journal of Combinatorics
Australas J Dermatol — Australasian Journal of Dermatology
Australas J Ecotoxicol — Australasian Journal of Ecotoxicology
Australas J Med Technol — Australasian Journal of Medical Technology
Australas J Phar — Australasian Journal of Pharmacy
Australas J Pharm — Australasian Journal of Pharmacy
Australas J Pharm Sci Suppl — Australasian Journal of Pharmacy. Science Supplement
Australas J Phil — Australasian Journal of Philosophy
Australas Leath Footwear Rev — Australasian Leather and Footwear Review
Australas Leath Trades Rev — Australasian Leather Trades Review
Australas Manuf — Australasian Manufacturer
Australas Manuf Eng — Australasian Manufacturing Engineer
Australas Med Congr — Australasian Medical Congress. Transactions
Australas Med Gaz — Australasian Medical Gazette
Australas Mfr — Australasian Manufacturer
Australas Mfr Plast Rev — Australasian Manufacturer. Plastics Review
Australas Nurses J — Australasian Nurses Journal
Australas Nurs J (Port Adelaide) — Australasian Nursing Journal (Port Adelaide)
Australas Oil Gas J — Australasian Oil and Gas Journal
Australas Oil Gas Rev — Australasian Oil and Gas Review
Australas Past Rev — Australasian Pastoralists' Review
Australas Pharm Notes News — Australasian Pharmaceutical Notes and News
Australas Photogr Rev — Australasian Photographic Review
Australas Photo Rev — Australasian Photo Review
Australas Photo Review — Australasian Photo Review
Australas Phys and Eng Sci Med — Australasian Physical and Engineering Sciences in Medicine
Australas Phys Eng Sci Med — Australasian Physical and Engineering Sciences in Medicine
Australas Phys Sci Med — Australasian Physical Sciences in Medicine [Later, *Australasian Physical and Engineering Sciences in Medicine*]
Australas Plant Pathol — APP. Australasian Plant Pathology
Australas Plat Finish — Australasian Plating and Finishing
Australas Poult Stock Feed Conv Proc — Australasian Poultry and Stock Feed Convention. Proceedings
Australas Print — Australasian Printer
Australas Printer — Australasian Printer
Australas Radiol — Australasian Radiology
Australas Symp Microcir — Australasian Symposium on the Microcirculation
Australas Text — Australasian Textiles
Australas Trade Rev — Australasian Trade Review and Manufacturers Journal
Australas Typogr J — Australasian Typographical Journal
Austral Beekeeper — Australian Beekeeper
Austral Comput J — Australian Computer Journal
Austral Comput Sci Comm — Australian Computer Science Communications
Austral Connoisseur & Colr — Australian Connoisseur and Collector
Austral Econ Hist R — Australian Economic History Review
Austral Econ Pap — Australian Economic Papers
Austral Fam Physician — Australian Family Physician
Austral For Aff Rec — Australian Foreign Affairs Record
Austral Forest Res — Australian Forest Research. Forest Research Institute
Austral For J — Australian Forestry Journal
Austral Fruitgrower — Australian Fruitgrower, Fertiliser, and Poultry Farmer
Austral Gard Field — Australian Garden and Field
Austral Hist Yb — Australian History Yearbook
Austral Hort Mag Gard Guide — Australian Horticultural Magazine and Garden Guide
Australian Acad and Res Lib — Australian Academic and Research Libraries
Australian and New Zealand Assoc Adv Sci Rept — Australian and New Zealand Association for the Advancement of Science. Report
Australian and NZ J Sociol — Australian and New Zealand Journal of Sociology
Australian J Econ Hist R — Australian Economic History Review
Australian Econ Hist Rev — Australian Economic History Review
Australian Econ Pas — Australian Economic Papers
Australian Econ R — Australian Economic Review
Australian For Affairs Rec — Australian Foreign Affairs Record
Australian For J — Australian Forestry Journal
Australian Garden History Soc Jnl — Australian Garden History Society. Journal
Australian Hist Bibliogr — Australian Historical Bibliography
Australian Inst Libn Proc — Australian Institute of Librarians. Proceedings
Australian J French Stud — Australian Journal of French Studies
Australian J Mgt — Australian Journal of Management
Australian J Mus Ed — Australian Journal of Music Education
Australian J Psychol — Australian Journal of Psychology
Australian J Statis — Australian Journal of Statistics

Australian Lib J — Australian Library Journal
Australian Math Teacher — Australian Mathematics Teacher
Australian Mineral Industry Q — Australian Mineral Industry. Quarterly
Australian M J — Australian Medical Journal
Australian New Zeal J Obstet Gynaecol — Australian and New Zealand Journal of Obstetrics and Gynaecology
Australian New Zeal J Surg — Australian and New Zealand Journal of Surgery
Australian Offic J Pat Pat Abridgments Suppl — Australian Official Journal of Patents, Trade Marks, and Designs. Patent Abridgments Supplement
Australian Soc Explor Geophys Bull — Australian Society of Exploration Geophysicists. Bulletin
Austral J A — Australian Journal of Art
Austral J Agr Econ — Australian Journal of Agricultural Economics
Austral J Agric Econ — Australian Journal of Agricultural Economics
Austral J Agric Res — Australian Journal of Agricultural Research
Austral J Appl Sci — Australian Journal of Applied Science
Austral J Bibl Archaeol — Australian Journal of Biblical Archaeology
Austral J Biol Sci — Australian Journal of Biological Sciences
Austral J Bot — Australian Journal of Botany
Austral J Chem — Australian Journal of Chemistry
Austral J Exp Agric Anim Husb — Australian Journal of Experimental Agriculture and Animal Husbandry
Austral J High Educ — Australian Journal of Higher Education
Austral J Hum Commun Dis — Australian Journal of Human Communication Disorders
Austral J Mar Freshwater Res — Australian Journal of Marine and Freshwater Research
Austral J Phys — Australian Journal of Physics
Austral J Polit Hist — Australian Journal of Politics and History
Austral J Sci Res Ser B Biol Sci — Australian Journal of Scientific Research. Series B. Biological Sciences
Austral J Soc Issues — Australian Journal of Social Issues
Austral J Statist — Australian Journal of Statistics
Austral Lilium Soc Bull — Australian Lilium Society Bulletin
Austral Lilum Soc Quart — Australian Lilum Society Quarterly
Austral M — Australian Mining
Austral Math Soc Gaz — Australian Mathematical Society. Gazette
Austral Math Soc Lect Ser — Australian Mathematical Society Lecture Series
Austral Med J — Australian Medical Journal
Austral Mus Mag — Australian Museum Magazine
Austral N — Australia Now
Austral Nat Hist — Australian Natural History
Austral Naturalist — Australian Naturalist. Journal and Magazine. New South Wales Naturalists' Club
Austral N Zealand J Sociol — Australian and New Zealand Journal of Sociology
Austral O — Australian Outlook
Austral Off J Pat — Australian Official Journal of Patents
Austral Orchid Rev — Australian Orchid Review
Austral Outlook — Australian Outlook
Austral Paint J — Australian Paint Journal
Austral Pkg — Australian Packaging
Austral Plan Inst J — Australian Planning Institute. Journal
Austral Pl Dis Rec — Australian Plant Disease Recorder
Austral Publ Aff Inform Serv — Australian Public Affairs Information Service
Austral Quart — Australian Quarterly
Austral Sci Index — Australian Science Index
Austral Sketcher — Australian Sketcher
Austral Sugar J — Australian Sugar Journal
Austral Sugar Year Book — Australian Sugar Year Book
Austral Teacher Deaf — Australian Teacher of the Deaf
Austral Tobacco Growers Bull — Australian Tobacco Grower's Bulletin
Austral Wild Life — Australian Wild Life
Austr BC — Australian Bankruptcy Cases
Austr Beek — Australasian Beekeeper
Austr Brew Wi J — Australian Brewing and Wine Journal
Austr Bus LR — Australian Business Law Review
Austr Chem Abstr — Australian Chemical Abstracts
Austr Chem Inst J Pr — Australian Chemical Institute. Journal and Proceedings
Austr Chem Met — Australasian Chemist and Metallurgist
Austr Civ Eng Constr — Australian Civil Engineering and Construction
Austr Cott Grow — Australian Cotton Grower
Austr Cott Grow Farm Dairym — Australian Cotton Grower, Farmer, and Dairyman
Austr Dent J — Australian Dental Journal
Austr Dent Mirr — Australian Dental Mirror
Aust Rd Index — Australian Road Index
Aust Rd Res — Australian Road Research
Aust Rd Res Progress — Australian Road Research in Progress
Aust Rd Res Rep — Australian Road Research. Reports
AUSTRE — Australian Scientific and Technological Reports
Aust Red Cross Q — Australian Red Cross Quarterly
Aust Refrig Air Cond Heat — Australian Refrigeration, Air Conditioning, and Heating
Aust Refrig Air Condit — Australian Refrigeration, Air Conditioning, and Heating
Aust Refrig Air Condit Heat — Australian Refrigeration, Air Conditioning, and Heating
Aust Refrig Air Con Heat — Australian Refrigeration, Air Conditioning, and Heating
Aust Refrig Rev — Australian Refrigeration Review
Austr Eng — Australasian Engineer
AUSTRE on COM — Australian Scientific and Technological Reports on COM
Aust Rep — Australian Reporter
Aust Represent Basins Program Rep Ser Rep — Australian Representative Basins Program Report. Series Report
Aust Reptile Park Rec — Australian Reptile Park. Records
Austr For — Australian Forestry
Austr For J — Australian Forestry Journal

Austr Geogr — Australian Geographer
Austr Geogr Soc Rep — Australian Geographical Society. Report
Austr Herb News — Australasian Herbarium News
Aust Rhodes R — Australian Rhodes Review
Austria Geol Bundesanst Verh — Austria. Geologische Bundesanstalt. Verhandlungen
Austria Geol Bunesanst Jahrb — Austria. Geologische Bundesanstalt. Jahrbuch
Austria Mach Steel — Austria. Machinery and Steel
Austrian Ital Yugosl Chem Eng Conf Proc — Austrian-Italian-Yugoslav Chemical Engineering Conference. Proceedings
Austrian J Oncol — Austrian Journal of Oncology
Austria Pat Doc — Austria. Patent Document
Austria Patentamt Oesterr Patentbl — Austria, Patentamt, Oesterreichisches Patentblatt
Austria Tabakwerke Fachliche Mitt — Austria Tabakwerke. Fachliche Mitteilungen
Austria Zentralanst Meteorol Geodynamik Arb — Austria. Zentralanstalt fuer Meteorologie und Geodynamik. Arbeiten
Austr Inst Aborig Stud Newsletter — Australian Institute of Aboriginal Studies. Newsletter
Austr J Agric Res — Australian Journal of Agricultural Research
Austr J Appl Sci — Australian Journal of Applied Science
Austr J Biol Sci — Australian Journal of Biological Sciences
Austr J Bot — Australian Journal of Botany
Austr J Chem — Australian Journal of Chemistry
Austr J Dent — Australian Journal of Dentistry
Austr J Derm — Australian [later, Australasian] Journal of Dermatology
Austr J Exp Biol Med Sci — Australian Journal of Experimental Biology and Medical Science
Austr J Instr Techn — Australian Journal of Instrument Technology
Austr J Mar Freshwat Res — Australian Journal of Marine and Freshwater Research
Austr J Pharm — Australian Journal of Pharmacy
Austr J Phys — Australian Journal of Physics
Austr J Psychol — Australian Journal of Psychology
Austr J Sci — Australian Journal of Science
Austr J St — Australian Journal of Statistics
Austr Jur — Australian Jurist
Austr J Zool — Australian Journal of Zoology
Austr Leath J — Australian Leather Journal
Austrl Fin — Australian Financial Review
Austr LJ — Australian Law Journal
Austr LT — Australian Law Times
Austr Mach Prod Eng — Australian Machinery and Production Engineering
Austr Mech Eng — Australian Mechanical Engineering
Austr Med Gaz — Australasian Medical Gazette
Austr Med J — Australian Medical Journal
Austr Min Ind Rev — Australian Mineral Industry. Review
Austr Min Ind Stat — Australian Mineral Industry. Statistics
Austr Mth Weath Rep — Australian Monthly Weather Report
Austr Mus Mag — Australian Museum. Magazine
Austr Nat — Australian Naturalist
Austr Neighb — Australia's Neighbours
Austr NZ Gen Pract — Australian and New Zealand General Practitioner
Austr NZ J Obst Gynaec — Australian and New Zealand Journal of Obstetrics and Gynaecology
Austr NZ J Surg — Australian and New Zealand Journal of Surgery
Aust Road Haulage J — Australian Road Haulage Journal
Aust Road Res — Australian Road Research
Aust Road Res Bd Bull — Australian Road Research Board. Bulletin
Aust Road Res Board ARR Rep — Australian Road Research Board. ARR Reports
Aust Road Res Board Bull — Australian Road Research Board. Bulletin
Aust Road Res Board Conf — Australian Road Research Board. Conference
Aust Road Res Board Proc Conf — Australian Road Research Board. Proceedings of the Conference
Aust Road Res Bp Spec Rep — Australian Road Research Board. Special Report
Aust Road Research — Australian Road Research
Aust Off J Pat — Australian Official Journal of Patents, Trade Marks, and Designs
Aust Rose A — Australian Rose Annual
Aust Rose Annu — Australian Rose Annual
Austr Past — Australian Pastoralist
Austr Past Rev — Australasian Pastoralists' Review
Austr Photogr J — Australian Photographic Journal
Austr Plast — Australian Plastics
Austr Plast All Trade Rev — Australian Plastics and Allied Trades Review
Austr Plast Rubb J — Australian Plastics and Rubber Journal
Austr Pl Dis Rec — Australian Plant Disease Recorder
Austr Q — Australian Quarterly
Austr Rad Rec — Australian Radiation Records
Austr Sci Abstr — Australian Science Abstracts
Austr Sci Ind — Australian Science Index
Austr Stand Q — Australian Standards Quarterly
Austr Statesm Min Stand — Australian Statesman and Mining Standard
Austr Sug J — Australian Sugar Journal
Austr Surv — Australian Surveyor
Austr Tax D — Australian Tax Decisions
Austr Tax R — Australian Tax Review
Austr Terr — Australian Territories
Austr Timb J — Australian Timber Journal
Austr Tob J — Australian Tobacco Journal
Aust Rubber — Australian Rubber
Austr Vet J — Australian Veterinary Journal
Austr Weld Eng — Australian Welding Engineer
Austr Wild Life — Australian Wild Life
Aust Saf N — Australian Safety News

Aust Saf News — Australian Safety News
Aust Sch L — Australian School Librarian
Aust Sch Lib — Australian School Librarian
Aust Sch Libr — Australian School Librarian
Aust Sch Librn — Australian School Librarian
Aust School Libr — Australian School Librarian
Aust Sci — Australian Scientist
Aust Sci Abstr — Australian Science Abstracts
Aust Science Teachers J — Australian Science Teachers' Journal
Aust Scient — Australian Scientist
Aust Scientist — Australian Scientist
Aust Sci Index — Australian Science Index
Aust Sci Newsl — Australian Science Newsletter
Aust Sci Teach J — Australian Science Teachers' Journal
Aust Seacraft — Australian Seacraft Magazine
Aust Seacraft — Australian Seacraft, Power, and Sail
Aust Seacraft Mag — Australian Seacraft Magazine
Aust Seed Prod Rev — Australian Seed Producers Review
Aust Shell News — Australian Shell News
Aust's Heritage — Australia's Heritage
Aust Ship Shipbuild — Australian Shipping and Shipbuilding
Aust Shorthorn — Australian Shorthorn
Aust Ski — Australian Ski Year Book
Aust Ski YB — Australian Ski Year Book
Austsn Cath Rec — Australasian Catholic Record
Austsn J Pharm — Australasian Journal of Pharmacy
Austsn J Philos — Australasian Journal of Philosophy
Austsn Meth Hist Soc J — Australasian Methodist Historical Society. Journal and Proceedings
Austsn Pr — Australasian Printer
Aust Soc Accountants SA Convention — Australian Society of Accountants. South Australian Division. Convention Reports
Aust Soc Anim Prod NSW Branch Bull — Australian Society of Animal Production. New South Wales Branch. Bulletin
Aust Soc Anim Prod Victorian Branch Fed Counc Bull — Australian Society of Animal Production. Victorian Branch. Federal Council. Bulletin
Aust Soc Dairy Technol Tech Pub — Australian Society of Dairy Technology. Technical Publication
Aust Soc Dairy Technol Tech Publ — Australian Society of Dairy Technology. Technical Publication
Aust Soc Dairy Techn Tech Publ — Australian Society of Dairy Technology. Technical Publication
Aust Soc Dairy Tech Tech Pub — Australian Society of Dairy Technology. Technical Publication
Aust Soc Explor Geophys Bull — Australian Society of Exploration Geophysicists. Bulletin
Aust Soc Soil Sci Soils News — Australian Society of Soil Science. Soils News
Aust Soc Study Lab Hist Bull — Australian Society for the Study of Labour History. Bulletin
Aust Soc Sugar Cane Technol Proc Conf — Australian Society of Sugar Cane Technologists. Proceedings of the Conference
Aust Soc Welfare — Australian Social Welfare
Aust South Dep Mines Geol Sur Bull — South Australia. Department of Mines. Geological Survey. Bulletin
Aust South Dep Mines Geol Surv Rep Invest — South Australia. Department of Mines. Geological Survey. Report of Investigations
Aust South Dep Mines Min Rev — South Australia. Department of Mines. Mining Review
Aust Spec Libr News — Australian Special Libraries News
Aust Stamp Bull — Australian Stamp Bulletin
Aust Stamp M — Australian Stamp Monthly
Aust Stamp Mo — Australian Stamp Monthly
Aust Stand — Australian Standard
Aust Stand Q — Australian Standards Quarterly
Aust Stand Specif — Australian Standard Specifications
Aust Stand Specif Stand Ass Aust — Australian Standard Specifications. Standards Association of Australia
Aust Statesm Min Stand — Australian Statesman and Mining Standard
Aust Stock Exchange J — Australian Stock Exchange Journal
Aust Stock Exch J — Australian Stock Exchange Journal
Aust Stud — Australian Student
Aust Stud & Farm M — Australian Stud and Farm Monthly
Aust Stud Legal Philos — Australian Studies in Legal Philosophy
Aust Stud Newsl — Australian Studies Newsletter
Aust Sugar J — Australian Sugar Journal
Aust Sugar Yr Bk — Australian Sugar Year Book
Aust Sug J — Australian Sugar Journal
Aust Sug Yb — Australian Sugar Yearbook
Aust Surv — Australian Surveyor
Aust Survey — Australian Surveyor
Aust Surveyor — Australian Surveyor
Aust Syst Bot — Australian Systematic Botany
Aust TAFE Teach — Australian TAFE [*Department of Technical and Further Education*] Teacher
Aust Tax D — Australasian Tax Decisions
Aust Tax Rev — Australasian Tax Review
Aust Tax Rev — Australian Tax Review
Aust T Deaf — Australian Teacher of the Deaf
Aust Teach — Australian Teacher
Aust Teach Deaf — Australian Teacher of the Deaf
Aust Teacher of the Deaf — Australian Teacher of the Deaf
Aust Teach Fed Rep — Australian Teachers' Federation. Report
Aust Teach J — Australian Technical Journal
Aust Technol Mag — Australian Technology Magazine
Aust Technol Rev — Australian Technology Review

Aust Telecomm Res — Australian Telecommunication Research
Aust Telecomm Research — Australian Telecommunication Research
Aust Telecommun Dev Assoc — Australian Telecommunications Development Association. Annual Report
Aust Telecommun Res — Australian Telecommunication Research
Aust Terr — Australian Territories
Aust Territ — Australian Territories
Aust Territories — Australian Territories
Aust Theatre Yrbk — Australian Theatre Yearbook
Aust Thermodyn Conf — Australian Thermodynamics Conference
Aust Timber J — Australian Timber Journal
Aust Timb J — Australian Timber Journal
Aust Timb J — Australian Timber Journal and Building Products Merchandiser
Aust Tobacco J — Australian Tobacco Journal
Aust Tob Grow Bull — Australian Tobacco Grower's Bulletin
Aust Tob J — Australian Tobacco Journal
Aust Today — Australia Today
Aust Tract Test — Australian Tractor Test
Aust Tract Test Comm Aust Tract Test — Australian Tractor Testing Committee. Australian Tractor Test
Aust Trade Chronicle — Australian Trade Chronicle
Aust Transp — Australian Transport
Aust Transport — Australian Transport
Aust Transport Inf Dir — Australian Transport Information Directory
Aust Travel Goods — Australian Travel Goods and Handbags and Accessories
Aust Traveller — Australian Traveller
Aust Univ — Australian University
Aust Uranium News — Australian Uranium News
Aust Urban Stud — Australian Urban Studies
Aust Vet J — Australian Veterinary Journal
Aust Vet Pr — Australian Veterinary Practitioner
Aust Vet Pract — Australian Veterinary Practitioner
Aust Vid Cin — Australian Video and Cinema
Aust Vid Comm — Australian Video and Communications
Aust Waste Conf — Australian Waste Conference
Aust Waste Disposal Conf — Australian Waste Disposal Conference
Aust Waste Manage Control Conf Pap — Australian Waste Management and Control Conference. Papers
Aust Water Resour Counc Conf Ser — Australian Water Resources Council. Conference Series
Aust Water Resour Counc Hydrol Ser — Australian Water Resources Council. Hydrological Series
Aust Water Resour Counc Occas Pap Ser — Australian Water Resources Council. Occasional Papers Series
Aust Water Resour Counc Stream Gauging Inf — Australian Water Resources Council. Stream Gauging Information
Aust Water Resour Counc Tech Pap — Australian Water Resources Council. Technical Paper
Aust Water Resour Coun Tech Pap — Australian Water Resources Council. Technical Paper
Aust Water Wastewater Assoc Fed Conv — Australian Water and Wastewater Association. Federal Convention
Aust Water Wastewater Assoc Int Conv — Australian Water and Wastewater Association. International Convention
Aust Water Wastewater Assoc Summer Sch — Australian Water and Wastewater Association. Summer School
Aust Water Well J — Australasian Water Well Journal
Aust Wat Resour Coun Hydrol Ser — Australian Water Resources Council. Hydrological Series
Aust Weapons Res Establ Tech Rep — Australia. Weapons Research Establishment. Technical Report
Aust Weed — Australian Weeds
Aust Weed Control Handb — Australian Weed Control Handbook
Aust Weeds — Australian Weeds
Aust Weeds Conf Proc — Australian Weeds Conference. Proceedings
Aust Weld — Australian Welder
Aust Weld Engr — Australian Welding Engineer
Aust Welding J — Australian Welding Journal
Aust Weld J — Australian Welding Journal
Aust Weld Res — Australian Welding Research
Aust Weld Res Ass Bull — Australian Welding Research Association. Bulletin
Aust (West) Dep Mines Annu Rep — Australia (Western). Department of Mines. Annual Report
Aust West Dep Mines Annu Rep Geol Surv — Western Australia. Department of Mines. Annual Report of the Geological Survey
Aust West Dep Mines Bull — Western Australia. Department of Mines. Bulletin
Aust West Dep Mines Miner Resour West Aust Bull — Australia (Western). Department of Mines. Mineral Resources of Western Australia. Bulletin
Aust (West) Dep Mines Rep Mineral Anal Chem — Australia (Western). Department of Mines. Report of the Mineralogist, Analyst, and Chemist
Aust West Geol Surv Bull — Western Australia. Geological Survey. Bulletin
Aust (West) Geol Surv Miner Resour Bull — Australia (Western). Geological Survey. Mineral Resources Bulletin
Aust (West) Rep Dir Gov Chem Lab — Australia (Western). Report of the Director of Government Chemical Laboratories
Aust Wildl Res — Australian Wildlife Research
Aust Wild R — Australian Wildlife Research
Aust Wine Brewing and Spir Rev — Australian Wine, Brewing, and Spirit Review
Aust Wine Brewing Spir Rev — Australian Wine, Brewing, and Spirit Review
Aust Wine Brew Spirit Rev — Australian Wine, Brewing, and Spirit Review
Aust Womens W — Australian Women's Weekly
Aust Wool Bd Rep — Australian Wool Board. Report
Aust Wool Bur Wool Stat Service — Australian Wool Bureau. Wool Statistical Service

Aust Wool Bur Wool Stat Service Aust Wool Stat Analysis — Australian Wool Bureau. Wool Statistical Service. Australian Wool. Statistical Analysis

Aust Wool Stat Analysis — Australian Wool. Statistical Analysis

Aust Wool Test Auth Text Test Bull — Australian Wool Testing Authority. Textile Testing Bulletin

Aust Workshop Adv Protein Electroph Tech — Australian Workshop on Advanced Protein Electrophoretic Techniques

Aust Workshop Coal Hydrogenation — Australian Workshop on Coal Hydrogenation

Aust YB Intl L — Australian Yearbook of International Law

Aust Yearbook Int L — Australian Yearbook of International Law

Aust Yr Bk IL — Australian Yearbook of International Law

Aust Yr Book Int Law — Australian Yearbook of International Law

Aust Zoo — Australian Zoologist

Aust Zool — Australian Zoologist

Aust Zoologist — Australian Zoologist

Aus Unterricht Forsch — Aus Unterricht und Forschung. Korrespondenzblatt der Hoeheren Schulen Wuertembergs. Neue Folge

Auswaert Politik — Auswaertige Politik

Auswahl Besten Ausl Geogr Statist Nachr Voelker Landesk — Auswahl der Besten Auslaendischen Geographischen und Statistischen Nachrichten zur Aufklaerung der Voelker- und Landeskunde

Auswahl Kleinen Schriften Arzneiwiss — Auswahl der Kleinen Schriften, Welche in der Arzneiwissenschaft, Chemie, Chirurgie, und Botanik Herausgekommen

Auswahl Med Aufsaetze Beob Nuernberg Gel Unterhandl — Auswahl der Medicinischen Aufsaetze und Beobachtungen aus den Nuernbergischen Gelehrten Unterhandlungen

Auswahl Oekon Abh Freya Oekon Ges St Petersburg — Auswahl Oekonomischer Abhandlungen. Welche die Freye Oekonomische Gesellschaft zu St. Petersburg in Teutscher Sprache Erhalten Hat

Aus Walde — Aus dem Walde

Aus Walde Mitt Niedersaechs Landesforstverwalt — Aus dem Walde. Mitteilungen aus der Niedersaechsischen Landesforstverwaltung

Auszuege Auslegeschr Patentschr — Auszuege Auslegeschriften Patentschriften

Auszuege Europ Patentschr — Auszuege aus den Europaeischen Patentschriften

Auszuege Protok Ges Natur Heilk Dresden — Auszuege aus den Protokollen der Gesellschaft fuer Natur- und Heilkunde in Dresden

Auszug Protoc Versamml Ersten Cl — Auszug aus den Protocollen ueber die Versammlungen der Ersten Classe. LeipzigerOekonomische Societaet

AUT — Analele. Universitatii din Timisoara. Seria Stiinte Filologice

AUT — Annales Universitatis Turkuensis

AUT — Annali. Universita Toscane

Aut — Aut Aut

Aut — Authentic Science Fiction

AUT — Auto + Motortechniek

Aut Eng — Automotive Engineering

AUTFAE — Ankara Universitesi. Tip Fakultesi. Mecmuasi

Auth Pub N V — Author/Publisher News and Views

Autisme Infant — Autisme Infantile

AUTMA — Automatizace

Auto Age — Automotive Age

Auto Agric — Automobile Agricole

Auto and Con — Automation and Control

Auto Aviat — Automobile-Aviation

Auto Belge — Automobile Belge

Auto Carr Bldrs J — Automobile and Carriage Builders' Journal

Auto Chem (Tokyo) — Auto Chemicals (Tokyo)

Auto Chn S — Automotive Chain Store

Auto Col N — Auto Collector News

Auto Cred — Automobile Credit

Auto Dig — Automobile Digest

Auto Dig Reg — Automobile Digest and Register</PHR> %

Auto Discuss — Automobile Discussions

Auto Elect — Automobile Electricity

Auto Elect Wir Diag — Automobile Electricity Wiring Diagram

Auto Eng — Automobile Engineer

Auto Engng — Automobile Engineering

Auto Engr — Automobile Engineer

Auto Engrg SAE — Automotive Engineering. Society of Automotive Engineers

Auto Engr UK — Automotive Engineer (UK)

Auto Fact Fig — Automobile Facts and Figures

Autogene Ind — Autogene Industrie

Autogene Metallbearb — Autogene Metallbearbeitung

Autogenous Ind — Autogenous Industry

Autogestion et Social — Autogestion et Socialisme

Autograph Collect J — Autograph Collectors Journal

Auto Highwy — Automotive Industries. Truck and Off Highway

Auto Housg — Automation in Housing and Systems Building News

Autoimmun Autoimmune Dis — Autoimmunity and Autoimmune Disease

Autoimmun Endocr Dis — Autoimmunity and Endocrine Disease

Auto Ind — Automobile Industry

Auto Ind — Automotive Industries

Auto Ind Napoli — Automobile nell'Industria, nel Commercio, nello Sport (Napoli)

Auto Ind Rep — Autotransaction Industry Report

Auto Inds — Automobile Industries

Auto L Rep CCH — Automobile Law Reports. Commerce Clearing House

Autom — Automatik

Autom Anal Drugs Other Subst Pharm Interest — Automated Analysis of Drugs and Other Substances of Pharmaceutical Interest

Autom and Control — Automation and Control

Automat Comput Appl Math — Automation Computers Applied Mathematics

Automat Control and Computer Sci — Automatic Control and Computer Sciences

Automat Control Comput Sci — Automatic Control and Computer Sciences

Automat Control Theory Appl — Automatic Control Theory and Applications

Automat Data Process Inform B — Automatic Data Processing Information Bulletin

Automat Document and Math Linguistics — Automatic Documentation and Mathematical Linguistics

Automat Elec Tech J — Automatic Electric Technical Journal

Automatica-J IFAC — Automatica: The Journal of IFAC

Automatic Control Theory Appl — Automatic Control Theory and Applications

Automation (Cleve) — Automation (Cleveland)

Automatisierungspraxis — Automatisierungspraxis fuer Grundlagen Geratebau und Betriebserfahrungen

Automat Monit Mea — Automatic Monitoring and Measuring

Automat Programming — Automatic Programming

Automat Reason Ser — Automated Reasoning Series

Automat Remote Contr — Automation and Remote Control

Automat Remote Control — Automation and Remote Control

Automat Weld (USSR) — Automatic Welding (USSR)

Automaz Automatismi — Automazione e Automatismi

Automaz Strument — Automazione e Strumentazione

Autom Constr — Automation in Construction

Autom Control — Automatic Control

Autom Control and Comput Sci — Automatic Control and Computer Sciences

Autom Control Comput Sci — Automatic Control and Computer Sciences

Autom Control Comput Sci (Engl Transl) — Automatic Control and Computer Sciences (English Translation)

Autom Control Pet Petrochem Desalin Ind Proc IFAC Workshop — Automatic Control in Petroleum, Petrochemical, and Desalination Industries. Proceedings. IFAC (International Federation of Automatic Control) Workshop

Autom Control Theory & Appl — Automatic Control Theory and Applications

Autom Data Process Inf Bull — Automatic Data Processing Information Bulletin

Autom Doc Math Linguist — Automatic Documentation and Mathematical Linguistics

Autom Doc Rech Reflexions — Automatisation Documentaire. Recherches et Reflexions

Autom Elec Tech J — Automatic Electric Technical Journal

Auto Merch — Auto Merchandising News

Autom et Inf Ind — Automatique et Informatique Industrielles

Autom Inform Ind — Automatique et Informatique Industrielles

Autom Instrum Proc Int Conv — Automation and Instrumentation. Proceedings. International Convention on Automation and Instrumentation

Autom Mach — Automatic Machining

Autom Manuf Rep — Automated Manufacturing Report

Autom Microbiol Immunol Pap Symp — Automation in Microbiology and Immunology. Papers. Symposium on Rapid Methods and Automation in Microbiology

Autom Monit and Meas — Automatic Monitoring and Measuring

Autom Monit Meas (Engl Transl) — Automatic Monitoring and Measuring (English Translation)

Automn Autom Equip News — Automation and Automatic Equipment News

Automn Express — Automation Express

Automn Ind — Automation in Industry

Automn Prog — Automation Progress

Automn Remote Control — Automation and Remote Control

Automob Eng — Automobile Engineer

Automobile Abs — Automobile Abstracts

Automobiltech Z — Automobiltechnische Zeitschrift

Automob Q — Automobile Quarterly

Automob Technol — Automobile Technology

Automot Abstr — Automotive Abstracts

Automot Aviat Ind — Automotive and Aviation Industries

Automot Des Dev — Automotive Design and Development

Automot Des Eng — Automotive Design Engineering

Automot Dig Cincinnati — Automotive Digest (Cincinnati)

Automot Dig Toronto — Automotive Digest (Toronto)

Automot Elect Engr — Automotive Electrical Engineer

Automot Electron Int Conf — Automotive Electronics. International Conference

Automot Eng — Automotive Engineering

Automot Eng (Lond) — Automotive Engineer (London)

Automot Engng — Automotive Engineering

Automot Eng (Pittsb) — Automotive Engineering (Pittsburgh)

Automot Engr — Automotive Engineer

Automot Ind — Automotive Industries

Automot Inds — Automotive Industries

Automotive & Aviation Ind — Automotive and Aviation Industries

Automotive Eng — Society of Automotive Engineers. Journal of Automotive Engineering

Automotive Ind — Automotive Industry

Automot Mfr — Automotive Manufacturer

Automot N — Automotive News

Automot News — Automotive News

Automot Serv News — Automotive Service News

Automot Top — Automotive Topics

Autom Remote Control — Automation and Remote Control

Autom Remote Control Proc Int Congr Int Fed Autom Control — Automatic and Remote Control. Proceedings. International Congress. International Federation of Automatic Control

Autom Schweissen — Automatisches Schweissen

Autom si Electron — Automatica si Electronica

Autom Strum — Automazione e Strumentazione

Autom Subj Citation Alert — Automatic Subject Citation Alert

Autom Syst Rizeni — Automatizovane Systemy Rizeni - Bulletin INORGA

Autom Telecommande C R Congr Int — Automatisme et Telecommande. Comptes-Rendus. Congres International

Autom Weld — Automatic Welding

Autom Weld (Engl Transl) — Automatic Welding (English Translation)

Auto News — Automotive News

Auton Neurosci — Autonomic Neuroscience

Autoradiogr Biol — Autoradiography for Biologists

Auto Rbldr — Automotive Rebuilder
AutoRdsch — Automobilrundschau
Autor Livr Rio — Autores e Livros. Suplemento Literario de A Manha (Rio de Janeiro)
Auto Sp Can — Auto Sport Canada
Auto Tech — Auto Technik
Autotech Mag — Autotech Magazine
Auto Tech Z — Automobiletechnische Zeitschrift .
AUTOTESCON Proc — AUTOTESCON Proceedings
Auto Turismo Lima — Auto Movilismo y Turismo (Lima)
Auto u Flugverk — Automobil- und Flugverkehr
Auto u MotFabr — Automobil- und Motorenfabrikation
Autoxid Antioxid — Autoxidation and Antioxidants
Auto Yr — Automobile Year
AUTRB — Australian Transport
Aut Remot (R) — Automation and Remote Control (USSR)
AUTUA — Annales Universitatis Turkuensis. Series A-I. Astronomica-Chemica-Physica-Mathematica
Aut Weld R — Automatic Welding (USSR)
AuU — Afrika und Uebersee
AUUASLU — Acta Universitatis Upsaliensis. Acta Societatis Linguisticae Upsaliensis
AUUHL — Acta Universitatis Upsaliensis. Historia Litterarum
AUUNBA — Acta Universitatis Upsaliensis. Nova Acta Regiae Societatis Scientiarum Upsaliensis. Series VC
AUUSAU — Acta Universitatis Upsaliensis. Studia Anglistica Upsaliensia
AUUSEU — Acta Universitatis Upsaliensis. Studia Ethnologica Upsaliensia
AUUSGU — Acta Universitatis Upsaliensis. Studia Germanistica Upsaliensia
AUUSRU — Acta Universitatis Upsaliensis. Studia Romanica Upsaliensia
AUUUDX — Acta Universitatis Upsaliensis. Symbolae Botanicae Upsalienses
AUV — Anales. Universidad de Valencia
Auvergne A Sc — Annales Scientifiques, Litteraires, et Industrielles de l'Auvergne, Publiees par l'Academie des Sciences, Belles-Lettres, et Arts de Clermont-Ferrand
Auvergne Litt — L'Auvergne Litteraire, Artistique, et Historique
AUVJA — Australian Veterinary Journal
AuvL — Auvergne Litteraire, Artistique, et Historique
AUvS — Annales Universiteit van Stellenbosch
AUW — Acta Universitatis Wratislaviensis
AUW — Aussenwirtschaft. Zeitschrift fuer Internationale Wirtschaftsbeziehungen
AUWEA — Automatic Welding (English Translation)
AUWEDT — Australian Weeds
AUWJA — Australian Welding Journal
AUWMD — ASCE [*American Society of Civil Engineers*] Urban Water Resources ResearchProgram. Technical Memorandum IHP
AUWPET — Agricultural University (Wageningen). Papers
AUWTB — ASCE [*American Society of Civil Engineers*] Urban Water Resources ResearchProgram. Technical Memorandum
Aux Front Spectrosc Laser Ec Ete Phys Theor — Aux Frontieres de la Spectroscopie Laser. Ecole d'Ete de Physique Theorique
AUY — Ankara Universitesi Yilligi
AUZ — Australian Packaging
AUZCA — Analele Stiintifice ale Universitatii Al. I. Cuza din Iasi. Sectiunea 1c. Chimie
AUZFA — Analele Stiintifice ale Universitatii Al. I. Cuza din Iasi. Sectiunea 1b. Fizica
AUZMA — Analele Stiintifice ale Universitatii Al. I. Cuza din Iasi. Sectiunea 1a. Matematica
AUZOA3 — Australian Zoologist
AV — Actualidades (Venezuela)
AV — Annales des Voyages
AV — Annales des Voyages de la Geographie et de l'Histoire
AV — Annales Valaisannes
AV — Archaeologische Veroeffentlichungen. Deutsches Archaeologisches Institut Cairo
AV — Archiv fuer Voelkerkunde
AV — Archivio Veneto
AV — Arheoloski Vestnik
AV — Artha Vijnana
AV — Ateneo Veneto
AV — Audio Visual
AV — Aus Aachens Vorzeit
AV — Auserlesene Griechische Vasenbilder
AV — A Vanguarda. Semanario Republicano Federal
AV — AV Communication Review
A VA — Arts in Virginia
A Vaerl — Arsskrift. Historisk Forening for Vaerlose Kommune
AVAGA — Avvenire Agricolo
Avalanche Mag — Avalanche Magazine
Av Aliment Mejora Anim — Avances en Alimentacion y Mejora Animal
Av Aliment Mejora Anim Supl — Avances en Alimentacion y Mejora Animal. Suplemento
Avances Aliment Mejora Anim — Avances en Alimentacion y Mejora Animal
A Van Leeuw — Antonie Van Leeuwenhoek Journal of Microbiology and Serology [*Later, Antonie Van Leeuwenhoek Journal of Microbiology*]
Avant Sc C — Avant-Scene Cinema
Avant Scene — Avant-Scene Cinema
Avant Sc Th — Avant Scene Theatre
AVAPA — Archivio "De Vecchi" per l'Anatomia Patologica e la Medicina Clinica
AVASAX — Acta Veterinaria. Academiae Scientiarum Hungaricae
AVBAAI — Agronomia y Veterinaria
AVBIB — Advances in the Biosciences
AVBIDB — Avian Biology
AVBNA — Arhiv Bioloskih Nauka
AVBNAN — Arhiv Bioloskih Nauka

AV Bul Malay — Audio-Visual Bulletin (Malaysia)
AVBWKN — Annalen der Vereeniging tot het Hevorderen van de Beoefening der Wetenschap Onder de Katholieken in Nederland
AVC — Acta Venezolana (Caracas)
AVC — Arquivo de Viana do Castelo
AVC — Victorian Conveyancing Law and Practice
Av Cas CCH — Aviation Cases. Commerce Clearing House
Avco Corp Res Rep — Avco Corporation. Research Reports
AV Comm R — AV Communication Review
AV Commun Rev — AV Communication Review
AVCPAY — Advances in Clinical Pharmacology
AVCR — AV Communication Review
AVDF — Archivos Venezolanos de Folklore
AVDIA — Avian Diseases
AV Ed — Audio-Visual Education
AVEIA — Archivio Veterinario Italiano
AVEIAN — Archivio Veterinario Italiano
Ave Mag — Avenue Magazine
A Ven — Archeologia Veneta
AVen — Archivio Veneto
A Ven — Arte Veneta
Avenir Agr — Avenir Agriculture
Avenir Med — Avenir Medical
Avenir Milit — Avenir Militaire
Av Ensenanza Invest Esc Nac Agric (Chapingo) — Escuela Nacional de Agricultura (Chapingo). Avances en la Ensenanza y la Investigacion
Avery — Avery Index to Architectural Periodicals
Avery Ind Archit Per — Avery Index to Architectural Periodicals of Columbia University
Avery Index Archit Period — Avery Index to Architectural Periodicals
Avery Index Archit Period Second Ed Revis Enlarged Suppl — Avery Index to Architectural Periodicals. Second Edition. Revised andEnlarged. Supplement
A Ves — Arheoloski Vestnik
A Ves L — Arheoloski Vestnik (Ljubljana)
Avesta Stainless Bull — Avesta Stainless Bulletin
AVETD — Atomno-Vodorodnaya Energetika i Tekhnologiya
AVEZA6 — Acta Vitaminologica et Enzymologica
AVF — Archivos Venezolanos de Folklore
AVFSAO — Archiv fuer Fischereiwissenschaft
AVG — Educational Screen and Audiovisual Guide [*Later, AV Guide: The Learning Media Magazine*]
AVGADC — Aktual'nye Voprosy Gastroenterologii
AVGH — Annales des Voyages de la Geographie et de l'Histoire
Av Hist Soc Aust J — Aviation Historical Society of Australia. Journal
Avh Norske Vid Akad — Avhandlinger. Utgitt av Det Norske Videnskaps-Akademi
Avh Norske Vidensk Akad Oslo Ser 1 Mat Naturvidensk Kl — Avhandlinger Utgitt av det Norske Videnskaps-Akademi i Oslo. Serie I. Matematisk-Naturvidenskapelig Klasse
Avh Norsk Vid-Akad Oslo I NS — Avhandlinger Utgitt av Norsk Videnskaps-Akademi I Oslo. I. Matematisk-Naturvidenskapelig Klasse. Ny Serie
Avh Nor Vidensk-Akad Oslo I — Avhandlinger Utgitt av Norsk Videnskaps-Akademi I Oslo. I. Matematisk-Naturvidenskapelig Klasse
AVHUEA — Acta Veterinaria Hungarica
Avh Utgitt Nor Vidensk-Akad Oslo Mat-Naturvidensk Kl — Avhandlinger Utgitt av Norsk Videnskaps-Akademi I Oslo. Matematisk-Naturvidenskapelig Klasse
Av I — Audiovisual Instruction
AVIAA — Aviation Age
Aviakosm Ekolog Med — Aviakosmicheskaia i Ekologicheskaia Meditsina
Avian Biol — Avian Biology
Avian Dis — Avian Diseases
Avian Endocrinol Proc Int Symp — Avian Endocrinology. Proceedings. International Symposium on Avian Endocrinology
Avian Mamm Wildl Toxicol Conf — Avian and Mammalian Wildlife Toxicology. Conference
Avian Pathol — Avian Pathology
Avian Pathol J WVPA — Avian Pathology. Journal. WVPA (World Veterinary Poultry Association)
Avian Physiol — Avian Physiology
Avian Res — Avian Research
Aviat Age — Aviation Age
Aviation Da — Aviation Daily
Aviation N — Aviation News
Aviation Q — United States Aviation Quarterly
Aviation W — Aviation Week
Aviat Kosmonavt — Aviatsiya i Kosmonavtika
Aviat Med — Aviation Medicine
Aviat Res Monogr — Aviation Research Monographs
Aviat Rev — Aviation Review
Aviats Khim — Aviatsiya i Khimiya
Aviat Sp — Aviation/Space
Aviat Space Environ Med — Aviation, Space, and Environmental Medicine
Aviat Spac Environ Med — Aviation, Space, and Environmental Medicine
Aviat Sp En — Aviation, Space, and Environmental Medicine
Aviats Promst — Aviatsionnaya Promyshlennost
Aviats Tekh — Aviatsionnaya Tekhnika
Aviat Tr — Aviation Trader
Aviat Week Space Technol — Aviation Week and Space Technology
Avia Week — Aviation Week and Space Technology
Avic Mag — Avicultural Magazine
Avicult Mag — Avicultural Magazine
Avicult Tec — Avicultura Tecnica
AVINB — Advances in Instrumentation
A-V Ind — Audio-Visual Index
Av Ing Quim — Avances en Ingenieria Quimica
AV Inst — Audiovisual Instruction

Av Instr — Audiovisual Instruction
AVIRA2 — Acta Virologica
AVISD — Avishkar
A Visual — Arte Visual
A Viva — Archeologia Viva
A Vivant — Art Vivant
AVKOA — Aviatsiya i Kosmonavtika
AV Libn — Audiovisual Librarian
A-V L J — Audio-Visual Language Journal
Av L Rep CCH — Aviation Law Reports. Commerce Clearing House
AV Mark Pl — Audiovisual Market Place
AVMEBI — Avtometriia
AVMED — Aviation Medicine
A-V Media — Audio-Visual Media
AVMGAN — Avicultural Magazine
AVMHB — Archives of Mechanics
AVMPAG — Archivos Venezolanos de Medicina Tropical y Parasitologia Medica
AVN — Annalen des Historischen Vereins fuer den Niederrhein
AVN — Aviation News
AVNAG — Annalen des Vereins fuer Nassauische Altertumskunde und Geschichtsforschung
AVNAKGF — Annalen des Vereins fuer Nassauische Altertumskunde und Geschichtsforschung
AVNDA — Avtomobil'nye Dorogi
AV News — Audio-Visual News
AVNP — Arviap Nipinga. Eskimo Point
AVNSBV — Advances in Neurosurgery
AVNUA2 — Archivos Venezolanos de Nutricion
Avocado Grow — Avocado Grower
Avoc Grow — Avocado Grower
Av Odontoestomatol — Avances en Odontoestomatologia
A Voices — Art Voices
AVOMBI — Advances in Ophthalmology
AvP — Alertuemer von Pergamon
AvP — Avant-Poste
AVPADN — Avian Pathology
AVPBC — Advances in Psychobiology
AVPBCP — Advances in Psychobiology
AVPCA — Advances in Pharmacology and Chemotherapy
AVPCCS — Archiv foer Pharmaci og Chemi. Scientific Edition
Av Periodoncia — Avances en Periodoncia
AVPI — Agricultural and Veterinary Products Index
AVPMAM — American Veterinary Medical Association. Scientific Proceedings of the Annual Meeting
AVPPAV — Archivos Venezolanos de Puericultura y Pediatria
AVPRA — Avtomobil'naya Promyshlennost
Av Prod Anim — Avances en Produccion Animal
AVPTA9 — Archivos Venezolanos de Patologia Tropical y Parasitologia Medica
AVPZAR — Archiv fuer Pflanzenschutz
AVR — Australian Video Review
AVRD — Audio Visual Review Digest
AVRTAJ — Acta Vertebratica
AvSc — Avant-Scene
AVSCA7 — Acta Veterinaria Scandinavica
AVSCB — Advances in Veterinary Science and Comparative Medicine
AvScC — Avant-Scene du Cinema
AVsL — Archiv des Vereins fuer Siebenbuergische Landeskunde
AVSLK — Archiv des Vereins fuer Siebenbuergische Landeskunde
AVsLund — Vetenskaps-Societeten i Lund. Aarsbok
AVSPAC — Acta Veterinaria Scandinavica. Supplementum
AVSRCK — Advances in Sleep Research
AVSTA — Advances in Space Science and Technology
AVSVA — Avtomaticheskaya Svarka
AVT — Archivio Veneto-Tridentino
AVTEA — Avtomatika i Telemekhanika
Av Tec Cenicafe — Avances Tecnicos Cenicafe
Av Ter — Avances en Terapeutica
AVThRw — Aufsaetze und Vortraege zur Theologie und Religionswissenschaft
Avto — Avtomobil'nyi
Avtodorozhnik Ukr — Avtodorozhnik Ukrainy
Avtog Delo — Avtogennoe Delo
Avtoklavn Betony Izdeliya Ikh Osn — Avtoklavnye Betony i Izdeliya na Ikh Osnove
Avtom — Avtomatika
Avtom & Vychisl Tekh — Avtomatika i Vychislitel'naya Tekhnika
Avtomatika — Akademija Nauk Ukrainskoi RSR. Institut Elektrotehniki Avtomatika
Avtomat i Telemeh — Akademija Nauk SSSR. Avtomatika i Telemehanika
Avtomat i Telemekh — Akademija Nauk SSSR. Avtomatika i Telemekhanika
Avtomat i Vychisl Tekhn — Avtomatika i Vychislitel'naya Tekhnika. Akademiya Nauk Latviiskoi SSR
Avtomat i Vychisl Tekhn — Avtomatika i Vychislitel'naya Tekhnika. Minskii Radiotekhnicheskii Institut
Avtomat i Vycisl Tehnika (Minsk) — Avtomatika i Vycislitel'naja Tehnika (Minsk)
Avtomat i Vycisl Tehn (Riga) — Avtomatika i Vycislitel'naja Tehnika (Riga)
Avtomat Izchisl Tekhn — Avtomatika i Izchislitelna Tekhnika
Avtomat Sistemy Upravlen — Leningradskii Gosudarstvennyi Universitet Avtomatizirovannye Sistemy Upravlenija
Avtomat Sistemy Upravlenija i Pribory Avtomat — Avtomatizirovannye Sistemy Upravlenija i Pribory Avtomatiki
Avtomat Upravlenie i Vychisl Tekhn — Avtomaticheskoe Upravlenie i Vychislitel'naya Tekhnika
Avtomat Upravl i Vycisl Tehnika — Avtomaticeskoe Upravlenie i Vycislitel'naja Tehnika
Avtometrija — Avtometrija Akademija Nauk SSSR
Avtom Khim Proizvod (Kiev) — Avtomatizatsiya Khimicheskikh Proizvodstv (Kiev)

Avtom Khim Proizvod (Moscow) — Avtomatizatsiya Khimicheskikh Proizvodstv (Moscow)
Avtom Khim Promsti — Avtomatizatsiya Khimicheskoi Promyshlennosti
Avtom Kompleksn Mekh Khim Tekhnol Protsessov — Avtomatizatsiya i Kompleksnaya Mekhanizatsiya Khimiko Tekhnologicheskikh Protsessov
Avtom Kontrol Metody Elektr Izmer Tr Vses Konf — Avtomaticheskii Kontrol i Metody Elektricheskikh Izmerenii. Trudy Vsesoyuznoi Konferentsii po Avtomaticheskomu Kontrolyu i Metodam Elektricheskikh Izmerenii
Avtom Kontrol Upr Obogashch Gidrometall Tsvetn Met — Avtomaticheskii Kontrol i Upravlenie pri Obogashchenii i Gidrometallurgii Tsvetnykh Metallov
Avtom Mekh Oborud Protsessov Tsellyul Bum Proizvod — Avtomatizatsiya, Mekhanizatsiya i Oborudovanie Protsessov Tsellyulozno-Bumazhnogo Proizvodstva
Avtom Mekh Protsessov Litya — Avtomatizatsiya i Mekhanizatsiya Protsessov Lit'ya
Avtom Mikrobiol Elektrofiziol Issled — Avtomatizatsiya Mikrobiologicheskikh i Elektrofiziologicheskikh Issledovanii
Avtom Nauchn Issled Khim — Avtomatizatsiya Nauchnykh Issledovanii v Khimii
Avtom Nauchn Issled Khim Khim Tekhnol Mater Vses Shk — Avtomatizatsiya Nauchnykh Issledovanii v Khimii i Khimicheskoi Tekhnologii. Materialy Vsesoyuznoi Shkoly
Avtom Nauchn Issled Mater Vses Shk — Avtomatizatsiya Nauchnykh Issledovanii. Materialy Vsesoyuznoi Shkoli po Avtomatizatsii Nauchnykh Issledovanii
Avtom Neftepererab Neftekhim Promsti — Avtomatizatsiya Neftepererabatyvayushchei i Neftekhimicheskoi Promyshlennosti
Avtomob Dorogi — Avtomobil'nye Dorogi
Avtomob Dorogi Dorozhne Budiv — Avtomobil ni Dorogi i Dorozhne Budivnitstvo
Avtomob Dorogi Dorozhn Stroit — Avtomobil'nye Dorogi i Dorozhnoe Stroitel'stvo
Avtomob Prom-St — Avtomobil'naya Promyshlennost
Avtomob Traktorostr — Avtomobile- i Traktorostroenie
Avtomob Trakt Promst — Avtomobil'naya i Traktornaya Promyshlennost
Avtomob Transp Dorogi — Avtomobil'nyi Transport i Dorogi
Avtomob Transp (Kiev) — Avtomobil'nyi Transport (Kiev)
Avtomob Transp (Moscow) — Avtomobil'nyi Transport (Moscow)
Avtomon Transp Kaz — Avtomobil'nyi Transport Kazakhstana
Avtom Priborostr — Avtomatizatsiya i Priborostroenie
Avtom Priborostr Inf Nauchno Tekh — Avtomatika i Priborostroenie. Informasionnyi Nauchno-Tekhnicheskii
Avtom Proekt Elektron — Avtomatizatsiya Proektirovaniya v Elektronike
Avtom Proizvod Protsessov — Avtomatizatsiya Proizvodstvennykh Protsessov
Avtom Proizvod Protsessov Mashinostr Priborostr (Lvov) — Avtomatizatsiya Proizvodstvennykh Protsessov v Mashinostroenii i Priborostroenii (Lvov)
Avtom Proizvod Protsessov Tsvetn Metall — Avtomatizatsiya Proizvodstvennykh Protsessov Tsvetnoi Metallurgii
Avtom Sist Upr Prib Avtom — Avtomatizirovannye Sistemy Upravlenija i Pribory Avtomatiki
Avtom Staleplavil'n Proizvod — Avtomatizatsiya Staleplavil'nogo Proizvodstva
Avtom Svarka — Avtomaticheskaya Svarka
Avtom Tekhnol Protsessov Khim Proizvod — Avtomatizatsiya Tekhnologicheskikh Protsessov Khimicheskikh Proizvodstv
Avtom Telemekh — Avtomatika i Telemekhanika
Avtom Telemekh Svyaz — Avtomatika, Telemekhanika, i Svyaz
Avtom Tsitol Diagn Opukholei — Avtomatizatsiya Tsitologicheskoi Diagnostiki Opukholei
Avtom Vychisl — Avtomatika i Vychislitel'naya Tekhnika
Avtotrakt Delo — Avtotraktornoe Delo
AVTRA — Avtomobil'nyi Transport
Avt Telemekh — Avtomatika i Telemekhanika
Avulso Div Fom Prod Miner (Braz) — Avulso. Divisao de Fomento da Producao Mineral (Brazil)
Avulso Lab Prod Miner (Braz) — Avulso. Laboratorio da Producao Mineral (Brazil)
AVUSAV — Aberdeen University. Studies
Avven Agr — Avvenire Agricolo
Avvenire Agric — Avvenire Agricolo
AVVTA — Avtomatika i Vychislitel'naya Tekhnika (1961-66)
AW — Air Wonder Stories
AW — All-Alaska Weekly
AW — Allgemeine Wochenzeitung der Juden in Deutschland
AW — Alliance Witness
AW — American West
AW — Annals of Wyoming
AW — Antike Welt
AW — Arrow
AW — Australian Workman
AW — Aviation Week
AW — [The] Arab World
Awamia Rev Rech Agron Maroc — Awamia. Revue de la Recherche Agronomique Marocaine
AWAN — AWA [Alberta Wilderness Association] Newsletter
Awards Nucl Med Radiopharmacol — Awards in Nuclear Medicine and Radiopharmacology
Awas — Awasis
AWAT — Archiv fuer Wissenschaftliche Erforschung des Alten Testaments
AWA Tech Rev — AWA [Amalgamated Wireless Australasia] Technical Review
AWBAbh — Koeniglich-Preussische Akademie der Wissenschaften (Berlin). Abhandlungen
AWBMA — Archiwum Budowy Maszyn
AWBSb — Koeniglich-Preussische Akademie der Wissenschaften (Berlin). Sitzungsberichte
AWC — Algemeen Weekblad voor Christendom en Cultuur
AWCH NSW Newsletter — Association for the Welfare of Children in Hospital. New South Wales. Newsletter
AWCM — Advances in Working Capital Management
AWCN — American Women Composers Newsletter

AWD — Recht der Internationalen Wirtschaft Aussenwirtschaftsdienst des Betriebsberaters

AW Dimock Lect NY State Coll Agric Life Sci Dep Plant Pathol — A. W. Dimock Lectures. New York State College of Agriculture and Life Sciences.Department of Plant Pathology

AWEG — Australian Writers and Editors' Guide

AWF Mitt — AWF [*Ausschuss fuer Wirtschaftliche Fertigung*] Mitteilungen

AWG Phk — Akademie der Wissenschaften in Goettingen. Philologisch-Historische Klasse

AWIFA — Angewandte Informatik/Applied Informatics

AWJ — Allgemeine Wochenzeitung der Juden in Deutschland

AWJD — Allgemeine Wochenzeitung der Juden in Deutschland

AWK — Australian Worker's Compensation Guide

A Wkbld — Artistiek Weekblad

A Wkly — Arts Weekly

AWL — The Arab World (London)

AWLM — Akademie der Wissenschaften und der Literatur (Mainz) Publications

AWLMA9 — Akademie der Wissenschaften und der Literatur in Mainz. Abhandlungen der Mathematisch-Naturwissenschaftlichen Klasse

AWLM AGSK — Akademie der Wissenschaften und der Literatur in Mainz. Abhandlungen der Geistes- und Sozialwissenschaftlichen Klasse

AWLMGS — Akademie der Wissenschaften und der Literatur in Mainz. Abhandlungen der Geistes- und Sozialwissenschaftlichen Klasse

AWLMML — Akademie der Wissenschaften und der Literatur in Mainz. Klasse der Literatur

AWLRAO — Australian Wildlife Research

AWM — Auskunftsblatt

AWMAbh — Akademie der Wissenschaften in Muenchen. Abhandlungen

AWMADF — Agricultural Water Management

AWMFAR — Acta Universitatis Wratislaviensis. Matematyka, Fizyka, Astronomia

AWMIA2 — Awamia. Revue de la Recherche Agronomique Marocaine

AWMMAE — Akademie der Wissenschaften und der Literatur in Mainz. Mathematisch-Naturwissenschaftliche Klasse. Mikrofauna des Meeresbodens

AWMSb — Akademie der Wissenschaften in Muenchen. Philosophisch-Historische Klasse. Sitzungsberichte

AWN — Allahabad Weekly Notes

AWN — Aramco World (New York)

AWO — Afrique Industrie Infrastructures

AWO — Average Monthly Weather Outlook

A Work — Art Work

A Workers Q — Art Workers' Quarterly

AWPAA — Angewandte Parasitologie

AWPE — Abstracts of Working Papers in Economics

AWPOA — Air and Water Pollution

AWPOAZ — Air and Water Pollution

A/WPR — Air/Water Pollution Report

AWR — Anglo-Welsh Review

AWRA Monogr Ser — AWRA Monograph Series

AWRE Rep O — AWRE (Atomic Weapons Research Establishment) Report O

AWRE Rep Ser NR UK At Energ Auth — AWRE (Atomic Weapons Research Establishment) Report. Series NR. United Kingdom Atomic Energy Authority

AWRE Rep Ser R UK At Energ Auth — AWRE (Atomic Weapons Research Establishment) Report. Series R. United Kingdom Atomic Energy Authority

AWRHA — Australian Water Resources Council. Hydrological Series

AWRTAQ — Australian Water Resources Council. Technical Paper

AWS — Air Wonder Stories

AWS — Aviation Week and Space Technology

AWSJ — Asian Wall Street Journal

AWSTA — Aviation Week and Space Technology

AWT Abwassertech — AWT Abwassertechnik

AWTEA — Allgemeine Waermetechnik

AWW — Australian Women's Weekly

AWW — Australian Writer's Workshop

AWWA Annu Conf Proc — AWWA [*American Water Works Association*] Annual Conference. Proceedings

AWWA Disinfect Semin Proc — AWWA [*American Water Works Association*] Disinfection Seminar. Proceedings

AWWA Fed Conv — AWWA (American Water Works Association) Federal Convention

AWWA Semin Control Inorg Contam — AWWA (American Water Works Association) Seminar on Control of Inorganic Contaminants

AWWA Semin Controlling Corros Water Syst Proc — AWWA [*American Water Works Association*] Seminar on Controlling Corrosion within Water Systems. Proceedings

AWWA Semin Minimizing Recycl Water Plant Sludge — AWWA (American Water Works Association) Seminar on Minimizing and Recycling Water Plant Sludge

AWWA Semin Ozonation — AWWA [*American Water Works Association*] Seminar on Ozonation. Recent Advances and Research Needs

AWWA Semin Proc Controlling Corros Water Syst — AWWA (American Water Works Association) Seminar Proceedings. Controlling Corrosion within Water Systems

AWWA Semin Strategies Control Trihalomethanes — AWWA (American Water Works Association) Seminar on Strategies for the Control of Trihalomethanes

AWWA Semin Water Chlorination Princ Pract — AWWA [*American Water Works Association*] Seminar on Water Chlorination Principles and Practices

AWWA Semin Water Disinfect Ozone Chloramines Chlorine Dioxide — AWWA (American Water Works Association) Seminar on Water Disinfection with Ozone, Chloramines, or Chlorine Dioxide

AWWA Semin Water Treat Waste Disposal Proc — AWWA (American Water Works Association) Seminar on Water Treatment Waste Disposal. Proceedings

AWWA Water Qual Technol Conf Proc — AWWA [*American Water Works Association*] Water Quality Technology Conference. Proceedings

AWWDs — Koenigliche Akademie der Wissenschaften (Wien). Denkschriften

AWWR — Alaska Wildlife Watcher's Report

AWWSb — Akademie der Wissenschaften in Wien. Sitzungsberichte

AX — Axis

AXB — Artha Vijnana

Axel Heiberg Isl Res Rep Geol McGill Univ — Axel Heiberg Island Research Reports. Geology. McGill University

A Xen — Actes de Xenophon

A Xer — Actes de Xeropotamou

AXL — Cartonnages et Emballages Modernes

AXT — Australian Sales Tax Guide

AXVMA — Archiv fuer Experimentelle Veterinaermedizin

AXVMAW — Archiv fuer Experimentelle Veterinaermedizin

AYA — Anuario. Facultad de Derecho

Ayasofia Muez Yil — Ayasofya Muezesi Yilligi

A Yb — Arts Yearbook

AYBIL — Australian Yearbook of International Law

AYE — Antropologia y Etnologia

AyL — Armas y Letras

AYLR — Aylesford Review

AY Purdue Univ Coop Ext Serv — AY. Purdue University Cooperative Extension Service

AYR — American Year Review

Ayrshire Archaeol Natur Hist Collect 2 Ser — Ayrshire Archaeological and Natural History Collections. Series 2

AZ — A la Luz

AZ — Archaeologische Zeitung

AZ — Archivalische Zeitschrift

AZ — Arizona Reports

AZ — Armeezeitung

AZA — Allgemeine Zeitung (Augsburg)

Azabu Juika Daigaku Kenkyu Hokoku Bull — Azabu Juika Daigaku Kenkyu Hokoku/Bulletin. Azabu Veterinary College

AZAF — Archivio per la Zoologia, l'Anatomia, e la Fisiologia

AZAg — Annals of Zoology (Agra)

AZARAO — Arizona. Agricultural Experiment Station. Research Report

AzAS — Aziia i Afrika Segodnia

AZATAU — Arizona. Agricultural Experiment Station. Technical Bulletin

AZBAZ — Arzneimittel-Forschung. Beiheft

AZBTAZ — Annotationes Zoologicae et Botanicae

AZBUD7 — Acta Zoologica Bulgarica

AZCRAY — Acta Zoologica Cracoviensia

AZDJ — Allgemeine Zeitung des Judentums

AZEAAR — Annales de Zoologie - Ecologie Animale

AZEG — Archives de Zoologie Experimentale Generale

AZEGAB — Archives de Zoologie Experimentale et Generale

Azerbaidzan Gos Univ Ucen Zap — Azerbaidzanskii Gosudarstvennyi Universitet Imeni M. Kirova. Ucenye Zapiski

Azerbaidzan Gos Univ Ucen Zap Ser Fiz-Mat Nauk — Azerbaidzanskii Gosudarstvennyi Universitet Imeni S. M. Kirova. Ucenye Zapiski.Serija Fiziko-Matematiceskih Nauk

Azerbaidzhan Med Zhurnal — Azerbaidzhanskii Meditsinskii Zhurnal

Azerbajdzansk Fil Akad Nauk SSSR — Azerbajdzanskij Filial Akademii Nauk SSSR. SSCI Elmler Aqademijasb Azerbajcan Filialb

Azerb Ak Heberleri — Azerbajdzan SSR Elmler Akademijasynyn Herberleri. Izvestija Akademii Nauk Azerbajdzanskoj SSR

Azerb Gos Med Inst Mater Nauchn Konf — Azerbaidzhanskii Gosudarstvennyi Meditsinskii Institut Materialy Nauchnoi Konferentsii

Azerb Gos Med Inst Uch Zap — Azerbaidzhanskii Gosudarstvennyi Meditsinskii Institut. Uchenye Zapiski

Azerb Gos Nauchno Issled Proektn Inst Neft Promsti Tr — Azerbaidzhanskii Gosudarstvennyi Nauchno-Issledovatel'skii i Proektnyi InstitutNeftyanoi Promyshlennosti. Trudy

Azerb Inst Nefti Khim Tr — Azerbaidzhanskii Institut Nefti i Khimii. Trudy

Azerb Khim Zh — Azerbaidzhanskii Khimicheskii Zhurnal

Azerb Med Zh — Azerbaidzhanskii Meditsinskii Zhurnal

Azerb Nauchno Issled Inst Gematol Pereliv Krovi Sb Nauchn Tr — Azerbaidzhanskii Nauchno-Issledovatel'skii Institut Gematologii i Perelivaniya Krovi. Sbornik Nauchnykh Trudov

Azerb Nauchno-Issled Inst Oftalmol Sb Tr — Azerbaidzhanskii Nauchno-Issledovatel'skii Institut Oftal'mologii. Sbornik Trudov

Azerb Nauchno Issled Inst Sadovod Vinograd Subtyrop Kult Tr — Azerbaidzhanskii Nauchno-Issledovatel'skii Institut Sadovodstva, Vinogradarstvai Subtropicheskikh Kul'tur. Trudy

Azerb Nauchno Issled Inst Shelkovod Tr — Azerbaidzhanskii Nauchno-Issledovatel'skii Institut Shelkovodstva. Trudy

Azerb Neft Khoz — Azerbajdzhanskoe Neftyanoe Khozyajstvo

Azerb Skh Inst S Agamaliogly Tr — Azerbaidzhanskii Sel'skokhozyaistvennyi Institut imeni S. Agamaliogly. Trudy

Azetylen Wiss Ind — Azetylen in Wissenschaft und Industrie

AZFEAA — Acta Zoologica Fennica

AZHIA — Arizona Highways

AZHUE4 — Acta Zoologica Hungarica

AZI — Archivio Zoologico Italiano

AZIH — Archiwum Zydowskiego Instytutu Historycznego

Azija i Afr Segodnja — Azija i Afrika Segodnja

AZIL — Arbeiten aus dem Zoologischen Institut der Universitaet Innsbruck

AZIMDI — Arnoldia Zimbabwe

AZJ — Allgemeine Zeitung des Judentums

AZKZA — Azerbajdzhanskii Khimicheskii Zhurnal

AZ L — Arizona Law Review

AZLGAC — Annals of Zoology

AZ LR — Arizona Law Review

AZMXAY — Acta Zoologica Mexicana

AZMZA — Azerbajdzhanskii Meditsinskii Zhurnal

AZO — Allgemeine Zionistische Organisation

AZOCAF — Acta Zoologica Cracoviensia

AZOF — Annales Zoologica Fennici

AZOFAO — Annales Zoologici Fennici
A Zog — Actes de Zographou
AZOGAR — Annales Zoologici
AZOGB — Australian and New Zealand Journal of Obstetrics and Gynaecology
AZOIAX — Archivio Zoologico Italiano
AZOJA2 — Annotationes Zoologicae Japonenses
AZOLA8 — Acta Zoologica Lilloana
AZOOAH — Annales de Zootechnie
AZOSAT — Acta Zoologica
AZOTAW — Archivos de Zootecnia
Azotul Agric — Azotul in Agricultura

AZP — Archiv fuer die Zivilistische Praxis
AzQ — Arizona Quarterly
AZRC — Arid Zone Research Centre
AZSHAG — Acta Zoologica. Academiae Scientiarum Hungaricae
AZSITE — Archaeological Sites Data Base
AZSPA6 — Arquivos de Zoologia do Estado de Sao Paulo
AZTh — Arbeiten zur Theologie
AZW — Annales Zoologici. Instytut Zoologiczny. Polska Akademia Nauk (Warsaw)
AZWBAI — Arizona. Game and Fish Department. Wildlife Bulletin
AZXNAP — Archives de Zoologie Experimentale et Generale. Notes et Revue
AZZFAB — Annales Zoologici. Societatis Zoologicae-Botanicae Fennicae "Vanamo"

B

B — Banker
B — Barcelona
B — Beiaard
B — Bibliofilia
B — Bibliotekarz
B — Biekorf
B — Bigaku
B — Bolero
B — Bookman
B — Brasilia. Instituto de Estudos Brasileiros. Faculdade de Letras de Coimbra
B — Brazda
B — Broadcasting
B — [*The*] Bulletin
B — Bund
B — Weekly Law Bulletin
Ba — Babel. International Journal of Translation
BA — Bach
Ba — Baconiana
BA — Baessler-Archiv
BA — Balkan Archiv
BA — Bank Administration
BA — Beitraege zur Assyriologie und Semitischen Sprachwissenschaft
BA — Belleten (Ankara)
BA — Berita Anthropologi
BA — Biblical Archaeologist
BA — Biblical Archaeology
BA — Bibliotheca Aegyptiaca
BA — Biological Abstracts
BA — Boletin Arqueologico
BA — Bollettino d'Arte
BA — Book of Awards
BA — Books Abroad
BA — Bracara Augusta. Revista Cultural da Camara Municipal de Braga
BA — Buenos Aires
BA — Business Administration
BA — Die Botschaft des Alten Testaments
BAA — Braunschweiger Anglistische Arbeiten
BAA — British Archaeological Abstracts
BAA — Bulletin. Association pro Aventico
BAA — Bulletin d'Archeologie Algerienne
BAA — Bulletin des Archives d'Anvers
BAA — Technisch Weekblad
BAAA — Bibliographie Analytique de l'Afrique Antique
BAAA — Bulletin de l'Association des Amis d'Alain
BAAAC — Bulletin. Association des Amis de l'Art Copte
BAABL — Boletin. Academia Argentina de Buenas Letras
BAAC — Boletin. Academia de Artes y Ciencias
BAAFB — Bulletin. Academie des Sciences Agricoles et Forestieres (Bucharest)
BAAFBT — Bulletin. Academie des Sciences Agricoles et Forestieres
BAAFLP — Bulletin. Association Amicale des Anciens Eleves de la Faculte des Lettres de Paris
BAAG — Association des Amis d'Andre Gide. Bulletin d'Informations
BAAI — Bollettino. Associazione degli Africanisti Italiani
BAAJ — British Archaeological Association. Journal
BAAL — Boletin. Academia Argentina de Letras
BAALA — Societe des Agricultures d'Algerie. Bulletin
BA Alg — Bulletin d'Archeologie Algerienne
BA Alger — Bulletin d'Archeologie Algerienne
BAAP — Beira Alta. Arquivo Provincial
BAAPA — Bulletin. American Association of Petroleum Geologists
BAAPG — Bulletin. American Association of Petroleum Geologists
BAAR — Bollettino. Associazione Archeologica Romana
BAARD — Bulletin. Association des Amis de Rabelais et de la Deviniere
BAAS — Report of the First Meeting of the British Association for the Advancement of Science
BAASB — British Association for American Studies. Bulletin
BAB — Academie Royale de Belgique. Bulletin. Classe des Lettres et des Sciences Morales et Politiques
BAB — Association des Bibliothecaires Francais. Bulletin
Bab — Babyloniaca. Etudes de Philologie Assyro-Babylonienne
BAB — Boletin de Arqueologia (Bogota)
BAB — Bremer Archaeologische Blaetter
BAB — Izvestiia na Arkheologicheskiia Institut. Bulgarska Akademiia na Naukite
BABA — Beitraege zur Aegyptischen Bauforschung und Altertumskunde
BABA — Boletin. Academia de Bellas Artes de Valladolid
BABAB — Bauplanung-Bautechnik

BA Barcel — Bulleti Informatiu. Institut de Prehistoria i Arqueologia. Diputacio Provincialde Barcelona
BABAT — Boletin. Academia de Bellas Artes y Ciencias Historicas de Toledo
B Abbeville — Bulletin. Societe d'Emulation Historique et Litteraire d'Abbeville
BABC — Boletin. Academia de Bellas Artes de Cordoba
BABCA — Bulletin of the American Business Communication Association
B Aberdeen Univ Afr Stud Group — Bulletin. Aberdeen University. African Studies Group
B A Besch — Bulletin van de Vereeniging tot Bevordering der Kennis van de Antike Beschaving
BAbh — Abhandlungen der Preussischen Akademie der Wissenschaften. Berlin
BABIEC — Biotechnology and Applied Biochemistry
Bab J A — Babel. Journal of the Australian Federation of Modern Language Teachers Association
BABL — Boletin. Real Academia de Buenas Letras de Barcelona
BABLB — Boletin. Real Academia de Buenas Letras de Barcelona
BABN — Bollettino. Archivio Storico del Banco di Napoli
BABO — Association of British Orientalists. Bulletin
BABO — Association of British Orientalists. Bulletin of Near Eastern and Indian Studies
BABO — Association of British Orientalists. Bulletin of Oriental Studies
BABSD — South African Bureau of Standards. Bulletin
BA Bull LA — Bar Association Bulletin, Los Angeles
BABV — Baessler-Archiv. Beitraege zur Voelkerkunde
Baby J — Baby John
Babyl — Babyloniaca. Etudes de Philologie Assyro-Babylonienne
BAC — Barclays Review
BAC — Biblioteca de Autores Cristianos
BAC — Boletim de Antropologia (Ceara)
BAC — Boletin. Academia Colombiana
BAC — Boletin. Real Academia de Cordoba
BAC — Bollettino di Archeologia Cristiana
BAC — Bulletin Archeologique. Comite des Travaux Historiques et Archeologiques
BACA — Bulleti. Associacio Catalana d'Antropologia
B Acad Ci Letras Artes Cordoba — Boletin. Real Academia de Ciencias. Buenas Letras y Bellas Artes de la Ciudad de Cordoba
B Acad Espan — Boletin. Real Academia Espanola
B Acad Gallega — Boletin. Real Academia Gallega
B Acad Hist — Boletin. Real Academia de la Historia
B Acad Letras Barcelona — Boletin. Real Academia de Buenas Letras de Barcelona
B Acad Med — Bulletin. Academie de Medecine
B Acad Nac Hist — Boletin. Academia Nacional de Historia
B Acad Roy Belg — Bulletin. Classe des Lettres et des Sciences Morales et Politiques. Academie Royale de Belgique
B Acad Roy Sci O Mer — Bulletin des Seances. Academie Royale des Sciences d'Outre-Mer
B Acad Sci — Bulletin. Academy of Sciences of the USSR. Division of Chemical Science
BACAEP — Butlleti. Associacio Catalana d'Antropologia, Etnologia, i Prehistoria
BACAP — Boletim. Associacao Central da Agricultura Portuguesa
BACB — Biblioteca de Autores Colombianos (Bogota)
B Ac Belg — Bulletins. Academie Royale de Belgique
BACBLNAC — Boletin. Academia de Ciencias, Bellas Letras, y Nobles Artes de Cordoba
BACD — Bulletin de l'Association Charles Dullin
BACF — Boletin de la Academia de Ciencias Fisicas, Matematicas, y Naturales [*Caracas*]
BACH — Boletin de la Academia Chilena de la Historia
B Ac Hist — Boletin. Real Academia de la Historia
BachJb — Bach-Jahrbuch
Bach of Arts — Bachelor of Arts
BACIE J — BACIE [*British Association for Commercial and Industrial Education*] Journal
Backgr Collect — Background to Collecting
Backgr Notes — Background Notes
Background Migraine Migraine Symp — Background to Migraine. Migraine Symposium
Background Pap Workshop Tropospheric Transp Pollut Ocean — Background Papers for a Workshop on the Tropospheric Transport of Pollutants tothe Ocean
Back Notes — Background Notes on the Countries of the World. US Department of State
Backpacking J — Backpacking Journal
Backyard — Your Big Backyard
BACL — Boletin. Academia Cubana de la Lengua
BACILg — Bulletin Semestriel. Association des Classiques de l'Universite de Liege

BACM — Bulletin. Academie pour l'Histoire de la Culture Materielle
B Ac N — Bulletin des Seances. Academie de Nimes
B Ac Nimes — Bulletin des Seances. Academie de Nimes
BACOAV — Bulletin. Agricultural Chemical Society of Japan
BACol — Boletin. Academia Colombiana
BA Coll Agric Mag — BA [*Bansilal Amritlal*] College of Agriculture Magazine
BA Copt — Bulletin. Societe d'Archeologie Copte
B Ac Pol — Bulletin International. Academie Polonaise des Sciences et des Lettres
BACPS — Boletin. Academia de Ciencias Politicas y Sociales
BA Cr — Bollettino di Archeologia Cristiana
B A Crist — Bullettino di Archeologia Cristiana
BACT — Bulletin Archeologique. Comite des Travaux Historiques et Scientifiques
Bact Bacteriophages Fungi — Bacteria, Bacteriophages, and Fungi
Bacteriol News — Bacteriological News
Bacteriol Proc — Bacteriological Proceedings
Bacteriol Rev — Bacteriological Reviews
Bacteriol Virusol Parazitol Epidemiol — Bacteriologia, Virusologia, Parazitologia, Epidemiologia
Bacteriol Virusol Parazitol Epidemiol (Buchar) — Bacteriologia, Virusologia, Parazitologia, Epidemiologia (Bucharest)
Bacteriophage Lambda Conf Pap — Bacteriophage Lambda. Conference. Papers
Bact Genet Syst — Bacterial Genetic Systems
BACTH — Bulletin Archeologique. Comite des Travaux Historiques et Scientifiques
BACTHS — Bulletin Archeologique. Comite des Travaux Historiques et Scientifiques
Bact Immunoglobulin Binding Proteins — Bacterial Immunoglobulin-Binding Proteins
Bact Infect Respir Gastrointest Mucosae — Bacterial Infections of Respiratory and Gastrointestinal Mucosae
Bact Proc — Bacteriological Proceedings
Bact Protein Toxins Eur Workshop — Bacterial Protein Toxins. European Workshop
Bact R — Bacteriological Reviews
Bact Rev — Bacteriological Reviews
Bact Rs — Bacteriological Reviews
Bact Transp — Bacterial Transport
B Ac (Zagr) — Bulletin International. Academie Yugoslave des Sciences et des Beaux-Arts et Belles-Lettres (Zagreb)
BAD — Bangkok Bank. Monthly Review
BAD — Bulletin. Academie Delphinale
BAD — Bulletino di Archeologia e Storia Dalmata
BAD — Magazine of Bank Administration
Badan Fizjogr Pol Zachod — Badania Fizjograficzne nad Polska Zachodnia. B. Biologia
BADE — Bulletin of the Association of Departments of English
Baden Heimat — Badener Heimat
Bad FB — Badische Fundberichte
Bad Fber — Badische Fundberichte
Bad Fu Ber — Badische Fundberichte
Bad Geol Abh — Badische Geologische Abhandlungen
Badger Pharm — Badger Pharmacist. Wisconsin Pharmaceutical Association
Bad Hersfelder Jh — Bad Hersfelder Jahresheft
Badische Hist Komm Neujahrsbl — Badische Historische Kommission. Neujahrsblaetter
BADL — Bonner Arbeiten zur Deutschen Literatur
Bad M — Badminton Magazine
Badminton Rev — Badminton Review
Bad N — Badener Neujahrsblaetter
Bad Not Z — Badische Notarszeitschrift
Bad Obst Gartenbau — Badischer Obst- und Gartenbau
Bad Rechtsprax — Badische Rechtspraxis
BADWS — Bayerische Akademie der Wissenschaften. Philosophisch-Historische Klasse. Sitzungsberichte
BAE — Bank of Jamaica. Bulletin
BAE — Biblioteca de Autores Espanoles
BAE — Boletin. Real Academia Espanola
BAEAD2 — Alabama. Agricultural Experiment Station. Bulletin (Auburn University)
BAEC — Bollettino. Amicizia Ebraico-Cristiana di Firenze
BAEC — Bulletin. Association des Amis des Eglises et de l'Art Coptes
Baecker Konditor — Baecker und Konditor
BAEM — Bulletin des Amis d'Emmanuel Mounier
BAEO — Boletin. Asociacion Espanola de Orientalistas
BAEPE — Boletin. Asociacion Europea de Profesores de Espanol
Baer Berl — Baer von Berlin
Baessler-Arch — Baessler-Archiv
Baessler-Arch — Baessler-Archiv. Beitraege zur Voelkerkunde
Baessler Arch — Baessler-Archiv. Beitraege zur Volkskunde
Baessler Archv — Baessler-Archiv. Beitraege zur Voelkerkunde
Baetica — Baetica; Estudios de Arte, Geografia, e Historia
BAF — Bamberger Abhandlungen und Forschungen
BAF — Bulletin. Association des Amis de Flaubert
BAF — Bulletin. Societe Nationale des Antiquaires de France
BAFA — Boletin. Asociacion Folklorica (Argentina)
BAFAS — Bulletin de l'Association Francaise pour l'Avancement des Sciences
BAFN — Boletim. Associacao de Filosofia Natural
BAfO — Beiheft. Archiv fuer Orientforschung
BAFOEG — Biotechnology in Agriculture and Forestry
BAFPD — Biogas and Alcohol Fuels Production
BAFS — Bulletin Annuel de la Fondation Suisse
BAG — Beitraege zur Alten Geschichte
BAG — Boletin. Academia Galega
BAG — Bovagblad
BAGB — Bulletin. Association Guillaume Bude
BAGB SC — Bulletin. Association Guillaume Bude. Supplement Critique
B Ag Econ Colon Auto Ter Afr — Bulletin. Agence Economique des Colonies Autonomes et des Territoires Africainssous Mandat

B Agenc Int Energie Atom — Bulletin. Agence Internationale de l'Energie Atomique
BAGF — Bulletin de l'Association des Geographes Francais
B Ag Gen Colon — Bulletin. Agence Generale des Colonies
Baghdader Mitt — Baghdader Mitteilungen. Deutsches Archaeologisches Institut. Abteilung Baghdad
Baghdad Mitt — Baghdader Mitteilungen
Baghdad Mitt Beihft — Baghdader Mitteilungen Beiheft
Baghdad Univ Coll Sci Bull — Baghdad University. College of Science. Bulletin
BaghMitt — Baghdader Mitteilungen des Deutschen Archaeologischen Instituts. Abteilung Baghdad
BAGN — Boletin. Archivo General de la Nacion
B Agricultura — Boletin de Agricultura. Diputacion Provincial de Baleares
BAGS — Bulletin. American Geographical Society
BAH — Amis du Hurepoix et des Arts de l'Yveline. Bulletin
BAH — Bibliotheque Archeologique et Historique. Institut Francais d'Archeologie de Beyrouth
BAH — Biological Agriculture and Horticulture
BAH — Boletin. Academia de la Historia
BAH — Bulletin. Academie d'Hippone
BAH — Business Archives and History
BAHAD — Bulletin of Animal Health and Production in Africa
BAHASA — Bulletin Archeologique, Historique, et Artistique. Societe Archeologique de Tarn-et-Garonne
BAHC — Bulletin. American Historical Collection
BAHD — Bulletin d'Archeologie et d'Histoire Dalmate
Bahia Bal E — Bahia. Balanco Energetico Consolidado
Bahia Braz Cent Estat Inf An Estat — Bahia, Brazil. Centro de Estatistica e Informacoes. Anuario Estatistico
Bahia Cent Pesqui Desenvolvimento Bol Tec — Bahia. Centro de Pesquisas e Desenvolvimento. Boletim Tecnico
Bahia Ener — Bahia. Annuario Energetico
BAHID — Basic and Applied Histochemistry
BAHIFAI — Bibliotheque Archeologique et Historique de l'Institut Francais d'Archeologie d'Istanbul
BAHist — Boletin. Real Academia de la Historia
BAHL — Boletin. Academia Hondurena de la Lengua
BahnA — Bahnarzt
BAHODP — Bangladesh Horticulture
BAHV — Boletin de la Academia de Historia del Valle de Cauca
BAHV — Bulletin. Association Internationale pour l'Histoire du Verre
BAI — Biological and Agricultural Index
BAI — Bulletin. American Institute of Swedish Arts, Literature, and Science
BAIBL — Bulletin. Academie des Inscriptions et Belles-Lettres
BAID — Black Americans Information Directory
BAIE — Boletin Antropologico. Instituto Etnologico. Universidad de Cauca
BAIEMA — Bulletin d'Information. Association Internationale pour l'Etude de la Mosaique Antique
Baier Akad Wiss Muenchen Meteorol Ephem — Der Baierischen Akademie der Wissenschaften in Muenchen. Meteorologische Ephemeriden
Baileys Ind Oil Fat Prod — Bailey's Industrial Oil and Fat Products
Baillieres Best Pract Res Clin Endocrinol Metab — Baillieres Best Practice & Research Clinical Endocrinology & Metabolism
Baillieres Clin Endocrinol Metab — Baillieres Clinical Endocrinology and Metabolism
Baillieres Clin Gastroenterol — Baillieres Clinical Gastroenterology
Baillieres Clin Haematol — Baillieres Clinical Haematology
Baillieres Clin Neurol — Baillieres Clinical Neurology
Baillieres Clin Obstet Gynaecol — Baillieres Clinical Obstetrics and Gynaecology
Baillieres Clin Rheumatol — Baillieres Clinical Rheumatology
BAIMR — United States Bureau of Animal Industry. Monthly Record
B Ain — Bulletin. Societe des Naturalistes et des Archeologues de l'Ain
BAINB — Bulletin. Astronomical Institutes of the Netherlands. Supplement Series
BAIS — Bulletin de l'Academie Imperiale des Sciences de St. Petersbourg
BAIU — Bulletin. Alliance Israelite Universelle
Bajan S Carib — Bajan and South Caribbean
BAK — Bakker. Actueel Vakblad voor de Broodbakkerij. Banketbakkerij
BAK — Beilage zur Anhalter Kurier
Bakasha LePat — Bakasha LePatent
Bakelite Rev — Bakelite Review
Baker Calif — Bakersfield Californian
Baker J T Chem Co Prod Bull — Baker, J. T., Chemical Company. Product Bulletin
Baker Millers J — Baker and Millers' Journal
Baker Millr J — Baker and Millers' Journal
Baker Prod — Bakery Production and Marketing
Baker's — Baker's Digest
Baker's Dig — Baker's Digest
BakerSJ — Baker Street Journal
Baker's Rev — Baker's Review
Baker's Tech Dig — Baker's Technical Digest
Bakers Wkly — Bakers Weekly
Bakery Ind — Bakery Industry
Baking Ind — Baking Industry
Baking Technol — Baking Technology
Bakish Mater Corp Publ — Bakish Materials Corporation. Publication
Bakkerij Wet — Bakkerij Wetenschap
Bakony Termeszettud Kutatas Eredm — A Bakony Termeszettudomanyi Kutatasanak Eredmenyei. Resultationes Investigationis Rerum Naturalium Montium Bakony
BAL — Berichte. Verhandlungen der Saechsischen Akademie der Wissenschaften zu Leipzig
BAL — Buenos Aires Literaria
BAL — Bulletin des Antiquites Luxembourgeoises
BALA — Bulletin. American Library Association

BALA — Bulletin. Association Lyonnaise de Recherches Archeologiques
BALAC — Bulletin d'Ancienne Litterature et d'Archeologie Chretienne
Balafon Mag — Balafon Magazine
Balai Penelitian Ind Bull Penelitian — Balai Penelitian Industri. Bulletin Penelitian
Balasov Gos Ped Inst Ucen Zap — Balasovkii Gosudarstvennyi Pedagogiceskii Institut. Ucenye Zapiski
Balaton Symp Part Phys — Balaton Symposium on Particle Physics
BALB — Academie Royale de Langue et de Litterature Francaise (Belgium). Bulletin
BALB — Boletin. Real Academia de Buenas Letras de Barcelona
BALC — Bulletin d'Ancienne Litterature Chretienne Latine
BALF — Black American Literature Forum
BALF — Bulletin. Academie Royale de Langue et de Litterature Francaises
Balgarska M — Balgarska Muzyka
Balg Etnogr — Balgarska Etnografiya
Balg Folkl — Balgarski Folklor
Balg Ovostarstvo Gradinarstvo — Balgarsko Ovostarstvo i Gradinarstvo
Bal Hist Foren — Ballerup og Omegns Historiske Forening. Egnsmuseet i Lindbjerggard. Arshefte
BALI — Bollettino dell'Atlante Linguistico Italiano
B A Liege — Bulletin. Institut Archeologique Liegeois
BALit — Biblioteka Analiz Literackich
Balkan Kutat Tud Eredm — Balkan-Kutatasainak Tudomanyos Eredmenyei
Balkan St — Balkan Studies
Balkan Stud — Balkan Studies
BalkE — Balkansko Ezikoznanije
Balk Ez — Balkansko Ezikoznanie
Balk Ezik — Balkansko Ezikoznanie
Balk J Med Genet — Balkan Journal of Medical Genetics
Balk St — Balkan Studies
Balk Stud — Balkan Studies
Ballade — Ballade Tidsskrift for Ny Musikk
Ball & Roller Bear Engng — Ball and Roller Bearing Engineering
Ball Bearing J — Ball Bearing Journal (English Edition)
Ball Bear J — Ball Bearing Journal
Ballet N — Ballet News
Ballet Rev — Ballet Review
Ballist Mater Penetration Mech — Ballistic Materials and Penetration Mechanics
Balloon Res Technol Symp — Balloon Research and Technology Symposium
Ball Roller Bear Eng — Ball and Roller Bearing Engineering
Ball State J — Ball State Journal for Business Educators
Ball St Bus Rev — Ball State Business Review
Ball St Monogr — Ball State Monographs
Ball St Uni — Ball State University Forum
BALM — Bollettino dell'Atlante Linguistico Mediterraneo
Balneol Bohem — Balneologia Bohemica
Balneol Pol — Balneologia Polska
Balneol Soc Japan Jour — Balneological Society of Japan. Journal
Bal R — Baltic Review
Ba LR — University of Baltimore. Law Review
Bal Sheet — Balance Sheet
Bal St — Balkan Studies
Bal St — Baltische Studien
Balston Conf Nucl Phys — Balston Conference on Nuclear Physics
Balt H — Baltische Hefte
Baltic Sea Environ Proc — Baltic Sea Environment. Proceedings
Baltimore Annu — Baltimore Annual
Baltimore B of Ed — Baltimore Bulletin of Education
Baltimore Journ Med — Baltimore Journal of Medicine
Baltimore Manuf Rec — Baltimore Manufacturers' Record
Baltimore Med Phys Rec — Baltimore Medical and Physical Recorder
Baltimore Munic J — Baltimore Municipal Journal
Baltimore Mus A Annu — Baltimore Museum of Art Annual
Baltimore Mus A News Q — Baltimore Museum of Art News Quarterly
Baltimore Mus Art N — Baltimore Museum of Art. News
Baltimore Mus N — Baltimore Museum of Art. News
Baltimr BJ — Baltimore Business Journal
Baltische Stud — Baltische Studien
Balt Mh — Baltische Monatschefte
Baltmr Sun — Sun (Baltimore)
Balt Mschr — Baltische Monatsschrift
Balt Recht — Baltisches Recht
Balt Rev — Baltic Review
Balt Revy — Baltisk Revy
Balt Stud — Baltische Studien
BaltW — Baltische Wochenschrift fuer Landwirtschaft, Gewerbefleiss, und Handel
BA Lux — Bulletin d'Archeologie Luxembourgeoise
Balwant Vidyapeeth J Agric Sci Res — Balwant Vidyapeeth Journal of Agricultural and Scientific Research
Balwant Vidyapeeth J Agr Sci Res — Balwant Vidyapeeth Journal of Agricultural and Scientific Research
BaM — Baghdader Mitteilungen
BAM — Basic and Applied Myology
BAM — Beitraege zur Saarlaendischen Archlichen Archaeologie des Mittelmeer-Kulturraumes
BAM — Boletim do Arquivo Municipal. Camara Municipal de Braga
BAM — Buenos Aires Musical
BAM — Bulletin d'Archeologie Marocaine
BAM — Bulletin of the American Museum of Natural History
BAM — Business America
BAMA — Bulletin d'Information. Association Internationale pour l'Etude de la Mosaique Antique
BAMAB — Battery Man
BAMalgache — Bulletin. Academie Malgache

BAM Amtsbl Mitteilungsbl — BAM Berlin Amtsblatt und Mitteilungsblatt der Bundesanstalt fuer Materialpruefung
BAM Amts Mitteilungsbl — BAM Amts- und Mitteilungsblatt
B Am Anth A — Bulletin. American Anthropological Association
BA Maroc — Bulletin d'Archeologie Marocaine
B Am Ass Petrol Geol — Bulletin. American Association of Petroleum Geologists
BAMBAM — Bookline Alert. Missing Books and Manuscripts
BAM-Ber — BAM-Berichte. Forschung und Entwicklung in der Bundesanstalt fuer Materialpruefung
Bamb Nf Gs B — Bericht des Naturforschenden Gesellschaft zu Bamberg
Bamboo J — Bamboo Journal
Bambou Paris — Bambou. Periodique Illustre (Paris)
BAM Bundesanst Materialpruef Forschungsber — BAM, Bundesanstalt fuer Materialpruefung. Forschungsbericht
BAMEG — Bulletin Annuel. Musee d'Ethnographie de la Ville de Geneve
B Amer School Orient — Bulletin. American Schools of Oriental Research
B Am Geogr Soc — Bulletin. American Geographical Society
B Am Hist Col — Bulletin. American Historical Collection
BAMIA — Bulletin. American Meteorological Society
BAmicEbrCr — Bollettino. Amicizia Ebraico-Cristiana di Firenze
Bamidgeh Bull Fish Cult Isr — Bamidgeh. Bulletin of Fish Culture in Israel
Ba Mitt — Baghdader Mitteilungen. Deutsches Archaeologisches Institut. Abteilung Baghdad
BAM Jahresber — BAM (Bundesanstalt Fuer Materialpruefung) Jahresbericht
B Am Math S — Bulletin. American Mathematical Society
B Am Meteor — Bulletin. American Meteorological Society
BAMNH — Bulletin of the American Museum of Natural History
BAMOA — Bulletin. American Mathematical Society
BA Montl — Bulletin Regional. Amis de Montlucon
B Am Pal — Bulletins of American Paleontology
B Am Phys S — Bulletin. American Physical Society
BAMPI — Bollettino d'Arte. Ministero della Pubblica Istruzione
B Am Pr Hist Res — Bulletin. American School of Prehistoric Research
BAMRAM — Bulletin. Academie de Medecine de Roumanie
BAMS — Bulletin. American Mathematical Society
BAMS — Bulletin. American Musicological Society
B Am Soc P — Bulletin. American Society of Papyrologists
B Am S Pap — Bulletin. American Society of Papyrologists
BAN — Banking Law Journal
BAN — Boletin. Archivo Nacional
BAN — Bullettino Archeologico Napoletano
Banach Center Publ — Banach Center. Publications
B Anal Hist Rom — Bulletin Analytique d'Histoire Romaine
B Analyt Hist Rom — Bulletin Analytique d'Histoire Romaine
Banaras LJ — Banaras Law Journal
Banaras Metall — Banaras Metallurgist
BA Narb — Bulletin. Commission Archeologique de Narbonne
Banater Z Landw — Banater Zeitschrift fuer Landwirthschaft, Handel, Kuenste, und Gewerbe
BANAZ — Boletin. Academia Aragonesa de Nobles y Bellas Artes de San Luis de Zaragoza
B An B — Babesch. Bulletin Antieke Beschaving
BANB — Boletin de la Academia Nacional de Historia (Buenos Aires)
Banb Erev Hamal — Banber Erevani Hamalsarani-Vestnik Erevanskogo Universiteta
Banbury Hist Soc — Banbury Historical Society
Banbury Rep — Banbury Report
Banca d'Italia Bol — Banca d'Italia. Bollettino
Banca Nazionale del Lavoro Q R — Banca Nazionale del Lavoro. Quarterly Review
Banca Naz Lav Quart R — Banca Nazionale del Lavoro. Quarterly Review
BANCC — Boletin de la Academia Nacional de Ciencias en Cordoba
B Anc Lit — Bulletin d'Ancienne Litterature et d'Archeologie Chretienne
Banc Nacl Habit Orca Plurian — Banco Nacional da Habitacao. Orcamento Plurianual
Banc Nacl Habit Relator Ativid — Banco Nacional da Habitacao. Relatorio de Atividades
Banco Angola Bol Trim — Banco de Angola. Boletim Trimestral
Banco Brasil Bol Trim — Banco do Brasil. Boletim Trimestral
Banco Central Bolivia Bol Estadistico — Banco Central de Bolivia. Boletin Estadistico
Banco Nacl — Banco Nacional de Comercio Exterior, SA, Mexico. Annual Report
Banco Nacl Panama Cuad — Banco Nacional de Panama
B Anc Or Mus — Bulletin. Ancient Orient Museum
Banco Roma — Banco Roma. Review of the Economic Conditions in Italy
Banco Vizcaya — Banco de Vizcaya. Revista Financiera
B & B — Bench and Bar
B&B — Books and Bookmen
B & C Rec — Brick and Clay Record
Bandeaux Or — Bandeaux d'Or
B and L — Brain and Language
BandO — Bandeaux d'Or
B and S — Bible and Spade
B&TS — Bible et Terre Sainte
B & W — Bibliothek und Wissenschaft
BANE — Bible and the Ancient Near East
Banff Conf Reprod Immunol — Banff Conference on Reproductive Immunology
BANGA — Bauingenieur
Bangabasi College Mag — Bangabasi College Magazine
Bangabasi Morning College Mag — Bangabasi Morning College Magazine
Bangalore Th F — Bangalore Theological Forum
B (Angers) — Bulletin. Centre de Recherches et d'Enseignement de l'Antiquite (Angers)
Bang J Bio Agri Sci — Bangladesh Journal of Biological and Agricultural Sciences
Bang J Bio Sci — Bangladesh Journal of Biological Science

Bang J Bot — Bangladesh Journal of Botany
Bang J Sci Ind Res — Bangladesh Journal of Scientific and Industrial Research
Bang J Sci Res — Bangladesh Journal of Scientific Research
Bang J Soc — Bangladesh Journal of Sociology
Bang J Soil Sci — Bangladesh Journal of Soil Science
Bang J Zoo — Bangladesh Journal of Zoology
Bangkok Bank Mo R — Bangkok Bank. Monthly Review
Bangkok R — Monthly Review (Bangkok)
Bangladesh Acad Sci J — Bangladesh Academy of Sciences. Journal
Bangladesh Agric Res Counc Soils Irrig Publ — Bangladesh Agricultural Research Council Soils and Irrigation Publication
Bangladesh Agric Sci Abstr — Bangladesh Agricultural Sciences Abstracts
Bangladesh Agr Sci Abstr — Bangladesh Agricultural Sciences Abstracts
Bangladesh CSIRL Chittagong Res Bull — Bangladesh Council of Scientific and Industrial Research Laboratories. Chittagong. Research Bulletin
Bangladesh Devel Stud — Bangladesh Development Studies
Bangladesh Dev Stud — Bangladesh Development Studies
Bangladesh Geol Surv Rec — Bangladesh Geological Survey. Records
Bangladesh Hortic — Bangladesh Horticulture
Bangladesh J Agric — Bangladesh Journal of Agriculture
Bangladesh J Agric Sci — Bangladesh Journal of Agricultural Sciences
Bangladesh J Anim Sci — Bangladesh Journal of Animal Sciences
Bangladesh J Biol Agric Sci — Bangladesh Journal of Biological and Agricultural Sciences [*Later,* Bangladesh Journal of Biological Sciences]
Bangladesh J Biol Sci — Bangladesh Journal of Biological Sciences
Bangladesh J Bot — Bangladesh Journal of Botany
Bangladesh J Jute Fibre Res — Bangladesh Journal of Jute and Fibre Research
Bangladesh J Sci Ind Res — Bangladesh Journal of Scientific and Industrial Research
Bangladesh J Sci Res — Bangladesh Journal of Scientific Research
Bangladesh J Soil Sci — Bangladesh Journal of Soil Science
Bangladesh J Zool — Bangladesh Journal of Zoology
Bangladesh Med Res Counc Bull — Bangladesh Medical Research Council. Bulletin
Bangladesh Pharm J — Bangladesh Pharmaceutical Journal
Bangladesh Vet J — Bangladesh Veterinary Journal
Bangla Dev Stud — Bangladesh Development Studies
Bangla Hist Stud — Bangladesh Historical Studies
Bang Lal Kal — Bangla Lalit Kala
Bang Lib Sci News — Bangladesh Library Science Newsbulletin
Bang Med Res Bul — Bangladesh Medical Research Council Bulletin
Bangor Dail — Bangor Daily News
Bang Pharm J — Bangladesh Pharmaceutical Journal
Bang Q — Bangladesh Quarterly
Bang Sugar J — Bangladesh Sugar Journal
Bang Today — Bangladesh Today
BANH — Boletin. Academia Nacional de la Historia
BANHQ — Boletin. Academia Nacional de la Historia (Quito)
Banjo N — Banjo Newsletter
Bank — Bankers' Magazine
Bank Admin — Magazine of Bank Administration
Bank Ad News — Bank Advertising News
BANKANAL — Bank Analysis System
Bank-Betr — Bank-Betrieb
Bank Can R — Bank of Canada. Review
Bank Comp — Bank Compliance
Bank Dir Can — Bank Directory of Canada
Bank England Q Bul — Bank of England. Quarterly Bulletin
Bank Eng QB — Bank of England. Quarterly Bulletin
Bank Eng Q Bull — Bank of England. Quarterly Bulletin
Banker-F — Banker-Farmer
Bankers Bus — Banker's Business
Bankers J — Bankers' Journal
Banker's LJ — Banker's Law Journal
Bankers' M — Bankers' Magazine
Bankers M — Bankers' Monthly
Bankers' Mag — Bankers' Magazine
Bankers Mag — Bankers Magazine of Australasia
Bankers Mag A'sia — Bankers Magazine of Australasia
Bankers Mag Aust — Bankers Magazine of Australasia
Bankers Mag Australas — Bankers Magazine of Australasia
Bankers M Australasia — Bankers Magazine of Australasia
Bankers' Mo — Bankers' Monthly
Bankers' Mon — Bankers' Monthly
Bank Exec Rep — Bank Executive's Report
Bank Finland Mo Bul — Bank of Finland. Monthly Bulletin
Bank Finland Mthly B — Bank of Finland. Monthly Bulletin
Bank Gaz — Bankruptcy Gazette
Bankhist Archiv — Bankhistorisches Archiv
Banking — ABA [*American Bankers Association*] Banking Journal
Banking Am Bankers Assn — Banking. American Bankers Association
Banking Law J — Banking Law Journal
Banking LJ — Banking Law Journal
Bank Install Lend Newsl — Bank Installment Lending Newsletter
Bank Isr Cur Bank Stat — Bank of Israel. Current Banking Statistics
Bank Law J — Banking Law Journal
Bank Law J Dig Fed Sup — Banking Law Journal Digest. Federal Supplement
Bank Lit Index — American Bankers Association. Banking Literature Index
Bank LJ — Banking Law Journal
Bank London and South Am R — Bank of London and South Abmerica. Review
Bank London South Amer R — Bank of London and South America. Review
Bank Mag — Bankers' Magazine
Bank Mag A'sia — Bankers Magazine of Australasia
Bank Mark — Bank Marketing
Bank Mark Rep — Bank Marketing Report

Bank Mktg M — Bank Marketing Magazine
Bank Mktg R — Bank Marketing Report
Bank M (L) — Bankers' Magazine (London)
Bank M (Lond) — Bankers' Magazine (London)
Bank M (NY) — Bankers' Magazine (New York)
Bank Montreal Bus R — Bank of Montreal. Business Review
Bank N — Bank News
Bank Nova Scotia Mo R — Bank of Nova Scotia. Monthly Review
Bank NSW R — Bank of New South Wales. Review
Bank NSW Re — Bank of New South Wales. Review
Bank NSW Rev — Bank of New South Wales. Review
Bank of Ghana Q Econ Bull — Bank of Ghana Quarterly Economic Bulletin
Bank of NSW R — Bank of New South Wales. Review
Bank of Sierra Leone Econ Rev — Bank of Sierra Leone Economic Review
Banko Janakari J For Inf Nepal — Banko Janakari. A Journal of Forestry Information for Nepal
Bankr L Rep — Bankruptcy Law Reports
Bank Sierra Leone Econ R — Bank of Sierra Leone. Economic Review
Bank Sudan Ec Fin Bull — Bank of Sudan. Economic and Financial Bulletin
Bank Sys — Bank Systems and Equipment
Bank Syst and Equip — Bank Systems and Equipment
Bank Thailand Mo Bul — Bank of Thailand. Monthly Bulletin
Bank Thailand Q Bul — Bank of Thailand. Quarterly Bulletin
BANLE — Boletin. Academia Norteamericana de la Lengua Espanola
Ban LJ — Banaras Law Journal
Ban LJ — Banking Law Journal
BANMAC — Bulletin. Academie Nationale de Medecine
B Ann Mus Ferr — Bollettino Annuale. Musei Ferraresi
B Annu Mus Ethnogr Geneve — Bulletin Annuel. Musee d'Ethnographie de la Ville de Geneve
BANQ — Biblionews and Australian Notes and Queries
BANQ — Boletin de la Academia Nacional de Historia. Quito
Banque Centrale Etats Afr Ouest Notes Info et Statis — Banque Centrale des Etats de l'Afrique de l'Ouest. Notes d'Information et Statistiques
Banque Centrale Madagascar Bul Mensuel Statis — Banque Centrale de Madagascar. Bulletin Mensuel de Statistiques
Banque Etats Afr Centrale Etud et Statis — Banque des Etats de l'Afrique Centrale. Etudes et Statistiques
Banque Franc Ital Amer Sud Et Econ — Banque Francaise et Italienne pour l'Amerique du Sud. Etudes Economiques
Banque Fr Bul Trim — Banque de France. Bulletin Trimestriel
Banque Marocaine du Commerce Exterieur Mo Info R — Banque Marocaine du Commerce Exterieur. Monthly Information Review
Banque Nat Belgique Bul — Banque Nationale de Belgique. Bulletin
Banque Nationale de Belgique Bul — Banque Nationale de Belgique. Bulletin
Banque Nat Paris R Econ — Banque Nationale de Paris. Revue Economique
Banque Repub Burundi Bul Mensuel — Banque de la Republique du Burundi. Bulletin Mensuel
Banque Repub Burundi Bul Trim — Banque de la Republique du Burundi. Bulletin Trimestriel
Banque Zaire Bul Trim — Banque du Zaire. Bulletin Trimestriel
Bansilal Amritlal Agric Coll Mag — Bansilal Amritlal Agricultural College. Magazine
Bansk Obz — Bansky Obzor
Banta's Greek Exch — Banta's Greek Exchange
B Ant Beschav — Babesch. Bulletin Antieke Beschaving
B Ant Fr — Bulletin. Societe Nationale des Antiquaires de France
B Anthropol Inst — Bulletin. Anthropological Institute
B Ant Lux — Bulletin des Antiquites Luxembourgeoises
Bantu Stud — Bantu Studies
Banyasz Kohasz Lap Banyasz — Banyaszati es Kohaszati Lapok. Banyaszat
Banyasz Kohasz Lapok — Banyaszati es Kohaszati Lapok
Banyasz Kohasz Lapok Banyasz — Banyaszati es Kohaszati Lapok. Banyaszat
Banyasz Kohasz Lapok Banyasz Kulonszam — Banyaszati es Kohaszati Lapok. Banyaszat Kulonszam
Banyasz Kohasz Lapok Koeolaj Foeldgaz — Banyaszati es Kohaszati Lapok. Koeolaj es Foeldgaz
Banyasz Kohasz Lapok Kohasz — Banyaszati es Kohaszati Lapok. Kohaszat
Banyasz Kohasz Lapok Mellek Alum — Banyaszati es Kohaszati Lapok. Melleklet. Aluminum
Banyasz Kohasz Lapok Ontode — Banyaszati es Kohaszati Lapok. Ontode
Banyasz Kut Intez Kozl — Banyaszati Kutato Intezet Kozlemenyei
Banyasz Kut Intez Kozlem — Banyaszati Kutato Intezet Kozlemenyei
Banyasz Kut Intez Kozl Kulonszam — Banyaszati Kutato Intezet Kozlemenyei. Kulonszam
Banyasz Lapok — Banyaszati Lapok
BANYB — Banyaszat
BANZ Antarct Exped Rep Ser B — BANZ [*British-Australian-New Zealand*] Antarctic Research Expedition. Report. Series B
BA on CD — Biological Abstracts on Compact Disc
BA Orange — Bulletin des Amis d'Orange
BAP — Biotechnology Action Programme
BAP — Boletin Antropologico. Popayan
BAP — Bulletin de l'Administration des Prisons
BA (Paris) — Bulletin Archeologique. Comite des Travaux Historiques et Scientifiques (Paris)
BAPBAN — Bulletin. Academie Polonaise des Sciences. Serie des Sciences Biologiques
BAPC — Bulletin. Academie Polonaise de Cracovie
BAPE — Boletim. Academia Portuguesa do Ex-Libris
BAPEL — Boletim. Academia Portuguesa do Ex-Libris
BAPH — Boletin. Academia Puertorriquena de la Historia
BAPI — Bollettino. Archivio Paleografico Italiano
BAPI — British Alternative Press Index
BapQ — Baptist Quarterly

BA Prov — Bulletin Archeologique de Provence
BAPSA — Bulletin. American Physical Society
BAPSL — Bulletin. Academie Polonaise des Sciences et des Lettres
Bapt B — Baptist Bulletin
Bapt H Heri — Baptist History and Heritage
Bapt Hist and Heritage — Baptist History and Heritage
Bapt Q — Baptist Quarterly
Bapt Q — Baptist Quarterly Review
Bapt Quar — Baptist Quarterly. Baptist Historical Society
Bapt Ref R — Baptist Reformation Review
BAPXB — Baupraxis
BAQ — Barclays Review
Bar — Baretti
Bar — Barrister
BAR — Barron's
BAR — Biblical Archaeology Review
BAR — Biblioteca dell'Archivum Romanicum
BAR — Book Arts Review
BAR — British Archaeological Reports
BAR — Broadcast Advertisers Reports
BAR — Bulletin. Association des Amis de Rabelais et de la Deviniere
BARAB — Bulletin. Academie Royale d'Archeologie de Belgique
Barat R — Barat Review
Barb — Barbacane. Revue des Pierres et des Hommes
Barb — Barbour's Supreme Court Reports
BARB — Broadcasters Audience Research Board
BARB — Bulletin. Academie Royale de Belgique
Barbados Annu Rep Dep Sci Agric — Barbados. Annual Report. Department of Science and Agriculture
Barbados Nurs J — Barbados Nursing Journal
Barbero Mun — Barbero Municipal
Bar Briefs — Bar Briefs. North Dakota State Bar Association
Bar Bul Boston — Bar Bulletin. Bar Association of the City of Boston [*Boston*]
Bar Bull Boston — Bar Bulletin of the Boston Bar Association
Bar Bull (NY County La) — Bar Bulletin, New York County Lawyers'
Bar Bull (NY County Law A) — New York County Lawyers Association. Bar Bulletin
Barcel Ac Bl — Boletin de la Real Academia de Ciencias y Artes de Barcelona
Barcel Ac Mm — Memorias de la Real Academia de Ciencias Naturales y Artes de Barcelona
BArchAlex — Bulletin. Societe Archeologique d'Alexandrie
B Arch Alg — Bulletin d'Archeologie Algerienne
B Archeol — Bulletin Archeologique du Comite des Travaux Historiques et Scientifiques. Ministere d'Education Nationale
Barc Inst Invest Geol Publ — Barcelona. Instituto de Investigaciones Geologicas. Publicaciones
Barc Inst Prov Paleontol Actividades — Barcelona. Instituto Provincial de Paleontologia. Actividades
Barc Inst Prov Paleontol Bol Inf — Barcelona. Instituto Provincial de Paleontologia. Boletin Informativo
Barc Inst Prov Paleontol Paleontol Evol — Barcelona. Instituto Provincial de Paleontologia. Paleontologia y Evolucion
Barclays R — Barclays Review
Barclays Rev — Barclays Review
BARC Soils Irrig Publ — BARC (Bangladesh Agricultural Research Council) Soils and Irrigation Publication
Barc Univ Fac Cienc Misc Alcobe — Barcelona Universidad. Facultad de Ciencias. Miscellanea Alcobe
Barc Univ Inst Geol Mem Commun — Barcelona Universidad. Instituto Geologia. Memorias y Communicaciones
BARD — Bulletin. Association des Amis de Rabelais et de la Deviniere
Bardsey Obs Rep — Bardsey Observatory Report
BARE — Bollettino dell'Associazione Romana di Entomologia
BAREA — Bacteriological Reviews
BAREDB — Baruka Rebyu
BA Rev — Black Academy Review
Bar Exam — Bar Examiner
Bar Ex Ann — Bar Examination Annual
Bar Ex J — Bar Examination Journal
Bar Ex Jour — Bar Examination Journal
Bargaining Rep — Bargaining Report
Bar Gaz — Bar Gazette
BARIDN — Agricultural Research Council. Meat Research Institute [*Bristol*]. Biennial Report
B Ariege — Bulletin. Societe Prehistorique de l'Ariege
Bari Int Conf — Bari International Conference
Barley Genet Newsl — Barley Genetics Newsletter
Barley Genet Proc Int Barley Genet Symp — Barley Genetics. Proceedings. International Barley Genetics Symposium
BARLLF — Bulletin. Academie Royale de Langue et de Litterature Francaises
BARMAW — Bulletin. Academie Royale de Medecine de Belgique
Bar Mus Hist Soc J — Barbados Museum and Historical Society. Journal
B Arn — Bibliotheca Arnamagnaeana
Barnaul Gos Ped Inst Ucen Zap — Barnaul'skii Gosudarstvennyi Pedagogiceskii Institut. Ucenye Zapiski
Barn Nob Cr — Barnes and Noble Critical Study Series
Baroda J Nutr — Baroda Journal of Nutrition
Baroid News Bull — Baroid News Bulletin
Barossa Hist Bull — Barossa Historical Bulletin
B A Rp — Report of the Meeting of the British Association for the Advancement of Science
B Arqueol — Boletin Arqueologico. Real Sociedad Arqueologica Tarraconense de la Comision Provincial de Monumentos y del Museo Arqueologico Provincial
Barricada Int — Barricada Internacional
BA/RRM — Biological Abstracts/Reports, Reviews, Meetings [*Formerly, BIOI*]

Barrons Ind — Barron's Index
Barrow FC Rp — Barrow Naturalists' Field Club and Literary and Scientific Association. Annual Report and Proceedings
Barrow (W J) Res Lab Publ — Barrow (W. J.) Research Laboratory. Publication
BARSDJ — North Carolina. Agricultural Research Service. Bulletin
B Arte — Bollettino d'Arte. Ministero della Pubblica Istruzione
Bartlett Tree Res Lab Bull — Bartlett Tree Research Laboratory. Bulletin
Bartonia Proc Phila Bot Club — Bartonia. Proceedings. Philadelphia Botanical Club
B Art Tournus — Bulletin. Amis des Arts et des Sciences de Tournus
Baryon Reson Conf — Baryon Resonances. Conference
BAS — Bancaria
BAS — Beitraege zur Assyriologie und Semitischen Sprachwissenschaft
BAS — Bochumer Anglistische Studien
BAS — Bombay Asiatic Society
BAS — Bulletin. ASIS
BAS — Bulletin of the Atomic Scientists
BAS — Business and Society
BASB — British Antarctic Survey. Bulletin
BASD — Bollettino di Archeologia e Storia Dalmata
BASD — British Antarctic Survey. Data
Baseb Can — Baseball Canada
Base Bleed Int Symp Spec Top Chem Propul — Base Bleed. International Symmposium on Special Topics in Chemical Propulsion
Baseb (Ott) — Baseball (Ottawa)
BASE Eur — Bulletin d'Archeologie Sud-Est Europeenne
Basel B — Bericht ueber die Verhandlungen der Naturforschenden Gesellschaft in Basel
Baselbiet Heimatb — Baselbieter Heimatbuch
Basel Inst Immunol Annu Rep — Basel Institute for Immunology. Annual Report
Basel Vh — Verhandlungen der Naturforschenden Gesellschaft in Basel
BASF Engl Ed — BASF (Badische Anilin- und Soda-Fabrik) (English Edition)
BASF Inf — BASF [*Badische Anilin- und Sodafabrik*] Information
BASF Mitt Landbau — BASF (Badische Anilin- und Soda-Fabrik) Mitteilungen fuer den Landbau
BASF Rev — BASF [*Badische Anilin- und Sodafabrik*] Review
BASF Rev (Engl Ed) — BASF (Badische Anilin- und Soda-Fabrik) Review (English Edition)
BASF Symp — BASF [*Badische Anilin- und Soda-Fabrik*] Symposium
BaSh — Ba Shiru
Bashk Gos Med Inst Sb Nauchn Tr — Bashkirskii Gosudarstvennyi Meditsinskii Institut. Sbornik Nauchnykh Trudov
Bashk Gos Univ Uch Zap — Bashkirskii Gosudarstvennyi Universitet. Uchenye Zapiski
Bashk Khim Zh — Bashkirskii Khimicheskii Zhurnal
Bashk Nauchno Issled Inst Stroit Tr — Bashkirskii Nauchno-Issledovatel'skii Institut po Stroitel'stvu. Trudy
Bashk Neft — Bashkirskaya Neft. Tekhnicheskii Byulleten
BASI — Bulletin. American Swedish Institute
B Asian Schol — Bulletin of Concerned Asian Scholars
BASIC — B.A.S.I.C. Key to the World's Biological Research. Biological Abstracts SubjectIndex. Biological Abstracts, Inc.
BASIC — Bulletin. American Society for Information Science
Basic and Clin Immunol — Basic and Clinical Immunology
Basic Appl Histochem — Basic and Applied Histochemistry
Basic Biol Color Ser — Basic Biology in Color Series
Basic Biol New Dev Biotechnol — Basic Biology of New Developments in Biotechnology
Basic Clin Aspects Neurosci — Basic and Clinical Aspects of Neuroscience
Basic Clin Cardiol — Basic and Clinical Cardiology
Basic Clin Dermatol — Basic and Clinical Dermatology
Basic Clin Endocrinol — Basic and Clinical Endocrinology
Basic Clin Nutr — Basic and Clinical Nutrition
Basic Clin Ther Aspects Alzheimers Parkinsons Dis — Basic, Clinical, and Therapeutic Aspects of Alzheimer's and Parkinson's Diseases
Basic Data Rep Md Geol Surv — Basic Data Report. Maryland. Geological Survey
Basic Data Rep WV Geol Econ Surv — Basic Data Report. West Virginia. Geological and Economic Survey
Basic Data Ser Ground Water Release Kans Geol Surv — Basic Data Series. Ground-Water Release. Kansas Geological Survey
Basic Doc World Fertil Surv — Basic Documentation/World Fertility Survey
Basic Environ Probl Man Space Proc Int Symp — Basic Environmental Problems of Man in Space. Proceedings. International Symposium
Basic Life Sci — Basic Life Sciences
Basic Neurochem 2nd Ed — Basic Neurochemistry. 2nd Edition
Basic Pharmacol Ther — Basic Pharmacology Therapeutics
Basic Plasma Processes Sun Proc Symp Int Astron Union — Basic Plasma Processes on the Sun. Proceedings. Symposium. International Astronomical Union
Basic Rec Rep LA Dep Public Works — Basic Records Report. Louisiana Department of Public Works
Basic Rec Rep US Dep Inter Geol Surv — Basic Record Report. United States Department of Interior. Geological Survey
Basic Res Cardiol — Basic Research in Cardiology
Basic Sci Diagn — Basic Science and Diagnosis
Basic Sci Princ Nucl Med — Basic Science Principles of Nuclear Medicine
Basic Sci Toxicol Proc Int Congr Toxicol — Basic Science in Toxicology. Proceedings. International Congress of Toxicology
Basic Sleep Mech — Basic Sleep Mechanisms
BASIDS — Biologiski Aktivo Savienojumu Kimijas Tehnologija Rigas Politehniskaja Instituta
Basilica Teres — Basilica Teresiana
Basin Plann Rep Allegheny Basin Reg Water Resour Plann Board — Basin Planning Report. Allegheny Basin Regional Water Resources Planning Board

Basin Plann Rep ARB NY State Dep Environ Conserv — Basin Planning Report ARB (Allegheny River Basin). New York State Department ofEnvironmental Conservation

Basin Plann Rep Black River Basin Reg Water Resour Plann Board — Basin Planning Report. Black River Basin Regional Water Resources Planning Board

Basin Plann Rep BRB NY State Dep Environ Conserv — Basin Planning Report BRB [Black River Basin]. New York State Department of Environmental Conservation

Basin Plann Rep East Oswego Basin Reg Water Resour Plann Board — Basin Planning Report. Eastern Oswego Basin Regional Water Resources Planning Board

Basin Plann Rep ENB NY State Water Resour Comm — Basin Planning Report ENB (Erie-Niagara Basin). New York State Water Resources Commission

Basin Plann Rep NY State Dep Environ Conserv ORB — Basin Planning Report. New York State Department of Environmental Conservation.Series ORB

Basin Plann Rep NY State Dept Environ Conserv ARB — Basin Planning Report. New York State Department of Environmental Conservation.Series ARB

Basin Plann Rep NY State Water Resour Comm ENB — Basin Planning Report. New York State Water Resources Commission. Series ENB

B As Int S Soc — Bulletin. Association Internationale de la Securite Sociale

BASIS — Bulletin. American Society for Information Science

Basis Individ Physiol — Basis of an Individual Physiology

Basis Pract Neuroanaesth — Basis and Practice of Neuroanaesthesia

BASKAV — Baskerville Chemical Journal

Baskerville Chem J — Baskerville Chemical Journal

Baskir Gos Univ Ucen Zap — Baskirskii Gosudarstvennyi Universitet. Ucenye Zapiski

BASL — Bochumer Arbeiten zur Sprach- und Literaturwissenschaft

BASLAY — Bulletin. Academie et Societe Lorraines des Sciences

Basl Beitr Ethnol — Basler Beitraege zur Ethnographie

Basler — Basler Jahrbuch fuer Historische Musikpraxis

Basler Beitr Chir — Basler Beitraege zur Chirurgie

Basler Beitr Ethnol — Basler Beitraege zur Ethnologie

Basler Beitr Geogr — Basler Beitraege zur Geographie

Basler Beitr Gesch Wiss — Basler Beitraege zur Geschichtswissenschaft

Basler Jb — Basler Jahrbuch

Basler Veroeffentl Gesch Med Biol — Basler Veroeffentlichungen zur Geschichte der Medizin und der Biologie

Basler Z Gesch Altertumskde — Basler Zeitschrift fuer Geschichte und Altertumskunde

Basler Z Gesch Altertumskunde — Basler Zeitschrift fuer Geschichte und Altertumskunde

Basler Z Gesch & Altertumsk — Basler Zeitschrift fuer Geschichte und Altertumskunde

Basl Jb — Basler Jahrbuch

Basl Kstver Ber — Basler Kunstverein. Bericht

Basl Kstver Berstatt — Basler Kunstverein. Berichterstattung

Basl Kstver Jber — Basler Kunstverein. Jahresbericht

BASLS — Bulletin. Academie et de la Societe Lorraines des Sciences

Basl Stadtb — Basler Stadtbuch

Basl Z Gesch & Altertknd — Basler Zeitschrift fuer Geschichte und Altertumskunde

BASM — Bollettino. Associazione per gli Studi Mediterranei

BASO — Bulletin. American Schools of Oriental Research in Jerusalem and Bagdad

BASOR — Bulletin. American Schools of Oriental Research

BASORSS — Bulletin. American Schools of Oriental Research. Supplementary Series

BASP — Bollettino. Reale Accademia de Scienze, Lettere, e Belle Arti di Palermo

BASP — Bulletin. Academie de Science de St. Petersbourg

BASP — Bulletin. American Society of Papyrologists

BASPR — Bulletin. American School of Prehistoric Research

BASR — Bulletin. Academie des Sciences de Russie

Basrah Nat Hist Mus Publ — Basrah Natural History Museum. Publication

Bas R Card — Basic Research in Cardiology

BASS — Beitraege zur Assyriologie und Semitischen Sprachwissenschaft

B Ass Av Sci — Bulletin. Association Francaise pour l'Avancement des Sciences

BAssBude — Bulletin. Association Guillaume Bude

B Ass Geogr Fr — Bulletin. Association de Geographes Francais

B Ass Geogr Franc — Bulletin. Association des Geographes Francais

B Ass Mos Ant — Bulletin d'Information. Association Internationale pour l'Etude de la Mosaique Antique

B Assoc Cadres Dir Industr Progres Soc Econ — Bulletin. Association de Cadres Dirigeants de l'Industrie pour le Progres Social et Economique

B Assoc Geogr Franc — Bulletin. Association des Geographes Francais

B Ass Pro Aventico — Bulletin. Association Pro Aventico

BASSR — British Antarctic Survey. Scientific Reports

Bass Sound — Bass Sound Post

Bastfaser Ind — Bastfaser-Industrie

B Astr I Cz — Bulletin. Astronomical Institutes of Czechoslovakia

BASU — Balkan Studies

BA Sud Est Eur — Bulletin d'Archeologie Sud-Est Europeenne

BASURSS — Bulletin. Academie des Sciences de l'URSS

BAT — Bataille

BAT — Biological Abstracts on Tape

BAT — Boletin Arqueologico de Tarragona

BAT — Bulletin. Analysis and Testing

Batav Gn Vh — Verhandelingen van het Bataviaasch Genootschap der Kunsten en Wetenschappen

Batav Ntk Ts — Natuurkunding Tijdschrift voor Nederlandsch-Indie

Bateman E — Bateman Eichler and Hill Richards. News Release

Bateman E — Bateman Eichler and Hill Richards. Research Report

BATF — Boletin. Asociacion Tucumana de Folklore

Bath Chron — Bath Chronicle

Bath FCP — Proceedings. Bath Natural History and Antiquarian Field Club

Bath Hist — Bath History

Baths Bath Eng — Baths and Bath Engineering

Bath S J — Journal of the Bath and West of England Society for the Encouragement of Agriculture, Arts, Manufactures, and Commerce

Baths Serv Rec Mgmt — Baths Service and Recreation Management

Batim Int — Batiment International

Batim Int Build Res Pract — Batiment International/Building Research and Practice

BATMA — Bulletin. Association Technique Maritime et Aeronautique

B Atom Sci — Bulletin of the Atomic Scientists

Baton Rou B — Greater Baton Rouge Business Report

BATRA — Battelle Technical Review

Bat Res News — Bat Research News

BATTDW — Batteries

Battelle Inf (Frankfurt) — Battelle Information (Frankfurt)

Battelle Inst Ber Frankfurt Main — Battelle-Institut. Bericht (Frankfurt/Main)

Battelle Inst Mater Sci Colloq — Battelle Memorial Institute. Materials Science Colloquia

Battelle Mem Inst Battelle Inst Mater Sci Colloq — Battelle Memorial Institute. Battelle Institute Materials Science Colloquia

Battelle Mem Inst DCIC Rep — Battelle Memorial Institute. Defense Ceramic Information Center. DCIC Report

Battelle Mem Inst DMIC Memo — Battelle Memorial Institute. Defense Metals Information Center. DMIC Memorandum

Battelle Mem Inst DMIC Rep — Battelle Memorial Institute. Defense Metals Information Center. DMIC Report

Battelle Meml Inst Def Met Inf Cent DMIC Rep — Battelle Memorial Institute. Defense Metals Information Center. DMIC Report

Battelle Mg — Battelle Monographs

Battelle Pac Northwest Lab Rep BNWL — Battelle Pacific Northwest Laboratories. Report BNWL

Battelle Pac Northwest Lab Tech Rep PNL — Battelle Pacific Northwest Laboratory. Technical Report PNL

Battelle Pac Northwest Lab Tech Rep PNL SA — Battelle Pacific Northwest Laboratory. Technical Report PNL-SA

Battelle Res Outlook — Battelle Research Outlook

Battelle T — Battelle Today

Battelle Tech R — Battelle Technical Review

Battelle Tech Rev — Battelle Technical Review

Battel R & D — Battelle Memorial Institute. Probable Levels of R and D Expenditures

Battery Bimon — Battery Bimonthly

Battery Counc Int Conv — Battery Council International Convention

Battery Counc Int Conv Proc — Battery Council. International Convention. Proceedings

Battery Counc Int Meet — Battery Council International Meeting

Battery Mater Symp Proc — Battery Material Symposium. Proceedings

Battery Mn — Battery Man

Battery Res Dev Conf Proc — Battery Research and Development Conference. Proceedings

BAUA — Universidad de Antioquia Boletin de Antropolia

BAUADE — US Department of Agriculture. Science and Education Administration. Bibliographies and Literature of Agriculture

Bau & Werk — Baukunst und Werkform

Bau & Werkkst — Bau und Werkkunst

BAUB — Beitraege zur Anthropologie und Urgeschichte Bayerns

Bau Betr — Bau und Betrieb

B Auckland Inst Mus — Bulletin. Auckland Institute and Museum

Bauelem Elektrotech — Bauelemente der Elektrotechnik

Bauen Landwirtsch — Bauen fuer die Landwirtschaft

Bauen Wirtsch — Bauen und Wirtschaft

BAUFO — Bauforschungsprojekte

B Aug — Bracara Augusta. Revista Cultural da Camara Municipal de Braga

BAUGA — Buecherei des Augenarztes

Baugesch Bauplan — Baugeschichte - Bauplanung

Bauginia Z Basler Botan Ges — Bauginia. Zeitschrift. Basler Botanische Gesellschaft

Bauhaus Z Bau & Gestalt — Bauhaus. Zeitschrift fuer Bau und Gestaltung

Bauinf Wiss Tech — Bauinformation. Wissenschaft und Technik

Bauing — Bauingenieur

Bauing Prax — Bauingenieur Praxis

Baukst & Werkform — Baukunst und Werkform. Monatsschrift fuer die Gebiete der Gestaltung

BAUMA — Baumeister

Baumasch Bautech — Baumaschine und Bautechnik

Baum B — Baum Bugle

BaumB — Baum Bugle: A Journal of Oz

Baumgartner Z — Zeitschrift fuer Physik, Mathematik, und Verwandte Wissenschaften. Baumgartner und von Ettingshausen

Baumwoll Ind — Baumwoll-Industrie

Bauplanung Bautech — Bauplanung-Bautechnik

B Aur — Boletin Auriense

Bausteine Tueb Universitaetsgesch — Bausteine zur Tuebinger Universitaetsgeschichte

Baustoffind Ausg A — Baustoffindustrie. Ausgabe A. Primaerbaustoffe

Baustoffind Ausg B — Baustoffindustrie. Ausgabe B. Bauelemente

Baustoffindustrie Ausg B — Baustoffindustrie. Ausgabe B. Bauelemente

Bautech-Arch — Bautechnik-Archiv

Bautechnik Ausg A — Bautechnik. Ausgabe A

Bautechnik Beil Zeitschriftenschau Gesamte Bauingenieurwes — Bautechnik, Beilage. Zeitschriftenschau fuer das Gesamte Bauingenieurwesen

Bauteile Rep — Bauteile Report

B Automatn — Business Automation

BAUVA — Bauverwaltung

B Auvergne — Bulletin Historique et Scientifique de l'Auvergne

Bauxite Symp — Bauxite Symposium

Bauztg Ungarn — Bauzeitung fuer Ungarn

BAV — Boletin. Academia Venezolana

BAV — Bulletin. Academie du Var
BAVA — Beitraege zur Allgemeinen und Vergleichenden Archaeologie
B Avalon — Bulletin. Societe d'Etudes d'Avallon
BAVC — Boletin. Academia Venezolana Correspondiente a la Espanola
BAVED — Bayerische Verwaltungsblaetter
BA Vexin — Bulletin Archeologique du Vexin Francais
BAVF — Bulletin Archeologique du Vexin Francais
BAVFAV — Bulletin. Academie Veterinaire de France
BAW — Banco Central. Boletin Informativo
BAW — Bibliothek der Alten Welt
BA Wb — Beitraege zum Assyrischen Woerterbuch
BAWM — Sitzungsberichte der Mathematisch-Physikalische-Klasse der Koeniglichen Bayerischen Akademie der Wissenschaften (Muenchen)
BAWOA — Bauen und Wohnen
BAW PHK — Bayerische Akademie der Wissenschaften. Philosophisch-Historische Klasse. Sitzungsberichte
BAWS — Bayerische Akademie der Wissenschaften. Philosophisch-Historische Klasse. Sitzungsberichte
BAWTA — Bauwelt
BAX — Management Facetten
Bax S — Arnold Bax Society. Bulletin
Bay — Bayou
Bay Cities Gard Monthy — Bay Cities Garden Monthly
BAYED — Bayerland
Bayer Aerztebl — Bayerisches Aerzteblatt
Bayer Akad d Wiss Philos-Philol u Hist Kl Abhandl — Bayerische Akademie der Wissenschaften. Philosophisch-Philologische und Historische Klasse. Abhandlungen
Bayer Akad Wiss Jahrb — Bayerische Akademie der Wissenschaften. Jahrbuch
Bayer Akad Wiss Math-Natur Kl Abh — Bayerische Akademie der Wissenschaften. Mathematisch-Naturwissenschaftliche Klasse. Abhandlungen
Bayer Akad Wiss Math-Natur Kl Abh NF — Bayerische Akademie der Wissenschaften. Mathematisch-Naturwissenschaftliche Klasse. Abhandlungen. Neue Folge
Bayer Akad Wiss Math-Natur Kl S-B — Bayerische Akademie der Wissenschaften. Mathematisch-Naturwissenschaftliche Klasse. Sitzungsberichte
Bayer Akad Wiss Math-Natur Kl Sitzungsber — Bayerische Akademie der Wissenschaften. Mathematisch-Naturwissenschaftliche Klasse. Sitzungsberichte
Bayer Akad Wiss Math-Naturw Abt Abh — Bayerische Akademie der Wissenschaften. Mathematisch-Naturwissenschaftliche Abteilung. Abhandlungen
Bayer Akad Wiss Math-Naturwiss Kl Abh — Bayerische Akademie der Wissenschaften. Mathematisch-Naturwissenschaftliche Klasse. Abhandlungen
Bayer Akad Wiss Math-Naturwiss Kl Sitzungsber — Bayerische Akademie der Wissenschaften. Mathematisch-Naturwissenschaftliche Klasse. Sitzungsberichte
Bayer Akad Wiss Philos-Hist Abt Abh — Bayerische Akademie der Wissenschaften. Philosophisch-Historische Abteilung. Abhandlungen
Bayer Akad Wiss Philos Hist Kl Sitzungsber — Bayerische Akademie der Wissenschaften. Philosophisch-Historische Klasse. Sintzungbericht
Bayer Berufsschule — Bayerische Berufsschule
Bayer Bienenztg — Bayerische Bienen-Zeitung
Bayer Bildungswesen — Bayerisches Bildungswesen
Bayer Color — Bayer Colorist
Bayer Farben Rev Spec Ed (USA) — Bayer Farben Revue. Special Edition (USA)
Bayer Gemeinde u Verwztg — Bayerische Gemeinde- und Verwaltungszeitung
Bayer Heimatschutz — Bayerische Heimatschutz
Bayerische Akad Wiss Jahrbuch — Bayerische Akademie der Wissenschaften. Jahrbuch
Bayerische Volksm — Bayerische Volksmusik
Bayer Jb Vlksknd — Bayerisches Jahrbuch fuer Volkskunde
Bayer Landesamt Dkmlpf — Bayerisches Landsamt fuer Denkmalpflege
Bayer Landwirt Jahrb — Bayerisches Landwirtschaftliches Jahrbuch
Bayer Landwirtschaftsrat Vierteljahresschr — Bayerischer Landwirtschaftsrat Vierteljahresschrift
Bayer Landwirtsch Jahrb — Bayerisches Landwirtschaftliches Jahrbuch
Bayer Landwirtsch Jahrb Sonderh — Bayerisches Landwirtschaftliches Jahrbuch. Sonderheft
Bayer Landwirtsch Jb — Bayerisches Landwirtschaftliches Jahrbuch
Bayer Landw Jb — Bayerisches Landwirtschaftliches Jahrbuch
Bayer Lit Merkantil Anz Literatur Kunstfr — Bayerischer Literaerischer und Markantilischer Anzeiger fuer Literatur-und Kunstfreunde. Im In- und Auslande
Bayer Mitt Gummi Ind — Bayer-Mitteilungen fuer die Gummi-Industrie
Bayer Mitt Gummi Ind (Engl Transl) — Bayer Mitteilungen fuer die Gummi Industrie (English Translation)
Bayer Nztg — Bayerische Nationalzeitung
Bayer Sitzb — Bayerische Akademie der Wissenschaften. Sitzungsberichte
Bayer Staatssamml Palaeontol Hist Geol Mitt — Bayerische Staatssammlung fuer Palaeontologie und Historische Geologie. Mitteilungen
Bayer Staatsztg Bayer Staatsanz — Bayerische Staatszeitung und Bayerischer Staatsanzeiger
Bayer-Symp — Bayer-Symposium
Bayer Szb — Sitzungsberichte der Bayerischen Akademie der Wissenschaften
Bayer Verwaltungsbl — Bayerische Verwaltungsblaetter
Bayer Verwbll — Bayerische Verwaltungsblaetter
Bayer Vorgeschbl — Bayerische Vorgeschichtsblaetter
Bayer Z Vermessungswesen — Bayerische Zeitschrift fuer Vermessungswesen
Bayeux Mm — Memoires de la Societe d'Agriculture, Sciences, Arts, et Belles-Lettres de Bayeux
Baylor Bus Stud — Baylor Business Studies
Baylor Bus Studies — Baylor Business Studies
Baylor Dent J — Baylor Dental Journal
Baylor Geol Stud Bull — Baylor Geological Studies. Bulletin
Baylor Law — Baylor Law Review
Baylor Law R — Baylor Law Review
Baylor L Rev — Baylor Law Review
Baylor Nurs Educ — Baylor Nursing Educator

Bay LR — Baylor Law Review
Bayr Beitr — Beitraege zur Anthropologie und Urgeschichte Bayerns
Bayreuther Hefte Erwachsenenbild — Bayreuther Hefte fuer Erwachsenenbildung
Bayreuth Math Schr — Bayreuther Mathematische Schriften
BayS — Sammlung der Entscheidungen des Bayerischen Obersten Landesgerichts
BAYSAH — Bayer-Symposium
Bay Sitz — Sitzungsberichte der Bayerischen Akademie der Wissenschaften
Bay State Libn — Bay State Librarian
Bay State Mo — Bay State Monthly
Bay St Librn — Bay State Librarian
Bay Vg Bl — Bayerische Vorgeschichtsblaetter
Bay Workr — Bay Area Worker
BayZ — Zeitschrift fuer Rechtspflege in Bayern
BaZ — Basler Zeitschrift fuer Geschichte und Altertumskunde
Bazele Fiz Chim Intaririi Liantilor Anorg — Bazele Fizico-Chimice ale Intaririi Liantilor Anorganici
Bazele Mat Cercetarii Oper — Bazele Matematice ale Cercetarii Operationale
BAZM — Beilage zur Allgemeine Zeitung (Muenchen)
BAZTA — Bauzeitung
BB — Bayreuther Blaetter
BB — Bermondsey Book
BB — Bezzenbergers Beitraege
BB — Bibliographie de Belgique
BB — Biblische Beitraege
Bb — Bijblad op het Staatsblad
BB — Billboard
BB — Boletin Bibliografico
BB — Bonner Beitraege
BB — Books and Bookmen
BB — Bossche Bijdragen
BB — British Business
BB — Bulletin du Bibliophile et du Bibliothecaire
BB — Bulletin du Bouquiniste
BB — Bulletin of Bibliography
BB — Bundesblatt
BB — Government Blue Book
BBA — Berliner Byzantinistische Arbeiten
BBA — Biochimica et Biophysica Acta
BBA — Bulletin des Bibliotheques et des Archives
BBA — Bulletin. Societe Scientifique et Litteraire des Basses-Alpes. Annales des Basses-Alpes
BBAA — Boletin Bibliografico de Antropologia Americana
BBAB — Babesch. Bulletin Antieke Beschaving
BBACA — Biochimica et Biophysica Acta
BBAE — Bulletin. Bureau of American Ethnology
BBALAJ — BBA [Biochimica et Biophysica Acta] Library
BBA Libr — BBA [Biochimica et Biophysica Acta] Library
B Banque Nat Belgique — Bulletin. Banque Nationale de Belgique
B Bar — Bench and Bar
BBASA6 — Chung Yang Yen Chiu Yuan Chih Wu Hsueh Hui K'an
B Baud — Bulletin Baudelairien
B Bayonne — Bulletin. Societe des Sciences, Lettres, et Arts de Bayonne
BBB — Banque de France. Bulletin Trimestriel
BBB — Boletin de Bibliotecas y Bibliografia
BBB — Bonner Biblische Beitraege
BBB — Bulletin du Bibliophile et du Bibliothecaire
BBBMB — Biochimica et Biophysica Acta. M. Biomembranes
BBBNS — Biblioteca Bio-Bibliografica della Terra Santa. Nova Serie
BBBr — Boletim Bibliografico Brasileiro
BBBRD — BBR. Brunnenbau, Bau von Wasserwerken, Rohrleitungsbau
BB Bul — BB [B'nai Brith in Australia] Bulletin
BBCBB — Berichte Biochemie und Biologie
BBC Eng — BBC [British Broadcasting Corporation] Engineering
BBC Eng Div Monogr — BBC [British Broadcasting Corporation] Engineering Division. Monograph
BBCNA — BBC [Brown, Boveri & Cie.] Nachrichten
BBC Nachr — BBC [Brown, Boveri & Cie.] Nachrichten
BBCNI — Bulletin Bimestriel de la Commission Nationale Iranienne pour l'UNESCO
BBCS — Bulletin. Board of Celtic Studies
BBDAA — Bulletin d'Information. Association Belge pour le Developpement Pacifique de l'Energie Atomique
B Bd Celt S — Bulletin. Board of Celtic Studies/Bwletin y Bwrdd Gwybodau Celtaidd
BBDI — Bulletin of Bibliography and Dramatic Index
B Beauvais — Bulletin. Societe Archeologique et Historique de Beauvais
B Bel Art — Boletin de Bellas Artes
B Belfort — Bulletin. Societe Belfortaine d'Emulation
B Belg Anthrop — Bulletin. Societe Royale Belge d'Anthropologie et de Prehistoire
BBEZA — Biochimica et Biophysica Acta. Enzymology
BBF — Bulletin des Bibliotheques de France
BBF — Bulletin des Bibliotheques de France et Bulletin de Documentation Bibliographique
BBG — Basler Beitraege zur Geschichtswissenschaft
BBG — Blaetter fuer das Bayerische Gymnasialschulwesen
BBGG — Bollettino della Badia Greca di Grottaferrata
BBGSB — Biochimica et Biophysica Acta. G. General Subjects
BBH — Bulletin Analytique de Bibliographie Hellenique
BBH — Notities over Europa
BBHCD — Bangason Bango Hakhoe Chi
BBHS — Australian Business Brief and Hansard Service
BBI — Balik ve Balikcilik (Istanbul)
BBI — Biomedical Business International
BBI — Bulletin. Byzantine Institute of America
BBib — Beschreibende Bibliographien
BBib — Boletin Bibliografico

BBIBA — Boletin. Biblioteca Americana y de Bellas Artes
BBibl — Bulletin du Bibliophile
B Bibl — Bulletin du Bibliophile et du Bibliothecaire
B Bibliogr Agricola — Boletin Bibliografico Agricola. Ministerio de Agricultura
B Bibliogr Antropol Americana — Boletin Bibliografico de Antropologia Americana
B Bibl M Pelayo — Boletin. Biblioteca Menendez Pelayo
B Bibl Mus Balaguer — Boletin. Biblioteca Museo Balaguer
BBICAW — BSBI [*Botanical Society of the British Isles*] Conference Reports
BBIJM — B'nai B'rith International Jewish Monthly
B Bimestr Soc Comptabil France — Bulletin Bimestriel. Societe de Comptabilite de France
BBJ — Boston Bar Journal
BBK — Bibliotekininkystes ir Bibliografijos Klausimai
BBK — Business Review (Bangkok)
BBKCA — Bruns' Beitraege zur Klinischen Chirurgie
BBKCA8 — Bruns' Beitraege zur Klinischen Chirurgie
BBKG — Beitraege zur Bayerischen Kirchengeschichte
Bbl — Biblica
BBL — Biblioteksbladet
BBL — Bulletin des Bibliophiles Liegeois
BBLA — Beitraege zur Biblischen Landes- und Altertumskunde
BBLAK — Beitraege zur Biblischen Landes- und Altertumskunde
BBLG — Basler Beitraege zur Deutschen Literatur- und Geistesgeschichte
BBM — Betriebs-Berater. Zeitschrift fuer Recht und Wirtschaft
BBM — Boletin Bibliografico Mexicano
BBM — Boletin Bibliografico (Mexico)
BBM — Bulletin. Brooklyn Museum
BBMB — Boletin. Biblioteca-Museo-Balaguer
BBMB — Bulletin Bibliographique. Musee Belge
BBME — Bulletin of the British Museum. Natural History. Entomology
BBMG — Bulletin of the British Museum. Natural History. Geology
BBMM — Bulletin of the British Museum. Natural History. Mineralogy
BBMN — Bulletin of Bibliography and Magazine Notes
BBMODN — Biologiya Baltiiskogo Morya
BBMP — Boletin Bibliografico Mexicano Porrua
BBMP — Boletin. Biblioteca de Menendez Pelayo
BBMPG — Baroda Museum and Picture Gallery. Bulletin
BBMSWK — Berliner Blaetter fuer Muenz-, Siegel- und Wappenkunde
BBMZ — Bulletin of the British Museum. Natural History. Zoology
BBN — Berliner Beitraege zur Namenforschung
BBN — British Book News
BBN — Bulletin d'Information et de Documentation. Banque Nationale
BBNL — Boletin. Biblioteca National (Lima)
BBNM — Boletin. Biblioteca National (Mexico)
BBNPA — Biochimica et Biophysica Acta. Nucleic Acids and Protein Synthesis
BBNQ — Boletin de la Biblioteca Nacional. Quito
BBOC — Bulletin. British Ornithologists' Club
BBOJ — Berks, Bucks, and Oxon. Archaeological Journal
BBP — Bank of Papua New Guinea. Quarterly Economic Bulletin
BBP — British Bulletin of Publications
BBP — Bulletin Bibliographique et Pedagogique du Musee Belge
BBPAD — Bano Biggyan Patrika
BBPCA — Berichte. Bunsengesellschaft fuer Physikalische Chemie
BBPMAT — Buletin Balai Penelitian Perkebunan Bedan
BBPMB — Bulletin Bibliographique. Musee Belge
BBPMM — Boletim da Biblioteca Publica Municipal de Matosinhos
BBPTB — Biochimica et Biophysica Acta. P. Protein Structure
BBR — Baylor Business Review
BBR — Beitraege zur Kenntnis der Babylonischen Religion
BBr — Books at Brown
BBR — Bothnian Bay Reports
BBR — Buletinul Bibliotecii Romane
BBR Brunnenbau Bau Wasserwerken — BBR. Brunnenbau, Bau von Wasserwerken, Rohrleitungsbau
BBRCA — Biochemical and Biophysical Research Communications
B Bretagne — Bulletin. Societe d'Histoire et d'Archeologie de Bretagne
BBR Impressum — BBR. Brunnenbau, Bau von Wasserwerken, Rohrleitungsbau. Impressum
B Br Mus — Bulletin. British Museum
BBROA — Baender, Bleche, Rohre
BBRP — Berliner Beitraege zur Romanischen Philologie
B Br Psycho — Bulletin. British Psychological Society
BBS — Bulletin of Baltic Studies
BBSAJ — Bulletin. British School of Archaeology, Jerusalem
BBSCDH — Behavioral and Brain Sciences
BBSIA — Bulletin Bibliographique. Societe Internationale Arthurienne
BBSM — Bullettino di Bibliografia e di Storia delle Scienze Matematiche e Fisiche
BBSNS — Bulletin of the Buffalo Society of Natural Sciences
BBSP — Botetourt Bibliographical Society. Publications
BBSPA — Biochimica e Biologia Sperimentale
BBST — Bibliotheque Bonaventurienne. Series "Textes"
BBSW — Die Beitraege des Staatsanzeiger fuer Wuertemburg
BBT — Bulletin of Black Theatre
BBU — British Business
B Buddhist Cult Inst Ryukoku Univ — Bulletin. Buddhist Cultural Institute. Ryukoku University
BBude — Bulletin. Association Guillaume Bude
B Bude Suppl — Bulletin. Association Guillaume Bude
B Bur Am Ethnol — Bulletin. Bureau of American Ethnology
B(Burgos) — Boletin. Institucion Fernan-Gonzalez (Burgos)
BBV — Berliner Beitraege zur Vor- und Fruehgeschichte
BBVF — Berliner Beitraege zur Vor- und Fruehgeschichte
BBY — Bankbedrijf en Effectenbedrijf
BBY — Britannica Book of the Year
B Byz — Bulletin. Byzantine Institute of America

BByzA — Berliner Byzantinistische Arbeiten. Deutsche Akademie der Wissenschaften zu Berlin
BByzI — Bulletin. Byzantine Institute
BBZ — Baylor Business Studies
BbZ — Biblische Zeitschrift
BC — Belastingsconsulent
BC — Bibliographia Cartographica
BC — Bibliotheca Celtica
BC — Bibliotheque Choisie
BC — Boletim Cultural. Camara Municipal do Porto
BC — Bollettino della Capitale
BC — Book Collector
BC — Brisbane Courier
B/C — Broadcasting
BC — Bulletin Critique
BC — Bulletin de Nos Communautes
BC — Bulletin des Contributions
BC — Bulletin of the Comediantes
BC — New South Wales Bankruptcy Cases
BCA — Blaetter fuer Christliche Archaeologie und Kunst
BCA — Capilla Alfonsina. Boletin
BCAC — Bollettino. Commissione Archeologica Comunale di Roma
BCA CCH — Board of Contract Appeals Decisions. Commerce Clearing House
BCACR — Bollettino. Commissione Archeologica Comunale di Roma
BC Admin — British Columbia Administrator
BCAF — Bulletin. Comite de l'Asie Francaise
BCA Lezoux — Bulletin. Comite Archeologique de Lezoux
BCALMA — Bulletin du Cange. Archivum Latinitatis Medii Aevi
BCAM — Bulletin. Cercle Archeologique, Litteraire, et Artistique de Malines
B Camuno St Pr Istor — Bollettino. Centro Camuno di Studi Preistorici
BCAN — Bulletin. Commission Archeologique de Narbonne
BCANA — Bulletin. International Union Against Cancer
B Cancer — Bulletin du Cancer
BCA News — BCA [*Business Committee for the Arts*] News
BCAR — Bollettino. Commissione Archeologica Comunale di Roma
BCARDD — Connecticut Arboretum Bulletin
BCARoma — Bullettino. Commissione Archeologica Communale di Roma
BC Art Teach Assn J — British Columbia Art Teachers' Association. Journal
BCASB — Bulletin of the College of Arts and Sciences (Baghdad)
BCA (Sic) — Beni Culturali e Ambientali (Sicilia)
BCASM — Bulletin. Commission des Antiquites de Seine-Maritime
BCASSI News — British Columbia Association of School Supervisors of Instruction. News
Bcast — Broadcast
BCB — BC [*British Columbia*] Business
BCB — Boletin Cultural y Bibliografico
BCB — Brinkman's Cumulatieve Catalogus van Boeken in Nederland en Vlaanderen Uitgegeven of Herdrukt met Aanvullingen over Voorafgaande Jaren
BCBA — Academie Royale de Belgique. Bulletin. Classe des Beaux-Arts
BCBIEQ — Biochemistry and Cell Biology
BCBJ — Monthly Bulletin. Central Bank of Jordan
BCBL — Bulletin. Cercle Belge de Linguistique
BC Build Trade — BC [*British Columbia*] Building Tradesman
BC Bus Ed Assn News — British Columbia Business Educators' Association. Newsletter
BC Bus Mag — BC [*British Columbia*] Business Magazine
BCC — Biblioteca di Cultura Contemporanea
BCCCD — Biweekly Cryogenics Current Awareness Service
BCCCN — Bollettino. Commemorazione del XVI Centenario del Concilio di Nicea
BCCF — Boletim de Comissao Catarinense de Folclore
BCCF — Bollettino Critico di Cose Francescane
BCCMP — Boletim Cultural. Camara Municipal do Porto
BC Couns — British Columbia Counsellor
BCCSP — Bollettino. Centro Camuno di Studi Preistorici
BCD — Bank fuer Gemeinwirtschaft. Aussenhandelsdienst
BCD — Bankruptcy Court Decisions
BCD — Bulletin des Contributions Directes
BCD — Business Conditions Digest
BC Dep Mines Annu Rep — British Columbia Department of Mines. Annual Report
BC Dep Mines Bull — British Columbia. Department of Mines. Bulletin
BC Dep Mines Non Met Miner Invest Rep — British Columbia. Department of Mines. Non Metallic Mineral Investigations Report
BC Dep Mines Pet Resour Bull — British Columbia. Department of Mines and Petroleum Resources. Bulletin
BC Dep Recreat Conserv Annu Rep — British Columbia. Department of Recreation and Conservation. Annual Report
BCDI — Bollettino della Carta dei Dialetti Italiani
BCEA — Boletin del Centro de Estudios Americanistas
BCEC — Bwletin Cymdeithas Emynau Cymru
B CECA — Bulletin. Communaute Europeenne du Charbon et de l'Acier
BCECC — Bulletin de Cultures Ethniques et de Civilisations Comparees
BC Econ Dev — BC [*British Columbia*] Economic Development
BCEDLFB — Bulletin. Centre d'Etudes et de Discussion de Litterature Francaise. Universite de Bordeaux
BCEE — Bulletin. Communaute Economique Europeenne
BCELA — British Communications and Electronics
B Celt St — Bulletin. Board of Celtic Studies
BCEN — Bulletin. Cercle d'Etudes Numismatiques
BC Engl Teach J — British Columbia English Teachers' Association. Journal
B Centre Docum Et Jur Econ Soc — Bulletin. Centre de Documentation d'Etudes Juridiques, Economiques, et Sociales
B Centre Europ Cult — Bulletin. Centre Europeen de la Culture
B Centre Inform Et Credit — Bulletin. Centre d'Information et d'Etude du Credit
B Centro Excursionista Els Blaus — Boletin. Centro Excursionista de Els Blaus
BC Env Aff LR — Boston College. Environmental Affairs Law Review

BC Environ Aff Law R — Boston College. Environmental Affairs Law Review
BC Envtl Aff L Rev — Boston College. Environmental Affairs Law Review
BCER — Bank of China. Economic Review
B Ceram RA Spec Publ — British Ceramic Research Association. Special Publications
B Ceram RA Tech Note — British Ceramic Research Association. Technical Notes
B Cercle Num — Bulletin. Cercle d'Etudes Numismatiques
B Cercl Num — Bulletin du Cercle d'Etudes Numismatiques
BCESS — Bibliotheque des Centres d'Etudes Superieures Specialisees
BCETA — Bulletin de Liaison. Centre International d'Etude des Textiles Anciens
BCETB — Bulletin d'Information. CETAMA
BCETCEHRS — Bibliotheque des Centres d'Etudes Superieures Specialisees. Travaux du Centre d'Etudes Superieures Specialisees d'Histoire de Religions de Strasbourg
BCF — Boletim Trimestral Subcomissao Catarinense de Folclore da Comissao Nacional Brasileira de Folclore do Instituto Brasileiro de Educacao, Ciencia, e Cultura
BCF — Business China
BC Farmw — BC [British Columbia] Farmways
BCFF — Bulletin. Comite Flamand de France
BC For Serv Annu Rep — British Columbia. Forest Service. Annual Report
BC For Serv Can For Serv Jt Rep — British Columbia Forest Service-Canadian Forestry Service. Joint Report
BC For Serv For Res Rev — British Columbia. Forest Service. Forest Research Review
BC For Serv Res Notes — British Columbia. Forest Service. Research Notes
BC For Serv Tech Publ — British Columbia. Forest Service. Technical Publication
BC Gaz — British Columbia Gazette
BCG Cancer Immunother Proc Int Symp — BCG (Bacillus Calmette-Guerin) in Cancer Immunotherapy. Proceedings. International Symposium
BCGI — Bollettino. Comitato Glaciologico Italiano
BCGP — Boletim Cultural da Guine Portuguesa
BCGuineP — Boletim Cultural da Guine Portuguesa
BCH — Bulletin. Commission Royale d'Histoire
BCH — Bulletin de Correspondance Hellenique
BCHAC — Bulletin. Cercle Historique et Archeologique de Courtrai
BCHAM — Bulletin. Commission Historique et Archeologique de la Mayenne
B Chem S J — Bulletin. Chemical Society of Japan
B Chi — Bastan Chenassi va Honar-Eiran
BC His Q — British Columbia Historical Quarterly
BC Hist — Bulletin. Commission Royale d'Histoire
BC Hist Q — British Columbia Historical Quarterly
BCHL — Bibliographical Contributions. Harvard University. Library
BCHS — Bulletin. Cincinnati Historical Society
BCH Supp — Bulletin de Correspondance Hellenique. Supplement
BCI — Nederlandse Chemische Industrie
BCIA — Critical Introduction to the Apocrypha
BCIAM — Boletin del Centro de Investigaciones Antropologicas de Mexico
BCIIS — Bulletin. Christian Institutes of Islamic Studies
BC Ind & Com L R — Boston College. Industrial and Commercial Law Review
BC Ind & Com L Rev — Boston College. Industrial and Commercial Law Review
BC Ind Com'l L Rev — Boston College. Industrial and Commercial Law Review
BC Indus & Com L Rev — Boston College. Industrial and Commercial Law Review
BC Int'l and Comp LJ — Boston College. International and Comparative Law Journal
BC Int'l and Comp L Rev — Boston College. International and Comparative Law Review
BCIP — Bibliotheque du Congres International de Philosophie
BCIRA Abstr Foundry Lit — BCIRA [British Cast Iron Research Association] Abstracts of Foundry Literature
BCIRA Abstr Int Foundry Lit — BCIRA [British Cast Iron Research Association] Abstracts of International Foundry Literature
BCIRA Abstr Int Lit Metal Cast Prod — BCIRA [British Cast Iron Research Association] Abstracts of International Literature on Metal Castings Production
BCIRA J — BCIRA [British Cast Iron Research Association] Journal
B Circ Num Nap — Bollettino. Circolo Numismatico Napoletano
BCIS — Bulletin of the Cranbrook Institute of Science
B Civico Ist Colombiano — Bolletino Civico. Istituto Colombiano
BC J Spec Ed — British Columbia Journal of Special Education
BCKGD — Backgrounder
BCL — Boston College. Law Review
BCLA Rept — BCLA [British Columbia Library Association] Reporter
BCLC — Bulletin. Cercle Linguistique de Copenhague
BCLEDT — Basic and Clinical Endocrinology
B Cleveland Mus Art — Bulletin. Cleveland Museum of Art
B Clev Mus — Bulletin. Cleveland Museum of Art
BCLF — Bulletin Critique du Livre Francais
B Cl Gr Lat — Bollettino dei Classici. Comitato per la Preparazione dell'Edizione Nazionale dei Classici Greci e Latini
BC Lib Q — British Columbia Library Quarterly
BCLIE8 — BOU [British Ornithologists' Union] Check-List
BCLQ — British Columbia Library Quarterly
BCLR — Boston College. Law Review
BCL Rev — Boston College. Law Review
BCLRS — Building and Construction Legal Reporting Service
BCLSMP — Academie Royale de Belgique. Bulletin. Classe des Lettres et des Sciences Morales et Politiques
BC Lumberm — British Columbia Lumberman
BCM — Banque Centrale des Etats de l'Afrique de l'Ouest. Notes d'Information et Statistiques
BCM — Biblioteca di Cultura Moderna
BCM — Book Collector's Market
BCM — Buletinul. Comisiunii Monumentelor Istorice
BCM — Courier-Mail (Brisbane)
BCMA — Bulletin. Cleveland Museum of Art

BC Mark N — BC [British Columbia] Market News
BCMB — Boletin. Comision de Monumentos de Burgos
BCMI — Buletinul Comisiunii Monumentelor Istorice a Romaniei
BC Minist Agric Publ — British Columbia. Ministry of Agriculture. Publications
BC Minist Energy Mines Pet Resour Bull — British Columbia. Ministry of Energy, Mines, and Petroleum Resources. Bulletin
BC Minist Energy Mines Pet Resour Pap — British Columbia. Ministry of Energy, Mines, and Petroleum Resources. Paper
BC Minist For For Res Rev — British Columbia. Ministry of Forests. Forest Research Review
BC Minist For Res Note — British Columbia. Ministry of Forests. Research Note
BC Minist Mines Pet Resour Annu Rep — British Columbia. Minister of Mines and Petroleum Resources. Annual Report
BC Minist Mines Pet Resour Bull — British Columbia. Ministry of Mines and Petroleum Resources. Bulletin
BCMIR — Buletinul Comisiunii Monumentelor Istorice a Romaniei
BCML — Boletin. Comision de Monumentos de Lugo
BCML — Boletin. Comision Provincial de Monumentos Historicos y Artisticos de Lugo
BCML — Bulletin du Club du Meilleur Livre
BCM Lugo — Boletin. Comision Provincial de Monumentos Historicos y Artisticos de Lugo
BCMO — Boletin. Comision Provincial de Monumentos Historicos y Artisticos de Orense
BCM Or — Boletin. Comision Provincial de Monumentos Historicos y Artisticos de Orense
BCMS — Bulletin. Commission Royale des Monuments et des Sites
BCMSB — Bulletin. Calcutta Mathematical Society
BCMU — BC [British Columbia] Musher
BC Mus Ed — British Columbia Music Educator
BCMV — Boletin. Comision de Monumentos de Valladolid
BCMVASA — Bulletin. Central Mississippi Valley American Studies Association
BCN — Bar Code News
BC (Newspr) (Q) — Brisbane Courier Reports (Newspaper) (Queensland)
BCNN — Bollettino del Circolo Numismatico Napolitano
BC (NSW) — New South Wales Bankruptcy Cases
BCNUDJ — Basic and Clinical Nutrition
BCO — Bibliotheca Classica Orientalis
BCOD — BC [British Columbia] Outdoors
BCol — Book Collector
B Co Leg J'nal — Beaver County Legal Journal
B Colon Comp — Bulletin de Colonisation Comparee
B Colon Inst Amst — Bulletin. Colonial Institute of Amsterdam
B Com — Bulletin of the Comediantes
B Comediant — Bulletin of the Comediantes
BComEtSulp — Bulletin. Comite d'Etudes. Compagnie de S. Sulpice
B Com Monum Hist Art Lugo — Boletin. Comision Provincial de Monumentos Historicos y Artisticos de la Ciudadde Lugo
B Comm Sicilia — Bullettino. Commissione di Antichita e Belle Arte in Sicilia
B Commun Europ — Bulletin des Communautes Europeennes
B Com Prov Monum Hist Art Orense — Boletin. Comision Provincial de Monumentos Historicos y Artisticos Orense
B Com Prov Monum Inst F Gonzalez Burgos — Boletin. Comision Provincial de Monumentos y de la Institucion Fernan Gonzalez de la Ciudad de Burgos
BCON — British Commonwealth Occupation News
B Con As Sc — Bulletin of Concerned Asian Scholars
B Concern As Schol — Bulletin of Concerned Asian Scholars
B Concerned Asian Scholars — Bulletin of Concerned Asian Scholars
B Conjonct Region — Bulletin de Conjoncture Regionale
B Conjoncture Suppl — Bulletin de Conjoncture Regionale. Supplement
B Copyrgt S — Bulletin. Copyright Society of the USA
B Corse — Bulletin. Societe des Sciences Historiques et Naturelles de la Corse
BCPAA — Beitraege zur Chemischen Physiologie und Pathologie
BCPCA — Biochemical Pharmacology
BCPCB7 — Buletinul de Cercetari Piscicole
BCPC Monogr — BCPC (British Crop Protection Council) Monograph
BCPC Symp Proc — BCPC (British Crop Protection Council) Symposium Proceedings
BCPE — Bollettino. Centro Internazionale per lo Studio dei Papiri Ercolanesi
BCPE — Bulletin. Centre Protestant d'Etudes
BCPEA — British Columbia Professional Engineer
BC Persp — BC [British Columbia] Perspectives
BCPG — Bulletin of Canadian Petroleum Geology
BCPGA — Bulletin of Canadian Petroleum Geology
BCPHBM — British Journal of Clinical Pharmacology
BCPMHAO — Boletin. Comision Provincial de Monumentos Historicos y Artisticos de Orense
BCPM Lugo — Boletin. Comision Provincial de Monumentos Historicos y Artisticos de Lugo
BCPM Orense — Boletin. Comision Provincial de Monumentos Historicos y Artisticos de Orense
BCPN — Boletin. Comision Provincial de Monumentos de Navarra
BCPO — Boletin. Comision Provincial de Monumentos de Orense
BCPOrense — Boletin. Comision Provincial de Monumentos de Orense
BCPPAB — Buletinul. Institutului de Cercetari si Proiectari Piscicole
BC Prof Eng — British Columbia Professional Engineer
BC Prov Mus Nat Hist Anthropol Handb — British Columbia Provincial Museum of Natural History and Anthropology. Handbook
BC Prov Mus Nat Hist Anthropol Rep — British Columbia Provincial Museum of Natural History and Anthropology. Report
BCPTA — British Chemical Engineering and Process Technology
BCQ — Book Collector's Quarterly
BCR — Bollettino. Commissione Archeologica Comunale di Roma
BCr — Bulletin Critique
BCr — Bulletin Critique du Livre Francais

BCR — Business Communications Review
BCRAA — Bulletin. Commissions Royales d'Art et d'Archeologie
BCRAD — BCRA [*British Carbonization Research Association*] Review
BCRA/EE — Ensayos Economicos. Banco Central de la Republica Argentina
BCRA Rev — BCRA [*British Carbonization Research Association*] Review
BCRBD — Boletim. Casa Regional da Beira-Douro
BCRCA — Boletim. Comissao Reguladora de Cereais do Arquipelago dos Acores
BCREA — Bulletin. Centre de Recherches et d'Essais de Chatou
BCRED — Bulletin. Centres de Recherches Exploration-Production ELF [*Essences et Lubrifiants de France*] - Aquitaine
B Cred Nat — Bulletin du Credit National
BC Res — BC [*British Columbia*] Research
BC Res — British Columbia Research
BC Res Counc Annu Rep — British Columbia. Research Council. Annual Report
BC Res Counc Tech Bull — British Columbia. Research Council. Technical Bulletin
B C Res Mus — Bulletin. Council for Research in Music Education
BC Rev Stat — Revised Statutes of British Columbia
BCRH — Bulletin. Commission Royale d'Histoire
BCRIUK — Bulletin of the Central Research Institute. University of Kerala
BCRTD — Bulletin. Commission Royale de Toponymie et de Dialectologie
BCRUD5 — Biology of Crustacea
BC Run — BC [*British Columbia*] Runner
BCS — Bulletin of Chinese Studies
BCS — Business Computer Systems
BCSA — Bollettino. Centro Internazionale di Studi d'Architettura Andrea Palladio
B CSAR Belg — Bulletin. Classe des Sciences. Academie Royale de Belgique
BCSCA — Bibliotheca Cardiologica (Switzerland)
BC Sch Couns News — British Columbia School Counsellors' Association. Newsletter
BC Sci Teach — BC [*British Columbia*] Science Teacher
BC Sea Ang G — BC [*British Columbia*] Sea Angling Guide
BCSF — Bollettino. Centro di Studi Filologici e Linguistici Siciliani
BCSFLS — Bollettino. Centro di Studi Filologici e Linguistici Siciliani
BC Shelf Maricult Newsl — BC [*British Columbia*] Shellfish Mariculture Newsletter
BCSic — Bollettino. Centro di Studi Filologici e Linguistici Siciliani
BCSIR Lab Chittagong Res Bull — BCSIR [*Banglaesh Council of Scientific and Industrial Research*] Laboratories. Chittagong. Research Bulletin
BCSJA — Bulletin. Chemical Society of Japan
BCSLA R — BCSLA [*British Columbia School Librarians' Association*] Reviews
BCSLA Reviews — BC [*British Columbia*] School Librarians Association. Reviews
BCSO — Bollettino. Centro di Studi Onomastici
BCSP — Bollettino. Centro di Studi di Poesia Italiana e Straniera
BCSS — Bollettino. Centro di Studi Filologici e Linguistici Siciliani
BCSSA — Bollettino. Centro di Studi per la Storia dell'Architettura
BCST — BC [*British Columbia*] Studies
BCSTA — Bulletin. Calcutta School of Tropical Medicine
BCSTB — Biochemical Society. Transactions
BC St Stor Archit — Bollettino. Centro di Studi per la Storia dell'Architettura
BCSV — Bollettino. Centro di Studi Vichiani
BCSYDM — Bristol-Myers Cancer Symposia
BCTA — Bulletin. Comite des Travaux Historiques et Scientifiques. Section d'Archeologie
BCTD — Bulletin. Commission Royale de Toponymie et de Dialectologie
BCTF News — British Columbia Teachers' Federation. Newsletter
BCTH — Bulletin Archeologique. Comite des Travaux Historiques
BCTH — Bulletin. Comite des Travaux Historiques et Scientifiques
BCTKA — Bromatologia i Chemia Toksykologiczna
BCTKAG — Bromatologia i Chemia Toksykologiczna
BC Track M — BC [*British Columbia*] Track Monthly
BCTRD6 — Breast Cancer Research and Treatment
BCu — Boletim Cultural
BCUBAS — Biological Sciences Curriculum Study. Bulletin
BC Univ Dep Geol Rep — British Columbia University. Department of Geology. Report
BCURA — British Coal Utilisation Research Association. Monthly Bulletin
BCURA Gaz — BCURA [*British Coal Utilization Research Association*] Gazette
BCURA Q Gaz — BCURA [*British Coal Utilisation Research Association*] Quarterly Gazette
BC Water Waste Assoc Proc Annu Conf — British Columbia Water and Waste Association. Proceedings of the Annual Conference
BC Water Waste Sch — British Columbia Water and Waste School
BCWL — Bulletin of Canadian Welfare Law
BC-X Can For Serv Pac For Res Cent — BC-X. Canadian Forestry Service. Pacific Forest Research Centre
BCYCD — BioCycle
BD — Bulletin du Cange
B d A — Boletim de Ariel
BDA — Bollettino d'Arte
BDA — Bullettino. Deputazione Abruzzesi di Storia Patria
Bd Agric and Fish Ann Rep Proc Dis Anim Acts (London) — Board of Agriculture and Fisheries. Annual Reports of Proceedings under the Diseases of Animals Acts (London)
BDAI — Bulletin of the Department of Anthropology. India
BDAPC — Bulletin. Debating Association of Pennsylvania Colleges
BDASI — Bulletin. Department of Antiquities of the State of Israel
BDASP — Bullettino. Deputazione Abruzzesi di Storia Patria
BDB — Borsenblatt fuer den Deutschen Buchhandel
BDB — Broadcasters Database
BDB — Bulletin de Documentation Bibliographique
BDB — Bulletin van de Directe Belastingen
BDBAD — Baumaschinendienst
BDBBDB — Departement de Biologie. College Bourget Rigaud. Bulletin
BDBG — Bericht der Deutschen Botanischen Gesellschaft
BDBHA — Boersenblatt fuer den Deutschen Buchhandel
BDC — Bulleti de Dialectologia Catalana

BDC — Bulletin. Deccan College Research Institute
BDCDA — Bulletin de Documentation. Centre d'Information du Chrome Dur
BDCGA — Berichte. Deutsche Chemische Gesellschaft
BDChG — Berichte der Deutschen Chemischen Gesellschaft
BDCNB — Bulletin. Centre de Compilation de Donnees Neutroniques
BDCSB — Building Design and Construction
BDE — Boletin de Dialectologia Espanola
BDEAAK — Estacion Experimental Agropecuaria Pergamino. Boletin de Divulgacion
BDEC — Bulletin. Department of English (Calcutta)
B Deccan Coll Res Inst — Bulletin. Deccan College Research Institute
BDEE — Boletin del Departamento de Estudios Etnograficos y Coloniales [*Santa Fe, Argentina*]
B Delph — Bulletin. Academie Delphinale
B de P — Bibliotheque de la Pleiade
B Dept Ag (Trinidad) — Bulletin. Department of Agriculture (Trinidad and Tobago)
B Dept Archaeol Anthropol — Bulletin. Department of Archaeology and Anthropology
B Dept Sociol (Okinawa) — Bulletin. Department of Sociology (Okinawa)
BDEVDI — Brain and Development
BdF — Boletim de Filologia
BDG — Scandinavian Economies. A Business Economic Report on Denmark, Finland, Norway,and Sweden
BDGAA — Bilten Dokumentacije
BDGAB — Boletin. Direccion General de Archivos y Bibliotecas
BDGHA — Bundesgesundheitsblatt
BDI — Beyond Infinity
BdI — Bollettino. Istituto di Corrispondenza Archeologica
BdI — Bullettino. Istituto di Diritto Romano. Vittorio Scialoja
BDial — Balgarska Dialektologija
Bd I Dir Rom — Bullettino. Istituto di Diritto Romano "Vittorio Scialoja"
BDIPD — Blaetter fuer Deutsche und Internationale Politik
B Direc Gen Arch Bibl — Boletin. Direccion General de Archivos y Bibliotecas
BDIS — Birth Defects Information Systems
B Divis Hum Relat — Bulletin. Division of Human Relations
BdJ — Barre du Jour
BDJOA — British Dental Journal
BDK — Beitraege zur Deutschen Klassik
BDKA — Beitraege zur Deutschen Klassik. Abhandlungen
BDKGA — Berichte. Deutsche Keramische Gesellschaft
BDL — Banque de Donnees Locales
BDL — Beleid en Maatschappij
BDL — Berichte zur Deutschen Landeskunde
BdL — Bulletin des Lettres
BDLG — Blaetter fuer Deutsche Landesgeschichte
BDLIC — Bolleti del Diccionari de la Llengua Catlana
BDLM — Bibliographien zur Deutschen Literatur des Mittelalters
BDM — Banque de Donnees Macroeconomique
BDM — Bollettino del Domus Mazziniana
BDN — Bausteine zum Deutschen Nationaltheater
BDN — Bulletin d'Information. Office de Commercialisation
BDNKA — Busushchee Nauki
BDO — Biblioteca del Oficial. Estado Mayor General de las Fuerzas Armadas [*Bogota*]
BDO — Business Eastern Europe
B Doc — Bulletin de Documentation
B Docum Prat Secur Soc Legisl Trav — Bulletin de Documentation Pratique de Securite Sociale et de Legislation du Travail
BDOGA — Bericht. Deutsche Ophthalmologische Gesellschaft
BDP — Beitraege zur Deutschen Philologie
BDP — Blaetter fuer Deutsche Philosophie
BDPH — Blaetter fuer Deutsche Philosophie. Zeitschrift der Deutsche Philosophische Gesellschaft
BDR — Bedrijfsdocumentaire; Magazine op het Gebied van Praktisch Management
B Draguignan — Bulletin. Societe d'Etudes Scientifiques et Archeologiques de Draguignan
B Drome — Bulletin. Societe d'Archeologie et de Statistique de la Drome
B Dr Tchecosl — Bulletin de Droit Tchecoslovaque
BDSekt — Bjulleten Dialektologiceskogo Sektora Instituta Russkogo Jazyka
BDSPU — Bollettino. Deputazione di Storia Patria per l'Umbria
BDT — Bibliografia, Documentacion, y Terminologia
Bd Trade Metropolitan Toronto J — Journal. Board of Trade of Metropolitan Toronto
BDU — Banque de Donnees Urbaines de Paris et de la Region d'Ile de France
BDU — Bollettino. Deputazione di Storia Patria per l'Umbria
BDUMAY — Duke University. Marine Station Bulletin
BDUZD8 — Universidad Nacional de Tucuman. Facultad de Agronomia y Zootecnia. Boletin de Divulgacion
BdV — Biennale di Venezia. Rivista Trimestrale di Arte, Cinema, Teatro, Musica, Moda
BDVA — Beitraege zur Deutschen Volks- und Altertumskunde
BDW — Bulletin du Dictionnaire Wallon
BDWK — Berichte ueber Verhandlungen der Deutschen Weinbau-Kongresse
BDZ — Business Europe. A Weekly Report to Managers. Europe, Middle-East, and Africa
BE — [*The*] Babylonian Expedition of the University of Pennsylvania. Series A: Cuneiform Texts
BE — Babylonian Expedition. University of Pennsylvania
BE — Balgarski Ezik
BE — Basic Education
Be — Bealoideas
BE — Bedrijfseconoom
Be — Belgrade
BE — Bibliografia Ecuatoriana
BE — Black Elegance
BE — Boletim de Etnografia

BE — Bulletin Epigraphique
BE — Business Economist
Bea — Beaver
BEA — Boletin de Estudios Asturianos
BEA — Building Economic Alternatives
BEA — Bulletin des Etudes Arabes
BEAD (Ankara Turkey) — Bati Edebiyatlari Arastirma Dergisi (Ankara, Turkey)
Bead J — Bead Journal
BEA J — Business Education Association of Metropolitan New York. Journal
BEAJA — BEAMA [*British Electrical and Allied Manufacturers Association*] Journal
BEAMA J — BEAMA [*British Electrical and Allied Manufacturers Association*] Journal
Beam Foil Spectros — Beam Foil Spectroscopy
Beam Foil Spectros Proc Int Conf — Beam Foil Spectroscopy. Proceedings of the International Conference on Beam Foil Spectroscopy
Beam Modif Mater — Beam Modification of Materials
BEAR — Bibliotheque des Ecoles Francaises d'Athenes et de Rome
Bears Bluff Lab Prog Rep — Bears Bluff Laboratories. Progress Report
Bear Steels Rating Nonmet Inclusion Symp — Bearing Steels; The Rating of Nonmetallic Inclusion. Symposium
Beaufortia Ser Misc Publ Zool Mus Univ Amsterdam — Beaufortia Series of Miscellaneous Publications. Zoological Museum. University of Amsterdam
Beaux A [*19th C*] — Beaux-Arts
Beaux A [*20th C*] — Beaux-Arts
Beaux A Chron A & Curiosite — Beaux-Arts. Chronique des Arts et de la Curiosite
Beaux A Rev Inf A — Beaux-Arts. Revue d'Information Artistique
Beaux-Arts Inst Des Bul — Beaux-Arts Institute of Design. Bulletin
BEAV — Beaver
Beaver — Beaver County Legal Journal
Beaver County LJ — Beaver County Legal Journal
Beaver County LJ (PA) — Beaver County Legal Journal (Pennsylvania)
BEB — Beitraege zur Entomologie (Berlin)
BEBEBP — Bioelectrochemistry and Bioenergetics
BEBMA — Byulleten' Eksperimental'noi Biologii i Meditsiny
BEBR — Bechtel Briefs
BEC — Bibliotheque de l'Ecole des Chartes
BEC — Boletim de Estudos Classicos
BEC — Bulletin of the European Communities
BEC — Business Economics
BECAN — Biomedical Engineering Current Awareness Notification
BECAN Biomechan Orthopaed — BECAN [*Bioengineering Current Awareness Notification*] Biomechnics and Orthopaedics
BECAN Electrod Med Biol — BECAN [*Bioengineering Current Awareness Notification*] Electrodes for Medicine and Biology
BECAN Equip Disabled Pop — BECAN [*Bioengineering Current Awareness Notification*] Equipment for the Disabled Population
BECAN Instr Tech Cardiol — BECAN [*Bioengineering Current Awareness Notification*] Instrumentation andTechniques in Cardiology
BECC — Bollettino Economico della Camera di Commercio, Industria, Artigianato, e Agricoltura
B Ec Cam Commerc Ravenna — Bollettino Economico. Camera di Commercio. Industria, Artigianato, e Agricoltura de Ravenna
BECC (Ravenne) — Bollettino Economico della Camera di Commercio, Industria, Artigianato, e Agricoltura (Ravenne)
BECD — Behavioural Sciences and Community Development
BECh — Bibliotheque de l'Ecole des Chartes
BeCHS — Berks County Historical Society. Papers
Bechuanaland Prot Geol Surv Dep Miner Resour Rep — Bechuanaland Protectorate. Geological Survey Department. Mineral Resources Report
Beckacite Nachr — Beckacite Nachrichten
BeckettC — Beckett Circle
Beck Isoliertech — Beck Isoliertechnik
Beckman Bull — Beckman Bulletin
Beckman Instrum Inc Tech Rep — Beckman Instruments, Incorporated. Technical Report
Beckman Rep — Beckman Report
Becks J Dec A — Beck's Journal of Decorative Art
B Ecole Fr Ex Or — Bulletin. Ecole Francaise d'Extreme-Orient
B Econ Afr — Bulletin Economique pour l'Afrique
B Econ Europe — Bulletin Economique pour l'Europe
B Econ Res — Bulletin of Economic Research
B Econ Soc Maroc — Bulletin Economique et Social du Maroc
BECRB — Beckman Report
BECSB — Bulletin. European Communities. Supplement
BECTA — Bulletin of Environmental Contamination and Toxicology
BED — Business Equipment Digest
BEDA — Bulletin of Epizootic Diseases of Africa
BED Amer Soc Mech Eng — BED (American Society of Mechanical Engineers)
BEDB — Bulletin of Endemic Diseases. Ministry of Health (Baghdad)
BEDBA — Berichte. Deutsche Botanische Gesellschaft
Bedford Arch J — Bedfordshire Archaeological Journal
Bedfordshire Archaeol J — Bedfordshire Archaeological Journal
Bedi Kart — Bedi Kartlisa
B Ednl Research J — British Educational Research Journal
Bedrijfsontwikkeling Ed Akkerbouw — Bedrijfsontwikkeling. Editie Akkerbouw. Maandblad voor Agrarische Produktie. Verwerking en Afzet
Bedrijfsontwikkeling Ed Tuinbouw — Bedrijfsontwikkeling. Editie Tuinbouw
Bedrijfsontwikkeling Ed Veehouderij — Bedrijfsontwikkeling. Editie Veehouderij
BEDS — Beitraege zur Erforschung der Deutschen Sprache
BEE — Berichten over de Buitenlandse Handel
BEE — Bulletin of Environmental Education
BEEB — Bulletin of the Egyptian Education Bureau
Beecham Colloq — Beecham Colloquium
Beecham Colloq Aspects Infect — Beecham Colloquium on Aspects of Infection
Beecham Colloq Infect — Beecham Colloquium on Infections

Beecham Symp — Beecham Symposium
Beef Cattle Sci Handb — Beef Cattle Science Handbook
Beef Res Rep — Beef Research Report
Beef Res Rep (Bur Agric Econ) — Beef Research Report (Bureau of Agricultural Economics)
Bee Genet Inf Bull — Bee Genetics Information Bulletin
BEEIA — Edison Electric Institute. Bulletin
Beekeep A — Bee-Keeping Annual
Beekeep Div Leafl (Tanganyika) — Beekeeping Division Leaflet. Forest Department (Tanganyika)
Beekeep Inf Coop Ext Serv (Ohio) — Beekeeping Information. Cooperative Extension Service (Ohio)
Beekeep (QD) — Beekeeping (Queensland)
Bee Kingdom Leafl — Bee Kingdom Leaflet
Beekprs Bull — Beekeepers Bulletin
Beekprs Mag — Bee-Keepers Magazine
Beekprs News — Bee-Keepers News
Beekprs Rec — Bee-Keepers Record
Beeldhouwkst Eeuw Rubens — Beeldhouwkunst in de Eeuw van Rubens
Beeld Kst — Beeldende Kunst
BEEMA — Association des Ingenieurs Electriciens Sortis de l'Institut Electrotechnique Montefiore. Bulletin
BEENA — Bergbau und Energiewirtschaft
BEEO — Bulletin. Ecole Francaise d'Extreme-Orient
Bee Sci — Bee Science
Beethoven J — Beethoven Journal
BeethovenJb — Beethoven-Jahrbuch
Beet Sugar Technol — Beet-Sugar Technology
Bee Wld — Bee World
BEF — Bank of England. Quarterly Bulletin
BEF — Boletin Eclesiastico de Filipinas
BEF — Bulletin des Etudes Francaises
BEFAR — Bibliotheque des Ecoles Francaises d'Athenes et de Rome
BEFBAZ — Berichte. Naturforschende Gesellschaft (Freiburg Im Breisgau)
BEFEO — Bulletin. Ecole Francaise d'Extreme-Orient
BEFPA — Bollettino. Istituto di Entomologia Agraria e Osservatorio di Fitopatologia di Palermo
BEFT — Beaufort Bulletin. Dome Petroleum Ltd.
Beg — Begegnung
BeG — Beitraege zur Geschichte der Deutschen Arbeiterbewegung
BEG — Belgische Kleding
BEG — Boletin de Estudios Germanicos
BEGAA — Bergbau-Archiv
BEGBA — Bulletin. Eidgenoessisches Gesundheitsamt. Beilage B
BegD — Begegnung Dorstale
Begg J Orthod Theory Treat — Begg Journal of Orthodontic Theory and Treatment
BEGHA — Bulletin of Engineering Geology and Hydrogeology
BEGIA — Bulletin. Institution of Engineers (India)
BEGMA — Beitraege zur Gerichtlichen Medizin
BEGOA — Gerlands Beitraege zur Geophysik
BEGUB — Bulletin EGU
BeGUE — Beitraege zur Geschichte der Universitaet Erturt
BEH — Boletin de Estudios Historicos [*Pasto*]
Behandl Industrieabwaessern — Behandlung von Industrieabwaessern
Behandl Rheumatoiden Arthritis D-Penicillamin Symp — Behandlungen der Rheumatoiden Arthritis mit D-Penicillamin. Symposion
Behandl Verwert Kommunaler Abwasserschlaemme — Behandlung und Verwertung Kommunaler Abwasserschlaemme
Behav — Behaviour
Behav Abstr — Behavioural Abstracts
Behav and Inf Technol — Behaviour and Information Technology
Behav and Soc Sci Libr — Behavioral and Social Sciences Librarian
Behav Assess — Behavioral Assessment
Behav Biol — Behavioral Biology
Behav Brain Res — Behavioural Brain Research
Behav Brain Sci — Behavioral and Brain Sciences
Behav Chem State Irradiat Ceram Fuels Proc Panel — Behaviour and Chemical State of Irradiated Ceramic Fuels. Proceedings. Panel
Behav Couns Quart — Behavioral Counseling Quarterly
Behav Ecol Sociobiol — Behavioral Ecology and Sociobiology
Behav Genet — Behavior Genetics
Behav Gr Ther — Behavioral Group Therapy
Behavioral & Social Sci Libn — Behavioral and Social Sciences Librarian
Behavioral Bio — Behavioral Biology
Behavioral Sci — Behavioral Science
Behavior Sci Notes — Behavior Science Notes
Behavior Ther — Behavior Therapy
Behaviour Inf Tech — Behaviour and Information Technology
Behaviour Res & Ther — Behaviour Research and Therapy
Behaviour Sci Res — Behaviour Science Research
Behav Med — Behavioral Medicine
Behav Med Abstr — Behavioral Medicine Abstracts
Behav Med Stress Man N — Behavioral Medicine and Stress Management News
Behav Med Upd — Behavioral Medicine Update
Behav Models Anal Drug Action Proc OHOLO Conf — Behavioral Models and the Analysis of Drug Action. Proceedings. OHOLO Conference
Behav Modif — Behavior Modification
Behav Neural Biol — Behavioral and Neural Biology
Behav Neurochem — Behavioral Neurochemistry
Behav Neurol — Behavioural Neurology
Behav Neuropsychiatry — Behavioral Neuropsychiatry
Behav Neurosci — Behavioral Neuroscience
Behav Pathol Aging Rhesus Monkeys — Behavior and Pathology of Aging in Rhesus Monkeys

Behav Pharm — Behavioural Pharmacology
Behav Pharmacol — Behavioral Pharmacology
Behav Pharmacol Curr Status — Behavioral Pharmacology. The Current Status
Behav Polit Anim Stud — Behavioural and Political Animal Studies
Behav Processes — Behavioural Processes
Behav Psychother — Behavioural Psychotherapy
Behav Res M — Behavior Research Methods and Instrumentation
Behav Res Methods Instrum — Behavior Research Methods and Instrumentation
Behav Res Methods Instrum & Comput — Behavior Research Methods, Instruments, and Computers
Behav Res Severe Dev Disabil — Behavior Research of Severe Developmental Disabilities
Behav Res T — Behaviour Research and Therapy
Behav Res Ther — Behaviour Research and Therapy
Behav Sc — Behavioral Science
Behav Sci — Behavioral Science
Behav Sci Com Dev — Behavioural Sciences and Community Development
Behav Sci Community Develop — Behavioural Sciences and Community Development
Behav Sci Law — Behavioral Sciences and the Law
Behav Sci N — Behavior Science Notes
Behav Sci R — Behavior Science Research
Behav Sci Res — Behavior Science Research
Behav Soc Sci Libr — Behavioral and Social Sciences Librarian
Behav Ther — Behavior Therapy
Behav Today — Behavior Today
Behav Toxicol — Behavioral Toxicology
BEHE — Bibliotheque de l'Ecole des Hautes Etudes Belfagor
BEH Et — Bibliotheque. Ecole des Hautes Etudes Sciences, Philologiques, et Historiques
BEHMA — Berg- und Huettenmaennische Monatshefte. Montanistische Hochschule in Leoben
Behring Inst Mitt — Behring Institute Mitteilungen
Behring Inst Res Commun — Behring Institute. Research Communications
Behringwerk Mitt — Behringwerk Mitteilungen
BEHSA — Behavioral Science
BEHSDV — Behavioral Assessment
Bei — Beiblatt zur Anglia
BEI — Benefits International
BEI — British Education Index
BEI — Review of the Economic Conditions in Italy
Beibl — Beiblatt zur Anglia
Beibl Ann Phys — Beiblaetter zu den Annalen der Physik
Beiblatt — Beiblatt zur Anglia
Beih Ber Naturhist Ges Hannover — Beihefte. Berichten der Naturhistorischen Gesellschaft zu Hannover
Beih Bot Centralbl — Beihefte zum Botanischen Centralblatt
Beihefte Arch Schiffs- u Tropen-Hyg — Beihefte. Archiv fuer Schiffs und Tropen-Hygiene
Beihefte Elem Math — Beihefte. Zeitschrift Elemente der Mathematik
Beihefte zur Zischr f Roman Philol — Beihefte zur Zeitschrift fuer Romanische Philologie
Beihft Ant Kst — Beiheft Antike Kunst
Beihft Mittelaltein Jb — Beiheft zum Mittelalteinischen Jahrbuch
Beihft Roem Jb Kstgesch — Beiheft des Roemischen Jahrbuchs fuer Kunstgeschichte
Beih Geol — Beihefte zur Geologie
Beih Geol Jahrb — Beihefte zum Geologischen Jahrbuch
Beihh Wiss AT — Beihefte zur Wissenschaft des Alten Testaments
Beih Int Z Vitam-Ernaehrungsforsch — Beiheft. Internationale Zeitschrift fuer Vitamin- und Ernaehrungsforschung
Beih Int Z Vitaminforsch — Beiheft zur Internationalen Zeitschrift fuer Vitaminforschung
Beih Jb Zent Anst Met Geodyn Wien — Beihefte zu den Jahrbuecher der Zentralanstalt fuer Meteorologie und Geodynamik (Wien)
Beih Mater Org — Beihefte zu Material und Organismen
Beih Mitt Saechs Thuer Ver Erdk — Beih zu den Mitteilungen des Saechsisch-Thueringischen Vereins fuer Erdkunde zu Halle an der Saale
Beih Nov Hedwigia — Beihefte zur Nova Hedwigia
Beih Pharmazie — Beihefte der Pharmazie
Beih Philo Nat — Beihefte zur Philosophia Naturalis
Beih Repert Spec Nov Regni Veg — Beihefte zum Repertorium Specierum Novarum Regni Vegetabilis
Beih Schweiz Bienenztg — Beihefte. Schweizerische Bienenzietung
Beih Sydowia — Beihefte zur Sydowia
Beih Sydowia Ann Mycol Ser II — Beihefte. Sydowia Annales. Mycologici. Serie II
Beih Tropenpfl — Beihefte zum Tropenpflanzer
Beih Tueb Atlas Vorderen Orients Reihe A Naturwiss — Beihefte. Tuebinger Atlas des Vorderen Orients. Reihe A. Naturwissenschaften
Beih Veroeff Naturschutz Landschaftspflege Baden Wuerttumb — Beihefte zu den Veroeffentlichungen fuer Naturschutz und Landschaftspflege in Baden-Wuerttemberg
Beih Vierteljahr Soz Wirtsch — Beihefte zur Vierteljahrsschrift fuer Sozial- und Wirtschaftsgeschichte
Beih Zbl Gewerbehyg — Beihefte. Zentralblatt fuer Gewerbehygiene und Unfallverhuetung
Beih Zentralbl Gewerbehyg Unfallverhuet — Beihefte. Zentralblatt fuer Gewerbehygiene und Unfallverhuetung
Beih Z Ernaehr — Beihefte zur Zeitschrift Ernaehrung
Beih Z Ges Kaelte Ind — Beihefte. Zeitschrift fuer die Gesamte Kaelte-Industrie
Beih Zn Schweiz Forstver — Beihefte zu den Zeitschriften des Schweizerischen Forstvereins
Beih Zn Ver Dt Chem — Beihefte zu den Zeitschriften des Vereins Deutscher Chemiker

Beih Z Schweiz Forstver — Beiheft. Zeitschriften des Schweizerischen Forstvereins
Beijing Int Symp Fast Neutron Phys — Beijing International Symposium on Fast Neutron Physics
Beijing Int Symp Hydrogen Syst — Beijing International Symposium on Hydrogen Systems
Beijing Int Symp Pyrotech Explos — Beijing International Symposium on Pyrotechnics and Explosives
Beijing R — Beijing Review
Beijing Rev — Beijing Review
Beil Graph Kst — Beilage der Graphischen Kunst
Beil WettKarte Schlesw — Beilage zur Wetterkarte (Wetteramt Schleswig)
Beil Z Med Laboratoriumsdiagn — Beilage der Zeitschrift fuer Medizinische Laboratoriumsdiagnostik
BEIND — Beratende Ingenieure
BeiP — Beitraege zur Philosophie
Beispiele Angew Forsch Fraunhofer Ges Foerd Angew Forsch — Beispiele Angewandter Forschung. Fraunhofer Gesellschaft zur Foerderung der Angewandten Forschung
Beit Kolon Uebersee — Beitrage zur Kolonial- und Ueberseegeschichte
Beitr — Beitraege zur Geschichte der Deutschen Sprache und Literatur
Beitr Abfallwirtsch — Beitraege zur Abfallwirtschaft
Beitraege Algebra Geom — Beitraege zur Algebra und Geometrie
Beitraege Anal — Beitraege zur Analysis
Beitraege Gesch Buchw — Beitraege zur Geschichte des Buchwesens
Beitraege Namen — Beitraege zur Namenforschung
Beitraege Numer Math — Beitraege zur Numerischen Mathematik
Beitraege z Neur Literaturgesch — Beitraege zur Neuren Literaturgeschichte
Beitr Aerztl Fortbild — Beitraege zur Aerztlichen Fortbildung
Beitr Aerztl Prax — Beitraege zur Aerztlichen Praxis
Beitrage Bf — Beitraege zur Aegyptischen Bauforschung und Altertumskunde
Beitr Agrargeogr — Beitraege zur Agrargeographie
Beitr Agrarwiss — Beitraege zur Agrarwissenschaft
Beitr Alexander von Humboldt Forsch — Beitraege zur Alexander-von-Humboldt-Forschung
Beitr Allg A — Beitraege zur Allgemeinen und Vergleichenden Archaeologie
Beitr Allg & Vergl Archaeol — Beitraege zur Allgemeinen und Vergleichenden Archaeologie
Beitr Allg Bot — Beitraege zur Allgemeinen Botanik
Beitr Altbayer Kirchgesch — Beitraege zur Altbayerischen Kirchengeschichte
Beitr Anat Funkt Syst — Beitraege zur Anatomie Funktioneller Systeme
Beitr Anat Physiol Path Ther Ohr Nase Hals — Beitraege zur Anatomie, Physiologie, Pathologie und Therapie des Ohres der Nase und des Halses
Beitr & Ber Staatl Kstsamml Dresden — Beitraege und Berichte der Staatlichen Kunstsammlungen Dresden
Beitr Angew Geophys — Beitraege zur Angewandten Geophysik
Beitr Anthrop Els Loth — Beitraege zur Anthropologie Elsass-Lothringens
Beitr Anthrop Urgesch Bayerns — Beitraege zur Anthropologie und Urgeschichte Bayerns
Beitr Anthr u Urgesch Bayern — Beitraege zur Anthropologie und Urgeschichte Bayerns
Beitr Augenheilk — Beitraege zur Augenheilkunde
Beitr Bauwiss — Beitraege zur Bauwissenschaft
Beitr Bez Naturkundemus Stralsund — Beitraege des Bezirks-Naturkundemuseums Stralsund
Beitr Biol Pfl — Beitraege zur Biologie der Pflanzen
Beitr Biol Pflanz — Beitraege zur Biologie der Pflanzen
Beitr Chem Physiol Path — Beitraege zur Chemischen Physiologie und Pathologie
Beitr Chem Physiol Pathol — Beitraege zur Chemischen Physiologie und Pathologie
Beitr Datenverarb Unternehmensforsch — Beitraege Datenverarbeitung und Unternehmensforschung
Beitr Deutsch Volks Altertumskunde — Beitraege zur Deutschen Volks- und Altertumskunde
Beitr Deut Volks Alter — Beitraege zur Deutschen Volks- und Altertumskunde
Beitr Dt Akad LandwWiss — Beitraege der Deutschen Akademie der Landwirtschaftswissenschaften
Beitr Engl u Nordamerikas — Beitraege zur Erforschung der Sprache und Kultur Englands und Nordamerikas
Beitr Ent — Beitraege zur Entomologie
Beitr Entomol — Beitraege zur Entomologie
Beitr Entwicklungsmech Anat Pflanz — Beitraege zur Entwicklungsmechanischen Anatomie der Pflanzen
Beitr Entwmech Anat Pfl — Beitraege zur Entwicklungsmechanischen Anatomie der Pflanzen
Beitr Erforsch Mecklenburg Naturschutzgeb — Beitraege zur Erforschung Mecklenburgischer Naturschutzgebiete
Beitr Erk Uranism — Beitraege zur Erkenntnis des Uranismus
Beitr Ethnomusik — Beitraege zur Ethnomusikologie
Beitr Exp Ther — Beitraege zur Experimentellen Therapie
Beitr Foerd Landeskult — Beitraege zur Foerderung der Landeskultur
Beitr Forens Med — Beitraege zur Forensischen Medizin
Beitr Forsch Stud & Mitt Antiqua Jacques Rosenthal — Beitraege zur Forschung. Studien und Mitteilungen aus dem Antiquariat Jacques Rosenthal
Beitr Forschungstech — Beitraege zur Forschungstechnologie
Beitr Forschungstechnol — Beitraege zur Forschungstechnologie
Beitr Forstwirtsch — Beitraege fuer die Forstwirtschaft
Beitr FortpflBiol Vogel — Beitraege zur Fortpflanzungsbiologie der Voegel mit Beruecksichtigung der Oologie
Beitr Freiburg Wiss U UnivGesch — Beitraege zur Freiburger Wissenschafts- und Universitaetsgeschichte
Beitr Geburtsh Gynaek — Beitraege zur Geburtshilfe und Gynaekologie
Beitr Geobot Landesaufn Schweiz — Beitraege Geobotanischen Landesaufnahme der Schweiz
Beitr Geogr — Beitraege zur Geographie, Geschichte, und Staatenkunde

Beitr Geol — Beitraege zur Geologie
Beitr Geol Karte Schweiz — Beitraege zur Geologischen Karte der Schweiz
Beitr Geol Schweiz — Beitraege zur Geologie der Schweiz
Beitr Geol Schweiz Geotech Ser — Beitraege zur Geologie der Schweiz. Geotechnische Serie
Beitr Geol Schweiz Kleinere Mitt — Beitraege zur Geologie der Schweiz. Kleinere Mitteilungen
Beitr Geol Thueringen — Beitraege zur Geologie von Thueringen
Beitr Geoph — Beitraege zur Geophysik
Beitr Geophysik — Beitraege zur Geophysik
Beitr Gerichtl Med — Beitraege zur Gerichtlichen Medizin
Beitr Gesch Bergaus Huettenwes — Beitraege zur Geschichte des Bergbaus und Huettenwesens
Beitr Gesch Bistums Regensburg — Beitraege zur Geschichte des Bistums Regensburg
Beitr Gesch Bwsns — Beitraege zur Geschichte des Buchwesens
Beitr Gesch Dortmunds & Grafsch Mark — Beitraege zur Geschichte Dortmunds und der Grafschaft Mark
Beitr Gesch Dt Kst — Beitraege zur Geschichte Deutscher Kunst
Beitr Gesch Dtsch Sprache — Beitraege zur Geschichte der Deutschen Sprache und Literatur
Beitr Gesch Kult Stadt Nuernberg — Beitraege zur Geschichte und Kultur der Stadt Nuernberg
Beitr Gesch Landwirtschaftswiss — Beitraege zur Geschichte der Landwirtschaftswissenschaften
Beitr Gesch Moenchtums Benediktinerordens — Beitraege zur Geschichte des Alten Moenchtums und des Benediktinerordens
Beitr Gesch Niederrheins — Beitraege zur Geschichte des Niederrheins
Beitr Gesch Pharm — Beitraege zur Geschichte der Pharmazie
Beitr Gesch Pharm Ihrer Nachbargeb — Beitraege zur Geschichte der Pharmazie und Ihrer Nachbargebiete
Beitr Gesch Phil Mittelalters — Beitraege zur Geschichte der Philosophie und Theologie des Mittelalters
Beitr Gesch Stadt Goslar — Beitraege zur Geschichte der Stadt Goslar
Beitr Gesch Staedte Mitteleuropas — Beitraege zur Geschichte der Staedte Mitteleuropas
Beitr Gesch Tech Ind — Beitraege zur Geschichte der Technik und Industrie. Jahrbuch des Vereines Deutscher Ingenieure
Beitr Gesch Top & Statistik Erzbistums Muenchen & Freising — Beitraege zur Geschichte, Topographie, und Statistik des Erzbistums Muenchen und Freising
Beitr Gesch Tyrol Vorarlberg — Beitraege zur Geschichte, Statistik, Naturkunde und Kunst von Tyrol und Vorarlberg
Beitr Gesch Univ Erfurt — Beitraege zur Geschichte der Universitaet Erfurt
Beitr Gesch Univ Halle-Wittenberg — Beitraege zur Geschichte der Universitaet Halle-Wittenberg
Beitr Heimatknd Niederbayern — Beitraege sur Heimatkunde von Niederbayern
BeitrHistTh — Beitraege zur Historischen Theologie
Beitr Hyg Epidemiol — Beitraege zur Hygiene und Epidemiologie
Beitr Indforsch — Beitraege zur Indienforschung
Beitr Infusionsther Klin Ernaehr — Beitraege zur Infusionstherapie und Klinische Ernaehrung
Beitr Infusionsther Klin Ernaehr Forsch Prax — Beitraege zur Infusionstherapie und Klinische Ernaehrung. Forschung und Praxis
Beitr Infusionsther Transfusionsmed — Beitraege zur Infusionstherapie und Transfusionsmedizin
Beitr Inkunabelk — Beitraege zur Inkunabelkunde. Gesellschaft fuer Typenkunde des 15 Jahrhunderts-Wiegendruck-Gesellschaft
Beitr Intensiv Notfallmed — Beitraege zur Intensiv und Notfallmedizin
Beitr Int Kongr Gesch Wiss — Beitraege zum Internationalen Kongress fuer Geschichte der Wissenschaft
Beitr Japan — Beitrage zur Japanologie
Beitr Klin Chir — Beitraege zur Klinischen Chirurgie
Beitr Klin Erforsch Tuberk Lungenkr — Beitraege zur Klinik und Erforschung der Tuberkulose und der Lungenkrankheiten
Beitr Klin Neurol Psychiatr — Beitraege zur Klinischen Neurologie und Psychiatrie
Beitr Klin Tuberk Spezif Tuber-Forsch — Beitraege zur Klinik der Tuberkulose und Spezifischen Tuberkulose-Forschung
Beitr Klin Tuberk Spezif Tuberk Forsch — Beitraege zur Klinik der Tuberkulose und Spezifischen Tuberkulose-Forschung
Beitr Klin Tuberkulose Spezif Tuberkulose Forsch — Beitraege zur Klinik der Tuberkulose und Spezifischen Tuberkulose-Forschung
Beitr Kolonialf Ergaenzungsband — Beitraege zur Kolonialforschung. Ergaenzungsband
Beitr Konfl — Beitraege zur Konfliktforschung
Beitr Konfliktforsch — Beitraege zur Konfliktforschung
Beitr Krebsforsch — Beitraege zur Krebsforschung
Beitr Kryptogamenflora Schweiz — Beitraege zur Kryptogamenflora der Schweiz
Beitr Kryptogamenfl Schweiz — Beitraege zur Kryptogamenflora der Schweiz
Beitr Krystallogr Mineral — Beitraege zur Krystallographie und Mineralogie
Beitr Kstgesch — Beitraege zur Kunstgeschichte
Beitr Kstgesch Schweiz — Beitraege zur Kunstgeschichte in der Schweiz
Beitr Kunde Preussens — Beitraege zur Kunde Preussens
Beitr Landespfl — Beitraege zur Landespflege
Beitr Math Informatik Nachrichtentech — Beitraege zur Mathematik, Informatik, und Nachrichtentechnik
Beitr Math-Naturwiss Unterr — Beitraege zum Mathematisch-Naturwissenschaftlichen Unterricht
Beitr Meer — Beitraege zur Meereskunde
Beitr Mineralogie u Petrographie — Beitraege zur Mineralogie und Petrographie
Beitr Miner Petrogr — Beitraege zur Mineralogie und Petrographie
Beitr Mittelstandsforsch — Beitraege zur Mittelstandsforschung
Beitr Morphol Physiol Pflanzenzelle — Beitraege zur Morphologie und Physiologie der Pflanzenzelle
Beitr Musik — Beitraege zur Musikwissenschaft
BeitrMw — Beitraege zur Musikwissenschaft

Beitr Namenforsch — Beitraege zur Namenforschung
Beitr Nam F — Beitraege zur Namenforschung
Beitr Naturgesch — Beitraege zur Naturgeschichte
Beitr Naturgesch Schweizerl — Beitraege zu der Naturgeschichte des Schweizerlandes
Beitr Natur Heilk Heilbronn — Beitraege zur Natur- und Heilkunde (Heilbronn)
Beitr Naturk — Beitraege zur Naturkunde
Beitr Naturkd Forsch Suedwestdtsch — Beitraege zur Naturkundlichen Forschung in Suedwestdeutschland
Beitr Naturkd Forsch Suedwestdtsch Beih — Beitraege zur Naturkundlichen Forschung in Suedwestdeutschland. Beihefte
Beitr Naturkd Forsch Suedwestdtschl — Beitraege zur Naturkundlichen Forschung in Suedwestdeutschland
Beitr Naturkd Forsch Suedwestdtschl Beih — Beitraege zur Naturkundlichen Forschung in Suedwestdeutschland. Beihefte
Beitr Naturkd Niedersachsens — Beitraege zur Naturkunde Niedersachsens
Beitr Naturkd Wetterau — Beitraege zur Naturkunde der Wetterau
Beitr Naturk Forsch Oberrheingeb — Beitraege zur Naturkundlichen Forschung im Oberrheingebiet
Beitr Naturk Forsch Suedwdtl — Beitraege zur Naturkundlichen Forschung in Suedwestdeutschland
Beitr Naturk Forsch Suedwestdeut — Beitraege zur Naturkundlichen Forschung in Suedwestdeutschland
Beitr Naturk Niedersachsens — Beitraege zur Naturkunde Niedersachsens
Beitr Naturk Preussens — Beitraege zur Naturkunde Preussens. Herausgegeben von der Koeniglichen Physikalisch-Oekonomischen Gesellschaft zu Koenigsberg
Beitr Neotrop Fauna — Beitraege zur Neotropischen Fauna
Beitr Neurochir — Beitraege zur Neurochirurgie
Beitr Numer Math — Beitraege zur Numerischen Mathematik
Beitr Onkol — Beitraege zur Onkologie
Beitr Orthop Traumatol — Beitraege zur Orthopaedie und Traumatologie
Beitr Palaeontol Oesterr — Beitraege zur Palaeontologie von Oesterreich
Beitr Path — Beitraege zur Pathologie
Beitr Path Anat u Allg Path — Beitraege zur Pathologischen Anatomie und zur Allgemeinen Pathologie
Beitr Pathol — Beitraege zur Pathologie
Beitr Pathol Anat Allg Pathol — Beitraege zur Pathologischen Anatomie und zur Allgemeinen Pathologie
Beitr Petrefacten Kunde — Beitraege zur Petrefacten-Kunde
Beitr Pflanzenzucht — Beitraege zur Pflanzenzucht
Beitr Phys Atmos — Beitraege zur Physik der Atmosphaere
Beitr Plasmaphys — Beitraege aus der Plasmaphysik
Beitr Pl Physik — Beitraege aus der Plasmaphysik
Beitr Radioastron — Beitraege zur Radioastronomie
Beitr Rhein Kstgesch & Dkmlpf — Beitraege zur Rheinischen Kunstgeschichte und Denkmalpflege
Beitr Rhein Naturgesch — Beitraege zur Rheinischen Naturgeschichte. Herausgegeben von der Gesellschaft fuer Befoerderung der Naturwissenschaften zu Freiburg im Breisgau
Beitr Rheumatol — Beitraege zur Rheumatologie
Beitr Saechs Kirchgesch — Beitraege zur Saechsischen Kirchengeschichte
Beitr Sexualforsch — Beitraege zur Sexualforschung
Beitr Silikose-Forsch — Beitraege zur Silikose-Forschung
Beitr Silikose-Forsch (Pneumokoniose) — Beitraege zur Silikose-Forschung (Pneumokoniose)
Beitr Silikose-Forsch Sonderb — Beitraege zur Silikose-Forschung. Sonderband
Beitr Sittenl — Beitraege zur Sittenlehre, Oekonomie, Arzneywissenschaft, Naturlehre, und Geschichte in Ihrem Allgemeinen Umfange
Beitr Stud Fund — Beitraege zum Studium Fundamentale
Beitr Suedasien Forsch — Beitraege zur Suedasien-Forschung
Beitr Tabakforsch — Beitraege zur Tabakforschung
Beitr Tabakforsch Int — Beitraege zur Tabakforschung International
Beitr Technikgesch Tirols — Beitraege zur Technikgeschichte Tirols
Beitr Theorie Kst 19 Jht — Beitraege zur Theorie der Kuenste im 19. Jahrhundert
Beitr Toxikol Forsch — Beitraege aus Toxikologischer Forschung
Beitr Trop Landwirtsch Veterinaermed — Beltraege zur Tropischen Landwirtschaft und Veterinaermedizin
Beitr Trop Subtrop Landwirtsch Tropenveterinaermed — Beitraege zur Tropischen und Subtropischen Landwirtschaft und Tropenveterinaermedizin
Beitr Urol — Beitraege zur Urologie
Beitr Vaterlandsk Inner Oesterreichs Einwohner — Beitraege zur Vaterlandskunde fuer Inner-Oesterreichs Einwohner
Beitr Verschiedenen Wiss — Beitraege zu Verschiedenen Wissenschaften von Einigen Oesterreichischen Gelehrten
Beitr Vogelkd — Beitraege zur Vogelkunde
Beitr Volksk Ungarndt — Beitraege zur Volkskunde der Ungarndeutschen
Beitr Wetterauischen Ges Gesammte Naturk Bot — Beitraege der Wetterauischen Gesellschaft fuer die Gesammte Naturkunde. Zur Botanik
Beitr Wirkstofforsch — Beitraege zur Wirkstofforschung
Beitr Wirtschaftsgesch Nuernbergs — Beitraege zur Wirtschaftsgeschichte Nuernbergs
Beitr Wirtsch U Wahrungsfragen U Bankgesch — Beitrage zu Wirtschafts- und Wahrungsfragen und zur Bankgeschichte
Beitr Wiss Bot Stuttgart — Beitraege zur Wissenschaftlichen Botanik (Stuttgart)
Beitr Wissenschaftsgesch — Beitraege zur Wissenschaftsgeschichte
Beitr Wuerttemb Apothekengesch — Beitraege zur Wuerttembergischen Apothekengeschichte
Beitr Z Gerichtl Med — Beitraege zur Gerichtlichen Medizin
Beitr z Land u Volk v Elsass-Loth — Beitraege zur Landes und Volkeskunde von Elsass-Lothringen
Beitr Zuechtungsforsch — Beitraege zur Zuechtungsforschung
Beitr Z Volks U Voelkerkunde — Beitraege zur Volks- und Voelkerkunde
Beit Sonderschulwesen Rehabilitationspaedagog — Beitraege zum Sonderschulwesen und zur Rehabilitationspaedagogik
BEJ — Business Education Journal

Be Jb — Beethoven-Jahrbuch
BEJUA — Behavioral Engineering
Bekanntm Staatsmin Soz Fuers — Bekanntmachung des Staatsministeriums fuer Soziale Fuersorge
Beke es Szocial — Beke es Szocializmus
Bekes Koezl — A Bekes Megyei Muzeumok Koezlemenyei
Bekes M K — Bekes Megyei Muzeumok Kozlemenyei
BEKOA — Berichte. Gesellschaft fuer Kohlentechnik
Bekr Verh Utrecht Genoot Kust Wet — Bekroonde Verhandelingen. Utrechtsch Genootschap voor Kunsten en Wetenschappen
BEL — Balgarski Ezik i Literatura
Bel — Belfagor
Bel — Belleten. Tuerk Tarih Kurumu
BEL — Bell Journal of Economics
BEL — Boletin de Estudios Latinoamericanos y del Caribe
BEL — Mededelingen. Verbond van Belgische Ondernemingen
Belarusk Med Dumka — Belaruskaia Medychnaia Dumka
Belas A — Belas Artes. Revista e Boletim da Academia Nacional de Belas Artes
Belastungsgrenzen Kunstst Bauteilen — Belastungsgrenzen von Kunststoff Bauteilen
Belehrende Herbarsbeil — Belehrende Herbarsbeilage
Beleid en Mij — Beleid en Maatschappij
Belfast Nat Fld Cl — Belfast Naturalists' Field Club
Belfast Nat Hist Phil Soc Proc — Belfast Natural History and Philosophical Society. Proceedings and Reports
Belfast NH S P — Report and Proceedings of the Belfast Natural History and Philosophical Society
Belfast NH S Rp & P — Report and Proceedings of the Belfast Natural History and Philosophical Society
Belg Ac Bull — Bulletins. Academie Royale de Belgique
Belg Apic — Belgique Apicole
Belg Arch — Belgisch Archief
Belg Auto — Belgique Automobile
Belg Chem Ind — Belgische Chemische Industrie
Belg Col — Belgique Coloniale et Commerce International
Belg Commr — Statistiques du Commerce Exterieur. Union Economique Belgo-Luxembourgeoise
Belg DiamFabr — Belgische Diamantfabrikant
Belg DiamNijv — Belgische Diamantnijverheid
Belg E & T — Belgium Economy and Technique
Belg Econ — Belgium. Economic and Technical Information. English Edition
Belg Fruit Rev — Belgische Fruit-Revue. Organ der Vlaamsche Pomologische Vereinigingen
Belgian R Internat Law — Belgian Review of International Law
Belgicatom Bull — Belgicatom Bulletin
Belgicatom Bull Inf — Belgicatom Bulletin d'Information
Belg Inst Verbetering Beit Driemaand Publ — Belgisch Institut tot Verbetering van de Beit Driemaandelijkse Publikatie
Belgique A & Litt — Belgique Artistique et Litteraire
Belgique Hort — La Belgique Horticole. Annales de Botanique et d'Horticulture
Belgique Med — Belgique Medicale
Belg J Food Chem Biotechnol — Belgian Journal of Food Chemistry and Biotechnology
Belg J Oper Res Statist Comput Sci — Belgian Journal of Operations Research Statistics and Computer Science
Belg Lait — Belgique Laitiere
Belg Med — Belgique Medicale
Belg Memo — Business Memo from Belgium
Belg Ned Kleiind — Belgische en Nederlandsche Kleiindustrie
Belg Ned Tijdschr Oppervlatke Tech Met — Belgisch-Nederlands Tijdschrift voor Oppervlatketechnieken van Metalen
Belg Plast — Belgian Plastics
Belgra — Belgravia
Belg Rev — Belgian American Trade Review
Belg Serv Geol Mem — Belgium. Service Geologique. Memoire
Belg Serv Geol Prof Pap — Belgium. Service Geologique. Professional Paper
Belg Stat A — Annuaire Statistique de la Belgique
Belg Tijdschr Fys Geneeskd Rehabil — Belgisch Tijdschrift voor Fysische Geneeskunde en Rehabilitatie
Belg Tijdschr Geneeskd — Belgisch Tijdschrift voor Geneeskunde
Belg Tijdschr Oudhdknd & Kstgesch — Belgisch Tijdschrift voor Oudheidkunde en Kunstgeschiedenis
Belg Tijdschr Radiol — Belgisch Tijdschrift voor Radiologie
Belg Tijdschr Reumatol Fys Geneeskd — Belgisch Tijdschrift voor Reumatologie en Fysische Geneeskunde
Belg Tijds Soc Zekerh — Belgisch Tijdschrift voor Sociale Zekerheid
Belize Today — Belize Today Magazine
Beliz Stud — Belizean Studies
Bel L — Belaruskaja Linhvistyka
BelL — Belles Lettres. Revue Mensuelle des Lettres Francaises
BELL — Bulletin. Societe des Etudes de Lettres (Lausanne)
Bellas A — Bellas Artes
Belle A — Belle Arti
Belle Glade AREC Res Rep EV Fla Univ Agric Res Educ Cent — Belle Glade AREC. Research Report EV. Florida University. Agricultural Researchand Education Center
Belle Glade EREC Res Rep EV Fla Univ Agric Res Educ Cent — Belle Glade EREC Research Report EV. Florida University Agricultural Research and Education Center
Belleten — Belleten Turk Tarih Kurumu
Belle W Baruch Libr Mar Sci — Belle W. Baruch Library in Marine Science
Belli LJ — Belli Law Journal
Bell J Econ — Bell Journal of Economics
Bell J Econ and Manage Sci — Bell Journal of Economics and Management Science [Later, Bell Journal of Economics]

Bell J Econ Manage Sci — Bell Journal of Economics and Management Science [Later, Bell Journal of Economics]
Bell J Econom — Bell Journal of Economics
Bell Lab Re — Bell Laboratories Record
Bell Lab Rec — Bell Laboratories Record
Bell Labs Rec — Bell Laboratories Record
Bell System Tech J — Bell System Technical Journal
Bell Syst T — Bell System Technical Journal
Bell Syst Tech J — Bell System Technical Journal
Bell Teleph Mag — Bell Telephone Magazine
Bell Telephone Mag — Bell Telephone Magazine
Bell Teleph Syst Tech Publ Monogr — Bell Telephone System. Technical Publications. Monographs
Bell Teleph Syst Tech Publs — Bell Telephone System Technical Publications
Bell Tele Q — Bell Telephone Quarterly
Bell Tel Mag — Bell Telephone Magazine
Bell Telph Q — Bell Telephone Quarterly
Bell Turk Tarih Kurumu — Belleten Turk Tarih Kurumu
Belmontia 1 Taxon — Belmontia. Miscellaneous Publications in Botany. I. Taxonomy
Belmontia 3 Hort — Belmontia. Miscellaneous Publications in Botany. III. Horticulture
Beloit — Beloit Poetry Journal
Beloit Poet — Beloit Poetry Journal
Beloruss Nauchn Konf Onkol Mater — Belorusskaya Nauchnaya Konferentsiya Onkologov. Materialy
Beloruss Nauchno Issled Inst Melior Vodn Khoz Tr — Belorusskii Nauchno-Issledovatel'skii Institut Melioratsii i Vodnogo Khozyaistva. Trudy
Beloruss Nauchno Issled Kozhno Venerol Inst Sb Nauchn Tr — Belorusskii Nauchno-Issledovatel'skii Kozhno-Venerologicheskii Institut. Sbornik Nauchnykh Trudov
Beloruss Rev — Belorussian Review
Bel Po J — Beloit Poetry Journal
BELR — Bell Laboratories Record
Beltsville Symp Agric Res — Beltsville Symposia in Agricultural Research
Belt Transm Tools Supplies — Belting Transmission, Tools, and Supplies
Beltz Monogr — Beltz Monographien
BEM — Bulletin Economique et Social du Maroc
BEMBA — Boletin de Estudios Medicos y Biologicos
Bemerk Kuhrpfaelz Phys Oekon Ges — Bemerkungen der Kuhrpfaelzischen Physikalisch-Oekonomischen Gesellschaft
BEMID — Bulletin. Electron Microscope Society of India
BEMS — Biomedical and Environmental Mass Spectrometry
BEMTA — Berliner und Muenchener Tieraerztliche Wochenschrift
Ben — Benedictina
BEN — Benelux
BEn — Black Enterprise
BEN — Bull's-Eye News
Bench & B — Bench and Bar
Bench and B Minn — Bench and Bar of Minnesota
Benchmark Pap Acoust — Benchmark Papers in Acoustics
Benchmark Pap Anal Chem — Benchmark Papers in Analytical Chemistry
Benchmark Pap Behav — Benchmark Papers in Behavior
Benchmark Pap Biochem — Benchmark Papers in Biochemistry
Benchmark Pap Biol Concep — Benchmark Papers in Biological Concepts
Benchmark Pap Ecol — Benchmark Papers in Ecology
Benchmark Pap Energy — Benchmark Papers on Energy
Benchmark Papers Electrical Engrg Comput Sci — Benchmark Papers in Electrical Engineering and Computer Science
Benchmark Pap Genet — Benchmark Papers in Genetics
Benchmark Pap Geol — Benchmark Papers in Geology
Benchmark Pap Hum Physiol — Benchmark Papers in Human Physiology
Benchmark Pap Inorg Chem — Benchmark Papers in Inorganic Chemistry
Benchmark Pap Microbiol — Benchmark Papers in Microbiology
Benchmark Pap Nucl Phys — Benchmark Papers in Nuclear Physics
Benchmark Pap Opt — Benchmark Papers in Optics
Benchmark Pap Org Chem — Benchmark Papers in Organic Chemistry
Benchmark Pap Phys Chem Phys — Benchmark Papers in Physical Chemistry and Chemical Physics
Benchmark Pap Polym Chem — Benchmark Papers in Polymer Chemistry
Benchmark Pap Soil Sci — Benchmark Papers in Soil Science
Benchmark Pap Syst Evol Biol — Benchmark Papers in Systematic and Evolutionary Biology
Benchmark Soils Proj Tech Rep Ser — Benchmark Soils Project. Technical Report Series
Bendix Radio Engr — Bendix Radio Engineer
Bendix Tech J — Bendix Technical Journal
Benedictine Hist Mon — Benedictine Historical Monographs
BENEDJ — Behavioral Neuroscience
Bened St M — Studien und Mitteilungen aus dem Benediktiner- und Zisterzienser-Orden
Benelux Geneal — Be-ne-lux Genealogist
Benelux (The Hague) — Union Economique Benelux (The Hague)
Beng Acad J — Bengali Academy Journal
Bengal Agric J — Bengal Agricultural Journal
Bengal P P — Bengal Past and Present
Bengal Public Health J — Bengal Public Health Journal
Bengal Vet — Bengal Veterinarian
Beng As S J — Journal of the Asiatic Society of Bengal
Beng As S P — Proceedings of the Asiatic Society of Bengal
Beng Forest Bull Silvicult Ser — Bengal Forest Bulletin. Silvicultural Series
Beng Forest Mag — Bengal Forest Magazine
Beng Immun Res Inst Pamph — Bengal Immunity Research Institute Pamphlets
Beng J As S — Journal of the Asiatic Society of Bengal
Beng Publ Hlth Bull — Bengal Public Health Bulletin

Beng Publ Hlth J — Bengal Public Health Journal
Beng Publ Hlth Rep — Bengal Public Health Report
Beng Tanng Inst Publs — Bengal Tanning Institute Publications
Benin R — Benin Review
Benin Rev — Benin Review
Benn Electron Exec — Benn Electronics Executive
Bennis Bull — Bennis Bulletin. Bennis Combustion Ltd
Benn Pr Dir Int — Benn's Press Directory International
BENPD — Building Energy Progress
Ben Rev Bd Serv MB — Benefits Review Board Service. Matthew Bender
BENSD — Biomass Energy Institute. Newsletter
B Ent — Black Enterprise
Bentley — Bentley's Miscellany
Bentleys Misc — Bentley's Miscellany
Bent Q — Bentley's Quarterly Review
B Ent Res — Bulletin of Entomological Research
BENV — Built Environment
B Envir Con — Bulletin of Environmental Contamination and Toxicology
Benzene Its Ind Deriv — Benzene and Its Industrial Derivatives
Benzene Mag — Benzene Magazine
Benzene Work Environ — Benzene in the Work Environment
Benzole Dig — Benzole Digest
Benzole Prod Ltd Inf Circ — Benzole Producers Limited. Information Circular
Benzole Prod Ltd Res Pap — Benzole Producers Limited. Research Paper
B e O — Bibbia e Oriente
BEO — Bulletin d'Etudes Orientales
Beobachtete Chromosph Erupt Freiburg — Beobachtete Chromospharische Eruptionen (Freiburg)
Beob Met Obs Bremen — Beobachtungen des Meteorologischen Observatoriums. Bremen
Beob Met Obs Univ Innsbruck — Beobachtungen des Meteorologischen Observatoriums der Universitaet Innsbruck
BEOD — Bulletin d'Etudes Orientales (Damascus)
BEOR — Bulletin d'Etudes Orientales. Institut Francais de Damas
Beor — Queensland Law Reports (Beor)
BEP — Beitraege zur Englischen Philologie
BEP — Bulletin des Etudes Parnassiennes
BEP — Bulletin des Etudes Portugaises. Institut Francais au Portugal
B Ep — Bulletin Epigraphique
BEPFA — Beitraege zur Biologie der Pflanzen
BEPh — Beitraege zur Englischen Philologie
BEPIF — Bulletin des Etudes Portugaises. Institut Francais au Portugal
B E Port — Bulletin des Etudes Portugaises
B Ep P — Bulletin Epigraphique (Paris)
BEPRD — Bulletin Europeen de Physiopathologie Respiratoire
BEQB — Bank of England. Quarterly Bulletin
BEQIDC — Bulletin. Equine Research Institute
Ber — Berichte. Deutsche Chemische Gesellschaft
BeR — Berkeley Review
BER — Bulletin of Economic Research
BER — Bulletin of Entomological Research
BER — Business and Economic Review
Ber Abh Clubs Naturk — Bericht und Abhandlungen des Clubs fuer Naturkunde. Section des Bruenner Lehrervereins
Ber Abh Klubs Naturk Bruenn — Bericht und Abhandlungen des Klubs fuer Naturkunde (Bruenn)
Ber Abh Wiss Ges Luftfahrt — Bericht und Abhandlungen der Wissenschaftlichen Gesellschaft fuer Luftfahrt
Ber Abwasser Abfalltech — Berichte zur Abwasser- und Abfalltechnik
Ber Abwassertech Ver — Berichte. Abwassertechnische Vereinigung
Ber Abwassertech Verein — Bericht. Abwassertechnische Vereinigung
Ber Aeromech VersAnst Wien — Bericht der Aeromechanischen Versuchsanstalt in Wien
Ber Afd Handelsmus Kolon Inst Amst — Bericht van de Afdeeling Handelsmuseum van het Koloniaal Instituut te Amsterdam
Ber Afd Trop Prod K Inst Trop — Berichten. Afdeling Tropische Producten van het Koninklijke Institut por de Tropen
Ber Akad Wiss Wien — Sitzungsberichte. Akademie der Wissenschaften in Wien
Ber Alg Proefst AVROS — Bericht. Algemeen Proefstation der AVROS
Ber Allg Aerztl Kongr Psychother — Bericht des Allgemeinen Aerztlichen Kongresses fuer Psychotherapie
Ber Allg Spez Path — Bericht ueber die Allgemeine und Spezielle Pathologie
Ber Amersfoort — Berichten Amersfoort
Ber & Mitt Altert Ver Wien — Berichte und Mitteilungen des Altertums-Vereines zu Wien
Ber Annaberg Buchholzer Verein Naturk — Bericht ueber den Annaberg-Buchholzer-Verein fuer Naturkunde
Ber Annaberg Buchholzer Ver Naturk — Bericht ueber den Annaberg-Buchholzer Verein fuer Naturkunde
Ber Arbeiten Math Phys Kl Koenigl Bayer Akad Wiss — Berichte ueber die Arbeiten an der Mathematisch-Physicalischen Klasse der Koeniglich Bayerischen Akademie der Wissenschaften
Ber Arbeitsgem Ferromagn — Berichte. Arbeitsgemeinschaft Ferromagnetismus
Ber Arbeitsgem Saechs Bot — Berichte. Arbeitsgemeinschaft Saechsischer Botaniker
Ber Arbeitsgruppe Math — Berichte der Arbeitsgruppe Mathematisierung
Ber Arbeitstag Arbeitsgem Saatzuchtleiter — Bericht. Arbeitstagung der Arbeitsgemeinschaft der Saatzuchtleiter
Ber Arb Vers U Lehranst Brau Berl — Bericht ueber die Arbeiten der Versuchs- und Lehranstalt fuer Brauerei in Berlin
Beratende Ing — Beratende Ingenieure
Ber ATWD Phys Tech Bundesanst — Bericht ATWD. Physikalisch-Technische Bundesanstalt
Ber Basler Mus Volkerk — Bericht. Basler Museum fuer Volkerkunde und Schweizerische Museum fuer Volkerkunde

Ber Basl Kstver — Bericht. Basler Kunstverein
Ber Bayer Bot Ges Erforsch Heim Flora — Berichte. Bayerische Botanische Gesellschaft zur Erforschung der Heimischen Flora
Ber Bekanntm Verh Koenigl Preuss Akad Wiss Berlin — Bericht ueber die zur Bekanntmachung Geeigneten Verhandlungen der Koeniglich Preussischen Akademie der Wissenschaften zu Berlin
Ber Bergische Univ Gesamthochsch Wuppertal Fachbereich 9 Phys — Bericht. Bergische Universitaet. Gesamthochschule Wuppertal. Fachbereich 9. Physikalische Chemie
Berbg Bohrtech U Erdoelztg — Bergbau-, Bohrtechniker-, und Erdoelzeitung
Ber Biochem Biol — Berichte Biochemie und Biologie
Ber Bl V Frue Gesch — Berliner Blaetter fuer Vor- und Fruehgeschichte
Ber Bonn Univ Poliklin Mund Zahn Kieferkr — Berichte aus der Bonner Universitatsklinik und Poliklinik fuer Mund-, Zahn-, und Kieferkrankheiten
Ber Bot Gard Bot Inst Bern — Bericht ueber den Botanischen Garten und das Botanische Institut in Bern
Ber Bot Gart Bot Inst Univ Bern — Bericht ueber den Botanischen Garten und das Botanische Institut der Universitaet Bern
Ber Bot Vereines Landshut — Bericht des Botanischen Vereines in Landshut. Bayern Anerkannter Verein
Ber Bot V Landshut — Bericht des Botanischen Vereins zu Landshut
Ber Bun Ges — Berichte. Bunsengesellschaft fuer Physikalische Chemie
Ber Bunsen Ges — Berichte. Bunsengesellschaft fuer Physikalische Chemie
Ber Bunsenges Phys Chem — Berichte. Bunsengesellschaft fuer Physikalische Chemie
Berc — Berceo
Ber Detmolder Studientage — Bericht ueber die Detmolder Studientage fuer Lehrer an Berufsbildenden Schulen
Ber Deu Bot — Berichte. Deutsche Botanische Gesellschaft
Ber Deut Ausschusses Stahlbau — Berichte. Deutscher Ausschuss fuer Stahlbau
Ber Deut Bot Ges — Berichte. Deutsche Botanische Gesellschaft
Ber Deut Chem Ges — Berichte. Deutsche Chemische Gesellschaft
Ber Deut Keram Gesell — Berichte. Deutsche Keramische Gesellschaft
Ber Deut Pharm Ges — Bericht der Deutschen Pharmazeutischen Gesellschaft
Ber Deutsch Bot Ges — Berichte der Deutschen Botanischen Gesellschaft
Ber Deutsch Orchideen Ges — Bericht der Deutschen Orchideen-Gesellschaft
Ber Deutsch Pharm Ges Ber Pharmacogn Lit Aller Laender — Berichte der Deutschen Pharmaceutischen Gesellschaft. Bericht ueber die Pharmacognostische Literatur aller Laender
Ber Deut Wetterdienst — Berichte. Deutscher Wetterdienst
Ber Dkmlpf Niedersachsen — Berichte zur Denkmalpflege Niedersachsen
Ber Dt Bot Ges — Berichte. Deutsche Botanische Gesellschaft
Ber Dt Chem Ges — Berichte. Deutsche Chemische Gesellschaft
Ber Dt Ker Ges — Berichte der Deutschen Keramischen Gesellschaft
Ber Dtsch Bot Ges — Berichte. Deutsche Botanische Gesellschaft
Ber Dtsch Chem Ges — Berichte. Deutsche Chemische Gesellschaft
Ber Dtsch Chem Ges A — Berichte. Deutsche Chemische Gesellschaft. Abteilung A. Vereins Nachrichten
Ber Dtsch Chem Ges B — Berichte. Deutsche Chemische Gesellschaft. Abteilung B. Abhandlungen
Ber Dtsch Ges Geol Wiss Reihe A — Berichte. Deutsche Gesellschaft fuer Geologische Wissenschaften. Reihe A. Geologie und Palaeontologie
Ber Dtsch Ges Geol Wiss Reihe B — Berichte. Deutsche Gesellschaft fuer Geologische Wissenschaften. Reihe B. Mineralogie und Lagerstaettenforschung
Ber Dtsch Ges Holzforsch — Berichte. Deutsche Gesellschaft fuer Holzforschung
Ber Dtsch Keram Ges — Berichte. Deutsche Keramische Gesellschaft
Ber Dtsch Landeskd — Bericht zur Deutschen Landeskunde
Ber Dtsch Ophthalmol Ges — Bericht. Deutsche Ophthalmologische Gesellschaft
Ber Dtsch Pharm Ges — Berichte. Deutsche Pharmazeutische Gesellschaft
Ber Dtsch Phys Ges — Berichte. Deutsche Physikalische Gesellschaft
Ber Dtsch Wetterdienstes — Berichte. Deutscher Wetterdienst
Ber Dtsch Wiss Ges Erdoel Erdgas Kohle Tagungsber — Berichte. Deutsche Wissenschaftliche Gesellschaft fuer Erdoel, Erdgas, und Kohle. Tagungsbericht
Ber Dtsch Wiss Komm Meeresforsch — Berichte. Deutscher Wissenschaftliche Kommission fuer Meeresforschung
Ber Durum Teigwaren Tag — Bericht ueber die Durum- und Teigwaren-Tagung
Ber Durum Teigwaren Tag Vortr — Bericht ueber die Durum-Teigwaren-Tagung. Vortraege
Ber D W Meer — Berichte. Deutsche Wissenschaftliche Kommission fuer Meeresforschung
Berdyanskii Opytn Neftemaslozavod Tr — Berdyanskii Opytnyi Neftemaslozavod. Trudy
BEREA — Bulletin of Entomological Research
Ber Eidg Anst Forstl Versuchswes — Berichte. Eidgenoessische Anstalt fuer das Forstliche Versuchswesen
Ber Ernst-Mach-Inst — Bericht. Ernst-Mach-Institut
Beret Faellesudvalget Statens Mejeri Husdyrbrugsfors (Den) — Beretning-Faellesudvalget for Statens Mejeri- og Husdyrbrugsforsoeg (Denmark)
Beret Faellesudvalget Statens Planteavls- Husdyrbrugsfors — Beretning fra Faellesudvalget foer Statens Planteavls- og Husdyrbrugsforsog
Beret Forsoegslab K Vet Landbohoejsk Landoekon Forsoegslab — Beretning fra Forsoegslaboratoriet Kungliga Veterinaer- og Landbohoejskoles Landoekonomiske Forsoegslaboratorium
Beret Forsoegslab Statens Husdyrbrugsudvalg — Beretning fra Forsoegslaboratoriet Udgivet af Statens Husdyrbrugsudvalg
Beret Forsoegslab — Beretning fra Forsoegslaboratoriet
Beretn d Biol S — Beretning til Ministeriet for Landbrug og Fiskeri fra Den Danske Biologiske Station
Beretn Forsogsl — Beretninger fra Forsogslaboratoriet
Beret Statsfrokontr (Denmark) — Beretning fra Statsfrokontrollen (Denmark)
Beret Statens Forogsmejeri — Beretning fra Statens Forogsmejeri
Beret Statens Husdyrbrugsfors — Beretning fra Statens Husdyrbrugsforsog
Ber Fachausschuesse Dtsch Glastech Ges — Berichte der Fachausschuesse. Deutsche Glastechnische Gesellschaft

Ber Folge Kohlenstaubaussch Reichskohl Rat — Berichtfolge des Kohlenstaubausschusses des Reichskohlenrates

Ber Forsch Inst Osten & Orient — Berichte des Forschungs-Instituts fuer Osten und Orient

Ber Forschungsinst Cech Zuckerind Prag — Bericht. Forschungsinstitut der Cechoslavakische Zuckerindustrie in Prag

Ber Forschungsinst Zuckerind Boehm Machren Prag — Bericht. Forschungsinstitut der Zuckerindustrie fuer Boehmen und Machren in Prag

Ber Forschungsstelle Nedri As Hveragerdi Isl — Berichte aus der Forschungsstelle Nedri As Hveragerdi Island

Ber Freien Vereinigung Pflanzengeogr — Bericht der Freien Vereinigung fuer Pflanzengeographie und Systematische Botanik

Berg — Bergonum

BERGA — Bergakademie

Bergamo A — Bergamo Arte

Bergb Arch — Bergbau-Archiv

Bergbau-Arch — Bergbau-Archiv

Bergbau Energiewirtsch — Bergbau und Energiewirtschaft

Bergbau Rohst Energ — Bergbau Rohstoffe Energie

Bergbau Rundsch — Bergbau Rundschau

Bergbau Wirtsch — Bergbau und Wirtschaft

Bergbauwiss — Bergbauwissenschaften

Bergbauwissen Verfahrenstech Bergbau Huettenwes — Bergbauwissenschaften und Verfahrenstechnik im Bergbau und Huettenwesen

Bergbauwiss Verfahrenstech Bergbau Huettenwes — Bergbauwissenschaften und Verfahrenstechnik im Bergbau und Huettenwesen

Bergb Rdsch — Bergbau-Rundschau

BERGD — Bergbau

Bergens Mus Ab — Bergens Museum Arbok

Bergens Mus Arbok Naturvitensk Rekke — Bergens Museums. Aarbok. Naturvitenskapelig Rekke

Bergens Mus Skr — Bergens Museums. Skrifter

Bergens Mus Skrifter — Universitetet i Bergen Skrifter

Bergens Sjofartsmus Aersh — Bergens Sjofartsmuseums Aershefte

Ber Geobot Forschungsinst Ruebel Zuerich — Bericht. Geobotanische Forschungsinstitut Ruebel in Zuerich

Ber Geobot Inst Eidg Tech Hochsch Stift Ruebel Zuer — Berichte. Geobotanische Institut der Eidgenoessischen Technischen Hochschule Stiftung Ruebel Zuerich

Ber Geol Ges DDR Gesamtgeb Geol Wiss — Berichte. Geologische Gesellschaft in der Deutschen Demokratischen Republik fuer das Gesamtgebiet der Geologischen Wissenschaft

Ber Geol Ges Dtsch Demokrat Repub Gesamtgeb Geol Wiss — Berichte. Geologische Gesellschaft in der Deutschen Demokratischen Republik fuer das Gesamtgebiet der Geologischen Wissenschaft

Berger Burger Newsl — Berger-Burger Newsletter

Ber Gesamte Biol Abt A Ber Wiss Biol — Berichte ueber die Gesamte Biologie. Abteilung A. Berichte ueber die Wissenschaftliche Biologie

Ber Gesamte Biol Abt B Ber Gesamte Physiol — Berichte ueber die Gesamte Biologie. Abteilung B. Berichte ueber die Gesamte Physiologie und Experimentelle Pharmakologie

Ber Gesamte Physiol Exp Pharmakol — Berichte ueber die Gesamte Physiologie und Experimentelle Pharmakologie

Ber Gesellsch Math Datenverarb — Berichte der Gesellschaft fuer Mathematik und Datenverarbeitung

Ber Ges Inn Med DDR — Bericht. Gesellschaft fuer Innere Medizin der Deutschen Demokratischen Republik

Ber Ges Kohlentech — Berichte. Gesellschaft fuer Kohlentechnik

Ber Gesundh Verh Nuernberg — Bericht ueber die Gesundheitsverhaeltnisse und Gesundheitsanstalten in Nuernberg

Ber Getreidechem-Tag (Detmold) — Bericht ueber die Getreidechemiker-Tagung (Detmold)

Ber Getreidetag (Detmold) — Bericht ueber die Getreidetagung (Detmold)

Berg Hm Ztg — Berg- und Huettenmaennische Zeitung. Mit Besonderer Beruecksichtigung der Mineralogie und Geologie. Hartmann

Berg Huettenmaenn Jahrb Montan Hochsch Leoben — Berg- und Huettenmaennisches Jahrbuch. Montanistische Hochschule in Leoben

Berg Huettenmaenn Monatsh — Berg- und Huettenmaennische Monatshefte

Berg Huettenmaenn Monatsh Montan Hochsch Leoben — Berg- und Huettenmaennische Monatshefte. Montanistische Hochschule in Leoben

Berg Huettenmaenn Monatsh Suppl — Berg- und Huettenmaennische Monatshefte. Supplementum

Berg Huttenmann Monatsh — Berg- und Huettenmaennische Monatshefte

Bergische Forschgg — Bergische Forschungen

Bergmann Mitt — Bergmann-Mitteilungen

Bergmann Schaefer Lehrb Experimentalphys — Bergmann Schaefer Lehrbuch der Experimentalphysik

Ber Gottfried Keller Stift — Berichte der Gottfried Keller Stiftung

Ber Gouv Kina Ondern Java — Berigt Nopens de Gouvernments Kina-Onderneming op Java

Berg Tech — Berg Technik

Berg U Huettenm — Berg- und Huettenmann

Berg u Huettenmaenn Jb Leoben — Berg- und Huettenmaennisches Jahrbuch Leoben

Berg U Huettenm Mh — Berg- und Huettenmaennische Monatshefte

Berg U Huettenm Rdsch — Berg- und Huettenmaennische Rundschau

Berg u Huettenm Ztg — Berg- und Huettenmaennische Zeitung

Bergwirtsch Mitt — Bergwirtschaftliche Mitteilungen

Bergwke Salin Niederrhein BergBez — Bergwerke und Salinen im Niederrheinischwestfaelische Bergbaubezirk

Ber Hahn Meitner Inst — Berichte des Hahn-Meitner-Institute

Ber Hahn-Meitner-Inst Kernforsch (Berlin) — Berichte des Hahn-Meitner-Instituts fuer Kernforschung (Berlin)

Ber Hamburg Mus Kunst Gew — Bericht ueber das Hamburgische Museum fuer Kunst und Gewerbe

Ber Hamburg Stn PflSchutz — Bericht der Hamburgischen Station fuer Pflanzenschutz

Ber Hauptvers Dt Forstver — Bericht ueber die Hauptversammlung des Deutschen Forstvereins

Ber Hist Gez Utrecht — Berigten van het Historisch Gezelschap te Utrecht

Ber Hist Ver Bamberg — Bericht des Historischen Vereins Bamberg

Ber Hyg Inst NahrMittelkontrolle Hamburg — Bericht des Hygienischen Instituts ueber die Nahrungsmittelkontrolle in Hamburg

Berichte — Berichte. Deutsche Chemische Gesellschaft

Berichte — Muenzen- und Medaillensammler Berichte aus allen Gebieten der Geld-, Muenzen-, und Medaillenkunde

Berichte Dtsch Wiss Komm Meeresforsch — Berichte. Deutsche Wissenschaftliche Kommission fuer Meeresforschung

Bericht Rom-Germ Komm — Berichte der Roemisch-Germanische Kommission des Deutschen Archaeologischen Instituts

Berichtsband EAST Kongr — Berichtsband ueber den EAST (European Academy of Surface Technology)-Kongress

Ber Indon Inst RubbOnderz — Bericht. Indonesisch Instituut voor Rubberonderzoek

Ber Inf Europ Gem — Berichte und Informationen. Europaeische Gemeinschaften

Ber Inf KEG — Berichte und Informationen. Kommission der Europaeischen Gemeinschaften

Ber Inform Forschungsgr — Bericht der Informatik-Forschungsgruppen

Bering Sea Oceanogr — Bering Sea Oceanography

Ber Inst Agrarraumforsch Berl — Bericht des Instituts fuer Agrarraumforschung der Humboldt-Universitaet zu Berlin

Ber Inst Festkoerpermech Fraunhofer-Ges — Bericht. Institut fuer Festkoerpermechanik der Fraunhofer-Gesellschaft

Ber Inst Gew Wasserw Luftreinh — Bericht des Instituts fuer Gewerbliche Wasserwirtschaft und Luftreinhaltung

Ber Inst Hochenergiephys (Wien) — Bericht. Institut fuer Hochenergiephysik. Oesterreichische Akademie der Wissenschaften (Wien)

Ber Inst Mech Technol Materialk — Bericht des Instituts fuer Mechanische Technologie und Materialkunde

Ber Inst Tabakforsch (Dresden) — Berichte. Institut fuer Tabakforschung (Dresden)

Ber Inst Tabakforsch Wohlsdorf-Biendorf — Berichte. Institut fuer Tabakforschung. Wohlsdorf-Biendorf

Ber Inst Tex Faserforsch (Stuttgart) — Berichte. Institut fuer Textil und Faserforschung (Stuttgart)

Ber Intern Kongr Phot — Berichte. Internationale Kongress fuer Photographie

Ber Int Ges Erhalt Wisents — Bericht der Internationalen Gesellschaft zur Erhaltung des Wisents

Ber Int Ges Getreidechem — Berichte. Internationale Gesellschaft fuer Getreidechemie

Ber Int Kongr Grenzflaechenaktive Stoffe — Berichte vom Internationalen Kongress fuer Grenzflaechenaktive Stoffe

Ber Int Met Kom — Bericht des Internationalen Meteorologischen Komitees

Ber Int Semin Kernstrukturphys Autom — Bericht ueber das Internationale Seminar Kernstrukturphysik und Automatisierung

Berita Balai Penjel Perusah Gula — Berita. Balai Penjelidikan Perusahaan Gula

Berita Biol — Berita Biologi

Berita Dep Keseh RI — Berita Departemen Kesehatan R.I

Berita Djaw Perik Laut — Berita dari Djawatan Perikanan Laut

Berita Gunung Berapi — Berita Gunung Berapi. Vulcanological Survey of Indonesia

Berita Hyg — Berita Hygiene

Berita Ind Gula — Berita Industri Gua

Berita ISPK — Berita I.S.P.K. (Ikatan Sardjana Pertanian dan Kehutanan)

Berita MIPI — Berita MIPI (Madjelis Ilmu Pengetahuan Indonesia)

Berita Perik — Berita Perikanan

Berita Pusat Djaw Kehew — Berita. Pusat Djawatan Kehewanan

Ber Jahrestag Dtsch Ges Arbeitsmed — Bericht ueber die Jahrestagung der Deutschen Gesellschaft fuer Arbeitsmedizin

Ber Jhb — Berliner Jahrbuch fuer Vor- und Fruehgeschichte

Ber J Soc — Berkeley Journal of Sociology

Berk — Berkeley

Berkala Ilmu Kedokt — Berkala Ilmu Kedokteran

Berkala Ilmu Kedokt Gadjah Mada — Berkala Ilmu Kedokteran

Berk Bud St — Berkeley Buddhist Studies Series

Berk Co LJ — Berks County Law Journal

Berkeley J Sociol — Berkeley Journal of Sociology

Berkeley Sci — Berkeley Scientific

Ber Kernforschungsanlage Juelich — Berichte. Kernforschungsanlage Juelich

Ber Kernforschungszentr Karlsruhe — Bericht. Kernforschungszentrum Karlsruhe

Ber Kfa Juelich — Berichte. Kernforschungsanlage Juelichgesellschaft mit Beschraenkter Haftung

Ber Knopf Mus — Bericht des Knopf-Museum Heinrich Waldes

Ber KohlStaubaussch ReichskohlRat — Bericht des Kohlenstaubausschusses des Reichskohlenrat

Ber Kom AbwassFrag Prag — Bericht des Komitees fuer Abwasserfragen (Prag)

Ber Kommn Geophys Forsch Prag — Bericht der Kommission fuer Geophysikalische Forschungen der Deutschen Gesellschaft der Wissenschaften und Kuenste fuer die Tschechoslowakische Republik (Prag)

Ber Kommn Ozeanogr Forsch — Bericht der Kommission fuer Ozeanographische Forschungen

Ber Kongr Dt Ges Psychol — Berichte ueber den 24 Kongress der Deutschen Gesellschaft fuer Psychologie

Ber Kongr Exp Psychol — Bericht ueber den Kongress fuer Experimentelle Psychologie

Ber Kongr Int Messtech Konfoed — Berichte der Kongresses der Internationalen Messtechnischen Konfoederation

Ber Kontaktstud Werkstoffkd Eisen Stahl — Berichte. Gehalten im Kontaktstudium "Werkstoffkunde Eisen und Stahl"

Ber KorrosTag Ver Dt Eisenhuettenl — Bericht ueber die Korrosionstagung. Verein Deutscher Eisenhuettenleute
Berk Relig — Berkeley Religious Studies Series
Berks — Berks County Law Journal
Berks AJ — Berkshire Archaeological Journal
Berks Co — Berks County Law Journal
BerksCoHS — Berks County Historical Society. Papers
Berkshire A J — Berkshire Archaeological Journal
Berkshire Archaeol J — Berkshire Archaeological Journal
Berkshire Arch J — Berkshire Archaeological Journal
Berkshire Hist Sc Soc — Berkshire Historical and Scientific Society
Berk Symp Math Stat Prob — Berkeley Symposia on Mathematical Statistics and Probability
Ber Kunsts — Berliner Museen. Berichte aus den Preusssischen Kunstsammlungen
BERLA — Bericht ueber Landwirtschaft
Berl Ab — Abhandlungen der Koeniglichen Akademie der Wissenschaften zu Berlin
Berl Aerzetbl — Berliner Aerzteblatt
Berl Aerztekorr — Berliner Aerztekorrespondenz
Berl Ak Ab — Abhandlungen der Koeniglichen Akademie der Wissenschaften zu Berlin
Berl Akad Nachr — Berliner Akademische Nachrichten
Berl Akad Wschr — Berliner Akademische Wochenschrift
Berl Ak Sb — Sitzungsberichte der Deutschen Akademie der Wissenschaften zu Berlin
Ber Land Forstw Deutsch Ostafrika — Berichte ueber Land- und Forstwirtschaft in Deutsch-Ostafrika
Ber Landtech — Bericht ueber Landtechnik
Ber Landw — Bericht ueber Landwirtschaft
Ber Landw Chem Vers U Samenkontrolstn Riga — Bericht der Landwirtschaftlich-Chemischen Versuchs- und Samen-Kontrol-Station
Ber Landwirt Bundes Min Ernaehr Landwirt Forsten — Berichte ueber Landwirtschaft. Bundes Ministerium fuer Ernaehrung, Landwirtschaft, und Forsten
Ber Landwirt N F — Berichte ueber Landwirtschaft. Neue Folge
Ber Landwirtsch — Berichte ueber Landwirtschaft
Ber Landwirtsch Sonderh — Berichte ueber Landwirtschaft. Sonderheft
Berl Anz — Berliner Anzeiger
Berl Archit Welt — Berliner Architekturwelt
Berl Astr Jb — Berliner Astronomisches Jahrbuch
Berl A Tel — Annalen der Telegraphie (Berlin)
Berl B — Berichte der Deutschen Chemischen Gesellschaft (Berlin)
Berl Beitr Archaeom — Berliner Beitraege zur Archaeometrie
Berl Ber — Monatsberichte der Preussischen Akademie der Wissenschaften zu Berlin
Ber Lehrerklubs Naturk — Bericht des Lehrerklubs fuer Naturkunde
Ber Leipz — Berichte ueber die Verhandlungen der Saechsischen Gesellschaft der Wissenschaftzu Leipzig
Berl Ent Z — Berliner Entomologische Zeitschrift
Berl Freie Univ FU Pressedienst Wiss — Berlin Freie Universitaet. FU Pressedienst Wissenschaft
Berl Geowissenschaftliche Abh Reihe A — Berliner Geowissenschaftliche Abhandlungen. Reihe A
Berl Gesell F Anthropol Verhandl — Berliner Gesellschaft fuer Anthropologie. Verhandlungen
Berl Griech Urkdn — Berliner Griechische Urkunden
Berl Gs Erdk Vh — Verhandlungen der Gesellschaft fuer Erdkunde zu Berlin
Berl Gsndhamt Arb — Arbeiten aus dem Kaiserlichen Gesundheitsamte
Berl Gs Nt Fr Mg — Magazin der Gesellschaft Naturforschender Freunde zu Berlin
Berl Gs Nt Fr N Schr — Neue Schriften der Gesellschaft Naturforschender Freunde zu Berlin
Ber Limnol Flusst Freudenthal Munden — Berichte. Limnologische Flusstation Freudenthal Munden
Berlin Abendbl — Berliner Abendblaetter
Berlin Abhandl — Abhandlungen der Koeniglichen Akademie der Wissenschaften in Berlin
Berlin Architwelt — Berliner Architekturwelt
Berlin Beitr Archaeom — Berliner Beitraege zur Archaeometrie
Berlin BI — Berlinische Blaetter
Berlin Blaett — Berlinische Blaetter
Berlin Brandenburgische Akad Wiss Ber Abh — Berlin-Brandenburgische Akademie der Wissenschaften. Berichte und Abhandlungen
Berlin Byz Arbeit — Berliner Byzantinische Arbeiten
Berlin Charivari — Berliner Charivari
Berliner Beytr Landwirthschaftswiss — Berliner Beytraege zur Landwirthschaftswissenschaft
Berliner Jahr Vor Fruehgesch — Berliner Jahrbuch fuer Vor- und Fruehgeschichte
Berliner Med Z — Berliner Medizinische Zeitschrift
Berliner Mh — Berliner Monatshefte fuer Internationale Aufklaerung
Berliner Mus — Berliner Museen. Berichte aus den Preusssischen Kunstsammlungen
Berliner Numism Ztschr — Berliner Numismatische Zeitschrift
Berliner Num Z — Berliner Numismatische Zeitschrift
Berliner Philol Wochenschr — Berliner Philologische Wochenschrift
Berliner Statis — Berliner Statistik
Berliner Tieraerztl Wochenschr — Berliner Tieraerztliche Wochenschrift
Berliner Wohlfahrtsbl — Berliner Wohlfahrtsblaetter
Berlin Heimat — Berliner Heimat
Berlin Illus Ztg — Berliner Illustrierte Zeitung
Berlin Indol Stud — Berliner Indologische Studien
Berlin Jahrb f Wiss Kritik — Jahrbuecher fuer Wissenschaftliche Kritik zu Berlin
Berlin Jb Vor & Fruehgesch — Berliner Jahrbuch fuer Vor- und Fruehgeschichte
Berlin Mag — Berlinisches Magazin, oder Gesammlete Schriften und Nachrichten fuer die Liebhaber der Arzneywissenschaft, Naturgeschichte und der Angenehmen Wissenschaften Ueberhaupt
Berlin Mschr — Berlinische Monatsschrift

Berlin Muenzbl — Berliner Muenzblaetter
Berlin Mus Ber Ehem Preuss Kstsamml — Berliner Museen. Berichte aus den Ehemaligen Preussischen Kunstsammlungen
Berlin Mus Ber Staatl Mus Preuss Kultbes — Berliner Museen. Berichte aus den Staatlichen Museen Preussischer Kulturbesitz
Berlin N Ztg — Berliner National-Zeitung
Berlin Samml Befoerd Arzneywiss — Berlinische Sammlungen zur Befoerderung der Arzneywissenschaft, der Naturgeschichte, der Haushaltungskunst, Cameralwissenschaft und der Dahin Einschlagenden Litteratur
Berlin Tagbl — Berliner Tageblatt
Berl Jahrb Pharm — Berlinisches Jahrbuch fuer die Pharmacie
Berl Jb f Vor-u Fruehgesch — Berliner Jahrbuch fuer Vor- und Fruehgeschichte
Berl KfmG J — Jahrbuch des Kaufmannsgerichts Berlin
Berl Klass Text — Berliner Klassiker Texte
Berl Klin Wchnschr — Berliner Klinische Wochenschrift
Berl Klin Wschr — Berliner Klinische Wochenschrift
Berl MB — Monatsberichte der Preussischen Akademie der Wissenschaften zu Berlin
Berl Mm — Memoires de l'Academie Royale des Sciences de Berlin
Berl Mm Ac — Memoires de l'Academie Royale des Sciences de Berlin
Berl Mt Gs Nf — Mittheilungen aus den Verhandlungen der Gesellschaft Naturforschender Freunde zu Berlin
Berl Muench Tieraerztl Wochenschr — Berliner und Muenchener Tieraerztliche Wochenschrift
Berl Muench Tieraerztl Wschr — Berliner und Muenchener Tieraerztliche Wochenschrift
Berl Mus — Berliner Museen
Berl Nf Fr Sb — Sitzungs-Berichte der Gesellschaft Naturforschender Freunde zu Berlin
Berl Num Z — Berliner Numismatische Zeitschrift
Berl Num Zeit — Berliner Numismatische Zeitschrift
Berl NZ — Berliner Numismatische Zeitschrift
Berl Philol Woch — Philologische Wochenschrift (Berlin)
Berl Phil Woch — Berliner Philologische Wochenschrift
Berl Pol Gs Vh — Verhandlungen der Polytechnischen Gesellschaft (Berlin)
Berl Pol Gs Vort — Vortraege in der Polytechnischen Gesellschaft zu Berlin
Berl Ps Gs Vh — Verhandlungen der Physikalischen Gesellschaft in Berlin
Berl Ps Reichsanst Ab — Wissenschaftliche Abhandlungen der Physikalisch-Technischen Reichsanstalt (Berlin)
Berl Sitz — Sitzungsberichte der Deutschen Akademie der Wissenschaften zu Berlin
Berl Stat — Berliner Statistik
Berl Strnw Beob Ergebn — Beobachtungs-Ergebnisse der Koeniglichen Sternwarte zu Berlin
Berl Studienreihe Math — Berliner Studienreihe zur Mathematik
Berl Tieraerztl Wchnschr — Berliner Tieraerztliche Wochenschrift
Berl Vh Md Gs — Verhandlungen der Berliner Medicinischen Gesellschaft
Berl Wetterkarte Suppl — Berliner Wetterkarte. Supplement
Berl Winck Prog — Berlin. Winckelmannsprogramm der Archaeologischen Gesellschaft
Berl Wirtschber — Berliner Wirtschaftsbericht
Ber Math — Berichte aus der Mathematik
Ber Math Statist Sekt Forschungsgesellsch Joanneum — Berichte der Mathematisch-Statistischen Sektion in der Forschungsgesellschaft Joanneum
Ber Math-Statist Sekt Forschungszentrum (Graz) — Berichte. Forschungszentrum. Mathematisch-Statistische Sektion (Graz)
Ber Max-Planck-Inst Stroemungsforsch — Bericht. Max-Planck-Institut fuer Stroemungsforschung
Ber Meded Genootsch Landb Utrecht — Berichten en Mededeelingen van het Genootschap Voor Landbouw en Kruidkunde te Utrecht
Berm Hist Q — Bermuda. Historical Quarterly
Ber MPI Kernphys (Heidelberg) — Bericht. Max-Planck-Institut fuer Kernphysik (Heidelberg)
Ber MPI Phys Astrophys Inst Extraterr Phys — Bericht. Max-Planck-Institut fuer Physik und Astrophysik. Institut fuer Extraterrestrische Physik
Ber MPI Plasmaphys Garching — Bericht. Max-Planck-Institut fuer Plasmaphysik. Garching bei Muenchen
Ber MPI Stroemungsforsch — Bericht. Max-Planck-Institut fuer Stroemungsforschung
Bermuda Biol Sta Res Contr — Bermuda Biological Station for Research. Contributions
Bermuda Biol Stn Res Spec Publ — Bermuda. Biological Station for Research. Special Publication
Bermuda Hist Soc Occas Publ — Bermuda Historical Society. Occasional Publications
Bermuda Rep Dir Agric Fish — Bermuda. Report of the Director of Agriculture and Fisheries
Ber Mus — Berliner Museen. Berichte aus den Preusssischen Kunstsammlungen
Ber Mus Francisco Carol — Bericht ueber das Museum Francisco-Carolinum
Ber Mus Francisco Carolinium — Bericht ueber das Museum Francisco-Carolinium
Ber Musikw Arb DDR — Bericht ueber die Musikcwissenschaftlichen Arbeiten in der DDR
Ber Mus Stadt Ulms — Berichte des Museums der Stadt Ulms
Ber Musver Judenburg — Berichte des Museumsvereins Judenburg
Ber Mus Vlkernd Leipzig — Bericht des Museums fuer Voelkerkunde in Leipzig
Ber Natf Ges Freiburg — Bericht der Naturforschenden Gesellschaft Freiburg
Ber Naturf Ges Freiburg — Berichte der Naturforschenden Gesellschaft zu Freiburg
Ber Naturf Ges Uri — Berichte der Naturforschenden Gesellschaft Uri
Ber Naturforsch Ges (Augsb) — Berichte. Naturforschende Gesellschaft (Augsburg)
Ber Naturforsch Ges (Bamberg) — Berichte. Naturforschende Gesellschaft (Bamberg)

Ber Naturforsch Ges (Freib I Br) — Berichte. Naturforschende Gesellschaft (Freiburg Im Breisgau)

Ber Naturforsch Ges (Freiburg) — Berichte. Naturforschende Gesellschaft (Freiburg)

Ber Naturforsch Ges (Freiburg Breisgau) — Berichte. Naturforschende Gesellschaft (Freiburg Im Breisgau)

Ber Naturhist Ges Hannover — Bericht. Naturhistorische Gesellschaft zu Hannover

Ber Naturiwss Vereines Aussig — Bericht des Naturwissenschaftlichen Vereines in Aussig

Ber Naturwiss Med Vereins Innsbruck — Bericht des Naturwissenschaftlich-Medizinischen Vereins Innsbruck

Ber Naturwiss-Med Ver Innsb — Berichte. Naturwissenschaftlich-Medizinischer Verein in Innsbruck

Ber Naturwiss Ver Bielefeld Umgegend EV — Bericht des Naturwissenschaftlichen Vereins fuer Bielefeld und Umgegend EV

Ber Naturwiss Vereines Regensburg — Bericht des Naturwissenschaftlichen Vereines zu Regensburg

Ber Naturwiss Vereins Dessau — Berichte des Naturwissenschaftlichen Vereins in Dessau

Ber Naturwiss Vereins Schwaben — Bericht des Naturwissenschaftlichen Vereins fuer Schwaben

Ber Naturwiss Vereins Schwaben Augsburg — Bericht des Naturwissenschaftlichen Vereins fuer Schwaben und Neuburg a.V. in Augsburg, fruerher Naturhistorischen Vereins in Augsburg

Ber Naturwiss Verein Zerbst — Bericht ueber den Naturwissenschaftlichen Verein zu Zerbst

Ber Naturwiss Ver Regensburg — Berichte des Naturwissenschaftlichen Vereins zu Regensburg

Ber Naturw Med Ver Innsbruck — Berichte. Naturwissenschaftlich-Medizinischer Verein in Innsbruck

Ber Natwiss Ver & Mus Natknd & Vorgesch Dessau — Berichte des Naturwissenschaftlichen Vereins und des Museums fuer Naturkunde und Vorgeschichte in Dessau

Bern Blaett Landw — Bernische Blaetter fuer Landwirthschaft

BERND — Bio-Energy Re-News

Berner Beitr Gesch Med Naturwiss — Berner Beitraege zur Geschichte der Medizin und der Naturwissenschaften

Ber Neth Plantenziektenkundige Dienst — Berichte. Netherlands. Plantenziektenkundige Dienst

Bernice Pauahi Bishop Museum Bull — Bernice Pauahi Bishop Museum. Bulletin

Bernice Pauahi Bishop Museum Bull Special Pub — Bernice Pauahi Bishop Museum. Bulletin. Special Publication

Bernice Pauahi Bishop Mus Oc P — Bernice Pauahi Bishop Museum. Occasional Papers

Bernice P Bishop Mus Spec Publ — Bernice Pauahi Bishop Museum. Special Publication

Bern Mt — Mittheilungen der Naturforschenden Gesellschaft in Bern

BEROA — Better Roads

Ber Oberhess Ges Nat Heikd Giessen Naturwiss Abt — Bericht. Oberhessische Gesellschaft fuer Natur und Heilkunde zu Giessen. Naturwissenschaftliche Abteilung

Ber Oekol Forsch — Berichte aus der Oekologischen Forschung

Ber Oesterr Lit Zool Bot — Bericht ueber die Oesterreichische Literatur der Zoologie, Botanik, und Paleontologie

Ber Oesterr Studienges Atomenerg — Berichte. Oesterreichische Studiengesellschaft fuer Atomenergie

Ber Offenbacher Vereins Naturkd — Bericht des Offenbacher Vereins fuer Naturkunde

Ber Offenbacher Vereins Naturk Thaetigk — Bericht des Offenbacher Vereins fuer Naturkunde ueber seine Thaetigkeit

Ber Ohara Inst Landw Biol — Berichte. Ohara Institut fuer Landwirtschaftliche Biologie

Ber Ohara Inst Landwirtsch Biol Okayama Univ — Berichte. Ohara Institut fuer Landwirtschaftliche Biologie. Okayama Universitaet

Ber Ohara Inst Landwirtsch Forsch Kurashiki — Berichte. Ohara Institut fuer Landwirtschaftliche Forschungen in Kurashiki

Ber Ohara Inst Landwirtsch Forsch Okayama Univ — Berichte. Ohara Institut fuer Landwirtschaftliche Forschungen. Okayama Universitaet

Ber Pet Ind — Berichte ueber die Petroleum Industrie

Ber Pharmakogn Litt Aller Laender — Berichte ueber die Pharmakognostische Litteratur Aller Laender, Herausgegeben von der Deutschen Pharmaceutischen Gesellschaft

Ber Phys Chem Unters Rheinwassers — Bericht ueber die Physikalisch-Chemische Untersuchung des Rheinwassers

Ber Physiol Lab Versuchsanst Landw Inst — Berichte aus dem Physiologischen Laboratorium und der Versuchsanstalt des Landwirthschaftlichen Instituts

Ber Physiol Lab Versuchsanst Landwirtsch Inst Univ Halle — Berichte. Physiologisches Laboratorium und der Versuchsanstalt des Landwirthschaftlichen Instituts der Universitaet Halle

Ber Phys-Med Ges Wuerzb — Berichte. Physikalisch-Medizinische Gesellschaft zu Wuerzburg

Ber Phys Tech Bundesanst Braunschweig Berlin — Berichte. Physikalisch-Technische Bundesanstalt, Braunschweig und Berlin

Ber Phys Tech Bundesanst PTB ATWD — Bericht. Physikalisch-Technische Bundesanstalt. PTB-ATWD

Ber Preuss Ak — Berichte der Preussischen Akademie der Wissenschaften

BerR — Berkeley Review

Ber Rassenkeuze — Bericht ueber Rassenkeuze

Ber Raumforsch & Raumplan — Berichte zur Raumforschung und Raumplanung

Ber Raumforsch und Raumplanung — Berichte zur Raumforschung und Raumplanung

Berr Dt Chem Ges — Berichte der Deutschen Chemischen Gesellschaft

Berr Ges Physiol — Berichte ueber die Gesamte Physiologie

Ber RGK — Bericht. Roemisch-Germanische Kommission

Ber RGKO — Berichte der Roemisch-Germanische Kommission des Deutschen Archaeologischen Instituts

Ber Rijksdienst Oudhdknd Bodemonderzoek — Berichten van de Rijksdienst voor het Oudheidkundig Bodemonderzoek

Ber Rijksd Oudh Bod — Berichten. Rijksdienst voor het Oudheidkundige Bodemonderzoek

Ber Roem Ger Komm — Bericht der Roemisch-Germanischen Kommission

Ber Roem Germ Kom — Berichte der Roemisch-Germanische Kommission des Deutschen Archaeologischen Instituts

Berr Vhdlgg Saechs Akad Wiss — Berichte ueber die Verhandlungen der Sachsischen Akademie der Wissenschaften

Ber Saarland — Bericht. Staatliche Denkmalpflege im Saarland

Ber Saechs Gesell — Berichte ueber die Verhandlungen der Saechsischen Gesellschaft der Wissenschaftzu Leipzig

Ber Saechs Ges Wiss — Berichte ueber die Verhandlungen der Saechsischen Gesellschaft der Wissenschaftzu Leipzig

Ber Schweiz Bot Ges — Berichte. Schweizerische Botanische Gesellschaft

Ber Schweiz Bot Ges Bull Soc Bot Suisse — Berichte. Schweizerische Botanische Gesellschaft/Bulletin de la Societe Botanique Suisse

Ber Senckenberg Naturf Ges — Bericht ueber die Senckenbergische Naturforschende Gesellschaft

Ber Senckenberg Naturforsch Ges — Bericht der Senckenbergischen Naturforschenden Gesellschaft

Ber Senckenbg Naturf Ges — Bericht der Senckenbergischen Naturforschenden Gesellschaft

Ber Sitzungen Joachim Jungius Gesellsch Wiss — Berichte aus den Sitzungen der Joachim Jungius-Gesellschaft der Wissenschaften

Ber Sitzungen Naturf Ges Halle — Bericht ueber die Sitzungen der Naturforschenden Gesellschaft zu Halle

Ber Staat Denkmaf Saarland — Bericht. Staatliche Denkmalpflege im Saarland. Beitrage zur Archaeologie und Kunstgeschichte

Berstatt Jahr Basl Kstver — Berichterstattung. Ueber das Jahr. Basler Kunstverein

Ber Studiengruppe Systemforsch (Heidelberg) — Bericht. Studiengruppe fuer Systemforschung (Heidelberg)

Ber Taetigkeit Naturwiss Ges Isis Bautzen — Bericht ueber die Taetigkeit der Naturwissenschaftlichen Gesellschaft Isis. Bautzen

Ber Taetigk Jahrb St Gallischen Naturwiss Ges — Bericht ueber die Taetigkeit Jahrbuch der St. Gallischen Naturwissenschaftlichen Gesellschaft

Ber Tag Baeckerei Technol — Bericht ueber die Tagung fuer Baeckerei-Technologie

Ber Tag Baeckerei-Technol Vortr Tag — Berichte ueber die Tagung fuer Baeckerei-Technologie. Vortraege, gehalten Anlaesslich der Tagung der Arbeitsgemeinschaft Getreideforschung

Ber Tag Getreidechem — Bericht ueber die Tagung fuer Getreidechemie

Ber Tag Lebensmittelrheol — Bericht ueber die Tagung fuer Lebensmittelrheologie

Ber Tag Muellerei Technol — Bericht ueber die Tagung fuer Muellerei Technologie

Ber Tag Muellerei-Technol Vortr Tag — Bericht ueber die Tagung fuer Muellerei-Technologie. Vortraege Gehalten Anlaesslich der Tagung der Arbeitsgemeinschaft Getreideforschung

Ber Tag Nordwestdtsch Forstver — Berichte ueber die Tagung im Nordwestdeutscher Forstverein

Ber Tech Akad Wuppertal — Berichte. Technische Akademie Wuppertal

Ber Tech Wiss Abt Verb Keram Gewerke Dtschl — Berichte. Technisch Wissenschaftliche Abteilung des Verbandes Keramischer Gewerke in Deutschland

Ber Thaetigk Naturwiss Vereins Lueneburg — Bericht ueber die Thaetigkeit des Naturwissenschaftlichen Vereins in Lueneburg

Ber Thaetigk Offenbacher Vereins Naturk — Bericht ueber die Thaetigkeit des Offenbacher Vereins fuer Naturkunde

BERUA — Berufs-Dermatosen

BERUAG — Dermatoses Professionnelles

Berufs-Derm — Berufs-Dermatosen

Ber Ukr Wiss Forsch Inst Phys Chem — Berichte. Ukrainische Wissenschaftliche Forschungs Institut fuer Physikalische Chemie

Ber Univ Jyvaeskyla Math Inst — Bericht. Jyvaeskylae Universitaet. Mathematisches Institut

Ber Vereines Schutze Pflege Alpenpfl — Bericht des Vereines zum Schutze und zur Pflege der Alpenpflanzen

Ber Vereins Erforsch Heimischen Pflanzenwelt Halle — Bericht des Vereins zur Erforschung der Heimischen Pflanzenwelt. Halle

Ber Vereins Naturk Fulda — Bericht des Vereins fuer Naturkunde zu Fulda

Ber Vereins Schutze Alpenpfl — Bericht des Vereins zum Schutze der Alpenpflanzen

Ber Verhand Koen Saechs Ges Wiss Leipzig Philol Hist Kl — Berichte ueber die Verhandlungen der Koeniglichen Saechsischen Gesellschaft der Wissenschaften zu Leipzig. Philologisch-Historische Klasse

Ber Verhandl Saechs Akad Wiss Leipzig Math Naturwiss Kl — Berichte. Verhandlungen der Saechsischen Akademie der Wissenschaftenzu Leipzig. Mathematisch-Naturwissenschaftliche Klasse

Ber Verhandl Saechs Akad Wiss Leipzig Philol Hist Kl — Berichte. Verhandlungen der Saechsischen Akademie der Wissenschaftenzu Leipzig. Philologisch-Historische Klasse

Ber Verhandl Saechs Ges Wiss Leipzig Philol Hist — Berichte. Verhandlungen der Saechsischen Gesellschaft der Wissenschaften zu Leipzig. Philologisch-Historische Klasse

Ber Verh Naturf Ges Basel — Bericht ueber die Verhandlungen der Naturforschenden Gesellschaft in Basel

Ber Verh Saechs Akad Wiss Leipzig Math-Naturwiss Kl — Berichte. Verhandlungen der Saechsischen Akademie der Wissenschaften zu Leipzig. Mathematisch-Naturwissenschaftliche Klasse

Ber Verh Saechs Akad Wiss Leipzig Math Phys Kl — Berichte. Verhandlungen der Saechsischen Akademie der Wissenschaften zu Leipzig. Mathematisch-Physische Klasse

Ber Ver Nat Heimat Naturhist Mus Luebeck — Berichte des Vereins Natur und Heimat und des Naturhistorischen Museums zu Luebeck

Ber Versamml Deutsch Forstmaenner — Berichte ueber die Versammlung Deutscher Forstmaenner

Ber Versamml Deutsch Naturf Aerzte — Berichte ueber die Versammlung Deutscher Naturforscher und Aerzte

Ber VetWes Sachs — Bericht ueber das Veterinaerwesen im Koenigreich Sachsen

Ber VF Naturk Fulda — Bericht des Vereines fuer Naturkunde in Fulda

Ber Vollversamm Dt VetRat — Bericht ueber die Vollversammlung des Deutschen Veterinaerrates

Ber Vortr Dt Akad LandWiss — Bericht und Vortraege der Deutschen Akademie de Landwirtschaftswissenschaften zu Berlin

Ber Wasserguete Abfallwirtsch Tech Univ Muenchen — Berichte aus Wasserguete- und Abfallwirtschaft. Technische Universitaet Muenchen

Ber Wiss Biol — Berichte ueber die Wissenschaftliche Biologie

Ber Wissenschaftsgesch — Berichte zur Wissenschaftsgeschichte

Ber Wiss Leist Geb Ent — Bericht ueber die Wissenschaftlichen Leistungen im Gebiete der Entomologie

Ber Wiss Leist NatGesch Med Tiere — Beriche ueber die Wissenschaftlichen Leistungen in der Naturgeschichte der Niederen Tiere

Ber Wiss Untern Dt Oest Alpenver — Bericht ueber die Wissenschaftlichen Unternehmungen des Deutsch-Oesterreichischen Alpenvereins

Berytus — Berytus Archaeological Studies

Ber Zent Verb Preuss Dampfk Ueberw Ber — Bericht des Zentralverbands Preussischer Dampfkessel-Ueberwachungsvereine

Ber Zool Ges Hamburg — Beriche. Zoologische Gesellschaft in Hamburg

Ber Zool Mus Berl — Bericht ueber das Zoologische Museum zu Berlin

Ber Zool St Inst Zool Mus Hamburg — Bericht. Zoologisches Staatsinstitut und Zoologisches Museum (Hamburg)

Ber Zuercherischen Bot Ges — Bericht der Zuercherischen Botanischen Gesellschaft

Ber Zusammenk Freien Vereinigung Syst Bot — Bericht ueber die Zusammenkunft der Freien Vereinigung der Systematischen Botaniker und Pflanzengeographen zu

Ber Zusammenkunft Dtsch Ophthalmol Ges — Bericht ueber die Zusammenkunft der Deutschen Ophthalmologischen Gesellschaft

Ber Zweit Geburtsh Gynaek Klin Wien — Bericht aus der Zweiten Geburtshuefflich Gynaekologischen Klinik in Wien

Bes — Besinnung

BESA — Bulletin of the Entomological Society of America

BESAA — Bulletin of the Ethnological Society. University College (Addis Ababa)

Besancon Univ Ann Sci Ser 3 — Besancon Universite. Annales Scientifiques. Serie 3. Geologie

BESC — Bulletin of the Egyptian Society of Cardiology

Beschr Rassenlijst Fruitgew — Beschrijvende Rassenlijst voor Fruitgewassen

Beschr Rassenlijst Groentegew — Beschrijvende Rassenlijst voor Groentegewassen

BESID — BS. Betriebssicherheit

Beskontaktn Elektr Mash — Beskontaktnye Elektricheskie Mashiny

B Esp A — Boletin. Asociacion Espanola de Amigos de la Arqueologia

B Esp Or — Boletin. Asociacion Espanola de Orientalistas

BESR — Bibliotheque de l'Ecole des Hautes Etudes. Sciences Religieuses

Bess — Bessarione

Best — Best Sellers

BEST — British Expertise in Science and Technology

BESTA — Beton- und Stahlbetonbau

Best Bus — Best of Business

B Est Econ — Boletin de Estudios de Economia. Universidad Comercial de Deusto

Bestimm Isotopenverteil Markierten Verbindungen — Bestimmung der Isotopenverteilung in Markierten Verbindungen

Best Life — Best's Review. Life/Health Insurance Edition

Best News Des — Best of Newspaper Design

Best Pract Res Clin Endocrinol Metab — Best Practice & Research. Clinical Endocrinology & Metabolism

Best Pract Res Clin Gastroenterol — Best Practice & Research. Clinical Gastroenterology

Best Pract Res Clin Haematol — Best Practice & Research. Clinical Haematology

Best Pract Res Clin Obstet Gynaecol — Best Practice & Research. Clinical Obstetrics & Gynaecology

Best Pract Res Clin Rheumatol — Best Practice & Research. Clinical Rheumatology

Best Sell — Best Sellers

Best's Ins N — Best's Insurance News

Best's Life — Best's Review. Life/Health Insurance Edition

Bests Prop — Best's Review. Property/Liability Edition

Bests R — Best's Review. Life/Health Insurance Edition

Best's Rev Life Health Insur Ed — Best's Review. Life/Health Insurance Edition

Best's Rev Prop/Casualty Insur Ed — Best's Review. Property/Casualty Insurance Edition

Bests R Life Ed — Best's Review. Life/Health Insurance Edition

Bests R Prop Ed — Best's Review. Property/Liability Edition

Best's R Property Ed — Best's Review. Property/Liability Edition

Beszamolo Vizgazdalkodasi Tud Kut Intez Munkajarol — Beszamolo a Vizgazdalkodasi Tudomanyos Kutato Intezet Munkajarol

BET — Bedrijf en Techniek

Beta Adrenerge Blocker Hochdruck Int Symp — Beta Adrenerge Blocker und Hochdruck Internationales Symposion

Beta Adrenergic Blockers Hypertens — Beta Adrenergic Blockers and Hypertension

Beta Aluminas Beta Batteries Proc Int Workshop — Beta-Aluminas and Beta Batteries. Proceedings. International Workshop

Betablocker Ggw Zukunft Int Symp — Betablocker Gegenwart und Zukunft Internationales Symposium

Beta Blocker Hypertonie Behandl — Beta Blocker in der Hypertonie Behandlung

Beta Blockers Present Status Future Prospects Int Symp — Beta Blockers. Present Status and Future Prospects. An International Symposium

Beta Phi Research Exch — Beta Phi Research Exchange

Betel — Betelgeuse. Cahier Trimestriel de Poesie

Beth Hamikra — Beth Hamikra. Bulletin of the Israel Society for Biblical Research and the World Jewish Biblical Society

Beth Israel Hosp Semin Med — Beth Israel Hospital. Seminars in Medicine

Beth Isr Hosp Semin Med — Beth Israel Hospital. Seminars in Medicine

Bet Hom & Gard — Better Homes and Gardens

BETKA — Bergbautechnik

Bet Libns — Between Librarians

Betongtek Publ — Betongtekniske Publikasjoner

Beton Herstellung Verwend — Beton, Herstellung, Verwendung

Betons Ind — Betons Industriels

Betonstein Zig — Betonstein Zeitung

Betontech Ber — Betontechnische Berichte

Betonwerk Fertigteil-Tech — Betonwerk und Fertigteil-Technik

B Et Or — Bulletin d'Etudes Orientales

B Et Orient — Bulletin d'Etudes Orientales

Betr-Berat — Betriebs-Berater. Zeitschrift fuer Recht und Wirtschaft

BETRC — British Engine Technical Reports

BETRD — Betrieb (Duesseldorf)

Betr Erz — Betrifft Erziehung

Betriebsraete Zeitsch F Funktionaere D Metallind — Betriebsraete-Zeitschrift fuer Funktionaere der Metallindustrie

Betriebswirt Mitt Wirtberater — Betriebswirtschaftliche Mitteilungen fuer den Wirtschaftsberater

Betriebswirtsch — Betriebswirtschaft

Betriebswirtsch Forsch Praxis — Betriebswirtschaftliche Forschung und Praxis

Betriebswirtsch Mitt Wirtschaftsberat — Betriebswirtschaftliche Mitteilungen fuer den Wirtschaftsberater

Betr-Oekon — Betriebs-Oekonom

Betr-Tech — Betriebs-Technik

BETS — Bulletin. Evangelical Theological Society [Later, Journal. Evangelical Theological Society]

Bett Crops Pl Fd — Better Crops with Plant Food

Bet-Tek — Beton-Teknik

Betterave Ind Agr — Betterave et les Industries Agricoles

Better Bus — Better Business

Better Ceram Chem Symp — Better Ceramics Through Chemistry. Symposium

Better Crops With Pl Food — Better Crops With Plant Food

Better F — Better Farming

Better Fruit — Better Fruit. Northwest Fruit Growers' Association

BETUA — Toyama Daigaku Kogakubu Kiyo

Betuwsche Rassenlijst Fruit — Betuwsche Rassenlijst voor Fruit van de Nederlandsche Fruittelers Organisatie

Between Spec J Ethics — Between the Species. A Journal of Ethics

Betw Libns — Between Librarians

Betz Indic — Betz Indicator

BEUP — [The] Babylonian Expedition of the University of Pennsylvania. Series A: Cuniform Texts

B Eur S Hum — Bulletin. European Society of Human Genetics

Beurtellungskriterien Chemother — Beurteilungskriterien fuer Chemotherapeutika

Bev — Beverage World

Bev Ann — Beverage Industry Annual Manual

Beverage — Beverage Industry

Beverage Ind — Beverage Industry

Bev Hills BAJ — Beverly Hills Bar Association. Journal

BEVOA — Beitraege zur Vogelkunde

BEVSA — Berichte. Verhandlungen der Saechsischen Akademie der Wissenschaften zu Leipzig. Mathematisch-Naturwissenschaftliche Klasse

BEvTh — Beitraege zur Evangelischen Theologie

BEvTSoc — Bulletin. Evangelical Theological Society [Later, Journal. Evangelical Theological Society]

Bev Wld — Beverage World

Bev Wld 100 — Beverage World 100

Bev Wld P — Beverage World Periscope. Late Breaking News and Analysis

Bewirtsch Fester Abfaelle Ber Int Kongr — Bewirtschaftung Fester Abfaelle Berichte Internationaler Kongress

B Exam — Bar Examiner

BEXBA — Bulletin of Experimental Biology and Medicine

BEXBB — Biochemistry and Experimental Biology

B Exp B Med — Bulletin of Experimental Biology and Medicine

Bey B — Beyond Baroque

Beytr Bot — Beytraege zur Botanik

Beytr Gesch Erfind — Beytraege zur Geschichte der Erfindungen

Beytr Natuerl Oekon Polit Gesch Ober Niederlausiz — Beytraege zur Natuerlichen Oekonomischen und Politischen Geschichte der Ober- und Niederlausiz

Beytr Naturk Herzogth Zelle — Beytraege zur Naturkunde des Herzogthums Zelle

B Ez — Balkansko Ezikoznanije

BEZEA — Betonstein Zeitung

BEZHDK — Beton i Zhelezobeton

Beziers S Sc Bll — Bulletin de la Societe d'Etude des Sciences Naturelles de Beziers

Bezop Gorn Rab — Bezopasnost Gornykh Rabot

Bezop Tr Proizvod Issled Ispyt Sprav Posobie 2-e Izd — Bezopasnost Truda na Proizvodstve Issledovaniya i Ispytaniya Spravochnoe Posobie 2-e Izdanie

Bezop Tr Prom-St — Bezopasnost Truda v Promyshlennosti

Bezpecnost Jad Energ — Bezpecnost Jaderne Energie

Bezzenb Beitr — Beitraege zur Kunde der Indogermanischen Sprachen (A. Bezzenberger, Editor)

BF — Badische Fundberichte

BF — Bibliofilia

BF — Bibliographie de la France

BF — Boletin de Filologia

BF — Book Forum

BF — Books from Finland

BFA — Benelumat Revue
BFA — Bulletin. Faculty of Arts. Fuad University. Arabic Section
BFA — Bulletin. Faculty of Arts. University of Egypt
BFA — Bulletin. Federation des Avoues de Belgique
BFAC — Bulletin. Faculty of Arts. University of Egypt (Cairo)
B Fac Dereito — Boletin. Facultade de Dereito
BFAgC — Bulletin of the Faculty of Agriculture. Cairo University
BFAM — Bulletin. Fogg Art Museum
BFBU — Beaufort Bulletin. Dome Petroleum Ltd.
BFC — Boletin. Instituto de Filologia. Universidad de Chile
BFC — Bollettino di Filologia Classica
BFCE — Breviarios del Fondo de Cultura Economica
BFCF — Bibliotheque de la Faune des Colonies Francaises
BFChTh — Beitraege zur Foerderung Christlicher Theologie
BFCL — Bulletin. Facultes Catholiques de Lyon
BFCTL — Bibliotheque de la Faculte Catholique de Theologie de Lyon
BFD — Bulletin for International Fiscal Documentation
BFDC — Boletin. Facultad de Derecho y Ciencias Sociales
BFdIF — Bulletin Folklorique de l'Ile-de-France
BFE — Boletin de Filologia Espanola
BFF — Beyond Fiction
BFf — Blodau'r Ffair
BFFC — Boletim da Faculdade de Filosofia, Ciencias, e Letras da Univercidade de Sao Paulo
BFFRAM — British Columbia. Ministry of Forests. Forest Research Review
BFG — Bibliotheque. Grenoble. Universite. Institut Francais de Florence. Collection d'Opuscules de Critique et d'Histoire
BFH — Bouwmarkt
BFHA — Bulletin. Friends Historical Association
BFIF — Bulletin Folklorique d'Ile-De-France
B Fil — Boletin de Filologia
BFIl — Bolletino Filosofico
B Fil Gr — Bollettino. Istituto di Filologia Greca
B Fil Gr Padova — Bollettino. Istituto di Filologia Greca. Universita di Padova
B Fil Ling Sic — Bollettino. Centro di Studi Filologici e Linguistici Siciliani
BFL — Bibliotheque. Liege. Universite. Faculte de Philosophie et de Lettres
BFL — Bulletin. Faculte des Lettres de Lille
BFLAV — Bulletin. Foreign Language Association of Virginia
BFLL — Bibliotheque. Faculte de Philosophie et Lettres. Universite de Liege
BFLM — Bulletin de la Faculte des Lettres de Mulhouse
BFLS — Bulletin. Faculte des Lettres de Strasbourg
BfM — Blaetter fuer Muenzfreunde und Muenzforschung
BfM — Blaetter fuer Musikfreunde
BFM — Boletin de Filologia (Montevideo)
BFM — Business Conditions Digest
BFMA — Bibliotheque Francaise du Moyen Age
BFMA — Bulletin. Fogg Museum of Art
BFMB — Bank of Finland. Monthly Bulletin
BFMUP — Bulletin of the Free Museum of Science and Arts. University of Pennsylvania
BFNJ — Bijdragen Uitgegeven door en Philosophische en Theologische Faculteiten der Noord- en Zuid-Nederlandse Jezuieten
BFNPT — Boletim da Federacao Nacional dos Produtores de Trigo
BFo — Biuletyn Fonograficzny
BFO — Business Forum
BFO — Steel News
Bf o Bv — Brandfare og Brandvaern
BFOL — Beaufort Outlook. Newsletter from the Northern Office of the Beaufort Sea Alliance
B Fon — Biuletyn Fonograficzny
BFOO — Berichte. Forschungsinstitut fuer Osten und Orient
B Forum — Book Forum
B Fougeres — Bulletin et Memoires. Societe Archeologique et Historique de l'Arrondisement deFougeres
BFPhLL — Bibliotheque de la Faculte de Philosophie et Lettres de l'Universite de Liege
BFPLUL — Bibliotheque de la Faculte de Philosophie et Lettres de l'Universite de Liege
BFPPE2 — Bulletin Francais de la Peche et de la Pisciculture
BFR — Bibliotheque Francaise et Romane
BFR — Boletin de Filologia (Rio De Janeiro)
B Friends Hist Ass — Bulletin. Friends' Historical Association
BFRNA2 — British Columbia. Ministry of Forests. Research Note
BFRPD — Biofuels Report
BFS — Bulletin. Faculte des Lettres de Strasbourg
BFSCU — Bulletin of the Faculty of Science. Cairo University
BFSGA — Bulletin. Federation des Societes de Gynecologie et d'Obstetrique de Langue Francaise
BfS ISH Ber — BfS-ISH-Berichte (Bundesamt fuer Strahlenschutz. Institut fuer Strahlenhygiene)
BFT — Bizarre Fantasy Tales
BFT — Bulgarian Foreign Trade
BFTADA — Bulletin. Fruit Tree Research Station. Series E
BFTh — Beitraege zur Foerderung Christlicher Theologie
BFTMB — Bundesministerium fuer Forschung und Technologie. Mitteilungen
BFTRA — Bois et Forets des Tropiques
BFU — Boletin de Filologia. Instituto de Estudios Superiores del Uruguay
BFUCH — Boletin de Filologia. Instituto de Filologia. Universidade de Chile
BFX — Overseas Business Reports
BG — Belastinggids
BG — Bijdragen tot de Geschiedenis
BG — Blue Guitar
BG — Bogoslovski Glasnik
BG — Bonner Geschichtsblaetter
BG — Boston Globe

BG — Botanical Gazette
BG — Brown Gold [*Woodworth, Wisconsin*]
BG — Bungaku
BG — Grosse Brockhaus
BGA — Bibliotheca Geographorum Arabicorum
BGA — Bonner Geographische Abhandlungen
BGAB — Boletim do Grupo Amigos de Braganca
BGA Mac — Bulletin. Groupement Archeologique du Maconnais
B GA Nogent — Bulletin. Groupe Archeologique du Nogentais
BGAOAT — Breviora Geologica Asturica
BGAS — Proceedings. Bristol and Gloucestershire Archaeological Society
BGA Schr — BGA (Bundesgesundheitsamt) Schriften
BGASM — Bulletin. Groupement Archeologique de Seine-et-Marn
BGAST — Transactions. Bristol and Gloucestershire Archaeological Society
BGAW — Beitraege zur Geschichte der Abtei Werden
BGB — Bulletin. Association Guillaume Bude
BGB — Bulletin. Groupe Belge des Auditeurs. Academie de Droit Internationalde La Haye
BGBH — Bijdragen voor de Geschiedenis van het Bisdom van Haarlem
BGBWD — Blaetter fuer Grundstuecks, Bau-, und Wohnungsrecht
BGCSS — Bulletin General Congregatio Santi-Spiritus
BGCTH — Bulletin. Section de Geographie. Comite des Travaux Historiques et Scientifiques
BGDM — Beitraege zur Geschichte Dortmunds und der Grafschaft Mark
BGDS — Beitraege zur Geschichte der Deutschen Sprache
BGDSL — Beitraege zur Geschichte der Deutschen Sprache und Literatur
BGDSLH — Beitraege zur Geschichte der Deutschen Sprache und Literatur (Halle)
BGDSLT — Beitraege zur Geschichte der Deutschen Sprache und Literatur (Tuebingen)
BGENA — Biologie et Gastro-Enterologie
B Geneve — Bulletin. Societe d'Histoire et d'Archeologie de Geneve
B Geogr Soc Phila — Bulletin. Geographical Society of Philadelphia
B Geol Soc Am — Bulletin. Geological Society of America
BGFND — Bulletin. Groupe Francais d'Humidimetrie Neutronique
BgG — Berichte ueber die Gesamte Gynaekologie und Geburtshilfe
BGGPB — Biofeedback and Self-Regulation
BGGUA — Bulletin. Groenlands Geologiske Undersoegelse
BGH — Beleggers Belangen
BGHB — Bijdragen tot de Geschiedenis Bijzonderlijk van het Aloude Hertogdom Brabant
BGHD — Bulletin de Geographie Historique et Descriptive
BGHDP — Bulletin de Geographie Historique et Descriptive (Paris)
BGIGA — Biuletyn Glownego Instytutu Gornictwa
BGIHB — Bijdragen tot de Geschiedenis Inzonderheid van het oud Hertogdom Brabant
BGL — Bibliographical Bulletin of the Greek Language
BGLD Hb — Burgenlaendische Heimatblaetter
BGLE — Bangladesh Development Studies
BGLRK — Beitraege zur Geschichte und Lehre der Reformierten Kirche
BGLS — Bausteine zur Geschichte der Literatur bei den Slaven
BGM — Biographoi. Vitarum Scriptores Graeci Minores
BGM — Bombay Geographical Magazine
BGMGAV — Background to Migraine. Migraine Symposium
BGMI — Biography and Genealogy Master Index
BGMIA — Boletin Geologico y Minero
BGN — Bijdragen voor de Geschiedenis der Nederlanden
BGNrh — Beitraege zur Geschichte des Niederrheins
BGNSA — Berufsgenossenschaft
Bgorm — Bogormen
BGPA — Berichtigungsliste der Griechischen Papyrusurkunden aus Aegypten
BGPMN — Bijdragen voor de Geschiedenis van de Provincie der Minderbroeders in de Nederlanden
BGPSum — Beitraege zur Geologie und Palaeontologie von Sumatra
BGPTM — Beitraege zur Geschichte der Philosophie und Theologie des Mittelalters
BGRLL — Bulletin. Groupes de Recherches Archeologiques du Departement de la Loire
BGROD — Bundesgesetzblatt fuer die Republik Oesterreich
B Grottaf — Bollettino. Badia Greca di Grottaferrata
B Group Seine Marne — Bulletin. Groupement Archeologique de Seine-Et-Marne
BGRS — Bungaku Ronshu
BGRSA — Bulletin. Groupement International pour la Recherche Scientifique en Stomatologie
BGSA — Bulletin. Geological Society of America
BGSGB — Bibliotheca Gastroenterologica
BGSP — Bulletin of the Geographical Society [*Philadelphia*]
BGSPD — Bulgarsko Geofizichno Spisanie
BGSSE — Beitraege zur Geschichte von Stadt und Stift Essen
BGST — Bulletin of the Geological Society of Turkey/Turkiye Jeoloji Kurumu
BGSTB — Biologist
BGU — Bluegrass Unlimited
BGU — Boletim Geral do Ultramar
Bg V — Bogens Verden
Bgv — Bogvennen
BGWK — Boekenschouw voor Godsdienst, Wetenschap en Kunst
BGWVAO — George Washington University. Bulletin
BH — Bear Hills Native Voice
BH — Bibliografia Hispanica
BH — Bibliotheque Historique
BH — Bulletin Hispanique
BH — Business History
BHA — Bibliography of the History of Art/Bibliographic d'Histoire d l'Art
BHA — Boletin de Historia y Antiguedades
BH Ac Roum — Bulletin. Section Historique. Academie Roumaine
BHAG — Bulletin. Societe d'Histoire et d'Archeologie de Gand
BHAGA — Bhagirath

Bhagirath Irrig Power Q — Bhagirath. The Irrigation and Power Quarterly
B'ham Post — Birmingham Post
BHAR — Bulletin. Section Historique. Academie Roumaine
Bhar Ma Q — Bharata Manisha Quarterly
B Hautes-Alpes — Bulletin. Societe d'Etudes Historiques, Scientifiques, et Litteraires des Hautes-Alpes
Bhavan's J — Bhavan's Journal
BHb — Baselbieter Heimatblaetter
BHB — Baselbieter Heimatbuch
BHB — Biblioteca Historica Brasileira
BHB — Bulletin d'Histoire Benedictine
BHb — Burgenlaendische Heimatblaetter
BHB — Nouvelles Economiques de Suisse
BHBLA — Behavioral Biology
BHBSA — Harvard Business School. Bulletin
BHC — Business in Thailand
BHCM — Boletin Historial. Cartagena and Medellin
BHDEA — Bulletin of the History of Dentistry
BHDL — Bulletin Historique. Diocese de Lyon
B He — Baltische Hefte
BHE — Barid Hollanda
BHEAT — Bulletin d'Histoire et Exegese de l'Ancien Testament
BHEP — Bosquejo Historico de Etnografia Portuguesa
B Hesbaye-Condroz — Bulletin. Cercle Archeologique Hesbaye-Condroz
BHET — Bulletin d'Histoire et Exegese de l'Ancien Testament
BHEW — Bulletin. Societe pour l'Histoire des Eglises Wallonnes
BHF — Bonner Historische Forschungen
BHFabrimetal — Bulletin Hebdomadaire Fabrimetal
BHFIA — Bulletin. Haffkine Institute
BHfV — Bayerische Hefte fuer Volkskunde
BHG — Bibliotheca Hagiographica Graeca
BHGDA — Better Homes and Gardens
BHGNA — Behavior Genetics
BHH — Baptist History and Heritage
BHH — Bibliotheca Humanitatis Historica
BHI — British Humanities Index
BHi — Bulletin Hispanique
BHI — Business History
BHI — Europe Outremer. Revue Internationale
BHIJA — Bulletin. Heart Institute (Japan)
BHipp — Bulletin. Academie d'Hippone
BHis — Biblioteca Hispana
BHisp — Bibliografia Hispanica
BHisp — Bulletin Hispanique
B Hispan — Bulletin Hispanique
B Hispan S — Bulletin of Hispanic Studies
BHist — Boletin Historico
B Hist Antig — Boletin de Historia Antigua. Academia Colombiana de Historia
B Hist Med — Bulletin of the History of Medicine
B Historical Res — Bulletin of Historical Research in Music Education
BHL — Bibliotheca Hagiographica Latina
BHLD — Bulletin d'Histoire, de Litterature, et d'Art Religieux du Diocese de Dijon
BHM — Bibliography of the History of Medicine
BHM — Bulletin of the History of Medicine
BHM — Bulletin. Societe Francaise d'Histoire de la Medecine
BHM Berg u Huttenm Mh — BHM. Berg- und Huttenmaennische Monatshefte
BHMMA — Berg- und Huettenmaennische Monatshefte
BHN — Biblioteca de Historia Nacional [*Bogota*]
BHN — Boosey & Hawkes Newsletter
BHNNA — Societe d'Histoire Naturelle de l'Afrique du Nord. Bulletin
BHO — Bibliotheca Hagiographica Orientalis
BHO — Business Horizons
B Hor — Business Horizons
BHPAS — Bulletin. National Research Institute of History and Philology. Academia Sinica
BHPCTHS — Bulletin Historique et Philologique. Comite des Travaux Historiques et Scientifiques
BHPF — Bulletin Historique et Litteraire. Societe de l'Histoire du Protestantisme Francais
BHP J — BHP [*Broken Hill Proprietary Ltd.*] Journal
BHP Jo — BHP [*Broken Hill Proprietary Ltd.*] Journal
B H Points — Bulletin of High Points
BHP R — BHP [*Broken Hill Proprietary Ltd.*] Review
BHP Res Div Inf Circ — Broken Hill Proprietary Ltd. Research Division. Information Circular
BHP Rev — BHP [*Broken Hill Proprietary Ltd.*] Review
BHPSO — Bulletin. Historical and Philosophical Society of Ohio
BHP Tech Bull — BHP [*Broken Hill Proprietary Ltd.*] Technical Bulletin
BHR — Bibliotheque d'Humanisme et Renaissance
BHR — British Hotelier and Restaurateur
BHR — Business History Review
BHren — Bibliotheque d'Humanisme et Renaissance
BHS — Biuletyn Historii Sztuki
BHS — Bombay Historical Society. Journal
Bh S — Bornholmske Samlinger
BHS — Bulletin of Hispanic Studies
BHSA — Bulletin Historique et Scientifique de l'Auvergne
BHSAM — Bulletin Historique. Societe des Antiquaires de la Morinie
BHSM — Bulletin. Historical Society of Montgomery County
BHSMCo — Bulletin. Historical Society of Montgomery County
BHS Prov — Bulletin. Societe d'Histoire et d'Archeologie de l'Arrondissement de Provins
BHTh — Beitraege zur Historischen Theologie
BHTP — Bulletin d'Histoire du Theatre Portugais
BhV — Bharatiya Vidya

BHV — Boletin Historico del Valle [*Cali*]
BHV — Business History Review
BHVBamberg — Bericht. Historischer Verein fuer das Fuerstbistum (Bamberg)
BHVFB — Bericht. Historischer Verein fuer das Fuerstbistum (Bamberg)
BHVG — Bonner Hefte zur Vorgeschichte
BHZ — Business Horizons
Bi — Biblica
Bi — Bibliofilia
Bi — Bibliografia Italiana
Bi — Bibliotheca Indica
Bi — Bibliotheca Islamica
Bi — Biblos
Bi — Bijdragen
Bi — Boletin Indigenista [*Mexico*]
Bi — Boletin Informativo
Bi — Books at Iowa
Bi — Bulletin Italien
Bi — Business Index
Bi — Business Insurance
BiA — Biblical Archaeologist
BIA — Bibliotheca Ibero-Americana
BIA — Boletin. Instituto de Antropologia
BIA — Bollettino. Istituto Nazzionale di Archeologia e Storia dell'Arte
BIA — Bollettino. Reale Istituto di Archeologia e Storia dell'Arte
BIA — Broadcasting in Australia
BIA — Bulletin. Institute of Arab-American Affairs
BIA — Bulletin. Institute of Archaeology
BIAA — Bollettino. Reale Istituto di Archeologia e Storia dell'Arte
BIAAD4 — Buletinul. Institutului Agronomic Cluj-Napoca. Seria Agricultura
BIAB — Bulletin. Institut Archeologique Bulgare
BIABE — Biomass Abstracts
BIA Bulg — Bulletin. Institut Archeologique Bulgare
BIACDA — Buletinul. Institutului Agronomic Cluj-Napoca
BIADDD — Biotechnology Advances
Biafra R — Biafra Review
BIAHA — Bulletin. International Association of Scientific Hydrology
BIAL — Bulletin. Institut Archeologique Liegeois
BIAL — Bulletin. Institute of Archaeology. University of London
BIALB — Boletim. Instituto de Tecnologia de Alimentos
BIA London — Bulletin. Institute of Archaeology. University of London
BIA Lux — Bulletin Trimestriel. Institut Archeologique du Luxembourg
BIAM — Banque d'Informations Automatisees sur les Medicaments
BIAMA — Bulletin International. Academie Polonaise des Sciences et des Lettres. Classe des Sciences Mathematiques et Naturelles. Serie A. Sciences Mathematiques
BIANA — Bibliotheca Anatomica
Bian & Nero — Bianco e Nero
Biann Rev Allergy — Bi-annual Review of Allergy
BIAO — Bulletin. Institut Francais d'Archeologie Orientale
BIAP — Bulletin International. Academie Polonaise des Sciences et des Lettres
BIAPSL — Bulletin International. Academie Polonaise des Sciences et des Lettres
BIAS — Bulletin in Applied Statistics
BIASA — Bollettino. Istituto Nazzionale di Archeologia e Storia dell'Arte
BIASC — Bulletin International de l'Academie des Sciences et des Lettres de Cracovie
BIATBP — Estacion Experimental Agricola de Tucuman. Boletin
BIAVDX — Buletinul. Institutului Agronomic Cluj-Napoca. Seria Zootehnie si Medicina Veterinara
BIB — Bank of Israel. Bulletin
Bib — Biblica
Bib — Biblio. Bibliographie des Ouvrages Parus en Langue Francaise dans le Monde Entier
Bib — Bibliofilia
Bib — Biblos
BIB — Boletin Informativo y Bibliografico
BIB — Bulletin. Institut International de Bibliographie
BIB — Open; Vaktijdschrift voor Bibliothecarissen, Literatuuronderzoekers, Bedrijfsarchivarissen, en Documentalisten
Bib A — Biblical Archeologist
BibAg — Bibliography of Agriculture
Bib Am Ling Am Soc Am — Bibliographie Americaniste. Linguistique Amerindienne. Societe desAmericanistes
Bib & Mus Neuchatel — Bibliotheques et Musees de Neuchatel
Bib & Wiss — Bibliothek und Wissenschaft
Bib Ar — Biblical Archaeologist
Bib Arch — Biblical Archaeologist
Bib Arch R — Biblical Archaeology Review
Bib Arch Rev — Biblical Archaeology Review
Bib Archv Romanicum — Biblioteca dell'Archivum Romanicum
BibB — Bibliophile Belge
Bib Bibliog It — Biblioteca di Bibliografia Italiana
BibC — Bibliographie Catholique
Bib Col — Bible Collector
Bib Cont Anx Fear Pain Dent — Bibliography for the Control of Anxiety, Fear, and Pain in Dentistry
Bib Deut Bib — Bibliographie der Deutschen Bibliographien
Bib Diffusion Mus Guimet — Bibliotheque de Diffusion du Musee Guimet
Bib Ecole France — Bibliotheque de l'Ecole de France
Bib Ecole Hautes Etud — Bibliotheque de l'Ecole des Hautes Etudes
Bib Ecoles Fr Athenes & Rome — Bibliotheque des Ecoles Francaises d'Athenes et de Rome
BIBEDL — Biologie du Comportement
Bib Ent Soc Am — Bibliographies. Entomological Society of America
Bib Forsch & Praxis — Bibliothek. Forschung und Praxis
Bib Francescana Sarda — Biblioteca Francescana Sarda

Bib Himalay — Bibliotheca Himalayica
Bib Hist Am — Bibliografia de Historia de America
Bib Hist Ville Paris — Bibliotheque Historique de la Ville de Paris
BibHT — Bibliotheque de la Societe des Historiens du Theatre
Bib Humanisme & Ren — Bibliotheque d'Humanisme et Renaissance
Bibl — Bibliotheque des Idees
BIBIA — Biotechnology and Bioengineering
Bib Inst Fr Etud Anat Istanbul — Bibliotheque de l'Institut Francais d'Etudes Anatoliennes d'Istanbul
Bib Inz Oprogram — Biblioteka Inzynierii Oprogramowania
Bib It G Lett Sci & A — Biblioteca Italiana Ossia Giornale di Letteratura, Scienze, ed Arti
Bibl — Biblica
BIBL — Bibliografia Espanola
Bibl — Bibliographer (London)
Bibl — Bibliographic Index
Bibl — Bibliographie Linguistique
BibL — Biblioteca del Leonardo
Bibl — Biblioteksbladet
BIBL — Bulletin of the Independent Biological Laboratories [*Kefar-Malal, Palestine*]
Bibl A — Biblical Archaeologist
Biblaa — Biblioteksaarbog
Bibl Anat — Bibliotheca Anatomica
Bibl Anatom — Bibliotheca Anatomica
Bibl & Ind Geol — Bibliography and Index of Geology
Bibl Arch — Biblical Archaeologist
Bibl Archaeolo — Biblical Archaeologist
Bibl Archaeologist — Biblical Archaeologist
Bibl Archaeol Rev — Biblical Archaeology Review
Bibl Archeol — Biblical Archeologist
Bibl Arch Roman Ser II Linguistica — Biblioteca dell'Archivum Romanicum. Serie II. Linguistica
Bibl Asiatica — Bibliographia Asiatica
Bibl Automat Inform Electron Management Ser Practica — Biblioteca de Automatica, Informatica, Electronica, Management. Seria Practica
BIBLB — Boletim Internacional de Bibliografia Luso-Brasileira
Bibl Bel — Bibliographie de Belgique
Bibl Biotheor — Bibliotheca Biotheoretica
BiblBot — Bibliotheca Botanica
Bibl Br Sci Arts — Bibliotheque Britannique. Sciences et Arts
Bibl Cardio — Bibliotheca Cardiologica
Bibl Cardiol — Bibliotheca Cardiologica
Bibl Clas Gredos — Biblioteca Clasica Gredos
Bibl Class Or — Bibliotheca Classica Orientalis
Bibl Class Orient — Bibliotheca Classica Orientalis
Bibl Crit d Lett Ital — Biblioteca Critica della Letteratura Italiana
Bibl Dedalo — Biblioteca Dedalo
Bibl de H Et — Bibliotheque de l'Ecole de Hautes Etudes
Bibl de la Pleiade — Bibliotheque de la Pleiade
Bibl de la R d C et Conf — Bibliotheque de la Revue des Cours et Conferences
Bibl de la R d Cours et Conf — Bibliotheque de la Revue des Cours et Conferences
Bibl de la Rev d C et Conf — Bibliotheque de la Revue des Cours et Conferences
Bibl de la Rev d Cours et Conf — Bibliotheque de la Revue des Cours et Conferences
Bibl de la Soc d Hist Eccl de la France — Bibliotheque de la Societe d'Histoire Ecclesiastique de la France
Bibl de l Ec H Et — Bibliotheque de l'Ecole de Hautes Etudes
Bibl de l Inst Franc a l Univ de Budapest — Bibliotheque de l'Institut Francais a l'Universite de Budapest
Bibl de l Inst Franc de Florence — Bibliotheque de l'Institut Francais de Florence
Bibl de Philos — Bibliotheque de Philosophie
Bibl de Philos Contemp — Bibliotheque de Philosophie Contemporaine
Bibl de RCC — Bibliotheque de la Revue des Cours et Conferences
Bibl d H et Ren — Bibliotheque d'Humanisme et Renaissance. Travaux et Documents
Bibl d Hist Litt et de Critique — Bibliotheque d'Histoire Litteraire et de Critique
Bibl Diatomol — Bibliotheca Diatomologica
Bibl di Crit Stor e Lett — Biblioteca di Critica Storica e Letteraria
Bibl di Cult — Biblioteca di Cultura
Bibl di Cult Mod — Biblioteca di Cultura Moderna
Bibl di Saggi e Lez Accad — Biblioteca di Saggi e Lezioni Accademiche
Bibl d Leonardo — Biblioteca del Leonardo
Bibl Docum Terminology — Bibliography, Documentation, Terminology
Bibl d Scuole Ital — Biblioteca delle Scuole Italiane
Bibl d Scuole Italiane — Biblioteca delle Scuole Italiane
Bibl d Soc Stor Subalpina — Biblioteca della Societa Storica Subalpina
Bibl du XV S — Bibliotheque du XV Siecle
Bibl du XV Siecle — Bibliotheque du XV Siecle
Biblebas — Biblebhashyam
Bibl Ec Chartes — Bibliotheque de l'Ecole des Chartes
Bibl Ec Franc — Bibliotheque des Ecoles Francaises d'Athenes et de Rome
Bibl Ec H Et — Bibliotheque de l'Ecole de Hautes Etudes
Bibl Ecole Chartes — Bibliotheque de l'Ecole des Chartes
Bibl Elzev — Bibliotheque Elzevirienne
Bibl Engl Lang & Lit — Bibliography of English Language and Literature
Bible T — Bible Today
Biblfia Ital Elettrotec — Bibliografia Italiana di Elettrotecnica
Biblfia Ital Idraul — Bibliografia Italiana di Idraulica
Biblfia Jugosl — Bibliografija Jugoslavije
Biblfia Maneggio Mecc Mater — Bibliografia sul Maneggio Meccanico dei Materiali
Biblfia Mat Ital — Bibliografia Matematica Italiana
Biblfia Med Argent — Bibliografia Medica Argentina
Biblfia Med Biol — Bibliografia Medico-Biologica
Biblfia Med Int — Bibliografia Medica Internacional

Biblfia Med Port — Bibliografia Medica Portuguesa
Biblfia Metal Mec — Bibliografia Metalurgica y Mecanica
Biblfia Met Ital — Bibliografia Meteorologica Italiana
Biblfia Obras Hidrol Repub Argent — Bibliografia de Obras sobre Hidrologia. Republica Argentina
Biblfia Ortop — Bibliografia Ortopedica
Biblfia Polarogr — Bibliografia Polarografica
Biblfia Prac Dziedz Ewol — Bibliografia Prac z Dziedziny Ewolucjonizmu
Biblfia Quim Argent — Bibliografia Quimica Argentina
Biblfia Scient Tec Ital — Bibliografia Scientifico-Tecnica Italiana
Biblfias Inst Biol Chapultepec — Bibliografias. Instituto de Biologia (Chapultepec, D.F.)
Biblfia Tess — Bibliografia Tessile
Biblfia Traff Citt — Bibliografia sul Traffico Cittadino
Biblfie Zemed Lesn Csl Lit — Bibliografie Zemedelska a Lesnicka. Ceskoslovenska Literatura
Bibl Filol — Bibliografia Filologica do Centro de Estudos Filologica de Lisboa
Biblfiya Kartogr Lit Kart — Bibliografiya Kartograficheskoi Literatury i Kart
Biblfiya Uslov Refleksam — Bibliografiya po Uslovnym Refleksam
Bibl Franc — Bibliotheque Francaise
Bibl Franc du M A — Bibliotheque Francaise du Moyen Age
Bibl Gastro — Bibliotheca Gastroenterologica
Bibl Gastroenterol — Bibliotheca Gastroenterologica
Bibl Gen CSIC — Biblioteca General del Consejo Superior de Invistigaciones Cientificas. BoletinSemestral
Bibl Gen Ill — Bibliotheque Generale Illustree
BiblGeo — Bibliography and Index of Geology
Bibl Gesch Dt Arbeiterbewegung — Bibliographie zur Geschichte der Deutschen Arbeiterbewegung
Bibl Gynaecol — Bibliotheca Gynaecologica
Bibl Haem — Bibliotheca Haematologica
Bibl Haemat — Bibliotheca Haematologica
Bibl Haematol — Bibliotheca Haematologica
Bibl Haematol Basel — Bibliotheca Haematologica (Basel)
BiblH & R — Bibliotheque d'Humanisme et Renaissance
Bibl Hist des Curiosites Litteraires — Bibliotheque Historique des Curiosites Litteraires
Bibl Hist Sci — Bibliotheque d'Histoire des Sciences
Bibl Hist Sueo-Gothica — Bibliotheca Historica Sueo-Gothica
Bibl Hist Vaudoise — Bibliotheque Historique Vaudoise
Bibl Humanisme Renaissance — Bibliotheque d'Humanisme et Renaissance
Bibl Hum et Ren — Bibliotheque d'Humanisme et Renaissance. Travaux et Documents
Bibl Hum Hist — Bibliotheca Humanitatis Historica
Bibl Hum R — Bibliotheque d'Humanisme et Renaissance
Bibl Hum Renaiss — Bibliotheque d'Humanisme et Renaissance. Travaux et Documents
Bibl Hum Renaissance — Bibliotheque d'Humanisme et Renaissance
Biblical Archaeol — Biblical Archaeologist
Biblical Rev — Biblical Review
Bibl IFAO — Bibliotheque d'Etudes. Institute Francais d'Archeologie Orientale
Bibl Ind — Bibliographic Index
Bibl Inz Oprogram — Biblioteka Inzynierii Oprogramowania
Biblio — Bibliofilia
Biblio France — Bibliographie de la France
Bibliog — Bibliographer
Bibliog Doc Terminology — Bibliography, Documentation, Terminology
Bibliog Fascista — Bibliografia Fascista
Bibliog Hisp — Bibliografia Hispanica
Bibliogr Afr Afr Bibliogr — Bibliographie Africaine/Afrikaanse Bibliografie
Bibliogr Agric — Bibliography of Agriculture
Bibliogr Agric Washington — Bibliography of Agriculture. US Department of Agriculture (Washington, DC)
Bibliogr Anal Afr Cent — Bibliographies Analytiques sur l'Afrique Centrale
Bibliogr Annu Madagascar — Bibliographie Annuelle de Madagascar
Bibliograph Hist Sci Tech — Bibliographies of the History of Science and Technology
Bibliogr Apprais Lit — Bibliography of Appraisal Literature
Bibliogr Arg Art Letr BA — Bibliografia Argentina de Artes y Letras (Buenos Aires)
Bibliogr Belgique — Bibliographie de la Belgique
Bibliogr Bestrahlung Lebensm — Bibliographie zur Bestrahlung von Lebensmitteln
Bibliogr Bibl Conmem Orton Inst Interamer Cienc Agr — Bibliografias. Biblioteca Conmemorativa Orton. Instituto Interamericano de Ciencias Agricolas
Bibliogr Biol — Bibliographie der Biologie. Internationales Institut fuer Bibliographie der Medizin und der Nachbargebiete
Bibliogr Books Child — Bibliography of Books for Children
Bibliogr Bras Odontol — Bibliografia Brasileira Odontologia
Bibliogr Bur Soils — Bibliography. Commonwealth Bureau of Soils
Bibliogr Carto — Bibliographia Cartographica
Bibliogr Chim — Bibliographia Chimica
Bibliogr Ci Hist — Bibliografia de Ciencias Historicas
Bibliogr Deutsch — Bibliographie von Deutschland
Bibliogr Doc Caracas — Bibliografia y Documentacion (Caracas)
Bibliogr Econ Geol — Bibliography of Economic Geology
Bibliogr Econ Mex — Bibliografia Economica de Mexico
Bibliog Reg — Bibliographical Register
Bibliogr Engl Lit — Bibliography of English Language and Literature
Bibliogr Engl Speak Carib — Bibliography of the English-Speaking Caribbean
Bibliog Res Stud Educ — Bibliography of Research Studies in Education
Bibliogr Farm — Bibliografica Farmaceutica
Bibliogr For Bur (Oxf) — Annotated Bibliography. Commonwealth Forestry Bureau (Oxford)
Bibliogr Forest — Bibliographia Forestalis. Forstliche Bibliographie der Internationalen Forstzentrale

Bibliogr Forest Forest Prod — Bibliography of Forestry and Forest Products/ Bibliographie des Forets et Products Forestieres/Bibliografia de la Silvicultura y Productos Forestale
Bibliogr Genet — Bibliographia Genetica
Bibliogr Genet Med — Bibliographica Genetica Medica
Bibliogr Geol Lit At Energy Raw Mater — Bibliography of Geological Literature on Atomic Energy Raw Materials
Bibliogr Geol Pol — Bibliografia Geologiczna Poliski
Bibliogr High Temp Chem Phys Gases Plasmas — Bibliography on the High Temperature Chemistry and Physics of Gases and Plasmas
Bibliogr High Temp Chem Phys Mater — Bibliography on the High Temperature Chemistry and Physics of Materials
Bibliogr High Temp Chem Phys Mater Condens State — Bibliography on the High Temperature Chemistry and Physics of Materials in the Condensed State
Bibliogr Hisp — Bibliografia Hispanica. Instituto Nacional del Libro Espanol
Bibliogr Hist Med — Bibliography of the History of Medicine
Bibliogr Index — Bibliographic Index
Bibliogr Index Geol — Bibliography and Index of Geology
Bibliogr Index Geol Exclus North Am — Bibliography and Index of Geology Exclusive of North America
Bibliogr Index Health Educ Period — Bibliographic Index of Health Education Periodicals. BIHEP
Bibliogr Index Micropaleontology — Bibliography and Index of Micropaleontology
Bibliogr Internaz Sci Art — Bibliografia Internazionale di Scienze ed Arti
Bibliogr Irradiat Foods — Bibliography in Irradiation of Foods
Bibliogr Lit Agric US Dep Agric Econ Stat Serv — Bibliographies and Literature of Agriculture. United States Department of Agriculture. Economics and Statistics Service
Bibliogr Med Biol — Bibliografia Medico-Biologica
Bibliogr Mex — Bibliografia (Mexico)
Bibliogr Mission — Bibliografia Missionaria
Bibliogr North Am Geol — Bibliography of North American Geology
Bibliogr Paint Technol — Bibliographies in Paint Technology
Bibliogr Pflanzenschutzlit — Bibliographie der Pflanzenschutzliteratur
Bibliogr Phil — Bibliographie Philosophie
Bibliogr Phytosociol Syntaxon — Bibliographia Phytosociologica Syntaxonomica
Bibliogr Reihe Kernforschungsanlage Juelich — Bibliographische Reihe der Kernforschungsanlage Juelich
Bibliogr Repert Inst Chret — RIC. Repertoire Bibliographique des Institutions Chretiennes
Bibliogr Reprod — Bibliography of Reproduction
Bibliogr Rev Chem — Bibliography of Reviews in Chemistry
Bibliogr S Afr Gov Publ — Bibliography of South African Government Publications
Bibliogr Schweiz Naturwiss Lit — Bibliographie der Schweizerischen Naturwissenschaftlichen Literatur. Bibliographie Scientifique Suisse
Bibliogr Sci Franc — Bibliographie Scientifique Francaise. Bureau Francais du Catalogue International de la Litterature Scientifique
Bibliogr Sci Ind Rep — Bibliography of Scientific and Industrial Reports
Bibliogr Ser IAEA — Bibliographical Series. International Atomic Energy Agency
Bibliogr Ser Inst Pap Chem — Bibliographic Series. Institute of Paper Chemistry
Bibliogr Ser Ore For Res Lab — Bibliographical Series. Oregon State University. Forest Research Laboratory
Bibliogr Ser Sci Libr Sci Mus — Bibliographical Series. Science Library. Science Museum
Bibliogr Stud — Bibliographien und Studien
Bibliogr Subj Index S Afr Geol — Bibliography and Subject Index of South African Geology
Bibliogr Syst Mycol — Bibliography of Systematic Mycology. Commonwealth Mycological Institute
Bibliogr Tech Rep — Bibliography of Technical Reports
Bibliogr Umweltradioakt Lebensm — Bibliographie zur Umweltradioaktivitaet in Lebensmitteln
Bibliogr Vostoka Moscow Leningrad — Bibliografija Vostoka. Bibliography of the Orient (Moscow and Leningrad)
Bibliog Soc — Bibliographical Society (London)
Bibliog Soc Amer — Bibliographical Society of America
Bibliog Soc Am Pa — Bibliographical Society of America. Papers
Bibliog Soc Am Pap — Bibliographical Society of America. Papers
Bibliog Soc Ir — Bibliographical Society of Ireland. Publications
Bibliog Soc Univ Virginia — Bibliographical Society. University of Virginia
Biblio Ital Educ Sordi — Bibliografia Italiana sull'Educazione dei Sordi
Biblio Sci Nat Helv — Bibliographia Scientiae Naturalis Helvetica
Biblio Soc Am — Bibliographical Society of America. Papers
Bibliot — Bibliotek 70
Biblioteca Nac Jose Marti R — Biblioteca Nacional Jose Marti. Revista
Biblioteca Scuole Ital — Biblioteca della Scuole Italiane
Bibliotec BA — Bibliotecologia (Buenos Aires)
Bibliot Farm — Bibliotheca de Farmacia, Chimica, Fisica, Medicina, Chirurgia, Terapeutica, Storia Naturale
Bibliot F Laeg — Bibliotek for Laeger
Bibliot German Lett — Biblioteca Germanica di Lettere, Arti, e Scienze
Biblioth Anz Auszuegen Kleiner Schriften — Bibliothek von Anzeigen und Auszuegen Kleiner, Meist Akademischer, Schriften
Biblioth Biotheor — Bibliotheca Biotheoretica
Biblioth Crit — Bibliotheca Critica
Biblioth Crit Nova — Bibliotheca Critica Nova
Biblioth de la Rev d Hist Eccles — Bibliotheque de la Revue d'Histoire Ecclesiastique
Bibliotheca Afr — Bibliotheca Africana
Bibliotheca Ind — Bibliotheca Indica
Bibliotheca Zool — Bibliotheca Zoologica
Biblioth Elzev — Bibliotheque Elzevirienne
Biblioth Franc — Bibliotheque Francaise
Biblioth Intern de Critique — Bibliotheque Internationale de Critique

Biblioth Ital Turin — Bibliotheque Italienne, ou Tableau des Progres des Sciences et des Arts en Italie (Turin)
Biblioth Litt de la Renaiss — Bibliotheque Litteraire de la Renaissance
Biblioth Litt de la Renaissance — Bibliotheque Litteraire de la Renaissance
Biblioth Litteraire de la Renais — Bibliotheque Litteraire de la Renaissance
Biblioth Litteraire de la Renaissance — Bibliotheque Litteraire de la Renaissance
Biblioth Lit Ver Stuttg — Bibliothek des Literarischen Vereins in Stuttgart
Biblioth Med Cassel — Bibliotheca Medica Cassel
Biblioth Med Phys N — Bibliotheque Medico-Physique du Nord
Biblioth Neuesten Phys Chem Lit — Bibliothek der Neuesten Physisch-Chemischen, Metallurgischen, Technologischen, und Pharmaceutischen Literatur
Biblioth Nicotiana — Bibliotheca Nicotiana
Biblioth Orient — Bibliotheca Orientalis
Biblioth Sci Int — Bibliotheque Scientifique Internationale
Biblioth SELAF — Bibliotheque. Societe pour l'Etude des Langues Africaines
Biblioth Universelle Agric — Bibliotheque Universelle. Agriculture
Bibliot Vrach — Biblioteka Vracha
Biblio Univ Grenoble Publ — Bibliotheque Universitaire. Grenoble. Publications
Bib Lit Fr Moy Age N Jou — Bibliographie de la Litterature Francaise du Moyen Age a Nos Jours
Bibl Jose Jeronimo Triana — Biblioteca Jose Jeronimo Triana
Bibl Klass Texte — Bibliothek Klassischer Texte
Bibl Laeger — Bibliotek for Laeger
Bibl Lg — Bibliotek for Laeger
Bibl Liberta — Biblioteca della Liberta
Bibl Lichenol — Bibliotheca Lichenologica
Bibl Litt de la Renaiss — Bibliotheque Litteraire de la Renaissance
Bibl Litt de la Renaissance — Bibliotheque Litteraire de la Renaissance
Bibl Litter de la Renais — Bibliotheque Litteraire de la Renaissance
Bibl Litter de la Renaissance — Bibliotheque Litteraire de la Renaissance
Bibl M — Bibliotheca Medica
Bibl Mat — Biblioteka Matematyczna
Bibl Mech Stos — Biblioteka Mechaniki Stosowanej
Bibl Med Can — Bibliotheca Medica Canadiana
Bibl Merida — Bibliotheca (Merida, Venezuela)
Bibl Meridionale — Bibliotheque Meridionale
Bibl Microbiol — Bibliotheca Microbiologica
Bibl Mondadori — Bibliotheca Mondadori
Bibl Mycol — Bibliotheca Mycologica
Bibl Nac De Crim Y Cienc Afines Bol — Biblioteca Nacional de Criminologie y Ciencias Afines. Boletin
Bibl Nat — Bibliotheque Nationale
Bibl Nauk Inz — Biblioteka Naukowa Inzyniera
Bibl Norm — Bibliotheca Normannica
Bibl Nuncius Studi Testi — Biblioteca di Nuncius. Studi e Testi
Bibl Nutr D — Bibliotheca Nutrito et Dieta
Bibl Nutr Dieta — Bibliotheca Nutrito et Dieta
Bibl Ophthalmol — Bibliotheca Ophthalmologica
Bibl Or — Bibliotheca Orientalis
Bibl Orient — Bibliotheca Orientalis
Bibl Oriental — Bibliotheca Orientalis
Bibl Oto-Rhino-Laryngol — Bibliotheca Oto-Rhino-Laryngologica
Bibl Paediatr — Bibliotheca Paediatrica
Bibl Pflanz — Bibliographie der Pflanzenschutzliteratur
Biblphia Biotheor — Bibliographia Biotheoretica
Biblphia Chim — Bibliographia Chimica
Biblphia For — Bibliographia Forestalis
Biblphia Genet — Bibliographia Genetica
Biblphia Geol — Bibliographia Geologica
Biblphia Med — Bibliographia Medica
Biblphia Med Csl — Bibliographia Medica Cechoslovaka
Biblphia Med Helv — Bibliographia Medica Helvetica
Biblphia Med Lat — Bibliographia Medica Latina
Biblphia Not Met Buc — Bibliographia si Notite Meteorologice (Bucuresti)
Biblphia Oceanogr — Bibliographia Oceanographica
Biblphia Odont — Bibliographia Odontologica
Biblphia Oto Rhino Lar Jap — Bibliographia Oto-Rhino-Laryngologica Japonica
Biblphia Phon — Bibliographia Phonetica
Biblphia Physiol — Bibliographia Physiologica
Biblphia Sci Nat Helv — Bibliografia Scientiae Naturalis Helvetica
Biblphical Bull US Dep Agric Libr — Bibliographical Bulletin. United States Department of Agriculture. Library
Biblphical Contr US Dep Agric Libr — Bibliographical Contributions. United States Department of Agriculture. Library
Biblphie Anat — Bibliographie Anatomique
Biblphie Inn Med — Bibliographie der Inneren Medizin
Biblphie Int Met Gen — Bibliographie Internationale de Meteorologie Generale
Biblphie Isl Forst u Holzw — Bibliographie der Islandischen Forst- und Holzwirtschaften
Biblphie Klima Mensch — Bibliographie Klima und Mensch
Biblphie Med Int — Bibliographie Meteorologique Internationale
Biblphie Mens Astr — Bibliographie Mensuelle de l'Astronomie
Biblphie Met — Bibliographie Meteorologique
Biblphie Meth Trimest Commun Eur Charb Acier — Bibliographie Methodique Trimestrielle. Communaute Europeenne du Charbon et de l'Acier
Biblphie Met Suisse — Bibliographie Meteorologique Suisse
Biblphien Dt Wetterd — Bibliographien des Deutschen Wetterdienstes
Biblphie Neurol Psychiat Berl — Bibliographie der Neurologie und Psychiatrie (Berlin)
Biblphie PflSchutzlit — Bibliographie der Pflanzenschutzliteratur
Biblphie Phil Psychol Lpz — Bibliographie der Philosophie und Psychologie (Leipzig)
Biblphies Armstrong Siddeley Mot — Bibliographies. Armstrong Siddeley Motors, Ltd

Biblphie Schweiz Landesk — Bibliographie der Schweizerischen Landeskunde

Biblphie Schweiz Naturw Geogr Lit — Bibliographie der Schweizerischen Naturwissenschaftlichen und Geographischen Literatur

Biblphie Scient — Bibliographie Scientifique

Biblphie Scient Fr — Bibliographie Scientifique Francaise

Biblphie Scient Suisse — Bibliographie Scientifique Suisse

Biblphie Sci Geol — Bibliographie des Sciences Geologiques

Biblphie Sci Ind — Bibliographie des Science et de l'Industrie

Biblphies Commonw Bur Anim Genet — Bibliographies. Commonwealth Bureau of Animal Genetics

Biblphies Commonw Bur Pl Genet — Bibliographies. Commonwealth Bureau of Plant Genetics

Biblphies Commonw Bur Soil Sci — Bibliographies. Commonwealth Bureau of Soil Science

Biblphies Hte Autor Commun Eur Charb Acier — Bibliographies de la Haute Autorite, Communaute Europeenne du Charbon et de l'Acier

Biblphie Signal Met Natn — Bibliographie Signaletique. Meteorologie Nationale

Biblphies Paint Technol — Bibliographies in Paint Technology

Biblphie Trav Scient — Bibliographie des Travaux Scientifiques

Biblphie Veroff Hyg Inst Hamb — Bibliographie der Veroffentlichungen. Hygienisches Institut der Hansestadt Hamburg und Akademie fuer Staatsmedizin

Biblphie VetMed — Bibliographie der Veterinarmedizin

Bibl Philos Louvain — Bibliotheque Philosophique de Louvain

Biblphische Mschr Int Z Ges Med — Bibliographische Monatsschrift. Internationale Zeitschrift fuer die Gesamte Medizin

Biblphisch Jber Soz Hyg — Bibliographischer Jahresbericht uber Soziale Hygiene. Demographie und Medizinalstatistik

Biblphisch SemBer Ersch Geb Neurol Psychiat — Bibliographischer Semesterbericht der Erscheinungen auf dem Gebiet der Neurologie und Psychiatrie

Bibl Phonet — Bibliotheca Phonetica

Bibl Phonetica — Bibliotheca Phonetica

Biblphy Agric (Wash) — Bibliography of Agriculture (Washington)

Biblphy Bee Research Ass — Bibliography. Bee Research Association

Bibl Phycol — Bibliotheca Phycologica

Biblphy Int Bee Res Ass — Bibliography. International Bee Research Association

Biblphy Soil Sci — Bibliography of Soil Science, Fertilizers, and General Agronomy

Biblphy Spectrophot Meth Analysis Inorg Ions — Bibliography of Spectrophotometric Methods of Analysis for Inorganic Ions

Biblphy Subj Index S Afr Geol — Bibliography and Subject Index of South African Geology

Biblphy System Mycol — Bibliography of Systematic Mycology

Biblphy Tech Libr Armstrong Siddeley Mot — Bibliography. Technical Library. Armstrong Siddeley Motors

Biblphy Tech Rep Wash — Bibliography of Technical Reports (Washington)

Biblphy Tidal Hydraul — Bibliography on Tidal Hydraulics

Biblphy Trace Elem Fds — Bibliography of Trace Elements in Foods. Ministry of Health

Biblphy Transl Russ Scient Tech Lit — Bibliography of Translations from Russian Scientific and Technical Literature

Biblphy Trop Agric — Bibliography of Tropical Agriculture

Biblphy Un Steel Co — Bibliography. United Steel Companies

Biblphy US Soil Conserv Serv — Bibliography. United States Soil Conservation Service

Bibl Primatol — Bibliotheca Primatologica

Bibl Problem — Biblioteka Problemow

Bibl Profes Mat — Biblioteca Profesorului de Matematica

Bibl Psych — Bibliotheca Psychiatrica

Bibl Psychiatr — Bibliotheca Psychiatrica

Bibl Psychiatr Neurol — Bibliotheca Psychiatrica et Neurologica

Bibl Radiol — Bibliotheca Radiologica

Bibl Repro — Bibliography of Reproduction

BiblRes — Biblical Research. Papers of the Chicago Society of Biblical Research

Bibl Rev Mat Iberoamericana — Biblioteca de la Revista Matematica Iberoamericana

Bibl Rio — Biblioteca (Rio de Janeiro)

Bibl RLC — Bibliotheque de la Revue de Litterature Comparee

Bibl Sac — Bibliotheca Sacra

Bibl Sacra — Bibliotheca Sacra

Bibl Sci Albert Blanchard — Bibliotheque Scientifique Albert Blanchard

Bibl Script Gr Rom Teub — Bibliotheca Scriptorum Graecorum et Romanorum Teubneriana

Bibl Selective Pubns Officielles Fr — Bibliographie Selective des Publications Officielles Francaises

Bibl Sel'sk Profsoiuznogo Akt — Bibliotechka Sel'skogo Profsoiuznogo Aktivista

Bibl Soc Am Pa — Bibliographical Society of America. Papers

Bibl Storia Sci — Biblioteca di Storia della Scienza

Bibl Stor T — Biblioteca Storica Toscana. Sezione di Storia del Risorgimento

BiblStud — Biblische Studien

Biblt — Bibliotekaren

Bibltca Antrop — Biblioteca de Antropologie

Bibltca Argent Cienc Nat — Biblioteca Argentina de Ciencias Naturales

Bibltca Boln Minas Petrol — Biblioteca del Boletin de Minas y Petroleo

Bibltca Cerc The — Biblioteca Cercului Tehnic

Bibltca Cient Obs Fis Cosm S Miguel — Biblioteca Cientifica del Observatorio de Fisica Cosmica. San Miguel

Bibltca Cient Obs S Miguel — Biblioteca Cientifica del Observatorio de San Miguel

Bibltca Geogr Ist Geogr de Agostini — Biblioteca Geografica dell'Istituto Geografico de Agostini

Bibltca Inst Agric Catalan — Biblioteca del Instituto Agricola Catalan de San Isidro

Bibltca Med — Biblioteca del Medico

Bibltca Pro Vulg Agric — Biblioteca Pro-Vulgarizacion Agricola

Bibltca Scient Sov — Biblioteca Scientifica Sovietica

Bibltca Sci Mod — Biblioteca di Scienze Moderne

Bibltca Soc Cient Parag — Biblioteca de la Sociedad Cientifica del Paraguay

Bibltca Soc Sti Mat Fiz — Biblioteca Societatii de Stiinte Matematice si Fizice din R.P.R

Bibltca Sti Evr — Biblioteca Stiinta Evreiasca

Bibltca Stud Colon — Biblioteca di Studi Coloniali

Bibltca Zootech — Biblioteca Zootechnica

Bibltchka Galvanotekh — Bibliotechka Gal'vanotekhnika

Bibltchka Zuboreza Nov — Bibliotechka Zuboreza-Novatora

Bibltczka Roln — Biblioteczka Rolnicza

Bibl Teubn — Bibliotheca Scriptorum Graecorum et Romanorum Teubneriana

Bibl Text Philos — Bibliotheque des Textes Philosophiques

Bibl Theatrale Ill — Bibliotheque Theatrale Illustree

Bibl Theol — Bibliotheque de Theologie. Serie 4. Histoire de la Theologie

Bibltka Warsz — Biblioteka Warszawska

Bibl Tuberc — Bibliotheca Tuberculosea

Bibl Tuberc Med Thorac — Bibliotheca Tuberculosea et Medicinae Thoracalis

Bibl Tub Me T — Bibliotheca Tuberculosea et Medicinae Thoracalis

Bibl Universelle Rev Suisse — Bibliotheque Universelle et Revue Suisse

Bibl Univers Geneve — Bibliotheque Universelle de Geneve

Bibl Univers Rev Gen — Bibliotheque Universelle et Revue de Geneve

Bibl Univers Rev Suisse — Bibliotheque Universelle et Revue Suisse

Bibl Univers Rev Suisse Etrang Nouv Periode — Bibliotheque Universelle et Revue Suisse et Etrangere. Nouvelle Periode

Bibl Univers Sci B L Arts Sci Arts — Bibliotheque Universelle des Sciences, Belles Lettres, et Arts. Sciences et Arts

Bibl Univ Prov Barc Bol Not — Biblioteca Universitaria y Provincial Barcelona. Boletin de Noticias

Bibl "Vita Hum" — Bibliotheca "Vita Humana"

Bibl Wirtschaftspresse — Bibliographie der Wirtschaftspresse

BiblZ — Biblische Zeitschrift

BibM — Bibliographe Moderne

Bib Mes — Bibliotheca Mesopotamica

Bib Mesop — Bibliotheca Mesopotamica

Bib N Eng Hist — Bibliographies of New England History

Bib Neuroendocr — Bibliographia Neuroendocrinologica

Bib N Madrid — Biblioteca Nacional de Madrid

Bib Not — Biblische Notizen. Beitraege zur Exegetischen Diskussion

BibO — Bibliotheca Orientalis

Bib Or — Bibbia e Oriente

Bib Orient — Bibliotheca Orientalis

Bib Or Pont — Biblica et Orientalia. Pontificum Institutum Biblicum

BibP — Bibliotheque de la Pleiade

Bib Padagog — Bibliographie Padagogik

Bib R — Biblical Review

BibR — Bibliotheca Romanica

BIBR — Bulletin. Institut Historique Belge de Rome

BIBRA Bull — BIBRA [*British Industrial Biological Research Association*] Bulletin

Bib Reden & Bild Kst — Bibliothek der Redenden und Bildenden Kuenste

Bib Res — Biblical Research

Bib Sac — Bibliotheca Sacra

Bib Sacra — Bibliotheca Sacra

Bib Sanctorum — Bibliotheca Sanctorum

Bib Soc Am — Bibliographical Society of America. Papers

Bibs of Aust Writers — Bibliographies of Australian Writers

Bib S Wiss & Frejen Kst — Bibliothek der Schoenen Wissenschaften und der Frejen Kuenste

BibTB — Biblical Theology Bulletin

Bib Th Bul — Biblical Theology Bulletin

Bib Transl — Bible Translator

Bib Tr No 1 No 3 — Bible Translator. Technical Papers. Numbers 1 and 3

Bib Tr No 2 No 4 — Bible Translator. Practical Papers. Numbers 2 and 4

Bib Tr P — Bible Translator. Practical Papers

Bib Tr T — Bible Translator. Technical Papers

Bl Bulg — Bulletin. Institut Archeologique Bulgare

Bib Univl — Bibliotheque Universelle. Revue Suisse et Etrangere

Bib Univl & Rev Suisse — Bibliotheque Universelle et Revue Suisse

Bib Univl Geneve — Bibliotheque Universelle de Geneve

Bib VC — Bible e Vie Chretienne

Bib Vulgarisation Mus Guimet — Bibliotheque de Vulgarisation du Musee Guimet

BibW — Bibliothek und Wissenschaft

Bib Warszaw — Biblioteka Warszawska

Bib World — Biblical World

Bib Z — Biblische Zeitschrift

Bib Zeit — Biblische Zeitschrift

BIC — Books in Canada

BIC — Bulletin Interieur des Cadres

BICA — Bollettino. Istituto di Corrispondenza Archeologica

BICA — Bulletin of Information on Computing in Anthropology

BICAER — Bulletin. International Committee on Urgent Anthropological and Ethnological Research

BICB — Institut Royal Colonial Belge. Bulletin des Seances

BICByz — Bulletin d'Information et de Coordination. Association Internationale desEtudes Byzantines

BICC — Boletin. Instituto Caro y Cuervo

BICEB — Bulletin d'Information des Centrales Electriques

BICED — Biologie Cellulaire

B I Cent Rest — Bollettino. Istituto Centrale del Restauro

Bic Forum — Bicycle Forum

BICH — Bulletin. International Committee of Historical Sciences

BICHA — Biochemistry

BICHB — Bioinorganic Chemistry

BICHS — Bulletin. International Committee of Historical Sciences

Bickel C M N — Bickel's Coin and Medal News. Munt en Medaljenuus

Bi Cl Or — Bibliotheca Classica Orientalis

BICMA — Bulletin. Institute of Chemistry. Academia Sinica

BICN — Boletin de Informaciones Cientificas Nacionales [*Quito*]
Bic N Can — Bicycling News Canada
BICOB — Biological Conservation
BICODM — Biologia Contemporanea
BICP — Institut Catholique de Paris. Bulletin
BICR — Bollettino. Istituto Centrale di Restauro
BICRA — Bulletin. Institute for Chemical Research. Kyoto University
BICS — Bulletin. Institute of Classical Studies. University of London
BICSL — Bulletin. Institute of Classical Studies. University of London
BICTA — Bibliotheca Tuberculosea
BICU — Bulletin of the International Committee on Urgent Anthropological and Ethnological Research
BICYA — Biological Cybernetics
Bicycles Bull — Bicycles Bulletin
BID — Bulletin International des Douanes
BIDCUS — Bibliotheque de l'Institut de Droit Canonique de l'Universite de Strasbourg
BIDE — Bulletin de l'Institut du Desert d'Egypte
BIDFD — Bulletin. International Dairy Federation
BIDICS (Bond Index Determinations Inorg Cryst Struct) — BIDICS (Bond Index to the Determinations of Inorganic Crystal Structures)
BIDID — Biosources Digest
BIDIEA — Bibliotheca Diatomologica
BIDR — Bollettino. Istituto di Diritto Romano
Bidrag Kundskab Naturvidensk — Bidrag Till Kundskab Over Naturvidenskaberne
Bidr Kaenned Finlds Nat — Bidrag till Kaennedom of Finlands Natur Och Folk
Bidr Kaennedom Finl Natur Folk — Bidrag till Kaennedom af Finlands Natur och Folk
BIDS — Moody's Bond Information Database Service
BIDZD — Boei Ika Daigakko Zasshi
BIE — Bijblad bij de Industriele Eigendom
BIE — Boletin. Instituto de las Espanas
BIE — Boletin. Instituto Espanol de Londres
BIE — Bulletin. Institut d'Egypte
BIEA — Boletin. Instituto de Estudios Asturianos
Biedermanns Zentralbl — Biedermanns Zentralblatt
Biedermanns Zentralbl Abt A — Biedermanns Zentralblatt. Abteilung A. Allgemeiner und Referierender Teil
Biedermanns Zentralbl Abt B — Biedermanns Zentralblatt. Abteilung B. Tierernaehrung
BIEG — Boletin. Instituto de Estudios Giennenses
BIEGB — Bulletin. International Association of Engineering Geology
BIE Gien — Boletin. Instituto de Estudios Giennenses
BIEH — Boletin. Instituto de Estudios Helenicos
Bielefeld Encount Phys Math — Bielefeld Encounters in Physics and Mathematics
Bielefelder Beitr Ausbildungsforsch Studienreform — Bielefelder Beitraege zur Ausbildungsforschung und Studienreform
BIEN — Boletin del Instituto Etnico Nacional [*Buenos Aires*]
Bienenbl Bundesgebiet — Bienen-Blatt fuer des Bundesgebiet
Bienenw Zbl — Bienenwirtschaftliches Zentralblatt
Bienen Ztg — Bienen-Zeitung
Bien-Etre Soc Canadien — Bien-Etre Social Canadien
Bienn Anaerobe Discuss Group Int Symp — Biennial Anaerobe Discussion Group International Symposium
Bienn Conf Carbon Ext Abstr Program — Biennial Conference. Carbon. Extended Abstracts and Program
Bienn Congr Int Deep Drawing Res Group — Biennial Congress. International Deep Drawing Research Group
Bienn Congr Int Sol Energy Soc — Biennial Congress. International Solar Energy Society
Bienn Int CODATA Conf — Biennial International CODATA [*Committee on Data for Science and Technology*] Conference
Bienn Low Rank Fuels Symp — Biennial Low-Rank Fuels Symposium
Bienn Rep Calif State Board Forest — Biennial Report. California State Board of Forestry
Bienn Rep Fla St Bd Conserv — Biennial Report. Florida State Board of Conservation
Bienn Rep For Div La — Biennial Report of the Forestry Division of the Louisiana Department of Conservation
Bienn Rep For Div New Hamp — Biennial Report. Forestry Division. Forestry and Recreation Commission. New Hampshire
Bienn Rep Forest Commnr Me — Biennial Report. Forest Commissioner. Maine
Bienn Rep Ga Dep For — Biennial Report. Georgia Department of Forestry
Bienn Rep Geol Surv Ill — Biennial Report of the Geological Survey. State of Illinois
Bienn Rep Hawaii Geophys — Biennial Report. Hawaii Institute of Geophysics
Bienn Rep Hawaii Inst Geophys — Biennial Report. Hawaii Institute of Geophysics
Bienn Rep Idaho St Bd Ld Commnrs — Biennial Report of the Idaho State Board of Land Commissioners
Bienn Rep Ill St Lab Nat Hist — Biennial Report. Illinois State Laboratory of Natural History
Bienn Rep Insp Coal Mines Mont — Biennial Report of the Inspector of Coal Mines of the State of Montana
Bienn Rep Iowa Bk Agric — Biennial Report of Iowa Book of Agriculture
Bienn Rep Kans Agric Exp Stn — Biennial Report of the Kansas State Board of Agriculture
Bienn Rep Kans St Bd Hlth — Biennial Report. Kansas State Board of Health
Bienn Rep Kans St Ent Commn — Biennial Report. Kansas State Entomological Commission
Bienn Rep Kans St Hort Soc — Biennial Report. Kansas State Horticultural Society
Bienn Rep Kans St Wat Commn — Biennial Report. Kansas State Water Commission
Bienn Rep Ky Bur Agric — Biennial Report. Kentucky Bureau of Agriculture
Bienn Rep Ky St Bd Hlth — Biennial Report. Kentucky State Board of Health

Bienn Rep La Dep Agric — Biennial Report. Louisiana Department of Agriculture and Immigration
Bienn Rep La Dep Conserv — Biennial Report of the Louisiana Department of Conservation
Bienn Rep La Rice Exp Stn — Biennial Report of the Louisiana Rice Experiment Station
Bienn Rep La St Bd Hlth — Biennial Report. Louisiana State Board of Health
Bienn Rep La St Crop Pest Commn — Biennial Report. Louisiana State Crop Pest Commission
Bienn Rep La St Dep Agric — Biennial Report of the Louisiana State Department of Agriculture
Bienn Rep La St Live Stk Sanit Bd — Biennial Report. Louisiana State Live Stock Sanitary Board
Bienn Rep La St Mus — Biennial Report of the Louisiana State Museum
Bienn Rep Mar Fishg Progm — Biennial Report of the Marine Fishing Program
Bienn Rep Mass Agric Exp Stn — Biennial Report of the Massachusetts Agricultural Experiment Station
Bienn Rep Me St Forest Serv — Biennial Report. Maine State Forest Service
Bienn Rep Mich Dep Agric — Biennial Report. Michigan Department of Agriculture
Bienn Rep Mich Dep Conserv — Biennial Report. Michigan Department of Conservation
Bienn Rep Mich St Bd Fish Commnrs — Biennial Report of the Michigan State Board of Fish Commissioners
Bienn Rep Minn Commnr Highw — Biennial Report. Minnesota Commissioner of Highways
Bienn Rep Minn Dep Conserv — Biennial Report. Minnesota Department of Conservation
Bienn Rep Minn Ind Commn — Biennial Report of the Minnesota Industrial Commission
Bienn Rep Minn St Dairy Fd Commnr — Biennial Report. Minnesota State Dairy and Food Commissioner
Bienn Rep Miss St Forest Park Serv — Biennial Report of the Mississippi State Forest and Park Service
Bienn Rep Miss St Geol Surv — Biennial Report of the Mississippi State Geological Survey
Bienn Rep Miss St Live Stk Sanit Bd — Biennial Report of the Mississippi State Live Stock Sanitary Board
Bienn Rev Anthropol — Biennial Review of Anthropology
Bienn Studi Stor Arte Med — Biennial. Studi Storia Arte Medicina
Bien Pub — Bien Public
Bien Rep Cal Waste Man Bd — Biennial Report. California Waste Management Board
Bien Rep Hawaii Agr Exp Sta — Biennial Report. Hawaii Agricultural Experiment Station
Bien Rep Iowa Book Agr — Biennial Report. Iowa. Book of Agriculture. Iowa State Department of Agriculture
Bien Rep Meat Res Ins — Biennial Report. Meat Research Institute
Bien Rep Nev State Dept Agr — Biennial Report. Nevada State Department of Agriculture
BIES — Bulletin. Israel Exploration Society
BIF — Boletin del Instituto de Folklore [*Caracas*]
BIF — Boletin. Instituto Frances
BIFAN — Bulletin de l'Institut Francais d'Afrique Noire
BIFAO — Bulletin. Institut Francais d'Archeologie Orientale
BIFAOr — Bibliotheque d'Etudes. Institute Francais d'Archeologie Orientale
BIFB — Budapest. Tudomany-Egyetem. Francia Intezet. Bibliotheque de l'Institut Francais
BIFD — Bulletin for International Fiscal Documentation
BIFG — Boletin. Institucion Fernan-Gonzalez
BIFG — Bollettino. Istituto di Filologia Greca. Universita di Padova
Bifidobact Microflora — Bifidobacteria and Microflora
BIFLTA — Bulletin. Illinois Foreign Language Teachers Association
BIFMC — Bulletin of International Folk Music Council
BIFP — Boletin. Instituto de Investigaciones Folkloricas. Universidad Interamericana (Panama)
BIFP — Bulletin et Memoires. Institut des Fouilles de Provence et des Prealpes
BIFR — Buletinul. Institutului de Filologie Romana "Alexandru Philippide"
BIFRI — Buletinul. Institutului de Filologie Romana "Alexandru Philippide" (Iasi)
BIFV — Boletin. Instituto de Folklore
BIGA — Boletin del Instituto Geografico Argentino
BIGBA — Buletinul. Institutului Politehnic "Gheorghe Gheorghiu-Dej" Bucuresti
Big D — Big Deal
BIGEB — Biochemical Genetics
BIGENA — Bibliography and Index of Geology Exclusive of North America
Big Farm Manage — Big Farm Management
BIGLA — Bioloski Glasnik
Big Mama — Big Mama Rag
Big Sky Econ Mont Stat Univ Coop Ext Serv — Big Sky Economics. Montana State University. Cooperative Extension Service
BiH — Bibliografia Hispanica
BiH — Bibliotheque d'Humanisme et Renaissance
BIHAA — Bibliotheca Haematologica
Bihang K Svenska Vetensk-Akad Handl (Stockholm) — Bihang till Kongliga Svenska Vetenskaps-Akademiens Handlingar (Stockholm)
Bihar Acad Agr Sci Proc — Bihar Academy of Agricultural Sciences. Proceedings
BIHBR — Bulletin. Institut Historique Belge de Rome
BIHEP — Bibliographic Index of Health Education Periodicals
B I Hist R — Bulletin. Institute of Historical Research
BIHIT — Boletim. Instituto Historico da Ilha Terceira
Bih LJ Rep — Bihar Law Journal Reports
BI Hochschultaschenb — BI [*Bibliographisches Institut*] Hochschultaschenbuecher
BIHP — Bulletin. Institute of History and Philology. Academia Sinica
BIHR — Bibliotheque d'Humanisme et Renaissance
BIHR — Bulletin. Institute of Historical Research
BII — Banque d'Information Industrielle

BII — Bulletin. Iranian Institute of America
BII — Business International Index
BIIA — Bulletin. Iranian Institute of America
BIIB — Boletin. Instituto de Investigaciones Bibliograficas
BIIDD — Bulletin. Institute for Industrial and Social Development
BIIH — Boletin. Instituto de Investigaciones Historicas
BIIL — Boletin. Instituto de Investigaciones Literarias
BIIN — Boletin. Instituto Inter-Americano del Nino
BIINA — Biuletyn. Instytutu Naftowego
BIIP — International Institute of Philosophy. Institut International de la Philosophie. Bulletin Trimestriel
BIIRHT — Bulletin d'Information. Institut de Recherche et d'Histoire des Textes
BIIV — Boletin Informativo. Departamento de Antropologia. Instituto Venezolano de Investigaciones Cientificas
BIIZDH — Instytut Zootechnik. Biuletyn Informacyjny
BIJ — Bialik Institute (Jerusalem)
Bijbl I E — Bijblad bij de Industriele Eigendom
Bijbl Ind Eig — Bijblad bij de Industriele Eigendom
Bijd Dierkunde — Bijdragen tot de Dierkunde
Bijd Kennis Boomsoorten Java — Bijdrage tot de Kennis der Boomsoorten van Java
Bijdr — Bijdragen. Tijdschrift voor Filosofie en Theologie
Bijdragen — Bijdragen tot de Taal-Land- en Volkenkunde
Bijdragen Dialectencommissie — Bijdragen en Mededeelingen der Dialectencommissie van de Koninklijke Akademie van Wetenschappen te Amsterdam
Bijdragen Nederl-Indie — Bijdragen tot de Taal-Land- en Volkenkunde van Nederlandsche-Indie
Bijdrag Taal-Land- Volkenk — Bijdragen tot de Taal-Land- en Volkenkunde
Bijdr & Meded Betreff Gesch Ned — Bijdragen en Mededelingen Betreffende de Geschiedenis der Nederlanden
Bijdr & Meded Hist Genoot Utrecht — Bijdragen en Mededelingen van het Historisch Genootschap te Utrecht
Bijdr & Meded Ver Gelre — Bijdragen en Mededelingen der Vereniging Gelre
Bijdr Dierk — Bijdragen tot de Dierkunde
Bijdr Dierkd — Bijdragen tot de Dierkunde
Bijdr Dierkhd — Bijdragen tot de Dierkunde
Bijdr Gesch Geneesk — Bijdragen tot de Geschiedenis der Geneeskunde. Nederlandsche Maatschappij tot Bevordering der Geneeskunst
Bijdr Gesch Kst Nederlanden — Bijdragen tot de Geschiedenis van de Kunst der Nederlanden
Bijdr Gesch Ndl — Bijdragen voor de Geschiedenis der Nederlanden
Bijdr Gesch Nederl — Bijdragen voor de Geschiedenis der Nederlanden
Bijdr Taalkde Nederl Indie — Bijdragen tot de Taal-, Land- en Volkenkunde van Nederlandsch-Indie
Bijdr Taal Land & Vlkenknd — Bijdragen tot de Taal-, Land-, en Volkenkunde
Bijdr Taal- Land-en Volkenk Nederl-Indie — Bijdragen tot de Taal-Land- en Volkenkunde van Nederlandsche-Indie
Bijdr Taal Land Volkenk — Bijdragen tot de Taal- Land- en Volkenkunde
BijdrTLV — Bijdragen tot de Taal-Land- en Volkenkunde
Bijd Volk — Bijdragen tot de Taal, Land- en Volkenkunde
Bijd Volk Ned Indie — Bijdragen tot de Taal- Land- en Volkenkunde van Nederlandsch-Indie
Bijl Hand Tw K der St Gen — Bijlagen bij de Handelingen van de Tweede Kamer der Staten Generaal
BIJOA — Biochemical Journal
BIJS — Bulletin. Institute of Jewish Studies
Bijv Stb — Bijvoegsel tot het Staatsblad
Bijzondere Publ Bosbouwproefstat — Bijzondere Publicaties van het Bosbouwproefstation/Pengumuman Isti Mewa Balai Penjelidiken Kehutanan
BIK — Biergrosshandel. Zeitschrift fuer den Gesamten Biergrosshandel und Getrankegrosshandel
Biken J — Biken Journal
BIKHD — Bioorganicheskaya Khimiya
BiKi — Bibel und Kirche
BIKJA — Biken Journal
BIKLEK — Biopolimery i Kletka
BIKOA — Biologiai Koezlemenyek
BiI — Bilychnis
BIL — Bollettino Internazionale di Informazioni sul Latino
BIL — Bulletin. Iranian League
BILA Bull — British Insurance Law Association. Bulletin
BILAL — Bulletin d'Information. Laboratoire d'Analyse Lexicologique
Bil Aspects Inorg Chem Symp — Biological Aspects of Inorganic Chemistry. Symposium
Bilateral Semin Int Bur — Bilateral Seminars. International Bureau
Bilateral Semin Int Bur — Bilateral Seminars of the International Bureau
BILC — Boletim. Instituto Luis de Camoes
BILD — Bibliographic Index of Library Documents
Bildhft Ger Nmus — Bildhefte des Germanischen Nationalmuseums
Bildhft Mus Kst & Gew Hamburg — Bilderhefte des Museums fuer Kunst und Gewerbe Hamburg
Bildhft Westfael Landesmus Kst & Kultgesch — Bilderhefte des Westfaelischen Landesmuseums fuer Kunst- und Kulturgeschichte
BildK — Bildenden Kuenste
Bild Kst — Bildende Kunst
Bild Kst Oesterreich — Bildende Kunst in Oesterreich
Bildner Erz Werkerziehung Textiles Gestalt — Bildnerische Erziehung/Werkerziehung/Textiles Gestalten
Bildung Erzieh — Bildung und Erziehung
Bild Wiss — Bild der Wissenschaft
BILE — Bollettino. Istituto di Lingue Estere
Bile Acid Meet Proc — Bile Acid Meeting. Proceedings
Bile Acid Metab Health Dis Proc Bile Acid Meet — Bile Acid Metabolism in Health and Disease. Proceedings of the Bile Acid Meeting

Bile Acids Ther Agents Proc Falk Symp — Bile Acids as Therapeutic Agents. From Basic Science to Clinical Practice. Proceedings. Falk Symposium
BiLeb — Bibel und Leben
BILEG — Bollettino. Istituto di Lingue Estere (Genova)
BILEUG — Bollettino. Istituto de Lingue Estere
BILEUG — Bollettino. Istituto di Lingue Estere (Genoa)
BILIA — Biologicke Listy
Biling Ed Pap Ser — Bilingual Education Paper Series
Biling Rev — Bilingual Review/Revista Bilingue
Bilirubin Metab Newborn Int Symp — Bilirubin Metabolism in the Newborn. International Symposium
BiLit — Bibel und Liturgie
Biljeske Inst Oceanogr Ribar (Split) — Biljeske. Institut za Oceanografiju i Ribarstvo (Split)
BILL — Boletin. Instituto de Literatura y Linguistica
BILLA — Billboard
Billboard Co Mus Sour — Billboard Country Music Sourcebook
Billboard Int Aud Vid Tape Dir — Billboard International Audio Video Tape Directory
Billboard Int Buy G — Billboard International Buyer's Guide
Billboard Int Rec Equip St Dir — Billboard International Recording Equipment and Studio Directory
Billboard Int Tal Tour Dir — Billboard International Talent and Touring Directory
Billings Geol Soc Annu Field Conf Guideb — Billings Geological Society. Annual Field Conference. Guidebook
Bill of Rights J — Bill of Rights Journal
Bill Rights J — Bill of Rights Journal
B III Wall — Bulletin Illustre de la Wallonie
BILPatr — Bulletin d'Information et de Liaison. Association Internationale des Etudes Patristiques
Bilt Dok — Bilten Dokumentacije
Bilten Drushtvo Mat Fiz Nar Repub Makedonija — Bilten. Drushtvo na Matematicharite i Fizicharite od Narodna Republika Makedonija
Bilt Farm Drus Maked — Bilten za Farmaceutskoto Drustvo za Makedonija
Bilt Farm Drus Soc Repub Makedonija — Bilten za Farmaceutskoto Drustvo za Socijalisticka Republika Makedonija
Bilt Hematol Transfuz — Bilten za Hematologiju i Transfuziju
Bilt Hmelj Sirak — Bilten za Hmelj i Sirak
Bilt Hmelj Sirak Lek Bilje — Bilten za Hmelj Sirak i Lekovito Bilje
Bilt Inst Nukl Nauke Vinca — Bilten Instituta za Nuklearne Nauke Vinca
Bilt Poslovnog Udruzenja Proizvodaca Biljnih Ulja Masti — Bilten Poslovnog Udruzenja Proizvodaca Biljnih Ulja i Masti
Bilt Sojuzot Zdruzenijata Farm Farm Teh SR Maked — Bilten za Sojuzot za Zdruzenijata za Farmacevtite i Farmacevtskite Tehnicari zaSR Makedonija
Bilt Udruz Ortodonata Jugosl — Bilten Udruzenja Ortodonata Jugoslavije
Bim — Bimestre
BIM — Boletin Interamericano de Musica
BIM — Brookings Papers on Economic Activity
Bi-M Bull N Dak Agric Exp Stn — Bi-Monthly Bulletin. North Dakota Agricultural Experiment Station
BIMC — Monthly Circular. Baltic and International Maritime Conference
BIMDA — Biochemical Medicine
BIMDB — Biomedicine
BIME — Bullettino. Istituto Storico Italiano per il Medio Evo e Archivio Muratorino
BIMEA — Biologie Medicale
BIMEB — Biomedical Engineering
BIMHEI — Butterworths International Medical Reviews. Hematology
BI Mid East Market Cond Egypt — BI [*Business International Corp.*] Middle East Marketing Conditions. Egypt
Bi M L R — Bi-Monthly Law Review
BIMOA — Biologiya Morya
Bi Mo Law R — Bi-Monthly Law Review
Bi-Mo L Rev — Bi-Monthly Law Review. University of Detroit
Bimon Bus Rev — Bimonthly Business Review
B Imp Inst — Bulletin. Imperial Institute
Bi-M Res Notes Canada Dep For — Bi-Monthly Research Notes. Canada Department of Forestry
BIMYDY — Bibliotheca Mycologica
BIN — Babylonian Inscriptions in the Collection of James B. Nies. Yale University
BIN — Billboard Information Network
BIN — Bollettino Italiano di Numismatica
BIN — Bulletin of International News
Binatl USA USSR Symp Laser Opt Condens Matter — Binational USA-USSR Symposium on Laser Optics of Condensed Matter
BIN Bibliogr Ser — BIN [*Boreal Institute for Northern Studies*] Bibliographic Series
B Indo Econ Stud — Bulletin of Indonesian Economic Studies
B Indones Econ Stud — Bulletin of Indonesian Economic Studies
BINEA — Biologia Neonatorum [*Later, Biology of the Neonate*]
BINEAA — Biologia Neonatorum [*Later, Biology of Neonate*]
BINED — BIOP [*Board on International Organizations and Programs*] Newletter
B Inf — Bulletin d'Information. Institut d'Etude Economique et Sociale des Classes Moyennes
B Inf Consejo Gener Col Veterinarios Esp — Boletin de Informacion. Consejo General de Colegios Veterinarios de Espana
B Inf Doc — Boletin de Informacion Documental
B Inf Doc BN — Bulletin d'Information et de Documentation. Banque Nationale
B Inf FNAMI — Bulletin d'Information. FNAMI
B Inform Centre Docum Educ Europe — Bulletin d'Information. Centre de Documentation pour l'Education en Europe
B Inform C N C — Bulletin d'Information. Centre National de la Cinematographie
B Inform Dept Econ Sociol Rur — Bulletin d'Information. Departement d'Economie et de Sociologie Rurales
B Inform Econ — Bulletin d'Informations Economiques
B Inform Econ Caisse Nat Marches Etat — Bulletin d'Information Economique de la Caisse Nationale des Marches de l'Etat

B Inform Haut Comite Et Inform Alcool — Bulletin d'Information. Haut Comite d'Etude et d'Information sur l'Alcoolisme

B Inform Region Champagne-Ardenne — Bulletin d'Information Regionale Champagne-Ardenne

B Inform Region Paris — Bulletin d'Information de la Region Parisienne

B Inf Zak Narod — Biuletyn Informacyjny. Zakladu Narodowego Ossolinskich Biblioteki Polskiej Akademii Nauk

Binnenschiffahrts-Nachr — Binnenschiffahrts-Nachrichten

B Inostr Kommerc Inform Priloz — Bjulleten Inostrannoj Kommerceskoj Informacii Prilozenie

B In Sci T — Bulletin d'Informations Scientifiques et Techniques. Commissariat a l'Energie Atomique

BINSCS — Boreal Institute for Northern Studies. Contribution Series

BINSOP — Boreal Institute for Northern Studies. Occasional Publication

B Inst — Bullettino. Instituto di Correspondenza Archeologica

B Inst A (London) — Bulletin. Institute of Archaeology (London)

B Inst Angola — Boletim. Instituto de Angola

BInstArch — Bulletin. Institute of Archaeology

B Inst Archaeol — Bulletin. Institute of Archaeology. University of London

B Inst Arch Bulg — Izvestiia na Arkheologicheskiia Institut. Bulgarska Akademiia na Naukite

B Inst Communication Res — Bulletin. Institute of Communication Research

B Inst Develop Stud — Bulletin. Institute of Development Studies

B Inst Econ Paris — Bulletin. Institut Economique de Paris

B Inst Est Asturianos — Boletin. Instituto de Estudios Asturianos

B Inst Est Hel — Boletin. Instituto de Estudios Helenicos

B Inst Est Hel — Boletin. Instituto de Estudios Helenicos. Universidad de Barcelona. Facultad deFilosofia y Letras

B Inst Ethnol Acad Sinica — Bulletin. Institute of Ethnology. Academia Sinica

B Inst F Gonzalez — Boletin. Institucion Fernan Gonzalez de Burgos. CSIC (Consejo Superior de Investigacion Cientificas)

B Inst Fondam Afr Noire — Bulletin. Institut Fondamental d'Afrique Noire

B Inst Fr Afr Noire — Bulletin. Institut Francais d'Afrique Noire

B Inst Franc Espagne — Bulletin. Institut Francais en Espagne

B Inst Franc Et Andines — Bulletin. Institut Francais d'Etudes Andines

B Inst Hist Belg Rom — Bulletin. Institut Historique Belge de Rome

B Inst Hist Med (Hyderabad) — Bulletin. Institute of History of Medicine (Hyderabad)

B Inst Hist Philol Acad Sinica — Bulletin. Institute of History and Philology. Academia Sinica

B Inst Int Adm Publ — Bulletin. Institut International d'Administration Publique

B Inst Jam Sci — Bulletin. Institute of Jamaica. Science Series

B Inst Mod Hist Acad Sinica — Bulletin. Institute of Modern History. Academia Sinica

B Inst Rech Econ — Bulletin. Institut de Recherches Economiques

B Inst Trad Cult — Bulletin. Institute of Traditional Cultures

Binsurance — Business Insurance

B Int Assoc Educ Vocat Guidance — Bulletin. International Association for Educational and Vocational Guidance

B Int Committee on Urg Anthropol Ethnol Res — Bulletin. International Committee on Urgent Anthropological and Ethnological Research

B Int Committee Urgent Anthro Ethno Res — Bulletin. International Committee on Urgent Anthropological and Ethnological Research

B Interminist Rational Choix Budget — Bulletin Interministeriel pour la Rationalisation des Choix Budgetaires

B Interparl — Bulletin Interparlementaire

B Int Fisc Docum — Bulletin for International Fiscal Documentation

B Int Fis D — Bulletin for International Fiscal Documentation

BINUA — Bulletin d'Instrumentation Nucleaire

BiO — Bibbia e Oriente

BIO — Bulletin. Institut Oceanographique

BioAb — Biological Abstracts

Bioact Mol — Bioactive Molecules

BioAg — Biological and Agricultural Index

Bioantioksidant Luchevom Porazhenii Zlokach Roste — Bioantioksidanty v Luchevom Porazhenii i Zlokachestvennom Roste

Biobehav Rev — Biobehavioral Reviews

BioC — Biologia Culturale

BIOCAS — BIOSIS/CAS Registry Number Concordance

Biocatal Biotransform — Biocatalysis and Biotransformation

Biocatal Ind — Biocatalysts for Industry

Bioc Biop A — Biochimica et Biophysica Acta

Bioc Biop R — Biochemical and Biophysical Research Communications

BIOCC — Bedford Institute of Oceanography. Collected Contributions

Bioceram Hum Body Proc Int Congr — Bioceramics and the Human Body. Proceedings. International Congress

Biochem — Biochemistry

Biochem Actions Horm — Biochemical Actions of Hormones

Biochem Acute Allerg React Int Symp — Biochemistry of the Acute Allergic Reactions. International Symposium

Biochem Adenosylmethionine Proc Int Symp — Biochemistry of Adenosylmethionine. Proceedings of an International Symposium on the Biochemistry of Adenosylmethionine

Biochem Anal Membr — Biochemical Analysis of Membranes

Biochem Anima Dev — Biochemistry of Animal Development

Biochem Arch — Biochemical Archives

Biochem Aspects Plant Parasite Relat Proc Symp — Biochemical Aspects of Plant Parasite Relationships. Proceedings of the Symposium

Biochem Bact Growth 2nd Ed — Biochemistry of Bacterial Growth. 2nd Edition

Biochem Befunde Differentialdiag Inn Kr — Biochemische Befunde in der Differentialdiagnose Innerer Krankheiten

Biochem Biophys Perspect Mar Biol — Biochemical and Biophysical Perspectives in Marine Biology

Biochem Biophys Res Commun — Biochemical and Biophysical Research Communications

Biochem Bull (NY) — Biochemical Bulletin (New York)

Biochem Cell Biol — Biochemistry and Cell Biology

Biochem Cell Differ — Biochemistry of Cell Differentiation

Biochem Cell Differ Fed Eur Biochem Soc Meet — Biochemistry of Cell Differentiation. Federation of European Biochemical Societies. Meeting

Biochem Centralbl — Biochemisches Centralblatt

Biochem Clin — Biochemical Clinics

Biochem Clin Aspects Pteridines — Biochemical and Clinical Aspects of Pteridines

Biochem Clin Bohemoslov — Biochemia Clinica Bohemoslovaca

Biochem Collagen — Biochemistry of Collagen

Biochem Copper — Biochemistry of Copper

Biochem Correl Brain Struct Funct — Biochemical Correlates of Brain Structure and Function

Biochem Cutaneous Epidermal Differ Proc Jpn US Semin — Biochemistry of Cutaneous Epidermal Differentiation. Proceedings of the Japan-US Seminar on Biochemistry of Cutaneous Epidermal Differentiation

Biochem Cytol Plant Parasite Interact Symp — Biochemistry and Cytology of Plant Parasite Interaction Symposium

Biochem Dev — Biochemistry of Development

Biochem Developing Brain — Biochemistry of the Developing Brain

Biochem Dis — Biochemistry of Disease

Biochem Dis (NY) — Biochemistry of Disease (New York)

Biochem Educ — Biochemical Education

Biochem Eff Environ Pollut — Biochemical Effects of Environmental Pollutants

Biochem Endocrinol — Biochemical Endocrinology

Biochem Eng — Biochemical Engineering

Biochem Eng J — Biochemical Engineering Journal

Biochem Eng Stuttgart Proc Int Symp — Biochemical Engineering. Stuttgart. Proceedings. International Symposium on Biochemical Engineering

Biochem Exercise Proc Int Symp — Biochemistry of Exercise. Proceedings of the International Symposium on Exercise Biochemistry

Biochem Exp Biol — Biochemistry and Experimental Biology

Biochem Folic Acid Relat Pteridines — Biochemistry of Folic Acid and Related Pteridines

Biochem Gen — Biochemical Genetics

Biochem Genet — Biochemical Genetics

Biochem Int — Biochemistry International

Biochem Interact Plants Insects — Biochemical Interaction between Plants and Insects

Biochemistry (Engl Transl Biokhimiya) — Biochemistry (English Translation of Biokhimiya)

Biochemistry Mosc — Biochemistry (Moscow)

Biochemistry Ser One — Biochemistry. Series One

Biochem J — Biochemical Journal

Biochem J Mol Asp — Biochemical Journal. Molecular Aspects

Biochem Life Sci Adv — Biochemistry. Life Science Advances

Biochem Lipids Lipoproteins Membr — Biochemistry of Lipids, Lipoproteins, and Membranes

Biochem Med — Biochemical Medicine

Biochem Med Metab Biol — Biochemical Medicine and Metabolic Biology

Biochem Membr Transp — Biochemistry of Membrane Transport

Biochem Methods Monit Risk Pregnancies — Biochemical Methods for Monitoring Risk Pregnancies

Biochem Mol Aspects Sel Cancers — Biochemical and Molecular Aspects of Selected Cancers

Biochem Mol Biol Fishes — Biochemistry and Molecular Biology of Fishes

Biochem Mol Biol Int — Biochemistry and Molecular Biology International

Biochem Mol Med — Biochemical and Molecular Medicine

Biochem Neurol Dis — Biochemistry and Neurological Disease

Biochem On Line — Biochemistry On-Line

Biochem Parasites Host Parasite Relat Proc Int Symp — Biochemistry of Parasites and Host Parasite Relationships. Proceedings of the International Symposium on the Biochemistry of Parasites and Host Parasite Relationships

Biochem Pathol Connect Tissue — Biochemistry and Pathology of Connective Tissue

Biochem Pept Antibiot — Biochemistry of Peptide Antibiotics

Biochem Pharmac — Biochemical Pharmacology

Biochem Pharmacol — Biochemical Pharmacology

Biochem Pharmacol Toxicol — Biochemical Pharmacology and Toxicology

Biochem Physiol Pflanz — Biochemie und Physiologie der Pflanzen

Biochem Physiol Pflanz BPP — Biochemie und Physiologie der Pflanzen. BPP

Biochem Physiol Subst Abuse — Biochemistry and Physiology of Substance Abuse

Biochem Plants Compr Treatise — Biochemistry of Plants. A Comprehensive Treatise

Biochem Prep — Biochemical Preparations

Biochem Probl Lipids Proc Int Conf — Biochemical Problems of Lipids. Proceedings. International Conference

Biochem Rev (Bangalore) — Biochemical Reviews (Bangalore)

Biochem Sens Funct — Biochemistry of Sensory Functions

Biochem Ser Monogr — Biochemistry: a Series of Monographs

Biochem Smooth Muscle Proc Symp — Biochemistry of Smooth Muscle. Proceedings of the Symposium

Biochem Soc Spec Publ — Biochemical Society. Special Publications

Biochem Soc Symp — Biochemical Society. Symposia

Biochem Soc Trans — Biochemical Society. Transactions

Biochem Spectros — Biochemical Spectroscopy

Biochem SSR — Biochemistry-USSR

Biochem Struct Dyn Cell Nucl — Biochemical and Structural Dynamics of the Cell Nucleus

Biochem Syst — Biochemical Systematics [*Later, Biochemical Systematics and Ecology*]

Biochem Syst Ecol — Biochemical Systematics and Ecology

Biochem Tarybu Lietuvoje — Biochemija Tarybu Lietuvoje

Biochem Women Clin Concepts — Biochemistry of Women. Clinical Concepts
Biochem Women Methods Clin Invest — Biochemistry of Women. Methods for Clinical Investigation
Biochem Z — Biochemische Zeitschrift
Biochim Appl — Biochimica Applicata
Biochim Biol Sper — Biochimica e Biologia Sperimentale
Biochim Biophys Acta — Biochimica et Biophysica Acta
Biochim Biophys Acta B — Biochimica et Biophysica Acta. B. Bioenergetics
Biochim Biophys Acta Bioenerg — Biochimica et Biophysica Acta. B. Bioenergetics
Biochim Biophys Acta Biomembranes — Biochimica et Biophysica Acta. M. Biomembranes
Biochim Biophys Acta BR — Biochimica et Biophysica Acta. BR. Reviews on Bioenergetics
Biochim Biophys Acta Enzymol — Biochimica et Biophysica Acta. Enzymology
Biochim Biophys Acta G — Biochimica et Biophysica Acta. G. General Subjects
Biochim Biophys Acta General Subjects — Biochimica et Biophysica Acta. G. General Subjects
Biochim Biophys Acta Int J Biochem Biophys — Biochimica et Biophysica Acta/International Journal of Biochemistry and Biophysics
Biochim Biophys Acta Libr — Biochimica et Biophysica Acta. Library
Biochim Biophys Acta Lipids Lipid Metab — Biochimica et Biophysica Acta. Lipids and Lipid Metabolism
Biochim Biophys Acta M — Biochimica et Biophysica Acta. M. Biomembranes
Biochim Biophys Acta MR — Biochimica et Biophysica Acta. MR. Reviews on Biomembranes
Biochim Biophys Acta Nucl Acids Protein Synth — Biochimica et Biophysica Acta. Nucleic Acids and Protein Synthesis
Biochim Biophys Acta P — Biochimica et Biophysica Acta. P. Protein Structure
Biochim Biophys Acta Protein Struct — Biochimica et Biophysica Acta. P. Protein Structure
Biochim Ter Sper — Biochimica e Terapia Sperimentale
Bioch Pharm — Biochemical Pharmacology
Bioch Soc T — Biochemical Society. Transactions
Bioclimat Numero Spec — Bioclimat Numero Special
Biocomplex Invest Kaz — Biocomplex Investigation in Kazakhstan
Bioconjugate Chem — Bioconjugate Chemistry
Bioconjug Chem — Bioconjugate Chemistry
Bio Cons — Biological Conservation
Biocontrol Sci — Biocontrol Science
Biocoord Chem — Biocoordination Chemistry. Coordination Equilibria in Biologically Active Systems
Bioc Phy Pf — Biochemie und Physiologie der Pflanzen
BIODA — Biodynamica
BioDef Shirizu — BioDefence Shirizu
Biodeterior Invest Tech — Biodeterioration Investigation Techniques
Biodeter Res Titles — Biodeterioration Research Titles
BIOEA — Biomedical Engineering
Bioelectr B — Bioelectrochemistry and Bioenergetics
Bioelectrochem Bioenerg — Bioelectrochemistry and Bioenergetics
Bioelectrochem Prin Pract — Bioelectrochemistry Principles and Practice
Bioen Dir — Bio-energy Directory
Bioeng Abstr — Bioengineering Abstracts
Bioeng Proc Northeast Conf — Bioengineering. Proceedings of the Northeast Conference
Bioeng Skin — Bioengineering and the Skin
Bioethics Q — Bioethics Quarterly
Bioethius Texte Abh Gesch Exakt Wissensch — Bioethius. Texte und Abhandlungen zur Geschichte der Exakten Wissenschaften
BIOFA — Biofizika
BIOFDL — Annual Research Reviews. Biofeedback
Biofeedback and Self-Regul — Biofeedback and Self-Regulation
Biofeedback Self-Regul — Biofeedback and Self-Regulation
Biofiz — Biofizika
Biofiz Biokhim Myshechnogo Sokrashcheniya — Biofizika i Biokhimiya Myshechnogo Sokrashcheniya
Biofizika — Biofizika. Akademija Nauk SSSR
Biofiz Radiobiol — Biofizika i Radiobiologiya
Biofiz Rast Mater Vses Simp Mol Prikl Biofiz Rast — Biofizika Rastenii. Materialy Vsesoyuznogo Simpoziuma po Molekulyarnoi i Prikladnoi Biofizike Rastenii
Biofiz Zhivoi Kletki — Biofizika Zhivoi Kletki
Bioforum Int — Bioforum International
Biofuels Rep — Biofuels Report
BIOG — Biografias
Biog Amine — Biogenic Amines
Biog Amines — Biogenic Amines
Biog & Rev — Biograph and Review
Biogas Alcohol Fuels Prod — Biogas and Alcohol Fuels Production
Biog Bl — Biographische Blaetter
Biogeochem Devils Lake ND — Biogeochemistry of Devils Lake, North Dakota
Biogeochemi — Biogeochemistry
Biogeogr Nauchn Konf Mater — Biogeograficheskaya Nauchnaya Konferentsiya Materialy
Biogeokhim Diageneza Osadkov Okeana — Biogeokhimiya Diageneza Osadkov Okeana
Biog Ind — Biography Index
Biog Jb & Dt Nekrol — Biographisches Jahrbuch und Deutscher Nekrolog
Biog Mem N Acad Sci — Biographical Memoirs. National Academy of Science
Biog Mem R Soc — Biographical Memoirs. Royal Society
Biograph Dir Am Pol Sci Ass — Biographical Directory. American Political Science Association
Biograph Hervorrag Naturwiss Tech Medizin — Biographien Hervorragender Naturwissenschaftler, Techniker, und Mediziner
Biogr Gr — Biographoi. Vitarum Scriptores Graeci Minores

Biogr Hervorragender Naturwiss Tech Med — Biographien Hervorragender Naturwissenschaftler, Techniker, und Mediziner
Biogr Index — Biography Index
Biogr Jb Altertskde — Biographisches Jahrbuch fuer Altertumskunde
Biogr Mem Fellows Roy Soc — Biographical Memoirs. Fellows of the Royal Society
Biogr Mem Fellows R Soc — Biographical Memoirs. Fellows of the Royal Society
Biogr Mem Nat Acad Sci (USA) — Biographical Memoirs. National Academy of Sciences (United States of America)
Biogr Mem Natl Acad Sci — Biographical Memoirs. National Academy of Sciences
Biogr Nat Acad Roy Belg — Biographie Nationale. Academie Royale des Sciences, des Lettres, et des Beaux-Arts de Belgique
BIOHA — Biokhimiya
Biol — Biography Index
BIOI — BioResearch Index [*Later, BA/RRM*]
Bioinorg Ch — Bioinorganic Chemistry
Bioinorg Chem — Bioinorganic Chemistry
BIOJA — Biophysical Journal
Bio-Joule Newsl — Bio-Joule Newsletter
BIOKA — Biometrika
Biokhim — Biokhimiya
Biokhim Aspekty Introd Otdalennoi Gibrid Filogenii Rast — Biokhimicheskie Aspekty Introduktsii Otdalennoi Gibridizatsii i Filogenii Rastenii
Biokhim Chain Prozvod — Biokhimiya Chainogo Proizvodstva
Biokhim Genet Ryb Mater Vses Soveshch — Biokhimicheskaya Genetika Ryb. Materialy Vsesoyuznogo Soveshchaniya po Biokhimicheskoi Genetike Ryb
Biokhim Issled Protsesse Sel Kukuruzy — Biokhimicheskie Issledovaniya v Protsesse Selektsii Kukuruzy
Biokhim Kul't Rast Mold — Biokhimiya Kul'turnykh Rastenii Moldavu
Biokhim Lit SSR Mater S'ezda Biokhim Lit SSR — Biokhimiya v Litovskoi SSR. Materialy S'ezda Biokhimikov Litovskoi SSR
Biokhim Metody Issled Gig — Biokhimicheskie Metody Issledovaniya v Gigiene
Biokhim Nasekomykh — Biokhimiya Nasekomykh
Biokhim Plodov Ovoshchei — Biokhimiya Plodov i Ovoshchei
Biokhim Rast — Biokhimiya Rastenii
Biokhim Tekhnol Protsessy Pishch Promsti — Biokhimicheskie i Tekhnologicheskie Protsessy v Pishchevoi Promyshlennosti
Biokhim Vinodel — Biokhimiya Vinodeliya
Biokhim Zerna Khlebopeeh — Biokhimiya Zerna i Khlebopeeheniya
Biokhim Zh — Biokhimichna Zhurnal
Biokhim Zhivotn Chel — Biokhimiya Zhivotnykh i Cheloveka
Biokompleksnye Issled Kaz — Biokompleksnye Issledovaniya v Kazakhstane
Biokon Rep — Biokon Reports
Biol — Biologia
Biol — O Biologico
Biol Abh — Biologische Abhandlungen
Biol Abs — Biological Abstracts
Biol Abstr — Biological Abstracts
Biol Abstr RRM — Biological Abstracts/RRM
Biol Abwasserreinig — Biologische Abwasserreinigung
Biol Actinomycetes Relat Org — Biology of the Actinomycetes and Related Organisms
Biol Actions Dimethyl Sulfoxide — Biological Actions of Dimethyl Sulfoxide
Biol Acuatica — Biologia Acuatica
Biol Afr — Biologia Africana
Biol Aging Dev — Biology of Aging and Development
Biol Agric & Hortic — Biological Agriculture and Horticulture
Biol Agric Hort Int J — Biological Agriculture and Horticulture. An International Journal
Biol Agric Index — Biological and Agricultural Index
Biol Akklim Obez'yan Mater Simp — Biologiya i Akklimatizatsiya Obez'yan. Materialy Simpoziuma
Biol Akt Nek Aminotiolov Aminosul'fidov — Biologicheskaya Aktivnost Nekotorykh Aminotiolov i Aminosul'fidov
Biol Akt Savienojumu Kim Tehnol Rigas Politeh Inst — Biologiski Aktivo Savienojumu Kimijas Tehnologija Rigas Politehniskaja Instituta
Biol Akt Soedin Rast Sib Flory — Biologicheski Aktivnye Soedineniya Rastenii Sibirskoi Flory
Biol Akt Veshchestva Mikroorg — Biologicheski Aktivnye Veshchestva Mikroorganizmov
Biol Akt Veshchestva Mikroorg Ikh Ispol'z — Biologicheski Aktivnye Veshchestva Mikroorganizmov i Ikh Ispol'zovanie
Biol Akt Veshchestva Zhizni Rast Zhivotn — Biologicheski Aktivnye Veshchestva v Zhizni Rastenii i Zhivotnykh
Biol Amplification Syst Immunol — Biological Amplification Systems in Immunology
Biol & Agr Ind — Biological and Agricultural Index
Biol & Philos — Biology and Philosophy
Biol Appl Electron Spin Reson — Biological Applications of Electron Spin Resonance
Biol Artif Membr Desalin Water Proceed Study Week — Biological and Artificial Membranes and Desalination of Water. Proceedings of the Study Week
Biol Aspects Brain Tumors Proc Nikko Brain Tumor Conf — Biological Aspects of Brain Tumors. Proceedings. Nikko Brain Tumor Conference
Biol Asymmetry Handedness — Biological Asymmetry and Handedness
Biol B — Biological Bulletin
Biol Baltic Sea — Biology of the Baltic Sea
Biol Balt Morya — Biologiya Baltiiskogo Morya
Biol Basis Clin Eff Bleomycin — Biological Basis of Clinical Effect of Bleomycin
Biol Behav — Biology of Behaviour
Biol Biochem Nitrogen Fixation — Biology and Biochemistry of Nitrogen Fixation
Biol Blood Marrow Transplant — Biology of Blood and Marrow Transplantation
Biol Board Can Bull — Biological Board of Canada. Bulletin
Biol Brain Dysfunct — Biology of Brain Dysfunction
Biol Brain Dysfunction — Biology of Brain Dysfunction

Biol (Bratislava) — Biologia (Bratislava)
Biol Bul — Biological Bulletin
Biol Bull — Biological Bulletin
Biol Bull Acad Sci USSR — Biology Bulletin. Academy of Sciences of the USSR
Biol Bull Dep Biol Coll Sci Tunghai Univ — Biological Bulletin. Department of Biology. College of Science. Tunghai University
Biol Bull India — Biological Bulletin of India
Biol Bull Mar Biol Lab (Woods Hole) — Biological Bulletin. Marine Biological Laboratory (Woods Hole)
Biol Bull Poznan — Biological Bulletin of Poznan
Biol Bull Russ Acad Sci Transl of Izvest Akad Nauk Ser Biol — Biology Bulletin of the Russian Academy of Sciences. Translation of Izvestiya Akademii Nauk. Seriya Biologich
Biol Bull St Johns Univ Shanghai — Biological Bulletin of St. John's University (Shanghai)
Biol Bull Wash Dep Game — Biological Bulletin. Washington Department of Game
Biol Bull (Woods Hole) — Biological Bulletin (Woods Hole)
Biol Bundesanst Land Forstwirtsch Merkbl — Biologische Bundesanstalt fuer Land- und Forstwirtschaft Merkblatt
Biol Cancer 2nd Ed — Biology of Cancer. 2nd Edition
Biol Carbohydr — Biology of Carbohydrates
Biol Cel — Biologie Cellulaire
Biol Cell — Biologie Cellulaire
Biol Cell — Biology of the Cell
Biol Cephalopods Proc Symp — Biology of Cephalopods. Proceedings of a Symposium
Biol Chem — Biological Chemistry
Biol Chem Eucaryotic Cell Surf Proc Miami Winter Symp — Biology and Chemistry of Eucaryotic Cell Surfaces. Proceedings. Miami Winter Symposia
Biol Chem Hoppe-Seyler — Biological Chemistry Hoppe-Seyler
Biol Chem Zivocisne Vyroby Vet — Biologizace a Chemizace Zivocisne Vyroby-Veterinaria
Biol Clin Appl Interleukin 2 Proc Meet — Biology and Clinical Applications of Interleukin-2. Proceedings. Meeting
Biol Clin Aspects Fetus — Biological and Clinical Aspects of the Fetus
Biol Clin Basis Radiosensitivity Rep Proc Conf — Biological and Clinical Basis of Radiosensitivity. Report. Proceedings. Conference
Biol Clin Hematol — Biologia y Clinica Hematologica
Biol Comport — Biologie du Comportement
Biol Conf "Oholo" Annu Meet — Biological Conference "Oholo." Annual Meeting
Biol Conser — Biological Conservation
Biol Conserv — Biological Conservation
Biol Contemp — Biologia Contemporanea
Biol Control Soil-Borne Plant Pathog Int Symp — Biology and Control of Soil-Borne Plant Pathogens. International Symposium on Factors Determining the Behavior of Plant Pathogens in Soil
Biol Counc Ser Drug Action Mol Level — Biological Council Series. Drug Action at the Molecular Level
Biol Crist Cours Dev Senescence Colloq — Biologie de Cristallin au Cours de Developpement et de la Senescence. Colloque
Biol Crustacea — Biology of Crustacea
Biol Culturale — Biologia Culturale
Biol Cybern — Biological Cybernetics
Biol Cybernet — Biological Cybernetics
Biol Cybernetics — Biological Cybernetics
Biol Cytoplasmic Microtubules Pap Conf — Biology of Cytoplasmic Microtubules. Papers. Conference
BIOLD5 — Biologia
Biol Deistvie Bystrykh Neitronov — Biologicheskoe Deistvie Bystrykh Neitronov
Biol Deistvie Gig Znach Atmos Zagryaz — Biologicheskoe Deistvie i Gigienicheskoe Znachenie Atmosfernykh Zagryaznenii
Biol Deistvie Radiats — Biologicheskoe Deistvie Radiatsii
Biol Deistvie Ul'trafiolet Izluch Dokl Vses Soveshch — Biologicheskoe Deistvie Ul'trafioletovogo Izlucheniya. Doklady Vsesoyuznoi Soveshchanii
Biol Diag Brain Disord Proc Int Conf — Biological Diagnosis of Brain Disorders. Proceedings. International Conference
Biol Diatoms — Biology of Diatoms
Biol Dig — Biology Digest
Biol Ecol Med — Biologie-Ecologie Mediterraneenne
Biol Eff Asbestos Proc Work Conf — Biological Effects of Asbestos. Proceedings. Working Conference
Biol Eff Heavy Met — Biological Effects of Heavy Metals
Biol Eff Light Proc Symp — Biologic Effects of Light. Proceedings of a Symposium
Biol Eff Low Level Exposures Chem Radiat — Biological Effects of Low Level Exposures to Chemicals and Radiation
Biol Eff Neutron Irradiat Proc Symp — Biological Effects of Neutron Irradiation. Proceedings. Symposium. Effects of Neutron Irradiation upon Cell Function
Biol Eff Nonioniz Radiat Conf — Biological Effects of Nonionizing Radiation. Conference
Biol Environ Eff Low Level Radiat Proc Symp — Biological and Environmental Effects of Low Level Radiation. Proceedings of a Symposium on Biological Effects of Low Level Radiation Pertinent to Protection ofMan and His Environment
Biol Fac Filos Univ Sao Paulo Bot — Boletim de Faculdade de Filosofia, Ciencias, e Letras. Universidade de Sao Paulo. Botanica
Biol Fak Univ Kiril Metod Skopje God Zb — Bioloshki Fakultet na Univerzitetot Kiril i Metodij Skopje Godishen Zbornik
Biol Fertil Soils — Biology and Fertility of Soils
Biol Flora Br Isl — Biological Flora of the British Isles
Biol Flora Mosk Obl — Biologicheskaya Flora Moskovskoi Oblasti
Biol Fraternity — Biological Fraternity
Biol Gabonica — Biologia Gabonica
Biol Gallo-Hell — Biologia Gallo-Hellenica
Biol Gallo-Hellenica — Biologia Gallo-Hellenica
Biol Gastro — Biologie et Gastro-Enterologie

Biol Gastro-Enterol — Biologie et Gastro-Enterologie
Biol Gen — Biologia Generalis
Biol Glas — Bioloski Glasnik
Biol Handb — Biological Handbooks
Biol Heilkunst — Biologische Heilkunst
Biol Hum Aff — Biology and Human Affairs
Biol Hum Fetal Growth — Biology of Human Fetal Growth
Biol Hystricomorph Rodents Proc Symp — Biology of Hystricomorph Rodents. Proceedings of a Symposium
Biol Identif Comput Proc Meet — Biological Identification with Computers. Proceedings of a Meeting
Biol Implic Met Environ Proc Annu Hanford Life Sci Symp — Biological Implications of Metals in the Environment. Proceedings of the AnnualHanford Life Sciences Symposium
Biol Ind — Biologia et Industria
Biol Inspired Phys — Biologically Inspired Physics
Biol Int — Biology International
Biol Invest Wat Purif Pl Calcutta — Biological Investigation of the Water Purification Plants of Calcutta Corporation
Biol Issled Sev Vostoke Evr Chasti SSSR — Biologicheskie Issledovaniya na Severo Vostoke Evropeiskoi Chasti SSSR
Biol Izv Gos Biol Nauchno Issled Inst K A Timiryazeva — Biologicheskie Izvestiya. Izdavaemye pri Gosudarstvennom Biologicheskom Nauchno-Issledovatel'skom Institute im K. A. Timiryazeva
Biol J — Biological Journal
Biol Jaarb — Biologisch Jaarboek
Biol Jb — Biologisch Jaarboek
Biol J Linn — Biological Journal. Linnean Society
Biol J Linn Soc — Biological Journal. Linnean Society
Biol J Linn Soc Lond — Biological Journal. Linnean Society of London
Biol J Nara Women's Univ — Biological Journal. Nara Women's University
Biol J Okayama Univ — Biological Journal. Okayama University
Biol J Univ St Andrews — Biological Journal. Biological Society of the University of St. Andrews
Biol Khim — Biologiya i Khimiya
Biol Khim Geogr — Biologiya Khimiya Geografiya
Biol Koezl — Biologiai Koezlemenyek
Biol Koezlem — Biologiai Koezlemenyek
Biol Koezlem Pars Biol — Biologiai Koezlemenyek. Pars Biologica
Biol Kozl — Biologiai Koezlemenyek
Biol Lab Owens Coll Stud — Biological Laboratory of Owens College. Manchester University. Studies
Biol Lab Rabbit — Biology of the Laboratory Rabbit
Biol Lab Zhivotn — Biologiya Laboratornykh Zhivotnykh
Biol Lat — Biologica Latina
Biol Listu — Biologickych Listu
Biol Listy — Biologicke Listy
Biol Luchistykh Gribkov — Biologiya Luchistykh Gribkov
Biol Macromol — Biological Macromolecules
Biol Macromol Assem — Biological Macromolecules and Assemblies
Biol Mag — Biological Magazine/Okinawa Seibutsu Gekhai
Biol Mag Univ St Andrews — Biological Magazine. University of St. Andrews
Biol Mass S — Biological Mass Spectrometry
Biol Mass Spectrom — Biological Mass Spectrometry
Biol Medd K Dan Vidensk Selsk — Biologiske Meddelelser Kongelige Danske Videnskabernes Selskab
Biol Meddr — Biologiske Meddelelser
Biol Med Milano Ed Ital — Biologie Medical Milano. Edizione per l'Italia
Biol Med (Niteroi Brazil) — Biologia Medica (Niteroi, Brazil)
Biol Med (Paris) — Biologie Medicale (Paris)
Biol Mem — Biological Memoirs
Biol Memb — Biologicheskie Membrany
Biol Membr — Biological Membranes
Biol Membr — Biologicheskie Membrany
Biol Mikroorg Ikh Ispol'z Nar Khoz — Biologiya Mikroorganizmov i Ikh Ispol'zovanie v Narodnom Khozyaistve
Biol Monit — Biological Monitoring
Biol Monit Exposure Chem Met — Biological Monitoring of Exposure to Chemicals. Metals
Biol Monit Water Effluent Qual Symp — Biological Monitoring of Water and Effluent Quality. Symposium
Biol Moria — Biologiia Moria
Biol Morya — Biologiya Morya
Biol Morya (Vladivost) — Biologiya Morya (Vladivostok)
Biol Nauka Sel'sk Lesn Khoz — Biologicheskaya Nauka. Sel'skomu i Lesnomu Khozyatsteu
Biol Nauki — Biologicheskie Nauki
Biol Neonat — Biologia Neonatorum [*Later, Biology of Neonate*]
Biol Neonat — Biology of the Neonate
Biol Neonate — Biology of the Neonate
Biol Neonatorum — Biologia Neonatorum [*Later, Biology of the Neonate*]
Biol Nitrogen Fixation — Biology of Nitrogen Fixation
Biol Nocardiae — Biology of the Nocardiae
Biol Notes — Biological Notes. Illinois Natural History Survey
Biol Notes Ill Nat Hist Surv — Biological Notes. Illinois Natural History Survey
Biol Notes Nat Hist Surv Div St Ill — Biological Notes. Natural History Survey Division. State of Illinois
Biol Oceanic Pac Proc Annu Biol Colloq — Biology of the Oceanic Pacific. Proceedings. Annual Biology Colloquium
Biol Oceanogr — Biological Oceanography
Biologia Bratisl — Biologia. Casopis Slovenskej Akademie vied Bratislava
Biologia Pl — Biologia Plantarum
Biologica Lat — Biologica Latina
Biol Osn Bor'by Obrastaniem — Biologicheskie Osnovy Bor'by s Obrastaniem

Biol Osn Oroshaemogo Zemled Mater Vses Soveshch — Biologicheskie Osnovy Oroshaemogo Zemledeliya. Materialy Vsesoyuznogo Soveshchaniya "Biologicheskie Osnovy Oroshaemogo Zemledeliya"

Biol Osn Povysh Prod Skh Rast — Biologicheskie Osnovy Povysheniya Produktivnosti Sel'skokhozyaistvennykh Rastenii

Biol Pap Univ Alaska — Biological Papers. University of Alaska

Biol Pap Univ Alaska Spec Rep — Biological Papers. University of Alaska. Special Report

Biol Pap Univ Minn — Biological Papers. University of Minnesota

Biol Peau Cours Francophone Annu — Biologie de la Peau. Cours Francophone Annuel

Biol Penguins — Biology of Penguins

Biol Pesq — Biologia Pesquera

Biol Pharmac — Biological Pharmacology

Biol Pharm Bull — Biological and Pharmaceutical Bulletin

Biol Plant — Biologia Plantarum

Biol Plant (Prague) — Biologia Plantarum (Prague)

Biol Povrezhdeniya Stroit Prom Mater — Biologicheskie Povrezhdeniya Stroitel'nykh i Promyshlennykh Materialov

Biol Pr — Biologicke Prace

Biol Prace Slov Akad Vied — Biologicke Prace, Slovenskej Akademie Vied

Biol Probl Sev Tezisy Dokl Simp — Biologicheskie Problemy Severa Tezisy Dokladov Simpozium

Biol Prod Freeze Drying Formulation Proc Symp — Biological Product Freeze-Drying and Formulation. Proceedings. Symposium

Biol Prod Protsessy Basseine Volgi — Biologicheskie Produktsionnye Protsessy v Basseine Volgi

Biol Prod Yuzhn Morei — Biologicheskaya Produktivnost Yuzhnykh Morei

Biol Prop Mamm Surf Membr Symp — Biological Properties. Mammalian Surface Membrane. Symposium

Biol Protsessy Miner Obmen Pochvakh Kol'sk Poluostrova — Biologicheskie Protsessy i Mineral'nyi Obmen v Pochvakh Kol'skogo Poluostrova

Biol Psych Bul — Biological Psychology Bulletin

Biol Psychi — Biological Psychiatry

Biol Psychiat — Biological Psychiatry

Biol Psychiatry — Biological Psychiatry

Biol Psychol — Biological Psychology

Biol Psychol Bull (Okla City) — Biological Psychology Bulletin (Oklahoma City)

Biol R — Biological Reviews

Biol Rdsch — Biologische Rundschau

Biol React Intermed Proc Int Conf — Biological Reactive Intermediates, Formation Toxicity, and Inactivation. Proceedings of an International Conference on Active Intermediates, Formation Toxicity, and Inactivation

Biol Rec Cave Res Grp Gt Br — Biological Records. Cave Research Group of Great Britain

Biol Regul Dev — Biological Regulation and Development

Biol Rep Dep Fish St Wash — Biological Reports. Department of Fisheries. State of Washington

Biol Reprod — Biology of Reproduction

Biol Reprod Kletok — Biologiya Reprodaksii Kletok

Biol Reprod Suppl — Biology of Reproduction. Supplement

Biol Res — Biological Research

Biol Res Nurs — Biological Research For Nursing

Biol Resour Nat Cond Mong People's Repub — Biological Resources and Natural Conditions. Mongolian People's Republic

Biol Res Pregnancy Perinatol — Biological Research in Pregnancy and Perinatology

Biol Res Rep Univ Jyvaeskylae — Biological Research Reports. University of Jyvaeskylae

Biol Resur Bodoemov Mold — Biologicheskie Resursy Bodoemov Moldavii

Biol Resur Prir Usloviya Mong Nar Resp — Biologicheskie Resursy i Prirodnye Usloviya Mongol'skoi Narodnoi Respubliki

Biol Rev — Biological Reviews. Cambridge Philosophical Society

Biol Rev Camb Philos Soc — Biological Reviews. Cambridge Philosophical Society

Biol Rev Cambridge Phil Soc — Biological Reviews. Cambridge Philosophical Society

Biol Rev City Coll NY — Biological Review. City College of New York

Biol Rev Cy Coll NY — Biological Review of the City College. New York

Biol Rhythm Res — Biological Rhythm Research

Biol Rhythms Neuroendocr Act — Biological Rhythms in Neuroendocrine Activity

Biol Role Porphyrins Relat Struct Pap Conf — Biological Role of Porphyrins and Related Structures. Papers. Conference

Biol Roles Sialic Acid — Biological Roles of Sialic Acid

Biol Rol Mikroelem Ikh Primen Sel'sk Khoz Med — Biologicheskaya Rol Mikroelementov i Ikh Primenenie v Sel'skom Khozyaistve i Meditsine

Biol Rs — Biological Reviews

Biol Rundsch — Biologische Rundschau

Biol Rundschau — Biologische Rundschau

Biol Sborn Slov Akad Vied — Biologicky Sbornik. Slovenskej Akademie Vied a Umeni

Biol Schizophr Proc Int Symp Tokyo Inst Psychiatry — Biology of Schizophrenia. Proceedings of the International Symposium of the Tokyo Institute of Psychiatry

Biol Sci — Biological Science

Biol Sci Bull Univ Arizona — Biological Science Bulletin. University of Arizona

Biol Sci Curric Study Bull — Biological Sciences Curriculum Study. Bulletin

Biol Sci Curriculum Study Bull — Biological Sciences Curriculum Study. Bulletin

Biol Sci Ser Okla Agric Mech Coll — Biological Science Series. Oklahoma Agricultural and Mechanical College

Biol Sci (Tokyo) — Biological Science (Tokyo)

Biol Seal Proc Symp — Biology of the Seal. Proceedings of the Symposium

Biol Sel Mikroorg — Biologiya i Selektsiya Mikroorganizmov

Biol Ser Cath Univ Am — Biological Series. Catholic University of America

Biol Ser Mich St Univ Agric Mus — Biological Series. Michigan State University of Agriculture Museum

Biol Ser Okla Agric Mech Coll — Biological Series. Oklahoma Agricultural and Mechanical College

Biol Shk — Biologiya Shkole

Biol Signals — Biological Signals

Biol Signals Proc Symp — Biological Signals. Proceedings of a Symposium

Biol Signals Recept — Biological Signals and Receptors

Biol Skr — Biologiske Skrifter

Biol Skr K Dan Vidensk Selsk — Biologiske Skrifter. Kongelige Dansk Videnskabernes Selskab

Biol Soc — Biology and Society

Biol Soc Nev Mem — Biological Society of Nevada. Memoirs

Biol Soc Nev Occas Pap — Biological Society of Nevada. Occasional Papers

Biol Soc Pak Monogr — Biological Society of Pakistan. Monograph

Biol Soc Washington Proc — Biological Society of Washington. Proceedings

Biol Soc Wash Proc — Biological Society of Washington. Proceedings

Biol Sol — Biologie du Sol. Bulletin International d'Informations

Biol Sol Microbiol — Biologie du Sol. Microbiologie

Biol Struct Morphog — Biological Structures and Morphogenesis

Biol Stud Catholic Univ Amer — Biological Studies. Catholic University of America

Biol Stud Cath Univ Am — Biological Studies. Catholic University of America

Biol Suppl Cave Res Grp Gt Br — Biological Supplement. Cave Research Group of Great Britain

Biol Svoistva Khim Soedin — Biologicheskie Svoistva Khimicheskikh Soedinenii

Biol Symp — Biological Symposia

Biol Szkole — Biologia w Szkole

Biol Trab Inst Biol "Juan Noe" Fac Med Univ Chile — Biologica. Trabajos. Instituto de Biologia "Juan Noe." Facultad de Medicina de la Universidad de Chile

Biol Trace Elem Res — Biological Trace Element Research

Biol Unserer Zeit — Biologie in Unserer Zeit

Biol Uterus — Biology of the Uterus

Biol Vestn — Bioloski Vestnik

Biol Vnutr Vod — Biologiya Vnutrennykh Vod

Biol Vnutr Vod Inf Byull — Biologiya Vnutrennykh Vod. Informatsionnyi Byulleten

Biol Vses Inst Eksp Vet — Biologicheskii i Vsesoyuzni Institut Eksperimental'noi Veterinarii

Biol Wastes — Biological Wastes

Biol World Res Ser — Biology of World Resources Series

Biolyumin Tikhom Okeane Mater Simp Tikhookean Nauchn Kongr — Biolyuminestsentsiya v Tikhom Okeane. Materialy SimpoziumaTikhookeanskogo Nauchnogo Kongressa

Biol Zakl Pol'nohospod — Biologike Zaklad Pol'nohospodarstvo

Biol Zbirn Lvov — Biologichnii Zbirnik. L'vivs'kii Derzhavnii Universitet. L'vov

Biol Zbl — Biologisches Zentralblatt

Biol Zb L'viv Derzh Univ — Biologichnii Zbirnik. L'vivs'kii Derzhaenii Universitet

Biol Zentralbl — Biologisches Zentralblatt

Biol Zh — Biologicheskii Zhurnal

Biol Zh Arm — Biologicheskii Zhurnal Armenii

Biol Zh Armenii — Biologicheskii Zhurnal Armenii

Biol Zhur — Biologicheskii Zhurnal

Biol Zh Zool Otd Imp Obshch Lyub Estest — Biologicheskii Zhurnal, Izdavaemyi Pri Zoologicheskom Otdielenii Imperatprskago Obshchestva Lyubitelei Estestvoznaniya, Antropologii i Etnografii

Biom — Biometrics

Biom — Biometrika

BIOMA — Biometrics

Biomass Bioenergy — Biomass and Bioenergy

Biomass Dig — Biomass Digest

Biomass Energy Environ Agric Ind Proc Eur Biomass Conf — Biomass for Energy, Environment, Agriculture, and Industry. Proceedings of the European Biomass Conference

Biomass Energy Ind Environ EC Conf — Biomass for Energy, Industry, and Environment. E.C. Conference

Biomass Energy Inst Newsl — Biomass Energy Institute. Newsletter

Biomass Pyrolysis Liq Upgrading Util — Biomass Pyrolysis Liquids Upgrading and Utilisation

Biomater — Biomaterials

Biomater Artif Cells Artif Organs — Biomaterials, Artificial Cells, and Artificial Organs

Biomater Artif Cells Immobilization Biotechnol — Biomaterials, Artificial Cells, and Immobilization Biotechnology

Biomater Med Dev Artif Organs — Biomaterials, Medical Devices, and Artificial Organs

Biomater Med Devices and Artif Organs — Biomaterials, Medical Devices, and Artificial Organs

Biomater Med Devices Artif Organs — Biomaterials, Medical Devices, and Artificial Organs

Bio-Math — Bio-Mathematics

Biomat Med — Biomaterials, Medical Devices, and Artificial Organs

Biom Bull — Biometrae Bulletin

Biom Chem Pharm Ind — Biometrie in der Chemisch-Pharmazeutischen Industrie

Biomech Symp Jt Appl Mech Fluids Eng Bioeng Conf — Biomechanics Symposium Presented at the Joint Applied Mechanics Fluids Engineering and Bioengineering Conference

Biomech Transp Processes — Biomechanical Transport Processes

Biomed Appl — Biomedical Applications

Biomed Appl Biotechnol — Biomedical Applications of Biotechnology

Biomed Appl Gas Chromatogr — Biomedical Applications of Gas Chromatography

Biomed Appl Immobilized Enzymes Proteins — Biomedical Applications of Immobilized Enzymes and Proteins

Biomed Appln Polym — Biomedical Applications of Polymers

Biomed Biochim Acta — Biomedica Biochimica Acta

Biomed Bull — Biomedical Bulletin

Biomed Chro — Biomedical Chromatography

Biomed Chromatogr — Biomedical Chromatography

Biomed Clin Aspects Coenzyme Q — Biomedical and Clinical Aspects of Coenzyme Q
Biomed Clin Aspects Coenzyme Q Proc Int Symp — Biomedical and Clinical Aspects of Coenzyme Q. Proceedings of the InternationalSymposium
Biomed Commun — Biomedical Communications
Biomed Elect — Biomedical Electronics
Biomed Eng — Biomedical Engineering
Biomed Eng Appl Basis Commun — Biomedical Engineering Applications Basis Communications
Biomed Eng (Berl) — Biomedical Engineering (Berlin)
Biomed Eng (Engl Transl) — Biomedical Engineering (English Translation)
Biomed Eng (Engl Transl Med Tekh) — Biomedical Engineering (English Translation of Meditsinskaya Tekhnika)
Biomed Eng (Lond) — Biomedical Engineering (London)
Biomed Engng Curr Aware Notif — Biomedical Engineering Current Awareness Notification
Biomed Eng (NY) — Biomedical Engineering (New York)
Bio Med Eng (Tokyo) — Bio-Medical Engineering (Tokyo)
Biomed Eng (USSR) — Biomedical Engineering (USSR)
Biomed Environ Mass Spectrom — Biomedical and Environmental Mass Spectrometry
Biomed Environ Sci — Biomedical and Environmental Sciences
Biomed Expr — Biomedicine Express
Biomed Express (Paris) — Biomedicine Express (Paris)
Biomed Health Res — Biomedical and Health Research
BIOMEDICAL LETT — BIOMEDICAL LETTERS
Bio Med Instrum — Bio Medical Instrumentation
Biomed Instrum Technol — Biomedical Instrumentation and Technology
Biomed Lab Tech Rep US Army Med Res Dev Command — Biomedical Laboratory Technical Report. United States Army Medical Research andDevelopment Command
Biomed Lett — Biomedical Letters
Biomed Mass — Biomedical Mass Spectrometry
Biomed Mass Spectrom — Biomedical Mass Spectrometry
Bio Med Mater Eng — Bio-Medical Materials and Engineering
Biomed Mater Eng — Bio-Medical Materials and Engineering
Biomed Mater Symp — Biomedical Materials Symposium
Biomed Pept Proteins Nucleic Acids — Biomedical Peptides, Proteins, and Nucleic Acids
Biomed Pharmacother — Biomedicine and Pharmacotherapy
Biomed Physiol Vitam B12 Proc Int Symp — Biomedicine and Physiology of Vitamin B12. Proceedings. International Symposium
Bio Med Preview — Bio-Medical Preview. National Society for Medical Research
Bio-Med Purv — Bio-Medical Purview
Bio-Med Rep 406 Med Lab — Bio-Medical Reports of the 406 Medical Laboratory
Biomed Res — Biomedical Research
Biomed Res Appl Scanning Electron Micros — Biomedical Research Applications of Scanning Electron Microscopy
Biomed Res Trace Elem — Biomedical Research on Trace Elements
Bio Med Rev — Bio Medical Reviews
Biomed Sci Instrum — Biomedical Sciences Instrumentation
Biomed Sci London — Biomedical Science (London)
Biomed Sci (Tokyo) — Biomedical Sciences (Tokyo)
Biomed Tech — Biomedizinische Technik
Biomed Tech (Berlin) — Biomedizinische Technik (Berlin)
Biomed Tech Biomed Eng — Biomedizinische Technik. Biomedical Engineering
Biomed Tech Rep Beckman Instrum Inc — Biomedical Technical Report. Beckman Instruments, Inc.
Biomed Thermol Proc Int Symp — Biomedical Thermology. Proceedings. International Symposium
Biomed Ther (Tokyo) — Biomedicine and Therapeutics (Tokyo)
Biomembr Lipids Proteins Recept Proc NATO Adv Study Inst — Biomembranes, Lipids, Proteins, and Receptors. Proceedings of a NATO Advanced Study Institute
Biometeorol Czlowieka — Biometeorologia Czlowieka
Biometeorol Res Cent (Leiden) Monogr Ser — Biometeorological Research Centre (Leiden). Monograph Series
Biomet-Praximet — Biometrie-Praximetrie
Biometrical J — Biometrical Journal
Biometrie Hum — Biometrie Humaine
Biometr-Praxim — Biometrie-Praximetrie
Biometr Z — Biometrische Zeitschrift
Biom Hum — Biometrie Humaine
Biom J — Biometrical Journal
Biom J — Biometrical Journal. Journal of Mathematical Methods of Biosciences
Biomol Eng — Biomolecular Engineering
Biom Z — Biometrische Zeitschrift
Biom Z — Biometrische Zeitschrift. Zeitschrift fuer Mathematische Methoden in den Biowissenschaften
Biom Zeit — Biometrische Zeitschrift
Bionika Mat Model Biol — Bionika i Matematicheskoe Modelirovanie v Biologii
Bioorg Chem — Bioorganic Chemistry
Bioorg Chem Front — Bioorganic Chemistry Frontiers
Bioorg Khim — Bioorganicheskaya Khimiya
Bioorg Mar Chem — Bioorganic Marine Chemistry
Bioorg Med Chem — Bioorganic and Medicinal Chemistry
Bioorg Med Chem Lett — Bioorganic and Medicinal Chemistry Letters
Bio Oriented Technol Res Adv Inst Techno News — Bio-oriented Technology Research Advancement Instution Techno News
BIOPA — Biophysics
BIOPAE — Biophysics
BIOPEI — Biology and Philosophy
Biopharm Drug Dispos — Biopharmaceutics and Drug Disposition
Biopharm Eur — Biopharm Europe
BioPharm Manuf — BioPharm Manufacturing

Biophys — Biophysics
Biophys Centralbl — Biophysikalisches Centralblatt
Biophys Ch — Biophysical Chemistry
Biophys Chem — Biophysical Chemistry
Biophysics (Engl Transl Biofizika) — Biophysics (English Translation of Biofizika)
Biophys J — Biophysical Journal
Biophys J Suppl — Biophysical Journal. Supplement
Biophys Membr Transp — Biophysics of Membrane Transport. School Proceedings. School onBiophysics of Membrane Transport
Biophys Soc Abstr Ann Meetings — Biophysical Society Abstracts. Annual Meetings
Biophys Soc Annu Meet Abstr — Biophysical Society. Annual Meeting. Abstracts
Biophys Soc Symp — Biophysical Society. Symposium
Biophys Str — Biophysics of Structure and Mechanism
Biophys Struct Mech — Biophysics of Structure and Mechanism
BIOP Newsl — BIOP [*Board of International Organizations and Programs*] Newsletter
Biopolim Kletka — Biopolimery i Kletka
Biopolym Cell — Biopolymers and Cell
Biopolym Symp — Biopolymers Symposia
Bioprocess Eng — Bioprocess Engineering
Bioprocess Technol — Bioprocess Technology
Bioquim Clin — Bioquimica Clinica
Bioquim Clini — Bioquimica Clinica
BIOQUIP — DECHEMA [*Deutshe Gesellschaft fuer Chemisches Apparatenesen, Chemische Technik, und Biotechnologie e V*] Biotechnology Equipment Suppliers
BIOr — Bibliotheca Orientalis
BIORA — Biochemistry
Biorem J — Bioremediation Journal
BioRes Index — BioResearch Index [*Later, BA/RRM*]
Bioresour Technol — Bioresource Technology
Biores Titles — Bioresearch Titles
Biorheol Suppl — Biorheology. Supplement
BIORS — Bedford Institute of Oceanography. Report Series
BIOS — British Institute for Organ Studies Journal
Bios Boissons Cond — Bios Boissons Conditionnement
BioSci — BioScience
BioSci Am Inst Biol Sci — BioScience. American Institute of Biological Sciences
Biosci Commun — Biosciences Communications
Bioscience & Ind — Bioscience and Industry
Biosci Microflora — Bioscience and Microflora
Biosci Rep — Bioscience Reports
Biosci Rep Abo Akad — Bioscience Report. Abo Akademi
BIOSE — Bio-Sciences
Biosens Bioelectron — Biosensors and Bioelectronics
Biosens Bioelectronics — Biosensors and Bioelectronics
Biosfera Chel Mater Vses Simp — Biosfera i Chelovek Materialy Vsesoyuznogo Simpoziuma
Bios Genoa — Bios. Rivista di Biologia Sperimentale e Generale (Genoa)
Biosint Sostoyanie Khlorofillov Rast — Biosintez i Sostoyanie Khlorofillov v Rastenii
Biosources Dig — Biosources Digest
Bios (Unadilla NY) — Bios (Unadilla, New York)
BIOSW — BIOS [*Baffin Island Oil Spill Project*] Working Report
Biosyn — Biosynthesis
Biosynth Antibiot — Biosynthesis of Antibiotics
Biosynth Biodegrad Cellul — Biosynthesis and Biodegradation of Cellulose
Biosynth Prod Cancer Chemother — Biosynthetic Products for Cancer Chemotherapy
Bio Syst — Bio Systems
Biota — Biota. Instituto Salesiano Pablo Albera
Biotech — Biotechnology International. Trends and Perspectives
Biotech Bio — Biotechnology and Bioengineering
Biotech Bioeng — Biotechnology and Bioengineering
BioTechForum Adv Mol Genet — BioTechForum. Advances in Molecular Genetics
Biotech His — Biotechnic and Histochemistry
Biotech Histochem — Biotechnic and Histochemistry
Biotechnol — Bio/Technology. The International Monthly for Industrial Biology
Biotechnol Adv — Biotechnology Advances
Biotechnol Agric — Biotechnology in Agriculture
Biotechnol Agric Chem — Biotechnology in Agricultural Chemistry
Biotechnol Agric For — Biotechnology in Agriculture and Forestry
Biotechnol Agric Ser — Biotechnology in Agriculture Series
Biotechnol Agron Soc Environ — Biotechnologie, Agronomie, Societe et Environnement
Biotechnol Annu Rev — Biotechnology Annual Review
Biotechnol Appl Biochem — Biotechnology and Applied Biochemistry
Biotechnol Bioeng — Biotechnology and Bioengineering
Biotechnol Bioeng Symp — Biotechnology and Bioengineering. Symposium
Biotechnol Bioind — Biotechnology and Bioindustry
Biotechnol Biotechnol Equip — Biotechnology and Biotechnological Equipment
Biotechnol Blood — Biotechnology of Blood
Biotechnol Bus News — Biotechnology Business News
Biotechnol Curr Prog — Biotechnology. Current Progress
Biotechnol Educ — Biotechnology Education
Biotechnol Genet Eng Rev — Biotechnology and Genetic Engineering Reviews
Biotechnol Handb — Biotechnology Handbooks
Biotechnol Law Rep — Biotechnology Law Report
Biotechnol Lett — Biotechnology Letters
Biotechnol Monogr — Biotechnology Monographs
Biotechnol News — Biotechnology News
Biotechnol Nutr Proc Int Symp — Biotechnology and Nutrition. Proceedings. International Symposium

Biotechnol Plant Prot — Biotechnology and Plant Protection. Viral Pathogenesis and Disease Resistance. Proceedings of the International Symposium
Biotechnol Polym Proc Am Chem Soc Symp Polym Biotechnol — Biotechnology and Polymers. Proceedings. American Chemical Society Symposium on Polymers from Biotechnology
Biotechnol Prog — Biotechnology Progress
Biotechnol Res Ser — Biotechnology Research Series
Biotechnol Ser — Biotechnology Series
Biotechnol Tech — Biotechnology Techniques
Biotechnol Ther — Biotechnology Therapeutics
Biotechn Pat Dig — Biotechnology Patent Digest
Biotech Pat News — Biotech Patent News
Biotecnol Apl — Biotecnologia Aplicada
Biotekhnol Biotekh — Biotekhnologiya i Biotekhnika
Biotekhnol Khim — Biotekhnologiya i Khimiya
Biotek Lab Tied (Valt Tek Tutkimuskeskus) — Biotekniikan Laboratorio, Tiedonanto (Valtion TeknillinenTutkimuskeskus)
Biotelemetr — Biotelemetry [Later, Biotelemetry and Patient Monitoring]
Biotelem Patient Monit — Biotelemetry and Patient Monitoring
Biotest Bull — Biotest Bulletin
Biother Today — Biotherapy Today
Bioticheskie Komponenty Nazemn Ekosistem Tyan Shanya — Bioticheskie Komponenty Nazemnykh Ekosistem Tyan Shanya
Biotrop Bull — Biotrop Bulletin
Biotypologie Bul Soc Typ — Biotypologie. Bulletin. Societe de Typologie
BIOVD — Biovigyanam
BIP — Best's Review. Property/Casualty Insurance Edition
BIPA — Bulletin. Institut Royal du Patrimoine Artistique
BIPAA — Bulletin. Institut Pasteur
BIPADB — Instituto de Pesquisas Agronomicas. Boletim Tecnico
B I Pasteur — Bulletin. Institut Pasteur
BIPCB — Biological Psychiatry
BIPED — Buletinul. Institutului Politehnic "Gheorghe Gheorghiu-Dej" Bucuresti. Seria Electrotehnica
BIPG — Bulletin. Institut de Phonetique de Grenoble
BIPGA — Buletinul. Institutului de Petrol, Gaze, si Geologie
BIPHDW — Bibliotheca Phycologica
BIPHEX — Biomedicine and Pharmacotherapy
BIPID — Bits and Pieces
BIPMA — Biopolymers
BIPNA — Bibliotheca Phonetica
Bipolar Disord — Bipolar Disorders
BIPSA — Books in Print South Africa
BIR — Banque d'Informations sur les Recherches
BiR — Biblical Research
BIRA — Boletin. Instituto Riva Agueero
B Iran Inst — Bulletin. Iranian Institute
Birbal Sahni Inst Palaeobot Birbal Sahni Mem Lect — Birbal Sahni Institute of Palaeobotany. Birbal Sahni Memorial Lecture
Birbal Sahni Inst Palaeobot Spec Publ — Birbal Sahni Institute of Palaeobotany. Special Publication
BIR Bull — BIR [British Institute of Radiology] Bulletin
BIRD — Base d'Information Robert Debre
BIRD — Business Information Desk Reference
Bird-Band — Bird-Banding
Bird Behav — Bird Behaviour
Bird Control Semin Proc — Bird Control Seminar. Proceedings
Bird E — Bird Effort
Bird Keeping — Bird Keeping in Australia
Bird L — Bird Lore
BIREB — Biology of Reproduction
BiRes — Biblical Research
BIRESUL — Bulletin. Institut de Recherches Economiques et Sociales. Universite de Louvain
Birla Archaeol Cult Res Inst Res Bull — Birla Archaeological and Cultural Research Institute. Research Bulletin
BIRMA — Birmingham University. Chemical Engineer
Birm AST — Transactions. Birmingham and Warwickshire Archaeological Society
Birmingham Archaeol Soc Transcr — Birmingham Archaeological Society Transcripts
Birmingham Hist J — Birmingham Historical Journal
Birmingham Ph Soc Pr — Birmingham [England] Philosophical Society. Proceedings
Birmingham Univ Chem Eng — Birmingham University. Chemical Engineer
Birmingham Univ Hist — Birmingham University. Historical Journal
Birm Ph S P — Proceedings of the Birmingham Philosophical Society
BIRODT — Butterworths International Medical Reviews. Otolaryngology
BIRPA — Bulletin. Institut Royal du Patrimoine Artistique
BIRS — Baptist Information Retrieval System
BIRS — British Institute of Recorded Sound. Bulletin
BIRSC — Bulletin. Institut de Recherches Scientifiques au Congo
BIRT — Bulletin d'Information. Institut de Recherche et d'Histoire des Textes
Birth Control R — Birth Control Review
Birth Defects — Birth Defects. Original Article Series
Birth Defects Orig Artic Ser — Birth Defects. Original Article Series
Birth Family J — Birth and the Family Journal
Birth Fam J — Birth and the Family Journal
BIRUA — Biologische Rundschau
BIS — Books in Series
BIS — Browning Institute. Studies
BIS — Bulletin. Institute for the Study of the USSR
BIS — Bulletin of Indonesian Economic Studies
BIS — Business Insurance
BISA — Bibliographic Information on Southeast Asia
BISchk — Buletin i Institutit te Shkencave

BIS Conf Rep — BIS [Brain Information Service] Conference Report
BISD — Bowker's International Serials Database
BISDP — Boletin Informativo. Seminario de Derecho Politico
BISDSL — Britische und Irische Studien zur Deutschen Sprache und Literatur
Biserica Ortod Romana — Biserica Ortodoxa Romana
Biser Ortdx Roman — Biserica Ortodoxa Romana
BISGM — Boletin Informativo. Secretaria General del Movimiento
Bishop Mus Occas Pap — Bishop Museum Occasional Papers
BISI — Bollettino. Istituto Storico Italiano
BISIAM — Bollettino. Istituto Storico Italiano e Archivio Muratoriano
BISIMAM — Bollettino. Istituto Storico Italiano per il Medioevo e Archivio Muratoriano
BISLDP — Sociedad Mexicana de Lepidopterologia. Boletin Informativo
BISLM — Bollettino. Istituto di Storia e di Arte del Lazio Meridionale
Bismuth Inst Bull (Brussels) — Bismuth Institute. Bulletin (Brussels)
BISN — Bulletin de l'Institut Royal de Sciences Naturelles de Belgique
BISNA — BioScience
BISO — Bulletin. Institut pour l'Etude de l'Europe Sud-Orientale
BISRA/BS — Belizean Studies. Belizean Institute of Social Research and Action and St. John's College
BISRA Open Rep — BISRA [British Iron and Steel Research Association] Open Report
BISRD — Boletim Informativo. Sociedade Brasileira de Radiologia
BISS — Bibliographie Internationale des Sciences Sociales
BISS — Boletin. Institucion Sancho el Sabio
BISSA — Bulletin of the International Social Security Association
B Ist C — Bollettino. Istituto di Correspondenza Archeologica
B Ist Rest — Bollettino. Istituto Centrale del Restauro
B Ist Sier — Bollettino. Istituto Sieroterapico Milanese
BISV — Bollettino. Istituto di Storia della Societa e dello Stato Veneziano
BISWA — Biuletyn. Instytuta Spawalnictwa. Gliwice
Bit — Bulletin Italien
BITAA — Bitumen, Teere, Asphalte, Peche
BItal — Bulletin Italien
B Ital Biol — Bollettino. Societa Italiana di Biologia Sperimentale
BITC — Bulletin. Institute of Traditional Cultures
BiTerS — Bible et Terre Sainte (Nouvelle Serie)
BITJA — Journal. Birla Institute of Technology and Science
Bitki Koruma Buelt — Bitki Koruma Bulteni
Bitki Koruma Bul — Bitki Koruma Bulteni
Bitki Koruma Bul Ek Yayin — Bitki Koruma Bulteni. Ek Yayin
Bitki Koruma Bul Plant Prot Bull — Bitki Koruma Bulteni. Plant Protection Bulletin
Bit Nord Tidskr Informationsbehandl — Bit Nordisk Tidskrift fuer Informationsbehandling
BITOA — Bild und Ton
BiTod — Bible Today
BiTr — Bible Translator
BiTrans — Bible Translator
BITUA — Bitumen
Bitum Coal Res Inc Tech Rep — Bituminous Coal Research, Incorporated. Technical Report
Bitumen Teere Asphalte Peche — Bitumen, Teere, Asphalte, Peche, und Verwandte Stoffe
Bitum Low Medium Level Radioact Wastes Proc Semin — Bituminization of Low and Medium Level Radioactive Wastes. Proceedings of a Seminar
BITYA — Byulleten' Informatsionnogo Tsentral'nogo po Yadernym Dannym
BIUGA — Biuletyn. Instytutu Geologicznego
Biul Bib Jagiellon — Biuletyn Biblioteki Jagiellonskiej
Biul Cent Inst Ochr Pr — Biuletyn Centralnogo Instytutu Ochrony Pracy
Biul Cent Lab Technol Przetworstwa Przechow Zboz Warszawie — Biuletyn Centralnego Laboratorium Technologii Przetworstwa iPrzechowalnictwa Zboz w Warszawie
Biul Cent Stacji Oceny Pasz Inst Zootech Pol — Biuletyn Centralnej Stacji Oceny Pasz. Instytut Zootechniki w Polsce
Biul Geol — Biuletyn Geologiczny
Biul Gl Bot Sada (Leningrad) — Biulleten Glavnogo Botanicheskogo Sada (Leningrad)
Biul Gl Inst Gorn — Biuletyn Glownego Instytutu Gornictwa
Biul Gl Inst Wlok — Biuletyn Glownego Instytutu Wlokiennictwa
Biul Gos Nikitsk Bot Sad — Biulleten Gosudarstvennyi Nikitskii Botanicheskii Sad
Biul Hist Sztuki — Biuletyn Historii Sztuki
Biul Hist Sztuki & Kult — Biuletyn Historii Sztuki i Kultury
Biul IB — Biuletyn. Instytutu Bibliograficznego
Biul IGS — Biuletyn. Instytutu Gospodarstwa Spolecznego
Biul Inf Barwniki Srodki Pomocnicze — Biuletyn Informacyjny. Barwniki i Srodki Pomocnicze
Biul Inf Cent Lab Przem Tytoniowego — Biuletyn Informacyjny. Centralnego Laboratorium Przemyslu Tytoniowego
Biul Inf Geol Geofiz Ekon Tech Prac Geol — Biuletyn Informacyjny. Geologia. Geofizyka oraz Ekonomika i Technika Prac Geologicznych
Biul Inf Gl Inst Elektrotech — Biuletyn Informacyjny. Glowny Instytut Elektrotechniki
Biul Inf Inst Badaw Proj Przem Farb Lakierow — Biuletyn Informacyjny. Instytut Badawezo Projektowy Przemyslu Farb i Lakierow
Biul Inf Inst Farb Lakierow — Biuletyn Informacyjny. Instytut Farb i Lakierow
Biul Inf Inst Lekow — Biuletyn Informacyjny. Instytutu Lekow
Biul Inf Inst Mater Ogniotrwalych — Biuletyn Informacyjny. Instytutu Materialow Ogniotrwalych
Biul Inf Inst Przem Tworzyw Farb — Biuletyn Informacyjny. Instytut Przemyslu Tworzyw i Farb
Biul Inf Inst Przem Wiazacych Mater Budow (Krakow) — Biuletyn Informacyjny. Instytut Przemyslu Wiazacych Materialow Budowlanych (Krakow)
Biul Inf Inst Tech Budow — Biuletyn Informacyjny. Instytut Techniki Budowlanej
Biul Inf Inst Tech Cieplnej — Biuletyn Informacyjny Instytutu Techniki Cieplnej

Biul Inf Inst Zbozowego Warszawie — Biuletyn Informacyjny. Instytutu Zbozowego w Warszawie

Biul Inf Kom Krystalogr PAN — Biuletyn Informacyjny. Komisji Krystalografii PAN

Biul Inf Mater Ogniotrwalych — Biuletyn Informacyjny. Materialow Ogniotrwalych

Biul Inf Nauk Tech Inst Tech Budow — Biuletyn Informacyjny. Naukowo Technicznej. Instytut Techniki Budowlanej

Biul Inform — Biuletyn Informacyjny

Biul Inform Inst Zboz Warszawie — Biuletyn Informacyjny. Instytutu Zbozowego w Warszawie

Biul Inf Osr Badaw Rozwoj Przem Barwnikow — Biuletyn Informacyjny. Osrodek Badawczo-Rozwojowy Przemyslu Barwnikow

Biul Inf Panst Inst Elektrotech — Biuletyn Informacyjny. Panstwowy Instytut Elektrotechniczny

Biul Inf Przem Farb Lakierow — Biuletyn Informacyjny Przemyslu Farb i Lakierow

Biul Inst Energ — Biuletyn. Instytutu Energetyki

Biul Inst Energ (Warsaw) — Biuletyn. Instytutu Energetyki (Warsaw)

Biul Inst Genet Hodowli Zwierzat Pol Akad Nauk — Biuletyn. Instytutu Genetyki i Hodowli Zwierzat Polskiej Akademii Nauk

Biul Inst Geol (Warsaw) — Biuletyn. Instytut Geologiczny (Warsaw)

Biul Inst Hodowii Rosl — Biuletyn Instytutu Hodowii i Aklimatyzacji Roslin

Biul Inst Hodowli Aklimat Ros (Warszawa) — Biuletyn. Instytutu Hodowli i Aklimatyzacji Roslin (Warszawa)

Biul Inst Hodowli Aklim Rosl — Biuletyn. Instytutu Hodowli i Aklimatyzacji Roslin

Biul Inst Masz Przepływ Pol Akad Nauk Gdansku — Biuletyn. Instytut Maszyn Przeplywowych Polskiej Akademii Nauk wGdansku

Biul Inst Mech Precyz — Biuletyn. Instytutu Mechaniki Precyzyjnej

Biul Inst Med Morsk Gdansk — Biuletyn. Instytutu Medycyny Morskiej w Gdansku

Biul Inst Med Morsk Gdansku — Biuletyn. Instytutu Medycyny Morskiej w Gdansku

Biul Inst Med Morsk Trop Akad Lek Gdansku — Biuletyn. Instytutu Medycyny Morskiej i Tropikalnej Akademii Lekarskiejw Gdansku

Biul Inst Med Morsk Trop Gdyni — Biuletyn. Instytutu Medycyny Morskiej i Tropikalne w Gdyni

Biul Inst Met Niezelaz — Biuletyn. Instytut Metali Niezelaznych

Biul Inst Naft — Biuletyn. Instytutu Naftowego

Biul Inst Naftowego — Biuletyn. Instytutu Naftowego

Biul Inst Nauk Badaw Przem Weglowego Komun — Biuletyn. Instytutu Naukowo-Badawczego Przemyslu Weglowego Komunikat

Biul Inst Ochr Rosl — Biuletyn. Instytutu Ochrony Roslin

Biul Inst Przem Cukrow — Biuletyn. Instytutu Przemyslu Cukrowniczego

Biul Inst Rosl Lecz — Biuletyn. Instytutu Roslin Leczniezych

Biul Inst Spawal (Gliwice) — Biuletyn. Instytutu Spawalnictwa (Gliwice)

Biul Inst Spawalnictwa — Biuletyn. Instytutu Spawalnictwa

Biul Inst Spawalnictwa (Gliwice) — Biuletyn. Instytutu Spawalnictwa (Gliwice)

Biul Inst Tech Drewna — Biuletyn. Instytutu Technologii Drewna

Biul Inst Weglowego Komun — Biuletyn. Instytutu Weglowego. Komunikat

Biul Inst Weter Pulawy — Biuletyn. Instytutu Weterynarny w Pulawy

Biul Inst Wlok — Biuletyn. Instytutu Wlokiennictwa

Biul Inst Ziemniaka — Biuletyn. Instytutu Ziemniaka

Biul Inst Ziemniaka (Koszalin Pol) — Biuletyn. Instytutu Ziemniaka (Koszalin, Poland)

Biul Koksownika — Biuletyn Koksownika

Biul Kwarant Ochr Ros Min Roln (Warszawa) — Biuletyn. Kwarantanny i Ochrony Roslin Ministerstwo Rolnictwa (Warszawa)

Biull Eksp Biol Med — Biulleten Eksperimentalnoi Biologii i Meditsiny

Biull Gl Bot Sada — Biulleten Glavnogo Botanicheskogo Sada

Biull Izobret — Biulleten Izobretenii

Biul Lubel Towarz Nauk Mat Fiz Chem — Biuletyn Lubelskiego Towarzystwa Naukowego. Matematyka-Fizyka-Chemia

Biul Lubel Tow Nauk Biol — Biuletyn Lubelskiego Towarzystwa Naukowego Biologia

Biul Lubel Tow Nauk Geogr — Biuletyn Lubelskiego Towarzystwa Naukowego. Geografia

Biul Lubel Tow Nauk Mat Fiz Chem — Biuletyn Lubelskiego Towarzystwa Naukowego. Matematyka-Fizyka-Chemia

Biul Lubel Tow Nauk Sect A-D Suppl — Biuletyn Lubelskiego Towarzystwa Naukowego. Sectio A-D. Supplement

Biul Lubel Tow Nauk Wydz 2 — Biuletyn Lubelskiego Towarzystwa Naukowego. Wydzial 2. Biologia

Biul Lubel Tow Nauk Wydz 3 — Biuletyn Lubelskiego Towarzystwa Naukowego. Wydzial 3. Geografia

Biull Vses Nauchno-Issled Inst Kukuruzy — Biulleten Vsesoiuznogo Nauchno-Issledovatel'skogo Instituta Kukuruzy

Biull Vsesoiuznogo Kardiol Nauchn Tsentr AMN SSSR — Biulleten Vsesoiuznogo Kardiologicheskogo Nauchnogo Tsentra AMN SSSR

Biul Nauchno Tekh Inf Agron Fiz — Biulleten Nauchno-Tekhnicheskoi Informatsii po Agronomicheskoi Fizike

Biul Nauchno Tekh Inf Maslichn Kult — Biulleten Nauchno-Tekhnicheskoi Informatsii po Maslichnym Kul'turam

Biul Nauchno-Tekh Inf Vses Nauchno-Issled Inst Risa — Biulleten Nauchno-Tekhnicheskoi Informatsii Vsesoiuznyi Nauchno-Issledovatel'skii Instituta Risa

Biul Nauchn Rabot Vses Nauchno Issled Inst Zhivotnovod — Biulleten Nauchno-Issledovatel'skii Institut Nauchnykh Rabot. Vsesoiuznyi Nauchno-Issledovatel'skii Institut Zhivotnovodstva

Biul Num — Biuletyn Numizmatyczny

Biul Panst Inst Nauk Leczn Surow Ros Poznaniu — Biuletyn. Panstwowy Instytut Naukowy Leczniczych Surowcow Roslinnych w Poznaniu

Biul Panstw Inst Geol — Biuletyn. Panstwowy Instytut Geologiczny

Biul Panstw Inst Med Morsk Trop Gdansku — Biuletyn. Panstwowy Instytutu Medycyny Morskiej i Tropikalnej w Gdansku

Biul Peryglac — Biuletyn Peryglacjalny

Biul PIK — Biuletyn Panstwowego Instytutu Ksiazki

Biul Pol Tow Farm — Biuletyn Polskiego Towarzystwa Farmaceutycznego

Biul Prod Pieczarek — Biuletyn Producenta Pieczarek

Biul Przem Inst Autom Pomiarow MERA PIAP — Biuletyn Przemyslowego Instytutu Automatyki i Pomiarow MERA-PIAP

Biul Sluzby Sanit Epidemiol Wojewodztwa Katowickiego — Biuletyn Sluzby Sanitarno Epidemiologicznej Wojewodztwa Katowickiego

Biul Tech Biura Proj Budownictwa — Biuletyn Techniczny Biura Projektowania Budownictwa

Biul Tech Elektrownie Elektrocieplownie — Biuletyn Techniczny, Elektrownie, i Elektrocieplownie

Biul Urb — Biuletyn Urbanistyczny

Biul Vses Inst Gel'mintol — Biulleten. Vsesoiuznyi Institut Gel'mintologii

Biul Vses Nauchno Issled Inst Zashch Rast — Biulleten Vsesoiuznyi Nauchno-Issledovatel'skii Institut Zashchity Rastenii

Biul Warzywniczy — Biuletyn Warzywniczy

Biul Wojsk Akad Med — Biuletyn Wojskowej Akademii Medycznej

Biul Wojsk Akad Tech — Biuletyn Wojskowej Akademii Technicznej Imienia Jaroslawa Dabrowskiego

Biul Wojsk Inst Chem Radiom — Biuletyn. Wojskowy Instytut Chemii I Radiometrii

Biul Zakl Badan Nauk Gornoslask Okregu Przem Pol Akad Nauk — Biuletyn Zaklad Badan Naukouyeh Gornoslaskiego Okregu Przemyslowego Polskiej Akademii Nauk

Biul Zakl Ochr Srodowiska Reg Przem Pol Akad Nauk — Biuletyn Zaklad Ochrony Srodowiska Regionow Przemyslowych Polskiej Akademii Nauk

Biul Zjednoczenia Przem Chem Gospod Pollena — Biuletyn Zjednoczenia Przemyslu Chemii Gospodarczej Pollena

Biul Zydowskiego Inst Hist — Biuletyn Zydowskiego Instytutu Historycznego

Biul Zydowskiego Inst Hist Pol — Biuletyn Zydowskiego Instytutu Historycznego w Polsci

BIUNA — Biologieunterricht

BIV — Boletin Indigenista Venezolano

BiViChr — Bible et Vie Chretienne

BiVieChr — Bible et Vie Chretienne

Bi W — Biblical World

BIWAA9 — Bulletin of Vegetable Crops Research Work

BiWelt — Die Bibel in der Welt

BIWIA — Bild der Wissenschaft

Biwkly Cryog Curr Aware Serv — Biweekly Cryogenics Current Awareness Service

Bi Wld — Biblical World

Bix — Bixen

BIX — BYTE Information Exchange

Biyokim Derg — Biyokimya Dergisi

BIZ — Berliner Illustrierte Zeitung

BiZ — Biblische Zeitschrift

BIZ — Billings Gazette

Biz — Bizarre Mystery Magazine

Biz — Bizarre [*Paris*]

BIZEA — Biochemische Zeitschrift

BIZEB — Biometrische Zeitschrift

BIZNA — Biologisches Zentralblatt

B I Zool AS — Bulletin. Institute of Zoology. Academia Sinica

BIZUT — Bollettino dell'Istituto Zoologica. Universita di Torino

BIZYAS — Chung Yang Yen Chiu Yuan T'ung Wu Yen Chiu So Chi K'an

BJ — Blue Jeans Magazine

BJ — Bonner Jahrbuecher

BJ — Bookman's Journal

BJ — La Sainte Bible. Traduit en Francais sous la Direction de l'Ecole Biblique de Jerusalem

BJA — British Journal of Administrative Management

BJA — British Journal of Aesthetics

BJAL — British Journal of Administrative Law

BJANA — British Journal of Anaesthesia

B Jap S S F — Bulletin. Japanese Society of Scientific Fisheries

BJAY — Blue Jay

BJAYAC — British Journal of Audiology

B JB — Bach-Jahrbuch

B Jb — Bonner Jahrbuecher des Rheinischen Landesmuseums in Bonn und des Vereins von Altertumsfreunden im Rheinlande

BJbb — Bonner Jahrbuecher

BJBB — Bulletin du Jardin Botanique de l'Etat (Brussels)

BJBNDL — Boletin. Jardin Botanico Nacional

BJBTB — Bangladesh Journal of Botany

BJCAAI — British Journal of Cancer

BJCEA — Boletin. Junta do Control de Energia Atomica

BJCP — British Journal of Clinical Practice

BJCPB — British Journal of Social and Clinical Psychology

BJCPBU — British Journal of Social and Clinical Psychology

BJCPDW — British Journal of Clinical Psychology

BJ Crim — British Journal of Criminology

B J Criminology — British Journal of Criminology

BJDCA — British Journal of Diseases of the Chest

BJDCAT — British Journal of Diseases of the Chest

BJDEAZ — British Journal of Dermatology

BJDEB — British Journal of Disorders of Communication

BJ Delinq — British Journal of Delinquency

BJDIAD — Bijdragen tot de Dierkunde

B J Disorders of Communication — British Journal of Disorders of Communication

BJDPE4 — British Journal of Developmental Psychology

BJDSA9 — British Journal of Dermatology. Supplement

BJEBA — British Journal of Experimental Biology

BJECD — Bell Journal of Economics

B J Ednl Psych — British Journal of Educational Psychology

B J Ednl Studies — British Journal of Educational Studies

B J Ednl Technology — British Journal of Educational Technology

BJEMA — Bell Journal of Economics and Management Science [*Later, Bell Journal of Economics*]

BJEMA — British Journal of Aesthetics
BJEP — British Journal of Educational Psychology
BJEPA — British Journal of Experimental Pathology
BJEPA5 — British Journal of Experimental Pathology
BJES — British Journal of Educational Studies
BJESA — British Journal of Educational Psychology
BJESAE — British Journal of Educational Psychology
B Jeun Fr — Bulletin. Jeunesse Prehistorique et Geologique de France
B Jew Pal Soc — Bulletin. Jewish Palestine Exploration Society
BJewPES — Bulletin. Jewish Palestine Exploration Society
BJF — Biblioteka Juznoslovenskog Filologa
BJF — Boletin. Institucion Fernan-Gonzales
BJFAO — Bulletin. Institut Francais d'Archeologie Orientale
BJFBE6 — Belgian Journal of Food Chemistry and Biotechnology
BJFPDD — British Journal of Family Planning
BJG — Bank of Japan. Monthly Economic Review
BJGL — Blaetter fuer Juedische Geschichte und Literatur
B J Guidance & Counseling — British Journal of Guidance and Counselling
BJGZ — Berliner Juedische Gemeinde-Zeitung
BJHEA — British Journal of Haematology
BJHEAL — British Journal of Haematology
BJHIL — Bibliographie zur Juedisch-Hellenistischen und Intertestamentarischen Literatur
BJHMA — British Journal of Hospital Medicine
BJHMAB — British Journal of Hospital Medicine
BJHS — British Journal for the History of Science
BJHSAT — British Journal for the History of Science
BJI — British Journal of Industrial Relations
BJI — Bulletin des Juridictions Indigenes
BJIMA — British Journal of Industrial Medicine
BJIMAG — British Journal of Industrial Medicine
BJ Ind Rel — British Journal of Industrial Relations
B J In-Service Ed — British Journal of In-Service Education
BJIR — British Journal of Industrial Relations
BJJTEC — Biblioteca Jose Jeronimo Triana
BJKG — Brettener Jahrbuch fuer Kultur und Geschichte
BJLS — British Journal of Law and Society
BJM — Basler Juristische Mitteilungen
BJM — Metropolitan Toronto Business Journal
B J Ma St Ps — British Journal of Mathematical and Statistical Psychology
B J Math & Stat Psych — British Journal of Mathematical and Statistical Psychology
BJMEAC — British Journal of Medical Education
BJMEDF — British Journal of Sexual Medicine
BJ Mental Subnormality — British Journal of Mental Subnormality
BJMPA — British Journal of Medical Psychology
BJMPAB — British Journal of Medical Psychology
BJMPs — British Journal of Medical Psychology
BJMRDK — Brazilian Journal of Medical and Biological Research
BJMSA — British Journal of Mathematical and Statistical Psychology
BJMSBL — British Journal of Mental Subnormality
BJMTD — British Journal of Music Therapy
BJNC — Boletim da Junta Nacional da Cortica
BJNTA — British Journal of Non-Destructive Testing
BJNUA — British Journal of Nutrition
BJNUAV — British Journal of Nutrition
BJOADD — Bangladesh Journal of Agriculture
BJOCA — British Journal of Occupational Safety
BJOGA — British Journal of Obstetrics and Gynaecology
BJOGAS — British Journal of Obstetrics and Gynaecology
B John Ryl — Bulletin. John Rylands Library. University of Manchester
BJOPA — British Journal of Ophthalmology
BJOPAL — British Journal of Ophthalmology
BJOSA — British Journal of Sociology
BJOSB — British Journal of Oral Surgery [*Later, British Journal of Oral and Maxillofacial Surgery*]
BJOSBV — British Journal of Oral Surgery [*Later, British Journal of Oral and Maxillofacial Surgery*]
BJOSEY — British Journal of Oral and Maxillofacial Surgery
BJOTA — Begg Journal of Orthodontic Theory and Treatment
BJP — British Journal of Photography
BJP — British Journal of Psychology
BJP — Business Japan
BJPCA — British Journal of Pharmacology and Chemotherapy [*Later, British Journal of Pharmacology*]
BJPCAL — British Journal of Pharmacology and Chemotherapy [*Later, British Journal of Pharmacology*]
BJPCB — British Journal of Pharmacology
BJPCBM — British Journal of Pharmacology
BJPEBS — British Journal of Physical Education
BJPES — Bulletin. Jewish Palestine Exploration Society
B J Physical Ed — British Journal of Physical Education
BJPIA5 — British Journal for the Philosophy of Science
BJPOAN — British Journal of Physiological Optics
BJPS — British Journal for the Philosophy of Science
BJPs — British Journal of Psychology
BJPSA — British Journal of Plastic Surgery
BJPSAZ — British Journal of Plastic Surgery
BJPSB — British Journal of Psychiatry
BJPSB2 — British Journal of Psychiatry. Special Publication
B J Psych — British Journal of Psychology
BJ Psychiatry — British Journal of Psychiatry
BJPVA — British Journal of Preventive and Social Medicine
BJPVAA — British Journal of Preventive and Social Medicine
BJPYA — British Journal of Psychiatry

BJPYAJ — British Journal of Psychiatry
BJR — Bulletin des Jeunes Romanistes
BJR — Bulletin. John Rylands Library. University of Manchester
BJRAA — British Journal of Radiology
BJRAAP — British Journal of Radiology
BJ Religious Ed — British Journal of Religious Education
BJRHDF — British Journal of Rheumatology
BJRL — Bulletin. John Rylands Library. University of Manchester
BJRLM — Bulletin. John Rylands Library. University of Manchester
BJRSAB — British Journal of Radiology. Supplement
BJR Suppl — BJR [*British Journal of Radiology*] Supplement
BJS — British Journal of Sociology
BJSCP — British Journal of Social and Clinical Psychology
BJSGA — British Journal of Psychology. General Section
BJSGAE — British Journal of Psychology
BJSIB — Bangladesh Journal of Scientific and Industrial Research
BJSIBL — Bangladesh Journal of Scientific and Industrial Research
BJSMAW — British Journal of Social Medicine
B JSME — Bulletin. JSME
B J Social and Clinical Psych — British Journal of Social and Clinical Psychology
B J Sociology — British Journal of Sociology
BJSPDA — British Journal of Social Psychology
BJSRDG — Bangladesh Journal of Scientific Research
B J Stat Psych — British Journal of Statistical Psychology
BJSUA — British Journal of Surgery
BJSUAM — British Journal of Surgery
BJTBA4 — British Journal of Tuberculosis
BJ Teach Ed — British Journal of Teacher Education
BJTUAR — British Journal of Tuberculosis and Diseases of the Chest
Bjull Akad Nauk Uz SSR — Bjulleten Akademiji Nauk Uzbekskoj SSR
Bjull Glavn Bot Sada — Bjulleten Glavnogo Botaniceskogo Sada
Bjull Gos Nikit Bot Sada — Bjulleten Gosudarstvennogo Nikitskogo Botaniceskogo Sada
Bjull Habarovsk Lesn Pitomn — Bjulleten' Habarovskogo Lesnogo Pitomnika
Bjull Inst Teoret Astronom — Bjulleten Instituta Teoreticeskoi Astronomii. Akademija Nauk Sojuza Sovetskih Socialisticeskih Respublik
Bjull Jarov — Bjulleten' Jarovizacii
Bjull Mosk Obsc Ispyt Prir Otd Biol — Bjulleten Moskovskogo Obscestva Ispytatelej Prirody. Otdel Biologiceskij
Bjull Moskovsk Obsc Isp Prir Otd Geol — Bjulleten' Moskovskogo Obscestva Ispytatelej Prirody. Otdel Geologiceskij/Bulletin. Societe des Naturalistes de Moscou. Section Geologique
Bjull Sibirsk Bot Sada — Bjulleten' Sibirskogo Botaniceskogo Sada
Bjull Tihookeansk Komiteta Akad Nauk SSSR — Bjulleten' Tihookeanskogo Komiteta Akademii Nauk SSSR/Bulletin. Pacific Committee. Academy of Sciences. USSR
Bjull Vsesojuzn Naucno Issl Inst Zasc Rast — Bjulleten' Vsesojuznogo Naucno-Issledovatel'skogo Instituta Zascity Rastenij
BJURA — British Journal of Urology
BJURAN — British Journal of Urology
BJV — Berliner Jahrbuch fuer Vor- und Fruehgeschichte
BJVDA — British Journal of Venereal Diseases
BJVDAK — British Journal of Venereal Diseases
BJVF — Berliner Jahrbuch fuer Vor- und Fruehgeschichte
BK — Bedi Kartlisa
BK — Biblischer Kommentar
BK — Bildende Kunst
Bk — Bookman
Bk Abroad — Books Abroad
Bk & Bkmen — Books and Bookmen
Bk & Pap Grp Annu — Book and Paper Group Annual
BKAT — Biblischer Kommentar. Altes Testament
BKB — Bank of Israel. Economic Review
BKBCB — Bulletin. Boris Kidric Institute of Nuclear Sciences. Chemistry
BKBGA4 — Brooklyn Botanic Garden. Annual Report
Bkbinding & Bk Production — Bookbinding and Book Production
Bkbird — Bookbird
BKBR — Beitraege zur Kenntnis der Babylonischen Religion
Bk Buyer — Book Buyer [*Later, Lamp*]
Bk Coll — Book Collector
Bk Collec — Book Collector
Bk Collecting & Lib Mo — Book Collecting and Library Monthly
Bk Collector — Book Collector
Bk Colr — Book Collector
BKCSD — Bulletin. Korean Chemical Society
Bk Egypt A — Central Bank of Egypt. Annual Report
BKEJA — Berichte. Kernforschungsanlage Juelich
BKEst — Beitraege zur Kunde Est-, Liv-, und Kurlands
Bk Forum — Book Forum
BKFSD — Bulletin. Korean Fisheries Technological Society
BKGP — Blaetter fuer Kirchengeschichte Pommerns
BKH — Baksteen. Tweemaandelijks Tijdschrift Gewijd aan de Technische en Esthetische Eigenschappen van Gebakken Kleiprodukten
Bk Hawaii — Bank of Hawaii. Monthly Review
Bk Hb — Book Handbook
BkIA — Books at Iowa
BKIDGRS — Beitraege zur Kunde der Indogermanischen Sprachen
BKIS — Beitraege zur Kunde der Indogermanischen Sprachen
BKISA — Bulletin. Boris Kidric Institute of Nuclear Sciences. Supplement
BKJ — Beitraege zur Kinder- und Jugendliteratur
BKK — Expovisie. Beurzen, Tentoonstellingen, Congressen, Hotellerie
Bkl — Booklist
BkL — Bookman (London)
Bklegger — Booklegger Magazine
BKIIKr — Beitraege zur Klinik der Infektionskrankheiten

Bklist — Booklist and Subscription Books Bulletin [*Later, Booklist*]
Bk LJ — Banking Law Journal
BKLKB — Banyaszati es Kohaszati Lapok. Kohaszat
Bklyn Mus Q — Brooklyn Museum Quarterly
BKM — Bankers' Monthly
BKM — Byzantina kai Metabyzantina
Bkman (Lond) — Bookman (London)
Bkmans J & Prt Colr — Bookman's Journal and Print Collector
Bkmark — Bookmark
Bkmark (Idaho) — Bookmark. University of Idaho
BKMGA — Blackwood's Magazine
BKMR — Beitraege zur Kulturgeschichte des Mittelalters und der Renaissance
BKN — Bank Negara Malaysia. Quarterly Economic Bulletin
Bk-News — Book-News
Bk Nigeria — Central Bank of Nigeria. Annual Report and Statement of Accounts
BKNOB — Bulletin. Koninklijke Nederlandse Oudheidkundige Bond
Bk Norm Commonw Bur Met — Book of Normals. Commonwealth Bureau of Meteorology (Melbourne)
BKO — Bank of Korea. Quarterly Economic Review
BKO — Beitraege zur Kenntnis des Orients
BKOAA — Byulleten' Komissii po Opredeleniyu Absolyutnogo Vozrasta Geologicheskikh Formatsii
Bk Old Edinburgh Club — Book of the Old Edinburgh Club
B Konan Women Coll — Bulletin. Konan Women's College
BKQ — Bakery Production and Marketing
BKR — Banker
BKRC — Bulletin. Korean Research Center
Bk Rev Dig — Book Review Digest
Bk Rev Ind — Book Review Index
Bk Rev Mo — Book Reviews of the Month
BKS — Bibel und Kircher (Stuttgart)
Bks Abrd Norman — Books Abroad (Norman, Oklahoma)
Bks Abroad — Books Abroad
Bks & Bkmn — Books and Bookmen
Bks & Libs — Books and Libraries at the University of Kansas
BKSCA — Black Scholar
Bks in Can — Books in Canada
BKstG — Beitraege zur Kunde Steiermaerkischer Geschichtsquellen
Bks Today — Books Today
BKSTS J — BKSTS [*British Kinematograph Sound and Television Society*] Journal
BKT — Berliner Klassiker Texte
Bk T — Book Times
BK Tech Rev — BK Technical Review
BKTLA — Book Trolley
Bk Trolley — Book Trolley
BKV — Bibliothek der Kirchenvaeter
BKW — Bakkerswereld
BKW — Book of Weird Tales
BkW — Book World
Bk Wk — Book Week
Bk World — Book World
BL — Bibel und Leben
BL — Bibliographie Linguistique
BL — Bibliotheekleven
Bl — Blackfriars
Bl — Black Perspective in Music
Bl — Blackwood's Magazine
BL — Booklist
BL — Book List. Society for Old Testament Studies
BL — Bookman (London)
BL — Brain and Language
BL — Bulletin des Lettres
BL — Bulletin Linguistique. Faculte des Lettres de Bucarest
BL — Business Lawyer
BL — Dois Distritos da Beira Litoral. Factos e Coisas do Nosso Tempo
BLA — Biblioteca de Linguistica Americana
BLA — Black Art
BLA — Business Latin America
B Labor Mus Louvre — Bulletin. Laboratoire du Musee de Louvre
BLAC — Bulletin d'Ancienne Litterature et d'Archeologie Chretiennes
Black — Blackwood's Magazine
Black Am L — Black American Literature Forum
Black Bus News — Black Business News
BlackCh — Black Church
Black Coal Aust — Black Coal in Australia
Black Col — Black Collegian
Black Coll — Black Collegian
Black Ent — Black Enterprise
Black Enterp — Black Enterprise
Blackf — Blackford
Black F — Black Forum
Black Fox Mag — Black Fox Magazine
Black Hills Eng — Black Hills Engineer
BlackI — Black Images: A Critical Quarterly on Black Arts and Culture
BlackIC — Black I: A Canadian Journal of Black Expression
Black Inf Index — Black Information Index
Black L J — Black Law Journal
Black Mag — Blackwood's Magazine
Black Mountain Coll Bull — Black Mountain College Bulletin
Black Mtn Rev — Black Mountain Review
Black Mus Jazz Rev — Black Music and Jazz Review
Black N Dig — Black News Digest
Black Per M — Black Perspective in Music
Black Perspective M — Black Perspective in Music
Black Pol Econ — Review of Black Political Economy

BlackR — Black Review
Black Rock For Bull — Black Rock Forest. Bulletin
Black Rock Forest Bull — Black Rock Forest. Bulletin
Black Rock For Pap — Black Rock Forest. Papers
Black Sacred Mus — Black Sacred Music
Black Sch — Black Scholar
Black Soc — Black Sociologist
Blackw — Blackwood's Magazine
Black W — Black World
Blackwell Newsl — Blackwell Newsletter
Blackwoods Edinburgh Mag — Blackwood's Edinburgh Magazine
Blackwood's Mag — Blackwood's Magazine
Bl Adm Pr — Blaetter fuer Administrative Praxis
Blaett Dtsche u Int Polit — Blaetter fuer Deutsche und Internationale Politik
Blaett Lit Unterhalt — Blaetter fuer Literarische Unterhaltung
Blaett Naturk Naturschutz — Blaetter fuer Naturkunde und Naturschutz
Blaett Obst Wein Gartenbau Kleintierzucht — Blaetter fuer Obst-, Wein-, Gartenbau, und Kleintierzucht
Blaett Pflanzenbau Pflanzenzuecht — Blaetter fuer Pflanzenbau und Pflanzenzuechtung
Blaett Technikgesch — Blaetter fuer Technikgeschichte
Blaett Vereins Landesk Niederoesterreich — Blaetter des Vereins fuer Landeskunde in Niederoesterreich
Blagoveshch Gos Med Inst Tr — Blagoveshchenskii Gosudarstvennyi Meditsinskii Institut. Trudy
Blagoveshch Skh Inst Tr — Blagoveshchenskii Sel'skokhozyaistvennyi Institut. Trudy
Bl Agric Chem Soc Jap — Bulletin. Agricultural Chemical Society of Japan
Blair & Ketchum's — Blair and Ketchum's Country Journal
Blake Ill Q — Blake; an Illustrated Quarterly
BlakeN — Blake Newsletter
Blake Newslett — Blake Newsletter
Blake Q — Blake; an Illustrated Quarterly
BlakeS — Blake Studies
Blake Stud — Blake Studies
BLAM — Boletin Latino-Americano de Musica
BLAM — Bulletin. Librairie Ancienne et Moderne
Bl Amer Lit Forum — Black American Literature Forum
Bl Am Phys Soc — Bulletin. American Physical Society
Bl & Bild — Blaetter und Bilder. Eine Zeitschrift fuer Dichtung, Musik, und Malerei
B Langres — Bulletin. Societe Historique et Archeologique de Langres
BLAP — Bibliotheque Linguistique Americaine (Paris)
BLAR — Bulletin of Latin American Research
Bl Assoc Chim — Bulletin. Association des Chimistes
Blast F & Steel Pl — Blast Furnace and Steel Plant
Blast Furn Coke Oven Raw Mater Proc — Blast Furnace, Coke Oven, and Raw Materials. Proceedings
Blast Furn Steel Plant — Blast Furnace and Steel Plant
B Lazio Merid — Bollettino. Istituto di Storia e di Arte del Lazio Meridionale
BLB — Bloembollenexport
BLB — Bulletin Legislatif Belge
BLB — Bulletin Linguistique. Faculte des Lettres de Bucarest
Bl Bayer Landesver Familienknd — Blaetter des Bayerischen Landesvereins fuer Familienkunde
Bl Belt Mag — Black Belt Magazine
Bl Bergakad Freiberg — Blaetter der Bergakademie Freiberg
Bl Bergshandteringens Vaenner — Blad foer Bergshandteringens Vaenner
BlBGym — Blaetter fuer das Bayerische Gymnasialschulwesen
BLBHAE — Balneologia Bohemica
BLBI — Bulletin. Leo Baeck Institute
BLBIA — Bluegrass
Bl Bks B — Black Books Bulletin
BLC — Bollettino di Legislazione Comparata
BLC — Bulletin de Litterature Chretienne
BLCED — Blood Cells
Bl Chem Soc Jap — Bulletin. Chemical Society of Japan
BLD — Bulletin Legislatif Dalloz
Bl Deut Phil — Blaetter fuer Deutsche Philosophie
Bl Deutsche Landesgesch — Blaetter fuer Deutsche Landesgeschichte
Bldg — Building
BLDGA — Buildings
Bldg Age — Building Age and National Builder
Bldg & Engin J — Building and Engineering Journal
Bldg & Engin J Australia & NZ — Building and Engineering Journal of Australia and New Zealand
Bldg & Environment — Building and Environment
Bldg Conserv — Building Conservation
Bldg Conservation — Building Conservation
Bldg Constr — Building Construction
Bldg Des — Building Design
Bldg Des & Bldg Constr — Building Design and Construction
Bldg Desgn — Building Design and Construction
Bldg Design — Building Design
Bldg Econ — Building Economist
Bldg Economist — Building Economist
Bldg Env — Building and Environment
Bldg Envir — Building and Environment
Bldg Environ — Building and Environment
Bldg Forum — Building Forum
Bldg Mater — Building Materials
Bldg Mater — Building Materials and Equipment
Bldg Mats List — Building Materials List
Bldg Mgmt Abs — Building Management Abstracts
Bldg News — Building News
Bldg Opr — Building Operating Management

Bldg Products — Building Products
Bldg Refurb — Building Refurbishment
Bldg Refurb & Maint — Building Refurbishment and Maintenance
Bldg Refurbishment & Maintenance — Building Refurbishment and Maintenance
Bldg Research & Practice — Building Research and Practice
Bldg Research Assocn New Zealand Bldg Information Bull — Building Research Association of New Zealand. Building Information Bulletin
Bldg Res Practice — Building Research and Practice
Bldg Res Stn Dig — Building Research Station Digest
Bldg Res (Washington DC) — Building Research (Washington, DC)
Bldg Rev — Building Review
Bldg Rev New Orl — Building Review (New Orleans)
Bldg Rev S Francisco — Building Review (San Francisco)
Bldgs — Buildings: the Construction and Building Management Journal
Bldg Sci — Building Science
Bldg Sci Abstr — Building Science Abstracts
Bldg Sci Quest Answ — Building Science Questions and Answers
Bldg Serv — Building Services
Bldg Serv Engin Res & Technol — Building Services Engineering Research and Technology
Bldg Serv Engr — Building Services Engineer
Bldg Serv Environ Engr — Building Services and Environmental Engineer
Bldg Services — Building Services
Bldg Services & Environmental Engineer — Building Services and Environmental Engineer
Bldg Services Engineer — Building Services Engineer
Bldg Services Environ Engnr — Building Services and Environmental Engineer
Bldg S Home — Building Supply and Home Centers
Bldg SN — Building Supply News
Bldg Soc Gaz — Building Societies Gazette
Bldg Specif — Building Specification
Bldg Specification — Building Specification
Bldg Stand Mon — Building Standards Monthly
Bldg Steel — Building with Steel
Bldg Study — Building Study
Bldg Study Div Bldg Res CSIRO — Building Study. Division of Building Research. Commonwealth Scientific and Industrial Research Organisation
Bldg Systems Design — Building Systems Design
Bldg Systm — Building Systems Design
Bldg Tech File — Building Technical File
Bldg Tech Mgmt — Building Technology and Management
Bldg Technol Mgmt — Building Technology and Management
Bldg Times — Building Times
Bldg Today — Building Today
Bldg Top — Building Topics
Bldg Trade — Building Trade
Bldg Trade News — Building Trade News
Bldg Trades J — Building Trades Journal
Bldg Trades Jnl — Building Trades Journal
Bldg with Steel — Building with Steel
Bldg Witn — Building Witness
Bldg Wld — Building World
BLDIA — Black Diamond
Bld Kenya — Build Kenya
Bl D Lg — Blaetter fuer Deutsche Landesgeschichte
Bl D Ph — Blaetter fuer Deutsche Philosophie
Bld Res Prac — Building Research and Practice
Bldrs J — Builder's Journal
Bldrs J & Archit Rec — Builder's Journal and Architectural Record
Bldrs Mag — Builder's Magazine
Bld Serv Enging Res Tech — Building Services Engineering Research and Technology
Bld Technol Mgmnt — Building Technology and Management
Bl Dte Philos — Blaetter fuer Deutsche Philosophie
Bl Dt Landesgesch — Blaetter fuer Deutsche Landesgeschichte
Bl Dtsch Int Polit — Blaetter fuer Deutsche und Internationale Politik
Bl Dt und Internat Pol — Blaetter fuer Deutsche und Internationale Politik
BIE — Black Experience
BLE — Bulletin de Litterature Ecclesiastique
BLE — Bulletin Linguistique et Ethnologique
Bleacher Finish Tex Chem — Bleacher, Finisher, and Textile Chemist
BLEND — Black Enterprise
BLESA — Bollettino. Laboratorio di Entomologia Agraria "Filippo Silvestri" di Portici
BLESAS — Bollettino. Laboratorio di Entomologia Agraria "Filippo Silvestri" di Portici
B Lezoux — Bulletin. Comite Archeologique de Lezoux
BLF — Bank of London and South America. Review
BlfH — Blaetter fuer Heimatkunde
BIFL — Blaetter fuer die Fortbildung des Lehrers
BLFSA — Blast Furnace and Steel Plant
BLFSB — Basic Life Sciences
Bl Gemaeldeknd — Blaetter fuer Gemaeldekunde
Bl Gemaeldeknd Beil — Blaetter fuer Gemaeldekunde Beilage
Bl Gesch Tech — Blaetter fuer Geschichte der Technik. Oesterreichisches Forschungsinstitut fuerGeschichte der Technik
Bl Grundstuecks Bau-Wohnungsrecht — Blaetter fuer Grundstuecks, Bau-, und Wohnungsrecht
BLGTB — Biologist
Bl Gymnasialschulwesen — Blaetter fuer das Bayerische Gymnasialschulwesen
BLH — Best's Review. Life/Health Insurance Edition
Bl H — Blaetter fuer Heimatkunde
BLH — Boletin de Estudios Latinoamericanos y del Caribe
BIH — Bulletin Hispanique
Bl Heimatkd — Blaetter fuer Heimatkunde
Bl HK — Blaetter fuer Heimatkunde. Historischer Verein fuer Steiermark

BLI — Banking Literature Index
BLI — Beitraege zur Linguistik und Informationsverarbeitung
B Liaison Inform Adm Centr Econ Finances — Bulletin de Liaison et d'Information. Administration Centrale de l'Economie et des Finances
B Liaison OCDE — Bulletin de Liaison (OCDE)
BLICD3 — Bibliotheca Lichenologica
Blick Mus — Blick ins Museum. Mitteilungen aus den Staatlichen Wissenschaftlichen Museen Dresden
Blick Wiss — Blick in die Wissenschaft
BLIJ — Burma Law Institute. Journal
B Limousin — Bulletin. Societe Archeologique et Historique du Limousin
Blind Vis Impair Deaf Blind — Blindness, Visual Impairment, Deaf-Blindness
BlIntPR — Blaetter fuer Internationales Privatrecht
B Lit E — Bulletin de Litterature Ecclesiastique
BLJ — Bihar Law Journal Reports
BLJ — British Library Journal
Blk Lib — Black Liberation
Blk Panth — Black Panther
Blk Schol — Black Scholar
BLL — Belaruskaia Litaratura
BLL — Bibliographie Linguistischer Literatur
Bll Bayer Gymnschulw — Blaetter fuer das Bayerische Gymnasialschulwesen
Bll Gymnschulw — Blaetter fuer das Gymnasialschulwesen
BLLIAX — Bratislavske Lekarske Listy
Bl LJ — Black Law Journal
Bll Klin Hydrotherap — Blaetter fuer Klinische Hydrotherapie und Verwandte Heilmethoden [*Wien undLeipzig*]
Bll Philharm — Konzertzeitung. Blaetter der Philharmonie
Bll Phm — Bulletin de Pharmacie. Parmentier
Bll Rechtspfl Thuering — Blaetter fuer Rechtspflege in Thueringen und Anhalt
BLL Rev — BLL [*British Library Lending Division*] Review
BLL Review — British Library. Lending Division. Review
Bll Sc Fr Blg — Bulletin Scientifique de la France et de la Belgique
Bll Sc Mth — Bulletin des Sciences Mathematiques
Bll Sc Mth As — Bulletin des Sciences Mathematiques et Astronomiques
Bll Sc Nord — Bulletin Scientifique, Historique, et Litteraire du Departement du Nord et des pays Voisins
Bll Staatsoper — Blaetter der Staatsoper
Bll Univ Tenn Agr Exp Sta — Bulletin. University of Tennessee. Agricultural Experiment Station
Bll Vt It — Bullettino del Vulcanismo Italiano
BIM — Blackwood's Magazine
BLM — Bolletini di Litteratura Moderna
BLM — Bonniers Litteraera Magasin
BLM — Bonniers Litterara Magasin
BLM — Book League Monthly
BLM — Boulainviller's Life of Mohammed
BLMag — Bonniers Litteraera Magasin
BLM (Bon Lit) — BLM (Bonniers Litterara Magasin)
BLMNR — Bureau of Land Management. Alaska. News Release
BLMRA J — BLMRA [*British Leather Manufacturers' Research Association*] Journal
Bl Muefreunde F — Blaetter fuer Muenzfreunde und Muenzforschung
Bl Muenzfreunde — Blaetter fuer Muenzfreunde
Bl Muenzfreunde Muenzforsch — Blaetter fuer Muenzfreunde und Muenzforschung
BLN — Banca Nazionale del Lavoro. Quarterly Review
BLN — Bottomline
BLND — Reading Material for the Blind and Physically Handicapped
BLOAA — Biologia
Blok Casop Umeni — Blok. Casopis pro Umeni
Blood Bank Technol 2nd Ed — Blood Bank Technology. 2nd Edition
Blood Cells Mol Dis — Blood Cells, Molecules, and Diseases
Blood Coagul Fibrinolysis — Blood Coagulation and Fibrinolysis
Blood Pres Cont — Blood Pressure Control
Blood Press — Blood Pressure
Blood Press Monit — Blood Pressure Monitoring
Blood Press Suppl — Blood Pressure. Supplement
Blood Pressure Suppl — Blood Pressure. Supplement
Blood Purif — Blood Purification
Blood Rev — Blood Reviews
Blood Ther J — Blood Therapy Journal
Blood Transfus Immunohaematol — Blood Transfusion and Immunohaematology
Blood Vess — Blood Vessels
Bl Orcl — Black Oracle
B Lorraine — Bulletin. Academie et Societe Lorraines des Sciences
BLOT — Book List. Society for Old Testament Studies
Bl Patentw — Blatt fuer Patent-, Muster-, und Zeichenwesen
BLPPD9 — Bulletin Lembaga Penelitian Peternakan
BLPYA — Biological Psychology
BLR — Baylor Law Review
BLR — Belorussian Review
BLR — Bodleian Library Record
BLR — Bulletin de Liaison Racinienne
BLR — Business and Law Review
BLR — Business Law Reports
BLR — Business Law Review
BLRCA — Bell Laboratories Record
B L Rev — Bluegrass Literary Review
BIRS — Blaetter fuer Religioesen Sozialismus
BIS — Black Scholar
BLS — Business Lawyer. Special Issue
BLS — Employee Relations
BLS 1892 — Labor and Material Requirements for Private Multi-Family Housing Construction. BLS Bulletin 1892. US Bureau of Labor Statistics

BLS 2070 — Handbook of Labor Statistics. BLS Bulletin 2070. US Bureau of Labor Statistics

BLS 2121 — Economic Projections to 1990. BLS Bulletin 2121. US Bureau of Labor Statistics

BLS 2128 — Productivity Measures for Selected Industries, 1954-80. BLS Bulletin 2128. USBureau of Labor Statistics

BLS 2175 — Handbook of Labor Statistics. BLS Bulletin 2175. US Bureau of Labor Statistics

BLS 2197 — Employment Projections for 1995. BLS Bulletin 2197. US Bureau of Labor Statistics

BLS 2202 — Occupational Projections and Training. BLS Bulletin 2202. US Bureau of Labor Statistics

BLS 2224 — Productivity Measures for Selected Industries, 1954-83. BLS Bulletin 2224. US Bureau of Labor Statistics

BLS 2253 — Employment Projections for 1995; Data and Methods. BLS Bulletin 2253. US Bureauof Labor Statistics

BLS 2256 — Productivity Measures for Selected Industries, 1958-84. BLS Bulletin 2256. US Bureau of Labor Statistics

BlSch — Black Scholar

BLS CPI — CPI [*Consumer Price Index*] Detailed Report. US and City Averages. US Bureau of Labor Statistics

BLSCR — Bollettino Linguistico per la Storia e la Cultura Regionale

Bl Soc Chim Belg — Bulletin. Societe Chimique de Belgique

Bl Soc Chim Ind — Bulletin. Societe de Chimie Industrielle

BLS PPI — United States. Bureau of Labor Statistics. Producer Prices and Price Indexes

BLS PPIA — Producer Prices and Price Indexes [*later, Producer Price Indexes*]. Supplement to Data for 1983. US Bureau of Labor Statistics

BLS Review — United States. Bureau of Labor Statistics. Monthly Labor Review

BLS Whole — Wholesale Prices and Price Indexes. US Bureau of Labor Statistics

BLS Whole A — Wholesale Prices and Price Indexes. Supplement. US Bureau of Labor Statistics

BLT — Belgie/Economische en Handelsvoorlichting

BLT — Brethren Life and Thought

BLTBAI — Folia Societatis Scientiarum Lublinensis. Biologia

Bl Technikgesch — Blaetter fuer Technikgeschichte. Forschungsinstitut fuer Technikgeschichte in Wien

BLTND — [*The*] Bulletin

BLTSG — Bulletin. Lutheran Theological Seminary

Blue Book Cat Ed Annu Buyers Guide — Blue Book and Catalog Edition. Annual Buyers' Guide

Blue Book Soap Sanit Chem — Blue Book of Soap and Sanitary Chemicals

Blue Chip — Blue Chip Economic Indicators

Blue Cloud Q — Blue Cloud Quarterly

Blue Cross Assoc Res Ser — Blue Cross Association. Research Series

Blue Cross Rep — Blue Cross Reports

Bluegrass — Bluegrass Unlimited

Bluegrass Lit Rev — Bluegrass Literary Review

Blueh Kakteen — Bluehende Kakteen. Deutsche Kakteengesellschaft

Blues — Blues Unlimited

Blue Sky L Rep CCH — Blue Sky Law Reports. Commerce Clearing House

B Lugo — Boletin. Comision Provincial de Monumentos Historicos y Artisticos de Lugo

BLUMA — Bollettino. Unione Matematica Italiana

Blumen Kalender — Blumen-Kalender

Blumen Zeitung — Blumen-Zeitung

B Lund — Bulletin. Societe de Lettres de Lund

Bl Unters Forsch Instrum — Blaetter fuer Untersuchungs- und Forschungs-Instrumente

Blut Sonderb — Blut. Sonderbaende

Blut Suppl — Blut. Supplement

BLux — Bulletin Linguistique et Ethnologique. Institut Granducal (Luxembourg)

BlverglR — Blaetter fuer Vergleichende Rechtswissenschaft

BLVS — Bibliothek des Literarischen Vereins (Stuttgart)

BL W — Black World

BLW — Business Lawyer

Blwd Mag — Blackwood's Magazine

Bl Wuerttemberg Kirchenges — Blaetter fuer Wuerttembergische Kirchengeschichte

Bl Wuerttemb Kirchengesch — Blaetter fuer Wuerttembergische Kirchengeschichte

BLZG — Bollettino del Laboratorio di Zoologia Generale e Agraria della Facolta Agraria in Portici. Naples

Bl Zuckerruebenbau — Blaetter fuer Zuckerruebenbau

BM — Baghdader Mitteilungen

BM — Baltische Monatsschrift

BM — Banber Matenadarani

BM — Bankers' Magazine

BM — Benediktinische Monatshefte

BM — Berliner Morgenpost

BM — Berliner Museen. Berichte aus den Preussischen Kunstsammlungen

BM — Beth Mikra

BM — Bibliotheca Mathematica

BM — Bibliotheca Mesopotamica

BM — Blackwood's Magazine

BM — Bluegrass Music News

BM — Bonniers Maenadstidning

Bm — Bookman

BM — British Museum. Quarterly

BM — Bulletin Monumental

BM — Bulletin Monumental. Societe Francaise d'Archeologie

BM — Burlington Magazine

BM — Business Monitor. Monthly Statistics

BM — Business Month

BMA — Bergens Museums. Aarbok

BMA — Bulletin of Mediterranean Archaeology

BM Aa — Bergens Museums. Aa

BMAAA — Byulleten' Mezhdunarodnykh Agenstv Atomnoi Energii

B Mad — Bulletin de Madagascar

BMAD — Bulletin Mensuel. Academie Delphinale

BMadagascar — Bulletin de Madagascar

B Madras Dev Sem Ser — Bulletin. Madras Development Seminar Series

BMAEA7 — Montana. Agricultural Experiment Station. Bulletin

BMAH — Bulletin. Musees Royaux d'Art et d'Histoire

BMAIU — Bulletin Mensuel. Alliance Israelite Universelle

BMALDV — Bollettino Malacologico

BMAN — Baltimore Museum of Art News

BM Angers — Bulletin. Musees de la Ville d'Angers

BMAP — BMA [*British Medical Association*] Press Cuttings Database

BMAP — Bulletin du Musee d'Anthropologie Prehistorique

BMAP Orense — Boletin. Musei Arqueologico Provincial de Orense

BMARB — Bergens Museums. Aarbok

B Marin Sci — Bulletin of Marine Science

B Maroc — Bulletin. Societe d'Histoire du Maroc

B M Arq Or — Boletin. Musei Arqueologico Provincial de Orense

BM Arq Or — Boletin. Museo Arqueologico Provincial de Orense

BM Arras — Bulletin. Societe des Amis du Musee d'Arras

BMASDI — Mississippi. Agricultural and Forestry Experiment Station. Bulletin

B Math Biol — Bulletin of Mathematical Biology

B Math Stat — Bulletin of Mathematical Statistics

B Maurienne — Bulletin. Societe d'Histoire et d'Archeologie de la Maurienne

BMAW — Berichte und Mittheilungen des Altertumsvereins in Wien

B Mayenne — Bulletin. Commission Historique et Archeologique de la Mayenne

BMB — Boston Museum. Bulletin

BMB — British Medical Bulletin

BMB — Bulletin Bibliographique. Musee Belge

BMB — Bulletin des Musees Royaux des Arts Decoratifs et Industriels a Bruxelles

BMB — Bulletin. Musee Basque

BMB — Bulletin. Musee de Beyrouth

B Mb — Bundner Monatsblatt. Zeitschrift fuer Bundnerische Geschichte, Heimat-und Volkskunde

BMBA — Bulletin. Musees Royaux des Beaux-Arts de Belgique

BMBAB — Bulletin. Musees Royaux des Beaux-Arts de Belgique

BMBB — Bulletin Museum Boymans van Beuningen

BMBe — Berliner Museen. Berichte aus den Preussischen Kunstsammlungen

BM Beyr — Bulletin. Musee de Beyrouth

BM Beyrouth — Bulletin. Musee de Beyrouth

BMBIA — Bulletin of Mathematical Biophysics

BMBL — Berliner Munzblaetter

BMBTA — Baumaschine und Bautechnik

BMBTAN — Baumaschine und Bautechnik

BMBUA — British Medical Bulletin

BMBUAQ — British Medical Bulletin

BMC — Biomedical Chromatography

BMC — Mayenne, Departement. Commission Historique et Archeologique. Bulletin

BMC Bronzes — British Museum Catalogs. Bronzes. Catalogue of the Bronzes, Greek, Roman, and Etruscan in the Department of Greek and Roman Antiquities

BMCCP — Bollettino Italiano di Numismatica e di Arte della Medaglia

BMC Emp — British Museum Catalogs. Coins. Roman Empire. Coins of the Roman Empire

BMCL — Bulletin of Medieval Canon Law

BMCMEB — Boletin. Museo de Ciencias Naturales y Antropologicas Juan Cornelio Moyano

BMCN — Boletin del Museo de Ciencias Naturales [*Caracas*]

BMCN — Book of the Month Club. News

BMCR — Bollettino. Museo della Civilta Romana

BMC Rom Emp — British Museum Catalogs. Coins. Roman Empire. Coins of the Roman Empire

BMC RR — British Museum. Catalogs. Coins. Roman Republic. Coins of the Roman Republic

BMCV — Bullettino dei Musei Civici Veneziani

BMC Venezia — Bollettino. Musei Civici Veneziani

BMD — Bijdragen en Mededeelingen der Dialectencommissie van de Koninklijke Akademie van Wetenschappen te Amsterdam

BMD — Boletin Mexicano de Derecho Comparado

BMD — Bulletin. Societe des Amis du Musee de Dijon

BMDIA — Bulletin. Mount Desert Island Biological Laboratory

BMDial — Bijdragen en Mededeelingen der Dialectencommissie van de Koninklijke Akademie van Wetenschappen te Amsterdam

BM Dijon — Bulletin. Societe des Amis du Musee de Dijon

BMDJA — Burma Medical Journal

BMDOA — Biomaterials, Medical Devices, and Artificial Organs

BM/E — Broadcast Management/Engineering

B Med Lib A — Bulletin. Medical Library Association

BMEEB — Bulletin of Mechanical Engineering Education

BMEGA — Bulletin. Mechanical Engineering Laboratory of Japan

BMEMDK — Biological Memoirs

B Mem Soc Anthr — Bulletins et Memoires. Societe d'Anthropologie de Paris

B Mem Soc Anthrop — Bulletins et Memoires. Societe d'Anthropologie

B Mem Soc Arch Bordeaux — Bulletin et Memoires. Societe Archeologique de Bordeaux

B Menninger — Bulletin. Menninger Clinic

B Mens Statist Trav Suppl — Bulletin Mensuel des Statistiques du Travail. Supplement

B Mens Stat O-Mer — Bulletin Mensuel de Statistique d'Outre-Mer

BMEPAQ — British Museum (Natural History). Economic Series

BMET — Bulletin du Musee d'Ethnographie du Trocadero

B Metr Mus — Bulletin. Metropolitan Museum of Art

B Metr Mus A — Bulletin. Metropolitan Museum of Art

BMF — Blaetter fuer Muenzfreunde und Muenzforschung
BMF — Bulletin. Musees de France
BMF — Musees de France
BMFA — Bulletin. Museum of Fine Arts
BMFAAK — British Museum (Natural History). Fossil Mammals of Africa
BMFAB — Bulletin. Museum of Fine Arts. Boston
BMFEA — Bulletin. Museum of Far Eastern Antiquities
BM Ferr — Bollettino. Musei Ferraresi
BMFJ — Bulletin. Maison Franco-Japonais
BMFR — Blaetter fuer Muenzfreunde
BMFT Mitt — BMFT [*Bundesministerium fuer Forschung und Technologie*] Mitteilungen
BMFT Mitteilungen — Bonn. Pressereferat des Bundesministeriums fuer Forschung und Technologie. Mitteilungen
BMG — Bulletin du Museum de Georgie
BMGC — British Museum. General Catalogue of Printed Books
BMGeire — Bijdragen en Mededeelingen Uitgegeven door de Vereeniging Geire
BM Geol Bull — British Museum. Geology Bulletin
BMGHA — Bamidgeh
BMGJW — Bijdragen en Mededeelingen van het Genootschap voor de Joodsche Wetenschap in Nederland
BMGLA — Bulletin. Societe des Sciences Medicales du Grand-Duche de Luxembourg
BMGM — Bulletin of the Madras Government Museum
BMGN — Bijdragen en Mededelingen Betreffende de Geschiedenis der Nederlanden
BMGS — Byzantine and Modern Greek Studies
BMH — Bulletin. Museum Haaretz
BMH — Handelsvoorlichting Bank Mees en Hope
BMHA — Bulletin pour la Conservation des Monuments Historiques d'Alsace
BMHB — Bulletin. Musee National Hongrois des Beaux-Arts
BMHBA — Bulletin. Musee Hongrois des Beaux Arts
BMHG — Bijdragen en Mededeelingen van het Historisch Genootschap
BMHM — Bulletin. Musee Historique de Mulhouse
BMHNAZ — Museo Nacional de Historia Natural. Boletin
BMHS — Bulletin. Missouri Historical Society
BMHS/J — Journal. Barbados Museum and Historical Society
BMI — BMI: The Many Worlds of Music
BMIA — Bulletin of the Minneapolis Institute of Arts
BMIC 8900 — Future Trends and Prospects for the Australian Mineral Processing Sector. Bureau of Mines Information Circular
BMIC 8917 — Aluminum Availability - Market Economy Countries. Bureau of Mines Information Circular
B Midwest M — Bulletin. Midwest Modern Language Association
BM Imp R — Bollettino. Museo dell'Impero Romana
B Minero E Ind — Boletin Minero e Industrial
B Min Inter — Bulletin. Ministere de l'Interieur
BMIPA — Bulletin et Memoires. Institut des Fouilles de Prehistoire et d'Archeologie desAlpes-Maritimes
BMIR — Bollettino. Museo dell'Impero Romano
BMISR — Botanicheskie Materialy Instituta Sporovykh Rastenii. Akademiia Nauk SSSR
B Miss Hist Soc — Bulletin. Missouri Historical Society
BMJ — British Medical Journal
BMJ — Brunei Museum Journal
BMJA — Bulletin. Museum of Jewish Antiquities
BMJ Br Med J — BMJ. British Medical Journal
BMJE — British Medical Journal Epitome
BM Jewell — Bulletin d'Archeologie Algerienne
BMJH — Boletin. Museo de Motivos Populares Argentinos Jose Hernandez
BMJOA — British Medical Journal
BMJOAE — British Medical Journal
BML — Bibliotheque du Museon (Louvain)
BML — Blackwood's Magazine (London)
BML — British Museum (London)
BMLA — Bulletin. Medical Library Association
BML Boll Microbiol Indag Lab — BML. Bollettino di Microbiologia e Indagini di Laboratorio
BMLF — Bulletin de la Maison du Livre Francais
BM Lyon — Bulletin des Musees et Monuments Lyonnais
BMM — Belaruskaia Mova. Mizhvuzauski Zbornik
BMM — Bibliography of Manichaean Materials
BMM — Biblioteca Moderna Mondadori
BMM — Bulletin. Metropolitan Museum of Art
BMMA — Bulletin. Metropolitan Museum of Art
BMMANY — Bulletin. Metropolitan Museum of Art (New York)
BMMBES — Biochemical Medicine and Metabolic Biology
BMMK — Bekes Megyei Muzeumok Kozlemenyei
BMMLA — Bulletin. Midwest Modern Language Association
BM (Monaco) — Bulletin. Musee d'Anthropologie Prehistorique (Monaco)
BMN — Boletim do Museu Nacional. Antropologia [*Rio de Janeiro*]
BMN — Building Material News
BMNADT — Bulletin. Museum National d'Histoire Naturelle. Section A. Zoologie, Biologie, et Ecologie Animales
BM Nat Hist Bull — British Museum. Natural History Bulletin
BMNB — Bulletin. Musee National de Burgas
BMNBDW — Bulletin. Museum National d'Histoire Naturelle. Section B. Adansonia Botanique.Phytochimie
BMNC — Boletin del Museo Nacional (Santiago de Chile)
BMNE — Bulletin. Museum of Mediterranean and Near Eastern Antiquities
BMNMDV — Bulletin. Museum National d'Histoire Naturelle. Section C. Sciences de la Terre. Paleontologie, Geologie, Mineralogie
BMNPA3 — British Museum (Natural History). Publication
BMNPD6 — Bulletin. Museum National d'Histoire Naturelle. Section B. Botanique, Biologie,et Ecologie Vegetales. Phytochimie

BMNRBA — British Museum (Natural History). Report
BMNV — Bulletin. Musee National de Varsovie
BMod — Bibliographie Moderne
BMOGA — Bollettino delle Malattie dell'Orecchio, della Gola, del Naso
B Mon — Bulletin Monumental
B Mon Ist — Buletinul Comisiunii Monumentelor Istorice a Romaniei
B Mon Mus Pont — Bollettino Monumenti. Musei e Gallerie Pontificie
B Montbeliard — Bulletin et Memoires. Societe d'Emulation de Montbeliard
B (Montreal) — Business Review (Montreal)
B Monument — Bulletin Monumental
BMOPDB — Butterworths International Medical Reviews. Ophthalmology
B Morbihan — Bulletin Mensuel. Societe Polymatique de Morbihan
BMORDH — Butterworths International Medical Reviews. Orthopaedics
BMP — Birmingham Post
BMP — Boletim Mensal. Sociedade de Lingua Portuguesa
BMP — Bulletin de la Societe des Amis de Marcel Proust et des Amis de Combray
BMP — Bulletin du Museum d'Histoire Naturelle (Paris)
BMPAE6 — Boletim. Museu Paraense Emilio Goeldi. Serie Antropologia
BMPBA — British Columbia. Department of Mines and Petroleum Resources. Bulletin
BMPBE9 — Boletim. Museu Paraense Emilio Goeldi. Serie Botanica
BMPEAE — Boletim. Museu Paraense Emilio Goeldi
BMPEG — Boletim do Museu Paraense Emilio Goeldi
BMPFr — Bulletin Mensuel des Publications Francaises
BMPG — Bulletin of the Museum and Picture Gallery [*Baroda*]
BMPGA — Byulleten' Moskovskogo Obshchestva Ispytatelei Prirody Otdel Geologicheskii
BMPMB — Bibliotheca Microbiologica
BMPS — Boletin del Ministerio de Prevision Social [*Quito*]
BMPSEQ — Brunner/Mazel Psychosocial Stress Series
BMPZED — Boletim. Museu Paraense Emilio Goeldi. Serie Zoologia
BMQ — Boston Medical Quarterly
BMQ — British Museum. Quarterly
BM Qu — British Museum. Quarterly
BMR — Bank Marketing
BMR — Black Music Research Journal
BMR — Monthly Bibliography of Medical Reviews
BMRAH — Bulletin. Musees Royaux d'Art et d'Histoire
BMRBA — Bulletin. Musees Royaux des Beaux-Arts
BMR Bull — BMR [*Bureau of Mineral Resources, Geology, and Geophysics*] Bulletin
BMRCDL — Butterworths International Medical Reviews. Cardiology
BMRED — Bureau of Mines. Research
BMR J — Black Music Research Journal
BMR J Aust Geol Geophys — BMR [*Australia. Bureau of Mineral Resources. Geology and Geophysics*] Journal of Australian Geology and Geophysics
BMRN — Bimonthly Research Notes. Canada Department of Environment
BMRNDK — Butterworths International Medical Reviews. Neurology
BMRNEL — Museo Regionale di Scienze Naturali. Bollettino
BMRODN — Butterworths International Medical Reviews. Obstetrics and Gynecology
BMRSA — Bulletin of Marine Science
BMS — Babylonian Magic and Sorcery
BMS — Benedictiner Monatsschrift
BMS — Mongolia Society. Bulletin
BMSA — Bulletins et Memoires. Societe d'Anthropologie
BMSAB — Bulletin et Memoires. Societe Archeologique de Bordeaux
BMSAF — Bulletin. Societe Nationale des Antiquaires de France
B M S Anthr — Bulletins et Memoires. Societe d'Anthropologie de Paris
BMSAO — Bulletin et Memoires. Societe des Antiquaires de l'Ouest
BMSAP — Bulletins et Memoires de la Societe d'Anthropologie de Paris
BMSF — Bulletin et Memoires. Societe Archeologique et Historique de l'Arrondisement deFougeres
BMSIA — Biomedical Sciences Instrumentation
BMSJ — British Medical Students Journal
BMSLP — Boletim Mensal. Sociedade de Lingua Portuguesa
BMSMA — Bulletins et Memoires. Societe Medicale des Hopitaux de Paris
BMSPM — Bulletin Mensuel. Societe Polymathique du Morbihan
BMSQ — Boston Medical and Surgical Quarterly
BMSSB — Bulletin Mathematique
BMSSD — Biomass Digest
BMSTA — Transactions. British Mycological Society
BMSYA — Biomedical Mass Spectrometry
BMT — Biomedical Technology Information Service
BMTBA — Bulletin of Mathematical Biology
BMTFA — Buletinul. Institutului Politehnic din Iasi. Sectia I. Matematica, Mecanica Teoretica, Fizica
B Mu — Berliner Museen
BMus — Berliner Museen
B Mus Anthropol Prehist — Bulletin. Musee d'Anthropologie Prehistorique
B Mus Art — Bulletin. Musees Royaux d'Art et d'Histoire
BMusB — Bulletin. Museum of Fine Arts (Boston)
BMusBeyr — Bulletin. Musee de Beyrouth
B Mus F A — Bulletin. Museum of Fine Arts
B Mus Far East Antiq — Bulletin. Museum of Far Eastern Antiquities
BMusFr — Bulletin. Musees de France
B Mus Hist Nat — Bulletin. Museum d'Histoire Naturelle
BMusHongr — Bulletin. Musee Hongrois des Beaux Arts
B Mus Imp — Bollettino. Museo dell'Impero Romano
B Mus (Monaco) — Bulletin. Musee d'Anthropologie Prehistorique (Monaco)
B Mus Mon Lyon — Bulletin des Musees et Monuments Lyonnais
B Mus Mulhouse — Bulletin. Musee Historique de Mulhouse
B Mus Natur Verona — Bollettino. Museo Civico di Storia Naturale di Verona
B Mus Padova — Bollettino. Museo Civico di Padova

B Mus Prov Bellas Artes Zaragoza — Boletin. Museo Provincial de Bellas Artes de Zaragoza
B Mus Vars — Bulletin. Musee National de Varsovie
B Muz — Belgarsko Muzikoznanie
BM Vases — British Museum. Catalogs. Vases. Catalogue of the Greek and Etruscan Vases
B Mw — Beitraege zur Musikwissenschaft
BMWEJ — Brotherhood of Maintenance of Way Employees. Journal
BM Yb — British Museum Yearbook
BMYBA — British Mycological Society. Bulletin
BMYSD2 — British Mycological Society. Symposium
BMZACT — Bollettino dei Musei di Zoologia e di Anatomia Comparata della (Reale) Universita di Torino
BMZTA — Biomedizinische Technik
BN — Beitraege zur Namenforschung
BN — Benelux Nieuws
BN — Bibliotheque Nationale
BN — Bibliotheque Norbertine
BN — Biography News
BN — Biuletyn Numizmatyczny
BN — Book Notes
BN — Borsen
BN — Botaniska Notiser
BN — Browning Newsletter
BN — Burke's Newsletter
BN — Byzantina Neerlandica
BNA — Tijdschrift. Nationale Bank van Belgie
BNA Admin Pract Man — BNA [*Bureau of National Affairs*] Administrative Practice Manual
BNAMC — Bulletin. National Association for Music Therapy
B Nancy — Bulletin. Academie et de la Societe Lorraines des Sciences (Nancy)
BN & R — Botswana Notes and Records
BNAP — Bulletin. National Association of Secondary-School Principals
B Narcotics — Bulletin on Narcotics
BNA Sec Reg — Securities Regulation and Law Reports (Bureau of National Affairs)
B Nat Geogr Soc India — Bulletin. National Geographical Society of India
B Nauk Inst Nauk Ekon Univ Warszaw — Biuletyn Naukowy Instytutu Nauk Ekonomicznych Uniwersytetu Warszawskiego
BNB — Boletin Nicaraguense de Bibliografia y Documentacion
BNB — Brazilian News Briefs
BNB — British National Bibliography
BNBE — Bibliografia Extranjera Depositada en la Biblioteca Nacional
BNBE — Economic Bulletin. National Bank of Egypt
BNBGAP — Bulletin. National Botanic Garden
BN Bian Ner — BN. Bianco e Nero
BNBID — Behavioral and Neural Biology
BNB/REN — Revista Economica do Nordeste. Banco do Nordeste do Brasil. Departamento de Estudos Economicos do Nordeste
BNBUD — Baroid News Bulletin
BNC — Business and Finance
Bnc Angola — Boletin Trimestral. Banco de Angola
BNCE/CE — Comercio Exterior. Banco Nacional de Comercio Exterior
Bnc Espana — Banco de Espana
BNCJ — Byzantinisch-Neugriechische Jahrbuecher
Bnc Lavoro — Italian Trends. Banco Lavoro
BNCPPS — Bulletin of the North Caucasian Plant Protection Station/Izvestiia Severno-Kavkazskoi Kraevoi Stantsii Zashchity Rastenii
BndM — Benediktinische Monatsschrift
BNDpfl — Beitraege zur Naturdenkmalpflege
BNDSA — Bibliotheca Nutrito et Dieta (Switzerland)
BNDSD — Bundesarbeitsblatt
BNEOB — Biology of the Neonate
BNEPB — Behavioral Neuropsychiatry
BNF — Beitraege zur Namenforschung
BNF Bull — BNF [*British Nutrition Foundation*] Bulletin
BNF Inf Bull — BNF [*British Nutrition Foundation*] Information Bulletin
BNF Nutr Bull — BNF [*British Nutrition Foundation*] Nutrition Bulletin
BNF Nutr Bull Br Nutr Found — BNF Nutrition Bulletin. British Nutrition Foundation
B Ng Jb — Byzantinisch-Neugriechische Jahrbuecher
BNGO — Bijdragen voor Nederlandsche Geschiedenis en Oudheidkunde
BNGrJb — Byzantinisch-Neugriechische Jahrbuecher
BNH — Beitraege zur Namenforschung (Heidelberg)
BNH Em Res — BNH [*Banco Nacional da Habitacao*] Em Resumo
BNHMB6 — Bulletin. Natural History Museum in Belgrade
BNHPDH — Basrah Natural History Museum. Publication
BNH Relat Atividad — BNH [*Banco Nacional da Habitacao*] Relatorio de Atividades
BNI — Bank van de Nederlandse Antillen. Quarterly Bulletin
BNI — Bibliografia Nazionale Italiana
BNIAA — Norinsho Kachiku Eisei Shikenjo Kenkyu Hokoku
B Nimes — Bulletin. Societe d'Etude des Sciences Naturelles de Nimes
BNISI — Bulletin of the National Institute of Sciences of India
BNIST Rapp Annu — BNIST [*Bureau National de l'Information Scientifique et Technique*] Rapport Annuel
BNJ — British Numismatic Journal, Including the Proceedings of the British NumismaticSociety
BNJ — Business News. Facts, Analysis, Information
BNJ — Byzantinisch-Neugriechische Jahrbuecher
B NJ Acad S — Bulletin. New Jersey Academy of Science
BNJb — Byzantinisch-Neugriechische Jahrbuecher
BN Jbb — Byzantinisch-Neugriechische Jahrbuecher
BNK — ABA [*American Bankers Association*] Banking Journal
BNK — Bank Reports
BNKAB — Bionika
BNKRB — Banker

BNL — Banca Nazionale del Lavoro. Quarterly Review
BNL — Beitraege zur Neueren Literaturgeschichte
BNLVAI — Brookhaven National Laboratory. Lectures in Science. Vistas in Research
BNM — Bank Marketing
BNMB — Bank Negara Malaysia. Bulletin
BNMFDC — New Mexico. Department of Game and Fish. Bulletin
BNN — Buggalo Nam Newsletter
BNo — Biblische Notizen
BNO — Biuletyn Nauczyciela Opolskiego
BNOB — Bulletin. Nederlandse Oudheidkundige Bond
B Nogent — Bulletin. Societe Historique et Archeologique de Nogent-sur-Marne et du Canton de Nogent
BNOTA — Belgisch-Nederlands Tijdschrift voor Oppervlaktetechnieken van Metalen
BNPL — Bulletin. New York Public Library
BNR — Bank Note Reporter
BNR — Brassey's Naval Record
BNrhGV — Berichte ueber die Versammlungen des Niederrheinischen Geologischen Vereins
BNRS — Registros Sonoros
BNS — Banque Nationale Suisse. Bulletin Mensuel
BNSCDX — Braunschweiger Naturkundliche Schriften
BNSDA — Bulletin. New York State Society of Dentistry for Children
BNSKA — Bunseki Kagaku
BNSMR — Bank of Nova Scotia. Monthly Review
BNT — Boreal Northern Titles
B Num — Biuletyn Numizmatyczny
B Num — Bulletin de Numismatique
B Num (Paris) — Bulletin. Societe Francaise de Numismatique (Paris)
BNUNA — Bulletin on Narcotics
BNV — Business Asia. Weekly Report to Managers of Asia/Pacific Operations
BNVUDY — Bericht des Naturwissenschaftlichen Vereins fuer Bielefeld und Umgegend EV
B NY Ac Med — Bulletin. New York Academy of Medicine
BNYLS — Bulletin. New York C. S. Lewis Society
BNYPL — Bulletin. New York Public Library
BNZ — Berliner Numismatische Zeitschrift
BNZED — Bulletin. New Zealand National Society for Earthquake Engineering
BO — Bibliotheca Orientalis
BO — Black Orpheus
Bo — Bohemia. Jahrbuch des Collegium Carolinum
BO — Boletin. Comision Provincial de Monumentos Historicos y Artisticos de Orense
BO — Boletin Oficial
Bo — Bolivar
BO — Bulletin Officiel du Congo Belge
BOA — Bibliography of Agriculture
BoAb — Boating Abstracts
Board Environ Stud Res Pap Univ Newcastle — University of Newcastle. Board of Environmental Studies. Research Paper
Board Greenkeeping Res Brit Golf Unions J — Board of Greenkeeping Research. British Golf Unions. Journal
Board Mfr — Board Manufacture and Practice
Board of Review Decisions — Decisions. Income Tax Board of Review
Boardroom — Boardroom Reports
BOAS — Bulletin. School of Oriental and African Studies
Boat Bus — Boating Business
Bo B — Bok og Bibliotek
BOB — By og Bygd. Norsk Folkemuseums Arbok
Bobbin Mag — Bobbin Magazine
BOC — Bulletin Officiel des Chemins de Fer
BOCAAD Bull Comput Aided Archit Des — BOCAAD. Bulletin of Computer-Aided Architectural Design
BOCDA — Building Official and Code Administrator
BOCES XVIII — Boletin. Centro de Estudios del Siglo XVIII, Oviedo
Docholt Quellen & Beitr — Booholtor Quollen und Beitraege
BOCKA — Bochu Kagaku
Bo Co — Bollettino. Commissione Archeologica Comunale di Roma
BOCVA — Boletin. Academia de Ciencias Fisicas, Matematicas, y Naturales (Caracas, Venezuela)
Bod Denkm Pfl Mecklenb — Jahrbuch der Bodendenkmalpflege in Mecklenburg
BODEA — Bodenkultur
Bode As Jb — Astronomisches Jahrbuch, nebst einer Sammlung der Neuesten in die Astronomischen Wissenschaften Einschlagenden Abhandlungen, Beobachtungen, und Nachrichten. Bode
Bode Jb — Astronomisches Jahrbuch, nebst einer Sammlung der Neuesten in die Astronomischen Wissenschaften Einschlagenden Abhandlungen, Beobachtungen, und Nachrichten. Bode
Bodenbiol Microbiol — Bodenbiologie Microbiologie
Bodenkd Pflanzenernaehr — Bodenkunde und Pflanzenernaehrung
Bodenk Forsch — Bodenkundliche Forschungen
Bodenk Pflanzenernaehr — Bodenkundliche und Pflanzenernaehrung
Bodensee-Chron — Bodensee-Chronik
Bodleian Lib Rec — Bodleian Library Record
Bodleian Libr Rec — Bodleian Library Record
Bodleian Q Rec — Bodleian Quarterly Record
Bodleian Quart Rec — Bodleian Quarterly Record
Bod Lib Rec — Bodleian Library Record
Bodl Libr Rec — Bodleian Library Record
BODO — Bauobjektdokumentation
Body Pol — Body Politic
BoE — Boletin de Estudios Historicos sobre San Sebastiano
BOE — Bulletin of Economic Research
BOE — Bureau of Explosives
BoeDB — Boersenblatt fuer den Deutschen Buchandel

BOEIA — Boei Eisei
Boek — Het Boek
BOEMA — Boletin. Instituto de Estudios Medicos y Biologicos. Universidad Nacional Autonoma de Mexico
Boergyogy Venerol Sz — Boergyogyaszati es Venerologiai Szemle
Boerhaave Ser Postgrad Med Educ — Boerhaave Series for Postgraduate Medical Education
Boersenbl Dtsch Buchhandel — Boersenblatt fuer den Deutschen Buchhandel
Boersen-Ztg — Boersen-Zeitung
Boethius Texte Abh Gesch Math Naturwiss — Boethius. Texte und Abhandlungen zur Geschichte der Mathematik und der Naturwiss
BOF — Bank of Finland. Monthly Bulletin
B Offic Ch Com (Bruxelles) — Bulletin Officiel. Chambre de Commerce (Bruxelles)
B Off Inst — Bulletin. Office Internationale. Instituts d'Archeologie et d'Histoire de l'Art
B Off Int — Bulletin. Office International des Instituts d'Archeologie et d'Histoirede l'Art
B Off Int Hyg Publ — Bulletin. Office International d'Hygiene Publique
B Off Int Vitic — Bulletin. Office International de la Viticulture
Bo Fi Cl — Bollettino di Filologia Classica
B of M — Books of the Month
B Of San Pa — Boletin. Oficina Sanitaria Panamericana
Bogazici U Derg Human Bilimler — Bogazici Universitesi Dergisi. Humaniter Bilimler
Bogazici Univ Derg Muhendislik — Bogazici Universitesi Dergisi. Muhendislik
Bogazici Univ Derg Temel Bilimler — Bogazici Universitesi Dergisi. Temel Bilimler
Bogazici Univ Derg Temel Bilimler Kim — Bogazici Universitesi Dergisi. Temel Bilimler. Kimya
Bogazici Univ J Eng — Bogazici Universitesi Journal. Engineering
Bogazici Univ J Sci — Bogazici Universitesi Journal. Sciences
Bogazici Univ J Sci Chem — Bogazici Universitesi Journal. Sciences. Chemistry
Boghazkoei Stud — Boghazkoei-Studien
BOGIA — Bollettino. Societa Geologica Italiana
Bog V — Bogens Verden
BoH — Boletin de Historia y Antiguedades
Bohemia Jb Coll Carolinum — Bohemia-Jahrbuch des Collegium Carolinum
Bohr Sprengprax — Bohr- und Sprengpraxis
Bohrtech Ztg — Bohrtechniker Zeitung
BOIA — Bulletin. Office International des Instituts d'Archeologie et d'Histoirede l'Art
BoiCl — Boite a Clous
BOIID — Boletin IIE
Boiler Eng — Boiler Engineer
Boiler Maker Plate Fabr — Boiler Maker and Plate Fabricator
Bois Forets Trop — Bois et Forets des Tropiques
Bois For Trop — Bois et Forets des Tropiques
BOJAAK — Boletim. Museu Nacional (Rio De Janeiro). Geologia
BOJODV — Biological Oceanography
BOK — Boekverkoper
Bok og Bibl — Bok og Bibliotek
Bol — Bolivar
Bola — Boletin. Academia Chilena de la Historia
BolA — Boletin. Academia Nacional de la Historia
Bol ABCP — Boletim ABCP
Bol Acad Arg Letr BA — Boletin. Academia Argentina de Letras (Buenos Aires)
Bol Acad B A — Boletin de la Academia de Bellas Artes
Bol Acad Buenas Letras Barcelona — Boletin. Real Academia de Buenas Letras de Barcelona
Bol Acad Chil Hist — Boletin de la Academia Chilena de Historia
Bol Acad Chil Hist Santiago — Boletin. Academia Chilena de Historia (Santiago)
Bol Acad Chil Santiago — Boletin. Academia Chilena (Santiago)
Bol Acad Cienc Cordoba — Boletin. Academia de Ciencias en Cordoba
Bol Acad Cienc Exactas Fis Nat — Boletin. Academia de Ciencias Exactas, Fisicas, y Naturales
Bol Acad Cienc Fis Mat Nat (Caracas) — Boletin. Academia de Ciencias Fisicas, Matematicas, y Naturales (Caracas, Venezuela)
Bol Acad Cienc Fis Mat Natur — Boletin. Academia de Ciencias Fisicas, Matematicas, y Naturales
Bol Acad Cienc (Repub Argent) — Boletin. Academia de Ciencias Fisicas (Republica Argentina)
Bol Acad Cien Fis Mat Nat Caracas — Boletin. Academia de Ciencias Fisicas, Matematicas, y Naturales (Caracas)
Bol Acad Cien Inst Chile — Boletin. Academia de Ciencias del Instituto de Chile
Bol Acad Ci Exact Madrid — Boletin. Academia de Ciencias Exactas, Fisicas, y Naturales de Madrid
Bol Acad Ci Nat Barcelona — Boletin. Academia de Ciencias Naturales y Artes de Barcelona
Bol Acad Col Bogota — Boletin. Academia Colombiana (Bogota)
Bol Acad Cordoba — Boletin. Real Academia de Ciencias, Bellas Letras, y Nobles Artes de Cordoba
Bol Acad Cubana Leng Hav — Boletin. Academia Cubana de la Lengua (Habana)
Bol Acad Galega Cienc — Boletin. Academia Galega de Ciencias
Bol Acad Hist — Boletin. Real Academia de la Historia
Bol Acad Hist Valle Cauca Cali — Boletin. Academia de Historia del Valle del Cauca (Cali, Colombia)
Bol Acad Nac Cienc (Argent) — Boletin. Academia Nacional de Ciencias (Argentina)
Bol Acad Nac Cienc (Cordoba) — Boletin. Academia Nacional de Ciencias (Cordoba)
Bol Acad Nac Farm — Boletim. Academia Nacional de Farmacia
Bol Acad Nac Hist Caracas — Boletin. Academia Nacional de la Historia (Caracas)
Bol Acad Nac Hist Quito — Boletin. Academia Nacional de Historia (Quito)
Bol Acad Nac Med — Boletim. Academia Nacional de Medicina
Bol Acad Nac Med (B Aires) — Boletim. Academia Nacional de Medicina (Buenos Aires)
Bol Acad Nac Med (Braz) — Boletim. Academia Nacional de Medicina (Brazil)

Bol Acad Nac Med (Rio De J) — Boletim. Academia Nacional de Medicina (Rio De Janeiro)
Bol Acad N B A — Boletim da Academia Nacional de Belas Artes
Bol Acad N Hist — Boletin de la Academia Nacional de Historia
Bol Acad Panamena Hist Panama — Boletin. Academia Panamena de la Historia (Panama)
Bol Acad Venez Corr Espanola Caracas — Boletin. Academia Venezolana. Correspondiente de la Espanola (Caracas)
Bol Ac Hist — Boletin. Real Academia de la Historia
Bol A de la H — Boletin. Real Academia de la Historia
Bol Adm Nac Agua (Argent) — Boletin. Administracion Nacional del Agua (Argentina)
Bol Aer Inst Panam Geo Hist — Boletin Aereo. Instituto Panamericano de Geografia e Historia
Bolaffi A — Bolaffi Arte
Bol Agencia Geral Colon — Boletin. Agencia Geral das Colonias
Bol Agr — Boletin de Agricultura, Mineria, e Industrias
Bol Agr Dept Prod Veg (Minas Gerais) — Boletin de Agricultura. Departamento de Producao Vegetal (Minas Gerais)
Bol Agr Dir Publ Agr (Sao Paulo) — Boletin. Agricultura. Directoria de Publicidade Agricola (Sao Paulo)
Bol Agric — Boletin Agricola. Sociedade Antioquena de Agricultores
Bol Agric Asoc Agric Rio Culiacan — Boletin Agricola. Asociacion de Agricultores del Rio Culiacan
Bol Agric (Belo Horizonte Braz) — Boletim de Agricultura (Belo Horizonte, Brazil)
Bol Agric (Belo Horizonte Brazil) — Boletim de Agricultura (Belo Horizonte, Brazil)
Bol Agric Estado Sao Paulo — Boletim de Agricultura do Estado de Sao Paulo
Bol Agric (Limburgerhof Ger) — Boletin Agricola (Limburgerhof, Germany)
Bol Agric (Mendoza Argent) — Boletin Agricola (Mendoza, Argentina)
Bol Agric Sao Paulo — Boletim de Agricultura (Sao Paulo)
Bol Agric Trop — Boletin de Agricultura Tropical
Bol Agric Zootech e Vet Bello Horizonte — Boletim de Agricultura, Zootechnia, e Veterinaria. Bello Horizonte
Bol Agro-Pec — Boletin Agro-Pecuario
Bol Agropecu Com Colomb Aliment Lacteos — Boletin Agropecuario. Compania Colombiana de Alimentos Lacteos
Bol Agr S Paulo — Boletim de Agricultura (Sao Paulo)
Bol Am Barcelona — Boletin Americanista (Barcelona)
Bol Amigos Porto — Boletim dos Amigos do Porto
Bol Antrop Amer — Boletin de Antropologia Americana
Bol Antrop Fortaleza — Boletin de Antropologia. Instituto de Antropologia. Universidade do Ceara (Fortaleza, Brazil)
Bol Antropol — Boletin de Antropologia
Bol Antrop Sucre — Boletin Antropologico. Publicacion. Museo de Arqueologia, Etnografia, y Folklore (Sucre)
Bol Anuar Bibliogr Cubano Hav — Boletin. Anuario Bibliografico Cubano (Habana)
Bol Arch Gen Gob Guat — Boletin. Archivo General del Gobierno (Guatemala)
Bol Arch Gen Nac Caracas — Boletin. Archivo General de la Nacion (Caracas)
Bol Arch Gen Nac C Trujillo S Domingo — Boletin. Archivo General de la Nacion (Ciudad Trujillo, Santo Domingo)
Bol Arch Gen Nac Mex — Boletin. Archivo General de la Nacion (Mexico)
Bol Arch Hist Jalisco — Boletin del Archivo Historico de Jalisco
Bol Arch Nac Hav — Boletin. Archivo Nacional (Habana)
Bol Arch Nac Hist Quito — Boletin. Archivo Nacional de Historia (Quito)
Bol Archv Gen Nacion — Boletin del Archivo General de la Nacion
Bol Argent For — Boletin Argentino Forestal
Bol (Argent) Serv Geol Nac — Boletin (Argentina). Servicio Geologico Nacional
Bol (Argent) Serv Nac Min Geol — Boletin (Argentina). Servicio Nacional Minero Geologico
Bol Arq — Boletin Arqueologico de Tarragona
Bol Arqu — Boletin Arqueologico
Bol Arqueol — Boletin de Arqueologia
Bol Arqueol Bogota — Boletin de Arqueologia (Bogota)
Bol Arquiv Distr Porto — Boletim do Arquivo Distrital do Porto
Bol Arquiv U Coimbra — Boletim do Arquivo da Universidade de Coimbra
Bol Arte — Bollettino d'Arte. Ministero della Pubblica Istruzione
Bol Arte Arq Valladolid — Boletin. Seminario de Estudios de Arte y Arqueologia
Bol Asoc A Concr Inven — Boletin de la Asociacion Arte Concreto Invencion
Bol Asoc Argent Electrotec — Boletin. Asociacion Argentina de Electrotecnicos
Bol Asoc Argent Odontol Ninos — Boletin. Asociacion Argentina de Odontologia para Ninos
Bol Asoc Chil Prot Fam — Boletin. Asociacion Chilena de Proteccion de la Familia
Bol Asoc Col Bibl Bogota — Boletin. Asociacion Colombiana de Bibliotecarios (Bogota)
Bol Asoc Costa Bibl S Jose — Boletin. Asociacion Costarricense de Bibliotecarios (San Jose)
Bol Asoc Cubana Bibl Hav — Boletin. Asociacion Cubana de Bibliotecarios (La Habana)
Bol Asoc Esp Entomol — Boletin. Asociacion Espanola de Entomologia
Bol Asoc Esp Orientalistas — Boletin de la Asociacion Espanola de Orientalistas
Bol Asoc Filat Bahia Blanca — Boletin. Asociacion Filatelica (Bahia Blanca, Argentina)
Bol Asoc Gen Agric Guatemala — Boletin. Asociacion General de Agricultures (Guatemala)
Bol Asoc Med PR — Boletin. Asociacion Medica de Puerto Rico
Bol Asoc Med Puerto Rico — Boletin. Asociacion Medica de Puerto Rico
Bol Asoc Mex Bibl Mex — Boletin. Asociacion Mexicana de Bibliotecarios (Mexico)
Bol Asoc Mex Geofis Explor — Boletin. Asociacion Mexicana de Geofisicos de Exploracion
Bol Asoc Mex Geol Pet — Boletin. Asociacion Mexicana de Geologos Petroleros
Bol Asoc Mex Geol Petrol — Boletin. Asociacion Mexicana de Geologos Petroleros
Bol Asoc Nac Ing Agron — Boletin. Asociacion Nacional de Ingenieros Agronomos
Bol Asoc Nac Ingen Agron — Boletin. Asociacion Nacional de Ingenieros Agronomos

Bol Asoc Peritos Forest — Boletin. Asociacion de Peritos Forestales

Bol Asoc Peruana Bibl Lima — Boletin. Asociacion Peruana de Bibliotecarios (Lima)

Bol Asoc Urug Prog Cienc — Boletin. Asociacion Uruguaya para el Progreso de la Ciencia

Bol Asoc Venez Enferm Prof — Boletin. Asociacion Venezolana de Enfermeras Profesionales

Bol Asoc Venez Geol Min Pet — Boletin. Asociacion Venezolana de Geologia, Mineria, y Petroleo

Bol Assist Med Indigen (Luanda) — Boletim de Assistencia Medicaos Indigenas e da Luta Contra a Moleatia do Sono (Luanda)

Bol Assoc Bras Fis Med — Boletim. Associacao Brasileira de Fisicos em Medicina

Bol Assoc Bras Normas Tec Rio — Boletim da Associacao Brasileira de Normas Tecnicas (Rio de Janeiro)

Bol Assoc Bras Pesqui Plant Aromat Oleos Essen — Boletim. Associacao Brasileira de Pesquisas sobre Plantas Aromaticas e Oleos Essenciais

Bol Assoc Bras Pesqui Plant Aromat Oleos Essenc — Boletim. Associacao Brasileira de Pesquisas sobre Plantas Aromaticas eOleos Essenciais

Bol Assoc Bras Pharm — Boletim. Associacao Brasileira de Pharmaceuticos

Bol Assoc Bras Quim — Boletim. Associacao Brasileira de Quimica

Bol Assoc Filos Nat (Portugal) — Boletim. Associacao de Filosofia Natural (Portugal)

Bol Assoc Quim Brasil — Boletim. Associacao Quimica do Brasil

Bol Assoc Tec Bras Celul Pap — Boletim. Associacao Tecnica Brasileira de Celulose e Papel

Bol A Toled — Boletin de Arte Toledano

Bol A U Malaga — Boletin de Arte de la Universidad de Malaga

Bol AVGMP — Boletin. AVGMP

Bol Azucar Mex — Boletin Azucarero Mexicano

Bol Banca Italia — Bollettino. Banca d'Italia

Bol Banco Cent Brasil — Boletim. Banco Central do Brasil

Bol Banco Cent Venez Caracas — Boletin. Banco Central de Venezuela (Caracas)

Bol B A Real Acad S Isabel Hungria — Boletin de Bellas Artes de la Real Academia de Santa Isabel de Hungria

Bol Bib Cer — Boletin Bibliografico Cerlal

Bol Bibl — Boletin Bibliografico Forestal

Bol Bibl Agric — Boletin para Bibliotecas Agricolas

Bol Bibl Antropol Amer — Boletin Bibliografico de Antropologia Americana

Bol Bibl Cam Deputados Rio Brasilia — Boletim da Biblioteca da Camara dos Deputados (Rio de Janeiro, Brasilia)

Bol Bibl Cent Univ Cato Santiago — Boletin. Biblioteca Central y de las Bibliotecas Departamentales. Universidad Catolica de Chile (Santiago)

Bol Bibl Col Abogad Lima — Boletin. Biblioteca del Colegio de Abogados (Lima)

Bol Bibl Gen Maracaibo — Boletin. Biblioteca General. Universidad del Zulia (Maracaibo, Venezuela)

Bol Bibl Ibero Am Bellas Art Mex — Boletin. Biblioteca Ibero Americana de Bellas Artes (Mexico)

Bol Bibliog Antropol Amer — Boletin Bibliografico de Antropologia Americana

Bol Bibliog Geofisica y Oceanografia Am — Boletin Bibliografico de Geofisica y Oceanografia Americanas

Bol Bibliog Agric Turrialba — Boletin Bibliografico Agricola (Turrialba, Costa Rica)

Bol Bibliogr Agrop Pasto — Boletin Bibliografico Agropecuario. Universidad de Narino (Pasto, Colombia)

Bol Bibliogr Antioq Medellin — Boletin de Bibliografia Antioquena (Medellin, Colombia)

Bol Bibliogr Antrop Am Mex — Boletin Bibliografico de Antropologia Americana (Mexico)

Bol Bibliogr Bahia Blanca — Boletin Bibliografico (Bahia Blanca, Argentina)

Bol Bibliogr Bibl Cam Diputados Lima — Boletin Bibliografico. Biblioteca. Camara de Diputados (Lima)

Bol Bibliogr Bibl Cent Min Trab Asunt Indig Lima — Boletin Bibliografico. Biblioteca Central. Ministerio de Trabajo y Asuntos Indigenas (Lima)

Bol Bibliogr Bibl Fac Cien Jur Soc La Plata — Boletin Bibliografico. Facultad de Ciencias Juridicas y Sociales. Universidad Nacional de La Plata (La Plata, Argentina)

Bol Bibliogr Bibl Univ S Marcos Lima — Boletin Bibliografico. Biblioteca. Universidad Mayor de San Marcos (Lima)

Bol Bibliogr Bot — Boletin de Bibliografia Botanica

Bol Bibliogr Bras Rio — Boletim Bibliografico Brasileiro (Rio de Janeiro)

Bol Bibliogr Dept Bibl Min Agr BA — Boletin Bibliografico. Departamento de Bibliotecas. Ministerio de Agricultura (Buenos Aires)

Bol Bibliogr Dom C Trujillo — Boletin Bibliografico Dominicano (Ciudad Trujillo)

Bol Bibliogr Fac Agron Univ Cent Venez — Boletin Bibliografico. Facultad de Agronomia. Universidad Central de Venezuela

Bol Bibliogr Geofis Oceano Am Mex — Boletin Bibliografico de Geofisica y Oceanografia Americanas (Mexico)

Bol Bibliogr Inst Forest Latinoamer Invest — Boletin Bibliografico. Instituto Forestal Latinoamericano de Investigacion y Capacitacion

Bol Bibliogr Mex Mex — Boletin Bibliografico Mexicano. Instituto Panamericana de Bibliografia y Documentacion (Mexico)

Bol Bibliogr Sec Hac Cred Publ Mex — Boletin Bibliografico. Secretaria de Hacienda y Credito Publico (Mexico)

Bol Bibliogr Semes Guat — Boletin Bibliografico Semestral. Publicacion. Banco de Guatemala

Bol Bibliogr S Paulo — Boletim Bibliografico. Biblioteca Publica Municipal (Sao Paulo)

Bol Bibliogr Yucat Merida — Boletin de Bibliografia Yucateca

Bol Biblio (Peru) — Boletin Bibliografico (Peru)

Bol Biblioteca — Boletin de Biblioteca

Bol Bibl Menendez Pelayo — Boletin. Biblioteca de Menendez Pelayo

Bol Bibl Nac Caracas — Boletin. Biblioteca Nacional (Caracas)

Bol Bibl Nac Guat — Boletin. Biblioteca Nacional (Guatemala)

Bol Bibl Nac Lima — Boletin. Biblioteca Nacional (Lima)

Bol Bibl Nac Mex — Boletin. Biblioteca Nacional (Mexico)

Bol Bibl Nac Quito — Boletin. Biblioteca Nacional (Quito)

Bol Bibl Nac Santiago — Boletin. Biblioteca Nacional (Santiago)

Bol Bibl Nac S Salvador — Boletin. Biblioteca Nacional (San Salvador)

Bol Bibl Trib D F Caracas — Boletin. Biblioteca de los Tribunales del Distrito Federal (Caracas)

Bol Bib Menendez Pelayo — Boletin Biblioteca Menendez Pelayo

Bol Bioestat Epidem — Boletim de Bioestatistica e Epidemiologia

Bol Biol — Boletin Biologico

Bol Biol (S Paulo) — Boletin Biologica (Sao Paulo)

Bol Bosques — Boletin de Bosques, Pesca i Caza

Bol Cam Com (Caracas) — Boletin. Camara de Comercio (Caracas)

Bol Catedra Fitopatol Univ Nac La Plata — Boletin. Catedra de Fitopatologia. Universidad Nacional La Plata

Bol Cear Agron — Boletim Cearense de Agronomia

Bol Cent A Granada — Boletin del Centro Artistico de Granada

Bol Cent Coop Cientif Monte — Boletin. Centro de Cooperacion Cientifica (Montevideo)

Bol Cent Estud Hosp Servidores Estado (Rio De J) — Boletim. Centro de Estudos do Hospital dos Servidores do Estado (Rio De Janeiro)

Bol Cent Estudiant Der Sucre — Boletin. Centro de Estudiantes de Derecho (Sucre)

Bol Cent Hist Larense Barquisimeto — Boletin. Centro de Historia Larense (Barquisimeto, Venezuela)

Bol Cent Invest Antrop Mex — Boletin. Centro de Investigaciones Antropologicas de Mexico (Mexico)

Bol Cent Invest Biol Univ Zulia — Boletin. Centro de Investigaciones Biologicas. Universidad del Zulia

Bol Cent Invest Hist & Estet Caracas — Boletin del Centro de Investigaciones Historicas y Esteticas de Caracas

Bol Cent Invest Hist Guayaquil — Boletin. Centro de Investigaciones Historicas (Guayaquil)

Bol Cent Lat Am Pesq Cien Soc Rio — Boletim do Centro Latino-Americano de Pesquisas em Ciencias Sociais (Rio de Janeiro)

Bol Cent Nac Aliment Nutr (Spain) — Boletin. Centro Nacional de Alimentacion y Nutricion (Spain)

Bol Cent Nav — Boletin. Centro Naval

Bol Cent Panam Fiebre Aftosa — Boletin. Centro Panamericano de Fiebre Aftosa

Bol Centro Invest Antropol Mexico — Boletin. Centro de Investigaciones Antropologicas de Mexico

Bol Chil Parasitol — Boletin Chileno de Parasitologia

Bol Chim Un Italiana Lb Prov Par Scien — Bollettino dei Chimici. Unione Italiana dei Laboratori Provinciali. Parte Scientifica

Bol Cia Adm Guano — Boletin. Compania Administradora del Guano

Bol Ciencias Econs — Boletim de Ciencias Economicas

Bol Ciencias Pol y Socs — Boletin de Ciencias Politicas y Sociales

Bol Cienc Mar — Boletim de Ciencias do Mar

Bol Cienc Tecnol Dep Asuntos Cult Union Panam — Boletin de Ciencia y Tecnologia. Departamento de Asuntos Culturales. Union Panamericana

Bol Cient BC Cent Energ Nucl Agric — Boletim Cientifico BC. Centro de Energia Nuclear na Agricultura

Bol Cient Cent Invest Oceanogr Hidrogr (Cartagena Colomb) — Boletin Cientifico. Centro de Investigaciones Oceanograficas eHidrograficas (Cartegena, Colombia)

Bol Cientif Lima — Boletin Cientifico. Compania Administradora del Guano (Lima)

Bol Ci Med Guadalajara — Boletin de Ciencias Medicas (Guadalajara, Mexico)

Bol Ci Soc Sanchez Oropeza — Boletin Cientifico. Sociedad Sanchez Oropeza

Bol Clac — Boletin Clacso

Bol Clin Endocrinol Metab — Boletin. Clinica de Endocrinologia y Metabolismo

Bol Clin Hosp Civis Lisb — Boletim Clinico dos Hospitals Civis de Lisboa

Bol Col Prof Enferm PR — Boletin. Colegio de Profesionales de la Enfermeria de Puerto Rico

Bol Col Prov Med Valladolid — Boletin del Colegio Provincial de Medicos (Valladolid)

Bol Col Quim PR — Boletin. Colegio de Quimicos de Puerto Rico

Bol Com Arch Hav — Boletin. Comite de Archivos (La Habana)

Bol Combust Petroquim — Boletin de Combustibles y Petroquimica

Bol Com Fom Min (Mex) — Boletin. Comision de Fomento Minero (Mexico)

Bol Com Geogr Geol Estado Sao Paulo — Boletim. Comissao Geografica e Geologica do Estado de Sao Paulo

Bol Comis Nac Panama UNESCO Panama — Boletin. Comision Nacional de Panama (UNESCO) (Panama)

Bol Commiss Geogr Estado Sao Paulo — Boletim. Commissao Geographica e Geologica do Estado de Sao Paulo

Bol Com Mnmts Navarros — Boletin de la Comision de Monumentos de Navarros

Bol Com Mnmts Vizcaya — Boletin de la Comision de Monumentos de Vizcaya

Bol Com Mun Turismo — Boletim da Comissao Municipal de Turismo

Bol Com Nac Energ Nucl (Braz) — Boletim. Comissao Nacional de Energia Nuclear (Brazil)

Bol Comp Admin Guano — Boletin. Compania Administradora del Guano

Bol Com Perm Asoc Acad Lengua Espan — Boletin. Comision Permanente de la Asociacion de Academias de la LenguaEspanola

Bol Com Prov Mnmts Burgos — Boletin de la Comision Provincial de Monumentos de Burgos

Bol Com Prov Mnmts Orense — Boletin de la Comision Provincial de Monumentos de Orense

Bol Comunic Hav — Boletin de Comunicaciones (La Habana)

Bol Cons Nac Pesqui (Braz) — Boletim. Conselho Nacional de Pesquisas (Brazil)

Bol Cons Nac Pesqui (Brazil) — Boletim. Conselho Nacional de Pesquisas (Brazil)

Bol Corp Venez Fomento — Boletin. Corporacion Venezolana de Fomento

Bol CPE Salvador — Boletim da Comissao de Planejamento Economico (Salvador, Brazil)

Bol Cuerpo Ing Minas Peru — Boletin. Cuerpo de Ingenieros de Minas del Peru

Bol Cult — Boletim Cultural

Bol Cult & Bib Bib Luis Angel Arango — Boletin Cultural y Bibliografico. Biblioteca Luis Angel Arango

Bol Cult Assembl Distr Lisboa — Boletim Cultural da Assembleia Distrital de Lisboa
Bol Cult Bibliogr Bogota — Boletin Cultural y Bibliografico (Bogota)
Bol Cult Camara Mun Porto — Boletim Cultural da Camara Municipal do Porto
Bol Cult Guine Port — Boletim Cultural da Guine Portuguesa
Bol Cult Guine Portug — Boletim Cultural da Guine Portuguesa
Bol De Crimin — Boletin de Criminologia
Bol del SEAA — Boletin. Seminario de Estudios de Arte y Arqueologia
Bol Del Sindacato Fascista Avvocati — Il Bollettino del Sindacato Fascista Avvocati e Procuratori di Napoli
Bol Demografico (Brazil) — Boletim Demografico (Brazil)
Bol Dent Oper — Boletim de Dentistica Operatoria
Bol Dent Urug — Boletin Dental Uruguayo
Bol Dep Biol Fac Cienc Univ Nac Colombia — Boletin. Departamento de Biologia. Facultad de Ciencias. Universidad Nacional de Colombia
Bol Dep Eng Quim Esc Politec Univ Sao Paulo — Boletim. Departamento de Engenharia Quimica. Escola Politecnica.Universidade de Sao Paulo
Bol Dep For (Uruguay) — Boletin. Departamento Forestal (Montevideo, Uruguay)
Bol Dep Geol Uni Son — Boletin. Departamento de Geologia. Universidad de Sonora
Bol Dep Mat Estat (Araraquara Braz) — Boletim. Departamento de Matematica e Estatistica (Araraquara, Brazil)
Bol Dep Nac Prod Miner (Brasil) — Boletim. Departamento Nacional da Producao Mineral (Brasil)
Bol Dep Quim Esc Politec Univ Sao Paulo — Boletim. Departamento de Quimica. Escola Politecnica. Universidadede Sao Paulo
Bol Dep Quim Inst Tecnol Estud Super (Monterrey) — Boletim. Departamento de Quimica. Instituto Tecnologico y de Estudios Superiores (Monterrey)
Bol Dept Eng Quim Esc Politec Univ Sao Paulo — Boletim. Departamento de Engenharia Quimica. Escola Politecnica. Universidade e de Sao Paulo
Bol Dept Estradas Rodagem S Paulo — Boletim do Departamento de Estradas de Rodagem (Sao Paulo)
Bol Dermatol Sanit — Boletin Dermatologico Sanitario
Bol Didat Esc Agron Eliseu Maciel (Pelotas Braz) — Boletim Didatico. Escola de Agronomia Eliseu Maciel (Pelotas, Brazil)
Bol Didat Esc Agron Eliseu Maciel (Pelotas Brazil) — Boletim Didatico. Escola de Agronomia Eliseu Maciel (Pelotas, Brazil)
Bol Dir Agric Ganad (Peru) — Boletin. Direccion de Agricultura y Ganaderia (Peru)
Bol Dir Gen Agric (Peru) — Boletin. Direccion General de Agricultura (Peru)
Bol Dir Gen Arch Bibl Madrid — Boletin. Direcion General de Archivos y Bibliotecas (Madrid)
Bol Dir Gen Forest Caza Mex — Boletin. Direccion General Forestal y de Caza (Mexico)
Bol Dir Gen Odontol (Santa Fe) — Boletin. Direccion General de Odontologia (Santa Fe)
Bol Malariol Saneamiento Ambiental — Boletin. Direccion de Malariologia y Saneamiento Ambiental
Bol Dir Nac Geol Min (Argent) — Boletin. Direccion Nacional de Geologia y Mineria (Argentina)
Bol Div Fom Prod Miner (Braz) — Boletin. Divisao de Fomento da Producao Mineral (Brazil)
Bol Div Nac Dermatol Sanit — Boletim. Divisao Nacional de Dermatologia Sanitaria
Bol Div Nac Lepra — Boletim. Divisao Nacional de Lepra
Bol Divul Estac Exp Agropec INTA (Pergamino) — Boletin de Divulgacion. Estacion Experimental Agropecuaria. Instituto Nacional de Tecnologia Agropecuaria (Pergamino, Argentina)
Bol Divulg Inst Nac Invest For (Mex) — Boletin Divulgativo. Instituto Nacional de Investigaciones Forestales (Mexico)
Bol Divulg Inst Oleos (Rio De Janeiro) — Boletim de Divulgacao. Instituto de Oleos (Rio De Janeiro)
Bol Divulg Minist Agric Ganad — Boletin Divulgativo. Ministerio de Agricultura y Ganaderia
Bol Divulg Tec Inst Patol Veg (B Aires) — Boletin de Divulgacion Tecnica. Instituto de Patologia Vegetal (Buenos Aires)
Bol Docum Fondo Invest Econ Soc — Boletin de Documentacion. Fondo para la Investigacion Economica y Social
Bol Do Inst De Crimin — Boletim do Instituto de Criminologia
Bol Eclesias Fil — Boletin Eclesiastico de Filipinas
Bol Econ Pubblica — Bollettino dell'Economia Pubblica
Bol Ed — Boletin de Edificacion
Bol Educ Paraguay Asuncion — Boletin de Educacion Paraguaya (Asuncion)
Bol Electroquim Corros — Boletim de Electroquimica e Corrosao
Bol Entomol Venez — Boletin de Entomologia Venezolana
Bol Epidemiol — Boletin Epidemiologico
Bol Epidemiol (Rio De J) — Boletim Epidemiologico (Rio De Janeiro)
Bol Equipe Odontol Sanit — Boletim da Equipe de Odontologia Sanitaria
Bol Esc Cienc Antrop Yucatan — Boletin de la Escuela de Ciencias Antropologicas de la Universidad de Yucatan
Bol Esc Farm (Coimbra) — Boletim. Escola de Farmacia (Coimbra)
Bol Esc Farm Univ Coimbra — Boletim. Escola de Farmacia. Universidade de Coimbra
Bol Esc Farm Univ Coimbra Ed Cien — Boletim. Escola de Farmacia. Universidade de Coimbra. Edicao Cientifica
Bol Esc Farm Univ Coimbra Ed Didact Not Farm — Boletim. Escola de Farmacia. Universidade de Coimbra. Edicao Didactica. Noticias Farmaceuticas
Bol Esc Nac Agr (Lima) — Boletin. Escuela Nacional de Agricultura (Lima)
Bol Esc Nac Ci Biol — Boletin. Escuela Nacional de Ciencias Biologicas
Bol Esc Nac Ing (Peru) — Boletin. Escuela Nacional de Ingenieros (Peru)
Bol Esc Super Agric "Luiz De Queiroz" Univ Sao Paulo — Boletim. Escola Superior de Agricultura "Luiz De Queiroz." Universidade de Sao Paulo
Bol Esc Super Farm Univ Lisboa — Boletim. Escola Superior de Farmacia. Universidade de Lisboa
Bol Escuela Nac Bibl Arch Mex — Boletin. Escuela Nacional de Bibliotecarios y Archivistas (Mexico)

Bol Estac Agric Exp Chihuahua — Boletin. Estacion Agricola Experimental (Chihuahua, Mexico)
Bol Estac Biol Mar Univ Ceara — Boletim. Estacao de Biologia Marinha. Universidade do Ceara
Bol Estac Biol Mar Univ Fed Ceara — Boletim. Estacao de Biologia Marinha. Universidade Federal do Ceara
Bol Estac Cent Ecol — Boletin. Estacion Central de Ecologia
Bol Estac Cent Ecol (Spain) — Boletin. Estacion Central de Ecologia (Spain)
Bol Estac Exp Agric "La Molina" — Boletin. Estacion Experimental Agricola "La Molina"
Bol Estac Exp Agric "La Molina" (Lima) — Boletin. Estacion Experimental Agricola "La Molina" (Lima)
Bol Estac Exp Agric (Rio Piedras PR) — Boletin. Estacion Experimental Agricola (Rio Piedras, Puerto Rico)
Bol Estac Exp Agric Tucuman — Boletin. Estacion Experimental Agricola de la Provincia de Tucuman
Bol Estac Exp Agric Tucuman — Boletin. Estacion Experimental Agricola de Tucuman
Bol Estac Exp Agr "La Molina" — Boletin. Estacion Experimental Agricola "La Molina"
Bol Estac Exp Agropec Pres Roque Saenz Pena (Argentina) — Boletin. Estacion Experimental Agropecuaria de Presidencia Roque Saenz Pena (Argentina)
Bol Estac Exp Agr "Tingo Maria" — Boletin. Estacion Experimental Agricola "Tingo Maria"
Bol Estadistica — Boletin de Estadistica
Bol Estadistico Trim (Argentina) — Boletin Estadistico Trimestral (Argentina)
Bol Estadistico Trim (Bolivia) — Boletin Estadistico Trimestral (Bolivia)
Bol Est Doc Serem — Boletin de Estudios y Documentacion del Serem
Bol Estud Econ — Boletin de Estudios Economicos
Bol Estud Geogr Mendoza — Boletin de Estudios Geograficos (Mendoza, Argentina)
Bol Estud Geogr Univ Nac Cuyo — Boletin de Estudios Geograficos. Universidad Nacional de Cuyo
Bol Estud Hist Pasto — Boletin de Estudios Historicos (Pasto, Colombia)
Bol Estud Latinoamer — Boletin de Estudios Latinoamericanos y del Caribe
Bol Estud Latinoam y Caribe — Boletin de Estudios Latinoamericanos y del Caribe
Bol Estud Med Biol — Boletin de Estudios Medicos y Biologicos
Bol Estud Med Biol Univ Nac Auton Mex — Boletin de Estudios Medicos y Biologicos. Universidad Nacional Autonoma de Mexico
Bol Estud Oaxaquenos — Boletin de Estudios Oaxaquenos
Bol Estud Oaxaquenos Oaxaca — Boletin de Estudios Oaxaquenos (Oaxaca, Mexico)
Bol Estud Pesca — Boletim de Estudos de Pesca
Bol Estud Pol Mendoza — Boletin de Estudios Politicos (Mendoza, Argentina)
Bol Estud Supt Desenvolvimento Nordeste Div Geol (Braz) — Boletim de Estudos. Superintendencia do Desenvolvimento do Nordeste. Divisao deGeologia (Brazil)
Bol Estud Teatro BA — Boletin de Estudios de Teatro (Buenos Aires)
Boletin IF — Boletin. Instituto de Folklore
Bolet R Acad Hist — Boletin. Real Academia de la Historia
Bol Exp Serv Agric Interam (La Paz) — Boletin Experimental. Servicio Agricola Interamericano (La Paz)
Bolex Rep — Bolex Reporter
Bolezni Rast — Bolezni Rastenij. Morbi Plantarum. Jahrbuch fuer Pflanzenkrankheiten
Bolezni Skh Zhivotn Sb SAO VASKhNIL — Bolezni Sel'skokhozyaistvennykh Zhivotnykh. Sbornik SAO VASKhNIL
Bolezni Skh Zhivotn Tr UzNIVI — Bolezni Sel'skokhozyaistvennykh Zhivotnykh. Trudy UzNIVI
Bol Fac Agron — Boletin. Facultad de Agronomia. Universidad de San Carlos
Bol Fac Agron Univ Repub (Montevideo) — Boletin. Facultad de Agronomia. Universidad de la Republica(Montevideo)
Bol Fac Agron Univ San Carlos Guatemala — Boletin. Facultad de Agronomia. Universidad de San Carlos de Guatemala
Bol Fac Cienc Agrar Para — Boletim. Faculdade de Ciencias Agrarias do Para
Bol Fac Cienc For Univ Los Andes — Boletin. Facultad de Ciencias Forestales. Universidad de Los Andes
Bol Fac Der Cienc Soc (Cordoba) — Boletin. Facultad de Derecho y Ciencias Sociales (Cordoba)
Bol Fac Der Cien Soc Cordoba — Boletin. Facultad de Derecho y Ciencias Sociales. Universidad Nacional de Cordoba (Cordoba, Argentina)
Bol Fac Dir (Coimbra) — Boletim. Faculdade de Direito (Coimbra)
Bol Fac Farm Coimbra (Coimbra) — Boletim. Faculdade de Farmacia. Universidade de Coimbra (Coimbra)
Bol Fac Farm Odontol Ribeirao Preto — Boletim. Faculdade de Farmacia e Odontologia de Ribeirao Preto
Bol Fac Farm Univ Coimbra Ed Cient — Boletim. Faculdade de Farmacia. Universidade de Coimbra. Edicao Cientifica
Bol Fac Farm Univ Coimbra Ed Didact Not Farm — Boletim. Faculdade de Farmacia. Universidade de Coimbra. Edicao Didactica. Noticias Farmaceuticas
Bol Fac Farm Univ Lisboa — Boletim. Faculdade de Farmacia. Universidade de Lisboa
Bol Fac Filos Cienc Let Univ Sao Paulo Bot — Boletim. Faculdade de Filosofia, Ciencias, e Letras. Universidade deSao Paulo. Serie Botanica
Bol Fac Filos Cienc Let Univ Sao Paulo Geol — Boletim. Faculdade de Filosofia, Ciencias, e Letras. Universidade deSao Paulo. Serie Geologia
Bol Fac Filos Cienc Let Univ Sao Paulo Mineral — Boletim. Faculdade de Filosofia, Ciencias, e Letras. Universidade deSao Paulo. Serie Mineralogia
Bol Fac Filos Cienc Let Univ Sao Paulo Quim — Boletim. Faculdade de Filosofia, Ciencias, e Letras. Universidade deSao Paulo. Serie Quimica
Bol Fac Filos Cienc Let Univ Sao Paulo Ser Bot — Boletim. Faculdade de Filosofia, Ciencias, e Letras. Universidade de Sao Paulo. Serie Botanica
Bol Fac Filos Cienc Let Univ Sao Paulo Ser Zool — Boletim. Faculdade de Filosofia, Ciencias, e Letras. Universidade de Sao Paulo. Serie Zoologia

Bol Fac Ing Agrimens Univ Repub — Boletin. Facultad de Ingenieria y Agrimensura. Universidad de la Republica

Bol Fac Ing Agrimensura Montevideo — Boletin. Facultad de Ingenieria y Agrimensura de Montevideo

Bol Fac Ing Montevideo — Boletin. Facultad de Ingenieria de Montevideo

Bol Fac Ing Ramas Anexas Univ Montevideo — Boletin. Facultad de Ingenieria y Ramas Anexas. Universidad deMontevideo

Bol Fac Ing Univ Repub — Boletin. Facultad de Ingenieria. Universidad de la Republica

Bol Fac Ing y Agrimensura Montevideo — Boletin. Facultad de Ingenieria y Agrimensura de Montevideo

Bol Fac Nac Agron — Boletin. Facultad Nacional de Agronomia

Bol Fac Odontol Piracicaba — Boletim. Faculdade de Odontologia de Piracicaba

Bol Fac Odontol Piracicaba Univ Estadual Campinas — Boletim. Faculdade de Odontologia de Piracicaba. Universidade Estadual de Campinas

Bol Farm Mil — Boletin de Farmacia Militar

Bol Fed Bras Assoc Bibl S Paulo — Boletim da Federacao Brasileira de Associacoes de Bibliotecarios (Sao Paulo)

Bol Fed Med Ecuador — Boletin. Federacion Medica del Ecuador

Bol Filol Monte — Boletin de Filologia (Montevideo)

Bol Filol Santiago — Boletin de Filologia (Santiago)

Bol Fisiol Anim (Sao Paulo) — Boletim de Fisiologia Animal (Sao Paulo)

Bol Fitossanit — Boletim Fitossanitario

Bol Fomento San Jose — Boletin de Fomento. Secretaria de Fomento y Agricultura (San Jose, Costa Rica)

Bol Forest Caracas — Boletin Forestal (Caracas)

Bol For Ind For Amer Lat FAO — Boletin Forestal y de Industrias Forestales para America Latina. Oficina Forestal Regional de la FAO

Bol Fund Goncalo Moniz — Boletim. Fundacao Goncalo Moniz

Bol Genet — Boletin Genetico

Bol Genet (Engl Ed) — Boletin Genetico (English Edition)

Bol Geocienc Petrobras — Boletim de Geociencias da Petrobras

Bol Geo Dir Geol (Venez) — Boletin de Geologia. Direccion de Geologia (Venezuela)

Bol Geog — Boletim Geografico

Bol Geogr — Boletim Geografico

Bol Geogr Rio — Boletim Geografico. Instituto Brasileiro de Geografia e Estatistica (Rio de Janeiro)

Bol Geol Bogota — Boletin Geologico (Bogota)

Bol Geol (Caracas) — Boletin de Geologia (Caracas)

Bol Geol (Caracas) Publ Espec — Boletin de Geologia (Caracas). Publicacion Especial

Bol Geol (Colomb) Inst Nac Invest Geol Min — Boletin Geologico (Columbia). Instituto Nacional de InvestigacionesGeologico-Mineras

Bol Geol Dir Geol (Venez) — Boletin de Geologia. Direccion de Geologia (Venezuela)

Bol Geol Ingeominas — Boletin Geologico Ingeominas

Bol Geol Inst Geogr Nac (Guatem) — Boletin Geologico. Instituto Geografico Nacional (Guatemala)

Bol Geol Inst Geol Nac (Colomb) — Boletin Geologico. Instituto Geologico Nacional (Colombia)

Bol Geol Min — Boletin Geologico y Minero

Bol Geol Miner — Boletin Geologico y Minero

Bol Geol Min (Esp) — Boletin Geologico y Minero (Espana)

Bol Geol Publ Espec — Boletin de Geologia. Publicacion Especial

Bol Geol Publ Espec Dir Geol (Venez) — Boletin de Geologia. Publicacion Especial. Direccion de Geologia (Venezuela)

Bol Geol Serv Geol Nac (Colomb) — Boletin Geologico. Servicio Geologico Nacional (Colombia)

Bol Geol Univ Fed Rio De Janeiro Inst Geocienc — Boletim de Geologia. Universidade Federal do Rio De Janeiro. Institutode Geociencias

Bol Geol Univ Ind Santander — Boletin de Geologia. Universidad Industrial de Santander

Bol Geol (Venez) Dir Geol — Boletin de Geologia (Venezuela). Direccion de Geologia

Bol GEOMINAS — Boletin. GEOMINAS

Bolg Fiz Zh — Bolgarskii Fizicheskii Zhurnal

Bolg Tab — Bolgarskii Tabak

Bol Hig Epidemiol — Boletin de Higiene y Epidemiologia

Bol Hist Antig Bogota — Boletin de Historia y Antiguedades (Bogota)

Bol Hist Caracas — Boletin Historico (Caracas)

Bol Hist Cartagena — Boletin Historial (Cartagena, Colombia)

Bol Hist Fund John Boulton — Boletin Historico de la Fundacion John Boulton

Bol Hist Monte — Boletin Historico (Montevideo)

Bol Hist Nat Soc "Felipe Poey" — Boletin de Historia Natural. Sociedad "Felipe Poey"

Bol Hist Nat Soc Felipe Poey Univ Habana — Boletin de Historia Natural. Sociedad Felipe Poey. Universidad de la Habana

Bol Hist Nat Soc F Poey Hav — Boletin de Historia Natural. Sociedad Felipe Poey (La Habana)

Bol Historia Nat — Boletin de Historia Natural

Bol Hist Valle Cali — Boletin Historico del Valle (Cali, Colombia)

Bol Hosp — Boletin de los Hospitales

Bol Hosp Civ San Juan De Dios (Quito) — Boletin. Hospital Civil de San Juan De Dios (Quito)

Bol Hosp Clin Fac Med Univ Bahia — Boletim. Hospital das Clinicas. Faculdade de Medicina. Universidade daBahia

Bol Hosp Fac Med Univ Bahia — Boletim. Hospital da Faculdade de Medicina. Universidade da Bahia

Bol Hosp Hosp Geral Santo Antonio Porto — Boletim. Hospital. Hospital Geral de Santo Antonio-Porto

Bol Hosp Oftalmol Nuestra Senora de la Luz — Boletin. Hospital Oftalmologico de Nuestra Senora de la Luz

Bol Hosp Prof Edgard Santos Fac Med Univ Bahia — Boletim. Hospital Prof. Edgard Santos. Faculdade de Medicina.Universidade da Bahia

Bol Hosp Vina del Mar — Boletin. Hospital de Vina del Mar

Bol Iberoam Cult Tec — Boletin Iberoamericano de Cultura Tecnica

Bol IG Univ Sao Paulo Inst Geocien — Boletim IG. Universidade de Sao Paulo. Instituto de Geociencias

Bol IIE — Boletin IIE

Bol INAH — Boletin del Instituto Nacional de Antropologia e Historia

Bol Ind Anim — Boletim de Industria Animal

Bol Ind Com Papel — Boletin de la Industria y Comercio del Papel

Bol Indig Mex — Boletin Indigenista (Mexico)

Bol Indig Venez — Boletin Indigenista Venezolano

Bol Indig Venez Caracas — Boletin Indigenista Venezolano (Caracas)

Bol INED — Boletin. INED

Bol Inf ABIA/SAPRO — Boletim Informativo ABIA/SAPRO

Bol Inf (Argent) Dir Nac Quim — Boletin Informativo (Argentina). Direccion Nacional de Quimica

Bol Inf Asoc Venez Geol Min Pet — Boletin Informativo. Asociacion Venezolana de Geologia, Mineria, y Petroleo

Bol Inf Bromatol — Boletin de Informacion Bromatologica

Bol Inf Cent Nac Invest Cafe — Boletin Informativo. Centro Nacional de Investigaciones de Cafe

Bol Inf Cient Nac — Boletin de Informaciones Cientificas Nacionales

Bol Inf Circ Farm — Boletin Informativo de Circular Farmaceutica

Bol Inf Cir Farm — Boletin Informativo de Circular Farmaceutica

Bol Inf Dent Ilustre Cons Gen Col Odontol Estomatol Esp — Boletin de Informacion Dental. Ilustre Consejo General de Colegiosde Odontologos y Estomatologos de Espana

Bol Inf Dent (Madr) — Boletin de Informacion Dental (Madrid)

Bol Inf Dep Quim Veg Patron Juan Cuerva — Boletin de Informacion. Departamento de Quimica Vegetal. Consejo Superior de Investigaciones Cientificas. Patronato Juan de la Cuerva

Bol Inf DNQ — Boletin Informativo. DNQ

Bol Inf Estac Exp Agri Tucuman — Boletin Informativo. Estacion Experimental Agricola de Tucuman

Bol Inf Inst Biol Marit — Boletim Informativo. Instituto de Biologia Maritima

Bol Inf Inst Bot — Boletim Informativo. Instituto de Botanica

Bol Inf Inst Cubano Invest Tecnol — Boletin Informativo. Instituto Cubano de Investigaciones Tecnologicas

Bol Info Jud — Boletin de Informacion Judicial

Bol Inform Bibl Fac Filos Letr Tucuman — Boletin Informativo. Biblioteca. Facultad de Filosofia y Letras. Universidad Nacional de Tucuman (Tucuman, Argentina)

Bol Inform Cientif Nac Quito — Boletin de Informaciones Cientificas Nacionales (Quito)

Bol Inform Inst Bras Bibliogr Doc Rio — Boletim Informativo do Instituto Brasileiro de Bibliografia e Documentacao (Riode Janeiro)

Bol Inform Inst Cacau Bahia — Boletim Informativo. Instituto de Cacau da Bahia

Bol Inform Inst For (Chile) — Boletin Informativo. Instituto Forestal (Santiago-De-Chile)

Bol Inform Inst Forest — Boletin Informativo. Instituto Forestal

Bol Inform Inst Interamer Ci Agric — Boletin Informativo. Instituto Interamericano de Ciencias Agricolas

Bol Inform Inst Nac Tec Agropec Inst Fitotec — Boletin Informativo. Instituto Nacional de Tecnologia Agropecuaria. Instituto de Fitotecnia

Bol Inform Ital — Bollettino di Informazioni Italiani

Bol Inform Minist Agric (Madrid) — Boletin de Informacion. Ministerio de Agricultura (Madrid)

Bol Inform Min Rel Ext Quito — Boletin Informativo. Ministerio de Relaciones Exteriores (Quito)

Bol Inform Petrol BA — Boletin de Informaciones Petroleras (Buenos Aires)

Bol Inform Petrol Yac Indus BA — Boletin de Informaciones Petroliferas, Yacimientos, e Industrias (Buenos Aires)

Bol Inform Santiago — Boletin Informativo (Santiago)

Bol Inform Tec Asoc Invest Tec Ind Madera — Boletin de Informacion Tecnica. Asociacion de Investigacion Tecnica de las Industrias de la Madera y Corcho

Bol Info Secretar Iberoam Mun — Boletin de Informacion. Secretariado Iberoamericano de Municipios

Bol Inf Parasit Chil — Boletin de Informaciones Parasitarias Chilenas

Bol Inf Pet — Boletin de Informaciones Petroleras

Bol Inf Soc Bras Radiol — Boletim Informativo. Sociedade Brasileira de Radiologia

Bol Inf Soc Colomb Quim Farm — Boletin Informativo. Sociedad Colombiana de Quimicos Farmaceuticos

Bol Inf Tec Dep Met No Ferreos — Boletin de Informacion Tecnica. Departamento de Metales No Ferreos.Patronato Juan de la Cierva de Investigacion Tecnica

Bol Inf Tec Dep Met No Ferreos CSIC (Spain) — Boletin de Informacion Tecnica. Departamento de Metales No Ferreos. Consejo Superior de Investigaciones Cientificas (Spain)

Bol Inf Tec Negromex SA Dep Serv Tec — Boletin de Informacion Tecnica. Negromex, SA. Departamento de ServicioTecnico

Bol Ing — Boletin de Ingenieros

Bol INPABO — Boletim do INBAPO (Instituto Paranaense de Botanica)

Bol INPA Bot — Boletim. INPA [*Instituto Nacional de Pesquisas da Amazonia*]. Botanica

Bol INPA Patol Trop — Boletim. INPA [*Instituto Nacional de Pesquisas da Amazonia*]. PatologiaTropical

Bol INPA Pat Trop — Boletim. INPA [*Instituto Nacional de Pesquisas da Amazonia*]. Patologia Tropical

Bol INPA Pesqui Florestais — Boletim. INPA [*Instituto Nacional de Pesquisas da Amazonia*]. PesquisasFlorestais

Bol INPA Tecnol — Boletim. INPA [*Instituto Nacional de Pesquisas da Amazonia*]. Tecnologia

Bol Inseminacao Artif — Boletim de Inseminacao Artificial

Bol Insemin Artif — Boletim de Inseminacao Artificial

Bol Inst Agric Trop Univ PR — Boletin. Instituto de Agricultura Tropical. Universidad de Puerto Rico

Bol Inst Agron Campinas — Boletim. Instituto Agronomico Campinas

Bol Inst Agron Estado Sao Paulo — Boletim. Instituto Agronomico do Estado de Sao Paulo

Bol Inst Agron (Sao Paulo) — Boletim. Instituto Agronomico (Sao Paulo)

Bol Inst Angola — Boletim. Instituto de Angola

Bol Inst Antrop Medellin — Boletin. Instituto de Antropologia (Medellin, Colombia)

Bol Inst Antropol — Boletin del Instituto de Antropologia

Bol Inst Antropol Univ Antioquia Medellin — Boletin. Instituto de Antropologia. Universidad de Antioquia, Medellin

Bol Inst Azeite Prod Oleaginosos — Boletim. Instituto do Azeite e Produtos Oleaginosos

Bol Inst Bacteriol Chile — Boletin. Instituto Bacteriologico de Chile

Bol Inst Biol Bahia — Boletim. Instituto Biologico da Bahia

Bol Inst Biol Mar — Boletin. Instituto de Biologia Marina. Universidades Nacionales de Buenos Aires

Bol Inst Biol Mar (Mar Del Plata) — Boletin. Instituto de Biologia Marina (Mar Del Plata)

Bol Inst Biol Mar Univ Fed Rio Grande Do Norte — Boletim. Instituto de Biologia Marinha. Universidade Federal do Rio Grande Do Norte

Bol Inst Biol Pesqui Tecnol — Boletim. Instituto de Biologia e Pesquisas Tecnologicas

Bol Inst Boliv Pet — Boletin. Instituto Boliviano del Petroleo

Bol Inst Bot (Sao Paulo) — Boletim. Instituto de Botanica (Sao Paulo)

Bol Inst Bot Univ Cent (Quito) — Boletin. Instituto Botanico. Universidad Central (Quito)

Bol Inst Bot Univ Quito — Boletin. Instituto Botanica. Universidad de Quito

Bol Inst Brasil Sci — Boletim. Instituto Brasileiro de Sciencias

Bol Inst Caro Cuervo Bogota — Boletin. Instituto Caro y Cuervo (Bogota)

Bol Inst Cent Biocienc Ser Bot — Boletim. Instituto Central de Biociencias. Serie Botanica

Bol Inst Centr Fomento Econ Bahia — Boletim. Instituto Central de Fomento Economica da Bahia

Bol Inst Cienc Biol Geocienc Commun Malacol — Boletim. Instituto de Ciencias Biologicas e de Geociencias. Communicacoes Malacologicas

Bol Inst Cienc Nat Univ Cent Ecuador — Boletin. Instituto de Ciencias Naturales. Universidad Central del Ecuador

Bol Inst Cienc Nat Univ Rio Grande Do Sul — Boletim. Instituto de Ciencias Naturais. Universidade do Rio Grande Do Sul

Bol Inst Clin Quir — Boletin. Instituto de Clinica Quirurgica

Bol Inst Der Comp Mex — Boletin. Instituto de Derecho Comparado de Mexico (Mexico, DF)

Bol Inst Der Comp Quito — Boletin. Instituto de Derecho Comparado (Quito)

Bol Inst Ecol Exp Agric — Boletim. Instituto de Ecologia e Experimentacao Agricolas

Bol Inst Esp Oceanogr — Boletin. Instituto Espanol de Oceanografia

Bol Inst Est Astur — Boletin. Instituto de Estudios Asturianos

Bol Inst Est Giennenses — Boletin. Instituto de Estudios Giennenses

Bol Inst Estud Astur — Boletin del Instituto de Estudios Asturianos

Bol Inst Estud Aymaras — Boletin del Instituto de Estudios Aymaras

Bol Inst Estud Econ Finan La Plata — Boletin. Instituto de Estudios Economicos y Financieros (La Plata, Argentina)

Bol Inst Estud Med Biol — Boletin. Instituto de Estudios Medicos y Biologicos

Bol Inst Estud Med Biol Univ Nac Mex — Boletin. Instituto de Estudios Medicos y Biologicos. Universidad Nacional de Mexico

Bol Inst Estud Polit — Boletin. Instituto de Estudios Politicos

Bol Inst Etnol & Flklore — Boletin del Instituto de Etnologia y Folklore

Bol Inst Fer Gonz — Boletin. Institucion Fernan-Gonzales

Bol Inst Fernan Gonzalez — Boletin del Institucion Fernan Gonzalez

Bol Inst Folk Caracas — Boletin. Instituto de Folklore (Caracas)

Bol Inst Fomento Algodonero — Boletin. Instituto de Fomento Algodonero

Bol Inst Forest Latinoamer Invest — Boletin. Instituto Forestal Latinoamericano de Investigacion y Capacitacion

Bol Inst Forest Latinoam Invest Capacit Merida — Boletin. Instituto Forestal Latino Americano de Investigacion y Capacitacion (Merida, Venezuela)

Bol Inst For Invest Exper (Madrid) — Boletin. Instituto Forestal de Investigaciones y Experiencias (Madrid)

Bol Inst For Invest Exp (Madrid) — Boletin. Instituto Forestal de Investigaciones y Experiencias (Madrid)

Bol Inst For Lat-Am Invest Capac — Boletin. Instituto Forestal Latino-Americano de Investigacion y Capacitacion

Bol Inst For Latino-Am Invest Capac — Boletin. Instituto Forestal Latino-Americano de Investigacion y Capacitacion

Bol Inst Genet Soc Nac Agrar (Lima) — Boletin. Instituto de Genetica. Sociedad Nacional Agraria (Lima)

Bol Inst Geocienc Astron Univ Sao Paulo — Boletim. Instituto de Geociencias e Astronomia. Universidade de Sao Paulo

Bol Inst Geogr Geol (Sao Paulo State) — Boletim. Instituto Geografico e Geologico (Sao Paulo State)

Bol Inst Geogr Lima — Boletin. Instituto de Geografia (Lima)

Bol Inst Geol — Boletin. Instituto de Geologia

Bol Inst Geol (Mex) — Boletin. Instituto de Geologia (Mexico)

Bol Inst Geol Min Esp — Boletin. Instituto Geologico y Minero de Espana

Bol Inst Geol Univ Nac Auton Mex — Boletin. Instituto de Geologia. Universidad Nacional Autonoma de Mexico

Bol Inst Geol Univ Recife Mineral — Boletim. Instituto de Geologia. Universidade de Recife. Mineralogia

Bol Inst Hist Arg BA — Boletin. Instituto de Historia Argentina Doctor Emilio Ravignani (Buenos Aires)

Bol Inst Hist Nat Curitiba Bot — Boletim. Instituto de Historia Natural Curitiba Botanica

Bol Inst Indig Nac Guat — Boletin. Instituto Indigenista Nacional (Guatemala)

Bol Inst Int Am Prot Infanc — Boletin. Instituto Internacional Americano de Proteccion a la Infancia

Bol Inst Interam Nino — Boletin. Instituto Interamericano del Nino

Bol Inst Invest Agron (Spain) — Boletin. Instituto de Investigaciones Agronomicas (Spain)

Bol Inst Invest Bibliogr — Boletin. Instituto de Investigaciones Bibliograficas

Bol Inst Invest Cient Angola — Boletin. Instituto de Investigacao Cientifica de Angola

Bol Inst Invest Cient Univ Nuevo Leon — Boletin. Instituto de Investigaciones Cientificas. Universidad de Nuevo Leon

Bol Inst Invest Electr — Boletin. Instituto de Investigaciones Electricas

Bol Inst Invest Geol (Chile) — Boletin. Instituto de Investigaciones Geologicas (Chile)

Bol Inst Invest Hist & Estet — Boletin del Instituto de Investigaciones Historicas y Esteticas

Bol Inst Invest Hist BA — Boletin. Instituto de Investigaciones Historicas (Buenos Aires)

Bol Inst Investig Cient Angola — Boletim. Instituto de Investigacao Cientifica de Angola

Bol Inst Invest Recur Mar (Callao) — Boletin. Instituto de Investigacion de los Recursos Marinos (Callao)

Bol Inst Invest Soc Econ Panama — Boletin. Instituto de Investigaciones Sociales y Economicas (Panama)

Bol Inst Invest Text Coop Ind Univ Politec Barcelona — Boletin. Instituto de Investigacion Textil y de CooperacionIndustrial. Universidad Politecnica de Barcelona

Bol Inst Invest Vet (Maracay) — Boletin. Instituto de Investigaciones Veterinarias (Maracay)

Bol Inst Invest Vet (Maracay Venez) — Boletin. Instituto de Investigaciones Veterinarias (Maracay,Venezuela)

Bol Inst J Nabuco Pesq Soc Recife — Boletim do Instituto Joaquim Nabuco de Pesquisas Sociais (Recife, Brazil)

Bol Inst Kuribara Ci Nat Brasil — Boletim. Instituto Kuribara de Ciencia Natural Brasileira

Bol Inst Legis Comp Der Intern Panama — Boletin. Instituto de Legislacion Comparada y Derecho Internacional (Panama)

Bol Inst Lit Chil Santiago — Boletin. Instituto de Literatura Chilena (Santiago)

Bol Inst Mar Peru (Callao) — Boletin. Instituto del Mar del Peru (Callao)

Bol Inst Mat Astron Fis — Boletin. Instituto de Matematica, Astronomia, y Fisica

Bol Inst Med Exp Estud Trat Cancer (Buenos Aires) — Boletin. Instituto de Medicina Experimental para el Estudio y Tratamiento del Cancer (Buenos Aires)

Bol Inst Mex Cafe — Boletin. Instituto Mexicana del Cafe

Bol Inst M F Suarez Medellin — Boletin. Instituto Marco Fidel Suarez (Medellin, Colombia)

Bol Inst Microbiol Univ Fed Rio Grande Do Sul — Boletim. Instituto de Microbiologia. Universidade Federal do Rio Grande Do Sul

Bol Inst Nac Aliment (Montevideo) — Boletin. Instituto Nacional de Alimentacion (Montevideo)

Bol Inst Nac Antropol Hist Mexico — Boletin. Instituto Nacional de Antropologia e Historia de Mexico

Bol Inst Nac Examen Diagn — Boletin. Institucion Nacional de Examen y Diagnostico

Bol Inst Nac Hig Alfonso XIII — Boletin. Instituto Nacional de Higiene de Alfonso XIII

Bol Inst Nac Hig (Caracas) — Boletin. Instituto Nacional de Higiene (Caracas)

Bol Inst Nac Invest Agron — Boletin. Instituto Nacional de Investigaciones Agronomicas

Bol Inst Nac Invest Agron (Madr) — Boletin. Instituto Nacional de Investigaciones Agronomicas (Madrid)

Bol Inst Nac Invest Agron (Spain) — Boletin. Instituto Nacional de Investigaciones Agronomicas (Spain)

Bol Inst Nac Invest Exper Agron For — Boletin. Instituto Nacional de Investigaciones y Experiencias Agronomicas y Forestales

Bol Inst Nac Invest Fom Min (Peru) — Boletin. Instituto Nacional de Investigacion y Fomento Mineros (Peru)

Bol Inst Nac Invest Ind Electroquim Corros (Port) — Boletim. Instituto Nacional de Investigacao Industrial. Electroquimicae Corrosao (Portugal)

Bol Inst Nac Mejia Quito — Boletin. Instituto Nacional Mejia (Quito)

Bol Inst Nac Neumol (Mex) — Boletin. Instituto Nacional de Neumologia (Mexico)

Bol Inst Nac Pesqui Amazonia Pesqui Florestais — Boletim. Instituto Nacional de Pesquisas da Amazonia. Pesquisas Florestais

Bol Inst Nac Pesqui Amazonia Tecnol — Boletim. Instituto Nacional de Pesquisas da Amazonia. Tecnologia

Bol Inst Nac Prev Soc BA — Boletin. Instituto Nacional de Prevision Social (Buenos Aires)

Bol Inst Nac Tecnol (Rio De Janeiro) — Boletim. Instituto Nacional de Tecnologia (Rio De Janeiro)

Bol Inst Num Hist San Nicolas — Boletin. Instituto de Numismatica e Historia de San Nicolas de los Arroyos

Bol Inst Oceanogr — Boletim. Instituto Oceanografico

Bol Inst Oceanogr (Cumana Venez) — Boletin. Instituto Oceanografico (Cumana, Venezuela)

Bol Inst Oceanogr Sao Paulo — Boletim. Instituto de Oceanografia. Sao Paulo Universidade (Sao Paulo)

Bol Inst Oceanogr Univ Oriente — Boletin. Instituto Oceanografico. Universidad de Oriente

Bol Inst Oceanogr Univ Oriente (Cumana) — Boletin. Instituto Oceanografico. Universidad de Oriente (Cumana)

Bol Inst Oceanogr Univ Sao Paulo — Boletim. Instituto Oceanografico. Universidade de Sao Paulo

Bol Inst Patol Med (Madrid) — Boletin. Instituto de Patologia Medica (Madrid)

Bol Inst Pesqui Cir (Rio De J) — Boletim. Instituto de Pesquisas Cirurgicas (Rio De Janeiro)

Bol Inst Pesqui Vet "Desiderio Finamor" — Boletim. Instituto de Pesquisas Veterinarias "Desiderio Finamor"

Bol Inst Prod Florestais Cortica — Boletim. Instituto dos Produtos Florestais - Cortica

Bol Inst Prod Florestais Madeiras Deriv — Boletim. Instituto dos Produtos Florestais. Madeiras e Derivados

Bol Inst Prod Florestais Resinosos — Boletim. Instituto dos Produtos Florestais. Resinosos
Bol Inst Psicopedagog Nac Lima — Boletin. Instituto Psicopedagogico Nacional (Lima)
Bol Inst Psiquiatr Fac Cienc Med Rosario — Boletin. Instituto Psiquiatrico. Facultad de Ciencias Medicas deRosario
Bol Inst Quim Agric (Rio De Janeiro) — Boletim. Instituto de Quimica Agricola (Rio De Janeiro)
Bol Inst Quim Mexico — Boletin. Instituto de Quimica. Universidad Nacional Autonoma de Mexico
Bol Inst Quim Univ Nac Auton Mex — Boletin. Instituto de Quimica. Universidad Nacional Autonoma de Mexico
Bol Instr Publ — Boletin de Instruccion Publica
Bol Inst Salud Publica Chile — Boletin. Instituto de Salud Publica de Chile
Bol Inst Sociol BA — Boletin. Instituto de Sociologia (Buenos Aires)
Bol Inst Sudam Pet (Montevideo) — Boletin. Instituto Sudamericano del Petroleo (Montevideo)
Bol Inst Sudam Petrol Monte — Boletin. Instituto Sudamericano del Petroleo (Montevideo)
Bol Inst Tecnol Aliment — Boletim. Instituto de Tecnologia de Alimentos
Bol Inst Tecnol Aliment (Campinas Braz) — Boletim. Instituto de Tecnologia de Alimentos (Campinas, Brazil)
Bol Inst Tecnol (Rio Grande Sul) — Boletim. Instituto Tecnologico (Rio Grande Do Sul)
Bol Inst Tecnol Rural Univ Ceara — Boletim. Instituto de Tecnologia Rural. Universidade do Ceara
Bol Inst Tonantzintla — Boletin. Instituto de Tonantzintla
Bol Inst Zimotec (Sao Paulo) — Boletim. Instituto Zimotecnico (Sao Paulo)
Bol Inter Am Child Inst Monte — Boletin. Instituto Inter-Americano del Nino (Montevideo)
Bol Interamer M — Boletin Interamericano de Musica/Inter-American Music Bulletin
Bol Interam Music Wash — Boletin Interamericano de Musica (Washington, DC)
Bol IPA PSM — Boletim. IPA [*Instituto de Pesquisas Agronomicas*]. PSM
Bol Ist Pato Lib — Bollettino. Istituto di Patologia del Libro
Bol Ist Stud Verdiani — Bollettino. Istituto di Studi Verdiani
Bolivia Dep Nac Geol Bol — Bolivia. Departamento Nacional de Geologia. Boletin
Bolivia Inst Nac Esstadist Bol Estadist Mens — Bolivia. Instituto Nacional de Estadistica. Boletin Estadistico Mensual
Bolivia Inst Nac Estadist Bol Estadist Trimest — Bolivia. Instituto Nacional de Estadistica. Boletin Estadistico Trimestral
Bolivia Minist Minas Pet Dep Nac Geol Bol — Bolivia. Ministerio de Minas y Petroleo. Departamento Nacional deGeologia. Boletin
Bolivia Serv Geol Bol — Bolivia. Servicio Geologico. Boletin
Bol Jard Bot Mexico City — Boletin. Jardin Botanico. Mexico City
Bol Jard Bot Nac — Boletin. Jardin Botanico Nacional
Bol Jard Bot Rio De Janeiro — Boletim do Jardim Botanico (Rio de Janeiro)
Bol Junta Control Energ At — Boletim. Junta do Control de Energia Atomica
Bol Junta Geral Distr Auton Ponta Delgada — Boletim. Junta Geral Distrito Autonomo Ponta Delgada
Bol Junta Nac Cortica — Boletim. Junta Nacional da Cortica
Bol Junta Patrn Mus Prov B A Murcia — Boletin de la Junta del Patronato de Museo Provincia de Bellas Artes de Murcia
Bol Junt Aux Soc Mex Geogr Estad Guadalajara — Boletin. Junta Auxiliar. Sociedad Mexicana de Geografia y Estadistica (Guadalajara, Mexico)
Boll A — Bollettino d'Arte
Bol Lab Clin "Luis Razetti" — Boletin. Laboratorio de la Clinica "Luis Razetti"
Bol Lab Paleontol Vertebr — Boletin. Laboratorio de Paleontologia de Vertebrados
Bol Lab Prod Miner (Braz) — Boletim. Laboratorio de Producao Mineral (Brazil)
Bol Lab Quim Nac — Boletin. Laboratorio Quimico Nacional
Bol Lab Quim Nac (Colomb) — Boletin. Laboratorio Quimico Nacional (Colombia)
Bol Lab Quim Nac (Colombia) — Boletin. Laboratorio Quimico Nacional (Colombia)
Boll Accad Euloti — Bollettino dell'Accademia degli Euloti
Boll Accad Euteleti Citta San Miniato — Bollettino dell'Accademia degli Euteleti della Citta di San Miniato
Boll Accad Med-Chir Bologna — Bollettino. Accademia Medico-Chirurgica di Bologna
Boll Accad Med Genova — Bollettino. Accademia Medica de Genova
Boll Accad Med Pistoiese Filippo Pacini — Bollettino. Accademia Medica Pistoiese Filippo Pacini
Boll Accad Svizz Sci Med — Bollettino. Accademia Svizzera delle Scienze Mediche
Boll A Indust & Curiosita Ven — Bollettino di Arti, Industrie, e Curiosita Veneziane
Boll A Min Educ N — Bollettino d'Arte del Ministero dell'Educazione Nazionale
Boll A Min Pub Istruzione — Bollettino d'Arte. Ministero della Pubblica Istruzione
Boll Annu — Bollettino Annuario
Boll Archaeol Crist — Bollettino di Archeologia Cristiana
Boll Archeol Crist Roma — Bollettino di Archeologia Cristiana di Roma
Boll Arte — Bollettino d'Arte
Boll Ass Arch Rom — Romana. Associazione Archeologica Romana
Boll Ass Int Stud Med — Bollettino. Associazione Internazionale degli Studi Mediterranei
Boll Ass It Dir Mar — Bollettino d'Informazioni. Associazione Italiana di Diritto Marittimo
Boll Ass Med March — Bollettino. Associazione Medica Marchigiana
Boll Ass Med Trid — Bollettino. Associazione Medica Tridentina
Boll Ass Med Triest — Bollettino. Associazione Medica Triestina
Boll Ass Min Ital — Bollettino. Associazione Mineraria Italiana
Boll Assoc African Ital — Bollettino. Associazione degli Africanisti Italiani
Boll Assoc Afr Ital — Bollettino. Associazione degli Africanisti Italiani
Boll Assoc Cult Ventaglio — Bollettino dell'Associazione Culturale il Ventaglio
Boll Assoc Ital Chim Tess Color — Bollettino. Associazione Italiana de Chimica Tessile e Coloristica
Boll Assoc Ital Ind Zucchero Alcool — Bollettino. Associazione Italiana delle Industrie delle Zucchero e dell'Alcool

Boll Assoc Ital Piante Med — Bollettino di Associazione Italiana Pro Piante Medicinali, Aromatiche, ed AltrePiante Utili
Boll Assoc Ital Piante Med Aromat Altre Piante Utili — Bollettino. Associazione Italiana pro Piante Medicinali Aromatiche ed Altre Piante Utili
Boll Assoc Ital Tec Ind Vernici Affini — Bollettino. Associazione Italiana Tecnici Industrie Vernici Affini
Boll Assoc Rom Entomol — Bollettino. Associazione Romana di Entomologia
Boll Ass Ott Ital — Bollettino. Associazione Ottica Italiana
Boll Atti Accad Med Roma — Bollettino ed Atti. Accademia Medica di Roma
Boll Atti R Accad Med Roma — Bollettino e Atti. Reale Accademia Medica di Roma
Boll Atti Soc Ital Endocrinol — Bollettino ed Atti. Societa Italiana de Endocrinologia
Boll Badia Greca Grottaferrata — Bolletino della Badia Greca di Grottaferrata
Boll Bibl — Bollettino Biblico
Boll Bibl Fac Archit U Stud Roma — Bollettino della Biblioteca. Facolta di Architettura dell'Universita degli Studi di Roma
Boll Bibliogr Bot Ital — Bollettino Bibliografico Della Botanica Italiana
Boll Bibliogr Stor Sci Mat — Bollettino di Bibliografia e Storia delle Scienze Matematiche
Boll Brev Invenz Modelli Marchi — Bollettino dei Brevetti per Invenzioni, Modelli, e Marchi
Boll Camera Agrum Messina — Bollettino Camera Agrumaria de Messina
Boll Cent Camuno Stud Preist — Bollettino del Centro Camuno di Studi Preistorici
Boll Cent Int Stud Archit Andrea Palladio — Bollettino del Centro Internazionale di Studi di Architettura Andrea Palladio
Boll Centro — Bollettino. Centro di Studi per la Storia dell'Architettura
Boll Centro Architettura — Bollettino. Centro di Studi per la Storia dell'Architettura
Boll Centro Camuno — Bollettino. Centro Camuno di Studi Preistorici
Boll Centro Int Beltrame Stor Spaz Tempo — Bollettino. Centro Internazionale A. Beltrame di Storia dello Spazio e del Tempo
Boll Centro Stud Vichiani — Bollettino. Centro di Studi Vichiani
Boll Cent Stud Stor Archit — Bollettino del Centro di Studi per la Storia dell'Architettura
Boll Chim Clin — Bollettino di Chimica Clinica
Boll Chim Farm — Bollettino Chimico Farmaceutico
Boll Chim Ig Parte Sci — Bollettino dei Chimici Igienisti. Parte Scientifica
Boll Chim Lab Prov — Bollettino dei Chimici dei Laboratori Provinciali
Boll Chim Unione Ital Lab Prov — Bollettino dei Chimici. Unione Italiana dei Laboratori Provinciali
Boll Chim Unione Ital Lab Prov Parte Sci — Bollettino dei Chimici. Unione Italiana dei Laboratori Provinciali.Parte Scientifica
Boll Chim Unione Ital Parte Sci — Bollettino dei Chimici. Unione Italiana dei Laboratori Provinciali. Parte Scientifica
Boll Circ Numi Napoletano — Bollettino del Circolo Numismatico Napoletano
Boll Circ Num Napoletano — Bollettino. Circolo Numismatico Napoletano
Boll CIRVI — Bollettino del CIRVI
Boll Citta Foligno — Bollettino Storico della Citta di Foligno
Boll Civ Bib Bergamo — Bollettino della Civica Biblioteca di Bergamo
Boll Civ Mus Ven A & Stor — Bollettino dei Civici Musei Veneziani d'Arte e di Storia
Boll Class — Bollettino dei Classici
Boll Clin — Il Bollettino delle Cliniche
Boll Coll Ingeg & Architetti Napoli — Bollettino del Collegio degli Ingegneri ed Architetti in Napoli
Boll Com — Bollettino. Comitato per la Preparazione dell'Edizione Nazionale dei Classici Greci e Latini
Boll Com Glaciol Ital Ser 3 — Bollettino. Comitato Glaciologico Italiano. Serie 3
Boll Comm — Bollettino. Commissione Archeologica Comunale di Roma
Boll Comm Archeol Com Roma — Bollettino della Commissione Archeologica Comunale di Roma
Boll Comm Archeol Mun Roma — Bollettino della Commissione Archeologica Municipale di Roma
Boll Comm Spec Ig Munic Roma — Bollettino della Commissione Speciale d'Igiene del Municipio di Roma
Boll Com Naz Ital Geod Geofis — Bollettino. Comitato Nazionale Italiano Geodetico-Geofisico
Boll Com Prep Ed Naz Class Greci Lat — Bollettino. Comitato per la Preparazione dell'Edizione Nazionale dei Classici Greci e Latini
Boll Com Prep Ed N Class Gr & Lat — Bollettino del Comitato per la Preparazione dell'Edizione Nazionale dei Classici Greci e Latini
Boll Cons Cagliari — Bollettino Economico. Consiglio Provinciale delle Corporazioni di Cagliari
Boll Corpo For — Bollettino. Corpo Forestale dello Stato
Boll Cost Parl — Bollettino d'Informazioni Costituzionali e Parlamentari
Boll Coton — Bollettino della Cotoniera
Boll Croc Period — Bollettino delle Crociere Periodiche
Boll d A — Bollettino d'Arte
Boll d'Arte — Bollettino d'Arte. Ministero della Pubblica Istruzione
Boll d'Arte MPI — Bollettino d'Arte. Ministero della Pubblica Istruzione
Boll dei Mus Is Biol Univ Genova — Bollettino. Musei e Istituti Biologici. Universita di Genova
Boll della Comm Arch Com di Roma — Bollettino. Commissione Archeologica Comunale di Roma
Boll Dem Met — Bollettino Demografico-Meteorico
Boll Demogr Met — Bollettino Demografico-Meteorico
Boll Docum Elettrotec — Bollettino di Documentazione Elettrotecnica
Boll Docum Tec — Bollettino di Documentazione Tecnica
Bol Leit — Boletim do Leite e Seus Derivados
Bol Leite — Boletim do Leite
Bol Leite Seus Deriv — Boletim do Leite e Seus Derivados
Boll Emat Quad Diet — Bollettino Ematologico e Quaderni di Dietetica
Boll Enol Tosc — Bollettino Enologico Toscano
Boll Ent Agr Patol Veg — Bollettino di Entomologia Agraria e Patologia Vegetale
Boll Epizooz — Bollettino delle Epizoozie

Boll Fac Agrar Univ Pisa — Bollettino. Facolta Agraria. Universita di Pisa
Boll F Cl — Bollettino di Filologia Classica
Boll Fed Int Assoc Chim Tess Color — Bollettino. Federazione Internazionale. Associazioni diChimica Tessile e Coloristica
Boll Fed Miner — Bollettino. Federazione Mineraria
Boll Fed Naz Brefotr — Bollettino. Federazione Nazionale fra i Brefotrofi
Boll Fed Naz Fasc Lotta Tuberc — Bollettino della Federazione Nazionale Fascista per la Lotta Contro la Tuberculosi
Boll Fil Cl — Bollettino di Filologia Classica
Boll Fil Class — Bollettino di Filologia Classica
Boll Fond Sen Pascale — Bollettino Fondazione Sen. Pascale
Boll Fond Sen Pascale Cent Diagn Cura Tumori — Bollettino. Fondazione Sen Pascale Centro per la Diagnosi e la Cura dei Tumori
Boll For — Bollettino Forense
Boll Gal Milione — Bollettino della Galleria del Milione
Boll Geod — Bollettino dei Geodesia e Scienze Affini
Boll Geodes — Bollettino di Geodesia e Scienze Affini
Boll Geod Sci Affini — Bollettino di Geodesia e Scienze Affini
Boll Geofis Teor Appl — Bollettino di Geofisica Teorica ed Applicata
Boll Geofis Teorica Appl — Bollettino di Geofisica Teorica ed Applicata
Boll Geof Teor Appl — Bollettino di Geofisica Teorica ed Applicata. Osservatorio Geofisico
Boll Geogr Gov Cirenaica — Bollettino Geografico. Governo della Cirenaica
Boll Geogr Uff Studi Tripolit — Bollettino Geografico. Ufficio di Studi, Tripolitania
Boll Giorn Uff Idrogr Po — Bollettino Giornaliero. Ufficio Idrografico del Po
Boll Gov — Bollettino. Commissione Archeologica de Governatorato di Roma
Boll ICR — Bollettino. Istituto Centrale del Restauro
Boll Idrobiol Cacc Pesca Afr Orient Ital — Bollettino di Idrobiologia, Caccia e Pesca dell' Africa Orientale Italiana
Boll Idrogr Bologna — Bollettino Idrografico. Bologna
Boll Idrogr Cagliari — Bollettino Idrografico. Cagliari
Boll Idrogr Catanzaro — Bollettino Idrografico. Catanzaro
Boll Idrogr Chieti — Bollettino Idrografico. Chieti
Boll Idrogr Napoli — Bollettino Idrografico. Napoli
Boll Idrogr Palermo — Bollettino Idrografico. Palermo
Boll Idrogr Pisa — Bollettino Idrografico. Pisa
Boll Idrogr Roma — Bollettino Idrografico. Roma
Boll Idrol Mens — Bollettino Idrologico Mensile
Boll Idrol Supp A — Bollettino Idrologico. Supplemento Annuale
Bol Liga Cancer — Boletin. Liga Contra el Cancer
Bol Lima — Boletin de Lima
Boll Ind Ital Carta — Bollettino delle Industrie Italiane della Carta, della Cencelleria, dell'Arredamento, dell'Ufficio
Boll Inf Brigata Aretina Amici Mnmt — Bolletino d'Informazione della Brigata Aretina degli Amici dei Monumenti
Boll Inf Cons Naz Ric — Bollettino d'Informazioni. Consiglio Nazionale delle Ricerche
Boll Inf Consoc Naz (Rome) — Bollettino d'Informazioni. Consociazione Nazionale Infermiere Professionali e Assistenti Sanitarie Visitatrici (Rome)
Boll Inf Ind Olearia Sapon — Bollettino d'Informazioni per l'Industria Olearia e Saponiera
Boll Inf Iscritti — Bollettino d'Informazioni agli Iscritti
Boll Inf Microriprod — Bollettino di Informazioni sulla Microriproduzione
Boll Inf Ord Ing Prov Torino — Bollettino d'Informazioni. Ordine degli Ingegneri della Provincia di Torino
Boll Ingeg — Bollettino degli Ingegneri
Boll Int Opere Scient Med — Bollettino Internazionale delle Opere Scientifiche Medicina
Boll Int Opere Sci Med — Bollettino Internazionale delle Opere Scientifiche Medicina
Boll Ist Aero Elettroter Torino — Bollettino dell'Istituto Aero-Elettroterapico di Torino pe la Cura delle Malattie dei Polmoni e del Cuore (Torino)
Boll Ist Agrar Scandicci — Bollettino. Istituto Agrario di Scandicci
Boll Ist Agr Scandicci — Bollettino dell'Istituto Agrario di Scandicci
Boll Ist Aliment Diet — Bollettino dell'Istituto di Alimentazione e Dietologia
Boll Ist Aliment Dietol — Bollettino. Istituto di Alimentazione e Dietologia
Boll Ist Arch St Arte — Bollettino. Istituto Nazzionale di Archeologia e Storia dell'Arte
Boll Ist Bot Palermo — Bollettino dell'Istituto Botanico (Palermo)
Boll Ist Cent Patol Libro Alfonso Gallo — Bollettino. Istituto Centrale per la Patologia del Libro AlfonsoGallo
Boll Ist Cent Rest — Bollettino dell'Istituto Centrale del Restauro
Boll Ist Dermatol S Gallicano — Bollettino. Istituto Dermatologico S. Gallicano
Boll Ist Ent Agr Oss Fitopat Palermo — Bollettino. Istituto di Entomologia Agraria e Osservatorio di Fitopatologia di Palermo
Boll Ist Entomol — Bollettino. Istituto di Entomologia
Boll Ist Entomol Agrar Osse Fitopatol Palermo — Bollettino. Istituto di Entomologia Agraria e Osservatorio di Fitopatologia di Palermo
Boll Ist Entomol Agrar Oss Fitopatol Palermo — Bollettino. Istituto di Entomologia Agraria e Osservatorio di Fitopatologia di Palermo
Boll Ist Entomol Univ Studi Bologna — Bollettino. Istituto dei Entomologia. Universita degli Studi di Bologna
Boll Ist Ent Univ Bologna — Bollettino. Istituto di Entomologia. Universita degli Studi di Bologna
Boll Ist Naz Arche St Arte — Bollettino. Istituto Nazzionale di Archeologia e Storia dell'Arte
Boll Ist Patol Libr — Bollettino. Istituto di Patologia del Libro Alfonso Gallo
Boll Ist Patol Libro — Bollettino. Istituto di Patologia del Libro
Boll Ist Patol Libro Alfonso Gallo — Bollettino. Istituto di Patologia del Libro Alfonso Gallo
Boll Ist Patologia Lib — Bollettino. Istituto di Patologia del Libro
Boll Ist Rest — Bollettino. Istituto Centrale del Restauro
Boll Ist Restauro — Bollettino. Istituto Centrale de Restauro
Boll Ist Sieroter Milan — Bollettino. Istituto Sieroterapico Milanese

Boll Ist Stor & A Lazio Merid — Bollettino dell'Istituto di Storia ed Arte del Lazio Meridionale
Boll Ist Stor A Orviet — Bollettino dell'Istituto Storico Artistico Orvietano
Boll Ist Stor Cult Arma Genio — Bollettino. Istituto Storico e di Cultura dell'Arma del Genio
Boll Ist Stor It — Bollettino. Istituto Storico Italiano per il Medioevo e Archivio Muratoriano
Boll Ist Stor Ital Arte Sanit — Bollettino. Istituto Storico Italiano dell'Arte Sanitaria
Boll Ist Stor Soc & Stato Veneziano — Bolletino dell'Istituto di Storia della Societa e dello Stato Veneziano
Boll Ist Tumori Napoli — Bollettino. Istituto dei Tumori di Napoli
Bol Lit Hisp Santa Fe — Boletin de Literaturas Hispanicas (Santa Fe, Argentina)
Boll Lab Chim Prov — Bollettino. Laboratori Chimici Provinciali
Boll Lab Entol Agr — Bollettino. Laboratorio di Entomologia Agraria
Boll Lab Entomol Agrar Filippo Silvestri — Bollettino. Laboratorio di Entomologia Agraria "Filippo Silvestri"
Boll Lab Entomol Agrar Portici — Bollettino. Laboratorio di Entomologia Agraria "Filippo Silvestri" di Portici
Boll Laboratori Chim Prov — Bollettino. Laboratori Chimici Provinciali
Boll Laniera — Bollettino della Laniera
Boll Ligustico Stor & Cult Reg — Bollettino Ligustico per la Storia e la Cultura Regionale
Boll Malacol — Bollettino Malacologico
Boll Malacol Unione Malacol Ital — Bollettino Malacologico. Unione Malacologica Italiana
Boll Mal Orecch Gola Naso — Bollettino delle Malattie dell'Orecchio, della Gola, del Naso
Boll Mal Orecchio Gola Naso — Bollettino delle Malattie dell'Orecchio, della Gola, del Naso
Boll Mat — Bollettino di Matematica
Boll Mathesis — Bollettino. Associazione Mathesis. Societa Italiana di Matematica
Boll MC — Bollettino dei Musei Comunali di Roma
Boll Med Svizz — Bollettino del Medici Svizzeri
Boll Mem Soc Piemont Chir — Bollettino e Memorie. Societa Piemontese de Chirurgia
Boll Mem Soc Tosco Umbro Emiliana Med Interna — Bollettino e Memorie. Societa Tosco Umbro Emiliana di Medicina Interna
Boll Mens Cam Com Ind Agr (Perugia) — Bollettino Mensile. Camera di Commercio Industria e Agricoltura (Perugia)
Boll Mens Inform Notiz Sta Patol Vegetale Roma — Bollettino Mensile d'Informazioni e Notizie. Reale Stazione di Patologia Vegetale di Roma e Reale Osservatorio Fitopatologico per la Provincia di Roma e gli Abruzzi
Boll Mens Soc Svizz Ind Gas Acqua Potabile — Bollettino Mensile. Societa Svizzera per l'Industria del Gas e dell'Acqua Potabile
Boll Metallogr — Bollettino Metallografico
Boll Meteorol Idrol Agrar — Bollettino di Meteorologia e di Idrologia Agraria
Boll Microbiol Indag Lab — Bollettino di Microbiologia e Indagini di Laboratorio
Boll Milione — Bollettino del Milione
Boll Mnmt Mus & Gal Pont — Bollettino dei Monumenti, Musei, e Gallerie Pontificie
Boll Mun Viterbo — Bollettino Municipale. Viterbo
Boll Mus Civ Bassano — Bollettino del Museo Civico di Bassano
Boll Mus Civico Padova — Bollettino. Museo Civico di Padova
Boll Mus Civ Padova — Bollettino del Museo Civico di Padova
Boll Mus Civ Stor Nat Ven — Bollettino. Museo Civico di Storia Naturale di Venezia
Boll Mus Civ Stor Nat Venezia — Bollettino. Museo Civico di Storia Naturale di Venezia
Boll Mus Civ Stor Nat Verona — Bollettino. Museo Civico di Storia Naturale di Verona
Boll Mus Civ Ven — Bollettino dei Musei Civici Veneziani
Boll Mus Com Roma — Bollettino dei Musei Comunali di Roma
Boll Musei Com Roma — Bollettino dei Musei Comunali di Roma
Boll Museo Civico Padova — Bollettino. Museo Civico di Padova
Boll Mus Ist Biol Univ Genova — Bollettino. Musei e Istituti Biologici. Universita di Genova
Boll Mus Zool Univ Torino — Bollettino. Museo di Zoologia. Universita di Torino
BolIN — Bollettino Numismatico di Luigi Simonetti
Boll Napol — Bollettino Archeologico Napoletano
Boll Oceanol Teor ed Appl — Bollettino di Oceanologia Teorica ed Applicata
Boll Ocul — Bollettino d'Oculistica
Boll Olii Grassi — Bollettino degli Olii e dei Grassi
Boll Oncol — Bollettino di Oncologia
Boll Ord Med Prov Firenze — Bollettino dell'Ordine dei Medici della Provincia di Firenze
Boll Ord Med Prov Napoli — Bollettino dell'Ordine dei Medici della Provincia di Napoli
Boll Ord Med Prov Torino — Bollettino dell'Ordine dei Medici della Provincia di Torino
Boll Ord Sanit Catanzaro — Bollettino dell'Ordine dei Sanitari di Catanzaro e Provincia
Boll Ord Sanit Citta Prov Parma — Bollettino dell'Ordine dei Sanitari della Citta e Provincia di Parma
Boll Ord Sanit Piacenza — Bollettino dell'Ordine dei Sanitari di Piacenza
Boll Ord Sanit Prov Teramo — Bollettino dell'Ordine dei Sanitari della Provincia di Teramo
Boll Ord Sanit Prov Trapani — Bollettino dell'Ordine dei Sanitari della Provincia di Trapani
Boll Orto Bot Napoli — Bollettino dell'Orto Botanico (Napoli)
Boll Osp Oftal Prov Roma — Bollettino dell'Ospedale Oftalmico della Provincia di Roma
Boll Oss Coll Pennisi — Bollettino dell'Osservatorio. Collegio Pennisi
Boll Pal — Bollettino Paleontologico Italiano
Boll Paletnol Ital — Bollettino di Paletnologia Italiana
Boll Pesca Piscic Idrobiol — Bollettino di Pesca, Piscicoltura, e Idrobiologia

Boll Pomol Fruttic — Bollettino di Pomologia e Frutticoltura
Boll Psicol App — Bollettino di Psicologia Applicata
Boll Psicol Appl — Bollettino di Psicologia Applicata
Boll Psicol Appl Inserto — Bollettino di Psicologia Applicata. Inserto
Boll Quind Com Agr Mantova — Bollettino Quindicinale del Comizio Agrario (Mantova)
Boll Quind Soc Agric Ital — Bollettino Quindicinale della Societa degli Agricoltori Italiani
Boll Quotid Tec Serv Met Aeronaut — Bollettino Quotidiano Tecnico. Servizio Meteorologico dell'Aeronautica
Boll R Accad Med Roma — Bollettino. Reale Accademia Medica di Roma
Boll Reale Deput Stor Patria Umbria — Bollettino della Reale Deputazione di Storia Patria per l'Umbria
Boll Reale Ist Archeol & Stor A — Bollettino del Reale Istituto di Archeologia e Storia dell'Arte
Boll Reale Ist Archit & Stor A — Bollettino del Reale Istituto di Architettura e Storia dell'Arte
Boll Reale Ist Bot Univ Parmense — Bolletino. Reale Istituto Botanico. Universita Parmense
Boll Reale Orto Bot Giardino Colon Palermo — Bollettino delle Reale Orto Botanico e Giardino Coloniale di Palermo
Boll Regia Stn Patol Veg (Rome) — Bollettino. Regia Stazione di Patologia Vegetale (Rome)
Boll Regia Stn Sper Ind Carta Stud Fibre Tess Veg — Bollettino. Regia Stazione Sperimentale per l'Industria della Carta e lo Studiodelle Fibre Tessili Vegetali
Boll Regia Stn Sper Ind Pelli Mater Concianti Napoli — Bollettino. Regia Stazione Sperimentale per l'Industria delle Pelli e delle Materie Concianti Napoli
Boll Regio Is Super Agrar Pisa — Bollettino. Regio Istituto Superiore Agrario di Pisa
Boll Regio Ist Super Agrar Pisa — Bollettino. Regio Istituto Superiore Agrario di Pisa
Boll Ric Cent Sper Enol F Paulson (Marsala) — Bollettino di Ricerche. Centro Sperimentale Enologico F. Paulson(Marsala)
Boll Ric Inf Cent Reg Sper Ind Enol F Paulsen (Marsala) — Bollettino di Ricerche e Informazioni. Centro Regionale Sperimentale per l'Industria Enologia F. Paulsen (Marsala)
Boll Ric Reg Sicil Cent Sper Enol F Paulsen (Marsala) — Bollettino di Ricerche. Regione Siciliana. Centro Sperimentale Enologia F. Paulsen (Marsala)
Boll Riv — Bollettino delle Riviste
BollS — Bolletino Storico-Bibliografico Subalpino
Boll Schermogr — Bollettino Schermografico
Boll Scient — Bollettino Scientifico
Boll Sci Fac Chim Ind Bologna — Bollettino Scientifico. Facolta di Chimica Industriale di Bologna
Boll Sci Fac Chim Ind Univ Bologna — Bollettino Scientifico. Facolta di Chimica Industriale.Universita di Bologna
Boll Sci Med — Bollettino delle Scienze Mediche
Boll Sc Med Bologna — Bollettino delle Scienze Mediche di Bologna
Boll Sedute Accad Gioenia Sci Nat Catania — Bollettino. Sedute della Accademia Gioenia di Scienze Naturali in Catania
Boll Senese Stor Patria — Bollettino Senese di Storia Patria
Boll Serv Geol Ital — Bollettino. Servizio Geologico d'Italia
Boll Sezione Novara — Bolletino di Sezione Novara
Boll Sez Ital Soc Int Microbiol — Bollettino. Sezione Italiana. Societa Internazionale diMicrobiologia
Boll Soc Adriat Sci (Trieste) — Bollettino. Societa Adriatica di Scienze (Trieste)
Boll Soc Adriat Sci (Trieste) Suppl — Bollettino. Societa Adriatica di Scienze (Trieste). Supplemento
Boll Soc Biol Sper — Bollettino. Societa di Biologia Sperimentale
Boll Soc Dant It — Bollettino della Societa Dantesca Italiana
Boll Soc Ent Ital — Bollettino. Societa Entomologica Italiana
Boll Soc Entomol Ital — Bollettino. Societa Entomologica Italiana
Boll Soc Eustachiana — Bollettino. Societa Eustachiana
Boll Soc Filol Romana — Bollettino della Societa Filologica Romana
Boll Soc Fot It — Bollettino della Societa Fotografica Italiana
Boll Soc Geog — Bollettino. Societa Geografica Italiana
Boll Soc Geogr It — Bolletino. Societa Geografica Italiana
Boll Soc Geogr Ital — Bollettino. Societa Geografica Italiana
Boll Soc Geol Ital — Bollettino. Societa Geologica Italiana
Boll Soc Int Microbiol Sez Ital — Bollettino. Societa Internazionale di Microbiologia. SezioneItaliana
Boll Soc Ital Biol Sper — Bollettino. Societa Italiana di Biologia Sperimentale
Boll Soc Ital Biol Sperim — Bollettino. Societa Italiana di Biologia Sperimentale
Boll Soc Ital Cardiol — Bollettino. Societa Italiana di Cardiologia
Boll Soc Ital Ematol — Bollettino. Societa Italiana di Ematologia
Boll Soc Ital Farm Osp — Bollettino. Societa Italiana di Farmacia Ospedaliera
Boll Soc Ital Fis — Bollettino. Societa Italiana di Fisica
Boll Soc Ital Patol — Bollettino. Societa Italiana di Patologia
Boll Soc Lett Verona — Bollettino della Societa di Lettere di Verona
Boll Soc Med Chir Brescia — Bollettino. Societa Medico-Chirurgica Bresciana
Boll Soc Med Chir Catania — Bollettino. Societa Medico-Chirurgica di Catania
Boll Soc Med Chir (Cremona) — Bollettino. Societa Medico-Chirurgica (Cremona)
Boll Soc Med Chir Modena — Bollettino. Societa Medico-Chirurgica di Modena
Boll Soc Med-Chir Osp Prov Cremona — Bollettino. Societa Medico-Chirurgica e Ospedali Provincia di Cremona
Boll Soc Med-Chir Pavia — Bollettino. Societa Medico-Chirurgica di Pavia
Boll Soc Med Chir Pisa — Bollettino. Societa Medico-Chirurgica di Pisa
Boll Soc Med Chir Prov Varese — Bollettino. Societa Medico-Chirurgica della Provincia di Varese
Boll Soc Med Chir Reggio Emilia — Bollettino. Societa Medico-Chirurgica di Reggio Emilia
Boll Soc Med Chir Salento — Bollettino. Societa di Medicina e Chirurgia del Salento
Boll Soc Med Lazzaro Spallanzani Reggio Emilia — Bollettino. Societa Medica Lazzaro Spallanzani con Sede in Reggio Emilia

Boll Soc Nat Napoli — Bollettino. Societa di Naturalisti di Napoli
Boll Soc Paleontol Ital — Bollettino. Societa Paleontologica Italiana
Boll Soc Pavese Stor Patria — Bollettino. Societa Pavese di Storia Patria
Boll Soc Piemont Archeol & B A — Bollettino della Societa Piemontese di Archeologia e Belle Arti
Boll Soc Piemontese — Bollettino. Societa Piemontese di Archeologia e di Belle Arti
Boll Soc Rom Stud Zool — Bollettino. Societa Romana per gli Studi Zoologici
Boll Soc Sarda Sci Nat — Bollettino. Societa Sarda di Scienze Naturali
Boll Soc Sismol Ital — Bollettino. Societa Sismologica Italiana
Boll Soc Studi Stor Prov Cuneo — Bollettino. Societa per gli Studi Storici, Archeologici, ed Artistici nella Provincia di Cuneo
Boll Soc Zool Ital — Bollettino. Societa Zoologica Italiana
Boll S P — Bollettino Storico Piacentino
Boll St A — Bollettino di Storia dell'Arte
Boll Sta Patol Veg — Bollettino. Stazione di Patologia Vegetale di Roma
Boll St Arte (Salerno) — Bollettino di Storia dell'Arte (Salerno)
Boll Stat Com Ferrara — Bollettino Statistico del Comune di Ferrara
Boll Staz Patol Veg Roma — Bollettino. Stazione di Patologia Vegetale di Roma
Boll St Cremonese — Bollettino Storico Cremonese
Boll St M — Bollettino. Associazione Internazionale degli Studi Mediterranei
Boll St Novara — Bollettino Storico per la Provincia di Novara
Boll Stn Patol Veg Roma — Bollettino. Stazione di Patologia Vegetale di Roma
Boll Stn Sper Ind Carta Stud Fibre Tess Veg — Bollettino. Regia Stazione Sperimentale per l'Industria della Carta e lo Studio delle Fibre Tessile Vegetali
Boll Stn Sper Ind Pelli Mater Concianti (Napoli Torino) — Bollettino. Stazione Sperimentale per l'Industria della Pelli e delle Materie Concianti (Napoli-Torino)
Boll Stor Bibliog Subalp — Bollettino Storico-Bibliografico Subalpino
Boll Stor Cat — Bollettino Storico Catanese
Boll Stor Crem — Bollettino Storico Cremonese
Boll Stor Cremon — Bollettino Storico Cremonese
Boll Stor Cremonese — Bollettino Storico Cremonese
Boll Stor Fil — Bolletino di Storia della Filosofia
Boll Storia Sci Mat — Bollettino di Storia delle Scienze Matematiche
Boll Stor Lucchese — Bollettino Storico Lucchese
Boll Stor Messin — Bollettino Storico Messinese
Boll Stor Novara — Bollettino Storico per la Provincia di Novara
Boll Stor Piacent — Bollettino Storico Piacentino
Boll Stor Pisa — Bollettino Storico Pisano
Boll Stor Pisano — Bollettino Storico Pisano
Boll Stor Pistoi — Bollettino Storico Pistoiese
Boll Stor Prov Novara — Bollettino Storico per la Provincia di Novara
Boll Stor Sci Mat — Bollettino di Storia della Scienze Matematiche
Boll Stor Svizzera It — Bollettino Storico della Svizzera Italiana
Boll Stor Svizzera Italiana — Bollettino Storico della Svizzera Italiana
Boll Stor Svizz Ital — Bollettino Storico della Svizzera Italiana
Boll St Patria Umbria — Bollettino. Deputazione di Storia Patria per l'Umbria
Boll St Piacentino — Bollettino Storico Piacentino
Boll Stran — Bollettino Universitario Italiano per Stranieri
Boll St Sv It — Bollettino Storico della Svizzera Italiana
Boll Svizzera It — Bollettino della Svizzera Italiana
Boll Svizz Mineral Petrogr — Bollettino Svizzero di Mineralogia e Petrografia
Boll Tec Dir Sper Aviaz — Bollettino Tecnico. Direzione Sperimentale dell'Aviazione
Boll Tec FINSIDER — Bollettino Tecnico FINSIDER
Boll Tec Lab Elettrotec Luigi Magrini — Bollettino Tecnico. Laboratorio Elettrotecnico Luigi Magrini
Boll Tec Ligure — Bollettino Tecnico Ligure
Boll Tecn Coltiv Tabacchi — Bollettino Tecnico della Coltivazione del Tabacchi
Boll Tec Regio Ist Sper Coltiv Tab Leonardo Angeloni — Bollettino Tecnico. Regio Istituto Sperimentale per la Coltivazione dei Tabacchi Leonardo Angeloni
Boll Tec Savigl — Bollettino Tecnico Savigliano
Boll Uff Ammin For Ital — Bollettino Ufficiale per l'Amministrazione Forestale Italiana
Boll Uff Ass Ortic Prof Ital — Bollettino Ufficiale dell'Associazione Orticola Professionale Italiana
Boll Uff Cent Serv Agr Libia — Bollettino. Ufficio Centrale per i Servizi Agrari della Libia
Boll Uff Com Agr Biell — Bollettino Ufficiale del Comizio Agrario Biellese
Boll Uff Controllo Chim Perm Ital — Bollettino Ufficiale del Controllo Chimico Permanente Italiano
Boll Uff Corpo For St — Bollettino Ufficiale. Corpo Forestale dello Stato
Boll Uffic Cam Com Ind Agr Udine — Bollettino Ufficiale. Camera di Commercio, Industria, e Agricoltura di Udine
Boll Uffic Geol Ital — Bollettino. Ufficio Geologico d'Italia
Boll Ufficiale Min Pub Istr — Bollettino Ufficiale del Ministero della Pubblica Istruzione
Boll Uffic Regia Stn Sper Seta (Italy) — Bollettino Ufficiale. Regia Stazione Sperimentale per la Seta (Italy)
Boll Uffic Stn Sper Ind Essenze Deriv Agrumi Reggio Calabria — Bollettino Ufficiale. Stazione Sperimentale per l'Industria delle Essenze e deiDerivati degli Agrumi in Reggio Calabria
Boll Uff Idrogr Venezia — Bollettino. Ufficio Idrografico. Venezia
Boll Uff Minist Agric Foreste — Bollettino Ufficiale del Ministero dell'Agricoltura e delle Foreste
Boll Uff Minist Agric Ind Comm — Bollettino Ufficiale del Ministero d'Agricoltura, Industria, e Commercio
Boll Unione Mat Ital — Bollettino. Unione Matematica Italiana
Boll Unione Mat Ital Ser IV — Bollettino. Unione Matematica Italiana. Series IV
Boll Un Mat Ital — Bollettino. Unione Matematica Italiana
Boll Un Mat Ital A — Bollettino. Unione Matematica Italiana. A
Boll Un Mat Ital A V — Unione Matematica Italiana. Bollettino. A. Serie V
Boll Un Mat Ital A VI — Unione Matematica Italiana. Bollettino. A. Serie VI

Boll Un Mat Ital B — Bollettino. Unione Matematica Italiana. B
Boll Un Mat Ital B VI — Unione Matematica Italiana. Bollettino. B. Serie VI
Boll Un Mat Ital C 5 — Bollettino. Unione Matematica Italiana. C. Serie V. Analisi Funzionale e Applicazioni
Boll Un Mat Ital Suppl — Unione Matematica Italiana. Bollettino. Supplemento
Boll Un Stor & A — Bollettino dell'Unione di Storia ed Arte
Boll Zool — Bollettino di Zoologia
Boll Zool Agrar Bachic — Bollettino di Zoologia Agraria e di Bachicoltura
Boll Zool Agrar Bachicolt — Bollettino di Zoologia Agraria e di Bachicoltura
Boll Zool Agr Bachic — Bollettino di Zoologia Agraria e di Bachicoltura
Boll Zool Agr Bachicolt — Bollettino di Zoologia Agraria e di Bachicoltura
Boll Zool (Napoli) — Bollettino di Zoologia (Napoli)
Bolm Acad Nac Farm Rio de J — Boletim da Academia Nacional de Farmacia (Rio de Janeiro)
Bolm Acad Nac Med Rio de J — Boletim da Academia Nacional de Medicina (Rio de Janeiro)
Bolm Actinom Port — Boletim Actinometrico de Portugal
Bolm Ag Ger Colon Ultramar — Boletim da Agencia Geral das Colonias do Ultramar
Bolm Agric Bahia — Boletim da Agricultura (Bahia, Brasil)
Bolm Agric Dep Prod Veg Belo Horiz — Boletim de Agricultura do Departamento de Producao Vegetal (Belo Horizonte)
Bolm Agric Lisb — Boletim de Agricultura (Lisboa)
Bolm Agric Loanda — Boletim de Agricultura (Loanda)
Bolm Agric Nova Goa — Boletim de Agricultura (Nova Goa)
Bolm Agric Pecuar Mocamb — Boletim Agricola e Pecuaria. Colonia de Mocambique
Bolm Agric S Paulo — Boletim de Agricultura (Sao Paulo)
Bolm Agric Zootech Vet Minas Geraes — Boletim de Agricultura, Zootechnia, e Veterinaria. Secretaria de Agricultura de Minas Geraes
Bolm Antrop — Boletim de Antropologia
Bolm Apic — Boletim Apicola
Bolm Ass Bras Farm — Boletim da Associacao Brasileira de Farmaceuticos
Bolm Ass Bras Metais — Boletim. Associacao Brasileira de Metais
Bolm Ass Bras Norm Tec — Boletim. Associacao Brasileira de Normas Tecnicas
Bolm Ass Bras Odont — Boletim da Associacao Brasileira de Odontologia
Bolm Ass Bras Quim — Boletim da Associacao Brasileira de Quimica
Bolm Ass Farm Pernambuco — Boletim da Associacao Farmaceutica de Pernambuco
Bolm Ass Filos Nat — Boletim da Associacao da Filosofia Natural
Bolm Ass Geogr Bras — Boletim da Associacao dos Geografos Brasileiros
Bolm Assist Med Indig Luanda — Boletim de Assistencia Medica aos Indigenas e da Luta Contra a Molestia do Sono (Luanda)
Bolm Ass Port Fotogram — Boletim da Associacao Portuguesa de Fotogrametria
Bolm Ass Quim Bras — Boletim da Associacao Quimica do Brasil
Bol Mat — Boletin de Matematicas
Bol Mat — Boletin Matematico
Bol Mat Dent — Boletim de Materias Dentarios
Bol Mat Estat Fis (Araraquara Braz) — Boletim de Matematica, Estatistica, e Fisica (Araraquara, Brazil)
Bol Mat Estat Fis (Araraquara Brazil) — Boletim de Matematica, Estatistica, e Fisica (Araraquara, Brazil)
Bol Mat Estatist Fis — Boletim de Matematica, Estatistica, e Fisica
Bolm Biblfico Acad Sci Lisb — Boletim Bibliografico. Academia das Sciencias de Lisboa
Bolm Biblfico Cent Docum Cient Angola — Boletim Bibliografico. Centro de Documentacao Cientifica. Instituto de Investigacao Cientifica de Angola
Bolm Biblfico Dir Estat Prod Rio de J — Boletim Bibliografico. Directoria de Estatistica da Produccao, Ministerio da Agricultura (Rio de Janeiro)
Bolm Biblfico Geofis Oceanogr Am — Boletim Bibliografico de Geofisica y Oceanografia Americanas
Bolm Bioestat Epidem — Boletim de Bioestatistica e Epidemiologia
Bolm Biol Clube Zool Bras — Boletim Biologico. Clube Zoologico do Brasil
Bolm Biol Lab Parasit Fac Med S Paulo — Boletim Biologico. Laboratorio de Parasitologia. Faculdade de Medicina de Sao Paulo
Bolm Carioca Geogr — Boletim Carioca de Geografia
Bolm Casa Dent Bras — Boletim da Casa do Dentista Brasileiro
Bolm Casa Douro — Boletim da Casa do Douro
Bolm Cent Estud Hosp Aeronaut Galeaa — Boletim. Centro de Estudos. Hospital da Aeronautica do Galeaa
Bolm Cent Estud Hosp Serv Estado — Boletim do Centro de Estudos do Hospital dos Servidores do Estado
Bolm Cent Estud Pesq Geod Univ Parana — Boletim. Centro de Estudos e Pesquisas de Geodesia. Universidade do Parana
Bolm Cent Estud Policlin Pesc — Boletim. Centro de Estudos da Policlinica de Pescadores
Bolm Cent Pesq Hermann von Ihering — Boletim do Centro de Pesquisas Hermann von Ihering
Bol Med — Boletin de Medicina
Bol Med Brit — Boletin Medico Britanico
Bol Med Chile — Boletin Medico de Chile
Bol Med Cirug Guayaquil — Boletin de Medicina y Cirugia (Guayaquil)
Bol Med Cirug y Farm (Madrid) — Boletin de Medicina, Cirugia, y Farmacia (Madrid)
Bol Med Hosp Inf — Boletin Medico. Hospital Infantil
Bol Med Hosp Infant Mex — Boletin Medico. Hospital Infantil de Mexico
Bol Med Hosp Infant Mex (Engl Ed) — Boletin Medico. Hospital Infantil de Mexico (English Edition)
Bol Med Hosp Infant Mex (Span Ed) — Boletin Medico. Hospital Infantil de Mexico (Spanish Edition)
Bol Med Inf — Boletin Medico Informativo
Bol Med Inst Mex Seg Soc — Boletin Medico. Instituto Mexicano del Seguro Social
Bol Med Quir — Boletin Medico-Quirurgico
Bol Med Soc — Boletin Medico-Social. Caja de Seguro Obligatorio

Bol Med Univ Auton Guadalajara — Boletin Medico. Universidad Autonoma de Guadalajara
Bol Med Univ Guad — Boletin Medico. Universidad Autonoma de Guadalajara
Bol Mensal Estatistica (Portugal) — Boletim Mensal de Estatistica (Portugal)
Bol Mens Estad Agri — Boletin Mensual de Estadisticas Agricolas
Bol Mens Estadist — Boletin Mensual de Estadistica
Bol Mensile Statis — Bollettino Mensile di Statistica
Bol Mens Inst Nac Aliment Montev — Boletin Mensual. Instituto Nacional de Alimentacion (Montevideo)
Bol Mens Inst Nac Aliment (Montevideo) — Boletin Mensual. Instituto Nacional de Alimentacion (Montevideo)
Bol Mens Obs Astr Met Col Est Puebla — Boletin Mensual. Observatorio Astronomico-Meteorologico del Colegio del Estado de Puebla
Bol Mens Obs Ebro — Boletin Mensual. Observatorio del Ebro
Bol Mens Obs Ebro Ser A — Boletin Mensual. Observatorio del Ebro. Seria A
Bol Mensual Estadistica — Boletin Mensual de Estadistica
Bol Mensual Estadistica Agraria — Boletin Mensual de Estadistica Agraria
Bol Mensual Estadisticas Agrics — Boletin Mensual de Estadisticas Agricolas
Bolm Esc Agric "Luiz Queiroz" — Boletim. Escola Agricola "Luiz De Queiroz"
Bol Met (Ecuad) — Boletin Meteorologico (Ecuador)
Bol Met Seism — Boletin Meteorologico y Seismologico
Bol (Mex) Com Fom Min — Boletin (Mexico). Comision de Fomento Minero
Bol (Mex) Cons Recur Nat No Renov — Boletin (Mexico). Consejo de Recursos Naturales No Renovables
Bol Mexic Der Comp — Boletin Mexicano de Derecho Comparado
Bol Mex Reumatol — Boletin Mexicano de Reumatologia
Bol Min Agr Indus Com Rio — Boletim do Ministerio da Agricultura, Industria e Commercio (Rio de Janeiro)
Bol Min Agr Rio — Boletim do Ministerio da Agricultura (Rio de Janeiro)
Bol Minas — Boletin de Minas
Bol Minas Ind Constr — Boletin de Minas, Industria, y Construcciones
Bol Minas Pet — Boletin de Minas y Petroleo
Bol Minas (Port Dir-Geral Minas Serv Geol) — Boletin de Minas (Portugal Direccao-Geral de Minas e Servicos Geologicos)
Bol Minas y Energia — Boletin de Minas y Energia
Bol Minas y Petroleo — Boletin de Minas y Petroleo
Bolm Ind Anim — Boletim de Industria Animal
Bol Mineral — Boletim Mineralogico
Bol Mineral (Mexico City) — Boletin de Mineralogia (Mexico City)
Bol Mineral (Recifec Braz) — Boletim Mineralogico (Recife, Brazil)
Bol Minero — Boletin Minero
Bol Min Geogr — Boletin Mineiro de Geografia
Bol Min Ind — Boletin Minero e Industrial
Bol Minist Agric Buenos Aires — Boletin. Ministerio de Agricultura (Buenos Aires)
Bol Minist Fomento — Boletin del Ministerio de Fomento
Bol Minist Sanid Asist Soc (Venez) — Boletin. Ministerio de Sanidad y Asisteneta Social (Venezuela)
Bol Min Justica — Boletin. Ministerio de Justica
Bol Min (Mexico City) — Boletin Minero (Mexico City)
Bol Min Petr — Boletin de Miras y Petroleo
Bol Min Rel Ext Monte — Boletin. Ministerio de Relaciones Exteriores (Montevideo)
Bolm Inst Angola — Boletim. Instituto de Angola
Bolm Inst Cent Fom Econ Bahia — Boletim do Instituto Central de Fomento Economica da Bahia
Bolm Inst Crim Lisb — Boletim do Instituto de Criminologia (Lisboa)
Bolm Inst Ecol Exp Agric Rio de J — Boletim do Instituto de Ecologia e Experimentacao Agricolos (Rio de Janeiro)
Bolm Inst Engen S Paulo — Boletim. Instituto de Engenharia (Sao Paulo)
Bolm Inst Exp Agric Rio de J — Boletim do Instituto de Experimentacao Agricola (Rio de Janeiro)
Bolm Inst Geogr Cadast Lisb — Boletim do Instituto Geografico e Cadastral (Lisboa)
Bolm Inst Geogr Geol Est S Paulo — Boletim do Instituto Geografico e Geologico do Estado de Sao Paulo
Bolm Inst Hist Nat Curitiba — Boletim do Instituto de Historia Natural (Curitiba, Parana)
Bolm Inst Hyg Fac Med Vet Univ S Paulo — Boletim do Instituto de Hygiene. Faculdade de Medicina Veterinaria. Universidade de Sao Paulo
Bolm Inst Oceanogr S Paulo — Boletim do Instituto Oceanografico (Sao Paulo)
Bolm Inst Paul Oceanogr — Boletim do Instituto Paulista de Oceanografia
Bolm Inst Pesq Technol S Paulo — Boletim do Instituto de Pesquisas Technologicas (Sao Paulo)
Bolm Inst Port Oncol — Boletim do Instituto Portugues de Oncologia
Bolm Inst Pueric Rio de J — Boletim do Instituto de Puericultura (Rio de Janeiro)
Bolm Inst Quim Agric Rio de J — Boletim do Instituto de Quimica Agricola (Rio de Janeiro)
Bolm Inst Sup Hig Dr Ricardo Jorge — Boletim do Instituto Superior de Higiene Doctor Ricardo Jorge
Bolm Inst Vital Braz — Boletim do Instituto Vital Brazil
Bol Min Trab Indus Com Rio — Boletim do Ministerio do Trabalho, Industria e Commercio (Rio de Janeiro)
Bolm Jard Bot Rio de J — Boletim do Jardim Botanico (Rio de Janeiro)
Bolm Jta Nac Cortica — Boletim. Junta Nacional da Cortica
Bolm Jta Nac Frutas — Boletim. Junta Nacional das Frutas
Bolm Lab Cent Prod Min Rio de J — Boletim do Laboratorio Central da Producao Mineral (Rio de Janeiro)
Bolm Mens Estat Demogr Sanit Belem — Boletim Mensal de Estatistica Demographo-Sanitaria de Belem
Bolm Mens Inf Lab Eng Civ Lisb — Boletim Mensal de Informacao. Laboratorio de Engenharia Civil (Lisboa)
Bolm Mens Inf Lab Nac Eng Civ Lisb — Boletim Mensal de Informacao. Laboratorio Nacional de Engenharia Civil (Lisboa)
Bolm Mens Obscoes Met Arquip Madeira — Boletim Mensal das Observacoes Meteorologicas no Arquipelago da Madeira

Bolm Mens Obscoes Met Lourenco Marq — Boletim Mensal das Observacoes Meteorologicas Feitas nos Postos da Colonia, Lourenco Marques

Bolm Mens Obscoes Met Serv Met Mocamb — Boletim Mensal das Observacoes Meteorologicas Organizad pelo Servico Meteorologico de Mocambique

Bolm Mens Obs Rio de J — Boletim Mensal do Observatorio de Rio de Janeiro

Bolm Mens Resumo a Inst Geofis Porto — Boletim Mensal e Resumo Anual. Instituto Geofisico. Universidade do Porto

Bolm Mens Resumo a Obs Serra Pilar — Boletim Mensal e Resumo Anual. Observatorio da Serra do Pilar

Bolm Mus Para Emilio Goeldi Bot — Boletim. Museu Paraense Emilio Goeldi. Nova Serie. Botanica

Bol Mnmts Hist — Boletin de Monumentos Historicos

Bolm Real Soc Esp Hist Nat Secc — Boletim. Real Sociedad Espanola de Historia Natural. Seccion Biologica

Bolm Soc Bras Ent — Boletim. Sociedade Brasileira de Entomologia

Bolm Soc Broteriana — Boletim. Sociedade Broteriana

Bolm Soc Cearense Agron — Boletim. Sociedade Cearense de Agronomia

Bolm Soc Ent Bras — Boletim da Sociedade Entomologica do Brasil

Bolm Soc Estud Mocamb — Boletim da Sociedade de Estudios da Colonia de Mocambique

Bolm Soc Geogr Lisb — Boletim da Sociedade de Geographia de Lisboa

Bolm Soc Geol Port — Boletim da Sociedade Geologica de Portugal

Bolm Soc Mat S Paulo — Boletim da Sociedade de Matematica de Sao Paulo

Bolm Soc Med Cirurg Rio de J — Boletim da Sociedade de Medicina e Cirurgia de Rio de Janeiro

Bolm Soc Med Cirurg S Paulo — Boletim da Sociedade de Medicina e Cirurgia de Sao Paulo

Bolm Soc Nac Hort Port — Boletim da Sociedade Nacional de Horticultura de Portugal

Bolm Soc Parana Mat — Boletim da Sociedade Paranaense de Matematica

Bolm Soc Paul Med Vet — Boletim da Sociedade Paulista de Medicina Veterinaria

Bolm Soc Port Cienc Nat — Boletim da Sociedade Portuguesa de Ciencias Naturais

Bolm Soc Port Oftal — Boletim da Sociedade Portuguesa de Oftalmologia

Bolm Suptdcia Serv Cafe S Paulo — Boletim da Superintendencia dos Servicos do Cafe (Sao Paulo)

Bolm Tec Inst Agron Est Campinas — Boletim Tecnico. Instituto Agronomico do Estado em Campinas

Bolm Tec Inst Agron Leste — Boletim Tecnico. Instituto Agronomico do Leste

Bolm Tec Inst Agron N — Boletim Tecnico, Instituto Agronomico do Norte

Bolm Tec Inst Agron NE — Boletim Tecnico. Instituto Agronomico do Nordeste

Bolm Tec Inst Agron S — Boletim Tecnico. Instituto Agronomico do Sul

Bolm Tec Inst Cacau Bahia — Boletim Tecnico. Instituto de Cacau da Bahia

Bolm Tec Inst Pesq Exp Agropecuar N — Boletim Tecnico. Instituto de Pesquisas e Experimentacao Agropecuarias do Norte

Bolm Ther — Boletim de Therapeutica

Bolm Trimest Clin Doenc Trop Hosp Pedro II — Boletim Trimestral da Clinica de Doencas Tropicais e da Nutricao do Hospital Pedro II

Bolm Univ Parana Botanica — Boletim da Universidade do Parana. Botanica

Bolm Univ Parana Geologia — Boletim da Universidade do Parana. Geologia

Bolm Univ Parana Zool — Boletim. Universidade Federal do Parana. Zoologia

Bol Mus A Barcelona — Boletin de los Museos de Arte de Barcelona

Bol Mus & Inst Camon Aznar — Boletin del Instituto y Museo Camon Aznar

Bol Mus Arqueol La Serena — Boletin. Museo Arqueologico de La Serena

Bol Mus Arqueol N Madrid — Boletin del Museo Arqueologico Nacional de Madrid

Bol Mus Arte Colonial Bogota — Boletin. Museo de Arte Colonial (Bogota)

Bol Mus Bibl Guat — Boletin de Museos y Bibliotecas de Guatemala

Bol Mus Bolivar Lima — Boletin. Museo Bolivariano (Lima)

Bol Mus Bot Munic (Curitiba) — Boletim. Museu Botanico Municipal (Curitiba)

Bol Mus Chil Arte Precolomb — Boletin del Museo Chileno de Arte Precolombino

Bol Mus Cienc Nat — Boletin. Museo de Ciencias Naturales

Bol Mus Cienc Nat Antropol Juan Cornelio Moyano — Boletin. Museo de Ciencias Naturales y Antropologicas Juan Cornelio Moyano

Bol Mus Cien Nat Caracas — Boletin. Museo de Ciencias Naturales (Caracas)

Bol Museo Civico Padova — Bollettino. Museo Civico di Padova

Bol Museus N A Ant — Boletim dos Museus Nacionais de Arte Antiga

Bol Mus Hist Nat Javier Prado — Boletin. Museo de Historia Natural Javier Prado

Bol Mus Hist Nat J Prado Lima — Boletin. Museo de Historia Natural Javier Prado (Lima)

Bol Mus Hist Nat UFMG Bot — Boletim. Museu de Historia Natural UFMG [*Universidade Federal de Minas Gerais*]. Botanica

Bol Mus Hist Nat UFMG Geol — Boletim. Museu de Historia Natural UFMG [*Universidade Federal de Minas Gerais*]. Geologia

Bol Mus Hist Nat UFMG Zool — Boletim. Museu de Historia Natural UFMG [*Universidade Federal de Minas Gerais*]. Zoologia

Bol Mus Hombre Domin — Boletin. Museo del Hombre Dominicano

Bol Music Art Vis Wash — Boletin de Musica y Artes Visuales (Washington, DC)

Bol Mus Lab Mineral Geol Fac Cienc Univ Lisboa — Boletim. Museu e Laboratorio Mineralogico e Geologicao. Faculdade de Ciencias. Universidade de Lisboa

Bol Mus Mun — Boletin del Museo Municipal

Bol Mus Munic Funchal — Boletim. Museu Municipal do Funchal

Bol Mus N A Ant — Boletim do Museu Nacional de Arte Antiga

Bol Mus Nac Antrop Rio — Boletim do Museu Nacional. Antropologia (Rio de Janeiro)

Bol Mus Nac Geol Rio — Boletim do Museu Nacional. Geologia (Rio de Janeiro)

Bol Mus Nac Hist Nat Santiago — Boletin. Museo Nacional de Historia Natural (Santiago)

Bol Mus Nac Rio — Boletim do Museu Nacional (Rio de Janeiro)

Bol Mus Nac (Rio De Janeiro) — Boletim. Museu Nacional (Rio De Janeiro)

Bol Mus Nac (Rio De Janeiro) Geol — Boletim. Museu Nacional (Rio De Janeiro). Geologia

Bol Mus Nac (Rio De J) Antropol — Boletim. Museu Nacional (Rio De Janeiro). Antropologia

Bol Mus Nac (Rio De J) Bot — Boletim. Museu Nacional (Rio De Janeiro). Botanica

Bol Mus Nac (Rio De J) Geol — Boletim. Museu Nacional (Rio De Janeiro). Geologia

Bol Mus Nac (Rio De J) Nova Ser Geol — Boletim. Museu Nacional (Rio De Janeiro). Nova Serie. Geologia

Bol Mus Nac (Rio De J) Zool — Boletim. Museu Nacional (Rio De Janeiro). Zoologia

Bol Mus Nac Zool Rio — Boletim do Museu Nacional. Zoologia (Rio de Janeiro)

Bol Mus N Arqueol Hist & Etnog — Boletin del Museo Nacional de Arqueologia, Historia, y Etnografia

Bol Mus Oro — Boletin del Museo del Oro

Bol Mus Oro Bogota — Boletin. Museo del Oro. Banco de la Republica (Bogota)

Bol Mus Para Emilio Goeldi — Boletim. Museu Paraense Emilio Goeldi

Bol Mus Para Emilio Goeldi Geol — Boletim. Museu Paraense Emilio Goeldi. Geologia

Bol Mus Para Emilio Goeldi Nova Ser Antropol — Boletim. Museu Paraense Emilio Goeldi. Nova Serie. Antropologia

Bol Mus Para Emilio Goeldi Nova Ser Bot — Boletim. Museu Paraense Emilio Goeldi. Nova Serie. Botanica

Bol Mus Para Emilio Goeldi Nova Ser Geol — Boletim. Museu Paraense Emilio Goeldi. Nova Serie. Geologia

Bol Mus Para Emilio Goeldi Nova Ser Zool — Boletim. Museu Paraense Emilio Goeldi. Nova Serie. Zoologia

Bol Mus Para Emilio Goeldi Ser Antrop — Boletim. Serie Antropologia. Museu Paraense Emilio Goeldi [*Belem*]

Bol Mus Para Emilio Goeldi Ser Antropol — Boletim. Museu Paraense Emilio Goeldi. Serie Antropologia

Bol Mus Para Emilio Goeldi Ser Bot — Boletim. Museu Paraense Emilio Goeldi. Serie Botanica

Bol Mus Para Emilio Goeldi Ser Zool — Boletim. Museu Paraense Emilio Goeldi. Serie Zoologia

Bol Mus Paraense E Goeldi Belem — Boletim do Museu Paraense Emilio Goeldi (Belem, Brazil)

Bol Mus Paraense E Goeldi NS Antrop Belem — Boletim. Museu Paraense Emilio Goeldi. Nova Serie. Antropologia (Belem)

Bol Mus Paraense Emilio Goeldi — Boletim. Museu Paraense Emilio Goeldi

Bol Mus Paraense Emilio Goeldi Nova Ser Antropol — Boletim. Museu Paraense Emilio Goeldi. Nova Serie. Antropologia

Bol Mus Paraense Emilio Goeldi Nova Ser Bot — Boletim. Museu Paraense Emilio Goeldi. Nova Serie. Botanica

Bol Mus Paraense Emilio Goeldi Nova Ser Geol — Boletim. Museu Paraense Emilio Goeldi. Nova Serie. Geologia

Bol Mus Paraense Hist Nat — Boletim do Museu Paraense de Historia Natural e Ethnographia

Bol Mus Prado — Boletin del Museo del Prado

Bol Mus Prov B A Valladolid — Boletin del Museo Provincial de Bellas Artes de Valladolid

Bol Mus Prov B A Zaragoza — Boletin del Museo Provincial de Bellas Artes de Zaragoza

Bol Mus Soc Argent — Boletin. Museo Social Argentino

Bol Mus Soc Arqueol la Serena — Boletin. Publicaciones del Museo y de la Sociedad Arqueologica de la Serena

Bol Mus Valp — Boletin. Museo de Valparaiso

Bolm Vet Porto Alegre — Boletim Veterinario (Porto Alegre)

Bolm Zool Univ S Paulo — Boletim de Zoologia. Universidade de Sao Paulo

Boln Acad Cienc Artes Barcelona — Boletin de la Academia de Ciencias y Artes de Barcelona

Boln Acad Cienc Exact Madr — Boletin de la Academia de Ciencias Exactas, Fisico-Quimicas, y Naturales de Madrid

Boln Acad Nac Cienc Cordoba — Boletin de la Academia Nacional de Ciencias en Cordoba

Boln Acad Nac Med B Aires — Boletin de la Academia Nacional de Medicina de Buenos Aires

Bol Nac Minas — Boletin Nacional de Minas

Boln Adm Nac Agua B Aires — Boletin de la Administracion Nacional del Agua (Buenos Aires)

Boln Adm Secr Minist Salud Publ Nac B Aires — Boletin Administrativo de la Secretaria. Ministerio de Salud Publica de la Nacion (Buenos Aires)

Boln Aeronaut — Boletin de Aeronautica

Boln Agric Ambato — Boletin de Agricultura (Ambato)

Boln Agric Andalucia Orient — Boletin Agricola de Andalucia Oriental

Boln Agric Camp Cub — Boletin Agricola para el Campesino Cubano

Boln Agric Ciudad Real — Boletin Agricola (Ciudad Real)

Boln Agric Mendoza — Boletin Agricola (Mendoza)

Boln Agric Palma — Boletin Agricola (Palma)

Boln Agric Reg Agron Levante — Boletin Agricola de la Region Agronomica de Levante

Boln Agric Reg Andalucia Occid — Boletin Agricola de la Region de Andalucia Occidental

Boln Cia Adm Guano — Boletin de la Compania Administradora del Guano

Boln Col of Med Tarragona — Boletin del Colegio Oficial de Medicos (Tarragona)

Boln Col Prov Vet Burgos — Boletin. Colegio Provincial de Veterinarios de Burgos

Boln Cols Pract Med Cirug — Boletin de los Colegios de Practicantes de Medicina y Cirugia

Boln Comn Cent Estud Tabard Mex — Boletin de la Comision Central para el Estudio del Tabardillo (Mexico)

Boln Comn Hon Lucha Antituberc Montev — Boletin. Comision Honoraria para la Lucha Antituberculosa (Montevideo)

Boln Comn Mapa Geol Esp — Boletin de la Comision del Mapa Geologico de Espana

Boln Comn Nac Errad Palud Mex — Boletin. Comision Nacional para la Erradicacion del Paludismo (Mexico)

Boln Cons Medic Alim Cosmet — Boletin. Consejo de Medicamentos, Alimentos, y Cosmeticos

Boln Cons Nac Hig Montev — Boletin del Consejo Nacional de Higiene (Montevideo)

Boln Cons Sup Hig Publ Santiago — Boletin del Consejo Superior de Higiene Publica (Santiago de Chile)

Boln Cons Sup Salubr Mex — Boletin del Consejo Superior de Salubridad (Mexico)

Boln Cons Sup Salubr S Salvador — Boletin del Consejo Superior de Salubridad (San Salvador)

Boln Consult Agric Ganad Mex — Boletin de Consultas Sobre Agricultura, Ganaderia, e Industrias Rurales (Mexico)

Boln Cuerpo Ing Camin Lima — Boletin del Cuerpo de Ingenieros de Caminos (Lima)

Boln Cuerpo Ing Civ Lima — Boletin del Cuerpo de Ingenieros Civiles de Lima

Boln Cuerpo Ing Minas Peru — Boletin del Cuerpo de Ingenieros de Minas del Peru

Boln Cult Inf Cons Gen Col Med Esp — Boletin Cultural e Informativo. Consejo General de Colegios Medicos de Espana

Boln Demogr Esp — Boletin Demografico de Espana

Boln Demogr Met S Luis Potosi — Boletin Demografico Meterologico (San Luis Potosi)

Boln Dent Argent — Boletin Dental Argentino

Boln Dent Urug — Boletin Dental Uruguayo

Boln Dep Agric Santiago — Boletin del Departamento de Agricultura (Santiago)

Boln Dep For Caza Pesca Mex — Boletin del Departamento Forestal y de Caza y Pesca de Mexico

Boln Dep Hig Cordoba — Boletin del Departamento de Higiene (Cordoba)

Boln Dep Minas Petrol Santiago — Boletin del Departamento de Minas y Petroleo (Santiago de Chile)

Boln Dep Salubr Publ Mex — Boletin del Departamento de Salubridad Publica (Mexico)

Boln Dep Sanid Veg Santiago — Boletin del Departamento de Sanidad Vegetal (Santiago de Chile)

Boln Dep Tec Inst Fom Algod Bogota — Boletin. Departamento Tecnico. Instituto de Fomento Algodonero (Bogota)

Boln Diaro Inst Cent Met — Boletin Diaro. Instituto Central Meteorologico

Boln Diaro Serv Met Nac — Boletin Diaro del Servicio Meteorologico Nacional

Boln Dir Agric Ganad Lima — Boletin de la Direccion de Agricultura, Ganaderia, y Colonizacion (Lima)

Boln Dir Estud Biol Mex — Boletin de la Direccion de Estudios Biologicos (Mexico)

Boln Dir Gen Aeronaut Civ Lima — Boletin de la Direccion General de Aeronautica Civil (Lima)

Boln Dir Gen Agric Mex — Boletin de la Direccion General de Agricultura (Mexico)

Boln Dir Gen Estadist Estud Geogr La Paz — Boletin. Direccion General de Estadistica y Estudios Geograficos (La Paz)

Boln Dir Gen For Caza Mex — Boletin de la Direccion General Forestal y de Caza (Mexico)

Boln Dir Gen Ganad Madr — Boletin de la Direccion General de Ganaderia (Madrid)

Boln Dir Gen Minas Geol Hidrol B Aires — Boletin de la Direccion General de Minas, Geologia, e Hidrologia (Buenos Aires)

Boln Dir Gen Serv Agric Santiago — Boletin. Direccion General de los Servicios Agricolas (Santiago de Chile)

Boln Dir Gen Serv Met Nac Montev — Boletin. Direccion General del Servicio Meteorologico Nacional (Montevideo)

Boln Divulg Ganad — Boletin de Divulgacion Ganadera

Boln Divulg (Pergamino) — Boletin de Divulgacion (Pergamino)

Boln Estac Exp Agric "Tingo Maria" — Boletin. Estacion Experimental Agricola "Tingo Maria"

Boln Gaz Botkina — Bol'nichnaya Gazeta Botkina

Boln Geol (Bogota) — Boletin Geologico. Instituto Geologico Nacional (Bogota, Colombia)

Boln Hosps Caracas — Boletin de los Hospitales (Caracas)

Boln Hosps Mun Caracas — Boletin de los Hospitales Municipales del Distrito Federal (Caracas)

Boln Iberoam Cult Tec — Boletin Iberoamericano de Cultura Tecnica

Bol Nicar Bibliog & Doc — Boletin Nicaraguense de Bibliografia y Documentacion

Boln Indig — Boletin Indigenista

Boln Inf Activid Eur Paleont Vertebr — Boletin Informativo. Actividades Europeas en Paleontologia de Vertebrados

Boln Inf Aerotec — Boletin Informativo Aerotecnico

Boln Inf Agron Reg La Serena — Boletin de Informaciones del Agronomo Regional de la la Zona (La Serena)

Boln Inf Asoc Med Peru — Boletin Informativo de la Asociacion Medica Peruana Daniel A. Carrion

Boln Inf Asoc Quim Esp Ind Cuero — Boletin Informativo. Asociacion Quimica Espanola de la Industria del Cuero

Boln Inf Cent Nac Invest Cafe Colombia — Boletin Informativo. Centro Nacional de Investigaciones de Cafe, Colombia

Boln Inf Col Nac Vet Esp — Boletin de Informacion. Colegio Nacional de Veterinarios de Espana

Boln Inf Cons Gen Col Vet Esp — Boletin de Informacion. Consejo General de Colegios Veterinarios de Espana

Boln Inf Dent — Boletin de Informacion Dental

Boln Inf Dir Ganad B Aires — Boletin Informativo de la Direccion de Ganaderia (Buenos Aires)

Boln Inf Dir Gen Arquit — Boletin de Informacion de la Direccion General de Arquitectura

Boln Inf Dir Nac Min B Aires — Boletin Informativo. Direccion Nacional de Mineria (Buenos Aires)

Boln Inf Dir Sanid Veg B Aires — Boletin Informativo de la Direccion de Sanidad Vegetal (Buenos Aires)

Boln Inf Docum Biblfica Esc of Telecomun Madr — Boletin de Informacion Documental y Bibliografica. Escuela Oficial de Telecomunicacion (Madrid)

Boln Inf Electron — Boletin de Informacion Electronica

Boln Inf Esc Nac Cienc Biol Mex — Boletin de Informacion de la Escuela Nacional de Ciencias Biologicas (Mexico)

Boln Inf Estac Exp Pergamino — Boletin Informativo. Estacion Experimental Pergamino

Boln Inf Estadist Agropec Caracas — Boletin Informativo de Estadisticas Agropecuarias (Caracas)

Boln Inf Inst Cub Invest Tecnol — Boletin Informativo. Instituto Cubano de Investigaciones Tecnologicas

Boln Inf Inst Fievre Aftosa Caracas — Boletin Informativo del Instituto de la Fievre Aftosa (Caracas)

Boln Inf Inst Fitotec Castelar — Boletin Informativo. Instituto de Fitotecnia (Castelar)

Boln Inf Inst Nac Carb Oviedo — Boletin Informativo. Instituto Nacional del Carbon. Oviedo

Boln Inf Lab Transp Mec Suelo Madr — Boletin de Informacion. Laboratorio del Transporte y Mecanica del Suelo (Madrid)

Boln Inf Minist Ind Agric Madr — Boletin de Informacion del Ministerio de Agricultura (Madrid)

Boln Infs Agron Reg Chillan — Boletin de Informaciones del Agronomo Regional de la 4a Zona (Chillan)

Boln Infs Agron Reg S Fernando — Boletin de Informaciones del Agronomo Regional de la 3a Zona (San Fernando)

Boln Infs Cient Nac Quito — Boletin de Informaciones Cientificas Nacionales (Quito)

Boln Infs Parasit Chil — Boletin de Informaciones Parasitarias Chilenas

Boln Infs Petrol — Boletin de Informaciones Petroleras

Boln Infs Servs Agric Santiago — Boletin de Informaciones de los Servicios Agricolas (Santiago de Chile)

Boln Inf Tec Dep Parasit Santiago — Boletin de Informacion Tecnica. Departamento de Parasitologia (Santiago)

Boln Inf Tec Estadist Dir Gen Minas Combust Madr — Boletin de Informacion Tecnica y Estadistica. Direccion General de Minas y Combustibles (Madrid)

Boln Inst Caro Cuerva — Boletin. Instituto Caro y Cuerva

Boln Latam Mus Inst Inter Amer Music — Boletin Latinoamericano de Musica

Boln Med Br — Boletin Medico Britanico

Boln Med Chile — Boletin Medico de Chile

Boln Med Farm Extrem — Boletin Medico-Farmaceutico Extremeno

Boln Med Guipuzcoa — Boletin Medico (Guipuzcoa)

Boln Med Hosp Infant Mex — Boletin Medico del Hospital Infantil (Mexico)

Boln Med Huesca — Boletin Medico (Huesca)

Boln Med Lerida — Boletin Medico (Lerida)

Boln Med Mex — Boletin Medico Mexicano

Boln Med N — Boletin Medico del Norte

Boln Med Quir — Boletin Medico-Quirurgico

Boln Med Soc — Boletin Medico-Social

Boln Mens Asist Publ Valparaiso — Boletin Mensual de la Asistencia Publica (Valparaiso)</PHR> %

Boln Mens Asoc Nac Med Vet Cuba — Boletin Mensual de la Asociacion Nacional de Medicina Veterinaria de Cuba

Boln Mens Cent Met Palma Mallorca — Boletin Mensual. Centro Meteorologico Palma de Mallorca

Boln Mens Clim Hidrol Caracas — Boletin Mensual Climatologico e Hidrologico (Caracas)

Boln Mens Clim Las Palmas — Boletin Mensual Climatologico (Las Palmas)

Boln Mens Clim Madr — Boletin Mensual Climatologico (Madrid)

Boln Mens Clim S Cruz Tenerife — Boletin Mensual Climatologico (Santa Cruz de Tenerife)

Boln Mens Clim Sidi Ifni — Boletin Mensual Climatologico (Sidi Ifni)

Boln Mens Clim Valencia — Boletin Mensual Climatologico (Valencia)

Boln Mens Clin Asoc Damas Covadonga — Boletin Mensual de la Clinica de la Asociacion de Damas de la Covadonga

Boln Mens Col Med Prov Gerona — Boletin Mensual del Colegio de Medicos de la Provincia de Gerona

Boln Mens Comn Nac Agr Mex — Boletin Mensual de la Comision Nacional Agraria (Mexico)

Boln Mens Def Agric Mex — Boletin Mensual. Defensa Agricola (Mexico)</PHR> %

Boln Mens Dir Algodon B Aires — Boletin Mensual. Direccion de Algodon (Buenos Aires)

Boln Mens Dir Ganad Montev — Boletin Mensual. Direccion de Ganaderia (Montevideo)

Boln Mens Dir Gen Econ Rur Agric Mex — Boletin Mensual de la Direccion General de Economia (Rural) Agricola (Mexico)

Boln Mens Estac Sism Cartuja — Boletin Mensual. Estacion Sismologia de Cartuja

Boln Mens Estadist Agric Mex — Boletin Mensual de Estadistica Agricola (Mexico)

Boln Mens Estadist Agropec B Aires — Boletin Mensual de Estadistica Agropecuaria (Buenos Aires)

Boln Mens Ests Un Mex Def Agric — Boletin Mensual dos Estados Unidos Mexicanos per la Defensa Agricola

Boln Mens Geoelect Met S Miguel — Boletin Mensual. Geoelectricidad y Meteorologia. Observatorio de Fisica Cosmica (San Miguel)

Boln Mens Heliofis S Miguel — Boletin Mensual. Heliofisica. Observatorio de Fisica Cosmica (San Miguel)

Boln Mens Inst Nac Fis Clim Montev — Boletin Mensual del Instituto Nacional Fisico-Climatologico de Montevideo

Boln Mens Jta Nac Algodon B Aires — Boletin Mensual. Junta Nacional de Algodon (Buenos Aires)

Boln Mens Liga Tuberc Cuba — Boletin Mensual de la Liga Contra la Tuberculosis en Cuba

Boln Mens Minist Ind Def Agric Montev — Boletin Mensual del Ministerio de Industrias. Defensa Agricola (Montevideo)

Boln Mens Obs Astr Met Quito — Boletin Mensual. Observatorio Astronomico y Meteorologico (Quito)

Boln Mens Obsnes Astr Microsism Obs Cartuja — Boletin Mensual-Observaciones Astronomicas y Microsismicas. Observatorio de Cartuja

Boln Mens Obsnes Met Obs Cartuja — Boletin Mensual-Observaciones Meteorologicas. Observatorio de Cartuja

Boln Mens Obsnes Sism Madr — Boletin Mensual de la Observaciones Sismicas (Madrid)

Boln Mens Obsnes Sism Obs Cartuja — Boletin Mensual-Observaciones Sismicas. Observatorio de Cartuja

Boln Mus Hist Nat Javier Prado — Boletin. Museo de Historia Natural "Javier Prado"

Boln Mus Nac Hist Nat (Chile) — Boletin. Museo Nacional de Historia Natural (Chile)

Boln Observs Tonantzintla Tacubaya — Boletin de los Observatorios Tonantzintla y Tacubaya

Boln Oceanogr Pesc — Boletin de Oceanografia y Pescas

Boln Odont Bogota — Boletin de Odontologia (Bogota)

Boln Odont Mex — Boletin Odontologico Mexicano

Boln Of Asoc Tec Azuc Cuba — Boletin Oficial de la Asociacion de Tecnicos Azucareros de Cuba

Boln Of CMVN Habana — Boletin Oficial del C.M.V.N. (La Habana)

Boln Of Col Farm Palencia — Boletin Oficial del Colegio de Farmaceuticos (Palencia)

Boln Of Col Farm Zaragoza — Boletin Oficial del Colegio de Farmaceuticos (Zaragoza)

Boln Of Col Med Almeria — Boletin Oficial del Colegio de Medicos (Almeria)

Boln Of Col Med Barcelona — Boletin Oficial del Colegio de Medicos (Barcelona)

Boln Of Cons Gen Col Odont Oviedo — Boletin Oficial des Consejo General de Colegios de Odontologos (Oviedo)

Boln Of Def Agric Tacubaya — Boletin. Oficina para la Defensa Agricola (Tacubaya)

Boln Of Estado — Boletin Oficial del Estado

Boln Of Fac Cienc Med Univ B Aires — Boletin Oficial. Facultad de Ciencias Medicas. Universidad de Buenos Aires

Boln Of Marc Pat Habana — Boletin Oficial de Marcas y Patentes (Habana)

Boln Of Minas Metal Madr — Boletin Oficial de Minas, Metalurgia, y Combustibles (Madrid)

Boln Of Minas Petrol Peru — Boletin Oficial de Minas y Petroleo. Peru

Boln Of Minist Fom Madr — Boletin Oficial del Ministerio de Fomento (Madrid)

Boln Of Patol Veg Habana — Boletin. Oficina de Patologia Vegetal (Habana)

Boln Of Sanid Nac Caracas — Boletin. Oficina de Sanidad Nacional (Caracas)

Boln Of Sanid Veg Habana — Boletin. Oficina de Sanidad Vegetal (Habana)

Boln Of Sanit Pan Am — Boletin de la Oficina Sanitaria Pan-Americana

Boln Of Secr Agric Com Trab Habana — Boletin Oficial de la Secretaria de Agricultura, Comercio, y Trabajo (Habana)

Boln Of Secr Agric Fom Mex — Boletin Oficial de la Secretaria de Agricultura y Fomento (Mexico)

Boln Of Secr Sanid Habana — Boletin Oficial de la Secretaria de Sanidad y Beneficiencia (Habana)

Boln Of Serv Met Habana — Boletin Oficial. Servicio Meteorologico, Climatologico, y de Cosechas de la Habana

Boln Oleicult Int — Boletin de Oleicultura Internacional

Boln Orient Prof Ind Revta Telecomun — Boletin de Orientacion Profesional y Industrial de la Revista de Telecomunicacion

Bol Not Inst Fom Algodonero (Bogota) — Boletin de Noticias. Instituto de Fomento Algodonero (Bogota)

Boln Paleont B Aires — Boletin Paleontologico de Buenos Aires

Boln Pan Am Sanid — Boletin Pan-Americano de Sanidad de la Oficina Sanitaria Internacional

Boln Patol Veg Ent Agric — Boletin de Patologia Vegetal y Entomologia Agricola

Boln Pesca Caza — Boletin de Pesca y Caza

Boln Pesca Minist Agric Cria Caracas — Boletin de Pesca. Ministerio de Agricultura y Cria (Caracas)

Boln Pescas — Boletin de Pescas. Instituto Espanol de Oceanografia

Boln Petrol Mex — Boletin del Petroleo (Mexico)

Boln Petrol Minas Mex — Boletin de Petroleo y Minas (Mexico)

Boln Platan Agric — Boletin Platanero y Agricola

Boln Polic Sanit Anim — Boletin de Policia Sanitaria de los Animales

Boln Pro Cult Reg SCL Mazatlan — Boletin de Pro-Cultura Regional S.C.L. Mazatlan

Boln Prod Fam Agric B Aires — Boletin de Produccion y Fomento Agricolo (Buenos Aires)

Boln R Soc Esp Hist Nat — Boletin. Real Sociedad Espanola de Historia Natural

Boln Rur Inst Nac Tecnol Agropec — Boletin Rural. Instituto Nacional de Tecnologia Agropecuaria

Boln Soc Ing Lima — Boletin de la Sociedad de Ingenieros (Lima)</PHR> %

Boln Soc Malag Cienc — Boletin de la Sociedad Malaguena de Ciencias

Boln Soc Mat Mex — Boletin de la Sociedad Matematica Mexicana

Boln Soc Med Cent Materno Infant Gen Maximino Avila Camacho — Boletin de la Sociedad Medica del Centro Materno-Infantil General Maximino Avila Camacho

Boln Soc Med Mendoza — Boletin de la Sociedad Medica de Mendoza

Boln Soc Mex Electro Radiol — Boletin de la Sociedad Mexicana de Electro-Radiologia

Boln Soc Michoac Geogr Estadist — Boletin de la Sociedad Michoacana de Geografia y Estadistica

Boln Soc Nac Agric C Rica — Boletin de la Sociedad Nacional de Agricultura de Costa Rica

Boln Soc Nac Agr Lima — Boletin de la Sociedad Nacional Agraria (Lima)

Boln Soc Peru Bot — Boletin de la Sociedad Peruana Te Botanica

Boln Soc Peru Hist Med — Boletin. Sociedad Peruana de Historia de la Medicina

Boln Soc Physis — Boletin de la Sociedad Physis para el Cultivo y Difusion de la Ciencias Naturales en la Argentina

Boln Soc Quim Peru — Boletin de la Sociedad Quimica del Peru

Boln Soc Taguato — Boletin de la Sociedad Taguato

Boln Soc Tipogr Bonaer — Boletin de la Sociedad Tipografica Bonaerense

Boln Soc Valenc Pediat — Boletin de la Sociedad Valenciana de Pediatria

Boln Soc Venez Cienc Nat — Boletin. Sociedad Venezolana de Ciencias Naturales

Boln Soc Venez Cirug — Boletin de la Sociedad Venezolana de Cirugia

Boln Subdir Tec Agropec Litoral — Boletin de la Subdireccion Tecnica Agropecuaria del Litoral

Boln Tab — Boletin de Tabaco

Boln Tabac — Boletin Tabacalero

Boln Tab Timb — Boletin de Tabaco y Timbres

Boln Taxon Lab Pesq Caiguire — Boletin Taxonomico del Laboratorio de Pesqueria de Caiguire

Boln Tec Asoc Quim Esp Ind Cuero — Boletin Tecnico. Asociacion Quimica Espanola de la Industria del Cuero

Boln Tec Cent Nac Agric S Pedro — Boletin Tecnico. Centro Nacional de Agricultura (San Pedro)

Boln Tec Cent Nac Invest Cafe Colombia — Boletin Tecnico. Centro Nacional de Investigaciones de Cafe. Colombia

Boln Tec Dep Genet Fitotec Santiago — Boletin Tecnico. Departamento de Genetica Fitotecnica (Santiago)

Boln Tec Dep Invest Agric Chili — Boletin Tecnico. Departamento de Investigaciones Agricoles. Chili

Boln Tec Dir Gen Ganad B Aires — Boletin Tecnico de la Direccion General de Ganaderia (Buenos Aires)

Boln Tec Dir Gen Sanid Madr — Boletin Tecnico de la Direccion General de Sanidad (Madrid)

Boln Tec Empr Petrol Fisc — Boletin Tecnico. Empresa Petrolera Fiscal

Boln Tec Fac Agron Univ Chile — Boletin Tecnico. Facultad de Agronomia. Universidad de Chile

Boln Tec Fac Cienc Agrar Univ Cuyo — Boletin Tecnico. Facultad de Ciencias Agrarias. Universidad Nacional de Cuyo

Boln Tec Fed Nac Cafet Colombia — Boletin Tecnico. Federacion Nacional de Cafeteros de Colombia

Boln Tec Inst Cient Paul Hnos — Boletin Tecnico. Instituto Cientifico Paul Hnos

Boln Tec Inst Fom Algod Bogota — Boletin Tecnico. Instituto de Fomento Algodonero (Bogota)

Bol Nucl — Boletin Nucleo

Bol Num (Brasil) — Boletim de Numismatica (Brasil)

Boln Univ (Montevideo) Fac Agron — Boletin. Universidad de la Republica. Faculdad de Agronomia (Montevideo)

Bol Obras Sanit Nac (Argent) — Boletin de Obras Sanitarias de la Nacion (Argentina)

Bol Obs Ebro Ser A — Boletin. Observatorio del Ebro. Serie A

Bol Obs Nac Habana — Boletin del Observatorio Nacional (Habana)

Bol Oceanogr Pesc — Boletin de Oceanografia y Pescas

Bol Odont — Boletin de Odontologia

Bol Odont Mex — Boletin Odontologico Mexicano

Bol Odontol (B Aires) — Boletin Odontologico (Buenos Aires)

Bol Odontol (Bogota) — Boletin de Odontologia (Bogota)

Bol Odontol Mex — Boletin Odontologico Mexicano

Bol Odont Paul — Boletim Odontologico Paulista

Bol Of Asoc Nac Ing Agron — Boletin Oficial. Asociacion Nacional de Ingenieros Agronomos

Bol Of Asoc Quim PR — Boletin Oficial. Asociacion de Quimicos de Puerto Rico

Bol Of Asoc Tec Azucar Cuba — Boletin Oficial. Asociacion de Tecnicos Azucareros de Cuba

Bol Of Col Quim PR — Boletin Oficial. Colegio Quimicos de Puerto Rico

Bol Of Dir Min Indus Lima — Boletin Oficial. Direccion de Minas e Industrias (Lima)

Bol Of Estado — Boletin Oficial del Estado

Bol Oficina Sanit Panam — Boletin. Oficina Sanitaria Panamericana

Bol Ofic Sanit Panam Engl Ed — Boletin. Oficina Sanitaria Panamericana. English Edition

Bol Ofic Sanit Panamer — Boletin. Oficina Sanitaria Panamericana

Bol Of Met Argent — Boletin de la Oficina Meteorologica Argentina

Bol Of Prop Ind 2 — Boletin Oficial. Propiedad Industrial. 2. Patentes y Modelos deUtilidad

Bol Of Sanit Panam — Boletin. Oficina Sanitaria Panamericana

Bol Of Sanit Panam Engl Ed — Boletin. Oficina Sanitaria Panamericana. English Edition

Bol Of Sanit Panam Wash — Boletin. Oficina Sanitaria Panamericana (Washington, DC)

Bol Oftal — Boletin Oftalmologico

Bologna Ac Mm — Memorie della Accademia delle Scienze dell' Istituto di Bologna

Bologna Ac Sc Mm — Memorie della Accademia delle Scienze dell' Istituto di Bologna

Bologna Med — Bologna Medica

Bologna Mm Ac — Memorie della Accademia delle Scienze dell' Istituto di Bologna

Bologna Mm Ac Sc — Memorie della Accademia delle Scienze dell' Istituto di Bologna

Bologna Mm I It — Memorie dell' Istituto Nazionale Italiano. Classe di Fisica e di Matematica (Bologna)

Bologna N A — Nuovi Annali delle Scienze Naturali. Alessandrini, Bertolini, Gherardi, e Ranzani (Bologna)

Bologna N Cm — Novi Commentarii Academiae Scientiarum Instituti Bononiensis

Bologna Opusc Sc — Opuscoli Scientifici (Bologna)

Bologna Opusc Sc N — Nuova Collezione d'Opuscoli Scientifici (Bologna)

Bologna Rd — Rendiconto delle Sessioni dell' Accademia delle Scienze dell' Istituto di Bologna

Bol Oncol — Boletim de Oncologia

Bol Ord Med — Boletim. Ordem dos Medicos

BolP — Boletin del Poeta

Bol Paleontol B Aires — Boletin Paleontologico de Buenos Aires

Bol Parana Geocienc — Boletim Paranaense de Geociencias

Bol Parana Geogr — Boletim Paranaense de Geografia

Bol Paran Geogr — Boletim Paranense de Geografia. Associacao dos Geografas Brasileiros. Seccao Regional do Parana

Bol Par Geogr — Boletim Paranaense de Geografia
Bol Patol Med — Boletin de Patologia Medica
Bol Patol Med (Madr) — Boletin de Patologia Medica (Madrid)
Bol Patol Veg Entomol Agric — Boletin de Patologia Vegetal y Entomologia Agricola
Bol Paul Geogr — Boletim Paulista de Geografia
Bol Paulista Geogr S Paulo — Boletim Paulista de Geografia. Associacao dos Geografos Brasileiros (Sao Paulo)
Bol Pecu — Boletim Pecuario
Bol Pecuar Dir Geral Serv Pecuar (Portugal) — Boletim Pecuario. Direccao Geral dos Servicos Pecuarios (Portugal)
Bol Pecu (Lisb) — Boletim Pecuario (Lisbon)
Bol (Peru) Com Carta Geol Nac — Boletin (Peru). Comision Carta Geologica Nacional
Bol Pesqui Cent Tecnol Agric Aliment EMBRAPA — Boletim de Pesquisa. Centro de Tecnologia Agricola e Alimentar EMBRAPA
Bol Pesqui EMBRAPA Cent Tecnol Agric Alimen — Boletim de Pesquisa. EMBRAPA [*Empresa Brasileira de Pesquisa Agropecuaria*]. Centro de Tecnologia Agricola e Alimentar
Bol Pet — Boletin del Petroleo
Bol Pet Minas — Boletin de Petroleo y Minas
Bol Petroleo — Boletin del Petroleo
Bol Planificacion — Boletin de Planificacion
Bol Popular Min Agric (Guatemala) — Boletin Popular. Direccion General de Agricultura de Guatemala. Ministerio de Agricultura (Guatemala)
Bol Prod Anim — Boletin de Produccion Animal
Bol Prod Fom Agric — Boletin de Produccion y Fomento Agricola
Bol Produc Fom Agri BA — Boletin de Produccion y Fomento Agricola (Buenos Aires)
Bol Protes — Boletin de Protesis
Bol Proy Bibliogr Lima — Boletin. Proyecto Bibliografico del Sur (Lima)
Bol Psicol — Boletim de Psicologia
Bol Psiquiatr — Boletin de Psiquiatria
Bol Quim Clin — Boletin de Quimica. Clinica
Bol Quim Peru — Boletin del Quimico Peruano
BolR — Boletin. Real Academia de la Historia
Bol R Ac Esp — Boletin. Real Academia Espanola
Bol R Ac Hist — Boletin. Real Academia de la Historia
Bol Radiact — Boletin de Radiactividad
Bol RAH — Boletin. Real Academia de la Historia
Bol Real Ac — Boletin. Real Academia de la Historia
Bol Real Acad B A — Boletin de la Real Academia de Bellas Artes
Bol Real Acad B A & Cienc Hist Toledo — Boletin de la Real Academia de Bellas Artes y Ciencias Historicas de Toledo
Bol Real Acad B Let — Boletin de la Real Academia de Buenas Letras [*Seville*]
Bol Real Acad B Let Barcelona — Boletin de la Real Academia de Buenas Letras de Barcelona
Bol Real Acad Cordoba Cienc B Let & Nob A — Boletin de la Real Academia de Cordoba de Ciencias, Bellas Letras, y Nobles Artes
Bol Real Acad Hist — Boletin. Real Academia de la Historia
Bol Real Soc Bascongadas Amigos Pais — Boletin de la Real Sociedad Bascongadas de los Amigos del Pais
Bol Real Soc Geogr — Boletin. Real Sociedad de Geografia
Bol Resenas Ser Agric — Boletin de Resenas. Serie Agricultura
Bol Resenas Ser Ganad — Boletin de Resenas. Serie Ganaderia (Havana)
Bol Resenas Suelos Agroquim — Boletin de Resenas. Suelos y Agroquimica
Bol Resenas Viandas Hortalizas Granos — Boletin de Resenas. Viandas, Hortalizas, y Granos
Bol Rev Peru Pediat — Boletin. Revista Peruana de Pediatria
Bol Rev Univ Madrid — Boletin. Revista. Universidad de Madrid
Bol R Soc Espan Hist Nat — Boletin. Real Sociedad Espanola de Historia Natural
Bol R Soc Esp Hist Nat — Boletin. Real Sociedad Espanola de Historia Natural
Bol R Soc Esp Hist Nat Secc Biol — Boletin. Real Sociedad Espanola de Historia Natural. Seccion Biologica
Bol R Soc Esp Hist Nat Secc Geol — Boletin. Real Sociedad Espanola de Historia Natural. Seccion Geologica
BOLS — Boreales. Revue du Centre de Recherches Inter-Nordiques
BOLSA — Bank of London and South America. Review
Bol Salubr Hig — Boletin de Salubridad e Higiene
Bol Salud Publica — Boletin de Salud Publica
Bol Sanat (Sao Lucas) — Boletim do Sanatorio (Sao Lucas)
Bol Sancho Sabio — Boletin. Institucion Sancho el Sabio
Bol Sanid Mil — Boletin de Sanidad Militar
Bolsa Rev — Bolsa Review
Bol Sec Indus Com BA — Boletin. Secretaria de Industria y Comercio (Buenos Aires)
Bol Secr Ind Comer (Argent) — Boletin. Secretaria de Industria y Comercio (Argentina)
Bol Secr Sal Publ — Boletin Administrativo. Secretaria de Salud Publica de la Nacion
Bol Sem Est Arte Arq — Boletin. Seminario de Estudios de Arte y Arqueologia
Bol Semin Cult Mex Mex — Boletin. Seminario de Cultura Mexicano (Mexico)
Bol Semin Der Publ Santiago — Boletin. Seminario de Derecho Publico (Santiago)
Bol Semin Estud A & Arqueol — Boletin del Seminario de Estudios de Arte y Arqueologia
Bol Semin Santa Fe — Boletin. Seminario (Santa Fe, Argentina)
Bol Ser D Estud Espec Inst Geol Miner Repub Peru — Boletin. Serie D. Estudios Especiales. Instituto de Geologia y Mineria. Republica del Peru
Bol Serv Def Contra Plagas Inspeccion Fitopatol (Spain) — Boletin. Servicio de Defensa Contra Plagas e Inspeccion Fitopatologica (Spain)
Bol Serv Geol Minas Angola — Boletim. Servicos de Geologia e Minas de Angola
Bol Serv Geol Minas (Mocambique) — Boletim. Servicos de Geologia e Minas (Mocambique)
Bol Serv Geol Nac Managua — Boletin. Servicio Geologico Nacional de Nicaragua (Managua)

Bol Serv Geol Nac (Nicar) — Boletin. Servicio Geologico Nacional (Nicaragua)
Bol Serv Geol Nac Nicaragua — Boletin. Servicio Geologico Nacional de Nicaragua
Bol Serv Med Nac Empl (Ch) — Boletin. Servicio Medico Nacional de Empleados (Chile)
Bol Serv Nac Pesq Agron — Boletim do Servico Nacional de Pesquisas Agronomicas
Bol Serv Nac Sal (Ch) — Boletin. Servicio Nacional de Salud (Chile)
Bol Serv Odontol Sanit (Porto Alegre) — Boletim. Servico de Odontologia Sanitaria. Secretaria da Saude. Rio Grande do Sul (Porto Alegre)
Bol Serv Plagas For — Boletin. Servicio de Plagas Forestales
Bol Serv Plagas Forest — Boletin. Servicio de Plagas Forestales
Bol Serv Plagas For (Spain) — Boletin. Servicio de Plagas Forestales (Spain)
Bol Soc Amigos A — Boletin de la Sociedad de los Amigos de Arte
Bol Soc Arg Angiol — Boletines. Sociedad Argentina de Angiologia
Bol Soc Arg Bot — Boletin. Sociedad Argentina de Botanica
Bol Soc Arg Botan La Plata BA — Boletin. Sociedad Argentina de Botanica (La Plata, Buenos Aires)
Bol Soc Arg Ciruj — Boletines y Trabajos. Sociedad Argentina de Cirujanos
Bol Soc Argent Angiol — Boletin. Sociedad Argentina de Angiologia
Bol Soc Argent Bot — Boletin. Sociedad Argentina de Botanica
Bol Soc Arg Est Gaea — Boletin. Sociedad Argentina de Estudios Geograficos Gaea
Bol Soc Arg Estud Geogr BA — Boletin. Sociedad Argentina de Estudios Geograficos GAEA (Buenos Aires)
Bol Soc Astr Mex — Boletin. Sociedad Astronomica de Mexico
Bol Soc Bibl Puerto Rico S Juan — Boletin. Sociedad de Bibliotecarios de Puerto Rico (San Juan)
Bol Soc Biol Concepcion — Boletin. Sociedad de Biologia de Concepcion
Bol Soc Biol Santiago De Chile — Boletin. Sociedad de Biologia de Santiago De Chile
Bol Soc Boliv Pediat — Boletin. Sociedad Boliviana de Pediatria
Bol Soc Botan Mex — Boletin. Sociedad Botanica de Mexico
Bol Soc Bot Estado Jalisco — Boletin. Sociedad Botanica del Estado de Jalisco
Bol Soc Bot Mex — Boletin. Sociedad Botanica de Mexico
Bol Soc Bras Agron — Boletim. Sociedade Brasileira de Agronomia
Bol Soc Bras Direito Intern Rio — Boletim da Sociedade Brasileira de Direito Internacional (Rio de Janeiro)
Bol Soc Bras Ent — Boletim. Sociedade Brasileira de Entomologia
Bol Soc Bras Geogr Rio — Boletim da Sociedade Brasileira de Geografia (Rio de Janeiro)
Bol Soc Bras Geol — Boletim. Sociedade Brasileira de Geologia
Bol Soc Brasil Mat — Boletim. Sociedade Brasileira de Matematica
Bol Soc Brasil Mat NS — Boletim da Sociedade Brasileira de Matematica. Nova Serie
Bol Soc Bras Mat — Boletin. Sociedade Brasileira de Matematica
Bol Soc Bras Med Vet — Boletim. Sociedade Brasileira de Medicina Veterinaria
Bol Soc Bras Tuberc — Boletim. Sociedade Brasileira de Tuberculose
Bol Soc Brot — Boletim da Sociedade Broteriana
Bol Soc Broteriana — Boletim. Sociedade Broteriana
Bol Soc Castell Cult — Boletin. Sociedad Castellonense de Cultura
Bol Soc Castell Excurs — Boletin de la Sociedad Castellana de Excursiones
Bol Soc Cast Leon Pediat — Boletin. Sociedad Castellano-Astur-Leonosa de Pediatria
Bol Soc Catal Pediat — Boletin. Sociedad Catalana de Pediatria
Bol Soc Cear Agron — Boletim. Sociedade Cearense de Agronomia
Bol Soc Cearense Agron — Boletim. Sociedade Cearense de Agronomia
Bol Soc Chil Obstet Ginec — Boletin. Sociedad Chilena de Obstetricia y Ginecologia
Bol Soc Chil Obstet Ginecol — Boletin. Sociedad Chilena de Obstetricia y Ginecologia
Bol Soc Chil Quim — Boletin. Sociedad Chilena Quimica
Bol Soc Chim Sao Paulo — Boletim. Sociedade de Chimica de Sao Paulo
Bol Soc Cient Hispano-Marroqui — Boletin. Sociedad Cientifica Hispano-Marroqui de Alcazarquivir
Bol Soc Ci Lit Artist — Boletin de la Sociedad Cientifica, Literaria, y Artistica
Bol Soc Cirug Chile — Boletin. Sociedad de Cirugia de Chile
Bol Soc Cirug Cord — Boletines y Trabajos. Sociedad de Cirugia de Cordoba
Bol Soc Cirug Urug — Boletin. Sociedad de Cirugia del Uruguay
Bol Soc Cir Urug — Boletin. Sociedad de Cirugia del Uruguay
Bol Soc Col Cienc Nat — Boletin. Sociedad Colombiana de Ciencias Naturales
Bol Soc Colomb Quim Farm — Boletin. Sociedad Colombiana de Quimicos Farmaceuticos
Bol Soc Cubana Dermatol Sifilogr — Boletin. Sociedad Cubana de Dermatologia y Sifilografia
Bol Soc Cub Derm Sif — Boletin. Sociedad Cubana de Dermatologia y Sifilografia
Bol Soc Dent Guatem — Boletin. Sociedad Dental de Guatemala
Bol Soc Eng Rio Grande Do Sul — Boletim. Sociedade de Engenharia do Rio Grande Do Sul
Bol Soc Esp Ceram — Boletin. Sociedad Espanola de Ceramica
Bol Soc Esp Ceram Vidr — Boletin. Sociedad Espanola de Ceramica y Vidrio
Bol Soc Esp Ceram Vidrio — Boletin. Sociedad Espanola de Ceramica y Vidrio
Bol Soc Esp Excurs — Boletin de la Sociedad Espanola de Excursiones
Bol Soc Esp Hist Farm — Boletin. Sociedad Espanola de Historia de la Farmacia
Bol Soc Esp Hist Med — Boletin. Sociedad Espanola de Historia de la Medicina
Bol Soc Estomatol Argent — Boletin. Sociedad Estomatologica Argentina
Bol Soc Estud Mocambique — Boletim. Sociedade de Estudos de Mocambique
Bol Soc Fom Fabril — Boletin. Sociedad de Fomento Fabril
Bol Soc Geogr Bogota — Boletin. Sociedad Geografica de Colombia (Bogota)
Bol Soc Geogr Hist Sucre — Boletin. Sociedad Geografica e Historica (Sucre, Bolivia)
Bol Soc Geogr La Paz — Boletin. Sociedad Geografica (La Paz)
Bol Soc Geogr Lima — Boletin. Sociedad Geografica de Lima
Bol Soc Geogr Lisboa — Boletim. Sociedade de Geografia de Lisboa
Bol Soc Geogr (Madrid) — Boletin. Real Sociedad de Geografia (Madrid)

Bol Soc Geogr Sucre — Boletin. Sociedad Geografica de Sucre (Bolivia)

Bol Soc Geog Sucre — Boletin de la Sociedad Geografica e Historica de Sucre

Bol Soc Geol Boliv — Boletin. Sociedad Geologica Boliviana

Bol Soc Geol Mex — Boletin. Sociedad Geologica Mexicana

Bol Soc Geol Peru — Boletin. Sociedad Geologica del Peru

Bol Soc Geol Port — Boletim. Sociedade Geologica de Portugal

Bol Soc Hist Aguascalientes — Boletin de la Sociedad de Historia, Geografia, y Estadistica de Aguascalientes

Bol Soc Invest Arte Rup Boliv — Boletin. Sociedad de Investigacion del Arte Rupestre de Bolivia

Bol Soc Ital Fis — Bollettino. Societa Italiana di Fisica

Bol Soc Mat Mexicana — Boletin. Sociedad Matematica Mexicana

Bol Soc Mat Mexicana 2 — Boletin. Sociedad Matematica Mexicana. Segunda Serie

Bol Soc Med Cent Materno Infant Gral Maximino Avila Camacho — Boletin. Sociedad Medica del Centro Materno Infantil Gral Maximino Avila Camacho

Bol Soc Med e Cirug S Paulo — Boletim. Sociedade de Medicina e Cirugia de Sao Paulo

Bol Soc Med Quir Centro Republ — Boletin. Sociedad Medico-Quirurgica del Centro de la Republica

Bol Soc Mex Geogr Estad Mex — Boletin. Sociedad Mexicana de Geografia y Estadistica (Mexico)

Bol Soc Mex Hist Filos Med — Boletin. Sociedad Mexicana de Historia y Filosofia de la Medicina

Bol Soc Mex Mico — Boletin. Sociedad Mexicana de Micologia

Bol Soc Mex Micol — Boletin. Sociedad Mexicana de Micologia

Bol Soc Nac Agrar — Boletin de la Sociedad Nacional Agraria

Bol Soc Nac Mineria Lima — Boletin. Sociedad Nacional de Mineria del Peru (Lima)

Bol Soc Nac Mineria Petrol — Boletin. Sociedad Nacional de Mineria y Petroleo

Bol Soc Nac Min (Peru) — Boletin. Sociedad Nacional de Mineria (Peru)

Bol Soc Nac Min Pet — Boletin. Sociedad Nacional de Mineria y Petroleo

Bol Soc Paran Mat 2 — Boletim. Sociedade Paranaense de Matematica. 2 Serie

Bol Soc Paul Med Vet — Boletim. Sociedade Paulista de Medicina Veterinaria

Bol Soc Peruana Bot — Boletin. Sociedad Peruana de Botanica

Bol Soc Port Cardiol — Boletim. Sociedade Portuguesa de Cardiologia

Bol Soc Port Cienc Nat — Boletim. Sociedade Portuguesa de Ciencias Naturais

Bol Soc Port Entomol — Boletim. Sociedade Portuguesa de Entomologia

Bol Soc Port Mat — Boletim de Sociedade Portuguesa de Matematica

Bol Soc Port Quim — Boletim. Sociedade Portuguesa de Quimica

Bol Soc Quim Peru — Boletin. Sociedad Quimica del Peru

Bol Soc St Vald — Bollettino. Societa di Studi Valdesi

Bol Soc Valencia Pediatr — Boletin. Sociedad Valenciana de Pediatria

Bol Soc Venez Cienc Nat — Boletin. Sociedad Venezolana de Ciencias Naturales

Bol Soc Venez Cien Nat Caracas — Boletin. Sociedad Venezolana de Ciencias Naturales (Caracas)

Bol Soc Venez Cir — Boletin. Sociedad Venezolana de Cirugia

Bol Soc Venez Espeleol — Boletin. Sociedad Venezolana de Espeleologia

Bol Soc Venez Geol — Boletin. Sociedad Venezolana de Geologos

Bol Suelos Deriv Cenizas Volcanicas — Boletin sobre Suelos Derivados de Cenizas Volcanicas

Bol Superin Serv Cafe S Paulo — Boletim da Superintendencia dos Servicos do Cafe (Sao Paulo)

Bol Supt Serv Cafe (Sao Paulo) — Boletim. Superintendencia dos Servicos do Cafe (Sao Paulo)

Bol Tec Arpel — Boletin Tecnico Arpel

Bol Tec Asoc Interam Bibl Doc Agric — Boletin Tecnico. Asociacion Interamericana de Bibliotecarios y Documentalistas Agricolas

Bol Tec Braz Dep Nac Obras Contra Secas — Boletim Tecnico. Brazil Departamento Nacional de Obras Contra as Secas

Bol Tec BT Cent Energ Nucl Agric — Boletim Tecnico BT. Centro de Energia Nuclear na Agricultura

Bol Tec Cent Invest Agric Alberto Boerger — Boletin Tecnico. Centro de Investigaciones Agricolas "Alberto Boerger"

Bol Tec Cent Pesqui Agropecu Trop Umido — Boletim Tecnico. Centro de Pesquisa Agropecuaria do Tropico Umido

Bol Tec Cent Pesqui Cacau (Itabuna Braz) — Boletim Tecnico. Centro de Pesquisa do Cacau (Itabuna, Braz)

Bol Tec Cent Pesqui Desenvolvimento (Estado Bahia) — Boletim Tecnico. Centro de Pesquisas e Desenvolvimento (Estado da Bahia)

Bol Tec Cent Tecnol Agric Aliment — Boletim Tecnico. Centro de Tecnologia Agricola e Alimentar

Bol Tec Cent Tecnol Agric Aliment (Rio De Janeiro) — Boletim Tecnico. Centro de Tecnologia Agricola e Alimentar (Rio De Janeiro)

Bol Tec Cient Univ Sao Paulo Esc Super Agri Luiz de Queiroz — Boletim Tecnico Cientifico. Universidade de Sao Paulo. Escola SuperiorAgricultura "Luiz de Queiroz"

Bol Tec COPERSUCAR — Boletim Tecnico COPERSUCAR

Bol Tec Dep Nac Obras Contra Secas — Boletim Tecnico. Departamento Nacional de Obras Contra as Secas

Bol Tec Dep Nac Obras Contra Secas (Braz) — Boletim Tecnico. Departamento Nacional de Obras Contra as Secas(Brazil)

Bol Tec Dep Prod Veg Secr Agric Parana — Boletim Tecnico. Departamento de Producao Vegetal Secretaria de Agricultura do Parana

Bol Tec Dept Invest Agr Min Agr Dir Agr Pesca (Chile) — Boletin Tecnico. Departamento de Investigacion Agricola. Ministerio de Agricultura. Direccion de Agricultura y Pesca (Chile)

Bol Tec Dir Gen Sanid — Boletin Tecnico. Direccion General de Sanidad

Bol Tec Div Pedol Fertil Solo (Braz) — Boletim Tecnico. Divisao de Pedologia e Fertilidade do Solo (Brazil)

Bol Tec Div Pesqui Pedol (Braz) — Boletim Tecnico. Divisao de Pesquisa Pedologica (Brazil)

Bol Tec Div Tecnol Agric Aliment (Braz) — Boletim Tecnico. Divisao de Tecnologia Agricola e Alimentar (Brazil)

Bol Tec Div Tecnol Agric Aliment (Brazil) — Boletim Tecnico. Divisao de Tecnologia Agricola e Alimentar (Brazil)

Bol Tec Equipe Pedol Fertil Solo (Braz) — Boletim Tecnico. Equipe de Pedologia e Fertilidade do Solo (Brazil)

Bol Tec Equipe Pedol Fertil Solo (Brazil) — Boletim Tecnico. Equipe de Pedologia e Fertilidade do Solo (Brazil)

Bol Tec Esc Ingen For Univ Chile — Boletin Tecnico. Escuela de Ingenieria Forestal. Universidad de Chile

Bol Tec Esc Nac Agr Chapingo — Boletin Tecnico. Escuela Nacional de Agricultura Chapingo

Bol Tec Esc Super Agric Antonio Narro Univ Coahuila Saltillo — Boletin Tecnico. Escuela Superior de Agricultura "Antonio Narro." Universidad de Coahuila (Saltillo)

Bol Tec Es Super Agric Antonio Narro Univ Coahuila Saltillo — Boletin Tecnico. Escuela Superior de Agricultura "Antonio Narro." Universidad de Coahuila (Saltillo)

Bol Tec Feder Nac Cafeteros (Colombia) — Boletin Tecnico. Federacion Nacional de Cafeteros (Colombia)

Bol Tec Fed Nac Cafeteros Colomb — Boletin Tecnico. Federacion Nacional de Cafeteros de Colombia

Bol Tec Fund Inst Agron Parana — Boletim Tecnico. Fundacao Instituto Agronomico do Parana

Bol Tec IAPAR — Boletim Tecnico IAPAR

Bol Tec Inst Agron — Boletim Tecnico. Instituto Agronomico

Bol Tec Inst Agron Leste (Cruz Das Almas) — Boletim Tecnico. Instituto Agronomico do Leste (Cruz Das Almas)

Bol Tec Inst Agron Nordeste — Boletim Tecnico. Instituto Agronomico do Nordeste

Bol Tec Inst Agron Norte — Boletim Tecnico. Instituto Agronomico do Norte

Bol Tec Inst Agron Norte (Belem) — Boletim Tecnico. Instituto Agronomico do Norte (Belem)

Bol Tec Inst Agron Sul — Boletim Tecnico. Instituto Agronomico do Sul

Bol Tec Inst Agron Sul (Braz) — Boletim Tecnico. Instituto Agronomico do Sul (Brazil)

Bol Tec Inst Agron Sul (Pelotas) — Boletim Tecnico. Instituto Agronomico do Sul (Pelotas)

Bol Tec Inst Agron Sul (Pelotas Brazil) — Boletim Tecnico. Instituto Agronomico do Sul (Pelotas, Brazil)

Bol Tec Inst Exp Invest Fom Agric Ganad (St Fe) — Boletin Tecnico. Instituto Experimental de Investigacion y FomentoAgricola-Ganadero (Sante Fe)

Bol Tec Inst Florest — Boletim Tecnico. Instituto Florestal

Bol Tec Inst Fom Algodonero (Bogota) — Boletin Tecnico. Instituto de Fomenta Algodonero (Bogota)

Bol Tec Inst For Chile — Boletin Tecnico. Instituto Forestal. Santiago-De-Chile

Bol Tec Inst Nac Invest For (Mex) — Boletin Tecnico. Instituto Nacional de Investigaciones Forestales (Mexico)

Bol Tec Inst Nac Tecnol Ind (Argent) — Boletin Tecnico. Instituto Nacional de Tecnologia Industrial(Argentina)

Bol Tec Inst Pesqui Agropecu Norte — Boletim Tecnico. Instituto de Pesquisa Agropecuaria do Norte

Bol Tec Inst Pesqui Exp Agropecu Norte — Boletim Tecnico. Instituto de Pesquisas e Experimentacao Agropecuarias do Norte

Bol Tec Inst Pesqui Exp Agropecu Sul (Braz) — Boletim Tecnico. Instituto de Pesquisas e Experimentacao Agropecuariasdo Sul (Brazil)

Bol Tec Inst Prov Agropecu — Boletin Tecnico. Instituto Provincial Agropecuario

Bol Tec Inst Prov Agropecu (Mendoza) — Boletin Tecnico. Instituto Provincial Agropecuario (Mendoza)

Bol Tec IPEAN — Boletim Tecnico. Instituto de Pesquisas e Experimentacao Agropecuarias do Norte

Bol Tec Min Agr (Colombia) — Boletin Tecnico. Ministerio de Agricultura (Colombia)

Bol Tec Min Agr (Guatemala) — Boletin Tecnico. Ministerio de Agricultura (Guatemala)

Bol Tec Minist Agric Ganad (Costa Rica) — Boletin Tecnico. Ministerio de Agricultura y Ganaderia (Costa Rica)

Bol Tec Minist Agric Ind (San Jose Costa Rica) — Boletin Tecnico. Ministerio de Agricultura e Industrias (San Jose, Costa Rica)

Bol Tecn Fac Ci Biol Univ Nuevo Leon — Boletin Tecnico. Facultad de Ciencias Biologicas. Universidad de Nuevo Leon

Bol Tecn Inst Agron Estado Sao Paulo — Boletim Tecnico. Instituto Agronomico do Estado de Sao Paulo

Bol Tecn Inst Fitotecn — Boletin Tecnico. Instituto de Fitotecnia

Bol Tecn Minist Agric — Boletin Tecnico. Ministerio de Agricultura y Cria

Bol Tecn Soc Agron Mex — Boletinos Tecnicos. Sociedad Agronomica Mexicana

Bol Tec Peru Serv Invest Promoc Agr — Boletin Tecnico. Peru. Servicio de Investigacion y Promocion Agraria

Bol Tec PETROBRAS — Boletim Tecnico. PETROBRAS

Bol Tec Serv Nac Levantamento Conserv Solos — Boletim Tecnico. Servico Nacional de Levantamento e Conservacao de Solos

Bol Tec S Jose — Boletin Tecnico (San Jose, Costa Rica)

Bol Tec Univ Cent Venez Inst Mater Modelos Estruct — Boletin Tecnico. Universidad Central de Venezuela. Instituto deMateriales y Modelos Estructurales

Bol Tec Univ Chile Fac Cienc For — Boletin Tecnico. Universidad de Chile. Facultad de Ciencias Forestales

Bol Tec Univ Fed Rural Rio De Janeiro Inst Agron Dep Solos — Boletim Tecnico. Universidade Federal Rural do Rio De Janeiro.Instituto de Agronomia. Departamento de Solos

Bolton Landing Conf Proc — Bolton Landing Conference. Proceedings

Bol Trab Soc Argent Cir — Boletines y Trabajos. Sociedad Argentina de Cirujanos

Bol Trab Soc Cir Buenos Aires — Boletines y Trabajos. Sociedad de Cirugia de Buenos Aires

Bol Trim Estad Munici Caracas — Boletin Trimestral de Estadistica Municipal (Caracas)

Bol Trimest Exp Agropecu — Boletin Trimestral de Experimentacion Agropecuaria

Bol Trimest Hosp Vina Del Mar — Boletin Trimestral. Hospital del Vina Del Mar

Bol U Compostelana — Boletin de la Universidad Compostelana

Bol Univ Chile — Boletin. Universidad de Chile

Bol Univ Fed Parana Bot — Boletim. Universidade Federal do Parana. Botanica

Bol Univ Fed Parana Fis Teor — Boletim. Universidade Federal do Parana. Fisica Teorica

Bol Univ Fed Parana Inst Geol Geol — Boletim. Universidade Federal do Parana. Instituto de Geologia. SerieGeologia

Bol Univ Fed Parana Zool — Boletim. Universidade Federal do Parana. Zoologia

Bol Univ Los Andes Fac Cienc For — Boletin. Universidad de Los Andes. Facultad de Ciencias Forestales

Bol Univ Nac Ing Lima — Boletin. Universidad Nacional de Ingenieria (Lima)

Bol Univ Nac Ing (Peru) — Boletin. Universidad Nacional de Ingenieria (Peru)

Bol Univ Parana Bot — Boletim. Universidade do Parana. Botanica

Bol Univ Parana Cons Pesqui Dep Med Pre Monogr — Boletim. Universidade do Parana. Conselho de Pesquisas. Departamento de Medicina Preventiva. Monografia

Bol Univ Parana Farm — Boletim. Universidade do Parana. Farmacognosia

Bol Univ Parana Farmacogn — Boletim. Universidade do Parana. Farmacognosia

Bol Univ Parana Geol — Boletim. Universidade do Parana. Geologia

Bol Univ Parana Inst Geol Geol — Boletim. Universidade do Parana. Instituto de Geologia. SerieGeologia

Bol Univ Parana Zool — Boletim. Universidade do Parana. Zoologia

Bol Univ Repub Fac Agron (Montevideo) — Boletin. Universidad de la Republica. Facultad de Agronomia (Montevideo)

Bol Univ Rio Grande Sul Esc Geol — Boletim. Universidade do Rio Grande Do Sul. Escola de Geologia

Bol Univ Sao Paulo Bot — Boletim da Universidade de Sao Paulo. Botanica

Bol Univ Sao Paulo Inst Geocien Astron — Boletim. Universidade de Sao Paulo. Instituto de Geociencias e Astronomia

Bol Univ Sao Paulo Inst Geocienc — Boletim. Universidade de Sao Paulo. Instituto de Geociencias

Bol Un Pan Wash — Boletin. Union Panamericana (Washington, DC)

Bol Urug Sociol — Boletin Uruguayo de Sociologia

Bolyai Soc Math Stud — Bolyai Society Mathematical Studies

Bol y Trab Soc Cirug Buenos Aires — Boletines y Trabajos. Sociedad de Cirugia de Buenos Aires

BolzePr — Praxis des Reichsgerichts (Bolze, Editor)

Bol Zool — Boletim de Zoologia

Bol Zool Biol Mar — Boletim de Zoologia e Biologia Marinha [*Later, Boletim de Zoologia*]

Bol Zool Biol Mar (Nova Ser) — Boletim de Zoologia e Biologia Marinha (Nova Serie) [*Later, Boletim de Zoologia*]

Bol Zool Mus Para Emilio Goeldi — Boletim de Zoologia. Museu Paraense Emilio Goeldi

Bol Zootec — Boletim de Zootecnia

Bombay Cott A — Bombay Cotton Annual

Bombay Geogr Mag — Bombay Geographical Magazine

Bombay Hosp J — Bombay Hospital Journal

Bombay L J — Bombay Law Journal

Bombay Med J — Bombay Medical Journal

Bombay Technol — Bombay Technologist

Bombay Univ J — Bombay University Journal

Bombay Vet Coll Mag — Bombay Veterinary College Magazine

BOMBB — Biomembranes

BOMDD — Bio Med

Bome S-Afr — Bome in Suid-Afrika

Bom LJ — Bombay Law Journal

BOMXA — Boletin. Asociacion Mexicana de Geologos Petroleros

B o N — Bog og Naal

Bone Ac Hip BII — Bulletin de l'Academie d'Hippone (Bone)

Bone Metab — Bone Metabolism

Bone Miner — Bone and Mineral

Bone Miner Res — Bone and Mineral Research

Bones Jt — Bones and Joints

Bone Tooth Proc Eur Symp — Bone and Tooth. Proceedings. European Symposium

BonG — Bonner Geschichtsblaetter

BONM — Bulletin. Office National Meteorologique

BONMOT — Sinnspruche, Aphorismen, und Lebensweisheiten

BONNA — Bollettino. Societa di Naturalisti di Napoli

Bonn Amer Stud — Bonner Amerikanistische Studien

Bonn Cor BI NH Vr — Correspondenzblatt des Naturhistorischen Vereins fuer Rheinland und Westphalen (Bonn)

Bonner Arbeiten — Bonner Arbeiten zur Deutschen Literatur

Bonner County Geneal Soc Quart — Bonner County Genealogical Society Quarterly

Bonner Energ-Rep — Bonner Energie-Report

Bonner J — Bonner Jahrbuecher des Rheinischen Landesmuseums in Bonn und des Vereins von Altertumsfreunden in Rheinlande

Bonner Jahrb — Bonner Jahrbuecher des Rheinischen Landesmuseums in Bonn und des Vereins von Altertumsfreunden in Rheinlande

Bonner Jb — Bonner Jahrbuecher

Bonner Math Schriften — Bonner Mathematische Schriften

Bonner Rechtswiss Abh — Bonner Rechtswissenschaftliche Abhandlungen

Bonn Geogr Abh — Bonner Geographische Abhandlungen

Bonn Hefte Vg — Bonner Hefte zur Vorgeschichte

Bonniers Litt Mag — Bonniers Litteraerae Magasin

Bonn Jahrb — Bonner Jahrbuecher des Rheinischen Landesmuseums in Bonn und des Vereins von Altertumsfreunden in Rheinlande

Bonn Jb — Bonner Jahrbuecher

Bonn Jbb — Bonner Jahrbuecher. Jahrbuecher des Vereins von Altertumsfreunden im Rheinlande

Bonn Jb Rhein Landesmus Bonn & Ver Altertfreund Rheinlande — Bonner Jahrbuecher des Rheinischen Landesmuseums in Bonn und des Vereins von Altertumsfreunden im Rheinlande

Bonn Jb Ver Altertfreund Rheinlande & Rhein Provmus Bonn — Bonner Jahrbuecher des Vereins von Altertumsfreunden im Rheinlande und des Rheinischen Provincialmuseums in Bonn

Bonn Jhb — Bonner Jahrbuecher des Rheinischen Landesmuseums in Bonn und des Vereins von Altertumsfreunden in Rheinlande

Bonn Litt Mag — Bonniers Litteraera Magasin

Bonn Math Schr — Bonner Mathematische Schriften

Bonn NH Vr Cor BI — Correspondenzblatt des Naturhistorischen Vereins fuer Rheinland und Westphalen (Bonn)

Bonn Niedr Gs Sb — Sitzungsberichte der Niederrheinischen Gesellschaft fuer Natur- und Heilkunde zu Bonn

Bonn NL Vr Vh — Verhandlungen des Naturhistorischen Vereins der Preussischen Rheinlande, Westfalens und des Reg.-Bezirks Osnabruek (Bonn)

Bonn Sb Niedr Gs — Sitzungsberichte der Niederrheinischen Gesellschaft fuer Natur- und Heilkunde zu Bonn

Bonn Univ Phys Inst Tech Rep BONN HE — Bonn University. Physikalisches Institut. Technical Report BONN-HE

Bonn Univ Phys Inst Tech Rep BONN IR — Bonn University. Physikalisches Institut. Technical Report BONN-IR

Bonn Vh NH Vr — Verhandlungen des Naturhistorischen Vereins der Preussischen Rheinlande, Westfalens und des Reg.-Bezirks Osnabruek (Bonn)

Bonn Zool Beitr — Bonner Zoologische Beitraege

Bonn Zool Monogr — Bonner Zoologische Monographien

Bonsai Bull New York — Bonsai Bulletin. Bonsai Society of Greater New York

Bonsai Bull Philadelphia — Bonsai Bulletin. Quarterly. Pennsylvania Bonsai Society (Philadelphia)

Bonsai J — Bonsai Journal

BOO — Banco de Guatemala. Informe Economico

Bo O Bo — Born og Boger

BOOCA — Bollettino d'Oculistica

Bo og Bo — Born og Boger

Book — Bookman

Book Abstr Int Conf At Spectrosc — Book of Abstracts. International Conference on Atomic Spectroscopy

Book ASTM Stand — Book of ASTM [*American Society for Testing and Materials*] Standards

Book Auct Rec — Book Auction Records

Book Coll — Book Collector

Book Collec — Book Collector

Book Collect — Book Collector

Book Coll Qtr — Book Collector's Quarterly

Book Fr — Books in French

Bookleger — Booklegger

Booklet SE — Bookletter Southeast

Bookl For Comm (Lond) — Booklet. Forestry Commission (London)

Bookl For Commn — Booklet. Forestry Commission (London)

Bookl Int Colloq Magn Films Surf — Booklet. International Colloquium on Magnetic Films and Surfaces

Booklist — American Library Association. Booklist

Booklist — Booklist and Subscription Books Bulletin [*Later, Booklist*]

Booklist and SBB — Booklist and Subscription Books Bulletin [*Later, Booklist*]

Bookl M — Booklovers' Magazine

Booklover's M — Booklover's Magazine

Bookl Ser Agric Org Soc — Booklet Series. Agricultural Organisation Society (London)

Bookl Timb Pres Assoc Aust — Booklet. Timber Preservers' Association of Australia

Bookm — Bookman

Bookmark — Bookmark. New York State Library

Book Met Soc — Book. Metals Society

Bookm (Lond) — Bookman (London)

Book Pap Am Assoc Text Chem Color Int Conf Exhib — Book of Papers. American Association of Textile Chemists and Colorists. International Conference and Exhibition

Book Pap Can Text Semin Int — Book of Papers. Canadian Textile Seminar International

Book Pap Int Conf Exhib AATCC — Book of Papers. International Conference and Exhibition. AATCC

Book Pap Int Tech Conf Am Assoc Tex Chem Color — Book of Papers. International Technical Conference. American Association of Textile Chemists and Colorists

Book Pap Natl Tech Conf AATCC — Book of Papers. National Technical Conference. AATCC

Book Pap Natl Tech Conf Am Assoc Text Chem Color — Book of Papers. National Technical Conference. American Association of Textile Chemists and Colorists

Book Pap Nat Tech Conf — Book of Papers. National Technical Conference

Book Pap Tech Symp Nonwovens Innovative Fabr Future — Book of Papers. Technical Symposium. Nonwovens. Innovative Fabrics for the Future

Book Proc Annu Ind Air Pollut Contam Contr Semin — Book of Proceedings. Annual Industrial Air Pollution/Contamination Control Seminar

Book Proc Annu Ind Air Pollut Control Semin — Book of Proceedings. Annual Industrial Air Pollution ControlSeminar

Book Proc Annu Ind Air Water Pollut Contam Control Semin — Book of Proceedings. Annual Industrial Air and Water Pollution/Contamination Control Seminar

Book Prod — Book Production Industry

Book Pub Dir — Book Publishers Directory

Book R — Book Reviews

Book Rev Digest — Book Review Digest

Book Revi Index — Book Review Index

Book Rev Index Soc Sci Period — Book Review Index to Social Science Periodicals
Book Rev Mon — Book Reviews of the Month
Books — Books Abroad
Books — New York Herald Tribune Books
Books Earth Sci Relat Top — Books in the Earth Sciences and Related Topics
Books in Library and Information Sci — Books in Library and Information Science
Books in Scot — Books in Scotland
Book Suppl J Child Psychol Psychiatr — Book Supplement. Journal of Child Psychology and Psychiatry
Boole Press Conf Ser — Boole Press Conference Series
Bo O Un — Born og Unge
BOP — Beitraege zur Oberpfalzforschung
BOP — Bibliographique Officiel des Imprimes Publies en Pologne. Bulletin
BOP — Bibliography of Philosophy
BOP — Bouwbedrijf
BOP — British Overseas Pharmacist
BophthG — Bericht ueber die Versammlung der Ophthalmologischen Gesellschaft [*Heidelberg*]
Bopp Reuther Tech Mitt — Bopp und Reuther. Technische Mitteilungen
BOPS — Balance of Payments Statistics
BOPSA — Bibliotheca Ophthalmologica
BOR — Babylonian and Oriental Record
BOR — Biserica Orthodoxa Romana
BOR — Business Owner
BOran — Bulletin Trimestriel des Antiquites Africaines Recueillies par les Soins de la Societe de Geographie et d'Archeologie de la Province d'Oran
Borasz Lapok Budapest — Boraszati Lapok (Budapest)
Borasz Lapok Pest — Boraszati Lapok (Pest)
Bor'ba Gazom Pyl'yu Ugol'n Shakhtakh — Bor'ba s Gazom i Pyl'yu v Ugol'nykh Shakhtakh
Bor'ba Tuberk — Bor'ba s Tuberkulezom
Bor Cipotech — Bor es Cipotechnika
Bor Cipotech Piac — Bor- es Cipotechnika, -Piac
Bordeaux Ac Act — Recueil des Actes de l'Academie des Sciences, Belles-Lettres, et Arts de Bordeaux
Bordeaux Ac Sc Pbl — Seances Publiques de l'Academie Royale des Sciences, Belles-Lettres, et Arts de Bordeaux
Bordeaux Ac Sc Se Pbl — Seances Publiques de l'Academie Royale des Sciences, Belles-Lettres, et Arts de Bordeaux
Bordeaux Act — Recueil des Actes de l'Academie des Sciences, Belles-Lettres, et Arts de Bordeaux
Bordeaux Act Ac Sc — Recueil des Actes de l'Academie des Sciences, Belles-Lettres, et Arts de Bordeaux
Bordeaux Chir — Bordeaux Chirurgicale
Bordeaux J Md — Journal de Medecine de Bordeaux
Bordeaux Med — Bordeaux Medical
Bordeaux Mm S Sc — Memoires de la Societe des Sciences Physiques et Naturelles de Bordeaux
Bordeaux Mm S Sc Ps — Memoires de la Societe des Sciences Physiques et Naturelles de Bordeaux
Bordeaux Obs A — Annales de l'Observatoire de Bordeaux
Bordeaux S L Act — Actes de la Societe Linneenne de Bordeaux
Bordeaux S Md Mm — Memoires et Bulletins de la Societe Medico-Chirurgicale des Hopitaux et Hospices de Bordeaux
Bordeaux S Sc Mm — Memoires de la Societe des Sciences Physiques et Naturelles de Bordeaux
Bordeaux S Sc PV — Proces-Verbaux des Seances de la Societe des Sciences Physiques et Naturelles de Bordeaux
Borden's Rev Nutr Res — Borden's Review of Nutrition Research
Borderl Neurol — Borderlands of Neurology
Borderl Psychiatry — Borderland of Psychiatry
Bord Med — Bordeaux Medical
Boreal Environ Res — Boreal Environment Research
Boreal Inst North Stud Univ Alberta Annu Rep — Boreal Institute for Northern Studies. University of Alberta. Annual Report
Boreal Inst North Stud Univ Alberta Occas Publ — Boreal Institute for Northern Studies. University of Alberta. Occasional Publication
Borehole Water J — Borehole Water Journal
Borgyogy Venerol Sz — Borgyogyaszati es Venerologiai Szemle
BORL — Boreal
B Orleans — Bulletin. Societe Archeologique et Historique de l'Orleannais
Borneo Res Bull — Borneo Research Bulletin
Bornholm Sam — Bornholmske Samlinger
Bor Poluch Strukt Svoistva Mater Mezhdunar Simp Boru — Bor. Poluchenie, Struktura, i Svoistva. Materialy Mezhdunarodnogo.Simpoziuma po Boru
Bor Res B — Borneo Research Bulletin
BORS — Bihar and Orissa Research Society. Journal
Borsod Szle — Borsodi Szemle
BORU — Bulletin Officiel de Ruanda-Urundi
BoRv — Book Review Digest
BOS — Bonner Orientalistische Studien
Bosai Soc Newslett — Bosai Society Newsletter
BoSBB — Booklist and Subscription Books Bulletin
Bos Bijdr — Bossche Bijdragen
Bosbou S-Afr — Bosbou in Suid-Afrika
Bosbouwproefstn TNO Korte Meded — Bosbouwproefstation TNO. Korte Mededeling
Bosb Suid-Afr — Bosbou in Suid-Afrika
Boschbouwk Tijdschr — Boschbouwkundig Tijdschrift
Bosch Tech Ber — Bosch Technische Berichte
BOSE — Bulletin of the Ophthalmological Society of Egypt
BOSFA — Bollettino. Societa Italiana di Fisica
BOSGA — Bollettino. Servizio Geologico d'Italia
Bos Pub Lib Q — Boston Public Library. Quarterly

Bo St — Boghazkoei-Studien
Bost — Bostonian
Bost Am Ac Mm — Memoirs of the American Academy of Arts and Sciences (Cambridge, Boston)
Bost Coll Ind L Rev — Boston College. Industrial and Commercial Law Review
Bost Her Am — Boston Herald American
Bost Med & Surg J — Boston Medical and Surgery Journal
Bost Mm Am Ac — Memoirs of the American Academy of Arts and Sciences (Cambridge, Boston)
Bost Mo — Boston Monthly Magazine
Bostn Glbe — Boston Globe
Bostn Glbe Ind — Boston Globe Index
Bost Obs — Boston Observer
Boston BJ — Boston Bar Journal
Boston Bsn — Boston Business Journal
Boston Col Environmental Affairs Law R — Boston College. Environmental Affairs Law Review
Boston Col Ind and Commer Law R — Boston College. Industrial and Commercial Law Review
Boston Col Ind Com L Rev — Boston College. Industrial and Commercial Law Review
Boston Col Int Comp L Rev — Boston College. International and Comparative Law Review
Boston Col Internat and Comparative Law R — Boston College. International and Comparative Law Review
Boston Col Int'l & Comp LJ — Boston College. International and Comparative Law Journal
Boston Col Law R — Boston College. Law Review
Boston Coll Env Aff Law Rev — Boston College Environmental Affairs Law Review
Boston Coll Environ Aff Law Rev — Boston College. Environmental Affairs Law Review
Boston Coll Press Anthrop Ser — Boston College Press Anthropological Series
Boston Col Stud Phil — Boston College. Studies in Philosophy
Boston J Nat Hist — Boston Journal of Natural History
Boston J N H — Boston Journal of Natural History
Boston J Ph — Boston Journal of Philosophy and the Arts
Boston M — Boston Magazine
Boston Med and S J — Boston Medical and Surgical Journal
Boston Med Q — Boston Medical Quarterly
Boston Med Surg J — Boston Medical and Surgical Journal
Boston Mus Bul — Boston Museum of Fine Arts. Bulletin
Boston Mus Bull — Boston Museum Bulletin
Boston Pub Lib Quar — Boston Public Library. Quarterly
Boston Publ Libr Quart — Boston Public Library Quarterly
Boston R — Boston Review
Boston Soc C E J — Boston Society of Civil Engineers. Journal
Boston Soc of Nat Hist Memoirs — Boston Society of Natural History. Memoirs
Boston Soc of Nat Hist Occ Papers — Boston Society of Natural History. Occasional Papers
Boston Soc of Nat Hist Proc — Boston Society of Natural History. Proceedings
Boston State Hosp Monogr Ser — Boston State Hospital. Monograph Series
Boston Studies Philos Sci — Boston Studies in the Philosophy of Science
Boston Stud Philos Sci — Boston Studies in the Philosophy of Science
Boston U LR — Boston University. Law Review
Boston UL Rev — Boston University. Law Review
Boston Univ Law R — Boston University. Law Review
Boston Univ Law Rev — Boston University Law Review
Boston U St — Boston University. Studies in Philosophy and Religion
Bost Q — Boston Quarterly
Bost R — Boston Review
Bost S Md Sc J — Journal of the Boston Society of Medical Sciences
Bost S NH P — Proceedings of the Boston Society of Natural History
Bost Soc Natur Hist Occ Pa — Boston Society of Natural History. Occasional Papers
Bost Soc Natur Hist Proc — Boston Society of Natural History. Proceedings
Bost Sym — Boston Symphony Orchestra. Program Notes
Bost Sym Concert Bul — Boston Symphony Orchestra. Concert Bulletin
Bo Stud — Bonner Studien zur Englischen Philologie
Bost UL Rev — Boston University. Law Review
Bost Univ Afr Lib Newsl — Boston University. Africana Libraries. Newsletter
Bost Univ Bus Rev — Boston University. Business Review
Bost Univ L R — Boston University Law Review
Bost Univ St Engl — Boston University. Studies in English
BOSUAN — Forestry in South Africa
Bos U J — Boston University. Journal
Bos U Law Rev — Boston University. Law Review
BOSYA — Bulletin. Ophthalmological Society of Egypt
BOT — Books of the Times
BoT — Books of Today
Bo T — Bornesagens Tidende
Bo T — Born i Tiden
Bot Abh — Botanische Abhandlungen aus dem Gebiet der Morphologie und Physiologie
Bot Abstr — Botanical Abstracts
Bot Acta — Botanica Acta
Bot Advertiser Rhode Island Rec Med Reform — Botanic Advertiser and Rhode Island Record of Modern Medical Reform
Botan B A S — Botanical Bulletin. Academia Sinica
Botan Gaz — Botanical Gazette
Botan J Lin — Botanical Journal. Linnean Society
Botan Mag — Botanical Magazine
Botan Marin — Botanica Marina
Botan Notis — Botaniska Notiser
Botan Rev — Botanical Review

Botan Tids — Botanisk Tidsskrift
Botany Bull Dep Agric Qd — Botany Bulletin. Department of Agriculture (Queensland)
Botany Curr Lit — Botany. Current Literature
Botany Icel — Botany of Iceland
Botany Pamph Carnegie Mus — Botany Pamphlet. Carnegie Museum
Botany Zool Tokyo — Botany and Zoology. Theoretical and Applied (Tokyo)
Bot Arch — Botanisches Archiv
Bot Arch Gartenbauges Oesterr Kaiserstaates — Botanisches Archiv der Gartenbaugesellschaft des Oesterreichischen Kaiserstaates
Bot Biol Veg — Botanique et Biologie Vegetale
Bot Blaett Befoerd Selbststud Pflanzenk — Botanische Blaetter zur Befoerderung des Selbststudiums der Pflanzenkunde auch Besonders fuer Frauenzimmer
Bot Bull — Botanical Bulletin
Bot Bull Acad Sinica — Botanical Bulletin. Academia Sinica
Bot Bull Acad Sinica Inst Bot New Ser — Botanical Bulletin. Academia Sinica. Institute of Botany. New Series
Bot Bull Acad Sin (Taipei) — Botanical Bulletin. Academia Sinica (Taipei)
Bot Bull Ac Sin — Botanical Bulletin. Academia Sinica
BotC — Botanisches Centralblatt
Bot Centralbl Beih 2 Abt — Botanisches Centralblatt. Beihefte. Zweite Abteilung-Systematik. Pflanzengeographie. Angewandte Botanik
Bot Centralbl Deutschl — Botanisches Centralblatt fuer Deutschland
Bot Chron — Botanists' Chronicle
Bot Echo Konigsb — Botanisches Echo. (Koenigsberg)
Bot Egl Montreal — Bottin Eglise de Montreal
Bot Exch Club Soc Brit Isles — Botanical Exchange Club and Society. British Isles
Bot Fem Prof Com — Bottin des Femmes Professionnelles et Commercantes
Bot Gard — Botanic Garden. Consisting of Highly Finished Representations of Hardy Ornamental Flowering Plants Cultivated in Great Britain
Bot Gard (Singapore) Annu Rep — Botanic Gardens (Singapore). Annual Report
Bot Gaz — Botanical Gazette
Bot Gaz (Chicago) — Botanical Gazette (Chicago)
Bot Gothob — Botanica Gothoburgensia. Acta Universitatis Gothoburgensis
Bot Gothob Acta Univ Gothob — Botanica Gothoburgensia. Acta Universitatis Gothoburgensis
Bot Haves Virksomhed Beret — Botanisk Haves Virksomhed Beretning
Bot Helv — Botanica Helvetica
Bot Inst Izv Bulg Akad Nauk — Botanicheski Institut. Izvestiya. Bulgarska Akademiya na Naukite
Bot Issled Beloruss Otd Vses Bot O-Va — Botanika. Issledovaniya. Belorusskoe Otdelenie Vsesoyuznogo Botanicheskogo Obshchestva
Bot J — Botanical Journal
Bot Jaarb — Botanisch Jaarboek
Bot Jahrb Jedermann — Botanisches Jahrbuch fuer Jedermann
Bot Jahrb Syst Pflanzengesch Pflanzengeogr — Botanische Jahrbuecher fuer Systematik Pflanzengeschichte und Pflanzengeographie
BOTJAT — British Orthoptic Journal
Bot Jb — Botanische Jahrbuecher fuer Systematik Pflanzengeschichte und Pflanzengeographie
Bot Jbb — Englers Botanische Jahrbuecher fuer Systematik, Pflanzengeschichte, und Pflanzengeographie
Bot J Boston — Botanic Journal (Boston)
Bot J Linn Soc — Botanical Journal. Linnean Society
Bot J Linn Soc (Lond) — Botanical Journal. Linnean Society (London)
BOT Jo — Board of Trade Journal
Bot Klausimai — Botanikos Klausimai
Bot Koezl — Botanikai Koezlemenyek
Bot Koezlem — Botanikai Koezlemenyek
Bot Kozl — Botanikai Koezlemenyek
BOTLA — Bollettino. Societa Italiana di Cardiologia
Bot Leafl — Botanical Leaflets. A Series of Studies in the Systematic Botany of Miscellaneous Dicotyledonous Plants
Bot Ledger Family J Health — Botanic Ledger and Family Journal of Health
Bot Lith — Botanica Lithuanica
Bot Mag — Botanical Magazine
Bot Mag Roemer Usteri — Botanisches Magazin. Edited by Roemer and Usteri
Bot Mag Spec Issue — Botanical Magazine. Special Issue
Bot Mag Tokyo — Botanical Magazine/Shokubutsu-Gaku Zasshi. Tokyo Botanical Society
Bot Mag (Tokyo) — Botanical Magazine (Tokyo)
Bot Mar — Botanica Marina
Bot Mar Suppl — Botanica Marina. Supplement
Bot Mater Gerb Bot Inst Akad Nauk — Botanicheskie Materialy Gerbariya Botanicheskogo Instituta. Akademii Nauk
Bot Mater Gerb Glavn Bot Sada SSSR — Botaniceskie Materialy Gerbarija Glavnogo Botaniceskogo Sada SSSR/Notulae Systematicae ex Herbario Horti Botanici Petropolitanae USSR
Bot Mater Gerb Inst Bot Akad Nauk Kaz — Botanicheskie Materialy Gerbariya Instituta Botaniki. Akademii Nauk Kazakhskoi
Bot Mater Gerb Inst Bot Akad Nauk Kaz SSR — Botanicheskie Materialy Gerbariya Instituta Botaniki. Akademii Nauk Kazakhskoi SSR
Bot Mater Gerb Inst Bot Akad Nauk Uzbeksk SSR — Botaniceskie Materialy Gerbarija Instituta Botaniki Akademii Nauk Uzbekskoj SSR
Bot Mater Otd Sporov Rast — Botaniceskie Materialy Otdela Sporovyh Rastenij/Notulae Systematicae e SectioneCryptogamica
Bot Med Rec — Botanico-Medical Recorder
Bot Med Reformer Mount Vernon — Botanico-Medical Reformer. Or a Course of Lectures Introductory to a Knowledge of True Medical Science (Mount Vernon, Ohio)
Bot Misc — Botanical Miscellany
Bot Mitt — Botanische Mitteilungen
Bot Mitt Tropen — Botanische Mitteilungen aus den Tropen
Bot Monogr (New Delhi) — Botanical Monographs (New Delhi)
Bot Monogr (Oxf) — Botanical Monographs (Oxford)

Bot Mus Leafl — Botanical Museum Leaflets. Harvard University
Bot Mus Leafl Harv Univ — Botanical Museum Leaflets. Harvard University
BOT (New York) — Books of the Times (New York)
Bot Not — Botaniska Notiser
Bot Notis — Botaniska Notiser
Bot Notiser — Botaniska Notiser
Bot Not Suppl — Botaniska Notiser. Supplement
BotO — Botteghe Oscure
Bot Obozr — Botaniceskoe Obozrenie. Conspectus Literaturae Botanicae
Bot Oecon — Botanica Oeconomica
Bot Phaenol Beob Boehmen — Botanisch-Phaenologische Beobachtungen in Boehmen
Bot R — Botanical Review
BOTRA — Beitraege zur Orthopaedie und Traumatologie
Bot Repos — Botanical Repository. For New and Rare Plants
Bot Rev — Botanical Review
Bot Rhedonica Ser A — Botanica Rhedonica. Serie A
Bot Sentinel Lit Gaz — Botanic Sentinel and Literary Gazette
Bot Soc Br Isl Proc — Botanical Society. British Isles Proceedings
Bot Soc Brit Isles Proc — Botanical Society. British Isles. Proceedings
Bot Soc Edinb Trans — Botanical Society of Edinburgh. Transactions
Bot Soc Edinburgh Trans — Botanical Society of Edinburgh. Transactions
Bot Stud — Botanische Studien
Bot Surv S Afr Mem — Botanical Survey of South Africa. Memoir
Botswana Geol Sur Dep Miner Resour Rep — Botswana. Geological Survey Department. Mineral Resources Report
Botswana Geol Surv Dep Bull — Botswana. Geological Survey Department. Bulletin
Botswana Geol Surv Dist Mem — Botswana. Geological Survey. District Memoir
Botswana Geol Surv Mines Dep Annu Rep — Botswana. Geological Survey and Mines Department. Annual Report
Botswana Mag — Botswana Magazine
Botswana Notes — Botswana Notes and Records
Botswana Notes Rec — Botswana Notes and Records
Botswana Notes Recs — Botswana Notes and Records
Botswana Rev — Botswana Review. A Pan-African Cultural Journal
Bot T — Botanisk Tidsskrift
Botteghe Osc — Botteghe Oscure
Bot Tidsskr — Botanisk Tidsskrift
Bottlers Yb — Bottlers' Year Book
Bot Trans Yorkshire Naturalists Union — Botanical Transactions. Yorkshire Naturalists Union
BoTU — Boghazkoei-Texte in Umschrift
Botucatu Cient Ser A — Botucatu Cientifica. Serie A. Ciencias Agrarias
Botucatu Cient Ser B — Botucatu Cientifica. Serie B. Ciencias Biomedicas
Bot Untersuch Berlin — Botanische Untersuchungen. Landwirthschaftliche Lehranstalt. Physiologisches Laboratorium (Berlin)
Bot Ver Ham EV Ber — Botanischer Verein zu Hamburg EV. Berichte
Bot Z — Botaniceskij Zurnal
Bot Zbl — Botanisches Zentralblatt
Bot Zblt — Botanisches Zentralblatt
Bot Zeitung 2 Abt — Botanische Zeitung. 2. Abteilung
Bot Zeitung Berlin — Botanische Zeitung (Berlin)
Bot Zh (Kiev) — Botanichnyi Zhurnal (Kiev)
Bot Zh (Leningr) — Botanicheskii Zhurnal (Leningrad)
Bot Zh (Moscow) — Botanicheskii Zhurnal (Moscow)
Bot Zh (SSSR) — Botanicheskii Zhurnal (SSSR)
Bot Ztg — Botanische Zeitung
Bot Zurn Kiev — Botanicnyj Zurnal/Journal Botanique. Academie des Sciences de la RSS d'Ukraine (Kiev)
Bot Zurn SSSR — Botaniceskij Zurnal SSSR/Journal Botanique de l'URSS
BOU — International Labour Review
BOU (Br Ornithol Union) Check-List — BOU (British Ornithologists' Union) Check-List
BouF — Bouquiniste Francais
BOUIS — Bulletin. Oxford University. Institute of Statistics
Boumajnaja Promst — Boumajnaja Promyshlennost
Boun — Boundary 2. A Journal of Postmodern Literature
Bound — Boundary 2
Boundary-Layer Meteorol — Boundary-Layer Meteorology
Bound Two — Boundary Two
Bourg Med — Bourgogne Medicale
Bourgogne Med — Bourgogne Medicale
Bourgogne Odont — Bourgogne Odontologique
Bourgogne Vinic — Bourgogne Vinicole
Bourgogne Vitic Agric Hort — Bourgogne Viticole, Agricole et Horticole
Bourne Soc Local Hist Rec — Bourne Society. Local History Records
Bourse Cuirs Belg — Bourse aux Cuirs de Belgique
Bout — Bouteille a la Mer
Bouwbedr & Openbare Werken — Bouwbedrijf en Openbare Werken
Bouwbedrijv Bouwmater — Bouwbedrijvigheid en Bouwmaterialen
Bouw Cent Wkbld Bouwwzn Nederland & Belgie — Bouw. Central Weekblad voor het Bouwwezen in Nederland en Belgie
Bouwdoin Coll Bull — Bowdoin College Bulletin
Bouwknd Bijdr — Bouwkundige Bijdragen
Bouwknd Tijdschr — Bouwkundig Tijdschrift
Bouwknd Wkbld — Bouwkundig Weekblad
Bouwknd Wkbld Archit — Bouwkundig Weekblad. Architectura
Bouwk Weekbl Archit — Bouwkundig Weekblad Architectura
Bouwsteenen J V N M — Bouwsteenen. Jaarboek der Vereeniging voor Nederlandsche Muziekgeschiedenis
Bouwstenen — Bouwstenen voor een Geschiedenis der Toonkunst in de Nederlanden
BoV — Bockernas Varld
Bovine Pract — Bovine Practitioner

BOVNDK — Bericht des Offenbacher Vereins fuer Naturkunde
B o W — Biochemistry of Wood
BOW — Kappersbondsnieuws
Bowater Pap — Bowater Papers
Bowdoin Sci Rev — Bowdoin Scientific Review. A Fortnightly Journal
Bowhunting Wld — Bowhunting World
BOWI — Bibliographie zur Offentlichen Unternehmung und Verwaltung
Bowker Ann — Bowker Annual of Library and Book Trade Information
Bowl Fenc G — Bowling-Fencing Guide
Bowl Gr St — Bowling Green Studies in Applied Philosophy
Bowl J — Bowlers Journal
Bowman Memor Lect — Bowman Memorial Lectures
Box — Boxspring
Boxbd Cont — Boxboard Containers
Boxbrd Con — Boxboard Containers
B Oxf Univ Inst Statist — Bulletin. Oxford University. Institute of Statistics
Box Mkrs J — Box Makers' Journal and Packaging Review
Boyce Thompson Inst Contrib — Boyce Thompson Institute. Contributions
Boyce Thompson Inst Plant Res Prof Pap — Boyce Thompson Institute for Plant Research. Professional Papers
Boydell Bull — Boydell Bulletin
Boyer Mus Coll — Boyer Museum Collection
Boyle Lect — Boyle Lectures
BOZAA — Bollettino di Zoologia Agraria e di Bachicoltura
Bozart — Bozart and Contemporary Verse
BOZED — Boersen-Zeitung
BP — Banasthali Patrika
BP — Beitraege zur Philosophie
BP — Bibliographie de la Philosophie
BP — Bijdragen van de Philosophische en Theologische Faculteiten der Nederlandsche Jezuieten
BP — Bisbabharati Patrika
BP — Biuletyn Polonistyczny
BP — Boletim Pecuario
BPAAA — Beitraege zur Pathologischen Anatomie und zur Allgemeinen Pathologie
BpAaP — Beitraege zur Pathologischen Anatomie und zur Allgemeinen Pathologie
BPABA — Biologia Plantarum
BPABAJ — Biologia Plantarum
BPABDM — Benchmark Papers in Biochemistry
BP Accel — BP [British Petroleum] Accelerator
BPAD — Bowker's Publisher Authority Database
BPAH — Bulletin. Pan American Health Organization
BPAHA3 — Boletin. Oficina Sanitaria Panamericana. English Edition
BPAIA — Bulletin of Pathology (Chicago, Illinois)
B Pan Am Un — Bulletin. Pan American Union
BP & R — British Plastics and Rubber
B Parl — Bulletin. Societe des Parlers de France
B Parthenay — Bulletin. Societe Historique et Archeologique. Les Amis des Antiquites de Parthenay
BPAS — Bulletin of the Philadelphia Anthropological Society
B Pas De Calais — Bulletin. Commission Departementale de Monuments Historiques du Pas-De-Calais
BPAU — Bulletin. Pan American Union
BPB — Biblioteca Pedagogica Brasileira
BPC — Biblioteca de la Presidencia de Colombia
BPC — Bibliotheque de Philosophie Contemporaine
BPC — Boletin de Politica Cultural
BP Calv — Bulletin des Parlers du Calvados
BPCBAT — Biological Psychology Bulletin
BPCC — Biblioteca Popular de la Cultura Colombiana
BPCCDZ — Biosynthetic Products for Cancer Chemotherapy
BPCMUS — Bulletin. Post-Graduate Committee in Medicine. University of Sydney
BPC/RE — Revista de Economia. Banco de la Provincia de Cordoba
BPCTH — Bulletin Philologique et Historique. Comite des Travaux Historiques et Scientifiques
BPDNA2 — SUDENE [Superintendencia do Desenvolvimento do Nordeste] GCDP Boletim de Estudos de Pesca
BPE — Brookings Papers on Economic Activity
BPEA — Brookings Papers on Economic Activity
B Peace Propos — Bulletin of Peace Proposals
BPEAD — Brookings Papers on Economic Activity
BPEC — Bollettino. Comitato per la Preparazione dell'Edizione Nazionale dei Classici Greci e Latini
BPECDB — Benchmark Papers in Ecology
B Pedag — Bulletin Pedagogique
BPEFA — Buletinul. Institutului Politehnic din Brasov. Seria B. Economie Forestiera
B Perigord — Bulletin. Societe Historique et Archeologique du Perigord
B Perm Int Ass Nav Congr — Bulletin. Permanent International Association of Navigation Congresses
BPES — Bibliotheca Patrum Ecclesiasticorum Selectissima
BPES — Bulletin. Palestine Exploration Society
BPF — Bulletin du Protestantisme Francais
BPF Compos Congr — BPF (British Plastics Federation) Composites Congress
B Pfl Z — Beitraege zur Pflanzenzucht
BPFRAO — Boletim. Universidade do Parana. Farmacognosia
BPGAAC — Boletim. Museu Paraense Emilio Goeldi. Nova Serie. Antropologia
BPGEDR — Benchmark Papers in Genetics
BPGEES — Benchmark Papers in Geology
BPGGA — Bulletin. Academie Polonaise des Sciences. Serie des Sciences Geologiques et Geographiques
BPGMD — Buletinul. Institutului Politehnic "Gheorghe Gheorghiu-Dej" Bucuresti. Seria Mecanica
BPGOU — Beitraege zur Palaeontologie und Geologie Oesterreich-Ungarns und des Orients
BPh — Bibliographie de la Philosophie

BPH — Botanico-Periodicum-Huntianum
BPH — Bulletin Philologique et Historique
BPHBA — BHP [Broken Hill Proprietary Ltd.] Technical Bulletin (Australia)
BPhC — Bibliotheca Philologica Classica
B Ph C — Bibliotheque de Philosophie Contemporaine
BPHCTHS — Bulletin Philologique et Historique. Comite des Travaux Historiques et Scientifiques
B Ph DI — Beitraege zur Philosophie des Deutschen Idealismus
B Ph Fr A — Beitraege zur Physik der Freien Atmosphaere
B Phila Mus — Bulletin. Philadelphia Museum of Art
BPHist — Bulletin Philologique et Historique
BPHJA — British Phycological Journal
BPHJAA — British Phycological Journal
B Phl — Beitraege zur Physiologie
BPhM — Bulletin. Societe Internationale pour l'Etude de la Philosophie Medievale
BPHP — Bulletin Philologique et Historique. Comite des Travaux Historiques et Scientifiques (Paris)
BPHPDV — Benchmark Papers in Human Physiology
BPhSC — Bulletin. Philological Society of Calcutta
BPhSJ — Bulletin. Phonetic Society of Japan
BPHUED — Bulletin Penelitian Hutan
BPhW — Berliner Philologische Wochenschrift
B Physiopa — Bulletin de Physiopathologie Respiratoire
BPI — Bollettino delle Pubblicazioni Italiane Ricevute per Diritto di Stampa
BPI — Bollettino delle Publicazione Italiane
BPI — Bollettino Paleontologico Italiano
BPI — Book Production Industry
BPI — Business Periodicals Index
BPIAS — Bulletin. Polish Institute of Arts and Sciences in America
B Picardie — Bulletins. Societe des Antiquaires de Picardie
BPiM — Black Perspectives in Music
BPIt — Bullettino di Paletnologia Italiana
BPJ — Beloit Poetry Journal
BPJSA — Biophysical Journal. Supplement
BPK — Berichte. Preussische Kunstsammlungen
BPKG — Blaetter fuer Pfaelzische Kirchengeschichte
BPKS — Berichte. Preussische Kunstsammlungen
BPKUD — BP [Benzin und Petroleum AG Hamburg] Kurier
BP Kur — BP [Benzin und Petroleum AG Hamburg] Kurier
B Plastics — British Plastics [Later, European Plastics News]
BP Lit — Boletin de Pastoral Liturgica
BPLNME — Bibliography of Periodical Literature on the Near and Middle East
BPLQ — Boston Public Library. Quarterly
BPM — Bulletin. Palestine Museum
BPMCM — Bulletins of the Public Museum of the City of Milwaukee
BPMGA — Berichte. Physikalisch-Medizinische Gesellschaft zu Wuerzburg
BPMIDZ — Benchmark Papers in Microbiology
BPN — Beitraege zur Psychiatrie und Neurologie
BPN — BPN
BPN — Building Products News
BPNS — Boletin de la Provincia de Neustra Senora de la Candelaria de Colombia de la Orden de Agustinos Recoletos
BPNSA — Bibliotheca Psychiatrica et Neurologica (Switzerland)
BPNSAX — Aktuelle Fragen der Psychiatrie und Neurologie
BPNSB — Bulletin. Psychonomic Society
BPO — Business Periodicals Ondisc
BPOEA — British Power Engineering
BPOJA — British Polymer Journal
B Pol — Biblioteka Polska
B Pol — Biuletyn Prasowy Polonia
B Pol Biol — Bulletin. Academie Polonaise des Sciences. Serie des Sciences Biologiques
B Pol Chim — Bulletin. Academie Polonaise des Sciences. Serie des Sciences Chimiques
B Pol Math — Bulletin. Academie Polonaise des Sciences. Serie des Sciences Mathematiques, Astronomiques, et Physiques
B Pol Sci T — Bulletin. Academie Polonaise des Sciences. Serie des Sciences de la Terre
B Pol Techn — Bulletin. Academie Polonaise des Sciences. Serie des Sciences Techniques
BPOPD — British Public Opinion
BPOSA — British Poultry Science
BPOSA4 — British Poultry Science
BPP — Beitraege zur Philosophie und Psychologie
BPP — Bengal Past and Present
BPP — Biblioteka Pisarzy Polskich i Obcych
BPP — Biochemie und Physiologie der Pflanzen
BPP — Bulletin of Plant Protection/Zashchita Rastenii ot Vreditelie
BPPHA — Beitraege aus der Plasmaphysik
BPPRA — Bulletin de Physiopathologie Respiratoire
BPPRD — Bulletin of Peace Proposals
BP Purdue Univ Coop Ext Serv — BP. Purdue University. Cooperative Extension Service
BPR — American Book Publishing Record
B Pr — Books in Print
BPR — Budapest Regisegei
BPR — Bulletin of Prosthetics Research
BPR — Butterworth's Property Reports
BPRCCS — Byrd Polar Research Center
Bp Reg — Budapest Regisegei. Budapesti Toerteneti Muzeum
B Pr Hist Fr — Bulletin. Societe Prehistorique Francaise. Etudes et Travaux
B Prince of Wales Mus West India — Bulletin. Prince of Wales Museum of Western India
BPRMA — Bibliotheca Primatologica

B (Providence) — Bulletin. Rhode Island School of Design. Museum Notes (Providence)

B Provins — Bulletin. Societe d'Histoire et d'Archeologie de l'Arrondissement de Provins

BPRRB — Bulletin of Prosthetics Research

BPS — Biblical and Patristic Studies

BPS — Birmingham Photographic Society. Journal

BPS — Bulletin. Psychonomic Society

BPSBA7 — British Pteridological Society. Bulletin

BPSBDA — Benchmark Papers in Systematic and Evolutionary Biology

BPSC — Bulletin. Philological Society of Calcutta

BP Shield Int — BP [*British Petroleum*] Shield International

B Psic Appl — Bollettino di Psicologia Applicata

BPSMLA — Bulletin. Pennsylvania State Modern Language Association

BPSP — Bollettino. Societa Pavese di Storia Patria

BPSPBG — Biologicheskie Provrezhdeniya Stroitel'nykh i Promyshlennykh Materialov

BPSR — PSR [*Pacific School of Religion*] Bulletin

BPSTBS — Bulletin. Academie Polonaise des Sciences. Serie des Sciences de la Terre

B Psychol — Bulletin de Psychologie

B Psychon S — Bulletin. Psychonomic Society

BPSYDB — Bibliographia Phytosociologica Syntaxonomica

Bp Szle — Budapesti Szemle

BPT — Journal of Contemporary Business

BPTBBD — Bericht. Physikalisch-Technische Bundesanstalt, Braunschweig und Berlin

BPT Ber — BPT [*Bereich Projekttraegerschaften*]-Bericht

BP Th — Beitraege zur Praktischen Theologie

BPTJ — Biuletyn Polskiego Towarzystwa Jezykoznawczego

BPTPM — Bulletin Professionel et Technique des Pecheurs Maritimes

BPUA — Biological Papers. University of Alaska

BPUASR — Biological Papers. University of Alaska. Special Report

BPUPBQ — Bilten Poslovnog Udruzenja Proizvodaca Biljnih Ulja i Masti

BPW — Berliner Philologische Wochenschrift

Bp W — Philologische Wochenschrift

BPWS — Berliner Philologische Wochenschrift

BPYBA3 — British Phycological Bulletin [*Later, British Phycological Journal*]

BPYCA — Rikagaku Kenkyusho Iho

BPYKA — Biophysik

BPZ — Berufspaedagogische Zeitschrift

BPZBA — Bulletin. Societe des Amis des Sciences et des Lettres de Poznan. Serie B. Sciences Mathematiques et Naturelles

BQ — Banknote Quarterly

BQ — Baptist Quarterly

BQL — Bank Markazi Iran. Bulletin

BQO — Belgian Business

BQR — Bodleian Quarterly Record

BQRP — Bulletin des Questions et Reponses Parlementaires

BQU — Bangladesh Bank. Bulletin

BQU — Business Quarterly

BR — Baltic Review

BR — Belorussian Review

BR — Benedictine Review

BR — Bennington Review

BR — Biblical Research

BR — Biblical Review

BR — Bibliotheca Romana

BR — Bibliotheque Raisonnee

BR — Bilingual Review

BR — Book Report

BR — Botanical Review

BR — Brooklyn Law Review

BR — Bucimul Romanu

BR — Budapest Regisegei

BR — Bullarium Romanum

BR — Business Review

BR — Business Review Weekly

BRA — Beitraege zur Religionsgeschichte des Altertums

BrA — Brasil Acucareiro

Brabant Agric Hortic — Brabant Agricole et Horticole

Brabant Flklore — Brabantse Folklore

Brabantse Folkl — De Brabantse Folklore

BRABLB — Boletin. Real Academia de Buenas Letras de Barcelona

Br Abstr — British Abstracts

Br Abstr A1 — British Abstracts A1. General, Physical, and Inorganic Chemistry

Br Abstr A2 — British Abstracts A2. Organic Chemistry

Br Abstr A3 — British Abstracts A3. Physiology and Biochemistry

Br Abstr B1 — British Abstracts B1. Chemical Engineering, Fuels, Metallurgy, Applied Electrochemistry, and Industrial Inorganic Chemistry

Br Abstr B2 — British Abstracts B2. Industrial Organic Chemistry

Br Abstr B3 — British Abstracts B3. Agriculture, Foods, Sanitation

Br Abstr C — British Abstracts C. Analysis and Apparatus

Br Abstr Med Sci — British Abstracts of Medical Sciences

BRAC — Boletin. Real Academia de Cordoba

BRACA2 — Brasil Acucareiro

Brac Aug — Bracara Augusta. Revista Cultural de Camara Municipal de Braga

BRACC — Boletin. Real Academia de Ciencias, Bellas Letras, y Nobles Artes de Cordoba

Br Acet Weld Ass — British Acetylene and Welding Association

Brackish Water Factor Dev — Brackish Water as a Factor in Development

Brac LJ — Bracton Law Journal

BRA Cor — Boletin. Real Academia de Ciencias, Bellas Letras, y Nobles Artes de Cordoba

BRA Cord — Boletin. Real Academia de Ciencias, Bellas Letras, y Nobles Artes de Cordoba

Bracton LJ — Bracton Law Journal

Bradea Bol Herb Bradeanum — Bradea. Boletim do Herbarium Bradeanum

Bradf — Bradford

Brad Fight — Bradley Fighting Vehicle. US Army White Paper, 1986

Bradford Ant — Bradford Antiquary

Bradford Antiq — Bradford Antiquary

Bradford Scient J — Bradford Scientific Journal

Bradleys Mag — Bradley's Magazine

BRAE — Boletin. Real Academia Espanola

BRAG — Boletin. Real Academia Gallega

Br Agric Bull — British Agricultural Bulletin

Br Agric Chem — British Agricultural Chemicals and Chemical Weed Control

BRAH — Boletin. Real Academia de la Historia

Brahms-Stud — Brahms-Studien

BRAIA — Brain. Journal of Neurology

Brain Behav — Brain, Behavior, and Evolution

Brain Behav Evol — Brain, Behavior, and Evolution

Brain Behav Immun — Brain, Behavior, and Immunity

Brain Behav Res Monogr Ser — Brain and Behavior Research Monograph Series

Brain Cogit — Brain and Cogitation

Brain Cogn — Brain and Cognition

Brain Dev — Brain and Development

Brain Dysfunct — Brain Dysfunction

Brain Dysfunct Infant Febrile Convulsions Symp — Brain Dysfunction in Infantile Febrile Convulsions. Symposium

Brain Edema Proc Int Symp — Brain Edema. Proceedings. International Symposium

Brain Endocr Interact — Brain-Endocrine Interaction

Brain Funct Proc Conf — Brain Function. Proceedings. Conference

Brain Inj — Brain Injury

Brain Lang — Brain and Language

Brain Metab Cereb Disord — Brain Metabolism and Cerebral Disorders

Brain/Mind — Brain/Mind Bulletin

Brain Pathol — Brain Pathology

Brain Pep — Brain Peptides

Brain Res — Brain Research

Brain Res Brain Res Protoc — Brain Research, Brain Research Protocols

Brain Res Brain Res Rev — Brain Research. Brain Research Reviews

Brain Res Bull — Brain Research Bulletin

Brain Res Cogn Brain Res — Brain Research. Cognitive Brain Research

Brain Res Cognit Brain Res — Brain Research. Cognitive Brain Research

Brain Res Dev Brain Res — Brain Research. Developmental Brain Research

Brain Res Mol Brain Res — Brain Research. Molecular Brain Research

Brain Res Protoc — Brain Research Protocols

Brain Res Rev — Brain Research Reviews

Brains Chem Eng — Brains of Chemical Engineer

Brain Stimul Reward Collect Pap Int Conf — Brain Stimulation Reward. Collection of Papers Prepared for the International Conference

Brain Topogr — Brain Topography

Brain Tumor Pathol — Brain Tumor Pathology

Br Aircr Ind Bull — British Aircraft Industry Bulletin

Brake FE — Brake and Front End

Br Alma Comp — British Almanac Companion

BraM — Braunschweigisches Magazin

B Ramakr Miss Inst — Bulletin. Ramakrishna Mission Institute of Culture

B Rama Miss Inst Cult — Bulletin. Ramakrishna Mission Institute of Culture

Brandenburg Jb — Brandenburgische Jahrbuecher

Brandschutz Dtsch Feuerwehrztg — Brandschutz Deutsche Feuerwehrzeitung

Brand Ship Forward — Brandon's Shipper and Forwarder

Brandstofnavorsingsinst S Afr Bull — Brandstofnavorsingsinstituut van Suid-Afrika. Bulletin

Branntwein Ind (Moscow) — Branntwein-Industrie (Moscow)

Branntweinwirt — Branntweinwirtschaft

Br Antarct Surv Bull — British Antarctic Survey. Bulletin

Br Antarct Surv Sci Rep — British Antarctic Survey. Scientific Reports

BRAR — British Rheumatism and Arthritis Association. Review

Br Arch Abs — British Archaeological Abstracts

Br Archaeol Abstr — British Archaeological Abstracts

Br Archt I Pp — Papers Read at the Royal Institute of British Architects

Br Archt I T — Transactions of the Institute of British Architects of London

Br Archt J — Journal of the Royal Institute of British Architects

Br Archt Pp — Papers Read at the Royal Institute of British Architects

Br Archt T — Transactions of the Institute of British Architects of London

BRA Rev — BRA [*British Rheumatic Association*] Review

Bras — Brasilia

Bras Acucareiro — Brasil Acucareiro

Bras Acuc Rio — Brasil Acucareiro (Rio de Janeiro)

Bras Flores — Brasil Florestal

Brasil Acucar — Brasil Acucareiro

Brasil Apic — Brasil Apicola

Brasiliana — Bibliotheca Pedagogica Brasiletra. Serie 5. Brasiliana

Bras-Med — Brasil-Medico

Bras Odont — Brasil Odontologico

Brasov Int Sch — Brasov International School

Brass & Wood Q — Brass and Woodwind Quarterly

Brass Ann Arm Forc Yb — Brassey's Annual and Armed Forces Yearbook

Brass B — Brass Bulletin

Brass Founder Finsh — Brass Founder and Finisher

Brass Fr — Brasseur Francais

Brass Malt — Brasserie et Malterie

Brass Nav A — Brassey's Naval Annual

Br Assoc Psychopharmacol Monogr — British Association for Psychopharmacology Monographs

Brass W — Brass World and Plater's Guide
Bras Text — Brasil Textil
Br Astron Assoc Circ — British Astronomical Association. Circular
Bratisl Lek Listy — Bratislavske Lekarske Listy
Brauerei Wiss Beil — Brauerei. Wissenschaftliche Beilage
Brau Getraenke Rundsch — Brauerei- und Getraenke-Rundschau
Brau Hopfen Ztg Gambrinus — Brauer- und Hopfen-Zeitung Gambrinus
Brau Ind — Brau Industrie
Brau Maelzer — Brauer und Maelzer
Brau Maelzer Lehrling — Brauer- und Maelzer-Lehrling
Brau Malzind — Brau- und Malzindustrie
Braun H — Braunschweigische Heimat
Braun J — Braunschweigisches Jahrbuch
Braunk — Braunkohle
Braunkohle Bergbautech — Braunkohle Bergbautechnik
Braunkohle Waerme Energ — Braunkohle, Waerme, und Energie
Braunschweiger Naturkd Schr — Braunschweiger Naturkundliche Schriften
Braunschweig Jb — Braunschweigisches Jahrbuch
Braunschweig Mag — Braunschweigisches Magazin
Braunschweig Wiss Ges Abh — Braunschweigische Wissenschaftliche Gesellschaft. Abhandlungen
Braunschw Jb — Braunschweigisches Jahrbuch
Braunschw Konserv Z — Braunschweigische Konserven-Zeitung
Braunschw Konserv Ztg — Braunschweigische Konserven-Zeitung
Braunschw Wiss Ges Sitzungsber Mitt Sonderh — Braunschweigische Wissenschaftliche Gesellschaft, Sitzungsberichte, und Mitteilungen. Sonderheft
BraunschwZ — Zeitschrift fuer Rechtspflege im Herzogtum Braunschweig
Brau Rundsch — Brauerei-Rundschau
Brauwiss — Brauwissenschaft
Braz Am Surv Rio — Brazilian American Survey (Rio de Janeiro)
Braz Com Nac Energ Nucl Bol — Brazil. Comissao Nacional de Energia Nuclear. Boletim
Braz Dep Nac Obras Secas Serv Piscic Publ Ser 1 C — Brazil. Departamento Nacional de Obras Contra as Secas. Servico de Piscicultura. Publicacao. Serie 1 C
Braz Dep Nac Prod Miner Anu Miner Bras — Brazil. Departamento Nacional da Producao Mineral. Anuario Mineral Brasileiro
Braz Dep Nac Prod Miner Bol — Brazil. Departamento Nacional da Producao Mineral. Boletim
Braz Dep Nac Prod Miner Div Aguas — Brazil. Departamento Nacional da Producao Mineral. Divisao de Aguas. Boletim
Braz Dep Nac Prod Miner Lab Prod Miner Bol — Brazil. Departamento Nacional da Producao Mineral. Laboratorio da Producao Mineral. Boletim
Braz Div Fom Prod Miner Avulso — Brazil. Divisao de Fomento da Producao Mineral. Avulso
Braz Div Fom Prod Miner Bol — Brazil. Divisao de Fomento da Producao Mineral. Boletim
Braz Div Fom Prod Miner Mem — Brazil. Divisao de Fomento da Producao Mineral. Memoria
Braz Div Geol Mineral Avulso — Brazil. Divisao de Geologia e Mineralogia. Avulso
Braz Div Geol Mineral Bol — Brazil. Divisao de Geologia e Mineralogia. Boletim
Braz Div Geol Mineral Monogr — Brazil. Divisao de Geologia e Mineralogica. Monografia
Braz Div Geol Mineral Notas Prelim Estud — Brazil. Divisao de Geologia e Mineralogia. Notas Preliminares e Estudos
Braz Div Pesqui Pedol Bol Tec — Brazil. Divisao de Pesquisa Pedologica. Boletim Tecnico
Braz Div Tecnol Agric Aliment Bol Tec — Brazil. Divisao de Tecnologia Agricola e Alimentar. Boletim Tecnico
Braz Econ — Brazilian Economy. Trends and Perspectives
Braz Econ Stud — Brazilian Economic Studies
Braz Equipe Pedol Fertil Solo Bol Tec — Brazil. Equipe de Pedologia e Fertilidade do Solo. Boletim Tecnico
Braz Escritorio Pesqui Exp Equipe Pedol Fertil Solo Bol Tec — Brazil. Escritorio de Pesquisas e Experimentacao. Equipe de Pedologia e Fertilidade da Solo. Boletim Tecnico
Braz Fund Serv Saude Publica Rev — Brazil. Fundacao Servicos de Saude Publica. Revista
Brazil Camara Deput Bibl Bol — Brazil. Camara dos Deputados. Biblioteca. Boletim
Brazil Camara Deput Document Inform — Brazil. Camara dos Deputados. Documentacao e Informacao
Brazil Cons Nac Petrol Relat — Brazil. Conselho Nacional do Petroleo. Relatorio
Brazil Dep Nac Prod Miner Lab Prod Miner Avulso — Brazil. Departamento Nacional da Producao Mineral. Laboratorio da Producao Mineral. Avulso
Brazil Div Geol Mineral Bol — Brazil. Divisao de Geologia e Mineralogia. Boletim
Brazil Div Geol Mineral Notas Prelim Estud — Brazil. Divisao de Geologia e Mineralogia. Notas Preliminares e Estudos
Brazilian Bus — Brazilian Business
Brazilian Econ Studies — Brazilian Economic Studies
Brazil-Med — Brazil-Medico
Brazil Minist Minas Energ Dep Nac Prod Miner Bol — Brazil. Ministerio das Minas e Energia. Departamento Nacional da Producao Mineral. Boletim
Brazil S — Brazilian Studies
Braz Inst Agron Nordeste Bol Tec — Brazil. Instituto Agronomico da Nordeste. Boletim Tecnico
Braz Inst Nac Propr Ind Rev Propr Ind — Brazil. Instituto Nacional da Propriedade Industrial. Revista da Propriedade Industrial
Braz Inst Oleos Bol — Brazil. Instituto de Oleos. Boletim
BRAZ Int J Adapt PE Res — Brazilian International Journal of Adapted Physical Education Research
Braz J Bot — Brazilian Journal of Botany
Braz J Chem Eng — Brazilian Journal of Chemical Engineering
Braz J Genet — Brazilian Journal of Genetics
Braz J Infect Dis — Brazilian Journal of Infectious Diseases

Braz J Med Biol Res — Brazilian Journal of Medical and Biological Research
Braz J Med Biol Res Rev Bras Pesqui Med Biol — Brazilian Journal of Medical and Biological Research/Revista Brasileira de Pesquisas Medicas e Biologicas
Braz J Phys — Brazilian Journal of Physics
Braz J Plant Physiol — Brazilian Journal of Plant Physiology
Braz J Sports Med — Brazilian Journal of Sports Medicine
Braz J Vet Res — Brazilian Journal of Veterinary Research
Braz Lab Prod Miner Avulso — Brazil. Laboratorio da Producao Mineral. Avulso
Braz Lab Prod Miner Bol — Brazil. Laboratorio da Producao Mineral. Boletim
Braz Med — Brazil-Medico
Braz Minist Agric Cent Tecnol Agric Aliment Bol Tec — Brazil. Ministerio da Agricultura. Centro de Tecnologia Agricola e Alimentar. Boletim Tecnico
Braz Minist Agric Dep Nac Prod Anim Rev — Brazil. Ministerio da Agricultura. Departamento Nacional da Producao Animal. Revista
Braz Minist Agric Dep Nac Prod Miner Div Aguas Bol — Brazil. Ministerio da Agricultura. Departamento Nacional da Producao Mineral. Divisao de Aguas. Boletim
Braz Minist Agric Dep Nac Prod Miner Div Fom Prod Miner Avuls — Brazil. Ministerio da Agricultura. Departamento Nacional da Producao Mineral. Divisao do Fomento da Producao Mineral. Avulso
Braz Minist Agric Dep Nac Prod Miner Div Fom Prod Miner Bol — Brazil. Ministerio da Agricultura. Departamento Nacional da Producao Mineral. Divisao do Fomento da Producao Mineral. Boletim
Braz Minist Agric Dep Nac Prod Miner Div Geol Mineral Avulso — Brazil. Ministerio da Agricultura. Departamento Nacional da Producao Mineral. Divisao de Geologia e Mineralogia. Avulso
Braz Minist Agric Dep Nac Prod Miner Div Geol Mineral Monogr — Brazil. Ministerio da Agricultura. Departamento Nacional da Producao Mineral. Divisao de Geologia e Mineralogia. Monografia
Braz Minist Agric Dep Nac Prod Miner Lab Prod Miner Avulso — Brazil. Ministerio da Agricultura. Departamento Nacional da Producao Mineral. Laboratorio da Producao Mineral. Avulso
Braz Minist Agric Dep Nac Prod Miner Lab Prod Miner Bol — Brazil. Ministerio da Agricultura. Departamento Nacional da Producao Mineral. Laboratorio da Producao Mineral. Boletim
Braz Minist Agric Inst Agron Nordeste Bol Tec — Brazil. Ministerio da Agricultura. Centro Nacional de Ensino e Pesquisas Agronomicas. Instituto Agronomico do Nordeste. Boletim Tecnico
Braz Minist Agric Inst Oleos Rio de Janiero Bol — Brazil. Ministerio da Agricultura. Instituto de Oleos (Rio de Janiero). Boletim
Braz Minist Agric Serv Inf Agric Estud Tec — Brazil. Ministerio da Agricultura. Servico de Informacao Agricola. Estudos Tecnicos
Braz Minist Minas Energ Dep Nac Prod Miner Bol — Brazil. Ministerio das Minas e Energia. Departamento Nacional da Producao Mineral. Boletim
Braz Minist Minas Energ Dep Nac Prod Miner Lab Prod Miner Bo — Brazil. Ministerio das Minas e Energia. Departamento Nacional da Producao Mineral. Laboratorio da Producao Mineral. Boletim
Braz Pat Doc — Brazil. Patent Document
Braz Serv Espec Saude Publica Rev — Brazil. Servico Especial de Saude Publica. Revista
Braz Serv Fom Prod Miner Avulso — Brazil. Servico de Fomento da Producao Mineral. Avulso
Braz Serv Fom Prod Miner Bol — Brazil. Servico de Fomento da Producao Mineral. Boletim
Braz Serv Geol Mineral Bol — Brazil. Servico Geologico e Mineralogico. Boletim
Braz Serv Inf Agric Estud Tee — Brazil. Servico de Informacao Agricola. Estudos Teemcos
Braz Supt Desenvolvimento Nordeste Div Geol Bol Estud — Brazil. Superintendencia do Desenvolvimento do Nordeste. Divisao de Geologia. Boletim de Estudos
Braz Supt Desenvolvimento Nordeste Div Geol Ser Espec — Brazil. Superintendencia do Desenvolvimento do Nordeste. Divisao de Geologia. Serie Especial
Braz Supt Desenvolvimento Nordeste Div Geol Ser Geol Econ — Brazil. Superintendencia do Desenvolvimento do Nordeste. Divisao de Geologia. Serie Geologia Economica
Braz Supt Desenvolvimento Nordeste Div Geol Ser Geol Espec — Brazil. Superintendencia do Desenvolvimento do Nordeste. Divisao de Geologia. Serie Geologia Especial
Braz Symp Theor Phys Proc — Brazilian Symposium on Theoretical Physics. Proceedings
BRBEBE — Brain, Behavior, and Evolution
Br Bee J — British Bee Journal
BRBI — Bulletin. Reserve Bank of India
BRBIDS — Bryophytorum Bibliotheca
Br Birds — British Birds
Br Bks Print — British Books in Print
Br BI — Bremer Archaeologische Blaetter
BRBOA — Brown Boveri Review
Br Br — Brunn-Bruckmann
BRBUD — Brain Research Bulletin
BRBUDU — Brain Research Bulletin
Br Bull Spectrosc — British Bulletin of Spectroscopy
Br Bus — British Business
Br Business — British Business
BRC — Banco de la Republica. Revista
Br Cactus & Succulent J — British Cactus and Succulent Journal
Br Cah JdP — Bruxelles. Cahiers du Journal des Poetes
Br Carbonization Res Assoc Spec Publ — British Carbonization Research Association. Special Publication
Br Car Suppl — British Caribbean Supplement of New Commonwealth
Br Cast Iron Res Assoc Bur Bull — British Cast Iron Research Association. Bureau Bulletin
Br Cast Iron Res Assoc J — British Cast Iron Research Association. Journal

Br Cast Iron Res Assoc J Res Dev — British Cast Iron Research Association. Journal of Research and Development

Br Cast Iron Res Assoc Jrna Res Dev — British Cast Iron Research Association. Journal of Research and Development

Br Cave Res Assoc Trans — British Cave Research Association. Transactions

BRCB — Boletim do Rotary Club de Braga

BRCC — Bibliotheque de la Revue des Cours et Conferences

BRCC — Broteria. Revista Contemporanea de Cultura

Br Ceram Abstr — British Ceramic Abstracts

Br Ceram Proc — British Ceramic Proceedings

Br Ceram Res Assoc Spec Publ — British Ceramic Research Association. Special Publication

Br Ceram Rev — British Ceramic Review

Br Ceram Soc Proc — British Ceramic Society. Proceedings

Br Ceram Trans — British Ceramic Transactions

Br Ceram Trans J — British Ceramic Transactions and Journal

Br Cer Res Assoc Spec Publ — British Ceramic Research Association. Special Publications

Br Ch — Brennstoff-Chemie

Br Chem Abstr A — British Chemical Abstracts. A. Pure Chemistry

Br Chem Abstr A1 — British Chemical Abstracts. A1

Br Chem Abstr B — British Chemical Abstracts. B. Applied Chemistry

Br Chem Dig — British Chemical Digest

Br Chem Eng — British Chemical Engineering

Br Chem Engng — British Chemical Engineering

Br Chem Engng Process Technol — British Chemical Engineering and Process Technology

Br Chem Eng Process Technol — British Chemical Engineering and Process Technology

Br Chem Physiol Abstr A1 — British Chemical and Physiological Abstracts. A1

Br Chem Physiol Abstr A3 — British Chemical and Physiological Abstracts. A3

Br Chem Physiol Abstr B — British Chemical and Physiological Abstracts. B

Br Chem Physiol Abstr B1 — British Chemical and Physiological Abstracts. B1

Br Chem Physiol Abstr B2 — British Chemical and Physiological Abstracts. B2

Br Chem Physiol Abstr B3 — British Chemical and Physiological Abstracts. B3

Br Chem Physiol Abstr C — British Chemical and Physiological Abstracts. C

BRCI — Bulletin. Research Council of Israel

Br Claywkr — British Clayworker

Br Clayworker — British Clayworker

Br Coal Util Res Ass Mon Bull — British Coal Utilisation Research Association. Monthly Bulletin

Br Colon Drug — British and Colonial Druggist

Br Columbia Col Barg Env — British Columbia Collective Bargaining Environment

Br Columbia Col Barg Outl — British Columbia Collective Bargaining Outlook

Br Columbia Col Barg Rev — British Columbia Collective Bargaining Review

Br Columbia Dec Week Headn — British Columbia Decisions Weekly Headnotes

Br Columbia Med J — British Columbia Medical Journal

Br Columbia West Liv — British Columbia's Western Living

Br Columbia Yukon Ter — British Columbia and Yukon Territory

Br Columb Libr Q — British Columbia Library Quarterly

Br Commun Electron — British Communications and Electronics

Br Constr Eng — British Constructional Engineer

Br Corrosion J — British Corrosion Journal

Br Corros J — British Corrosion Journal

Br Council News — British Council News

BRCPA — Biological Reviews. Cambridge Philosophical Society

Br Crop Prot Conf Pests Dis Proc — British Crop Protection Conference. Pests and Diseases. Proceedings

Br Crop Prot Conf Weeds Proc — British Crop Protection Conference. Weeds. Proceedings

Br Crop Prot Counc Monogr — British Crop Protection Council. Monograph

BRCSDT — Australia. Commonwealth Scientific and Industrial Research Organisation. Land Resources Laboratories. Division of Soils. Biennial Report

BRD — Book Review Digest

BRDAA — Beitraege zur Radioastronomie

BRDB — Book Review Data Base

Brdcstng — Broadcasting

Br Decorator — British Decorator

Br Den Annu — British Dental Annual

Br Dental J — British Dental Journal

Br Dent J — British Dental Journal

Br Dent Nurs J — British Dental Nurses Journal

Br Dent Surg Assist — British Dental Surgery Assistant

BRDGAT — Brewers Digest

BRDIA — Bulletin on Rheumatic Diseases

BRDSPL — Bollettino. Regia Deputazione di Storia Patria per la Liguria

BRDSPU — Bollettino. Regia Deputazione di Storia Patria per l'Umbria

Bread Manuf WA — Bread Manufacturer and Pastrycook of Western Australia

B Real Acad — Boletin. Real Academia de la Historia

B Real Acad — Boletin. Real Academia Espanola

Breast Cancer Adv Res Treat — Breast Cancer. Advances in Research and Treatment

Breast Cancer Res — Breast Cancer Research

Breast Cancer Res Treat — Breast Cancer Research and Treatment

Breast Dis — Breast Disease

Breast Dis Breast — Breast. Diseases of the Breast

Breast Feed Mother — Breast Feeding and the Mother

Breast J — Breast Journal

BrechaM — Brecha (Montevideo)

BrechtH — Brecht Heute - Brecht Today

Brecht J — Brecht-Jahrbuch

Br Ecol Soc Symp — British Ecological Society. Symposium

BRE Dig — BRE [*Building Research Establishment*] Digest

Br Educ Index — British Education Index

Br Educ Res J — British Educational Research Journal

Breeder's Gaz — Breeder's Gazette

Breed Sci — Breeding Science

BREF — Book Review Editors File

BReg — Besluit van de Regent

Breifny Antiq Soc J — Breifny Antiquarian Society Journal

Br Elect Lab Mem — British Electricity Laboratories Memoirs

Br Electr Allied Manuf Assoc J — British Electrical and Allied Manufacturers' Association Journal

Brem A Bl — Bremer Archaeologische Blaetter

Bremer Arch Bl — Bremer Archaeologische Blaetter

Bremer Beitr Naturwiss — Bremer Beitraege zur Naturwissenschaft

Bremer Briefe Chem — Bremer Briefe zur Chemie

Br Emp Confect — British and Empire Confectioner

Brem Verdische Biblioth — Brem- und Verdische Bibliothek, Worin zur Aufnahme der Wissenschaften. AllerleyBrauchbare Abhandlungen und Anmerkungen Mitgetheilet Werden

Bren — Brenner. Halbmonatsschrift fuer Kunst und Kultur

Br Engine Tech Rep — British Engine Technical Reports

Br Engng — British Engineering

Br Engng Export J — British Engineering Export Journal

Br Engng Int — British Engineering International

Br Engng Stand Cod Lists — British Engineering Standards Coded Lists

Br Engng Transp — British Engineering and Transport

Br Engr — British Engineer

Br Engrs Home Export J — British Engineers' Home and Export Journal

Br Eng Tech Rep — British Engine Technical Reports

Brennerei Ztg — Brennerei Zeitung

Brennkrafttech Ges Jahrb — Brennkrafttechnische Gesellschaft. Jahrbuch

Brennst-Chem — Brennstoff-Chemie

Brennstoff u Waermewirtsch — Brennstoff- und Waermewirtschaft

Brennst-Waerme-Kraft — Brennstoff-Waerme-Kraft

Brennst Waermewirtsch — Brennstoff- und Waermewirtschaft

Brenns-Waerme-Kraft — Brennstoff-Waerme-Kraft

Brenn-Waerme — Brennstoff-Waerme-Kraft

Bren-S — Brenner-Studien

B Rens Agr — Bulletin de Renseignements Agricoles

Brent Unempl Bull — Brent Unemployment Bulletin

BRep — Bourgogne Republicaine

Br Epilepsy Ass J — British Epilepsy Association Journal

Brera Not — Brera Notizie

BRERD — Brain Research Reviews

BRERD2 — Brain Research Reviews

Brescia Cm — Commentarj della Accademia di Scienze, Lettere, Agricultura, ed Arti del Dipartimento del Mella (Brescia)

Brescia Cm Aten — Commentarj della Accademia di Scienze, Lettere, Agricultura, ed Arti del Dipartimento del Mella (Brescia)

Brescia Cm Aten — Commentarj dell' Ateneo di Brescia

BResClsr — Bulletin. Research Council of Israel

B Res Council Isr — Bulletin. Research Council of Israel

BRESD — Biomedical Research

B Res Hum — Bulletin of Research in the Humanities

Bresl AK — Zeitschrift der Anwaltskammer Breslau

Bresl Jbr Schl Gs — Jahresbericht der Schlesischen Gesellschaft fuer Vaterlaendische Cultur

Bresl Schl Gs Jbr — Jahresbericht der Schlesischen Gesellschaft fuer Vaterlaendische Cultur

Bresl Schl Gs Uebs — Uebersicht der Arbeiten und Veraenderungen der Schlesischen Gesellschaft fuer Vaterlaendische Cultur (Breslau)

Brest S Ac Bll — Bulletin de la Societe Academique de Brest

B Rethel — Bulletin Archeologique, Historique, et Folklorique. Musee du Rethelois et du Porcien

Breth Life — Brethren Life and Thought

Brett J — Brettener Jahrbuch fuer Kultur und Geschichte

Br Eur Airw Mag — British European Airways Magazine

Brev — Biblical Review

Brev Can — Brevet Canadien

Brev Can Brev Redelivrance — Brevet Canadien. Brevet de Redelivrance

Brev Import Belg — Brevet d'Importation (Belgium)

Brev Invent (Belg) — Brevet d'Invention (Belgium)

Brev Invent (Fr) — Brevet d'Invention (France)

Brev Invenz Ind (Italy) — Brevetto per Invenzione Industriale (Italy)

Breviora Geol Asturica — Breviora Geologica Asturica

Brev Perfect Belg — Brevet de Perfectionnement (Belgium)

Brev Spec Med Fr — Brevet Special de Medicament (France)

Brew Chem News Lett — Brewing Chemists' News Letter

Brew Dig — Brewers Digest

Brew Distill Int — Brewing and Distilling International

Brew Guardian — Brewers' Guardian

Brew Guild J — Brewers' Guild Journal

Brew Ind — Brewing Industry

Brew J — Brewers Journal

Brew J Chicago — Brewers' Journal (Chicago)

Brew J Hop Malt Trades Rev — Brewers' Journal and Hop and Malt Trades' Review

Brew J (London) — Brewers' Journal (London)

Brew J NY — Brewers' Journal (New York)

Brew J (Philadelphia) — Brewers Journal (Philadelphia)

Brew J West Brew — Brewer's Journal. Western Brewer

Brew Malting Allied Processes — Brewing, Malting, and Allied Processes

Brew Maltster — Brewer and Maltster

Brew Rev — Brewing Review

Brew Sci — Brewing Science

Brew Tech Rev — Brewers Technical Review

Brew Trade Rev — Brewing Trade Review

Brew Trade Rev Suppl — Brewing Trade Review. Supplement

Br Export J — British Export Journal
BRF — Bulletin. Rabinowitz Fund for the Exploration of Ancient Synagogues
Br Farmer Stockbreed — British Farmer and Stockbreeder
Br Fd J — British Food Journal and Hygienic Review
Br Fd Mach Export J — British Food Machinery Export Journal
Br Fern Gaz — Brill Fern Gazette
Br Film J — British Film Journal
BRFLUC — Biblios. Revista da Faculdade de Letras da Universidade de Coimbra
Br Fm Mechanis — British Farm Mechanisation
Br Fmr — British Farmer
Br Fmr J Agric — British Farmer and Journal of Agriculture
Br Food J — British Food Journal
Br Food J Hyg Rev — British Food Journal and Hygienic Review
Br Food Manuf Ind Res Assoc Sci Tech Surv — British Food Manufacturing Industries Research Association. Scientific and Technical Surveys
Br For Confect — British and Foreign Confectioner
Br Foundrym — British Foundryman
Br Foundryman — British Foundryman
Br Fries J — British Friesian Journal
Br Fur Fmr — British Fur Farmer
Br Furnish — British Furnishing
Br Fur Trad — British Fur Trade
Br Fur Trade Yb — British Fur Trade Year Book
BRG — Blaetter der Rilke-Gesellschaft
Br Gas Res Technol Div Midlands Res Stn Report MRS E — British Gas. Research and Technology Division. Midlands Research Station. Report MRS E
Br Geol — British Geologist
Br Geol Lit New Ser — British Geological Literature. New Series
Br Geomorphol Res Group Tech Bull — British Geomorphological Research Group. Technical Bulletin
BRGIAG — Brewers' Guild Journal
BRGK — Bericht. Roemisch-Germanische Kommission
Br Glass Pckr — British Glass Packer
Br Grassl Soc Occas Symp — British Grassland Society. Occasional Symposium
BRgT — Beitraege zur Rechtsgeschichte Tirols
BRgt — Besluit van de Regent
BRGTAF — Bragantia
BRGUAI — Brewers' Guardian
Br Guiana Dep Agric Sugar Bull — British Guiana. Department of Agriculture. Sugar Bulletin
Br Guiana Geol Surv Dep Bull — British Guiana. Geological Survey Department. Bulletin
Br Guiana Geol Surv Dep Miner Resour Pam — British Guiana. Geological Survey Department. Mineral Resources Pamphlet
Br Guiana Geol Surv Dep Rep — British Guiana. Geological Survey Department. Report
Br Guiana Med A — British Guiana Medical Annual and Hospital Reports
Br Guiana Timb — British Guiana Timbers
Br Gui Med Annual — British Guiana Medical Annual
Br Gynaec J — British Gynaecological Journal
BRH — Bulletin of Research in the Humanities
BRH Bull — BRH [*Bureau of Radiological Health*] Bulletin
BRHE — Bibliotheque de la Revue d'Histoire Ecclesiastique
Br Heart J — British Heart Journal
Br Herb Doct — British Herb Doctor
Br H I — British Humanities Index
Br Hist Illus — British History Illustrated
BRHLA — Biorheology
Br Hlth Rev — British Health Review
Br Honduras Dep Agric Annu Rep — British Honduras. Department of Agriculture. Annual Report
Br Honduras Dep Agric Fish Annu Rep — British Honduras. Department of Agriculture and Fisheries. Annual Report
Br Humanit Index — British Humanities Index
BRI — BioResearch Index [*Later, BA/RRM*]
BRI — British Journal of Industrial Relations
BRI — Buddhist Research Information
Briar Q — Briarcliff Quarterly
BRICA — Bulletin. Research Council of Israel. Section C. Technology
Brickb — Brickbuilder
Brick Bull — Brick Bulletin
Brick Clay Rec — Brick and Clay Record
Brick Dev Res Inst Tech Notes Clay Prod — Brick Development Research Institute. Technical Notes on Clay Products
Brick Tech Note — Brick Technical Note
Bridge Eng — Bridge Engineering
Bridge Eng Conf — Bridge Engineering Conference
Brief Bioinform — Briefings in Bioinformatics
Brief Case — Legal Aid Brief Case
Brief Clin Lab Observations — Brief Clinical and Laboratory Observations
Briefing CVCP — Briefing. Committee of Vice-Chancellors and Principals
Brief Pap Aust Dev Stud — Briefing Paper. Australian Development Studies Network
BRIFB — Berichte und Informationen. Europaeische Gemeinschaften
Brigant — Brigantium. Museo Arqueologico e Historico
Brigham You — Brigham Young University. Studies
Brigham Young U L Rev — Brigham Young University. Law Review
Brigham Young Univ Geol Stud — Brigham Young University. Geology Studies
Brigham Young Univ L Rev — Brigham Young University. Law Review
Brigham Young Univ Res Stud Geol Ser — Brigham Young University. Research Studies. Geology Series
Brigham Young Univ Sci Bull Biol Ser — Brigham Young University. Science Bulletin. Biological Series
Brigham Young Univ Stud — Brigham Young University Studies
Brigham YULR — Brigham Young University. Law Review

Brighton Crop Prot Conf Pests Dis — Brighton Crop Protection Conference. Pests and Diseases
Brighton NH S Rp — Brighton and Sussex Natural Nistory and Philosophical Society. Annual Report
Brig Yo ULR — Brigham Young University. Law Review
Brill Mag — Brill Magazine
BRIMD7 — Brimleyana
Brimst Brevities — Brimstone Brevities
Br Ind Finish (Leighton Buzzard Engl) — British Industrial Finishing (Leighton Buzzard, England)
Br Ind Finish (London) — British Industrial Finishing (London)
Brink Boeken — Brinkman's Cumulatieve Catalogus van Boeken
Br Ink Maker — British Ink Maker
Br Ink Mkr — British Ink Maker
Br Insectic Fungic Conf Proc — British Insecticide and Fungicide Conference. Proceedings
Br Inst Radiol Spec Rep — British Institute of Radiology. Special Report
Br Int Law — British Yearbook of International Law
BRI Occ Rep — BRI [*Building Research Institute*] Occasional Report
Br Iron Steel Res Assoc Open Rep — British Iron and Steel Research Association. Open Report
BRISD — Bulletin. Rhode Island School of Design. Museum Notes
BRISDMN — Bulletin. Rhode Island School of Design. Museum Notes
Br Isles Bee Breeders' News — British Isles Bee Breeders' Association. News
BRISMES Bull — British Society for Middle East Studies Bulletin
Bristol Med-Chir J — Bristol Medico-Chirurgical Journal
Bristol-Myers Cancer Symp — Bristol-Myers Cancer Symposia
Bristol-Myers Nutr Symp — Bristol-Myers Nutrition Symposia
Bristol Myers Squibb Cancer Symp — Bristol-Myers Squibb Cancer Symposia
Bristol Myers Squibb Mead Johnson Nutr Symp — Bristol-Myers Squibb/Mead Johnson Nutrition Symposia
Bristol Nat Soc Proc — Bristol Naturalists' Society. Proceedings
Bristol Nt S P — Proceedings of the Bristol Naturalists' Society
Bristol Q — Bristol Quarterly
Bristol Rev — Bristol Review
Bristol Siddeley J — Bristol Siddeley Journal
Bristol Univ Dep Agric Hortic Bull — Bristol University. Department of Agriculture and Horticulture. Bulletin
Bristol Univ Spelaeol Soc Proc — Bristol University. Spelaeological Society. Proceedings
Bristol Univ Spel Soc Proc — Bristol University. Proceedings. Speleological Society
Brit — British
Brit AA — British Archaeological Abstracts
Brit Abstr Med Sci — British Abstracts of Medical Sciences
Brit Acad Proc — British Academy [*London*]. Proceedings
Brit Agric Bull — British Agricultural Bulletin
Britains Rds — Britain's Roads</PHR> %
Brit Amended — British Amended
Brit Am Tr N — British-American Trade News
Brit & For Evang R — British and Foreign Evangelical Review
Brit & For R — British and Foreign Review
Britannica R For Lang Educ — Britannica Review of Foreign Language Education
Brit Arch Ab — British Archaeological Abstracts
Brit Archaeol Assoc Confer Trans — British Archaeology Association Conference Transactions
Brit Archaeol Rep — British Archaeological Reports
Brit Architect — British Architect
Brit As Rp — British Association for the Advancement of Science. Report
Brit Assn Adv Sci Rpt — British Association for the Advancement of Science. Report
Brit Assoc Am Studies Bull — British Association for American Studies. Bulletin
Brit Bee J — British Bee Journal and Beekeepers' Adviser
Brit Beet Grower — British Beet Grower and Empire Producer
Brit Birds — British Birds
Brit Bk N — British Book News
Brit Bk N C — British Book News. Children's Supplement
Brit Bk News — British Book News
Brit Bk Yr — Britannica Book of the Year
Brit Bryol Soc Trans — British Bryological Society. Transactions
Brit Bull Spectrosc — British Bulletin of Spectroscopy
Brit Busin — British Business
Brit Busn — British Business
Brit Cave Res Ass Trans — British Cave Research Association. Transactions
Brit Cer Abstr — British Ceramic Abstracts
Brit Chem Abstr — British Chemical Abstracts
Brit Chem Abstr Coll Ind — British Chemical Abstracts. Collective Index
Brit Chem Eng — British Chemical Engineering
Brit Chem Phys Abstr — British Chemical and Physiological Abstracts
Brit Clayw — British Clayworker
Brit Coal Util Res Assoc Gaz — British Coal Utilisation Research Association. Gazette
Brit Col Med J — British Columbia Medical Journal
Brit Colon Pharm — British and Colonial Pharmacist
Brit Col Print — British and Colonial Printer and Stationer
Brit Columbia Dep Mines Petrol Resour Bull — British Columbia. Department of Mines and Petroleum Resources. Bulletin
Brit Columbia Hist Quart — British Columbia Historical Quarterly
Brit Columbia Lib Q — British Columbia Library Quarterly
Brit Constr Steelworks Ass Publ — British Constructional Steelworks Association. Publications
Brit Corrosion J — British Corrosion Journal
Brit Corros J — British Corrosion Journal
Brit Critic — British Critic
Brit Deaf News — British Deaf News

Brit Def T — British Defence Technology
Brit Delphinium Soc Yearb — British Delphinium Society's Yearbook
Brit Dent J — British Dental Journal
Brit Ecol Soc Symp — British Ecological Society. Symposium
BritEdI — British Education Index
Brit Eng — British Engineer
Brit Eng — British Engineering
Brit Engine Boiler Elec Ins Co Tech Rep — British Engine, Boiler, and Electrical Insurance Company. Technical Report
Brit Engin Export J — British Engineers Export Journal
Brit Europ Airw Mag — British European Airways Magazine
Brit Florist — British Florist
Brit Food J — British Food Journal and Hygienic Review [*Later, British Food Journal*]
Brit Foreign Med Chir Rev London — British and Foreign Medico-Chirurgical Review (London)
Brit Foreign Sci Mag — British and Foreign Scientific Magazine and Journal of Scientific Inventions
Brit Foundrym — British Foundryman
Brit Gas Corp Ext Rep Res Commun MRS Rep — British Gas Corporation External Reports. Research Communications and Midlands Research Station Reports
Brit Granite Whinstone Fed J — British Granite and Whinstone Federation. Journal
Brit Grassland Soc J — British Grassland Society. Journal
Brit Guiana Med Annals — British Guiana Medical Annals
Brit Gui Med Ann — British Guiana Medical Annual and Hospital Reports
Brit Gyn J — British Gynaecological Journal
BritH — British Heritage
Brit Heart J — British Heart Journal
Brit Hist Illus — British History Illustrated
Brit Hosp Soc Serv J — British Hospital and Social Service Journal
Brit Hum — British Humanities Index
Brit Ink Maker — British Ink Maker
British Acad Classical Medieval Logic Texts — British Academy Classical and Medieval Logic Texts
British Archaeological Assocn Conference Trans — British Archaeological Association. Conference Transactions
British Ceramic Soc Trans — British Ceramic Society. Transactions
British Columbia Dept Mines Ann Rept Bull — British Columbia. Department of Mines. Annual Report. Bulletin
British Columbia Univ Dept Geology Rept — British Columbia University. Department of Geology. Report
British J Math Statist Psych — British Journal of Mathematical and Statistical Psychology
British J Math Statist Psychology — British Journal of Mathematical and Statistical Psychology
British J Philos Sci — British Journal for the Philosophy of Science
British J Pol Science — British Journal of Political Science
British Mus (Nat History) Bull Geology — British Museum (Natural History). Bulletin. Geology
British Nat Biblio — British National Bibliography
British R Econ Issues — British Review of Economic Issues
British Reports Transl & Theses — British Reports, Translations, and Theses
British Tax R — British Tax Review
Brit J 18th Cent Stud — British Journal for Eighteenth-Century Studies
Brit J 18th C Stud — British Journal for 18th-Century Studies
Brit J Addict — British Journal of Addiction
Brit J Admin Law — British Journal of Administrative Law
Brit J Adm L — British Journal of Administrative Law
Brit J Aes — British Journal of Aesthetics
Brit J Aesth — British Journal of Aesthetics
Brit J Aesthet — British Journal of Aesthetics
Brit J Aesthetics — British Journal of Aesthetics
Brit J Anaesth — British Journal of Anaesthesia
Brit J Ap Phys — British Journal of Applied Physics
Brit J Appl Phys — British Journal of Applied Physics
Brit J Audiol — British Journal of Audiology
Brit J Cancer — British Journal of Cancer
Brit J Child Dis — British Journal of Children's Diseases
Brit J Clin Pract — British Journal of Clinical Practice
Brit J Crim — British Journal of Criminology
Brit J Criminol — British Journal of Criminology
Brit J Criminology — British Journal of Criminology
Brit J Delinq — British Journal of Delinquency
Brit J Dermat — British Journal of Dermatology
Brit J Dermatol — British Journal of Dermatology
Brit J Dev Psychol — British Journal of Developmental Psychology
Brit J Dis Chest — British Journal of Diseases of the Chest
Brit J Dis Commun — British Journal of Disorders of Communication
Brit J Disord Commun — British Journal of Disorders of Communication
Brit J Ed Psychol — British Journal of Educational Psychology
Brit J Ed Studies — British Journal of Educational Studies
Brit J Educ Psychol — British Journal of Educational Psychology
Brit J Educ Stud — British Journal of Educational Studies
Brit J Exper Path — British Journal of Experimental Pathology
Brit J Haemat — British Journal of Haematology
Brit J Herpe — British Journal of Herpetology
Brit J Hist Sci — British Journal for the History of Science
Brit J Hosp Med — British Journal of Hospital Medicine
Brit J Ind Med — British Journal of Industrial Medicine
Brit J Ind Rel — British Journal of Industrial Relations
Brit J Indust Med — British Journal of Industrial Medicine
Brit J Industr Med — British Journal of Industrial Medicine
Brit J Industr Relat — British Journal of Industrial Relations

Brit J Inebriety — British Journal of Inebriety
Brit J Int'l L — British Journal of International Law
Brit J Int Stud — British Journal of International Studies
Brit J L & Soc — British Journal of Law and Society
Brit JL & Soc'y — British Journal of Law and Society
Brit J Law & Soc — British Journal of Law and Society
Brit Jl Photogr — British Journal of Photography
Brit J Math & Stat Psychol — British Journal of Mathematical and Statistical Psychology
Brit J Med Psychol — British Journal of Medical Psychology
Brit J Ment Subnorm — British Journal of Mental Subnormality
Brit J M Psychol — British Journal of Medical Psychology
Brit J Mus Ed — British Journal of Music Education
Brit J Non-Destruct Test — British Journal of Non-Destructive Testing
Brit J Nutr — British Journal of Nutrition
Brit J Nutr Proc Nutr Soc — British Journal of Nutrition. Proceedings of the Nutrition Society
Brit J of Crimin — British Journal of Criminology
Brit J Ophth — British Journal of Ophthalmology
Brit J Ophthalmol — British Journal of Ophthalmology
Brit Jour Radiol — British Journal of Radiology
Brit Jour Sociol — British Journal of Sociology
Brit J Pharmacol — British Journal of Pharmacology
Brit J Pharmacol — British Journal of Pharmacology and Chemotherapy
Brit J Pharmacol Chemother — British Journal of Pharmacology and Chemotherapy [*Later, British Journal of Pharmacology*]
Brit J Philos Sci — British Journal for the Philosophy of Science
Brit J Phil Sci — British Journal for the Philosophy of Science
BritH J Phot — British Journal of Photography
Brit J Photo — British Journal of Photography
Brit J Plast Surg — British Journal of Plastic Surgery
Brit J Polit Sci — British Journal of Political Science
Brit J Pol Sci — British Journal of Political Science
Brit J Prev Soc Med — British Journal of Preventive and Social Medicine
Brit J Psych — British Journal of Psychiatry
Brit J Psychiat — British Journal of Psychiatry
Brit J Psychol — British Journal of Psychology
Brit J Psych Soc Work — British Journal of Psychiatric Social Work
Brit J Radiol — British Journal of Radiology
Brit J Soc — British Journal of Sociology
Brit J Social & Clin Psychol — British Journal of Social and Clinical Psychology
Brit J Social Psychiat — British Journal of Social Psychiatry
Brit J Sociol — British Journal of Sociology
Brit J Soc Work — British Journal of Social Work
Brit J Surg — British Journal of Surgery
Brit J Tuberc — British Journal of Tuberculosis
Brit J Urol — British Journal of Urology
Brit J Ven Dis — British Journal of Venereal Diseases
Brit J Vener Dis — British Journal of Venereal Diseases
Brit Kinemat — British Kinematography
Brit Kinematogr Sound Telev — British Kinematography, Sound, and Television
Brit Kinemat Sound and Telev — British Kinematography, Sound, and Television
Brit Lib Assoc — Library Association of the United Kingdom. Monthly Notes
Brit Lib J — British Library Journal
Brit Lib Res Dev Newsletter — British Library Research and Development Newsletter
Brit Libr J — British Library Journal
Brit Lithographer — British Lithographer
Brit M Bull — British Medical Bulletin
Brit Med J — British Medical Journal
Brit MJ — British Medical Journal
Brit Museum Nat Hist Bull Zool — Bulletin. British Museum. Natural History. Zoology
Brit Mus (Nat Hist) Econom Ser — British Museum (Natural History). Economic Series
Brit Mus Q — British Museum. Quarterly
Brit Mus Quart — British Museum. Quarterly
Brit Mus Quarterly — British Museum. Quarterly
Brit Mus Subj Index — British Museum. Subject Index
Brit Mus Yearb — British Museum. Yearbook
Brit Mycol Soc Trans — British Mycological Society. Transactions
Brit Numi J — British Numismatic Journal
Brit Numis J — British Numismatic Journal
Brit Orth J — British Orthoptic Journal
Brit Osteop J — British Osteopathic Journal
Brit Osteop Rev — British Osteopathic Review
Brit Overs Pharm Yb — British and Overseas Pharmacist's Yearbook
Brit Pat Abs Sect CH Chem — British Patent Abstracts. Section CH. Chemical
Brit Petr Equipm — British Petroleum Equipment
Brit Petr Equipm Ne — British Petroleum Equipment News
Brit Phycol Bull — British Phycological Bulletin
Brit Plast — British Plastics [*Later, European Plastics News*]
Brit Plast Rubb — British Plastics and Rubber
Brit Plast Yb — British Plastics Yearbook
Brit Polit Sociol Yb — British Political Sociology. Yearbook
Brit Polym J — British Polymer Journal
Brit Poultry Sci — British Poultry Science
Brit Poult Sci — British Poultry Science
Brit Print — British Printer
Brit Printer — British Printer
Brit Psychol Soc Bull — Bulletin. British Psychological Society
Brit Q — British Quarterly Review
Brit Quar Rev — British Quarterly Review
Brit Racehorse — British Racehorse
Brit Repts Transl Theses — British Reports, Translations, and Theses

Brit Rheum Ass Rev — British Rheumatic Association. Review
Brit Sch Athens Ann — British School at Athens. Annual
Brit Sch at Rome Papers — British School at Rome. Papers
Brit Sci News — British Science News
Britsh Ink — British Ink Maker
Brit Soc Fran Stud — British Society of Franciscan Studies
Brit Soc Middle E Stud Bull — British Society for Middle Eastern Studies Bulletin
Brit Sov Archaeol Newslett — British-Soviet Archaeological Newsletter
Brit Stand — British Standard Specification
Brit Stand Inst Brit Stand — British Standards Institution. British Standard
Brit Steelmaker — British Steelmaker
Brit Stud Mon — British Studies Monitor
Brit Sug Beet Rev — British Sugar Beet Review
Brit Tax Rev — British Tax Review
Brit Techl — British Technology Index [*Later, Current Technology Index*]
Brit Telec — British Telecom Journal
Brit UK Pat Appl — British UK Patent Application
Brit Vet J — British Veterinary Journal
Brit Weld J — British Welding Journal
Brit Yb Int Law — British Yearbook of International Law
Brit Yb Int'l L — British Yearbook of International Law
Brit Y Book — British Year Book of International Law
Brit Yearb Internat Law — British Yearbook of International Law
Brit Yearbook Int L — British Yearbook of International Law
BRJ — Bill of Rights Journal
BrJ — Braunschweiger Jahrbuch
Br J Actinother — British Journal of Actinotherapy
Br J Actinother Physiother — British Journal of Actinotherapy and Physiotherapy
Br J Addict — British Journal of Addiction
Br J Adm L — British Journal of Administrative Law
Br J Aesth — British Journal of Aesthetics
Br J Alcohol Alcohol — British Journal on Alcohol and Alcoholism
Br J Anaest — British Journal of Anaesthesia
Br J Anaesth — British Journal of Anaesthesia
Br J Anim Behav — British Journal of Animal Behaviour
Br J Appl Phys — British Journal of Applied Physics
Br J Appl Phys Suppl — British Journal of Applied Physics. Supplement
Br J Audiol — British Journal of Audiology
Br J Audiology — British Journal of Audiology
Br J Audiol Suppl — British Journal of Audiology. Supplement
Br Jb — Bremisches Jahrbuch
Br J Biomed Sci — British Journal of Biomedical Science
Br J Canc — British Journal of Cancer
Br J Cancer — British Journal of Cancer
Br J Cancer Suppl — British Journal of Cancer. Supplement
Br J Clin Equip — British Journal of Clinical Equipment
Br J Clin P — British Journal of Clinical Practice
Br J Clin Pharmacol — British Journal of Clinical Pharmacology
Br J Clin Pract — British Journal of Clinical Practice
Br J Clin Pract Symp Suppl — British Journal of Clinical Practice. Symposium Supplement
Br J Clin Prat — British Journal of Clinical Practice
Br J Clin Psychol — British Journal of Clinical Psychology
Br J Cl Ph — British Journal of Clinical Pharmacology
Br J Community Nurs — British Journal of Community Nursing
Br J Crimin — British Journal of Criminology
Br J Criminology — British Journal of Criminology
Br J Dent Sci Prosthetics — British Journal of Dental Science and Prosthetics
Br J Derm — British Journal of Dermatology
Br J Dermatol — British Journal of Dermatology
Br J Dermatol Suppl — British Journal of Dermatology. Supplement
Br J Dermatol Syph — British Journal of Dermatology and Syphilis
Br J Dev Psychol — British Journal of Developmental Psychology
Br J Dis Ch — British Journal of Diseases of the Chest
Br J Dis Chest — British Journal of Diseases of the Chest
Br J Dis Co — British Journal of Disorders of Communication
Br J Ed Psy — British Journal of Educational Psychology
Br J Educ Psychol — British Journal of Educational Psychology
Br J Educ S — British Journal of Educational Studies
Br J Educ Stud — British Journal of Educational Studies
Br J Educ T — British Journal of Educational Technology
Br J Educ Tech — British Journal of Educational Technology
Br J Eighteenth Century Stud — British Journal for Eighteenth Century Studies
Br J Ex Pat — British Journal of Experimental Pathology
Br J Exp Bio — British Journal of Experimental Biology
Br J Exp Biol — British Journal of Experimental Biology
Br J Exp Path — British Journal of Experimental Pathology
Br J Exp Pathol — British Journal of Experimental Pathology
BRJFA — British Journal of Photography
Br J Fam Plann — British Journal of Family Planning
Br J Gen Pract — British Journal of General Practice
Br J Guid Couns — British Journal of Guidance and Counselling
Br J Haem — British Journal of Haematology
Br J Haematol — British Journal of Haematology
Br J Haematology — British Journal of Haematology
Br J Herpetol — British Journal of Herpetology
Br J Hist S — British Journal for the History of Science
Br J Hist Sci — British Journal for the History of Science
Br J Hosp Med — British Journal of Hospital Medicine
Br J Ind Me — British Journal of Industrial Medicine
Br J Ind Med — British Journal of Industrial Medicine
Br J Ind Medicine — British Journal of Industrial Medicine
Br J Ind Relations — British Journal of Industrial Relations
Br J Ind Saf — British Journal of Industrial Safety
Br J Inebriety — British Journal of Inebriety

Br J Inserv Educ — British Journal of Inservice Education
Br J Int Stud — British Journal of International Studies
Br J Law Soc — British Journal of Law and Society
Br J Math S — British Journal of Mathematical and Statistical Psychology
Br J Math Stat Psychol — British Journal of Mathematical and Statistical Psychology
Br J Med Educ — British Journal of Medical Education
Br J Med Ps — British Journal of Medical Psychology
Br J Med Psychol — British Journal of Medical Psychology
Br J Ment S — British Journal of Mental Subnormality
Br J Ment Subnorm — British Journal of Mental Subnormality
Br J Mid East Stud — British Journal of Middle Eastern Studies
BRJNA — Building Research
Br J Neurosurg — British Journal of Neurosurgery
Br J Non-Destr Test — British Journal of Non-Destructive Testing
Br J Nutr — British Journal of Nutrition
Br J Obstet Gynaecol — British Journal of Obstetrics and Gynaecology
Br J Obst G — British Journal of Obstetrics and Gynaecology
Br J Occup Saf — British Journal of Occupational Safety
Br J Ophth — British Journal of Ophthalmology
Br J Ophthalmol — British Journal of Ophthalmology
Br J Oral Maxillofac Surg — British Journal of Oral and Maxillofacial Surgery
Br J Oral S — British Journal of Oral Surgery [*Later, British Journal of Oral and Maxillofacial Surgery*]
Br J Oral Surg — British Journal of Oral Surgery [*Later, British Journal of Oral and Maxillofacial Surgery*]
Br J Orthod — British Journal of Orthodontics
BrJP — British Journal of Political Science
BR J PE — British Journal of Physical Education
Br J Perioper Nurs — British Journal of Perioperative Nursing
Br J Pharm — British Journal of Pharmacology
Br J Pharmac — British Journal of Pharmacology
Br J Pharmac Chemother — British Journal of Pharmacology and Chemotherapy [*Later, British Journal of Pharmacology*]
Br J Pharmacol — British Journal of Pharmacology
Br J Pharmacol Chemother — British Journal of Pharmacology and Chemotherapy [*Later, British Journal of Pharmacology*]
Br J Pharm Pract — British Journal of Pharmaceutical Practice
Br J Philos Sci — British Journal for the Philosophy of Science
Br J Phil S — British Journal for the Philosophy of Science
Br J Photogr — British Journal of Photography
Br J Photogr Ann — British Journal of Photography. Annual
Br J Phys Ed — British Journal of Physical Education
Br J Physiol Opt — British Journal of Physiological Optics
Br J Phys Med — British Journal of Physical Medicine
Br J Phys O — British Journal of Physiological Optics
Br J Plast Surg — British Journal of Plastic Surgery
Br J Pl Sur — British Journal of Plastic Surgery
Br J Poli S — British Journal of Political Science
Br J Polit Sci — British Journal of Political Science
Br J Prev S — British Journal of Preventive and Social Medicine
Br J Prev Soc Med — British Journal of Preventive and Social Medicine
Br J Psych — British Journal of Psychiatry
Br J Psychi — British Journal of Psychiatry
Br J Psychiat — British Journal of Psychiatry
Br J Psychiatry — British Journal of Psychiatry
Br J Psychiatry Spec Publ — British Journal of Psychiatry. Special Publication
Br J Psychiatry Suppl — British Journal of Psychiatry. Supplement
Br J Psychiat Soc Wk — British Journal of Psychiatric Social Work
Br J Psycho — British Journal of Psychology
Br J Psychol — British Journal of Psychology
Br J Psychol Med Sect — British Journal of Psychology. Medical Section
Br J Psychol Statist Sect — British Journal of Psychology. Statistical Section
Br J Psych Res — British Journal of Psychical Research
Br J Radiesth Radion — British Journal of Radiesthesia (and Radionics)
Br J Radiol — British Journal of Radiology
Br J Radiol BIR Sect — British Journal of Radiology. British Association of Radio and Physiotherapy Section
Br J Radiol Rontg Soc Sect — British Journal of Radiology. Rontgen Society Section
Br J Radiol Spec Rep — British Journal of Radiology. Special Report
Br J Radiol Suppl — British Journal of Radiology. Supplement
Br J Rheumatol — British Journal of Rheumatology
BrJS — British Journal of Sociology
Br J Sex Med — British Journal of Sexual Medicine
Br J Soc — British Journal of Sociology
Br J Soc Cl — British Journal of Social and Clinical Psychology
Br J Soc Clin Psychol — British Journal of Social and Clinical Psychology
Br J Sociol — British Journal of Sociology
Br J Sociol Educ — British Journal of the Sociology of Education
Br J Sociology — British Journal of Sociology
Br J Soc Med — British Journal of Social Medicine
Br J Soc Ps — British Journal of Social Psychiatry
Br J Soc Psychol — British Journal of Social Psychology
Br J Soc W — British Journal of Social Work
Br J Soc Wk — British Journal of Social Work
Br J Sports Med — British Journal of Sports Medicine
Br J Statist Psychol — British Journal of Statistical Psychology
Br J Surg — British Journal of Surgery
Br J Tuberc — British Journal of Tuberculosis
Br J Tuberc Dis Chest — British Journal of Tuberculosis and Diseases of the Chest
Br J Urol — British Journal of Urology
Br J Ven Dis — British Journal of Venereal Diseases
Br J Vener Dis — British Journal of Venereal Diseases

BRKIA — British Kinematography
Br Kinematogr — British Kinematography, Sound, and Television
Br Kinematogr Sound and Telev — British Kinematography, Sound, and Television
BRKM — Bulletin of the Rama Krishna Mission. Institute of Culture
Br Knitting Ind — British Knitting Industry
BRL — Biblisches Reallexikon
BRL — Bulletin. John Rylands Library. University of Manchester
BRLC — Bibliotheque de la Revue de Litterature Comparee
BRLGA — Brain and Language
BRLI — Bright Lights
Br Lib Inf Sci — British Librarianship and Information Science
Br Libr News — British Library News
Br Libr Res Dev Rep — British Library Research and Development Reports
Br Limemaster — British Limemaster
Br Lithium Congr — British Lithium Congress
Br LR — Brooklyn Law Review
BRLTD — Bulletin. Research Laboratory for Nuclear Reactors. Tokyo Institute of Technology
BRM — Bulletin. Council for Research in Music Education
Br Mach Gaz — British Machinery Gazette
Br Machst Pat — British Machinist and Patents
Br Mach Tool Engng — British Machine Tool Engineering
Br Malaya — British Malaya
BRMA Rev — BRMA [*British Rubber Manufacturers' Association Ltd.*] Review
Br MB — Brooklyn Museum. Bulletin
BRMCEW — Behavior Research Methods
BRMEA — Bruxelles Medical
BRMEAY — Bruxelles Medical
Br Med B — British Medical Bulletin
Br Med Bklist — British Medical Booklist
Br Med Bull — British Medical Bulletin
Br Med J — British Medical Journal
Br Med J Pract Obs — British Medical Journal. Practice Observed Edition
BRMIA — Behavior Research Methods and Instrumentation
BRMIC — Ramarkrishna Mission Institute of Culture [*Calcutta*]. Bulletin
Br Min — British Mining
BRMMLA — Bulletin. Rocky Mountain Modern Language Association
BrMQ — British Museum. Quarterly
Br MQ — Brooklyn Museum. Quarterly
Br M Qu — British Museum. Quarterly
BRMRA5 — Brasil-Medico
Br Mus Mag — British Museum Magazine
Br Mus (Nat Hist) Bull — British Museum (Natural History). Bulletin. Geology
Br Mus (Nat Hist) Bull Geol — British Museum (Natural History). Bulletin. Geology
Br Mus (Nat Hist) Bull Zool — British Museum (Natural History). Bulletin. Zoology
Br Mus (Nat Hist) Econ Ser — British Museum (Natural History). Economic Series
Br Mus (Nat Hist) Fossil Mammals Afr — British Museum (Natural History). Fossil Mammals of Africa
Br Mus (Nat Hist) Mineral Leafl — British Museum (Natural History). Mineralogy Leaflet
Br Mus (Nat Hist) Palaeontol Leafl — British Museum (Natural History). Palaeontology Leaflet
Br Mus (Nat Hist) Publ — British Museum (Natural History). Publication
Br Mus (Nat Hist) Rep — British Museum (Natural History). Report
Br Mus Occas Pap — British Museum Occasional Paper
Br Mus Q — British Museum Quarterly
Br Mus Yearbook — British Museum. Yearbook
Br Mycol Soc Symp — British Mycological Society. Symposium
Br Mycol Soc Trans — British Mycological Society. Transactions
BrN — Brugger Neujahrsblaetter. Kulturgesellschaft des Bezirks Brugg
Br Nat Bibliography — British National Bibliography
BRNLDT — Australia. Commonwealth Scientific and Industrial Research Organisation. National Measurement Laboratory. Biennial Report
BRNNRC — Building Research News. National Research Council of Canada
Br Non Ferrous Met Res Assoc Ann Rep — British Non-Ferrous Metals Research Association. Annual Report
Br Non Ferrous Met Res Assoc Bull — British Non-Ferrous Metals Research Association. Bulletin
Br Non Ferrous Met Res Assoc Res Monogr — British Non-Ferrous Metals Research Association. Research Monograph
Brno Univ Prirod Fak Scr Geol — Brno. Universita. Prirodovedecka Fakulta. Scripta Geologia
BRNR — Borden Review of Nutrition Research
BRNSBE — Brenesia
Br Nucl Energy Conf J — British Nuclear Energy Conference Journal
Br Nucl Energy Soc Symp Adv Gas Cooled React Pap — British Nuclear Energy Society. Symposium. Advanced Gas-Cooled Reactor. Papers
Br Numismatic J — British Numismatic Journal
Br Nutr Found Bull — British Nutrition Foundation. Bulletin
Br Nutr Found Inf Bull — British Nutrition Foundation. Information Bulletin
Br Nutr Found Nutr Bull — British Nutrition Foundation. Nutrition Bulletin
BRNWA — Brennstoff- und Waermewirtschaft
Bro — Broteria
Broad — Broadside Series
Broadcast — Broadcasting Magazine
Broadcast Bank — Broadcast Banking
Broadcast Engng Tokyo — Broadcast Engineering (Tokyo)
Broadcast Equip Today — Broadcast Equipment Today
Broadcasting Bus — Broadcasting Business
Broadcast Syst and Oper — Broadcasting Systems and Operations
Broadcast Technol — Broadcast Technology
Broad Datab — Broadcast Databook
Broadsheet R Coll Pathol Aust — Broadsheet. Royal College of Pathologists of Australia

Broadw — Broadway
Broad Way Clin Suppl — Broad Way Clinical Supplement
Broadway J — Broadway Journal
BROB — Berichten. Rijksdienst voor het Oudheidkundige Bodemonderzoek
BROBA — Brookings Bulletin
Bro CC — Brown's Chancery Cases
Broch Anchor Chem Co — Brochure. Anchor Chemical Co.
Broch Applic Mec Therm — Brochure. Applications Mecaniques et Thermiques S.A.
Broch Asph Ass — Brochure. Asphalt Association
Brock Univ Dep Geol Sci Res Rep Ser — Brock University. Department of Geological Sciences. Research Report Series
Brodil'naya Prom — Brodil'naya Promyshlennost
Broil Grow — Broiler Growing
Brolga R — Brolga Review
BROM — Bulletin. Royal Ontario Museum. Art and Archaeology Division
BROMA — Bulletin. Royal Ontario Museum. Art and Archaeology Division
Bromatol Chem Toksykol — Bromatologia i Chemia Toksykologiczna
Bromley Local Hist — Bromley Local History
Bromma Hembygds-Foren Arsskr — Bromma Hembygds-Forenings Arsskrift
Brompt Hosp Rep — Brompton Hospital Reports
BRONA — Bronches
BRONA3 — Bronches
Broncho Pneumol — Broncho-Pneumologie
Brook Bul — Brookings Bulletin
Brookgreen Bul — Brookgreen Bulletin
Brookhaven Conf Rep — Brookhaven Conference Report
Brookhaven Natl Lab Lect Sci Vistas Res — Brookhaven National Laboratory. Lectures in Science. Vistas in Research
Brookhaven Natl Lab Natl Neutron Cross Sect Cent Rep BNL NCS — Brookhaven National Laboratory. National Neutron Cross Section Center. Report. BNL-NCS
Brookhaven Natl Lab Natl Nucl Data Cent Rep — Brookhaven National Laboratory. National Nuclear Data Center. Report
Brookhaven Natl Lab Rep BNL — Brookhaven National Laboratory. Report. BNL
Brookhaven Symp Biol — Brookhaven Symposia in Biology
Brookh Symp Biol — Brookhaven Symposia in Biology
Brookings — Brookings Papers on Economic Activity
Brookings Ann Rep — Brookings Annual Report
Brookings Bull — Brookings Bulletin
Brookings P — Brookings Papers on Economic Activity
Brookings Pa Econ Activ — Brookings Papers on Economic Activity
Brookings Pap Econ Activ — Brookings Papers on Economic Activity
Brookings Pas Econ Activity — Brookings Papers on Economic Activity
Brookings R — Brookings Review
Brook J Int L — Brooklyn Journal of International Law
Brookl Bot Gard Rec — Brooklyn Botanic Garden. Record
Brookl J Int L — Brooklyn Journal of International Law
Brookl L Rev — Brooklyn Law Review
Brookl M Bu — Brooklyn Museum Bulletin
Brookl Med J — Brooklyn Medical Journal
Brookl Mus Ann — Brooklyn Museum. Annual
Brookl Mus Bull — Brooklyn Museum. Bulletin
Brookl Mus J — Brooklyn Museum. Journal
Brookl Mus Quart — Brooklyn Museum. Quarterly
Brook Lodge Conf Lung Cells Dis Proc — Brook Lodge Conference on Lung Cells in Disease. Proceedings
Brook LR — Brooklyn Law Review
Brookl Rec — Brooklyn Daily Record
Brooklyn Bar — Brooklyn Barrister
Brooklyn Bot Gard Annu Rep — Brooklyn Botanic Garden. Annual Report
Brooklyn Bot Gard Mem — Brooklyn Botanic Garden. Memoirs
Brooklyn Bot Gard Rec — Brooklyn Botanic Garden. Record
Brooklyn Bot Gard Rec Plants Gard — Brooklyn Botanic Garden. Record. Plants and Gardens
Brooklyn Bot Gdn Rec — Brooklyn Botanic Garden Record
Brooklyn Daily Rec — Brooklyn Daily Record
Brooklyn Hosp J — Brooklyn Hospital. Journal
Brooklyn J Int L — Brooklyn Journal of International Law
Brooklyn J Intl L — Brooklyn Journal of International Law
Brooklyn Law R — Brooklyn Law Review
Brooklyn L R — Brooklyn Law Review
Brooklyn L Re — Brooklyn Law Review
Brooklyn L Rev — Brooklyn Law Review
Brooklyn Med J — Brooklyn Medical Journal
Brooklyn Mus Ann — Brooklyn Museum. Annual
Brooklyn Mus Annu — Brooklyn Museum Annual
Brooklyn Mus Bul — Brooklyn Institute of Arts and Sciences. Museum Bulletin
Brooklyn Mus Bull — Brooklyn Museum Bulletin
Brooklyn Mus J — Brooklyn Museum Journal
Brooklyn Mus Q — Brooklyn Museum Quarterly
Brook Mus Q — Brooklyn Museum. Quarterly
Brookng R — Brookings Review
Brook Pap Econ Act — Brookings Papers on Economic Activity
Brook S Bio — Brookhaven Symposia in Biology
Brookville Soc N H B — Brookville Society of Natural History. Bulletin
Broom Broom Corn News — Broom and Broom Corn News
Broom Corn Rev — Broom Corn Review
BROPD — Bjulleteni Rukopisnogo Otdela Puskinskogo Doma
BRORAF — Broteria. Serie Trimestral. Ciencias Naturais
Br Orthopt J — British Orthoptic Journal
Brosches Zeitschr — Zeitschrift fuer Natur- und Heilkunde (Brosche, Editor)
Brosche Z — Zeitschrift fuer Natur- und Heilkunde. Brosche, Carus, Choulant
Brot — Broteria
BROTA — Brot und Gebaeck

BROTAL — Brot und Gebaeck
Broteria Genet — Broteria Genetica
Broteria Ser Cienc Nat — Broteria. Serie de Ciencias Naturais
Broteria Ser Trimest Cienc Nat — Broteria. Serie Trimestral. Ciencias Naturais
Brot Gebaeck — Brot und Gebaeck
Brown Am — Brown American
Brown Bayleys J — Brown Bayley's Journal
Brown Boveri Cie Nachr — Brown Boveri und Cie Nachrichten
Brown Boveri Mitt — Brown Boveri Mitteilungen
Brown Boveri Rev — Brown Boveri Review
Brown Boveri Symp Corros Power Gener Equip — Brown Boveri Symposium on Corrosion in Power Generating Equipment
Brown Boveri Symp Nonemissive Electoopt Disp — Brown Boveri Symposium on Nonemissive Electrooptic Displays
Brown Boveri Symp Surges High Voltage Networks — Brown Boveri Symposium on Surges in High-Voltage Networks
Brown Bov R — Brown Boveri Review
Browning In — Browning Institute. Studies
Browning Inst Stud — Browning Institute. Studies
Brown Sequard J Pl — Journal de la Physiologie de l'Homme et des Animaux. Brown-Sequard
Brownson — Brownson's Quarterly Review
Brownsons Q R — Brownson's Quarterly Review
Brown Univ Hum Dev Let — Brown University. Human Development Letter
BRP — Beitraege zur Romanischen Philologie
BRP — Bollettino. Reale Universita Italiana per Stranieri di Perugia
Br Pap Board Makers Assoc Proc Tech Sect — British Paper and Board Makers Association. Proceedings of the Technical Section
Br Pest Control Conf — British Pest Control Conference
Br Pet Equip News — British Petroleum Equipment News
BRPFD — Blech, Rohre, Profile
BRPGDO — Brooklyn Botanic Garden. Record. Plants and Gardens
BRPh — Beitraege zur Romanischen Philologie
Br Pharmacol Soc 50th Anniv Meet — British Pharmacological Society. 50th Anniversary Meeting
Br Phycol Bull — British Phycological Bulletin [Later, British Phycological Journal]
Br Phycol J — British Phycological Journal
Br PIP — British Paperbacks in Print
BRPLA — British Plastics [Later, European Plastics News]
Br Plant Growth Regul Group Monogr — British Plant Growth Regulator Group. Monograph
Br Plast — British Plastics [Later, European Plastics News]
Br Plast Fed Reinf Plast Tech Conf — British Plastics Federation. Reinforced Plastics Technical Conference
Br Plastics Rubber — British Plastics and Rubber
Br Plast Moulded Prod Trader — British Plastics and Moulded Products Trader
Br Plast Moulded Prod Trader Suppl — British Plastics and Moulded Products Trader. Supplement
Br Plast Rubber — British Plastics and Rubber
BRPNDB — Broncho-Pneumologie
Br Polym J — British Polymer Journal
Br Portland Cem Res Assoc Pam — British Portland Cement Research Association. Pamphlets
Br Poult Sc — British Poultry Science
Br Poult Sci — British Poultry Science
Br Power Eng — British Power Engineering
BRPPDH — Biological Research in Pregnancy and Perinatology
BRPRA Techn Bull — BRPRA [British Rubber Producers' Research Association] Technical Bulletin
BRPRD — Bulletin of Radiation Protection
Br Print — British Printer
Br Psych Soc Bull — British Psychological Society. Bulletin
BRPT — Biasutti, R. Le Razze e i Popoli della Terra [Torino]
BRPT — Briarpatch. Saskatchewan's Independent Monthly Newsmagazine
Br Pteridol Soc Bull — British Pteridological Society. Bulletin
Br Public Opin — British Public Opinion
BRQ — Book Research Quarterly
BRR — Barron's Financial Weekly
BRR — Brazilian Economic Studies
BRR — Brookings Review
BRRAB — Brain Research Bulletin
Br Rayon Silk J — British Rayon and Silk Journal
BR/RB — Bilingual Review/Revista Bilingue
BRREA — Brain Research
BRREAP — Brain Research
Br Reg Geol — British Regional Geology
Br Rep Transl Theses — British Reports, Translations, and Theses
Br Rubber Prod Res Assoc Tech Bull — British Rubber Producers' Research Association. Technical Bulletin
BRRUD — Brauerei-Rundschau
BRS — Bihar Research Society. Journal
Br S Afr Co Publ Mazoe Citrus Exp Stn — British South Africa Company. Publication. Mazoe Citrus Experimental Station
BRS Bull — BRS [Bibliographic Retrieval Services] Bulletin
BRSCB — Building Research Station. Current Papers
Br Sci News — British Science News
BRSG — Boletin. Real Sociedad Geografica
BRSGI — Bollettino. Reale Societa Geografica Italiana
BrSM — British Studies Monitor
Br Small Anim Vet Assoc Congr Proc — British Small Animal Veterinary Association. Congress. Proceedings
BRSNAN — Feddes Repertorium. Specierum Novarum Regni Vegetabilis. Beihefte
BRSOA — British Steel Corporation. Open Report
Br Soap Manuf — British Soap Manufacturer

Br Soc Anim Prod Occas Publ — British Society of Animal Production. Occasional Publication
Br Soc Anim Prod Proc — British Society of Animal Production. Proceedings
Br Soc Cell Biol Symp — British Society for Cell Biology. Symposium
Br Soc Dev Biol Symp — British Society for Developmental Biology Symposium
Br Soc Parasitol Symp — British Society for Parasitology. Symposia
BRSRA — Bibliotheca Radiologica
Br Stan Yrbk — British Standards Yearbook
BRSTB — British Steel
Br Steel — British Steel
Br Steel Corp Gen Steels Div Rep — British Steel Corporation. General Steels Division. Report
Br Steel Corp Open Rep — British Steel Corporation. Open Report
Br Steel Corp Rep — British Steel Corporation. Reports
Br Steelmaker — British Steelmaker
Br Stud Monit — British Studies Monitor
BRSUAA — British Sugar Beet Review
Br Sugar Beet Rev — British Sugar Beet Review
Br Sug Beet Rev — British Sugar Beet Review
Br Sulphur Corp Q Bull — British Sulphur Corporation Ltd. Quarterly Bulletin
BRSV — Boletin. Real Sociedad Vascongada de Amigos del Pais
BRSVAP — Boletin. Real Sociedad Vascongada de Amigos del Pais
Brs Z — Breslauer Zeitung
BRT — Behavior Research and Therapy
BrT — Britain Today
BRTAAN — Brittonia
BR Tax R — British Tax Review
Br Technol Index — British Technology Index [Later, Current Technology Index]
Br Telecom Engng — British Telecommunications Engineering
Br Telecom J — British Telecom Journal
Br Telecommun Eng — British Telecommunications Engineering
Br Territ Borneo Annu Rep Geol Sur Dep — British Territories in Borneo. Annual Report. Geological Survey Department
Br Territ Borneo Geol Surv Dep Annu Rep — British Territories in Borneo. Geological Survey Department. Annual Report
Br Territ Borneo Geol Surv Dep Bull — British Territories in Borneo. Geological Survey Department. Bulletin
Br Territ Borneo Geol Surv Dep Rep — British Territories in Borneo. Geological Survey Department. Report
BRTHA — Behavior Research and Therapy
Br Thomson Houston Act — British Thomson-Houston Activities
Br Thorac Tuber Assoc Rev — British Thoracic and Tuberculosis Association. Review
Brt Lgts — Bright Lights
Br Travel News — British Travel News
Bruel & Kjaer Tech Rev — Bruel and Kjaer Technical Review
Bruenn Jh Nw Sect — Jahresheft der Naturwissenschaftlichen Section der Kaiserlich-Koeniglichen Maehrisch-Schlesischen Gesellschaft fuer Ackerbau, Natur- und Landes-Kunde (Bruenn)
Bruenn Mt — Mittheilungen der Kaiserlich-Koeniglichen Maehrisch-Schleslschen Gesellschaft zur Befoerderung des Ackerbaues, der Natur- und Landeskunde in Bruenn
Bruenn Notb — Notizen-Blatt der Historisch-Statistischen Section der Kaiserlich-Koeniglichen Maehrisch-Schlesischen Gesellschaft zur Befoerderung des Ackerbaues, der Natur- und Landes-Kunde in Bruenn
Bruennow As Not — Astronomical Notices. Bruennow
Bruenn Vb — Verhandlungen des Naturforschenden Vereins zu Bruenn
Brugnatelli G — Giornale di Fisica, Chimica, e Storia Naturale. Brugnatelli
Bruker Rep — Bruker Report
BRUND2 — Brunonia
Brunei Mus J — Brunei Museum Journal
BR UNESCO — Bulletin. Commission Nationale de la Republique Populaire Roumaine pour l'UNESCO
Brun Mus J — Brunei Museum. Journal
Brunnenbau Bau Rohrleitungsbau — Brunnenbau Bau von Wasserwerken Rohrleitungsbau
Brunner/Mazel Psychosoc Stress Ser — Brunner/Mazel Psychosocial Stress Series
Bruns' Beitr Klin Chir — Bruns' Beitraege zur Klinischen Chirurgie
BrunsBtr — Bruns Beitraege zur Klinischen Chirurgie
BRUSEI — US Fish and Wildlife Service. Biological Report
Brush & P — Brush and Pencil
Brus Museum — Brussels Museum of Musical Instruments. Bulletin
Brus Mus Roy Beaux Arts Bull — Brussels. Musees Royaux des Beaux-Arts Belgiques. Bulletin
B Russell Mem Lect Phil Sci — Bertrand Russell Memorial Lecture in Philosophy and Science
Brussels Museum M Instruments Bul — Brussels Museum of Musical Instruments. Bulletin
Brussels Mus Roy Bul — Brussels. Musees Royaux d'Art et d'Histoire. Bulletin
Brux Ac Bll — Bulletins de l'Academie Royale des Sciences de Belgique (Bruxelles)
Brux Ac Cent Anniv — Centieme Anniversaire de Fondation (1772-1872) de l'Academie Royale de Belgique (Bruxelles)
Brux Ac Md Bll — Bulletin de l'Academie Royale de Medecine de Belgique a Bruxelles
Brux Ac Md Mm Sav Etr — Memoires de l'Academie Royale de Medecine de Belgique. Memoires des Concours et des Savants Etrangers (Bruxelles)
Brux Ac Mm — Memoires de l'Academie Royale des Sciences, des Lettres, et des Beaux-Arts de Belgique (Bruxelles)
Brux Ac Sc Mm — Memoires de l'Academie Royale des Sciences, des Lettres, et des Beaux-Arts de Belgique (Bruxelles)
Brux A Tr Pbl — Annales des Travaux Publics de Belgique (Bruxelles)
Brux A Un — Annales des Universites de Belgique (Bruxelles)

Brux Bll Ac — Bulletins de l'Academie Royale des Sciences de Belgique (Bruxelles)
Brux Bll Pht — Bulletin Belge de la Photographie (Bruxelles)
Bruxelles Med — Bruxelles Medical
Brux J S Ag — Journal de la Societe Centrale d'Agriculture de Belgique (Bruxelles)
Brux Med — Bruxelles Medical
Brux Mm Ac Sc — Memoires de l'Academie Royale des Sciences, des Lettres, et des Beaux-Arts de Belgique (Bruxelles)
Brux Mm Cour — M moires Couronn s et M moires des Savants Etrangers, publi s par l'Acad mie Royale des Sciences, des Lettres et des Beaux-Arts de Belgique. 4to (Bruxelles)
Brux Mm Cour 4 — M moires Couronn s et M moires des Savants Etrangers, publi s par l'Acad mie Royale des Sciences, des Lettres, et des Beaux-Arts de Belgique. 4to (Bruxelles)
Brux Mm Cour 8 — M moires Couronn s et M moires des Savants Etrangers, publi s par l'Acad mie Royale des Sciences, des Lettres et des Beaux-Arts de Belgique. 8vo (Bruxelles)
Brux S Blg As Bll — Bulletin de la Societe Belge d'Astronomie. Comptes Rendus des Seances Mensuelles de la Societe et Revue des Sciences d'Observation, Astronomie, Meteorologie, Geodesie et Physique du Globe (Bruxelles)
Brux S Blg Gl Bll — Bulletin de la Societe Belge de Geologie, de Paleontologie, et d'Hydrologie (Bruxelles)
Brux S Blg Mcr A — Annales de la Societe Belge de Microscopie (Bruxelles)
Brux S Blg Mcr Bll — Bulletin de la Societe Belge de Microscopie (Bruxelles, Paris)
Brux S Sc A — Annales de la Societe Scientifique de Bruxelles
BRV — Brookings Review
Br Vest — Bratskij Vestnik
Br Vet J — British Veterinary Journal
BRVRAG — Breviora
BRVWA — Business Review. University of Washington
BRW — Business Review
BRW — Business Review Weekly
Br Wat Supply — British Water Supply
BRWE — Business Review Weekly
Br Weed Control Conf Proc — British Weed Control Conference. Proceedings
Br Weld J — British Welding Journal
Br Westinghouse Gaz — British Westinghouse Gazette
Br Wire J — British Wire Journal
BRWJA — British Welding Journal
Br Wood Preserv Assoc Rec Annu Conv — British Wood Preserving Association. Record of the Annual Convention
BRX — Brazil. A Monthly Publication on Trade and Industry
Br Yb Agric — British Year Book of Agriculture
BRYGAW — Brygmesteren
Brygm — Brygmesteren
BRYOA — Bryologist
BRYOAM — Bryologist
Bryol — Bryologist
Bryophytorum Bibl — Bryophytorum Bibliotheca
BS — Bantu Studies
BS — Basler Stadtbuch
BS — Behavioral Science
BS — Belgisch Staatsblad
BS — Best Sellers
BS — Biblioteka Slovesnika
BS — Bibliotheca Sacra
BS — Bijvoegsel tot het Staatsblad
BS — Black Scholar
BS — Bogoslovska Smotra
BS — Bollettino Salesiano
BS — Bollettino Senese
BS — Bollingen Series
BS — Bombay Secretariat
BS — Botanische Studien
BS — Brixia Sacra
BS — Building Science
BS — Bukowiner Schule
BS — Bulletin Signaletique
BS — Bulletin. Sommaires des Periodiques Francais et Etrangers
BS — Business Systems and Equipment
BS — Byzantino-Slavica
BS 101 — Bulletin Signaletique 101. Sciences de l'Information. Documentation
BSa — Bibliotheca Sacra
BSA — British School at Athens. Annual
BSA — Buletinul Stiintifice. Academia Romana. Sectia de Stiinte Isotrice, Filozofice si Economice
BSA — Bulletin. Societe des Amis de Vienne
BSAA — Boletin de la Sociedad Argentina de Antropologia
BSAA — Boletin. Seminario de Estudios de Arte y Arqueologia
BSAA — Bulletin Signaletique. Art et Archeologie
BSAA — Bulletin. Societe Archeologique d'Alexandrie
BSA Al — Bulletin. Societe d'Archeologie d'Alexandrie
BSA Alex — Bulletin. Societe d'Archeologie d'Alexandrie
BSA Aube — Bulletin. Societe Academique d'Agriculture des Sciences, Arts, et Belles-Lettres du Departement de l'Aube
BSAAV — Boletin. Seminario de Estudios de Arte y Arqueologia. Universidad de Valladolid
BSAB — Bulletin de la Societe des Americanistes de Belgique
BSAB — Bulletin. Societe Archeologique Bulgare
BSAB — Bulletin. Societe Archeologique de Bordeaux
BSAB — Bulletin. Societe d'Anthropologie (Brussels)
BSAC — Bulletin. Societe d'Archeologie Copte
BSAC — Bulletin. Societe d'Archeologie Champenoise
BSA Copt — Bulletin. Societe d'Archeologie Copte

BSACorreze — Bulletin. Societe Archeologique de la Correze
BSACP — Bulletin de la Societe des Amis de Colette en Puisaye
BSAE — British School of Archaeology in Egypt. Publications
BSAE — Bulletin der Schweizerischen Gesellschaft fuer Anthropologie und Ethnologie
BSaechsKG — Beitraege fuer Saechsische Kirchengeschichte
BSAEL — Bulletin. Societe Archeologique d'Eure-et-Loir
BSA Eur Bul — BSA [*Building Societies Association*] European Bulletin
BSAF — Bulletin. Societe Nationale des Antiquaires de France
BSA Fin — Bulletin. Societe Archeologique du Finstere
BSA Finistere — Bulletin. Societe Archeologique du Finistere
BSAFrance — Bulletin. Societe Nationale des Antiquaires de France
BSAFS — Bibliographical and Special Series of the American Folklore Society
BSAG — Bulletin. Societe Archeologique, Historique, Litteraire, et Scientifique du Gers
BSAHB — Bulletin. Societe Archeologique et Historique de Beauvis
BSAHDL — Bulletin. Societe d'Art et d'Histoire du Diocese de Liege
BSAHG — Bulletin. Societe Archeologique, Historique, Litteraire, et Scientifique du Gers
BSAHL — Bulletin. Societe Archeologique et Historique du Limousin
BSAH Liege — Bulletin. Societe d'Art et d'Histoire du Diocese de Liege
BSAHLimousin — Bulletin. Societe Archeologique et Historique du Limousin
BSAHNantes — Bulletin. Societe Archeologique et Historique de Nantes et de Loire-Atlantique
BSAH Noy — Bulletin. Societe Archeologique et Scientifique de Noyon
BSAHO — Bulletin. Societe Archeologique et Historique de l'Orleannais
BSAHT — Bulletin Annuel. Societe d'Archeologie et d'Histoire du Tonnerrois
BSAHW — Bulletin d'Information. Societe d'Archeologie et d'Histoire de Waremme et Environs
BSAI — Bollettino della Societa Africana d'Italia
BSAIO — Boletin. Sociedad Argentina de Investigacion Operativa
BSA/J — Journal. British Sociological Association
BSAK — Beitraege zur Saarlaendischen Archaeologie und Kunstgeschichte
BSAL — Bolleti. Societat Arqueologica Lubliana
BSAL — Bulletin. Societe Archeologique du Limousin
BSAL — Bulletin. Societe d'Anthropologie (Lyon)
BSAM — Bulletin. Societe Archeologique du Midi de la France
BSAM — Bulletin. Societe des Amis de Montaigne
BSAM — Bulletin Trimestriel. Societe Academique des Antiquaires de la Morinie
BSAMA — Bulletin. Schweizerische Akademie der Medizinischen Wissenschaften
BSAMA5 — Bulletin. Academie Suisse des Sciences Medicales
BSAMF — Bulletin. Societe Archeologique du Midi de la France
BSAMorinie — Bulletin Trimestriel. Societe Academique des Antiquaires de la Morinie
BSAN — Bulletin. Societe des Antiquaires de Normandie
BSANormandie — Bulletin. Societe des Antiquaires de Normandie
B Sante P — Bulletin de la Sante Publique
BSAO — Bulletin. Societe des Antiquaires de l'Ouest
BSAO — Bulletin. Societe des Antiquaires de l'Ouest et des Musees de Poitiers
BSAOuest — Bulletin. Societe des Antiquaires de l'Ouest et des Musees de Poitiers
BSAP — Bibliographical Society of America. Papers
BSAP — Bulletin de la Societe d'Anthropologie (Paris)
BSAP — Bulletin. Societe des Amis de Marcel Proust et de Combray
BSAP — Bulletin Trimestriel. Societe des Antiquaires de Picardie
BSAPicardie — Bulletin Trimestriel. Societe des Antiquaires de Picardie
BSAP Occas Publ Occas Publ Br Soc Anim Prod — BSAP Occasional Publication. An Occasional Publication. British Society of Animal Production
BSAPR — Bulletin. Societe des Amis de Port-Royal
BSARPR — Buletin Stiintific. Academia Republicii Populare Romine
BSAS — Bulletin. Seattle Anthropological Society
BSAS — Bulletin. Societe Archeologique de Sens
BSA Sarthe — Bulletin. Societe d'Agriculture, Sciences, et Arts de la Sarthe
BSASD — Bulletin. Societe Archeologique et Statistique de la Drome
BSAT — Bulletin. Societe Archeologique de Touraine
BSA Touraine — Bulletin Trimestriel. Societe Archeologique de Touraine
BSAU — Boletin de la Sociedad de Antropologia del Uruguay
BSAV — Boletin. Seminario de Estudios de Arte y Arqueologia. Universidad de Valladolid
BSAV — Bulletin. Societe Archeologique, Scientifique, et Litteraire du Vendomois
B Saverne — Bulletin. Societe d'Histoire et d'Archeologie de Saverne et des Environs
BSA Vienne — Bulletin. Societe des Amis de Vienne
BSAW — Berichte. Verhandlungen der Saechsischen Akademie der Wissenschaften
BSAWL — Berichte. Verhandlungen der Saechsischen Gesellschaft der Wissenschaftzu Leipzig
BSB — Ball State Business Review
BSBAP — Bulletin. Societe Royale Belge d'Anthropologie et de Prehistoire
BSBB — Bulletin. Societe des Bibliophiles Belges Seant a Mons
BSBBM — Bulletin. Societe des Bibliophiles Belges Seant a Mons
BSBC — Boletin de la Sociedad de Biologia (Concepcion)
BSBE — Bulletin. Societe Belfortaine d'Emulation
BSBF — Bulletin de la Societe Botanique de France
BSBF — Bulletin. Societe des Bibliolatres de France
BSBFA — Bulletin. Societe Botanique de France
BSBG — Berichte. Schweizerische Botanische Gesellschaft
BSBG — Bulletin. Societe des Bibliophiles de Guyenne
BSBG — Bulletin de la Societe Royal Belge de Geographie
BSBG — Bulletin Societe Bretonne de Geographie
BSBGA — Berichte. Schweizerische Botanische Gesellschaft
BSBGD — Bulletin. Societe Belge de Geologie
BSBIA — Brookhaven Symposia in Biology
BSBIAW — Brookhaven Symposia in Biology
BSBI Conf Rep — BSBI [*Botanical Society of the British Isles*] Conference Reports
BSBL — Bulletin. Societe des Bibliophiles Liegeois
BS BI — Bundessteuerblatt

BS Borda — Bulletin. Societe de Borda
B S Bot Fr I — Bulletin. Societe Botanique de France. Premiere Partie
BSBPA — Bulletin. Societe Belge de Geologie, de Paleontologie, et d'Hydrologie [Later, Bulletin. Societe Belge de Geologie]
BSBPP — Bulletin. Societe Bibliographique des Publications Populaires
BSBQA — Bulletin. Societes Chimiques Belges
BSBR — Bollettino Sistematico di Bibliografia Romana
BSBS — Bollettino Storico-Bibliografico Subalpino
BSB Subalpino — Bollettino Storico-Bibliografico Subalpino
BSC — Bibliotheque de Sociologie Contemporaine
BSC — Bollettino Storico Catanese
BSC — Bollettino Storico Cremonese
BSC — Bulletin et Memoires. Societe Archeologique et Historique de la Charente (Angouleme)
BSC — Bulletin. Societe Chateaubriand
B Sc Ak Med — Bulletin. Schweizerische Akademie der Medizinischen Wissenschaften
BSCAM — Bulletin des Seances. Cercle Archeologique de Mons
BSCat — Bollettino Storico Catanese
BSCC — Boletin. Sociedad Castellonense de Cultura
BSCFA — Bulletin. Societe Chimique de France
B Sch — Black Scholar
BSCh — Bulletin de la Societe Chateaubriand
B S Ch Fr I — Bulletin. Societe Chimique de France. Premiere Partie
B S Ch Fr II — Bulletin. Societe Chimique de France. Deuxieme Partie
B S Chim Be — Bulletin. Societes Chimiques Belges
B Sch Or Afr Stud — Bulletin. School of Oriental and African Studies
B Sch Orien — Bulletin. School of Oriental and African Studies
B Sch Orient Afr Stud — Bulletin. School of Oriental and African Studies
BSci — Behavioral Science
BSCIA — Bulletin. Societe de Chimie Biologique
B Sci Math — Bulletin des Sciences Mathematiques
BSCJ — Ball State Commerce Journal
BSCJA — Bristol Chamber of Commerce. Journal
BSCL — Business Service Checklist
BSCLA — Bulletin Annuel. Societe Suisse de Chronometrie et Laboratoire Suisse de Recherches Horlogeres
BScM — Bulletin des Sciences Mathematiques
BSCNA — Bulletin. Societe de Chimie Industrielle
B Sc Nat — Bulletin des Sciences Naturelles et de Geologie
BSCo — Bulletin. Societe des Lettres, Sciences, et Arts de la Correze
BSCP — Boletin de la Sociedad Cientifica del Paraguay y del Museo Dr. Andres Barbero Etnografico e Historico Natural [Asuncion]
BSCP Commun — BSCP [Biological Sciences Communication Project] Communique
BS Cr — Bollettino Storico Cremonese
BSCSD2 — British Society for Cell Biology. Symposium
BSC Stat — British Sulphur Corporation Ltd. Statistical Supplement
BSD — Bulletin. Societe d'Etudes Scientifiques et Archeologiques de Draguignan
BSD — Business Software Database
BSDP — Boletin del Seminario de Derecho Publico de la Escuela de Ciencias Juridicas y Sociales [Santiago de Chile]
BSDSL — Basler Studien zur Deutschen Sprache und Literatur
BSE — Bank Systems and Equipment
BSE — Brno Studies in English
BSE — Recherches Economiques de Louvain
BSEA — Boletin. Seminario de Estudios de Arte y Arqueologia
BSEAA — Boletin. Seminario de Estudios de Arte y Arqueologia
BSE Abb — Bulletin. Societe d'Emulation Historique et Litteraire d'Abbeville
B Seances Acad Roy Sci O-Mer — Bulletin des Seances. Academie Royale des Sciences d'Outre-Mer
BSE Aude — Bulletin. Societe d'Etudes Scientifiques de l'Aude
BSE Av — Bulletin. Societe d'Etudes d'Avallon
BSE Bour — Bulletin. Societe d'Emulation du Bourbonnais
BSE Bourbonn — Bulletin. Societe d'Emulation du Bourbonnais
BSEBourbonnais — Bulletin. Societe d'Emulation du Bourbonnais
BSEC — Bulletin. Societe d'Etudes Camerounaises
BSECA — Bollettino. Societa d'Esplorazione Commerciale
B Sec GP — Bulletin. Section de Geographie de Paris. Congres des Societies Savantes. Congres de Strasbourg
B Secretar — Boletin del Secretariado Tecnico
B Sect Geogr Soc Sav — Bulletin. Section de Geographie. Actes du 96e Congres National des Societes Savantes
BSED — Bulletin. Societe d'Etudes Dantesques. Centre Universitaire Mediterraneen
BSEDEIS — Bulletin SEDEIS
BSEE — Boletin. Sociedad Espanola de Excursiones
BSEE — Bulletin de la Societe Entomologique d'Egypte
BSEEAZ — Bulletin. Entomological Society of Egypt
BSEEH — Boletin de la Sociedad Ecuatoriana de Estudios Historicos Americanos
BSEF — Boletim. Sociedade de Estudios Filologicos
BSEF — Bulletin de la Societe Entomologique de France
BSEG — Bibliotheque de la Societe des Etudes Germaniques
BSEI — Bollettino della Societa Entomologica Italiana
BSEI — Bulletin. Societe des Etudes Indochinoises
BSEIC — Bulletin. Societe des Etudes Indochinoises
BSEIS — Bulletin de la Societe d'Etudes Indochinoises (Saigon)
B Seis S Am — Bulletin. Seismological Society of America
B Sel — Bombay Selections
BSEL — Bulletin. Societe des Etudes de Lettres de Lausanne
BSELB — Berita Selulosa
BSELot — Bulletin. Societe des Etudes Litteraires, Scientifiques, et Artistiques du Lot
BSEM — Boletim. Sociedade de Estudos de Macambique
BSEM — Bulletin de la Societe Entomologique de Mulhouse

B Sem EAA (Valladolid) — Boletin. Seminario de Estudios de Arte y Arqueologia (Valladolid)
B Sem Est Arte Arqueol Valladolid — Boletin. Seminario de Estudios de Arte y Arqueologia de Valladolid
BSEn — Bol'shaia Sovietskaia Entsiklopediia (2nd ed.)
BSEND — Building Services and Environmental Engineer
BSEO — Bulletin. Societe d'Etudes Oceaniennes
BSEPC — Bulletin. Societe d'Etudes de la Province de Cambrai
BSEPE4 — Baltic Sea Environment. Proceedings
BSEPT — Bulletin Scientifique. Ecole Polytechnique de Timisoara
BSEQA — Business Systems and Equipment
Bser — Bollingen Series
BSER — Bulletin. Societe Ernest Renan
B Serv Carte Geol — Bulletin. Service de la Carte Geologique de la France
B Serv Carte Geol Alg — Bulletin. Service de la Carte Geologique de l'Algerie
B Serv Carte Phytogeogr — Bulletin. Service de la Carte Phytogeographique
B Serv Soc Caisses Assur Malad — Bulletin. Service Social des Caisses d'Assurance Maladie
B Serv Tunis Statist — Bulletin. Service Tunisien des Statistiques
BSESD — Bulletin. School of Engineering and Architecture of Sakarya
BSES News — British Schools Exploring Society. News
BSESNN — Bulletin. Societe d'Etude des Sciences Naturelles de Nimes
B Sete — Bulletin. Societe d'Etudes Scientifiques de Sete et de la Region
BSF — Bulletin. Societe Francaise d'Archeologie Classique
BSF — Bulletin. Societe Francaise d'Egyptologie
BSF — Bulletin. Societe Francaise de Numismatique
BSFA Bull — BSFA [British Steel Founders' Association] Bulletin
BSFAC — Bulletin. Societe Francaise d'Archeologie Classique
BSFCA — Bollettino Scientifico. Facolta di Chimica Industriale di Bologna
BSFE — Bulletin de la Societe Fouad I d'Entomologie
BSFE — Bulletin. Societe Francaise d'Egyptologie
BSFEA — Bulletin. Societe Francaise des Electriciens
BSFEM — Bulletin. Societe Francaise d'Etudes Mariales
BSFF — Bollettino. Societa Filologica Friulana
BSFIA — Bulletin. Sport Fishing Institute
BSFN — Bulletin. Societe Francaise de Numismatique
BSFP — Bulletin. Societe Francaise de Philosophie
BSFR — Bollettino. Societa Filologica Romana
B S Fr Cer — Bulletin. Societe Francaise de Ceramique
B S Fr D Sy — Bulletin. Societe Francaise de Dermatologie et de Syphiligraphie
B S Fr Min — Bulletin. Societe Francaise de Mineralogie et de Cristallographie
BSFRS — Bulletin. Sea Fisheries Research Station [Caesarea, Israel]
BSG — Buletinul. Societatii Geografice Romine
BSG — Bulletin. Societe de Geographie
BSGA — Bulletin. Societe de Geographie d'Anvers
BSGAE — Boletin. Sociedad General de Autores de Espana
BSGAE — Bulletin der Schweizerischen Gesellschaft fuer Anthropologie und Ethnologie
BSGAO — Bulletin. Societe de Geographie et d'Archeologie d'Oran
BSGB — Boletin de la Sociedad Geografica de Colombia (Bogota)
BSGC — Bulletin de la Societe de Geographie Commerciale de Paris
BSGCH — Bulletin. Societe de Geographie Commerciale du Havre
BSGCP — Bulletin. Societe de Geographie Commerciale de Paris
BSGE — Bulletin. Societe de Geographie d'Egypte
BSGE — Bulletin. Societe Royale de Geographie d'Egypte
BSGEN — Bulletin. Societe Geographie de l'Est (Nancy)
BSGF — Bulletin. Societe Geologique de France
BSGG — Bolletino. Societa Geographica (Genoa)
BSGHSC — Boletin de la Sociedad Geographica e Historica de Santa Cruz [Bolivia]
BSGI — Bollettino. Societa Geografica Italiana
BSGIA — Bollettino. Societa Geografica Italiana
BSGL — Boletim. Sociedade de Geografia de Lisboa
BSGL — Boletin de la Sociedad de Geografia de Lima
BSGL — Bulletin. Societe de Geographie de Lyon
BSGLi — Bulletin. Societe de Geographie de Lille
BSGLP — Boletin de la Sociedad Geografica de La Paz
BSGM — Boletin de la Sociedad Geografica de Madrid
BSGM — Boletin. Sociedad Geografica Nacional (Madrid)
BSGP — Boletim da Sociedade de Geografia de Lisboa
BSGP — Boletim. Sociedade Geologica de Portugal
BSGP — Bulletin. Societe de Geographie de Paris
BSGQ — Bulletin. Societe de Geographie de Quebec
BSGR — Buletinul. Societatii de Geografie al Romaniei
BSGR — Buletinul Societatii Geografice din Republica Socialista Romania
BSGR — Buletinul Societatii Geografice Romane
BSGR — Bulletin. Societe de Geographie de Rochefort
BSGRE — Bulletin. Societe Geographie de l'Egypte
BSGRSR — Buletinul Societatii Geografice din Republica Socialista Romania
BSGS — Boletin de la Sociedad Geografica de Sucre
BSGW — Berichte. Verhandlungen der Saechsischen Gesellschaft der Wissenschaften
BSH — Bulletin. Section Historique. Academie Roumaine
BSHA — Bulletin. Societe de l'Histoire de l'Art Francais
BSHAB — Bulletin. Societe d'Histoire et d'Archeologie de Beaucaire
BSHA Br — Bulletin. Societe d'Histoire et d'Archeologie de Bretagne
BSHAF — Bulletin. Societe de l'Histoire de l'Art Francais
BSHA Geneve — Bulletin. Societe d'Histoire et d'Archeologie de Geneve
BSHAM — Societes d'Histoire et d'Archeologie de la Meuse
BSHA Maur — Bulletin. Societe d'Histoire et d'Archeologie de la Maurienne
BSHAN — Bulletin. Societe Historique et Archeologique de Nogent-sur-Marne et du Canton de Nogent
BSHA Or — Bulletin. Societe Historique et Archeologique de l'Orne
BSHAP — Bulletin. Societe Historique et Archeologique du Perigord
BSHAP — Provincia. Bulletin de la Societe d'Histoire et d'Archeologie de Marseille et de la Provence

BSHA Par — Bulletin. Societe Historique et Archeologique. Les Amis des Antiquites de Parthenay
BSHAPerigord — Bulletin. Societe Historique et Archeologique du Perigord
BSHAR — Bulletin. Section Historique. Academie Roumaine
BSHAV — Bulletin. Societe d'Histoire et d'Archeologie de Vichy et des Environs
BSH Corbeil — Bulletin. Societe Historique et Archeologique de Corbeil, d'Etampes et du Hurepoix
BSH Correze — Bulletin. Societe Scientifique, Historique, et Archeologique de la Correze
BSHDS — Bulletin. Societe Historique et Scientifique des Deaux-Sevres
BSHEW — Bulletin. Societe pour l'Histoire des Eglises Wallonnes
BSH Gien — Bulletin. Societe Historique, Archeologique, et Artistique du Giennois
BSHM — Bulletin. Societe d'Histoire de la Medecine
BSHM — Bulletin. Societe d'Histoire Moderne
BSHM — Bulletin. Societe Francaise d'Histoire de la Medecine et de ses Filiales
BSH Maroc — Bulletin. Societe d'Histoire du Maroc
BSHMC — Bulletin. Section d'Histoire Moderne et Contemporaine
BSHNA — Bulletin de la Societe d'Histoire Naturelle de l'Afrique du Nord
BSHNT — Bulletin de la Societe d'Histoire Naturelle de Toulouse
BSHP — Bulletin. Societe de l'Histoire du Protestantisme Francais
BSHPF — Bulletin. Societe de l'Histoire du Protestantisme Francais
BSHPIF — Bulletin. Societe Historique de Paris et de l'Ile de France
BSHS — Bulletin. Societe d'Histoire et de Geographie de la Region de Setif
BSHSL — Bulletin Signaletique. Histoire et Science de la Litterature
BSHST — Bulletin Signaletique. Histoire des Sciences et des Techniques
BSHT — Bulletin. Societe d'Histoire du Theatre
BSHY — Bulletin. Societe des Sciences Historiques de l'Yonne
BSI — Bollettino Storico della Svizzera Italiana
BSI — Bulletin Social des Industriels
BSI — Bulletin. Societe des Etudes Indochinoises
BSIAD — Bulletin. South African Institute of Assayers and Analysts
BSIBA — Bollettino. Societa Italiana di Biologia Sperimentale
BSIC — Bulletin. Societe des Etudes Indochinoises
B Siena — Bullettino Sienese di Storia Patria
Bsig — Bulletin Signaletique
B Sign — Bulletin Signaletique
BSignHum — Bulletin Signaletique. Sciences Humaines, Etc.
BSII — Bollettino degli Studi Inglesi in Italia
BSINA — BSI [*British Standards Institution*] News
BSI News — BSI [*British Standards Institution*] News
BSIPA — Buletinul Stiintific. Institutului Politehnic
BSIS — Society for Italian Studies
BSI Sales Bull — BSI [*British Standards Institution*] Sales Bulletin
BSJ — Baker Street Journal
BSJKH — Bulletin de la Societe J.-K. Huysmans
BSKG — Beitraege zur Saechsischen Kirchengeschichte
BSKG — Bulletin. Societe Khedivale de Geographie
BSL — Bollettino Storico Livornese
BSL — Bulletin. Societe de Linguistique de Paris
BSL — Bulletin. Societe Scientifique et Litteraire du Limbourg
BSL — Byzantino-Slavica
BSLAM — Bulletin. St. Louis City Art Museum
BSLELEP — Bulletin. Societe Lorraine des Etudes Locales dans l'Enseignement Public
BSLLW — Bulletin. Societe de Langue et Litterature Wallonnes
BSLP — Bulletin. Societe de Linguistique de Paris
BSM — Beitraege zur Schweizerdeutschen Mundartforschungen
BSM — Bollettino. Associazione Internazionale degli Studi Mediterranei
BSM — Bollettino di Studi Mediterranei
BSM — Bollettino Storico Mantovano
BSM — British Studies Monitor
BSM — Bulletin des Sciences Mathematiques
BSM — Bulletin Statistique Mensuel
BSMA — Boletin de la Sociedad Cientifica de Paraguay y del Museo Andres Barbero (Asuncion)
BS Mar — Bollettino. Societa Storica Maremmana
B S Math Fr — Bulletin. Societe Mathematique de France
BSMHA — Bulletins et Memoires. Societe Medicale des Hopitaux de Paris
BSMHB — Biophysics of Structure and Mechanism
BSMMDY — Boletin. Sociedad Mexicana de Micologia
BSN — Buletinul. Societatii Numismatice Romane
BSNA — Bulletin. Societe Nationale des Antiquaires de France
BSNAF — Bulletin. Societe Nationale des Antiquaires de France
BSN Ain — Bulletin. Societe des Naturalistes et des Archeologiques de l'Ain
BSNAP — Bulletin. Societe Normande d'Archeologie Prehistorique et Historique
Bsn Atlant — Business Atlanta
BSNG — Bulletin de la Societe Neuchateloise de Geographie
BSNG — Bulletin des Sciences Naturelles et de Geologie
BSNM — Bulletin de la Societe des Naturalistes de Moscou
BSNotes — Browning Society. Notes
BSNR — Buletinul Societatii Naturalistilor din Romania
BSNR — Buletinul. Societatii Numismatice Romane
BSNRB — Binnenschiffahrts-Nachrichten
Bsn Record — Business Record
BSNS — Bollettino della Sezione di Novara della Regia Deputazione Subalpina di Storia Patria
Bsns Abroad — Business Abroad
Bsns & Tech Sources — Business and Technology Sources
Bsns Automation — Business Automation
BSNSDN — Boletim Tecnico. Servico Nacional de Levantamento e Conservacao de Solos
Bsns Ed Forum — Business Education Forum
Bsns Ed World — Business Education World
Bsns Hist R — Business History Review
Bsns Lit — Business Literature

Bsns Mgt — Business Management
Bsns Mgt (London) — Business Management (London)
Bsns Revw — Business Review
Bsns W — Business Week
Bsns W — Business World
Bsn SW Fla — Business View of Southwest Florida
BSO — Business Owner
BSO — Monthly Bulletin of Statistics
BSOA — Bulletin. School of Oriental and African Studies
BSOAS — Bulletin. School of Oriental and African Studies
B Soc A Champ — Bulletin. Societe d'Archeologique Champenoise
B Soc Anthrop — Bulletin. Societe d'Anthropologie
B Soc Anthropol Paris — Bulletins et Memoires. Societe d'Anthropologie de Paris
B Soc Arch Al — Bulletin. Societe d'Archeologie d'Alexandrie
B Soc Archeol Hist Limousin — Bulletin. Societe Archeologique et Historique du Limousin
B Soc Arch Eure-Et-Loir — Bulletin. Societes Archeologiques d'Eure-Et-Loir
B Soc Arch HCH — Bulletin. Societe Archeologique et Historique des Hauts Cantons de l'Herault
B Soc Arqueol Luliana — Boletin. Sociedad Arqueologica Luliana
B Soc Belge Et Exp — Bulletin. Societe Belge d'Etudes et d'Expansion
B Soc Belge Et Geogr — Bulletin. Societe Belge d'Etudes Geographiques
B Soc Belge Geol Paleont Hydrol — Bulletin. Societe Belge de Geologie, de Paleontologie, et d'Hydrologie [*Later,Bulletin. Societe Belge de Geologie*]
B Soc Bulg — Bulletin. Societe Archeologique Bulgare
B Soc Castell Cult — Boletin. Sociedad Castellonense de Cultura
B Soc Catalana Est Hist — Butlleti de la Societat Catalana d'Estudis Historics
B Soc Espan Amigos Castillos — Boletin. Sociedad Espanola de Amigos de los Castillos
B Soc Espan Excurs — Boletin. Sociedad Espanola de Excursiones
B Soc Ethnogr Limousin Marche — Bulletin. Societe d'Ethnographie du Limousin et de la Marche
B Soc Et Indoch — Bulletin. Societe des Etudes Indochinoises
B Soc Et Indochinoises — Bulletin. Societe des Etudes Indochinoises
B Soc Et Ocean — Bulletin. Societe d'Etudes Oceaniennes
B Soc Et Sci Aude — Bulletin. Societe d'Etudes Scientifiques de l'Aude
B Soc Franc Sociol — Bulletin. Societe Francaise de Sociologie
BSocFrEg — Bulletin. Societe Francaise d'Egyptologie
B Soc Fr Hist Nat Ant — Bulletin. Societe Francaise d'Histoire Naturelle des Antilles
B Soc Fr Min Crist — Bulletin. Societe Francaise de Mineralogie et de Cristallographie
B Soc Geogr — Boletin. Real Sociedad Geografica
B Soc Geogr — Bulletin. Societe de Geographie de Lille
B Soc Geogr Comml Paris — Bulletin. Societe de Geographie Commerciale de Paris
B Soc Geogr Eg — Bulletin. Societe de Geographie d'Egypte
B Soc Geogr Etud Colon Mars — Bulletin. Societe de Geographie et d'Etudes Coloniales de Marseille
B Soc Geogr Hellen — Bulletin. Societe de Geographie Hellenique
B Soc Geogr Mars — Bulletin. Societe de Geographie de Marseille
B Soc Geogr Paris — Bulletin. Societe de Geographie de Paris
B Soc Geogr Toul — Bulletin. Societe de Geographie de Toulouse
B Soc Geol Belg — Bulletin. Societe Geologique de Belgique
B Soc Geol Fr — Bulletin. Societe Geologique de France
B Soc Geol Fr Notes Mem — Bulletin. Societe Geologique de France. Notes et Memoires
B Soc Langued Gegr — Bulletin. Societe Languedocienne de Geographie
B Soc Ling P — Bulletin. Societe de Linguistique de Paris
B Soc Linguist Paris — Bulletin. Societe de Linguistique de Paris
B Soc Linn — Bulletin. Societe Linneenne
B Soc Litt Hist Brie — Bulletin. Societe Litteraire et Historique de la Brie
B Soc Myth Franc — Bulletin. Societe de Mythologie de France
B Soc Neuch Geogr — Bulletin. Societe Neuchatelloise de Geographie
B Soc Oceanogr Fr — Bulletin. Societe d'Oceanographie de France
B Soc Path Exot — Bulletin. Societe de Pathologie Exotique
B Soc Path Exot Fil — Bulletin. Societe de Pathologie Exotique et de ses Filiales
B Soc Prehist Fr — Bulletin. Societe Prehistorique Francaise
B Soc Prehist Franc — Bulletin. Societe Prehistorique Francaise
B Soc Prehist Franc C R Mens — Bulletin. Societe Prehistorique Francaise. Comptes Rendus Mensuels
B Soc Roy Belge Anthropol — Bulletin. Societe Royale Belge d'Anthropologie
B Soc Roy Belge Anthropol Prehis — Bulletin. Societe Royale Belge d'Anthropologie et de Prehistoire
B Soc Roy For Belge — Bulletin. Societe Royale Forestiere Belge
B Soc Sci Nat Tunisie — Bulletin. Societe des Sciences Naturelles de Tunisie
B Soc Suisse Am — Bulletin. Societe Suisse des Americanistes
B Soc Suisse American — Bulletin. Societe Suisse des Americanistes
B Soc Thanatologie — Bulletin. Societe de Thanatologie
B Soc Vascongada — Boletin. Real Sociedad Vascongada de Amigos del Pais
B Soc Vosg — Bulletin. Societe Philomatique Vosgienne
BSONA — Byulleten' Stantsii Opticheskogo Nablyudeniya Iskusstvennykh Sputnikov Zemli
BSOS — Bulletin. School of Oriental Studies
BSOSt — Bulletin. School of Oriental and African Studies. University of London
BSP — Bibliographical Society of America. Papers
BSP — Bibliographical Society [*London*]. Publications
BSP — Bollettino Storico Piacentino
BSP — Bollettino Storico Pistoiese
BSP — British Space Fiction Magazine
BSP — Bulletin des Sciences Politiques
BSPA — Bollettino. Societa Piemontese di Archeologia
BSPABA — Bollettino. Societa Piemontese di Archeologia e Belle Arti
BSPar — Bulletin. Societe de l'Histoire de Paris et de l'Ile-de-France
BSPBA — Bulletin. Societe de Pharmacie de Bordeaux

BSPC — Bulletin de la Societe Paul Claudel
BSPEA — Bulletin. Societe de Pathologie Exotique et de Ses Filiales
BSPEEQ — Boletim. Sociedade Portuguesa de Entomologia
BSPF — Bulletin. Societe Prehistorique Francaise
BSPFA — Bulletin de la Societe des Professeurs Francais en Amerique
B S Ph — Bulletin. Societe Francaise de Philosophie
BSPi — Bollettino Storico Pistoiese
BSPI — Bulletin. Societe de l'Histoire de Paris et de l'Ile-de-France
BSPIA — Bollettino. Societa Paleontologica Italiana
BSPiac — Bollettino di Storia Piacentina
BS Piem — Bollettino. Societa Piemontese di Archeologia e di Belli Arti
BSPis — Bollettino Storico Pisano
BSPL — Biological Society of Pakistan (Lahore)
BSPL — Bulletin. Societe Polonaise de Linguistique
BSPM — Bulletin. Societe de Prehistoire du Maroc
BSPN — Bollettino Storico per la Provincia de Novara
BSPR — Bulletin. Societe des Amis de Port-Royal
BSPS — Bollettino. Societa Pavese di Storia Patria
BSPSP — Bollettino. Societa Pavese di Storia Patria
BSPTA — Buletinul Stiintific si Tehnic. Institutului Politehnic (Timisoara)
BSPTR — Beaufort Sea Project. Technical Report
BSPU — Bollettino. Regia Deputazione di Storia Patria per l'Umbria
BSQ — Business Quarterly
BSR — British School of Archaeology at Rome. Papers
BSR — Buletinul Statistic al Romaniei
BSR — Papers. British School at Rome
BSRA — Bulletin de la Societe Royale d'Anthropologie et de Prehistoire
BSRAA — Bulletin. Societe Royale d'Archeologie d'Alexandrie
BSRBAP — Bulletin. Societe Royale Belge d'Anthropologie et de Prehistoire
BSRBG — Bulletin de la Societe Royale Belge de Geographie
BSRGA — Bulletin. Societe Royale de Geographie d'Anvers
BSRGE — Bulletin. Societe Royale de Geographie d'Egypte
BSRIA — Southern Research Institute. Bulletin
BSRMA — Bulletin. Institut National de la Sante et de la Recherche Medicale
BSRP — Papers. British School at Rome
BSR Papers — Papers. British School at Rome
BSRV-L — Bulletin. Societe Royale de Vieux-Liege
BSS — Birger Sjoberg Sallskapet
BSS — Buletin per Shkencat Shoqerore
BSS — Bulletin de Statistique Suisse
BSS — Bulletin of Spanish Studies
BSS — Bulletin. Societe des Sciences Historiques et Naturelles de Semur-en-Auxois
BSS — Business and Society
BSSA — Bulletin de la Societe Suisse des Americanistes
BSSAD — Business SA
BSSAEO — Bulletin. Societe Suisse des Amis de l'Extreme-Orient
BSSAT — Bollettino di Studi Storici ed Archeologici di Tivoli e Regione
BS Sci Ed — Bulletin Signaletique. Sciences de l'Education
BS Sci L — Bulletin Signaletique. Sciences du Langage
B S Sci Med — Bulletin. Societe des Sciences Medicales du Grand-Duche de Luxembourg
BS Sci R — Bulletin Signaletique. Sciences Religieuses
BSSG — Bulletin. Societe Sultanieh de Geographie
BSSGC — Buletinul. Societatii de Stiinte Geologice din Republica Socialista Romania
BSSHC — Bulletin. Societe des Sciences Historiques et Naturelles de la Corse
BSSHN — Bulletin. Societe des Sciences Historiques et Naturelles de la Corse
BSSHNY — Bulletin. Societe des Sciences Historiques et Naturelles de l'Yonne
BSSHS — Bulletin. Societe des Sciences Historiques et Naturelles de Semur-en-Auxois
BSSI — Bollettino Storico della Svizzera Italiana
BSSI — Bulletin. Societe Libre d'Emulation du Commerce et de l'Industrie de la Seine-Inferieure
BSSIA — Byulleten' Sovet po Seismologii
BSSL — Bibliographien zum Studium der Deutschen Sprache und Literatur
BSSL — Bulletin. Societe des Sciences et des Lettres de Lodz
BSSLL — Bulletin. Societe Scientifique et Litteraire du Limbourg
BSSNB — National Bureau of Standards. Building Science Series
BSSNN — Bulletin. Societe d'Etude des Sciences Naturelles de Nimes
BS Soc Ethn — Bulletin Signaletique. Sociologie-Ethnologie
BSSP — Bollettino Senese di Storia Patria
BSSS — Bulletin Mensuel. Societe des Sciences de Semur
BSSV — Bollettino. Societa di Studi Valdesi
BSSY — Bulletin. Societe des Sciences Historiques de l'Yonne
BSSYA — Biochemical Society. Symposia
B St — Balkan Studies
BSt — Berliner Studien fuer Klassische Philologie und Archaeologie
BSt — Biblische Studien
BST — Biocontrol Science and Technology
BST — Bronte Society. Transactions
BST — Bulletin. Societe Toulousaine d'Etudes Classiques
B St Ac — Buletinul Stiintifice. Academia Romana. Sectia de Stiinte Isotrice, Filozofice,si Economice
B Statec — Bulletin du Statec
B Statist (Bruxelles) — Bulletin de Statistique (Bruxelles)
B Stat M — Bollettino Mensile di Statistica
BStB — Beitraege zur Statistik des Koenigreichs Bayern
BSTCA — Bulletin. Standard Oil Company of California
BSTCF — Ball State Teachers College Forum [Later, Ball State University Forum]
BSTEA — British Steelmaker
BSTEC — Bulletin. Societe Toulousaine d'Etudes Classiques
BSt(F) — Biblische Studien (Freiburg)
BSTG — Bulletin. Societe Theophile Gautier
BSTGA — Bulletin. South Texas Geological Society

BSTIS — Biweekly Scientific and Technical Intelligence Summary
BSTJ — Bell System Technical Journal
BSTJA — Bell System Technical Journal
B St KPA — Berliner Studien fuer Klassische Philologie und Archeologie
B St Lat — Bollettino di Studi Latini
BStM — Bollettino. Associazione Internazionale degli Studi Mediterranei
BSTPP — Bulletin. Societe Tournaisienne de Paleontologie et de Prehistoire
BStud Lat — Bollettino di Studi Latini
B Stupefiants — Bulletin des Stupefiants
BSU — Transport Echo. The Benelux Transport Magazine
BSUCA — Buletinul Stiintific al Universitatii Craiova
BSUF — Ball State University Forum
BSUSSR — Bulletin. Institute for the Study of the USSR
BSVAH — Bulletin. Societe Vervietoise d'Archeologie et d'Histoire
BSVasc — Boletin. Real Sociedad Vascongada de Amigos del Pais
BSVCN — Boletin de la Sociedad Venezolana de Ciencias Naturales
BSVPB — Bulletin. Slovenskej Pol'nohospodarskej Akademie. Vyskumneho Ustavu Potravinarskeho
BSVSAQ — Kongelige Danske Videnskabernes Selskab. Biologiske Skrifter
BSW — Bank of New South Wales. Review
Bs Worcstr — Business Worcester
BSY — Bank Systems and Equipment
BSYSA — Bulletin Scientifique. Conseil des Academies des Sciences et des Arts de la RSFde Yougoslavie. Section A. Sciences Naturelles, Techniques, et Medicales
B Sz — Budapesti Szemle
B S Zool Fr — Bulletin. Societe Zoologique de France
BT — Berlingske Tidende
BT — Bible Today
BT — Bible Translator
BT — Bibliotheque de Theologie
BT — Big Table
BT — Bioprocessing Technology
BT — Bio/Technology
BT — Black Times
BT — Bulletin of Tibetology
BT — Business Traveler Magazine
BTA — Beteram (Tel Aviv)
BTAED — BMWI Tagesnachrichten
BTA J — Business Teachers Association of New York State. Journal
BTAM — Bulletin de Theologie Ancienne et Medievale
BTAPB — Bitumen, Teere, Asphalte, Peche, und Verwandte Stoffe
BTAQAO — Universidade de Sao Paulo. Escola Superior de Agricultura Luiz De Queiroz. Boletim Tecnico Cientifico
B Tarn-et-Garone — Bulletin Archeologique, Historique, et Artistique. Societe Archeologique de Tarn-et-Garonne
BTAS — Bulletin. Texas Archaeological Society
BTB — Biblical Theology Bulletin
BTBCA — Bulletin. Torrey Botanical Club
BTBib — Bulletin de Theologie Biblique
BTBVA — Bulletin Technique. Bureau Veritas
BTCAB — Boletim Tecnico. Centro de Tecnologia Agricola e Alimentar (Brazil)
Bt Cb — Botanisches Centralblatt
BTCCDT — Centro Nacional de Investigaciones de Cafe. Boletin Tecnico
BTCHDA — Bio-Technology
BTD — Bank of Thailand. Monthly Bulletin
BTD — Bulletin. Commission Royale de Toponymie et de Dialectologie
BTE — Belfast Telegraph
BTEKA — Byulleten' Tekhniko-Ekonomicheskoi Informatsii
BTERD — Biological Trace Element Research
B Tex Agric Exp Stn — Bulletin. Texas Agricultural Experiment Station
B Textil Anc — Bulletin de Liaison. Centre International d'Etude des Textiles Anciens
BTF — Betriebswirtschaftliche Forschung und Praxis
BTFCA — Bulletin Technique. Societe Francaise des Constructions Babcock et Wilcox
BTFFA — Bulletin Technique des Mines de Fer de France
BTFIA — Bollettino Tecnico FINSIDER
BTG — Butterworths Tax Guide
Bt Gz — Botanical Gazette
BTH — Bibliotheque de Theologie Historique
BTh — Bulletin de Theologie Ancienne et Medievale
BTH Act — BTH [British Thomson-Houston Co.] Activities
BTHDA — Birth Defects. Original Article Series
BTHG — Business Traveler Hotel Guide [National Association of Business Travel Agents]
BThom — Bulletin Thomiste
BTI — Boletim do Trabalho Industrial
BTI — British Technology Index [Later, Current Technology Index]
BTI — Buddhist Text Information
BTI — Business Traveler International
BTIAL — Bulletin Trimestriel. Institut Archeologique du Luxembourg
BTIALux — Bulletin Trimestriel. Institut Archeologique du Luxembourg
B Tibetol — Bulletin of Tibetology
BTIDA — Byulleten' Tsentra po Yadernym Dannym
BTIIA6 — Bulletin Technique d'Information des Ingenieurs des Services Agricoles
BTIPAR — Instituto de Pesquisa Agropecuaria do Norte [IPEAN]. Boletim Tecnico
BTITA — Bulletin. Tokyo Institute of Technology
BTJ — British Business
BTL — Bottomline
BTLV — Bijdragen tot de Taal-Land- en Volkenkunde
BTLVNI — Bijdragen tot de Taal-Land- en Volkenkunde van Nederlandsche-Indie
BTMDA — Bulletin. Tokyo Medical and Dental University
BTMG — Blaetter der Thomas Mann Gesellschaft
BTMNA — Bitamin

BTMSD — Bio Times
BTN — Bibliotheca Theologica Norvegica
BTN — British Travel News
BTNKA — Biotechniek
Bt Not — Botaniska Notiser
BTNQA — Botanique
BTONA — Beton, Herstellung, Verwendung
B Tor Bot C — Bulletin. Torrey Botanical Club
B Tournal — Bulletin. Societe Tournaisienne de Paleontologie et de Prehistoire
B Tours — Bulletin Trimestriel. Societe Archeologique de Touraine
BTP — Bibliotheque des Textes Philosophiques
BTPC — Bulletin des Tribunaux de Police Congolais
BTPGA — Beitraege zur Pathologie
BTQ — Banque de Terminologie du Quebec
BTQSA — Bulletin Technique de la Suisse Romande
BTR — British Tax Review
BTR — Business Trends. A Concise and Systematic Weekly Report to Management on the Argentine Economy
Btr Allg Bot — Beitraege zur Allgemeinen Botanik
Btr An Pl — Beitraege zur Anatomie und Physiologie. Eckhard. Giessen
Btr Anthropol Bayern — Beitraege zur Anthropologie und Urgeschichte Bayerns
Btr Bayer Kirchgesch — Beitraege zur Bayerischen Kirchengeschichte
Btr Diplomat — Beitraege zur Diplomatik
Btr Geol Erforsch Dt Schutzgeb — Beitraege zur Geologischen Erforschung der Deutschen Schutzgebiete
Btr Geops — Beitraege zur Geophysik
Btr Gesch Abtei Werden — Beitraege zur Geschichte der Abtei Werden
Btr Gesch Dt Spr — Beitraege zur Geschichte der Deutschen Sprache und Literatur
Btr Gesch Dt Spr — Paul und Braunes Beitraege zur Geschichte der Deutschen Sprache und Literatur
Btr Gesch Rostock — Beitraege zur Geschichte der Stadt Rostock
B Trim Banque France — Bulletin Trimestriel. Banque de France
B Trim Ecole Nat Sante Publ — Bulletin Trimestriel. Ecole Nationale de la Sante Publique
B Tr Int Ch Fer — Bulletin des Transports Internationaux par Chemins de Fer
Btr Kde Indogerm Spr — Beitraege zur Kunde der Indogermanischen Sprachen
Btr Klin Chir — Bruns Beitraege zur Klinischen Chirurgie
Btr Klin Tuberk — Beitraege zur Klinik der Tuberkulose
Btr Natdenkmalpfl — Beitraege zur Naturdenkmalpflege
BTROA — Biotropica
Btr Pflanzenzucht — Beitraege zur Pflanzenzucht
Btr Rechtsgesch Tirols — Beitraege zur Rechtsgeschichte Tirols
Btr Turn u Sportwiss — Beitraege zur Turn- und Sportwissenschaft
BTS — Business Times. An Economic and Business Review
BTSAAM — Bulletin Trimestriel. Societe Academique des Antiquaires de la Morinie
BTSAP — Bulletin Trimestriel. Societe des Antiquaires de Picardie
BTSCB — Bulletin Technique de Securite et Salubrite. Institut National des Industries Extractives
BTSEAA — El Salvador. Direccion General de Investigaciones Agronomicas. Seccion de Entomologia. Boletin Tecnico
BTSZ — Belgisch Tijdschrift voor Sociale Zekerheid
BTTA — Journal. British Thoracic and Tuberculosis Association
BTTA Rev — BTTA [*British Thoracic and Tuberculosis Association*] Review
BTTCA9 — Inter-American Tropical Tuna Commission. Bulletin
BT Technol J — BT Technology Journal
BTTK — Belleten. Tuerk Tarih Kurumu
BTUPA — Bulletin. Union des Physiciens
BTVVA — Bulletin Technique Vevey
BTZBA — Beton i Zhelezobeton
Bt Ztg — Botanische Zeitung
BU — Blues Unlimited
BuA — Bulletin. Academie Royale de Belgique. Classe des Lettres et des Sciences Morales et Politiques
BUA — Bulletin. Universite l'Aurore
BuAJR — Bulletin des Amis de Jacques Riviere et Alain-Fournier
BUAM — Bibliotheque de l'Universite d'Aix-Marseille
BUAMD — Business America
BUAT — Toulouse. Universite. Bulletin de l'Universite et de l'Academie de Toulouse
BUB — Boletin. Unesco para las Bibliotecas
BuB — Buecherei und Bildung
BuB — Bulletin de la Societe des Amis de Georges Bernanos
BUBBA — Bundesbaublatt
BUBEA — Bulletin Belgicatom
BUBFA — Bulletin Biologique de la France et de la Belgique
BUBL — Building Blocks. Aboriginal Rights and Constitutional Update
BuBl — Burschenschaftliche Blaetter
BUC — Boletin. Universidad de Chile
BUCAB — Bulletin du Cancer
Buccal Nasal Adm Altern Parenter Adm Minutes Eur Symp — Buccal and Nasal Administration as an Alternative to Parenteral Administration.Minutes. European Symposium
BUCDA — Bulletin. Georgia Academy of Science
Buch & Schr — Buch und Schrift
Buchar- Univ- An Geol — Bucharest. Universitatea. Analele. Geologie
Buchar Univ An Ser Stiint Nat — Bucharest. Universitatea. Analele. Seria Stiintele Naturii
Buch Augenarzt — Bucherei des Augenarztes
Buch Ct App Cape G H — Buchanan's Appeal Court Reports, Cape Of Good Hope
Buchr Atomkenenerg — Buchreihe Atomkernenergie
Buchr Cusanus Ges — Buchreihe der Cusanus-Gesellschaft
BuCHS — Bucks County Historical Society. Papers
Buch und Bibl — Buch und Bibliothek
Bucknell Re — Bucknell Review
Bucknell Rev — Bucknell Review

BucksCoHS — Bucks County Historical Society. Papers
Bucks Records — Records of Buckinghamshire
BU Comp — Boletin. Universidad de Santiago de Compostela
Budapesti Magyar Kir Allami Vetoem Allomas Evi Muek — A Budapesti Magyar Kiralyi Allami Vetoemagvizsgalo Allomas Evi Muekoedese
Budapesti Musz Egy Elemiszerkem Tansz Kozl — Budapesti Muszaki Egyetem Elemiszerkemiai Tanszekenek Kozlemenyei
Budapesti Musz Egy Mezogazd Kem Technol Tansz Evk — Budapesti Muszaki Egyetem Mezogazdasagi Kemiai Technologiai Tanszekenek Evkonyve
Budapesti Musz Egy Mezogazd Kem Technol Tansz Kozl — Budapesti Muszaki Egyetem Mezogazdasagi Kemiai Technologiai Tanszekenek Kozlemenyei
Budapest Reg — Budapest Regisegei
Budavox Telecommun Rev — Budavox Telecommunication Review
Buddhica Brit — Buddhica Britannica
Bude — Collection des Universites de France. Association Guillaume Bude
Budget — Budget of the US Government
Budget Program Newsl — Budget and Program Newsletter
Budget SA — Budget of the US Government. Special Analyses
Budiv Mater Konstr — Budivel'ni Materialy i Konstruktsii
Budownictwo Roln — Budownictwo Rolnicze
BudR — Budapest Regisegei. Budapesti Toerteneti Muzeum
Bud Reg — Budapest Regisegei
BudS — Bulletin. Societe de l'Histoire du Protestantisme Francais
BUE — Bulletin. Faculty of Arts. University of Egypt
BueBpfl — Buecherei und Bildungspflege
BUECD — Bulletin d'Ecologie
Buech Augenarzt — Buecherei des Augenarztes
Buecher Arch Bienenk — Buecher des Archiv fuer Bienenkunde
Buecherei Bienenk — Buecherei fuer Bienenkunde
Buecher Wirt — Buecher fuer die Wirtschaft
Buech Fachlicher Wiss Schr Tech Hochsch Brno — Buecherei Fachlicher und Wissenschaftlicher Schriften der Technischen Hochschule in Brno
Buech Fachlicher Wiss Schr Tech Hochsch Brno A — Buecherei Fachlicher und Wissenschaftlicher Schriften der Technischen Hochschule in Brno. A
Buech Fachlicher Wiss Schr Tech Hochsch Brno B — Buecherei Fachlicher und Wissenschaftlicher Schriften der Technischen Hochschule in Brno. B
Buech Frauenarztes — Buecherei des Frauenarztes
Buendner Jb — Buendner Jahrbuch
Buendner Mbl — Buendner Monatsblatt
Buenos Aires M — Buenos Aires Musical
Buenos Aires Mus — Buenos Aires Musical
Buenos Aires (Prov) Com Invest Cient Monogr — Buenos Aires (Province). Comision de Investigaciones Cientificas. Monografias
Buerotech — Buerotechnik
Buerotech Autom & Organ — Buerotechnik Automation und Organisation
Buerotech und Org — Buerotechnik und Organisation
BUESD — Buerger im Staat
BueW — Buehne und Welt
Buf Bul — Buffalo Bulletin
Buffalo Gal Notes — Buffalo Fine Arts Academy. Albright Art Gallery. Notes
Buffalo Hist Soc Publ — Buffalo Historical Society. Publications
Buffalo L Rev — Buffalo Law Review
Buffalo Nw — Buffalo News
Buffalo Phil — Buffalo Philharmonic. Program Notes
Buffalo Soc Nat Sci Bull — Buffalo Society of Natural Sciences. Bulletin
Buffalo Soc N Sc B — Buffalo Society of Natural Sciences. Bulletin
BUFFB — Boletim. Universidade Federal do Parana. Fisica Teorica (Brazil)
Buff Law R — Buffalo Law Review
Buff LR — Buffalo Law Review
Buff L Rev — Buffalo Law Review
BUFORA Bull — BUFORA (British Unidentified Flying Object Research Association) Bulletin
BUFSA — Bulletin. Association Francaise pour l'Etude du Sol
BUG — Boletin. Universidad de Granada
BUGGA — Bulletin. Geological Survey of Great Britain
BuGL — Bulletin de la Guilde du Livre
BUGMAF — Geological Society of America. Bulletin
BUGTA — Bulletin of Grain Technology
BuH — Bulletin. History of Medicine
BuHB — Bulletin Henri Bosco
BuHT — Bulletin des Historiens du Theatre
BuI — Bulletin. Institute of Modern History. Academica Sinica
BUI — Nederland USSR Instituut. Maandberichten
BUIAA — Bulletin d'Informations Scientifiques et Techniques. Commissariat a l'Energie Atomique
BUIDD — Building Ideas
Build — Builder
Build — Building
Build & Archit — Building and Architecture
Build & Cons — Building and Construction
Build & Cons (VIC) — Building and Construction and Cazaly's Contract Reporter (Melbourne, Victoria)
Build & Decorating Materials — Building and Decorating Materials
Build & Eng — Building and Engineering
Build & Manuf — Building and Manufacturing
Build Arch Contr Eng — Builder Architect Contractor Engineer
Build Briefs Div Build Res CSIRO — Building Briefs. Division of Building Research. Commonwealth Scientific and Industrial Research Organisation
Build Cont Tex — Building Construction in Texas
Build Cont J Ir — Building and Contract Journal for Ireland
Build Decorating Mat — Building and Decorating Materials
Build Des Constr — Building Design and Construction
Build Des Jnl — Building Design Journal
Build Dig — Building Digest
Build Econ — Building Economist

Build Econ Let — Building Economics Letter
Build Ed — Buildings for Education
Build En Conserv — Buildings Energy Conservation
Build Energy Prog — Building Energy Progress
Build Eng Rev — Building and Engineering Review
Build Environ — Building and Environment
Builder (NSW) — Builder (New South Wales)
Builders Timber Merchants J — Builders and Timber Merchants Journal
Build Forum — Building Forum
Build (Hobart) — Building (Hobart)
Build Ideas — Building Ideas
Build Inf Bull — Building Information Bulletin
Building & Arch — Building and Architecture
Building Ltg and Engng — Building, Lighting, and Engineering
Building Ltg Engng — Building, Lighting, and Engineering
Building Sci Ser Nat Bur Stand US — Building Science Series. United States National Bureau of Standards
Build Int (Engl Ed) — Build International (English Edition)
Build J — Builders' Journal
Build Jnl — Buildings Journal
Build Light Eng — Building, Lighting, and Engineering
Build Ltg Engng — Building, Lighting, and Engineering
Build Mach Constr Methods — Building Machinery and Construction Methods
Build Maint — Building Maintenance
Build Mat — Building Materials, Components, and Equipment
Build Mat Dig — Building Materials Digest
Build Mater — Building Materials
Build Mater — Building Materials and Equipment
Build Mater & Equip — Building Materials and Equipment
Build Mater (Chicago) — Building Materials (Chicago)
Build Mater Equip (Syd) — Building Materials and Equipment (Sydney)
Build Materials — Building Materials
Build Mater Mag — Building Materials Magazine
Build Mater Moscow — Building Materials (Moscow)
Build Mon — Building Monthly
Build Note Natl Res Counc Can Div Build Res — Building Note. National Research Council of Canada. Division of Building Research
Build NSW — Builder NSW
Build Off Code Adm — Building Official and Code Administrator
Build Oper Manage — Building Operating Management
Build Own Man — Building Owner and Manager
Build Perm — Building-Permit Activity
Build Prod News — Building Products News
Build Prod Rep — Building Products Report
Build Res — Building Research
Build Res Assoc NZ Tech Pap P — Building Research Association of New Zealand. Technical Paper P
Build Res Establ Dig — Building Research Establishment. Digest
Build Res Estab (Sta) Digest — Building Research Establishment (Station). Digest
Build Res Inst Q — Building Research Institute Quarterly
Build Res News — Building Research News
Build Res Note Natl Res Counc Can Div Build Res — Building Research Note. National Research Council of Canada. Division of Building Research
Build Res Pract — Building Research and Practice
Build Res Stn Curr Pap — Building Research Station. Current Papers
Build Sci — Building Science
Build Sci Ser Natl Bur Stand — Building Science Series. United States National Bureau of Standards
Build Sci Ser Natl Bur Stand US — Building Science Series. United States National Bureau of Standards
Build Seals Sealants — Building Seals and Sealants
Build Serv — Building Services
Build Serv Eng — Building Services Engineer
Build Serv Eng Res — Building Services Engineering Research and Technology
Build Serv Eng Res and Technol — Building Services Engineering Research and Technology
Build Serv Environ (Eng) — Building Services and Environmental Engineer (England)
Build Stand — Building Standards
Build Steel — Building with Steel
Build Sup N — Building Supply News
Build Syst Des — Building Systems Design
Build Technol Manage — Building Technology and Management
Build Worker — Building Worker
Built Env — Built Environment
Built Envir — Built Environment
Built Environ — Built Environment
BUIMB — Bollettino. Unione Matematica Italiana. Series IV
BUIND — Business India
BUJ — Bombay University. Journal
BUJ — Boston University. Journal
BUJ — Business Japan
BUJPA — Bulletin. Japan Petroleum Institute
Bujq Soc — Bujqesia Socialiste
B u K — Bibel und Kirche
BUKEA — Busseiron Kenkyu
BUKKA — Bunko Kenkyu
Bukowin Landw Bl — Bukowinaer Landwirtschaftliche Blaetter
Bukow Landw Bl Czernowitz — Bukowinaer Landwirtschaftliche Blaetter (Czernowitz)
BUL — Boston University. Law Review
BUL — B + U. Bouw en Uitvoering van Gemeentewerken; Maandblad voor Functionarissen van de Diensten van Publieke en Openbare Werken
Bul — [The] Bulletin
BUL — Bulletin. Universite de Lyon

Bul Acad De Med Paris — Bulletin de l'Academie de Medecine de Paris
Bul Acad Inalte Stud Agron Cluj — Buletinul Academiei de Inalte Studii Agronomice din Cluj
Bul Acad Stiinte Repub Mold Stiinte Biol Chim — Buletinul Academiei de Stiinte a Republicii Moldova. Stiinte Biologice si Chimice
Bul Acad Stiinte RSS Mold Stiinte Biol Chim — Buletinul Academiei de Stiinte a RSS Moldovenesti. Stiinte Biologice si Chimice
Bul Ac Int — Bulletin. Groupe Belge des Auditeurs et Anciens Auditeurs. Academie deDroit International de La Haye
Bul Ac R — Bulletin. Academie Royale de Belgique. Classe des Lettres et desSciences Morales et Politiques
Bul Admin Penitentiaire — Bulletin. Administration Penitentiaire
Bul Afr Noire — Bulletin de l'Afrique Noire
Bul Agric Congo Belge — Bulletin Agricole du Congo Belge
Bul Akad Stiince RSS Moldoven — Buletinul Akademiei. Stiince a RSS Moldovenest
Bul ALO — Bulletin. Commission Royale des Anciennes Lois et Ordonnances deBelgique
Bul Am Acad Psy and L — Bulletin. American Academy of Psychiatry and the Law
Bul Am Cong Surv Map — Bulletin. American Congress on Surveying and Mapping
Bul Amnesty Int Can Sect — Bulletin. Amnesty International. Canadian Section
Bul/AMQ — Bulletin. Association Mathematique du Quebec
Bul Am Repub — Bulletin. International Bureau of the American Republics
Bul Am Soc Inf Sci — Bulletin of the American Society for Information Sciences
Bul Analytique Docum — Bulletin Analytique de Documentation Politique, Economique, et Sociale Contemporaine
Bul Anthro Surv India — Bulletin. Anthropological Survey of India
Bul Apic — Buletinul Apicultorilor
Bul Arab Chret — Bulletin d'Arabe Chretien
Bul Arch Maroc — Bulletin d'Archeologie Marocaine
Bul Arco — Bulletin de l'Arco
Bul Art Inst Chic — Bulletin. Art Institute of Chicago
Bul ASE — Bulletin d'Archeologie Sud-Est Europeenne
Bul Asoc Gen Ing Rom — Buletinul Asociatiei Generale a Inginerilor din Romania
Bul Asoc Gen Med Rom — Buletinul Asociatiunei Generale a Medicilor din Romania
Bul Asoc Gen Med Vet Rom — Buletinul Asociatiei Generale a Medicilor Veterinari din Romania
Bul Ass — Bulletin des Assurances
Bul Ass Guil Bude — Bulletin. Association Guillaume Bude
Bul Assoc Franc Etud Chin — Bulletin. Association Francaise d'Etudes Chinoises
Bul Assoc Lit Ling Comp — Bulletin. Association for Literary and Linguistic Computing
Bul Assoc Mine Am Quebec — Bulletin. Association des Mines d'Amiante du Quebec
Bul Atomic Sci — Bulletin of the Atomic Scientists
Bul Aust Asian Assn of Vic — Bulletin. Australian-Asian Association of Victoria
Bul Aust Assn Occupational Therapists — Bulletin. Australian Association of Occupational Therapists
Bul Aust Ind — Bulletin for Australian Industry
Bul Aust Industry — Bulletin for Australian Industry
Bul Aust Soc Stud Lab Hist — Bulletin. Australian Society for the Study of Labour History
Bul B — Bulletin of Bibliography
Bul Balai Penelitian Perkebunan Medan — Buletin Balai Penelitian Perkebunan Medan
Bul Belg — Bulletin. Banque Nationale de Belgique
Bul Bibl — Bulletin Bibliographique
Bul Bibl de France — Bulletin des Bibliotheques de France
Bul Bibliog — Bulletin of Bibliography
Bul Bibl Romane — Buletinul Bibliotecii Romane
Bul Black Theatre — Bulletin of Black Theatre
Bul BN — Bulletin d'Information et de Documentation. Banque Nationale
Bul Br Columbia Police Com — Bulletin. British Columbia Police Commission
Bul Bude — Bulletin. Association Guillaume Bude
Bul Build Assoc India — Bulletin. Builders Association of India
Bul Bus Res — Bulletin of Business Research
Bul Bus Research Ohio State Univ — Bulletin of Business Research. Ohio State University
Bul Cailor Fer — Buletinul Cailor Ferate
Bul Calif Acad Sci — Bulletin. California Academy of Sciences
Bul Can Celt Art Assoc — Bulletin. Canadian Celtic Arts Association
Bul Can Corp — Bulletin. Canada Corporations
Bul Can Corp Bankrupt Insolv — Bulletin. Canada Corporations. Bankruptcy and Insolvency
Bul Can Folk Mus Soc — Bulletin. Canadian Folk Music Society
Bul Can Stud — Bulletin of Canadian Studies
Bul Card Res Cent — Bulletin. Cardiovascular Research Center
Bul Carignan — Bulletin de Carignan
Bul Cent Bank Ceylon — Bulletin. Central Bank of Ceylon
Bul Cent Leisure Stud Acadia Univ — Bulletin. Centre of Leisure Studies. Acadia University
Bul Cent Mar Blanch — Bulletin. Centre Marin des Blanchons
Bul Central Res Inst Fukuoka Univ — Bulletin of Central Research Institute Fukuoka University
Bul Cercet Piscic — Buletinul de Cercetari Piscicole
Bul Cerc Gabriel Marcel — Bulletin. Cercle Gabriel-Marcel
Bul Cerc Juif — Bulletin. Cercle Juif
Bul Chambre Com Francaise — Bulletin. Chambre de Commerce Francaise et Organe Officiel du Tourisme Francaise en Australie
Bul Child Bks — Bulletin. Center for Children's Books
Bul Chr Inst Islamic St — Bulletin. Christian Institutes of Islamic Studies
Bul Christ Assoc Psych Stud — Bulletin. Christian Association for Psychological Studies

Bul Citoyen — Bulletin du Citoyen
Bul Cl Lo — Bulletin. Institute of Classical Studies. University of London
Bul Col Comp — Bulletin de Colonisation Comparee
Bul Com Arch Un Ch Can — Bulletin. Committee on Archives. United Church of Canada
Bul Com Electrotech Rom — Buletinul. Comitatul Electrotechnic Roman
Bul Comite D Etudes Hist Et Sci De L Afrique Occid Fr — Bulletin du Comite d'Etudes Historiques et Scientifiques de l'Afrique Occidentale Francaise
Bul Com Mnmt Istor — Buletinul Comisiunii Monumentelor Istorice
Bul Com Mon Ist — Buletinul Comisiunii Monumentelor Istorice a Romaniei
Bul Conc Asia Sch — Bulletin of Concerned Asian Scholars
Bul Confed Gen Pub — Bulletin. Confederation Generale de la Publicite
Bul Confed Gen Pub Eng Ed — Bulletin. Confederation Generale de la Publicite. English Edition
Bul Corresp Hellenique — Bulletin de Correspondance Hellenique
Bul Council Stud Rel — Bulletin. Council on the Study of Religion
Bul Cult Ferment Tutun — Buletinul Cultivarei si Fermentarei Tutunului
Bul Cult Res Inst — Bulletin of the Cultural Research Institute
Bul Cult Tutun — Buletinul Culturii Tutunului
BULDB — Building
Bul D Cpr — Bulletin. Institut Belge de Droit Compare
Bul De Dr Tchecoslovaque — Bulletin de Droit Tchecoslovaque
Bul Demogr Rom — Buletinul Demografic al Romaniei
Bul Dept Labor — Bulletin. Department of Labor
Bul Dept Zoo Univ Punjab — Bulletin of the Department of Zoology of the University of the Punjab
Bul Dir Gen Serv Sanit — Buletinul Directiunii Generale a Serviciului Sanitar
Bul Dir Gen Zooteh Sanit Vet — Buletinul Directiei Generale Zootehnice si Sanitare Veterinare
Bul Doc Bibliog — Bulletin de Documentation Bibliographique
Bul Docum — Bulletin de Documentation
Bul Docum Econ — Bulletin de Documentation Economique
Bul Docum Teh — Buletinul de Documentare Tehnica
Bul D Rech Hist — Bulletin des Recherches Historiques
Bul Ec — Bulletin. Institut des Sciences Economiques
Bul Econ et Fin — Bulletin Economique et Financier
Bul Econ et Soc Maroc — Bulletin Economique et Social du Maroc
Bul Econ Research (England) — Bulletin of Economic Research (England)
Bul Ed & Res — Bulletin of Education and Research
Bul Enf — Bulletin. Association Internationale pour la Protection de l'Enfance
Bul Ent Res — Bulletin of Entomological Research
Bul Erb Inst Bot Buc — Buletinul Erbarului Institutului Botanic din Bucuresti
Bul Erb Inst Bot Bucuresti — Buletinul Erbarului Institutului Botanic din Bucuresti
Bulet Cluj — Buletinul. Societatii de Stiinte din Cluj
Buletin Shkenc Nat — Buletin per Shkencat Natyrore
Buletin Sti Acad Repub Pop Rom — Buletin Stiintific. Academia Republicii Populare Romane (Romine)
Buletinul Soc Geogr Rom — Buletinul Societatii Geografice Romane
Buletin Univ Shtet Tiranes Shkencat Nat — Buletin. Universiteti Shteteror te Tiranes. Seria Shkencat Natyrore
Bul Fac Agron Cluj — Buletinul Facultatii de Agronomie din Cluj
Bul Fac Sti Cernauti — Buletinul Facultatii de Stiinte din Cernauti
Bul Fac Stiinte Cernauti — Buletinul Facultatii de Stiinte din Cernauti
Bul Fed Femmes Quebec — Bulletin. Federation des Femmes du Quebec
Bul Fiz — Buletin Fizik
Bul Florida St Univ Tallahassee — Bulletin. Florida State University. Tallahassee
Bul for Psych — Bulletin for Psychologists
Bul Franc Piscicul — Bulletin Francais de Pisciculture
Bulg Acad Sci Commun Dep Chem — Bulgarian Academy of Sciences. Communications. Department of Chemistry
Bulg Akad Nauk Dokl — Bulgarska Akademiya na Naukite. Doklady
Bulg Akad Nauk Geol Inst Izv Ser Inzh Geol Khidrogeol — Bulgarska Akademiya na Naukite. Geologicheski Institut. Izvestiya. Seriya Inzhenerna Geologiya i Khidrogeologiya
Bulg Akad Nauk Geol Inst Izv Ser Paleontol — Bulgarska Akademiya na Naukite. Geologicheski Institut. Izvestiya. Seriya Paleontologiya
Bulg Akad Nauk Inst Okeanogr Ribno Stop Izv — Bulgarska Akademiya na Naukite. Institut po Okeanografiya i Ribno Stopanstvo Izvestiya
Bulg Akad Nauk Izv Inst Zhivotnovud — Bulgarska Akademiya na Naukite. Izvestiya na Instituta za Zhivotnovudstvo
Bulg Akad Nauk Izv Khim Inst — Bulgarska Akademiya na Naukite. Izvestiya na Khimicheskiya Institut
Bulg Akad Nauk Izv Med Inst — Bulgarska Akademiya na Naukite. Izvestiya na Meditsinskite Instituti
Bulg Akad Nauk Izv Mikrobiol Inst — Bulgarska Akademiya na Naukite. Izvestiya na Mikrobiologicheskiya Institut
Bulg Akad Nauk Izv Tekh Inst — Bulgarska Akademiya na Naukite. Izvestiya na Tekhnicheskiya Institut
Bulg Akad Nauk Otd Geol Geogr Khim Nauki Izv Geol Inst — Bulgarska Akademiya na Naukite. Otdelenie za Geologo-Geografski i Khimicheski Nauki. Izvestiya na Geologicheskiya Institut
Bulg Akad Nauk Otd Khim Nauki Izv — Bulgarska Akademiya na Naukite. Otdelenie za Khimicheski Nauki. Izvestiya
Bulg Akad Nauk Zool Inst Muz Izv — Bulgarska Akademiya na Naukite. Otdelenie za Biologichni Nauki. Zoologicheski Institut si Muzey. Izvestiya
Bulgar J Phys — Bulgarian Journal of Physics
Bulgar Math Monographs — Bulgarian Mathematical Monographs
Bulgar Muz — Bulgarska Muzika
Bulgarsko Muz — Bulgarsko Muzikoznanie
Bul GB For Com — Bulletin. Great Britain Forestry Commission
Bul Geol S — Bulletin of the Geological Society of Denmark
Bul Geol Tutkimuslaitos (Fin) — Bulletin. Geologinen Tutkimuslaitos (Finland)
Bulg Ez — Bulgarski Ezik
Bulg F — Bulgarian Films
Bulg Geofiz Spis — Bulgarsko Geofizichno Spisanie

Bulg Geol Druzh Spis — Bulgarsko Geologichesko Druzhestvo. Spisanie
Bulg Geophys J — Bulgarian Geophysical Journal
Bulg Hist — Bulgarian Historical Review/Revue Bulgare d'Histoire
Bulg J Phys — Bulgarian Journal of Physics
Bulg J Plant Physiol — Bulgarian Journal of Plant Physiology
Bulg Muzik Bulg Akad Nauk Inst Muzik — Bulgarsko Muzikoznanie. Bulgarska Akademiia na Naukite. Institut za Muzikoznanie
Bulg Phot — Bulgarian Photo
Bulg Spis Fiziol Rast — Bulgarsko Spisanie po Fiziologiya na Rasteniyata
Bulg Tab — Bulgarische Tabak
Bulg Tiutiun — Bulgarski Tiutiun
Bulg Tob — Bulgarian Tobacco
Bulg Tyutyun — Bulgarski Tyutyun
Bul Halte — Bulletin Halte
Bul Hel — Bulletin de Correspondance Hellenique
Bul Hisp — Bulletin Hispanique
BULIB — Bulletin on Inventions
BULID — Business Librarian
Bul IEC — Bulletin. Institut d'Etudes Centrafricaines
Bul Ind Dev Assoc Can — Bulletin. Industrial Developers Association of Canada
Bul Indonesian Econ Studies — Bulletin of Indonesian Economic Studies
Bul Ind Psychol — Bulletin for Industrial Psychology and Personnel Practice
Bul Inf Acad Stiinte Agric Silvice — Buletinul Informativ al Academiei de Stiinte Agricole si Silvice
Bul Inf Chine — Bulletin d'Information sur la Chine
Bul Inf Invent Marci — Buletin de Informare pentru Inventii si Marci
Bul Inf Lab Cent Color — Buletin Information. Laboratorul Central Coloristic
Bul Info — Bulletin d'Information. Departement d'Economie et de Sociologie Rurales
Bul Info Anthro Med Psych Transcult — Bulletin d'Information en Anthropologie Medicale et en Psychiatrie Transculturelle
Bul Info Corp Prof Cons Orient Quebec — Bulletin d'Information. Corporation Professionnelle des Conseillers d'Orientation du Quebec
Bul Info Lab Coop — Bulletin d'Information. Laboratoire Cooperatif
Bul Info Off Assoc Pharm Etablis Sante Quebec — Bulletin d'Information Officiel. Association des Pharmaciens des Etablissementsde Sante du Quebec
Bul Info Region Parisienne — Bulletin d'Information de la Region Parisienne
Bul Inform Soc Nat Romania — Buletinul de Informatii al Societatii Naturalistilor din Romania
Bul Inst Agron Cluj Napoca — Buletinul. Institutului Agronomic Cluj-Napoca
Bul Inst Agron Cluj Napoca Inst Agron Dr Petru Groza — Buletinul. Institutului Agronomic Cluj-Napoca. Institutul Agronomic "Dr. Petru Groza"
Bul Inst Agron Cluj Napoca Ser Agric — Buletinul. Institutului Agronomic Cluj-Napoca. Seria Agricultura
Bul Inst Agron Cluj-Napoca Ser Zooteh Med Vet — Buletinul Institutului Agronomic Cluj-Napoca. Seria Zootehnie si Medicina Veterinara
Bul Inst Cercet Piscic — Buletinul Institutului de Cercetari Piscicole
Bul Inst Cercet Proiect Piscic — Buletinul. Institutului de Cercetari si Proiectari Piscicole
Bul Inst Pet Gaze Geol — Buletinul. Institutului de Petrol, Gaze, si Geologie
Bul Inst Polit Brasov Ser B Econ For — Buletinul. Institutului Politehnic din Brasov. Seria B. Economie Forestiera
Bul Inst Politeh Brasov A — Buletinul. Institutului Politehnic din Brasov. Seria A. Mecanica
Bul Inst Politeh Bucur — Buletinul. Institutului Politehnic Bucuresti
Bul Inst Politeh Bucuresti — Buletinul. Institutului Politehnic Bucuresti
Bul Inst Politeh Bucuresti Ser Chim — Buletinul Institutului Politehnic Bucuresti. Seria Chimie
Bul Inst Politeh Bucuresti Ser Chim Metal — Buletinul. Institutului Politehnic "Gheorghe Gheorghiu-Dej" Bucuresti. Seria Chimie-Metalurgie
Bul Inst Politeh Bucuresti Ser Mec — Buletinul. Institutului Politehnic "Gheorghe Gheorghiu-Dej" Bucuresti. Seria Mecanica
Bul Inst Politeh Bucuresti Ser Metal — Buletinul Institutului Politehnic Bucuresti. Seria Metalurgie
Bul Inst Politeh Chim-Metal — Buletinul. Institutului Politehnic "Gheorghe Gheorghiu-Dej" Bucuresti. Seria Chimie-Metalurgie
Bul Inst Politeh Gheorghe Gheorghiu Dej Bucur — Buletinul. Institutului Politehnic "Gheorghe Gheorghiu-Dej" Bucur
Bul Inst Politeh Gheorghe Gheorghiu Dej Bucuresti — Buletinul. Institutului Politehnic "Gheorghe Gheorghiu-Dej" Bucuresti
Bul Inst Politeh Gheorghe Gheorghiu Dej Bucuresti Ser Chim — Buletinul. Institutului Politehnic "Gheorghe Gheorghiu-Dej" Bucuresti. SeriaChimie
Bul Inst Politeh Gheorghe Gheorghiu Dej Bucuresti Ser Chim M — Buletinul Institutului Politehnic. Gheorghe Gheorghiu-Dej. Bucuresti. Seria Chimie-Metalurgie
Bul Inst Politeh Gheorghe Gheorghiu Dej Bucuresti Ser Electro — Buletinul Institutului Politehnic. Gheorghe Gheorghiu-Dej. Bucuresti. Seria Electrotechnica
Bul Inst Politeh Gheorghe Gheorghiu Dej Bucuresti Ser Mec — Buletinul. Institutului Politehnic "Gheorghe Gheorghiu-Dej" Bucuresti. Seria Mecanica
Bul Inst Politeh Gheorghe Gheorghiu Dej Bucuresti Ser Metal — Buletinul Institutului Politehnic. Gheorghe Gheorghiu-Dej. Bucuresti. Seria Metalurgie
Bul Inst Politeh Gheorghe Gheorghiu Dej Chim-Metal — Buletinul. Institutului Politehnic "Gheorghe Gheorghiu-Dej." Seria Chimie-Metalurgie
Bul Inst Politeh Gheorghe Gheorghiu Dej Electroteh — Buletinul. Institutului Politehnic "Gheorghe Gheorghiu-Dej." Seria Electrotehnica
Bul Inst Politeh Gheorghe Gheorghiu Dej Mec — Buletinul. Institutului Politehnic "Gheorghe Gheorghiu-Dej." Seria Mecanica
Bul Inst Politeh Iasi — Buletinul. Institutului Politehnic din Iasi
Bul Inst Politeh Iasi I — Buletinul. Institutului Politehnic din Iasi. Sectia I. Matematica, Mecanica Teoretica, Fizica
Bul Inst Politeh Iasi III — Buletinul. Institutului Politehnic din Iasi. Sectia III. Electrotehnica, Electronica Automatizari
Bul Inst Politeh Iasi Sect 2 Chim — Buletinul Institutului Politehnic din Iasi. Sectia 2. Chimie

Bul Inst Politeh Iasi Sect 2 Chim Ing Chim — Buletinul Institutului Politehnic din Iasi. Sectia 2. Chimie si Inginerie Chimica

Bul Inst Politeh Iasi Sect 5 — Buletinul Institutului Politehnic din Iasi. Sectia 5. Constructii Arhit ectura

Bul Inst Politeh Iasi Sect 6 — Buletinul Institutului Politehnic din Iasi. Sectia 6. Imbunatatiri Funciare

Bul Inst Politeh Iasi Sect 7 — Buletinul Institutului Politehnic din Iasi. Sectia 7. Textile, Pielarie

Bul Inst Politeh Iasi Sect I — Buletinul. Institutului Politehnic din Iasi. Sectia I. Matematica, Mecanica Teoretica, Fizica

Bul Inst Politeh Iasi Sect II — Buletinul. Institutului Politehnic din Iasi. Sectia II. Chimie

Bul Inst Politeh Iasi Sect III — Buletinul. Institutului Politehnic din Iasi. Sectia III. Electrotehnica, Electronica Automatizari

Bul Inst Politeh Iasi Sect IV — Buletinul. Institutului Politehnic din Iasi. Sectia IV. Mecanica Tehnica

Bul Inst Politeh Iasi Sect V — Buletinul. Institutului Politehnic din Iasi. Sectia V

Bul Inst Politeh Mec — Buletinul. Institutului Politehnic "Gheorghe Gheorghiu-Dej" Bucuresti. Seria Mecanica

Bul Inst Politehn Bucuresti — Buletinul. Institutului Politehnic Bucuresti

Bul Inst Politehn Bucuresti Ser Automat Calc — Buletinul Institutului Politehnic Bucuresti. Seria Automatica-Calculatoare

Bul Inst Politehn Bucuresti Ser Chim-Metal — Buletinul. Institutului Politehnic "Gheorghe Gheorghiu-Dej" Bucuresti. Seria Chimie-Metalurgie

Bul Inst Politehn Bucuresti Ser Construc Mas — Buletinul Institutului Politehnic Bucuresti. Seria Constructii de Masini

Bul Inst Politehn Bucuresti Ser Electron — Buletinul Institutului Politehnic Buchuresti. Seria Electronica

Bul Inst Politehn Bucuresti Ser Electrotehn — Buletinul. Institutului Politehnic "Gheorghe Gheorghiu-Dej" Bucuresti. Seria Electrotehnica

Bul Inst Politehn Bucuresti Ser Energet — Buletinul Institutului Politehnic Buchuresti. Seria Energetica

Bul Inst Politehn Bucuresti Ser Mec — Institutului Politehnic Gheorghe Gheorghiu Dej Bucuresti. Buletinul. Seria Mecanica

Bul Inst Politehn Bucuresti Ser Transport Aeronave — Buletinul Institutului Politehnic Bucuresti. Seria Transporturi-Aeronave

Bul Inst Politehn Iasi — Buletinul. Institutului Politehnic din Iasi. Seria Noua

Bul Inst Politehn Iasi NS — Buletinul. Institutului Politehnic din Iasi. Seria Noua

Bul Inst Politehn Iasi Sect I — Institutului Politehnic din Iasi. Buletinul. Sectia I

Bul Inst Stud & Proj Energ — Buletinul. Institutului de Studii si Projectari Energetice

Bul Inst Stud si Project Energ — Buletinul. Institutului de Studii si Projectari Energetice

Bul Int — Bulletin. Ministere de l'Interieur

Bul Int De La Protec De L Enf — Bulletin International de la Protection de l'Enfance

Bul Internat Fiscal Docum — Bulletin for International Fiscal Documentation

Bul Internat Fiscal Documentation — Bulletin for International Fiscal Documentation

Bul Int Fiscal Doc — Bulletin for International Fiscal Documentation

Bul Int Fisc Docu — Bulletin of International Fiscal Documentation

Bul Int Pac Salmon Fish Com — Bulletin. International Pacific Salmon Fisheries Commission

Bul Int Union Tuber — Bulletin of the International Union Against Tuberculosis

Bul Invent Marci — Buletin pentru Inventii si Marci

Bul Istanbul Tek Univ Nukl Enerji Enst — Bulten. Istanbul Teknik Universitesi Nukleer Enerji Enstitusu

Bul Jap Soc Sci Fish — Bulletin of the Japanese Society of Scientific Fisheries

Bul J Rylands — Bulletin. John Rylands Library. University of Manchester

Bul Jur I — Bulletin des Juridictions Indigenes du Droit Coutumier

Bul Kebun Raya Bot Gard Indones — Buletin Kebun Raya. Botanical Gardens of Indonesia

Bulk Solids Handl — Bulk Solids Handling

Bulk Syst Int — Bulk Systems International

Bull A Ariz Univ Ext Serv — Bulletin A. University of Arizona. Extension Service

Bull A Ass Chim Ind Text — Bulletin Annuel de l'Association des Chimistes de l'Industrie Textile

Bull A Ass Fr Ponts Charp — Bulletin Annuel de l'Association Francaise des Ponts et Charpentes

Bull A Ass Lutte Anti Tuberc Savoie — Bulletin Annuel de l'Association pour la Lutte Anti-Tuberculeuse en Savoie

Bull A Assoc Indianapolis — Bulletin of the Art Association of Indianapolis

Bull Aberd N Scotl Coll Agric — Bulletin. Aberdeen and North of Scotland College of Agriculture

Bul Lab Etud Polit Admin — Bulletin. Laboratoire d'Etudes Politiques et Administratives

Bul Laborat — Buletinul Laboratoarelor

Bull ABTPL — Bulletin. Association of British Theological and Philosophical Libraries

Bull Acad Agric Aube — Bulletin. Societe Academique d'Agriculture des Sciences, Arts, et Belles-Lettres du Departement de l'Aube

Bull Acad Chir Dent (Paris) — Bulletin. Academie de Chirurgie Dentaire (Paris)

Bull Acad Delph — Bulletin. Academie Delphinale

Bull Acad Dent Handicap — Bulletin. Academy of Dentistry for the Handicapped

Bull Acad Dent (Paris) — Bulletin. Academie Dentaire (Paris)

Bull Acad Ebroic — Bulletin. Academie Ebroicienne

Bull Academ Belg — Bulletin. Academie de Belgique. Classe des Lettres et des SciencesMorales et Politiques

Bull Acad Gen Dent — Bulletin. Academy of General Dentistry

Bull Acad Imp Sci Petrograd — Bulletin. Academie Imperiale des Sciences de Petrograd

Bull Acad Imp Sci St Petersbourg — Bulletin. Academie Imperiale des Sciences de St. Petersbourg

Bull Acad Imp Sc St Petersb — Bulletin. Academie Imperiale des Sciences de St. Petersbourg

Bull Acad Int — Bulletin. Academie Internationale de Geographie Botanique

Bull Acad M — Bulletin. American Academy of Medicine

Bull Acad Malg — Bulletin. Academie Malgache

Bull Acad Malgache — Bulletin. Academie Malgache

Bull Acad Med Belg — Bulletin. Academie Royale de Medecine de Belgique

Bull Acad Med (Paris) — Bulletin. Academie de Medecine (Paris)

Bull Acad Med Roum — Bulletin. Academie de Medecine de Roumanie

Bull Acad Med Sci USSR — Bulletin. Academy of Medical Sciences. USSR

Bull Acad Med Tol — Bulletin. Academy of Medicine of Toledo

Bull Acad Med Toledo — Bulletin. Academy of Medicine of Toledo and Lucas County

Bull Acad Med Toledo Lucas Cty — Bulletin of the Academy of Medicine of Toledo and Lucas County

Bull Acad Med Tor — Bulletin. Academy of Medicine of Toronto

Bull Acad Med Toronto — Bulletin. Academy of Medicine of Toronto

Bull Acad Mil Med Sci — Bulletin. Academy of Military Medical Sciences

Bull Acad Natl Chir Dent — Bulletin de l'Academie Nationale de Chirurgie Dentaire

Bull Acad Natl Med — Bulletin. Academie Nationale de Medecine

Bull Acad Natl Med (Paris) — Bulletin. Academie Nationale de Medecine (Paris)

Bull Acad Nat Med — Bulletin. Academie Nationale de Medecine

Bull Acad Polon Paris — Academie Polonaise des Sciences et des Lettres. Centre Polonais de Recherches Scientifiques de Paris. Bulletin

Bull Acad Polon Sci Ser Sci Biol — Bulletin. Academie Polonaise des Sciences. Serie des Sciences Biologiques

Bull Acad Polon Sci Ser Sci Math — Academie Polonaise des Sciences. Bulletin. Serie des Sciences Mathematiques

Bull Acad Polon Sci Ser Sci Math Astronom Phys — Bulletin. Academie Polonaise des Sciences. Serie des Sciences Mathematiques, Astronomiques, et Physiques

Bull Acad Polon Sci Ser Sci Phys Astronom — Academie Polonaise des Sciences. Bulletin. Serie des Sciences Physiques et Astronomiques

Bull Acad Polon Sci Ser Sci Tech — Bulletin. Academie Polonaise des Sciences. Serie des Sciences Techniques

Bull Acad Pol Sci — Bulletin. Academie Polonaise des Sciences

Bull Acad Pol Sci Biol — Bulletin. Academie Polonaise des Sciences. Serie des Sciences Biologiques

Bull Acad Pol Sci Cl 2 — Bulletin. Academie Polonaise des Sciences. Classe 2. Agrobiologie, Biologie, Sciences Medicales

Bull Acad Pol Sci Cl 3 — Bulletin. Academie Polonaise des Sciences. Classe 3. Mathematique, Astronomie, Physique, Chimie, Geologie, et Geographie

Bull Acad Pol Sci Ser Sci Biol — Bulletin. Academie Polonaise des Sciences. Serie des Sciences Biologiques

Bull Acad Pol Sci Ser Sci Chim — Bulletin. Academie Polonaise des Sciences. Serie des Sciences Chimiques

Bull Acad Pol Sci Ser Sci Chim Geol Geogr — Bulletin. Academie Polonaise des Sciences. Serie des Sciences Chimiques, Geologiques, et Geographiques

Bull Acad Pol Sci Ser Sci Geol Geogr — Bulletin. Academie Polonaise des Sciences. Serie des Sciences Geologiques et Geographiques

Bull Acad Pol Sci Ser Sci Math Astron et Phys — Bulletin. Academie Polonaise des Sciences. Serie des Sciences Mathematiques, Astronomiques, et Physiques

Bull Acad Pol Sci Ser Sci Math Astron Phys — Bulletin. Academie Polonaise des Sciences. Serie des Sciences Mathematiques, Astronomiques, et Physiques

Bull Acad Pol Sci Ser Sci Math Astr Phys — Bulletin de l'Academie Polonaise des Sciences. Serie des Sciences Mathematiques, Astronomiques, et Physiques

Bull Acad Pol Sci Ser Sci Phys Astron — Bulletin. Academie Polonaise des Sciences. Serie des Sciences Physiques etAstronomiques

Bull Acad Pol Sci Ser Sci Phys et Astron — Bulletin. Academie Polonaise des Sciences. Serie des Sciences Physiques et Astronomiques

Bull Acad Pol Sci Ser Sci Tech — Bulletin. Academie Polonaise des Sciences. Serie des Sciences Techniques

Bull Acad Pol Sci Ser Sci Terre — Bulletin. Academie Polonaise des Sciences. Serie des Sciences de la Terre

Bull Acad R Belg — Bulletin. Academie Royale de Belgique

Bull Acad R Belg Cl Sci — Bulletin. Academie Royale de Belgique. Classe des Sciences

Bull Acad R Med Belg — Bulletin. Academie Royale de Medecine de Belgique

Bull Acad Royale Archeol Belgique — Bulletin de l'Academie Royale d'Archeologie de Belgique

Bull Acad Royale Belgique — Bulletin de l'Academie Royale de Belgique

Bull Acad Royale Sci Lett & B A Belgique — Bulletins de l'Academie Royale des Sciences, des Lettres, et des Beaux-Arts de Belgique

Bull Acad Roy Belg — Bulletins. Academie Royale de Belgique

Bull Acad Roy Belg Cl — Bulletin. Academie Royale de Belgique. Classe des Sciences

Bull Acad Roy Belg Cl Beaux Arts — Bulletin. Academie Royale de Belgique. Classe des Beaux-Arts

Bull Acad Roy Belg Cl Lett — Bulletin. Academie Royale de Belgique. Classe des Lettres et des Sciences Morales et Politiques

Bull Acad Roy Belgique Cl Lett Sci Moral Polit — Bulletin. Academie Royale de Belgique. Classe des Lettres et des Sciences Morales et Politiques

Bull Acad Roy Belgique Cl Sci — Bulletin. Academie Royale de Belgique. Classe des Sciences

Bull Acad Roy Med Belgique — Bulletin. Academie Royale de Medecine de Belgique

Bull Acad Roy Med (Paris) — Bulletin. Academie Royale de Medecine (Paris)

Bull Acad Roy Sci Belgique — Bulletins. Academie Royale des Sciences, des Lettres, et des Beaux Arts de Belgique

Bull Acad Roy Sci Belgique Cl Sci — Bulletins de l'Academie Royale des Sciences, des Lettres, et des Beaux Arts de Belgique. Classe des Sciences

Bull Acad Sci Agric For — Bulletin. Academie des Sciences Agricoles et Forestieres

Bull Acad Sci Agric For Bucharest — Bulletin. Academie des Sciences Agricoles et Forestieres (Bucharest)

Bull Acad Sci Arm SSR Nat Sci — Bulletin. Academy of Sciences. Armenian SSR. Natural Sciences

Bull Acad Sci Arts Belles Lett Caen — Bulletin de l'Academie des Sciences, Arts, et Belles-Lettres de Caen

Bull Acad Sci Azerb SSR — Bulletin. Academy of Sciences. Azerbaidjan SSR

Bull Acad Sci Belles Lett Arts Besancon — Bulletin de l'Academie des Sciences, Belles-Lettres, et Arts de Besancon

Bull Acad Sci DPR Korea — Bulletin. Academy of Sciences. DPR [*Democratic People's Republic*] Korea

Bull Acad Sci Ga SSR — Bulletin. Academy of Sciences of the Georgian SSR

Bull Acad Sci Georgia — Bulletin. Academy of Sciences of Georgia

Bull Acad Sci Georgian SSR — Bulletin. Academy of Sciences. Georgian SSR

Bull Acad Sci Inscript Belles Lett Toulouse — Bulletin de l'Academie des Sciences, Inscriptions, et Belles-Lettres de Toulouse

Bull Acad Sci Lett Montpellier — Bulletin. Academie des Sciences et Lettres de Montpellier

Bull Acad Sci Math Nat Acad R Serbe A — Bulletin. Academie des Sciences Mathematiques et Naturelles. Academie Royale Serbe. Serie A. Sciences Mathematiques et Physiques

Bull Acad Sci Math Nat Acad R Serbe B — Bulletin. Academie des Sciences Mathematiques et Naturelles. Academie Royale Serbe. Serie B. Sciences Naturelles

Bull Acad Sci Math Natur (Belgrade) A — Bulletin. Academie des Sciences Mathematiques et Naturelles. Academie Royale Serbe. Serie A. Sciences Mathematiques et Physiques (Belgrade)

Bull Acad Sci Russ — Bulletin. Academie des Sciences de Russie

Bull Acad Sci St Louis — Bulletin. Academy of Sciences of St. Louis

Bull Acad Sci St Petersbourg — Bulletin. Academie des Sciences de St. Petersbourg

Bull Acad Sci United Prov Agra Oudh India — Bulletin. Academy of Sciences of the United Provinces of Agra and Oudh, India

Bull Acad Sci Un Prov Agra Oudh — Bulletin of the Academy of Sciences of the United Provinces of Agra and Oudh

Bull Acad Sci URSS — Bulletin. Academie des Sciences de l'URSS

Bull Acad Sci URSS Cl Sci Chim — Bulletin. Academie des Sciences de l'URSS. Classe des Sciences Chimiques

Bull Acad Sci URSS Cl Sci Math Nat — Bulletin. Academie des Sciences de l'URSS. Classe des Sciences Mathematiques etNaturelles

Bull Acad Sci URSS Cl Sci Phys Math — Bulletin. Academie des Sciences de l'URSS. Classe des Sciences Physico-Mathematiques

Bull Acad Sci URSS Cl Sci Tech — Bulletin. Academie des Sciences de l'URSS [*Union des Republiques SocialistesSovietiques*]. Classe des Sciences Techniques

Bull Acad Sci URSS Ser Biol — Bulletin. Academie des Sciences de l'URSS [*Union des Republiques SocialistesSovietiques*]. Serie Biologique

Bull Acad Sci URSS Ser Geogr Geophys — Bulletin. Academie des Sciences de l'URSS. Serie Geographique et Geophysique

Bull Acad Sci URSS Ser Geol — Bulletin. Academie des Sciences de l'URSS. Serie Geologique

Bull Acad Sci URSS Ser Phys — Bulletin. Academie des Sciences de l'URSS. Serie Physique

Bull Acad Sci USSR Div Chem Sci — Bulletin. Academy of Sciences of the USSR. Division of Chemical Science

Bull Acad Sci USSR Div Chem Sci Engl Transl — Bulletin. Academy of Sciences of the USSR. Division of Chemical Science [*English Translation*]

Bull Acad Sci USSR Geol Ser — Bulletin. Academy of Sciences of the USSR. Geologic Series

Bull Acad Sci USSR Geophys Ser — Bulletin. Academy of Sciences. USSR. Geophysics Series

Bull Acad Sci USSR Phys Sci — Bulletin. Academy of Sciences of the USSR. Physical Sciences

Bull Acad Sci USSR Phys Ser — Bulletin. Academy of Sciences of the USSR. Physical Series

Bull Acad Sci USSR Phys Ser (Columbia Tech Transl) — Bulletin. Academy of Sciences of the USSR. Physical Series (Columbia Technical Translations)

Bull Acad Sci USSR Phys Ser (Engl Transl) — Bulletin. Academy of Sciences of the USSR. Physical Series (English Translation)

Bull Acad Serbe Sci Arts Classe Sci Tech — Bulletin. Academie Serbe des Sciences et des Arts. Classe des Sciences Techniques

Bull Acad Serbe Sci Arts Cl Sci Math Nat — Bulletin. Academie Serbe des Sciences et des Arts. Classe des Sciences Mathematiques et Naturelles

Bull Acad Serbe Sci Arts Cl Sci Math Nat Sci Nat — Bulletin. Academie Serbe des Sciences et des Arts. Classe des Sciences Mathematiques et Naturelles. Sciences Naturelles

Bull Acad Serbe Sci Arts Cl Sci Math Natur — Bulletin. Academie Serbe des Sciences et des Arts. Classe des Sciences Mathematiques et Naturelles

Bull Acad Serbe Sci Arts Cl Sci Math Natur NS — Bulletin. Academie Serbe des Sciences et des Arts. Classe des Sciences Mathematiques et Naturelles. Nouvelle Serie

Bull Acad Serbe Sci Arts Cl Sci Math Natur Sci Math — Bulletin. Academie Serbe des Sciences et des Arts. Classe des Sciences Mathematiques et Naturelles. Sciences Mathematiques

Bull Acad Serbe Sci Arts Cl Sci Med — Bulletin. Academie Serbe des Sciences et des Arts. Classe des Sciences Medicales

Bull Acad Serbe Sci B Sci Nat — Bulletin. Academie Serbe des Sciences. B. Sciences Naturelles

Bull Acad Serbe Sci Cl Sci Math Nat — Bulletin. Academie Serbe des Sciences. Classe des Sciences Mathematiques et Naturelles

Bull Acad Serbe Sci Cl Sci Math Nat Sci Nat — Bulletin. Academie Serbe des Sciences. Classe des Sciences Mathematiques et Naturelles. Sciences Naturelles

Bull Acad Serbe Sci Cl Sci Med — Bulletin de l'Academie Serbe des Sciences. Classe des Sciences Medicales

Bull Acad Serbe Sci Cl Sci Tech — Bulletin de l'Academie Serbe des Sciences. Classe des Sciences Techniques

Bull Acad Serbe Sci et Arts Cl Sci Tech — Bulletin. Academie Serbe des Sciences et des Arts. Classe des Sciences Techniques

Bull Acad Soc Lorraines Sci — Bulletin. Academie et Societe Lorraines des Sciences

Bull Acad Sui Sci Med — Bulletin. Academie Suisse des Sciences Medicales

Bull Acad Suisse Sci Med — Bulletin. Academie Suisse des Sciences Medicales

Bull Acad Tchec Agric — Bulletin. Academie Tchecoslovaque d'Agriculture

Bull Acad Veterin France — Bulletin de l'Academie Veterinaire de France

Bull Acad Vet Fr — Bulletin. Academie Veterinaire de France

Bull Acad Vet France — Bulletin. Academie Veterinaire de France

Bull Ac Belgique — Bulletins. Academie Royale de Belgique

Bull Acet Soud Autogene — Bulletin de l'Acetylene et de la Soudure Autogene

Bull Acheson Colloids — Bulletin. Acheson Colloids Ltd

Bull Acid Open Hearth Res Ass — Bulletin. Acid Open Hearth Research Association

Bull Acid Open Hearth Res Assoc — Bulletin. Acid Open Hearth Research Association

Bull ACLS — Bulletin. American Council of Learned Societies

Bull Ac Malg — Bulletin. Academie Malgache

Bull A Commn Dep Met Rhone — Bulletin Annuel. Commission Departementale de Meteorologie du Rhone

Bull A Commn Met Cotes Du N — Bulletin Annuel de la Commission Meteorologique des Cotes-du-Nord

Bull A Commn Met Dep Bouches Du Rhone — Bulletin Annuel de la Commission de Meteorologie du Departement des Bouches-du-Rhone

Bull A Commn Met Dep Sarthe — Bulletin Annuel de la Commission Meteorologique du Departement de la Sarthe

Bull A Commn Met Hte Loire — Bulletin Annuel de la Commission Meteorologique de la Houte-Loire

Bull A Commn Met Yonne — Bulletin Annuel de la Commission de Meteorologie de l'Yonne

Bull A Cotons — Bulletin Annuel des Cotons et des Graines de Coton

Bull Acoust Mater Ass — Bulletin. Acoustical Materials Association

Bull Ac Polon Sci — Bulletin. Academie Polonaise des Sciences

Bull Actinom Int — Bulletin Actinometrique International

Bull Act Inst Geol Subsurf Res — Bulletin. Activity of the Institute for Geology and Subsurface Research

Bull Adler Mus Hist Med — Bulletin. Adler Museum of the History of Medicine

Bull Adm Pr — Bulletin de l'Administration des Prisons

Bull Advis Counc Sci Ind Res (Can) — Bulletin. Advisory Council for Scientific and Industrial Research (Canada)

Bull Advis C Sci I R (Can) — Bulletin. Advisory Council for Scientific and Industrial Research (Canada)

Bull Aeronaut Res Inst Univ Tokyo — Bulletin. Aeronautical Research Institute. University of Tokyo

Bull AFG — Bulletin. Association Francaise de Gemmologie

Bull Afghan Geol Miner Surv — Bulletin. Afghan Geological and Mineral Survey

Bull Afr Inst S Afr — Bulletin. Africa Institute of South Africa

Bull Afr Stud Assoc — Bulletin. African Studies Association of the United Kingdom

Bull Afr Stud Canada — Bulletin of African Studies in Canada

Bull Age Gen Colon — Bulletin de l'Agence Generale des Colonies

Bull Agence Econ Colon Auton Territ Afr Mandat (Fr) — Bulletin. Agence Economique des Colonies Autonomes et des Territoires Africainssous Mandat (France)

Bull Agence Gen Colon (Fr) — Bulletin. Agence Generale des Colonies (France)

Bull Agency Ind Sci Technol Jpn — Bulletin. Agency of Industrial Science and Technology (Japan)

Bull Agr CB — Bulletin Agricole du Congo Belge

Bull Agr Chem Soc Jap — Bulletin. Agricultural Chemical Society of Japan

Bull Agr Congo — Bulletin Agricole du Congo

Bull Agric — Bulletin Agricole

Bull Agric Chem Insp Stn — Bulletin. Agricultural Chemicals Inspection Station

Bull Agric Chem Insp Stn Jpn — Bulletin. Agricultural Chemicals Inspection Station. Japan

Bull Agric Chem Insp Stn (Tokyo) — Bulletin. Agricultural Chemicals Inspection Station (Tokyo)

Bull Agric Chem Soc Jpn — Bulletin. Agricultural Chemical Society of Japan

Bull Agric Coll Suwon — Bulletin. Agricultural and Forestry College. Suwon

Bull Agric Cong Belg — Bulletin Agricole du Congo Belge

Bull Agric Congo — Bulletin Agricole du Congo

Bull Agric Congo Belg — Bulletin Agricole du Congo Belge

Bull Agric Dep (Assam) — Bulletin. Agricultural Department (Assam)

Bull Agric Dep (Tasm) — Bulletin. Agricultural Department (Tasmania)

Bull Agric Exp Sta Kungchuling — Bulletin. Agricultural Experiment Station. Kungchuling/Manchukuo Kung Chu Ling Noji Shikenjo Hokoku

Bull Agric Exp Stn Ala Polytech Inst — Bulletin. Agricultural Experiment Station. Alabama Polytechnic Institute

Bull Agric Exp Stn Fla — Bulletin. Agricultural Experiment Stations. Florida

Bull Agric Exp Stn Ga — Bulletin. Agricultural Experiment Stations. Georgia

Bull Agric Exp Stn Ill — Bulletin. Agriculture Experiment Station. Illinois

Bull Agric Exp Stn NC — Bulletin. Agricultural Experiment Station. North Carolina

Bull Agric Exp Stn ND State Univ — Bulletin. Agricultural Experiment Station. North Dakota State University

Bull Agric Exp Stn (Rehovoth) — Bulletin. Agricultural Experiment Station (Rehovoth)

Bull Agric Exp Stn Rio Piedras PR — Bulletin. Agricultural Experiment Station. Rio Piedras, Puerto Rico

Bull Agric Exp Stn SD State Univ — Bulletin. Agricultural Experiment Station. South Dakota State University

Bull Agric Exp Stn (Tahreer Prov) — Bulletin. Agricultural Experiment Station (Tahreer Province)

Bull Agric Hort — Bulletin de l'Agriculture et de l'Horticulture

Bull Agric Inst Sci Indochine — Bulletin Agricole. Institut Scientifique de l'Indochine

Bull Agric Intell Plant Dis Mon — Bulletin. Agricultural Intelligence and Plant Diseases. Monthly

Bull Agric Mech Coll Texas — Bulletin. Agricultural and Mechanical College of Texas

Bull Agric Mech Coll Tex Tex Eng Exp Stn Bull — Bulletin. Agricultural and Mechanical College of Texas. Texas Engineering Experiment Station. Bulletin

Bull Agric Res Inst Iregszemcse Hung — Bulletin. Agricultural Research Institute. Iregszemcse, Hungary

Bull Agric Res Inst Kanagawa Prefect — Bulletin. Agricultural Research Institute of Kanagawa Prefecture

Bull Agric Rwanda — Bulletin Agricole du Rwanda

Bull Agric Sci (Hung) — Bulletin. Agricultural Science (Hungary)

Bull Agric Sci Pract Mon — Bulletin. Agricultural Science and Practice. Monthly

Bull Agric Soc Agric Bas Phin — Bulletin Agricole de la Societe d'Agriculture et des Quatre Comices du Bas-Rhin/Neue Ackerbau-Zeitung der Ackerbau-Gesellschaft und der Vier Comitien des Niederrheins

Bull Agric Soc Agric Dep Bas Rhin — Bulletin Agricole. Societe d'Agriculture et des Quatre Comices du Departement du Bas-Rhin

Bull Agric Soc Cairo Tech Sect — Bulletin. Agricultural Society. Cairo. Technical Section

Bull Agri Eng Res Stn — Bulletin. Agricultural Engineering Research Station. Nogyo Doboku Shikenjo Hokou

Bull Agrogeol Instn Finl — Bulletin of the Agrogeological Institution of Finland

Bull Agron Inst Rech Agron Trop Cult Vivrieres — Bulletin Agronomique. Institut de Recherches Agronomiques Tropicales et des Cultures Vivrieres

Bull Agron Minist Fr D Outre Mer — Bulletin Agronomique. Ministere de la France d'Outre Mer

Bull Agr Res Inst (Pusa) — Bulletin. Agricultural Research Institute (Pusa)

Bull Agr Res Sta (Rehovat) — Bulletin. Agricultural Research Station (Rehovat)

Bull Aichi Agr Exp Sta — Bulletin. Aichi Agricultural Experiment Station

Bull Aichi Environ Res Cent — Bulletin. Aichi Environmental Research Center

Bull Aichi Gakugei Univ — Bulletin. Aichi Gakugei University

Bull Aichi Gakugei Univ Nat Sci — Bulletin. Aichi Gakugei University. Natural Science

Bull Aichi Inst Technol — Bulletin. Aichi Institute of Technology

Bull Aichi Inst Technol Part B — Bulletin. Aichi Institute of Technology. Part B

Bull Aichi Ken Agric Exp Stn — Bulletin. Aichi-Ken Agricultural Experiment Station

Bull Aichi ken Agric Res Cent Ser A — Bulletin. Aichi-ken Agricultural Research Center. Series A. Food Crop

Bull Aichi ken Agric Res Cent Ser B — Bulletin. Aichi-ken Agricultural Research Center. Series B. Horticulture

Bull Aichi ken Agric Res Cent Ser D — Bulletin. Aichi-ken Agricultural Research Center. Series D. Sericulture

Bull Aichi Prefect Agric Exp Sta — Bulletin. Aichi Prefecture Agricultural Experiment Station/Aichi-Ken Nogyo Shikenjo Iho

Bull Aichi Univ Ed Natur Sci — Bulletin. Aichi University of Education. Natural Science

Bull AIEA — Bulletin. Agence Internationale de l'Energie Atomique

Bull AIEMA — Bulletin d'Information. Association Internationale pour l'Etude de la Mosaique Antique

Bull AI Et SE Eur — Bulletin. Association Internationale d'Etudes du Sud-Est Europeen

Bull AIM — Bulletin de l'Aide a l'Implantation Monastique

Bull A Inst Chicago — Bulletin of the Art Institute of Chicago

Bull Air Bd Can — Bulletin. Air Board. Canada

Bull Air Leag Br Emp — Bulletin. Air League of the British Empire

Bull Airpl Engng Dep USA — Bulletin of the Airplane Engineering Department U.S.A.

Bull Akad Serbe Sci Cl Sci Med — Bulletin. Akademie Serbe des Sciences. Classe des Sciences Medicales

Bull Akita Agric Exp Stn — Bulletin. Akita Agricultural Experiment Station

Bull Akita Fruit Tree Exp Stn — Bulletin. Akita Fruit-Tree Experiment Station

Bull Akita Prefect Coll Agric — Bulletin. Akita Prefectural College of Agriculture

Bull Akron Dent Soc — Bulletin. Akron Dental Society

Bull Ala Agr Exp Sta — Bulletin. Alabama Agricultural Experiment Station. Auburn University

Bull Ala Agric Exp Sta — Bulletin. Alabama Agricultural Experiment Station. Auburn University

Bull Ala Agric Exp Stn — Bulletin. Alabama Agricultural Experiment Station. Auburn University

Bull Ala Agric Exp Stn Agric Mech Coll Auburn — Bulletin. Alabama Agricultural Experiment Station of the Agricultural and Mechanical College. Auburn

Bull Ala Dent Ass — Bulletin of the Alabama Dental Association

Bull Ala Dep Agric Ind — Bulletin. Alabama Department of Agriculture and Industries

Bull Ala Engng Exp Stn — Bulletin. Alabama Engineering Experiment Station

Bull Ala Geol Surv — Bulletin. Alabama. Geological Survey

Bull Alameda-Contra Costa Med Assoc — Bulletin. Alameda-Contra Costa Medical Association

Bull Alameda Cty Dent Soc — Bulletin. Alameda County Dental Society

Bull Alameda Cty Distr Dent Soc — Bulletin of the Alameda County District Dental Society

Bull Ala Polytech Inst Engng Exp Stn — Bulletin. Alabama Polytechnic Institute Engineering Experiment Station

Bull Alaska Agr Exp Sta — Bulletin. Alaska Agricultural Experiment Station

Bull Alaska Agric Exp Stn — Bulletin. Alaska Agricultural Experiment Station

Bull Ala St Bd Hlth — Bulletin of the Alabama State Board of Health

Bull Ala St Commn For — Bulletin. Alabama State Commission of Forestry

Bull Ala St Mine Exp Stn — Bulletin. Alabama State Mine Experiment Station School of Mines

Bull Alberta Res Counc — Bulletin. Alberta Research Council

Bull Alex — Bulletin. Societe Archeologique d'Alexandrie

Bull Alexander Blain Hosp — Bulletin. Alexander Blain Hospital

Bull Alexandria Fac Med — Bulletin. Alexandria Faculty of Medicine

Bull Alexandria Univ Fac Arts — Bulletin. Faculty of Arts. Alexandria University

Bull Alger Cancer — Bulletin Algerien de Cancerologie

Bull Alger Carcin — Bulletin Algerien de Carcinologie

Bull Alger Carcinol — Bulletin Algerien de Carcinologie

Bull Alg Proefstat Landb — Bulletin van het Algemeen Proefstation voor de Landbouw

Bull A Liaison Orgs Met Dep — Bulletin Annuel de Liaison des Organisations Meteorologiques Departementales et des Correspondants du Reseau Climatologique Francais

Bull Allahabad Math Soc — Bulletin of the Allahabad Mathematical Society

Bull Allahabad Univ Math Ass — Bulletin. Allahabad University Mathematical Association

Bull Allegheny County Med Soc — Bulletin. Allegheny County Medical Society

Bull Allen Mem A Mus — Bulletin of the Allen Memorial Art Museum

Bull ALLF — Bulletin. Academie Royale de Langue et de Litterature Francaises

Bull Alliance A — Bulletin de l'Alliance des Arts

Bull Alloy Phase Diagrams — Bulletin of Alloy Phase Diagrams

Bull All Union Inst Agric Microbiol — Bulletin. All-Union Institute of Agricultural Microbiology

Bull All Union Inst Exp Med — Bulletin. All-Union Institute of Experimental Medicine

Bull All Union Sci Res Cotton Inst — Bulletin. All-Union Scientific Research Cotton Institute

Bull All Union Sci Res Inst Fert Agro Soil Sci Leningrad Dep — Bulletin. All-Union Scientific Research Institute of Fertilizers and Agro-Soil Science. Leningrad Department

Bull Allyn Mus — Bulletin. Allyn Museum

Bull Alox Corp — Bulletin. Alox Corporation

Bull Alp Gdn Soc — Bulletin of the Alpine Garden Society of Great Britain

Bull Alumni Assoc Utsunomiya Agric Coll — Bulletin. Alumni Association. Utsunomiya Agricultural College

Bull Am Acad Dermatol — Bulletin. American Academy of Dermatology

Bull Am Acad Med — Bulletin of the American Academy of Medicine

Bull Am Acad Ophthal Otolar — Bulletin. American Academy of Ophthalmology and Otolaryngology

Bull Am Acad Orthopaedic Surg — Bulletin. American Academy of Orthopaedic Surgeons

Bull Am Acad Psychiatr Law — Bulletin. American Academy of Psychiatry and the Law

Bull Am Acad Psychiatry Law — Bulletin. American Academy of Psychiatry and the Law

Bull Am Acad Rel — Bulletin. American Academy of Religion

Bull Am Acad Tuberc Physns — Bulletin of the American Academy of Tuberculosis Physicians

Bull Am Agric Chem Co — Bulletin. American Agricultural Chemical Company

Bull Am Anthr Ass — Bulletin. American Anthropological Association

Bull Am Anthrop Ass — Bulletin of the American Anthropological Association

Bull Am Arch Co — Bulletin. American Arch Co

Bull Am Ass Conserv Vision — Bulletin of the American Association for the Conservation of Vision

Bull Am Ass Ind Physns Surg — Bulletin of the American Association of Industrial Physicians and Surgeons

Bull Am Ass Med Rec Librr — Bulletin. American Association of Medical Record Librarians

Bull Am Ass Nurse Anaesth — Bulletin. American Association of Nurse Anaesthetists

Bull Am Assoc Bot Gard Arboreta — Bulletin. American Association of Botanical Gardens and Arboreta

Bull Am Assoc Dent Ed — Bulletin. American Association of Dental Editors

Bull Am Assoc Hosp Dent — Bulletin. American Association of Hospital Dentists

Bull Am Assoc Nurse Anesth — Bulletin. American Association of Nurse Anesthetists

Bull Am Assoc Pet Geol — Bulletin. American Association of Petroleum Geologists

Bull Am Assoc Variable Star Obs — Bulletin. American Association of Variable Star Observers

Bull Am Ass Petrol Geol — Bulletin. American Association of Petroleum Geologists

Bull Am Ass Publ Hlth Dent — Bulletin. American Association of Public Health Dentists

Bull Am Ass Publ Hlth Phys — Bulletin. American Association of Public Health Physicians

Bull Am Ass Univ Prof — Bulletin. American Association of University Professors

Bull Am Astron Soc — Bulletin. American Astronomical Society

Bull Amat Ent Soc — Bulletin of the Amateur Entomologists Society

Bull Amat Orchid Grow Soc — Bulletin of the Amateur Orchid Growers' Society

Bull Ambul Proct — Bulletin of Ambulant Proctology

Bull Am Cancer Soc — Bulletin. American Cancer Society

Bull Am Ceram Soc — Bulletin. American Ceramic Society

Bull Am Cer Soc — Bulletin. American Ceramic Society

Bull Am Coll Nurse Midwifery — Bulletin. Americana College of Nurse-Midwifery

Bull Am Coll Physicians — Bulletin. American College of Physicians

Bull Am Coll Surg — Bulletin. American College of Surgeons

Bull Am Dahlia Soc — Bulletin. American Dahlia Society

Bull Am Dent Ass — Bulletin. American Dental Association

Bull Amer Acad Arts Sci — Bulletin. American Academy of Arts and Sciences

Bull Amer Acad Benares — Bulletin of the American Academy of Benares

Bull Amer Assoc Petrol Geol — Bulletin. American Association of Petroleum Geologists

Bull Amer Astron Soc — Bulletin. American Astronomical Society

Bull Amer A Un — Bulletin of the American Art Union

Bull Amer Counc Learned Soc — Bulletin. American Council of Learned Societies

Bull Amer Dahlia Soc — Bulletin. American Dahlia Society

Bull Amer Fuchsia Soc — Bulletin American Fuchsia Society

Bull Amer Group IIC — Bulletin of the American Group IIC [*International Institute for Conservation*]

Bull Amer Hort Soc — Bulletin. American Horticultural Society

Bull Amer Inst Conserv Hist & A Works — Bulletin of the American Institute for Conservation of Historic and Artistic Works

Bull Amer Inst Iran A & Archaeol — Bulletin of the American Institute for Iranian Art and Archaeology
Bull Amer Inst Min Eng — Bulletin. American Institute of Mining Engineers
Bull Amer Math Soc — Bulletin. American Mathematical Society
Bull Amer Math Soc NS — Bulletin. American Mathematical Society. New Series
Bull Amer Meteorol Soc — Bulletin. American Meteorological Society
Bull Amer Mus Nat Hist — Bulletin of the American Museum of Natural History
Bull Amer Orient — Bulletin. American Schools of Oriental Research
Bull Amer Poinsettia Soc — Bulletin. American Poinsettia Society
Bull Amer Pomol Soc — Bulletin. American Pomological Society
Bull Amer Railw Eng Assoc — Bulletin. American Railway Engineering Association
Bull Amer Sch Orient Res — Bulletin. American Schools of Oriental Research
Bull Amer Sch Prehist Res — Bulletin of the American School of Prehistoric Research
Bull Amer Soc Bakery Eng — Bulletin. American Society of Bakery Engineers
Bull A Met Natn Tunis — Bulletin Annuel. Meteorologie Nationale (Tunis)
Bull Am Foundrymen's Assoc — Bulletin. American Foundrymen's Association
Bull Am Game Protect Ass — Bulletin. American Game Protective Association
Bull Am Group IIC — Bulletin. American Group. International Institute for Conservation of Historic and Artistic Works
Bull Am Hosta Soc — Bulletin. American Hosta Society
Bull Am Inst Chem Eng — Bulletin. American Institute of Chemical Engineers
Bull Am Inst Min Metall Eng — Bulletin. American Institute of Mining and Metallurgical Engineers
Bull Amis Gustave Courbet — Bulletin des Amis de Gustave Courbet
Bull Amis Laos — Bulletin des Amis de Laos
Bull Amis Mnmts Rouen — Bulletin des Amis des Monuments Rouennais
Bull Amis Mus Poitiers — Bulletin des Amis des Musees de Poitiers
Bull Amis Mus Rennes — Bulletin des Amis du Musee de Rennes
Bull Amis Mus Rouen — Bulletin des Amis du Musee de Rouen
Bull Amis Sevres — Bulletin des Amis de Sevres
Bull Amis Vieux Hue — Bulletin des Amis du Vieux Hue
Bull Am Malacol Union Inc — Bulletin. American Malacological Union, Incorporated
Bull Am Math Soc — Bulletin. American Mathematical Society
Bull Am Meteorol Soc — Bulletin. American Meteorological Society
Bull Am Mus Nat Hist — Bulletin. American Museum of Natural History
Bull Am Orchid Soc — Bulletin. American Orchid Society
Bull Am Paleontol — Bulletins of American Paleontology
Bull Am Paleontology — Bulletins of American Paleontology
Bull Am Pharm Assoc — Bulletin. American Pharmaceutical Association
Bull Am Phys Soc — Bulletin. American Physical Society
Bull Am Prot Hosp Assoc — Bulletin. American Protestant Hospital Association
Bull Am Sch Prehist Res — Bulletin. American School of Prehistoric Research
Bull Am Sch Prehist Research — Bulletin. American School of Prehistoric Research
Bull Am Soc Hosp Pharm — Bulletin. American Society of Hospital Pharmacists
Bull Am Soc Inform Sci — Bulletin. American Society for Information Science
Bull Am Soc Inf Sci — Bulletin. American Society for Information Science
Bull Am Soc Pap — Bulletin. American Society of Papyrologists
Bull Am Soc Vet Clin Pathol — Bulletin. American Society of Veterinary Clinical Pathologists
Bull Am Wood Preserv Assoc — Bulletin. American Wood Preservers' Association
Bull Am Zinc Inst — Bulletin. American Zinc Institute
Bull Anal d Hist Rom — Bulletin Analytique d'Histoire Romaine
Bull Anal Ent Med Vet — Bulletin Analytique d'Entomologie Medical et Veterinaire
Bull Anal Entomol Med Vet — Bulletin Analytique d'Entomologie Medicale et Veterinaire
Bull Anal Test — Bulletin of Analysis and Testing
Bull Anc Eleves Ec Fr Meun — Bulletin. Anciens Eleves de l'Ecole Francaise de Meunerie
Bull Anc Eleves Ec Meun ENSMIC — Bulletin des Anciens Eleves de l'Ecole de Meunerie ENSMIC
Bull Anciens Eleves Ecole Franc Meun — Bulletin. Anciens Eleves de l'Ecole Francaise de Meunerie
Bull Anc Ind Hist & Archaeol — Bulletin of Ancient Indian History and Archaeology
Bull Anc Lois et Ord Belg — Bulletin. Commission Royale des Anciennes Lois et Ordonnances deBelgique
Bull Anc Orient Mus — Bulletin of the Ancient Orient Museum
Bull & Nieuws Bull Kon Ned Oudhdknd Bond — Bulletin en Nieuws-Bulletin Koninklijke Nederlandse Oudheidkundige Bond
Bull Anglo Egypt Sudan Geol Surv — Bulletin of the Anglo-Egyptian Sudan Geological Survey
Bull Anglo Israel Archaeol Soc — Bulletin of the Anglo-Israel Archaeological Society
Bull Anglo-Sov LA — Bulletin. Anglo-Soviet Law Association
Bull Anim Behav — Bulletin of Animal Behavior
Bull Anim Health Prod Afr — Bulletin of Animal Health and Production in Africa
Bull Anim Health Prod Afr Bull Sante Prod Anim Afr — Bulletin of Animal Health and Production in Africa/Bulletin de la Sante et de la Production Animales en Afrique
Bull Anim Hlth Serv Tasm — Bulletin. Animal Health Service. Tasmania
Bull Anim Hlth Stn Yeerongpilly — Bulletin of the Animal Health Station. Yeerongpilly, Queensland
Bull Annexe Annls Minist Agric — Bulletin-Annexe des Annales du Ministere de l'Agriculture [Paris]
Bull Annls CR Soc Belge Ingrs Ind — Bulletin. Annales et Comptes Rendus de la Societe Belge des Ingenieurs et des Industriels
Bull Annls Soc R Ent Belg — Bulletin et Annales. Societe Royale Entomologique de Belgique
Bull Ann Soc Entomol Belg — Bulletin et Annales. Societe Entomologique de Belgique
Bull Ann Soc R Belge Entom — Bulletin et Annales. Societe Royale Belge d'Entomologie

Bull Ann Soc R Entomol Belg — Bulletin et Annales. Societe Royale d'Entomologie de Belgique
Bull Ann Soc Roy Entomol Belg — Bulletin et Annales. Societe Royale d'Entomologie de Belgique
Bull Ann Soc Suisse Chronom et Lab Suisse Rech Horlogeres — Bulletin Annuel. Societe Suisse de Chronometrie et Laboratoire Suisse de Recherches Horlogeres
Bull Annu Fed Int Lait — Bulletin Annuel. Federation Internationale de Laiterie
Bull Annu Mus Ethnog — Bulletin Annuel. Musee d'Ethnographie
Bull Annu Soc Suisse Chronom Lab Suisse Rech Horlog — Bulletin Annuel. Societe Suisse de Chronometrie et Laboratoire Suisse de Recherches Horlogeres
Bull Annu Stn Met Salonique — Bulletin Annuaire de la Station Meteorologique du Gymnase Bulgare de Garcons St. Cyrille et Methode (Salonique)
Bull Ant B — Babesch. Bulletin Antieke Beschaving
Bull Ant Besch — Babesch. Bulletin Antieke Beschaving
Bull Ant Besch — Bulletin Antieke Beschaving
Bull Ant Fr — Bulletin. Societe Nationale des Antiquaires de France
Bull Anthrop — Bulletin of Anthropology
Bull Anthrop — Bulletin. Societe d'Anthropologie de Paris
Bull Antivenin Inst Am — Bulletin. Antivenin Institute of America
Bull Antwerp Ver Bodem & Grotonderzoek — Bulletin van der Antwerpse Vereniging van Bodem- en Grotonderzoek
Bull A Obs Met Semin Coll St Martial — Bulletin Annuel. Observatoire Meteorologique. Seminaire-College St. Martial (Port-au-Prince)
Bull A Off Natn Met — Bulletin Annuel. Office Nationale Meteorologique
Bull Aomori Agr Exp Sta — Bulletin. Aomori Agricultural Experiment Station
Bull Aomori Agric Exp Stn — Bulletin. Aomori Agricultural Experiment Station
Bull Aomori Apple Exp Sta — Bulletin. Aomori Apple Experiment Station/Aomori-Ken Ringo Shikenjo Hokoku
Bull Aomori Apple Exp Stn — Bulletin. Aomori Apple Experiment Station
Bull Aomori Prefect Inst Public Health Environ — Bulletin. Aomori Prefectural Institute of Public Health and Environment
Bull A Pa Bur Topogr Geol Surv — Bulletin A. Pennsylvania Bureau of Topographic and Geologic Survey
Bull A Phys Soc — Bulletin. American Physical Society
Bull Apic — Bulletin Apicole
Bull Apic Doc Sci Tech Inf — Bulletin Apicole de Documentation Scientifique et Technique et d'Information
Bull Apic Inf Doc Sci Tech — Bulletin Apicole d'Information et de Documentation Scientifique et Technique
Bull Apic Inf Docum Scient Tech — Bulletin Apicole d'Information et de Documentation Scientifique et Technique
Bull APM Forests — Bulletin. APM [Australian Paper Manufacturers] Forests Proprietary Ltd.
Bull Appl Bot Genet Plant Breed — Bulletin. Applied Botany. Genetics and Plant Breeding
Bull Appl Bot Genet Plant Breed Ser C — Bulletin. Applied Botany. Genetics and Plant Breeding. Series C. Supplement
Bull Appl Bot Plant Breed — Bulletin. Applied Botany and Plant Breeding
Bull Aquat Biol — Bulletin of Aquatic Biology
Bull Aquatic Biol — Bulletin of Aquatic Biology
BullArch — Bulletin Archeologique. Comite des Travaux Historiques et Scientifiques
Bull Archaeol Inst America — Bulletin of the Archaeological Institute of America
Bull Arch Alg — Bulletin d'Archeologie Algerienne
Bull Arch Comite — Bulletin Archeologique. Comite des Travaux Historiques et Scientifiques
Bull Archeol — Bulletin Archeologique
Bull Archeol — Bulletin Archeologique, Historique, et Artistique. Societe Archeologique de Tarn-et-Garonne
Bull Archeol Alg — Bulletin d'Archeologie Algerienne
Bull Archeol Assoc Bret — Bulletin Archeologique de l'Association Bretonne
Bull Archeol Crist — Bullettino di Archeologia Cristiana
Bull Archeol Cte Trav Hist & Sci — Bulletin Archeologique du Comite des Travaux Historiques et Scientifiques
Bull Archeol Maroc — Bulletin d'Archeologie Marocaine
Bull Archeol Mus Guimet — Bulletin Archeologique du Musee Guimet
Bull Archeol Tarn — Bulletin Archeologique, Historique, et Artistique. Societe Archeologique de Tarn-et-Garonne
Bull Arch Hist — Bulletin Archeologique, Historique, et Artistique. Societe Archeologique de Tarn-et-Garonne
Bull Arch Maroc — Bulletin d'Archeologie Marocaine
Bull Arch Nap — Bullettino Archeologico Napoletano
Bull Arch Sens — Bulletin. Societe Archeologique de Sens
Bull ARERS — Bulletin. Association Regionale pour l'Etude et la Recherche Scientifiques
Bull Argic Exp Stn N Carol St Univ — Bulletin. Agricultural Experiment Station. North Carolina State University
Bull Ariegeois — Bulletin Annuel. Societe Ariegeoise des Sciences, Lettres, et Arts
Bull Ariz Agr Exp Sta — Bulletin. Arizona Agricultural Experiment Station
Bull Ariz Agr Exp Sta Coop Ext Serv — Bulletin. Arizona Agricultural Experiment Station. Cooperating Extension Service
Bull Ariz Agric Exp Stn — Bulletin. Arizona Agricultural Experiment Station
Bull Ariz Water Comm — Bulletin. Arizona Water Commission
Bull Ark Agr Exp Sta — Bulletin. Arkansas Agricultural Experiment Station
Bull Ark Agric Exp Stn — Bulletin. Arkansas Agricultural Experiment Station
Bull Arkansas Agric Exp Stn — Bulletin. Arkansas Agricultural Experiment Station
Bull Arm Branch Acad Sci USSR — Bulletin. Armenian Branch. Academy of Sciences. USSR
Bull Arts Sci Div Ryukyu Univ — Bulletin of Arts and Science Division. Ryukyu University/Ryukyu Daigaku Bunrui Gakubu Kiyo
Bull Arts Sci Div Univ Ryukyus Math Natur Sci — Bulletin. Arts and Science Division. University of the Ryukyus. Mathematics andNatural Sciences
Bull A Serv Met Cote Fr Somalis — Bulletin Annuel. Service Meteorologique de la Cote Francaise des Somalis

Bull A Serv Met Metrop Afr N — Bulletin Annuel. Service Meteorologique Metropole et de l'Afrique du Nord

Bull A Serv Met Obs Geophys Martinique — Bulletin Annuel. Service Meteorologique et Observatoire Geophysique, Martinique

Bull Asia Inst — Bulletin of the Asia Institute

Bull Asian Inst MI — Bulletin of the Asian Institute. Michigan

Bull A Soc Astr Met Port Au Prince — Bulletin Annuel. Societe Astronomique et Meteorologique de Port-au-Prince

Bull A Soc Jersiaise — Bulletin Annuel de la Societe Jersiaise

Bull A Soc Pomol Ernee — Bulletin Annuel de la Societe Pomologique d'Ernee

Bull A Soc Prof Spec Agric Gannat — Bulletin Annuel de la Societe des Professeurs Speciaux d'Agriculture (Gannat)

Bull A Soc Suisse Chronom — Bulletin Annuel de la Societe Suisse de Chronometrie et du Laboratoire Suisse de Recherches Horlogeres

Bull Ass — Bulletin des Assurances

Bull Ass Anat (Paris) — Bulletin. Association des Anatomistes (Paris)

Bull Ass Bude — Bulletin. Association Guillaume Bude

Bull Ass Can Bibliot Lang Fr — Bulletin. Association Canadienne des Bibliothecaires de Langue Francaise

Bull Ass Dipl Microbiol Nancy — Bulletin. Association des Diplomes de Microbiologie. Faculte de Pharmacie de Nancy

Bull Ass Diplomes Microbiol Fac Pharm Nancy — Bulletin. Association des Diplomes de Microbiologie. Faculte de Pharmacie de Nancy

Bull Ass Franc Avance Sci — Bulletin. Association Francaise pour l'Avancement des Sciences

Bull Ass Franc Canc — Bulletin. Association Francaise pour l'Etude du Cancer

Bull Ass Fr Etude Sol — Bulletin. Association Francaise pour l'Etude du Sol

Bull Ass Geogr Fr — Bulletin. Association des Geographes Francais

Bull Ass Guillaume Bude — Bulletin. Association Guillaume Bude

Bull Ass Int Hydrol Scient — Bulletin. Association Internationale d'Hydrologie Scientifique

Bull Ass Int Sec Soc — Bulletin. Association Internationale de la Securite Sociale

Bull Ass Jur Eur — Bulletin. Association des Juristes Europeens

Bull Ass Languedoc Hort Prat — Bulletin de l'Association Languedocienne d'Horticulture Pratique

Bull Ass Magn Terr — Bulletin. Association de Magnetisme Terrestre

Bull Ass Marit — Bulletin de l'Association Maritime

Bull Ass Med Belge Accid Trav — Bulletin de l'Association Medicale Belge des Accidents du Travail

Bull Ass Med Chir Accid Trav — Bulletin de l'Association Medico-Chirurgicale des Accidents du Travail

Bull Ass Med Corp — Bulletin. Association Medicale Corporative

Bull Ass Med Hait — Bulletin. Association Medicale Haitienne

Bull Ass Med Haiti — Bulletin de l'Association Medicale Haitienne

Bull Ass Med Int Notre Dame De Lourdes — Bulletin de l'Association Medicale Internationale de Notre-Dame de Lourdes

Bull Ass Med Lang Fr — Bulletin. Association des Medecins de Langue Francaise

Bull Ass Med Lang Fr Am N — Bulletin de l'Association des Medecins de Langue Francaise de l'Amerique du Nord

Bull Ass Med Libr — Bulletin of the Association of Medical Librarians

Bull Ass Membr Corps Facs Med Lyon — Bulletin de l'Association des Membres du Corps Enseignant des Facultes de Medicine (Lyon)

Bull Ass Nat Levall Perret — Bulletin de l'Association des Naturalistes de Levallois-Perret

Bull Ass Nat Vall Loing — Bulletin de l'Association des Naturalistes de la Vallee du Loing

Bull Ass Normande Accid Trav — Bulletin de l'Association Normande pour Prevenir les Accidents du Travail

Bull Assoc Anat — Bulletin. Association des Anatomistes

Bull Assoc Anat (Nancy) — Bulletin. Association des Anatomistes (Nancy)

Bull Assoc Anc Eleves Inst Ind Ferment Bruxelles — Bulletin. Association des Anciens Eleves de l'Institut des Industries de Fermentation de Bruxelles

Bull Assoc Anc Eleves Inst Super Ferment Gand — Bulletin. Association des Anciens Eleves de l'Institut Superieur des Fermentations de Gand

Bull Assoc Anc Eleves Super Ferment Gand — Bulletin. Association des Anciens Eleves de l'Institut Superieur des Fermentations de Gand

Bull Assoc Anc Etud Brass Univ Louv — Bulletin. Association des Anciens Etudiants de l'Ecole Superieure de Brasserie de l'Universite de Louvain

Bull Assoc Anc Etud Brass Univ Louvain — Bulletin. Association des Anciens Etudiants en Brasserie de l'Universite de Louvain

Bull Assoc Anc Etud Ec Super Brass Univ Louv — Bulletin. Association des Anciens Etudiants de l'Ecole Superieure de Brasserie de l'Universite de Louvain

Bull Assoc Anc Etud Ec Super Brass Univ Louvain — Bulletin. Association des Anciens Etudiants de l'Ecole Superieure de Brasserie de l'Universite de Louvain

Bull Assoc Anciens Eleves Ecole Fr Meun — Bulletin. Association des Anciens Eleves de l'Ecole Francaise de Meunerie

Bull Assoc Biochim Hop Que — Bulletin. Association des Biochimistes des Hopitaux du Quebec

Bull Assoc Chim — Bulletin. Association des Chimistes

Bull Assoc Chim Sucr Distill Fr Colon — Bulletin. Association des Chimistes de Sucrerie et de Distillerie de France et des Colonies

Bull Assoc Chim Sucr Distill Ind Agric Fr Colon — Bulletin. Association des Chimistes de Sucrerie, de Distillerie, et des Industries Agricoles de France et des Colonies

Bull Assoc Difesa Firenze Ant — Bullettino dell'Associazione per la Difesa di Firenze Antica

Bull Assoc Diplomes Microbiol Fac Pharm Nancy — Bulletin. Association des Diplomes de Microbiologie. Faculte de Pharmacie de Nancy

Bull Ass Oceanogr Phys — Bulletin. Association d'Oceanographie Physique

Bull Assoc Eng Geol — Bulletin. Association of Engineering Geologists

Bull Assoc Engng Geol — Bulletin. Association of Engineering Geologists

Bull Assoc Enseign Math Ser B — Bulletin. Association des Enseignants de Mathematiques. Serie B

Bull Assoc F A Yale U — Bulletin of the Associates in Fine Arts at Yale University

Bull Assoc Fr Chim Ind Cuir Doc Sci Tech Ind Cuir — Bulletin de l'Association Francaise des Chimistes des Industries du Cuir et Documents Scientifiques et Techniques des Industries du Cuir

Bull Assoc Fr Etude Cancer — Bulletin. Association Francaise pour l'Etude du Cancer

Bull Assoc Fr Etude Sol — Bulletin. Association Francaise pour l'Etude du Sol

Bull Assoc Fr Etude Sol Suppl — Bulletin. Association Francaise pour l'Etude du Sol. Supplement

Bull Assoc Fr Etud Sol — Bulletin. Association Francaise pour l'Etude du Sol

Bull Assoc Fr Ing Chim Tech Ind Cuir Doc Inf Cent Tech Cuir — Bulletin. Association Francaise des Ingenieurs, Chimistes, et Techniciens des Industries du Cuir et Documents et Informations du Centre Technique du Cuir

Bull Assoc Fr Ing Tech Cinema — Bulletin. Association Francaise des Ingenieurs et Techniciens du Cinema

Bull Assoc Fr Rech & Etud Cameroun — Bulletin de l'Association Francaise pour les Recherches et Etudes Camerounaises

Bull Assoc Fr Tech Pet — Bulletin. Association Francaise des Techniciens du Petrole

Bull Assoc Guillaume Bude — Bulletin. Association Guillaume Bude

Bull Assoc Gynecol Obstet Lang Fr — Bulletin. Association des Gynecologues et Obstetriciens de Langue Francaise

Bull Assoc Int Doc — Bulletin. Association Internationale des Documentalistes

Bull Assoc Int Doc Tech Inf — Bulletin. Association Internationale des Documentalistes et Techniciens de l'Information

Bull Assoc Int Etud S E Eur — Bulletin. Association International d'Etudes du Sud-Est Europeen

Bull Assoc Int Explor Hist Asie Cent & Extreme Orient — Bulletin de l'Association Internationale pour l'Exploration Historique de l'Asie Centrale et de l'Extreme-Orient

Bull Assoc Int Froid Mon — Bulletin. Association Internationale du Froid. Monthly

Bull Assoc Int Geol Ing — Bulletin. Association Internationale de Geologie de l'Ingenieur

Bull Assoc Int Hist Verre — Bulletin de l'Association Internationale pour l'Histoire du Verre

Bull Assoc Kinet India — Bulletin. Association of Kineticists of India

Bull Assoc Minn Entomol — Bulletin. Association of Minnesota Entomologists

Bull Assoc Napol Med — Bullettino di Associazione Napolitana di Medici e Naturalisti

Bull Assoc Perm Congr Belg Route — Bulletin. Association Permanente des Congres Belges de la Route

Bull Assoc Philom Alsace Lorraine — Bulletin. Association Philomatique d'Alsace et de Lorraine

Bull Assoc Preserv Technol — Bulletin of the Association for Preservation Technology

Bull Assoc Pyren Echange Pl — Bulletin de l'Association Pyreneenne pour l'Echange des Plantes

Bull Assoc R Anc Etud Brass Univ Louv — Bulletin. Association Royal des Anciens Etudiants en Brasserie de l'Universite de Louvain

Bull Assoc R Anc Etud Brass Univ Louvain — Bulletin. Association Royale des Anciens Etudiants en Brasserie de l'Universitede Louvain

Bull Assoc Reg Etude Rech Sci — Bulletin. Association Regionale pour l'Etude et la Recherche Scientifiques

Bull Assoc Rus Ric Sci Prague — Bulletin de l'Association Russe pour les Recherches Scientifiques a Prague

Bull Assoc Sci Alger — Bulletin. Association Scientifique Algerienne

Bull Assoc Sci Math Educ Penang — Bulletin. Association for Science and Mathematics Education Penang

Bull Assoc State Eng Soc — Bulletin. Associated State Engineering Societies

Bull Assoc State Eng Soc Yearb — Bulletin. Associated State Engineering Societies. Yearbook

Bull Assoc Suisse Electr — Bulletin. Association Suisse des Electriciens

Bull Assoc Suisse Geol Ing Pet — Bulletin. Association Suisse des Geologues et Ingenieurs du Petrole

Bull Assoc Tech Anim Hyg — Bulletin. Association of the Technic for Animal Hygiene

Bull Assoc Tech Fonderie — Bulletin. Association Technique de Fonderie

Bull Assoc Tech Ind Papet — Bulletin. Association Technique de l'Industrie Papetiere

Bull Assoc Tech Mar Aeronaut — Bulletin. Association Technique Maritime et Aeronautique

Bull Assoc Tech Marit Aeronaut — Bulletin. Association Technique Maritime et Aeronautique

Bull Assoc Trop Biol — Bulletin. Association for Tropical Biology

Bull Ass Oper Millers — Bulletin. Association of Operative Millers

Bull Ass Ordre Natn Merite Agric — Bulletin de l'Association de l'Ordre National du Merite Agricole

Bull Ass Philomath — Bulletin de l'Association Philomathique

Bull Ass Philomath Alsace et Lorraine — Bulletin. Association Philomathique d'Alsace et de Lorraine

Bull Ass Philomath Als Lorr — Bulletin. Association Philomathique d'Alsace et de Lorraine

Bull Ass Plrs Caoutch — Bulletin de l'Association des Planteurs de Caoutchouc et Autres Produits Tropicaux

Bull Ass Presse Med Fr — Bulletin de l'Association de la Presse Medicale Francaise

Bull Ass Prof Math Paris — Bulletin de l'Association des Professeurs de Mathematiques de l'Enseignement Publics (Paris)

Bull Ass Prov Archit Fr — Bulletin de l'Association Provinciale des Architectes Francais

Bull Ass Psychiat Roum — Bulletin de l'Association des Psychiatres Roumaines

Bull Ass Pyren Ech Pl — Bulletin de l'Association Pyreneenne pour l'Echange des Plantes

Bull Ass Rec Libr N Am — Bulletin. Association of Record Librarians of North America

Bull Ass Reg Dev Rech Paleont Lyon — Bulletin de l'Association Regionale pour le Developpement des Recherches de Paleontologie et Prehistoire (Lyon)

Bull Ass Reg Etude Rech Scient Reims — Bulletin. Association Regionale pour l'Etude et la Recherche Scientifique (Reims)

Bull Ass Reg Ingrs Als Lorr — Bulletin de l'Association Regionale des Ingenieurs d'Alsace et Lorraine

Bull Ass Scient Alger — Bulletin de l'Association Scientifique Algerienne

Bull Ass Scient Wkrs Sth Afr — Bulletin of the Association of Scientific Workers of Southern Africa

Bull Ass Suisse El — Bulletin. Association Suisse des Electriciens

Bull Ass Suisse Elec — Bulletin. Association Suisse des Electriciens

Bull Ass Tech Fo — Bulletin. Association Technique de Fonderie

Bull Ass Tech Fond Liege — Bulletin de l'Association Technique de Fonderie de Liege

Bull Ass Tech Ind Pap — Bulletin. Association Technique de l'Industrie Papetiere

Bull Ass Tech Marit Aeronaut — Bulletin de l'Association Technique Maritime et Aeronautique

Bull Ass Tech Prod Util Energ Nucl — Bulletin. Association Technique pour la Production et l'Utilisation de l'Energie Nucleaire

Bull Astr — Bulletin Astronomique

Bull Astr Inst Neth — Bulletin. Astronomical Institutes of the Netherlands

Bull Astron — Bulletin Astronomique

Bull Astron Inst Czech — Bulletin. Astronomical Institutes of Czechoslovakia

Bull Astron Inst Neth — Bulletin. Astronomical Institutes of the Netherlands

Bull Astron Inst Neth Suppl Ser — Bulletin. Astronomical Institutes of the Netherlands. Supplement Series

Bull Astron Observ Belg — Bulletin Astronomique. Observatoire Royale de Belgique

Bull Astronom Inst of Czechoslovakia — Bulletin. Astronomical Institutes of Czechoslovakia

Bull Astron Soc India — Bulletin. Astronomical Society of India

Bull A Synd Piscic Fr — Bulletin Annuel du Syndicat des Pisciculteurs de France

Bull At Energy Res Inst Korea — Bulletin. Atomic Energy Research Institute of Korea

Bull Atmos Radioactiv — Bulletin of Atmospheric Radioactivity

Bull Atom Sci — Bulletin of the Atomic Scientists

Bull Atom Scient — Bulletin of the Atomic Scientists

Bull At Sci — Bulletin of the Atomic Scientists

Bull Auburn Univ Eng Exp Stn — Bulletin. Auburn University. Engineering Experiment Station

Bull Auckl Inst Mus — Bulletin. Auckland Institute and Museum

Bull Audiophonol — Bulletin d'Audiophonologie

Bull A Univ Ariz Coop Ext Serv — Bulletin A. University of Arizona. Cooperative Extension Service

Bull Aust Math Soc — Bulletin. Australian Mathematical Society

Bull Aust Miner Dev Lab — Bulletin. Australian Mineral Development Laboratories

Bull Australas Inst Min Metall — Bulletin. Australasian Institute of Mining and Metallurgy

Bull Austral Math Soc — Bulletin. Australian Mathematical Society

Bull Aust Road Res Bd — Bulletin. Australian Road Research Board

Bull Aust Soc Explor Geophys — Bulletin. Australian Society of Exploration Geophysicists

Bull Aust Soc Stud Lab Hist — Bulletin. Australian Society for the Study of Labour History

Bull Aust Weld Res Assoc — Bulletin. Australian Welding Research Association

Bull Av — Bulletin. Federation des Avoues

Bull Aventico — Bulletin pro Aventico

Bull Ayer Clin Lab PA Hosp — Bulletin. Ayer Clinical Laboratory of the Pennsylvania Hospital

Bull Azabu Univ Vet Med — Bulletin. Azabu University of Veterinary Medicine

Bull Azabu Vet Coll — Bulletin. Azabu Veterinary College

Bull B A — Bulletin des Beaux-Arts

Bull BA — Bulletin. Musee National Hongrois des Beaux-Arts

Bull Balai Penelitian Perkebunan Medan — Bulletin Balai Penelitian Perkebunan Medan

Bull Baroda Mus & Pict Gal — Bulletin of the Baroda Museum and Picture Gallery

Bull Baroda State Mus & Pict Gal — Bulletin of the Baroda State Museum and Picture Gallery

Bull Basic Sci Res — Bulletin of Basic Science Research

Bull Basic Sci Res Inst Inha Univ — Bulletin. Basic Science Research Institute. Inha University

Bull Basrah Nat Hist Mus — Bulletin. Basrah Natural History Museum

Bull Bas Sci Res — Bulletin of Basic Science Research

Bull BC Dep Mines Pet Resour — Bulletin. British Columbia Department of Mines and Petroleum Resources

Bull BC Minist Energy Mines Pet Resour — Bulletin. British Columbia. Ministry of Energy, Mines, and Petroleum Resources

Bull BC Minist Mines Pet Resour — Bulletin. British Columbia. Ministry of Mines and Petroleum Resources

Bull BCS — Bulletin. Board of Celtic Studies

Bull Bd Agric Isle Man — Bulletin. Board of Agriculture. Isle of Man

Bull Bd Celtic Studies — Bulletin. Board of Celtic Studies

Bull Bd Commnrs Agric For Hawaii Div Ent — Bulletin. Board of Commissioners of Agriculture and Forestry. Hawaii. Division of Entomology

Bull Bd Commnrs Agric For Hawaii Div For — Bulletin. Board of Commissioners of Agriculture and Forestry. Hawaii. Division of Forestry

Bull Bd Sci Art NZ — Bulletin. Board of Science and Art. New Zealand

Bull Belfort — Bulletin. Societe Belfortaine d'Emulation

Bull Belgicatom — Bulletin Belgicatom

Bull Belg Math Soc Simon Stevin — Bulletin of the Belgian Mathematical Society. Simon Stevin

Bull Belg Metrol — Bulletin Belge de Metrologie

Bull Belg Phys Soc — Bulletin. Belgian Physical Society

Bull Belg Ver Geol — Bulletin van de Belgische Vereniging voor Geologie

Bull Belg Ver Geol Paleontol Hydrol — Bulletin van de Belgische Vereniging voor Geologie. Paleontologie en Hydrologie

Bull Bell Mus Pathobiol — Bulletin. Bell Museum of Pathobiology

Bull Benelux — Bulletin. Benelux

Bull Bergen Cty Dent Soc — Bulletin. Bergen County Dental Society

Bull Bernice P Bishop Mus — Bulletin. Bernice P. Bishop Museum

Bull Beziers — Bulletin. Societe Archeologique, Scientifique, et Litteraire de Beziers

Bull Bibl — Bulletin of Bibliography

Bull Bibl de France — Bulletin des Bibliotheques de France

Bull Bibl Fr — Bulletin des Bibliotheques de France

Bull Bibl France — Bulletin des Bibliotheques de France

Bull Bibliog — Bulletin of Bibliography

Bull Bibliogr Boston — Bulletin of Bibliography (Boston)

Bull Bibliogr Mag Notes — Bulletin of Bibliography and Magazine Notes

Bull Bibliogr Pedag Musee Belge — Bulletin Bibliographique et Pedagogique du Musee Belge

Bull Biblioph — Bulletin du Bibliophile

Bull Biblioph & Bibliothecaire — Bulletin du Bibliophile et du Bibliothecaire

Bull Biblioph Belge — Bulletin du Bibliophile Belge

Bull Biblioth Fr — Bulletin des Bibliotheques de France

Bull Bibl Natl — Bulletin. Bibliotheque Nationale

Bull Biblphique Pedol ORSTOM — Bulletin Bibliographique de Pedologie. Office de la Recherche Scientifique et Technique d'Outre-Mer

Bull Bibl Soc Rencesvals — Bulletin Bibliographique. Societe Rencesvals

Bull Bib Royale Belgique — Bulletin de la Bibliotheque Royale de Belgique

Bull Bime — Bulletin Bimestriel

Bull Bimens Soc Linn Lyon — Bulletin Bimensual. Societe Linneenne de Lyon

Bull Bimest INACOL — Bulletin Bimestriel. INACOL

Bull Bimest Inst Natl Amelior Conserves Legumes (Belg) — Bulletin Bimestriel. Institut National pour l'Amelioration des Conserves de Legumes (Belgium)

Bull Bingham Oceanogr Collect — Bulletin. Bingham Oceanographic Collection

Bull Bingham Oceanogr Collect Yale Univ — Bulletin. Bingham Oceanographic Collection. Yale University

Bull Biochem Res Lab Bulg Acad Sci — Bulletin. Biochemical Research Laboratory. Bulgarian Academy of Sciences

Bull Bio Farma — Bulletin Bio-Farma

Bull Biogeogr Soc Japan — Bulletin. Biogeographical Society of Japan

Bull Biogeogr Soc Jpn — Bulletin. Biogeographical Society of Japan

Bull Biol Assoc Univ Amoy — Bulletin. Biological Association. University of Amoy/Hsia-Ta Shengwu-Hsueeh-HuiCh'i K'an

Bull Biol (Beijing) — Bulletin. Biology (Beijing)

Bull Biol Board Can — Bulletin. Biological Board of Canada

Bull Biol France et Belgique — Bulletin Biologique de la France et de la Belgique

Bull Biol Fr Belg — Bulletin Biologique de la France et de la Belgique

Bull Biol Med Exp URSS — Bulletin de Biologie et de Medecine Experimentale de l'URSS

Bull Biol Pharm — Bulletin des Biologistes Pharmaciens

Bull Biol Pharmns — Bulletin des Biologistes Pharmaciens

Bull Biol Res Cent (Baghdad) — Bulletin. Biological Research Centre (Baghdad)

Bull Biol Res Cent Publ (Baghdad) — Bulletin. Biological Research Centre. Publication (Baghdad)

Bull Biol Soc Hiroshima Univ — Bulletin. Biological Society of Hiroshima University

Bull Biol Soc Wash — Bulletin. Biological Society of Washington

Bull Bismuth Inst — Bulletin. Bismuth Institute

Bull Bismuth Inst Brussels — Bulletin. Bismuth Institute (Brussels)

Bull Bitum Rds Dev Grp — Bulletin. Bituminous Roads Development Group

Bull Blue Hill Met Obs — Bulletin. Blue Hill Meteorological Observatory

Bull BN — Bulletin. Banque Nationale

Bull BNL — Bulletin. Benelux

Bull Board Celtic Stud — Bulletin. Board of Celtic Studies

Bull Board Sci Art (NZ) — Bulletin. Board of Science and Art (New Zealand)

Bull B Okla Agric Exp Stn — Bulletin B. Oklahoma Agricultural Experiment Station

Bull Borda — Bulletin. Societe de Borda

Bull Boris Kidric Inst Nucl Sci — Bulletin. Boris Kidric Institute of Nuclear Sciences

Bull Boris Kidric Inst Nucl Sci Biol — Bulletin. Boris Kidric Institute of Nuclear Sciences. Biology

Bull Boris Kidric Inst Nucl Sci Ceram Metall — Bulletin. Boris Kidric Institute of Nuclear Sciences. Ceramics and Metallurgy

Bull Boris Kidric Inst Nucl Sci Chem — Bulletin. Boris Kidric Institute of Nuclear Sciences. Chemistry

Bull Boris Kidric Inst Nucl Sci Electron — Bulletin. Boris Kidric Institute of Nuclear Sciences. Electronics

Bull Boris Kidric Inst Nucl Sci Nucl Eng — Bulletin. Boris Kidric Institute of Nuclear Sciences. Nuclear Engineering

Bull Boris Kidric Inst Nucl Sci Phys — Bulletin. Boris Kidric Institute of Nuclear Sciences. Physics

Bull Boris Kidric Inst Nucl Sci Suppl — Bulletin. Boris Kidric Institute of Nuclear Sciences. Supplement

Bull Boston Mycol Club — Bulletin of the Boston Mycological Club

Bull Boston Soc Nat Hist — Bulletin. Boston Society of Natural History

Bull Boston Soc Psychic Res — Bulletin. Boston Society for Psychic Research

Bull Bot Dep Jamaica — Bulletin. Botanical Department. Jamaica

Bull Bot Gard Buitenzorg — Bulletin. Botanic Gardens of Buitenzorg

Bull Bot Gdns Buitenz — Bulletin of the the Botanic Gardens. Buitenzorg

Bull Bot Lieg — Bulletin de Botanique Liegeoise

Bull Bot Soc Beng — Bulletin of the Botanical Society of Bengal

Bull Bot Soc Bengal — Botanical Society of Bengal

Bull Bot Soc Coll Sci (Nagpur) — Bulletin. Botanical Society. College of Science (Nagpur)

Bull Bot Soc Gov Sci Coll (Jabalpur (MP) India) — Bulletin. Botanical Society. Government Science College (Jabalpur (MP) India)

Bull Bot Soc Univ Saugar — Bulletin. Botanical Society. University of Saugar

Bull Bot Surv India — Bulletin. Botanical Survey of India

Bull B Psych Soc — Bulletin. British Psychological Society
Bull Brackishwater Aquacult Dev Cent — Bulletin. Brackishwater Aquaculture Development Centre
Bull Bradford Nat Hist Microsc Soc — Bulletin of the Bradford Natural History and Microscopical Society
Bull Br Antarct Surv — Bulletin. British Antarctic Survey
Bull Br Arachnol Soc — Bulletin. British Arachnological Society
Bull Br Ass Chem — Bulletin. British Association of Chemists
Bull Br Astr Ass NSW Brch — Bulletin. British Astronomical Association. New South Wales Branch
Bull Br Bak Ind Res Ass — Bulletin. British Baking Industries Research Association
Bull Br Beekprs Ass Res Comm — Bulletin. British Bee-Keepers Association. Research Committee
Bull Br Bur Non Ferr Metal Statist — Bulletin of the British Bureau of Non-Ferrous Metal Statistics
Bull Br Carnat Soc — Bulletin. British Carnation Society
Bull Br Cast Iron Res Ass — Bulletin of the British Cast Iron Research Association
Bull Br Cast Iron Res Assoc — Bulletin. British Cast Iron Research Association
Bull Br Coke Res Ass — Bulletin. British Coke Research Association
Bull Br Colomb Snow Surv — Bulletin. British Columbia Snow Survey
Bull Br Columb Dep Hlth — Bulletin. British Columbia Department of Health and Welfare
Bull Br Columb Ent Soc — Bulletin of the British Columbia Entomological Society
Bull Br Comm Gas Ass — Bulletin of the British Commercial Gas Association
Bull Brev Budapest — Bulletin des Brevets (Budapest)
Bull Brev Bull Cent Marques — Bulletin des Brevets et Bulletin Central des Marques
Bull Brew Malt Barley Res Inst — Bulletin. Brewing and Malting Barley Research Institute
Bull Brew Sci — Bulletin of Brewing Science
Bull Brew Soc Jpn — Bulletin. Brewing Society (Japan)
Bull Br Gelat Glue Res Ass — Bulletin. British Gelatine and Glue Research Association
Bull Br Hydromech Res Ass — Bulletin. British Hydromechanics Research Association
Bull Brie — Bulletin. Societe Litteraires et Historiques de la Brie
Bull Br Interplanet Soc — Bulletin. British Interplanetary Society
Bull Brit Carnation Soc — Bulletin. British Carnation Society
Bull Brit Mus Natur Hist — Bulletin. British Museum (Natural History)
Bull Brit Mus Natur Hist Bot Ser — Bulletin. British Museum. Natural History. Botany Series
Bull Brit Mus Natur Hist Geol — Bulletin. British Museum (Natural History). Geology
Bull Brit Psychol Soc — Bulletin. British Psychological Society
Bull Brit Soc Hist Sci — Bulletin. British Society for the History of Science
Bull Br Mus (Nat Hist) Bot — Bulletin. British Museum (Natural History). Botany
Bull Br Mus (Nat Hist) Entomol — Bulletin. British Museum (Natural History). Entomology
Bull Br Mus (Nat Hist) Entomol Suppl — Bulletin. British Museum (Natural History). Entomology. Supplement
Bull Br Mus (Nat Hist) Geol — Bulletin. British Museum (Natural History). Geology
Bull Br Mus (Nat Hist) Geol Suppl — Bulletin. British Museum (Natural History). Geology. Supplement
Bull Br Mus (Nat Hist) Hist Ser — Bulletin. British Museum (Natural History). Historical Series
Bull Br Mus Nat Hist Mineral — Bulletin. British Museum (Natural History). Mineralogy
Bull Br Mus (Nat Hist) Zool — Bulletin. British Museum (Natural History). Zoology
Bull Br Mus (Nat Hist) Zool Suppl — Bulletin. British Museum (Natural History). Zoology. Supplement
Bull Br Mycol Soc — Bulletin. British Mycological Society
Bull Br Non Ferrous Met Res Assoc — Bulletin. British Non-Ferrous Metals Research Association
Bull Bromeliad Soc — Bulletin. Bromeliad Society
Bull Bronx Cty Dent Soc — Bulletin. Bronx County Dental Society
Bull Brooklyn Entomol Soc — Bulletin. Brooklyn Entomological Society
Bull Brooklyn Ent Soc — Bulletin. Brooklyn Entomological Society
Bull Brooklyn Mus — Bulletin of the Brooklyn Museum
Bull Br Ornithol Club — Bulletin. British Ornithologists' Club
Bull Br Soc Rheol — Bulletin. British Society of Rheology
Bull Bude — Bulletin. Association Guillaume Bude
Bull Buffalo Gen Hosp — Bulletin. Buffalo General Hospital
Bull Buffalo Naturalists Field Club — Bulletin. Buffalo Naturalists' Field Club
Bull Buffalo Soc Nat Sci — Bulletin. Buffalo Society of Natural Sciences
Bull Bur Agnew Bot — Trudy Bjuro Prikl Bot
Bull Bur Agric Intell Plant Des — Bulletin. Bureau of Agricultural Intelligence and Plant Diseases
Bull Bur Bio Technol — Bulletin. Bureau of Bio Technology
Bull Bur Chem US Dep Agric — Bulletin. Bureau of Chemistry. United States Department of Agriculture
Bull Bureau Animal Indust US Dept Agric — Bulletin. Bureau of Animal Industry. United States Department of Agriculture
Bull Bur Ent US Dep Agric — Bulletin. Bureau of Entomology. United States Department of Agriculture
Bull Bur Ethnol Port Au Prince — Bulletin. Bureau d'Ethnologie (Port-au-Prince)
Bull Bur Fish Wash — Bulletin of the Bureau of Fisheries (Washington)
Bull Bur For Philipp Isl — Bulletin of the Bureau of Forestry. Philippine Islands
Bull Bur Geol Topogr (NJ) — Bulletin. Bureau of Geology and Topography (New Jersey)
Bull Bur Gov Labs Philipp Isl — Bulletin of the Bureau of Government Laboratories. Philippine Islands
Bull Bur Hort Insp NY St — Bulletin of the Bureau of Horticultural Inspection. New York State Department of Agriculture
Bull Bur Int Edn Mec — Bulletin. Bureau International de l'Edition Mecanique

Bull Bur Int Repress Fraud Aliment Pharm — Bulletin du Bureau International de la Repression des Fraudes Alimentaires et Pharmaceutiques
Bull Burma Hist Comm — Bulletin of the Burma Historical Commission
Bull Bur Met Melb — Bulletin. Bureau of Meteorology (Melbourne)
Bull Bur Met Queb — Bulletin. Bureau de Meteorologie (Quebec)
Bull Bur Miner Resour Geol Geophys — Australia. Bureau of Mineral Resources. Geology and Geophysics. Bulletin
Bull Bur Miner Resour Geol Geophys (Aust) — Bulletin. Bureau of Mineral Resources. Geology and Geophysics (Australia)
Bull Bur Mines Br Columb — Bulletin of the Bureau of Mines. British Columbia
Bull Bur Mines Geol (State Montana) — Bulletin. Bureau of Mines and Geology (State of Montana)
Bull Bur Mines Geol Surv Indones — Bulletin of the Bureau of Mines and the Geological Survey in Indonesia
Bull Bur Mines Ont — Bulletin of the Bureau of Mines. Ontario
Bull Bur Mines Philipp Isl — Bulletin. Bureau of Mines. Philippine Islands
Bull Bur Mines Univ Ariz — Bulletin. Bureau of Mines. University of Arizona
Bull Bur Natn Ethnol Haiti — Bulletin du Bureau National d'Ethnologie (Haiti)
Bull Bur Perm Interafr Tsetse — Bulletin du Bureau Permanent Interafricain de la Tsetse et de la Trypanosomiase
Bull Bur Pl Ind Philipp Isl — Bulletin. Bureau of Plant Industry. Philippine Islands
Bull Bur Pl Ind US Dep Agric — Bulletin. Bureau of Plant Industry. United States Department of Agriculture
Bull Bur Rech Geol Min — Bulletin. Bureau de Recherches Geologiques et Minieres
Bull Bur Rech Geol Min Fr — Bulletin. Bureau de Recherches Geologiques et Minieres (France)
Bull Bur Rech Geol Minieres — Bulletin. Bureau de Recherches Geologiques et Minieres
Bull Bur Rech Geol Minieres Deuxieme Ser Sect 2 — Bulletin. Bureau de Recherches Geologiques et Minieres. Deuxieme Serie. Section2. Geologie des Gites Mineraux
Bull Bur Rech Geol Minieres Deuxieme Ser Sect 3 — Bulletin. Bureau de Recherches Geologiques et Minieres. Deuxieme Serie. Section3. Hydrogeologie - Geologie de l'Ingenieur
Bull Bur Rech Geol Minieres (Fr) Sect 1 — Bulletin. Bureau de Recherches Geologiques et Minieres (France). Section 1. Geologie de la France
Bull Bur Rech Geol Minieres (Fr) Sect 2 — Bulletin. Bureau de Recherches Geologiques et Minieres (France). Section 2. Geologie Appliquee
Bull Bur Rech Geol Minieres (Fr) Sect 3 — Bulletin. Bureau de Recherches Geologiques et Minieres (France). Section 3. Hydrogeologie - Geologie de l'Ingenieur
Bull Bur Rech Geol Minieres (Fr) Sect 4 — Bulletin. Bureau de Recherches Geologiques et Minieres (France). Section 4. Geologie Generale
Bull Bur Rech Geol Minieres Sec 2 Geol Appl — Bulletin. Bureau de Recherches Geologiques et Minieres (France). Section 2. Geologie Appliquee
Bull Bur Rech Geol Minieres Ser 2 Sect 1 — Bulletin. Bureau de Recherches Geologiques et Minieres. Serie 2. Section 1
Bull Bur Rech Geol Minieres Ser 2 Sect 2 — Bulletin. Bureau de Recherches Geologiques et Minieres. Serie 2. Section 2
Bull Bur Rech Geol Minieres Ser 2 Sect 3 — Bulletin. Bureau de Recherches Geologiques et Minieres. Serie 2. Section 3
Bull Bur Rech Geol Minieres Ser 2 Sect 4 — Bulletin. Bureau de Recherches Geologiques et Minieres. Serie 2. Section 4
Bull Bur Rech Geol Min Sect 1 Fr — Bulletin. Bureau de Recherches Geologiques et Minieres. Section 1. Geologie de la France
Bull Bur Rech Geol Min Sect 2 Geol Appl Chron Mines (Fr) — Bulletin. Bureau de Recherches Geologiques et Minieres. Section 2. Geologie Appliquee. Chronique des Mines (France)
Bull Bur Rech Geol Min Sect 2 Geol Appl (Fr) — Bulletin. Bureau de Recherches Geologiques et Minieres. Section 2. Geologie Appliquee (France)
Bull Bur Rech Geol Min Sect 2 Geol Gites Miner (Fr) — Bulletin. Bureau de Recherches Geologiques et Minieres. Section 2. Geologie desGites Mineraux (France)
Bull Bur Rech Geol Min Sect 3 (Fr) — Bulletin. Bureau de Recherches Geologiques et Minieres. Section 3. Hydrogeologie - Geologie de l'Ingenieur (France)
Bull Bur Rech Geol Min Sect 4 Fr — Bulletin du Bureau de Recherches Geologiques et Minieres. Section 4. Geologie Generale (France)
Bull Bur Rech Geol Min Sect II Geol Appl — Bulletin. Bureau de Recherches Geologiques et Minieres. Section II. Geologie Appliquee
Bull Bur Rech Min Alger — Bulletin. Bureau de Recherches Minieres de l'Algerie
Bull Bur Scient Res Div Conserv Ohio — Bulletin. Bureau of Scientific Research. Division of Conservation. Department of Agriculture. Ohio
Bull Bur Sci Philipp Isl — Bulletin. Bureau of Science. Philippine Islands
Bull Bur Stand US — Bulletin. Bureau of Standards (US)
Bull Bur Stand Wash — Bulletin of the Bureau of Standards (Washington)
Bull Bur Sug Exp Stns Qd — Bulletin of the Bureau of Sugar Experiment Stations. Queensland
Bull Bur Sug Exp Stns Qd Div Ent — Bulletin. Bureau of Sugar Experiment Stations. Queensland. Division of Entomology
Bull Bur Sug Exp Stns Qd Div Path — Bulletin. Bureau of Sugar Experiment Stations. Queensland. Division of Pathology
Bull Bus Archs Coun Aust — Business Archives Council of Australia. Bulletin
Bull Bus FA — Bulletin. Museum of Fine Arts. Boston
Bull Bus Hist Soc — Bulletin. Business Historical Society
Bull Bussey Inst — Bulletin. Bussey Institution
Bull B Wyo Agric Exp Stn — Bulletin B. Wyoming Agricultural Experiment Station
Bull Byz Inst — Bulletin of the Byzantine Institute
Bull Cairo — Bulletin. Institut Francais d'Archeologie Orientale (Cairo)
Bull Calc Chlor Ass — Bulletin. Calcium Chloride Association
Bull Calcutta Math Soc — Bulletin. Calcutta Mathematical Society
Bull Calcutta Psych Soc — Bulletin. Calcutta Psychical Society
Bull Calcutta Sch Trop Med — Bulletin. Calcutta School of Tropical Medicine
Bull Calif Agr Exp Sta — Bulletin. California Agricultural Experiment Station

Bull Calif Agric Exp Stn — Bulletin. California Agricultural Experiment Station

Bull Calif Dep Agric — Bulletin. California Department of Agriculture

Bull Calif Dept Agr — Bulletin. California Department of Agriculture

Bull Calif Dep Water Resour — Bulletin. California. Department of Water Resources

Bull Calif Div Mines Geol — Bulletin. California. Division of Mines and Geology

Bull Calif Insect Surv — Bulletin of the California Insect Survey

Bull Calif State Min Bur — Bulletin. California State Mining Bureau

Bull Canada Dept Agric — Bulletin. Dominion of Canada. Department of Agriculture

Bull Canad Petrol Geol — Bulletin. Canadian Petroleum Geology

Bull Can Biochem Soc — Bulletin. Canadian Biochemical Society

Bull Cancer — Bulletin du Cancer

Bull Cancer Inst Okayama Univ Med Sch — Bulletin. Cancer Institute. Okayama University Medical School

Bull Cancer (Paris) — Bulletin du Cancer (Paris)

Bull Cancer Radiother — Bulletin du Cancer. Radiotherapie

Bull Can Inst Min Metall — Bulletin. Canadian Institute of Mining and Metallurgy

Bull Can Min Inst — Bulletin. Canadian Mining Institute

Bull Can Pet Geol — Bulletin of Canadian Petroleum Geology

Bull Can Petrol Geol — Bulletin of Canadian Petroleum Geology

Bull Can Soc Dec A — Bulletin of the Canadian Society of Decorative Arts

Bull Canton Christian Coll — Bulletin. Canton Christian College

Bull Can Welfare L — Bulletin of Canadian Welfare Law

Bull Can Wheat Board — Bulletin. Canadian Wheat Board

Bull Caoutch Inst Colon Marseille — Bulletin des Caoutchoucs de l'Institut Colonial de Marseille

Bull Caoutch Inst Fr Outre Mer — Bulletin. Caoutchoucs de l'Institut Francais d'Outre-Mer

Bull Cardiovas Res Cent (Houston) — Bulletin. Cardiovascular Research Center (Houston)

Bull Carnegie Inst Technol Min Metall Invest — Bulletin. Carnegie Institute of Technology. Mining and Metallurgical Investigations

Bull Carnegie Mus Nat Hist — Bulletin. Carnegie Museum of Natural History

Bull Carte Veg Provence Alpes Sud — Bulletin de la Carte et de la Vegetation de la Provence et des Alpes du Sud

Bull Cathedrale Strasbourg — Bulletin de la Cathedrale de Strasbourg

Bull Cathol Res Inst Med Sci Cathol Univ Korea — Bulletin of the Catholic Research Institutes of Medical Science. Catholic University of Korea

Bull CCB — Bulletin. Center for Children's Books

Bull Cent Asia Sci Res Cotton Inst — Bulletin. Central Asia Scientific Research Cotton Institute

Bull Cent Belge Etude Doc Eaux — Bulletin. Centre Belge d'Etude et de Documentation des Eaux

Bull Cent Build Res Inst (Roorkee India) — Bulletin. Central Building Research Institute (Roorkee, India)

Bull Cent Compilation Donnees Neutroniques — Bulletin. Centre de Compilation de Donnees Neutroniques

Bull Cent Etud Rech Sci (Biarritz) — Bulletin. Centre d'Etudes et de Recherches Scientifiques (Biarritz)

Bull Cent Excellence Geol Univ Peshawar — Bulletin. Centre of Excellence in Geology. University of Peshawar

Bull Cent Food Technol Res Inst (Mysore) — Bulletin. Central Food Technological Research Institute (Mysore)

Bull Cent Genev Anthrop — Bulletin du Centre Genevois d'Anthropologie

Bull Cent Glass Ceram Res Inst (Calcutta) — Bulletin. Central Glass and Ceramic Research Institute (Calcutta)

Bull Cent Helminthol Lab Bulg Acad Sci — Bulletin. Central Helminthological Laboratory. Bulgarian Academy of Sciences

Bull Cent Insp Inst Weights Meas (Tokyo) — Bulletin. Central Inspection Institute of Weights and Measures (Tokyo)

Bull Cent Int Engrais Chim — Bulletin. Centre International des Engrais Chimiques

Bull Cent Leather Res Inst (Madras) — Bulletin. Central Leather Research Institute (Madras)

Bull Cent Mar Fish Res Inst — Bulletin. Central Marine Fisheries Research Institute

Bull Cent Phys Nucl Univ Lib Bruxelles — Bulletin. Centre de Physique Nucleaire. Universite Libre de Bruxelles

Bull Cent Phys Nucl Univ Libre Bruxelles — Bulletin. Centre de Physique Nucleaire. Universite Libre de Bruxelles

Bull Central Res Lab OIT — Bulletin. Central Research Laboratory. Osaka Institute of Technology

Bull Cent Rech Elf Explor Prod — Bulletin du Centre de Recherches Elf Exploration Production

Bull Cent Rech Essais Chatou — Bulletin. Centre de Recherches et d'Essais de Chatou

Bull Cent Rech Explor ELF Aquitaine — Bulletin. Centres de Recherches Exploration-Production ELF [*Essences et Lubrifiants de France*] - Aquitaine

Bull Cent Rech Explor Prod ELF Aquitaine — Bulletin. Centres de Recherches Exploration-Production ELF [*Essences et Lubrifiants de France*] - Aquitaine

Bull Cent Rech Pau — Bulletin. Centre de Recherches de Pau

Bull Centre Inform — Bulletin of Centre for Informatics

Bull Centre Pol Rech Sci Paris — Bulletin. Centre Polonais de Recherches Scientifiques de Paris

Bull Cent Res Inst Univ Kerala (India) Ser C Nat Sci — Bulletin. Central Research Institute. University of Kerala (India). Series C. Natural Science

Bull Cent Res Inst Univ Kerala (Trivandrum) Ser C — Bulletin. Central Research Institute. University of Kerala (Trivandrum). SeriesC. Natural Science

Bull Cent Res Inst Univ Trav — Bulletin. Central Research Institute. University of Travancore

Bull Centres Rech Explor-Prod ELF-Aquitaine — Bulletin. Centres de Recherches Exploration-Production ELF [*Essences et Lubrifiants de France*] - Aquitaine

Bull Centr Rech Agron Bingerville — Bulletin. Centre de Recherches Agronomiques de Bingerville

Bull Cent Text Controle Rech Sci — Bulletin. Centre Textile de Controle et de Recherche Scientifique

BullCER — Bulletin. Cercle Ernest Renan

Bull Cerc Archeol Litt & A Malines — Bulletin du Cercle Archeologique, Litteraire, et Artistique de Malines

Bull Cerc Archeol Litt & A Malines Hand Kon Kring Oudhdknd Le — Bulletin du Cercle Archeologique, Litteraire, et Artistique de Malines/ Handelingen van de Koninklijke Kring voor Oudheidkunde, Letteren, en Kunst van Mechelen

Bull Cerc Arch Hesbaye-Condroz — Bulletin. Cercle Archeologique Hesbaye-Condroz

Bull Cerc Benel Hist Pharm — Bulletin. Cercle Benelux d'Histoire de la Pharmacie

Bull Cercle Benelux Hist Pharm — Bulletin. Cercle Benelux d'Histoire de la Pharmacie

Bull Cercle Etud Met — Bulletin. Cercle d'Etudes des Metaux

Bull Cercle Etud Metaux — Bulletin. Cercle d'Etudes des Metaux

Bull Cercle Gen Hort — Bulletin. Cercle General d'Horticulture

Bull Cercle Vaud Bot — Bulletin du Cercle Vaudois de Botanique

Bull Cercle Zool Congolais — Bulletin. Cercle Zoologique Congolais

Bull CETA — Bulletin. Centres d'Etudes Techniques Agricoles

Bull CETIOM Cent Tech Interprof OI Metrop — Bulletin CETIOM. Centre Technique Interprofessionnel des Oleagineux Metropolitains

Bull Ceyl Fish — Bulletin. Ceylon Fisheries. Ceylon Department of Fisheries

Bull Ceylon Geogr Soc — Bulletin of the Ceylon Geographical Society

Bull Ceylon Plrs Soc — Bulletin. Ceylon Planters' Society

Bull Ceylon Rubb Res Scheme — Bulletin of the Ceylon Rubber Research Scheme

Bull CFL — Bulletin. Cercle Francois Laurent

Bull Chamber Hort — Bulletin of the Chamber of Horticulture

Bull Chamb Fr Agric Rabat — Bulletin de la Chambre Francaise d'Agriculture de Rabat, du Rharb et d'Ouezzane (Rabat)

Bull Chamb Synd Ind Aeronaut — Bulletin Chambre Syndicale des Industries Aeronautiques

Bull Chamb Synd Mecns — Bulletin de la Chambre Syndicale des Mecaniciens, Chaudronniers, Fondeurs

Bull Chamb Synd Pharmns Forez — Bulletin de la Chambre Syndicale des Pharmaciens du Forez

Bull Chamb Synd Pharmns Gironde — Bulletin de la Chambre Syndicale des Pharmaciens de la Gironde

Bull Chamb Synd Prod Chim Paris — Bulletin de la Chambre Syndicale des Produits Chimiques de Paris

Bull Chamb Synd Siderurg — Bulletin de la Chambre Syndicale de la Siderurgie

Bull Chamb Synd Soc Prevoy Pharmns Paris — Bulletin de la Chambre Syndicale et Societe de Prevoyance des Pharmaciens de Paris

Bull Charact Fig Sol Phenom — Bulletin for Character Figures of Solar Phenomena

Bull Charleston Mus — Bulletin. Charleston Museum

Bull Chekiang Prov Fish Exp Stn — Bulletin. Chekiang Provincial Fisheries Experiment Station

Bull Chem Dep Univ III — Bulletin. Chemistry Department. University of Illinois

Bull Chem Res Inst Non-Aqueous Solutions Tohoku Univ — Bulletin. Chemical Research Institute of Non-Aqueous Solutions. Tohoku University

Bull Chem Res Inst Non Aqueous Solut Tohoku Univ — Bulletin of the Chemical Research Institute of Non-Aqueous Solutions. Tohoku University

Bull Chem Soc Jap — Bulletin. Chemical Society of Japan

Bull Chem Soc Japan — Bulletin. Chemical Society of Japan

Bull Chem Soc Univ Allahabad — Bulletin of the Chemical Society of the University of Allahabad

Bull Chem Technol Macedonia — Bulletin. Chemists and Technologists of Macedonia

Bull Chem Thermodyn — Bulletin of Chemical Thermodynamics

Bull Chem Warf Fld Serv — Bulletin. Chemical Warfare Field Service

Bull Cheng Kung Univ Sci Eng — Bulletin of Cheng Kung University. Science and Engineering

Bull Chest Dis Res Inst Kyoto Univ — Bulletin. Chest Disease Research Institute. Kyoto University

Bull Cheyenne Mtn Mus — Bulletin of the Cheyenne Mountain Museum

Bull Chiba Agric — Bulletin. Chiba College of Agriculture

Bull Chiba Coll Agric — Bulletin of the Chiba College of Agriculture

Bull Chiba Coll Hort — Bulletin. Chiba College of Horticulture/Chiba Koto Engeigakko Gakujutsu Hokoku

Bull Chiba-Ken Agr Exp Sta — Bulletin. Chiba-ken Agricultural Experiment Station

Bull Chiba Prefect Agri Exp Stn — Bulletin. Chiba Prefecture Agricultural Experiment Station

Bull Chiba Prefect Res Inst Environ Pollut — Bulletin. Chiba Prefectural Research Institute for Environmental Pollution

Bull Chiba Seric Exp Stn — Bulletin. Chiba Sericultural Experiment Station

Bull Chic Acad Sci — Bulletin. Chicago Academy of Sciences

Bull Chicago Acad — Bulletin of the Chicago Academy of Sciences

Bull Chicago Dent Soc — Bulletin of the Chicago Dental Society

Bull Chicago Munic Tuberc Sanat — Bulletin of the Chicago Municipal Tuberculosis Sanatorium

Bull Chicago Sch Sanit Instruct — Bulletin. Chicago School of Sanitary Instruction

Bull Chicago Tuberc Inst — Bulletin. Chicago Tuberculosis Institute

Bull Chic Herpetol Soc — Bulletin. Chicago Herpetological Society

Bull Chichibu Mus Nat Hist — Bulletin. Chichibu Museum of Natural History

Bull Chim Clin — Bulletin de Chimie Clinique

Bull Chim Text — Bulletin de Chimie Textile

Bull Chin Acad Geol Sci — Bulletin of the Chinese Academy of Geological Sciences

Bull Chin Ass Advmt Sci — Bulletin of the Chinese Association for the Advancement of Science

Bull Chin Assoc Advancem Sci — Bulletin. Chinese Association for the Advancement of Science

Bull Chin Assoc Adv Sci — Bulletin. Chinese Association for the Advancement of Science

Bull Chin Bot Soc — Bulletin. Chinese Botanical Society
Bull Chin Inst Min Metall Eng — Bulletin. Chinese Institute of Mining and Metallurgical Engineers
Bull Chin Mater Med — Bulletin of Chinese Materia Medica
Bull Chin Stud — Bulletin of Chinese Studies/Chung Kuo Wen Hua Yen Chin Hui Kan
Bull Chir Accid Trav — Bulletin Chirurgical des Accidents du Travail
Bull Chir Cannes — Bulletin Chirurgical de Cannes et de la Region du Sud-Est
Bull Chir Dent Indep — Bulletin des Chirurgiens Dentistes Independents
Bull Christmas Isl Nat Hist Soc — Bulletin of the Christmas Island Natural History Society
Bull Chubu Inst Technol — Bulletin. Chubu Institute of Technology
Bull Chugoku Agr Exp Sta — Bulletin. Chugoku National Agricultural Experiment Station
Bull Chugoku Agr Exp Sta Ser A Ser D Ser E — Bulletin. Chugoku Agricultural Experiment Station. Series A, D, and E
Bull Chugoku Natl Agric Exp Stn Ser A — Bulletin. Chugoku National Agricultural Experiment Station. Series A (Crop Division)
Bull Chugoku Natl Agric Exp Stn Ser A (Crop Div) — Bulletin. Chugoku National Agricultural Experiment Station. Series A (Crop Division)
Bull Chugoku Natl Agric Exp Stn Ser B — Bulletin. Chugoku National Agricultural Experiment Station. Series B (LivestockDivision)
Bull Chugoku Natl Agric Exp Stn Ser B (Livest Div) — Bulletin. Chugoku National Agricultural Experiment Station. Series B (Livestock Division)
Bull Chugoku Natl Agric Exp Stn Ser E — Bulletin. Chugoku National Agricultural Experiment Station. Series E (Environment Division)
Bull Chugoku Natl Agric Exp Stn Ser E (Environ Div) — Bulletin. Chugoku National Agricultural Experiment Station. Series E (Environment Division)
Bull Chukyo Women's Coll — Bulletin. Chukyo Women's College
Bull Chukyo Women's Univ — Bulletin. Chukyo Women's University
Bull Chungking Inst Ind Res — Bulletin. Chungking Institute of Industrial Research
Bull CIMAB — Bulletin. Centre d'Information du Material et des Articles de Bureau
Bull Cinci Dent Soc — Bulletin. Cincinnati Dental Society
Bull City Hosp Akr — Bulletin. City Hospital of Akron
Bull Civ I — Bulletin des Arrets de la Cour de Cassation. Chambres Civiles. PremiereSection Civile
Bull Civ II — Bulletin des Arrets de la Cour de Cassation. Chambres Civiles. DeuxiemeSection Civile
Bull Civ III — Bulletin des Arrets de la Cour de Cassation. Chambres Civiles.Troisieme Section Civile
Bull Claremont Pomol Club — Bulletin. Claremont Pomological Club
Bull Classe Sci Acad Roy Belg — Bulletin. Classe des Sciences. Academie Royale de Belgique
Bull Classific Soc — Bulletin. Classification Society
Bull Cl B A Acad Royale Sci Lett & B A Belgique — Bulletin de la Classe des Beaux-Arts. Academie Royale des Sciences, des Lettres, et des Beaux-Arts de Belgique
Bull Clemson Agr Exp Sta — Bulletin. Clemson Agricultural Experiment Station
Bull Clemson Univ Coop Ext Serv — Bulletin. Clemson University. Cooperative Extension Service
Bull Cleve Dent Soc — Bulletin. Cleveland Dental Society
Bull Cleveland Med Libr — Bulletin. Cleveland Medical Library
Bull Cleveland Mus A — Bulletin of the Cleveland Museum of Art
Bull Cleveland Museum — Bulletin. Cleveland Museum of Art
Bull Cleveland Sci Tech Inst — Bulletin. Cleveland Scientific and Technical Institution
Bull Cleve Med Libr Assoc — Bulletin. Cleveland Medical Library Association
Bull Clin Neurosci — Bulletin of Clinical Neurosciences
Bull Cl Phys Math Acad Imp Sci St Petersbourg — Bulletin. Classe Physico-Mathematique. Academie Imperiale des Sciences de St. Petersbourg
Bull Cl Sci Acad R Belg — Bulletin. Classe des Sciences. Academie Royale de Belgique
Bull Cl Sci Acad R Belg 5e Ser — Bulletin. Classe des Sciences. Academie Royale de Belgique. 5e Serie
Bull Cl Sci Acad Royale Belg — Bulletin. Classe des Sciences. Academie Royale de Belgique
Bull Club Fr Medaille — Bulletin du Club Francais de la Medaille
Bull Cocon Res Inst (Cey) — Bulletin. Coconut Research Institute (Ceylon)
Bull Cocon Res Inst (Ceylon) — Bulletin. Coconut Research Institute (Ceylon)
Bull Coll Agr Forest Univ Nanking — Bulletin. College of Agriculture and Forestry. University of Nanking
Bull Coll Agric Res Cent Wash State Univ — Bulletin. College of Agriculture. Research Center. Washington State University
Bull Coll Agric Res Cent Wash St Univ — Bulletin. College of Agriculture. Research Center. Washington State University
Bull Coll Agric Sci (Mosonmagyarovar Hung) — Bulletin. College of Agricultural Sciences (Mosonmagyarovar, Hungary)
Bull Coll Agric Tokyo Imp Univ — Bulletin. College of Agriculture. Tokyo Imperial University
Bull Coll Agric Univ Teheran — Bulletin. College of Agriculture. University of Teheran
Bull Coll Agric Utsunomiya Univ — Bulletin. College of Agriculture. Utsunomiya University
Bull Coll Agric Vet Med Nihon Univ — Bulletin. College of Agriculture and Veterinary Medicine. Nihon University
Bull Coll Agr Utsunomiya Univ — Bulletin. College of Agriculture. Utsunomiya University
Bull Coll Art Ass — Bulletin. College Art Association of America
Bull Coll Arts Baghdad — Bulletin. College of Arts and Sciences. Baghdad
Bull College Liberal Arts Kyushu Sangyo Univ — Bulletin of the College of Liberal Arts Kyushu Sangyo University
Bull College Sci (Baghdad) — Bulletin. College of Science (Baghdad)
Bull College Sci Univ Ryukyus — University of the Ryukyus. College of Science. Bulletin
Bull Coll Eng Hosei Univ — Bulletin. College of Engineering. Hosei University

Bull Coll Eng Natl Taiwan Univ — Bulletin. College of Engineering. National Taiwan University
Bull Coll Foreign Stud (Yokohama) Nat Sci — Bulletin. College of Foreign Studies (Yokohama). Natural Science
Bull Coll Gen Educ Nagoya City Univ Nat Sci Sect — Bulletin. College of General Education. Nagoya City University. Natural ScienceSection
Bull Coll Sci 1 — Bulletin. College of Science. Part 1
Bull Coll Sci Univ Baghdad — Bulletin. College of Science. University of Baghdad
Bull Coll Sci Univ Ryukyus — Bulletin. College of Science. University of the Ryukyus
Bull Coll Wm & Mary — William and Mary College. Bulletin
Bull Colo Agr Exp Sta — Bulletin. Colorado Agricultural Experiment Station
Bull Colo Agric Exp Stn — Bulletin. Colorado Agricultural Experiment Station
Bull Colo Dept Agr — Bulletin. Colorado Department of Agriculture
Bull Colorado Agric Coll Colorado Exp Sta — Bulletin Colorado Agricultural College. Colorado Experiment Station
Bull Colorado State Univ Exp Sta — Bulletin. Colorado State University Experiment Station
Bull Colo State Univ Agr Exp Sta — Bulletin. Colorado State University. Agricultural Experiment Station
Bull Colo State Univ Exp Stn — Bulletin. Colorado State University. Experiment Station
Bull Colo St Univ Agric Exp Stn — Bulletin. Colorado State University. Agricultural Experiment Station
Bull Colo Vet Med Ass — Bulletin. Colorado Veterinary Medical Association
Bull Colo Vet Med Assoc — Bulletin. Colorado Veterinary Medical Association
Bull Com — Bullettino Comunale
BullComEt — Bulletin. Comite d'Etudes
Bull Com Etud Hist & Sci A O F — Bulletin du Comite des Etudes Historiques et Scientifiques de l'Afrique Occidentale Francaise
Bull Com For — Bulletin. Comite des Forets
Bull Comite Centr Ind — Bulletin. Comite Central Industriel de Belgique
Bull Comite Etud Hist Sci Afr Occident Franc — Bulletin. Comite d'Etudes Historiques et Scientifiques de l'Afrique OccidentaleFrancaise
Bull Comite Trav Hist Sect Hist — Bulletin du Comite des Travaux Historiques et Scientifiques. Section de Histoire
Bull Comm Ant Dept Seine Inferieure — Bulletin de la Commission des Antiquites du Departement de la Seine-Inferieure
Bull Comm Ant Sic — Bullettino. Commissione di Antichita e Belle Arte in Sicilia
Bull Comm Archeol Com Roma — Bullettino della Commissione Archeologica Comunale di Roma
Bull Comm Archeol Indochine — Bulletin de la Commission Archeologique de l'Indochine
Bull Comm Archeol Mun Com Roma — Bullettino della Commissione Archeologica Municipale Comunale di Roma
Bull Comm Archeol Narbonne — Bulletin de la Commission Archeologique de Narbonne
Bull Comm Arch Narbonne — Bulletin. Commission Archeologique de Narbonne
Bull Comm Autom Train Control — Bulletin. Committee on Automatic Train Control
Bull Comm Belge Bibl — Bulletin. Commission Belge de Bibliographie
Bull Comm Distrib Astr Lit Harv Coll Obs — Bulletin. Committee for the Distribution of Astronomical Literature. Harvard College Observatory
Bull Comm Geol Finl — Bulletin. Commission Geologique de Finlande
Bull Comm Hist Archeol Mayenne — Bulletin. Commission Historique et Archeologique de la Mayenne
Bull Commiss Int Explor Sci Mer Medit — Bulletin. Commission Internationale pour l'Exploration Scientifique de la Mer Mediterranee
Bull Comm Malnutr — Bulletin. Committee Against Malnutrition
Bull Commn Actinom Perm Leningrad — Bulletin de la Commission Actinometrique Permanente (Leningrad)
Bull Commn Furth Study Sol Terr Relat — Bulletin of the Commission Appointed to Further the Study of Solar and Terrestrial Relationships
Bull Commn Geol Finl — Bulletin de la Commission Geologique de la Finlande
Bull Commn Int Congr Chem De Fer — Bulletin de la Commimssion Internationale du Congres des Chemins de Fer
Bull Commn Int Explor Scient Mer Mediterr — Bulletin de la Commission Internationale pour l'Exploration Scientifique de la Mer Mediterranee
Bull Commn Int Perm Etude Mal Prof — Bulletin. Commission Internationale Permanente pour l'Etude des Maladies Professionelles
Bull Commn Met Dep Seine Et Marne — Bulletin de la Commission Meteorologique du Departement de Seine-et-Marne
Bull Commn Met Deux Sevres — Bulletin de la Commission Meteorologique des Deux-Sevres
Bull Commn Met Doubs — Bulletin de la Commission Meteorologique du Doubs
Bull Commn Met Ille Et Vilaine — Bulletin de la Commission Meteorologique d'Ille-et-Vilaine
Bull Commn Met Loiret — Bulletin de la Commission Meteorologique du Loiret
Bull Commn Met Lozere — Bulletin de la Commission Meteorologique de la Lozere
Bull Commn Met Marne — Bulletin de la Commission Meteorologique de la Marne
Bull Commn Met Nievre — Bulletin. Commission Meteorologique de la Nievre
Bull Commn Met Somme — Bulletin de la Commission Meteorologique de la Somme
Bull Commonw Bur Met — Bulletin. Commonwealth Bureau of Meteorology
Bull Commonw Bur Past Fld Crops — Bulletin. Commonwealth Bureau of Pastures and Field Crops
Bull Commonw Bur Pastures Field Crops — Bulletin. Commonwealth Bureau of Pastures and Field Crops
Bull Commonw Scient Ind Res Org — Bulletin. Commonwealth Scientific and Industrial Research Organisation
Bull Commonw Sci Ind Res Org — Bulletin. Commonwealth Scientific and Industrial Research Organisation
Bull Commonw Sci Industr Res Organ (Aust) — Bulletin. Commonwealth Scientific and Industrial Research Organisation (Australia)

Bull Comm Royale Mnmts & Sites — Bulletin de la Commission Royale des Monuments et des Sites

Bull Comm Royales A & Archeol — Bulletin des Commissions Royales d'Art et d'Archeologie

Bull Comm Study Spec Dis — Bulletin of the Committee for the Study of Special Diseases

Bull Com Perm Congr Int Accid Trav — Bulletin du Comite Permanent du Congres International des Accidents du Travail

Bull Com Perm Congr Int Actu — Bulletin. Comite Permanent des Congres Internationaux d'Actuaires

Bull Comp L — American Bar Association. Comparative Law Bureau. Bulletin

Bull Comp Lab Rel — Bulletin of Comparative Labour Relations

Bull Compr Gas Man Ass — Bulletin. Compressed Gas Manufacturers Association

Bull Com Roma — Bullettino. Commissione Archeologica Comunale di Roma

Bull Com Scient Tech Ind Chauff Vent — Bulletin. Comite Scientifique et Technique de l'Industrie du Chauffage et de la Ventilation

Bull Com Tech Incend — Bulletin du Comite Technique Contre l'Incendie

Bull Comunale — Bullettino. Commissione Archeologica Comunale di Roma

Bull Conn Agr Exp Sta — Bulletin. Connecticut Agricultural Experiment Station

Bull Conn Agric Exp Sta — Bulletin. Connecticut Agricultural Experiment Station

Bull Conn Agric Exp Stn New Haven — Bulletin. Connecticut Agricultural Experiment Station. New Haven

Bull Connecticut Agr Exp Sta — Bulletin. Connecticut Agriculture Experiment Station

Bull Connecticut Arbor — Bulletin. Connecticut Arboretum

Bull Conn Hist Soc — Bulletin. Connecticut Historical Society

Bull Conn St Geol Nat Hist Surv — Bulletin. Connecticut State Geological and Natural History Survey

Bull Contr — Bulletin des Contributions

Bull Contrib Dir — Bulletin des Contributions Directes

Bull Co-Op Ext Serv Coll Agric Univ Idaho — Bulletin. Co-Operative Extension Service. College of Agriculture. University of Idaho

Bull Coop Ext Serv Colo State Univ — Bulletin. Cooperative Extension Service. Colorado State University

Bull Coop Ext Serv Montana State Univ — Montana State University. Cooperative Extension Service. Bulletin

Bull Coop Ext Serv Mont State Univ — Bulletin. Cooperative Extension Service. Montana State University

Bull Coop Ext Serv Ohio St Univ — Bulletin. Cooperative Extension Service. Ohio State University

Bull Coop Ext Serv Univ Conn — Bulletin. Cooperative Extension Service. University of Connecticut

Bull Coop Ext Serv Univ GA Coll Agric — Bulletin. Cooperative Extension Service. University of Georgia. College of Agriculture

Bull Copper Brass Res Assoc — Bulletin. Copper and Brass Research Association

Bull Cop Soc — Bulletin. Copyright Society of the USA

Bull Copte — Bulletin. Societe d'Archeologie Copte

Bull Copyright Soc'y — Bulletin. Copyright Society of the USA

Bull Copyright Soc'y USA — Bulletin. Copyright Society of the USA

Bull Cor Arch — Bullettino. Instituto di Correspondenza Archeologica

Bull Cornell Univ Agric Exp Stn — Bulletin. Cornell University. Agricultural Experiment Station

Bull Cornell Univ Eng Exp St — Bulletin. Cornell University. Engineering Experiment Station

Bull Corresp Hellen — Bulletin de Correspondance Hellenique

Bull Corr Hell — Bulletin de Correspondance Hellenique

Bull Corr Hellenique — Bulletin de Correspondance Hellenique

Bull Council Res Mus Educ — Bulletin. Council for Research in Music Education

Bull C'right Soc'y — Bulletin. Copyright Society of the USA

Bull Crim — Bulletin des Arrets de la Chambre Criminelle de la Cour de Cassation

Bull Crim — Bulletin des Arrets de la Cour de Cassation. Chambre Criminelle

Bull Crimean Astrophys Obs — Bulletin. Crimean Astrophysical Observatory

Bull Crit — Bulletin Critique

Bull Cr Soc — Bulletin. Copyright Society of the USA

Bull CSIRO — Australia. Commonwealth Scientific and Industrial Research Organisation. Bulletin

Bull Curr Doc — Bulletin of Current Documentation

Bull Czech L — Bulletin of Czechoslovak Law

Bull Czech Med Ass Great Brit — Bulletin. Czechoslovak Medical Association in Great Britain

Bull Dahlia Soc Michigan — Bulletin. Dahlia Society of Michigan

Bull Daito Bunka Univ — Bulletin. Daito Bunka University

Bull Dalm — Vjesnik za Arheologiju i Historiju Dalmatinsku

Bull de ALCAM — Bulletin de Atlas Linguistique du Cameroun

Bull Deccan Coll Res Inst — Bulletin. Deccan College Research Institute

Bull de Droit Nucl — Bulletin de Droit Nucleaire

Bull de Droit Tchecoslovaque — Bulletin de Droit Tchecoslovaque

Bull de l Acad Roy de Belgique — Bulletin de l'Academie Royale de Belgique

Bull de l'Ac Roy de Belg Cl Let — Bulletins. Academie Royale de Belgique. Classe des Lettres, des Sciences Morales et Politiques

Bull Del Agric Exp Stn — Bulletin. Delaware Agricultural Experiment Station

Bull de la Soc de l Hist de Paris et de l Ile de France — Bulletin de la Societe de l'Histoire de Paris et de l'Ile-de-France

Bull Delaware County Med Soc — Bulletin. Delaware County Medical Society

Bull Del Geol Surv — Bulletin. Delaware. Geological Survey

Bull de Liaison Cent Univ Rech Dev Abidjan — Bulletin de Liaison du Centre Universitaire de Recherches de Developpement. Universite d'Abidjan

Bull Deli Proefstat Medan — Bulletin. Deli Proefstation Medan

Bull de Litt Eccles — Bulletin de Litterature Ecclesiastique

Bull de Madagascar — Bulletin de Madagascar

Bull Dent — Bulletin Dentaire

Bull Dent Guid Counc Cereb Palsy — Bulletin. Dental Guidance Council for Cerebral Palsy

Bull Dep Agric Alberta — Bulletin. Department of Agriculture. Alberta

Bull Dep Agric Bermuda — Bulletin. Department of Agriculture. Bermuda

Bull Dep Agric Bihar Orissa — Bulletin. Department of Agriculture. Bihar and Orissa

Bull Dep Agric (Br Columb) — Bulletin. Department of Agriculture (British Columbia)

Bull Dep Agric Br E Afr — Bulletin. Department of Agriculture. British East Africa

Bull Dep Agric Br E Afr Div Ent — Bulletin. Department of Agriculture. British East Africa. Division of Entomology

Bull Dep Agric Burma — Bulletin of the Department of Agriculture. Burma

Bull Dep Agric Can Ent Brch — Bulletin of the Department of Agriculture. Canada. Entomological Branch

Bull Dep Agric Can Fruit Brch — Bulletin. Department of Agriculture. Canada. Fruit Branch

Bull Dep Agric Can Live Stk Brch — Bulletin. Department of Agriculture. Canada. Live Stock Branch

Bull Dep Agric Can Seed Brch — Bulletin. Department of Agriculture. Canada. Seed Branch

Bull Dep Agric Cape Gd Hope — Bulletin of the Department of Agriculture. Cape of Good Hope

Bull Dep Agric Cent Prov — Bulletin of the Department of Agriculture. Central Provinces

Bull Dep Agric (Ceyl) — Bulletin. Department of Agriculture (Ceylon)

Bull Dep Agric Ceylon — Bulletin of the Department of Agriculture. Ceylon

Bull Dep Agric Colony Gambia — Bulletin. Department of Agriculture. Colony of the Gambia

Bull Dep Agric (Cyp) — Bulletin. Department of Agriculture (Cyprus)

Bull Dep Agric Cyprus — Bulletin. Department of Agriculture. Cyprus

Bull Dep Agric (Dom Can) — Bulletin. Department of Agriculture (Dominion of Canada)

Bull Dep Agric Fiji — Bulletin of the Department of Agriculture. Fiji

Bull Dep Agric FMS — Bulletin of the Department of Agriculture. Federated Malay States

Bull Dep Agric For (Un S Afr) — Bulletin. Department of Agriculture and Forestry (Union of South Africa)

Bull Dep Agric Gold Cst — Bulletin. Department of Agriculture. Gold Coast Colony

Bull Dep Agric Hlth Anim Brch — Bulletin. Department of Agriculture. Canada. Health of Animals Branch

Bull Dep Agric Indes Neerl — Bulletin du Departement de l'Agriculture aux Indes Neerlandaises

Bull Dep Agric (Madras) — Bulletin. Department of Agriculture (Madras)

Bull Dep Agric NW Terr — Bulletin. Department of Agriculture. North-West Territories

Bull Dep Agric (NZ) — Bulletin. Department of Agriculture (New Zealand)

Bull Dep Agric Peche Seychelles — Bulletin du Departement de l'Agriculture et de la Peche. Seychelles

Bull Dep Agric (Queb) — Bulletin. Department of Agriculture (Quebec)

Bull Dep Agric Res Campbell Soup Co — Bulletin. Department of Agricultural Research. Campbell Soup Company

Bull Dep Agric Res R Trop Inst (Amsterdam) — Bulletin. Department of Agricultural Research. Royal Tropical Institute (Amsterdam)

Bull Dep Agric Res Trop Inst (Amst) — Bulletin. Department of Agricultural Research. Royal Tropical Institute (Amsterdam)

Bull Dep Agric (Tas) — Bulletin. Department of Agriculture (Tasmania)

Bull Dep Agric (Tasm) — Bulletin. Department of Agriculture (Tasmania)

Bull Dep Agric Tech Serv (S Afr) — Bulletin. Department of Agricultural Technical Services (South Africa)

Bull Dep Agric Tech Serv (Transv) — Bulletin. Department of Agricultural Technical Services (Transvaal)

Bull Dep Agric (West Aust) — Bulletin. Department of Agriculture (Western Australia)

Bull Dep Anthrop Taiwan — Bulletin of the Department of Anthropology (Taiwan)

Bull Dep Civ Engng QD Univ — Bulletin. Department of Civil Engineering. University of Queensland

Bull Dep Civ Eng Queensl Univ — Bulletin. Department of Civil Engineering. University of Queensland

Bull Dep Ent Kans St Univ — Bulletin. Department of Entomology. Kansas State University

Bull Dep Ent Neb St Univ — Bulletin. Department of Entomology. Nebraska State University

Bull Dep Fish Baroda — Bulletin. Department of Fisheries. Baroda State

Bull Dep Fish Beng — Bulletin of the Department of Fisheries. Bengal

Bull Dep Fish Game St Calif — Bulletin. Department of Fish and Game. State of California

Bull Dep Fish Israel — Bulletin. Department of Fisheries. Israel

Bull Dep For Br N Borneo — Bulletin. Department of Forestry. British North Borneo

Bull Dep For Can — Bulletin of the Department of Forestry. Canada

Bull Dep For Pa — Bulletin. Department of Forestry. Pennsylvania

Bull Dep For (S Afr) — Bulletin. Department of Forestry (Pretoria, South Africa)

Bull Dep For Stephen F Austen St Coll Tex — Bulletin. Department of Forestry. Stephen F. Austen State College, Texas

Bull Dep For Univ Adelaide — Bulletin. Department of Forestry. University of Adelaide

Bull Dep For Univ Ibadan — Bulletin. Department of Forestry. University of Ibadan

Bull Dep For Un S Afr — Bulletin. Department of Forestry. Union of South Africa

Bull Dep Gen Educ Tokyo Med Dent Univ — Bulletin. Department of General Education. Tokyo Medical and Dental University

Bull Dep Geol Heb Univ (Jerusalem) — Bulletin. Department of Geology. Hebrew University (Jerusalem)

Bull Dep Geol S Barbara Mus Nat Hist — Bulletin. Department of Geology. Santa Barbara Museum of Natural History

Bull Dep Geol Surv Nth Rhod — Bulletin. Department of Geological Surveys. Northern Rhodesia

Bull Dep Geol Univ Alberta — Bulletin. Department of Geology. University of Alberta

Bull Dep Hlth Aust — Bulletin of the Department of Health. Australia

Bull Dep Hlth Welf Br Columb — Bulletin. Department of Health and Welfare. British Columbia

Bull Dep Home Econ Kyoritsu Womens Jr Coll — Bulletin. Department of Home Economics. Kyoritsu Women's Junior College

Bull Dep Ind Res Pittsburgh Univ — Bulletin of the Department of Industrial Research. Pittsburg University

Bull Dep Inds Beng — Bulletin. Department of Industries. Bengal

Bull Dep Inds Bihar Orissa — Bulletin of the Department of Industries. Bihar and Orissa

Bull Dep Inds Bombay — Bulletin of the Department of Industries. Bombay

Bull Dep Inds Comm Unit Prov Agra Oudh — Bulletin. Department of Industries and Commerce. United Provinces of Agra and Oudh

Bull Dep Inds Hyderabad — Bulletin of the Department of Industries. Hyderabad

Bull Dep Inds Madras — Bulletin of the Department of Industries. Madras

Bull Dep Inds S Aust — Bulletin of the Department of Industries. South Australia

Bull Dep Landb Proefstn Suriname — Bulletin. Departement-Landbouwproefstation in Suriname

Bull Dep Landb Suriname — Bulletin. Departement van den Landbouw. Suriname

Bull Dep Ld Rec Agric Beng — Bulletin of the Department of Land Records and Agriculture. Bengal

Bull Dep Ld Rec Agric Bombay — Bulletin of the Department of Land Records and Agriculture. Bombay

Bull Dep Ld Rec Agric Madras — Bulletin of the Department of Land Records and Agriculture. Madras

Bull Dep Lds Forests Nova Scotia — Bulletin. Department of Lands and Forests. Nova Scotia

Bull Dep Lds Forests Ottawa Silvic — Bulletin. Department of Lands and Forests. Ottawa. Silviculture Series

Bull Dep Math Brown Univ — Bulletin of the Department of Mathematics of Brown University

Bull Dep Mines (Br Columbia) — Bulletin. Department of Mines (British Columbia)

Bull Dep Mines Fed Malaya — Bulletin. Department of Mines. Federation of Malaya

Bull Dep Mines Miner Resour West Aust — Bulletin of the Department of Mines and Mineral Resources. Western Australia

Bull Dep Mines Petrol Resour Br Columb — Bulletin. Department of Mines and Petroleum Resources. British Columbia

Bull Dep Sci Ind Res (NZ) — Bulletin. Department of Scientific and Industrial Research (New Zealand)

Bull Dept Agr Econ Univ Manchester — Bulletin. Department of Agricultural Economics. University of Manchester

Bull Dept Agric and Indust (West Australia) — Bulletin. Department of Agriculture and Industries (Western Australia)

Bull Dept Agric Gov Res Inst Formosa — Bulletin. Department of Agriculture. Government Research Institute. Formosa/Taiwan Sotokufu Chuo Kenkyu Jo, Nogyo-Bu Iho

Bull Dept Agric Kingston — Bulletin. Department of Agriculture (Kingston)

Bull Dept Agr (Mysore) Entomol Ser — Bulletin. Department of Agriculture (Mysore State). Entomology Series

Bull Dept Agron Mosonmagyarovar Coll Agr Sci — Bulletin. Department of Agronomy. Mosonmagyarovar College of Agricultural Sciences

Bull Dept Agr (Tanganyika) — Bulletin. Department of Agriculture (Tanganyika)

Bull Dept Agr Tech Serv (Repub S Afr) — Bulletin. Department of Agricultural Technical Services (Republic of South Africa)

Bull Dept Biol Yenching Univ — Bulletin. Department of Biology. Yenching University/Yen Ta Sheng Wu Pu Ts'ung K'an

Bull Dept Gen Ed College Sci Tech Nihon Univ — Bulletin. Department of General Education. College of Science and Technology. Nihon University

Bull Dept Gen Educ Nagoya City Univ Nat Sci Sect — Bulletin. Department of General Education. Nagoya City University. Natural Science Section

Bull Dept Heat Vent Engng Univ Coll Lond — Bulletin of the Department of Heating and Ventilating Engineering. University College, London

Bull Dept Hlth Ky — Bulletin of the Department of Health. Kentucky

Bull Dept Land Rec Madras — Bulletin. Department of Land Records and Agriculture (Madras)

Bull Dep Zool Univ Panjab New Ser — Bulletin. Department of Zoology. University of the Panjab. New Series

Bull Dep Zool Univ Punjab — Bulletin of the Department of Zoology. University of the Punjab

Bull des Avoues — Bulletin. Federation des Avoues

Bull des Cereales Plant Fecule — Bulletin des Cereales et des Plantes a Fecule

Bull Detroit Inst A — Bulletin of the Detroit Institute of Arts

Bull d Inst Corr Arch — Bullettino. Instituto di Corrispondenza Archeologica

Bull di Paletn Ital — Bullettino di Paletnologia Italiana

Bull Dir Bel — Bulletin van de Directe Belastingen

Bull Direction Etudes Recherches Ser C Math Informat — Bulletin. Direction des Etudes et Recherches. Serie C. Mathematiques. Informatique

Bull Direction Etudes Rech Ser C Math Inform — Electricite de France. Bulletin de la Direction des Etudes et Recherches. SerieC. Mathematiques-Informatique

Bull Dir Etud & Rech A — Bulletin. Direction des Etudes et Recherches. Serie A

Bull Dir Etud & Rech B — Bulletin. Direction des Etudes et Recherches. Serie B

Bull Dir Etud & Rech C — Bulletin. Direction des Etudes et Recherches. Serie C

Bull Dir Etud & Rech Ser A — Bulletin. Direction des Etudes et Recherches. Serie A

Bull Dir Etud & Rech Ser B — Bulletin. Direction des Etudes et Recherches. Serie B

Bull Dir Etud & Rech Ser C — Bulletin. Direction des Etudes et Recherches. Serie C

Bull Dir Etud Rech Electr Fr — Bulletin. Direction des Etudes et Recherches. Electricite de France. Serie B. Reseaux Electriques Materiels Electriques

Bull Dir Etud Rech Electr Fr — Bulletin. Direction des Etudes et Recherches. Electricite de France. Serie C. Matematiques, Informatiques

Bull Dir Etud Rech Electr Fr Ser A — Bulletin. Direction des Etudes et Recherches. Electricite de France. Serie A. Nucleaire, Hydraulique, Thermique

Bull Dir Gen Miner Resour Saudi Arabia — Bulletin. Directorate General of Mineral Resources (Saudia Arabia)

Bull Dir Mines Geol (Afr Equa) — Bulletin. Direction des Mines et de la Geologie (Afrique Equatoriale)

Bull Div Miner Resour (VA) — Bulletin. Division of Mineral Resources (Virginia)

Bull Div Plant Ind NSW Dept Agr — Bulletin. Division of Plant Industry. New South Wales Department of Agriculture

Bull Div Pl Pathol Agric Exp Sta Formosa — Bulletin. Division of Plant Pathology. Agricultural Experiment Station. Formosa/Taiwan Nosakubutsu Byogai Mokuroku

Bull Div Silv Dep For Papua & N Guinea — Bulletin. Division of Silviculture. Department of Forests of Papua and New Guinea

Bull Div Veg Physiol Path US Dep Agric — Bulletin. Division of Vegetable Physiology and Pathology. United States Department of Agriculture

Bull Doc Bibliog — Bulletin de Documentation Bibliographique

Bull Doc Cent Inf Chrome Dur — Bulletin de Documentation. Centre d'Information du Chrome Dur

Bull Doc Int Superphosphate Mfr Ass Agr Comm — Bulletin of Documentation. International Superphosphate Manufacturers Association. Agricultural Committee

Bull Docum Ass Int Fabr Superphos — Bulletin de Documentation. Association Internationale des Fabricants de Superphosphates

Bull Docum Bur Etud Ind Fernand Courtoy — Bulletin de Documentation. Bureau d'Etudes Industrielles Fernand Courtoy

Bull Docum Cent Etud Rech Ind Liants Hydraul — Bulletin de Documentation. Centre d'Etudes et de Recherches de l'Industrie des Liants Hydrauliques

Bull Docum Cent Etud Rech Mach Agric — Bulletin de Documentation. Centre d'Etudes et de Recherches du Machinisme Agricole

Bull Docum Cent Tech Mach Agric — Bulletin de Documentation. Centre Technique du Machinisme Agricole

Bull Docum Inf Synd Constr Fr — Bulletin de Documentation et d'Information. Syndicat des Constructeurs Francais

Bull Docum Inst Hyg Mines ASBL — Bulletin de Documentation. Institut d'Hygiene des Mines. A.S.B.L

Bull Docum Med Inst Hyg Mines ASBL — Bulletin de Documentation Medicale. Institut d'Hygiene des Mines. A.S.B.L

Bull Docum Sante Publ Pop — Bulletin de Documentation de la Sante Publique et de la Population

Bull Docum Soc Controle Exploit Transp Auxil — Bulletin de Documentation. Societe de Controle et d'Exploitation de Transports Auxiliaires

Bull Docum Soud — Bulletin de Documentation de la Soudure et des Techniques Connexes

Bull Docum Tech Cent Tech Ind Fond — Bulletin de Documentation Technique. Centre Technique des Industries de la Fonderie

Bull Docum Tech Inst Hyg Mines ASBL — Bulletin de Documentation Technique. Institut d'Hygiene des Mines. A.S.B.L

Bull Docum Un Int Chem De Fer — Bulletin de Documentation. Union Internationale des Chemins de Fer

Bull Dom Grain Res Lab Winnipeg — Bulletin of the Dominion Grand Research Laboratory. Winnipeg

Bull Dom Mus Wellington — Bulletin of the Dominion Museum (Welllington)

Bull Dom Obs NZ — Bulletin. Dominion Observatory. New Zealand

Bull Dom Wat Pwr Reclam Serv Irrig Ser — Bulletin of the Dominion Water Power and Reclamation Service. Irrigation Series

Bull Dosente — Bulletin vir Dosente

Bull d Paleont — Bullettino di Paleontologia Italiana

Bull Drog Fed Fr — Bulletin de la Droguerie Federale de France

Bull Droit Nucl — Bulletin de Droit Nucleaire

Bull Drome — Revue Dromoise

Bull Drugg Res Bur — Bulletin. Druggists' Research Bureau

Bull Dry Fmg Congr — Bulletin. Dry Farming Congress

Bull d Soc Filol Rom — Bullettino della Societa Filologica Romana

Bull du Bibl — Bulletin du Bibliophile et du Bibliothecaire

Bull du Biblioph — Bulletin du Bibliophile et du Bibliothecaire

Bull Duke Univ Mar Stn — Bulletin. Duke University Marine Station

Bull Duke Univ Sch For — Bulletin. Duke University School of Forestry

Bull du Mus d Anthrop Prehistorique de Monaco — Bulletin. Musee d'Anthropologie Prehistorique de Monaco

Bull E A — Bulletin of Eastern Art

Bull E Angl Inst Agric — Bulletin. East Anglian Institute of Agriculture

Bull Earth Miner Sci Exp Sta PA State Univ — Bulletin. Earth and Mineral Sciences Experiment Station. Pennsylvania State University

Bull Earth Miner Sci Exp Stn PA State Univ — Bulletin. Earth and Mineral Sciences Experiment Station. Pennsylvania State University

Bull Earthq Invest Comm Tokyo — Bulletin of the Earthquake Investigation Committee (Tokyo)

Bull Earthq Res Inst Tokyo Univ — Bulletin of the Earthquake Research Institute. Tokyo University

Bull Earthquake Res Inst Univ Tokyo — Bulletin. Earthquake Research Institute. University of Tokyo

Bull Earth Sci Fac Ege Univ (Izmir) — Bulletin. Earth Science Faculty. Ege University (Izmir)

Bull East Scotl Coll Agric — Bulletin. East of Scotland College of Agriculture

Bull Ecc — Bulletin de Litterature Ecclesiastique

Bull Ec Fr Extr Orient — Bulletin de l'Ecole Francaise d'Extreme-Orient

Bull Eclect Med Univ Kans Cy — Bulletin of Eclectic Medical University (Kansas City)

Bull Ec Meun Belge — Bulletin. Ecole de la Meunerie Belge

Bull Ec Natl Super Agron Ind Aliment — Bulletin. Ecole Nationale Superieure d'Agronomie et des Industries Alimentaires

Bull Ec Natl Super Agron Nancy — Bulletin. Ecole Nationale Superieure Agronomique de Nancy

Bull Ec Natn Sup Agron Nancy — Bulletin. Ecole Nationale Superieure Agronomique de Nancy

Bull Ec Nat Super Agron Ind Aliment — Bulletin. Ecole Nationale Superieure d'Agronomie et des Industries Alimentaires

Bull Ecol — Bulletin d'Ecologie
Bull Ecole Franc Extreme-Orient — Bulletin. Ecole Francaise d'Extreme-Orient
Bull Ecole Fr Extreme Orient — Bulletin de l'Ecole Francaise d'Extreme-Orient
Bull Ecole Nat Super Agron Nancy — Bulletin. Ecole Nationale Superieure Agronomique de Nancy
Bull Ecole Super Agr Tunis — Bulletin. Ecole Superieure d'Agriculture de Tunis
Bull Ecol Res Comm-NFR (Statens Naturvetensk Forskningsrad) — Bulletins. Ecological Research Committee-NFR (Statens Naturvetenskapliga Forskningsrad)
Bull Ecol Soc Amer — Bulletin. Ecological Society of America
Bull Econ et Soc Maroc — Bulletin Economique et Social du Maroc
Bull Econom — Bulletin Economique Mensuelle
Bull Ec Sup Aeronaut Paris — Bulletin de l'Ecole Superieure d'Aeronautique et de Construction Mecanique (Paris)
Bull Edinburgh Sch Agr — Bulletin. Edinburgh School of Agriculture
Bull Educ Dev & Res — Bulletin of Educational Development and Research
Bull Educ Res Inst Fac Educ Univ Kagoshima — Bulletin. Educational Research Institute. Faculty of Education. University of Kagoshima
Bull Effort Mod — Bulletin de l'Effort Moderne
Bul Leg Dalloz — Bulletin Legislatif Dalloz
Bull Egyp Semin — Bulletin of the Egyptological Seminar
Bull Egypt Univ Fac Arts — Bulletin. Faculty of Arts. Egyptian University
Bull Ehime Agr Exp Sta — Bulletin. Ehime Agricultural Experiment Station
Bull Ehime Prefect Agric Exp Stn — Bulletin. Ehime Prefectural Agricultural Experiment Station
Bull Ehime Univ For — Bulletin. Ehime University Forest
Bull Eidgenoess Gesundh Beil B — Bulletin. Eidgenoessisches Gesundheitsamt. Beilage B
Bulleid Mem Lect — Bulleid Memorial Lectures
Bull E I Du Pont De Nemours — Bulletin. E.I. Du Pont de Nemours and Company
Bull Eighth Dist Dent Soc — Bulletin. Eighth District Dental Society
Bull Electron Microsc Soc India — Bulletin. Electron Microscope Society of India
Bull Electrotech Lab — Bulletin. Electrotechnical Laboratory
Bull Electrotech Lab (Tokyo) — Bulletin. Electrotechnical Laboratory (Tokyo)
Bull Eleventh Dist Dent Soc NY — Bulletin. Eleventh District Dental Society
Bull Endem Dis — Bulletin of Endemic Diseases
Bull Endem Dis (Baghdad) — Bulletin of Endemic Diseases (Baghdad)
Bull Endemic Diseases — Bulletin of Endemic Diseases
Bull Eng Exp Stn Oreg State Coll — Bulletin. Engineering Experiment Station. Oregon State College
Bull Eng Geol Hydrogeol (Engl Transl) — Bulletin of Engineering Geology and Hydrogeology (English Translation)
Bull Engrais — Bulletin des Engrais
Bull Eng Res Inst Kyoto Univ — Bulletin. Engineering Research Institute of Kyoto University
Bull Enseign Public Gouvernement Cherifien — Bulletin. Enseignement Public du Gouvernement Cherifien
Bull Entomol — Bulletin of Entomology
Bull Entomol Res — Bulletin of Entomological Research
Bull Entomol Soc Am — Bulletin. Entomological Society of America
Bull Entomol Soc Amer — Bulletin. Entomological Society of America
Bull Entomol Soc Egypt — Bulletin. Entomological Society of Egypt
Bull Entomol Soc Egypt Econ Ser — Bulletin. Entomological Society of Egypt. Economic Series
Bull Entomol Soc Nigeria — Bulletin. Entomological Society of Nigeria
Bull Ent Res — Bulletin of Entomological Research
Bull Ent Soc Am — Bulletin. Entomological Society of America
Bull Ent Soc Egypt Econ Ser — Bulletin. Entomological Society of Egypt. Economic Series
Bull Envir Contam Toxic — Bulletin of Environmental Contamination and Toxicology
Bull Environ Contam — Bulletin of Environmental Contamination and Toxicology
Bull Environ Contam Toxicol — Bulletin of Environmental Contamination and Toxicology
Bull Environ Pollut Control Res Cent Shizuoka Prefect — Bulletin. Environmental Pollution Control and Research Center. Shizuoka Prefecture
Bull Environ Sci — Bulletin of Environmental Sciences
Bull Environ Sci — Bulletin of Environmental Sciences. Hanyang University
Bull Ep — Bulletin Epigraphique
Bull Epigr — Bulletin Epigraphique
Bull Epigraph — Bulletin Epigraphique
Bull Epigr Gaule — Bulletin Epigraphique de la Gaule
Bull Epizoot Dis Afr — Bulletin of Epizootic Diseases of Africa
Bull Equine Res Inst — Bulletin. Equine Research Institute
Bull Escher Wyss — Bulletin Escher Wyss
Bull Essex Cty Dent Soc — Bulletin. Essex County [New Jersey] Dental Society
Bullet dell Inst Arch — Bullettino. Instituto di Corrispondenza Archeologica
Bull Ethnogr Mus Beograd — Bulletin of the Ethnographic Museum in Beograd
BullETHS — Bulletin. Evangelical Theological Society [Later, Journal. Evangelica l Theological Society]
Bulletin-AQQUA — Bulletin. Association Quebecoise pour l'Etude du Quaternaire
Bulletin Comp L — Bulletin. Comparative Law Bureau
Bulletin de Liaison — Bulletin de Liaison. Centre d'Etudes des Peintures Murales Romaines
Bulletin San Quentin — Bulletin. California State Prison (San Quentin)
Bulletin Singapore Natl Inst Chem — Bulletin. Singapore National Institute of Chemistry
Bull et Mem Soc Anat Paris — Bulletins et Memoires. Societe Anatomique de Paris
Bull et Mem Soc Centr Med Vet — Bulletins et Memoires. Societe Centrale de Medecine Veterinaire
Bull et Mem Soc Chir Paris — Bulletins et Memoires. Societe de Chirurgie de Paris
Bull et Mem Soc Med Hop Bucarest — Bulletins et Memoires. Societe Medicale des Hopitaux de Bucarest

Bull et Mem Soc Med Hop Paris — Bulletins et Memoires. Societe Medicale des Hopitaux de Paris
Bull et Mem Soc Nat Chir (Paris) — Bulletins et Memoires. Societe Nationale de Chirurgie (Paris)
Bull et Mem Soc Therap — Bulletins et Memoires. Societe de Therapeutique
Bullet Mus Belge — Bulletin Bibliographique et Pedagogique du Musee Belge
Bull Et Orient — Bulletin d'Etudes Orientales
Bullet Soc Nat Fr — Bulletin. Societe Nationale des Antiquaires de France
Bullett Commiss Archeol Comun Roma — Bullettino della Commissione Archeologica Communale di Roma
Bullettino Archeol Crist — Bullettino di Archeologia Cristiana
Bullett Istit Dir Rom — Bulletino. Istituto di Diritto Romano
Bull Etud Commun Mediter — Bulletin de l'Etude en Commun de la Mediterranee
Bull Etudes Orient — Bulletin d'Etudes Orientales
Bull Etud Or — Bulletin d'Etudes Orientales. Institut Francais de Damas
Bull Etud Orient — Bulletin d'Etudes Orientales
Bull Etud Rech Tech — Bulletin d'Etudes et de Recherches Techniques
Bull Eur Assoc Theor Comput Sci — Bulletin. European Association for Theoretical Computer Science
Bull Eur Chiro Union — Bulletin. European Chiropractors' Union
Bull Eur Communities — Bulletin. European Communities
Bull Eur Communities Suppl — Bulletin. European Communities. Supplement
Bull Eur Physiopathol Respir — Bulletin Europeen de Physiopathologie Respiratoire
Bull Eur South Obs — Bulletin. European Southern Observatory
Bull Exp Anim — Bulletin of the Experimental Animals
Bull Exp Biol Med — Bulletin of Experimental Biology and Medicine
Bull Exp Biol Med (Eng Transl Byull Eksp Biol Med) — Bulletin of Experimental Biology and Medicine (English Translation of Byulleten' Eksperimental'noi Biologii i Meditsiny)
Bull Exp Biol Med USSR — Bulletin of Experimental Biology and Medicine. USSR
Bull Exp Farm Coll Agr Ehime Univ — Bulletin. Experimental Farm College of Agriculture. Ehime University
Bull Exp Fms Brch Dep Agric (Can) — Bulletin. Experimental Farms Branch. Department of Agriculture (Canada)
Bull Exp Forests Tokyo Univ Agric — Bulletin of the Experimental Forests. Tokyo University of Agriculture
Bull Exp For Natl Taiwan Univ — Bulletin. Experimental Forest of National Taiwan University
Bull Exp For Tokyo Univ Agric Technol — Bulletin of the Experiment Forest. Tokyo University of Agriculture and Technology
Bull Exp Sta Tuskegee Normal Industr Inst — Bulletin. Experiment Station. Tuskegee Normal and Industrial Institute. Tuskegee Institute, Alabama
Bull Exp Stn Horse Breed (Slatinany) — Bulletin. Experimental Station for Horse Breeding (Slatinany)
Bull Ext — Bulletin Exterieur
Bull Eyesight Conserv Coun Am — Bulletin of the Eyesight Conservation Council of America
Bull Fac A Alexandria — Bulletin of the Faculty of Arts (Alexandria)
Bull Fac A Fouad I U — Bulletin of the Faculty of Arts. Fouad I University
Bull Fac Agric Ain Shams Univ — Bulletin. Faculty of Agriculture. Ain Shams University
Bull Fac Agric Alberta Univ — Bulletin of the Faculty of Agriculture. Alberta University</PHR> %
Bull Fac Agric Cairo Univ — Bulletin. Faculty of Agriculture. Cairo University
Bull Fac Agric Hirosaki Univ — Bulletin. Faculty of Agriculture. Hirosaki University
Bull Fac Agric Hort Univ Reading — Bulletin of the Faculty of Agriculture and Horticulture. University of Reading
Bull Fac Agric Kagoshima Univ — Bulletin. Faculty of Agriculture. Kagoshima University
Bull Fac Agric Meiji Univ — Bulletin. Faculty of Agriculture. Meiji University
Bull Fac Agric Mie Univ — Bulletin. Faculty of Agriculture. Mie University
Bull Fac Agric Miyazaki Univ — Bulletin. Faculty of Agriculture. Miyazaki University
Bull Fac Agric Niigata Univ — Bulletin. Faculty of Agriculture. Niigata University
Bull Fac Agric Saga Univ — Bulletin. Faculty of Agriculture. Saga University
Bull Fac Agric Sci (Mosonmagyarovar Hung) — Bulletin. Faculty of Agricultural Sciences (Mosonmagyarovar, Hungary)
Bull Fac Agric Shimane Univ — Bulletin. Faculty of Agriculture. Shimane University
Bull Fac Agric Shinshu Univ — Bulletin. Faculty of Agriculture. Shinshu University/ Shinshu Daigaku Nogakubu Gakujitsu Hokoku
Bull Fac Agric Shizuoka Univ — Bulletin. Faculty of Agriculture. Shizuoka University
Bull Fac Agric Tamagawa Univ — Bulletin. Faculty of Agriculture. Tamagawa University
Bull Fac Agric Tokyo Univ Agric Technol — Bulletin. Faculty of Agriculture. Tokyo University of Agriculture and Technology
Bull Fac Agric Tottori Univ — Bulletin. Faculty of Agriculture. Tottori University
Bull Fac Agric Transv Univ Coll — Bulletin. Faculty of Agriculture. Transvaal University College
Bull Fac Agric Univ Miyazaki — Bulletin. Faculty of Agriculture. University of Miyazaki
Bull Fac Agric Univ Pretoria — Bulletin. Faculty of Agriculture. University of Pretoria
Bull Fac Agric Yamaguchi Univ — Bulletin of the Faculty of Agriculture. Yamaguchi University
Bull Fac Agric Yamaguti Univ — Bulletin. Faculty of Agriculture. Yamaguti University
Bull Fac Agr Kagoshima Univ — Bulletin. Faculty of Agriculture. Kagoshima University
Bull Fac Agr Meiji Univ — Bulletin. Faculty of Agriculture. Meiji University
Bull Fac Agr Niigata Univ — Bulletin. Faculty of Agriculture. Niigata University
Bull Fac Agr Shimane Univ — Bulletin. Faculty of Agriculture. Shimane University
Bull Fac Agr Shizuoka Univ — Bulletin. Faculty of Agriculture. Shizuoka University

Bull Fac Agr Univ Miyazaki — Bulletin. Faculty of Agriculture. University of Miyazaki

Bull Fac Agr Yamaguchi Univ — Bulletin. Faculty of Agriculture. Yamaguchi University

Bull Fac Bioresour Mie Univ — Bulletin. Faculty of Bioresources. Mie University

Bull Fac Ed Kagoshima Univ Natur Sci — Bulletin. Faculty of Education. Kagoshima University. Natural Science

Bull Fac Educ Chiba Univ — Bulletin. Faculty of Education. Chiba University

Bull Fac Educ Hirosaki Univ — Bulletin. Faculty of Education. Hirosaki University

Bull Fac Educ Hiroshima Univ — Bulletin. Faculty of Education. Hiroshima University

Bull Fac Educ Hiroshima Univ Part 3 (Sci Tech) — Bulletin. Faculty of Education. Hiroshima University. Part 3 (Science and Technology)

Bull Fac Educ Kanazawa Univ Nat Sci — Bulletin. Faculty of Education. Kanazawa University. Natural Science

Bull Fac Educ Kobe Univ — Bulletin. Faculty of Education. Kobe University

Bull Fac Educ Kochi Univ Ser 3 — Bulletin. Faculty of Education. Kochi University. Series 3

Bull Fac Educ Univ Kagoshima Nat Sci — Bulletin. Faculty of Education. University of Kagoshima. Natural Science

Bull Fac Educ Utsunomiya Univ Sect 2 — Bulletin. Faculty of Education. Utsunomiya University. Section 2

Bull Fac Educ Wakayama Univ Nat Sci — Bulletin. Faculty of Education. Wakayama University. Natural Science

Bull Fac Educ Yamaguchi Univ — Bulletin. Faculty of Education. Yamaguchi University

Bull Fac Ed Univ Kagoshima — Bulletin. Faculty of Education. University of Kagoshima

Bull Fac Ed Utsunomiya Univ Sect 2 — Bulletin. Faculty of Education. Utsunomiya University. Section 2

Bull Fac Ed Wakayama Univ Natur Sci — Wakayama University. Faculty of Education. Bulletin. Natural Science

Bull Fac Eng Alexandria Univ — Bulletin. Faculty of Engineering. Alexandria University

Bull Fac Eng Cairo Univ — Bulletin. Faculty of Engineering. Cairo University

Bull Fac Eng Hiroshima Univ — Bulletin. Faculty of Engineering. Hiroshima University

Bull Fac Eng Hokkaido Univ — Bulletin. Faculty of Engineering. Hokkaido University

Bull Fac Eng Ibaraki Univ — Bulletin. Faculty of Engineering. Ibaraki University

Bull Fac Eng Kyushu Sangyo Univ — Bulletin. Faculty of Engineering. Kyushu Sangyo University

Bull Fac Eng Miyazaki Univ — Bulletin. Faculty of Engineering. Miyazaki University

Bull Fac Engng Ibaraki Univ — Bulletin of the Faculty of Engineering. Ibaraki University

Bull Fac Engng Yokohama Natn Univ — Bulletion of the Faculty of Engineering. Yokohama National University

Bull Fac Engrg Hiroshima Univ — Bulletin. Faculty of Engineering. Hiroshima University

Bull Fac Engrg Miyazaki Univ — Bulletin. Faculty of Engineering. Miyazaki University

Bull Fac Eng Tokushima Univ — Bulletin. Faculty of Engineering. Tokushima University

Bull Fac Eng Toyama Univ — Bulletin. Faculty of Engineering. Toyama University

Bull Fac Eng Univ Alexandria Chem Eng — Bulletin. Faculty of Engineering. University of Alexandria. Chemical Engineering

Bull Fac Eng Yokohama Natl Univ — Bulletin. Faculty of Engineering. Yokohama National University

Bull Fac Eng Yokohama Univ — Bulletin. Faculty of Engineering. Yokohama University

Bull Fac F A Tokyo N U F A & Music — Bulletin of the Faculty of Fine Arts. Tokyo National University of Fine Arts and Music

Bull Fac F A Tokyo U A — Bulletin of the Faculty of Fine Arts. Tokyo University of the Arts

Bull Fac Fish Hokkaido Univ — Bulletin. Faculty of Fisheries. Hokkaido University

Bull Fac Fish Mie Univ — Bulletin. Faculty of Fisheries. Mie University

Bull Fac Fish Nagasaki Univ — Bulletin. Faculty of Fisheries. Nagasaki University

Bull Fac For Univ BC — Bulletin. Faculty of Forestry. University of British Columbia

Bull Fac Gen Ed Gifu Univ — Gifu University. Faculty of General Education. Bulletin

Bull Fac Gen Educ Utsunomiya Univ Sect 2 — Bulletin. Faculty of General Education. Utsunomiya University. Section 2

Bull Fac Home Econ Hiroshima Womens Univ — Bulletin of the Faculty of Home Economics. Hiroshima Women's University

Bull Fac Home Econ Kobe Women's Univ — Bulletin of the Faculty of Home Economics. Kobe Women's University

Bull Fac Home Life Sci Fukuoka Women's Univ — Bulletin. Faculty of Home Life Science. Fukuoka Women's University

Bull Fac Hort Univ Sci Agric — Bulletin. Faculty of Horticulture and Viticulture. University of Agriculture

Bull Fac Hum Environ Sci Fukuoka Womens Univ — Bulletin of the Faculty of Human Environmental Science. Fukuoka Women's University

Bull Fac Hum Life Environ Sci Hiroshima Womens Univ — Bulletin of the Faculty of Human Life and Environmental Science. Hiroshima Women's University

Bull Fac Lib Arts Ibaraki Univ (Nat Sci) — Bulletin. Faculty of Liberal Arts. Ibaraki University (Natural Science)

Bull Fac Liberal Arts Chukyo Univ — Bulletin of the Faculty of the Liberal Arts Chukyo University

Bull Fac Liberal Arts Shiga Univ Pt 2 Nat Sci — Bulletin. Faculty of Liberal Arts and Education. Shiga University. Part 2. Natural Science/Shiga Daigaku Gakugeibu Kenkyu Ranshu

Bull Fac Med Istanbul — Bulletin. Faculte de Medecine d'Istanbul

Bull Fac Med Osaka Univ — Bulletin. Faculty of Medicine. Osaka University

Bull Fac Pharm Cairo Univ — Bulletin. Faculty of Pharmacy. Cairo University

Bull Fac Pharm Kinki Univ — Bulletin. Faculty of Pharmacy. Kinki University

Bull Fac Sch Educ Hiroshima Univ Part I — Bulletin. Faculty of School Education. Hiroshima University. Part I

Bull Fac Sch Educ Hiroshima Univ Part II — Bulletin. Faculty of School Education. Hiroshima University. Part II

Bull Fac School Ed Hiroshima Univ Part II — Bulletin. Faculty of School Education. Hiroshima University. Part II

Bull Fac Sci Alexandria Univ — Bulletin. Faculty of Science. Alexandria University

Bull Fac Sci Assiut Univ — Bulletin. Faculty of Science. Assiut University

Bull Fac Sci Assiut Univ B Chem — Bulletin of the Faculty of Science. Assiut University. B. Chemistry

Bull Fac Sci Assiut Univ C — Bulletin of the Faculty of Science. Assiut University. C. Mathematics

Bull Fac Sci (Cairo) — Bulletin. Faculty of Science (Cairo)

Bull Fac Sci Cairo Univ — Bulletin. Faculty of Science. Cairo University

Bull Fac Sci Egypt Univ — Bulletin of the Faculty of Science. Egyptian University

Bull Fac Sci Eng Chuo Univ — Bulletin. Faculty of Science and Engineering. Chuo University

Bull Fac Sci Engrg Chuo Univ — Bulletin. Faculty of Science and Engineering. Chuo University

Bull Fac Sci Engrg Chuo Univ Ser I Math — Bulletin of the Faculty of Science and Engineering Chuo University. Seres I. Mathematics

Bull Fac Sci Ibaraki Univ Ser A — Bulletin. Faculty of Science. Ibaraki University. Series A. Mathematics

Bull Fac Sci Ibaraki Univ Series A — Bulletin. Faculty of Science. Ibaraki University. Series A. Mathematics

Bull Fac Sci King Abdul Aziz Univ — Bulletin. Faculty of Science. King Abdul Aziz University

Bull Fac Sci Riyad Univ — Bulletin. Faculty of Science. Riyad University. Series II

Bull Fac Sci Univ Fr Chin Peiping — Bulletin. Faculte des Sciences. Universite Franco-Chinoise de Peiping

Bull Fac Text Fib Kyoto Univ Ind Arts — Bulletin of the Faculty of Textile Fibers. Kyoto University of Industrial Arts and Textile Fibers

Bull Fac Textile Fibers Kyoto Univ Ind Arts Textile Fibers — Bulletin. Faculty of Textile Fibers. Kyoto University of Industrial Arts and Textile Fibers

Bull Fan Meml Inst Biol — Bulletin of the Fan Memorial Institute of Biology

Bull Far Eastern Antiquities — Bulletin. Museum of Far Eastern Antiquities

Bull Farm Manage Land Util Ser H — Bulletin. Farm Management and Land Utilization. Series H

Bull Farouk I Univ Fac Arts — Bulletin. Farouk I University. Faculty of Arts

Bull Far Seas Fish Res Lab (Shimizu) — Bulletin. Far Seas Fisheries Research Laboratory (Shimizu)

Bull Fed Belg Soc Sci — Bulletin. Federation Belge des Societes de Sciences Mathematiques, Physiques, Chimiques, Naturelles, Medicales, et Appliquees

Bull Fed Ind Chim Bel — Bulletin. Federation des Industries Chimiques de Belgique

Bull Fed Int Assoc Chim Text Couleur — Bulletin. Federation Internationale des Associations des Chimistes du Textile et de la Couleur

Bull Fed Int Lait — Bulletin. Federation Internationale de Laiterie

Bull Fed Min Agr (Salisbury) — Bulletin. Federal Ministry of Agriculture (Salisbury)

Bull Fed Soc Gynecol Obstet Lang Fr — Bulletin. Federation des Societes de Gynecologie et d'Obstetrique de Langue Francaise

Bull Fed Soc Hist Nat Franche-Comte — Bulletin. Federation des Societes d'Histoire Naturelle de Franche-Comte

Bull Fed Soc Hort Belgique — Bulletin. Federation des Societes d'Horticulture de Belgique

Bull FIB — Bulletin. Federation des Industries Belges

Bull Fiber Text Res Found — Bulletin. Fiber and Textile Research Foundation

Bull Field Geol Club South Aust — Bulletin. Field Geology Club of South Australia

Bull Fifth Dist Dent Soc (Fresno) — Bulletin. Fifth District Dental Society (Fresno)

Bull Fifth Dist Dent Soc State NY — Bulletin. Fifth District Dental Society of the State of New York

Bull Fil Soc Biol Paris — Bulletin. Filiales de la Societe de Biologie de Paris

Bull First Agron Div Tokai-Kinki Nat Agr Exp Sta — Bulletin. First Agronomy Division. Tokai-Kinki National Agricultural ExperimentStation

Bull First Agron Div Tokai-Kinki Natl Agric Exp Stn — Bulletin. First Agronomy Division. Tokai-Kinki National Agricultural ExperimentStation

Bull Fish Exp Stn Gov Gen Chosen Ser B — Bulletin. Fishery Experiment Station. Government General of Chosen. Series B

Bull Fish Res Board Can — Bulletin. Fisheries Research Board of Canada

Bull Fish Res Dev — Bulletin of Fisheries Research and Development

Bull Fish Res Stn (Ceylon) — Bulletin. Fisheries Research Station (Ceylon)

Bull Fla Agr Exp Sta — Bulletin. Florida Agricultural Experiment Station

Bull Fla Agric Exp Stn — Bulletin. Florida Agricultural Experiment Station

Bull Fla Agric Ext Serv — Bulletin. Florida Agricultural Extension Service

Bull Fla Coop Ext Serv Univ Fla — Bulletin. Florida Cooperative Extension Service. University of Florida

Bull Fla Dep Agric — Bulletin. Florida Department of Agriculture

Bull Fla Dept Agr Div Plant Ind — Bulletin. Florida Department of Agriculture. Division of Plant Industry

Bull Fla State Mus Biol Sci — Bulletin. Florida State Museum. Biological Sciences

Bull Fla Univ Agr Exp Sta — Bulletin. Florida University. Agricultural Experiment Station

Bull Florida Nurserymen Growers Assoc — Bulletin. Florida Nurserymen and Growers Association

Bull Fogg A Mus — Bulletin of the Fogg Art Museum

Bull Fogg Art Mus — Bulletin. Fogg Art Museum

Bull Fonds Rech For Univ Laval — Bulletin. Fonds de Recherches Forestieres. Universite Laval

Bull Food Ind Exp Stn Hiroshima Prefect — Bulletin. Food Industrial Experiment Station. Hiroshima Prefecture

Bull For Comm (Lond) — Bulletin. Forestry Commission (London)

Bull For Comm Tasm — Bulletin. Forestry Commission of Tasmania

Bull For Comm Vict — Bulletin. Forests Commission of Victoria

Bull For Dep Nigeria — Bulletin. Forestry Department. Nigeria

Bull For Dep Tasm — Bulletin. Forestry Department. Tasmania
Bull For Dep (Uganda) — Bulletin. Forest Department. Kampala (Uganda)
Bull For Dep Univ Edinb — Bulletin of the Forestry Department. University of Edinburgh
Bull For Dep W Aust — Bulletin. Forests Department of Western Australia
Bull For Dep West Aust — Bulletin. Forests Department of Western Australia
Bull Ford For Cent — Bulletin. Ford Forestry Center
Bull Forest Comm Vict — Bulletin. Forests Commission of Victoria
Bull Forest Dep WA — Bulletin. Forests Department of Western Australia
Bull Forest Exp Sta Gov Taiwan — Bulletin of Forest Experiment Station. Government of Taiwan/Taiwan Ringyo Shikenjo Hokoku
Bull Forest Res Inst — Bulletin of Forest Research Institute
Bull Forests Commn Victoria — Bulletin. Forests Commission. Victoria
Bull Forests Comm Tasm — Bulletin. Forests Commission of Tasmania
Bull Forests Dep West Aust — Bulletin. Forests Department of Western Australia
Bull Forest Soc Korea — Bulletin. Forestry Society of Korea/Chosen Sanrin-Kaiho
Bull For Exp Sta (Meguro) — Bulletin. Government Forest Experiment Station (Meguro)
Bull For Exp Stn Chosen — Bulletin. Forestry Experiment Station. Chosen
Bull For For Prod Res Inst — Bulletin. Forestry and Forest Products Research Institute
Bull for Internat Fiscal Docum — Bulletin for International Fiscal Documentation
Bull for Int'l Fisc Doc — Bulletin for International Fiscal Documentation
Bull Formosa Agric Exp Stn — Bulletin of the Formosa Agricultural Experiment Station
Bull Formosa Bur Prod Ind — Bulletin. Formosa Bureau of Productive Industry
Bull For Prod Res (Lond) — Bulletin. Forest Products Research. Ministry of Technology (London)
Bull For Timb Bur — Bulletin. Forestry and Timber Bureau
Bull For Timb Bur (Aust) — Bulletin. Forestry and Timber Bureau (Canberra, Australia)
Bull Fouad I Univ Fac Arts — Bulletin. Fouad I University. Faculty of Arts
Bull Foundry Abstr Br Cast Iron Res Assoc — Bulletin and Foundry Abstracts. British Cast Iron Research Association
Bull Foxboro Co — Bulletin. Foxboro Company
Bull Foxboro Yoxall — Bulletin. Foxboro-Yoxall Ltd
Bull Franc Piscicult — Bulletin Francais de Pisciculture
Bull Franz Theodore Stone Lab — Bulletin. Franz Theodore Stone Laboratory
Bull Free Mus Sci Art Univ Pa — Bulletin of the Free Museum of Science and Art of the University of Pennsylvania
Bull Freshwater Fish Res Lab (Tokyo) — Bulletin. Freshwater Fisheries Research Laboratory (Tokyo)
Bull Freshwat Fish Res Lab Tokyo — Bulletin. Freshwater Fisheries Research Laboratory (Tokyo)
Bull Freshw Fish Res Lab (Tokyo) — Bulletin. Freshwater Fisheries Research Laboratory (Tokyo)
Bull Friends Hist Ass — Bulletin. Friends Historical Association
Bull Frnds Hist Assn — Bulletin. Friends Historical Association
Bull Fr Peche Piscic — Bulletin Francais de la Peche et de la Pisciculture
Bull Fr Piscic — Bulletin Francais de Pisciculture
Bull Fruit Tree Res Stn Minist Agric For Ser E (Akitsu) — Bulletin. Fruit Tree Research Station. Ministry of Agriculture and Forestry. Series E (Akitsu)
Bull Fruit Tree Res Stn Ser A (Hiratsuka) — Bulletin. Fruit Tree Research Station. Series A (Hiratsuka)
Bull Fruit Tree Res Stn Ser A (Yatabe) — Bulletin. Fruit Tree Research Station. Series A (Yatabe)
Bull Fruit Tree Res Stn Ser B (Okitsu) — Bulletin. Fruit Tree Research Station. Series B (Okitsu)
Bull Fruit Tree Res Stn Ser C (Morioka) — Bulletin. Fruit Tree Research Station. Series C (Morioka)
Bull Fruit Tree Res Stn Ser D (Kuchinotsu) — Bulletin. Fruit Tree Research Station. Series D (Kuchinotsu)
Bull Fruit Tree Res Stn Ser E (Akitsu) — Bulletin. Fruit Tree Research Station. Series E (Akitsu)
Bull Ft Wayne Med Soc — Bulletin. Fort Wayne Medical Society
Bull Fuel Res Inst Japan — Bulletin of the Fuel Research Institute. Japan
Bull Fuel Res Inst S Afr — Bulletin. Fuel Research Institute of South Africa
Bull Fuji Women's Coll — Bulletin. Fuji Women's College
Bull Fukui Prefect Text Eng Res Inst — Bulletin. Fukui Prefectural Textile Engineering Research Institute
Bull Fukuoka Agr Exp Stn — Bulletin. Fukuoka Agricultural Experiment Station
Bull Fukuokaken For Exp Sta — Bulletin. Fukuokaken Forest Experiment Station
Bull Fukuoka Pref Agr Exp Sta — Bulletin. Fukuoka Prefectural Agricultural Experiment Station
Bull Fukuoka Ringyo Shikenjo — Bulletin. Fukuoka. Ringyo Shikenjo
Bull Fukuoka Univ Ed 3 — Bulletin. Fukuoka University of Education. Part 3. Natural Sciences
Bull Fukuoka Univ Educ Part 3 Math Nat Sci Technol — Bulletin. Fukuoka University of Education. Part 3. Mathematics, Natural Sciences, and Technology
Bull Fukuoka Univ Educ Part 3 Nat Sci — Bulletin. Fukuoka University of Education. Part 3. Natural Sciences
Bull Fukushima Prefect Fish Exp Stn — Bulletin. Fukushima Prefectural Fisheries Experimental Station
Bull Fusion Weld Corp — Bulletin of the Fusion Welding Corporation
Bull GA Acad Sci — Bulletin. Georgia Academy of Science
Bull GA Agr Exp Sta — Bulletin. Georgia Agricultural Experiment Station
Bull GA Agric Exp Stn — Bulletin. Georgia Agricultural Experiment Station
Bull Ga Agric Ext Serv — Bulletin. Georgia Agricultural Extension Service
Bull Ga Bd Hlth — Bulletin. Georgia Board of Health
Bull Ga Coll Agric — Bulletin. Georgia College of Agriculture
Bull Ga Cst Plain Exp Stn — Bulletin. Georgia Coastal Plain Experiment Station
Bull Ga Dep Agric — Bulletin of the Georgia Department of Agriculture
Bull Ga Dep Ent — Bulletin. Georgia Department of Entomology
Bull Ga Dep Game Fish — Bulletin. Georgia Department of Game and Fish
Bull Galenica — Bulletin Galenica

Bull Gard Club Amer — Bulletin. Garden Club of America
Bull Gas Eng Fm Pwr Ass Chicago — Bulletin. Gas Engine and Farm Power Association (Chicago)
Bull Ga St Dent Soc — Bulletin of the Georgia State Dental Society
Bull Ga St Engng Exp Stn — Bulletin. Georgia State Engineering Experiment Station
Bull Gaud — Bulletin de Gaud
Bull Gaz — Bulletin du Gaz
Bull GB For Prod Res — Bulletin. Great Britain Forest Products Research
Bull G Bude — Bulletin. Association Guillaume Bude
Bull Geisinger Med Cent — Bulletin. Geisinger Medical Center
Bull Gen Ed Dokkyo Univ School Medicine — Bulletin of General Education. Dokkyo University. School of Medicine
Bull Genessee County Med Soc — Bulletin. Genessee County Medical Society
Bull Genet — Bulletin of Genetics
Bull Gen Fr Moulin Soie — Bulletin General Francais du Moulinage de la Soie
Bull Gen Res Pat Inf Ass Br Insectic Mfrs — Bulletin of General Research and Patent Information. Association of British Insecticide Manufacturers
Bull Gen Therap (Paris) — Bulletin General de Therapeutique Medicale, Chirurgicale, et Obstetricale (Paris)
Bull Gen Ther Med Chir — Bulletin General de Therapeutique Medicale, Chirurgicale, Obstetricale, et Pharmaceutique
Bull Gen Universel Annonces Nouv Sci — Bulletin General et Universel des Annonces et des Nouvelles Scientifiques
Bull Geochem Soc India — Bulletin. Geochemical Society of India
Bull Geod — Bulletin Geodesique
Bull Geodesique — Bulletin Geodesique
Bull Geogr Aix Marseille — Bulletin de Geographie d'Aix-Marseille
Bull Geogr Archeol Prov Oran — Bulletin de Geographie et d'Archeologie de la Province d'Oran
Bull Geogr Bot — Bulletin de Geographie Botanique
Bull Geogr Hist — Bulletin de Geographie Historique et Descriptive
Bull Geogr Hist Descr — Bulletin de Geographie Historique et Descriptive
Bull Geogr Soc Am — Bulletin of the Geographical Society of America
Bull Geogr Soc Chicago — Bulletin of the Geographic Society of Chicago
Bull Geogr Soc Ire — Bulletin of the Geographical Society of Ireland
Bull Geogr Soc Phila — Bulletin. Geographical Society of Philadelphia
Bull Geogr Soc Philad — Bulletin. Geographical Society of Philadelphia
Bull Geogr Surv Inst — Bulletin. Geographical Survey Institute
Bull Geogr Surv Inst Tokyo — Bulletin of the Geographical Survey Institute (Tokyo)
Bull Geol Comm Hokkaido — Bulletin of the Geological Committee of Hokkaido
Bull Geol Dep Hebrew Univ — Bulletin. Geological Department of the Hebrew University
Bull Geol Inst Bulg Acad Sci Ser Geotecton — Bulletin. Geological Institute. Bulgarian Academy of Sciences. Series Geotectonics
Bull Geol Inst Univ Upps — Bulletin. Geological Institutions of the University of Uppsala
Bull Geol Inst Univ Ups — Bulletin. Geologiska Institut. Universitet Upsala
Bull Geol Miner Resour Dep (Sudan) — Bulletin. Geological and Mineral Resources Department (Sudan)
Bull Geol Min Metall Soc India — Bulletin. Geological, Mining, and Metallurgical Society of India
Bull Geol Min Metall Soc Liberia — Bulletin. Geological, Mining, and Metallurgical Society of Liberia
Bull Geol Nat Hist Surv — Bulletin. Geological and Natural History Survey
Bull Geol Soc Am — Bulletin. Geological Society of America
Bull Geol Soc Amer — Bulletin. Geological Society of America
Bull Geol Soc Am Part 1 — Bulletin. Geological Society of America. Part 1
Bull Geol Soc China — Bulletin. Geological Society of China
Bull Geol Soc Den — Bulletin. Geological Society of Denmark
Bull Geol Soc Denmark — Bulletin. Geological Society of Denmark
Bull Geol Soc Finl — Bulletin. Geological Society of Finland
Bull Geol Soc Greece — Bulletin. Geological Society of Greece
Bull Geol Soc Malays — Bulletin. Geological Society of Malaysia
Bull Geol Soc Turk — Bulletin. Geological Society of Turkey
Bull Geol Surv Can — Bulletin. Geological Survey of Canada
Bull Geol Surv Dep (Botswana) — Bulletin. Geological Survey Department (Republic of Botswana)
Bull Geol Surv Dep (Malawi) — Bulletin. Geological Survey Department (Malawi)
Bull Geol Surv Div (Jamaica) — Bulletin. Geological Survey Division (Jamaica)
Bull Geol Surv Div (Solomon Isl) — Bulletin. Geological Survey Division (Solomon Islands)
Bull Geol Surv G — Bulletin. Geological Survey of Georgia
Bull Geol Surv GB — Bulletin. Geological Survey of Great Britain
Bull Geol Surv Georgia — Bulletin. Geological Survey of Georgia
Bull Geol Surv Gr Brit — Bulletin. Geological Survey of Great Britain
Bull Geol Surv Greenland — Bulletin. Geological Survey of Greenland
Bull Geol Surv Guyana — Bulletin. Geological Survey of Guyana
Bull Geol Surv India A — Bulletin. Geological Survey of India. Series A. Economic Geology
Bull Geol Surv India Ser B — Bulletins. Geological Survey of India. Series B. Engineering Geology and GroundWater
Bull Geol Surv Indones — Bulletin. Geological Survey of Indonesia
Bull Geol Surv Irel — Bulletin. Geological Survey of Ireland
Bull Geol Surv Israel — Bulletin. Geological Survey of Israel
Bull Geol Surv Jap — Bulletin. Geological Survey of Japan
Bull Geol Surv Jpn — Bulletin. Geological Survey of Japan
Bull Geol Surv NSW — Bulletin. Geological Survey of New South Wales
Bull Geol Surv Prague — Bulletin. Geological Survey of Prague
Bull Geol Surv Rhod — Bulletin. Geological Survey of Rhodesia
Bull Geol Surv S Afr — Bulletin. Geological Survey of South Africa
Bull Geol Surv S Aust — Bulletin. Geological Survey of South Australia
Bull Geol Surv South Aust — Geological Survey of South Australia. Bulletin
Bull Geol Surv Taiwan — Bulletin. Geological Survey of Taiwan

Bull Geol Surv Tanz — Bulletin. Geological Survey of Tanzania
Bull Geol Surv Tas — Geological Survey of Tasmania. Bulletin
Bull Geol Surv Tasm — Geological Survey of Tasmania. Bulletin
Bull Geol Surv Vic — Geological Survey of Victoria. Bulletin
Bull Geol Surv Vict — Geological Survey of Victoria. Bulletin
Bull Geol Surv West Aust — Bulletin. Geological Survey of Western Australia
Bull Geol Warsaw — Bulletin of Geology (Warsaw)
Bull Geophys — Bulletin de Geophysique
Bull Geophys Natl Cent Univ Taiwan — Bulletin of Geophysics. National Central University (Taiwan)
Bull Geophys Obs Haile Sellassie I Univ — Bulletin. Geophysical Observatory. Haile Sellassie I University
Bull Georg Acad Sci — Bulletin of the Georgian Academy of Science
Bull George Foster Peabody Sch For — Bulletin. George Foster Peabody School of Forestry
Bull Georgetown Univ Med Cent — Bulletin. Georgetown University Medical Center
Bull George Wash Univ — Bulletin of the George Washington University
Bull Georgian Acad Sci — Bulletin of the Georgian Academy of Sciences
Bull Geotech Comm Govt Rlys Japan — Bulletin. Geotechnical Committee. Government Railways of Japan
Bull Geotek Inst — Bulletin. Geoteknisk Institut
Bull Geotek Inst (Copenhagen) — Bulletin- Geoteknisk Institut (Copenhagen)
Bull Geotherm Resour Counc (Davis Calif) — Bulletin. Geothermal Resources Council (Davis, California)
Bull Geranium Soc — Bulletin. Geranium Society
Bull Gers — Bulletin. Societe Archeologique, Historique, Litteraire, et Scientifique du Gers
Bull Ghana Geogr Ass — Bulletin of the Ghana Geographical Association
Bull Ghana Geol Surv — Bulletin. Ghana Geological Survey
Bull Gifu College E — Bulletin. Gifu College of Education
Bull Gifu College Ed — Bulletin. Gifu College of Education
Bull Gilde St Thomas & St Luc — Bulletin de la Gilde de Saint Thomas et de Saint Luc
Bull Glass Res Ass — Bulletin. Glass Research Association
Bull Goldbergs Lab Precis Wk — Bulletin. Goldberg's Laboratory for Precision Work
Bull Gold Cst Dep Soil Ld Use Surv — Bulletin. Gold Coast Department of Soil and Land-Use Survey
Bull Gold Cst Geogr Ass — Bulletin of the Gold Coast Geographical Association
Bull Gov Chem Lab West Aust — Western Australia. Government Chemical Laboratories. Bulletin
Bull Gov Forest Exp Sta — Bulletin. Government Forest Experiment Station
Bull Gov For Exp Stn (Tokyo) — Bulletin. Government Forest Experiment Station (Tokyo)
Bull Gov Ind Res Inst (Osaka) — Bulletin. Government Industrial Research Institute (Osaka)
Bull Gov Mus New Ser Nat Hist Sect — Bulletin. Government Museum. New Series. Natural History Section
Bull Govt Chem Jamaica — Bulletin of the Government Chemist. Jamaica
Bull Govt Chem Labs West Aust — Western Australia. Government Chemical Laboratories. Bulletin
Bull Govt Forest Exp Stn Meguro — Bulletin of the Government Forest Experiment Station. Meguro
Bull Govt Forest Expt Sta — Bulletin. Government Forest Experiment Station
Bull Govt Hosp Insane Wash — Bulletin. Government Hospital for the Insane (Washington)
Bull Govt Mus Madras — Bulletin of the Government Museum. Madras
Bull Govt Res Inst Taihoku — Bulletin of the Government Research Institute (Taihoku, Formosa)
Bull Grad Sch Soc Cult Stud Kyushu Univ — Bulletin of the Graduate School of Social and Cultural Studies. Kyushu University
Bull Grain Technol — Bulletin of Grain Technology
Bull Gravure Tech Ass — Bulletin. Gravure Technical Association
Bull Gr Cons — Bulletin du Grand Conseil des Veterinaires de France
Bull Greek Math Soc — Bulletin of the Greek Mathematical Society
Bull Greene County Med Soc — Bulletin. Greene County Medical Society
Bull Green Sect US Golf Ass — Bulletin of the Green Section of the United States Golf Association
Bull Greenville County Med Soc — Bulletin. Greenville County Medical Society
Bull Gr Masse — Bulletin de la Grand Masse
Bull Groenl Geol Unders — Bulletin. Groenlands Geologiske Undersoegelse
Bull Gronl Geol Unders — Groenlands Geologiske Undersoegelse
Bull Group Archeol Seine et Marne — Bulletin du Groupement Archeologique de Seine-et-Marne
Bull Groupe Fr Argiles — Bulletin. Groupe Francais des Argiles
Bull Groupe Fr Humidimetrie Neutron — Bulletin. Groupe Francais d'Humidimetrie Neutronique
Bull Groupe Fr Humidimetrie Neutronique — Bulletin. Groupe Francais d'Humidimetrie Neutronique
Bull Groupe Trav Etud Equilib Foret-Gibier — Bulletin. Groupe de Travail pour l'Etude de l'Equilibre Foret-Gibier
Bull Groupe Trav Etud Equilibre Foret-Gibier — Bulletin. Groupe de Travail pour l'Etude de l'Equilibre Foret-Gibier
Bull Group Eur Rech Sci Stomatol Odontol — Bulletin. Groupement Europeen pour la Recherche Scientifique en Stomatologie etOdontologie
Bull Group Int Rech Sci Stomatol — Bulletin. Groupement International pour la Recherche Scientifique en Stomatologie
Bull Group Int Rech Sci Stomatol Odontol — Bulletin. Groupement International pour la Recherche Scientifique en Stomatologie et Odontologie
Bull Grpe Etud Scient — Bulletin du Groupe d'Etudes Scientifiques
Bull Grpe Fr Argiles — Bulletin du Groupe Francais des Argiles
Bull Grpe Fr Argiles — Bulletin. Groupe Francais des Argiles
Bull Grpmt Ass Fr Propr Appar Vap — Bulletin. Groupement des Associations Francaises de Proprietaires d'Appareils a Vapeur

Bull Grpmt Int Rech Scient Stomat — Bulletin du Groupement International pour la Recherche Scientifique en Stomatologie
Bull GTV (Group Tech Vet) Dossiers Tech Vet — Bulletin des GTV (Groupements Techniques Veterinaires). Dossiers Techniques Veterinaires
Bull Guam Agric Exp Stn — Bulletin. Guam Agricultural Experiment Station
Bull Guerre Biol Pharm — Bulletin de Guerre des Biologistes Pharmaciens
Bull Gulf Biol Stn — Bulletin of the Gulf Biologic Station
Bull Hadley Clim Lab — Bulletin of the Hadley Climatological Laboratory of the University of New Mexico
Bull Haffkine Inst — Bulletin. Haffkine Institute
Bull Hakodate Mar Observ — Bulletin. Hakodate Marine Observatory
Bull Halifax Riv Bird Club — Bulletin. Halifax River Bird Club
Bull Hannah Dairy Res Inst — Bulletin. Hannah Dairy Research Institute
Bull Hardy Pl Soc — Bulletin. Hardy Plant Society
Bull Harper Adams Agric Coll — Bulletin of the Harper-Adams Agricultural College
Bull Harpswell Lab — Bulletin. Harpswell Laboratory
Bull Harvard Forest Club — Bulletin. Harvard Forestry Club
Bull Harvard Med Alumni Ass — Bulletin. Harvard Medical Alumni Association
Bull Hatano Tob Exp Stn — Bulletin. Hatano Tobacco Experiment Station
Bull Hear Inst (Jpn) — Bulletin. Heart Institute (Japan)
Bull Heart Inst (Jpn) — Bulletin. Heart Institute (Japan)
Bull Hell Vet Med Soc — Bulletin. Hellenic Veterinary Medical Society
Bull Hemlock Arbor — Bulletin. Hemlock Arboretum at Far Country
Bull Hennepin County Med Soc — Bulletin. Hennepin County Medical Society
Bull Herb Boissier — Bulletin de l'Herbier Boissier
Bull Highw Res Bd — Bulletin. Highway Research Board
Bull Hiroshima Agric Coll — Bulletin. Hiroshima Agricultural College
Bull Hiroshima Food Res Inst — Bulletin. Hiroshima Food Research Institute
Bull Hiroshima Jogakuin Coll — Bulletin. Hiroshima Jogakuin College
Bull Hiroshima Prefect Agric Exp Stn — Bulletin. Hiroshima Prefectural Agricultural Experiment Station
Bull Hiroshima Prefect Food Technol Res Cent — Bulletin. Hiroshima Prefectural Food Technological Research Center
Bull Hiroshima Prefect Inst Public Health — Bulletin. Hiroshima Prefectural Institute of Public Health
Bull Hiruzen Res Inst Okayama Univ Sci — Bulletin of the Hiruzen Research Institute. Okayama University of Science
Bull Hisp — Bulletin Hispanic
Bull Hisp — Bulletin Hispanique
Bull Hispanique — Bulletin Hispanique
Bull Hist — Bulletin Historique
Bull Hist Chem — Bulletin for the History of Chemistry
Bull Hist Dent — Bulletin of the History of Dentistry
Bull Hist Dioc Lyon — Bulletin Historique du Diocese de Lyon
Bull Hist Haute-Loire — Bulletin Historique, Scientifique, Litteraire, Artistique et Agricole. Societe Academique du Puy et de la Haute-Loire
Bull Hist Med — Bulletin of the History of Medicine
Bull Hist Medic — Bulletin of the History of Medicine
Bull Hist Metal Group — Bulletin. Historical Metallurgy Group
Bull Hist Nat Soc Linn Bordeaux — Bulletin. Histoire Naturelle. Societe Linneenne de Bordeaux
Bull Histol Appl — Bulletin d'Histologie Appliquee
Bull Hoblitzelle Agric Lab Tex Res Found — Bulletin. Hoblitzelle Agricultural Laboratory. Texas Research Foundation
Bull Hoblitzelle Agr Lab Tex Res Found — Bulletin. Hoblitzelle Agricultural Laboratory. Texas Research Foundation
Bull Hokkaido Agric Exp Sta — Bulletin. Hokkaido Agricultural Experiment Station/ Hokkaido Noji Shikenjo Iho
Bull Hokkaido For Exp Stn — Bulletin. Hokkaido Forest Experiment Station
Bull Hokkaido Pref Agr Exp Sta — Bulletin. Hokkaido Prefectural Agricultural Experiment Station
Bull Hokkaido Prefect Agric Exp Stn — Bulletin. Hokkaido Prefectural Agricultural Experiment Station
Bull Hokkaido Reg Fish Res Lab — Bulletin. Hokkaido Regional Fisheries Research Laboratories
Bull Hokkaido Underground Resour Invest — Bulletin of Hokkaido Underground Resource Investigation
Bull Hokuriku Natl Agric Exp Stn — Bulletin. Hokuriku National Agricultural Experiment Station
Bull Holly Soc Amer — Bulletin. Holly Society of America
Bull Hortic (Liege) — Bulletin Horticole (Liege)
Bull Hortic Res Stn (Minist Agric For) Ser A (Hiratsuka) — Bulletin. Horticultural Research Station (Ministry of Agriculture and Forestry). Series A (Hiratsuka)
Bull Hortic Res Stn (Minist Agric For) Ser B (Okitsu) — Bulletin. Horticultural Research Station (Ministry of Agriculture and Forestry). Series B (Okitsu)
Bull Hortic Res Stn (Minist Agric For) Ser C (Morioka) — Bulletin. Horticultural Research Station (Ministry of Agriculture and Forestry). Series C (Morioka)
Bull Hortic Res Stn (Minist Agric For) Ser D (Kurume) — Bulletin. Horticultural Research Station (Ministry of Agriculture and Forestry). Series D (Kurume)
Bull Hort Res Sta Ser A Hiratsuka — Bulletin. Horticultural Research Station. Series A. Hiratsuka/Engei Shikenjo Hokoku. A. Hiratsuka
Bull Hort Res Sta Ser D Kurume — Bulletin. Horticultural Research Station. Series D. Kurume/Engei Shikenjo Hokoku. D. Kurume
Bull Hosp Joint Dis — Bulletin. Hospital for Joint Diseases
Bull Hosp Jt Dis — Bulletin. Hospital for Joint Diseases
Bull Hosp Jt Dis Orthop Inst — Bulletin. Hospital for Joint Diseases. Orthopaedic Institute
Bull Hot Spring Res Inst Kanagawa Prefect — Bulletin. Hot Spring Research Institute. Kanagawa Prefecture
Bull H Shaw Sch Bot — Bulletin. H. Shaw School of Botany
Bull Hudson Cty Dent Soc — Bulletin. Hudson County Dental Society
Bull Hum Body Meas — Bulletin of Human Body Measurement
Bull Hunan Med Coll — Bulletin. Hunan Medical College
Bull Hunan Med Univ — Bulletin. Hunan Medical University
Bull Hydrobiol Res — Bulletin of Hydrobiological Research

Bull Hyg — Bulletin of Hygiene
Bull Hyg Lab Tokyo — Bulletin of the Hygiene Laboratory (Tokyo)
Bull Hyg Lab US Mar Hosp Serv — Bulletin. Hygienic Laboratory. United States Marine Hospital Service
Bull Hyg Lab US Pub Health and Mar Hosp Serv — Bulletin. Hygienic Laboratory. United States Public Health and Marine Hospital Service
Bull Hyg Lab US Pub Health Serv — Bulletin. Hygienic Laboratory. United States Public Health Service
Bull Hyg Prof — Bulletin de l'Hygiene Professionnelle
Bull Hyogo Pref Agr Exp Sta — Bulletin. Hyogo Prefectural Agricultural Experiment Station
Bull Hyogo Prefect Agric Cent Exp Ext Educ — Bulletin. Hyogo Prefectural Agricultural Center for Experiment, Extension, and Education
Bull Hyogo Prefect Agric Exp Sta — Bulletin. Hyogo Prefectural Agricultural Experiment Station/Hyogo-Kenritsu Nogyo Shikenjo Kenkyu Hokoku
Bull Hyogo Prefect Agric Inst — Bulletin. Hyogo Prefectural Agricultural Institute
Bull Hyogo Prefect For Exp Stn — Bulletin. Hyogo Prefectural Forest Experiment Station
Bul Liaison et Info — Bulletin de Liaison et d'Information
Bull IBA — Bulletin. International Bar Association
Bull Ibaraki Prefect For Exp Stn — Bulletin. Ibaraki Prefectural Forest Experiment Station
Bull ICID — Bulletin. International Commission on Irrigation and Drainage
Bull ICJ — Bulletin. International Commission of Jurists
Bull Idaho Agr Exp Sta — Bulletin. Idaho Agricultural Experiment Station
Bull Idaho Agric Exp Stn — Bulletin. Idaho Agricultural Experiment Station
Bull Idaho Bur Mines Geol — Bulletin. Idaho Bureau of Mines and Geology
Bull Idaho For Wildl Range Exp Stn — Bulletin. Idaho Forest, Wildlife, and Range Experiment Station
Bull Idaho Oreg Wash Agr Exp Sta US Dept Agr — Bulletin. Idaho, Oregon, and Washington Agricultural Experiment Stations and USDepartment of Agriculture
Bull IDR — Bullettino. Istituto di Diritto Romano Vittorio Scialoja
Bull IFAL — Bulletin. Institut Francais d'Amerique Latine
Bull IFAN — Bulletin. Institut Francais d'Afrique Noire
Bull IFAO — Bulletin. Institut Francais d'Archeologie Orientale
Bull IFAOC — Bulletin. Institut Francais d'Archeologie Orientale
Bull IGPL — Bulletin of the Interest Group in Pure and Applied Logics
Bull III — Bulletin. Institut Intermediaire International
Bull III Agr Exp Sta — Bulletin. Illinois Agricultural Experiment Station
Bull III Agric Exp Sta — Bulletin. University of Illinois. Agricultural Experiment Station
Bull III Coop Crop Rep Serv — Bulletin. Illinois Cooperative Crop Reporting Service
Bull III Dep Agric — Bulletin of the Illinois Department of Agriculture
Bull III Fd Dairy Commn — Bulletin. Illinois Food and Dairy Commission
Bull III Highw Commn — Bulletin. Illinois Highway Commission
Bull Illinois Nat Hist Surv — Bulletin. Illinois Natural History Survey
Bull III Miners Mech Inst — Bulletin. Illinois Miners' and Mechanics' Institute
Bull III Nat Hist Surv — Bulletin. Illinois Natural History Survey
Bull III State Geol Surv — Bulletin. Illinois State Geological Survey
Bull III St Dent Soc — Bulletin of the Illinois State Dental Society
Bull III St Flor Ass — Bulletin. Illinois State Florists' Association
Bull III St Geol Surv — Bulletin. Illinois State Geological Survey
Bull III St Lab Nat Hist — Bulletin. Illinois State Laboratory of Natural History
Bull III St Nat Hist Surv — Bulletin of the Illinois State Natural History Survey
Bull III Univ Engng Exp Stn — Bulletin. Illinois University Engineering Experiment Station
Bull Immed Inf Conn Agric Exp Stn — Bulletin of Immediate Information. Connecticut Agricultural Experiment Station
Bull Imp — Bullettino. Museo dell'Impero Romana
Bull Imp Agric Exp Stn Japan — Bulletin of the Imperial Agricultural Experiment Station of Japan
Bull Imp Bur Pastures Forage Crops — Bulletin. Imperial Bureau of Pastures and Forage Crops
Bull Imp Bur PI Genet Herb — Bulletin. Imperial Bureau of Plant Genetics. Herbage
Bull Imp Cent Agric Exp Stn Japan — Bulletin of the Imperial Central Agricultural Experiment Station. Japan
Bull Imp Coll Agric For Morioka — Bulletin. Imperial College of Agriculture and Forestry (Morioka, Japan)
Bull Impero — Bullettino. Museo dell'Impero Romana
Bull Imp Forest Exp Sta — Bulletin. Imperial Forest Experiment Station/Ringyo Shiken Hokoku
Bull Imp Inst — Bulletin. Imperial Institute
Bull Imp Inst Gr Brit — Bulletin. Imperial Institute of Great Britain
Bull Imp Inst (London) — Bulletin. Imperial Institute (London)
Bull Imp PI Quarant Stn Yokohama — Bulletin of the Imperial Plant Quarantine Station. Yokohama
Bull Imp Seric Coll Tokyo — Bulletin of the Imperial Sericultural College (Tokyo)
Bull Imp Seric Stn (Tokyo) — Bulletin. Imperial Sericultural Station (Tokyo)
Bull Imp Zootech Exp Stn Chiba Shi — Bulletin of the Imperial Zootechnical Experiment Station. Chiba-Shi
Bull Indep Biol Lab (Kefar-Malal) — Bulletin. Independent Biological Laboratories (Kefar-Malal)
Bull Indep Biol Labs Palest — Bulletin. Independent Biological Laboratories. Palestine
Bull Indian Ass Cult Sci — Bulletin. Indian Association for the Cultivation of Science
Bull Indian Cent Cocon Comm — Bulletin. Indian Central Coconut Committee
Bull Indian Cent Cott Comm — Bulletin. Indian Central Cotton Committee
Bull Indian Coun Agric Res — Bulletin. Indian Council of Agricultural Research
Bull Indian Geol Ass — Bulletin. Indian Geologists' Association
Bull Indian Ind Res — Bulletins. Indian Industrial Research
Bull Indian Inst Hist Med — Bulletin. Indian Institute of the History of Medicine
Bull Indian Natl Sci Acad — Bulletin. Indian National Science Academy

Bull Indian Phytopathol Soc — Bulletin. Indian Phytopathological Society
Bull Indian Soc Earthqu Technol — Bulletin. Indian Society of Earthquake Technology
Bull Indian Soc Malar Commun Dis — Bulletin. Indian Society for Malaria and Other Communicable Diseases
Bull Indian Soc Soil Sci — Bulletin. Indian Society of Soil Science
Bull India Sect Electrochem Soc — Bulletin. India Section. Electrochemical Society
Bull Ind Res Cent Ehime Prefect — Bulletin. Industrial Research Center of Ehime Prefecture
Bull Ind Res Inst Ehime Prefect — Bulletin. Industrial Research Institute of Ehime Prefecture
Bull Ind Res Inst Kanagawa Prefect — Bulletin. Industrial Research Institute of Kanagawa Prefecture
Bull Ind Techn — Bulletin of Industrial Technology
Bull Inf ANSEAU — Bulletin d'Information. ANSEAU
Bull Inf Appl Ind Radioelem — Bulletin d'Information sur les Applications Industrielles des Radioelements
Bull Inf Archit — Bulletin d'Informations Architecturales
Bull Inf Assoc Belge Dev Pac Energ At — Bulletin d'Information. Association Belge pour le Developpement Pacifique de l'Energie Atomique
Bull Inf Assoc Nat Serv Eau (Belg) — Bulletin d'Information. Association Nationale des Services d'Eau (Belgium)
Bull Inf Assoc Tech Energ Nucl — Bulletin d'Information. Association Technique pour l'Energie Nucleaire
Bull Inf Ass Tech Prod Util Energ Nucl — Bulletin d'Information. Association Technique pour la Production et l'Utilisation de l'Energie Nucleaire
Bull Inf ATEN — Bulletin d'Information. ATEN
Bull Inf ATEN Suppl — Bulletin d'Information. ATEN [*Association Technique pour l'Energie Nucleaire*]. Supplement
Bull Inf Bibliogr — Bulletin d'Information et de Bibliographie
Bull Inf Bur Natl Metrol — Bulletin d'Information. Bureau National de Metrologie
Bull Inf Cent Electr — Bulletin d'Information des Centrales Electriques
Bull Inf Cent Natl Exploit Oceans — Bulletin d'Information. Centre National pour l'Exploitation des Oceans
Bull Inf Centre Donnees Stellaires — Bulletin d'Information. Centre de Donnees Stellaires
Bull Inf CNEEMA (Cent Natl Etud Exp Mach Agric) — Bulletin d'Information. CNEEMA (Centre National d'Etudes et d'Experimentation de Machinisme Agricole)
Bull Inf Generateurs Isot — Bulletin d'Information sur les Generateurs Isotopiques
Bull Inf INEAC — Bulletin d'Information. Institut National pour l'Etude Agronomique du CongoBelge
Bull Inf Inst N Hist A — Bulletin d'Information de l'Institut National d'Histoire de l'Art
Bull Inf Inst Text Fr Nord — Bulletin d'Information. Institut Textile de France Nord
Bull Infirm Cathol Can — Bulletin. Infirmieres Catholiques du Canada
Bull Inf ITF Nord — Bulletin d'Information. ITF [*Institut Textile de France*] Nord
Bull Inf Mens Archvs Archit Mod — Bulletin d'Information Mensuel des Archives de l'Architecture Moderne
Bull Inf Minist Agric — Bulletin d'Information. Ministere de l'Agriculture
Bull Inform CORESTA — Bulletin d'Information CORESTA. Centre de Co-operation pour les Recherches Scientifiques Relatives au Tabac
Bull Inform Cybernet — Bulletin of Informatics and Cybernetics
Bull Inform Inst Etude Agron Congo — Bulletin d'Information de l'Institut pour l'Etude Agronomique du Congo
Bull Inform Inst Nat Etud Agron Congo (INEAC) — Bulletin d'Information. Institut National pour l'Etude Agronomique du Congo Belge (INEAC)
Bull Inform Inst Rebois Tunis — Bulletin d'Information. Institut de Reboisement de Tunis
Bull Inform Tech Centre Tech Bois — Bulletin d'Informations Techniques. Centre Technique du Bois
Bull Inf Rizic Fr — Bulletin d'Information des Riziculteurs de France
Bull Inf Sci & Tech (Paris) — Bulletin d'Informations Scientifiques et Techniques (Paris)
Bull Inf Sci Tech — Bulletin d'Informations Scientifiques et Techniques
Bull Inf Sci Tech Commis Energ At — Bulletin d'Informations Scientifiques et Techniques. Commissariat a l'Energie Atomique
Bull Inf Stn Exp Avic Ploufragan — Bulletin d'Information. Station Experimentale d'Aviculture de Ploufragan
Bull Inf Tech Charbon Fr — Bulletin d'Informations Techniques. Charbonages de France
Bull Inf UGGI — Bulletin d'Information. UGGI
Bull Inst Agric Res Rolling Land (Tokyo) — Bulletin. Institute for Agricultural Research on Rolling Land (Tokyo)
Bull Inst Agric Res Tohoku Univ — Bulletin. Institute for Agricultural Research. Tohoku University
Bull Inst Agron Gembloux — Bulletin. Institut Agronomique et Stations de Recherches de Gembloux
Bull Inst Agron Sta Rech Gembloux — Bulletin. Institut Agronomique et Stations de Recherches de Gembloux
Bull Inst Agron Stn Rech Gembloux — Bulletin. Institut Agronomique et Stations de Recherches de Gembloux
Bull Inst Agron Stn Rech Gembloux Hors Ser — Bulletin. Institut Agronomique et Stations de Recherches de Gembloux. HorsSerie
Bull Inst Agron Stns Rech Gembloux — Bulletin. Institut Agronomique et Stations de Recherches de Gembloux
Bull Inst Agr Res Tohoku Univ — Bulletin. Institute for Agricultural Research. Tohoku University
Bull Inst Appl Geol King Abdulaziz Univ — Bulletin. Institute of Applied Geology. King Abdulaziz University
Bull Inst Arch — Bulletin. Institute of Archaeology
Bull Inst Archaeol Univ London — Bulletin. Institute of Archaeology. University of London
Bull Inst Archeol Liege — Bulletin de l'Institut Archeologique Liegeois

Bull Inst Archeol Liegeois — Bulletin. Institut Archeologique Liegeois

Bull Inst Arch Liegeois — Bulletin. Institut Archeologique Liegeois

Bull Inst At Energ Kyoto Univ — Bulletin. Institute of Atomic Energy. Kyoto University

Bull Inst At Energy Kyoto Univ — Bulletin. Institute of Atomic Energy. Kyoto University

Bull Inst Balneother — Bulletin. Institute of Balneotherapeutics

Bull Inst Basic Sci Inha Univ — Bulletin. Institute for Basic Science. Inha University

Bull Inst Bulg — Izvestiia na Arkheologicheskiia Institut. Bulgarska Akademiia na Naukite

Bull Inst Chem Acad Sin — Bulletin. Institute of Chemistry. Academia Sinica

Bull Inst Chem Prep Agric Acad Agric Sci Bulg — Bulletin. Institute for Chemical Preparations in Agriculture. Academy of Agricultural Sciences. Bulgaria

Bull Inst Chem React Sci Tohoku Univ — Bulletin. Institute for Chemical Reaction Science. Tohoku University

Bull Inst Chem Res Kyoto Univ — Bulletin. Institute for Chemical Research. Kyoto University

Bull Inst China Bord Area Stud — Bulletin of the Institute of China Border Area Studies

Bull Inst Classic Stud — Bulletin. Institute of Classical Studies. University of London

Bull Inst Class Studies — Bulletin. Institute of Classical Studies

Bull Inst Class Stud U London — Bulletin of the Institute of Classical Studies of the University of London

Bull Inst Class Stud U London Suppl Pap — Bulletin of the Institute of Classical Studies of the University of London. Supplementary Papers

Bull Inst Cl St — Bulletin. Institute of Classical Studies. University of London

Bull Inst Combin Appl — Bulletin of the Institute of Combinatorics and its Applications

Bull Inst Const Med Kumamoto Univ — Bulletin. Institute of Constitutional Medicine. Kumamoto University

Bull Inst Corros Sci Technol — Bulletin. Institute of Corrosion Science and Technology

Bull Inst Desert Egypte — Bulletin. Institut du Desert d'Egypte

Bull Inst Econ Soc — Bulletin. Institut de. Recherches Economiques et Sociales

Bull Inst Eg — Bulletin. Institut d'Egypte

Bull Inst Egyp — Bulletin de l'Institut Egyptien

Bull Inst Egypt — Bulletin. Institut d'Egypte

Bull Inst Egypt — Bulletin. Institut Egyptien

Bull Inst Egypte — Bulletin. Institut d'Egypte

Bull Inst Email Vitrifie — Bulletin. Institut de l'Email Vitrifie

Bull Inst Eng — Bulletin. Institution of Engineers

Bull Inst Eng (India) — Bulletin. Institution of Engineers (India)

Bull Inst Ethnol Acad Sinica — Bulletin of the Institute of Ethnology. Academica Sinica

Bull Inst Ethnol Taipei — Bulletin of the Institute of Ethnology (Taipei)

Bull Inst Etudes Centrafr — Bulletin. Institut d'Etudes Centrafricaines

Bull Inst Filip Geol — Bulletin. Institute of Filipino Geologists

Bull Inst Fondam Afr Noire — Bulletin. Institut Fondamental d'Afrique Noire

Bull Inst Fondam Afr Noire Ser A Sci Nat — Bulletin. Institut Fondamental d'Afrique Noire. Serie A. Sciences Naturelles

Bull Inst Fr Afrique Noire — Bulletin de l'Institut Francais d'Afrique Noire

Bull Inst Fr Afr Noire — Bulletin. Institut Francais d'Afrique Noire

Bull Inst Fr Afr Noire Ser A — Bulletin. Institut Francais d'Afrique Noire. Serie A

Bull Inst Fr Afr Noire Ser A Sci Nat — Bulletin. Institut Francais d'Afrique Noire. Serie A. Sciences Naturelles

Bull Inst Fr Amer — Bulletin de l'Institut Franco-Americain

Bull Inst Franc — Bulletin. Institut Francais d'Archeologie Orientale

Bull Inst Franc Afrique Noire — Bulletin de l'Institut Francaise d'Afrique Noire

Bull Inst Franc Archeol Orient — Bulletin. Institut Francais d'Archeologie Orientale

Bull Inst Fr Archeol Orient — Bulletin de l'Institut Francais d'Archeologie Orientale

Bull Inst Fr Archeol Orient — Bulletin. Institut Francais d'Archeologie Orientale

Bull Inst Fr Cafe Cacao — Bulletin. Institut Francais du Cafe et du Cacao

Bull Inst Fr Etud And — Bulletin de l'Institut Franaais d'Etudes Andines

Bull Inst Gas Technol — Bulletin. Institute of Gas Technology

Bull Inst Gen Comp Pathol Bulg Acad Sci — Bulletin. Institute of General and Comparative Pathology. Bulgarian Academy of Sciences

Bull Inst Gen Psychol — Bulletin. Institut General Psychologique

Bull Inst Geol Bassin Aquitaine — Bulletin. Institut de Geologie du Bassin d'Aquitaine

Bull Inst Geol Geophys Res (Belgrade) Ser A — Bulletin. Institute for Geological and Geophysical Research (Belgrade). Series A. Geology

Bull Inst Geol Geophys Res (Belgrade) Ser B — Bulletin. Institute for Geological and Geophysical Research (Belgrade). Series B. Engineering Geology and Hydrogeology

Bull Inst Geol Geophys Res (Belgrade) Ser C — Bulletin. Institute for Geological and Geophysical Research (Belgrade). Series C. Applied Geophysics

Bull Inst Geol Geophys Res Ser A (Engl Transl) — Bulletin. Institute for Geological and Geophysical Research. Series A. Geology (English Translation)

Bull Inst Geol Geophys Res Ser B (Engl Trans) — Bulletin. Institute for Geological and Geophysical Research. Series B. Engineering Geology and Hydrogeology (English Translation)

Bull Inst Geol Geophys Res Ser C (Eng Trans) — Bulletin. Institute for Geological and Geophysical Research. Series C. Applied Geophysics (English Translation)

Bull Inst Geol Sci — Bulletin. Institute of Geological Sciences

Bull Inst Geol Univ Louis Pasteur Strasbourg — Bulletin. Institut de Geologie. Universite Louis Pasteur de Strasbourg

Bull Inst Geophys Natl Cent Univ — Bulletin. Institute of Geophysics. National Central University

Bull Inst Hist & Archaeol Acad Sinica — Bulletin of the Institute of History and Archaeology. Academia Sinica

Bull Inst Hist Belge — Bulletin. Institut Historique Belge de Rome

Bull Inst Hist Belg Rome — Bulletin. Institut Historique Belge de Rome

Bull Inst Hist Med — Bulletin. Institute of History of Medicine

Bull Inst Hist Med Johns Hopk Univ — Bulletin. Institute of History of Medicine. Johns Hopkins University

Bull Inst Hist Res — Bulletin. Institute of Historical Research

Bull Inst Hist Res LU — Bulletin. Institute of Historical Research (London University)

Bull Inst Immunol Sci Hokkaido Univ — Bulletin. Institute of Immunological Science. Hokkaido University

Bull Inst Indochin Etude Homme — Bulletin de l'Institut Indochinois pour l'Etude de l'Homme

Bull Inst Ind Soc Dev — Bulletin. Institute for Industrial and Social Development

Bull Inst Int Adm Publique — Bulletin. Institut International d'Administration Publique

Bull Inst Int Bibliogr — Bulletin. Institut International de Bibliographie

Bull Inst Int Chateaux Hist — Bulletin de l'Institut International des Chateaux Historiques

Bull Inst Internat Statist — Bulletin. Institut International de Statistique

Bull Inst Int Froid — Bulletin. Institut International du Froid

Bull Inst Int Froid Annexe — Bulletin. Institut International du Froid. Annexe

Bull Inst Int Stat — Bulletin. Institut International de Statistique

Bull Inst Jam Sci Ser — Bulletin. Institute of Jamaica, Science Series

Bull Inst Jew St — Bulletin. Institute of Jewish Studies

Bull Inst Likovne Umjetnosti JAZU — Bulletin Instituta za Likovne Umjetnosti Yugoslavenske Akademije Znanosti i Umjetnosti

Bull Inst Marit Trop Med Gdynia — Bulletin. Institute of Maritime and Tropical Medicine in Gdynia

Bull Inst Mar Med Gdansk — Bulletin. Institute of Marine Medicine in Gdansk

Bull Inst Mar Trop Med Gdynia — Bulletin. Institute of Maritime and Tropical Medicine in Gdynia

Bull Inst Mater Sci Eng Fac Eng Fukui Univ — Bulletin. Institute for Material Science and Engineering. Faculty of Engineering. Fukui University

Bull Inst Math Acad Sinica — Bulletin. Institute of Mathematics. Academia Sinica

Bull Inst Math Appl — Bulletin. Institute of Mathematics and Its Applications

Bull Inst Med — Bulletin. Instituts de Medecine

Bull Inst Med Exp — Bulletin. Institut de Medecine Experimentale

Bull Inst Med Research FMS — Bulletin. Institute for Medical Research. Federated Malay States

Bull Inst Med Res Fed Malaya — Bulletin. Institute for Medical Research. Federation of Malaya

Bull Inst Med Res (Kuala Lumpur) — Bulletin. Institute for Medical Research (Kuala Lumpur)

Bull Inst Med Res Malaya — Bulletin. Institute for Medical Research of Malaya

Bull Inst Med Res Univ Madr — Bulletin. Institute for Medical Research. University of Madrid

Bull Inst Met — Bulletin. Institute of Metals

Bull Inst Met Finish — Bulletin. Institute of Metal Finishing

Bull Inst Miner Deposits Chin Acad Geol Sci — Bulletin. Institute of Mineral Deposits. Chinese Academy of Geological Sciences

Bull Inst Min Metall — Bulletin. Institution of Mining and Metallurgy

Bull Inst Nat Educ Shiga Heights — Bulletin. Institute of Natural Education in Shiga Heights

Bull Inst Nat Genevois — Bulletin. Institut National Genevois

Bull Inst Natl Hyg (Paris) — Bulletin. Institut National d'Hygiene (Paris)

Bull Inst Natl Sante Rech Med (Paris) — Bulletin. Institut National de la Sante et de la Recherche Medicale (Paris)

Bull Inst Natl Sci Rech Oceanogr Peche — Bulletin. Institut National Scientifique et Technique d'Oceanographie et de Peche

Bull Inst Natl Sci Tech Oceanogr Peche Salammbo — Bulletin. Institut National Scientifique et Technique d'Oceanographie et de Peche de Salammbo

Bull Inst Nutr Bulg Acad Sci — Bulletin. Institute of Nutrition. Bulgarian Academy of Sciences

Bull Inst Obs Phys Globe Puy De Dome — Bulletin. Institut et Observatoire Physique du Globe du Puy De Dome

Bull Inst Oceanogr Fish — Bulletin. Institute of Oceanography and Fisheries

Bull Inst Oceanogr (Monaco) — Bulletin. Institut Oceanographique (Monaco)

Bull Inst Oinoue Rech Agron — Bulletin. Institut Oinoue de Recherches Agronomiques et Biologiques/Oinoue Rinogaku Kenkyusho. Kenkyu Hokoku

Bull Inst Pap Chem — Bulletin. Institute of Paper Chemistry

Bull Inst Pasteur — Bulletin. Institut Pasteur

Bull Inst Pasteur (Paris) — Bulletin. Institut Pasteur (Paris)

Bull Inst Peches Marit Maroc — Bulletin. Institut des Peches Maritimes du Maroc

Bull Inst Phys Chem Res — Bulletin. Institute of Physical and Chemical Research

Bull Inst Phys (Lond) — Bulletin. Institute of Physics (London)

Bull Inst Phys (Malays) — Bulletin. Institute of Physics (Malaysia)

Bull Inst Phys Univ Libre Bruxelles — Bulletin. Institut de Physique. Universite Libre de Bruxelles

Bull Inst Pin — Bulletin. Institut du Pin

Bull Inst Polytech Ivanovo Vosniesensk — Bulletin. Institut Polytechnique a Ivanovo-Vosniesensk

Bull Inst Post Grad Med Educ Res — Bulletin. Institute of Post Graduate Medical Education and Research

Bull Inst Prov Coop Agr — Bulletin. Institut Provincial de Cooperation Agricole

Bull Inst Public Health (Tokyo) — Bulletin. Institute of Public Health (Tokyo)

Bull Inst Radiat Breed — Bulletin. Institute of Radiation Breeding

Bull Inst Royal Patrm A — Bulletin de l'Institut Royal du Patrimoine Artistique

Bull Inst Roy Sci Nat Belgique — Bulletin de l'Institut Royal des Sciences Naturelles de Belgique/Koninklijk Belgisch Instituut voor Natuurwetenschappen. Mededelingen

Bull Inst R Sci Nat Belg — Bulletin. Institut Royal des Sciences Naturelles de Belgique

Bull Inst R Sci Nat Belg Biol — Bulletin. Institut Royal des Sciences Naturelles de Belgique. Biologie

Bull Inst R Sci Nat Belg Entomol — Bulletin. Institut Royal des Sciences Naturelles de Belgique. Entomologie

Bull Inst R Sci Nat Belg Sci Terre — Bulletin. Institut Royal des Sciences Naturelles de Belgique. Sciences dela Terre

Bull Instrum Nucl — Bulletin d'Instrumentation Nucleaire
Bull Inst Sanit Eng — Bulletin. Institution of Sanitary Engineers
Bull Inst Sci Natur Belg — Bulletin. Institut Royal des Sciences Naturelles de Belgique
Bull Inst Sci (Rabat) — Bulletin. Institut Scientifique (Rabat)
Bull Inst Sociol Solvay — Bulletin. Institut de Sociologie Solvay
Bull Inst Space Aeronaut Sci Univ Tokyo — Bulletin. Institute of Space and Aeronautical Science. University of Tokyo
Bull Inst Space & Aeronaut Sci Univ Tokyo A — Bulletin. Institute of Space and Aeronautical Science. University of Tokyo. A
Bull Inst Space & Aeronaut Sci Univ Tokyo B — Bulletin. Institute of Space and Aeronautical Science. University of Tokyo. B
Bull Inst Study USSR — Bulletin. Institute for the Study of the USSR
Bull Inst Tech Porc — Bulletin. Institut Technique du Porc
Bull Inst Text Fr — Bulletin. Institut Textile de France
Bull Inst Tropen Afd Agrar Onderz — Bulletin. Instituut voor de Tropen Afdeling Agrarisch Onderzoek
Bull Inst Verre — Bulletin. Institut du Verre
Bull Inst Vitreous Enamellers — Bulletin. Institute of Vitreous Enamellers
Bull Inst Zool Acad Sin (Taipei) — Bulletin. Institute of Zoology. Academia Sinica (Taipei)
Bull Inst Zool Mus Acad Bulg Sci — Bulletin. Institut de Zoologie et Musee. Academie Bulgare des Sciences
Bull Int Acad Croate Sci Cl Sci Math — Bulletin International. Academie Croate des Sciences et des Beaux-Arts. Classe des Sciences Mathematiques et Naturelles
Bull Int Acad Pol Sci Lett Cl Sci Math Nat Ser A — Bulletin International. Academie Polonaise des Sciences et des Lettres. Classe des Sciences Mathematiques et Naturelles. Serie A. Sciences Mathematiques
Bull Int Acad Pol Sci Lett Cl Sci Math Nat Ser B — Bulletin International. Academie Polonaise des Sciences et des Lettres. Classe des Sciences Mathematiques et Naturelles. Serie B. Sciences Naturelles
Bull Int Acad Pol Sci Lett Cl Sci Math Nat Ser B 1 — Bulletin International. Academie Polonaise des Sciences et des Lettres. Classe des Sciences Mathematiques et Naturelles. Serie B-1. Botanique
Bull Int Acad Pol Sci Lett Cl Sci Math Nat Ser B-2 — Bulletin International. Academie Polonaise des Sciences et des Lettres. Classe des Sciences Mathematiques et Naturelles. Serie B-2. Zoologie
Bull Int Acad Sci Cracovie — Bulletin International. Academie des Sciences du Cracovie
Bull Int Acad Sci Cracovie Cl Sci Math Natur — Bulletin International. Academie des Sciences du Cracovie. Classe des Sciences Mathematiques et Naturelles
Bull Int Acad Sci Cracovie Cl Sci Math Natur Ser A — Bulletin International. Academie des Sciences du Cracovie. Classe des Sciences Mathematiques et Naturelles. Serie A. Sciences Mathematiques
Bull Int Acad Sci Lett Cracovie — Bulletin International. Academie des Sciences et des Lettres du Cracovie
Bull Int Acad Sci Lett Cracovie Ser A — Bulletin International. Academie des Sciences et des Lettres du Cracovie. SerieA
Bull Int Acad Yougoslave Cl Sci Math Natur — Bulletin International. Academie Yougoslave des Sciences et des Beaux-Arts. Classe des Sciences Mathematiques et Naturelles
Bull Int Acad Yougoslave Sci Beaux-Arts Cl Sci Math Nat — Bulletin International. Academie Yougoslave des Sciences et des Beaux-Arts. Classe des Sciences Mathematiques et Naturelles
Bull Int Acad Yougoslave Sci Cl Sci Math — Bulletin International. Academie Yougoslave des Sciences et des Beaux-Arts. Classe des Sciences Mathematiques et Naturelles
Bull Int Ass Med Mus — Bulletin. International Association of Medical Museums
Bull Int Assoc Eng Geol — Bulletin. International Association of Engineering Geology
Bull Int Assoc Med Mus — Bulletin. International Association of Medical Museums
Bull Int Assoc Sci Hydrol — Bulletin. International Association of Scientific Hydrology
Bull Int Assoc Shell Spat Struct — Bulletin. International Association for Shell and Spatial Structures
Bull Int Ass Sci Hydrol — Bulletin. International Association of Scientific Hydrology
Bull Int Ass Shell Struct — Bulletin. International Association for Shell Structures
Bull Int Ass Wood Anatomists — Bulletin. International Association of Wood Anatomists
Bull Int Cent Heat Mass Transf — Bulletin. International Centre for Heat and Mass Transfers
Bull Int Comm Hist Sci — Bulletin. International Committee of Historical Sciences
Bull Int Comm on Urgent Anthrop Ethnol Res — Bulletin. International Committee on Urgent Anthropological and Ethnological Research
Bull Int Comm Urgent Anthrop Res — Bulletin of the International Committee on Urgent Anthropological and Ethnological Research
Bull Intern Assocn Paper Hist — Bulletin. International Association of Paper Historians
Bull Internat Comm Hist Sci — Bulletin. International Committee of Historical Sciences
Bull Internat Inst Soc Hist — Bulletin. International Institute for Social History
Bull Intern Com Anthrop Ethnol Res Vienna — Bulletin. International Committee on Urgent Anthropological Research (Vienna)
Bull Int Fisc Doc — Bulletin for International Fiscal Documentation
Bull Int Inst Ref — International Institute of Refrigeration. Bulletin
Bull Int Inst Refrig — Bulletin. International Institute of Refrigeration
Bull Int Off Epizoot — Bulletin. International Office of Epizootics
Bull Int Peat Soc — Bulletin. International Peat Society
Bull Int Potash Inst — Bulletin. International Potash Institute
Bull Int Ry Congr Ass — Bulletin. International Railway Congress Association
Bull Int Sc Soc — Bulletin International des Sciences Sociales
Bull Int Ser Sante Armees Terre Mer Air — Bulletin International. Services de Sante des Armees de Terre, de Mer, et de l'Air
Bull Int Soc Trop Ecol — Bulletin. International Society for Tropical Ecology

Bull Int Tin Res — Bulletin. International Tin Research and Development Council
Bull Int Union Cancer — Bulletin. International Union Against Cancer
Bull Int Union Tuberc — Bulletin. International Union Against Tuberculosis
Bull Int Un Tub — Bulletin. International Union Against Tuberculosis
Bull Invent — Bulletin on Inventions
Bull Io Agric Exp St — Bulletin. Iowa Agricultural Experiment Station
Bull Iowa Agr Exp Sta — Bulletin. Iowa Agricultural Experiment Station
Bull Iowa Nurses Assoc — Bulletin. Iowa Nurses Association
Bull Iowa State Univ Sci Technol Eng Exp Stn — Bulletin. Iowa State University of Science and Technology. Engineering Experiment Station
Bull Iranian Math Soc — Bulletin. Iranian Mathematical Society
Bull Iranian Petrol Inst — Bulletin. Iranian Petroleum Institute
Bull Iran Pet Inst — Bulletin. Iranian Petroleum Institute
Bull Iraq Nat Hist Mus (Univ Baghdad) — Bulletin. Iraq Natural History Museum (University of Baghdad)
Bull IRCB — Bulletin des Seances. Institut Royal Colonial Belge
Bull Irish Georg Soc — Bulletin of the Irish Georgian Society
Bull IRO (Aust) — Bulletin. Commonwealth Scientific and Industrial Research Organisation (Australia)
Bull Iron Steel Inst — Bulletin. Iron and Steel Institute
Bull Isaac Ray Med Libr — Bulletin. Isaac Ray Medical Library
Bull Ishikawa-Ken Agric Exp Stn — Bulletin. Ishikawa-Ken Agricultural Experiment Station
Bull Ishikawa Prefect Coll Agric — Bulletin. Ishikawa Prefecture College of Agriculture
Bull Ishinomaki Senshui Univ — Bulletin of Ishinomaki Senshu University
Bull Islam Stud — Bulletin of Islamic Studies
Bull (Israel) Res Counc — Bulletin. Research Council (Israel)
Bull Isr Chem Soc — Bulletin. Israel Chemical Society
Bull Isr Phys Soc — Bulletin. Israel Physical Society
Bull Isr Soc Spec Libr & Inf Cent — Bulletin. Israel Society of Special Libraries and Information Centres
Bull ISSA — Bulletin. International Social Security Association
Bull Istanbul Tech Univ — Bulletin. Istanbul Technical University
Bull Ist Corr Archeol — Bullettino dell'Istituto di Corrispondenza Archeologica
Bull Ist Dir Rom — Bullettino. Istituto di Diritto Romano Vittorio Scialoja
Bull Ist Stor It Med Evo & Archv Murator — Bullettino dell'Istituto Storico Italiano per il Medio Evo e Archivio Muratoriano
Bull It — Bulletin Italien
Bull Ital — Bulletin Italien
Bull Iwate-Ken Agr Exp Sta — Bulletin. Iwate-Ken Agricultural Experiment Station
Bull Iwate Univ For — Bulletin. Iwate University Forests
Bull Jacks Mem Hosp — Bulletin. Jackson Memorial Hospital and the School of Medicine of the University of Florida
Bull JAG — Bulletin. Judge Advocate General of the Army
Bull Jam Geol Surv — Bulletin. Jamaica Geological Survey
Bull Japan Pet Inst — Bulletin. Japan Petroleum Institute
Bull Japan Soc Mech Engrs — Bulletin. Japanese Society of Mechanical Engineers
Bull Japan Soc Precis Engng — Bulletin. Japan Society of Precision Engineering
Bull Jap Pet Inst — Bulletin. Japan Petroleum Institute
Bull Jap Soc Grinding Eng — Bulletin. Japan Society of Grinding Engineers
Bull Jap Soc Mech E — Japan Society of Mechanical Engineers. Bulletin
Bull Jap Soc Precis Eng — Bulletin. Japan Society of Precision Engineering
Bull Jap Soc Sci Fish — Bulletin. Japanese Society of Scientific Fisheries
Bull Jard Bot Buitenzorg — Bulletin. Jardin Botanique de Buitenzorg
Bull Jard Bot Etat — Bulletin du Jardin Botanique de l'Etat / Bulletin van den Rijksplantentuin
Bull Jard Bot Etat Brux — Bulletin. Jardin Botanique de l'Etat a Bruxelles
Bull Jard Bot Natl Belg — Bulletin. Jardin Botanique National de Belgique
Bull Jard Bot Natn Belg — Bulletin. Jardin Botanique National de Belgique
Bull J Ass Gen Dent S E Fr — Bulletin-Journal de l'Association Generale des Dentistes du Sud-Est de la France
Bull Jealott's Hill Res St — Bulletin. Jealott's Hill Research Station
Bull Jersey Soc — Bulletin. Jersey Society
Bull Jew Hosp — Bulletin. Jewish Hospital
Bull Jew Pal Expl Soc — Bulletin. Jewish Palestine Exploration Society
Bull J Fabr Pap — Bulletin-Journal des Fabricants de Papier
Bull JKH — Bulletin. Societe J. K. Huysmans
Bull J NY Archaeol Ass — Bulletin. Journal of the New York State Archaeologicl Association
Bull John Herron A Inst — Bulletin John Herron Art Institute
Bull John Rylands Lib — Bulletin of the John Rylands Library
Bull John Rylands Libr — Bulletin. John Rylands Library
Bull John Rylands Univ Libr Manchester — Bulletin. John Rylands University Library. Manchester
Bull John Ryl Libr — John Rylands Library. Bulletin
Bull Johns Hopk Hosp — Bulletin. Johns Hopkins Hospital
Bull Johns Hopkins Hosp — Bulletin. Johns Hopkins Hospital
Bull Josai Dent Univ — Bulletin. Josai Dental University
Bull Josselyn Bot Soc Maine — Bulletin. Josselyn Botanical Society of Maine
Bull Journees Int Verre — Bulletin des Journees Internationales du Verre
Bull Jpn Electron Mater Soc — Bulletin. Japan Electronic Materials Society
Bull Jpn Entomol Acad — Bulletin. Japan Entomological Academy
Bull Jpn Inst Met — Bulletin. Japan Institute of Metals
Bull Jpn Min Ind Assoc — Bulletin. Japan Mining Industry Association
Bull Jpn Pet Inst — Bulletin. Japan Petroleum Institute
Bull Jpn Sea Reg Fish Res Lab — Bulletin. Japan Sea Regional Fisheries Research Laboratories
Bull Jpn Soc Mech Eng — Bulletin. Japan Society of Mechanical Engineers
Bull Jpn Soc Phycol — Bulletin. Japanese Society of Phycology
Bull Jpn Soc Precis Eng — Bulletin. Japan Society of Precision Engineering
Bull Jpn Soc Sci Fish — Bulletin. Japanese Society of Scientific Fisheries
Bull Jpn Soc Tuberc — Bulletin. Japanese Society of Tuberculosis
Bull J Rylands Libr — Bulletin. Johns Rylands Library Manchester

Bull J Ryl Libr — Bulletin. John Rylands Library
Bull JSAE — Bulletin. JSAE
Bull JSME — Bulletin. JSME
Bull Jurid Indig — Bulletin des Juridictions Indigenes
Bull Jur Immob — Bulletin de la Jurisprudence Immobiliere et de la Construction
Bull Jur Indig & Droit Coutumier Congol — Bulletin des Juridictions Indigenes et du Droit Coutumier Congolais
Bull Kagawa Agr Exp Sta — Bulletin. Kagawa Agricultural Experiment Station
Bull Kagawa Agric Exp Stn — Bulletin. Kagawa Agricultural Experiment Station
Bull Kagawa Prefect Agric Exp Stn — Bulletin. Kagawa Prefecture Agricultural Experiment Station
Bull Kagoshima Imp Coll Agric — Bulletin. Kagoshima Imperial College of Agriculture and Forestry
Bull Kagoshima Prefect Jr Coll Nat Sci — Bulletin. Kagoshima Prefectural Junior College. Natural Sciences
Bull Kagoshima Univ For — Bulletin. Kagoshima University Forest
Bull Kanagawa Agric Exp Stn — Bulletin. Kanagawa Agricultural Experiment Station
Bull Kanagawa Hort Exp Stn — Bulletin. Kanagawa Horticultural Experiment Station
Bull Kanagawa Hortic Exp Stn — Bulletin. Kanagawa Horticultural Experiment Station
Bull Kanagawa Ken Agric Exp Sta — Bulletin. Kanagawa-Ken Agricultural Experiment Station/Kanagawa Ken Noji ShikenSeiseki
Bull Kanagawa Prefect Environ Cent — Bulletin. Kanagawa Prefectural Environmental Center
Bull Kanagawa Prefect Mus Nat Sci — Bulletin. Kanagawa Prefectural Museum of Natural Science
Bull Kans Agr Exp Sta — Bulletin. Kansas Agricultural Experiment Station
Bull Kans Agric Exp Stn — Bulletin. Kansas Agricultural Experiment Station
Bull Kansas City Vet Coll Quart — Bulletin. Kansas City Veterinary College. Quarterly
Bull Kans Eng Exp Stn — Bulletin. Kansas Engineering Experiment Station
Bull Kans St Agric Coll — Bulletin. Kansas State Agricultural College
Bull Kans State Geol Surv — Bulletin. Kansas State Geological Survey
Bull Karachi Geogr Soc — Bulletin. Karachi Geographical Society
Bull K Belg Bot Ver — Bulletin. Koninklijke Belgische Botanische Vereniging
Bull K Belg Inst Natuurwet Aardwet — Bulletin van het Koninklijke Belgische Instituut voor Natuurwetenschappen. Aardwetenschappen
Bull K Belg Inst Natuurwet Biol — Bulletin van het Koninklijke Belgische Instituut voor Natuurwetenschappen. Biologie
Bull K Belg Inst Natuurwet Entomol — Bulletin van het Koninklijke Belgische Instituut voor Natuurwetenschappen. Entomologie
Bull Kent Agr Exp St — Bulletin. Kentucky Agricultural Experiment Station
Bull Kent Agric Exp St — Bulletin. Kentucky Agricultural Experiment Station
Bull Kent County Med Soc — Bulletin. Kent County Medical Society
Bull Kent Geol Surv — Bulletin. Kentucky Geological Survey
Bull Kentucky Geol Surv — Bulletin. Kentucky Geological Survey
Bull Kern County Med Soc — Bulletin. Kern County Medical Society
Bull Kesennuma Miyagi Prefect Fish Exp Stn — Bulletin. Kesennuma Miyagi Prefectural Fisheries Experiment Station
Bull King County Med Soc — Bulletin. King County Medical Society
Bull Kisarazu Tech Coll — Bulletin. Kisarazu Technical College
Bull KNOB — Bulletin. Koninklijke Nederlandse Oudheidkundige Bond
Bull Kobayasi Inst Phys Res — Bulletin. Kobayasi Institute of Physical Research
Bull Kobe Med Coll — Bulletin. Kobe Medical College
Bull Kobe Women's Coll — Bulletin. Kobe Women's College
Bull Kobe Women's Coll Domest Sci Dep — Bulletin. Kobe Women's College. Domestic Science Department
Bull Kobe Women's Univ Fac Home Econ — Bulletin. Kobe Women's University. Faculty of Home Economics
Bull Koch Cancer Fdn — Bulletin. Koch Cancer Foundation
Bull Kochi Tech Coll — Bulletin. Kochi Technical College
Bull Kochi Womens Coll — Bulletin of Kochi Women's College/Kochi Joshi Daigaku Kiyo
Bull Kodaikanal Obs — Bulletin. Kodaikanal Observatory
Bull Kolar Gold Fld Min Metall Soc — Bulletin of the Kolar Gold Field Mining and Metallurgical Society
Bull Kolon Mus Haarlem — Bulletin van het Koloniaal Museum te Haarlem
Bull Kon Ned Oudhdknd Bond — Bulletin van de Koninklijke Nederlandse Oudheidkundige Bond
Bull Korean Acad Sci — Bulletin. Korean Academy of Science
Bull Korean Chem Soc — Bulletin. Korean Chemical Society
Bull Korean Fish Soc — Bulletin. Korean Fisheries Society
Bull Korean Fish Technol Soc — Bulletin. Korean Fisheries Technological Society
Bull Korean Inst Met — Bulletin. Korean Institute of Metals
Bull Korean Inst Met Mater — Bulletin. Korean Institute of Metals and Materials
Bull Korean Math Soc — Bulletin. Korean Mathematical Society
Bull Korea Ocean Res & Dev Inst — Bulletin. Korea Ocean Research and Development Institute
Bull Koshien Univ B — Bulletin of Koshien University. B
Bull Kwangsi Agric Exp Stn — Bulletin. Kwangsi Agricultural Experiment Station
Bull Kwasan Observ — Bulletin. Kwasan Observatory
Bull KY Agr Exp Sta — Bulletin. Kentucky Agricultural Experiment Station
Bull KY Agric Exp Stn — Bulletin. Kentucky Agricultural Experiment Station
Bull Ky Bur Agric — Bulletin of the Kentucky Bureau of Agriculture
Bull Ky Dep Geol For — Bulletin of the Kentucky Department of Geology and Forestry
Bull Kyoto Daigaku Inst Chem Res — Bulletin. Kyoto Daigaku Institute for Chemical Research
Bull Kyoto Gakugei Univ Ser B Math Nat Sci — Bulletin. Kyoto Gakugei University. Series B. Mathematics and Natural Science
Bull Kyoto Prefect Univ For — Bulletin. Kyoto Prefectural University Forests
Bull Kyoto Univ Ed Ser B — Bulletin. Kyoto University of Education. Series B. Mathematics and Natural Science

Bull Kyoto Univ Educ Ser B Math Nat Sci — Bulletin. Kyoto University of Education. Series B. Mathematics and Natural Science
Bull Kyoto Univ For — Bulletin. Kyoto University Forests
Bull Kyo Univ Obs — Bulletin. Kyoto University Observatory
Bull Kyushu Agr Exp Sta — Bulletin. Kyushu Agricultural Experiment Station
Bull Kyushu Agric Exp Sta — Bulletin. Kyushu Agricultural Experiment Station/Kyushu Nogyo Shikenjo Iho
Bull Kyushu Agric Exp Stn — Bulletin. Kyushu Agricultural Experiment Station
Bull Kyushu Inst Tech Math Natur Sci — Bulletin. Kyushu Institute of Technology. Mathematics and Natural Science
Bull Kyushu Inst Technol — Bulletin. Kyushu Institute of Technology
Bull Kyushu Inst Technol Math Nat Sci — Bulletin. Kyushu Institute of Technology. Mathematics and Natural Science
Bull Kyushu Inst Technol Sci & Technol — Bulletin. Kyushu Institute of Technology. Science and Technology
Bull Kyushu Univ For — Bulletin. Kyushu University Forests
Bull Kyushu Univ Forests — Bulletin. Kyushu University Forests/Kyushu Daigaku Nogaku-Bu Enshurin Hokoku
Bull Kyus Inst Technol — Bulletin. Kyushu Institute of Technology
Bull LA Agr Exp Sta — Bulletin. Louisiana Agricultural Experiment Station
Bull LA Agric Exp Stn — Bulletin. Louisiana Agricultural Experiment Station
Bull Lab Biol Appl (Paris) — Bulletin. Laboratoire de Biologie Appliquee (Paris)
Bull Lab Cent Energ Acad Bulg Sci — Bulletin. Laboratoire Central d'Energie. Academie Bulgare des Sciences
Bull Lab Food Technol Hachinohe Inst Technol — Bulletin of Laboratory of Food Technology. Hachinohe Institute of Technology
Bull Lab Geol Fac Sci Caen — Bulletin. Laboratoire de Geologie. Faculte des Sciences de Caen
Bull Lab Geol Mineral Geophys Mus Geol Univ Laus — Bulletin. Laboratoires de Geologie, Mineralogie, Geophysique, et Musee Geologique. Universite de Lausanne
Bull Lab Geol Mineral Geophys Mus Geol Univ Lausanne — Bulletin. Laboratoires de Geologie, Mineralogie, Geophysique, et Musee Geologique. Universite de Lausanne
Bull Lab Louvre — Bulletin. Laboratoire du Musee du Louvre
Bull Lab Marit Dinard — Bulletin. Laboratoire Maritime de Dinard
Bull Lab Mus Louvre — Bulletin du Laboratoire du Musee du Louvre
Bull Lab Nat Hist Iowa State Univ — Bulletin. Laboratories of Natural History. Iowa State University
Bull Lab Orto Bot Reale Univ Siena — Bulletino del Laboratorio ed Orto Botanico della Reale Universita di Siena
Bull Lab Ponts Chaussees — Bulletin des Laboratoires des Ponts et Chaussees
Bull Lab Prof — Bulletin du Laboratoire Professionnel
Bull LA Co Mus A — Bulletin of the Los Angeles County Museum of Art
Bull LA Coop Ext Serv — Bulletin. Louisiana Cooperative Extension Service
Bull La Libr Assoc New Orleans — Bulletin. Louisiana Library Association (New Orleans)
Bull Landbproefstn Suriname — Bulletin. Landbouwproefstation in Suriname
Bull LA Neurol Soc — Bulletin. Los Angeles Neurological Societies
Bull Latin Amer Res — Bulletin of Latin American Research
Bull Leg Dev — Bulletin of Legal Developments
Bull Lembaga Penelitian Peternakan — Bulletin Lembaga Penelitian Peternakan
Bull Liaison Cent Int Etud Textiles Anc — Bulletin de Liaison du Centre International d'Etude des Textiles Anciens
Bull Liaison Dir Reg Affaires Cult Picardie — Bulletin de Liaison de la Direction Regionale des Affaires Culturelles de Picardie
Bull Liaison Groupe Polyphenols — Bulletin de Liaison. Groupe Polyphenols
Bull Liaison Lab Lab Prof Pein Bitry Thiais (Fr) — Bulletin de Liaison du Laboratoire. Laboratoire de la Profession des Peintures Bitry Thiais (France)
Bull Liaison Lab Ponts Chaussees — Bulletin de Liaison des Laboratoires des Ponts et Chaussees
Bull Liaison Rech Inform Automat — Bulletin de Liaison de la Recherche en Informatique et Automatique
Bull Liberia Geol Surv — Bulletin. Liberia Geological Survey
Bull Lloyd Libr Bot Pharm Mater Med — Bulletin. Lloyd Library of Botany, Pharmacy, and Materia Medica
Bull London Math Soc — Bulletin. London Mathematical Society
Bull Long Island Hort Soc — Bulletin. Long Island Horticultural Society
Bull Los Ang Cty Mus Nat Hist Sci — Bulletin. Los Angeles County Museum of Natural History. Contributions in Science
Bull Los Angeles County Med Ass — Bulletin. Los Angeles County Medical Association
Bull Los Angeles Dent Soc — Bulletin. Los Angeles Dental Society
Bull Los Angeles Neurol Soc — Bulletin. Los Angeles Neurological Societies
Bull Los Ang Neurol Soc — Bulletin. Los Angeles Neurological Societies
Bull Lot — Bulletin. Societe des Etudes Litteraires, Scientifiques et Artistiques du Lot
Bull L Sci and Tech — Bulletin of Law, Science, and Technology
Bull Lucknow Natl Bot Gard — Bulletin. Lucknow National Botanic Gardens
Bull Maatsch — Bulletin Maatschappij
Bull Maatsch Gesch Oudhdknd Gent — Bulletin van de Maatschappij voor Geschiedenis en Oudheidkunde te Gent
Bull Madagascar — Bulletin de Madagascar
Bull Madhya Pradesh Agric Dep — Bulletin. Madhya Pradesh Agriculture Department
Bull Madjelis Ilmu Penges Indonesia — Bulletin. Madjelis Ilmu Pengetahuan Indonesia
Bull Madras Gov Mus Nat Hist Sect — Bulletin. Madras Government Museum. Natural History Section
Bull Madras Govt Mus — Bulletin of the Madras Government Museum
Bull Madras Govt Mus New Ser — Bulletin of the Madras Government Museum. New Series
Bull Magn Inst Geophys Natn Tchecosl — Bulletin Magnetique. Institut Geophysique National Tchecoslovaque
Bull Maine Geol Surv — Bulletin. Maine Geological Survey

Bull Maine Life Sci Agric Exp Stn — Bulletin. Maine Life Sciences and Agriculture Experiment Station

Bull Maison Franco Jap — Bulletin. Maison Franco-Japonaise

Bull Maison Med — Bulletin de la Maison du Medecin

Bull Malay Dent Ass — Bulletin. Malayan Dental Association

Bull Malaysian Math Soc — Bulletin. Malaysian Mathematical Society

Bull Malaysian Math Soc (2) — Bulletin. Malaysian Mathematical Society. Second Series

Bull Malaysian Min Agric Rural Dev — Bulletin. Malaysian Ministry of Agriculture and Rural Development

Bull Malays Kementerian Pertanian — Bulletin. Malaysia Kementerian Pertanian

Bull Malays Minist Agric Rural Dev — Bulletin. Malaysia Ministry of Agriculture and Rural Development

Bull Mammal Soc Br Isl — Bulletin. Mammal Society of the British Isles

Bull Manchr Interplan Soc — Bulletin. Manchester Interplanetary Society

Bull Manchur Sci Mus — Bulletin. Manchurian Science Museum

Bull Manila Cent Obs Weath Bur — Bulletin. Manila Central Observatory. Weather Bureau

Bull Manila Med Soc — Bulletin. Manila Medical Society

Bull Manitoba Agric Coll — Bulletin of the Manitoba Agricultural College

Bull Mar Biol Stn Asamushi — Bulletin. Marine Biological Station of Asamushi

Bull Mar Dep NZ Fish — Bulletin. Marine Department. New Zealand. Fisheries

Bull Mar Ecol — Bulletins of Marine Ecology

Bull Margaret Hague Matern Hosp — Bulletin of the Margaret Hague Maternity Hospital

Bull Margaret Hague Maternity Hospital — Bulletin. Margaret Hague Maternity Hospital

Bull Marine Sci — Bulletin of Marine Science

Bull Marine Sci Gulf and Caribbean — Bulletin of Marine Science of the Gulf and Caribbean [Later, Bulletin of Marine Science]

Bull Mar Sci — Bulletin of Marine Science

Bull Mar Sci Gulf Caribb — Bulletin of Marine Science of the Gulf and Caribbean [Later, Bulletin of Marine Science]

Bull Mar Sci Gulf Caribbean — Bulletin of Marine Science of the Gulf and Caribbean. University of Miami Marine Laboratory

Bull Mason Clinic — Bulletin. Mason Clinic

Bull Mass Agr Exp Sta — Bulletin. Massachusetts Agricultural Experiment Station

Bull Mass Agric Exp Sta — Bulletin. Massachusetts Agricultural Experiment Station

Bull Mass Audubon Soc — Bulletin. Massachusetts Audubon Society

Bull Mass Nat Hist — Bulletin of Massachusetts Natural History

Bull Mass Nurses Assoc — Bulletin. Massachusetts Nurses Association

Bull Mat Biophys — Bulletin of Mathematical Biophysics

Bull Mater Sci — Bulletin of Materials Science

Bull Mater Sci (India) — Bulletin of Materials Science (India)

Bull Math — Bulletin Mathematique

Bull Math — Bulletin of Mathematics

Bull Math Assoc India — Bulletin. Mathematical Association of India

Bull Math Biol — Bulletin of Mathematical Biology

Bull Math Biology — Bulletin of Mathematical Biology

Bull Math Biophys — Bulletin of Mathematical Biophysics

Bull Math Soc Sci Math RS Roumanie — Bulletin Mathematique. Societe des Sciences Mathematiques de la Republique Socialiste de Roumanie

Bull Math Soc Sci Math RS Roumanie NS — Bulletin Mathematique. Societe des Sciences Mathematiques de la Republique Socialiste de Roumanie. Nouvelle Serie

Bull Math Statist — Bulletin of Mathematical Statistics

Bull Matieres Grasses Inst Colon Marseille — Bulletin des Matieres Grasses. Institut Colonial de Marseille

Bull Mat Sci — Bulletin of Materials Science

Bull McKillip Vet Coll — Bulletin of the McKillip Veterinary College

Bull MD Agr Exp Sta — Bulletin. Maryland Agricultural Experiment Station

Bull MD Agric Exp Stn — Bulletin. Maryland Agricultural Experiment Station

Bull MD Herpetol Soc — Bulletin. Maryland Herpetological Society

Bull Md Off Anim Health Consum Serv — Bulletin. Maryland Office of Animal Health and Consumer Services

Bull ME Agric Exp Sta — Bulletin. Maine University Agricultural Experiment Station

Bull ME Agric Exp Stn — Bulletin. Maine Agricultural Experiment Station

Bull Mech Eng Educ — Bulletin of Mechanical Engineering Education

Bull Mech Eng Lab — Bulletin. Mechanical Engineering Laboratory

Bull Mech Engng Educ — Bulletin of Mechanical Engineering Education

Bull Med — Bulletin Medical

Bull Med Coll V — Bulletin. Medical College of Virginia

Bull Med Coll VA — Bulletin. Medical College of Virginia

Bull Medel — Bulletin. Medelhausmuseet

Bull Me Dep Agric — Bulletin of the Maine Department of Agriculture

Bull Me Dep St Lds For — Bulletin of the Maine Department of State Lands and Forestry

Bull Me Dept Hlth — Bulletin. Maine Department of Health

Bull Mediev Canon L — Bulletin of Medieval Canon Law

Bull Med Katanga — Bulletin Medical du Katanga

Bull Med Leg Toxicol Med — Bulletin de Medecine Legale et de Toxicologie Medicale

Bull Med Leg Toxicol Urgence Med Cent Anti Poisons — Bulletin Medecine Legale, Toxicologie, Urgence Medicale. Centre Anti-Poisons

Bull Med Libr Ass — Bulletin. Medical Library Association

Bull Med Libr Assoc — Bulletin. Medical Library Association

Bull Med Nord — Bulletin Medical du Nord

Bull Med (Paris) — Bulletin Medical (Paris)

Bull Med Res Natl Soc Med Res — Bulletin for Medical Research. National Society for Medical Research

Bull Med Science Philad — Bulletin of Medical Science (Philadelphia)

Bull Med Staff Methodist Hosp Dallas — Bulletin. Medical Staff of Methodist Hospitals of Dallas

Bull Med Suisses — Bulletin des Medecins Suisses

Bull ME For Dep — Bulletin. Maine Forestry Department

Bull Me Forest Serv — Bulletin of the Maine Forest Service

Bull Meiji Coll Pharm — Bulletin. Meiji College of Pharmacy

Bull Mem Acad R Med Belg — Bulletin et Memoires. Academie Royale de Medecine de Belgique

Bull Mem Bordeaux — Bulletin et Memoires. Societe Archeologique de Bordeaux

Bull Mem Ec Natl Med Pharm Dakar — Bulletins et Memoires. Ecole Nationale de Medecine et de Pharmacie de Dakar

Bull Mem Ec Prep Med Pharm Dakar — Bulletins et Memoires. Ecole Preparatoire de Medecine et de Pharmacie de Dakar

Bull Mem Fac Med Pharm Dakar — Bulletins et Memoires. Faculte de Medecine et de Pharmacie de Dakar

Bull Mem Fac Natl Med Pharm Dakar — Bulletins et Memoires. Faculte Nationale de Medecine et de Pharmacie de Dakar

Bull Meml Hosp Treat Cancer — Bulletin of the Memorial Hospital for the Treatment of Cancer and Allied Diseases

Bull Mem Soc Anat Paris — Bulletin et Memoires de la Societe Anatomique de Paris

Bull Mem Soc Anthropol Paris — Bulletins et Memoires. Societe d'Anthropologie de Paris

Bull Mem Soc Anthrop Paris — Bulletin et Memoires de la Societe d'Anthropologie de Paris

Bull Mem Soc Antiqua Ouest — Bulletin et Memoires de la Societe des Antiquaires de l'Ouest

Bull Mem Soc Arch Bordeaux — Bulletin et Memoires. Societe Archeologique de Bordeaux

Bull Mem Soc Archeol Bordeaux — Bulletin et Memoires de la Societe Archeologique de Bordeaux

Bull Mem Soc Archeol Hist Charente — Bulletin et Memoires. Societe Archeologique et Historique de la Charente

Bull Mem Soc Belge Orthoped — Bulletin et Memoires de la Societe Belge d'Orthopedie et de Chirurgie de l'Appareil Moteur

Bull Mem Soc Cent Med Vet — Bulletin et Memoires. Societe Centrale de Medecine Veterinaire

Bull Mem Soc Chir Buc — Bulletin et Memoires de la Societe de Chirurgie de Bucarest

Bull Mem Soc Chirgns Paris — Bulletin et Memoires de la Societe des Chirurgiens de Paris

Bull Mem Soc Chir Marseille — Bulletin et Memoires de la Societe de Chirurgie de Marseille

Bull Mem Soc Chir Paris — Bulletin et Memoires. Societe des Chirurgiens de Paris

Bull Mem Soc Electroradiol Med Fr — Bulletin et Memoires de la Societe d'Electroradiologie Medicale de France

Bull Mem Soc Emul Cotes Du N — Bulletin et Memoires de la Societe d'Emulation des Cotes-du-Nord

Bull Mem Soc Fr Ophtal — Bulletin et Memoires de la Societe Francaise d'Ophtalmologie

Bull Mem Soc Fr Ophtalmol — Bulletins et Memoires. Societe Francaise d'Ophtalmologie

Bull Mem Soc Fr Otol — Bulletin et Memoires de la Societe Francaise d'Otologie

Bull Mem Soc Lar Otol Rhinol Paris — Bulletin et Memoires de la Societe de Laryngologie, d'Otologie, et de Rhinologie de Paris

Bull Mem Soc Med Chir Bordeaux — Bulletin et Memoires de la Societe de Medecine et de Chirurgie de Bordeaux

Bull Mem Soc Med Clim Nice — Bulletin et Memoires de la Societe de Medecine et de Climatologie de Nice

Bull Mem Soc Med Hop Buc — Bulletin et Memoires de la Societe Medicale des Hopitaux de Bucarest

Bull Mem Soc Med Hop Paris — Bulletin et Memoires de la Societe Medicale des Hopitaux de Paris

Bull Mem Soc Med Paris — Bulletin et Memoires. Societe de Medecine de Paris

Bull Mem Soc Med Passy — Bulletin et Memoires de la Societe Medicale de Passy

Bull Mem Soc Med Vaucluse — Bulletin et Memoires de la Societe de Medecine de Vaucluse

Bull Mem Soc Natl Chir — Bulletins et Memoires. Societe Nationale de Chirurgie

Bull Mem Soc Neurol Psychiat Psychopath Jassy — Bulletin et Memoires de la Societe de Neurologie, Psychiatrie, et Psychopathie de Jassy

Bull Mem Soc Radiol Med Fr — Bulletin et Memoires de la Societe de Radiologie Medicale de France

Bull Mem Soc Ther — Bulletin et Memoires de la Societe de Therapeutique

Bull Menninger Clin — Bulletin. Menninger Clinic

Bull Mens Acad Clermont — Bulletin Mensuel de l'Academie de Clermont

Bull Mens Acad Sci Bell Lett Arts Angers — Bulletin Mensuel de l'Academie des Sciences, Belles-Lettres, et Arts d'Angers

Bull Mens Acad Sci Lett Montpellier — Bulletin Mensuel de l'Academie des Sciences et Lettres de Montpellier

Bull Mens Acad Vaucluse — Bulletin Mensuel de l'Academie de Vaucluse

Bull Mens Ag Econ Afr Occid Fr — Bulletin Mensuel de l'Agence Economique de l'Afrique Occidentale Francais

Bull Mens Ass Doct Pharm Univ Fr — Bulletin Mensuel de l'Association des Docteurs en Pharmacie des Universites de France

Bull Mens Ecole Super Agr Viticult Angers — Bulletin Mensuel. Ecole Superieure d'Agriculture et de Viticulture d'Angers

Bull Mens Inf — Bulletin Mensuel d'Informations

Bull Mens Nat Belg — Bulletin Mensuel des Naturalistes Belges

Bull Mens Off Int Hyg Publique — Bulletin Mensuel. Office International d'Hygiene Publique

Bull Mens Soc Linn Lyon — Bulletin Mensuel. Societe Linneenne de Lyon

Bull Mens Soc Linn Soc Bot Lyon — Bulletin Mensuel. Societe Linneenne et des Societes Botanique de Lyon, d'Anthropologie, et de Biologie de Lyon Reunies

Bull Mens Soc Med Mil Fr — Bulletin Mensuel. Societe de Medecine Militaire Francaise

Bull Mens Soc Nant Amis Hort — Bulletin Mensuel. Societe Nantaise des Amis de l'Horticulture

Bull Mens Soc Natl Hortic Fr — Bulletin Mensuel. Societe Nationale d'Horticulture de France
Bull Mens Soc Nat Luxemb — Bulletin Mensuel de la Societe des Naturalistes Luxemburgeois
Bull Mens Soc Natur Luxembourgeois — Bulletin Mensuel. Societe des Naturalistes Luxembourgeois
Bull Mens Soc Orn Mammal Fr — Bulletin Mensuel de la Societe Ornithologique et Mammalogique de France
Bull Mens Soc Scient Pharmns Aveyron — Bulletin Mensuel de la Societe Scientifique des Pharmaciens de l'Aveyron et du Centre
Bull Mens Soc Sci Nancy — Bulletin Mensuel de la Societe des Sciences de Nancy
Bull Mens Soc Sci Nat Toulon — Bulletin Mensuel de la Societe des Sciences Naturelles de Toulon
Bull Mens Soc Secours Blesses Milit — Bulletin Mensuel de la Societe de Secours aux Blesses Militaires
Bull Mens Soc Vet Prat Fr — Bulletin Mensuel de la Societe Veterinaire Pratique de France
Bull Mens Soc Vet Prat France — Bulletin Mensuel. Societe Veterinaire Pratique de France
Bull Mens Stn Met Port Au Prince — Bulletin Mensuel. Station Meteorologique. Port-au-Prince
Bull Mens Synd Gen Agric Sud Ouest — Bulletin Mensuel du Syndicat General des Agriculteurs du Sud-Ouest
Bull Mens Synd Gen Cuirs Peaux Fr — Bulletin Mensuel du Syndicat General des Cuirs et Peaux de France
Bull Mens Synd Gen Prod Chim — Bulletin Mensuel du Syndicat General des Produits Chimiques
Bull Met — Bulletin of the Metropolitan Museum of Art
Bull Metall Dep Ontario Res Fdn — Bulletin of the Metallurgical Department of the Ontario Research Foundation
Bull Met Dep Herault — Bulletin Meteorologique du Departement de l'Herault
Bull Met Indo Chine — Bulletin Meteorologique de l'Indo-Chine
Bull Met Inst Scient Cherif — Bulletin Meteorologique. Institut Scientifique Cherifien
Bull Met Journ Vietnam — Bulletin Meteorologique Journalier. Vietnam
Bull Met Maroc — Bulletin Meteorologique du Maroc
Bull Met Med Leysin — Bulletin Meteorologique et Medical de Leysin
Bull Met Mens Obs Tananarive — Bulletin Meteorologique Mensuel de l'Observatoire de Tananarive
Bull Met Mens Yougosl — Bulletin Meteorologique Mensuel. Yougoslavie
Bull Met Mus — Bulletin. Metals Museum
Bull Met N — Bulletin Meteorologique du Nord
Bull Met Nijni Oltchedaef — Bulletin Meteorologique. Nijni-Oltchedaef
Bull Met Obs Cent Beogr — Bulletin Meteorologique. Observatoire Central (Beograd)
Bull Met Obs Ksara — Bulletin Meteorologique. Observatoire de Ksara
Bull Met Obs Met Beogr — Bulletin Meteorologique. Observatoire Meteorologique (Beograd)
Bull Met Quot Mex — Bulletin Meteorologique Quotidien du Mexique
Bull Metr Mus — Bulletin. Metropolitan Museum of Art
Bull Metr Mus Art — Bulletin. Metropolitan Museum of Art
Bull Metrol — Bulletin de Metrologie
Bull Metrop Mus Art — Metropolitan Museum of Art. Bulletin
Bull Met Seism Magn Istanbul — Bulletin Meteorologique, Seismique et Magnetique (Istanbul)
Bull Met Soc Res Tohoku Distr — Bulletin of the Meteorological Society for Research of Tohoku District
Bull Meun Fr — Bulletin Meunerie Francaise
Bull Me Univ Technol Exp Stn — Bulletin. Maine University Technology Experiment Station
Bull MFA — Bulletin. Museum of Fine Arts
Bull Mfrs Ass New Jers — Bulletin. Manufacturers' Association of New Jersey
Bull Mich Agric Coll — Bulletin. Michigan Agricultural College
Bull Mich Agric Coll Exp Stn — Bulletin. Michigan Agricultural College. Experiment Station
Bull Mich Dent Hyg Assoc — Bulletin. Michigan Dental Hygienists Association
Bull Mich State Dent Soc — Bulletin. Michigan State Dental Society
Bull Mich St Univ — Bulletin. Michigan State University
Bull Micr Appl — Bulletin de Microscopie Appliquee
Bull Microbiol — Bulletin of Microbiology
Bull Microscopie Appl — Bulletin de Microscopie Appliquee
Bull Microsc Soc Can — Bulletin. Microscopical Society of Canada
Bull Mid E Stud Ass — Bulletin. Middle East Studies Association of North America
Bull Mie Agric Tech Cent — Bulletin. Mie Agricultural Technical Center
Bull Millard Fillmore Hosp — Bulletin. Millard Fillmore Hospital
Bull Min Agr (Egypt) — Bulletin. Ministry of Agriculture (Egypt)
Bull Min Agr Land (Jamaica) — Bulletin. Ministry of Agriculture and Lands (Jamaica)
Bull Mineral — Bulletin de Mineralogie
Bull Mineral Res Explor Inst (Turkey) — Bulletin. Mineral Research and Exploration Institute (Turkey). Foreign Edition
Bull Miner Ind Exp Stn PA State Univ — Bulletin. Mineral Industries Experiment Station. Pennsylvania State University
Bull Miner Res Explor Inst (Turk) — Bulletin. Mineral Research and Exploration Institute (Turkey)
Bull Miner Res Explor Inst (Turk) Foreign Ed — Bulletin. Mineral Research and Exploration Institute (Turkey). Foreign Edition
Bull Minist Agric (Egypt) Tech Scient Serv — Bulletin. Ministry of Agriculture (Egypt) Technical and Scientific Service
Bull Minist Agric Fish Fd — Bulletin. Ministry of Agriculture, Fisheries, and Food
Bull Minist Agric Fish Fd (Lond) — Bulletin. Ministry of Agriculture, Fisheries, and Food (London)
Bull Minist Agric Fish Food (GB) — Bulletin. Ministry of Agriculture, Fisheries, and Food (Great Britain)

Bull Minist Agric Fish (NZ) — Bulletin. Ministry of Agriculture and Fisheries (New Zealand)
Bull Minist Agric (Queb) — Bulletin. Ministry of Agriculture (Quebec)
Bull Minist Agric Rural Dev (Malays) — Bulletin. Ministry of Agriculture and Rural Development (Malaysia)
Bull Minist Educ — Bulletin. Ministry of Education/Chiao-Yue Kung Pao
Bull Min Met Soc Am — Bulletin. Mining and Metallurgical Society of America
Bull Minneapolis Inst A — Bulletin of the Minneapolis Institute of Arts
Bull Minn Geol Surv — Bulletin. Minnesota Geological Survey
Bull Misaki Mar Biol Inst — Bulletin. Misaki Marine Biological Institute. Kyoto University
Bull Misaki Mar Biol Inst Kyoto Univ — Bulletin. Misaki Marine Biological Institute. Kyoto University
Bull Misc Inf (Kew) — Bulletin of Miscellaneous Information. Royal Botanic Gardens (Kew)
Bull Misc Inform Dept Agric Imp Coll Agric — Bulletin of Miscellaneous Information. Department of Agriculture. Imperial College of Agriculture
Bull Misc Inform Roy Bot Gard (Kew) — Bulletin of Miscellaneous Information. Royal Botanic Gardens (Kew)
Bull Misc Inf R Bot Gard — Bulletin of Miscellaneous Information. Royal Botanic Gardens
Bull Miss Agric Exp Sta — Bulletin. Mississippi State University. Agricultural Experiment Station
Bull Miss Agric Exp Stn — Bulletin. Mississippi Agricultural Experiment Station
Bull Miss Agric For Exp Stn — Bulletin. Mississippi Agricultural and Forestry Experiment Station
Bull Miss Agric Mech Coll — Bulletin. Mississippi Agricultural and Mechanical College
Bull Mississippi Geol Econ Topogr Surv — Bulletin. Mississippi Geological, Economic, and Topographical Survey
Bull Miss Sch Min Tech Ser — Bulletin. Missouri School of Mines. Technical Series
Bull Miss State Univ Agr Exp Sta — Bulletin. Mississippi State University. Agricultural Experiment Station
Bull Miyagi Agr Coll — Bulletin. Miyagi Agricultural College
Bull Miyagi Agric Coll — Bulletin. Miyagi Agricultural College
Bull Miyazaki Agr Exp Sta — Bulletin. Miyazaki Agricultural Experiment Station
Bull Mizunami Fossil Mus — Bulletin. Mizunami Fossil Museum
Bull MMA — Bulletin. Metropolitan Museum of Art
Bull M Nat Varsovie — Bulletin. Musee National de Varsovie
Bull Mnmt Istor — Bulletin Monumentelor Istorice
Bull Mnmtl — Bulletin Monumental
Bull Mnmts — Bulletin des Monuments
Bull MO Acad Sci Suppl — Bulletin. Missouri Academy of Science. Supplement
Bull MO Bot Gdn — Bulletin. Missouri Botanical Garden
Bull MO Hist Soc — Bulletin. Missouri Historical Society
Bull Mol Biol Med — Bulletin of Molecular Biology and Medicine
Bull MOMA NY — Bulletin of the Museum of Modern Art. New York
Bull Mon — Bulletin Monumental
Bull Monmouth Cty Dent Soc — Bulletin. Monmouth County [New Jersey] Dental Society
Bull Monroe County Med Soc — Bulletin. Monroe County Medical Society
Bull Mont Agr Exp Sta — Bulletin. Montana Agricultural Experiment Station
Bull Montana Agric Exp Stn — Bulletin. Montana Agricultural Experiment Station
Bull Montana State Univ Biol Ser — Bulletin. Montana State University. Biological Series
Bull Montg-Bucks Dent Soc — Bulletin. Montgomery-Bucks Dental Society
Bull Montreal Bot Gard — Bulletin. Montreal Botanical Gardens
Bull Mont State Coll Agric Exp Stn — Bulletin. Montana State College. Agricultural Experiment Station
Bull Mont State Coll Coop Ext Serv — Bulletin. Montana State College. Cooperative Extension Service
Bull Monum — Bulletin Monumental
Bull Morioka Tob Exp Stn — Bulletin. Morioka Tobacco Experiment Station
Bull Mt Desert Isl Biol Lab — Bulletin. Mount Desert Island Biological Laboratory
Bull Mukogawa Women's Univ — Bulletin of Mukogawa Women's University
Bull Mukogawa Womens Univ Food Sci — Bulletin. Mukogawa Women's University. Food Science
Bull Mukogawa Women's Univ Nat Sci — Bulletin. Mukogawa Women's University. Natural Science
Bull Mukogawa Women's Univ Pharm Sci — Bulletin of Mukogawa Women's University. Pharmaceutical Sciences
Bull Mun Officiel Ville Paris — Bulletin Municipal Officiel de la Ville de Paris
Bull Murithienne — Bulletin de la Murithienne
Bull Mus — Bullettino. Museo dell'Impero Romana
Bull Mus A & Archaeol U MI — Bulletin. Museums of Art and Archaeology. University of Michigan
Bull Mus & Archaeol U P — Bulletin. Museums and Archaeology in Uttar Pradesh
Bull Mus & Mnmts Lyon — Bulletin des Musees et Monuments Lyonnais
Bull Mus Anthrop Prehist Monaco — Bulletin du Musee d'Anthropologie Prehistorique de Monaco
Bull Mus Anthr Prehist (Monaco) — Bulletin. Musee d'Anthropologie Prehistorique (Monaco)
Bull Mus A RI Sch Des — Bulletin of the Museum of Art. Rhode Island School of Design
Bull Mus Art Hist Geneve — Bulletin. Musee d'Art et d'Histoire de Geneve
Bull Mus Augustins — Bulletin du Musee des Augustins
Bull Mus B A Alger — Bulletin du Musee des Beaux-Arts d'Alger
Bull Mus Barbier Mueller — Bulletin du Musee Barbier-Mueller
Bull Mus Belge — Bulletin Bibliographique et Pedagogique. Musee Belge
Bull Mus Beyrouth — Bulletin. Musee de Beyrouth
Bull Mus Boymans — Bulletin. Museum Boymans
Bull Mus Boymans van Beuningen — Bulletin. Museum Boymans-van Beuningen
Bull Mus Carnavalet — Bulletin du Musee Carnavalet
Bull Mus Comp Zool — Bulletin. Museum of Comparative Zoology

Bull Mus Comp Zool Harv — Bulletin. Museum of Comparative Zoology at Harvard University

Bull Mus Comp Zool Harv Univ — Bulletin. Museum of Comparative Zoology at Harvard University

Bull Mus Dijon — Bulletin des Musees de Dijon

Bull Musees Royaux — Bulletin. Musees Royaux d'Art et d'Histoire

Bull Mus Ermitage — Bulletin du Musee de l'Ermitage

Bull Museum (Boston) — Bulletin. Museum of Fine Arts (Boston)

Bull Mus F A Boston — Bulletin. Museum of Fine Arts. Boston

Bull Mus Far E Ant — Bulletin of the Museum of Far Eastern Antiquities

Bull Mus Far East Antiquities — Bulletin. Museum of Far Eastern Antiquities

Bull Mus Fi A — Museum of Fine Arts. Bulletin

Bull Mus Fine Arts (Boston) — Bulletin. Museum of Fine Arts (Boston)

Bull Mus France — Bulletin des Musees de France

Bull Mus Hist Mulhouse — Bulletin. Musee Historique de Mulhouse

Bull Mus Hist Nat Belg — Bulletin. Musee Royal d'Histoire Naturelle de la Belgique

Bull Mus Hist Nat Mars — Bulletin. Museum d'Histoire Naturelle de Marseille

Bull Mus Hist Nat Marseille — Bulletin. Musee d'Histoire Naturelle de Marseille

Bull Mus Hist Nat Paris — Bulletin du Museum d'Histoire Naturelle (Paris)

Bull Mus Hist Nat Pays Serbe — Bulletin. Museum d'Histoire Naturelle du Pays Serbe

Bull Mus Hist Natur Belg — Bulletin. Musee Royal d'Histoire Naturelle de la Belgique

Bull Mus Hong — Bulletin. Musee Hongrois des Beaux-Arts

Bull Mus Hong B A — Bulletin du Musee Hongrois des Beaux-Arts

Bull Mus Imp — Bullettino. Museo dell'Impero Romana

Bull Mus Imp Rom — Bullettino. Museo dell'Impero Romana

Bull Mus Ingres — Bulletin du Musee Ingres

Bull Mus Lyon — Bulletin. Musees et Monuments Lyonnais

Bull Mus Mon Lyonn — Bulletin des Musees et Monuments Lyonnais

Bull Mus Nat Hist Nat (Paris) — Bulletin. Museum National d'Histoire Naturelle (Paris)

Bull Mus Nat Hist Univ Oregon — Bulletin. Museum of Natural History. University of Oregon

Bull Mus Natl Hist Nat — Bulletin. Museum National d'Histoire Naturelle

Bull Mus Natl Hist Nat Bot — Bulletin. Museum National d'Histoire Naturelle. Botanique

Bull Mus Natl Hist Nat Ecol Gen — Bulletin. Museum National d'Histoire Naturelle. Ecologie Generale

Bull Mus Natl Hist Nat Sci Terre — Bulletin. Museum National d'Histoire Naturelle. Serie 3. Sciences de la Terre

Bull Mus Natl Hist Nat Sect A Zool Biol Ecol Anim — Bulletin. Museum National d'Histoire Naturelle. Section A. Zoologie, Biologie, et Ecologie Animales

Bull Mus Natl Hist Nat Sect B Andansonia Bot Phytochim — Bulletin. Museum National d'Histoire Naturelle. Section B. Andansonia Botanique. Phytochimie

Bull Mus Natl Hist Nat Sect B Bot Biol Ecol Veg Phytochim — Bulletin. Museum National d'Histoire Naturelle. Section B. Botanique, Biologie,et Ecologie Vegetales. Phytochimie

Bull Mus Natl Hist Nat Ser 3 Sci Terre — Bulletin. Museum National d'Histoire Naturelle. Serie. 3. Sciences de la Terre

Bull Mus Natl Hist Nat Zool — Bulletin. Museum National d'Histoire Naturelle. Zoologie

Bull Mus N Hong B A — Bulletin du Musee National Hongrois des Beaux-Arts

Bull Mus N Varsovie Biul Muz N Warszaw — Bulletin du Musee National de Varsovie/Biuletyn Muzeum Narodowego w Warszawie

Bull Mus R Hist Nat Belg — Bulletin. Musee Royal d'Histoire Naturelle de la Belgique

Bull Mus Roy Art et Hist — Bulletin. Musees Royaux d'Art et d'Histoire

Bull Mus Royaux A & Hist — Bulletin des Musees Royaux d'Art et d'Histoire

Bull Mus Royaux A Dec & Indust — Bulletin des Musees Royaux des Arts Decoratifs et Industriels

Bull Mus Royaux Cinquantenaire — Bulletin des Musees Royaux du Cinquantenaire

Bull Mus Roy Beaux Arts Belg — Bulletin. Musees Royaux des Beaux-Arts de Belgique

Bull Mus Roy Bruxelles — Bulletin. Musees Royaux d'Art et d'Histoire (Brussels)

Bull Mycol — Bulletin of Mycology

Bull Mysore Geol Assoc — Bulletin. Mysore Geologists Association

Bull Nagano Agr Exp Sta — Bulletin. Nagano Agricultural Experiment Station

Bull Nagaoka Munic Sci Mus — Bulletin. Nagaoka Municipal Science Museum

Bull Nagoya City Univ Dep Gen Educ Nat Sci Sect — Bulletin. Nagoya City University. Department of General Education. Natural Science Section

Bull Nagoya Inst Tech — Bulletin. Nagoya Institute of Technology

Bull Nagoya Inst Technol — Bulletin. Nagoya Institute of Technology

Bull N A G S Australia — Bulletin of the National Art Gallery of South Australia

Bull Naikai Reg Fish Res Lab — Bulletin. Naikai Regional Fisheries Research Laboratory

Bull N Am Gladiolus Counc — Bulletin. North American Gladiolus Council

Bull Naniwa Univ Ser A — Bulletin. Naniwa University. Series A. Engineering and Natural Sciences

Bull Naniwa Univ Ser B — Bulletin. Naniwa University. Series B. Agricultural and Natural Science

Bull Nanjing Inst Geol Miner Resour — Bulletin. Nanjing Institute of Geology and Mineral Resources

Bull Nansei Reg Fish Res Lab — Bulletin. Nansei Regional Fisheries Research Laboratories

Bull Nap — Bullettino Archeologico Napoletano

Bull Napol — Bullettino Archeologico Napoletano

Bull Nara Agric Exp Stn — Bulletin. Nara Agricultural Experiment Station

Bull Nara Univ Ed Natur Sci — Bulletin. Nara University of Education. Natural Science

Bull Nara Univ Educ Nat Sci — Bulletin. Nara University of Education. Natural Science

Bull Narc — Bulletin on Narcotics

Bull Narcotics — Bulletin on Narcotics

Bull Nat Assoc Wool Manuf — Bulletin. National Association of Wool Manufacturers

Bull Nat Ass Watch Clock Collect — Bulletin. National Association of Watch and Clock Collectors

Bull Nat Club Shanghai — Bulletin of the Naturalists' Club of Shanghai

Bull Nat Dist Heat Assoc — Bulletin. National District Heating Association

Bull Nat Formul Comm — Bulletin. National Formulary Committee

Bull Nat Geophys Res Inst (India) — Bulletin. National Geophysical Research Institute (India)

Bull Nat His Mus Belgr Ser A Mineral Geol Paleontol — Bulletin. Natural History Museum in Belgrade. Series A. Mineralogy, Geology, Paleontology

Bull Nat Hist Mus — Bulletin. Natural History Museum, Balboa Park

Bull Nat Hist Mus Balboa Pk — Bulletin. Natural History Museum. Balboa Park

Bull Nat Hist Mus Belgr — Bulletin. Natural History Museum in Belgrade

Bull Nat Hist Mus Belgrade B — Bulletin. Natural History Museum in Belgrade. Series B. Biological Sciences

Bull Nat Hist Mus Belgr Ser B Biol Sci — Bulletin. Natural History Museum in Belgrade. Series B. Biological Sciences

Bull Nat Hist Res Cent Univ Baghdad — Bulletin. Natural History Research Center. University of Baghdad

Bull Nat Hist Soc Br Columb — Bulletin. Natural History Society of British Columbia

Bull Nat Hist Soc British Columbia — Bulletin. Natural History Society of British Columbia

Bull Nat Hist Soc Md — Bulletin. Natural History Society of Maryland

Bull Nat Hist Soc New Br — Bulletin. Natural History Society of New Brunswick

Bull Nat Hist Soc New Brunswick — Bulletin of the Natural History Society of New Brunswick

Bull Nat Hist Surv Chicago Acad Sci — Bulletin. Natural History Survey. Chicago Academy of Sciences

Bull Nat Hist Surv St La — Bulletin of the Natural History Survey. State of Louisiana

Bull Nat Inst Anim Ind — Bulletin. National Institute of Animal Industry

Bull Nat Inst Geol Min (Bandung Indonesia) — Bulletin. National Institute of Geology and Mining (Bandung, Indonesia)

Bull Nat Inst Hyg Sci — Bulletin. National Institute of Hygienic Sciences

Bull Nat Inst Sci India — Bulletin. National Institute of Sciences of India

Bull Natl Anti Vivisection Soc — Bulletin. The National Anti-Vivisection Society

Bull Natl Bot Gard — Bulletin. National Botanic Garden

Bull Natl Bot Gard (Lucknow) — Bulletin. National Botanic Garden (Lucknow)

Bull Natl Chrysanthemum Soc — Bulletin. National Chrysanthemum Society

Bull Natl Fish Univ Pusan Nat Sci — Bulletin of National Fisheries. University of Pusan. Natural Sciences

Bull Natl Geophys Res Inst (India) — Bulletin. National Geophysical Research Institute (India)

Bull Natl Grassl Res Inst — Bulletin. National Grassland Research Institute

Bull Natl Hyg Lab (Tokyo) — Bulletin. National Hygienic Laboratory (Tokyo)

Bull Natl Inst Agric Sci Ser A — Bulletin. National Institute of Agricultural Sciences. Series A (Physics and Statistics)

Bull Natl Inst Agric Sci Ser A (Phys Stat) — Bulletin. National Institute of Agricultural Sciences. Series A (Physics and Statistics) (Japan)

Bull Natl Inst Agric Sci Ser B (Soils Fert) (Japan) — Bulletin. National Institute of Agricultural Sciences. Series B (Soils and Fertilizers) (Japan)

Bull Natl Inst Agric Sci Ser C (Plant Pathol Entomol) — Bulletin. National Institute of Agricultural Sciences. Series C (Plant Pathology and Entomology) (Japan)

Bull Natl Inst Agric Sci Ser D (Physiol Genet) (Japan) — Bulletin. National Institute of Agricultural Sciences. Series D (Physiology andGenetics) (Japan)

Bull Natl Inst Agric Sci Ser D Plant Physiol Genet Crops Gen — Bulletin. National Institute of Agricultural Sciences. Series D (Plant Physiology, Genetics, and Crops in General)

Bull Natl Inst Agric Sci Ser E Hort — Bulletin. National Institute of Agricultural Sciences. Series E. Horticulture/Nogyo Gijutsu Kenkyusho Hokoku. E. Engei

Bull Natl Inst Agric Sci Ser G (Anim Husb) — Bulletin. National Institute of Agricultural Sciences. Series G (Animal Husbandry) (Japan)

Bull Natl Inst Agri Sci Ser C — Bulletin. National Institute of Agricultural Sciences. Series C

Bull Natl Inst Agrobiol Resour — Bulletin. National Institute of Agrobiological Resources

Bull Natl Inst Agro Environ Sci Jpn — Bulletin. National Institute of Agro-Environmental Sciences (Japan)

Bull Natl Inst Anim Health (Jpn) — Bulletin. National Institute of Animal Health (Japan)

Bull Natl Inst Anim Ind (Chiba) — Bulletin. National Institute of Animal Industry (Chiba)

Bull Natl Inst Anim Ind (Ibaraki) — Bulletin. National Institute of Animal Industry (Ibaraki)

Bull Natl Inst Health Sci Jpn — Bulletin of National Institute of Health Sciences (Japan)

Bull Natl Inst Hyg Sci (Tokyo) — Bulletin. National Institute of Hygienic Sciences (Tokyo)

Bull Natl Inst Oceanogr (India) — Bulletin. National Institute of Oceanography (India)

Bull Natl Inst Pollut Resour — Bulletin. National Research Institute for Pollution and Resources

Bull Natl Inst Sci India — Bulletin. National Institute of Sciences of India

Bull Natl Med Dent Assoc Natl Advocates Soc — Bulletin. National Medical and Dental Association and National Advocates Society

Bull Natl Mus (Singapore) — Bulletin. National Museum (Singapore)

Bull Natl Pearl Res Lab — Bulletin. National Pearl Research Laboratory

Bull Natl Plant Belg — Bulletin. Nationale Plantentuin van Belgie

Bull Natl Res Cent Egypt — Bulletin of the National Research Centre (Egypt)

Bull Natl Res Council Philipp — Bulletin. National Research Council. Philippines

Bull Natl Res Counc Philipp — Bulletin. National Research Council of the Philippines

Bull Natl Res Inst Aquacult — Bulletin. National Research Institute of Aquaculture

Bull Natl Res Inst Fish Eng — Bulletin. National Research Institute of Fisheries Engineering

Bull Natl Res Inst Pollut Resour Jpn — Bulletin. National Research Institute for Pollution and Resources (Japan)

Bull Natl Res Inst Tea — Bulletin. National Research Institute of Tea

Bull Natl Res Inst Veg Ornamental Plants Tea Ser B Kanaya — Bulletin. National Research Institute of Vegetables, Ornamental Plants, and Tea. Series B. Kanaya

Bull Natl Res Inst Veg Ornamental Plants Tea Ser B Tea — Bulletin. National Research Institute of Vegetables, Ornamental Plants, and Tea. Series B. Tea

Bull Natl Res Lab Metrol — Bulletin. National Research Laboratory of Metrology

Bull Natl Res Lab Metrology — Bulletin. National Research Laboratory of Metrology

Bull Natl Sci Found — Bulletin. National Science Foundation

Bull Natl Sci Mus Ser A (Zool) — Bulletin. National Science Museum. Series A (Zoology) (Japan)

Bull Natl Sci Mus Ser B (Bot) — Bulletin. National Science Museum. Series B (Botany) (Japan)

Bull Natl Sci Mus Ser C (Geol) — Bulletin. National Science Museum. Series C (Geology) [Later, Bulletin. National Science Museum. Series C. (Geology and Paleontology)] (Japan)

Bull Natl Sci Mus Ser C (Geol Paleontol) — Bulletin. National Science Museum. Series C (Geology and Paleontology)

Bull Natl Sci Mus Ser D (Anthropol) — Bulletin. National Science Museum. Series D (Anthropology)

Bull Natl Sci Mus Ser E Tokyo — Bulletin. National Science Museum. Series E. Physical Sciences and Engineering (Tokyo)

Bull Natl Sci Mus (Tokyo) — Bulletin. National Science Museum (Tokyo)

Bull Natl Speleol Soc — Bulletin. National Speleological Society

Bull Natl Tuberc Assoc — Bulletin. National Tuberculosis Association

Bull Natl Tuberc Respir Dis Assoc — Bulletin. National Tuberculosis Respiratory Disease Association

Bull Nat Mons — Bulletin des Naturalistes de Mons et du Borinage

Bull Natn Inst Agric Sci (Tokyo) — Bulletin. National Institute of Agricultural Sciences (Tokyo)

Bull Natn Inst Hyg Sci (Tokyo) — Bulletin. National Institute of Hygienic Sciences (Tokyo)

Bull Natn Inst Sci India — Bulletin. National Institute of Sciences of India

Bull Natn Muse Ethnol Osaka Spec Issue — Bulletin of the National Museum of Ethnology (Osaka). Special Issue

Bull Natn Mus Ethnol — Bulletin. National Museum of Ethnology

Bull Natn Mus Ethnol Osaka — Bulletin of the National Museum of Ethnology (Osaka)

Bull Natn Mus Nat Sci Taichung — Bulletin of the National Museum of Natural Science (Taichung)

Bull Natn Sci Mus (Tokyo) — Bulletin. National Science Museum (Tokyo)

Bull Natn Sci Mus Tokyo Ser D Anthrop — Bulletin of the National Science Museum (Tokyo). Series D. Anthropology

Bull Natn Soc India Malar — Bulletin of the National Society of India for Malaria and other Mosquito Borne Disease

Bull Nat Pearl Res Lab (Jpn) — Bulletin. National Pearl Research Laboratory (Japan)

Bull Nat Res Counc (US) — Bulletin. National Research Council (US)

Bull Nat Res Lab Metrology — Bulletin. National Research Laboratory of Metrology

Bull Nat Resour Res Inst Univ Wyo — Bulletin. Natural Resources Research Institute. College of Engineering. University of Wyoming

Bull Nat Sci Brd — Bulletin. National Science Board, Philippine Islands

Bull Nat Sci (Wellington) — Bulletin of Natural Sciences (Wellington)

Bull Nat Soc Ind Malar — Bulletin. National Society of India for Malaria and Other Mosquito Borne Disease

Bull Nat Spel Soc — Bulletin. National Speleological Society

Bull Nat Tax Assoc — Bulletin. National Tax Association

Bull Nat Tub Ass — Bulletin. National Tuberculosis Association

Bull Naut Geogr Roma — Bulletino Nautico e Geografico di Roma

Bull N Carol Coll Agric — Bulletin. North Carolina College of Agriculture and Mechanic Arts

Bull N Carol Dent Soc — Bulletin of the North Carolina Dental Society

Bull N Carol Dep Agric — Bulletin of the North Carolina Department of Agriculture

Bull N Carol Dep Conserv Dev — Bulletin. North Carolina Department of Conservation and Development

Bull N Carol Engng Exp Stn — Bulletin. North Carolina Engineering Experiment Station

Bull N Carol Geol Econ Surv — Bulletin of the North Carolina Geological and Economic Survey

Bull N Carol St Univ Agric Exp Stn — Bulletin. North Carolina State University. Agricultural Experiment Station

Bull NC Div Miner Resour — Bulletin. North Carolina Division of Mineral Resources

Bull NC Div Resour Plann Eval Miner Resour Sect — Bulletin. North Carolina Division of Resource Planning and Evaluation. Mineral Resources Section

Bull NC Mus A — Bulletin. North Carolina Museum of Art

Bull N Dak Agr Exp Sta — Bulletin. North Dakota Agricultural Experiment Station

Bull N Dak Agric Exp St — Bulletin. North Dakota Agricultural Experimental Station

Bull N Dak Agric Exp Stn — Bulletin. North Dakota Agricultural Experiment Station

Bull N Dak Geol Surv — Bulletin of the North Dakota Geological Survey

Bull N Dak Univ Sch Mines — Bulletin of the North Dakota University School of Mines

Bull N East Wood Util Coun — Bulletin. Northeastern Wood Utilization Council

Bull Neb Bd Agric — Bulletin of the Nebraska Board of Agriculture

Bull Nebr Agric Exp St — Bulletin. Nebraska Agricultural Experiment Station

Bull Neb St Ent — Bulletin. Nebraska State Entomologist

Bull Neb St Mus — Bulletin. Nebraska State Museum

Bull Ned Oudhdknd Bond — Bulletin van den Nederlandschen Outheidkundigen Bond

Bull Needle & Bobbin Club — Bulletin of the Needle and Bobbin Club

Bull Neuesten Wissenswuerd Naturwiss — Bulletin des Neuesten und Wissenswuerdigsten aus der Naturwissenschaft, so wie den Kuensten, Manufakturen, Technischen Gewerben, der Landwirthschaft der Buergerlichen Haushaltung

Bull Neurol Inst NY — Bulletin. Neurological Institute of New York

Bull Nev Agr Exp St — Bulletin. Nevada Agricultural Experiment Station

Bull Nev Bur Mines Geol — Bulletin. Nevada Bureau of Mines and Geology

Bull Newark Dent Club — Bulletin. Newark [New Jersey] Dental Club

Bull New Engl Med Cent — Bulletin. New England Medical Center

Bull New Hamps Agric Exp Stn — Bulletin. New Hampshire Agricultural Experiment Station

Bull New Jers Agric Exp St — Bulletin. New Jersey Agricultural Experiment Station

Bull New Jers Agric Exp Stn — Bulletin. New Jersey Agricultural Experiment Station

Bull New Jers St Soil Conserv Comm — Bulletin. New Jersey State Soil Conservation Committee

Bull New Mex Agric Exp Stn — Bulletin. New Mexico Agricultural Experiment Station

Bull New Ser Rep Agric Exp Sta Agric Coll — Bulletin. New Series. Report. Agricultural Experiment Station. Agricultural andMechanical College

Bull New York Acad Med — Bulletin. New York Academy of Medicine

Bull New York Bot Gard — Bulletin. New York Botanical Garden

Bull N G Prague — Bulletin of the National Gallery of Prague

Bull NH Agric Exp Stn — Bulletin. New Hampshire Agricultural Experiment Station

Bull N Hampshire Agric Exper Station — Bulletin. New Hampshire Agricultural Experiment Station

Bull Niger For Dep — Bulletin. Nigerian Forestry Departments

Bull Nigerian For Dep — Bulletin. Nigerian Forestry Departments

Bull Niigata Univ For — Bulletin. Niigata University Forests

Bull Nimes — Bulletin des Seances. Academie de Nimes

Bull Ninth Dist Dent Soc — Bulletin. Ninth District Dental Society

Bull Nippon Agric Res Inst — Bulletin. Nippon Agricultural Research Institute/ Nihon Nogyo Kenkyusho Hokoku

Bull Nippon Dent Coll Gen Educ — Bulletin. Nippon Dental College. General Education

Bull Nippon Dent Univ Gen Educ — Bulletin. Nippon Dental University. General Education

Bull Nippon Vet Zootech Coll — Bulletin. Nippon Veterinary and Zootechnical College

Bull NJ Acad Sci — Bulletin. New Jersey Academy of Science

Bull NJ Agr Exp Sta — Bulletin. New Jersey Agricultural Experiment Station

Bull NJ Bur Geol Topogr — Bulletin. New Jersey Bureau of Geology and Topography

Bull NJ Soc Dent Child — Bulletin. New Jersey Society of Dentistry for Children

Bull N Mex Agr Exp Sta — Bulletin. New Mexico Agricultural Experiment Station

Bull N Mus New Delhi — Bulletin of the National Museum. New Delhi

Bull N Negros Sug Co — Bulletin. North Negros Sugar Co. Inc., Manapla and Victorias Milling Co.

Bull Norg Geol Unders — Bulletin. Norges Geologiske Undersokelse

Bull Northampt Cty Coun Fm Inst — Bulletin. Northampton County Council Farm Institute

Bull North Carolina Bd Health — Bulletin. North Carolina Board of Health

Bull North Dist Dent Soc — Bulletin. Northern District Dental Society

Bull North Scotl Coll Agric — Bulletin. North of Scotland College of Agriculture

Bull Northumb Co Agric Exp Stn — Bulletin. Northumberland County Agricultural Experiment Station. Cockle Park

Bull Nova Scotia Dep Nat Resour — Bulletin. Nova Scotia Department of Natural Resources

Bull NRDC — Bulletin. National Research Development Corporation

Bull N Rhodesia Dept Agr — Bulletin. Northern Rhodesia Department of Agriculture

Bull NRLM — Bulletin. NRLM

Bull N Scot Coll Agr — Bulletin. North of Scotland College of Agriculture

Bull N Scotl Coll Agric — Bulletin. North of Scotland College of Agriculture

Bull N Scotl Coll Agric Beekeep Dep — Bulletin. North of Scotland College of Agriculture. Beekeeping Department

Bull N Staffs Min Stud Ass — Bulletin. North Staffordshire Mining Students' Association

Bull Nth Terr Aust — Bulletin of the Northern Territory of Australia

Bull N Terr Austr — Bulletin of the Northern Territory of Australia

Bull Number Theory Related Topics — Bulletin of Number Theory and Related Topics

Bull Nutr Inst UAR — Bulletin. Nutrition Institute of the United Arab Republic

Bull N West Univ Med Sch — Bulletin of the Northwestern University Medical School

Bull NW Line Elev Ass — Bulletin. North-West Line Elevator Association [Winnipeg]

Bull NY Acad Med — Bulletin. New York Academy of Medicine

Bull NY Acad Medic — Bulletin of the New York Academy of Medicine

Bull NY Agr Exp Sta — Bulletin. New York Agricultural Experiment Station

Bull NY Agric Exp Stn Ithaca — Bulletin. New York. Agricultural Experiment Station (Ithaca)

Bull NY Cty Dent Soc — Bulletin. New York County Dental Society

Bull NY Med Coll Flower Fifth Ave — Bulletin. New York Medical College. Flower and Fifth Avenue

Bull NYPL — Bulletin. New York Public Library

Bull NY Pub Lib — Bulletin. New York Public Library

Bull NY Public Libr — Bulletin. New York Public Library

Bull NY Publ Libr — Bulletin. New York Public Library

Bull NY St Agric Exp St — Bulletin. New York State Agricultural Experiment Station

Bull NY St Agric Exp Stn — Bulletin. New York State Agricultural Experiment Station

Bull NY State Flower Ind — Bulletin. New York State Flower Industries

Bull NY State Mus — Bulletin. New York State Museum

Bull NY State Mus Sci Serv — Bulletin. New York State Museum and Science Service
Bull NY State Soc Anesthesiol — Bulletin. New York State Society of Anesthesiologists
Bull NY St Conserv Dep — Bulletin. New York State Conservation Department
Bull NY St Dep Agric — Bulletin. New York State Department of Agriculture
Bull NY St Mus — Bulletin. New York State Museum
Bull NY St Mus Sci Serv — Bulletin. New York State Museum and Science Service
Bull NY Zool Soc — Bulletin. New York Zoological Society
Bull NZ A Hist — Bulletin of New Zealand Art History
Bull NZ Astr Soc — Bulletin. New Zealand Astronomical Society. Variable Star Section
Bull NZ Dep Scient Ind Res — Bulletin. New Zealand Department of Scientific and Industrial Research
Bull NZ Dept Sci Ind Res — Bulletin. New Zealand Department of Scientific and Industrial Research
Bull NZ Geol Surv — Bulletin. New Zealand Geological Survey
Bull NZ Geol Surv New Ser — Bulletin. New Zealand Geological Survey. New Series
Bull NZ Natl Soc Earthq Eng — Bulletin. New Zealand National Society for Earthquake Engineering
Bull NZ Soc Earthquake Eng — Bulletin. New Zealand Society for Earthquake Engineering
Bull NZ Soc Periodontol — Bulletin. New Zealand Society of Periodontology
Bull O — Weekly Law Bulletin
Bull Oberlin Coll Lab — Bulletin of the Oberlin College Laboratory
Bull Obs Astr Belgr — Bulletin de l'Observatoire Astronomique de Belgrade
Bull Obs Astr Libau — Bulletin de l'Observatoire Astronomique de Libau
Bull Obs Astr Lisb Tapada — Bulletin de l'Observatoire Astronomique de Lisbonne, Tapada
Bull Obs Carlier — Bulletin de l'Observatoire Carlier a la Tour Moncade d'Orthez
Bull Obs Hop Pau — Bulletin de l'Observatoire de l'Hopital de Pau
Bull Obs Lyon — Bulletin de l'Observatoire de Lyon
Bull Obs Met Port Au Prince — Bulletin. Observatoire Meteorologique. Seminaire College St. Martial (Port-au-Prince)
Bull Obsns Magn Met Obs Jers — Bulletin des Observations Magnetiques et Meteorologiques faites a l'Observatoire de Jersey
Bull Obsns Met Commn Met Hte Loire — Bulletin des Observations Meteorologiques. Commission Meteorologique de la Haute Loire
Bull Obsns Met Dep Nievre — Bulletin des Observations Meteorologiques faites dans le Departement de la Nievre
Bull Obsns Obs Zi Ka Wei — Bulletin des Observations. Observatoire de Zi-Ka-Wei
Bull Obsn Upp Air Curr — Bulletin of the Observation of Upper Air Current
Bull Obs Puy De Dome — Bulletin. Observatoire du Puy De Dome
Bull Oceanogr Inst — Bulletin. Oceanographical Institute of Taiwan
Bull Ocean Res Inst Univ Tokyo — Bulletin. Ocean Research Institute. University of Tokyo
Bull OEPP — Bulletin OEPP
Bull Oerlikon — Bulletin Oerlikon
Bull of Computer Aided Archtl Design — Bulletin of Computer Aided Architectural Design
Bull Off Ass Med Dent Fr — Bulletin Officiel. Association des Medecins Dentistes de France
Bull Off Dir Rech Sci Ind Inv (Fr) — Bulletin Officiel. Direction des Recherches Scientifiques et Industrielles et des Inventions (France)
Bull Offic — Bulletin Officiel de la Propriete Industrielle
Bull Office Exper Stations US Dept Agric — Bulletin. Office of Experiment Stations. United States Department of Agriculture
Bull Office Surg Gen US War Dept — Bulletins. Office of the Surgeon General. United States War Department
Bull Offic Propriete Ind (Fr) — Bulletin Officiel de la Propriete Industrielle (France)
Bull Off Int Epizoot — Bulletin. Office International des Epizooties
Bull Off Int Hyg Publ — Bulletin Mensuel. Office International d'Hygiene Publique
Bull Off Int Vin — Bulletin de l'Office International de la Vigne et du Vin
Bull Off Off Int Cacao Choc — Bulletin Officiel. Office International du Cacao et du Chocolat
Bull Off Propr Ind Abr — Bulletin Officiel de la Propriete Industrielle. Abreges
Bull Off Propr Ind Brev Invent Abr Listes — Bulletin Officiel de la Propriete Industrielle. Brevets d'Invention, Abreges, et Listes
Bull Off Soc Fr Electrotherap — Bulletin Officiel. Societe Francaise d'Electrotherapie et de Radiologie
Bull Off Soc Int Psycho Proph Obstet — Bulletin Officiel. Societe Internationale de Psychoprophylaxie Obstetricale
Bull Ogata Inst Med Chem Res — Bulletin. Ogata Institute for Medical and Chemical Research
Bull (Ohio) — Weekly Law Bulletin (Ohio)
Bull Ohio Agr Exp Sta — Bulletin. Ohio Agricultural Experiment Station
Bull Ohio Agr Exp St — Bulletin. Ohio Agricultural Experiment Station
Bull Ohio Agric Exp Stn — Bulletin. Ohio Agricultural Experiment Station
Bull Ohio Biol Surv — Bulletin. Ohio Biological Survey
Bull Ohio Eng Exp St — Bulletin. Ohio Engineering Experiment Station
Bull Ohio State Univ Coop Ext Serv — Bulletin. Ohio State University. Cooperative Extension Service
Bull Ohio St Univ Co-Op Ext Serv — Bulletin. Ohio State University. Co-Operative Extension Service
Bull Oil Nat Gas Comm — Bulletin. Oil and Natural Gas Commission
Bull Oil Natur Gas Comm (India) — Bulletin. Oil and Natural Gas Commission (India)
Bull Oita Inst Technol — Bulletin. Oita Institute of Technology
Bull OIV — Bulletin de l'OIV
Bull Oji Inst Forest Tree Improv — Bulletin. Oji Institute for Forest Tree Improvement
Bull Oji Inst For Tree Impr — Bulletin. Oji Institute for Forest Tree Improvement
Bull Okayama Coll Sci — Bulletin. Okayama College of Science

Bull Okayama Tob Exp Stn — Bulletin. Okayama Tobacco Experiment Station
Bull Okayama Univ Sci — Bulletin. Okayama University of Science
Bull Okayama Univ Sci A Nat Sci — Bulletin. Okayama University of Science. A. Natural Science
Bull Okayama Univ Sci B Hum Sci — Bulletin. Okayama University of Science. B. Human Sciences
Bull Okinawa Prefect Agric Exp Sta — Bulletin. Okinawa Prefectural Agricultural Experiment Station/Okinawa Kenritsu Noji Shikenjo
Bull Okla Agric Exp St — Bulletin. Oklahoma Agricultural Experiment Station
Bull Okla Agric Exp Stn — Bulletin. Oklahoma Agricultural Experiment Station
Bull Okla Anthrop Soc — Bulletin. Oklahoma Anthropological Society
Bull Okla Dent Ass — Bulletin. Oklahoma State Dental Association
Bull Okla Geol Surv — Bulletin. Oklahoma Geological Survey
Bull Oklahoma Geol Surv — Bulletin. Oklahoma Geological Survey
Bull Okla Ornithol Soc — Bulletin. Oklahoma Ornithological Society
Bull Okla State Univ Agr Exp Sta — Bulletin. Oklahoma State University. Agricultural Experiment Station
Bull ONAF — Bulletin. Office National de Coordination des Allocations Familiales
Bull Ont Agric Coll — Bulletin. Ontario Agricultural College
Bull Ont Coll Pharm — Bulletin. Ontario College of Pharmacy
Bull Ont Dep Agric — Bulletin. Ontario Department of Agriculture
Bull Ont Med Ass — Bulletin. Ontario Medical Association
Bull Oper Res Soc Am — Bulletin. Operations Research Society of America
Bull Ophthalmol Soc Egypt — Bulletin. Ophthalmological Society of Egypt
Bull Ophth Soc Eg — Bulletin. Ophthalmological Society of Egypt
Bull Op Res Soc Am — Bulletin. Operations Research Society of America
Bull Oran — Bulletin Trimestriel. Societe de Geographie et d'Archeologie de la Province d'Oran
Bull Orange County Med Assoc — Bulletin. Orange County Medical Association
Bull Ordre Natl Pharm — Bulletin. Ordre National des Pharmaciens
Bull Ordre Pharm (Brussels) — Bulletin. Ordre des Pharmaciens (Brussels)
Bull Ore Agric Coll — Bulletin. Oregon Agricultural College
Bull Ore Agric Exp Stn — Bulletin. Oregon Agricultural Experiment Station
Bull Ore Ent Soc — Bulletin. Oregon Entomological Society
Bull Ore For Res Lab — Bulletin. Oregon State University. Forest Research Laboratory
Bull Oreg Agr Exp Sta — Bulletin. Oregon Agricultural Experiment Station
Bull Oreg Agric Exp St — Bulletin. Oregon Agricultural Experiment Station
Bull Organ Int Metrol Leg — Bulletin. Organisation Internationale de Metrologie Legale
Bull Organismes Off Pet Elev Hainaut — Bulletin des Organismes Officiels de Petit Elevage du Hainaut
Bull Organ Natuurw Onderz Indonesiee — Bulletin. Organisatie voor Natuurwetenschappelijk Onderzoek in Indonesiee/Bulletin. Organization for Scientific Research in Indonesia
Bull Org Int Metrol Leg — Bulletin. Organisation Internationale de Metrologie Legale
Bull Org Mond Sante — Bulletin. Organisation Mondiale de la Sante
Bull Org Natuurw Onderz — Bulletin. Organisatie voor Natuurwetenschappelijk Onderzoek
Bull Orient Cer Soc Hong Kong — Bulletin of the Oriental Ceramic Society of Hong Kong
Bull Orn Romand — Bulletin Ornithologique Romand
Bull Orn Soc Japan — Bulletin of the Ornithological Society of Japan
Bull Orn Soc NZ — Bulletin. Ornithological Society of New Zealand
Bull ORSA — Bulletin. Operations Research Society of America
Bull Orthop Brux — Bulletin d'Orthopedie (Bruxelles)
Bull Orton Soc — Bulletin. Orton Society
Bull Osaka Agric Res Cent — Bulletin. Osaka Agricultural Research Center
Bull Osaka Ind Res Inst — Bulletin. Osaka Industrial Research Institute
Bull Osaka Int Univ Women — Bulletin of the Osaka International University for Women
Bull Osaka Kun'ei Women's Jr Coll — Bulletin of Osaka Kun'ei Women's Junior College
Bull Osaka Med Coll — Bulletin of the Osaka Medical College
Bull Osaka Med Sch — Bulletin. Osaka Medical School
Bull Osaka Med Sch Suppl — Bulletin. Osaka Medical School. Supplement
Bull Osaka Munic Mus Nat Hist — Bulletin of the Osaka Municipal Museum of Natural History
Bull Osaka Munic Tech Res Inst — Bulletin. Osaka Municipal Technical Research Institute
Bull Osaka Mus Nat Hist — Bulletin. Osaka Museum of Natural History
Bull Osaka Prefect College Tech — Bulletin of Osaka Prefectural College of Technology
Bull Osaka Prefect Tech College — Bulletin. Osaka Prefectural Technical College
Bull Osaka Prefect Univ Ser A — Bulletin of Osaka Prefecture University. Series A. Engineering and Natural Sciences
Bull Osaka Prefect Univ Ser B — Bulletin of Osaka Prefecture University. Series B. Agriculture and Life Sciences
Bull Os Med Sch — Bulletin. Osaka Medical School
Bull Ostreic Marit Quart Marennes — Bulletin Ostreicole et Maritime du Quartier de Marennes
Bull Otago Catchm Bd — Bulletin. Otago Catchment Board
Bull Oto Lar Clins Beth Israel Hosp — Bulletin of the Oto-Laryngological Clinics of the Beth-Israel Hospital
Bull Oto Rhino Lar Paris — Bulletin d'Oto-Rhino-Laryngologie (Paris)
Bull Oxf Univ Explor Club — Bulletin. Oxford University Exploration Club
Bull Oxf Univ Inst Stat — Bulletin. Oxford University. Institute of Statistics
Bull Oxf Univ Inst Statist — Bulletin of the Oxford University Institute of Statistics
Bull PA Agr Exp Sta — Bulletin. Pennsylvania Agricultural Experiment Station
Bull PA Agric Exp Stn — Bulletin. Pennsylvania Agricultural Experiment Station
Bull Pac Coast Soc Orthod — Bulletin. Pacific Coast Society of Orthodontists
Bull Pacif Cst Soc Orthod — Bulletin of the Pacific Coast Society of Orthodontists
Bull Pacif Mar Fish Commn — Bulletin of the Pacific Marine Fisheries Commission
Bull Pacif Orchid Soc Haw — Bulletin. Pacific Orchid Society of Hawaii

Bull Pacif Rock Soc — Bulletin. Pacific Rocket Society

Bull Pac Orchid Soc Hawaii — Bulletin. Pacific Orchid Society of Hawaii

Bull Pac Trop Bot Gard — Bulletin. Pacific Tropical Botanical Garden

Bull Pa Flower Grow — Bulletin. Pennsylvania Flower Growers

Bull Paint Mfrs All Trades Ass — Bulletin. Paint Manufacturers' and Allied Trades Association

Bull Paint Mfrs Ass US Scient Sect — Bulletin. Paint Manufacturers' Association of the United States. Scientific Section

Bull Pal — Bullettino di Paletnologia Italiana

Bull Paleot Ital — Bullettino di Paleontologia Italiana

Bull Paletnol It — Bullettino di Paletnologia Italiana

Bull Palplanches — Bulletin des Palplanches

Bull Pan Amer Un — Bulletin of the Pan American Union

Bull Pan Am Health Organ — Bulletin. Pan American Health Organization

Bull Pan Am Sanit Bur — Bulletin of the Pan American Sanitary Bureau

Bull Pan Am Un Wash — Bulletin. Pan American Union (Washington, DC)

Bull Parasit Sheep — Bulletin. Parasites of Sheep

Bull Parent Drug Ass — Bulletin of the Parenteral Drug Association

Bull Parenter Drug Assoc — Bulletin. Parenteral Drug Association

Bull Passaic Cty Dent Soc — Bulletin. Passaic County Dental Society

Bull PA State Univ Agr Exp Sta — Bulletin. Pennsylvania State University. Agricultural Experiment Station

Bull Pasteur Inst — Bulletin of the Pasteur Institute

Bull Pasteur Inst Sth India — Bulletin of the Pasteur Institute of Southern India

Bull Pathol (Chicago) — Bulletin of Pathology (Chicago, Illinois)

Bull Patna Sci Coll Philos Soc — Bulletin. Patna Science College Philosophical Society

Bull Peab Mus Nat Hist — Bulletin. Peabody Museum of Natural History

Bull Peace Propos — Bulletin of Peace Proposals

Bull Peak Dist Mines Hist Soc — Bulletin. Peak District Mines Historical Society

Bull Peking Soc Nat Hist — Bulletin. Peking Society of Natural History

Bull Penns Agric Exp St — Bulletin. Pennsylvania Agricultural Experiment Station

Bull Penns St Dent Soc — Bulletin. Pennsylvania State Dental Society

Bull Peony News — Bulletin of Peony News. American Peony Society

Bull Perma Int Ass Navig Congr — Bulletin. Permanent International Association of Navigation Congresses

Bull Permanent Int Assoc Navigation Congresses — Bulletin. Permanent International Association of Navigation Congresses

Bull Perm Int Assoc Navig Congr — Bulletin. Permanent International Association of Navigation Congresses

Bull Pewter Colrs Club America — Bulletin of the Pewter Collectors' Club of America

Bull Pharm — Bulletin of Pharmacy

Bull Pharmacol (Beijing) — Bulletin of Pharmacology (Beijing)

Bull Pharm (Istanbul) — Bulletin of Pharmacy (Istanbul)

Bull Pharm Res Inst (Osaka) — Bulletin. Pharmaceutical Research Institute (Osaka)

Bull Pharm Sud Est — Bulletin de Pharmacie du Sud-Est

Bull Phila Cty Dent Soc — Bulletin. Philadelphia County Dental Society

Bull Philadelphia Astronaut Soc — Bulletin. Philadelphia Astronautical Society

Bull Philadelphia Mus A — Bulletin. Philadelphia Museum of Art

Bull Phila Herpetol Soc — Bulletin. Philadelphia Herpetological Society

Bull Philipp Biochem Soc — Bulletin. Philippine Biochemical Society

Bull Phil Mediev — Bulletin de Philosophie Medievale

Bull Philol & Hist Cte Trav Hist & Sci — Bulletin Philologique et Historique du Comite des Travaux Historiques et Scientifiques

Bull Philol Hist — Bulletin Philologique et Historique

Bull Philol Hist — Bulletin Philologique et Historique. Comite des Travaux Historiques et Scientifiques

Bull Phil Soc Wash — Bulletin. Philosophical Society of Washington

Bull Phot Club Paris — Bulletin du Photo-Club de Paris

Bull Photogramm — Bulletin de Photogrammetrie

Bull Phys Fitness Res Inst — Bulletin. Physical Fitness Research Institute

Bull Physio Pathol Respir — Bulletin de Physio-Pathologie Respiratoire

Bull Physiopathol Respir (Nancy) — Bulletin de Physiopathologie Respiratoire (Nancy)

Bull Pittsb Univ — Bulletin. Pittsburgh University

Bull Plankton Soc Jpn — Bulletin. Plankton Society of Japan

Bull Plant Bd Fla — Bulletin. Plant Board of Florida

Bull Plant Physiol (Beijing) — Bulletin. Plant Physiology (Beijing)

Bull P NSW Dep Agric Div Plant Ind — Bulletin P. New South Wales Department of Agriculture. Division of Plant Industry

Bull Pol Acad Sci Biol — Bulletin. Polish Academy of Sciences. Biology

Bull Pol Acad Sci Biol Sci — Bulletin. Polish Academy of Sciences. Biological Sciences

Bull Pol Acad Sci Chem — Bulletin. Polish Academy of Sciences. Chemistry

Bull Pol Acad Sci Earth Sci — Bulletin. Polish Academy of Sciences. Earth Sciences

Bull Pol Inst Arts Sci Am — Bulletin. Polish Institute of Arts and Sciences in America

Bull Pol Inst Arts Sci Amer — Bulletin. Polish Institute of Arts and Sciences in America

Bull Pol Inst Arts Sci America — Bulletin. Polish Institute of Arts and Sciences in America

Bull Polish Acad Sci Math — Bulletin of the Polish Academy of Sciences. Mathematics

Bull Polish Acad Sci Tech Sci — Bulletin of the Polish Academy of Sciences. Technical Sciences

Bull Pol Med Sci Hist — Bulletin of Polish Medical Science and History

Bull Popular Inform Arnold Arbor — Bulletin of Popular Information. Arnold Arboretum Harvard University

Bull Postgrad Inst Med Educ Res (Chandigarh) — Bulletin. Postgraduate Institute of Medical Education and Research (Chandigarh)

Bull Poznan Tow Przyjaciol Nauk Ser D — Bulletin. Poznanskie Towarzystwo Przyjaciol Nauk. Serie D

Bull Preh — Bulletin. Societe Prehistorique de France

Bull Pres Hist Soc Ir — Bulletin. Presbyterian Historical Society of Ireland

Bull Presse- Informationsamt Bundesregier — Bulletin. Presse- und Informationsamt der Bundesregierung

Bull Press Exchange Documn Cent Apimondia — Bulletin. Press Exchange and Documentation Centre of Apimondia

Bull Primary Tungsten Assoc — Bulletin. Primary Tungsten Association

Bull Proefstat Cacao Salatiga — Bulletin van het Proefstation voor Cacao te Salatiga

Bull Proefstn JavasuikInd Tech Afd — Bulletin. Proefstation voor de Javasuikerindustrie, Technische Afdeeling

Bull Proefstn Suikerreit W Java Kagok — Bulletin. Proefstation voor Suikerriet in West-Java, Kagok

Bull Prosthet Res — Bulletin of Prosthetics Research

Bull Protect Veg — Bulletin de la Protection des Vegetaux

Bull Prot Veg — Bulletin de la Protection des Vegetaux

Bull Provis Int Comput Cent — Bulletin of the Provisional International Computation Centre

Bull Psychiat Rehab — Bulletin on Psychiatric Rehabilitation

Bull Psychol Paris — Bulletin de Psychologie (Paris)

Bull Psycho Magn — Bulletin Psycho-Magnetique

Bull Psychon Soc — Bulletin. Psychonomic Society

Bull Publ Hlth Mar Hosp Serv — Bulletin of the Public Health and Marine-Hospital Service

Bull Public Health Inst Hyogo Prefect — Bulletin. Public Health Institute of Hyogo Prefecture

Bull Publ Libr NY — Bulletin. New York Public Library (New York)

Bull Publs Pwr Fuel — Bulletin of Publications dealing with Power and Fuel [Tokyo]

Bull Pub Mus City Milwaukee — Bulletin of the Public Museum of the City of Milwaukee

Bull Puerto Rico Agric Exp Stn Insular Stn (Rio Piedras) — Bulletin. Puerto Rico Agricultural Experiment Station. Insular Station (Rio Piedras)

Bull Puget Sound Mar Stn — Bulletin. Puget Sound Marine Station

Bull Punjab Agric Univ — Bulletin. Punjab Agricultural University

Bull Pure Appl Sci — Bulletin of Pure and Applied Sciences

Bull Pure Appl Sci Sec B — Bulletin of Pure and Applied Sciences. Section B. Plant Sciences

Bull Pure Appl Sci Sec E Math — Bulletin of Pure and Applied Sciences. Section E. Mathematics

Bull Pusan Fish Coll (Nat Sci) — Bulletin. Pusan Fisheries College (Natural Sciences)

Bull Quarant Serv Melb — Bulletin of the Quarantine Service (Melbourne)

Bull Que Soc Crim — Bulletin. Quebec Society of Criminology

Bull Quest Rep Parlem — Bulletin des Questions et Reponses Parlementaires

Bull Quetta Fruit Exp Stn — Bulletin of the Quetta Fruit Experiment Station

Bull Quezon Inst (Manila) — Bulletin. Quezon Institute (Manila)

Bull Quot Etud Off Natn Met — Bulletin Quotidien d'Etudes. Office National Meteorologique

Bull Quot Inst Cent Met Dan — Bulletin Quotidien del'Institut Central Meteorologique Danois

Bull Quot Int Off Natn Met — Bulletin Quotidien International. Office National Meteorologique

Bull Quot Obsns Met Natn — Bulletin Quotidien d'Observations. Meteorologie National

Bull Quot Obs R Belg — Bulletin Quotidien. Observatoire Royale de Belgique

Bull Quot Renseign Maroc Serv Met — Bulletin Quotidien de Renseignements du Maroc. Service Meteorologique

Bull Quot Renseign Met Afr N — Bulletin Quotidien de Renseignements Meteorologiques de l'Afrique du Nord

Bull Quot Renseign Off Natn Met — Bulletin Quotidien de Renseignements. Office National Meteorologique

Bull Quot Temps Athene — Bulletin Quotidien du Temps (Athene)

Bull Radiat Prot — Bulletin of Radiation Protection

Bull Radio Electr Eng Div Natl Res Counc Can — Bulletin. Radio and Electrical Engineering Division. National Research Council of Canada

Bull Radio Electr Eng Div Nat Res Counc Can — Bulletin. Radio and Electrical Engineering Division. National Research Council of Canada

Bull Radio Induct Interfer Ottawa — Bulletin. Radio Inductive Interference. Radio Branch. Department of Marine and Fisheries (Ottawa)

Bull Radioisot Res Inst Tokyo Univ Agric — Bulletin. Radioisotope Research Institute. Tokyo University of Agriculture

Bull Raffles Mus — Bulletin. Raffles Museum

Bull Rayon Silk Ass — Bulletin. Rayon and Silk Association

Bull R Col Psychiatr — Bulletin. Royal College of Psychiatrists

Bull Reading Publ Mus — Bulletin. Reading Public Museum and Art Gallery

Bull Rech Agron Gembloux — Bulletin des Recherches Agronomiques de Gembloux

Bull Rech Hist — Bulletin des Recherches Historiques

Bull Reg Res Lab (Jammu) — Bulletin. Regional Research Laboratory (Jammu)

Bull Reinf Concr Dep Fac Engng Egypt Univ — Bulletin. Reinforced Concrete Department. Faculty of Engineering. Egyptian University

Bull Relat Scient Inst Int Coop Intell — Bulletin des Relations Scientifiques. Institut International de Cooperation Intellectuelle

Bull Rem Sens Soc Aust — Remote Sensing Association of Australia. Bulletin

Bull Renseign Chamb Synd Maitr Verr Fr — Bulletin de Renseignements. Chambre Syndicale des Maitres de Verrerie de France

Bull Repub Inst Prot Nat Mus Nat Hist Titograd — Bulletin. Republic Institution for the Protection of Nature and the Museum of Natural History in Titograd

Bull Res Cent Archaeol Indonesia — Bulletin of the Research Centre of Archaeology of Indonesia

Bull Res Coll Agric Vet Sci Nihon Univ — Bulletin of Research. College of Agriculture and Veterinary Science. Nihon University

Bull Res Coll Agr Vet Med Nihon Univ — Bulletin of Research. College of Agriculture and Veterinary Medicine. Nihon University

Bull Res Council Israel — Bulletin. Research Council of Israel

Bull Res Council Israel Sect D Bot — Bulletin. Research Council of Israel. Section D. Botany

Bull Res Counc Isr — Bulletin. Research Council of Israel

Bull Res Counc Isr Sect A Chem — Bulletin. Research Council of Israel. Section A. Chemistry

Bull Res Counc Isr Sect A Math Phys Chem — Bulletin. Research Council of Israel. Section A. Mathematics, Physics, and Chemistry

Bull Res Counc Isr Sect B Biol Geol — Bulletin. Research Council of Israel. Section B. Biology and Geology

Bull Res Counc Isr Sect B Zool — Bulletin. Research Council of Israel. Section B. Zoology

Bull Res Counc Isr Sect C Technol — Bulletin. Research Council of Israel. Section C. Technology

Bull Res Counc Isr Sect D Bot — Bulletin. Research Council of Israel. Section D. Botany

Bull Res Counc Isr Sect E Exp Med — Bulletin. Research Council of Israel. Section E. Experimental Medicine

Bull Res Counc Isr Sect F — Bulletin. Research Council of Israel. Section F. Mathematics and Physics

Bull Res Counc Isr Sect G — Bulletin. Research Council of Israel. Section G. Geo-Sciences

Bull Res Counc Isr Sect G Geo-Sci — Bulletin. Research Council of Israel. Section G. Geo-Sciences

Bull Res Coun Israel — Bulletin. Research Council of Israel

Bull Reserve Bank — Bulletin. Reserve Bank of New Zealand

Bull Res Hum — Bulletin of Research in the Humanities

Bull Res Humanit — Bulletin of Research in the Humanities

Bull Res Inst Appl Electr — Bulletin. Research Institute of Applied Electricity

Bull Res Inst Appl Mech Kyushu Univ — Bulletin. Research Institute for Applied Mechanics. Kyushu University

Bull Res Inst Bioresour Okayama Univ — Bulletin. Research Institute for Bioresources. Okayama University

Bull Res Inst Diathetic Med Kumamoto Univ — Bulletin. Research Institute for Diathetic Medicine. Kumamoto University

Bull Res Inst Electron Shizuoka Univ — Bulletin. Research Institute of Electronics. Shizuoka University

Bull Res Inst Ferment Yamanashi Univ — Bulletin. Research Institute of Fermentation. Yamanashi University

Bull Res Inst Food Sci Kyoto Univ — Bulletin. Research Institute for Food Science. Kyoto University

Bull Res Inst Mater Sci Eng Fac Eng Fukui Univ — Bulletin. Research Institute for Material Science and Engineering. Faculty of Engineering. Fukui University

Bull Res Inst Min Dressing Metall — Bulletin. Research Institute of Mineral Dressing and Metallurgy

Bull Res Inst Miner Dressing Metall Tohoku Univ — Bulletin. Research Institute of Mineral Dressing and Metallurgy. Tohoku University

Bull Res Inst Nat Sci Okayama Univ Sci — Bulletin of Research Institute of Natural Sciences. Okayama University of Scienc

Bull Res Inst Polymers Textiles — Bulletin. Research Institute for Polymers and Textiles

Bull Res Inst Sci Meas Tohoku Univ — Bulletin. Research Institute for Scientific Measurements. Tohoku University

Bull Res Inst Sumatra Plant Assoc — Bulletin. Research Institute. Sumatra Plantations Association

Bull Res Inst Univ Kerala (Trivandrum) Ser A — Bulletin. Research Institute. University of Kerala (Trivandrum). Series A. Physical Sciences

Bull Res Lab Nucl React Tokyo Inst Technol — Bulletin. Research Laboratory for Nuclear Reactors. Tokyo Institute of Technology

Bull Res Lab Precis Mach and Electron — Bulletin. Research Laboratory of Precision Machinery and Electronics

Bull Res Lab Precis Mach Electron — Bulletin. Research Laboratory of Precision Machinery and Electronics

Bull Res Lab Precis Mach Electron Tokyo Inst Technol — Bulletin. Research Laboratory of Precision Machinery and Electronics. Tokyo Institute of Technology

Bull Res Music Ed — Bulletin of Research in Music Education

Bull Rheum Dis — Bulletin on Rheumatic Diseases

Bull Rhode Isl Agric Exp Stn — Bulletin. Rhode Island Agricultural Experiment Station

Bull Rhod Geol Surv — Bulletin. Rhodesia Geological Survey

Bull RI Agric Exp Stn — Bulletin. Rhode Island Agricultural Experiment Station

Bull Richmond County Med Soc — Bulletin. Richmond County Medical Society

Bull Rijksmus — Bulletin. Rijksmuseum

Bull RILEM — Bulletin R.I.L.E.M (Reunion Internationale des Laboratoires d'Essais et de Recherches sur les Materiaux et les Constructions)

Bull Riverside County Med Assoc — Bulletin. Riverside County Medical Association

Bull Rly Loco Hist Soc — Bulletin of the Railway and Locomotive Historical Society

Bull Rly Tech Lab Tokyo — Bulletin of the Railway Technical Laboratory (Tokyo)

Bull ROM — Bulletin. Royal Ontario Museum. Art and Archaeology Division

Bull Roum — Academie Roumaine. Bulletin de la Section Historique

Bull Roy Soc New Zealand — Bulletin. Royal Society of New Zealand

Bull Rubber Grow Assoc — Bulletin. Rubber Growers Association

Bull Rubber Res Inst Malaya — Bulletin. Rubber Research Institute of Malaya

Bull Rur Econ Sociology — Bulletin of Rural Economics and Sociology

Bull Rylands Libr — Bulletin. John Rylands Library

Bull S A D G — Bulletin de la Societe des Architectes Diplomes par le Gouvernement

Bull S Afr Cult Hist Mus — Bulletin. South African Cultural History Museum

Bull S Afr Inst Assayers Anal — Bulletin. South African Institute of Assayers and Analysts

Bull Saga Agr Exp Sta — Bulletin. Saga Agricultural Experiment Station

Bull Saga Agric Exp Sta — Bulletin. Saga Agricultural Experiment Station/Saga-Ken Nogyo Shikenjo Kenkyu Hokoku

Bull Saginaw County Med Soc — Bulletin. Saginaw County Medical Society

Bull Saitama Hortic Exp Stn — Bulletin. Saitama Horticultural Experiment Station

Bull Salesian Polytech — Bulletin. Salesian Polytechnic

Bulls Am Paleontology — Bulletins of American Paleontology

Bull Sandal Spike Invest Comm — Bulletin. Sandal Spike Investigation Committee

Bull San Diego Cty Dent Soc — Bulletin. San Diego County Dental Society

Bull Sanit Alger — Bulletin Sanitaire de l'Algerie

Bull Sanit Brux — Bulletin Sanitaire (Bruxelles)

Bull Sanit Constantinople — Bulletin Sanitaire de Constantinople

Bull Sanit Montreal — Bulletin Sanitaire (Montreal)

Bull Sanit Paris — Bulletin Sanitaire (Paris)

Bull San Mateo County Med Soc — Bulletin. San Mateo County Medical Society

Bull San Mateo Cty Dent Soc — Bulletin. San Mateo [*California*] County Dental Society

Bull Santa Clara County Med Soc — Bulletin. Santa Clara County Medical Society

Bull Sante Prod Anim Afr — Bulletin des Sante et Production Animales en Afrique

Bull Sante Publ Brux — Bulletin de la Sante Publique (Bruxelles)

Bull Sanyo Gakuen Coll — Bulletin of Sanyo Gakuen College

Bull Sanyo Gakuen Jr Coll — Bulletin of Sanyo Gakuen Junior College

Bull Sapporo Branch Forest Exp Sta — Bulletin. Sapporo Branch. Forestry Experiment Station/Hokkaido Ringyo Shiken Hokoku

Bull Sapporo Brch Govt Forest Exp Stn — Bulletin of the Sapporo Branch of the Government Forest Experiment Station

Bull Sarajevo — Glasnik Zemaljskog Muzeja Bosne i Hercegovine u Sarajevu

Bull Sask Univ Coll Agric Ext Dep — Bulletin. Saskatchewan University College of Agriculture. Extension Department

Bull SC Acad Sci — Bulletin. South Carolina Academy of Science

Bull SC Agric Exp Stn — Bulletin. South Carolina Agricultural Experiment Station

Bull S Cal Acad Sci — Bulletin. Southern California Academy of Sciences

Bull Sch Agric For Taihoku Imp Univ — Bulletin of the School of Agriculture and Forestry. Taihoku Imp. University

Bull Sch Fish Hokkaido Imp Univ — Bulletin of the School of Fishery. Hokkaido Imperial Univerisity

Bull Sch For Agric Exp Stn Univ Minn — Bulletin. School of Forestry Agricultural Experiment Station. University of Minnesota

Bull Sch For Conserv Univ Mich — Bulletin of the School of Forestry and Conservation. University of Michigan

Bull Sch For Duke Univ — Bulletin. School of Forestry. Duke University

Bull Sch For Montana St Univ — Bulletin. School of Forestry. Montana State University

Bull Sch For Mont St Univ — Bulletin. School of Forestry. Montana State University

Bull Sch For S F Austin St Coll — Bulletin. School of Forestry. Stephen F. Austin State College

Bull Sch For Univ Idaho — Bulletin. School of Forestry. University of Idaho

Bull Sch For Univ Melb — Bulletin. School of Forestry. University of Melbourne

Bull Sch For Yale Univ — Bulletin. School of Forestry. Yale University

Bull Sch Med Univ MD — Bulletin. School of Medicine. University of Maryland

Bull Sch Med Wash Univ — Bulletin of the School of Medicine. Washington University

Bull School Eng Archit Sakarya — Bulletin. School of Engineering and Architecture of Sakarya

Bull School Orient African Stud — Bulletin. School of Oriental and African Studies

Bull Sch Orient Afr Stud — Bulletin. School of Oriental and African Studies

Bull Sch Orient Afr Stud Lond — Bulletin of the School of Oriental and African Studies (London)

Bull Sch Oriental Afr Stud — Bulletin. School of Oriental and African Studies

Bull Sch Orient Stud — Bulletin. School of Oriental Studies

Bull Schweiz Akad Med Wiss — Bulletin. Schweizerische Akademie der Medizinischen Wissenschaften

Bull Schweiz Electrotech Ver — Bulletin. Schweizerischer Elektrotechnischer Verein

Bull Schweiz Ges Anthropol Ethnol — Bulletin. Schweizerische Gesellschaft fuer Anthropologie und Ethnologie

Bull Schweiz GesundhAmt — Bulletin des Schweizerischen Gesundheitsamtes

Bull Schweiz Verein Krebsbekaempf — Bulletin der Schweizerischen Vereinigung fuer Krebsbekaempfung

Bull Sci Acad Imp Sci Saint Petersbourg — Bulletin Scientifique. Academie Imperiale des Sciences de Saint Petersbourg

Bull Sci Assoc Ing Electr Inst Electrotech (Montefiore) — Bulletin Scientifique. Association des Ingenieurs Electriciens Sortis de l'Institut Electrotechnique (Montefiore)

Bull Sci Bourgogne — Bulletin Scientifique de Bourgogne

Bull Sci Clubs India — Bulletin. Science Clubs of India

Bull Sci Cons Acad RSF Yougosl — Bulletin Scientifique. Conseil des Academies de la RSF de Yougoslavie

Bull Sci Cons Acad RSF Yougosl Sect A Sci Nat Tech Med — Bulletin Scientifique. Conseil des Academies de la RSF de Yougoslavie. Section A. Sciences Naturelles, Techniques, et Medicales

Bull Sci Cons Acad Sci Arts RSF Yougosl Sect A — Bulletin Scientifique. Conseil des Academies des Sciences et des Arts de la RSFde Yougoslavie. Section A. Sciences Naturelles, Techniques, et Medicales

Bull Sci Conseil Acad RSF Yougoslav Sect A — Bulletin Scientifique. Conseil des Academies de la RSF de Yougoslavie. Section A

Bull Sci Dep Nord Pays Voisins — Bulletin Scientifique, Historique, et Litteraire du Department du Nord et des Pays Voisins

Bull Sci Ecole Polytech Timisoara — Bulletin Scientifique. Ecole Polytechnique de Timisoara. Comptes Rendus des Seances. Societe Scientifique de Timisoara

Bull Sci Econ Bur Rech Minieres Alger — Bulletin Scientifique et Economique. Bureau de Recherches Minieres de l'Algerie

Bull Sci Eng Res Lab Waseda Univ — Bulletin. Science and Engineering Research Laboratory. Waseda University

Bull Sci Engrg Div Univ Ryukyus Math Natur Sci — Bulletin. University of the Ryukyus. Science and Engineering Division. Mathematics and Natural Sciences

Bull Scient France et Belgique — Bulletin Scientifique de la France et de la Belgique

Bull Scient Fr Belg — Bulletin Scientifique de la France et de la Belgique

Bull Sci Geogr — Bulletin des Sciences Geographiques, Economie Publique, Voyages

Bull Sci Geol — Bulletin des Sciences Geologiques

Bull Sci Hist Auvergne — Bulletin Scientifique et Historique de l'Auvergne

Bull Sci Ind Maison Roure Bertrand Fils — Bulletin Scientifique et Industriel de la Maison Roure Bertrand Fils

Bull Sci Inst Text Fr — Bulletin Scientifique. Institut Textile de France

Bull Sci ITF — Bulletin Scientifique. Institut Textile de France

Bull Sci Lab Denison Univ — Bulletin. Scientific Laboratories of Denison University

Bull Sci Math — Bulletin des Sciences Mathematiques

Bull Sci Math (2) — Bulletin des Sciences Mathematiques (2e Serie)

Bull Sci Pharmacol — Bulletin des Sciences Pharmacologiques

Bull Sci Phys Nat Neerl — Bulletin des Sciences Physiques et Naturelles en Neerlande

Bull Sci Res Alumni Assoc Morioka Coll Agric — Bulletin. Scientific Researches. Alumni Association. Morioka College of Agriculture and Forestry/Morioka Kono Dosokai Gakujutsu Iho

Bull Sci Roumain — Bulletin Scientifique Roumain

Bull Sci Sect A — Bulletin Scientifique. Section A. Sciences Naturelles, Techniques, et Medicales

Bull Sci Ser — Bulletin's Science Series

Bull Sci Tech Doc Cent (Egypt) — Bulletin. Scientific and Technical Documentation Centre (Egypt)

Bull Sci Tech Inst Polytech Timisoara — Bulletin de Science et Technique. Institut Polytechnique de Timisoara

Bull Sci Technol Agency — Bulletin. Science and Technology Agency

Bull Sci Technol Soc — Bulletin of Science, Technology, and Society

Bull Sci Terre Univ Poitiers — Bulletin. Sciences de la Terre. Universite de Poitiers

Bull Scot Georg Soc — Bulletin of the Scottish Georgian Society

Bull Scott Assoc Geogr Teach — Bulletin. Scottish Association of Geography Teachers

Bull Scott Georgian Soc — Bulletin. Scottish Georgian Society

Bull Scripps Inst Oceanogr Univ Calif — Bulletin. Scripps Institution of Oceanography of the University of California

Bull Sc Soc Philomat Paris — Bulletin des Sciences. Societe Philomathique de Paris

Bull SC State Dev Board — Bulletin. South Carolina. State Development Board

Bull S Dak Agr Exp Sta — Bulletin. South Dakota Agricultural Experiment Station

Bull S Dak Agric Exp St — Bulletin. South Dakota Agricultural Experiment Station

Bull S Dak Sch Mines — Bulletin of the South Dakota School of Mines

Bull SD Geol Surv — Bulletin. South Dakota Geological Survey

Bull S Diego Cty Dent Soc — Bulletin of the San Diego County Dental Society

Bull Sean Acad Roy Sci Outre-Mer — Bulletin des Seances. Academie Royale des Sciences d'Outre-Mer

Bull Seanc Acad R Sci Outre Mer — Bulletin des Seances. Academie Royale des Sciences d'Outre-Mer

Bull Seances Acad Roy Sci Outre Mer — Bulletin des Seances. Academie Royale des Sciences d'Outre-Mer

Bull Seances Acad R Sci Outre-Mer (Brussels) — Bulletin des Seances. Academie Royale des Sciences d'Outre-Mer (Brussels)

Bull Seances Inst Roy Colon Belge — Bulletin des Seances. Institut Royal Colonial Belge/Bulletin der Zittingen. Koninklijk Belgisch Koloniaalinstitut

Bull Seances IRCB — Bulletin des Seances. Institut Royal Colonial Belge

Bull Seanc Soc Sci Nancy — Bulletin des Seances. Societe des Sciences de Nancy et Reunion Biologique de Nancy

Bull S East Un Scient Socs — Bulletin of the South Eastern Union of Scientific Societies

Bull Sea View Hosp — Bulletin. Sea View Hospital

Bull Sec Agron Div Tokai-Kinki Natl Agric Exp Stn — Bulletin. Second Agronomy Division. Tokai-Kinki National Agricultural Experiment Station

Bull Second Agron Div Tokai-Kinki Nat Agr Exp Sta — Bulletin. Second Agronomy Division. Tokai-Kinki National Agricultural Experiment Station

Bull Second Dist Dent Soc — Bulletin. Second District Dental Society

Bull Sect Geogr Comite Trav Hist Sci — Bulletin. Section de Geographie. Comite des Travaux Historiques et Scientifiques. Ministere de l'Instruction Publique et des Beaux Arts. Ministere de l'Education Nationale

Bull Sect Hist Acad Roumaine — Bulletin. Section Historique. Academie Roumaine

Bull Sect Hist Mod Contemp — Bulletin. Section d'Histoire Moderne et Contemporaine. Comite des Travaux Historiques et Scientifiques

Bull Sect Log — Bulletin. Section of Logic

Bull Sect Logic Univ Lodz — University of Lodz. Department of Logic. Bulletin of the Section of Logic

Bull Sect Sc Ac Roum — Bulletin. Section Scientifique. Academie Roumaine

Bull Sect Sci Acad Roum — Bulletin. Section Scientifique. Academie Roumaine

Bull Seikai Reg Fish Res Lab — Bulletin. Seikai Regional Fisheries Research Laboratory

Bull Seishin Igaku Inst — Bulletin. Seishin Igaku Institute

Bull Seishin Igaku Inst (Seishin Igaku Kenkyusho Gyosekishu) — Bulletin. Seishin Igaku Institute (Seishin Igaku Kenkyusho Gyosekishu)

Bull Seism Obs Weston Coll — Bulletin. Seismological Observatory. Weston College

Bull Seismol Soc Am — Bulletin. Seismological Society of America

Bull Seismol Soc Amer — Bulletin. Seismological Society of America

Bull Seismol Soc America — Bulletin of Seismological Society of America

Bull Seismol (Warsaw) — Bulletin Seismologique (Warsaw)

Bull Seism Soc Am — Bulletin. Seismological Society of America

Bull Seism Stn Harvard — Bulletin of the Seismological Station. Harvard

Bull Seism Stn Ivigtut — Bulletin of the Seismological Station. Ivigtut

Bull Seism Stn Nord — Bulletin of the Seismological Station Nord

Bull Seism Stn Scoresby Sund — Bulletin of the Seismological Station. Scoresby-Sund

Bull Semest Huil Essent — Bulletin Semestriel des Huiles Essentielles, Parfums Synthetiques

Bull Semest Obs Met Semin Coll St Martial — Bulletin Semestriel de l'Observatoire Meteorologique du Seminaire College Saint-Martial

Bull Semest Off Natn Anti Acrid — Bulletin Semestriel de l'Office National Anti-Acridien

Bull Semet Solvay — Bulletin of the Semet-Solvay and Piette Coke Oven Co., Ltd.

Bull Sen Stor Patria — Bullettino Senese di Storia Patria

Bull Seoul Natl Univ For — Bulletin. Seoul National University Forests

Bull Seoul Natl Univ For Seoul Taehakyo Yonsuplim Pogo — Bulletin. Seoul National University Forests/Seoul Taehakkyo Yonsuplim Pogo

Bull Ser Br Rlys Perform Effic Tests — Bulletin Series. British Railways. Performance and Efficiency Tests

Bull Ser C Soc Geol Mineral Bretagne — Bulletin. Serie C. Societe Geologique et Mineralogique de Bretagne

Bull Ser Exp Stn Gov Gen Chosen — Bulletin. Sericultural Experiment Station. Government General of Chosen

Bull Ser Fla Engng Ind Exp Stn — Bulletin Series. Florida Engineering and Industrial Experiment Station

Bull Seric Exp Stn Gov Gen Chosen — Bulletin. Sericultural Experiment Station. Government-General of Chosen

Bull Seric Exp Stn Japan — Bulletin of the Sericultural Experiment Station. Japan

Bull Seric Exp Stn Miyagi Prefect — Bulletin. Sericultural Experimental Station of Miyagi Prefecture

Bull Seric Exp Stn (Tokyo) — Bulletin. Sericultural Experiment Station (Tokyo)

Bull Seric Exp Stn Tsukuba gun Jpn — Bulletin. Sericultural Experiment Station (Tsukuba-gun, Japan)

Bull Seric Fr — Bulletin Sericicole Francais

Bull Seric Silk Ind — Bulletin. Sericulture and Silk Industry

Bull Serol Mus New Brunsw — Bulletin. Serological Museum (New Brunswick)

Bull Ser Ore St Coll Engng Exp Stn — Bulletin Series. Oregon State College Engineering Experiment Station

Bull Ser S Afr Orn Un — Bulletin Series. South African Ornithologists' Union

Bull Ser Technol Dir Agric Elev Forets Sect Tech Agric Trop — Bulletin. Serie Technologique. Direction de l'Agriculture, de l'Elevage et des Forets. Section Technique d'Agriculture Tropicale

Bull Serum Antituberc Dr Aiguilere — Bulletin du Serum Antituberculeux du Dr. Aiguillere

Bull Ser Univ Ill Engng Exp Stn — Bulletin Series. University of Illinois Engineering Experiment Station

Bull Serv Agric Tunis — Bulletin. Service de l'Agriculture de Tunisie

Bull Serv Arboric Prov Queb — Bulletin du Service de l'Arboriculture de la Province de Quebec

Bull Serv Biogeogr Univ Montreal — Bulletin du Service de Biogeographie. Universite de Montreal

Bull Serv Bot Agron Tunis — Bulletin. Service Botanique et Agronomique de Tunisie

Bull Serv Carte Geol Alger — Bulletin. Service de la Carte Geologique de l'Algerie

Bull Serv Carte Geol Alger Ser 1 — Bulletin. Service de la Carte Geologique. Algerie. Serie 1. Paleontologie

Bull Serv Carte Geol Alger Ser 2 — Bulletin. Service de la Carte Geologique de l'Algerie. Serie 2. Stratigraphie

Bull Serv Carte Geol Alger Ser 3 — Bulletin. Service de la Carte Geologique de l'Algerie. Serie 3. Geologie Appliquee

Bull Serv Carte Geol Alger Ser 4 — Bulletin. Service de la Carte Geologique. Algerie. Serie 4. Geophysique

Bull Serv Carte Geol Alger Ser 5 — Bulletin. Service de la Carte Geologique de l'Algerie. Serie 5. Petrographie

Bull Serv Carte Geol Alger Ser 6 — Bulletin. Service de la Carte Geologique de l'Algerie. Serie 6. Metallogenie

Bull Serv Carte Geol Alger Trav Rec — Bulletin du Service de la Carte Geologique de l'Algerie. Travaux Recents des Collaborateurs

Bull Serv Carte Geol Alsace Lorraine — Bulletin du Service de la Carte Geologique d'Alsace et de Lorraine

Bull Serv Carte Geol Als Lorr — Bulletin. Service de la Carte Geologique d'Alsace et de Lorraine

Bull Serv Carte Geol Fr — Bulletin. Service de la Carte Geologique de la France

Bull Serv Carte Geol Fr Topogr Souterr — Bulletin. Services de la Carte Geologique de la France et des Topographies Souterraines

Bull Serv Carte Phytogeogr Ser A — Bulletin du Service de la Carte Phytogeographique. Ser. A. Carte de la Vegetation

Bull Serv Carte Phytogeogr Ser B — Bulletin du Service de la Carte Phytogeographique. Ser. B. Carte des Groupements Vegetaux

Bull Serv Cult Etud Peuplier et Saule — Bulletin. Service de Culture et d'Etudes du Peuplier et du Saule

Bull Serv Eaux Forets Alger — Bulletin. Service des Eaux et Forets en Algerie

Bull Serv Elect Inst Phys Univ Brux — Bulletin. Service d'Electricite. Institut de Physique. Universite Libre de Bruxelles

Bull Serv Ent Queb — Bulletin du Service d'Entomologie (Quebec)

Bull Serv Et — Bulletin. Service des Etudes et de la Documentation Economiques. Office de la Statistique Generale

Bull Serv For Queb — Bulletin. Service Forestier (Quebec)

Bull Serv Geol Geophys RP Serbie — Bulletin. Service Geologique et Geophysique. RP de Serbie

Bull Serv Geol Luxemb — Bulletin. Service Geologique du Luxembourg

Bull Serv Geol Pol — Bulletin Service Geologique de Pologne

Bull Serv Geol (Rwanda) — Bulletin. Service Geologique (Rwanda)

Bull Serv Geol Rwandaise — Bulletin. Service Geologique de la Republique Rwandaise

Bull Serv Instrum Mes — Bulletin. Service des Instruments de Mesure

Bull Serv Med Trav — Bulletin. Service Medical du Travail

Bull Serv Mines Cameroun Territ — Bulletin de Service des Mines. Cameroun, Territoire

Bull Ser Weld Res Coun — Bulletin Series. Welding Research Council
Bull S Essex Nat Hist Soc — Bulletin. South Essex Natural History Society
Bull Sete — Bulletin. Societe d'Etudes Scientifiques de Sete et de la Region
Bulls et Mem Soc Anthrop Paris — Bulletins et Memoires. Societe d'Anthropologie de Paris
Bull SEV — Bulletin. Schweizerischer Elektrotechnischer Verein
Bull SFN — Bulletin. Societe Francaise de Numismatique
Bull Shanghai Sci Inst — Bulletin. Shanghai Science Institute
Bull Shemane Agric Exp Stn — Bulletin. Shemane Agricultural Experiment Station
Bull Shenyang Inst Geol Miner Resour — Bulletin. Shenyang Institute of Geology and Mineral Resources
Bull Shiga Pref Agr Exp Sta — Bulletin. Shiga Prefectural Agricultural Experiment Station
Bull Shiga Prefect Agric Exp Stn — Bulletin. Shiga Prefecture Agricultural Experiment Station
Bull Shiga Prefect Livest Res Improv Inst — Bulletin of the Shiga Prefectural Livestock Research and Improvement Institute
Bull Shih Yen Pao Kao Taiwan For Res Inst — Bulletin. Shih Yen Pao Kao. Taiwan Forest Research Institute
Bull Shikoku Agr Exp Sta — Bulletin. Shikoku Agricultural Experiment Station
Bull Shikoku Agric Exp Stn — Bulletin. Shikoku Agricultural Experiment Station
Bull Shikoku Natl Agric Exp Stn — Bulletin. Shikoku National Agricultural Experiment Station
Bull Shikoku Natl Agric Exp Stn Extra Issue — Bulletin. Shikoku National Agricultural Experiment Station. Extra Issue
Bull Shimane Agr Coll — Bulletin. Shimane Agricultural College
Bull Shimane Agr Exp Sta — Bulletin. Shimane Agricultural Experiment Station
Bull Shimane Agric Coll — Bulletin. Shimane Agricultural College
Bull Shimane Agric Exp Stn — Bulletin. Shimane Agricultural Experiment Station
Bull Shimane Prefect For Exp Stn — Bulletin. Shimane Prefecture Forestry Experiment Station
Bull Shimane Univ Nat Sci — Bulletin. Shimane University. Natural Science
Bull Shinshu Univ For — Bulletin. Shinshu University Forests
Bull Shinshu Univ Forest — Bulletin. Shinshu University Forest/Shinshu Daigaku Nogaku-Bu Enshurin Hokoku
Bull Shizuoka Agr Exp Sta — Bulletin. Shizuoka Agricultural Experiment Station
Bull Shizuoka Daigaku Nogaku-Bu — Bulletin. Shizuoka Daigaku Nogaku-Bu
Bull Shizuoka Inst Environ Hyg — Bulletin of Shizuoka Institute of Environment and Hygiene
Bull Shizuoka Pref Agr Exp Sta — Bulletin. Shizuoka Prefectural Agricultural Experiment Station
Bull Shizuoka Prefect Agric Exp Sta — Bulletin of Shizuoka Prefecture Agricultural Experiment Station/Shizuoka-Ken Nogyo Shikenjo Kenkyu Hokoku
Bull Shizuoka Prefect Fish Exp Stn — Bulletin. Shizuoka Prefectural Fisheries Experiment Station
Bull Shizuoka Prefect For Exp Stn — Bulletin. Shizuoka Prefecture Forestry Experiment Station
Bull Shizuoka Prefect Inst Public Health — Bulletin. Shizuoka Prefecture Institute of Public Health
Bull Shizuoka Prefect Inst Public Health Environ Sci — Bulletin. Shizuoka Prefecture Institute of Public Health and Environmental Science
Bull SHPF — Bulletin. Societe de l'Histoire du Protestantisme Francais
Bull Shrimp Cult Res Cent — Bulletin. Shrimp Culture Research Center
Bull Signal — Bulletin Signaletique
Bull Signal 17 Biol Physiol Veg — Bulletin Signaletique. Section 17. Biologie et Physiologie Vegetales
Bull Signal 221 — Bulletin Signaletique 221. Gitologie Economie Miniere
Bull Signal Ent Med Vet — Bulletin Signaletique. Entomologie Medicale et Veterinaire
Bull Sign Polym Peint Bois Cuirs — Bulletin Signaletique. Polymeres, Peintures, Bois, Cuirs
Bull Sinai Hosp Detroit — Bulletin. Sinai Hospital of Detroit
Bull S Indian Med Un — Bulletin of the South Indian Medical Union
Bull Singapore Natl Inst Chem — Bulletin. Singapore National Institute of Chemistry
Bull S Juan de Dios Hosp Manila — Bulletin of the San Juan de Dios Hospital of Manila
Bull Skloprojektu — Bulletin Skloprojektu
Bull SL — Bulletin. Societe de Linguistique de Paris
Bull Sloane Hosp Women Columbia-Presbyt Med Cent — Bulletin. Sloane Hospital for Women in the Columbia-Presbyterian Medical Center
Bull Slov Chem Soc — Bulletin. Slovene Chemical Society
Bull Slov Pol'nohospod Akad Vysk Ustavu Potravin — Bulletin. Slovenskej Pol'nohospodarskej Akademie. Vyskumneho Ustavu Potravinarskeho
Bull Small Scale Ind in Afr — Bulletin of Small Scale Industry in Africa
Bull S NSW Dep Agric — Bulletin S. New South Wales Department of Agriculture
Bull SOAS — Bulletin. School of Oriental and African Studies
Bull Soc A & Hist Dioc Liege — Bulletin de la Societe d'Art et d'Histoire du Diocese de Liege
Bull Soc Acad Antiqua Morinie — Bulletin de la Societe Academique des Antiquaires de la Morinie
Bull Soc Acad Laon — Bulletin de la Societe Academique de Laon
Bull Soc Acad Sci Agric A & B Lett Dept Var — Bulletin de la Societe Academique des Sciences, Agricultures, Arts, et Belles-Lettres du Departement du Var
Bull Soc Acup — Bulletin. Societe d'Acupuncture
Bull Soc A E — Bulletin des Societes Artistiques de l'Est
Bull Soc A Fr — Bulletin de la Societe de l'Art Francais
Bull Soc Afr Church Hist — Bulletin. Society for African Church History
Bull Soc Africanistes — Bulletin de la Societe des Africanistes
Bull Soc Agric Alg — Bulletin. Societe d'Agriculture d'Alger
Bull Soc Agric Dep Ardeche — Bulletin de la Societe d'Agriculture du Department de l'Ardeche
Bull Soc Agric Fr — Bulletin. Societe des Agriculteurs de France
Bull Soc Agricrs Fr — Bulletin. Societe des Agriculteurs de France

Bull Soc Agric Sarthe — Bulletin. Societe d'Agriculture, Sciences, et Arts de la Sarthe
Bull Soc Agr Sci Arts Sarthe — Bulletin. Societe d'Agriculture, Sciences, et Arts de la Sarthe
Bull Soc Alex — Bulletin. Societe d'Archeologie d'Alexandrie
Bull Soc Alsac Constr Mec — Bulletin. Societe Alsacienne de Construction Mecanique
Bull Soc Amis A Dept Eure — Bulletin de la Societe des Amis d'Art du Departement de l'Eure
Bull Soc Amis Andre-Marie Ampere — Bulletin. Societe des Amis d'Andre-Marie Ampere
Bull Soc Amis Bibl Ecole Polytech — Societe des Amis de la Bibliotheque de l'Ecole Polytechnique. Bulletin
Bull Soc Amis Chateau Pau — Bulletin de la Societe des Amis du Chateau de Pau
Bull Soc Amis Mnmts Paris — Bulletin de la Societe des Amis des Monuments Parisiens
Bull Soc Amis Mnmts Rouen — Bulletin de la Societe des Amis des Monuments Rouennais
Bull Soc Amis Mus Barbier Mueller — Bulletin de la Societe des Amis du Musee Barbier-Mueller
Bull Soc Amis Mus Dijon — Bulletin de la Societe des Amis du Musee de Dijon
Bull Soc Amis Sci Lett Poz — Bulletin. Societe des Amis des Sciences et des Lettres de Poznan
Bull Soc Amis Sci Lett Poznan Ser B — Bulletin. Societe des Amis des Sciences et des Lettres de Poznan. Serie B. Sciences Mathematiques et Naturelles
Bull Soc Amis Sci Lett Poznan Ser C — Bulletin. Societe des Amis des Sciences et des Lettres de Poznan. Serie C. Medecine
Bull Soc Amis Sci Lett Poznan Ser D — Bulletin. Societe des Amis des Sciences et des Lettres de Poznan. Serie D. Sciences Biologiques
Bull Soc Amis Sci Lett Poznan Ser D Sci Biol — Bulletin. Societe des Amis des Sciences et des Lettres de Poznan. Serie D. Sciences Biologiques
Bull Soc Amis Sci Nat Rouen — Bulletin de la Societe des Amis des Sciences Naturelles de Rouen
Bull Soc Amis Sci Nat Vienne — Bulletin de la Societe des Amis des Sciences Naturelles de Vienne
Bull Soc Amis Sci Poznan Ser B — Bulletin. Societe des Amis des Sciences de Poznan. Serie B. Sciences Mathematiques et Naturelles
Bull Soc Amis Univ Lyon — Bulletin de la Societe des Amis de l'Universite de Lyon
Bull Soc Amis Vienne — Bulletin de la Societe des Amis de Vienne
Bull Soc Amis Vieux Chinon — Bulletin de la Societe des Amis du Vieux Chinon
Bull Soc Analyt Chem — Bulletin. Society for Analytical Chemistry
Bull Soc Anat Clin Bordeaux — Bulletin de la Societe Anatomo-Clinique de Bordeaux
Bull Soc Anat Clin Lille — Bulletin de la Societe Anatomo-Clinique de Lille
Bull Soc Anat Nantes — Bulletin de la Societe Anatomique de Nantes
Bull Soc Anat Paris — Bulletin. Societe Anatomique de Paris
Bull Soc Anat Pathol — Bulletin. Societe d'Anatomie Pathologique
Bull Soc Anat Physiol Norm Path Bordeaux — Bulletin de la Societe d'Anatomie et de Physiologie Normales et Pathologiques de Bordeaux
Bull Soc Ant — Bulletin. Societe Nationale des Antiquaires de France
Bull Soc Ant France — Bulletin. Societe Nationale des Antiquaires de France
Bull Soc Anthrop Biol Lyon — Bulletin de la Societe d'Anthropologie et de Biologie de Lyon
Bull Soc Anthrop Brux — Bulletin de la Societe d'Anthropologie de Bruxelles
Bull Soc Anthropol — Bulletin de la Societe d'Anthropologie
Bull Soc Anthropol — Bulletins et Memoires. Societe d'Anthropologie de Paris
Bull Soc Anthropol Bruxelles — Bulletin de la Societe d'Anthropologie de Bruxelles
Bull Soc Anthropol Paris — Bulletin. Societe d'Anthropologie de Paris
Bull Soc Anthrop Paris — Bulletin et Memoires. Societe d'Anthropologie de Paris
Bull Soc Anthr Paris — Bulletin et Memoires. Societe d'Anthrolopogie de Paris
Bull Soc Antiq Picardie — Bulletin. Societe des Antiquaires de Picardie
Bull Soc Antiqua France — Bulletin de la Societe des Antiquaires de France
Bull Soc Antiquaires Ouest — Bulletin. Societe des Antiquaires de l'Ouest
Bull Soc Antiqua Normandie — Bulletin de la Societe des Antiquaires de Normandie
Bull Soc Antiqua Ouest — Bulletin de la Societe des Antiquaires de l'Ouest
Bull Soc Antiqua Picardie — Bulletin de la Societe des Antiquaires de Picardie
Bull Soc Ant Ouest — Bulletin. Societe des Antiquaires de l'Ouest et des Musees de Poitiers
Bull Soc Apic Alpes-Marit — Bulletin. Societe d'Apiculture des Alpes-Maritimes
Bull Soc Arch Champenoise — Bulletin. Societe d'Archeologique Champenoise
Bull Soc Arch Copte — Bulletin. Societe d'Archeologie Copte
Bull Soc Arch du Midi de la France — Bulletin. Societe Archeologique du Midi de la France
Bull Soc Archeol Alexandr — Bulletin. Societe Archeologique Alexandrine
Bull Soc Archeol Alexandrie — Bulletin de la Societe Archeologique d'Alexandrie
Bull Soc Archeol & Hist Chatillon — Bulletin de la Societe Archeologique et Historique du Chatillonnais
Bull Soc Archeol & Hist Limousin — Bulletin de la Societe Archeologique et Historique du Limousin
Bull Soc Archeol & Hist Nantes & Loire Atlantique — Bulletin de la Societe Archeologique et Historique de Nantes et de Loire-Atlantique
Bull Soc Archeol Chatillon — Bulletin de la Societe Archeologique du Chatillonnais
Bull Soc Archeol Copte — Bulletin de la Societe d'Archeologie Copte
Bull Soc Archeol Finistere — Bulletin. Societe Archeologique du Finistere
Bull Soc Archeol Hist Artist Vieux Pap — Bulletin. Societe Archeologique, Historique, et Artistique de Vieux Papier
Bull Soc Archeol Hist Scient Reg Bonnieres — Bulletin de la Societe Archeologique, Historique, et Scientifique de la Region de Bonnieres
Bull Soc Archeol Hist Scient Soissons — Bulletin de la Societe Archeologique, Historique, et Scientifique de Soissons

Bull Soc Archeol Lorraine — Bulletin de la Societe d'Archeologie Lorraine

Bull Soc Archeol Midi France — Bulletin de la Societe Archeologique du Midi de la France

Bull Soc Archeol Orlean — Bulletin de la Societe Archeologique de l'Orleanais

Bull Soc Archeol Sci Dep Seine et Marne — Bulletin de la Societe d'Archeologie, Sciences, Lettres, et Arts du Departement de Seine-et-Marne

Bull Soc Archeol Scient Litt Beziers — Bulletin de la Societe Archeologique, Scientifique, et Litteraire de Beziers

Bull Soc Archeol Scient Litt Sens — Bulletin de la Societe Archeologique, Scientifique, et Litteraire de Sens

Bull Soc Archeol Scient Litt Sousse — Bulletin de la Societe Archeologique, Scientifique, et Litteraire de Sousse

Bull Soc Archeol Scient Litt Vendomois — Bulletin de la Societe Archeologique, Scientifique, et Litteraire du Vendomois

Bull Soc Archeol Sci Litt Vendomois — Bulletin. Societe Archeologique, Scientifique, e Litteraire du Vendomois

Bull Soc Archeol Tarn et Garonne — Bulletin de la Societe Archeologique de Tarn-et-Garonne

Bull Soc Archeol Touraine — Bulletin de la Societe Archeologique de Touraine

Bull Soc Arch Hist Chatillonnais — Bulletin. Societe Archeologique et Historique du Chatillonnais

Bull Soc Arch Sci Lettr de Beziers — Bulletin. Societe Archeologique, Scientifique, et Litteraire de Beziers

Bull Soc Arieg Sci Lett Arts — Bulletin de la Societe Ariegoise des Sciences, Lettres, et Arts

Bull Soc Arts Mass Inst Technol — Bulletin. Society of Arts. Massachusetts Institute of Technology

Bull Soc Astr Amien — Bulletin de la Societe Astronomique Amienoise

Bull Soc Astr Bordeaux — Bulletin de la Societe Astronomique de Bordeaux

Bull Soc Astr Flammarion Geneve — Bulletin de la Societe Astronomique Flammarion de Geneve

Bull Soc Astr Fr — Bulletin de la Societe Astronomique de France

Bull Soc Astr Pop Toulouse — Bulletin de la Societe d'Astronomie Populaire de Toulouse

Bull Soc Astr Rhone — Bulletin de la Societe Astronomique du Rhone

Bull Soc Avic Fr — Bulletin de la Societe des Aviculteurs Francais

Bull Soc B A Caen — Bulletin de la Societe des Beaux-Arts de Caen

Bull Soc Belfort Emul — Bulletin de la Societe Belfortaine d'Emulation

Bull Soc Belge Astr — Bulletin de la Societe Belge d'Astronomie

Bull Soc Belge Derm Syph — Bulletin. Societe Belge de Dermatologie et de Syphiligraphie

Bull Soc Belge Etudes Colon — Bulletin de la Societe Belge d'Etudes Coloniales

Bull Soc Belge Etud Geogr — Bulletin de la Societe Belge des Etudes Geographiques

Bull Soc Belge Etud Napoleon — Bulletin. Societe Belge d'Etudes Napoleoniennes

Bull Soc Belge Geol — Bulletin. Societe Belge de Geologie

Bull Soc Belge Geol Paleontol Hydrol — Bulletin. Societe Belge de Geologie, de Paleontologie, et d'Hydrologie

Bull Soc Belge Geom Anvers — Bulletin de la Societe Belge des Geometres a Anvers

Bull Soc Belge Gynec Obstet — Bulletin de la Societe Belge de Gynecologie et d'Obstetrique

Bull Soc Belge Ing Ind — Bulletin. Societe Belge des Ingenieurs et des Industriels

Bull Soc Belge Ophtal — Bulletin de la Societe Belge d'Ophtalmologie

Bull Soc Belge Ophtalmol — Bulletin. Societe Belge d'Ophtalmologie

Bull Soc Belge Orthop — Bulletin de la Societe Belge d'Orthopedie et de Chirurgie de l'Appareil Moteur

Bull Soc Belge Otol Lar Rhinol — Bulletin de la Societe Belge d'Otologie, de Laryngologie, et de Rhinologie

Bull Soc Belge Photogramm — Bulletin de la Societe Belge de Photogrammetrie

Bull Soc Belge Phys — Bulletin. Societe Belge de Physique

Bull Soc Belge Geol Paleontol Hydrol — Bulletin. Societe Belge de Geologie, de Paleontologie, et d'Hydrologie [Later, Bulletin. *Societe Belge de Geologie*]

Bull Soc Borda — Bulletin. Societe de Borda

Bull Soc Bot Belg — Bulletin. Societe Royale de Botanique de Belgique

Bull Soc Bot Fr — Bulletin. Societe Botanique de France

Bull Soc Bot Fr Actual Bot — Bulletin. Societe Botanique de France. Actualites Botaniques

Bull Soc Bot France — Bulletin. Societe Botanique de France

Bull Soc Bot Fr Lett Bot — Bulletin. Societe Botanique de France. Lettres Botaniques

Bull Soc Bot Fr Mem — Bulletin. Societe Botanique de France. Memoires

Bull Soc Bot Geneve — Bulletin. Societe Botanique de Geneve

Bull Soc Bot N Fr — Bulletin. Societe de Botanique du Nord de la France

Bull Soc Bot Nord Fr — Bulletin. Societe de Botanique du Nord de la France

Bull Soc Bot Suisse — Bulletin. Societe Botanique Suisse

Bull Soc Can Biochim — Bulletin. Societe Canadienne de Biochimie

Bull Soc Catalana Mat — Bulleti de la Societat Catalana de Matematiques

Bull Soc Cent Architectes — Bulletin de la Societe Centrale des Architectes

Bull Soc Cent For Belg — Bulletin. Societe Centrale Forestiere de Belgique

Bull Soc Centr Agric Dep Herault — Bulletin. Societe Centrale d'Agriculture du Departement de l'Herault

Bull Soc Centr Forest Belgique — Bulletin de la Societe Centrale Forestiere de Belgique

Bull Soc Centr Med Vet — Bulletin. Societe Centrale de Medecine Veterinaire

Bull Soc Chateaubriand — Bulletin de la Societe Chateaubriand

Bull Soc Chim — Bulletin. Societe Chimique de France

Bull Soc Chim Belg — Bulletin. Societes Chimiques Belges

Bull Soc Chim (Beogr) — Bulletin. Societe Chimique (Beograd)

Bull Soc Chim (Beograd) — Bulletin. Societe Chimique (Beograd)

Bull Soc Chim Biol — Bulletin. Societe de Chimie Biologique

Bull Soc Chim de France — Bulletin. Societe Chimique de France

Bull Soc Chim Fr — Bulletin. Societe Chimique de France

Bull Soc Chim Fr 1 — Bulletin. Societe Chimique de France. Premiere Partie. Chimie Analytique, Chimie Minerale, Chimie Physique

Bull Soc Chim Fr 2 — Bulletin. Societe Chimique de France. Deuxieme Partie

Bull Soc Chim France — Bulletin. Societe Chimique de France

Bull Soc Chim Fr Doc — Bulletin. Societe Chimique de France. Documentation

Bull Soc Chim Fr Mem — Bulletin. Societe Chimique de France. Memoires

Bull Soc Chim Fr Part 1 — Bulletin. Societe Chimique de France. Premiere Partie. Chimie Analytique, Chimie Minerale, Chimie Physique

Bull Soc Chim Fr Part 2 — Bulletin. Societe Chimique de France. Deuxieme Partie. Chimie Organique, Biochimie

Bull Soc Chim Ind — Bulletin. Societe de Chimie Industrielle

Bull Soc Chim Repub Pop Bosnie Herzeqovine — Bulletin. Societe de Chimistes. Republique Populaire de Bosnie et Herzeqovine

Bull Soc Chim Roy Yougosl — Bulletin. Societe Chimique du Royaume de Yougoslavie

Bull Soc Chir Paris — Bulletin. Societe de Chirurgie de Paris

Bull Soc Conserv Monum Hist Als — Bulletin. Societe pour la Conservation des Monuments Historiques d'Alsace

Bull Soc Cons Mon Hist Alsace — Bulletin. Societe pour la Conservation des Monuments Historiques d'Alsace

Bull Soc Dunoise — Bulletin de la Societe Dunoise

Bull Soc Egyp Geneve — Bulletin de la Societe d'Egyptologie (Geneve)

Bull Soc Emul Bourbon — Bulletin de la Societe d'Emulation du Bourbonnais

Bull Soc Encour Ind Natl — Bulletin. Societe d'Encouragement pour l'Industrie Nationale

Bull Soc Encour Indust N — Bulletin de la Societe d'Encouragement pour l'Industrie Nationale

Bull Soc Encour Industr Natl — Bulletin. Societe d'Encouragement pour l'Industrie Nationale

Bull Soc Ent Egypte — Bulletin. Societe Entomologique d'Egypte

Bull Soc Ent Fr — Bulletin. Societe Entomologique de France

Bull Soc Ent Mulhouse — Bulletin. Societe Entomologique de Mulhouse

Bull Soc Entomol Egypte — Bulletin. Societe Entomologique d'Egypte

Bull Soc Entomol Fr — Bulletin. Societe Entomologique de France

Bull Soc Entomol Suisse — Bulletin. Societe Entomologique Suisse

Bull Soc Ethnozootech — Bulletin. Societe d'Ethnozootechnie

Bull Soc Et Lot — Bulletin. Societe des Etudes du Lot

Bull Soc Etudes Sci Angers — Bulletin de la Societe d'Etudes Scientifiques d'Angers

Bull Soc Etudes Sci Lyon — Bulletin. Societe d'Etudes Scientifiques de Lyon

Bull Soc Etud Hist & Sci Oise — Bulletin de la Societe d'Etudes Historiques et Scientifiques de l'Oise

Bull Soc Etud Indochin — Bulletin de la Societe des Etudes Indochinoises

Bull Soc Etud Ocean — Bulletin de la Societe des Etudes Oceaniennes

Bull Soc Etud Oceaniennes — Bulletin. Societe d'Etudes Oceaniennes

Bull Soc Etud Scient Tuberc — Bulletin de la Societe d'Etudes Scientifiques sur la Tuberculose

Bull Soc Etud Vulg Zool Agric Bordeaux — Bulletin de la Societe d'Etudes et de Vulgarisation de la Zoologie Agricole (Bordeaux)

Bull Soc Etud XVIIe Siecle — Bulletin de la Societe d'Etudes du XVIIe Siecle

Bull Soc Fed Pharmns Fr — Bulletin de la Societe Federale des Pharmaciens de France

Bull Soc For Belg — Bulletin. Societe Royale Forestiere de Belgique

Bull Soc For Franche-Comte — Bulletin. Societe Forestiere de Franche-Comte et Belfort

Bull Soc For Franche-Comte — Bulletin Trimestriel. Societe Forestiere de Franche-Comte et des Provinces de l'Est

Bull Soc Fouad I Ent — Bulletin de la Societe Fouad 1er d'Entomologie

Bull Soc Fouad I Entomol — Bulletin. Societe Fouad I d'Entomologie

Bull Soc Fr Amis Arbres — Bulletin de la Societe Francaise des Amis des Arbres

Bull Soc Franc Hyg — Bulletin. Societe Francaise d'Hygiene

Bull Soc Franco Jap Paris — Bulletin. Societe Franco-Japonaise de Paris

Bull Soc Franc Phot — Bulletin. Societe Francaise de Photographie

Bull Soc Franc Physiol Veg — Bulletin. Societe Francaise de Physiologie Vegetale

Bull Soc Fr Bot Courrensan — Bulletin de la Societe Francaise de Botanique de Courrensan

Bull Soc Fr Ceram — Bulletin. Societe Francaise de Ceramique

Bull Soc Fr Dahlia — Bulletin de la Societe Francaise du Dahlia

Bull Soc Fr Dermatol Syphiligr — Bulletin. Societe Francaise de Dermatologie et de Syphiligraphie

Bull Soc Fr Derm Syph — Bulletin de la Societe Francaise de Dermatologie et de Syphiligraphie

Bull Soc Fr Ech Pl Vasc — Bulletin. Societe Francaise pour l'Echange des Plantes Vasculaires

Bull Soc Fr Econ Rur — Bulletin de la Societe Francaise d'Economie Rurale

Bull Soc Fr Egyp — Bulletin de la Societe Francaise d'Egyptologie

Bull Soc Fr Electr — Bulletin. Societe Francaise des Electriciens

Bull Soc Fr Fouilles Tanis — Bulletin de la Societe Francaise des Fouilles de Tanis

Bull Soc Fr Hist Hop — Bulletin. Societe Francaise d'Histoire des Hopitaux

Bull Soc Fr Hist Med — Bulletin. Societe Francaise d'Histoire de la Medecine

Bull Soc Fr Hort — Bulletin de la Societe Francaise d'Horticulture

Bull Soc Fribourg Hort — Bulletin de la Societe Fribourgeoise d'Horticulture

Bull Soc Fribourg Sci Nat — Bulletin de la Societe Fribourgeoise des Sciences Naturelles

Bull Soc Frib Sci Nat — Bulletin. Societe Fribourgeoise des Sciences Naturelles

Bull Soc Fr Ingrs Colon — Bulletin de la Societe Francaise des Ingenieurs Coloniaux

Bull Soc Fr Jpn Sci Pures Appl — Bulletin. Societe Franco-Japonaise des Sciences Pures et Appliquees

Bull Soc Fr Micros — Bulletin. Societe Francaise de Microscopie

Bull Soc Fr Mineral — Bulletin. Societe Francaise de Mineralogie

Bull Soc Fr Mineral Cristallogr — Bulletin. Societe Francaise de Mineralogie et de Cristallographie

Bull Soc Fr Mineral et Cristallogr — Bulletin. Societe Francaise de Mineralogie et de Cristallographie

Bull Soc Fr Miner Cristallogr — Bulletin. Societe Francaise de Mineralogie et de Cristallographie

Bull Soc Fr Mycol Med — Bulletin. Societe Francaise de Mycologie Medicale

Bull Soc Fr Num Paris — Bulletin. Societe Francaise de Numismatique (Paris)

Bull Soc Fr Oto Rhino Lar — Bulletin. Societe Francaise d'Oto-Rhino-Laryngologie

Bull Soc Fr Parasitol — Bulletin. Societe Francaise de Parasitologie

Bull Soc Fr Phil — Bulletin. Societe Francaise de Philosophie

Bull Soc Fr Phlebol — Bulletin de la Societe Francaise de Phlebologie

Bull Soc Fr Phot — Bulletin de la Societe Francaise de Photographie

Bull Soc Fr Photogr — Bulletin de la Societe Francaise de Photographie et de Cinematographie

Bull Soc Fr Photogramm — Bulletin. Societe Francaise de Photogrammetrie [Later, Bulletin. Societe Francaise de Photogrammetrie et de Teledetection]

Bull Soc Fr Photogramm et Teledetect — Bulletin. Societe Francaise de Photogrammetrie et de Teledetection

Bull Soc Fr Physiol Veg — Bulletin. Societe Francaise de Physiologie Vegetale

Bull Soc Fr Physiother — Bulletin de la Societe Francaise de Physiotherapie

Bull Soc Fr Prophyl Sanit Mor — Bulletin de la Societe Francaise de Prophylaxie Sanitaire et Morale

Bull Soc Fr Repr MSS Peint — Bulletin de la Societe Francaise de Reproductions de Manuscrits a Peintures

Bull Soc Fr Urol — Bulletin de la Societe Francaise d'Urologie

Bull Soc Gens Sci — Bulletin de la Societe des Gens de Science

Bull Soc Geog — Bulletin de la Societe Geographique

Bull Soc Geogr Afr Occid Fr — Bulletin de la Societe de Geographie de l'Afrique Occidentale Francaise

Bull Soc Geogr Ain — Bulletin de la Societe de Geographie de l'Ain

Bull Soc Geogr Aisne — Bulletin de la Societe de Geographie de l'Aisne

Bull Soc Geogr Alger Afr N — Bulletin de la Societe de Geographie d'Alger et de l'Afrique du Nord

Bull Soc Geogr Anvers — Bulletin de la Societe de Geographie d'Anvers

Bull Soc Geographie — Bulletin. Societe de Geographie

Bull Soc Geogr Comm Bordeaux — Bulletin de la Societe de Geographie Commerciale de Bordeaux

Bull Soc Geogr Comm Havre — Bulletin de la Societe de Geographie Commerciale du Havre

Bull Soc Geogr Comm Nantes — Bulletin de la Societe de Geographie Commerciale de Nantes

Bull Soc Geogr Comm Paris — Bulletin de la Societe de Geographie Commerciale de Paris

Bull Soc Geogr Comm Paris Sect Tunis — Bulletin de la Societe de Geographie Commerciale de Paris. Section Tunisienne

Bull Soc Geol Belg — Bulletin. Societe Geologique de Belgique

Bull Soc Geol Fr — Bulletin. Societe Geologique de France

Bull Soc Geol France — Bulletin. Societe Geologique de France

Bull Soc Geol Fr Suppl — Bulletin. Societe Geologique de France. Supplement. Compte Rendu Sommaire des Seances

Bull Soc Geol Mineral Bretagne — Bulletin. Societe Geologique et Mineralogique de Bretagne

Bull Soc Geol Mineral Bretagne Ser C — Bulletin. Societe Geologique et Mineralogique de Bretagne. Serie C

Bull Soc Geol Normandie — Bulletin. Societe Geologique de Normandie

Bull Soc Hist A Fr — Bulletin de la Societe de l'Histoire de l'Art Francais

Bull Soc Hist & Archeol Corbeil Est & Hurepoix — Bulletin de la Societe Historique et Archeologique de Corbeil, d'Estampes, et du Hurepoix

Bull Soc Hist & Archeol Gand — Bulletin de la Societe d'Histoire et d'Archeologie de Gand

Bull Soc Hist & Archeol Nimes & Gard — Bulletin de la Societe Historique et Archeologique de Nimes et du Gard

Bull Soc Hist & Archeol Orne — Bulletin de la Societe Historique et Archeologique de l'Orne

Bull Soc Hist & Archit Geneve — Bulletin de la Societe d'Histoire et d'Architecture de Geneve

Bull Soc Hist Archeol Arrond Provins — Bulletin de la Societe d'Histoire et d'Archeologie de l'Arrondissement de Provins

Bull Soc Hist Archeol Perigord — Bulletin. Societe Historique et Archeologique du Perigord

Bull Soc Hist Ile Maurice — Bulletin. Societe de l'Histoire de l'Ile Maurice

Bull Soc Hist Maroc — Bulletin. Societe d'Histoire du Maroc

Bull Soc Hist Mod — Bulletin. Societe d'Histoire Moderne

Bull Soc Hist Nat Afr Nord — Bulletin. Societe d'Histoire Naturelle de l'Afrique du Nord

Bull Soc Hist Nat Autun — Bulletin. Societe d'Histoire Naturelle d'Autun

Bull Soc Hist Nat Colmar — Bulletin de la Societe d'Histoire Naturelle de Colmar

Bull Soc Hist Nat Doubs — Bulletin. Societe d'Histoire Naturelle du Doubs

Bull Soc Hist Nat Metz — Bulletin. Societe d'Histoire Naturelle de Metz

Bull Soc Hist Nat Sci Biol Energ — Bulletin. Societe d'Histoire Naturelle et des Sciences Biologiques et Energetiques

Bull Soc Hist Nat Toulouse — Bulletin. Societe d'Histoire Naturelle de Toulouse

Bull Soc Hist Natur Afr Nord — Bulletin. Societe d'Histoire Naturelle de l'Afrique du Nord

Bull Soc Hist Paris & Ile de France — Bulletin de la Societe de l'Histoire de Paris et de l'Ile-de-France

Bull Soc Hist Protestantisme Fr — Bulletin de la Societe de l'Histoire du Protestantisme Francais

Bull Soc Hist VIIIe & XVIIe Arrond Paris — Bulletin. Societe Historique des VIIIe et XVIIe Arrondissements de Paris

Bull Soc Hort Maroc — Bulletin. Societe d'Horticulture et d'Acclimation du Maroc

Bull Soc Hort Sarthe — Bulletin de la Societe d'Horticulture de la Sarthe

Bull Soc Huysmans — Bulletin de la Societe Joris-Karl Huysmans

Bull Soc Hyg Aliment — Bulletin. Societe Scientifique d'Hygiene Alimentaire et d'Alimentation Rationnelle de l'Homme

Bull Societe Ind Mulhouse — Bulletin. Societe Industrielle de Mulhouse

Bull Soc Imp Nat Moscou — Bulletin. Societe Imperiale des Naturalistes de Moscou

Bull Soc Ind — Bulletin Social des Industriels. Association des Patrons et IngenieursCatholiques de Belgique

Bull Soc Ind Amiens — Bulletin. Societe Industrielle d'Amiens

Bull Soc Ind Miner St Etienne — Bulletin. Societe de l'Industrie Minerale de St. Etienne

Bull Soc Ind Mulhouse — Bulletin. Societe Industrielle de Mulhouse

Bull Soc Ind Rouen — Bulletin. Societe Industrielle de Rouen

Bull Soc Indust Mulhouse — Bulletin de la Societe Industrielle de Mulhouse

Bull Soc Ing Civ Fr — Bulletin. Societe des Ingenieurs Civils de France

Bull Soc Int Chir — Bulletin. Societe Internationale de Chirurgie

Bull Soc Int Electr — Bulletin. Societe Internationale des Electriciens

Bull Soc Int Et Phil Med — Bulletin. Societe Internationale pour l'Etude de la Philosophie Medievale

Bull Soc Khediv Geogr — Bulletin. Societe Khediviale de Geographie

Bull Soc Languedoc Geog — Bulletin de la Societe Languedocienne de Geographie

Bull Soc Lat Am Stud — Bulletin. Society for Latin American Studies

Bull Soc Lepid Fr — Bulletin. Societe des Lepidopteristes Francais

Bull Soc Linguistique Paris — Bulletin. Societe de Linguistique de Paris

Bull Soc Linn Bord — Bulletin. Societe Linneenne de Bordeaux

Bull Soc Linn Bordeaux — Bulletin. Societe Linneenne de Bordeaux

Bull Soc Linn Lyon — Bulletin. Societe Linneenne de Lyon

Bull Soc Linn N France — Bulletin de la Societe Linneenne du Nord de la France

Bull Soc Linn Normandie — Bulletin. Societe Linneenne de Normandie

Bull Soc Linn Provence — Bulletin. Societe Linneenne de Provence

Bull Soc Lorraine Sci — Bulletin. Societe Lorraine des Sciences

Bull Soc Lorraine Sci Mem — Bulletin. Societe Lorraine des Sciences. Memoires

Bull Soc Math Belg — Bulletin. Societe Mathematique de Belgique

Bull Soc Math Belg Ser A — Bulletin. Societe Mathematique de Belgique. Serie A

Bull Soc Math Belg Ser B — Bulletin. Societe Mathematique de Belgique. Serie B

Bull Soc Math Fr — Bulletin. Societe Mathematique de France

Bull Soc Math France — Bulletin. Societe Mathematique de France

Bull Soc Math France Mem — Societe Mathematique de France. Bulletin, Memoire

Bull Soc Math France Suppl Mem — Societe Mathematique de France. Bulletin, Supplement, Memoire

Bull Soc Math Fr Mem — Bulletin. Societe Mathematique de France. Memoire

Bull Soc Math Grece — Bulletin. Societe Mathematique de Grece

Bull Soc Math Grece NS — Bulletin. Societe Mathematique de Grece. Nouvelle Serie

Bull Soc Math Phys Macedoine — Bulletin. Societe des Mathematiciens et des Physiciens de la Republique Populaire de Macedoine

Bull Soc Med Afr Noire — Bulletin. Societe Medicale d'Afrique Noire de Langue Francaise

Bull Soc Med Afr Noire de Langue Fr — Bulletin. Societe Medicale d'Afrique Noire de Langue Francaise

Bull Soc Med Afr Noire Lang Fr — Bulletin. Societe Medicale d'Afrique Noire de Langue Francaise

Bull Soc Med Alger — Bulletin de la Societe de Medecine d'Alger

Bull Soc Med Amiens — Bulletin de la Societe Medicale d'Amiens

Bull Soc Med Angers — Bulletin de la Societe de Medecine d'Angers

Bull Soc Med Bas Rhin — Bulletin de la Societe de Medecine du Bas-Rhin

Bull Soc Med Bayonne — Bulletin de la Societe Medicale de Bayonne-Biarritz et de la Cote Basque

Bull Soc Med Belge Temper — Bulletin de la Societe Medicale Belge de Temperance

Bull Soc Med Charleroi — Bulletin de la Societe Medicale de Charleroi

Bull Soc Med Chir Athenes — Bulletin de la Societe Medico-Chirurgicale d'Athenes

Bull Soc Med Chir Drome — Bulletin de la Societe Medico-Chirurgicale de la Drome et de l'Ardeche

Bull Soc Med Chir Fr Ouest Afr — Bulletin. Societe Medico-Chirurgicale Francaise de l'Ouest Africain

Bull Soc Med-Chir Indo-Chine — Bulletin. Societe Medico-Chirurgicale de l'Indo-Chine

Bull Soc Med Chir La Rochelle — Bulletin de la Societe de Medecine et de Chirurgie de La Rochelle

Bull Soc Med Chir Paris — Bulletin de la Societe Medico-Chirurgicale de Paris

Bull Soc Med Dep Sarthe — Bulletin de la Societe de Medecine du Departement de la Sarthe

Bull Soc Med Educ Phys — Bulletin de la Societe Medicale d'Education Physique et de Sport

Bull Soc Med Haiti — Bulletin de la Societe de Medecine d'Haiti

Bull Soc Med Hist — Bulletin de la Societe Medico-Historique

Bull Soc Med Hop Lyon — Bulletin. Societe Medicale des Hopitaux de Lyon

Bull Soc Med Hop Pa — Bulletins et Memoires. Societe Medicale des Hopitaux de Paris

Bull Soc Med Hop Paris — Bulletins et Memoires. Societe Medicale des Hopitaux de Paris

Bull Soc Med Hop Univ Quebec — Bulletin. Societe Medicale des Hopitaux Universitaires de Quebec

Bull Soc Med Ile Maurice — Bulletin de la Societe Medicale de l'Ile Maurice

Bull Soc Med Leg Fr — Bulletin de la Societe de Medecine Legale de France

Bull Soc Med Loiret — Bulletin. Societe de Medecine de Loiret

Bull Soc Med Ment Belg — Bulletin de la Societe de Medecine Mentale de Belgique

Bull Soc Med Nancy — Bulletin. Societe de Medecine de Nancy

Bull Soc Medns Dispens Antituberc Dep Seine — Bulletin de la Societe des Medecins des Dispensaires Antituberculeux de l'Office Public d'Hygiene Sociale du Departement de la Seine

Bull Soc Med Par — Bulletin et Memoires. Societe de Medecine de Paris

Bull Soc Med Pau — Bulletin de la Societe Medicale de Pau

Bull Soc Med Pratns Lille — Bulletin de la Societe de Medecine des Praticiens de Lille

Bull Soc Med Rouen — Bulletin de la Societe de Medecine de Rouen
Bull Soc Med Sanit Marit — Bulletin de la Societe de Medecine Sanitaire Maritime
Bull Soc Med Toulouse — Bulletin de la Societe de Medecine de Toulouse
Bull Soc Med Vet Basses Pyren — Bulletin de la Societe de Medecine Veterinaire des Basses-Pyrenees
Bull Soc Med Vet Dep Oise — Bulletin de la Societe de Medecine Veterinaire du Departement de l'Oise
Bull Soc Med Vet Deps Cent — Bulletin de la Societe de Medecine Veterinaire des Departements du Centre
Bull Soc Med Vet Eure et Loir — Bulletin de la Societe de Medecine Veterinaire d'Eure-et-Loir
Bull Soc Med Vet Lot et Gar — Bulletin de la Societe de Medecine Veterinaire de Lot-et-Garonne
Bull Soc Med Vet Lyon — Bulletin de la Societe de Medecine Veterinaire de Lyon et du Sud-Est
Bull Soc Med Vet Prat — Bulletin de la Societe de Medecine Veterinaire Pratique
Bull Soc Med Vet Somme — Bulletin de la Societe de Medecine Veterinaire de la Somme
Bull Soc Med Vienne — Bulletin de la Societe de Medecine de la Vienne
Bull Soc Med Yonne — Bulletin de la Societe Medicale de l'Yonne
Bull Soc Microsc Can — Bulletin. Societe de Microscopie du Canada
Bull Soc Min Colomb Br — Bulletin de la Societe Miniere de Colombie Britannique
Bull Soc Mycol — Bulletin. Societe Mycologique de Geneve
Bull Soc Mycol Fr — Bulletin. Societe Mycologique de France
Bull Soc N Antiqua France — Bulletin de la Societe Nationale des Antiquaires de France
Bull Soc Nat Antiq Fr — Bulletin. Societe Nationale des Antiquaires de France
Bull Soc Nat Antiqu France — Bulletin. Societe Nationale des Antiquaires de France
Bull Soc Nat Archeol Ain — Bulletin. Societe des Naturalistes et des Archeologues de l'Ain
Bull Soc Nat Fr — Bulletin. Societe Nationale des Antiquaires de France
Bull Soc Nat Lux — Bulletin. Societe des Naturalistes Luxembourgeois
Bull Soc Nat Moscou Sect Biol — Bulletin. Societe des Naturalistes de Moscou. Section Biologique
Bull Soc Nat Moscou Sect Geol — Bulletin. Societe des Naturalistes de Moscou. Section Geologique
Bull Soc Naturalistes Dinantais — Bulletin de la Societe des Naturalistes Dinantais
Bull Soc Naturalistes Parisiens — Bulletin. Societe les Naturalistes Parisiens
Bull Soc Nat Voroneje — Bulletin. Societe des Naturalistes de Voroneje
Bull Soc Nav Archit Mar Eng — Bulletin. Society of Naval Architects and Marine Engineers
Bull Soc Neuchatel Geog — Bulletin de la Societe Neuchateloise de Geographie
Bull Soc Neuchatel Sci Nat — Bulletin. Societe Neuchatelloise des Sciences Naturelles
Bull Soc Nivernaise — Bulletin. Societe Nivernaise des Lettres, Sciences, et Arts
Bull Soc Nivernaise Lett Sci & A — Bulletin de la Societe Nivernaise des Lettres, Sciences, et Arts
Bull Soc Norm Arch Prehist Hist — Bulletin. Societe Normande d'Archeologie Prehistorique et Historique
Bull Soc NZ — Bulletin. Royal Society of New Zealand
Bull Soc Obst Gynec — Bulletin. Societe d'Obstetrique et de Gynecologie de Paris
Bull Soc Ophtal Egy — Bulletin. Societe d'Ophtalmologie d'Egypte
Bull Soc Ophtal Fr — Bulletin. Societes d'Ophtalmologie de France
Bull Soc Ophtalmol Fr — Bulletin. Societes d'Ophtalmologie de France
Bull Soc Ophtalmol Paris — Bulletin. Societe d'Ophtalmologie de Paris
Bull Soc Path Exot — Bulletin. Societe de Pathologie Exotique
Bull Soc Path Exot — Bulletin. Societe de Pathologie Exotique et de Ses Filiales
Bull Soc Pathol Exot — Bulletin. Societe de Pathologie Exotique
Bull Soc Pathol Exot Filiales — Bulletin. Societe de Pathologie Exotique et de Ses Filiales
Bull Soc Pathol Exotique — Bulletin. Societe de Pathologie Exotique
Bull Soc Pathol Exot Ses Fil — Bulletin. Societe de Pathologie Exotique et de Ses Filiales
Bull Soc Pediat Paris — Bulletin. Societe de Pediatrie de Paris
Bull Soc Pharmacol Environ Pathol — Bulletin. Society of Pharmacological and Environmental Pathologists
Bull Soc Pharm Bord — Bulletin. Societe de Pharmacie de Bordeaux
Bull Soc Pharm Bordeaux — Bulletin. Societe de Pharmacie de Bordeaux
Bull Soc Pharm Bruxelles — Bulletin. Societe de Pharmacie de Bruxelles
Bull Soc Pharm Lille — Bulletin. Societe de Pharmacie de Lille
Bull Soc Pharm Mars — Bulletin. Societe de Pharmacie de Marseille
Bull Soc Pharm Marseille — Bulletin. Societe de Pharmacie de Marseille
Bull Soc Pharm Nancy — Bulletin. Societe de Pharmacie de Nancy
Bull Soc Pharm Strasb — Bulletin. Societe de Pharmacie de Strasbourg
Bull Soc Pharm Strasbourg — Bulletin. Societe de Pharmacie de Strasbourg
Bull Soc Philomath Paris — Bulletin. Societe Philomathique de Paris
Bull Soc Philomat Paris — Bulletin. Societe Philomatique de Paris
Bull Soc Philom Perpignan — Bulletin. Societe Philomatique de Perpignan
Bull Soc Philom Vosg — Bulletin. Societe Philomatique Vosgienne
Bull Soc Photogr Sci Technol Jpn — Bulletin. Society of Photographic Science and Technology of Japan
Bull Soc Phycol Fr — Bulletin. Societe Phycologique de France
Bull Soc Pl Ecol — Bulletin. Society of Plant Ecology/Shokubutsu Seitai-Gaku Kaiho
Bull Soc Polymath Morbihan — Bulletin Mensuel. Societe Polymathique du Morbihan
Bull Soc Port Sci Nat — Bulletin. Societe Portugaise des Sciences Naturelles
Bull Soc Portugaise Sc Nat — Bulletin. Societe Portugaise des Sciences Naturelles
Bull Soc Poussin — Bulletin de la Societe Poussin
Bull Soc Prehist — Bulletin. Societe Prehistorique de France
Bull Soc Prehist Ariege — Bulletin. Societe Prehistorique de l'Ariege

Bull Soc Prehist Ariege Pyrenees — Bulletin de la Societe Prehistorique de l'Ariege-Pyrenees
Bull Soc Prehist Fr — Bulletin. Societe Prehistorique Francaise
Bull Soc Prehist France — Bulletin. Societe Prehistorique Francaise
Bull Soc Prehist Fr C R Seances Mens — Bulletin de la Societe Prehistorique Francaise. Comptes Rendus des Seances Mensuelles
Bull Soc Prehist Fr Etud & Trav — Bulletin de la Societe Prehistorique Francaise. Etudes et Travaux
Bull Soc Preserv New England Ant — Bulletin of the Society for the Preservation of New England Antiquities
Bull Soc Prof Hist Geogr — Bulletin. Societe des Professeurs d'Histoire et de Geographie
Bull Soc Promot Eng Educ — Bulletin. Society for the Promotion of Engineering Education
Bull Soc Prot Pays Esthet Gen France — Bulletin de la Societe pour la Protection des Paysages et de l'Esthetique Generale de la France
Bull Soc R Belge Anthrop et Prehist — Bulletin. Societe Royale Belge d'Anthropologie et de Prehistoire
Bull Soc R Belge Electr — Bulletin. Societe Royale Belge des Electriciens
Bull Soc R Belge Gynecol Obstet — Bulletin. Societe Royale Belge de Gynecologie et d'Obstetrique
Bull Soc R Belge Ing Ind — Bulletin. Societe Royale Belge des Ingenieurs et des Industriels
Bull Soc R Bot Belg — Bulletin. Societe Royale de Botanique de Belgique
Bull Soc Rech Congol Brazzaville — Bulletin de la Societe des Recherches Congolaises (Brazzaville)
Bull Soc R Entomol Egypte — Bulletin. Societe Royale Entomologique d'Egypte
Bull Soc R For Belg — Bulletin. Societe Royale Forestiere de Belgique
Bull Soc R For Belg Tijdschr K Belg Bosbouwmaatsch — Bulletin. Societe Royale Forestiere de Belgique/Tijdschrift van de Koninklijke Belgische Bosbouwmaatschappij
Bull Soc Romande Apic — Bulletin. Societe Romande d'Apiculture
Bull Soc Roum Neurol Psychiatr Psychol Endocrinol — Bulletin. Societe Roumaine de Neurologie, Psychiatrie, Psychologie, et Endocrinologie
Bull Soc Roy Agric Mans — Bulletin. Societe Royale d'Agriculture, Sciences, et Arts du Mans
Bull Soc Royale Archeol Alexandrie — Bulletin de la Societe Royale d'Archeologie (Alexandrie)
Bull Soc Royale Archeol Bruxelles — Bulletin de la Societe Royale d'Archeologie de Bruxelles
Bull Soc Royale Belge Anth Prehist — Bulletin de la Societe Royale Belge d'Anthropologie et de Prehistoire
Bull Soc Royale Vieux Liege — Bulletin de la Societe Royale du Vieux-Liege
Bull Soc Roy Belg Anthr Prehist — Bulletin. Societe Royale Belge d'Anthropologie et de Prehistoire
Bull Soc Roy Belg Elec — Bulletin. Societe Royale Belge des Electriciens
Bull Soc Roy Pharm Bruxelles — Bulletin. Societe Royale de Pharmacie de Bruxelles
Bull Soc Roy Sci Liege — Bulletin. Societe Royale des Sciences de Liege
Bull Soc R Pharm Bruxelles — Bulletin. Societe Royale de Pharmacie de Bruxelles
Bull Soc R Sci Liege — Bulletin. Societe Royale des Sciences de Liege
Bull Soc Salt Sci Jpn — Bulletin. Society of Salt Science. Japan
Bull Soc Schongauer — Bulletin de la Societe Schongauer
Bull Soc Sci Anc — Bulletin. Societe des Sciences Anciennes
Bull Soc Sci Anciennn — Bulletin. Societe des Sciences Anciennes
Bull Soc Sci Arts Bayonne — Bulletin de la Societe des Sciences et Arts de Bayonne
Bull Soc Sci Arts Belles Lett Dep Tarn — Bulletin de la Societe des Sciences, Arts, et Belles-Lettres du Departement du Tarn
Bull Soc Sci Arts Ile Reunion — Bulletin de la Societe des Sciences et Arts de l'Ile de la Reunion
Bull Soc Sci Arts Rochechouart — Bulletin de la Societe des Sciences et Arts de Rochechouart
Bull Soc Sci Arts Vitry le Franc — Bulletin de la Societe des Sciences et Arts de Vitry-le-Francois
Bull Soc Sci Bretagne — Bulletin. Societe Scientifique de Bretagne
Bull Soc Sci Cluj Roum — Bulletin. Societe des Sciences de Cluj. Roumanie
Bull Soc Sci Dep Bas Rhin — Bulletin. Societe des Sciences, Agriculture, et Arts du Departement du Bas-Rhin
Bull Soc Scient Artist Litt Chalon S Saone — Bulletin de la Societe Scientifique, Artistique, et Litteraire de Chalon-sur-Saone
Bull Soc Scient Bretagne — Bulletin. Societe Scientifique de Bretagne
Bull Soc Scient Med Ouest — Bulletin. Societe Scientifique et Medicale de l'Ouest
Bull Soc Sci Geol Repub Soc Roum — Bulletin. Societe des Sciences Geologiques. Republique Socialiste de Roumanie
Bull Soc Sci Hist & Nat Yonne — Bulletin de la Societe des Sciences Historiques et Naturelles de l'Yonne
Bull Soc Sci Hist Nat Corse — Bulletin de la Societe des Sciences Historiques et Naturelles de la Corse
Bull Soc Sci Hist Nat Semur — Bulletin de la Societe des Sciences Historiques et Naturelles de Semur-en-Auxois
Bull Soc Sci Hyg Aliment — Bulletin. Societe Scientifique d'Hygiene Alimentaire
Bull Soc Sci Hyg Aliment Aliment Ration — Bulletin. Societe Scientifique d'Hygiene Alimentaire et d'Alimentation Rationnelle
Bull Soc Sci Hyg Aliment Aliment Ration Homme — Bulletin. Societe Scientifique d'Hygiene Alimentaire et d'Alimentation Rationnelle de l'Homme
Bull Soc Sci Lett & A Bayonne — Bulletin de la Societe des Sciences, Lettres, et Arts de Bayonne
Bull Soc Sci Lett Beaux Arts Cholet — Bulletin de la Societe des Sciences, Lettres, et Beaux-Arts de Cholet
Bull Soc Sci Lett Lodz — Bulletin. Societe des Sciences et des Lettres de Lodz
Bull Soc Sci Lett Lodz Cl 3 — Bulletin. Societe des Sciences et des Lettres de Lodz. Classe 3. Sciences Mathematiques et Naturelles

Bull Soc Sci Lett Lodz Cl 4 — Bulletin. Societe des Sciences et des Lettres de Lodz. Classe 4. Sciences Medicales

Bull Soc Sci Lett Lodz Ser Rech Deform — Bulletin de la Societe des Sciences et des Lettres de Lodz. Serie. Recherches sur les Deformations

Bull Soc Sci Lettres Lodz — Bulletin. Societe des Sciences et des Lettres de Lodz

Bull Soc Sci Med Biol Montpellier — Bulletin de la Societe des Sciences Medicales et Biologiques de Montpellier et du Languedoc Mediterraneen

Bull Soc Sci Med Constantine — Bulletin de la Societe des Sciences Medicales de Constantine

Bull Soc Sci Med Grand-Duche Luxemb — Bulletin. Societe des Sciences Medicales du Grand-Duche de Luxembourg

Bull Soc Sci Med Gr-Duche Luxemb — Bulletin. Societe des Sciences Medicales du Grand-Duche de Luxembourg

Bull Soc Sci Med Lille — Bulletin de la Societe des Sciences Medicales de Lille

Bull Soc Sci Med Madagascar — Bulletin. Societe des Sciences Medicales de Madagascar

Bull Soc Sci Nancy — Bulletin. Societe des Sciences de Nancy

Bull Soc Sci Nat — Bulletin. Societe des Sciences Naturelles

Bull Soc Sci Nat Archeol Ain — Bulletin de la Societe des Sciences Naturelles et d'Archeologie de l'Ain

Bull Soc Sci Nat Ardeche — Bulletin de la Societe des Sciences Naturelles et Historiques de l'Ardeche

Bull Soc Sci Nat Arts St Etienne — Bulletin de la Societe des Sciences Naturelles et Arts de St-Etienne

Bull Soc Sci Nat Autun — Bulletin de la Societe des Sciences Naturelles d'Autun

Bull Soc Sci Nat Charente Infer — Bulletin de la Societe des Sciences Naturelles de la Charente-Inferieure

Bull Soc Sci Nat Hte Marne — Bulletin de la Societe des Sciences Naturelles de la Haute-Marne

Bull Soc Sci Nat Macon — Bulletin de la Societe des Sciences Naturelles de Macon

Bull Soc Sci Nat Mar — Bulletin. Societe des Sciences Naturelles du Maroc

Bull Soc Sci Nat Maroc — Bulletin. Societe des Sciences Naturelles du Maroc

Bull Soc Sci Nat Med Seine et Oise — Bulletin de la Societe des Sciences Naturelles et Medicales de Seine-et-Oise

Bull Soc Sci Nat Neuchatel — Bulletin. Societe des Sciences Naturelles de Neuchatel

Bull Soc Sci Nat Ouest Fr — Bulletin. Societe des Sciences Naturelles de l'Ouest de la France

Bull Soc Sci Nat Ouest France — Bulletin. Societe des Sciences Naturelles de l'Ouest de la France

Bull Soc Sci Nat Phys Mar — Bulletin. Societe des Sciences Naturelles et Physiques du Maroc

Bull Soc Sci Nat Phys Maroc — Bulletin. Societe des Sciences Naturelles et Physiques du Maroc

Bull Soc Sci Nat Phys Montpellier — Bulletin de la Societe des Sciences Naturelles et Physiques de Montpellier

Bull Soc Sci Nat Rouen — Bulletin de la Societe des Sciences Naturelles de Rouen

Bull Soc Sci Nat Saone et Loire — Bulletin de la Societe des Sciences Naturelles de Saone-et-Loire

Bull Soc Sci Nat Sud E — Bulletin de la Societe des Sciences Naturelles du Sud-Est

Bull Soc Sci Nat Tarare — Bulletin de la Societe des Sciences Naturelles de Tarare

Bull Soc Sci Nat Tun — Bulletin. Societe des Sciences Naturelles de Tunisie

Bull Soc Sci Nat Tunis — Bulletin. Societe des Sciences Naturelles de Tunisie

Bull Soc Sci Photogr Jpn — Bulletin. Society of Scientific Photography of Japan

Bull Soc Sci Phys Algerie — Bulletin. Societe des Sciences Physiques, Naturelles, et Climatologiques de l'Algerie

Bull Soc Sci Phys Nat Toulouse — Bulletin de la Societe des Sciences Physiques and Naturelles de Toulouse

Bull Soc Sci Vet Lyon — Bulletin. Societe des Sciences Veterinaires de Lyon

Bull Soc Sci Vet Med Comp Lyon — Bulletin. Societe des Sciences Veterinaires et de Medecine Comparee de Lyon

Bull Soc Sc Vet Lyon — Bulletin. Societe des Sciences Veterinaires de Lyon

Bull Soc Sea Water Sci (Jpn) — Bulletin. Society of Sea Water Science (Japan)

Bull Soc Semur — Bulletin. Societe des Sciences Historiques et Naturelles de Semur-en-Auxois

Bull Soc Statistiques Sci Nat & A Indust Depts Isere — Bulletin de la Societe des Statistiques, Sciences Naturelles, et Arts Industriels des Departements de l'Isere

Bull Soc Stiinte Geol Repub Soc Rom — Buletinul. Societatii de Stiinte Geologice din Republica Socialista Romania

Bull Soc Suisse American — Bulletin de la Societe Suisse des Americanistes

Bull Soc Suisse Am Geneva — Bulletin. Societe Suisse des Americanistes (Geneva)

Bull Soc Suisse Amis Extreme Orient — Bulletin de la Societe Suisse des Amis de l'Extreme-Orient

Bull Soc Turq Med — Bulletins. Societe Turque de Medecine

Bull Soc Vaudoise Sci Nat — Bulletin. Societe Vaudoise des Sciences Naturelles

Bull Soc Vaud Sci Nat — Bulletin. Societe Vaudoise des Sciences Naturelles

Bull Soc Vector Ecol — Bulletin. Society of Vector Ecologists

Bull Soc Vet Hell — Bulletin. Societe Veterinaire Hellenique

Bull Soc Vieux Papier — Bulletin. Societe de Vieux Papier

Bull Soc Zool Anvers — Bulletins. Societe de Zoologie d'Anvers

Bull Soc Zool Fr — Bulletin. Societe Zoologique de France

Bull Soc Zool France — Bulletin. Societe Zoologique de France

Bull Soc Zool Fr Suppl — Bulletin. Societe Zoologique de France. Supplement

Bull Soies Kinugasa — Bulletin des Soies Kinugasa

Bull Soil Bur (NZ) — Bulletin. Soil Bureau Department of Scientific and Industrial Research (New Zealand)

Bull Soil Surv Gt Br — Bulletin. Soil Survey of Great Britain

Bull Sonoma County Med Assoc — Bulletin. Sonoma County Medical Association

Bull South Calif Acad Sci — Bulletin. Southern California Academy of Sciences

Bull South Pac Gen Hosp — Bulletin. Southern Pacific General Hospital

Bull South Res Inst — Bulletin. Southern Research Institute

Bull South Tex Geol Soc — Bulletin. South Texas Geological Society

Bull Soviet Econ Dev — Bulletins on Soviet Economic Development

Bull Sov Sect Int Pedol Assoc — Bulletin. Soviet Section. International Pedologists Association

Bull Spec Astrophys Obs (North Caucasus) — Bulletin. Special Astrophysical Observatory (North Caucasus)

Bull Spec Com Tech Soc Hydrotech Fr — Bulletin Special. Comite Technique. Societe Hydrotechnique de France

Bull Spec Libr Coun Phila — Bulletin. Special Libraries Council of Philadelphia and Vicinity

Bull Spec Serv Sante Hyg Publ Brux — Bulletin Special du Service de Sante et de l'Hygiene Publique (Bruxelles)

Bull Spectrum Analysis — Bulletin of Spectrum Analysis

Bull Speleol Soc DC — Bulletin. Speleological Society of the District of Columbia

Bull SPF — Bulletin. Societe Prehistorique Francaise

Bull Spokane County Med Soc — Bulletin. Spokane County Medical Society

Bull Sport Fish Inst — Bulletin. Sport Fishing Institute

Bull Springfield Mus Nat Hist — Bulletin of the Springfield Museum of Natural History

Bull Spring Washer Ind — Bulletin. Spring Washer Industry

Bull SSI — Bulletin. Shanghai Science Institute

Bull Stand Oil Co Calif — Bulletin. Standard Oil Company of California

Bull State Agric Exp Sta Alabama — Bulletin. State Agricultural Experiment Station (Auburn, Alabama)

Bull State Biol Surv Kans — Bulletin. State Biological Survey of Kansas

Bull State Board Agric Dover Del — Bulletin. State Board of Agriculture. Dover, Delaware

Bull State Fruit Exp Stn Southwest MO State Univ (Mt Grove) — Bulletin. State Fruit Experiment Station. Southwest Missouri State University (Mountain Grove)

Bull State Geol Surv Kansas — Bulletin. State Geological Survey of Kansas

Bull State Geol (Wyo) — Bulletin. State Geologist (Wyoming)

Bull State Inst Agric Microbiol Leningrad — Bulletin. State Institute of Agricultural Microbiology (Leningrad)

Bull State Inst Mar Trop Med Gdansk — Bulletin. State Institute of Marine and Tropical Medicine in Gdansk

Bull State Nikita Bot Gard — Bulletin. State Nikita Botanical Gardens

Bull State Plant Board Fla — Bulletin. State Plant Board of Florida

Bull State Univ Iowa — Bulletin. State University of Iowa

Bull Statist Soc NSW — Bulletin. Statistical Society of New South Wales

Bull St Bd Hlth Ky — Bulletin of the State Board of Health of Kentucky

Bull S Tex Geol Soc — Bulletin. South Texas Geological Society

Bull St Francis Hosp Sanat (Roslyn NY) — Bulletin. St. Francis Hospital and Sanatorium (Roslyn, New York)

Bull St Francis Sanat Roslyn NY — Bulletin. St. Francis Sanatorium. Roslyn, New York

Bull Sth Calif Acad Sci — Bulletin. Southern California Academy of Sciences

Bull Sticht Oude Holland Kerken — Bulletin van der Stichting Oude Hollandse Kerken

Bull St Louis A Mus — Bulletin of St. Louis Art Museum

Bull St Marianna Univ Sch Med Gen Educ — Bulletin. St. Marianna University. School of Medicine. General Education

Bull St Mens Com Forg Fr — Bulletin Statistique Mensuel. Comite des Forges de France

Bull Stn Agric Pas de Calais — Bulletin de la Station Agricole du Pas de Calais

Bull Stn Agric Peche Castiglione — Bulletin. Station d'Agriculture et de Peche de Castiglione

Bull Stn Agron Dep Aisne — Bulletin de la Station Agronomique du Departement de l'Aisne

Bull Stn Agron Etat Gembloux — Bulletin de la Station Agronomique de l'Etat a Gembloux

Bull Stn Agron Guadeloupe — Bulletin. Station Agronomique de Guadeloupe

Bull Stn Agron Lab Dep Finistere — Bulletin. Station Agronomique et Laboratoire Departemental de Finistere

Bull Stn Agron Loire Infer — Bulletin de la Station Agronomique de la Loire-Inferieure

Bull Stn Agron Maurice — Bulletin de la Station Agronomique de Maurice

Bull Stn Agron Somme — Bulletin de la Station Agronomique de la Somme

Bull Stn Exp Agric Hong A — Bulletin. Stations d'Experimentation Agricole Hongroises. A. Production Vegetale

Bull Stn Exp Agric Hong B — Bulletin des Stations d'Experimentation Agricole Hongroises. B. Elevage

Bull Stn Exp Agric Hong C — Bulletin. Stations d'Experimentation Agricole Hongroises. C. Horticulture

Bull Stomatol Kyoto Univ — Bulletin of Stomatology. Kyoto University

Bull Storrs Agric Exp Stn Univ Conn — Bulletin. Storrs Agricultural Experiment Station. University of Connecticut

Bull Storrs Agric Stn — Bulletin. Storrs Agricultural Station

Bull Strasb — Bulletin. Faculte des Lettres de Strasbourg

Bull Strashimir Dimitrov Inst Geol Bulg Acad Sci — Bulletin. Strashimir Dimitrov Institute of Geology. Bulgarian Academy of Sciences

Bull Stud Philos & Hist A U Tsukuba — Bulletin of the Study of Philosophy and History of Art in the University of Tsukuba

Bull Sugadaira Biol Lab — Bulletin. Sugadaira Biological Laboratory

Bull Sugar Beet Res — Bulletin of Sugar Beet Research

Bull Sugar Beet Res Suppl — Bulletin of Sugar Beet Research. Supplement

Bull Suicidol — Bulletin of Suicidology

Bull Suisse Mineral Petrogr — Bulletin Suisse de Mineralogie et Petrographie

Bull Suisse Mycol — Bulletin Suisse de Mycologie

Bull Sung Yuan Stud — Bulletin of Sung-Yuan Studies

Bull Suzugamine Women's Coll Nat Sci — Bulletin. Suzugamine Women's College. Natural Science

Bull SW Ass Petrol Geol — Bulletin. Southwestern Association of Petroleum Geologists

Bull Swazild Dep Agric — Bulletin. Swaziland Department of Agriculture
Bull Swed Corros Inst — Swedish Corrosion Institute
Bull S West Ass Petrol Geol — Bulletin of the Southwestern Association of Petroleum Geologists
Bull S West Univ Med Coll — Bulletin of the Southwestern University Medical College
Bull Symbolic Logic — Bulletin of Symbolic Logic
Bull Synd Apic — Bulletin. Union Syndicale des Apiculteurs
Bull Taichung Dist Agric Improv Stn — Bulletin. Taichung District Agricultural Improvement Station
Bull Taipei Med Coll — Bulletin. Taipei Medical College
Bull Taiwan Agric Res Inst — Bulletin. Taiwan Agricultural Research Institute
Bull Taiwan Forestry Res Inst — Bulletin. Taiwan Forestry Research Institute
Bull Taiwan For Res Inst — Bulletin. Taiwan Forestry Research Institute
Bull Taiwan For Res Inst Co Op Taiwan For Bur — Bulletin of Taiwan Forestry Research Institute in Co-Operation with Taiwan Forest Bureau
Bull Tall Timbers Res Stn — Bulletin. Tall Timbers Research Station
Bull Tama A Sch — Bulletin of Tama Art School
Bull Tamagawa-Gakuen Women's Jr Coll — Bulletin. Tamagawa-Gakuen Women's Junior College
Bull Tas For Comm — Tasmanian Forest Commission. Bulletin
Bull Tea Div Tokai Kinki Agric Stn — Bulletin. Tea Division. Tokai Kinki Agricultural Station
Bull Tea Res Sta Minist Agric — Bulletin. Tea Research Station. Ministry of Agriculture and Forestry/Chagyo Shikenjo Kenkyu Hokoku
Bull Tea Res Stn (Kanaya Jpn) — Bulletin. Tea Research Station (Kanaya, Japan)
Bull Tea Res Stn Minist Agric For — Bulletin. Tea Research Station. Ministry of Agriculture and Forestry
Bull Tech Agric Exp Stn Fla — Bulletin (Technical). Agricultural Experiment Stations (Florida)
Bull Tech AIBr — Bulletin Technique AIBr
Bull Tech Api — Bulletin Technique Apicole
Bull Tech Apic — Bulletin Technique Apicole
Bull Tech Assoc Graphic Arts Jpn — Bulletin. Technical Association of Graphic Arts of Japan
Bull Tech Bur Veri — Bulletin Technique. Bureau Veritas
Bull Tech Cent Rech Zootech Vet Theix — Bulletin Technique. Centre de Recherches Zootechniques et Veterinaires de Theix
Bull Tech Chambre Synd Mines Fer Fr — Bulletin Technique. Chambre Syndicale des Mines de Fer de France
Bull Tech Dep Genet Anim — Bulletin Technique. Departement de Genetique Animale
Bull Tech Div Sols Queb Minist Agric — Bulletin Technique. Division des Sols. Province de Quebec Ministere de l'Agriculture
Bull Tech For Acad — Bulletin. Technical Forest Academy
Bull Tech Gattefosse — Bulletin Technique. Gattefosse
Bull Tech Gattefosse Rep — Bulletin Technique/Gattefosse Report
Bull Tech Genie Rural — Bulletin Technique du Genie Rural
Bull Tech Houille Deriv Inst Natl Ind Charbon — Bulletin Technique de l'Houille et Derives. Institut National de l'Industrie Charbonniere
Bull Tech Inf — Bulletin Technique d'Information
Bull Tech Inf Ingrs Servs Agric — Bulletin Technique d'Information des Ingenieurs des Services Agricoles
Bull Tech Inf Ing Serv Agric — Bulletin Technique d'Information des Ingenieurs des Services Agricoles
Bull Tech Inf Min Agric (France) — Bulletin Technique d'Information. Ministere de l'Agriculture (France)
Bull Tech Inform Min Agr (France) — Bulletin Technique d'Information. Ministere de l'Agriculture (France)
Bull Tech Inst Email Vitrifie — Bulletin Technique de l'Institut de l'Email Vitrifie
Bull Tech Mines Fer Fr — Bulletin Technique des Mines de Fer de France
Bull Tech Mines Inst Natn Ind Charb — Bulletin Technique. Mines. Institut National de l'Industrie Charbonniere
Bull Technol Inst Plant Prod Athens — Bulletin. Technological Institute of Plant Products. Athens
Bull Technol Lab Indian Cent Cott Comm — Bulletin. Technological Laboratory. Indian Central Cotton Committee
Bull Technol Mus Sydney — Bulletin of the Technological Museum (Sydney)
Bull Techn Soc Stand Petroles — Bulletin Technique. Societe Standard Francaise des Petroles
Bull Techn Suisse Rom — Bulletin Technique de la Suisse Romande
Bull Tech Polym — Bulletin Technique Polymeres
Bull Tech Prep Miner Inst Natn Ind Charb — Bulletin Technique. Preparation des Minerais. Institut National de l'Industrie Charbonniere
Bull Tech PTT — Bulletin Technique PTT
Bull Tech Route Silic — Bulletin Technique de la Route Silicatee
Bull Tech Secur Salubr Inst Natl Ind Extr — Bulletin Technique de Securite et Salubrite. Institut National des Industries Extractives
Bull Tech Seric Stn Rech Seric Ales — Bulletin Technique Sericicole. Station de Recherches Sericicoles (Ales)
Bull Tech Serv Tech Aerotech — Bulletin Technique du Service Technique de l'Aerotechnique
Bull Tech Soc Belge Radio Elect — Bulletin Technique de la Societe Belge Radio-Electrique
Bull Tech Soc Fr Constr Babcock et Wilcox — Bulletin Technique. Societe Francaise des Constructions Babcock et Wilcox
Bull Tech Soc Fr Constr Babcock Wilcox — Bulletin Technique. Societe Francaise des Constructions Babcock et Wilcox
Bull Tech Soc Rateau — Bulletin Technique. Societe Rateau
Bull Tech Soc R Belge Ing Ind — Bulletin Technique. Societe Royale Belge des Ingenieurs et des Industriels
Bull Tech Soc Standard Fr Petrol — Bulletin Technique. Societe Standard Francaise des Petroles
Bull Tech Stn Agron Guadeloupe — Bulletin Technique. Station Agronomique de la Guadeloupe

Bull Tech Suisse Romande — Bulletin Technique de la Suisse Romande
Bull Tech Trimest Un Prof Insp Tech Chem de Fer Belg — Bulletin Technique Trimestriel. Union Professionnelle des Inspecteurs Techniques et des Chefs de Section des Chemins de Fer Belges
Bull Tech Un Ingrs Ec Spec Louvain — Bulletin Technique de l'Union des Ingenieurs Sortis des Ecoles Speciales de Louvain
Bull Tech Un Ingrs Tech Inst Gramme Liege — Bulletin Technique. Union des Ingenieurs Techniques Sortis de l'Institut Gramme de Liege
Bull Tech Union Suisse Lithogr Soc Suisse Patrons Lithogr — Bulletin Technique. Edite par l'Union Suisse des Lithographes et la Societe Suisse des Patrons Lithographes
Bull Tech Univ Brno — Bulletin. Technical University Brno
Bull Tech Univ Istanbul — Bulletin. Technical University of Istanbul
Bull Tech Valorisation Util Combust Inst Natl Ind Extr — Bulletin Technique. Valorisation et Utilisation des Combustibles. Institut National des Industries Extractives
Bull Tech Vevey — Bulletin Technique Vevey
Bull Teikoku Gakuen — Bulletin of Teikoku-Gakuen
Bull Telecommun Engng Bur Jpn — Bulletin of the Telecommunication Engineering Bureau of Japan
Bull Teletype Print Telegr Syst — Bulletin. Teletype Printing Telegraph Systems
Bull Temps Obs R Belg — Bulletin du Temps. Observatoire Royale de Belgique
Bull Tenn Agric Exp Stn — Bulletin. Tennessee Agricultural Experiment Station
Bull Tenn Bd Ent — Bulletin. Tennessee Board of Entomology
Bull Tenn Div Geol — Bulletin. Tennessee. Division of Geology
Bull Tenn Nurses Assoc — Bulletin. Tennessee Nurses Association
Bull Tenn St Hort Soc — Bulletin of the Tennessee State Horticultural Society
Bull Tenn Univ Engng Exp Stn — Bulletin. Tennessee University Engineering Experiment Station
Bull Tenth Dist Dent Soc (Rockville Centre) — Bulletin. Tenth District Dental Society (Rockville Centre)
Bull Terminol — Bulletin de Terminologie
Bull Tex Agr Exp Sta — Bulletin. Texas Agricultural Experiment Station
Bull Tex Agric Exp St — Bulletin. Texas Agricultural Experiment Station
Bull Tex Agric Exp Stn — Bulletin. Texas Agricultural Experiment Station
Bull Tex Mem Mus — Bulletin. Texas Memorial Museum
Bull Tex Nurses Assoc — Bulletin. Texas Nurses Association
Bull Tex Ornithol Soc — Bulletin. Texas Ornithological Society
Bull Text Anc — Bulletin de Liaison. Centre International d'Etude des Textiles Anciens
Bull Text Inst Fac Eng Yamagata Univ — Bulletin. Textile Institute. Faculty of Engineering. Yamagata University
Bull Text Res Inst Fac Eng Fukui Univ — Bulletin. Textile Research Institute. Faculty of Engineering. Fukui University
Bull Text Res Inst (Jpn) — Bulletin. Textile Research Institute (Japan)
Bull Thermodyn & Thermochem — Bulletin of Thermodynamics and Thermochemistry
Bull Tob Res Inst — Bulletin. Tobacco Research Institute
Bull Tob Res Inst Taiwan Tob Wine Monop Bur — Bulletin. Tobacco Research Institute. Taiwan Tobacco and Wine Monopoly Bureau
Bull Tochigi Agr Exp Sta — Bulletin. Tochigi Agricultural Experiment Station
Bull Tochigi Prefect Dairy Exp Inst — Bulletin. Tochigi Prefectural Dairy Experimental Institute
Bull Tohoku Inst Technol Sect B — Bulletin. Tohoku Institute of Technology. Section B. Sciences
Bull Tohoku Nat Agr Exp Sta — Bulletin. Tohoku National Agricultural Experiment Station
Bull Tohoku Natl Agric Exp Sta — Bulletin. Tohoku National Agricultural Experiment Station/Tohoku Nogyo ShikenjoKenkyu Hokoku
Bull Tohoku Natl Agric Exp Stn — Bulletin. Tohoku National Agricultural Experiment Station
Bull Tohoku Natn Agric Exp Stn — Bulletin. Tohoku National Agricultural Experiment Station
Bull Tohoku Natol Agr Exp Stn (Morioka) — Bulletin. Tohoku National Agricultural Experiment Station (Morioka)
Bull Tohoku Reg Fish Res Lab — Bulletin. Tohoku Regional Fisheries Research Laboratory
Bull Tokai-Kinki Agr Exp Sta — Bulletin. Tokai-Kinki National Agricultural Experiment Station
Bull Tokai-Kinki Nat Agr Exp Sta — Bulletin. Tokai-Kinki National Agricultural Experiment Station
Bull Tokai-Kinki Natl Agric Exp Stn — Bulletin. Tokai-Kinki National Agricultural Experiment Station
Bull Tokai Reg Fish Res Lab — Bulletin. Tokai Regional Fisheries Research Laboratory
Bull Tokyo Coll Domest Sci — Bulletin. Tokyo College of Domestic Science
Bull Tokyo Coll Photogr — Bulletin. Tokyo College of Photography
Bull Tokyo Dent Coll — Bulletin. Tokyo Dental College
Bull Tokyo Gakugei Univ — Bulletin. Tokyo Gakugei University
Bull Tokyo Gakugei Univ Ser 4 — Bulletin. Tokyo Gakugei University. Series 4
Bull Tokyo Imp Univ Forests — Bulletin. Tokyo Imperial University Forests/Nogaku-Bu Enshurin Hokoku
Bull Tokyo Inst Technol — Bulletin. Tokyo Institute of Technology
Bull Tokyo Inst Technol Ser A — Bulletin. Tokyo Institute of Technology. Series A
Bull Tokyo Kasei Daigaku — Bulletin. Tokyo Kasei Daigaku
Bull Tokyo Med Coll — Bulletin of Tokyo Medical College
Bull Tokyo Med Dent Univ — Bulletin. Tokyo Medical and Dental University
Bull Tokyo Metrop Isot Res Cent — Bulletin. Tokyo Metropolitan Isotope Research Center
Bull Tokyo Metro Rehab Cent Phys Ment Handcp — Bulletin. Tokyo Metropolitan Rehabilitation Center of the Physically and Mentally Handicapped
Bull Tokyo Sci Mus — Bulletin. Tokyo Science Museum
Bull Tokyo Univ For — Bulletin. Tokyo University Forests
Bull Toledo Dent Soc — Bulletin. Toledo [Ohio] Dental Society
Bull Toronto East Med Assoc — Bulletin. Toronto East Medical Association

Bull Torr Bot Club — Bulletin. Torrey Botanical Club
Bull Torrey Bot Club — Bulletin. Torrey Botanical Club
Bull Tottori Agr Exp Sta — Bulletin. Tottori Agricultural Experiment Station
Bull Tottori Agric Exp Stn — Bulletin. Tottori Agricultural Experiment Station
Bull Tottori Fruit Tree Exp Sta — Bulletin. Tottori Fruit Tree Experiment Station/ Tottori-Ken Kaju Shikenjo Kenkyu Hokoku
Bull Tottori Tree Fruit Exp Stn — Bulletin. Tottori Tree Fruit Experiment Station
Bull Tottori Univ For — Bulletin. Tottori University Forests
Bull Tottori Univ Forests — Bulletin. Tottori University Forests/Tottori Daigaku Nogaku-Bu Fusoku Enshurin Hokoku
Bull Tottori Veg Ornamental Crops Exp Stn — Bulletin. Tottori Vegetable and Ornamental Crops Experiment Station
Bull Toyama Agric Exp Stn — Bulletin. Toyama Agricultural Experiment Station
Bull Toyama Food Res Inst — Bulletin of Toyama Food Research Institute
Bull Toyama Prefect Livest Exp Stn — Bulletin. Toyama Prefectural Livestock Experiment Station
Bull Train — Bulletin on Training
Bull Transilvania Univ Brasov Ser B — Bulletin of the Transilvania University of Brasov. Series B. Mathematics, Economic Sciences, Philology, Medicine, Physics, Chemistry, Sports
Bull Transilv Univ Brasov Ser A NS — Transilvania University of Brasov. Bulletin. Series A. New Series
Bull Transilv Univ Brasov Ser B NS — Transilvania University of Brasov. Bulletin. Series B. New Series
Bull Transylv Univ Brasov Ser C — Bulletin of the Transylvania University of Brasov. Seria C. Mathematics. Physics. Chemistry
Bull Tra Soc Pharm Lyon — Bulletin des Travaux. Societe de Pharmacie de Lyon
Bull Trav Dep Chim Inst Hyg Etat Warsaw — Bulletin des Travaux. Department de Chimie. Institut d'Hygiene d'Etat (Warsaw)
Bull Trav Inst Pharm Etat (Warsaw) — Bulletin des Travaux de l'Institut Pharmaceutique d'Etat (Warsaw)
Bull Trav Soc Pharm Bordeaux — Bulletin des Travaux. Societe de Pharmacie de Bordeaux
Bull Trav Soc Pharm Lyon — Bulletin des Travaux. Societe de Pharmacie de Lyon
Bull Trib Pol Cong — Bulletin des Tribunaux de Police Congolais
Bull Tri Cty Dent Soc — Bulletin. Tri-County Dental Society
Bull Trim Ass Cent Vet — Bulletin Trimestriel. Association Centrale des Veterinaires
Bull Trimest Acad Malgache — Bulletin Trimestriel de l'Academie Malgache
Bull Trimest Assoc Anc Eleves Ec Super Brass Univ Louvain — Bulletin Trimestriel de l'Association des Anciens Eleves de l'Ecole Superieure de Brasserie de l'Universite de Louvain
Bull Trimest CEBEDEAU — Bulletin Trimestriel du CEBEDEAU
Bull Trimest Cent Text Controle Rech Sci — Bulletin Trimestriel. Centre Textile de Controle et de Recherche Scientifique
Bull Trimest Credit Com Belgique — Bulletin Trimestriel du Credit Communal de Belgique
Bull Trimest INACOL — Bulletin Trimestriel INACOL
Bull Trimest Inf Carbure Calcium Acetylene — Bulletin Trimestriel d'Information du Carbure de Calcium et de l'Acetylene
Bull Trimest Inst Natl Amelior Conserves Legumes (Belg) — Bulletin Trimestriel. Institut National pour l'Amelioration des Conserves de Legumes (Belgium)
Bull Trimestriel Amis Mus Oceanogr Monaco — Bulletin Trimestriel. Les Amis du Musee Oceanographique de Monaco
Bull Trimestriel Soc Forest Franc Amis Arbres — Bulletin Trimestriel de la Societe Forestiere Francaise des Amis des Arbres
Bull Trimest Soc Hist Nat Amis Mus Autun — Bulletin Trimestriel. Societe d'Histoire Naturelle des Amis du Museum d'Autun
Bull Trimest Soc Hist Nat Sci Biol Energ — Bulletin Trimestriel. Societe d'Histoire Naturelle et des Sciences Biologiques et Energetiques
Bull Trimest Soc Mycol Fr — Bulletin Trimestriel. Societe Mycologique de France
Bull Trimest Soc R Belge Electr — Bulletin Trimestriel. Societe Royale Belge des Electriciens
Bull Trimest Soc Sci Lett Arts Pau — Bulletin Trimestriel de la Societe des Sciences, Lettres, et Arts de Pau
Bull Trimest Soc Vet Lorr — Bulletin Trimestriel de la Societe des Veterinaires Lorrains
Bull Trimest Soc Vet N — Bulletin Trimestriel de la Societe des Veterinaires du Nord
Bull Trimest Synd Fabr Sucre — Bulletin Trimestriel du Syndicat des Fabricants de Sucre
Bull Trimest Synd Med Angers — Bulletin Trimestriel du Syndicat Medical d'Angers
Bull Trimest Synds Med Dep Maine et Loire — Bulletin Trimestriel des Syndicats Mediaux du Departement du Maine-et-Loire
Bull Trimest Un Coord Prod Transp Elect — Bulletin Trimestriel de l'Union pour la Coordination de la Production et du Transport de l'Electricite
Bull Trimest Un Socs Fr Hist Nat — Bulletin Trimestriel. Union des Societes Francaises d'Histoire Naturelle
Bull Trim Inst Arch Luxembourg — Bulletin Trimestriel. Institut Archeologique du Luxembourg
Bull Trim Soc Mycol Fr — Bulletin Trimestriel. Societe Mycologique de France
Bull Trop Pl Res Fdn — Bulletin. Tropical Plant Research Foundation
Bull Tufts Coll — Bulletin. Tufts College
Bull Tufts Dent Club NY — Bulletin of the Tufts Dental Club of New York
Bull Tufts N Engl Med Cent — Bulletin. Tufts New England Medical Center
Bull Tufts New Engl Med Cent — Bulletin. Tufts New England Medical Center
Bull Tulane Med Fac — Bulletin. Tulane Medical Faculty
Bull Tulane Univ Med Fac — Bulletin. Tulane University Medical Faculty
Bull Turk Med Soc — Bulletin. Turkish Medical Society
Bull Turk Phys Soc — Bulletin. Turkish Physical Society
Bull Tuskegee Normal Industr Inst Exp Sta — Bulletin. Tuskegee Normal and Industrial Institute Experiment Station
Bull Uganda Soc — Bulletin. Uganda Society

Bull UICN — Bulletin UICN (Union Internationale pour la Conservation de la Nature et de sesResources)
Bull Ukr Sci Res Inst Grain Cult — Bulletin. Ukrainian Scientific Research Institute of Grain Culture
Bull Umeno Ent Lab — Bulletin of the Umeno Entomological Laboratory
Bull U Mus — Bulletin of the University Museum
Bull Un Agric Caledon — Bulletin de l'Union Agricole Caledonienne
Bull Un Agric Jodoigne — Bulletin de l'Union Agricole de Jodoigne
Bull Agricrs Egypte — Bulletin de l'Union des Agriculteurs d'Egypte
Bull Un Cent Synds Soc Agricrs Fr — Bulletin de l'Union Centrale des Syndicats de la Societe des Agriculteurs de France
Bull Un Charb Mines Us Metall Prov Liege — Bulletin de l'Union de Charbonnages, Mines, et Usines Metallurgiques de la Province de Liege
Bull Un Chin Nat Haiti — Bulletin de l'Union des Chimistes et Naturalistes d'Haiti
Bull Un Colon Fr — Bulletin. Union Coloniale Francaise
Bull UNESCO Reg Off Sci Technol Arab States UNESCO SC/ROSTAS — Bulletin. UNESCO Regional Office for Science and Technology for the Arab States(UNESCO SC/ROSTAS)
Bull Un Exploit Elect Belg — Bulletin de l'Union des Exploitations Electriques en Belgique
Bull Un Geod Geophys Int — Bulletin. Union Geodesique et Geophysique Internationale
Bull Un Geogr N Fr — Bulletin de l'Union Geographique du Nord de la France
Bull Un Int Chem de Fer — Bulletin de l'Union Internationale des Chemins de Fer
Bull Un Int Tub — Bulletin. Union Internationale Contre la Tuberculose
Bull Union Agric Egypte — Bulletin. Union des Agriculteurs d'Egypte
Bull Union Cty Dent Soc — Bulletin. [New Jersey] County Dental Society
Bull Union Med Balk — Bulletin. Union Medicale Balkanique
Bull Union Oceanogr Fr — Bulletin. Union des Oceanographes de France
Bull Union Physiciens — Bulletin. Union des Physiciens
Bull Union Synd Agric Egypte — Bulletin. Union Syndicale des Agriculteurs d'Egypte
Bull Union Synd Apic Picards — Bulletin. Union Syndicale des Apiculteurs Picards
Bull Uniprojektu — Bulletin Uniprojektu
Bull United Bible Soc — Bulletin. United Bible Societies
Bull United Plant Assoc South India Tea Sci Dep — Bulletin. United Planters' Association of Southern India. Tea Scientific Department
Bull United Plant Assoc South Ind Sci Dep — Bulletin. United Planters' Association of Southern India. Scientific Department
Bull Univ Agric Sci Godollo Hung — Bulletin. University of Agricultural Sciences. Godollo, Hungary
Bull Univ Alberta — Bulletin. University of Alberta
Bull Univ Asie Cent — Bulletin de l'Universite de l'Asie Centrale
Bull Univ Brasov Ser C — Bulletin de l'Universite de Brasov. Serie C
Bull Univ Calif Div Agric Sci — Bulletin. University of California. Division of Agricultural Sciences
Bull Univ Cape Town Chamber Mines Precambrian Res Unit — Bulletin. University of Cape Town. Chamber of Mines Precambrian Research Unit
Bull Univ Coll Med (Calcutta) — Bulletin. University College of Medicine (Calcutta)
Bull Univ Coll Med Calcutta Univ — Bulletin. University College of Medicine. Calcutta University
Bull Univ Electro Comm — Bulletin of the University of Electro-Communications
Bull Univ Etat Asie Cent — Bulletin. Universite d'Etat de l'Asie Centrale
Bull Univ Fla Agric Ext Serv — Bulletin. University of Florida. Agricultural Extension Service
Bull Univ Fla Coop Ext Serv — Bulletin. University of Florida. Cooperative Extension Service
Bull Univ Fla Fla Coop Ext Serv — Bulletin. University of Florida. Florida Cooperative Extension Service
Bull Univ Fla Gainesville Inst Food Agric Sci Agric Exp Stn — Bulletin. University of Florida, Gainesville. Institute of Food and Agricultural Experiment Stations
Bull Univ Forest Kyushu Imp Univ — Bulletin. University Forest. Kyushu Imperial University
Bull Univ GA Coll Agr Coop Ext Serv — Bulletin. University of Georgia. College of Agriculture. Cooperative Extension Service
Bull Univ Idaho Coll Agr Ext Serv — Bulletin. University of Idaho. College of Agriculture. Extension Service
Bull Univ Ill Eng Exp Stat — Bulletin. University of Illinois. Engineering Experiment Station
Bull Univ Iowa Inst Agr Med — Bulletin. University of Iowa. Institute of Agricultural Medicine
Bull Univ KY Off Res Eng Serv — Bulletin. University of Kentucky. Office of Research and Engineering Services
Bull Univ Lg — Bulletin. Association des Amis de l'Universite de Liege
Bull Univ Lyon — Bulletin. Universite de Lyon
Bull Univ MD Coop Ext Serv — Bulletin. University of Maryland. Cooperative Extension Service
Bull Univ MD Sch Med — Bulletin. University of Maryland. School of Medicine
Bull Univ Miami Sch Med — Bulletin. University of Miami School of Medicine and Jackson Memorial Hospital
Bull Univ Miami Sch Med Jackson Mem Hosp — Bulletin. University of Miami School of Medicine and Jackson Memorial Hospital
Bull Univ Minn Eng Exp Stat — Bulletin. University of Minnesota. Institute of Technology. Engineering Experiment Station
Bull Univ Minn Inst Technol — Bulletin. University of Minnesota. Institute of Technology
Bull Univ MO Coll Agr Exp Sta — Bulletin. University of Missouri. College of Agriculture. Experiment Station
Bull Univ Mo Eng Exp Stn Ser — Bulletin. University of Missouri. Engineering Experiment Station Series
Bull Univ MO Rolla Tech Ser — Bulletin. University of Missouri at Rolla. Technical Series
Bull Univ Mo Sch Mines Metall — Bulletin. University of Missouri School of Mines and Metallurgy

Bull Univ Nebr State Mus — Bulletin. University of Nebraska State Museum

Bull Univ Neb St Mus — Bulletin. University of Nebraska State Museum

Bull Univ Osaka Prefect Ser A — Bulletin. University of Osaka Prefecture. Series A. Sakai

Bull Univ Osaka Prefect Ser B — Bulletin. University of Osaka Prefecture. Series B. Agriculture and Biology

Bull Univ Osaka Prefect Ser B Agric Biol — Bulletin. University of Osaka Prefecture. Series B. Agriculture and Biology

Bull Univ Osaka Prefecture Ser A — Bulletin. University of Osaka Prefecture. Series A. Engineering and Natural Sciences

Bull Univ Osaka Pref Ser B — Bulletin. University of Osaka Prefecture. Series B

Bull Univ Otago Sch Min Metall — Bulletin of the University of Otago School of Mining and Metallurgy

Bull Univ PR Agric Exp Stn Rio Piedras — Bulletin. University of Puerto Rico. Agricultural Experiment Station. Rio Piedras

Bull Univ RI Agric Exp Stn — Bulletin. University of Rhode Island. Agricultural Experiment Station

Bull Univ RI Coop Ext Serv — Bulletin. University of Rhode Island. Cooperative Extension Service

Bull Univ S Carol — Bulletin. University of South Carolina

Bull Univ Tehran Agric Coll — Bulletin. University of Tehran Agricultural College

Bull Univ Tenn Agric Exp Stn — Bulletin. University of Tennessee. Agricultural Experiment Station

Bull Univ Tex Bur Econ Geol Technol — Bulletin. University of Texas. Bureau of Economic Geology and Technology

Bull Univ Tex Med Ser — Bulletin. University of Texas. Medical Series

Bull Univ Tex Miner Surv Ser — Bulletin. University of Texas. Mineral Survey Series

Bull Univ Tex Scient Ser — Bulletin. University of Texas. Scientific Series

Bull Univ Toronto Sch Engng Res — Bulletin. University of Toronto. School of Engineering Research

Bull Univ Utah Biol Ser — Bulletin of the University of Utah. Biological Series

Bull Univ Utah Geol Ser — Bulletin of the University of Utah. Geological Series

Bull Univ Vt Agric Exp Stn — Bulletin. University of Vermont. Agricultural Experiment Station

Bull Univ Wash Eng Exp Stat — Bulletin. University of Washington. Engineering Experiment Station

Bull Univ Wisconsin Sci Ser — Bulletin. University of Wisconsin. Science Series

Bull Univ Wisconsin Stud Sci — Bulletin. University of Wisconsin. Studies in Science

Bull Univ Wyo Agric Exp Stn — Bulletin. University of Wyoming. Agricultural Experiment Station

Bull Un Synd Architectes Fr — Bulletin de l'Union Syndicale des Architectes Francais

Bull Upp Air Curr Obsns Shanghai — Bulletin of the Upper Air Current Observations. Academia Sinica (Shanghai)

Bull Urb Ld Inst — Bulletin. Urban Land Institute [*Chicago*]

Bull Us — Bulletin Usuel des Lois et Arretes

Bull US Army Med Dep — Bulletin. United States Army Medical Department

Bull US Bur Fish — Bulletin. United States Bureau of Fisheries

Bull US Bur Min — Bulletin. United States Bureau of Mines

Bull US Bur Mines — Bulletin. United States Bureau of Mines

Bull US Cst Geod Surv — Bulletin. United States Coast and Geodetic Survey

Bull US Dept Agric — Bulletin. United States Department of Agriculture

Bull US Geol Surv — Bulletin. United States Geological Survey

Bull US Golf Assoc Green Comm — Bulletin. United States Golf Association. Green Committee

Bull Usin Elect — Bulletin des Usines Electriques

Bull Usin Guerre — Bulletin des Usines de Guerre

Bull Usin Renault — Bulletin des Usines Renault

Bull US Natl Mus — Bulletin. United States National Museum

Bull US Nat Mus — Bulletin. United States National Museum

Bull US Natn Mus — Bulletin. United States National Museum

Bull USSR Inst Agric Microbiol — Bulletin. USSR Institute of Agricultural Microbiology

Bull Utah Agr Exp Sta — Bulletin. Utah Agricultural Experiment Station

Bull Utah Agric Coll — Bulletin of Utah Agricultural College

Bull Utah Agric Exp Stn — Bulletin. Utah Agricultural Experiment Station

Bull Utah Crop Pest Commn — Bulletin. Utah Crop Pest Commission

Bull Utah Eng Exp Stn — Bulletin. Utah Engineering Experiment Station

Bull Utah Geol Miner Surv — Bulletin. Utah Geological and Mineral Survey

Bull Utah Hlth Bd — Bulletin of Utah Health Board

Bull Utah Idaho Sug Co — Bulletin. Utah-Idaho Sugar Co

Bull Utah St Live Stk Bd — Bulletin. Utah State Live Stock Board

Bull Utsunomiya Agric Coll Sect A — Bulletin. Utsunomiya Agricultural College. Section A. Agricultural Sciences and Forestry

Bull Utsunomiya Agric Coll Ser A — Bulletin. Utsunomiya Agricultural College. Series A. Agricultural Sciences, Forestry, Veterinary Science, Agricultural Engineering, Agricultura Chemistry

Bull Utsunomiya Agric Coll Ser B — Bulletin. Utsunomiya Agricultural College. Series B. Agricultural and Forest Economics

Bull Utsunomiya Tob Exp Stn — Bulletin. Utsunomiya Tobacco Experiment Station

Bull Utsunomiya Univ For — Bulletin. Utsunomiya University Forests

Bull Utsunomiya Univ Sect 2 — Bulletin. Utsunomiya University. Section 2

Bull UV Spectrom Group — Bulletin. UV Spectrometry Group

Bull VA Agr Exp Sta — Bulletin. Virginia Agricultural Experiment Station

Bull VA Agric Exp Stn — Bulletin. Virginia Agricultural Experiment Station

Bull VA Agric Ext Serv — Bulletin. Virginia Agricultural Extension Service

Bull Va Div Miner Resour — Bulletin. Virginia Division of Mineral Resources

Bull Vadodara Mus & Pict Gal — Bulletin of the Vadodara Museum and Picture Gallery

Bull VA Geol Surv — Bulletin. Virginia Geological Survey

Bull Val Dent Soc — Bulletin. Valley Dental Society

Bull Vanc Med Ass — Bulletin. Vancouver Medical Association

Bull Vancouver Med Assoc — Bulletin. Vancouver Medical Association

Bull V & A — Bulletin of the Victoria and Albert Museum

Bull Vanderbilt Mar Mus — Bulletin of the Vanderbilt Marine Museum

Bull Vanderbilt Oceanogr Mus — Bulletin of the Vanderbilt Oceanographic Museum

Bull VA Polytech Inst Agr Ext Serv — Bulletin. Virginia Polytechnic Institute. Agricultural Extension Service

Bull Va Polytech Inst Eng Exp Stn Ser — Bulletin. Virginia Polytechnic Institute. Engineering Experiment Station Series

Bull VA Polytech Inst State Univ VA Water Resources Cent — Bulletin. Virginia Polytechnic Institute and State University. Virginia Water Resources Research Center

Bull Va Polytech Inst State Univ Water Resour Res Cent — Bulletin. Virginia Polytechnic Institute and State University. Water Resources Research Center

Bull VA Sect Amer Chem Soc — Bulletin. Virginia Sections of the American Chemical Society

Bull VA Water Resour Res Cent — Bulletin. Virginia Water Resources Research Center

Bull Veg Crops Res Inst Kecskemet Hung — Bulletin. Vegetable Crops Research Institute (Kecskemet, Hungary)

Bull Veg Crops Res Work — Bulletin of Vegetable Crops Research Work

Bull Veg Ornamental Crops Res Stn Ser A — Bulletin. Vegetable and Ornamental Crops Research Station. Series A

Bull Veg Ornamental Crops Res Stn Ser B (Morioka) — Bulletin. Vegetable and Ornamental Crops Research Station. Series B (Morioka)

Bull Veg Ornamental Crops Res Stn Ser C — Bulletin. Vegetable and Ornamental Crops Research Station. Series C

Bull Veg Ornamental Crops Res Stn Ser C (Kurume) — Bulletin. Vegetable and Ornamental Crops Research Station. Series C (Kurume)

Bull Ver Bevord Kennis Ant Besch — Bulletin van de Vereniging tot Bevordering der Kennis van de Antieke Beschaving

Bull Verm Agric Exp St — Bulletin. Vermont Agricultural Experiment Station

Bull Ver Schweiz Pet-Geol Ing — Bulletin. Vereinigung der Schweizerischen Petroleum-Geologen und -Ingenieure

Bull Ver Schweiz Petrol Geol-Ing — Bulletin. Vereinigung der Schweizerischen Petroleum-Geologen und -Ingenieure

Bull Vet — Bulletin Veterinaire

Bull Vet Inst Infect Parasit Dis Acad Agric Sci Bulg — Bulletin. Veterinary Institute of Infectious and Parasitic Diseases. Academy ofAgricultural Sciences. Bulgaria

Bull Vet Inst Pulawy — Bulletin. Veterinary Institute in Pulawy

Bull Vet (Lisb) — Bulletin Veterinaire (Lisbon)

Bull Vet Res Lab Anyang South Korea — Bulletin. Veterinary Research Laboratory (Anyang, South Korea)

Bull Vet Virus Res Inst Acad Agric Sci Bulg — Bulletin. Veterinary Virus Research Institute. Academy of Agricultural Sciences. Bulgaria

Bull Vexin — Bulletin Archeologique du Vexin Francais

Bull Vict Inst Educ Res — Bulletin. Victorian Institute of Educational Research

Bull Vict Mem Mus — Bulletin. Victoria Memorial Museum of the Geological Survey of Canada

Bull Vie A — Bulletin de la Vie Artistique

Bull Vieux Monthey — Bulletin du Vieux-Monthey

Bull Vijnana Parishad India — Vijnana Parishad of India. Bulletin

Bull Virg Agric Exp St — Bulletin. Virginia Agricultural Experiment Station

Bull Virg Dent Ass — Bulletin. Virginia State Dental Association

Bull V Luna Gen Hosp Med Soc — Bulletin V. Luna General Hospital Medical Society

Bull Volcan — Bulletin Volcanologique

Bull Volcanic Eruptions (Tokyo) — Bulletin of Volcanic Eruptions (Tokyo)

Bull Volcanol — Bulletin Volcanologique

Bull Volcanol Heidelberg — Bulletin of Volcanology (Heidelberg)

Bull Volcanol Rome — Bulletin Volcanologique (Rome)

Bull Volcanol Soc Jpn — Bulletin. Volcanological Society of Japan

Bull VSS — Bulletin Vereinigung Schweizerischer Spitzenmacherinnen

Bull VT Agric Exp Stn — Bulletin. Vermont Agricultural Experiment Station

Bull Vt Geol Surv — Bulletin. Vermont. Geological Survey

Bull Vysk Ustavu Pap Celul — Bulletin. Vyskumneho Ustavu Papieru a Celulozy

Bull Vysk Ustavu Potravin — Bulletin. Vyskumneho Ustavu Potravinarskeho

Bull Vysk Ustavu Priem Celul — Bulletin. Vyskumneho Ustavu Priemyslu Celulozy

Bull W Afr Mus Proj — Bulletin of the West African Museums Project

Bull Wagner Free Inst Sci — Bulletin. Wagner Free Institute of Science

Bull Wakayama Fruit Tree Exp Stn — Bulletin. Wakayama Fruit Tree Experiment Station

Bull Walters A G — Bulletin of the Walters Art Gallery

Bull War Med — Bulletin of War Medicine

Bull Waseda Appl Chem Soc — Bulletin. Waseda Applied Chemical Society

Bull Waseda Univ Inst of Comp Law — Waseda University. Institute of Comparative Law. Bulletin

Bull Wash Agr Exp Sta — Bulletin. Washington Agricultural Experiment Station

Bull Wash Agric Exp St — Bulletin. Washington Agricultural Experiment Station

Bull Wash Agric Exp Stn — Bulletin. Washington Agricultural Experiment Station

Bull Wash Div Geol Earth Resour — Bulletin. Washington. Division of Geology and Earth Resources

Bull Wash Div Mines Geol — Bulletin. Washington. Division of Mines and Geology

Bull Wash Geol Surv — Bulletin. Washington Geological Survey

Bull Washington Agric Exp Stn — Bulletin. Washington Agricultural Experiment Station

Bull Wash State Inst Technol — Bulletin. Washington State Institute of Technology

Bull Wash State Univ Agric Res Cent — Bulletin. Washington State University. Agricultural Research Center

Bull Wash State Univ Coll Agric Res Cent — Bulletin. Washington State University. College of Agriculture Research Center

Bull Wash State Univ Coll Eng — Bulletin. Washington State University. College of Engineering

Bull Wash St Coll Ext Serv — Bulletin. Washington State College Extension Service

Bull Water Resour Res Cent Blacksburg Va — Bulletin. Water Resources Research Center (Blacksburg, Virginia)
Bull Wat Res Fdn Aust — Bulletin. Water Research Foundation of Australia
Bull Wds For Dep S Aust — Bulletin. Woods and Forests Department of South Australia
Bull Weld Res Counc — Bulletin. Welding Research Council
Bull Welsh Pl Breed Stn — Bulletin. Welsh Plant Breeding Station. University College of Wales
Bull West Aust For Dep — Bulletin. Western Australia. Forests Department
Bull West Soc Eng — Bulletin. Western Society of Engineers
Bull Wheat Sunflower Res Inst Tolbouhin Acad Agric Sci Bulg — Bulletin. Wheat and Sunflower Research Institute. Tolbouhin. Academy of Agricultural Sciences. Bulgaria
Bull WHO — Bulletin. World Health Organization
Bull Wildl Dis — Bulletin. Wildlife Disease Association
Bull Wildl Dis Assoc — Bulletin. Wildlife Disease Association
Bull Wis Agr Exp Sta — Bulletin. Wisconsin Agricultural Experiment Station
Bull Wis Agric Exp Stn — Bulletin. Wisconsin Agricultural Experiment Station
Bull Wisc Agric Exp St — Bulletin. Wisconsin Agricultural Experiment Station
Bull Wisconsin Nat Hist Soc — Bulletin. Wisconsin Natural History Society
Bull Wis St Conserv Commn — Bulletin. Wisconsin State Conservation Commission
Bull Wistar Inst Anat — Bulletin of the Wistar Institute of Anatomy [*Philadelphia*]
Bull Wld Engng Conf — Bulletin of the World Engineering Conference [*Paris*]</PHR> %
Bull Wld Engng Conf Br Sect — Bulletin of the World Engineering Conference. British Section
Bull Wld Fed Ment Hlth — Bulletin of the World Federation for Mental health
Bull Wld Hlth Org — Bulletin. World Health Organization
Bull Wld Med Ass — Bulletin. World Medical Association
Bull Wld Non Ferr Metal Statist — Bulletin. World Non-Ferrous Metal Statistics
Bull Wollongong Univ Coll — Wollongong University College. Bulletin
Bull Womans Hosp NY — Bulletin of the Woman's Hospital. Cathedral Parkway (New York)
Bull Womans Med Coll Philad — Bulletin of the Woman's Medical College (Philadelphia)
Bull Wom Aux Amer Med Ass — Bulletin. Woman's Auxiliary to American Medical Association
Bull Wood Res Inst Kyoto — Bulletin Wood Research Institute. Kyoto University
Bull Wood Res Lab VA Polyt Inst — Bulletin. Wood Research Laboratory. Virginia Polytechnic Institute
Bull Woods For Dep South Aust — South Australia. Woods and Forests Department. Bulletin
Bull Woods Forests Dep S Aust — Bulletin. Woods and Forests Department of South Australia
Bull Woods Forests Dep S Aust — South Australia. Woods and Forests Department. Bulletin
Bull Woods Forests Dep West Aust — Bulletin of the Woods and Forests Department. Western Australia
Bull Wool Inds Res Ass — Bulletin. Woollen Industries Research Association [*Leeds*]
Bull World Health Organ — Bulletin. World Health Organization
Bull W Scotl Agric Coll — Bulletin. West of Scotland Agricultural College
Bull W Va Agric Exp Sta — Bulletin. West Virginia University. Agricultural Experiment Station
Bull W Va Geol Econ Surv — Bulletin. West Virginia Geological and Economic Survey
Bull W Va Univ Agr Exp Sta — Bulletin. West Virginia University. Agricultural Experiment Station
Bull Wyo Agr Exp Sta — Bulletin. Wyoming Agricultural Experiment Station
Bull Wyo Agric Exp Stn — Bulletin. Wyoming Agricultural Experiment Station
Bull Wyo Agric Ext Serv — Bulletin. Wyoming Agricultural Extension Service
Bull Wyo Dept Agr Div Statist Inform — Bulletin. Wyoming Department of Agriculture. Division of Statistics and Information
Bull Wyo Exp Stn — Bulletin. Wyoming Experiment Station
Bull Wyo Game Fish Commn — Bulletin. Wyoming Game and Fish Commission
Bull Wyo Game Fish Dep — Bulletin. Wyoming Game and Fish Department
Bull Wyo St Geol — Bulletin of the Wyoming State Geologist
Bull Wyo Univ Coop Ext Serv — Bulletin. Wyoming University. Cooperative Extension Service
Bull Wyo Univ Sch Mines Petrol Ser — Bulletin. Wyoming University School of Mines. Petroleum Series
Bull Yale Coll Obs — Bulletin. Yale College Observatory
Bull Yale Sch For — Bulletin. Yale University School of Forestry
Bull Yale Univ — Bulletin of Yale University
Bull Yale Univ Sch For — Bulletin. Yale University. School of Forestry
Bull Yama Fms Mycol Club — Bulletin of the Yama Farms Mycological Club
Bull Yamagata Agric Coll — Bulletin. Yamagata Agricultural College/Yamagata Kenritsu Norin Senmon Gakko Kenkyu Hokoku
Bull Yamagata Univ Agric Sci — Bulletin. Yamagata University. Agricultural Science
Bull Yamagata Univ Eng — Bulletin. Yamagata University. Engineering
Bull Yamagata Univ Med Sci — Bulletin. Yamagata University. Medical Science
Bull Yamagata Univ Nat Sci — Bulletin. Yamagata University. Natural Science
Bull Yamagata Univ Natur Sci — Bulletin. Yamagata University. Natural Science
Bull Yamaguchi Agric Exp Stn — Bulletin. Yamaguchi Agricultural Experiment Station
Bull Yamaguchi Med Sch — Bulletin. Yamaguchi Medical School
Bull Yamaguchi Prefect Poult Breed Stn — Bulletin. Yamaguchi Prefectural Poultry Breeding Station
Bull Yamaguchi Womens Univ Sect 2 — Bulletin of Yamaguchi Women's University. Section 2. Natural Science
Bull Yamanashi Agric Exp Stn — Bulletin. Yamanashi Agricultural Experiment Station

Bull Yamanashi Agric Res Cent — Bulletin. Yamanashi Agricultural Research Center
Bull Yamanashi For Exp Sta — Bulletin. Yamanashi Prefectural Forest Experiment Station
Bull Yamanashi Fruit Tree Exp Stn — Bulletin. Yamanashi Fruit Tree Experiment Station
Bull Yamanashi Pref Agr Exp Sta — Bulletin. Yamanashi Prefectural Agricultural Experiment Station
Bull Yamanashi Prefect Agric Exp Sta — Bulletin. Yamanashi Prefectural Agricultural Experiment Station/Yamanashi-Ken Nogyo Shikenjo Hokoku
Bull Yell Fev Inst Wash — Bulletin. Yellow Fever Institute (Washington)
Bull Yerkes Obs — Bulletin. Yerkes Observatory. University of Chicago
Bull Yichang Inst Geol Miner Resour — Bulletin. Yichang Institute of Geology and Mineral Resources
Bull Yichang Inst Geol Miner Resour Chin Acad Geol Sci — Bulletin. Yichang Institute of Geology and Mineral Resources. Chinese Academy of Geological Sciences
Bull Y Natl Fert Dev Cent (US) — Bulletin Y. National Fertilizer Development Center (United States)
Bull Yokohama City Univ Nat Sci — Bulletin of Yokohama City University. Natural Science
Bull York Inst Archit Study — Bulletin. York Institute of Architectural Study
Bull (Zagreb) — Bulletin International. Academie Yougoslave (Zagreb)
Bull Zambia Language Grp — Bulletin. Zambia Language Group
Bull Zimbabwe Geol Surv — Bulletin. Zimbabwe Geological Survey
Bull Zool — Bulletin of Zoology
Bull Zool Mus Univ Amsterdam — Bulletin. Zoologisch Museum Universitet van Amsterdam
Bull Zool Nom — Bulletin of Zoological Nomenclature
Bull Zool Nomencl — Bulletin of Zoological Nomenclature
Bull Zool Soc Coll Sci (Nagpur) — Bulletin. Zoological Society College of Science (Nagpur)
Bull Zool Soc Egypt — Bulletin. Zoological Society of Egypt
Bull Zool Soc India — Bulletin of the Zoological Society of India
Bull Zool Soc Philad — Bulletin. Zoological Society of Philadelphia
Bull Zool Soc S Diego — Bulletin of the Zoological Society of San Diego
Bull Zool Surv India — Bulletin. Zoological Survey of India
Bul Man Consult Inst — Bulletin. Management Consulting Institute
Bul Med Paris — Bulletin Medical (Paris)
Bul Mens Banque Roy Can — Bulletin Mensuel. Banque Royale du Canada
Bul Mens Bur Relat Pub Ind Sucriere — Bulletin Mensuel. Bureau des Relations Publiques de l'Industrie Sucriere
Bul Mens Com Exter Un Econ Belg Lux — Bulletin Mensuel du Commerce Exterieur. Union EconomiqueBelgo-Luxembourgeoise
Bul Mens Stat Indust — Bulletin Mensuel de Statistiques Industrielles
Bul Mensuel Statis (Cameroon) — Bulletin Mensuel des Statistiques (Cameroon)
Bul Mensuel Statis (Congo People's Republic) — Bulletin Mensuel des Statistiques (Congo People's Republic)
Bul Mensuel Statis (France) — Bulletin Mensuel de Statistique (France)
Bul Mensuel Statis (Gabon) — Bulletin Mensuel de Statistique (Gabon)
Bul Mensuel Statis (Ivory Coast) — Bulletin Mensuel de Statistique (Ivory Coast)
Bul Mensuel Statis Trav — Bulletin Mensuel des Statistiques du Travail
Bul Mensuel Statis (Tunisia) — Bulletin Mensuel de Statistique (Tunisia)
Bul Merkaz Volkani (Bet Dagan Isr) — Buletin. Merkaz Volkani (Bet Dagan, Israel)
Bul Midw MLA — Bulletin. Midwest Modern Language Association
Bul Mon Ist — Buletinul Comisiunii Monumentelor Istorice a Romaniei
Bul Mon Ist — Buletinul Monumentelor Istorica
Bul Mor Mus Found — Bulletin. Moravian Music Foundation
Bul Musashino Academia M — Bulletin. Musashino Academia Musicae
Bul Narcotics (UN) — Bulletin on Narcotics (United Nations)
Bul Nat Clearh Poison Cont Cent — Bulletin. National Clearinghouse for Poison Control Centers
Bul Nat Gallery of SA — Bulletin. National Gallery of South Australia
Bul NE Rose Soc — Bulletin. New England Rose Society
Bul NHPL — Bulletin. New Hampshire Public Libraries
Bul NJ Assoc Osteopath Phys Surg — Bulletin. New Jersey Association of Osteopathic Physicians and Surgeons
Bul NYPL — Bulletin. New York Public Library
Bul of Bibliography — Bulletin of Bibliography and Dramatic Index
Bul Of Propr Ind Sect Invent — Buletin Oficial de Proprietate Industriala. Sectiunea Inventii
Bul OPE — Bulletin. Office de la Protection de l'Enfance
Bul Pan Am Union — Bulletin. Pan American Union
Bul Pat Tradem Inst Can — Bulletin. Patent and Trademark Institute of Canada
Bul Penelitian Hutan — Buletin Penelitian Hutan
Bul Penelitian Teknol Hasil Pertanian — Buletin Penelitian Teknologi Hasil Pertanian
Bul Persat Geol Malays — Buletin Persatuan Geologi Malaysia
Bul Pol — Bulletin des Sciences Politiques
Bul Politeh Gh Asachi Iasi — Buletinul Politehnicii "Gh. Asachi" din Iasi
Bul Polit Liberal — Bulletin sur les Politiques Liberales
Bul Polytec Ecole Polytech Montreal — Bulletin Polytec. Ecole Polytechnique de Montreal
Bul Post-Graduate Ctee in Medicine Univ of Syd — Bulletin. Post-Graduate Committee in Medicine. University of Sydney
Bul PPTM — Buletin PPTM
Bul Prod — Bulletin aux Producteurs
Bul Pusat Pengembangan Teknol Miner — Buletin Pusat Pengembangan Teknologi Mineral
Bul Quebec Asbest Min Assoc — Bulletin. Quebec Asbestos Mining Association
BULR — Boston University. Law Review
Bu LR — Buffalo Law Review
Bul Recherches Hist — Bulletin des Recherches Historiques
Bul Repr — Bulletin of Reprints
BU L Rev — Boston University. Law Review

Bul Sci AIM — Bulletin Scientifique. Association des Ingenieurs Electriciens Sortis de l'Institut Electrotechnique (Montefiore)

Bul Sect Piscic Minist Ind Aliment Rom — Buletinul Sectorului Piscicol. Ministerul Industriei Alimentare. Romania

Bul S/EEJA — Bulletin of Soviet and East European Jewish Affairs

Bul Septuagint St — Bulletin. International Organization for Septuagint and Cognate Studies

Bul Shken Bujqesore — Buletini i Shkencave Bujqesore

Bul Shken Bujqesore Tirana Inst Larte Shteteror Bujqesise — Buletini i Shkencave Bujqesore Tirana. Institute i Larte Shteteror i Bujqesise

Bul Shkencat Biol — Buletin peer Shkencat Biologijke

Bul Shkencat Shoqerore — Buletin per Shkencat Shoqerore

Bul Shkencave Bujqesore — Buletini i Shkencave Bujqesore

Bul Shkencave Gjeol — Buletini i Shkencave Gjeologjike

Bul Shkencave Mjekesore — Buletin i Shkencave Mjekesore

Bul Shkencave Nat — Buletin i Shkencave Natyrore

Bul si Mem Soc Med Vet Bucuresti — Buletinul si Memorie. Societatii de Medicina Veterinaria din Bucuresti

BulSNTS — Bulletin. Studiorum Novi Testamenti Societas

Bul Soc Can Rel Publ — Bulletin. Societe Canadienne des Relations Publiques

Bul Soc Ent Ital — Bulletino della Societa Entomologia Italiana

Bul Soc Ind — Bulletin Social des Industriels

Bul Soc Lang Geog — Bulletin. Societe Languedocienne de Geographie

Bul Soc Liegeoise Musicol — Bulletin. Societe Liegeoise de Musicologie

Bul Soc Naturalistilor Romania — Buletinul Societatii Naturalistilor din Romania

Bul Soc Rom Geogr — Buletinul. Societatii Regale Romane de Geografie

Bul Soc Stiinte Cluj — Buletinul. Societatii de Stiinte din Cluj

Bul Soc Stiinte Geol Repub Soc Rom — Buletinul Societatii de Stiinte Geologice din Republica Socialista Romania

Bul Solidar — Bulletin Solidarnosc

Bul S Res Inst — Bulletin. Southern Research Institute

Bul Stand — Buletinul de Standardizare

Bul Stat Agr — Bulletin des Statistiques Agricoles

Bul Static — Bulletin du Static

Bul Statis Agric — Bulletin Statistique Agricole

Bul Statis (Belgium) — Bulletin de Statistique (Belgium)

Bul Statis et Docum — Bulletin de Statistique et de Documentation

Bul Statis et Econ — Bulletin Statistique et Economique

Bul Statis Mensuel (Lebanon) — Bulletin Statistique Mensuel (Lebanon)

Bul Statis (Rwanda) — Bulletin de Statistique (Rwanda)

Bul Statist Romaniei — Buletinul Statistal Romaniei

Bul Stat Off Plan Stat Off High Com — Bulletin of Statistics. Office of Planning and Statistics. Office of the High Commissioner

Bul Sti Acad Republ Populare Romane — Buletin Stiintific. Academia Republicii Populare Romane/Bulletin Scientifique. Academie de la Republique Populaire Roumaine/Naucnyj Vestnik. Akademija Rumynskoj Narodnoj Respubliki

Bul Sti Inst Politehn (Cluj) — Buletinul Stiintific. Institutului Politehnic (Cluj)

Bul Sti Inst Politehn (Cluj) Ser Construc — Buletinul Stiintific. Institutului Politehnic (Cluj). Seria Constructii

Bul Sti Inst Politehn (Cluj) Ser Electromec — Buletinul Stiintific. Institutului Politehnic (Cluj). Seria Electromecanica

Bul Sti Inst Politehn (Cluj) Ser Mec — Buletinul Stiintific. Institutului Politehnic (Cluj). Seria Mecanica

Bul Stiint Acad Repub Pop Rom — Buletin Stiintific. Academia Republicii Populare Romine

Bul Stiinta Teh Inst Politeh Timisoara — Buletinul de Stiinta si Tehnica al Institutului Politehnic din Timisoara

Bul Stiint Inst Constr (Bucuresti) — Buletinul Stiintific. Institutul de Constructii (Bucuresti)

Bul Stiint Inst Pedagog (Baia Mare) Ser B — Buletin Stiintific. Institutul Pedagogic (Baia Mare). Seria B. Biologie, Fizico- Chimie, Matematica

Bul Stiint Inst Politeh (Cluj) — Buletinul Stiintific. Institutului Politehnic (Cluj)

Bul Stiint Inst Politeh (Cluj-Napoca) — Buletinul Stiintific. Institutului Politehnic (Cluj-Napoca)

Bul Stiint Inst Politeh Cluj Napoca Ser Electroteh Energ Inf — Buletinul Stiintific al Institutului Politehnic Cluj-Napoca. Seria. Electrotehnica, Energetica, Informatica

Bul Stiint Inst Politeh (Cluj) Ser Electromec — Buletinul Stiintific. Institutului Politehnic (Cluj). Seria Electromecanica

Bul Stiint Inst Politehn Cluj-Napoca Ser Arhitect-Construc — Institutului Politehnic Cluj-Napoca. Buletinul Stiintific. Seria Arhitectura-Constructii

Bul Stiint Inst Politehn Cluj-Napoca Ser Chim Metal — Institutului Politehnic Cluj-Napoca. Buletinul Stiintific. Seria Chimie-Metalurgie

Bul Stiint Inst Politehn Cluj-Napoca Ser Construc Mas — Institutului Politehnic Cluj-Napoca. Buletinul Stiintific. Seria Constructii deMasini

Bul Stiint Inst Politehn Cluj Napoca Ser Electrotehn Energet — Buletinul Stiintific. Institutului Politehnic Cluj-Napoca. Seria Electrotehnica-Electrotechnica-Energetica-Informatica

Bul Stiint Inst Politehn Cluj Napoca Ser Mat Apl Mec — Buletinul Stiintific al Institutului Politehnic Cluj-Napoca. Seria Matematica Aplicada, Mecanica

Bul Stiint Inst Politehn Cluj-Napoca Ser Mat-Fiz-Mec Apl — Institutului Politehnic Cluj-Napoca. Buletinul Stiintific. Seria Matematica-Fizica-Mecanica Aplicata

Bul Stiint Inst Politehn (Cluj) Ser Construc — Institutului Politehnic (Cluj). Buletinul Stiintific. Seria Constructii

Bul Stiint Inst Politehn (Cluj) Ser Electromec — Buletinul Stiintific. Institutului Politehnic (Cluj). Seria Electromecanica

Bul Stiint Inst Politehn (Cluj) Ser Mec — Buletinul Stiintific. Institutului Politehnic (Cluj). Seria Mecanica

Bul Stiint Teh Inst Politeh (Timisoara) — Buletinul Stiintific si Tehnic. Institutului Politehnic (Timisoara)

Bul Stiint Teh Inst Politeh Traian Vuia Timisoara — Buletinul Stiintific si Tehnic al Institutului Politehnic Traian Vuia Timisoara

Bul Stiint Teh Inst Politeh Traian Vuia Timisoara Ser Mat Fiz — Buletinul Stiintific si Tehnic al Institutului Politehnic Traian Vuia Timisoara. Seria Matematica-Fizica

Bul Stiint Tehn Univ Tehn Timisoara Mat Fiz — Universitatii Tehnice din Timisoara. Buletinul Stiintific si Tehnic. Matematica-Fizica

Bul Stiint Univ Craiova — Buletinul Stiintific al Universitat. Universitatii Craiova

Bul Stiint Univ Politech Timisoara Rom Ser Chim Ind Ing Mediului — Buletinul Stiintific al Universitatii Politechnica din Timisoara Romania. Seria Chimie Industriala si Ingineria Mediului

Bul Stiint Univ Tehn Timosoara Mat Fiz — Universitatii Tehnice din Timisoara. Buletinul Stiintific. Matematica-Fizica

Bul St Inst Iowa — Bulletin of State Institutions (Iowa)

Bul Stl Tehn Inst Politehn "Traian Vuia" (Timisoara) — Buletinul Stiintific si Tehnic. Institutului Politehnic "Traian Vuia" (Timisoara)

Bul Suicidol — Bulletin of Suicidology

Bul Tax Tarif — Bulletin de Taxes et Tarifs

Bul Teh Inf Cent Cercet Mater Prot — Buletin Tehnico-Informativ. Central de Cercetari pentru Materiale de Protectie

Bul Teh Inf Lab Cent Cercet Lacuri Cerneluri Bucuresti — Buletin Tehnico-Informativ. Laboratorului Central de Cercetari pentru Lacuri siCerneluri Bucuresti

Bulteni Istanbul Tek Univ — Istanbul Teknik Universitesi Bulteni

Bul Th Africa — Bulletin de Theologie Africaine

Bul Thailand Nat Com UNESCO — Bulletin. Thailand National Commission for UNESCO

Bul Trimest Ban Cent Mali — Bulletin Trimestriel. Banque Centrale du Mali

Bul Tutunului — Buletinul Tutunului

Bul UNESCO Reg Off Ed Asia — Bulletin. UNESCO Regional Office for Education in Asia

Bul Univ Brasov — Buletinul. Universitatea din Brasov

Bul Univ Brasov Ser A Mec Apl — Buletinul. Universitatii din Brasov. Seria A. Mecanica Aplicata Constructii de Masini

Bul Univ Brasov Ser C — Buletinul. Universitatea din Brasov. Seria C

Bul Univ Brasov Ser C Mat Fiz Chim Sti Natur — Buletinul. Universitatii din Brasov. Seria C. Matematica, Fizica, Chimie, Stiinte Naturale

Bul Univ Galati Fasc 2 — Buletinul Universitatii din Galati. Fascicula 2. Matematica, Fizica, Mecanica Teoretica

Bul Univ Galati Fasc 4 — Buletinul Universitatii din Galati. Fascicula 4. Constructii de Masini. Frigotehnie. Constructii Navale

Bul Univ Galati Fasc 5 — Buletinul Universitatii din Galati. Fascicula 5. Tehnologii in Constructia de Masini. Metalurgie

Bul Univ Galati Fasc 6 — Buletinul Universitatii din Galati. Fascicula 6. Tehnologia si Chimia Produselor Alimentare

Bul Univ Galati Fasc II Mat Fiz Mec Teoret — Universitatea din Galati Buletinul Fascicula II Matematica Fizica. Mecanica Teoretica

Bul Univ Galati Fasc VI Techn Chim Prod Aliment — Buletinul Universitatii din Galati. Fascicula VI. Technologia si Chimia Produselor Alimentare

Bul Univ Iowa Mus Art — Bulletin. University of Iowa. Museum of Art

Bul Univ Shteteror Tiranes Ser Shkencat Mjekesore — Buletin. Universiteti Shteteror te Tiranes. Seria Shkencat Mjekesore

Bul Univ Shteteror Tiranes Ser Shkencat Nat — Buletin. Universiteti Shteteror te Tiranes. Seria Shkencat Natyrore

Bul Univ Shteteror Tiranes Shk Nat — Buletin. Universiteti Shteteror te Tiranes. Fakulteti i Shkencave te Natyres

Bul Univ Tiranes Enver Hoxha Ser Shkencat Mjekesore — Buletin i Universitetit te Tiranes Enver Hoxha. Seria Shkencat Mjekesore

Bul Univ V Babes Bolyai (Cluj) Ser Stiint Nat — Buletinul Universitatilor "V Babes" si "Bolyai" (Cluj). Seria Stiintele Natura

Bul Un L — Bulletin. Association des Amis de l'Universite de Liege

Bul Van — Bulletin de Vanier

Bul Vie M Belge — Bulletin. Vie Musicale Belge

Bul VIER — Bulletin. Victorian Institute of Educational Research

Bul WHO — Bulletin of the World Health Organization

BUM — Boletin. Universidad de Madrid

Bumagodel Mashinostr — Bumagodelatel'noe Mashinostroenie

Bumazh Prom — Bumazhnaya Promyshlennost

Bumaz Prom — Bumazhnaya Promyshlennost

Bum Derevoobrab Promst — Bumazhnaya i Derevoobrabatyvayushchaya Promyshlennost

BuMH — Bulletin. Missouri Historical Society

BUMMB — Building Materials Magazine

BUMP — Bulletin of the University Museum. University of Pennsylvania (Philadelphia)

BUMPA — Bumazhnaya Promyshlennost

Bum Promst — Bumazhnaya Promyshlennost

BUMSD — Bulletin of Materials Science

BUMTAW — Bulletin. Academie Malgache

BUMYDG — Bulletin of Mycology

Bunda Coll Agric Res Bull — Bunda College of Agriculture. Research Bulletin

BUNDD — Bundesrat - Drucksache

Bundesamt Strahlenschutz Inst Strahlenhyg Ber — Bundesamt fuer Strahlenschutz. Institut fuer Strahlenhygiene Berichte

Bundesanst Arbeitsschutz Schriftenr Gefaehrliche Arbeitsst — Bundesanstalt fuer Arbeitsschutz. Schriftenreihe. Gefaehrliche Arbeitsstoffe

Bundesanst Arbeitsschutz Unfallforsch Dortmund Forschungsber — Bundesanstalt fuer Arbeitsschutz und Unfallforschung. Dortmund. Forschungsbericht

Bundesanst Arbeitsschutz Unfallforsch Schriftenr Arbeitsschutz — Bundesanstalt fuer Arbeitsschutz und Unfallforschung. Schriftenreihe Arbeitsschutz

Bundesanst Forst Holzwirtsch Merkbl — Bundesanstalt fuer Forst- und Holzwirtschaft. Merkblaetter

Bundesanst Materialforsch Pruef Berlin Amts Mitteilungsbl — Bundesanstalt fuer Materialforschung und -Pruefung. Berlin. Amts- und Mitteilungsblatt

Bundesanst Materialpruef Ber — Bundesanstalt fuer Materialpruefung-Berichte

Bundesanst Materialpruef Forschungsber — Bundesanstalt fuer Materialpruefung. Forschungsbericht

Bundesanst Materialpruef Jahresber — Bundesanstalt fuer Materialpruefung. Jahresbericht

Bundesanst Pflanzenschutz Flugbl — Bundesanstalt fuer Pflanzenschutz Flugblatt
Bundesanst Wasserbau Mitteilungsbl Fed Repub Ger — Bundesanstalt fuer Wasserbau. Mitteilungsblatt (Federal Republic of Germany)
Bundesanzeiger Beil — Bundesanzeiger. Beilage
Bundesapothekerkammer Wiss Fortbild Schriftenr Gelbe Reihe — Bundesapothekerkammer zur Wissenschaftlichen Fortbildung. Schriftenreihe. GelbeReihe
Bundesapothekerkammer Wiss Fortbild Schriftenr Gruene Reihe — Bundesapothekerkammer zur Wissenschaftlichen Fortbildung. Schriftenreihe. Gruene Reihe
Bundesapothekerkammer Wiss Fortbild Schriftenr Weisse Reihe — Bundesapothekerkammer zur Wissenschaftlichen Fortbildung. Schriftenreihe. Weisse Reihe
Bundesarbeitsbl — Bundesarbeitsblatt
Bundesforschungsanst Ernaehr Ber — Bundesforschungsanstalt fuer Ernaehrung. Berichte
Bundesforschungsanst Fisch Inst Kuesten Binnenfisch Veroeff — Bundesforschungsanstalt fuer Fischerei. Institut fuer Kuesten- und Binnenfischerei. Veroeffentlichungen
Bundesges — Bundesgesundheitsblatt
Bundesgesetzbl — Bundesgesetzblatt
Bundesgesetzbl Repub Oesterr — Bundesgesetzblatt fuer die Republik Oesterreich
Bundesgesundheitsamt Ber — Bundesgesundheitsamt. Berichte
Bundesgesundheitsamt BGA Schr — Bundesgesundheitsamt. BGA Schriften
Bundesminist Bild Wiss Forschungsber — Bundesministerium fuer Bildung und Wissenschaft. Forschungsbericht
Bundesminist Bild Wiss Forschungsber Kernforsch — Bundesministerium fuer Bildung und Wissenschaft. Forschungsbericht. Kernforschung
Bundesminist Bild Wiss Forschungsber Weltraumforsch — Bundesministerium fuer Bildung und Wissenschaft. Forschungsbericht. Weltraumforschung
Bundesminister Verteidigung Forschungsber Wehrmed — Bundesministerium der Verteidigung. Forschungsbericht aus der Wehrmedizin
Bundesminister Verteidigung Forschungsber Wehrtech — Bundesministerium der Verteidigung. Forschungsbericht aus der Wehrtechnik
Bundesminist Forsch Technol Forschungsber DV — Bundesministerium fuer Forschung und Technologie. Forschungsbericht DV. Datenverarbeitung
Bundesminist Forsch Technol Forschungsber Hum Arbeitslebens — Bundesministerium fuer Forschung und Technologie. Forschungsbericht. Humanisierung des Arbeitslebens
Bundesminist Forsch Technol Forschungsber K — Bundesministerium fuer Forschung und Technologie. Forschungsbericht K. Kernforschung
Bundesminist Forsch Technol Forschungsber Kernforsch — Bundesministerium fuer Forschung und Technologie. Forschungsbericht. Kernforschung
Bundesminist Forsch Technol Forschungsber M — Bundesministerium fuer Forschung und Technologie. Forschungsbericht M. Meeresforschung
Bundesminist Forsch Technol Forschungsber Meeresforsch — Bundesministerium fuer Forschung und Technologie. Forschungsbericht. Meeresforschung
Bundesminist Forsch Technol Forschungsber T — Bundesministerium fuer Forschung und Technologie. Forschungsbericht T. Technologische Forschung und Entwicklung
Bundesminist Forsch Technol Forschungsber W — Bundesministerium fuer Forschung und Technologie. Forschungsbericht W. Weltraumforschung
Bundesminist Forsch Technol Forschungsber Weltraumforsch — Bundesministerium fuer Forschung und Technologie. Forschungsbericht W. Weltraumforschung
Bundesminist Wiss Forsch Forschungsber K 69 03 Kernforsch — Bundesministerium fuer Wissenschaftliche Forschung. Forschungsbericht K 69-03. Kernforschung
Bundes Vers Inst Kulturtech Tech Bodenk — Bundesversuchsinstitut fuer Kulturtechnik und Technische Bodenkunde
BundJb — Bunder Jahrbuch
BUNDMB — Bundnerisches Monatsblatt
Bund Oesterreich Ksterzieher — Bund Oesterreichischer Kunsterzieher
B UNESCO Reg Off Educ — Bulletin. UNESCO [*United Nations Educational, Scientific, and Cultural Organization*] Regional Office for Education in Asia
B Universities Annual — British Universities Annual
B Univ Granada — Boletin. Universidad de Granada
B Univ Santiago — Boletin. Universidad de Santiago de Compostela
Bunseki Kag — Bunseki Kagaku
Bunsen Ges Phys Chem Ber — Bunsen-Gesellschaft fuer Physikalische Chemie. Berichte
BUnt — Biblische Untersuchungen
Bunting Lyon — Bunting and Lyon's Guide to Private Schools
BUOPD — Osaka Prefecture University (Saikai). Bulletin. Series D
BUP — Boletin de la Union Panamericana
BUP — Bulletin. University of Pittsburgh
BUPFA5 — Commonwealth Bureau of Pastures and Field Crops. Hurley Berkshire Bulletin
BUPRD — Budget and Program Newsletter
BUR — Bibliotheque Universelle des Romans
BuR — Bucknell Review
BUR — Bureaucrat
Bur Am Ethn — Bureau of American Ethnology. Bulletin
Bur Am Ethnol Annual Report — Bureau of American Ethnology. Annual Report
Burdekin-Townsville Reg QD Resour Ser — Burdekin-Townsville Region, Queensland. Resource Series
Bureau Amer Ethnol Bull — Bureau of American Ethnology Bulletin
Bureau of Steel Manuf — Bureau of Steel Manufacturers of Australia. Paper Presented at the Annual Meeting
Bur Econ Geol Univ Tex Austin Miner Resour Circ — Bureau of Economic Geology. University of Texas at Austin. Mineral Resource Circular

Buren Ispyt Neft Gazov Skvazhin Oslozhennykh Usloviyakh Uzb — Burenie i Ispytanie Neftyanykh i Gazovykh Skvazhin v Oslozhennykh Usloviyakh Uzbekistana
Bur Farmer — Bureau Farmer
BURG — Bibliotheque Universelle et Revue de Geneve
Burgenlaend Bienenzucht — Burgenlaendische Bienenzucht
Burgenl Heimatbl — Burgenlaendische Heimatblaetter
Burgenl Heim Bl — Burgenlaendische Heimatblaetter
Burgers Med Chem — Burger's Medicinal Chemistry
BurgHb — Burgenlaendische Heimatblaetter
Burg Hbl — Burgenlaendische Heimatblaetter
Burg Monographs in Sci — Burg Monographs in Science
Buridava — Buridava Studii si Materiale
Bur Inform — Bureau et Informatique
Bur Insp Test Commer Commod (China) Bull — Bureau for Inspecting and Testing Commercial Commodities (China). Bulletin
BURJL — Bulletin Ustavu Russkeho Jazyka a Literatury
Burlington Mag — Burlington Magazine
Burl M — Burlington Magazine
Burl Mag — Burlington Magazine
BurM — Burlington Magazine
Burma For Bull — Burma Forest Bulletin
Burma For Dep Burma For Bull — Burma. Forest Department. Burma Forest Bulletin
Burma Law Inst J — Burma Law Institute. Journal
Burma L Inst J — Burma Law Institute. Journal
Burma Med J — Burma Medical Journal
Bur Miner Resour Geol Geophys Bull (Aust) — Bureau of Mineral Resources. Geology and Geophysics. Bulletin (Australia)
Bur Miner Resour Geol Geophys Bull (Canberra) — Bureau of Mineral Resources, Geology, and Geophysics. Bulletin (Canberra)
Bur Miner Resour Geol Geophys Rep (Aust) — Bureau of Mineral Resources. Geology and Geophysics. Report (Australia)
Bur Miner Resour Geol Geophys Rep (Canberra) — Bureau of Mineral Resources, Geology, and Geophysics. Report (Canberra)
Bur Miner Resour J Aust Geol Geophys — Bureau of Mineral Resources Journal of Australian Geology and Geophysics
Bur Mines Inf Circ — Bureau of Mines. Information Circular
Bur Mines Open File Rep US — Bureau of Mines Open File Report (United States)
Bur Mines Rep Invest — Bureau of Mines. Report of Investigations
Bur Mines Res — Bureau of Mines. Research
Bur Mines Technol News — Bureau of Mines. Technology News
Bur Mines Tech Prog Rep US — Bureau of Mines Technical Progress Report (United States)
Burns Chron — Burns Chronicle
Burns Incl Therm Inj — Burns, Including Thermal Injury
Bur Pl Industr Libr Curr Author Entries — Bureau of Plant Industry Library. Current Author Entries
Bur Rech Geol Min Bull Sect 2 Geol Gites Miner (Fr) — Bureau de Recherches Geologiques et Minieres. Bulletin. Section 2. Geologie desGites Mineraux (France)
Bur Rech Geol Min Doc (Fr) — Bureau de Recherches Geologiques et Minieres. Documents (France)
Bur Rech Geol Min Mem Fr — Bureau de Recherches Geologiques et Minieres. Memoire (France)
Burrell — Burrelle's Hispanic Media Directory
Bur River — Burning River News
Burroughs Clear House — Burroughs Clearing House
BURS — Bibliotheque Universelle et Revue Suisse
Burschensch Bll — Burschenschaftliche Blaetter
Bursian — Bursians Jahresbericht ueber die Fortschritte der Klassischen Altertumswissenschaft
Bur Stand J Res — Bureau of Standards Journal of Research
Bur Stand (US) Bull — Bureau of Standards (United States). Bulletin
Bur Stand (US) Cir — Bureau of Standards (United States). Circular
Bur Stand US Handb — US Bureau of Standards. Handbook
Bur Stand US J Res — US Bureau of Standards. Journal of Research
Bur Stand US Misc Publ — Bureau of Standards (United States). Miscellaneous Publication
Bur Stand US Sci Pap — Bureau of Standards (US). Scientific Papers
Bur Stand US Technol Pap — Bureau of Standards (US). Technologic Papers
Bur Sugar Exp Stn (Brisbane) Annu Rep — Bureau of Sugar Experiment Stations (Brisbane). Annual Report
Bur Sugar Exp Stn (Brisbane) Tech Commun — Bureau of Sugar Experiment Stations (Brisbane). Technical Communications
Bur Sugar Exp St Queensl Tech Commun — Bureau of Sugar Experiment Stations. Queensland Technical Communications
Bur Sug Exp Sta Tech Commun — Queensland. Bureau of Sugar Experiment Stations. Technical Communication
Bur Sug Exp Stat Tech Commun — Queensland. Bureau of Sugar Experiment Stations. Technical Communication
Burton Hist Coll Leaflet — Burton Historical Collection Leaflet. Detroit Public Library
Bur Vet Med Tech Rep FDA BVM US Food Drug Adm — Bureau of Veterinary Medicine. Technical Report FDA/BVM (US Food and Drug Administration)
BUS — Brown University. Studies
BUS — Bucknell University Studies
BUS — Bulletin. Universite de Strasbourg
Bus — Busara
BUS — Business and Society Review
BUS — Industrial Management
BuSA — Bulletin. Society for African Church History
BUSAB — Business Administration
Bus Adm — Business Administration
Bus Admin (Great Britain) — Business Administration (Great Britain)

Bus Am — Business America
Bus and Econ Dim — Business and Economic Dimensions
Bus and Econ Dimensions — Business and Economic Dimensions
Bus and Econ Perspectives — Business and Economic Perspectives
Bus and Econ R (Univ SC) — Business and Economic Review (University of South Carolina)
Bus and Fin (Ireland) — Business and Finance (Ireland)
Bus and Public Affairs — Business and Public Affairs
Bus & Scty — Business and Society
Bus & Scty R — Business and Society Review
Bus & Soc — Business and Society Review
Bus and Society — Business and Society
Bus and Society R — Business and Society Review
Bus & Soc R — Business and Society Review
Bus and Socy Rev — Business and Society Review
Busan Women's Univ J — Busan Women's University. Journal
Bus Arch & Hist — Business Archives and History
Bus Arch Cncl Aust Bull — Business Archives Council of Australia. New South Wales Branch. Bulletin
Bus Archives Council Aust Bul — Business Archives Council of Australia. Bulletin
Bus Archives Council Aust Pub — Business Archives Council of Australia. Publications
Bus Archs Hist — Business Archives and History
Bus Asia — Business Asia
Bus Barometer — Business Barometer of Central Florida
Bus Brief — Business Briefing
BUSC — Boletin. Universidad de Santiago de Compostela
BUSCA — Bollettino delle Scienze Mediche
BUSCB — Building Science
Bus China — Business China
Bus Chron — Business Chronicle
BuschsZ — Zeitschrift fuer Deutschen Zivilprozess (Begriff von Busch)
Bus Comm — Business Communications Review
Bus Commer Aviat — Business and Commercial Aviation
Bus Comp Sys — Business Computer Systems
Bus Comput Commun — Business Computing and Communications
Bus Cond Dig — Business Conditions Digest
Bus Conditions Dig — Business Conditions Digest
BUSE — Boston University. Studies in English
BUSEB — Byulleten' Sovetskoi Antarkticheskoi Ekspeditsii
Bus Econ — Business Economics
Bus Econ Fin Ser — Business Economics and Finance Series
Bus Economist — Business Economist
BUSED — Base and User
Bus Ed Forum — Business Education Forum
Bus Ed J — Business Education Journal
Bus Ed News — Business Education Council. Newsletter
Bus Ed Observer — New Jersey Business Education Observer
Bus Educ Forum — Business Education Forum
Bus Educ Ind — Business Education Index
Bus Educ Index — Business Education Index
Bus Ed World — Business Education World
Bus E Eur — Business Eastern Europe
Bus Europe — Business Europe
Bus Exch — Business Exchange
Bus Fin Rev — Business Finance Review
Bus Form Rep — Business Forms Reporter
Bus Forum — Business Forum
Bus Franchise Guide CCH — Business Franchise Guide. Commerce Clearing House
Bus Grad — Business Graduate
Bus Health — Business and Health
Bus Hist — Business History
Bus History — Business History
Bus Hist R — Business History Review
Bus Hist Rev — Business History Review
Bus Hist Soc Bull — Business History Society. Bulletin
Bus Horiz — Business Horizons
Bus Horizn — Business Horizons
Bus Horizons — Business Horizons
BusI — Business Periodicals Index
BUSIB — Bussei
Bus in Brief — Business in Brief
Bus India — Business India
Busin Econ — Business Economics
Busin Economist — Business Economist
Busines NC — Business North Carolina
Busines NJ — Southern New Jersey Business Digest
Business Autmn — Business Automation
Business Equip Dig — Business Equipment Digest
Business Hist — Business History
Business Hist Rev — Business History Review
Business Hist Soc Bul — Business Historical Society. Bulletin
Business Insur — Business Insurance
Business LJ — Business Law Journal
Business LR — Business Law Review
Business Org Agen Dir — Business Organizations and Agencies Directory
Business Q — Business Quarterly
Business R — Business Review
Business Rev — Business Review
Bus Inf — Business Information
Bus Inf Technol — Business Information Technology
Busin Monitor Rubb — Business Monitor. Rubber
Busin Monitor Synth — Business Monitor. Synthetic Resins and Plastics Materials
Busin R — Business Review

Busin Soc R — Business and Society Review
Bus Insur — Business Insurance
Bus Int Ind — Business International Index
Bus Int Mo — Business International. Money Report
Bus Intnl — Business International
Bus Ja — Business Japan
Bus Jap — Business Japan
Bus Japan — Business Japan
Bus J (Manila) — Business Journal (Manila)
Bus Jpn — Business Japan
Bus Jrl NJ — Business Journal of New Jersey
Bus J (San Jose) — Business Journal (San Jose, California)
BUSKA — Bulletin. Schweizerischer Elektrotechnischer Verein
BUSKB — Bussei Kenkyu
Bus L — Business Lawyer
BUSL — Business Life
BUSLA — Bulletin International. Academie Yougoslave des Sciences et des Beaux-Arts. Classe des Sciences Mathematiques et Naturelles
Bus Lanka — Business Lanka
B Us L Ar — Bulletin Usuel des Lois et Arretes
Bus Latin A — Business Latin America
Bus Law — Business Lawyer
Bus Law — Businessman's Law
Bus Law Memo — Business Law Memo
Bus Law R — Business Law Review
Bus Laws Oman — Business Laws of Oman
Bus Lawyer — Business Lawyer
Bus Lit — Business Literature
Bus LJ — Business Law Journal
Bus Loc File — Business Location File
Bus LR — Business Law Review
Bus L Rev — Business Law Review
Bus L Rev (Butterworths) — Business Law Review (Butterworths)
Bus Mag — Business Magazine
Bus Mark — Business Marketing
Bus Matters — Business Matters
Bus Media — Business and the Media
Bus Mexico — Business Mexico
Bus Mktg — Business Marketing
BUSN — Business North
BUSNM — Bulletin. United States National Museum
Busn Times — Business Times
Bus Overseas — Business Overseas
Bus Period Index — Business Periodicals Index
Bus Print — Business Printer
Bus Prof Ethics J — Business and Professional Ethics Journal
Bus Pub Ind Abst — Business Publications Index and Abstracts
Bus Publ — Business Publisher
Bus Q — Business Quarterly
Bus Radio Buy G — Business Radio Buyers' Guide
Bus R (Bangkok) — Business Review (Bangkok)
Bus Rev — Business Review
Bus Rev Kobe Univ — Business Review. Kobe University
Bus Rev Wash Univ — Business Review. Washington University
Bus Rev Wkly — Business Review Weekly
BUSS — Buletin i Universitetit Shteteror te Tiranes. Seria Shkencat Shoqerore
BuSSAC — Bulletin de la Societe Scientifique et Artistique de Clamecy
Bus Scotland — Business Scotland
Bus Scr — Business Screen
Bus Soc — Business and Society
Bus Soc Rev — Business and Society Review
Bus Software Rev — Business Software Review
Bus Stat — Business Statistics. US Department of Commerce
BuSSY — Bulletin de la Societe des Sciences Historiques et Naturelles de l'Yonne
Bus Syst — Business Systems
Bus Syst & Equip — Business Systems and Equipment
Bus Syst Update — Business Systems Update
BUST — Buletin i Universitetit Shteteror te Tiranes. Seria Shkencat Shoqerore
Bus Taiwan — Business and Industry Taiwan
Bus Tech Video — Business and Technology Videolog
Bus Today — Business Today
Bus Track Trans — Bus and Track Transport
Bus Trade — Business and Trade
Bus Transp — Bus Transportation
Bus Trav — Business Traveler
Bus Trav Rep — Business Traveler's Report
Bus Tr Surv — Business Trends Survey
Bus Unix Jnl — Business Unix Journal
Bus Update — Business Update
Bus Venezuela — Business Venezuela
Bus W — Business Week
Bus Week — Business Week
Bus Week Ind Technol Ed — Business Week. Industrial/Technology Edition
BUT — Buletin. Universiteti Shteteror te Tiranes. Seria Shkencat Shoqerore
BUT — Bulletin. Universite de Toulouse
BUT — Business International
Butl Bib Catalunya — Butlleti de la Biblioteca de Catalunya
Butl Cent Excurs Catalunya — Butlleti del Centre Excursionista de Catalunya
Butler — Butler's Money Fund Report
Butler Univ Bot Stud — Butler University Botanical Studies
Butl Inf Cer — Butlleti Informatiu de Ceramica
Butl Inst Catalana Hist Nat — Butlleti. Institucio Catalana d'Historia Natural
Butl Soc Catalana Pediatr — Butlleti. Societat Catalana de Pediatria
Butl Mus A Barcelona — Butlleti dels Museus d'Art de Barcelona
Butl Mus N A Catalunya — Butlleti del Museu Nacional d'Art de Catalunya

Butl Sec Mat — Butlleti de la Seccio de Matematiques
Butl Sec Mat Soc Catalana Cienc Fis Quim Mat — Butlleti. Seccio de Matematiques. Societat Catalana de Ciencies Fisiques, Quimiques, i Matematiques
Butl Soc Catalana Cienc Fis Quim Mat 2 — Butlleti. Societat Catalana de Ciencies Fisiques, Quimiques, i Matematiques. Segona Epoca
Butl Soc Catalana Mat — Butlleti de la Societat Catalana de Matematiques
BUTMB — Building Technology and Management
BUTPA — Butane Propane
Butsuri Phys Soc Jap — Butsuri. Physical Society of Japan
Butter & Cheese J — Butter and Cheese Journal
Butter Cheese Milk Prod J — Butter, Cheese, and Milk Products Journal
Butterworth Heinemann Int Med Rev Neurol — Butterworth-Heinemann International Medical Reviews. Neurology
Butterworth Heinemann Ser Chem Engrg — Butterworth-Heinemann Series in Chemical Engineering
Butterworths Int Med Rev Cardiol — Butterworths International Medical Reviews. Cardiology
Butterworths Int Med Rev Clin Endocrinol — Butterworths International Medical Reviews. Clinical Endocrinology
Butterworths Int Med Rev Clin Pharmacol Ther — Butterworths International Medical Reviews. Clinical Pharmacology and Therapeutics
Butterworths Int Med Rev Gastroenterol — Butterworths International Medical Reviews. Gastroenterology
Butterworths Int Med Rev Hematol — Butterworths International Medical Reviews. Hematology
Butterworths Int Med Rev Neurol — Butterworths International Medical Reviews. Neurology
Butterworths Int Med Rev Obstet Gynecol — Butterworths International Medical Reviews. Obstetrics and Gynecology
Butterworths Int Med Rev Ophthalmol — Butterworths International Medical Reviews. Ophthalmology
Butterworths Int Med Rev Orthop — Butterworths International Medical Reviews. Orthopaedics
Butterworths Int Med Rev Otolaryngol — Butterworths International Medical Reviews. Otolaryngology
Butterworths Int Med Rev Pediatr — Butterworths International Medical Reviews. Pediatrics
Butterworths Int Med Rev Rheumatol — Butterworths International Medical Reviews. Rheumatology
Butterworths Int Med Rev Surg — Butterworths International Medical Reviews. Surgery
Butterworths Int Med Rev Urol — Butterworths International Medical Reviews. Urology
Butterworth's SA Law Review — Butterworth's South African Law Review
Butterworth's South Afr L Rev — Butterworth's South African Law Review
Butt SA Law Rev — Butterworth's South African Law Review
BUV — Biblioteca de la Universidad del Valle [*Cali*]
BUVOA — Bulletin Volcanologique
BUVSA — Bulletin. Vereinigung der Schweizerischen Petroleum-Geologen und -Ingenieure
BuW — Buhne und Welt
BUW — Business Week
BUWEA — Business Week
BUX — Greece's Weekly for Business and Finance
Buy Farm — Buying for the Farm
BUYRA — Bulletin. Parenteral Drug Association
Buzz E J — Buzzworm's Earth Journal
BV — Bharatiya Vidya
BV — Biblical Viewpoint
BV — Bilder Griechischen Vasen
BV — Bogens Verden
BV — Bogoslovni Vestnik
BV — Bratskii Vestnik
BV — Bulletin Volcanologique
BV — Bundesverfassung
BV — Byzantina Vindobonensia
BVAB — Bulletin van de Vereeniging tot Bevordering der Kennis van de Antike Beschaving
B Vallad — Boletin. Seminario de Estudios de Arte y Arqueologia. Universidad de Valladolid
BVAOD — Byulleten' Vil'nyusskoi Astronomicheskoi Observatorii
B Var — Bulletin. Academie du Var
BVB — Bont. Maandblad voor het Bontbedrijf
BVBHAG — Bergbauwissenschaften und Verfahrenstechnik im Bergbau und Huettenwesen
BVBI — Bayerische Vorgeschichtsblaetter
BVC — Bericht des Vereins Carnuntum in Wien
BVC — Bible et Vie Chretienne
B Vendome — Bulletin. Societe Archeologique, Scientifique, et Litteraire du Vendomois
BVG — Bijdragen voor Vaderlandsche Geschiedenis en Oudheidskunde
BVGO — Bijdragen voor Vaderlandsche Geschiedenis en Oudheidskunde
BVGPA — Boletin Informativo. Asociacion Venezolana de Geologia, Mineria, y Petroleo
B Vgzh — Bulletin van Volksgezondheid
BVHUA — Bibliotheca "Vita Humana"
BVI — Venezolaans Nederlandse Kamer van Koophandel en Industrie. Bulletin
BVIBA — Biologiya Vnutrennykh Vod. Informatsionnyi Byulleten
B Vichy — Bulletin. Societe d'Histoire et d'Archeologie de Vichy et des Environs
B Victoria Mem — Bulletin. Victoria Memorial Museum of the Geological Survey of Canada
BVIRA — Byulleten' Vsesoyuznogo Nauchno-Issledovatel'skogo Instituta Rastenievodstva Imeni N. I. Vavilova
BVJ — British Veterinary Journal

BVJOA — British Veterinary Journal
BVJOA9 — British Veterinary Journal
BVL — Beitraege zur Vogelkunde (Leipzig)
BVM — Buvoha Mededelingen
BVmB — Bulletin de la Vie Musicale Belge
BVNLDN — Berichte des Vereins Natur und Heimat und des Naturhistorischen Museums zu Luebeck
BVP — Business Venture Profiles
BVP — Personenvervoer
BVR — Bausteine zur Volkskunde und Religionswissenschaft
BVR — Beroepsvervoer
BVR — Byggvaruregistret
BVSAW — Berichte. Verhandlungen der [*Koeniglich*] Saechsischen Akademie der Wissenschaften zu Leipzig
BVSAWL — Berichte. Verhandlungen der Saechsischen Akademie der Wissenschaften zu Leipzig
BVSGW — Berichte. Verhandlungen der Saechsischen Gesellschaft der Wissenschaften
BVSRJL — Bulletin Vysoke Skoly Russkeho Jazyka a Literatury
BVUPD — Bulletin. Vyskumneho Ustavu Potravinarskeho
BVZ — Berliner Volks-Zeitung
BW — Bankwissenschaft
BW — Between Worlds
BW — Biblical World
BW — Blick durch die Wirtschaft
BW — Blues World
BW — Books and Writers
BW — Book Week
BW — Book World
BW — Brass and Wind News
BW — Buecherei Winter
BW — Business Week
BWA — Business Venezuela
BWANT — Beitraege zur Wissenschaft vom Alten und Neuen Testament
B Waremme — Bulletin d'Information. Societe d'Archeologie et d'Histoire de Waremme et Environs
BWAT — Beitraege zur Wissenschaft vom Alten Testament
BWATA — Biuletyn Wojskowej Akademii Technicznej Imienia Jaroslawa Dabrowskiego
BWAuNT — Beitraege zur Wissenschaft vom Alten und Neuen Testament
BWB — Berliner Wirtschaftsbericht
BWB — Burma Weekly Bulletin
BWCSA — Broad Way Clinical Supplement
BWDEB — Boden Wand und Decke
BWE — Business Week
BWESA — Berliner Wetterkarte. Supplement
BWF — Business Review. Wells Fargo Bank
BWG — Bouw. Onafhankelijk Weekblad voor de Bouw
B WHO — Bulletin. World Health Organization
B Wi — Bankwirtschaft
B Wi — Bankwissenschaft
B Wirtsch B — Berliner Wirtschaftsbericht
B Wk — Book Week
BWK — Brennstoff-Waerme-Kraft
BWKG — Blaetter fuer Wuerttembergische Kirchengeschichte
BWL — Bouwbelangen
BWO — Bibliographie der Wirtschaftspresse
BWPA News Sheet — BWPA [*British Wood Preserving Association*] News Sheet
BWpBZV — Bericht des Westpreussischen Botanisch-Zoologischen Vereines
B W Pr — Wickelmannsprogramm der Archaeologischen Gesellschaft zu Berlin
BWQ — Brass and Woodwind Quarterly
Bw R — Betriebswirtschaftliche Rundschau
BWR — Black Warrior Review
BWR — Bouwkroniek. Weekblad voor de Bouwvakken en Aanverwante Vakken. Aanbestedingsbulletin voor Alle Werken en Leveringen
BWT — Bestuurswetenschappen
BWTSA — Bauwirtschaft
BWUJD — Busan Women's University. Journal
BWVACET — Bulletin. West Virginia Association of College English Teachers
BW (WP) — Book World (Washington Post)
BWWSAP — Branntweinwirtschaft
BWX — Berliner Wirtschaft; Mitteilungen der Industriekammer und Handelskammer zu Berlin
BWY — Bouw/Werk. De Bouw in Feiten, Cijfers, en Analyses
B Wyo Agric Exp Stn — Bulletin. Wyoming Agricultural Experiment Station
BxA — Beaux-Arts
BXD — Bulletin de Documentation Rhenane
BXK — Bank Leumi Le-Israel. Economic Review
BXTJA — Bendix Technical Journal
BXV — Boxboard Containers
BY — British Yearbook of International Law
BYA — Beleidsanalyse
B Yale — Bulletin. Yale University Art Gallery
B Yale U — Bulletin. Yale University Art Gallery
BYB — British Yearbook of International Law
BYB — Maandstatistiek Bouwnijverheid
BYBBA — Brigham Young University. Science Bulletin. Biological Series
BYBBAJ — Brigham Young University. Science Bulletin. Biological Series
By Bygd — By og Bygd
BYDAA — Baylor Dental Journal
Bydgoskie Tow Nauk Pr Wydz Nauk Tech Ser A — Bydgoskie Towarzystwo Naukowe. Prace Wydzialu Nauk Technicznych. Seria A
Bydgoskie Tow Nauk Wydz Nauk Przyr Pr Ser A — Bydgoskie Towarzystwo Naukowe. Wydzial Nauk Przyrodniczych. Prace. Seria A

Bydgoskie Tow Nauk Wydz Nauk Przyr Pr Ser B — Bydgoskie Towarzystwo Naukowe. Wydzial Nauk Przyrodniczych. Prace. Seria B
Bydgoskie Tow Nauk Wydz Nauk Tech Pr Ser B — Bydgoskie Towarzystwo Naukowe Wydzial Nauk Technicznych. Prace. Seria B
ByF — Biblia y Fe
BYGEA — Byggmestern
Byg F — Bygge Forum
Bygind — Byggeindustrien
Bygkst — Byggekunst
Bygm — Bygmesteren
Bygnin Medd — Bygningsstatiske Meddelelser
Bygn M — Bygningsstatiske Meddelelser
BYGSA — Brigham Young University. Geology Studies
BYH — Bulletin. Europese Gemeenschappen. Europese Gemeenschap voor Kolen en Staal, Europese Economische Gemeenschap, Europese Gemeenschap voor Atoomenergie
BYIL — British Yearbook of International Law
BYILDJ — Biology International
ByJ — Byzantinisch-Neugriechische Jahrbuecher
BYL — Bulletin van de Generale Bankmaatschappij
Bylg Plodove Zelenchutsi Konserv — Bylgarski Plodove Zelenchutsi i Konservi
BYLJA — Bayerisches Landwirtschaftliches Jahrbuch
By LR — Baylor Law Review
BYM — Bell Journal of Economics
BYMEA — Bygningsstatiske Meddelelser
BYMOA — Byulleten' Moskovskogo Obshchestva Ispytatelei Prirody Otdel Biologicheskii
B Yokohama City Univ — Bulletin. Yokohama City University
B Yonne — Bulletin. Societe des Sciences Historiques et Naturelles de l'Yonne
Byron J — Byron Journal
Byrsa — Cahiers de Byrsa
Bysl — Byzantino-Slavica
BYSTA — Byulleten' Stroitel'noi Tekhniki
ByT — Barrasiha-Ye Tarikhi
BYT — Byte
BYTE Spcl — BYTE. The Small Systems Journal. Special IBM Issue
Bytova Kult — Bytova Kultura
Bytraf — Bytrafik
BYU — BYU [*Brigham Young University*] Law Review
Byul Brashovskogo Univ Ser C — Byuleten Brashovskogo Universiteta. Seriya C
Byul Gl Upr Stroit Voiski (Sofia) — Byulleten'. Glavno Upravlenie na Stroitelnite Voiski (Sofia)
Byul Inst Stuklo Fina Keram — Byuletin. Institut po Stuklo i Fina Keramika
Byull Abastumanskaya Astrofiz Obs Akad Nauk Gruz SSR — Byulleten' Abastumanskaya Astrofizicheskaya Observatoriya Akademiya Nauk Gruzinskoi SSR
Byull Akad Nauk Gruz SSR Abastumanskaya Astrofiz Obs — Byulleten' Akademiya Nauk Gruzinskoi SSR Abastumanskaya Astrofizicheskaya Observatoriya
Byull Akad Nauk Uzb SSR — Byulleten' Akademii Nauk Uzbekskoi SSR
Byull Astron Inst Chekh — Byulleten' Astronomicheskikh Institutov Chekhoslovakii
Byull Azerb Nauchno Issled Inst Khlopkovod — Byulleten' Azerbaidzhanskogo Nauchno Issledovatel'skogo Instituta Khlopkovodstva
Byull Belogo Morya — Byulleten' Belogo Morya
Byull Bot Sada Akad Nauk Arm SSR — Byulleten' Botanicheskogo Sada Akademii Nauk Armyanskoi SSR
Byull Bot Sada Erevan — Byulleten' Botanicheskogo Sada Erevan
Byull Eksp Biol Med — Byulleten' Eksperimental'noi Biologii i Meditsiny
Byull Fiziol Rast — Byulleten' po Fiziologii Rastenii
Byull Geogr Inst — Byulleten' Geograficheskogo Instituta
Byull Gidrotekhstroya — Byulleten Gidrotekhstroya
Byull Gipromeza — Byulleten Gipromeza
Byull Glav Bot Sada — Byulleten Glavnogo Botanicheskogo Sada
Byull Glavn Bot Sada (Leningr) — Byulleten' Glavnogo Botanicheskogo Sada (Leningrad)
Byull Glavn Kom Delam Bumazh Prom — Byulleten' Glavnogo Komiteta po Delam Bumazhnoi Promyshlennosti i Torgovli pri Vysshom Sovete Narodnago Khozyaistva
Byull Glavn Kom Vses Sel Khoz Vyst — Byulleten' Glavnogo Komiteta Vsesoyuznoi Sel'skokhozyaistvennoi Vystavki
Byull Glavn Uprav Nauch Khudozh Muz Uchrezh — Byulleten' Glavnogo Upravleniya Nauchnykh, Khudozhestvennykh i Muzeinykh Uchrezhdenii Akademicheskogo Tsentra Narkomprosa
Byull Glavn Voenno Vet Kom — Byulleten' Glavnogo Voenno-Veterinarnago Komiteta
Byull Gl Bot Sada — Byulleten' Glavnogo Botanicheskogo Sada
Byull Gos Makeev Nauchno Issled Inst Bezop Rab Gorn Promsti — Byulleten. Gosudarstvennyi Makeevskii Nauchno-Issledovatel'skii Institut po Bezopasnosti Rabot v Gornoi Promyshlennosti
Byull Gos Nikitsk Bot Sada — Byulleten' Gosudarstvennogo Nikitskogo Botanicheskogo Sada
Byull Gosplana — Byulleten Gosplana
Byull Gosud Astr Inst Shternberga — Byulleten' Gosudarstvennogo Astronomicheskogo Instituta imeni Shternberga
Byull Gosud Kom Elektrif Ross — Byulleten' Gosudarstvennoi Komissii po Elektrifikatsii Rossii
Byull Gosud Nikitsk Opyt Bot Sad — Byulleten' Gosudarstvennogo Nikitskogo Opytnogo Botanicheskogo Sada
Byull Gosud Okeanogr Inst — Byulleten' Gosudarstvennogo Okeanograficheskogo Instituta
Byull Inf Tsentra Yad Dannym — Byulleten' Informatsionnogo Tsentral'nogo po Yadernym Dannym
Byull Inf Tsentr Genet Lab Im I V Michurina — Byulleten' Informatsii Tsentralnoi Geneticheskoi Laboratorii Imeni I. V. Michurina

Byull Inst Astrofiz Akad Nauk Tadzh — Byulleten' Instituta Astrofiziki Akademiya Nauk Tadzhikskoi SSR
Byull Inst Astrofiz Akad Nauk Tadzh SSR — Byulleten' Instituta Astrofiziki Akademiya Nauk Tadzhikskoi SSR
Byull Inst Astrofiz Stalinabad — Byulleten' Instituta Astrofiziki (Stalinabad)
Byull Inst Biol Akad Nauk Beloruss SSR — Byulleten Instituta Biologii Akademii Nauk Belorusskoi SSR
Byull Inst Biol Akad Nauk B SSR — Byulleten' Instituta Biologiya Akademii Nauk Belorusskoi SSR
Byull Inst Biol Mlnsk — Byulleten' Instituta Biologii. Belaruskaya Akademiya Navuk (Minsk)
Byull Inst Biol Vodokhran — Byulleten' Instituta Biologii Vodokhranilishcha
Byull Inst Biol Vodokhran Akad Nauk SSSR — Byulleten Instituta Biologii Vodokhranilishch. Akademiya Nauk SSSR
Byull Inst Epidem Mikrobiol Tashkent — Byulleten' Instituta Epidemiologii i Mikrobiologii i Nauchnogo Obshchestva Epidemiologov, Mikrobiologov, Parazitologov i Sanitarnykh Vrachei (Tashkent)
Byull Inst Mekhaniz Sel Khoz — Byulleten' Instituta Mekhanizatsii Sel'skogo Khozyaistva
Byull Inst Metallokeram Spets Splavov Akad Nauk Ukr SSR — Byulleten' Instituta Metallokeramiki i Spetsial'nykh Splavov Akademiya Nauk Ukrainskoi SSR
Byull Inst Morsk Med Gdanske — Byulleten Instituta Morskoi Meditsiny v Gdan'ske
Byull Inst Morsk Trop Med Gdyne — Byulleten Instituta Morskoi i Tropicheskoi Meditsiny v Gdyne
Byull Inst Teor Astron — Byulleten' Instituta Teoreticheskoi Astronomii
Byull Inst Teor Astron Akad Nauk SSSR — Byulleten' Instituta Teoreticheskoi Astronomii Akademiya Nauk SSSR
Byull Inst Teoret Astronom — Akademiya Nauk SSSR. Byulleten Instituta Teoreticheskoi Astronomii
Byull Inst Zern Khoz Yugo Vost SSSR — Byulleten' Instituta Zernovogo Khozyaistva Yugo-Vostoka SSSR
Byull Ivanov Nauchno Issled Inst Khlopchatobum Promsti — Byulleten Ivanovskogo Nauchno-Issledovatel'skogo Instituta Khlopchatobumazhnoi Promyshlennosti
Byull Izobr — Byulleten' Izobretenii
Byull Izobret — Byulleten Izobretenii
Byull Izobret Tovarnykh Znakov — Byulleten Izobretenii i Tovarnykh Znakov
Byull Kavk Inst Miner Syrya — Byulleten' Kavkazskogo Instituta Mineral'nogo Syr'ya
Byull Kazan Okruga Put Soobshch — Byulleten' Kazanskago Okruga Putei Soobshcheniya
Byull Kharkov Obshch Lyub Prir — Byulleten' Khar'kovskago Obshchestva Lyubitelei Prirody
Byull Khlopkovod Koop — Byulleten' Khlopkovodcheskoi Kooperatsii
Byull Kiev Politekh Obshch Inzh Agron — Byulleten' Kievskago Politekhnicheskago Obshchestva Inzhenerov i Agronomov
Byull Kirgiz Nauch Issled Inst Zemled — Byulleten' Kirgizskogo Nauchno-Issledovatel'skogo Instituta Zemledeliya
Byull Kirgiz Nauchno-Issled Inst Zeml — Byulleten' Kirgizskogo Nauchno-Issledovatel'skogo Instituta Zemledeliya
Byull Kirg Nauchno Issled Inst Zemled — Byulleten' Kirgizskogo Nauchno-Issledovatel'skogo Instituta Zemledeliya
Byull Koll Nablyud Mosk Obshch Lyub Astr — Byulleten' Kollektiva Nablyudatelei Moskovskogo Obshchestva Lyubitelei Astronomii
Byull Kom Issled Sol — Byulleten' Komissii po Issledovaniyu Solntsa
Byull Kom Izuch Chetvertichn Perioda Akad Nauk SSSR — Byulleten' Komissii po Izucheniyu Chetvertichnogo Perioda Akademiya Nauk SSSR
Byull Kom Kometam Meteoram Astron Sov Akad Nauk SSSR — Byulleten' Komissii po Kometam i Meteoram Astronomicheskogo Sovieta Akademii Nauk SSSR
Byull Kom Opred Absol Geol Form — Byulleten' Komissii po Opredeleniyu Absolyutnogo Vozrasta Geologicheskikh Formatsii
Byull Kom Opred Absol Vozrasta Geol Form Akad Nauk SSSR — Byulleten' Komissii po Opredeleniyu Absolyutnogo Vozrasta Geologicheskikh Formatsii Akademiya Nauk SSSR
Byull Kraev Derm Venerol Inst Kaz — Byulleten. Kraevoi Dermato-Venerologicheskii Institut Kazakhstana
Byull Leningr Inst Organ Okhr Tr — Byulleten' Leningradskii Institut Organizatsii i Okhrany Truda
Byull Leningr Otd Inst Udobr Agropochvoved — Byulleten' Leningradskogo Otdeleniya Institut Udobrenii i Agropochvovedeniya
Byull Mezhdunar O-Va Torfu — Byulleten' Mezhdunarodnogo Obshchestva po Torfu
Byull Mosk Obshch Isp Prir Otd Biol — Byulleten Moskovskoho Obshchestva Ispytatelei Prirody. Otdel Biologicheskii
Byull Mosk Obshch Ispyt Prir — Byulleten' Moskovskogo Obshchestva Ispytatelei Prirody Otdel Biologicheskii
Byull Mosk Ova Ispyt Prir Kalinin Otd — Byulleten' Moskovskogo Obshchestva Ispytatelei Prirody Kalininskii Otdel
Byull Mosk Ova Ispyt Prir Otd Biol — Byulleten' Moskovskogo Obshchestva Ispytatelei Prirody Otdel Biologicheskii
Byull Mosk Ova Ispyt Prir Otd Geol — Byulleten' Moskovskogo Obshchestva Ispytatelei Prirody Otdel Geologicheskii
Byull Nauch-Issled Inst Malyarii Med Parazitol — Byulleten' Nauchno-Issledovatel'skogo Instituta Malyarii i Meditsinskoi Parazitologii
Byull Nauchn Avtomot Inst — Byulleten Nauchnogo Avtomotornogo Instituta
Byull Nauchno Issled Inst Chain Promsti — Byulleten Nauchno-Issledovatel'skogo Instituta Chainoi Promyshlennosti
Byull Nauchno Issled Inst Khlopkovod — Byulleten Nauchno-Issledovatel'skogo Instituta po Khlopkovodstvu
Byull Nauchno Issled Inst Malyarii Med Parazitol — Byulleten' Nauchno Issledovatel'skogo Instituta Malyarii i Meditsinskoi Parazitologii

Byull Nauchno Issled Khim Farm Inst — Byulleten' Nauchno Issledovatel'skogo Khimiko Farmatsevticheskogo Instituta

Byull Nauchno-Tekh Inf — Byulleten' Nauchno-Tekhnicheskoi Informatsii

Byull Nauchno-Tekh Inf Agron Fiz — Byulleten' Nauchno-Tekhnicheskoi Informatsii po Agronomicheskoi Fizike

Byull Nauchno Tekh Inf Arm Nauchno Issled Inst Zemled — Byulleten' Nauchno-Tekhnicheskoi Informatsii Armyanskogo Nauchno-Issledovatel'skogo Instituta Zemledeliya

Byull Nauchno Tekh Inf Beloruss Nauchno Issled Inst Zemled — Byulleten' Nauchno-Tekhnicheskoi Informatsii Belorusskogo Nauchno-Issledovatel'skogo Instituta Zemledeliya

Byull Nauchno Tekh Inf Gos Geol Kom SSSR — Byulleten' Nauchno-Tekhnicheskoi Informatsii Gosudarstvennyi Geologicheskii Komitet SSSR

Byull Nauchno Tekh Inf Inst — Byulleten' Nauchno-Tekhnicheskoi Informatsii Nauchno-Issledovatel'skogo Instituta Pchelovodstva

Byull Nauchno Tekh Inf Litov Nauchno Issled Inst Zhivotnovod — Byulleten' Nauchno-Tekhnicheskoi Informatsii Litovskogo Nauchno-Issledovatel'skogo Instituta Zhivotnovodstva

Byull Nauchno Tekh Inf Maslichn Kult — Byulleten' Nauchno-Tekhnicheskoi Informatsii po Maslichnym Kulturam

Byull Nauchno Tekh Inf Minist Geol Okhr Nedr SSSR — Byulleten' Nauchno-Tekhnicheskoi Informatsii Ministerstvo Geologii i Okhrany Nedr SSSR

Byull Nauchno Tekh Inf Minist Geol SSSR — Byulleten' Nauchno-Tekhnicheskoi Informatsii Ministerstvo Geologii SSSR

Byull Nauchno Tekh Inf ONTI VIEMS — Byulleten Nauchno-Tekhnicheskoi Informatsii ONTI VIEMS

Byull Nauchno Tekh Inf Sib Nauchno Issled Inst Zhivotnovod — Byulleten Nauchno-Tekhnicheskoi Informatsii Sibirskogo Nauchno-Issledovatel'skogo Instituta Zhivotnovodstva

Byull Nauchno-Tekh Inf S-Kh Mikrobiol — Byulleten' Nauchno-Tekhnicheskoi Informatsii po Sel'skokhozyaistvennoi Mikrobiologii

Byull Nauchno-Tekh Inf (Sumskaya Gos Skh Opytn Stn) — Byulleten' Nauchno-Tekhnicheskoi Informatsii (Sumskaya Gosudarstvennaya Sel'skokhozyaistvennaya Opytnaya Stantsiya)

Byull Nauchno Tekh Inf Tadzh Nauchno Issled Inst Sel'sk Khoz — Byulleten' Nauchno-Tekhnicheskoi Informatsii Tadzhikskogo Nauchno-Issledovatel'skogo Instituta Sel'skogo Khozyaistva

Byull Nauchno Tekh Inf Tsentr Torfobolotnoi Opytn Stant — Byulleten' Nauchno-Tekhnicheskoi Informatsii Tsentralnoi Torfobolotnoi Opytnoi Stantsii

Byull Nauchno Tekh Inf Tsentr Torfobolotnoi Opytn Stn — Byulleten Nauchno-Tekhnicheskoi Informatsii Tsentral'noi Torfobolotnoi Opytnoi Stantsii

Byull Nauchno Tekh Inf Turkm Nauchno Issled Inst Zemled — Byulleten' Nauchno-Tekhnicheskoi Informatsii Turkmenskogo Nauchno-Issledovatel'skogo Instituta Zemledeliya

Byull Nauchno Tekh Inf Ukr Nauchno Issled Inst Met — Byulleten' Nauchno-Tekhnicheskoi Informatsii Ukrainskii Nauchno-Issledovatel'skii Institut Metallov

Byull Nauchno Tekh Inf Ukr Nauchno Issled Inst Ogneuporov — Byulleten' Nauchno-Tekhnicheskoi Informatsii Ukrainskogo Nauchno-Issledovatel'skogo Instituta Ogneuporov

Byull Nauchno Tekh Inf Ukr Nauchno Issled Trubn Inst — Byulleten Nauchno-Tekhnicheskoi Informatsii. Ukrainskii Nauchno-Issledovatel'skii Trubnyi Institut

Byull Nauchno Tekh Inf Ukr Nauchno Issled Uglekhim Inst — Byulleten' Nauchno-Tekhnicheskoi Informatsii Ukrainskii Nauchno-Issledovatel'skii Uglekhimicheskii Institut

Byull Nauchno Tekh Inf Ural Nauchno Issled Inst Chern Met — Byulleten' Nauchno-Tekhnicheskoi Informatsii Ural'skogo Nauchno-Issledovatel'skogo Instituta Chernykh Metallov

Byull Nauchno Tekh Inf Vses Inst Gelmintol — Byulleten Nauchno-Tekhnicheskoi Informatsii Vsesoyuznogo Instituta Gel'mintologi

Byull Nauchno Tekh Inf Vses Nauchno Issled Inst Ogneuporov — Byulleten Nauchno-Tekhnicheskoi Informatsii Vsesoyuznogo Nauchno-Issledovatel'skogo Instituta Ogneuporov

Byull Nauchno Tekh Inf Vses Nauchno Issled Trub Inst — Byulleten Nauchno-Tekhnicheskoi Informatsii Vsesoyuznyi Nauchno-Issledovatel'skii Trubnyi Institut

Byull Nauchno Tekh Inf Zashch Rast — Byulleten Nauchno-Tekhnicheskoi Informatsii po Zashchite Rastenii

Byull Nauchno Tekh Sov Metall Legk Met — Byulleten' Nauchno-Tekhnicheskogo Soveta po Metallurgii Legkikh Metallov

Byull Nauchno-Tekh Sov Metall Tyazh Tsvetn Met — Byulleten' Nauchno-Tekhnicheskogo Soveta po Metallurgii Tyazhilykh Tsvetnykh Metallov

Byull Nauchno-Tekh Sov Obogashch Rud Tsvetn Met — Byulleten' Nauchno-Tekhnicheskogo Soveta po Obogashcheniyu Rud Tsvetnykh Metallov

Byull Nauchno-Tekh Sov Obrab Tsvetn Met Vtorichnoi Metall — Byulleten' Nauchno-Tekhnicheskogo Soveta po Obrabotke Tsvetnykh Metallov i Vtorichnoi Metallurgii

Byull Nauchn Stud Ova Kaz Gos Univ — Byulleten' Nauchnogo Studencheskogo Obshchestva Kazakhskii Gosudarstvennyi Universitet

Byull NIKhFI — Byulleten NIKhFI

Byull Obmena Opytom Lakokras Promsti — Byulleten' Obmena Opytom Lakokrasochnoi Promyshlennosti

Byull Otd Zemled Gos Inst Opytn Agron — Byulleteni Otdela Zemledeliya. Gosudarstvennyi Institut Opytnoi Agronomii

Byull Ova Estestvoispyt Voronezh Gos Univ — Byulleten' Obshchestva Estestvoispytatelei pri Voronezhskom Gosudarstvennom Universitete

Byull Ovoshchevod — Byulleten' po Ovoshchevodstvu

Byull Poch Inst im V V Dokuchaeva — Byulleten Pochvennogo Instituta imeni V.V. Dokuchaeva

Byull Pochvoveda — Byulleten' Pochvoveda

Byull Rybn Khoz — Byulleten Rybnogo Khozyaistva

Byull Sakharotresta — Byulleten' Sakharotresta

Byull Sov Antarkt Eksped — Byulleten' Sovetskoi Antarkticheskoi Ekspeditsii

Byull Sov Seismol — Byulleten' Sovet po Seismologii

Byull Sredneaziat Gos Univ — Byulleten' Sredneaziatskogo Gosudarstvennogo Universiteta

Byull Sredneaziat Nauchno Issled Inst Khlopkovod — Byulleten Sredneaziatskogo Nauchno-Issledovatel'skogo Instituta po Khlopkovodstvu

Byull Stn Opt Nablyudeniya Iskusstvennykh Sputnikov Zemli — Byulleten' Stantsii Opticheskogo Nablyudeniya Iskusstvennykh Sputnikov Zemli

Byull Stroit Tekh — Byulleten' Stroitel'noi Tekhniki

Byull Stud Nauchn Ova Kaz Gos Univ — Byulleten' Studencheskogo Nauchnogo Obshchestva Kazakhskii Gosudarstvennyi Universitet

Byull Stud Nauchn Ova Leningr Gos Univ — Byulleten' Studencheskogo Nauchnogo Obshchestva Leningradskii Gosudarstvennyi Universitet

Byull Tekh-Ehkon Inf Gos Nauchno-Issled Inst Nauchn Tekh Inf — Byulleten' Tekhniko-Ehkonomicheskoj Informatsii. Gosudarstvennyj Nauchno-Issledovatel'skij Institut Nauchnoj i Tekhnicheskoj Informatsii

Byull Tekh Ekon Inf — Byulleten' Tekhniko-Ekonomicheskoi Informatsii

Byull Tekh-Ekon Inf Gos Nauchno-Issled Inst Nauchn Tekh Inf — Byulleten' Tekhniko-Ekonomicheskoi Informatsii Gosudarstvennyi Nauchno-Issledovatel'skii Institut Nauchnoi i Tekhnicheskoi Informatsii

Byull Tekh Ekon Inf Minist Morsk Flota — Byulleten Tekhniko-Ekonomicheskoi Informatsii. Ministerstvo Morskogo Flota

Byull Tekh Ekon Inf Mork Flota — Byulleten' Tekhniko-Ekonomicheskoi Informatsii Morskogo Flota

Byull Tekh Ekon Inf Morsk Flota — Byulleten Tekhniko-Ekonomicheskoi Informatsii Morskogo Flota

Byull Tekh Ekon Inf Mosk Obl Sovnarkhoz — Byulleten Tekhniko-Ekonomicheskoi Informatsii. Moskovskii Oblastnoi Sovnarkhoz

Byull Tekh Ekon Inf Sov Nar Khoz Bryansk Ekon Adm Raiona — Byulleten Tekhniko-Ekonomicheskoi Informatsii. Sovet Narodnogo Khozyaistva Bryanskogo Ekonomicheskogo Administrativnogo Raiona

Byull Tekh Ekon Inf Sov Nar Khoz B SSR — Byulleten' Tekhniko-Ekonomicheskoi Informatsii Sovet Narodnogo Khozyaistva Belorusskoi SSR

Byull Tekh Ekon Inf Sov Nar Khoz Ivanov Ekon Adm Raiona — Byulleten Tekhniko-Ekonomicheskoi Informatsii. Sovet Narodnogo Khozyaistva Ivanovskogo Ekonomicheskogo Administrativnogo Raiona

Byull Tekh Ekon Inf Sov Nar Khoz Khark Ekon Adm Raiona — Byulleten Tekhniko-Ekonomicheskoi Informatsii. Sovet Narodnogo Khozyaistva Khar'kovskogo Ekonomicheskogo Administrativnogo Raiona

Byull Tekh Ekon Inf Sov Nar Khoz Rostov Ekon Adm Raiona — Byulleten Tekhniko-Ekonomicheskoi Informatsii. Sovet Narodnogo Khozyaistva Rostovskogo Ekonomicheskogo Administrativnogo Raiona

Byull Tekh Ekon Inf Sov Nar Khoz Stalingr Ekon Adm Raiona — Byulleten Tekhniko-Ekonomicheskoi Informatsii. Sovet Narodnogo Khozyaistva Stalingradskogo Ekonomicheskogo Administrativnogo Raiona

Byull Tekh Ekon Inf Sov Nar Khoz Stalinskogo Ekon Adm Raiona — Byulleten' Tekhniko-Ekonomicheskoi Informatsii Sovet Narodnogo Khozyaistva Stalinskogo Ekonomicheskogo Administrativnogo Raiona

Byull Tekh Inf Sov Nar Khoz Kursk Ekon Adm Raiona — Byulleten' Tekhnicheskoi Informatsii Sovet Narodnogo Khozyaistva Kurskogo Ekonomicheskogo Administrativnogo Raiona

Byull Tekh Inf Stroit — Byulleten' Tekhnicheskoi Informatsii po Stroitel'stvu

Byull Tsentra Yad Dannym — Byulleten' Tsentra po Yadernym Dannym

Byull Tsentr Inst Inf Chern Metall — Byulleten. Tsentral'nyi Institut Informatsii Chernoi Metallurgii

Byull Tsentr Inst Inf Tsvetn Metall — Byulleten. Tsentral'nyi Institut Informatsii Tsvetnoi Metallurgii

Byull Tsentr Nauchno Issled Inst Tekhnol Mashinostr — Byulleten. Tsentral'nyi Nauchno-Issledovatel'skii Institut Tekhnologii i Mashinostroeniya

Byull Tsvetn' Metall — Byulleten' Tsvetnoi Metallurgii

Byull Ural Otd Mosk Ova Ispyt Prir — Byulleten' Ural'skogo Otdeleniya Moskovskogo Obshchestva Ispytatelei Prirody

Byull Vil'nyus Astron Obs — Byulleten' Vil'nyusskoi Astronomicheskoi Observatorii

Byull Vost Sib Fenol Kom — Byulleten' Vostochno Sibirskoi Fenologicheskoi Komissii

Byull Vses Astron Geod Ova — Byulleten' Vsesoyuznogo Astronomo-Geodezicheskogo Obshchestva

Byull Vses Inst Eksp Med — Byulleten Vsesoyuznogo Instituta Eksperimental'noi Meditsiny

Byull Vses Inst Eksp Vet — Byulleten' Vsesoyuznogo Instituta Eksperimental'noi Veterinarii

Byull Vses Inst Gel'mintol — Byulleten' Vsesoyuznogo Instituta Gel'mintologii

Byull Vses Inst Rastenievod — Byulleten' Vsesoyuznogo Instituta Rastenievodstva

Byull Vses Kardiol Nauchn Tsentra AMN SSSR — Byulleten' Vsesoyuznogo Kardiologicheskogo Nauchnogo Tsentra AMN SSSR

Byull Vses Koord Kom Mikroelem — Byulleten' Vsesoyuznoi Koordinatsionnoi Komissee po Mikroelementam

Byull Vses Koord Kom Mikroelem Akad Nauk Latv SSR — Byulleten Vsesoyuznoi Koordinatsionnoi Komissii po Mikroelementam. Akademiya Nauk Latviiskoi SSR

Byull Vses Nauchno Issled Geol Inst — Byulleten' Vsesoyuznogo Nauchno-Issledovatel'skogo Geologicheskogo Instituta

Byull Vses Nauchno-Issled Inst Agrolesomelior — Byulleten' Vsesoyuznogo Nauchno-Issledovatel'skogo Instituta Agrolesomelioratsii

Byull Vses Nauchno Issled Inst Chain Promsti — Byulleten' Vsesoyuznogo Nauchno-Issledovatel'skogo Instituta Chainoi Promyshlennosti

Byull Vses Nauchno Issled Inst Chain Promsti Subtrop Kult — Byulleten Vsesoyuznogo Nauchno-Issledovatel'skogo Instituta Chainoi Promyshlennosti i Subtropicheskikh Kul'tur

Byull Vses Nauchno-Issled Inst Chaya Subtrop Kul't — Byulleten' Vsesoyuznogo Nauchno-Issledovatel'skogo Instituta Chaya i Subtropicheskikh Kul'tur

Byull Vses Nauchno Issled Inst Eksp Vet Im Ya R Kovalenko — Byulleten' Vsesoyuznogo Nauchno-Issledovatel'skogo Instituta Eksperimental'noi Veterinarii Imeni Ya. R. Kovalenko

Byull Vses Nauchno-Issled Inst Fiziol Biokhim Skh Zhivotn — Byulleten. Vsesoyuznogo Nauchno-Issledovatel'skogo Instituta Fiziologii i Biokhimii i Pitaniya Sel'skokhozyaistvennykh Zhivotnykh

Byull Vses Nauchno Issled Inst Khlopkovod — Byulleten Vsesoyuznogo Nauchno-Issledovatel'skogo Instituta po Khlopkovodstvu

Byull Vses Nauchno-Issled Inst Kukuruzy — Byulleten' Vsesoyuznogo Nauchno-Issledovatel'skogo Instituta Kukuruzy

Byull Vses Nauchno Issled Inst Ovtsevod Kozovod — Byulleten Vsesoyuznogo Nauchno-Issledovatel'skogo Instituta Ovtsevodstva i Kozovodstva

Byull Vses Nauchno-Issled Inst Rastenievod Im N I Vavilova — Byulleten' Vsesoyuznogo Nauchno-Issledovatel'skogo Instituta Rastenievodstva Imeni N. I. Vavilova

Byull Vses Nauchno Issled Inst Tsem — Byulleten' Vsesoyuznogo Nauchno-Issledovatel'skogo Instituta Tsementov

Byull Vses Nauchno Issled Inst Udobr Agropochvoved — Byulleten' Vsesoyuznogo Nauchno-Issledovatel'skogo Instituta Udobrenii i Agropochvovedeniya

Byull Vses Nauchno-Issled Inst Zashch Rast — Byulleten' Vsesoyuznogo Nauchno-Issledovatel'skogo Instituta Zashchity Rastenii

Byull Vses Ordena Lenina Inst Eksp Vet — Byulleten' Vsesoyuznogo Ordena Lenina Instituta Eksperimental'noi Veterinarii

Byull Vulkanol Stn Akad Nauk SSSR — Byulleten' Vulkanologicheskikh Stantsii Akademiya Nauk SSSR

Byull Vulkanol Stn Kamchatke Akad Nauk SSSR — Byulleten' Vulkanologicheskikh Stantsii na Kamchatke Akademiya Nauk SSSR

Byul Nauk Inf Zemlerob — Byulleten' Naukovoi Informatsii po Zemlerobstvu

Byul Nauk Tekh Inf Zemlerob — Byuleten Naukova-Tekhnichnoi Informatsii po Zemlerobstvu

BYU LR — Brigham Young University. Law Review

BYU L Rev — Brigham Young University. Law Review

BYUS — Brigham Young University. Studies

Byz — Byzantina

ByZ — Byzantinische Zeitschrift

Byz — Byzantion

Byz & Mod Gr Stud — Byzantine and Modern Greek Studies

Byzant — Byzantion; Revue Internationale des Etudes Byzantines

Byzantinak — Byzantina kai Metabyzantina

Byzantine M — Byzantine and Modern Greek Studies

Byzantine S — Byzantine Studies

Byzantinische Z — Byzantinische Zeitschrift

Byzantinosl — Byzantino-Slavica

Byzantin Z — Byzantinische Zeitschrift

Byzantin Ztschr — Byzantinische Zeitschrift

Byzant Z — Byzantinische Zeitschrift

Byz Arch — Byzantinisches Archiv

Byz Bul — Byzantino-Bulgarica

Byz-Bulg — Byzantino-Bulgarica

Byz F — Byzantinische Forschungen

Byz Forsch — Byzantinische Forschungen

Byz J — Byzantinisch-Neugriechische Jahrbuecher

Byz Jb — Byzantinisch-Neugriechische Jahrbuecher

Byz-Met — Byzantina-Metabyzantina

ByzMetabyz — Byzantina-Metabyzantina

Byz Neer — Byzantina Neerlandica

Byz Neerl — Byzantina Neerlandica

Byz Neerland — Byzantina Neerlandica

Byz Neugriech Jb — Byzantinisch-Neugriechische Jahrbuecher

Byz-Neugr Jahrb — Byzantinisch-Neugriechische Jahrbuecher

BYZNGJB — Byzantinisch-Neugriechische Jahrbuecher

BYZOA — Byulleten' Izobretenii

Byz Pap — Byzantine Papers

ByzS — Byzantino-Slavica

ByzSl — Byzantino-Slavica

Byz Slav — Byzantino-Slavica. Sbornik pro Studium Byzantskoslovanskych Vztahu

ByzZ — Byzantinische Zeitschrift

Byz Zeitschr — Byzantinische Zeitschrift

Byz Zeitschrift — Byzantinische Zeitschrift

Byz Zs — Byzantinische Zeitschrift

BZ — Berliner Zeitung

BZ — Biblische Zeitschrift

BZ — Borsen Zeitung

BZ — Byzantinische Zeitschrift

BZA — Berichte ueber Landwirtschaft. Zeitschrift fuer Agrarpolitik und Landwirtschaft

B Zambia Lang Group — Bulletin of the Zambia Language Group

BZAW — Beihefte. Zeitschrift fuer die Alttestamentliche Wissenschaft

B Zb — Bayerisches Zahnaerzteblatt

BZB — Bonner Zoologische Beitraege

BZ Bl — Bayerisches Zahnaerzteblatt

BZ Bl — Bundeszollblatt

BzDB — Bibliographien zur Deutsche Barockliteratur

BZE — Bankers' Magazine

BZF — Biblische Zeitfragen

BZfR — Bayerische Zeitschrift fuer Realschulwesen

B Zfr — Biblische Zeitfragen

BZG — Basler Zeitschrift fuer Geschichte und Altertumskunde

BZG — Beitraege zur Geschichte der Deutschen Arbeiterbewegung

BZGA — Basler Zeitschrift fuer Geschichte und Altertumskunde

BZGAK — Basler Zeitschrift fuer Geschichte und Altertumskunde

BZHM — Berliner Zahnaerztliche Halbmonatsschrift

BZIH — Biuletyn Zydowskiego Instytutu Historycznego

BzJA — Beihefte zum Ja

BZM — Berliner Zeitung am Mittag

BZM — Beton, Herstellung, Verwendung

BZM — Botanicheskii Zhurnal (Moscow)

BzMW — Beitraege zur Musikwissenschaft

BZN — Beitraege zur Namenforschung

BZN — Bulletin of Zoological Nomenclature

B z Nf — Beitraege zur Namenforschung

BzNH — Bizantion-Nea Hellas

BZNW — Beihefte. Zeitschrift fuer die Neutestamentliche Wissenschaft und die Kunde der Alteren Kirche

BZR Gg — Beihefte. Zeitschrift fuer Religions und Geistesgeschichte

BZRP — Beihefte. Zeitschrift fuer Romanische Philologie

BZSE — Bulletin of the Zoological Society of Egypt

B Ztfr — Biblische Zeitfragen

BZThS — Bonner Zeitschrift fuer Theologie und Seelsorge

BZTS — Bonner Zeitschrift fuer Theologie und Seelsorge

BZWW — Beihefte. Zeitschrift Wirkendes Wort

BZX — Bank of Tanzania. Economic Bulletin

C

C — Campaign
C — Canada. Department of the Environment. Fisheries and Marine Service. Technical Report Series
C — Candela
C — Castrum Peregrini
C — Cenobio
C — Century
C — Chemisches Zentralblatt
C — Codex Juris Civilis
C — Coimbra
C — Collier's
C — Columbia Journalism Review
C — Comment
C — Commonweal
C — Corpus Inscriptionum Latinarum
C — Correspondent
C — Cosmos
C — Critica
C — Criticism
C — Critique
C$_1$ Mol Chem — C$_1$ Molecule Chemistry
C77 — Cinema 77
C 83 — Cinema 83
C22-83-9 — Construction Reports. C22-83-9. Housing Completions
C25-83-9 — Construction Reports. C25-83-9. New One-Family Houses Sold and for Sale
C40-85-5 — Construction Reports. C40-85-5. Housing Units Authorized by Building Permits and Public Contracts
CA — Beaux Arts. Chronique des Arts et de la Curiosite
CA — CA. A Bulletin of Cancer Progress
CA — CA. A Cancer Journal for Clinicians
CA — Cahiers Archeologiques. Fin de l'Antiquite et Moyen-age
CA — Carmina
CA — Casa de las Americas
CA — Cercetari Arheologice
CA — Chemical Abstracts
C A — Chemical Age
CA — Church Administration
CA — Communication Arts
CA — Critica d'Arte
CA — Cuadernos Americanos
CA — Cuadernos de Aragon
CA — Current Anthropology
CA — Recueils de Jurisprudence. Cour d'Appel
CAA — Camara de Industria y Comercio Argentino-Alemana
CAA — Chinese Astronomy and Astrophysics
CAA — Ciencias Administrativas (Argentina)
CAA — Commonwealth Arbitration Awards and Determinations
CA A & Archit — California Arts and Architecture
CAAAP/AP — Amazonia Peruana. Centro Amazonico de Antropologia y Aplicacion Practica. Departamento de Documentacion y Publicaciones
CAAB — Canadian Archaeological Association. Bulletin
CAAGB — Canada Agriculture
CAAH — Cahiers Alsaciens d'Archeologie, d'Art, et d'Histoire
CAA J — Civil Aeronautics Administration. Journal
CAANA — Comptes Rendus. Association des Anatomistes
CAANB — Cahiers d'Anesthesiologie
Ca Ar — Cahiers Archeologiques
CAAR — Calgary Archaeologist. University of Calgary
CAARA — Canadian Architect
CA Architect & Bldg News — California Architect and Building News
CAAS Bull — Canadian Association for American Studies. Bulletin
CAB — Cahiers d'Archeologie Biblique
CAB — Cercetari Arheologice in Bucuresti
CAB — Commentari dell'Ateneo di Brescia
CAB — Current Affairs Bulletin
CAB — Current Awareness Bulletin
Cab Amat & Antiqua — Cabinet de l'Amateur et de l'Antiquaire
Cabanis Journ — Journal fuer Ornithologie (Von Jean Cabanis)
CAB Annot Bibliogr — Commonwealth Agricultural Bureaux. Annotated Bibliography
CABCD — Cancer Biochemistry - Biophysics
CABCD4 — Cancer Biochemistry - Biophysics
CABD — Canadian Building Digest
CABFR — Commonwealth Agricultural Bureaux. Farnham Royal [Slough, Buckinghamshire, England]

Cab Int — Cababe. Interpleader and Attachment of Debts
CABIOS Comput Appl Biosci — CABIOS. Computer Applications in the Biosciences
Ca Bi Q — Catholic Biblical Quarterly
Cablecast Cable TV Eng — Cablecasting, Cable TV Engineering
Cab Lecture — Cabinet de Lecture
Cable Lib — Cable Libraries
Cable Mktg — Cable Marketing
Cable Rpt — Cable Report
Cables & Transm — Cables et Transmission
Cables Transm — Cables et Transmission
Cable Telev Eng — Cable Television Engineering
Cable TV Adv — Cable TV Advertising
Cable TV B — Cable Television Business
Cable TVBD — Cable Television Business Directory. CATV Suppliers Phone Book
Cable TV Fin — Cable TV Finance
Cable TV Pro — Cable TV Programming
Cable TV Reg — Cable TV Regulation
Cable TV Sec — Cable TV Security
CABLIS — Current Awareness Bulletin for Librarians and Information Scientists
Cabl Transm — Cables et Transmission
Cab Modes — Cabinet des Modes
CABN — Caribou News
Cab Nat Hist Amer Rural Sports — Cabinet of Natural History and American Rural Sports
CaboV — Cabo Verde
C A Brescia — Commentari. Accademia di Brescia
CABS — Current Awareness in Biological Sciences
CABSAF — Catholic University of America. Biological Studies
CABUA — Canadian Business
CA Bull — CA. A Bulletin of Cancer Progress
CA Bull Cancer Prog — CA. A Bulletin of Cancer Progress
CaC — Cahiers CEDAF (Centre d'Etudes et de Documentation Africaines)
CAC — Computer-Assisted Composition Journal
CAC — Constitutional Acts of Canada
CAC — Corporate Accounting
CAC — Cuadernos de Arte Colonial
CAC — Current Abstracts of Chemistry
CACAA — Cafe, Cacao, The
CA Cancer J Clin — CA. A Cancer Journal for Clinicians
CAC & IC — Current Abstracts of Chemistry and Index Chemicus
Cacao Choc Suikerwerken — Cacao Chocolade en Suikerwerken
Cacao Choc SuikWkn — Cacao-Chocolade-Suikerwerken
Cacao Colomb — Cacao en Colombia
Cacao Inf Bull — Cacao Information Bulletin
Cacau Atual — Cacau Atualidades
CACBB — Annual Reports on the Progress of Chemistry. Section B. Organic Chemistry
CACBB4 — Annual Reports on the Progress of Chemistry. Section B. Organic Chemistry
Cacciat Ital — Cacciatore Italiano
Cacciatore Ital — Cacciatore Italiano
Cacciatore Trent — Cacciatore Trentino
Cacciat Trent — Cacciatore Trentino
CACEEG — Cancer Cells
CACH — Canadian Churchman
CaCM — Cahiers Charles Maurras
CACM — Communications. ACM
CaCo — Cahiers du Communisme
CACO — Canadian Conservationist
CACOD — Canadian Consumer
CACP — Cahiers de l'Amitie Charles Peguy
CACS — Canada. Climatological Studies
CACS Forum — CACS (Chemical Analysis Center. Saitama University) Forum
Cactaceas Sucul Mex — Cactaceas y Suculentas Mexicanas
Cact Digest — Cactus Digest. Henry Shaw Cactus Society
Cact J — Cactus Journal
Cact J Croydon — Cactus Journal (Croydon, England)
Cact Succ J — Cactus and Succulent Journal
Cact Succ J Gr Br — Cactus and Succulent Journal of Great Britain
Cact Succ J Gr Brit — Cactus and Succulent Journal of Great Britain
Cact Succ J Woollahra — Cactus and Succulent Journal. Cactus and Succulent Society of New South Wales (Woollahra, Australia)
Cact Suc Mex — Cactaceas y Suculentas Mexicanas
Cact Suculentas Mex — Cactaceas y Suculentas Mexicanas
Cactus J — Cactus Journal

Cactus Mont St Amaud — Cactus. Bulletin Bimestriel (Mont St. Amaud, France)
Cactussen Vetpl — Cactussen en Vetplanten
Cactus Succ J — Cactus and Succulent Journal
Cactus Succ J Gt Br — Cactus and Succulent Journal of Great Britain
Cactus Succ J Los Ang — Cactus and Succulent Journal (Los Angeles)
Cactus Succulent J — Cactus and Succulent Journal
Cactus Succulent J GB — Cactus and Succulent Journal of Great Britain
Ca Cu — Boletin. Instituto Caro y Cuervo
CACUL Newsl — Canadian Association of College and University Libraries. Newsletter
CACYA4 — Cancer Cytology
Cad — Cadence
Cad — Caducee
Cad — Caduceo. Revista Grafica Espanola Economico Financiera
Cad — Caduceus
CaD — Cahiers des Dix
CAD — Canadian Annual Digest
CAD — Computer Applications Digest
CAD — Crime and Delinquency
Cadalyte Serv Bull — Cadalyte Service Bulletin. Grasselli Chemical Company
Cad Amazonia — Cadernos da Amazonia
Cadastro Oleic Registo Port — Cadastro Oleicola. Registo Portugues
CadB — Cadernos Brasileiros
Cad Bibliotecon — Cadernos de Biblioteconomia
Cad Brasil — Cadernos Brasileiros
Cad Brasil Arquit — Cadernos Brasileiros de Arquitectura
Cad Bras Rio — Cadernos Brasileiros (Rio de Janeiro)
CAD/CAM Tech — CAD/CAM [Computer-Aided Design/Computer-Aided Manufacturing] Technology
Cad Cient — Cadernos Cientificos. Instituto Pasteur de Lisboa
Cad Deb — Cadernos de Debate
CADEC — Computer-Aided Design of Electronic Circuits
Cadence — Cadence Magazine
Cadern Cient Inst Pasteur Lisb — Cadernos Cientificos. Instituto Pasteur de Lisboa
Cad Estud Sociais — Cadernos de Estudos Sociais
Cad Hist & A Ebor — Cadernos de Historia e Arte Eborense
Cad Hist Filos Cienc — Cadernos de Historia e Filosofia da Ciencia
CADIDW — Cardiovascular Diseases Bulletin. Texas Heart Institute
Cadiz Med — Cadiz Medico
Cadiz Period M Ci — Periodico Mensual de Ciencias Matematicas y Fizicas (Cadiz)
C Adm — Code Administratif
Cad Med — Cadiz Medico
Cad Mens Estat Inf Inst Vinho Porto — Cadernos Mensais de Estatistica e Informacao. Editados pelo Instituto da Vinho da Porto
Cadmium Abstr — Cadmium Abstracts
CADOD — Cahiers de l'Analyse des Donnees
Cad Omega — Caderno Omega
Cad Omega Univ Fed Rural Pernambuco — Caderno Omega. Universidade Federal Rural de Pernambuco
CADRDP — Cardiovascular Drugs
CADRE — Cumulative Abstracts of Defence Readings
Cadres et Profes — Cadres et Professions
CaE — Cahiers d'Etudes Africaines
CAE — Canadian Entomologist
CAE — Cercle Archeologique d'Enghien. Annales
CAE — Critica (Espana)
CAEAn — Cercle Archeologique d'Enghien. Annales
CAE Comput Aided Eng — CAE. Computer-Aided Engineering
CAED Rep Iowa State Univ Sci Tech Center Agr Econ Develop — CAED Report. Iowa State University of Science and Technology. Center for Agricultural and Economic Development
CAEEA — Canadian Electronics Engineering
CAEF — Cahiers. Association Internationale des Etudes Francaises
CAELB — Atomic Energy Law Reports
CAEN — Canadian Energy News
CAENA — Canadian Entomologist
Caen Ac Mm — Memoires de l'Academie des Sciences, Arts, et Belles-lettres de Caen
Caen Mm Ac — Memoires de l'Academie des Sciences, Arts, et Belles-lettres de Caen
Caen Mm S L — Memoires de la Societe Linneene du Calvados de Normandie (Caen)
Caen S L BlI — Bulletin de la Societe Linneenne de Normandie (Caen)
Caen Tr — Precis des Travaux de la Societe d'Agriculture de Caen
CAES — Canadian Ethnic Studies
Caesaraug — Caesaraugusta. Seminario de Arqueologia y Numismatica Aragonesas
Caes Leop Ac N Acta — Nova Acta Physico-Medica Academiae Caes. Leopoldino-Carolinae Naturae Curiosorum
CAETB — Canadian Aeronautic and Space Institute. Transactions
CAF — Captain Future
CAF — Comicorum Atticorum Fragmenta
Cafe — Cafe Solo
Cafe Peruano — Cafe Peruano. Comite Cafetalero del Peru
Cafe Salvador S Salvador — Cafe de El Salvador. Revista. Asociacion Cafetalera de El Salvador (San Salvador)
Caffer Com It Caffe — Caffer. Comitato Italiano Caffe e del Bureau Europeen du Cafe
CAFGA — California Fish and Game
CAFN — Canadian Field-Naturalist
CAFNA — Canadian Field-Naturalist
CAFO — Canadian Forum
CAFODQ — Cancer Forum
CAFOER — Cancer Focus

CAfr — Congo-Afrique
C Afr Adm Publ — Cahiers Africains d'Administration Publique
C Afr Secur Soc — Cahiers Africains de la Securite Sociale
CAFSB2 — Congres. Association Francaise pour l'Avancement des Sciences
CAG — Commentaria in Aristotelem Graeca
CAG — Communication Age
CAG/CG — Canadian Geographer/Le Geographe Canadien. Canadian Association of Geographers
Cage Birds A — Cage Birds Annual
CAGIB — Chemical Age International
CAGQ — Cahiers de Geographie de Quebec
CAGR — Carte Archeologique de la Gaule Romaine
CAGRA — California Agriculture
CAGYAO — Cardiology
Cah — Cahier
Ca H — Cahiers d'Histoire
CAH — Cambridge Ancient History
CAHA — Cahiers Alsaciens d'Archeologie d'Art et d'Histoire
Cah A — Cahiers Archeologiques
CAHA — Cahiers d'Archeologie et d'Histoire d'Alsace
Cah A — Cahiers d'Art
CahA — Cahiers d'Aujourd'hui
CahAAM — Cahiers de l'Association des Amis de Milosz
Cah A & Essai — Cahiers d'Art et d'Essai
Cah A & Tech Afrique N — Cahiers des Arts et Techniques de l'Afrique du Nord
Cah A & Trad Pop — Cahiers des Arts et Traditions Populaires
Cah Abbaye Sainte Croix — Cahiers de l'Abbaye Sainte-Crois
Cah Acad Auquetin — Cahiers de l'Academie Auquetin
CahACF — Cahiers de l'Academie Canadienne Francaise
Cah Acoust — Cahiers d'Acoustique
CahAD — Cahiers d'Art Dramatique
Cah Aerod — Cahiers d'Aerodynamique
Cah Aerodyn — Cahiers d'Aerodynamique
Cah Afr Adm Publ Afr Adm Stud — Cahiers Africains d'Administration Publique
Cah Agric Econ Ec Natn Agric Grignon — Cahiers Agricoles et Economiques de l'Ecole Nationale d'Agriculture de Grignon
CahAHB — Cahiers de l'Amitie Henri Bosco
CahAl — Cahiers de l'Alpe
CahAL — Cahiers des Ameriques Latines. Serie Arts et Litteratures
Cah Albert Le Grand — Cahiers Albert Le Grand
Cah Albert Roussel — Cahiers Albert Roussel
CahALC — Cahiers Algeriens de Litterature Comparee
Cah Alger Sante — Cahiers Algeriens de la Sante
Cah Alg San — Cahiers Algeriens de la Sante
Cah Als — Cahiers Alsaciens d'Archeologie, d'Art, et d'Histoire
Cah Alsac Archeol A & Hist — Cahiers Alsaciens d'Archeologie, d'Art, et d'Histoire
Cah Alsac Archeol Art Hist — Cahiers Alsaciens d'Archeologie, d'Art, e d'Histoire
Cah Alsaciens — Cahiers Alsaciens d'Archeologie d'Art et d'Histoire
Cah Als Arch — Cahiers Alsaciens d'Archeologie, d'Art, et d'Histoire
Cah Als Arch Art Hist — Cahiers Alsaciens d'Archeologie d'Art et d'Histoire
Cah Am Ch P — Cahiers de l'Amitie Charles Peguy
Cah Amer Latin — Cahiers des Ameriques Latines
Cah Am Lat — Cahiers des Ameriques Latines
Cah Am Latines Ser Sciences Homme — Cahiers des Ameriques Latines. Serie Sciences de l'Homme
Cah Anal — Cahiers pour l'Analyse
Cah Anal Text — Cahiers d'Analyse Textuelle
Cah Anesth — Cahiers d'Anesthesiologie
Cah Anesthesiol — Cahiers d'Anesthesiologie
Cah Anim Spirit — Cahiers d'Animation Spirituelle
Cah Ann — Cahiers des Annales
Cah Ann Norm — Cahier des Annales de Normandie
Cah Anthrop Biometr Hum — Cahiers d'Anthropologie et Biometrie Humaine
Cah Anthropol Biom Hum — Cahiers d'Anthropologie et Biometrie Humaine
Cah Apic — Cahiers Apicoles
Cah A R — Cahiers de l'Actualite Religieuse
Cah Arbeidsgeneeskd — Cahiers voor Arbeidsgeneeskunde
Cah Arch — Cahiers Archeologiques
Cah Archeol — Cahiers Archeologiques
Cah Archeol Amerique S — Cahiers d'Archeologie d'Amerique du Sud
Cah Archeol & Hist Alsace — Cahiers d'Archeologie et d'Histoire d'Alsace
Cah Archeol Hist Berry — Cahiers d'Archeologie et d'Histoire du Berry
Cah Archeol Romande — Cahiers d'Archeologie Romande
Cah Arch et Hist Alsace — Cahiers Alsaciens d'Archeologie d'Art et d'Histoire
Cah Arch Hist Berry — Cahiers d'Archeologie et d'Histoire du Berry
Cah Arch Subaqu — Cahiers d'Archeologie Subaquatique
Cah Armee Rom — Cahiers. Groupe de Recherches sur l'Armee Romaine et les Provinces
Cah Art — Cahiers d'Art
Cah Art Sacre — Cahiers de l'Art Sacre
Cah Art Trad Pop — Cahiers des Arts et Traditions Populaires
Cah As Se — Cahiers de l'Asie du Sud-Est
Cah Ass Int Et Fr — Cahiers. Association Internationale des Etudes Francaises
Cah Assoc Interuniv Est — Cahiers. Association Interuniversitaire de l'Est
Cah Assoc Int Etud Fr — Cahiers de l'Association Internationale des Etudes Francaises
Cah A Subaqu — Cahiers d'Archeologie Subaquatique
CahAT — Cahiers d'Analyse Textuelle
Cah AUPELF — Cahiers. Association des Universites Parliellement ou Entierement de Langue Francaise
CahAVL — Cahiers des Amis de Valery Larbaud
CAHB — Cahiers d'Archeologie et d'Histoire du Berry
Cah Bazadais — Cahiers du Bazadais
CahBC — Cahiers Bourbonnais et du Centre
Cah Bedrijfsgeneeskd — Cahiers voor Bedrijfsgeneeskunde

Cah Berry — Cahiers d'Archeologie et d'Histoire du Berry
CahBil — Cahiers de la Biloque
Cah Biloque — Cahiers de la Biloque
Cah Biol Mar — Cahiers de Biologie Marine
Cah Bio Mar — Cahiers de Biologie Marine
CahBl — Cahiers Blancs
Cah B Lett — Cahiers de Belles-Lettres
Cah Bleus Vet — Cahiers Bleus Veterinaires
Cah Bordeaux — Cahiers de Bordeaux
Cah Bretagne Occident — Cahiers de Bretagne Occidentale
Cah Bruges — Cahiers de Bruges
Cah Brux — Cahiers Bruxellois
Cah Bruxell — Cahiers Bruxellois
Cah Bur Univ Rech Oper Univ Paris — Cahiers. Bureau Universitaire de Recherche Operationnelle. Universite de Paris
Cah Byr — Cahiers de Byrsa. Tunis. Musee Lavigerie
Cah Byrsa — Cahiers de Byrsa
CahC — Cahiers du Communisme
CAHC — Cuadernos de Arqueologia e Historia de la Ciudad
Cah CACEF — Cahier du Centre d'Action Culturel de la Communaute d'Expression Francaise
Cah Cambre — Cahiers de la Cambre
Cah Canadiens M — Cahiers Canadiens de Musique
CahCC — Cahiers Canadien Claudel
CahCD — Cahiers Charles Du Bos
CahCe — Cahiers Cesairiens
Cah Cent — Cahiers de Centreau
Cah Cent Etud et Rech Ethnol — Cahiers du Centre d'Etudes et de Recherches Ethnologiques
Cah Cent Etud Rech Oper — Cahiers. Centre d'Etudes de Recherche Operationnelle
Cah Cent Etud Reg Ant Guy — Cahiers du Centre d'Etudes Regionales (Antilles-Guyane)
Cah Cent Rech Dev Econ — Cahier. Centre de Recherches en Developpement Economique
Cah Cent Rech Etud Oceanogr — Cahiers du Centre de Recherches et Etudes Oceanographiques
Cah Centre Tech Bois — Cahier. Centre Technique du Bois
Cah Centr Etudes Rech Biol — Cahiers du Centre d'Etudes et de Recherches de Biologie et d'Oceanographie Medicale
Cah Cent Scient Tech Batim — Cahiers du Centre Scientifique et Technique du Batiment
Cah Cent Sci Tech Batim — Cahiers. Centre Scientifique et Technique du Batiment
Cah Cent Tech Bois — Cahiers. Centre Technique du Bois
Cah CERBOM — Cahiers. CERBOM
CahCerclERenan — Cahiers. Cercle Ernest Renan
Cah Cer Egyp — Cahiers de la Ceramique Egyptienne
CahCERM — Cahiers du Centre d'Etudes et Recherches Marxistes
Cah Cer Verre & A Feu — Cahiers de la Ceramique, du Verre, et des Arts du Feu
CahCh — Cahiers du Chemin
Cah Ch Foucauld — Cahiers Charles De Foucauld
Cah Chim Org — Cahiers de Chimie Organique
Cah Chir — Cahiers de Chirurgie
Cah Cinema — Cahiers du Cinema
Cah Civilisation Medievale — Cahiers de Civilisation Medievale
Cah Civilis Med — Cahiers de Civilisation Medievale
Cah Civ Med — Cahiers de Civilisation Medievale
Cah Civ Mediev — Cahiers de Civilisation Medievale
CahCM — Cahiers Charles Maurras
Cah CM — Cahiers de Civilisation Medievale Xe-XIIe Siecles
CahCo — Cahiers du Contadour
Cah Coll Med Hop Paris — Cahiers. College de Medecine des Hopitaux de Paris
Cah Communisme — Cahiers du Communisme
Cah Com Prev Batim Trav Publics — Cahiers. Comites de Prevention du Batiment et des Travaux Publics
Cah Congol Anthropol & Hist — Cahiers Congolais d'Anthropologie et d'Histoire
Cah Coptes — Cahiers Coptes
Cah Corps Maitres Stage Hop Univ Libre Bruxelles — Cahier du Corps des Maitres de Stage des Hopitaux. Universite Libre de Bruxelles
CahCP — Cahiers du College de Pataphysique
Cah Debussy — Cahiers Debussy
Cah de Droit Eur — Cahiers de Droit Europeen
Cah de Droit (Quebec) — Cahiers de Droit (Quebec)
Cah de la Fac de Droit Nancy — Cahiers. Faculte de Droit et des Sciences Economiques de Nancy
Cah Del Archeol Fr Iran — Cahiers de la Delegation Archeologique Francaise en Iran
Cah Del Fr Iran — Cahiers. Delegation Francaise en Iran
Cah d'Et Afr — Cahiers d'Etudes Africaines. Revue Trimestrielle
Cah de Tunisie — Cahiers de Tunisie
CahdM — Cahiers des Midis
Cah Docum — Cahiers de la Documentation
Cah d Outre Mer — Cahiers d'Outre-Mer
CahdP — Cahiers de Paris
Cah Dr Eur — Cahiers de Droit Europeen
CahDS — Cahiers Dada Surrealisme
Cah du CEDAF — Cahiers du CEDAF
Cah du Cinema — Cahiers du Cinema
Cah E — Cahiers de l'Est
CAHE — Canadian Heritage
Cah Econ Br — Cahiers Economiques de Bruxelles
Cah Econ Brux — Cahiers Economiques de Bruxelles
Cah Econs Bruxelles — Cahiers Economiques de Bruxelles
Cah Econs et Monetaires — Cahiers Economiques et Monetaires

Cah Econs et Soc — Cahiers Economiques et Sociaux
Cah Econ Soc — Cahiers Economiques et Sociaux
Cah Educ Civ — Cahiers d'Education Civique
Cah Elis — Cahiers Elisabethains
Cah Enf — Cahiers de l'Enfance
Cah ENSBANA — Cahiers de l'ENSBANA
CahEq — Cahiers de l'Equipe
CahER — Cahiers des Etudiants Romanistes
Cah Et Afr — Cahiers d'Etudes Africaines
Cah Et Cath — Cahiers d'Etudes Cathares
Cah Ethnol — Cahiers Ethnologiques
Cah Etoile — Cahiers de l'Etoile
Cah Etud Af — Cahiers d'Etudes Africaines
Cah Etud Afr — Cahiers d'Etudes Africaines
Cah Etud Anc — Cahiers des Etudes Anciennes
Cah Etud Biol — Cahiers d'Etudes Biologiques
Cah Etud Mediev — Cahiers d'Etudes Medievales
Cah Etud Mongol & Siber — Cahiers d'Etudes Mongoles et Siberiennes
Cah Expansion Reg — Cahiers de l'Expansion Regionale
Cah Extreme Asie — Cahiers d'Extreme Asie
Cah Fac Sci Univ Mohammed Ser Bio Anim — Cahiers. Faculte des Sciences. Universite Mohammed 5. Serie Biologie Animale
Cah Fanjeaux — Cahiers du Fanjeaux
Cah Fr — Cahiers Francais
CahGB — Cahiers Gaston Baty
Cah Geogr Phys — Cahiers de Geographie Physique
Cah Geol — Cahiers Geologiques
Cah Geol Thoiry — Cahiers Geologiques de Thoiry
CahGFM — Cahiers du Groupe Francais Minkowska
Cah Groupe Fr Etud Rheol — Cahier. Groupe Francais d'Etudes de Rheologie
Cah Groupe Fr Rheol — Cahiers. Groupe Francais de Rheologie
CahH — Cahiers de l'Herne
Cah Haute Loire — Cahiers de la Haute-Loire
Cah Haut Marnais — Cahiers Haut-Marnais
Cah Herm — Cahiers d'Hermes
CahHF — Cahiers d'Histoire et de Folklore
Cah Hist — Cahiers d'Histoire
Cah Hist A Contemp Doc — Cahiers d'Histoire d'Art Contemporain; Documents
Cah Hist Arch — Cahiers d'Histoire et d'Archeologie
Cah Hist Eg — Cahiers d'Histoire Egyptienne
Cah Hist M — Cahiers d'Histoire Mondiale/Journal of World History
Cah Hist Mond — Cahiers d'Histoire Mondiale/Journal of World History
Cah Hist Mondiale — Cahiers d'Histoire Mondiale
Cah Hist Mond J Wld Hist — Cahiers d'Histoire Mondiale/Journal of World History/ Cuadernos de Historia Mundial
Cah Hist Soc Hist Que — Cahiers d'Histoire. Societe Historique de Quebec
Cahl — Cahiers de l'Iroise
Cahier Dr Fiscal — Cahiers de Droit Fiscal International
Cahiers — Cahiers de Droit
Cahiers — Cahiers du Cinema
Cahiers Alsaciens — Cahiers Alsaciens d'Archeologie d'Art et d'Histoire
Cahiers Arch — Cahiers Archeologiques. Fin de l'Antiquite et Moyen-age
Cahiers Archeol — Cahiers Archeologiques. Fin de l'Antiquite et Moyen-age
Cahiers Arch et Hist Alsace — Cahiers Alsaciens d'Archeologie d'Art et d'Histoire
Cahiers C — Cahiers Cesairiens
Cahiers Centre Etudes Recherche Oper — Cahiers. Centre d'Etudes de Recherche Operationnelle
Cahiers Centre Etudes Rech Oper — Cahiers. Centre d'Etudes de Recherche Operationnelle
Cahiers Centre Logique — Cahiers du Centre de Logique
Cahiers Cinematheque — Cahiers de la Cinematheque
Cahiers CSTB — Cahiers. Centre Scientifique et Technique du Batiment
Cahiers de la Rev d Hist et de Philos Religieuses — Cahiers de la Revue d'Histoire et de Philosophie Religieuses Publies par la Faculte de Theologie Protestante de l'Universite de Strasbourg
Cahiers d'Hist Mond — Cahiers d'Histoire Mondiale
Cahiers Droit — Quebec [City]. Universite Laval. Faculte de Droit. Cahiers de Droit
CahiersE — Cahiers Elisabethains
CahiersF — Cahiers Francophones
Cahiers Geog Quebec — Cahiers de Geographie de Quebec
Cahiers Geol — Cahiers Geologiques
Cahiers Herne — Cahiers de l'Herne
Cahiers Hist Mond Paris — Cahiers d'Histoire Mondiale (Paris)
Cahiers Hist Philos Sci Nouvelle Ser — Cahiers d'Histoire et de Philosophie des Sciences. Nouvelle Serie
Cahiers Hist Philos Sci Nouv Ser — Cahiers d'Histoire et de Philosophie des Sciences. Nouvelle Serie
Cahiers I — Cahiers Irlandais
Cahiers in Eng — Cahiers du Cinema in English
Cahiers Lig Prehist Arch — Cahiers Ligures de Prehistoire et d'Archeologie
Cahiers Math — Cahiers Mathematiques
Cahiers Math Ecole Polytech Fed Lausanne — Cahiers Mathematiques de l'Ecole Polytechnique Federale de Lausanne
Cahiers Math Montpellier — Cahiers Mathematiques Montpellier. Universite des Sciences et Techniques du Languedoc
Cahiers Num — Cahiers Numismatiques
Cahiers ORSTOM Pedologie — Cahiers. ORSTOM [Office de la Recherche Scientifique et Technique d'Outre-Mer]. Serie Pedologie
Cahiers R — Cahiers Renaniens
Cahiers S — Cahiers Staeliens
Cahiers Sci — Cahiers Scientifiques
Cahiers Sci (Suppl Bois Forets Trop) — Cahiers Scientifiques (Supplement to Bois et Forets des Tropiques)
Cahiers Sem Hist Math Ser 2 — Cahiers du Seminaire d'Histoire des Mathematiques. Serie 2

Cahiers Techniques — Cahiers Techniques de l'Art
Cahiers Topologie Geom Differentielle — Cahiers de Topologie et Geometrie Differentielle
Cahiers Topologie Geom Differentielle Categ — Cahiers de Topologie et Geometrie Differentielle Categoriques
Cah I F A L — Cahiers. Institut Francais d'Amerique Latine
CahIMT — Cahiers de l'Institut Maurice Thorez
Cah Inf Bur Eurisotop — Cahier d'Information du Bureau Eurisotop
Cah Inf Dep Oceanogr Univ Que Rimouski — Cahier d'Information. Departement d'Oceanographie. Universite du Quebec a Rimouski
Cah Inf Stn Biol Mar Grande-Riviere — Cahiers d'Information Station de Biologie Marine de Grande-Riviere
Cah Inf Tech Rev Metall — Cahiers d'Informations Techniques/Revue de Metallurgie
Cah Inf Univ Que Rimouski Dep Oceanogr — Cahier d'Information. Universite du Quebec a Rimouski. Departement d'Oceanographie
Cah Ing Agron — Cahiers des Ingenieurs Agronomes
Cah Ingnrs Agron — Cahiers des Ingenieurs Agronomes
Cah Inst Et Pol Belg — Cahiers de l'Institut d'Etudes Polonaises en Belgique
Cah Inst Moyen Age Grec & Lat — Cahiers de l'Institut du Moyen-Age Grec et Latin
Cah Int — Cahiers Internationaux
Cah Internat — Cahiers Internationaux. Revue Internationale du Monde du Travail
Cah Internat Resistance — Cahiers Internationaux de la Resistance
Cah Internat Sociol — Cahiers Internationaux de Sociologie
Cah Int Soc — Cahiers Internationaux de Sociologie
Cah Int Sociol — Cahiers Internationaux de Sociologie
Cah Int Sociologie — Cahiers Internationaux de Sociologie
Cah Iroise — Cahiers de l'Iroise
CahIS — Cahiers Internationaux de Symbolisme
CahISoc — Cahiers Internationaux de Sociologie
Ca Hist — Cahiers d'Histoire
Cah Ivoiriens de Rech Econ et Sociale — Cahiers Ivoiriens de Recherche Economique et Sociale
Cah Ivoiriens Rech Econ et Soc — Cahiers Ivoiriens de Recherche Economique et Sociale
CahJ — Cahiers des Jeunes
CAHJ — CAHPER [*Canadian Association for Health, Physical Education, and Recreation*] Journal
Cah Jaunes — Cahiers Jaunes
Cah JKH — Cahiers J. K. Huysmans
CahJT — Cahiers Jean Tousseul
Cah Juridiques Electr Gaz — Cahiers Juridiques de l'Electricite et du Gaz
Cah Kinesither — Cahiers de Kinesitherapie
CahL — Cahiers de la Licorne
Cah Lab Hydrobiol Montereau — Cahiers. Laboratoire d'Hydrobiologie de Montereau
Cah Leopold Delisle — Cahiers Leopold Delisle
Cah Lex — Cahiers de Lexicologie
CahLib — Cahiers de la Liberation
Cah Lig — Cahiers Ligures de Prehistoire et d'Archeologie
Cah Ling — Cahiers de Linguistique Theorique et Appliquee
Cah Ling As Or — Cahiers de Linguistique Asie Orientale
CahLit — Cahiers Litteraires
Cah Litt Orale — Cahiers de Litterature Orale
CahLO — Cahiers Litteraires de l'ORTF
Cah Lor — Cahiers Lorrains
CaHM — Cahiers d'Histoire Mondiale
Cah Maboke — Cahiers de la Maboke
Cah Mariemont — Cahiers de Mariemont
CAHMB — Cahiers de Medecine
Cah Med — Cahiers de Medecine
Cah Med — Cahiers Medicaux
Cah Med — Cahiers Meduliens
Cah Med Assises Med — Cahiers de Medecine. Assises de Medecine
Cah Med Eur Med — Cahiers de Medecine. Europa Medica
Cah Med Interprof — Cahiers de Medecine Interprofessionnelle
Cah Med Lyon — Cahiers Medicaux Lyonnais
Cah Med Lyon Enseign Post Univ — Cahiers Medicaux Lyonnais d'Enseignement Post Universitaire
Cah Med Paris — Cahiers de Medecine (Paris)
Cah Med Trav — Cahiers de Medecine du Travail
Cah Medul — Cahiers Meduliens
Cah Med Vet — Cahiers de Medecine Veterinaire
Cah Micropaleontol — Cahiers de Micropaleontologie
CahMN — Cahiers du Monde Nouveau
CahMNo — Cahiers Marie Noel
Cah M Nouv — Cahiers du Monde Nouveau
Cah Monde Hisp Luso-Bresil — Cahiers du Monde Hispanique et Luso-Bresilien
Cah Monde Rus & Sov — Cahiers du Monde Russe et Sovietique
Cah Monde Russ Soviet — Cahiers du Monde Russe et Sovietique
Cah Mon Rus — Cahiers du Monde Russe et Sovietique
Cah Mus A & Essai — Cahiers du Musee d'Art et d'Essai
Cah Mus & Mnmts Nimes — Cahiers des Musees et Monuments de Nimes
Cah Mus Forezien — Cahiers. Musee Forezien
Cah Mus N A Mod — Cahiers du Musee National d'Art Moderne
Cah Mus Poche — Cahiers du Musee de Poche
CahN — Cahiers de Neuilly
CahN — Cahiers Numismatiques
Cah Nat — Cahiers des Naturalistes
Cah Naturalistes — Cahiers des Naturalistes
CahNC — Cahiers du Nivernais et du Centre
CahNJ — Cahiers de la Nouvelle Journee
CahNo — Cahiers du Nord
Cah Nord Est — Cahiers d'Archeologie du Nord-Est

Cah Notes Doc — Cahiers de Notes Documentaires
Cah Notes Doc — Cahiers de Notes Documentaires. Securite et Hygiene du Travail
Cah Notes Doc Secur Hyg Trav — Cahiers de Notes Documentaires. Securite et Hygiene du Travail
Cah Notre Dame Rouen — Cahiers Notre Dame de Rouen
Cah Nouv Journee — Cahiers de la Nouvelle Journee
Cah Nouv Rev Theol — Cahiers de la Nouvelle Revue Theologique
Cah Num — Cahiers Numismatiques
Cah Nurs — Cahiers du Nursing
Cah Nutr Diet — Cahiers de Nutrition et de Dietetique
CahO — Cahiers de l'Occident
CAHOA — Canadian Hospital
CAHOAX — Canadian Hospital
Cah Oceanogr — Cahiers Oceanographiques
Cah Oceanogr Suppl — Cahiers Oceanographiques. Supplement
Cah Odonto-Stomatol — Cahiers d'Odonto-Stomatologie
Cah Odontostomatol (Touraine) — Cahiers Odontostomatologiques (Touraine)
CahOF — Cahiers de l'Ordre Francais
Cah Off Rech Sci Tech Outre-Mer Ser Pedol — Cahiers. Office de la Recherche Scientifique et Technique d'Outre-Mer. Serie Pedologie
Cah OM — Cahiers d'Outre-Mer
Cah O-Mer — Cahiers d'Outre-Mer
Cah ONAREST — Cahiers de l'ONAREST (Office National de la Recherche Scientifique et Techniquedu Cameroun)
Cah Or — Cahiers de l'Oronte
Cah ORL — Cahiers d'ORL
Cah ORST Hy — Cahiers. ORSTOM [*Office de la Recherche Scientifique et Technique d'Outre-Mer*]. Hydrobiologie
Cah ORST Oc — Cahiers. ORSTOM [*Office de la Recherche Scientifique et Technique d'Outre-Mer*]. Oceanographie
Cah ORSTOM — Cahiers. Office de la Recherche Scientifique et Technique d'Outre-Mer
Cah ORSTOM Physiol Plant Trop Cult — Cahiers. ORSTOM [*Office de la Recherche Scientifique et Technique d'Outre-Mer*]. Physiologie des Plantes Tropicales Cultivees
Cah ORSTOM Physiol Pl Trop Cult — Cahiers ORSTOM. Physiologie des Plantes Tropicales Cultivees. Office de la Recherche Scientifique et Technique d'Outre-Mer
Cah ORSTOM Sci Hum — Cahiers. Office de la Recherche Scientifique et Technique pour l'Outre-Mer. Serie Sciences Humaines
Cah ORSTOM Ser Biol — Cahiers. ORSTOM [*Office de la Recherche Scientifique et Technique d'Outre-Mer*]. Serie Biologie
Cah ORSTOM Ser Entomol Med — Cahiers. ORSTOM [*Office de la Recherche Scientifique et Technique d'Outre-Mer*]. Serie Entomologie Medicale
Cah ORSTOM Ser Entomol Med Parasitol — Cahiers. ORSTOM [*Office de la Recherche Scientifique et Technique d'Outre-Mer*]. Serie Entomologie Medicale et Parasitologie
Cah ORSTOM Ser Geol — Cahiers ORSTOM [*Office de la Recherche Scientifique et Technique Outre-Mer. France*] Serie Geologie
Cah ORSTOM Ser Hydrobiol — Cahiers. ORSTOM [*Office de la Recherche Scientifique et Technique d'Outre-Mer*]. Serie Hydrobiologie
Cah ORSTOM Ser Hydrol — Cahiers. ORSTOM [*Office de la Recherche Scientifique et Technique d'Outre-Mer*]. Serie Hydrologie
Cah ORSTOM Ser Oceanogr — Cahiers. ORSTOM [*Office de la Recherche Scientifique et Technique d'Outre-Mer*]. Serie Oceanographie
Cah ORSTOM Ser Pedol — Cahiers. ORSTOM [*Office de la Recherche Scientifique et Technique d'Outre-Mer*]. Serie Pedologie
Cah ORSTOM Ser Physiol Plant Trop Cultiv — Cahiers ORSTOM. [*Office de la Recherche Scientifique et Technique Outre-Mer.France*] Serie Physiologie des Plantes Tropicales Cultivees
Cah ORSTOM Ser Sci Hum — Cahiers. ORSTOM [*Office de la Recherche Scientifique et Technique d'Outre-Mer*]. Serie Sciences Humaines
Cah Oto Rhino Laryngol Suppl — Cahiers d'Oto-Rhino-Laryngologie. Supplement
Cah Outre-Mer — Cahiers d'Outre-Mer
CahP — Cahiers de la Pleiade
Cah Pac — Cahiers du Pacifique
CahPC — Cahiers Paul Claudel
CahPE — Cahiers Paul Eluard
Cah Pedol ORSTOM — Cahiers de Pedologie. Office de la Recherche Scientifique et Technique d'Outre-Mer
Cah Pedopsych — Cahiers Pedopsychiatriques
Cah Pensee & Hist Archit — Cahier de Pensee et d'Histoire de l'Architecture
CAHPER J — CAHPER [*Canadian Association for Health, Physical Education, and Recreation*] Journal
Cah P et CP — Cahiers Points et Contrepoints
Cah Phil Afr — Cahiers Philosophiques Africains
Cah Phys — Cahiers de Physique
Cah Phys — Cahiers de Physique. Theorie, Syntheses, et Mises au Point
Cah P L — Cahiers Pierre Loti
Cah Pleiade — Cahiers de la Pleiade
Cah Pologne Allemagne — Cahiers Pologne-Allemagne
CahPr — Cahiers Protestants
Cah Presse Fr — Cahiers de la Presse Francaise
Cah Prot — Cahiers Protestants
Cah Prothese — Cahiers de Prothese
Cah Psych — Cahiers de Psychiatrie
CahQ — Cahiers de la Quinzaine
CaHQ — California Historical Quarterly
Cah Quebecois Demographie — Cahiers Quebecois de Demographie
Cah Quentovic — Cahiers de Quentovic
CahR — Cahiers Raciniens
CahR — Cahiers Rationalistes
CAHR — Canadian Historical Review
Cah Rac — Cahiers Raciniens
Cah Rationalistes — Cahiers Rationalistes

Cah Readapt — Cahiers de Readaptation
Cah Rech Agron — Cahiers de la Recherche Agronomique
Cah Rech Agron Inst Rech Agron (Morocco) — Cahiers de la Recherche Agronomique. Institut National de la Recherche Agronomique (Morocco)
Cah Rech Archit — Cahiers de la Recherche Architecturale
CahREL — Cahiers Roumains d'Etudes Litteraires
Cah Relig Afr — Cahiers des Religions Africaines
Cah Religions Afr — Cahiers des Religions Africaines
Cah Rene de Lucinge — Cahiers Rene de Lucinge
CahRh — Cahiers du Rhone
Cah Rotonde — Cahiers de la Rotonde
CahRR — Cahiers Romain Rolland
CahS — Cahiers du Sud
CAHS — CAHS [*Canadian Aviation Historical Society*] Journal
CahSa — Cahiers des Saisons. Revue Bimestrielle de Litterature
Cah Saint Michel de Cuxa — Cahiers de Saint-Michel de Cuxa
Cah Saint Simon — Cahiers Saint-Simon
Cah San Commun — Cahiers de Sante Communautaire
Cah Sar — Cahiers Sarregueminois
Cah Sci Appl — Cahiers de Science Appliquee
Cah Sem Econ — Cahiers du Seminaire d'Econometrie
Cah Seminar Hist Math — Cahiers. Seminar d'Histoire des Mathematiques
Cah Sexol Clin — Cahiers de Sexologie Clinique
CahSion — Cahiers Sioniens
CahSM — Cahiers de Sainte Marie
Cah Soc — Cahiers Socialistes
Cah Soc Chim Org Biol — Cahier de la Societe de Chimie Organique et Biologique
Cah Soc Ec — Cahiers de Sociologie Economique
Cah Sociol Demogr Med — Cahiers de Sociologie et de Demographie Medicales
Cah Sociol Econ — Cahiers de Sociologie Economique
Cah Staeeliens — Cahiers Staeeliens
Cah Sticht Bio-Wet Maatsch — Cahiers van de Stichting Bio-Wetenschappen en Maatschappij
Cah St Michel — Cahiers de Saint-Michel de Cuxa
Cah Sud — Cahiers du Sud
Cah Synth Org — Cahiers de Synthese Organique
CAHT — Cahiers de Tunisie
CahTD — Cahiers. Groupe Francois-Thureau-Dangin. I
Cah Tech — Cahiers Techniques de l'Art
Cah Tech Cent Nat Coord Etud Rech Nutr Aliment — Cahiers Techniques. Centre National de Coordination des Etudes et Recherches sur la Nutrition et l'Alimentation
Cah Therm — Cahiers de la Thermique
Cah Toxicol Clin Exp — Cahiers de Toxicologie Clinique et Experimentale
Cah Tun — Cahiers de Tunisie
Cah Tunis — Cahiers de Tunisie
Cah Tunisie — Cahiers de Tunisie
CahUC — Cahiers Universitaires Catholiques
Cah U Lyon II Inst Hist A — Cahiers. Universite de Lyon II. Institut d'Histoire de l'Art
CahUQ — Cahiers de l'Universite du Quebec
Cah Vaudois — Cahiers Vaudois
Cah Vict Ed — Cahiers Victoriens et Edouardiens
Cah Victoriens Edouardiens — Cahiers Victoriens et Edouardiens
Cah Vieux Dijon — Cahiers du Vieux-Dijon
Cah Vilfredo Pareto — Cahiers Vilfredo Pareto. Revue Europeenne des Sciences Sociales
Cah V Paret — Cahiers Vilfredo Pareto
CahXXs — Cahiers du XXe Siecle
Cah Zair Et Polit Soc — Cahiers Zairois d'Etudes Politiques et Sociales
Cah Zairois Etud Pol et Soc — Cahiers Zairois d'Etudes Politiques et Sociales
Cah Zairois Etud Polit et Soc — Cahiers Zairois d'Etudes Politiques et Sociales
Cah Zairois Rech et Dev — Cahiers Zairois de la Recherche et du Developpement
CAI — CAIC [*Computer Assisted Instruction Center*] Technical Memo. Florida StateUniversity
CAI — Cuba Internacional
CAIBL — Comptes Rendus. Academie des Inscriptions et Belles Lettres
CAIEF — Cahiers. Association Internationale des Etudes Francaises
CAIIAK — Centro de Investigaciones Agricolas del Noreste. Informe de Investigacion Agricola
CAIL — Academie des Inscriptions et Belles-Lettres. Comptes Rendus des Seances
CAIN — Cancer Investigation
CAIN — Comite Arctique International. Newsletter
CAIN — Computerized AIDS Information Network
CAIRDG — Cardiovascular and Interventional Radiology
Cairo St Engl — Cairo Studies in English
Cairo Univ Fac Agric Bull — Cairo University. Faculty of Agriculture. Bulletin
Cairo Univ Fac Pharm Bull — Cairo University. Faculty of Pharmacy. Bulletin
Cairo Univ Fac Sci Bull — Cairo University. Faculty of Science. Bulletin
Cairo Univ Herb Publ — Cairo University. Herbarium. Publications
Cairo Univ Med J — Cairo University. Medical Journal
CaIS — Cahiers Internationaux de Sociologie
CaiSE — Cairo Studies in English
CAIU — Cahiers. Alliance Israelite Universelle
CAIUM — Cahiers. Alliance Israelite Universelle
CAJ — Central Asiatic Journal
CAJ — College Art Journal
CAJMA3 — Central African Journal of Medicine
CAJOB — Canadian Journal of Ophthalmology
CAJOBA — Canadian Journal of Ophthalmology
CAJOD — Cato Journal
CAKCAC — Communications. Faculte des Sciences. Universite d'Ankara. Serie C. Sciences Naturelles
C A L — Cahiers. Academie Luxembourgeoise

CAL — Cahiers des Ameriques Latines
Cal — Caliban
Cal — Caliche
CAL — California Law Review
Cal — California Reports
CaL — Campus Life
CAL — Current Antarctic Literature
CAL — Romance Writers of America. Chapter Advisory Letter
Cal Ac Sc — California Academy of Sciences
Cal Ac Sc Mem — California Academy of Sciences. Memoirs
Cal Ac Sc Oc P — California Academy of Sciences. Occasional Papers
Cal Ac Sc Pr — California Academy of Sciences. Proceedings
Cal Admin Code — California Administrative Code
Cal Admin Notice Reg — California Administrative Notice Register
Cal Adv Leg Serv (Deering) — California Advance Legislative Service (Deering)
Cal Ag Exp — University of California. College of Agriculture. Agricultural Experiment Station. Publications
Cal Agr — California Agriculture
Cal App — California Appellate Reports
Cal Astr Obs Astr La Plata — Calendario Astronomico del Observatorio Astronomico de la Plata [*Buenos Aires*]
Cal Astr Parte Austral Am S — Calendario Astronomico para le Parte Austral de la America del Sur [*Buenos Aires*]
Cal Atlante Agostini — Calendario Atlante de Agostini [*Novara*]
CAL Bull — Association of the Bar of the City of New York. Committee on Amendment of the Law. Bulletin
CALC — Cahiers Algeriens de Litterature Comparee
Calc — Calculi. Department of Classics. Dartmouth
Calcif Tiss — Calcified Tissue Research [*Later, Calcified Tissue International*]
Calcif Tissue Int — Calcified Tissue International
Calcif Tissue Res — Calcified Tissue Research [*Later, Calcified Tissue International*]
Calcif Tissues Proc Eur Symp — Calcified Tissues. Proceedings of the European Symposium
Calcitonin Proc Int Symp — Calcitonin Proceedings. International Symposium
Cal Citrograph — California Citrograph
Calcium Cell Funct — Calcium and Cell Function
Calc J M — Calcutta Journal of Medicine
Calc LJ — Calcutta Law Journal
Calc Med Rev — Calcutta Medical Review
Cal Code (Deering) — Deering's Annotated California Code
Cal Code (West) — West's Annotated California Code
CALCON — California Connections
Cal Countryman — California Countryman
Calc Rev — Calcutta Review
Calc Tiss Res — Calcified Tissue Research [*Later, Calcified Tissue International*]
Cal Cultivator — California Cultivator
Calcut St — Calcutta Statistical Association. Bulletin
Calcutta Hist J — Calcutta Historical Journal
Calcutta J Nat Hist — Calcutta Journal of Natural History and Miscellany of the Arts and Sciences in India
Calcutta LJ — Calcutta Law Journal
Calcutta Med J — Calcutta Medical Journal
Calcutta R — Calcutta Review
Calcutta Rev — Calcutta Review
Calcutta Statist Ass Bull — Calcutta Statistical Association Bulletin
Calcutta Statist Assoc Bull — Calcutta Statistical Association. Bulletin
Calcutta WN — Calcutta Weekly Notes
Calc Var Partial Differential Equations — Calculus of Variations and Partial Differential Equations
Calc WN — Calcutta Weekly Notes
Cal Dairym — California Dairyman
Cald Med — Caldas Medico
CalE — California English
Caled Med J — Caledonian Medical Journal
Caledonian M J — Caledonian Medical Journal [*Glasgow*]
Caledon Med J — Caledonian Medical Journal [*Glasgow*]
CALEDQ — Cancer Letters
Calendar Met Off — Calendar. Meteorological Office
Calendrier A Obs Zi Ka Wei — Calendrier Annuaire. Observatoire de Zi-Ka-Wei [*Chang-Hai*]
Cal Engl J — California English Journal
Cal Fi Ga — California Fish and Game
CALF News Concern Am Livest Feeders — CALF News. Concerning America's Livestock Feeders
Cal Folkl Q — California Folklore Quarterly
Cal For For Prod — California Forestry and Forest Products
Cal For Ital — Calendario Forestale Italiano
Cal Gen Laws Ann (Deering) — Deering's California General Laws Annotated
Cal Geogr — California Geography
CALGIR — Community and Local Government Information Review
Cal Hist J — Calcutta Historical Journal
Cal Hist Soc Quar — California Historical Society. Quarterly
Cal Hlth — California's Health
CALICO J — CALICO [*Computer-Assisted Language Learning and Instruction Consortium*] Journal
Calicut Univ Res J — Calicut University Research Journal
Calif Acad Sci Mem — California Academy of Sciences. Memoirs
Calif Acad Sci Occasional Paper Proc — California Academy of Sciences. Occasional Papers and Proceedings
Calif Ag Bul — California. Department of Agriculture. Bulletin
Calif Agr — California Agriculture
Calif Agric — California Agriculture
Calif Agric Calif Agric Exp Stn — California Agriculture. California Agricultural Experiment Station

Calif Agric Exp Stn Bull — California. Agricultural Experiment Station. Bulletin
Calif Agric Ext Serv Circ — California. Agricultural Extension Service. Circular
Calif Air Environ — California Air Environment
Calif Air Qual Data — California Air Quality Data
Calif Anthropol — California Anthropologist
Calif Art Nat — California Art and Nature
Calif Avocado Assoc Yearb — California Avocado Association Yearbook
Calif Avocado Soc Yearb — California Avocado Society Yearbook
Calif Bee Times — California Bee Times
Calif Birds — California Birds
Calif Bus — California Business
Calif Bus Ed J — California Business Education Journal
Calif Cattleman — California Cattleman
Calif Cit News — California Citation News
Calif Citrogr — California Citrograph
Calif Coop Oceanic Fish Invest Atlas — California Cooperative Oceanic Fisheries Investigations. Atlas
Calif Coop Oceanic Fish Invest Rep — California Cooperative Oceanic Fisheries Investigations. Reports
Calif Cult — California Culturist. A Journal of Agriculture, Horticulture, Mechanism, and Mining
Calif Dep Agric Bienn Rep — California. Department of Agriculture. Biennial Report
Calif Dep Agric Bull — California. Department of Agriculture. Bulletin
Calif Dep Agric Bur Entomol Occas Pap — California. Department of Agriculture. Bureau of Entomology. Occasional Papers
Calif Dep Agric Mon Bull — California. Department of Agriculture. Monthly Bulletin
Calif Dep Conserv Div Mines Geol Spec Rep — California. Department of Conservation. Division of Mines and Geology. Special Report
Calif Dep Fish Game Fish Bull — California. Department of Fish and Game. Fish Bulletin
Calif Dep Fish Game Game Bull — California. Department of Fish and Game. Game Bulletin
Calif Dep Food Agric Lab Serv-Entomol Occas Pap — California. Department of Food and Agriculture. Laboratory Services-Entomology.Occasional Papers
Calif Dep Nat Resour Div Mines Bull — California. Department of Natural Resources. Division of Mines. Bulletin
Calif Dep Nat Resour Div Mines Spec Rep — California. Department of Natural Resources. Division of Mines. Special Report
Calif Dep Nat Resour Div Soil Conserv Bull — California. Department of Natural Resources. Division of Soil Conservation. Bulletin
Calif Dept Agric Bur Entomol Occas Pap — California. Department of Agriculture. Bureau of Entomology. Occasional Papers
Calif Dept Nat Res Div Mines Bull — California. Department of Natural Resources. Division of Mines. Bulletin
Calif Dept Nat Res Div Mines Econ Mineral Map — California. Department of Natural Resources. Division of Mines. Economic Mineral Map
Calif Dept Nat Res Div Mines Mineral Inf Service — California. Department of Natural Resources. Division of Mines. Mineral Information Service
Calif Dept Nat Res Div Mines Rept State Mineralogist — California. Department of Natural Resources. Division of Mines. Report of StateMineralogist
Calif Dept Nat Res Div Mines Special Rept — California. Department of Natural Resources. Division of Mines. Special Report
Calif Dep Public Works Div Water Res Bull — California. Department of Public Works. Division of Water Resources. Bulletin
Calif Dep Public Works Div Water Res Water Quality Inv Rept — California. Department of Public Works. Division of Water Resources. Water Quality Investigations Report
Calif Dept Water Res Bull — California. Department of Water Resources. Bulletin
Calif Dept Water Res Div Res Plan Bull — California. Department of Water Resources. Division of Resources. Planning Bulletin
Calif Dept Water Res Rept — California. Department of Water Resources. Report
Calif Dep Water Resour Bull — California. Department of Water Resources. Bulletin
Calif Div For Fire Control Exp — California. Division of Forestry. Fire Control Experiments
Calif Div For Fire Control Notes — California. Division of Forestry. Fire Control Notes
Calif Div Mines Geol Bull — California. Division of Mines and Geology. Bulletin
Calif Div Mines Geol Cty Rep — California. Division of Mines and Geology. County Report
Calif Div Mines Geol Geol Data Map — California. Division of Mines and Geology. Geologic Data Map
Calif Div Mines Geol Map Sheet Ser — California. Division of Mines and Geology. Map Sheet Series
Calif Div Mines Geol Rep — California. Division of Mines and Geology. County Report
Calif Div Mines Geol Rep State Geol — California. Division of Mines and Geology. Report of the State Geologist
Calif Div Mines Geol Spec Publ — California. Division of Mines and Geology. Special Publication
Calif Div Mines Geol Spec Rep — California. Division of Mines and Geology. Special Report
Calif Div Oil Gas Annu Rep — California. Division of Oil and Gas. Annual Report
Calif Ecl Med J — Californa Eclectic Medical Journal [*Los Angeles*]
Calif Ed — California Education
Calif El Sch Adm Assn Mon — California Elementary School Administrators Association. Monographs
Calif El Sch Adm Assn Yearbook — California Elementary School Administrators Association. Yearbook
Calif Farmer — California Farmer
Calif Farmer Cent Ed — California Farmer. Central Edition
Calif Feeders Day — California Feeders' Day
Calif Fire Control Note Calif Div For — California Fire Control Notes. California Division of Forestry

Calif Fire Prev Note Calif Div For — California Fire Prevention Notes. California Division of Forestry
Calif Fish — California Fish and Game
Calif Fish Game — California Fish and Game
Calif Florist — California Florist
Calif Fmr — California Farmer [*Los Angeles*]
Calif Fm Reptr — California Farm Reporter [*Santa Clara*]
Calif Folklore Qu — California Folklore Quarterly
Calif For — California Forestry [*Berkeley*]
Calif For & For Prod Calif For Prod Lab — California Forestry and Forest Products. University of California. Forest Products Laboratory
Calif Forest — California Forestry
Calif For For Prod — California Forestry and Forest Products
Calif For For Prod — California Forestry and Forest Products [*Berkeley*]
Calif For Note — California Forestry Note
Calif Fruit Grape Grow — California Fruit and Grape Grower [*San Francisco*]
Calif Fruit Grow — California Fruit Grower [*San Francisco*]
Calif Fruit News — California Fruit News [*San Francisco*]
Calif Geogr — California Geographer
Calif Geol — California Geology
Calif Grape Grow — California Grape Grower [*San Francisco*]
Calif Grow — California Grower [*San Francisco*]
Calif Grower — California Grower
Calif Grow Rancher Sacramento Val Ed — California Grower and Rancher. Sacramento Valley Edition
Calif Health — California's Health
Calif Highw & Pub Wks — California Highways and Public Works
Calif Highw Patrol — California Highway Patrolman
Calif Highw Public Works — California Highways and Public Works
Calif Highw Publ Wks — California Highways and Public Works [*Sacramento*]
Calif Hist — California History
Calif Hist Courier — California Historical Courier
Calif Hist Q — California Historical Quarterly
Calif Hist Soc Q — California Historical Society. Quarterly
Calif Hist Soc Quar — California Historical Society. Quarterly
Calif Hort Fl Mag — California Horticulturist and Floral Magazine
Calif Hortic J — California Horticultural Journal
Calif Hosp — California Hospitals
Calif Hous — California Housing Outlook
Calif Inst Technol Earthquake Eng Res Lab (Rep) EERL — California Institute of Technology. Earthquake Engineering Research Laboratory (Report) EERL
Calif Inst Technol Jet Propul Lab Publ — California Institute of Technology. Jet Propulsion Laboratory. Publication
Calif Inst Technol Jet Propul Lab Spec Publ JPL SP — California Institute of Technology. Jet Propulsion Laboratory. Special Publication JPL SP
Calif Inst Technol Jet Propul Lab Tech Memo — California Institute of Technology. Jet Propulsion Laboratory. Technical Memorandum
Calif Inst Technol Jet Propul Lab Tech Rep — California Institute of Technology. Jet Propulsion Laboratory. Technical Report
Calif Inst Technology Div Geol Sci Contr — California Institute of Technology. Division of Geological Sciences. Contributions
Calif J Dev — California Journal of Development [*San Francisco*]
Calif J Development — California Journal of Development
Calif J Ed Res — California Journal of Educational Research
Calif J Edu — California Journal of Educational Research
Calif J El Ed — California Journal of Elementary Education
Calif J El Educ — California Journal of Elementary Education
Calif J Mines Geol — California Journal of Mines and Geology
Calif Jnl Teach Educ — California Journal of Teacher Education
Calif Jour Mines and Geology — California Journal of Mines and Geology
Calif J Sec Ed — California Journal of Secondary Education
Calif J Sec Educ — California Journal of Secondary Education
Calif J Technol — California Journal of Technology
Calif Landscape Manage — California Landscape Management
Calif Leag Women Voters Bul — California League of Women Voters. Bulletin
Calif Libn — California Librarian
Calif Librn — California Librarian
Calif Lib Stat Dir — California Library Statistics and Directory
Calif Livestk News — California Livestock News [*San Francisco*]
Calif L R — California Law Review
Calif L Rev — California Law Review
Calif M — Californian Illustrated Magazine
Calif Mag — California Magazine
Calif Manag — California Management Review
Calif Management Rev — California Management Review
Calif Manage Rev — California Management Review
Calif Manag R — California Management Review
Calif Med — California Medicine
Calif Med Bull — California Medical Bulletin [*San Francisco*]
Calif Med J — California Medical Journal [*San Francisco*]
Calif Mgt R — California Management Review
Calif Min Bus Ent Dir — California Minority Business Enterprises Directory
Calif Min J — California Mining Journal
Calif Mosq Control Assoc Proc Pap Annu Conf — California Mosquito Control Association. Proceedings and Papers of the Annual Conference
Calif Mosq Vector Control Assoc Proc Pap Annu Conf — California Mosquito and Vector Control Association. Proceedings and Papers of the Annual Conference
Calif Nat Hist Guides — California Natural History Guides
Calif Nurs — California Nurse
Calif Nurse — California Nurse
Calif Oil Fields — California Oil Fields
Calif Oil World — California Oil World
Calif Oil World Pet Ind — California Oil World and Petroleum Industry
Calif Olive Industr News — California Olive Industry News

California Acad Sci Proc — California Academy of Sciences. Proceedings
California Dept Water Resources Bull — California. Department of Water Resources. Bulletin
California Div Mines and Geology Bull — California. Division of Mines and Geology. Bulletin
California Div Mines and Geology Map Sheet — California. Division of Mines and Geology. Map Sheet
California Div Mines and Geology Mineral Inf Service — California. Division of Mines and Geology. Mineral Information Service
California Div Mines and Geology Spec Rept — California. Division of Mines and Geology. Special Report
California Geol — California Geology
California Med — California Medicine
Californian Law Rev — Californian Law Review
California Slav Stud — California Slavic Studies
California Stud Hist Sci — California Studies in the History of Science
California Univ Pubs Geol Sci — California University. Publications in Geological Sciences
California Univ Water Resources Center Rept — California University. Water Resources Center. Report
California West L Rev — California Western Law Review
California West Med — California and Western Medicine
Californium 252 Prog — Californium-252 Progress
Calif Pal Leg Hon Bul — California Palace of the Legion of Honor. Museum Bulletin
Calif Poult Lett Univ Calif Coop Ext — California Poultry Letter. University of California Cooperative Extension
Calif Pub Lib Sal Surv — California Public Library Salary Survey
Calif Q — California Quarterly
Calif S B — State Bar of California. Journal
Calif SBJ — California State Bar Journal
Calif SBJ — State Bar of California. Journal
Calif Sch — California Schools
Calif Sch Lib — California School Libraries
Calif Sch Libr — California School Libraries
Calif Schs — California Schools
Calif Sewage Works J — California Sewage Works Journal
Califs Hlth — California's Health
Calif Slavic Stud — California Slavic Studies
Calif Social — California Socialist
Calif State Dep Public Health Mon Bull — California. State Department of Public Health. Monthly Bulletin
Calif State Dep Public Health Q Bull — California. State Department of Public Health. Quarterly Bulletin
Calif State Dep Public Health Wkly Bull — California. State Department of Public Health. Weekly Bulletin
Calif State Dept Education Bull — California State Department of Education. Bulletin
Calif State J Med — California State Journal of Medicine
Calif State Univ (Chico) Reg Programs Monogr — California State University (Chico). Regional Programs Monograph
Calif State Water Pollut Control Board Publ — California State Water Pollution Control Board. Publication
Calif State Water Pollution Control Board Pub — California State Water Pollution Control Board. Publication
Calif State Water Qual Control Board Publ — California. State Water Quality Control Board. Publication
Calif State Water Res Board Bull — California State Water Resources Board. Bulletin
Calif State Water Resour Control Board Publ — California State Water Resources Control Board. Publication
Calif St Bar Jnl — California State Bar Journal
Calif St B J — California State Bar. Journal
Calif St B Proc — California State Bar. Proceedings
Calif St Cl Ant — California Studies in Classical Antiquity
Calif St Emp — California State Employee
Calif St J Med — California State Journal of Medicine
Calif St Sheriff Assn Proc — California State Sheriff Association. Proceedings
Calif Turfgrass Cult Calif Univ Berkeley Coop Ext Serv — California Turfgrass Culture. California University. Berkeley Cooperative Extension Service
Calif Univ Agr Expt Sta Ground Water Studies — California University. Agricultural Experiment Station. Ground Water Studies
Calif Univ Agric Exp Stn Bull — California. University. Agricultural Experiment Station. Bulletin
Calif Univ Agric Exp Stn Circ — California. University. Agricultural Experiment Station. Circular
Calif Univ (Berkeley) Water Resour Cent Desalin Rep — California University (Berkeley). Water Resources Center. Desalination Report
Calif Univ Chron — California University. Chronicle
Calif Univ Inst Transp and Traffic Eng Inf Circ — California University. Institute of Transportation and Traffic Engineering. Information Circular
Calif Univ Mem — California University. Memoirs
Calif Univ Publ Geol Sci — California University. Publications in Geological Sciences
Calif Univ Pubs Astronomy — California University. Publications in Astronomy
Calif Univ Pubs Geography — California University. Publications in Geography
Calif Univ Pubs Geol Sci — California University. Publications in Geological Sciences
Calif Univ Pubs Zoology — California University. Publications in Zoology
Calif Univ (Riverside) Campus Mus Contrib — California University (Riverside). Campus Museum. Contributions
Calif Univ Scripps Inst — California University. Scripps Institution of Oceanography. Reference Series
Calif Univ Scripps Inst Oceanogr Annu Rep — California University. Scripps Institution of Oceanography. Annual Report

Calif Univ Scripps Inst Oceanography Bull — California University. Scripps Institution of Oceanography. Bulletin
Calif Univ Scripps Inst Oceanography SIO Reference — California University. Scripps Institution of Oceanography. SIO Reference
Calif Univ Scripps Inst Oceanography Submarine Geology Rept — California University. Scripps Institution of Oceanography. Submarine Geology Report
Calif Univ Scripps Inst Oceanogr Contrib — California University. Scripps Institution of Oceanography. Contributions
Calif Univ Scripps Inst Oceanogr Ref Ser — California University. Scripps Institution of Oceanography. Reference Series
Calif Univ Water Res Center Archives Archives Ser Rept Contr — California University. Water Resources Center Archives. Archives Series Report.Contributions
Calif Univ Water Resour Cent Contrib — California. University. Water Resources Center. Contribution
Calif Univ Water Resour Cent Rep — California University. Water Resources Center. Report
Calif Vector Views — California Vector Views
Calif Vet — California Veterinarian
Calif Water Pollut Control Assoc Bull — California Water Pollution Control Association. Bulletin
Calif Water Resour Cent Rep — California Water Resources Center Report
Calif Weed Conf Proc — California Weed Conference. Proceedings
Calif Western Int L J — California Western International Law Journal
Calif Western L Rev — California Western Law Review
Calif West Int'l LJ — California Western International Law Journal
Calif West L Rev — California Western Law Review
Calif West Med — California and Western Medicine
Calif West States Grape Grow — California and Western States Grape Grower
Calif W Int Law J — California Western International Law Journal
Calif W Int'l LJ — California Western International Law Journal
Calif WL Rev — California Western Law Review
Calif Wool Grow — California Wool Grower
Cali His Nugget — California History Nugget
Cali Hist Soc Special Pub — California Historical Society. Special Publication
Calitatea Prod & Metrol — Calitatea Productiei si Metrologie
Cal J — California Journal
CALJ — Canadian Alpine Journal
Cal J Dev — California Journal of Development
Cal J Educ Res — California Journal of Educational Research
Cal J Min — California Journal of Mines and Geology
Cal J Tech — California Journal of Technology
Cal J Techn — California Journal of Technology
CALL — Current Awareness-Library Literature
Cal Law — California Lawyer
Cal Law R — California Law Review
Cal Law Rev — California Law Review. University of California
Cal Legis Serv (West) — California Legislative Service (West)
Cal Libr — California Librarian
Callig Idea Exch — Calligraphy Idea Exchange
Cal LJ — Calcutta Law Journal Reports
Cal LJ — California Law Journal
Cal LR — California Law Review
Cal L Rev — California Law Review
Cal Man Rev — California Management Review
Cal M As — California Miners' Association
Cal Med — California Medicine
Cal Med Bull — California Medical Bulletin
Cal Med J — California Medical Journal
Cal Med Surg Rep — California Medical and Surgical Reporter
Cal Ment Hlth Ne — California Mental Health News
Cal Meteoro Fenol Madr — Calendario Meteoro-Fenologico. Servicio Meteorologico Nacional [*Madrid*]
Cal Mgmt Rev — California Management Review
Cal Mgt R — California Management Review
CalN — Calabria Nobilissima
Cal Neva TL — Cal-Neva Token Ledger
Cal Nob — Calabria Nobilissma. Periodico di Arte, Storia, e Letteratura Calabrese
CALOA — Calore
CALOD — Calorie
Calore Tecnol — Calore e Tecnologia
Calorim Therm Anal — Calorimetry and Thermal Analysis
CALPHAD Comput Coupling Phase Diagrams and Thermochem — CALPHAD. Computer Coupling of Phase Diagrams and Thermochemistry
Cal Phys Geog Club B — California Physical Geography Club. Bulletin
Cal Pioneers Soc Quar — Society of California Pioneers. Quarterly
Cal Polyt J — California Polytechnic Journal
Cal Poult J — California Poultry Journal
Cal Poult Trib — California Poultry Tribune
Cal Publ Class Arch — California Publications in Classical Archaeology
Cal Public Employee Relations — California Public Employee Relations
Cal Q — California Quarterly
Cal Q Sec Ed — California Quarterly of Secondary Education
CalR — Calcutta Review
CA LR — California Law Review
Cal R — California Reporter
Cal R Oss Astr Coll Romano Roma — Calendario del Reale Osservatorio Astronomico al Collegio Romano in Roma
Cal Rptr — West's California Reporter
Cal Saf Ne — California Safety News
Cal Savings and Loan J — California Savings and Loan Journal
Cal SBJ — California State Bar Journal
Cal Sew WJ — California Sewage Works Journal
Cal Sl St — California Slavic Studies
Cal SS — California Slavic Studies

Cal Stat — Statutes of California
Cal State Comm Hort B — California State Commission of Horticulture. Monthly Bulletin
Cal St BJ — California State Bar Journal
Cal St Class Ant — California Studies in Classical Antiquity
Cal St J Med — California State Journal of Medicine
Cal St M Bur — California State Mining Bureau
Cal St M Bur An Rp B — California State Mining Bureau. Annual Report. Bulletin
Caltex Lubric — Caltex Lubrication
Cal Th J — Calvin Theological Journal
Cal Univ Chron — University of California Chronicle
Cal Univ Dp G B — California University. Publications. Department of Geology. Bulletin
Cal Univ Pub — California University [*Berkeley*]. Publications in Agricultural Science
Cal Univ Pub Geog — California University. Publications in Geography
Cal Univ Seism Sta B — California University. Publications. Seismography Stations. Bulletin
Cal Unrep — California Unreported Cases
Calv Theol J — Calvin Theological Journal
CalvTJ — Calvin Theological Journal
CalwerH — Calwer Hefte zur Foerderung Biblischen Glaubens und Christlichen Lebens
Cal Western Law R — California Western Law Review
Cal W Int LJ — California Western International Law Journal
Cal W Int'l LJ — California Western International Law Journal
Cal W LR — California Western Law Review
Cal WL Rev — California Western Law Review
Cal WN — Calcutta Weekly Notes
Cal WR — Calcutta Weekly Reporter
CaM — Cahiers du Monde Russe et Sovietique
CAM — CA [*Chartered Accountant*] Magazine
CAm — Casa de las Americas
CAM — Contemporary Australian Management
CAM — Corsica Antica e Moderna
CAM — Critica. Revista Hispano-Americana de Filosofia (Mexico)
Cam 35 — Camera 35
Cam Abs — Cambridge Abstracts
CA Mag — California's Magazine
CA Mag — CA [*Chartered Accountant*] Magazine
CA Magazin — CA [*Chemical Abstracts*] Magazine
CA Mag J Commer Art — CA Magazine. Journal of Commercial Art
CAMAn — Cercle Archeologique de Mons. Annales
Camara Comer Bogota R — Camara de Comercio de Bogota. Revista
Camara Text Mex — Camara Textil de Mexico
Camara Text Mex Rev Tec — Camara Textil de Mexico. Revista Tecnica
Cam Austria — Camera Austria. Zeitschrift fuer Fotografie
CAMB — Cincinnati Art Museum Bulletin
Camb And Dubl Mth J — Cambridge and Dublin Mathematical Journal. Thomson and Ferrers
Camb Anthrop — Cambridge Anthropology
Camb Archaeol J — Cambridge Archaeological Journal
Camb ASP — Cambridge Antiquarian Society. Proceedings
Camb Bibliog Soc — Cambridge Bibliographical Society
Camb Biol Stud — Cambridge Biological Studies
CAMBDM — Cambridge Studies in Modern Biology
Camb Engng Tracts — Cambridge Engineering Tracts
Camb Hist J — Cambridge Historical Journal
Camb J — Cambridge Journal
Camb L J — Cambridge Law Journal
Camb M Mth M — Mathematical Monthly. Runkle (Cambridge, Massachusetts)
Camb Mod Hist — Cambridge Modern History
Camb Monogr Exp Biol — Cambridge Monographs in Experimental Biology
Camb Mountg — Cambridge Mountaineering
Camb Mth J — Cambridge Mathematical Journal
Camb Opera J — Cambridge Opera Journal
Camborne Sch Mines J — Camborne School of Mines Journal
Camborne Sch Mines Mag — Camborne School of Mines Magazine
Camb Pap Soc Anthrop — Cambridge Papers in Social Anthropology
Camb Philos Soc Trans — Cambridge Philosophical Society. Transactions
Camb Ph S P — Proceedings of the Cambridge Philosophical Society
Camb Ph S T — Transactions of the Cambridge Philosophical Society
Camb Phys Tracts — Cambridge Physical Tracts
Camb Q — Cambridge Quarterly
Camb Q Healthc Ethics — Cambridge Quarterly of Healthcare Ethics
Cambr Anc Hist — Cambridge Ancient History
Cambr Bibl Soc Trans — Cambridge Bibliographical Society. Transactions
Cambr Biol Stud — Cambridge Biological Studies
Cambria — Cambria County Legal Journal
Cambria Co LJ — Cambria County Legal Journal
Cambria Co (PA) — Cambria County Legal Journal
Cambrian Archaeol Ass Monogr Collect — Cambrian Archaeological Association. Monographs and Collections
Cambrian Law R — Cambrian Law Review
Cambrian LR — Cambrian Law Review
Cambrian L Rev — Cambrian Law Review
Cambrian Nat Obsr — Cambrian Natural Observer
Cambridge Anthrop — Cambridge Anthropology
Cambridge Anthropol — Cambridge Anthropology
Cambridge Antiqua Soc Proc — Cambridge Antiquarian Society Proceedings
Cambridge Archeol J — Cambridge Archeological Journal
Cambridge Comput Sci Texts — Cambridge Computer Science Texts
Cambridge Econ Policy Rev — Cambridge Economic Policy Review
Cambridge Econ Pol R — Cambridge Economic Policy Review

Cambridge Ed Works Immanuel Kant — Cambridge Edition of the Works of Immanuel Kant
Cambridge Environ Chem Ser — Cambridge Environmental Chemistry Series
Cambridge Hist J — Cambridge Historical Journal
Cambridge Hist Jour — Cambridge Historical Journal
Cambridge Hist Sci Ser — Cambridge History of Science Series
Cambridge Inst Ed Bulletin — Cambridge Institute of Education. Bulletin
Cambridge Internat Ser Parallel Comput — Cambridge International Series on Parallel Computation
Cambridge J — Cambridge Journal
Cambridge J Econ — Cambridge Journal of Economics
Cambridge J Economics — Cambridge Journal of Economics
Cambridge J Ed — Cambridge Journal of Education
Cambridge J Educ — Cambridge Journal of Education
Cambridge Lecture Notes Phys — Cambridge Lecture Note in Physics
Cambridge LJ — Cambridge Law Journal
Cambridge Math Lib — Cambridge Mathematical Library
Cambridge Math Textbooks — Cambridge Mathematical Textbooks
Cambridge Medieval Celtic Stud — Cambridge Medieval Celtic Studies
Cambridge Mongraphs Math Phys — Cambridge Monographs on Mathematical Physics
Cambridge Monographs Mech Appl Math — Cambridge Monographs on Mechanics and Applied Mathematics
Cambridge Monographs Phys — Cambridge Monographs on Physics
Cambridge Monogr Appl Comput Math — Cambridge Monographs on Applied and Computational Mathematics
Cambridge Monogr Mech — Cambridge Monographs on Mechanics
Cambridge Monogr Mech Appl Math — Cambridge Monographs on Mechanics and Applied Mathematics
Cambridge Nonlinear Sci Ser — Cambridge Nonlinear Science Series
Cambridge Opera J — Cambridge Opera Journal
Cambridge Philos Soc Biol Rev — Cambridge Philosophical Society. Biological Reviews
Cambridge Philos Soc Math Proc — Cambridge Philosophical Society. Mathematical Proceedings
Cambridge Philos Soc Proc — Cambridge Philosophical Society. Proceedings
Cambridge Ph Soc Pr — Cambridge Philosophical Society. Proceedings
Cambridge Q — Cambridge Quarterly
Cambridge Sci Classics — Cambridge Science Classics
Cambridge Stud Adv Math — Cambridge Studies in Advanced Mathematics
Cambridge Stud Math Biol — Cambridge Studies in Mathematical Biology
Cambridge Stud Mod Opt — Cambridge Studies in Modern Optics
Cambridge Stud Philos — Cambridge Studies in Philosophy
Cambridge Stud Probab Induc Decis Theory — Cambridge Studies in Probability, Induction, and Decision Theory
Cambridge Stud Soc Anthropology — Cambridge Studies in Social Anthropology
Cambridge Texts Appl Math — Cambridge Texts in Applied Mathematics
Cambridge Tracts in Math — Cambridge Tracts in Mathematics
Cambridge Tracts Theoret Comput Sci — Cambridge Tracts in Theoretical Computer Science
Cambridge Univ Eng Dep Rep CUED A Turbo — Cambridge University. Engineering Department. Report CUED/A-Turbo
Cambridge Univ Eng Dep Rep CUED C MATS — Cambridge University. Engineering Department. Report CUED/C/MATS
Cambridge Univ Med Soc Mag — Cambridge University Medical Society. Magazine
Cambridge Urban Architect Stud — Cambridge Urban and Architectural Studies
Cambr LJ — Cambridge Law Journal
Cambr Or Ser — Cambridge Oriental Series
Cambr Tr Math — Cambridge Tracts in Mathematics and Mathematical Physics [*Later, Cambridge Tracts in Mathematics*]
Cambr Univ Agr Soc Mag — Cambridge University Agricultural Society. Magazine
Cambr Univ Eng Aeronaut — Cambridge University Engineering and Aeronautical Societies. Journal
Cambr Univ Eng Soc J — Cambridge University Engineering Society. Journal
Cambr Univ Med Soc Mag — Cambridge University Medical Society. Magazine
Cambs Antiqua Soc 8vo Pubns — Cambridge Antiquarian Society Octavo Publications
Camb Stud Biol Anthropol — Cambridge Studies in Biological Anthropology
Camb Stud Biotechnol — Cambridge Studies in Biotechnology
Camb Stud Mod Biol — Cambridge Studies in Modern Biology
Camb Texts Physiol Sci — Cambridge Texts in the Physiological Sciences
Camb Tracts Math — Cambridge Tracts in Mathematics and Mathematical Physics
CAMBull — Cercle Archeologique de Malines. Bulletin
Camb Univ Agric Soc Mag — Cambridge University Agricultural Society Magazine
Camb Univ Engng Aeronaut Socs J — Cambridge University Engineering and Aeronautical Societies Journal
Camb Univ Engng Soc J — Cambridge University Engineering Society Journal
Camb Univ Lib Bull — Cambridge University Library Bulletin
Camb Univ Med Soc Mag — Cambridge University Medical Society Magazine
Camb US Mth M — Mathematical Monthly. Runkle (Cambridge, Massachusetts)
Camb Wire — Cambridge Wire
CAMCA — CA. A Cancer Journal for Clinicians
Cam Club — Camera Club
CAMCORE Bull Trop For — CAMCORE Bulletin on Tropical Forestry
Camden Co Hist Soc Pub — Camden County Historical Society. Camden History
CAMEA — California Medicine
CAMEEW — Cardiovascular Medicine
Camellia J — Camellia Journal
Camellian S Carolina — Camellian. South Carolina Camellia Society
Camellia Rev — Camellia Review. Publication. Southern California Camellia Society
CAmer — Curioso Americano
Camera — Camera and Cine
Camera Club J — Camera Club Journal
Camera Dark Rm — Camera and Dark Room

Camera (Engl Ed) — Camera (English Edition)
Camera Int Z Phot & Film — Camera. Internationale Zeitschrift fuer Photographie und Film
Camera Mag — Camera Magazine
Camera News Tech — Camera News and Technique
Camera Obsc — Camera Obscura
Cameras Equip — Cameras and Equipment
Camera Wld — Camera World
C Amer Lat — Cahiers des Ameriques Latines
C Amer Lat Ser Sci Homme — Cahiers des Ameriques Latines. Serie Sciences de l'Homme
Cameron Synth Fuels Rep — Cameron Synthetic Fuels Report
Cameron Bull Dir Mines Geol — Cameroon. Bulletin. Direction des Mines et de la Geologie
Cameroon Natl Off Sci Tech Res Cameroon Onarest Sci Pap — Cameroon. National Office for Scientific and Technical Research of Cameroon. Onarest Scientific Papers
Cameroon P — Plan Quinquennal de Developpement Economique, Social, et Culturel, 1981-1986 (Cameroon)
Cameroons Fr Bull Dir Mines Geol — Cameroons. French. Bulletin. Direction des Mines et de la Geologie
Cameroun Agric Pastor For — Cameroun Agricole, Pastoral, et Forestier
Cameroun Dir Mines Geol Act Minieres Cameroun — Cameroun. Direction des Mines et de la Geologie. Activites Minieres au Cameroun
Cameroun Territ Bull Dir Mines Geol — Cameroun Territoire. Bulletin de la Direction des Mines et de la Geologie
CAMI — Canadian Mineralogist
CAMIA — Canadian Mineralogist
Caminos Mex — Caminos de Mexico
CamJ — Cambridge Journal
CAMJ — Canadian Mining Journal
CAMJA — Canadian Mining Journal
Cam J Educ — Cambridge Journal of Education
Cam Mainichi — Camera Mainichi
CAMN — Canadian Directory of Completed Master's Theses in Nursing
Cam Not — Camera Notes
Cam Notes — Camera Notes. Official Organ of the Camera Club of New York
Cam Obs — Camera Obscura
Campagne Antipalud — Campagne Antipaludique
Campagne Hareng — Campagne Harenguiere
Campaign — Campaigner
CAMPB — Comments on Atomic and Molecular Physics
Campbell L Rev — Campbell Law Review
Campbell Soup Co Dep Agric Res Bull — Campbell Soup Company. Department of Agricultural Research. Bulletin
Campbell Soup Co Dep Agric Res Res Monogr — Campbell Soup Company. Department of Agricultural Research. Research Monograph
Campbell Soup Dep Agric Res Bull — Campbell Soup Company. Department of Agricultural Research. Bulletin
Campbell Soup Dep Agric Res Res Monogr — Campbell Soup Company. Department of Agricultural Research. Research Monograph
Camping — Camping Magazine
Camp Mag — Camping Magazine
Campo La Paz — Campo. Banco Agricola de Bolivia (La Paz)
Campo Porto Alegre — Campo. Diarios e Emissoras Associadas do Rio Grande do Sul (Porto Alegre)
Campo Suelo Argent — Campo y Suelo Argentino
CAMP Rpt — CAMP [*Cable Advertising, Merchandising, and Programming*] Report
CamQ — Cambridge Quarterly
CAMQA — Canadian Metallurgical Quarterly
CamR — Cambridge Review
CAMT — Canada. Meteorological Translations
CAMT — Corpus des Mosaieques de Tunisie
CamW — Camera Work. A Photographic Quarterly
Cam Work — Camera Work
CAMZA — CA Magazine. Journal of Commercial Art
CAN — Cahiers Francais; Revue Periodique de l'Actualite Politique, Economique, Sociale, et Culturelle de la France
CaN — Calabria Nobilissima
Can — Canadiana
Can — Canadian. Patent Document
Can — Candide. Grand Hebdomadaire Parisien et Litteraire
Can — Canoniste
CAN — Canticle
CAn — Correo de los Andes
CANA — California Association of Nurse Anesthetists
Can A — Canadian Art
Can Acoust Acoust Can — Canadian Acoustics/Acoustique Canadienne
Canada Ag — Canada. Department of Agriculture. Publication
Canada Bus — Canadian Business Magazine
Canada Defence Research Board Handb — Canada Defence Research Board. Handbook
Canada Dept Mines and Tech Surveys Geog Br Bibl Ser — Canada. Department of Mines and Technical Surveys. Geographical Branch. Bibliographical Series
Canada Dept Mines and Tech Surveys Geog Bull — Canada. Department of Mines and Technical Surveys. Geographical Bulletin
Canada Dept Mines and Tech Surveys Geog Paper — Canada. Department of Mines and Technical Surveys. Geographical Paper
Canada Dept Mines and Tech Surveys Mem — Canada. Department of Mines and Technical Surveys. Memoir
Canada Dept Mines and Tech Surveys Misc Paper Ser — Canada. Department of Mines and Technical Surveys. Miscellaneous Paper Series
Canada Dominion Observatory Contr Pub — Canada Dominion Observatory Contributions. Publications
Canada Geol Survey Bull — Canada. Geological Survey. Bulletin

Canada Geol Survey Econ Geology Rept — Canada. Geological Survey. Economic Geology Report
Canada Geol Survey Geophysics Paper — Canada. Geological Survey. Geophysics Paper
Canada Geol Survey Map — Canada. Geological Survey. Map
Canada Geol Survey Mem — Canada. Geological Survey. Memoir
Canada Geol Survey Paper — Canada. Geological Survey. Paper
Canada Geol Survey Prelim Ser Map — Canada. Geological Survey. Preliminary Series. Map
Canad Alpine Jour — Canadian Alpine Journal. Alpine Club of Canada
Canada Med J — Canada Medical Journal and Monthly Record of Medical and Surgical Science
Canada Med Surg J — Canada Medical and Surgical Journal
Canad Anaesth Soc J — Canadian Anaesthetists' Society. Journal
Canada Natl Mus Bull Nat History Paper Special Contr — Canada. National Museum Bulletin. Natural History Paper. Special Contributions
Canad Antiq Numis J — Canadian Antiquarian and Numismatic Journal
Canada O & G — Canadian Oil and Gas Handbook
Canad Appl Math Quart — Canadian Applied Mathematics Quarterly
Canada Rpt — Report on Canada, 1985
Canad Ass Afr Stud Newsl — Canadian Association of African Studies Newsletter
Canad Bankers Assoc Jour — Canadian Bankers' Association. Journal
Canad Bar Rev — Canadian Bar Review
Canad Bee J — Canadian Bee Journal
Canad Bookm — Canadian Bookman
Canad Cath Hist Assoc Rep — Canadian Catholic Historial Association Report
Canad Chem Process — Canadian Chemical Processing
Canad Dairy Ice Cream J — Canadian Dairy and Ice Cream Journal
Canad Defence Quar — Canadian Defence Quarterly
Canad Doctor — Canadian Doctor
Canad Ent — Canadian Entomologist
Canad Entom — Canadian Entomologist
Canad Ethnic Stud — Canadian Ethnic Studies
Canad Fam Physician — Canadian Family Physician
Canad Fld-Nat — Canadian Field-Naturalist
Canad For Ind — Canadian Forest Industries
Canad Forum — Canadian Forum
Canad Fruitgrower — Canadian Fruitgrower
Canad Geog J — Canadian Geographical Journal [*Later, Canadian Geographic*]
Canad Geogr J — Canadian Geographical Journal
Canad Geol Survey Bul — Geological Survey of Canada. Bulletin. Anthropological Series
Canad Gladiolus Soc Quart — Canadian Gladiolus Society Quarterly
Canad Hist Assn Rep — Canadian Historical Association. Report
Canad Hist Rev — Canadian Historical Review
Canad Hort Mag — Canadian Horticultural Magazine
Canad Hosp — Canadian Hospital
Canadian Alpine Jour — Canadian Alpine Journal
Canadian Arcsht — Canadian Architect
Canadian Assoc Geographers Education Comm Bull — Canadian Association of Geographers. Education Committee. Bulletin
Canadian Bldg Digest — Canadian Building Digest
Canadian Ceramic Soc Jour — Canadian Ceramic Society. Journal
Canadian Geotech Jour — Canadian Geotechnical Journal
Canadian Hist Rev — Canadian Historical Review
Canadian Inst Mining and Metallurgy Trans — Canadian Institute of Mining and Metallurgy. Transactions
Canadian Inst Mining Met Bulletin — Canadian Institute of Mining and Metallurgy. Bulletin
CanadianJTH — Canadian Journal of Theology
Canadian Lib Assn Bul — Canadian Library Association. Bulletin
Canadian Shipp & Mar Engng — Canadian Shipping and Marine Engineering
Canad J — Canadian Journal of Industry
Canad J Afr Stud — Canadian Journal of African Studies
Canad J Agric Econ — Canadian Journal of Agricultural Economics
Canad J Archaeol — Canadian Journal of Archaeology
Canad J Biochem — Canadian Journal of Biochemistry and Physiology
Canad J Bot — Canadian Journal of Botany
Canad J Chem — Canadian Journal of Chemistry
Canad J Chem Engng — Canadian Journal of Chemical Engineering
Canad J Econ — Canadian Journal of Economics
Canad J Econ Polit Sci — Canadian Journal of Economics and Political Science
Canad J Industr — Canadian Journal of Industry, Science, and Art
Canad J Math — Canadian Journal of Mathematics
Canad J Med Sc — Canadian Journal of Medical Science
Canad J Med Tech — Canadian Journal of Medical Technology
Canad J Med Technol — Canadian Journal of Medical Technology
Canad J Microbiol — Canadian Journal of Microbiology
Canad J Native Stud — Canadian Journal of Native Studies
Canad Jour — Canadian Journal of Linguistics
Canad Jour L — Canadian Journal of Linguistics
Canad Jour Medicine And Surgery — Canadian Journal of Medicine and Surgery
Canad J Phys — Canadian Journal of Physics
Canad J Physiol Pharmacol — Canadian Journal of Physiology and Pharmacology
Canad J Pl Sci — Canadian Journal of Plant Science
Canad J Polit Sci — Canadian Journal of Political Science
Canad J Polit Soc Theory — Canadian Journal of Political and Social Theory
Canad J Psychiatr — Canadian Journal of Psychiatry
Canad J Psychiatr Nurs — Canadian Journal of Psychiatric Nursing
Canad J Psychol — Canadian Journal of Psychology
Canad J Public Health — Canadian Journal of Public Health
Canad J Radiogr Radiother Nucl Med — Canadian Journal of Radiography, Radiotherapy, Nuclear Medicine
Canad J Soil Sci — Canadian Journal of Soil Science
Canad J Statist — Canadian Journal of Statistics

Canad J Surg — Canadian Journal of Surgery
CanadJT — Canadian Journal of Theology
Canad J Zool — Canadian Journal of Zoology
Canad J Zoology — Canadian Journal of Zoology
Canad Law Times R — Canadian Law Times and Review
Canad Lib — Canadian Library
Canad Lib Assn Bul — Canadian Library Association. Bulletin
Canad Lib Assn Feliciter — Canadian Library Association. Feliciter
Canad Lib J — Canadian Library Journal
Canad M — Canadian Magazine
Canad Mag — Canadian Magazine
Canad MAJ — Canadian Medical Association. Journal
Canad Math Soc Ser Monographs Adv Texts — Canadian Mathematical Society Series of Monographs and Advanced Texts
Canad Med Assn J — Canadian Medical Association. Journal
Canad Med Assoc J — Canadian Medical Association. Journal
Can Admin — Canadian Administrator
Canad Mo — Canadian Monthly
Canad Nat Sci News — Canadian Natural Science News
Canad Naturalist Geol — Canadian Naturalist and Geologist
Canad Nurse — Canadian Nurse
Canad Person Industr Relat J — Canadian Personnel and Industrial Relations Journal (Including the Canadian Training Digest)
Canad Plast — Canadian Plastics
Canad Pract — Canadian Practitioner
Canad Pract and Rev — Canadian Practitioner and Review
Canad Psychiat AJ — Canadian Psychiatric Association. Journal
Canad Psychiat Ass J — Canadian Psychiatric Association. Journal
Canad Publ Adm — Canadian Public Administration/Administration Publique du Canada
Canad Publ Pol — Canadian Public Policy
Canad Rec Nat Hist Geol — Canadian Record of Natural History and Geology. With Proceedings. Natural History Society of Montreal
Canad Rev Sociol Anthrop — Canadian Review of Sociology and Anthropology
Canad Rose Annual — Canadian Rose Annual
Canad R Sociol Anthropol — Canadian Review of Sociology and Anthropology
Canad Slavonic Pap — Canadian Slavonic Papers
Canad Soc Lab Technol Bull — Canadian Society of Laboratory Technologists. Bulletin
Canad Vet Rec — Canadian Veterinary Record
Canad Yb Int Law — Canadian Yearbook of International Law
Can Aeronaut and Space J — Canadian Aeronautics and Space Journal
Can Aeronaut J — Canadian Aeronautical Journal
Can Aeronaut Space Inst Trans — Canadian Aeronautic and Space Institute. Transactions
Can Aeronaut Space J — Canadian Aeronautics and Space Journal
Can Aeron J — Canadian Aeronautical Journal
Can Aer Spa — Canadian Aeronautics and Space Journal
Can Agr — Canadian Agriculture
Can Agr Eng — Canadian Agricultural Engineering
Can Agric — Canada Agriculture
Can Agric Eng — Canadian Agricultural Engineering
Can Agric Insect Pest Rev — Canadian Agricultural Insect Pest Review
Can Aircr Ind — Canadian Aircraft Industries
Can Al J — Canadian Alpine Journal
Can Amer Slav Stud — Canadian-American Slavic Studies
Can Am Rev Hung Stud — Canadian-American Review of Hungarian Studies
Can-Am Slav — Canadian-American Slavic Studies
Can Am Sl Stud — Canadian-American Slavic Studies
Can Anae S J — Canadian Anaesthetists' Society. Journal
Can Anaesth Soc J — Canadian Anaesthetists' Society. Journal
Can & World — Canada and the World
Can Ant Art Deal Ybk — Canadian Antiques and Art Dealers Yearbook
Can Ant Coll — Canadian Antiques Collector
Can Arch — Canadian Architect
Can Architect — Canadian Architect
Can Architect & Bldr — Canadian Architect and Builder
Can Arch Ybk — Canadian Architect Yearbook
Can Arct Land Use Res Program Rep ALUR — Canada. Arctic Land Use Research Program. Report ALUR
Can Arct Land Use Res Prog Rep — Canada. Arctic Land Use Research Program Report
Can Art — Canadian Art
Can Assoc Lab Anim Sci Proc — Canadian Association for Laboratory Animal Science. Proceedings
Can Assoc Radiol J — Canadian Association of Radiologists Journal
Can Aud — Canadian Audubon
Can Audubon — Canadian Audubon
Can Auth & Book — Canadian Author and Bookman
Can Automot Trade — Canadian Automotive Trade
Can Av — Canadian Aviation
Can BA — Canadian Bar Association. Proceedings
Can BAJ — Canadian Bar Association. Journal
Can Bank — Canadian Banker [*Formerly, Canadian Banker and ICB Review*]
Can Banker — Canadian Banker [*Formerly, Canadian Banker and ICB Review*]
Can Banker & ICB R — Canadian Banker and ICB [*Institute of Canadian Bankers*] Review
Can Banker ICB Rev — Canadian Banker and ICB [*Institute of Canadian Bankers*] Review
Can Bank R — Canadian Bankruptcy Reports
Can Bankr — Canadian Bankruptcy Reports
Can Bankr Rep — Canadian Bankruptcy Reports
Can Bar AJ — Journal. Canadian Bar Association
Can Bar Assoc Cont Educ Sem — Canadian Bar Association. Continuing Education Seminars

Can Bar J — Canadian Bar Journal
Can Bar J (NS) — Canadian Bar Journal. New Series
Can Bar R — Canadian Bar Review
Can Bar Rev — Canadian Bar Review
Can Bar Year Book — Year Book. Canadian Bar Association
Can B Assn Proc — Canadian Bar Association. Proceedings
Canb Comments — Canberra Comments
Can Bee J — Canadian Bee Journal
Can Beekeep — Canadian Beekeeping
Canberra Anthrop — Canberra Anthropology
Canberra Anthropol — Canberra Anthropology
Canberra Surv — Canberra Survey
Canb Hist Soc Add — Canberra and District Historical Society. Addresses
Canb Hist Soc News — Canberra and District Historical Society. Newsletter
Can Biochem Soc Bull — Canadian Biochemical Society. Bulletin
Can B J — Canadian Bar Journal
Can Bkman — Canadian Bookman
Canb Letter — Canberra Letter
Can Board Grain Comm Grain Res Lab Annu Rep — Canada. Board of Grain Commissioners. Grain Research Laboratory. Annual Report
Can BPI — Canadian Business Periodicals Index [*Later, Canadian Business Index*]
Can BR — Canadian Bar Review
Can B Rev — Canadian Bar Review
Canb Survey — Canberra Survey
Can Build Dig — Canadian Building Digest
Can Build News — Canadian Building News
Can Bull Fish Aquat Sci — Canadian Bulletin of Fisheries and Aquatic Sciences
Can Bull Nutr — Canadian Bulletin on Nutrition
Canb Univ Col Gaz — Canberra University College. Gazette
Canb Univ Coll Gaz — Canberra University College. Gazette
Can Bus — Canadian Business
Can Bus Econ — Canadian Business Economics
Can Bus Index — Canadian Business Index
Can Bus LJ — Canadian Business Law Journal
Can Bus Mag — Canadian Business Magazine
Can Bus Period Index — Canadian Business Periodicals Index [*Later, Canadian Business Index*]
Can Bus R — Canadian Business Review
Can Bus Rev — Canadian Business Review
Can Bus Tr M Ind — Canadian Business Trends. Monthly Indicators
Can Bus Tr Q Ind — Canadian Business Trends. Quarterly Indicators
Canb Viewpoint — Canberra Viewpoint
Canb Weekly — Canberra Weekly
Can B Year Book — Canadian Bar Association. Year Book
Can C — Canoniste Contemporain
Can Camp — Canadian Camping
CANCAM Proc Can Congr Appl Mech — CANCAM Proceedings. Canadian Congress of Applied Mechanics
Can Cancer Conf — Canadian Cancer Conference
Can Cancer Conf Proc — Canadian Cancer Conference. Proceedings
Can Cap Mark — Canadian Capital Markets
Can Cartogr — Canadian Cartographer
CANCAS Coll Acad NC Acad Sci — CANCAS. Collegiate Academy of the North Carolina Academy of Sciences
Can Cases L Torts — Canadian Cases on the Law of Torts
Can Cattlemen — Canadian Cattlemen
Canc Bioc B — Cancer Biochemistry - Biophysics
Canc Bull — Cancer Bulletin
Can CC — Canadian Criminal Cases
Canc Chemoth Abstr — Cancer Chemotherapy Abstracts
Canc Chemother Rep — Cancer Chemotherapy Reports
Canc Chemother Rep Suppl — Cancer Chemotherapy Reports. Supplement
Canc Ch P 1 — Cancer Chemotherapy Reports. Part 1
Canc Ch P 2 — Cancer Chemotherapy Reports. Part 2
Canc Ch P 3 — Cancer Chemotherapy Reports. Part 3
Canc Curr Lit Ind — Cancer Current Literature Index
Canc Drug D — Cancer Drug Delivery
Canc Drug Del — Cancer Drug Delivery
Can Cem Concr Rev — Canadian Cement and Concrete Review
Can Cent Inland Waters Inland Waters Dir Rep Ser — Canada Centre for Inland Waters. Inland Waters Directorate. Report Series
Can Cent Miner Energy Technol CANMET Rep — Canada Centre for Mineral and Energy Technology. CANMET Report
Can Cent Miner Energy Technol Publ — Canada. Centre for Mineral and Energy Technology. Publications
Can Cent Miner Energy Technol Sci Bull — Canada. Centre for Mineral and Energy Technology. Scientific Bulletin
Can Cent Miner Energy Technol Spec Publ — Canada Centre for Mineral and Energy Technology. Special Publication
Can Cent Rech For Laurentides Rapp Inf LAUX Ed Fr — Canada. Centre de Recherches Forestieres des Laurentides. Rapport d'InformationLAU-X (Edition Francaise)
Can Cent Ser — Canadian Centenary Series
Can Cent Terminol Bull Terminol — Canada. Centre de Terminologie. Bulletin de Terminologie
Can Ceram Q — Canadian Ceramics Quarterly
Can Ceram Soc J — Canadian Ceramic Society. Journal
Cancer Biochem Biophys — Cancer Biochemistry - Biophysics
Cancer Biol Biosynth — Cancer Biology and Biosynthesis
Cancer Biol Rev — Cancer Biology Reviews
Cancer Biother — Cancer Biotherapy
Cancer Biother Radiopharm — Cancer Biotherapy and Radiopharmaceuticals
Cancer Bull — Cancer Bulletin
Cancer Causes Control — Cancer Causes and Control
Cancer Cel — Cancer Cells

Cancer Chemother Biol Response Modif — Cancer Chemotherapy and Biological Response Modifiers
Cancer Chemother Pharmacol — Cancer Chemotherapy and Pharmacology
Cancer Chemother Rep — Cancer Chemotherapy Reports
Cancer Chemother Rep Part 1 — Cancer Chemotherapy Reports. Part 1
Cancer Chemother Rep Part 2 — Cancer Chemotherapy Reports. Part 2
Cancer Chemother Rep Part 3 — Cancer Chemotherapy Reports. Part 3
Cancer Chemother Rep Suppl — Cancer Chemotherapy Reports. Supplement
Cancer Chemother Screening Data — Cancer Chemotherapy Screening Data
Cancer Chem Rep — Cancer Chemotherapy Reports
Cancer Clin Trials — Cancer Clinical Trials
Cancer Commun — Cancer Communications
Cancer Cytol — Cancer Cytology
Cancer Detect Prev — Cancer Detection and Prevention
Cancer Det Prev — Cancer Detection and Prevention
Cancer Drug Deliv — Cancer Drug Delivery
Cancer Epidemiol Biomarkers Prev — Cancer Epidemiology, Biomarkers, and Prevention
Cancer Genet Cytogenet — Cancer Genetics and Cytogenetics
Cancer Gene Ther — Cancer Gene Therapy
Cancer Immunol Immunother — Cancer Immunology and Immunotherapy
Cancer Invest — Cancer Investigation
Cancer J — Cancer Journal
Cancer J Sci Am — Cancer Journal from Scientific American
Cancer Lett — Cancer Letters
Cancer Lett Shannon Irel — Cancer Letters (Shannon, Ireland)
CANCERLIT — Cancer Literature
Cancer Metastasis Rev — Cancer and Metastasis Reviews
Cancer Mol Biol — Cancer Molecular Biology
Cancer Nurs — Cancer Nursing
Cancer Nurs Let — Cancer Nursing Letter
Cancer Nutr — Cancer and Nutrition
Cancer Progr — Cancer Progress
CANCERPROJ — Cancer Research Projects
Cancer Rehabil — Cancer Rehabilitation
Cancer Res — Cancer Research
Cancer Res Campaign Annu Rep — Cancer Research Campaign. Annual Report
Cancer Res Clin Oncol — Cancer Research and Clinical Oncology
Cancer Res Inst Slovak Acad Sci Annu Rep — Cancer Research Institute. Slovak Academy of Sciences. Annual Report
Cancer Res Monogr — Cancer Research Monographs
Cancer Res Suppl — Cancer Research. Supplement
Cancer Rev — Cancer Reviews
Cancer Semin — Cancer Seminar
Cancer Suppl — Cancer Supplement
Cancer Surv — Cancer Surveys
Cancer T R — Cancer Treatment Reviews
Cancer Treat Rep — Cancer Treatment Reports
Cancer Treat Res — Cancer Treatment and Research
Cancer Treat Rev — Cancer Treatment Reviews
Cancer Treat Symp — Cancer Treatment Symposia
Cancer Very Young Child Proc Conf — Cancer in the Very Young Child. Proceedings. Conference
C Anc H — Cambridge Ancient History
Can Chart Acc — Canadian Chartered Accountant [*Later, CA Magazine*]
Can Chart Account — Canadian Chartered Accountant [*Later, CA Magazine*]
Can Chart Acct — Canadian Chartered Accountant [*Later, CA Magazine*]
Can Chem & Met — Canadian Chemistry and Metallurgy
Can Chem & Process Ind — Canadian Chemistry and Process Industries
Can Chem Educ — Canadian Chemical Education
Can Chem J — Canadian Chemical Journal
Can Chem J — Cancer Chemical Journal
Can Chem Met — Canadian Chemistry and Metallurgy
Can Chem Metall — Canadian Chemistry and Metallurgy
Can Chem News — Canadian Chemical News
Can Chem Proc — Canadian Chemical Processing
Can Chem Process — Canadian Chemical Processing
Can Chem Process — Canadian Chemistry and Process Industry
Can Chem Process Ind — Canadian Chemistry and Process Industry
Can Chem Reg — Canadian Chemical Register
Can Child Lit — Canadian Children's Literature
Can Civ Aircr Reg — Canadian Civil Aircraft Register
Canc J — Cancer Journal
Can CL — Canadian Current Law
Can Clay Ceram Q — Canadian Clay and Ceramics Quarterly
Canc Met Rev — Cancer Metastasis Reviews
Canc NJ — Cancer News Journal
Can Collector — Canadian Collector
Can Coll Sp Sc — Canadian Colleges Sport Scene
Can Color Text Process — Canadian Colorist and Textile Processor
Can Colr — Canadian Collector
Can Com LJ — Canadian Community Law Journal
Can Commer — Canada Commerce
Can Commerce — Canada Commerce
Can Commun Dis Rep — Canada Communicable Disease Report
Can Community LJ — Canadian Community Law Journal
Can Commun Power Conf Proc — Canadian Communications and Power Conference. Proceedings
Can Comp — Canadian Composer
Can Competition Pol — Canadian Competition Policy Record
Can Composer — Canadian Composer
Can Conserv Inst Tech Bull — Canadian Conservation Institute [*CCI/ICC*] Technical Bulletin
Can Cons Regs — Consolidated Regulations of Canada
Can Consult Eng — Canadian Consulting Engineer

Can Consum — Canadian Consumer
Can Consumer — Canadian Consumer
Can Contract Rep Hydrogr Ocean Sci — Canadian Contractor Report of Hydrography and Ocean Sciences
Can Controls & Instrum — Canadian Controls and Instrumentation
Can Controls Instrum — Canadian Controls and Instrumentation
Can Controls Instruments — Canadian Controls and Instruments
Can Copper — Canadian Copper
CanCorp — Canadian Corporations
Can Coun — Canadian Counsellor
Can Couns/Cons Can — Canadian Counsellor/Conseiller Canadien
Can Courant — Canadian Courant
Can Crafts — Canada Crafts
Canc Res — Cancer Research
Canc Res Campaign Annu Rep — Cancer Research Campaign. Annual Report
Canc Res Inst Slovak Acad Annu Rep — Cancer Research Institute. Slovak Academy of Sciences. Annual Report
Canc Rev — Cancer Review
(Can) Crim — Criminal Reports (Canada)
Can Crit Care Nurs J — Canadian Critical Care Nursing Journal
Canc Ther Abst — Cancer Therapy Abstracts
Canc Treat Symp — Cancer Treatment Symposia
Can Cyc — Canadian Cyclist
Can Dairy Ice Cream J — Canadian Dairy and Ice Cream Journal
C & AR — Colonial and Asiatic Review
Can Data — Canadian Datasystems
Can Data Rep Fish Aquat Sci — Canadian Data Report of Fisheries and Aquatic Sciences
Can Data Rep Hydrogr Ocean Sci — Canadian Data Report of Hydrography and Ocean Sciences
Can Datasyst — Canadian Datasystems
C & C — Cameron and Carroll
C & C — Case and Comment
C & C — Christianity and Crisis
C & CA Tech Rep — C & CA [*Cement and Concrete Association*] Technical Report
C & E — Conferences and Exhibitions [*Later, Conferences and Exhibitions International*]
C & EN — Chemical and Engineering News
C & E News — Chemical and Engineering News
Can Dent Assoc J — Canadian Dental Association. Journal
Can Dent Hyg — Canadian Dental Hygienist
Can Dep Agric Annu Rep — Canada. Department of Agriculture. Annual Report
Can Dep Agric Bull — Canada. Department of Agriculture. Bulletin
Can Dep Agric Circ — Canada. Department of Agriculture. Circular
Can Dep Agric Ext Circ — Canada. Department of Agriculture. Extension Circular
Can Dep Agric Farmers Bull — Canada. Department of Agriculture. Farmers' Bulletin
Can Dep Agric Plant Res Inst Agro-Meteorol Sect Tech Bull — Canada. Department of Agriculture. Plant Research Institute. Agrometeorology Section. Technical Bulletin
Can Dep Agric Publ — Canada. Department of Agriculture. Publication
Can Dep Agric Res Branch Monogr — Canada. Department of Agriculture. Research Branch Monograph
Can Dep Agric Res Branch Rep — Canada. Department of Agriculture. Research Branch Report
Can Dep Agric Tech Bull — Canada. Department of Agriculture. Technical Bulletin
Can Dep Energy Mines Resources Earth Phys Br Mem — Canada. Department of Energy, Mines, and Resources. Earth Physics Branch. Memoir
Can Dep Energy Mines Resources Earth Phys Br Mineral Rep — Canada. Department of Energy, Mines, and Resources. Earth Physics Branch. Mineral Report
Can Dep Energy Mines Resources Earth Sci Br Inform Circ — Canada. Department of Energy, Mines, and Resources. Earth Science Branch. Information Circular
Can Dep Energy Mines Resources Rep — Canada. Department of Energy, Mines, and Resources. Report
Can Dep Energy Mines Resour Geol Surv Can Bull — Canada. Department of Energy, Mines, and Resources. Geological Survey of Canada. Bulletin
Can Dep Energy Mines Resour Geol Surv Can Geol Surv Pap — Canada. Department of Energy, Mines, and Resources. Geological Survey of Canada. Geological Survey Paper
Can Dep Energy Mines Resour Miner Resour Div Miner Inf Bull — Canada. Department of Energy, Mines, and Resources. Mineral Resources Division. Mineral Information Bulletin
Can Dep Energy Mines Resour Mines Branch Inf Circ — Canada. Department of Energy, Mines, and Resources. Mines Branch. Information Circular
Can Dep Energy Mines Resour Mines Branch Invest Rep — Canada. Department of Energy, Mines, and Resources. Mines Branch. Investigation Report
Can Dep Energy Mines Resour Mines Branch Monogr — Canada. Department of Energy, Mines, and Resources. Mines Branch. Monograph
Can Dep Energy Mines Resour Mines Branch Res Rep — Canada. Department of Energy, Mines, and Resources. Mines Branch. Research Report
Can Dep Energy Mines Resour Mines Branch Tech Bull — Canada. Department of Energy, Mines, and Resources. Mines Branch. Technical Bulletin
Can Dep Environ Can For Ser North For Res Cent Inf Rep — Canada. Department of the Environment. Canadian Forestry Service. Northern Forest Research Centre. Information Report
Can Dep Environ Can For Serv North For Res Cent Inf Rep NORX — Canada. Department of the Environment. Canadian Forestry Service. Northern Forest Research Centre. Information Report NOR-X
Can Dep Environ For Serv Inf Rep CCX — Canada. Department of Environment. Forestry Service Information Report CC-X
Can Dep Environ Inland Waters Branch Rep Ser — Canada. Department of the Environment. Inland Waters Branch. Report Series

Can Dep Environ Inland Waters Branch Sci Ser — Canada. Department of the Environment. Inland Waters Branch. Scientific Series

Can Dep Environ Inland Waters Dir Sediment Data Can Rivers — Canada. Department of the Environment. Inland Waters Directorate. Sediment Datafor Canadian Rivers

Can Dep Environ Mar Sci Dir Manuscr Rep Ser — Canada. Department of the Environment. Marine Sciences Directorate. Manuscript Report Series

Can Dep Fish Annu Rep — Canada. Department of Fisheries. Annual Report

Can Dep Fish For Annu Rep — Canada. Department of Fisheries and Forestry. Annual Report

Can Dep Fish For Bimon Res Notes — Canada. Department of Fisheries and Forestry. Bimonthly Research Notes

Can Dep Fish For Can For Ser Inf Rep — Canada. Department of Fisheries and Forestry. Canadian Forestry Service. Information Report

Can Dep Fish For Can For Serv Inf Rep FF-X — Canada. Department of Fisheries and Forestry. Canadian Forestry Service. Information Report FF-X

Can Dep Fish For Can For Serv Publ — Canada. Department of Fisheries and Forestry. Canadian Forestry Service. Publication

Can Dep Fish For For Branch Dep Publ — Canada. Department of Fisheries and Forestry. Forestry Branch Departmental Publication

Can Dep Fish For For Branch Publ — Canada. Department of Fisheries and Forestry. Forestry Branch Publication

Can Dep Fish Oceans Can Spec Publ Fish Aquat Sci — Canada. Department of Fisheries and Oceans. Canadian Special Publication of Fisheries and Aquatic Sciences

Can Dep Fish Oceans Ocean Dumping Rep — Canada. Department of Fisheries and Oceans. Ocean Dumping Report

Can Dep Fish Trade News — Canada. Department of Fisheries. Trade News

Can Dep For For Entomol Pathol Branch Bi-Mon Prog Rep — Canada. Department of Forestry. Forest Entomology and Pathology Branch. Bi-Monthly Progress Report

Can Dep For Publ — Canada. Department of Forestry. Publication

Can Dep For Rural Dev Annu Rep — Canada. Department of Forestry and Rural Development. Annual Report

Can Dep For Rural Dev Annu Rep For Insect Dis Surv — Canada. Department of Forestry and Rural Development. Annual Report. Forest Insect and Disease Survey

Can Dep For Rural Dev Bi-Mon Res Notes — Canada. Department of Forestry and Rural Development. Bi-Monthly Research Notes

Can Dep For Rural Dev For Branch Dep Publ — Canada. Department of Forestry and Rural Development. Forestry Branch. Department Publication

Can Dep For Rural Dev For Branch Inf Rep FF-X — Canada. Department of Forestry and Rural Development. Forestry Branch. Information Report FF-X

Can Dep For Rural Dev Publ — Canada. Department of Forestry and Rural Development. Publication

Can Dep Indian Aff North Dev Environ Stud — Canada. Department of Indian Affairs and Northern Development. Environmental Studies

Can Dep Indian North Aff Arct Land Use Res Program Rep ALUR — Canada. Department of Indian and Northern Affairs. Arctic Land Use Research Program. Report ALUR

Can Dep Mines Geol Surv Econ Geol Ser — Canada. Department of Mines. Bureau of Economic Geology. Geological Survey. Economic Geology Series

Can Dep Mines Mines Branch Memo Ser — Canada Department of Mines. Mines Branch. Memorandum Series

Can Dep Mines Mines Branch Rep — Canada Department of Mines. Mines Branch. Report

Can Dep Mines Resour Bur Geol Topogr Econ Geol Ser — Canada. Department of Mines and Resources. Mines and Geology Branch. Bureau of Geology and Topography. Economic Geology Series

Can Dep Mines Resour Bur Mines Memo Ser — Canada. Department of Mines and Resources. Bureau of Mines Memorandum Series

Can Dep Mines Resour Geol Surv Can Pap — Canada. Department of Mines and Resources. Geological Survey of Canada. Paper

Can Dep Mines Tech Surv Geol Surv Can Bull — Canada. Department of Mines and Technical Surveys. Geological Survey of Canada.Bulletin

Can Dep Mines Tech Surv Geol Surv Can Econ Geol Rep — Canada. Department of Mines and Technical Surveys. Geological Survey of Canada.Economic Geology Report

Can Dep Mines Tech Surv Geol Surv Can Mem — Canada. Department of Mines and Technical Surveys. Geological Survey of Canada. Memoir

Can Dep Mines Tech Surv Geol Surv Can Pap — Canada. Department of Mines and Technical Surveys. Geological Survey of Canada.Paper

Can Dep Mines Tech Surv Miner Inf Bull — Canada. Department of Mines and Technical Surveys. Mineral Information Bulletin

Can Dep Mines Tech Surv Miner Resour Div Miner Inf Bull — Canada. Department of Mines and Technical Surveys. Mineral Resources Division. Mineral Information Bulletin

Can Dep Mines Tech Surv Miner Resour Div Miner Rep — Canada. Department of Mines and Technical Surveys. Mineral Resources Division. Mineral Report

Can Dep Mines Tech Surv Miner Resour Div Miner Resour Inf Circ — Canada. Department of Mines and Technical Surveys. Mineral Resources Division. Mineral Resources Information Circular

Can Dep Mines Tech Surv Mines Branch Invest Rep — Canada. Department of Mines and Technical Surveys. Mines Branch. Investigation Report

Can Dep Mines Tech Surv Mines Branch Memo Ser — Canada. Department of Mines and Technical Surveys. Mines Branch. Memorandum Series

Can Dep Mines Tech Surv Mines Branch Monogr — Canada. Department of Mines and Technical Surveys. Mines Branch. Monograph

Can Dep Mines Tech Surv Mines Branch Radioact Div Top Rep — Canada. Department of Mines and Technical Surveys. Mines Branch. Radioactivity Division. Topical Report

Can Dep Mines Tech Surv Mines Branch Rep — Canada. Department of Mines and Technical Surveys. Mines Branch. Report

Can Dep Mines Tech Surv Mines Branch Res Rep — Canada. Department of Mines and Technical Surveys. Mines Branch. Research Report

Can Dep Mines Tech Surv Mines Branch Tech Bull — Canada. Department of Mines and Technical Surveys. Mines Branch. Technical Bulletin

Can Dep Mines Tech Surv Mines Branch Tech Pap — Canada. Department of Mines and Technical Surveys. Mines Branch. Technical Paper

Can Dep Mines Tech Surv Water Resour Branch Water Resour Pap — Canada. Department of Mines and Technical Surveys. Water Resources Branch. Water Resources Paper

Can Dep Resour Dev For Branch For Prod Lab Div Tech Note — Canada. Department of Resources and Development. Forestry Branch. Forest Products Laboratory Division. Technical Note

Can Dep Resour Dev Natl Parks Branch Natl Mus Can Bull — Canada. Department of Resources and Development. National Parks Branch. National Museum of Canada. Bulletin

Can Dept Forestry Bimo Res Note — Canada. Department of Fisheries and Forestry. Bimonthly Research Notes

Can Dept Forestry Disease Surv — Canada. Department of Fisheries and Forestry. Annual Report of the Forest Insect and Disease Survey

Can Dept Forestry Publ — Canada. Department of Fisheries and Forestry. Departmental Publications

Can Dept Forestry Res News — Canada. Department of Fisheries and Forestry. Research News

Can Dep Trade Commer Board Grain Comm Grain Res Lab Annu Rep — Canada. Department of Trade and Commerce. Board of Grain Commissioners. Grain Research Laboratory. Annual Report

Candid — Candid Quarterly Review of Public Affairs

Can Dimen — Canadian Dimension

Can Dir Hyg Milieu Rapp DHM — Canada. Direction de l'Hygiene de Milieu. Rapport DHM

Can Dist Ret — Canadian Distributor and Retailer

C & J — Crime and Justice Bulletin

Cand J St — Canadian Journal of Statistics

C and L — Christianity and Literature

C & M — Classica et Mediaevalia

CAN DO — Computer Analyzed Newspaper Data On-line

Can Doct — Canadian Doctor

Can Dom Grain Res Lab Annu Rep — Canada. Dominion Grain Research Laboratory. Annual Report

Can Dp Interior Rp Chief Astronomer — Canada. Department of the Interior. Report of the Chief Astronomer

Can Dp Interior Sup Mines Rp — Canada. Department of the Interior. Superintendent of Mines. Report

Can DQ — Canadian Defence Quarterly

C & RL — College and Research Libraries

Can Drug — Canadian Druggist

C & S — Cultura e Scuola

C & S App — Clifford and Stephens' English Locus Standi Reports, Appendix

C & SLib — Church and Synagogue Libraries

C & SLJ — Company and Securities Law Journal

C & T — Culture and Tradition

C & U — College and University

C and V — Counseling and Values

C & W — Christentum und Wissenschaft

C&W — Cumberland and Westmorland Antiquarian and Archaeological Society. Transactions

C & W — Transactions. Cumberland and Westmorland Antiquarian and Archaeological Society

C & W Trans — Cumberland and Westmorland Antiquarian and Archaeological Society. Transactions

Can Dyer Color User — Canadian Dyer and Color User

Candy Ind — Candy and Snack Industry

Candy Ind Confect J — Candy Industry and Confectioners Journal

Candy Snack Ind — Candy and Snack Industry

CANE — Cahier d'Archeologie du Nordest

CanE — Canard Enchaine. Journal Satirique

Can Earth Phys Branch Publ — Canada. Earth Physics Branch. Publications

Canebrake Agric Exp Sta Bull — Canebrake Agricultural Experiment Station Bulletin

CanEdI — Canadian Education Index

Can Ed Res Digest — Canadian Education and Research Digest

Can Educ Index — Canadian Education Index

Can Educ Res Dig — Canadian Education and Research Digest

Cane Growers Q Bul — Cane Growers Quarterly Bulletin

Cane Grow Q Bull — Cane Growers Quarterly Bulletin

Cane Gr Quart Bull — Cane Growers Quarterly Bulletin

Can Electr Assoc Trans Eng Oper Div — Canadian Electrical Association. Transactions of the Engineering and Operating Division

Can Electr Eng J — Canadian Electrical Engineering Journal

Can Electron Eng — Canadian Electronics Engineering

Can Energy News — Canadian Energy News

Can Eng — Canadian Engineer

Can Ent — Canadian Entomologist

Can Entm — Canadian Entomologist

Can Entom — Canadian Entomologist

Can Entomol — Canadian Entomologist

Can Environ — Canadian Environment

Can Environ Conserv Dir Solid Waste Manage Branch Rep EPS — Canada. Environmental Conservation Directorate. Solid Waste Management Branch. Report EPS

Can Environ Health Dir Rep EHD — Canada. Environmental Health Directorate. Report EHD

Can Environ Law News — Canadian Environmental Law News

Can Environ Prot Serv Econ Tech Rev Rep — Canada. Environmental Protection Service. Economic and Technical Review Report

Can Environ Prot Serv Econ Tech Rev Rep EPS 3 — Canada. Environmental Protection Service. Economic and Technical Review Report EPS 3

Can Environ Prot Serv Solid Waste Manage Branch Rep EPS — Canada. Environmental Protection Service. Solid Waste Management Branch. ReportEPS

Can Environ Prot Serv Surveill Rep EP — Canada. Environmental Protection Service. Surveillance Report EP

Can Environ Prot Serv Technol Dev Rep — Canada. Environmental Protection Service. Technology Development Report

Can Environ Prot Serv Technol Dev Rep EPS 4 — Canada. Environmental Protection Service. Technology Development Report EPS 4

Can Essay Lit Index — Canadian Essay and Literature Index

Canestrini Archiv — Archivio per la Zoologia, l'Anatomia, e la Fisiologia (Da G. Canestrini) [*Genova*]</PHR> %

Can Ethnic Stud — Canadian Ethnic Studies

Can Ethnic Studies — Canadian Ethnic Studies

Can Ethnol Serv Pap — Canadian Ethnology Service Paper

Can F — Canadian Forum

Can Fam Physician — Canadian Family Physician

Can Farm Ec — Canadian Farm Economics

Can Farm Econ — Canadian Farm Economics

Can Fd Bull — Canadian Food Bulletin [*Ottawa*]

Can Fd Ind — Canadian Food Industries [*Quebec*]

Can Fd J — Canadian Food Journal

Can Fd Pack — Canadian Food Packer [*Quebec*]

Can Fed Biol Soc Proc — Canadian Federation of Biological Societies. Proceedings

Can Feed Grain J — Canadian Feed and Grain Journal

Can Fic Mag — Canadian Fiction Magazine

Can Fi Cu — Canadian Fish Culturist

Can Field-Nat — Canadian Field-Naturalist

Can Field-Natur — Canadian Field-Naturalist

Can Fie Nat — Canadian Field-Naturalist

Can Fish Cult — Canadian Fish Culturist

Can Fish Environ Can Occas Pap — Canada. Fisheries and Environment Canada. Occasional Paper

Can Fisherm — Canadian Fisherman

Can Fisherman — Canadian Fisherman

Can Fish Exp — Canadian Fisheries. Exports

Can Fish Game — Canadian Fish and Game [*Toronto*]

Can Fish Imp — Canadian Fisheries. Imports

Can Fish Mar Serv Data Rep Ser Cen-D — Canada. Fisheries and Marine Service. Data Report. Series Cen-D

Can Fish Mar Serv Ind Rep — Canada. Fisheries and Marine Service. Industry Report

Can Fish Mar Serv Manuscr Rep — Canada. Fisheries and Marine Service. Manuscript Report

Can Fish Mar Serv Misc Spec Publ — Canada. Fisheries and Marine Service. Miscellaneous Special Publication

Can Fish Mar Serv Resour Branch Marit Reg Inf Publ MAR-N — Canada. Fisheries and Marine Service Resource Branch. Maritimes Region. Information Publication MAR-N

Can Fish Mar Serv Resour Dev Branch Halifax Prog Rep — Canada. Fisheries and Marine Service Resource Development Branch. Halifax Progress Report

Can Fish Mar Serv Resour Dev Branch Marit Reg Rep — Canada. Fisheries and Marine Service Resource Development Branch. Maritimes Region. Report

Can Fish Mar Serv Tech Rep — Canada. Fisheries and Marine Service. Technical Report

Can Fish Mar Serv Tech Rep Ser Cen-T — Canada. Fisheries and Marine Service. Technical Report. Series Cen-T

Can Fish Rep — Canadian Fisheries Reports

Can Fish Res Board Biol Stn St Andrews NB Gen Ser Circ — Canada. Fisheries Research Board. Biological Station. St. Andrews, NB GeneralSeries Circular

Can Fish Res Board J — Canada. Fisheries Research Board. Journal

Can Fish Res Board Tech Rep — Canada. Fisheries Research Board. Technical Report

Can Fish Serv Resour Dev Branch Halifax Prog Rep — Canada. Fisheries Service. Resource Development Branch. Halifax Progress Report

Can Fld Nat — Canadian Field-Naturalist

Can Flklore Can — Canadian Folklore Canadien

Can Folk B — Canada Folk Bulletin

Can Folk Mus — Canadian Folk Music Journal

Can Folk Mus Bulletin — Canadian Folk Music Bulletin

Can Food Bull — Canadian Food Bulletin

Can Food Ind — Canadian Food Industries

Can Food Pack — Canadian Food Packer

Can Food Packer — Canadian Food Packer

Can For Branch Dep Publ — Canada. Forestry Branch. Departmental Publication

Can For Branch Publ — Canada. Forestry Branch Publication

Can Forces Dent Serv Q — Canadian Forces Dental Services Quarterly

Can For Entomol Pathol Branch Annu Rep — Canada. Forest Entomology and Pathology Branch. Annual Report

Can Forester — Canadian Forester [*Guelph*]

Can For Ind — Canadian Forest Industries

Can For J — Canadian Forestry Journal

Can For M — Canadian Forestry Magazine

Can For Prod Res Branch Annu Rep — Canada. Forest Products Research Branch. Annual Report

Can For Prod Res Branch Tech Note — Canada. Forest Products Research Branch. Technical Note

Can For Res Branch Annu Rep — Canada. Forest Research Branch. Annual Report

Can For Ser For Fire Res Inst Info Rep — Canada. Forestry Service. Forest Fire Research Institute. Information Report

Can For Serv Annu Rep For Insect Dis Surv — Canadian Forestry Service. Annual Report of the Forest Insect and Disease Survey

Can For Serv Bi-Mon Res Notes — Canada. Forestry Service. Bi-Monthly Research Notes

Can For Serv Chem Control Res Inst File Rep — Canadian Forestry Service. Chemical Control Research Institute. File Report

Can For Serv Chem Control Res Inst Inf Rep CCX — Canada. Forestry Service. Chemical Control Research Institute. Information Report CC-X

Can For Serv Chem Control Res Inst Rep CC-X — Canadian Forestry Service. Chemical Control Research Institute. Report CC-X

Can For Serv Dep Environ Intern Rep CC 16 — Canada. Forestry Service. Department of the Environment. Internal Report CC-16

Can For Serv For Fire Res Inst Inf Rep FF-X — Canadian Forestry Service. Forest Fire Research Institute. Information Report FF-X

Can For Serv For Fire Res Inst Misc Rep FF-X — Canadian Forestry Service. Forest Fire Research Institute. Miscellaneous ReportFF-X

Can For Serv For Manage Inst Inf Rep FMR-X — Canadian Forestry Service. Forest Management Institute. Information Report FMR-X

Can For Serv For Pest Manage Inst Inf Rep FPM-X — Canadian Forestry Service. Forest Pest Management Institute. Information ReportFPM-X

Can For Serv For Pest Manage Inst Rep FPM-X — Canadian Forestry Service. Forest Pest Management Institute. Report FPM-X

Can For Serv For Tech Rep — Canadian Forestry Service. Forestry Technical Report

Can For Serv Gt Lakes For Cent Inf Rep O-X — Canadian Forestry Service. Great Lakes Forestry Centre. InformationReport O-X

Can For Serv North For Res Cent For Rep — Canadian Forestry Service. Northern Forest Research Centre. Forestry Report

Can For Serv North For Res Cent Inf Rep NOR-X — Canadian Forestry Service. Northern Forest Research Centre. Information Report NOR-X

Can For Serv Pac For Res Cent BC-P — Canadian Forestry Service. Pacific Forest Research Centre BC-P

Can For Serv Pac For Res Cent For Pest Leafl — Canadian Forestry Service. Pacific Forest Research Centre. Forest Pest Leaflet

Can For Serv Pac For Res Cent Inf Rep BC-X — Canadian Forestry Service. Pacific Forest Research Centre. Information Report BC-X

Can For Serv Pac For Res Cent Rep BC-R — Canadian Forestry Service. Pacific Forest Research Centre. Report BC-R

Can For Serv Pac For Res Cent Rep BC-X — Canadian Forestry Service. Pacific Forest Research Centre. Report BC-X

Can For Serv Petawawa Natl For Inst Inf Rep PI-X — Canadian Forestry Service. Petawawa National Forestry Institute. Information Report PI-X

Can For Serv Publ — Canadian Forestry Service. Publication

Can Forum — Canadian Forum

Can Foundry J — Canada's Foundry Journal

Can Foundryman — Canadian Foundryman

Can Foundryman Electroplat — Canadian Foundryman and Electroplater

Can Foundryman Met Ind — Canadian Foundryman and Metal Industry

Can Foundrym Metal Ind — Canadian Foundryman and Metal Industry [*Toronto*]

CanFr — Canada-Francais

Can Franc — Canada Francais

Can Fruitgrower — Canadian Fruitgrower

Can Gas J — Canadian Gas Journal

Can Gaz — Canadian Gazette

Can Gaz Part I — Canada Gazette. Part I

Can Gaz Part II — Canada Gazette. Part II

Can Geneal — Canadian Genealogist

Can Geog — Canadian Geographer

Can Geog J — Canadian Geographical Journal [*Later, Canadian Geographic*]

Can Geogr — Canadian Geographer

Can Geogr — Canadian Geographic

Can Geogr — Canadian Geography

Can Geographer — Canadian Geographer

Can Geographic — Canadian Geographic

Can Geogr J — Canadian Geographical Journal [*Later, Canadian Geographic*]

Can Geol Surv Bull — Canada. Geological Survey. Bulletin

Can Geol Surv Econ Geol Rep — Canada. Geological Survey. Economic Geology Report

Can Geol Surv Map — Canada. Geological Survey. Map

Can Geol Surv Mem — Canada. Geological Survey. Memoir

Can Geol Surv Misc Rep — Canada. Geological Survey. Miscellaneous Report

Can Geol Surv Pap — Canada. Geological Survey. Paper

Can Geoph Bull — Canadian Geophysical Bulletin

Can Geophys Bull — Canadian Geophysical Bulletin

Can Geotech Conf — Canadian Geotechnical Conference

Can Geotech J — Canadian Geotechnical Journal

CanGJ — Canadian Geographical Journal

Can Gov Publ Q — Canadian Government Publications Quarterly

Can Gov Ser — Canadian Government Series

Can Grain J — Canadian Grain Journal [*Winnipeg*]

Can Grain Res Lab Annu Rep — Canadian Grain Research Laboratory. Annual Report

Can Grain Res Lab Rep — Canadian Grain Research Laboratory. Report

Can Grow — Canadian Grower [*Toronto*]

Can Grow Q Bull — Cane Growers Quarterly Bulletin

Can G S — Canada. Geological Survey

Can G S An Rp — Canada. Geological Survey. Annual Report

Can G S Mem — Canada. Geological Survey. Memoir

Can G S Mus B — Canada. Geological Survey. Museum Bulletin

Can G S Sum Rp — Canada. Geological Survey. Summary Report

Can Health Welfare Rep EHD — Canada. Health and Welfare. Report EHD

Can Heritage — Canadian Heritage

Can His R — Canadian Historical Review

Can Hist Ass Ann Rep — Canadian Historical Association. Annual Report

Can Hist Assn — Canadian Historical Association. Historical Papers

Can Hist Assn Rep — Canadian Historical Association. Report

Can Hist Assoc Ann Rep — Canadian Historical Association. Annual Report

Can Hist Mag — Canada. An Historical Magazine
Can Hist R — Canadian Historical Review
Can Hist Rev — Canadian Historical Review
Can Home Ec J — Canadian Home Economics Journal
Can Home Econ J Rev Can Econ Familiale — Canadian Home Economics Journal/Revue Canadienne d'Economie Familiale
Can Homes & Gdns — Canadian Homes and Gardens
Can Honorary Advis Counc Sci Ind Res Rep — Canada. Honorary Advisory Council Scientific and Industrial Research. Report
Can Honorary Advis CSIR Bull — Canada. Honorary Advisory Council for Scientific and Industrial Research. Bulletin
Can Hort — Canadian Horticulture and Home Magazine
Can Hort Beek — Canadian Horticulturist and Beekeeper
Can Hort Home Mag — Canadian Horticulture and Home Magazine
Can Hortst Beekeep — Canadian Horticulturist and Beekeeper
Can Hosp — Canadian Hospital
CanHR — Canadian Historical Review
CanI — Canadian Periodical Index
Can I Food — Canadian Institute of Food Science and Technology. Journal
Can Impl Trade Pwr Fmg Equip J — Canadian Implement Trade and Power Farming Equipment Journal [*Toronto*]
Can Ind — Canadian Periodical Index
Can Ind Geosci Data — Canadian Index to Geoscience Data
Can Indian North Aff Environ Stud — Canada. Indian and Northern Affairs. Environmental Studies
Can Ind Rep Fish Aquat Sci — Canadian Industry Report of Fisheries and Aquatic Sciences
Canine Pract — Canine Practice
Can Inland Waters Branch Rep Ser — Canada. Inland Waters Branch. Report Series
Can Inland Waters Branch Sci Ser — Canada. Inland Waters Branch. Scientific Series
Can Inland Waters Dir Rep Ser — Canada. Inland Waters Directorate. Report Series
Can Inland Waters Dir Sci Ser — Canada. Inland Waters Directorate. Scientific Series
Can Inland Waters Dir Sediment Data Can Rivers — Canada. Inland Waters Directorate. Sediment Data for Canadian Rivers
Can Inland Waters Dir Tech Bull — Canada. Inland Waters Directorate. Technical Bulletin
Can Inland Waters Dir Water Qual Interpret Rep — Canada. Inland Waters Directorate. Water Quality Interpretive Report
Can Inland Waters Lands Dir Sci Ser — Canada. Inland Waters/Lands Directorate. Scientific Series
Can Insect Pest Rev — Canadian Insect Pest Review
Can Inst Food Sci Technol J — Canadian Institute of Food Science and Technology. Journal
Can Inst Food Sci Technol J J Inst Can Sci Technol Aliment — Canadian Institute of Food Science and Technology Journal/Journal de l'Institute Canadien de Science et Technologie Alimentaire
Can Inst Food Technol J — Canadian Institute of Food Technology. Journal
Can Inst Int Aff — Canadian Institute of International Affairs
Can Inst Min Metall Bull — Canadian Institute of Mining and Metallurgy. Bulletin
Can Inst Min Metall Min Soc NS Trans — Canadian Institute of Mining and Metallurgy and the Mining Society of Nova Scotia. Transactions
Can Inst Min Metall Pet Soc Annu Tech Meet — Canadian Institute of Mining and Metallurgy. Petroleum Society. Annual Technical Meeting
Can Inst Min Met Spec Vol — Canadian Institute of Mining and Metallurgy. Special Volume
Can Inst Part Phys Summer Sch Proc — Canada Institute of Particle Physics Summer School. Proceedings
Can Inst Pr — Canadian Institute Proceedings
Can Int Educ — Canadian and International Education
Can Inter Ed/Ed Can — Canadian and International Education/Education Canadienne et Internationale
Can Interiors — Canadian Interiors
Can J — Canadian Journal
CANJA — Canadian Anaesthetists' Society. Journal
CanJA — Canadian Journal of African Studies
Can J Afr S — Canadian Journal of African Studies
Can J Afr Stud — Canadian Journal of African Studies
Can J Afr Studies — Canadian Journal of African Studies
Can J Ag Ec — Canadian Journal of Agricultural Economics
Can J Agr Econ — Canadian Journal of Agricultural Economics
Can J Agric Econ — Canadian Journal of Agricultural Economics
Can J Agric Econ Rev Can Econ Rurale — Canadian Journal of Agricultural Economics/Revue Canadienne d'Economie Rurale
Can J Agric Sci — Canadian Journal of Agricultural Science
Can J Agr Sci — Canadian Journal of Agricultural Science
Can J Ag Sci — Canadian Journal of Agricultural Science
Can J Anaesth — Canadian Journal of Anaesthesia
Can J Anal Sci Spectrosc — Canadian Journal of Analytical Sciences and Spectroscopy
Can J Anim — Canadian Journal of Animal Science
Can J Anim Sci — Canadian Journal of Animal Science
Can J Anthropol — Canadian Journal of Anthropology
Can J Appl Physiol — Canadian Journal of Applied Physiology
Can J Appl Spectrosc — Canadian Journal of Applied Spectroscopy
Can J Appl Sport Sci — Canadian Journal of Applied Sport Sciences
Can J Appl Sport Sciences — Canadian Journal of Applied Sport Sciences
Can J Behav Sci — Canadian Journal of Behavioural Science
Can J Beh S — Canadian Journal of Behavioural Science
Can J Beh Sc/R Can Sc Comport — Canadian Journal of Behavioural Science/Revue Canadienne des Sciences du Comportement
Can J Bioch — Canadian Journal of Biochemistry

Can J Biochem — Canadian Journal of Biochemistry
Can J Biochem Cell Biol — Canadian Journal of Biochemistry and Cell Biology
Can J Biochem Physiol — Canadian Journal of Biochemistry and Physiology
Can J Bot — Canadian Journal of Botany
Can J Bot J Can Bot — Canadian Journal of Botany/Journal Canadien de Botanique
Can J Cardiol — Canadian Journal of Cardiology
Can J Chem — Canadian Journal of Chemistry
Can J Chem Eng — Canadian Journal of Chemical Engineering
Can J Chem Engng — Canadian Journal of Chemical Engineering
Can J Ch En — Canadian Journal of Chemical Engineering
Can J Civ Eng — Canadian Journal of Civil Engineering
Can J Civ Engng — Canadian Journal of Civil Engineering
Can J Civ Eng/Rev Can Genie Civ — Canadian Journal of Civil Engineering/Revue Canadienne de Genie Civil
Can J Clin — Cancer Journal for Clinicians
Can J Clin Pharmacol — Canadian Journal of Clinical Pharmacology/Journal Canadien de Pharmacologie Clinique
Can J Com M — Canadian Journal of Comparative Medicine
Can J Community Dent — Canadian Journal of Community Dentistry
Can J Comp Med — Canadian Journal of Comparative Medicine
Can J Comp Med Vet Sci — Canadian Journal of Comparative Medicine and Veterinary Science [*Later, Canadian Journal of Comparative Medicine*]
Can J Corr — Canadian Journal of Corrections [*Later, Canadian Journal of Criminology*]
Can J Correct — Canadian Journal of Corrections
Can J Correction — Canadian Journal of Corrections [*Later, Canadian Journal of Criminology*]
Can J Crim — Canadian Journal of Criminology and Corrections [*Later, Canadian Journal of Criminology*]
Can J Crim & Correct — Canadian Journal of Criminology and Corrections [*Later, Canadian Journal of Criminology*]
Can J Criminol — Canadian Journal of Criminology
Can J Criminology — Canadian Journal of Criminology
Can J Criminology & Corr — Canadian Journal of Criminology and Corrections [*Later, Canadian Journal of Criminology*]
Can J Development Studies — Canadian Journal of Development Studies
Can J Development Studies (Ottawa) — Canadian Journal of Development Studies (Ottawa)
Can J Diet Pract Res — Canadian Journal of Dietetic Practice and Research
Can J Earth — Canadian Journal of Earth Sciences
Can J Earth Sci — Canadian Journal of Earth Sciences
Can J Ec — Canadian Journal of Economics
Can J Econ — Canadian Journal of Economics
Can J Econ & Pol Sci — Canadian Journal of Economics and Political Science [*Later, Canadian Journal of Economics*]
Can J Econ Polit Sci — Canadian Journal of Economics and Political Science [*Later, Canadian Journal of Economics*]
Can J Econ Pol Sci — Canadian Journal of Economics and Political Science [*Later, Canadian Journal of Economics*]
Can J Econ Rev Can Econ Univ Toronto Press Can Econ Assoc — Canadian Journal of Economics/Revue Canadienne d'Economique. University of Toronto Press. Canadian Economics Association
Can J Ed — Canadian Journal of Education
Can J Ed Comm — Canadian Journal of Educational Communication
Can J Electr Comput Eng — Canadian Journal of Electrical and Computer Engineering
Can J Exp Psychol — Canadian Journal of Experimental Psychology
Can J Fabr — Canadian Journal of Fabrics
Can J Family Law — Canadian Journal of Family Law
Can J Fam L — Canadian Journal of Family Law
Can J Fish Aquatic Sci — Canadian Journal of Fisheries and Aquatic Sciences
Can J Fish Aquat Sci — Canadian Journal of Fisheries and Aquatic Sciences
Can J Fish Aquat Sci J Can Sci Halieutiques Aquat — Canadian Journal of Fisheries and Aquatic Sciences. Journal Canadien des Sciences Halieutiques et Aquatiques
Can J Forest Res — Canadian Journal of Forest Research
Can J For Res — Canadian Journal of Forest Research
Can J For Res J Can Rech For — Canadian Journal of Forest Research/Journal Canadien de Recherche Forestiere
Can J Gastroenterol — Canadian Journal of Gastroenterology
Can J Gen Cyt — Canadian Journal of Genetics and Cytology
Can J Genet — Canadian Journal of Genetics and Cytology
Can J Genet Cytol — Canadian Journal of Genetics and Cytology
CanJH — Canadian Journal of History
Can J Higher Ed — Canadian Journal of Higher Education
Can J His — Canadian Journal of History
Can J Hist — Canadian Journal of History
Can J Hist Sport — Canadian Journal of History of Sport
Can J Hist Sport Phys Educ — Canadian Journal of History of Sport and Physical Education [*Later, Canadian Journal of History of Sport*]
Can J Hosp Pharm — Canadian Journal of Hospital Pharmacy
Can J Info Science — Canadian Journal of Information Science
Can J Ital — Canadian Journal of Italian Studies
Can J L — Canadian Journal of Linguistics
Can J Ling — Canadian Journal of Linguistics
Can J Lingu — Canadian Journal of Linguistics
Can J Math — Canadian Journal of Mathematics
Can J Med Sci — Canadian Journal of Medical Science
Can J Med Surg — Canadian Journal of Medicine and Surgery
Can J Med T — Canadian Journal of Medical Technology
Can J Med Techn — Canadian Journal of Medical Technology
Can J Med Technol — Canadian Journal of Medical Technology
Can J Ment Hyg — Canadian Journal of Mental Hygiene
Can J Micro — Canadian Journal of Microbiology

Can J Microb — Canadian Journal of Microbiology
Can J Microbiol — Canadian Journal of Microbiology
Can J Nat Ed — Canadian Journal of Native Education
Can J Neurol Sci — Canadian Journal of Neurological Sciences
Can Jnl Biochem Cell Biol — Canadian Journal of Biochemistry and Cell Biology
Can Jnl Engl Lang Arts — Canadian Journal of English Language Arts
Can Jnl Except Child — Canadian Journal for Exceptional Children
Can Jnl/His — Canadian Journal of History
Can Jnl Ment Ret — Canadian Journal on Mental Retardation
Can Jnl Nat Stud — Canadian Journal of Native Studies
Can Jnl Res Semiot — Canadian Journal of Research in Semiotics
Can J Occup Ther — Canadian Journal of Occupational Therapy
Can J Oncol — Canadian Journal of Oncology
Can J Ophth — Canadian Journal of Ophthalmology
Can J Ophthalm — Canadian Journal of Ophthalmology
Can J Ophthalmol — Canadian Journal of Ophthalmology
Can J Optom — Canadian Journal of Optometry
Can J Otolaryngol — Canadian Journal of Otolaryngology
Can Jour Hist — Canadian Journal of History
Can J Pharm Sci — Canadian Journal of Pharmaceutical Sciences
Can J Phil — Canadian Journal of Philosophy
Can J Ph Sc — Canadian Journal of Pharmaceutical Sciences
Can J Phys — Canadian Journal of Physics
Can J Physiol Pharm — Canadian Journal of Physiology and Pharmacology
Can J Physiol Pharmacol — Canadian Journal of Physiology and Pharmacology
Can J Physl — Canadian Journal of Physiology and Pharmacology
Can J Plant — Canadian Journal of Plant Science
Can J Plant Pathol — Canadian Journal of Plant Pathology
Can J Plant Pathol Rev Can Phytopathol — Canadian Journal of Plant Pathology/ Revue Canadienne de Phytopathologie
Can J Plant Sci — Canadian Journal of Plant Science
Can J Plant Sci Rev Can Phytotech — Canadian Journal of Plant Science/Revue Canadienne de Phytotechnie
Can J Pl Sci — Canadian Journal of Plant Science
Can J Pol and Soc Theory — Canadian Journal of Political and Social Theory
Can J Poli — Canadian Journal of Political Science
Can J Pol Sc — Canadian Journal of Political Science
Can J Pol Sci — Canadian Journal of Political Science
Can J Pol Science — Canadian Journal of Political Science
Can J Pol Science (Ont) — Canadian Journal of Political Science (Ontario)
Can J Psych — Canadian Journal of Psychology
Can J Psychiatr Nurs — Canadian Journal of Psychiatric Nursing
Can J Psychiatry — Canadian Journal of Psychiatry
Can J Psychol — Canadian Journal of Psychology
Can J Publ — Canadian Journal of Public Health
Can J Publ Hlth — Canadian Journal of Public Health
Can J Public Health — Canadian Journal of Public Health
Can J Radiogr Radiother Nucl Med — Canadian Journal of Radiography, Radiotherapy, Nuclear Medicine
Can J Radiogr Radiother Nucl Med (Engl Ed) — Canadian Journal of Radiography, Radiotherapy, Nuclear Medicine (English Edition)
Can J Rel Thought — Canadian Journal of Religious Thought
Can J Remote Sens — Canadian Journal of Remote Sensing
Can J Remote Sensing — Canadian Journal of Remote Sensing
Can J Res — Canadian Journal of Research
Can J Res Sect A — Canadian Journal of Research. Section A. Physical Sciences
Can J Res Sect B — Canadian Journal of Research. Section B. Chemical Sciences
Can J Res Sect C — Canadian Journal of Research. Section C. Botanical Sciences
Can J Res Sect C Bot Sci — Canadian Journal of Research. Section C. Botanical Sciences
Can J Res Sect D — Canadian Journal of Research. Section D. Zoological Sciences
Can J Res Sect D Zool Sci — Canadian Journal of Research. Section D. Zoological Sciences
Can J Res Sect E — Canadian Journal of Research. Section E. Medical Sciences
Can J Res Sect E Med Sci — Canadian Journal of Research. Section E. Medical Sciences
Can J Res Sect F — Canadian Journal of Research. Section F. Technology
Can J Sci — Canadian Journal of Science, Literature, and History
Can J Soil — Canadian Journal of Soil Science
Can J Soil Sci — Canadian Journal of Soil Science
Can J Spect — Canadian Journal of Spectroscopy
Can J Spectrosc — Canadian Journal of Spectroscopy
Can J Spectry — Canadian Journal of Spectroscopy
Can J Sport Sci — Canadian Journal of Sport Sciences
Can J Statis — Canadian Journal of Statistics
Can J Surg — Canadian Journal of Surgery
Can JT — Canadian Journal of Theology
Can J Technol — Canadian Journal of Technology
Can J Th — Canadian Journal of Theology
Can J Univ Cont Ed — Canadian Journal of University Continuing Education
Can J Urol — Canadian Journal of Urology
Can J Vet Res — Canadian Journal of Veterinary Research
Can J Vet Res Rev Can Rech Vet — Canadian Journal of Veterinary Research/ Revue Canadienne de Recherche Veterinaire
Can J Zool — Canadian Journal of Zoology
Can L — Canadian Literature
Can Lab — Canadian Labour
Can Labour — Canadian Labour
Can Lanc — Canada Lancet and Practitioner
Can Law — Canadian Lawyer
Can Lawyer — Canadian Lawyer
Can Lbr — Canadian Labour
Can Legal Aid Bul — Canadian Legal Aid Bulletin
Can Lib — Canadian Library

Can Lib Assn Bul — Canadian Library Association. Bulletin
Can Lib Bull — Canadian Library Bulletin
Can Lib J — Canadian Library Journal
Can Libr J — Canadian Library Journal
Can Lit — Canadian Literature
Can Lit Mag — Canadian Literary Magazine
Can LJ — Canada Law Journal
Can LJ NS — Canada Law Journal, New Series
Can LS — Canadian Legal Studies
Can Lugano — Cantonette Lugano
Can M — Canadian Magazine
Can Mach Manu News — Canadian Machinery and Manufacturing News
Can Mach Metalwork — Canadian Machinery and Metalworking
Can Mach Mfg News — Canadian Machinery and Manufacturing News
Can Mag — Canadian Magazine
Can Mag Polit Sci Art Lit — Canadian Magazine of Politics, Science, Art, and Literature
Can MAJ — Canadian Medical Association. Journal
CANMAN — Casopis Narodniho Muzea
Can Manuscr Rep Fish Aquat Sci — Canadian Manuscript Report of Fisheries and Aquatic Sciences
CAN/MARC — Canadian Machine-Readable Cataloging
Can Mark Data Ind — Canadian Market Data Index
Can M Assn J — Canadian Medical Association. Journal
Can Math B — Canadian Mathematical Bulletin
Can Math Bull — Canadian Mathematical Bulletin
Can Math Teach — Canadian Mathematics Teacher
Can Med A J — Canadian Medical Association. Journal
Can Med Ass J — Canadian Medical Association. Journal
Can Med Assn J — Canadian Medical Association. Journal
Can Med Assoc J — Canadian Medical Association. Journal
Can Mental Health — Canada's Mental Health
Can Ment He — Canada's Mental Health
Can Ment Health — Canada's Mental Health
Can Ment Hlth — Canada's Mental Health
Can Met — Canadian Metals
Can Metall Q — Canadian Metallurgical Quarterly
Can Metal Q — Canadian Metallurgical Quarterly
Can Metalwork — Canadian Metalworking
Can Metalwork/Mach Prod — Canadian Metalworking/Machine Production
Can Metalwork Prod — Canadian Metalworking Production
Can Met Metall Ind — Canadian Metals and Metallurgical Industries
Can Met Quart — Canadian Metallurgical Quarterly
CANMET Rep — CANMET [Canada Centre for Mineral and Energy Technology] Report
CANMET Spec Publ — CANMET [Canada Centre for Mineral and Energy Technology] Special Publication
Can Milling Feed — Canadian Milling and Feed Journal
Can Milling Feed J — Canadian Milling and Feed Journal
Can Milling Grain J — Canadian Milling and Grain Journal
Can Min & Metallurg Bull — Canadian Mining and Metallurgical Bulletin
Can Min & Met Bul — Canadian Mining and Metallurgical Bulletin
Can Mineral — Canadian Mineralogist
Can Miner Ind Rev — Canadian Mineral Industry. Review
Can Miner Process Annu Meet — Canadian Mineral Processors. Annual Meeting
Can Miner Resour Branch Miner Bull — Canada. Mineral Resources Branch. Mineral Bulletin
Can Miner Resour Branch Miner Inf Bull — Canada. Mineral Resources Branch. Mineral Information Bulletin
Can Miner Resour Branch Miner Rep — Canada. Mineral Resources Branch. Mineral Report
Can Miner Resour Div Miner Bull — Canada. Mineral Resources Division. Mineral Bulletin
Can Miner Resour Div Oper List — Canada. Mineral Resources Division. Operators List
Can Miner Yearb — Canadian Minerals Yearbook
Can Mines Branch Inf Circ — Canada. Mines Branch. Information Circular
Can Mines Branch Invest Rep — Canada. Mines Branch. Investigation Report
Can Mines Branch Memo Ser — Canada. Mines Branch. Memorandum Series
Can Mines Branch Monogr — Canada. Mines Branch. Monograph
Can Mines Branch Radioact Div Top Rep — Canada. Mines Branch. Radioactivity Division. Topical Report
Can Mines Branch Rapp Div Mines — Canada. Mines Branch. Rapports. Division des Mines
Can Mines Branch Rep — Canada. Mines Branch. Report
Can Mines Branch Res Rep — Canada. Mines Branch. Research Report
Can Mines Branch Tech Bull — Canada. Mines Branch. Technical Bulletin
Can Mines Branch Tech Pap — Canada. Mines Branch. Technical Paper
Can Mines Br Sum Rp — Canada. Department of Mines. Mines Branch. Summary Report
Can Mining J — Canadian Mining Journal
Can Mining Met Bul — Canadian Mining and Metallurgical Bulletin
Can Min Inst Bull — Canadian Mining Institute. Bulletins
Can Min J — Canadian Mining Journal
Can Min Met — Canadian Mining and Metallurgical Bulletin
Can Min Metall Bull — Canadian Mining and Metallurgical Bulletin
Can Ml J — Canadian Military Journal
Can-Mong R — Canada-Mongolia Review
Can M Rv — Canadian Mining Review
Can Munic Util — Canadian Municipal Utilities
Can Mus — Canadian Musician
Can Mus Bk — Canada Music Book
Can Mus Ed — Canadian Music Educator
Can Mus J — Canadian Music Journal

Can Nat — Canadian Naturalist and Geologist and Proceedings of the Natural History Society of Montreal

Can Nat Comm Ment Hyg Bul — Canadian National Commission on Mental Hygiene. Bulletin

Can Natl Aeronaut Establ Mech Eng Rep — Canada. National Aeronautical Establishment. Mechanical Engineering Report

Can Natl Aeronaut Establ Mech Eng Rep MS — Canada. National Aeronautical Establishment. Mechanical Engineering Report MS

Can Natl Power Alcohol Conf — Canadian National Power Alcohol Conference

Can Natl Res Counc Div Mech Eng Lab Tech Rep — Canada. National Research Council. Division of Mechanical Engineering. Laboratory Technical Report

CANNB — Canadian Nurse

Canner Pckr — Canner/Packer

Canners Bull — Canners' Bulletin. Fruit and Vegetable Preservation Research Station

Canners Inf Lett Br Fd Mfg Ind Res Ass — Canners' Information Letter. British Food Manufacturing Industries Research Association

Canners J (Tokyo) — Canners Journal (Tokyo)

Can News Index — Canadian News Index

Cann Ind — Canning Industry

Canning H Libr Bull London — Canning House Library Bulletin (London)

Can North For Res Cent Inf Rep NOR-X — Canada. Northern Forest Research Centre. Information Report NOR-X

Cann Pack — Canning and Packing

Cann Trade — Canning Trade

Can Nucl — Canada Nucleaire

Can Nucl Assoc Annu Int Conf — Canadian Nuclear Association. Annual International Conference

Can Nucl Assoc Annu Int Conf (Pro) — Canadian Nuclear Association. Annual International Conference (Proceedings)

Can Nucl Assoc Rep CNA — Canadian Nuclear Association. Report CNA

Can Nucl Assoc Report — Canadian Nuclear Association. Report

Can Nucl Soc Annu Conf Proc — Canadian Nuclear Society. Annual Conference. Proceedings

Can Nucl Soc Annu Conf Trans — Canadian Nuclear Society. Annual Conference. Transactions

Can Nucl Soc Trans — Canadian Nuclear Society. Transactions

Can Nucl Technol — Canadian Nuclear Technology

Can Numi J — Canadian Numismatic Journal

Can Nurse — Canadian Nurse

CANO — Canoma. Canada Department of Energy, Mines, and Resources

Canoe — Canoe & Kayak

Canoe — Canoe Magazine

Can Oil Gas Ind — Canadian Oil and Gas Industries

Canon Law — Canon Law Abstracts

Canon Law Abstr — Canon Law Abstracts

Can Oper Res Soc J — Canadian Operational Research Society. Journal

Can Oper Room Nurs J — Canadian Operating Room Nursing Journal

Can Opt — Canadian Optician

CANP — Canadian Association of Native Peoples. Bulletin

Can Pac For Res Cent Rep BC X — Canada. Pacific Forest Research Centre. Report. BC X

Can/Pack — Canner Packer World

Can Packag — Canadian Packaging

Can Paint Finish — Canadian Paint and Finishing

Can Paint Varn — Canadian Paint and Varnish

Can Pap Rural Hist — Canadian Papers in Rural History

Can Pat — Canadian Patent

Can Pat Doc — Canada. Patent Document

Can Pat Office Rec — Canadian Patent Office. Record

Can Pat Office Recd — Canadian Patent Office. Record

Can Pat Off Pat Off Rec — Canada. Patent Office. Patent Office Record

Can Pat Reissue — Canadian Patent. Reissue

Can Pat Rep — Canadian Patent Reporter

Can Peat Soc B — Canadian Peat Society. Bulletin

Can Pen Cong Proc — Canadian Penal Congress. Proceedings

Can Period Index — Canadian Periodical Index

Can Pers — Canadian Personnel and Industrial Relations Journal (Including the Canadian Training Digest)

Can Persp — Canadian Perspective

Can Pest Manage Soc Proc Annu Meet — Canadian Pest Management Society. Proceedings of the Annual Meeting

Can Pet — Canadian Petroleum

Can Pet Eng — Canadian Petro Engineering

Can Petro Eng — Canadian Petro Engineering

Can Petrol — Canadian Petroleum

Can Pharm J — Canadian Pharmaceutical Journal

Can Phil Rev — Canadian Philosophical Reviews

Can Phot J — Canadian Photographic Journal

Can Pkg — Canadian Packaging

Can Plains Proc — Canadian Plains Proceedings

Can Plant Dis Surv — Canadian Plant Disease Survey

Can Plast — Canadian Plastics

Can Plastics — Canadian Plastics

CanPlast Proc Conf Soc Plast Ind Can — CanPlast. Proceedings. Conference. Society of the Plastics Industry of Canada

Can Po — Canadian Poetry

Can Pod — Canadian Podiatrist

Can Poetry — Canadian Poetry

Can Police Bul — Canadian Police Bulletin

Can Poult Rev — Canadian Poultry Review

Can Poultry Rev — Canadian Poultry Review

Can Power Eng — Canadian Power Engineering

Can Power Eng Plant Maint — Canadian Power Engineering and Plant Maintenance

Can P R — Canadian Patent Reporter

Can Printer Publ — Canadian Printer and Publisher

Can Psl & Ind Rel J — Canadian Personnel and Industrial Relations Journal (Including the Canadian Training Digest)

Can Psychi — Canadian Psychiatric Association. Journal

Can Psychiatr Assoc J — Canadian Psychiatric Association. Journal

Can Psychol — Canadian Psychologist

Can Psychology — Canadian Psychology

Can Psychol Rev — Canadian Psychological Review

Can Psych Psych Can — Canadian Psychology/Psychologie Canadienne

Can Psych R — Canadian Psychological Review

Can Pub Admin — Canadian Public Administration/Administration Publique du Canada

Can Publ Ad — Canadian Public Administration/Administration Publique du Canada

Can Public Admin — Canadian Public Administration

Can Public Health J — Canadian Public Health Journal

Can Public Policy — Canadian Public Policy

Can Public Policy (Guelph) — Canadian Public Policy (Guelph)

Can Pub Pol — Canadian Public Policy

Can Pub Policy — Canadian Public Policy

Can Pulp Pap Assoc Tech Sect Annu Meet Prepr Pap — Canadian Pulp and Paper Association. Technical Section. Annual Meeting.Preprints of Papers

Can Pulp Pap Assoc Tech Sect Prepr Pap Annu Meet — Canadian Pulp and Paper Association. Technical Section. Preprints ofPapers. Annual Meeting

Can Pulp Pap Assoc Tech Sect Trans — Canadian Pulp and Paper Association. Technical Section. Transactions

Can Pulp Paper Ind — Canadian Pulp and Paper Industry

Can Quill — Canadian Quill

Can R Am St — Canadian Review of American Studies

Can R Com L — Canadian Review of Comparative Literature/Revue Canadienne de Litterature Comparee

Can Rec N H — Canadian Record of Natural History and Geology

Can Rec Sc — Canadian Record of Science

Can Renewable Energy News — Canadian Renewable Energy News

Can Res — Canadian Research

Can Res Dev — Canadian Research and Development [*Later, Canadian Research*]

Can Res Inst Launderers Clean — Canadian Research Institute of Launderers and Cleaners. TechnicalReport

Can Res Inst Launders Clean Tech — Canadian Research Institute of Launderers and Cleaners. Technical Report

Can Resour Dev Branch Fish Ser Halifax Prog Rep — Canada. Resource Development Branch. Fisheries Service. Halifax Progress Report

Can Rev — Canadian Review

Can Rev Amer Stud — Canadian Review of American Studies

Can Rev Am Stud — Canadian Review of American Studies

Can Rev Comp Lt — Canadian Review of Comparative Literature/Revue Canadienne de Litterature Comparee

Can Rev Sociol Anthropol — Canadian Review of Sociology and Anthropology

Can Rev Stud Natl — Canadian Review of Studies in Nationalism

Can R Soc — Canadian Review of Sociology and Anthropology

Can R Soc A — Canadian Review of Sociology and Anthropology

Can R Soc Anthr — Canadian Review of Sociology and Anthropology

Can R Sociol & Anthrop — Canadian Review of Sociology and Anthropology

Can R Sociol Anth — Canadian Review of Sociology and Anthropology

Can R Studies Nationalism — Canadian Review of Studies in Nationalism

Can R Stud Nat — Canadian Review of Studies in Nationalism

Can Run — Canadian Runner

CANS — Canada - North of 60

CanS — Canadian Slavic Studies

Can Sales Tax Rep CCH — Canadian Sales Tax Reports. Commerce Clearing House

Can Sch Exec — Canadian School Executive

Can Sci — Canadian Scientist

Can Sc Mo — Canadian Science Monthly

Can Semicond Technol Conf — Canadian Semiconductor Technology Conference

Can Serv Med J — Canadian Services Medical Journal

CanSIS — Canadian Soil Information System

Can Slavonic Pa — Canadian Slavonic Papers

Can Slavonic Pap — Canadian Slavonic Papers

Can Slav P — Canadian Slavonic Papers

Can Slav Stud — Canadian-American Slavic Studies

Can Sl P — Canadian Slavonic Papers

Can's Mental Health — Canada's Mental Health

CANSN — Canada - North of 60. Newsletter

Can Soc Forensic Sci J — Canadian Society of Forensic Science. Journal

Can Soc Pet Geol Mem — Canadian Society of Petroleum Geologists. Memoir

CanSP — Canadian Slavonic Papers

Can Spec Publ Fish Aquat Sci — Canadian Special Publication of Fisheries and Aquatic Sciences

Can Spectrosc — Canadian Spectroscopy

Can Spectry — Canadian Spectroscopy

CanSS — Canadian-American Slavic Studies

CANSTAN — Canadian Standards

Can Stand Ass CSA Stand — Canadian Standards Association. CSA Standard

Can Stat Can Biscuits Confect — Canada. Statistics Canada. Biscuits and Confectionery

Can Stat Can Coarse Grains Rev — Canada. Statistics Canada. Coarse Grains Review

Can Stat Can Coastwise Shipping Stat — Canada. Statistics Canada. Coastwise Shipping Statistics

Can Stat Can Consumer Credit — Canada. Statistics Canada. Consumer Credit

Can Stat Can Consumption Rubber — Canada. Statistics Canada. Consumption, Production and Inventories of Rubber

Can Stat Can Honey — Canada. Statistics Canada. Honey Production and Value. Production Forecast

Can Stat Can Index Farm Prod — Canada. Statistics Canada. Index of Farm Production
Can Stat Can New Manuf — Canada. Statistics Canada. New Manufacturing Establishments in Canada
Can Stat Can Shorn Wool — Canada. Statistics Canada. Shorn Wool Production
Can Stat Can Tuberc Stat — Canada. Statistics Canada. Tuberculosis Statistics
Can Statis R — Canadian Statistical Review
Can Statis Rev WS — Canadian Statistical Review. Weekly Supplement
Can Stat Rev — Canadian Statistical Review
Canstatts Jahresber Fortschr Pharm Verwandten Wiss — Canstatt's Jahresbericht ueber die Fortschritte in der Pharmacie und VerwandtenWissenschaften
Can St Ec — Canadian Studies in Economics
Cansteiner Kolloq — Cansteiner Kolloquium
Can Struct Eng Conf — Canadian Structural Engineering Conference
Can Stud — Canadian Student
Can Stud Bul — Canadian Studies Bulletin
Can Studies Population — Canadian Studies in Population
Can Sulfur Symp — Canadian Sulfur Symposium
Can Surv — Canadian Surveyor
Can Surveyor — Canadian Surveyor
Can Symp Catal Prepr — Canadian Symposium on Catalysis. Preprints
Can Symp Nonwovens Disposables — Canadian Symposium on Nonwovens and Disposables
Can Symp Remote Sensing Proc — Canadian Symposium of Remote Sensing. Proceedings
Can Symp Water Pollut Res — Canadian Symposium on Water Pollution Research
Can Taxation — Canadian Taxation
Can Tax J — Canadian Tax Journal
Can Tax J Tax Policy — Canadian Taxation. A Journal of Tax Policy
Can Tax LJ — Canadian Tax Law Journal
Can Tax News — Canadian Tax News
Can Tax Rep CCH — Canadian Tax Reports. Commerce Clearing House
Can Tech Asphalt Assoc Proc Annu Conf — Canadian Technical Asphalt Association. Proceedings of the AnnualConference
Can Tech Rep Fish Aquat Sci — Canadian Technical Report of Fisheries and Aquatic Sciences
Can Tech Rep Hydrogr Ocean Sci — Canadian Technical Report of Hydrography and Ocean Sciences
Canteras Explot — Canteras y Explotaciones
Canterbury Cathedral Chron — Canterbury Cathedral Chronicle
Canterbury Chamber Commer Agric Bull — Canterbury Chamber of Commerce. Agricultural Bulletin
Canterbury Eng J — Canterbury Engineering Journal
Canterbury L Rev — Canterbury Law Review
Can Text J — Canadian Textile Journal
Can Text Semin Int Book Pap — Canadian Textile Seminar. International Book of Papers
CAnth — Current Anthropology
Can Theat R — Canadian Theatre Review
Can Theatre R — Canadian Theatre Review
Can Theosophist — Canadian Theosophist
Can Theses — Canadian Theses
CAnthr — Current Anthropology
C Anthropol Ecol Hum — Cahiers d'Anthropologie et d'Ecologie Humaines
C Antiq — Carmarthenshire Antiquary
C Antiq FPL — Coins and Antiquities Ltd. Fixed Price List
Cant Mount — Canterbury Mountaineer
Cant Mus Bull — Canterbury Music Bulletin
Can Tob Grower — Canadian Tobacco Grower
Canto Greg — Canto Gregoriano
Canto Lib — Canto Libre
Can Transp — Canadian Transportation [*Later, Canadian Transportation and Distribution Management*]
Cantrill's F — Cantrill's Filmnotes
Cantrill's Fmnts — Cantrill's Filmnotes
CANU — Canadian Nurse
CANUA — Canadian Nurse
CANUC:H — Canadian Union Catalogue of Library Materials for the Handicapped
CANUDG — Comparative Animal Nutrition
Can U Mus R — Canadian University Music Review
Ca Nurs — Cancer Nursing
Can-US Law J — Canada-United States Law Journal
Can-US LJ — Canada-United States Law Journal
Can Vending — Canadian Vending
Can Vet J — Canadian Veterinary Journal
Can Vet Record — Canadian Veterinary Record
Can Victoria Mem Mus B — Canada. Victoria Memorial Museum. Bulletin
Can Voc J — Canadian Vocational Journal
CANW — Canada Now Social Studies Magazine for Schools
Can W — Canada Weekly
CANW — Cancer News
CANWA — Chemia Analityczna (Warszawa)
Can Water Resour Branch Water Resour Pap — Canada. Water Resources Branch. Water Resources Paper
Can Water Resour Branch Water Resour Pap S — Canada. Water Resources Branch. Water Resources Paper S. Sediment
Can Water Resour J — Canadian Water Resources Journal
Can Wel — Canadian Welfare
Can Welder Fabr — Canadian Welder and Fabricator
Can Welfare — Canadian Welfare
Can West For Prod Lab Inf Rep VP X — Canada. Western Forest Products Laboratory. Information Report VP-X
Can Wildl Serv — Canadian Wildlife Service
Can Wildl Serv Occas Pap — Canadian Wildlife Service. Occasional Papers

Can Wildl Serv Prog Notes — Canadian Wildlife Service. Progress Notes
Can Wildl Serv Rep Ser — Canadian Wildlife Service. Report Series
Can WI Mag — Canada-West Indies Magazine
Can Woodl Rev — Canadian Woodlands Review
CANWP — Canadian Network Papers. National Library of Canada
Can W Rev — Canadian Weather Review
Can YBIL — Canadian Yearbook of International Law
Can YB Int'l L — Canadian Yearbook of International Law
Can Yb of Internat — Canadian Yearbook of International Law
Cany C News — Canyon Cinema News
Can Yearb Int Law — Canadian Yearbook of International Law
Can Yearbook Int L — Canadian Yearbook of International Law
CANZLLI — Current Australian and New Zealand Legal Literature Index
CAO — Cabinet Maker and Retail Furnisher
CaO — Choir and Organ
CaOM — Cahiers d'Outre-Mer
Caoutch Gutta Percha — Caoutchouc et la Gutta Percha
Caoutch Latex Artif — Caoutchoucs et Latex Artificiels
Caoutch Mod — Caoutchouc Moderne
Caoutch Plast — Caoutchoucs et Plastiques
Caoutchs Latex Artif — Caoutchoucs et Latex Artificiels
Caoutchs Plast — Caoutchoucs et Plastiques
Cap — Capitole
Cap — Capitoli
Cap — Capitolium
CAP — Computers and People
CAP — Cuadernos de Arte y Poesia
Cap Ann — Capuchin Annual
CAPBAY — Catalogue of American Amphibians and Reptiles
CAPBBZ — Colorado. Agricultural Experiment Station. Bulletin
Cap Chem — Capital Chemist
Cap Dist Bs — Capital District Business Review
CAPE — Canadian Petroleum
Cape Astrogr Zones — Cape Astrographic Zones. Royal Observatory
Cape Exped Ser Bull — Cape Expedition Series Bulletin. Department of Scientific and Industrial Research
Cape Good Hope Dep Nat Conserv Rep — Cape Of Good Hope. Department of Nature Conservation. Report
Cape Law J — Cape Law Journal
Cape Librn — Cape Librarian
Cape LJ — Cape Law Journal
Cape Mimeogr — Cape Mimeograms
Cape Nat — Cape Naturalist
Cape Of Good Hope Dep Nat Conserv Invest Rep — Cape Of Good Hope. Department of Nature Conservation. Investigational Report
Cape Of Good Hope Dep Nat Conserv Rep — Cape Of Good Hope. Department of Nature Conservation. Report
Ca Per — Castrum Peregrini
Cape Town Univ Dep Geol Precambrian Res Unit Annu Rep — Cape Town. University. Department of Geology. Precambrian Research Unit. AnnualReport
CAPF — Chemical Age Project File
Capi — Capitoli. Revue Literraire Franco-Italienne
Capil Alfonsina Bol — Capilla Alfonsina Boletin
Capillarity Today Proc Adv Workshop Capillarity — Capillarity Today. Proceedings. Advanced Workshop on Capillarity
Capit — Capitolium
Capital — Capital and Class
Capital Goods R — Capital Goods Review
Capital ULR — Capital University. Law Review
Capital U L Rev — Capital University. Law Review
Capital Univ L Rev — Capital University. Law Review
Capita Zool — Capita Zoologica
Capitol Stud — Capitol Studies
CaPL — Cahiers de la Pleiade
CAPL — Chronique Archeologique du Pays de Liege
CAPLD — Carolina Planning
Cap Libn — Cape Librarian
Cap Nurs — Capital Nursing
CAPPA — Centralblatt fuer Allgemeine Pathologie und Pathologische Anatomie
Cappers Fmr — Capper's Farmer
CAPPS — Chemicals and Polymers Production Statistics
CAPRI — Computerized Administration of Patent Documents Reclassified According to the IPC
CAPSAH — Canadian Psychologist
Cap Stud — Capitol Studies
Capsule Inf Ser Mont Agric Exp Stn — Capsule Information Series. Montana Agricultural Experiment Station
Captv Insur — Captive Insurance Concept
Capuchin Annu — Capuchin Annual
Cap U LR — Capital University. Law Review
Cap UL Rev — Capital University. Law Review
CAPWAn — Cercle Archeologique du Pays de Waes. Annales
CaQ — California Quarterly
CAQDA — California Air Quality Data
CA Qtrly — CA Quarterly. Facts and Figures on Austria's Economy
CAR — Cahiers d'Archeologie Regionale
CaR — Cakavska Ric
CAR — Canadian Annual Review
CAR — Caravan Kampeersport. Maandblad voor Caravan/Kampeerliefhebbers
Car — Caravelle
Car — Carinthia. Zeitschrift fuer Vaterlanskunde, Belehrung, und Unterhaltung
Car — Carmelus
Car — Carovana
Car — Carrefour
Car — Carrefour. La Semaine en France et Dans le Monde

CAR — Central Asian Review
CAR — Chile-America (Roma)
CAR — Commonwealth Arbitration Reports
Car A and E J — Cardozo Arts and Entertainment Journal
Car & Dr — Car and Driver
CARB — Current Australian Reference Books
Carbide Eng — Carbide Engineering
Carbide J — Carbide Journal
Carbide Tool J — Carbide and Tool Journal
Carb Ne — Carbon News
Carbohydr Chem — Carbohydrate Chemistry
Carbohydr Chem Subst Biol Interest Proc Int Congr Biochem — Carbohydrate Chemistry of Substances of Biological Interest. Proceedings. International Congress of Biochemistry
Carbohydr Compr Biochem — Carbohydrate. Comprehensive Biochemistry
Carbohyd Res — Carbohydrate Research
Carbohydr Lett — Carbohydrate Letters
Carbohydr Metab Compr Biochem — Carbohydrate Metabolism. Comprehensive Biochemistry
Carbohydr Metab Pregnancy Newborn Int Colloq — Carbohydrate Metabolism in Pregnancy and the Newborn. InternationalColloquium
Carbohydr Metab Quant Physiol Math Model — Carbohydrate Metabolism. Quantitative Physiology and Mathematical Modeling
Carbohydr Polym — Carbohydrate Polymers
Carbohydr Res — Carbohydrate Research
Carbohy Res — Carbohydrate Research
Carbon Dio — Carbon Dioxide and Climate. A Second Assessment
Carbon Dioxide Rev — Carbon Dioxide Review
Carbonization Res Rep — Carbonization Research Report
Carbon Rev — Carbon Review
CARC — Censo de Archivos
CARC — Central Asian Research Centre. London, in Association with St. Anthony's College, Oxford
C Arcad Riv Mens Lett Sci & A — Giornale Arcadico. Rivista Mensile di Lettere, Scienze, e Arti
CARCBE — Annual Report. Central and Regional Arecanut Research Stations
CArch — Cahiers Archeologiques
Carcinog Abst — Carcinogenesis Abstracts
Carcinog Compr Surv — Carcinogenesis: A Comprehensive Survey
Carcinog Tech Rep Ser US Natl Cancer Inst — Carcinogenesis Technical Report Series. United States National Cancer Institute
CARCMYS — Canadian Arctic Resources Committee. Monograph. Yukon Series
Car Commn Mon Inf B — Caribbean Commission. Monthly Information Bulletin
Card — Cardiologia
CARDAG — Cardiologia
CARDDJ — Cardiologia
Cardil Hung — Cardiologia Hungarica
Cardio Dr R — Cardiovascular Drug Reviews
Cardiol Bull — Cardiologisches Bulletin
Cardiol Clin — Cardiology Clinics
Cardiol Int Perspect Proc World Congr — Cardiology. An International Perspective. Proceedings. World Congress of Cardiology
Cardiol Prat — Cardiologia Pratica
Cardiol Proc World Congr — Cardiology. Proceedings of the World Congress of Cardiology
Cardiol Rev — Cardiology in Review
Cardio Res — Cardiovascular Research
Cardiovasc Clin — Cardiovascular Clinics
Cardiovasc Dis Bull Tex Heart Inst — Cardiovascular Diseases Bulletin. Texas Heart Institute
Cardiovasc Diuretic Rev — Cardiovascular Diuretic Review
Cardiovasc Drug Rev — Cardiovascular Drug Reviews
Cardiovasc Drugs — Cardiovascular Drugs
Cardiovasc Drugs Ther — Cardiovascular Drugs and Therapy
Cardiovasc Drug Ther Hahnemann Symp — Cardiovascular Drug Therapy. The Hahnemann Symposium
Cardiovasc Flow Dyn Meas (NATO Adv Study Inst) — Cardiovascular Flow Dynamics and Measurements (North Atlantic Treaty Organization. Advanced Study Institute on Cardiovascular Flow Dynamics)
Cardiovasc Interventional Radiol — Cardiovascular and Interventional Radiology
Cardiovasc Intervent Radiol — Cardiovascular and Interventional Radiology
Cardiovasc J S Afr — Cardiovascular Journal of South Africa
Cardiovasc Med — Cardiovascular Medicine
Cardiovasc Med (NY) — Cardiovascular Medicine (New York)
Cardiovasc Nurs — Cardiovascular Nursing
Cardiovasc Pathobiol — Cardiovascular Pathobiology
Cardiovasc Pathol — Cardiovascular Pathology
Cardiovasc Physiol — Cardiovascular Physiology
Cardiovasc Radiat Med — Cardiovascular Radiation Medicine
Cardiovasc Radiol — Cardiovascular Radiology
Cardiovasc Res — Cardiovascular Research
Cardiovasc Res Cent Bull — Cardiovascular Research Center. Bulletin
Cardiovasc Res Cent Bull (Houston) — Cardiovascular Research Center. Bulletin (Houston)
Cardiovasc Surg — Cardiovascular Surgery
Cardiovasc Syst — Cardiovascular System
Cardiovasc Ther — Cardiovascular Therapy
Cardiovasc Toxic Cocaine Underlying Mech — Cardiovascular Toxicity of Cocaine. Underlying Mechanisms
Cardiovas Dis (Houston) — Cardiovascular Diseases (Houston)
Cardiovas Res — Cardiovascular Research
Cardiovas Res Suppl — Cardiovascular Research. Supplement
Cardiovas Rev — Cardiovascular Review
Car Dis Ab — Careers and the Disabled
Card Nat Hist Bull — Cardiganshire Natural History Bulletin

Card Ne Let — Cardiac News Letter. Chest and Heart Association
Card Nt S T — Cardiff Naturalists' Society. Reports and Transactions
Cardozo L Rev — Cardozo Law Review
Card Pract — Cardiac Practice
Card Prat — Cardiologia Pratica
CARD Rep — CARD [Center for Agricultural and Rural Development] Report
CAREBK — Caries Research
Car Econ Rev — Caribbean Economic Review
Career Dev Bul — Career Development Bulletin
Careers Bull — Careers Bulletin
Careers Guid Teach — Careers and Guidance Teacher
Careers J — Careers Journal
CAREL — Cascadian Regional Library
Car Eng — Carbide Engineering
CA Rep Tech Assoc Pulp Pap Ind — CA [Committee Assignment] Report. Technical Association of the Pulp and Paper Industry
Carey — Manitoba Reports, by Carey
Carey's Mus — Carey's American Museum
Car For — Caribbean Forester
Cargese Lect Phys — Cargese Lectures in Physics
Cargill Crop Bull — Cargill Crop Bulletin
Cargo Syst Int — Cargo Systems International
Car Hist Rev — Caribbean Historical Review
CARHS — Canadian-American Review of Hungarian Studies
Carl — Carrefour des Idees
CARIAV — Caribbean Forester
Caribb Agr — Caribbean Agriculture
Caribb Agric — Caribbean Agriculture
Carib Basin Econ Surv — Caribbean Basin Economic Survey
Caribb Bus — Caribbean Business
Caribbean Agric — Caribbean Agriculture
Caribbean Forest — Caribbean Forester
Caribbean J Math — Caribbean Journal of Mathematics
Caribbean J Math Comput Sci — Caribbean Journal of Mathematical and Computing Sciences
Caribbean Jour Sci — Caribbean Journal of Science
Caribbean J Sci Math — Caribbean Journal of Science and Mathematics
Caribbean R — Caribbean Review
Caribbean S — Caribbean Studies
Caribbean Stud — Caribbean Studies
Caribb For — Caribbean Forester
Carib Geol Conf Trans — Caribbean Geological Conference. Transactions
Caribb Isl Water Resour Congr — Caribbean Islands Water Resources Congress
Caribb J Sci — Caribbean Journal of Science
Caribb J Sci Math — Caribbean Journal of Science and Mathematics
Caribb Med J — Caribbean Medical Journal
Caribb Q — Caribbean Quarterly
Caribb Stud — Caribbean Studies
Caribb Technol Abstr — Caribbean Technological Abstracts
Carib Bul — Caribbean Monthly Bulletin
Caribb Yb Int Relat — Caribbean Yearbook of International Relations
Carib Forest Rio Piedras — Caribbean Forester (Rio Piedras, Puerto Rico)
Carib Jour Sc Mayaguez — Caribbean Journal of Sciences (Mayaguez, Puerto Rico)
Carib J Rel St — Caribbean Journal of Religious Studies
Carib LJ — Caribbean Law Journal
Carib Med J — Caribbean Medical Journal
Carib Q — Caribbean Quarterly
Carib Quart Kingston Port of Spain — Caribbean Quarterly (Kingston, Jamaica, Port of Spain, Trinidad)
Carib Rev — Caribbean Review
Carib Stud — Caribbean Studies
Carib Updat — Caribbean Update
Caricom Persp — Caricom Perspective
Caridad Cienc Arte — Caridad Ciencia y Arte
Caries Res — Caries Research
Carindex Soc Sci — Carindex Social Sciences
Carinthia — Carinthia. Mitteilungen des Geschichtsverein fuer Kaernten
Carinthia 2 Sonderh — Carinthia 2. Sonderheft
CARIS — Current Agricultural Research Information System
CarJos — Cahiers de Josephologie
Car J Pharm — Carolina Journal of Pharmacy
Car J Sci — Caribbean Journal of Science
CARLD — Chicorel Abstracts to Reading and Learning Disabilities
Carle Clin Carle Found Sel Pap — Carle Clinic and Carle Foundation. Selected Papers
Carle Hosp Clin Carle Found Sel Pap — Carle Hospital Clinic and Carle Foundation. Selected Papers
Carle Sel Pap — Carle Selected Papers
Carleton Misc — Carleton Miscellany
Carleton Ottawa Math Lecture Note Ser — Carleton-Ottawa Mathematical Lecture Note Series
Carleton Univ Dep Geol Geol Pap — Carleton University. Department of Geology. Geological Paper
Carleton Univ Dept Geology Geol Paper — Carleton University. Department of Geology. Geological Paper
Car LJ — Carolina Law Journal
Carl Mis — Carleton Miscellany
CarlN — Carleton Newsletter
Carl Rpm — Repertorium fuer Physikalische Technik, fuer Mathematik und Astronomische Instrumentenkunde. Carl
Carlsbergfond Beret — Carlsbergfondet, Frederiksborgmuseet, Ny Carlsbergfondet. Beretning
Carlsbergfondet Arsskr — Carlsbergfondet, Frederiksborgmuseet, Ny Carlsbergfondet. Arsskrift

Carlsbergfond Frederiksborgmus NyCarlsbergfond Aaskr — Carlsbergfondet, Frederiksborgmuseet, NyCarlsbergfond, Aarskrift

Carlsberg Res Commun — Carlsberg Research Communications

Carlsruhe Vh Nw Vr — Verhandlungen des Naturwissenschaftlichen Vereins (Carlsruhe)

Carlyle Newslett — Carlyle Newsletter

CarM — Carleton Miscellany

Carmarthenshire Antiq — Carmarthenshire Antiquary

Car Mech — Car Mechanics

Car Med J — Caribbean Medical Journal

Carm Lat Epigr — Carmina Latina Epigraphica

CARN — Cairn. Archives of the Canadian Rockies Newsletter

CARN — Carnets de l'Enfance/Assignment Children

Carnation Craft ACS — Carnation Craft. American Carnation Society

Carnation Nutr Educ Ser — Carnation Nutrition Education Series

Carnegie Coll Physical Ed Research Papers — Carnegie College of Physical Education (Leeds). Research Papers in Physical Education

Carnegie Inst Technol Bull Coal Min Invest — Carnegie Institute of Technology. Bulletin. Coal Mining Investigations

Carnegie Inst Technol Coal Res Lab Contri — Carnegie Institute of Technology. Coal Research Laboratory. Contribution

Carnegie Inst Technol Coal Res Lab Contrib — Carnegie Institute of Technology. Coal Research Laboratory. Contributions

Carnegie Inst Technol Coop Bull Min Metall Invest — Carnegie Institute of Technology. Cooperative Bulletin. Mining and Metallurgical Investigations

Carnegie Inst Washington Pap Geophys Lab — Carnegie Institution of Washington. Papers from the Geophysical Laboratory

Carnegie Inst Washington Yb — Carnegie Institution of Washington Yearbook

Carnegie Inst Wash Pap Geophys Lab — Carnegie Institution of Washington. Papers from the Geophysical Laboratory

Carnegie Inst Wash Publ — Carnegie Institution of Washington. Publication

Carnegie Inst Wash Year Book — Carnegie Institution of Washington. Year Book

Carnegie Mag — Carnegie Magazine

Carnegie-Mellon Univ TRI Res Rep — Carnegie-Mellon University, Pittsburgh. Transportation Research Institute. TRI Research Report

Carnegie Mus An Mem — Carnegie Museum of Natural History. Annals. Memoirs

Carnegie Mus Annals — Carnegie Museum of Natural History. Annals

Carnegie Mus Bot Pam — Carnegie Museum Botany Pamphlet

Carnegie Mus Nat Hist Annu Rep — Carnegie Museum of Natural History. Annual Report

Carnegie Mus Nat Hist Spec Publ — Carnegie Museum of Natural History. Special Publication

Carnegie Res Papers — Carnegie Research Papers

Carnegie Scholarship Mem — Carnegie Scholarship Memoirs

Carn Enfance — Carnets de l'Enfance/Assignment Children

Carnes Merc — Carnes y Mercados

Carnet Artistes — Carnet des Artistes. Art Ancien, Art Moderne, Arts Appliques

Carnet Mus — Carnet Musical

Carnet Sem — Carnet de la Semaine

Carnets Enfance — Carnets de l'Enfance/Assignment Children

Carnets Enfance Assignment Child — Carnets de l'Enfance/Assignment Children

Carnets Zool — Carnets de Zoologie

Carniv Genet Newsl — Carnivore Genetics Newsletter

Carnivore Genet Newsl — Carnivore Genetics Newsletter

Carn Jb — Carnuntum Jahrbuch

CarnM — Carnegie Magazine

Carn Mag — Carnegie Magazine

Carn SE — Carnegie Series in English

Carn Ser Am Educ — Carnegie Series in American Education

Carnuntum Jb — Carnuntum-Jahrbuch

Caro — Carovana. Rassegna Bimestrale di Cultura

CAROEJ — Carolinea

Carol Biol Readers — Carolina Biology Readers

Carol Camellias — Carolina Camellias

Carolim Anal Therm — Carolimetrie et Analyse Thermique

Carolina Lecture Ser — Carolina Lecture Series

Carolina Q — Carolina Quarterly

Carol J Pharm — Carolina Journal of Pharmacy

Carol Plann — Carolina Planning

Carol Q — Carolina Quarterly

Carol Tips — Carolina Tips

Carotenoid Chem Biochem Proc Int Symp Carotenoids — Carotenoid Chemistry and Biochemistry. Proceedings of the InternationalSymposium on Carotenoids

Carotenoids Photosynth — Carotenoids in Photosynthesis

Carousel Q — Carousel Quarterly

CarP — Carolina Playbook

Carpet Rev — Carpet Review

CarQ — Caribbean Quarterly

CAR Q — Carolina Quarterly

Car Quart — Caribbean Quarterly

CarR — Caribbean Review

Carrobbio — Carrobbio; Rivista di Studi Bolognesi

Carroll Bus Bul — Carroll Business Bulletin

CarS — Caribbean Studies

CARSCT — Canada. Agrometeorology Research and Service. Chemistry and Biology Research Institute. Research Branch Technical Bulletin

Car Stud — Caribbean Studies

Carswell's Prac — Carswell's Practice Cases

Carswell's Prac Cases — Carswell's Practice Cases

Cart — Cartel; Review of Monopoly Development and Consumer Protections

C Art — Connaissance des Arts

Carta (Chile) Inst Invest Geol — Carta (Chile). Instituto de Investigaciones Geologicas

Carta Geol Chile — Carta Geologica de Chile

Carta Geol Chile Inst Invest Geol — Carta Geologica de Chile. Instituto de Investigaciones Geologicas

Carta Mens Rio — Carta Mensal (Rio de Janeiro)

Carta Sem Mex — Carta Semanal (Mexico, DF)

Carte — Carte Segrete

Cart J — Cartographic Journal

Cartogr — Cartography

Cartogr Geograph Inf Syst — Cartography and Geographic Information System

Cartogr J — Cartographic Journal

Cart Sax — Cartularium Saxonicum

Carus Math Monogr — Carus Mathematical Monographs

Carus Math Monographs — Carus Mathematical Monographs

CarV — Carnets Viatoriens

CARV — Carnivore. Carnivore Research Institute

Carvao Inf Pesqui — Carvao, Informacao, e Pesquisa

Car Wom — Career Woman

CARYAB — Caryologia

Cary Part — Cary. Partnership

CAS — Canadian Business Review

CAS — Central Asiatic Studies

CAS — Chemical Abstracts Service. Report

CAS — Christelijk Arbeidssecretariaat

CAS — Current Australian Serials

CASA — Cronache di Archeologia e di Storia dell'Arte

CasaA — Casa de las Americas

Casa Am Hav — Casa de las Americas (La Habana)

Casabella Cont — Casabella Continuita

Casabella Costr — Casabella-Costruzione

Casa Cult Equat Quito — Casa de la Cultura Ecuatoriana (Quito)

CASAE — Cahier. Supplement aux Annales du Service des Antiquites de l'Egypte

Cas Ceskeho Mus — Casopis Ceskeho Museum

Cas Ceske Spol Ent — Casopis Ceske Spolecnosti Entomologicke

Cas Cesk Lek — Casopis Ceskenho Lekarstnitva

Cas Ceskoslov Lekarn — Casopis Ceskoslovenskeho Lekarnictva

Cas Cesk Spolecnosti Entomol — Casopis Ceskoslovenske. Spolecnosti Entomologicke

Cas Cesk Spol Entomol — Casopis Ceskoslovenske. Spolecnosti Entomologicke

CaSE — Carnegie Series in English

CASEA — Cancer Seminar

Case & Com — Case and Comment

Casella Reidel Arch Wiss Reihe Cerebrum — Casella-Reidel Archiv. Wissenschaftliche Reihe. Cerebrum I

Case Stud At Phys — Case Studies in Atomic Physics

Case Stud Dent Emerg — Case Studies in Dental Emergencies

Case Stud Health Adm — Case Studies in Health Administration

Case West J Int Law — Case Western Reserve. Journal of International Law

Case West Reserve — Case Western Reserve University. Studies in Anthropology

Case West Reserve J Int Law — Case Western Reserve Journal of International Law

Case West Reserve L Rev — Case Western Reserve. Law Review

Case West Reserve Univ Dep Mech Aerosp Eng Tech Rep — Case Western Reserve University. Department of Mechanical and AerospaceEngineering. Technical Report FTAS/TR

Case West Res J Int'l L — Case Western Reserve. Journal of International Law

Case West Res L Rev — Case Western Reserve. Law Review

Case W Res — Case Western Reserve. Journal of International Law

Case W Reserve Law R — Case Western Reserve. Law Review

Case W Reserve L Rev — Case Western Reserve. Law Review

Case W Res J Int L — Case Western Reserve. Journal of International Law

Case W Res L Rev — Case Western Reserve. Law Review

Casflow C — Cashflow Classics

Cashflow — Cashflow Magazine

Cashflow M — Cashflow Magazine

CASI Trans — CASI [Canadian Aeronautics and Space Institute] Transactions

CASJ — Catgut Acoustical Society Journal

CAsJ — Central Asiatic Journal

CASJ — Chester and North Wales Architectural, Archaeological, and Historical Society. Journal

Cas Lek Cesk — Casopis Lekaru Ceskych

CASL Rev Cient — CASL [Centro Academico Sarmento Leite] Revista Cientifica

Cas Matice Morav — Casopis Matice Moravske

Cas Mineral Geol — Casopis pro Mineralogii a Geologii

Cas Morav Mus (Brne) — Casopis Moravskeho Musea (Brne)

Cas Morav Mus Vedy Prir — Casopis Moravskeho Musea. Vedy Prirodni

Cas Morav Mus Zemsk — Casopis Moravskeho Musea Zemskeho. Acta Musei Moraviensis

CASNAH — Casopis Slezskeho Muzea. Serie A. Vedy Prirodni

Cas Nar Muz Oddil Priroddoved — Casopis Narodniho Muzea. Oddil Priroddovedny

Cas Nar Muz (Prague) — Casopis Narodniho Muzea (Prague)

Cas Nar Muz Praze Rada Prirodoved — Casopis Narodniho Muzea v Praze. Rada Prirodovedna

Cas Narod Muz — Casopis Narodniho Muzea. Historicke Muzeum Rocnik

Casopis — Casopis pro Pestovani Mathematiky a Fysiky

Casopis Moravskeho Musea — Casopis Moravskeho Musea. Vedy Spolcenske

Casopis Pest Mat — Ceskoslovenska Akademie Ved. Casopis pro Pestovani Matematiky

Casopis Vlast Spolku Olomouci — Casopis Vlasteneckeho Spolku Muzejniho v Olomouci

Casop Matice Morav — Casopis Matice Moravske

Casop Morav Muz — Casopis Moravskeho Muzea

Casop Pro Pravni A Statni Vedu — Casopsis pro Pravni a Statni Vedu

Casop Spolecnosti Pratel Starozitnosti — Casopis Spolecnosti Pratel Starozitnosti

C A Source Index — Chemical Abstracts Service. Source Index Quarterly

Casove Otaz Zemed — Casove Otazky Zemedelske
Casove Spisky Minist Zemed — Casove Spisky. Ministerstvo Zemedelstvi
Cas Ovocn Spolku Kral Ceske — Casopis Ovocnickeho Spolku Pro Kralovstvi Ceske
CASPA — Canadian Spectroscopy
Cas Prac Lek — Casopis Pracovniho Lekarstvi
Cas Prum Chem — Casopis pro Prumysl Chemicky
CAsR — Central Asian Review
CASR — Chemical Activity Status Report
CASRAT — Colorado State University. Annual Report
CASRBU — Connecticut. Storrs Agricultural Experiment Station. Research Report
Cass — Arret de la Cour de Cassation de Belgique
CASS — Canadian-American Slavic Studies
CASS — Computer Applications in Shipping and Shipbuilding
Cassava Prog Ann Rep — Cassava Program Annual Report
CASSAW — Cassinia
Cass Ch Reun — Cour de Cassation. Chambres Reunies
Cass Civ 1re — Cour de Cassation. Premiere Section Civile
Cass Civ 2e — Cour de Cassation. Deuxieme Section Civile
Cass Crim — Cour de Cassation. Criminelle
Cassella Riedel Arch Cerebrum 1 — Cassella Riedel Archiv Cerebrum 1
Cassel Salt Bath Furnaces Data Sh — Cassel Salt Bath Furnaces Data Sheet
CASSI — Chemical Abstracts Service Source Index
Cassier — Cassier's Magazine
Cassiers Engng Mon — Cassier's Engineering Monthly
Cassiers Ind Mgmt — Cassier's Industrial Management
Cassiers M — Cassier's Magazine
Cassiers Mag — Cassier's Magazine
Cassiers Mech Handl — Cassier's Mechanical Handling, Works Management, and Equipment
Cassinia J Ornithol East Penn South NJ Del — Cassinia. A Journal of Ornithology of Eastern Pennsylvania, Southern New Jersey, and Delaware
Cas Slez Mus Ser A Hist Nat — Casopis Slezskeho Musea. Serie A. Historia Naturalis. Acta Musei Silesiae
Cas Slezskeho Muz Ser A Sci Nat — Casopis Slezskeho Muzea. Serie A. Scientiae Naturales
Cas Slezskeho Muz Ser A Vedy Prir — Casopis Slezskeho Muzea. Serie A. Vedy Prirodni
Cas Slezskeho Muz Vedy Prir Acta Mus Silesiae Ser A Sci Nat — Casopis Slezskeho Muzea. Vedy Prirodni (Acta Musei Silesiae. Series A. Scientiae Naturales)
Cas Slezske Muz — Casopis Slezskeho Muzea
Cas Sl Muz — Casopis Slezskeho Muzea
Cassoe Nesl — Cassoe Newsletter
Cass Req — Cour de Cassation. Requetes
Cass Soc — Cour de Cassation. Sociale
CASTA — Colorado State University. Agricultural Experiment Station. Technical Bulletin
CASTAZ — Colorado State University. Experiment Station. Technical Bulletin
Castella Med — Castella Medica
Cast Eng — Casting Engineering
Cast Eng/Foundry World — Casting Engineering/Foundry World
Cast Forg — Casting and Forging
Cast Forg Heat Treat (Osaka) — Casting, Forging, and Heat Treatment (Osaka)
Cast Forg (Osaka) — Casting and Forging (Osaka)
Cast Forg Steel — Casting and Forging of Steel
Cast Met — Cast Metals
Cast Met Inst Electr Ironmelting Conf — Cast Metals Institute. Electric Ironmelting Conference
Cast Met Res J — Cast Metals Research Journal
CA St Michel de Cuxa — Cahiers de Saint-Michel de Cuxa
Cast Stone Archit — Cast Stone Architecture and Concrete Design
CA Stud Class Ant — California Studies in Classical Antiquity
CASU — Canadian Surveyor
CASUA — Canadian Surveyor
Casualt Un J — Casualties Union Journal
Casualty Simul — Casualty Simulation
C A Subaqu — Cahiers d'Archeologie Subaquatique
CASUD7 — Cancer Surveys
Casuist Med Chir — Casuistica Medico-Chirurgica
CASURSS — Comptes Rendus. Academie des Sciences de l'Union des Republiques Sovietiques Socialistes
Cas W Res L Rev — Case Western Reserve. Law Review
CasZ — Casopis za Zgodovino in Narodopisje
Cas Zemsk Spolku Step Kral Ceske — Casopis Zemskeho Spolku Steparskeho Pro Kralovstvi Ceske. Zeitschrift des Landes-Obstbaumzucht-Vereines fuer das Koenigreich Boehmen
CAT — Cahiers d'Analyse Textuelle. Les Belles Lettres
Cat — Catacomb
Cat — Catalyst
Cat — Catechistes
CAT — Commentaire de l'Ancien Testament
CaT — Computers and Translation
Cata — Catalyst
Cat Act Volc Wld — Catalogue of the Active Volcanoes of the World including Solftara Fields. International Volcanological Association
Cat A Exhib Scient Instrum — Catalogue of the Annual Exhibition of Scientific Instruments. Physical Society
Catal Chem — Catalysts in Chemistry
Catal Cod Hag Gr B — Catalogus Codicum Hagiographicorum Graecorum Bibliothecae Nationalis Parisiensis
Catal Cod Hag Gr Ger — Catalogus Codicum Hagiographicorum Graecorum Germaniae, Gelgii, Angliae

Catal Cod Hag La Ant — Catalogus Codicum Hagiographicorum Latinorum Antiquiorum Saeculo XVI qui Asservantur in Bibliotheca Nationalis Parisiensis
Catal Cod Hag Lat — Catalogus Codicum Hagiograhicorum Latinorum Bibliothecarum Romanorum Praeter quam Vaticanae
Catal Environ Qual — Catalyst for Environmental Quality
Catal Graec Germ — Catalogus Codicum Hagiographicorum Graecorum Germaniae, Gelgii, Angliae
Catal Graec Vatic — Catalogus Codicum Hagiographicorum Graecorum Bibliothecae Vaticanae
Catal Gr Paris — Catalogus Codicum Hagiographicorum Graecorum Bibliothecae Nationalis Parisiensis
Catal Lat Brux — Catalogus Codicum Hagiographicorum Bibliothecae Regiae Bruxellensis
Catal Lat Rom — Catalogus Codicum Hagiograhicorum Latinorum Bibliothecarum Romanorum Praeter quam Vaticanae
Catal Lett — Catalysis Letters
Catal Lett Suppl — Catalysis Letters. Supplement
Catal Met Complexes — Catalysis by Metal Complexes
Catal Org React — Catalysis of Organic Reactions
Catal Org Synth — Catalysis in Organic Syntheses
Catal Proc Int Congr — Catalysis. Proceedings of the International Congress on Catalysis
Catal Rev — Catalysis Reviews
Catal Rev Sci Eng — Catalysis Reviews. Science and Engineering
Catal Sci Technol Proc Tokyo Conf — Catalytic Science and Technology. Proceedings. Tokyo Conference on Advanced Catalytic Science and Technology
Catal Today — Catalysis Today
Catalyst Envir Qual — Catalyst for Environmental Quality
Cat Am Amphib Reptiles — Catalogue of American Amphibians and Reptiles
Cat and Classif Q — Cataloging and Classification Quarterly
Catania Ac Gioen At — Atti dell' Accademia Gioenia di Scienze Naturali in Catania
Catania Ac Gioen Bll — Bullettino Mensile della Accademia Gioenia di Scienze Naturali in Catania
Catania At Ac Gioen — Atti dell' Accademia Gioenia di Scienze Naturali in Catania
Cat Br Off Publications — Catalogue of British Official Publications
Cat Calcareous Nannofossils — Catalogue of Calcareous Nannofossils. Edizioni Tecnoscienza
Cat Charts Cst Pilots Tide Tables Wash — Catalogue of Charts, Coast Pilots, and Tide Tables (Washington)
Cat Cod Astr Gr — Catalogus Codicum Astrologorum Graecorum
Cat Disturb Ionosph — Catalogue of Disturbances in Ionosphere, Geomagnetic Field, Field Intensity of Radio Wave, Cosmic Ray, Solar Phenomena, and Other Related Phenomena
Cateques Latinoamer — Catequesis Latinoamericana
Cater — Catering
Cat Ess Helices — Catalogue d'Essais d'Helices. Grande Soufflerie de Paris
Cat Expos Instrum Mater Scient — Catalogue de l'Exposition d'Instruments et Materiel Scientifiques. Societe Francaise de Physique
Cat Faunae Austriae — Catalogus Faunae Austriae
Cat Faunae Pol — Catalogus Faunae Poloniae
Cat Fossilium Austriae — Catalogus Fossilium Austriae
CATGD4 — Centro Internacional de Agricultura Tropical [CIAT]. Series GE
Cath — Catholica
CatH — Catholic Historical Review
Cath — Catholicisme. Hier, Aujourd'hui, Demain
CATHA4 — Carinthia 2
Cath Anthropol Confer Pubns — Catholic Anthropological Conference Publications
Cath Bibl Q — Catholic Biblical Quarterly
Cath Bib Q — Catholic Biblical Quarterly
Cath Charis — Catholic Charismatic
Cath Char R — Catholic Charities Review [New York]
Cath Choirmaster — Catholic Choirmaster
Cath Doc — Catholic Documentation
Cath Ed R — Catholic Educational Review
Cath Educ Assn Bul — Catholic Educational Association. Bulletin
Cath Educ R — Catholic Educational Review
Cath Educ Rev — Catholic Educational Review
Cath Ency — Catholic Encyclopedia
Cathet Cardiovasc Diagn — Catheterization and Cardiovascular Diagnosis
Catheterization Cardiovasc Diagn — Catheterization and Cardiovascular Diagnosis
Cath His R — Catholic Historical Review
Cath Hist R — Catholic Historical Review
Cath Hist Rev — Catholic Historical Review
Cath Hosp — Catholic Hospital
CathHR — Catholic Historical Review
Cathl — Catholic Periodical and Literature Index
Cath Law — Catholic Lawyer
Cath Lawyer — Catholic Lawyer
Cath Libr Wld — Catholic Library World
Cath Lib W — Catholic Library World
Cath Lib World — Catholic Library World
Cath M — Catholic Mind
Cath Mind — Catholic Mind
Cathol Hist Rev — Catholic Historical Review
Cathol Hosp — Catholic Hospital
Catholic Doc — Catholic Documentation
Catholic Law — Catholic Lawyer
Catholic Trust — Catholic Trustee
Catholic UALR — Catholic University of America. Law Review
Catholic ULR — Catholic University. Law Review
Catholic U L Rev — Catholic University. Law Review
Catholic Univ Amer Biol Ser — Catholic University of America. Biological Series
Catholic Univ L Rev — Catholic University. Law Review

Catholic W — Catholic Weekly
Cathol Libr World Glen Ellyn — Catholic Library World (Glen Ellyn, III)
Cathol Nurse (Wallsend) — Catholic Nurse (Wallsend)
Cathol Period Index — Catholic Periodical Index
Cathol Period Lit Index — Catholic Periodical and Literature Index
Cathol Univ Am Biol Stud — Catholic University of America. Biological Studies
Cath-Presb — Catholic-Presbyterian
Cath Rec Soc — Catholic Record Society
Cath Rec Soc Pub — Catholic Record Society. Publications
Cath Sch J — Catholic School Journal
Cath UALR — Catholic University of America. Law Review
Cath U Law — Catholic University of America. Law Review
Cath ULR — Catholic University. Law Review
Cath UL Rev — Catholic University. Law Review
Cath Univ Am Biol Stud — Catholic University of America. Biological Studies
Cath Univ Bull — Catholic University. Bulletin
Cath Univ Bull — Catholic University of America. Bulletin
Cath Univ Law Rev — Catholic University of America. Law Review
Cath Univ Stud Am Church Hist — Catholic University of America. Studies in American Church History
CathW — Catholic World
Cath Work — Catholic Worker
Cath World — Catholic World
Cat Index — Catalogue and Index. Library Association Cataloguing and Indexing Group
Cat Invertebres Suisse Mus Hist Nat Geneve — Catalogue des Invertebres de la Suisse. Museum d'Histoire Naturelle de Geneve
Cations Biol Significance — Cations of Biological Significance
Cat Life Pol — Catholic Life in Poland
CATNI — Catchword and Trade Name Index
Cato J — Cato Journal
CATRAY — Canning Trade
CATRB — Calcified Tissue Research [Later, Calcified Tissue International]
CATS — Computer Assisted Trading System
Cat Show Merch — Catalog Showroom Merchandiser
CATSS — UTLAS [University of Toronto Library Automation System] Catalogue SupportSystem
Cattaneo Bb Farm — Biblioteca di Farmacia, Chimica. Cattaneo
Cattaneo G Farm — Giornale di Farmacia (Cattaneo)
Cat Tel — Catholic Telegraph
Cattlemen Beef Mag — Cattlemen. The Beef Magazine
Cat Trans C — Catalogus Translationum et Commentariorum/Medieval and Renaissance Latin Translations and Commentaries
Cat Type Invertebr Fossils Geol Surv Can — Catalogue of Type Invertebrate Fossils. Geological Survey of Canada
CATUA — Chimica Acta Turcica
CAU — Construccion Arquitectura Urbanismo
Caucas Rev — Caucasian Review
CAUTA — Canadian Automotive Trade
CAUT ACPU Bul — Canadian Association of University Teachers/Association Canadienne des Professeurs d'Universite. Bulletin
CAV — Chambre de Commerce et d'Industrie d'Anvers. Bulletin
Cava Crist Svizz — Cava-Cristallas Svizzer
Cavalry J — Cavalry Journal
Cavalry Jour — Cavalry Journal. United States Cavalry Association. Journal
Caveat — Caveat Emptor
Cave Geol — Cave Geology
Cave Res Group GB Trans — Cave Research Group of Great Britain. Transactions
Cave Res Group Great Britain Trans — Cave Research Group of Great Britain. Transactions
Cave Res Group News — Cave Research Group of Great Britain. Newsletter
Cave Sci — Cave Science
CAVOAZ — Contribuicoes Avulsas. Instituto Oceanografico Sao Paulo
CaVS — Cahiers du Vingtieme Siecle
CaW — Catholic World
CAW — China Aktuell
CAWE — Canada West
CA WILJ — California Western International Law Journal
CA WLR — California Western Law Review
Cawthron Inst (Nelson NZ) Rep — Cawthron Institute (Nelson, New Zealand). Report
Cawthron Inst Publs — Cawthron Institute. Publications
Cax — Caxton Magazine
CAXPAE — Connecticut. Storrs Agricultural Experiment Station. Progress Report
CAYBAB — Clean Air Year Book
CB — Cahiers Bruxellois
CB — Cahiers de Bruges
CB — Cahiers de Byrsa
CB — Caiman Barbudo
CB — Canadian Business
CB — Christian Businessman
CB — Classical Bulletin
CB — Collection des Universites de France. Association Guillaume Bude
CB — Commentationes Balticae
CB — Congress Bulletin
CB — Correspondentieblad. Orgaan der Centrale van Hogere Rijks- en Gemeente-Ambtenaren
CB — Cuadernos Bibliograficos
CB — Cultura Biblica
CB — Cumulative Bulletin
CB — Current Bibliography on African Affairs
CB — Current Biography
CB — Customs Bulletin
CB — US Consulate [Hong Kong]. Current Background
C Ba — Cahiers du Bazadais

CBA — Comentarios Bibliograficos Americanos
CBA — COMLINE Business Analysis
CBA — Cronaca delle Belle Arti
CBA — Current Biotechnology Abstracts
CBA — Maandstatistiek van Bevolking en Volksgezondheid
CBAA — Current Bibliography on African Affairs
CBAC — Chemical-Biological Activities
CBAIAL — Contributions. Arctic Institute. Catholic University of America
CBalt — Commentationes Balticae
CBAND5 — Clinical and Biochemical Analysis
CBAQAB — Contribuciones Cientificas. Facultad de Ciencias Exactas y Naturales. Universidad de Buenos Aires. Serie Quimica
CBA Res Rep — CBA [Council for British Archaeology] Research Report
CBASA — Ciba Symposia
CBASF — Current Bibliography for Aquatic Sciences and Fisheries
CBB — Commercial Bank of Greece. Economic Bulletin
CBBAA2 — Communications in Behavioral Biology. Part A. Original Articles
CBBMA4 — Contributions. Institut de Botanique. Universite de Montreal
CBBMC — Ciencia Biologica
CB Bul — Conference Board. Information Bulletin
CBC — Cahiers Benjamin Constant
CBC — Cesare Barbieri Courier
CBCA — Canadian Business and Current Affairs
CB Cap A — Conference Board. Manufacturing Investment Statistics. Capital Appropriations
CB Cap Inv — Conference Board. Manufacturing Investment Statistics. Capital Investment and Supply Conditions
CBC (Citizens Budget Comm) Q — CBC (Citizens Budget Commission) Quarterly
CBCDO — Catalogue of Byzantine Coins in the Dumbarton Oaks Collection and in the Whittemore Collection
CBCNS — CBC [Canadian Broadcasting Corporation] Northern Service Press Releases
CB Corp Con — Conference Board. Report 869. Annual Survey of Corporate Contributions
CBCPA — Comparative Biochemistry and Physiology
CBCPAI — Comparative Biochemistry and Physiology
CBD — Commerce Business Daily
CBDB — Conference Board Data Base
CBE — Sociale Maandstatistiek
CB Ec 1990 — Conference Board. Report 864. US Economy to 1990
CBerry — Cahiers d'Archeologie et d'Histoire du Berry
CBESD — Caribbean Basin Economic Survey
CBF — Cell Biochemistry and Function
CBFAS — Canadian Bulletin of Fisheries and Aquatic Sciences
CBFL — Critical Bibliography of French Literature
CBFMA — Combustion and Flame
CBFMAO — Combustion and Flame
CBFSDB — Canadian Bulletin of Fisheries and Aquatic Sciences
CBFUDH — Cell Biochemistry and Function
CBG — Collationes Brugenses et Gandavenses
CBH Byz — Corpus Bruxellense Historiae Byzantinae
CBI — Canadian Banker [Formerly, Canadian Banker and ICB Review]
CBI — Canadian Business Index
CBI — Cumulative Book Index
CBI — Current Bibliographic Information
Cbib — Cabinet des Bibliophiles
CBIB — Censo de Bibliotecas
CBib — Cuba Bibliotecologica
CBI (Confederation British Industry) R — CBI (Confederation of British Industry) Review
CBI Forsk — CBI [Cement- och Betonginstitutet] Forskning
CBI Ind Trends — CBI [Confederation of British Industry] Industrial Trends
CBI Ind Trends Surv — CBI [Confederation of British Industry] Industrial Trends Survey
CBIMA — Cahiers de Biologie Marine
CBINA — Chemico-Biological Interactions
CB Index — Conference Board. Cumulative Index
CBI News — Confederation of British Industry. News
CBIOD — Cell Biophysics
CBIP — Canadian Books in Print
CBI Rapp — CBI [Cement- och Betonginstitutet] Rapporter
CBI Rep — CBI [Cement- och Betonginstitutet] Reports
CBI Res — CBI [Cement- och Betonginstitutet] Research
CB Iris — Correspondenzblatt des Entomologischen Vereins Iris zu Dresden
CBJ — Canadian Business Law Journal
CBJ — Connecticut Bar Journal
CBJ — Koopkracht. Blad voor de Konsument
CBJNA — Carbide Journal
CBK — Economies et Societes
CBKK — Chuban Kenkyu
CBL — Canadian Business Law Journal
CBL — Collectanea Biblica Latina
CBL — Cumulative Book List
CBL — Journal of Commercial Bank Lending
CBLBA — Ciba Lectures in Microbial Biochemistry
Cbl Brsch Not Ned — Correspondentieblad van de Broederschap der Notarissen in Nederland
CBLGA2 — Chronobiologia
Cbl Ges Forstw — Centralblatt fuer das Gesamte Forstwesen
CBLKAE — Contributions. Biological Laboratory. Kyoto University
CBLLAH — Contributions. Bears Bluff Laboratories
Cb LR — Columbia Law Review
CBl Rw — Centralblatt fuer Rechtswissenschaft
CBMDAW — Computers in Biology and Medicine
Cb Md Ws — Centralblatt fuer die Medicinischen Wissenschaften

CB Merger — Conference Board. Announcements of Mergers and Acquisitions

Cb Mn — Centralblatt fuer Mineralogie, Geologie, und Palaeontologie

CBMODY — Cell Biology Monographs

CBMRB7 — Computers and Biomedical Research

CBMW — Cypriote Bronzework in the Mycenaean World

CBN — Colonial Building Notes [*Watford, England*]

CBN — Correspondentieblad van de Broederschap der Notarissen in Nederland

CBNB — Chemical Business NewsBase

CBO Def S — Defense Spending and the Economy. Congressional Budget Office Study

CBO Med Ben — Changing the Structure of Medicare Benefits. Issues and Options. Congressional Budget Office

CBO Nat Gas — Understanding Natural Gas Price Control. Congressional Budget Office Study

CBP — CB Review (Philippines)

CBPAB5 — Comparative Biochemistry and Physiology. A. Comparative Physiology

CBPBB — Comparative Biochemistry and Physiology. B. Comparative Biochemistry

CBPBB8 — Comparative Biochemistry and Physiology. B. Comparative Biochemistry

CBPCBB — Comparative Biochemistry and Physiology. C. Comparative Pharmacology [*Later, Comparative Biochemistry and Physiology. C. Comparative Pharmacology and Toxicology*]

CBPCD — Ciments, Betons, Platres, Chaux

CBPCEE — Comparative Biochemistry and Physiology. C. Comparative Pharmacology and Toxicology

CBPI — Canadian Business Periodicals Index [*Later, Canadian Business Index*]

Cb Pl — Centralblatt fuer Physiologie

CBPRA — Cerebral Palsy Review

CBQ — Catholic Biblical Quarterly

CBr — Cadernos Brasileiros

CBR — Canadian Bar Review

CBR — China Business Report

CBR — China Business Review

CBR — Computer Book Review

CBRA — Canadian Book Review Annual

CBRBAH — Comunicaciones. Museo Argentino de Ciencias Naturales "Bernardino Rivadavia" e Instituto Nacional de Investigacion de las Ciencias Naturales. Ciencias Botanicas

CBRC — Current Book Review Citations

CB Review — Canadian Business Review

CBRI — Children's Book Review Index

CBRPDS — Cell Biology International Reports

CB Rpt 814 — Conference Board. Report 814. Managing the International Company. Building a Global Perspective

CB Rpt 815 — Conference Board. Report 815. Corporate Directorship Practices. Compensation

CB Rpt 818 — Conference Board. Report 818. Compensating Foreign Service Personnel

CB Rpt 820 — Conference Board. Report 820. Corporate Contributions Function

CB Rpt 821 — Conference Board. Report 821. Who Is Top Management

CB Rpt 823 — Conference Board. Report 823. Impact of Social Welfare Policies in the United States

CB Rpt 824 — Conference Board. Report 824. Insurance Deregulation. Issues and Perspectives

CB Rpt 825 — Conference Board. Report 825. Regional Perspectives on Energy Issues

CB Rpt 826 — Conference Board. Report 826. Planning for Staff and Support Units

CB Rpt 831 — Conference Board. Report 831. Flexible Employee Benefit Plans. Companies' Experiences

CB Rpt 832 — Conference Board. Report 832. Corporate Voluntary Contributions in Europe

CB Rpt 834 — Conference Board. Report 834. Corporate Aid Programs in Twelve Less-Developed Countries

CB Rpt 835 — Conference Board. Report 835. Adapting Products for Export

CB Rpt 837 — Conference Board. Report 837. Organizing and Managing for Energy Efficiency

CB Rpt 838 — Conference Board. Report 838. Managing Business-State Government Relations

CB Rpt 839 — Conference Board. Report 839. New Patterns in Organizing for Financial Management

CB Rpt 842 — Conference Board. Report 842. Research and Development. Key Issues for Management

CB Rpt 844 — Conference Board. Report 844. Manufacturing. New Concepts and New Technology toMeet New Competition

CB Rpt 845 — Conference Board. Report 845. Organizing Corporate Marketing

CB Rpt 846 — Conference Board. Report 846. Economic Overview 1983. Medium-Term Corporate Forecasts

CB Rpt 847 — Conference Board. Report 847. Developing Strategic Leadership

CB Rpt 849 — Conference Board. Report 849. Innovations in Managing Human Resources

CB Rpt 850 — Conference Board. Report 850. Managing National Accounts

CB Rpt 851 — Conference Board. Report 851. From Owner to Professional Management. Problems in Transition

CB Rpt 852 — Conference Board. Report 852. Regulating International Data Transmission. Impact on Managing International Business

CB Rpt 853 — Conference Board. Report 853. International Patterns of Inflation. A Study in Contrasts

CB Rpt 855 — Conference Board. Report 855. Federal Budget Deficits and the US Economy

CB Rpt 859 — Conference Board. Report 859. Inflation Adjustment of the Individual Income Tax. Indexation or Legislation

CB Rpt 860 — Conference Board. Report 860. Managing Older Workers. Company Policies and Attitudes

CB Rpt 861 — Conference Board. Report 861. Managing International Public Affairs

CB Rpt 863 — Conference Board. Report 863. Corporate R & D Strategy. Innovation and Funding Issues

CB Rpt 865 — Conference Board. Report 865. New Look in Wage Policy and Employee Relations

CB Rpt 867 — Conference Board. Report 867. Facing Strategic Issues. New Planning Guides and Practices

CB Rpt 868 — Conference Board. Report 868. Corporations and Families. Changing Practices andPerspectives

CB Rpt 870 — Conference Board. Report 870. Trends in Corporate Education and Training

CB Rpt 872 — Conference Board. Report 872. World Economy in the 1980's

CB Rpt 873 — Conference Board. Report 873. Refocusing the Company's Business

CB Rpt 874 — Conference Board. Report 874. Developing New Leadership in a Multinational Environment

CB Rpt 876 — Conference Board. Report 876. Competitive Leverage

CB Rpt 881 — Conference Board. Report 881. Meeting Human Needs. Corporate Programs and Partnerships

CB Rpt 882 — Conference Board. Report 882. Annual Survey of Corporate Contributions. 1986 Edition

CB Rpt 883 — Conference Board. Report 883. Corporate Strategies for Controlling Substance Abuse

CB Rpt 886 — Conference Board. Report 886. Board Committees in European Companies

CB Rpt 887 — Conference Board. Report 887. Screening Requests for Corporate Contributions

CBR Retail — Current Business Reports. Annual Retail Trade

CBR Retl A — Current Business Reports. Advanced Monthly Retail Sales

CBR Retl M — Current Business Reports. Monthly Retail Trade Sales and Inventories

CBR Retl S — Current Business Reports. Revised Monthly Retail Sales and Inventories for January, 1974 - December, 1983

CBRS — Children's Book Review Service

CBR Whsl S — Current Business Reports. Revised Monthly Wholesale Trade Sales and Inventoriesfor January, 1975 - December, 1984

CBR Whsl TM — Current Business Reports. Monthly Wholesale Trade Sales and Inventories

CBS — Canadian Business Magazine

CBS — Chugoku No Bunka To Shakai

CB Stat — Conference Board. Statistical Bulletin

CBSTB — Combustion Science and Technology

CBTIAE — Contributions. Boyce Thompson Institute

CBTNAT — Comunicari de Botanica

CBU — Canada's Business Climate

CBU — Canadian Business Review

CBU — Coal Age

C Bun H — Chugoku Bungaku Ho

CBV — Comenius-Blaetter fuer Volkserziehung

CBW — Centralblatt fuer Bibliothekwesen

CBW — Citibase-Weekly

CBW — Congress Bi-Weekly

C B Worldbus — Conference Board. Worldbusiness

CC — Cahiers du Cinema

CC — Careers and Courses

CC — Christian Century

CC — Cine Cubano

CC — Civilta Cattolica

CC — Code Civil Suisse

CC — Codice Civile Svizzero

CC — Codigo Civil

CC — Codrul Cosminului

CC — Computers and Composition

CC — Contemporary China

CC — Corpus Christianorum

CC — Cross Currents

CC — Currency Collector

CC — Current Contents

CC — Trabajos del Congreso Cientifico Latino-Americano

CCA — Cancer Chemotherapy Abstracts

CCA — Cancer Chemotherapy Annual

CCa — Civilta Cattolica

CCA — Computer and Control Abstracts

CC/A & H — Current Contents/Arts and Humanities

CCAB — Corsi di Cultura sull'Arte Ravennate e Bizantina

CC/AB & ES — Current Contents/Agriculture, Biology, and Environmental Sciences

CCACA — Croatica Chemica Acta

CCACB — CRC [*Chemical Rubber Company*] Critical Reviews in Analytical Chemistry

CCAG — Catalogus Codicum Astrologorum Graecorum

CCAJAV — Coffee and Cacao Journal

CCALA — Cry California

CCAM Info — CCAM [*Chambre de Commerce et d'Industrie de Marseille*] Information

C Can — Cinema Canada

CCanC — Cahier Canadien Claudel

CC & T Rpt — Corporate Controller's and Treasurer's Report

CCAODF — INTA [*Instituto Nacional de Tecnologia Agropecuaria*] Coleccion Cientifica

CCARB — Corso di Cultura dell'Arte Ravennate e Bizantina

CCARJ — Central Conference of American Rabbis. Journal

CCARY — CCAR [*Central Conference of American Rabbis*] Yearbook

CCAR/YB — Central Conference of American Rabbis. Year Book

CCATAR — Clinica Chimica Acta

CCatt — Civilta Cattolica

CCB — Center for Children's Books. Bulletin

C CB — Chemisches Central-Blatt

CCB-B — Center for Children's Books. Bulletin
CCBCAF — Computers in Chemical and Biochemical Research
CCBEA — Contamination Control. Biomedical Environments
CCBEAL — Contamination Control. Biomedical Environments
CCB Rev Choc Confect Bakery — CCB. Review for Chocolate Confectionery and Bakery
CCBUC — Cursos y Conferencias. Biblioteca de Universidade de Coimbra
CCBZAG — Contribuciones Cientificas. Facultad de Ciencias Exactas y Naturales. Universidad de Buenos Aires. Serie Zoologia
CCC — Canadian Criminal Cases
CCC — Chinese Cooperative Catalog
CCC — Citeaux. Commentarii Cistercienses
CCC — Civilta Classica e Cristiana
CCC — College Composition and Communication
CCCA — Corpus Cultus Cybelae Attidisque
CCCBAH — Canterbury Chamber of Commerce. Agricultural Bulletin
CCC Bul — Canterbury Chamber of Commerce. Bulletin
CCC Bull — Bulletin. Committee on Criminal Courts' Law and Procedure. Association of the B ar. City of New York
CCCCAK — Collection of Czechoslovak Chemical Communications
CCC Hist Bldg Ctee Min — Cumberland County Council. Historic Buildings Committee. Minutes
CCCist — Citeaux. Commentarii Cistercienses
CC/CP — Current Contents Clinical Practice
CCCQDV — CCQ. Critical Care Quarterly
CCCQDV — Critical Care Quarterly
CCD — Chambre de Commerce de Tunis. Bulletin
CCD — Commonwealth Employees Compensation Decisions
CCD — Computing Canada
CCDF — Codigo Civil para el Distrito Federal
CCDIDC — Catheterization and Cardiovascular Diagnosis
CCDS — Corpus Cultus Deae Syriae
CCE — Contributions to Canadian Economics
CCE — Cuadernos de Cultura Espanola
CCEA Newsl — Commonwealth Council for Educational Administration. Newsletter
CCEA SEA — Commonwealth Council for Educational Administration. Studies in Educational Administration
CCECA — CRC [*Chemical Rubber Company*] Critical Reviews in Environmental Control
CCEGP — Celtica. Caderno de Estudos Galaico-Portugueses
CCEI — Cahiers. Centre d'Etudes Irlandaises
CCELCN — Canadian Committee on Ecological Land Classification. Newsletter
CCEM — Construction, Civil Engineering, Mining
C Cent — Christian Century
C Centre Et Coutumes — Cahiers. Centre d'Etudes des Coutumes
CCER — Cahiers. Cercle Ernest Renan pour Libres Recherches d'Histoire du Christianisme
C Cer — Cahiers de la Ceramique, du Verre, et des Arts du Feu
CCE/RA — Revista de Antropologia. Casa de la Cultura Ecuatoriana, Nucleo del Azuay
CCERO — Cahiers. Centre d'Etudes de Recherche Operationnelle
CCF — Cahiers Economiques et Monetaires
CCF — Cesky Casopis Filologicky
CCFCSP — Canadian Centre for Folk Culture Studies Papers. National Museum of Man MercurySeries
CCFDD — CFI [*Ceramic Forum International*] Berichte der Deutschen Keramischen Gesellsch aft
CCFFAA — Contributions. Cushman Foundation for Foraminiferal Research
CCFS — Contributions of the Cushman Foundation (Sharon, Massachusetts and Washington, D.C.)
C C Furnas Meml Conf — C. C. Furnas Memorial Conference
C Ch — Corpus Christianorum
CCHCDE — Chung-Hua Chieh Heh Heh Hu Hsi Hsi Chi Ping Tsa Chih
(CCH) CLC — Company Law Cases (Commerce Clearing House)
CCHHAQ — Chishitsu Chosajo Hokoku
CCHI — Crain's Chicago Business
CCH Inh Est & Gift Tax Rep — Inheritance, Estate, and Gift Tax Reports (Commerce Clearing House)
CCHMD — Clinics in Chest Medicine
CCHNDD — Cell and Chromosome Newsletter
CCHNEE — Canadian Chemical News
CCHP — Chung Chi Hsueh-Pao
CCHPA — Jianzhu Xuebao
CChr — Corpus Christianorum
CCHR — Correspondentieblad van de Centrale voor Hogere Rijksambtenaren
CCI — Bulletin. Comite Central Industriel
CCIBAD — Coconut Research Institute. Bulletin
CCIEP — Courrier du Centre International des Etudes Poetiques
C Cinema — Cahiers du Cinema
CCISA — Canadian Controls and Instrumentation
CCist — Collectanea Cisterciensia
CCIWD — Canada. Centre for Inland Waters. Data Report Series
CCIWF — Canada. Centre for Inland Waters. Field Report Series
CCIWM — Canada. Centre for Inland Waters. Manuscript Report Series
CCIWT — Canada. Centre for Inland Waters. Technical Note Series
CCJ — Chung Chi Journal
CCJ — Communicator's Journal
CCJDA — Journal. Chemical Society. Section D. Chemical Communications
CCL — Canadian Children's Literature
CCL — Clinical Chemistry Lookout
CCL — Consumer Credit Letter
CCL — Crown Colonist (London)
CCL — Management Accounting
CCLA Record — CCLA [*Correspondence Chess League of Australia*] Record
CCLat — Corpus Christianorum. Series Latina

CCLC — Cuadernos del Congreso por la Libertad de la Cultura
CCLCDY — Chinese Journal of Oncology
CCLE — Crain's Cleveland Business
CCLIB — Cardiovascular Clinics
CCLP — Contents of Current Legal Periodicals
CCLP Contents Curr Leg Period — CCLP. Contents of Current Legal Periodicals
CCLT — Canadian Cases on the Law of Torts
CCLTDH — Controlled Clinical Trials
CCM — Cahiers de Civilisation Medievale
CCM — Casopis Ceskenho Musea
CCM — Clays and Clay Minerals
CCM — Colby College. Monographs
CCM — Collection des Chefs-d'Oeuvre Meconnus
CCM — Conseiller du Commerce Exterieur
CCM — Critical Care Medicine
CCMDA — Cahiers. College de Medecine des Hopitaux de Paris
CCMDC — Critical Care Medicine
CCMe — Cahiers de Civilisation Medievale
CCMJ — Contents of Contemporary Mathematical Journals
CCML — Comprehensive Core Medical Library
CCMS Rep — CCMS [*North Atlantic Treaty Organization. Committee on the Challenges of Modern Society*] Report
CCN — Christian College News
CCN — Commonwealth Employees Compensation Notes
CCNB — Counciline Newsletter. Canadian Council for Native Business
CCNED — Chishitsu Chosasho Nenpo
CCNS — Christian College News Service
CCNTB — Current Concepts in Nutrition
CCO — Caribe Contemporaneo
C Co — Codigo Comercial
CCOD — Consultants and Consulting Organizations Directory
CCOMA — Chemical Communications
C Comm — Codice di Commercio
C Communisme — Cahiers du Communisme
CCont — Cuba Contemporanea
CCOP Newsl — Committee for Co-Ordination of Joint Prospecting for Mineral Resources in AsianOff-Shore Areas. Newsletter
C-CORE — C-CORE [*Centre for Cold Ocean Resources Engineering*] Publications
CCP — Checkout. Management im Modernen Handel
CCP — Current Commonwealth Publications
CCPBA — Cahiers. Comites de Prevention du Batiment et des Travaux Publics
CCPHDZ — Cancer Chemotherapy and Pharmacology
CCPPD — Canadian Communications and Power Conference. Proceedings
CCPRA — Canadian Chemical Processing
CCPTAY — Contraception
CCPYAF — Comments on Contemporary Psychiatry
CCQ — Critical Care Quarterly
CCQ Crit Care Q — CCQ: Critical Care Quarterly
CCQUA8 — Cleveland Clinic. Quarterly
CCQUD — Cataloging and Classification Quarterly
Ccr — Carnet Critique
CCR — Center City Report
CCR — Claflin College. Review
CCR — Company Credit Reports
CCRB — Cahiers de la Compagnie Madeleine Renaud-Jean Louis Barrault
CCRB — Compagnie Madeleine Renaud-Jean-Louis Barrault. Cahiers
CCRBES — CRC [*Chemical Rubber Company*] Critical Reviews in Biocompatibility
CCRCAR — Cancer Chemotherapy Screening Data
CCRCDU — Contributions. Central Research Institute for Food Crops
CCREE3 — Cell and Chromosome Research
C C Rev — Comparative Civilizations Review
CCRHEC — CRC [*Chemical Rubber Company*] Critical Reviews in Oncology/ Hematology
CCRHOS — Canadian Contractor Report of Hydrography and Ocean Sciences
CCRIDE — CRC [*Chemical Rubber Company*] Critical Reviews in Immunology
CCRIS — Chemical Carcinogenesis Research Information System
C Crit — Comparative Criticism
CCRNEU — CRC [*Chemical Rubber Company*] Critical Reviews in Clinical Neurobiology
CCROBU — Cancer Chemotherapy Reports. Part 1
CCRSEB — Canadian Contractor Report of Hydrography and Ocean Sciences
CCR (VIC) — County Court Reports (Victoria)
CCS — Cambridge Classical Studies
CCS — Cincinnati Classical Studies
CCS — Collectanea Commissionis Synodalis
CCS Cent Cienc Saude — CCS: Centro de Ciencias da Saude
CCS Cienc Cult Saude — CCS. Ciencia, Cultura, Saude
CCSN — Center for Cuban Studies Newsletter
CCSUBJ — Cancer Chemotherapy Reports. Part 2
CCSUDL — Carcinogenesis: A Comprehensive Survey
CCT — Cuadernos de Cultura Teatral
CCTC — Cambridge Classical Texts and Commentaries
CCTE — Conference of College Teachers of English of Texas. Proceedings
CCT Occ Pap — Canadian College of Teachers. Occasional Papers
CCTRDH — Cancer Clinical Trials
CCU — Cuadernos de la Catedra de Unamuno
C Cubano — Cine Cubano
CCUHCL — Cahiers. Centre Universitaire d'Histoire Contemporaine de Louvain
C Cul — Chinese Culture
CCult — Cronache Culturali
CCur — Cross Currents
CCV — Centro de Cultura Valenciana
CCX — Cinquante Millions de Consommateurs
CCYPBY — Cancer Chemotherapy Reports. Part 3
CCZ — Camara de Comercio de Bogota. Revista

CD — Cairo Document
CD — Candle
C/D — Car and Driver
CD — Child Development
CD — Ciudad de Dios
CD — Climatological Data
CD — Coleccion de Documentos Ineditos para la Historia de Ibero-America
CD — Comparative Drama
CD — Computer Design
CD — Comunidad
CD — Cuadernos para el Dialogo
CD — Current Digest
CdA — Camp de l'Arpa
CDA — Correo de los Andes (Argentina)
CdA — Cronache di Archeologia e di Storia dell'Arte
CDAB — Child Development Abstracts and Bibliography
CDAFI — Cahiers de la Delegation Archeologique Francaise. Iran
Cda Forest — Canada's Domestic Consumption of Forest Products, 1960-2000
CDA J — California Dental Association. Journal
CDAL — Cahiers des Ameriques Latines
CDALB — Concise Dictionary of American Literary Biography
CDAPAM — Conserve e Derivati Agrumari
CDAS — Computer Design and Architecture Series
CDB — Colecao Documentos Brasileiros
CDB — Community Development Bulletin
CdBv — Centralblatt der Bauverwaltung
C d Byrsa — Cahiers de Byrsa. Tunis. Musee Lavigerie
CDC — Centers for Disease Control. Publications
CDCP — Comparative Drama Conference. Papers
CdD — Ciudad de Dios
CDDED7 — Cancer Drug Delivery
CDDR — CD Data Report
CDE — Cahiers de Droit Europeen
CdE — Chronique d'Egypte
C de D — Cahiers de Droit
C d Eg — Chronique d'Egypte
CDEGA — Chiba Daigaku Engeigakubu Gakujutsu Hokoko
CDESDK — Contraceptive Delivery Systems
CDET — Crain's Detroit Business
CdF — Cuadernos de Filologia
CDFKAW — Annual Report. Institute of Food Microbiology. Chiba University
CDG — Cuadernos del Guayas
C Dgst — Catholic Digest
CDHA Jnl — CDHA [*California Dental Hygienists Association*] Journal
CDHBAF — Contributions. Dudley Herbarium
CDHF — Collection de Documents Inedits sur l'Histoire de France
CDHS — Canberra Historical Journal
CDHSDZ — Canadian Data Report of Hydrography and Ocean Sciences
CDHSDZ — Rapport Statistique Canadien sur l'Hydrographie et les Sciences Oceaniques
CDI — Commander's Digest
CDI — Cuadernos del Idioma
CDIF — Consumer Drug Information
CDIG — Coleccion de Documentos Ineditos sobre la Geografia y la Historia de Colombia. A.B.Cuervo [*Bogota*]
CDIH — Coleccion de Documentos Ineditos para la Historia de Espana [*Madrid*]
CDIHC — Coleccion de Documentos Ineditos para la Historia de Chile [*Santiago*]
CdIL — Cahiers. Institut de Linguistique de Louvain
CDIR — Coleccion de Documentos Ineditos Relativos al Descubrimiento, Conquista y Organizacion de las Posesiones Espanolas en America y Oceania [*Madrid*]
CDJM — Canadian Journal of Mathematics
CDKKA — Chiba Daigaku Kogakubu Kenkyu Hokoku
CdL — Cahiers de Lexicologie
CDL — Canadian Labour
CDL — Conferenze. Deselec Lefebvre
CDL — Le Commerce du Levant
CDL — Sainte-Beuve. Causeries du Lundi [*monograph*]
CDLA — Casa de las Americas
CdLF — Chronique des Lettres Francaises
CDM — Connaissance du Monde [*Paris*]
CDMBA — California. Division of Mines and Geology. Bulletin
CDMI — Canadian Dun's Market Identifiers
CDMI Bul — Centre de Documentation de Musique Internationale. Bulletin
CDMUAT — Contributions. Dudley Museum
CDN — Chicago Daily News
Cdn Aviat — Canadian Aviation
Cdn Bnk Rv — Canadian Banker and ICB [*Institute of Canadian Bankers*] Review
CD NC Agric Ext Serv — CD. North Carolina Agricultural Extension Service
Cdn Chem N — Canadian Chemical News
Cdn Chem P — Canadian Chemical Processing
Cdn Contrl — Canadian Controls and Instrumentation
Cdn Data — Canadian Datasystems
Cdn Elec E — Canadian Electronics Engineering
Cdn Elec P — Electronics Product News. Supplement to Canadian Electronics Engineering
Cdn Forest — Canadian Forest Industries
Cdn J ECE — Canadian Journal of Early Childhood Education
Cdn Mach D — Canadian Machinery and Metalworking Directory and Buying Guide
Cdn Machin — Canadian Machinery and Metalworking
Cdn Mine H — Canadian Mines Handbook
CDNOPT — Canadian Stock Options
CDNP — Chicago Daily News. Panorama
Cdn P & L — Future Population and Labour Force of Canada. Projections to the Year 2051
Cdn P & P — Canadian Pulp and Paper Industry

Cdn Pkg — Canadian Packaging
Cdn Pkg Mk — Statistical Report on Canada's Packaging Market
Cdn Plast — Canadian Plastics
Cdn Plast D — Canadian Plastics Directory and Buyer's Guide
CdO — Courrier d'Orleans
C Docum Ch Com Marseille — Cahiers de Documentation de la Chambre de Commerce et d'Industrie de Marseille
CDOEAP — Community Dentistry and Oral Epidemiology
CDP — Cahiers de Paris
CDP — Computer Products Directory
CdP — Cri de Paris
CDP Press Inf — Committee of Directors of Polytechnics Press. Information
CDPRD — Cancer Detection and Prevention
CDPRD4 — Cancer Detection and Prevention
CDR — Communicable Disease Report
CDR — Communications and Distributed Resources Report
CDr — Comparative Drama
C Dr Entreprise — Cahiers de Droit de l'Entreprise
CDREOR — Canada. Defence Research Establishment. Ottawa. Reports
C Dr Europ — Cahiers de Droit Europeen
CD ROM Prof — CD-ROM Professional
CD-ROM Rev — CD-ROM [*Compact Disc Read Only Memory*] Review
CDR Rev — CDR (Communicable Disease Report) Review
CDR Wkly (Online) — CDR Weekly (Online)
CDS — Cahiers du Sud
CdS — Corriere della Sera
CDS — Country Dance and Song
CDSEA — Chuo Daigaku Rikogakubu Kiyo
CDSKAT — Annual Report. Research Institute for Chemobiodynamics. Chiba University
CDSP — Current Digest of the Soviet Press
CDS Rev — Chicago Dental Society. Review
CDSS N — Country Dance and Song Society. News
CDU — Centre de Documentation Universitaire
CDU — Cronica de la UNESCO
CduC — Cahiers du Cinema
CDX — WVC Documentatie. Systematisch Overzicht met Samenvattingen van Nieuwe Boeken, Tijdschriftartikelen, Parlementaire Stukken
CE — Cahiers Evangiles
CE — Canadian Engineer
CE — Carmina Latina Epigraphica
CE — Catholic Encyclopedia
Ce — Celtica
CE — Central Opera Service. Bulletin
CE — Ceylon Economist
CE — Chemistry in Ecology
CE — Chief Executive
CE — Childhood Education
CE — Choice
CE — Christian East
CE — Chronique d'Egypte
CE — College English
CE — Comptes Economiques
CE — Construction and Engineering
CE — Consumer Electronics
CE — Corno Emplumado
CE — Correio Elvense
CE — Correo Erudito
C/E — Creation/Evolution
CE — Current Endocrinology
CEA — Cahiers des Etudes Anciennes
CEA — CEA [*College English Association*] Critic
CEA — Chemical Engineering Abstracts
CEA — Contributions to Economic Analysis
CEAAN — Center for Editions of American Authors. Newsletter
CEAC — CEA [*College English Association*] Chap Book
CEAC — CEA [*College Education Association*] Critic
CEA (Chem Eng Aust) — CEA (Chemical Engineering in Australia)
CEACrit — CEA [*College English Association*] Critic
CEAEA — Canadian Electrical Association. Transactions of the Engineering and Operating Division
CEAF — CEA [*College English Association*] Forum
CEAfr — Cahiers d'Etudes Africaines
CEAGD5 — Centro Agricola
CEAL — Centro Editor de America Latina
CE and S — Commonwealth Essays and Studies
CEA News — Canadian Education Association. Newsletter
CEA Notes Inf — CEA [*Cahiers d'Etudes Anciennes*] Notes d'Information
CEAPAT — Contribuicoes para o Estudo da Antropologia Portuguesa
CEAZD — Centro Azucar
CEB — Caribbean Educational Bulletin
CEB — Chronique d'Egypte. Bulletin Periodique de la Fondation Egyptologique Reine Elisabeth (Brussels)
CEBAL — Copenhagen School of Economics and Business Administration. Language DepartmentPublications
CEBCMT — Cidade de Evora. Boletim da Comissao Municipal de Turismo
CEBEA — Centre Belge d'Etude et de Documentation des Eaux. Bulletin Mensuel
CEBIEH — Cell Biology Monographs
CEBUD — Ceramika Budowlana
CEC — Cahiers d'Etudes Cathares
CEC — Cayapos e Carajas. Conceicao do Araguaya
CEC — Conselho Estadual de Cultura
CECEB — Chemical Economy and Engineering Review
CECED9 — Commission des Communautes Europeennes/Commissione delle Comunita Europee/Commission of the European Communities. Eur Report

CECED9 — Kommission der Europaeischen Gemeinschaften
Ceceno-Ingus Gos Ped Inst Ucen Zap — Ceceno-Ingusskii Gosudarstvennyi Pedagogiceskii Institut. Ucenye Zapiski
CECHAF — Cereal Chemistry
Cech Arch Dermatol Syph — Cechoslovakisches Archiv fuer Dermatologie und Syphilis
CECIAI — Cecidologia Indica
Cecidol Indica — Cecidologia Indica
Cecidol Int — Cecidologia Internationale
CECJA — Civil Engineering, Construction, and Public Works Journal
CECN — Canadian Environmental Control Newsletter
CECOB — Cement and Concrete
C Econ Bretagne — Cahiers Economiques de Bretagne
C Econ Bruxelles — Cahiers Economiques de Bruxelles
C Econ Monet — Cahiers Economiques Monetaires
C Econ Soc — Cahiers Economiques et Sociaux
CECRA — CEC [Consolidated Electrodynamics Corporation] Recordings
CECTA — Cellulose Chemistry and Technology
CECTBI — CEPLAC [Comissao Executiva do Plano da Lavoura Cacaueira] Comunicacao Tecnica
CECU — Concursos y Certamenes Culturales
C Ed — Childhood Education
CEd — Communication Education
CEDAD2 — Clinical and Experimental Dialysis and Apheresis
CEDB — Currency Exchange Database
CEDEDE — Clinical and Experimental Dermatology
CEDLA/B — Boletin de Estudios Latinoamericanos. Centro de Estudios y Documentacion Latinoamericanos
CEDMB2 — Clinics in Endocrinology and Metabolism
CED Newsl — CED [Committee for Economic Development] Newsletter
CEDP — Centre d'Etudes et de Documentation Paleontologiques
CEE — Commerce Exterieur Albanais
CEEGAM — Clinical Electroencephalography
CEEN — Cuadernos de Etnologia y Etnografia de Navarra
CEER — Chemical Economy and Engineering Review
CEER (Chem Econ Eng Rev) — CEER (Chemical Economy and Engineering Review)
CEESTEM/TM — Tercer Mundo y Economia Mundial. Centro de Estudios Economicos y Sociales del Tercer Mundo
CeF — Ce Fastu
CEF — Coleccion Etnografia y Folklore [La Paz]
CE Focus — Continuing Education in Nursing Focus
C Eg — Chronique d'Egypte
CEG — Competitive Events Guidelines
CEG — Cuadernos de Estudios Gallegos
CEGB Abs — CEGB [Central Electricity Generating Board] Abstracts
CEGB Cent Electr Generating Board — CEGB (Central Electricity Generating Board) Research
CEGB Dig — CEGB [Central Electricity Generating Board] Digest
CEGB Res — CEGB [Central Electricity Generating Board] Research
CEGB Tech Disclosure Bull — CEGB [Central Electricity Generating Board] Technical Disclosure Bulletin
CEGFA — Centralblatt fuer das Gesamte Forstwesen
CEGJB — Canterbury Engineering Journal
CEGOAM — Clinical and Experimental Obstetrics and Gynecology
CEGPAP — CEGS [Council on Education in the Geological Sciences] Programs Publication
CEGS Programs Publ — CEGS [Council on Education in the Geological Sciences] Programs Publication
CEGYA — Ceskoslovenska Gynekologie
CEH — Central European History
CEH — Chromatography of Environmental Hazards
CEHADM — Clinical and Experimental Hypertension. Part A. Theory and Practice
CEHSJ — Church of England Historical Society. Journal
CEHSMO — Historia Obrera. Centro de Estudios Historicos del Movimiento Obrero Mexicano
CEHYDQ — Clinical and Experimental Hypertension
CEI — Canadian Education Index
CEI — Chemical Engineering Index
CEI — Conferences and Exhibitions International
CEIAA — Centro di Studi per l'Ingegneria Agraria. Memorie ed Atti
CEIADR — Commission of the European Communities. Information on Agriculture
CEIED — Chemical Engineering (International Edition)
CEIND — Ceramurgia International
CEINEX — Cecidologia Internationale
CE I P — Minutes of Proceedings of the Institution of Civil Engineers, containing Abstracts of the Papers and of the Discussions
CE I T — Transactions of the Institution of Civil Engineers
CEJ — California English Journal
CEJ — Christian Educators Journal
CEJL — Current Events in Jewish Life
CEK — Cahiers Economiques de Bruxelles
CEL — China Trade and Economic Newsletter
CELA Newsletter — Canadian Environmental Law Association. Newsletter
CELBA — Conti Elektro Berichte
CELCA — Commutation et Electronique
Celestial Mech — Celestial Mechanics
Celestial Mech Dynam Astronom — Celestial Mechanics and Dynamical Astronomy
Celest Mech — Celestial Mechanics
Celfan R — Revue Celfan/Celfan Review
Celjabinsk Gos Ped Inst Trudy — Celjabinskii Gosudarstvennyi Pedagogiceskii Institut. Trudy
CELLA4 — Cellule
Cell Adhes Commun — Cell Adhesion and Communication

Cell Biochem Biophys — Cell Biochemistry and Biophysics
Cell Biochem Funct — Cell Biochemistry and Function
Cell Biol Commun — Cell Biology Communications
Cell Biol Int — Cell Biology International
Cell Biol Int Rep — Cell Biology International Reports
Cell Biol Monogr — Cell Biology Monographs
Cell Biol Ser Monogr — Cell Biology: a Series of Monographs
Cell Biol T — Cell Biology and Toxicology
Cell Biol Toxicol — Cell Biology and Toxicology
Cell Biol Uterus — Cellular Biology of the Uterus
Cell Biophys — Cell Biophysics
Cell Chem T — Cellulose Chemistry and Technology
Cell Chromosome Newsl — Cell and Chromosome Newsletter
Cell Chromosome Res — Cell and Chromosome Research
Cell Commun Ocul Dev Pap Symp — Cellular Communication during Ocular Development. Papers. Symposium
Cell Cult Its Appl Int Cell Cult Congr — Cell Culture and Its Application. International Cell Culture Congress
Cell Cult Methods Mol Cell Biol — Cell Culture Methods for Molecular and Cell Biology
Cell Cytokine Networks Tissue Immun Proc Int RES Congr — Cellular and Cytokine Networks in Tissue Immunity. Proceedings. International RES Congress
Cell Death Diff — Cell Death and Differentiation
Cell Death Differ — Cell Death and Differentiation
Cell Differ — Cell Differentiation
Cell Differ Dev — Cell Differentiation and Development
Cell Eng — Cellular Engineering
Cell Growth & Differ — Cell Growth and Differentiation
Cell Immun — Cellular Immunology
Cell Immunol — Cellular Immunology
Cell Interact — Cellular Interactions
Cell Interact Proc Lepetit Colloq — Cell Interactions. Proceedings. Lepetit Colloquium
Cell Membr (NY) — Cell Membranes (New York). Methods and Reviews
Cell Messengers Fert Proc Symp Br Soc Dev Biol Soc Study Fert — Cell Messengers at Fertilization. Proceedings. Symposium. British Society for Developmental Biology and the Society for the Study of Fertility
Cell Microbiol — Cellular Microbiology
Cell Mol Aspects React Proc Congr Int Endotoxin Soc — Cellular and Molecular Aspects of Endotoxin Reactions. Proceedings. Congress. International Endotoxin Society
Cell Mol Biol — Cellular and Molecular Biology
Cell Mol Biol Lett — Cellular and Molecular Biology Letters
Cell Mol Biol Materno Fetal Relat Proc Meet Reprod Immunol — Cellular and Molecular Biology of the Materno-Fetal Relationship. Proceedings. Meeting on Reproductive Immunology
Cell Mol Biol Res — Cellular and Molecular Biology Research
Cell Mol Life Sci — Cellular and Molecular Life Sciences
Cell Mol Mech Inflammation — Cellular and Molecular Mechanisms of Inflammation
Cell Mol Neurobiol — Cellular and Molecular Neurobiology
Cell Mol Physiol Cell Vol Regul — Cellular and Molecular Physiology of Cell Volume Regulation [monograph]
Cell Monogr Ser — Cell Monograph Series
Cell Motil — Cell Motility
Cell Motil Cytoskeleton — Cell Motility and the Cytoskeleton
Cell Muscle Motil — Cell and Muscle Motility
Cell Pharmacol — Cellular Pharmacology
Cell Physiol Biochem — Cellular Physiology and Biochemistry
Cell Polym — Cellular Polymers
Cell Polym Pap Three Day Int Conf — Cellular Polymers. Papers from a Three-Day International Conference
Cell Prolif — Cell Proliferation
Cell Regul — Cell Regulation
Cell Res — Cell Research (Beijing)
Cell Senescence Somatic Cell Genet — Cellular Senescence and Somatic Cell Genetics
Cell Signal — Cellular Signalling
Cell Signalling — Cellular Signalling
Cells Mater — Cells and Materials
Cells Mater Suppl — Cells and Materials. Supplement
Cell Sol — Cellules Solaires
Cell Struct Funct — Cell Structure and Function
Cell Surf Rev — Cell Surface Reviews
Cell Technol (Tokyo) — Cell Technology (Tokyo)
Cell Tis Re — Cell and Tissue Research
Cell Tiss K — Cell and Tissue Kinetics
Cell Tissue Kinet — Cell and Tissue Kinetics
Cell Tissue Res — Cell and Tissue Research
Cell Transplant — Cell Transplantation
Cellul Carta — Cellulosa e Carta
Cellul Chem — Cellulose-Chemie
Cellul Chem Technol — Cellulose Chemistry and Technology
Cellul Commun — Cellulose Communications
Cellul Ind — Cellulose Industry
Celluloid Plast — Celluloid und Plastische Massen
Celluloid Plast Massen — Celluloid und Plastische Massen
Cellulose Chem Technol — Cellulose Chemistry and Technology
Celosloven Geol Konf Mater — Celoslovenska Geologicka Konferencia. Materialy
Celostatna Konf Term Anal — Celostatna Konferencia o Termickej Analyze
Celostatna Konf Term Anal Zb — Celostatna Konferencia o Termickej Analyze. Zbornik
Celostatne Dni Tepelneho Spracovania Konf Zahr Ucastou — Celostatne Dni Tepelneho Spracovania. Konferencia so ZahranicnouUcastou

Celostatni Konf Makrotest Sb Prednasek — Celostatni Konference "Makrotest". Sbornik Prednasek
Celovek i Obsc — Celovek i Obscestvo
CelR — Celtic Review
Celt — Celtiberia
Celtic R — Celtic Review
Celt Mag — Celtic Magazine
Celul Hartie — Celuloza si Hartie
Celul Hirtie — Celuloza si Hirtie
Celuloza Hirt — Celuloza si Hirtie
Celul Pap Grafika — Celuloza, Papir, Grafika
CEM — Cahiers d'Etudes Medievales
CEM — Chemical Engineering Monographs
CEM — Clinical and Experimental Metastasis
CEM — Comercio Exterior de Mexico
CEm — Corno Emplumado
CEM — Cuadernos de Estudios Manchegos
Cem Age — Cement Age
Cem Armato — Cemento Armato
Cem Assoc Jpn Rev Gen Meet Tech Sess — Cement Association of Japan. Review of General Meeting. Technical Session
Cem Betong — Cement och Betong
Cem Betonginst Forsk — Cement- och Betonginstitutet. Forskning
CEMC — Centro de Estudios Mayas-Cuadernos
Cem Cem Manuf — Cement and Cement Manufacture
Cem Compos — Cement Composites
Cem Concr Aggregates — Cement, Concrete, and Aggregates
Cem Concr Assoc Tech Rep — Cement and Concrete Association. Technical Report
Cem Concr Compos — Cement and Concrete Composites
Cem Concr (Delhi) — Cement and Concrete (Delhi)
Cem Concrete Ass Res Rep — Cement and Concrete Association. Research Report
Cem Concr Res — Cement and Concrete Research
Cem Concr (Tokyo) — Cement and Concrete (Tokyo)
Cement Concrete Res — Cement and Concrete Research
Cement (Engl Transl) — Cement (English Translation of Tsement)
Cem Era — Cement Era
CEMF — Collected Essays by the Members of the Faculty
Cem Hormigon — Cemento-Hormigon
Cem Ind (Tokyo) — Cement Industry (Tokyo)
CEMLA/M — Monetaria. Centro de Estudios Monetarios Latinoamericanos
Cem Lime Grav — Cement, Lime, and Gravel
Cem Lime Gravel — Cement, Lime, and Gravel
Cem Lime Manuf — Cement and Lime Manufacture
Cem Lime Mf — Cement and Lime Manufacture
Cem Mill Quarry — Cement Mill and Quarry
Cem Rec — Cement Record
Cem Res Inst India Monogr MS — Cement Research Institute of India. Monograph MS
Cem Res Inst India RB — Cement Research Institute of India. Research Bulletin
Cem Res Prog — Cements Research Progress
Cem Technol — Cement Technology
Cem Vapno Azbestocem Sadra — Cement. Vapno, Azbestocement, Sadra
CEMW — Columbia Essays on Modern Writers
Cem Wapno Beton — Cement-Wapno-Beton
Cem Wapno Gips — Cement Wapno Gips
CEN — Bulletin du Cercle d'Etudes Numismatiques
CEN — Canada. Department of the Environment. Fisheries and Marine Service. Data Report Series
Cen — Cenobio. Rivista Mensile di Cultura
CEN — Chemische Industrie. Zeitschrift fuer die Deutsche Chemiewirtschaft
CeN — Classici e Neo-Latini
CEn — Colecao Ensaio
CEN — Construction Equipment News
CENB — Cercle d'Etudes Numismatiques. Bulletin
CENCBM — Carnets de l'Enfance/Assignment Children
CENCN — Centre d'Etudes Nordiques. Collection Nordicana. University of Laval
CEN Constr Equip News — CEN. Construction Equipment News
CenE — Central European History
CENEA — Chemical and Engineering News
Cen Eur Hist — Central European History
CENIA5 — Cenicafe
Cenicafe — Cenicafe. Centro Nacional de Investigaciones de Cafe
Cenicafe Av Tec — Cenicafe. Avances Tecnicos
CENMD — Chemical Engineering Monographs
CENN — Center News
Cenni Storici Mus Civico Storia Nat Trieste — Cenni Storici. Museo Civico di Storia Naturale di Trieste
Cenni Stor Mus Civ Stor Nat Trieste — Cenni Storici del Museo Civico di Storia Naturale di Trieste
CENSAC — Census Access System
Censorship Mag — Censorship Magazine
Cent — Centaure
Cent — Centaurus
Cent — Century Magazine
Cent Actual Sci Tech INSA Monogr — Centre d'Actualisation Scientifique et Technique de l'INSA [*Institut National des Sciences Appliques. France*] Monographies
Cent Adv Study Geol Publ (Chandigarh India) — Centre of Advanced Study in Geology. Publication (Chandigarh, India)
Cent Afr J Med — Central African Journal of Medicine
Cent Agric — Centro Agricola
Cent Agric Publ Doc (Wageningen) Annu Rep — Centre for Agricultural Publications and Documentation (Wageningen). Annual Report

Cent Arecanut Res St Tech Bull — Central Arecanut Research Station. Technical Bulletin
Cent Asia J — Central Asiatic Journal
Cent Asian Rev — Central Asian Review
Cent Asiat J — Central Asiatic Journal
Cent Azucar — Centro Azucar
Cent BA — Centro (Buenos Aires)
Cent Belge Etude Corros Rapp Tech — Centre Belge d'Etude de la Corrosion. Rapport Technique
Cent Belge Etude Doc Eaux Bull Mens — Centre Belge d'Etude et de Documentation des Eaux. Bulletin Mensuel
Cent Belge Etude Doc Eaux J Mens — Centre Belge d'Etude et de Documentation des Eaux. Journal Mensuel
Centbl Bauverwalt — Centralblatt der Bauverwaltung
Centbl Bibwsn — Centralblatt fuer Bibliothekswesen
Centbl Ges Forstw — Centralblatt fuer das Gesamte Forstwesen
Cent Cercet Mater Prot Bul Teh Inf — Centrul de Cercetare pentru Materiale de Protectie. BuletinTehnico-Informativ
Cent Cienc Biomed Rev Univ Fed St Maria — Centro de Ciencias Biomedicas. Revista. Universidade Federal de SantaMaria
Cent Cienc Educ Bol — Centro de Ciencias da Educacao. Boletim
Cent Cienc Rurais Rev Univ Fed St Maria — Centro de Ciencias Rurais. Revista. Universidade Federal de SantaMaria
Cent Cienc Saude Rev Univ Fed St Maria — Centro de Ciencias Saude. Revista. Universidade Federal de Santa Maria
Cent Cient Trop Estud Ocas — Centro Cientifico Tropical. Estudio Ocasional
Cent Cient Trop Estud Ocas (San Jose, Costa Rica) — Centro Cientifico Tropical. Estudio Ocasional (San Jose, Costa Rica)
Cent Creative Phot — Center for Creative Photography
Cent Cult Sci Rev (Pelotas, Brazil) — Centro de Cultura Scientifica. Revista (Pelotas, Brazil)
Cent D — Century Dictionary
Cent Doc Sider Circ Inf Tech — Centre de Documentation Siderurgique. Circulaire d'Informations Techniques
Cent Doc Sider Cir Inf Tech — Centre de Documentation Siderurgique. Circulaire d'Informations Techniques
Cent Edafol Biol Apl Salamanca Anu — Centro de Edafologia y Biologia Aplicada de Salamanca. Anuario
Cent Electr Gener Board CEGB Res — Central Electricity Generating Board. CEGB [*Central Electricity Generating Board. London*] Research
Cent Energ Nucl Agric Bol Cient BC — Centro de Energia Nuclear na Agricultura. Boletim Cientifico BC
Cent Energ Nucl Agric Bol Tec BT — Centro de Energia Nuclear na Agricultura. Boletim Tecnico BT
Centen Mag — Centennial Magazine
Centennial Mag — Centennial Magazine
Centennial Rev — Centennial Review
Centen Rev — Centennial Review
Center — Center Magazine
Center Child Bk Bull — Center for Children's Books. Bulletin
Center J — Center Journal
Center J Archit America — Center. A Journal for Architecture in America
Center M — Center Magazine
Center Mag — Center Magazine
Cent Estud Recur Odontol Nino — Centro de Estudios de Recursos Odontologicos para el Nino
Cent Estud Zool Univ Brasil Avulso — Centro de Estudos Zoologicos. Universidade do Brasil. Avulso
Cent Etude Azote — Centre d'Etude de l'Azote
Cent Etude Energ Nucl BLG — Centre d'Etude de l'Energie Nucleaire. Rapport. BLG
Cent Etude Rech Essais Sci Genie Univ Liege Mem — Centre d'Etude, de Recherches, et d'Essais Scientifiques du Genie Civil. Universite de Liege. Memoires
Cent Etud Nucl Saclay Ser Bibliogr — Centre d'Etudes Nucleaires de Saclay. Serie Bibliographies
Cent Etud Rech Essais Sci Genie Civ Univ Liege Mem — Centre d'Etudes, de Recherches, et d'Essais Scientifiques du Genie Civil. Universite de Liege. Memoires
Cent Etud Rech Sci (Biarritz) Bull — Centre d'Etudes et de Recherches Scientifiques (Biarritz). Bulletin
Cent Etud Super Sider Fr Rapp — Centre d'Etudes Superieures de la Siderurgie Francaise. Rapport
Cent Eur Fed — Central European Federalist
Cent Eur H — Central European History
Cent Eur Hist — Central European History
Cent Eur J Immunol — Central-European Journal of Immunology
Cent Eur J Public Health — Central European Journal of Public Health
Cent European Obs — Central European Observer [*Prague*]
Cent Form Tech Perfect Bull — Centre de Formation Technique et de Perfectionnement. Union des Fabricants de Biscuits, Biscottes, Aliments Dietetiques, et Divers. Bulletin
Cent Geomorphol Caen Bull — Centre de Geomorphologie de Caen. Bulletin
Cent Glass Ceram Res Inst Bull — Central Glass and Ceramic Research Institute. Bulletin
Cent Great Lakes Stud Univ Wis Milwaukee Spec Rep — Center for Great Lakes Studies. University of Wisconsin-Milwaukee. Special Report
Cent High-Energy Form Pro — Center for High-Energy Forming. Proceedings. International Conference
Cent High Energy Form Proc Int Conf — Center for High-Energy Forming. Proceedings. InternationalConference
Cent High Res Res Rep Tex Austin — Center for Highway Research. Research Report. University of Texas at Austin
Cent Highw Res Res Rep Univ Tex Austin — Center for Highway Research. Research Report. University of Texas atAustin

Cent Hist Chem News — Center for History of Chemistry News

Cent Inf Chrome Dur Bull Doc — Centre d'Information du Chrome Dur. Bulletin de Documentation

Cent Inf Nickel Toutes Appl Tech Ind Ser A — Centre d'Information du Nickel pour Toutes Applications Techniques et Industrielles. Serie A. Alliages

Cent Inf Nickel Toutes Appl Tech Ind Ser C — Centre d'Information du Nickel pour Toutes Applications Techniques et Industrielles. Serie C. Fontes au Nickel

Cent Inf Nickel Toutes Appl Tech Ind Ser D — Centre d'Information du Nickel pour Toutes Applications Techniques et Industrielles. Serie D. Nickelage

Cent Inf Nickel Toutes Appl Tech Ind Ser X — Centre d'Information du Nickel pour Toutes Applications Techniques et Industrielles. Serie X. Applications du Nickel

Cent Inland Fish Res Inst (Barrackpore) Annu Rep — Central Inland Fisheries Research Institute (Barrackpore). Annual Report

Cent Inland Fish Res Inst (Barrackpore) Bull — Central Inland Fisheries Research Institute (Barrackpore). Bulletin

Cent Inland Fish Res Inst (Barrackpore India) Surv Rep — Central Inland Fisheries Research Institute (Barrackpore, India). Survey Report

Cent Inland Fish Res Inst (Barrackpore) Misc Contri — Central Inland Fisheries Research Institute (Barrackpore). Miscellaneous Contribution

Cent Inland Fish Res Inst (Barrackpore) Misc Contrib — Central Inland Fisheries Research Institute (Barrackpore). Miscellaneous Contribution

Cent Inland Fish Res Inst (Barrackpore) Surv Rep — Central Inland Fisheries Research Institute (Barrackpore). Survey Report

Cent Inst Mater Onderz Afd Corr Medede — Centraal Instituut voor Materiaal Onderzoek. Afdeling Corrosie. Mededeling

Cent Inst Mater Onderz Afd Corros Circ — Centraal Instituut voor Materiaal Onderzoek. Afdeling Corrosie.Circulaire

Cent Inst Mater Onderz Afd Corros Meded — Centraal Instituut voor Materiaal Onderzoek. Afdeling Corrosie.Mededeling

Cent Inst Mater Onderz Afde Corros Circ — Centraal Instituut voor Materiaal Onderzoek. Afdeling Corrosie. Circulaire

Cent Inst Mater Onderz Afd Hout Circ — Centraal Instituut voor Materiaal Onderzoek. Afdeling Hout. Circulaire

Cent Inst Mater Onderz Afd Verf Circ — Centraal Instituut voor Materiaal Onderzoek. Afdeling Verf. Circulaire

Cent Inst Phys Inst Phys Nucl Eng Rep (Romania) — Central Institute of Physics. Institute for Physics and Nuclear Engineering. Report (Romania)

Cent Inst Phys Rep (Bucharest) — Central Institute of Physics. Report (Bucharest)

Cent Inst Phys Top Theor Phys — Central Institute of Physics Topics in Theoretical Physics

Cent Int Agric Trop Annu Rep — Centro Internacional de Agricultura Tropical [*CIAT*]. Annual Report

Cent Int Agric Trop (CIAT) Ser CE — Centro Internacional de Agricultura Tropical (CIAT). Series CE

Cent Int Agric Trop (CIAT) Ser EE — Centro Internacional de Agricultura Tropical (CIAT). Series EE

Cent Int Agric Trop (CIAT) Ser FE — Centro Internacional de Agricultura Tropical (CIAT). Series FE

Cent Int Agric Trop (CIAT) Ser GE — Centro Internacional de Agricultura Tropical (CIAT). Series GE

Cent Int Agric Trop (CIAT) Ser JE — Centro Internacional de Agricultura Tropical (CIAT). Series JE

Cent Int Agric Trop Ser CE — Centro Internacional de Agricultura Tropical [*CIAT*]. Series CE

Cent Int Agric Trop Ser EE — Centro Internacional de Agricultura Tropical [*CIAT*]. Series EE

Cent Int Agric Trop Ser FE — Centro Internacional de Agricultura Tropical [*CIAT*]. Series FE

Cent Int Agric Trop Ser GE — Centro Internacional de Agricultura Tropical [*CIAT*]. Series GE

Cent Int Agric Trop Ser Semin — Centro Internacional de Agricultura Tropical [*CIAT*]. Series Seminars

Cent Int Agric Trop Tech Bull — Centro Internacional de Agricultura Tropical [*CIAT*]. Technical Bulletin

Cent Int Engrais Chim Assem Gen Rapp — Centre International des Engrais Chimiques. Assemblee Generale.Rapports

Cent Int Engrais Chim Symp — Centre International des Engrais Chimiques. Symposium

Cent Interdiscip Cienc Mar Invest Mar — Centro Interdisciplinario de Ciencias Marinas. Investigaciones Marinas

Cent Int Etud Romanes Bull Trimest — Centre International d'Etudes Romanes. Bulletin Trimestriel

Cent Invest Agric Alberto Boerger Bol Tec — Centro de Investigaciones Agricolas Alberto Boerger. Boletin Tecnico

Cent Invest Agric Noreste Inf Invest Agric — Centro de Investigaciones Agricolas del Noreste. Informe de Investigacion Agricola

Cent Invest Agron Maracay Monogr — Centro de Investigaciones Agronomicas Maracay. Monografia

Cent Invest Agropecu Reg Cent Occident Bol Tec — Centro de Investigaciones Agropecuarias de la Region Centro Occidental.Boletin Tecnico

Cent Invest Baja Calif Scripps Inst Oceanogr Trans — Centros de Investigacion de Baja California and Scripps Institution ofOceanography. Transactions

Cent Invest Biol Mar Contrib Tec — Centro de Investigacion de Biologia Marina. Contribucion Tecnica

Cent Invest Desarrollo Tecnol Pint An — Centro de Investigacion y Desarrollo en Tecnologia de Pinturas. Anales

Cent Invest Oceanogr Hidrogr Bol Cient (Cartagena, Colomb) — Centro de Investigaciones Oceanograficas e Hidrograficas. BoletinCientifico (Cartagena, Colombia)

Cent Invest Tecnol Inf Invest (Pando Urug) — Centro de Investigaciones Tecnologicas. Informe de Investigacion(Pando, Uruguay)

Cent Invest Tecnol Publ (Pando, Urug) — Centro de Investigaciones Tecnologicas. Publicacion (Pando, Uruguay)

Cent Issues Anthrop — Central Issues in Anthropology

Cent Ital Smalti Porcellanati Not — Centro Italiano Smalti Porcellanati. Notiziario

Cent Ital Smalti Porcellanati Not Inf — Centro Italiano Smalti Porcellanati. Notiziario Informativo

Cent Jpn J Orthop Traumatic Surg — Central Japan Journal of Orthopaedic and Traumatic Surgery

Cent Lab Ochron Radiol Rap — Centralne Laboratorium Ochrony Radiologicznej. Raport

Cent Lab Ochr Radiol Rap — Centralne Laboratorium Ochrony Radiologicznej. Raport

Cent Lab Ochr Radiol Rap Tech — Centralne Laboratorium Ochrony Radiologicznej. Raport Techniczny

Cent Lab Przem Tytoniowego Biul Inf — Centralne Laboratorium Przemyslu Tytoniowego. Biuletyn Informacyjny

Cent Lab Radiol Prot Warsaw Rep — Central Laboratory for Radiological Protection. Warsaw. Report

Cent Lab Radiol Prot Warsaw Tech Rep — Central Laboratory for Radiological Protection. Warsaw. Technical Report

Cent Landbouwdoc Literatuuroverz — Centrum voor Landbouwdocumentatie. Literatuuroverzicht

Cent Landbouwpubl Landbouwdoc Literatuuroverz — Centrum voor Landbouwpublikaties en Landbouwdocumentatie Literatuuroverzicht

Cent Law J — Central Law Journal

Cent Linceo Interdiscip Sci Mat Loro Appl Contrib — Centro Linceo Interdisciplinare di Scienze Matematiche e LoroApplicazioni. Contributi

Cent L J — Central Law Journal

Cent LJ — Central Law Journal

Cent L Mo — Central Law Monthly

Cent Luzon State Univ Sci J — Central Luzon State University. Scientific Journal

Cent Mag — Center Magazine

Cent Mag — Century Magazine

Cent Mar Fish Res Inst Bull — Central Marine Fisheries Research Institute. Bulletin

Cent Mar Fish Res Inst CMFRI Bull — Central Marine Fisheries Research Institute. CMFRI Bulletin

Cent Med J Semin Rep (Moscow) — Central Medical Journal. Seminar Reports (Moscow)

Cent Mus Utrecht Meded — Centraal Museum Utrecht Mededelingen

Cent Nac Agric (Costa Rica) Bol Tec — Centro Nacional de Agricultura (Costa Rica). Boletin Tecnica

Cent Nac Aliment Nutr (Spain) Bol — Centro Nacional de Alimentacion y Nutricion (Spain). Boletin

Cent Nac Invest Cafe Av Tec — Centro Nacional de Investigaciones de Cafe. Avances Tecnicos

Cent Nac Invest Cafe Bol Tec (Chinchin) — Centro Nacional de Investigaciones de Cafe. Boletin Tecnico (Chinchina)

Cent Nac Invest Cient Rev CENIC Cienc Biol — Centro Nacional de Investigaciones Cientificas. Revista CENIC. Ciencias Biologicas

Cent Nac Invest Cient Rev CENIC Cienc Fis — Centro Nacional de Investigaciones Cientificas. Revista CENIC. CienciasFisicas

Cent Nac Invest Cient Rev CENIC Cienc Quim — Centro Nacional de Investigaciones Cientificas. Revista CENIC. CienciasQuimicas

Cent Nat Exploit Oceans Publ Ser Rapp Sci Tech (Fr) — Centre National pour l'Exploitation des Oceans. Publications. Serie Rapports Scientifiques et Techniques (France)

Cent Natl Coord Etud Rech Nutr Aliment Cah Tech — Centre National de Coordination des Etudes et Recherches sur laNutrition et l'Alimentation. Cahiers Techniques

Cent Natl Doc Sci Tech Rap Act — Centre National de Documentation Scientifique et Technique. Rapport d'Activite

Cent Natl Exploit Oceans Publ Ser Actes Colloq (Fr) — Centre National pour l'Exploitation des Oceans. Publications. Serie Actes de Colloques (France)

Cent Natl Exploit Oceans Publ Ser Rapp Sci Tech (Fr) — Centre National pour l'Exploitation des Oceans. Publications. Serie Rapports Scientifiques et Techniques (France)

Cent Natl Exploit Oceans Rapp Annu — Centre National pour l'Exploitation des Oceans. Rapport Annuel

Cent Natl Rech Metall Mem — Centre National de Recherches Metallurgiques. Memoires

Cent Natl Rech Metall Metall Rep — Centre National de Recherches Metallurgiques. Metallurgical Reports

Cent Natl Rech Sci Tech Ind Cimentiere Rapp Rech — Centre National de Recherches Scientifiques et Techniques pour l'Industrie Cimentiere. Rapport de Recherche

Cent Nat Rech Sci — Centre National de la Recherche Scientifique

Cent Nat Rech Sci Groupe Fr Argiles R Reun Etude — Centre National de la Recherche Scientifique. Groupe Francais des Argiles. Compte Rendu des Reunions d'Etudes

Cent Nerv Syst Behav Trans Conf — Central Nervous System and Behavior. Transactions. Conference on the Central Nervous System and Behavior

Cent Nerv Syst Pharmacol Ser — Central Nervous System Pharmacology Series

Cent Nerv Syst Trauma — Central Nervous System Trauma

Cent Nucl TRICO Rapp Rech — Centre Nucleaire TRICO [*Training, Research, Isotope Production Reactor. Congo*]. Rapport de Recherche

CENTO Conf Ld Classif Non-Irrig Lds — CENTO [*Central Treaty Organization*] Conference on Land Classification for Non-Irrigated Lands

CENTO Sci Programme Rep — CENTO [*Central Treaty Organization*] Scientific Programme. Report

Cent Overseas Pest Res Misc Rep — Centre for Overseas Pest Research. Miscellaneous Report

Cent Overseas Pest Res Rep — Centre for Overseas Pest Research. Report

Cent Pesqis Agropecu Trop Umido Bol Tec — Centro de Pesquisa Agropecuaria do Tropico Umido. Boletim Technico

Cent Pesqui Agropecu Trop Umido — Centro de Pesquisa Agropecuaria do Tropico Umido EMBRAPA

Cent Pesqui Cacau Bol Tec Itabuna Braz — Centro de Pesquisas do Cacau. Boletim Tecnico (Itabuna, Brazil)

Cent Pesqui Desenvolvimento Bol Tec (Estado Bahia) — Centro de Pesquisas e Desenvolvimento. Boletim Tecnico (Estado da Bahia)

Cent Phar J — Central Pharmaceutical Journal

Cent Plant Crops Res Inst (Kasaragod) Annu Rep — Central Plantation Crops Research Institute (Kasaragod). Annual Report

Cent Public Health Eng Res Inst Nagpur India Bull — Central Public Health Engineering Research Institute. Nagpur. India. Bulletin

Cent Quim Ind Buenos Aires Publ — Centro de Quimicos Industriales. Buenos Aires. Publicacion

Cent Quim Ind Buenos Aires Rev — Centro de Quimicos Industriales. Buenos Aires. Revista

CentR — Centennial Review

Central African J Med — Central African Journal of Medicine

Central Bank Barbados Q Rept — Central Bank of Barbados. Quarterly Report

Central Bank Ireland Q Bul — Central Bank of Ireland. Quarterly Bulletin

Central Bank Libya Econ Bul — Central Bank of Libya. Economic Bulletin

Central Bank Malta QR — Central Bank of Malta. Quarterly Review

Central Bank Nigeria Econ and Fin R — Central Bank of Nigeria. Economic and Financial Review

Central Bank Trinidad and Tobago Q Econ Bul — Central Bank of Trinidad and Tobago. Quarterly Economic Bulletin

Centralbl Agrikulturchem Ration Wirtschaftsbetr — Centralblatt fuer Agrikulturchemie und Rationellen Wirtschaftsbetrieb

Centralbl Allg Path u Path Anat — Centralblatt fuer Allgemeine Pathologie und Pathologische Anatomie

Centralbl Bakteriol — Centralblatt fuer Bakteriologie und Parasitenkunde

Centralbl Bakteriol 1 Abt Originale — Centralblatt fuer Bakteriologie, Parasitenkunde, und Infektionskrankheiten. Erste Abteilung. Medizinisch-Hygienische Bakteriologie Virusforschung, und Tierische Parasitologie. Originale

Centralbl Bakteriol 1 Abt Ref — Centralblatt fuer Bakteriologie, Parasitenkunde, und Infektionskrankheiten. Erste Abteilung. Medizinisch-Hygienische Bakteriologie, Virusforschung, und Tierische Parasitologie. Referate

Centralbl Bakteriol Parasitenk 2 Abt — Centralblatt fuer Bakteriologie und Parasitenkunde. Zweite Abteilung

Centralbl Chir — Centralblatt fuer Chirurgie

Centralbl Gesammte Landescult In Ausl — Centralblatt fuer die Gesammte Landescultur des In- und Auslandes

Centralbl Gesamte Forstwes — Centralblatt fuer das Gesamte Forstwesen

Centralbl Innere Med — Centralblatt fuer Innere Medicin

Centralbl Maehr Landwirthe — Centralblatt fuer die Maehrischen Landwirthe

Centralbl Miner — Centralblatt fuer Mineralogie, Geologie, und Palaeontologie

Central European J Oper Res Econom — Central European Journal for Operations Research and Economics

Central Law J — Central Law Journal

Central LJ — Central Law Journal

Central Ohio Sc As Pr — Central Ohio Scientific Association of Urbana, Ohio. Proceedings

Central Opera — Central Opera Service. Bulletin

Central Q Herald — Central Queensland Herald

Centr Asian Rev — Central Asian Review

Centr Asiat J — Central Asiatic Journal

Centr Bank Ireland Annu Rep — Central Bank of Ireland. Annual Report

Centr Bank Ireland Quart B — Central Bank of Ireland. Quarterly Bulletin

Cent Rech Agron Etat Gembloux Note Tech — Centre de Recherches Agronomiques de l'Etat. Gembloux. Note Technique

Cent Rech Archeol Cah — Centre de Recherches Archeologiques Cahier

Cent Rech Ecol Phytosociol Gembloux Commun — Centre de Recherches Ecologiques et Phytosociologiques de Gembloux. Communication

Cent Rech Etud Oceanogr Trav — Centre de Recherches et d'Etudes Oceanographiques. Travaux

Cent Rech Explor Prod Elf Aquitaine Bull — Centres de Recherches Exploration-Production Elf-Aquitaine. Bulletin

Cent Rech Fer Blanc Bull (Thionville Fr) — Centre de Recherches du Fer-Blanc. Bulletin (Thionville, France)

Cent Rech For Laurentides Rapp Inf LAU X Ed Fr — Centre de Recherches Forestieres des Laurentides. Rapport d'Information LAU-X (Edition Francaise)

Cent Rech Ind Afr Cent Sci Tech Inf CRIAC — Centre de Rechereches Industrielles en Afrique Centrale. Sciences. Techniques. Informations CRIAC

Cent Rech Metall Metall Rep — Centre de Recherches Metallurgiques. Metallurgical Reports

Cent Rech Oceanogr (Abidjan) Doc Sci — Centre de Recherches Oceanographiques (Abidjan). Documents Scientifiques

Cent Rech Oceanogr (Abidjan) Doc Sci Provisoire — Centre de Recherches Oceanographiques (Abidjan). Document Scientifique Provisoire

Cent Rech Pau Bull — Societe Nationale des Petroles d'Aquitaine. Centre de Recherches de Pau. Bulletin. [Later, Bulletin. Centres de Recherches Exploration-Production ELF Aquitaine]

Cent Rech Routieres CR CR (Brussels) — Centre de Recherches Routieres. Comptes Rendus CR (Brussels)

Cent Rech Routieres Methode Mes Brussels — Centre de Recherches Routieres. Methode de Mesure (Brussels)

Cent Rech Sci Tech Ind Fab Met Sect Fonderie Rep FD — Centre de Recherches Scientifiques et Techniques de l'Industrie des Fabrications Metalliques. Section. Fonderie. Report FD

Cent Rech Sci Tech Ind Fabr Met Sect Plast Rep PL — Centre de Recherches Scientifiques et Techniques de l'Industrie des Fabrications Metalliques. Section Plastiques. Report PL

Cent Rech Zootech Vet Theix Bull Tech — Centre de Recherches Zootechniques et Veterinaires de Theix. Bulletin Technique

Centr Econ Plan — Centraal Economisch Plan

Centre Docum Siderurg — Centre de Documentation Siderurgique

Centre Et Docum Soc (Liege) — Centre d'Etudes et de Documentation Sociales (Liege)

Centre Etud Emploi Cah — Centre d'Etudes de l'Emploi. Cahiers

Centre Etud et Docum Socs Bul — Centre d'Etudes et de Documentation Sociales. Bulletin Mensuel

Centre Reg Etud Nucl Kinshasa Rapp Rech — Centre Regional d'Etudes Nucleaires de Kinshasa. Rapport de Recherche

Centre Info et Etud Credit Bul — Centre d'Information et d'Etudes du Credit. Bulletin

Centre Inform Chrome Dur Bull Doc — Centre d'Information du Chrome Dur. Bulletin de Documentation

Centre Nat Rech Sci Tech Ind Cimentiere Rapp Rech — Centre National de Recherches Scientifiques et Techniques pour l'Industrie Cimentiere. Rapport de Recherche

Centre Pure Appl Differential Geom PADGE — Centre for Pure and Applied Differential Geometry (PADGE)

Centre Recherches Pau Bull — Centre de Recherches de Pau. Bulletin

Centre Sci & Tech Constr Note Inf Tech — Centre Scientifique et Technique de la Construction. Note d'Information Technique

Cent Res Inst Agric Contrib (Bogor Indones) — Central Research Institute for Agriculture. Contributions (Bogor, Indonesia)

Cent Res Inst Electr Power Ind Rep Tokyo — Central Research Institute of Electric Power Industry. Report (Tokyo)

Cent Res Inst Electr Power Ind Tech Rep (Tokyo) — Central Research Institute of Electric Power Industry. Technical Report (Tokyo)

Cent Res Inst Phys Rep KFKI — Central Research Institute for Physics. Report KFKI

Cent Reumatol Boll Osp Riuniti Roma — Centro di Reumatologia. Bollettino. Ospedali Riuniti di Roma

Centr LJ — Central Law Journal

Centro Am Intelect — Centro-America Intelectual. Revista Cientifico-Literaria

Centro Estud Demograficos R — Centro de Estudos Demograficos. Revista

Centro Estud Rurais e Urbanos Cad — Centro de Estudos Rurais e Urbanos. Cadernos

Centro Investigacion y Accion Soc R — Centro de Investigacion y Accion Social. Revista

Centro Pirenaico Biolog Exp — Publicaciones. Centro Pirenaico de Biologia Experimental

Centro pro Un Bul — Centro pro Unione. Bulletin

CENTRO Ser Azucar — CENTRO. Serie. Azucar. Revista Cientifica. Universidad Central de Las Villas

CENTRO Ser Constr Maquinaria — CENTRO Serie. Construccion de Maquinaria. Revista Cientifica. Universidad Central de Las Villas (Cuba)

CENTRO Ser Quim Tecnol Quim — CENTRO. Serie. Quimica y Tecnologia Quimica. Revista Cientifica. Universidad Central de las Villas

Cent Rubberstn Meded — Centraal Rubberstation. Mededeeling

Cent Sci Res Inst Leather Ind Coll Pap — Central Scientific Research Institute of the Leather Industry. Collection of Papers

Cent S L Potosi — Centro (San Luis Potosi, Mexico)

Cent Soil Salinity Res Inst Bull — Central Soil Salinity Research Institute. Bulletin

Cent Sper Agric For Pubbl — Centro di Sperimentazione Agricola e Forestale. Pubblicazioni

Cent SS RR — Center for Settlement Studies. University of Manitoba. Research Reports

Cent St Spe — Central States Speech Journal

Cent Stud Citogenet Veg Pubbl — Centro di Studio per la Citogenetica Vegetale. Consiglio Nazionale delle Richerche. Pubblicazioni

Cent Studi Lotta Antitermitica Pubbl — Centro di Studi per la Lotta Antitermitica. Pubblicazione

Cent Stud Ing Agrar Mem Atti — Centro di Studi per l'Ingegneria Agraria. Memorie ed Atti

Cent Stud Lunensi Quad — Centro di Studi Lunensi. Quaderni

Cent Stud Stor Cer Merid — Centro di Studi per la Storia della Ceramica Meridionale

CentStyr Hastavelsforb Finl Publr — Centralstyrelsens for Hastavelsforbunden i Finland Publikationer

Cent Tech For Trop (Nogent Sur Marne Fr) Note Tech — Centre Technique Forestier Tropical (Nogent Sur Marne, France). Note Technique

Cent Tech For Trop (Nogent Sur Marne Fr) Publ — Centre Technique Forestier Tropical (Nogent Sur Marne, France). Publication

Cent Tech Ind Mec Mem Tech — Centre Technique des Industries Mecaniques. Memoires Techniques

Cent Tech Inst TNO Afd Warmtetech Versl — Centraal Technisch Instituut TNO. Afdeling Warmtetechniek. Verslag

Cent Tech Inst TNO Versl — Centraal Technisch Instituut TNO. Verslag

Cent Tech Interprof Ol Metrop Bull CETIOM — Centre Technique Interprofessionnel des Oleagineux Metropolitains. Bulletin CETIOM

Cent Tech Interprof Ol Metrop Inf Tech — Centre Technique Interprofessionnel des Oleagineux Metropolitains. Informations Techniques

Cent Tech Union Bull — Centre Technique de l'Union. Bulletin

Cent Ted Stud Ven Quad — Centro Tedesco di Studi Veneziani. Quaderni

Cent Text Controle Rech Sci Bull — Centre Textile de Controle et de Recherche Scientifique. Bulletin

Cent Treaty Organ Sci Programme Rep — Central Treaty Organization Scientific Programme. Report

Cent Unit Environ Pollut Pollut Pap G B — Central Unit on Environmental Pollution. Pollution Paper (Great Britain)

Century Wks Q Rev — Century Works Quarterly Review. Engineering Supplement

CENUA — Courrier des Etablissements Neu

CEO — Central European Observer

CEO — Courrier de l'Extreme-Orient

CEOABL — Centre National pour l'Exploitation des Oceans. Rapport Annuel

CEOFA — Ceskoslovenska Oftalmologie

Ceol — Ceol. Journal of Irish Music

CEOTA — Ceskoslovenska Otolaryngologie

CEP — Chemical Engineering Progress

CEP — Country Economic Profiles

CEP — Czechoslovak Economic Papers
CEPAL — CEPAL (Comision Economica para America Latina) Review
CEPAL Rev — CEPAL [*Comision Economica para America Latina*] Review
CEPBA — Cerebral Palsy Bulletin
CEPCAV — Centre de Recherches Ecologiques et Phytosociologiques de Gembloux. Communication
CEPEA — Ceskoslovenska Pediatrie
CEPEC Inf Tec — CEPEC [*Centro de Pesquisas do Cacau*] Informe Tecnico
CEPED — Civil Engineering for Practicing and Design Engineers
CEPHDF — Cephalalgia
C Epigr — Carmina Latina Epigraphica
CEPLAC Bol Tec — CEPLAC [*Comissao Executiva do Plano da Lavoura Cacaueira*] Boletim Tecnico
CEPLAC Comun Tec — CEPLAC [*Comissao Executiva do Plano da Lavoura Cacaueira*] Comunicacao Tecnica
CEPLAO — CEPLAC [*Comissao Executiva do Plano da Lavoura Cacaueira*] Boletim Tecnico
CEPND — CEP [*Council on Economic Priorities*] Newsletter
CEP Newsl — CEP [*Council on Economic Priorities*] Newsletter
CEPR — Cambridge Economic Policy Review
CEPRA — Chemical Engineering Progress
CEPS — Canadian Journal of Economics and Political Science
CEPS — Computerized Equipment Pricing System
CEPSA — Chemical Engineering Progress. Symposium Series
CEPSB — Ceskoslovenska Psychologie
CEPYA — Ceskoslovenska Psychiatrie
CEQ — Central Bank of Barbados. Quarterly Report
CER — Cahiers d'Etudes Romanes
CER — Catholic Educational Review
CeR — Centennial Review
CER — Comparative Education Review
CERAB — Ceskoslovenska Radiologie
Ceram Abstr — Ceramic Abstracts
Ceram Age — Ceramic Age
Ceram Awareness Bull — Ceramic Awareness Bulletin
Ceram Budow — Ceramika Budowlana
Ceram Bull — Ceramic Bulletin
Ceram Carbon Matrix Compos — Ceramic- and Carbon-Matrix Composites
Ceram Chem Conf Sil Anal — Ceramic Chemists' Conference on Silicate Analysis
Ceram Crist — Ceramica y Cristal
Ceram Cult Maya — Ceramica de Cultura Maya
Ceram Energy Appl Proc Inst Energy Conf — Ceramics in Energy Applications. New Opportunities. Proceedings. Institute of Energy Conference
Ceram Eng Sci Proc — Ceramic Engineering and Science Proceedings
Ceram Films Coat — Ceramic Films and Coatings
Ceram Forum Int — Ceramic Forum International
Ceram Glass Moscow — Ceramics and Glass (Moscow)
Ceram Glass Sci Technol — Ceramics and Glass. Science and Technology
Ceramic Abstr — Ceramic Abstracts
Ceramic Dig — Ceramic Digest
Ceramic Ind — Ceramic Industry
Ceramic R — Ceramic Review
Ceramics Art Ind — Ceramics in Art and Industry
Ceramic S B — American Ceramic Society. Bulletin
Ceramics Int — Ceramics International
Ceramics Mo — Ceramics Monthly
Ceram Ind — Ceramic Industry
Ceram Ind Chicago — Ceramic Industry (Chicago)
Ceram Ind J — Ceramics Industries Journal
Ceram Ind Sao Paulo — Ceramica Industrial (Sao Paulo)
Ceram Ind (Sevres Fr) — Ceramiques Industrielles (Sevres, France)
Ceram Int — Ceramics International
Ceram Int News — Ceramics International News
Ceramique Archit — Ceramique et Architecture
Ceramique Mater Constr — Ceramique et les Materiaux de Construction
Ceramique Mod — Ceramique Moderne
Ceramique Verr — Ceramique et Verrerie
Ceramique Verr Emaill — Ceramique, Verrerie, Emaillerie
Ceram Jap — Ceramics Japan
Ceram Jpn — Ceramics Japan
Ceram Laterizi — Ceramichte e Laterizi
Ceram Mag — Ceramics Magazine
Ceram Mater Ogniotrwale — Ceramika. Materialy Ogniotrwale
Ceram Mo — Ceramics Monthly
Ceram Monogr — Ceramic Monographs
Ceram Powder Process Sci Proc Int Conf — Ceramic Powder Processing Science. Proceedings. International Conference
Ceram Powder Sci — Ceramic Powder Science
Ceram Pr Kom Ceram Pol Akad Nauk Oddzial Krak — Ceramika Prace Komisji Ceramicnyj Polska Akademie Nauk Oddzial w Krakowie
Ceram Process Sci Technol — Ceramic Processing Science and Technology
Ceram Res Inst Tokoname Aichi Prefect News — Ceramic Research Institute. Tokoname. Aichi Prefecture. News
Ceram Severe Environ Proc Univ Conf Ceram Sci — Ceramics in Severe Environments. Proceedings. University Conference on Ceramic Science
Ceram Supercond Proc Winter Meet Low Temp Phys — Ceramic Superconductors. Proceedings. Winter Meeting on Low Temperature Physics
Ceram Supercond Res Update — Ceramic Superconductors. Research Update
Ceram Trns — Ceramic Transactions
Ceramurgia Int — Ceramurgia International
Ceramurgia Tec Ceram — Ceramurgia, Tecnologia Ceramica
Ceramurg Int — Ceramurgia International
Ceram Verrerie — Ceramique et Verrerie
Ceram Verrerie Emaill — Ceramique, Verrerie, Emaillerie
Ceram Vidrio — Ceramica y Vidrio

CERB — Congresso e Exposicao Regional das Beiras
CERBD — Chemical Engineering Research Bulletin (Dacca)
Cerberus Elektron — Cerberus Elektronik
Cerberus R — Cerberus Report
CERBOM Rapp Act — CERBOM [*Centre d'Etudes et de Recherches de Biologie et d'Oceanographie Medicale*] Rapport d'Activite
Cerc & Carre — Cercle et Carre
Cercet Agron Moldova — Cercetari Agronomice in Moldova
Cercet Arh Buc — Cercetari Arheologice in Bucuresti
Cercetari Muzicol — Cercetari de Muzicologie
Cercet Domeniul Constr Hidroteh — Cercetari in Domeniul Constructiilor Hidrotehnice
Cercet Ist — Cercetari Istorice
Cercet Ist (Iasi) — Cercetari Istorice (Iasi)
Cercet Met — Cercetari Metalurgice
Cercet Metal — Cercetari Metalurgice
Cercet Metal Inst Cercet Metal (Bucharest) — Cercetari Metalurgice. Institutul de Cercetari Metalurgice (Bucharest)
Cercet Min — Cercetari Miniere
Cercet Miniere Inst Cercet Miniere — Cercetari Miniere. Institutul de Cercetari Miniere
Cercet Num — Cercetari Numismatice
Cerc Ist — Cercetari Istorice
Cerc Ist (Buch) — Cercetari Istorice (Bucharest)
Cerc Num — Cercetari Numismatice. Muzeul de Istorie
Cer Cult Maya — Ceramica de Cultura Maya
CERDA — Chemie der Erde
Cereal Chem — Cereal Chemistry
Cereal Chem Bull — Cereal Chemists Bulletin
Cereal Crop Ser Indian Counc Agr Res — Cereal Crop Series. Indian Council of Agricultural Research
Cereal Foods World — Cereal Foods World
Cereal F W — Cereal Foods World
Cereal Res Commun — Cereal Research Communications
Cereal Rusts Bull — Cereal Rusts Bulletin
Cereal Sci Today — Cereal Science Today
Cereb Circ Metab — Cerebral Circulation and Metabolism
Cereb Cir Metab Pap Int Symp Cereb Blood Flow — Cerebral Circulation and Metabolism. Papers. International Symposium on Cerebral Blood Flow
Cereb Cortex — Cerebral Cortex
Cereb Dis — Cerebrovascular Diseases
Cereb Palsy J — Cerebral Palsy Journal
Cereb Palsy Rev — Cerebral Palsy Review
Cerebrovasc Brain Metab Rev — Cerebrovascular and Brain Metabolism Reviews
Cerebrovasc Dis — Cerebrovascular Diseases
Cerebrovasc Dis Princeton Stroke Conf — Cerebrovascular Diseases. Princeton Stroke Conference
Cerebr Palsy Bull — Cerebral Palsy Bulletin
Ccreb Vas Dis — Cerebral Vascular Diseases
Cereb Vas Dis Int Conf — Cerebral Vascular Diseases. International Conference
Cereb Vas Dis Proc Int Salzburg Conf — Cerebral Vascular Disease. Proceedings. International Salzburg Conference
CERED — CEGB [*Central Electricity Generating Board*] Research
Cere Vasc Dis Trans Conf — Cerebral Vascular Diseases. Transactions of the Conference
Cerevisia Biotechnol — Cerevisia and Biotechnology
Cerf — Cerf Volant. Cahier Litteraire
CERI J Ed — CERI (Central Research Institute) Journal of Education
Cer Ind — Ceramic Industry
CERMA — Cermica
CERMB — Cercetari Metalurgice
Cer Mthly — Ceramics Monthly
CERN Accel Sch Appl Geod Part Accel — CERN (Conseil Europeen pour la Recherche Nucleaire) Accelerator School. AppliedGeodesy for Particle Accelerators
CERN Accel Sch Gen Accel Phys Course — CERN [*Conseil Europeen pour la Recherche Nucleaire*] Accelerator School. General Accelerator Physics Course
CERN High Energy React Anal Group Rep — CERN [*Conseil Europeen pour la Recherche Nucleaire*] High Energy ReactionAnalysis Group Report
CERN JINR Sch Phys — CERN-JINR [*Conseil Europeen pour la Recherche Nucleaire. Joint Institute of Nuclear Research*] School of Physics
CERN Rep — CERN [*Conseil Europeen pour la Recherche Nucleaire*] Report
CERN Sch Phys Proc — CERN (Conseil Europeen pour la Recherche Nucleaire) School of Physics. Proceedings
CERN Symp High Energy Pion Phys Proc — CERN (Conseil Europeen pour la Recherche Nucleaire) Symposium on High Energy Accellerators and Pion Physics. Proceedings
CERP — Cities of the Eastern Roman Provinces
Cerrahpasa Tip Fak Derg — Cerrahpasa Tip Fakultesi Dergisi
Cer Rev — Ceramic Review
CER-T — Cahiers d'Etudes de Radio-Television
CERT — CERT. Civil Engineering and Road Transport
Certif Addit Brev Invent Fr — Certificat d'Addition au Brevet d'Invention (France)
Certif Addit Brev Spec Med Fr — Certificat d'Addition a un Brevet Special Medicament (France)
Certif Addit Certif Util Fr — Certificat d'Addition au Certificat d'Utilite (France)
Certif Adicion (Spain) — Certificado de Adicion (Spain)
Certifd Engr — Certificated Engineer
Certif Dent Tec — Certified Dental Technician
Certif Eng — Certificated Engineer
Certif Eng — Certified Engineer
Certified Milk Confs — Certified Milk Conferences. American Association of Medical Milk Commissioners
Certif Milk — Certified Milk

Certifs Rep Agric Mach Test Comm — Certificates and Reports. Agricultural Machinery Testing Committee
Certif Util Fr — Certificat d'Utilite (France)
CES — Chinese Economic Studies
CES — Comparative Ethnographical Studies [*Goeteborg*]
CES — Computer Enhanced Spectroscopy
CeS — Cultura e Scuola
CES A — Ceskoslovenska Stomatologie
CESARS — Chemical Evaluation Search and Retrieval System
CESBBA — Connecticut. Agricultural Experiment Station. Department of Entomology. SpecialBulletin
CesC — Ceskoslovensky Casopis Historicky
CESCA — Chemical Engineering Science
CES (Centre Environmental Studies) R — CES (Centre Environmental Studies) Review
CES Comput Enhanced Spectrosc — CES. Computer Enhanced Spectroscopy
CES Conf Paps — Centre for Environmental Studies. Conference Papers
CESGA — Comments on Earth Sciences. Geophysics
CES Inf Paps — Centre for Environmental Studies. Information Papers
Ceska Derm — Ceska Dermatologie
Ceska Dermatol — Ceska Dermatologie
Ceska Gynekol — Ceska Gynekologie
Ceska Hospod — Ceska Hospodyne
Cesk Akad Ved Geogr Ustav Zpr — Ceskoslovenska Akademie Ved. Geograficky Ustav Zpravy
Cesk Akad Ved Lab Radiol Dozim Rep LRD — Ceskoslovenska Akademie Ved. Laborator Radiologicke Dozimetrie. Report LRD
Cesk Akad Ved Publ — Ceskoslovenska Akademie Ved. Publikace
Cesk Akad Ved Stud Geophys Geod — Ceskoslovenska Akademie Ved. Studia Geophysica et Geodaetica
Cesk Akad Ved Ustav Dozim Zareni Vyzk Zpr UDC CSAV — Ceskoslovenska Akademie Ved. Ustav Dozimetrie Zareni. Vyzkumna Zprava UDZ CSAV
Cesk Akad Ved Ustav Fyz Plazmatu Res Rep IPPCZ — Ceskoslovenska Akademie Ved. Ustav Fyziky Plazmatu. Research Report IPP CZ
Cesk Akad Ved Ustav Jad Fyz Rep — Ceskoslovenska Akademie Ved. Ustav Jaderne Fyziky. Report.
Cesk Akad Ved Ved Inf CSAV — Ceskoslovenska Akademie Ved. Vedecke Informace CSAV
Cesk Akad Zemed Ustav Vedeckotech Inf Metod Zavadeni Vysledku — Ceskoslovenska Akademie Zemedelska. Ustav Vedeckotechnickych Informaci. Metodiky pro Zavadeni Vysledku Vyzkumu do Praxe
Cesk Akad Zemed Ustav Vedeckotech Inf Zemed Sb Potravin Vedy — Ceskoslovenska Akademie Zemedelska. Ustav Vedeckotechnickych Informaci pro Zemedelstvi. Sbornik. Potravinarske Vedy
Ceska Mykol — Ceska Mykologie
Ceska Rev — Ceska Revue
Ceska Slov Farm — Ceska a Slovenska Farmacie
Ceska Slov Gastroenterol — Ceska a Slovenska Gastroenterologie
Ceska Slov Psychiatr — Ceska a Slovenska Psychiatrie
Cesk Biol — Ceskoslovenska Biologie
Cesk Cas Fys — Ceskoslovensky Casopis pro Fysiku. Sekce A
Cesk Cas Fys A — Ceskoslovensky Casopis pro Fysiku. Sekce A
Cesk Cas Fys Sekce A — Ceskoslovensky Casopis pro Fysiku. Sekce A
Cesk Cas Hist — Ceskoslovensky Casopis Historicky
Cesk C Fys — Ceskoslovensky Casopis pro Fysiku. Sekce A
Cesk Dermatol — Ceskoslovenska Dermatologie
Ceske Lesn Rozhl — Ceske Lesnicke Rozhledy
Ceske Museum Filol — Ceske Museum Filologicke
Cesk Epidemiol Mikrobiol Immunol — Ceskoslovenska Epidemiologie, Mikrobiologie, Immunologie
Ceske Vys Uceni Tech Praze Pr I — Ceske Vysoke Uceni Technicke v Praze. Prace. I. Stavebni
Ceske Vys Uceni Tech Praze Pr Rada 3 — Ceske Vysoke Uceni Technicke v Praze. Prace. Rada 3. Elektrotechnicka
Ceske Vys Uceni Tech Praze Pr Rada 4 — Ceske Vysoke Uceni Technicke v Praze. Prace. Rada 4. Technicko-Teoreticka
Cesk Farm — Ceskoslovenska Farmacie
Cesk Farm Spol Sb Prednasek Sjezdu — Ceskoslovenska Farmaceuticka Spolecnost. Sbornik Prednasek Sjezdu
Cesk Fysiol — Ceskoslovenska Fysiologie
Cesk Gastroenterol Vyz — Ceskoslovenska Gastroenterologie a Vyziva
Cesk Gynekol — Ceskoslovenska Gynekologie
Cesk Hyg — Ceskoslovenska Hygiena
Cesk Hyg Epidemiol Mikrobiol Imunol — Ceskoslovenska Hygiena Epidemiologie, Mikrobiologie, Imunologie
Cesk Inf — Ceskoslovenska Informatika. Teorie a Praxe
Cesk Inf Teor a Praxe — Ceskoslovenska Informatika. Teorie a Praxe
Cesk Kozarstvi — Ceskoslovenska Kozarstvi
Cesk Lit — Ceska Literatura
Cesk Mikrobiol — Ceskoslovenska Mikrobiologie
Cesk Morfol — Ceskoslovenska Morfologie
Cesk Neurol — Ceskoslovenska Neurologie [*Later, Ceskoslovenska Neurologie a Neurochirurgie*]
Cesk Neurol Neurochir — Ceskoslovenska Neurologie a Neurochirurgie
Cesko Architekt — Ceskoslovensky Architekt
Cesk Oftalmol — Ceskoslovenska Oftalmologie
Cesk Onkol — Ceskoslovenska Onkologie
Ceskoslov Bot Listy — Ceskoslovenske Botanicke Listy
Ceskoslovensk Akad Ved Geog Ustav (Brno) Studia Geog — Ceskoslovenska Akademie Ved. Geograficky Ustav (Brno). Studia Geographica
Cesko Slov Epidemiol Mikrobiol Imunol — Cesko-Slovenska Epidemiologie, Mikrobiologie, Imunologie
Cesko Slov Farm — Cesko-Slovenska Farmacie
Cesko Slov Gastroenterol Vyz — Cesko-Slovenska Gastroenterologie a Vyziva
Cesko Slov Hyg — Cesko-Slovenska Hygiena

Ceskoslov Mikrobiol — Ceskoslovenska Mikrobiologie
Cesk Otolaryngol — Ceskoslovenska Otolaryngologie
Cesk Parasitol — Ceskoslovenska Parasitologie
Cesk Patol — Ceskoslovenska Patologie
Cesk Patol Priloha — Ceskoslovenska Patologie. Priloha.
Cesk Pediatr — Ceskoslovenska Pediatrie
Cesk Psychiatr — Ceskoslovenska Psychiatrie
Cesk Psycho — Ceskoslovenska Psychologie
Cesk Psychol — Ceskoslovenska Psychologie
Cesk Radiol — Ceskoslovenska Radiologie
Cesk Rentgenol — Ceskoslovenska Rentgenologie
Cesk Stand — Ceskoslovenska Standardizace
Cesk Stomatol — Ceskoslovenska Stomatologie
Cesky Vcel — Cesky Vcelar
Cesk Zdrav — Ceskoslovenske Zdravotnictvi
CES Occ Paps — Centre for Environmental Studies. Occasional Papers
Ces Odontol — Ces Odontologia
CES Policy Series — Centre for Environmental Studies. Policy Series
CES Res Paps — Centre for Environmental Studies. Research Papers
CES Res Series — Centre for Environmental Studies. Research Series
CES Rev — Centre for Environmental Studies. Review
CESRL Rep Univ Tex Austin Dep Civ Eng Struct Res Lab — CESRL Report. University of Texas at Austin. Department of Civil Engineering. Structures Research Laboratory
CESSA — Catalogue of Egyptian Scarabs, Scaraboids, Seals, and Amulets in the Palestine Archeological Museum
CESSDT — Cambridge Texts in the Physiological Sciences
CESSID Cent Etud Super Sider Fr Rapp — CESSID. Centre d'Etudes Superieures de la Siderurgie Francaise. Rapport
Ce Sta — Ceskoslovenska Stomatologie
CESTD — Ceskoslovenska Standardizace
CE Studies — Canadian Ethnic Studies/Etudes Ethniques au Canada
CES Univ Wkng Paps — Centre for Environmental Studies. University Working Papers
CES Wkng Paps — Centre for Environmental Studies. Working Papers
C Et Afr — Cahiers d'Etudes Africaines
CETDA — CEGB [*Central Electricity Generating Board*] Technical Disclosure Bulletin
CETIM Informations — CETIM Informations. Centre Technique des Industries Mechaniques
CEU — Consensus. Informatietijdschrift over Energie Mol
CEUFA — Central European Federalist
CEURBY — Coeur
C Europ — Cahiers Europeens
CEW Chem Eng World — CEW. Chemical Engineering World
CEWOA — Chemical Engineering World
CEX — Chief Executive
CEXIA — Clinical and Experimental Immunology
CEXIAL — Clinical and Experimental Immunology
CEXMD2 — Clinical and Experimental Metastasis
CEXPB — Clinical and Experimental Pharmacology and Physiology
CEXSBI — Colorado State University. Experiment Station. Bulletin
CEY — Cuba Economic News
Cey J Hist Soc Stud — Ceylon Journal of Historical and Social Studies
Cey Lab LJ — Ceylon Labour Law Journal
Ceyl LJ — Ceylon Law Journal
Ceyl LW — Ceylon Law Weekly
Ceylon Antiqua & Lit Register — Ceylon Antiquary and Literary Register
Ceylon Assoc Adv Sci Proc Annu Sess — Ceylon Association for the Advancement of Science. Proceedings of the Annual Session
Ceylon Coconut J — Ceylon Coconut Journal
Ceylon Coconut Plant Rev — Ceylon Coconut Planters' Review
Ceylon Coconut Q — Ceylon Coconut Quarterly
Ceylon Dent J — Ceylon Dental Journal
Ceylon Dep Fish Bull — Ceylon. Department of Fisheries. Bulletin
Ceylon Dep Fish Fish Res Stn Bull — Ceylon. Department of Fisheries. Fisheries Research Station. Bulletin
Ceylon Dep Mineral Geol Surv Ceylon Mem — Ceylon. Department of Mineralogy. Geological Survey of Ceylon. Memoir
Ceylon Fish Res St Prog Rep Biol Technol — Ceylon. Fisheries Research Station. Progress Reports. Biological and Technological
Ceylon For — Ceylon Forester
Ceylon Forest — Ceylon Forester
Ceylon Geol Surv Mem — Ceylon. Geological Survey. Memoir
Ceylon Hist J — Ceylon Historical Journal
Ceylon Inst Sci Ind Res Nat Prod Sect Nat Prod Tech Notes Ser — Ceylon Institute of Scientific and Industrial Research. Natural Products Section. Natural Products Technical Notes Series
Ceylon J Hist & Soc Stud — Ceylon Journal of Historical and Social Studies
Ceylon J Med Sci — Ceylon Journal of Medical Science
Ceylon J Sci — Ceylon Journal of Science
Ceylon J Sci Anthropol — Ceylon Journal of Science. Anthropology
Ceylon J Sci Biol Sci — Ceylon Journal of Science. Biological Sciences
Ceylon J Sci Med Sci — Ceylon Journal of Science. Medical Science
Ceylon J Sci Sect A — Ceylon Journal of Science. Section A. Botany
Ceylon J Sci Sect A Bot — Ceylon Journal of Science. Section A. Botany
Ceylon J Sci Sect B — Ceylon Journal of Science. Section B. Zoology
Ceylon J Sci Sect B Zool — Ceylon Journal of Science. Section B. Zoology
Ceylon J Sci Sect C — Ceylon Journal of Science. Section C. Fisheries
Ceylon J Sci Sect C Fish — Ceylon Journal of Science. Section C. Fisheries
Ceylon J Sci Sect D — Ceylon Journal of Science. Section D. Medical Science
Ceylon J Sci Sect D Med Sci — Ceylon Journal of Science. Section D. Medical Science
Ceylon L Soc J — Ceylon Law Society. Journal
Ceylon Med J — Ceylon Medical Journal

Ceylon Natl Mus Adm Rep Dir Part IV Educ Sci Art (E) — Ceylon. National Museums Administration. Report of the Director. Part IV. Education, Science, and Art (E)

Ceylon Natl Mus Ethnogr Ser — Ceylon National Museums. Ethnographic Series

Ceylon Nat Mus Adm Rep Dir Part IV Educ Sci Art — Ceylon. National Museums Administration. Report of the Director. Part IV. Education, Science, and Art

Ceylon NLR — New Law Reports (Ceylon)

Ceylon N Rev — Ceylon National Review

Ceylon Rubber Res Scheme Q Circ — Ceylon Rubber Research Scheme. Quarterly Circular

Ceylon Trade J — Ceylon Trade Journal

Ceylon Vet J — Ceylon Veterinary Journal

CF — Canada Francais

CF — Canadian Forum

CF — Captain Future

CF — Catalunya Franciscana [Barcelona]

CF — Ce Fastu

CF — Classical Folia

CF — Collectanea Franciscana

CF — Computer Fraud

CF — Confluence

CF — Constituicao Federal

CFA — Central Bank of the Bahamas. Quarterly Review

CFA — City Facts and Abstracts

CFABEW — Communications. Faculte des Sciences. Universite d'Ankara. Serie C. Biologie

C Fantas — Cinefantastique

CFB — Across the Board

CFBTAJ — Commonwealth Forestry Bureau. Technical Communication

CFBUBN — Clemson University. Department of Forestry. Forestry Bulletin

CFC — Contemporary French Civilization

CFC — Cuadernos de Filologia Clasica

CFCA — Challenge for Change. Access. National Film Board of Canada

CFCD — Canadian Federal Corporations and Directors

CfCh — Centralblatt fuer Chirurgie

CFD — Canadian Financial Database

CFE — Economic Road Maps

CFEKA7 — Chirurgisches Forum fuer Experimentelle und Klinische Forschung

CFEM Ser Tec — CFEM [Comision Forestal del Estado de Michoacan] Serie Tecnica

CFeng — Ching Feng

CFF — Codigo Fiscal de la Federacion

CFFAn — Comite Flamand de France. Annales

CFHB — Corpus Fontium Historiae Byzantinae

CFI — CBI Newsbulletin

CFIAAV — Conferencia Interamericana de Agricultura

CFI Ceram Forum Int — CFI. Ceramic Forum International. Berichte der Deutschen Keramischen Gesellschaft

CFI Ceram Forum Int Beih — CFI Ceramic Forum International. Beihefte

CFI (Ceram Forum Int) Ber Dtsch Keram Ges — CFI (Ceramic Forum International). Berichte der Deutschen Keramischen Gesellschaft

CFI(Ceram Forus Int) Ber DKG — CFI (Ceramic Forum International). Berichte der Deutschen Keramischen Gesellschaft

CFI (Commonw For Inst) Occas Pap — CFI (Commonwealth Forest Institute) Occasional Papers

CFIl — Cuadernos de Filologia

Cfil — Cuadernos Filosoficos

C Filos — Cuadernos de Filosofia

CFIRBF — Colorado Fisheries Research Review

CFKEA — Commercial Fisheries Review [Later, Marine Fisheries Review]

CFL — Cashflow

Cfl — Confluence

CFM — Canadian Fiction Magazine

CFM — Club Francais de la Medaille

CFM — Credit and Financial Management

CFMA — Classiques Francais du Moyen Age

CFMCBO — Central Inland Fisheries Research Institute (Barrackpore). Miscellaneous Contribution

C F Mgmt — Credit and Financial Management

CFMJ — Canadian Folk Music Journal

CFMSMSP — Canada. Department of the Environment. Fisheries and Marine Service. Miscellaneous Special Publication

CFMSTR — Canada. Department of the Environment. Fisheries and Marine Service. Technical Report

CFOCCRH — Canada. Fisheries and Oceans. Canadian Contractor Report of Hydrography and Ocean Sciences

CFOI — Canadian Forest Industries

CFO J — CFO [Colorado Field Ornithologists] Journal

CFol — Classical Folia

CFOPB5 — Canadian Forestry Service. Publication

Cfor — Canadian Forum

CFORAA — Colorado Field Ornithologist

C Forum — Cineforum

CForum — Cultural Forum

CFOTNS — Canada. Fisheries and Oceans. Ocean Science and Surveys. Technical Note Series

Cf Pa — Centralblatt fuer Pathologie

CFPC — Codigo Federal de Procedimientos Civiles

CFPFDG — Canadian Forestry Service. Pacific Forest Research Abentre. Report BC-P

CFPIAM — Canada. Department of Forestry. Forest Entomology and Pathology Branch. Annual Report. Forest Insect and Disease Survey

CFPME4 — US Forest Service. Northern Region. Cooperative Forestry and Pest Management Report

CFPOB — Chaud-Froid-Plomberie

CFPP — Codigo Federal de Procedimientos Penales

CFPQAC — Australia. Commonwealth Scientific and Industrial Research Organisation. Food Preservation Quarterly

CFPSA — Confinia Psychiatrica

CFPSAI — Confinia Psychiatrica/Confins de la Psychiatrie

CFP XXI — Report of the Twenty-First Congress of Flemish Philologists [Louvain, 1955]

CFQ — California Folklore Quarterly

Cfr — Collectanea Friburgensia

CFR — Commerce Franco-Suisse

CFR — Commercial Fisheries Review

C Franc — Cahiers Francais

CFREAK — Commercial Fisheries Review [Later, Marine Fisheries Review]

CFR/FA — Foreign Affairs. Council on Foreign Relations

CFRMB — Chantiers de France

CFRQAM — Australia. Commonwealth Scientific and Industrial Research Organisation. Food Research Quarterly

CFRTBW — Canadian Forestry Service. Northern Forest Research Centre. Forestry Report

CFRV — Commercial Fisheries Review [Later, Marine Fisheries Review]

CFS — Cahiers Ferdinand de Saussure

CFSA — Communications de la Faculte des Sciences de l'Universite d'Ankara

CFSBDJ — Communications. Faculte des Sciences. Universite d'Ankara. Serie C2. Botanique

CFS Cour Forschungsinst Senckenberg — CFS. Courier Forschungsinstitut Senckenberg

CFSFP — Canadian Forestry Service. Forestry Publication

CFSFTR — Canadian Forestry Service. Forestry Technical Report

CFSGDY — Communications. Faculte des Sciences. Universite d'Ankara. Serie C1. Geologie

CFSR — Canadian Forestry Service. Research News

CFSTB3 — Canadian Institute of Food Science and Technology. Journal

CFSXAE — Contraception-Fertilite-Sexualite

CFSZDN — Communications. Faculte des Sciences. Universite d'Ankara. Serie C3. Zoologie

CFT — China's Foreign Trade

CFTPB — Californium-252 Progress

CFTTA — Chemiefasern und Textil-Anwendungstechnik/Textil-Industrie

CFTXA — Chemiefasern/Textil-Industrie

CFW — Cereal Foods World

CFWODA — Cereal Foods World

CFX — Confectie. Sociaal, Economisch, en Technisch Maandblad voor de Confectie Industrie in de Beneluxlanden

CG — Canadian Geographic

CG — Chugoku Gogaku

CG — Classiques Garnier

CG — Collationes Gandavenses

CG — Common Ground

CG — Courrier Graphique

CGB — Colecao General Benicio

CGB — Global Church Growth Bulletin

CGBCA9 — Colloquium. Gesellschaft fuer Biologische Chemie in Mosbach

CGBLB — Colorado. Geological Survey. Bulletin

CGBMA — Coal, Gold, and Base Minerals of Southern Africa

CGBUA — Canadian Geophysical Bulletin

CGCPA — Geological Survey of Canada. Paper

CGCPAJ — Geological Survey of Canada. Paper

CGCYD — Cancer Genetics and Cytogenetics

CGCYDF — Cancer Genetics and Cytogenetics

CGD — Commonwealth Government Directory

CGDT — Coleccion General de Documentos. Tocantes a la Persecucion Que los Regulares de la Compania Suscitaron y Siguieron [Madrid]

CGEJ — Canadian Geographical Journal [Later, Canadian Geographic]

CGEPAT — Comunicacoes. Servicos Geologicos de Portugal

CGF — Comicorum Graecorum Fragmenta

CGF — Computer Graphics Forum

CGFE — Commission Geologique de Finlande. Bulletin

CGF Pap — Comicorum Graecorum Fragmenta i Papyri Reperta

CGFPAY — Colorado. Division of Game, Fish, and Parks. Special Report

CGFPR — Comicorum Graecorum Fragmenta i Papyri Reperta

CGFTD — Cahiers. Groupe Francois-Thureau-Dangin

CGGFA9 — Congres pour l'Avancement des Etudes de Stratigraphie et de Geologie du Carbonifere. Compte Rendu

CGHCA — Chongi Hakhoe Chi

CGHHAK — Contributions. Gray Herbarium. Harvard University

CGHRBH — Cape Of Good Hope. Department of Nature Conservation. Report

CGI — Creative Guitar International

CGIB — Comitato Glaciologico Italiano. Bollettino

CGIJD — Chinetsu Gijutsu

Cg Int Chron — Congres International de Chronometrie. Comptes Rendus des Travaux, Proces-Verbaux, Rapports et Memoires

Cg Int Hyg C R — Congres International d'Hygiene et de Demographie. Comptes-Rendus Arbeiten, Transactions, Actas

Cg Int Md C R — Comptes-Rendus Atti, Verhandlungen, Transactions du Congres International de Medecine

CGIRAL — Cape Of Good Hope. Department of Nature Conservation. Investigational Report

CGJ — Canadian Geographic

CGJ — Canadian Geographical Journal

CGJ — Caribbean Geography (Jamaica)

CGJO — Canadian Geotechnical Journal

CGJOA — Canadian Geotechnical Journal

CGL — Catalogues of the Gennadius Library

CGL — Choristers Guild. Letters

CGLC — Cambridge Greek and Latin Classics

CGLIA9 — Conchiglie

C Gl Lat — Corpus Glossariorum Latinorum a G. Loewe Incohatum

CGM — Centro Grafico. Lerici's Foundation of the Engineering School of Milan

Cg Md Int At — Comptes-Rendus Atti, Verhandlungen, Transactions du Congres International de Medecine

CGMJ — Christoph Gottlieb von Murr Journal zur Kunstgeschichte und zur Allgemeinen Litteratur [*Nuernberg*]

CGMR — Colonial Geology and Mineral Resources [*London*]

CGN — Cahiers Gerard De Nerval

CGN — Carnivore Genetics Newsletter

CGNWAR — Carnivore Genetics Newsletter

CGOBD6 — Contributions to Gynecology and Obstetrics

CGOMA — Canada. Geological Survey. Map

CGP — Carleton Germanic Papers

CGP — Central Gaulish Potters

CGP — Current Geographical Publications

CGPBA8 — Collection "Les Grands Problemes de la Biologie." Monographie

CGPCAB — Colloquium. Gesellschaft fuer Physiologische Chemie

CGPQA — Canadian Government Publications Quarterly

CGr — Collection "Grandeurs"

CGRAR — Cahiers. Groupe de Recherches. Armee Romaine et les Provinces

CGRRAW — Colorado Game Research Review

CGS — Cults of the Greek States

CGSFAZ — Citrus Grower and Sub-Tropical Fruit Journal

CGSPBW — Contributions to Geology. Special Paper

CGSTA — Clinics in Gastroenterology

CGSTA9 — Clinics in Gastroenterology

CGSTB — Cognition

CGT — Cambridge Greek Testament for Schools and Colleges

CGTNAU — Cognition

C Guild Hobby Horse — Century Guild Hobby Horse

CGURL — Cultura de Guatemala Universidad Rafael Landivar

C Gz — Chemical Gazette

CH — Cabinet Historique

CH — Cahiers d'Histoire

CH — Carmarthenshire Historian

Ch — Channels of Communications

Ch — Choice

CH — Christian Herald

CH — Church History

CH — Commentary on Herodotus

CH — Community Health

CH — Connchord

CH — Critica Hispanica

CH — Cuadernos Hispanoamericanos

CH — Cuadernos Latinoamericanos

CH — Current History

CHA — Cahiers d'Histoire et d'Archeologie

CHA — Challenge. Magazine of Economic Affairs

CHA — Chasqui

CHA — Commerce International

CHA — Correspondance Historique et Archeologique

CHA — Cuadernos de Historia y Arqueologia [*Guayaquil*]

CHA — Cuadernos Hispanoamericanos

CHAC — Cercle Historique et Archeologique de Courtrai. Bulletin

Chacaras Quint — Chacaras e Quintais

CHACBull — Cercle Historique et Archeologique de Courtrai. Bulletin

Ch Acc Aust — Chartered Accountant in Australia

CHAC Rev — Catholic Health Association of Canada. Review

CHAGA — Chemical Age

Ch Agric — Chambres d'Agriculture

Chagyo Shikenjo Kenkyu Hokoku Bull Natl Res Inst Tea — Chagyo Shikenjo Kenkyu Hokoku. Bulletin. National Research Institute of Tea

CHAIA — Chemical Age of India

Cha Ind — Chaleur et Industrie

Chain Drug R — Chain Drug Review. Reporter for the Chain Drug Store Industry

Chain React — Chain Reaction

Chain Store Age Adm Ed — Chain Store Age. Administration Edition

Chain Store Age Exec — Chain Store Age. Executive Edition

Chain Store Age Gen Merch Ed — Chain Store Age. General Merchandise Edition [*Later, Chain Store Age. General Merchandise Trends*]

Chain Store Age Supermark — Chain Store Age Supermarkets

Chal Clim — Chaleur et Climats

Chal Climats — Chaleur et Climats

Chal Ind — Chaleur et Industrie

Challenge in Ed Admin — Challenge in Educational Administration

Challenges Mod Med — Challenges of Modern Medicine

Challenges Mont Agr — Challenges to Montana Agriculture

Chalmers Tek Hoegsk Handl — Chalmers Tekniska Hoegskola. Handlingar

Chalmers Tek Hoegsk Inst Vattenfoersoerjnings Avloppstek Pub — Chalmers Tekniska Hoegskola. Institutionen foer Vattenfoersoerjnings-och Avloppsteknik. Publikation

Chalmers Tek Hogsk Publ B — Chalmers Tekniska Hoegskola. Publikation B

Chalmers Tek Hogsk Doktorsavh — Chalmers Tekniska Hoegskola. Doktorsavhandlingar

Chamber Comm St NY M Bul — Chamber of Commerce of the State of New York. Monthly Bulletin

Chamber Mines J — Chamber of Mines. Journal

Chamber Mines Newsl — Chamber of Mines. Newsletter

Chamber Mus — Chamber Music

Chamber of Ag Vic Yrbk — Chamber of Agriculture of Victoria. Yearbook

Chambers J — Chambers Journal

Chambery Mm Ac Sav — Memoires de la Societe Academique de Savoie (Chambery)

Chamb J — Chamber's Edinburgh Journal

Chamb Mines Newsl — Chamber of Mines. Newsletter

Chambre Commer Fr Can R — Chambre de Commerce Francaise au Canada. Revue

Chambre Commer Gabon Bul — Bulletin. Chambre de Commerce d'Agriculture, d'Industrie, et des Mines du Gabon

Chambre Commer Repub Cote D'Ivoire Bul Mensuel — Chambre de Commerce. Republique de Cote D'Ivoire. Bulletin Mensuel

Chambre de Commerce Francaise Bul — Chambre de Commerce Francaise en Australie. Bulletin

Champignon Netherlands — Champignon. Algemene Nederlandse Champignon-Kwekers Vereniging (Netherlands)

Champignonteelt — Champignonteelt. Voorlichtingsblad voor de Nederlandse Champignonkwekers

Chan — Chantiers

CHANA — Chemist-Analyst

Ch & H — Church and Home

Chang Ed — Changing Education

Change (Par) — Change (Paris)

Changes — Changes Socialist Monthly

Chang Gung Med J — Chang Gung Medical Journal

Changing T — Changing Times

Chang Scene — Changing Scene

Chang Times — Changing Times

Channel Isles Annu Anthol — Channel Isles Annual Anthology

Chanoyu Q — Chanoyu Quarterly

Chantiers Fr — Chantiers de France

Chantiers Mag — Chantiers Magazine

Chantiers Monde — Chantiers dans le Monde

Chapingo Soc Alum Esc Nac Agric — Chapingo. Sociedad de Alumnos. Escuela Nacional de Agricultura

Chapman and Hall Comput — Chapman and Hall Computing

Chapman and Hall Math Ser — Chapman and Hall Mathematics Series

Char — Charisma

Char — Charities

CHAR — Committee for High Arctic Scientific Research Liaison and Information Exchange [*CHARLIE*]. News Bulletin

Char Acctnt Aust — Chartered Accountant in Australia

Charact Adv Mater Proc Int Metallogr Soc Symp — Characterization of Advanced Materials. Proceedings. International Metallographic Society Symposium

Character & Personality — Character and Personality

Character Person — Character and Personality

Charact Treat Use Sewage Sludge Proc Symp — Characterization, Treatment, and Use of Sewage Sludge. Proceedings. European Symposium

Charb Chauff — Charbon et Chauffage

Ch Arch Liege — Chronique Archeologique du Pays de Liege

Charged Part Tracks Solids Liq Proc L H Gray Conf — Charged Particle Tracks in Solids and Liquids. Proceedings. L. H. Gray Conference

Charged React Polym — Charged and Reactive Polymers

Charge Field Eff Biosyst 3 Int Symp — Charge and Field Effects in Biosystems-3. International Symposium on Charge andField Effects in Biosystems

Charite Ann — Charite-Annalen

Charles Babbage Inst Newslett — Charles Babbage Institute Newsletter

Charles Babbage Inst Reprint Ser Hist Comput — Charles Babbage Institute Reprint Series for the History of Computing

Charles Rennie Mackintosh Soc Newsletter (Glasgow) — Charles Rennie Mackintosh Society. Newsletter (Glasgow)

Charleston Med J R — Charleston Medical Journal and Review

Charlot Obs — Charlotte Observer

Charlotte Med J — Charlotte Medical Journal

Charlotte N — Charlotte News

Charlstn G — Charleston Gazette

CharP — Character and Personality

Char R — Charities Review

Chart Acc in Aust — Chartered Accountant in Australia

Chart Accnt in Aust — Chartered Accountant in Australia

Chart Accountant in Aust — Chartered Accountant in Australia

Chart Acct — Chartered Accountant in Australia

Chart Build — Chartered Builder

Chart Builder — Chartered Builder

Chart Eng — Chartered Engineer

Chartered Accountant Aust — Chartered Accountant in Australia

Chartered Inst Transport J — Chartered Institute of Transport. Journal

Chartered Surveyor Bldg & Quantity Surveying Qly — Chartered Surveyor. Building and Quantity Surveying Quarterly

Chartered Surveyor Urban Qly — Chartered Surveyor. Urban Quarterly

Chart Inst Transp J — Chartered Institute of Transport. Journal

Chart Land Surv Chart Miner Surv — Chartered Land Surveyor/Chartered Minerals Surveyor

Chart Mech E — Chartered Mechanical Engineer

Chart Mech Eng — Chartered Mechanical Engineer

Chart Mech Engr — Chartered Mechanical Engineer

Chart Munic Eng — Chartered Municipal Engineer

Chart Quant Surv — Chartered Quantity Surveyor

Chart Sec — Chartered Secretary

Chart Surv — Chartered Surveyor [*Later, Chartered Surveyor Weekly*]

Chart Surv Land Hydrogr Miner Q — Chartered Surveyor. Land Hydrographic and Minerals Quarterly

Chart Surv Rural Q — Chartered Surveyor. Rural Quarterly

Chart Surv Wkly — Chartered Surveyor Weekly

CHAS — Cambridgeshire and Huntingdonshire Archaeological Society

Chase Coal — Coal Situation (Chase Bank)

Chase Diam — Chase Diamond

Chase Econ Bul — Chase Economic Bulletin

Chase Econ Observer — Chase Economic Observer

Chase Fin — Chase Manhattan Bank. International Finance

Chase Obsv — Chase Economic Observer
Chatel Guyon J — Chatel-Guyon Journal
Cha Ti — Changing Times
Chaucer R — Chaucer Review
Chaucer Rev — Chaucer Review
Chaucer Soc — Chaucer Society
Chaudesaigues Therm — Chaudesaigues Thermal
Chaud Froid Plomb — Chaud-Froid-Plomberie
Chaudronn Tolerie — Chaudronnerie-Tolerie
Chauff Ind Mod — Chauffage Industriel Moderne
Chauff Ind Sanit — Chauffage et Industries Sanitaires
Chauff Mazout — Chauffage au Mazout
Chauff Mod Prat — Chauffage Moderne Pratique
Chauff Vent — Chauffage et Ventilation
Chauff Vent Con — Chauffage, Ventilation, Conditionnement
Chauff Vent Condit — Chauffage-Ventilation-Conditionnement
Chauf Vent Cond — Chauffage, Ventilation, Conditionnement
ChauR — Chaucer Review
Chaut — Chautauquan
CHAVB — Chemie-Anlagen und Verfahren
Chayanica Geol — Chayanica Geologica
CHB — Cooperative Housing Bulletin
CHBEA — Chemische Berichte
CHBIE4 — Chronobiology International
CHC — Chile Economic Report
ChC — Chinese Culture
CHC — Christian Century
CHC — Church History (Chicago)
CHC — Coleccion de Historiadores de Chile
ChCen — Christian Century
Ch Century — Christian Century
CHCGA — Chishitsu Chosajo Geppo
CHCGAX — Chishitsu Chosajo Geppo
CHC J — Children's Health Care. Journal of the Association for the Care of Children's Health
CHCLG — Cahiers d'Histoire Publies par les Universites de Clermont-Lyon-Grenoble
CHCOD — Chemical Concepts
CHCRISP — Courrier Hebdomadaire. Centre de Recherche et d'Information Socio-Politiques
Ch D — Christian Doctrine
CHDCA — Comptes Rendus des Seances. Academie des Sciences. Serie C. Sciences Chimiques
CHDDA — Comptes Rendus des Seances. Academie des Sciences. Serie D. Sciences Naturelles
CHDEA — Child Development
CHDEDZ — Contributions to Human Development
CHDID — Chimica Didactica
CHE — Cahiers d'Histoire Egyptienne
Che — Chesterian
ChE — Chiake Epitheoresis
CHE — Chief Executive
CHE — Chronicle of Higher Education
CHE — Cuadernos de Historia de Espana
ChEC Ser Chem Eng Comput — ChEC Series on Chemical Engineering Computing
C H Ed — Chronicle of Higher Education
CHEDA — Chemical Engineering Education
CHEDC — Chemie. Experiment und Didaktik
ChED Chem Exp Didakt — ChED. Chemie. Experiment + Didaktik
CHEEA — Chemical Engineering
Cheese Abstr — Cheese Abstracts
Chef Nyt — Chef Nyt/Kontor Nyt
Cheiron Tamil Nadu J Vet Sci Anim Husb — Cheiron. The Tamil Nadu Journal of Veterinary Science and Animal Husbandry
CHEJ — Canadian Home Economics Journal
Cheju Univ J — Cheju University. Journal
Cheju Univ J Nat Sci — Cheju University Journal. Natural Sciences
CHEKAL — Chung-Hua Min Kuo Hsiao Erh K'o I Hsueh Hui Tsa Chi
Chek Fiz Zh — Chekhoslovatskii Fizicheskii Zhurnal
Chekh Biol — Chekhoslovatskaya Biologiya
Chekh Fiziol — Chekhoslovatskaya Fiziologiya
Chekh Med Obozr — Chekhoslovatskoe Meditsinskoe Obozrenie
Chekhoslov Biol — Chekhoslovatskaya Biologiya
Chek Zh Gig Tr Prof Zabol — Chekhoslovatskii Zhurnal Gigieny Truda i Professional'nykh Zabolevanii
Chel — Chelsea
Chelates Anal Chem — Chelates in Analytical Chemistry
Chel Biosfera — Chelovek i Biosfera
Chelovek Prir — Chelovek i Priroda
Cheltenham Mag — Cheltenham Magazine
Chelyab Med Inst Sb Nauchn Tr — Chelyabinskii Meditsinskii Institut. Sbornik Nauchnykh Trudov
Chelyab Politekh Inst Tr — Chelyabinskii Politekhnicheskii Institut. Trudy
Chem — Chemins du Monde
Chem — Chemistry
CHEM — Community Health Education Monographs
ChemAb — Chemical Abstracts
Chem Abs Macromol — Chemical Abstracts. Macromolecular Sections
Chem Abst Phy Anal Chem Sect — Chemical Abstracts. Physical and Analytical Chemistry Section
Chem Abstr — Chemical Abstracts
Chem Abstr Cum Subj Index — Chemical Abstracts. Decennial Cumulative Subject Index
Chem Abstr Jpn — Chemical Abstracts of Japan

Chem Abstr Serv Source Index — Chemical Abstracts Service. Source Index
Chem Abstr Subj Ind — Chemical Abstracts. Annual Subject Index
Chem Ackersmann — Chemische Ackersmann
Chem Adhes — Chemistry and Adhesion
Chem Age — Chemical Age
Chem Age India — Chemical Age of India
Chem Age Int — Chemical Age International
Chem Age (Lond) — Chemical Age (London)
Chem Age London Suppl — Chemical Age (London). Supplement
Chem Age (NY) — Chemical Age (New York)
Chem Agric — Chemicals in Agriculture
Chem Agric Int Congr — Chemistry in Agriculture. International Congress
Chem Ag Sv — Chemical Age Survey
Chem Amidines Imidates — Chemistry of Amidines and Imidates
Chem Anal and Biol Fate Polynucl Aromat Hydrocarbons Int Sym — Chemical Analysis and Biological Fate. Polynuclear Aromatic Hydrocarbons. International Symposium
Chem Anal (New York) — Chemical Analysis. A Series of Monographs on Analytical Chemistry and Its Applications (New York)
Chem Anal NY — Chemical Analysis (New York). A Series of Monographs
Chem Anal Reagent — Chemical Analysis and Reagent
Chem Anal Ser Monogr Anal Chem Appl — Chemical Analysis. A Series of Monographs on Analytical Chemistry and Its Applications
Chem Anal (Warszawa) — Chemia Analityczna (Warszawa)
Chem Analyse — Chemische Analyse
Chem and Engin News — Chemical and Engineering News
Chem & Eng N — Chemical and Engineering News
Chem & Engng News — Chemical and Engineering News
Chem & Ind — Chemistry and Industry
Chem & Met Eng — Chemical and Metallurgical Engineering
Chem & Pet Engng — Chemical and Petroleum Engineering
Chem and Process Eng — Chemical and Process Engineering
Chem & Process Engng — Chemical and Process Engineering [Later, Process Engineering]
Chem-Anlagen Verfahren — Chemie-Anlagen und Verfahren
Chem Ann Freunde Naturl — Chemische Annalen fuer die Freunde der Naturlehre, Arzneygelahrtheit, Haushaltungskunst, Manufacturen
Chem Appar — Chemische Apparatur
Chem Apparatebau — Chemischer Apparatebau
Chem Appar Suppl — Chemische Apparatur. Supplement
Chem Appl Nonlinear Raman Spectrosc — Chemical Applications of Nonlinear Raman Spectroscopy [monograph]
Chem Arb Werk Labor — Chemie Arbeit in Werk und Labor
Chem Aust — Chemistry in Australia
Chem Automot Ind — Chemicals for the Automotive Industry
Chem Ber — Chemische Berichte
Chem Ber Recl — Chemische Berichte/Recueil
Chem Ber Recl — Chemische Berichte/Recueil. Inorganic and Organometallic Chemistry
Chem Biochem Amino Acids Pept Proteins — Chemistry and Biochemistry of Amino Acids, Peptides, and Proteins
Chem Biochem Appl Lasers — Chemical and Biochemical Applications of Lasers [monograph]
Chem Biochem Eng Q — Chemical and Biochemical Engineering Quarterly
Chem Biochem Environ Fiber Sens — Chemical, Biochemical, and Environmental Fiber Sensors
Chem Biochem Plant Pig — Chemistry and Biochemistry of Plant Pigments
Chem Biochem Walnut Trees — Chemistry and Biochemistry of Walnut Trees
Chem-Bio In — Chemico-Biological Interactions
Chem Biol — Chemistry and Biology [London]
Chem Biol Action Radiat — Chemical and Biological Action of Radiation
Chem Biol Beta Lactam Antibiot — Chemistry and Biology of Beta-Lactam Antibiotics
Chem Biol Hydroxamic Acids Proc Int Symp — Chemistry and Biology of Hydroxamic Acids. Proceedings. International Symposiumon Chemistry and Biology of Hydroxamic Acids
Chem-Biol Interact — Chemico-Biological Interactions
Chem-Biol Interactions — Chemico-Biological Interactions
Chem Biol Pept Proc Am Pept Symp — Chemistry and Biology of Peptides. Proceedings. American Peptide Symposium
Chem Biol (Tokyo) — Chemistry and Biology (Tokyo)
Chem Biomed and Environ Instrum — Chemical, Biomedical, and Environmental Instrumentation
Chem Biomed Environ Inst — Chemical, Biomedical, and Environmental Instrumentation
Chem Biomed Environ Instrum — Chemical, Biomedical, and Environmental Instrumentation
Chem Bk Econ — Chemical Bank. Weekly Economic Package
Chem Bk Frct — Chemical Bank. Economic Forecast Summary
Chem Br — Chemistry in Britain
Chem Brit — Chemistry in Britain
Chem Bull — Chemical Bulletin
Chem Bull (Beijing) — Chemical Bulletin (Beijing)
Chem Bull Politeh Univ Timisoara — Chemical Bulletin of the Politehnica University of Timisoara
Chem Bull Polytech Inst Traian Vuia Timisoara — Chemical Bulletin of the Polytechnic Institute Traian Vuia of Timisoara
Chem Bull Tech Univ Timisoara — Chemical Bulletin of the Technical University Timisoara
Chem Bus — Chemical Business
Chem Can — Chemistry in Canada
Chem Carbon Carbon Triple Bond — Chemistry of the Carbon-Carbon Triple Bond
Chem Carcinog — Chemical Carcinogens
Chem Cda — Chemistry in Canada

Chem Cem Proc Int Symp — Chemistry of Cement. Proceedings. International Symposium
Chem Changes Food Process Proc Basic Symp — Chemical Changes in Food during Processing. Proceedings. Basic Symposium
Chem Charact Proc Semin — Chemical Characterisation. Proceedings. Seminar
Chem Chem Eng — Chemistry and Chemical Engineering
Chem Chem Ind — Chemistry and Chemical Industry
Chem Chem Ind J Hanoi — Chemical and Chemical Industry Journal (Hanoi)
Chem Chem Technol Kauno Politech Inst Jubiliejines Mokslines — Chemija ir Chemine Technologija. Kauno-Politechnikos Instituto Jubiliejines Mokslines-Technines Konferencijos. Darbai
Chem Chron — Chemika Chronika
Chem Chron A — Chemika Chronika. Section A
Chem Chron B — Chemika Chronika. Section B
Chem Chron Epistem Ekdosis — Chemika Chronika. Epistemonike Ekdosis
Chem Chron Genike Ekdosis — Chemika Chronika. Genike Ekdosis
Chem Coat Conf Powder Coat Sess Tech Pap — Chemical Coatings Conference. Powder Coatings Session. Technical Papers
Chem Coat Conf Tech Pap — Chemical Coatings Conference. Technical Papers
Chem Coaters Assoc Annu Natl Tech Semin — Chemical Coaters Association. Annual National Technical Seminar
Chem Color Oil Daily — Chemical, Color, and Oil Daily
Chem Color Oil Rec — Chemical, Color, and Oil Record
Chem Commun — Chemical Communications
Chem Commun Cambridge — Chemical Communications (Cambridge)
Chem Commun J Chem Soc — Chemical Communications. Journal of the Chemical Society
Chem Communs — Chemical Communications
Chem Commun Univ Stockholm — Chemical Communications. University of Stockholm
Chem Concepts — Chemical Concepts
ChemConf 96 New Initiatives Chem Educ — ChemConf '96. New Initiatives in Chemical Education
Chem Conf Proc — Chemists' Conference. Proceedings
Chem Congr North Am Cont — Chemical Congress of the North American Continent
Chem Control Res Inst (Ottawa) Inf Rep — Chemical Control Research Institute (Ottawa). Information Report
Chem Control Res Inst Ottawa Inf Rep CC X — Chemical Control Research Institute. Ottawa. Information Report CC-X
Chem Control Res Inst Ottawa Int Rep CC 16 — Chemical Control Research Institute. Ottawa. Internal Report CC-16
Chem Corps J — Chemical Corps Journal
Chem Corr — Chemical Correspondence
CHEMD — Chemsa
Chem De Fer — Chemins de Fer
Chem Depend — Chemical Dependencies
Chem Digest — Chemurgic Digest
Chem Div Trans Am Soc Qual Control — Chemical Division Transactions. American Society for Quality Control
Chem Drug — Chemist and Druggist
Chem Drug Export Rev — Chemist and Druggist Export Review
Chem Dydakt Ekol — Chemia, Dydaktyka, Ekologia
Chem Dyn Evol Our Galaxy Proc IAU Colloq — Chemical and Dynamical Evolution of Our Galaxy. Proceedings. IAU [International Astronomical Union] Colloquium
Chem Ecol — Chemistry and Ecology
Chem Econ — Chemical Economy and Engineering Review
Chem Econ Eng Rev — Chemical Economy and Engineering Review
Chem Ed (Seoul) — Chemical Education (Seoul)
Chem Ed Tokyo — Chemical Education (Tokyo)
Chem Educ — Chemical Education
Chem Educ — Chemical Educator [Electronic Publication]
Chem Eng — Chemical Engineer
Chem Eng — Chemical Engineering
Chem Eng & Min R — Chemical Engineering and Mining Review
Chem Eng and Min Rev — Chemical Engineering and Mining Review
Chem Eng (Aust) — Chemical Engineering (Australia)
Chem Eng Aust — Chemical Engineering in Australia
Chem Eng Birmingham Univ — Chemical Engineer. Birmingham University
Chem Eng Changing World Proc Plenary Sess World Congr Chem E — Chemical Engineering in a Changing World. Proceedings. Plenary Sessions. World Congress on Chemical Engineering
Chem Eng China — Chemical Engineering (China)
Chem Eng Comm — Chemical Engineering Communications
Chem Eng Commun — Chemical Engineering Communications
Chem Eng Costs Q — Chemical Engineering Costs Quarterly
Chem Eng Data Ser — Chemical and Engineering Data Series
Chem Eng Dep Monash Univ Rep — Chemical Engineering Department. Monash University. Report
Chem Eng Dig (Tokyo) — Chemical Engineer's Digest (Tokyo)
Chem Eng Educ — Chemical Engineering Education
Chem Eng Fundam — Chemical Engineering Fundamentals
Chem Eng Group Soc Chem Ind London Proc — Chemical Engineering Group. Society of Chemical Industry. London. Proceedings
Chem Eng (Int Ed) — Chemical Engineering (International Edition)
Chem Eng J — Chemical Engineering Journal
Chem Eng J Biochem Eng J — Chemical Engineering Journal and Biochemical Engineering Journal
Chem Eng (Jpn) — Chemical Engineering (Japan)
Chem Eng London — Chemical Engineer (London)
Chem Eng Mach Lanzhou Peoples Repub China — Chemical Engineering and Machinery (Lanzhou, People's Republic of China)
Chem Eng Monogr — Chemical Engineering Monographs
Chem Eng News — Chemical and Engineering News

Chem Eng New York — Chemical Engineering (New York)
Chem Engng — Chemical Engineering
Chem Engng (Aust) — Chemical Engineering (Australia)
Chem Engng Commun — Chemical Engineering Communications
Chem Engng Communications — Chemical Engineering Communications
Chem Engng J — Chemical Engineering Journal
Chem Engng Journal — Chemical Engineering Journal
Chem Engng Min Rev — Chemical Engineering and Mining Review
Chem Engng Prog — Chemical Engineering Progress
Chem Engng Progress — Chemical Engineering Progress
Chem Engng Res Des — Chemical Engineering Research and Design
Chem Engng Sci — Chemical Engineering Science
Chem Engng Science — Chemical Engineering Science
Chem Engng World — Chemical Engineering World
Chem Engn News — Chemical and Engineering News
Chem Eng (NY) — Chemical Engineering (New York)
Chem Eng P — Chemical Engineering Progress
Chem Eng Pr — Chemical Engineering Progress
Chem Eng Process — Chemical Engineering and Processing
Chem Eng Prog — Chemical Engineering Progress
Chem Eng Prog Monogr Ser — Chemical Engineering Progress. Monograph Series
Chem Eng Progr — Chemical Engineering Progress
Chem Eng Progr Symp Ser — Chemical Engineering Progress. Symposium Series
Chem Eng Prog Symp Ser — Chemical Engineering Progress. Symposium Series
Chem Engr — Chemical Engineer
Chem Engr Diary & Process Ind News — Chemical Engineer Diary and Process Industries News
Chem Eng Res and Des — Chemical Engineering Research and Design
Chem Eng Res Bul — Chemical Engineering Research Bulletin
Chem Eng Res Bull Dhaka — Chemical Engineering Research Bulletin (Dhaka)
Chem Eng Res Des Part A Trans Inst Chem Eng — Chemical Engineering Research and Design. Part A. Transactions of the Institute of Chemical Engineers
Chem Engrg J — Chemical Engineering Journal
Chem Engr (Lond) — Chemical Engineer (London)
Chem Eng (Rugby) — Chemical Engineer (Rugby)
Chem Eng S — Chem Show Guide. Special Advertising Supplement from Chemical Engineering
Chem Eng Sc — Chemical Engineering Science
Chem Eng Sci — Chemical Engineering Science
Chem Eng Supercrit Fluid Cond — Chemical Engineering at Supercritical Fluid Conditions
Chem Eng Technol — Chemical Engineering and Technology
Chem Eng Technol For Prod Process — Chemical Engineering Technology in Forest Products Processing [monograph]
Chem Eng (Tokyo) — Chemical Engineering (Tokyo)
Chem Eng Works Chem — Chemical Engineering and the Works Chemist
Chem Eng World — Chemical Engineering World
Chem Environ Res — Chemical and Environmental Research
Chem Environ Sci — Chemical and Environmental Science
Chem Equip News — Chemical Equipment News
Chem Equip Preview — Chemical Equipment Preview
Chem Era — Chemical Era
Chem Erde — Chemie der Erde
Chem Eur J — Chemistry. A European Journal
Chem Evol Early Precambrian College Park Colloq — Chemical Evolution of the Early Precambrian. College Park Colloquium on Chemical Evolution
Chem Exp Didakt — Chemie. Experiment und Didaktik
Chem Express — Chemistry Express. Journal. Kinki Chemical Society
Chem Exp Technol — Chemie. Experiment und Technologie
Chem Fab — Chemische Fabrik
Chem Fabr — Chemische Fabrik
Chem Fact (Tokyo) — Chemical Factory (Tokyo)
Chem Farming — Chemical Farming
Chemfasern — Chemiefasern/Textil-Industrie
Chem Fert Proc Int Congr — Chemical Fertilizers. Proceedings. International Congress
Chem Foods Beverages Recent Def — Chemistry of Foods and Beverages. Recent Developments
Chem Future Proc IUPAC Congr — Chemistry for the Future. Proceedings. IUPAC Congress
Chem Geol — Chemical Geology
Chem Geology — Chemical Geology
Chem Ges DDR Mitteilungsbl — Chemische Gesellschaft der Deutschen Demokratischen Republik. Mitteilungsblatt
Chem G Eur — Chemical Guide to Europe
Chem Health Saf — Chemical Health and Safety
Chem Heterocycl Comp — Chemistry of Heterocyclic Compounds
Chem Heterocycl Compd (Engl Transl) — Chemistry of Heterocyclic Compounds (English Translation)
Chem Heterocycl Compd NY — Chemistry of Heterocyclic Compounds (New York)
Chem Heterocycl Compd Proc Symp — Chemistry of Heterocyclic Compounds. Proceedings. Symposium on Chemistry of Hetercyclic Compounds
Chem Heterocycl Comp (USSR) — Chemistry of Heterocyclic Compounds (USSR)
Chem High Polym — Chemistry of High Polymers
Chem Hydrazo Azo Azoxy Groups — Chemistry of the Hydrazo, Azo, and Azoxy Groups
Chemia Analit — Chemia Analityczna
Chemia Politech Szczecin — Chemia (Politechnika Szczecinska)
Chemical Engnr — Chemical Engineer
Chemica Scr — Chemica Scripta
Chemico-Biol Interactions — Chemico-Biological Interactions
Chemico Bull — Chemico Bulletin
Chemie Einzeldarst — Chemie in Einzeldarstellungen

Chemiefasern Text-Anwendungstech — Chemiefasern und Textil-Anwendungstechnik [*Later, Chemiefasern/Textil-Industrie*]
Chemiefasern + Text-Anwendungstech Text Ind — Chemiefasern und Textil-Anwendungstechnik/Textil-Industrie
Chemiefasern/Textilind — Chemiefasern/Textilindustrie
Chemiefasern/Text-Ind — Chemiefasern/Textil-Industrie
Chemie Ind — Chemie en Industrie
Chemie-Ingr-Tech — Chemie-Ingenieur-Technik
Chemie Labor Betrieb — Chemie fuer Labor und Betrieb
Chemie Med — Chemie und Medizin
Chemie Rdsch — Chemie-Rundschau
Chemie Tech — Chemie en Techniek
Chemie Tech Gegenw — Chemie en Technik der Gegenwart
Chemie Tech Landw — Chemie und Technik in der Landwirtschaft
Chemikerztg — Chemiker-Zeitung [*Coethen*]
Chem Immunol — Chemical Immunology
Chem in Br — Chemistry in Britain
Chem in Britain — Chemistry in Britain
Chem Ind — Chemical Industries
Chem Ind — Chemical Industry and Engineering
Chem Ind — Chemistry and Industry
Chem Ind and Engng — Chemical Industry and Engineering
Chem Ind (Berlin) — Chemische Industrie (Berlin)
Chem Ind (Berlin) Gemeinschaftsausg — Chemische Industrie (Berlin). Gemeinschaftsausgabe
Chem Ind (Berlin) Nachrichtenausg — Chemische Industrie (Berlin). Nachrichtenausgabe
Chem Ind Dev — Chemical Industry Developments
Chem Ind Dev Ann — Chemical Industry Developments. Annual
Chem Ind Dig — Chemical Industry Digest
Chem Ind (Duesseldorf) — Chemische Industrie (Duesseldorf)
Chem Ind Duesseldorf Suppl — Chemische Industrie (Duesseldorf). Supplementum
Chem Ind Eng — Chemical Industry and Engineering
Chem Ind Eng (Beijing) — Chemical Industry and Engineering (Beijing)
Chem Ind Engl Ed — Chemische Industrie. English Edition
Chem Ind Eng Prog Beijing — Chemical Industry and Engineering Progress (Beijing)
Chem Ind Eng Tianjin — Chemical Industry and Engineering (Tianjin)
Chem Ind Facts Book — Chemical Industry Facts Book [*monograph*]
Chem Ind For Prod — Chemistry and Industry of Forest Products
Chem Ind Int — Chemische Industrie International
Chem Ind Int (Engl Transl) — Chemische Industrie International (English Translation)
Chem Ind Jahrb — Chemische Industrie. Jahrbuch
Chem Ind (Jpn) — Chemical Industry (Japan)
Chem Ind (Jpn) Suppl — Chemical Industry (Japan). Supplement
Chem Ind (Lond) — Chemistry and Industry (London)
Chem Ind London — Chemistry and Industry (London)
Chem Ind Maclean Hunter — Chemical Industries (Maclean-Hunter)
Chem Ind (NY) — Chemical Industries (New York)
Chem Ind NZ — Chemistry and Industry in New Zealand
Chem Ind Peking — Chemical Industry (Peking)
Chem Ind Rev — Chemistry and Industry Review
Chem Ind Shanghai — Chemical Industry (Shanghai)
Chem Ind (Tenali India) — Chemical Industry (Tenali, India)
Chem Indus — Chemistry and Industry
Chem Ind Week — Chemical Industries Week
Chem Inf — Chemical Information. Information in Chemistry, Pharmacology, and Patents
Chem Infd — Chemischer Informationsdienst
Chem Inf Dienst — Chemischer Informationsdienst
Chem Influences Behav — Chemical Influences on Behaviour [*monograph*]
Chem Info — Chemical Information and Computer Sciences. Journal
ChemInform — Chemischer Informationsdienst
Chem Informationsdienst — Chemischer Informationsdienst
Chem Informationsdienst Anorg Phys Chem — Chemischer Informationsdienst. Anorganische und Physikalische Chemie
Chem Informationsdienst Org Chem — Chemischer Informationsdienst. Organische Chemie
Chem Inf Sys — Chemical Information Systems
Chem-Ing-T — Chemie-Ingenieur-Technik
Chem-Ing-Tech — Chemie-Ingenieur-Technik
Chem Inhib Corros Control Proc Int Symp — Chemical Inhibitors for Corrosion Control. Proceedings. International Symposium
Chem Inorg Ring Syst — Chemistry of Inorganic Ring Systems
Chem Insgt — Chemical Insight
Chem Inst Can J Conf Am Chem Soc Abstr Pap — Chemical Institute of Canada. Joint Conference with the American Chemical Society. Abstracts of Papers
Chem Instr — Chemical Instrumentation
Chem Instrum — Chemical Instrumentation
Chem Instrum Leiden — Chemie und Instrument (Leiden)
Chem Int — Chemistry International
Chem Intell — Chemical Intelligencer
Chem Interfaces Proc Eur Conf — Chemistry of Interfaces. Proceeding. European Conference
Chem Inz Chem — Chemia i Inzynieria Chemiczna
Chem Inz Ekol — Chemia i Inzynieria Ekologiczna
Chemiosmotic Proton Circuits Biol Membr — Chemiosmotic Proton Circuits in Biological Membranes
Chemioter Antimicrob — Chemioterapia Antimicrobica
Chemioter Oncol — Chemioterapia Oncologica
Chemische — Chemische Industrie
Chemistry (Kyoto) Suppl — Chemistry (Kyoto). Supplement

Chem Jaarb Ned — Chemisch Jaarboekje voor Nederland, Belgie, en Nederlandsch Indie
Chem J Arm — Chemical Journal of Armenia
Chem J Chin Univ — Chemical Journal of Chinese Universities
Chem J Freunde Natur — Chemisches Journal fuer die Freunde der Naturlehre
Chem Jrl — Chemicals and Petro-Chemicals Journal
Chem Kraftwerk — Chemie im Kraftwerk
Chem Kunst Aktuell — Chemie Kunststoffe Aktuell
Chem Lab Betr — Chemie fuer Labor und Betrieb
Chem Lab Rep Dep Mines (NSW) — Chemical Laboratory Report. Department of Mines (New South Wales)
Chem Lab Rep Hiroshima — Chemical Laboratory Report (Hiroshima)
Chem Lab Rep NSW Dep Mines — Chemical Laboratory Report. New South Wales. Department of Mines
Chem Leafl — Chemistry Leaflet
Chem Lett — Chemistry Letters
Chem Lide — Chemie a Lide
Chem Life — Chemistry and Life
Chem Life — Chemistry of Life
Chem Lignans — Chemistry of Lignans
Chem Listy — Chemicke Listy
Chem Listy Vedu Prum — Chemicke Listy pro Vedu a Prumysl
Chem Mach — Chemical Machinery
Chem Mag — Chemie Magazine
Chem Mag Leuven — Chemie Magazine (Leuven)
Chem Mag Rijswijk Neth — Chemisch Magazine (Rijswijk, Netherlands)
Chem Mag The Hague — Chemisch Magazine (The Hague)
Chem Mark — Chemical Markets
Chem Market Reptr — Chemical Marketing Reporter
Chem Mark Newspaper — Chemical Marketing Newspaper
Chem Mark Rep — Chemical Marketing Reporter
Chem Mark Rep — Chemical Market Reporter
Chem Mar Sediments — Chemistry of Marine Sediments
Chem Mater — Chemistry of Materials
Chem Mercury — Chemistry of Mercury [*monograph*]
Chem Metall Eng — Chemical and Metallurgical Engineering
Chem Metall Z — Chemisch Metallurgische Zeitschrift
Chem Met CVD — Chemistry of Metal CVD (Chemical Vapor Deposition) [*monograph*]
Chem Met Eng — Chemical and Metallurgical Engineering
Chem Mikrobiol Technol Lebensm — Chemie, Mikrobiologie, Technologie der Lebensmittel
Chem Mktg Rep — Chemical Marketing Reporter
Chem Mkt R — Chemical Marketing Reporter
Chem Mkt Rept — Chemical Marketing Reporter
Chem Modif Oxide Surf Proc Chem Modif Surf Symp — Chemically Modified Oxide Surfaces. Proceedings. Chemically Modified Surfaces Symposium
Chem Modif Surf — Chemically Modified Surfaces
Chem Modif Surf Proc Symp — Chemically Modified Surfaces. Proceedings. Symposium on Chemically Modified Surfaces
Chem Mon — Chemical Monthly
Chem Mutagen Mamm Man — Chemical Mutagenesis in Mammals and Man [*monograph*]
Chem Mutagens — Chemical Mutagens
Chem N — Chemical News
Chem Nachr — Chemische Nachrichten
Chem Nat Compd — Chemistry of Natural Compounds
Chem Nat Compd Engl Transl — Chemistry of Natural Compounds (English Translation)
Chem Nat Compounds — Chemistry of Natural Compounds
Chem Nat Protein Fibers — Chemistry of Natural Protein Fibers [*monograph*]
Chem News — Chemical News
Chem News — Chemical News and Journal of Industrial Science
Chem News J Ind Sci — Chemical News and Journal of Industrial Science
Chem News J Phys Sci — Chemical News and Journal of Physical Science
Chem Nichtwaessrigen Ionis Loesungsm — Chemie in Nichtwaessarigen Ionisierenden Loesungsmitteln
Chem Non Aqueous Solvents — Chemistry of Non-Aqueous Solvents
Chem Novit — Chemische Novitaeten
Chem Nowych Urzadzeniach — Chemik o Nowych Urzadzeniach
Chem Nukl Entsorgung — Chemie der Nuklearen Entsorgung
Chem NZ — Chemistry in New Zealand
Chem Obz — Chemicke Obzor
Chem Oceanogr — Chemical Oceanography [*monograph*]
Chem Oil Gas Rom — Chemistry, Oil, and Gas in Romania
Chem Oil Ind Proc Int Symp — Chemicals in the Oil Industry. Proceedings. International Symposium
Chemom Intell Lab Syst — Chemometrics and Intelligent Laboratory Systems
Chemom Species Identif — Chemometrics and Species Identification
Chemorecept Carotid Body Int Workshop — Chemoreception in the Carotid Body. International Workshop
Chemorecept Mar Org — Chemoreception in Marine Organisms
Chem Organophosphorus Compd — Chemistry of Organophosphorus Compounds
Chem Org Selenium Tellurium Compd — Chemistry of Organic Selenium and Tellurium Compounds
Chem Org Sulfur Compd — Chemistry of Organic Sulfur Compounds
Chemorheol Thermosetting Polym Symp — Chemorheology of Thermosetting Polymers. Symposium
Chemothera — Chemotherapy
Chemother Fact Sheet — Chemotherapy Fact Sheet
Chemother Immun — Chemotherapy and Immunity
Chemother Infect Dis — Chemotherapy of Infectious Disease [*monograph*]
Chemother J — Chemotherapie Journal

Chemother Proc Int Congr Chemother — Chemotherapy. Proceedings. International Congresss of Chemotherapy

Chemother Pro Int Congr Chemother — Chemotherapy. Proceedings of the International Congress of Chemotherapy

Chem Oxid — Chemical Oxidation. Technologies for the Nineties. Proceedings of the International Symposium

Chem Pap — Chemical Papers

Chem Papermaking Conf Proc — Chemistry of Papermaking. Conference Proceedings

Chem Pept Proteins — Chemistry of Peptides and Proteins

Chem Peroxides — Chemistry of Peroxides [*monograph*]

Chem Pet Eng — Chemical and Petroleum Engineering

Chem Pet Eng (Engl Transl) — Chemical and Petroleum Engineering (English Translation)

Chem Pet Hydrocarbons — Chemistry of Petroleum Hydrocarbons [*monograph*]

Chem Petro-Chem J — Chemicals and Petro-Chemicals Journal

Chem Pharm — Chemical and Pharmaceutical Bulletin

Chem Pharmacol Drugs — Chemistry and Pharmacology of Drugs

Chem Pharmacol Synapse — Chemical Pharmacology of the Synapse [*monograph*]

Chem Pharm Bull — Chemical and Pharmaceutical Bulletin

Chem Pharm Bull (Tokyo) — Chemical and Pharmaceutical Bulletin (Tokyo)

Chem Pharm Centralbl — Chemisch-Pharmaceutisches Centralblatt

Chem Pharm Tech (Dordrecht Neth) — Chemische en Pharmaceutische Technik (Dordrecht, Netherlands)

Chem Phy Fract — Chemistry and Physics of Fracture

Chem Phys — Chemical Physics

Chem Phys Appl Surf Act Subst Proc Int Congr — Chemistry, Physics, and Application of Surface Active Substances. Proceedings. International Congress on Surface Active Substances

Chem Phys Carbon — Chemistry and Physics of Carbon

Chem Phys Chem Appl Surf Act Subst Proc Int Congr — Chemistry, Physical Chemistry, and Applications of Surface Active Substances. Proceedings. International Congress on Surface Active Substances

Chem Phys L — Chemistry and Physics of Lipids

Chem Phys Lett — Chemical Physics Letters

Chem Phys Lipids — Chemistry and Physics of Lipids

Chem Phy Solid Surf — Chemistry and Physics of Solid Surfaces

Chem Phys Processes Combust — Chemical and Physical Processes in Combustion

Chem Phys Prod Aspects Tob Smoke Tob Chem Res Conf — Chemical, Physical, and Production Aspects of Tobacco and Smoke. Tobacco Chemists' Research Conference

Chem Phys Solids Their Surf — Chemical Physics of Solids and Their Surfaces

Chem Phys Technol Kunst Einzeldarst — Chemie, Physik, und Technologie der Kunststoffe in Einzeldarstellungen

Chem Plant Prot — Chemistry of Plant Protection

Chem Plant (Tokyo) — Chemical Plant (Tokyo)

Chem P Lett — Chemical Physics Letters

Chem Polym Rubber Plast Ind News — Chemicals, Polymers, Rubber, and Plastics Industry News

Chem Prax — Chemische Praxis

Chem Pretreat Nucl Waste Disposal Proc Am Chem Soc Symp — Chemical Pretreatment of Nuclear Waste for Disposal. Proceedings of an AmericanChemical Society Symposium

Chem Preview — Chemical Preview

Chem Probl Connected Stab Explos — Chemical Problems Connected with the Stability of Explosives

Chem Process — Chemical Processing

Chem Process Adv Mater — Chemical Processing of Advanced Materials

Chem Process Chicago — Chemical Processing (Chicago)

Chem Process Control CPC Proc Int Conf Chem Process Control — Chemical Process Control. CPC. Proceedings. International Conference on Chemical Process Control

Chem Process Control Proc Eng Found Conf — Chemical Process Control. Proceedings. Engineering Foundation Conference

Chem Process Eng — Chemical and Process Engineering

Chem Process Eng Annu (Bombay) — Chemical Processing and Engineering. Annual (Bombay)

Chem Process Eng At World — Chemical and Process Engineering and Atomic World

Chem Process Eng (Bombay) — Chemical Processing and Engineering (Bombay)

Chem Process Eng London — Chemical and Process Engineering (London)

Chem Process Hazards Spec Ref Plant Des Int Symp — Chemical Process Hazards with Special Reference to Plant Design. International Symposium

Chem Processing — Chemical Processing

Chem Process (London) — Chemical Processing (London)

Chem Process Rev — Chemical Processing Review

Chem Process (Sydney) — Chemical Processing (Sydney)

Chem Proc (Sydney) — Chemical Processing (Sydney)

Chem Prod — Chemische Produktion

Chem Prod Aerosol News — Chemical Products and Aerosol News

Chem Prod Chem News — Chemical Products and the Chemical News

Chem Prog Bull — Chemicals in Progress Bulletin

Chem Progr — Chemical Progress

Chem Prop Biomol Syst — Chemistry and Properties of Biomolecular Systems

Chem Propul Inf Agency CPIA Publ — Chemical Propulsion Information Agency. CPIA Publication

Chem Prot Environ Proc Int Conf — Chemistry for Protection of the Environment. Proceedings. International Conference

Chem Prum — Chemicky Prumysl

Chem Prum Priloha — Chemicky Prumysl. Priloha

Chem Purch — Chemical Purchasing

Chem Q — Chemists Quarterly

Chem Qual Ser Kans Geol Surv — Chemical Quality Series. Kansas Geological Survey

Chem R — Chemical Reviews

Chem Rdsch Mitteleur — Chemische Rundschau fuer Mitteleuropa und der Balkan

Chem React Eng Houston Int Symp — Chemical Reaction Engineering. Houston. International Symposium on Chemical Reaction Engineering

Chem React Eng Int Symp — Chemical Reaction Engineering. International Symposium on Chemical Reaction Engineering

Chem React Eng Plenary Lect Int Symp — Chemical Reaction Engineering. Plenary Lectures. Based on the International Symposium on Chemical Reaction Engineering

Chem React Eng Proc Eur Symp — Chemical Reaction Engineering. Proceedings. European Symposium

Chem React Eng Rev Houston Int Symp Chem React Eng — Chemical Reaction Engineering Reviews. Houston. International Symposium on Chemical Reaction Engineering

Chem React Eng Rev Int Symp — Chemical Reaction Engineering Reviews. International Symposium on Chemical Reaction Engineering

Chem React Eng Technol — Chemical Reaction Engineering and Technology

Chem React Liq Proc Int Meet Soc Fr Chim Div Chim Phys — Chemical Reactivity in Liquids. Fundamental Aspects. Proceedings. InternationalMeeting. Societe Francaise de Chimie. Division de Chimie Physique

Chem Rec-Age — Chemical Record-Age

Chem Reg Rep BNA — Chemical Regulation Reporter. Bureau of National Affairs

Chem Regulat Pl — Chemical Regulation in Plants/Shokubutsu no Kagaku Chosetsu/The Society of Chemical Regulation of Plants

Chem Regul Rep — Chemical Regulation Reporter

Chem Reihe — Chemische Reihe

Chem Res Appl — Chemical Research and Application

Chem Res Chin Univ — Chemical Research in Chinese Universities

Chem Res Kaifeng Peoples Repub China — Chemical Researches (Kaifeng, People's Republic of China)

Chem Res Toxicol — Chemical Research in Toxicology

Chem Rev — Chemical Reviews

Chem Rev Deddington UK — Chemistry Review (Deddington, United Kingdom)

Chem Rev Fett Harz Ind — Chemische Revue ueber die Fett und Harz Industrie

Chem Rev (Jpn) — Chemical Review (Japan)

Chem Rev Washington DC — Chemical Reviews (Washington, D.C.)

Chem Rund — Chemische Rundschau

Chem Rundschau — Chemische Rundschau

Chem Rundsch Farbbeilage — Chemische Rundschau. Farbbeilage

Chem Rundsch Mag — Chemische Rundschau Magazine

Chem Rundsch (Solothurn) — Chemische Rundschau (Solothurn)

Chem Saf Data Sheet — Chemical Safety Data Sheet

CHEMSAFE — Chemical Industry Scheme for Assistance in Freight Emergencies

Chems Brtn — Chemistry in Britain

Chem Sch — Chemie in der Schule

Chem Scr — Chemica Scripta

Chem Scripta — Chemica Scripta

Chem Semin Honours Stud Univ Singapore — Chemistry Seminar for Honours Students. University of Singapore

Chem Sens — Chemical Senses

Chem Sens — Chemical Sensors

Chem Senses — Chemical Senses

Chem Senses — Chemical Senses and Flavor

Chem Sens Technol — Chemical Sensor Technology

Chem Sep Dev Sel Pap Int Conf Sep Sci Technol — Chemical Separations. Developed from Selected Papers Presented at theInternational Conference on Separations Science and Technology

Chem Sierra Leone — Chemistry in Sierra Leone

Chem Signals Vertebr Aquat Invertebr Proc Symp — Chemical Signals. Vertebrates and Aquatic Invertebrates. Proceedings of the Symposium

Chem Soc Agric — Chemisation of Socialistic Agriculture

Chem Soc Ethiop Bull — Chemical Society of Ethiopia. Bulletin

Chem Soc Faraday Discuss — Chemical Society. Faraday Discussions

Chem Soc Faraday Symp — Chemical Society. Faraday Symposia

Chem Soc J — Chemical Society. Journal

Chem Soc Pak J — Chemical Society of Pakistan. Journal

Chem Soc Re — Chemical Society. Reviews

Chem Soc Rev — Chemical Society. Reviews

Chem Soc Spec Publ — Chemical Society. Special Publication

Chem Software — Chemistry and Software

Chem Space — Chemistry in Space

Chem Speciation Bioavailability — Chemical Speciation and Bioavailability

Chem Spec Manuf Assoc Proc Annu Meet — Chemical Specialities Manufacturers Association. Proceedings. Annual Meeting

Chem Spec Manuf Assoc Proc Mid-Year Meet — Chemical Specialties Manufacturers Association. Proceedings of the Mid-Year Meeting

Chem Sri Lanka — Chemistry in Sri Lanka

Chem Stosow — Chemia Stosowana

Chem Stosow Ser A — Chemia Stosowana. Seria A

Chem Stosow Ser B — Chemia Stosowana. Seria B

Chem Strojir Stavitelstvi Pristrojova Tech — Chemicke Strojirenstvi. Stavitelstvi a Pristrojova Technika

Chem Sulphinic Acids Esters Their Deriv — Chemistry of Sulphinic Acids, Esters, and Their Derivatives

Chem Sustainable Dev — Chemistry for Sustainable Development

Chem Szk — Chemia Szkole

Chem Take-Off — Chemical Take-Off

Chem Tech — Chemical Technology

Chem Tech — Chemische Technik

Chem Tech (Amsterdam) — Chemie en Techniek (Amsterdam)

Chem Tech Berlin — Chemische Technik (Berlin)

Chem Tech Fabr — Chemisch Technische Fabrikant

Chem Tech Fuels Oils — Chemistry and Technology of Fuels and Oils

Chem Tech (Heidelberg) — Chemische Technik (Heidelberg)
Chem Tech Ind — Chemisch-Technische Industrie
Chem Tech Inst Tech Hochsch Karlsruhe Mitt — Chemisch-Technisches Institut der Technischen Hochschule Karlsruhe. Mitteilungen
Chem Tech Landwirt — Chemie und Technik in der Landwirtschaft
Chem Tech Leipzig — Chemische Technik (Leipzig)
Chem Technol — Chemical Technology
Chem Technol — Chemical Technology, a Series of Monographs
Chem Technol Chem — Chemia i Technologia Chemiczna
Chem Technol Eur — Chemical Technology Europe
Chem Technol Fuels Oils — Chemistry and Technology of Fuels and Oils
Chem Technol Fuels Oils Engl Transl — Chemistry and Technology of Fuels and Oils (English Translation)
Chem Technol Makromol Stoffe Kolloq — Chemie und Technologie Makromolekularer Stoffe. Kolloquium
Chem Technol Pectin — Chemistry and Technology of Pectin
Chem Tech Rev — Chemical Technology Review
Chem Tech Rev — Chemie und Technik Revue
Chem Tech Rev Bijl — Chemie and Techniek Revue. Bijlage
Chem Tech Rundsch Anz Chem Ind — Chemisch Technische Rundschau und Anzeiger der Chemischen Industrie
Chem Tech Rundsch (Berlin) — Chemisch-Technische Rundschau (Berlin)
Chem Tech Rundsch Solothurn Switz — Chemisch-Technische Rundschau (Solothurn, Switzerland)
Chem Tech Uebers — Chemisch Technische Uebersicht
Chem Tech Umsch — Chemisch-Technische Umschau
Chemtech (US) — Chemtech (United States) [*Formerly, Chemical Technology*]
Chem Tech Ztg — Chemiker- und Techniker-Zeitung. Allgemeine-Oesterreichische
Chem Thermodyn — Chemical Thermodynamics
Chem Times (Athens) B — Chemical Times (Athens). Section B
Chem Times Trends — Chemical Times and Trends
Chem Titles — Chemical Titles
Chem Titles Chicago Psychoanal Lit Index — Chemical Titles. Chicago Psychoanalytic Literature Index
Chem Today — Chemistry Today
Chemtracts Anal Phys Chem — Chemtracts. Analytical and Physical Chemistry
Chemtracts Anal Phys Inorg Chem — Chemtracts. Analytical, Physical, and Inorganic Chemistry
Chemtracts Biochem Mol Biol — Chemtracts. Biochemistry and Molecular Biology
Chemtracts Inorg Chem — Chemtracts. Inorganic Chemistry
Chemtracts Macromol Chem — Chemtracts. Macromolecular Chemistry
Chemtracts Org Chem — Chemtracts. Organic Chemistry
Chem Trade J Chem Eng — Chemical Trade Journal and Chemical Engineer
Chem Trade Mag — Chemical Trade Magazine
Chem Umsch Geb Fette Oele Wachse Harze — Chemische Umschau auf dem Gebiete der Fette, Oele, Wachse, und Harze
Chem Unserer Zeit — Chemie in Unserer Zeit
Chemurg Dig — Chemurgic Digest
Chemurgic Dig — Chemurgic Digest
Chemurg Pap — Chemurgic Papers
Chem Use Organophosphorus Compd Trans Conf — Chemistry and Use of Organophosphorus Compounds. Transactions. Conference
Chem Uses Molybdenum Proc Int Conf — Chemistry and Uses of Molybdenum. Proceedings. International Conference
Chem Vap Deposition Int Conf — Chemical Vapor Deposition. International Conference
Chem Vapor Deposition — Chemical Vapor Deposition
Chem Verteidigung — Chemie und Verteidigung
Chem Vlakna — Chemicke Vlakna
Chem W — Chemical Week
Chem Warf — Chemical Warfare
Chem Warf Bull — Chemical Warfare Bulletin
Chem Water Wastewater Treat Proc Gothenburg Symp — Chemical Water and Wastewater Treatment. Proceedings. Gothenburg Symposium
Chem Week — Chemical Week
Chem Weekbl — Chemisch Weekblad [*Later, Chemisch Weekblad/Chemische Courant*]
Chem Weekb Mag — Chemisch Weekblad Magazine [*Later, Chemisch Magazine*]
Chem Wkly — Chemical Weekly
Chem Wkr — Chemical Worker
Chem World — Chemical World
Chem World (Shanghai) — Chemical World (Shanghai)
Chemy Ind — Chemistry and Industry
Chemy Life — Chemistry and Life
Chem Zeit — Chemiker-Zeitung
Chem-Zeitun — Chemiker-Zeitung
Chem Zeitung — Chemiker-Zeitung
Chem Zelle Gewebe — Chemie der Zelle und Gewebe
Chem Zent Bl — Chemisches Zentralblatt
Chem Zentr — Chemisches Zentralblatt
Chem Zentralbl — Chemisches Zentralblatt
Chem Zool — Chemical Zoology
Chem-Ztg — Chemiker-Zeitung
Chem Ztg Beil — Chemiker-Zeitung. Beilage
Chem-Ztg Chem Appar — Chemiker-Zeitung. Chemische Apparatur
Chem Ztg Chem Appar Verfahrenstech — Chemiker-Zeitung. Chemische Apparatur. Verfahrenstechnik
Chem Zvesti — Chemicke Zvesti
C Her — Christian Herald
Cherb S Sc Nt Mm — Memoires de la Societe Imperiale des Sciences Naturelles de Cherbourg
CHERD — Chemical Era
Chern Metall — Chernaya Metallurgiya
Chesapeake Bay Inst Johns Hopkins Univ Tech Rep — Chesapeake Bay Institute. Johns Hopkins University. Technical Report

Chesapeake Sci — Chesapeake Science
Chess L — Chess Life
Chester & N Wales Archaeol Soc — Chester and North Wales Archaeological Society
Chesterton Rev — Chesterton Review
Chest Heart Stroke J — Chest, Heart, and Stroke Journal
Chest Surg Clin N Am — Chest Surgery Clinics of North America
CHETA — Chung-Hua Erh K'o Tsa Chih
CHETAE — Chung-Hua Erh K'o Tsa Chih
ChET Chem Exp Technol — ChET. Chemie. Experiment und Technologie
Chet Soc — Chetham Society
Chetvertichn Period — Chetvertichnyi Period
Chev Troie — Cheval de Troie
CHEYAT — Chung-Hua Erh Pi Yen Hou K'o Tsa Chih
CHF — Cahiers d'Histoire et de Folklore
CHFCA — Chung-Hua Fu Ch'an K'o Tsa Chih
CHFCA2 — Chung-Hua Fu Ch'an K'o Tsa Chih
Chf Engrs Rep Br Eng Boil Elect Insur Co — Chief Engineer's Reports of the British Engine Boiler and Electrical Insurance Co
CHFMA — Classiques de l'Histoire de France du Moyen Age
CHFSAG — Chung-Hua Fang She Hsueh Tsa Chih
CHGEA — Chemical Geology
CHGLA — Chemik
CHGP — Collection Historique des Grands Philosophes
CHGSAL — Chromatographic Science Series
CHH — Chronos. Vakblad voor de Uurwerkbranche
ChH — Church History
CHH — Cuadernos de Historia Habanera
CHHCDF — Chung-Hua Hsin Hsuch Kuan Ping Tsa Chih
Ch Her — Church Herald
Ch Hist — Church History
CHHNA — Chung-Hua Nei K'o Tsa Chih
CHHNAB — Chinese Journal of Internal Medicine
CHHOAE — Chronica Horticulturae
CHHPA — Ch'ing Hua Ta Hsueh Hsueh Pao
CHHTAT — Chung-Hua I Hsueh Tsa Chih
CHI — Chemical Hazards in Industry
CHI — China Newsletter
CHIA — Cahiers. Institut d'Amenagement et d'Urbanisme de la Region d'Ile-De-France
Chiang Mai Med Bull — Chiang Mai Medical Bulletin
Chiangmai Univ Sci Fac J — Chiangmai University. Science Faculty. Journal
Chiba Found Colloq Ageing — Chiba Foundation. Colloquia on Ageing
Chiba Med J — Chiba Medical Journal
Chi BA Rec — Chicago Bar Association. Record
Chi B Rec — Chicago Bar Record
Chicag Chem Bull — Chicago Chemical Bulletin
Chicago Acad Sci Bull Nat History Misc — Chicago Academy of Sciences. Bulletin. Natural History Miscellanea
Chicago Anthrop Exch — Chicago Anthropology Exchange
Chicago Archit J — Chicago Architectural Journal
Chicago Archtl Jnl — Chicago Architectural Journal
Chicago Art Inst Bul — Chicago Art Institute. Bulletin
Chicago Art Inst Cal — Chicago Art Institute. Calendar
Chicago Art Inst Q — Chicago Art Institute. Quarterly
Chicago Bar Rec — Chicago Bar Record
Chicago Bd Options Ex Guide CCH — Chicago Board Options Exchange Guide. Commerce Clearing House
Chicago B Rec — Chicago Bar Record
Chicago Bs — Crain's Chicago Business
Chicago Dairy Prod — Chicago Dairy Produce
Chicago Fld Mus Nat Hist — Chicago Field Museum of Natural History
Chicago Herpetol Soc Newsl — Chicago Herpetological Society. Newsletter
Chicago His — Chicago History of Science and Medicine
Chicago Hist Sci Med — Chicago History of Science and Medicine
Chicago J Theoret Comput Sci — Chicago Journal of Theoretical Computer Science
Chicago-Kent L Rev — Chicago-Kent Law Review
Chicago LB — Chicago Law Bulletin
Chicago Lectures in Math — Chicago Lectures in Mathematics
Chicago Lectures Phys — Chicago Lectures in Physics
Chicago Leg News — Chicago Legal News
Chicago Leg News (Ill) — Chicago Legal News
Chicago LJ — Chicago Law Journal
Chicago Med — Chicago Medicine
Chicago Med Exam — Chicago Medical Examiner
Chicago Med Rec — Chicago Medical Record
Chicago Med Recorder — Chicago Medical Recorder
Chicago Med Sch Q — Chicago Medical School Quarterly
Chicago Med Times — Chicago Medical Times
Chicago Nat — Chicago Naturalist
Chicago Nat Hist Mus Bull — Chicago Natural History Museum Bulletin
Chicago Psychoanal Lit Ind — Chicago Psychoanalytic Literature Index
Chicago Psychoanal Lit Index — Chicago Psychoanalytic Literature Index
Chicago R — Chicago Review
Chicago Rev — Chicago Review
Chicago Sch J — Chicago Schools Journal
Chicagos Hlth — Chicago's Health
Chicago Stds — Chicago Studies
Chicago Studs — Chicago Studies
Chicago Trib — Chicago Tribune
Chicago Univ Dept Geography Research Paper — Chicago. University. Department of Geography. Research Paper
Chicago Univ Rec — University Record. University of Chicago
Chicano L Rev — Chicano Law Review

Chic Banker — Chicago Banker
Chic B Rec — Chicago Bar Record
Chicg Trib — Chicago Tribune
Chic Hist Soc Proc — Chicago Historical Society. Proceedings
Chic Kent R — Chicago-Kent Review
Chic LB — Chicago Law Bulletin
Chic Leg News — Chicago Legal News
Chic LJ — Chicago Law Journal
Chic Med Sch Q — Chicago Medical School Quarterly
Chic Nat Hist Mus Annu Rep — Chicago Natural History Museum. Annual Report
Chicorel Abst Read Learn Disab — Chicorel Abstracts to Reading and Learning Disabilities
Chicorel Abstr Read Learn Disabil — Chicorel Abstracts to Reading and Learning Disabilities
Chic R — Chicago Review
Chic Sch J — Chicago Schools Journal
ChicSt — Chicago Studies
ChicTSemReg — Chicago Theological Seminary. Register
Chic Univ Dep Geogr Res Pap — Chicago. University. Department of Geography. Research Paper
CHID — Combined Health Information Database
Chief Constables Assn Can Proc — Chief Constables Association of Canada. Proceedings
Chief Coun — Chief Counsel. Annual Report. United States Internal Revenue Service
Chief Executive Mon — Chief Executive Monthly
Chiesa Quart — Chiesa e Quartiere
CHIHA — Chi'i Hsiang Hsueh Pao
Chih Wu Fen Liu Hsueeh Pao — Journal of Botanical Analysis/Chih-Wu Fen-Liu Hsueh-Pao
Chih Wu Hsueeh Pao — Acta Botanica Taiwanica. Science Reports. National Taiwan University. Chih Wu Hsueh Pao
Chih Wu Hsueh Pao Acta Bot Sin — Chih Wu Hsueh Pao. Acta Botanica Sinica
CHIIA — Chemische Industrie International
Chi Jrl R — Chicago Journalism Review
CHIKD — Chi Kuang
Chi-Kent LR — Chicago-Kent Law Review
Chi-Kent L Rev — Chicago-Kent Law Review
Chi-Kent Rev — Chicago-Kent Law Review
Chikyukagaku (Geochem) — Chikyukagaku (Geochemistry) Nagoya
Chilandar Zborn — Chilandarski Zbornik
Chi LB — Chicago Law Bulletin
Child Abuse Negl — Child Abuse and Neglect
Child Adolesc Psychiatr Clin N Am — Child and Adolescent Psychiatric Clinics of North America (Philadelphia, PA)
Child Alcohol — Children of Alcoholics
Child & Youth Serv — Child and Youth Services
Child Behav Ther — Child Behaviour Therapy
Child Care — Child Care Quarterly
Child Care Health Dev — Child Care Health and Development
Child Care Inf Exch — Child Care Information Exchange
Child Care Q — Child Care Quarterly
Child Contemp Soc — Children in Contemporary Society
Child D — Children's Digest
Child Dev — Child Development
ChildDevAb — Child Development Abstracts
Child Dev Abstr Bibliogr — Child Development Abstracts and Bibliography
Child Dev Abstr Biblphy — Child Development Abstracts and Bibliography
Child Devel — Child Development
Child Developm Absts Biblio — Child Development Abstracts and Bibliography
Child Ed — Childhood Education
Child Environ Adult Dis — Childhood Environment and Adult Disease
Child Exercise — Children and Exercise
Child Exercise Proc Int Symp — Children and Exercise. Proceedings. International Symposium
Child Guid Inter Clin Confs — Child Guidance Inter-Clinic Conferences. National Association for Mental Health
Child Health Care — Children's Health Care
Child Health Dev — Child Health and Development
Child Health M — Child Health Magazine
Childh Educ — Childhood Education
Child Hlth Bull — Child Health Bulletin
Child Hlth Mag — Child Health Magazine
ChildL — Children's Literature
Child Legal Rights J — Children's Legal Rights Journal
Child Legal Rts J — Children's Legal Rights Journal
Child Lib News — Children's Libraries Newsletter
Child Lit — Children's Literature
Child Lit Abstr — Children's Literature Abstracts
Child Lit Educ — Children's Literature in Education
Child Mag Guide — Children's Magazine Guide
Child Maltreat — Child Maltreatment
Child Nephr — Child Nephrology and Urology
Childns Mus Bull Brooklyn — Children's Museum Bulletin (Brooklyn, New York)
Childns Mus News Brooklyn — Children's Museum News (Brooklyn, New York)
Child Obes — Childhood Obesity
Child Par M — Children. The Parents' Magazine
Child Prot Serv NY St Ann Rep — Child Protective Services in New York State. Annual Report
Child Psych — Child Psychiatry and Human Development
Child Psych & Human Devel — Child Psychiatry and Human Development
Child Psychiatry Hum Dev — Child Psychiatry and Human Development
Child Psychol — Child Psychology. Bulletin of the Institute of Child Psychology
Child Psy Q — Child Psychiatry Quarterly
Childrens Lib News — Children's Libraries Newsletter

Childr Lit — Children's Literature
Childs Bsn — Children's Business
Childs Nerv Syst — Child's Nervous System
Child St J — Child Study Journal
Child Stud J — Child Study Journal
Child Theat Rev — Children's Theatre Review
Child Today — Children Today
Child Trop (Engl Ed) — Children in the Tropics (English Edition)
Child Wel — Child Welfare
Child Welf — Child Welfare
Child Welf Leag Am Bul — Child Welfare League of America. Bulletin
Child Youth Care Q — Child and Youth Care Quarterly
Child Youth Serv — Child and Youth Services
Chile Econ — Chile Economic Report
Chile Econ N — Chile Economic News
Chile Mader — Chile Maderero
Chile Univ Fac Cienc Fis Mat Inst Geol Publ — Chile. Universidad. Facultad de Ciencias Fisica y Matematicas. Instituto de Geologia. Publicacion
Chi Lib Sys Com — Chicago Library System Communicator
Chili S Sc Act — Actes de la Societe Scientifique du Chili. Sociedad Cientifica de Chile
Chi LJ — Chicago Law Journal
Chillan Chile Estac Exp Bol Tec — Chillan, Chile. Estacion Experimental. Boletin Tecnico
Chil Nitrate Agric Serv Inf — Chilean Nitrate Agricultural Service. Information
Chilton Automot Ind — Chilton's Automotive Industries
Chilton MF — Chilton Market Forecast
Chiltons Food Eng — Chilton's Food Engineering
Chiltons Food Eng Int — Chilton's Food Engineering International
Chiltons I&CS — Chilton's I&CS. Instrumentation and Control Systems
Chilton Tract J — Chilton Tractor Journal
Chim — Chimica
Chim Acta Turc — Chimica Acta Turcica
Chim Actual — Chimie Actualites
Chim Agric — Chimie et Agriculture
Chim Agric — Chimizarea Agriculturii
Chim Anal (Bucharest) — Chimie Analitica (Bucharest)
Chim Anal (Paris) — Chimie Analytique (Paris)
Chim Analyt — Chimie Analytique
Chim Batim — Chimie et Batiment
Chim Chim Phys Appl Agents Surf CR Congr Int Deterg — Chimie, Chimie Physique, et Applications des Agents de Surface. Compte-Rendu. Congres International de la Detergence
Chim Chron — Chimika Chronika
Chim Chron A — Chimika Chronika. Section A
Chim Chron (Athens) — Chimika Chronika (Athens)
Chim Chron B — Chimika Chronika. Section B
Chim Chron Epistem Ekdosis — Chimika Chronika. Epistemonike Ekdosis
Chim Chron Gen Ed — Chimika Chronika. General Edition
Chim Didact — Chimica Didactica
Chim Hautes Temp Colloq Natl — Chimie des Hautes Temperatures. Colloque National
Chim Htes Temp — Chimie des Hautes Temperatures. Compte Rendu du Colloque National, Centre National de la Recherche Scientifique
Chimica e Ind — Chimica e l'Industria
Chimica Ind — Chimica Industriale
Chimica Ind Agric Biol — Chimica nell'Industria nell'Agricoltura, nella Biologia, e altre sue Applicazioni
Chimica Ind Appl — Chimica Industriale e Applicata
Chimica Ind (Milano) — Chimica e l'Industria (Milano)
Chimica Ind S Paulo — Chimica e Industria (Sao Paulo)
Chimica Med Mod — Chimica e la Medicina Moderna
Chimico Ital — Chimico Italiano
Chimie Act — Chimie Actualites
Chimie & Ind — Chimie et Industrie
Chimie Mag — Chimie Magazine
Chimie Peint — Double Liaison. Chimie des Peintures
Chim Ind — Chimica e l'Industria
Chim Ind Agric Biol Realizz Corp — Chimica nell Industria, nell Agricultura, nella Biologia e nelle Realizzazioni Corporative
Chim Ind Financ — Chimie Industrielle et Financiere
Chim Ind - Genie Chim — Chimie et Industrie - Genie Chimique
Chim Ind Milan — Chimica e l'Industria (Milan)
Chim Ind Milan Suppl — Chimica e l'Industria (Milan). Supplemento
Chim Ind Milan Suppl Quad Ing Chim Ital — Chimica e l'Industria (Milan). Supplemento. Quaderni dell'Ingegnere Chimico Italiano
Chim Ind (Paris) — Chimie et Industrie (Paris)
Chim Ind (Paris) Suppl Mens — Chimie et Industrie (Paris). Supplement Mensuel
Chim Ing — Chimica e Ingegneria
Chim Macromol — Chimie Macromoleculaire
Chim Med — Chimie Medicale
Chim Microbiol Technol Aliment — Chimie, Microbiologie, Technologie Alimentaire
Chim Mod — Chimie Moderne
Chim Mondo — Chimica nel Mondo
Chim Nouv — Chimie Nouvelle
Chim Oggi — Chimica Oggi
Chim Pein Encres Plast Adhes Leurs Composants — Chimie des Peintures, des Encres, des Plastiques, des Adhesifs, et de Leurs Composants
Chim Peint — Chimie des Peintures
Chim Peint Vernis — Chimie des Peintures et Vernis
Chim Phys Appl Prat Agents Surf CR Congr Int Deterg — Chimie, Physique, et Applications Pratiques des Agents de Surface. Compte-Rendu. Congres International de la Detergence
Chim Pitture Vernici Smalti — Chimica delle Pitture-Vernici e Smalti

Chim Pure Appl — Chimie Pure et Appliquee
Chim Sc — Chimica nella Scuola
Chim Subst Nat — Chimie des Substances Naturelles
Chim Tech — Chimie et Technique
Chim Ther — Chimica Therapeutica
Chim Ther — Chimie Therapeutique
China Agri — China Agriculture to the Year 2000
China Brew — China Brewing
China Bus R — China Business Review
China Bus Trade — China Business and Trade
China Chem Rep — China Chemical Reporter
China Chem Week — China Chemical Week
China Clay Trade Rev — China Clay Trade Review
China Cotton J — China Cotton Journal/Shang Ch'ang Ho Chi Hua Sha Lien Hui K'an
China Dly — China Daily
China Dly Bus Wkly — China Daily Business Weekly
China Dly North Am Ed — China Daily (North American Edition)
China Earth Sci — China Earth Sciences
Chin AEC Bull — Chinese AEC (Atomic Energy Council) Bulletin
China Econ — China Economic Model and Projections
China Econ Rept — China Economic Report
China Environ Sci — China Environmental Science
China Fish Mon — China Fisheries Monthly
China For Tr — China's Foreign Trade
China Geog — China Geographer
Chin Agric Sci — Chinese Agricultural Science
China Internat Bus — China International Business
China J — China Journal
China J Chin Mater Med — China. Journal of Chinese Materia Medica
China Jpn US Trilateral Semin Organomet Chem — China-Japan-United States Trilateral Seminar on Organometallic Chemistry
China J Sci & A — China Journal of Science and Arts
China J Sci Arts — China Journal of Science and Arts
China Law Rev — China Law Review
China Long — China Long-Term Development Issues and Options
China L Rep — China Law Reporter
China Med — China's Medicine
China Med J — China Medical Journal
China Med Miss J — China Medical Missionary Journal
Chin Am J Comm Rural Reconstr Plant Ind Ser — Chinese-American Joint Commission on Rural Reconstruction. Plant Industry Series
Chin Am J Comm Rural Reconstr (Taiwan) Spec Bull — Chinese-American Joint Commission on Rural Reconstruction (Taiwan). Special Bulletin
Chin Am Jt Comm Rural Reconstr (Taiwan) Spec Bull — Chinese-American Joint Commission on Rural Reconstruction (Taiwan) Special Bulletin
China News Anal — China News Analysis
Chin Anim Husb J — Chinese Animal Husbandry Journal
Chin Anim Husb Vet Med — Chinese Animal Husbandry and Veterinary Medicine
China Pict — China Pictorial
China Pulp Pap — China Pulp and Paper
China Q — China Quarterly
China Quart — China Quarterly
China Recon — China Reconstructs
China Reconstr — China Reconstructs
China Rep — China Report
China Rep Sci Technol — China Report. Science and Technology
China Rev — China Review
China Rubber Ind — China Rubber Industry
China's — China's Screen
China's Ceram — China's Ceramics
China Sci & Technol Abstr Ser III — China Science and Technology Abstracts. Series III. Industry Technology
China Sci Tech Abstracts — China Science and Technology Abstracts
China Sci Tech Abstracts Ser I Math Astronom Phys — China Science and Technology Abstracts. Series I. Mathematics, Astronomy, Physics
China Sci Technol Abstr Ser II — China Science and Technology Abstracts. Series II. Chemistry, Earth Science, Energy Sources
China's Med — China's Medicine
China's Med (Peking) — China's Medicine (Peking)
Chinas Refract — China's Refractories
Chin Astron — Chinese Astronomy [Later, Chinese Astronomy and Astrophysics]
China Surfactant Deterg Cosmet — China Surfactant Detergent and Cosmetics
China T — China Today
Chin At Energy Counc Bull — Chinese Atomic Energy Council. Bulletin
China Trade Rep — China Trade Report
China Weld — China Welding
China Wkly Rev — China Weekly Review
China W R — China Weekly Review
China Ybk — China Yearbook
CHINB — Chemical Instrumentation
Chin Bee J — Chinese Bee Journal
Chin Biochem J — Chinese Biochemical Journal
Chin Biochem Soc J — Chinese Biochemical Society. Journal
Chin Biosci — Chinese Bioscience
Chin Chem Ind Eng — Chinese Chemical Industry and Engineering
Chin Chem Soc Peking J — Chinese Chemical Society. Peking. Journal
Chinchilla Anal Hist Med Gen Bio Bib — Chinchilla. Anales Historicos de la Medicina en General y Biografico-Bibliograficos de la Espanola en Particular
Chin Cult — Chinese Culture
Chin Econ J — Chinese Economic Journal
Chin Econ Monthly — Chinese Economic Monthly
Chin Econ S — Chinese Economic Studies
Chin Econ Stud — Chinese Economic Studies
Chin Educ — Chinese Education

Chinese Ann Math — Chinese Annals of Mathematics
Chinese Ann Math Ser A — Chinese Annals of Mathematics. Series A. Shuxue Niankan
Chinese Ann Math Ser B — Chinese Annals of Mathematics. Series B. Shuxue Niankan
Chinese Astronom — Chinese Astronomy [Later, Chinese Astronomy and Astrophysics]
Chinese Astronom Astrophys — Chinese Astronomy and Astrophysics
Chinese Cult — Chinese Culture
Chinese Econ Studies — Chinese Economic Studies
Chinese J Appl Mech — Chinese Journal of Applied Mechanics
Chinese J Appl Probab Statist — Chinese Journal of Applied Probability and Statistics
Chinese J Contemp Math — Chinese Journal of Contemporary Mathematics
Chinese J Math — Chinese Journal of Mathematics
Chinese J Numer Math Appl — Chinese Journal of Numerical Mathematics and Applications
Chinese J Oper Res — Chinese Journal of Operations Research
Chinese J Phys (Peking) — Chinese Journal of Physics (Peking)
Chinese L & Govt — Chinese Law and Government
Chinese Law Gvt — Chinese Law and Government
Chinese M — Chinese Music
Chinese MJ — Chinese Medical Journal
Chinese Mus — Chinese Music
Chinese Phys — Chinese Physics
Chinese Phys Lett — Chinese Physics Letters
Chinese Quart J Math — Chinese Quarterly Journal of Mathematics
Chinese Sci Bull — Chinese Science Bulletin
Chinese Soc'y Int'l L Annals — Annals. Chinese Society of International Law
Chinese Stud Hist — Chinese Studies in History
Chin For Sci — Chinese Forestry Science
Chin Int Summer Sch Phys — Chinese International Summer School of Physics
Chin J Anesthesiol — Chinese Journal of Anesthesiology
Chin J Anim Husb — Chinese Journal of Animal Husbandry
Chin J Anim Sci — Chinese Journal of Animal Science
Chin J Antibiot — Chinese Journal of Antibiotics
Chin J Appl Chem — Chinese Journal of Applied Chemistry
Chin J Appl Ecol — Chinese Journal of Applied Ecology
Chin J Appl Physiol — Chinese Journal of Applied Physiology
Chin Jap Repos Facts Events Sci — Chinese and Japanese Repository of Facts and Events in Science, History, and Art Relating to Eastern Asia
Chin J Archaeol — Chinese Journal of Archaeology
Chin J At Mol Phys — Chinese Journal of Atomic and Molecular Physics
Chin J Biochem Mol Biol — Chinese Journal of Biochemistry and Molecular Biology
Chin J Biochem Pharm — Chinese Journal of Biochemical Pharmaceutics
Chin J Biomed Eng — Chinese Journal of Biomedical Engineering
Chin J Biotechnol — Chinese Journal of Biotechnology
Chin J Cardiol — Chinese Journal of Cardiology
Chin J Cardiol (Beijing) — Chinese Journal of Cardiology (Beijing)
Chin J Cell Biol — Chinese Journal of Cell Biology
Chin J Chem Eng — Chinese Journal of Chemical Engineering
Chin J Chromatogr — Chinese Journal of Chromatography
Chin J Clin Oncol — Chinese Journal of Clinical Oncology
Chin J Clin Pharmacol — Chinese Journal of Clinical Pharmacology
Chin J Comput — Chinese Journal of Computers
Chin J Dent Res — Chinese Journal of Dental Research
Chin J Dermatol — Chinese Journal of Dermatology
Chin J Disinfect — Chinese Journal of Disinfection
Chin J Endocrinol Metab — Chinese Journal of Endocrinology and Metabolism
Chin J Environ Sci — Chinese Journal of Environmental Science
Chin J Epidemiol — Chinese Journal of Epidemiology
Chin J Exp Clin Virol — Chinese Journal of Experimental and Clinical Virology
Chin J Explos & Propellants — Chinese Journal of Explosives and Propellants
Chin J Geochem — Chinese Journal of Geochemistry
Chin J Gynecol Obstet — Chinese Journal of Gynecology and Obstetrics
Chin J Hematol — Chinese Journal of Hematology
Chin J High Pressure Phys — Chinese Journal of High Pressure Physics
Chin J Histochem Cytochem — Chinese Journal of Histochemistry and Cytochemistry
Chin J Immunol — Chinese Journal of Immunology
Chin J Ind Hyg Occup Dis — Chinese Journal of Industrial Hygiene and Occupational Diseases
Chin J Infrared Res — Chinese Journal of Infrared Research
Chin J Infrared Res A — Chinese Journal of Infrared Research. A
Chin J Intern Med — Chinese Journal of Internal Medicine
Chin J Lasers — Chinese Journal of Lasers
Chin J Low Temp Phys — Chinese Journal of Low Temperature Physics
Chin J Magn Reson — Chinese Journal of Magnetic Resonance
Chin J Mar Drugs — Chinese Journal of Marine Drugs
Chin J Mater Sci — Chinese Journal of Materials Science
Chin J Mech — Chinese Journal of Mechanics
Chin J Mech Eng — Chinese Journal of Mechanical Engineering
Chin J Med Chem — Chinese Journal of Medicinal Chemistry
Chin J Med Lab Technol Beijing — Chinese Journal of Medical Laboratory Technology (Beijing)
Chin J Met Sci Technol — Chinese Journal of Metal Science and Technology
Chin J Microbiol — Chinese Journal of Microbiology [Later, Chinese Journal of Microbiology and Immunology]
Chin J Microbiol Immunol (Beijing) — Chinese Journal of Microbiology and Immunology (Beijing)
Chin J Microbiol Immunol (Taipei) — Chinese Journal of Microbiology and Immunology (Taipei)
Chin J Neurol Psychiatry — Chinese Journal of Neurology and Psychiatry
Chin J Nonferrous Met — Chinese Journal of Nonferrous Metals

Chin J Nucl Med — Chinese Journal of Nuclear Medicine
Chin J Nucl Phys — Chinese Journal of Nuclear Physics
Chin J Nutr — Chinese Journal of Nutrition
Chin J Obstet Gynecol — Chinese Journal of Obstetrics and Gynecology
Chin J Oceanol Limnol — Chinese Journal of Oceanology and Limnology
Chin J Oncol — Chinese Journal of Oncology
Chin J Ophthalmol — Chinese Journal of Ophthalmology
Chin J Ophthalmology — Chinese Journal of Ophthalmology
Chin J Org Chem — Chinese Journal of Organic Chemistry
Chin J Orthop — Chinese Journal of Orthopedics
Chin J Otorhinolaryngol — Chinese Journal of Otorhinolaryngology
Chin J Parasit Dis Commun Dis — Chinese Journal of Parasitic Diseases and Communicable Diseases
Chin J Parasit Infect Dis — Chinese Journal of Parasitic and Infectious Diseases
Chin J Pathol — Chinese Journal of Pathology
Chin J Pathophysiol — Chinese Journal of Pathophysiology
Chin J Pediatr — Chinese Journal of Pediatrics
Chin J Peoples Health — Chinese Journal of People's Health
Chin J Pharm — Chinese Journal of Pharmaceuticals
Chin J Pharmacol Toxicol — Chinese Journal of Pharmacology and Toxicology
Chin J Pharm Anal — Chinese Journal of Pharmaceutical Analysis
Chin J Phys — Chinese Journal of Physics
Chin J Phys Beijing — Chinese Journal of Physics (Beijing)
Chin J Physiol — Chinese Journal of Physiology
Chin J Physiol Beijing — Chinese Journal of Physiology (Beijing)
Chin J Physiol Metab Ser — Chinese Journal of Physiology. Metabolism Series
Chin J Physiol Rep Ser — Chinese Journal of Physiology. Report Series
Chin J Physiol (Taipei) — Chinese Journal of Physiology (Taipei)
Chin J Phys (New York) — Chinese Journal of Physics (New York)
Chin J Phys (Peking) — Chinese Journal of Physics (Peking)
Chin J Phys (Taipei) — Chinese Journal of Physics (Taipei)
Chin Jpn Electron Microsc Sem Proc — Chinese-Japanese Electron Microscopy Seminar. Proceedings
Chin J Polar Res — Chinese Journal of Polar Research
Chin J Polym Sci — Chinese Journal of Polymer Science
Chin J Power Sources — Chinese Journal of Power Sources
Chin J Prev Med — Chinese Journal of Preventive Medicine
Chin J Public Health — Chinese Journal of Public Health
Chin J Quantum Electron — Chinese Journal of Quantum Electronics
Chin J Radiol — Chinese Journal of Radiology
Chin J Radiol Med Prot — Chinese Journal of Radiological Medicine and Protection
Chin J Sci Agr — Chinese Journal of the Science of Agriculture
Chin J Sci Instrum — Chinese Journal of Scientific Instrument
Chin J Semicond — Chinese Journal of Semiconductors
Chin J Space Sci — Chinese Journal of Space Science
Chin J Spectrosc Lab — Chinese Journal of Spectroscopy Laboratory
Chin J Stomatol — Chinese Journal of Stomatology
Chin J Surg — Chinese Journal of Surgery
Chin J Traumatol — Chinese Journal of Traumatology
Chin J Tuber — Chinese Journal of Tuberculosis
Chin J Tuberc Respir Dis — Chinese Journal of Tuberculosis and Respiratory Diseases
Chin J Vet Med — Chinese Journal of Veterinary Medicine
Chin J Vet Sci — Chinese Journal of Veterinary Science
Chin J Virol — Chinese Journal of Virology
Chin J Zool — Chinese Journal of Zoology
ChinL — Chinese Literature
Chin L and Gov — Chinese Law and Government
Chin Law G — Chinese Law and Government
Chin Law Govt — Chinese Law and Government
Chin Lit — Chinese Literature
Chin Lit Es — Chinese Literature. Essays, Articles, Reviews
Chin Med J — Chinese Medical Journal
Chin Med J (Engl Ed) — Chinese Medical Journal (English Edition)
Chin Med J (Peking) — Chinese Medical Journal (Peking)
Chin Med J Taipei — Chinese Medical Journal (Taipei)
Chin Med Sci J — Chinese Medical Sciences Journal
Chin Pen — Chinese Pen
Chin Pharm Bull — Chinese Pharmaceutical Bulletin
Chin Pharm J (Beijing) — Chinese Pharmaceutical Journal (Beijing)
Chin Pharm J Taipei — Chinese Pharmaceutical Journal (Taipei)
Chin Phys — Chinese Physics
Chin Phys L — Chinese Physics Letters
Chin Repub Stud — Chinese Republic Studies. Newsletter
Chin Sci — Chinese Science
Chin Sci Bull — Chinese Science Bulletin
Chin Sci Tech — Chinese Science and Technology
Chin Silicate Soc J — Chinese Silicate Society Journal
Chin Soc A — Chinese Sociology and Anthropology
Chin Social & Pol Sci R — Chinese Social and Political Science Review
Chin Sociol Anthro — Chinese Sociology and Anthropology
Chin St Lit — Chinese Studies in Literature
Chin St Ph — Chinese Studies in Philosophy
Chin Stud — Chinese Studies in History
Chin Stud Archaeol — Chinese Studies in Archaeology
Chin Stud Hist — Chinese Studies in History
Chin Stud Monthly — Chinese Students' Monthly. Chinese Students Alliance of Eastern States, USA
Chin Stud Phil — Chinese Studies in Philosophy
Chin Stud Philo — Chinese Studies in Philosophy
Chin Tradit Herb Drugs — Chinese Traditional and Herbal Drugs
Chin Vet J — Chinese Veterinary Journal
Chip Snack — Chipper Snacker
ChiQ — China Quarterly

CHIQ — Concordia Historical Institute. Quarterly
ChiR — Chicago Review
Chir Aktuell — Chirurgie Aktuell
Chiral Dyn Theory Exp Proc Workshop — Chiral Dynamics. Theory and Experiment. Proceedings of the Workshop
CHIRAS — Der Chirurg
Chir Dent F — Chirurgien-Dentiste de France
Chir-Dent Fr — Chirurgien-Dentiste de France
Chir Forum Exp Klin Forsch — Chirurgisches Forum fuer Experimentelle und Klinische Forschung
Chir Gastroenterol (Engl Ed) — Chirurgia Gastroenterologica (English Edition)
Chir Gen — Chirurgia Generale
Chir Ital — Chirurgia Italiana
Chir Main — Chirurgie de la Main
Chir Maxillofac Plast — Chirurgia Maxillofacialis et Plastica
Chir Narzadow Ruchu Ortop Pol — Chirurgia Narzadow Ruchu i Ortopedia Polska
Chiro Hist — Chiropractic History
Chiropractic Sports Med — Chiropractic Sports Medicine
Chir Organi Mov — Chirurgia degli Organi di Movimento
Chir Org Movimento — Chirurgia degli Organi di Movimento
Chir Patol Sper — Chirurgia e Patologia Sperimentale
Chir Pediatr — Chirurgie Pediatrique
Chir Plast — Chirurgia Plastica
Chir Plast Reconstr — Chirurgia Plastica et Reconstructiva
Chir Prax — Chirurgische Praxis
Chir Ther Mammakarzinoms Oesterr Chirurgentag — Chirurgische Therapie des Mammakarzinoms, Oesterreichische Chirurgentagung
Chir Torac — Chirurgia Toracica
Chir Vet Ref Abstr — Chirurgia Veterinaria Referate. Abstracts
Chisa Main Lect Int Congr Chem Eng Equip Des Autom — Chisa. Main Lectures. International Congress on Chemical Engineering, EquipmentDesign, and Automation
Chisholm Gaz — Chisholm Gazette
Chislennye Metody Din Razrezh Gazov — Chislennye Metody v Dinamike Razrezhennykh Gazov
Chislennye Metody Mekh Sploshnoi Sredy — Chislennye Metody Mekhaniki Sploshnoi Sredy
Chisl Metody Mekh Sploshn Sredy — Akademiya Nauk SSSR. Sibirskoe Otdelenie. Vychislitelnyi Tsentr. Chislennye Metody Mekhaniki Sploshnoi Sredy
CHISS Cah — CHISS [Centre Haitien d'Investigation en Science Sociales] Cahiers
C Hist — Catholic Historical Review
CHist — Church History
CHist — Corse Historique
C Hist Arch — Cahiers d'Histoire et d'Archeologie
C Hist Inst Maurice Thorez — Cahiers d'Histoire. Institut Maurice Thorez
Chi Sym — Chicago Symphony Orchestra. Program Notes
CHITAY — Chirurgia Italiana
ChiTBW — Chicago Tribune Book World
Chi T M — Chicago Tribune Magazine
Chittagong Univ Stud Part II Sci — Chittagong University. Studies. Part II. Science
Chitt Univ Stud — Chittagong University Studies
Chitty LJ — Chitty's Law Journal
Chitty's L J — Chitty's Law Journal
CHIUA — Chemische Industrie
CHJ — Cambridge Historical Journal
ChJ — Choral Journal
CHJ — Cooperative Housing Journal
Ch J Forum — Chicago Jewish Forum
CHJIA — Chitaniumu Jirukoniumu
CHJL — Cambridge Historical Journal (London)
CHJPB — Chinese Journal of Physics
CHJZ — Cuadernos de Historia. Jeronimo Zurita
CHK — Caterer and Hotelkeeper
Ch K — Christliche Kunstblaetter
CHKAD — Chiiki Kaihatsu
Ch Kal — Chemiker-Kalender
CHKSex — Centralblatt fuer die Krankheiten der Harn- und Sexualorgane
CHKWA — Chijil Kwa Chiri
CHL — Cahiers de la Haute-Loire
CHL — Challenge
Ch L — Chartae Latinae Antiquiores
CHL — Christian Liberty
CHL — Commentationes Humanarum Litterarum. Societas Scientiarum Fennica [Helsingfors]
CHL — Cuadernos del Hombre Libre
Ch L — University of Chicago. Law Review
ChLA — Chartae Latinae Antiquiores
Ch L B — Charles Lamb Bulletin
CHLBA — Chemie fuer Labor und Betrieb
CHLGB — Challenge
Ch Lib Newsl — Children's Libraries Newsletter
ChLit — Chinese Literature
Chlorine Coal Proc Int Conf — Chlorine in Coal. Proceedings. International Conference
Ch LR — University of Chicago. Law Review
CHLSA — Chemicke Listy
CHLSSF — Commentationes Humanarum Litterarum. Societas Scientiarum Fennica
CHM — Cahiers d'Histoire Mondiale/Journal of World History
ChM — Chamber Music
CHM — Chemisch Magazine
Chm — Churchman
CHMAD — Chemie Magazine
CHMEB — China's Medicine
CHMEBA — China's Medicine
Chmel Listy — Chmelarske Listy

CHMGA — Chartered Mechanical Engineer
Ch Mis I — Church Missionary Intelligencer
CHMJB — Chamber of Mines. Journal
Chmn — Churchman
CHMNA — Chantiers Magazine
Ch Mnmts — Church Monuments
CHMond — Cahiers d'Histoire Mondiale/Journal of World History
CHMTB — Chemical Technology
Ch Music — Church Music
CHNCDB — Journal of Agricultural Research of China
CHNHA — Chung-Hua Nung Hsueh Hui Pao
CHNHAN — Journal. Agricultural Association of China. New Series
Ch NI — Christian News from Israel
Chn Merch — Chain Merchandiser
Chn Mktg — Chain Marketing and Management
Chn Stor D — Chain Store Age. Drug Store Edition. Annual Report of the Chain Drug Industry
Chn Store — Chain Store Age
Chn Str GM — Chain Store Age. General Merchandise Trends Edition
CHNYB — Chishitsu Nyusu
CHO — Choice
Choc Confiserie Fr — Chocolaterie. Confiserie de France
Choices Mag Food Farm Resour Issues — Choices. The Magazine of Food, Farm, and Resource Issues
ChOIDR — Chteniia v Imperatorskom Obshchestve Istorii i Drevnostei Rossisskikh
ChOLDP — Chteniia v Moskovskom Obshchestve Liubiteli Dukhovnogo Prosveshcheniia
Cholinergic Neurotransm Funct Clin Aspects Proc Nobel Symp — Cholinergic Neurotransmission. Functional and Clinical Aspects. Proceedings. Nobel Symposium
CHOMA9 — Chirurgia degli Organi di Movimento
C Home — Christian Home
CHOMS — Canadian Hydrological Operational Multipurpose Subprogramme
CHONDF — Contemporary Hematology/Oncology
Chonnam Med J — Chonnam Medical Journal
Choral G — Choral and Organ Guide
Choral J — Choral Journal
Chosen Bull — Chosen Bulletin/Chosen Iho
Chosen M Assn J — Chosen Medical Association. Kaijo Imperial University. Journal
CHOVA2 — Commissie voor Hydrologisch Onderzoek TNO
Chowder — Chowder Review
CHP — Cuadernos de Historia Primitiva
CHPAAC — Chirurgia e Patologia Sperimentale
CHPAD — Journal. Korean Academy of Maxillofacial Radiology
CHPCA — Chemical Processing (Chicago)
CHPHD — Chinese Physics
CHPI — Christian Periodical Index
CHPLB — Chemical Physics Letters
CHPRD — Chemische Produktlon
CHPUA — Chemicky Prumysl
CHPXBE — Chirurgische Praxis
CHQ — California Historical Quarterly
Ch Q — Church Quarterly
Ch Q — Church Quarterly Review
Ch Q R — Church Quarterly Review
CHR — Canadian Historical Review
CHR — Canadian Hotel and Restaurant
CHR — Caribbean Historial Review
CHR — Catholic Historical Review
CHR — China Business Review
CHR — Correspondentieblad van Hogere Rijksambtenaren
CHR — Current Housing Reports
Chr & Cr — Christianity and Crisis
Chr & Crisis — Christianity and Crisis
CHRAQ — Cornell Hotel and Restaurant Administration Quarterly
CHRA Rec — CHRA [*Canadian Health Record Association*] Recorder
CHRBAP — Chronica Botanica
Chr C — Christian Century
Chr Cent — Christian Century
Chr Cris — Christianity and Crisis
Chrd'Eg — Chronique 'Egypte
Chr Disc — Christian Disciple
ChrE — Chronique d'Egypte
CHREA — Chemical Reviews
Chr Eg — Chronique d'Egypte
Chr Exam — Christian Examiner
CHRF — Cahiers d'Histoire de la Revolution Francaise
CHRGA6 — Chirurgia Gastroenterologica
CHRGB7 — Chromatographia
ChrGem — Die Christengemeinschaft
CHRIP — Comision Honoraria de Reducciones de Indios. Publicaciones [*Buenos Aires*]
CHRIS — Chemical Hazards Response Information System
Chris Art — Christian Art
Chris Q — Christian Quarterly Review
Chris Sc Mon — Christian Science Monitor
Christ Brothers Stud — Christian Brothers Studies
Christ Cen — Christian Century
ChristCent — Christian Century
Christ Dkml — Christliche Denkmale
Christiana Albertina Kiel Univ Z — Christiana Albertina. Kieler Universitaets Zeitschrift
Christian Cent — Christian Century
Christian Exam — Christian Examiner

Christiania F — Fordhanlinger i Videnskabs-Selskabet i Christiania
Christiania Skr Mth Nt Kl — Skrifter Udgivne af Videnskabsselskabet i Christiania. Mathematisk-Naturvidenskabelig Klasse
Christian Lit — Christian Literature
Christian Q — Christian Quarterly
Christian Q Spec — Christian Quarterly Spectator
Christian Reg — Christian Register
Christian Sci Mon — Christian Science Monitor
Christian Sci Monitor — Christian Science Monitor
Christian Sci Mon Mag — Christian Science Monitor. Magazine Section
Christies Int Mag — Christie's International Magazine
Christ Inq Can Ed — Christian Inquirer. Canadian Edition
Christ Kst — Christliche Kunst
Christ Kstbl — Christliche Kunstblaetter
Christ Lead Let — Christian Leadership Letter
Christ Libr — Christian Librarian
Christ Lit — Christianity and Literature
Christl Orient — Christliche Orient in Vergangenheit und Gegenwart
Christl Paedag Bll — Christlich-Paedagogische Blaetter
Christ Man Rev — Christian Management Review
Christmas Tree Grow J — Christmas Tree Growers Journal
Christ Nurse — Christian Nurse
Christ Oosten — Het Christelijk Oosten en Hereniging
Christ Period Index — Christian Periodical Index
Christ Sch Rev — Christian Scholar's Review
Christ Sci Mon — Christian Science Monitor
Christ Sci Monitor — Christian Science Monitor
ChristTod — Christianity Today
Christ U Wiss — Christentum und Wissenschaft
ChrJF — Christlich-Juedisches Forum
Chr Lit — Christian Literature
Chr Ministry — Christian Ministry
ChRMJ — Chinese Recorder and Missionary Journal
Chr Mo Spec — Christian Monthly Spectator
ChrNIsrael — Christian News from Israel
ChrO — Chronicles of Oklahoma
CHROAU — Chromosoma
Chr Obs — Christian Observer
CHROD — Chronolog
Chro E — Chronique d'Egypte
Chromatin Chromosomal Protein Res — Chromatin and Chromosomal Protein Research
Chromatog Bull — Chromatography Bulletin
Chromatogr — Chromatographia
Chromatography Newsl — Chromatography Newsletter
Chromatogr Biochem Med Environ Res Proc Int Symp — Chromatography in Biochemistry, Medicine, and Environmental Research. Proceedings. International Symposium on Chromatography in Biochemistry, Medicine, and Environmental Research
Chromatogr Colonne Reun Int Methodes Sep — Chromatographie sur Colonne. Reunion Internationale sur les Methodes de Separation
Chromatogr Commun — Chromatography Communications
Chromatogr Electrophor Symp Int — Chromatographie, Electrophorese. Symposium International
Chromatogr Isol Insect Horm Pheromones Proc Int Symp — Chromatography and Isolation of Insect Hormones and Pheromones. Proceedings. International Symposium
Chromatogr Methods — Chromatographic Methods
Chromatogr Newsl — Chromatography Newsletter
Chromatogr Rev — Chromatographic Reviews
Chromatogr Sci — Chromatographic Science
Chromatogr Sci Ser — Chromatographic Science Series
Chromatogr Soc Int Symp Chiral Sep — Chromatographic Society International Symposium on Chiral Separations
Chromatogr Symp — Chromatographie. Symposium
Chromatogr Symp Ser — Chromatography Symposia Series
Chromat Rev — Chromatographic Reviews
Chromo Inf Serv — Chromosome Information Service
Chromos — Chromosoma
Chromos Inform Serv (Tokyo) — Chromosome Information Service (Tokyo)
Chromosome Inf Serv (Tokyo) — Chromosome Information Service (Tokyo)
Chromosome Res — Chromosome Research
Chromosome Sci — Chromosome Science
Chromosome Var Hum Evol — Chromosome Variations in Human Evolution
Chron — Chronology of Mycenaean Pottery
Chron A — Chronique des Arts
Chron A & Curiosite — Chronique des Arts et de la Curiosite
Chron A Ass Cul — Chronique Archeologique. Association Culturelle du Groupe Total
Chron Actual — Chroniques d'Actualite
Chron Actual SEDEIS — Chroniques d'Actualite de la SEDEIS
Chron Alum — Chronique Aluminum
Chron Aust Ed — Chronicle of Australian Education
Chron Bot — Chronica Botanica
Chron Chim — Chronache di Chimica
Chron Cult — Chronicles of Culture
Chron d'Eg — Chronique d'Egypte
Chron Dermatol — Chronica Dermatologica
Chron Eg — Chronique d'Egypte
Chron Egypte — Chronique d'Egypte
Chron Higher Educ — Chronicle of Higher Education
Chron Hortic — Chronica Horticulturae
Chron Hydrogeol — Chronique d'Hydrogeologie
Chronic Dis Can — Chronic Diseases in Canada
Chronicles Okla — Chronicles of Oklahoma

Chron Int Com — Chronicle of International Communication
Chronique Arch Liege — Chronique Archeologique du Pays de Liege
Chron Lind — Lindische Tempelchronik
Chron Med — Chronique Medicale
Chron Mens Soc Fr Photogr Cinematogr — Chronique Mensuelle de la Societe Francaise de Photographie et de Cinematographie
Chron Mens Tech Ass Gen Chim Ind Text — Chronique Mensuelle Technique de l'Association Generale des Chimistes de l'Industrie Textile
Chron Merid — Chroniques Meridionales
Chron Min Colon — Chronique Miniere Coloniale
Chron Mines Colon — Chronique des Mines Coloniales
Chron Mines D Outre Mer — Chronique des Mines d'Outre Mer
Chron Mines Outre Mer — Chronique des Mines d'Outre-Mer
Chron Mines Outre Mer Rech Min — Chronique des Mines d'Outre-Mer et de la Recherche Miniere
Chron Mines Rech Min — Chronique des Mines et de la Recherche Miniere
Chron MP — Chronology of Mycenaean Pottery
Chron Mus A Dec Cooper Un — Chronicle of the Museum of the Arts of Decoration of the Cooper Union
Chronmy Przyr Ojcz — Chronmy Przyrode Ojczysta
Chronmy Przyr Ojczysta — Chronmy Przyrode Ojczysta
Chron Nat — Chronica Naturae
Chron Nicotiana — Chronica Nicotiana
Chronobiol Int — Chronobiology International
Chronobiologia Organ Int Soc Chronobiology — Chronobiologia. Organ of the International Society for Chronobiology
ChronOkla — Chronicles of Oklahoma
Chron Oklahoma — Chronicles of Oklahoma. Oklahoma Historical Society
Chron OMS — Chronique. Organisation Mondiale de la Sante
Chron Or — Chroniques d'Orient
Chron Paris — Chronique de Paris
Chron Pol Etrang — Chronique de Politique Etrangere
Chron Pol Etrangere — Chronique de Politique Etrangere
Chron Polit Etr — Chronique de Politique Etrangere
Chron Politique Etrangere — Chronique de Politique Etrangere
Chron Port Royal — Chroniques de Port-Royal. Bulletin de la Societe des Amis de Port-Royal
Chron Przyr Ojczysta — Chronmy Przyrode Ojczysta
Chron Rech Min — Chronique de la Recherche Miniere
Chron Rech Miniere — Chronique de la Recherche Miniere
Chrons Actualite — Chroniques d'Actualite
Chron Soc Fr — Chronique Sociale de France
Chron Soc France — Chronique Sociale de France
Chron Social Fr — Chronique Sociale de France
Chron UGGI — Chronique de l'U.G.G.I. Union Geodesique et Geophysique Internationale
Chron Vervielfalt Kst — Chronik fuer Vervielfaltigende Kunst
Chron WHO — Chronicle. World Health Organization
Chron WI Comm — Chronicle. West India Committee
ChrOost — Het Christelijk Oosten
ChrPer — Christian Perspectives
Chr Per Ind — Christian Periodical Index
Chr Pol Et — Chronique de Politique Etrangere
Chr Q — Christian Quarterly
Chr Q R — Church Quarterly Review
Chr Q Spec — Christian Quarterly Spectator
Chr R — Christian Review
Chr Rem — Christian Remembrance
ChrS — Christianisme Social
Chr Sch — Christliche Schule
Chr Sch R — Christian Scholar's Review
Chr Sci Mon — Christian Science Monitor
Chr Sci Monit Mag — Christian Science Monitor Magazine
Chr Sci Monitor — Christian Science Monitor
Chr T — Christianity Today
CHRTB — Chromosomes Today
CHRTBC — Chromosomes Today
Chr Today — Christianity Today
CHRU — Christian Union
CHRUA — Chemische Rundschau
Chr Un — Christian Union
Chr World — Christ to the World
Chry — Chrysalis Review
CHRYA — Chemistry
Chrysanth Dahlia — Chrysanthemum and Dahlia
Chrysanth Yb — Chrysanthemum Year Book
CHS — Baghdad Chamber of Commerce. Commercial Bulletin. Bi-Weekly
CHS — Chain Store Age. Executive Edition
ChS — Christian Scholar
CHSB — Cincinnati Historical Society. Bulletin
CHSB — Connecticut Historical Society. Bulletin
CHSCD — Changing Scene
Ch Sec — Chartered Secretary
CHS Fac Rev — CHS Faculty Review
Ch Soc — Church and Society
C H Soc Q — California Historical Society. Quarterly
CHSOP — Canadian Historic Sites. Occasional Papers in Archaeology and History
CHSQ — California Historical Society. Quarterly
Ch S R — Christian Scholar's Review
ChSRev — Christian Scholar's Review
CHSTA — Child Study Journal
CHSUA — Chartered Surveyor [*Later, Chartered Surveyor Weekly*]
Ch T — Chamber Tombs at Mycenae
CHT — Christelijk Historisch Tijdschrift
ChT — Church Teachers

CHTCB5 — Enfant en Milieu Tropical
CHTED — Chemtech
ChTh — Choses de Theatre
CHTHA — Chung-Shan Ta Hsueh Hsueh Pao. Tzu Jan K'o Hsueh
C Ht M — Cahiers Haut-Marnais
CHTRD — Chicago Tribune
CHTTA — Chuko To Tanko
CHTZA — Chishitsugaku Zasshi
CHTZA5 — Chishitsugaku Zasshi
CHU — Christelijk-Historische Unie
ChU — Christian Union
Chu — Church Music
Chugoku Agric Res — Chugoku Agricultural Research/Chugoku Nogyo Kenkyu
Chugoku Agr Res — Chugoku Agricultural Research
Chugoku Shikoku Dist J Jpn Soc Obstet Gynecol — Chugoku and Shikoku Districts Journal. Japan Society of Obstetrics and Gynecology
CHUIAR — Chung-Ang Uihak
CHum — Computers and the Humanities
Chung-Ang J Med — Chung-Ang Journal of Medicine
Chung Hua Lin Hsueh Chi K'an Q J Chin For — Chung-Hua Lin Hsueh Chi K'an. Quarterly Journal of Chinese Forestry
Chung-Hua Nung Yeh Yen Chiu J Agric Res China — Chung-Hua Nung Yeh Yen Chiu/Journal of Agriculture Research of China
Chung-Kuo Lin Yeh K'o Hsueh Chin For Sci — Chung-Kuo Lin Yeh K'o Hsueh/Chinese Forestry Science
Chung-Kuo Nung Yeh Hua Hsueh Hui Chih J Chin Agric Chem Soc — Chung-Kuo Nung Yeh Hua Hsueh Hui Chih/Journal of the Chinese Agriculture Chemical Society
Chung-Kuo Nung Yeh K'o Hsueh Sci Agric Sin — Chung-Kuo Nung Yeh K'o Hsueh/Scientia Agricultura Sinica
Chungnam J Sci — Chungnam Journal of Sciences
Chungnam Med J — Chungnam Medical Journal
Chungnam Natl Univ Res Inst Chem Spectrosc Rep — Chungnam National University. Research Institute of Chemical Spectroscopy. Reports
Chungnam Natl Univ Res Inst Phys Chem Rep — Chungnam National University. Research Institute of Physics and Chemistry. Reports
Chung-Shan Univ J Nat Sci Ed — Chung-Shan University Journal. Natural Sciences Edition
Chung Yuan J — Chung Yuan Journal
ChunY — Chung-yang Yen-chiu Yuean Chin-tai Shih Yen-chiu So Chi-k'an
Church Bldr — Church Builder
Church Eng Hist Soc J — Church of England Historical Society. Journal
Church Hist — Church History
Churchills J Mod Prod Pract — Churchill's Journal of Modern Production Practice
Church Mis R — Church Missionary Review
Church Mus (London) — Church Music (London)
Church Mus (St L) — Church Music (St. Louis)
Church Q — Church Quarterly Review
Church Q R — Church Quarterly Review
Church Qtr Rev — Church Quarterly Review
Church Quartl Revw — Church Quarterly Review
Church Quart Rev — Church Quarterly Review
Church R — Church Review
ChurH — Church History
Churn Bull — Churn Bulletin
Chuv Skh Inst Sb Nauchn Rab Molodykh Uch — Chuvashskii Sel'skokhozyaistvennyi Institut. Sbornik Nauchnykh Rabot Molodykh Uchenykh
CHVCA — Chauffage, Ventilation, Conditionnement
CHW — Chemisch Weekblad/Chemische Courant
Ch W — Chercheurs de la Wallonie
ChW — Christliche Welt
CHWCA — Chung-Hua Wai K'o Tsa Chih
CHWCAJ — Chinese Journal of Surgery
CHWEA — Chemisch Weekblad [*Later, Chemisch Weekblad/Chemische Courant*]
CHWHA — Chih Wu Hsueh Pao
CHWHAY — Acta Botanica Sinica
CHWKA — Chemical Week
CHWOD — Chevron World
CHX — Chemische Rundschau. Europaeische Wochenzeitung fuer Chemie, Pharmazeutik, und die Lebensmittelindustrie
CHY — Current History
CHYCDW — Chinese Journal of Preventive Medicine
Chymia Ind — Chymia et Industria
CI — Canadian Insurance
CI — Canadian Interiors
CI — Cancer Investigation
CI — Chemistry International
CI — Ciencia Interamericana
CI — City Invincible
CI — Commercial Intelligencer
CI — Critical Inquiry
CI — Cuadernos del Idioma
CIA — Congres International d'Anthropologie
CIA — Contributi. Istituto di Archeologia. Universita Milan
CIA — Corpus Inscriptionum Arabicorum
CIA — Corpus Inscriptionum Atticarum
CIAAP — Congres International d'Anthropologie et d'Archeologie Prehistorique
CIAC — Canadian Indian Artcrafts. National Indian Arts and Crafts Advisory Committee
CIACDL — Centro Internacional de Agricultura Tropical [*CIAT*]. Series CE
CIADI — Clinically Important Adverse Drug Interactions
CIAH — Culture, Illness, and Healing
CIAMAE — Centro de Investigaciones Agronomicas Maracay. Monografia
Cianc Trop — Ciancia and Tropico
CIARAT — Cawthron Institute [*Nelson, New Zealand*]. Report

CIAT Annu Rep — CIAT [*Centro Internacional de Agricultura Tropical*] Annual Report
CIATB2 — Centro Internacional de Agricultura Tropical [*CIAT*]. Annual Report
CIATC3 — Centro Internacional de Agricultura Tropical [*CIAT*]. Technical Bulletin
CIAT Ser Semin — CIAT [*Centro Internacional de Agricultura Tropical*] Series Seminars
CI Att — Corpus Inscriptionum Atticarum
CIB — Commercial and Industrial Bulletin
Ciba — Ciba Symposia
Ciba Bl — Ciba-Blaetter
Ciba Clin Symp — Ciba Clinical Symposia
Ciba Collect Med Illus — Ciba Collection of Medical Illustrations
Ciba Fdn Colloq Ageing — Ciba Foundation Colloquia on Ageing
Ciba Fdn Colloq Endocr — Ciba Foundation Colloquia on Endocrinology
Ciba Fdn Study Grps — Ciba Foundation Study Groups
Ciba Fdn Symp — Ciba Foundation. Symposium
Ciba Found Colloq Endocrinol — Ciba Foundation. Colloquia on Endocrinology
Ciba Found Colloq Endocrinol Proc — Ciba Foundation Colloquia on Endocrinology. Proceedings
Ciba Found Study Group — Ciba Foundation. Study Group
Ciba Found Symp — Ciba Foundation. Symposium
Ciba Geig Rev — Ciba-Geigy Review
Ciba Geigy J — Ciba-Geigy Journal
Ciba Geigy Q — Ciba-Geigy Quarterly
Ciba-Geigy Tech Notes — Ciba-Geigy Technical Notes
Ciba J — Ciba Journal
Ciba Lect Microb Biochem — Ciba Lectures in Microbial Biochemistry
Ciba R — Ciba Review
Ciba Rdsch — Ciba-Rundschau
Ciba Rev — Ciba Review
Ciba Rundsch — Ciba Rundschau
Ciba Symp — Ciba Symposia
Ciba Z — Ciba Zeitschrift
CIBCASIO Trans — CIBCASIO (Centros de Investigacion de Baja California and Scripps Institution of Oceanography) Transactions
CIB Congr — CIB [*Conseil International du Batiment pour la Recherche, l'Etude, et la Documentation*] Congress
CIBMAJ — Centro de Investigacion de Biologia Marina. Contribucion Tecnica
CIBMBK — Commonwealth Institute of Biological Control. Miscellaneous Publication
CibS — Ciba Symposium
CIBSB — Ciba Foundation. Symposium
CIB VIII — Eighth International Botanical Congress. Paris, 1954, Proceedings
Cic — Cicerone
CICF — Current Issues in Commerce and Finance
CICIAMS Nouv — CICIAMS [*Comite International Catholique des Infirmieres et Assistantes Medico-Sociales*] Nouvelles
CIC Inform B Inform Gen — CIC Informations. Bulletin d'Informations Generales
Ciclo Combust U Th Congr Nucl — Ciclo Combustible U-Th. Simposio. Congresso Nucleare
CICNEV — Contemporary Issues in Clinical Nutrition
CICR — Carta Informativa (Costa Rica)
CICRD8 — Colloque Scientifique International sur le Cafe
CICSA — Clinical Symposia
CID — Computer Industry Daily
CIDE — Caisse Israelite de Demarrage Economique
CIDG — Current Intelligence Digest
CIDI Quad — CIDI (Centro de Iniziativa Democratica degli Insegnanti) Quaderni
Cidrerie Fr — Cidrerie Francaise
CIDS — Centro Intercultural de Documentacion. Sondeos
CIE — Cambio Internacional (Ecuador)
CIE — Catering Industry Employee
CIE — Corpus Inscriptionum Etruscarum
CIE — Cuestiones Indigenas del Ecuador
CIEA Preclin Rep — CIEA [*Central Institute for Experimental Animals*] Preclinical Reports
Cie Fr Pet Notes Mem — Compagnie Francaise des Petroles. Notes et Memoires
CIEH — Contributions to Indian Economic History
Ciel Terre — Ciel et Terre. Societe Belge d'Astronomie
CIEMDT — Clinical and Experimental Immunoreproduction
Cien Admin La Plata — Ciencias Administrativas (La Plata, Argentina)
Cien Biol Ser C Biol Mol Cel — Ciencia Biologica. Serie C. Biologia Molecular e Celular
Cienc — Ciencia
Cienc Adm — Ciencias Administrativas
Cienc Aeronaut — Ciencia Aeronautica
Cienc Agric — Ciencias de la Agricultura
Cienc Agron — Ciencia Agronomica
Cienc Agrotecnol — Ciencia e Agrotecnologia
Cienc & Tec — Ciencia y Tecnica
Cienc Biol — Ciencia Biologica
Cienc Biol Acad Cienc Cuba — Ciencias Biologicas. Academia de Ciencias de Cuba
Cienc Biol B — Ciencia Biologica. B. Ecologia e Sistematica
Cienc Biol Biol Mol Cel — Ciencia Biologica. Biologia Molecular e Cellular
Cienc Biol (Coimbra) — Ciencia Biologica (Coimbra)
Cienc Biol Ecol Sist — Ciencia Biologica, Ecologia, e Sistematica
Cienc Biol (Luanda) — Ciencias Biologicas (Luanda)
Cienc Biol Mol Cell Biol — Ciencia Biologica. Molecular and Cellular Biology
Cienc Cult (Maracaibo) — Ciencia y Cultura (Maracaibo)
Cienc Cult (Sao Paulo) — Ciencia e Cultura (Sao Paulo)
Cienc Cult (Sao Paulo) Supl — Ciencia e Cultura (Sao Paulo). Suplemento
Cienc Cult Saude — Ciencia, Cultura, Saude
Cienc Cult Simp Sao Paulo — Ciencia e Cultura. Simposios (Sao Paulo)
Cienc Cult Soc Bras Progr Cienc — Ciencia e Cultura. Sociedade Brasileira para o Progresso da Ciencia

Cienc Cult (S Paulo) — Ciencia e Cultura (Sao Paulo)
Cienc Desarrollo — Ciencia y Desarrollo
Cienc Eng — Ciencia & Engenharia
Cienc For — Ciencia Forestal
Ciencia Botucatu Braz — Ciencia (Botucatu, Brazil). Revista do Centro Academico Piraja da Silva
Ciencia e Tec Fiscal — Ciencia e Tecnica Fiscal
Ciencia Info — Ciencia da Informacao
Ciencias Madrid — Ciencias. Asociacion Espanola por el Progreso de las Ciencias (Madrid)
Ciencias Ser 1 Mat — Ciencias. Serie 1. Matematica
Ciencias Ser 3 — Ciencias. Serie 3.
Ciencias Ser 5 — Ciencias. Serie 5. Bioquimica Farmaceutica
Ciencia Tecnol — Ciencia y Tecnologia
Ciencia y Soc — Ciencia y Sociedad
Cienc Ind Farm — Ciencia e Industria Farmaceutica
Cienc Interam — Ciencia Interamericana
Cienc Invest — Ciencia e Investigacion
Cienc Invest Agrar — Ciencia e Investigacion Agraria
Cienc Invest (B Aires) — Ciencia e Investigacion (Buenos Aires)
Cienc Mar — Ciencias Marinas
Cienc Mat — Ciencias Matematicas
Cienc Nat — Ciencia y Naturaleza
Cienc Nat Bol R Soc Vascongada Amigos Pais Suppl — Ciencias Naturales. Boletin. Real Sociedad Vascongada de Amigos del Pais. Supplemento
Cienc Nat (Quito) — Ciencia y Naturaleza (Quito)
Cienc Nat (S Maria Braz) — Ciencia e Natura (Santa Maria, Brazil)
Cienc Neurol — Ciencias Neurologicas
Cienc Pediatr — Ciencia Pediatrika
Cienc Prat — Ciencia e Pratica
Cienc Ser 4 Cienc Biol (Havana) — Ciencias. Serie 4. Ciencias Biologicas (Havana)
Cienc Ser 8 Invest Mar (Havana) — Ciencias. Serie 8. Investigaciones Marinas (Havana)
Cienc Ser 10 Bot (Havana) — Ciencias. Serie 10. Botanica (Havana)
Cienc Tec Agric Ganado Porcino — Ciencia y Tecnica en la Agricultura. Ganado Porcino
Cienc Tec Agric Prot Plant — Ciencia y Tecnica en la Agricultura. Proteccion de Plantas
Cienc Tec Agric Vet — Ciencia y Tecnica en la Agricultura. Veterinaria
Cienc Tec (Buenos Aires) — Ciencia y Tecnica (Buenos Aires)
Cienc Tec Fis Mat — Ciencias Tecnicas Fisicas y Matematicas
Cienc Tec Mar — Ciencia y Tecnologia del Mar. Comite Oceanografico Nacional
Cienc Tec Mundo — Ciencia y Tecnica en el Mundo
Cienc Tecn — Ciencia y Tecnologia
Cienc Tecnol Aliment — Ciencia e Tecnologia de Alimentos
Cienc Tecnol Aliment Int — Ciencia y Tecnologia de Alimentos Internacional
Cienc Tecnol Nucl — Ciencia y Tecnologia Nuclear
Cienc Tecnol (San Jose Costa Rica) — Ciencia y Tecnologia (San Jose, Costa Rica)
Cienc Tecnol Washington DC — Ciencia y Tecnologia (Washington, DC)
Cienc Tec Pet Sec Eng Reservatorios — Ciencia - Tecnica - Petrolea. Secao Engenharia de Reservatorios
Cienc Tec Pet Sec Quim — Ciencia - Tecnica - Petroleo. Secao Quimica
Cienc Tec Quito — Ciencia y Tecnica (Quito)
Cienc Tec Soldadura (Madrid) — Ciencia y Tecnica de la Soldadura (Madrid)
Cienc Tec Vitivini — Ciencia e Tecnica Vitivinicola
Cienc Terra — Ciencias da Terra
Cienc Tierra Espacio — Ciencias de la Tierra y del Espacio
Cienc Tomista — Ciencia Tomista
Cien Cult Maracaibo — Ciencia y Cultura (Maracaibo, Venezuela)
Cienc Vet — Ciencias Veterinarias
Cienc Vet Aliment Nutr Anim — Ciencias Veterinarias y Alimentas y Nutricion Animal
Cienc Vet Maracay Venez — Ciencias Veterinarias (Maracay, Venezuela)
Cienc Vet Mexico City — Ciencias Veterinarias (Mexico City)
Cien Econ Medellin — Ciencias Economicas. Facultad de Ciencias Economicas. Universidad de Antioquia (Medellin, Colombia)
Cien Econ Soc — Ciencias Economicas Sociais
Cien Fe S Miguel — Ciencia y Fe (San Miguel, Argentina)
Ci Eng — Civil Engineering
Cien Invest BA — Ciencia e Investigacion (Buenos Aires)
Cien Mex — Ciencia (Mexico)
Cien Natur Quito — Ciencia y Naturaleza (Quito)
Cien Pol Soc Mex — Ciencias Politicas y Sociales (Mexico)
Cien Soc Cumana — Ciencias Sociales (Cumana, Venezuela)
Cien Soc Wash — Ciencias Sociales (Washington, DC)
Cien Tom — Ciencia Tomista
Cien Tomista — Ciencia Tomista
Cieplownictwo Ogrzewnictwo Went — Cieplownictwo, Ogrzewnictwo, Wentylacja
Ciep Ogrz Went — Cieplownictwo, Ogrzewnictwo, Wentylacja
Cieta Bull — Cieta Bulletin
CIETD — Ciencias da Terra
CIFA (Comm Inland Fish Afr) Tech Pap — CIFA (Committee for Inland Fisheries of Africa) Technical Paper
CIFA Tech Pap — CIFA (Committee for Inland Fisheries of Africa) Technical Paper
CIFBA6 — Central Inland Fisheries Research Institute (Barrackpore). Bulletin
CIFCA9 — Communications. Instituti Forestalis Cechosloveniae
CiFe — Ciencia y Fe
CIFJAU — Canadian Institute of Food Technology. Journal
CIFM — Contributi. Istituto di Filologia Moderna
CIFRBL — Central Inland Fisheries Research Institute (Barrackpore). Annual Report
CIFRI (Cent Inland Fish Res Inst) Semin — CIFRI (Central Inland Fisheries Research Institute) Seminar
CIFSBO — Central Inland Fisheries Research Institute (Barrackpore). Survey Report

CIF-SP — Congresso Internacional de Filosofia. Anais (Sao Paulo)
CIFW — Institut Francais de Washington. Historical Documents. Cahiers
CIG — Congres International de Geographie
CIG — Corpus Inscriptionum Graecarum [*A collection of Greek inscriptions*]
CIGC — Congres International de Geographie (Cairo)
CIG Cryog Indus Gases — CIG. Cryogenics and Industrial Gases
CI Gr — Corpus Inscriptionum Graecarum
CIGR XVI — Sixteenth International Congress of Geographers. Lisbon, 1949
CIG XIX — Nineteenth International Geological Congress. Algiers, 1952
CIG XVIII — Eighteenth International Geological Congress. London, 1948
CIG XX — Twentieth International Geological Congress. Mexico City, 1956
CIH — Cincinnati Historical Society Bulletin
CIH — Computers in Healthcare
CIHB — Canadian Inventory of Historic Building
CIHMBG — Congreso Internacional de Hematologia. Conferencias
CIHS — Cuadernos del Instituto de Historia. Serie Antropologica [*Mexico*]
CII — Corpus Inscriptionum Iranicarum
CII — Corpus Inscriptionum Iudaicarum
CIICBP — Convenio IICA-ZN-ROCAP [*Instituto Interamericano de Ciencias Agricolas-Zona Norte-Regional Organization for Central America and Panama*] Bibliografia
CIIG Bull — CIIG [*Construction Industry Information Group*] Bulletin
CIIMDN — Cancer Immunology and Immunotherapy
CIINAN — Citrus Industry
CI Ins — Corpus Inscriptionum Insularum Celticarum
Ci Interamer — Ciencia Interamericana. Departamento de Asuntos Cientificos. Union Panamericana
Ci Invest — Ciencias e Investigacion
CIIS — Corporate Integrated Information System
CIJ — Canada Commerce
CIJ — Commercial Investment Journal
CIJ — Criminology an Interdisciplinary Journal
CIJE — Current Index to Journals in Education
CIJED4 — Centro Internacional de Agricultura Tropical [*CIAT*]. Series JE
CIL — Caribbean Insight (London)
CiL — Cite Libre
CIL — Congo Illustre
CIL — Congres International de Linguistes. Actes
CIL — Contemporary Indian Literature
CIL — Corpus Inscriptionum Latinarum [*A collection of Latin inscriptions*]
CIL — Crain's Illinois Business
CILA B — CILA [*Centre Internationale de Linguistique Appliquee*] Bulletin
CILBA2 — Contributions. Institute of Low Temperature Science. Hokkaido University. Series B
CILH — Cuadernos para Investigacion de la Literatura Hispanica
CILJDT — Contact and Intraocular Lens Medical Journal
CILL — Current Inquiry into Language and Linguistics
C Illus — Century Illustrated
CILP — Conferences. Institut de Linguistique de Paris
CILP — Current Index to Legal Periodicals
Ci LR — Cincinnati Law Review
CILT — Amsterdam Studies in the Theory and History of Linguistic Science. Series IV. Current Issues in Linguistic Theory
CILUL — Cahiers. Institut de Linguistique. Universite Louvain
CIM — COMLINE Industrial Monitor
CIMA — Cahiers. Institut du Moyen-Age Grec et Latin. Universitaire Copenhagen
CIMAGL — Cahiers. Institut du Moyen Age Grec et Latin
CIMA Outlk — Construction Industry Manufacturers Association. Outlook
CIMB — CIM [*Canadian Institute of Mining and Metallurgy*] Bulletin
Cimbebasia Mem — Cimbebasia. Memoir
Cimbebasia Ser A — Cimbebasia. Series A
Cim Beton — Ciment si Beton
Cim Betons Platres Chaux — Ciments, Betons, Platres, Chaux
CIM Bull — CIM [*Canadian Institute of Mining and Metallurgy*] Bulletin
CIM Bulletin — Canadian Institute of Mining and Metallurgy. Bulletin
CIME — Computers in Mechanical Engineering
Cimento Bul — Cimento Bulteni
Cimento Mustahsilleri Bul — Cimento Mustahsilleri Bulteni
CIMGL — Cahiers. Institut du Moyen-Age Grec et Latin
CIMIDV — Comparative Immunology, Microbiology, and Infectious Diseases
CIM Mag — CIM [*Computer Integrated Manufacturing*] Magazine
CIMMYT News — Centro Internacional de Mejoramiento de Maiz y Trigo. News
CIMNDC — Clinical Immunology Newsletter
CIMOA — Chimie Moderne
CimR — Cimarron Review
CIMRDO — Clinical Immunology Reviews
CIMRM — Corpus Inscriptionum et Monumentorum Religionis Mithriacae
CIMS — Canada. Industrial Meteorology Studies. Environment Canada. Atmospheric Environment
CIN — Actes. Congres International de Numismatique
CIN — Canadian Insurance
CIN — Chemical Industry Notes
Cin — Cinema
CINAHL — Cumulative Index to Nursing and Allied Health Literature
Cin Art B — Cincinnati Art Museum. Bulletin
Cin BAJ — Cincinnati Bar Association. Journal
Cinci Dent Soc Bull — Cincinnati Dental Society. Bulletin
Cincin BJ — Cincinnati Business Journal
Cincin Bsn — Cincinnati Business Courier
Cincin Enq — Cincinnati Enquirer
Cincinnati A Mus Bull — Cincinnati Art Museum Bulletin
Cincinnati Class Stud — Cincinnati Classical Studies
Cincinnati Dent Soc Bull — Cincinnati Dental Society Bulletin
Cincinnati J Med — Cincinnati Journal of Medicine
Cincinnati Med — Cincinnati Medicine

Cincinnati Mus Bull — Cincinnati Art Museum. Bulletin
Cincinnati Mus Bul NS — Cincinnati Art Museum. Bulletin. New Series
Cincinnati Mus N — Cincinnati Art Museum. News
Cincinnati Quart J Sci — Cincinnati Quarterly Journal of Science
Cincinnati Univ Law Rev — University of Cincinnati Law Review
Cincin S NH J — Journal of the Cincinnati Society of Natural History
Cinc L Bul — Cincinnati Law Bulletin
Cinc Sym Prog Notes — Cincinnati Symphony Orchestra. Program Notes
CINDA — Computer Index of Neutron Data
CINE — Cinematografia
Cinegram — Cinegram Magazine
Cinema Can — Cinema Canada
Cinema J — Cinema Journal
Cinema P — Cinema Papers
Cinemateca Rev — Cinemateca Revista
Cinematgr — Cinematographe
Cineradiogr Photons Part Eur Conf — Cineradiography with Photons or Particles. European Conference
CinF — Cine-France
C Inform Chef Personnel — Cahiers d'Information du Chef de Personnel
C Ingen Agron — Cahiers des Ingenieurs Agronomes
CinJ — Cinema Journal
CINL — Cumulative Index to Nursing and Allied Health Literature
Cin Law Bul — Cincinnati Law Bulletin
Cin Law Bull — Weekly Cincinnati Law Bulletin
Cin Law Rev — University of Cincinnati. Law Review
Cin L Rev — University of Cincinnati. Law Review
CINMDE — Colloque. INSERM
CINND — Ceramics International
CINP — CINEP/PLUS. Bulletin du Centre d'Ingenierie Nordique de l'Ecole Polytechnique
Cin Regional Police Assn J — Cincinnati Regional Police Association. Journal
C Inst Amenag Urb Region Paris — Cahiers. Institut d'Amenagement et d'Urbanisation de la Region Parisienne
Cin Sym — Cincinnati Symphony Orchestra. Program Notes
CInt — Cuba Intelectual
CINTD — Communications International
C Int Sociol — Cahiers Internationaux de Sociologie
CINUD — Computers in Industry
CINVA — Publicaciones del Centro Interamericano de Vivienda. Serie Resumenes de Clase [*Bogota*]
CINVD7 — Cancer Investigation
CIO Let — CIO [*Chief Information Officer*] Letter
CIO Mo — CIO [*Chief Information Officer*] Monthly
CIOP XI — Eleventh International Ornithological Congress. Basel, 1954. Proceedings
CIOVD — Cistota Ovzdusia
CIO XXII — Twenty-second International Congress of Orientalists. Istanbul, 1951. Proceedings
CIO XXIV — Twenty-fourth International Congress of Orientalists. Munich, 1957
CIP — Congres International de Philosophie
CIPAC Monogr — CIPAC [*Collaborative International Pesticides Analytical Council*] Monograph
CIP Circ Int Potato Cent — CIP [*Centre International de la Pomme de Terre*] Circular. International Potato Center
CIPC VI — Sixieme Congres International de Pathologie Comparee. Madrid, 1952
CIPED — Carvao, Informacao, e Pesquisa
CIPMAL — Clarke Institute of Psychiatry. Monograph Series
CIP Newsl — CIP [*Capital Improvement Project*] Newsletter
CIPPS IV — Fourth International Congress of Prehistoric and Protohistoric Sciences. Madrid, 1954. Acts
CIPRA2 — Canadian Insect Pest Review
CIPS Rev — CIPS [*Canadian Information Processing Society*] Review
CIPVDH — Comunicaciones. INIA [*Instituto Nacional de Investigaciones Agrarias*]. Serie Produccion Vegetal
CIR — Communications Industries Report
CIRAA — CIRP [*College International pour l'Etude Scientifique des Techniques de Production Mecanique*] Annals
CIRADW — Contributions. Central Research Institute for Agriculture
Cir Bucal — Cirugia Bucal
Circ Aff Etr — Circulaire. Ministre des Affaires Etrangeres
Circ Agric Exp Stn Purdue Univ — Circular. Agricultural Experiment Station. Purdue University
Circ Agric Ext Serv Univ Ark — Circular. Agricultural Extension Service. University of Arkansas
Circ Agric Ext Serv Wash St Univ — Circular. Agricultural Extension Service. Washington State University
Circ Ala Agr Exp Sta — Circular. Alabama Agricultural Experiment Station
Circ Ala Geol Surv — Circular. Alabama Geological Survey
Circ Ala Polytech Inst Ext Serv — Circular. Alabama Polytechnic Institute. Extension Service
Circ Alaska Agric Exp Stn — Circular. Alaska. Agricultural Experiment Station
Circ Alaska Agric Exp Stns — Circular. Alaska Agricultural Experiment Stations
Circ Alaska Agric Exp Stn Sch Agric Land Resour Manage — Circular. Alaska Agricultural Experiment Station. School of Agriculture and Land Resources Management
Circ Alaska Game Commn — Circular. Alaska Game Commission
Circ Am Agric Chem Co — Circular. American Agricultural Chemical Company
Circ Am Paint Varn Manuf Assoc Sci Sect — Circulars. American Paint and Varnish Manufacturers' Association. Scientific Section
Circ A N Dak State Univ Agr Appl Sci Ext Serv — Circular A. North Dakota State University of Agriculture and Applied Science. Extension Service
Circ & Cuadrado — Circulo y Cuadrado
Circ ANR Ala Coop Ext Serv Auburn Univ — Circular ANR [*Agricultural and Natural Resources*] Alabama Cooperative Extension Service. Auburn University

Circ Argent Odontol Bol — Circulo Argentino de Odontologia. Boletin
Circ Ariz Agric Ext Serv — Circular. Arizona Agricultural Extension Service
Circ Ariz Bur Mines — Circular. Arizona Bureau of Mines
Circ Ark St Pl Bd — Circular. Arkansas State Plant Board
Circ Asph Ass — Circular. Asphalt Association
Circ Asph Inst — Circular. Asphalt Institute
Circ Ass Hawaii Pineapple Cann Exp Stn — Circular. Association of Hawaiian Pineapple Canners Experiment Station
Circ Assoc Mine Managers S Afr — Circular. Association of Mine Managers of South Africa
Circ Astr Inst Univ Amst — Circular of the Astronomical Institute of the University of Amsterdam
Circ Astr Obs Harv — Circular. Astronomical Observatory of Harvard College
Circ Atlant Biol Stn — Circular. Atlantic Biological Station. General Series
Circ Auburn Univ Agr Ext Serv — Circular. Auburn University. Agricultural Extension Service
Circ Aust Mus — Circular. Australian Museum
CIRCAZ — Circulation
Circ Bd Agric For Hawaii — Circular. Board of Agriculture and Forestry. Territory of Hawaii
Circ Bd Agric Trin — Circular. Board of Agriculture. Trinidad and Tobago
Circ Br Astr Ass — Circular of the British Astronomical Association
Circ Br Lichen Soc — Circular. British Lichen Society
Circ Br Mosq Control Inst — Circular. British Mosquito Control Institute
Circ Br Rheol Club — Circular. British Rheologists' Club
Circ Br Westinghouse Elect Co — Circular of the British Westinghouse Electric Company
Circ Br Wood Preserv Ass — Circular. British Wood Preserving Association
Circ Bull Oreg Agric Exp Stn — Circular Bulletin. Oregon Agricultural Experiment Station
Circ Bur Ent US Dep Agric — Circular. Bureau of Entomology. United States Department of Agriculture
Circ Calif Agr Ext Serv — Circular. California Agricultural Extension Service
Circ Calif Agric Exp Stn — Circular. California Agricultural Experiment Station
Circ Can Beekprs Coun — Circular. Canadian Beekeepers' Council
Circ Cent Insp Inst Weights Meas — Circular. Central Inspection Institute of Weights and Measures
Circ Cent Invest Agr El Bajio (CIAB) — Circular. Centro de Investigaciones Agricolas de El Bajio (CIAB)
Circ Cent Invest Agr Noroeste (CIANO) — Circular. Centro de Investigaciones Agricolas del Noroeste (CIANO)
Circ Cent Invest Agr Sudeste — Circular. Centro de Investigaciones Agricolas del Sudeste
Circ Cent Invest Basicas (CIB) — Circular. Centro de Investigaciones del Basicas (CIB)
Circ Clemson Agr Coll Ext Serv — Circular. Clemson Agricultural College. Extension Service
Circ Clemson Univ Coop Ext Serv — Circular. Clemson University Cooperative Extension Service
Circ Coll Agric Res Cent Wash State Univ — Circular. College of Agriculture Research Center. Washington State University
Circ Coll Agric Univ Ill — Circular. College of Agriculture. University of Illinois
Circ Conn Agric Exp Stn New Haven — Circular. Connecticut Agricultural Experiment Station. New Haven
Circ Control — Circulation Control
Circ Coop Ext Serv Max C Fleischmann Coll Agric Nevada Univ — Circular. Nevada University. Max C. Fleischmann College of Agriculture. Cooperative Extension Service
Circ Coop Ext Serv N Dak St Univ — Circular. Cooperative Extension Service. North Dakota State University
Circ Coop Ext Serv Univ GA — Circular. Cooperative Extension Service. University of Georgia
Circ Coop Ext Serv Univ Hawaii — Circular. Cooperative Extension Service. University of Hawaii
Circ Coop Ext Serv Univ Ill — Circular. Cooperative Extension Service. University of Illinois
Circ Def Nat — Circulaire. Ministre de la Defense Nationale
Circ Dep Agric Can — Circular. Department of Agriculture. Canada
Circ Div Fd Res CSIRO — Circular. Division of Food Research. Commonwealth Scientific and Industrial Research Organisation
Circ Div Fish Oceanogr CSIRO — Circular. Division of Fisheries and Oceanography. Commonwealth Scientific and Industrial Research Organisation
Circ Div Mech Eng CSIRO — Circular. Division of Mechanical Engineering. Commonwealth Scientific and Industrial Research Organisation
CIRCE — Catalogo Italiano Riviste su Calcolatore Elettronico
Circ Electrotech Lab — Circulars. Electrotechnical Laboratory
Circ Electrotech Lab (Tokyo) — Circulars. Electrotechnical Laboratory (Tokyo, Japan)
Circ Electrotech Lab (Tokyo Japan) — Circulars. Electrotechnical Laboratory (Tokyo, Japan)
Circ Engng Exp Stn Ore St Coll — Circular. Engineering Experiment Station. Oregon State College
Circ Engng Exp Stn Purdue — Circular. Engineering Experiment Station. Purdue University
Circ Engng Ext Dep Purdue — Circular. Engineering Extension Department. Purdue University
Circ Engng Sect Am Railr Ass — Circular of the Engineering Section. American Railroad Association
Circ Engng Sect CSIRO Aust — Circular. Engineering Section. Commonwealth Scientific and Industrial Research Organization. Australia
Circ Eng Sec CSIRO — Circular. Engineering Section. Commonwealth Scientific and Industrial Research Organisation
Circ Ent Dep Rhode Isl Bd Agric — Circular. Entomological Department. Rhode Island Board of Agriculture

Circ E Okla State Univ Coop Ext Serv — Circular. E. Oklahoma State University. Cooperative Extension Service
Circ Estac Exp Agric Canete — Circular. Estacion Experimental Agricola. Canete
Circ Estac Exp Agric La Molina — Circular. Estacion Experimental Agricola La Molina
Circ Estac Exp Agric Soc Nac Agr Lima — Circular. Estacion Experimental Agricola de la Sociedad Nacional Agraria (Lima)
Circ Estac Exp Agric Tucuman — Circular. Estacion Experimental Agricola de Tucuman
Circ Estac Exp Agrofor S Lorenzo — Circular. Estacion Experimental Agroforestal de San Lorenzo
Circ Estac Exp Agron Cuba — Circular. Estacion Experimental Agronomica de Cuba
Circ Estac Exp Quinta Normal Ambato — Circular. Estacion Experimental. Quinta Normal (Ambato)
Circ EX Ala Coop Ext Serv Auburn Univ — Circular EX. Alabama Cooperative Extension Service. Auburn University
Circ Exp Fms Can — Circular. Experimental Farms of Canada
Circ Ext Div Minn Univ Coll Agric — Circular. Extension Division. Minnesota University College of Agriculture
Circ Ext Inst Prod Anim Univ Cent Venez — Circular de Extension. Instituto de Produccion Animal. Universidad Central de Venezuela
Circ Ext Serv Ext Agric Mayaguez — Circular de Extension. Servicio de Extension Agricola (Mayaguez)
Circ Ext Serv Minist Natn Econ Syria — Circular. Extension Service. Ministry of National Economy. Syria
Circ Fac Agric Alberta Univ — Circular of the Faculty of Agriculture. Alberta University
Circ Farm — Circular Farmaceutica
Circ Farm Bol Inf — Circular Farmaceutica. Boletin Informativo
Circ Fin — Circulaire. Ministre des Finances
Circ Fla Agric Exp Stn — Circular. Florida Agricultural Experiment Station
Circ Fla Agric Ext Serv — Circular. Florida Agricultural Extension Service
Circ Fla Coop Ext Serv — Circular. Florida Cooperative Extension Service
Circ Fla Univ Agr Ext Serv — Circular. Florida University. Agricultural Extension Service
Circ GA Agr Exp Sta — Circular. Georgia Agricultural Experiment Stations
Circ Geol Surv Ala — Circular. Geological Survey of Alabama
Circ Geol Surv GA — Circular. Geological Survey of Georgia
Circ Hawaii Div Water Land Dev — Circular. Hawaii. Division of Water and Land Development
Circ HE Ala Coop Ext Serv Auburn Univ — Circular HE. Alabama Cooperative Extension Service. Auburn University
Circ Hort Biol Serv Nova Scot Dep Agric Mktg — Circular. Horticulture and Biology Service. Nova Scotia Department of Agriculture and Marketing
Circ Ill Dep Agric — Circular. Illinois Department of Agriculture
Circ Illinois State Geol Surv — Circular. Illinois State Geological Survey
Circ Ill Nat Hist Surv — Circular. Illinois Natural History Survey
Circ Ill Natur Hist Surv — Circular. Illinois Natural History Survey
Circ Ill State Geol Surv Div — Circular. Illinois State Geological Survey Division
Circ Ill State Water Surv — Circular. Illinois State Water Survey
Circ Inf Agric Exp Stn Oreg State Univ — Circular of Information. Agricultural Experiment Station. Oregon State University
Circ Inform Oreg State Coll Agr Exp Sta — Circular of Information. Oregon State College. Agricultural Experiment Station
Circ Inf Tech Cent Doc Sider — Circulaire d'Informations Techniques. Centre de Documentation Siderurgique
Circ Inst Agron — Circular. Instituto Agronomico
Circ Inst Agron (Campinas Braz) — Circular. Instituto Agronomico (Campinas, Brazil)
Circ Inst Agron Estado Sao Paulo — Circular. Instituto Agronomico do Estado de Sao Paulo
Circ Inst Agron Norte Braz — Circular. Instituto Agronomico do Norte (Brazil)
Circ Inst Agron Norte (Brazil) — Circular. Instituto Agronomico do Norte (Brazil)
Circ Inst Agron Sul (Pelotas) — Circular. Instituto Agronomico do Sul (Pelotas)
Circ Inst Agron Sul Pelotas Braz — Circular. Instituto Agronomico do Sul (Pelotas, Brazil)
Circ Inst Pesq Exp Agropecuar N — Circular. Instituto de Pesquisas e Experimentacao Agropecuarias do Norte
Circ Inst Pesqui Agron Pernambuco — Circular. Instituto de Pesquisas Agronomicas de Pernambuco
Circ Inst Pesqui Agropecu Norte — Circular. Instituto de Pesquisas Agropecuarias do Norte
Circ Inst Pesqui Agropecu Sul — Circular. Instituto de Pesquisas Agropecuarias do Sul
Circ Inst Pesqui Agropecu Sul (Braz) — Circular. Instituto de Pesquisas Agropecuarias do Sul (Brazil)
Circ Inst Pesqui Exp Agropecu Norte Braz — Circular. Instituto de Pesquisas e Experimentacao Agropecuarias do Norte (Brazil)
Circ Inst Pesqui Exp Agropecu Sul Braz — Circular. Instituto de Pesquisas e Experimentacao Agropecuarias do Sul (Brazil)
Circ Int — Circulaire. Ministre de l'Interieur
Cir Cir — Cirugia y Cirujanos
Cir Cirujanos — Cirugia y Cirujanos
Circ Just — Circulaire. Ministre de la Justice
Circ Kans Agr Exp Sta — Circular. Kansas Agricultural Experiment Station
Circ Kans Agric Exp Stn — Circular. Kansas Agricultural Experiment Station
Circ Kans State Univ Agr Appl Sci Ext Serv — Circular. Kansas State University of Agriculture and Applied Science. ExtensionService
Circ Kans St Ent Commn — Circular. Kansas State Entomological Commission
Circ Kans Univ Ext Serv — Circular. Kansas University Extension Service
Circ KY Agric Exp Stn — Circular. Kentucky Agricultural Experiment Station
Circ KY Univ Agr Ext Serv — Circular. Kentucky University. Agricultural Extension Service
Circ LA Agr Exp Sta — Circular. Louisiana Agricultural Experiment Station

Circ Line Elevators Farm Serv — Circular. Line Elevators Farm Service

Circ Metab Cerveau — Circulation et Metabolisme du Cerveau

Circ Min — Circulaire Ministerielle

Circ Mont Agr Exp Sta — Circular. Montana Agricultural Experiment Station

Circ Mont State Coll Coop Ext Serv — Circular. Montana State College. Cooperative Extension Service

Circ Mont State Univ Coop Ext Serv — Circular. Montana State University. Cooperative Extension Service

Circ MO Univ Coll Agr Ext Serv — Circular. Missouri University. College of Agriculture. Extension Service

Circ Natl Bur Stand (US) — Circular. National Bureau of Standards (United States)

Circ Natl Paint Varn Lacquer Assoc Sci Sect — Circulars. National Paint, Varnish, and Lacquer Association. Scientific Section

Circ Natl Varn Manuf Assoc — Circulars. National Varnish Manufacturers' Association

Circ N Carol Agric Ext Serv — Circular. North Carolina Agricultural Extension Service

Circ N Dak Agr Coll Agr Ext Serv — Circular. North Dakota Agricultural College. Agricultural Extension Service

Circ New Jers Agric Exp Stn — Circular. New Jersey Agricultural Experiment Station

Circ New Jers Dep Agric — Circular. New Jersey Department of Agriculture

Circ New Mex Bur Mines Miner Resour — Circular. New Mexico Bureau of Mines and Mineral Resources

Circ New Mex St Bur Mines Miner Resour — Circular. New Mexico State Bureau of Mines and Mineral Resources

Circ New York State Mus — Circular. New York State Museum

Circ NJ Agr Exp Sta — Circular. New Jersey Agricultural Experiment Station

Circ NJ Agric Exp Stn — Circular. New Jersey Agricultural Experiment Station

Circ NM Bur Mines Miner Resour — Circular. New Mexico. Bureau of Mines and Mineral Resources

Circ N Mex State Univ Agr Ext Serv — Circular. New Mexico State University. Agricultural Extension Service

Circ NM State Univ Coop Ext Serv — Circular. New Mexico State University. Cooperative Extension Service

Circ Odontol San Martin Tres Febr — Circulo Odontologico de San Martin y Tres de Febrero

Circ Okla Agric Exp Stn — Circular. Oklahoma Agricultural Experiment Station

Circ Okla Geol Surv — Circular. Oklahoma Geological Survey

Circ Oklahoma Geol Surv — Circular. Oklahoma Geological Survey

Circ Okla State Univ Agr Appl Sci Agr Ext Serv — Circular. Oklahoma State University of Agriculture and Applied Science. Agricultural Extension Service

Circ Ont Agric Coll — Circular. Ontario Agricultural College

Circ Ont Dep Agric — Circular. Ontario Department of Agriculture

Circ Ore Agric Exp Stn — Circular. Oregon Agricultural Experiment Station

Circ Oreg State Coll Eng Exp — Circular. Oregon State College. Engineering Experiment Station

Circ Oreg State Coll Eng Exp Stn — Circular. Oregon State College. Engineering Experiment Station

Circ Oreg State Univ Eng Exp St — Circular. Oregon State University. Engineering Experiment Station

Circ Osseuse CR Symp Int — Circulation Osseuse. Compte Rendu du Symposium International sur la Circulation Osseuse

Circ PA Agric Exp Stn — Circular. Pennsylvania Agricultural Experiment Station

Circ Paint Manuf Assoc US Educ Bur Sci Sect — Circulars. Paint Manufacturers' Association of the United States. Educational Bureau. Scientific Section

Circ Pa State Univ Agric Ext Serv — Circular. Pennsylvania State University. Agricultural Extension Service

Circ PA State Univ Earth Miner Sci Exp St — Circular. Pennsylvania State University. Earth and Mineral Sciences Experiment Station

Circ PA Univ Ext Serv — Circular. Pennsylvania University Extension Service

Circ Purdue Univ Agric Exp Stn — Circular. Purdue University. Agricultural Experiment Station

Circ Regul Factors Neuroendocr Funct — Circulating Regulatory Factors and Neuroendocrine Function

Circ Res — Circulation Research

Circ Res Suppl — Circulation Research. Supplement

Circ Rubber Res Inst Malaya — Circular. Rubber Research Institute of Malaya

Circ Sask Res Counc Geol Div — Circular. Saskatchewan Research Council. Geology Division

Circ SC Agric Exp Stn — Circular. South Carolina Agricultural Experiment Station

Circ SD Agric Exp Stn — Circular. South Dakota. Agricultural Experiment Station

Circ S Dak Agr Exp Sta — Circular. South Dakota Agricultural Experiment Station

Circ Secr Agr Secc Inform Publ Agr (Porto Alegre) — Circular. Secretaria da Agricultura. Seccao de Informacoes e Publicidade Agricola (Porto Alegre)

Circ Ser Oreg State Coll Eng Exp Stn — Circular Series. Oregon State College. Engineering Experiment Station

Circ Ser W Va Geol Econ Sur — Circular Series. West Virginia Geological and Economic Survey

Circ S Fla Agric Exp Stn — Circular. South Florida Agricultural Experiment Station

Circ S Fla Agric Exp Stn Inst Food Agric Sci Univ Fla — Circular S. Florida Agricultural Experiment Stations. Institute of Food and Agricultural Sciences. University of Florida

Circ S Fla Univ Agr Exp Sta — Circular S. Florida University Agricultural Experiment Station

Circ Shock — Circulatory Shock

Circ Shock (Suppl) — Circulatory Shock (Supplement)

Circ Speleol Rom Not — Circolo Speleologico Romano. Notiziario

Circ Suppl — Circulation. Supplement

Circ Syst Signal Process — Circuits, Systems, and Signal Processing

Circ Tex Agric Exp Stn — Circular. Texas Agricultural Experiment Station

Circ Tex For Serv — Circular. Texas Forest Service

Circ to Sch — Circular to Schools

Circuits Manuf — Circuits Manufacturing

Circuits Mfg — Circuits Manufacturing

Circuits Syst — Circuits and Systems

Circular Com Parasitol Agric (Mexico) — Circular. Comision de Parasitologia Agricola (Mexico)

Circular Illinois Agric Exper Station — Circular. Illinois Agricultural Experiment Station

Circular Univ Fla Coop Ext Serv — Circular. University of Florida. Cooperative Extension Service

Circular West Virginia Agric Exper Station — Circular. West Virginia Agricultural Experiment Station

Circulation Res — Circulation Research

Circulation Suppl — Circulation. Supplement

Circum Pac Counc Energy Miner Resour Earth Sci Ser — Circum-Pacific Council for Energy and Mineral Resources Earth Science Series

Circ Univ Fla Agric Ext Serv — Circular. University of Florida. Agricultural Extension Service

Circ Univ GA Coll Agr Coop Ext Serv — Circular. University of Georgia. College of Agriculture. Cooperative Extension Service

Circ Univ Ill Coll Agr Coop Ext Serv — Circular. University of Illinois. College of Agriculture. Cooperative ExtensionService

Circ Univ Ill Coop Ext Serv — Circular. University of Illinois. Cooperative Extension Service

Circ Univ KY Agr Ext Serv — Circular. University of Kentucky. Agricultural Extension Service

Circ Univ Ky Agric Exp Stn — Circular. University of Kentucky Agricultural Experiment Station

Circ Univ Nebr Coll Agr Home Econ Agr Exp Sta — Circular. University of Nebraska. College of Agriculture and Home Economics. Agricultural Experiment Station

Circ Univ Nev Max C Fleischmann Coll Agr Agr Ext Serv — Circular. University of Nevada. Max C. Fleischmann College of Agriculture. Agricultural Extension Service

Circ Univ Tenn Agric Exp Stn — Circular. University of Tennessee. Agricultural Experiment Station

Circ Univ Wis Coll Agr Ext Serv — Circular. University of Wisconsin. College of Agriculture. Extension Service

Circ USDA — Circular. United States Department of Agriculture

Circ US Dep Agric — Circular. United States Department of Agriculture

Circ US Geol Surv — Circular. United States Geological Survey

Circ US Natn Bur Stand — Circular. United States National Bureau of Standards

Circ Utah Agric Exp Stn — Circular. Utah Agricultural Experiment Station

Circ Utah Geol Miner Surv — Circular. Utah Geological and Mineral Survey

Circ VA Polytech Inst Agr Ext Serv — Circular. Virginia Polytechnic Institute. Agricultural Extension Service

Circ Verfinst TNO — Circulaire. Verfinstituut TNO

Circ Wash Agr Exp Sta — Circular. Washington Agriculture Experiment Station

Circ Wash State Univ Coll Eng — Circular. Washington State University. College of Engineering

Circ Wash State Univ Coop Ext Serv — Circular. Washington State University. Cooperative Extension Service

Circ Wild Fl Preserv Soc — Circular. Wild Flower Preservation Society

Circ Wis Univ Agric Ext Serv — Circular. Wisconsin University of Agriculture. Extension Service

Circ WV Agric Exp Stn — Circular. West Virginia. Agricultural Experiment Station

Circ W Va Univ Agric For Exp Stn — Circular. West Virginia University Agricultural and Forestry Experiment Station

Circ WV Geol Econ Surv — Circular. West Virginia. Geological and Economic Survey

Circ Wy Agric Exp Stn — Circular. Wyoming. Agricultural Experiment Station

Circ Wyo Agric Ext Serv — Circular. Wyoming Agricultural Extension Service

CIR DIB917 — Current Industrial Reports. DIB-917. Copper-Base Mill and Foundry Products

Cir Div Food Res CSIRO — Circular. Division of Food Research. Commonwealth Scientific and Industrial Research Organisation

CIREJ — Commercial Investment Real Estate Journal

Cir Esp — Cirugia Espanola

CIRFAS — Canadian Industry Report of Fisheries and Aquatic Sciences

Cir Ginecol Urol — Cirurgia, Ginecologia, y Urologia

CIRIBK — Congres International de Reproduction Animale et Insemination Artificielle

CIR ITA991 — Current Industrial Reports. ITA-991. Titanium Mill Products, Ingots, and Castings

Cirk Jordbrukstek Inst — Cirkulaer. Jordbrukstekniska Institutet

CIRM — Corpus Inscriptionum et Monumentorum Religionis Mithriacae

CIR M20A — Current Industrial Reports. M20A. Flour Milling Products

CIR M20J — Current Industrial Reports. M20J. Fats and Oils, Oilseed Crushings

CIR M20K — Current Industrial Reports. M20K. Fats and Oils. Production, Consumption, and Warehouse Stocks

CIR M22A — Current Industrial Reports. M22A. Finished Fabrics. Production, Inventories, and Unfilled Orders

CIR M22D — Current Industrial Reports. M22D. Consumption on the Woolen and Worsted Systems

CIR M22P — Current Industrial Reports. M22P. Cotton, Manmade Fiber Staple, and Linters

CIR M23I — Current Industrial Reports. M23I. Men's, Women's, Misses', and Juniors' Selected Apparel

CIR M28A — Current Industrial Reports. M28A. Inorganic Chemicals

CIR M28B — Current Industrial Reports. M28B. Inorganic Fertilizer Materials and Related Products

CIR M28C — Current Industrial Reports. M28C. Industrial Gases

CIR M28F — Current Industrial Reports. M28F. Paint, Varnish, and Lacquer

CIR M30E — Current Industrial Reports. M30E. Plastic Bottles

CIR M3-1 — Current Industrial Reports. M3-1. Manufacturers' Shipments, Inventories, and Orders

CIR M31A — Current Industrial Reports. M31A. Footwear

CIR M32D — Current Industrial Reports. M32D. Clay Construction Products

CIR M32G — Current Industrial Reports. M32G. Glass Containers
CIR M33A — Current Industrial Reports. M33A. Iron and Steel Castings
CIR M33E — Current Industrial Reports. M33E. Nonferrous Castings
CIR M33K — Current Industrial Reports. M33K. Inventories of Brass and Copper Wire Mill Shapes
CIR M34H — Current Industrial Reports. M34H. Closures for Containers
CIR M35S — Current Industrial Reports. M35S. Tractors, except Garden Tractors
CIR M36D — Current Industrial Reports. M36D. Electric Lamps
CIR M37G — Current Industrial Reports. M37G. Complete Aircraft and Aircraft Engines
CIR M37L — Current Industrial Reports. M37L. Truck Trailers
CIR M332 — Current Industrial Reports. M33-2. Aluminum Ingot and Mill Products
CIR M333 — Current Industrial Reports. M33-3. Inventories of Steel Mill Shapes
CIR MA20D — Current Industrial Reports. MA-20D. Confectionery, Including Chocolate Products
CIR MA20O — Current Industrial Reports. MA-20O. Manufacturers' Pollution Abatement CapitalExpenditures and Operating Costs
CIR MA22F1 — Current Industrial Reports. MA-22F1. Textured Yarn Production
CIR MA22F2 — Current Industrial Reports. MA-22F2. Spun Yarn Production
CIR MA22G — Current Industrial Reports. MA-22G. Narrow Fabrics
CIR MA22S — Current Industrial Reports. MA-22S. Finished Broadwoven Fabric Production
CIR MA23E — Current Industrial Reports. MA-23E. Men's and Boys' Outerwear
CIR MA23F — Current Industrial Reports. MA-23F. Women's and Children's Outerwear
CIR MA23G — Current Industrial Reports. MA-23G. Underwear and Nightwear
CIR MA23J — Current Industrial Reports. MA-23J. Brassieres, Corsets, and Allied Garments
CIR MA24F — Current Industrial Reports. MA-24F. Hardwood Plywood
CIR MA24H — Current Industrial Reports. MA-24H. Softwood Plywood
CIR MA25H — Current Industrial Reports. MA-25H. Manufacturers' Shipments of Office Furniture
CIR MA26A — Current Industrial Reports. MA-26A. Pulp, Paper, and Board
CIR MA26B — Current Industrial Reports. MA-26B. Selected Office Supplies and Accessories
CIR MA26F — Current Industrial Reports. MA-26F. Converted Flexible Materials for Packaging and Other Uses
CIR MA28A — Current Industrial Reports. MA-28A. Inorganic Chemicals
CIR MA28B — Current Industrial Reports. MA-28B. Sulfuric Acid
CIR MA28C — Current Industrial Reports. MA-28C. Industrial Gases
CIR MA28F — Current Industrial Reports. MA-28F. Paint and Allied Products
CIR MA28G84 — Current Industrial Reports. MA-28G(84)-1. Pharmaceutical Preparations, except Biologicals
CIR MA30A — Current Industrial Reports. MA-30A. Rubber Production Shipments and Stocks
CIR MA30B — Current Industrial Reports. MA-30B. Rubber and Plastics Hose and Belting
CIR MA30D — Current Industrial Reports. MA-30D. Shipments of Selected Plastic Products
CIR MA31A — Current Industrial Reports. MA-31A. Footwear Production by Manufacturers' Selling Price
CIR MA32C — Current Industrial Reports. MA-32C. Refractories
CIR MA32E — Current Industrial Reports. MA-32E. Consumer, Scientific, Technical, and Industrial Glassware
CIR MA32J — Current Industrial Reports. MA-32J. Fibrous Glass
CIR MA33B — Current Industrial Reports. MA-33B. Steel Mill Products
CIR MA33G — Current Industrial Reports. MA-33G. Magnesium Mill Products
CIR MA33L — Current Industrial Reports. MA-33L. Insulated Wire and Cable
CIR MA34N — Current Industrial Reports. MA-34N. Heating and Cooking Equipment
CIR MA34P — Current Industrial Reports. MA-34P. Aluminum Foil Converted
CIR MA35A — Current Industrial Reports. MA-35A. Farm Machines and Equipment
CIR MA35D — Current Industrial Reports. MA-35D. Construction Machinery
CIR MA35F — Current Industrial Reports. MA-35F. Mining Machinery and Mineral Processing Equipment
CIR MA35J — Current Industrial Reports. MA-35J. Selected Air Pollution Equipment
CIR MA35L — Current Industrial Reports. MA-35L. Internal Combustion Engines
CIR MA35M — Current Industrial Reports. MA-35M. Air-Conditioning and Refrigeration Equipment
CIR MA35N — Current Industrial Reports. MA-35N. Fluid Power Products Including Aerospace
CIR MA35P — Current Industrial Reports. MA-35P. Pumps and Compressors
CIR MA35R — Current Industrial Reports. MA-35R. Office, Computing, and Accounting Machines
CIR MA35U — Current Industrial Reports. MA-35U. Vending Machines Coin Operated
CIR MA36A — Current Industrial Reports. MA-36A. Switchgear, Switchboard Apparatus, Relays, and Industrial Controls
CIR MA36E — Current Industrial Reports. MA-36E. Electric Housewares and Fans
CIR MA36F — Current Industrial Reports. MA-36F. Major Household Appliances
CIR MA36G — Current Industrial Reports. MA-36G. Transformers
CIR MA36H — Current Industrial Reports. MA-36H. Motors and Generators
CIR MA36K — Current Industrial Reports. MA-36K. Wiring Devices and Supplies
CIR MA36L — Current Industrial Reports. MA-36L. Electric Lighting Fixtures
CIR MA36M — Current Industrial Reports. MA-36M. Home-Type Radio Receivers and TV Sets, AutoRadios, Phonos, and Record Players
CIR MA36N — Current Industrial Reports. MA-36N. Selected Electronic and Associated Products
CIR MA37D — Current Industrial Reports. MA-37D. Aerospace Industry Orders, Sales, and Backlog
CIR MA37E — Current Industrial Reports. MA-37E. Aircraft Propellers
CIR MA38B — Current Industrial Reports. MA-38B. Selected Instruments and Related Products
CIR MA38Q — Current Industrial Reports. MA-38Q. Selected Atomic Energy Products

CIR MA39A — Current Industrial Reports. MA-39A. Pens, Pencils, and Marking Devices
CIR MA350 — Current Industrial Reports. MA-35O. Antifriction Bearings
CIRMA/M — Mesoamerica. Centro de Investigaciones Regionales de Mesoamerica
CIR MQ22Q — Current Industrial Reports. MQ-22Q. Carpets and Rugs
CIR MQ22T — Current Industrial Reports. MQ-22T. Broadwoven Fabrics
CIR MQ23X — Current Industrial Reports. MQ-23X. Sheets, Pillowcases, and Towels
CIR MQ32A — Current Industrial Reports. MQ-32A. Flat Glass
CIR MQ32C — Current Industrial Reports. MQ-32C. Refractories
CIR MQ34E — Current Industrial Reports. MQ-34E. Plumbing Fixtures
CIR MQ34K — Current Industrial Reports. MQ-34K. Steel Shipping Drums and Pails
CIR MQ35D — Current Industrial Reports. MQ-35D. Construction Machinery
CIR MQ35W — Current Industrial Reports. MQ-35W. Metalworking Machinery
CIR MQ36B — Current Industrial Reports. MQ-36B. Electric Lamps
CIR MQ36C — Current Industrial Reports. MQ-36C. Fluorescent Lamp Ballasts
CIR MQ-C1 — Current Industrial Reports. MQ-C1. Survey of Plant Capacity
CIRND3 — Comunicaciones. INIA [*Instituto Nacional de Investigaciones Agrarias*]. Serie Recursos Naturales
Cir Od NWP — Circular Orders, Northwestern Provinces
CIRP Ann — CIRP [*College International pour l'Etude Scientifique des Techniques de Production Mecanique*] Annals
CIRPB7 — Rapports et Proces-Verbaux des Reunions. Commission Internationale pour l'Exploration Scientifique de la Mer Mediterranee
Cir Pediatr — Cirugia Pediatrica
CIRPHO — CIRPHO [*Cercle International de Recherches Philosophiques par Ordinateur*]Review
CIRQNS — Centre for International Relations. Queen's University. Northern Studies Series
CIRQNSS — Centre for International Relations. Queen's University. Northern Studies Series
CIRR — Corporate and Industry Research Reports
CIRR — Corporate and Industry Research Reports Index
Cir Ser Oreg State Coll Eng Exp Stn — Circular Series. Oregon State College. Engineering Experiment Station
CIRUAL — Circulation Research
Cir Urug — Cirugia del Uruguay
CIS — Cahiers Internationaux de Sociologie
CIS — Career Information System
CIS — Computer and Information Systems
CIS — Corpus Inscriptionum Semiticarum
CIS — Current Index to Statistics
CISA — Contributi. Istituto di Storia Antica
CIS Abstr — CIS [*Congressional Information Service*] Abstracts on Cards
CISAE IV — Quatrieme Congres International des Sciences Anthropologiques et Ethnologiques. Vienna, 1952. Actes
CIS Chromosome Inf Serv — CIS. Chromosome Information Service
CI Sem — Corpus Inscriptionum Semiticarum
CISE Newsl — Library Association. University and Research Section. Colleges, Institutes, andSchools of Education Subsection. Newsletter
CISGDL — Comunicaciones. INIA [*Instituto Nacional de Investigaciones Agrarias*]. Serie General
CISI — CIS [*Congressional Information Service*] Index
CISIDR — Comunicaciones. INIA [*Instituto Nacional de Investigaciones Agrarias*]. Serie Proteccion Vegetal
CIS Ind — CIS [*Congressional Information Service*] Index
CIS/Index Publ US Congr — CIS [*Congressional Information Service*] Index to Publications of the United States Congress
Cisl Metody Meh Splosn Stredy — Cislennye Metody Mehaniki Splosnoi Stredy
CI Soc — Cahiers Internationaux de Sociologie
C Ist — Cercetari Istorice
C Ista Milano — Contributi. Istituto di Archeologia. Universita Milan
CistC — Cistercienserchronik
CISTDQ — Comunicaciones. INIA [*Instituto Nacional de Investigaciones Agrarias*]. Serie Tecnologia Agraria
CISTISER — CISTI [*Canada Institute for Scientific and Technical Information*] Serials
Cist Stud — Cistercian Studies
CIS XV — Fifteenth International Congress of Sociology. Istanbul, 1952
CIS XVII — Seventeenth International Congress of Sociology. Beirut, 1956. Proceedings
CIT — Canadian Import Tribunal
CiT — Ciencia Tomista
Cit — Citeaux
Cit — Cithara
CIT — Commerce International
CITAC7 — Coletanea. Instituto de Tecnologia de Alimentos
Cit Bul — Citizens Bulletin
CITE — CITES Reports. Convention on International Trade in Endangered Species of Wild Fauna and Flora
CITEA — Chemie-Ingenieur-Technik
Citeaux Comment Cisterc — Citeaux Commentarii Cistercienses
Citeaux Comment Cisterc Stud & Doc — Citeaux Commentarii Cistercienses. Studia et Documenta
CITE N — CITE [*Construction Information-Training Education Project*] News
Cite Tech — Cite et Technique
CITGAN — Citrograph
Cit God — City of God
Cith — Cithara
Citibank — Citibank. Monthly Economic Letter
Citibank Mo Econ Letter — Citibank. Monthly Economic Letter
Citin Gos Ped Inst Ucen Zap — Citinskii Gosudarstvennyi Pedagogiceskii Institut. Ucenye Zapiski
CITJD — Chartered Institute of Transport. Journal
CITMD — Cahiers d'Informations Techniques/Revue de Metallurgie

CitN — Citeaux in de Nederlande
CitN — Cite Nouvelle. Revue Catholique d'Etude et d'Action
CiTom — La Ciencia Tomista
Ci Tomista — Ciencia Tomista. Publicacion Trimestral de los P.P. Dominicos Espanoles
Citrus Eng Conf Trans — Citrus Engineering Conference. Transactions
Citrus Grow — Citrus Grower
Citrus Grow Orlando Fla — Citrus Grower (Orlando, Florida)
Citrus Grow Sub-Trop Fruit J — Citrus Grower and Sub-Tropical Fruit Journal
Citrus Grow Uitenhage S Afr — Citrus Grower (Uitenhage, South Africa)
Citrus Ind — Citrus Industry
Citrus Ind Mag — Citrus Industry Magazine
Citrus Industr — Citrus Industry
Citrus J — Citrus Journal
Citrus Mag — Citrus Magazine
Citrus Subtrop Fruit J — Citrus and Subtropical Fruit Journal
Citrus Veg Mag — Citrus and Vegetable Magazine
City Adelaide Munic Yb — Adelaide. City. Municipal Year Book
City Civ Ct Act — New York City Civil Court Act
City Club Bul Chic — City Club Bulletin (Chicago)
City Coll Vector — City College Vector
City Crim Ct Act — New York City Criminal Court Act
City Stoke-On-Trent Mus Archaeol Soc Rep — City of Stoke-On-Trent Museum. Archaeological Society. Reports
Citzn Reg — Citizen Register
C Iust — Codex Iustinianus
Civ & Military LJ — Civil and Military Law Journal
Civ and Mil LJ — Civil and Military Law Journal
Civ Brux — Jugement du Tribunal Civil de Bruxelles
CivC — Civilita Cattolica
Civ C — Quaderni di Civilta Cinese
CivCatt — La Civilta Cattolica
Civ Cattol — Civilta Cattolica
Civ Cl Crist — Civilta Classica e Cristiana
Civ Def — Civilian Defense
Civ Def Bull — Civil Defence Bulletin
Civ Develop — Civic Development
Civ Eng — Civil Engineering
Civ Eng Constr Public Works J — Civil Engineering, Construction, and Public Works Journal
Civ Eng Contract — Civil Engineering Contractor
Civ Engin & Architects J — Civil Engineer and Architect's Journal
Civ Eng Jpn — Civil Engineering in Japan
Civ Eng (London) — Civil Engineering (London)
Civ Engng — Civil Engineering
Civ Engng ASCE — Civil Engineering. American Society of Civil Engineers
Civ Engn (GB) — Civil Engineering (Great Britain)
Civ Engng (Lond) — Civil Engineering (London)
Civ Engng Pract & Des Engrs — Civil Engineering for Practicing and Design Engineers
Civ Engng Publ Wks Rev — Civil Engineering and Public Works Review
Civ Engng Trans — Civil Engineering Transactions. Institution of Engineers of Australia
Civ Engng Trans Instn Engrs Aust — Civil Engineering Transactions. Institution of Engineers of Australia
Civ Eng (NY) — Civil Engineering (New York)
Civ Eng (Peking) — Civil Engineering (Peking)
Civ Eng Public Works Rev — Civil Engineering and Public Works Review
Civ Eng Pub Works Rev — Civil Engineering and Public Works Review
Civ Eng S Afr — Civil Engineering in South Africa
Civ Eng Trans — Civil Engineering Transactions. Institution of Engineers of Australia
Civ Eng Trans Inst Eng Aust — Civil Engineering Transactions. Institution of Engineers of Australia
Civic Aff — Civic Affairs. University of Southern California
Civic Alliance Bul — Civic Alliance Bulletin
Civic Dev — Civic Development
Civil Aero J — Civil Aeronautics Administration. Journal
Civil Ambrosiana — Civilta Ambrosiana
Civil Catt — Civilta Cattolica
Civil Defence Bul — Civil Defence Bulletin
Civil Eng — Civil Engineering
Civil Engineering ASCE — Civil Engineering. American Society of Civil Engineers
Civil Enging — Civil Engineering
Civil Enging Practicing Des Engrs — Civil Engineering for Practicing and Design Engineers
Civil Enging Surv — Civil Engineering Surveyor
Civilis Malgache — Civilisation Malgache
Civil Liberties R — Civil Liberties Review
Civil Liberties Rev — Civil Liberties Review
Civil Macchine — Civilta delle Macchine
Civil Mant — Civilta Mantovana
Civil Rights Dig — Civil Rights Digest
Civil Rights Research R — Civil Rights Research Review
Civil Romana — Civilta Romana
Civil Serv Assem US & Can N Lett — Civil Service Assembly of United States and Canada. News Letter
Civil Serv Assem US & Can Proc — Civil Service Assembly of United States and Canada. Proceedings
Civil Serv Obs — Civil Service Observer. Civil Service Assembly of the United States and Canada. Western Regional Conference
Civilta Catt — Civilta Cattolica
Civilta Cattol — Civilta Cattolica
Civilta Macch — Civilta delle Macchine
Civil Veron — Civilta Veronese

Civil War H — Civil War History
Civil War Hist — Civil War History
Civing — Civilingenieur. Zeitschrift fuer das Ingenieurwesen
CIVITEXT — Civic Information and Techniques Exchange
Civ Lib Rev — Civil Liberties Review
Civ Lib Rptr — Civil Liberties Reporter
Civ Mod — Civilta Moderna
Civ Rights Digest — Civil Rights Digest
Civ Rts — Civil Rights
Civ Rts Dig — Civil Rights Digest
Civ Serv J — Civil Service Journal
CIVTA4 — Congres International de la Vigne du Vin
Civ War Hist — Civil War History
Civ War T Illus — Civil War Times Illustrated
Civ War Times Illus — Civil War Times Illustrated
CIW — Civil War History
CIWDSS — Canada. Inland Waters Directorate. Scientific Series
CIWDSSS — Canada. Inland Waters Directorate. Social Science Series
CIWDTB — Canada. Inland Waters Directorate. Technical Bulletin
CIWPAV — Carnegie Institution of Washington. Publication
CIWQIR — Canada. Inland Waters Directorate. Water Quality Interpretive Reports
CIWYAO — Carnegie Institution of Washington. Year Book
CIZSAL — Conseil International pour l'Exploration de la Mer. Zooplankton Sheet
CIZ XIV — Fourteenth International Congress of Zoology. Copenhagen, 1956
CIZ XV — Fifteenth International Congress of Zoology. London, 1958
CJ — Cambridge Journal
CJ — Canadian Journal of Economics
CJ — Catholic Journalist
CJ — Chamber's Journal
CJ — Chelsea Journal
CJ — Choral Journal
CJ — Cinema Journal
CJ — Classical Journal
CJ — Computer Journal
CJ — Concordia Journal
CJ — Conservative Judaism
CJ — Contemporary Japan
C/J — Contemporary Jewry
CJ — Coyote's Journal
CJ — Critica Juridica
CJ — Curriculum Journal
CJA — Canadian Journal of Archaeology
CJA — Changing Japanese Attitudes Toward Modernization
CJA — Chinese Journal of Administration
CJA — Christlich-Juedisches Arbeitsgemeinschaft
CJa — Cizi Jazyky ve Skole
CJACS — Chemical Journals. American Chemical Society
CJAfS — Caribbean Journal of African Studies
CJAOAC — Chemical Journal. Association of Official Analytical Chemists
CJap — Contemporary Japan
CJAS — Canadian Journal of African Studies
CJB — Columbia Journal of World Business
CJBBDU — Canadian Journal of Biochemistry and Cell Biology
CJBIA — Canadian Journal of Biochemistry
CJBIAE — Canadian Journal of Biochemistry
CJBO — Canadian Journal of Botany
CJBOA — Canadian Journal of Botany
CJBOAW — Canadian Journal of Botany
CJBPAZ — Canadian Journal of Biochemistry and Physiology
CJBSAA — Canadian Journal of Behavioural Science
CJC — Cahiers Jean Cocteau
CJCE — Canadian Journal of Civil Engineering
CJCEA — Canadian Journal of Chemical Engineering
CJCh — Canadian Jewish Chronicle
CJCHA — Canadian Journal of Chemistry
CJCHAG — Canadian Journal of Chemistry
CJCMA — Canadian Journal of Comparative Medicine
CJCMAV — Canadian Journal of Comparative Medicine
CJD — Canadian Journalism Database
CJD — Canadian Journal of Economics
CJE — Canadian Journal of Economics
CJE — Canadian Journal of Economics and Political Science [Later, Canadian Journal of Economics]
CJECB — Canadian Journal of Economics
CJEPS — Canadian Journal of Economics and Political Science [Later, Canadian Journal of Economics]
CJES — Canadian Journal of Earth Sciences
CJESA — Canadian Journal of Earth Sciences
CJESAP — Canadian Journal of Earth Sciences
CJF — Chicago Jewish Forum
CJFA — Canadian Journal of Fisheries and Aquatic Sciences
CJFR — Canadian Journal of Forest Research
CJFRAR — Canadian Journal of Forest Research
CJFSDX — Canadian Journal of Fisheries and Aquatic Sciences
CJG — Cahiers Jean Giraudoux
CJH — Canadian Journal of History
CJHi — Canadian Journal of History
CJHPAV — Canadian Journal of Hospital Pharmacy
CJHSJ — Canadian Jewish Historical Society. Journal
CJHSS — Ceylon Journal of Historical and Social Studies
CJI — Corpus Inscriptionum Iudaicarum
CJIS — Canadian Journal of Irish Studies
C J It S — Canadian Journal of Italian Studies
CJL — Canadian Journal of Linguistics
CJL — Cesky Jazyk a Literatura

CJL — Columbia Journal of Law and Social Problems
CJLACS — Canadian Journal of Latin American and Caribbean Studies
CJLit — Cesky Jazyk a Literatura
CJMAA — Canadian Journal of Mathematics
CJ(Malta) — Classical Journal (Malta)
CJMBAE — Chinese Journal of Microbiology [*Later, Chinese Journal of Microbiology and Immunology*]
CJMED — Chung-Ang Journal of Medicine
CJMEDQ — Chung-Ang Journal of Medicine
CJMGA — California Journal of Mines and Geology
CJMIA — Canadian Journal of Microbiology
CJMIAZ — Canadian Journal of Microbiology
CJMSAV — Canadian Journal of Medical Science
CJMTA — Canadian Journal of Medical Technology
CJMTAY — Canadian Journal of Medical Technology
CJN — Canadian Jewish News
CJN — Canadian Journal of Anthropology
CJN — Collection Jadis et Naguere
CJN — Croissance de Jeunes Nations
CJNE — Canadian Journal of Native Education
CJNS — Canadian Journal of Native Studies
CJNSA2 — Canadian Journal of Neurological Sciences
CJOA — Canadian Journal on Aging
CJOL — Chinese Journal of Oceanology and Limnology
CJOLAK — Canadian Journal of Otolaryngology
CJOPA — Chinese Journal of Physics
CJORD — Columbia Journalism Review
CJOSD — Chungnam Journal of Sciences
CJP — Canadian Journal of Psychology
CJPEA — Canadian Journal of Public Health
CJPEA4 — Canadian Journal of Public Health
CJPH — Canadian Journal of Public Health
CJPHA — Canadian Journal of Physics
CJPHAD — Canadian Journal of Physics
CJPhil — Canadian Journal of Philosophy
CJPI — Criminal Justice Periodical Index
CJPPA — Canadian Journal of Physiology and Pharmacology
CJPPA3 — Canadian Journal of Physiology and Pharmacology
CJPS — Canadian Journal of Political Science
CJPs — Canadian Journal of Psychology
CJPSA — Canadian Journal of Psychology
CJPSAC — Canadian Journal of Psychology
CJPST — Canadian Journal of Political and Social Theory
CJPYA — Chinese Journal of Physiology
CJR — Chicago Journalism Review
CJR — Christian Jewish Relations
CJR — Columbia Journalism Review
CJR — Contemporary Jewish Record
CJRC/B — Czech Jewish Representative Committee/Bulletin
CJRMD7 — Canadian Journal of Radiography, Radiotherapy, Nuclear Medicine
CJRS — Canadian Journal of Research in Semiotics
CJRSC — Chemical Journals. Royal Society of Chemistry
CJS — Cizi Jazyky ve Skole
CJSCDG — Canadian Journal of Applied Sport Sciences
CJSPAI — Canadian Journal of Spectroscopy
CJSR — Classical Journal and Scholars Review
CJSSA — Canadian Journal of Soil Science
CJSSAR — Canadian Journal of Soil Science
CJSUA — Canadian Journal of Surgery
CJSUAX — Canadian Journal of Surgery
CJT — Canadian Journal of Theology
CJU — Conjuntura Economica
CJUADK — Contact. Journal of Urban and Environmental Affairs
C Jud — Code Judiciaire
C Jur Ind — Code des Juridictions Indigenes
CJVCH — Chemical Journals. VCH Verlagsgesellschaft
CJVS — Cizi Jazyky ve Skole
CJW — Columbia Journal of World Business
CJWB — Columbia Journal of World Business
CJWILEY — Chemical Journal of John Wiley and Sons
CJZ — Canadian Journal of Zoology
CJZOA — Canadian Journal of Zoology
CJZOAG — Canadian Journal of Zoology
CK — Chicago-Kent Law Review
C Kans State Univ Coop Ext Serv — C. Kansas State University. Cooperative Extension Service
CKCFA — Ceskoslovensky Casopis pro Fysiku
CKCKD — Chung-Kuo Kung Ch'eng Hsueh K'an
CKD — Casopis Katolickeko Duckovenstva a Prilohou
CKD — Chambre de Commerce et d'Industrie. Republique Populaire du Benin. Bulletin Hebdomadaire d'Information et de Documentation
CKHMA — Chung-Kuo Hsu Mu Shou I
CKI — Central Bank of Ireland. Quarterly Bulletin
CKKKA — Cho-Koon Kenkyu
CKLR — Chicago-Kent Law Review
CKN — Chambre de Commerce, d'Agriculture, et d'Industrie du Niger. Bulletin
CKNHA — Chung-Kuo Nung Yeh Hua Hsueh Hui Chih
CKNKD — Chikyukagaku (Nippon Chikyu Kagakkai)
CKNKDM — Geochemistry
CKNSA — Chiba-Ken Nogyo Shikenjo Kenkyu Hokoku
CKNYA — Chung-Kuo Nung Yeh K'o Hsueh
CKP — Central Bank of Cyprus. Bulletin
CKSCDN — Journal. Chinese Society of Veterinary Science
CKTND — Chayon Kwahak Taehak Nomunjip
CKTNDR — Proceedings. College of Natural Sciences

CKWCD9 — Chinese Journal of Microbiology and Immunology
CKYW — Chung-Kuo Yu-Wen
CL — Cahiers Lorrains
CL — Cambridge Left
CL — Ceska Literatura
CL — Chinese Literature
CL — Christian Life
Cl — Clavier
Cl — Clavileno
C/L — Coloquio. Revista de Artes e Letras
CL — Comparative Literature
CL — Correspondance Litteraire
CL — Country Life
CL — Cuadernos de Literatura
CL — Current Law Year Book
CLA — Chartae Latinae Antiquiores
CLA — Children's Literature Abstracts
Cla — Clavier
CLA — Collections Litteratures Africaines
CLA — College Language Association. Journal
CLA — University of California at Los Angeles. Law Review
CLAA Bulletin — Commercial Law Association of Australia. Bulletin
CLAB — Commercial Law Association. Bulletin
CLA Bull — Colorado Library Association. Bulletin
CLA Bulletin — Commercial Law Association. Bulletin
CLACSO/ERL — Estudios Rurales Latinoamericanos. Consejo Latinoamericano de Ciencias Sociales. Secretaria Ejecutiva y la Comision de Estudios Rurales
Cl Act Rep — Class Action Reports
CLADA — Crystal Lattice Defects [*Later, Crystal Lattice Defects and Amorphous Materials*]
CLADEC — Cladistics
Cladistics Int J Willi Hennig Soc — Cladistics. International Journal. Willi Hennig Society
Clae — Classica et Mediaevalia
ClaF — Classical Folia
CLAGB — Clinical Allergy
CLAGBI — Clinical Allergy
CLAJ — CLA [*College Language Association*] Journal
CLA J — CLA Journal. Official Quarterly Publication. College Language Association
ClaJ — Classical Journal
CLAND — Computer Languages
CL & CL Comput Linguist Comput Lang — CL & CL. Computational Linguistics and Computer Languages
Clan Gunn Soc Mag — Clan Gunn Society. Magazine
Clan MacLeod Mag — Clan MacLeod Magazine
Clan Munro Mag — Clan Munro Magazine
CLANN — Australian College Libraries Activities Network
Cl Antiq — Classical Antiquity
CLAO (Contact Lens Assoc Ophthalmol) J — CLAO (Contact Lens Association of Ophthalmologists) Journal
CLAO J — CLAO [*Contact Lens Association of Ophthalmologists*] Journal
CLAQ — Children's Literature Association. Quarterly
Clar — Clarinet
Clarendon Lib Logic Philos — Clarendon Library of Logic and Philosophy
Clare Q — Claremont Quarterly
Clarice Cliff Colrs Club Rev — Clarice Cliff Collector's Club Review
Claridad — Claridad Weekly
Clark Col Law — Clark. Colonial Law
Clarke Inst Psychiatry Monogr Ser — Clarke Institute of Psychiatry. Monograph Series
Clark (PA) — Clark's Pennsylvania Law Journal Reports
Clarks Dig Annot — Clark's Digest-Annotator
Clart Synd — Clartes Syndicales. Revue de Pensee et d'Action Syndicale
CLAS — Canadian Labour Arbitration Summaries
CLAS — College Language Association Journal
CLAS — Criminal Law Audio Series
Clas Cienc — Classicos de la Ciencias
Clas Pensam — Clasicos del Pensamiento
Class America — Classical America
Class B — Classical Bulletin
ClassBull — Classical Bulletin
Classic — Classic Images
Classical J — Classical Journal
Classical Mus Mag — Classical Music Magazine
Classical Philol — Classical Philology
Classical Q — Classical Quarterly
Classical Quantum Gravity — Classical and Quantum Gravity
Classic F Col — Classic Film Collector
Classic Jnl — Classical Journal
Classics Appl Math — Classics in Applied Mathematics
Classics Math — Classics in Mathematics
Classics Soviet Math — Classics of Soviet Mathematics
Classic World — Classical World
Classif — Journal of Classification
Classified Abstr Arch Alcohol Lit — Classified Abstract Archive of the Alcohol Literature
Class J — Classical Journal
Class J — Classical Journal and Scholars Review
Class J (C) — Classical Journal (Chicago)
Class J (L) — Classical Journal (London)
Class Journ — Classical Journal
Class Journ — Classical Journal and Scholars Review
Class J SR — Classical Journal and Scholars Review
ClassMed — Classica et Mediaevalia
Class Mod L — Classical and Modern Literature

Class Out — Classical Outlook
ClassPh — Classical Philology
Class Phil — Classical Philology
Class Philol — Classical Philology
Class Prepartoires Ecoles Sci — Classes Preparatoires aux Grandes Ecoles Scientifiques
Class Q — Classical Quarterly
Class Quart — Classical Quarterly
Class Quartl — Classical Quarterly
Class R — Classical Review
Class Rev — Classical Review
Class Rev N Ser — Classical Review. New Series
Class R NS — Classical Review. New Series
Classr Res Mater Ser — Classroom Resource Materials Series
Class Sci — Classici della Scienza
Class Soc Bull — Classification Society. Bulletin
Class Verts — Classiques Verts
ClassW — Classical Weekly
Class W — Classical World
Class World — Classical World
CLATDP — Compendium de Investigaciones Clinicas Latinoamericanas
ClaudelN — Claudel Newsletter
ClaudelS — Claudel Studies
Claudel St — Claudel Studies
Clausthaler Geol Abh — Clausthaler Geologische Abhandlungen
Clausthaler Hefte Lagerstaettenk Geochemie Miner Rohst — Clausthaler Hefte zur Lagerstaettenkund und Geochemie der Mineralischen Rohstoffe
Clav — Clavileno
CLAVA — Clavier
CLAWA — Clarinet
C Lawyer — Catholic Lawyer
Clay Clay M — Clays and Clay Minerals
Clay Constr Prod Curr Ind Rep — Clay Construction Products (Current Industrial Reports)
Claycraft Struct Ceram — Claycraft and Structural Ceramics
Clay Ind — Clay-Industry
Clay Miner — Clay Minerals
Clay Miner Bull — Clay Minerals. Bulletin [*Later, Clay Minerals*]
Clay Prod J — Clay Products Journal of Australia
Clay Prod J Aust — Clay Products Journal of Australia
Clay Prod J Austr — Clay Products Journal of Australia
Clay Prod News Ceram Rec — Clay Products News and Ceramic Record
Clay Rec — Clay Record
Clay Res — Clay Research
Clay Resour Bull La Geol Surv — Clay Resources Bulletin. Louisiana Geological Survey
Clay Sci (Tokyo) — Clay Science (Tokyo)
Clays Clay Miner — Clays and Clay Minerals
Clays Clay Miner Proc Conf — Clays and Clay Minerals. Proceedings. Conference
Clay Work — Clay-Worker
CLB — Cellular Business
Cl B — Classical Bulletin
CLB — Commercial Law Bulletin
CLB — Commonwealth Law Bulletin
CLB — Communications Law Bulletin
CLBCBB — Cardiologisches Bulletin
CLB Chem Labor Betr — CLB. Chemie fuer Labor und Betrieb
CLB Chem Labor Betr Beil — CLB. Chemie fuer Labor und Betrieb. Beilage. Lernen und Leisten
CLBIA — Clinical Biochemistry
CLBIAS — Clinical Biochemistry
CLBU — China Law and Business Update
CLBUA — Clinical Bulletin
CLBUAU — Clinical Bulletin
Cl Bull — Classical Bulletin
Cl Bull C — Classical Bulletin (Chicago)
CLC — Clarte (superseded by Luttes des Classes)
CLC — Columbia Library. Columns
CLC — Company Law Cases
CLC — Cuadernos de Literatura Contemporanea
CLCAA9 — Cellulosa e Carta
CLCADC — Clinical Cardiology
CLCEA — Casopis Lekaru Ceskych
CLCEAL — Casopis Lekaru Ceskych
CLCHA — Clinical Chemistry
CLCHAU — Clinical Chemistry
CLCHD — Climatic Change
CLCHDX — Climatic Change
CLCL — Computational Linguistics and Computer Languages
CLCNB — Clinician
CLCYAD — Clinical Cytology: Series of Monographs
CLD — Cahiers Leoppold Delisle. Societe Parisienne d'Histoire et d'Archeologi e Norman des
CLD — California Library Directory
CLD — Central Bank of Malta. Quarterly Review
CLD — Coleccion de Libros y Documentos Referentes a la Historia de America [*Madrid*]
CLDFAT — Cell Differentiation
CLDID7 — Clinica Dietologica
CLDR — Coleccion de Libros y Documentos Referentes a la Historia del Peru. H.H.Urteaga and C.A.Romero [*Lima*]
CLe — Cahiers de Lexicologie
CLE — Cahiers. Ligue Catholique de l'Evangile
CLE — Carmina Latina Epigraphica
Cle — Connaissance des Lettres

Clean Air Conf Proc — Clean Air Conference. Proceedings
Clean Air J — Clean Air Journal
Clean Air Spec Ed — Clean Air. Special Edition
Clean Dyeing World — Cleaning and Dyeing World
Clean Dyers Advert — Cleaners and Dyers Advertiser
Clean Fuels Biomass Wastes Symp Pap — Clean Fuels from Biomass and Wastes. Symposium Papers
Cleaning Maint Big Bldg Mgmt — Cleaning Maintenance and Big Building Management
Clean Laundry World (Chicago) — Cleaning and Laundry World (Chicago)
Clean Technol — Clean Technology
CLEAR — Chinese Literature. Essays, Articles, Reviews
Clear H — Clearing House
Clearing H — Clearing House
Clearing House J — Clearing House Journal
Clearinghouse R — Clearinghouse Review
Clearinghouse Rev — Clearinghouse Review
Clearing Hse L A Soc Serv Res — Clearing House for Local Authority Social Services Research
Clear R — Clearinghouse Review
CLEB — Comunidad Latinoamericana de Escritores. Boletin
CLECA — Clinical Endocrinology
CLECAP — Clinical Endocrinology
Clef Pal CR — Cleft Palate Craniofacial Journal
Clef Pal J — Cleft Palate Journal
Cleft Palate Craniofac J — Cleft Palate-Craniofacial Journal
Cleft Palate J — Cleft Palate Journal
CleM — [*The*] Clergy Monthly
CLEM — Contact List of Electronic Music
Clemson Agric Coll Agron Dept Mimeogr Ser — Clemson Agricultural College. Agronomy Department. Mimeographed Series
Clemson Agric Exp Sta Annual Rep — Clemson Agricultural College of South Carolina. Agricultural Experiment Station. Annual Report
Clemson Agric Exp Sta Misc Ser — Clemson Agricultural College of South Carolina. Agricultural Experiment Station. Miscellaneous Series
Clemson Univ Coll Eng Eng Exp Sta Bull — Clemson University. College of Engineering. Engineeri ng Experiment Station. Bulletin
Clemson Univ Coll For Recreat Resour Dep For For Res Ser — Clemson University. College of Forest and Recreation Resources. Department of Forestry. Forest Research Series
Clemson Univ Dep For For Bull — Clemson University. Department of Forestry. Forestry Bulletin
Clemson Univ Dep For For Res Ser — Clemson University. Department of Forestry. Forest Research Series
Clemson Univ Dep For Tech Pap — Clemson University. Department of Forestry. Technical Paper
Clemson Univ Rev Ind Manage Text Sci — Clemson University. Review of Industrial Management and Textile Science
Clemson Univ Water Resour Res Inst Rep — Clemson University. Water Resources Research Institute. Report
Clemson Univ Water Resour Res Inst Tech Rep — Clemson University Water Resources Research Institute. Technical Report
CLENDR — Clinical Engineering
CL Ep — Carmina Latina Epigraphica
CleR — Clergy Review
ClergyM — [*The*] Clergy Monthly
ClergyR — [*The*] Clergy Review
Clergy Rev — Clergy Review
Clermont Mm Ac Sc — Memoires de l'Academie des Sciences, Belles Lettres, et Arts de Clermont-Ferrand
Clermont Univ Ann Sci Geol Mineral — Clermont. Universite. Annales Scientifiques. Geologie et Mineralogie
C Let Dram — Cineschedario-Letture Drammatiche
Cl et Med — Classica et Medievalia
Clev B A J — Cleveland Bar Association. Journal
Clev Bar Ass'n J — Cleveland Bar Association. Journal
Clev B Assn J — Cleveland Bar Association. Journal
Clev BJ — Journal. Cleveland Bar Association
Cleve Busn — Crain's Cleveland Business
Cleve Clin J Med — Cleveland Clinic. Journal of Medicine
Cleve Clin Q — Cleveland Clinic. Quarterly
Cleveland City Rec — Cleveland City Record
Cleveland Clin Cardiovasc Consult — Cleveland Clinic. Cardiovascular Consultations
Cleveland Clin Q — Cleveland Clinic. Quarterly
Cleveland Clin Quart — Cleveland Clinic. Quarterly
Cleveland Inst Eng Proc — Cleveland Institution of Engineers. Proceedings
Cleveland Med J — Cleveland Medical Journal
Cleveland Mus Bull — Cleveland Museum of Art. Bulletin
Cleveland Mus Nat History Mus News — Cleveland Museum of Natural History. Museum News
Cleveland Mus Nat History Sci Pubs — Cleveland Museum of Natural History. Science Publications
Cleveland SLJ — Cleveland State Law Journal
Cleveland Symp Macromol — Cleveland Symposium on Macromolecules
Cleve LR (Ohio) — Cleveland Law Reporter (Ohio)
Clev-Mar L Rev — Cleveland-Marshall Law Review
Clev Orch — Cleveland Orchestra. Program Notes
Clev St L R — Cleveland State Law Review
Clev St L Rev — Cleveland State Law Review
CLex — Cahiers de Lexicologie
CLEYDQ — Butterworths International Medical Reviews. Clinical Endocrinology
CLF — Chronique des Lettres Francaises
CLF — Club du Livre Francais
CLGAAT — Colorado. Agricultural Experiment Station. Annual Report

CLGEB8 — Clinica Geral
CLGEDA — Clinical Gerontologist
Clgh Bull Res Hum Organ — Clearinghouse Bulletin of Research in Human Organization
CLGNA — Clinical Genetics
CLGNAY — Clinical Genetics
CLGR — Clinical Gerontologist
CLGUA — Colliery Guardian
CLH — Canadian Library Handbook
CLHMB3 — Clinics in Haematology
CLHMD — Cahiers. Laboratoire d'Hydrobiologie de Montereau
CLi — Christian Librarian
CLI — Commercial Liability Insurance
CLI — Computer Literature Index
CLi — Cuadernos de Literatura
CLid — Cesky Lid
C Life — Christian Life
C Ligures Prehist Archeol — Cahiers Ligures de Prehistoire et d'Archeologie
CLIIA — Clinical Immunology and Immunopathology
CLIIAT — Clinical Immunology and Immunopathology
Clima Comm Internat — Clima Commerce International
Clim Arc Alaska Sci Conf — Climate of the Arctic. Alaska Science Conference
Climat Data — Climatological Data
Climax Int Conf Chem Uses Molybdenum — Climax International Conference on the Chemistry and Uses of Molybdenum
CLIMB8 — Cellular Immunology
Clim Change — Climatic Change
Clim Control — Climate Control
CLin — Cercetari de Linguistica
Clin Allergy — Clinical Allergy
Clin Allergy Immunol — Clinical Allergy and Immunology
Clin All-Round — Clinic All-Round
Clin Anaesthesiol — Clinics in Anaesthesiology
Clin Anat — Clinical Anatomy
Clin & Exp Metastasis — Clinical and Experimental Metastasis
Clin Androl — Clinics in Andrology
Clin Anesth — Clinical Anesthesia
Clin Appl Thromb Hemost — Clinical and Applied Thrombosis/Hemostasis
Clin Approaches Probl Child — Clinical Approaches to Problems of Childhood
Clin Aspects Metab Bone Dis Proc Int Symp Clin Aspects Metab — Clinical Aspects of Metabolic Bone Disease. Proceedings. International Symposium on Clinical Aspects of Metabolic Bone Disease
Clin Auton Res — Clinical Autonomic Research
Clin Bacteriol (Tokyo) — Clinical Bacteriology (Tokyo)
Clin Behav Ther — Clinical Behavior Therapy
Clin Behav Therapy Rev — Clinical Behavior Therapy Review
Clin Bioch — Clinical Biochemistry
Clin Biochem — Clinical Biochemistry
Clin Biochem (Amsterdam) — Clinical Biochemistry (Amsterdam)
Clin Biochem Anal — Clinical and Biochemical Analysis
Clin Biochem Aspects Intern Dis — Clinical-Biochemical-Aspects of Internal Diseases
Clin Biochem Cancer — Clinical Biochemistry of Cancer
Clin Biochem Domest Anim — Clinical Biochemistry of Domestic Animals [*monograph*]
Clin Biochem Elderly — Clinical Biochemistry of the Elderly
Clin Biochem Hepatobiliary Dis Proc Int Satell Symp — Clinical Biochemistry in Hepatobiliary Diseases. Proceedings. International Satellite Symposium
Clin Biochem Nutr Aspects Trace Elem — Clinical, Biochemical, and Nutritional Aspects of Trace Elements
Clin Biochem Ottawa — Clinical Biochemistry (Ottawa)
Clin Biochem Rev (NY) — Clinical Biochemistry Reviews (New York)
Clin Biofeedback Health — Clinical Biofeedback and Health
Clin Biomech — Clinical Biomechanics
Clin Biomech Briston Avon — Clinical Biomechanics (Briston, Avon)
Clin Bull — Clinical Bulletin
Clin Bull (Mem Sloan-Kettering Cancer Cent) — Clinical Bulletin (Memorial Sloan-Kettering Cancer Center)
Clin Calcium — Clinical Calcium
Clin Cancer Chemother — Clinical Cancer Chemotherapy [*monograph*]
Clin Cardiol — Clinical Cardiology
Clin Cardiovasc Physiol — Clinical Cardiovascular Physiology [*monograph*]
Clin Cell Immunol Mol Ther Rev — Clinical Cellular Immunology. Molecular and Therapeutic Reviews
Clin Chem — Clinical Chemistry
Clin Chem Annu Lect Ser — Clinical Chemistry. Based on the Annual Lecture Series
Clin Chem Chem Toxicol Met Proc Int Symp — Clinical Chemistry and Chemical Toxicology of Metals. Proceedings. International Symposium
Clin Chem Lab Med — Clinical Chemistry and Laboratory Medicine
Clin Chem Monoamines — Clinical Chemistry of Monoamines
Clin Chem Newsl — Clinical Chemistry Newsletter
Clin Chem NY — Clinical Chemist (New York)
Clin Chem Princ Tech — Clinical Chemistry. Principles and Technics [*monograph*]
Clin Chem (Winston Salem North Carolina) — Clinical Chemistry (Winston-Salem, North Carolina)
Clin Chest Med — Clinics in Chest Medicine
Clin Child Fam Psychol Rev — Clinical Child and Family Psychology Review
Clin Chim A — Clinica Chimica Acta
Clin Chim Acta — Clinica Chimica Acta
Clin Conf Cancer — Clinical Conference on Cancer
Clin Cornerstone — Clinical Cornerstone
Clin Crit Care Med — Clinics in Critical Care Medicine
Clin Cytol Ser Monogr — Clinical Cytology: Series of Monographs
Clin Decis Obstet Gynecol — Clinical Decisions in Obstetrics and Gynecology

Clin Dermatol — Clinics in Dermatology
Clin Dev Med — Clinics in Developmental Medicine
Clin Diagn Lab Immunol — Clinical and Diagnostic Laboratory Immunology
Clin Diagn Ultrasound — Clinics in Diagnostic Ultrasound
Clin Diagn Virol — Clinical and Diagnostic Virology
Clin Dial Transplant Forum Proc — Clinical Dialysis and Transplant Forum. Proceedings
Clin Dietol — Clinica Dietologica
Clin Disord Fluid Electrolyte Metab — Clinical Disorders of Fluid and Electrolyte Metabolism
Clin Disord Pediatr Nutr — Clinical Disorders in Pediatric Nutrition
Clin Drug Invest — Clinical Drug Investigation
Clin Drug Ther — Clinics and Drug Therapy
Clin Drug Trials Tribulations — Clinical Drug Trials and Tribulations
Clin Dysmorphol — Clinical Dysmorphology
Clin Echocardiogr — Clinical Echocardiography
Clin Ecol — Clinical Ecology
Clin EEG — Clinical Electroencephalography
Clin Electr — Clinical Electroencephalography
Clin Electroencephalogr — Clinical Electroencephalography
Clin End Me — Clinics in Endocrinology and Metabolism
Clin Endocr — Clinical Endocrinology
Clin Endocrinol — Clinical Endocrinology
Clin Endocrinol London — Clinical Endocrinology (London)
Clin Endocrinol Metab — Clinical Endocrinology and Metabolism
Clin Endocrinol NY — Clinical Endocrinology (New York)
Clin Endocrinol (Oxford) — Clinical Endocrinology (Oxford)
Clin Eng — Clinical Engineering
Clin Engineer — Clinical Engineer
Clin Eng Inf Serv — Clinical Engineering Information Service
Clin Eng News — Clinical Engineering News
Clin Enzymol — Clinical Enzymology
Clin Enzymol Symp — Clinical Enzymology Symposia
Clin Eur — Clinica Europa
Clin Evid — Clinical Evidence
Clin Exp Al — Clinical and Experimental Allergy
Clin Exp Allergy — Clinical and Experimental Allergy
Clin Exp Dermatol — Clinical and Experimental Dermatology
Clin Exp Dial Apheresis — Clinical and Experimental Dialysis and Apheresis
Clin Experiment Ophthalmol — Clinical & Experimental Ophthalmology
Clin Exper Immunol — Clinical and Experimental Immunology
Clin Exp Gnotobiotics Proc Int Symp — Clinical and Experimental Gnotobiotics. Proceedings. International Symposium onGnotobiology
Clin Exp Hypertens — Clinical and Experimental Hypertension
Clin Exp Hypertens A — Clinical and Experimental Hypertension. Part A. Theory and Practice
Clin Exp Hypertens B — Clinical and Experimental Hypertension. Part B. Hypertension in Pregnancy
Clin Exp Hypertens Part A — Clinical and Experimental Hypertension. Part A. Theory and Practice
Clin Exp Hypertens Part A Theory Pract — Clinical and Experimental Hypertension. Part A. Theory and Practice
Clin Exp Hypertens Part B — Clinical and Experimental Hypertension. Part B. Hypertension in Pregnancy
Clin Exp Im — Clinical and Experimental Immunology
Clin Exp Immunol — Clinical and Experimental Immunology
Clin Exp Immunoreprod — Clinical and Experimental Immunoreproduction
Clin Exp Med — Clinical and Experimental Medicine
Clin Exp Metastasis — Clinical and Experimental Metastasis
Clin Exp Nephrol — Clinical and Experimental Nephrology
Clin Exp Neurol — Clinical and Experimental Neurology
Clin Exp Nutr — Clinical and Experimental Nutrition
Clin Exp Obstet Gynecol — Clinical and Experimental Obstetrics and Gynecology
Clin Exp Ph — Clinical and Experimental Pharmacology and Physiology
Clin Exp Pharmacol Physiol Suppl — Clinical and Experimental Pharmacology and Physiology. Supplement
Clin Exp Pharmcol Physiol — Clinical and Experimental Pharmacology and Physiology
Clin Exp Psychiatry — Clinical and Experimental Psychiatry
Clin Exp Rheumatol — Clinical and Experimental Rheumatology
Clin Exp Stud Gastroenterol Hematol Pap — Clinical and Experimental Studies in Gastroenterology and Hematology. Papers
Clin Exp Stud Immunother Proc Int Symp — Clinical and Experimental Studies in Immunotherapy. Proceedings. International Symposium
C Ling — Cercetari de Linguistica
Clin Gastro — Clinics in Gastroenterology
Clin Gastroenterol — Clinical Gastroenterology
Clin Gastroenterol — Clinics in Gastroenterology
Clin Gastroenterol Suppl — Clinics in Gastroenterology. Supplement
Clin Genet — Clinical Genetics
Clin Genet Semin — Clinical Genetics Seminar
Clin Geral (Sao Paulo) — Clinica Geral (Sao Paulo)
Clin Geriatr Med — Clinics in Geriatric Medicine
Clin Gerontol — Clinical Gerontologist
Clin Ginecol — Clinica Ginecologica
Cling Peach Quart — Cling Peach Quarterly. California Canning Peach Association
Clin Gynecol Obstet (Tokyo) — Clinical Gynecology and Obstetrics (Tokyo)
Clin Haemat — Clinics in Haematology
Clin Haematol — Clinics in Haematology
Clin Hemorh — Clinical Hemorheology
Clin Hemorheol — Clinical Hemorheology
Clin Hemorheol Microcirc — Clinical Hemorheology and Microcirculation
Clin Hig Hidrol — Clinica Higiene e Hidrologia
Clin Hop Enfants — Clinique des Hopitaux des Enfants et Revue Retrospective Medico-Chirugicale et Hygienique

Clinica Chim Acta — Clinica Chimica Acta
Clinical J Sport Med — Clinical Journal of Sport Medicine
Clinical Kines — Clinical Kinesiology
Clinica Pediat — Clinica Pediatrica
Clinica Terap — Clinica Terapeutica
Clin Imaging — Clinical Imaging
Clin Immun — Clinical Immunology and Immunopathology
Clin Immunobiol — Clinical Immunobiology
Clin Immunol Allergy — Clinics in Immunology and Allergy
Clin Immunol Immunopathol — Clinical Immunology and Immunopathology
Clin Immunol Newsl — Clinical Immunology Newsletter
Clin Immunol Proc IUIS Conf — Clinical Immunology. Proceedings. IUIS [*International Union of ImmunologicalSocieties*] Conference on Clinical Immunology
Clin Immunol Rev — Clinical Immunology Reviews
Clin Immunotoxicol — Clinical Immunotoxicology
Clin Important Adverse Drug Interact — Clinically Important Adverse Drug Interactions
Clin Infect Dis — Clinical Infectious Diseases
Clin Invest — Clinical and Investigative Medicine
Clin Invest — Clinical Investigator
Clin Invest Med — Clinical and Investigative Medicine
Clin J — Clinical Journal
Clin J Pain — Clinical Journal of Pain
Clin Jpn — Clinics of Japan
Clin J Sport Med — Clinical Journal of Sport Medicine
Clin Lab — Clinical Laboratory
Clin Lab — Clinica y Laboratoria
Clin Lab Annu — Clinical Laboratory Annual
Clin Lab Assays Pap Annu Clin Lab Assays Conf — Clinical Laboratory Assays. New Technology and Future Directions. Papers presented at the Annual Clinical Laboratory Assays Conference
Clin Lab Haematol — Clinical and Laboratory Haematology
Clin Lab Med — Clinics in Laboratory Medicine
Clin Lab Rome — Clinica e Laboratorio (Rome)
Clin Lab Zaragoza Spain — Clinica y Laboratorio (Zaragoza, Spain)
Clin Latina — Clinica Latina
Clin Law Jnl Newsl — Clinical Law Journal and Newsletter
Clin Libr Q — Clinical Librarian Quarterly
Clin Liver Dis — Clinics in Liver Disease
Clin Manage Phys Ther — Clinical Management in Physical Therapy
Clin Mater — Clinical Materials
Clin Med — Clinical Medicine
Clin Med Ital — Clinica Medica Italiana
Clin Med Surg — Clinical Medicine and Surgery
Clin Microbiol Infect — Clinical Microbiology and Infection
Clin Microbiol Rev — Clinical Microbiology Reviews
Clin Microbiol Tokyo — Clinical Microbiology (Tokyo)
Clin Mol Pathol — Clinical Molecular Pathology
Clin Mon Hemat — Clinical Monographs in Hematology
Clin Nephrol — Clinical Nephrology
Clin Neurol — Clinical Neurology and Neurosurgery
Clin Neurol Neurosurg — Clinical Neurology and Neurosurgery
Clin Neurol (Tokyo) — Clinical Neurology (Tokyo)
Clin Neuropathol — Clinical Neuropathology
Clin Neuropharmacol — Clinical Neuropharmacology
Clin Neuropsychol — Clinical Neuropsychologist [*Netherlands*]
Clin Neuropsychol — Clinical Neuropsychology
Clin Neurosci — Clinical Neuroscience
Clin Neurosurg — Clinical Neurosurgery
Clin Notes Respir Dis — Clinical Notes on Respiratory Diseases
Clin Nucl Med — Clinical Nuclear Medicine
Clin Nuova — Clinica Nuova
Clin Nutr — Clinical Nutrition
Clin Nutr Health Dis — Clinical Nutrition in Health and Disease
Clin Nutr (Phila) — Clinical Nutrition (Philadelphia)
Clin Obstet Gynaecol Suppl — Clinics in Obstetrics and Gynaecology. Supplement
Clin Obstet Gynecol — Clinical Obstetrics and Gynecology
Clin Obst Gynec — Clinical Obstetrics and Gynecology
Clin Oculist — Clinica Oculistica
Clin Odontoiatr — Clinica Odontoiatrica
Clin Odonto Protes — Clinica Odonto-Protesica
Clin Oncol — Clinical Oncology
Clin Oncol R Coll Radiol — Clinical Oncology. Royal College of Radiologists
Clin Oncol (Tianjin) — Clinical Oncology (Tianjin)
Clin Ophtalmol — Clinique Ophtalmologique
Clin Orthod R — Clinical Orthodontics and Research
Clin Orthop — Clinical Orthopaedics
Clin Orthop — Clinical Orthopaedics and Related Research
Clin Orthopaedics — Clinical Orthopaedics
Clin Orthop Relat Res — Clinical Orthopaedics and Related Research
Clin Orthop Surg — Clinical Orthopedic Surgery
Clin Ortop — Clinica Ortopedica
Clin Ostet Ginecol — Clinica Ostetrica e Ginecologica
Clin Otolaryngol — Clinical Otolaryngology
Clin Otolaryngol Allied Sci (Oxf) — Clinical Otolaryngology and Allied Sciences (Oxford)
Clin Otolaryngol (Oxf) — Clinical Otolaryngology (Oxford)
Clin Otorinolaringoiatr — Clinica Otorinolaringoiatrica
Clin Otorinolaringoiatr (Catania) — Clinica Otorinolaringoiatrica (Catania)
Clin Pediat — Clinical Pediatrics
Clin Pediat — Clinica Pediatrica
Clin Pediatr — Clinical Pediatrics
Clin Pediatr Bologna — Clinica Pediatrica (Bologna)
Clin Pediatr NY — Clinical Pediatrics (New York)

Clin Pediatr (Phila) — Clinical Pediatrics (Philadelphia)
Clin Pediatr (Philadelphia) — Clinical Pediatrics (Philadelphia)
Clin Perinatol — Clinics in Perinatology
Clin Pharm — Clinical Pharmacology and Therapeutics
Clin Pharm — Clinical Pharmacy
Clin Pharmacokinet — Clinical Pharmacokinetics
Clin Pharmacol — Clinical Pharmacology
Clin Pharmacol Biotechnol Prod Proc Esteve Found Symp — Clinical Pharmacology of Biotechnology Products. Proceedings. Esteve FoundationSymposium
Clin Pharmacol Drug Epidemiol — Clinical Pharmacology and Drug Epidemiology
Clin Pharmacol (NY) — Clinical Pharmacology (New York)
Clin Pharmacol Res — Clinical Pharmacology Research
Clin Pharmacol Ther — Clinical Pharmacology and Therapeutics
Clin Pharmacol Therap — Clinical Pharmacology and Therapeutics
Clin Pharmacol Ther London — Clinical Pharmacology and Therapeutics (London)
Clin Pharmacol Ther Proc Interam Congr — Clinical Pharmacology and Therapeutics. Proceedings. Interamerican Congress of Clinical Pharmacology and Therapeutics
Clin Pharmacol Ther Ser — Clinical Pharmacology and Therapeutics Series
Clin Pharmacol Ther St Louis — Clinical Pharmacology and Therapeutics (St. Louis)
Clin Pharmacol Ther Toxicol — Clinical Pharmacology, Therapy, and Toxicology
Clin Pharm Educ Patient Educ Proc Eur Symp Clin Pharm — Clinical Pharmacy Education and Patient Education. Proceedings. European Symposium on Clinical Pharmacy
Clin Pharm Symp — Clinical Pharmacy Symposium
Clin Phys and Physiol Meas — Clinical Physics and Physiological Measurement
Clin Physiol — Clinical Physiology
Clin Physiol Biochem — Clinical Physiology and Biochemistry
Clin Physiol (Oxf) — Clinical Physiology (Oxford)
Clin Physiol (Tokyo) — Clinical Physiology (Tokyo)
Clin Plast Surg — Clinics in Plastic Surgery
Clin Pod — Clinics in Podiatry
Clin Podiatr Med Surg — Clinics in Podiatric Medicine and Surgery
Clin Podiatry — Clinics in Podiatry
Clin Pract Guidel Quick Ref Guide Clin — Clinical Practice Guideline. Quick Reference Guide for Clinicians
Clin Prev Dent — Clinical Preventive Dentistry
Clin Prevent Dent — Clinical Preventive Dentistry
Clin Proc (Cape Town) — Clinical Proceedings (Cape Town)
Clin Proc Child Hosp DC — Clinical Proceedings. Children's Hospital of the District of Columbia [*Later, Clinical Proceedings. Children's Hospital National Medical Center*]
Clin Proc Child Hosp Natl Med Cent — Clinical Proceedings. Children's Hospital National Medical Center
Clin Prod Rev — Clinical Products Review
CLINPROT — Clinical Protocols
Clin Psychiatr — Clinical Psychiatry
Clin Psychiatry (Tokyo) — Clinical Psychiatry (Tokyo)
Clin Psychol Rev — Clinical Psychology Review
Clin Radiol — Clinical Radiology
Clin Rehabil — Clinical Rehabilitation
Clin Rep — Clinical Report
Clin Reprod Fertil — Clinical Reproduction and Fertility
Clin Reprod Neuroendocrinol Int Semin — Clinical Reproductive Neuroendocrinology. International Seminar on ReproductivePhysiology and Sexual Endocrinology
Clin Res — Clinical Research
Clin Res Cent Symp — Clinical Research Centre Symposium
Clin Res Cent Symp (Harrow Engl) — Clinical Research Centre. Symposium (Harrow, England)
Clin Respir Organs — Clinics of Respiratory Organs
Clin Respir Physiol — Clinical Respiratory Physiology
Clin Res Pract Drug Regul Aff — Clinical Research Practices and Drug Regulatory Affairs
Clin Res Proc — Clinical Research Proceedings
Clin Res Rev — Clinical Research Reviews
Clin Rev Allergy — Clinical Reviews in Allergy
Clin Rev Allergy Immunol — Clinical Reviews in Allergy and Immunology
Clin Rev Res Notes — Clinical Review and Research Notes
Clin Rheumatol — Clinical Rheumatology
Clin Rheum Dis — Clinics in Rheumatic Diseases
Clin Sc — Clinical Science
Clin Sci — Clinical Science
Clin Sci Colch — Clinical Science (Colchester)
Clin Sci (Lond) — Clinical Science (London)
Clin Sci Mol Med — Clinical Science and Molecular Medicine
Clin Sci Mol Med Suppl — Clinical Science and Molecular Medicine. Supplement
Clin Sci (Oxf) — Clinical Science (Oxford) [*Later, Clinical Science and Molecular Medicine*]
Clin Sci Suppl — Clinical Science. Supplement
Clin Sc Mol — Clinical Science and Molecular Medicine
Clin Sociol Rev — Clinical Sociology Review
Clin Sports Med — Clinics in Sports Medicine
Clin Stud — Clinical Studies
Clin Superv — Clinical Supervisor. The Journal of Supervision in Psychotherapy and Mental Health
Clin Surg — Clinical Surgery
Clin S Work — Clinical Social Work Journal
Clin Symp — Clinical Symposia
Clin Tech Rep Beckman Instrum Inc — Clinical Technical Report. Beckman Instruments, Inc.
Clin Ter — Clinica Terapeutica
Clin Ter Rome — Clinica Terapeutica (Rome)

Clin Ter Sao Paulo — Clinica e Terapeutica (Sao Paulo)
Clin Ter Suppl — Clinica Terapeutica. Supplemento
Clin Ther — Clinical Therapeutics
Clinton Lab Tech Pap — Clinton Laboratories. Technical Paper
Clin Toxic — Clinical Toxicology
Clin Toxicol — Clinical Toxicology
Clin Toxicol Bull — Clinical Toxicology Bulletin
Clin Toxicol Consult — Clinical Toxicology Consultant
Clin Transpl — Clinical Transplants
Clin Transplant — Clinical Transplantation
Clin Trials J — Clinical Trials Journal
Clin Vet — Clinica Veterinaria
Clin Vet (Milan) — Clinica Veterinaria (Milan)
Clin Virginia Mason Hosp — Clinics of the Virginia Mason Hospital
Clin Virol Tokyo — Clinical Virology (Tokyo)
CLIOAD — Clinique Ophtalmologique
Clio Med — Clio Medica
CLit — Ceska Literatura
Clit — Comparative Literature
CLit — Convorbiri Literare
CLit — Correo Literario
CLJ — Calcutta Law Journal
CLJ — California Law Journal
CLJ — Cambridge Law Journal
CLJ — Canada Law Journal
CLJ — Canadian Library Journal
CLJ — Cape Law Journal
CLJ — Central Law Journal
CLJ — Ceylon Law Journal
CLJ — Chicago Law Journal
CLJ — Classical Journal
ClJ — Classical Journal and Scholars Review
CLJ — Colonial Law Journal Reports
CLJ — Commercial Law Journal
CLJ — Cornell Library Journal
CLJ — Criminal Law Journal
CLJ — Criminal Law Journal of India
CLJ & Lit Rev — California Law Journal and Literary Review
Cl Journ — Classical Journal. Virgil Society. Malta Branch
Cl Journ (C) — Classical Journal (Chicago)
Clk's Mag — Clerk's Magazine
CLL — Clinical Lab Letter
CLLA — Cahiers de Litterature et de Linguistique Appliquee
CLLAAK — Clinica y Laboratoria
CLLAN — Collection Langues et Litteratures de l'Afrique Noire
CLLC — Coleccion de Leyes, Decretos, Resoluciones i Otros Documentos Oficiales Referentes al Departamento de Loreto Formado de Orden Supremo por el Doctor Carlos Larrabure i Correa [Lima]
CLLR — Crown Lands Law Reports
CLM — Catequesis Latinoamericana (Mexico)
CLM — Chinese Literature Monthly
CIM — [The] Clergy Monthly
CLM — Computer Language Magazine
CLM — Current Law Monthly
CLMBB — College Music Symposium
CLMDAY — Clio
CLMEA3 — Clinical Medicine
Cl Med — Classica et Mediaevalia
Cl Mediaev — Classica et Mediaevalia
CLMJA — California Mining Journal
CLMNDX — Colemania
CLMO — Climate Monitor. Climatic Research Unit. University of East Anglia
CLM Rep UK At Energy Auth — CLM [Culham Laboratory Reports] Report. United Kingdom Atomic Energy Authority
CIMthly — [The] Clergy Monthly
Cl Mus — Classical Museum
CLN — Chemical and Engineering News
CLN — Children's Libraries Newsletter
CLN — Clinica World Medical Device News
CLN — Commercial Lending Newsletter
CLNAAU — Clinica
CLNABV — Clean Air
CLNEA — Clinical Neurosurgery
CLNEDB — Clinical Neuropharmacology
CLNHBI — Clinical Nephrology
CLNL — Comparative Literature News-Letter
CLNPDA — Clinical Neuropathology
CLNSAG — Contributions. Department of Limnology. Academy of Natural Sciences of Philadelphia
CLNUEQ — Clinical Nutrition
CLNYD3 — Clinical Neuropsychology
CLO — Cahiers Linguistiques d'Ottawa
CIO — Clair-Obscur
Cl O — Classical Outlook
Clogher Rec — Clogher Record
CLOND — Clinical Oncology
CLOND9 — Clinical Oncology
Cloth & Textiles Res J — Clothing and Textiles Research Journal
Clothing Text Res J — Clothing and Textiles Research Journal
Cloth Res Jnl — Clothing Research Journal
Cl Outlook — Classical Outlook. Journal. American Classical League
CLP — Classical Philology
CLP — Current Legal Problems
CLPA — Cahiers Ligures de Prehistoire et d'Archeologie

CLPCA — Chung-Kuo K'o-Hsueh-Yuan Lan-Chou Hua-Hsueh Wu-Li Yen-Chiu-So Yen-Chiu Pao-Kao Chi-K An
CLPCBD — Clinical Approaches to Problems of Childhood
CLPED — Clinics in Perinatology
CLPEDL — Clinics in Perinatology
Cl Ph — Classical Philology
CLPHDU — Clinical Physiology
CLPHEV — Clinical Pharmacology
Cl Phil — Classical Philology
Cl Philol — Classical Philology
Cl Phy — Classical Philology
CLPJA — Cleft Palate Journal
CLPNAB — Collective Phenomena
CLPS — Climatic Perspectives
CLPTA — Clinical Pharmacology and Therapeutics
CLPTAT — Clinical Pharmacology and Therapeutics
Cl Q — Classical Quarterly
CLQ — Colby Library. Quarterly
CLQ — Cornell Law Quarterly
CL (Q) — Crown Lands Law Reports (Queensland)
Cl Qu — Classical Quarterly
Cl Quart — Classical Quarterly
CLR — Children's Literature Review
CLR — Civil Liberties Review
Cl R — Classical Review
ClR — [The] Clergy Review
CLR — Columbia Law Review
CLR — Commonwealth Law Reports
CLR — Cornell Law Review
CLR — Crown Lands Law Reports
CLRA — Inter-Corporate Ownership
CLRAA — Clinical Radiology
CLRAAG — Clinical Radiology
CLR (Aust) — Commonwealth Law Reports (Australia)
CLRC — Coleccion de Libros Raros o Curiosos Que Tratan de America [Madrid]
CLRDA — CLR [Council on Library Resources] Recent Developments
CLREA — Clinical Research
CLREAS — Clinical Research
CL Rev — California Law Review
Cl Rev — Classical Review
CIRh — Clara Rhodos
CLR Recent Devt — CLR [Council on Library Resources] Recent Developments
CLS — California Library Statistics
CLS — Charles Lamb Society. Bulletin
CLS — Comparative Literature Studies
CLSAP — Canon Law Society of America. Proceedings
CLSB — Charles Lamb Society. Bulletin
CLSJ — Company and Securities Law Journal
CLSOAT — Contact Lens Society of America. Journal
CLS Q — CLS [Christian Legal Society] Quarterly
CLSU Sci J — CLSU (Central Luzon State University) Scientific Journal
CLSU Sci Jnl — Central Luzon State University Science Journal
CLT — Consolidacao das Leis do Trabalho
Clt — Culture
CLT — Cuttack Law Times
CLTA — Cahiers de Linguistique Theorique et Appliquee
CLTE — Commissao de Linhas Telegraphicas Estrategicas de Matto Grosso ao Amazonas. Publicacao
CLTEA4 — Clinica Terapeutica
CLTHDG — Clinical Therapeutics
CLTPD — Chi Lin Ta Hsueh Hsueh Pao. Tzu Jan K'o Hsueh Pan
CLTS — Contributions. Institute of Low Temperature Science
CLU — Capitol Line-Up
CLU — CLU [Chartered Life Underwriters] Journal
CLU — Corporate Library Update
Club Ser Univ NC State Coll Agr Eng Agr Ext Serv — Club Series. University of North Carolina. State College of Agriculture and Engineering. Agricultural Extension Service
CLU J — CLU [Chartered Life Underwriters] Journal
Cluj Med — Clujul Medical
Clujul Med — Clujul Medical
CLUQ — Cahiers de Linguistique. Universite du Quebec
Clustering Phenom Nuclei — Clustering Phenomena in Nuclei
CLV — Classical Views
CLVEAE — Clinica Veterinaria
CLW — Catholic Library World
CLW — Ceylon Law Weekly
CIW — Classical Weekly
Cl W — Classical World
Cl Weekly — Classical Weekly
Cl World — Classical World
CLY — Current Law Year Book
CLYB — Current Law Year Book
CM — Cahiers de Mariemont
CM — Cahiers Maynard
CM — Camden Miscellany
CM — Canadian Materials
CM — Canadian Mining Journal
CM — Canberra Income Tax Circular Memorandum
CM — Carleton Miscellany
CM — Century Magazine
CM — Church Musician
CM — Ciencia Revista Hispanoamericana de Ciencias Puras y Aplicadas (Mexico)
CM — Civilta Moderna
CM — Classica et Mediaevalia

CM — Cleveland-Marshall Law Review
CM — Clio Medica
CM — Club Management
CM — CM. Canadian Materials for Schools and Libraries
CM — Coins, Incorporating Coins and Medals
CM — Colloquia Mathematica. Societatis Janos Bolyai
CM — Colorado Magazine
CM — Congress Monthly
CM — Construction Management
CM — Contemporaries and Makers
CM — Contemporary Musicians
CM — Cornhill Magazine
CMA — Canadian Manager
CMA — Catalogue des Manuscrits Alchimiques Grecs
CMA — Criminalia
CMA — MMS Currency Market Analysis
CMAG — Catalogue des Manuscrits Alchimiques Grecs
C Mag — Center Magazine
C Mag — Century Magazine
CMAGD — Chemisch Magazine
C Magic — Cinemagic
CMAI — Contributions from the Museum of the American Indian. Heye Foundation [New York]
CMAJ — Canadian Medical Association. Journal
CMAJA — Canadian Medical Association. Journal
CMAJAX — Canadian Medical Association. Journal
CMAL — Catalogue des Manuscrits Alchimiques Latins
CMA Lat — Catalogue des Manuscrits Alchimiques Latins
CMAnnual — Coins Annual
CMAPAH — Collana di Monografie. Ateneo Parmense
CMAUA — Chemoautomatyka
CMAZAD — Comunicaciones. Museo Argentino de Ciencias Naturales "Bernardino Rivadavia" e Instituto Nacional de Investigacion de las Ciencias Naturales. Zoologia
CMB — Caribbean Monthly Bulletin
CMBBBF — Collection de Monographies de Botanique et de Biologie Vegetale
CMBI — Commentationes Biologicae. Societas Scientiarum Fennica
CMBID4 — Cellular and Molecular Biology
CMBUA — Canadian Mathematical Bulletin
CMBUC5 — Australia. Commonwealth Scientific and Industrial Research Organisation. MarineBiochemistry Unit. Annual Report
CMC — Coins, Medals, and Currency Weekly
CMC — Crosscurrents/Modern Critiques
C Mc — Current Musicology
CMCB — Comments on Molecular and Cellular Biophysics
CMCD — Coins, Medals, and Currency Digest and Monthly Catalogue
CMCEA — Commerce
CMCHA — Canadian Machinery and Metalworking
Cmcl Law Assoc Bull — Commercial Law Association. Bulletin
Cmcl Space — Commercial Space
CMCPDU — Comunicacoes. Museu de Ciencias. PUCRGS
CMCS — Cambridge Medieval Celtic Studies
CMCS — Coloquios sobre Metodologia das Ciencias Sociais [Lisboa]
CMCYEO — Cell Motility and the Cytoskeleton
CMD — California Management Review
Cmd — Command Paper
CM/D — Dialogos. Colegio de Mexico
CMDCDU — Congressi Italiani di Medicina
CMdF — Courrier Musical de France
CME — Chartered Mechanical Engineer
CMEALL — Cooper Monographs on English and American Language and Literature
CME Chart Mech Eng — CME. Chartered Mechanical Engineer
C Med — Cahiers Meduliens
Cmed — Chronique Medicale
CMEDD4 — Cardiovascular Medicine
C Med H — Cambridge Medieval History
CMEDSTR — Canada. Marine Environmental Data Service. Technical Report
CMENA — Chemical and Metallurgical Engineering
CMens — Correspondance Mensuelle
CMERBN — Catalogue des Monnaies de l'Empire Romain. Bibliotheque Nationale
CME Reprnt — Chemical Marketing and Economics Reprints
CMEW — Comparative Medicine East and West
CMEWDR — Comparative Medicine East and West
CMF — Casopis pro Moderni Filologii
CMF — Ceske Museum Filologicke
CMF — Collection des Moralistes Francais
CMF — Courrier Musical de France
CMF — Crosscurrents/Modern Fiction
CMF — Yugoslavia Export
CMFAAV — Communications. Faculte des Sciences. Universite d'Ankara
CMFBD3 — CMFRI [Central Marine Fisheries Research Institute] Bulletin
CM/FI — Foro Internacional. El Colegio de Mexico
CMFL — Casopis pro Moderni Filologii a Literatury
CMFRI Bull — CMFRI [Central Marine Fisheries Research Institute] Bulletin
CMG — Consumentengids
CMG — Corpus Medicorum Graecorum
CMGEA — Geological Survey of Canada. Bulletin
CMGEAE — Geological Survey of Canada. Bulletin
CMGPA — Centralblatt fuer Mineralogie, Geologie, und Palaeontologie
CMG Proc — CMG (Computer Measurement Group) Proceedings
C M Gr — Convegno di Studi sulla Magna Graeca
CMG Trans — CMG (Computer Measurement Group) Transactions
CMH — Cambridge Mediaeval History
CMHJAY — Community Mental Health Journal
CMHLB — Cahiers du Monde Hispanique et Luso-Bresilien

CMHPAI — Acta Veterinaria et Zootechnica Sinica
CMI — Canadian Magazine Index
CMI — Chemical Week
CMI — China Market Intelligence
CMI — Church Missionary Intelligencer
CMI — Coping with Medical Issues
CMICA — Canada. Mines Branch. Information Circular
CMIDB — Chemischer Informationsdienst
CMI Descr Pathog Fungi Bact — CMI [Commonwealth Mycological Institute] Descriptions of Pathogenic Fungi and Bacteria
CMIFAR — CMI [Commonwealth Mycological Institute] Descriptions of Pathogenic Fungiand Bacteria
CMIMAE — Commonwealth Mycological Institute. Mycological Papers
CMIMBF — Contributions to Microbiology and Immunology
C Min — Christian Ministry
C Mind — Catholic Mind
CMIPB — Cahiers de Medecine Interprofessionnelle
CMIS — Change to Metric Information Service
CMJ — Canadian Mining Journal
CMJ — Christian Medical Society. Journal
CMJ — Communicator's Journal
CMJ — Compensation Planning Journal
CMJ — Computer Music Journal
CMJ — Czechoslovak Mathematical Journal
CMJODS — Chinese Medical Journal
CMJPB — Community and Junior College Journal
CMJUA9 — Caribbean Medical Journal
CMK — Compendium. Dagelijks Overzicht van de Buitenlandse Pers
CMKRA — Chemical Marketing Reporter
CMKZA — Chemiker-Zeitung
CML — Chambre de Commerce France-Amerique Latine
CML — Change
CML — Classical and Modern Literature. Quarterly
CML — Club du Meilleur Livre
CML — Commercial Law Journal
CML — Cornhill Magazine (London)
CML — Corpus Medicorum Latinorum
CML — Cronica Medica (Lima)
CMLC — Classical and Medieval Literature Criticism
CMLR — Canadian Modern Language Review
CMLR — Cleveland-Marshall Law Review
CMLR — Common Market Law Reports
CMLR — Common Market Law Review
CML Rev — Common Market Law Review
CMLS — Computer Multiple Listing Service
CMM — Cape Monthly Magazine
CMM — Casopis Matice Moravske
CMM — Chemical Engineering. Chemical Technology for Profit Minded Engineers
CM Mag — CM Magazine
CMMB — Casopis. Moravskeho Musea v Brne
CMMBA — Canadian Mining and Metallurgical Bulletin
CMMBE5 — Cell Culture Methods for Molecular and Cell Biology
CMMI Congr — CMMI (Council of Mining and Metallurgical Institutions) Congress
CMMS — Corpus der Minoischen und Mykenischen Siegel
CMMSC — Chislennye Metody Mekhaniki Sploshnoi Sredy
Cmmty Serv — Community Service Newsletter
CMN — Cellular and Molecular Neurobiology
CMN — Common Market News
CMNEDI — Cellular and Molecular Neurobiology
CMNH — Comunicaciones del Museo Nacional de Historia Natural de Buenos Aires
CMNLD — Chamber of Mines. Newsletter
CMO — Computers and Operations Research
CMo — Creative Moment
C Monde Hisp Luso-Bresil — Cahiers du Monde Hispanique et Luso-Bresilien
C Monde Russe Sov — Cahiers du Monde Russe et Sovietique
CMONDG — Computer Monographs
CMonth — Coin Monthly
C Monthly Mag — Century Monthly Magazine
CMOPAJ — Casopis Narodniho Muzea v Praze. Rada Prirodovedna
CMORA — Computers and Operations Research
CMORAP — Computers and Operations Research
CMOTDY — Cell Motility
C Mo Univ Coop Ext Serv — C. Missouri University. Cooperative Extension Service
CMP — CMP Newsletter
CMP — Congresso do Mundo Portugues
CMP — Current Mathematical Publications
CMPBEK — Computer Methods and Programs in Biomedicine
CMPHA — Communications in Mathematical Physics
CMPLDF — Complement
CMPMA — Compositio Mathematica
CMPN — Campaign
CMPRB — Coal Mining and Processing
CMPSD — Culture, Medicine, and Psychiatry
CMPYAH — Commonwealth Mycological Institute. Phytopathological Papers
CMPZBL — Comunicacoes. Museu de Ciencias. PUCRGS [Pontificia Universidade Catolica doRio Grande Do Sul]. Serie Zoologia
CMQ — Tijdschrift voor Marketing
CMR — California Management Review
CMR — California Manufacturers Register
CMR — Capital Markets Report
CMR — Christian Management Report
CMR — Church Missionary Review
CMR 17 — Centre Meridional de Recherche sur le Dix-Septieme Siecle
CMRAD — Camera

CMR Chem Bus — Chemical Business (Supplement to Chemical Marketing Reporter)
CMRDM — Corpus Monumentorum Religionis Dei Menis
CM/RE — Relaciones. Colegio de Michoacan
CMRFAS — Canadian Manuscript Report of Fisheries and Aquatic Sciences
CMRPD3 — Cardiovascular Medicine
CMRS — Cahiers du Monde Russe et Sovietique
C MRS Int Symp Proc — C-MRS (Chinese Materials Research Society) International Symposia Proceedings
CMS — College Music Symposium
CMS — Corpus der Minoischen und Mykenischen Siegel
CMSCA — Contributions in Marine Science
CMSCAY — Contributions in Marine Science
CMS Cmp (Bah) — Country Market Survey. Computers and Peripheral Equipment (Bahrain)
CMS Cmp (Cda) — Country Market Survey. Computers and Peripheral Equipment (Canada)
CMS Cmp (Emi) — Country Market Survey. Computers and Peripheral Equipment (United Arab Emirates)
CMS Cmp (Fra) — Country Market Survey. Computers and Peripheral Equipment (France)
CMS Cmp (Jpn) — Country Market Survey. Computers and Peripheral Equipment (Japan)
CMS Cmp (Kuw) — Country Market Survey. Computers and Peripheral Equipment (Kuwait)
CMS Cmp (Sau) — Country Market Survey. Computers and Peripheral Equipment (Saudi Arabia)
CMS Cmp (Sin) — Country Market Survey. Computers and Peripheral Equipment (Singapore)
CMS Cmp (Swe) — Country Market Survey. Computers and Peripheral Equipment (Sweden)
CMS Cmp (Tai) — Country Market Survey. Computers and Peripheral Equipment (Taiwan)
CMS Cmp (UK) — Country Market Survey. Computers and Peripheral Equipment (United Kingdom)
CMS Cmp (Yug) — Country Market Survey. Computers and Peripheral Equipment (Yugoslavia)
CMSDMR — Canada. Marine Sciences Directorate. Department of Fisheries and Oceans. Manuscript Report
CMS EIC (Aut) — Country Market Survey. Electronic Components (Austria)
CMS EIC (Mex) — Country Market Survey. Electronic Components (Mexico)
CMS EIC (Phl) — Country Market Survey. Electronic Components (Philippines)
CMS EIC (Swi) — Country Market Survey. Electronic Components (Switzerland)
CMS EIC (Tai) — Country Market Survey. Electronic Components (Taiwan)
CMS EPS (Col) — Country Market Survey. Electric Power Systems (Colombia)
CMS EPS (Egy) — Country Market Survey. Electric Power Systems (Egypt)
CMS EPS (Nig) — Country Market Survey. Electric Power Systems (Nigeria)
CMS EPS (Phi) — Country Market Survey. Electric Power Systems (Philippines)
CMS EPS (Sau) — Country Market Survey. Electric Power Systems (Saudi Arabia)
CMS EPS (Spa) — Country Market Survey. Electric Power Systems (Spain)
CMS EPS (Tha) — Country Market Survey. Electric Power Systems (Thailand)
CMS EPS (Yug) — Country Market Survey. Electric Power Systems (Yugoslavia)
CMS FPP (Tha) — Country Market Survey. Food Processing Packaging Equipment (Thailand)
CMS GIE (Aus) — Country Market Survey. Graphic Industries Equipment (Australia)
CMS GIE (Jpn) — Country Market Survey. Graphic Industries Equipment (Japan)
CMS GIE (Mex) — Country Market Survey. Graphic Industries Equipment (Mexico)
CMS GIE (Net) — Country Market Survey. Graphic Industries Equipment (Netherlands)
CMS GIE (Soa) — Country Market Survey. Graphic Industries Equipment (South Africa)
CMS GIE (UK) — Country Market Survey. Graphic Industries Equipment (United Kingdom)
CMS/IMR — International Migration Review. Center for Migration Studies
CMS IPC (Aus) — Country Market Survey. Industrial Process Controls (Australia)
CMS IPC (Bra) — Country Market Survey. Industrial Process Controls (Brazil)
CMS IPC (Fra) — Country Market Survey. Industrial Process Controls (France)
CMS IPC (Sin) — Country Market Survey. Industrial Process Controls (Singapore)
CMS IPC (Sok) — Country Market Survey. Industrial Process Controls (South Korea)
CMS IPC (Spa) — Country Market Survey. Industrial Process Controls (Spain)
CMS IPC (Tai) — Country Market Survey. Industrial Process Controls (Taiwan)
CMS Lab (Jpn) — Country Market Survey. Laboratory Instruments (Japan)
CMS Lab (Spa) — Country Market Survey. Laboratory Instruments (Spain)
CMS MED (Arg) — Country Market Survey. Medical Equipment (Argentina)
CMS MED (Aus) — Country Market Survey. Medical Equipment (Australia)
CMS MED (Bra) — Country Market Survey. Medical Equipment (Brazil)
CMS MED (Can) — Country Market Survey. Medical Equipment (Canada)
CMS MED (Jpn) — Country Market Survey. Medical Equipment (Japan)
CMS MIE (Pak) — Country Market Survey. Mining Industry Equipment (Pakistan)
CMS MIE (Zai) — Country Market Survey. Mining Industry Equipment (Zaire)
CMS MTL (Por) — Country Market Survey. Machine Tools (Portugal)
CMS PCE (Isr) — Country Market Survey. Pollution Instrumentation and Equipment (Israel)
CMS PCE (Phl) — Country Market Survey. Pollution Instrumentation and Equipment (Philippines)
CMS PCE (Tai) — Country Market Survey. Pollution Instrumentation and Equipment (Taiwan)
CMS PCE (W Ge) — Country Market Survey. Pollution Instrumentation and Equipment (West Germany)
CMSRAB — Communications. Research Institute of the Sumatra Planters' Association. RubberSeries
CMSS — Casopis Musealnej Slovenskej Splocnosti
CMS SGR (Arg) — Country Market Survey. Sporting and Recreational Equipment (Argentina)

CMS SGR (Sau) — Country Market Survey. Sporting and Recreational Equipment (Saudi Arabia)
CMS SGR (Swe) — Country Market Survey. Sporting and Recreational Equipment (Sweden)
CMS SGR (Swi) — Country Market Survey. Sporting and Recreational Equipment (Switzerland)
CMS SGR (UK) — Country Market Survey. Sporting and Recreational Equipment (United Kingdom)
CMS TCE (Arg) — Country Market Survey. Telecommunications Equipment (Argentina)
CMS TCE (Chn) — Country Market Survey. Telecommunications Equipment (China)
CMS TCE (Emi) — Country Market Survey. Telecommunications Equipment (United Arab Emirates)
CMS TCE (Fra) — Country Market Survey. Telecommunications Equipment (France)
CMS TCE (Ger) — Country Market Survey. Telecommunications Equipment (Germany)
CMS TCE (Kuw) — Country Market Survey. Telecommunications Equipment (Kuwait)
CMS TCE (Pak) — Country Market Survey. Telecommunications Equipment (Pakistan)
CMS TCE (Phl) — Country Market Survey. Telecommunications Equipment (Philippines)
CMS TCE (Sau) — Country Market Survey. Telecommunications Equipment (Saudi Arabia)
CMS TCE (Spa) — Country Market Survey. Telecommunications Equipment (Spain)
CMS TCE (Tha) — Country Market Survey. Telecommunications Equipment (Thailand)
CMS Workshop Lect — CMS (Clay Minerals Society) Workshop Lectures
CMT — Courrier Musical et Theatral
CMTBB — Canada. Mines Branch. Technical Bulletin
CMTLBX — Food Chemistry, Microbiology, Technology
CMTS — Clarendon Medieval and Tudor Series
C Mu — Classical Museum
CMUC — Commentationes Mathematicae. Universitatis Carolinae
CMUE B — Council for Research in Music Education. Bulletin
CMUED — Contributions to Music Education
CMUJST — CMU [*Central Mindanao University*] Journal of Science and Technology
CMUMD9 — Cell and Muscle Motility
CMUS — Censo de Museos de Espana
CMUTB — Chemieunterricht
CMW — Communication World
CMXPAU — Chirurgia Maxillofacialis et Plastica
CMYBA — Canadian Minerals Yearbook
C Mz — Cercetari de Muzicologie
CN — Cahiers Numismatiques
CN — Calcoin News
Cn — Center Magazine
C N — Chemical News and Journal of Physical Science
CN — Classici e Neo-Latini
CN — Clinical Nephrology
CN — CN
CN — Comunicacion
CN — Consultants News
CN — Cornishman
CN — Cultura Neolatina
CN — Current Notes
CNA — Canadian Advertising Rates and Data
CNA — China News Analysis
CNA — Cronica. Congreso Nacional de Arqueologia
CNA — Cronica Numismatica si Arheologica
CNABAG — Connecticut. Agricultural Experiment Station. Bulletin
CNA Bull — California Nurses Association. Bulletin
CNACAJ — Connecticut. Agricultural Experiment Station. Circular
CNAIB — Clean Air (Brighton, England)
CNAIB4 — Clean Air
CNAM — Canadian Corporate Names
CNA Rep — CNA (Canadian Nuclear Association) Report
CNASAX — Chugoku Nogyo Shikenjo Hokoku. A. Sakumotsu-Bu
CNat — Cahiers des Naturalistes
C Nav — Codice della Navigazione
CNBUAA — Connecticut. Storrs Agricultural Experiment Station. Bulletin
CNC — Confluencia (Caracas)
CNCBAQ — Comunicaciones. Instituto Nacional de Investigacion de las Ciencias Naturales. Ciencias Botanicas
CNCCA — Canadian Cancer Conference
CNCF — Collection Nationale des Classiques Francais
CNCNAS — Contamination Control
CNCRA6 — Cancer Chemotherapy Reports
CNDBA — Bulletin. Cincinnati Dental Society
CNDIB — Cahiers de Notes Documentaires
CNDLAR — Candollea
CNEA Inf — CNEA (Argentina. Comision Nacional de Energia Atomica) Informe
CNE Commun Navig Electron — CNE. Communication/Navigation Electronics
CNEKAT — Chugoku Nogyo Shikenjo Hokoku. E. Kankyo-Bu
CNEN RT BIO Italy Com Naz Energ Nucl — CNEN-RT/BIO (Italy. Comitato Nazionale Energia Nucleare)
CNEN RT FIMA Italy Com Naz Energ Nucl — CNEN-RT/FIMA (Italy. Comitato Nazionale Energia Nucleare)
CNEN RT ING Italy Com Naz Energ Nucl — CNEN-RT/ING (Italy. Comitato Nazionale Energia Nucleare)
CNEP Bol — CNEP [*Comision Nacional para la Erradicacion del Paludismo*] Boletin
CNEP (Com Nac Errad Palud) Bol — CNEP (Comision Nacional para la Erradicacion del Paludismo) Boletin
CNEPDD — Contributions to Nephrology

CNET Ann Telecommun — CNET (France. Centre National d'Etudes des Telecommunications) Annales des Telecommunications
CNeu — Cahiers de Neuilly
CNew — Carlyle Newsletter
CNEWA — Chemical News
C News — Cinemanews
CNF — Consudel. Maandblad voor de Benelux, Gewijd aan de Belangen van Industrie en Handel op het Gebied van Cacao, Chocolade, Suikerwerken, Koek, Banket, Biscuit Enz
CNFI — Christian News from Israel
CNFRA Com Nat Fr Rech Antarct — CNFRA. Comite National Francais des Recherches Antarctiques
CNFS Commer News For Serv — CNFS. Commercial News for the Foreign Service
CNG — Change
CNGGA — Canadian Geographer
CNGGAR — Canadian Geographer
CNGTA — Changing Times
CNH — Courier. European Community, Africa, Caribbean, Pacific
CNHABF — Carnegie Museum of Natural History. Annual Report
CNHP — Congreso Nacional de Historia del Peru
CNI — Canadian News Index
CNI — Christian News from Israel
CNI — Columbus News Index
CNIE — Commonwealth Novel in English
Cn I P — Proceedings of the Canadian Institute
Cn I T — Transactions of the Canadian Institute
CNJ — Cahiers de la Nouvelle Journee
Cn J — Canadian Journal of Industry, Science, and Art
CNJ — Canadian Numismatic Journal
CNJGA — Canadian Journal of Genetics and Cytology
CNJGA8 — Canadian Journal of Genetics and Cytology
CNJMAQ — Canadian Journal of Comparative Medicine and Veterinary Science [*Later, Canadian Journal of Comparative Medicine*]
CNJNA — Canadian Journal of Animal Science
CNJNAT — Canadian Journal of Animal Science
Cn Jour — Canadian Journal of Political and Social Theory
CNJPA — Canadian Journal of Pharmaceutical Sciences
CNJPAZ — Canadian Journal of Pharmaceutical Sciences
CNL — Central Bank of Nigeria. Economic and Financial Review (Lagos)
CNLB — Canadian Native Law Bulletin. Native Law Centre. University of Saskatchewan
CNLMA2 — Contact Lens Medical Bulletin
CNLR — Canadian Native Law Reporter. Native Law Centre. University of Saskatchewan
CNLR — Council on National Literatures. Quarterly World Report
CNM — Canadian Manager
CNM — Casopis Narodniho Muzea
CNM — Contemporary Poland
CNMAD — Construction News Magazine
CNMBB — Canada. Mineral Resources Branch. Mineral Bulletin
CNMEAH — Connecticut Medicine
CNMED — Clinical Nuclear Medicine
CNMEDK — Clinical Nuclear Medicine
CNN — Common Market Business Reports
CNNS — Canadian Native News Service
CNNSBV — Clinical Neurology and Neurosurgery
Cn Nt — Canadian Naturalist and Geologist, and Proceedings of the Natural History of Montreal
CNNU — Colleccao de Noticias para a Historia e Geographia das Nacoes Ultramarinas, Que Vivem nos Dominios Portuguezes, ou Que Lhes Sao Visinhas [*Lisboa*]
CNOL — Clinical Notes On-Line
CNOR — Canada. Northern Forest Research Centre. Information Reports
CNP — France Pays Bas
CNPI — Consejo Nacional de Protecao aos Indios. Publicacao [*Rio de Janeiro*]
CNPIA — Canadian Pulp and Paper Industry
CNPPA — Comments on Nuclear and Particle Physics
CNPRA3 — Canadian Poultry Review
CNQBAS — Cane Growers Quarterly Bulletin
CNRCA2 — Canadian Journal of Research. Section C. Botanical Sciences
CNRCB — Clinical Notes on Respiratory Diseases
Cn Rc Sc — Canadian Record of Science, Including the Proceedings of the Natural History of Montreal, and Replacing the Canadian Naturalist
CNRD — Clinical Notes on Respiratory Diseases
CNRDA5 — Canadian Journal of Research. Section D. Zoological Sciences
CNREA8 — Cancer Research
C N Report — Computer Negotiations Report
CNRM — CNRM [*Centre National de Recherches Metallurgiques*]. Metallurgical Reports
CNRM — CONRIM [*Committee on Natural Resource Information Management*] Newsletter
CNRMAW — Canadian Journal of Research. Section E. Medical Sciences
CNRM (Cent Natl Rech Metall) Metall Rep — CNRM (Centre National de Recherches Metallurgiques). Metallurgical Reports
CNRM Metall Rep — CNRM (Centre National de Recherches Metallurgiques) Metallurgical Reports
CNROA4 — Chirurgia Narzadow Ruchu i Ortopedia Polska
CNRS Colloq Int — Centre National de la Recherche Scientifique. Colloques Internationaux
CNRS Groupe Fr Argiles Bull — Centre National de la Recherche Scientifique. Groupe Francais des Argiles. Bulletin
CNRS Groupe Fr Argiles CR Reun Etud — Centre National de la Recherche Scientifique. Groupe Francais des Argiles. Compte Rendu des Reunions d'Etudes

Cn R S P & T — Proceedings and Transactions of the Royal Society of Canada
CNRS Res — CNRS (Centre National de la Recherche Scientifique) Research (New York)
CNRXAV — Canadian Forestry Service. Northern Forest Research Centre. Information Report NOR-X
CNS — Center for North Atlantic Studies. Newsletter
CNSBB5 — Chugoku Nogyo Shikenjo Hokoku. B. Chikusan-Bu
CNS Drug Rev — CNS Drug Reviews
CNSLAY — Consultant
CNSRG — Canada. Northern Science Research Group. Reports
CNSRGSSN — Canada. Northern Science Research Group. Social Science Notes
CNSRNN — Center for Northern Studies and Research. McGill University. News Notes
CNSSEP — Central Nervous System. Pharmacology Series
CNST — Cardiff Naturalist's Society. Transactions
CNSVAU — Conservationist
CNSVC — Center for Northern Studies (Wolcott, Vermont). Contributions
CNTA — Contact
CNTEBJ — Congreso Nacional de Tuberculosis y Enfermedades Respiratorias
CNTIB — Constructii (Bucharest)
Cntry Wom — Country Women
CNU — Financial Executive
C Nuovo — Cinema Nuovo
CNUTA — Canadian Nuclear Technology
CNV — Collegiate News and Views
CNV — Cum Notis Variorum
CNVJA9 — Canadian Veterinary Journal
CNVMDL — Clinical and Investigative Medicine
CNW — Canada News-Wire
CNWHA8 — Contributions. New South Wales National Herbarium
CNY — Commentary (New York)
CNYB — Crain's New York Business
C NY Bs Rv — Central New York Business Review
CO — Cahiers de l'Oronte
CO — Cahiers de l'Ouest
CO — Chronicles of Oklahoma
CO — Classical Outlook
Co — Code de Commerce
CO — Code des Obligations
CO — Codice delle Obligazioni
CO — Colorado Journal of Research in Music Education
Co — Composer
Co — Comprendre
CO — Computing
Co — Conference
Co — Corona
CO2 Metab Plant Prod Proc Annu Harry Steenbock Symp — CO2 Metabolism and Plant Productivity. Proceedings. Annual Harry Steenbock Symposium
COA — Coal Miner
CoA — Coat of Arms
COA — Corporate Accounting
COABER — Computer Applications in the Biosciences
Coach & Ath Dir — Scholastic Coach and Athletic Director
Coach and Athl — Coach and Athlete
Coach Clin — Coaching Clinic
Coach Clinic — Coaching Clinic
Coaching J Bus Rev — Coaching Journal and Bus Review
Coach Rev — Coaching Review
Coach Sci Update — Coaching Science Update
Coach Women's Athl — Coaching Women's Athletics
Coach Women's Athletics — Coaching Women's Athletics
COAD — Company Facts and Addresses
Coagulation Blood Transfus Proc Annu Symp Blood Transfus — Coagulation and Blood Transfusion. Proceedings. Annual Symposium on Blood Transfusion
CoAJ — College Art Journal
Coal Abstr — Coal Abstracts
Coal Base Miner South Afr — Coal and Base Minerals of Southern Africa
Coal Can Foc — Coal Canada Focus
Coal Coke Sess Can Chem Eng Conf — Coal and Coke Sessions. Canadian Chemical Engineering Conference
Coal Conference and Expo — Coal Conference and Exposition
Coal Convers — Coal Conversion
Coal Conv Sess Pap Set 4 Coal Prep — Coal Convention. Session Papers. Set 4. Coal Preparation
COALDATA — European Coal Data Bank
Coal Energy Q — Coal and Energy Quarterly
Coal Geol Bul — Coal Geology Bulletin
Coal Geol Bull WV Geol Econ Surv — Coal Geology Bulletin. West Virginia Geological and Economic Survey
Coal Gold Base Miner South Afr — Coal, Gold, and Base Minerals of Southern Africa
Coal Gold Base Miner Sthn Afr — Coal, Gold, and Base Minerals of Southern Africa
Coal Ind — Coal Industry
Coal Ind N — Coal Industry News
Coal Int Redhill Engl — Coal International (Redhill, England)
Coal Iron Kharkov — Coal and Iron (Kharkov)
Coal Liq Mixtures Eur Conf — Coal Liquid Mixtures. European Conference
Coal Manage Symp — Coal Management Symposium
Coal Manage Tech Symp — Coal Management Techniques Symposia
Coal M & P — Coal Mining and Processing
Coal Min (Chicago) — Coal Mining (Chicago)
Coal Mine Drain Res Symp — Coal Mine Drainage Research Symposia
Coal Min Process — Coal Mining and Processing
Coal Min Technol — Coal Mining Technology

Coal Obs — Coal Observer
Coal Oper — Coal Operator
Coal Outlk — Coal Outlook
Coal Prep — Coal Preparation
Coal Prep (Gordon & Breach) — Coal Preparation (Gordon & Breach)
Coal Prep Symp — Coal Preparation Symposia
Coal Prep Thunderbird Enterp — Coal Preparation (Thunderbird Enterprises)
Coal Prep (Tokyo) — Coal Preparation (Tokyo)
Coal Prep Util Symp — Coal Preparation and Utilization Symposium
Coal Process Technol — Coal Processing Technology
Coal Q — Coal Quarterly
Coal Rep — Coal Report
Coal Res CSIRO — Coal Research in CSIRO
Coal Sci Chem — Coal Science and Chemistry
Coal Sci Technol — Coal Science and Technology
Coal Sci Technol (Peking) — Coal Science Technology (Peking)
Coal Situat — Coal Situation
Coal Slurry Fuels Prep Util Proc Int Symp — Coal Slurry Fuels Preparation and Utilization. Proceedings. International Symposium
Coal Tar (Tokyo) — Coal Tar (Tokyo)
Coal Technol — Coal Technology
Coal Technol Eur — Coal Technology Europe
Coal Technol (Houston) — Coal Technology (Houston)
Coal Technol NY — Coal Technology (New York)
Coal Technol Rep — Coal Technology Report
Coal Test Conf Proc — Coal Testing Conference. Proceedings
Coal Util — Coal Utilization
Coal Util Symp — Coal Utilization Symposia
Coal Wk I — Coal Week International
COANB — Coal News
CO & G — Clinical Obstetrics and Gynecology
Co & Sec Law Journal — Company and Securities Law Journal
COASB — Comments on Astrophysics and Space Physics [Later, Comments on Astrophysics]
COAST — Canada. Ocean and Aquatic Sciences Central Region. Technical Notes
Coastal Bend Med — Coastal Bend Medicine
Coastal Eng — Coastal Engineering
Coastal Eng Japan — Coastal Engineering in Japan
Coastal Eng Jpn — Coastal Engineering in Japan
Coastal Engng — Coastal Engineering
Coastal Engng Japan — Coastal Engineering in Japan
Coastal Res — Journal of Coastal Research
Coastal Res Gulf Bothnia — Coastal Research in the Gulf of Bothnia
Coastal Res Notes — Coastal Research Notes
Coastal Water Res Proj Bienn Rep South Calif — Coastal Water Research Project Biennial Report (Southern California)
Coastal Zone Manage J — Coastal Zone Management Journal
Coastal Zone Mgt J — Coastal Zone Management Journal
Coast Artillery J — Coast Artillery Journal
Coast Artillery Jour — Coast Artillery Journal. Coast Artillery School
Coast Zone Manage J — Coastal Zone Management Journal
Coat Community Car Int Conf — Coatings, Community, and Care. International Conference
Coat Conf Proc — Coating Conference. Proceedings
COB — Cobouw. Dagblad voor de Bouwwereld
COBAA — Cobalt
Cobalt Cobalt Abstr — Cobalt and Cobalt Abstracts
Cobalt Engl Ed — Cobalt (English Edition)
Cobalt Fr Ed — Cobalt (French Edition)
Cobble — Cobblestone
COBD — Commerce Business Daily
COBGA — Commentationes Biologicae. Societas Scientiarum Fennica
COBGA9 — Commentationes Biologicae. Societas Scientiarum Fennica
COBIEJ — Comunicaciones Biologicas
COBLAO — Coleopterists' Bulletin
COBLES — Continental Birdlife
CoBINVR — Correspondenzblatt des Naturforschervereins zu Riga
CoblZH — Coblenzer Zeitschrift fuer Heimatkunde
COBOAX — Collectanea Botanica
Cobra Bull Coord Invest A — Cobra. Bulletin pour la Coordination des Investigations Artistiques
Cobra Rev Int A Expermntl — Cobra. Revue Internationale de l'Art Experimental
COBRD — Communication and Broadcasting
Coburg Gothaischen Landen Heimatblaetter — Aus den Coburg-Gothaischen Landen Heimatblaetter
COC — Computer Communications
COC — Criterio (Colombia)
COCA — Conservation Canada
COCBAX — Coconut Bulletin
Coccidioidomycosis Proc Int Conf — Coccidioidomycosis. Proceedings. International Conference on Coccidioidomycosis
COCHDK — Computers in Chemistry
Cochin LJ — Cochin Law Journal
Cochlear Res Symp — Cochlear-Research. Symposium
Cockerill — Cockerill Sambre Acier
COCN — Community Contact
Cocoa Res Inst CSIR Annu Rep — Cocoa Research Institute. Council for Scientific and Industrial Research. Annual Report
Cocoa Res Inst Ghana Acad Sci Annu Rep — Cocoa Research Institute. Ghana Academy of Sciences. Annual Report
Cocoa Res Inst Ghana Tech Bull — Cocoa Research Institute. Ghana. Technical Bulletin
Cocoa Res Inst Tafo Ghana Tech Bull — Cocoa Research Institute. Tafo, Ghana. Technical Bulletin
Cocobro Jaarb — Cocobro-Jaarboekje

Coconut Bull — Coconut Bulletin
Coconut Res Inst Bull — Coconut Research Institute. Bulletin
COCR — Collectanea Ordinis Cisterciensium Reformatorum
Cocuk Sagligi Hastaliklari Derg — Cocuk Sagligi ve Hastaliklari Dergisi
CoD — Comparative Drama
COD — Corporate Design
CODATA Bull — CODATA [Committee on Data for Science and Technology] Bulletin
CODATA Newsl — CODATA [Committee on Data for Science and Technology] Newsletter
CODATA Spec Rep — CODATA [Committee on Data for Science and Technology] Special Report
Cod Civ — Codigo Civil
Cod Com — Codigo de Comercio
Cod Dip — Codex Diplomaticus
Codd Lat Ant — Codices Latini Antiquiores
CODE — Cable On-line Data Exchange
Code Crim Proc — New York Code of Criminal Procedure
CODEDG — Contact Dermatitis
Code Fed Reg — Code of Federal Regulations
Code J — Code of Justinian
Code Th — Code of Theodosius
Co Dir — Company Director and Professional Administrator
Co Dir Prof Adm — Company Director and Professional Administrator
Cod Man — Codices Manuscripti
Cod MSS — Codices Manuscripti
CODOC — Cooperative Documents Network Project
Cod Pen — Codigo Penal
Cod Proc Civ y Com — Codigo Procesal Civil y Comercial de la Nacion
Cod Proc Pen — Codigo Procedimiento en Materia Penal de la Nacion
CODR — Coleccion de Obras y Documentos Relativos a la Historia Antigua y Moderna de las Provincias del Rio de la Plata
CODSBM — Centre de Recherches Oceanographiques [Abidjan]. Document Scientifique Provisoire
Coedwigwr Univ Col Wales — Coedwigwr. The Forester. Magazine. Forestry Society. University College of North Wales
Co Engl — College English
COEQD — CoEvolution Quarterly
Coeur Med I — Coeur et Medecine Interne
Coeur Med Interne — Coeur et Medecine Interne
Coeur Toxiques CR Reun Cent Poisons — Coeur et Toxiques. Compte-Rendu. Reunion des Centres de Poisons
Coevol Anim Plants Symp 5 Five Int Congr Syst Evol Biol — Coevolution of Animals and Plants. Symposium 5 (Five). International Congress of Systematic and Evolutionary Biology
CoEvolution Qly — CoEvolution Quarterly
CoEvolutn — CoEvolution Quarterly
CoEv Q — CoEvolution Quarterly
C of E Hist Soc J — Church of England Historical Society. Journal
Coffee Brew Inst Publ — Coffee Brewing Institute. Publication
Coffee Cacao J — Coffee and Cacao Journal
Coffee Res Found (Kenya) Annu Rep — Coffee Research Foundation (Kenya). Annual Report
Coffee Tea Ind Flavor Field — Coffee and Tea Industries and the Flavor Field
COFR — Commercial Fisheries Review [Later, Marine Fisheries Review]
Cog — Cognition
COGCA — Chemistry, Oil, and Gas in Romania
Cogenic Rep — Cogenic Report
COGLAC Newsl — COGLAC [Coal Gasification, Liquefaction, and Conversion to Electricity]Newsletter
Cognit Brain Res — Cognitive Brain Research
Cognit Defects Dev Ment Illness Proc Int Symp Kittay Sci Found — Cognitive Defects in the Development of Mental Illness. Proceedings. International Symposium. Kittay Scientific Foundation
Cognitive Psychol — Cognitive Psychology
Cognitive Sci Ser — Cognitive Science Series
Cognit Rehabil — Cognitive Rehabilitation
Cognit Sci — Cognitive Science
Cognit Ther Res — Cognitive Therapy and Research
Cog Psyc — Cognitive Psychology
Cog Psychol — Cognitive Psychology
CoGr — Courrier Graphique
COGYA — Clinical Obstetrics and Gynecology
COGYAK — Clinical Obstetrics and Gynecology
COH — Christelijk Oosten en Hereniging
COH — Commentary on Herodotus
COHAJ — Canadian Oral History Association. Journal/Societe Canadienne d'Histoire Orale.Journal
COHEB — Community Health (Bristol)
COHEBY — Community Health
Coherence Quantum Opt — Coherence and Quantum Optics
Coherent Technol Fiber Opt Syst — Coherent Technology in Fiber Optic Systems
COI — Coin Slot Location
Coil Coat Rev — Coil Coating Review
Coil Winding Int — Coil Winding International
COIMAS — Coimbra Medica
Coimbra — O Instituto, Jornal Scientifico e Litterario (Coimbra)
Coimbra Med — Coimbra Medica
Coimbra Med Rev Mens Med Cir — Coimbra Medica. Revista Mensal de Medicina e Cirurgia
Coimbra Univ Mus Lab Mineral Geol Mem Not — Coimbra. Universidade. Museu e Laboratorio Mineralogico e Geologico. Memorias eNoticias.
COIMDV — Comprehensive Immunology
COIMEW — Concepts in Immunopathology
Coin — Co-Incidences

COIN — Coordinated Occupational Information Network Database
COINAV — Colloques Internationaux. Centre National de la Recherche Scientifique
Coin Medal Bull — Seaby's Coin and Medal Bulletin
COIN Rep — COIN [*Communication and Information Technology*] Reports
Coin Rev — Coin Review
Coin W — Coin World
Coir Q J — Coir Quarterly Journal
COJ — Commodity Journal
COJOA — Colloid Journal of the USSR
Cojo Ilus — Cojo Ilustrado
COJPA8 — Colorado Journal of Pharmacy
COKCA — Coke and Chemistry USSR
Coke Chem R — Coke and Chemistry USSR
Coke Chem USSR — Coke and Chemistry USSR
Coke Chem USSR Engl Transl — Coke and Chemistry USSR (English Translation)
Coke Coal Chem Mon Energy Data Rep — Coke and Coal Chemicals Monthly. Energy Data Report
Coke Res Rep — Coke Research Report
Coke Smokeless Fuel Age — Coke and Smokeless-Fuel Age
COKRA — Coke Research Report
Col — Colloquium. Freien Universitaet
COL — Colorado Music Educator
COL — Cornell Linguistic Contributions
ColA — Coloquio Artes
COLAA — Coal Age
Col and Research Libs — College and Research Libraries
Col and Research Libs News — College and Research Libraries News
Col & Res Lib — College and Research Libraries
Col & Univ — College and University
Col & Univ Bsns — College and University Business
Col & Univ J — College and University Journal
Col Anthro — Colorado Anthropologist
ColBG — Collationes Brugenses et Gandavenses
ColBiQ — College of the Bible. Quarterly
Colburn — Colburn's New Monthly Magazine
Col Bus Rev — Colorado Business Review
Colby Lib Qtr — Colby Library Quarterly
Colby Libr — Colby Library. Quarterly
ColcFranc — Collectanea Franciscana
Colchester Archaeol Group Annu Bull — Colchester Archaeological Group. Annual Bulletin
ColCM — Colby College. Monographs
Col Comp & Comm — College Composition and Communication
ColctCist — Collectanea Cisterciensa
ColctTFujen — Collectanea Theologica Universitatis Fujen
ColctMech — Collectanea Mechlinensia
ColctT — Collectanea Theologica
Col Diplom Galicia Hist — Coleccion Diplomatica de Galicia Historica
Cold Reg Sci Technol — Cold Regions Science and Technology
Cold S Harb — Cold Spring Harbor Symposia on Quantitative Biology
Cold Spr Harb Symp — Cold Spring Harbor Symposia on Quantitative Biology
Cold Spring Harbor Conf Cell Proliferation — Cold Spring Harbor Conference on Cell Proliferation
Cold Spring Harbor Lab Banbury Cent Banbury Rep — Cold Spring Harbor Laboratory. Banbury Center. Banbury Report
Cold Spring Harbor Monogr Ser — Cold Spring Harbor Monograph Series
Cold Spring Harbor Rep Neurosci — Cold Spring Harbor Reports in the Neurosciences
Cold Spring Harbor Symp Quant Biol — Cold Spring Harbor Symposia on Quantitative Biology
Cold Spring Harbor Symp Quantit Biol — Cold Spring Harbor Symposia on Quantitative Biology
Cold Spring Harb Symp Quant Biol — Cold Spring Harbor Symposia on Quantitative Biology
Cold Storage Prod Rev — Cold Storage and Produce Review
Colec Agropec Inst Nac Tec Agropec (Argentina) — Coleccion Agropecuaria. Instituto Nacional de Tecnologia Agropecuaria (Argentina)
Colec Al Andalus — Coleccion Al-Andalus
Colecao — Colecao das Leis
Colecc Diario Navarra — Coleccion Diario de Navarra
Colec Cienc Fisico Quim Mat — Colecciones Ciencias Fisico-Quimicas y Matematicas
Coleccion Estud CIEPLAN — Coleccion Estudios CIEPLAN
Colecc Monogr Org Int Energ At — Coleccion de Monografias. Organismo Internacional de Energia Atomica
Colecc Textos Agron Vet — Coleccion de Textos de Agronomia y Veterinaria
Colec Enrique Perez Arbelaez — Coleccion Enrique Perez Arbelaez
Colec Estadist — Coleccion Estadistica
Colec Monograf — Coleccion Monografias
Colec Monograf Mem Mat — Coleccion de Monografias y Memorias de Matematicas
Colec Montano — Coleccion Montano
ColeF — Còllege et Famille
ColeFranc — Collectanea Franciscana
Colegio Bibl Col Medellin — Colegio de Bibliotecarios Colombianos (Medellin, Colombia)
Colegio De Abogados Buenos Aires R — Colegio de Abogados de Buenos Aires. Revista
ColEng — College English
Coleopt Bull — Coleopterists' Bulletin
Coleopts Bull — Coleopterists' Bulletin
ColeT — Collectanea Theologica
Coletanea Inst Tecnol Aliment — Coletanea. Instituto de Tecnologia de Alimentos
Colet Inst Tecnol Alim — Coletanea. Instituto Tecnologia de Alimentos
Colet Inst Tecnol Aliment — Coletanea. Instituto Tecnologia de Alimentos

Colet Inst Tecnol Aliment Campinas Braz — Coletanea do Instituto de Tecnologia de Alimentos (Campinas, Brazil)
ColetMech — Collectanea Mechlinensia
COLF — Chefs-d'Oeuvre de la Litterature Francaise
ColF — Columbia Forum
Colfarit Symp — Colfarit-Symposion
Col Farm — Colegio Farmaceutico
ColG — Collationes Gandavenses
ColGer — Colloquia Germanica
Col Hist Soc Mono Ser — Colorado Historical Society. Monograph Series
Col Hist Soc Rec — Columbia Historical Society. Records
Col Hum RL Rev — Columbia Human Rights Law Review
Col Hu Ri LR — Columbia Human Rights Law Review
CoLi — Comparative Literature
Col Interam Defensa R — Colegio Interamericano de Defensa Revista
Co LJ — Cochin Law Journal
Co LJ — Colonial Law Journal
Col J Environ L — Columbia Journal of Environmental Law
Col J Env L — Columbia Journal of Environmental Law
Col J L and Soc Prob — Columbia Journal of Law and Social Problems
Col JL & Soc Probl — Columbia Journal of Law and Social Problems
Col Jour Rev — Columbia Journalism Review
ColJR — Columbia Journalism Review
Col J Transnat'l L — Columbia Journal of Transnational Law
Col J Tr L — Columbia Journal of Transnational Law
Col J World Bus — Columbia Journal of World Business
Coll — Collegium
Col(L) — Coloquio (Lisbon)
Collab Int Pestic Anal Counc Monogr — Collaborative International Pesticides Analytical Council. Monograph
Collab Proc Ser Int Inst Appl Syst Anal — Collaborative Proceedings Series. International Institute for Applied Systems Analysis
Collage Mag — Collage Magazine
Collagen Relat Res — Collagen and Related Research
Collagen Relat Res — Collagen and Related Research. Clinical and Experimental
Coll Aggiorn Cult Mat — Collana di Aggiornamento e Cultura Matematica
Coll Agric (Nagpur) Mag — College of Agriculture (Nagpur). Magazine
Coll Agric Nat Taiwan Univ Spec Publ — College of Agriculture. National Taiwan University. Special Publication
Coll Agric Res Cent Wash State Univ Circ — College of Agriculture Research Center. Washington State University. Circular
Coll Agric Univ Tehran Bull — College of Agriculture. University of Tehran. Bulletin
Coll A J — College Art Journal
Coll Alex — Collectanea Alexandrina. Reliquiae Minores Poetarum Graecorum Aetatis Ptolemaicae 323-146 A.C. Epicorum, Elegiacorum, Lyricorum, Ethicorum
Coll Amis Hist — Collection. Amis de l'Histoire
Coll Am Pathol Aspen Conf Diagn Immunol — College of American Pathologists. Aspen Conference on Diagnostic Immunology
Coll Am Statis Assn — Collections. American Statistical Association
Collana Accad Accad Patav Sci Lett Arti — Collana Accademica. Accademia Patavina di Scienze, Lettere, ed Arti
Collana Atti Congr — Collana Atti di Congressi
Collana Monogr Ateneo Parmense — Collana di Monografie. Ateneo Parmense
Collana Monogr Oli Essenz Sui Deri Agrum — Collana di Monografie sugli Oli Essenziali e Sui Derivati Agrumari
Collana Monogr Rass Med Sarda — Collana di Monografie di Rassegna Medica Sarda
Collana Monogr Vet Ital — Collana di Monografie di Veterinaria Italiana
Collana Verde Minist Agric For (Roma) — Collana Verde. Ministero dell'Agricoltura e della Foreste (Roma)
Coll & Res Lib — College and Research Libraries
Coll & Res Lib N — College and Research Libraries News
Coll & Univ — College and University
Coll & Univ Bus — College and University Business
Coll & Univ J — College and University Journal
Coll Antropol — Collegium Antropologicum
Coll Art J — College Art Journal
ColLat — Collection Latomus
Col Law Rev — Columbia Law Review
Col Law Review — Columbia Law Review
Coll Bd R — College Board Review
CollBrugGand — Collationes Brugenses et Gandavenses
Coll CC — Collyer's Chancery Cases Tempore Bruce, V-C
Coll Cist — Collectanea Cisterciensia
Coll Comp & Comm — College Composition and Communication
Coll Composition & Commun — College Composition and Communication
Coll Courant — College Courant
Collct Franciscana — Collectanea Franciscana
Collct Ordinis Cisterc Reformatorum — Collectanea Ordinis Cisterciensium Reformatorum
Coll Czech — Collection of Czechoslovak Chemical Communications
Coll Czech Chem Communications — Collection of Czechoslovak Chemical Communications
Coll d Aut Franc — Collection d'Auteurs Francais
Coll d'Ecologie — Collection d'Ecologie
Coll de la Soc de l Hist de France — Collection de la Societe de l'Histoire de France
Coll de la Soc de l Histoire de France — Collection de la Societe de l'Histoire de France
Coll des Class Populaires — Collection des Classiques Populaires
Coll de Tourisme Litt et Histor — Collection de Tourisme Litteraire et Historique
Coll de Trav — Collection de Travaux. Academie Internationale d'Histoire des Sciences
Coll Dir Etudes Rech Elec France — Collection. Direction des Etudes et Recherches d'Electricite de France

Coll Dir Etudes Rech Elect France ESE — Collection de la Direction des Etudes et Recherches d'Electricite de France ESE

CollE — College English

Collec Czechosl Chem Commun — Collection of Czechoslovak Chemical Communications

Coll Ecole Norm Sup Jeunes Filles — Collection. Ecole Normale Superieure de Jeunes Filles

Collect Acad Pt Etrangere — Colletion Academique. Composee des Memoires, Actes, ou Journaux des Plus Celebres Academies and Societes Litteraires. Partie Etrangere

Collect Alea Saclay Monogr Texts Statist Phys — Collection Alea-Saclay. Monographs and Texts in Statistical Physics

Collect Artic Int Soil Sci Congr — Collection of Articles to the International Soil Scientists Congress

Collect Biol Evol — Collection de Biologie Evolutive

Collect Biol Mol — Collection de Biologie Moleculaire

Collect Blain Faye Martin — Collection Blain Faye Martin

Collect Bot (Barc) — Collectanea Botanica (Barcelona)

Collect Breed — Collecting and Breeding

Collect Chaire Aisenstadt — Collection de la Chaire Aisenstadt

Collect Colloq Semin Inst Fr Pet — Collection. Colloques et Seminaires. Institut Francais du Petrole

Collect Commissariat Energ Atom Ser Sci — Collection du Commissariat a l'Energie Atomique. Serie Scientifique

Collect Czech Chem Commun — Collection of Czechoslovak Chemical Communications

Collect Czechoslovak Chem Commun — Collection of Czechoslovak Chemical Communications

Collect Didact — Collection Didactique

Collect Dir Etudes Rech Elec France — Collection. Direction des Etudes et Recherches d'Electricite de France

Collect Dunod Inform — Collection Dunod Informatique

Collecteanea Francisc — Collecteanea Franciscana

Collect Ec Fr Rome — Collection. Ecole Francaise de Rome

Collect Ecole Norm Sup Jeunes Filles — Collection. Ecole Normale Superieure de Jeunes Filles

Collect Ecologie — Collection d'Ecologie

Collect Econom Statist Av — Collection Economie et Statistiques Avancees

Collected Studies Ser — Collected Studies Series

Collect Eff Condens Media Winter Sch Theor Phys — Collective Effects in Condensed Media. Winter School of Theoretical Physics

Collect Enseignement Sci — Collection Enseignement des Sciences

Collect Episteme — Collection Episteme

Collect Grands Probl Biol Monogr — Collection "Les Grands Problemes de la Biologie." Monographie

Collect Improv Husb Trade — Collection for Improvement of Husbandry and Trade

Collect Invited Pap Int Conf Phenom Ioniz Gases — Collection of Invited Papers Presented at the International Conference on Phenomena in Ionized Gases

Collective Bargaining Negot & Cont BNA — Collective Bargaining, Negotiations, and Contracts. Bureau of NationalAffairs

Collect Lang Algorithmes Inform — Collection Langages et Algorithmes de l'Informatique

Collect Lect Int Symp Furan Chem — Collection of Lectures. International Symposium of Furan Chemistry

Collect Maitrise Math Pures — Collection Maitrise de Mathematiques Pures

Collect Major — Collection Major

Collect Math — Collectanea Mathematica

Collect Math Appl Maitrise — Collection Mathematiques Appliquees pour la Maitrise

Collect Med Leg Toxicol Med — Collection de Medecine Legale et de Toxicologie Medicale

Collect Methodes — Collection Methodes

Collect Methods Accel Pap Int Conf — Collective Methods of Acceleration. Papers Presented. International Conference on Collective Methods of Acceleration

Collect Monogr Agence Int Energ At — Collection Monographies. Agence Internationale de l'Energie Atomique

Collect Monogr Bot Biol Veg — Collection de Monographies de Botanique et de Biologie Vegetale

Collect Notes Internes Dir Etud Rech Electr Fr — Collection de Notes Internes. Direction des Etudes et Recherches. Electricite de France

Collect Pap Annu Conf Glass Probl — Collected Papers. Annual Conference on Glass Problems

Collect Pap Annu Symp Fundam Cancer Res — Collection of Papers Presented at the Annual Symposium on Fundamental Cancer Research

Collect Pap Changchun Inst Appl Chem Acad Sin — Collected Papers. Changchun Institute of Applied Chemistry. Academia Sinica

Collect Pap Earth Sci Nagoya Univ Dep Earth Sci — Collected Papers on Earth Sciences. Nagoya University. Department of Earth Sciences

Collect Papers Lister Inst Prevent Med — Collected Papers. Lister Institute of Preventive Medicine

Collect Papers Math Soc Wakayama Univ — Collected Papers. Mathematical Society. Wakayama University

Collect Papers School Hyg and Pub Health Johns Hopkins Univ — Collected Papers. School of Hygiene and Public Health. Johns Hopkins University

Collect Pap Fac Sci Osaka Imp Univ Ser A — Collected Papers. Faculty of Science. Osaka Imperial University. Series A. Mathematics

Collect Pap Fac Sci Osaka Imp Univ Ser B — Collected Papers. Faculty of Science. Osaka Imperial University. Series B. Physics

Collect Pap Fac Sci Osaka Imp Univ Ser C — Collected Papers. Faculty of Science. Osaka Imperial University. Series C. Chemistry

Collect Pap Fac Sci Osaka Univ Ser B — Collected Papers. Faculty of Science. Osaka University. Series B. Physics

Collect Pap Fac Sci Osaka Univ Ser C — Collected Papers. Faculty of Science. Osaka University. Series C. Chemistry

Collect Pap Inst Appl Chem Acad Sin — Collected Papers. Institute of Applied Chemistry. Academia Sinica

Collect Pap Inst Appl Chem Chin Acad Sci — Collected Papers. Institute of Applied Chemistry. Chinese Academy of Sciences

Collect Pap Inst Chem Acad Sin — Collected Papers. Institute of Chemistry. Academia Sinica

Collect Pap Inst Miner Raw Mater Kutna Hora — Collected Papers. Institute of Mineral Raw Materials in Kutna Hora

Collect Pap Int Conf Electron Prop Two Dimens Syst — Collection of Papers. International Conference on Electronic Properties of Two-Dimensional Systems

Collect Pap Int Congr Glass — Collected Papers. International Congress on Glass

Collect Pap Inter Am Conf Toxicol Occup Med — Collection of Papers Presented at Inter-American Conferences on Toxicology and Occupational Medicine

Collect Pap Int Symp Anim Toxins — Collection of Papers Presented. International Symposium on Animal Toxins

Collect Pap Int Symp Mol Beam Epitaxy Relat Clean Surf Tech — Collected Papers of International Symposium on Molecular Beam Epitaxy and Related Clean Surface Techniques

Collect Pap Jpn Soc Civ Eng — Collected Papers. Japan Society of Civil Engineers

Collect Pap Macaulay Inst Soil Res — Collected Papers. Macaulay Institute for Soil Research

Collect Pap Mayo Clin Mayo Found — Collected Papers. Mayo Clinic and Mayo Foundation

Collect Pap Med Mayo Clin Mayo Found — Collected Papers in Medicine. Mayo Clinic and Mayo Foundation

Collect Pap Med Res Lab Parke Davis Co — Collected Papers from the Medical Research Laboratory of Parke, Davis and Company

Collect Pap Med Sci Fukuoka Univ — Collected Papers on Medical Science. Fukuoka University

Collect Pap Res Lab Parke Davis Co — Collected Papers. Research Laboratory of Parke, Davis & Company

Collect Pap Surg Mayo Clin Mayo Found — Collected Papers in Surgery. Mayo Clinic and Mayo Foundation

Collect Pap Symp At Interact Space Phys — Collection of Papers Presented. Symposium on Atomic Interactions and Space Physics

Collect Pap Technol Sci Fukuoka Univ — Collected Papers on Technological Sciences. Fukuoka University

Collect Pharm Suec — Collectanea Pharmaceutica Suecica

Collect Phenom — Collective Phenomena

Collect Points Ser Sci — Collection Points. Serie Sciences

Collect Prop Phys Syst Proc Nobel Symp — Collective Properties of Physical Systems. Proceedings. Nobel Symposium

Collect Regards Sci — Collection Regards sur la Science

Collect Rem Bot Spectantia Zurich — Collectanea ad Omnem Rem Botanicam Spectantia (Zurich)

Collect Rep Nat Sci Fac Palacky Univ (Olomouc) — Collected Reports. Natural Science Faculty. Palacky University (Olomouc)

Collect Res Works Pap Pulp Ind — Collection of Research Works from the Paper and Pulp Industry

Collect Reuse Waste Oils Proc Eur Congr Waste Oils — Collection and Reuse of Waste Oils. Proceedings. European Congress on Waste Oils

Collect Ryukyu Forest Exp Sta — Collections. Ryukyu Forestry Experiment Station/Ryukyu Ringyo Shikenjo Shuho

Collect Sci Commun Charles Univ Fac Med Hradec Kralove — Collection of Scientific Communications. Charles University. Faculty of Medicine. Hradec Kralove

Collect Sci Hist — Collection Sciences dans l'Histoire

Collect Sci Pap Commem 20th Anniv Found Shizuoka Coll Pharm — Collection of Scientific Papers Commemorating the 20th Anniversary of the Foundation of the Shizuoka College of Pharmacy

Collect Sci Pap Econ Agric Univ (Ceske Budejovice) Biol Part — Collection of Scientific Papers. Economic Agricultural University (Ceske Budejovice). Biological Part

Collect Sci Tech Pet — Collection Science et Technique du Petrole

Collect Sci Works Charles Univ Fac Med Hradec Kralove — Collection of Scientific Works. Charles University Faculty of Medicine in Hradec Kralove

Collect Sci Works Est Res Inst Anim Breed Vet Sci — Collection of Scientific Works. Estonian Research Institute of Animal Breeding and Veterinary

Collect Sci Works Fac Med Charles Univ (Hradec Kralove) — Collection of Scientific Works. Faculty of Medicine. Charles University (Hadec Kralove)

Collect Soc Fr Tuber Mal Respir — Collection. Societe Francaise de la Tuberculose et des Maladies Respiratoires

Collect Struct Mater Compos — Collection Structures et Materiaux Composites

Collect Studies Ser — Collected Studies Series

Collect Tech Av Inform — Collection Techniques Avancees de l'Informatique

Collect Tech Pap AIAA/ASME/SAE Struct Dyn Mater Conf — Collection of Technical Papers. AIAA/ASME/SAE Structural Dynamics and Materials Conference

Collect Tech Pap AIAA ASME SAE Struct Struct Dyn Mater Conf — Collection of Technical Papers. AIAA/ASME/SAE Structures, Structural Dynamics, and Materials Conference

Collect Tech Pap AIAA ASME Struct Struct Dyn Mater Conf — Collection of Technical Papers. AIAA/ASME Structures, Structural Dynamics, and Materials Conference

Collect Tech Sci Telecomm — Collection Technique et Scientifique des Telecommunications

Collect Theses Kwang Woon Inst Technol — Collection of Theses. Kwang Woon Institute of Technology

Collect Trav Acad Int Hist Sci — Collection des Travaux. Academie Internationale d'Histoire des Sciences

Collect Travaux Acad Internat Hist Sci — Collection des Travaux. Academie Internationale d'Histoire des Sciences

Collect Trav Chim Tchec — Collection des Travaux Chimiques de Tchecoslovaquie

Collect Trav Chim Tcheques — Collection des Travaux Chimiques Tcheques
Collect Trav Univ Brazzaville — Collection des Travaux. Universite de Brazzaville
Collect Treatises Fac Hum Univ Fukuoka — Collection of Treatises Published by the Faculty of Humanity. University of Fukuoka
Collect Tschech Chem Forschungsarb — Collection Tschechischer Chemischer Forschungsarbeiten
Collect Univ France — Collection des Universites de France
Collect Works Cardio-Pulm Dis — Collected Works on Cardio-Pulmonary Disease
College Can — College Canada
College L Dig Natl Assn College & Univ Attys — College Law Digest. National Association of College and UniversityAttorneys
College Math J — College Mathematics Journal
College M Symposium — College Music Symposium
College Mus — College Music Symposium
College Park Colloq Chem Evol Proc — College Park Colloquium on Chemical Evolution. Proceedings
Coll Eng — College English
Coll Engl — College English
Coll Enseignement Sci — Collection Enseignement des Sciences
Coll Fr — Collectionneur Francais
Coll Fran — Collectanea Franciscana
Coll G — Colloquia Germanica
Coll Hawaii Publ Bull — College of Hawaii Publications. Bulletins
Coll Hist des Grands Philosophes — Collection Historique des Grands Philosophes
Coll Hist Inst Et Slav — Collection Historique de l'Institut d'Etudes Slaves
Coll Histor — Collection Historique
Coll Hist Sci — Collection d'Histoire des Sciences
Collier Bankr — Collier's Law of Bankruptcy
Collier Bankr Cas 2d MB — Collier Bankruptcy Cases. Second Series. Matthew Bender
Collier's — Collier's National Weekly
Collier's Yrbk — Collier's Encyclopedia Yearbook
Colliery Eng — Colliery Engineering
Colliery Eng (London) — Colliery Engineering (London)
Colliery Eng Met Monir — Colliery Engineer and Metal Monitor
Colliery Eng (Scranton PA) — Colliery Engineer (Scranton, Pennsylvania)
Colliery Eng Suppl — Colliery Engineering. Supplement
Colliery Guard — Colliery Guardian
Colliery Guardian J Coal Iron Trades — Colliery Guardian and Journal of the Coal and Iron Trades
Colliery Guardian J Coal Iron Trades Suppl — Colliery Guardian and Journal. Coal and Iron Trades. Supplement
Coll Int Neuro Psychopharmacol — Collegium Internationale Neuro-Psychopharmacologicum
Coll Int Neuro Psychopharmacol Congr — Collegium Internationale Neuro-Psychopharmacologicum. Congress
Coll Int Neuro Psychopharmacol Proc Congr — Collegium Internationale Neuro-Psychopharmacologicum. Proceedings. Congress
Collisions Half Collisions Lasers Tavola Rotonda — Collisions and Half-Collisions with Lasers. Tavola Rotonda
Collision Spectrosc — Collision Spectroscopy
Col Lit — College Literature
Col LJ — Colonial Law Journal
Col LJNZ — Colonial Law Journal (New Zealand)
Coll L — College Literature
Coll Latomus — Collection Latomus
Coll Lit — College Literature
Coll Logicum Ann Kurt Goedel Soc — Collegium Logicum. Annals of the Kurt-Goedel Society
CollM — Collegiate Microcomputer
Coll Manage — Collection Management
Coll Mass Hist Soc — Collections. Massachusetts Historical Society
Coll Mat — Collana di Matematica
Coll Math — Colloquium Mathematicum
CollMech — Collectanea Mechlinensia
Coll Med Ann (Mosul) — College of Medicine. Annals (Mosul)
Coll Media Dir Newsl — College Media Director Newsletter
Coll Mgt — College Management
Coll Music — College Music Symposium
Coll Musician — College Musician
Coll N & V — Collegiate News and Views
Colln Czech Chem Commun — Collection of Czechoslovak Chemical Communications
Colln Etud Mus Vie Wallonne — Collection d'Etudes Publiee par le Musee de la Vie Wallonne
Coll News — College News
Collns INSEE Ser C — Collections. Institut National de la Statistique et des Etudes Economiques. Serie C. Comptes et Planification
Collns INSEE Ser D — Collections. Institut National de la Statistique et des Etudes Economiques. Serie D. Demographie et Emploi
Collns INSEE Ser E — Collections. Institut National de la Statistique et des Etudes Economiques. Serie E. Entreprises
Collns INSEE Ser M — Collections. Institut National de la Statistique et des Etudes Economiques. Serie M. Menages
Collns INSEE Ser R — Collections. Institut National de la Statistique et des Etudes Economiques. Serie R. Regions
Colloidal Surf Act Agents — Colloidal Surface-Active Agents
Colloid Chem — Colloid Chemistry
Colloides Biol Clin Ther — Colloides en Biologie. Clinique et Therapeutique
Colloid Interface Sci Pro Int Conf — Colloid and Interface Science. Proceedings of the International Conference on Colloids and Surfaces
Colloid J — Colloid Journal of the USSR

Colloid J Transl of Kolloidn Zh — Colloid Journal (Translation of Kolloidnyi Zhurnal)
Colloid J USSR — Colloid Journal of the USSR
Colloid J USSR Engl Transl — Colloid Journal. USSR. English Translation
Colloid Polymer Sci — Colloid and Polymer Science
Colloid Polym Sci — Colloid and Polymer Science
Colloid Polym Sci Suppl — Colloid and Polymer Science. Supplement
Colloid P S — Colloid and Polymer Science
Colloids and Surf — Colloids and Surfaces
Colloid Sci — Colloid Science
Colloids Surf — Colloids and Surfaces
Colloids Surf B Biointerfaces — Colloids and Surfaces B. Biointerfaces
Colloids Surf Physicochem Eng Aspects — Colloids and Surfaces A. Physicochemical and Engineering Aspects
Colloid Surf Sci Symp — Colloid Surface Science Symposium
Colloid Symp Annu — Colloid Symposium Annual
Colloid Symp Monogr — Colloid Symposium Monograph
Colloq Amino Acid Anal — Colloquium on Amino Acid Analysis
Colloq Appl Fabr Technol Plast — Colloquium on Application and Fabrication Technology of Plastics
Colloq Art — Colloquies on Art and Archaeology in Asia
Colloq Atomspektrom Spurenanal — Colloquium Atomspektrometrische Spurenanalytik
Colloq Biol Saclay — Colloque de Biologie de Saclay
Colloq Biol Sci — Colloquium in Biological Sciences
Colloq Biol Sci Blood Brain Transfer — Colloquium in Biological Sciences. Blood-Brain Transfer
Colloq Biol Sci Cell Signal Transduction — Colloquium in Biological Sciences. Cellular Signal Transduction
Colloq Biosynth Aromat Compd — Colloquium. Biosynthesis of Aromatic Compounds
Colloq Club Jules Gonin — Colloque. Club "Jules Gonin"
Colloq Conserv Probl Antarct Proc — Colloquium on Conservation Problems in Antarctica. Proceedings
Colloq Dtsch Ges Physiol Chem — Colloquium der Deutschen Gesellschaft fuer Physiologische Chemie
Colloq Electron Filters — Colloquium on Electronic Filters
Colloq Electroplat — Colloquium on Electroplating
Colloq Endocrinol Rapp — Colloque d'Endocrinologie. Rapports
Colloq For Fert — Colloquium on Forest Fertilization
Colloq Geol Aegean Reg Proc — Colloquium on the Geology of the Aegean Region. Proceedings
Colloq Ger — Colloquia Germanica
Colloq Ges Biol Chem — Colloquium der Gesellschaft fuer Biologische Chemie
Colloq Ges Biol Chem Mosbach — Colloquium. Gesellschaft fuer Biologische Chemie in Mosbach
Colloq Ges Physiol Chem — Colloquium. Gesellschaft fuer Physiologische Chemie
Colloq Group Av Biochim Mar GABIM — Colloque. Groupement pour l'Avancement de la Biochimie Marine (GABIM)
Colloq Inf Chim CR — Colloque sur l'Information en Chimie. Compte Rendu
Colloq INRA — Colloques de l'INRA (Institut National de la Recherche Agronomique)
Colloq INSERM (Inst Natl Sante Rech Med) — Colloque. INSERM (Institut National de la Sante et de la Recherche Medicale)
Colloq Inst Natl Rech Agron — Colloques. Institut National de la Recherche Agronomique
Colloq Inst Natl Sante Rech Med — Colloque. Institut National de la Sante et de la Recherche Medicale
Colloq Int Appl Sci Tech Vide Revetements Etats Surf — Colloque International sur les Applications des Sciences et Techniques du Vide aux Revetements et Etats de Surface
Colloq Int Astrophys — Colloque International d'Astrophysique
Colloq Int Astrophys Commun — Colloque International d'Astrophysique. Communications
Colloq Int Bacteriol Mar — Colloque International de Bacteriologie Marine
Colloq Int Berthelot Vieille Mallard Le Chatelier Actes — Colloque International Berthelot-Vieille-Mallard-Le Chatelier. Actes
Colloq Int Biol Saclay — Colloque International de Biologie de Saclay
Colloq Int Blennorragie — Colloque International sur la Blennorragie. Comptes Rendus
Colloq Int Blennorragie CR — Colloque International sur la Blennorragie. Comptes Rendus
Colloq Int Cent Natl Rech Sci — Colloques Internationaux. Centre National de la Recherche Scientifique
Colloq Int Chim Cafes C R — Colloque International sur la Chimie des Cafes. Comptes Rendus
Colloq Int CNRS — Colloques Internationaux. Centre National de la Recherche Scientifique
Colloq Int Electr Sol — Colloque International sur l'Electricite Solaire. Comptes Rendus
Colloq Int Electr Sol CR — Colloque International sur l'Electricite Solaire. Comptes Rendus
Colloq Internat CNRS — Colloques Internationaux. Centre National de la Recherche Scientifique
Colloq Int Essais Bitumes Mater Bitum — Colloque International Consacre aux Essais sur Bitumes et Materiaux Bitumineux
Colloq Int Mater Granulaires CR — Colloque International sur les Materiaux Granulaires. Comptes Rendus
Colloq Int Methodes Anal Rayonnem X CR — Colloque International sur les Methodes Analytiques par Rayonnement X. ComptesRendus
Colloq Int Photogr Corpusc — Colloque International de Photographie Corpusculaire
Colloq Int Phys Chim Surf — Colloque International de Physique et Chimie des Surfaces

Colloq Int Plant Aromat Med Maroc — Colloque International sur les Plantes Aromatiques et Medicinales du Maroc

Colloq Int Potash Inst — Colloquium. International Potash Institute

Colloq Int Potash Inst Proc — Colloquium. International Potash Institute. Proceedings

Colloq Int Prev Risques Mal Prof Ind Chim CR — Collque International sur la Prevention des Risques et des Maladies Professionnelles dans l'Industrie Chimique. Compte Rendu

Colloq Int Prev Trait Toxicomanies Conf — Colloque International sur la Prevention et le Traitement des Toxicomanies. Conferences

Colloq Int Probl Biochim Lipides — Colloque International sur les Problemes Biochimiques des Lipides

Colloq Int Propr Util Struct MIS CR — Colloque International sur les Proprietes et l'Utilisation des Structures MIS. Comptes Rendus

Colloq Int Pulverisation Cathod Ses Appl — Colloque International sur la Pulverisation Cathodique et ses Applications

Colloq Int Refract — Colloque International sur les Refractaires

Colloq Int Soudage Fusion Faisceau Electrons — Colloque International. Soudage et Fusion par Faisceau d'Electrons

Colloq Int Spectrochim CR — Colloque International de Spectrochimie. Comptes Rendus

Colloq Int Spettrochim Rend — Colloquio Internazionale di Spettrochimica. Rendiconti

Colloq Int Technol — Colloque International de Technologie

Colloq Low Level Counting — Colloquy on Low-Level Counting

Colloq Mater Energy Conserv Powder Metall Rep Pap — Colloquium on Material and Energy Conservation in Powder Metallurgy. Reports and Papers

Colloq Math — Colloquium Mathematicum

Colloq Math Soc Janos Bolyai — Colloquia Mathematica. Societatis Janos Bolyai

Colloq Med Nucl Lang Fr — Colloque de Medecine Nucleaire de Langue Francaise

Colloq Metall — Colloque de Metallurgie

Colloq Metall Saclay — Colloque de Metallurgie de Saclay

Colloq Myoglobin — Colloquium on Myoglobin

Colloq Nationaux CNRS — Colloques Nationaux du Centre National de la Recherche Scientifique

Colloq Nationaux CNRS Chim Hautes Temp — Colloques Nationaux du Centre National de la Recherche Scientifique. Chimie desHautes Temperatures

Colloq Nationaux CNRS Colloq Natl Phys Theor — Colloques Nationaux du Centre National de la Recherche Scientifique. Colloque National de Physique Theorique

Colloq Nationaux CNRS Comportement Homeothermes Stimulus Froid — Colloques Nationaux du Centre National de la Recherche Scientifique. Comportement des Homeothermes vis-a-vis du Stimulus Froid

Colloq Nationaux CNRS Struct Chim Proteines — Colloques Nationaux du Centre National de la Recherche Scientifique. Structure Chimique des Proteines

Colloq Natl Hyg Environ Collect CR — Colloque National d'Hygiene de l'Environnement et des Collectivites. Comptes Rendus

Colloq Natl Inf Chim CNIC — Colloque National sur l'Information en Chimie CNIC

Colloq Pedobiologiae — Colloquium Pedobiologiae

Colloq Pflanzenphysiol Humboldt Univ Berlin — Colloquia Pflanzenphysiologie. Humboldt-Universitaet zu Berlin

Colloq Phys — Colloque de Physique

Colloq Phytosociol — Colloques Phytosociologiques

Colloq Pollut Prot Eaux Reg Rhone Alpes CR — Colloque sur la Pollution et la Protection des Eaux de la Region Rhone-Alpes. Comptes Rendus

Colloq Procede Conf Int Met Lourds Environ — Colloque Procede. Conference Internationale sur les Metaux Lourds dans l'Environnement

Colloq Proc Potassium Inst — Colloquium Proceedings. Potassium Institute

Colloq Prot Reg Eaux Souterr Journ Tech Com Natl Fr AIH — Colloque la Protection Regionale des Eaux Souterraines. Journee Technique du Comite National Francais de l'AIH

Colloq Rupture Mater CR — Colloque sur la Rupture des Materiaux. Comptes Rendus

Colloq Sci Fac Med Univ Carol Congr Morphol Symp Pap — Colloquium Scientificum Facultatis Medicae Universitatis Carolinae et Congressus Morphologicus Symposia. Papers

Colloq Sci Int Cafe — Colloque Scientifique International sur le Cafe

Colloq Sci Int Cafe CR — Colloque Scientifique International sur le Cafe. Comptes Rendus

Colloq Soc Catalana Biol — Colloquis. Societat Catalana de Biologia

Colloq Soc Fr Microbiol — Colloque. Societe Francaise de Microbiologie

Colloq Soc Fr Microbiol Sect Microbiol Ind Biotechnol — Colloque. Societe Francaise de Microbiologie. Section de Microbiologie Industrielle et de Biotechnologie

Colloq Sodalizio — Colloqui del Sodalizio

Colloq Spectro Int Pro — Colloquium Spectroscopicum Internationale. Proceedings

Colloq Spectrosc Int Acta — Colloquium Spectroscopicum Internationale. Acta

Colloq Spectrosc Int CR — Colloquium Spectroscopicum Internationale. Comptes Rendus

Colloq Spectrosc Int Gesamtausg Vortr Ref — Colloquium Spectroscopicum Internationale. Gesamtausgabe der Vortraege und Referate

Colloq Spectrosc Int Keynote Lect — Colloquium Spectroscopicum Internationale. Keynote Lectures

Colloq Spectrosc Int Plenary Lect Rep — Colloquium Spectroscopicum Internationale. Plenary Lectures and Reports

Colloq St Jans Hosp Bruges Belg — Colloquium St. Jans Hospital. Bruges, Belgium

Colloq Tech Appl Plast Their Process Technol — Colloquium on Technical Application of Plastics and Their Processing Technologies

Colloq Top Quest Biochem Proc Int Congr Biochem — Colloquia on Topical Questions in Biochemistry. Proceedings. International Congress of Biochemistry

Colloques Int Cent Natn Rech Scient — Colloques Internationaux. Centre National de la Recherche Scientifique

Colloques Internat CNRS — Colloques Internationaux. Centre National de la Recherche Scientifique

Colloques Int Path Insectes — Colloques Internationaux de la Pathologie des Insectes

Colloques Nat CNRS — Colloques Nationaux. Centre National de la Recherche Scientifique

Colloqui Sod — Colloqui del Sodalizio

Colloquiumsber Inst Gerbereichem Tech Hochsch (Darmstadt) — Colloquiumsberichte. Instituts fuer Gerbereichemie. Technischen Hochschule (Darmstadt)

Colloq Use Iodinated Density Gradient Media Biol Sep — Colloquium on Use of Iodinated Density-Gradient Media for Biological Separations

Colloq Weyl — Colloque Weyl

Coll Phil — Collection Philosophica

Coll Physicians Philadelphia Trans Stud — College of Physicians of Philadelphia. Transactions and Studies

Coll Phys Surg Ont Int Rep — College of Physicians and Surgeons of Ontario. Interim Report

Coll Plasma Phys — College on Plasma Physics

Coll Polym Sci — Colloid and Polymer Science

Coll Press — College Press Service

Coll Programmation Rech Oper Appl — Collection. Programmation Recherche Operationnelle Appliquee

Col LR — Columbia Law Review

Coll Rech Interdiscip — Collection Recherches Interdisciplinaires

Coll Relat Res — Collagen and Related Research

Coll Res Li — College and Research Libraries

Coll Res Libr — College and Research Libraries

Col L Rev — Columbia Law Review

Coll Sci Mat — Collana di Scienze Matematiche

Coll Sci Philos Arabes — Collection Sciences et Philosophie Arabes

Coll Statist Agric Et — Collections de Statistique Agricole. Etudes

Coll Studi — Collana di Studi

Coll Stud J — College Student Journal

Coll Stud Pers Abstr — College Student Personnel Abstracts

Coll Surfaces — Colloids and Surfaces

CollT — College Teaching

Coll Travaux Acad Internat Hist Sci — Collection des Travaux. Academie Internationale d'Histoire des Sciences

Coll Trop Agric Misc Publ Univ Hawaii — College of Tropical Agriculture. Miscellaneous Publication. University of Hawaii

Coll UNESCO Oeuvres Represent Ser Persane — Collection UNESCO D'Oeuvres Representatives Serie Persane

Coll Vet — Collegium Veterinarium

Coll Works Cardio-Pulm Dis — Collected Works on Cardio-Pulmonary Disease

ColM — Colorado Magazine

COLMA9 — Colorado Medicine

Colmar S H Nt BII — Bulletin de la Societe d'Histoire Naturelle de Colmar

ColMech — Collectanea Mechlinensia

Col Med — Colegio Medico

Col Med Vida Med — Colegio Medico Vida Medica

Colmena Univ — Colmena Universitaria

Colmen Esp — Colmenero Espanol

Col Mgt — College Management

Col Monograf Mem Mat — Coleccion de Monografias y Memorias de Matematicas

CoIN — Colonial Newsletter

Col Nac Mem — Memoria. El Colegio Nacional

COLO — Colorado Business Magazine

Colo — Colorado Reports

Colo A&M News — Colorado A&M News

Colo Ag Exp — Colorado. Agricultural Experiment Station. Publications

Colo Agric Exp Stn Annu Rep — Colorado. Agricultural Experiment Station. Annual Report

Colo Agric Exp Stn Bull — Colorado. Agricultural Experiment Station. Bulletin

Colo Agric Exp Stn Pop Bull — Colorado. Agricultural Experiment Station. Popular Bulletin

Colo Agric Exp Stn Tech Bull — Colorado. Agricultural Experiment Station. Technical Bulletin

Colo Agric Mech Coll Colo Agric Exp Stn Annu Rep — Colorado Agricultural and Mechanical College. Colorado Agricultural Experiment Station. Annual Report

Colo Agric Mech Coll Colo Agric Exp Stn Bull — Colorado Agricultural and Mechanical College. Colorado Agricultural Experiment Station. Bulletin

Colo App — Colorado Court of Appeals Reports

COLOB — Colourage

Colo Bar Assn — Colorado Bar Association

Colo B Assn Rep — Colorado Bar Association. Report

Colo Bur Mines Ann Rept — Colorado. Bureau of Mines. Annual Report

Colo Bus — Colorado Business

Colo Bus R — Colorado Business Review

Colo Code Regs — Code of Colorado Regulations

Colo Country Life — Colorado Country Life

Colo Dep Game Fish Parks Spec Rep — Colorado. Department of Game, Fish, and Parks. Special Report

Colo Div Game Fish Parks Fish Res Rev — Colorado. Division of Game, Fish, and Parks. Fisheries Research Review

Colo Div Game Fish Parks Game Res Rev — Colorado Division of Game, Fish, and Parks. Game Research Review

Colo Div Game Fish Parks Spec Rep — Colorado. Division of Game, Fish, and Parks. Special Report

Colo Div Game Parks Game Res Rev — Colorado. Division of Game, Fish, and Parks. Game Research Review

Colo Div Wildl Div Rep — Colorado. Division of Wildlife. Division Report

Colo Div Wildl Spec Rep — Colorado. Division of Wildlife. Special Report

Colo Div Wildl Tech Publ — Colorado. Division of Wildlife. Technical Publication

Colo Energy Factbook — Colorado Energy Factbook

Colo Engineer — Colorado Engineer
Colo Farm & Home Res — Colorado Farm and Home Research
Colo Field Ornithol — Colorado Field Ornithologist
Colo Fish Res Rev — Colorado Fisheries Research Review
Colo Game Fish Parks Dep Spec Rep — Colorado. Game, Fish, and Parks Department. Special Report
Colo Game Res Rev — Colorado Game Research Review
Colo Geol Surv Bull — Colorado. Geological Survey. Bulletin
Colo Geol Surv Inf Ser — Colorado Geological Survey. Information Series
Colo Geol Surv Map Ser — Colorado. Geological Survey. Map Series
Colo Geol Surv Resour Ser — Colorado Geological Survey. Resource Series
Colo Geol Surv Spec Publ — Colorado. Geological Survey. Special Publication
Colo Ground Water Basic Data Rep — Colorado Ground Water Basic Data Report
Colo Ground Water Circ — Colorado Ground Water Circular
Colo J Pharm — Colorado Journal of Pharmacy
Colo J Res Mus Ed — Colorado Journal of Research in Music Education
Colo Law — Colorado Lawyer
Colo Lib Assn Bul — Colorado Library Association. Bulletin
ColoM — Colorado Magazine
Colo Mag — Colorado Magazine
Colomb Armada Nac Cent Invest Oceanogr Hidrogr Bol Cient — Colombia. Armada Nacional. Centro de Investigaciones Oceanograficas e Hidrograficas. Boletin Cientifico
Colomb Inst Geogr Agustin Codazzi Dep Agrol Publ — Colombia. Instituto Geografico "Agustin Codazzi." Departamento Agrologico. Publicaciones
Colomb Inst Geogr Agustin Codazzi Dir Agrol Publ — Colombia. Instituto Geografico "Agustin Codazzi." Direccion Agrologica. Publicaciones
Colomb Inst Geol Nac Compil Estud Geol Of Colomb — Colombia. Instituto Geologica Nacional. Compilacion de los Estudios Geologicos Oficiales en Colombia
Colomb Inst Nac Invest Geol Min Bol Geol — Colombia. Instituto Nacional de Investigaciones Geologico-Mineras. Boletin Geologico
Colomb Minist Agric Div Invest Inf Tec — Colombia. Ministerio de Agricultura. Division de Investigacion. Informacion Tecnica
Colomb Minist Minas Energ Mem — Colombia. Ministerio de Minas y Energia. Memoria
Colomb Minist Minas Pet Inst Nac Invest Geol Min Bol Geol — Colombia. Ministerio de Minas y Petroleas. Instituto Nacional de Investigaciones Geologico-Mineras. Boletin Geologico
Colomb Minist Minas Pet Serv Geol Nac Bol Geol — Colombia. Ministerio de Minas y Petroleos. Servicio Geologico Nacional. BoletinGeologico
Colombo LJ — Colombo Law Journal
Colombo L Rev — Colombo Law Review
Colomb Repub Minist Minas Pet Bol Minas — Republica de Colombia. Ministerio de Minas y Petroleos. Boletin de Minas
Colomb Repub Minist Minas Pet Bol Nac Minas — Republica de Colombia. Ministerio de Minas y Petroleos. Boletin Nacional de Minas
Colomb Repub Minist Minas Pet Lab Quim Nac Bol — Colombia Republica. Ministerio de Minas y Petroleos. Laboratorio Quimico Nacional. Boletin
Colomb Serv Geol Nac Compil Estud Geol Of Colomb — Colombia. Servicio Geologico Nacional. Compilacion de los Estudios Geologicos Oficiales en Colombia
Colo Med — Colorado Medicine
Colo Med J — Colorado Medical Journal
Colo Min Assoc Min Year Book — Colorado Mining Association. Mining Year Book
Colo Munic — Colorado Municipalities
Colon Auton — Colonies Autonomes
Colon Geol Miner Resour — Colonial Geology and Mineral Resources
Colon Geol Miner Resour Suppl Bull Suppl — Colonial Geology and Mineral Resources. Supplement Series. Bulletin Supplement
Colon Geol Miner Resour Suppl Ser Bull Suppl — Colonial Geology and Mineral Resources. Supplement Series. Bulletin Supplement
Colon Geol Miner Rsrc — Colonial Geology and Mineral Resources
Colonial Geology and Mineral Res — Colonial Geology and Mineral Resources
Colonial Research Pub — Colonial Research Publications
Colonic Carcinog — Colonic Carcinogenesis
Colon Mar — Colonies et Marine
Colon Pl Anim Prod — Colonial Plant and Animal Products
Colon Plant Anim Prod — Colonial Plant and Animal Products
Colon Soc MA — Colonial Society of Massachusetts
Colo Nurse — Colorado Nurse
Colo Nurse Update — Colorado Nurse Update
Colon Waterbirds — Colonial Waterbirds
Colon Williamsburg — Colonial Williamsburg. The Journal of the Colonial Williamsburg Foundation
Colony Fiji Agric J — Colony of Fiji. Agricultural Journal
Colony Prot Kenya Dep Agric Bull — Colony and Protectorate of Kenya. Department of Agriculture. Bulletin
Colo Outdoors — Colorado Outdoors
ColoQ — Colorado Quarterly
Coloq A — Coloquio Artes. Revista de Artes Visuais Musica e Bailado
Coloq Cient Int Cafe — Coloquio Cientifico Internacional Sobre el Cafe
Coloq Estratigr Paleogeogr Triasico Permico Esp — Coloquio de Estratigrafia y Paleogeografia del Triasico y Permico de Espana
Coloq Hisp Fr Trat Combust Irradiados Quim Plutonio — Coloquio Hispano-Frances sobre Tratamiento de Combustibles Irradiados y la Quimica del Plutonio
Coloq Invest Recur Mar Caribe Reg Adyacentes Contrib — Coloquio sobre Investigaciones y Recursos del Mar Caribe y Regiones Adyacentes.Contribuciones
Coloq Quim Cafes Atas — Coloquio sobre a Quimica dos Cafes. Atas
Coloquio — Coloquio Letras
Colorado Exp Sta Bull — Colorado Experiment Station Bulletin
Colorado Farm Home Res — Colorado Farm and Home Research. Colorado Agricultural Experiment Station

Colorado Mag — Colorado Magazine. State Historical and Natural History Society of Colorado
Colorado Med — Colorado Medicine
Colorado School Mines Prof Contr — Colorado School of Mines. Professional Contributions
Colorado Seed Lab Bull — Colorado Seed Laboratory Bulletin. Colorado Agricultural Experiment Station
Colorado Univ Stud — University of Colorado Studies
Colorado-Wyoming Acad Sci Jour — Colorado-Wyoming Academy of Science. Journal
Colo Rancher Farmer — Colorado Rancher and Farmer
Color Cent Cryst Lumin Proc Int Conf — Color Centers and Crystal Luminescence. Proceedings. International Conference
Color Des — Color Design
Colo Reg — Colorado Register
Color Eng — Color Engineering
Colores Pint — Colores y Pinturas. Revista Tecnica de Pinturas y Afines
Colo Rev Stat — Colorado Revised Statutes
Color Mater — Color Materials
Color Res and Appl — Color Research and Application
Color Res Appl — Color Research and Application
Color Sch Mines Q Bull — Colorado School of Mines. Quarterly Bulletin
Color Trade J — Color Trade Journal
Color Tr J — Color Trade Journal and Textile Chemist
Colo Sch Mines Alumni Mag — Colorado School of Mines. Alumni Magazine
Colo Sch Mines Mag — Colorado School of Mines. Magazine
Colo Sch Mines Mineral Energy Resources Bul — Colorado School of Mines. Mineral and Energy Resources Bulletin
Colo Sch Mines Miner Ind Bull — Colorado School of Mines. Mineral Industries Bulletin
Colo Sch Mines Prof Contrib — Colorado School of Mines. Professional Contributions
Colo Sch Mines Q — Colorado School of Mines. Quarterly
Colo Sch Mines Quart — Colorado School of Mines. Quarterly
Colo Sci Soc Proc — Colorado Scientific Society. Proceedings
Colo Sci Soc Yearb — Colorado Scientific Society. Yearbook
Colo Sc S P — Proceedings of the Colorado Scientific Society
Colo Sess Laws — Session Laws. Colorado
Colo State Univ Agric Exp Stn Annu Rep — Colorado State University. Agricultural Experiment Station. Annual Report
Colo State Univ Agric Exp Stn Bull — Colorado State University. Agricultural Experiment Station. Bulletin
Colo State Univ Agric Exp Stn Tech Bull — Colorado State University. Agricultural Experiment Station. Technical Bulletin
Colo State Univ Annu Rep — Colorado State University. Annual Report
Colo State Univ Colo Water Resour Res Inst Inf Ser — Colorado State University. Colorado Water Resources Research Institute. Information Series
Colo State Univ Environ Resour Cent Inf Ser — Colorado State University. Environmental Resources Center. Information Series
Colo State Univ Exp Stn Bull — Colorado State University. Experiment Station. Bulletin
Colo State Univ Exp Stn Tech Bull — Colorado State University. Experiment Station. Technical Bulletin
Colo State Univ Expt Sta Bull — Colorado State University. Experiment Station. Bulletin
Colo State Univ (Fort Collins) Hydrol Pap — Colorado State University (Fort Collins). Hydrology Papers
Colo State Univ (Fort Collins) Proj Themis Tech Rep — Colorado State University (Fort Collins). Project Themis Technical Reports
Colo State Univ News — Colorado State University News
Colo State Univ Range Sci Dep Range Sci Ser — Colorado State University. Range Science Department. Range Science Series
Colo State Univ Range Sci Dep Sci Ser — Colorado State University. Range Science Department. Range Science Series
Colo Univ Eng Expt Sta Circ Highway Ser Studies Gen Ser — Colorado University. Engineering Experiment Station Circular. Highway Series. Studies. General Series
Colo Univ Stud — Colorado University Studies
Colo Univ Stud Ser Chem Pharm — Colorado. University Studies. Series in Chemistry and Pharmacy
Colour Annu — Colourage Annual
Colour Rev — Colouristical Review
Colour Soc J — Colour Society. Journal
Co Louth Archaeol Hist J — County Louth Archaeological and Historical Journal
Colo Water Conserv Board Ground Water Ser Basic Data Rep — Colorado Water Conservation Board. Ground Water Series. Basic Data Report
Colo Water Conserv Board Ground-Water Ser Bull Circ — Colorado Water Conservation Board. Ground-Water Series Bulletin. Circular
Colo Water Conserv Board Ground Water Ser Circ — Colorado. Water Conservation Board. Ground Water Series. Circular
Colo Water Resour Circ — Colorado Water Resources Circular
Colo Water Resour Res Inst Inf Ser — Colorado Water Resources Research Institute. Information Series
Colo Water Resour Res Inst Tech Rep — Colorado Water Resources Research Institute. Technical Report
Colo-Wyo Acad Sci Jour — Colorado-Wyoming Academy of Science. Journal
Col-Pa Madr Univ Fac Cienc — Col-Pa. Coloquios de la Catedra de Paleontologia. Madrid, Universidad, Facultade Ciencias
Col Phys Ed Assn Proc — College Physical Education Association. Proceedings
Col Press — College Press Service
COLPS — Center for Oceans Law and Policy. University of Virginia. Oceans Policy Studies
ColQ — Colorado Quarterly
Col Quim-Farm — Colegio Quimico-Farmaceutico

Col Quim Ing Quim Costa Rica Rev — Colegio de Quimicos e Ingenieros Quimicos de Costa Rica. Revista
Col Quim PR Rev — Colegio de Quimicos de Puerto Rico. Revista
ColR — Columbia Review
Col Soc Mass Publ — Colonial Society of Massachusetts. Publications
Col Soc Mass Trans — Colonial Society of Massachusetts. Transactions
Colston Pap — Colston Papers
Colston Res Soc Proc Symp — Colston Research Society. Proceedings of the Symposium
ColStuAb — College Student Personnel Abstracts
Colt — Coltivazione
Colt — Coltman's Registration Appeal Cases
Colt G Vinic Ital — Coltivatore e Giornale Vinicolo Italiano
Coltiv Giorn Vinicolo Ital — Coltivatore e Giornale Vinicolo Italiano
Coltiv G Vinic Ital — Coltivatore e Giornale Vinicolo Italiano
Colt News — Colt Newsletter
Coltons J Geogr Collat Sci — Colton's Journal of Geography and Collateral Sciences. A Record of Discovery, Exploration, and Survey
Colt Prot — Colture Protette
Colt Protette — Colture Protette
Columb Bsn — Columbus Business Journal
Columbia Hist Soc Rec — Columbia Historical Society. Records
Columbia J-Ism R — Columbia Journalism Review
Columbia J Law and Social Problems — Columbia Journal of Law and Social Problems
Columbia J of L and Soc Probl — Columbia Journal of Law and Social Problems
Columbia Journalism Rev — Columbia Journalism Review
Columbia J Transnational Law — Columbia Journal of Transnational Law
Columbia J Transnat Law — Columbia Journal of Transnational Law
Columbia J Wld Busin — Columbia Journal of World Business
Columbia J World Bus — Columbia Journal of World Business
Columbia Law R — Columbia Law Review
Columbia Law Rev — Columbia Law Review
Columbia Lib C — Columbia Library. Columns
Columbia Libr Col — Columbia Library. Columns
Columbia Libr Columns — Columbia Library. Columns
Columbia Univ Contrib To Anthrop — Columbia University Contributions to Anthropology
Columbia Univ Stud — Columbia University Studies in History, Economics, and Public Law
Columbia U Q — Columbia University. Quarterly
Columb J L — Columbia Journal of Law and Social Problems
Columb Jrl — Columbia Journal of World Business
Columb J Tr — Columbia Journal of Transnational Law
Columb J W — Columbia Journal of World Business
Columb Law — Columbia Law Review
Columbus Dent Soc Bull — Columbus [Ohio] Dental Society. Bulletin
Columbus Gal Bul — Columbus Gallery of Fine Arts. Bulletin
Columbus Med Bul — Columbus Medical Bulletin
Colum Disp — Columbus Dispatch
Colum Forum — Columbia Forum
Colum His S — Columbia Historical Society. Records
Colum Human Rights L Rev — Columbia Human Rights Law Review
Colum Hum Rts L Rev — Columbia Human Rights Law Review
Colum J Environ L — Columbia Journal of Environmental Law
Colum J Envtl L — Columbia Journal of Environmental Law
Colum J Int'l Aff — Columbia Journal of International Affairs
Colum J L & Soc Prob — Columbia Journal of Law and Social Problems
Colum J Law & Soc Prob — Columbia Journal of Law and Social Problems
Colum Journalism R — Columbia Journalism Review
Colum J Transnat L — Columbia Journal of Transnational Law
Colum J Transnat'l Law — Columbia Journal of Transnational Law
Colum J World Bus — Columbia Journal of World Business
Colum L R — Columbia Law Review [New York]
Colum L Rev — Columbia Law Review
Colum LT — Columbia Law Times
Column Chromatogr Int Symp Sep Methods — Column Chromatography. International Symposium on Separation Methods
Colum Soc'y Int'l L Bull — Columbia Society of International Law. Bulletin
Colum Univ Q — Columbia University. Quarterly
Col Univ — College and University
Col Univ Gerona Secc Cien An — Colegio Universitario de Gerona. Seccion de Ciencias. Anales
COM — Cambio (Mexico)
COM — Chronique d'Outre-Mer
COM — Comet Stories
Com — Commentari
COM — Commentary
Com — Commercial
Com — Comoedia
COM — Composer
COM — Cost and Management
ComA — Communaute Algerienne
ComAb — Computer Abstracts
COMA Bull Conf Mus Anthrop — COMA. Bulletin of the Conference of Museum Anthropologists of Australia
Com Amer — Commerce America
Com & Electronics — Communication and Electronics
Com and Fin Chr — Commercial and Financial Chronicle. Statistical Section
Com & Jr Coll — Community and Junior College Journal
Com & Jr Coll J — Community and Junior College Journal
Com and L — Communications and the Law
Com & Law — Communications and the Law

Com Applic Meth Isotop Rech Agron — Rapport. Comite d'Application des Methodes Isotopiques aux Recherches Agronomiques, Organise Sous les Auspices de l'I.R.S.I.A. Section de Gemblaux
Com Archeol Senlis C R & Mem — Comite Archeologique de Senlis. Comptes-Rendus et Memoires
Comb — Combat. Hebdomadaire du Mouvement de Liberation Francaise
COMBA — Combustion
Comb Chem — Combinatorial Chemistry
Comb Chem High Throughput Screen — Combinatorial Chemistry & High Throughput Screening
Comb Chem High Throughput Screening — Combinatorial Chemistry and High Throughput Screening
Comb Cumul Index Pediatr — Combined Cumulative Index to Pediatrics
Comb Eng — Combustion Engineering
Comb Expl (R) — Combustion, Explosion, and Shock Waves (USSR)
Comb Flame — Combustion and Flame
Combin Probab Comput — Combinatorics, Probability, and Computing
Com Bologna — Comune di Bologna
Comb Proc Int Plant Propagators Soc — Combined Proceedings. International Plant Propagators' Society
Comb Sci T — Combustion Science and Technology
Combust and Flame — Combustion and Flame
Combust Combust — Combustione e Combustibile
Combust Eng Assoc Doc — Combustion Engineering Association. Document
Combust Engines Reduct Frict Wear Int Conf — Combustion Engines. Reduction of Friction and Wear. International Conference
Combust Explos Shock Waves — Combustion, Explosion, and Shock Waves
Combust Explos Shock Waves Engl Transl — Combustion, Explosion, and Shock Waves (English Translation)
Combust Flame — Combustion and Flame
Combust Inst Can Sect Spring Tech Meet — Combustion Institute. Canadian Section. Spring Technical Meeting
Combust Inst East Sect Fall Tech Meet — Combustion Institute. Eastern Section. Fall Technical Meeting
Combustion Sci Tech — Combustion Science and Technology
Combust React Kinet — Combustion and Reaction Kinetics
Combust Sci Technol — Combustion Science and Technology
Combust Sci Technol Book Ser — Combustion Science and Technology. Book Series
Combust Theory Modell — Combustion Theory and Modelling
Combust Toxicol — Combustion Toxicology
Com Canada — Commerce Canada
ComCh — Communaute Chretienne
Com Challenges of Mod Soc Air Pollution — Committee on the Challenges of Modern Society. Air Pollution
Com Col Can — Community Colleges of Canada
Com Coll Front — Community College Frontiers
Com Coll R — Community College Review
Com Com — Journal of Community Communications
Com Con Psy — Comments on Contemporary Psychiatry
Com Consult Definition Metre Rapp — Comite Consultatif pour la Definition du Metre. Rapport
Com Consult Definition Metre Trav — Comite Consultatif pour la Definition du Metre. Travaux
Com Consult Electr Trav — Comite Consultatif d'Electricite. Travaux
Com Consult Etalons Mes Radiat Ionis Trav — Comite Consultatif pour les Etalons de Mesure des RadiationsIonisantes. Travaux
Com Consult Etalons Mes Rayonnem Ionis Sect 1 — Comite Consultatif pour les Etalons de Mesure des RayonnementsIonisants. Section 1. Rayons X et Y. Electrons
Com Consult Etalons Mes Rayonnem Ionis Sect 2 — Comite Consultatif pour les Etalons de Mesure des RayonnementsIonisants. Section 2. Mesure des Radionucleides
Com Consult Etalons Mes Rayonnem Ionis Sect 3 — Comite Consultatif pour les Etalons de Mesure des RayonnementsIonisants. Section 3. Mesures NeutronIques
Com Consult Etalons Mes Rayonnem Ionis Sect 4 — Comite Consultatif pour les Etalons de Mesure des RayonnementsIonisants. Section 4. Etalons d'Energie Alpha
Com Consult Photom Trav — Comite Consultatif de Photometrie. Travaux
Com Consult Thermom Sess — Comite Consultatif de Thermometrie. Session
Com Crew — Combat Crew
COMD — Countermedia. Alaska Journalism Review and Supplement
Com Des — Comercio y Desarrollo
Com Develop J — Community Development Journal
Com Dev J — Community Development Journal
Com Dev Pancha Raj D — Community Development and Panchayati Raj Digest
Com Dir Invest Recur Miner (Mex) Bol — Comite Directivo para la Investigacion de los Recursos Minerales(Mexico). Boletin
COMEAO — Concours Medical
ComEd — Communication Education
Comen — Commentario
C O-Mer — Cahiers d'Outre-Mer
Comercio Exterior de Mexico — Comercio Exterior de Mexico
Comercio Prod — Comercio y Produccion
Comer e Mercados — Comercio e Mercados
Comer Exterior Mexico — Comercio Exterior de Mexico
ComErm — Communications. Musee National de l'Ermitage
Comer y Produccion — Comercio y Produccion
Com Et Coop — Commerce et Cooperation
Com Ext Mexico — Comercio Exterior de Mexico
Com Ext Tchecosl — Commerce Exterieur Tchecoslovaque
Com Fac Sci Univ Ankara Ser A3 Astronom — Universite d'Ankara. Faculte des Sciences. Communications. Serie A3. Astronomie
Com Fish — Commercial Fishing

Com Fom Min Bol (Mex) — Comision de Fomento Minera. Boletin (Mexico)
Com For Rev — Commonwealth Forestry Review
Com Geol (Rom) Stud Teh Econ — Comitetul Geologic (Romania). Studii Tehnice si Economice
Com Glaciol Ital Boll Ser 2 — Comitato Glaciologico Italiano. Bollettino. Serie Seconda
Com Hlth Serv Bul — Community Health Services Bulletin
Com Hort — Commercial Horticulture
Com Inst Agron Sul — Comunicado. Instituto Agronomico do Sul
Com Interam Atun Trop Bol — Comision Interamericana del Atun Tropical. Boletin
Com Internaz — Communita Internazionale
Com Int Etude Bauxites Alumine Alum Trav — Comite International pour l'Etude des Bauxites, de l'Alumine, et d'Aluminium. Travaux
Com Int Etude Bauxites Oxydes Hydroxydes Alum Trav — Comite International pour l'Etude des Bauxites, des Oxydes, et des Hydroxydes d'Aluminium. Travaux
Com Int Poids Mes Com Consult Definition Metre Trav — Comite International des Poids et Mesures. Comite Consultatif pour laDefinition du Metre. Travaux
Com Int Poids Mes Com Consult Def Metre Trav — Comite International des Poids et Mesures. Comite Consultatif pour la Definition du Metre. Travaux
Com Int Poids Mes Com Consult Electr Trav — Comite International des Poids et Mesures. Comite Consultatif d'Electricite. Travaux
Com Int Poids Mes Com Consult Etalons Mes Radiat Ionis Trav — Comite International des Poids et Mesures. Comite Consultatif pour les Etalons de Mesure des Radiations Ionisantes. Travaux
Com Int Poids Mes Com Consult Photom Trav — Comite International des Poids et Mesures. Comite Consultatif de Photometrie. Travaux
Com Int Poids Mes Com Consult Thermom Sess — Comite International des Poids et Mesures. Comite Consultatif deThermometrie. Session
Com Int Poids Mes Com Consult Thermom Trav — Comite International des Poids et Mesures. Comite Consultatif de Thermometrie. Travaux
Com Int Poids Mes PV Seances — Comite International des Poids et Mesures. Proces-Verbaux des Seances
Com Int Thermodyn Cinet Electrochim CR — Comite International de Thermodynamique et de CinetiqueElectrochimiques. Comptes Rendus
Com Int Thermodyn Cinet Electrochim CR Reun — Comite International de Thermodynamique et de CinetiqueElectrochimiques. Comptes Rendus de la Reunion
Com Invest Cient Prov Buenos Aires Inf — Comision de Investigaciones Cientificas. Provincia de Buenos Aires. Informes
Com Invest Cient Prov Buenos Aires Monogr — Comision de Investigaciones Cientificas de la Provincia de Buenos Aires.Monografias
Com Invest Cient Prov Buenos Aires Publ — Comision de Investigaciones Cientificas de la Provincia de Buenos Aires.Publicacion
Com Invest Jnl — Commercial Investment Journal
Comision Nac Valores Bol — Comision Nacional de Valores. Boletin
Comiss Linhas Telegr Estrateg Mato Grosso Amazonas — Comissao das Linhas Telegraficas Estrategicas Mato Grosso ao Amazonas
Comitato Naz Energia Nucleare Notiz — Comitato Nazionale per l'Energia Nucleare. Notiziario
COMJD — Commodity Journal
Com LA — Commercial Law Annual
Com L Assoc Bull — Commercial Law Association. Bulletin
Com Law — Communications and the Law
Com Law Ann — Commercial Law Annual
Com Law Jnl — Commercial Law Journal
Com L J — Commercial Law Journal
Com L League J — Commercial Law League. Journal
Com LQ — Commercial Law Quarterly
Com LR — Commonwealth Law Review
Comm — Commonweal
Comm — Communication. Kodak Research Laboratories
Com M — Communication Monographs
Comm — Communications. Ecole Pratique des Hautes Etudes. Paris
Comm — Community
Comm ACM — Communications. ACM
Comm Algeb — Communications in Algebra
Comm Algebra — Communications in Algebra
Comm Alkali React Concr Nat Prog Rep H — Committee on Alkali Reactions in Concrete. Danish National Institute of Building Research and the Academy of Technical Sciences. Progress Report. Series H. Methods of Evaluation of Alkali Reactions
Comm Alkali React Concr Prog Rep A — Committee on Alkali Reactions in Concrete. Danish National Institute of Building Research and the Academy of Technical Sciences. Progress Report. Series A. Alkali Reactions in Concrete. General
Comm Alkali React Concr Prog Rep D — Committee on Alkali Reactions in Concrete. Danish National Institute of Building Research and the Academy of Technical Sciences. Progress Report. Series D. Aggregate Types of Denmark
Comm Alkali React Concr Prog Rep F — Committee on Alkali Reactions in Concrete. Danish National Institute of Building Research and the Academy of Technical Sciences. Progress Report. Series F. Alkali Contents of Concrete Components
Comm Alkali React Concr Prog Rep H — Committee on Alkali Reactions in Concrete. Danish National Institute ofBuilding Research and the Academy of Technical Sciences. Progress Report. SeriesH. Methods of Evaluation of Alkali Reactions
Comm Alkali React Concr Prog Rep I — Committee on Alkali Reactions in Concrete. Danish National Institute of Building Research and the Academy of Technical Sciences. Progress Report. Series I. Inhibition of Alkali Reactions by Admixtures
Comm Alkali React Concr Prog Rep L — Committee on Alkali Reactions in Concrete. Danish National Institute ofBuilding Research and the Academy of Technical Sciences. Progress Report. SeriesL. Inhibition of Alkali Reactions by Admixtures

Comm Alkali React Concr Prog Rep N — Committee on Alkali Reactions in Concrete. Danish National Institute of Building Research and the Academy of Technical Sciences. Progress Report. Series N. Observed Symptoms of Deterioration
Comm Anal Geom — Communications in Analysis and Geometry
Comm Anal Theory Contin Fractions — Communications in the Analytic Theory of Continued Fractions
Comm and Dist Res — Communications and Distributed Resources Report
Comm & Fin — Commerce and Finance
Comm & Fin Chr — Commercial and Financial Chronicle
Comm & Fin Chron — Commercial and Financial Chronicle
Comman Dig — Commander's Digest
Comm Appl Math Comput — Communication on Applied Mathematics and Computation
Comm Appl Nonlinear Anal — Communications on Applied Nonlinear Analysis
Comm Appl Numer Methods — Communications in Applied Numerical Methods
Comma Prospettive Cult — Comma. Prospettive di Cultura
Comm AR — Commonwealth Arbitration Reports
Comm Archives Centrales Orgue — Communications. Archives Centrales de l'Orgue/Mededelingen. Centraal Orgelarchief
Comm Assignment Rep CAR Tech Assoc Pulp Pap Ind — Committee Assignment Report CAR. Technical Association of the Pulp andPaper Industry
Comm Bibl Hist Med Hungar — Communicationes. Bibliotheca Historiae Medicae Hungarica
Comm Broadc — Communication and Broadcasting
Comm Brux — Jugement du Tribunal de Commerce de Bruxelles
Comm Bul — Commercial Bulletin for Teachers in Secondary Schools
Comm Cognition — Communication and Cognition
Comm Cognition Monograph — Communication and Cognition Monographies
Comm Communautes Eur — Commission des Communautes Europeennes
Comm Comunita Eur — Commissione delle Comunita Europee
Comm Control Engrg Ser — Communication and Control Engineering Series
Commctn Age — Communication Age
Comm Data Sci Technol Bull — Committee on Data for Science and Technology. Bulletin
Comm Data Sci Technol Spec Rep (ICSU) — Committee on Data for Science and Technology. Special Report (International Council of Scientific Unions)
Comm Den Or — Community Dentistry and Oral Epidemiology
Comm Dev J — Community Development Journal
Comm Dublin Inst Adv Stud Geophys Bull — Communications. Dublin Institute of Advanced Studies. Geophysical Bulletin
Comm Dublin Inst Adv Studies Ser A — Communications. Dublin Institute for Advanced Studies. Series A
Comm Ed — Commercial Education
Comm Educ — Communication Education
Commen — Commentary
Comm Energie At (Fr) Serv Doc Ser Bibliogr — Commissariat a l'Energie Atomique (France). Service de Documentation. Serie Bibliographie
Com Men Health J — Community Mental Health Journal
Comment Accad Sci Dip Mella — Commentarj. Accademia di Scienze, Lettere, Agricultura, ed Arti del Dipartimento del Mella
Commentat Biol — Commentationes Biologicae
Commentat Biol Soc Sci Fenn — Commentationes Biologicae. Societas Scientiarum Fennica
Comment Ateneo Brescia — Commentari dell'Ateneo di Brescia
Commentat Phys-Math — Commentationes Physico-Mathematicae
Commentat Phys Math Diss — Commentationes Physico-Mathematicae. Dissertationes
Commentat Phys-Math Suppl — Commentationes Physico-Mathematicae. Supplement
Commentat Pontif Acad Sci — Commentationes Pontificiae. Academiae Scientiarum
Commentat Soc Phys Med Univ Lit Caes Mosq — Commentationes Societatis Physico-Medicae Apud Universitatem Literarum Caesaream Mosquensem Institutae
Comment Balt — Commentationes Balticae
Com Ment Health J — Community Mental Health Journal
Comment Math Helv — Commentarii Mathematici Helvetici
Comment Math Prace Mat — Roczniki Polskiego Towarzystwa Matematycznego. Seria I. Commentationes Mathematicae Prace Matematyczne
Comment Math Special Issue — Commentationes Mathematicae. Special Issue
Comment Math Univ Carolin — Commentationes Mathematicae. Universitatis Carolinae
Comment Math Univ Carolinae — Commentationes Mathematicae. Universitatis Carolinae
Comment Math Univ St Paul — Commentarii Mathematici. Universitatis Sancti Pauli
Comment on Ed — Comment on Education
Comment Phys Math Chem Med — Societas Scientiarum Fennica. Commentationes Physico-Mathematicae et Chemico-Medicae
Comment Phys Math Soc Sci Fenn — Commentationes Physico-Mathematicae. Societas Scientiarum Fennica
Comment Plant Sci — Commentaries in Plant Science
Comment Pontif Acad Sci — Commentario. Pontificia Academia Scientiarum
Comment Res Breast Dis — Commentaries on Research in Breast Disease
Comments Agric Food Chem — Comments on Agricultural and Food Chemistry
Comments Astrophys — Comments on Astrophysics
Comments Astrophys Comments Mod Phys Part C — Comments on Astrophysics. Comments on Modern Physics. Part C
Comments Astrophys Space Phys — Comments on Astrophysics and Space Physics [Later, Comments on Astrophysics]
Comments At Mol Phys — Comments on Atomic and Molecular Physics
Comments Condens Matter Phys — Comments on Condensed Matter Physics
Comments Contemp Psychiatry — Comments on Contemporary Psychiatry
Comments Earth Sci Geophys — Comments on Earth Sciences. Geophysics

Comments Inorg Chem — Comments on Inorganic Chemistry
Comments Mod Biol — Comments on Modern Biology
Comments Mod Chem — Comments on Modern Chemistry
Comments Mod Chem Part B — Comments on Modern Chemistry. Part B
Comments Mod Phys — Comments on Modern Physics
Comments Mod Phys Part B — Comments on Modern Physics. Part B
Comments Mod Phys Part D — Comments on Modern Physics. Part D
Comments Mol and Cell Biophys Comments Mod Biol Part A — Comments on Molecular and Cellular Biophysics. Comments on Modern Biology. PartA
Comments Mol Cell Biophys — Comments on Molecular and Cellular Biophysics
Comments Nucl & Part Phys — Comments on Nuclear and Particle Physics
Comments Nucl Part Phys — Comments on Nuclear and Particle Physics
Comments Nucl Part Phys Suppl — Comments on Nuclear and Particle Physics. Supplement
Comment Soc Regiae Sci Gott — Commentarii Societatis Regiae Scientiarum Gottingensis
Comments Plasma Phys & Controlled Fusion — Comments on Plasma Physics and Controlled Fusion
Comments Plasma Phys Controlled Fusion — Comments on Plasma Physics and Controlled Fusion
Comments Plasma Phys Controll Fus — Comments on Plasma Physics and Controlled Fusion
Comments Solid State Phys — Comments on Solid State Physics
Comments Toxicol — Comments on Toxicology
Commer Am — Commerce America
Commer Appl Precis Manuf Sub Micron Level — Commercial Applications of Precision Manufacturing at the Sub-Micron Level
Commer Bank Australia Econ R — Commercial Bank of Australia. Economic Review
Commerc A — Commercial Art
Commerc A & Indust — Commercial Art and Industry
Commer Car J — Commercial Car Journal
Commerce et Coop — Commerce et Cooperation
Commerce Ind & Min R — Commerce, Industrial, and Mining Review
Commerce Int — Commerce International
Commercial — Commercial Appeal
Commercium Lit Rei Med et Sc Nat — Commercium Litterarium ad Rei Medicae et Scientiae Naturali Incrementum Institutum
Commer Fert — Commercial Fertilizer
Commer Fert Plant Food Ind — Commercial Fertilizer and Plant Food Industry
Commer Fert Plant Food Ind Yearb — Commercial Fertilizer and Plant Food Industry. Yearbook
Commer Fert Yearb — Commercial Fertilizer Yearbook
Commer Fin J — Commercial Finance Journal
Commer Fish Abstr — Commercial Fisheries Abstracts
Commer Fish Rev — Commercial Fisheries Review [*Later, Marine Fisheries Review*]
Commer Ind — Commercial Index
Commer Ind & Min Rev — Commerce, Industrial, and Mining Review
Commer Letter Can Imperial Bank Commer — Commercial Letter. Canadian Imperial Bank of Commerce
Commer Levant — Commerce du Levant
Commer Motor — Commercial Motor
Commer News USA — Commercial News USA
Commer Pan Am Wash — Commercial Pan America (Washington, DC)
Commer Rabbit — Commercial Rabbit
Commer Stand Mon — Commercial Standards Monthly
Commer Today — Commerce Today
Commer W — Commercial West
Comm Eur Communities Eurisotop Off Inf Bookl — Commission of the European Communities. Eurisotop Office. InformationBooklet
Comm Eur Communities Eurosotop Off ITE Rep — Commission of the European Communities. Eurosotop Office. ITF-Report
Comm Eur Communities Eur Rep — Commission of the European Communities. Eur Report
Comm Eur Communities Inf Agric — Commission of the European Communities. Information on Agriculture
Comm Eur Communities Rep EUR — Commission of the European Communities. Report EUR
Comm Eur Communities Rep EUR 12448 — Commission. European Communities. Report EUR 12448
Comm Eur Communities Rep EUR 12540 — Commission. European Communities. Report EUR 12540
Comm Eur Communities Rep EUR 12642 — Commission. European Communities. Report EUR 12642
Comm Eur Communities Rep EUR 12806 — Commission. European Communities. Report EUR 12806
Comm Fac Sci Univ Ankara Ser A — Communications. Faculte des Sciences. Universite d'Ankara. Serie A. Mathematiques-Physique-Astronomie
Comm Fert — Commercial Fertilizer
Comm Fish Newsl — Commercial Fishing Newsletter
Comm Fut L Rep CCH — Commodity Futures Law Reports. Commerce Clearing House
Comm Heal S — Community Health Studies
Comm Health — Community Health
Comm Hist Art Med — Communicationes de Historia Artis Medicinae
Comm Hydrol Onderz TNO Versl Meded — Commissie voor Hydrologisch Onderzoek TNO [*Nederlandse Centrale Organisatie voor Toegepast Natuurwetenschappelijk Onderzoek*]. Verslagen en Mededelingen
Comm Hydrol Onderz TNO Versl Tech Bijeenkomst — Commissie voor Hydrologisch Onderzoek TNO [*Nederlandse Centrale Organisatievoor Toegepast Natuurwetenschappelijk Onderzoek*]. Verslag van de Technische Bijeenkomst

Comm Hydrol Onderz TNO Versl Tech Bijeenkomsten — Commissie voor Hydrologisch Onderzoek TNO [*Nederlandse Centrale Organisatie voor Toegepast Natuurwetenschappelijk Onderzoek*]. Verslag van de Technische Bijeenkomst
Comm Hydrol Res TNO (Cent Organ Appl Sci Res Neth) Proc Inf — Committee for Hydrological Research TNO (Central Organization for Applied Scientific Research in the Netherlands). Proceedings and Informations
Comm Hydrol Res TNO Proc Inf — Committee for Hydrological Research TNO [*Central Organization for Applied Scientific Research in the Netherlands*]. Proceedings and Information
Comm (India) — Commerce (India)
Comm Ind Rep — Communications Industry Report
Comm Inland Fish Afr Tech Pap — Committee for Inland Fisheries of Africa. Technical Paper
Comm Int Explor Sci Mer Mediterr Rapp PV Reun — Commission Internationale pour l'Exploration Scientifique de la Mer Mediterranee. Rapports et Proces-Verbaux des Reunions
Comm Int Ind Agric Aliment Symp Int — Commission Internationale des Industries Agricoles et Alimentaires.Symposium International
Comm Intnl — Communications International
Comm Int Prot Acque Italo-Svizz Rapp — Commissione Internazionale per la Protezione delle Acque. Italo-Svizzere Rapporti
Comm Int Tech Sucr CR Assem Gen — Commission Internationale Technique de Sucrerie. Comptes Rendus del'Assemblee Generale
Commis Energ At Clefs — Commissariat a l'Energie Atomique. Clefs
Commis Energ At (Fr) Bull Inf Sci Tech — Commissariat a l'Energie Atomique (France). Bulletin d'Informations Scientifiques et Techniques
Commis Energ At (Fr) Rapp — Commissariat a l'Energie Atomique (France). Rapport
Commis Energ At (Fr) Serv Doc Ser Bibliogr — Commissariat a l'Energie Atomique (France). Service de Documentation. Serie Bibliographie
Commis Energ At Note CEA N (Fr) — Commissariat a l'Energie Atomique. Note CEA-N (France)
Commis Energ At Rapp CEA CONF (Fr) — Commissariat a l'Energie Atomique. Rapport CEA-CONF (France)
Comm Ital Com Int Geofis Pubbl — Commissione Italiana del Comitato Internazionale di Geofisica. Pubblicazioni
Comm Ital Geofis Pubbl — Commissione Italiana per la Geofisica. Pubblicazioni
Comm Jap — Communications in Japan
Comm Jud J — Commonwealth Judicial Journal
Comm L Assoc Bull — Commercial Law Association. Bulletin
Comm LB — Commonwealth Law Bulletin
Comml Grow — Commercial Grower
Comm L J — Commercial Law Journal
Comm L Law — Common Law Lawyer
Comm L Leag J — Commercial Law League Journal
Comm LR — Commonwealth Law Reports
Comm M — Commerce Monthly
Comm Market L Rev — Common Market Law Review
Comm Math H — Commentarii Mathematici Helvetici
Comm Math P — Communications in Mathematical Physics
Comm Math Phys — Communications in Mathematical Physics
Comm Ment H — Community Mental Health Journal
Comm Mkt LR — Common Market Law Reports
Comm Mkt L Rep — Common Market Law Reports
Comm Mkt L Rev — Common Market Law Review
Comm Mod — Commerece Moderne
Comm Mon — Communication Monographs
Comm Monogr — Communication Monographs
Comm Mot — Commercial Motor
Comm Murals Mag — Community Murals Magazine
Comm News — Communications News
Comm Numer Methods Engrg — Communications in Numerical Methods in Engineering
Com Mod — Commerce Moderne
Commod Bul Dep Agric NSW Div Mark Econ — Commodity Bulletin. Department of Agriculture of New South Wales. Division of Marketing and Economics
Commodities M — Commodities Magazine
Commod J — Commodity Journal
Commod Jrl — Commodity Journal
Commod Mag — Commodities Magazine
Common — Common Sense
Common Agric — Commonwealth Agriculturist
Common Cause M — Common Cause Membership
Commoner Glass Work — Commoner and Glass Worker
Common Exp Build Stn NSB — Australia. Commonwealth Experimental Building Station. Notes on the Science of Building
Common Market Law R — Common Market Law Review
Common Mkt L Rev — Common Market Law Review
Common Mkt Rep CCH — Common Market Reports. Commerce Clearing House
Commons J — Commons Journals
Commonw Agric — Commonwealth Agriculturist
Commonw Bur Anim Breed Genet Tech Commun — Commonwealth Bureau of Animal Breeding and Genetics. Technical Communication
Commonw Bur Anim Health Rev Ser — Commonwealth Bureau of Animal Health. Review Series
Commonw Bur Anim Nutr Tech Commun — Commonwealth Bureau of Animal Nutrition. Technical Communication
Commonw Bur Dairy Sci Technol Tech Commun — Commonwealth Bureau of Dairy Science and Technology. TechnicalCommunication
Commonw Bur Hortic Plant Crops (GB) Tech Commun — Commonwealth Bureau of Horticulture and Plantation Crops (Great Britain). Technical Communication
Commonw Bur Nutr Tech Commun — Commonwealth Bureau of Nutrition. Technical Communication

Commonw Bur Pastures Field Crops Bull — Commonwealth Bureau of Pastures and Field Crops. Bulletin

Commonw Bur Pastures Field Crops (GB) Rev Ser — Commonwealth Bureau of Pastures and Field Crops (Great Britain). Review Series

Commonw Bur Pastures Field Crops Hurley Berkshire Bull — Commonwealth Bureau of Pastures and Field Crops. Hurley Berkshire Bulletin

Commonw Bur Plant Breed Genet Tech Commun — Commonwealth Bureau of Plant Breeding and Genetics. Technical Communication

Commonw Bur Soil Sci Tech Commun — Commonwealth Bureau of Soil Science. Technical Communication

Commonw Bur Soils Spec Publ — Commonwealth Bureau of Soils. Special Publication

Commonw Bur Soils Tech Commun — Commonwealth Bureau of Soils. Technical Communication

Commonw Dev — Commonwealth Development

Commonwealth Club Calif Tr — Commonwealth Club of California. Transactions

Commonwealth Club Cal Transactions — Commonwealth Club of California. Transactions

Commonwealth J — Commonwealth Journal

Commonwealth Phytopathol — Commonwealth Phytopathological News

Commonwealth R — Commonwealth Review. University of Oregon

Commonwealth Road Trans Index — Commonwealth Road Transport Index

Commonw Eng — Commonwealth Engineer

Commonw Engr — Commonwealth Engineer

Commonw Exp Build Stat Bull — Australia. Commonwealth Experimental Building Station. Bulletin

Commonw Exp Build Stat RF — Australia. Commonwealth Experimental Building Station. CEBS Researchers and Facilities

Commonw Exp Build Stat SR — Australia. Commonwealth Experimental Building Station. Special Report

Commonw Exp Build Stat TS — Australia. Commonwealth Experimental Building Station. Technical Study

Commonw Fert — Commonwealth Fertilizer

Commonw For Bur Tech Commun — Commonwealth Forestry Bureau. Technical Communication

Commonw Forest Rev — Commonwealth Forestry Review

Commonw For Rev — Commonwealth Forestry Review

Commonw Geol Liaison Off Liaison Rep — Commonwealth Geological Liaison Office. Liaison Report

Commonw Geol Liaison Off Spec Liaison Rep — Commonwealth Geological Liaison Office. Special Liaison Report

Commonw Inst Biol Control Misc Publ — Commonwealth Institute of Biological Control. Miscellaneous Publication

Commonw Inst Helminthol (Albans) Tech Commun — Commonwealth Institute of Helminthology (Saint Albans). Technical Communication

Commonw J — Commonwealth Journal

Commonw J Soc Growing Austral Pl — Commonwealth Journal. Society for Growing Australian Plants

Commonw L Rep — Commonwealth Law Reports

Commonw L Rev — Commonwealth Law Review

Commonw Min Metall Congr Proc — Commonwealth Mining and Metallurgical Congress. Proceedings

Commonw Mycol Inst Descr Pathog Fungi Bact — Commonwealth Mycological Institute. Descriptions of Pathogenic Fungi and Bacteria

Commonw Mycol Inst Mycol Pap — Commonwealth Mycological Institute. Mycological Papers

Commonw Mycol Inst Phytopathol Pap — Commonwealth Mycological Institute. Phytopathological Papers

Commonw Phytopath News — Commonwealth Phytopathological News

Commonw Sci Ind Res Organ — Commonwealth Scientific and Industrial Research Organization

Comm Part D — Communications in Partial Differential Equations

Comm Partial Differential Equations — Communications in Partial Differential Equations

Comm Penit Int Bul — Commission Penitentiaire Internationale. Bulletin

Comm Phys-M — Commentationes Physico-Mathematicae

Comm Phytopathol News — Commonwealth Phytopathological News

Comm Probl Drug Depend Proc Annu Sci Meet US Nat Res Counc — Committee on Problems of Drug Dependence. Proceedings of the Annual Scientific Meeting. United States National Research Council

Comm Prop J — Community Property Journal

Comm Pure Appl Math — Communications on Pure and Applied Mathematics

Comm Q — Communication Quarterly

Comm Rec — Commonwealth Record

Comm Rep — Commerce Reports

Comm Reporter — Committee Reporter

Comm Reps — Commerce Reports. US Government Printing Office

Comm Res — Communication Research

Comm Res Trends — Communication Research Trends

Comm Roy Soc Edinburgh Phys Sci — Communications. Royal Society of Edinburgh. Physical Sciences

Comm Saf Nucl Install Rep — Committee on the Safety of Nuclear Installations. Report

Comms N — Communications News

Comm Soc — Communicatio Socialis

Comm Soil S — Communications in Soil Science and Plant Analysis

Comm St A — Communications in Statistics. Part A. Theory and Methods

Comm Standards M — Commercial Standards Monthly [*Washington, D.C.*]

Comm Statis — Communications in Statistics

Comm Statist A Theory Methods — Communications in Statistics. Part A. Theory and Methods

Comm Statist B Simulation Comput — Communications in Statistics. Part B. Simulation and Computation

Comm Statist Econometric Rev — Communications in Statistics. Econometric Reviews

Comm Statist Sequential Anal — Communications in Statistics. Part C. Sequential Analysis

Comm Statist Simulation Comput — Communications in Statistics. Part B. Simulation and Computation

Comm Statist Stochastic Models — Communications in Statistics. Stochastic Models

Comm Statist Theory Methods — Communications in Statistics. Part A. Theory and Methods

Comm St B — Communications in Statistics. Part B. Simulation and Computation

Comm Tech Co Op Afr Publ — Commission for Technical Co-Operation in Africa. Publication

Comm Theoret Phys — Communications in Theoretical Physics

Comm Theoret Phys Allahabad — Communications in Theoretical Physics (Allahabad)

Comm Th Phy — Communications in Theoretical Physics

Comm Today — Commerce Today

Comm Trad Dig — Commodity Trading Digest

Commu LB — Communications Law Bulletin

Commun — Communio. International Catholic Review

Commun — Communion

Commun Abstr — Communication Abstracts

Commun Abstr Int Congr Int Union Crystallogr — Communicated Abstracts. International Congress. International Union of Crystallography

Commun ACM — Communications. ACM

Commun Action — Community Action

Commun Algebra — Communications in Algebra

Commun All Russ Inst Met — Communications. All-Russian Institute of Metals

Commun Am Ceram Soc — Communications. American Ceramic Society

Commun and Cybernet — Communication and Cybernetics

Commun & Law — Communications and the Law

Commun Appl Cell Biol — Communications in Applied Cell Biology

Commun Archaeol Hung — Communicationes Archaeologicae Hungariae

Commun Artistiques Hist Congr Int Verre — Communications Artistiques et Historiques. Congres International duVerre

Commun Arts Mag — Communication Arts Magazine

Commun Assoc Int Limnol Theor Appl — Communications. Association Internationale de Limnologie Theoretique etAppliquee

Commun Aust — Communications Australia

Communaute Eur Energ At EURATOM Rapp — Communaute Europeenne de l'Energie Atomique. EURATOM Rapport

Commun Balai Penjelidikan Pemakaian Karet — Communication. Balai Penjelidikan dan Pemakaian Karet

Commun Behav Biol Part A Orig Artic — Communications in Behavioral Biology. Part A. Original Articles

Commun Biohist — Occasional Communications. Utrecht University. Biohistorical Institute

Commun Broadc — Communication and Broadcasting

Commun Broadcast — Communication and Broadcasting

Commun Care — Community Care

Commun Cent Rech Zootech Univ Louv — Communication. Centre de Recherches Zootechniques. Universite de Louvain

Commun Child — Communicating with Children

Commun Chin Biochem Soc — Communications. Chinese Biochemical Society

Commun Coal Res Inst (Prague) — Communications. Coal Research Institute (Prague)

Commun Conf Internat Hist Econ — Conference Internationale d'Histoire Economique. Communications

Commun Conf Int Planif Gestion Eaux — Communications. Conference International sur la Planification et laGestion des Eaux

Commun Cybern — Communication and Cybernetics

Commun Czech Pol Colloq Chem Thermodyn Phys Org Chem — Communications. Czech-Polish Colloquium on Chemical Thermodynamics and PhysicalOrganic Chemistry

Commun Dep Agric Res R Trop Inst (Amst) — Communication. Department of Agricultural Research. Royal Tropical Institute (Amsterdam)

Commun Dep Anat Univ Lund (Swed) — Communication. Department of Anatomy. University of Lund (Sweden)

Commun Dep Chem Bulg Acad Sci — Communications. Department of Chemistry. Bulgarian Academy of Sciences

Commun Dev J — Community Development Journal

Commun Dis Intell — Communicable Diseases Intelligence (Canberra)

Commun Dis Public Health — Communicable Disease and Public Health [*London*]

Commun Dis Rep CDR Rev — Communicable Disease Report. CDR Review

Commun Dis Rep CDR Wkly — Communicable Disease Report. CDR Weekly

Commun Dublin Inst Adv Stud A — Communications. Dublin Institute for Advanced Studies. Series A

Commun Dublin Inst Adv Stud Ser A — Communications. Dublin Institute for Advanced Studies. Series A

Commun Dublin Inst Adv Stud Ser D — Communications. Dublin Institute for Advanced Studies. Series D. Geophysical Bulletin

Commun Ec Med Vet Univ Etat Gand — Communications. Ecole de Medecine Veterinaire. Universite del'Etat a Gand

Commun Electron — Communications and Electronics

Commun Eng — Communication Engineering

Commun Eng Int — Communications Engineering International

Commun Equip & Syst Des — Communications Equipment and Systems Design

Commun Equip Manu — Communications Equipment Manufacturers

Commun Fac Med Vet Univ Etat Gand — Communications. Faculte de Medecine Veterinaire. Universite de l'Etat Gand

Commun Fac Sci Univ Ankara — Communications. Faculte des Sciences. Universite d'Ankara

Commun Fac Sci Univ Ankara Ser A — Communications. Faculte des Sciences. Universite d'Ankara. Serie A. Mathematiques-Physique-Astronomie

Commun Fac Sci Univ Ankara Ser A2 — Communications. Faculte des Sciences. Universite d'Ankara. Serie A2. Physique

Commun Fac Sci Univ Ankara Ser B — Communications. Faculte des Sciences. Universite d'Ankara. Serie B. Chimie

Commun Fac Sci Univ Ankara Ser B Chem Chem Eng — Communications. Faculte des Sciences. Universite d'Ankara. Series B. Chemistry and Chemical Engineering

Commun Fac Sci Univ Ankara Ser C — Communications. Faculte des Sciences. Universite d'Ankara. Serie C. Sciences Naturelles

Commun Fac Sci Univ Ankara Ser C Biol — Communications. Faculte des Sciences. Universite d'Ankara. Serie C. Biologie

Commun Fac Sci Univ Ankara Ser C I Geol — Communications. Faculte des Sciences. Universite d'Ankara. Serie C-I. Geologie

Commun Fac Sci Univ Ankara Ser C II Bot — Communications. Faculte des Sciences. Universite d'Ankara. Serie C-II. Botanique

Commun Fac Sci Univ Ankara Ser C III Zool — Communications. Faculte des Sciences. Universite d'Ankara. Serie C-III. Zoologie

Commun Fac Sci Univ Ankara Ser C Sci Nat — Communications. Faculte des Sciences. Universite d'Ankara. Serie C. Sciences Naturelles

Commun Fac Vet Med State Univ (Ghent) — Communications. Faculty of Veterinary Medicine. State University (Ghent)

Commun Fond Caoutch (Delft) — Communications. Fondation du Caoutchouc (Delft)

Commun Forest Res Inst — Communication. Forest Research Institute

Communic A — Communication Arts

Communicable Disease Rep — Communicable Disease Report

Communic Afr — Communications Africa

Communications in Afr — Communications in Africa

Communication Studies Bull — Communication Studies Bulletin

Communication Tech Impact — Communications Technology Impact

Communic et Lang — Communication et Langages

Communic Proy Puebla Tlaxcala — Communicaciones Proyecto Puebla-Tlaxcala

Communic Rei Cret Rom Faut — Communicationes Rei Cretariae Romanae Fautores

Commun Indones Rubber Res Inst — Communications. Indonesian Rubber Research Institute

Commun Inst For Cech — Communicationes. Instituti Forestalis Cechosloveniae

Commun Inst For Csl — Communicationes. Instituti Forestalis Cechosloveniae

Commun Inst Forest Cechosloveniae — Communicationes Instituti Forestalis Cechosloveniae

Commun Inst For Fenn — Communicationes. Instituti Forestalis Fenniae

Commun Inst For Res Agric Univ (Wageningen) — Communication. Institute of Forestry Research. Agricultural University (Wageningen)

Commun Inst Gas Eng — Communications. Institution of Gas Engineers

Commun Inst Mar Biol Far East Sci Cent Acad Sci USSR — Communications. Institute of Marine Biology. Far Eastern Scientific Center. Academy of Sciences. USSR

Commun Inst Rech Charbon (Prague) — Communications. Institut des Recherches sur le Charbon (Prague)

Commun Inst Therm Appl Ec Polytech Fed Lausanne — Communication. Institut de Thermique Appliquee. Ecole Polytechnique Federale de Lausanne

Commun Int — Communications International

Commun Int Assoc Theor Appl Limnol — Communications. International Association of Theoretical and Applied Limnology

Communist China Dig — Communist China Digest

Communist Chin Sci Abstr — Communist Chinese Scientific Abstracts

Communist R — Communist Review

Communist Rev — Communist Review

Communit — Communities

Communit Health S Afr — Community Health in South Africa

Community Anal Stud — Community Analysis Studies

Community and Junior Coll Libr — Community and Junior College Libraries

Community Dent Health — Community Dental Health

Community Dent Oral Epidemiol — Community Dentistry and Oral Epidemiology

Community Dev Abstr — Community Development Abstracts

Community Dev B — Community Development Bulletins

Community Devel J — Community Development Journal

Community Develop J — Community Development Journal

Community Development J — Community Development Journal

Community Dev J — Community Development Journal

Community Econ Univ Wis Dep Agric Econ Coop Ext Serv — Community Economics. University of Wisconsin. Department of Agricultural Economics. Cooperative Extension Service

Community Educ Newsl — Community Education Newsletter

Community Health Stud — Community Health Studies

Community Hlth — Community Health

Community Jr Coll J — Community and Junior College Journal

Community Med — Community Medicine

Community Ment Health J — Community Mental Health Journal

Community Ment Health Rev — Community Mental Health Review [*Later, Prevention in Human Services*]

Community Ment Hlth J — Community Mental Health Journal

Community Nurs — Community Nursing

Community Nutr — Community Nutritionist

Community Prop J — Community Property Journal

Commun Jajasan Penjelidikan Pemakain Karet — Communications. Jajasan Penjelidikan dan Pemakain Karet

Commun J Inst Nucl Res (Dubna) — Communications. Joint Institute for Nuclear Research (Dubna)

Commun Kamerlingh Onnes Lab Univ Leiden — Communications. Kamerlingh Onnes Laboratory. University of Leiden

Commun Kamerlingh Onnes Lab Univ Leiden Suppl — Communications. Kamerlingh Onnes Laboratory. University of Leiden. Supplement

Commun K Ned Springstoffenfabr — Communication. NV [*Naamloze Vennootschap*] Koninklijke Nederlandsche Springstoffenfabrieken

Commun Lang Etrang Inst Rech Ressour Hydraul (Budapest) — Communications en Langues Etrangeres. Institut de Recherches desRessources Hydrauliques (Budapest)

Commun Lunar & Planet Lab — Communications. Lunar and Planetary Laboratory

Commun Math Inst Rijksuniv Utrecht — Communications. Mathematical Institute. Rijksuniversiteit Utrecht

Commun Math Phys — Communications in Mathematical Physics

Commun Neth Indies Rubber Res Inst — Communications. Netherlands Indies Rubber Research Institute

Commun News — Communications News

Commun Newsl — Communique Newsletter

Commun Nurs Res — Communicating Nursing Research

Commun NV K Ned Springstoffenfabr — Communication. NV [*Naamloze Vennootschap*] Koninklijke Nederlandsche Springstoffenfabrieken

Commun Off Assoc Int Sci Sol — Communications Officielles. Association Internationale de la Science duSol

Commun Part Differ Equ — Communications in Partial Differential Equations

Commun Phys — Communications on Physics

Commun Phys Hanoi — Communications in Physics (Hanoi)

Commun Phys Lab Univ Leiden — Communications. Physical Laboratory. University of Leiden

Commun Plast Dep Rubber Found Delft — Communications. Plastics Department. Rubber Foundation. Delft

Commun Psychopharmacol — Communications in Psychopharmacology

Commun Pure Appl Math — Communications on Pure and Applied Mathematics

Commun Quart — Communication Quarterly

Commun R Dutch Explos Manuf — Communication. Royal Dutch Explosive Manufactories

Commun Res Inst SPA Rubber Ser — Communications. Research Institute of the Sumatra Planters' Association.Rubber Series

Commun Res Inst Sumatra Plant Assoc Rubber Ser — Communications. Research Institute of the Sumatra Planters' Association. RubberSeries

Commun R Soc Edinburgh — Communications. Royal Society of Edinburgh

Commun R Soc Edinburgh Phys Sci — Communications. Royal Society of Edinburgh. Physical Sciences

Commun Rubber Found Amsterdam — Communications. Rubber Foundation. Amsterdam

Commun Rubber Found (Delft) — Communications. Rubber Foundation (Delft)

Commun Rubber Res Inst Malays — Communication. Rubber Research Institute of Malaysia

Commun Sci & Tech Inf — Communicator of Scientific and Technical Information [*Later, Communicator*]

Commun Sci Pract Brew Wallerstein Lab — Communications on the Science and Practice of Brewing. WallersteinLaboratory

Commun Sect Bot Soc Biol Hung B Sect — Communications Sectionis Botanicae Societatis Biologicae Hungariae. BSectio

Commun Sect Matieres Plast Fond Caoutch (Delft) — Communications. Section de Matieres Plastiques. Fondation duCaoutchouc (Delft)

Communs Electron (Lond) — Communications and Electronics (London)

Communs Fac Sci Univ Ankara — Communications. Faculte des Sciences. Universite d'Ankara. Serie C

Commun Soc Ceram Tchec — Communications. Societe Ceramique Tchecoslovaque

Commun Soil Sci Plant Anal — Communications in Soil Science and Plant Analysis

Commun Stat — Communications in Statistics

Commun Stat A — Communications in Statistics. Part A. Theory and Methods

Commun Stat B — Communications in Statistics. Part B. Simulation and Computation

Commun Statist Theory Method — Communications in Statistics. Theory and Method

Commun Stat Part A Theory Methods — Communications in Statistics. Part A. Theory and Methods

Commun Stat Part B — Communications in Statistics. Part B. Simulation and Computation

Commun Stat Simulation and Comput — Communications in Statistics. Part D. Simulation and Computation

Commun Stat Theory and Methods — Communications in Statistics. Part A. Theory and Methods

Commun Stell Corp Tech Rev — Communications Satellite Corporation Technical Review

Commun Sugar Milling Res Inst — Communications. Sugar Milling Research Institute

Commun Swed Sugar Corp — Communications. Swedish Sugar Corporation

Commun Sys — Communication Systems

Commun Syst and Manage — Communications Systems and Management

Commun Tech Inf — Communicator of Technical Information [*Later, Communicator*]

Commun Theor Phys — Communications in Theoretical Physics

Commun Transport Q — Community Transport Quarterly

Commun Vet — Communicationes Veterinariae

Commun Vet Coll State Univ Ghent — Communications. Veterinary College. State University of Ghent

Commun Wool Res Organ NZ — Communication. Wool Research Organisation of New Zealand

Commun World Fert Congr — Communications. World Fertilizer Congress

Commutat & Electron — Commutation et Electronique

Commutat and Transm — Commutation and Transmission

Commutation Electron — Commutation et Electronique

Commuter W — Commuter World

Comm Veh — Commercial Vehicles

CommViat — Communio Viatorum. A Theological Quarterly

Commw Arb — Commonwealth Arbitration Reports

Commw Art — Commonwealth Arbitration Reports

Commw Exp Build Stat NSB — Commonwealth Experimental Building Station. Notes on the Science of Building
Commw Jud J — Commonwealth Judicial Journal
Commw LB — Commonwealth Law Bulletin
Commw LR — Commonwealth Law Reports
Commwth Eng — Commonwealth Engineer
Com Nac Energ At (Argent) Inf — Comision Nacional de Energia Atomica (Argentina). Informe
Com Nac Energ Nucl (Braz) Bol — Comissao Nacional de Energia Nuclear (Brazil). Boletim
Com Nac Energ Nucl (Braz) Publ — Comissao Nacional de Energia Nuclear (Brazil). Publicacao
Com Nac Energ Nucl (Mex) Publ — Comision Nacional de Energia Nuclear (Mexico). Publicacion
Com Nac Errad Palud Bol — Comision Nacional para le Erradicacion del Paludismo. Boletin
Com Naz Energ Nucl Not — Comitato Nazionale per l'Energia Nucleare. Notiziario
Com Naz Energ Nucl Not (Italy) — Comitato Nazionale per l'Energia Nucleare. Notiziario (Italy)
Com Naz Energ Nucl Rapp Tec CNEN-RT/BIO (Italy) — Comitato Nazionale per l'Energia Nucleare. Rapporto Tecnico CNEN-RT/BIO (Italy)
Com Naz Energ Nucl Rapp Tec CNEN-RT/CHI (Italy) — Comitato Nazionale per l'Energia Nucleare. Rapporto Tecnico CNEN-RT/CHI (Italy)
Com Naz Energ Nucl Rapp Tec CNEN-RT/DISP (Italy) — Comitato Nazionale per l'Energia Nucleare. Rapporto Tecnico CNEN-RT/DISP (Italy)
Com Naz Energ Nucl Rapp Tec CNEN-RT/FARE SDI — Comitato Nazionale per l'Energia Nucleare. Rapporto Tecnico CNEN-RT/FARE-SDI
Com Naz Energ Nucl Rapp Tec CNEN-RT/FARE SIN — Comitato Nazionale per l'Energia Nucleare. Rapporto Tecnico CNEN-RT/FARE-SIN
Com Naz Energ Nucl Rapp Tec CNEN-RT/FI (Italy) — Comitato Nazionale per l'Energia Nucleare. Rapporto Tecnico CNEN-RT/FI (Italy)
Com Naz Energ Nucl Rapp Tec CNEN-RT/FIMA (Italy) — Comitato Nazionale per l'Energia Nucleare. Rapporto Tecnico CNEN-RT/FIMA (Italy)
Com Naz Energ Nucl Rapp Tec CNEN-RT/ING (Italy) — Comitato Nazionale per l'Energia Nucleare. Rapporto Tecnico CNEN-RT/ING (Italy)
Com Naz Energ Nucl Rapp Tec CNEN-RT/MET (Italy) — Comitato Nazionale per l'Energia Nucleare. Rapporto Tecnico CNEN-RT/MET (Italy)
Com Naz Energ Nucl Rapp Tec CNEN-RT/PROT (Italy) — Comitato Nazionale per l'Energia Nucleare. Rapporto Tecnico CNEN-RT/PROT (Italy)
Com Naz Energ Nucl Rapp Tec RT/AI (Italy) — Comitato Nazionale per l'Energia Nucleare. Rapporto Tecnico RT/AI (Italy)
Com Naz Energ Nucl Rapp Tec RT/BIO (Italy) — Comitato Nazionale per l'Energia Nucleare. Rapporto Tecnico RT/BIO (Italy)
Com Naz Energ Nucl Rapp Tec RT/CHI (Italy) — Comitato Nazionale per l'Energia Nucleare. Rapporto Tecnico RT/CHI (Italy)
Com Naz Energ Nucl Rapp Tec RT/DISP (Italy) — Comitato Nazionale per l'Energia Nucleare. Rapporto Tecnico RT/DISP (Italy)
Com Naz Energ Nucl Rapp Tec RT/EC (Italy) — Comitato Nazionale per l'Energia Nucleare. Rapporto Tecnico RT/EC (Italy)
Com Naz Energ Nucl Rapp Tec RT/EL (Italy) — Comitato Nazionale per l'Energia Nucleare. Rapporto Tecnico RT/EL (Italy)
Com Naz Energ Nucl Rapp Tec RT/FI (Italy) — Comitato Nazionale per l'Energia Nucleare. Rapporto Tecnico RT/FI (Italy)
Com Naz Energ Nucl Rapp Tec RT/FIMA (Italy) — Comitato Nazionale per l'Energia Nucleare. Rapporto Tecnico RT/FIMA (Italy)
Com Naz Energ Nucl Rapp Tec RT/GEN (Italy) — Comitato Nazionale per l'Energia Nucleare. Rapporto Tecnico RT/GEN (Italy)
Com Naz Energ Nucl Rapp Tec RT/GEO (Italy) — Comitato Nazionale per l'Energia Nucleare. Rapporto Tecnico RT/GEO (Italy)
Com Naz Energ Nucl Rapp Tec RT/GIU (Italy) — Comitato Nazionale per l'Energia Nucleare. Rapporto Tecnico RT/GIU (Italy)
Com Naz Energ Nucl Rapp Tec RT/ING (Italy) — Comitato Nazionale per l'Energia Nucleare. Rapporto Tecnico RT/ING (Italy)
Com Naz Energ Nucl Rapp Tec RT/MET (Italy) — Comitato Nazionale per l'Energia Nucleare. Rapporto Tecnico RT/MET (Italy)
Com Naz Energ Nucl Rapp Tec RT/PROT (Italy) — Comitato Nazionale per l'Energia Nucleare. Rapporto Tecnico RT/PROT (Italy)
Com Naz Energ Nucl Repr — Comitato Nazionale per l'Energia Nucleare. Reprints
Com Naz Ric Nucl (Italy) Not — Comitato Nazionale per le Ricerche Nucleari (Italy). Notiziario
Com Naz Ric Nucl Rapp Tec (Italy) — Comitato Nazionale per le Ricerche Nucleari. Rapporto Tecnico (Italy)
Com Naz Ric Sviluppo Energ Nucl Energ Altern Not — Comitato Nazionale per la Ricerca e per lo Sviluppo dell'Energia Nucleare e delle Energie Alternative. Notiziario
COMNB — Commentary
Comnty — Community Newspapers
Comny — Commentary
Comoedia — Comoedia Illustre
ComP — Comparative Politics
Comp — Compass
COMPA — Compost Science [Later, Bio Cycle]
Compaction Qual Control Train Proc Powder Metall Conf Exhib — Compaction, Quality Control, and Training. Proceedings. Powder Metallurgy Conference and Exhibition
Comp Admin Sci Q — Comparative Administrative Science Quarterly
Comp Ad New — Computer Advertising News, Incorporated into Adweek's Computer and Electronics Marketing
Compagn Franc Petrol Notes Mem — Compagnie Francaise des Petroles. Notes et Memoires
Comp Air — Compressed Air
Comp Air Mag — Compressed Air Magazine
Compalloy Proc Int Congr Compat React Polym Alloying — Compalloy. Proceedings. International Congress on Compatibilizers and Reactive Polymer Alloying

Com P A Math — Communications on Pure and Applied Mathematics
COMPAN — Compost Science [Later, Bio Cycle]
Comp & Automation — Computers and Automation [Later, Computers and People]
Comp & Educ — Computers and Education
Comp & Int LJ South Africa — Comparative and International Law Journal of Southern Africa
Comp & Int'l LJS Afr — Comparative and International Law Journal of Southern Africa
Comp & L — Computers and Law
Comp and Maths with Appls — Computers and Mathematics with Applications
Comp & Med — Computers and Medicine
Comp & People — Computers and People
Comp and Sec — Computers and Security
Comp Anim Nutr — Comparative Animal Nutrition
Companion Anim Pract — Companion Animal Practice
Companion Bot Mag — Companion to the Botanical Magazine
Companion Microbiol — Companion to Microbiology
Company Law — Company Lawyer
Comparative Ed — Comparative Education
Comparative Educ R — Comparative Education Review
Comparative Pol Studies — Comparative Political Studies
Compare — Journal. Comparative Education Society in Europe (British Section)
Compar Educ — Comparative Education
Compar Educ Rev — Comparative Education Review
Compar Pol Stud — Comparative Political Studies
Comp Arquit A & Archit — Composicion Arquitectonica/Art and Architecture
COMPASS — Automotive Competitive Assessment Data Bank
Compass Proc Annu Conf Comput Assur — COMPASS. Proceedings of the Annual Conference on Computer Assurance
Comp Bioc A — Comparative Biochemistry and Physiology. A. Comparative Physiology
Comp Bioc B — Comparative Biochemistry and Physiology. B. Comparative Biochemistry
Comp Bioc C — Comparative Biochemistry and Physiology. C. Comparative Pharmacology [Later, Comparative Biochemistry and Physiology. C. Comparative Pharmacology and Toxicology]
Comp Biochem Mol Evol Compr Biochem — Comparative Biochemistry. Molecular Evolution. Comprehensive Biochemistry
Comp Biochem Physiol — Comparative Biochemistry and Physiology
Comp Biochem Physiol A Comp Physiol — Comparative Biochemistry and Physiology. A. Comparative Physiology
Comp Biochem Physiol A Mol Integr Physiol — Comparative Biochemistry and Physiology. Part A. Molecular and Integrative Physiology
Comp Biochem Physiol A Physiol — Comparative Biochemistry and Physiology. Part A. Physiology
Comp Biochem Physiol B — Comparative Biochemistry and Physiology. B. Comparative Biochemistry
Comp Biochem Physiol B Biochem Mol Biol — Comparative Biochemistry and Physiology. Part B. Biochemistry and Molecular Biology
Comp Biochem Physiol B Comp Biochem — Comparative Biochemistry and Physiology. B. Comparative Biochemistry
Comp Biochem Physiol Biochem Mol Biol — Comparative Biochemistry and Physiology. Biochemistry and Molecular Biology
Comp Biochem Physiol C — Comparative Biochemistry and Physiology. C. Comparative Pharmacology [Later, Comparative Biochemistry and Physiology. C. Comparative Pharmacology and Toxicology]
Comp Biochem Physiol C Comp Pharmacol — Comparative Biochemistry and Physiology. C. Comparative Pharmacology [Later, Comparative Biochemistry and Physiology. C. Comparative Pharmacology and Toxicology]
Comp Biochem Physiol C Comp Pharmacol Toxicol — Comparative Biochemistry and Physiology. C. Comparative Pharmacology and Toxicology
Comp Biochem Physiol C Pharmacol Toxicol Endocrinol — Comparative Biochemistry and Physiology. Part C. Pharmacology, Toxicology, and Endocrinology
Comp Biochem Physiol Part A Mol Integr Physiol — Comparative Biochemistry and Physiology. Part A. Molecular & Integrative Physiology
Comp Biochem Physiol Pharmacol Toxicol Endocrinol — Comparative Biochemistry and Physiology. Pharmacology, Toxicology, and Endocrinology
Comp Biochem Physiol Physiol — Comparative Biochemistry and Physiology. Physiology
Comp Biochem Physiol Transp Proc Meet Int Conf — Comparative Biochemistry and Physiology of Transport. Proceedings ofthe Meeting. International Conference on Biological Membranes
Comp Bul — Computer Bulletin
Comp Bus — Computing for Business
CompC — Composition Chronicle
Comp Cda — Computing Canada
Comp Cda F — Computing Canada Focus
Comp Chem — Computers and Chemistry
Comp Chem Biochem Res — Computers in Chemical and Biochemical Research
Comp Civ R — Comparative Civilizations Review
Comp Comm — Computer Communications
Comp Compacts — Computer Compacts
Comp Crit — Comparative Criticism
CompD — Comparative Drama
Comp Data — Computer Data
Comp Data Rep — Comparative Data Report
Comp Dec — Computer Decisions
Comp Decisions — Computer Decisions
Comp Des — Computer Design
CompDr — Comparative Drama
Comp Drama — Comparative Drama
Comp Ed — Comparative Education
Comp Ed R — Comparative Education Review
Comp Educ — Comparative Education

Comp Educ R — Comparative Education Review
Comp Edu Re — Comparative Education Review
COMPEL Int J Comput Math Electr Electron Eng — COMPEL. The International Journal for Computation and Mathematics in Electrical and Electronic Engineering
Compend Contin Educ Dent — Compendium of Continuing Education in Dentistry
Compend Contin Educ Pract Vet — Compendium on Continuing Education for the Practicing Veterinarian
Compend Dtsch Ges Mineraloelwiss Kohlechem — Compendium. Deutsche Gesellschaft fuer Mineraloelwissenschaft und Kohlechemie
Compend Invest Clin Latinoam — Compendium de Investigaciones Clinicas Latinoamericanas
Comp Endocrinol Proc Columbia Univ Symp — Comparative Endocrinology. Proceedings. Columbia University Symposium on Comparative Endocrinology
Comp Endocrinol Proc Int Symp — Comparative Endocrinology. Proceedings. International Symposium on Comparative Endocrinology
Compend Pap Natl Conv Can Manuf Chem Spec Assoc — Compendium of Papers Presented. National Convention. CanadianManufacturers of Chemical Specialties Association
Compend Tech Pap Annu Meet Inst Transp Eng — Compendium of Technical Papers. Annual Meeting. Institute of Transportation Engineers
Compens Benefits Rev — Compensation and Benefits Review
Compens Med — Compensation Medicine
Compens R — Compensation Review
Compens Rev — Compensation Review
Comp Fluids — Computers and Fluids
Comp Focus — Computerworld Focus
Comp Gen Pharmacol — Comparative and General Pharmacology
Comp Gra Forum — Computer Graphics Forum
Comp Graphics — Computer Graphics
Comp Graph Technol — Computer Graphics Technology
Comp Graph Wrld — Computer Graphics World
Comp G Wld — Computer Graphics World
Comp Haematol Int — Comparative Haematology International
Compil Estud Geol Of Colomb Inst Geol Nac (Colomb) — Compilacion de los Estudios Geologicos Oficiales en Colombia. InstitutoGeologico Nacional (Colombia)
Compil Res Work Accomplished Weld Res Inst (Bratislava) — Compilation of Research Work Accomplished in the Welding Research Institute (Bratislava)
Compil Res Work Weld Res Inst Bratislava — Compilation of Research Work Accomplished. Welding Research Institute. Bratislava
Comp Immunol Microbiol Infect Dis — Comparative Immunology, Microbiology, and Infectious Diseases
Comp Ind Rpt — Computer Industry Report
Comp Indus — Computers in Industry
Comp in Ed — Computers in Education
Comp Int Law J South Afr — Comparative and International Law Journal of Southern Africa
Comp Int Law J Sth Afr — Comparative and International Law Journal of Southern Africa
Comp J — Computer Journal
Comp Jurid Rev — Comparative Juridical Review
Comp Jur Rev — Comparative Juridical Review
Comp L — Comparative Literature
CompL — Computational Linguistics
Comp Lab Law — Comparative Labor Law
Com Plan R — Community Planning Review
Comp Law — Computer Law and Tax Report
Comp Law J — Computer/Law Journal
Comp Lawy — Company Lawyer
Complement Dis Proc Complement Dis Workshop — Complement in Disease. Proceedings. Complement in Disease Workshop
Complement Inflammation — Complement and Inflammation. Laboratory and Clinical Research
Complete Abstr Jpn Chem Lit — Complete Abstracts of Japanese Chemical Literature
Complete Chem Abstr Jpn — Complete Chemical Abstracts of Japan
Complete Specif (Aust) — Complete Specification (Australia)
Complete Specif (India) — Complete Specification (India)
Complete Texts Lect Congr Apimondia Prague Transl — Complete Texts of Lectures of Congress of Apimondia in Prague.Translations
Complexation Chromatogr — Complexation Chromatography
Complex Chem — Complex Chemistry
Complex Chem React Syst Proc Workshop — Complex Chemical Reaction Systems. Mathematical Modelling and Simulation. Proceedings. Workshop
Complex Invest Water Reservoirs — Complex Investigations of Water Reservoirs
Complexity Chaos Biol Evol — Complexity, Chaos, and Biological Evolution
Complexity Int — Complexity International [*Electronic Publication*]
Complex Variables Theory Appl — Complex Variables. Theory and Application
Comp Lit — Comparative Literature
Comp Lit Index — Computer Literature Index
Comp Lit St — Comparative Literature Studies
Comp Lit Stud — Comparative Literature Studies
Comp LJ — Computer/Law Journal
Comp L Rev — Comparative Law Review
Comp L Rev Japan Inst — Comparative Law Review. Japan Institute of Comparative Law
Comp L Ser — Comparative Law Series. United States Bureau of Foreign and Domestic Commerce. General Legal Bulletin
Comp L Yb — Comparative Law Yearbook
Comp Manage — Computer Management
Comp Master Marin Aust J — Company of Master Mariners of Australia. Journal
Comp Math — Compositio Mathematica
Comp Math Sci Educ — Computers in Mathematical Sciences Education
Comp Med — Comparative Medicine

Comp Med East West — Comparative Medicine East and West
Comp Merch — Computer Merchandising
Comp Methods Appl Mech Eng — Computer Methods in Applied Mechanics and Engineering
Comp Methods Geosci — Computer Methods in the Geosciences
Comp Mgmt — Computer Management
Comp Net — Computer Networks
Comp News-Rec — Composers News-Record
Components Rep — Components Report
Component Technol — Component Technology
Comp Oper Res — Computers and Operations Research
Compos Arquit — Composicion Arquitectonica
Compos Eng — Composites Engineering
Compos Interfaces Proc Int Conf — Composite Interfaces. Proceedings. International Conference on Composite Interfaces
Composites (Guildford UK) — Composites (Guildford, United Kingdom)
Composites Technol Rev — Composites Technology Review
Compositio Math — Compositio Mathematica
Compos Manuf — Composites Manufacturing
Compos Manuf Technol — Composite Manufacturing Technology
Compos Mater — Composite Materials
Compos Mater Lect Inst Metall Refresher Course — Composite Materials. Lectures Delivered at the Institution ofMetallurgists Refresher Course
Compos Mater Offshore Oper Proc Int Workshop — Composite Materials for Offshore Operations. Proceedings of the International Workshop
Compos Mater Ser — Composite Materials Series
Compos Polym — Composite Polymers
Compos Proc Int Conf Compos Mater — Composites. Design, Manufacture, and Application. Proceedings. International Conference on Composite Materials
Compos Sci Technol — Composites Science and Technology
Compos Struct — Composite Structures
Compos Struct Proc Int Conf — Composite Structures. Proceedings. International Conference on Composite Structures
Compos Struct Proc Int Conf Compos Struct — Composite Structures. Proceedings. International Conference onComposite Structures
Compos Technol Rev — Composites Technology Review
Compost Sci — Compost Science [*Later, Bio Cycle*]
Compost Sci Land Util — Compost Science/Land Utilization [*Later, Bio Cycle*]
Compos Wood — Composite Wood
Comp Pathobiol — Comparative Pathobiology
Comp Pathol Bull — Comparative Pathology Bulletin
Comp Perf — Computer Performance
Comp Pers — Computer Personnel
Comp Phys Comm — Computer Physics Communications
Comp Physiol — Comparative Physiology
Comp Physiol Ecol — Comparative Physiology and Ecology
Comp Plan Jnl — Compensation Planning Journal
Comp Pol — Comparative Politics
Comp Poli S — Comparative Political Studies
Comp Polit — Comparative Politics
Comp Politics — Comparative Politics
Comp Polit Stud — Comparative Political Studies
Comp Pol Stud — Comparative Political Studies
Comp Pract Sp Rep — Computing Practices Special Reports
Comp Psychi — Comprehensive Psychiatry
Comp R — Compensation Review
Compr — Comprendre
Compr Anal Chem — Comprehensive Analytical Chemistry
Compr Anal Environ Proc Sov Am Symp — Comprehensive Analysis of the Environment. Proceedings. Soviet-American Symposium
Comprehensive Ed — Comprehensive Education
Comprehensive Nurs Mon (Tokyo) — Comprehensive Nursing Monthly (Tokyo)
Comprehensive Psychiat — Comprehensive Psychiatry
Compr Endocrinol — Comprehensive Endocrinology
Compres Air — Compressed Air
Comp Resell — Computer Reseller News
Compress Air — Compressed Air
Compressed Air Mag — Compressed Air Magazine
Compressed Gas Assoc Annu Rep — Compressed Gas Association. Annual Report
Compressed Gas Assoc Tech Suppl Annu Rep — Compressed Gas Association. Technical Supplement to the Annual Report
Comp Rev — Compensation Review
Comp Rev — Computing Reviews
Compr Immunol — Comprehensive Immunology
Compr Nurs Q — Comprehensive Nursing Quarterly
Com Prof — Commonwealth Professional
Com Prov Mnmts Hist & A Alicante — Comision Provincial de Monumentos Historicos y Artisticos de Alicante
Compr Pediatr Nurs — Comprehensive Pediatric Nursing
Compr Psychiatry — Comprehensive Psychiatry
Compr Ther — Comprehensive Therapy
Comp Rtl — Computer Retail News. The Newspaper for Systems and Software Retailing
Compr Virol — Comprehensive Virology
Comp Sci T — Composites Science and Technology
Comp Stan — Computers and Standards
Comp Stand — Computers and Standards
Comp Strat — Comparative Strategy
Comp Stud S — Comparative Studies in Society and History
Comp Stud Soc & Hist — Comparative Studies in Society and History
Comp Stud Soc Hist — Comparative Studies in Society and History
Comp Stud Social — Comparative Studies in Sociology
Comp Studs Soc Hist — Comparative Studies in Society and History
Comp Surv — Computing Surveys

Comp Talk — Computer Talk
Comp Tech Rev — Composites Technology Review
Comptes Rend — Comptes Rendus. Academie des Sciences
Comptes Rend Bell Let — Comptes-Rendus des Seances. Academie des Inscriptions et Belles-Lettres
Comptes Rendus — Comptes Rendus Hebdomadaires des Seances. Academie des Sciences
Comptes Rendus (Paris) — Comptes Rendus des Seances. Academie des Inscriptions et Belles-Lettres (Paris)
Comp Transfus Med — Comparative Transfusion Medicine
Compt Rend Acad — Comptes Rendus des Seances. Academie des Inscriptions et Belles-Lettres
Compt Rend Acad Agr France — Comptes Rendus. Academie d'Agriculture de France
Compt Rend Acad Bulg Sci — Comptes Rendus. Academie Bulgare des Sciences
Compt Rend Acad Inscript Belles Lett — Comptes Rendus. Academie des Inscriptions et Belles-Lettres
Compt Rend Acad Sci — Comptes Rendus. Academie des Sciences
Compt Rend Acad Sci Outre-Mer — Comptes Rendus Trimestriels des Seances. Academie des Sciences d'Outre-Mer
Compt Rend Acad Sc (Paris) — Comptes Rendus Hebdomadaires des Seances. Academie des Sciences (Paris)
Compt Rend Assoc Strasbourg Amis Hist Nat — Compte-Rendu de l'Association Strasbourgeoise des Amis de l'Histoire Naturelle
Compt Rend Cong Internat Med Trop et Hyg — Comptes Rendus. Congres International de Medecine Tropicale et d'Hygiene
Compt Rend Congr Nat Soc Savant Sect Sci — Comptes Rendus. Congres National des Societes Savantes. Section des Sciences
Compt Rend Hebd Seances Mem Soc Biol — Comptes-Rendus Hebdomadaires des Seances et Memoires. Societe de Biologie
Compt Rend Seances Commun Acad Sci Colon — Comptes-Rendus des Seances. Communications de l'Academie des Sciences Coloniales
Compt Rend Seances Publiques Inst Roy Pays Bas — Comptes Rendus des Seances Publiques. Institut Royal des Pays-Bas
Compt Rend Soc Biol (Paris) — Comptes Rendus des Seances. Societe de Biologie et de Ses Filiales et Associees (Paris)
Compt Rend Soc Sci Wroclaw — Comptes Rendus. Societe des Sciences et des Lettres de Wroclaw
Compt Rend Trav Carlsberg Lab — Comptes-Rendus des Travaux du Carlsberg Laboratoriet
Compt Rend Trav Soc Agric Lyon — Compte Rendu des Travaux. Societe d'Agriculture, Histoire Naturelle, et Arts Utiles de Lyon
Compt Rend Trav Soc Natl Havraise Etudes Diverses — Compte Rendu des Travaux de la Societe Nationale Havraise d'Etudes Diverses
Comp Urb Res — Comparative Urban Research
Comput — Computer
Comput Abstr — Computer Abstracts
Comput Acquis Syst Ser — Computerized Acquisitions Systems Series
Comput Age — Computer Age
Comput Aided Chem Eng — Computer-Aided Chemical Engineering
Comput Aided Des — Computer-Aided Design
Comput Aided Des Compos Mater Technol Int Conf — Computer Aided Design in Composite Material Technology. International Conference
Comput Aided Geom Des — Computer Aided Geometric Design
Comput Aided Geom Design — Computer Aided Geometric Design
Comput Aided Surg — Computer Aided Surgery
Comput Anal Thermochem Data — Computer Analysis of Thermochemical Data
Comput and Autom and People — Computers and Automation and People
Comput and Biomed Res — Computers and Biomedical Research
Comput & Chem Eng — Computers and Chemical Engineering
Comput & Contr Abstr — Computer and Control Abstracts
Comput and Data Process Technol — Computer and Data Processor Technology
Comput and Educ — Computers and Education
Comput & Electr Eng — Computers and Electrical Engineering
Comput and Fluids — Computers and Fluids
Comput & Geosci — Computers and Geosciences
Comput & Graphics — Computers and Graphics
Comput & Human — Computers and the Humanities
Comput & Humanities — Computers and the Humanities
Comput and Ind Eng — Computers and Industrial Engineering
Comput & Info Sys — Computer and Information Systems
Comput and Math Ser — Computers and Math Series
Comput & Math with Appl — Computers and Mathematics with Applications
Comput and Medieval Data Process — Computers and Medieval Data Processing
Comput & Oper Res — Computers and Operations Research
Comput and People — Computers and People
Comput and Secur — Computers and Security
Comput and Soc — Computers and Society
Comput and Struct — Computers and Structures
Comput and Structures — Computers and Structures
Comput Appl — Computer Applications
Comput Appl — Computers and Their Applications
Comput Appl Archaeol — Computer Applications in Archaeology
Comput Appl Biosci — Computer Applications in the Biosciences
Comput Appl Chem (China) — Computers and Applied Chemistry (China)
Comput Appl Eng Educ — Computer Applications in Engineering Education
Comput Appl Lab — Computer Applications in the Laboratory
Comput Appl Nat and Soc Sci — Computer Applications in the Natural and Social Sciences
Comput Appl New Ser — Computer Applications. New Series
Comput Appl Serv — Computer Applications Service
Comput Arch Elektron Rechn — Computing. Archiv fuer Elektronisches Rechnen
Comput Arch Inf Num — Computing. Archiv fuer Informatik und Numerik
Comput Archit News — Computer Architecture News
Comput Artificial Intelligence — Computers and Artificial Intelligence

Comput Aspects Study Biol Macromol Nucl Magn Reson Spectrosc — Computational Aspects of the Study of Biological Macromolecules by Nuclear Magnetic Resonance Spectroscopy
Comput Autom — Computers and Automation [*Later, Computers and People*]
Comput Biol and Med — Computers in Biology and Medicine
Comput Biol Med — Computers in Biology and Medicine
Comput Biom — Computers and Biomedical Research
Comput Biomed Res — Computers and Biomedical Research
Comput Bull — Computer Bulletin
Comput Busn — Computer Business News
Comput Bus News — Computer Business News
Comput Cardiol — Computers in Cardiology
Comput Cat Syst Ser — Computerized Cataloging Systems Series
Comput Chem — Computers and Chemistry
Comput Chem Biochem Res — Computers in Chemical and Biochemical Research
Comput Chem Educ Res Proc Int Conf — Computers in Chemical Education and Research. Proceedings. International Conference on Computers in Chemical Research, Education, and Technology
Comput Chem Eng — Computers and Chemical Engineering
Comput Chem Instrum — Computers in Chemistry and Instrumentation
Comput Chem Singapore — Computational Chemistry (Singapore). Reviews of Current Trends
Comput Circ Syst Ser — Computerized Circulation Systems Series
Comput Civ Eng New York — Computing in Civil Engineering (New York)
Comput Commun — Computer Communications
Comput Commun Rev — Computer Communication Review
Comput Complexity — Computational Complexity
Comput Contrib — Computer Contributions
Comput Control Abstr — Computer and Control Abstracts
Comput Control Abstracts — Computer and Control Abstracts
Comput Control Eng J — Computing and Control Engineering Journal
Comput Control Inf Theory — Computers, Control, and Information Theory
Comput Data — Computer Data
Comput Decis — Computer Decisions
Comput Des — Computer Design
Comput Econom — Computational Economics
Comput Ed Math Sci Engrg — Computation in Education. Mathematics, Science, and Engineering
Comput Educ — Computer Education
Comput Electr Eng — Computers and Electrical Engineering
Comput Electr Engrg — Computers and Electrical Engineering
Comput Electron Agric — Computers and Electronics in Agriculture
Comput Elem Syst — Computer Elements and Systems
Comput Eng Proc Int Conf Exhib — Computers in Engineering. Proceedings of the International Conference and Exhibit
Comput Engrg Ser — Computer Engineering Series
Comput Enhanced Anal Spectrosc — Computer-Enhanced Analytical Spectroscopy
Comput Enhanced Spectrosc — Computer Enhanced Spectroscopy
Comput Enhanc Spectrosc — Computer Enhanced Spectroscopy
Comput Environ Urban Syst — Computers, Environment, and Urban Systems
Comput Equip Rev — Computer Equipment Review
Computer Aided Des — Computer-Aided Design
Computer D — Computer Digest
Computer Educ — Computer Education
Computer Engrg Ser — Computer Engineering Series
Computer Hu — Computers and the Humanities
Computer J — Computer Journal
Computer LJ — Computer Law/Journal
Computer Mus J — Computer Music Journal
Computer Pe — Computers and People
Computer Ph — Computer Physics Communications
Computer Pr — Computer Programs in Biomedicine
Computers & Chem Engng — Computers and Chemical Engineering
Computers and Ed — Computers and Education
Computers and Educ — Computers and Education
Computers and L — Computers and Law
Computers Geosci — Computers and Geosciences
Computers Mech Engrg — Computers in Mechanical Engineering
Computers Mus Res — Computers in Music Research
Computers Struc — Computers and Structures
Computer Wkly — Computer Weekly
Comput Fluids — Computers and Fluids
Comput Fraud and Secur Bull — Computer Fraud and Security Bulletin
Comput Geol — Computers and Geology
Comput Geom — Computational Geometry
Comput Geosci — Computers and Geosciences
Comput Geotech — Computers and Geotechnics
Comput Graphics — Computers and Graphics
Comput Graphics ACM — Computer Graphics (ACM)
Comput Graphics and Art — Computer Graphics and Art
Comput Graphics and Image Process — Computer Graphics and Image Processing
Comput Graphics Forum — Computer Graphics Forum
Comput Graphics Image Process — Computer Graphics and Image Processing
Comput Graphics World — Computer Graphics World
Comput Healthc — Computers in Healthcare
Comput Hosp — Computers in Hospitals
Comput Hum — Computers and the Humanities
Comput Hum Behav — Computers in Human Behavior
Comput Imaging Vision — Computational Imaging and Vision
Comput Ind — Computers in Industry
Comput Ind Eng — Computers and Industrial Engineering
Comput Inf — Computer Information

Comput Inf Syst — Computer and Information Systems
Comput Inf Syst Abstr J — Computer and Information Systems Abstracts Journal
Computing J Abs — Computing Journal Abstracts
Computing Suppl — Computing. Supplementum
Comput Integr Manuf Syst — Computer Integrated Manufacturing Systems
Comput Intell — Computational Intelligence
Comput Intelligence — Computational Intelligence
Comput J — Computer Journal
Comput L — Computational Linguistics
Comput Lang — Computer Languages
Comput/Law J — Computer/Law Journal
Comput Linguist and Comput Lang — Computational Linguistics and Computer Languages
Comput Mach Fi — Computing Machinery Field
Comput Mach Field — Computing Machinery Field
Comput Manage — Computer Management
Comput Marketplace — Computer Marketplace
Comput Mater Sci — Computational Materials Science
Comput Math Anal Ser — Computational Mathematics and Analysis Series
Comput Math Appl — Computers and Mathematics with Applications
Comput Math Math Phys — Computational Mathematics and Mathematical Physics
Comput Math Model — Computational Mathematics and Modeling
Comput Mech — Computational Mechanics. Solids, Fluids, Engineered Materials, Aging Infrastructure, Molecular Dynamics, Heat Transfer, Manufacturing Processes, Optimization, Fracture and Integrity
Comput Mech Adv — Computational Mechanics Advances
Comput Med — Computers and Medicine
Comput Med Imaging Graph — Computerized Medical Imaging and Graphics
Comput Med Imaging Graphics — Computerized Medical Imaging and Graphics
Comput Method Program Biomed — Computer Methods and Programs in Biomedicine
Comput Methods Appl Mech & Eng — Computer Methods in Applied Mechanics and Engineering
Comput Methods Appl Mech & Engng — Computer Methods in Applied Mechanics and Engineering
Comput Methods Appl Mech Eng — Computer Methods in Applied Mechanics and Engineering
Comput Methods Appl Mech Engrg — Computer Methods in Applied Mechanics and Engineering
Comput Methods Biomech Biomed Engin — Computer Methods in Biomechanics and Biomedical Engineering
Comput Methods Macromol Sequence Anal — Computer Methods for Macromolecular Sequence Analysis
Comput Methods Prog Biomed — Computer Methods and Programs in Biomedicine
Comput Methods Programs Biomed — Computer Methods and Programs in Biomedicine
Comput Mgmt — Computer Management
Comput Microelectron — Computational Microelectronics
Comput Model Corros — Computer Modeling in Corrosion
Comput Model Polym — Computational Modeling of Polymers
Comput Models Cognition Percept — Computational Models of Cognition and Perception
Comput Model Simul Eng — Computer Modeling and Simulation in Engineering
Comput Model Simul Engrg — Computer Modeling and Simulation in Engineering
Comput Monogr — Computer Monographs
Comput Mus — Computer Music Journal
Comput Music J — Computer Music Journal
Comput Networks — Computer Networks
Comput Networks ISDN Syst — Computer Networks and ISDN Systems
Comput News — Computer News
Comput Newsl Schools Bus — Computing Newsletter for Schools of Business
Comput Nonlinear Mech Aerosp Eng — Computational Nonlinear Mechanics in Aerospace Engineering
Comput Nurs — Computers in Nursing
Comput OA — Computerworld Office Automation
Comput OC — Computerworld on Communications
Comput Oper Res — Computers and Operations Research
Comput Optim Appl — Computational Optimization and Applications
Comput Performance — Computer Performance
Comput Peripherals Rev — Computer Peripherals Review
Comput Pers — Computer Personnel
Comput Phys — Computers in Physics
Comput Phys Comm — Computer Physics Communications
Comput Phys Commun — Computer Physics Communications
Comput Phys Proc Int Conf — Computational Physics. Proceedings of the International Conference on Computational Physics
Comput Phys Rep — Computer Physics Reports
Comput Polym Sci — Computational Polymer Science
Comput Prax — Computer Praxis
Comput Program Abstr — Computer Program Abstracts
Comput Programs Biomed — Computer Programs in Biomedicine
Comput Programs Chem — Computer Programs for Chemistry
Comput Psychiatry/Psychol — Computers in Psychiatry/Psychology
Comput Radiol — Computerized Radiology
Comput Ramblings Ext Comput Serv SD State Univ Coop Ext Serv — Computer Ramblings. Extension Computer Services. South Dakota State University.Cooperative Extension Service
Comput Rep Dep Archit Sci Syd Univ — Computer Report. Department of Architectural Science. University of Sydney
Comput Rev — Computing Reviews
Comput Rev Bibliogr Subj Index Curr Comput Lit — Computing Reviews. Bibliography and Subject Index of Current ComputingLiterature
Computrwld — Computerworld
Computrwl X — Computerworld Extra

Computrwoc — Computerwoche
Comput S Afr — Computing South Africa
Comput Sch — Computers in Schools
Comput Sci — Computers in Science
Comput Sci and Inf — Computer Science and Informatics
Comput Sci Appl Math — Computer Science and Applied Mathematics
Comput Sci Classics — Computer Science Classics
Comput Sci Econom Management — Computer Science in Economics and Management
Comput Sci J Moldova — Computer Science Journal of Moldova
Comput Sci Monographs (Tokyo) — Computer Science Monographs (Tokyo)
Comput Sci Sci Comput — Computer Science and Scientific Computing
Comput Sci Sci Comput Pro ICASE Conf — Computer Science and Scientific Computing. Proceedings. ICASE[*Institute for Computer Applications in Systems Engineering*] Conference on Scientific Computing
Comput Sci Texts — Computer Science Texts
Comput Sci Workbench — Computer Science Workbench
Comput Secur — Computers and Security
Comput Ser Syst Ser — Computerized Serials Systems Series
Comput Software Engrg Ser — Computer Software Engineering Series
Comput Speech Lang — Computer Speech and Language
Comput Stand Interfaces — Computer Standards and Interfaces
Comput Stat and Data Anal — Computational Statistics and Data Analysis
Comput Statist — Computational Statistics
Comput Struct — Computers and Structures
Comput Stud Hum & Verbal Behav — Computer Studies in the Humanities and Verbal Behavior
Comput Suppl — Computing. Supplementum
Comput Surv — Computer Survey
Comput Surv — Computing Surveys
Comput Survey — Computing Surveys
Comput Surveys — Computing Surveys
Comput Syst — Computer Systems
Comput Syst Eng Int J — Computing Systems in Engineering. An International Journal
Comput Syst Sci Eng — Computer Systems Science and Engineering
Comput Syst Sthn Afr — Computer Systems in Southern Africa
Comput Talk — Computer Talk
Comput Tech — Computational Techniques
Comput Technol Rev — Computer Technology Review
Comput Terminals Rev — Computer Terminals Review
Comput Theor Polym Sci — Computational and Theoretical Polymer Science
Comput Times with Computacards — Computer Times with Computacards
Comput Today — Computing Today
Comput Tomogr — Computerized Tomography
Comput Vienna New York — Computing (Vienna/New York)
Comput Vis Appl Meet Challenges AIPR Workshop — Computer Vision Applications. Meeting the Challenges. AIPR Workshop
Comput Vision Graphics and Image Process — Computer Vision. Graphics and Image Processing
Comput Week — Computer Week
Comput Wkly — Computer Weekly
Comput Wkly Int — Computer Weekly International
Comput World — Computer World
Computwrld — Computerworld
Comp Wkly — Computer Weekly
Comp Wld BG — Computerworld Buyer's Guide
Compwrld OA — Computerworld Office Automation
Compwrld on Comm — Computerworld on Communications
ComQ — Commonwealth Quarterly
ComQ — Communication Quarterly
ComR — Communication Research
Comrc Intl — Commerce International
COMRDW — Computerized Radiology
Com Rep — Commerce Reporter
ComRev — Computing Reviews
ComS — Comparative Studies in Society and History
COMSAT Tech Rev — COMSAT [*Communications Satellite Corp.*] Technical Review
Com Spec Katanga Ann Ser Mines Ser Geogr Geol — Comite Special du Katanga. Annales du Service des Mines et du Service Geographique et Geologique
Com Stat Energ Nucl Inst Fiz At Rep (Rom) — Comitetul de Stat pentru Energia Nucleara. Institutul de Fizica Atomica. Report(Romania)
Comt — Commentary
Com Today — Commerce Today
Comun Acad Rep Pop Romine — Comunicarile. Academiei Republicii Populare Romine
Comun Acad Republ Populare Romine — Comunicarile Academiei Republicii Populare Romine
Comun Acad Repub Pop Rom — Comunicarile. Academiei Republicii Populare Romine
Comun Biol — Comunicaciones Biologicas
Comun Bot — Comunicari de Botanica
Comun Bot Mus Hist Nat Montev — Comunicaciones Botanicas. Museo de Historia Natural de Montevideo
Comun Coloq Invest Agua — Comunicaciones Presentadas al Coloquio de Investigaciones sobre el Agua
Comun Dis Rep CDR Suppl — Communicable Disease Report. CDR Supplement
Comunicacao e Soc — Comunicacao e Sociedade
Comunicari Bot — Comunicari de Botanica
Comunic S Salvador — Comunicaciones. Instituto Tropical de Investigaciones Cientificas (San Salvador)
Comun INIA (Inst Nac Invest Agrar) Ser Gen — Comunicaciones. INIA (Instituto Nacional de Investigaciones Agrarias). Serie General

Comun INIA (Inst Nac Invest Agrar) Ser Prod Anim — Comunicaciones. INIA (Instituto Nacional de Investigaciones Agrarias). Serie Produccion Animal

Comun INIA (Inst Nac Invest Agrar) Ser Tecnol — Comunicaciones. INIA (Instituto Nacional de Investigaciones Agrarias). Serie Tecnologia

Comun INIA (Inst Nac Invest Agrar) Ser Tecnol Agrar — Comunicaciones. INIA (Instituto Nacional de Investigaciones Agrarias). Serie Tecnologia Agraria

Comun INIA Prot Veg — Comunicaciones. INIA [*Instituto Nacional de Investigaciones Agrarias*]. Serie Proteccion Vegetal

Comun INIA Ser Prod Anim (Spain) — Comunicaciones. INIA [*Instituto Nacional de Investigaciones Agrarias*] Serie Produccion Animal (Spain)

Comun INIA Ser Prod Veg — Comunicaciones. INIA [*Instituto Nacional de Investigaciones Agrarias*]. Serie Produccion Vegetal

Comun INIA Ser Prod Veg Inst Nac Invest Agrar — Comunicaciones. INIA [*Instituto Nacional de Investigaciones Agrarias*]. Serie Production Vegetal

Comun INIA Ser Prot Veg — Comunicaciones. INIA [*Instituto Nacional de Investigaciones Agrarias*]. Serie Proteccion Vegetal

Comun INIA Ser Pro Veg (Spain) — Comunicaciones. INIA [*Instituto Nacional de Investigaciones Agrarias*]. Serie Proteccion Vegetal (Spain)

Comun INIA Ser Recur Nat — Comunicaciones. INIA [*Instituto Nacional de Investigaciones Agrarias*]. Serie Recursos Naturales

Comun Inst Cienc Nat Mat Univ El Salvador — Comunicaciones. Instituto de Ciencias Naturales y Matematicas. Universidad de El Salvador

Comun Inst For Invest Exp (Madrid) — Comunicacion. Instituto Forestal de Investigaciones y Experiencias (Madrid)

Comun (Inst Nac Invest Agrar) Ser Hig Sanid Anim (Spain) — Comunicaciones. INIA(Instituto Nacional de Investigaciones Agrarias). SerieHigiene y Sanidad Animal (Spain)

Comun (Inst Nac Invest Agrar) Ser Prod Anim (Spain) — Comunicaciones. INIA(Instituto Nacional de Investigaciones Agrarias). SerieProduccion Animal (Spain)

Comun (Inst Nac Invest Agrar) Ser Prot Veg (Spain) — Comunicaciones. INIA(Instituto Nacional de Investigaciones Agrarias). SerieProteccion Vegetal (Spain)

Comun (Inst Nac Invest Agrar) Ser Tecnol Agrar (Spain) — Comunicaciones. INIA(Instituto Nacional de Investigaciones Agrarias). SerieTecnologia Agraria (Spain)

Comun Inst Nac Invest Cienc Nat Cienc Bot — Comunicaciones. Instituto Nacional de Investigacion de las Ciencias Naturales. Ciencias Botanicas

Comun Inst Nac Invest Ci Nat Ser Ci Bot — Comunicaciones del Instituto Nacional de Investigaciones de las Ciencias Naturales Anexo al Museo Argentino de Ciencias Naturales Bernardino Rivadavia. Serie Ciencias Botanicas

Comun Inst Trop Invest Cient — Comunicaciones. Instituto Tropical de Investigaciones Cientificas

Comun Inst Trop Invest Ci Univ El Salvador — Comunicaciones. Instituto Tropical de Investigaciones Cientificas, Universidad de El Salvador

Comun Intern — Comunita Internazionale

Comunita Int — Comunita Internazionale

Comunita Internaz — Comunita Internazionale

Comun Jorn Com Esp Deterg — Comunicaciones Presentadas a las Jornadas del Comite Espanol de laDetergencia

Comun Missao Estud Agron Ultramar (Lisb) — Comunicacao-Missao de Estudos Agronomicos do Ultramar (Lisbon)

Comun Mus Cienc PUCRGS (Pontif Univ Catol Rio Grande Do Sul) — Comunicacoes. Museu de Ciencias. PUCRGS (Pontificia Universidade Catolica doRio Grande Do Sul)

Comun Paleontol Mus Hist Nat Montev — Comunicaciones Paleontologicas. Museo de Historia Natural de Montevideo

Comun Progr Antrop Social Rio — Comunicaaao. Programa de Pos-Graduaaao em Antropologia Social

Comun Reun Cient Soc Esp Mineral — Comunicaciones de las Reuniones Cientificas de la Sociedad Espanola deMineralogia

Comun Serv Geol Port — Comunicacoes. Servicos Geologicos de Portugal

Comun Soc Malacol Urug — Comunicaciones. Sociedad Malacologica del Uruguay

Comun Stiint Ses Cent Cercet Metal Inst Politeh Bucuresti — Comunicari Stiintifice Prezentate la Sesiunea. Centrul de Cercetaripentru Metalurgie. Institutul Politehnic Bucuresti

Comun Stiint Simp Biodeterior Clim — Comunicari Stiintifice. Simpozion de Biodeteriorare si Climatizare

Comun Tec EMBRAPA Cent Pesqui Agropecu Trop Umido — Comunicado Tecnico. EMBRAPA [*Empresa Brasileira de Pesquisa Agropecuaria*] Centro de Pesquisa Agropecuaria do Tropico Umido

Comun Tec Empresa Pesqui Agropecu Bahia — Comunicado Tecnico. Empresa de Pesquisa Agropecuaria da Bahia

Comun Tec Empresa Pesqui Agropecu Estado Rio De J — Comunicado Tecnico. Empresa de Pesquisa Agropecuaria do Estado do Rio De Janeiro

Comun Tec Inst Ecol Exp Agric — Comunicados Tecnicos. Instituto de Ecologia e Experimentacao Agricolas

Comun Tec Inst Nac Carbon Sus Deri Francisco Pintado Fe — Comunicacion Tecnica. Instituto Nacional del Carbon y Sus Derivados"Francisco Pintado Fe"

Comun Univ El Salvador Inst Cienc Nat Mat — Comunicaciones. Universidad de El Salvador. Instituto de Ciencias Naturales y Matematicas

Comun y Cult — Comunicacion y Cultura

Comun Zool — Comunicari de Zoologie

Comun Zool Mus Hist Nat Montev — Comunicaciones Zoologicas. Museo de Historia Natural de Montevideo

Com Via — Communio Viatorum

Comw — Commonweal

Con — Confluence

Con — Connaissance. Revue de Lettres et d'Idees

CON — Conservator. Vaktijdschrift voor de Iisfrica Branche

Con — Constitutionnel

Con — Contact

Con — Contour

CON — Contribuciones

Con — Convivium

ConA — Connaissance des Arts

CONAEL — Contaminacion Ambiental

CONA J — CONA [*Canadian Orthopaedic Nurses Association*] Journal

Con BJ — Connecticut Bar Journal

Conc — Concilium. Internationale Zeitschrift fuer Theologie

Concast Technol News — Concast Technology News

Concept Immunopathol — Concepts in Immunopathology

Concepts Magn Reson — Concepts in Magnetic Resonance

Concepts Pediatr Neurosurg — Concepts in Pediatric Neurosurgery

Concepts Toxicol — Concepts in Toxicology

Concern Bull — Concern Bulletin

Conciliation Courts R — Conciliation Courts Review

Concimi Concimaz — Concimi e Concimazione

Concl — Conclusions du Ministere Public

Conc Milk Ind — Concentrated Milk Industries

Concor — Concordia Theological Monthly

Concord Theol Mthl — Concordia Theological Monthly

Concor H Inst Q — Concordia Historical Institute. Quarterly

Concor J — Concordia Journal

Concor Th Q — Concordia Theological Quarterly

Concours Med — Concours Medical

ConcPo — Concerning Poetry

Conc Poet — Concerning Poetry

Concr Abstr — Concrete Abstracts

Concr & Constr Engin — Concrete and Constructional Engineering

Concr Cem Age — Concrete Cement Age

Concr Constr — Concrete Construction

Concr Constr Eng — Concrete and Constructional Engineering

Concr Constr Eng Suppl — Concrete and Constructional Engineering. Supplement

Concr Constru Eng — Concrete and Constructional Engineering

Concr Eng — Concrete Engineering

Concr Eng Eng Archit Contract — Concrete Engineering for Engineers, Architects, and Contractors

Concrete P — Concrete Products

Concrete Q — Concrete Quarterly

Concrete Qly — Concrete Quarterly

Concrete Wks — Concrete Works

Concr Inst Aust News — Concrete Institute of Australia. News

Concr Int — Concrete International

Concr Int Des Constr — Concrete International. Design and Construction

Concr J — Concrete Journal

Concr Plant Prod — Concrete Plant and Production

Concr Precast Plant Technol — Concrete Precasting Plant and Technology

Concr Quart — Concrete Quarterly

Concr Res Technol — Concrete Research and Technology

Concr Soc Tech Rep — Concrete Society. Technical Report

Concr Technol Des — Concrete Technology and Design

Conc Theol Mthly — Concordia Theological Monthly

ConcTM — Concordia Theological Monthly

Conc Trid — Concilium Tridentinum

Concurrency Pract Exper — Concurrency Practice and Experience

Condens Matter News — Condensed Matter News

Condens Matter Phys — Condensed Matter Physics

Condens Matter Phys Aspects Electrochem Proc Conf — Condensed Matter Physics Aspects of Electrochemistry. Proceedings. Conference

Condens Matter Stud Nucl Methods Proc Zakopane Sch Phys — Condensed Matter Studies by Nuclear Methods. Proceedings. Zakopane School on Physics

Condens Matter Theor — Condensed Matter Theories

Condens Syst Low Dimens — Condensed Systems of Low Dimensionality

Con Des Temps — Connaissance des Temps, a l'Usage des Astronomes et des Navigateurs

CondH — Connaissance des Hommes

Condiment Sci Technol — Condiment Science and Technology

Condition — Conditions

Condiz dell'Aria — Condizionamneto dell'Aria

Cond Monit Diagn Technol — Condition Monitoring and Diagnostic Technology

Condotta Med — Condotta Medica

Cond Refl — Conditional Reflex

Cond Reflex — Conditional Reflex

CONEAT — Confinia Neurologica

Conegl Scuola Vit En A — Annali della Reale Scuola di Viticoltura e di Enologia in Conegliano

CONF — Conferences in Energy, Physics, and Mathematics

Conf — Conferencia

Conf — Conflict. An International Journal

Conf — Confluence

Conf — Confluent

CONFA — Confructa

Conf Adrenal Cortex Trans — Conference on Adrenal Cortex. Transactions

Conf Adv Compos — Conference on Advanced Composites

Conf Adv Magn Mater Their Appl — Conference on Advances in Magnetic Materials and Their Applications

Conf Afr Geol — Conference on African Geology

Conf Anaerobic Dig Solids Handl Proc — Conference on Anaerobic Digestion and Solids Handling. Proceedings

Conf Anal Cem Assoc Silic Mate Proc — Conference on the Analysis of Cement and Associated Silicate Materials.Proceedings

Conf Anal Chem Energy Technol — Conference on Analytical Chemistry in Energy Technology

Conf Appl Chem Unit Oper Processes — Conference on Applied Chemistry. Unit Operations and Processes

Conf Appl Crystallogr Proc — Conference on Applied Crystallography. Proceedings

Conf Appl Sci Technol Benefit Less Devel Areas UN — Conference on Application of Science and Technology for the Benefit of Less Developed Areas. United Nations

Conf Appl Small Accel — Conference on Application of Small Accelerators

Conf Assoc Cult It — Conferenze dell'Associazione Culturale Italiana

Conf Atmos Radiat Prepr — Conference on Atmospheric Radiation. Preprints

Conf Aust Fract Group Proc — Australian Fracture Group Conference. Proceedings

Conf Australas Corros Assoc — Conference. Australasian Corrosion Association

Conf Avic Eur — Conference Avicole Europeenne

Conf Avic Eur Atti — Conferenza Avicola Europea. Atti

CONFAW — Confructa

Conf Bd Bsns Mgt Rec — Conference Board. Business Management Record

Conf Bd Bsns Rec — Conference Board. Business Record

Conf Bd Rec — Conference Board. Record

Conf Betons Refract — Conference sur Betons Refractaires

Conf Biol Antioxid Trans — Conference on Biological Antioxidants. Transactions

Conf Biol Waste Treat Proc — Conference on Biological Waste Treatment. Proceedings

Conf Bioquim — Conferencias de Bioquimica

Conf Blood Clotting Allied Probl Trans — Conference on Blood Clotting and Allied Problems. Transactions

Conf Board Rec — Conference Board. Record

Conf Board Util Invest Rep — Conference Board Utility Investment Report

Conf Brd — Across the Board

ConfC — Conferences du Cenacle

Conf Capturing Sun Bioconver Pro — Conference on Capturing the Sun through Bioconversion. Proceedings

Conf Carbon Ext Abstr Program — Conference on Carbon. Extended Abstracts and Program

Conf Catal Org Symth — Conference on Catalysis in Organic Syntheses

Conf Ceram Electron — Conference on Ceramics for Electronics

Conf Char and Correc — National Conference of Charities and Correction. Proceedings

Conf Circompolaire Ecol Nord R — Conference Circompolaire sur l'Ecologie du Nord. Compte Rendu

Conf City Govt — National Conference for Good City Government. Proceedings

Conf City Planning — National Conference on City Planning. Proceedings

Conf Clay Mineral Petrol Proc — Conference on Clay Mineralogy and Petrology. Proceedings

Conf Clim Impact Assess Program Proc — Conference on the Climatic Impact Assessment Program. Proceedings

Conf Colloid Chem — Conference on Colloid Chemistry

Conf Colloq Int Prev Trait Alcool — Conferences Presentees au Colloque International sur la Prevention etle Traitement de l'Alcoolisme

Conf Colloq Int Prev Trait Toxicomanies — Conferences Presentees au Colloque International sur la Prevention etle Traitement des Toxicomanies

Conf Compat Propellants Explos Pyrotech Plast Addit — Conference on Compatibility of Propellants, Explosives, and Pyrotechnics with Plastics and Additives

Conf Connect Tissues Trans — Conference on Connective Tissues. Transactions

Conf Control Gaseous Sulphur Nitrogen Comp Emiss — Conference on the Control of Gaseous Sulphur and Nitrogen Compound Emission

Conf Coord Chem — Conference on Coordination Chemistry

Conf Coord Chem Proc — Conference on Coordination Chemistry. Proceedings

Conf Copper Coord Chem — Conference on Copper Coordination Chemistry

Conf Cotton Grow Probl Rep Summ Proc — Conference on Cotton Growing Problems. Report and Summary of Proceedings

Conf Cult Mar Invertebr Anim Proc — Conference on Culture of Marine Invertebrate Animals. Proceedings

Conf Cutaneous Toxic — Conference on Cutaneous Toxicity

Conf Dig IEEE Semicond Laser Conf — Conference Digest. IEEE International Semiconductor Laser Conference

Conf Dig Inst Phys (London) — Conference Digest. Institute of Physics (London)

Conf Dig Int Conf Infrared Millimeter Waves — Conference Digest. International Conference on Infrared and Millimeter Waves

Conf Dig Int Electr Electron Conf Expo — Conference Digest. International Electrical, Electronics Conference Exposition

Conf Dimens Strength Cal — Conference on Dimensioning and Strength Calculations

Confe — Conferencia

Confect Manuf — Confectionery Manufacture

Confect Prod — Confectionery Production

Confederazione Gen Ind Ital Notiz — Confederazione Generale dell'Industria Italiana Notiziario

Confed Nac Com — Confederacao Nacional do Comercio

Confed Nat Mutualite Coop Cred Agric Congres — Confederation Nationale de la Mutualite de la Cooperation et du Credit Agricoles Congres

Conf Elastoplast Technol Pap — Conference on Elastoplastics Technology. Papers

Conf Electr Insul Dielectr Phenom Annu Rep — Conference on Electrical Insulation and Dielectric Phenomena. AnnualReport

Conf Electron Beam Melting Refin State of the Art — Conference on Electron Beam Melting and Refining. State of the Art

Conf Environ Aspects Non Conv Energy Resour — Conference on Environmental Aspects of Non-Conventional EnergyResources

Conf Environ Chem Hum Anim Health Proc — Conference on Environmental Chemicals. Human and Animal Health. Proceedings

Conf Environ Impact Water Chlorination — Conference on the Abnvironmental Impact of Water Chlorination

Conference Bd Rec — Conference Board. Record

Confer Sem Mat Univ Bari — Conferenze. Seminario di Matematica. Universita di Bari

Conf e Studi Accad Polacca Sci Bibl Centro Studi Roma — Conferenze e Studi. Accademia Polacca delle Scienze. Biblioteca e Centro di Studi a Roma

Conf Eur Avic — Conference Europeenne de l'Aviculture

Conf Eur Microcirc — Conference Europeenne sur la Microcirculation

Conf Eur Microcirc — Conferenza Europea di Microcirculazione

Conf Eur Plast Caoutch CR — Conference Europeenne des Plastiques et des Caoutchoucs. Comptes Rendus

Conf Eur Soc Comp Physiol Biochem — Conference. European Society for Comparative Physiology and Biochemistry

Conf Exhib Int — Conferences and Exhibitions International

Conf Exp Med Surg Primates — Conference on Experimental Medicine and Surgery in Primates

Conf Extremely High Temp Proc — Conference on Extremely High Temperatures. Proceedings

Conf Factors Regul Blood Pressure Trans — Conference on Factors Regulating Blood Pressure. Transactions

Conf Fis Quim Org — Conferencia de Fisico-Quimica Organica

Conf Fluid Mach Proc — Conference on Fluid Machinery. Proceedings

Conf For Interafr Commun — Conference Forestiere Interafricaine. Communications

Conf Geol Caraibes Publ — Conference Geologique des Caraibes. Publication

Conf Ger Biochem Soc — Conference. German Biochemical Society

Conf Ges Aerosolforsch — Conference. Gesellschaft fuer Aerosolforschung

Conf Ges Biol Chem — Conference. Gesellschaft fuer Biologische Chemie

Conf Glass Probl — Conference on Glass Problems

Conf Great Lakes Res Proc — Conference on Great Lakes Research. Proceedings

Conf Halophilic Microorg — Conference on Halophilic Microorganisms

Conf Hemoglobin Switching — Conference on Hemoglobin Switching

Conf High Mol Compd — Conference on High Molecular Compounds

Conf Hist Medec — Conferences d'Histoire de la Medecine

Conf Hum Rel Ind Proc — Conference on Human Relations in Industry. Proceedings

Conf Hung Ther Invest Pharmacol — Conferentia Hungarica pro Therapia et Investigatione in Pharmacologia

Conf Hung Ther Invest Pharmacol Soc Pharmacol Hung — Conferentia Hungarica pro Therapia et Investigatione in Pharmacologia.Societas Pharmacologica Hungarica

Conf Ind Carbon Graphite Pap — Conference on Industrial Carbon and Graphite. Papers Read at theConference

Conf Ind Energy Conserv Technol — Conference on Industrial Energy Conservation Technology

Confinement Radioact Util Energ Nucl Actes Congr Int — Confinement de la Radioactivite dans l'Utilisation de l'Energie Nucleaire. Actes du Congres International

Confinia Neurol — Confinia Neurologica

Confin Neurol — Confinia Neurologica

Confin Psychiat — Confinia Psychiatrica

Confin Psychiatr — Confinia Psychiatrica

Conf In Situ Compos Proc — Conference on In Situ Composites. Proceedings

Confins Psychiatr — Confins de la Psychiatrie

Conf Install Eng — Conference on Installation Engineering

Conf Inst Nac Invest Agron Min Agr (Spain) — Conferencias. Instituto Nacional de Investigaciones Agronomicas. Ministerio Agricultura (Spain)

Conf Inst Nac Invest Agron (Spain) — Conferencias. Instituto Nacional de Investigaciones Agronomicas (Spain)

Conf Instrum Iron Steel Ind — Conference on Instrumentation for the Iron and Steel Industry

Conf Int Crudos Pesados Arena Bitum — Conferencia Internacional sobre Crudos Pesados y Arenas Bituminosas

Conf Interafr Sols — Conference Interafricaine des Sols

Conf Interam Agric (Caracas) — Conferencia Interamericana de Agricultura (Caracas)

Conf Interam Ensenanza Quim — Conferencia Interamericana sobre la Ensenanza de la Quimica

Conf Interam Radioquim — Conferencia Interamericana de Radioquimica

Conf Inter Am Tecnol Mater — Conferencia Inter-Americana en Tecnologia de Materiales

Conf Int Invest Cacao Mem — Conferencia Internacional de Investigaciones en Cacao. Memorias

Conf Int Met — Conference Internationale de Metallisation

Conf Int Metall Beryllium Commun — Conference Internationale sur la Metallurgie du Beryllium.Communications

Conf Int Meteorol Carpates — Conference Internationale sur la Meteorologie des Carpates

Conf Int Met Lourds Environ Colloq Procede — Conference Internationale sur les Metaux Lourds dans l'Environnement. Colloque Procede

Conf Int Pergelisol — Conference Internationale sur le Pergelisol

Conf Int Pesqui Cacau Mem — Conferencia Internacional de Pesquisas em Cacau. Memorias

Conf Int Pet Lourds Bruts Sables Bitum — Conference Internationale sur les Petroles Lourds Bruts et les SablesBitumineux

Conf Int Phenom Ionis Gaz CR — Conference Internationale sur les Phenomenes d'Ionisation dans les Gaz. Comptes Rendus

Conf Int Phys Chim Miner Amiante Resumes Commun — Conference Internationale sur la Physique et la Chimie des Minerauxd'Amiante. Resumes des Communications

Conf Int Phys Nuages Commun — Conference Internationale sur la Physique des Nuages. Communications

Conf Int Prod Thermo Ionique Energ Electr — Conference Internationale sur la Production Thermo-Ionique d'Energie Electrique

Conf Int Prot React — Conference Internationale sur la Protection des Reacteurs

Conf Int Rech Cacaoyeres Mem — Conference Internationale sur les Recherches Cacaoyeres. Memoires

Conf Int Sources Ions CR — Conference Internationale sur les Sources d'Ions. Comptes Rendus

Conf Int Spectrosc Raman — Conference Internationale de Spectroscopie Raman

Conf Int Thermodyn Chim CR — Conference Internationale de Thermodynamique Chimique. Compte Rendu

Conf Invitees Table Ronde Int Symp Int Chim Plasmas — Conferences Invitees. Table Ronde Internationale. SymposiumInternational de Chimie des Plasmas

Confl — Confluences. Revue des Lettres et des Arts

Conflict Mgt and Peace Science — Conflict Management and Peace Science

Conflict Q — Conflict Quarterly

Conf Liver Inj Trans — Conference on Liver Injury. Transactions

Conf Local Comput Networks — Conference on Local Computer Networks

Conf Macromol Synth — Conference on Macromolecular Synthesis

Conf Mar Transp Handl Storage Bulk Chem Proc — Conference on the Marine Transportation, Handling, and Storage of BulkChemicals. Proceedings

Conf Mater Coal Convers Util Proc — Conference on Materials for Coal Conversion and Utilization. Proceedings

Conf Mater Eng — Conference on Materials Engineering

Conf Math Finite Elem Appl Proc — Conference on the Mathematics of Finite Elements and Applications.Proceedings

Conf Mes Electromagn Precis — Conference sur les Mesures Electromagnetiques de Precision

Conf Metab Aspects Convalescence Trans — Conference on Metabolic Aspects of Convalescence. Transactions

Conf Metab Interrelat Trans — Conference on Metabolic Interrelations. Transactions

Conf Methods Air Pollut Ind Hyg Stud Plenary Sess — Conference on Methods in Air Pollution and Industrial Hygiene Studies. Plenary Session

Conf Min Coking Coal — Conference on the Mining and Coking of Coal

Conf Mol Spectrosc Proc — Conference on Molecular Spectroscopy. Proceedings

Conf Mond Energ CR — Conference Mondiale de l'Energie. Compte Rendu

Conf Mononucl Phagocytes — Conference on Mononuclear Phagocytes

Conf Natl Assoc Corros Eng Proc — Conference. National Association of Corrosion Engineers. Proceedings

Conf Nerve Impulse Trans — Conference on Nerve Impulse. Transactions

Conf Neuropharmacol Trans — Conference on Neuropharmacology. Transactions

Conf on Char Found NYU Proc — Conference on Charitable Foundations. New York University. Proceedings

Conf on Read (Univ Pittsburgh) Rep — Conference on Reading (University of Pittsburgh). Report

Conf Opt Fiber Sens Based Smart Mater Struct — Conference on Optical Fiber Sensor-Based Smart Materials and Structures

Conf Orig Congr Int Deterg — Conferences Originales. Congres International de la Detergence

Conform Anal Pap Int Symp — Conformational Analysis. Scope and Present Limitations Papers Presented at the International Symposium

Conform Forces Protein Folding — Conformations and Forces in Protein Folding

Conf Palais Decouverte Ser A — Conferences. Palais de la Decouverte. Serie A

Conf Pap Annu Conf Mater Coal Convers Util — Conference Papers. Annual Conference on Materials for Coal Conversionand Utilization

Conf Pap Appl Phys Sci — Conference Papers in Applied Physical Sciences

Conf Pap Eur Ind Res Manage Assoc — Conference Papers. European Industrial Research Management Association

Conf Pap Inst Metall Tech (London) — Conference Papers. Institute of Metallurgical Technicians (London)

Conf Pap Int Coal Util Conf Exhib — Conference Papers. International Coal Utilization Conference and Exhibition

Conf Pap Int Cosmic Ray Conf — Conference Papers. International Cosmic Ray Conference

Conf Pap Int Pipeline Technol Conv — Conference Papers. International Pipeline Technology Convention

Conf Pap Int Semin Mod Synth Methods — Conference Paper. International Seminar on Modern Synthetic Methods

Conf Pap Jt Conf Appl Air Pollut Meteorol — Conference Papers. Joint Conference on Applications of Air Pollution Meteorology

Conf Pers Fin LQR — Conference on Personal Finance Law. Quarterly Report

Conf Pers Fin L Q Rep — Conference on Personal Finance Law. Quarterly Report

Conf Plasma Phys Controlled Nucl Fusion Res — Conference on Plasma Physics and Controlled Nuclear Fusion Research

Conf Plenieres Princ Sect Congr Int Chim Pure Appl — Conferences Plenieres et Principales aux Sections Presentees au CongresInternational de Chimie Pure et Appliquee

Conf Polysaccharides Biol Trans — Conference on Polysaccharides in Biology. Transactions

Conf Precis Electromagn Meas CPEM Dig — Conference on Precision Electromagnetic Measurements. CPEM Digest

Conf Probl Aging Trans — Conference on Problems of Aging. Transactions

Conf Probl Conscious Trans — Conference on Problems of Consciousness. Transactions

Conf Probl Early Infancy Trans — Conference on Problems of Early Infancy. Transactions

Conf Probl Infancy Child Trans — Conference on Problems of Infancy and Childhood. Transactions

Conf Proc Am Assoc Contam Control Annu Tech Meet — Conference Proceedings. American Association for Contamination Control.Annual Technical Meeting

Conf Proc Annu Conv Wire Assoc Int — Conference Proceedings. Annual Convention. Wire AssociationInternational

Conf Proc Annu Phoenix Conf — Conference Proceedings. Annual Phoenix Conference

Conf Proc Annu Semicond Pure Water Chem Conf — Conference Proceedings. Annual Semiconductor Pure Water and Chemicals Conference

Conf Proc Annu Symp Comput Archit — Conference Proceedings. Annual Symposium on Computer Architecture

Conf Proc Eur Conf Controlled Fusion Plasma Phys — Conference Proceedings. European Conference on Controlled Fusion and Plasma Physics

Conf Proc Eur Microwave Conf — Conference Proceedings. European Microwave Conference

Conf Proc Ferrous Div Meet Wire Assoc Int — Conference Proceedings. Ferrous Divisional Meeting. Wire AssociationInternational

Conf Proc IEEE Appl Power Electron Conf Expo APEC — Conference Proceedings. IEEE Applied Power Electronics Conference and Exposition. APEC

Conf Proc IEEE SOUTHEASTCON — Conference Proceedings. IEEE SOUTHEASTCON

Conf Proc Int Conf Fire Saf — Conference Proceedings. International Conference on Fire Safety

Conf Proc Int Conf Nondestr Test — Conference Proceedings. International Conference on Nondestructive Testing

Conf Proc Intersoc Energy Convers Eng Conf — Conference Proceedings. Intersociety Energy Conversion Engineering Conference

Conf Proc Int Symp Plasma Chem — Conference Proceedings. International Symposium on Plasma Chemistry

Conf Proc Ital Phys Soc — Conference Proceedings. Italian Physical Society

Conf Proc Jt Conf Sens Environ Pollut — Conference Proceedings. Joint Conference on Sensing of EnvironmentalPollutants

Conf Proc Laser Electr Optic Soc Annu Meet — Conference Proceedings. Lasers and Electro-Optics Society Annual Meeting

Conf Proc Lecture Notes Algebraic Geom — Conference Proceedings and Lecture Notes in Algebraic Geometry

Conf Proc Lecture Notes Geom Topology — Conference Proceedings and Lecture Notes in Geometry and Topology

Conf Proc Lecture Notes Math Phys — Conference Proceedings and Lecture Notes in Mathematical Physics

Conf Proc Ocean Energy Conf — Conference Proceedings. Ocean Energy Conference

Conf Proc OFS Int Conf Opt Fiber Sens — Conference Proceedings OFS. International Conference on Optical Fiber Sensors

Conf Proc Purdue Agric Comput Conf — Conference Proceedings. Purdue Agricultural Computing Conference

Conf Proc Recycl World Congr — Conference Proceedings. Recycling World Congress

Conf Proc UK Sect Int Sol Energy Soc — Conference Proceedings. UK Section. International Solar Energy Society

Conf Proc World Hydrogen Energy Conf — Conference Proceedings. World Hydrogen Energy Conference

Conf Prod Prop Test Aggregates Pap — Conference on the Production, Properties, and Testing of Aggregates. Papers

Conf Prostaglandins Fertil Control — Conference on Prostaglandins in Fertility Control

Conf Psych — Confinia Psychiatrica

Conf Publ Inst Mech Eng — Conference Publications. Institution of Mechanical Engineers

Conf Publiques Univ Damas — Conferences Publiques. Universite de Damas

Conf Pulverized Fuel Proc Conf — Conference on Pulverized Fuel. Proceedings at the Conference

Confr — Confrontation

Conf Radiat Prot Accel Environ Proc — Conference on Radiation Protection in Accelerator Environments. Proceedings

Conf Radioprot Anticarcinog — Conference on Radioprotectors and Anticarcinogens

Conf Read (Univ Chicago) — Conference on Reading (University of Chicago). Proceedings

Conf Reanim Med Urgence Hop Raymond Poincare — Conferences de Reanimation et de Medecine d'Urgence de l'Hopital Raymond Poincare

Conf Rec Annu ACM Symp Princ Program Lang — Conference Record of the Annual ACM Symposium on Principles of Programming Languages

Conf Rec Annu Pulp Pap Ind Tech Conf — Conference Record. Annual Pulp and Paper Industry Technical Conference

Conf Rec Asilomar Conf Circuits Syst Comput — Conference Record. Asilomar Conference on Circuits Systems and Computers

Conf Rec Recent Adv Adapt Sens Mater Their Appl — Conference on Recent Advances in Adaptive and Sensory Materials and Their Applications

Conf Rec IAS Annu Meet — Conference Record. IAS [*IEEE Industry Applications Society*] Annual Meeting

Conf Rec IEEE Instrum Meas Technol Conf — Conference Record. IEEE Instrumentation and Measurement Technology Conference

Conf Rec IEEE Int Symp Electr Insul — Conference Record of IEEE International Symposium on Electrical Insulation

Conf Rec IEEE Photovoltaic Spec Conf — Conference Record. IEEE [*Institute of Electrical and Electronics Engineers*] Photovoltaic Specialists Conference

Conf Rec Int Conf Conduct Breakdown Dielectr Liq — Conference Record. International Conference on Conduction and Breakdownin Dielectric Liquids

Conf Refract Concr — Conference on Refractory Concretes

Conf Renal Funct Trans — Conference on Renal Function. Transactions

Conf Rep Bot Soc Brit Isles — Conference Reports. Botanical Society. British Isles

Conf Rep R Aust Inst Parks Rec — Conference Report. Australian Institute of Parks and Recreation

Conf Res Radiother Cancer Proc — Conference on Research on the Radiotherapy of Cancer. Proceedings

Conf Restor Coastal Veg Fla Proc — Conference on the Restoration of Coastal Vegetation in Florida. Proceedings

Conf Role Poisson Aliment Doc Trav — Conference sur le Role du Poisson dans l'Alimentation. Documents de Travail

Confrontat — Confrontation

Confront Pharmacol — Confrontations Pharmacologiques

Confront Radio-Anatomo-Clin — Confrontations Radio-Anatomo-Cliniques

Confructa Stud — Confructa-Studien

Conf Saf Tech Chem Process Agric Proc — Conference on the Safety Techniques of Chemical Processing in Agriculture. Proceedings

Conf Semi Insul III V Mater — Conference on Semi-Insulation III-V Materials

Conf Ser Australas Inst Min Metall — Conference Series. Australasian Institute of Mining and Metallurgy

Conf Ser Aust Water Resour Counc — Conference Series. Australian Water Resources Council

Conf Ser Inst Phys — Conference Series. Institute of Physics

Conf Shock Circ Homeostasis Trans — Conference on Shock and Circulatory Homeostasis. Transactions

Conf Silic Ind Silic Sci — Conference on Silicate Industry and Silicate Science

Conf Software Maint — Conference on Software Maintenance

Conf Solid State Devices Mater — Conference on Solid State Devices and Materials

Conf Solid State Devices Proc — Conference on Solid State Devices. Proceedings

Conf Spectrosc Its Appl Proc — Conference on Spectroscopy and Its Applications. Proceedings

Conf Stand Methodol Water Pollut Proc — Conference on the Standardization of Methodology of Water Pollution.Proceedings

Conf Supercond Appl — Conference on Superconductivity and Applications

Conf Supercond D F Band Met — Conference on Superconductivity in D- and F-Band Metals

Conf Superionic Conduct Chem Phys Appl Pro — Conference on Superionic Conductors. Chemistry, Physics, and Applications. Proceedings

Conf Tests Electroweak Theor Polariz Processes Other Phenom — Conference on Tests of Electroweak Theories. Polarized Processes and Other Phenomena

Conf Text Inst Manchester Engl — Conference. Textile Institute (Manchester, England)

Conf Therm Conduct Proc — Conference on Thermal Conductivity. Proceedings

Conf Thermodyn Natl Energy Probl Rep — Conference on Thermodynamics and National Energy Problems. Report

Conf Tin Consumption Pap — Conference on Tin Consumption. Papers

Conf Trace Subst Environ Health — Conference on Trace Substances in Environmental Health

Conf Transp Theory Proc — Conference on Transport Theory. Proceedings

Conf Tribol Lect — Conference on Tribology. Lectures

Conf Trisannuelle Assoc Eur Rech Pomme Terre — Conference Trisannuelle. Association Europeenne pour la Recherche sur la Pomme de Terre

Conf UK Sect Int Sol Energy Soc UK ISES — Conference. UK Section. International Solar Energy Society (UK-ISES)

Conf Union Int Chim CR — Conference. Union Internationale de Chimie. Comptes Rendus

Conf Uranium Min Technol Proc — Conference on Uranium Mining Technology. Proceedings

Conf Urethanes Environ Prepr — Conference on Urethanes and the Environment. Preprints

Conf Util Fly Ash — Conference on Utilization of Fly Ash

Conf Vitam C — Conference on Vitamin C

Conf Water Chlorination Environ Impact Health Eff — Conference on Water Chlorination. Environmental Impact and Health Effects

Conf Weather Modif Am Meteorol Soc Prepr — Conference on Weather Modification. American Meterological Society. Preprints

Conf Weld — Conference on Welding

Conf West Afr Agric Off — Conference of West African Agricultural Officers

Conf Wood Gluing Proc — Conference on Wood Gluing. Proceedings

Conf Zinc Coat All Their Aspects Pap — Conference on Zinc Coatings in All Their Aspects. Papers

Cong — Congregationalist

Cong and Presidency — Congress and the Presidency

Cong Braz De Geog — Congresso Brazileiro de Geografia

Cong Cient Mexicano Mem Cienc Fisicas y Matematicas — Congreso Cientifico Mexicano. Memoria. Ciencias Fisicas y Matematicas

Cong De Hist Nac Annaes — Congresso de Historia Nacional. Annaes

Cong Dig — Congressional Digest

Cong Digest — Congressional Digest

Congenital Anom — Congenital Anomalies

Congenital Dis Child Med Socio Med Aspects Symp — Congenital Diseases in Childhood. Medical and Socio-Medical Aspects. Symposium

Congenital Disord Erythropoiesis Symp — Congenital Disorders of Erythropoiesis. Symposium

Congenital Disord Urea Cycle Ammonia Detoxication — Congenital Disorders of the Urea Cycle and Ammonia Detoxication

Congenital Malform Proc Int Conf — Congenital Malformations. Proceedings. International Conference

Cong Globe — Congressional Globe

Cong Int De Dermat Et De Syph — Congres International de Dermatologie et de Syphilis

Cong Int De Med — Congres International de Medecine

Cong Internat Med C R — Congres International de Medecine. Comptes Rendus

Congiunt Econ Lombarda — Congiuntura Economica Lombarda

Congiuntura Econ Laziale — Congiuntura Economica Laziale

Congiuntura Ital — Congiuntura Italiana

Cong M — Congregational Magazine

Cong M — Congress Monthly

Cong Mo — Congregationalist Monthly Review

Cong Nazion — Cong Nazionale

Congo Belge Ruanda Urundi Serv Geol Mem — Congo Belge et Ruanda-Urundi. Service Geologique. Memoire

Cong of Q Coop — Congress of Queensland Cooperatives. Papers and Proceedings

Cong Q — Congregational Quarterly

Cong Q W Rept — Congressional Quarterly. Weekly Report

Cong R — Congregational Review

Congr Aeronaut Eur CR — Congres Aeronautique Europeen. Comptes Rendus

Congr A Fr — Congres Archeologique de France

Congr AMPERE Magn Reson Relat Phenom Proc — Congress AMPERE on Magnetic Resonance and Related Phenomena. Proceedings

Congr Annu Soc Nucl Can — Congres Annuel. Societe Nucleaire Canadienne

Congr Anu ABM — Congresso Anual da ABM

Congr Anu Reg Trop Soc Am Cienc Hortic — Congreso Anual de la Region Tropical. Sociedad Americana de Ciencias Horticolas

Congr Anu Soc Am Cienc Hortic Reg Trop — Congreso Anual. Sociedad Americana de Ciencias Horticolas. Region Tropical

Congr Archeol France — Congres Archeologique de France

Congr Assoc Eur Amelior Plant — Congres. Association Europeenne pour l'Amelioration des Plantes

Congr Assoc Fr Av Sci (Nancy) — Congres. Association Francaise pour l'Avancement des Sciences (Nancy)

Congr Assoc Geol Carpatho Balk — Congres. Association Geologique Carpatho-Balkanique

Congr Assoc Geol Carpatho-Balkan Bull — Congres. Association Geologique Carpatho-Balkanique. Bulletin

Congr Assoc Int Gerontol — Congresso della Associazione Internazionale di Gerontologia

Congr Assoc Pediatr Lang Fr Rapp — Congres. Association des Pediatres de Langue Francaise. Rapports

Congr Assoc Tech Fonderie CR — Congres de Association Technique de Fonderie. Comptes Rendus

Congr Av Etud Stratigr Geol Carbonif CR — Congres pour l'Avancement des Etudes de Stratigraphie et de Geologie du Carbonifere. Compte Rendu

Congr Av Etud Stratigr Geol Carbonifere C R — Congres pour l'Avancement des Etudes de Stratigraphie et de Geologie du Carbonifere. Compte Rendu

Congr Biofarm Farmacocinet — Congreso de Biofarmacia y Farmacocinetica

Congr Bras Apic — Congresso Brasileiro de Apicultura

Congr Bras Ceram — Congresso Brasileiro de Ceramica

Congr Bras Energ — Congresso Brasileiro de Energia

Congr Bulg Microbiol — Congress of Bulgarian Microbiologists

Congr Chem Agric — Congress Chemistry in Agriculture

Congr Chil Obstet Ginecol — Congreso Chileno de Obstetricia y Ginecologia

Congr Chim Biol CR — Congres de Chimie Biologique. Comptes Rendus

Congr Coll Fr Pathol Vas — Congres de College Francais de Pathologie Vasculaire

Congr Coll Int Neuro Psychopharmacol Proc — Congress. Collegium Internationale Neuro-Psychopharmacologicum. Proceedings

Congr Colloq Univ Liege — Congres et Colloques. Universite de Liege

Congr Conv Simp Sci C N R — Congressi. Convegni e Simposi Scientifici. Consiglio Nazionale delle Richerche

Congr Conv Simp Sci CNR — Congressi. Convegni e Simposi Scientifici. Consiglio Nazionale delle Richerche

Congr Corros Prot Yacimientos Gas Pet — Congreso de Corrosion y Proteccion en Yacimientos de Gas y Petroleo

Congr Counc Min Metall Inst — Congress. Council of Mining and Metallurgical Institutions

Congr Dev Biophys Methods — Congress on Developments in Biophysical Methods

Congr Dev Comp Immunol — Congress of Developmental and Comparative Immunology

Congr Dig — Congressional Digest

Congre — Congregationalist

Cong Rec — Congressional Record

Congreg R — Congregational Review

Congres Archeol — Congres Archeologique de France

Congres Archeol de France — Congres Archeologique de France

Congresb Wereldcongr Oppervlaktebehandel Met — Congresboek. Wereldcongres voor Oppervlaktebehandeling van Metalen

Congres des Rel Ind — Congres des Relations Industrielles. Universite Laval. Rapport

Congres Pomol — Congres Pomologique

Congres Prehist France — Congres Prehistorique de France. Compte Rendu

Congress Numer — Congressus Numerantium

Congress St — Congressional Studies

Congr Eur Assoc Res Plant Breed — Congress. European Association for Research on Plant Breeding

Congr Eur Assoc Vet Pharmacol Toxicol — Congress. European Association for Veterinary Pharmacology and Toxicology

Congr Eur Biopharm Pharmacocinet — Congres Europeen de Biopharmacie et Pharmacocinetique

Congr Eur Cent Lutte Poisons Rapp Commun — Congres Europeen. Centres de Lutte Contre les Poisons. Rapports et Communications

Congr Eur Fed Corros — Congress. European Federation of Corrosion

Congr Eur Fed Corros Prepr — Congress. European Federation of Corrosion. Preprints

Congr Eur Groupes Sang Polymorphisme Biochem Anim — Congres Europeen sur les Groupes Sanguins et le Polymorphisme Biochimique des Animaux

Congr Eur Med Aeronaut Spaz — Congresso Europeo di Medicina Aeronautica e Spaziale

Congr Eur Soc Exp Surg Abst — Congress. European Society for Experimental Surgery. Abstracts

Congr Eur Soc Parenter Enteral Nutr — Congress. European Society of Parenteral and Enteral Nutrition

Congr Eur Soc Photobiol — Congress. European Society for Photobiology

Congr Eur Spectrosc Mol Biol — Congres Europeen de Spectroscopie des Molecules Biologiques

Congr Expert Chim Vol Spec Conf Commun — Congres d'Expertise Chimique. Volume Special des Conferences et Communications

Congr Fed Asian Oceanian Biochem — Congress. Federation of Asian and Oceanian Biochemists

Congr Fed Asian Oceanian Biochem Proc — Congress. Federation of Asian and Oceanian Biochemists. Proceedings

Congr Fed Eur Corros Prepr — Congress. Federation Europeenne de la Corrosion. Preprints

Congr Fed Int Diabete CR — Congres. Federation Internationale du Diabete. Comptes Rendus

Congr Fed Int Precontrainte Pro — Congres. Federation Internationale de la Precontrainte. Procedes

Congr Fr Acoust — Congres Francais d' Acoustique

Congr Fr Anesthesiol Rapp — Congres Francais d'Anesthesiologie. Rapports

Congr Fr Med Rapp — Congres Francais de Medecine. Rapports

Congr Fr Med Rapp Agregation Plaquettaire — Congres Francais de Medecine. Rapports. l'Agregation Plaquettaire

Congr Fr Med Rapp Prostaglandines — Congres Francais de Medecine. Rapports. Les Prostaglandines

Congr Fr Oto Rhino Laryngol CR Seances — Congres Francais d'Oto-Rhino-Laryngologie. Comptes Rendus des Seances

Congr Geol Argent Relat — Congreso Geologico Argentino. Relatorio

Congr Geol Int CR — Congres Geologique International. Comptes Rendus

Congr Ger Soc Hematol — Congress. German Society of Hematology

Congr Group Av Methodes Anal Spectrogr Prod Metall — Congres du Groupement pour l'Avancement des Methodes d'Analyse Spectrographiquedes Produits Metallurgiques

Congr Heterocycl Chem — Congress of Heterocyclic Chemistry

Congr Hig Ind — Congreso de Higiene Industrial

Congr Hung Pharmacol Soc Pro — Congress. Hungarian Pharmacological Society. Proceedings

Congr IABG Free Pap — Congress of IABG. Free Papers

Congr Ibero-Am Geol Econ — Congreso Ibero-Americano de Geologia Economica

Congr Ibero Am Geol Econ Mem — Congreso Ibero-Americano de Geologia Economica. La Geologia en el Desarrollo delos Pueblos. Memorias

Congr Ibero Lat Am Dermatol Mem — Congreso Ibero Latino Americano de Dermatologia. Memorias

Congr ILAFA Carbon — Congreso ILAFA-Carbon (Instituto Latinoamericano del Fierro y el Acero)

Congr ILAFA Colada Continua Metal Cuchara — Congreso ILAFA [*Instituto Latinoamericano del Fierro y el Acero*]-Colada Continua y Metalurgia en Cuchara

Congr Ind Gaz CR — Congres de l'Industrie du Gaz. Compte Rendu

Congr Industr Chem — Compte Rendu. Congres International de Chemie Industrielle

Congr Int Air Pur CR — Congres International de l'Air Pur. Compte Rendu

Congr Int Alteration Conserv Pierre — Congres International sur l'Alteration et la Conservation de la Pierre

Congr Int Alum Rapp — Congres International de l'Aluminium. Rapports

Congr Int Annu Assoc Nucl Can — Congres International Annuel. Association Nucleaire Canadienne

Congr Int Assoc Soc Natl Eur Mediterr Gastro Enterol — Congres International. Association des Societes Nationales Europeennes et Mediterraneennes de Gastro-Enterologie

Congr Int Ass Seed Crushers — Congress. International Association of Seed Crushers

Congr Int Astronaut CR — Congres International d'Astronautique. Compte Rendu

Congr Int Beton Manuf CR — Congres International du Beton Manufacture. Comptes Rendus

Congr Int Biochim CR — Congres International de Biochimie. Compte Rendu

Congr Int Biochim Rapp Symp — Congres International de Biochimie. Rapports des Symposiums

Congr Int Biochim Resumes Commun — Congres International de Biochimie. Resumes des Communications

Congr Int Bot Colloq Anal Plant Probl Engrais Miner — Congres International de Botanique. Colloque Analyse des Plantes et Problemes des Engrais Mineraux

Congr Int Bot Rapp Commun — Congres International de Botanique. Rapports et Communications

Congr Int Bot Rapp Commun — Congres International de Botanique. Rapports et Communications Parvenus avant le Congres

Congr Int Carbone — Congres International sur le Carbone

Congr Int Chauffage Ind Therm Thermodyn Appl CR — Congres International da Chauffage Industriel. Thermique et Thermodynamique Appliquees. Comptes Rendus

Congr Int Chim Cim — Congres International de la Chimie des Ciments

Congr Int Chim Cim Proc — Congres International de la Chimie des Ciments. Procedes

Congr Int Chim Pure Appl — Congres International de Chimie Pure et Appliquee

Congr Int Cienc Fisiol Simp Conf — Congreso Internacional de Ciencias Fisiologicas. Simposios y Conferencias

Congr Int Colza — Congres International sur le Colza

Congr Int Comm Opt — Congress. International Commission for Optics

Congr Int Composes Phosphores Actes — Congres International sur les Composes Phosphores. Actes

Congr Int Corros Mar Incrustaciones — Congreso Internacional de Corrosion Marina e Incrustaciones

Congr Int Corros Mar Salissures — Congres International de la Corrosion Marine et des Salissures

Congr Int Corros Met — Congres International de Corrosion Metallique

Congr Int Counc Aeronaut Sci — Congress. International Council. Aeronautical Sciences

Congr Int Cybern Actes — Congres International de Cybernetique. Actes

Congr Int Deriv Tensio Actifs — Congres International des Derives Tensio-Actifs

Congr Int Dermatol — Congressus Internationalis Dermatologiae

Congr Int Deterg — Congres International de la Detergence

Congr Int Electrost CR — Congres International de l'Electrostatique. Comptes Rendus

Congr Int Electrothermie — Congres International d'Electrothermie

Congr Int Email Vitrifie — Congres International de l'Email Vitrifie

Congr Int Entomol PV — Congres International d'Entomologie. Proces-Verbaux

Congr Int Essai Mater — Congres International pour l'Essai des Materiaux

Congr Int Estud Pirenaicos Resumen Comun — Congreso Internacional de Estudios Pirenaicos. Resumen de las Comunicaciones

Congr Int Fed Soc Cosmet Chem Prepr Sci Pap — Congress of International Federation of Societies of Cosmetic Chemists. Preprint of Scientific Papers

Congr Int Fenom Ioniz Gas Rend — Congresso Internazionale sui Fenomeni d'Ionizzazione nei Gas. Rendiconti

Congr Int Fonderie — Congres International de Fonderie

Congr Int Fucinatura — Congresso Internationale della Fucinatura

Congr Int Gastro Enterol — Congres International de Gastro-Enterologie

Congr Int Gaz Nat Liquefie Mem — Congres International sur le Gaz Naturel Liquefie. Memoires

Congr Int Geoquim Org Actas — Congreso Internacional de Geoquimica Organica. Actas

Congr Int Gerontol — Congres International de Gerontologie

Congr Int Grosse Forge — Congres International de la Grosse Forge

Congr Int Hematol Conf — Congreso Internacional de Hematologia. Conferencias

Congr Int Histochim Cytochim — Congres International d'Histochimie et de Cytochimie

Congr Int Huiles Essent — Congres International des Huiles Essentielles

Congr Int Hydrogene Mater — Congres International Hydrogene et Materiaux

Congr Int Ind Agric Actas — Congreso Internacional de Industrias Agricolas. Actas

Congr Int Ind Agric CR — Congres International des Industries Agricoles. Comptes Rendus

Congr Int Ind Gaz — Congres International de l'Industrie du Gaz

Congr Int Inf Genie Chim — Congres International Informatique et Genie Chimique

Congr Int Jus Fruits — Congres International des Jus de Fruits

Congr Int Lait — Congres International de Laiterie

Congr Int Lait Rapp Congr — Congres International de Laiterie. Rapport du Congres

Congr Int Lait Ses Deriv — Congres International sur le Lait et Ses Derives

Congr Int Latte Deriv — Congresso Internazionale sul Latte e Derivati

Congr Int Leche Sus Deriv — Congreso Internacional de la Leche y Sus Derivados

Congr Int Maconnerie Briques — Congres International sur la Maconnerie en Briques

Congr Int Mal Betail — Congres International sur les Maladies du Betail

Congr Int Mal Infect Commun — Congres International pour les Maladies Infectieuses. Communications

Congr Int Mal Infett Commun — Congresso Internazionale per le Malattie Infettive. Communicazioni

Congr Int Mal Thorax — Congres International des Maladies du Thorax

Congr Int Mec Roches — Congres International de Mecanique des Roches

Congr Int Med Trav — Congres International de Medicine du Travail

Congr Int Metall Dent — Congres International de Metallurgie Dentaire

Congr Int Met Legers — Congres International des Metaux Legers

Congr Int Microbiol CR — Congres International de Microbiologie. Compte Rendu

Congr Int Microsc Electron CR — Congres International de Microscopie Electronique. Comptes Rendus

Congr Int Mineralurgie CR — Congres International de Mineralurgie. Compte Rendu

Congr Int Mines Metall Geol Appl CR — Congres International des Mines, de la Metallurgie, et de la Geologie Appliquee. Comptes Rendus

Congr Int Neurol Rapp Discuss — Congres International de Neurologie. Rapports et Discussions

Congr Int Oleos Essenc — Congresso Internacional de Oleos Essenciais

Congr Int Opt Rayons X Microanal — Congres International sur l'Optique des Rayons X et la Microanalyse

Congr Int Pain — Congres International du Pain

Congr Int Panif Atti — Congresso Internazionale di Panificazione. Atti

Congr Int Pathol Infect Commun — Congres International de Pathologie Infectieuse. Communications

Congr Int Patol Comp Actas — Congreso Internacional de Patologia Comparada. Actas

Congr Int Patol Infect Commun — Congres International de Patologie Infectiouse. Communicari

Congr Int Patol Infett Commun — Congresso Internazionale di Patologia Infettiva. Communicazioni

Congr Int Pediatr — Congreso Internacional de Pediatria

Congr Int Pharm CR — Congres International de Pharmacie. Comptes Rendus

Congr Int Phenom Contact Electr — Congres International sur les Phenomenes de Contact Electrique

Congr Int Potash Inst — Congress. International Potash Institute

Congr Int Prep Minerais CR — Congres International de la Preparation de Minerais. Compte Rendu

Congr Int Primatol Soc — Congress. International Primatological Society

Congr Int Quim Cimento An — Congresso Internacional de Quimica do Cimento. Anais

Congr Int Radiat Prot Soc — Congress. International Radiation Protection Society

Congr Int Rech Text Lainiere — Congres International de la Recherche Textile Lainiere

Congr Int Reprod Anim Insemin Artif — Congres International de Reproduction Animale et Insemination Artificielle

Congr Int Reprod Anim Insemin Artif — Congreso Internacional de Reproduccion Animal e Inseminacion Artificial

Congr Int Reprod Anim Insemination Artif — Congres International de Reproduction Animale et Insemination Artificielle

Congr Int Salud Ocup — Congreso Internacional Sobre Salud Ocupacional

Congr Int Sci Anthropol Ethnol — Congres International des Sciences Anthropologiques et Ethnologiques

Congr Int Sci Neurol — Congres International des Sciences Neurologiques

Congr Int Smalto Porcellano — Congresso Internazionale dello Smalto Porcellanto

Congr Int Soc Blood Transfus — Congress. International Society of Blood Transfusion

Congr Int Soc Fr Radioprot — Congres International. Societe Francaise de Radioprotection

Congr Int Soc Study Hypertens Pregnancy — Congress. International Society for the Study of Hypertension in Pregnancy

Congr Int Sol Energy Soc — Congress. International Solar Energy Society

Congr Int Spectrom Absorpt Fluoresc At — Congres International de Spectrometrie d'Absorption et de Fluorescence Atomique

Congr Int Stereol Rapp — Congres International de Stereologie. Rapport

Congr Int Stratigr Geol Carbonif CR — Congres International de Stratigraphie et de Geologie du Carbonifere. Compte Rendu

Congr Int Stratigr Geol Carbonifere C R — Congres International de Stratigraphie et de Geologie du Carbonifere. Compte Rendu

Congr Int Studi Carciofo — Congresso Internazionale di Studi sul Carciofo

Congr Int Tech Chim Ind Agric CR — Congres International Technique et Chimique des Industries Agricoles. Comptes Rendus

Congr Int Technol Pharm Expo — Congres International de Technologie Pharmaceutique. Exposes

Congr Int Tech Vide CR — Congres International des Techniques du Vide. Comptes Rendus

Congr Int Text Artif Synth — Congres International des Textiles Artificiels et Synthetiques

Congr Int Ther — Congres International de Therapeutique

Congr Int Ther CR — Congres International de Therapeutique. Compte Rendu

Congr Int Ther Rapp Commun — Congres International de Therapeutique. Rapports et Communications

Congr Int Trait Therm Mater — Congres International sur les Traitements Thermiques des Materiaux

Congr Int Transfert Chal — Congres International sur le Transfert de Chaleur

Congr Int Union Electrodeposition Surf Finish Proc — Congress. International Union for Electrodeposition and Surface Finishing. Proceedings

Congr Int Union Int Soc Chim Ind Cuir CR — Congres International. Union Internationale des Societes de Chimistes des Industries du Cuir. Comptes Rendus

Congr Int Union Physiol Sci — Congress. International Union of Physiological Sciences

Congr Int Verre Commun Artistiques Hist — Congres International du Verre. Communications Artistiques et Historiques

Congr Int Verre Commun Sci Tech — Congres International du Verre. Communications Scientifiques et Techniques

Congr Int Verre CR Trav — Congres International du Verre. Compte Rendu des Travaux

Congr Int Vigne Vin — Congres International de la Vigne du Vin

Congr Int Vigne Vin CR — Congres International de la Vigne et du Vin. Comptes Rendus

Congr Int Water Supply Assoc — Congress. International Water Supply Association

Congr Ital Assoc Study Liver — Congress. Italian Association for the Study of the Liver

Congr Ital Med — Congressi Italiani di Medicina

Congr Lat Am Eng Equip Ind Pet Petroquim — Congresso Latino-Americano de Engenharia e Equipamentos para as Industrias de Petroleo e Petroquimica

Congr Latinoam Petroquim — Congreso Latinoamericano de Petroquimica

Congr Latinoam Sider Mem Tec — Congreso Latinoamericano de Siderurgia. Memoria Tecnica

Congr Leather Ind — Congress. Leather Industry

Congr Luso Esp Farm — Congresso Luso-Espanhol de Farmacia

Congr Mater Test — Congress on Material Testing

Congr Mater Test Lect — Congress on Material Testing. Lectures

Congr Mediterr Ing Quim Actas — Congreso Mediterraneo de Ingenieria Quimica. Actas

Congr Microbiol Mater Congr Bulg Microbiol — Congress of Microbiology. Materials. Congress of Bulgarian Microbiologists

Congr Mond Aliment Anim — Congres Mondial d'Alimentation Animale

Congr Mond Filtr — Congres Mondial de la Filtration

Congr Mond Gastroenterol CR — Congres Mondial de Gastroenterologie. Comptes Rendus

Congr Mond Med Aeronaut — Congres Mondial de Medecine Aeronautique

Congr Mond Pet Actes Doc — Congres Mondial du Petrole. Actes et Documents

Congr Mond Rech Agron — Congres Mondial de la Recherche Agronomique

Congr Mond Recyclage Textes Conf — Congres Mondial du Recyclage. Textes de la Conference

Congr Mond Sci Tab — Congres Mondial Scientifique du Tabac

Congr Mond Sper Agrar — Congresso Mondiale della Sperimentazione Agraria

Congr Mond Vet Rapp — Congres Mondial Veterinaire. Rapports

Congr Morphol Symp — Congressus Morphologicus Symposia

Congr Mostra Int Ind Conserve Aliment — Congressi, Mostra Internazionale delle Industrie per le Conserve Alimentari

Congr Mund Aliment Anim — Congreso Mundial de Alimentacion Animal

Congr Mund Contam Aire Actas — Congreso Mundial sobre Contaminacion del Aire. Actas

Congr Mund Etol Apl Zootec Ses Plenarias Mesas Redondas — Congreso Mundial de Etologia Aplicada a la Zootecnia. Sesiones Plenarias y Mesas Redondas

Congr Mund Gastroenterol Inf — Congreso Mundial de Gastroenterologia. Informe

Congr Mund Invest Agron — Congreso Mundial de la Investigacion Agronomica

Congr Mund Vet Actas — Congreso Mundial de Veterinaria. Actas

Congr Nac Arq — Cronica. Congreso Nacional de Arqueologia

Congr Nac Biofarm Farmacocinet Actas — Congreso Nacional de Biofarmacia y Farmacocinetica. Actas

Congr Nac Cienc Tecnol Metal — Congreso Nacional de Ciencia y Technologia Metalurgicas

Congr Nac Farm Ind Actas — Congreso Nacional de Farmaceuticos en la Industria. Actas

Congr Nac Med Hig Segur Trab — Congreso Nacional de Medicina, Higiene, y Seguridad del Trabajo

Congr Nac Metal An — Congreso Nacional de Metalurgia. Anales

Congr Nac Petroquim — Congreso Nacional de Petroquimica

Congr Nac Tuberc Enferm Respir — Congreso Nacional de Tuberculosis y Enfermedades Respiratorias

Congr Natl Electrolyse Trait Surf — Congres National de l'Electrolyse et des Traitements de Surface

Congr Natl Sci Med Commun Invites Etrang — Congres National des Sciences Medicales. Communications des Invites Etrangers

Congr Natl Soc Savantes CR Sect Sci — Congres National des Societes Savantes. Comptes Rendus. Section des Sciences

Congr Natl Soc Savantes Sect Sci C R — Congres National. Societes Savantes. Section des Sciences. Comptes Rendus

Congr Natl Tuberc Mal Respir — Congres National de la Tuberculose et des Maladies Respiratoires

Congr Naz Assoc Ital Fis Sanit Prot Radiaz Atti — Congresso Nazionale. Associazione Italiana di Fisica Sanitaria e di Protezione contro le Radiazioni. Atti

Congr Naz Chim Inorg Atti — Congresso Nazionale di Chimica Inorganica. Atti

Congr Naz Chim Lab Prov Ig Profil — Congresso Nazionale dei Chimici dei Laboratori Provinciali di Igiene Profilassi

Congr Naz Elettron Quantistica Plasmi — Congresso Nazionales. Elettronica Quantistica e Plasmi

Congr Naz Fis Commun — Congresso Nazionale di Fisica. Communicazioni

Congr Naz Soc Ital Studi Fertil Steril Atti — Congresso Nazionale. Societa Italiana per gli Studi sulla Fertilita e la Sterilita. Atti

Congr Naz Stor Arte — Congresso Nazionale di Storia dell'Arte

Congr Neurol Surg — Congress of Neurological Surgeons

Congr Nucl — Congresso Nucleare

Congr Nucl Atti Uffic Congr Int Energ Nucl — Congresso Nucleare. Atti Ufficiali. Congresso Internazionale per l'Energia Nucleare

Congr Nucl Roma Atti — Congresso Nucleare di Roma. Atti

Congr Numer — Congressus Numerantium

Congr Occup Health — Congress on Occupational Health

Congr Pap Int Foundry Congr — Congress Papers. International Foundry Congress

Congr Print — Congress in Print

Congr Proc Int Congr Anim Reprod Artif Insemin — Congress Proceedings. International Congress on Animal Reproduction and Artificial Insemination

Congr Proc Recycl World Congr — Congress Proceedings. Recycling World Congress

Congr Quim Cont Am Norte — Congreso de Quimica del Continente de America del Norte

Congr Rec — Congressional Record

Congr Rec Dly — Congressional Record. Daily Edition

Congr Sci Farm Conf Comun — Congresso di Scienze Farmaceutiche. Conferenze e Comunicazioni

Congr Sci France — Congres Scientifiques de France

Congr Sci Int Tab — Congres Scientifique International du Tabac

Congr Sci Int Tab Actes — Congres Scientifique International du Tabac. Actes

Congr Ser Sudan Med Assoc — Congress Series. Sudan Medical Association

Congr Singapore Soc Microbiol — Congress. Singapore Society for Microbiology

Congr Soc Eur Hematol — Congres. Societe Europeenne d'Hematologie

Congr Soc Forensic Haemogenet — Congress. Society for Forensic Haemogenetics

Congr Soc Fr Phys Actes — Congres. Societe Francaise de Physique. Actes

Congr Soc Pharm Fr CR — Congres des Societes de Pharmacie de France. Comptes Rendus

Congr Tech Int Ind Peint Ind Assoc CR — Congres Technique International de l'Industrie des Peintures et des Industries Associees. Compte Rendu

Congr Union Ther Int CR — Congres. Union Therapeutique Internationale. Comptes Rendus

Congr Util Steel Constr Work — Congress on the Utilization of Steel in Construction Work

Congr Venez Cir — Congreso Venezolano de Cirugia

Congr World Fed Hemophilia — Congress. World Federation of Hemophilia

Congr Yellow Book — Congressional Yellow Book

ConH — Concordia Historical Institute Quarterly

ConHS — Connecticut Historical Society Bulletin

Con Int Explor Mer Bull Stat Peches Marit — Conseil International pour l'Exploration de la Mer. Bulletin Statistique des Peches Maritimes

Conj — Conjunction

Conjonct Econ Lorr — Conjoncture Economique Lorraine

Conjonct Econ Maroc — Conjoncture Economique Marocaine

Conjoncture Econ Maroc — Conjoncture Economique au Maroc

Con Jud — Conservative Judaism

Conjugated Plant Horm Proc Int Symp — Conjugated Plant Hormones. Structure, Metabolism, and Function. Proceedings. International Symposium

Conjugation React Drug Biotransform Proc Symp — Conjugation Reactions in Drug Biotransformation. Proceedings. Symposium

Conjunt Econ — Conjuntura Economica

Conjuntura Econ — Conjuntura Economica

ConL — Contemporary Literature

Con Life — Consecrated Life

ConLit — Contemporary Literature

ConLit — Convorbiri Literare

Con LR — Connecticut Law Review

Con L Rev — Connecticut Law Review

Con Mus Ed — Contribution to Music Education

Conn — Connaissance

Conn — Connecticut Reports

Conn — Connexions

Conn — Connoisseur

Conn — Connotation

Conn A — Connaissance des Arts

Conn Acad Arts & Sci Mem (New Haven) — Connecticut Academy of Arts and Sciences. Memoirs (New Haven)

Conn Acad Arts & Sci Trans — Connecticut Academy of Arts and Sciences. Transactions

Conn Acts (Reg Spec Sess) — Connecticut Public and Special Acts (Regular and Special Sessions)
Conn Agencies Regs — Regulations of Connecticut State Agencies
Conn Agr Expt Sta Bull — Connecticut. Agricultural Experiment Station. Bulletin
Conn Agric Exp Stn Bull (New Haven) — Connecticut. Agricultural Experiment Station. Bulletin (New Haven)
Conn Agric Exp Stn Dep Entomol Spec Bull — Connecticut. Agricultural Experiment Station. Department of Entomology. SpecialBulletin
Conn Agric Exp Stn (New Haven) Circ — Connecticut. Agricultural Experiment Station. Circular (New Haven)
Conn Agric Exp Stn Storrs Bull — Connecticut. Agricultural Experiment Station. Storrs. Bulletin
Conn Agric Exp Stn (Storrs) Misc Publ — Connecticut. Agricultural Experiment Station (Storrs). Miscellaneous Publication
Conn Agric Exp Stn (Storrs) Res Rep — Connecticut. Agricultural Experiment Station (Storrs). Research Report
Connais Art — Connaissance des Arts
Connaiss Arts — Connaissance des Arts
Connaiss Loire — Connaissance de la Loire
Connaiss Plast — Connaissance des Plastiques
Connaiss Vigne Vin — Connaissance de la Vigne et du Vin
Connaitre Sous Sol Atout Amenagement Urbain Colloq Natl — Connaitre le Sous-Sol. Un Atout pour l'Amenagement Urbain. Colloque National
Conn App — Connecticut Appellate Reports
Conn Arbor Bull — Connecticut Arboretum Bulletin
Conn Arts — Connaissance des Arts
Conn Bar J — Connecticut Bar Journal
Conn B J — Connecticut Bar Journal
Conn Busn — Connecticut Business
Conn Cir Ct — Connecticut Circuit Court Reports
Conn Dent Stud J — Connecticut Dental Student Journal
Connecticut Agric Exp Sta Forest Publ — Connecticut Agricultural Experiment Station. Forestry Publication
Connecticut L Rev — Connecticut Law Review
Connecticut Med — Connecticut Medicine
Connecticut Water Resources Bull — Connecticut Water Resources Bulletin
Connections J — Connections Journal
Connector Symp Proc — Connector Symposium. Proceedings
Connect Tis — Connective Tissue Research
Connect Tissue — Connective Tissue
Connect Tissue Dis — Connective Tissue Diseases
Connect Tissue Health Dis — Connective Tissue in Health and Disease
Connect Tissue Res — Connective Tissue Research
Connect Tissue Res Proc Eur Connect Tissue Clubs Meet — Connective Tissue Research. Chemistry, Biology, and Physiology. Proceedings. European Connective Tissue Clubs Meeting
Connect Tissues Biochem Pathophysiol — Connective Tissues. Biochemistry and Pathophysiology
Connect Tissues Trans Conf — Connective Tissues. Transactions. Conference
Connect Tissue Thromb Atheroscler Proc Conf — Connective Tissue, Thrombosis, and Atherosclerosis. Proceedings. Conference
Conn Gen Stat — General Statutes of Connecticut
Conn Gen Stat Ann (West) — Connecticut General Statutes, Annotated (West)
Conn Geol Natur Hist Surv Bull — Connecticut. Geological and Natural History Survey. Bulletin
Conn Govt — Connecticut Government
Conn Greenhouse Newsl Univ Conn Coop Ext Ser — Connecticut Greenhouse Newsletter. University of Connecticut. Cooperative Extension Service
Conn Health Bull — Connecticut Health Bulletin
Conn His S — Connecticut Historical Society. Collections
Conn Hist Soc Bull — Connecticut Historical Society. Bulletin
Conn Hist Soc Coll — Connecticut Historical Society. Collections
Conn Hlth Bull — Connecticut Health Bulletin
ConnHSB — Connecticut Historical Society. Bulletin
Conn Ind — Connecticut Industry
Conn Israel — Connaissance d'Israel
Conn Juv Prob Bul — Connecticut Juvenile Probation Bulletin
Conn Lab Dep Bull — Connecticut Labor Department. Bulletin
Conn Legis Serv — Connecticut Legislative Service
Conn Lib — Connecticut Libraries
Conn Lib Assn Bul — Connecticut Library Association. Bulletin
Conn LJ — Connecticut Law Journal
Conn LR — Connecticut Law Review
Conn L Rev — Connecticut Law Review
Conn M — Connecticut Magazine
Conn Med — Connecticut Medicine
Conn Med J — Connecticut Medicine Journal
Conn Mineral Folio — Connecticut. Mineral Folios
Conn Mm Sc — Memoirs of the Connecticut Academy of Arts and Sciences
Conn Nurs News — Connecticut Nursing News
Connoisseur Yb — Connoisseur Yearbook
Conn Per Ind — Connecticut Periodical Index
Conn Pub Acts — Connecticut Public Acts
Conn R — Connecticut Review
Conn Rev — Connecticut Review
Conn Roussillon — Connaissance du Roussillon
Con(NS) — Convivium (New Series)
Conn Spec Acts — Connecticut Special Acts
Conn State Ag Exp — Connecticut. State Agricultural Experiment Station. Publications
Conn State Geol Nat Hist Surv Bull — Connecticut. State Geological and Natural History Survey. Bulletin
Conn State Geol Nat Hist Surv Misc Ser — Connecticut. State Geological and Natural History Survey. Miscellaneous Series
Conn State Geol Nat Hist Surv Quadrangle Rep — Connecticut. State Geological and Natural History Survey. Quadrangle Report
Conn State Geol Nat Hist Surv Rep Invest — Connecticut. State Geological and Natural History Survey. Report of Investigations
Conn State Med J — Connecticut State Medical Journal
Conn Storrs Agric Exp Stn Bull — Connecticut. Storrs Agricultural Experiment Station. Bulletin
Conn Storrs Agric Exp Stn Misc Publ — Connecticut. Storrs Agricultural Experiment Station. Miscellaneous Publication
Conn Storrs Agric Exp Stn Prog Rep — Connecticut. Storrs Agricultural Experiment Station. Progress Report
Conn Storrs Agric Exp Stn Res Rep — Connecticut. Storrs Agricultural Experiment Station. Research Report
Conn Storrs Agric Stn Bull — Connecticut. Storrs Agricultural Station. Bulletin
Conn Supp — Connecticut Supplement
Conn Tiss — Connective Tissues
Conn Tiss Res — Connective Tissue Research
Conn Univ Agric Exp Stn Res Rep — Connecticut. University. Agricultural Experiment Station. Research Report
Conn Univ Eng Exp Stn Bull — Connecticut. University Engineering Experiment Station. Bulletin
Conn Urban Res Rep — Connecticut Urban Research Report
Conn Veg Grow Assoc Proc Annual Meet — Connecticut Vegetable Growers' Association. Proceedings. Annual Meeting
Conn Water Res Comm Conn Water Res Bull — Connecticut Water Resources Commission. Connecticut Water Resources Bulletin
Conn Water Resour Bull — Connecticut Water Resources Bulletin
Conn Woodl — Connecticut Woodlands
Conn Woodlands — Connecticut Woodlands
ConO — Conferences Faites aux Matinees Classiques du Theatre National de l'Odeon
Con Occup Ther Bull — Connecticut Occupational Therapy Bulletin
ConP — Concerning Poetry
Con P — Contemporary Poetry
CONQAV — Conquest
Conqu — Conquest
Conquest Bact Dis Dr Albert Wander Gedenkvorlesung — Conquest of Bacterial Disease. Dr. Albert Wander-Gedenkvorlesung
Conquest J Res Def Soc — Conquest. Journal of the Research Defence Society
ConR — Contemporary Review
Conrad — Conradiana
Con Res Mag — Consumers' Research Magazine
Cons — Conscience
CONS — Conservation News. National Wildlife Federation
Cons — Consigna
ConS — Contrat Social. Revue Historique et Critique des Faits et des Idees
Conscious Cogn — Consciousness and Cognition
Cons Com Ext — Conseiller du Commerce Exterieur
Cons Com Exter — Conseiller du Commerce Exterieur
Cons Congol — Conseiller Congolais
Cons Econ Wallon R — Conseil Economique Wallon. Revue
Conseil Int Chim — Conseil International de Chimie
Consejo Sup Invest Cient Bibl Bol — Consejo Superior de Investigaciones Cientificas. Biblioteca General. Boletin
Consensus Dev Conf Summ Natl Inst Health — Consensus Development Conference Summaries. National Institutes of Health
Conser Ser Dep Cap T — Conservation Series. Department of the Capital Territory
Conserv — Conservationist
Conserv & Recycling — Conservation and Recycling
Conservation Found Letter — Conservation Foundation Letter
Conserv Cotton — Conservation of Cotton
Conserve Deriv Agrum — Conserve e Derivati Agrumari
Conserver Soc Notes — Conserver Society Notes
Conserv Found Lett — Conservation Foundation Letter
Conserv M — Conservation Magazine
Conserv Nat — Conservation of Nature
Conserv News — Conservation News
Conserv Pap — Conservation Paper
Conserv Prod Nat Waters Proc Symp — Conservation and Productivity of Natural Waters. Proceedings. Symposium
Conserv R — Conservative Review
Conserv Reclam Water Proc Symp — Conservation and Reclamation of Water. Proceedings. Symposium
Conserv Recycl — Conservation and Recycling
Conserv Recycling — Conservation and Recycling
Conserv Res Rep US Agr Res Serv — Conservation Research Report. US Agricultural Research Service
Conserv Res Rep US Dep Agric — Conservation Research Report. United States Department of Agriculture
Conserv Res Rep US Dep Agric Agric Res Serv — Conservation Research Report. United States Department of Agriculture. Agricultural Research Service
Conserv Ser Dep Cap T — Conservation Series. Department of the Capital Territory
Conserv Stone Proc Int Symp — Conservation of Stone. Proceedings. International Symposium
Conserv Volunteer — Conservation Volunteer
Consfatuire Sudura Incercari Met — Consfatuire de Sudura si Incercari de Metale
Consfatuire Teh Stiint Ind Usoare Culegere Ref Text — Consfatuire Tehnico-Stiintifica a Industriei Usoare. Culegere de Referate Textile
Cons Gen Peches Mediterr Debata Doc Tech — Conseil General des Peches pour la Mediterranee, Debata et Documents Techniques
Cons Hawai — Construction in Hawaii
Cons Int Explor Mer Bull Stat Peches Marit — Conseil International pour l'Exploration de la Mer. Bulletin Statistique des Peches Maritimes

Cons Int Explor Mer Zooplankton Sheet — Conseil International pour l'Exploration de la Mer. Zooplankton Sheet
Cons Jud — Conservative Judaism
Cons L Today — Consumer Law Today
Consmr BG — Consumer Reports Buying Guide
Consmr Elc — Consumer Electronics Annual Review
Consmr Rpt — Consumer Reports
Cons N — Consumer News
Cons Nac De Hig Bol — Consejo Nacional de Higiene. Boletin
Cons Natl Rech Can Bull — Conseil National de Recherches du Canada. Bulletin
Cons Natl Rech Can Div Genie Mec Rapp Tech Lab — Conseil National de Recherches du Canada. Division de Genie Mecanique. Rapport Technique de Laboratoire
Cons Natl Rech Can Programme Stand Chim Anal Mar Rapp — Conseil National de Recherches Canada. Programme de Standards de Chimie Analytique Marine. Rapport
Cons Natl Rech Can Rapp Annu — Conseil National de Recherches du Canada. Rapport Annuel
Consol Frt Classif — Consolidated Freight Classification
Consortium Q — Consortium Quarterly
Consort Newsl — Consortium Newsletter
Conspect Hist — Conspectus of History
Cons Perm — Conseil Permanent International Pour l'Exploration de la Mer
Cons Rech Dev For Que Etude — Conseil de la Recherche et du Developpement Forestiers du Quebec. Etude
Cons Recur Nat No Renov Publ (Mex) — Consejo de Recursos Naturales No Renovables. Publicacion (Mexico)
Cons Rep — Consumer Reports
Cons Res Mag — Consumers' Research Magazine
Cons Sci Afr Sud Sahara Publ — Conseil Scientifique pour l'Afrique au Sud du Sahara. Publication
Cons Sci Int Rech Trypanosomiases — Conseil Scientifique International de Recherches sur les Trypanosomiases
Cons Sci Int Rech Trypanosomiases Controle — Conseil Scientifique International de Recherche sur les Trypanosomiases et leurControle
Cons Super Invest Cient — Consejo Superior de Investigaciones Cientificas
Const Endocr Metab — Constituicao, Endocrinologie, e Metabolismo
Constitutional and Parliamentary Info — Constitutional and Parliamentary Information
Const Prop Steels — Constitution and Properties of Steels
Const R — Constitutional Review
Constr — Construction
Constr — Construire
Constr & Engin J — Constructional and Engineering Journal
Constr Approx — Constructive Approximation
Constr Contracting — Construction Contracting
Constr Eng Res Lab Tech Rep — Construction Engineering Research Laboratory. Technical Report
Const Rev — Constitutional Review
Const Rev — Constitutional Review. National Association for Constitutional Government
Const Rev — Construction Review
Constr Forum — Constructivist Forum
Constr Frct — Construction Industry Forecast
Constr Glues Plywood Laminating Prefabricating Joining Assem — Construction Glues for Plywood, Laminating, Prefabricating, Joining, and Assembly
Constrl Rev — Constructional Review
Constrl Rev Tech Suppl — Constructional Review. Technical Supplement
Constr Mach — Construction Machinery
Constr Mach Equip — Construction Machinery and Equipment
Constr Mas — Constructia de Masini
Constr Mech (Tokyo) — Construction Mechanization (Tokyo)
Constr Met — Construction Metallique
Constr Metal — Construction Metallique
Constr Meth — Construction Methods
Constr Methods Equip — Construction Methods and Equipment
Constr Mex — Construccion Mexicana
Constr Mod — Construcao Moderna
Constr Mod — Construction Moderne
Constr Nav Compos Colloq — Construction Navale en Commposites. Colloque
Constr News — Construction News
Constr News (London) — Construction News (London)
Constr News Mag — Construction News Magazine
Constr News Magazine — Construction News Magazine
Constr Paps — Construction Papers
Constr Plant & Equip — Construction Plant and Equipment
Constr Plant Equip — Construction Plant and Equipment
Constr Q — Constructive Quarterly
Constr R — Construction Review
Constr Ref — Construction References
Constr Repair — Construction Repair
Constr Rev — Constructional Review
Constr Rev — Construction Review
Constr Road Trans — Construction and Road Transport
Constr S Afr — Construction in Southern Africa
Constr Sao Paulo — Construcao Sao Paulo
Constr South Afr — Construction in Southern Africa
Constr Specifier — Construction Specifier
Constr Steel User Maker Proc Conf — Constructing in Steel. The User and the Maker. Proceedings. Conference
Constr Sthn Afr — Construction in Southern Africa
Constr Tech Bull — Construction Technical Bulletin
Construct-Amenag — Construction-Amenagement
Constructional R — Constructional Review

Construction Law — Construction Lawyer
Construction R — Construction Review
Constru Masini — Constructia de Masini
Constr W — Contruction Week
Consultatio Universali Commercio Litt — Consultatio de Universali Commercio Litterario
Consult En — Consulting Engineer
Consult Eng — Consulting Engineer
Consult Eng (Barrington, Illinois) — Consulting Engineer (Barrington, Illinois)
Consult Eng (London) — Consulting Engineer (London)
Consult Engr — Consulting Engineer
Consult Eng (St Joseph Mich) — Consulting Engineer (St. Joseph, Michigan)
Consult Genet Predispos Toxic Eff Chem — Consultation on Genetic Predisposition to Toxic Effects of Chemicals
Consultor Bibliogr Mex — Consultor Bibliografico (Mexico)
Consult Specif Eng — Consulting-Specifying Engineer
Consum Aff Newsl — Consumer Affairs Newsletter
Consum Brief Summ — Consumer Briefing Summary
Consum Credit Let — Consumer Credit Letter
Consumer Buying Prosp — Consumer Buying Prospects
Consumer N — Consumer News
Consumer Rep — Consumer Reports
Consumers Res Mag — Consumers' Research Magazine
Consum Health Perspect — Consumer Health Perspectives
Consum Ind — Consumer's Index
Consum Index Prod Eval Inf Source — Consumers Index to Product Evaluations and Information Sources
Consum Mark Upd — Consumer Markets Update
Consum Prod Flammability — Consumer Product Flammability
Consum Rep — Consumer Reports
Consum Rep (Consum Union US) — Consumer Reports (Consumers Union of United States, Inc.)
Consum Res Mag — Consumers' Research Magazine
Cont — Contact
CONT — Contact. Journal of Urban and Environmental Affairs
Cont — Contemporaneo
Cont — Continuo
Contabilidad Admin — Contabilidad. Administracion
Contact Intraocul Lens Med J — Contact and Intraocular Lens Medical Journal
Contact J Urban Environ Aff — Contact. Journal of Urban and Environmental Affairs
Contact Lens Med Bull — Contact Lens Medical Bulletin
Contact Lens Soc Am J — Contact Lens Society of America. Journal
Containerisation Int — Containerisation International
Containment Dispersion Gases Water Sprays — Containment and Dispersion of Gases by Water Sprays
Contam Ambiental — Contaminacion Ambiental
Contam Control — Contamination Control
Contam Control Biomed Environ — Contamination Control. Biomedical Environments
Contam Prev — Contaminacion y Prevencion
Contam Sediments — Contaminants and Sediments
Contam Soil 90 Int KfK TNO Conf — Contaminated Soil '90. International KfK/TNO Conference
Contam Soil Int TNO Conf — Contaminated Soil. International TNO Conference on Contaminated Soil
Contam Soils — Contaminated Soils
Cont & Packag — Containers and Packaging
Cont Appl St — Contributions to Applied Statistics
ContAS — Contributions to Asian Studies
Cont Birdlife — Continental Birdlife
Cont Cas Fed CCH — Contracts Cases, Federal. Commerce Clearing House
Cont Crises — Contemporary Crises
Cont Drug P — Contemporary Drug Problems
Cont Dyn — Continental Dynamics
Conte — Contempora. A Literary Magazine
Cont Ed — Contemporary Education
Cont Educ — Contemporary Education
Conte Inst Ser — Conte Institute Series
Contemp — Contemporaneo
Contemp — Contemporary Review
Contemp Adm — Contemporary Administrator
Contemp Adm Long Term Care — Contemporary Administrator for Long-Term Care
Contemp Agric — Contemporary Agriculture
Contemp Anesth Pract — Contemporary Anesthesia Practice
Contemp A Pakistan — Contemporary Arts in Pakistan
Contemp A Soc Broadsheet — Contemporary Art Society Broadsheet
Contemp As R — Contemporary Asia Review
Contemp Biophys — Contemporary Biophysics
Contemp China — Contemporary China
Contemp Concepts Phys — Contemporary Concepts in Physics
Contemp Crises — Contemporary Crises
Contemp Designers — Contemporary Designers
Contemp Drug — Contemporary Drug Problems
Contemp Drug Prob — Contemporary Drug Problems
Contemp Drug Problems — Contemporary Drug Problems
Contemp Ed — Contemporary Education
Contemp Educ — Contemporary Education
Contemp Educ Psychol — Contemporary Educational Psychology
Contemp Educ Rev — Contemporary Education Review
Contemp Endocrinol — Contemporary Endocrinology
Contemp Eval Res — Contemporary Evaluation Research
Contemp Hematol Oncol — Contemporary Hematology/Oncology

Contemp Inorg Mater Proc Ger Yugosl Meet — Contemporary Inorganic Materials. Proceedings. German-Yugoslav Meeting on Materials Science and Development

Contemp Inorg Mater Proc Yugosl Ger Meet Mater Sci Dev — Contemporary Inorganic Materials. Proceedings. Yugoslav-German Meeting on Materials Science and Development

Contemp Issues Clin Biochem — Contemporary Issues in Clinical Biochemistry

Contemp Issues Clin Nutr — Contemporary Issues in Clinical Nutrition

Contemp Issues Fetal Neonat Med — Contemporary Issues in Fetal and Neonatal Medicine

Contemp Issues Infect Dis — Contemporary Issues in Infectious Diseases

Contemp Issue Small Anim Pract — Contemporary Issues in Small Animal Practice

Contemp Issues Nephrol — Contemporary Issues in Nephrology

Contemp Jap Agric — Contemporary Japanese Agriculture/Atarashi Nihon No Nogoyo

Contemp Jewish Rec — Contemporary Jewish Record

Contemp Lit — Contemporary Literature

Contemp Longterm Care — Contemporary Longterm Care

Contemp M — Contemporary Marxism

Contemp Manchuria — Contemporary Manchuria [*Dairen*]

Contemp Mathematicians — Contemporary Mathematicians

Contemp Metab — Contemporary Metabolism

Contemp Microb Ecol Proc Int Symp — Contemporary Microbial Ecology. Proceedings. International Symposium on Microbial Ecology

Contemp Nephrol — Contemporary Nephrology

Contemp Neurol Ser — Contemporary Neurology Series

Contemp Nurs Ser — Contemporary Nursing Series

Contemp Nutr — Contemporary Nutrition

Contemp Ob Gyn — Contemporary Ob/Gyn

Contemp Ophthalmol — Contemporary Ophthalmology

Contemp Org Synth — Contemporary Organic Synthesis

Contemp Orthop — Contemporary Orthopaedics

Contemp Pacif — Contemporary Pacific

Contemp Pacific — Contemporary Pacific

Contemp Pharm Pract — Contemporary Pharmacy Practice

Contemp Phot — Contemporary Photography

Contemp Phys — Contemporary Physics

Contemp Phys Trieste Symp Proc Int Symp — Contemporary Physics. Trieste Symposium. Proceedings. International Symposium on Contemporary Physics. International Centre for Theoretical Physics

Contemp Poland — Contemporary Poland

Contemp Polit — Contemporary Politics

Contemp Probl Cardiol — Contemporary Problems in Cardiology

Contemp Probl Neuromorphol — Contemporary Problems of Neuromorphology

Contemp Psychoanal — Contemporary Psychoanalysis

Contemp Psychol — Contemporary Psychology

Contemp R — Contemporary Review

Contemp Rad — Contemporary Radiology

Contemp Res Top Nucl Phys Proc Workshop — Contemporary Research Topics in Nuclear Physics. Proceedings. Workshop

Contemp Rev — Contemplative Review

Contemp Rev — Contemporary Review

Contemp Scripts — Contemporary Scripts

Contemp Soc — Contemporary Sociology

Contemp Sociol — Contemporary Sociology

Contemp Sociology — Contemporary Sociology

Contemp Soviet Math — Contemporary Soviet Mathematics

Contemp Stud Khoisan — Contemporary Studies on Khoisan

Contemp Surg — Contemporary Surgery

Contemp Themes Biochem Proc Fed Asian Oceanian Biochem Congr — Contemporary Themes in Biochemistry. Proceedings. Federation of Asian and Oceanian Biochemists Congress

Contemp Top Anal Clin Chem — Contemporary Topics in Analytical and Clinical Chemistry

Contemp Top Immunobiol — Contemporary Topics in Immunobiology

Contemp Top Immunochem — Contemporary Topics in Immunochemistry

Contemp Top Lab Anim Sci — Contemporary Topics in Laboratory Animal Science

Contemp Top Mol Immunol — Contemporary Topics in Molecular Immunology

Contemp Top Polym Sci — Contemporary Topics in Polymer Science

Contemp Trends Diuretic Ther Proc Symp — Contemporary Trends in Diuretic Therapy. Proceedings. Symposium

Contents Contemp Math J — Contents of Contemporary Mathematical Journals

Contents Contemp Math J New Publ — Contents of Contemporary Mathematical Journals and New Publications

Contents Curr Leg Period — Contents of Current Legal Periodicals

Contents Pages Manage — Contents Pages in Management

Contents Recent Econ J — Contents of Recent Economics Journals

Contests Math — Contests in Mathematics

Cont Fr Civ — Contemporary French Civilization

Cont Hum De — Contributions to Human Development

Conti Elektro Ber — Conti Elektro Berichte

Contin Atti R Accad Econ Agrar Georgofili Firenze — Continuazione degli Atti. Reale Accademia Economico-Agraria dei Georgofili di Firenze

Contin Cast Steel Proc Process Technol Conf — Continuous Casting of Steel. Proceedings. Process Technology Conference

Contin Cult Cells — Continuous Cultures of Cells [*monograph*]

Contin Cultiv Microorg Proc Symp — Continuous Cultivation of Microorganisms. Proceedings. Symposium on Continuous Cultivation of Microorganisms

Contin Educ — Continuing Education in New Zealand

Contin Edu Lect (Soc Nucl Med Southeast Chapter) — Continuing Education Lectures (Society of Nuclear Medicine. Southeastern Chapter)

Continentl — Continental Comment

Contin Mech Thermodyn — Continuum Mechanics and Thermodynamics

Contin Mo — Continental Monthly

Contin Plat Semin Proc — Continuous Plating Seminar. Proceedings

Contin Transcutaneous Blood Gas Monit Int Symp — Continuous Transcutaneous Blood Gas Monitoring. International Symposium

Continuing Ed Fam Physician — Continuing Education for the Family Physician

Continuing Educ for the Fam Physician — Continuing Education for the Family Physician

Continuing Med Educ Newsletter — Continuing Medical Education Newsletter

Continuum Mech Thermodyn — Continuum Mechanics and Thermodynamics

Continuum Models Discrete Syst Proc Int Conf — Continuum Models of Discrete Systems. Proceedings. International Conference on Continuum Models of Discrete Systems

Cont Jew Rec — Contemporary Jewish Record

Cont Keybd — Contemporary Keyboard

Contl & I — Control and Instrumentation

Cont Learning — Continuous Learning

Contl Eng S — Control Products Specifier. Special Issue of Control Engineering

Cont Lit — Contemporary Literature

ConTM — Concordia Theological Monthly

Cont Marx — Contemporary Marxism

Cont Metall Chem Eng — Continental Metallurgical and Chemical Engineering

Cont Mus R — Contemporary Music Review

Cont P — Contemporary Poetry

Cont Paint Resin News — Continental Paint and Resin News

Cont Philos — Contemporary Philosophy

Cont Phys — Contemporary Physics

Cont Psycha — Contemporary Psychoanalysis

Cont Psycho — Contemporary Psychology

Cont R — Contemporary Review

Contr — Contrordre

Contracept — Contraception

Contracept Delivery Syst — Contraceptive Delivery Systems

Contracept-Fertil-Sex — Contraception-Fertilite-Sexualite

Contra Costa Dent Bull — Contra Costa Dental Bulletin

Contract — Contractor

Contract & Constr Eng — Contracting and Construction Engineer

Contracting — Contracting and Construction Equipment

Contracting — Contracting and Public Works

Contract Int — Contract Interiors

Contract Inter — Contract Interiors

Contract J — Contract Journal

Contract Jnl — Contract Journal

Contract Rec — Contract Record

Contract Rec Eng Rev — Contract Record and Engineering Review

Contract Rep Eur Space Res Organ — Contractor Report. European Space Research Organization

Contract Rep US Army Eng Waterw Exp Stn — Contract Report. US Army Engineer Waterways Experiment Station

Contr Ames Bot Lab — Contributions. Ames Botanical Laboratory

Contr Anthropol Papuan Region Bot — Contributions to the Anthropology, Botany, Geology, and Zoology of the Papuan Region. Botany

Contrat Soc — Contrat Social

Contr Biol Lab Chin Assoc Advancem Sci — Contributions from the Biological Laboratory. Chinese Association for the Advancement of Science

Contr Biol Lab Chin Assoc Advancem Sci Sect Bot — Contributions. Biological Laboratory. Chinese Association for the Advancement of Science. Section Botany

Contr Bot Cluj Timisoara — Contributiuni Botanice din Cluj la Timisoara/ Contributions Botaniques de Cluj aTimisoara

Contr Bot Lab Johns Hopkins Univ — Contributions. Botanical Laboratory. Johns Hopkins University

Contr Bot Vermont — Contributions to the Botany of Vermont

Contr Boyce Thompson Inst Pl Res — Contributions. Boyce Thompson Institute for Plant Research

Contr Canada Dep For Forest Res Brch — Contribution. Canada Department of Forestry. Forest Research Branch

Contr Centr Rech Etudes Oceanogr — Contributions du Centre de Recherches et d'Etudes Oceanographiques

Contr Cryptog Lab Harvard Univ — Contributions. Cryptogamic Laboratory. Harvard University

Contr Dep Hort Univ Ill — Contributions. Department of Horticulture. University of Illinois

Contr Drama — Contributions in Drama and Theatre Studies

Contre — Contrepoint

Contr Eng — Control Engineering

Contrep — Contrepoints. Une Revue de Musique

Cont Rev — Contemporary Review

Contr Fonds Rech For Univ Laval — Contribution. Fonds de Recherches Forestieres. Universite Laval

Contr Gray Herb — Contributions. Gray Herbarium of Harvard University

Contr Henry Shaw School Bot — Contributions. Henry Shaw School of Botany. Washington University

Contr Herb Aust — Contributions. Herbarium Australiense

Contr Hort Inst Taihoku Imp Univ — Contributions. Horticultural Institute. Taihoku Imperial University/Taihoku Teikoku Daigaku Rinogakubu Engeigaku Kyoshitsu Kiyo

Contrib Alberta Res — Contribution. Alberta Research

Contrib Am Entomol Inst (Ann Arbor) — Contributions. American Entomological Institute (Ann Arbor)

Contrib Am Inst Min Metall Eng — Contributions. American Institute of Mining and Metallurgical Engineers

Contrib Arct Inst Cathol Univ Am — Contributions. Arctic Institute. Catholic University of America

Contrib Asian St — Contributions to Asian Studies

Contrib Asian Stud — Contributions to Asian Studies

Contrib As Stud — Contributions to Asian Studies

Contrib Atmos Phys — Contributions to Atmospheric Physics

Contrib Avulsas Inst Oceanogr Sao Paulo — Contribuicoes Avulsas. Instituto Oceanografico Sao Paulo

Contrib Bears Bluff Lab — Contributions. Bears Bluff Laboratories

Contrib Biol Lab Kyoto Univ — Contributions. Biological Laboratory. Kyoto University

Contrib Biol Lab Sci Soc China Bot Ser — Contributions. Biological Laboratory. Science Society of China. Botanical Series

Contrib Biol Lab Sci Soc China Zool Ser — Contributions. Biological Laboratory. Science Society of China. Zoological Series

Contrib Bot — Contributii Botanice

Contrib Bot Cluj — Contributii Botanice din Cluj

Contrib Bot Univ Babes Bolyai Cluj Napoca Gradina Bot — Contributii Botanice. Universitatea Babes-Bolyai din Cluj-Napoca. Gradina Botanica

Contrib Boyce Thompson Inst — Contributions. Boyce Thompson Institute for Plant Research

Contrib Can Biol Fish — Contributions to Canadian Biology and Fisheries

Contrib Can Mineral — Contributions to Canadian Mineralogy

Contrib Cent Linceo Interdiscip Sci Mat Loro Appl — Contributi del Centro Linceo Interdisciplinare di Scienze Matematiche e Loro Applicazioni

Contrib Cent Res Inst Agric (Bogor) — Contributions. Central Research Institute for Agriculture (Bogor)

Contrib Cent Res Inst Agric Bogor Indones — Contributions. Central Research Institute for Agriculture (Bogor, Indonesia)

Contrib Cent Res Inst Food Crops — Contributions. Central Research Institute for Food Crops

Contrib Centro Linceo Interdisc Sci Mat Appl — Contributi. Centro Lindeo Interdisciplinare di Scienze Matematiche e loro Applicazioni

Contrib Cient Fac Cienc Exactas Nat Univ B Aires Ser Bot — Contribuciones Cientificas. Facultad de Ciencias Exactas y Naturales. Universidad de Buenos Aires. Serie Botanica

Contrib Cient Fac Cienc Exactas Nat Univ B Aires Ser Geol — Contribuciones Cientificas. Facultad de Ciencias Exactas y Naturales. Universidad de Buenos Aires. Serie Geologia

Contrib Cient Fac Cienc Exactas Nat Univ B Aires Ser Quim — Contribuciones Cientificas. Facultad de Ciencias Exactas y Naturales. Universidad de Buenos Aires. Serie Quimica

Contrib Cient Fac Cienc Exactas Nat Univ B Aires Ser Zool — Contribuciones Cientificas. Facultad de Ciencias Exactas y Naturales. Universidad de Buenos Aires. Serie Zoologia

Contrib Cient Tecnol — Contribuciones Cientificas y Tecnologicas

Contrib Cient Univ Buenos Aires Fac Cienc Exactas Nat Ser C — Contribuciones Cientificas. Facultad de Ciencias Exactas y Naturales. Universidad de Buenos Aires. Serie C. Quimica

Contrib Curr Res Geophys — Contributions to Current Research in Geophysics

Contrib Cushman Found Foraminiferal Res — Contributions. Cushman Foundation for Foraminiferal Research

Contrib Dan Pharmacopoeia Comm — Contributions. Danish Pharmacopoeia Commission

Contrib Dep Biol Univ Laval (Que) — Contributions. Departement de Biologie. Universite Laval (Quebec)

Contrib Dep Geol Mineral Niigata Univ — Contributions. Department of Geology and Mineralogy. Niigata University

Contrib Dep Limnol Acad Nat Sci Phila — Contributions. Department of Limnology. Academy of Natural Sciences of Philadelphia

Contrib Dep Phys Fac Sci Univ Tokyo — Contributions from the Department of Physics. Faculty of Science. University of Tokyo

Contrib Dudley Herb — Contributions. Dudley Herbarium

Contrib Dudley Mus — Contributions. Dudley Museum

Contrib Econom Anal — Contributions to Economic Analysis

Contrib Epidemiol Biostat — Contributions to Epidemiology and Biostatistics

Contrib Estud Cienc Fis Mat Ser Mat Fis — Contribucion al Estudio de las Ciencias Fisicas y Matematicas. Serie MatematicoFisica

Contrib Estud Cienc Fis Mat Ser Tec — Contribucion al Estudio de las Ciencias Fisicas y Matematicas. Serie Tecnica

Contrib Estudo Antropol Port — Contribuicoes para o Estudo da Antropologia Portuguesa

Contrib Eur Fusion Theory Conf — Contributions to European Fusion Theory Conference

Contrib Fac Sci Haile Selassie I Univ Ser C Zool — Contributions. Faculty of Science. Haile Selassie I University. Series C. Zoology

Contrib Fac Sci Univ Coll Addis Ababa (Ethiop) Ser C Zool — Contributions. Faculty of Science. University College of Addis Ababa (Ethiopia). Series C. Zoology

Contrib FL Site Mus — Contributions of the Florida Site Museum

Contrib Gen Agric Res Stn (Bogor) — Contributions. General Agricultural Research Station (Bogor)

Contrib Geol — Contributions to Geology

Contrib Geol Spec Pap — Contributions to Geology. Special Paper

Contrib Geol Univ Wyo — Contributions to Geology. University of Wyoming

Contrib Geophys Inst Kyoto Univ — Contributions. Geophysical Institute. Kyoto University

Contrib Geophys Inst Slovak Acad Sci — Contributions. Geophysical Institute. Slovak Academy of Sciences

Contrib Geophys Inst Slovak Acad Sci Ser Meteorol — Contributions. Geophysical Institute. Slovak Academy of Sciences. Series of Meteorology

Contrib Geophys Obs Haile Sellassie I Univer Ser A — Contributions. Geophysical Observatory. Haile Sellassie I University. Series A

Contrib Gray Herb Harv Univ — Contributions. Gray Herbarium. Harvard University

Contrib Gynecol Obstet — Contributions to Gynecology and Obstetrics

Contrib Herb Aust — Contributions. Herbarium Australiense

Contrib HKBA — Contributions of HKBA (Hong Kong Biochemical Association)

Contrib Hong Kong Biochem Assoc — Contributions. Hong Kong Biochemical Association

Contrib Hum Dev — Contributions to Human Development

Contrib Ind Sociol — Contributions to Indian Sociology

Contrib Infusion Ther Clin Nutr — Contributions to Infusion Therapy and Clinical Nutrition

Contrib Infusion Ther Transfus Med — Contributions to Infusion Therapy and Transfusion Medicine

Contrib Inst Antarct Argent — Contribuciones. Instituto Antartico Argentino

Contrib Inst Antart Argent — Contribuciones. Instituto Antartico Argentino

Contrib Inst Bot Univ Montreal — Contributions. Institut de Botanique. Universite de Montreal

Contrib Inst Chem Nat Acad Peiping — Contributions. Institute of Chemistry. National Academy of Peiping

Contrib Inst Geol Paleontol Tohoku Univ — Contributions. Institute of Geology and Paleontology. Tohoku University

Contrib Inst Low Temp Sci A — Contributions. Institute of Low Temperature Science. Series A

Contrib Inst Low Temp Sci Hokkaido Univ — Contributions. Institute of Low Temperature Science. Hokkaido University

Contrib Inst Low Temp Sci Hokkaido Univ B — Contributions. Institute of Low Temperature Science. Hokkaido University. Series B

Contrib Inst Low Temp Sci Hokkaido Univ Ser A — Contributions. Institute of Low Temperature Science. Hokkaido University. Series A

Contrib Inst Low Temp Sci Hokkaido Univ Ser B — Contributions. Institute of Low Temperature Science. Hokkaido University. Series B

Contrib Inst Low Temp Sci Ser A — Contributions. Institute of Low Temperature Science. Series A

Contrib Inst Phys Nat Acad Peiping — Contributions. Institute of Physics. Natural Academy of Peiping

Contrib Iowa Corn Res Inst — Contributions. Iowa Corn Research Institute

Contrib Istanbul Sci Clin — Contributions d'Istanbul a la Science Clinique

Contrib Ist Ric Agrar Milano — Contributi. Istituto di Ricerche Agrarie Milano

Contrib Ist Stor A Med & Mod — Contributi dell'Istituto di Storia dell'Arte Medioevale e Moderna

Contrib Kans State Univ Dep Chem Eng — Contribution. Kansas State University. Department of Chemical Engineering

Contrib Lab Hist — Contributions in Labor History

Contrib Lab Vertebr Biol Univ Mich — Contributions. Laboratory of Vertebrate Biology. University of Michigan

Contrib Lunar Sci Inst — Contributions. Lunar Science Institute

Contrib Maced Acad Sci Arts Sect Biol Med Sci — Contributions. Macedonian Academy of Sciences and Arts. Section of Biological and Medical Sciences

Contrib Maced Acad Sci Arts Sect Nat Sci Math — Contributions. Macedonian Academy of Sciences and Arts. Section of Natural Sciences and Mathematics

Contrib Mar Sci — Contributions in Marine Science

Contrib Med Hist — Contributions in Medical History

Contrib Med Psychol — Contributions to Medical Psychology

Contrib Meteorit Soc — Contributions. Meteoritical Society

Contrib Microb Geochem — Contributions in Microbial Geochemistry

Contrib Microbiol Immunol — Contributions to Microbiology and Immunology

Contrib Mil Hist — Contributions in Military History

Contrib Mineral & Petrol — Contributions to Mineralogy and Petrology

Contrib Mineral Petrol — Contributions to Mineralogy and Petrology

Contrib Mineral Petrol Beitr Mineral Petrol — Contributions to Mineralogy and Petrology/Beitraege zur Mineralogie und Petrologie

Contrib Mineral Petrology — Contributions to Mineralogy and Petrology

Contrib Mus Amer Ind — Contributions from the Museum of the American Indian

Contrib Mus Amer Ind Heye Found — Contributions of the Museum of the American Indian. Heye Foundation

Contrib Mus Am Indn — Contributions. Museum of the American Indian

Contrib Mus Paleontol Univ Mich — Contributions. Museum of Paleontology. University of Michigan

Contrib Nat Res Inst Geol Acad Sin — Contributions. National Research Institute of Geology. Academia Sinica

Contrib Nepal Stud — Contributions to Nepalese Studies

Contrib Nephrol — Contributions to Nephrology

Contrib NSW Herb — Contributions. New South Wales National Herbarium

Contrib NSW Natl Herb — Contributions. New South Wales National Herbarium

Contrib NSW Natl Herb Flora Ser — Contributions. New South Wales National Herbarium. Flora Series

Contrib Oncol — Contributions to Oncology

Contrib Paleolimnol Lake Biwa Jpn Pleistocene — Contribution on the Paleolimnology of Lake Biwa and the Japanese Pleistocene

Contrib Pap Am Inst Min Metall Eng — Contribution Papers. American Institute of Mining and Metallurgical Engineers

Contrib Pap Eur Conf Controlled Fusion Plasma Phys — Contributed Papers. European Conference on Controlled Fusion and Plasma Physics

Contrib Pap Int Conf Phenom Ioniz Gases — Contributed Papers. International Conference on Phenomena in Ionized Gases

Contrib Pap Workshop ECR Ion Sources — Contributed Papers. Workshop on ECR Ion Sources

Contrib Pap Yugosl Symp Summer Sch Phys Ioniz Gases — Contributed Papers. Yugoslav Symposium and Summer School on the Physics of Ionized Gases

Contrib Perkins Obs — Contributions. Perkins Observatory

Contrib Perkins Obs Ser 1 — Contributions. Perkins Observatory. Series 1

Contrib Perkins Obs Ser 2 — Contributions. Perkins Observatory. Series 2

Contrib Phys Chem Petrol — Contributions to Physico-Chemical Petrology

Contrib Plasma Phys — Contributions to Plasma Physics

Contrib Primatol — Contributions to Primatology

Contrib Qd Herb — Contributions. Queensland Herbarium

Contrib Queensl Herb — Contributions. Queensland Herbarium

Contrib Res Counc Alberta — Contribution. Research Council of Alberta

Contrib Sci Dev Text Ind Jt Conf — Contributions of Science to the Development of the Textile Industry. Joint Conference

Contrib Sci (Los Ang) — Contributions in Science (Los Angeles)

Contrib Sci Neurol Psychopharmacol Syst Mot Colloq Int — Contribution des Sciences Neurologiques a la Psychopharmacologie et le Systeme Moteur. Colloques Internationaux

Contrib Scripps Inst Oceanogr — Contributions. Scripps Institution of Oceanography

Contrib Sedimentology — Contributions to Sedimentology

Contrib Sens Physiol — Contributions to Sensory Physiology

Contrib Shanghai Inst Entomol — Contributions. Shanghai Institute of Entomology

Contrib Soc Res Meteorites — Contributions. Society for Research on Meteorites

Contrib Statist — Contributions to Statistics

Contrib Stn Biol St Laurent Can — Contributions. Station Biologique du St. Laurent, Canada

Contrib Symp Immunol — Contributions to the Symposium on Immunology

Contrib Symp Immunol Ges Allerg Immunitaetsforsch — Contributions. Symposium on Immunology. Gesellschaft fuer Allergie und Immunitaetsforschung

Contrib Univ Calif San Diego Scripps Inst Oceanogr — Contributions. University of California, San Diego. Scripps Institution of Oceanography

Contrib Univ Calif Water Resour Cent — Contribution. University of California. Water Resources Center

Contrib Univ Mass Dep Geol Geogr — Contribution. University of Massachusetts. Department of Geology and Geography

Contrib Univ Mich Herb — Contributions. University of Michigan Herbarium

Contrib Univ Mich Herbar — Contributions. University of Michigan Herbarium

Contrib Univ Tec Estado Santiago — Contribuciones. Universidad Tecnica del Estado. Santiago

Contrib US Natl Herb — Contributions. United States National Herbarium

Contrib Va Geol — Contributions to Virginia Geology

Contrib Vertebr Evol — Contributions to Vertebrate Evolution

Contrib Welder Wildl Found — Contribution. Welder Wildlife Foundation

Contrib Zool — Contributions to Zoology

Contr Indian Sociol — Contributions to Indian Sociology

Contr Inst Antarc Argent — Contribuciones del Instituto Antarctico Argentino

Contr Inst Bot Natl Acad Peiping — Contributions. Institute of Botany. National Academy of Peiping

Contr Inst Bot Univ Montreal — Contributions. Institut de Botanique. Universite de Montreal

Contr Inst For Prod Univ Wash — Contribution. Institute of Forest Products. University of Washington. College of Forest Resources

Contr Inst Geol Tohoku Univ — Contributions from the Institute of Geology and Paleontology. Tohoku University

Contr Inst Met Belg — Contributions. Institut Royal de Meteorologie de Belgique

Contr Instr — Control and Instrumentation

Contr Instrum — Control and Instrumentation

Contr Iowa Corn Res Inst — Contributions. Iowa Corn Research Institute

Contr Jard Bot Rio J — Contributions. Jardin Botanique de Rio De Janeiro

Contr Jeff Phys Lab Harv — Contributions. Jefferson Physical Laboratory of Harvard University

Contr Lab Bot Natl Acad Peiping — Contributions from the Laboratory of Botany. National Academy of Peiping

Contr Lab Mar Biol Assoc — Contributions from the Laboratory. Marine Biological Association

Contr Lab Vertebr Biol — Contributions. Laboratory of Vertebrate Biology. University of Michigan

Contr Lab Vertebr Genet Univ Mich — Contributions. Laboratory of Vertebrate Genetics. University of Michigan

Contrl Eng — Control Engineering

Contr Life Sci Roy Ontario Mus — Contributions. Life Sciences. Royal Ontario Museum

Contr Mar Biol Univ Wales — Contributions to Marine Biology. University of Wales

Contr Marine Sci — Contributions in Marine Science

Contr Mar S — Contributions in Marine Science

Contr Min P — Contributions to Mineralogy and Petrology

Contr Mus Geol — Contributions. Museum of Geology. University of Michigan

Contr Mus Paleont — Contributions. Museum of Paleontology. University of Michigan

Contr New South Wales Natl Herb — Contributions. New South Wales National Herbarium

Contr New York Bot Gard — Contributions. New York Botanical Garden

Contr NSW Natn Herb — Contributions. New South Wales National Herbarium

Control Abstr — Control Abstracts

Control and Comput — Control and Computers

Control & Cybern — Control and Cybernetics

Control and Instrum — Control and Instrumentation

Control Antibiot Resist Bact Beecham Colloq — Control of Antibiotic-Resistant Bacteria. Beecham Colloquium

Control Automat Process — Control and Automation Process

Control Cibern & Autom — Control Cibernetica y Automatizacion

Control Clin Trials — Controlled Clinical Trials

Control Cybern — Control and Cybernetics

Control Cybernet — Control and Cybernetics

Control Diarrhoea Clin Pract Proc Int Symp — Control of Diarrhoea in Clinical Practice. Proceedings. International Symposium

Control Dynam Systems Adv Theory Appl — Control and Dynamic Systems. Advances in Theory and Applications

Control Dyn Syst — Control and Dynamic Systems. Advances in Theory and Applications

Controle Aliment Plant Cultiv Colloq Eur Mediterr — Controle de l'Alimentation des Plantes Cultivees. Colloque Europeen et Mediterraneen

Control Eng — Control Engineering

Control Engng — Control Engineering

Control Eng Pract — Control Engineering Practice

Control Feed Behav Biol Brain Protein-Calorie Malnutr — Control of Feeding Behavior and Biology of the Brain in Protein-Calorie Malnutrition

Control Gaseous Sulphur Nitrogen Compd Emiss Pap Int Conf — Control of Gaseous Sulphur and Nitrogen Compound Emission. Papers presented at the International Conference

Control Gene Expression Proc Annu Oholo Biol Conf — Control of Gene Expression. Proceedings. Annual Oholo Biological Conference

Control Glycogen Metab Proc Meet Fed Eur Biochem Soc — Control of Glycogen Metabolism. Proceedings. Meeting. Federation of European Biochemical Societies

Control Hazard Mater Spills Proc Natl Conf — Control of Hazardous Material Spills. Proceedings. National Conference on Control of Hazardous Material Spills

Control Instrum — Control and Instrumentation

Control Instrum Chem Ind — Control and Instruments in Chemical Industry

Controlled Clin Trials — Controlled Clinical Trials

Controlled Release Bioact Mater — Controlled Release of Bioactive Materials

Controlled Release Pestic Pharm Proc Int Symp — Controlled Release of Pesticides and Pharmaceuticals. Proceedings. International Symposium on Controlled Release of Bioactive Materials

Control Pig Reprod Proc Int Conf — Control of Pig Reproduction. Proceedings. International Conference on Pig Reproduction

Control Power Syst Conf Expo Conf Rec — Control of Power Systems Conference and Exposition. Conference Record

Control Rev — Control Review

Control Ser Bull Mass Agric Exp Stn Univ Mass — Control Series Bulletin. Massachusetts Agricultural Experiment Station. University of Massachusetts

Control Ser VA Polytech Inst State Univ Coop Ext Serv — Control Series. Virginia Polytechnic Institute and State University CooperativeExtension Service

Controls Opt Syst — Controls for Optical Systems

Control Specific Toxic Pollut — Control of Specific (Toxic) Pollutants

Control Sulphur Other Gaseous Emiss Int Symp — Control of Sulphur and Other Gaseous Emissions. International Symposium

Control Sys — Control Systems

Control Technol Cent US Environ Prot Agency Rep EPA — Control Technology Center. United States Environmental Protection Agency. Report EPA

Control Theory Adv Tech — Control Theory and Advanced Technology

Control Theory Appl — Control Theory and Applications

Control Tissue Damage Strangeways Res Lab 75th Anniv Symp — Control of Tissue Damage. Strangeways Research Laboratory 75th Anniversary Symposium

Control Virus Dis Pap Int Conf Comp Virol — Control of Virus Diseases. Papers. International Conference on Comparative Virology

Contr Palaeont — Contributions to Palaeontology

Contr Pl Genet — Contributions on Plant Genetics

Contr Prim — Contributions to Primatology

Contr Qd Herb — Contributions. Queensland Herbarium

Contr Sc — Contributions in Science

Contr Sci — Contributions in Science

Contr Sci Prat Migl Conosc Util Legno — Contributi Scientifico. Pratici per una Migliore Conoscenza ed Utilizzazione del Legno

Contr SE Asia Ethnogr — Contributions to Southeast Asian Ethnography

Contr Ser Bull Mass Agr Exp Sta — Control Series Bulletin. Massachusetts Agricultural Experiment Station

Contr Seto Mar Biol Lab — Contributions. Seto Marine Biological Laboratory. Kyoto University

Contr Soc — Contrat Social. Revue Historique et Critique des Faits et des Idees

Contr Tennessee Univ Bot Lab — Contributions. Tennessee University. Botanical Laboratory

Contr US Nat Herb — Contributions. United States National Herbarium

Contr US Natl Herb — Contributions from the United States National Herbarium. Smithsonian Institution

Cont Shelf Res — Continental Shelf Research

Cont Sociol — Contemporary Sociology

conv — Conveyancer and Property Lawyer

Conv — Convivium

Conv Addresses Natl Shellfish Assoc — Convention Addresses. National Shellfisheries Association

Conv and Prop Law — Conveyancer and Property Lawyer

Conv Battery Counc Int — Convention. Battery Council International

CONVDF — Convergence

Convegno Riv Lett & Tutte A — Convegno. Rivista di Letteratura e di Tutte le Arti

Conv Electr Electron Eng Isr Proc — Convention of Electrical and Electronics Engineers in Israel. Proceedings

Conven Proc Agric Vet Chem Assoc Aust — Convention Proceedings. Agricultural and Veterinary Chemicals Association of Australia

Convergences Med — Convergences Medicales

Conversation Biomol Stereodyn — Conversation in Biomolecular Stereodynamics

Conversation Discip Biomol Stereodyn — Conversation in the Discipline Biomolecular Stereodynamics

Convers Refuse Energy Int Conf Tech Exhib — Conversion of Refuse to Energy. International Conference and Technical Exhibition

Converting Technol — Converting Technology

Convey — Conveyancer and Property Lawyer

Convey NS — Conveyancer and Property Lawyer. New Series

Conv IICA-ZN-ROCAP Bibliogr — Convenio IICA-ZN-ROCAP [*Instituto Interamericano de Ciencias Agricolas-ZonaNorte-Regional Organization for Central America and Panama*] Bibliografia

Conv IICA-ZN-ROCAP Publ Misc — Convenio IICA-ZN-ROCAP [*Instituto Interamericano de Ciencias Agricolas-ZonaNorte-Regional Organization for Central America and Panama*] Publicacion Miscelanea

Conv Int Acque Sotterranee Atti — Convegno Internazionale sulle Acque Sotterranee. Atti. Ente Sviluppo Agricolo in Sicilia

Conv Int Geom Diff — Convegno Internazionale di Geometria Differenziale

Conv Int Idrocarb — Convegno Internazionale sugli Idrocarburi

Conv Ital Sci Macromol Atti — Convegno Italiano di Scienza delle Macromolecole. Atti

ConvLit — Convorbiri Literare
Conv Non Conv Proteins Capri Vet Workshop — Conventional and Non Conventional Proteins. Capri Veterinary Workshop
Conv (NS) — Conveyancer and Property Lawyer. New Series
Convorbiri Lit — Convorbiri Literare
Conv Rec IRE — Convention Record. IRE
Conv Rev — Conveyancing Review
Conv Salute Ereditarieta Ambiente Aliment — Convegno della Salute. Ereditarieta, Ambiente, Alimentazione
Conv Sc Caratt Mol Polim Atti — Convegno-Scuola su Caratterizzazione Molecolare di Polimeri. Atti
Conv Sc Crist Polim Atti — Convegno-Scuola su Cristallizzazione dei Polimeri. Atti
Conv Sc Fondam Transform Mater Polim Polym Process — Convegno-Scuola su Fondamenti della Transformazione dei Materiali Polimerici Polymer Processing
Conv Sc Sint Polim — Convegno-Scuola su Sintesi di Polimeri
Convulsive Ther — Convulsive Therapy
Convuls Ther — Convulsive Therapy
Conv Vitam Giornata Sci — Convegno sulle Vitamine. Giornata della Scienza
Conv Vol Indian Assoc Water Pollut Control — Convention Volume. Indian Association for Water Pollution Control
Conv YB — Conveyancers' Year Book
Con W — Congress Weekly
COO — Chronicles of Oklahoma
COOFA — Cahiers Oceanographiques (France)
COOLBM — Coolia
Cooleys Anemia Symp — Cooley's Anemia Symposium
Coombe Lodge Rep — Coombe Lodge Reports
Coombe Lodge Repts — Coombe Lodge Reports
Coop — Cooperation
Coop — Cooperation des Idees
COOP — Co-Op North
Coop Agr — Cooperation Agricole
Coop Agric — Cooperation Agricole
Coop Agric Coop Fed Que — Cooperateur Agricole la Cooperative Federee de Quebec
Coop and Conflict — Cooperation and Conflict
Coop Bogota — Cooperativa (Bogota)
Co-Op Bull Taiwan For Res Inst — Co-Operative Bulletin. Taiwan Forestry Research Institute
Co Op Bull Taiwan For Res Inst Co Op Jt Comm Rural Reconstr — Co-Operative Bulletin of Taiwan Forestry Research Institute in Co-Operation with the Joint Commission on Rural Reconstruction
Coop Can — Cooperation Canada
Coop Conflict — Cooperation and Conflict
Coop Consum — Cooperative Consumer
Coop Dent (B Aires) — Cooperador Dental (Buenos Aires)
Coop-Distrib-Consom — Cooperation-Distribution-Consommation
Co-Op Econ Insect Rep — Cooperative Economic Insect Report
Co-Op Electr Res — Co-Operative Electrical Research
Cooper Un Bull — Cooper Union Bulletin. Engineering and Science Series
Cooper Union Bull Eng Sci Ser — Cooper Union Bulletin. Engineering and Science Series
Cooper Union Chron — Cooper Union Museum Chronicle
Coop et Dev — Cooperation et Developpement
Coop et Development — Cooperation et Developpement
Coop Ext Serv Coll Agric Univ Conn Bull — Cooperative Extension Service. College of Agriculture. University of Connecticut. Bulletin
Coop Fr — Cooperateur de France
Coop Grain Quart — Coop Grain Quarterly
Coop Inf — Cooperation Information
Coop Inf Int Labor Off — Co-Operative Information. International Labor Office
Coop Internat — Cooperation Internationale. Culturelle, Scientifique, Technique
Coop Manager & F — Cooperative Manager and Farmer
Coop Meat Trade D — Cooperatives Meat Trade Digest
Coop Mediterr Energ Sol Rev Int Heliotech — Cooperation Mediterraneenne pour l'Energie Solaire. Revue Internationale d'Heliotechnique
Co-Op News — Co-Operative News
Coop News — Co-Operative News Digest
Coop Phenom Biol — Cooperative Phenomena in Biology
Coop Pl Rest Rep — Cooperative Plant Pest Report
Coop Resour Rep III State Water Survey III State Geol Surv — Cooperative Resources Report. Illinois State Water Survey and Illinois State Geological Survey
Coop Res Rep Int Counc Explor Sea Ser A — Cooperative Research Report. International Council for the Exploration of the Sea. Series A
Coop Res Rep Int Council Explor Sea — Cooperative Research Report. International Council for the Exploration of the Sea
Coop Rev — Co-Operative Review
Coop Tech — Cooperation Technique
Coop y Desarrollo — Cooperativesmo y Desarrollo
Coord Chem — Coordination Chemistry
Coord Chem Rev — Coordination Chemistry Reviews
Coord Ch Re — Coordination Chemistry Reviews
Coord Guidel Wildl Habitats US For Serv Calif Reg — Coordination Guidelines for Wildlife Habitats. United States Forest Service. California Region
Coordinating Council Bul — Coordinating Council Bulletin
Coord Regul Gene Expression Proc Int Workshop — Coordinated Regulation of Gene Expression. Proceedings. International Workshop on Coordinated Regulation of Gene Expression
Coord Res Counc CRC Rep — Coordinating Research Council. CRC Report
Coord Res Counc Inc Rep — Coordinating Research Council, Inc. Report
COOUA — Colorado Outdoors
COP — Computermarkt
Cop — Copeia

COPAAR — Copeia
Copenhagen Univ Mineralog Geol Mus Contr Mineralogy — Copenhagen University. Mineralogical and Geological Museum. Contributions to Mineralogy
COPMBU — Computer Programs in Biomedicine
COPNDZ — Concepts in Pediatric Neurosurgery
Copp All Bull — Copper Alloy Bulletin
Copper Abstr — Copper Abstracts
Copper Dev Assoc Tech Rep — Copper Development Association. Technical Report
Copper Dev Assoc Tech Sur — Copper Development Association. Technical Survey
Copper Development Assocn Information Sheet — Copper Development Association. Information Sheet
Copper Environ — Copper in the Environment [*monograph*]
Copper Ind Washington DC — Copper Industry (Washington, D.C.)
Copper Prod Washington (DC) — Copper Production (Washington, DC)
Copper Stud — Copper Studies
Copper US Washington DC — Copper in the United States (Washington, DC)
Copper Yugosl — Copper Yugoslavia
COPS — Canadian Operating Statistics
Coptic Ch R — Coptic Church Review
Coptic Stu — Coptic Studies
COPYA — Comprehensive Psychiatry
COPYAV — Comprehensive Psychiatry
Copy Rep — Copyright Reporter
Copyright Bul — Copyright Bulletin
Copyright Bull — UNESCO Copyright Bulletin
Copyright L Dec CCH — Copyright Law Decisions. Commerce Clearing House
Copyright L Sym (ASCAP) — Copyright Law Symposium. American Society of Composers, Authors, and Publishers
Copy Soc Aust News — Copyright Society of Australia. Newsletter
Copy Soc Bull — Bulletin. Copyright Society of the USA
COR — Business America
C Or — Chroniques d'Orient
CoR — Contemporary Review
Cor — Cornell Law Review
COR — Corporation Law Review
Cor — Correspondant [*Paris*]
Cor — Correspondent
CORAD6 — Corax
Coral Gables Conf Fundam Interact High Energy — Coral Gables Conference on Fundamental Interactions at High Energy
Cor-Bl Naturf-Ver Riga — Correspondenzblatt. Naturforscher-Verein zu Riga
Cord — Corduroy
Cord Med — Cordoba Medica
Cordulia Suppl — Cordulia. Supplement
CORE — Construction Review
CoRe — Contemporary Review
COREBG — Conditional Reflex
Core J Obst/Gyn — Core Journals in Obstetrics/Gynecology
Core J Pediatr — Core Journals in Pediatrics
CORFDL — Coral Reefs
Corfu Anthol — Corfu Anthology
C Org Jud — Code de l'Organisation Judiciaire du Congo
Cor Int LJ — Cornell International Law Journal
Cork Hist & Archaeol Soc J — Cork Historical and Archaeological Society Journal
Cork Hist Arch Soc J — Cork Historical and Archaeological Society. Journal
CorL — Correo Literario
Cor LQ — Cornell Law Quarterly
Cor LR — Cornell Law Review
Corm — Cormosa Newsletter
CorM — Cornhill Magazine
Cormosea Newsl — Cormosea Newsletter
Corn A — Cornish Archaeology
Corn Ann — Corn Annual
Corn Annu — Corn Annual
Cornelis Floris Jb — Cornelis Floris Jaarboek
Cornell Ag Exp — Cornell University. Agricultural Experiment Station. Publications
Cornell Agric Waste Manage Conf — Cornell Agricultural Waste Management Conference
Cornell Agric Waste Manage Conf Proc — Cornell Agricultural Waste Management Conference. Proceedings
Cornell Electr Eng Conf Proc — Cornell Electrical Engineering Conference. Proceedings
Cornell Eng — Cornell Engineer
Cornell Eng Q — Cornell Engineerng Quarterly
Cornell Ext Bull — Cornell Extension Bulletin
Cornell Ext Bull NY State Coll Agr Ext Serv — Cornell Extension Bulletin. New York State College of Agriculture. Extension Service
Cornell Feed Serv NY State Coll Agr Ext Serv — Cornell Feed Service. New York State College of Agriculture. Extension Service
Cornell Hist Sci Ser — Cornell History of Science Series
Cornell Hotel & Rest Adm Q — Cornell Hotel and Restaurant Administration Quarterly
Cornell Hotel & Restau Adm Q — Cornell Hotel and Restaurant Administration Quarterly
Cornell Hotel and Restaurant Admin Q — Cornell Hotel and Restaurant Administration Quarterly
Cornell Hotel Restaur Adm Q — Cornell Hotel and Restaurant Administration Quarterly
Cornell Hotel Restaurant Adm Q — Cornell Hotel and Restaurant Administration Quarterly
Cornell I J — Cornell International Law Journal
Cornell Int Agric Bull — Cornell International Agriculture Bulletin

Cornell Int Agric Dev Bull — Cornell International Agricultural Development Bulletin
Cornell Internat Law J — Cornell International Law Journal
Cornell Internat LJ — Cornell International Law Journal
Cornell Int L J — Cornell International Law Journal
Cornell Intl LJ — Cornell International Law Journal
Cornell Int Symp Workshop Hydrogen Econ — Cornell International Symposium and Workshop on the Hydrogen Economy
Cornell Jnl Soc Rel — Cornell Journal of Social Relations
Cornell J S — Cornell Journal of Social Relations
Cornell J Soc Rel — Cornell Journal of Social Relations
Cornell J Soc Relat — Cornell Journal of Social Relations
Cornell Law Q — Cornell Law Quarterly
Cornell Law Quar — Cornell Law Quarterly
Cornell Law Quart — Cornell Law Quarterly
Cornell Law R — Cornell Law Review
Cornell Law Rev — Cornell Law Review
Cornell LF — Cornell Law Forum
Cornell Lib J — Cornell Library Journal
Cornell L Q — Cornell Law Quarterly
Cornell L R — Cornell Law Review
Cornell L Rev — Cornell Law Review
Cornell Med J — Cornell Medical Journal
Cornell Misc Bull — Cornell Miscellaneous Bulletin
Cornell Nutr Conf Feed Manuf Proc — Cornell Nutrition Conference for Feed Manufacturers. Proceedings
Cornell Plant — Cornell Plantations
Cornell Plantat — Cornell Plantations
Cornell R — Cornell Review
Cornell Univ Agric Exp Sta Bull — Cornell University Agricultural Experiment Station. Bulletin
Cornell Univ Agric Exp Sta Circ — Cornell University Agricultural Experiment Station Circular
Cornell Univ Agric Exp Stn Mem — Cornell University. Agricultural Experiment Station. Memoirs
Cornell Univ Conf Agric Waste Manage — Cornell University Conference on Agricultural Waste Management
Cornell Univ Dep Struc Eng Rep — Cornell University. Department of Structural Engineering. Report
Cornell Univ Lib Bull — Cornell University Libraries. Bulletin
Cornell Univ Mem — Cornell University Memoirs
Cornell Vet — Cornell Veterinarian
Cornell Veterin — Cornell Veterinarian
Cornell Vet Suppl — Cornell Veterinarian. Supplement
Cornh — Cornhill Magazine
Cornhill M — Cornhill Magazine
Cornhill Mag — Cornhill Magazine
Corning Res — Corning Research
Corn Inst Eng Trans — Cornish Institute of Engineers. Transactions
Cornish Arch — Cornish Archaeology
Cornish Archaeol — Cornish Archaeology
Corn J Soc Rel — Cornell Journal of Social Relations
Corn Mimeogr Tex Res Found — Corn Mimeograph. Texas Research Foundation
Cornwall Gl S T — Transactions of the Royal Geological Society of Cornwall
Cornwall Pol S Rp — Reports and Transactions of the Royal Polytechnic Society of Cornwall
Cornwall Pol S T — Reports and Transactions of the Royal Polytechnic Society of Cornwall
Coron Artery Dis — Coronary Artery Disease
Coron Heart Dis (Stuttgart) — Coronary Heart Disease (Stuttgart). International Symposium
CORPA — Clinical Orthopaedics
Corp Ant Amer — Corpus Antiquitatum Americanensium
Corp Bulletin — Bureau of Corporate Affairs. Bulletin
Corp Christ — Corpus Christianorum
Corp Comment — Corporate Commentary
Corp Counsel Rev J Corp Counsel Section St B Tex — Corporate Counsel Review. Journal of the Corporate Counsel Section. State Bar of Texas
Corp Dir — Corporate Directorship
Corp Fit and R — Corporate Fitness and Recreation
Corp Forms (P-H) — Corporation Forms (Prentice-Hall, Inc.)
Corp Gl — Corpus Glossariorum Latinorum a G. Loewe Incohatum
Corp Gr Christl Inschr — Corpus der Griechisch-Christlichen Inschriften von Hellas
Corp Guide P-H — Corporation Guide. Prentice-Hall
Corp Inscr Attic — Corpus Inscriptionum Atticarum
Corp Inscr Et — Corpus Inscriptionum Etruscarum
Corp Inscr Lat — Corpus Inscriptionum Latinarum
Corp Inscr Semit — Corpus Inscriptionum Semiticarum
Corp J — Corporation Journal
Corp L Guide — Corporation Law Guide
Corp LR — Corporation Law Review
Corp L Rev — Corporation Law Review
Corp Med Graec — Corpus Medicorum Graecorum
Corp Med Lat — Corpus Medicorum Latinorum
Corp Mgt Tax Conf — Corporate Management Tax Conference
Corp Month — Corporate Monthly
Corp Nummorum It — Corpus Nummorum Italicorum
Corporate Rept — Corporate Report
Corp Papyr Hermopol — Corpus Papyrorum Hermopolitanorum
Corp Philanth — Corporate Philanthropy
Corp Poet Lat — Corpus Poetarum Latinorum
Corp Prac Com — Corporate Practice Commentator
Corp Prac Comm — Corporate Practice Commentator
Corp Prac Comment — Corporate Practice Commentator
Corp Prac Rev — Corporate Practice Review

Corp Prac Ser (BNA) — Corporate Practice Series (Bureau of National Affairs)
Corp Pract Comment — Corporate Practice Commentator
Corp Reorg & Am Bank Rev — Corporate Reorganization and American Bankruptcy Review
Corp Sc Eccl Lat — Corpus Scriptorum Ecclesiasticorum Latinorum
Corp Script Christ Or — Corpus Scriptorum Christianorum Orientalium
Corps Gras Ind — Corps Gras Industriels
Corps Med (Ettelbruck) — Corps Medical (Ettelbruck)
Corpus Astronom Byzantins — Corpus des Astronomes Byzantins
Corpus Christi Geol Soc Bull — Corpus Christi Geological Society. Bulletin
Corpus Inscript Graec — Corpus Inscriptionum Graecarum
Corr — Correspondant
Corr Blad — Correspondentieblad van de Broederschap der Notarissen in Nederland
Corr Bl Dt Ges Anthropol Ethnol & Urgesch — Correspondenz-Blatt der Deutschen Gesellschaft fuer Anthropologie, Ethnologie, und Urgeschichte
Corr Brux — Jugement du Tribunal Correctionnel de Bruxelles
Corr Ceram — Corriere dei Ceramisti
Corr Dir Acad France — Correspondance des Directeurs de l'Academie de France a Rome
Correc Educ — Correctional Education. American Prison Association
Correct Mag — Corrections Magazine
Correct Today — Corrections Today
Correio Agric — Correio Agricola
Correio Med Lisb — O Correio Medico de Lisboa
Corr Eng — Corrosion Engineer
Correo Erud — Correo Erudito
Correo Hond Tegucigalpa — Correo de Honduras (Tegucigalpa)
Corresp Bl Schweiz Aerzte — Correspondenz Blatt fuer Schweizer Aerzte
Correspondance Munic — Correspondance Municipale
Correspondentiebl Dienste Florist Veg Onderz Ned — Correspondentieblad ten Dienste van de Floristiek en het Vegetatie-Onderzoek van Nederland
Correspondenzbl Naturf Vereins Riga — Correspondenzblatt des Naturforschenden Vereins zu Riga
Correspondenzbl Naturhist Vereines Preuss Rheinl — Correspondenzblatt des Naturhistorischen Vereines fuer die Preussischen Rheinlande
Corresp Orient Et — Correspondance d'Orient. Etudes
Corr Farm — Corriere del Farmacista
Corr Farmac — Corriere del Farmacista
Corr Fotogr — Corriere Fotografico
Corr Fotogr Sudam — Correo Fotografico Sudamericano
Corrie Herring Hooks Ser — Corrie Herring Hooks Series
Corriere Cer — Corriere dei Ceramisti
Corr Mater Prot — Corrosion and Material Protection
Corr Met Finish (S Afr) — Corrosion and Metal Finishing (South Africa)
Corr Mil — Correspondencia Militar
Corros Abstr — Corrosion Abstracts
Corros Anti-Corros — Corrosion et Anti-Corrosion
Corros Australas — Corrosion Australasia
Corros Bull — Corrosion Bulletin
Corros Bull Karaikudi India — Corrosion Bulletin (Karaikudi, India)
Corros Coat S Afr — Corrosion and Coatings South Africa
Corros Control Org Coat Pap Conf — Corrosion Control by Organic Coatings. Papers presented at a Conference
Corros Degrad Implant Mater Symp — Corrosion and Degradation of Implant Materials. Symposium
Corros Electron Magn Mater — Corrosion of Electronic and Magnetic Materials
Corros Eng (Tokyo) — Corrosion Engineering (Tokyo)
Corros Erosion Lubr Symp Pap — Corrosion Erosion and Lubrication Symposium. Papers
Corros Fatigue Proc USSR UK Semin Corros Fatigue Met — Corrosion Fatigue. Proceedings. USSR-UK Seminar on Corrosion Fatigue of Metals
Corros Inst TNO Circ — Corrosie-Instituut TNO. Circulaire
Corros Inst TNO Meded — Corrosie-Instituut TNO. Mededeling
Corrosion Prev Contr — Corrosion Prevention and Control
Corrosion Prev Control — Corrosion Prevention and Control
Corrosion Prevention — Corrosion Prevention and Control
Corrosion Sci — Corrosion Science
Corros Its Prev — Corrosion and Its Prevention
Corros Maint — Corrosion and Maintenance
Corros Mar Environ — Corrosion in Marine Environment
Corros Mar Environ Int Sourceb — Corrosion in Marine Environment. International Sourcebook
Corros Mar Fouling — Corrosion Marine-Fouling
Corros Mater — Corrosion and Materials
Corros Mater Prot — Corrosion and Material Protection
Corros Met Finish S Afr — Corrosion and Metal Finishing. South Africa
Corros Pre Contr — Corrosion Prevention and Control
Corros Prev Control — Corrosion Prevention and Control
Corros Prev Process Ind Proc NACE Int Symp — Corrosion Prevention in the Process Industries. Proceedings. NACE (National Association of Corrosion Engineers) International Symposium
Corros Prot — Corrosion y Proteccion
Corros Prot Mater — Corrosao e Proteccao de Materiais
Corros Rev — Corrosion Reviews
Corros Sci — Corrosion Science
Corros Sci Eng Proc Int Symp — Corrosion Science and Engineering. Proceedings. International Symposium
Corros Technol — Corrosion Technology
Corros Technol NY — Corrosion Technology (New York)
Corros Test Eval Silver Anniv Vol — Corrosion Testing and Evaluation. Silver Anniversary Volume
Corros Trait Prot Finition — Corrosion, Traitements, Protection, Finition
Corros Week Manifestation Eur Fed Corros — Corrosion Week. Manifestation. European Federation of Corrosion

Corr Soc Ps — Corrective and Social Psychiatry
Corrugated Containers Conf Prepr — Corrugated Containers Conference. Preprints
Corrugated Newsl — Corrugated Newsletter
Corse Hist — Corse Historique. Etudes et Documents
Corse Hist Arch Lit Sci — Corse Historique, Archeologique, Litteraire, Scientifique
Corse Med — Corse Medicale
Corse Mediterr Med — Corse Mediterranee Medicale
Corsi Cult A Ravenn & Biz — Corsi di Cultura sull'Arte Ravennate e Bizantina
Corsi Ravenna — Corso di Cultura dell'Arte Ravennate e Bizantina
Corsi Semin Chim — Corsi e Seminari di Chimica. Consiglio Nazionale delle Ricerche e Fondazione "F. Giordani"
CORS J — CORS [*Canadian Operational Research Society*] Journal
Corso Teor Prat Util Colt Cell Indag Tossicol — Corso Teorico-Pratico sull'Utilizzazione delle Colture Cellulari nell'Indagine Tossicologica
C ORSTOM Ser Sci Hum — Cahiers. ORSTOM [*Office de la Recherche Scientifique et Technique d'Outre-Mer*]. Serie Sciences Humaines
CORTB — Clinical Orthopaedics and Related Research
CORTBR — Clinical Orthopaedics and Related Research
CORTDT — Contemporary Orthopaedics
Cortisone Invest — Cortisone Investigator
CorUV — Correspondance de l'Union pour la Verite
Cos — Cosmic Stories
COS — Cosmopolitan
Cos — Cosmos Science Fiction and Fantasy Magazine
Cos & Toil — Cosmetics and Toiletries
COSB — Central Opera Services Bulletin
Cos Chem — Cosmetic Chemists. Journal of the Society
COSE — Common Sense. Journal of Information for Environmentally Concerned Citizens. Kootenay Environmental Institute
COSHB — Cahiers. ORSTOM [*Office de la Recherche Scientifique et Technique d'Outre-Mer*]. Hydrologie
Cos Intnl — Cosmetics International
Cosm — Cosmic Science Fiction
Cosmet & Toiletries — Cosmetics and Toiletries
Cosmet J — Cosmetic Journal
Cosmet Med (Tokyo) — Cosmetic Medicine (Tokyo)
Cosmet News — Cosmetic News
Cosmet Perfum — Cosmetics and Perfumery
Cosmet Sci London — Cosmetic Science (London)
Cosmet Technol — Cosmetic Technology
Cosmet Toiletries Ed Ital — Cosmetics and Toiletries. Edizione Italiana
Cosmet Toiletry Fragrance Assoc Cosmet J — Cosmetic, Toiletry, and Fragrance Association. Cosmetic Journal
Cosmic Electrodyn — Cosmic Electrodynamics
Cosmic Ray Conf Pap Int Conf Cosmic Rays — Cosmic Ray Conference Papers. International Conference on Cosmic Rays
Cosmic Ray Lab CRL Rep Univ Tokyo — Cosmic Ray Laboratory. CRL-Report (University of Tokyo)
Cosmic Rays Proc Int Conf — Cosmic Rays. Proceedings. International Conference
Cosmic Res — Cosmic Research
Cosmic Res Engl Transl — Cosmic Research (English Translation)
Cosmic Subatomic Phys Rep — Cosmic and Subatomic Physics Report
Cosmic Subatomic Phys Rep LUIP Univ Lund Dep Phys — Cosmic and Subatomic Physics Report LUIP. University of Lund. Department of Physics
Cosmop — Cosmopolitan
Cosmopol — Cosmopolitan
Cosmopolitan A J — Cosmopolitan Art Journal
COSPAR Colloq Ser — COSPAR (Committee on Space Research) Colloquia Series
COSPAR Inf Bull — COSPAR [*Committee on Space Research*] Information Bulletin
COSPAR Space Res — COSPAR (Committee on Space Research) Space Research
COSPB — Comments on Solid State Physics
Costa Azzurra Agric Fl — Costa Azzurra Agricola-Floreale. Rivista Mensile di Floricoltura ed Orticoltura
Cost Accounting Stand Guide CCH — Cost Accounting Standards Guide. Commerce Clearing House
Cost and Man — Cost and Management
Cost & Mgt — Cost and Management
Costa Rica B Fomento — Costa Rica. Boletin de Fomento
Costa Rica Centro de Estudios Sismologicos An — Costa Rica. Centro de Estudios Sismologicos. Anales
Costa Rica Inst Geog Informe Semestral Informe Trimestral — Costa Rica. Instituto Geografico. Informe Semestral. Informe Trimestral
Costa Rica Minist Agric Ganad Bol Misc — Costa Rica. Ministerio de Agricultura y Ganaderia. Boletin Miscelaneo
Costa Rica Minist Agric Ganad Bol Tec — Costa Rica. Ministerio de Agricultura y Ganaderia. Boletin Tecnico
Cost Bul — Cost Bulletin
Cost Bull — Cost Bulletin
Cost Eng — Cost Engineering
Costerus Es — Costerus. Essays in English and American Language and Literature. New Series
Cost Fed — Costituzione Federale
Cost Manage — Cost and Management
Costr Met — Costruzioni Metalliche
COSUD — Colloids and Surfaces
COSUD3 — Colloids and Surfaces
Cos Wld N — Cosmetic World News
COT — Colombia Today
COTED — Coal Technology

Cote d Azur Agric Hort — Cote d'Azur Agricole et Horticole et la Revue Oleicole. Societe Centrale d'Agriculture, Horticulture, et d'Acclimatation de Nice et des Alpes-Maritimes
COTHD3 — Comprehensive Therapy
COTH Rep — COTH [*Council of Teaching Hospitals*] Report
COTOEP — Concepts in Toxicology
Coton Fibres Trop — Coton et Fibres Tropicales
Coton Fibres Trop Bull Anal — Coton et Fibres Tropicales. Bulletin Analytique
Coton Fibres Trop Engl Ed — Coton et Fibres Tropicales. English Edition
Coton Fibres Trop Fr Ed — Coton et Fibres Tropicales (French Edition)
Coton Fibr Trop — Coton et Fibres Tropicales
COTSD2 — Clinical Otolaryngology and Allied Sciences
Cott Impr Conf — Cotton Improvement Conference
Cotton Cts — Cotton Counts Its Customers. Quantity of Cotton Consumed in Final Uses in the United States
Cotton Dev — Cotton Development
Cotton Dig — Cotton Digest
Cotton Dust Res Conf Proc — Cotton Dust Research Conference. Proceedings
Cotton Growing Rev — Cotton Growing Review. Journal. Cotton Research Corporation
Cotton Grow Rev — Cotton Growing Review
Cotton Int — Cotton International
Cotton Int Ed — Cotton International Edition
Cotton Res Corp Cotton Res Rep — Cotton Research Corporation. Cotton Research Reports
Cotton Res Corp Prog Rep Exp Stn — Cotton Research Corporation. Progress Reports from Experiment Stations
Cotton Res Inst Sindos Sci Bull New Ser — Cotton Research Institute. Sindos Science Bulletin. New Series
Cotton Rev — Cotton. Monthly Review of the World Situation
Cotton States Assoc Comm Agric Proc — Cotton States Association of Commissioners of Agriculture. Proceedings
Cotton Wool Situat CWS US Dep Agric Econ Stat Serv — Cotton and Wool Situation. CWS. United States Department of Agriculture. Economics and Statistics Service
Cotton WS — Cotton. World Statistics
COU — Contacto (Uruguay)
COU — Courrier des Pays de l'Est. Mensuel d'Informations Economiques
Coulom Anal Conf — Coulometric Analysis. Conference
Counc Agric Sci Technol Rep — Council for Agricultural Science and Technology. Report
Counc Brit Archaeol Annu Rep — Council for British Archaeology. Annual Report
Counc Brit Archaeol Res Rep — Council for British Archaeology. Research Reports
Counc Econ Prior Newsl — Council on Economic Priorities. Newsletter
Counc Eur For — Council of Europe Forum
Council Anthropol Educ Qu — Council on Anthropology and Education. Quarterly
Council Eur Inf Bull — Council of Europe. Information Bulletin
Council Int Aff Nanking Inf Bull — Council of International Affairs. Information Bulletin (Nanking)
Council Legal Educ Prof Resp Newsl — Council on Legal Education for Professional Responsibility. Newsletter
Council Research M Education Bul — Council for Research in Music Education. Bulletin
Counc Miner Technol Rep — Council for Mineral Technology. Report
Counc Min Metall Inst Congr — Council of Mining and Metallurgical Institutions Congress
Counc Notes — Council Notes
Counc Ont Univ Quad Rev — Council of Ontario Universities Quadrennial Review
Counc Sci Indones Publ — Council for Sciences of Indonesia. Publication
Counc Sci Ind Res S Afr — Council for Scientific and Industrial Research (South Africa)
Couns Ed Su — Counselor Education and Supervision
Counsel & Values — Counseling and Values
Counsel Ed & Sup — Counselor Education and Supervision
Counsel Educ & Superv — Counselor Education and Supervision
Counsel Val — Counseling and Values
Couns For — Counsellor's Forum
Couns Mag — Counsellors' Magazine
Couns Psych — Counseling Psychologist
Counterpt — Counterpoint
Countrmsrs — Electronic, Electro-Optic, and Infrared Countermeasures
Country — Country Kids
Country Cal — Country Calendar
Country Gent — Country Gentleman
Country Gent Dublin — Country Gentleman (Dublin)
Country Gent Philadelphia — Country Gentleman (Philadelphia)
Country Hour J — Country Hour Journal
Country Life Annu — Country Life Annual
Country Life London — Country Life. Journal for All Interested in Country Life and Country Pursuits (London)
Countryman's Mag — (Western Mail) Countryman's Magazine
Country Side — Country-Side. Journal. British Naturalists' Association
Countryside Comm J — Countryside Commission. Journal
Countryside M — Countryside Magazine
Countryside M — Countryside Magazine and Suburban Life
Country Traders R — Country Traders' Review
County Employ Rep — County Employment Reporter
County Newsl — County Newsletter
COUR — Courier-Journal
COURA — Clinica Otorinolaringoiatrica
COURAZ — Clinica Otorinolaringoiatrica
Cour CNRS — Courrier du CNRS
Cour CNRS Suppl — Courrier du CNRS [*Centre National de la Recherche Scientifique*]. Supplement

Cour Forschungsinst Senckenb — Courier Forschungsinstitut Senckenberg
CourGB — Courrier Georges Bernanos
Cour Graph — Courrier Graphique
Courier Jl — Courier-Journal
CourMF — Courrier Musical de France
Cour Mus France — Courrier Musical de France
Courr Apic — Courrier Apicole
Courr Centre Int Enfance — Courrier. Centre International pour l'Enfance
Courr Etabl Neu — Courrier des Etablissements Neu
Courr Extr-Orient — Courrier de l'Extreme-Orient
Courr Hebd du CRISP — Courrier Hebdomadaire du CRISP (Centre de Recherche et d'Information Socio-Politiques)
Courrier — Courrier Revue Medico-Sociale de l'Enfance
Courrier A — Courrier de l'Art
Courrier du CNRS — Courrier du Centre National de la Recherche Scientifique
Courrier Fr — Courrier Francais
Courrier Graph — Courrier Graphique
Courrier M France — Courrier Musical de France
Courrier Pays Est — Courrier des Pays de l'Est
Courrier Phytochim — Courrier Phytochimique
Courr Nat — Courrier de la Nature
Courr Norm — Courrier de la Normalisation
Courr Pays Est — Courrier des Pays de l'Est
Courr UNESCO — Courrier. UNESCO
Cours Anal Ecole Roy Polytech — Cours d'Analyse de l'Ecole Royale Polytechnique
Cours Doc Bil — Cours et Documents de Biologie
Cours Doc Biol — Cours et Documents de Biologie
Cours Geom Fac Sci — Cours de Geometrie de la Faculte des Sciences
Cours Perfect Pediatr Prat — Cours de Perfectionnement en Pediatrie pour le Practicien
Cours Perfect Soc Suisse Psychiatr — Cours de Perfectionnement. Societe Suisse de Psychiatrie
Cours Spec — Cours Specialises
Court Inst Illus Archvs — Courtauld Institute Illustration Archives
Court J & Dist Ct Rec — Court Journal and District Court Record
Court Man Jnl — Court Management Journal
Court Mgt J — Court Management Journal
COUTA — Coal Utilization
COVAAN — Cor et Vasa
Coventry Eng Soc J — Coventry Engineering Society. Journal
COVPAY — Centre for Overseas Pest Research. Report
Cov Q — Covenant Quarterly
Covrt Act — Covert Action
COWA — Current Work in Old World Archaeology
COWA — Surveys and Bibliographies. Council for Old World Archaeology. Department of Sociology and Anthropology. Boston University
COWA CW — COWA [Council for Old World Archaeology] Survey. Current Work in Old World Archaeology
COWAEW — Colonial Waterbirds
Cow Moos Newsl Md Dairymen Md Univ Coop Ext Serv — Cow Moos. Newsletter for Maryland Dairymen. Maryland University. Cooperative Extension Service
COWPA — California Oil World and Petroleum Industry
Cox Anc L — Cox. Law and Science of Ancient Lights
Cox Mag Cas — Cox's Magistrates' Cases
Coyunt Econ — Coyuntura Economica
Coyuntura Econ — Coyuntura Economica
COZE — Coastal Zone. Informal Newsletter of the Resources of the Pacific and Western Arctic Coasts of Canada
COZOAH — Comunicari de Zoologie
CP — Castrum Peregrini
CP — China Pictorial
CP — Classical Philology
CP — Clinical Physiology
CP — Code Penal Suisse
CP — Codice Penale
CP — Codice Penale Svizzero
CP — Codigo Penal
CP — Commodity Prices
CP — Concerning Poetry
CP — Contemporary Psychology
CP — Cosmos (Paris)
CP — Coyoti Prints. Caribou Tribal Council Newsletter
CP — Crop Protection
CP — Cuadernos Politicos
CP — Cultura Politica
CPA — Chemical Propulsion Abstracts
CPA — Computer Program Abstracts
CPA — CPA [American Institute of Certified Public Accountants] Journal
CPA — Criminology and Penology Abstracts
CPAA — Current Physics Advance Abstracts
CPA Comp Rep — CPA [Certified Public Accountant] Computer Report
CPAJ — CPA [American Institute of Certified Public Accountants] Journal
CPAJA — Canadian Psychiatric Association. Journal
CPAMA — Communications on Pure and Applied Mathematics
CP & P — Computer Publishers and Publications
CPAOD — Chongqing Daxue Xuebao
CPAPA4 — Colonial Plant and Animal Products
C Papers — Cinema Papers
CPAP I — First Pan-African Congress on Prehistory. Nairobi, 1947. Proceedings
C Par — Corpus Scriptorum Latinorum Paravianum
CPARD — Cerpadla Potrubi Armatury
CPASAD — Commentationes Pontificiae. Academiae Scientiarum
CPASTATS — Canadian Petroleum Association Statistics

CPATBH — Canada. Department of Agriculture. Plant Research Institute. Agrometeorology Section. Technical Bulletin
CPB — China Phone Book and Business Directory
CPB — Clinical Physiology and Biochemistry
CPB — Cyprus Popular Bank Newsletter
CPBIDP — Clinical Physiology and Biochemistry
CPBLAV — Comparative Pathology Bulletin
CPBTA — Chemical and Pharmaceutical Bulletin (Tokyo)
CPC — Canadian Packaging
CPC — Canadian Public Administration
CPC — Carswell's Practice Cases
CPC — Codice de Procedura Civile
CPC — Codigo de Processo Civil
CPC — Current Papers on Computers and Control
CPCA — University of California. Publications in Classical Archaeology
CPCEAF — Canine Practice
CPCHAO — Clinical Proceedings. Children's Hospital of the District of Columbia [Later, Clinical Proceedings. Children's Hospital National Medical Center]
CPCIAR — CEPEC [Centro de Pesquisas do Cacau] Informe Tecnico
CPCJD — Chemicals and Petro-Chemicals Journal
CP Corris Prot — CP. Corrosion y Proteccion
CPCP — University of California. Publications in Classical Philology
CPCR — Crop Protection Chemicals Reference
CPD — Collection de Petrarque a Descartes
CPD — Commonwealth Parliamentary Debates
CpD — Cuadernos para el Dialogo
CPDE — Clinical Pharmacology and Drug Epidemiology
CPDF — Codigo Penal para el Distrito Federal
CPD (HR) — Commonwealth Parliamentary Debates (House of Representatives)
CPD (R) — Commonwealth Parliamentary Debates (House of Representatives)
CPDRD — Current Problems in Diagnostic Radiology
CPD (S) — Commonwealth Parliamentary Debates (Senate)
CPDSAS — Canadian Plant Disease Survey
CP du N — Cours de Perfectionnement du Notariat
CPe — Castrum Peregrini
CPE — Chronique de Politique Etrangere
CPE — Current Papers in Electrical and Electronics Engineering
CPECD — Comparative Physiology and Ecology
CPECDM — Comparative Physiology and Ecology
CPEDA — Clinical Pediatrics
C Pedag — Cahiers Pedagogiques
C Pedag Inst Et Occitanes — Cahiers Pedagogiques. Institut d'Etudes Occitanes
CPEDAM — Clinical Pediatrics
CPEDDP — Chirurgie Pediatrique
CPEGA — Canadian Petro Engineering
CPEGL — Corpusculum Poesis Epicae Graecae Ludibundae
CPEM Dig — CPEM (Conference on Precision Electromagnetic Measurements) Digest
CPENA — Chemical and Process Engineering
CPENB — Chemical Processing and Engineering
CPES/RPS — Revista Paraguaya de Sociologia. Centro Paraguayo de Estudios Sociologicos
CPETA — Canadian Petroleum
CPF — Congres Prehistorique de France. Compte Rendu
CPFIA8 — Canadian Forestry Service. Pacific Forest Research Centre. Information Report BC-X
CPFLBI — Computers and Fluids
CPFO — Parliamentary Papers. Foreign Office Command Paper
CPG — Canadian Plastics
CPG — Clavis Patrum Graecorum
CPGPAY — Comparative and General Pharmacology
CPh — Classical Philology
Cph — Classiques de la Philosophie
CPH — Colecao Poetas de Hoje
CPH — Cuadernos Prehispanicos
CPH — Czsaopismo Prawno-Historyczne
CPHADV — Clinical Pharmacy
CPHB — Coleccion de Publicaciones Historicas de la Biblioteca del Congresso Argentino [Madrid]
CPHCA — Chemistry and Physics of Carbon
CPHCC — Computers and the Humanities
CPHERI Bull — CPHERI (Central Public Health Engineering Research Institute. Nagpur, India) Bulletin
C P Herm — Corpus Papyrorum Hermopolitanorum
C Phil — Classical Philology
CPHMA — Commentationes Physico-Mathematicae
CPHPA — Chieh P'ou Hsueh Pao
CPHPA5 — Acta Anatomica Sinica
CPHRDE — Clinical Pharmacology Research
CPHRDE — International Journal of Clinical Pharmacology Research
CPHYDZ — Colloques Phytosociologiques
CPI — Canadian Periodicals Index
CPI — Conference Papers Index
CPI — Conference Proceedings Index
CPI — Consumer Price Index
CPI — Current Physics Index
CPI — Current Protocols in Immunology
CPIAAX — Central Plantation Crops Research Institute [Kasaragod]. Annual Report
CPI Mgmt — CPI [Current Physics Index] Management Service
CPJ — Canadian Pharmaceutical Journal
CPJ — Chambre de Commerce et d'Industrie de Nouvelle Caledonie. Bulletin
CPJ — Collision Parts Journal
CPJ — Contemporary Psychology
CPJ Equip Rep — CPJ Equipment Reporter
CPJI — Cour Permanente de Justice Internationale

CPJI-A — Cour Permanente de Justice Internationale. Serie A. Recueil des Arrets
CPJI-A/B — Cour Permanente de Justice Internationale. Serie A/B. Recueil desArrets. Avis Consultatifs et Ordonnances
CPJI-B — Cour Permanente de Justice Internationale. Serie B. Recueil des AvisConsultatifs
CPJO — Circumpolar Journal
CPJOAC — Canadian Pharmaceutical Journal
CP Jud — Corpus Papyrorum Judaicorum
CPKNDH — Clinical Pharmacokinetics
CPI — Cahiers de la Pleiade
CPL — Conveyancer and Property Lawyer. New Series
CPL — Corpus Papyrorum Latinorum
CPLI — Catholic Periodical and Literature Index
C PI Phys C Fus — Comments on Plasma Physics and Controlled Fusion
CPLRBW — Chirurgia Plastica et Reconstructiva
CPLSA — Canadian Journal of Plant Science
CPLSAY — Canadian Journal of Plant Science
CPM — Current Physics Microform
CPMAA — Cuoio, Pelli, Materie Concianti
CPMB — Current Protocols in Molecular Biology
CpMF — Casopis pro Moderni Filologii
CPMHA6 — Comunicaciones Paleontologicas. Museo de Historia Natural de Montevideo
CPMJ — Canadian Paper Money Journal
CPMMAL — Collected Papers in Medicine. Mayo Clinic and Mayo Foundation
CPMP — California. University. Publications in Modern Philology
CPMSB6 — Colloid and Polymer Science
CPMSR — Canada. Fisheries and Marine Service. Pacific Marine Science Report
CPMYAN — Contributions to Primatology
CPN — Canadian Press Network
CPN — Contractor Profit News
CPN — Crime Prevention News
CPNMAQ — Clinical Proceedings. Children's Hospital National Medical Center
CPo — Comparative Politics
CPOEA — Canadian Power Engineer
CPOEB — Canadian Power Engineering and Plant Maintenance
C Pop Q — Century. A Popular Quarterly
CPP — Codigo de Processo Penal
CPP — Commonwealth Parliamentary Papers
CPP — Conference of Actuaries in Public Practice. Proceedings
CPP — Contemporary Poetry and Prose
CPP — Corpus of Dated Palestinian Pottery
CPP — Current Papers in Physics
CPPA Newsprint Data — CPPA [Canadian Pulp and Paper Association] Newsprint Data
CPPA Newsprint Rept — CPPA [Canadian Pulp and Paper Association] Monthly Newsprint Report
CPPA Press Dig — CPPA [Canadian Pulp and Paper Association] Press Digest
CPPA Ref Tables — CPPA [Canadian Pulp and Paper Association] Reference Tables
CPPA Tech Sect Proc — CPPA [Canadian Pulp and Paper Association] Technical Section. Proceedings
CPPM — Clinical Physics and Physiological Measurement
CPPMD5 — Clinical Physics and Physiological Measurement
CPPS — Critique Philosophique, Politique, Scientifique, et Litteraire
CPPSBL — Contemporary Psychoanalysis
CPR — Canadian Patent Reporter
CPR — Claridad (Puerto Rico)
CPR — Copper. Quarterly Report
CPR — Cumberland Poetry Review
CPR — Current Population Reports
CPR 20 — Current Population Reports. Population Characteristics. Series P-20
CPR 23 — Current Population Reports. Special Studies. Series P-23
CPR 25 — Current Population Reports. Population Estimates and Projections. Series P-25
CPR 26 — Current Population Reports. Federal-State Cooperative Program for Population Estimates. Series P-26
CPR 27 — Current Population Reports. Farm Population. Series P-27
CPR 28 — Current Population Reports. Special Censuses. Series P-28
CPR 60 — Current Population Reports. Consumer Income. Series P-60
CPR 65 — Current Population Reports. Consumer Buying Indicators. Series P-65
CPR 27-57 — Current Population Reports. Farm Population of the US. Series P-27-57
CPR 20-398 — Current Population Reports. Household and Family Characteristics. Series P20-398
CPR 25-986 — Current Population Reports. Population Estimates and Projections.Households and Families, 1986-2000. Series P-25. No.986
CPR 60-146 — Current Population Reports. Money Income of Households, Families, and Persons in the US. Series P-60-146
CPR 60-147 — Current Population Reports. Characteristics of the Population below the PovertyLevel. Series P-60-147
CPR 60-148 — Current Population Reports. Characteristics of Households and Persons ReceivingSelected Noncash Benefits. Series P-60-148
CPR 60-149 — Current Population Reports. Money, Income, Poverty Status of Familiesand Persons in the US. Series P-60-149
CprAh — Centralblatt fuer Praktische Augenheilkunde
C Pratiq — Cinema Pratique
CPRDDM — Clinical Preventive Dentistry
CPREDP — Canadian Psychological Review
CPRMBD — Centre for Overseas Pest Research. Miscellaneous Report
CPro — Cuba Profesional
CPROA — Chemical Processing
C Pr Pen — Code de Procedure Penale
CPR Proc — Computer Personnel Research Proceedings
CPS — Comparative Political Studies

CPS — Comparative Politics
CPSAR — Commonwealth Public Service Arbitration Reports
CPSGD2 — Canadian Psychology
CPSMBI — Collected Papers in Surgery. Mayo Clinic and Mayo Foundation
CPSOA — Composites
CPSR — Commonwealth Public Service Arbitration Reports
CPSTB — Current Psychiatric Therapies
CPSUA — Current Problems in Surgery
CPsy — Cognitive Psychology
CPSZDP — Communications in Psychopharmacology
CPTEA — Chemical and Petroleum Engineering
CPTHA — Component Technology
CPTHDA — Butterworths International Medical Reviews. Clinical Pharmacology and Therapeutics
Cpt Rend Commiss Archeol — Compte Rendu. Commission Imperiale Archeologique [St. Petersbourg]
Cpt Rend Seanc Acad Inscr — Comptes Rendus des Seances. Academie des Inscriptions et Belles-Lettres
CPU — CPU-Estudios Sociales
CPUG — Cuadernos de Prehistoria. Universidad de Granada
CPUIR — Coloquios de Politica Ultramarina Internacionalmente Relevante
CPUP — Catalogo Colectivo de Publicaciones Periodicas
CPW — Confectionery Production
CPZOAO — Chronmy Przyrode Ojczysta
CQ — Cambridge Quarterly
CQ — Caribbean Quarterly
CQ — Carolina Quarterly
CQ — China Quarterly
CQ — Classical Quarterly
CQ — Critical Quarterly
CQ — Crozer Quarterly
CQB — Cornell Hotel and Restaurant Administration Quarterly
CQCQA — CQ [Call to Quarters]. Radio Amateur's Journal
CQFMAR — Colegio Quimico-Farmaceutico
CQG — Chain Store Age
CQK — Conjunctuur
CQMTA — Colloque de Metallurgie
CQO — China Quarterly
CQR — Church Quarterly Review
CQR — Classical Quarterly Review
CQ Radio Amat J — CQ [Call to Quarters]. Radio Amateur's Journal
C Qu — Classical Quarterly
C Quebec — Cinema Quebec
CR — Calcutta Review
CR — Carnegie-Rochester Conference Series on Public Policy
CR — Centennial Review
CR — China Reconstructs
CR — Clara Rhodos
CR — Classical Review
CR — Columbia Law Review
CR — Commonwealth Record
CR — Compte Rendu des Seances de la Chambre des Deputes du Grand-Duche deLuxembourg
C R — Comptes Rendus Hebdomadaires des Seances de l'Academie des Sciences
CR — Computing Reviews
CR — Congressional Record
CR — Congresso Ribatejano [Santarem]
CR — Consumer Reports
CR — Consumer Research Bulletin
CR — Contemporary Review
Cr — Crimen. Tijdschrift voor Criminologie en Criminalistiek
CR — Criminal Reports
Cr — Crisis
CR — Criterio
Cr — Criterion
CR — Critical Review
Cr — Critique. Revue Generale des Publications Francaises et Etrangeres
CR — Crop Research
Cr — Crux
CR 3d — Criminal Reports. Third Series. Annotated
CRa — Cahiers Raciniens
CRA — Compte-Rendu Analytique des Travaux du Conseil Colonial. Puis Conseilde Legislation
CRAABull — Commissions Royales d'Art et d'Archeologie. Bulletin
CRABB — Current Affairs Bulletin
Crabb Eng Law — Crabb's History of the English Law
C R Ac — Comptes-Rendus des Seances. Academie des Inscriptions et Belles-Lettres
CR Acad Agric Fr — Comptes Rendus des Seances. Academie d'Agriculture de France
CR Acad Agric France — Comptes Rendus Hebdomadaires des Seances. Academie d'Agriculture de France
CR Acad Agric Georgi Dimitrov — Comptes Rendus. Academie Agricole Georgi Dimitrov
CR Acad Agric (Sofia) — Comptes Rendus. Academie Agricole Georgi Dimitrov (Sofia)
CR Acad Bulgare Sci — Comptes Rendus. Academie Bulgare des Sciences
CR Acad Bulg Sci — Comptes Rendus. Academie Bulgare des Sciences
CR Academie Sci Ser IIa Sci Terre Planetes — Comptes Rendus de l'Academie des Sciences. Serie IIa. Sciences de la Terre et des Planetes
CR Academie Sci Ser IIb Mec Phys Chim Astron — Comptes Rendus de l'Academie des Sciences. Serie IIb. Mecanique Physique, Chimie, Astronomie
CR Acad Insc — Comptes Rendus des Seances. Academie des Inscriptions et Belles-Lettres

C R Acad Inscr — Comptes-Rendus des Seances. Academie des Inscriptions et Belles-Lettres

CR Acad Sci — Comptes Rendus. Academie des Sciences

CR Acad Sci — Comptes Rendus Hebdomadaires des Seances. Academie des Sciences

CR Acad Sci Agric Bulg — Comptes Rendus. Academie des Sciences Agricoles en Bulgarie

CR Acad Sci III — Comptes Rendus. Academie des Sciences. Serie III. Sciences de la Vie

CR Acad Sci (Paris) — Comptes Rendus. Academie des Sciences (Paris)

CR Acad Sci (Paris) Ser A-B — Comptes Rendus Hebdomadaires des Seances. Academie des Sciences (Paris). Serie A et B

CR Acad Sci (Paris) Ser III Sci Vie — Comptes Rendus des Seances. Academie des Sciences (Parls). Serie III. Sciences de la Vie

CR Acad Sci (Paris) Ser II Mec Phys Chim Sci — Comptes Rendus des Seances. Academie des Sciences (Paris). Serie II. Mecanique,Physique, Chimie, Sciences de la Terre, Sciences de l'Univers

CR Acad Sci (Paris) Ser I Math — Comptes Rendus des Seances. Academie des Sciences (Paris). Serie I. Mathematique

CR Acad Sci (Paris) Vie Academique — Comptes Rendus Hebdomadaires des Seances. Academie des Sciences. Vie Academique(Paris) [*Later, Comptes Rendus des Seances. Academie des Sciences. Vie Academique*]

CR Acad Sci Russ Ser A — Comptes Rendus. Academie des Sciences de Russie. Serie A

CR Acad Sci Ser 1 — Comptes Rendus. Academie des Sciences. Serie 1

CR Acad Sci Ser 2 — Comptes Rendus. Academie des Sciences. Serie 2. Mecanique, Physique, Chimie, Sciences de l'Univers, Sciences de la Terre

CR Acad Sci Ser 3 — Comptes Rendus. Academie des Sciences. Serie 3. Sciences de la Vie

CR Acad Sci Ser Gen Vie Sci — Comptes Rendus. Academie des Sciences. Serie Generale. La Vie des Sciences

CR Acad Sci Ser IIa Sci Terre Planetes — Comptes Rendus de l'Academie des Sciences. Serie IIa. Sciences de la Terre et des Planetes

CR Acad Sci Ser IIb Mec Phys Chim Astron — Comptes Rendus de l'Academie des Sciences. Serie IIb. Mecanique, Physique, Chimie, Astronomie

C R Acad Sci Ser IIc Chim — Comptes Rendus de l'Academie des Sciences. Serie IIc. Chimie

CR Acad Sci Ser III — Comptes Rendus de l'Academie des Sciences. Serie III. Sciences de la Vie

CR Acad Sci Ser II Mec Phys — Comptes Rendus de Seances. Academie des Sciences. Serie II. Mecanique, Physique, Chimie, Sciences de la Terre, Sciences de l'Univers

C R Acad Sci Ser II Mec Phys Chim Astron — Comptes Rendus de l'Academie des Sciences. Serie II. Mecanique, Physique, Chimie, Astronomie

C R Acad Sci Ser II Mec Phys Chim Sci Terre Univers — Comptes Rendus de l'Academie des Sciences. Serie II. Mecanique, Physique, Chimie, Sciences de la Terre et de l'Univers

C R Acad Sci Ser II Sci Terre Planetes — Comptes Rendus de l'Academie des Sciences. Serie II. Sciences de la Terre et des Planetes

CR Acad Sci URSS — Comptes Rendus. Academie des Sciences de l'URSS

CR Acad Sci URSS Ser A — Comptes Rendus. Academie des Sciences de l'URSS. Serie A

CRAcl — Comptes Rendus. Academie des Inscriptions et Belles Lettres

CR Ac Inscr — Comptes Rendus des Seances. Academie des Inscriptions et Belles Lettres

CR Ac Sci A — Comptes Rendus Hebdomadaires des Seances. Academie des Sciences. Serie A. Sciences Mathematiques

CR Ac Sci B — Comptes Rendus Hebdomadaires des Seances. Academie des Sciences. Serie B. Sciences Physiques

CR Ac Sci C — Comptes Rendus Hebdomadaires des Seances. Academie des Sciences. Serie C. Sciences Chimiques

CR Ac Sci D — Comptes Rendus Hebdomadaires des Seances. Academie des Sciences. Serie D. Sciences Naturelles

CR Act Inst Rech Ressour Hydraul — Compte-Rendu. Activite. Institut de Recherches des Ressources Hydrauliques

Craft A — Craft Australia

Craft Aust — Craft Australia

Craft Australia Yb — Craft Australia Yearbook

Craft Hor — Craft Horizons

Craft Horiz — Craft Horizons

Craft Int — Craft International

Crafts Rep — Crafts Report

CRAGAP — Caribbean Agriculture

CRAI — Comptes Rendus. Academie des Inscriptions et Belles Lettres

CRAIBL — Comptes Rendus. Academie des Inscriptions et Belles Lettres

Crain Detro — Crain's Detroit Business

Crain Illin — Crain's Illinois Business

Crains NY — Crain's New York Business

CRAL — Compte Rendu. Association Lyonnaise de Recherches Archeologiques

Cramp Mag — Crampton's Magazine

Cranberry World — Cranberry World. American Cranberry Exchange, Inc

Cranbrook Inst Sci Bull — Cranbrook Institute of Science. Bulletin

Cranbrook Inst Sci Bull News Letter — Cranbrook Institute of Science. Bulletin. News Letter

CraneR — Crane Review

Cranfield Int Symp Ser — Cranfield International Symposium Series

Crank Sibley J Eng — Crank. Sibley Journal of Engineering

CRAP — Comptes Rendus. Academie Polonaise des Sciences et des Lettres

Crap — Crapouillot. Magazine Non-Conformiste

Cr Arch — Cronache di Archeologia e di Storia dell'Arte

CRAS — Canadian Review of American Studies

CRAS — Centennial Review of Arts and Sciences [*Later, Centennial Review*]

CRAS — Comptes Rendus Hebdomaidaires des Seances. Academie des Sciences

CRASR — Comptes Rendus. Academie des Sciences de Russie

CRASR — Comptes Rendus de l'Academie des Sciences de l'URSS

CR Assem Comm Int Tech Sucr — Compte Rendu. Assemblee. Commission Internationale Technique de Sucrerie

CR Assem Gen Annu Groupe Polyphenols — Compte Rendu. Assemblee Generale Annuelle. Groupe Polyphenols

CR Assem Gen Comm Int Tech Sucr — Comptes Rendus. Assemblee Generale. Commission Internationale Technique de Sucrerie

CR Assoc Anat — Comptes Rendus. Association des Anatomistes

CR Assoc Belgo Neerl Etude Cereales — Comptes Rendus. Association Belgo-Neerlandaise pour l'Etude des Cereales

CR Assoc Int Essais Semences — Comptes Rendus. Association Internationale d'Essais de Semences

Crassulacean Acid Metab Proc Annu Symp Bot — Crassulacean Acid Metabolism. Proceedings. Annual Symposium in Botany

Craw Co Leg J (PA) — Crawford County Legal Journal

Crawford Co Leg Jour — Crawford County Legal Journal

CRB — Cahiers de la Compagnie Madeleine Renaud-Jean Louis Barrault

CRB — Cahiers de la Revue Biblique

CRB — China Report

CRB — Ciba Rundschau (Basel)

CRB — Courier de la Bourse et de la Banque

CrB — Critisch Bulletin

CRBDDO — Commentaries on Research in Breast Disease

CRBEDR — CRC [*Chemical Rubber Company*] Reviews in Biomedical Engineering

CRBL-A — Carre Bleu

CRBRAT — Carbohydrate Research

CRBTE5 — CRC [*Chemical Rubber Company*] Critical Reviews in Biotechnology

CRC — Calcutta Review (Calcutta)

CRC — Centre (Canada)

CRC — World Development

CRCAA — Comissao Reguladora dos Cereais do Arquipelago dos Acores

Crc Ac Sc BII — Bulletin International de l'Academie des Sciences de Cracovie

CR Carlsb L — Comptes Rendus des Travaux du Laboratoire Carlsberg. Serie Chimique et Serie Physiologique

CRCBAK — Cardiovascular Research Center. Bulletin

CRC Critical Reviews in Environmental Control — Chemical Rubber Company. Critical Reviews in Environmental Control

CRC Crit Rev Anal Chem — CRC [*Chemical Rubber Company*] Critical Reviews in Analytical Chemistry

CRC Crit Rev Biochem — CRC [*Chemical Rubber Company*] Critical Reviews in Biochemistry

CRC Crit Rev Biochem Mol Biol — CRC Critical Reviews in Biochemistry and Molecular Biology

CRC Crit Rev Biocompat — CRC [*Chemical Rubber Company*] Critical Reviews in Biocompatibility

CRC Crit Rev Bioeng — CRC [*Chemical Rubber Company*] Critical Reviews in Bioengineering

CRC Crit Rev Biomed Eng — CRC [*Chemical Rubber Company*] Critical Reviews in Biomedical Engineering

CRC Crit Rev Biotechnol — CRC [*Chemical Rubber Company*] Critical Reviews in Biotechnology

CRC Crit Rev Clin Lab Sci — CRC [*Chemical Rubber Company*] Critical Reviews in Clinical Laboratory Sciences

CRC Crit Rev Clin Neurobiol — CRC [*Chemical Rubber Company*] Critical Reviews in Clinical Neurobiology

CRC Crit Rev Clin Radiol Nucl Med — CRC [*Chemical Rubber Company*] Critical Reviews in Clinical Radiology and Nuclear Medicine

CRC Crit Rev Diagn Imaging — CRC [*Chemical Rubber Company*] Critical Reviews in Diagnostic Imaging

CRC Crit Rev Environ Control — CRC [*Chemical Rubber Company*] Critical Reviews in Environmental Control

CRC Crit Rev Food Sci Nutr — CRC [*Chemical Rubber Company*] Critical Reviews in Food Science and Nutrition

CRC Crit Rev Food Technol — CRC [*Chemical Rubber Company*] Critical Reviews in Food Technology

CRC Crit Rev Immunol — CRC [*Chemical Rubber Company*] Critical Reviews in Immunology

CRC Crit Rev Microbiol — CRC [*Chemical Rubber Company*] Critical Reviews in Microbiology

CRC Crit Rev Neurobiol — CRC Critical Reviews in Neurobiology

CRC Crit Rev Oncol/Hematol — CRC [*Chemical Rubber Company*] Critical Reviews in Oncology/Hematology

CRC Crit Rev Plant Sci — CRC [*Chemical Rubber Company*] Critical Reviews in Plant Sciences

CRC Crit Rev Radiol Sci — CRC [*Chemical Rubber Company*] Critical Reviews in Radiological Sciences

CRC Crit Rev Solid Sci — CRC [*Chemical Rubber Company*] Critical Reviews in Solid State Sciences

CRC Crit Rev Solid State Mater Sci — CRC [*Chemical Rubber Company*] Critical Reviews in Solid State and Materials Sciences

CRC Crit Rev Solid State Sci — CRC Critical Reviews in Solid States Sciences

CRC Crit Rev Ther Drug Carrier Syst — CRC [*Chemical Rubber Company*] Critical Reviews in Therapeutic Drug Carrier Systems

CRC Crit Rev Toxicol — CRC [*Chemical Rubber Company*] Critical Reviews in Toxicology

CRC Crit R Microbiol — CRC [*Chemical Rubber Company*] Critical Reviews in Microbiology

CRC C R NEU — CRC [*Chemical Rubber Company*] Critical Reviews in Clinical Neurobiology

CRCFA — Crescendo International

CRCFBSR — Community Research Center. Fairbanks North Star Borough. Special Report

CRC Handb Chromatogr Lipids — CRC Handbook of Chromatography. Lipids

CRC Handb Exp Aspects Oral Biochem — CRC [*Chemical Rubber Company*] Handbook of Experimental Aspects of Oral Biochemistry

CRC Handb Foodborne Dis Biol Origin — CRC Handbook of Foodborne Diseases of Biological Origin

CRC Handb HPLC Sep Amino Acids Pept Proteins — CRC Handbook of HPLC (High Performance Liquid Chromatography) for the Separation

CRC Handb Laser Sci Technol — CRC Handbook of Laser Science and Technology

CRC Handb Lasers Sel Data Opt Technol — CRC Handbook of Lasers with Selected Data on Optical Technology

CRC Handb Nat Occurring Food Toxicants — CRC [*Chemical Rubber Company*] Handbook of Naturally Occurring Food Toxicants

CRC Handb Nat Pestic Methods — CRC Handbook of Natural Pesticides. Methods

CRC Handb Neurohypophyseal Horm Analogs — CRC Handbook of Neurohypophyseal Hormone Analogs

CRC Handb Nutr Suppl — CRC [*Chemical Rubber Company*] Handbook of Nutritional Supplements

CRC Handb Pharmacol Methodol Study Neuroendocr Syst — CRC Handbook of Pharmacologie Methodologies for the Study of the NeuroendocrineSystem

CRC Handb Stereoisomers Drugs Psychopharmacol — CRC [*Chemical Rubber Company*] Handbook of Stereoisomers. Drugs in Psychopharmacology

CRC Handb Thermoelectr — CRC Handbook of Thermoelectrics

CRCIDA — CRIEPI [*Central Research Institute of Electric Power Industry*] Report

CRCL — Canadian Review of Comparative Literature/Revue Canadienne de Litterature Comparee

CRC Math Model Ser — CRC Mathematical Modelling Series

CRCMC — Creem Magazine

CRCMCL — Cereal Research Communications

CRCODS — Carlsberg Research Communications

CR Colloq AEN Radioecol Mar — Compte Rendue. Colloque de l'AEN sur la Radioecologie Marine

CR Colloq ARTEP — Comptes Rendus. Colloque de l'ARTEP

CR Colloq Etud Annu — Comptes Rendus du Colloque Etudiant Annuel

CR Colloq Fr Esp Trait Combust Irradies — Compte Rendu du Colloque Franco-Espagnol sur le Traitement des Combustibles Irradies

CR Colloq Inf Chim — Compte Rendu. Colloque sur l'Information en Chimie

CR Colloq Int Astrophys Liege — Comptes Rendus. Colloques Internationaux d'Astrophysique de Liege

CR Colloq Int Electron Nucl — Comptes Rendus. Colloque International sur l'Electronique Nucleaire

CR Colloq Int Spectrochim — Comptes Rendus. Colloque International de Spectrochimie

CR Colloq Med Nucl Lang Fr — Comptes Rendus. Colloque de Medecine Nucleaire de Langue Francaise

CR Colloq Natl Inf Chim CNIC — Compte Rendu. Colloque National sur l'Information en Chimie CNIC

CR Colloq Reg Inst Int Potasse — Comptes Rendus. Colloque Regional. Institut International de la Potasse

CR Conf COLUMA — Compte Rendu. Conference du COLUMA (Comite Francais de Lutte contre les Mauvaises Herbes)

CR Conf Interafr Sols — Comptes Rendus. Conference Interafricaine des Sols

CR Conf Int Mes — Comptes Rendus. Conference Internationale de la Mesure

CR Conf Int Metall Plutonium — Comptes Rendus. Conference Internationale sur la Metallurgie du Plutonium

CR Conf Int Pergelisol — Compte Rendu. Conference Internationale sur le Pergelisol

CR Conf Int Prot React — Comptes Rendus. Conference Internationale sur la Protection des Reacteurs

CR Conf Int Spectrosc Raman — Compte Rendu. Conference Internationale de Spectroscopie Raman

CR Conf Int Spectrosc Raman — Comptes Rendus. Conference Internationale de Spectroscopie Raman. Processus Lineaires et Non Lineaires

CR Conf Mond Energ — Compte Rendu. Conference Mondiale de l'Energie

CR Conf Sante Secur Prof — Compte-Rendu. Conference sur la Sante et la Securite Professionnelles

CR Conf Trienn Assoc Eur Rech Pomme Terre — Comptes Rendus. Conference Triennale. Association Europeenne pour la Recherche sur la Pomme de Terre

CR Conf Union Int Chim Pure Appl — Comptes Rendus. Conference. Union Internationale de Chimie Pure et Appliquee

CR Congr Annu Soc Nucl Can — Comptes Rendus. Congres Annuel. Societe Nucleaire Canadienne

CR Congr Assoc Sci Pays Ocean Indien — Comptes Rendus. Congres. Association Scientifique des Pays de l'Ocean Indien

CR Congr Can Mec Appl — Comptes Rendus. Congres Canadien de Mecanique Appliquee

CR Congr Confed Int Mes — Compte Rendu. Congres. Confederation Internationale de la Mesure

CR Congr Eur Biopharm Pharmacocinet — Comptes Rendus. Congres Europeen de Biopharmacie et Pharmacocinetique

CR Congr Ind Gaz — Compte Rendu. Congres de l'Industrie du Gaz

CR Congr Int Angeiol — Comptes Rendus. Congres International d'Angeiologie

CR Congr Int Arrieration Ment — Comptes Rendus du Congres International d'Arrieration Mentale

CR Congr Int Biochim — Compte Rendu. Congres International de Biochimie

CR Congr Int Chim Ind — Comptes Rendus. Congres Internationaux de Chimie Industrielle

CR Congr Int Chim Pure Appl — Compte Rendu des Congres International de Chimie Pure et Appliquee

CR Congr Int Deterg — Compte-Rendu. Congres International de la Detergence

CR Congr Int Froid — Comptes Rendus du Congres International du Froid

CR Congr Int Genet — Comptes Rendus. Congres International de Genetique

CR Congr Int Ind Gaz — Compte Rendu. Congres International de l'Industrie du Gaz

CR Congr Int Lutte Ennemis Plant — Comptes Rendus. Congres International de Lutte Contre les Ennemis des Plantes

CR Congr Int Mec Roches — Comptes Rendus. Congres International de Mecanique des Roches

CR Congr Int Mec Sols Trav Fond — Comptes Rendus du Congres International de Mecanique des Sols et des Travaux deFondations

CR Congr Int Microbiol — Compte Rendu. Congres International de Microbiologie

CR Congr Int Nephrol — Comptes Rendus. Congres International de Nephrologie

CR Congr Int Phenom Contact Electr — Comptes Rendus. Congres International sur les Phenomenes de Contact Electrique

CR Congr Int Psychother — Comptes Rendus. Congres International de Psychotherapie

CR Congr Int Sci Sol — Comptes Rendus. Congres International de la Science du Sol

CR Congr Int Tech Chim Ind Agric — Comptes Rendus. Congres International Technique et Chimique des Industries Agricoles

CR Congr Int Vide — Comptes Rendus Congres International du Vide

CR Congr Mond Psychiatr — Comptes Rendus. Congres Mondial de Psychiatrie

CR Congr Mond Trait Surf Met — Comptes Rendus. Congres Mondial du Traitement de Surface des Metaux

CR Congr Natl Soc Savantes Sect Sci — Comptes Rendus du Congres National des Societes Savantes. Section des Sciences

CR Congr Natl Transfus Sang — Compte Rendu. Congres National de Transfusion Sanguine

CR Congr Phys Chim Sider — Compte-Rendu du Congres. Physico-Chimie et Siderurgie

CR Congr Soc Eur Hematol — Comptes Rendus. Congres. Societe Europeenne d'Hematologie

CR Congr Soc Savantes Paris Dep Sect Sci — Comptes Rendus du Congres des Societes Savantes de Paris et des Departments. Section des Sciences

CR Congr Union Int Inst Rech For — Comptes Rendus. Congres. Union Internationales des Instituts des Recherches Forestieres

CR Congr Union Phytopathol Mediterr — Comptes Rendus. Congres de l'Union Phytopathologique Mediterraneenne

CRC Press Ser Discrete Math Appl — CRC Press Series on Discrete Mathematics and its Applications

Cr Crafts — Creative Crafts

CRC Rep — CRC (Coordinating Research Council) Report

CRC Ser Comput Mech Appl Anal — CRC Series in Computational Mechanics and Applied Analysis

Cr Cu — Cross Currents

CR Cycle Int Conf PRO AQUA — Compte Rendu. Cycle International de Conferences PRO AQUA

CRD — College Recruitment Database

CRD — Corporate Director

Cr d'A — Critica d'Arte

CRDACA — Atti. Centro Richerche Documentazione sull'Antichita Classica

CR Definitif Assem Int Rech Better — Compte Rendu Definitif. Assemblee. Institut International de Recherches Betteravieres

CRdGLECS — Comptes Rendus. Groupe Linguistique d'Etudes Chamito-Semitiques

CRDIDF — CRC [*Chemical Rubber Company*] Critical Reviews in Diagnostic Imaging

CRDMBP — Chronica Dermatologica

CRD Newsl US Dep Agric Ext Community Rural Dev — CRD Newsletter. United States Department of Agriculture. Science and Education Administration. Extension, Community, and Rural Development

CR (Dokl) Acad Sci URSS — Comptes Rendus (Doklady). Academie des Sciences de l'Union des Republiques Sovietiques Socialistes

CRDS — Chemical Reactions Documentation Service

CRDVA — Canadian Research and Development [*Later, Canadian Research*]

CRE — Compensation Review

CRE — Construction Review

CRE — Creacion de Rerchesches Caraibes

CRE — Credit

Crea — Creation

C Read — Christian Reader

Creamery J — Creamery Journal

Creamery Milk Plant Mon — Creamery and Milk Plant Monthly

Creat Crafts — Creative Crafts

Creat Detect Excited State — Creation and Detection of the Excited State

Creation Res Soc Q — Creation Research Society. Quarterly

Creative A — Creative Art

Creative Cam — Creative Camera

Creative Cam Annu — Creative Camera Annual

Creative Child Adult Q — Creative Child and Adult Quarterly

Creative Comput — Creative Computing

Creative Photogr — Creative Photography

Creat Photogr — Creative Photography

Creat Res Soc Q — Creation Research Society. Quarterly

Creatv Comp — Creative Computing

CReB — Ciba Review (Basel) [*English Edition*]

CRECD — Conservation and Recycling

CRECD2 — Conservation and Recycling

CREDIF — Bulletin Bibliographique de CREDIF [*Centre de Recherche et d'Etude pour la Diffusion du Francais*] Service de Documentation

Credit & Fin Man — Credit and Financial Management

Credit & Fin Mgt — Credit and Financial Management

Creditanst-Bankverein Wirtschaftsber — Creditanstalt-Bankverein. Wirtschaftsberichte

Credit Communal Belgique Bul Trim — Credit Communal de Belgique. Bulletin Trimestriel

Credit Financ Manage — Credit and Financial Management

Credit M — Credit Monthly

Credit Suisse Bul — Credit Suisse. Bulletin

Credit Suisse Bul (Zurich) — Credit Suisse. Bulletin (Zurich)

Credit Union M — Credit Union Magazine

Credit Wld — Credit World

Cred Rur — Credito Rural

Cred Suisse B — Credit Suisse. Bulletin
Creem M — Creem Magazine
Creep Charact Damage Life Assess Proc Int Conf Creep Mater — Creep. Characterization, Damage, and Life Assessments. Proceedings. International Conference on Creep of Materials
Creep Fract Eng Mater Struct Proc Int Conf — Creep and Fracture of Engineering Materials and Structures. Proceedings of the International Conference
Creep Struct Symp — Creep in Structures. Symposium
CREF — Crisis. Revista Espanola de Filosofia
Creighton L Rev — Creighton Law Review
CREJ — Contents of Recent Economics Journals
CREL — Cahiers Roumains d'Etudes Litteraires
Crell C A — Chemische Annalen fuer die Freunde der Naturlehre. Crell
Crelle J — Journal fuer die Reine und Angewandte Mathematik. Crelle
Crelle J Bauk — Journal fuer die Baukunst. Crelle
Crelle J Mth — Journal fuer die Reine und Angewandte Mathematik. Crelle
Cre LR — Creighton Law Review
CRen — Collection Rencontres
CRep — China Report
Cres — Cresset
Crescendo & Jazz Mus — Crescendo & Jazz Music
Crescendo Int — Crescendo International
Cress Ins Ca — Cresswell's Insolvency Cases
Crest Colect — Cresterea Colectiilor. Caiet Selectiv de Informare Bibliotecii Academii Republicii Socialiste Romania
Crest Patr Muz Bul — Cresterea Patrimoniului Muzeal Buletin
Cretaceous Res — Cretaceous Research
Cretacico Peninsula Iber — Cretacico de la Peninsula Iberica
CRETB — Current
C Rev — Chesterton Review
Crev — Contemporary Review
C Rev AS — Canadian Review of American Studies
C Rev B — Conch Review of Books
C Revue — Cine Revue
CRF — Consumer Reports
CRFABX — Coffee Research Foundation [*Kenya*]. Annual Report
CRFEDD — Clinical Reproduction and Fertility
CRFSDL — Rapport a l'Industrie Canadien sur les Sciences Halieutiques et Aquatiques
CRFW — Catalyst Resource on the Work Force and Women
CRGAA3 — Chirurgia
CRGAB4 — Cocoa Research Institute. Ghana Academy of Sciences. Annual Report
CRGIA — Ceramurgia, Tecnologia Ceramica
CR Groupe Linguistique Etud Chamito Semitiques — Comptes Rendus du Groupe Linguistique d'Etudes Chamito-Semitiques
CRGS — Chemical Regulations and Guidelines System
CRh — Cahiers du Rhone
C Rh — Clara Rhodos
Cr H — Craft Horizons
CRH Acad Sci Ser A Sci Math — Comptes Rendus Hebdomadaires des Seances. Academie des Sciences. Serie A. Sciences Mathematiques
CRH Acad Sci Ser B Sci Phys — Comptes Rendus Hebdomadaires des Seances. Academie des Sciences. Serie B. Sciences Physiques
CRH Acad Sci Ser C Sci Chim — Comptes Rendus Hebdomadaires des Seances. Academie des Sciences. Serie C. Sciences Chimiques
CRH Acad Sci Ser D Sci Natur — Comptes Rendus Hebdomadaires des Seances. Academie des Sciences. Serie D. Sciences Naturelles
CRHBull — Commission Royale d'Histoire. Bulletin
CRHDDK — Clinics in Rheumatic Diseases
CR Hebd Acad Sci Ser 2 — Comptes Rendus Hebdomadaires des Seances. Academie des Sciences. Serie 2. Mecanique-Physique, Chimie, Sciences de l'Univers, Sciences de la Terre
CR Hebd Acad Sci Ser D — Academie des Sciences. Comptes Rendus Hebdomadaires des Seances. Serie D. Sciences Naturelles
CR Hebd Seanc Acad Sci — Comptes Rendus Hebdomadaires des Seances. Academie des Sciences
CR Hebd Seanc Acad Sci Jekaterinoslaw — Compte Rendu Hebdomadaire des Seances. Academie des Sciences de Jekaterinoslaw
CR Hebd Seanc Acad Sci (Paris) D — Comptes Rendus Hebdomadaires des Seances. Academie des Sciences (Paris). Serie D. Sciences Naturelles
CR Hebd Seances Acad Agric Fr — Comptes Rendus Hebdomadaires des Seances. Academie d'Agriculture de France
CR Hebd Seances Acad Sci — Comptes Rendus Hebdomadaires des Seances. Academie des Sciences
CR Hebd Seances Acad Sci Ser 2 — Comptes Rendus Hebdomadaires des Seances. Academie des Sciences. Serie 2. Mecanique-Physique, Chimie, Sciences de l'Univers, Sciences de la Terre
CR Hebd Seances Acad Sci Ser 3 — Comptes Rendus Hebdomadaires des Seances. Academie des Sciences. Serie 3. Sciences de la Vie
CR Hebd Seances Acad Sci Ser A — Comptes Rendus Hebdomadaires des Seances. Academie des Sciences. Serie A. Sciences Mathematiques
CR Hebd Seances Acad Sci Ser A Sci Math — Comptes Rendus Hebdomadaires des Seances. Academie des Sciences. Serie A. Sciences Mathematiques
CR Hebd Seances Acad Sci Ser B — Comptes Rendus Hebdomadaires des Seances. Academie des Sciences. Serie B. Sciences Physiques
CR Hebd Seances Acad Sci Ser C — Comptes Rendus Hebdomadaires des Seances. Academie des Sciences. Serie C. Sciences Chimiques
CR Hebd Seances Acad Sci Ser C Sci Chim — Comptes Rendus Hebdomadaires des Seances. Academie des Sciences. Serie C. Sciences Chimiques
CR Hebd Seances Acad Sci Ser D — Comptes Rendus Hebdomadaires des Seances. Academie des Sciences. Serie D. Sciences Naturelles
CR Hebd Seances Acad Sci Ser D Sci Nat — Comptes Rendus Hebdomadaires des Seances. Academie des Sciences. Serie D. Sciences Naturelles
CR Hebd Seances Acad Sci Ser II — Comptes Rendus Hebdomadaires des Seances. Academie des Sciences. Serie II

CR Hebd Seances Mem Soc Biol Ses Fil — Comptes Rendus Hebdomadaires des Seances et Memoires. Societe de Biologie et des Ses Filiales
CRHK — China Review (Hong Kong)
C Rhod — Clara Rhodos
CRHPR — Cahiers de la Revue d'Histoire et de Philosophie Religieuses
CRI — Caribbean Review
CRI — Ceramic Industry
CRI — Credit
Cri — Criterion
CRI Abstr — Cement Research Institute of India. Abstracts
Criador Paul — O Criador Paulista. Publicacao Official da Secretaria da Agricultura, Commercio, e Obras Publicas. Estado de Sao Paulo
CRIA/W — Worldview. Council on Religion and International Affairs
CRIEH — Centre de Recherches. Institut d'Etudes Hispaniques
CRIEPI (Cent Res Inst Electr Power Ind) Rep — CRIEPI (Central Research Institute of Electric Power Industry) Report
CRIGB — Cryogenic and Industrial Gases
CRIJA — Ceramic Industries Journal
CRIL — Colorado Research in Linguistics
Crim — Criminology
CrimAb — Abstracts on Criminology and Penology
Crim & Delin — Crime and Delinquency
Crim App — Law Reports. Criminal Appeal Reports
Crim Def — Criminal Defense
Crime — Crime in the United States
Crime & Delin — Crime and Delinquency
Crime & Delin'cy — Crime and Delinquency
Crime & Delinq — Crime and Delinquency
Crime and Just — Crime and Justice
Crime & Soc Just — Crime and Social Justice
Crime Conf Mich Proc — Crime Conference of Michigan. Proceedings
Crime Delin — Crime and Delinquency
Crime Delinq Abstr — Crime and Delinquency Abstracts
Crime Delinq Lit — Crime and Delinquency Literature
Crime Prev News — Crime Prevention News
Crimin — Criminology
Criminal Justice Q — Criminal Justice Quarterly
Criminal Justice R — Criminal Justice Review
Criminal Law Bul — Criminal Law Bulletin
Criminal LQ — Criminal Law Quarterly
Criminal Mex — Criminalia. Organo. Academia Mexicana de Ciencias Penales (Mexico)
Crim Inj Comp — Criminal Injuries Compensation
Crim J and Beh — Criminal Justice and Behavior
Crim Just — Crime and Social Justice
Crim Just & Behav — Criminal Justice and Behavior
Crim Just B — Criminal Justice and Behavior
Crim Just Chicago — Criminial Justice (Chicago)
Crim Just Ethics — Criminal Justice Ethics
Crim Justice Abstr — Criminal Justice Abstracts
Crim Justice Period Index — Criminal Justice Periodical Index
Crim Just J — Criminal Justice Journal
Crim Just Newsl — Criminal Justice Newsletter
Crim Law Bul — Criminal Law Bulletin
Crim Law Q — Criminal Law Quarterly
Crim Law R — Criminal Law Review
Crim L Bul — Criminal Law Bulletin
Crim L Bull — Criminal Law Bulletin
Crim LJ — Criminal Law Journal
Crim LJI — Criminal Law Journal of India
Crim LJ Ind — Criminal Law Journal of India
Crim L J India — Criminal Law Journal of India
Crim LJ (Sydney) — Criminal Law Journal (Sydney)
Crim L Mag — Criminal Law Magazine
Crim L Q — Criminal Law Quarterly
Crim L R — Criminal Law Review
Crim L Rep — Criminal Law Reporter
Crim L Rep BNA — Criminal Law Reporter. Bureau of National Affairs
Crim L Rev — Criminal Law Review
Crim L Rev (England) — Criminal Law Review (England)
Crim L Rptr — Criminal Law Reporter
Crim Penol Abstr — Criminology and Penology Abstracts
Crim R (Can) — Criminal Reports (Canada)
Crim Rep — Criminal Reports
Crim Rep NS — Criminal Reports. New Series
CRINBJ — Annual Report. Nigeria Cocoa Research Institute
CR Ind Gaz Congr Int — Compte Rendu. Industrie du Gaz. Congress International
CRI Newsl — CRI [*Carpet and Rug Institute*] Newsletter
CRIPEL — Cahiers de Recherches. Institut de Papyrologie et d'Egyptologie de Lille
CRIS — Current Research Information System
CRIS-CAR — Current Information System (USDA)/Canadian Agricultural Research Council
Crisia — Crisia Culegere de Materiale si Studii
CRISP — Computer Retrieval of Information on Scientific Projects
Criss-Cross — Criss-Cross Art Communications
Cristianismo Soc — Cristianismo y Sociedad
Crist Suisse — Cristallier Suisse
Crist y Soc — Cristianismo y Sociedad
Crit — Criterio
Crit — Criterion
Crit — Criterium. Letterkundig Maandblad
Crit — Critic
Crit — Critica
Crit — Criticism. A Quarterly for Literature and the Arts
Crit — Critique. A Review of Contemporary Art

Crit — Critique: Studies in Modern Fiction
Crit A — Critica d'Arte
Crit A Afr — Critica d'Arte Africana
Crit Anthrop — Critique of Anthropology
Crit Ar — Critica d'Arte
Crit Arte — Critica d'Arte
Crit Arts — Critical Arts
CritB — Critisch Bulletin. Maanblad voor Letterkundige Critiek
Crit Bull — Critisch Bulletin
Crit Care Clin — Critical Care Clinics
Crit Care (Lond) — Critical Care
Crit Care Med — Critical Care Medicine
Crit Care Nurse — Critical Care Nurse
Crit Care Q — Critical Care Quarterly
Crit Care Update — Critical Care Update
Crit C Nurse — Critical Care Nurse
Crit Concerns Field Drug Abuse Proc Natl Drug Abuse Conf — Critical Concerns in the Field of Drug Abuse. Proceedings. National Drug Abuse Conference
Crit Contem Caracas — Critica Contemporanea (Caracas)
Crit CQ — Critical Care Quarterly
Crit Curr Limitations High Temp Supercond Proc Int Workshop — Critical Current Limitations in High Temperature Superconductors. Proceedings. International Workshop
Crit Curr Supercond — Critical Currents in Superconductors
Crit d A — Critica d'Arte
Crit Econ Polit — Critiques de l'Economie Politique
Criterio Econ — Criterio Economico
Crit Eval Some Equil Constants Involv Alkylammonium Extr — Critical Evaluation of Some Equilibrium Constants Involving Alkylammonium Extractants
Crit Fascista — Critica Fascista
Crit I — Critical Inquiry
Critical Soc Policy — Critical Social Policy
Crit Inq — Critical Inquiry
Critiq — Critique
Critique Anthrop — Critique of Anthropology
Critique of Anthropol — Critique of Anthropology
Critique Reg — Critique Regionale
Critique S — Critique: Studies in Modern Fiction
Critiques Econ Pol — Critiques de l'Economie Politique
Crit List — Critical List
Critm — Criticism
Crit Marx — Critica Marxista
Crit Mass J — Critical Mass Journal
Crit Pen — Critica Penale
Crit Perspe — Critical Perspectives
Crit Pol — Critica Politica
Crit Q — Critical Quarterly
Critq — Critique
Crit Quart — Critical Quarterly
Crit R — Critical Review
Crit Rep Appl Chem — Critical Reports on Applied Chemistry
Crit Rev — Critical Review
Crit Rev Anal Chem — Critical Reviews in Analytical Chemistry
Crit Rev Biochem — Critical Reviews in Biochemistry
Crit Rev Biochem Mol Biol — Critical Reviews in Biochemistry and Molecular Biology
Crit Rev Biocompat — Critical Reviews in Biocompatibility
Crit Rev Bioeng — Critical Reviews in Bioengineering
Crit Rev Biomed Eng — Critical Reviews in Biomedical Engineering
Crit Rev Biotechnol — Critical Reviews in Biotechnology
Crit Rev Clin Lab Sci — Critical Reviews in Clinical Laboratory Sciences
Crit Rev Clin Neurobiol — Critical Reviews in Clinical Neurobiology
Crit Rev Clin Radiol Nucl Med — Critical Reviews in Clinical Radiology and Nuclear Medicine
Crit Rev Diagn Imaging — Critical Reviews in Diagnostic Imaging
Crit Rev Environ Control — Critical Reviews in Environmental Control
Crit Rev Eukaryot Gene Expr — Critical Reviews in Eukaryotic Gene Expression
Crit Rev Food Sci Nutr — Critical Reviews in Food Science and Nutrition
Crit Rev Food Technol — Critical Reviews in Food Technology
Crit Rev Immunol — Critical Reviews in Immunology
Crit Rev Microbiol — Critical Reviews in Microbiology
Crit Rev Neurobiol — Critical Reviews in Neurobiology
Crit Rev Oncog — Critical Reviews in Oncogenesis
Crit Rev Oncol/Hematol — Critical Reviews in Oncology/Hematology
Crit Rev Opt Sci Technol — Critical Reviews of Optical Science and Technology
Crit Rev Oral Biol Med — Critical Reviews in Oral Biology and Medicine
Crit Rev Plant Sci — Critical Reviews in Plant Sciences
Crit Rev Radiol Sci — Critical Reviews in Radiological Sciences
Crit Rev Solid State Mater Sci — Critical Reviews in Solid State and Materials Sciences
Crit Rev Solid State Sci — Critical Reviews in Solid State Sciences
Crit Rev Surf Chem — Critical Reviews in Surface Chemistry
Crit Rev Ther Drug Carrier Syst — Critical Reviews in Therapeutic Drug Carrier Systems
Crit Rev Toxicol — Critical Reviews in Toxicology
CritS — Critical Survey
CritS — Critique Sociale
Crit Soc — Critica Sociale
Crit Social (Paris) — Critique Socialiste (Paris)
Crit Sociol (Roma) — Critica Sociologica (Roma)
Crit Stor — Critica Storica
CRJ — Contemporary Religions in Japan
CR Journ Electron — Comptes Rendus des Journees d'Electronique

CR Journ Etud Herb Conf COLUMA — Compte Rendu. Journees d'Etudes sur les Herbicides. Conference du COLUMA
CR Journ Int Etud Piles Combust — Comptes Rendus. Journees Internationales d'Etude des Piles a Combustible
CR Journ Natl Compos — Comptes Rendus des Journees Nationales sur les Composites
CRJSA4 — Caribbean Journal of Science
Cr Just — Criminal Justice
CRL — Classical Roman Law
CRL — College and Research Libraries
CRL — Critical Review of Theological and Philosophical Literature
Cr Law Mag — Criminal Law Magazine
Cr Law Rep — Criminal Law Reporter
Cr LJ — Criminal Law Journal of India
CRLM — CRREL [*Cold Regions Research and Engineering Laboratory*] Monograph Series
Cr L Mag — Criminal Law Magazine
CRLN — Comparative Romance Linguistics Newsletter
Cr LR — Criminal Law Reporter
CRL Rep Univ Tokyo Cosmic Ray Lab — CRL [*Cosmic Ray Laboratory*] Report. University of Tokyo. Cosmic Ray Laboratory
CRM — Caucasian Review. Institute for the Study of the USSR (Munich)
CRM — Construction Risk Management
CRM — Credit Management
CR Mag — CR [*Chemische Rundschau*] Magazin
CRM Boletin de Informacion — Consejo de Recursos Minerales. Boletin de Informacion
CRME — Council for Research in Music Education. Bulletin
CR Mens Seanc Acad Sci Colon — Comptes Rendus Mensuels des Seances. Academie des Sciences Coloniales
CRM Metall Rep — CRM [*Centre de Recherches Metallurgiques*] Metallurgical Reports
Cr NA — Cronica Numismatica si Arheologica
CRNGDP — Carcinogenesis
CRNIA — Current Notes on International Affairs
CRNS — Criminal Reports. New Series
CRNSBP — Chironomus
CRNVD2 — Carnivore
Croat Chem — Croatica Chemica Acta
Croat Chem A — Croatica Chemica Acta
Croat Geol Congr — Croatian Geological Congress
Croatia Pr — Croatia Press
CROCB — Chronache di Chimica
CRODAI — Centre de Recherches Oceanographiques [*Abidjan*]. Documents Scientifiques
CRodSpol — Casopis Rodopisne Spolecnosti Ceskoslovenske
CROEA — Cronache Economiche
CRom — Cuget Romanesc
C (Romania) — Cinema (Romania)
Cron — Cronos
Cron A — Cronache d'Arte
Cronache Econ — Cronache Economiche
Cron Agric — Cronica Agricola
Cron Arch — Cronache di Archeologia e di Storia dell'Arte
Cron Archeol — Cronache di Archeologia
Cron Archeol & Stor A — Cronache di Archeologia e di Storia dell'Arte
Cron A Stor Art — Cronache di Archeologia e di Storia dell'Arte
Cron Biz — Cronaca Bizantina
Cron Catania — Cronache di Archeologia e di Storia dell'Arte. Universita de Catania
Cron Chim — Cronache de Chimica
Cron Dent — Cronica Dental
Cron Econ — Cronache Economiche
Cron Erc — Cronache Ercolanesi
Cron Ercol — Cronache Ercolanesi
Cron Ercolanesi — Cronache Ercolanesi
Croner's — Croner's Export Digest
Croner's Ref Book Employ — Croner's Reference Book for Employers
Croner's Ref Book Export — Croner's Reference Book for Exporters
Cron Farm — Cronache Farmaceutiche
Cronica Caracas Caracas — Cronica de Caracas (Caracas)
Cron Med — Cronica Medica
Cron Med (Lima) — Cronica Medica (Lima)
Cron Med Mex — Cronica Medica Mexicana
Cron Med Mexicana — Cronica Medica Mexicana
Cron Med Quir — Cronica Medico-Quirurgica
Cron Med-Quir Habana — Cronica Medico-Quirurgica de La Habana
Cron Pomp — Cronache Pompeiane
Cron Pompeiane — Cronache Pompeiane
Cron Vin Cer — Cronica de Vinos y Cereales
Croom Helm Philos Focus Ser — Croom Helm Philosophers in Focus Series
Crop Bull Can Board Grain Comm — Crop Bulletin. Canada Board of Grain Commissioners
Crop Bull Grain Res Lab (Can) — Crop Bulletin. Grain Research Laboratory (Canada)
Crop Improv — Crop Improvement
Crop Improv Induced Mutat Rep Symp — Crop Improvements by Induced Mutation. Report of Symposium
Crop Prod — Crop Production
Crop Prod Budapest — Crop Production (Budapest)
Crop Prod Conf Rep Crop Qual Counc — Crop Production Conference Report. Crop Quality Council
Crop Prod (Pretoria) — Crop Production (Pretoria)
Crop Prod Sci — Crop Production Science
Crop Prot — Crop Protection

Crop Prot North Br — Crop Protection in Northern Britain
Crop Res — Crop Research
Crop Res ARS — Crops Research ARS
Crop Res News Dep Sci Ind Res (NZ) — Crop Research News. New Zealand Department of Scientific and Industrial Research
Crop Res News NZ Dep Sci Ind Res — Crop Research News. New Zealand Department of Scientific and Industrial Research
Crop Resour Proc Annu Meet Soc Econ Bot — Crop Resources. Proceedings. Annual Meeting. Society for Economic Botany
Crop Sci — Crop Science
Crop Sci Tianjin — Crop Science (Tianjin)
Crop Soil NC State Univ — Crop Soils. North Carolina State University
Crops Soils Mag — Crops and Soils Magazine
Croquis Archit — Croquis d'Architecture
Cross & Cr — Cross and Crown
Cross C — Cross Currents
Cross Crucible — Cross and Crucible
Cross Cur — Cross Currents
Cross Curr — Cross Currents
Crossref Hum Resour Manage — Cross-Reference on Human Resources Management
Cross Tie Bull — Cross Tie Bulletin
Crown Agents QR — Crown Agents Quarterly Review
Crown Ag R — Crown Agents Review
Crown Col — Crown Colonist
Crown Colon — Crown Colonist
Crown C Rev — Crown Counsel's Review
Crowther FPL — D. J. Crowther Ltd. Fixed Price List
Croydon Mcr Cl P & T — Proceedings and Transactions of the Croydon Microscopical and Natural History Club
Crozer Quar — Crozer Quarterly. Crozer Theological Seminary
CRPADH — Clinical Research Practices and Drug Regulatory Affairs
CRPD — Clinical Research Practices and Drug Regulatory Affairs
CR (Petersb) — Compte Rendu. Commission Imperiale Archeologique (St. Petersbourg)
CRPh — Cahiers de Royaumont. Philosophie
Crp Rpt KC — Corporate Report Kansas City
Crp Rpt MN — Corporate Report Minnesota
CRPSA — Crop Science
CRPSD3 — CRC [*Chemical Rubber Company*] Reviews in Plant Sciences
CR PV Mem Ass Breton — Compte Rendu. Proces-Verbaux et Memoires. Association Bretonne
CrQ — Critical Quarterly
CRR — Canadian Regulatory Reporter
CRR — Coinage of the Roman Republic
CRR — Compte Rendu. Rencontre Assyriologique Internationale
Cr R — Criminal Reports
CRRA — Compte Rendu. Rencontre Assyriologique Internationale
CRRAI — Compte Rendu. Rencontre Assyriologique Internationale
Cr R Anal C — Critical Reviews in Analytical Chemistry
CR Rapp Congr Int Matieres Plast — Comptes Rendus et Rapports. Congres International des Matieres Plastiques
Cr R Bioche — Critical Reviews in Biochemistry and Molecular Biology
Cr R Biomed — Critical Reviews in Biomedical Engineering
Cr R Biotec — Critical Reviews in Biotechnology
Cr R Cl Lab — Critical Reviews in Clinical Laboratory
CRRDB — CRC [*Chemical Rubber Company*] Critical Reviews in Radiological Sciences
Cr R Diagn — Critical Reviews in Diagnostic Imaging
CR Rech Bibl Immigr — Comptes Rendus de Recherches et Bibliographie sur l'Immigration
CR Rech Inst Encour Rech Sci Ind Agric — Comptes Rendus de Recherches. Institut pour l'Encouragement de la Recherche Scientifique dans l'Industrie et l'Agriculture
CR Rech IRSIA — Comptes Rendus de Recherches. IRSIA (Institut pour l'Encouragement de la Recherche Scientifique dans l'Industrie et l'Agriculture)
CR Rech Tchec Fonderie — Compte-Rendu des Recherches Tchecoslovaques de la Fonderie
CRRED — Carbonization Research Report
CRREL — CRREL [*Cold Regions Research and Engineering Laboratory*] Report
CRRELDT — CRREL [*Cold Regions Research and Engineering Laboratory*] Draft Translation
CRREL Monograph — Cold Regions Research and Engineering Laboratory. Monograph
CRRELR — CRREL [*Cold Regions Research and Engineering Laboratory*] Report
CRREL Rep — CRREL [*Cold Regions Research and Engineering Laboratory*] Report
CRREL Report — Cold Regions Research and Engineering Laboratory. Report
CRRELRR — CRREL [*Cold Regions Research and Engineering Laboratory*] Research Reports
CRRELSR — CRREL [*Cold Regions Research and Engineering Laboratory*] Special Report
CRRELTR — CRREL [*Cold Regions Research and Engineering Laboratory*] Technical Reports
CR Rencontre Moriond — Compte Rendu de la Rencontre de Moriond
Cr R Env C — Critical Reviews in Environmental Control
Cr Rep — Criminal Reports
CRRERI — Commonwealth Regional Renewable Energy Resources Index
CR Reun Annu Soc Chim Phys — Comptes Rendus. Reunion Annuelle. Societe de Chimie Physique
CR Reun Assoc Anat — Comptes Rendus. Reunion. Association des Anatomistes
CR Reun Cent Poisons — Compte Rendu. Reunion des Centres de Poisons
Cr R F Sci — Critical Reviews in Food Science and Nutrition
Cr R Immun — Critical Reviews in Immunology
Cr R Microb — Critical Reviews in Microbiology

Cr R Neur — Critical Reviews in Neurobiology
Cr R Onc H — Critical Reviews in Oncology/Hematology
Cr R Plant — Critical Reviews in Plant Sciences
CRRSDD — Cretaceous Research
Cr R Ther — Critical Reviews in Therapeutic Drug Carrier Systems
Cr R Toxic — Critical Reviews in Toxicology
CRRVAJ — Chromatographic Reviews
CrS — Cristianesimo nella Storia
CrS — Critical Survey
CrS — Critica Storica
CRSA — Canadian Review of Sociology and Anthropology
CRSAIBL — Comptes Rendus des Seances. Academie des Inscriptions et Belles-Lettres
CRSBA — Comptes Rendus des Seances. Societe de Biologie et de Ses Filiales
CRSBP — Comptes Rendus de la Societe de Biogeographie (Paris)
CR Seance Publ Ann Acad Pharm — Comptes Rendus de la Seance Publique Annuelle. Academie de la Pharmacie
CR Seances Acad Agric Fr — Comptes Rendus des Seances. Academie d'Agriculture de France
CR Seances Acad Sci III — Comptes Rendus des Seances. Academie des Sciences. Serie III. Sciences de la Vie
CR Seances Acad Sci Roum — Comptes Rendus des Seances. Academie des Sciences de Roumanie
CR Seances Acad Sci Ser 2 — Comptes Rendus des Seances. Academie des Sciences. Serie 2. Mecanique-Physique,Chimie, Sciences de l'Univers, Sciences de la Terre
CR Seances Acad Sci Ser A — Comptes Rendus des Seances. Academie des Sciences. Serie A. Sciences Mathematiques
CR Seances Acad Sci Ser B — Comptes Rendus des Seances. Academie des Sciences. Serie B. Sciences Physiques
CR Seances Acad Sci Ser C — Comptes Rendus des Seances. Academie des Sciences. Serie C. Sciences Chimiques
CR Seances Acad Sci Ser D — Comptes Rendus des Seances. Academie des Sciences. Serie D. Sciences Naturelles
CR Seances Acad Sci Ser I — Comptes Rendus de Seances. Academie des Sciences. Serie I. Mathematique
CR Seances Acad Sci Ser II — Comptes Rendus des Seances. Academie des Sciences. Serie II. Mecanique, Physique, Chimie, Sciences de la Terre, Sciences de l'Univers
CR Seances Acad Sci Ser III — Comptes Rendus des Seances. Academie des Sciences. Serie III. Sciences de la Vie
CR Seances Acad Sci Ser III Sci Vie — Comptes Rendus de Seances. Academie des Sciences. Serie III. Sciences de la Vie
CR Seances Acad Sci Vie Acad — Comptes Rendus des Seances. Academie des Sciences. Vie Academique
CR Seances Colloq Int Methodes Anal Rayonnem X — Compte Rendu des Seances. Colloque International sur les Methodes Analytiques par Rayonnements X
CR Seances Congr Fr Oto Rhino Laryngol — Comptes Rendus des Seances. Congres Francais d'Oto-Rhino-Laryngologie
CR Seances Inst Geol Geophys Rom — Comptes Rendus des Seances. Institut de Geologie et de Geophysique (Romania)
CR Seances Inst Geol Roum — Comptes Rendus des Seances. Institut Geologique de Roumanie
CR Seances Inst Geol Roum Fr Ed — Comptes Rendus des Seances. Institut Geologiques de Roumanie (French Edition)
CR Seances Inst Sci Roum Anc Acad Sci Roum — Comptes Rendus des Seances. Institut des Sciences de Roumanie. Ancienne Academie des Sciences de Roumanie
CR Seances Mem Soc Biol Ses Fil — Comptes Rendus des Seances et Memoires. Societe de Biologie et des Ses Filiales
CR Seances Mens Soc Sci Nat Phys Maroc — Comptes Rendus des Seances Mensuelles. Societe des Sciences Naturelles et Physiques du Maroc
CR Seances Repub Pop Roum Com Geol — Comptes Rendus des Seances. Republique Populaire Roumaine. Comite Geologique
CR Seances Soc Biogeogr — Compte Rendu des Seances. Societe de Biogeographie
CR Seances Soc Biol Fil — Comptes Rendus des Seances. Societe de Biologie et de Ses Filiales
CR Seances Soc Biol (Paris) — Comptes Rendus des Seances. Societe de Biologie (Paris)
CR Seances Soc Phys Hist Nat Geneve — Compte Rendu des Seances. Societe de Physique et d'Histoire Naturelle deGeneve
CR Seances Soc Pol Phys — Comptes Rendus des Seances. Societe Polonaise de Physique
CR Seances Soc Serbe Geol — Compte Rendu des Seances. Societe Serbe de Geologie
CR Seanc Mens Soc Sci Nat Phys Maroc — Comptes Rendus des Seances Mensuelles. Societe des Sciences Naturelles et Physiques du Maroc
CR Seanc Soc Biol — Comptes Rendus des Seances. Societe de Biologie
CR Seanc Soc Biol Fil — Comptes Rendus des Seances. Societe de Biologie et de Ses Filiales
CR Sem Geol Com Nat Malgache Geol — Comptes Rendus de la Semaine Geologique. Comite National Malgache de Geologie
CR Semin Controle Effluents Radioact — Compte Rendu. Seminaire sur le Controle des Effluents Radioactifs
CR Semin Exper Degagement Chal In Situ Form Geol — Compte Rendu du Seminaire sur des Experiences de Degagement de Chaleur In Situ dans les Formations Geologiques
CR Semin R D Bioenerg — Compte Rendu. Seminaire R and D Bioenergetique
CRSG — Comptes-Rendus. Societe de Geographie
CRSGF — Compte Rendu Sommaire des Seances de la Societe Geologique de France
CRSHA — Circulatory Shock
CRSHAG — Circulatory Shock

CRSIGR — Comptes Rendus des Seances. Institut de Geologie Roumaine

CRSL — Comptes Rendus. Societe des Sciences et des Lettres de Lodz

CRSLub — Comptes Rendus. Societe des Sciences et des Lettres. Universite Catholique de Lublin

CRSOA — Crops and Soils

CR Soc Biol — Comptes Rendus des Seances. Societe de Biologie et de Ses Filiales

CR Soc Biol (Paris) — Comptes Rendus des Seances. Societe de Biologie (Paris)

CR Soc Franc Gynec — Comptes Rendus. Societe Francaise de Gynecologie

CR Soc Fr Gynecol — Comptes Rendus. Societe Francaise de Gynecologie

CR Soc Geol Finl — Comptes Rendus. Societe Geologique de Finlande

CR Soc Geol Fr — Comptes Rendus. Societe Geologique de France

CR Soc Geol Fr — Comptes Rendus Sommaire des Seances. Societe Geologique de France

CR Soc Phys Hist Nat Geneve — Compte Rendu des Seances. Societe de Physique et d'Histoire Naturelle de Geneve

CR Soc Physiol Suisses — Comptes Rendus. Societe des Physiologistes Suisses

CR Soc Phys Warsaw — Comptes Rendus des Seances. Societe de Physique (Warsaw)

CR Soc Roy Econ Pol — Comptes Rendus des Travaux. Societe Royale d'Economie Politique de Belgique

CR Soc Sci Lett Wroclaw — Comptes Rendus. Societe des Sciences et des Lettres de Wroclaw

CR Soc Sci Nat Phys Maroc — Comptes Rendus des Seances Mensuelles. Societe des Sciences Naturelles et Physiques du Maroc

CR Somm Seances Soc Geol Fr — Compte Rendu Sommaire des Seances. Societe Geologique de France

CR Somm Seanc Soc Biogeogr — Compte Rendu Sommaire des Seances. Societe de Biogeographie

CR Som Seances Soc Geol Fr — Comptes Rendus Sommaire des Seances. Societe Geologique de France

CRSP — Comptes Rendus. Societe des Sciences et des Lettres de Poznan

CRSQ — Creation Research Society. Quarterly

Crst — Cahiers Rationalistes

CRST — Cold Regions Science and Technology

Cr St — Cristianesimo nella Storia

CrSt — Critica Storica

CRSTB — Proceedings. Conference on Remote Systems Technology

CRSTD — Cold Regions Science and Technology

CRSVa — Comptes Rendus. Societe des Sciences et des Lettres de Varsovie

CRSW — Comptes Rendus. Societe des Sciences et des Lettres de Wroclaw

CR Symp Eur Antiprotons — Comptes Rendus du Symposium Europeen sur les Antiprotons

CR Symp Int Decharges Isol Electr Vide — Comptes-Rendus du Symposium International sur les Decharges et l'Isolement Electrique dans le Vide

CR Symp Int Jets Mol — Comptes Rendus. Symposium International sur les Jets Moleculaires

CR Symp Trait Eaux Usees — Comptes Rendus. Symposium sur le Traitement des Eaux Usees

CRTD — Cold Regions Technical Digest

CRTED — Crystal Research and Technology

CR Ther Pharmacol Clin — Comptes Rendus de Therapeutique et de Pharmacologie Clinique

CR Trav Carlsb — Comptes Rendus des Travaux. Laboratoire Carlsberg

CR Trav Congr Int Aeronaut — Compte Rendu des Travaux du Congres International Aeronautique

CR Trav Congr Int Biochim — Comptes Rendus des Travaux du Congres International de Biochimie

CR Trav Congr Int Verre — Compte Rendu des Travaux. Congres International du Verre

CR Trav Fac Sci Univ Aix Marseille — Comptes Rendus des Travaux. Faculte des Sciences. Universite de l'Aix Marseille

CR Trav Lab Carlsberg — Comptes Rendus des Travaux. Laboratoire Carlsberg

CR Trav Lab Carlsberg Ser Chim — Comptes Rendus des Travaux. Laboratoire Carlsberg. Serie Chimique

CR Trav Lab Carlsberg Ser Physiol — Comptes Rendus des Travaux. Laboratoire Carlsberg. Serie Physiologique

CR Trim Acad Sci O-Mer — Comptes Rendus Trimestriels. Academie des Sciences d'Outre-Mer

CR Trim Seances Acad Sci Outre Mer — Comptes Rendus Trimestriels des Seances. Academie des Sciences d'Outre-Mer

CR Tr Lab C — Comptes Rendus des Travaux. Laboratoire Carlsberg

CRTSEO — CRC [*Chemical Rubber Company*] Critical Reviews in Therapeutic Drug Carrier Systems

CRTXA — Cortex

CRu — Ceskoslovenska Rusistika

Cruciferae Newsl — Cruciferae Newsletter

Crude Pet Pet Prod Nat Gas Liq — Crude Petroleum, Petroleum Products, and Natural Gas Liquids

Cruise Rep Geol Surv Jap — Cruise Report. Geological Survey of Japan

CRus — Ceskoslovenska Rusistika

CRUSA — Crustaceana

Crush Grind Min Quarr J — Crushing, Grinding, Mining, and Quarrying Journal

Crushing Grinding Min Quarrying J — Crushing, Grinding, Mining, and Quarrying Journal

Crushing Grinding Trades J — Crushing and Grinding Trades Journal

Crustaceana Suppl (Leiden) — Crustaceana. Supplement (Leiden)

Cruz Sur Caracas — Cruz del Sur (Caracas)

CRV — Creditanstalt-Bankverein. Wirtschaftsberichte

CRVMAC — CRC [*Chemical Rubber Company*] Critical Reviews in Microbiology

CRVR — Computerized Register of Voice Research

CRWSD4 — West Virginia University. Agricultural and Forestry Experiment Station. CurrentReport

Cr Wtg — Creative Writing

CRYBA — Cryobiology

Crybiol — Cryobiology

Cry Calif — Cry California

CRYOA — Cryogenics

Cryog — Cryogenics

Cryog & Ind Gases — Cryogenic and Industrial Gases

Cryog Eng — Cryogenic Engineering

Cryog Eng News — Cryogenic Engineering News

Cryog Eng Present Status Future Dev — Cryogenic Engineering. Present Status and Future Development

Cryog Opt Syst Instrum — Cryogenic Optical Systems and Instruments

Cryog Pure Appl — Cryogenic Pure et Appliquee

Cryog Suppl — Cryogenics. Supplement

Cryog Technol — Cryogenic Technology

Cryo Lett — Cryo Letters

Cryptogam Algol — Cryptogamie: Algologie

Cryptogam Bryol Lichenol — Cryptogamie: Bryologie et Lichenologie

Cryptogamica Helv — Cryptogamica Helvetica

Cryptogam Mycol — Cryptogamie: Mycologie

Cryptogam Stud — Cryptogamic Studies

Crys Lattice Defects — Crystal Lattice Defects [*Later, Crystal Lattice Defects and Amorphous Materials*]

Cryst — Crystallographica

Crystal Eng — Crystal Engineering

Crystallogr Comput Proc Int Summer Sch — Crystallographic Computing. Proceedings of an International Summer School

Crystallogr Comput Tech Proc Int Summer Sch — Crystallographic Computing Techniques. Proceedings of an International Summer School

Crystallogr Cryst Chem Mater Layered Struct — Crystallography and Crystal Chemistry of Materials with Layered Structures

Crystallogr Cryst Perfect Proc Symp — Crystallography and Crystal Perfection. Proceedings of a Symposium

Crystallogr Mol Biol — Crystallography in Molecular Biology

Crystallogr Rep Transl Kristallografiya — Crystallography Reports (Translation of Kristallografiya)

Crystallogr Res Cent Inst Protein Res Osaka Univ Rep — Crystallographic Research Center. Institute for Protein Research. Osaka University. Report

Crystallogr Rev — Crystallography Reviews

Crystallogr (Sov Phys) — Crystallography (Soviet Physics)

Cryst Chem Non-Met Mater — Crystal Chemistry of Non-Metallic Materials

Cryst Field Eff Met Alloys (Proc Int Conf) — Crystal Field Effects in Metals and Alloys (Proceedings of the International Conference on Crystal Field Effects in Metals and Alloys)

Cryst Growth Charact Polytype Struct — Crystal Growth and Characterization of Polytype Structures

Cryst Growth Charact Proc Int Spring Sch Cryst Growth — Crystal Growth and Characterization. Proceedings. International Spring School on Crystal Growth

Cryst Growth Prop Appl — Crystals. Growth, Properties, and Applications

Cryst Growth Space Relat Opt Diagn — Crystal Growth in Space and Related Optical Diagnostics

Cryst Latt — Crystal Lattice Defects [*Later, Crystal Lattice Defects and Amorphous Materials*]

Cryst Lattice Defects — Crystal Lattice Defects [*Later, Crystal Lattice Defects and Amorphous Materials*]

Cryst Lattice Defects Amorphous Mater — Crystal Lattice Defects and Amorphous Materials

Cryst Lattice Defects and Amorphous Mater — Crystal Lattice Defects and Amorphous Materials

Cryst Mater Growth Charact — Crystalline Materials. Growth and Characterization

CRYSTMET — Metals Crystallographic Data File

Cryst Prop Prep — Crystal Properties and Preparation

Cryst Res and Technol — Crystal Research and Technology

Cryst Res Technol — Crystal Research and Technology

Cryst Struct Clay Miner Their X Ray Identif — Crystal Structures of Clay Minerals and Their X-Ray Identification

Cryst Struct Commun — Crystal Structure Communications

CRZLAT — Communication. Centre de Recherches Zootechniques. Universite de Louvain

CS — Cahiers du Sud

CS — Cahiers Sioniens

CS — Camden Society. Publications

CS — Caribbean Studies

CS — Cathedral Series

CS — Christian Scholar

CS — Christopher Street

CS — Clinical Studies

CS — Computers and Standards

CS — Contemporary Sociology

CS — Cornish Studies

CS — Corriere della Sera

CS — Cretan Seals

CS — Critica Storica

CS — Croatia Sacra

CS — Cuban Studies/Estudios Cubanos

CS — Cue Sheet

CS — Cultura e Scuola

CS — Current Scene

CS — Recueil de Jurisprudence. Cour Superieure

CSA — Cahiers. Societe Asiatique

CSA — Calcutta Statistical Association. Bulletin

CSA — Central Bank of Trinidad and Tobago. Quarterly Economic Report

CSA — Chinese Sociology and Anthropology

CSA — Colegas (Antioquia, Colombia)

CSAAA — Annual Reports on the Progress of Chemistry. Section A. General, Physical, and Inorganic Chemistry

CSA Bull — CSA [*Canadian Standards Association*] Bulletin

CSACJ — CSAC [*Civil Service Association of Canada*] Journal

CSAE — Columbia Studies in Archeology and Ethnology [*New York*]

CSAKA — Chemia Stosowana. Seria A. Kwartalnik Poswiecony Zagadnieniom Technologii Chemicznej

CSAN — Coin, Stamp, and Antique News

CS & M — Cellular Sales and Marketing

CSA Neurosci Abstr — CSA [*Cambridge Scientific Abstracts*] Neurosciences Abstracts

CSAPC — Case Studies in Atomic Physics

CSA Publ — CSA (Scientific Council for Africa South of the Sahara). Publication

CSARCX — Cancer Research Institute. Slovak Academy of Sciences. Annual Report

CSATD6 — Department of the Capital Territory. Conservation Series

Csatornamue Inf — Csatornamue Informacio

CSAV — Ceskoslovenska Akademie Ved

CSB — Cataloging Service Bulletin

CSB — Cathedral Service Book

CSB — Common Market Business Reports (Spain)

CSB — Companies and Securities Bulletin

CSB — Corpus Scriptorum Historiae Byzantinae

CSB — Current Science (Bangalore)

CSBIED — Cambridge Studies in Biotechnology

CSBKA — Chemia Stosowana. Seria B. Kwartalnik Poswiecony Zagadnieniom Inzynierii i Aparatury Chemicznej

CSBL-A — Casabella

CSBW — Chicago Sun Book Week

C Sc — Cognitive Science

CSC — Coins, Stamps, and Collecting

CSC — CSC. Bulletin Mensuel. Confederation des Syndicats Chretiens deBelgique

CSCA — California Studies in Classical Antiquity

CSCh — Cahier Special des Charges

CSCH — Ceskoslovensky Casopis Historicky

CSch — Christian Scholar

CSCL — Columbia University Studies in Comparative Literature

CSCO — Corpus Scriptorum Christianorum Orientalium

CSCP — Church of Scotland Committee on Publications

CSCP — Cornell Studies in Classical Philology

CSCPC3 — Australia. Commonwealth Scientific and Industrial Research Organisation. Division of Chemical Physics. Annual Report

CSCRS — Calcutta Sanskrit College Research Series

CSCT — Columbia Studies in the Classical Tradition

CSD — Crystallographic Structural Database

CSDIR — Centro Studi e Documentazione sull'Italia Romana

CSE — Carnegie Series in English

CSE — Cornell Studies in English

CSE — Cosmetics International

CSE — Cost Engineering

CSEB — Canadian Society of Environmental Biologists. Newsletter/Bulletin

CSEC Newsl — CSEC [*Cesareans, Support, Education and Concern*] Newsletter

CSeg — Carte Segrete

CSEL — Corpus Scriptorum Ecclesiasticorum Latinorum

CSELT Rappo Tec — CSELT [*Centro Studi e Laboratori Telecomunicazioni*] Rapporti Tecnici

CSELT Rapp Tec — CSELT [*Centro Studi e Laboratori Telecomunicazioni*] Rapporti Tecnici

CSELT Tech Rep — CSELT [*Centro Studie e Laboratori Telecomunicazioni*] Technical Reports

CSEn — Cornell Studies in English

Cs Epidem — Ceskoslovenska Epidemiologie, Mikrobiologie, Immunologie

CSEV — Climatological Studies. Environment Canada. Atmospheric Environment

CSF — Cambridge Studies in French

CSF — Commentationes Humanarum Litterarum. Societas Scientiarum Fennica

CSF — Cuadernos Salmantinos de Filosofia

CS Faraday Transactions 1 — Chemical Society. Faraday Transactions 1

Cs Farm — Ceskoslovenska Farmacie

CSFDL — Collection Scientifique de la Faculte de Droit de l'Universite de Liege

CSFJA — Citrus and Subtropical Fruit Journal

CSFJAW — Citrus and Subtropical Fruit Journal

CSFRD — Cameron Synthetic Fuels Report

CSFSD — Ciencias Forestales

CSFUDY — Cell Structure and Function

Cs Fysiol — Ceskoslovenska Fysiologie

Cs Gastrent Vyz — Ceskoslovenska Gastroenterologie a Vyziva

CSGCAG — Congres International de Stratigraphie et de Geologie du Carbonifere. Compte Rendu

CSGEA — Compass. Sigma Gamma Epsilon

CSGH — Chosen Gakuno

CSGLL — Canadian Studies in German Language and Literature

CSGP — Comunicacoes. Servicos Geologicos de Portugal

CSGP — Congres. Societe Geographique de Paris

CSGP — Corpus Scriptorum Graecorum Paravianum

CSGYAF — Contemporary Surgery

Cs Gynek — Ceskoslovenska Gynekologie

CsH — Celuloza si Hirtie

CSH — Chinese Studies in History

CSHB — Corpus Scriptorum Historiae Byzantinae

CSH Byz — Corpus Scriptorum Historiae Byzantinae

CSHCAL — Cold Spring Harbor Conferences on Cell Proliferation

CSHSA — Cold Spring Harbor Symposia on Quantitative Biology

CSHSAZ — Cold Spring Harbor Symposia on Quantitative Biology

CSHVB — Computer Studies in the Humanities and Verbal Behavior

CSI — CSIRO [*Commonwealth Scientific and Industrial Research Organisation*] Index

CSi — Cuba Si

CSIC Cent Edafol Biol Apl Anu — Consejo Superior de Investigaciones Cientificas. Centro de Edafologia y Biologia Aplicada. Anuario

CSIC Estud Geol — Consejo Superior de Investigaciones Cientificas. Estudios Geologicos

CSIC Inst Nac Carbon Sus Deriv Francisco Pintado Fe Inf Tec — Consejo Superior de Investigaciones Cientificas. Instituto Nacional del Carbon y Sus Derivados Francisco Pintado Fe. Informe Tecnico

CSIC Patronato Juan De La Cierva Invest Tec Cuad — Consejo Superior de Investigaciones Cientificas. Patronato Juan De La Cierva deInvestigaciones Tecnicas. Cuaderno

CSIC Workshop SUSY Grand Unification — CSIC Workshop on SUSY [*Supersymmetry*] and Grand Unification. From Stringsto Collider Phenomenology

CSIO Commun — CSIO [*Central Scientific Instruments Organisation*] Communications

CSion — Cahiers Sioniens

CSIR — Corpus Signorum Imperii Romani

CSIR Air Pollut Res Group Rep APRG (S Afr) — Council for Scientific and Industrial Research. Air Pollution Research Group. Report APRG (South Africa)

CSIRB4 — Suid-Afrikaanse Wetenskaplike en Nywerheidnavorsingsraad Navorsingsverslag

CSIR (Counc Sci Ind Res S Afr) Ann Rep — CSIR (Council for Scientific and Industrial Research, South Africa) Annual Report

CSIR Dep Mines Asbestos Min Ind Asbestosis Res Proj Annu Rep — Council for Scientific and Industrial Research and Department of Mines and the Asbestos Mining Industry. Asbestosis Research Project. Annual Report

CSIR Natl Build Res Inst Rep BOU S Afr — Council for Scientific and Industrial Research. National Building Research Institute. Report BOU (South Africa)

CSIR Natl Timber Res Inst Spec Rep S Afr — Council for Scientific and Industrial Research. National Timber Research Institute. Special Report (South Africa)

CSIR News (India) — CSIR [*Council for Scientific and Industrial Research*] News (India)

CSIRO Abstr — CSIRO [*Commonwealth Scientific and Industrial Research Organisation*] Abstracts

CSIRO An Health Div TP — CSIRO [*Commonwealth Scientific and Industrial Research Organisation*] Division of Animal Health and Production. Technical Paper

CSIRO Annu Rep — CSIRO [*Commonwealth Scientific and Industrial Research Organisation*] Annual Report

CSIRO An Res Labs TP — CSIRO [*Commonwealth Scientific and Industrial Research Organisation*] Animal Research Laboratories. Technical Paper

CSIRO Aust Div Appl Phys Tech Pap — Commonwealth Scientific and Industrial Research Organization. Australia. Division of Applied Physics Technical Paper

CSIRO Aust Div Trop Crops Pastures Tech Pap — CSIRO [*Commonwealth Scientific and Industrial Research Organisation*] Australia. Division of Tropical Crops and Pastures. Technical Paper

CSIRO Bio Mem News — Bio Membrane News CSIRO [*Commonwealth Scientific and Industrial Research Organisation*] Biomembrane Committee

CSIRO Build Res Div Building Study — CSIRO [*Commonwealth Scientific and Industrial Research Organisation*] Division of Building Research. Building Study

CSIRO Build Res Div Rep — CSIRO [*Commonwealth Scientific and Industrial Research Organisation*] Division of Building Research. Report

CSIRO Build Res Div Tech Pap — CSIRO [*Commonwealth Scientific and Industrial Research Organisation*] Division of Building Research. Technical Paper

CSIRO Build Res Div TP — CSIRO [*Commonwealth Scientific and Industrial Research Organisation*] Division of Building Research. Technical Paper

CSIRO Bull — CSIRO [*Commonwealth Scientific and Industrial Research Organisation*] Bulletin

CSIRO Chem Res Labs TP — CSIRO [*Commonwealth Scientific and Industrial Research Organisation*] Chemical Research Laboratories. Technical Paper

CSIRO Chem Res Lab Tech Pap — CSIRO [*Commonwealth Scientific and Industrial Research Organisation*] Chemical Research Laboratories. Technical Paper

CSIRO Coal Res Div Ref TC — CSIRO [*Commonwealth Scientific and Industrial Research Organisation*] Division of Coal Research. Reference TC

CSIRO Coal Res Div Tech Commun — CSIRO [*Commonwealth Scientific and Industrial Research Organisation*] Division of Coal Research. Technical Communication

CSIRO Coal Res Lab Invest Rep — CSIRO [*Commonwealth Scientific and Industrial Research Organisation*] CoalResearch Laboratory. Division of Mineral Chemistry. Investigation Report

CSIRO Coal Res Lab Tech Commun — CSIRO [*Commonwealth Scientific and Industrial Research Organisation*] CoalResearch Laboratory. Division of Mineral Chemistry. Technical Communication

CSIRO Computing Res Sect Memo — CSIRO [*Commonwealth Scientific and Industrial Research Organisation*] Computing Research Section. Memorandum

CSIRO Consumer Liaison Ser Leaflet — Consumer Liaison Service Leaflet CSIRO [*Commonwealth Scientific and Industrial Research Organisation*]. Division of Food Research

CSIRO Dig of Curr Act — CSIRO [*Commonwealth Scientific and Industrial Research Organisation*] Digest of Current Activities

CSIRO Div Anim Genet Ann Rep — CSIRO [*Commonwealth Scientific and Industrial Research Organisation*] Division of Animal Genetics. Annual Report

CSIRO Div Appl Geomech Prog Circ — Computer Program Users Manual CSIRO

CSIRO Div Appl Organic Chem Res Rep — CSIRO [*Commonwealth Scientific and Industrial Research Organisation*] Division of Applied Organic Chemistry. Research Report

CSIRO Div Atmos Phys Tech Pap — CSIRO [*Commonwealth Scientific and Industrial Research Organisation*] Division of Atmospheric Physics. Technical Paper

CSIRO Div Build Res Publ — CSIRO [*Commonwealth Scientific and Industrial Research Organisation*] Division of Building Research. Publications

CSIRO Div Build Res Tech Pap — Commonwealth Scientific and Industrial Research Organisation. Division of Building Research. Technical Paper

CSIRO Div Chem Phys Ann Rep — CSIRO [*Commonwealth Scientific and Industrial Research Organisation*] Division of Chemical Physics. Annual Report

CSIRO Div Chem Phys Annu Rep — CSIRO [*Commonwealth Scientific and Industrial Research Organisation*] Division of Chemical Physics. Annual Report

CSIRO Div Chem Technol Res Rev — Commonwealth Scientific and Industrial Research Organisation. Division of Chemical Technology. Research Review

CSIRO Div Chem Technol Tech Pap — CSIRO [*Commonwealth Scientific and Industrial Research Organisation*] Division of Chemical Technology. Technical Paper

CSIRO Div Entomol Annu Rep — CSIRO [*Commonwealth Scientific and Industrial Research Organisation*] Division of Entomology. Annual Report

CSIRO Div Fish Oceanogr Rep — CSIRO [*Commonwealth Scientific and Industrial Research Organisation*] Division of Fisheries and Oceanography. Report

CSIRO Div Fish Oceanogr Rep (Aust) — CSIRO [*Commonwealth Scientific and Industrial Research Organisation*] Division of Fisheries and Oceanography. Report (Australia)

CSIRO Div Food Proc Tech Pap — Commonwealth Scientific and Industrial Research Organisation. Division of Food Processing. Technical Paper

CSIRO Div Food Res Rep Res — CSIRO [*Commonwealth Scientific and Industrial Research Organisation*] Division of Food Research. Report of Research

CSIRO Div Forest Prod Technol Paper — CSIRO [*Commonwealth Scientific and Industrial Research Organisation*] Division of Forest Products. Technological Paper

CSIRO Div For Res Ann Rep — CSIRO [*Commonwealth Scientific and Industrial Research Organisation*] Division of Forest Research. Annual Report

CSIRO Div Land Use Res Publ — CSIRO [*Commonwealth Scientific and Industrial Research Organisation*] Division of Land Use Research. Publications

CSIRO Div Mech Eng Info Serv Leafl — CSIRO [*Commonwealth Scientific and Industrial Research Organisation*] Division of Mechanical Engineering. Information Service Leaflet

CSIRO Div Mineral Invest Rep — CSIRO [*Commonwealth Scientific and Industrial Research Organisation*] Division of Mineralogy. Investigation Report

CSIRO Div Mineral Tech Commun — CSIRO [*Commonwealth Scientific and Industrial Research Organisation*] Division of Mineralogy. Technical Communication

CSIRO Div Miner Chem Invest Rep — CSIRO [*Commonwealth Scientific and Industrial Research Organisation*] Division of Mineral Chemistry. Investigation Report

CSIRO Div Miner Phys Invest Rep — CSIRO [*Commonwealth Scientific and Industrial Research Organisation*] Division of Mineral Physics. Investigation Report

CSIRO Div Plant Ind Field Stn Rec Aust — Australia. Commonwealth Scientific and Industrial Research Organisation. Division of Plant Industry. Field Station Record

CSIRO Div Plant Ind Rep — Commonwealth Scientific and Industrial Research Organisation. Division of PlantIndustry. Report

CSIRO Div Soils Tech Pap — Commonwealth Scientific and Industrial Research Organisation. Division of Soils. Technical Papers

CSIRO Div Text Phys Ann Rep — CSIRO [*Commonwealth Scientific and Industrial Research Organisation*] Division of Textile Physics. Annual Report

CSIRO Div Trop Agron Annu Rep — CSIRO [*Commonwealth Scientific and Industrial Research Organisation*] Division of Tropical Agronomy. Annual Report

CSIRO Div Trop Crops Pastures Tech Pap — Commonwealth Scientific and Industrial Research Organization. Division of Tropical Crops and Pastures Technical Paper

CSIRO Div Trop Crops Pastures Trop Agron Tech Memo — CSIRO [*Commonwealth Scientific and Industrial Research Organisation*] Division of Tropical Crops and Pastures. Tropical Agronomy Technical Memorandum

CSIRO Div Water Res Res Nat Res Ser — Commonwealth Scientific and Industrial Research Organisation. Division of WaterResources Research. Natural Resources Series

CSIRO Engng Sect C — CSIRO [*Commonwealth Scientific and Industrial Research Organisation*] Engineering Section. Circular

CSIRO Engng Sect Int Rept — CSIRO [*Commonwealth Scientific and Industrial Research Organisation*] Engineering Section. Internal Report

CSIRO Entomol Div Tech Pap — CSIRO [*Commonwealth Scientific and Industrial Research Organisation*] Division of Entomology. Technical Paper

CSIRO Entomol Div TP — CSIRO [*Commonwealth Scientific and Industrial Research Organisation*] Division of Entomology. Technical Paper

CSIRO Fd Pres Div Circ — CSIRO [*Commonwealth Scientific and Industrial Research Organisation*] Division of Food Preservation. Circular

CSIRO Fd Preserv Div Tech Pap — CSIRO [*Commonwealth Scientific and Industrial Research Organisation*] Division of Food Preservation. Technical Paper

CSIRO Fd Preserv Q — CSIRO [*Commonwealth Scientific and Industrial Research Organisation*] FoodPreservation Quarterly

CSIRO Fd Res Q — CSIRO [*Commonwealth Scientific and Industrial Research Organisation*] FoodResearch Quarterly

CSIRO Fish Div C — CSIRO [*Commonwealth Scientific and Industrial Research Organisation*] Division of Fisheries and Oceanography. Circular

CSIRO Fish Div Fish Synopsis — CSIRO [*Commonwealth Scientific and Industrial Research Organisation*] Division of Fisheries and Oceanography. Fisheries Synopsis

CSIRO Fish Div Oceanogrl Cruise Rep — CSIRO [*Commonwealth Scientific and Industrial Research Organisation*] Division of Fisheries and Oceanography. Oceanographical Cruise Report

CSIRO Fish Div Oceanogrl Stn List — CSIRO [*Commonwealth Scientific and Industrial Research Organisation*] Division of Fisheries and Oceanography. Oceanographical Station List

CSIRO Fish Div Oceanogr Station List — CSIRO [*Commonwealth Scientific and Industrial Research Organisation*] Division of Fisheries and Oceanography. Oceanographical Station List

CSIRO Fish Div Rep — CSIRO [*Commonwealth Scientific and Industrial Research Organisation*] Division of Fisheries and Oceanography. Report

CSIRO Fish Div Tech Pap — CSIRO [*Commonwealth Scientific and Industrial Research Organisation*] Division of Fisheries and Oceanography. Technical Paper

CSIRO Fish Div TP — CSIRO [*Commonwealth Scientific and Industrial Research Organisation*] Division of Fisheries and Oceanography. Technical Paper

CSIRO Food Pres Div C — CSIRO [*Commonwealth Scientific and Industrial Research Organisation*] Division of Food Preservation. Circular

CSIRO Food Pres Div TP — CSIRO [*Commonwealth Scientific and Industrial Research Organisation*] Division of Food Preservation. Technical Paper

CSIRO Food Preserv Q — CSIRO [*Commonwealth Scientific and Industrial Research Organisation*] Food Preservation Quarterly

CSIRO Food Res Q — CSIRO [*Commonwealth Scientific and Industrial Research Organisation*] Division of Food Research. Food Research Quarterly

CSIRO Food Res Q Suppl Ser — CSIRO [*Commonwealth Scientific and Industrial Research Organisation*] Division of Food Research. Food Research Quarterly. Supplementary Series

CSIRO Forest Prod Newsl — CSIRO [*Commonwealth Scientific and Industrial Research Organisation*] Forest Products Newsletter

CSIRO For Prod Div Technol P — CSIRO [*Commonwealth Scientific and Industrial Research Organisation*] Division of Forest Products. Technological Paper

CSIRO For Prod Div Technol Pap — CSIRO [*Commonwealth Scientific and Industrial Research Organisation*] Division of Forest Products. Technological Paper

CSIRO For Prod Newsl — CSIRO [*Commonwealth Scientific and Industrial Research Organisation*] Division of Forest Products. Forest Products Newsletter

CSIRO For Prod Newslett — CSIRO [*Commonwealth Scientific and Industrial Research Organisation*] Forest Products Newsletter

CSIRO For Prod Newsletter — CSIRO [*Commonwealth Scientific and Industrial Research Organisation*] Forest Products Newsletter

CSIRO For Prod Tech Notes — CSIRO [*Commonwealth Scientific and Industrial Research Organisation*] Division of Forest Products. CSIRO Forest Products Technical Notes

CSIRO Ind Res News — CSIRO [*Commonwealth Scientific and Industrial Research Organisation*] Industrial Research News

CSIRO Inst Earth Resour Invest Rep — CSIRO [*Commonwealth Scientific and Industrial Research Organisation*] Institute of Earth Resources. Investigation Report

CSIRO Inst Earth Resour Tech Commun — CSIRO [*Commonwealth Scientific and Industrial Research Organisation*] Institute of Earth Resources. Technical Communication

CSIRO Inst Energ Earth Resour Tech Commun — CSIRO [*Commonwealth Scientific and Industrial Research Organization*] Institute of Energy and Earth Resources. Technical Communication

CSIRO Irrig Res Stat TP — CSIRO [*Commonwealth Scientific and Industrial Research Organisation*] Irrigation Research Stations. Technical Paper

CSIRO Land Res Regional Surv Div Tech Pap — CSIRO [*Commonwealth Scientific and Industrial Research Organisation*] Division of Land Research and Regional Survey. Technical Paper

CSIRO Land Res Regional Surv Div TP — CSIRO [*Commonwealth Scientific and Industrial Research Organisation*] Division of Land Research and Regional Survey. Technical Paper

CSIRO Land Res Ser — CSIRO [*Commonwealth Scientific and Industrial Research Organisation*] LandResearch Series

CSIRO Leaflet Ser — CSIRO [*Commonwealth Scientific and Industrial Research Organisation*] Leaflet Series

CSIRO Mar Biochem Unit Annu Rep — CSIRO [*Commonwealth Scientific and Industrial Research Organisation*] Marine Biochemistry Unit. Annual Report

CSIRO Marine Biochem Unit Ann Rep — CSIRO [*Commonwealth Scientific and Industrial Research Organisation*] Marine Biochemistry Unit. Annual Report

CSIRO Mar Lab Fish Sit Rep — Commonwealth Scientific and Industrial Research Organisation. Marine Laboratories. Fishery Situation Report

CSIRO Mar Lab Rep — CSIRO [*Commonwealth Scientific and Industrial Research Organization*] Marine Laboratories. Report

CSIRO Math Statist Div Tech Pap — CSIRO [*Commonwealth Scientific and Industrial Research Organisation*] Division of Mathematical Statistics. Technical Paper

CSIRO Math Statist Div TP — CSIRO [*Commonwealth Scientific and Industrial Research Organisation*] Division of Mathematical Statistics. Technical Paper

CSIRO Mech Engng Div Circ — CSIRO [*Commonwealth Scientific and Industrial Research Organisation*] Division of Mechanical Engineering. Circular

CSIRO Mech Engng Div Rep — CSIRO [*Commonwealth Scientific and Industrial Research Organisation*] Division of Mechanical Engineering. Report

CSIRO Met Phys Div Tech Pap — CSIRO [*Commonwealth Scientific and Industrial Research Organisation*] Division of Meteorological Physics. Technical Paper

CSIRO Minerag Investig TP — CSIRO [*Commonwealth Scientific and Industrial Research Organisation*] Mineragraphic Investigations. Technical Paper

CSIRO Minerag Invest Tech Pap — CSIRO [*Commonwealth Scientific and Industrial Research Organisation*] Mineragraphic Investigations. Technical Paper

CSIRO Miner Phys Sect Invest Rep — CSIRO [*Commonwealth Scientific and Industrial Research Organisation*] Mineral Physics Section. Investigation Report

CSIRO Miner Res Lab Ann Rep — CSIRO [*Commonwealth Scientific and Industrial Research Organisation*] Minerals Research Laboratories. Annual Report

CSIRO Miner Res Lab Annu Rep — CSIRO [*Commonwealth Scientific and Industrial Research Organisation*] Minerals Research Laboratories. Annual Report

CSIRO Miner Res Lab Div Mineral Tech Commun — CSIRO [*Commonwealth Scientific and Industrial Research Organisation*] Minerals Research Laboratories. Division of Mineralogy. Technical Communication

CSIRO Miner Res Lab Invest Rep — CSIRO [*Commonwealth Scientific and Industrial Research Organisation*] Minerals Research Laboratories. Investigation Report

CSIRO Miner Res Lab Res Rev — CSIRO [*Commonwealth Scientific and Industrial Research Organisation*] Minerals Research Laboratories. Research Review

CSIRO Miner Res Lab Tech Commun — CSIRO [*Commonwealth Scientific and Industrial Research Organisation*] Minerals Research Laboratories. Technical Communication

CSIRO Natl Meas Lab Bienn Rep — CSIRO [*Commonwealth Scientific and Industrial Research Organisation*] National Measurement Laboratory. Biennial Report

CSIRO Natl Meas Lab Tech Pap — CSIRO [*Commonwealth Scientific and Industrial Research Organisation*] National Measurement Laboratory. Technical Paper

CSIRO Natl Measure Lab Biennial Rep — CSIRO [*Commonwealth Scientific and Industrial Research Organisation*] National Measurement Laboratory. Biennial Report

CSIRO Natl Stand Lab Bienn Rep — CSIRO [*Commonwealth Scientific and Industrial Research Organisation*] National Standards Laboratory. Biennial Report

CSIRO Nat Stand Lab Div Appl Phys Test Pamph — CSIRO [*Commonwealth Scientific and Industrial Research Organisation*] National Standards Laboratory. Division of Applied Physics. Test Pamphlet

CSIRO Nat Stands Lab Circ — CSIRO [*Commonwealth Scientific and Industrial Research Organisation*] National Standards Laboratory. Circular

CSIRO Nat Stands Lab Tech Pap — CSIRO [*Commonwealth Scientific and Industrial Research Organisation*] National Standards Laboratory. Technical Paper

CSIRO Nat Stands Lab Test Pamphl — CSIRO [*Commonwealth Scientific and Industrial Research Organisation*] National Standards Laboratory. Test Pamphlet

CSIRO Nat Stands Lab TP — CSIRO [*Commonwealth Scientific and Industrial Research Organisation*] National Standards Laboratory. Technical Paper

CSIROOA Bul — CSIROOA Bulletin. Journal of the Association of Officers of the Commonwealth Scientific and Industrial Research Organisation

CSIRO Phys Met Sec Tech Pap — CSIRO [*Commonwealth Scientific and Industrial Research Organisation*] Physical Metallurgy Section. Technical Paper

CSIRO Plant Ind Div Field Sta Rec — CSIRO [*Commonwealth Scientific and Industrial Research Organisation*] Division of Plant Industry. Field Station Record

CSIRO Plant Ind Div Field Stn Rec — CSIRO [*Commonwealth Scientific and Industrial Research Organisation*] Division of Plant Industry. Field Station Record

CSIRO Plant Ind Div Tech Pap — CSIRO [*Commonwealth Scientific and Industrial Research Organisation*] Division of Plant Industry. Technical Paper

CSIRO Plant Ind Div TP — CSIRO [*Commonwealth Scientific and Industrial Research Organisation*] Division of Plant Industry. Technical Paper

CSIRO Plant Ind TP — CSIRO [*Commonwealth Scientific and Industrial Research Organisation*] Division of Plant Industry. Technical Paper

CSIRO Radiophys Div Rept — CSIRO [*Commonwealth Scientific and Industrial Research Organisation*] Division of Radiophysics. Report

CSIRO Sci Index — CSIRO [*Commonwealth Scientific and Industrial Research Organisation*] Science Index

CSIRO Soil Mechanics Sect Geotech Rep — CSIRO [*Commonwealth Scientific and Industrial Research Organisation*] SoilMechanics Section. Geotechnical Report

CSIRO Soil Mechanics Sect Tech Rep — CSIRO [*Commonwealth Scientific and Industrial Research Organisation*] SoilMechanics Section. Technical Report

CSIRO Soil Mech Div Tech Pap — CSIRO [*Commonwealth Scientific and Industrial Research Organisation*] Division of Soil Mechanics. Technical Paper

CSIRO Soil Mech Div Tech Rep — CSIRO [*Commonwealth Scientific and Industrial Research Organisation*] Division of Soil Mechanics. Technical Report

CSIRO Soil Mech Sect Tech Rep — CSIRO [*Commonwealth Scientific and Industrial Research Organisation*] SoilMechanics Section. Technical Report

CSIRO Soil Pub — CSIRO [*Commonwealth Scientific and Industrial Research Organisation*] SoilPublications

CSIRO Soils Div SLU — CSIRO [*Commonwealth Scientific and Industrial Research Organisation*] Division of Soils. Soils and Land Use Series

CSIRO Text Ind Div Rep — CSIRO [*Commonwealth Scientific and Industrial Research Organisation*] Division of Textile Industry. Report

CSIRO Text News — CSIRO [*Commonwealth Scientific and Industrial Research Organisation*] WoodResearch Laboratory. Textile News

CSIRO Text Phys Div Rep — CSIRO [*Commonwealth Scientific and Industrial Research Organisation*] Division of Textile Physics. Report

CSIRO Trop Pastures Div TP — CSIRO [*Commonwealth Scientific and Industrial Research Organisation*] Division of Tropical Pastures. Technical Paper

CSIRO Wheat Res Unit Annu Rep — CSIRO [*Commonwealth Scientific and Industrial Research Organisation*] Wheat Research Unit. Annual Report

CSIRO Wildl Res — CSIRO [*Commonwealth Scientific and Industrial Research Organisation*] Wildlife Research

CSIRO Wildl Res Div Tech Pap — CSIRO [*Commonwealth Scientific and Industrial Research Organisation*] Division of Wildlife Research. Technical Paper

CSIRO Wildl Res Div TP — CSIRO [*Commonwealth Scientific and Industrial Research Organisation*] Division of Wildlife Research. Technical Paper

CSIRO Wildl Surv Sect TP — CSIRO [*Commonwealth Scientific and Industrial Research Organisation*] Wildlife Survey Section. Technical Paper

CSIRO Wool Text News — CSIRO [*Commonwealth Scientific and Industrial Research Organisation*] Division of Textile Industry. Wool Textile News

CSIRO Wool Text Res Labs Rep — CSIRO [*Commonwealth Scientific and Industrial Research Organisation*] WoolTextile Research Laboratories. Report

CSIRO Wool Text Res Labs TC — CSIRO [*Commonwealth Scientific and Industrial Research Organisation*] WoolTextile Research Laboratories. Trade Circular

CSIRO Wool Text Res Labs TP — CSIRO [*Commonwealth Scientific and Industrial Research Organisation*] WoolTextile Research Laboratories. Technical Paper

CSIR Rep BOU — CSIR [*South African Council for Scientific and Industrial Research*] Report BOU

CSIR Rep CENG — CSIR (South African Council for Scientific and Industrial Research) Report CENG

CSIR Res Rep — CSIR [*Council for Scientific and Industrial Research*] Research Report

CSIR Res Rep BOU — CSIR (South African Council for Scientific and Industrial Research) Research Report BOU

CSIR Res Rev — CSIR [*Council for Scientific and Industrial Research*] Research Review

CSIR Spec Rep BOU — CSIR (South African Council for Scientific and Industrial Research) Special Report Series BOU

CSIR Spec Rep CENG — CSIR [*South African Council for Scientific and Industrial Research*] Special Report. Series CENG

CSIR Spec Rep FIS — CSIR [*Council for Scientific and Industrial Research*] Special Report FIS

CSIR Spec Rep HOUT — CSIR [*South African Council for Scientific and Industrial Research*] Special Report HOUT

CSIR Spec Rep WISK — CSIR (South African Council for Scientific and Industrial Research) Special Report. Series WISK

CSIR Zool Monogr — CSIR [*Council for Scientific and Industrial Research*] Zoological Monograph

CSIS (Cent Strategic Int Stud) Energy Policy Ser — CSIS (Center for Strategic and International Studies) Energy Policy Series

CSISRS — Cross Section Information Storage and Retrieval System

CSJ — Casopis pro Slovanske Jazyky, Literaturu, a Dejiny SSSR

CSJ — Christian Science Journal

CSJ — Civil Service Journal

CSJ — Computer Security Journal

CSJ — Crime and Social Justice

C S J — Quarterly Journal of the Chemical Society of London

CSJP — Cahiers Saint-John Perse

CSJR — Contemporary Sociology. Journal of Reviews

CSKKA — Chikusan Shikenjo Kenkyu

CSKNA — Ceskoslovenska Neurologie [*Later, Ceskoslovenska Neurologie a Neurochirurgie*]

CSL — Cambridge Studies in Linguistics

CSL — Columbia University Studies in Literature

CSL — Corpus Scriptorum Ecclesiasticorum Latinorum

CSL — Scanshore

CSLBull — C. S. Lewis Society. Bulletin

CSLHA — Chartered Surveyor. Land Hydrographic and Minerals Quarterly

CSLJa — Casopis pro Slovanske Jazyky, Literaturu, a Dejiny SSSR

Cslka Derm — Ceskoslovenska Dermatologie

Cslka Farm — Ceskoslovenska Farmacie

Cslka Fysiol — Ceskoslovenska Fysiologie

Cslka Stomat — Ceskoslovenska Stomatologie

CSLN — California State Library Newsletter

CSLP — Canadian Slavonic Papers

CSLR — Cleveland State Law Review

CSM — Casopis Slezskeho Muzea

CSM — Christian Science Monitor

CSMA Proc Mid Year Meet — CSMA. Proceedings. Mid-Year Meeting

CSMBDC — Cambridge Studies in Mathematical Biology

CSMC — Ciencias Sociales. Colombia (Medillin)

CSMDA — Canadian Services Medical Journal

CSMDAF — Canadian Services Medical Journal

CSMIA — Mineral Industries Bulletin. Colorado School of Mines

CSM J — CSM (Camborne School of Mines) Journal

CSMJAX — Connecticut State Medical Journal

CSMLA5 — Comunicaciones. Sociedad Malacologica del Uruguay

CSMLT — Cambridge Studies in Medieval Life and Thought

C S Mm — Memoirs and Proceedings of the Chemical Society of London

CSMMCA — Clinical Science and Molecular Medicine

CSMMS — Christian Science Monitor. Magazine Section

C S Mon Mag — Christian Science Monitor. Magazine Section

CSMQD — Colorado School of Mines. Quarterly

CSMRCP — Australia. Commonwealth Scientific and Industrial Research Organisation. Minerals Research Laboratories. Annual Report

CSMSF XII — Duodecimo Convegno di Scienze Morali, Storiche, e Filogiche. Oriente ed Occidente nel Medio Evo. Rome, 1956. Publications

CSN — Caribbean Studies Newsletter

CSN — Cuban Studies Newsletter

Cs Neur — Ceskoslovenska Neurologie [*Later, Ceskoslovenska Neurologie a Neurochirurgie*]

CSNI Rep — CSNI (Committee on the Safety of Nuclear Installation) Report

CSNI Spec Meet Saf Aspects Fuel Behav Off Norm Accid Cond — CSNI [*Committee on the Safety of Nuclear Installation*] Specialist Meetingon Safety Aspects of Fuel Behaviour in Off-Normal and Accident Conditions

CSNI Spec Meet Transient Two Phase Flow — CSNI (Committee on the Safety of Nuclear Installation) Specialist Meeting on Transient Two-Phase Flow

CSNSAV — Australia. Commonwealth Scientific and Industrial Research Organisation. National Standards Laboratory. Biennial Report

CSO — Cuba Socialista

CSO — Maandstatistiek Financiewezen

CSoc — Cuba Socialista

C Soc — Current Sociology

C Soc Dem Med — Cahiers de Sociologie et de Demographie Medicales

C Soc Econ — Cahiers de Sociologie Economique

C Societa — Cinema Societa

C Sociol Demogr Medic — Cahiers de Sociologie et de Demographie Medicales

Cs Oft — Ceskoslovenska Oftalmologie

C Sol St Phys — Comments on Solid State Physics

Cs Onkol — Ceskoslovenska Onkologie

CSOPAR — Casopis Ceskoslovenske. Spolecnosti Entomologicke

CSOSA — Communications in Soil Science and Plant Analysis

CSOSA2 — Communications in Soil Science and Plant Analysis

CSov — Cultura Sovietica

CSP — Cahiers du Seminaire Ch. Gide

CSP — Cahiers Sextil Puscariu

CSP — California State Publications

CSP — Canadian Slavonic Papers
CSP — Catholic School Paper
CSp — Ceskoslovensky Spisovatel
CSP — Chinese Studies in Philosophy
CSP — Contents of Selected Periodicals
CSP — Cuban Studies (Pittsburgh)
C S P — Proceedings of the Chemical Society
CSPADO — Comunicaciones. INIA [*Instituto Nacional de Investigaciones Agrarias*]. Serie Produccion Animal
Cs Parasit — Ceskoslovenska Parasitologie
Cs Pediat — Ceskoslovenska Pediatrie
CSPG Mem — CSPG [*Canadian Society of Petroleum Geologists*] Memoir
CSPG Reservoir — Canadian Society of Petroleum Geologists. Reservoir
CSPh — Cornell Studies in Classical Philology
CSPHA — Contributions to Sensory Physiology
CSPHA8 — Contributions to Sensory Physiology
CSPJA — Canadian Aeronautics and Space Journal
CSPM — Catalogue of Egyptian Scarabs, Scaraboids, Seals, and Amulets in the Palestine Archeological Museum
CSPMBO — Conseil International pour l'Exploration de la Mer. Bulletin Statistique des Peches Maritimes
CSPSD — Canadian Special Publication of Fisheries and Aquatic Sciences
CSPSDA — Canadian Special Publication of Fisheries and Aquatic Sciences
CSPSR — Chinese Social and Political Science Review
Cs Psych — Ceskoslovenska Psychiatrie
Cs Psych — Ceskoslovenska Psychologie
CSP-T — Contents of Selected Periodicals - Technical
CSQ — Christian Science Quarterly
CSQ Comput Statist Quart — Computational Statistics Quarterly
CSR — Cell Surface Reviews
CsR — Ceskoslovenska Rusistika
CSR — Christian Scholar's Review
CSR — Continental Shelf Research
CSR Agric Circ — CSR [*Colonial Sugar Refining Company Limited*] Agricultural Circular
C S R Bul — Council on the Study of Religion. Bulletin
CSREDC — Cell Surface Reviews
Cs Rentgen — Ceskoslovenska Rentgenologie
CSRG — Commission for Scientific Research in Greenland. Newsletter
CSRL — Cambridge Studies in Russian Literature
CSRP — Columbia University Studies in Romance Philology and Literature
CSRPB — Chemica Scripta
CSRQA — Chartered Surveyor. Rural Quarterly
CSRSAH — Colorado State University. Range Science Department. Range Science Series
CSRVB — Chemical Society. Reviews
CSS — California Slavic Studies
CSS — Canadian Slavic Studies
CSSA Spec Publ — CSSA [*Crop Science Society of America*] Special Publication
CSSCD — Communications in Statistics. Part B. Simulation and Computation
CSSH — Comparative Studies in Society and History
CSSI — Centro di Studi e Scambi Internationali [*Rome*]
CSSJ — Central States Speech Journal
CSSOP — Center for Settlement Studies. University of Manitoba. Series 5. Occasional Papers
CSSP — Circuits, Systems, and Signal Processing
CSSRR — Center for Settlement Studies. University of Manitoba. Series 2. Research Reports
CST — Chicago Sunday Tribune
CST — Coal Science and Technology
CSt — Colecao Studium
C St — Comunicazioni i Studi
CST — Constitution Federale
CST — Contemporary Studies in Theology
CST — Cost and Management
CSTA Can Soc Tech Agric Rev — CSTA (Canadian Society of Technical Agriculturists) Review
C Stand — Christian Standard
CSTA R — CSTA [*Canadian Society of Technical Agriculturists*] Review
CSTA Rev — CSTA [*Canadian Society of Technical Agriculturists*] Review
CSTB — Cahiers. Centre Scientifique et Technique du Batiment
CSTBC — Concelho de Santo Tirso. Boletim Cultural
CSTC — Ceskoslovensky Terminologicky Casopis
CST Combust Sci Technol — CST. Combustion Science and Technology
CSTC Rev — CSTC [*Centre Scientifique et Technique de la Construction*] Revue
CSTC Trim — Revue Trimestrielle. Centre Scientifique et Technique de la Construction
CSTHBT — Special Report. National Institute of Animal Industry
CSTM — Chicago Sunday Tribune Magazine
CSTNAC — Castanea
C Stor — Critica Storica
CSTRC — COMSAT [*Communications Satellite Corp.*] Technical Review
CSTWA — Chemia Stosowana
CSU — Consumers' Research Magazine
CSU — Cultura. UNESCO
CSUCA/ESC — Estudios Sociales Centroamericanos. Consejo Superior de Universidades Centroamericanas, Confederacion Universitaria Centroamericana, Programa Centroamericano de Ciencias Sociales
C Succ — Code des Droits de Succession
Csud — Cinemasud
CSVAH — Chronique. Societe Vervietoise d'Archeologie et d'Histoire
CSW — Cahiers Simone Weil
CSW — Chartered Surveyor Weekly
CSW — Computer Sports World
CSWPA — Chung-Kuo Shui Sheng Wu Hui Pao

CSWQ — Quarterly of the National Writing Project and the Center for the Study of Writing
CSY — CSCE [*Centre Senegalais du Commerce Exterieur*] Informations
CSYIB — Cargo Systems International
Cs Zdrav — Ceskoslovenske Zdravotnictvi
CT — Cahiers de Tunisie
CT — Cahiers Thomistes
CT — Canadian Token
CT — Canberra Times
CT — Catering Times
CT — Chamber Tombs at Mycenae
CT — Chemical Titles
CT — Chicago Tribune
CT — Children Today
CT — China To-Day
CT — Christianity Today
CT — Ciencia Tomista
CT — Circle Track
CT — Code des Droits de Timbre
CT — Collectanea Theologica
CT — Journal of Computed Tomography
CTA — Computer and Telecommunications Acronyms
CTAIHS — Collection de Travaux. Academie Internationale d'Histoire des Sciences [*Paris*]
CTAIR — Code des Taxes Assimilees aux Impots sur les Revenus
CTA J — CTA [*Cine Technicians' Association*] Journal
CT & FCD Circ — C.T. and F.C.D. (Office of Cotton, Truck, and Forest Crop Disease) Circular
CT Antiqua — Connecticut Antiquarian
CTA Q — CTA [*Chicago Transit Authority*] Quarterly
Ctary — Commentary
CTASD — China Science and Technology Abstracts
CTBR — Commonwealth Taxation Board of Review Decisions
CTBR NS — Commonwealth Taxation Board of Review Decisions. New Series
CTBROS — Commonwealth Taxation Board of Review Decisions. Old Series
CTC — Catalogus Translationum et Commentariorum. Medieval and Renaissance Latin Translations and Commentaries. Annotated Lists and Guides
CTC — Ceskoslovensky Terminologicky Casopis
CTC — Contract Journal
CTCEA — Current Therapeutic Research. Clinical and Experimental
Ct Cl Act — New York Court of Claims Act
CTCP — Clinical Toxicology of Commercial Products
CTCPD — Changchun Dizhi Xueyuan Xuebao
CTCRA — Current Topics in Cellular Regulation
CTCRDH — Australia Commonwealth Scientific and Industrial Research Organisation. Tropical Crops and Pastures. Divisional Report
CTD — Cahiers. Groupe Francois-Thureau-Dangin
CTD — Canadian Transportation and Distribution Management
C Td — Ceylon Today
CTD — Collana di Testi e Documenti per lo Studio dell'Antichita
CTD — Commission de Toponymie et Dialectologie
CTD — Corporate Technology Database
CTD — Cultuurtechnische Dienst
CTDBA — Current Topics in Developmental Biology
CTDS — Canadian Transportation Documentation System
CTEAA7 — Comunicados Tecnicos. Instituto de Ecologia e Experimentacao Agricolas
CTEEA — Current Topics in Experimental Endocrinology
CTEGA — Cutting Tool Engineering
Ctenija Obscestve Istorii Moskovsk Univers — Ctenija v Obscestve Istorii i Drevnostej Rossijskich pri Moskovskom Universitetie
CTER — Cuadernos de Trabajos. Escuela Espanola de Historia y Arqueologia. Roma
CTF — Continentaler Stahlmarkt (Frankfurt Am Main)
CTFA Cosmet J — CTFA [*Cosmetic, Toiletry, and Fragrance Association*] Cosmetic Journal
CTFA Sci Monogr Ser — CTFA (Cosmetic, Toiletry, and Fragrance Association) Scientific Monograph Series
CTFMD — Ciencias Tecnicas Fisicas y Matematicas
CTGAAH — Citrus Grower
CTH — Catalogue des Textes Hittites
CTHAAM — Contributions. Herbarium Australiense
CTHBAr — Comite des Travaux Historiques et Scientifiques. Bulletin Archeologique
CTHBull — Comite des Travaux Historiques et Scientifiques. Bulletin Archeologique
CTHBullH — Comite des Travaux Historiques et Scientifiques. Bulletin Historique et Philologique
CT Hist Soc Bull — Connecticut Historical Society Bulletin
CThM — Concordia Theological Monthly
CTI — Communication Technology Impact
CTI — Current Technology Index
CTI — Documentatieblad van het Centraal Orgaan van de Landelijke Opleidingsorganen van het Bedrijfsleven
CTIBBV — Contemporary Topics in Immunobiology
CTICD2 — Catalogue of Type Invertebrate Fossils. Geological Survey of Canada
CTI Commun Technol Impact — CTI. Communication Technology Impact
CTI J — CTI (Cooling Tower Institute) Journal
CTIPB5 — Carolina Tips
CTIX — Canadian Trade Index
CTJ — Calvin Theological Journal
CTJ — Canadian Tax Journal
CTJ — Canadian Textile Journal
CTJ — Cato Journal
CTJ — Concerned Theater of Japan
CTJ Can Text J — CTJ. Canadian Textile Journal
CT J Comput Tomogr — CT. Journal of Computed Tomography

CT J Comput Tomography — CT. Journal of Computed Tomography
CTJOA — Canadian Textile Journal
CTKIAR — Cell and Tissue Kinetics
CTL — Cahiers - Theatre Louvain
CTLF — Cuttlefish. Unalaska City School. Unalaska
CTLMAA — Cattleman
CTM — Concordia Theological Monthly
CTM — Contract Management
CTMIA — Current Topics in Microbiology and Immunology
CTMIA3 — Ergebnisse der Mikrobiologie und Immunitaetsforschung
CTMIB4 — Contemporary Topics in Molecular Immunology
CTMMEJ — Current Topics in Medical Mycology
CTMS — Current Topics in Materials Science
CTMTA2 — Current Topics in Membranes and Transport
CTN — China Trade Report
CTN — Codigo Tributario Nacional
CTNEEY — Current Topics in Neuroendocrinology
CTNOR — Canada. Task Force on Northern Oil Development. Report
C Today — Christianity Today
C Tom — Ciencia Tomista
CTOMD — Computerized Tomography
CTOMDS — Computerized Tomography
CTOXA — Clinical Toxicology
CTOXAO — Clinical Toxicology
CTP — Customs Tariff Proposals
CTPHBG — Ergebnisse der Pathologie
CTQ — Computable. Automatiseringsvakblad voor de Benelux
CTQ — Contemporary Thought Quarterly
CTR — Canadian Theatre Review
CTr — Code du Travail
CTR — COMSAT [*Communications Satellite Corp.*] Technical Review
C Tracts — Cine Tracts
C Trav — Code du Travail
CTRED — Cancer Treatment Reviews
CTREDJ — Cancer Treatment Reviews
CTRFAS — Canadian Technical Report of Fisheries and Aquatic Sciences
CTRHOS — Canadian Technical Report of Hydrography and Ocean Sciences
CTRMA6 — Citrus Magazine
CTRQA — Current Topics in Radiation Research. Quarterly
CTRR — Current Topics in Radiation Research
CTRRA — Current Topics in Radiation Research
CTRRD — Cancer Treatment Reports
CTRRDO — Cancer Treatment Reports
CTRSDR — Rapport Technique Canadien des Sciences Halieutiques et Aquatiques
CTRSES — Current Topics in Research on Synapses
Ctry Demogr Profiles — Country Demographic Profiles
Ctry Gentleman — Country Gentleman
Ctry J — Country Journal
Ctry Landowner — Country Landowner
Ctry Life — Country Life
Ctry Life Am — Country Life in America
Ctry Mag — Country Magazine
Ctry Profiles — Country Profiles
Ctry Women — Country Women
CTS — Centralized Title Service
CTSAP — Catholic Theological Society of America. Proceedings
CTSRC — Cell and Tissue Research
CTSRCS — Cell and Tissue Research
CTS Reg — Chicago Theological Seminary. Register
CTSYEH — Cancer Treatment Symposia
CTUBDP — Collection des Travaux. Universite de Brazzaville
C Tunisie — Cahiers de Tunisie
CTUSA5 — Comunicaciones. Instituto Tropical de Investigaciones Cientificas
CTV — Computer Trade Video
CTV — Cotton. Monthly Review of the World Situation
CTVMDT — Current Topics in Veterinary Medicine
CTXBA3 — Clinical Toxicology Bulletin
CTY — Caribbean Today
CTYKA — Ch'uan-Kuo Ti-I-Chieh Yeh-Chin Kuo-Ch Eng Wu-Li Hua-Hsueh Hsueh-Shu Pao-Kao-HuiLun-Wen Chi
Cty Rep Calif Div Mines Geol — County Report. California. Division of Mines and Geology
Cty Rep Idaho Bur Mines Geol — County Report. Idaho. Bureau of Mines and Geology
Cty Rep K Geol Surv — County Report. Kentucky Geological Survey
Cty Rep Miss Board Water Comm — County Report. Mississippi Board of Water Commissioners
Cty Resour Ser Geol Surv Wyo — County Resource Series. Geological Survey of Wyoming
CTZ — Capital. Das Deutsche Wirtschaftsmagazin
CU — Canadian Underwriter
CU — Cultura Universitaria
Cu A — Cuadernos Americanos
CUA — Cuadernos. Universidad del Aire
CUA/AQ — Anthropological Quarterly. Catholic University of America. Catholic Anthropological Conference
CUAB — Catholic University of America. Bulletin
CUAD — Cuadernos del Congreso
Cuad A (Barcel) — Cuadernos de Arqueologia e Historia de la Ciudad (Barcelona)
Cuad A Colon — Cuadernos de Arte Colonial
Cuad Actual Tec Asoc Argent Consorcios Reg Exp Agric — Cuaderno de Actualizacion Tecnica. Asociacion Argentina de Consorcios Regionales de Experimentacion Agricola
Cuad Afr Or — Cuadernos Africanos y Orientales
Cuad Alhambra — Cuadernos de la Alhambra

Cuad Am — Cuadernos Americanos. La Revista del Nuevo Mundo
Cuad Amer — Cuadernos Americanos
Cuad Am Mex — Cuadernos Americanos (Mexico)
Cuad Antrop — Cuadernos de Antropologia
Cuad Antrop Guat — Cuadernos de Antropologia (Guatemala)
Cuad Antropol — Cuadernos de Antropologia
Cuad Antrop Social — Cuadernos de Antropologia Social
Cuad Area Cienc Mar — Cuadernos da Area de Ciencias Marinas
Cuad Arqueol Hist Ciudad — Cuadernos de Arqueologia e Historia de la Ciudad
Cuad Arquit — Cuadernos de Arquitectura
Cuad Arquit & Conserv Patrm A — Cuadernos de Arquitectura y Conservacion del Patrimonio Artistico
Cuad Arquit & Urb — Cuadernos de Arquitectura y Urbanismo
Cuad Arquit Mesoamer — Cuadernos de Arquitectura Mesoamericana
Cuad Arquit Urban — Cuadernos de Arquitectura y Urbanismo
Cuad Art Poesia Quito — Cuadernos de Arte y Poesia (Quito)
Cuad A U Granada — Cuadernos de Arte de la Universidad de Granada
Cuad Bell Art Mex — Cuadernos de Bellas Artes (Mexico)
Cuad Bibliog — Cuadernos Bibliograficos
Cuad Catedra M Unamuno — Cuadernos. Catedra Miguel de Unamuno
Cuad Cienc Biol Univ Granada — Cuadernos de Ciencias Biologicas. Universidad de Granada
Cuad Cirug — Cuadernos de Cirugia
Cuad Congr Liber Cult — Cuadernos del Congreso por la Libertad de la Cultura
Cuad Cult — Cuaderno Cultural
Cuad Cult — Cuadernos de la Cultura
Cuad Cult Pop — Cuadernos de Cultura Popular
Cuad CVF — Cuadernos de la Corporacion Venezolana de Fomento
Cuad Dominicanos Cult — Cuadernos Dominicanos de Cultura
Cuad Econ (Barcelona) — Cuadernos de Economia (Barcelona)
Cuad Econ (Santiago) — Cuadernos de Economia (Santiago)
Cuadern Algebra — Cuadernos de Algebra
Cuadern Inst Mat Beppo Levi — Cuadernos. Instituto de Matematica Beppo Levi
Cuadernos Cristianismo Soc — Cuadernos de Cristianismo y Sociedad
Cuadernos H — Cuadernos Hispanoamericanos
Cuadernos Hist Prim — Cuadernos de Historia Primitiva
Cuadernos Preh Granada — Cuadernos de Prehistoria. Universidad de Granada
Cuadernos Preh Granada — Cuadernos de Prehistoria. Universidad de Granda
Cuadern Teorema — Cuadernos Teorema
Cuad Est Afr — Cuadernos de Estudios Africanos
Cuad Est Africanos — Cuadernos de Estudios Africanos
Cuad Est Gallegos — Cuadernos de Estudios Gallegos
Cuad Est Manchegos — Cuadernos de Estudios Manchegos
Cuad Estud Borjanos — Cuadernos de Estudios Borjanos
Cuad Estud Gallegos — Cuadernos de Estudios Gallegos
Cuad Estud Manchegos — Cuadernos de Estudios Manchegos
Cuad Estud Yucat Merida — Cuadernos de Estudios Yucatecos (Merida, Yucatan)
Cuad Etnol & Etnog Navarra — Cuadernos de Etnologia y Etnografia de Navarra
Cuad Fac Panama — Cuadernos de las Facultades. Universidad de Panama (Panama)
Cuad Fil — Cuadernos de Filosofia
Cuad Fil Cl — Cuadernos de Filologia Clasica
Cuad Filo Clas — Cuadernos de Filologia Clasica
Cuad Filol Cl — Cuadernos de Filologia Clasica
Cuad Filosof — Cuadernos de Filosofia
Cuad Gall — Cuadernos de Estudios Gallegos
Cuad Gallegos — Cuadernos de Estudios Gallegos
Cuad Geogr Col Bogota — Cuadernos de Geografia de Colombia (Bogota)
Cuad Geogr Colom — Cuadernos de Geografia de Colombia
Cuad Geol Iber — Cuadernos de Geologia Iberica
Cuad Geol Univ Granada — Cuadernos de Geologia. Universidad de Granada
Cuad (Granada) — Cuadernos de Prehistoria (Universidad de Granada)
Cuad Hisp — Cuadernos Hispanoamericanos
Cuad Hisp Am — Cuadernos Hispanoamericanos. Instituto de Cultura Hispanica
Cuad Hispamer — Cuadernos Hispanoamericanos
Cuad Hist & Arqueol — Cuadernos de Historia y Arqueologia
Cuad Hist Arqueol Guayaquil — Cuadernos de Historia y Arqueologia (Guayaquil)
Cuad Hist Art Mendoza — Cuadernos de Historia del Arte (Mendoza, Argentina)
Cuad Hist Econ Cataluna — Cuadernos de Historia de la Economia Catuluna
Cuad Hist Esp — Cuadernos de Historia de Espana
Cuad Hist Espan — Cuadernos de Historia de Espana
Cuad Hist Med Esp — Cuadernos de Historia de la Medicina Espanola
Cuad Hist Med Espan — Cuadernos de Historia de la Medicina Espanola
Cuad Hist Primit — Cuadernos de Historia Primitiva
Cuad Hist Salud Publica — Cuadernos de Historia de la Salud Publica
Cuad Hist Sanit — Cuadernos de Historia Sanitaria
Cuad Idioma BA — Cuadernos del Idioma (Buenos Aires)
Cuad Inform Econ Caracas — Cuadernos de Informacion Economica. Corporacion Venezolana de Fomento (Caracas)
Cuad Inform Econ Sociol — Cuadernos de Informacion Economica y Sociologica
Cuad Inst Antrop B Aires — Cuadernos del Instituto Nacional de Antropologia (Buenos Aires)
Cuad Inst Hist (Mex) — Cuadernos. Instituto de Historia (Mexico)
Cuad Inst Hist Ser Antr — Cuadernos. Instituto de Historia. Seria Antropologica
Cuad Inst Nac Antrop BA — Cuadernos. Instituto Nacional de Antropologia (Buenos Aires)
Cuad Inst Nac Antropol — Cuadernos. Instituto Nacional de Antropologia
Cuad Inst Nac Invest Folk BA — Cuadernos. Instituto Nacional de Investigaciones Folkloricas (Buenos Aires)
Cuad Int Hist Psicosoc Arte — Cuadernos Internacionales de Historia Psicosocial del Arte
Cuad Invest IETCC — Cuadernos de Investigacion. IETCC
Cuad Invest Inst Eduardo Torroja Constr Cem — Cuaderno de Investigacion. Instituto Eduardo Torroja de la Construccion y del Cemento
Cuad Laborales — Cuadernos Laborales

Cuad Latinoam Econ Humana Monte — Cuadernos Latinoamericanos de Economia Humana (Montevideo)
Cuad Lima — Cuadernos. Centro de Estudiantes de Antropologia. Universidad Mayor de San Marcos (Lima)
Cuad Literatura — Cuadernos de Literatura. CSIC (Consejo Superior de Investigaciones Cientificas)
Cuad Manch — Cuadernos de Estudios Manchegos
Cuad Marcha — Cuadernos de Marcha
Cuad Med — Cuadernos Medicos
Cuad Med Divulg Cient — Cuadernos Medicos y de Divulgacion Cientifico
Cuad Min Geol Univ Tuc — Cuadernos de Mineralogia y Geologia. Universidad de Tucuman
Cuad Num — Cuadernos de Numismatica
Cuad Oceanogr Univ Oriente (Cumana) — Cuadernos Oceanograficos. Universidad de Oriente (Cumana)
Cuad Orient — Cuadernos de Orientacion
Cuad Paris — Cuadernos (Paris)
Cuad P Arq Cast — Cuadernos de Prehistoria y Arqueologia Castellonense
Cuad Ped — Cuadernos de Pedagogia
Cuad Pol — Cuadernos Politicos
Cuad Pol Int — Cuadernos de Politica Internacional
Cuad Prehispan — Cuadernos Prehispanicos
Cuad Prehist & Arqueol Castellonenses — Cuadernos de Prehistoria y Arqueologia Castellonenses
Cuad Pr Hist A — Cuadernos de Prehistoria y Arqueologia
Cuad Realidades Socs — Cuadernos de Realidades Sociales
Cuad Rom — Cuadernos de Trabajos. Escuela Espanola de Historia y Arqueologia en Roma
Cuad Ruedo Iber — Cuadernos de Ruedo Iberico
Cuad Seminario Hist Lima — Cuadernos. Seminario de Historia (Lima)
Cuad Sind — Cuadernos. Centro de Estudios Sindicales
Cuad Spain Inst Nac Invest Agron — Cuaderno. Spain. Instituto Nacional de Investigaciones Agronomicas
Cuad Sur — Cuadernos del Sur
Cuad Teol — Cuadernos Teologicos
Cuad U — Cuadernos Universitarios
Cuad Univ Leon — Cuadernos Universitarios (Leon, Nicaragua)
Cuad Urb — Cuadernos de Urbanismo
CuaH — Cuadernos Hispanoamericanos
CUALR — Catholic University of America. Law Review
CUAN — Current Anthropology
CUAPS — Catholic University of America. Patristic Studies
CUAS — Catholic University of America. Anthropological Series
CUASRL — Catholic University of America. Studies in Romance Languages and Literatures
CUASRLL — Catholic University of America. Studies in Romance Languages and Literatures
CUB — Catholic University. Bulletin
CUBA — College and University Business Administration, Administrative Service
Cuba — Cubatimes
Cuba Agric — Cuba Agricola
Cuba Bibl — Cuba Bibliotecologica
Cuba Bibliotec Hav — Cuba Bibliotecologica (La Habana)
Cuba Bibliotecol — Cuba Bibliotecologica. Colegio Nacional de Bibliotecarios Universitarios
Cuba Contemp — Cuba Contemporanea
Cuba Dir Montes B Minas — Cuba. Direccion de Montes y Minas. Boletin de Minas
Cubal — Cuba Internacional
CubaL — Cuba Literaria
Cuba Min Agric Jur Bol — Cuba Ministerio de la Agricultura Juridico. Boletin
Cuba Min Com Ext Rev — Cuba Ministerio del Commerco Exterior. Revista
CubaN — Cuba Nueva
Cuban J Agric Sci — Cuban Journal of Agricultural Science
Cuba Not Econ — Cuba Noticias Economicas
Cuban Stud — Cuban Studies/Estudios Cubanos
CubaR — Cuba Review
Cuba Revw — Cuba Review
Cuba Soc — Cuba Socialista
CUBBA2 — Contribuciones Cientificas. Facultad de Ciencias Exactas y Naturales. Universidad de Buenos Aires. Serie Botanica
Cu Bi — Cultura Biblica
CuBib — Cultura Biblica
CUC — Cahiers Universitaires Catholiques
CUC — Cultura Universitaria (Caracas)
CUCA — Columbia University. Contributions to Anthropology
CuCanI — Cuadernos Canarios de Investigacion
CUCB — Colegio Universitario de Cayey. Boletin
CUCD Bulletin — Bulletin. Council of University Classical Departments
CUC Gaz — Canberra University College. Gazette
CU Chemieunterr — CU. Der Chemieunterricht
CUC News — C.U.C. (Coal Utilisation Council) News
CuCo — Cursos y Conferencias
Cudd Copyh — Cuddon. Copyhold Acts
CUDPB — Chile. Universidad. Departamento de Astronomia. Publicaciones
CUE — Corpus delle Urne Etrusche di Eta Ellenistica
CUE — Credit Union Executive
Cue — Cue Sheet
Cu EG — Cuadernos de Estudios Gallegos
CUE J — Computer Using Educators of BC [British Columbia] Journal
Cu EM — Cuadernos de Estudios Manchegos
CUF — Collection des Universites de France. Association Guillaume Bude
CUF — Columbia University. Forum
CUFRB3 — Clemson University. Department of Forestry. Forest Research Series
CUFTA8 — Clemson University. Department of Forestry. Technical Paper

CUG — Credit Union Magazine
CUG — Cuadernos Universitarios (Guatemala)
CUGS — Columbia University. Germanic Studies
CUH — Caribe Universidad de Hawaii
CuH — Cuadernos Hispanoamericanos
Cu H — Current History
Cuir Tech — Cuir Technique
Cuir Tech Suppl — Cuir Technique. Supplement
CUIVA — Cuivre, Laitons, Alliages
CUJ — CPCU [Chartered Property and Casualty Underwriters] Journal
CU/JIA — Journal of International Affairs. Columbia University. School of International Affairs
CUJSD — Cheju University. Journal (South Korea)
CUK — Cuir. Journal Trihebdomadaire d'Informations du Cuir et de la Chaussure
CUKOA — Cukoripar
Cukoripar Mellek — Cukoripar, Melleklet
Cukorip Kutatointez Kozl — Cukoripari Kutatointezet Kozlemenyel
Cukurova Univ Tip Fak Derg — Cukurova Universitesi Tip Fakultesi Dergisi
CUL — Cultura
Cul — Culture
Cul — Culture. Revue Trimestrielle, Sciences Religieuses et Sciences Profanes au Canada
Cul Dair Prod J — Cultured Dairy Products Journal
CULE — Cultura (Ecuador)
CulEA — Cultural Events in Africa
Culegere Articole Consfatuire Tara Mater Electroteh — Culegere de Articole de la Consfatuire pe Tara de Materiale Electrotehnice
Culegere Lucr Meteorol Inst Meteorol Hidrol — Culegere de Lucrari de Meteorologie ale Institutului de Meteorologie si Hidrologie
CulF — Culture Francaise
CulFP — Culture Francaise (Paris)
CulH — Cultural Hermeneutics
Culham Lab UK At Energy Auth Rep CLM R — Culham Laboratory. United Kingdom Atomic Energy Authority. Report CLM-R
CULP — California Union List of Periodicals
CULR — Catholic University. Law Review
Cul Stud Cerc (Brasov) — Culegere de Studii si Cercetari (Brasov)
Cult — Cultura
Cult — Culture
Cult & Soc — Culture et Societe. Revue des Civilisations
Cult Anthrop — Cultural Anthropology
Cult Anthrop Meth Newsl — CAM the Cultural Anthropology Methods Newsletter
Cult Atesina — Cultura Atesina
Cult B — Cultura Biblica
CultBib — Cultura Biblica
CultBibl — Cultura Biblica
Cult Biblica — Cultura Biblica
Cult Boliviana Oruro — Cultura Boliviana (Oruro, Bolivia)
Cult Corr — Cultural Correspondence
Cult Dairy Prod J — Cultured Dairy Products Journal
Cult Divers Ment Health — Cultural Diversity and Mental Health
Cult Dynam — Cultural Dynamics
Cult Energ Biomassa — Culturas Energeticas. Biomassa
Cult Esp — Cultura Espanola
Cult et Authenticite — Culture et Authenticite. Revue Zairoise d'Orientation Culturelle
Cult et Devel — Cultures et Developpement
Cult Forum — Cultural Forum
Cult Fr — Culture Francaise
Cult Franc — Culture Francaise
Cult Guat — Cultura de Guatemala
Cult Hermen — Cultural Hermeneutics
Cult Hist — Culture and History
Cult Hombre Soc — Cultura, Hombre, Sociedad
Cult Indie — Cultureel Indie
Cultivator NY Agri Soc — Cultivator. New York State Agricultural Society
Cultiv Indus La Plata — Cultivos Industriales (La Plata, Argentina)
Cultiv Mod — Cultivador Moderno
Cult Jb Prov Oostvlaanderen — Cultureel Jaarboek voor de Provincie Oostvlaanderen
Cult Med — Cultura Medica
Cult Med Mod — Cultura Medica Moderna
Cult Med Psych — Culture, Medicine, and Psychiatry
Cult Med Psychiatry — Culture, Medicine, and Psychiatry
Cult Mex Mex — Cultura Mexico (Mexico)
Cult Mod — Cultivador Moderno
Cult Mod — Cultura Moderna
Cult Neol — Cultura Neolatina
Cult Neolat — Cultura Neolatina
Cult Peru — Cultura Peruana
Cult Pol Rio — Cultura Politica (Rio de Janeiro)
Cult Pop Alban — Culture Populaire Albanaise
Cult Resour Rep US For Serv Southwest Reg — Cultural Resource Report. United States Forest Service. Southwestern Region
Cult Sc — Cultura e Scuola
Cult Sci — Cultura Scientifica
Cult Scu — Cultura e Scuola
Cult Scuol — Cultura e Scuola
Cult S Salvador — Cultura (San Salvador)
Cult Stomat — Cultura Stomatologica
Cult Stud — Cultural Studies
Cult Surv — Cultural Survival Newsletter
Cult Survival Q — Cultural Survival Quarterly
Cult Trad — Culture and Tradition
Cult Tunja — Cultura (Tunja, Colombia)

Cult Univ — Cultura Universitaria
Cult Universitaria — Cultura Universitaria. Universidad Central de Venezuela
Cultural Cor — Cultural Correspondence
Cultura Med Mod — Cultura Medica Moderna
Cultur Divers Ethni Minor Psychol — Cultural Diversity & Ethnic Minority Psychology
Cultures au Zaire et en Afr — Cultures au Zaire et en Afrique
Cultures et Dev — Cultures et Developpement
CulZ — Culture de Zaiere et d'Afrique
CUM — Credit Union Management
Cumana Univ Oriente Inst Oceanogr Bol — Cumana. Universidad de Oriente. Instituto Oceanografico. Boletin
Cumb — Cumberland Law Journal
Cumb and West AAST — Cumberland and Westmorland Antiquarian and Archaeological Society. Transactions
CUMBB — Currents in Modern Biology
Cumberland LJ (PA) — Cumberland Law Journal
Cumberland L Rev — Cumberland Law Review
Cumberland-Samford — Cumberland-Samford Law Review
Cumberland-Samford L Rev — Cumberland-Samford Law Review
Cumberland Sem — Cumberland Seminarian
Cumber-Sam L Rev — Cumberland-Samford Law Review
Cum B Ind — Cumulative Book Index
Cumb Law Jrnl — Cumberland Law Journal
Cumb L Rev — Cumberland Law Review
Cum Book — Cumulative Book Index
Cumb Q — Cumberland Presbyterian Quarterly Review
Cum Bull — Cumulative Bulletin
Cum Comput Abstr — Cumulative Computer Abstracts
CUMFID — Cahiers des Utilisateurs des Machines a des Fins d'Information et de Documentation
CUMHDA — Contributions. University of Michigan Herbarium
CUMIA — Coeur et Medecine Interne
CUMIAA — Coeur et Medecine Interne
Cumidava — Cumidava Culegere de Studii si Cercetari
Cum LR — Cumberland Law Review
Cum L Rev — Cumberland Law Review
CUMOA — Cultivador Moderno
CUMR — Canadian University. Music Review
Cum-Sam — Cumberland-Samford Law Review
Cumul Index Med — Cumulated Index Medicus
Cumul Index Nurs Allied Health Lit — Cumulative Index to Nursing and Allied Health Literature
Cumul Index Nurs Lit — Cumulative Index to Nursing Literature
CUN — Cours de l'Universite Nouvelle
CUN — Cuadernos Universitarios (Nicaragua)
Cu N — Cultura Neolatina
CUn — Cultura Universitaria
CUNESCO — Cuba en la UNESCO
C Univ Nev Coop Ext Serv Max C Fleischmann Coll Agric — C. University of Nevada. Cooperative Extension Service. Max C. Fleischmann College of Agriculture
Cunobelin — Cunobelin Yearbook. British Association of Numismatic Societies
CUNY/CP — Comparative Politics. City University of New York, Political Science Program
CUNZA — Chemie in Unserer Zeit
CUO — Current Sociology
Cuore Circ — Cuore e Circolazione
Cuore Circol — Cuore e Circolazione
CUP — Cupey
CUPAD — Current Energy Patents
Cupola Oper State of the Art Proc AFS CMI Conf — Cupola Operation. State of the Art. Proceedings of AFS-CMI (American Foundrymen's Society. Cast Metals Institute) Conference
CUQ — Columbia University. Quarterly
CUR — University of Colorado. Law Review
CURABA — Current Archives Bibliography Australia
Cur Accts — Current Accounts
Cur Anthro — Current Anthropology
Cur Anthrop — Current Anthropology
Cur Anthropol — Current Anthropology
Cur Backg — Current Background
Cur Bibliog African Affairs — Current Bibliography on African Affairs
Cur Biog — Current Biography
Cur Biog Yrbk — Current Biography Yearbook
Cur Brit For Pol — Current British Foreign Policy
Cur Carib Bibliogr Port Of Spain — Current Caribbean Bibliography (Port of Spain, Trinidad)
Cur C Clin Prac — Current Contents Clinical Practice
Cur Ev — Current Events
CurH — Current History
Cur Health — Current Health
Cur His — Current History
Cur Hist — Current History
Cur Hist M NY Times — Current History Magazine of the New York Times
Curierul Farm — Curierul Farmaceutic
Curiosita & Ric Stor Subalp — Curiosita e Ricerche di Storia Subalpina
Cur Issues Higher Ed — Current Issues in Higher Education
Cur Issues Higher Educ Ann Ser — Current Issues in Higher Education. Annual Series
Cur J Rec — Current Jewish Record
CURL — Children's Understanding of Reading Language
Cur Lab Dev — Current Labour Developments
Cur Leg Thought — Current Legal Thought [*New York*]
Cur Lit — Current Literature

Cur Muni Prob — Current Municipal Problems
Cur Opinion — Current Opinion
Cur Pod — Current Podiatry
Cur Psychol Res — Current Psychological Research
Cur Psychol Rev — Current Psychological Reviews
Cur R — Curriculum Review
Curr Abstr Chem Index Chem — Current Abstracts of Chemistry and Index Chemicus
Curr Adv Androl Proc Int Congr Androl — Current Advances in Andrology. Proceedings of the International Congress of Andrology
Curr Adv Genet — Current Advances in Genetics
Curr Adv Mech Des Prod Proc Int Conf — Current Advances in Mechanical Design and Production. Proceedings. International Conference
Curr Adv Plant Sci — Current Advances in Plant Science
Curr Adv Plant Sci Comp — Current Advances in Plant Science. Compilations
Curr Affairs Bull — Current Affairs Bulletin
Curr Aff B — Current Affairs Bulletin
Curr Aff Bull — Current Affairs Bulletin
Curr Afr Issues — Current African Issues
Curr Agric — Current Agriculture
Curr Agric Res — Current Agricultural Research
Curr Alcohol — Currents in Alcoholism
Curr Am Gov — Current American Government
Curr Anthr — Current Anthropology
Curr Anthrop — Current Anthropology
Curr Anthropol — Current Anthropology
Curr Appl Radiopharmacol Proc Int Symp Radiopharmacol — Current Applications in Radiopharmacology. Proceedings. International Symposiumon Radiopharmacology
Curr Approaches Toxicol — Current Approaches in Toxicology
Curr Archaeol — Current Archaeology
Curr Aspects Neurosci — Current Aspects of the Neurosciences
Curr Atheroscler Rep — Current Atherosclerosis Reports
Curr Aus NZ Leg Lit Ind — Current Australian and New Zealand Legal Literature Index
Curr Aust New Z Leg Lit Index — Current Australian and New Zealand Legal Literature Index
Curr Aware Biol Sci CABS — Current Awareness in Biological Sciences. CABS
Curr Awareness Bull — Current Awareness Bulletin
Curr Awareness Libr Lit CALL — Current Awareness - Library Literature. CALL
Curr Bibl Afr Affairs — Current Bibliography on African Affairs
Curr Bibl Aquatic Sci & Fish — Current Bibliography for Aquatic Sciences and Fisheries
Curr Bibliogr Fish Sci — Current Bibliography for Fisheries Science. Food and Agriculture Organization
Curr Bibliogr Middle East Geol — Current Bibliography of Middle East Geology
Curr Biol — Current Biology
Curr Book Rev Citations — Current Book Review Citations
Curr Bus — Survey of Current Business
Curr Cardiovasc Top — Current Cardiovascular Topics
Curr Chemother Immunother Proc Int Congr Chemother — Current Chemotherapy and Immunotherapy. Proceedings. International Congress of Chemotherapy
Curr Chemother Infect Dis Proc Int Congr Chemother — Current Chemotherapy and Infectious Disease. Proceedings. International Congress of Chemotherapy
Curr Chemother Proc Int Congr Chemother — Current Chemotherapy. Proceedings. International Congress of Chemotherapy
Curr Chem Pap — Current Chemical Papers
Curr Clin Pract Ser — Current Clinical Practice Series
Curr Clin Top Infect Dis — Current Clinical Topics in Infectious Diseases
Curr Commun Cell & Mol Biol — Current Communications in Cell and Molecular Biology
Curr Commun Cell Mol Biol — Current Communications in Cell and Molecular Biology
Curr Concepts Cerebrovasc Dis Stroke — Current Concepts of Cerebrovascular Disease: Stroke
Curr Concepts Cutaneous Toxic Proc Conf — Current Concepts in Cutaneous Toxicity. Proceedings. Conference on Cutaneous Toxicity
Curr Concepts Emerg Med — Current Concepts in Emergency Medicine
Curr Concepts Hosp Pharm Manage — Current Concepts in Hospital Pharmacy Management
Curr Concepts Migraine Res — Current Concepts in Migraine Research
Curr Concepts Nutr — Current Concepts in Nutrition
Curr Concepts Plant Taxon — Current Concepts in Plant Taxonomy
Curr Concepts Surfactant Res Int Symp — Current Concepts in Surfactant Research. International Symposium on Surfactant Research
Curr Concepts Treat Parkinsonism Proc Symp — Current Concepts in the Treatment of Parkinsonism. Proceedings. Symposium
CurrCont — Current Contents
Curr Contents — Current Contents
Curr Contents Agric Biol Environ Sci — Current Contents/Agriculture, Biology, and Environmental Sciences
Curr Contents Behav Soc Educ Sci — Current Contents/Behavioral, Social, and Educational Sciences
Curr Contents Behav Soc Manage Sci — Current Contents/Behavioral, Social, and Management Sciences
Curr Contents Clin Med — Current Contents/Clinical Medicine
Curr Contents Clin Pract — Current Contents/Clinical Practices
Curr Contents Educ — Current Contents/Education
Curr Contents Eng Tech Appl Sci — Current Contents/Engineering, Technology, and Applied Sciences
Curr Contents Eng Technol — Current Contents/Engineering and Technology
Curr Contents Life Sci — Current Contents/Life Sciences
Curr Contents Pharm Publ — Current Contents of Pharmaceutical Publications

Curr Contents Phys Chem Earth Sci — Current Contents/Physical, Chemical, and Earth Sciences

Curr Contents Soc Behav Sci — Current Contents/Social and Behavioral Sciences

Curr Corros Res Scand Lect Scand Corros Congr — Current Corrosion Research in Scandinavia. Lectures held at the Scandinavian Corrosion Conference

CURRD — Current

Curr Dev Biol Nitrogen Fixation — Current Developments in Biological Nitrogen Fixation

Curr Dev Opt Des Eng — Current Developments in Optical Design and Engineering

Curr Dev Opt Eng — Current Developments in Optical Engineering

Curr Dev Opt Eng Diffr Phenom — Current Developments in Optical Engineering and Diffraction Phenomena

Curr Dev Psychopharmacol — Current Developments in Psychopharmacology

Curr Dev Yeast Res Proc Int Yeast Symp — Current Developments in Yeast Research. Proceedings. International Yeast Symposium

Curr Dig Sov Press — Current Digest of the Soviet Press

Curr Dir Autoimmun — Current Directions in Autoimmunity

Curr Discussions Theol — Current Discussions in Theology

Curr Doc Ger Dem Rep — Current Documents from the German Democratic Republic

Curr Drug Metab — Current Drug Metabolism

Curr Drug Targets — Current Drug Targets

Curr Econ Bus Aspects Wine Ind Symp — Current Economics and Business Aspects of the Wine Industry. Symposium

Curr Econ Comm — Current Economic Comment

Curr Endocr Concepts — Current Endocrine Concepts

Curr Energy Pat — Current Energy Patents

Curr Eng Pract — Current Engineering Practice

Current — Against the Current

Current Accts — Current Accounts

Current Adv Plant Sci — Current Advances in Plant Science

Current Affairs Bul — Current Affairs Bulletin

Current Anthr — Current Anthropology

Current Anthropol — Current Anthropology

Current Archaeol — Current Archaeology

Current Chem Transl — Current Chemical Translations

Current Dig Soviet Pr — Current Digest of the Soviet Press

Current Hist — Current History

Current Index Statist Appl Methods Theory — Current Index to Statistics; Applications-Methods-Theory

Current Ind Rept — Current Industrial Reports

Current Inf Constr Ind — Current Information in the Construction Industry

Current L — Current Law

Current L & Soc Probl — Current Law and Social Problems

Current Law — Current Law and Social Problems

Current Legal Prob — Current Legal Problems

Current Lit — Current Literature

Current Lit Traff Transp — Current Literature in Traffic and Transportation

Current LYB — Current Law Year Book

Current Math Publ — Current Mathematical Publications

Current Med — Current Medicine for Attorneys

Current Mun Prob — Current Municipal Problems

Current Mus — Current Musicology

Current Musicol — Current Musicology

Current Notes — Current Notes on International Affairs

Current Sci — Current Science

Current Sociol (Sage) — Current Sociology (Sage Publications Ltd.)

Current Tech Index — Current Technology Index

Curr Eur Dir — Current European Directories

Curr Eye Res — Current Eye Research

Curr Farm Econ — Current Farm Economics

Curr Farm Econ Agric Exp Stn Div Agric Okla State Univ — Current Farm Economics. Agricultural Experiment Station. Division of Agriculture. Oklahoma State University

Curr Gastroenterol — Current Gastroenterology

Curr Genet — Current Genetics

Curr Genet Clin Morphol Probl — Current Genetic, Clinical, and Morphologic Problems

Curr Hemat Onco — Current Hematology and Oncology

Curr Hepatol — Current Hepatology

Curr Hist — Current History

Curric & Research Bul — Curriculum and Research Bulletin

Curric Aust — Curriculum Australia

Curric Inq — Curriculum Inquiry

Curric Inquiry — Curriculum Inquiry

Curric News — Curriculum News

Curric R — Curriculum Review

Curric Stud and Ed Res B — Curriculum Study and Educational Research Bulletin

Curric Theo — Curriculum Theory Network

Curriculum Perspect — Curriculum Perspective

Curriculum Res Bull — Curriculum and Research Bulletin

Currier Gal A Bull — Currier Gallery of Art Bulletin

Curr Ind Commonw Leg Per — Current Index to Commonwealth Legal Periodicals

Curr Index Commonw Leg Period — Current Index to Commonwealth Legal Periodicals

Curr Index J Educ — Current Index to Journals in Education. CIJE

Curr Index Stat — Current Index to Statistics

Curr Index Stat Appl Methods Theory — Current Index to Statistics; Applications-Methods-Theory

Curr Indian Stat — Current Indian Statutes

Curr Ind Rep Alum Ingot Mill Prod — Current Industrial Reports. Aluminum Ingot and Mill Products

Curr Ind Rep Clay Constr Prod — Current Industrial Reports. Clay Construction Products

Curr Ind Rep Copper Controlled Mater — Current Industrial Reports. Copper Controlled Materials

Curr Ind Rep Fats Oils Oilseed Crushings — Current Industrial Reports. Fats and Oils-Oilseed Crushings

Curr Ind Rep Fats Oils Prod Consumption Stocks — Current Industrial Reports. Fats and Oils-Production, Consumption, and Stocks

Curr Ind Rep Flat Glass — Current Industrial Reports. Flat Glass

Curr Ind Rep Ind Gases — Current Industrial Reports. Industrial Gases

Curr Ind Rep Inorg Chem — Current Industrial Reports. Inorganic Chemicals

Curr Ind Rep Inorg Fert Mater Relat Prod — Current Industrial Reports. Inorganic Fertilizer Materials and Related Products

Curr Ind Rep Iron Steel Cast — Current Industrial Reports. Iron and Steel Castings

Curr Ind Rep Nonferrous Cast — Current Industrial Reports. Nonferrous Castings

Curr Ind Rep Refract — Current Industrial Reports. Refractories

Curr Ind Rep Sel Ind Air Pollut Control Equip — Current Industrial Reports. Selected Industrial Air Pollution Control Equipment

Curr Ind Rep Ser BCDF 84 — Current Industrial Reports. Series BCDF-84

Curr Ind Rep Ser BCDF 263 — Current Industrial Reports. Series BCDF-263

Curr Ind Rep Ser Copper Base Mill Foundry Prod — Current Industrial Reports. Series. Copper-Base Mill and Foundry Products

Curr Ind Rep Ser DIB 917 — Current Industrial Reports. Series DIB-917

Curr Ind Rep Ser DIB 991 — Current Industrial Reports. Series DIB-991

Curr Ind Rep Ser DIB 9008 — Current Industrial Reports. Series DIB-9008

Curr Ind Rep Ser ITA 991 — Current Industrial Reports. Series ITA-991

Curr Ind Rep Ser ITA 9008 — Current Industrial Reports. Series ITA-9008

Curr Ind Rep Ser M20J — Current Industrial Reports. Series M20J

Curr Ind Rep Ser M20K — Current Industrial Reports. Series M20K

Curr Ind Rep Ser M26A — Current Industrial Reports. Series M26A

Curr Ind Rep Ser M28A — Current Industrial Reports. Series M28A

Curr Ind Rep Ser M28C — Current Industrial Reports. Series M28C

Curr Ind Rep Ser M28F — Current Industrial Reports. Series M28F

Curr Ind Rep Ser M32D — Current Industrial Reports. Series M32D

Curr Ind Rep Ser M33A — Current Industrial Reports. Series M33A

Curr Ind Rep Ser M33E — Current Industrial Reports. Series M33E

Curr Ind Rep Ser M33 2 — Current Industrial Reports. Series M33-2

Curr Ind Rep Ser MA 35J — Current Industrial Reports. Series MA-35J

Curr Ind Rep Ser MQ 32A — Current Industrial Reports. Series MQ-32A

Curr Ind Rep Ser MQ 32C — Current Industrial Reports. Series MQ-32C

Curr Ind Rep Ser Pulp Pap Board — Current Industrial Reports. Series. Pulp, Paper, and Board

Curr Ind Rept Footwear — Current Industrial Reports. M31A. Footwear

Curr Ind Rep Titanium Mill Prod Ingot Cast — Current Industrial Reports. Titanium Mill Products, Ingot, and Castings

Curr Ind Rept Plast Bottles — Current Industrial Reports. M30E. Plastic Bottles

Curr Induced React Int Summer Inst Theor Part Phys — Current Induced Reactions. International Summer Institute on Theoretical Particle Physics

Curr Inform Ser Univ Idaho Coll Agr Ext Serv — Current Information Series. University of Idaho. College of Agriculture. Agricultural Extension Service

Curr Inf Ser Coop Ext Serv Univ Idaho — Current Information Series. Cooperative Extension Service. University of Idaho

Curr Inf Ser Idaho Agric Exp Stn — Idaho. Agricultural Experiment Station. Current Information Series

Curr Innovations Mol Biol — Current Innovations in Molecular Biology

Curr Issues Mol Biol — Current Issues in Molecular Biology

Curr Issues Psychoanal Pract — Current Issues in Psychoanalytic Practice

Curr Issues Stud US Nat Res Counc — Current Issues and Studies. United States National Research Council

Curr J Food Nutr Health — Currents. The Journal of Food, Nutrition, and Health

Curr Jod Lit — Current Jodine Literature

Curr Jpn Mater Res — Current Japanese Materials Research

Curr Lab Pract — Current Laboratory Practice

Curr Law Case Cit — Current Law Case Citator

Curr Law Cit — Current Law Citator

Curr Law Index — Current Law Index

Curr Law Soc Probl — Current Law and Social Problems

Curr Law Statut Cit Index — Current Law Statute Citator and Index

Curr Leather Lit — Current Leather Literature

Curr Leg Probl — Current Legal Problems

Curr Lit Aging — Current Literature on Aging

Curr Lit Blood — Current Literature of Blood

Curr Lit Vener Dis — Current Literature on Venereal Disease

Curr LSP — Current Law and Social Problems

Curr LYB — Current Law Year Book

Curr Math Publ — Current Mathematical Publications

Curr Med — Current Medicine

Curr Med Abstr Practit — Current Medical Abstracts for Practitioners

Curr Med Chem — Current Medicinal Chemistry

Curr Med Dig — Current Medical Digest

Curr Med Drugs — Current Medicine and Drugs

Curr Med Info Termin — Current Medical Information and Terminology

Curr Med Pract — Current Medical Practice

Curr Med Pract (India) — Current Medical Practice (India)

Curr Med Res — Current Medical Research

Curr Med Res Opin — Current Medical Research and Opinion

Curr Microbiol — Current Microbiology

Curr Mod Biol — Currents in Modern Biology

Curr Mod Biol Biosyst — Currents in Modern Biology. Biosystems

Curr Mun Pr — Current Municipal Problems

Curr Music — Current Musicology

Curr Nephrol — Current Nephrology

Curr Neurosurg Pract — Current Neurosurgical Practice

Curr No Int Aff — Current Notes on International Affairs

Curr Notes — Current Notes on International Affairs

Curr Notes Int Aff — Current Notes on International Affairs
Curr Notes Int Affairs — Current Notes on International Affairs
Curr Obstet Gynecol Diagn Treat — Current Obstetric and Gynecologic Diagnosis and Treatment
Curr Oncol Rep — Current Oncology Reports
Curr Op Im — Current Opinion in Immunology
Curr Opin — Current Opinion
Curr Opin Biotechnol — Current Opinion in Biotechnology
Curr Opin Cardiol — Current Opiinion in Cardiology
Curr Opin Cell Biol — Current Opinion in Cell Biology
Curr Opin Chem Biol — Current Opinion in Chemical Biology
Curr Opin Clin Nutr Metab Care — Current Opinion in Clinical Nutrition and Metabolic Care
Curr Opin Colloid Interface Sci — Current Opinion in Colloid and Interface Science
Curr Opin Crit Care — Current Opinion in Critical Care
Curr Opin Drug Discov Devel — Current Opinion in Drug Discovery & Development
Curr Opin Drug Discovery Dev — Current Opinion in Drug Discovery and Development
Curr Opin Endocrinol Diabetes — Current Opinion in Endocrinology and Diabetes
Curr Opin G — Current Opinion in Gastroenterology
Curr Opin Gastroenterol — Current Opinion in Gastroenterology
Curr Opin Genet Dev — Current Opinion in Genetics and Development
Curr Opin Gen Surg — Current Opinion in General Surgery
Curr Opin Hematol — Current Opinion in Hematology
Curr Opin Immunol — Current Opinion in Immunology
Curr Opin Infect Dis — Current Opinion in Infectious Diseases
Curr Opin Investig Drugs — Current Opinion in Investigational Drugs
Curr Opin Lipidol — Current Opinion in Lipidology
Curr Opin Microbiol — Current Opinion in Microbiology
Curr Opin Mol Ther — Current Opinion in Molecular Therapeutics
Curr Opin Nephrol Hypertens — Current Opinion in Nephrology and Hypertension
Curr Opin Neurobiol — Current Opinion in Neurobiology
Curr Opin Neurol — Current Opinion in Neurology
Curr Opin Obstet Gynecol — Current Opinion in Obstetrics and Gynecology
Curr Opin Oncol — Current Opinion in Oncology
Curr Opin Ophthalmol — Current Opinion in Ophthalmology
Curr Opin Pediatr — Current Opinion in Pediatrics
Curr Opin Plant Biol — Current Opinion in Plant Biology
Curr Opin Pulm Med — Current Opinion in Pulmonary Medicine
Curr Opin Radiol — Current Opinion in Radiology
Curr Opin Rheumatol — Current Opinion in Rheumatology
Curr Opin Solid State Mater Sci — Current Opinion in Solid State and Materials Science
Curr Opin Struct Biol — Current Opinion in Structural Biology
Curr Opin Ther Pat — Current Opinion in Therapeutic Patents
Curr Opin Urol — Current Opinion in Urology
Curr Org Chem — Current Organic Chemistry
Curr Pain Headache Rep — Current Pain and Headache Reports
Curr Pap Aeronaut Res Counc (UK) — Current Papers. Aeronautical Research Council (United Kingdom)
Curr Pap Build Res Establ — Current Paper. Building Research Establishment
Curr Papers Phys — Current Papers in Physics
Curr Pap Kyoto Univ Dep Aeronaut Eng — Current Papers. Kyoto University. Department of Aeronautical Engineering
Curr Pap Phys — Current Papers in Physics
Curr P Card — Current Problems in Cardiology
Curr Perspect Cancer Ther — Current Perspectives in Cancer Therapy
Curr Perspect Microb Ecol Proc Int Symp — Current Perspectives in Microbial Ecology. Proceedings. International Symposium on Microbial Ecology
Curr Perspect Nitrogen Fixation Proc Int Symp — Current Perspectives in Nitrogen Fixation. Proceedings. International Symposiumon Nitrogen Fixation
Curr Pharm Biotechnol — Current Pharmaceutical Biotechnology
Curr Pharm Des — Current Pharmaceutical Design
Curr Photosynth Proc West Eur Conf — Currents in Photosynthesis. Proceedings. Western-Europe Conference on Photosynthesis
Curr Phys Index — Current Physics Index
Curr Plant Sci Biotechnol Agric — Current Plant Science and Biotechnology in Agriculture
Curr Pollut Res India — Current Pollution Researches in India
Curr Pop Rep — Current Population Reports
Curr Pop Rep Special Studies — Current Population Reports. Special Studies. Series P-23
Curr Popul Rep Consum Income — Current Population Reports. Consumer Income. Series P-60
Curr Popul Rep P-26 — Current Population Reports. Series P-26. Federal-State Cooperative Program for Population Estimates
Curr Popul Rep Popul Charact — Current Population Reports. Population Characteristics. Series P-20
Curr Popul Rep Popul Estim Proj — Current Population Reports. Population Estimates and Projections. Series P-25
Curr Popul Rep Spec Censuses — Current Population Reports. Special Censuses. Series P-28
Curr Popul Rep Spec Stud — Current Population Reports. Special Studies. Series P-23
Curr Pract Environ Eng — Current Practices in Environmental Engineering
Curr Pract Environ Sci Eng — Current Practices in Environmental Science and Engineering
Curr Pract Gerontol Nurs — Current Practice in Gerontological Nursing
Curr Pract Obstet Gynecol Nurs — Current Practice in Obstetric and Gynecologic Nursing
Curr Pract Orthop Surg — Current Practice in Orthopaedic Surgery
Curr Pract Pediatr Nurs — Current Practice in Pediatric Nursing
Curr Prob Dermatol — Current Problems in Dermatology

Curr Probl — Current Problems
Curr Probl Anesth Crit Care Med — Current Problems in Anesthesia and Critical Care Medicine
Curr Probl Cancer — Current Problems in Cancer
Curr Probl Cardiol — Current Problems in Cardiology
Curr Probl Clin Biochem — Current Problems in Clinical Biochemistry
Curr Probl Derm — Current Problems in Dermatology
Curr Probl Dermatol — Current Problems in Dermatology
Curr Probl Diagn Radiol — Current Problems in Diagnostic Radiology
Curr Probl Electrophotogr Eur Colloq — Current Problems in Electrophotography. European Colloquium
Curr Probl Epilepsy — Current Problems in Epilepsy
Curr Probl Immunol Bayer Symp — Current Problems in Immunology. Bayer-Symposium
Curr Probl Obstet Gynecol Fertil — Current Problems in Obstetrics, Gynecology, and Fertility
Curr Probl Ped — Current Problems in Pediatry
Curr Probl Pediatr — Current Problems in Pediatrics
Curr Probl Rad — Current Problems in Radiology
Curr Probl Surg — Current Problems in Surgery
Curr P Surg — Current Problems in Surgery
Curr Psychiatr Ther — Current Psychiatric Therapies
Curr Psychiatry Rep — Current Psychiatry Reports
Curr Psychol — Current Psychology
Curr Psychol Res — Current Psychological Research
Curr Psychol Res & Rev — Current Psychological Research and Reviews
Curr Psychol Res Rev — Current Psychological Research and Reviews
Curr Psychol Rev — Current Psychological Reviews
Curr Pulmonol — Current Pulmonology
Curr Radiol — Current Radiology
Curr Rep W Va Agric Exp Stn — Current Report. West Virginia. Agricultural Experiment Station
Curr Rep W Va Univ Agr Exp Sta — Current Report. West Virginia University. Agricultural Experiment Station
Curr Rep W Va Univ Agric For Exp Stn — Current Report. West Virginia University. Agricultural and Forestry Experiment Station
Curr Res — Current Research
Curr Res Anesth Analg — Current Researches in Anesthesia and Analgesia
Curr Res Canc Chemoth — Current Research in Cancer Chemotherapy
Curr Res Des Trends Spec Conf Cold Formed Steel Struct — Current Research and Design Trends. Specialty Conference on Cold-Formed Steel Structures
Curr Res Geol Surv Can — Current Research. Geological Survey of Canada
Curr Res Geol Surv Isr — Current Research. Geological Survey of Israel
Curr Res Med Aromat Plants — Current Research on Medicinal and Aromatic Plants
Curr Res Med Arom Plants — Current Research on Medicinal and Aromatic Plants
Curr Res Nephrol Jpn — Current Research in Nephrology in Japan
Curr Res Neth Biol — Current Research in the Netherlands. Biology
Curr Res Photosynth Proc Int Conf Photosynth — Current Research in Photosynthesis. Proceedings. International Conference on Photosynthesis
Curr Res Rep — Current Research Reporter
Curr Res Univ Agric Sci Bangalore — Current Research. University of Agricultural Sciences. Bangalore
Curr Rev Agr Cond Can — Current Review of Agricultural Conditions in Canada
Curr Rev Biomed — Current Reviews in Biomedicine
Curr Rev Nurse Anesth — Current Reviews for Nurse Anesthetists
Curr Rev Recov Room Nurses — Current Reviews for Recovery Room Nurses
Curr Rev Respir Ther — Current Reviews in Respiratory Therapy
Curr Rheumatol R — Current Rheumatology Reports
Curr Sc — Current Science
Curr Sci — Current Science
Curr Sep — Current Separations
Curr Sociol — Current Sociology
Curr Status Future Prospects Diffr Proc Jpn USA Jt Meet — Current Status and Future Prospects of Diffraction. Proceedings. Japan-USA Joint Meeting
Curr Status Mod Ther — Current Status of Modern Therapy
Curr Stud Hematol Blood Transfus — Current Studies in Hematology and Blood Transfusion
Curr Surg — Current Surgery
Curr Swed — Current Sweden
Curr Themes Trop Sci — Current Themes in Tropical Science
Curr Theory Res Motiv Nebr Symp Motiv — Current Theory and Research in Motivation. Nebraska Symposium on Motivation
Curr Ther — Current Therapy
Curr Ther Endocrinol Metab — Current Therapy in Endocrinology and Metabolism
Curr Ther (Phila) — Current Therapy (Philadelphia)
Curr Ther R — Current Therapeutic Research. Clinical and Experimental
Curr Ther Res — Current Therapeutic Research
Curr Ther Res Clin Exp — Current Therapeutic Research. Clinical and Experimental
Curr Tit Electrochem — Current Titles in Electrochemistry
Curr Titles Electrochem — Current Titles in Electrochemistry
Curr Titles Turk Sci — Current Titles in Turkish Science
Curr T M — Currents in Theology and Mission
Curr Top Biochem — Current Topics in Biochemistry
Curr Top Bioenerg — Current Topics in Bioenergetics
Curr Top Cardiol — Current Topics in Cardiology
Curr Top Cell Regul — Current Topics in Cellular Regulation
Curr Top Chin Sci Sect D Biol — Current Topics in Chinese Science. Section D. Biology
Curr Top Chin Sci Sect G Med Sci — Current Topics in Chinese Science. Section G. Medical Science
Curr Top Clin Chem — Current Topics in Clinical Chemistry
Curr Top Clin Comm Psych — Current Topics in Clinical and Community Psychology

Curr Top Colloid Interface Sci — Current Topics in Colloid and Interface Science
Curr Top Comp Pathobiol — Current Topics in Comparative Pathobiology
Curr Top Coron Res Pap Symp — Current Topics in Coronary Research. Papers. Symposium
Curr Top Crit Care Med — Current Topics in Critical Care Medicine
Curr Top Cryst Growth Res — Current Topics in Crystal Growth Research
Curr Top Dev Biol — Current Topics in Developmental Biology
Curr Top Devel Biol — Current Topics in Developmental Biology
Curr Top Electrochem — Current Topics in Electrochemistry
Curr Top Electron Syst — Current Topics in Electronics and Systems
Curr Top Exp Endocrinol — Current Topics in Experimental Endocrinology
Curr Top Eye Res — Current Topics in Eye Research
Curr Top Hematol — Current Topics in Hematology
Curr Topics Bioenerget — Current Topics in Bioenergetics
Curr Topics Developm Biol — Current Topics in Developmental Biology
Curr Top Immunol Ser — Current Topics In Immunology Series
Curr Top Intensive Care Med — Current Topics in Intensive Care Medicine
Curr Top Mater Sci — Current Topics in Materials Science
Curr Top Med Chem — Current Topics in Medicinal Chemistry
Curr Top Med Mycol — Current Topics in Medical Mycology
Curr Top Membr — Current Topics in Membranes
Curr Top Membranes Transp — Current Topics in Membranes and Transport
Curr Top Membr Transp — Current Topics in Membranes and Transport
Curr Top Microbiol Immunol — Current Topics in Microbiology and Immunology
Curr Top Mol Endocrinol — Current Topics in Molecular Endocrinology
Curr Top Mol Simul — Current Topics in Molecular Simulation
Curr Top Nerve Muscle Res Sel Pap Symp Int Congr Neuromuscul — Current Topics in Nerve and Muscle Research. Selected Papers. Symposia held at the International Congress on Neuromuscular Diseases
Curr Top Neurobiol — Current Topics in Neurobiology
Curr Top Neurochem — Current Topics in Neurochemistry
Curr Top Neuroendocrinol — Current Topics in Neuroendocrinology
Curr Top Neuropathol — Current Topics in Neuropathology
Curr Top Nutr Dis — Current Topics in Nutrition and Disease
Curr Top Pain Res Ther Proc Int Symp Pain — Current Topics in Pain Research and Therapy. Proceedings. International Symposium on Pain
Curr Top Pathol — Current Topics in Pathology
Curr Top Pharmacol — Current Topics in Pharmacology
Curr Top Photovoltaics — Current Topics in Photovoltaics
Curr Top Plant Biochem Physiol — Current Topics in Plant Biochemistry and Physiology. Proceedings. Annual Plant Biochemistry and Physiology Symposium
Curr Top Plant Physiol — Current Topics in Plant Physiology
Curr Top Pulm Pharmacol Toxicol — Current Topics in Pulmonary Pharmacology and Toxicology
Curr Top Radiat Res — Current Topics in Radiation Research
Curr Top Radiat Res Q — Current Topics in Radiation Research. Quarterly
Curr Top Reprod Endocrinol — Current Topics in Reproductive Endocrinology
Curr Top Res Synapses — Current Topics in Research on Synapses
Curr Top Solution Chem — Current Topics in Solution Chemistry
Curr Top Surg Res — Current Topics in Surgical Research
Curr Top Synth Struct Polym IUPAC Int Symp — Current Topics in Synthesis and Structure of Polymers. Presented at IUPAC International Symposium
Curr Top Thyroid Res Proc Int Thyroid Conf — Current Topics in Thyroid Research. Proceedings of the International Thyroid Conference
Curr Top Tumor Cell Physiol Positron Emiss Tomogr — Current Topics in Tumor Cell Physiology and Positron-Emission Tomography
Curr Top Vet Med — Current Topics in Veterinary Medicine
Curr Top Vet Med Anim Sci — Current Topics in Veterinary Medicine and Animal Science
Curr Toxicol — Current Toxicology
Curr Toxicol Ther — Current Toxicology and Therapy
Curr Trends Heterocycl Chem Proc Symp — Current Trends in Heterocyclic Chemistry. Proceedings of a Symposium
Curr Trends Histocompat — Current Trends in Histocompatibility
Curr Trends Lithium Rubidium Ther Proc Int Symp — Current Trends in Lithium and Rubidium Therapy. Proceedings of an International Symposium
Curr Trends Morphol Tech — Current Trends in Morphological Techniques
Curr Trends Opt Invited Pap Meet — Current Trends in Optics. Invited Papers from the ICO [*International Commission for Optics*] Meeting
Curr Trends Org Synth Proc Int Conf — Current Trends in Organic Synthesis. Proceedings. International Conference
Curr Trends Polym Sci — Current Trends in Polymer Science
Curr US Gov Per Mfiche — Current US Government Periodicals on Microfiche
Curr Vet Ther — Current Veterinary Therapy. Small Animal Practice
Curr Views Gastroenterol Symp Round Table Conf Int Congr — Current Views in Gastroenterology. Symposia and Round Table Conferences. International Congress of Gastroenterology
Curr Work Hist Med — Current Work in the History of Medicine
Cur Scene — Current Scene
Cur Sci — Current Science
Cursillos Conf Inst Lucas Mallada — Cursillos y Conferencias. Instituto Lucas Mallada
Curso Esc Opt Cuantica — Curso. Escuela de Optica Cuantica
Curso Reson Magn Nucl Reson Magn Nucl Pulsos Alta Resoluc — Curso de Resonancia Magnetica Nuclear. Resonancia Magnetica Nuclear de Pulsos. Alta Resolucion
Curso Roso de Luna Invest Econ Recur Geol Min Actas — Curso Roso de Luna. Investigacion y Economia de los Recursos Geologico-Mineros. Actas
Cursos Conf BA — Cursos y Conferencias (Buenos Aires)
Cursos Congr Univ Santiago De Compostela — Cursos y Congresos. Universidad de Santiago de Compostela
Cur Sov Lead — Current Soviet Leaders
Curtis's Bot Mag New Ser — Curtis's Botanical Magazine. New Series
C (US) — Cinema (United States)
CUSCA — Current Science

CUSCDP — Chittagong University. Studies. Part II. Science
Cushman Found Foraminiferal Res Spec Publ — Cushman Foundation for Foraminiferal Research. Special Publication
Cushman Found Foram Research Contr — Cushman Foundation for Foraminiferal Research. Contributions
Cushman Found Foram Research Contr Special Pub — Cushman Foundation for Foraminiferal Research. Contributions. Special Publication
CUSM — Cuadernos. Universidad de San Marcos [*Lima*]
CUSQ — Cultural Survival Quarterly
CUSR — Catholic University of America. Studies in Romance Languages and Literatures
Cust B & Dec — Customs Bulletin and Decisions
Custom Tar J — Customs Tariff Schedule for Japan, 1986
Cutaneous Ocul Toxicol — Cutaneous and Ocular Toxicology
CUTBA — Current Topics in Bioenergetics
Cuticle Tech Arthropods — Cuticle Techniques in Arthropods
Cut LT — Cuttack Law Times
CuTM — Currents in Theology and Mission
Cuttington Res J — Cuttington Research Journal
Cutting Tool Eng — Cutting Tool Engineering
Cutting Tool Mater Proc Int Conf — Cutting Tool Materials. Proceedings of an International Conference
Cutt LT — Cuttack Law Times
Cut Tool En — Cutting Tool Engineering
CUUCV — Cultura Universitaria. Universidad Central de Venezuela
Cuvas Gos Ped Inst Ucen Zap — Cuvasskii Gosudarstvennyi Pedagogiceskii Institut Imeni I. Ja. Jakovleva UcenyeZapiski
Cuvas Gos Univ I Cuvas Gos Ped Inst Ucen Zap — Cuvasskii Gosudarstvennyi Universitet Imeni I. N. Ul'janova Cuvasskii Gosudarstvennyi Pedagogiceskii Institut Imeni I. Ja. Jakovleva Ucenyi Zapiski
CuW — Christentum und Wissenschaft
CUWPL — Columbia University. Working Papers in Linguistics
Cuy — Cuyo. Anuario de Historia del Pensamiento Argentino
Cuyper Rv Un — Revue Universelle des Mines, de la Metallurgie. De Cuyper
CV — Caravel
CV — Caritas. Zeitschrift des Schweizerischen Caritasverbandes
CV — Cerf-Volant
CV — Citta di Vita
CV — Civilta Fascista
CV — Classical Views
CV — Commentationes Vindobonenses
CV — Communio Viatorum
CV — Crkoven Vestnik
CV — Luttenberg's Chronologische Verzameling
CVA — Corpus Vasorum Antiquorum
CVCHD — Chonnam Medical Journal
CVE — Cahiers Victoriens et Edouardiens
CVEGA — Civil Engineering
CVETAA — Communicationes Veterinariae
CVETB — Civil Engineering Transactions. Institution of Engineers of Australia
CVEVDJ — Contributions to Vertebrate Evolution
CVGIP — Computer Vision Graphics and Image Processing
CVGIP Graph — CVGIP (Computer Vision Graphics and Image Processing) Graphical Models and Image Processing
CVGIP Graphical Models Image Process — CVGIP. Graphical Models and Image Processing
CVGIP Imag — CVGIP (Computer Vision Graphics and Image Processing) Image Understanding
CVGMAX — Citrus and Vegetable Magazine
CVH — Corpus Vasorum Hispanorum
CVI — Printing World
C Vind — Commentationes Vindobonenses
CVNS — Conveyance News
CVP — Cardiovascular and Pulmonary Technology. Journal
CVP J Cardiovasc Pulm Technol — CVP. Journal of Cardiovascular and Pulmonary Technology
CVREAU — Cardiovascular Research
CVS — Classiques du XXe Siecle
CVSMO — Casopis Vlasteneckeho Spolku Musejniho v Olomouci
CVT — Collection of Voyages and Travels by J. Churchill
CVTJA — Ceylon Veterinary Journal
CVTRBC — Connective Tissue Research
CVVIDV — Connaissance de la Vigne et du Vin
CVZOAW — Congreso Venezolano de Cirugia
CW — Canadian Welfare
CW — Catholic World
CW — China Weekly
CW — Christliche Welt
CW — Christ und Welt
CW — Classical Weekly
CW — Classical World
CW — Coin World
CW — Commonwealth
CW — Composite Wood
CW — Computer Weekly
CW — Computerworld
CW — Congress Weekly
CWA — Container News
CWAHAT — Commonwealth Bureau of Animal Health. Review Series
CWAPAJ — Commonwealth Bureau of Horticulture and Plantation Crops. Technical Communication
CWAT — Transactions. Cumberland and Westmorland Antiquarian and Archaeological Society
CWB — Canadian Weekly Bulletin
CWB — Czernowitzer Wochenblatt

CWBSAX — Commonwealth Bureau of Soils. Technical Communication
CW-Can Welf — CW-Canadian Welfare
CWCBAL — Connecticut Water Resources Bulletin
CWCDA — Collected Works on Cardio-Pulmonary Disease
CWCDAR — Collected Works on Cardio-Pulmonary Disease
CWCP — Contemporary Writers in Christian Perspective
Cwd — Catholic World
CWD — Credit World
CWE — Chemical Week
Cweal — Commonweal
Cwealth — Commonwealth
Cwealth Agriculturist — Commonwealth Agriculturist
Cwealth Eng — Commonwealth Engineer
Cwealth Jeweller — Commonwealth Jeweller and Watchmaker
Cwealth Jeweller and Watchmaker — Commonwealth Jeweller and Watchmaker
Cwealth Pub Serv Board Bul — Commonwealth Public Service Board. Bulletin
CWFN — Canadian Wildlife and Fisheries Newsletter
CWFRA — Commonwealth Forestry Review
CWFRAG — Commonwealth Forestry Review
CWGV — Chronik. Wiener Goetheverein
CWH — Civil War History
CWHFAO — Contributions. New South Wales National Herbarium. Flora Series
CWHM — Current Work in the History of Medicine
CWI — Commerce
CWIC — Chronicle. West Indian Committee
Cwiczenia Lab Kinet Procesowej — Cwiczenia Laboratoryjne z Kinetyki Procesowej
CWI Newslett — Centrum voor Wiskunde en Informatica. Newsletter
CWL — Case Western Reserve. Law Review
Cwl — Commonwealth
CWLM — Chung-Wai Literary Monthly
CWLR — California Western Law Review
CWLSBG — Canadian Wildlife Service
Cwlth Record — Commonwealth Record
CWM — Cashflow Magazine
CWN — Calcutta Weekly Notes
CWN — Congress Weekly (New York)
CWN — Cosmetic World News
CWODAJ — Connecticut Woodlands
CWON — Canadian Women of Note
CWOPAL — Canadian Wildlife Service. Occasional Papers
CWPBA — California Water Pollution Control Association. Bulletin
CWPL — Cornell Working Papers in Linguistics
CWPNBL — Canadian Wildlife Service. Progress Notes
CWR — Ceylon Weekly Reporter
CWRJ — Canadian Water Resources Journal
CWR J Int L — Case Western Reserve. Journal of International Law
CWR LR — Case Western Reserve. Law Review
CWRSBC — Canadian Wildlife Service. Report Series
CWRUAH — Australia Commonwealth Scientific and Industrial Research Organisation. Wheat Research Unit. Annual Report
CWS — Metropolitan Chamber of Commerce and Industry. Chamber News
CWSOP — Canadian Wildlife Service. Occasional Papers
CWSPA7 — Colorado. Division of Wildlife. Special Report
CWSPN — Canadian Wildlife Service. Progress Notes
CWSRS — Canadian Wildlife Service. Report Series
CWW — California's Wine Wonderland
CWWFAV — Contribution. Welder Wildlife Foundation
CXA — Chambre de Commerce, d'Agriculture, et d'Industrie de la Republique Togolaise. Bulletin Mensuel
CXE — China Informatie
CXG — Commerce in Belgium
CXNHAX — Contributions. United States National Herbarium
CXT — Banco Nacional de Comercio Exterior. Comercio de Exterior
CY — Cayey
Cy — Crawdaddy
CyA — Cuba y America
Cyanamid Int Mitt — Cyanamid International. Mitteilungen
Cyanamid Int Vet Bull — Cyanamid International. Veterinary Bulletin
Cyanamid Int Vet News — Cyanimid International Veterinary News
Cyanamid Mag — Cyanamid Magazine
Cyanam New Prod Bull — Cyanamid New Product Bulletin
Cyan Compd Biol — Cyanide Compounds in Biology
CYB — Commodity Year Book
Cyb — Cybernetica
Cyb — Cybernetics
Cyb — Cybium. Bulletin de l'Association des Amis du Laboratoire des Peches Coloniales
Cybern and Syst — Cybernetics and Systems
Cybernet Systems — Cybernetics and Systems
Cybernet Systems Anal — Cybernetics and Systems Analysis
Cybern Syst — Cybernetics and Systems
CYBNA — Cybernetics
CyC — Cursos y Conferencias
CYCLA — Cycles
Cycl Anat and Physiol — Cyclopaedia of Anatomy and Physiology
Cycle Aust — Cycle Australia
Cycle Perfect Genie Chim — Cycle de Perfectionnement en Genie Chimique
Cyclic Deform Fract Nondestr Eval Adv Mater — Cyclic Deformation, Fracture, and Nondestructive Evaluation of Advanced Materials
Cycling Sci — Cycling Science
CyE — Cuba y Espana
CYENA — Cryogenic Engineering News
CyF — Contabilidad y Finanzas
CyL — Cylchgrawn Llyfrgell Genedlaethol Cymru

CYLPDN — Acta Pharmacologica Sinica
Cym Trans — Honourable Society of Cymmrodorion. Transactions
CyP — Contaminacion y Prevencion
Cyp — Cypher
CYP — CYP. Revista de Contaminacion y Prevencion
Cypr Agric J — Cyprus Agricultural Journal
Cypr Med J — Cyprus Medical Journal
Cypr Orn Soc Bull — Cyprus Ornithological Society. Bulletin
Cypr Publ Hlth — Cyprus Public Health
Cyprus Agric J — Cyprus Agricultural Journal
Cyprus Agric Res Inst Annu Rep — Cyprus Agricultural Research Institute. Annual Report
Cyprus Agric Res Inst Misc Publ — Cyprus Agricultural Research Institute. Miscellaneous Publications
Cyprus Agric Res Inst Prog Rep — Cyprus Agricultural Research Institute. Progress Report
Cyprus Agric Res Inst Tech Bull — Cyprus Agricultural Research Institute. Technical Bulletin
Cyprus Agric Res Inst Tech Pap — Cyprus Agricultural Research Institute. Technical Paper
Cyprus Dep Agric Annu Rep — Cyprus Department of Agriculture. Annual Report
Cyprus Geol Surv Dep Bull — Cyprus Geological Survey Department. Bulletin
Cyprus Geol Surv Dep Mem — Cyprus Geological Survey Department. Memoir
Cyprus Ind — Cyprus Industrial Journal
Cyprus J — Cyprus Journal
Cyprus Repub Minist Commer Ind Geol Surv Dep Bull — Cyprus. Republic. Ministry of Commerce and Industry. Geological Survey Department. Bulletin
CyR — Cruz y Raya
CYS — Cristianismo y Sociedad
CYSYDH — Cybernetics and Systems
CYTBA — Cytobios
CYTEA — Cryogenic Technology
CYTGA — Cytogenetics
CYTOA — Cytologia
Cytobiologie Z Exp Zellforsch — Cytobiologie; Zeitschrift fuer Experimentelle Zellforschung
Cytobiol Reprod Sex Plant Ovulees Colloq Int — Cytobiologie de la Reproduction Sexuee des Plantes Ovulees. Collque International
Cytobiol Rev — Cytobiologische Revue
Cytochem Compr Biochem — Cytochemistry. Comprehensive Biochemistry
Cytog C Gen — Cytogenetics and Cell Genetics
Cytogen — Cytogenetics
Cytogenet Cell Genet — Cytogenetics and Cell Genetics
Cytokine Growth Factor Rev — Cytokine and Growth Factor Reviews
Cytokines Cell & Mol Ther — Cytokines, Cellular, and Molecular Therapy
Cytokines Hemopoiesis Oncol AIDS — Cytokines in Hemopoiesis, Oncology, and AIDS [monograph]
Cytokines Mol Ther — Cytokines and Molecular Therapy
Cytol — Cytologia
Cytol Genet — Cytology and Genetics
Cytol Genet (Engl Transl) — Cytology and Genetics (English Translation)
Cytol Genet (Engl Transl Tsitol Genet) — Cytology and Genetics (English Translation of Tsitologiya i Genetika)
Cytol Neurol Stud Fac Med Univ Kanazawa — Cytological and Neurological Studies. Faculty of Medicine. University of Kanazawa
Cytologia Int J Cytol — Cytologia. International Journal of Cytology
Cytol Stud Kanaz — Cytological Studies. Faculty of Medicine. University of Kanazawa
Cytometry Suppl — Cytometry Supplement
Cyto Prot Biol — Cyto-protection and Biology
Cytoprot Cytobiol Proc Symp Cytoprot — Cytoprotection and Cytobiology. Proceedings. Symposium on Cytoprotection
CYTZA — Cytobiologie
CZ — Cela Zimes
Cz — Czytelnik
C Zair Et Polit Soc — Cahiers Zairois d'Etudes Politiques et Sociales
C Zair Rech Develop — Cahiers Zairois de la Recherche et du Developpement
Czas Geogr — Czasopismo Geograficzne
Czas Praw Hist — Czasopismo Prawno-Historyczne
Czas Roln — Czasopismo Rolnicze
Czas Stomat — Czasopismo Stomatologiczne
Czas Stomatol — Czasopismo Stomatologiczne
Czas Tech (Krakow) — Czasopismo Techniczne (Krakow)
Czas Tech M — Czasopismo Techniczne. M. Mechanika
Czas Tow Aptek (L) — Czasopismo Towarzystwa Aptekarskiego (Lwow)
CZCAA — Chemiker-Zeitung. Chemische Apparatur
CZ Chem-Tech — CZ Chemie-Technik
CZE — Czechoslovak Foreign Trade
Czech — Czechoslovakian Patent Document
Czech Acad Sci Bot Inst Hydrobiol Lab Annu Rep — Czechoslovak Academy of Sciences. Botanical Institute. Hydrobiological Laboratory. Annual Report
Czech Acad Sci Inst Landscape Ecol Hydrobiol Lab Annu Rep — Czechoslovak Academy of Sciences. Institute of Landscape Ecology. Hydrobiological Laboratory. Annual Report
Czech Acad Sci Inst Landscape Ecol Sect Hydrobiol Annu Rep — Czechoslovak Academy of Sciences. Institute of Landscape Ecology. Section of Hydrobiology. Annual Report
Czech Acad Sci Inst Plasma Phys Res Rep IPPCZ — Czechoslovak Academy of Sciences. Institute of Plasma Physics. Research Report IPPCZ
Czech Bibliogr Ind Hyg Occup Dis — Czechoslovak Bibliography on Industrial Hygiene and Occupational Diseases
Czech Conf Electron Vac Phys Proc — Czechoslovak Conference on Electronics and Vacuum Physics. Proceedings
Czech Conf Electron Vac Phys Texts Contrib Pap — Czechoslovak Conference on Electronics and Vacuum Physics. Texts. Contributed Papers

Czech Conf Electron Vac Phys Texts Surv Pap — Czechoslovak Conference on Electronics and Vacuum Physics. Texts. Survey Papers

Czech Congr Gastroenterol — Czechoslovak Congress of Gastroenterology

Czech F — Czechoslovak Film

Czech Fg T — Czechoslovak Foreign Trade

Czech Glass Rev — Czechoslovak Glass Review

Czech Heavy Ind — Czechoslovak Heavy Industry

Czech J Anim Sci — Czech Journal of Animal Science

Czech J Food Sci — Czech Journal of Food Sciences

Czech J Occup Med — Czechoslovak Journal of Occupational Medicine

Czech J Phys — Czechoslovak Journal of Physics

Czech J Phys Sect A — Czechoslovak Journal of Physics. Section A

Czech J Phys Sect B — Czechoslovak Journal of Physics. Section B

Czech Life — Czechoslovak Life

Czech Math J — Czechoslovak Mathematical Journal

Czech Med — Czechoslovak Medicine

Czechosl Econ Pap — Czechoslovak Economic Papers

Czechoslovak Econ Dig — Czechoslovak Economic Digest

Czechoslovak J Phys — Czechoslovak Journal of Physics

Czechoslovak J Phys B — Czechoslovak Journal of Physics. Section B

Czechoslovak Math J — Czechoslovak Mathematical Journal

Czech Pol Colloq Chem Thermodyn Phys Org Chem Commun — Czech-Polish Colloquium on Chemical Thermodynamics and Physical Organic Chemistry. Communications

Czech Pol Colloq Chem Thermodyn Phys Org Chem Lect — Czech-Polish Colloquium on Chemical Thermodynamics and Physical Organic Chemistry. Lectures

Czech Res Inst Crop Prod Annu Rep — Czechoslovakia. Research Institutes for Crop Production. Annual Report

Czech Res W — Czechoslovak Research Work

Czech Rev Tuberc Pulm Dis — Czechoslovak Review of Tuberculosis and Pulmonary Diseases

Czech Semin Plasma Phys Technol — Czechoslovak Seminar on Plasma Physics and Technology

Czech Tr J — Czechoslovak Trade Journal

Czech Urad Pat Vynalezy Vestn — Czechoslovakia. Urad pro Patenty a Vynalezy. Vestnik

Czech Urad Vynalezy Objevy Vestn — Czechoslovakia. Urad pro Vynalezy a Objevy. Vestnik

Czec J Phys — Czechoslovak Journal of Physics. Section B

Czec Math J — Czechoslovak Mathematical Journal

CZHIA — Czechoslovak Heavy Industry

CZI — Chemiker-Zeitung. Chemie, Technische Chemie, Chemiewirtschaft; mit Chemie-Borseund Bezugsquellen fuer die Chemische Industrie

CZMJA — Czechoslovak Mathematical Journal

CZMJB — Coastal Zone Management Journal

CZMMAN — Comunicaciones Zoologicas. Museo de Historia Natural de Montevideo

CZN — Casopis za Zgodovino in Narodopisje

CZOOA5 — Carnets de Zoologie

Cz PH — Czasopismo Prawno-Historyczne

CZSTA — Czasopismo Stomatologiczne

C Ztg — Chemiker-Zeitung. Central-Organ fuer Chemiker, Apotheker, Techniker, Ingenieure, Fabrikanten

C (Zurich) — Cinema (Zurich)

CZYPA — Czechoslovak Journal of Physics

D

D — Dacoromania
D — Dance
D — December
D — Demain
D — Dial
D — Dialectica
D — Dickensian
D — Diogenes
D — Director
D — Discovery
D — Dissonances. Revue Musicale Independante
D — Doxographi Graeci
D — Drammaturgia
DA — Deutsches Archiv
DA — Deutsches Archiv fuer Erforschung des Mittelalters
DA — Deutschtum und Ausland
DA — Dictionary of Americanisms
DA — Dictionnaire des Antiquites Grecques et Romaines
DA — Diorama
DA — Direct Action
d/a — Direct Advertising [Later, Printing Paper Quarterly]
DA — Dissertation Abstracts [Later, Dissertation Abstracts International]
DA — Documentation Abstracts
DAA — Dedications from the Athenian Akropolis
DAA — Denkmaeler Antiker Architektur
DAAL — Directory of Australian Academic Libraries
DAAN — Doklady Azerbajdzanskogo Filiala. Akademii Nauk SSSR
DAAPPP — Data Archive on Adolescent Pregnancy and Pregnancy Prevention
DAB — Development of Attic Black-Figure
DAB — Dictionary of American Biography
DAB — Dictionnaire d'Archeologie Biblique
DAb — Dissertation Abstracts [Later, Dissertation Abstracts International]
DAB — Dun and Bradstreet Reports
DABAA — Dissertation Abstracts International. Section A
DABAWAS — Datenbank fuer Wassergefahrdende Stoffe
DABBB — Dissertation Abstracts International. Section B. Sciences and Engineering
DABSAQ — Dissertation Abstracts International. Section B. Sciences and Engineering
Dac — Dacia
Dac — Dacoromania
DAC — Dictionary of the Apostolic Church
DAC — Dictionnaire d'Archeologie Chretienne et de Liturgie
DAC — Directory of Associations in Canada [Micromedia, Ltd.]
DACAS — Drug Abuse Current Awareness System
Dacca Univ Bull — Dacca University. Bulletin
Dacca Univ J — Dacca University. Journal
Dacca Univ Or Publ Ser — Dacca University. Oriental Publications Series
Dacca Univ St — Dacca University. Studies
Dacca Univ Stud — Dacca University. Studies
Dacca Univ Stud Arts Sci — Dacca University Studies. Arts and Sciences
Dacca Univ Stud Part A — Dacca University. Studies. Part A
Dacca Univ Stud Part B — Dacca University. Studies. Part B
Dacca U Stud — Dacca University. Studies
Dacia — Dacia. Revue d'Archeologie et d'Histoire Ancienne
DACL — Dictionnaire d'Archeologie Chretienne et de Liturgie
Dacor — Dacoromania
DACP — Dossiers Acenonetes du College de 'Pataphysique
Dac Terr — Dacotah Territory
Dactyl — Dactylography
DAD — Data Automation Digest
Dada — Dada/Surrealism
DadaS — Dada/Surrealism
DADE — Drugs and Drug Abuse Education
Da Dend A — Dansk Dendrologisk Arsskrift
DADG — Danish Arctic Station of Disko Island, Greenland. Publications
D A Dif Ambientale — DA. Difesa Ambientale
D Ad W — Jahrbuch der Deutschen Akademie der Wissenschaften zu Berlin
Dae — Daedalus
DAE — Developments in Agricultural Engineering
DAE — Dictionary of American English
DAE Circ LA Agr Exp Sta Dept Agr Econ — DAE Circular. Louisiana Agricultural Experiment Station. Department of Agricultural Economics
Daed — Daedalus
DAEDA — Daedalus

Daedalus J Amer Acad Arts Sci — Daedalus. Journal. American Academy of Arts and Sciences
Daedalus Tek Mus Arsb — Daedalus Tekniska Museets Arsbok
DAEM — Deutsches Archiv fuer Erforschung des Mittelalters
Daen Biblioth — Daenische Bibliothek Oder Sammlung von Alten und Neuen Gelehrten Sachen aus Daenemark
DAENDT — Developments in Agricultural Engineering
DAE Res Rep Dep Agric Econ Agribusiness LA State Univ — DAE Research Report. Department of Agricultural Economics and Agribusiness. Louisiana State University
Da Erhvervsfj — Dansk Erhvervsfjerkrae
DAES — Proceedings. Devon Archaeological Exploration Society
DaF — Deutsch als Fremdsprache
DAFA — Memoires. Delegation Archeologique Francaise d'Afghanistan
Daffodil Tulip Year Book — Daffodil and Tulip Year Book. Royal Horticultural Society
Daffod Tul Yb — Daffodil and Tulip Year Book
Daffod Yb — Daffodil Yearbook
DAFI — Cahiers. Delegation Archeologique Francaise en Iran
DAFR — Documents on American Foreign Relations
DAFT — Dansk Ornithologisk Forenings Tidsskrift
Da Fysiot — Danske Fysioterapeuter
DAG — Dialects of Ancient Gaul
Dagbl — Dagbladet
Dagestan Gos Univ Ucen Zap — Dagestanskii Gosudarstvennyi Universitet Imeni V. I. Lenina Ucenyi Zapiski
Dagest Nauchno Issled Vet Inst Sb Nauchn Rab — Dagestanskii Nauchno-Issledovatel'skii Veterinarnyi Institut. Sbornik NauchnykhRabot
Dagest Skh Inst Tr — Dagestanskii Sel'skokhozyaistvennyi Institut. Trudy
DAGM — Deutsches Archiv fuer Geschichte des Mittelalters
DagN — Dagens Nyheter [newspaper]
DAGR — Dictionnaire des Antiquites Grecques et Romaines
Dahlem Workshop Rep Life Sci Res Rep — Dahlem Workshop Reports. Life Sciences Research Report
Dahlem Workshop Rep Phys Chem Earth Sci Res Rep — Dahlem Workshop Reports. Physical, Chemical, and Earth Sciences Research Report
Dahlia News Boston — Dahlia News. New England Dahlia Society (Boston)
Dahl Yb — Dahlia Year Book
DAHV — De Aarde en Haar Volken [Haarlem]
DAI — Dairy Industries International
DAI — Dissertation Abstracts International
DAI — Documenti Antichi dell'Africa Italiana
DAI Athens — Mitteilungen. Deutsches Archaeologische Institut. Athenische Abteilung
DAIJ — Jahrbuch des Deutschen Archaeologischen Instituts
Dail Deb — Dail Debates
Daily Leg News (PA) — Daily Legal News (Pennsylvania)
Daily Leg (PA) — Daily Legal Record
Daily L N — Daily Legal News
Daily L R — Daily Legal Record
Daily News — Daily News Record
Daily Oil Bull — Daily Oil Bulletin
Daily Oklah — Daily Oklahoman
Daily Trans — New York Daily Transcript, Old and New Series
Daily Transc — New York Daily Transcript
Daily Wld — Daily World
DAiM — Deutsches Archiv fuer Innere Medizin
DAIMM — Madrider Mitteilungen. Deutsches Archaeologisches Institut. Madrider Abteilung
Da Ind — Dansk Industri
Dainichi-Nippon Cables Rev — Dainichi-Nippon Cables Review
Dai Reg — New York Daily Register
DAIRI — Dissertation Abstracts International. Retrospective Index
Dairy and Ice Cream Fld — Dairy and Ice Cream Field
Dairy Annu — Dairy Farming Annual
Dairy Counc Dig — Dairy Council Digest
Dairy Cow Future Int Semin — Dairy Cow of the Future. International Seminar
Dairy Creamery J — Dairy and the Creamery Journal
Dairy Dairy Shopkeepers J — Dairy and Dairy Shopkeepers Journal
Dairy Effluents Proc Int Dairy Fed Semin — Dairy Effluents. Proceedings. International Dairy Federation Seminar
Dairy Eng — Dairy Engineering
Dairy F — Dairy Farmer
Dairy Farm — Dairy Farmer
Dairyfarm Annu — Dairyfarming Annual
Dairy Farmer Dairy Beef Prod — Dairy Farmer and Dairy Beef-Producer

Dairyfarming Dig — Dairyfarming Digest
Dairyfmg Dig — Dairyfarming Digest
Dairy Food Environ Sanit — Dairy, Food, and Environmental Sanitation
Dairy Goat J — Dairy Goat Journal
Dairy Guidelines Va Polytech Inst State Univ Ext Div — Dairy Guidelines. Virginia Polytechnic Institute and State University ExtensionDivision
Dairy Herd Manage — Dairy Herd Management
Dairy Herd Mgt — Dairy Herd Management
Dairy Ind — Dairy Industries [Later, Dairy Industries International]
Dairy Ind — Dairy Industries International
Dairy Ind Int — Dairy Industries International
Dairy Inds — Dairy Industries International
Dairy Ind Soc Int Bull — Dairy Industries Society International. Bulletin
Dairy Indus — Dairy Industries [Later, Dairy Industries International]
Dairy Info Bul — Dairy Information Bulletin
Dairymen's Digest South Reg Ed — Dairymen's Digest. Southern Region Edition
Dairymen's Dig North Cent Reg Ed — Dairymen's Digest. North Central Region Edition
Dairy Prod — Dairy Produce
Dairy Prom Rev — Dairy Promotion Review
Dairy Rec — Dairy Record
Dairy Res Rep — Dairy Research Report
Dairy Res Rep Dep Agric Fish — Dairy Research Report. South Australia Department of Agriculture and Fisheries
Dairy Res Rep La Agric Exp Stn — Dairy Research Report. Louisiana Agricultural Experiment Station
Dairy Sci Abstr — Dairy Science Abstracts
Dairy Sci Handb — Dairy Science Handbook
Dairy Soc Int Bull — Dairy Society International. Bulletin
Dairy Starter Cult — Dairy Starter Cultures [monograph]
Dairy Tales Calif Univ Berkeley Coop Ext Serv — Dairy Tales. California University, Berkeley. Cooperative Extension Service
Dairy Tales Univ Calif Berkeley Coop Ext Serv — Dairy Tales. University of California. Berkeley. Cooperative Extension Service
Dairy World Br Dairy Farmer — Dairy World and the British Dairy Farmer
DaiT — Daily Telegraph [London newspaper]
DAITA — Database of Antiviral and Immunomodulatory Therapies for AIDS
Daiwa — Daiwa Investment Monthly
DAJ — Derbyshire Archaeological Journal
DAJO — Danish Journal
DA Jur — Dalloz Analytique. Jurisprudence
Dakar Med — Dakar Medical
DAKEA — Dansk Kemi
Dak Law Rev — Dakota Law Review
Dak L Rev — Dakota Law Review
DAKMAJ — Deutsches Archiv fuer Klinische Medizin
Dakota — Dakota Reports
Dakota F — Dakota Farmer
Dakota Law Rev — Dakota Law Review
Dakota L R — Dakota Law Review
D Akvbl — Dansk Akvarieblad. Akvarie- og Terrarietidsskrift
DAL — Dalloz Analytique. Legislation
DAL — Dictionnaire d'Archeologie Chretienne et de Liturgie
DALB — Dictionary of American Library Biography
Dalgetys Annual Wool D — Dalgetys Annual Wool Digest
Dalgetys Annual Wool R — Dalgetys Annual Wool Review
Dalhousie Dent J — Dalhousie Dental Journal
Dalhousie L J — Dalhousie Law Journal
Dalhousie R — Dalhousie Review
Dalhousie Rev — Dalhousie Review
Dalhousie Univ Inst Pub Aff Occ Pap — Dalhousie University. Institute of Public Affairs. Occasional Papers
Dalhous Rev — Dalhousie Review
Dalh Rev — Dalhousie Review
Dalian Inst Technol J — Dalian Institute of Technology. Journal
DALIS — Directory of Automated Library and Information Systems in Australia
Dallam — Dallam's Opinions
Dallas Med J — Dallas Medical Journal
Dallas New — Dallas Morning News
Dallas Sym — Dallas Symphony Orchestra. Program Notes
Dal LJ — Dalhousie Law Journal
Dall Med J — Dallas Medical Journal
Dall R — Dallas Reports
Dalls FW B — Dallas/Fort Worth Business Journal
Dalnevost Akust Sb — Dal'nevostochnyi Akusticheskii Sbornik
Dal'nevost Fiz Sb — Dal'nevostochnyi Fizicheskii Sbornik
Dalnevost Nauchno Issled Inst Lesn Khoz Sb Tr — Dal'nevostochnyi Nauchno-Issledovatel'skii Institut Lesnogo Khozyaistva. Sbornik Trudov
Dalnevost Nauchno Issled Inst Selsk Khoz Tr — Dal'nevostochnyi Nauchno-Issledovatel'skii Institut Sel'skogo Khozyaistva. Trudy
Dal'nevost Nauchno Issled Inst Stroit Sb Nauchn Rab — Dal'nevostochnyi Nauchno-Issledovatel'skii Institut po Stroitel'stvu Sbornik Nauchnykh Rabot
Dal Nevostocn Gos Univ Ucen Zap — Dal'nevostocnyi Gosudarstvennyi Universitet Ucenyi Zapiski Serija Fiziko-Matematiceskih Nauk
Dal'nevostocn Mat Sb — Dal'nevostochnyi Matematiceskii Sbornik
Dalnevost Petrogr Reg Sovshchanie — Dal'nevostochnoe Petrograficheskoe Regional'noe Sovshchanie
Dalnevost Petrogr Soveshch — Dal'nevostochnoe Petrograficheskoe Soveshchanie
Dalnevost Politekh Inst im V V Kuibysheva Tr — Dal'nevostochnyi Politekhnicheskii Institut imeni V. V. Kuibysheva. Trudy
Dal R — Dalhousie Review
Dal Rev — Dalhousie Review
Dalton Trans — Dalton Transactions
DALV — Deutsches Archiv fuer Landes und Volksforschung

DAM — Dansk Aarbog foer Musikforskning
Damas Mitt — Damaszener Mitteilungen
DAMDD5 — Dakar Medical
DAME — Developments in Agricultural and Managed-Forest Ecology
DAMJA — Dallas Medical Journal
DAMSEL — Directory of Australian Manufactured Scientific Equipment and Laboratoryware
Dan — Danish Patent Document
DAN — Doklady Akademii Nauk SSSR
DANA — Doklady Akademii Nauk Armianskoi SSR
Dan Acad Tech Sci Trans — Danish Academy of Technical Sciences. Transactions
Dan AEC Res Establ Risoe Rep Risoe M — Danish Atomic Energy Commission. Research Establishment Risoe. Report Risoe-M
Dan AEC Res Establ Risoe Risoe Rep — Danish Atomic Energy Commission. Research Establishment Risoe. Risoe Report
Dan AEC Res Establ Riso Rep — Danish Atomic Energy Commission. Research Establishment. Risoe Report
Dan Arct Res — Danish Arctic Research
Dana-Rep — Dana-Report. Carlsberg Foundation
Dana-Rep Carlsberg Found — Dana-Report. Carlsberg Foundation
Dan Atomenergikomm Forsoegsanlaeg Risoe Rep — Dansk Atomenergikommissionens Forsoegsanlaeg Risoe. Report
Dan Audiol — Dansk Audiolopaedi
DANAz — Doklady Akademii Nauk Azerbaidzhanskoi SSR
DAN Bolg — Doklady Bolgarskoi Akademii Nauk
Dan Bot Ark — Dansk Botanisk Arkiv
Dan Brygg Tid — Dansk Bryggeritidende
Dance — Dance Magazine
Dance Chron — Dance Chronicle
Dance in Can — Dance in Canada
Dance Index Mag — Dance Index Magazine
Dance Mag — Dance Magazine
Dance N — Dance News
Dance Notat Rec — Dance Notation Record
Dance Per — Dance Perspectives
Dance Persp — Dance Perspectives
Dance Res A — Dance Research Annual
Dance Res An — Dance Research Annual
Dance Res J — Dance Research Journal
Dance Sco — Dance Scope
Dancing Tim — Dancing Times
D & A — Defense & Armament Magazine
D & B Pr Pr — Dodd and Brook. Probate Practice
D & B Rpts — D and B [Dun and Bradstreet] Reports
D & C Ind — Drug and Cosmetic Industry
Dan Dendrol Arsskr — Dansk Dendrologisk Arsskrift
D & FA Daily — Defense and Foreign Affairs Daily
D & FA Week — Defense and Foreign Affairs Weekly
D & G Trans — Transactions. Dumfriesshire and Galloway Natural History and Antiquarian Society
D & S — Dollars & Sense
D & T — Drama and Theatre
Dan Dyrlaegeforen Medlemsb — Danske Dyrlaegeforening. Medlemsblad
Dan Erhvervsfjerkrae — Dansk Erhvervsfjerkrae
Daneshgah e Tehran Daneshkade ye Darusazi Maj — Daneshgah-e Tehran. Daneshkade-ye Darusazi. Majallah
DanF — Danske Folkemaal
Dan Farm Aarb — Dansk Farmaceutisk Aarbog
Dan Fisk Havunders Medd — Danmarks Fiskeri-og Havundersoegelser. Meddelelser
Dan Fisk Tid — Dansk Fiskeritidende
Dan Flkeminder — Danmarks Folkeminder
Danfoss J — Danfoss Journal
Dan Geol Unders Afh Raekke 1 — Danmarks Geologiske Undersoegelse. Afhandlinger. Raekke 1
Dan Geol Unders Afh Raekke 2 — Danmarks Geologiske Undersoegelse. Afhandlinger. Raekke 2
Dan Geol Unders Afh Raekke 3 — Danmarks Geologiske Undersoegelse. Afhandlinger. Raekke 3
Dan Geol Unders Afh Raekke 4 — Danmarks Geologiske Undersoegelse. Afhandlinger. Raekke 4
Dan Geol Unders Afh Raekke 5 — Danmarks Geologiske Undersoegelse. Afhandlinger. Raekke 5
Dan Geol Unders Arbog — Danmarks Geologiske Undersoegelse. Arbog
Dan Geol Unders III Raekke — Danmarks Geologiske Undersoegelse. III Raekke
Dan Geol Unders II Raekke — Danmarks Geologiske Undersoegelse. II Raekke
Dan Geol Unders IV Raekke — Danmarks Geologiske Undersoegelse. IV Raekke
Dan Geol Unders Rapp — Danmarks Geologiske Undersoegelse. Rapport
Dan Geol Unders Ser A — Danmarks Geologiske Undersoegelse. Serie A
Dan Geol Unders Ser B — Danmarks Geologiske Undersoegelse. Serie B
Dan Haveb — Dansk Havebrug
Dan Havetid — Dansk Havetidende
Dania Rep — Dania Reports. Carlsberg Foundation
Dan Ingeniorforen Spildevandskom Skr — Dansk Ingeniorforening Spildevandskomiteen Skrift
DANIS — Datennachweis Informationssystem
Danish M Bull — Danish Medical Bulletin
Danish Yearb Phil — Danish Yearbook of Philosophy
Dan J Plant Soil Sci — Danish Journal of Plant and Soil Science
DANKA — Doklady Akademii Nauk SSR
Dan Kemi — Dansk Kemi
Dan Landbr — Dansk Landbrug
Dan Mag — Danske Magazin
Danmarks Geol Undersoegelse — Danmarks Geologiske Undersoegelse
Dan Med B — Danish Medical Bulletin

Dan Med Bull — Danish Medical Bulletin
Dan Med Bull Suppl — Danish Medical Bulletin. Supplement
Dan Medicinhist Arbog — Dansk Medicinhistorisk Arbog
Danm Geol Undersoeg — Danmarks Geologiske Undersoegelse
DANN — Dannzha
Dan Naturfr — Dansk Naturfredning
Dan Naturfredning — Dansk Naturfredning
Dan Naturfredningsforen Arsskr — Danmarks Naturfredningsforenings Arsskrift
Dan Ornithol Foren Feltornithol — Dansk Ornithologisk Forening. Feltornithologen
Dan Ornithol Foren Fuglevaern — Dansk Ornithologisk Forening. Fuglevaern
Dan Ornithol Foren Tidsskr — Dansk Ornithologisk Forenings Tidsskrift
Dan Patenttid — Dansk Patenttidende
Dan Pelsdyravl — Dansk Pelsdyravl
Dan Pelsdyrbl — Dansk Pelsdyrblad
Dan Pest Infest Lab Annu Rep — Danish Pest Infestation Laboratory. Annual Report
Dan Psykolognyt — Dansk Psykolognyt
Dan Rev Game Biol — Danish Review of Game Biology
Dansalan Q — Dansalan Quarterly
Dan Selsk Bygningsstatik Bygningsstatiske Medd — Dansk Selskab foer Bygningsstatik, Bygningsstatiske Meddelelser
Dansk Aarbog Mf — Dansk Aarbog for Musikforskning
Dansk Audiol — Dansk Audiologopaedi
Dansk Bog — Dansk Bogfortegnelse
Dansk Botan — Dansk Botanisk Arkiv
Dansk Dendrol Arsskr — Dansk Dendrologisk Arsskrift
Danske Bnk — Bank Letter den Danske Landsmandsbank
Danske Vid Selsk Mat-Fys Medd — Det Kongelige Danske Videnskabernes Selskab. Matematisk-Fysiske Meddelelser
Danske Vid Selsk Skrift — Kongelige Danske Videnskabernes Selskabs Skrifter
Dansk Geol Foren Medd — Dansk Geologisk Forening Meddelelser
Dansk Geol Foren Meddel — Dansk Geologisk Forening Meddelelser
Dansk Mt — Dansk Musiktidsskrift
Dansk Mus — Dansk Musiktidsskrift
Dan Skovforen Tidsskr — Dansk Skovforenings Tidsskrift
Dansk Rad Ind — Dansk Radio Industri
Dansk Tekn Tidsskr — Dansk Teknisk Tidsskrift
Dansk T Farm — Dansk Tidsskrift foer Farmaci
Dansk Tidssk Farm — Dansk Tidsskrift foer Farmaci
Dansk Tidsskr — Dansk Tidsskrift
Dansk Ugeskr — Dansk Ugeskrift
Dansk Vid Selsk — Historisk-Filosofiske Meddelelser. Dansk Videnskabernes Selskab
DAN SSSR — Doklady Akademii Nauk SSSR
Dan Tdsskr Farm — Dansk Tidsskrift foer Farmaci
Dan Tek Tidsskr — Dansk Teknisk Tidsskrift
Dante Soc America Annu Rep — Dante Society of America. Annual Report
Dante Stud — Dante Studies
D Anthropol Gesell Korrespondenzbl — Deutsche Anthropologische Gesellschaft. Korrespondenzblatt
Dan Tidsskr Farm — Dansk Tidsskrift foer Farmaci
Dan Tidsskr Farm Suppl — Dansk Tidsskrift for Farmaci. Supplementum
Dan Tidsskr Farm Supple — Dansk Tidsskrift foer Farmaci. Supplementum
Dan Tss Museumsformidl — Dan Tidsskrift for Museumsformidling
DanTTs — Dansk Teologisk Tidsskrift
DanU — Dansk Udsyn
Dan Udsyn — Dansk Udsyn
Danvers Hist Soc Coll — Danvers Historical Society. Historical Collections
Dan Veterinaertidsskr — Dansk Veterinaertidsskrift
Danv Q — Danville Quarterly Review
Dan Yrbk Phil — Danish Yearbook of Philosophy
Danz AZ — Danzers Armeezeitung [Wien]
Danziger Statist Mitt — Danziger Statistische Mitteilungen
Danzig Schr — Schriften der Naturforschenden Gesellschaft in Danzig
Danzig Uniw Wydz Biol Nauk Ziemi Zesz Nauk Geogr — Danzig. Uniwersytet. Wydzial Biologii i Nauk o Ziemi. Zeszyty Naukowe. Geografia
DAOD — Defending All Outdoors. Alberta Fish and Game Association
DAOREO — Diseases of Aquatic Organisms
DAP — Deutsche Aussenpolitik
DAP — Quarterly. Department of Antiquities in Palestine
DAPBAB — Data Acquisition and Processing in Biology and Medicine
Da Pelsdyr — Dansk Pelsdyravl
Daphn — Daphnis. Zeitschrift fuer Mittlere Deutsche Literatur
Dapim Refu — Dapim Refuiim
DAPJD4 — Date Palm Journal
DAPNA — Doklady Akademii Pedagogicheskikh Nauk RSFSR
DAPOAG — Deutsche Apotheker
D Apoth Ztg — Deutsche Apotheker-Zeitung
DAPSAS — Developments in Applied Spectroscopy
Da R — Dalhousie Review
Dar al Athar al Islamiyyah Newslett — Dar al-Athar al-Islamiyyah Newsletter
D Arb — Dansk Arbejde
Darbai Liet Vet Akad — Darbai. Lietuvos Veterinarijos Akademijos
D Arch — Dialoghi di Archeologia
D Arch — Dodekanesiakon Archeion
D Arch Klin Med — Deutsches Archiv fuer Klinische Medizin
DArChr — Dictionnaire d'Archeologie Chretienne et de Liturgie
DArChrL — Dictionnaire d'Archeologie Chretienne et de Liturgie
DARE — Dictionary of American Regional English
Daresbury Lab Prepr DL/P — Daresbury Laboratory. Preprint DL/P
Daresbury Lab Prepr DL/SRF/P — Daresbury Laboratory. Preprint DL/SRF/P
Daresbury Lab Rep — Daresbury Laboratory. Report
Daresbury Lab Rep DL NUC R — Daresbury Laboratory. Report DL/NUC/R
Daresbury Lab Rep DL R — Daresbury Laboratory. Report DL/R
Daresbury Lab Rep DL SRF R — Daresbury Laboratory. Report DL/SRF/R

Daresbury Lab Tech Memo — Daresbury Laboratory. Technical Memorandum
Daresbury Nucl Phys Lab Rep — Daresbury Nuclear Physics Laboratory. Report
Daresbury Nucl Phys Lab Rep DNPL R — Daresbury Nuclear Physics Laboratory. Report DNPL/R
Daresbury Nucl Phys Lab Tech Memo — Daresbury Nuclear Physics Laboratory. Technical Memorandum
Daresbury Synchrotron Radia Lect Note Ser — Daresbury Synchrotron Radiation Lecture Note Series
Dar Es Salaam Med J — Dar Es Salaam Medical Journal
Dar es Salaam Univ Law J — Dar es Salaam University Law Journal
Darl — Darshana International
Darien Inst Technol J — Darien Institute of Technology. Journal
DARIS — Detroit Art Registration Information System
Dari Seama Sedintelor Com Stat Geol (Rom) — Dari de Seama ale Sedintelor. Comitetul de Stat al Geologiei (Romania)
Dari Seama Sedintelor Inst Geol Bucharest — Dari de Seama ale Sedintelor. Institutul Geologic (Bucharest)
Dari Seama Sedintelor Inst Geol Geofiz Bucharest — Dari de Seama ale Sedintelor. Institutul de Geologie si Geofizica (Bucharest)
Dari Seama Sedintelor Inst Geol (Rom) — Dari de Seama ale Sedintelor. Institutul Geologie (Romania)
Dari Seama Sedintelor Repub Pop Rom Com Geol — Dari Seama Sedintelor. Republica Populara Romana. Comitetul Geologic
Dari Seama Sedint RPR Com Geol — Dari de Seama ale Sedintelor. Republica Populara Romana Comitetul Geologic
Darken Conf Proc — Darken Conference. Proceedings
Darkroom Photogr — Darkroom Photography
DAR Mag — Daughters of the American Revolution. Magazine
Darmstaedt Echo — Darmstaedter Echo
Darmstaedter Beitr Neuen M — Darmstaedter Beitraege zur Neuen Musik
Darmst Notb — Notizblatt des Vereins fuer Erdkunde und Verwandte Wissenschaften zu Darmstadt und des Mittelrheinischen Geologischen Vereins
DAR Rep — National Society of the Daughters of the American Revolution. Annual Report
Dar Sag — Dictionnaire des Antiquites Grecques et Romaines (Daremberg and Saglio)
Darshana Int — Darshana International
Darstell Wuerttemberg Gesch — Darstellungen aus der Wuerttembergischen Geschichte
DART — Directory of American Research and Technology
Dart Bi-Mo — Dartmouth Bi-Monthly
Dartm Coll Bull — Dartmouth College. Bulletin
Dartmouth Alumni Mag — Dartmouth Alumni Magazine
D Art-T — Dansk Artilleri-Tidsskrift
Daru J Sch Pharm Tehran Univ Med Sci Health Serv — Daru. Journal of the School of Pharmacy. Tehran University of Medical Sciences and Health Services
Darulfunun Edebiyat Fak Mecmuasi — Darulfunun Edebiyat Fakultesi Mecmuasi
DARWAG — Darwiniana
Darwin — Darwiniana. Revista del Instituto de Botanica Darwinion
DAS — Developments in Atmosphere Science
DAS — Dictionary of American Scholars
DAS — Dictionary of American Slang
DASD — Deutsche Akademie fuer Sprache und Dichtung (Darmstadt). Jahrbuch
DASDJ — Deutsche Akademie fuer Sprache und Dichtung (Darmstadt). Jahrbuch
DASHAA — Symposium for the Salivary Gland
Dasika Hron — Dasika Hronika
DASJA — Journal. Dental Association of South Africa
Dasonomia Interamer — Dasonomia Interamericana. Instituto Interamericano de Ciencias Agricolas
DaSt — Dante Studies
DAT — Datamation
Data Acquis Process Biol Med — Data Acquisition and Processing in Biology and Medicine
Data Acquis Process Biol Med Proc Rochester Conf — Data Acquisition and Processing in Biology and Medicine. Proceedings of the Rochester Conference
Data Anal Astron — Data Analysis in Astronomy
Data At Power — Data of Atomic Power
Database J — Database Journal
Database Jrnl — Database Journal
Data Base News — Data Base Newsletter
Database Sys — ACM [Association for Computing Machinery] Transactions on Database Systems
Data Bus — Data Business
Data C — Data Communications
Data Chan — Data Channels
D Atache — Defence Attache
Data Comm — Data Communications
Data Commun — Data Communications
Data C Xtra — Data Communications Extra
Data Dyn — Data Dynamics
Data Ed — Data Education
Data Hand Sci Technol — Data Handling in Science and Technology
Data Knowl Eng — Data and Knowledge Engineering
Data Manage — Data Management
Data Mgmt — Data Management
Data Mgt — Data Management
Datam NR — Datamation News Release
Data Proc — Data Processing
Data Proc Dig — Data Processing Digest
Data Proces — Data Processing
Data Process — Data Processing
Data Process — Data Processing Digest
Data Process Dig — Data Processing Digest
Data Process Educ — Data Processing for Education

Data Process Mag — Data Processing Magazine
Data Process Manage — Data Processing for Management
Data Process Med — Data Processing in Medicine
Data Process Pract — Data Processing Practitioner
Datapro Com Sol — Datapro Communications Solutions
Datapro Man Sm Comp Sys — Datapro Management of Small Comuter Systems
Datapro Rep Data Commun — Datapro Reports on Data Communications
Datapro Rep Minicomput — Datapro Reports on Minicomputers
Datapro Rep Office Syst — Datapro Reports on Office Systems
Data Rec Oceanogr Obs Explor Fish (Hokkaido) — Data Record of Oceanographic Observations and Exploratory Fishing (Hokkaido)
Data Rep — Data Report
Data Rep Virginia Inst Mar Sci — Data Report. Virginia Institute of Marine Science
Datas Ecol Morphol — Datas on Ecological Morphology
Data Ser Des Inst Phys Prop Data — Data Series. Design Institute for Physical Property Data
Data Sys — Data Systems
Data Syst — Data Systems
Data Systems N — Data Systems News
Data Trng — Data Training
Data User Ns — Data Users News
DATE — Directory of Australian Tertiary Education
Date Grow Inst Rep — Date Growers' Institute. Report
Daten Dok Umweltschutz — Daten und Dokumente zum Umweltschutz
Datenverarb Med — Datenverarbeitung in der Medizin
Datenverarb Recht — Datenverarbeitung im Recht
Date Palm J — Date Palm Journal
DATJBM — Datenjournal
DATPR — Domestic Air Transport Policy Review
Datum Collect Tokai Reg Fish Res Lab — Datum Collection. Tokai Regional Fisheries Research Laboratory
DAU — Datamation
DAUK — Deutsche Arbeiten der Universitaet Koeln
Dauph Med — Dauphine Medical
Dav — Davar. Revista Literaria
DAVEDJ — Dansk Veterinaertidsskrift
Davenport Acad Sci Proc — Davenport Academy of Sciences. Proceedings
Davis Land Ct Dec (Mass) — Davis' Land Court Decisions (Massachusetts)
Davos Symp — Davos Symposium
DAVS — Developments in Animal and Veterinary Sciences
DAVSDR — Developments in Animal and Veterinary Sciences
DAW — Denkschriften der Akademie der Wissenschaften in Wien
DAWAK — Mitteilungen des Deutschen Archaeologischen Instituts. Abteilung Kairo
DAWB — Deutsche Akademie der Wissenschaften zu Berlin
DAWBIDSL — Deutsche Akademie der Wissenschaften zu Berlin. Institut fuer Deutsche Sprache und Literatur
DAWBM — Monatsberichte der Deutschen Akademie der Wissenschaften zu Berlin
Dawe Dig — Dawe Digest
DAWRA — Mitteilungen des Deutschen Archaeologischen Instituts. Roemische Abteilung
DAWW — Denkschriften der Akademie der Wissenschaften in Wien
Dax S Borda Bll — Bulletin de la Societe de Borda a Dax
Day Care & Early Educ — Day Care and Early Education
Dayton — University of Dayton. Intramural Law Review
Dayton A Inst Bull — Dayton Art Institute Bulletin
Dayton Med — Dayton Medicine
DAZ — Deutsche Allgemeine Zeitung
DAZ — Deutsche Angler-Zeitung
DAZ — Deutsche Apotheker-Zeitung
DAZEA2 — Deutsche Apotheker-Zeitung
DB — Daybooks for Knossos
DB — Der Betrieb
DB — Deutsche Bibliographie
DB — Deutsche Buehne
DB — Developments in Biochemistry
DB — Dialektolohicnyi Bjuleten
DB — Dictionnaire de la Bible
DB — Doitsu Bungaku
Db — Downbeat
DBA — Baumarkt. Zeitschrift fuer Wirtschaftliche Unternehmensfuehrung
DBA — Dansk Botanisk Arkiv
DBB — Deutsche Bibliographie. Das Deutsche Buch. Auswahl Wichtiger Neuerscheinungen
DBB — Developments in Bioenergetics and Biomembranes
DBCRB2 — Diabetologia Croatica
DBDK — Daito Bunka Daigaku Kiyo
DBDKK — Daito Bunka Daigaku Kangakkaishi
DBE — Dictionary of Bahamian English
DBED — Diabetes Educator
D Bei — Deutsche Beitraege
DBEU — Deutsche Blaetter fuer Erziehenden Unterricht
DBF — Dictionnaire de Biographie Francaise
DBF — Distributie Vandaag. Maandblad over Verkooppromotie en Moderne Handelstechniek
DB Film Orienter — DB Film/Orientering
DBGGA — Dopovidi Akademii Nauk Ukrains'koi RSR. Seriya B. Geologiya, Geofizika, Khimiya, ta Biologiya
DBGU — Deutsche Beitraege zur Geistigen Ueberlieferung
DBHVA — Deutsche Bibliographie. Halbjahres-Verzeichnis
DBI — Defense Budget Intelligence
DBIA — Weekblad der Directe Belastingen, Invoerrechten en Accijnzen
D Bien Zt — Deutsche Bienenzeitung
DB II — Dun and Bradstreet Dunserve II
DBIOA — Doklady Biochemistry
DBIR — Directory of Biotechnology Information Resources

DBJ — Duke Bar Journal
DBJb — Deutsches Biographisches Jahrbuch
Dble Dealer — Double Dealer
DBLRA — Doklady Akademii Nauk BSSR
DBM — Dun's Business Month
DBMAD — Auerbach Data Base Management
DBNM — Darmstaedter Beitraege zur Neuen Musik
DBO — Directors and Boards
D Bot A — Dansk Botanisk Arkiv
D Bot Ms — Deutsche Botanische Monatsschrift
DBR — Dialectes Belgo-Romans
DBR Pap Natl Res Counc Can Div Build Res — DBR Paper (National Research Council of Canada. Division of Building Research)
DBSch — Deutsche Berufsschule
DB Sound Eng Mag — DB. The Sound Engineering Magazine
Dbt — Downbeat
DBTEAD — Diabete [Later, Diabete et Metabolisme]
DBTGAJ — Diabetologia
DBUS — Dun and Bradstreet United States
DBW — Denkmalpflege in Baden-Wuerttemberg
DBW — Dresdner Bank Wirtschaftsbericht
DBWBD — Deutsche Bibliographie. Woechentliches Verzeichnis. Reihe B
DBWCD — Deutsche Bibliographie. Woechentliches Verzeichnis. Reihe C
DBWVA — Deutsche Bibliographie. Woechentliches Verzeichnis. Reihe A
DBZ — Deutsche Bauzeitung
DBZT-A — Deutsche Bauzeitung
DC — [The] Daily Chronicle
DC — De Colores. Journal of Emerging Raza Philosophies
DC — Developments in Crop Science
DC — Documentation Catholique
DC — Treasury Department Circular
DCA — Diario de Centro America
DCA — Dictionary of Christian Antiquities
DCan — Dictionary of Canadianisms
DCB — Developments in Cell Biology
DCB — Dictionary of Christian Biography
DCB J — DC Bar Journal
DCCN — Dimensions of Critical Care Nursing
DC Code Ann — District of Columbia Code. Annotated
DCD — Kredietwaardigheden
DCDI — Dairy Council Digest
DCE — Developments in Civil Engineering
DCF — Daniell. Forms and Precedents in Chancery
DCF — Direction Commerciale Francaise
DCG — Dictionary of Christ and the Gospels
D Ch — Deutsche Chirurgie
DCHTA — Doklady Chemical Technology
DCI — Deuxieme Conference Internationale d'Histoire Economique
DCIMDQ — Developmental and Comparative Immunology
DCINA — Drug and Cosmetic Industry
DC Jur — Dalloz Critique. Jurisprudence
DCKHDL — Denryoku Chuo Kenkyusho Hokoku
DCL — Dalloz Critique. Legislation
DC Lib — District of Columbia Libraries
D Clin North America — Dental Clinics of North America
DCLR — District Court Law Reports
DCMS — Deccan College. Monograph Series
DC Mun Regs — DC [District of Columbia] Municipal Regulations
DCN — Daily Commercial News and Shipping List
DCN — Daily Consumer News
DCNAA — Dental Clinics of North America
DCNAAC — Dental Clinics of North America
DCNNAH — Decheniana
DCNQ — Devon and Cornwall. Notes and Queries
DC Nurs Action — District of Columbia Nursing Action
DCO — DnC Monthly Survey of Norwegian Trade, Industry, and Finance
Dcom — Doctor Communis
DCR — Developments in Cancer Research
DCR — District Court Reports
DC Reg — District of Columbia Register
DCRI — Deccan College Postgraduate and Research Institute. Bulletin
DCR (NSW) — District Court Reports (New South Wales)
DCS — Defects in Crystalline Solids
DCSCDC — Developments in Crop Science
DC Stat — District of Columbia Statutes at Large
DD — Dance and Dancers
DD — Decachord
DD — Deutsche Dialektgeographie
DD — Development Digest
DD — Diskussion Deutsch
DdA — Dialoghi di Archeologia
D d A — Droit d'Auteur
DDB — Der Deutsche Beamte
DdB — Distrito de Braga
DDB — Dortmund Data Bank
DDBP — Dance Data Base Project
DDC — Dictionnaire de Droit Canonique
DDD Diffus Defect Data — DDD. Diffusion and Defect Data
D Dev Rd — Deutsche Devisen-Rundschau
DDG — Deutsche Dialektgeographie
DDH — Dialogo Dor Haemshej
DDI — Derecho de Integracion
DDI — Documenti Diplomatici Italiani
DDIAEW — Dialogue on Diarrhoea
DDJ — Deutsches Dante-Jahrbuch

DDJ — Dr. Dobb's Journal
D DI M — Dansk Maanedsskrift for Dyrlaeger
DdO — Defense de l'Occident
DDO — Der Deutsche Oekonomist
D d O — Digest des Ostens
DDP — Die Deutsche Post
D Dr — Deutsche Drama
DDR — Developments in Diabetes Research
DDREDK — Drug Development Research
DDRKA — Doshisha Daigaku Rikogaku Kenkyu Hokoku
DDR-Med-Rep — DDR-Medizin-Report
DDS — Digest of Dental Science
DDS — Digital Design
DDSB — Duke Divinity School. Bulletin [Later, Duke Divinity School. Review]
DDSCD — Digestive Diseases and Sciences
DDSCDJ — Digestive Diseases and Sciences
DDT — Darling Downs Times
D d W — Dialectes de Wallonie
DDZ — Dokumentation der Zeit
DDZZA — DDZ. Das Deutsche Zahnaerzteblatt
DE — Daily Express
DE — Debate
DE — DE. Journal of Dental Engineering
DE — Dene Express. Fort Good Hope
DE — Deutsche Erde
DE — Developing Economies
DE — Diritto Ecclesiastico
DE — Divulgaciones Etnologicas [Barranquilla]
DE — Dope
DE — Dynamic Economics
DE — Excavations at Dura Europos
DE — Journal of Dental Engineering
DE — Journal of Drug Education
De 8 & Opbouw — De Acht en Opbouw
DEA — Daily Engineering Articles
DEA — Desarrollo Economico (Argentina)
Deaconess Hosp Med Bull — Deaconess Hospital. Medical Bulletin
Deact Poisoning Catal — Deactivation and Poisoning of Catalysts
Deafness Res & Train Cent — Deafness Research and Training Center
Dealerscop — Dealerscope Merchandising
DEAR — Dizionario Epigrafico di Antichita Romane
Dearborn Ind — Dearborn Independent
Dearborn Indep — Dearborn Independent
Dearsl Cr Pr — Dearsley's Criminal Process
DEASA — Dental Assistant
Death Educ — Death Education
Death Pen Rep — Death Penalty Reporter
Death Stud — Death Studies
DEB — Department of State. Bulletin
DEB — Dictionnaire Encyclopedique de la Bible
DEBEAC — Decheniana Beihefte
DEBEDF — Deviant Behavior
De Beers Duesseldorf Conf Pap — De Beers Duesseldorf-Conference. Papers
DEBFDI — Developments in Environmental Biology of Fishes
DEBIAO — Developmental Biology
DEBIDR — Developments in Biochemistry
DEBI — Deutsch-Evangelische Blaetter
DEBII — Deutsch-Evangelische Blaetter
De Bow — De Bow's Commercial Review
De Bows R — De Bow's Review
Debrecceni Mezogazd Akad Tud Evk — Debrecceni Mezogazdasagi Akademia Tudomanyos Evkonyve
Debrecceni Sz — Debrecceni Szemle
Debreceni Mezoegazd Kiserl Intez Evk — Debreceni Mezoegazdasagi Kiserleti Intezet Evkoenyve
Debreceni Mezogazd Akad Tud Evk — Debreceni Mezogazdasagi Akademia Tudomanyos Evkonyve
Debreceni Tisza Istvan Tud Tars 2 Orv Termeszettud Oszt Munka — Debreceni Tisza Istvan Tudomanyos Tarsasag II. Orvos-Termeszettudomanyi Osztalyanak Munkai
Debrec Muz Evk — Debreceni Deri Muzeum Evokoenyve
Debre Muz Evk — Debreceni Deri Muzeum Evkoenyve
DEBSAK — Developmental Biology. Supplement
DEBZA — Deutsche Bauzeitschrift. Fachblatt fuer Entwurf und Ausfuehrung
Dec — Decade of Short Stories
DEC — Decision Sciences
DEC — Deutscher Baustellen Informationsdienst
DEC — Developing Economies
DEC — Development and Change
DECAA — Dental Cadmos
Decade Egypt — Decade Egyptienne
Decalogue J — Decalogue Journal
Dec A Soc J — Decorative Arts Society Journal
Decc Geogr — Deccan Geographer
Decen Dig — American Digest (Decennial Edition)
DECHEMA Monogr — DECHEMA [Deutsche Gesellschaft fuer Chemisches Apparatewesen, Chemische Technik, und Biotechnologie eV] Monographien
Decheniana B Biol Abt — Decheniana. Verhandlungen des Naturhistorischen Vereins der Rheinlande und Westerfalens. B. Biologische Abteilung
Decheniana Beih — Decheniana Beihefte
Decid Fruit Grow — Deciduous Fruit Grower
Decid Fruit Grow Sagtevrugteboer — Deciduous Fruit Grower. Die Sagtevrugteboer
Deciduous Fruit Grow — Deciduous Fruit Grower
Decimal Research Bul — Decimal Research Bulletin

Decis Geogr Bd Can — Decisions. Geographic Board of Canada
Decis Sci — Decision Sciences
Decis Support Syst — Decision Support Systems
Decis US Geogr Bd — Decisions. United States Geographic Board
De Coll Age Bull Aktuel Ideen — De-Coll/Age. Bulletin Aktueller Ideen
Decontam Decomm Nucl Facil Proc Am Nucl Soc Top Meet — Decontamination and Decommissioning of Nuclear Facilities. Proceedings. American Nuclear Society Topical Meeting
DECOR — DECHEMA [Deutshe Gesellschaft fuer Chemisches Apparatenesen, Chemische Technik, und Biotechnologie e V] Corrosion Data Base
Decorative Arts Soc Jnl — Decorative Arts Society. Journal
Decorator — Decorator and Painter for Australia and New Zealand
DECRDP — Drugs under Experimental and Clinical Research
Decs — Decision
Ded — Dedalo
DEDIA — Dental Digest
DE Dom Eng — DE. Domestic Engineering [Formerly, DE Journal]
DeEc — De Economist
DEECAL — Dental Echo
DEED — Death Education. Pedagogy, Counseling, Care
Deep Delta Q — Deep Delta Quarterly
Deeper Pathways High Energy Phys — Deeper Pathways in High-Energy Physics
Deep Inelastic Fusion React Heavy Ions Proc Symp — Deep-Inelastic and Fusion Reactions with Heavy Ions. Proceedings. Symposium
Deep Sea Drill Proj Initial Rep — Deep Sea Drilling Project. Initial Reports
Deep-Sea Oceanogr Abstr — Deep-Sea Research and Oceanographic Abstracts
Deep Sea Re — Deep-Sea Research [Later, Deep-Sea Research with Oceanographic Literature Review]
Deep Sea Res — Deep-Sea Research [Later, Deep-Sea Research with Oceanographic Literature Review]
Deep Sea Res & Oceanogr Abstr — Deep Sea Research and Oceanographic Abstracts
Deep Sea Res Oceanogr Abstr — Deep Sea Research and Oceanographic Abstracts
Deep-Sea Res Part A — Deep-Sea Research. Part A. Oceanographic Research Papers [Later, Deep-Sea Research with Oceanographic Literature Review]
Deep-Sea Res Part A Oceanogr Res Pap — Deep-Sea Research. Part A. Oceanographic Research Papers [Later, Deep-Sea Research with Oceanographic Literature Review]
Deep Sea Res Part B Oceanogr Lit Rev — Deep Sea Research. Part B. Oceanographic Literature Review
Deep-Sea Res Pt A Oceanogr Res Pap — Deep-Sea Research. Part A. Oceanographic Research Papers [Later, Deep-Sea Research with Oceanographic Literature Review]
Deep-Sea Res Pt B Oceanogr Lit Rev — Deep-Sea Research. Part B. Oceanographic Literature Review
Deer Farm — Deer Farmer
Def Aer — Defence Aerienne
Defarmhera — Defense and Armament Heracles International
DEFAZET Dtsche Farben Z — DEFAZET. Deutsche Farben Zeitschrift
Def Daily — Defense Daily
Defect Complexes Semicond Struct Proc Int Sch — Defect Complexes in Semiconductor Structures. Proceedings. International School
Defect Diffus Forum — Defect and Diffusion Forum
Defects Insul Cryst Proc Int Conf — Defects in Insulating Crystals. Proceedings. International Conference
Defects Radiat Eff Semicond Invited Contrib Pap Int Conf — Defects and Radiation Effects in Semiconductors. Invited and Contributed Papersfrom the International Conference on Defects and Radiation Effects in Semiconductors
Defects Semicond Proc Mater Res Soc Annu Meet — Defects in Semiconductors. Proceedings. Materials Research Society Annual Meeting
Defects Silicon 2 Proc Symp — Defects in Silicon 2. Proceedings. Symposium on Defects in Silicon
Defect Struct Morphol Prop Deposits Proc Symp — Defect Structure, Morphology and Properties of Deposits. Proceedings of a Symposium
DEFEDZ — Defenders
Defektol — Defektologija
Defektosk — Defektoskopiya
Defektoskopiya Met — Defektoskopiya Metallov
Def Elect — Defense Electronics
Def Electron — Defense Electronics
Defence Sci J — Defence Science Journal
Defenders Wildl — Defenders of Wildlife Magazine [Later, Defenders]
Defenders Wildl Int — Defenders of Wildlife International
Defenders Wildl News — Defenders of Wildlife News
Defense A — Defense Africa and the Middle East
Defense Jpn — Defense of Japan, 1984
Defense L J — Defense Law Journal
Defense Mgt J — Defense Management Journal
Defense Nat — Defense Nationale
Defense Ns — Defense News
Defense Sci J — Defense Science Journal
Defense Veg — Defense des Vegetaux
Defens R & D — Defense R and D Update. Space, Aeronautics, and Electronic Systems
Defesa Nac Rio — A Defesa Nacional (Rio de Janeiro)
DEFGA — Deciduous Fruit Grower
Def Heli W — Defense Helicopter World
Defic Ment Jeunes Colloq — Deficience Mentale chez les Jeunes. Colloque
Defining Lab Anim Symp — Defining the Laboratory Animal. Symposium
Def J — Defence Journal
Def Latin A — Defensa Latino Americana
Def Law J — Defense Law Journal
Def L J — Defense Law Journal
Def Man J — Defense Management Journal

Def Mark Technol — Defense Markets and Technology
Def Med Soc — Defensa Medico Social
Def Ment — Deficience Mentale
Def Met Inf Cent Battelle Meml Inst DMIC Rep — Defense Metals Information Center. Batelle Memorial Institute. DMICReport
Def Mntr — Defense Monitor
Def Nat — Defense Nationale
Def Natl — Defense Nationale
Def Natn — Defense Nationale. Problemes Politiques Economiques, Scientifiques, Militaires
Def Nucl Agency Rep DNA (US) — Defense Nuclear Agency. Report DNA (United States)
Def Occident — Defense de l'Occident
De For Af — Defense and Foreign Affairs
Deform Met — Deformacion Metalica
Deform Razrushenie Neravnomernykh Temp Polyakh — Deformatsiya i Razrushenie v Neravnomernykh Temperaturnykh Polyakh
Def Plant — Defense des Plantes
Def Res Abs Contractors Edn — Defence Research Abstracts. Contractors Edition
Def Sci — Defense Science 2001
Def Sci J — Defence Science Journal
Def Sci Technol Organ Tech Note DSTO TN — Defence Science and Technology Organisation. Technical Note DSTO-TN
Def Sci Technol Organ Tech Rep DSTO-GD — Defence Science and Technology Organisation. Technical Report DSTO-GD
Def Stand Lab DSL Rep — Australia. Defence Standards Laboratories. DSL Report
Def Stand Lab Rep — Australia. Defence Standards Laboratories. Report
Def Stand Lab Tech Memo — Australia. Defence Standards Laboratories. Technical Memorandum
Def Stand Lab Tech Note — Australia. Defence Standards Laboratories. Technical Note
Def Sys Rv — Defense Systems Review and Military Communications
Def Syst Man Rev — Defense Systems Management Review
Def Tech Inf Cent Dig — Defense Technical Information Center. Digest
Def Tech Int — Defense Technology International
Def Today — Defense Today
Def Transp J — Defense Transportation Journal
Def Veg — Defense des Vegetaux
Def Wildl — Defenders of Wildlife
Def Wildl Int — Defenders of Wildlife International
Def Wildl News — Defenders of Wildlife News
Deg — Degres. Revue de Synthese a Orientation Semiologique
DEG — Design
DEG — Developments in Economic Geology
De G & J — De Gex and Jones' English Chancery Reports
De G & J By — De Gex and Jones' English Bankruptcy Appeals
De G & Sm — De Gex and Smale's English Chancery Reports
DEGEA3 — Deutsche Gesundheitswesen
De Gids — De Gids op Maatschappelijk Gebied
DEG Inf Ser UK At Energy Auth Dev Eng Group — DEG Information Series. United Kingdom Atomic Energy Authority. Development andEngineering Group
Degrad Stab Mater Pap Arab Int Conf Mater Sci — Degradation and Stabilization of Materials. Papers presented at the Arab International Conference in Materials Science
De Gruyter Exp Math — De Gruyter Expositions in Mathematics
De Gruyter Ser Nonlinear Anal Appl — De Gruyter Series in Nonlinear Analysis and Applications
De Gruyter Stud Math — De Gruyter Studies in Mathematics
DeH — De Homine
DeH — Delaware History
DEHEA8 — Dental Health
DEHYD3 — Developments in Hydrobiology
DEI — Dizionario Etimologico Italiano
DEIMD6 — Developments in Immunology
DE/J — DE Journal [*Later, DE. Domestic Engineering*]
DE J Dent Eng — DE. Journal of Dental Engineering
Dejiny Ved Tech — Dejiny Ved a Techniky
DeKalb — DeKalb Literary Arts Journal
DeKalb Lit — DeKalb Literary Arts Journal
Dek Isk — Dekorativnoye Iskusstvo
Dek Isk SSSR — Dekorativnoye Iskusstvo SSSR
Dek Iskusstvo — Dekorativnoe Iskusstvo SSSR
Dek Kst — Dekorative Kunst
Dekor Isk SSSR — Dekorativnoe Iskusstvo SSSR
Del — Delaware Supreme Court Reports
DEL — Dictionnaire Etymologique de la Langue Latine
Del Ag Exp — Delaware. Agricultural Experiment Station. Publications
Del Agric Exp Stn Bull — Delaware. Agricultural Experiment Station. Bulletin
Del Agric Exp Stn Circ — Delaware. Agricultural Experiment Station. Circular
Dela Inst Biol Slov Akad Znan — Dela Institut za Biologijo. Slovenska Akad. Znanosti in Umietnosti. Opera. Institutum Biologicum. Academia Scientiarum et Artium Slovenica
Delaware Co Inst Sc Pr — Delaware County Institute of Science. Proceedings
Delaware Hist Soc Papers — Delaware Historical Society. Papers
Delaware J Corp L — Delaware Journal of Corporate Law
Del Cas — Delaware Cases
Del Ch — Delaware Chancery Reports
Del-Chem Bull — Del-Chem Bulletin
Del Code Ann — Delaware Code. Annotated
Del Co L J (PA) — Delaware County Law Journal
Del Cty Farm Home News — Delaware County Farm and Home News
Delft Ec Pol A — Annales de l'Ecole Polytechnique de Delft
Delft Hydrosci Abstr — Delft Hydroscience Abstracts
Delft Prog Rep — Delft Progress Report
Delft Prog Report — Delft Progress Report

Delft Prog Rep Ser A — Delft Progress Report. Series A. Chemistry and Physics, Chemical and Physical Engineering
Delft Prog Rep Ser B — Delft Progress Report. Series B. Electrical, Electronic, and Information Engineering
Delft Prog Rep Ser C — Delft Progress Report. Series C. Mechanical and Aeronautical Engineering and Shipbuilding
Delft Prog Rep Ser D — Delft Progress Report. Series D. Architecture, Industrial Design, Social Sciences
Delft Prog Rep Ser E — Delft Progress Report. Series E. Geosciences
Delft Prog Rep Ser F — Delft Progress Report. Series F. Mathematical Engineering, Mathematics, and Information Engineering
Delft Progress Rep Ser F — Delft Progress Report. Series F. Mathematical Engineering, Mathematics, and Information Engineering
Delft Stud — Delftse Studien
Del Geol Surv Bull — Delaware. Geological Survey. Bulletin
Del Geol Survey Ann Rept Bull Rept Inv — Delaware. Geological Survey. Annual Report. Bulletin. Report of Investigations
Del Geol Surv Rep Invest — Delaware. Geological Survey. Report of Investigations
DelH — Delaware History
Delhi Alum Patrika — Delhi Aluminium Patrika
Delhi L R — Delhi Law Review
Delhi L Rev — Delhi Law Review
Delhi L Times — Delhi Law Times
Del Hist — Delaware History
Del Hlth News — Delaware Health News
Deliberations Soc R Can — Deliberations. Societe Royale du Canada
Delin — Delineator
Delineavit & Sculp — Delineavit et Sculpsit
Delin N Lett — Delinquency News Letter. University of Michigan
Delius — Delius Society. Journal
Del J Corp L — Delaware Journal of Corporate Law
Delkeletdunantuli Mezogazd Kiserl Intez Kozl — Delkeletdunantuli Mezogazdasagi Kiserleti Intezet Kozlemenye
DELL — Dictionnaire Etymologique de la Langue Latine
Del Laws — Laws of Delaware
Del L R — Delhi Law Review
Del Med J — Delaware Medical Journal
DelN — Delaware Notes
Del Note — Delaware Notes
Del Notes — Delaware Notes
Del Nurs — Delaware Nurse
Delos — Explorations Archeologiques de Delos
Delphinium Soc Yearb — Delphinium Society Yearbook
Delpinoa NS — Delpinoa. Nuova Serie del Bulletino dell'Orto Botanico. Universita di Napoli
Del Sea Grant Tech Rep DEL-SG — Delaware Sea Grant Technical Report. DEL-SG
Del State Bar Assn — Delaware State Bar Association
Del State Med J — Delaware State Medical Journal
Del St Med J — Delaware State Medical Journal
Del St M J — Delaware State Medical Journal
Delt — Archaiologikon Deltion
Delta ES — Delta. Revue du Centre d'Etudes et de Recherche sur les Ecrivains du Sud aux Etats-Unis
Delt Agrotikes Trapezes — Deltion Agrotikes Trapezes
Delta J Sci — Delta Journal of Science
Delta Kappa Gamma Bull — Delta Kappa Gamma Bulletin
Delta Pi Epsilon J — Delta Pi Epsilon Journal
Delt Arch — Deltion Archaiologikon
Delt Bibl Melet — Deltion Biblikon Meleton
Delt Chr — Deltion tes Christianikes Archaiologikes Hetaireias
Delt Ell Mikrobiol Etair — Deltio Ellenikes Mikrobiologikes Etaireias
Delt Hellen Mikrobiol Hyg Hetair — Deltion Hellenikes Mikrobiologikes kai Hygieinologikes Hetaireias
Delt Hell Geogr Het — Deltion Hellenikes Geografikes Hetaireias
Delt Hell Geol Hetair — Deltion tes Hellenikes Geolokne Hetaireias
Delt Hell Kteniatr Hetair — Deltion tes Hellenikes Kteniatrikes Hetaireias
Delt Hell Mikr Hyg Het — Deltion Hellenikes Mikrobiologikes kai Hygieinologikes Hetaireias
Delt Hell Mikrobiol Hetair — Deltion Hellenikes Mikrobiologikes Hetaireias
Delt Hell Mikrobiol Hygieinol Hetair — Deltion Hellenikes Mikrobiologikes kai Hygieinologikes Hetaireias
Delt IKA — Deltion Hidrymatos Koinonikon Asphaliseon
Delt Inst Technol Phytikon Proionton — Deltion tou Institoutou Technologias Phytikon Proionton
Deltion — Archaiologikon Deltion
Deltion Archaiol — Deltion Archaiologikon
Deltion Christ — Deltion tes Christianikes Archaiologikes Hetaireias
Deltion Christ Archaiol Etaireias — Deltion tis Christianikis Archaiologikis Etaireias
Deltion Istor & Ethnol Etaireias — Deltion tis Istorikis kai Ethnologikis Etaireias
Del Univ Agric Exp Stn Bull — Delaware. University. Agricultural Experiment Station. Bulletin
Del Univ Agric Exp Stn Circ — Delaware University. Agricultural Experiment Station. Circular
Del Univ Sea Grant Program Annu Rep — Delaware University. Sea Grant Program. Annual Report
Del Univ Water Resour Semin Proc — Delaware University. Water Resources Seminars. Proceedings
Del Val Bus D — Delaware Valley Business Digest
Dem — Democratie 60-62
Dem — Demografia
DEM — Developments in Environmental Modelling
DEMAB — Dental Management
DEMAEP — Dental Materials
Demag Nachr — Demag Nachrichten

Demande Brev Eur — Demande de Brevet Europeen
Demande Brev Invent (Fr) — Demande de Brevet d'Invention (France)
Demande Certif Addit (Fr) — Demande de Certificat d'Addition (France)
Demande Certif Util (Fr) — Demande de Certificat d'Utilite (France)
Dem Dir — Democrazia e Diritto
Dementia Geriatr Cognit Disord — Dementia and Geriatric Cognitive Disorders
Dementia Rev — Dementia Reviews
Demo — Democracy
DEMO — Demography
Demo & Chr — Democrat and Chronicle
Democratic R — Democratic Review
Democr e Dir — Democrazia e Diritto
Demogr — Demografia
Demogr — Demography
Demografia y Econ — Demografia y Economia
Demogr Bull — Demographic Bulletin
Demogr Dev Dig — Demography and Development Digest
Demogr y Econ — Demografia y Economia
Demokr Recht — Demokratie und Recht
Demo Left — Democratic Left
Demo Left — Newsletter of the Democratic Left
Demonstratio Math — Demonstratio Mathematica
Dempa Dig — Dempa Digest
Dem R — Democratic Review
DemStud — Demotische Studien
Den BA Rec — Denver Bar Association. Record
Dendritic Cells Fundam Clin Immunol — Dendritic Cells in Fundamental and Clinical Immunology
DENED7 — Developmental Neuroscience
DENFA7 — Dendroflora
Den'gi i Kred — Den'gi i Kredit
Deniliquin Hist Soc News — Deniliquin Historical Society. Newsletter
Denison Univ Sci Lab Jour — Denison University. Scientific Laboratories. Journal
Denison Univ Sc Lab B — Denison University. Scientific Laboratories. Bulletin
Denison Un Sc Lb Bll — Bulletin of the Scientific Laboratories of Denison University
Denitrif Soil Sediment — Denitrification in Soil and Sediment
Den JILP — Denver Journal of International Law and Policy
Den J Int L and Pol — Denver Journal of International Law and Policy
Den J Int'l L & Pol'y — Denver Journal of International Law and Policy
Denki Kag — Denki Kagaku
Denkm Aeg — Denkmaeler aus Aegypten und Aethiopien
Denkmaeler Ant — Denkmaeler Antiker Architektur
Denkmaeler Mal — Denkmaeler der Malerei des Altertums
Denkmaeler Skulpt — Denkmaeler Griechischer und Roemischer Skulptur
Denkmal Baden Wuerttemberg — Denkmalpflege in Baden-Wuerttemberg
Denkm Dt Tonkunst — Denkmaeler Deutscher Tonkunst
Denkm Klass — Denkmaeler des Klassischen Altertums zur Erlaeuterung des Lebens der Griechen und Roemer in Religion, Kunst, und Sitte
Denkm Pfl Bad Wuert — Denkmalpflege in Baden-Wuerttemberg
Denk Pfl Rhein Pfalz — Denkmalpflege in Rheinland-Pfalz
Denkschr Ak Wiss Wien — Denkschriften der Kaiserlichen Akademie der Wissenschaften (Wien)
Denkschr Allg Schweiz Ges Gesammte Naturwiss — Denkschriften der Allgemeinen Schweizerischen Gesellschaft fuer die Gesammten Naturwissenschaften
Denkschriften (Wien) — Oesterreichische Akademie der Wissenschaften. Philosophisch-Historische Klasse.Denkschriften (Wien)
Denkschriften Wien Ak — Denkschriften der Oesterreichischen Akademie der Wissenschaften. Philosophisch-Historische Klasse
Denkschr Kaiserl Akad Wiss Math Naturwiss Kl — Denkschriften der Kaiserlichen Akademie der Wissenschaften. Mathematisch-Naturwissenschaftliche Klasse
Denkschr Koenigl Bayr Bot Ges Regensburg — Denkschriften der Koeniglichen Bayrischen Botanischen Gesellschaft in Regensburg
Denkschr Russ Geogr Ges St Petersburg — Denkschriften der Russischen Geographischen Gesellschaft zu St. Petersburg
Denkschr Schweiz Natf Ges — Denkschriften der Schweizerischen Naturforschenden Gesellschaft
Denkschr Schweiz Naturforsch Ges — Denkschriften. Schweizerische Naturforschende Gesellschaft
Denkschr Vaterl Ges Aerzte Schwabens — Denkschriften der Vaterlaendischen Gesellschaft der Aerzte und Naturforscher Schwabens
Den LCJ — Denver Law Center. Journal
Den L J — Denver Law Journal
Den L N — Denver Legal News
Denmark Gronlands Geol Undersogelse Rapp — Denmark. Groenlands Geologiske Undersoegelse Rapport
DENN — Dene Nation Newsletter
DENPA3 — Dental Progress
Den Q — Denver Quarterly
Den Res Establ Risoe Rep — Denmark. Research Establishment Risoe. Report
Den Res Establ Risoe Rep Risoe M — Denmark. Research Establishment Risoe. Report Risoe-M
Den Res Establ Risoe Risoe Rep — Denmark. Research Establishment Risoe. Risoe Report
Den Risoe Natl Lab Rep Risoe M — Denmark. Risoe National Laboratory. Report Risoe-M
DENS — Denosa. Department of Northern Saskatchewan
Den Statens Husholdningsraad Tek Medd — Denmark. Statens Husholdningsraad. Tekniske Meddelelser
Dent Abstr — Dental Abstracts
Dent Anaesth Sedat — Dental Anaesthesia and Sedation
Dent Angles — Dental Angles
Dent Assist — Dental Assistant

Dent Assoc S Afr J — Dental Association of South Africa. Journal
Dent Bull — Dental Bulletin
Dent Bull Osaka Univ — Dental Bulletin. Osaka University
Dent Cadm — Dental Cadmos
Dent Cadmos — Dental Cadmos
Dent Clin N — Dental Clinics of North America
Dent Clin N Am — Dental Clinics of North America
Dent Clin North Am — Dental Clinics of North America
Dent Conc — Dental Concepts
Dent Concepts — Dental Concepts
Dent Cosm — Dental Cosmos
Dent Cosmos — Dental Cosmos
Dent Delin — Dental Delineator
Dent Dialogue — Dental Dialogue
Dent Dig — Dental Digest
Dent Dimens — Dental Dimensions
Dent Discourse — Dental Discourse
Dent Echo — Dental Echo
Den Tech Univ Struct Res Lab Rep — Denmark. Technical University. Structural Research Laboratory. Report
Dent Econ — Dental Economics
Dent Econ — Dental Economics - Oral Hygiene
Dent Fabr — Dental Fabrikant
Dent Fr — Dentiste de France
Dent Health (Lond) — Dental Health (London)
Dent Hyg — Dental Hygiene
Dent Images — Dental Images
Dent Ind — Dental Literature Index
Dent Items Interest — Dental Items of Interest
Dent J — Dental Journal
Dent J Aust — Dental Journal of Australia
Dent J Austr — Dental Journal of Australia
Dent J Malaysia Singapore — Dental Journal of Malaysia and Singapore
Dent J Nihon Univ — Dental Journal. Nihon University
Dent Jpn (Tokyo) — Dentistry in Japan (Tokyo)
Dent Lab Bl — Dental Laboratorie Bladet
Dent Labor (Munch) — Dental Labor (Munich)
Dent Lab Rev — Dental Laboratory Review
Dent Mag — Dental Magazine
Dent Mag — Dental Magazine and Oral Topics
Dent Mag — Dentists' Magazine
Dent Mag Oral Top — Dental Magazine and Oral Topics
Dent Manage — Dental Management
Dent Mater — Dental Materials
Dent Mater J — Dental Materials Journal
Dent Mirror (Atlanta) — Dental Mirror (Atlanta)
Dent Mirror (Quezon City) — Dental Mirror (Quezon City)
Dent News — Dentist News
Dent Obs — Dental Observer
Dento Maxillo Fac Radiol — Dento Maxillo Facial Radiology
Dent Outlook — Dental Outlook
Dent Pract — Dental Practitioner
Dent Pract (Cincinnati) — Dental Practice (Cincinnati)
Dent Pract Dent Rec — Dental Practitioner and Dental Record
Dent Pract (Ewell) — DP. Dental Practice (Ewell)
Dent Pract Manage — Dental Practice Management
Dent Press — Dental Press
Dent Prog — Dental Progress
Dent Qu — Dental Quarterly
Dent Radiogr Photogr — Dental Radiography and Photography
Dent Rec — Dental Record
Dent Refl — Dental Reflector
Dent Res Grad Study Q — Dental Research and Graduate Study Quarterly. Northwestern University
Dent Rev — Dental Revue
Dent Sci J Austr — Dental Science Journal of Australia
Dent Stud — Dental Student
Dent Surg — Dental Surgeon
Dent Surv — Dental Survey
Dent Tech — Dental Technician
Dent Ther Newsl — Dental Therapeutics Newsletter
Dent Update — Dental Update
Dent Wld — Dental World
Denver Bus — Denver Business
Denver J Internat Law and Policy — Denver Journal of International Law and Policy
Denver J Int L & Pol — Denver Journal of International Law and Policy
Denver J Int Law Policy — Denver Journal of International Law and Policy
Denver J Int'l L — Denver Journal of International Law
Denver Law — Denver Law Journal
Denver LCJ — Denver Law Center. Journal
Denver L J — Denver Law Journal
Denver L N — Denver Legal News
Denver Med Bull — Denver Medical Bulletin
Denver Med Times — Denver Medical Times
Denver Mus Nat History Mus Pictorial Pop Ser Proc — Denver Museum of Natural History. Museum Pictorial Popular Series. Proceedings
DenverQ — Denver Quarterly
Denver West Roundup — Denver Western Roundup
Denv Med Tim — Denver Medical Times
Denvr Post — Denver Post
DENZAX — Deutsche Entomologische Zeitschrift
DEOPDB — Developments in Ophthalmology
DeP — DePaul Law Review
DEP — Division of Electronic Products

DeP — Maandblad de Pacht

Dep Aeronaut Eng Kyoto Univ Curr Pap — Department of Aeronautical Engineering. Kyoto University. CurrentPapers

Dep Agric (Brisbane Queensl) Bur Sugar Exp Stn Tech Commun — Department of Agriculture (Brisbane, Queensland). Bureau of SugarExperiment Stations. Technical Communications

Dep Agric (NSW) Tech Bull — Department of Agriculture (New South Wales). Technical Bulletin

Dep Agric Straits Settlements Fed Malay States Econ Ser — Department of Agriculture. Straits Settlements and Federated Malay States. Economic Series

Dep Agric Straits Settlements Fed Malay States Gen Ser — Department of Agriculture. Straits Settlements and Federated Malay States. General Series

Dep Agric Straits Settlements Fed Malay States Sci Ser — Department of Agriculture. Straits Settlements and Federated Malay States. Scientific Series

Dep Agric (Victoria Aust) Tech Bull — Department of Agriculture (Victoria, Australia). Technical Bulletin

Dep Agric Victoria Tech Rep Ser — Department of Agriculture. Victoria Technical Report Series

Dep Appl Math Theor Phys Univ Cambridge Rep DAMTP — Department of Applied Mathematics and Theoretical Physics. Universityof Cambridge. Report DAMTP

De Paul L Rev — De Paul Law Review

DEPBA — Developmental Psychobiology

DEPBA5 — Developmental Psychobiology

Dep Biol Coll Bourget Rigaud Bull — Departement de Biologie. College Bourget Rigaud. Bulletin.

Dep Bull US Dep Agric — Department Bulletin. United States Department of Agriculture

Dep Cap Territ Conserv Ser (Canberra) — Department of the Capital Territory. Conservation Series (Canberra)

Dep Circ US Dep Agric — Department Circular. United States Department of Agriculture

Dep Def Aeronaut Res Lab Mech Eng Rep (Aust) — Department of Defence. Aeronautical Research Laboratories. Mechanical Engineering Report (Australia)

Dep Energy Environ Meas Lab Environ Q (US) — Department of Energy. Environmental Measurements Laboratory.Environmental Quarterly (US)

Dep Energy Indirect Liquefaction Contract Rev Meet — Department of Energy. Indirect Liquefaction Contractors' Review Meeting

Dep Energy Nucl Airborne Waste Manage Air Clean Conf (US) — Department of Energy. Nuclear Airborne Waste Management and Air Cleaning Conference (US)

Dep Energy Nucl Air Clean Conf Proc (US) — Department of Energy. Nuclear Air Cleaning Conference. Proceedings (US)

Dep Energy Symp Ser — Department of Energy. Symposium Series (US)

Dep Eng Sci Rep Univ Oxford — Department of Engineering. Science Report. University of Oxford

Dep Environ Fire Res St Fire Res Tech Pap (UK) — Department of the Environment. Fire Research Station. Fire Research Technical Paper (United Kingdom)

Dep For (Queensl) Res Note — Department of Forestry (Queensland). Research Note

Dep For (Queensl) Res Pap — Department of Forestry (Queensland). Research Paper

Dep For Tech Pap Clemson Univ — Department of Forestry Technical Paper. Clemson University

Dep Harb Mar (Queensl) Fish Notes — Department of Harbours and Marine (Queensland). Fisheries Notes

Dep Harbours Mar Queensl Fish Notes — Queensland Department of Harbours and Marine. Fisheries Notes

Dep Health Educ Welfare Natl Inst Health Publ — Department of Health, Education, and Welfare. National Institutes of Health. Publication

Dep Health Educ Welfare Natl Inst Occup Saf Health Publ (US) — Department of Health, Education, and Welfare. National Institute for Occupational Safety and Health. Publication (United States)

Dep Health Educ Welfare Publ (Health Serv Adm) (US) — Department of Health, Education, and Welfare. Publication (Health Services Administration) (United States)

De Phil — De Philosophia

Dep Ind (Bombay) Bull — Department of Industries (Bombay). Bulletin

Dep Ind (Prov Bombay) Bull — Department of Industries (Province of Bombay). Bulletin

DeP LR — DePaul Law Review

Dep Nac Agric (Costa Rica) Bol Tec — Departamento Nacional de Agricultura (Costa Rica). Boletin Tecnica

Dep Primary Ind Brisbane Fish Branch Fish Notes (New Ser) — Department of Primary Industries. Brisbane Fisheries Branch. Fisheries Notes (New Series)

Dep Primary Ind Fish Res Annu Rep (Port Moresby) — Department of Primary Industries. Fisheries Research Annual Report (Port Moresby)

Depressive Illness Ser — Depressive Illness Series

Dep State US Bull — Department of State US Bulletin

Dep St B — Department of State Bulletin

Dep St Bull — US Department of State. Bulletin

Dept Agric Bot Div Annual Rep — Department of Agriculture. Botany Division. Annual Report

Dept Agric Bot Div Bull — Department of Agriculture. Botanical Division. Bulletin

Dept Agric Forest Div Rep Chief Forest Div — Department of Agriculture. Forestry Division. Report. Chief of the Forestry Division

Dept Agric Microscop Div Food Prod — Department of Agriculture. Microscopy Division. Food Products

Dept Agric Rep Forest — Department of Agriculture. Report on Forestry

Dept Agric Special Rep — Department of Agriculture. Special Report

Dept Bull US Dept Agric — Department Bulletin. United States Department of Agriculture

Dep Tech Rep Tex Agric Exp Stn — Departmental Technical Report. Texas Agricultural Experiment Station

Dept Econ et Sociol Rurales Bul Info — Departement d'Economie et de Sociologie Rurales. Bulletin d'Information

Dept El Sch Prin B — Department of Elementary School Principals. Bulletin

Dept Employment Gaz (Gt Britain) — Department of Employment. Gazette (Great Britain)

Dept of Ed and Science Repts — Department of Education and Science: Reports on Education

Dept Sec Sch Prin B — Department of Secondary School Principals. Bulletin

Dept S Fct — Department Store Sales Fact File

Dept Sta Bul — Department of State. Bulletin

Dept Sta Nl — Department of State. Newsletter

Dept State Bul — Department of State. Bulletin

Dept State Bull — Department of State. Bulletin

Dept State Newsletter — Department of State. Newsletter

Dept St Bull — Department of State. Bulletin

DEQUIP — DECHEMA [*Deutsche Gesellschaft fuer Chemisches Apparatenesen, Chemische Technik, und Biotechnologie e V*] Equipment Suppliers Data Base

DERA — Directory of Education Research and Research in Australia

DERAAC — Dermatologica

Derbys Archaeol J — Derbyshire Archaeological Journal

Derbyshire Archaeol J — Derbyshire Archaeological Journal

Derbyshire Arch J — Derbyshire Archaeological Journal

Derdap Sveske — Derdapske Sveske

Derecho Reforma Agrar Rev — Derecho y Reforma Agraria Revista

Derecho Vivo — Actas Procesales del Derecho Vivo

DEREES — Developmental Review

De Re Met Min Met — De Re Metallica de la Mineria y los Metales

DERES — DECHEMA [*Deutshe Gesellschaft fuer Chemisches Apparatenesen, Chemische Technik, und Biotechnologie e V*] Research Institutes Databank

Derevoobrab Prom-St — Derevoobrabatyvaiushchaia Promyshlennost

Derevopererab Lesokhim Promst — Derevopererabatyvayushchaya i Lesokhimicheskaya Promyshlennost

Derev Prom — Derevoobrabatyvaiushchaia Promyshlennost

Derg Rev Fac For Univ Istanbul Ser A — Dergisi. Review of the Faculty of Forestry. University of Istanbul. Series A

DERIA — Dermatologia Internationalis

DERIA2 — Dermatologia Internationalis

Deri Muz Ev — Deri Muzeum Evkoenyve

Der Integr — Derecho de la Integracion

Derm — Dermatologia

DERMAE — Dermatologia

Dermatol Clin — Dermatologic Clinics

Dermatol Int — Dermatologia Internationalis

Dermatol Monatsschr — Dermatologische Monatsschrift

Dermatolog — Dermatologica

Dermatologica Suppl — Dermatologica Supplementum

Dermatol Online J — Dermatology Online Journal

Dermatol Surg — Dermatologic Surgery

Dermatol Syphilol Urol — Dermatologia, Syphilologia, et Urologia

Dermatol Trop — Dermatologica Tropica

Dermatol Trop Ecol Geogr — Dermatologia Tropica et Ecologia Geographica

Dermatol Update — Dermatology Update

Dermatol Venereol — Dermatology and Venereology

Dermatol Venerol — Dermatologiya i Venerologiya

Dermatol Venerol (Sofia) — Dermatologiya i Venerologiya (Sofia)

Dermatol Wochenschr — Dermatologische Wochenschrift

Dermatol Z — Dermatologische Zeitschrift

Dermatoses Prof — Dermatoses Professionnelles

Dermato-Vener — Dermato-Venerologie

Dermat Wchnschr — Dermatologische Wochenschrift

Dermat Wochnschr — Dermatologische Wochenschrift

Derm Beruf Umwelt — Dermatosen in Beruf und Umwelt

Derm Ib Lat Amer — Dermatologia Ibero Latino-Americana

Dermos — Dermosifilografo

Derm St — Dermatologische Studien

Derm Vener — Dermato-Venerologie

Derm Venerol — Dermato-Venerologie

Der Nt — Der Naturforscher

DERVA7 — Dermato-Venerologie

Derwent Archaeol Soc Res Rep — Derwent Archaeological Society. Research Reports

Des Abst Int — Design Abstracts International

Desalinatn — Desalination

Des & Envmt — Design and Environment

Des Anti AIDS Drugs — Design of Anti-AIDS Drugs

Desarr Econ — Desarrollo Economico

Desarr Indoamer — Desarrollo Indoamericano

Desarrollo Econ — Desarrollo Economico

Desarrollo Indoam — Desarrollo Indoamericano

Desarrollo y Soc — Desarrollo y Sociedad

Desarr Rural Am — Desarrollo Rural en las Americas

Desarr Rur Amer — Desarrollo Rural en las Americas

Des Arts Educ — Design for Arts in Education

DESB — Delta Epsilon Sigma Bulletin

Des Codes Cryptogr — Designs, Codes, and Crytography

Des Compon Engn — Design and Components in Engineering

Descrip Appl Ling — Descriptive and Applied Linguistics

DES Diesel Equip Supt — DES. Diesel Equipment Superintendent

Des Econ — Desarrollo Economico

Des Electron — Design Electronics

Des Eng — Design Engineering

Des Engng (GB) — Design Engineering (Great Britain)

Des Engng (USA) — Design Engineering (United States of America)

Des Eng (NY) — Design Engineering (New York)

Des Eng (Toronto) — Design Engineering (Toronto)

Desenvol Conjun Rio — Desenvolvimento e Conjuntura (Rio de Janeiro)
Desert Bot Gard (Phoenix) Sci Bull — Desert Botanical Garden (Phoenix). Science Bulletin
Desertification Control Bull — Desertification Control Bulletin
Desert Inst Bull — Desert Institute. Bulletin
Desert Inst Bull ARE — Desert Institute. Bulletin ARE
Desert Locust Control Organ E Afr Tech Rep — Desert Locust Control Organization for Eastern Africa. Technical Report
Desert Mag — Desert Magazine
Desert Pl Life — Desert Plant Life
Des Greece — Design in Greece
Design — Design Magazine
Design & Manage Resour Recovery — Design and Management for Resource Recovery
Designers J — Designers Journal
Design for Ind — Design for Industry
Design Ind — Design for Industry
Design Q — Design Quarterly
Design Qly — Design Quarterly
Design Qly (Heery) — Design Quarterly (Heery)
Design Sci Collect — Design Science Collection
Des Indus — Design for Industry
Desinfekt Gesundheitswes — Desinfektion und Gesundheitswesen
Desinfekt Schaedlingsbekaempf — Desinfektion und Schaedlingsbekaempfung
Desinfekt Schaedlingsbekaempf Ausg A — Desinfektion und Schaedlingsbekaempfung. Ausgabe A. Desinfektion
Desinfekt Schaedlingsbekaempf Ausg B — Desinfektion und Schaedlingsbekaempfung. Ausgabe B.Schaedlingsbekaempfung
Des in Steel — Design in Steel
Des Inst Phys Prop Data Data Ser — Design Institute for Physical Property Data. Data Series
Desk Comp — Desktop Computing
Des Manage Resour Recovery — Design and Management for Resource Recovery
Des Moines Anal — Analyst. A Monthly Journal of Pure and Applied Mathematics [*Des Moines*]
Des Monomers Polym — Designed Monomers and Polymers
Des News — Design News
DESP — Primeros Puestoss del Deporte Espanol
Des Prod Appln — Design Products and Applications
Des Q — Design Quarterly
DESRAY — Deep-Sea Research [*Later, Deep-Sea Research with Oceanographic Literature Review*]
D Es S LJ — Dar Es Salaam Law Journal
Des Special Needs — Design for Special Needs
Des Stud — Design Studies
D Es S ULJ — Dar Es Salaam University. Law Journal
DESTA — Deutsche Stomatologie
DESTA6 — Deutsche Stomatologie
Destill Lehrling — Destillateur Lehrling
Destill Likoerfabr — Destillateur Likoerfabrikant
DESUA9 — Dental Survey
Desv Journ — Journal de Botanique. Redige par une Societe de Botanistes (Desvaux, Editor)
DESY — Deutsches Elektronen-Synchrotron
DESY J — DESY [*Deutches Elektronen-Synchroton*] Journal
Detailman Inf — Detailman Information
Detali Mash (Kiev) — Detali Mashin (Kiev)
Detali Mash Podemno Transp Mash — Detali Mashin i Pod'emno Transportnye Mashiny
Det CLR — Detroit College of Law. Review
Det CL Rev — Detroit College of Law. Review
Det Coll LR — Detroit College of Law. Review
Det Coll L Rev — Detroit College of Law. Review
DETEQ — DECHEMA [*Deutshe Gesellschaft fuer Chemisches Apparatenesen, Chemische Technik, und Biotechnologie e V*] Environmental Technology Equipment Databank
Deterg Age — Detergent Age
Deterg Spec — Detergents and Specialties
Determ Org Struct Phys Methods — Determination of Organic Structures by Physical Methods
DETHERM — DECHEMA [*Deutshe Gesellschaft fuer Chemisches Apparatenesen, Chemische Technik, und Biotechnologie e V*] Thermophysical Property Data Bank
DETJA — Defense Transportation Journal
Det Law — Detroit Lawyer
Det Leg N — Detroit Legal News
Det Lit — Detskaya Literatura
Det LJ — Detroit Law Journal
Det L Rev — Detroit Law Review
Detr Med Ne — Detroit Medical News
Detr MJ — Detroit Medical Journal
Detroit Acad Nat Sci Occasional Paper — Detroit Academy of Natural Sciences. Occasional Papers
Detroit Chem — Detroit Chemist
Detroit Dent Bull — Detroit Dental Bulletin
Detroit Inst Bul — Detroit Institute of Arts. Bulletin
Detroit Law — Detroit Lawyer
Detroit L J — Detroit Law Journal
Detroit L Rev — Detroit Law Review
Detroit Med Journ — Detroit Medical Journal
Detroit Med News — Detroit Medical News
Detroit Nw — Detroit News
Detroit Perspect — Detroit in Perspective
Detroit Rev Med and Pharm — Detroit Review of Medicine and Pharmacy

Detroit Sym — Detroit Symphony Orchestra. Program Notes
Deuc — Deucalion. Cahiers de Philosophie
Deu E — Deutschlands Erneuerung
DEUPD7 — Dermatology Update
DeuR — Deutsche Rundschau
DeuS — Deutsche Studien
DeutA — Deutschland Archiv
Deut Agrartech — Deutsche Agrartechnik
Deut Apoth Z — Deutsche Apotheker-Zeitung
Deut Arch Erforsch Mittelalt — Deutsches Archiv fuer Erforschung des Mittelalters Namens Monumenta Germaniae Historica
Deut Ausschuss Stahlbeton — Deutscher Ausschuss fuer Stahlbeton
Deutch Archaeol Inst Jahrb — Deutsches Archaeologisches Institut. Jahrbuch
Deut Entomol Z — Deutsche Entomologische Zeitschrift
Deut Geod Komm Veroeff Reihe E Gesch Entwickl Geod — Deutsche Geodaetische Kommission. Veroeffentlichungen. Reihe E. Geschichte und Entwicklung der Geodaesie
Deut Geog Blaetter — Deutsche Geographische Blaetter
Deut Landwirt — Deutsche Landwirtschaft
Deut Lebensm Rundsch — Deutsche Lebensmittel Rundschau
Deut Luft Raumfahrt Forschungsber — Deutsche Luft- und Raumfahrt. Forschungsbericht
Deut Med Wo — Deutsche Medizinische Wochenschrift
Deut Mueller Ztg — Deutsche Mueller Zeitung
Deut Muenzbl — Deutsche Muenzblaetter
Deut Oesterr Alpen-Ver Zs — Deutscher und Oesterreichischer Alpen-Verein. Zeitschrift
Deut Papierwirtsch — Deutsche Papierwirtschaft
DeutR — Deutsche Revue
Deut Rundschau — Deutsche Rundschau
Deutsch Am Geschichtsblaetter — Deutsch-Amerikanische Geschichtsblaetter. German American Historical Society of Illinois
Deutsch Archaeol Ins Jahrb — Jahrbuch des Deutschen Archaeologischen Instituts
Deutsch Archaeol Inst Roem Mitt — Deutsches Archaeologisches Institut. Mitteilungen. Roemische Abteilung
Deutsch Dante Jahrb — Deutsches Dante-Jahrbuch
Deutsch-Dominikan Tropenforschungsinstitut Veroeff — Deutsch-Dominikanisches Tropenforschungsinstitut Veroeffentlichungen
Deutsche Aerzte-Ztg — Deutsche Aerztezeitung
Deutsche Akad Wissen Berlin Schr — Deutsche Akademie der Wissenschaften zu Berlin. Schriften der Sektion fuer Vor-und Fruehgeschichte
Deutsche Aquarien Terrar Z — Deutsche Aquarien- und Terrarien-Zeitschrift
Deutsche Bundesbank — Monthly Report. Deutsche Bundesbank
Deutsche Bundesbank Mo Rept — Deutsche Bundesbank. Monthly Report
Deutsche Chir — Deutsche Chirurgie
Deutsche Entomol Z — Deutsche Entomologische Zeitschrift
Deutsche Entom Ztschr "Iris" — Deutsche Entomologische Zeitschrift "Iris"
Deutsche Forsch Versuchsanst Luft Raumfahrt Forschungsber — Deutsche Forschungs- und Versuchsanstalt fuer Luft- und Raumfahrt. Forschungsbericht
Deutsche Gaertn Verbands Zeitung — Deutsche Gaertner-Verbands-Zeitung
Deutsche Geol Gesell Zeitschr — Deutsche Geologische Gesellschaft. Zeitschrift
Deutsche Hochschulschrift — Deutsche Hochschulschriften
Deutsche Hydrogr Z — Deutsche Hydrographische Zeitschrift
Deutsche Iris Ges Berlin Dahlem Nachrichtenbl — Deutsche Iris-Gesellschaft e. V. Berlin-Dahlem. Nachrichtenblaetter
Deutsche Iris Lilienges Jahrb — Deutsche Iris- und Liliengesellschaft Jahrbuch
Deutsche Jahrb Wiss Kunst — Deutsche Literaturzeitung
Deutsche Keramische Gesell Ber — Deutsche Keramische Gesellschaft. Berichte
Deutsche Med Wochenschr — Deutsche Medizinische Wochenschrift
Deutsche Med-Ztg — Deutsche Medizinal-Zeitung
Deutsche Mineralog Gesell Fortschr Mineralogie — Deutsche Mineralogische Gesellschaft. Fortschritte der Mineralogie
Deutsche Oper — Deutsche Oper am Rhein
Deutscher Geographentag Verh — Deutscher Geographentag Verhandlungen
Deutsche Rundschau Geogr — Deutsche Rundschau fuer Geographie
Deutsches Arch Klin Med — Deutsches Archiv fuer Klinische Medizin
Deutsche Schlacht-u Viehhof-Ztg — Deutsche Schlacht- und Viehhof-Zeitung
Deutsches Institut fuer Wirtschaftsforschung Econ Bul — Deutsches Institut fuer Wirtschaftsforschung. Economic Bulletin
Deutsche Tieraerztl Wochenschr — Deutsche Tieraerztliche Wochenschrift
Deutsche Ztschr Chir — Deutsche Zeitschrift fuer Chirurgie
Deutsche Ztschr Nervenh — Deutsche Zeitschrift fuer Nervenheilkunde
Deutsch Gart — Deutscher Garten
Deutsch Gesell Geol Wiss Ber — Deutschen Gesellschaft fuer Geologische Wissenschaften. Berichte
Deut Schiffahrtsarch — Deutsches Schiffahrtsarchiv. Zeitschrift des Deutschen Schiffartsmuseums
Deutsch Jahrb Musikw — Deutsches Jahrbuch fuer Musikwissenschaft
Deutsch Kam — Deutsche Kameramann
Deutschl Erneuerung — Deutschlands Erneuerung
Deutsch Mag — Deutsches Magazin
Deutsch Mag Garten Blumenk — Deutsches Magazin fuer Garten- und Blumenkunde
Deutsch Nationalbiblio Reihe A — Deutsche Nationalbibliographie. Reihe A
Deutsch Nationalbiblio Reihe B — Deutsche Nationalbibliographie. Reihe B
Deutschoesterr Monatsschr Naturwiss Fortbild — Deutschoesterreichische Monatsschrift fuer Naturwissenschaftliche Fortbildung
Deutschoesterr Spirit Ztg — Deutschoesterreichische Spirituisen-Zeitung
Deutschoesterr Tieraerztl Wchnschr — Deutschoesterreichische Tieraerztliche Wochenschrift
Deutsch Shakespeare Ges West Jahrb — Deutsch Shakespeare Gesellschaft West. Jahrbuch
Deutsch-Taschenb — Deutsch-Taschenbuecher
Deutschtum Ausl — Deutschtum im Ausland

Deutsch Verein Kunstwis Z — Deutscher Verein fuer Kunstwissenschaft. Zeitschrift
Deutsch Zool Ges Verh — Deutsche Zoologische Gesellschaft. Verhandlungen
Deut Vier L — Deutsche Vierteljahrsschrift fuer Literaturwissenschaft und Geistesgeschichte
Deut Vier Lit — Deutsche Vierteljahrsschrift fuer Literaturwissenschaft und Geistesgeschichte
Deut Vierteljahrsschr Literaturwiss Geistesgesch — Deutsche Vierteljahrsschrift fuer Literaturwissenschaft und Geistesgeschichte
Deut Zeitsch F Nervenh — Deutsche Zeitschrift fuer Nervenheilkunde
Deut Zeitsch F Wohlfahrtspfl — Deutsche Zeitschrift fuer Wohlfahrtspflege
Deut Z Phil — Deutsche Zeitschrift fuer Philosophie
Deu Viertel — Deutsche Vierteljahrsschrift fuer Literaturwissenschaft und Geistesgeschichte
DEV — Development News
Dev — Devoir
Dev — Devotee
DEvA — Deutsch-Evangelisch im Auslande
Dev Adhes — Developments in Adhesives
Dev Agric Econ — Developments in Agricultural Economics
Dev Agric Eng — Developments in Agricultural Engineering
Dev Agric Managed For Ecol — Developments in Agricultural and Managed-Forest Ecology
Dev Anim Vet Sci — Developments in Animal and Veterinary Sciences
Dev Anthrop Netwk — Development Anthropology Network
Dev Appl Spectrosc — Developments in Applied Spectroscopy
Dev Aquacult Fish Sci — Developments in Aquaculture and Fisheries Science
Dev Atmos Sci — Developments in Atmospheric Science
DevB — Devil's Box
Dev Biochem — Developments in Biochemistry
Dev Biodegrad Hydrocarbons — Developments in Biodegradation of Hydrocarbons
Dev Bioenerg Biomembr — Developments in Bioenergetics and Biomembranes
Dev Biol — Developmental Biology
Dev Biol (Basel) — Developments in Biologicals
Dev Biol Stand — Developments in Biological Standardization
Dev Biol Suppl — Developmental Biology. Supplement
Dev Block Copolym — Developments in Block Copolymers
Dev Brain Res — Developmental Brain Research
Dev Cancer Res — Developments in Cancer Research
Dev Cardiovasc Med — Developments in Cardiovascular Medicine
Dev Cell Biol — Developmental and Cell Biology
Dev Cell Biol (Amsterdam) — Developments in Cell Biology (Amsterdam)
Dev Cell Biol (London) — Developments in Cell Biology (London)
Dev Ceram Met Matrix Compos Proc Symp — Developments in Ceramic and Metal-Matrix Composites. Proceedings. Symposium
Dev Change — Development and Change
Dev Chem Eng Miner Process — Developments in Chemical Engineering and Mineral Processing
Dev Chromatogr — Developments in Chromatography
Dev Clin Biochem — Developments in Clinical Biochemistry
Dev Comp Immunol — Developmental and Comparative Immunology
Dev Compos Mater — Developments in Composite Materials
Dev Crop Sci — Developments in Crop Science
Dev Cryst Polym — Developments in Crystalline Polymers
Dev Dairy Chem — Developments in Dairy Chemistry
Dev Dialogue — Development Dialogue
Dev Disab Abstr — Developmental Disabilities Abstracts
Dev Dyn — Developmental Dynamics
DEVEAA — Defense des Vegetaux
Dev Econ — Developing Economies
Dev Econ Geol — Developments in Economic Geology
Dev Educ — Developing Education
Devel Biol — Developmental Biology
Devel Civ — Developpement et Civilisation
Devel Dig — Development Digest
Devel Ind Microbiol — Developments in Industrial Microbiology
Develop and Change — Development and Change
Develop Bio — Developmental Biology
Develop Biol — Developmental Biology
Develop Cha — Development and Change
Develop Civ Engrg — Developments in Civil Engineering
Develop Civ Found Engrg — Developments in Civil and Foundation Engineering
Develop Dialogue — Development Dialogue
Develop Eco — Developing Economies
Develop Econ — Developing Economies
Develop Electromagnet Theory Appl — Developments in Electromagnetic Theory and Applications
Develop et Civilis — Developpement et Civilisation
Develop Gr — Development, Growth, and Differentiation
Develop in Cell Biology — Developments in Cell Biology
Develop in Mech — Developments in Mechanics
Develop in Statist — Developments in Statistics
Developm Biol — Developmental Biology
Develop Med — Developmental Medicine and Child Neurology
Develop Med Child Neurol — Developmental Medicine and Child Neurology
Development — Development Forum
Developmental Med Child Neurol — Developmental Medicine and Child Neurology
Development & Materials Bull — Development and Materials Bulletin
Develop Progres Socio Econ — Developpement et Progres Socio-Economique
Develop Psy — Developmental Psychobiology
Develop Psychol — Developmental Psychology
Develop Sci Sources Hist Sci — Development of Science. Sources for the History of Science
Develop VIC — Develop Victoria Journal

Develop VIC J — Develop Victoria Journal
Devel Psych — Developmental Psychology
Devel Psychobiol — Development Psychobiology
Dev Endocrinol (Amersterdam) — Developments in Endocrinology (Amsterdam)
Dev Endocrinol (The Hague) — Developments in Endocrinology (The Hague)
Dev Environ Biol Fishes — Developments in Environmental Biology of Fishes
Dev Environ Control Public Health — Developments in Environmental Control and Public Health
Dev Environ Modell — Developments in Environmental Modelling
Dev et Civilisations — Developpement et Civilisations
Dev Food Anal Tech — Developments in Food Analysis Techniques
Dev Food Colours — Developments in Food Colours
Dev Food Eng Proc Int Congr Eng Food — Developments in Food Engineering. Proceedings of the International Congress on Engineering and Food
Dev Food Microbiol — Developments in Food Microbiology
Dev Food Packag — Developments in Food Packaging
Dev Food Preserv — Developments in Food Preservation
Dev Food Preservation — Developments in Food Preservation
Dev Food Preservatives — Developments in Food Preservatives
Dev Food Proteins — Developments in Food Proteins
Dev Food Sci — Development in Food Science
Dev Forum — Development Forum
Dev Genes Evol — Development Genes and Evolution
Dev Genet — Developmental Genetics
Dev Genet (Amsterdam) — Developments in Genetics (Amsterdam)
Dev Genet (NY) — Developmental Genetics (New York)
Dev Geochem — Developments in Geochemistry
Dev Geotech Eng — Developments in Geotechnical Engineering
Dev Geotectonics — Developments in Geotectonics
Dev Grow Differ — Development, Growth, and Differentiation
Dev Growth Differ — Development, Growth, and Differentiation
Dev Growth Differ (Nagoya) — Development, Growth, and Differentiation (Nagoya)
Dev Halophilic Microorg — Developments in Halophilic Microorganisms
Dev Halophilic Microorganisms — Developments in Halophilic Microorganisms
Dev Heat Exch Technol — Developments in Heat Exchanger Technology
Dev Heat Transfer — Developments in Heat Transfer
Dev Hematol — Developments in Hematology
Dev Hydrobiol — Developments in Hydrobiology
Deviant Behav — Deviant Behavior
Dev Immunol — Developments in Immunology
Dev Ind Microbiol — Developments in Industrial Microbiology
Dev Ind Microbiol Ser — Developments in Industrial Microbiology Series
Dev Ind Sci — Developpement Industriel et Scientifique
Dev Injection Moulding — Developments in Injection Moulding
Dev Innovation Aust Process Ind Pap Aust Chem Eng Conf — Development and Innovation for Australian Process Industries. Papers of the Australian Chemical Engineering Conference
Dev Ionic Polym — Developments in Ionic Polymers
Devl Biol — Developmental Biology
Dev Mamm — Development in Mammals
Dev Mar Biol — Developments in Marine Biology
Dev Mat Bull — Development and Materials Bulletin
Dev Meat Sci — Developments in Meat Science
Dev Mech — Developments in Mechanics
Dev Med Child Neurol — Developmental Medicine and Child Neurology
Dev Med Child Neurol Suppl — Developmental Medicine and Child Neurology. Supplement
Dev Miner Process — Developments in Mineral Processing
Dev Mol Cell Biochem — Developments in Molecular and Cellular Biochemistry
Dev Mol Virol — Developments in Molecular Virology
Dev Nephrol — Developments in Nephrology
Dev Neuropathol Schizophr — Developmental Neuropathology of Schizophrenia
Dev Neuropsychol — Developmental Neuropsychology
Dev Neurosci — Developmental Neuroscience
Dev Neurosci (Amsterdam) — Developments in Neuroscience (Amsterdam)
Dev Neurosci (Basel) — Developmental Neuroscience (Basel)
Dev Newsl — Development Newsletter
Dev Nucl Med — Developments in Nuclear Medicine
Dev Nutr Metab — Developments in Nutrition and Metabolism
Dev Obstet Gynecol — Developments in Obstetrics and Gynecology
Devon & Cornwall Rec Soc — Devon and Cornwall Record Society
Devon Archaeol Soc — Devon Archaeological Society
Devon As T — Reports and Transactions of the Devonshire Association for the Advancement of Science, Literature, and Art
Dev Oncol — Developments in Oncology
Devon Hist — Devon Historian
Devonshire Assoc — Devonshire Association
Dev Ophthalmol — Developments in Ophthalmology
Dev Opt Compon Coat — Developments in Optical Component Coatings
Dev Opt Process — Devices for Optical Processing
Dev Oriented Polym — Developments in Oriented Polymers
DEVPA — Developmental Psychology
DEVPA9 — Developmental Psychology
Dev Palaeontol Stratigr — Developments in Palaeontology and Stratigraphy
Dev Perinat Med — Developments in Perinatal Medicine
Dev Period Med — Development Period Medicine
Dev Pet Geol — Developments in Petroleum Geology
Dev Petrol — Developments in Petrology
Dev Pet Sci — Developments in Petroleum Science
Dev Pharmacol — Developments in Pharmacology
Dev Pharmacol Ther — Developmental Pharmacology and Therapeutics
Dev Plant Biol — Developments in Plant Biology
Dev Plant Genet Breed — Developments in Plant Genetics and Breeding
Dev Plant Soil Sci — Developments in Plant and Soil Sciences
Dev Plast Technol — Developments in Plastics Technology

Dev Polym — Developments in Polymerisation
Dev Polym Charact — Developments in Polymer Characterisation
Dev Polym Degrad — Developments in Polymer Degradation
Dev Polym Fract — Developments in Polymer Fracture
Dev Polym Photochem — Developments in Polymer Photochemistry
Dev Polym Stab — Developments in Polymer Stabilisation
Dev Polyurethane — Developments in Polyurethane
Dev Precambrian Geol — Developments in Precambrian Geology
Dev Psychiatry — Developments in Psychiatry
Dev Psychobiol — Developmental Psychobiology
Dev Psychol — Developmental Psychology
Dev Psychol Monogr — Developmental Psychology. Monograph
Dev Psychopathol — Development and Psychopathology
Dev PVC Prod Process — Developments in PVC Production and Processing
Dev Rail — Developing Railways
Dev Reinf Plast — Developments in Reinforced Plastics
Dev Rev — Developmental Review
Dev Rev Outl — Development Review and Outlook
Dev Rubber Rubber Compos — Developments in Rubber and Rubber Composites
Dev Rubber Technol — Developments in Rubber Technology
Devs Biol Standardiz — Developments in Biological Standardization
Dev Sci Technol Compos Mater Eur Conf Compos Mater — Developments in the Science and Technology of Composite Materials. European Conference on Composite Materials
Dev Sedimentol — Developments in Sedimentology
Dev Soft Drinks Technol — Developments in Soft Drinks Technology
Dev Soil Sci — Developments in Soil Science
Dev Stat — Developments in Statistics
Dev Stud — Development Studies
Dev Stud (Sthn Afr) — Development Studies (Southern Africa)
Dev Suppl — Development. Supplement
Dev Toxicol Environ Sci — Developments in Toxicology and Environmental Science
Dev Vet Virol — Developments in Veterinary Virology
DEWTA — DEW [*Deutsche Edelstahlwerke*] Technische Berichte
DEW Tech Ber — DEW [*Deutsche Edelstahlwerke*] Technische Berichte
D Exp — Dairy Exporter
DEZB — Deutsche Entomologische Zeitschrift (Berlin)
DF — Dandke Folkemaal
DF — Deutschland-Frankreich
DF — Duisberger Forschungen. Schriftenreihe fuer Geschichte und Heimatkunde Duisburges
DFA — Drammatic Festivals of Athens
DFA — Droguerie Francaise. La Couleur
DFBO Mitt — DFBO [*Deutsche Forschungsgesellschaft fuer Blechverarbeitung und Oberflaechenbehandlung*] Mitteilungen
DFFNAW — Differentiation
DFG Mitt — DFG Mitteilungen. Deutsche Forschungsgemeinschaft
DFIFAO — Documents de Fouilles. Institut Francais d'Archeologie Orientale du Caire
DFIRAP — Deutsche Fischerei-Rundschau
DFL — Defense de la Langue Francaise
DFL Ber — DFL [*Deutsche Forschungsanstalt fuer Luftfahrt*] Bericht
DFM — Dansk Folkemal
DFMhe — Deutsch-Franzoesische Monatshefte
DFO — Danish Journal. A Magazine about Denmark
D Fo — Danske Folkemaal
D For O J — Danish Foreign Office Journal
D Fot T — Dansk Fotografisk Tidsskrift
DFP — Dun's Financial Profiles Report
DFR — Deutsch-Franzoesische Rundschau
D Fro — Dansk Froavl
DFR Plus — Dun's Financial Records Plus
DFS — Developments in Food Science
DFSCDX — Developments in Food Science
D Fskt — Dansk Fiskeritidende
D Fs T — Dansk Forsikrings Tidende
DFSZAV — Deutsche Fischerei Zeitung
DFW — Dokumentation Fachbibliothek Werksbuecherei
DFZg — Deutsche Fortszeitung
DG — Daily Graphic
DG — Daily Guardian
DG — Developments in Geotectonics
Dg — Dialog
DG — Dictionnaire des Noms Geographiques Contenus dans les Textes Hieroglyphiques
DG — Doxographi Graeci
DG — Dublin Gazette
DG — Duerener Geschichtsblaetter
DG — Dumfriesshire and Galloway Natural History and Antiquarian Society. Transactions
DGABAC — Deutsche Gartenbau
DGB — Drogistenweekblad. Onafhankelijk Vakblad voor de Drogisterijbranche
DGBI — Deutsche Geographische Blaetter
DG BI — Deutsche Geschichtsblaetter
DGC — Deutsche Gaststatte. Deutsche Hotelzeitung
DGC — Developments in Geochemistry
DGDFA5 — Development, Growth, and Differentiation
DGE — Developments in Geotechnical Engineering
DGE — Diccionario Griego-Espanol
D Gefl Ztg — Deutsche Gefluegel-Zeitung
DGEND — Developments in Geotechnical Engineering
D Geog BI — Deutsche Geographische Blaetter
D Geogr BI — Deutsche Geographische Blaetter
D Geol F A — Dansk Geologisk Forening. Arsskrift

D Geol Unders — Danmarks Geologiske Undersogelse. Arbog
D Geschichtbl — Deutsche Geschichtsblaetter
D Gesell F Anthropol Korrespondenzbl — Deutsche Gesellschaft fuer Anthropologie. Korrespondenzblatt
DGF — Danmarks Gamle Folkeviser
DGIN — Dagens Industri
DGKRA — Denki Gakkai Ronbunshi. A
D GI Gs Z — Zeitschrift der Deutschen Geologischen Gesellschaft
DGM — Developments in Geomathematics
DGMK Tagungsber — DGMK [*Deutsche Wissenschaftliche Gesellschaft fuer Erdoel, Erdgas, und Kohle*] Tagungsbericht
DGMTAO — Deutsche Gewaesserkundliche Mitteilungen
DGNSAQ — Diagnostica
DGNTDW — Developmental Genetics
DGRBB — Denki Gakkai Ronbunshi. B
DGRCA — Denki Gakkai Ronbunshi. C
DGRHA — Doboku Gakkai Ronbun Hokokushu
DGRS — Denkmaeler Griechischer und Roemischer Skulptur
D Gs Ostas Mt — Mittheilungen der Deutschen Gesellschaft fuer Natur- und Voelkerkunde Ostasiens
Dgt Bypass — Digital Bypass Report
DGTPA — Diesel and Gas Turbine Progress [*Later, Diesel Progress North American*]
DGUAB8 — Geological Survey of Denmark. Yearbook
DGUADA — Geological Survey of Denmark. Serie A
DGUBAA — Geological Survey of Denmark. II Series
DGUBDD — Geological Survey of Denmark. Serie B
DGUCAD — Geological Survey of Denmark. III Series
DGU (Geol Surv Den) Ser C — DGU (Geological Survey of Denmark) Series C
DGURBP — Geological Survey of Denmark. Report
DGV/ZE — Zeitschrift fuer Ethnologie. Deutsche Gesellschaft fuer Voelkerkunde
DGZAA — Denki Gakkai Zasshi
DH — Delaware History
DH — Derniere Heure
DH — Deutsches Handwerksblatt
DH — Documents d'Histoire
DHA — Dialogos Hispanicos de Amsterdam
DHA — Dialogues d'Histoire Ancienne
D Haa — Danmarks Haandvaerk
Dhaka Univ J Sci — Dhaka University Journal of Science
Dhaka Univ Stud Part B — Dhaka University Studies. Part B
DHBAA — Dock and Harbour Authority
DHBI — Deutsche Handwerksblatt
DHC — Dimension Historica de Chile
DHC — Documents Relatifs a l'Histoire des Croisades
DHEHH — Deltion tes Historikes kai Ethnologikes Hetaireias tes Hellados
DHEW NIOSH Publ (US) — DHEW [*Department of Health, Education, and Welfare*] NIOSH Publication (US)
DHEW Publ ADM (US) — DHEW [*Department of Health, Education, and Welfare*] Publication ADM (US)
DHEW Publ HSA (US) — DHEW [*Department of Health, Education, and Welfare*] Publication. HSA (US)
DHEW Publ NIH (US) — DHEW [*Department of Health, Education, and Welfare*] Publication. NIH (US)
DHGE — Dictionnaire d'Histoire et de Geographie Ecclesiastique
DHHS NIOSH Publ (US) — DHHS [*Department of Health and Human Services*] Publication. NIOSH (US)
DHHS Publ ADM (US) — DHHS [*Department of Health and Human Services*] Publication. ADM (US)
D H Lawren — D. H. Lawrence Review
D H Lawrence R — D. H. Lawrence Review
DHLR — D. H. Lawrence Review
DHM — Description Historique des Monnaies Frapees sous l'Empire Romain Comunement Appelees Medailles Imperiales
DHM — Developments in Halophilic Microorganisms
DHR — Duquesne Hispanic Review
DHS — Deutsches Handwerksblatt
DHS — Dix-Huitieme Siecle
DHSTEV — Data Handling in Science and Technology
DHStL — Deutsch-Hebraeische Sterbeliste
DHT — Dvar Hashavua (Tel Aviv)
DHW — Deutsche Handelsschulwarte
DHYZA7 — Deutsche Hydrographische Zeitschrift
DHZ — Deutsche Hochschulzeitung
D Hz — Die Holzzucht
DI — Der Islam
DI — Desarrollo Indoamericano
DI — Developments in Immunology
DI — Diagnostic Immunology
Di — Dial. A Magazine for Literature, Philosophy, and Religion
Di — Dialog
Di — Dialoghi
Di — Diapason
Di — Didaskaleion
DI — Dissertationes Inaugurales
DI — Dissertations International
DI — Drvna Industrija
DI — Educational Documentation and Information Bulletin
DI — Sammlung der Griechischen Dialekinschriften
Dia — Dialog
Dia — Dialoghi
Dia — Dialogues [*Paris*]
Dia — Diapason
DIA — Documents on International Affairs
Diab — Diabete [*Later, Diabete et Metabolisme*]

Diab Abstr — Diabetes Abstracts
Diabet — Diabetes
Diabet — Diabetologia
Diabet Dig — Diabetic Digest
Diabete Met — Diabete et Metabolisme
Diabete Metab — Diabete et Metabolisme
Diabete Nutr — Diabete et Nutrition
Diabetes Annu — Diabetes Annual
Diabetes Care — Diabetes Care
Diabetes Educ — Diabetes Educator
Diabetes Forecast — Diabetes Forecast
Diabetes Front — Diabetes Frontier
Diabetes J — Diabetes Journal
Diabetes Lit Index — Diabetes Literature Index
Diabetes Mellitus Diagn Treat — Diabetes Mellitus. Diagnosis and Treatment
Diabetes Metab — Diabetes and Metabolism
Diabetes Metab Rev — Diabetes/Metabolism Reviews
Diabetes Metab Review — Diabetes/Metabolism Reviews
Diabetes Nutr & Metab — Diabetes, Nutrition, and Metabolism
Diabetes Obes Metab — Diabetes, Obesity & Metabolism
Diabetes Res — Diabetes Research
Diabetes Res Clin Prac — Diabetes Research and Clinical Practice
Diabetes Res Clin Pract — Diabetes Research and Clinical Practice
Diabetes Technol Ther — Diabetes Technology & Therapeutics
Diabetic J of Aust — Diabetic Journal of Australia
Diabet J — Diabetic Journal
Diabet Med — Diabetic Medicine
Diabetol Croat — Diabetologia Croatica
Diabetolog — Diabetologia
Diab Lit Ind — Diabetes Literature Index
DIA Bol Divulg — DIA [Division de Investigaciones Agropecuarias] Boletin de Divulgacion
DIA Bol Tec — DIA [Division de Investigaciones Agropecuarias] Boletin Tecnico
Diac — Diacritics. A Review of Contemporary Criticism
Diadora — Diadora Glasilo Arheoloskoga Muzeja u Zadru
DIAEAZ — Diabetes
Diaetetische Lebensm Prax Wiss — Diaetetische Lebensmittel in Praxis und Wissenschaft
Diaframma Fot It — Diaframma Fotografia Italiana
Diag E Tecn Di Lab — Diagnostica e Tecnica di Laboratorio
Diagn — Diagnostica
Diagn Contemp Fusion Exp Proc Workshop — Diagnostics for Contemporary Fusion Experiments. Proceedings. Workshop
Diagn Cytopathol — Diagnostic Cytopathology
Diagn Enzymol — Diagnostic Enzymology
Diagn Gynecol Obstet — Diagnostic Gynecology and Obstetrics
Diagn Histopathol — Diagnostic Histopathology
Diagn Imag Clin Med — Diagnostic Imaging in Clinical Medicine
Diagn Imaging — Diagnostic Imaging
Diagn Imaging Clin Med — Diagnostic Imaging in Clinical Medicine
Diagn Immunol — Diagnostic Immunology
Diagn Intell — Diagnostics Intelligence. Monthly Intelligence for the Medical Diagnostics Industry
Diagn Intensivmed — Diagnostik und Intensivmedizin
Diagn Intensivther — Diagnostik und Intensivtherapie
Diagn Lab — Diagnostyka Laboratoryjna
Diagn Lab Clin — Diagnosi Laboratorio e Clinica
Diagn Labor — Diagnose und Labor
Diagn Med — Diagnostic Medicine
Diagn Microbiol Infect Dis — Diagnostic Microbiology and Infectious Disease
Diagn Mol Pathol — Diagnostic Molecular Pathology
Diagnosi Pisa — Diagnosi (Pisa)
Diagnosticos APEC — Diagnosticos APEC. Associacao Promotora de Estudos de Economia
Diagn Plazmy — Diagnostika Plazmy
Diagn Radiol Ser — Diagnostic Radiology Series
Diagn Tec Lab — Diagnostica e Tecnica di Laboratorio
Diagn Ther — Diagnosis and Therapy
Diagn Trait — Diagnostics et Traitements
Diagn Treat — Diagnosis and Treatment
Dial — Dialectica
Dial — Dialog
Dial — Dialoghi
Dial — Dialogo
Dial — Dialogos. Problemi della Scuola Italiana
Dial — Dialogues. Cahiers de Litterature et de Linguistique
Dial A — Dialoghi di Archeologia
Dial Anthro — Dialectical Anthropology
Dial Ar — Dialoghi di Archeologia
Dial Arch — Dialoghi di Archeologia
Dial Archeol — Dialoghi di Archeologia. Rivista Semestrale
DialB — Dialektolohicnyi Bjuleten
Dial Belg-Rom — Dialectes Belgo-Romans
DialC — Dialogue. Canadian Philosophical Review
Dial (Ch) — Dial (Chicago)
Dial di Arch — Dialoghi di Archeologia
Dialec — Dialectica
Dialec — Dialectiques
Dial Ec — Dialogo Ecumenico
Dialec Hum — Dialectics and Humanism
Dialect Anthrop — Dialectical Anthropology
Dialect Hum — Dialectics and Humanism
Dialectical Anthrop — Dialectical Anthropology
DialEcum — Dialogo Ecumenico

Dialektika Ob'ekt Sub'ekt Poznanie Prakt Dejatel'nosti — Dialektika Ob'ektivnogo i Sub'ektivnogo v Poznanie i Prakticeskoj Dejatel'nosti
Dial Hist Anc — Dialogues d'Histoire Ancienne
Dial Notes — Dialect Notes
Dialog Fairleigh Dickinson Univ Sch Dent — Dialog. Fairleigh Dickinson University. School of Dentistry
Dialogue C — Dialogue. Canadian Philosophical Review
Dialogue (Canada) — Dialogue. Canadian Philosophical Review
Dialogue (M) — Dialogue (Milwaukee)
Dialogue (PST) — Dialogue (Phi Sigma Tau)
Dialog (W) — Dialog (Warsaw)
DialS — Dialog: Teatertidskrift (Stockholm)
Dial Transplant — Dialysis and Transplantation
Dial Transplant Nephrol — Dialysis, Transplantation, Nephrology
Dial Transplant Nephrol Pro Congr Eur Dial Transplant Assoc — Dialysis, Transplantation, Nephrology. Proceedings. Congress of the European Dialysis and Transplant Association
DIA Med — DIA [Division de Investigaciones Agropecuarias] Medico
DIA Med Urug — DIA [Division de Investigaciones Agropecuarias] Medico Uruguayo
Diamond Abrasives Eng — Diamond and Abrasives Engineering
Diamond Films Technol — Diamond Films and Technology
Diamond News and SA Jeweller — Diamond News and SA [South African] Jeweller
Diamond Relat Mater — Diamond and Related Materials
Diamond Res — Diamond Research
Diap — Diapason
Diario Ilus — Diario Ilustrado
Diario N — Diario Nacional
Diario Of Mex — Diario Oficial (Mexico)
Diario Of Minist Mar — Diario Oficial. Ministerio de Marina
Diario Of Rio — Diario Oficial (Rio de Janeiro)
DIATAC — DIA [Division de Investigaciones Agropecuarias] Boletin Tecnico
Diatomic Research Bull — Diatomic Research Bulletin
DIB — Daily Intelligence Bulletin
DIB — Defence Information Bulletin
DIB — Defense Industry Bulletin
DIB — Documentatie en Informatie over Toerisme
DIBLAR — Desert Institute. Bulletin ARE
DIBOD5 — Dissertationes Botanicae
DIBtn — Defense Industry Bulletin
DICEA — Die Casting Engineer
DICHA — Diseases of the Chest
DICHAK — Diseases of the Chest
Dicht & Vlkstum — Dichtung und Volkstum
Dicht u Volkst — Dichtung und Volkstum
Dick — Dickensian
Dickens — Dickensian
Dickens St — Dickens Studies Newsletter
Dicken Stud Newsl — Dickens Studies Newsletter
Dickinson L R — Dickinson Law Review
Dickinson L Rev — Dickinson Law Review
DickinsonR — Dickinson Review
Dickinson S — Dickinson Studies
Dick L R — Dickinson Law Review
Dick L Rev — Dickinson Law Review
DickQ — Dickens Quarterly
DICMD4 — Diagnostic Imaging in Clinical Medicine
DICP Ann Ph — DICP (Drug Intelligence and Clinical Pharmacy) The Annals of Pharmacotherapy
DICP Ann Pharmacother — DICP (Drug Intelligence and Clinical Pharmacy) Annals ofPharmacotherapy
DICPB — Drug Intelligence and Clinical Pharmacy
DICRA — Diseases of the Colon and Rectum
DICRAG — Diseases of the Colon and Rectum
Dic S — Dickinson Studies
Dict — Dictionnaire des Antiquites Grecques et Romaines
Dict Ant — Dictionnaire des Antiquites Grecques et Romaines
Dict Apol — Dictionnaire Apologetique
Dict Bibl — Dictionnaire de la Bible
Dict Class Hist Nat — Dictionnaire Classique d'Histoire Naturelle
DIC Tech Rev — DIC [Dainippon Ink and Chemicals] Technical Review
Dict Etym — Dictionnaire Etymologique de la Langue Latine
Dict Geog — Dictionnaire Geographique de l'Ancienne Egypte
Dict Limb Rom — Dictionarul Limbii Romane
Dict Sp — Dictionnaire de Spiritualite Ascetique et Mystique, Doctrine et Histoire
Dict Theol Cath — Dictionnaire de Theologie Catholique
Did — Didaskaleion
DID — Drug Induced Diseases
Didasc — Didascalia
Didask — Didaskalos
Diderot Stud — Diderot Studies
DIDIEW — Digestive Diseases
Did S — Diderot Studies
DIE — Developments in Endocrinology
Die Cast — Die Castings
Die Cast Eng — Die Casting Engineer
Diecasting Met Moulding — Diecasting and Metal Moulding
Diecast Met Mould — Diecasting and Metal Moulding
Diehlektr Poluprovodn — Diehlektriki i Poluprovodniki
Dielectr Mater Meas Appl Int Conf — Dielectric Materials, Measurements, and Applications. International Conference
Dielectr Opt Aspects Intermol Interact — Dielectric and Optical Aspects of Intermolecular Interactions
Dielectr Prop Heterog Mater — Dielectric Properties of Heterogeneous Materials

Dielectr Relat Mol Processes — Dielectric and Related Molecular Processes
Dielektr Opt Aspekty Oddzialywan Miedzyczasteczkowych — Dielektryczne i Optyczne Aspekty Oddzialywan Miedzyczasteczkowych
Dielektr Poluprovodn — Dielektriki i Poluprovodniki
DIEQA — Differential Equations
Diergeneesk Memo — Diergeneeskundig Memorandum
Diesel — Diesel and Gas Turbine Progress [*Later, Diesel Progress North American*]
Diesel Eng — Diesel Engineering
Diesel Eng Us Ass Report — Diesel Engineers and Users Association. Reports
Diesel Eng Users Ass Publ — Diesel Engineers and Users Association. Publication
Diesel Equip Supt — Diesel Equipment Superintendent
Diesel Gas Turbine Prog — Diesel and Gas Turbine Progress [*Later, Diesel Progress North American*]
Diesel Gas Turbine Progr — Diesel and Gas Turbine Progress [*Later, Diesel Progress North American*]
Diesel Gas Turbine Worldwide — Diesel and Gas Turbine Worldwide
Diesel Gas Turb Prog Worldwide — Diesel and Gas Turbine Progress Worldwide [*Later, Diesel and Gas Turbine Worldwide*]
Diesel Power Diesel Transp — Diesel Power and Diesel Transportation
Diesel Prog — Diesel Progress
Diesel Prog — Diesel Progress North American
Diesel Prog Engines Drives — Diesel Progress Engines and Drives
Diesel Prog N Amer — Diesel Progress North American
Diesel Prog North Am — Diesel Progress North American
Dies Rail Tract — Diesel Railway Traction
Diet Collect — Dietetique et Collectivites
Diet Curr — Dietetic Currents
Diet Currents — Dietetic Currents
Diet et Nutr — Dietetique et Nutrition
Diet Gaz — Dietetic Gazette
Diet Hyg Gaz — Dietetic and Hygienic Gazette
Diet Nutr — Dietetique et Nutrition
Dietol Dietoter — Dietologia e Dietoterapia
Diet Sante — Dietetique et Sante
Dietsk Med — Dietskaia Meditsina
DieuV — Dieu Vivant. Perspectives Religieuses et Philosophiques
DIF — Drug Information Fulltext
Dif Ambientale — Difesa Ambientale
DIFDA — Diffusion Data [*Later, Diffusion and Defect Data*]
Differencial'nye Uravnenija i Vycisl Mat — Differencial'nye Uravnenija i Vycislitelnaja Matematika
Differentia — Differentiation
Differ Equations — Differential Equations
Differ Uravn — Differentsial'nye Uravneniya
Differ Uravn Primen — Differentsial'nye Uravneniya i Ikh Primenenie
Diffus Data — Diffusion Data [*Later, Diffusion and Defect Data*]
Diffus Defect Data — Diffusion and Defect Data
Diffus Defect Data Pt A — Diffusion and Defect Data. Solid State Data. Part A. Defect and Diffusion Forum
Diffus Defect Data Pt B — Diffusion and Defect Data. Solid State Data. Part B. Solid State Phenomena
Diffus Defect Monogr Ser — Diffusion and Defect Monograph Series
Diffuz Met Splavakh Tr Vses Konf — Diffuziya v Metallakh i Splavakh. Trudy Vsesoyuznoi Konferentsii
Diffuz Nasyshchenie Pokrytiya Met — Diffuzionnoe Nasyshchenie i Pokrytiya na Metallakh
Diffuz Soedin Vak Met Splavov Nemet Mater — Diffuzionnoe Soedinenie v Vakuume Metallov. Splavov i NemetallicheskikhMaterialov
Diffuz Svarka Vak Met Splavov Nemet Mater — Diffuzionnaya Svarka v Vakuume Metallov. Splavov i Nemetallicheskikh Materialov
Dif Soc — Difesa Sociale
Difusion Econ — Difusion Economica
DIG — Developments in Genetics
Dig Absorpt (Tokyo) — Digestion and Absorption (Tokyo)
Dig Agric Econ — Digest of Agricultural Economics
Dig Chiro Econ — Digest of Chiropractic Economics
Dig Dis — Digestive Diseases
Dig Dis Sci — Digestive Diseases and Sciences
DIGEB — Digestion
DIGEBW — Digestion
Digeste Soc — Digeste Social
Digest Mod Teach — Digest of Modern Teaching
Dig Int Conf Med Biol Eng — Digest. International Conference on Medical and Biological Engineering
Dig Intermag Conf — Digests. Intermag Conference
Digital DD — Digital Design. Computer Compatible Directory and Technology Review
Digital Des — Digital Design
Digital Dn — Digital Design
Digitale Bilddiagn — Digitale Bilddiagnostik
Digital Syst Ind Autom — Digital Systems for Industrial Automation
Digital Tech J — Digital Technical Journal
Digit Comp Newsl — Digital Computer Newsletter
Digit Process — Digital Processes
Dig Lit Dielec — Digest of Literature on Dielectrics
Dig Lit Dielect — Digest of Literature on Dielectrics
Dig Liver Dis — Digestive and Liver Disease
Dig Metab Ruminant Proc Int Symp — Digestion and Metabolism in the Ruminant. Proceedings of the International Symposium on Ruminant Physiology
Dig Neurol Psychiat — Digest of Neurology and Psychiatry
Dig Neurol Psychiatry — Digest of Neurology and Psychiatry
Dig Ophthal Otolaryng — Digest of Ophthalmology and Otolaryngology
Dig Org Immunol — Digestive Organ and Immunology

Dig Pap COMPCON IEEE Comput Soc Int Conf — Digest of Papers. COMPCON. IEEE Computer Society International Conference
Dig Pap IEEE Comput Soc Int Conf — Digest of Papers. IEEE Computer Society International Conference
Dig Pap IEEE Microwave Millim Wave Monolithic Circuits Symp — Digest of Papers. IEEE Microwave and Millimeter-Wave Monolithic Circuits Symposium
Dig Pap IEEE Symp Mass Storage Syst — Digest of Papers. IEEE Symposium on Mass Storage Systems
Dig Pap Int Symp Fault Tolerant Comput — Digest of Papers. International Symposium on Fault-Tolerant Computing
Dig Pap Int Test Conf — Digest of Papers. International Test Conference
Dig Pap Semicond Test Symp — Digest of Papers. Semiconductor Test Symposium
Dig Proc Annu Conf Autom Control — Digest. Proceedings. Annual Conference on Automatic Control
DIGRD — Discipline and Grievances
Dig Stat ICAO — Digest of Statistics. International Civil Aviation Organization
Dig Surg — Digestive Surgery
Dig Tech Pap IEEE Int Conf Consum Electron — Digest of Technical Papers. IEEE International Conference on Consumer Electronics
Dig Tech Pap IEEE Int Solid State Circuits Conf — Digest of Technical Papers. IEEE International Solid State Circuits Conference
Dig Tech Pap IEEE MTTS Int Microwave Symp — Digest of Technical Papers. IEEE MTTS International Microwave Symposium
Dig Tech Pap Int Quantum Electron Conf — Digest of Technical Papers. International Quantum Electronics Conference
Dig Tech Pap Symp VLSI Technol — Digest of Technical Papers. Symposium on VLSI Technology
Dig Treatm — Digest of Treatment
DIHEA — District Heating
DIHIDH — Diagnostic Histopathology
DIIA — Daily Industrial Index Analyzer
DIIMD — Diagnostic Imaging
DIIMDY — Diagnostic Imaging
DIIMEZ — Diagnostic Immunology
DiJ — Dzis i Jutro
Dijon Ac Mm — Memoires de l'Academie des Sciences, Arts, et Belles-Lettres de Dijon
Dijon Ac Sc Mm — Memoires de l'Academie des Sciences, Arts, et Belles-Lettres de Dijon
Dijon Mm Ac — Memoires de l'Academie des Sciences, Arts, et Belles-Lettres de Dijon
Dijon Se Ac — Seances Publiques de l'Academie des Sciences, Arts, et Belles-Lettres de Dijon
Dijon Seances Acad — Academie des Sciences, Arts et Belles-Lettres de Dijon. Seance Publique
D i K — Den'gi i Kredit
DIKNAA — Annual Report. National Veterinary Assay Laboratory
Dikorastushchie Introd Polezn Rast Bashk — Dikorastushchie i Introdutsiruemye Poleznye Rasteniya v Bashkirii
DiIR — Diliman Review
Dilthey Jahrb — Dilthey-Jahrbuch fuer Philosophie und Geschichte der Geisteswissenschaften
DIM — Diamant. Maandelijks Tijdschrift voor de Studie van het Diamantbedrijf
DIM — Direct Marketing
DIMACS Ser Discrete Math Theoret Comput Sci — DIMACS Series in Discrete Mathematics and Theoretical Computer Science
DIMCAL — Developments in Industrial Microbiology
DIME — Dialogue in Instrumental Music Education
DIMEAR — DIA [*Division de Investigaciones Agropecuarias*] Medico
Dim Econ Bourgogne — Dimensions Economiques de la Bourgogne
DIMEDU — Diabete et Metabolisme
Dimen NBS — Dimensions. [*US*] National Bureau of Standards
Dimens — Dimensioni. Revista Abruzzese di Cultura e d'Arte
Dimens Crit Care Nurs — Dimensions of Critical Care Nursing
Dimens Health Serv — Dimensions in Health Service
Dimension — Canadian Dimension
Dimensions NBS — Dimensions. [*US*] National Bureau of Standards
Dimens Oncol Nurs — Dimensions in Oncology Nursing
DIMIA — DIN [*Deutsches Institut fuer Normung*] Mitteilungen
D Imm — Deutsche Immobilien
DIMOA — DM/Disease-a-Month
DIMS — Dimensions. Ontario Metis and Non-Status Indian Association
DIN — Developments in Neurology
DIN — Dialogue North
Dinamika Sploshn Sredy — Dinamika Sploshnoj Sredy. Institut Gidrodinamiki Sibirskogo Otdeleniya AkademiiNauk SSSR
Dinamo Futur — Dinamo Futurista
DINC — Dialogue North. Combined Edition
DINE — Dialogue North. Eastern Arctic Edition
DINEE2 — Drug Interactions Newsletter
Dingler — Polytechnisches Journal. Dingler
Dinglers Polytech J — Dinglers Polytechnisches Journal
DINM — Developments in Nutrition and Metabolism
DIN Mitt — DIN [*Deutsches Institut fuer Normung*] Mitteilungen
Din Prochn Mash — Dinamika i Prochnost Mashin
Din Prochn Mashin — Dinamika i Prochnost Mashin
D Inschr — Sammlung der Griechischen Dialekinschriften
Din Sploshn Sredy — Dinamika Sploshnoj Sredy
DIN Taschenb — DIN [*Deutsches Institut fuer Normung*] Taschenbuch
Din Tepl Protsessov Mater Resp Semin — Dinamika Teplovykh Protsessov. Materialy Respublikanskogo Seminara
DINW — Dialogue North. Western Arctic Edition
Dio — Diogenes
Dioez Archv Schwaben — Dioezesan-Archiv fuer Schwaben

Diog — Revue Diogene

Diogenes Int Z Wiss Menschen — Diogenes. Internationale Zeitschrift fuer die Wissenschaft von Menschen

Diog Int — Diogenes. International Council for Philosophy and Humanistic Studies

Dion — Dioniso

Diopt Optol Rev — Dioptric and Optological Review

Diopt Rev Br J Physiol Opt — Dioptric Review and British Journal of Physiological Optics

Diosk — Dioskuren. Jahrbuch fuer Geisteswissenschaft

Dioxin Perspect — Dioxin Perspectives. A Pilot Study on International Information Exchange on Dioxins and Related Compounds

DIP — Developments in Psychiatry

DIP — Dokumentations und Informationssystem fuer Parlamentsmaterial

Dipl Dan — Diplomattirium Danicum

Dipl Hist — Diplomatic History

Diplomat Kurier — Diplomatischer Kurier

DIPOA — Diesel Power

DIPPR Data Ser — DIPPR (Design Institute for Physical Property Data) Data Series

DIPRDG — Discourse Processes

Diquiu Huaxue Engl Ed — Diqiu Huaxue (English Edition)

DIR — Director

DIR — Documente Privind Isotria Romaniei

DIR — Florida Music Director

Dir Ancient Monum Hist Bldgs Occas Pap — Directorate of Ancient Monuments and Historic Buildings. Occasional Papers

Dir Annu Rep United Dent Hosp Sydney Inst Dent Res — Director's Annual Report. United Dental Hospital of Sydney. Institute of DentalResearch

Dir Appl Nutr — Directions in Applied Nutrition

Dirasat J Coll Educ Univ Riyadh — Dirasat. Journal of the College of Education. University of Riyadh

Dirasat Med Biol Sci — Dirasat. Medical and Biological Sciences

Dirasat Nat Engrg Sci — Dirasat. Natural and Engineering Sciences

Dirasat Nat Eng Sci — Dirasat. Natural and Engineering Sciences

Dirasat Nat Sci (Amman) — Dirasat/Natural Science (Amman)

Dirasat Nat Sci Univ Jordan — Dirasat/Natural Science. University of Jordan

Dirasat Ser B Pure Appl Sci — Dirasat. Series B. Pure and Applied Sciences

Dirasat Univ Jordan — Dirasat. University of Jordan

Dirasat Univ Jordan Ser B — Dirasat. University of Jordan. Series B. Pure and Applied Sciences

Dirasat Univ Of Jordan Ser B — Dirasat. University of Jordan. Series B. Pure and Applied Sciences

DIRAT — Documents Illustrating the Reigns of Augustus and Tiberius

Dir Aut — Diritti d'Autore

Dir Aut — Diritto Automobilistico

Dir Boards — Directors and Boards

Dir Chaos — Directions in Chaos

Dir Cinem — Diritto Cinematografico

Dir Condensed Matter Phys — Directions in Condensed Matter Physics

Dir Crim — Diritto Criminale e Criminologia

Dir Del Lavoro — Diritto del Lavoro

Direc — Direction

Dir Eccl — Diritto Ecclesiastico

Dir Ec Nucl — Diritto ed Economia Nucleare

Direct Brd — Directors and Boards

Direct Curr — Direct Current

Direct Curr & Power Electron — Direct Current and Power Electronics

Direct Inf Nuklearmed — Direct Information. Nuklearmedizin

Direct Inf Strahlenschutz — Direct Information. Strahlenschutz

Direct Mark — Direct Marketing

Direct Midrex — Direct from Midrex

Direct Mkt — Magazine of Direct Marketing

Direct Obs Imperfections Cryst Proc Tech Conf — Direct Observation of Imperfections in Crystals. Proceedings. Technical Conference

Directors and Bds — Directors and Boards

Dir e Giur — Diritto e Giurisprudenza

Direito Nucl — Direito Nuclear

Dir e Prat Trib — Diritto e Pratica Tributaria

Dir et Gestion — Direction et Gestion des Entreprises

Dir Etud Rech Electr Fr Bull Ser A — Direction des Etudes et Recherches. Electricite de France. Bulletin. Serie A. Nucleaire, Hydraulique, Thermique

Dir Etud Rech Electr Fr Bull Ser B — Direction des Etudes et Recherches. Electricite de France. Bulletin. Serie B. Reseaux Electriques, Materiels Electriques

Dir Etud Rech Electr Fr Collect — Direction des Etudes et Recherches d'Electricite de France. Collection

Dir fr Cu — Direct from Cuba

Dir Gen Agric (Peru) Divulg Inf — Direccion General de Agricultura (Peru). Divulgaciones e Informaciones

Dir Gen Bol — Direccion General de Archivos y Bibliotecas. Boletin

Dir Geneal Per — Directory of Genealogical Periodicals

Dir Gen Geol Minas Rev Ecuador — Direccion General de Geologia y Minas. Revista (Ecuador)

Dir Gen Inventario Nac For Publ — Direccion General del Inventario Nacional Forestal. Publicacion

Dir Gen Invent Nac For Publ — Direccion General del Inventario Nacional Forestal. Publicacion

Dir Geol Minas Pet Costa Rica Inf Tec Notas Geol — Direccion de Geologia, Minas y Petroleo (Costa Rica). Informes Tecnicos y NotasGeologias

Dir Geol Publ Tek Seri Geol Ekon Indones — Direktorat Geologi. Publikasi Teknik. Seri Geologi Ekonomi (Indonesia)

Dir Gestion — Direction et Gestion

Dir Gestion Entr — Direction et Gestion des Entreprises

Dir Gov — Directions in Government

DIRH — Directions in Health, Physical Education, and Recreation. Monograph Series

Dir High Tech Corp Suppl — Directory of High Technology Corporations. Supplement

Dir Indiana Crop Impr Ass Seed Certif Serv — Directory. Indiana Crop Improvement Association. Seed Certification Service

Dir Int — Diritto Internazionale. Rivista Trimestrale di Dottrina e Documentazione

Dir Interact Nucl React Mech Proc Conf — Direct Interactions and Nuclear Reaction Mechanisms. Proceedings. Conference

Diritto Lav — Diritto del Lavoro

Dir LR — Directors Law Reporter

Dir Marit — Diritto Marittimo

Dir Nac Propiedad Ind (Argent) — Direccion Nacional de la Propiedad Industrial (Argentina)

Dir Nac Quim Bol Inf Argent — Direccion Nacional de Quimica. Boletin Informativo (Argentina)

Dir Online Databases — Directory of Online Databases

Dir Prat Ass — Diritto e Pratica dell'Assicurazione

Dir Prat Trib — Diritto e Pratica Tributaria

Dir Pubbl Reg Sicil — Diritto Pubblico della Regione Siciliana

Dir Publ Proc — Directory of Published Proceedings

Dir Publ Proc SEMT — Directory of Published Proceedings. Series SEMT. Science, Engineering, Medicine, and Technology

Dir San Mod — Diritto Sanitario Moderno

Dir Scol — Diritto Scolastico

Dir Unpubl Exp Ment Meas — Directory of Unpublished Experimental Mental Measures

DiS — Dickens Studies

Dis — Discourse. A Review of the Liberal Arts

DIS — Dislocations in Solids

Dis — Dissent

DIS — Distrifood. Weekblad voor de Betaillist en Groothandel in Food en Nonfood

DIS — Drilling Information Services

DisA — Dissertation Abstracts [*Later, Dissertation Abstracts International*]

Disabil Rehabil — Disability and Rehabilitation

Dis Abst — Dissertation Abstracts [*Later, Dissertation Abstracts International*]

DISA Inf — DISA [*Danske Industri Syndikat A/S*] Information

Dis Aquat Org — Diseases of Aquatic Organisms

Dis Archit — Disegno di Architettura

Disarm — Disarmament

Disarm & Arms Control — Disarmament and Arms Control

Disaster Manage — Disaster Management

Disaster Prev Res Inst Annu — Disaster Prevention Research Institute. Annual

Disaster Prev Res Inst Kyoto Univ Bull — Disaster Prevention Research Institute. Kyoto University. Bulletin

Disc — Discovery

DISCA — Discovery

DISCAH — Discovery

DISCBI — Discovery

Disc Egyp — Discussions in Egyptology

Disc Excav (Scot) — Discovery and Excavation (Scotland)

Disc Far Soc — Discussions. Faraday Society

Discharges Electr Insul Vac Proc Int Symp — Discharges and Electrical Insulation in Vacuum. Proceedings. International Symposium on Discharges and Electrical Insulation in Vacuum

Dis Chest — Diseases of the Chest

Disch Plann Update — Discharge Planning Update

Discip Grievances — Discipline and Grievances

Disc L and Proc Adv Sheets — Disciplinary Law and Procedure Advance Sheets

Discn Faraday Soc — Discussions. Faraday Society

Disco Forum — Discographical Forum

Dis Colon Rectum — Diseases of the Colon and Rectum

Dis Col Rec — Diseases of the Colon and Rectum

Discoteca — Discoteca alta Fedalta I

Discount M — Discount Merchandiser

Discov — Discovery

Discoveries Pharmacol — Discoveries in Pharmacology

Discoveries Plant Biol — Discoveries in Plant Biology

Discover New World Instrum Proc Jt Symp — Discover the New World of Instrumentation. Proceedings. Joint Symposium

Discovery Excav (Scot) — Discovery and Excavation (Scotland)

Discovery Rep — Discovery Reports

Discov Rep — Discovery Reports

Discrete Appl Math — Discrete Applied Mathematics

Discrete Comput Geom — Discrete and Computational Geometry

Discrete Contin Dynam Systems — Discrete and Continuous Dynamical Systems

Discrete Dyn Nat Soc — Discrete Dynamics in Nature and Society

Discrete Event Dyn Syst Theory Appl — Discrete Event Dynamic Systems. Theory and Applications

Discrete Geom Convexity — Discrete Geometry and Convexity

Discrete Math — Discrete Mathematics

Discrete Math Appl — Discrete Mathematics and Applications

Discrete Math Theoret Comput Sci — Discrete Mathematics and Theoretical Computer Science

Discr Math — Discrete Mathematics

Discurs Contestacio Reial Acad Farm Barcelona — Discurs de Contestacio. Reial Academia de Farmacia de Barcelona

Discurs Reial Acad Farm Barcelona — Discurs. Reial Academia de Farmacia de Barcelona

Discuss Alphabet — Discussion sur l'Alphabetisation

Discuss Annu Conf Steel Cast Res Trade Assoc — Discussion Held at the Annual Conference. Steel Castings Research and Trade Association. Steel Foundry Practice

Discuss Faraday Soc — Discussions. Faraday Society

Discuss Farad Soc — Discussions. Faraday Society

Discuss Math — Discussiones Mathematicae

Discuss Math Algebra Stochastic Methods — Discussiones Mathematicae. Algebra and Stochastic Methods

Discuss Math Differential Incl — Discussiones Mathematicae. Differential Inclusions

Discuss Math Graph Theory — Discussiones Mathematicae. Graph Theory

Dis Esophagus — Diseases of the Esophagus

Dishek Alemi — Dishekimligi Alemi

Dishekim Derg — Dishekimligi Dergisi

DISI Bull — DISI (Dairy Industries Society, International) Bulletin

Dis Jud Des — Discoveries in the Judaean Desert

Diskret Anal Issled Oper — Diskretnyi Analiz i Issledovanie Operatsii

Diskret Analiz — Diskretnyi Analiz. Sbornik Trudov

Diskret Mat — Diskretnaya Matematika

Diskussionsforum Med Ethik — Diskussionsforum Medizinische Ethik

Diskussionstag Forschungskreis Ernaehrungsind — Diskussionstagung - Forschungskreis der Ernaehrungsindustrie e. V

Dis Liver — Diseases of the Liver

Dislocat Mech Prop Cryst Int Conf — Dislocations and Mechanical Properties of Crystals. International Conference

Dislocat Modell Phys Syst Proc Int Conf — Dislocation Modelling of Physical Systems. Proceedings. International Conference

Dislocat Solids Proc Yamada Conf — Dislocations in Solids. Proceedings. Yamada Conference

Dis Marker — Disease Markers

Dis Markers — Disease Markers

DISMDG — Documents. Institut Scientifique

Dis Metab — Diseases of Metabolism [*monograph*]

Dis Mon — Disease-a-Month

Dis Ner Sys — Diseases of the Nervous System

Dis Nerv Syst — Diseases of the Nervous System

Dis Nerv System — Diseases of the Nervous System

DISO — Dictionnaire des Inscriptions Semitiques de l'Ouest

DISOAJ — Difesa Sociale

Disodium Cromoglycate Allerg Airways Dis Proc Symp — Disodium Cromoglycate in Allergic Airways Disease. Proceedings. Symposium

Disord Carbohydr Metab Proc Conf — Disorders of Carbohydrate Metabolism. Proceedings. Conference

Disord Eat Nutr Treat Brain Dis — Disorders of Eating and Nutrients in Treatment of Brain Diseases

Disord Fract — Disorder and Fracture

Disord Miner Metab — Disorders of Mineral Metabolism

Disord Mot Unit Proc Int Meet — Disorders of the Motor Unit. Proceedings. International Meeting

Disord Respir Syst — Disorders of the Respiratory System

Disord Semicond — Disordered Semiconductors

Disord Sex Differ Etiol Clin Delin — Disorders of Sexual Differentiation. Etiology and Clinical Delineation [*monograph*]

Disord Thrombin Form — Disorders of Thrombin Formation

DISP — DISP. Dokumentations- und Informationsstelle fuer Planungsfragen

Disp — Displays

Dispergirovanie Zhidk Emulgiruyushchikh Appar Skh Proizvod — Dispergirovanie Zhidkostei v Emul'giruyushchikh Aparatakh Sel'skokhozyaistvennogo Proizvodstva

Dispergirovannye Met Plenki — Dispergirovannye Metallicheskie Plenki

Dispersion Polym Org Media — Dispersion Polymerization in Organic Media [*monograph*]

Dispersnye Sist Buren — Dispersnye Sistemy v Burenii

Dispersnye Sist Energokhim Protsessakh — Dispersnye Sistemy v Energokhimicheskikh Protsessakh

Dispersnye Sist Ikh Povedenie Elektr Magn Polyakh — Dispersnye Sistemy i Ikh Povedenie v Elektricheskikh i Magnitnykh Polyakh

Disp Imaging — Display and Imaging

Disposal Decontam Pestic Symp — Disposal and Decontamination of Pesticides. Symposium

Disposal Radioact Waste Proc Inf Meet — Disposal of Radioactive Waste. Proceedings. Information Meeting

Disposal Radioact Wastes Ground Proc Symp — Disposal of Radioactive Wastes into the Ground. Proceedings. Symposium

Disposal Radioact Wastes Proc Sci Conf — Disposal of Radioactive Wastes. Proceedings. Scientific Conference

Disposal Radioact Wastes Seas Oceans Surf Waters Proc Symp — Disposal of Radioactive Wastes into Seas, Oceans, and Surface Waters. Proceedings. Symposium

Disposal Sewage Sludge Sanit Landfill — Disposal of Sewage Sludge into a Sanitary Landfill [*monograph*]

Dispos Intern — Disposables International and Nonwoven Fabric Review

Disp Syst Opt — Display System Optics

Disp Technol and Appl — Displays. Technology and Applications

Disquis Math Hungar — Disquisitiones Mathematicae Hungaricae

Diss Abs — Dissertation Abstracts [*Later, Dissertation Abstracts International*]

Diss Abstr — Dissertation Abstracts [*Later, Dissertation Abstracts International*]

Diss Abstr A — Dissertation Abstracts. A. Humanities and Social Sciences

Diss Abstr B — Dissertation Abstracts. B. Sciences and Engineering

Diss Abstr B Sci Eng — Dissertation Abstracts. B. Sciences and Engineering

Diss Abstr Int — Dissertation Abstracts International

Diss Abstr Int B — Dissertation Abstracts International. Section B. Sciences and Engineering

Diss Abstr Int B Sci Eng — Dissertation Abstracts International. Section B. Sciences and Engineering

Diss Abstr Int C — Dissertation Abstracts International. C. European Abstracts

Diss Abstr Int Sec B — Dissertation Abstracts International. Section B. Sciences and Engineering

Diss Abstr Int Sect B — Dissertation Abstracts International. Section B. Sciences and Engineering

Diss Abstr Int Sect C — Dissertation Abstracts International. Section C. European Dissertations

Diss Arch — Dissertationes Archaeologicae

Diss Arch Gand — Dissertationes Archaeologicae Gandenses

Diss Bot — Dissertationes Botanicae

Diss Chalmers Tek Hoegsk — Dissertation. Chalmers Tekniska Hoegskola

Dissert Abs Internat — Dissertation Abstracts International

Dissert Abstr Int — Dissertation Abstracts International

Dissertationes Math (Rozprawy Mat) — Dissertationes Mathematicae (Rozprawy Matematyczny)

Diss Hohenheim Landwirt Hochsch — Dissertation. Hohenheim Landwirtschaftliche Hochschule

Diss Johannes Kepler Univ Linz — Dissertationen der Johannes Kepler. Universitaet Linz

Diss Pan — Dissertationes Pannonicae

Diss Pannon — Dissertationes Pannonicae

Diss Pharm — Dissertationes Pharmaceuticae

Diss Pharm Pharmacol — Dissertationes Pharmaceuticae et Pharmacologicae

Diss Pont Accad Romana Archeol — Dissertazione della Pontificia Accademia Romana di Archeologia

Diss Techn Univ Wien — Dissertationen der Technischen Universitaet Wien

DissUW — Dissertationen der Universitaet (Wien)

Diss Wirtschaftsuniv Wien — Dissertationen der Wirtschaftsuniversitaet Wien

Distance Educ — Distance Education

Dist Braga — Distrito de Braga

Dist Council Rev — District Council Review

Dist Drum — Distant Drummer

Dist Heat — District Heating

Dist Heat Int — District Heating International

Dist Heat NZ Proc Semin — District Heating for New Zealand. Proceedings. Seminar

Distill Feed Res Counc Conf Proc — Distillers Feed Research Council. Conference Proceedings

Distill Final Rep — Distillation. Final Report by the ABCM/BCPMA (Association of British Chemical Manufacturers/British Chemical Plant Manufacturers Association) Distillation Panel

Distill Fuel Stab Cleanliness Symp — Distillate Fuel Stability and Cleanliness. Symposium

Distill Int Symp — Distillation. International Symposium

Disting Diss Comput Sci — Distinguished Dissertations in Computer Science

Distinguished Lect Ser Soc Gen Physiol — Distinguished Lecture Series. Society of the General Physiologists

Dist Mem Geol Surv Botswana — District Memoir. Geological Survey of Botswana

Dist Mem Geol Surv Malays — District Memoir. Geological Survey of Malaysia

Dist Mem Geol Surv Malaysia — District Memoir. Geological Survey of Malaysia

Dist Mem Geol Surv West Malays — District Memoir. Geological Survey of West Malaysia

Dist Nurs — District Nursing

Dist Proc — Distributed Processing Newsletter

Distr — Distribution

Distrbutn — Distribution

Distr Col BAJ — District of Columbia Bar Association. Journal

Distr Heat — District Heating

Distr Heat Ass J — District Heating Association. Journal

Distrib Age — Distribution Age

Distrib Comput — Distributed Computing

Distrib El — Distribution of Electricity

Distrib Mgr — Distribution Manager

Distrib Parallel Databases — Distributed and Parallel Databases

Distributive Wkr — Distributive Worker

Distrib Water Proc Eur Reg Conf — Distribution of Water. Proceedings. European Regional Conference

Distrib Worldwide — Distribution Worldwide

District Law — District Lawyer

District Law (DC) — District Lawyer (District of Columbia)

Distr Man — Distribution Management

Distr Mod — Distrubuzione Moderna

Distr Worldwide — Distribution Worldwide

Disturbances Neurog Control Circ — Disturbances in Neurogenic Control of the Circulation

Disturbances Water Electrolyte Metab Symp Nephrol — Disturbances of Water and Electrolyte Metabolism. Symposium on Nephrology

DISUD6 — Digestive Surgery

DisV — Disque Vert

Ditchley J — Ditchley Journal

Ditillin Opyt Ego Klin Primen — Ditillin i Opyt Ego Klinicheskogo Primeneniya [*monograph*]

Diureseforsch Fortschr Geb Inn Med Symp — Diureseforschung. Fortschritte auf dem Gebiete der Inneren Medizin. Symposion

Diuretic Rev — Diuretic Review

Diuretics Chem Pharmacol Clin Appl Proc Int Conf Diuretics — Diuretics. Chemistry, Pharmacology, and Clinical Applications. Proceedings. International Conference on Diuretics

Div — Divan

Div — Divinitas

DIV — Divisions

Div Appl Chem Tech Pap Aust CSIRO — Division of Applied Chemistry Technical Paper (Australia. Commonwealth Scientific and Industrial Research Organization)

Div Appl Chem Tech Pap CSIRO Aust — Australia. Commonwealth Scientific and Industrial Research Organisation. Division of Applied Chemistry. Technical Paper

Div Appl Org Chem Tech Pap Aust CSIRO — Division of Applied Organic Chemistry Technical Paper (Australia. Commonwealth Scientific and Industrial Research Organization)

Div Appl Org Chem Tech Pap CSIRO Aust — Australia. Commonwealth Scientific and Industrial Research Organisation. Division of Applied Organic Chemistry. Technical Paper

Div Atmos Phys Tech Pap Aust CSIRO — Australia. Commonwealth Scientific and Industrial Research Organisation. Division of Atmospheric Physics. Technical Paper

Div Build Res Pap Natl Res Counc Can — Division of Building Research Paper (National Research Council of Canada)

Div Build Res Technol Pap For Prod Lab CSIRO Aust — Division of Building Research Technological Paper. Forest Products Laboratory. Commonwealth Scientific and Industrial Research Organization. Australia

Div Build Res Tech Pap Aust CSIRO — Division of Building Research Technical Paper (Australia. Commonwealth Scientific and Industrial Research Organization)

Div Chem Technol Tech Pap (Aust CSIRO) — Division of Chemical Technology Technical Paper (Australia. Commonwealth Scientific and Industrial Research Organization)

Div Chem Technol Tech Pap CSIRO Aust — Australia. Commonwealth Scientific and Industrial Research Organisation. Division of Chemical Technology. Technical Paper

Div Eng Res Bull La State Univ — Division of Engineering Research. Bulletin. Louisiana State University

Div Entomol Tech Pap Aust CSIRO — Division of Entomology Technical Paper (Australia. Commonwealth Scientific and industrial Research Organization)

Diverse Off Natl Etud Rech Aeronaut Fr — Diverse. Office National d'Etudes et de Recherches Aeronautiques (France)

Diversity Environ Biogeochem — Diversity of Environmental Biogeochemistry

Div Fish Oceanogr Tech Pap Aust CSIRO — Division of Fisheries and Oceanography. Technical Paper. Australia CommonwealthScientific and Industrial Research Organisation

Div Food Preserv Tech Pap Aust CSIRO — Division of Food Preservation Technical Paper (Australia. Commonwealth Scientific and Industrial Research Organization)

Div Food Res Tech Pap (Aust CSIRO) — Division of Food Research Technical Paper (Australia. Commonwealth Scientific and Industrial Research Organization)

Div For Prod Technol Pap Aust CSIRO — Division of Forest Products Technological Paper (Australia. Commonwealth Scientific and Industrial Research Organization)

DIVID — Divice

Div Invest Colomb Bol Tec — Division de Investigaciones (Colombia). Boletin Tecnico

Div Land Resour Manage Tech Pap (Aust CSIRO) — Division of Land Resources Management Technical Paper (Australia. Commonwealth Scientific and Industrial Research Organization)

Div Land Resour Manage Tech Pap CSIRO Aust — Australia. Commonwealth Scientific and Industrial Research Organisation. Division of Land Resources Management. Technical Paper

Div Land Res Reg Surv Tech Pap Aust CSIRO — Division of Land Research and Regional Survey Technical Paper (Australia. Commonwealth Scientific and Industrial Research Organization)

Div Land Res Tech Pap CSIRO Aust — Australia. Commonwealth Scientific and Industrial Research Organisation. Division of Land Research. Technical Paper

Div Land Use Res Tech Pap Aust CSIRO — Division of Land Use Research. Technical Paper. Australia Commonwealth Scientific and Industrial Research Organisation

Div Land Use Res Tech Pap CSIRO Aust — Australia. Commonwealth Scientific and Industrial Research Organisation. Division of Land Use Research. Technical Paper

Divl Rep Dep Agric Br Guiana — Divisional Reports. Department of Agriculture. British Guiana

Div Math Stat Tech Pap Aust CSIRO — Division of Mathematical Statistics Technical Paper (Australia. Commonwealth Scientific and Industrial Research Organization)

Div Meteorol Phys Tech Pap Aust CSIRO — Division of Meteorological Physics Technical Paper (Australia. Commonwealth Scientific and Industrial Research Organization)

Div Nutr Food Res TNO Rep — Division for Nutrition and Food Research TNO. Report

Divorce Actes Congr Int — Divorce. Actes du Congres International

Div Pesqui Pedol Bol Tec (Braz) — Divisao de Pesquisa Pedologica. Boletim Tecnico (Brazil)

Div Plant Ind Tech Pap Aust CSIRO — Division of Plant Industry Technical Paper (Australia. Commonwealth Scientific and Industrial Research Organization)

Div Rep Aust CSIRO Div Soils — Division Report. Australia. Commonwealth Scientific and Industrial Research Organization. Division of Soils

Div Rep Div Soils CSIRO — Divisional Report. Division of Soils. Commonwealth Scientific and Industrial Research Organisation

Div Soil Res Tech Pap Aust CSIRO — Division of Soil Research Technical Paper (Australia. Commonwealth Scientific and Industrial Organization)

Div Soils Div Rep (Aust CSIRO) — Division of Soils Divisional Report (Australia. Commonwealth Scientific and Industrial Research Organization)

Div Soils Div Rep CSIRO Aust — Australia. Commonwealth Scientific and Industrial Research Organisation. Division of Soils. Divisional Report

Div Soils Tech Pap Aust CSIRO — Division of Soils Technical Paper (Australia. Commonwealth Scientific and Industrial Research Organization)

Div Soils Tech Pap CSIRO Aust — Australia. Commonwealth Scientific and Industrial Research Organisation. Division of Soils. Technical Paper

Div Tech Conf Soc Plast Eng Tech Pap — Divisional Technical Conference. Society of Plastics Engineers. Technical Papers

DIVTEC Tech Pap Soc Plast Eng Eng Prop Struct Div — DIVTEC. Technical Papers (Society of Plastics Engineers. Engineering Propertiesand Structures Division)

Div Trop Agron Tech Pap CSIRO (Aust) — Division of Tropical Agronomy. Technical Paper. Commonwealth Scientific and Industrial Research Organisation (Australia)

Div Trop Crops Pastures Tech Pap CSIRO (Aust) — Division of Tropical Crops and Pastures. Technical Paper. Commonwealth Scientific and Industrial Research Organisation (Australia)

Div Trop Pastures Tech Pap CSIRO Aust — Australia. Commonwealth Scientific and Industrial Research Organisation. Division of Tropical Pastures. Technical Paper

Divul Agri Lima — Divulgaciones Agricolas (Lima)

Divul Etnol Barranquilla — Divulgaciones Etnologicas (Barranquilla, Colombia)

Divulg Cult Odontol — Divulgacion Cultural Odontologica

Divulg Dent — Divulgacion Dental

Divulg Hist — Divulgacion Historica

Divulg Mat — Divulgaciones Matematicas

Divulg Pesq (Bogota) — Divulgacion Pesquera (Bogota)

Divulg Pesq Dir Gen Pesca (Bogota) — Divulgacion Pesquera. Direccion General de Pesca (Bogota)

Divul Hist Mex — Divulgacion Historica (Mexico)

DIW — Visual Merchandising

Dix-Huit Siecle — Dix-Huitieme Siecle

Dixie Bus — Dixie Business

Dix-Sept S — Dix-Septieme Siecle

D-I-Y — Do-It-Yourselfer

DIZ — Deutsche Instrumentanbau Zeitung

DIZ — Deutsche Internierten Zeitung

DIZ — Deutsch-Israelitische Zeitung

Diz Epigr — Dizionario Epigrafico di Antichita Romane

Dizion Vet — Dizionario Veterinario

DJ — Denver Law Journal

DJ — Deutsches Dante-Jahrbuch

DJ — Die Justiz

DJ — Discipleship Journal

DJ — Dzis i Jutro

DJA — Davidson Journal of Anthropology

DJAS — Davidson Journal of Anthropology (Seattle, Washington)

D Jb — Duessseldorfer Jahrbuch. Beitraege zur Geschichte des Niederrheins

DJbN — Deutsches Jahrbuch fuer Numismatik

D Jb Num — Deutsches Jahrbuch fuer Numismatik

DJBR — Development of the James Bay Region/Societe de Developpement de la Baie James

DjbVk — Deutsches Jahrbuch fuer Volkskunde

DJC — Delaware Journal of Corporate Law

DJCL — Delaware Journal of Corporate Law

DJD — Discoveries in the Judaean Desert

DJE — Dictionary of Jamaican English

Djela Jugoslav Akad Znan — Djela Jugoslavenske Akademije Znanosti i Umjetnosti. Opera Academiae Scientiarum et Artium Slavorum Meridionalium

DJGKN — Doshida Joshidaigaku Gakujutsu Kenkyu Nenpo

D Jgt — Dansk Jagt

D Jgt — Dansk Jagttidende

DJM — Dentsu Japan Marketing/Advertising Yearbook

DJN — Dow Jones News

DJNEWS — Dow Jones News Wire

DJNR — Dow Jones News Retrieval Service

D Jour — Danish Journal

DJS — Slagersambacht

DJ St — Deutsche Justiz-Statistik

DJT — Digest of Japanese Industry and Technology

DJU — Diario de Justica da Uniao

D Jur — Dalloz. Jurisprudence

DJurZ — Deutsche Juristenzeitung

DJV — Deutsches Jahrbuch fuer Volkskunde

DJZ — Deutsche Juristenzeitung

DK — Deutsche Kolonialzeitung

DK — Die Kultur

DK — Dukovna Kultura

DkA — Deutschkundliche Arbeiten

DKath — De Katholick

DKAW — Denkschriften der Kaiserlichen Akademie der Wissenschaften. Mathematisch-Naturwissenschaftliche Klasse

DKAW — Denkschriften. Koenigliche Akademie der Wissenschaften [Vienna]

D Kbl — Deutsches Kunstblatt

DKBSA — Doklady Biological Sciences

DKBSB — Doklady Botanical Sciences

DKCHA — Doklady Chemistry

DKD — Deutsche Kunst und Denkmalpflege

DKDP — Deutsche Kunst und Denkmalpflege

D Kem — Dansk Kemi

DKESA — Doklady. Earth Sciences Sections

DKF — Dokumentation Kraftfahrwesen

DKHHD — Denryoku Chuo Kenkyusho Hokoku. Sogo Hokoku

D Kirkes A — Dansk Kirkesangs Arsskrift

DKKIB — Denpa Kenkyusho Kiho

Dk LR — Dickinson Law Review

DK Mitt — DK Mitteilungen

Dkmlpf & Forsch Westfalen — Denkmalpflege und Forschung in Westfalen

Dkmlpf & Heimatschutz — Denkmalpflege und Heimatschutz

Dkmlpf Baden Wuerttemberg — Denkmalpflege in Baden-Wuerttemberg

Dkmlpf Rheinland Pfalz Jber — Denkmalpflege in Rheinland-Pfalz, Jahresberichte

DKNHDO — Denryoku Chuo Kenkyusho Noden Kenkyusho Hokoku

Dk of Bay — Dock of the Bay

D Kolonialzeitung — Deutsche Kolonialzeitung

D Kom — Dansk Kommuner

DKPCA — Doklady Physical Chemistry

D Kred — Den'gi i Kredit
D Krkl — Dansk Kirkeliv Mens Tiderne Skifter
D Ku Denkm Pfl — Deutsche Kunst und Denkmalpflege
D Kunsth — Dansk Kunsthaandvaerk
DKVS — Det Kongelige Videnskapers Selskap
DKV Statusber Dtsch Kaelte Klimatech Ver — DKV-Statusbericht des Deutschen Kaelte- und Klimatechnischen Vereins
DKV Tagungsber — DKV [*Deutscher Kaelte- und Klimatechnischer Verein*] Tagungsbericht
DKZ — Deutsche Kolonialzeitung
DL — Dalloz. Legislation
DL — Darkenu (London)
DL — Detskaya Literatura
DL — Deus Loci
DL — Deutsche Literaturzeitung
DL — Die Literatur
DL — Dienstreglement Loodswezen
DL — Doctrine and Life
DL — Douro Litoral
DL — Droit et Liberte, Contre le Racisme, l'Antisemitisme, pour la Paix
DLA — Diario de Centroamerica
DLAJ — DeKalb Literary Arts Journal
D Landw Tz — Deutsche Landwirtschaftliche Tierzucht
DL Bl — Deutsches Literaturblatt
DLD — Deutsche Literaturdenkmale
D Ldb — Dansk Landburg
DLevZ — Deutsche Levante-Zeitung
DLF — Defense de la Langue Francaise
DLF — Dictionnaire des Lettres Francaises. Dix-Septieme Siecle
DLG Mit Dtsch Landwirtsch Ges — DLG. Mitteilungen. Deutsch Landwirtschafts Gesellschaft
DLI — Diabetes Literature Index
DLine — Direction Line
DLit — Deutsche Literatur
D Lit — Deutsche Literaturzeitung
DLit — Deutsche Literaturzeitung fuer Kritik der Internationalen Wissenschaft
D Literatur Z — Deutsche Literaturzeitung fuer Kritik der Internationalen Wissenschaft
DLJ — University of Detroit. Law Journal
DLJNAQ — Diagnostyka Laboratoryjna
DLL — Dictionnaire de la Langue Louvite
DLM — Developments in Landscape Management and Urban Planning
DI MI Gs Nb — Nachrichtsblatt der Deutschen Malakozoologischen Gesellschaft
DLMov — Doslidzennja z Literaturoznavstava ta Movoznavstva
DLN — Daily Legal News
DLN — Doris Lessing Newsletter
DLP — Douro Litoral (Portugal)
DI Planet — Daily Planet
DLPNAM — Delpinoa
DLQ — Drexel Library Quarterly
DLR — Dickinson Law Review
DLR — Directors Law Reporter
DLR — Dominion Law Reports
DLR 2d — Dominion Law Reports. Second Series
DLR 2d (Can) — Dominion Law Reports. Second Series (Canada)
DLR 3d — Dominion Law Reports. Third Series
DLRB — Digest of Decisions of the National Labor Relations Board
DLR (Can) — Dominion Law Reports (Canada)
DLRED — Duquesne Law Review
DL Rep — DL [*Dominion Laboratory*] Report
DLR Mitt — DLR-Mitteilungen
DLRUAJ — Deutsche Lebensmittel Rundschau
DLS — Deutsche Literatur und Sprachstudien
DLSPDC — Distinguished Lecture Series. Society of the General Physiologists
DLTPAE — Dialysis and Transplantation
DLTRBL — Desert Locust Control Organization for Eastern Africa. Technical Report
DLtz — Deutsche Literaturzeitung
DLTZA — DLZ. Die Landtechnische Zeitschrift
DLW — Deutsches Lesewerk
D Lw Pr — Deutsche Landwirtschaftliche Presse
D Lwsch — Deutsche Landwirtschaft
DLZ — Deutsche Lehrerzeitung
DLZ — Deutsche Literaturzeitung
D Lz — Deutsche Literaturzeitung fuer Kritik der Internationalen Wissenschaft
DLZ — Deutsche Lotto-Zeitung
DLZ — Die Landtechnische Zeitschrift
DLZ Deut Landtech Z — DLZ. Deutsche Landtechnische Zeitschrift
DLZ Die Landtech Z — DLZ. Die Landtechnische Zeitschrift
DL Zg — Deutsche Literarische Zeitung
DM — Daily Mail
DM — Daily Mirror
DM — Dance Magazine
DM — Danske Magazin
DM — Daybooks for Knossos
DM — Debater's Magazine
DM — Developments in Mammals
DM — Dialogos (Mexico)
DM — Direct Marketing
DM — DM/Disease-a-Month
DM — Dublin Magazine
D Ma — Det Danske Marked
DMA — MMS Debt Market Analysis
D Mag — Danske Magazin, Indeholdende Bidrag til den Danske Histories Oplysning
DMAGAZ — Durban Museum and Art Gallery. Annual Report
DMAMDM — Development in Mammals

D Manage J — Defense Management Journal
DMB — Danish Medical Bulletin
DMB — Developments in Marine Biology
DmB — Driemaandelijkse Bladen
DMB Dan Med Bull — DMB. Danish Medical Bulletin
DMB Dan Med Bull Suppl — DMB. Danish Medical Bulletin. Supplement
DM BI — Deutsche Muenzblaetter
DMBUA — Danish Medical Bulletin
DMC — Deutsches Monatsschrift fuer Chile
DMC — Merkblaetter fuer den Aussenhandel
DMCBDX — Developments in Molecular and Cellular Biochemistry
DMCNA — Developmental Medicine and Child Neurology
DMCNAW — Developmental Medicine and Child Neurology
DMCSAD — Developmental Medicine and Child Neurology. Supplement
DMDGA — DECHEMA [*Deutsche Gesellschaft fuer Chemisches Apparatewesen, Chemische Technik, und Biotechnologie eV*] Monographien
DM Dis Mon — DM/Disease-a-Month
DMDSAI — Drug Metabolism and Disposition
DME — Debreceni Deri Muzeum Evkoenyve
D Med Wochens — Deutsche Medizinische Wochenschrift
D Meere Jbr — Jahresbericht der Commission zur Wissenschaftlichen Untersuchung der Deutschen Meere in Kiel
D Mg — Danske Magazin
DMG — Data Management
DMG — De Maasgouw. Orgaan voor Limbrugsche Geschiedenis, Taal-en Letterkunde
DMG — Deutsche Morgenlaendische Gesellschaft
DMG — Deutsches Mozartfest der Deutschen Mozart-Gesellschaft
DMG — Documents in Mycenaean Greek
DMG-DRS J — DMG-DRS [*Design Methods Group - Design Research*] Journal
DMGMAF — Mitteilungen der Deutschen Malakozoologischen Gesellschaft
DMGYA — Demography
DMI — Dun's Market Identifiers
DMICP — Danish Meteorological Institute. Climatological Papers
DMID — Diagnostic Microbiology and Infectious Disease
DMIDDZ — Diagnostic Microbiology and Infectious Disease
D Militaeraerztl Kal Hamburg — Deutscher Militaeraerztlicher Kalender fuer die Sanitaetsoffiziere der Armee
DMIM — Danske Meteorologiske Institut. Meddelelser
D Miss — Dansk Missionsblad
DMIWAL — Deutsche Milchwirtschaft
DMIWSR — Danish Meteorological Institute. Weather Service Report
DMJ — Defense Management Journal
DMJB — Deutsches Meteorologisches Jahrbuch fuer Bayern
DMJOA2 — Deutsches Medizinisches Journal
DMJOB — Defense Management Journal
DMKHMT ERI — Dolgozatok a Magyar Kiralyi Horthy Miklos Tudomany-Egyetem Regisegtudomanyi Intezeteboel
DMKK — Deutsche Monatsschrift fuer Kolonialpolitik und Kolonisation
Dmkp — Danmarksposten
DMMRB — Daily Missouri-Mississippi River Bulletin
DMN — Dallas Morning News
DMNHA — Dimensions in Health Service
DMNOAM — Durban Museum Novitates
DMO — Dun's Marketing Online
DMOA — Documenta et Monumenta Orientis Antiqui
DMONBP — Dermatologische Monatsschrift
D Morgenl Gesell Zeits — Deutsche Morgenlaendische Gesellschaft. Zeitschrift
DMov — Doslidzennja z Movoznavstva Zbirnyk Statej Aspirantiv i Dysertantiv
DMP — Developments in Mineral Processing
DMP Durvoobrab Mebelna Promst — DMP. Durvoobrabotvashta i Mebelna Promishlenost
DMR — Daily Market Report
DMR — Diabetes/Metabolism Reviews
DMREEG — Diabetes/Metabolism Reviews
DMRRDK — Design and Management for Resource Recovery
DMS — De Militaire Spectator
DMS — Discount Merchandiser
DMt — Dansk Musiktidsskrift
D Mth Vr Jbr — Jahresbericht der Deutschen Mathematiker-Vereinigung
D Mtr — Defence Material
DMTRA — Drug Metabolism Reviews
DMTRAR — Drug Metabolism Reviews
DMUkrM — Doslidzennja i Materijaly z Ukrjins'koji Movy
D Mus — Dansk Musiktidsskrift
DMW — Deutsche Medizinische Wochenschrift
DMW Dtsch Med Wochenschr — DMW. Deutsche Medizinische Wochenschrift
DMWOAX — Deutsche Medizinische Wochenschrift
DMZ — Deutsche Medizinische Zeitung
DMZ Dtsch Molk Ztg — DMZ. Deutsche Molkerei-Zeitung
DMZ Lebensmittelind Milchwirtsch — DMZ (Deutsche Molkerei-Zeitung) Lebensmittelindustrie und Milchwirtschaft
DN — Dagens Nyheter
DN — Daily Nation
DN — Daily News
DN — Dance News
DN — Detroit News
DN — Developments in Neuroscience
DN — Dialect Notes
DN — Disraeli Newsletter
DN — Dreiser Newsletter
DN — Druzba Narodov
DNA Cell Biol — DNA [*Deoxyribonucleic Acid*] and Cell Biology
DNA Damage Repair Hum Tissues — DNA Damage and Repair in Human Tissues
D Na D Sk — Dansk Natur - Dansk Skole

DNAL — Diario de Noticias (Lisbon, Portugal)
DNA Repair Its Inhib — DNA Repair and Its Inhibition
DNA Res — DNA Research
DNA Seq — DNA Sequence
DNA Synth in Vitro Proc Annu Harry Steenbock Symp — DNA Synthesis in Vitro. Proceedings. Annual Harry Steenbock Symposium
D Natfr — Dansk Naturfredning
D Natl — Defense Nationale
DnatMus — Denkschrift des Naturhistorischen Museums. Wien
DNA US Def Nucl Agency — DNA. United States Defense Nuclear Agency
DNav — De Navorscher
DNB — Dictionary of National Biography
DNBSB — Dimensions. [*US*] National Bureau of Standards
DNCPA — Dental Concepts
DND — Development News Digest [*Later, Development Dossier*]
DND — NASA [*National Aeronautics and Space Administration*] Directory of Numerical D atabases
DNDJA — Dainichi Nippon Densen Jiho
DNE — Dictionary of Newfoundland English
Dnevn Vserossijsk Sezda Russk Bot — Dnevnik Vserossijskogo S'ezda Russkih Botanikov
DNF — Denmark Review
D Nf B — Bericht ueber die Versammlung der Deutschen Naturforscher und Aerzte
D Nf Festschr — Festschrift fuer die 59. Versammlung Deutscher Naturforscher und Aerzte
D Nf Tbl — Tageblatt der Versammlung Deutscher Naturforscher und Aerzte
DNFV — Dansk Naturhistorisk Forening. Videnskabelige Meddelelser
D Nf Vh — Verhandlungen der Gesellschaft Deutscher Naturforscher und Aerzte
D Nf Vsm B — Bericht ueber die Versammlung der Deutschen Naturforscher und Aerzte
DNG — De Nederlandse Gemeente
DNG — Dictionnaire des Noms Geographiques
DNHYAT — Dental Hygiene
DNIND4 — Drug-Nutrient Interactions
DNK — Doklady na Naucnych Konferencijach
DNKHAR — Deltion tes Hellenikes Kteniatrikes Hetaireias
DNL — Die Neue Literatur
Dn LJ — Denver Law Journal
DNO — Der Neue Orient
DNR Notes Wash State Dep Nat Resour — DNR [*Department of Natural Resources*] Notes. Washington (State) Department of Natural Resources
DNRPAI — Dana-Report. Carlsberg Foundation
DNS — Daily News
DNS — Die Neueren Sprachen
DNSYA — Diseases of the Nervous System
DNSYAG — Diseases of the Nervous System
DNT — De Nieuwe Taglalgids
DNUND — Dopovidi Akademii Nauk Ukrains'koi RSR. Seriya A. Fiziko-Tekhnichni ta Matematichni Nauki
Dn Vd Selsk Skr — Kongelige Danske Videnskabernes Selskabs Skrivter
DNVS — Det Norske Videnskapers Selskap
DNW — Der Neue Weg
DO — Dance Observer
DO — Demotic Ostraca from the Collections at Oxford, Paris, Berlin, and Cairo
DO — Diario Oficial
DO — Dispositivo
DOA — Abstracts on Tropical Agriculture
Doane Inf Cent Index Syst Subj Index — DICIS. Doane Information Center Indexing System. Subject Index
Doanes Agr Rep — Doane's Agricultural Report
Doanes Bus Mag Amer Agr — Doane's Business Magazine for American Agriculture
DOAW — Denkschriften der Oesterreichischen Akademie der Wissenschaften
DOB — Dictionary of the Bible
Dobuts Zasshi — Dobutsugaku Zasshi
Dobycha Obogashch Rud Tsvetn Met — Dobycha i Obogashchenie Rud Tsvetnykh Metallov
Dobycha Pererab Goryuch Slantsev — Dobycha i Pererabotka Goryuchikh Slantsev
Dobycha Pererab Nerudn Stroit Mater — Dobycha i Pererabotka Nerudnykh Stroitel'nykh Materialov
DOC — Catalogue of Byzantine Coins in the Dumbarton Oaks Collection and Whittemore Collection
DOC — Dictionary of Organic Compounds
Doc Abstr — Documentation Abstracts
Doc Abstr Inf Sci Abstr — Documentation Abstracts and Information Science Abstracts
Doc Actividad Contemp — Documentos de Actividad Contemporanea
Doc Alb — Documenta Albana
Doc A Merid — Documents d'Archeologie Meridionale
Doc & Mem Hist Porto — Documento e Memorias para a Historia do Porto
Doc & Per Dada — Documenti e Periodici Dada
Doc & Rap Soc Paleontol & Archeol — Documents et Rapports de la Societe Paleontologique et Archeologique
Doc Ant dell Afr Ital — Documenti Antichi dell'Africa Italiana
Doc A Oggi — Documenti d'Arte Oggi
Doc Archeol — Document Archeologie. Tresor des Ages
Doc Art du XV S — Documents Artistiques du XV Siecle
Doc Bibl — Documentacion Bibliotecologica
Doc Biol — Documents on Biology
Doc Biol Pract — Documentation du Biologiste Practicien
Docbl Werkgroep 18e Eeuw — Documentatieblad Werkgroep Achttiende Eeuw
Doc BRGM — Documents du BRGM
Doc Bull Natl Res Cent (Egypt) — Documentation Bulletin. National Research Centre (Egypt)

Doc Bull Nat Res Cent (UAR) — Documentation Bulletin. National Research Centre (United Arab Republic)
Doc Bur Geol Malagasy — Documentation du Bureau Geologique (Malagasy)
DocC — Documentation Catholique
Doc Cartogr Ecol — Documents de Cartographie Ecologique
Doc Cath — Documentation Catholique
Doc Centre Et Revenus Couts — Documents. Centre d'Etude des Revenus et des Couts
Doc CEPESS — Documents CEPESS
Doc Charleroi — Documents et Rapports. Societe Paleontologique et Archeologique de l'Arrondissement Judiciaire de Charleroi
Doc Chem Yugosl — Documenta Chemica Yugoslavica
Doc Combust Eng Assoc — Document. Combustion Engineering Association
Doc Coop — Documenti Cooperativi
Doc Crit Iberoam Sevilla — Documentacion Critica Iberoamericana (Sevilla)
Doc d'Et Droit Const — Documents d'Etudes. Droit Constitutionnel et Institutions Politiques
Doc d'Et Droit Internat Publ — Documents d'Etudes. Droit International Public
Doc Econ — Documentation Economique
Doc et Bibl — Documentation et Bibliotheques
Doc Eur Abwasser Abfallsymp — Documentation. Europaeisches Abwasser- und Abfallsymposium
Doc Eur Abwasser Abfall Symp EAS — Documentation. Europaeisches Abwasser- und Abfall-Symposium EAS
Doc Eur Sewage Refuse Symp EAS — Documentation. European Sewage and Refuse Symposium EAS
Doc Geogr — Documentatio Geographica
Doc Haematol (Bucharest) — Documenta Haematologica (Bucharest)
Doc Hist A Andalucia — Documentos para la Historia del Arte en Andalucia
Doc Hist Archaeol & Archit — Documents d'Histoire, d'Archeologie, et d'Architecture
Doc Hist Can Art — Documents in the History of Canadian Art
Doc Ill Dep Energy Nat Resour — Document. Illinois Department of Energy and Natural Resources
Doc Ill Inst Environ Qual — Document. Illinois Institute for Environmental Quality
Doc Inform Gestion — Documents d'Information et de Gestion
Doc Inst Nat Resour (Ill) — Document. Institute of Natural Resources (Illinois)
Doc Inst Sci (Rabat) — Documents. Institut Scientifique (Rabat)
Doc Invest Hidrol — Documentos de Investigacion Hidrologica
Dock & Harbour — Dock and Harbour Authority
Dock Harb Auth — Dock and Harbour Authority
Dock Harbour Auth — Dock and Harbour Authority
Doc Lab Geol Fac Sci Lyon — Documents des Laboratoires de Geologie de la Faculte des Sciences de Lyon
Doc Man — Document Management
Doc Math — Documenta Mathematica
Doc Med — Documentation Medicale. Comite International de la Croix-Rouge
Doc Med Geogr Trop — Documenta de Medicina Geographica et Tropica
Doc Neerl Indones Morb Trop — Documenta Neerlandica et Indonesica de Morbis Tropicis
Doc Ophthal — Documenta Ophthalmologica
Doc Ophthalmol — Documenta Ophthalmologica
Doc Ophthalmol Proc Ser — Documenta Ophthalmologica. Proceedings Series
DOCPAL — Sistema de Documentacion sobre Poblacion en America Latina
Doc Parl — Documents Parlementaires
Doc Pedozool — Documents Pedozoologiques
Doc Physiogr Pol — Documenta Physiographica Poloniae
Doc Phytosociol — Documents Phytosociologiques
Doc Polit — Documentos Politicos
Doc Public Adm — Documentation in Public Administration
Doc Rheum — Documenta Rheumatologica
Doc Rom — Documente Privind Isotria Romaniei
Docs Aug Tib — Documents Illustrating the Reigns of Augustus and Tiberius
Docs CEPESS — Documents. CEPESS
Doc Sci — Documentation Scientifique
Doc Sci XVe Siecle — Documents Scientifiques du XVe Siecle
Doc Seance — Document de Seance. Rapport Parlementaire au Parlement Europeen
Doc Swed Counc Build Res — Document. Swedish Council for Building Research
DoctCom — Doctor Communis
Doct Comm — Doctor Communis
Doct Diss Amer Univ — Doctoral Dissertations Accepted by American Universities
Doc Tech Charbon Fr — Documents Techniques. Charbonnages de France
Doc Tec Hidrol — Documentos Tecnicos de Hidrologia
Doc Tech Inst Natl Rech Agron Tunis — Documents Techniques. Institut National de la Recherche Agronomique de Tunisie
Doc Tech SCPA (Soc Commer Potasses Azote) — Document Technique de la SCPA (Societe Commerciale des Potasses et de l'Azote)
Doc Textilia — Documenta Textilia
Doc Travail — Document de Travail
DoctrLife — Doctrine and Life
Doc Ukr Sam — Documents of Ukrainian Samvydav
Docum Adm — Documentacion Administrativa
Docum Admin — Documentacion Administrativa
Docum Cath — Documentation Catholique
Docum Centre Nat Rech For — Document. Centre National de Recherches Forestieres
Docum Econ — Documentacion Economica
Docum Econ Colombiana — Documentacion Economica Colombiana
Docum Econ (Paris) — Documentation Economique (Paris)
Documen — Documentation Etc.
Documentatiebl Werkgr 18E-eeuw — Documentatieblad Werkgroep 18E-eeuw
Documents CEGM — Documents. Centre d'Etudes Geologiques et Minieres
Docum et Biblio — Documentation et Bibliotheques
Docum Europ — Documentation Europeenne

Docum Europe Centr — Documentation sur l'Europe Centrale
Docum Eur Ser Syndicale et Ouvriere — Documentation Europeenne. Serie Syndicale et Ouvriere
Docum Franc Illustr — Documentation Francaise Illustree
Docum Inform Pedag — Documentation et Information Pedagogiques
Docum Jur — Documentacion Juridica
Docum Legis Afr — Documentation Legislative Africaine
Docum Med Geogr Trop — Documenta de Medicina Geographica et Tropica
Docum Ned Indo Morbis Trop — Documenta Neerlandica et Indonesica de Morbis Tropicis
Docum Ophthal — Documenta Ophthalmologica
Docum Paesi Est — Documentazione sui Paesi de l'Est
Docums Cent Rech Anthrop Mus Homme — Documents. Centre de Recherche d'Anthropologie. Musee de l'Homme
Docums Tech INRAT — Documents Techniques. Institut National de la Recherche Agronomique de Tunisie
DocVdO — Documents du Val d'Or
Doc Vet — Documenta Veterinaria
Doc Vet Brno — Documenta Veterinaria (Brno)
Doc Vita It — Documenti di Vita Italiana
DOD — Dictionary of Drugs
Dod — Dod's Parliamentary Companion. Annual
Dodge — Dodge/Sweet's Construction Outlook
DOD NR — Department of Defense. News Release
D Oe — Deutsch-Oesterreich
D Oe B — Der Oesterreichische Betriebswirt
DOE Chem Hydrogen Energy Contract Rev Syst Proc — DOE [*Department of Energy*] Chemical/Hydrogen Energy Contractor Review Systems. Proceedings
D Oe D — Der Oeffentliche Dienst
DOE Nucl Airborne Waste Manage Air Clean Conf — DOE Nuclear Airborne Waste Management and Air Cleaning Conference
DOE Nucl Air Clean Conf Proc — DOE (US Department of Energy) Nuclear Air Cleaning Conference. Proceedings
DOE Pat Available Licens — DOE [*US Department of Energy*] Patents Available for Licensing
DOE Symp Ser — DOE (Department of Energy) Symposium Series
DOE TIC US Dep Energy Tech Inf Cent — DOE/TIC (United States. Department of Energy. Technical Information Center)
DOE Transp Lib Bull — DOE [*US Department of Energy*] and Transport Library Bulletin
DoetW — Deutsch-Oesterreichische Tieraerztliche Wochenschrift
DOE (US Dep Energy) Symp Ser — DOE (US Department of Energy) Symposium Series
DOFTAB — Dansk Ornithologisk Forenings Tidsskrift
DOG — Documentation sur l'Europe Centrale
Doga Bilim Derg Seri A — Doga Bilim Dergisi. Seri A
Doga Bilim Derg Seri A1 — Doga Bilim Dergisi. Seri A1
Doga Bilim Derg Seri A2 — Doga Bilim Dergisi. Seri A2
Doga Bilim Derg Seri B — Doga Bilim Dergisi. Seri B. Muhendislik ve Cevre
Doga Bilim Derg Seri D — Doga Bilim Dergisi. Seri D. Veterinerlik Hayvancilik ve Tarim Ormancilik
Doga Bilim Derg Seri D1 — Doga Bilim Dergisi. Seri D1
Doga Bilim Derg Seri D2 — Doga Bilim Dergisi. Seri D2
Doga Bilim Derg Seri D Vet Hayvancilik Tarim Ormancilik — Doga Bilim Dergisi. Seri D. Veterinerlik Hayvancilik ve Tarim Ormancilik
Doga Biyol Serisi — Doga Biyoloji Serisi
Doga Fiz Astrofiz Serisi — Doga Fizik Astrofizik Serisi
Doga Kim Serisi — Doga Kimya Serisi
Doga Mat — Doga. Turk Matematik Dergisi
Doga Mat Serisi — Doga Matematik Serisi
Doga Muhendislik Cevre Bilimleri — Doga. Muhendislik ve Cevre Bilimleri
Doga Ser A Math Phys Biol Sci — Doga. Serie A. Mathematical, Physical, and Biological Sciences
Doga Ser B Eng — Doga. Serie B. Engineering
Doga Ser C Med Sci — Doga. Serie C. Medical Sciences
Doga Ser D Agric Anim Husb — Doga. Serie D. Agriculture and Animal Husbandry
Doga Tarim Ormancilik Ser — Doga. Tarim ve Ormancilik Serisi
Doga Turk Biyol Derg — Doga. Turk Biyoloji Dergisi
Doga Turk Bot Derg — Doga. Turk Botanik Dergisi
Doga Turk Fiz Astrofiz Derg — Doga. Turk Fizik ve Astrofizik Dergisi
Doga Turk J Phys — Doga. Turkish Journal of Physics
Doga Turk Kim Derg — Doga. Turk Kimya Dergisi
Doga Turk Muhendislik Cevre Bilimleri Derg — Doga. Turk Muhendislik ve Cevre Bilimleri Dergisi
Doga Turk Tarim Ormancilik Derg — Doga. Turk Tarim ve Ormancilik Dergisi
Doga Turk Tip Eczacilik Derg — Doga. Turk Tip ve Eczacilik Dergisi
Doga Turk Vet Hayvancilik Derg — Doga. Turk Veterinerlik ve Hayvancilik Dergisi
Doga Turk Yerbilimleri Derg — Doga. Turk Yerbilimleri Dergisi
Doga Turk Zool Derg — Doga. Turk Zooloji Dergisi
Doga Vet Hayvancilik Ser — Doga. Veterinerlik ve Hayvancilik Serisi
DOGE — Gestion des Entreprises
DOGI — Dottrina Guiridica
Dogwoods Bark — Dogwood's Bark. A Bulletin of Wild Flower Notes and Outings
DOGWV — Wissenschaftliche Veroeffentlichungen der Deutschen Orientgesellschaft
DOGYDY — Developments in Obstetrics and Gynecology
DOH — Dock and Harbour Authority
Dohanykut Intez Kozl — Dohanykutato Intezet Kozlemenyei
DOHNA — Domestic Heating News
Doi B — Doitsu Bungaku
Doit Bung Ronko — Doitsu Bungaku Ronko
Doits — Doitsugo
DOJb — Deutsches Orient-Jahrbuch
DOK — Die Ortskrankenkasse
Dok — Dokumentation
Dok — Dokumente

DOK — Oesterreich Nederland
Dok Arbeitsmed — Dokumentation Arbeitsmedizin
DOKBA — Doklady Biophysics
DOKEA — Dokumenteshon Kenkyu
Dokembr Dokl Sov Geol Mezhdunar Geol Kongr — Dokembrii. Doklady Sovetskikh Geologov. Mezhdunarodnyi Geologicheskii Kongress
Dok Fachbibl Werkbuech — Dokumentation Fachbibliothek Werkbuecherei
Dok/Inf — Dokumentation/Information
Dokkyo J Med Sci — Dokkyo Journal of Medical Sciences
Dokl Acad Sci Belarus — Doklady. Academy of Sciences of Belarus
Dokl Acad Sci BSSR — Doklady. Academy of Sciences. BSSR
Dokl Acad Sci USSR Earth Sci Sect — Doklady Academy of Sciences of the USSR. Earth Science Sections
Dokl Acad Sci USSR Oceanol Sect — Doklady. Academy of Sciences. USSR. Oceanology Sections
Dokl Akad Nauk — Doklady Akademii Nauk
Dokl Akad Nauk Arm — Doklady Akademii Nauk Armenii
Dokl Akad Nauk Arm SSR — Doklady Akademii Nauk Armyanskoi SSR
Dokl Akad Nauk Azerb — Doklady. Akademiya Nauk Azerbaidzhana
Dokl Akad Nauk Azerbaidzhana — Doklady Akademiya Nauk Azerbaidzhana
Dokl Akad Nauk Azerb SSR — Doklady Akademii Nauk Azerbajdzanskoj SSR
Dokl Akad Nauk Az SSR — Doklady Akademii Nauk Azerbajdzanskoj SSR
Dokl Akad Nauk Belarusi — Doklady Akademii Nauk Belarusi
Dokl Akad Nauk Beloruss SSR — Doklady Akademii Nauk Belorusskoi SSR
Dokl Akad Nauk B SSR — Doklady Akademii Nauk Belorusskoi SSR
Dokl Akad Nauk Resp Kaz — Doklady Akademii Nauk Respubliki Kazakhstan
Dokl Akad Nauk Resp Tadzh — Doklady Akademii Nauk Respubliki Tadzhikistan
Dokl Akad Nauk Respub Tadzhikistan — Doklady Akademiya Nauk Respubliki Tadzhikistan
Dokl Akad Nauk SSR Biochem Sect (Engl Transl) — Doklady Akademii Nauk SSSR. Biochemistry Section (English Translation)
Dokl Akad Nauk SSR Bot Sci Sect (Engl Transl) — Doklady Akademii Nauk SSSR. Botanical Sciences Section (English Translation)
Dokl Akad Nauk SSSR — Doklady Akademii Nauk SSSR
Dokl Akad Nauk SSSR Biochem Sect (Engl Transl) — Doklady Akademii Nauk SSSR. Biochemistry Section (English Translation)
Dokl Akad Nauk SSSR Biol Sci Sect (Engl Transl) — Doklady Akademii Nauk SSSR. Biological Sciences Section (English Translation)
Dokl Akad Nauk SSSR Bot Sci Sect (Engl Transl) — Doklady Akademii Nauk SSSR. Botanical Sciences Section (English Translation)
Dokl Akad Nauk SSSR Engl Transl Biochem Sect — Doklady Akademii Nauk SSSR. English Translation. Biochemistry Section
Dokl Akad Nauk SSSR Engl Transl Biophys Sect — Doklady Akademii Nauk SSSR. English Translation. Biophysics Section
Dokl Akad Nauk SSSR Engl Transl Bot Sci Sect — Doklady Akademii Nauk SSSR. English Translation. Botanical Sciences Sections
Dokl Akad Nauk SSSR Engl Transl Chem Sect — Doklady Akademii Nauk SSSR. English Translation. Chemistry Section
Dokl Akad Nauk SSSR Engl Transl Chem Technol Sect — Doklady Akademii Nauk SSSR. English Translation. Chemical Technology Section
Dokl Akad Nauk SSSR Engl Transl Earth Sci Sect — Doklady Akademii Nauk SSSR. English Translation. Earth Sciences Sections
Dokl Akad Nauk SSSR Engl Transl Phys Chem Sect — Doklady Akademii Nauk SSSR. English Translation. Physical Chemistry Section
Dokl Akad Nauk SSSR Engl Transl Phys Sect — Doklady Akademii Nauk SSSR. English Translation. Physics Sections
Dokl Akad Nauk SSSR Engl Transl Pure Math Sect — Doklady Akademii Nauk SSSR. English Translation. Pure Mathematics Section
Dokl Akad Nauk SSSR Engl Transl Soil Sci Sect — Doklady Akademii Nauk SSSR. English Translation. Soil Science Section
Dokl Akad Nauk SSSR Ser A — Doklady Akademii Nauk SSSR. Seriya A
Dokl Akad Nauk SSSR Ser Biol — Doklady Akademii Nauk SSSR. Seriya Biologiya
Dokl Akad Nauk SSSR Ser Fiz Khim — Doklady Akademii Nauk SSSR. Seriya Fizicheskoj Khimii
Dokl Akad Nauk SSSR Ser Geol — Doklady Akademii Nauk SSSR. Seriya Geologiya
Dokl Akad Nauk SSSR Ser Khim — Doklady Akademii Nauk SSSR. Seriya Khimiya
Dokl Akad Nauk SSSR Ser Mat Fiz — Doklady Akademii Nauk SSSR. Seriya Matematika Fizika
Dokl Akad Nauk Tadzh SSR — Doklady Akademii Nauk Tadzhikskoi SSR
Dokl Akad Nauk Ukr — Doklady Akademii Nauk Ukrainy
Dokl Akad Nauk Ukrain SSR Ser A — Akademija Nauk Ukrainskoi SSR. Doklady. Serija A. Fiziko-Matematiceskie i Tehniceskie Nauki
Dokl Akad Nauk Ukr SSR — Doklady Akademii Nauk Ukrainskoi SSR
Dokl Akad Nauk Ukr SSR Ser B — Doklady Akademii Nauk Ukrainskoi SSR. Seriya B. Geologicheskie, Khimicheskie, iBiologicheski Nauki
Dokl Akad Nauk Ukr SSR Ser B Geol Khim Biol Nauki — Doklady Akademii Nauk Ukrainskoi SSR. Seriya B. Geologicheskie, Khimicheskie, iBiologicheski Nauki
Dokl Akad Nauk Uzbek SSR — Doklady Akademii Nauk Uzbekskoi SSR
Dokl Akad Nauk Uzb SSR — Doklady Akademii Nauk Uzbekskoi SSR
Dokl Akad Nauk UzSSR — Doklady Akademii Nauk Uzbekskoi SSR
Dokl Akad Pedagog Nauk RSFSR — Doklady Akademii Pedagogicheskikh Nauk RSFSR
Dokl Akad Skh Nauk Bolg — Doklady Akademii Sel'skokhozyaistvennykh Nauk v Bolgarii
Dokl Ak N Arm SSR — Doklady Akademii Nauk Armyanskoi SSR
Dokl Ak N Az SSR — Doklady Akademii Nauk Azerbajdzanskoj SSR
Dokl Ak N Bel SSR — Doklady Akademii Nauk Belorusskoi SSR
Dokl Ak SSSR — Doklady Akademii Nauk SSSR
Dokl Biochem — Doklady Biochemistry
Dokl Biochem Akad Nauk SSSR — Doklady. Biochemistry. Akademilia Nauk SSSR

Dokl Biochem (Engl Transl Dokl Akad Nauk SSSR Ser Biokhim) — Doklady Biochemistry (English Translation of Doklady Akademii Nauk SSSR. SeriyaBiokhimiya)

Dokl Biol Sci — Doklady Biological Sciences

Dokl Biol Sci Akad Nauk SSSR — Doklady. Biological Sciences. Akademilia Nauk SSSR

Dokl Biol Sci (Engl Transl Dokl Akad Nauk SSSR) — Doklady Biological Sciences (English Translation of Doklady Akademii Nauk SSSR)

Dokl Biol Sci (Engl Transl Dokl Akad Nauk SSSR Ser Biol) — Doklady Biological Sciences (English Translation of Doklady Akademii Nauk SSSR.Seriya Biologiya)

Dokl Biophys — Doklady Biophysics

Dokl Biophys Akad Nauk SSSR — Doklady. Biophysics. Akademilia Nauk SSSR

Dokl Biophys (Engl Transl Dokl Akad Nauk SSSR) — Doklady Biophysics (English Translation of Doklady Akademii Nauk SSSR)

Dokl Biophys (Engl Transl Dokl Akad Nauk SSSR Ser Biofiz) — Doklady Biophysics (English Translation of Doklady Akademii Nauk SSSR. Seriya Biofizika)

Dokl Bolg Akad Nauk — Doklady Bolgarskoi Akademii Nauk

Dokl Bot Sci — Doklady Botanical Sciences

Dokl Bot Sci Akad Nauk SSSR — Doklady. Botanical Sciences. Akademilia Nauk SSSR

Dokl Bot Sci (Engl Transl Dokl Akad Nauk SSSR) — Doklady Botanical Sciences (English Translation of Doklady Akademii Nauk SSSR)

Dokl Bot Sci (Engl Transl Dokl Akad Nauk SSSR Ser Bot) — Doklady Botanical Sciences (English Translation of Doklady Akademii Nauk SSSR. Seriya Botanika)

Dokl Bulg Akad Nauk — Dokladi na Bulgarskata Akademiya na Naukite/Reports. Bulgarian Academy of Sciences

Dokl Chekh Liteinogo Nauchn Issled — Doklady Chekhoslovatskogo Liteinogo Nauchnogo Issledovaniya

Dokl Chem — Doklady Chemistry

Dokl Chem Engl Transl — Doklady Chemistry (English Translation)

Dokl Chem Technol — Doklady Chemical Technology. Academy of Sciences of the USSR. Chemical Technology Section

Dokl Chem Technol Engl Transl — Doklady Chemical Technology (English Translation)

Dokl Geogr Ova SSSR — Doklady Geograficheskogo Obshchestva SSSR

Dokl Inst Geogr Sib Dal'nego Vostoka — Doklady Instituta Geografii Sibiri i Dal'nego Vostoka

Dokl Inst Geogr Sib Dal'n Vost — Doklady Instituta Geografii Sibiri i Dal'nego Vostoka

Dokl Irkutsk Protivochumn Inst — Doklady Irkutskogo Protivochumnogo Instituta

DoklIIRuJa — Doklady i Soobscenija Instituta Russkogo Jazyka

Dokl Kom Aerosemki Fotogrametrii Geogr Obs SSR — Doklady Komissii Aeros'emki i Fotogrametrii Geograficheskogo Obshchestva SSR

Dokl Kom Aeros'emki Fotogr Geogr O-Va SSR — Doklady Komissii Aeros'emki i Fotogrametrii Geograficheskogo Obshchestva SSR

Dokl Konf Elem Khim Reakts — Doklady Konferentsii po Elementarnym Khimicheskim Reaktsiyam

Dokl Konf Fiz Plazmy Probl Upr Termoyad Reakts — Doklady Konferentsii po Fizike Plazmy i Probleme Upravlyaemykh Termoyadernykh Reaktsii

Dokl Konf Fiz Plazmy Probl Upr Termoyad Sint — Doklady Konferentsii po Fizike Plazmy i Probleme Upravlyaemogo Termoyadernogo Sinteza

Dokl Konf Vopr Tsito Gistokhim — Doklady Konferentsiya po Voprosam Tsito- i Gistokhimii

Dokl Konf Vysokomol Soedin — Doklady k Konferentsii po Vysokomolekulyarnym Soedineniyam

Dokl Konf Vysokoprochn Nemagn Stalyam — Doklady Konferentsii po Vysokoprochnym Nemagnitnym Stalyam

Dokl L'vov Politekh Inst — Doklady L'vovskogo Politekhnicheskogo Instituta

Dokl L'vov Politekh Inst Khim Khim Tekhnol — Doklady L'vovskogo Politekhnicheskogo Instituta Khimiya i Khimicheskaya Tekhnologiya

Dokl Mezhdunar Geokhim Kongr — Doklady. Mezhdunarodnyi Geokhimicheskii Kongress

Dokl Mezhdunar Geol Kongr — Doklady. Mezhdunarodnyi Geologicheskii Kongress

Dokl Mezhdunar Konf Limnol Izuch Dunaya — Doklady Mezhdunarodnoi Konferentsii po Limnologicheskomu Izucheniyu Dunaya

Dokl Mezhdunar Kongr Mekh Gruntov Fundamentostr — Doklady k Mezhdunarodnomu Kongressu po Mekhanike Gruntov i Fundamentostroeniyu

Dokl Mezhdunar Kongr Pochvovedov — Doklady k Mezhdunarodnomu Kongressu Pochvovedov

Dokl Mezhdunar Kongr Teor Prikl Khim — Doklady na Mezhdunarodnom Kongresse Teoreticheskoi i Prikladnoi Khimii

Dokl Mezhdunar Neft Kongr — Doklady na Mezhdunarodnom Neftyanom Kongresse

Dokl Mezhdunar Simp Teor Elektron Obolochek At Mol — Doklady Mezhdunarodnogo Simpoziuma po Teorii Elektronnykh Obolochek Atomov i Molekul

Dokl Mezhvuz Konf Fiz Mat Model — Doklady Mezhvuzovskoi Konferentsii po Fizicheskomu i Matematicheskomu Modelirovaniya

Dokl Mezhvuz Konf Khim Org Kompleksn Soedin — Doklady Mezhvuzovskoi Konferentsii po Khimii Organicheskikh Kompleksnykh Soedinenii

Dokl Minist Nauki Akad Nauk Resp Kaz — Doklady Ministerstva Nauki-Akademii Nauk Respubliki Kazakhstan

Dokl Mosk Inst Inzh Skh Proizvod — Doklady Moskovskogo Instituta Inzhenerov Sel'skokhozyaistvennogo Proizvodstva

Dokl Mosk Ord Lenina Selskokhoz Akad Im Timiryazeva — Doklady Moskovskaya Ordena Lenina Sel'skokhozyaistvennaya Akademiya Imeni K. A.Timiryazeva

Dokl Mosk Ova Ispyt Prir Obshch Biol — Doklady Moskovskogo Obshchestva Ispytatelei Prirody Obshchaya Biologiya

Dokl Mosk Sel'Khoz Akad K A Timiryazeva — Doklady Moskovskoi Sel'skokhozyaistvennoi Akademii Imeni K. A. Timiryazeva

Dokl Mosk Skh Akad — Doklady Moskovskaya Sel'skokhozyaistvennaya Akademiya Imeni K. A. Timiryazeva

Dokl Mosk S-Kh Akad Im K A Timiryazeva — Doklady Moskovskoi Sel'skokhozyaistvennoi Akademii Imeni K. A. Timiryazeva

DoklMU — Doklady i Soobscenija Filologoceskogo Fakul'teta Moskovskogo Universiteta

Dokl Nats Akad Nauk Belarusi — Doklady Natsional'noi Akademii Nauk Belarusi

Dokl Nats Akad Nauk Resp Kaz — Doklady Natsional'noi Akademii Nauk Respubliki Kazakhstan

Dokl Nats Konf At Spektrosk — Doklady. Natsional'naya Konferentsiya po Atomnoi Spektroskopii s Mezhdunarodnym Uchastiem

Dokl Nats Nauchno Tekh Konf Zavaryavane Stroit Montazha — Dokladi. Natsionalna Nauchno-Tekhnicheska Konferentsiya po Zavaryavane v Stroitelstvoto i Montazha

Dokl Nauchn Konf Leningr Inzh Stroit Inst — Doklady na Nauchnoi Konferentsii. Leningradskii Inzhenerno-Stroitel'nyi Institut

Dokl Nauchn Konf Novokuz Gos Pedagog Inst Biol Naukam — Doklady Nauchnoi Konferentsii Novokuznetskogo Gosudarstvennogo PedagogicheskogoInstituta po Biologicheskim Naukam

Dokl Nauchn Konf Rab Ashinskimi Fosforitami — Doklady na Nauchnoi Konferentsii. Posvyashchennoi Rabotam s Ashinskimi Fosforitami

Dokl Nauchn Konf Yarosl Gos Pedagog Inst — Doklady na Nauchnykh Konferentsiyakh Yaroslavskii Gosudarstvennyi Pedagogicheskii Institut

Dokl Nauchn Konf Yarosl Gosud Pedagog Inst — Doklady na Nauchnykh Konferentsiyakh Yaroslavskii Gosudarstvennyi Pedagogicheskii Institut

Dokl Nauchno Tekh Konf Tekh Prog Mashinostr — Doklady Nauchno-Tekhnicheskoi Konferentsii Tekhnicheskii Progress v Mashinostroenii

Dokl Nauchno Tekh Konf Tomsk Politekh Inst — Doklady Nauchno-Technicheskoi Konferentsii. Tomskii Politekhnicheskii Institut

Dokl Nauchn Sess Probl Zharoprochn Met Splavov — Doklady na Nauchnoi Sessii po Problemam Zharoprochnykh Metallov i Splavov

Dokl Nauchn Soobshch Lvov Politekh Inst — Doklady i Nauchnye Soobshcheniya. L'vovskii Politekhnicheskii Institut

Dokl Ostrav Gorno Metall Inst Ser Gorno Geol — Doklady Ostravskogo Gorno-Metallurgicheskogo Instituta. Seriya Gorno-Geologicheskaya

Dokl Ostrav Gorno Metall Inst Ser Mashinostroit — Doklady Ostravskogo Gorno-Metallurgicheskogo Instituta. Seriya Mashinostroitel'naya

Dokl Ostrav Gorno Metall Inst Ser Metall — Doklady Ostravskogo Gorno-Metallurgicheskogo Instituta. Seriya Metallurgicheskaya

Dokl Otd Kom Geogr O-Va SSSR — Doklady Otdelov i Komissii Geograficheskogo Obshchestva SSSR

Dokl Partsionalnoe Zased Mirovaya Energ Konf — Doklad. Partsional'noe Zasedanie. Mirovaya Energeticheskaya Konferentsiya

Dokl Phys Chem (Engl Transl) — Doklady Physical Chemistry (English Translation)

Dokl Plenarnogo Zased Konf Svarke Stroit — Doklady Plenarnogo Zasedaniya. Konferentsiya po Svarke v Stroitel'stve

Dokl Plenarnykh Zased Mezhdunar Kongr Miner Udobr — Doklady na Plenarnykh Zasedaniyakh. Mezhdunarodnyi Kongress po Mineral'nym Udobreniyam

Dokl Resp Nauchno Tekh Konf Neftekhim — Doklady Respublikanskoi Nauchno-Tekhnicheskoi Konferentsii po Neftekhimii

Dokl Ross Akad Nauk Ser A — Doklady Rossiiskoi Akademii Nauk. Seriya A. Doklady Fiziko-Matematicheskogo i Estestvenno-Istoricheskogo Kharaktera

Dokl Ross Akad Skh Nauk — Doklady Rossiiskoi Akademii Sel'skokhozyaistvennykh Nauk

Dokl Ross S-Kh Akad Im K A Timiryazeva — Doklady Rossiiskoi Sel'skokhozyaistvennoi Akademii Imeni K. A. Timiryazeva

Dokl Sess Probl Zharoprochn — Doklady na Sessii po Probleme Zharoprochnosti

Dokl Sezd Arm Fiziol Ova — Doklady. S'ezd Armyanskogo Fiziologicheskogo Obshchestva

Dokl Simp Mezhdunar Biofiz Kongr — Doklady Simpoziumov. Mezhdunarodnyi Biofizicheskii Kongress

Dokl Skh Akad Im Geogiya Dimitrova — Doklady Sel'skokhozyaistvennoj Akademii Imeni Geogiya Dimitrova

Dokl Skh Akad Sofia — Doklady Sel'skokhozyaistvennoi Akademii imeni Georgiya Dimitrova (Sofia)

Dokl Sochinskogo Otd Geogr Ova SSSR — Doklady Sochinskogo Otdela Geograficheskogo Obshchestva SSSR

Dokl Soil Sci (Engl Transl) — Doklady Soil Science (English Translation)

Dokl Soobshch Kormoproizvod — Doklady i Soobshcheniya po Kormoproizvodstvu

Dokl Soobshch Lvov Gos Univ — Doklady i Soobshcheniya L'vovskii Gosudarstvennyi Universitet

Dokl Soobshch Mezhdunar Konf Merzlotoved — Doklady i Soobshcheniya. Mezhdunarodnaya Konferentsiya po Merzlotovedeniyu

Dokl Soobshch Mezhdunar Kongr Vinograd Vinodel Sekts Vinodel — Doklady i Soobshcheniya. Mezhdunarodnyi Kongress po Vinogradarstvu i Vinodeliyu. Sektsiya Vinodelie

Dokl Soobshch Mezhdunar Kongr Zashch Rast — Doklady i Soobshcheniya. Mezhdunarodnyi Kongress po Zashchite Rastenii

Dokl Soobshch Uzhgorod Gos Univ Ser Biol — Doklady i Soobshcheniya Uzhgorodskogo Gosudarstvennogo Universiteta. Seriya Biologicheskaya

Dokl Soobshch Uzhgorod Gos Univ Ser Fiz Mat Khim — Doklady i Soobshcheniya Uzhgorodskogo Gosudarstvennogo Universiteta. Seriya Fiziko. Matematicheskaya i Khimicheskaya

Dokl Soobshch Uzhgorod Gos Univ Ser Fiz Mat Nauk — Doklady i Soobshcheniya Uzhgorodskogo Gosudarstvennogo Universiteta. Seriya Fiziko. Matematicheskikh Nauk

Dokl Soobshch Vses Lateksnoi Konf — Doklady i Soobshcheniya Vsesoyuznoi Lateksnoi Konferentsii

Dokl Soobshch Vses Nauch Issled Inst Ekon Selskokhoz — Doklady i Soobshcheniya. Vsesoyuznyi Nauchno-Issledovatel'skii Institut Ekonomiki Sel'skogo Khozyaistva

Dokl Sooshch Uzhgorod Gos Univ Ser Khim — Doklady i Soobshcheniya Uzhgorodskogo Gosudarstvennogo Universiteta. Seriya Khimicheskaya

Dokl Soveshch Biol Prod Vodoemov Sib — Doklady Soveshchaniya po Biologicheskoi Produktivnosti Vodoemov Sibiri

Dokl Soveshch Fiz Metodam Izuch Miner Osad Porod — Doklady Soveshchaniya po Fizicheskim Metodam Izucheniya Mineralov Osadochnykh Porod

Dokl Soveshch Teor Prikl Magn Gidrodin — Doklady. Prochitannye na Soveshchanii po Teoreticheskoi i Prikladnoi Magnitnoi Gidrodinamike

Dokl Sov Geol Mezhdunar Geol Kongr — Doklady Sovetskikh Geologov Mezhdunarodnyi Geologicheskii Kongress

Dokl Sov Geol Sess Mezhdunar Geol Kongr — Doklady Sovetskikh Geologov na Sessii Mezhdunarodnogo Geologicheskogo Kongressa

Dokl Sov Geol Sess Mezhdunar Geol Kongr Geokhim Mineral Petrol — Doklady Sovetskikh Geologov na Sessii Mezhdunarodnogo Geologicheskogo Kongressa. Geokhimlya, Mineralogiya, Potrologiya

Dokl Sov Geol Sess Mezhdunar Geol Kongr Geol Inf Mat Geol — Doklady Sovetskikh Geologov na Sessii Mezhdunarodnogo Geologicheskogo Kongressa. Geologicheskaya Informatsiya i Matematicheskaya Geologiya

Dokl Sov Geol Sess Mezhdunar Geol Kongr Goryuch Iskop — Doklady Sovetskikh Geologov na Sessii Mezhdunarodnogo Geologicheskogo Kongressa. Goryuchie Iskopaemye

Dokl Sov Geol Sess Mezhdunar Geol Kongr Paleontol Morsk Geol — Doklady Sovetskikh Geologov na Sessii Mezhdunarodnogo Geologicheskogo Kongressa. Paleontologiya, Morskaya Geologiya

Dokl Sov Geol Sess Mezhdunar Geol Kongr Probl 1 — Doklady Sovetskikh Geologov na Sessii Mezhdunarodnogo Geologicheskogo Kongressa. Problema 1

Dokl Sov Geol Sess Mezhdunar Geol Kongr Probl 2 — Doklady Sovetskikh Geologov na Sessii Mezhdunarodnogo Geologicheskogo Kongressa. Problema 2

Dokl Sov Geol Sess Mezhdunar Geol Kongr Probl 3 — Doklady Sovetskikh Geologov na Sessii Mezhdunarodnogo Geologicheskogo Kongressa. Problema 3

Dokl Sov Geol Sess Mezhdunar Geol Kongr Probl 4 — Doklady Sovetskikh Geologov na Sessii Mezhdunarodnogo Geologicheskogo Kongressa. Problema 4

Dokl Sov Geol Sess Mezhdunar Geol Kongr Probl 5 — Doklady Sovetskikh Geologov na Sessii Mezhdunarodnogo Geologicheskogo Kongressa. Problema 5

Dokl Sov Geol Sess Mezhdunar Geol Kongr Probl 7 — Doklady Sovetskikh Geologov na Sessii Mezhdunarodnogo Geologicheskogo Kongressa. Problema 7

Dokl Sov Geol Sess Mezhdunar Geol Kongr Probl 8 — Doklady Sovetskikh Geologov na Sessii Mezhdunarodnogo Geologicheskogo Kongressa. Problema 8

Dokl Sov Geol Sess Mezhdunar Geol Kongr Probl 10 — Doklady Sovetskikh Geologov na Sessii Mezhdunarodnogo Geologicheskogo Kongressa. Problema 10

Dokl Sov Geol Sess Mezhdunar Geol Kongr Probl 11 — Doklady Sovetskikh Geologov na Sessii Mezhdunarodnogo Geologicheskogo Kongressa. Problema 11

Dokl Sov Geol Sess Mezhdunar Geol Kongr Probl 12 — Doklady Sovetskikh Geologov na Sessii Mezhdunarodnogo Geologicheskogo Kongressa. Problema 12

Dokl Sov Geol Sess Mezhdunar Geol Kongr Probl 13b — Doklady Sovetskikh Geologov na Sessii Mezhdunarodnogo Geologicheskogo Kongressa. Problema 13b

Dokl Sov Geol Sess Mezhdunar Geol Kongr Probl 14 — Doklady Sovetskikh Geologov na Sessii Mezhdunarodnogo Geologicheskogo Kongressa. Problema 14

Dokl Sov Geol Sess Mezhdunar Geol Kongr Simp 1 — Doklady Sovetskikh Geologov na Sessii Mezhdunarodnogo Geologicheskogo Kongressa. Simpozium 1

Dokl Sov Pochvovedov Mezhdunar Kongr SShA — Doklady Sovetskikh Pochvovedov k Mezhdunarodnomu Kongressu v SShA

Dokl Sov Uchastnikov Kongr Mezhdunar Kongr Miner Udobr — Doklady Sovetskikh Uchastnikov Kongressa. Mezhdunarodnyi Kongress po Mineral'nym Udobreniyam

Dokl Tbilis Nauchn O-Va Anat Gistol Embriol — Doklady Tbilisskogo Nauchnogo Obshchestva Anatomii, Gistologii, i Embriologii

Dokl Timiryazevsk S-Kh Akad — Doklady Timiryazevskaya Sel'skokhozyaistvennaya Akademiya

Dokl TSKHA — Doklady Timiryazevskaya Sel'skokhozyaistvennaya Akademiya

Dokl TSKhA Timiriazevsk S-Kh Akad — Doklady TSKhA. Timiriazevskaia Sel'skokhoziaistvennaia Akademiia

Dokl Vses Akad Sel'khoz Nauk — Doklady Vsesoyuznoi Akademii Sel'skokhozyaistvennykh Nauk Imeni V. I. Lenina

Dokl Vses Akad Selskokhoz Nauk V I Lenina — Doklady Vsesoyuznoi Akademii Sel'skokhozyaistvennykh Nauk Imeni V. I. Lenina

Dokl Vses Akad Skh Nauk — Doklady Vsesoyuznoi Akademii Sel'skokhozyaistvennykh Nauk

Dokl Vses Akad S-Kh Nauk Im V I Lenina — Doklady Vsesoyuznoi Akademii Sel'skokhozyaistvennykh Nauk Imeni V. I. Lenina

Dokl Vses Akust Konf — Doklady. Vsesoyuznaya Akusticheskaya Konferentsiya

Dokl Vses Geol Ugoln Soveshch — Doklady Vsesoyuznogo Geologicheskogo Ugol'nogo Soveshchaniya

Dokl Vses Konf "Fiz Khrupkogo Razrusheniya" — Doklady Vsesoyuznoi Konferentsii "Fizika Khrupkogo Razrusheniya"

Dokl Vses Konf Fotosint — Doklady na Vsesoyuznoi Konferentsii po Fotosintezu

Dokl Vses Konf Khim Atsetilena — Doklady Vsesoyuznoi Konferentsii po Khimii Atsetilena

Dokl Vses Konf Liteishchikov — Doklady Vsesoyuznoi Konferentsii Liteishchikov

Dokl Vses Konf Molochn Delu — Doklady Vsesoyuznoi Konferentsii po Molochnomu Delu

Dokl Vses Konf Neirokhim — Doklady na Vsesoyuznoi Konferentsii po Neirokhimii

Dokl Vses Konf Teplofiz Svoistvam Veshchestv — Doklady Vsesoyuznoi Konferentsii po Teplofizicheskim Svoistvam Veshchestv

Dokl Vses Mezhvuz Konf Khim Org Kompleksn Soedin — Doklady Vsesoyuznoi Mezhvuzovskoi Konferentsii po Khimii Organicheskikh Kompleksnykh Soedinenii

Dokl Vses Nauchn Tekh Konf Vozobnovlyaemym Istochnikam Energ — Doklady Vsesoyuznoi Nauchno-Tekhnicheskoi Konferentsii po Vozobnovlyaemym Istochnikam Energii

Dokl Vses Obedin Sess Zakonomern Razmeshcheniya Polezn Iskop — Doklady Vsesoyuznoi Ob'edinennoi Sessii po Zakonomernostyam Razmeshcheniya Poleznykh Iskopaemykh i Prognoznym Kartam

Dokl Vsesojuzn Ordena Lenina Akad Selskohoz Nauk Lenina — Doklady Vsesojuznoj Ordena Lenina Akademii Sel'skohozjajstvennyh Nauk Imeni V. I. Lenina

Dokl Vses Ordena Lenina Akad S-Kh Nauk Im V I Lenina — Doklady Vsesoyuznoi Ordena Lenina Akademii Sel'skokhozyaistvennykh Nauk Imeni V. I. Lenina

Dokl Vses Semin Org Veshchestvu Sovrem Iskop Osadkov — Doklady Vsesoyuznogo Seminara po Organicheskomu Veshchestvu Sovremennykh I Iskopaemykh Osadkov

Dokl Vses Semin Prikl Elektrokhim — Doklady Vsesoyuznogo Seminara po Prikladnoi Elektrokhimii

Dokl Vses Simp Impulsnym Davleniyam — Doklady Vsesoyuznogo Simpoziuma po Impul'snym Davleniyam

Dokl Vses Simp Vychisl Metodam Teor Perenosa Izluch — Doklady Vsesoyuznogo Simpoziuma po Vychislitel'nym Metodam v Teorii Perenosa Izlucheniya

Dokl Vses Soveshch Khim Kinet Reakts Sposobn — Doklady k Vsesoyuznomu Soveshchaniyu po Khimicheskoi Kinetike i Reaktsionnoi Sposobnosti

Dokl Vses Soveshch Mikroelem — Doklady Vsesoyuznogo Soveshchaniya po Mikroelementam

Dokl Vses Soveshch Plan Eksp — Doklady. Vsesoyuznoe Soveshchanie po Planirovaniyu Eksperimenta

Dokl Vses Soveshch Teplo Massoperenosu — Doklady Vsesoyuznogo Soveshchaniya po Teplo- i Massoperenosu

Dokl Vtoroi Mezhvuz Konf Khim Org Kompleksn Soedin — Doklady Vtoroi Mezhvuzovskoi Konferentsii po Khimii Organicheskikh KompleksnykhSoedinenii

Dokl Vyezdnoi Sess Otd Nauk Zemle Akad Nauk SSSR — Doklady na Vyezdnoi Sessii Otdeleniya Nauk o Zemle Akademii Nauk SSSR

Dokl Yubileinata Nauchna Ses Vissh Mash Elektrotekh Inst — Dokladi na Yubileinata Nauchna Sesiya po Sluchai 25 Godishninata na Instituta. Vissh Mashino-Elektrotekhnicheski Institut

Dokl Yubileinogo Mendeleevsk Sezda — Doklady Yubileinogo Mendeleevskogo S'ezda

Dokl Zarub Uchastnikov Mezhdunar Kongr Miner Udobr — Doklady Zarubezhnykh Uchastnikov. Mezhdunarodnyi Kongress po Mineral'nym Udobreniyam

Dokl Zased Issled Kom Mezhdunar Fed Dok Teor Osn Nauchn Inf — Doklady Zasedaniya Issledovatel'skogo Komiteta Mezhdunarodnoi Federatsii po Dokumentatsii Teoreticheskie Osnovy Nauchnoi Informatsii

Dok Raum — Dokumentation zur Raumentwicklung

Dok Raumentwickl — Dokumentation zur Raumentwicklung

Dok Schriftenr Wiss Prax Abwassertech Ver — Dokumentation und Schriftenreihe aus Wissenschaft und Praxis (Abwassertechnische Vereinigung)

Dok Str — Dokumentation Strasse

Doktorsavh Chalmers Tek Hoegsk — Doktorsavhandlingar vid Chalmers Tekniska Hoegskola

Dokum As Mitt — Dokumentationsdienst Asien Mitteilungen

Dokumentat d Zeit — Dokumentation der Zeit

Dokumente Gesch Math — Dokumente zur Geschichte der Mathematik

Dokum Ostmitteleur (NF) — Dokumentation Ostmitteleuropa (Neue Folge)

Dokum Raumentwicklung — Dokumentation zur Raumentwicklung

Dok Vortr Technicon Symp — Dokumentationen der Vortraege des Technicon Symposium

DOKWA — Dokumentation Wasser

Dok Wasser — Dokumentation Wasser

Dok Wissenschaftsgesch — Dokumente der Wissenschaftsgeschichte

Dok Zemed Lesn — Dokumentace Zemedelska a Lesnicka

Dok Zemed Lesn Zahr Lit — Dokumentace Zemedelska a Lesnicka. Zahranicni Literatura

Dol — Dolphin

Dolands Med Dir — Doland's Medical Directory. New York Metropolitan Area Edition

Dolciani Math Exp — [The] Dolciani Mathematical Expositions

Dolg Erd Nem Muz Erem Reg — Dolgozatok az Erdelyi Nemzeti Muzeum Erem-Es Regisegtarabol

Doll & Sen — Dollars and Sense

Dollars — Dollars and Sense

Dolmetsch B — Bulletin. Dolmetsch Foundation

Dom — Dominicana

DOMA — Dokumentation Maschinenbau

DOMC — Dictionary of Organometallic Compounds

Dom Comm — Domestic Commerce

Dom Eng — Domestic Engineering

Dom Engr — Dominion Engineer

Domennoe Proizvod — Domennoe Proizvodstvo

Domeny Cylindryczne Szk Zimowa Nowe Mater Magn — Domeny Cylindryczne. Szkola Zimowa Nowe Materialy Magnetyczne

Domest Anim Endocrinol — Domestic Animal Endocrinology

Domest Eng Heat Vent — Domestic Engineering. Heat and Ventilation

Domest Heat News — Domestic Heating News

Domestic Heat Air Cond News — Domestic Heating and Air Conditioning News

Dom Foundrym — Dominion Foundryman

DOMH — Demotic Ostraca from Medinet Habu

Dominion Observatory (Ottawa) Contr — Dominion Observatory (Ottawa). Contributions

Dominion Observatory Seismol Ser — Dominion Observatory. Seismological Series
Dominion Tax Cas CCH — Dominion Tax Cases. Commerce Clearing House
Dom LR — Dominion Law Reports
Dom Med — Domus Medici
Dom Med J — Dominion Medical Journal
Dom Mus Bull — Dominion Museum Bulletin
Dom Mus Monogr — Dominion Museum Monographs
Dom Mus Rec Entomol (Wellington) — Dominion Museum Records in Entomology (Wellington)
Dom Mus Rec Ethnol — Dominion Museum Records in Ethnology
Dom Mus Rec Zool (Wellington) — Dominion Museum Records in Zoology (Wellington)
Dom Obs Pamph — Dominion Observatory Pamphlet
Dom St — Dominican Studies
Domus Med — Domus Medici
Donauraum — Zeitschrift fuer Donauraum-Forschung
Donders Arch — Archiv fuer die Hollaendischen Beitraege zur Natur- und Heilkunde. Donders
Donders Ndl Gast Oogl Vs — Jaarlijksch Verslag Betrekkelijk de Verpleging en 't Onderwijs in het Nederlandsch Gasthuis voor Ooglijders. Donders
Donegal Ann — Donegal Annual
Donegal Hist Soc J — County Donegal Historical Society. Journal
Donetsk Nauchno Issled Inst Chern Metall Sb Tr — Donetskii Nauchno-Issledovatel'skii Institut Chernoi Metallurgii. Sbornik Trudov
Dong-A Ronchong Dong-A Univ — Dong-A Ronchong. Dong-A University
Dongguk J — Dongguk Journal
Donld — Donauland
Donnees Sediments Rivieres Can — Donnees sur les Sediments. Rivieres Canadiennes
Donnees Statist Limousin — Donnees Statistiques du Limousin
DOOPA — Documenta Ophthalmologica
Doopsgezinde Bijdr — Doopsgezinde Bijdragen
Doors Lat Am Gainesville — Doors to Latin America (Gainesville, Florida)
DOP — Dumbarton Oaks Papers
Dop Akad Nauk Ukr RSR — Dopovidi Akademii Nauk Ukrains'koi RSR
Dop Akad Nauk Ukr RSR Ser Fiz-Tekh Mat — Dopovidi Akademii Nauk Ukrains'koi RSR. Seriya A. Fiziko-Tekhnichni ta Matematichni Nauki
DOPapers — Dumbarton Oaks Papers
DOPGAM — Deutsche Ophthalmologische Gesellschaft. Bericht
DOPHDS — Documents Phytosociologiques
DOPOA — Dornier-Post
Dopov Akad Nauk Ukr — Dopovidi Akademii Nauk Ukraini
Dopov Akad Nauk Ukrajinsk RSR — Dopovidi Akademiji Nauk Ukrajins'koji RSR/Reports. Academy of Sciences. Ukrainian SSR/Doklady Akademii Nauk Ukrainskoj SSR
Dopov Akad Nauk Ukr RSR — Dopovidi Akademii Nauk Ukrains'koi RSR
Dopov Akad Nauk Ukr RSR B — Dopovidi Akademii Nauk Ukrains'koi RSR. Seriya B. Geologiya, Geofizika, Khimiya, ta Biologiya
Dopov Akad Nauk Ukr RSR Ser A Fiz — Dopovidi Akademii Nauk Ukrainskoj RSR. Seriya A. Fiziko-Tekhnichni i Matematichni Nauki
Dopov Akad Nauk Ukr RSR Ser A Fiz Mat Tekh Nauki — Dopovidi Akademii Nauk Ukrains'koi RSR. Seriya A. Fiziko-Matematichni ta Tekhnichni Nauki
Dopov Akad Nauk Ukr RSR Ser A Fiz Tekh Mat Nauki — Dopovidi Akademii Nauk Ukrains'koi RSR. Seriya A. Fiziko-Tekhnichni ta Matematichni Nauki
Dopov Akad Nauk Ukr RSR Ser B Geol — Dopovidi Akademii Nauk Ukrainskoj RSR. Seriya B. Geologiya, Geofizika, Khimiya, ta Biologiya
Dopov Akad Nauk Ukr RSR Ser B Geol Geofiz Khim Biol — Dopovidi Akademii Nauk Ukrains'koi RSR. Seriya B. Geologiya, Geofizika, Khimiya, ta Biologiya
Dopov Akad Nauk Ukr RSR Ser B Geol Khim Biol Nauki — Dopovidi Akademii Nauk Ukrains'koi RSR. Seriya B. Geologichni, Khimichni, ta Biologichni Nauki
Dopov Akad Nauk Ukr RSR Ser B Heol Heofiz Khim Biol — Dopovidi Akademiyi Nauk Ukrayins'koyi RSR. Seriya B. Heolohiya, Heofizyka, Khimiya, ta Biolohiya
Dopov Akad Nauk Ukr RSR Ser B Heol Khim Biol Nauky — Dopovidi Akademiyi Nauk Ukrayins'koyi RSR. Seriya B. Heolohichni, Khimichni, taBiolohichni Nauky
Dopov Akad Nauk Uk RSR Ser A — Dopovidi Akademii Nauk Ukrains'koi RSR. Seriya A. Fiziko-Tekhnichni ta Matematichni Nauki
Dopovidi Akad Nauk Ukrain RSR Ser A — Dopovidi Akademii Nauk Ukrains'koi RSR. Seriya A. Fiziko-Tekhnichni ta Matematichni Nauki
Dopovidi Akad Nauk Ukrain RSR Ser B — Dopovidi Akademii Nauk Ukrains'koi RSR. Seriya B. Geologiya, Geofizika, Khimiya, ta Biologiya
Dopov Lviv Derzh Pedagog Inst — Dopovidi. L'vivs'kii Derzhavnii Pedagogichnii Institut
Dopov Nats Akad Nauk Ukr — Dopovidi Natsional'noi Akademii Nauk Ukraini
Dopov Povidomlenniya L'viv Derzh Univ — Dopovidi ta Povidomlenniya L'vivs'koho Derzhavnoho Universytetu
Dopov Povidomlennya L'viv Derzh Pedagog Inst Sekts Biol Khim — Dopovidi ta Povidomlennya L'vivs'kii Derzhvnii Institut. Sektsiya Biologii Khi mii
Dopov Povidom Lvivsk Derzh Univ — Dopovidi ta Povidomlenniya L'vivs'koho Derzhavnoho Universytetu
Dopov Ukr Akad Sil's'kogospod Nauk — Dopovidi Ukrains'koi Akademii Sil's'kogospodars'kikh Nauk
Dop Ukr A — Dopovidi Akademii Nauk Ukrains'koi RSR. Seriya A. Tekhnichni Matematichni Nauki
Dop Ukr B — Dopovidi Akademii Nauk Ukrains'koi RSR. Seriya B. Geologiya, Geofizika, Khimiya, ta Biologiya
DOPW — Dumbarton Oaks Papers (Washington, D.C.)
DoR — Downside Review
DOR — Reproduktie
Dordrechts Mus Bull — Dordrechts Museum Bulletin
DORIS — Demographic Online Retrieval Information System
D Orn FT — Dansk Ornithologisk Forenings Tidsskrift
Dorogi Mosty Dokl Nauchn Konf Leningr Inzh Stroit Inst — Dorogi i Mosty. Doklady Nauchnoi Konferentsii Leningradskii Inzhenerno-Stroitel'nyi Institut
Dorpat Sb — Sitzungsberichte der Naturforscher-Gesellschaft zu Dorpat

Dorpat Schr — Schriften Herausgegeben von der Naturforscher-Gesellschaft bei der Universitaet Dorpat
Dorset FC P — Proceedings of the Dorset Natural History and Antiquarian Field Club
Dortm Beitr Wasserforsch — Dortmunder Beitraege zur Wasserforschung
Dortmund Mag — Dortmundisches Magazin
DOS — Dictionary of Steroids
DOS — Dumbarton Oaks Studies
Doshisha Eng Rev — Doshisha Engineering Review
Doshisha L — Doshisha Literature
Doshisha LJ — Doshisha Law Journal. International Edition
Doshisha Womens Coll Lib Arts Annu Rep Stud — Doshisha Women's College of Liberal Arts. Annual Reports of Studies
Dosieren Kunststofftech — Dosieren in der Kunststofftechnik
Dosim Eff Biol Campi Elettromagn Radiofreq — Dosimetria ed Effetti Biologici dei Campi Elettromagnetici a Radiofrequenza
Dosl Tvarinnitstvi — Doslidzhennya v Tvarinnitstvi
Dosl Zootekh L'vivskoho Zootekh Vet Inst — Doslidzhennya Zootekhniki L'vivskoho Zootekhnicheskoho Veterinars'koho Instituta
Doss Acenonetes Coll Pataphys — Dossiers Acenonetes du College de Pataphysique
Doss Alet — Dossiers. Centre Regional Archeologique d'Alet
Doss A (Paris) — Dossiers de l'Archeologie (Paris)
Doss Arch — Histoire et Archeologie. Dossiers
Doss Archeol — Dossiers de l'Archeologie
Doss Archeologie — Histoire et Archeologie. Dossiers
Doss Bis Jeune Afr Econ — Dossiers Bis Jeune Afrique et Economia
Doss Econ Lorraine — Dossiers de l'Economie Lorraine
Doss Hist & Archeol — Dossiers d'Histoire et Archeologie
Dossiers Archeol — Dossiers Archeologiques
Dossiers Sci Inst Fr Nutr — Dossiers Scientifiques de l'Institut Francais pour la Nutrition
Dossier Tech Assoc Natl Prot Incendie — Dossier Technique. Association Nationale pour la Protection contre l'Incendie
Doss Mundo — Dossier Mundo
Doss Mus Orsay — Dossiers du Musee d'Orsay
Doss Polit Agric Commune — Dossiers de la Politique Agricole Commune
DOST — Dictionary of the Older Scottish Tongue
Dostizh Biol Nauki — Dostizheniya Biologicheskoi Nauki
Dostizh Biol Skh Proizvod Mater Nauchn Konf — Dostizheniya Biologii v Sel'skokhozyaistvennoe Proizvodstvo. Materialy NauchnoiKonferentsii
Dostizh Efirnomaslichn Proizvod NR Bolg Mold SSR — Dostizheniya v Efirnomaslichnom Proizvodstve NR (Narodnaya Respublika) Bolgariii Moldavskoi SSR
Dostizh Eterichnomaslenoto Proizvod NR Bulg Mold SSR — Dostizheniya v Eterichnomaslenoto Proizvodstva na NR Bulgariya i Moldavska SSR
Dostizh Metall SSSR Zagr — Dostizheniya Metallurgii v SSSR i Zagranitsei
Dostizh Nauki Peredovogo Opyta Selsk Khoz — Dostizheniya Nauki i Peredovogo Opyta v Sel'skom Khozyaistve
Dostizh Nauki Peredovoi Opyt Sveklovod — Dostizheniya Nauki i Peredovoi Opyt po Sveklovodstvu
Dostizh Nauki Proizvod — Dostizheniya Nauki v Proizvodstvo
Dostizh Nauki Tekh Peredovoi Opyt Promsti Stroit — Dostizheniya Nauki i Tekhniki i Peredovoi Opyt v Promyshlennosti i Stroitel'stve
Dostizh Nauki Zhivotnovod — Dostizheniya Nauki v Zhivotnovodstve
Dostizh Nefrol — Dostizheniya Nefrologii
Dostizh Obl Sozdaniya Primen Kleev Promsti Mater Semin — Dostizheniya v Oblasti Sozdaniya i Primeneniya Kleev v Promyshlennosti. Materialy Seminara
Dostizh Razvit Nov Metodov Khim Anal — Dostizheniya v Razvitii Novykh Metodov Khimicheskogo Analiza
Dostizh Sov Mikrobiol — Dostizheniya Sovetskoi Mikrobiologii
Dostizh Sovrem Farmakol — Dostizheniya Sovremennoi Farmakologii
Dostizh Sovrem Kardiol — Dostizheniya Sovremennoi Kardiologii
Dostizh Sovrem Neirofarmakol — Dostizheniya Sovremennoi Neirofarmakologii
Dostizh Spektrosk Sezd Spektrosk — Dostizheniya Spektroskopii. S'ezd po Spektroskopii
Dostizh Vet Gelmintol Prakt — Dostizheniya Veterinarnoi Gel'mintologii v Praktiku
Dostizh Vet Nauki Peredovogo Opyta Zhivotnovod — Dostizheniya Veterinarnoi Nauki i Peredovogo Opyta. Zhivotnovodstvu
DOT — Dumbarton Oaks Texts
DOTS — Direction of Trade Statistics
Dottore Sci Agrar For — Il Dottore in Scienze Agrarie Forestali
Douai Mm S Ag — Memoires de la Societe d'Agriculture, de Sciences, et de Arts du Departement du Nord Seant a Douai
DouB — Double Bouquet. Prose et Vers
Double Liaison Chim Peint — Double Liaison. Chimie des Peintures
Double Liaison Phys Chim Peint Adhes — Double Liaison. Physique and Chimie des Peintures et Adhesifs
Double Liason Phys Chim Econ Peint Adhes — Double Liaison Physique, Chimie et Economie des Peintures et Adhesifs
Doubs S Mm — Memoires et Comptes Rendus de la Societe Libre d'Emulation du Doubs
DOVEB — Documenta Veterinaria (Brno)
Dover Books Adv Math — Dover Books on Advanced Mathematics
DOW — Deutsche Optische Wochenschrift
DOWM — Database of Offsite Waste Management
Down Bt — Down Beat
Down Con Hist Soc J — Down and Connor Historical Society. Journal
Down Earth — Down to Earth
DownR — Downside Review
Downside Rev — Downside Review
Downs Syndr Res Pract — Downs Syndrome Research and Practice
DowR — Downside Review
Dox Gr — Doxographi Graeci
Dox Graec — Doxographi Graeci

DOZ Dtsch Optikerztg — DOZ. Deutsche Optikerzeitung
Dozim Ioniz Izluch — Dozimetriya Ioniziruyushchikh Izluchenii
Dozim Radiats Protsessy Dozim Sist — Dozimetriya i Radiatsionnye Protsessy v Dozimetricheskikh Sistemakh
DP — Dance Perspectives
DP — Dawson Packet
DP — Delegation en Perse. Memoires
DP — Deutsche Philologie
DP — Developmental Psychology
DP — Developments in Petrology
DP — Die Presse
DP — Discourse Processes
DP — Maandblad de Pacht
DPAA — Dissertazioni. Pontificia Accademia Roman di Archeologia
D Paed T — Dansk Paedagogisk Tidsskrift
DPALD — DOE [*US Department of Energy*] Patents Available for Licensing
DPANZ — Decorator and Painter for Australia and New Zealand
DPAS — Developments in Palaeontology and Stratigraphy
DPB — Developments in Plant Biology
DPC — Dredging and Port Construction
DPCPDS — Divulgacion Pesquera
DPDroh — Dopovidi ta Povidomlennja. Materialy Konferencij Drohobyc'koho Derzavnoho Pedahohicnoho Instytutu Imeni I. Ja. Franka. Serija Filolohicnych Nauk. Drohobyc
DPfBl — Deutsches Pfarrerblatt
DPG — Developments in Precambrian Geology
DPGB — Digest of Public General Bills
DPHA — Descripcion del Patrimonio Historico-Artistico Espanol
DphBl — Deutsches Philologen-Blatt
DPHFA — Dissertationes Pharmaceuticae et Pharmacologicae
DPHSDS — Drugs and the Pharmaceutical Sciences
DPIF — Drug Products Information File
DPL — De Proprietatibus Litterarum
DPLR — De Paul Law Review
DPMAA — Data Processing Magazine
DPO — Directory of Periodicals Online
DPOA — Epigraphie. Documents du Proche-Orient Ancien
DPPNGL — Data Papers in Papua New Guinea Languages
DPPSA — Directory of Published Proceedings
DPR — Dialogos Revista. Departamento de Filosofia. Universidad de Puerto Rico
DPr — Discourse Processes
DPR — Economic Progress Report
DPRAC — Delft Progress Report. Series A. Chemistry and Physics, Chemical and Physical Engineering
DPRBA — Delft Progress Report. Series B. Electrical, Electronic, and Information Engineering
DPRCB — Delft Progress Report. Series C. Mechanical and Aeronautical Engineering and Shipbuilding
DPRED — Delft Progress Report
DPRPB — Delft Progress Report. Series A-F
DPS — Developments in Petroleum Science
D Ps Bs Vh — Verhandlungen der Deutschen Physikalischen Gesellschaft
DPST — Denver Post
DPTHDL — Developmental Pharmacology and Therapeutics
DPW Dtsch Papierwirtsch — DPW. Deutsche Papierwirtschaft
DQ — Denver Quarterly
DQ — Design Quarterly
DQR — Dutch Quarterly Review of Anglo-American Letters
DR — Dalhousie Review
DR — Deutsche Revue
DR — Deutsche Rundschau
DR — Diliman Review
DR — Double Reed
DR — Downside Review
DR — Drake Law Review
DR — Drama: The Quarterly Theatre Review
Dr — Dreikland
DR — Drum. Inuvik
DR — Drumworld
DR — Dublin Review
DR — Dun's Review
DR — Duquesne Review
DRA — Derechos y Reforma Agraria
D Rad I — Dansk Radio Industri
DRAE — Diccionario de la Real Academia Espanola
DRAEA — Draegerheft
Draegerh — Draegerheft. Mitteilungen der Draegerwerk AG
Draeger Rev — Draeger Review
Dr Aerien — Droit Aerien
Drag — Dragonfly
Dragoco Ber Engl Edn — Dragoco Berichte. English Edition
Dragoco Rep Engl Ed — Dragoco Report. English Edition
Dragoco Rep Engl Flavor Ed — Dragoco Report (English Flavoring Edition)
Dragoco Rep Flavor Inf Serv — Dragoco Report. Flavoring Information Service
Dragoco Rep Ger Ed — Dragoco Report. German Edition
Dragotsennye Tsvetn Kamni Polezn Iskop — Dragotsennye i Tsvetnye Kamni kak Poleznoe Iskopaemoe
Drag Reduct Pap Int Conf — Drag Reduction. Papers presented at the International Conference
Drag Reduct Polym Solutions Pap Symp — Drag Reduction in Polymer Solutions. Papers. Symposium
Drake Law R — Drake Law Review
Drake LR — Drake Law Review
Drake L Rev — Drake Law Review
Dram — Drammaturgia

Drama R — Drama Review
Drama Rev — Drama Review
Drama Surv — Drama Survey
DramC — Drama Critique
DramR — Drama Review
DramS — Drama Survey
Draper — Draper of Australasia
Draper Fund Rep — Draper Fund Report
Draper Fund Rept — Draper Fund Report
Draper World Population Fund Rept — Draper World Population Fund Report
DRB — Director. Journal of Business Leadership
DRB — Downside Review (Bath)
DRBIA — Drill Bit
DRCAC — Doxa. Rassegna Critica di Antichita Classica
DR Charl — Documents et Rapports. Societe Paleontologique et Archeologique de l'Arrondissement Judiciaire de Charleroi
DRCPE9 — Diabetes Research and Clinical Practice
DRCWDT — Colorado. Division of Wildlife. Division Report
DRD — Deltawerken. Driemaandelijks Bericht
DRDCD — Drilling - DCW
Dr Dobb's J — Dr. Dobb's Journal
Dr Dobb's J Comput Calisthenics and Orthod — Dr. Dobb's Journal of Computer Calisthenics and Orthodontia [*Later, Dr. Dobb's Journal of Software Tools*]
Dr Dobbs J Software Tools Prof Program — Dr. Dobb's Journal of Software Tools for Professional Programmer
Dredged Mater Res — Dredged Material Research
Dredging & Port Constr — Dredging and Port Construction
Dreijahrestagung Eur Ges Kartoffelforsch — Dreijahrestagung der Europaeischen Gesellschaft fuer Kartoffelforschung
DreiN — Dreiser Newsletter
DREOR — Defence Research Board of Canada. Defence Research Establishment Ottawa. Reports
DREPR — Defence Research Board of Canada. Defence Research Establishment Pacific. Reports
Dresden Ausz Protokol — Auszuege aus den Protokollen der Gesellschaft fuer Natur- und Heilkunde in Dresden
Dresden Erdk Jbr — Jahresbericht des Vereins fuer Erdkunde zu Dresden
Dresden Isis Festschr — Festschrift der Naturwissenschaftlichen Gesellschaft Isis in Dresden
Dresden Isis Sb — Sitzungsberichte der Naturwissenschaftlichen Gesellschaft Isis in Dresden
Dresden Jbr Nt Heilk — Jahresberichte Sitzungsberichte der Gesellschaft fuer Natur- und Heilkunde (Dresden)
Dresden Lndw V St — Landwirthschaftlichen Versuchs-Stationen. Organ fuer Wissenschaftliche Forschungen auf dem Gebiete der Landwirthschaft (Dresden, Chemnitz)
Dresden Sb Isis — Sitzungsberichte der Naturwissenschaftlichen Gesellschaft Isis in Dresden
Dresden Sb Nt Heilk — Jahresberichte Sitzungsberichte der Gesellschaft fuer Natur- und Heilkunde (Dresden)
Dresdn Anz — Dresdner Anzeiger
Dresdner Journ — Dresdner Journal
Dresdner Kunstbl — Dresdner Kunstblaetter. Monatsschrift. Staatliche Kunstsammlungen Dresden
Dresdner Reihe Forsch — Dresdner Reihe zur Forschung
Dresdn Geschbl — Dresdner Geschichtsblaetter
Dresdn Hft 10 — Dresdner Hefte 10
Dresdnisches Mag — Dresdnisches Magazin, Oder Ausarbeitungen und Nachrichten zum Behuf der Naturlehre, der Arzneykunst, der Sitten, und der Schoenen Wissenschaften
Dresdn Kstb — Dresdner Kunstbuch
Dresdn Kstbl — Dresdner Kunstblaetter
Dresdn Nachr — Dresdner Nachrichten
DRETN — Defence Research Board of Canada. Defence Research Establishment Ottawa. Technical Note
DRev — Deutsche Revue
Drev Vysk — Drevarsky Vyskum
Drev Vyskum — Drevarsky Vyskum
Drexel Lib Q — Drexel Library Quarterly
Drexel Libr Q — Drexel Library Quarterly
Drexel Tech J — Drexel Technical Journal
Drex Lib Q — Drexel Library Quarterly
DRF — Doctorate Records File
Dr Fisc — Journal Pratique de Droit Fiscal et Financier
DRFUD4 — Drugs of the Future
DRG — Directory of Research Grants
DrG — Drew Gateway
DRGBAH — Danish Review of Game Biology
DrGBL — Dresdner Geschichts-Blaetter
DRGS — Deutsche Rundschau fuer Geographie und Statistik
DRI-CEI — DRI Current Economic Indicators
DRICOM — DRI Commodities
Driemaand Bull Antwerp — Driemaandelijks Bulletin
Driemaand Publ K Belg Inst Verbetering Biet — Driemaandelijkse Publikatie. Koninklijk Belgisch Instituut tot Verbetering van de Biet
DRIFACS — DRI Financial and Credit Statistics
Driftprobl Avloppsreningsverk Nord Symp Vattenforsk — Driftproblem vid Avloppsreningsverk. Nordiska Symposiet om Vattenforskning
DRILA — Drilling
Drill Conf Proc — Drilling Conference. Proceedings
Drilling Contract — Drilling Contractor
Drill News — Drilling News
Drill Prod Pract — Drilling and Production Practice
Drills Pharmacol Med — Drill's Pharmacology in Medicine
DRINA — Drvna Industrija

Drip Trickle Irrig — Drip/Trickle Irrigation
Dritte Welt Mag — Dritte Welt Magazin
Driver Ed Bul — Driver Education Bulletin
Drives and Controls Int — Drives and Controls International
DRK — Dansk Rode Kors
D Rkl — Dansk Reklame
Dr LR — Drake Law Review
Dr Marit — Droit Maritime
Dr Marit Franc — Droit Maritime Francais
DRMGAS — Drugs Made in Germany
DrN — Druzba Narodov
DRO — Drogist. Vakblad voor Schoonheid, Gezondheid, en Hygiene
DROAAK — Deep Sea Research and Oceanographic Abstracts
DROFAZ — Data Record of Oceanographic Observations and Exploratory Fishing
DROGA — Drogownictwo
Drog Kozl — Drogista Kozlony
Droit et Pratique Commer Internat — Droit et Pratique du Commerce International
Droperidol Fentanyl Schock Ber Bremer Neuroleptanalg Symp — Droperidol und Fentanyl beim Schock. Bericht ueber das Bremer Neuroleptanalgesie-Symposion
Drought Lect Sess WMO Exec Comm — Drought. Lectures Presented at the Session. WMO [*World Meteorlogical Organization*] Executive Committee
Dr Ouvr — Droit Ouvrier
Drozhzhevaya Promst Nauchno Tekh Ref Sb — Drozhzhevaya Promyshlennost. Nauchno-Tekhnicheskii Referativnyi Sbornik
DRPPD5 — Deep-Sea Research. Part A. Oceanographic Research Papers [*Later, Deep-Sea Research with Oceanographic Literature Review*]
Dr Pratique Com Int — Droit et Pratique du Commerce International
DRPRB — Druck Print
DrR — Drama Review
DRR — Drug Research Reports: The Blue Sheet
DRS — CCH [*Commerce Clearing House*] Dominion Report Service
DRS — Data Resources Series
DRs — Deutsche Rundschau
DRS — Dominion Report Service
Dr Sanit Soc — Droit Sanitaire et Social
DRSEDL — Diagnostic Radiology Series
D Rsk — Den Danske Realskole
DRSN — Drug Survival News
Dr Soc — Droit Social
DRSPA — Druckspiegel
DRSPAAJC — Documents et Rapports. Societe Paleontologique et Archeologique de l'Arrondissement Judiciaire de Charleroi
DRSW — Documentary Relations of the South West
DRT — Director
DRTBB — Drug and Therapeutics Bulletin
DRTOBK — Drugs of Today
Dr Trav — Droit du Travail: Revue Mensuelle
DRTRD — Director
DRu — Deutsche Rundschau
Drudea Mitt Geobot Sachsen-Th — Drudea. Mitteilungen des Geobotanischen Arbeitskreises Sachsen-Thueringen
Drudes Ann — Drude's Annalen
Drug Absorpt Dispos Stat Consid Symp — Drug Absorption and Disposition. Statistical Considerations. Based on a Symposium
Drug Abu MS — Drug Abuse Council. Monograph Series
Drug Abu PPS — Drug Abuse Council. Public Policy Series
Drug Abuse & Alcohol Rev — Drug Abuse and Alcoholism Review
Drug Abuse LR — Drug Abuse Law Review
Drug Abuse L Rev — Drug Abuse Law Review
Drug Abuse Pregnancy Neonat Eff — Drug Abuse in Pregnancy and Neonatal Effects
Drug Abuse Prev Rep — Drug Abuse Prevention Report
Drug Abuse Soc Issues Int Symp — Drug Abuse and Social Issues. International Symposium on Drug Abuse
Drug Action Drug Resist Bact — Drug Action and Drug Resistance in Bacteria
Drug Action Mol Level Rep Symp — Drug Action at the Molecular Level. Report. Symposium
Drug Alcohol Abuse Rev — Drug and Alcohol Abuse Reviews
Drug Alcohol Depend — Drug and Alcohol Dependence
Drug Alert — Nurse's Drug Alert
Drug Allied Ind — Drug and Allied Industries
Drug and Cosmetic Ind — Drug and Cosmetic Industry
Drug Anesth Eff Membr Struct Funct — Drug and Anesthetic Effects on Membrane Structure and Function
Drug Bull — Drug Bulletin
Drug Carriers Biol Med — Drug Carriers in Biology and Medicine
Drug Chem Exports — Drug and Chemical Exports
Drug Chem Toxicol — Drug and Chemical Toxicology
Drug Circ — Druggists Circular
Drug Conc Neuropsychiatry — Drug Concentrations in Neuropsychiatry
Drug Cosmet — Drug and Cosmetic Industry
Drug Cosmet Ind — Drug and Cosmetic Industry
Drug Deliv — Drug Delivery
Drug Delivery Syst — Drug Delivery System
Drug Delivery Syst Dev Int Conf — Drug Delivery System Development. International Conference
Drug Delivery Syst Proc Int Conf — Drug Delivery Systems. Proceedings. International Conference
Drug Depend — Drug Dependence
Drug Des Delivery — Drug Design and Delivery
Drug Des Discov — Drug Design and Discovery
Drug Des Discovery — Drug Design and Discovery
Drug Dev — Drug Development [*monograph*]
Drug Dev C — Drug Development Communications

Drug Dev Commun — Drug Development Communications
Drug Dev Eval — Drug Development and Evaluation
Drug Dev Ind Pharm — Drug Development and Industrial Pharmacy
Drug Dev Res — Drug Development Research
Drug Dig — Drug Digests
Drug Discovery Technol — Drug Discovery Technologies
Drug Enf — Drug Enforcement
Drug Enforce — Drug Enforcement
Drug Enzyme Targeting Part A — Drug and Enzyme Targeting. Part A
Drug Enzyme Targeting Part B — Drug and Enzyme Targeting. Part B
Drug Fate Metab — Drug Fate and Metabolism
Drug Forum J Human Issues — Drug Forum. Journal of Human Issues
Drug Induced Clin Toxic — Drug Induced Clinical Toxicity
Drug Induced Dis — Drug Induced Diseases
Drug Induced Disord — Drug-Induced Disorders
Drug Induced Heart Dis — Drug-Induced Heart Disease
Drug Induced Liver Inj — Drug-Induced Liver Injury
Drug Induced Pathol — Drug-Induced Pathology
Drug Inf Bull — Drug Information Bulletin
Drug Inf Health Prof — Drug Information for the Health Professions
Drug Inf J — Drug Information Journal
Drug Inf News (Hiroshima) — Drug Information News (Hiroshima)
Drug Intel — Drug Intelligence and Clinical Pharmacy
Drug Intel Clin Pharm — Drug Intelligence and Clinical Pharmacy
Drug Intell — Drug Intelligence [*Later, Drug Intelligence and Clinical Pharmacy*]
Drug Intell Clin Pharm — Drug Intelligence and Clinical Pharmacy
Drug Interact — Drug Interactions [*monograph*]
Drug Interact Newsl — Drug Interactions Newsletter
Drug Interact Symp — Drug Interactions. Symposium
Drug Invest — Drug Investigation
Drug Manuf Technol Ser — Drug Manufacturing Technology Series
Drug Meas Drug Eff Lab Health Sci Int Colloq Prospect Biol — Drug Measurement and Drug Effects in Laboratory Health Science. International Colloquium on Prospective Biology
Drug Merch — Drug Merchandising
Drug Metab — Drug Metabolism Reviews
Drug Metab Dispos — Drug Metabolism and Disposition
Drug Metab Dispos Biol Fate Chem — Drug Metabolism and Disposition. The Biological Fate of Chemicals
Drug Metab Disposition — Drug Metabolism and Disposition
Drug Metab Drug Interact — Drug Metabolism and Drug Interactions
Drug Metab Drug Toxic — Drug Metabolism and Drug Toxicity
Drug Metab Isol Determ — Drug Metabolite Isolation and Determination
Drug Metab Microbe Man Symp — Drug Metabolism. From Microbe to Man. Symposium
Drug Metab Mol Man Eur Drug Metab Workshop — Drug Metabolism. From Molecules to Man. European Drug Metabolism Workshop
Drug Metab Proc Eur Workshop — Drug Metabolism. Molecular Approaches and Pharmacological Implications. Proceedings. European Workshop on Drug Metabolism
Drug Metab Rev — Drug Metabolism Reviews
Drug Meta D — Drug Metabolism and Disposition
Drug News & Perspect — Drug News and Perspectives
Drug-Nutr — Drug-Nutrient Interactions
Drug-Nutrient Interact — Drug-Nutrient Interactions
Drug-Nutr Interact — Drug-Nutrient Interactions
Drug Plast Interact Parenter Drug Adm Proc Workshop — Drug-Plastic Interactions in Parenteral Drug Administration. Proceedings. Workshop
Drug Recept Dyn Processes Cells Proc Alfred Benzon Symp — Drug Receptors and Dynamic Processes in Cells. Proceedings. Alfred Benzon Symposium
Drug Recept Interact Antimicrob Chemother Symp — Drug Receptor Interactions in Antimicrobial Chemotherapy. Symposium
Drug Recept Their Eff Rep Symp — Drug Receptors and Their Effectors. Report. Symposium
Drug Relat Damage Respir Tract — Drug-Related Damage to the Respiratory Tract
Drug Res — Drug Research
Drug Resist Biochem Target Cancer Chemother — Drug Resistance of a Biochemical Target in Cancer Chemotherapy
Drug Resist Mech Reversal Int Annu Pezcoller Symp — Drug Resistance. Mechanisms and Reversal. International Annual Pezcoller Symposium
Drug Resist Updat — Drug Resistance Updates
Drugs Abuse Chem Pharmacol Immunol AIDS — Drugs of Abuse. Chemistry, Pharmacology, Immunology, and AIDS
Drug Saf — Drug Safety
Drugs Affecting Cent Nerv Syst — Drugs Affecting the Central Nervous System
Drugs Behav — Drugs and Behavior [*monograph*]
Drugs Cardiol — Drugs in Cardiology
Drugs Cereb Funct Symp — Drugs and Cerebral Function. Symposium
Drugs Cereb Palsy Symp — Drugs in Cerebral Palsy. Symposium
Drugs Cholinergic Mech CNS Proc Conf — Drugs and Cholinergic Mechanisms in the CNS. Proceedings. Conference
Drugs Dev — Drugs in Development
Drugs Dev Cereb Funct Annu Cereb Funct Symp — Drugs, Development, and Cerebral Function. Annual Cerebral Function Symposium
Drugs Dis — Drugs and Diseases
Drugs Elderly Proc Symp — Drugs and the Elderly. Perspectives in Geriatric Clinical Pharmacology. Proceedings. Symposium
Drugs Enzymes Proc Int Pharmacol Meet — Drugs and Enzymes. Proceedings. International Pharmacological Meeting
Drugs Exp Clin Res — Drugs under Experimental and Clinical Research
Drugs Future — Drugs of the Future
Drugs Health Care — Drugs in Health Care
Drugs Hematol React Hahnemann Symp — Drugs and Hematologic Reactions. Hahnemann Symposium

Drugs Made Ger — Drugs Made in Germany
Drugs Neuro — Drugs in Neurology
Drugs Pharm Sci — Drugs and the Pharmaceutical Sciences
Drugs R D — Drugs in R&D
Drugs Resp Dis — Drugs in Respiratory Diseases
Drugs Sens Funct — Drugs and Sensory Functions
Drug Stab — Drug Stability
Drug Stand — Drug Standards
Drugs Today (Barcelona) — Drugs of Today (Barcelona)
Drug Stor N — Drug Store News
Drug Ther — Drug Therapy
Drug Ther Biomed Inf Corp — Drug Therapy (Biomedical Information Corporation)
Drug Ther Bull — Drug and Therapeutics Bulletin
Drug Ther Elderly — Drug Therapy for the Elderly
Drug Ther Hosp Ed — Drug Therapy. Hospital Edition
Drug Ther Prescr Pract Probl — Drug Therapy. Prescribing Practices and Problems
Drug Ther Rev — Drug Therapy Reviews
Drug Topic A — Annual Consumer Expenditures Survey (Supplement to Drug Topics)
Drug Vitam Allied Ind — Drug, Vitamin, and Allied Industries
DRUIA — Drug Intelligence [*Later, Drug Intelligence and Clinical Pharmacy*]
D Rund — Deutsche Rundschau
D Rundschau — Deutsche Rundschau
Drury Coll Bradley G Field Sta B — Drury College. Bradley Geological Field Station. Bulletin
Druzh N — Druzhba Narodov. Ezhemesiachnyi Literaturno-Khudozhestvennyi i Obshchestvenno-Politicheskii Zhurnal
D Rv — Deutsche Revue
Drvna Ind — Drvna Industrija
DRVYA — Drevarsky Vyskum
DRW — Repro en Druk
DRWEA — Draht-Welt
Dry — Dryade
Dry Goods Econ — Dry Goods Economist [*New York*]
Drying Technol — Drying Technology
Dryland Agric — Dryland Agriculture
Dry Valley Drill Proj Bull — Dry Valley Drilling Project. Bulletin. Northern Illinois University. Departmentof Geology
DRZg — Deutsche Richterzeitung
DS — Danske Studier
DS — Deutsche Studien
DS — Developments in Sedimentology
DS — Diacritics
DS — Diderot Studies
DS — Difesa Sociale
DS — Dokumentation Schweisstechnik
DS — Dominican Studies
DS — Drama Survey
DS — Dynamic Stories
D Sa — Dansk Sang
DSA — Dickens Studies Annual
DSAM — Dictionnaire de Spiritualite Ascetique et Mystique, Doctrine et Histoire
DSARDS — Dante Studies with the Annual Report of the Dante Society
DSASDE — Alabama. Agricultural Experiment Station. Auburn University. Agronomy and SoilsDepartmental Series
D'scape — Designscape
DSchNG — Denkschriften der Schweizerischen Naturforschenden Gesellschaft
DSCOA9 — Duquesne Science Counselor
DSE — Data Systems Engineering
DSec — Degre Second. Studies in French Literature
DSECEL — DGU [*Geological Survey of Denmark*] Series C
DSEG — Developments in Solid Earth Geophysics
DSF — Dynamic Science Fiction
DSFNS — Deutsche-Slawische Forschungen zur Namenkunde und Siedlungsgeschichte
DSFT — Dansk Skovforenings Tidsskrift
DSFTA — Dansk Skovforenings Tidsskrift
DSFTA5 — Dansk Skovforenings Tidsskrift
DSG — Deutsche Studien zur Geistesgeschichte
DSGEAX — Desinfektion und Gesundheitswesen
Dsgn Eng — Design Engineering
DSGRD7 — Delaware Sea Grant Technical Report Del-SG
DSGW — Deutsche Shakespeare-Gesellschaft (West Germany)
DSH — DSH [*Deafness, Speech, and Hearing*] Abstracts
DSHA — DSH [*Deafness, Speech, and Hearing*] Abstracts
DSH Abstr — DSH [*Deafness, Speech, and Hearing*] Abstracts
DSHIP — Digest of Selected Health and Insurance Plans
DSI — Danish Scientific Investigations in Iran
DSI — Decision Sciences
DSI Bull — DSI [*Dairy Society International*] Bulletin
DSIJa — Doklady i Soobscenija Instituta Jazykozanija Akademiji Nauk SSSR
DSIR Bull NZ — DSIR [*Department of Scientific and Industrial Research*] Bulletin (New Zealand)
DSIR Chem Rep CD — DSIR (New Zealand. Department of Scientific and Industrial Research) Chemistry. Report CD (Chemisty Division)
DSIR Inf Ser — DSIR [*Department of Scientific and Industrial Research*] Information Series
DSJOA — Defence Science Journal
DSJOAA — Defence Science Journal
DS Jur — Dalloz-Sirey. Jurisprudence
D Skf T — Dansk Skovforenings Tidsskrift
DSKSAR — Denki Seirigaku Kenkyu
D Sksl — Dansk Skoleslojd
DSL — Dalloz-Sirey. Legislation

DSL — Danske Sprog-og Literaturselskab
DSL — Dictionary of the Scottish Language
DSLL — Duquesne Studies in Language and Literature
D Smbl — Dansk Seminarieblad
DSMHA — Discrete Mathematics
DSMJA — Delaware Medical Journal
DSMJBB — Dar Es Salaam Medical Journal
DSN — Dickens Studies Newsletter
DSNGA6 — Denkschriften. Schweizerische Naturforschende Gesellschaft
DSNJDI — Dirasat/Natural Science
DSNQ — Design Quarterly
D Sof — Dansk Sofartstidende
DSOL — Defects in Solids
DSp — Deutsche Sprache
DSP — Dialogo Social (Panama)
DSpir — Dictionnaire de Spiritualite
DSPP — Digest of Selected Pension Plans
DSPS — Duquesne Studies. Philological Series
DSR — Deep-Sea Research [*London*]
DSRAB9 — Desarrollo Rural en las Americas
DSS — Design Studies
DSS — Developments in Soil Science
DSS — Dynamic Science Stories
DSS — XVIIe Siecle
DSSCDM — Developments in Soil Science
DSSSS — Developments in Solar System and Space Science
DSt — Danske Studier
DST — Dansk Skovforenings Tidsskrift
D St — Dermatologische Studien
DSt — Deutsche Studien
DSTB — Danmarks Statistiks TidsseriedataBank
D St R — Deutsches Steuerrecht
D St R — Deutsche Steuer-Rundschau
DSTS — Duquesne Studies. Theological Series
D Studies — Dostoevsky Studies. Journal of the International Dostoevsky Society
D St Z — Deutsche Steuerzeitung
DStZg — Deutsche Steuerzeitung
D St Zt — Deutsche Steuerzeitung
DSUzU — Doklady i Soobscenija Uzgorodskogo Universiteta
DSz — Dunantuli Szemle
DT — Daily Telegraph
DT — Daily Times
DT — Deutsche Tagespost
DT — Developments in Toxicology and Environmental Science
DT — Divus Thomas
DT — Duscepoleznie Tchtenie
DTA — Defixionum Tebellae Atticae
Dt Aerztbl Aerztl Mitt — Deutsches Aerzteblatt/Aerztliche Mitteilungen
Dt Aerzteztg — Deutsche Aerzte-Zeitung
Dt Allg Ztg — Deutsche Allgemeine Zeitung
Dt Apoth — Deutsche Apotheker
Dt Apoth Post — Deutsche Apotheker Post
Dt ApothZtg — Deutsche Apotheker-Zeitung
Dt Arbeit — Deutsche Arbeit. Zeitschrift des Volksbundes fuer das Deutschtum im Ausland
Dt Arb Univ Koeln — Deutsche Arbeiten der Universitaet Koeln
Dt Arch Erforsch Mittelalter — Deutsches Archiv fuer Erforschung des Mittelalters
Dt Arch Gesch Mittelalter — Deutsches Archiv fuer Geschichte des Mittelalters
Dt Arch Inn Med — Deutsches Archiv fuer Innere Medizin
Dt Archit — Deutsche Architektur
Dt Arch Klin Med — Deutsches Archiv fuer Klinische Medizin
Dt Arch Landes U Volksforsch — Deutsches Archiv fuer Landes- und Volksforschung
Dt Archv Erforsch Mittelalters — Deutsches Archiv fuer Erforschung des Mittelalters
Dt Archv Gesch Mittelalters — Deutsches Archiv fuer Geschichte des Mittelalters
Dt Archv Landes & Vlksforsch — Deutsches Archiv fuer Landes- und Volksforschung
Dt Aussenpolitik — Deutsche Aussenpolitik
DTB — Denkmaeler der Tonkunst in Bayern
DTB — Distribution
Dt Bauern Techn — Deutsche Bauerntechnik
Dt Bauz — Deutsche Bauzeitschrift
Dt Bauztg — Deutsche Bauzeitung
Dt Beitr — Deutsche Beitraege. Eine Zweimontsschrift
Dt Berufs & Fachsch — Deutsche Berufs- und Fachschule
Dt Berufsschule — Deutsche Berufsschule
Dt Bienenkal — Deutsche Bienenkalender
Dt Bienenztg — Deutsche Bienenzeitung
Dt Bienenzucht — Deutsche Bienenzucht
Dt Biog Jb — Deutsches Biographisches Jahrbuch
DTBSD — Database
Dt Buehne — Deutsche Buehne
DTBWAZ — Deutsche Bienenwirtschaft
DTC — CCH [*Commerce Clearing House*] Dominion Tax Cases
DTC — Dictionnaire de Theologie Catholique
DTCFA — Documents Techniques. Charbonnages de France
DTCFD — Dil ve Tarih-Cografya Fakueltesi Dergisi
DTD — Documentieblad. Nieuwe Reeks
Dt Dante Jb — Deutsches Dante-Jahrbuch
D T Dial Transplant — D & T. Dialysis and Transplantation
DTDRA — Denki Tsushin Daigaku Gakuho
DTE — Database
DTE — Down to Earth
DTEGA2 — Dermatologia Tropica et Ecologia Geographica

D Tekn T — Dansk Teknisk Tidsskrift
D Tel — Daily Telegraph
D Telegraph — Daily Telegraph
Dt Ent Z — Deutsche Entomologische Zeitschrift
Dteol T — Dansk Teologisk Tidsskrift
DTESD — Developments in Toxicology and Environmental Science
Dt Evgl Kirchztg — Deutsche Evangelische Kirchenzeitung
DTF — Divus Thomas (Freiburg)
DTFAA — Dansk Tidsskrift foer Farmaci
DTFAAN — Dansk Tidsskrift foer Farmaci
Dt Familienarch — Deutsches Familienarchiv
D T Farm — Dansk Tidsskrift for Farmaci
Dt Forsch Osten — Deutsche Forschung im Osten
Dt Forsch Ungarn — Deutsche Forschung in Ungarn
DTGDA — Denshi Tsushin Gakkai Rombunshi. Part D
Dt Gemeindeztg — Deutsche Gemeinde-Zeitung
DTGHD — Denshi Tsushin Gakkai Gijutsu Kenkyu Hokoku
DTGZA — Denki Tsushin Gakkai Zasshi
DTh — Deutsche Theologie: Monatsschrift fuer die Deutsche Evangelische Kirche
DTh — Divus Thomas
Dt Handelsschullehrztg — Deutsche Handelsschullehrer-Zeitung
D Th C — Dictionnaire de Theologie Catholique
Dt Hochschule — Deutsche Hochschule
Dt Ill Bienenztg — Deutsche Illustrierte Bienenzeitung
DTIMD9 — INTA [*Instituto Nacional de Tecnologia Agropecuaria*] Divulgacion Tecnica
Dt Imkerfuehrer — Deutsche Imkerfuehrer
Dt Imkerkal — Deutscher Imkerkalender
Dt Imkerztg — Deutsche Imkerzeitung
Dt Im Osten — Deutsche Im Osten
Dt Indinst Ber Wirtpol — Berichte. Deutsches Industrielinstitut zur Wirtschaftspolitik
Dt Inst Wirtschaftsforsch Wochenber — Deutsches Institut fuer Wirtschaftsforschung. Wochenbericht
DtlsrZtg — Deutsche Israelitische Zeitung
Dt Jaegerztg — Deutsche Jaegerzeitung
Dt Jb Numi — Deutsches Jahrbuch fuer Numismatik
Dt Jb Numismat — Deutsches Jahrbuch fuer Numismatik
Dt Jb Volkskde — Deutsches Jahrbuch fuer Volkskunde
Dt Justizstatist — Deutsche Justiz-Statistik
Dt Kolonbl — Deutsches Kolonialblatt
Dt Kolonialbl — Deutsches Kolonialblatt
Dt Konkurrenzen — Deutsche Konkurrenzen
Dt Kst & Dek — Deutsche Kunst und Dekoration. Illustrierte Monatshefte
Dt Kst & Dkmlpf — Deutsche Kunst- und Denkmalpflege
Dt Kstbl — Deutsches Kunstblatt
DTKTA — Dansk Teknisk Tidsskrift
Dt Kult Leben Voelker — Deutsche Kultur im Leben der Voelker
Dt Landwirt — Deutsche Landwirtschaft
Dt Landwirt (Berlin) — Deutsche Landwirtschaft (Berlin)
Dtl Arch — Deutschland Archiv
Dt LebensmittRdsch — Deutsche Lebensmittel Rundschau
Dt Lichtbild — Deutsches Lichtbild
Dt Litdenkm — Deutsche Literaturdenkmale
Dt Litztg — Deutsche Literaturzeitung
DTM — Deutsche Texte des Mittelalters
DTM — Directory of Texas Manufacturers
Dt Med J — Deutsches Medizinisches Journal
Dt Med Wschr — Deutsche Medizinische Wochenschrift
Dt Mh — Deutsche Monatschefte
Dt Mh Polen — Deutsche Monatschefte in Polen
Dt Milchwirt — Deutsche Milchwirtschaft
DTMNA — Datamation
Dt Mschr Ges Leben Gegenw — Deutsche Monatsschrift fuer das Gesamte Leben der Gegenwart
Dt Munzbl — Deutsche Muenzblaetter
Dt Mus — Deutsches Museum
DT (Newspr) (Tas) — Daily Telegraph Reports (Newspaper) (Tasmania)
Dt Notariatsztg — Deutsche Notariats-Zeitung
D To — Dansk Toldtidende
DTP — Divus Thomas (Piacenza)
Dt PH — Deutsch-Polnische Hefte
Dt Philologenbl — Deutsches Philologen-Blatt
Dt Pol H — Deutsch-Poinische Hefte
DTR — Drug Therapy Reviews
Dt Rdsch — Deutsche Rundschau
Dt Rdsch Geogr Statist — Deutsche Rundschau fuer Geographie und Statistik
Dt Recht — Deutsches Recht. Vereinigt mit Juristische Wochenschrift
DTREDU — Drug Therapy Reviews
Dt Rev — Deutsche Revue
Dt Richterztg — Deutsche Richterzeitung
D Trns J — Defense Transportation Journal
Dt Rs — Deutsche Rundschau
DTS — Diarium Terrae Sanctae
Dtsch Aerztebl — Deutsches Aerzteblatt. Aerztliche Mitteilungen
Dtsch Agrartech — Deutsche Agrartechnik
Dtsch Akad Landwirtschaftwiss Berl Tagungber — Deutsche Akademie der Landwirtschaftwissenschaften zu Berlin. Tagungberichte
Dtsch Akad Wiss Berlin Vortr Schr — Deutsche Akademie der Wissenschaften zu Berlin. Vortraege und Schriften
Dtsch Akad Wiss Berlin Zentralinst Phys Erde Veroeff — Deutsche Akademie der Wissenschaften zu Berlin. Zentralinstituts Physik der Erde. Veroeffentlichungen
Dtsch Am Brau J — Deutsches und Amerikanisches Brauer. Journal
Dtsch Apoth — Deutsche Apotheker
Dtsch Apoth Biogr — Deutsche Apotheker-Biographie

Dtsch Apoth-Ztg — Deutsche Apotheker-Zeitung
Dtsch Apoth Ztg Beil Apothekenhelferin — Deutsche Apotheker-Zeitung. Beilage. Apothekenhelferin
Dtsch Apoth Ztg Beil Apothekerprakt Pharm Tech Assist — Deutsche Apotheker-Zeitung. Beilage. Apothekerpraktikant und Pharmazeutisch-Technischer Assistent
Dtsch Apoth Ztg Beil Neue Arzneim Spez — Deutsche Apotheker-Zeitung. Beilage. Neue Arzneimittel und Spezialitaeten
Dtsch Apoth Ztg Beil Neue Arzneim Spez Geheimm — Deutsche Apotheker-Zeitung. Beilage. Neue Arzneimittel, Spezialitaeten, und Geheimmittel
Dtsch Apoth Ztg Beil Pharm Heute — Deutsche Apotheker-Zeitung. Beilage. Pharmazie Heute
Dtsch Apoth Ztg Beil Praktikantenbriefe — Deutsche Apotheker-Zeitung. Beilage. Praktikantenbriefe
Dtsch Apoth Ztg Beil PTA Heute — Deutsche Apotheker-Zeitung. Beilage. PTA Heute
Dtsch Archit — Deutsches Architektenblatt
Dtsch Arch Klin Med — Deutsches Archiv fuer Klinische Medizin
Dtsch Atomforum Schriftenr — Deutsches Atomforum. Schriftenreihe
Dtsch Ausschuss Stahlbeton Schriftenr — Deutscher Ausschuss fuer Stahlbeton. Schriftenreihe
Dtsch Aussenpolitik — Deutsche Aussenpolitik
Dtsch Baumsch — Deutsche Baumschule
Dtsch Bauz — Deutsche Bauzeitschrift. Fachblatt fuer Entwurf und Ausfuehrung
Dtsch Bauz Fachbl Entwurf Ausfuhrung — Deutsche Bauzeitschrift. Fachblatt fuer Entwurf und Ausfuehrung
Dtsch Beitr Geotech — Deutsche Beitraege zur Geotechnik
Dtsch Bibliogr Halbjahres Verzeichnis — Deutsche Bibliographie. Halbjahres-Verzeichnis
Dtsch Bibliogr Woech Verzeichnis A — Deutsche Bibliographie. Woechentliches Verzeichnis. Reihe A
Dtsch Bibliogr Woech Verzeichnis B — Deutsche Bibliographie. Woechentliches Verzeichnis. Reihe B
Dtsch Bibliogr Woech Verzeichnis C — Deutsche Bibliographie. Woechentliches Verzeichnis. Reihe C
Dtsch Bienenwirtsch — Deutsche Bienenwirtschaft
Dtsch Bienenwirtsch Teil 2 — Deutsche Bienenwirtschaft. Teil 2
Dtsch Bot Ges Ber — Deutsche Botanische Gesellschaft. Berichte
Dtsch Brau — Deutsche Brauerei
Dtsch Brauwirtschaft Beil — Deutsche Brauwirtschaft. Beilage
Dtsch Bundespost Forschungsinst FTZ Tech Ber — Deutsche Bundespost. Forschungsinstitut beim FTZ. Technischer Bericht
Dtsch Bundestag Drucks — Deutscher Bundestag. Drucksache
Dtsch Chem — Deutsche Chemiker
Dtsch Chem Z — Deutsche Chemiker-Zeitschrift
Dtsch Dendrol Ges Kurzmitt — Deutsche Dendrologische Gesellschaft. Kurzmitteilungen
Dtsch Destill Ztg — Deutsche Destillateur Zeitung
Dtsch Druckgewerbe — Deutsche Druckgewerbe
Dtsche A — Deutsche Annalen
Dtsche Aussenpolit — Deutsche Aussenpolitik
Dtsch Edelstahlwerke Tech Ber — Deutsche Edelstahlwerke Technische Berichte
Dtsche Ges Bevoelkerungswiss — Deutsche Gesellschaft fuer Bevoelkerungswissenschaft an der Universitaet Hamburg
Dtsche Ges Mineraloelwiss Kohlechem — Deutsche Gesellschaft fuer Mineraloelwissenschaft und Kohlechemie
Dtsch Eisenbahntech — Deutsche Eisenbahntechnik
Dtsch Elektrotech — Deutsche Elektrotechnik
Dtsch Engl Med Rundsch — Deutsche-Englische Medizinische Rundschau
Dtsch Entomol Z — Deutsche Entomologische Zeitschrift
Dtsches Inst Wirtsch Forsch Wber — Deutsches Institut fuer Wirtschaftsforschung Wochenbericht
Dtsch Essigind — Deutsche Essigindustrie
Dtsche Steuer Z — Deutsche Steuer-Zeitung
Dtsche Stud — Deutsche Studien. Vierteljahreshefte fuer Vergleichende Gegenwartskunde
Dtsche Z Philos — Deutsche Zeitschrift fuer Philosophie
Dtsch Faerber Kal — Deutscher Faerber-Kalender
Dtsch Faerber Ztg — Deutsche Faerber-Zeitung
Dtsch Faerber Ztg Beil — Deutsche Faerber-Zeitung. Beilage
Dtsch Farben Z — Deutsche Farben Zeitschrift
Dtsch Faserst Spinnpflanzen — Deutsche Faserstoffe und Spinnpflanzen
Dtsch Fischereirundsch — Deutsche Fischereirundschau
Dtsch Fisch Rundsch — Deutsche Fischerei-Rundschau
Dtsch Fischwirtsch — Deutsche Fischwirtschaft
Dtsch Fisch Ztg — Deutsche Fischerei Zeitung
Dtsch Flugtech — Deutsche Flugtechnik
Dtsch Flungtec — Deutsche Flungtechnik
Dtsch Forschungsanst Luft Raumfahrt DFL Ber — Deutsche Forschungsanstalt fuer Luft- und Raumfahrt. DFL-Bericht
Dtsch Forschungsdienst Sonderber Kernenerg — Deutscher Forschungsdienst. Sonderbericht Kernenergie
Dtsch Forschungsgem Farbst Komm Mitt — Deutsche Forschungsgemeinschaft Farbstoff Kommission Mitteilung
Dtsch Forschungsgem Farbstoffkomm Mitt — Deutsche Forschungsgemeinschaft. Farbstoffkommission. Mitteilung
Dtsch Forschungsgem Komm Erforsch Luftverunreinig Mitt — Deutsche Forschungsgemeinschaft. Kommission zur Erforschung der Luftverunreinigung. Mitteilung
Dtsch Forschungsgem Komm Erforsch Luftverunreinigung Mitt — Deutsche Forschungsgemeinschaft Kommission zur Erforschung der Luftverunreinigung. Mitteilung
Dtsch Forschungsgem Komm Geowiss Gemeinschaftsforsch Mitt — Deutsche Forschungsgemeinschaft Kommission fuer Geowissenschaftliche Gemeinschaftsforschung Mitteilung

Dtsch Forschungsgem Komm Pruef Fremder Stoffe Lebensm Mitt — Deutsche Forschungsgemeinschaft Kommission zur Pruefung Fremder Stoffe bei Lebensmitteln Mitteilung

Dtsch Forschungsgem Komm Pruef Rueckstaenden Lebensm Mitt — Deutsche Forschungsgemeinschaft. Kommission zur Pruefung von Rueckstaenden in Lebensmitteln. Mitteilung

Dtsch Forschungsgem Komm Wasserforsch Mitt — Deutsche Forschungsgemeinschaft. Kommission fuer Wasserforschung. Mitteilung

Dtsch Forschungsgem Mitt — Deutsche Forschungsgemeinschaft Mitteilungen

Dtsch Forschungsgem Senatskomm Wasserforsch Mitt — Deutsche Forschungsgemeinschaft. Senatskommission fuer Wasserforschung. Mitteilung

Dtsch Forschungsgem Wolle Schriftenr — Deutsche Forschungsgemeinschaft Wolle. Schriftenreihe

Dtsch Forschungsges Druck Reproduktionstech Forschungsber — Deutsche Forschungsgesellschaft fuer Druck- und Reproduktionstechnik. Forschungsbericht

Dtsch Forschungsges Druck Reproduktionstech Mitt — Deutsche Forschungsgesellschaft fuer Druck- und Reproduktionstechnik. Mitteilungen

Dtsch Forsch Versuchsanst Luft Raumfahrt Forschungsber — Deutsche Forschungs- und Versuchsanstalt fuer Luft- und Raumfahrt. Forschungsbericht

Dtsch Forsch Versuchsanst Luft Raumfahrt Mitt — Deutsche Forschungs- und Versuchsanstalt fuer Luft- und Raumfahrt. Mitteilung

Dtsch Forsch Versuchsanst Luft Raumfahrt Nachr — Deutsche Forschungs- und Versuchsanstalt fuer Luft und Raumfahrt. Nachrichten

Dtsch Forstm — Deutsche Forstmann

Dtsch Gaertnerboerse — Deutsche Gaertnerboerse

Dtsch Gartenbau — Deutsche Gartenbau

Dtsch Geod Komm Bayer Akad Wiss Reihe B — Deutsche Geodaetische Kommission bei der Bayerischen Akademie der Wissenschaften. Reihe B. Angewandte Geodaesie

Dtsch Geod Komm Bayer Akad Wiss Reihe C — Deutsche Geodaetische Kommission bei der Bayerischen Akademie der Wissenschaften. Reihe C. Dissertationen

Dtsch Geod Komm Veroeff Reihe B — Deutsche Geodaetische Kommission. Veroeffentlichungen. Reihe B. Angewandte Geodaesie

Dtsch Geol Ges Nachr — Deutsche Geologische Gesellschaft. Nachrichten

Dtsch Geol Ges Z — Deutsche Geologische Gesellschaft. Zeitschrift

Dtsch Ges Angiol Jahrestag — Deutsche Gesellschaft fuer Angiologie. Jahrestagung

Dtsch Ges Arbeitsmed Jahrestag — Deutsche Gesellschaft fuer Arbeitsmedizin. Jahrestagung

Dtsch Ges Chem Apparatewes Chem Tech Biotechnol Monogr — Deutsche Gesellschaft fuer Chemisches Apparatewesen, Chemische Technik, und Biotechnologie-Monographien

Dtsch Ges Ernaehr Symp — Deutsche Gesellschaft fuer Ernaehrung. Symposium

Dtsch Ges Herz Kreislaufforsch Verh — Deutsche Gesellschaft fuer Herz- und Kreislaufforschung. Verhandlungen

Dtsch Ges Holzforsch Ber — Deutsche Gesellschaft fuer Holzforschung Bericht

Dtsch Ges Luft Raumfahrt DGLR Fachbuch — Deutsche Gesellschaft fuer Luft- und Raumfahrt. DGLR-Fachbuchreihe

Dtsch Ges Metallkd Fachber — Deutsche Gesellschaft fuer Metallkunde Fachberichte

Dtsch Ges Metallkd Hauptversamml — Deutsche Gesellschaft fuer Metallkunde. Hauptversammlung

Dtsch Ges Mineraloelwiss Kohlechem Ber — Deutsche Gesellschaft fuer Mineraloelwissenschaft und Kohlechemie. Berichte

Dtsch Ges Mineraloelwiss Kohlechem Compend — Deutsche Gesellschaft fuer Mineraloelwissenschaft und Kohlechemie. Compendium

Dtsch Ges Qualitaetsforsch Pflanz Nahrungsm Congr — Deutsche Gesellschaft fuer Qualitaetsforschung (Pflanzliche Nahrungsmittel). Congress

Dtsch Ges Qualitaetsforsch Pflanz Nahrungsm Vortragstag — Deutsche Gesellschaft fuer Qualitaetsforschung (Pflanzliche Nahrungsmittel). Vortragstagung

Dtsch Ges Sonnenenerg Mitteilungsbl — Deutsche Gesellschaft fuer Sonnenenergie. Mitteilungsblatt

Dtsch Ges Tech Zusammenarb Schriftenr — Deutsche Gesellschaft fuer Technische Zusammenarbeit. Schriftenreihe

Dtsch Gesundheitsw — Deutsche Gesundheitswesen

Dtsch Gesundheitswes — Deutsche Gesundheitswesen

Dtsch Ges Wiss Angew Kosmet Symp — Deutsche Gesellschaft fuer Wissenschaftliche und Angewandte Kosmetik. Symposium

Dtsch Gewaesserkd Mitt — Deutsche Gewaesserkundliche Mitteilungen

Dtsch Goldschmiede Z — Deutsche Goldschmiede-Zeitung

Dtsch Haematologenkongr — Deutscher Haematologenkongress

Dtsch Handels Arch — Deutsches Handels-Archiv

Dtsch Hebe Foerdertech — Deutsche Hebe und Foerdertechnik

Dtsch Hydrogr Inst Jahresber — Deutsches Hydrographisches Institut. Jahresbericht

Dtsch Hydrogr Z — Deutsche Hydrographische Zeitschrift

Dtsch Inst Weiterbild Med Tech Assist J — Deutsches Institut zur Weiterbildung Medizinisch-Technischer Assistenten. Journal

Dtsch Inst Wirtschaftsforsch Wochenber — Deutsches Institut fuer Wirtschaftsforschung. Wochenbericht

Dtsch Kaelte Klimatech Ver Abh — Deutscher Kaelte und Klimatechnischer Verein. Abhandlungen

Dtsch Kaelte Klimatech Ver DKV Statusber — Deutscher Kaelte- und Klimatechnischer Verein. DKV-Statusbericht

Dtsch Kaelte Klimatech Ver Tagungsber — Deutscher Kaelte- und Klimatechnischer Verein-Tagungsbericht

Dtsch Kaeltetech Ver Abh — Deutscher Kaeltetechnischer Verein. Abhandlungen

Dtsch Kautsch Ges Vortragstag Dok — Deutsche Kautschuk-Gesellschaft Vortragstagung. Dokumenten

Dtsch Kautsch Ges Vortragstag Vortr — Deutsche Kautschuk-Gesellschaft Vortragstagung. Vortraege

Dtsch Keram Ges Ber — Deutsche Keramische Gesellschaft. Berichte

Dtsch Keram Ges Fachausschussber — Deutsche Keramische Gesellschaft Fachausschussbericht

Dtsch Kongr Perinat Med — Deutscher Kongress fuer Perinatale Medizin

Dtsch Kraftfahrtforsch Strassenverkehrstech — Deutsche Kraftfahrtforschung Strassenverkehrstechnik

Dtsch Krankenpflegez — Deutsche Krankenpflegezeitschrift

Dtsch Kunstseiden Ztg Spezialorgan Zellwolle — Deutsche Kunstseiden Zeitung und Spezialorgan fuer Zellwolle

Dtsch Landtech Z — Deutsche Landtechnische Zeitschrift

Dtsch Landwirtsch — Deutsche Landwirtschaft

Dtsch Landwirtsch Ges Mitt — Deutsche Landwirtschafts-Gesellschaft Mitteilungen

Dtsch Landwirtsch Rundsch — Deutsche Landwirtschaftliche Rundschau

Dtsch Landwirtsch Tierz — Deutsche Landwirtschaftliche Tierzucht

Dtsch Lebensm Rundsch — Deutsche Lebensmittel Rundschau

Dtsch Licht Wasserfach Ztg — Deutsche Licht- und Wasserfach Zeitung

Dtsch Luftfahrt Raumfahrt Forschungsber — Deutsche Luft- und Raumfahrt. Forschungsbericht

Dtsch Luftfahrt Raumfahrt Mitt — Deutsche Luft- und Raumfahrt. Mitteilung

Dtsch Luft Raumfahrt Mitt — Deutsche Luft- und Raumfahrt. Mitteilung

Dtsch Luftwacht Luftwissen — Deutsche Luftwacht. Ausgabe Luftwissen

Dtschl-Union-Dienst — Deutschland-Union-Dienst

Dtsch Mech Ztg — Deutsche Mechaniker-Zeitung

Dtsch Med Forsch — Deutsche Medizinische Forschung

Dtsch Med J — Deutsches Medizinisches Journal

Dtsch Med Wochenschr — Deutsche Medizinische Wochenschrift

Dtsch Med Wochenschr Sonderbeil — Deutsche Medizinische Wochenschrift. Sonderbeilage

Dtsch Med Wschr — Deutsche Medizinische Wochenschrift

Dtsch Metallwaren Ind — Deutsche Metallwaren Industrie

Dtsch Meteorol Tag — Deutsche Meteorologen-Tagung

Dtsch Milchwirtsch — Deutsche Milchwirtschaft

Dtsch Milchwirtsch (Gelsenkirchen) — Deutsche Milchwirtschaft (Gelsenkirchen)

Dtsch Milchwirtsch (Leipzig) — Deutsche Milchwirtschaft (Leipzig)

Dtsch Mineralwasser Ztg — Deutsche Mineralwasser-Zeitung

Dtsch Molkerei Ztg — Deutsche Molkerei-Zeitung

Dtsch Molk Fettwirtsch — Deutsche Molkerei- und Fettwirtschaft

Dtsch Molk Ztg — Deutsche Molkerei-Zeitung

Dtsch Mot Z — Deutsche Motor-Zeitschrift

Dtsch Muellerei — Deutsche Muellerei

Dtsch Mus Abh Ber — Deutsches Museum. Abhandlungen und Berichte

Dtsch Nahrungsm Rundsch — Deutsche Nahrungsmittel. Rundschau

Dtsch Ophthalmol Ges Ber — Deutsche Ophthalmologische Gesellschaft. Bericht

Dtsch Ophthalmol Ges Heidelberg Ber Zusammenkunft — Deutsche Ophthalmologische Gesellschaft in Heidelberg. Bericht ueber die Zusammenkunft

Dtsch Optikerztg — Deutsche Optikerzeitung

Dtsch Opt Wochenschr Cent Ztg Opt Mech — Deutsche Optische Wochenschrift und Central-Zeitung fuer Optik und Mechanik

Dtsch Opt Wochenschrift — Deutsche Optische Wochenschrift

Dtsch Papierwirtsch — Deutsche Papierwirtschaft

Dtsch Parfuem Ztg — Deutsche Parfuemerie-Zeitung

Dtsch Pelztierz — Deutsche Pelztierzuchter

Dtsch Pflanzenschutz Tag — Deutsche Pflanzenschutz-Tagung

Dtsch Roheisen — Deutsches Roheisen

Dtsch Schiffahrtsarch — Deutsches Schiffahrtsarchiv

Dtsch Schwarzbunte — Deutsche Schwarzbunte

Dtsch Schwed Symp Photomed Verhandlungsber — Deutsch-Schwedisches Symposion ueber Photomedizin. Verhandlungsbericht

Dtsch Skand Symp — Deutsch-Skandinavisches Symposium

Dtsch Sonnenforum — Deutsches Sonnenforum

Dtsch Sow Arbeitstag Fragen Strahlenschutzes — Deutsch-Sowjetische Arbeitstagung zu Fragen des Strahlenschutzes

Dtsch Sportaerztekongr — Deutscher Sportaerztekongress

Dtsch Stomatol — Deutsche Stomatologie

Dtsch Symp O Beta Hydroxyethyl Rutoside — Deutsches Symposium ueber O-(Beta-Hydroxyethyl)-Rutoside

Dtsch Tab Ztg — Deutsche Tabak Zeitung

Dtsch Tech — Deutsche Technik

Dtsch Textilgewerbe — Deutsche Textilgewerbe

Dtsch Textiltech — Deutsche Textiltechnik

Dtsch Textilwirtsch — Deutsche Textilwirtschaft

Dtsch Tieraerztl Wochenschr — Deutsche Tieraerztliche Wochenschrift

Dtsch Tieraerztl Wochenschr Beil Lebensmitteltierarzt — Deutsche Tieraerztliche Wochenschrift. Beilage. Lebensmitteltierarzt

Dtsch Tieraerztl Wochenschr Tieraerztl Rundsch — Deutsche Tieraerztliche Wochenschrift Tieraerztliche Rundschau

Dtsch Tierarztebl — Deutsches Tierarzteblatt

Dtsch Toepfer Ziegler Ztg — Deutsche Toepfer und Ziegler Zeitung

Dtsch Tropenmed Z — Deutsche Tropenmedizinische Zeitschrift

Dtsch Tuberk Bl — Deutsches Tuberkulose-Blatt

Dtsch Verb Schweisstech Ber — Deutscher Verband fuer Schweisstechnik. Berichte

Dtsch Verb Wasserwirtsch Kulturbau Mater — Deutscher Verband fuer Wasserwirtschaft und Kulturbau. Materialien

Dtsch Verb Wasserwirtsch Kulturbau Schriftenr — Deutscher Verband fuer Wasserwirtschaft und Kulturbau. Schriftenreihe

Dtsch Ver Gas Wasserfaches Schriftenr Wasser — Deutscher Verein des Gas- und Wasserfaches. Schriftenreihe. Wasser

Dtsch Ver Gas Wasserfachmaennern Schriften Gas — Deutscher Verein von Gas- und Wasserfachmaennern. Schriftenreihe. Gas

Dtsch Versuchsanst Luft Raumfahrt Ber — Deutsche Versuchsanstalt fuer Luft- und Raumfahrt. Bericht

Dtsch Verwaltungsbl Verwaltungsarch — Deutsches Verwaltungsblatt und Verwaltungsarchiv

Dtsch Veterinaermed Ges Tag Arbeitsgeb Lebensmittelhyg — Deutsche Veterinaermedizinische Gesellschaft. Tagung des Arbeitsgebietes Lebensmittelhygiene

Dt Schwed Jb — Deutsch-Schwedisches Jahrbuch

Dtsch Weinbau — Deutsche Weinbau

Dtsch Weinbau Wiss Beih — Deutsche Weinbau. Wissenschaftliche Beihefte

Dtsch Wein Ztg — Deutsche Wein-Zeitung

Dtsch Wirker Ztg — Deutsche Wirker Zeitung

Dtsch Wiss Ges Erdoel Erdgas Kohle Ber — Deutsche Wissenschaftliche Gesellschaft fuer Erdoel, Erdgas, und Kohle. Berichte

Dtsch Wiss Ges Erdoel Erdgas Kohle Ber Tagungsber — Deutsche Wissenschaftliche Gesellschaft fuer Erdoel, Erdgas,und Kohle. Berichte. Tagungsbericht

Dtsch Wiss Komm Meeresforsch Ber — Deutsche Wissenschaftliche Kommission fuer Meeresforschung. Berichte

Dtsch Wollen Gewerbe — Deutsche Wollen Gewerbe

Dtsch Wollforschungsinst Tech Hochsch Aachen Schriftenr — Deutsches Wollforschungsinstitut an der Technischen Hochschule Aachen. Schriftenreihe

Dtsch Zahnaerztl Wochenschr — Deutsche Zahnaerztliche Wochenschrift

Dtsch Zahnaerztl Z — Deutsche Zahnaerztliche Zeitschrift

Dtsch Zahn- Mund- Kieferheilkd — Deutsche Zahn- Mund- und Kieferheilkunde

Dtsch Zahn Mund Kieferheilkd Zentralbl Gesamte — Deutsche Zahn-, Mund-, und Kieferheilkunde mit Zentralblatt fuer die Gesamte Zahn-, Mund-, und Kieferheilkunde

Dtsch Z Chir — Deutsche Zeitschrift fuer Chirurgie

Dtsch Zentralbl Krankenpfl — Deutsches Zentralblatt fuer Krankenpflege

Dtsch Z Gesamte Gerichtl Med — Deutsche Zeitschrift fuer die Gesamte Gerichtliche Medizin

Dtsch Z Mund Kiefer Gesichtschir — Deutsche Zeitschrift fuer Mund-, Kiefer-, und Gesichtschirurgie

Dtsch Z Nervenheilkd — Deutsche Zeitschrift fuer Nervenheilkunde

Dtsch Zool Ges Verh — Deutsche Zoologische Gesellschaft. Verhandlungen

Dtsch Z Sportmed — Deutsche Zeitschrift fuer Sportmedizin

Dtsch Zuckerind — Deutsche Zuckerindustrie

Dtsch Z Verdau Stoffwechselkr — Deutsche Zeitschrift fuer Verdauungs- und Stoffwechselkrankheiten

Dtsch Z Verdau Stoffwechselkrankh — Deutsche Zeitschrift fuer Verdauungs- und Stoffwechselkrankheiten

DTS Direct — DTS [Digital Termination Systems] Directory

DTSERD — Driver and Traffic Safety Education Research Digest

Dt Statist Zbl — Deutsches Statistisches Zentralblatt

Dt Stud — Deutsche Studien

Dt Studien — Deutsche Studien

Dt Suedpolarexp — Deutsche Suedpolarexpedition

DTT — Dansk Teologisk Tidsskrift

Dt Texte Mittelalt — Deutsche Texte des Mittelalters

Dt Th — Deutsche Theologie

DTTIAF — Deutsche Tieraerztliche Wochenschrift

DTTid — Dansk Teologisk Tidsskrift

Dt Tieraerztl Wschr — Deutsche Tieraerztliche Wochenschrift

Dt Tonkuenstlerztg — Deutsche Tonkuenstlerzeitung

DTTP — Documents to the People

Dt Tub Bl — Deutsches Tuberkulose-Blatt

Dt Univ Ztg — Deutsche Universitaetszeitung

Dt Unterr — Deutschunterricht. Arbeitshefte zu Seiner Praktischen Gestaltung

D Tur Aa — Turistforeningen for Danmark. Aarbog

Dt Verw Bl — Deutsches Verwaltungsblatt

DtVis — Deutsche Vierteljahrsschrift fuer Literaturwissenschaft und Geistesgeschichte

Dt Vischr — Deutsche Vierteljahrsschrift fuer Literaturwissenschaft und Geistesgeschichte

Dt Vjschr Lit Wiss Geistesgesch — Deutsche Vierteljahresschrift fuer Literaturwissenschaft und Geistesgeschichte

Dt Vlkskal — Deutscher Volkskalender

DTW — Deutsche Technische Warte

DTW — DTW. Deutsche Tieraerztliche Wochenschrift

Dt Waldenser — Deutsche Waldenser

Dt Wass Wirt — Deutsche Wasserwirtschaft

DTWBA9 — Deutsche Weinbau

DTW Dtsch Tierarztl Wochenschr — DTW. Deutsche Tierarztliche Wochenschrift

Dt Wein Rd — Deutsche Weinrundschau

Dt Wein Zt — Deutsche Weinzeitung

Dt Wirtinst Forschhft — Deutsches Wirtschaftsinstitut Forschungshefte

Dt Wiss Z Polen — Deutsche Wissenschaftliche Zeitschrift fuer Polen

Dt Wiss Z Warthel — Deutsche Wissenschaftliche Zeitschrift im Wartheland

Dt Wochenbl — Deutsches Wochenblatt

DTZ — Deutsche Tonkuenstlerzeitung

Dt Zahnaerztebl — Deutsches Zahnaerzteblatt

Dt Zahnhkd — Deutsche Zahnheilkunde

Dt Z Chir — Deutsche Zeitschrift fuer Chirurgie

Dt Z f Ph — Deutsche Zeitschrift fuer Philosophie

D T Zg — Deutsche Tiefbauzeitung

Dt Z Maltechnik — Deutsche Zeitschrift fuer Maltechnik

Dt Z Philos — Deutsche Zeitschrift fuer Philosophie

Dt Zs Akup — Deutsche Zeitschrift fuer Akupunktur

Dt Zs Geschwiss — Deutsche Zeitschrift fuer Geschichtswissenschaft

Dt Zs Philos — Deutsche Zeitschrift fuer Philosophie

Dt Ztg — Deutsche Zeitung

DU — Dansk Udsyn

DU — Deutschunterricht

DUA — Deutschunterricht fuer Auslaender

DUABA8 — Delaware. Agricultural Experiment Station. Bulletin

DUBID3 — Dutch Birding

Dublin Bldr — Dublin Builder

Dublin Hist Rec — Dublin Historical Record

Dublin J — Dublin Journal

Dublin J Med Sci — Dublin Journal of Medical Science

Dublin Mag — Dublin Magazine

Dublin Med Press — Dublin Medical Press

Dublin Pen — Dublin Penny Journal

Dublin Philos J Sci Rev — Dublin Philosophical Journal and Scientific Review

Dublin Q J Med Sc — Dublin Quarterly Journal of Medical Science

Dublin Q J Sc — Dublin Quarterly Journal of Science

Dublin Qtr J Med Sci — Dublin Quarterly Journal of Medical Science

Dublin Quart J Med Sci — Dublin Quarterly Journal of Medical Science

Dublin R — Dublin Review

DublinRev — Dublin Review

Dublin ULJ — Dublin University. Law Journal

Dublin UL Rev — Dublin University. Law Review

Dublin Univ Bot Sch Trinity Coll Notes — Dublin University. Botanical School of Trinity College. Notes

Dublin Univ Law Rev — Dublin University Law Review

Dublin U Rev — Dublin University Review

Dubl J Med Sci — Dublin Journal of Medical Science

Dubl Mag — Dublin Magazine

Dubl Re — Dublin Review

Dubl R S J — Journal of the Royal Dublin Society

Dubl S J — Transactions and Journal of the Dublin Society

Dubl S Sc P — Scientific Proceedings of the Royal Dublin Society

Dubl S Sc T — Scientific Transactions of the Royal Dublin Society

Dubl S T — Transactions and Journal of the Dublin Society

Dubl Univ Mag — Dublin University Magazine

DUBMAC — Deutsche Baumschule

Dub Mag — Dublin Magazine

DubR — Dublin Review

Dub Rev — Dublin Review

DUBSDX — Dhaka University Studies. Part B

Dub Univ — Dublin University Magazine

D Ud — Dansk Udsyn

DuD Fachbeitr — DuD Fachbeitraege

Dudley Ednl J — Dudley Educational Journal

Dudley Obs Rep — Dudley Observatory Reports

DuE — Dichtung und Erkenntnis

Duelmener Hb — Duelmener Heimatblaetter

DUEMEV — Directory of Unpublished Experimental Mental Measures

Dueng Ernte — Duengung und Ernte

Duer Gesch Bl — Duerener Geschichtsblaetter

Duesseldorfer Jahrb — Duesseldorfer Jahrbuch

DuessJ — Duesseldorfer Jahrbuch

Duf Bently Rep — Duffy and Bently Report

Duinen — De Duinen. Bulletin du Centre Scientifique et Culturel de l'Abbaye des Dunes et du Westhoek

Duits Geog Bl — Duits Geographische Blaetter

Duits Q — Duits Quarterly

DUJ — Durham University. Journal

DUKAB — Dopovidi Akademii Nauk Ukrains'koi RSR. Seriya A. Fiziko-Tekhnichni ta Matematichni Nauki

Duke BAJ — Duke Bar Association. Journal

Duke BA Jo — Duke University Bar Association. Journal

Duke Bar J — Duke Bar Journal

Duke B Assn J — Duke Bar Association. Journal

Duke B J — Duke Bar Journal

Duke Div R — Duke Divinity School. Review

Duke Law J — Duke Law Journal

Duke L J — Duke Law Journal

Duke Math J — Duke Mathematical Journal

Dukes Physiol Domest Anim — Dukes' Physiology of Domestic Animals

Duke Univ Hist Pap — Duke University Historical Papers

Duke Univ Lib Newsl — Duke University Library Newsletter

Duke Univ Mar Stn Bull — Duke University. Marine Station Bulletin

Duke Univ Math Ser — Duke University Mathematics Series

Duke Univ Pub — Duke University Publications

DUKRA — Dopovidi Akademii Nauk Ukrains'koi RSR

Du Kunstz — Du Kunstzeitschrift

Dulcimer — Dulcimer Players News

Du LJ — Duke Law Journal

DULN — Duke University Library Notes

DULR — Dublin University. Law Review

DULR — Duquesne University. Law Review

DUM — Dublin University Magazine

Dumbarton Oaks Pap — Dumbarton Oaks Papers

Dumbarton OP — Dumbarton Oaks Papers

DumbOaksP — Dumbarton Oaks Papers

Dumb Pap — Dumbarton Oaks Papers

Dumfriesshire Galloway Nat Hist Antiq Soc Trans — Dumfriesshire and Galloway Natural History Antiquarian Society. Transactions

DUMJA — Duke Mathematical Journal

DUMP HEAP — Journal of Diverse Unsung Miracle Plants for Healthy Evolution among People

DUN — Dun's Business Month

Dunai Vasmu Musz Gazdasagi Kozl — Dunai Vasmu Muszaki-Gazdasagi Kozlemenyei

DUNDIS — Directory of United Nations Databases and Information Systems

Dunl (Ct of Sess) — Dunlop, Bell, and Murray's Scotch Court of Session Cases, Second Series

DunR — [The] Dunwoodie Review

Duns — Dun's Business Month

Dun's — Dun's Review

Duns Bus M — Dun's Business Month

Dun's Bus Mon — Dun's Business Month

Dun's Int R — Dun's International Review
Dun's R — Dun's Review
Duns Rev — Dun's Review
Dun's Stat R — Dun's Statistical Review
DUODA — Duodecim
DUODAG — Duodecim
Duodecim Suppl — Duodecim. Supplementum
DuPage Busi — DuPage Woodfield Business News
DUPMA — Du Pont Magazine
DuPont — DuPont Magazine
Du Pont Mag — Du Pont Magazine
Du Pont Mag Eur Edn — Du Pont Magazine. European Edition
Du Pont Mod Met Finish — Du Pont Modern Metal Finishing
Du Pont Tech Bull — Du Pont Technical Bulletin
DUPR — Dialogo (Puerto Rico)
Duq — Duquesne Law Review
Duq LR — Duquesne Law Review
Duq L Rev — Duquesne Law Review
Duq R — Duquesne Review
Duquesne L Rev — Duquesne Law Review
Duquesne Sci Couns — Duquesne Science Counselor
Duquesne U L Rev — Duquesne University. Law Review
DuR — Dublin Review
DuR — Durham Research Review
Durabilite Betons Colloq Int Rapp Prelim — Durabilite des Betons. Colloque International. Rapport Preliminaire
Durabilite Betons Rapp — Durabilite des Betons. Rapport
Durability Adhes Bonded Struct — Durability of Adhesive Bonded Structures
Durability Aging Geosynth Pap — Durability and Aging of Geosynthetics. Papers
Durability Build Mater — Durability of Building Materials
Durability Concr Final Rep — Durability of Concrete. Final Report
Durability Concr Int Conf — Durability of Concrete. International Conference
Durability Concr Int Symp Prelim Rep — Durability of Concrete. International Symposium. Preliminary Report
Durability Concr Prelim Rep — Durability of Concrete. Preliminary Report
Durability Concr Proc Symp — Durability of Concrete. Proceedings. Symposium
Durban Mus Art Gallery Annu Rep — Durban Museum and Art Gallery. Annual Report
Durban Mus Novit — Durban Museum Novitates
Durener Geschbl — Durener Geschichtsblaetter
Durferrit Hausmitt — Durferrit Hausmitteilungen
Durham Res — Durham Research Review
Durham Univ — Durham University. Journal
Durham Univ Biol Soc J — Durham University Biological Society. Journal
Durham Univ Dep Geogr Occas Publ New Ser — Durham University. Department of Geography. Occasional Publications. New Series
Durham Univ J — Durham University. Journal
Durham Un Ph S P — Proceedings of the University of Durham Philosophical Society
Durlacher Tagbl — Durlacher Tagblatt
Dur Newc Res Rev — Durham and Newcastle Research Review
DurU — Durham University Journal
DurUJ — Durham University. Journal
Durvoobrab Mebelna Promst — Durvoobrabotvashta i Mebelna Promishlenost
Durzh Inst Kontrol Lek Sredstva Izv — Durzhaven Institut za Kontrol na Lekarstveni Sredstva. Izvestiya
Durzh Vestn — Durzhaven Vestnik
DUS — Dacca University. Studies
Dusanbin Gos Ped Inst Ucen Zap — Dusanbinskii Gosudarstvennyi Pedagogiceskii Institut Imeni T. G. Sevcenko Ucenyi Zapiski
DUSEA5 — Dusenia
Dushanb Gos Pedagog Inst im T G Shevchenko Uch Zap — Dushanbinskii Gosudarstvennyi Pedagogicheskii Institut imeni T. G. Shevchenko. Uchenye Zapiski
Dusseldorf Jb — Dusseldorfer Jahrbuch
Dusseldorf Kultkal — Dusseldorfer Kulturkalender
Dusseldorf Monatshefte — Dusseldorfer Monatshefte
Dust Top — Dust Topics
Du Sz — Dunantuli Szemle
DuszpPZ — Duszpasterz Polski Zagranica
Dut A & Archit Today — Dutch Art and Architecture Today
Dutch Art & Archre Today — Dutch Art and Architecture Today
Dutch Boy Painter Mag — Dutch Boy Painter Magazine
Dutch Boy Q — Dutch Boy Quarterly
Dutchess Co Hist Soc Yr Bk — Dutchess County Historical Society. Year Book
Dutch Nitrogenous Fert Rev — Dutch Nitrogenous Fertilizer Review
Dutch Q Rev — Dutch Quarterly Review of Anglo-American Letters
DutchS — Dutch Studies
Dutch Settlers Soc Albany Yr Bk — Dutch Settlers Society of Albany. Year Book
Dutch S (The Hague Netherlands) — Dutch Studies (The Hague, Netherlands)
Dut Crossing — Dutch Crossing
DuU — Durham University Journal
DUULD5 — Annual Research Reviews. Duodenal Ulcer
DuV — Dichtung und Volkstum
Duv & Boc — Collection Complete, Decrets, Ordonnances, Reglements, et Avis duConseil d'Etat (Duvergier et Bocquet)
DuW — Dichtung und Wirklichkeit
Duxbury Ser Statist Decis Sci — Duxbury Series in Statistics and Decision Sciences
DUZ — Deutsche Universitaetszeitung
DV — David
DV — Deutsche Vierteljahrsschrift
DV — Dichtung und Volkstum
DV — Dieu Vivant
DVA — Development and Change

DVA — Directory of Visual Arts Organizations
DVASA — Doklady Vsesoyuznoi Akademii Sel'skokhozyaistvennykh Nauk Imeni V. I. Lenina
DVBSA3 — Developments in Biological Standardization
DVCBAP — Developmental and Cell Biology
DVDSAD — Davidsonia
DVE — Developing Economies
DVEC-A — Developing Economies
D Vejt — Dansk Vejtidsskrift
DVENA3 — Dermatologiya i Venerologiya
D Vet — Dansk Veterinaer Tidsskrift
DVGW Schriftenr Gas — DVGW [*Deutscher Verein Gas- und Wasserfachmaenner*] -Schriftenreihe. Gas
DVGW Schriftenr Wasser — DVGW-Schriftenreihe. Wasser
DVI — Development Forum. Business Edition
Dvigateli Vnutr Sgoraniya (Kharkov) — Dvigateli Vnutrennego Sgoraniya (Kharkov)
Dvigateli Vnutr Sgoraniya Omsk — Dvigateli Vnutrennego Sgoraniya (Omsk)
D Vildtf — Dansk Vildtforskning
DVIOJ — Deutsche Vereinigung fuer die Interessen der Osteuropaeischen Juden
Dvizhenie Geterog Sred Silnykh Magn Polyakh — Dvizhenie Geterogennykh Sred v Sil'nykh Magnitnykh Polyakh
DVJB — Danmarks Veterinaer- og Jordbrugsbase
DVJS — Deutsche Vierteljahrsschrift fuer Literaturwissenschaft und Geistesgeschichte
D Vjschr Gsndhpfl — Deutsche Vierteljahrsschrift fuer Oeffentliche Gesundheitspflege
DVK — De Duisburgse Vrachtkonvenie
DVLG — Deutsche Vierteljahrsschrift fuer Literaturwissenschaft und Geistesgeschichte
DVM — De Vierde Macht
DVMMB7 — Datenverarbeitung in der Medizin
DVN — Dan Viet Nam
DVo — Deutsches Volkstum. Monatsschrift fuer das Deutsche Geistesleben
Dvoinoi Sloi Adsorbts Tverd Elektrodakh — Dvoinoi Sloi i Adsorbtsiya na Tverdykh Elektrodakh
DVPMAL — Developmental Psychology. Monograph
DVPSD8 — Developments in Plant and Soil Sciences
DVS — Development Forum
DVSB — Danske Videnskabernes Selskabs Biologiske. Skrifter
DVS Ber — DVS [*Deutscher Verband fuer Schweisstechnik*] Berichte
DVSBM — Kongelige Danske Videnskabernes Selskab. Biologiske Meddelelser
DVSHFM — Kongelige Danske Videnskabernes Selskab Historisk-Filologiske Meddelelser
DVSM — Det Kongelige Danske Videnskabernes Selskab. Historisk-Filologiske Meddelelser
DVSS — Danske Videnskabernes Selskabs Skrifter
DVT — Dejiny Ved a Techniky
DVT-Dejiny Ved a Techniky — Dejiny Ved a Techniky. Spolecnost pro Dejiny Ved a Techniky
DVWK Mater — DVWK (Deutscher Verband fuer Wasserwirtschaft und Kulturbau) Materialien
DVZ Dtsch Verkehrs-Ztg — DVZ Deutsche Verkehrs-Zeitung
DW — Dahlmann-Waitz. Quellenkunde der Deutschen Geschichte
DW — Deutsche Woche
DW — Die Welt
DW — Die Weltliteratur
DWA — Denkschriften der Oesterreichischen Akademie der Wissenschaften. Philosophisch-Historische Klasse
DW & RB — Daily Weather and River Bulletin
DWB — Deutsche Warande en Belfort
DWb — Deutsche Weinbau
DWD — Deutsche Wissenschaftlicher Dienst
DWD — Dream World
DWEV — Deutsche Wissenschaft, Erziehung, und Volksbildung
DWI — Die Welt des Islams
Dwights J Mus — Dwight's Journal of Music
DWINAU — Defenders of Wildlife News
DWLIAU — Defenders of Wildlife Magazine [*Later, Defenders*]
DWS — Developments in Water Science
DWZP — Deutsche Wissenschaftliche Zeitschrift fuer Polen
DY — Demography
Dyason House Pap — Dyason House Papers
Dyason H P — Dyason House Papers
DYB — Dynamic Business
DYE — Demografia y Economia
Dye Ind — Dyeing Industry
Dyeing Finish Nippon Senshoku Kako Kenkyukai — Dyeing and Finishing. Nippon Senshoku Kako Kenkyukai
Dyeing Ind — Dyeing Industry
Dyeing Res (Kyoto) — Dyeing Research (Kyoto)
Dyer Text Printer Bleacher Finish — Dyer, Textile Printer, Bleacher, and Finisher
Dyes Chem Tech Bull — Dyes and Chemicals Technical Bulletin. Paper Industry Issue
Dyes Chem Tech Bull Pap Ind Issue — Dyes and Chemicals Technical Bulletin. Paper Industry Issue
Dyes Hist & Archaeol Textiles — Dyes on Historical and Archaeological Textiles
Dyes Pigm — Dyes and Pigments
Dyest Chem — Dyestuffs and Chemicals
Dyn — Dynamite
Dynam Contin Discrete Impuls Systems — Dynamics of Continuous, Discrete, and Impulsive Systems
Dynam Control — Dynamics and Control
Dynamic Econom Theory and Appl — Dynamic Economics. Theory and Applications

Dynam Psych — Dynamische Psychiatrie

Dynam Report Expositions Dynam Systems NS — Dynamics Reported. Expositions in Dynamical Systems (New Series)

Dynam Systems Appl — Dynamic Systems and Applications

Dynatech Rep — Dynatech Report

Dyn Atmos & Oceans — Dynamics of Atmospheres and Oceans

Dyn Brain Edema Pro Int Workshop — Dynamics of Brain Edema. Proceedings of the International Workshop on Dynamic Aspects of Cerebral Edema

Dyn Control — Dynamics and Control

Dyn Heavy Ion Collisions Proc Adriat Europhys Study Conf — Dynamics of Heavy-Ion Collisions. Proceedings. Adriatic EurophysicsStudy Conference

Dyn Magn Fluctuations High Temp Supercond — Dynamics of Magnetic Fluctuations in High-Temperature Superconductors

Dyn Mass Spectrom — Dynamic Mass Spectrometry

Dyn Membr Assem — Dynamics of Membrane Assembly

Dyn Mol Cryst Proc Int Meet Soc Fr Chem Div Chim Phys — Dynamics of Molecular Crystals. Proceedings. International Meeting. Societe Francaise de Chemie. Division de Chimie Physique

Dyn Ovarian Funct Bienn Ovary Workshop — Dynamics of Ovarian Function. Biennial Ovary Workshop

Dyn Processes Ordering Solid Surf Proc Taniguchi Symp — Dynamical Processes and Ordering on Solid Surfaces. Proceedings. Taniguchi Symposium

Dyn Processes Solid State Opt Tokyo Summer Inst Theor Phys — Dynamical Processes in Solid State Optics. Tokyo Summer Institute ofTheoretical Physics

Dyn Prop Solids — Dynamical Properties of Solids

Dyn Psychiatr — Dynamische Psychiatrie

Dyn Psychiatry — Dynamic Psychiatry

Dyn Solids Liq Neutron Scattering (1977) — Dynamics of Solids and Liquids by Neutron Scattering (1977)

Dyn Stab Syst — Dynamics and Stability of Systems

Dyn Star Clusters Proc Symp Int Astron Union — Dynamics of Star Clusters. Proceedings. Symposium. International Astronomical Union

Dyn Supervision — Dynamic Supervision

D Y Ph — Danish Yearbook of Philosophy

DYPSAQ — Dynamic Psychiatry

DYPSAQ — Dynamische Psychiatrie

Dyreven — Dyrevennen

Dysmorphol Annu Rev Birth Defects — Dysmorphology. Annual Review of Birth Defects

Dysmorphol Clin Gen — Dysmorphology and Clinical Genetics

DYSUD — Dynamic Supervision

Dyv — Dyrevennen

DYWIDAG Ber — DYWIDAG [*Dyckerhoff und Widmann AG*] Berichte

DZ — Dermatologische Zeitschrift

DZCW — Deutsche Zeitschrift fuer Christliche Wissenschaft und Christliches Leben

DzD — Dzejas Diena

DZfKr — Deutsche Zeitschrift fuer Kirchenrecht

DZGGAK — Deutsche Zeitschrift fuer die Gesamte Gerichtliche Medizin

DZGW — Deutsche Zeitschrift fuer Geschichtswissenschaft

DZI — Zuckerindustrie. Landwirtschaft, Technik, Chemie, Wirtschaft

Dziennik Roln — Dziennik Rolniczy

DzKarSt — Dzveli Kartuli Enis K'atedris Stomebi

DZKR — Deutsche Zeitschrift fuer Kirchenrecht

Dz Lit — Dziennik Literacki

DZMKAS — Deutsche Zahn- Mund- und Kieferheilkunde

DZNEAF — Deutsche Zeitschrift fuer Nervenheilkunde

DZ Nh — Deutsche Zeitschrift fuer Nervenheilkunde

D Zoll B — Deutsche Zollbeamte

Dz P — Dziennik Polski

DZ Ph — Deutsche Zeitschrift fuer Philosophie

DZ Ph B — Deutsche Zeitschrift fuer Philosophie. Beiheft

DZRw — Dorpater Zeitschrift fuer Rechtswissenschaft

D Zs N Hk — Deutsche Zeitschrift fuer Nervenheilkunde

DZT — Deutsche Zeitschrift

DZT — Deutsche Zeitung

D Z Thmd — Deutsche Zeitschrift fuer Thiermedicin und Vergleichende Pathologie

DZTK — Dorpater Zeitschrift fuer Theologie und Kirche

Dz Ust — Dziennik Ustaw

Dz Z — Dziennik Zachodni

DZZEA — Deutsche Zahnaerztliche Zeitschrift

DZZEA7 — Deutsche Zahnaerztliche Zeitschrift

E

E — Economist
E — Einheit
E — Encounter
E — English
E — Eolus. A Review for New Music
E — Eos. Commentarii Societatis Philologae Polonorum
E — Erasmus
E — Escorial
E — Esploratore
E — Esprit
E — Ethnohistory
E — Ethnos
E — Etnografija
E — Europa
EA — Eastern Anthropologist
E A — Eastern Art
EA — Economica
EA — Economie Appliquee
EA — Efrydiau Athronyddol
EA — Eidgenoessische Abschiede
EA — Ekklesiastike Aletheia
EA — El-Amarna Tafeln. Vorderasiatische Bibliothek
EA — Encyclopaedia Americana
EA — Enkomi-Alasia. Publications. Mission Archeologique Francaise et de la Mission du Gouvernement de Chypre a Enkomi
EA — Environmental Abstracts
EA — Ephemeris Archaiologike
EA — Erbe und Auftrag
EA — Estudios Afrocubanos
EA — Estudios Americanos
EA — Etudes Anglaises
EA — Etudes Asiatiques
EA — Europa-Archiv. Europaeischer Austauschdienst
EA — Executive Agreement. US State Department Series
EAA — Educational Administration Abstracts
EAA — Enciclopedia dell'Arte Antica, Classica, e Orientale
E Aa — Erhvervshistorisk Aarbog
EAA — Estudios de Arqueologia Alavesa
EAA — Estudos Anglo-Americanos
EAAED — Electrotehnica, Electronica, si Automatica. Seria Automatica si Electronica
EAAJA5 — East African Agricultural Journal
EAANAH — Eastern Anthropologist
EAAPAN — European Association for Animal Production. Publication
EAAP Publ — EAAP [European Association for Animal Production] Publication
EAASN — EAAS [European Association for American Studies] Newsletter
EAB — Era of Arnold Bennett
EAB — Quarterly Review of Economics and Business
EABH & B — Encyclopedia of American Business History and Biography
EABM — Erde und Auftrag. Benediktinische Monatsschrift. Erzabtei Beuroner Verlag
EABMD — Energy Advisory Bulletin for Texas Manufacturers
EABS — Euro Abstracts
EABUB — Electronic Applications Bulletin
E Abul — Estudios Abulenses
EAC — Enciclopedia di Autori Classici
EAC — Entretiens sur l'Antiquite Classique
EAC — EPRI [Electric Power Research Institute] Journal
EAC — Etudes d'Archeologie Classique
Ea Ch Qu — Eastern Churches Quarterly
EACS — East Asian Cultural Studies
EACSS — East Asian Cultural Studies Series
EAD — Explorations Archeologiques de Delos
EA Delos — Explorations Archeologiques de Delos
EADL — Erlanger Arbeiten zur Deutschen Literatur
EADT — East Anglia Daily Times
EaE — East European Quarterly
EAE — Economic Bulletin for Asia and the Pacific
EAE — Excavaciones Arqueologicas en Espana
EAECA — Eastern Economist
EAEG — Ergebnisse der Anatomie und Entwicklungsgeschichte
EAEHL — Encyclopaedia of Archaeological Excavations in the Holy Land
EAENA3 — Advances in Anatomy, Embryology, and Cell Biology
EAER — Eastern Africa Economic Review
EAEWAU — Edinburgh School of Agriculture. Experimental Work
EAf — Estudios Afrocubanos

EAF — Ethnographisch-Archaeologische Forschungen
EAFJAU — East African Agricultural and Forestry Journal
EAFNA8 — East African Agriculture and Forestry Research Organization. Forestry TechnicalNote
EAFOAB — East African Common Services Organization. East African Marine Fisheries Research Organization. Annual Report
EAFOBC — East African Freshwater Fisheries Research Organization. Annual Report
E Afr Agr Forest J — East African Agricultural and Forestry Journal
E Afr Agric For J — East African Agricultural and Forestry Journal
E Afr Agric J — East African Agricultural Journal
E Afr Annu — East African Annual
E Afr Econ — Eastern Africa Economic Review
E Afr Ec Rev — East African Economic Review
E Afr Farmer Plant — East African Farmer and Planter
E Afric Agric & For J — East African Agricultural and Forestry Journal
E African Agric Forest J — East African Agricultural and Forestry Journal
E African LJ — East African Law Journal
E African M J — East African Medical Journal
E Afr J — East Africa Journal
E Afr J Rur Dev — East African Journal of Rural Development
E Afr Law J — East African Law Journal
E Afr Libr Ass Bull — East African Library Association Bulletin
E Afr Med J — East African Medical Journal
E Afr Mgmt J — East African Management Journal
E Afr Stud — East African Studies
E Afr Wildlife J — East African Wildlife Journal
E Afr Wildl J — East African Wildlife Journal
EAGAB9 — Escola de Agronomia da Amazonia. Boletim
EAGRD — Experimental Aging Research
EAH — Ergon tes Archaiologikes Hetaireias
EAH — Essex Archaeology and History
EAI — England-Amerika-Institut
EAIABJ — East African Institute for Medical Research. Annual Report
EAIND — Electronique et Applications Industrielles
EAIS — Columbia University. East Asian Institute. Studies
EAISR — East African Institute of Social Research Conference Papers
EAJ — East Africa Journal
EAJ Criminol — East African Journal of Criminology
EAJKAJ — East African Agricultural Journal of Kenya, Tanganyika, Uganda, and Zanzibar
EAL — Early American Literature
EAL — Eastern Anthropologist (Lucknow)
EAI — Erbe der Alten
EALJ — East African Law Journal
EALN — Early American Literature. Newsletter
EAL Rev — Eastern Africa Law Review
EAM — Electro-Acoustic Music
EAM — Enlace (Mexico)
EAm — Estudios Americanos
EAM — Estudos do Alto Minho
EAMG — Estudios Antropologicas Publicados en Homenaje al Doctor Manual Gamio [Mexico]
EAMJA — East African Medical Journal
EAMJAV — East African Medical Journal
EAmL — Early American Literature
EAMRAL — East African Common Services Organization. East African Institute for Medical Research. Annual Report
EAn — Etudes Anglaises
E & G — Eiszeitalter und Gegenwart. Jahrbuch der Deutschen Quartaervereinigung
E & Ger St — English and Germanic Studies
E and G Stud — English and Germanic Studies
E & H — Economy and History
E & ITV — Education and Industrial Television
E & M Jour — Engineering and Mining Journal
E & MM — Electronics & Music Maker Magazine
E & MR — Energy and Mineral Resources
E & MS Exp Stn Circ Pa State Univ — E & MS [Earth and Mineral Sciences Experiment Station] Experiment StationCircular. Pennsylvania State University
E & P — Editor and Publisher
E & S — Essays and Studies
E&S — Essays and Studies by Members of the English Association [Oxford]
E & Th — Eglise et Theologie
E & W — East and West
E Anglian — East Anglian
E Anglian Archaeol — East Anglian Archaeology

431

EANHAU — EANHS [*East Africa Natural History Society*] Bulletin
EANHS Bull — EANHS [*East Africa Natural History Society*] Bulletin
EA Nimes — Ecole Antique de Nimes. Bulletin Annuel
E Anth — Eastern Anthropologist
E Anthropol — Eastern Anthropologist
EANWA — Energieanwendung
EAO — Etudes d'Archeologie Orientale
EAORAV — East African Common Services Organization. East African Agricultural and Forestry Research Organization. Record of Research
EAP — Economie Appliquee
EAP — English Association Pamphlets
EAP — Estudios Andinos (Peru)
EAPD — EAP [*Employee Assistance Program*] Digest
EAPR — East Asian Pastoral Review
EAPR Abstr Conf Pap — EAPR [*European Association for Potato Research*] Abstracts of Conference Papers
EAPR Proc — EAPR Proceedings
EAPTA8 — INTA [*Instituto Nacional de Tecnologia Agropecuaria*]. Estacion Experimental Regional Agropecuaria . Informe Tecnico
EAQNA — Earthquake Notes
EAQR — Imperial and Asiatic Quarterly Review
EAQUDJ — Eau du Quebec
EAR — China Market
EAR — EAR. Edinburgh Architectural Research
Ear — Ear Magazine
EAR — Encyclopedia of American Religions
EARBL — Erbe und Auftrag der Reformation in den Boehmischen Laendern
EArch — Etudes Archeologiques
Ear Clin Int — Ear Clinics International
E A Rep — Eastern Art Report
Ear Hear — Ear and Hearing
Earlham Coll Sci Bull — Earlham College. Science Bulletin
Early Am L — Early American Literature
Early Am Lit — Early American Literature
Early Child Bull — Early Childhood Bulletin
Early Child Dev Care — Early Child Development and Care
Early Child Ed — Early Childhood Education
Early Diabetes Early Life Proc Int Symp — Early Diabetes in Early Life. Proceedings. International Symposium
Early Diabetes Int Symp — Early Diabetes. International Symposium on Early Diabetes
Early Eff Radiat DNA — Early Effects of Radiation on DNA
Early Engl Text Soc — Early English Text Society
Early Hum Dev — Early Human Development
Early Key J — Early Keyboard Journal
EarlyM — Early Music
Early Mus — Early Music
Early Mus America — Early Music America
Early Mus G — Early Music Gazette
Early Mus Gaz — Early Music Gazette
Early Mus Today — Early Music Today
Early Obs Universe Diffuse Backgrounds Moriond Astrophys Meet — Early Observable Universe from Diffuse Backgrounds. Moriond Astrophysics Meetings
Early Pregnancy Biol Med — Early Pregnancy: Biology and Medicine
Early Yrs — Early Years
Ear Mag — Ear Magazine
EArmS — Erevanskij Armjanskij Gosudarstvennyk Pedagogiceskij Institut Imeni Chacatur Abovjana. Sbornik Naucnych Trudov. Serija Russkogo Jazyka
Ear Nose Throat J — Ear, Nose, and Throat Journal
EARRD — European Applied Research Reports. Nuclear Science and Technology Section
Ear Res (Jpn) — Ear Research (Japan)
Earth and Planet Sci Lett — Earth and Planetary Science Letters
Earth Evol Sci — Earth Evolution Sciences
Earth Extraterr Sci — Earth and Extraterrestrial Sciences. Conference Reports and Professional Activities
Earth Gar — Earth Garden
Earth Inf Bul — Earthquake Information Bulletin
Earth Interact — Earth Interactions
Earth Law J — Earth Law Journal
Earth Life Sci Ed — Earth and Life Science Editing
Earth L J — Earth Law Journal
Earth Miner Sci — Earth and Mineral Sciences
Earth Miner Sci Exp Stn Circ Pa State Univ — Earth and Mineral Sciences Experiment Station Circular. Pennsylvania State University
Earthmover & Civ Contrac — Earthmover and Civil Contractor
Earth Phys Branch (Can) Publ — Earth Physics Branch (Canada). Publications
Earth Plan — Earth and Planetary Science Letters
Earth Planetary Sci Lett — Earth and Planetary Science Letters
Earth Planet Sci Lett — Earth and Planetary Science Letters
Earthq Engng Struct Dynam — Earthquake Engineering and Structural Dynamics
Earthquake Engng & Struct Dyn — Earthquake Engineering and Structural Dynamics
Earthquake Engrg Struc Dynam — Earthquake Engineering and Structural Dynamics
Earthquake Eng Struct Dyn — Earthquake Engineering and Structural Dynamics
Earthquake Inf Bull — Earthquake Information Bulletin
Earthquake Inform Bull — Earthquake Information Bulletin. US Department of the Interior. Geological Survey
Earthquake Not — Earthquake Notes
Earthquake US — Earthquakes in the United States
Earthq Inf Bull — Earthquake Information Bulletin
Earthqu Notes — Earthquake Notes
Earth Res — Earth Research
Earth Res (Moscow) — Earth Research (Moscow)

Earth Resour Obs Inf Anal Syst Conf Tech Pap — Earth Resources Observation and Information Analysis System Conference. Technical Papers
Earth S — Earth Science
Earthscan Bull — Earthscan Bulletin
Earth Sci — Earth Science
Earth Sci Bull — Earth Science Bulletin
Earth Sci Dig — Earth Science Digest
Earth Sci Digest — Earth Science Digest
Earth Sci Hist — Earth Sciences History. Journal. History of the Earth Sciences Society
Earth Sci Inst Special Pub — Earth Science Institute. Special Publication
Earth Sci J — Earth Science Journal
Earth Sci Jour — Earth Science Journal
Earth Sci R — Earth Science Reviews
Earth Sci Relat Inf Sel Annot Titles — Earth Science and Related Information. Selected Annotated Titles
Earth Sci Rep Alberta Res Counc — Earth Sciences Report. Alberta Research Council
Earth Sci Rep Coll Lib Arts Kyoto Univ — Earth Science Report. College of Liberal Arts. Kyoto University
Earth Sci Rev — Earth Science Reviews
Earth Sci Ser Houston — Earth Science Series (Houston)
Earth Sci (Tokyo) — Earth Science (Tokyo)
Earth Sci (Wuhan Peoples Repub China) — Earth Science (Wuhan, People's Republic of China)
Earth Shelter Dig Energy Rep — Earth Shelter Digest and Energy Report
Earth Surf Process — Earth Surface Processes
Earth Surf Processes — Earth Surface Processes
Earth Surf Processes and Landforms — Earth Surface Processes and Landforms
EAS — Essays in Arts and Sciences
EAS — Ethnologischer Anzeiger (Stuttgart)
EASCD — Earth Sciences
EASCON Rec — EASCON Record. IEEE Electronics and Aerospace Systems Convention
E Asian Executive Rep — East Asian Executive Reports
EASJ Th — East Asia Journal of Theology
EASMD — Engineering Aspects of Magnetohydrodynamics
East — Eastern Reporter
East Afr Agric For J — East African Agricultural and Forestry Journal
East Afr Agric For Res Organ Annu Rep — East African Agricultural and Forestry Research Organization. Annual Report
East Afr Agric For Res Organ For Tech Note — East African Agriculture and Forestry Research Organization. Forestry TechnicalNote
East Afr Agric For Res Organ Rec Res Annu Rep — East African Agriculture and Forestry Research Organization. Record of Research. Annual Report
East Afr Agric J — East African Agricultural Journal
East Afr Agric J Kenya Tanganyika Uganda Zanzibar — East African Agricultural Journal of Kenya, Tanganyika, Uganda, and Zanzibar
East Afr Agric Res Inst Amani Annu Rep — East African Agricultural Research Institute. Amani. Annual Report
East Afr Agric Res Stn (Amani) Annu Rep — East African Agricultural Research Station (Amani). Annual Report
East Afr Common Serv Organ East Afr Inst Med Res Annu Rep — East African Common Services Organization. East African Institute for Medical Research. Annual Report
East Afr Econ Rev — Eastern Africa Economic Review
East Afr Freshw Fish Res Org Annu Rep — East African Freshwater Fisheries Research Organization. Annual Report
East Afr Geogr R — East African Geographical Review
East Afr Inst Malaria Vector-Borne Dis Annu Rep — East African Institute of Malaria and Vector-Borne Diseases. Annual Report
East Afr Inst Med Res Annu Rep — East African Institute for Medical Research. Annual Report
East Afr J Criminol — East African Journal of Criminology
East Afr J Med Res — East African Journal of Medical Research
East Afr J Rur Develop — Eastern Africa Journal of Rural Development
East Afr Law Jnl — East Africa Law Journal
East Afr Law Rev — East Africa Law Review
East Afr LJ — East African Law Journal
East Afr LR — Eastern Africa Law Review
East Afr L Rev — Eastern Africa Law Review
East Afr Med J — East African Medical Journal
East Afr Nat Resour Res Counc Annu Rep — East African Natural Resources Research Council. Annual Report
East Afr Rep Trade Ind — East African Report on Trade and Industry
East Afr Trypanosomiasis Res Organ Annu Rep — East African Trypanosomiasis Research Organization. Annual Report
East Afr Trypanosomiasis Res Organ Rep — East African Trypanosomiasis Research Organization. Report
East Afr Tuberc Invest Cent Annu Rep — East African Tuberculosis Investigation Centre. Annual Report
East Afr Vet Res Organ Annu Rep — East African Veterinary Research Organization. Annual Report
East Afr Virus Res Inst Rep — East African Virus Research Institute. Report
East Afr Weed Control Conf Proc — East Arfican Weed Control Conference. Proceedings
East Afr Wildl J — East African Wildlife Journal
East Anal Symp Adv Graphite Furn At Absorpt Spectrom — Eastern Analytical Symposium. Advances in Graphite Furnace AtomicAbsorption Spectrometry
East Anal Symp Reson Raman Spectrosc Anal Tool — Eastern Analytical Symposium. Resonance Raman Spectroscopy as an Analytical Tool
East Anal Symp Therm Methods Polym Anal — Eastern Analytical Symposium. Thermal Methods in Polymer Analysis
East Anthro — Eastern Anthropologist
East Anthrop — Eastern Anthropologist

East Anthropol — Eastern Anthropologist
East Arch Opthalmol — Eastern Archives of Ophthalmology
East As Cult Stud — East Asian Cultural Studies
East Asian R — East Asian Review
East As R — East Asian Review
East Bay — East Bay Voice
Eastbourne NH S Pp & T — Papers (Transactions) of the Eastbourne Natural History Society with Annual Report
Eastbourne NH S T — Papers (Transactions) of the Eastbourne Natural History Society with Annual Report
East Buddhist — Eastern Buddhist
East Cent Eur — East Central Europe
East China J Agric Sci — East China Journal of Agricultural Science
EastChQ — Eastern Churches Quarterly
East Ch R — Eastern Churches Review
East Churches Quart — Eastern Churches Quarterly
East Coal — Eastern Coal
East Econ — Eastern Economist
East Economist — Eastern Economist
East End Environ — East End Environment
Easter Annu — Easter Annual
Eastern Africa Econ R — Eastern Africa Economic Review
Eastern Africa J Rural Development — Eastern Africa Journal of Rural Development
Eastern Anthropol — Eastern Anthropologist
Eastern Eur Econ — Eastern European Economics
Eastern J Int L — Eastern Journal of International Law
Eastern J In'tl L — Eastern Journal of International Law
Eastern J of Internat L — Eastern Journal of International Law
Easter Sch Agric Sci Univ Nottingham Proc — Easter School in Agricultural Science. University of Nottingham. Proceedings
East Europ Quart — East European Quarterly
East Eur Q — East European Quarterly
East Eur Quart — East European Quarterly
East For Prod Lab (Can) Rep — Eastern Forest Products Laboratory (Canada). Report
East For Prod Lab Tech Rep Forintek Can Corp — Eastern Forest Products Laboratory. Technical Report. Forintek Canada Corporation
East Fruit Grow — Eastern Fruit Grower
East Ger Amt Erfindungs Patentwes Bekanntm — East Germany. Amt fuer Erfindungs- und Patentwesen. Bekanntmachungen
East Grape Grow Winery News — Eastern Grape Grower and Winery News
East Horiz — Eastern Horizon
East J Approx — East Journal of Approximations
East J Int L — Eastern Journal of International Law
East Lab Tech Rep Forintek Can Corp — Eastern Laboratory Technical Report. Forintek Canada Corporation
East Librn — Eastern Librarian
East Malays Geol Surv Rep — East Malaysia Geological Survey. Report
East Malling Res Stn Annu Rep — East Malling Research Station. Annual Report
East Malling Res Stn Kent Annu Rep — East Malling Research Station. Kent. Annual Report
East Malling Res Stn (Maidstone England) Rep — East Malling Research Station (Maidstone, England). Report
Eastman Org Chem Bull — Eastman Organic Chemical Bulletin
East Mediterr Health J — Eastern Mediterranean Health Journal
East Met Rev — Eastern Metals Review
East Midl Geogr — East Midland Geographer
East Pakistan Ed Ex Cen Bul — East Pakistan Education Extension Centre Bulletin
East Pharm — Eastern Pharmacist
East Pharmst — Eastern Pharmacist
East Quart — Eastern Quarterly
East Rev — Eastern Review
East Sib State Univ Stud — East Siberian State University Studies
East Tenn Hist Soc Pub — East Tennessee Historical Society. Publications
East Tenn Hist Soc Publ — East Tennessee Historical Society. Publications
East Turkic Rev — East Turkic Review
East Underw — Eastern Underwriter
East West — East West Journal
East West Bus Trade — East/West Business and Trade
East West J Numer Math — East-West Journal of Numerical Mathematics
East West Perspect — East West Perspectives
East West Technol Dig — East/West Technology Digest
East Wkr — Eastern Worker
EaT — East Tennessee Historical Society
EAT — Economic Inquiry
EAT — Economic Review. Federal Reserve Bank of Atlanta
EAT — El-Armarna-Tafeln
EATBA8 — East African Tuberculosis Investigation Centre. Annual Report
EATCAB — Estacion Experimental Agricola de Tucuman. Circular
EATMA7 — Estacion Experimental Agricola de Tucuman. Publicacion Miscelanea
EATRAM — East African Trypanosomiasis Research Organization. Annual Report
Eat Weight Disord — Eating and Weight Disorders
Eau Air Plans Amenagement CR Cycle Int Conf PRO AQUA — Eau et Air dans les Plans d'Amenagement. Compte Rendu du Cycle International de Conferences PRO AQUA
Eau Amenag Reg Provencale — Eau et Amenagement de la Region Provencale
Eau Ind — Eau et l'Industrie
Eau Ind Nuisances — Eau, l'Industrie, les Nuisances
EAUMAC — Ecological Society of Australia. Memoirs
Eau Que — Eau du Quebec
E Aux — Echo d'Auxerre
EAVRBX — East African Veterinary Research Organization. Annual Report
EaW — East and West

EaW — Eastern World
EAW — Einleitung in die Altertumswissenschaft
EAW — Environmental Policy and Law
EAW — Estadistica (Washington, D. C.)
EAWJAD — East African Wildlife Journal
EAZ — Ethnographisch-Archaeologische Zeitschrift
EA Zeits — Ethnographisch-Archaeologische Zeitschrift
EB — Eastern Buddhist
EB — Educational Broadcasting
EB — Encyclopaedia Britannica
EB — Environment and Behavior
EB — Estudios Biblicos
EB — Etudes Balkaniques
EB — Etudes Balzaciennes
EB — Etudes Bernanosiennes
EB — Etudes Bibliques
EB — Everybody's Magazine
EB — Revue des Etudes Byzantines
EBA — Entomologische Berichten (Amsterdam)
EBADAS — Endocrine Bioassay Data
EBAFE — Economic Bulletin for Asia and the Far East [Later, Economic Bulletin for Asiaand the Pacific]
EBALD — Energy at Booz-Allen
Ebara Eng Rev — Ebara Engineering Review
Ebara Infilco Eng Rev — Ebara-Infilco Engineering Review
EBB — Economic Analysis and Workers' Management (Belgrade)
EBB — Economic Bulletin Board
EBB — Eibei Bungaku
EBB — Evangelische Blaetter aus Bethlehem
EBBI — Enciclopedia Biografica e Bibliografica Italiana
EBBSAA — Entomologische Blaetter fuer Biologie und Systematik der Kaefer
EBC — Economic Bulletin/Warta Cafi
EBE — Economic Bulletin for Europe
EBE — Economic Outlook
EBEH — Environment and Behavior
EBEUA — Economic Bulletin for Europe
EBI — Educational Broadcasting International
EBI — Electronic Business
EBI — Energy Bibliography and Index
EBI — Estudios Biblicos
EBIB — Encyclopaedia Biblica
EBIb — Estudios Biblicos
E Bibl — Estudios Biblicos
EBIP — European Biotechnology Information Project Bibliographic Database
EBIPA — Enka Biniiru To Porima
EBIS — Employee Benefits Infosource
EBIS — ESCAP [United Nations Economic and Social Commission for Asia and the Pacific] Bibliographic Information System
EBJ — Employee Benefits Journal
EBJP — Estremadura. Boletim da Junta de Provincia
EBLA — Bourgeois, Emile, and Louis Andre. Sources de l'Histoire de France
EBMOA — Elektronika Bol'shikh Moshchnostei
EBn — Enchiridion Biblicum. Editionis Napoli/Roma
EBN — Essobron
EBNA — Economisch Bulletin Nederlandse Antillen
EBPR — Employee Benefit Plan Review
EBR — Educational Broadcasting Review
EBR — Employee Benefit Research Institute. Research Report
EBr — Encyclopaedia Britannica
EBra — Estudos Brasileiros
E Brit — Encyclopaedia Britannica
EBRSDP — Experimental Brain Research. Supplementum
EBS Bulletin — Bulletin. Experimental Building Station
EBSC — Eibungaku Shicho
Ebsco Bull Ser Changes — Ebsco Bulletin of Serials Changes
EBSE — Ezegodnik Bolsoj Sovetskoj Enciklopedii
EBSK — Erlanger Beitrage zur Sprach- und Kunstwissenschaft
EBST — Edinburgh Bibliographical Society. Transactions
EBT — Etudes Balkaniques Tchecoslovaques
EBTA J — EBTA [Eastern Business Teachers Association] Journal
EBTA Y — EBTA [Eastern Business Teachers Association] Yearbook
E B Tch — Etudes Balkaniques Tchecoslovaques
EBU — Economic Bulletin for Europe
EBU — Electronic Business
E Bud — Eastern Buddhist
E Buddhist — Eastern Buddhist
EBU Rev — EBU [European Broadcasting Union] Review
EBU Rev A — EBU [European Broadcasting Union] Review. Part A
EBU Rev Part A — EBU [European Broadcasting Union] Review. Part A. Technical
EBU Rev Tech — EBU [European Broadcasting Union] Review. Part A. Technical
EBYLA2 — Embryologia
EByz — Etudes Byzantines
EC — Ecology
EC — Economica
EC — Economist
EC — Education and Culture
EC — Egypte Contemporaine
EC — Enciclopedia Cattolica
EC — Essays in Criticism
EC — Estudios Clasicos
EC — Etudes Celtiques
EC — Etudes Classiques
EC — Etudes Cretoises
EC — Journal of Educational Computing Research
Eca — Economica

ECA — Economic Information on Argentina
ECA — Estudios Centroamericanos
ECA — Expositor and Current Anecdotes
E (Callao) — Estudios (Callao, Argentina)
Ec An — Economic Analysis
Ec Ant Nimes — Ecole Antique de Nimes. Bulletin Annuel
Ec Appl — Economie Appliquee
Ecarbica J — Ecarbica Journal. Official Journal. East and Central Africa Regional Branch. International Council on Archives
ECarm — Ephemerides Carmeliticae
E Catt — Enciclopedia Cattolica
ECB — Echo de la Bourse
ECB — Encontros com a Civilizacao Brasileira Editora Civilizacao Brasileira
ECB — English Catalogue of Books
ECB — Estudos de Castelo Branco
ECB — Quarterly Review of Economics and Business
ECBA — English Catalogue of Books. Annual Issue
ECBC — English Catalogue of Books. Cumulative Issue
ECBOA — Economic Botany
ECBOA5 — Economic Botany
ECBU — Economic Bulletin. Bank of Norway
ECBUAN — Eczacilik Bulteni
ECBUDQ — Ecological Bulletins - NFR
Ec Bul Eur — Economic Bulletin for Europe
Ecc — Ecclesia
ECC — Economic Commentary. Federal Reserve Bank of Cleveland
ECCAD5 — EORTC [European Organization for Research on Treatment of Cancer] Cancer Chemotherapy Annual
Eccl — Ecclesia. Encyclopedie Populaire des Connaissances Religieuses
Eccles Rev — Ecclesiastical Review
Eccl Rev — Ecclesiastical Review
ECCND — Electric Comfort Conditioning News
EC Coop Ext Serv Univ Nebr — EC. Cooperative Extension Service. University of Nebraska
Ec Cred — Economia e Credito
EcCSC — Ecole. Classes de Second Cycle
ECCVBW — Ecologie et Conservation
ECCVBW — Ecology and Conservation
EcD — Economic Development and Cultural Change
ECDC — Early Child Development and Care
ECDCAD — Early Child Development and Care
Ec Dev Cult Change — Economic Development and Cultural Change
ECDIN — Environmental Chemicals Data and Information Network
ECE — (El) Caribe
ECE — L'Esplorazione Commerciale e l'Esploratore
ECEA — Exceptional Child Education Abstracts [Later, ECER]
ECE Chem — Annual Review of the Chemical Industry, 1981. Economic Commission for Europe
ECelt — Etudes Celtiques
EC Energy Mon — EC Energy Monthly
E Cent — Eighteenth Century
E Cent Eur — East Central Europe
ECER — Exceptional Child Education Resources
Ec Ete Phys Part — Ecole d'Ete de Physique des Particules
Ec Ete Phys Part CR — Ecole d'Ete de Physique des Particules. Compte Rendu
Ec Ete Phys Theor — Ecole d'Ete de Physique Theorique
Ec Ete Phys Theor Les Houches — Ecole d'Ete de Physique Theorique. Les Houches
Ec Ete Roscoff — Ecole d'Ete de Roscoff
ECETOC Monogr — ECETOC (European Centre for Ecotoxicology and Toxicology of Chemicals) Monograph
ECETOC Spec Rep — ECETOC (European Centre for Ecotoxicology and Toxicology of Chemicals) Special Report
ECETOC Tech Rep — ECETOC (European Chemical Industry Ecology and Toxicology Centre) Technical Report
ECF — Ecrits du Canada Francais
ECFNBN — Ecology of Food and Nutrition
Ec Fr Maghrebine Printemps Biol Mol CR — Ecole Franco-Maghrebine de Printemps de Biologie Moleculaire. CompteRendu
ECG — Economic Geography
ECG — Egyptian Cotton Gazette
ECGEA — Economic Geography
ECGLA — Economic Geology and the Bulletin of the Society of Economic Geologists
ECGR — Empire Cotton Growing Review [London]
ECGT — Ecologist
ECGWAK — Empire Cotton Growing Corporation. Review
ECGYA — Ecology
EcH — Economic History Review
ECh — Enseignement Chretien
Echanges Int Develop — Echanges Internationaux et Developpement
Echang Univ — Echangiste Universel. Revue Mensuelle des Collectionneurs de Timbres et des Numismates
ECHC — Etudes Carmelitaines Historiques et Critiques
Echinoderm Stud — Echinoderm Studies
Ec Hist R — Economic History of Rome
ECHMB — Electrochemistry
ECHMBU — Specialist Periodical Reports. Electrochemistry
Echo — Echo Magazine
EchO — Echos d'Orient
E Ch O — Ergebnisse der Chirurgie und Orthopaedie
Echo B A — Echo des Beaux Arts
Echo Brass — Echo de la Brasserie
Echo Med Nord — Echo Medical du Nord
Echo Mines Metall — Echo des Mines et de la Metallurgie

Echo Min Met — Echo des Mines et de la Metallurgie
EchoP — Echo de Paris [newspaper]
Echo Rech — Echo des Recherches
Echos A — Echos d'Art
Echos Med — Echos de la Medecine
Echo Vet — Echo Veterinaire
E Ch Q — Eastern Churches Quarterly
Ec HR — Economic History Review
EChr — Enseignement Chretien
E Church Rev — Eastern Church Reviews
ECI — Economist
ECIME4 — Experimental and Clinical Immunogenetics
ECIN — Economic Indicators
ECIND — Economic Inquiry
EC Index — European Communities Index
ECINE7 — Ear Clinics International
ECIWDSS — Environment Canada. Inland Waters Directorate. Scientific Series
ECJ — Economic Journal
ECJOA — Economic Journal
ECJPA — Endocrinologia Japonica
ECJPAE — Endocrinologia Japonica
Eck — Eckart
ECK — Economic and Commercial News
Eckart J — Eckart Jahrbuch
Eck J — Eckart Jahrbuch
EcL — Ecole Liberatrice
ECL — Edward Cadbury Lectures
E Cl — Estudios Clasicos
E Cl — Etudes Classiques
ECLA — Etudes Classiques
Eclair Elect — Eclairage Electrique
Eclaireur Agric Hort — Eclaireur Agricole et Horticole. Revue Pratique des Cultures Meriodionales et de l'Afrique du Nord et des Industries Annexes
EClas — Estudios Clasicos
EClass — Les Etudes Classiques
ECLED — Economics Letters
Ecl Engin — Eclectic Engineering Magazine
EcLet — Ecole des Lettres. Second Cycle
Ecletica Quim — Ecletica Quimica
Eclet Quim — Ecletica Quimica
Ecl Geol Helv — Eclogae Geologicae Helvetiae
E-C Life — Eighteenth-Century Life
Ecl J Sci — Eclectic Journal of Science
Ecl M — Eclectic Magazine
Ecl Mus — Eclectic Museum
Eclogae Geol Helv — Eclogae Geologicae Helvetiae
Ecl R — Eclectic Review
E Cl T — Estudios Clasicos. Suplement Serie de Textos
E Cl Tr — Estudios Clasicos. Suplement Serie de Traducciones
ECM — Econometrica
ECM — Estudios de Cultura Maya
ECMAA — Economie et Medecine Animales
ECMAAI — Economie et Medecine Animales
ECMCC — Encyclopedie Medico-Chirurgicale
ECM Electr Constr Maint — EC&M. Electrical Construction and Maintenance
ECMM — Etudes Carmelitaines Mystiques et Missionnaires
ECMM — Extracts from China Mainland Magazines
ECMOA — Ecological Monographs
ECMOAQ — Ecological Monographs
ECMODT — Ecological Modelling
ECMP — Union Catalog of Medical Periodicals
ECMSC6 — Estuarine and Coastal Marine Science
ECMTA — Econometrica
ECN — Economist
ECN — Estudios de Cultura Nahuatl
ECN — European Chemical News
Ec Natl Super Biol Appl Nutr Aliment Cah — Ecole Nationale Superieure de Biologie Appliquee a la Nutrition et al'Alimentation. Cahiers
Ec N Bulg — Economic News of Bulgaria
ECNEA — Electroencephalography and Clinical Neurophysiology
ECNEAZ — Electroencephalography and Clinical Neurophysiology
EC Nebr Univ Coop Ext Serv — EC. Cooperative Extension Service. University of Nebraska
ECN Rep — ECN [Stichting Energieonderzoek Centrum Nederland] Report
ECNSB — Electrical Consultant
ECN Sup — European Chemical News. Supplement
ECO — Economica
ECO — Environment Centre Outlook
ECo — Etudes Corses
Eco Argent — Economic Information on Argentina
ECOBDY — Eisenhower Consortium. Bulletin
Eco Cient — Eco Cientifico
ECODOC — Economic Generale
ECOe — Etudes du Conseil Oecumenique
Eco Farm — Eco Farmaceutico
Eco Forcst — Economic Forecasts. A Worldwide Survey
ECOGA — Ecologist
ECOGAC — Ecologist
ECOGDF — Ecologia
Eco Ind — Eco Industry
ECOL — Ecology
ECOLA — Ecology
Ecol Abstr — Ecological Abstracts
Ecol Action Newsl — Ecology Action Newsletter
Ecol Agrar — Ecologia Agraria. Instituto de Ecologia Agraria. Universita di Perugia

Ecol Approaches Environ Chem Proc Int Symp — Ecological Approaches of Environmental Chemicals. Proceedings. International Symposium
ECOLAR — Ecology
Ecol Bull — Ecological Bulletins
Ecol Bull - NFR (Statens Naturvetensk Forskningsrad) — Ecological Bulletins - NFR (Statens Naturvetenskapliga Forskningsrad)
Ecol Chem — Ecological Chemistry
Ecol Chem Russ Ed — Ecological Chemistry (Russian Edition)
Ecol Consequences Global Clim Change — Ecological Consequences of Global Climate Change
Ecol Conserv — Ecology and Conservation
Ecol Dis — Ecology of Disease
Ecole Ant Nimes — Ecole Antique de Nimes
Ecole Nat Sup Agron Ind Aliment Bull — Ecole Nationale Superieure d'Agronomie et des Industries Alimentaires. Bulletin
Ecol Ent — Ecological Entomology
Ecol Entom — Ecological Entomology
Ecol Entomol — Ecological Entomology
Ecol Environ Conserv — Ecology, Environment, and Conservation
Ecol Food Nutr — Ecology of Food and Nutrition
Ecol Indic — Ecological Indicators
Ecol Law Q — Ecology Law Quarterly
Ecol LQ — Ecology Law Quarterly
Ecol L Quart — Ecology Law Quarterly
Ecol Mediterr — Ecologia Mediterranea
Ecol Model — Ecological Modelling
Ecol Monogr — Ecological Monographs
Ecologist Quart — Ecologist Quarterly
Ecologn Fd Nutr — Ecology of Food and Nutrition
Ecology (Engl Transl Ekologiya) — Ecology (English Translation of Ekologiya)
Ecology L Q — Ecology Law Quarterly
Ecol Phys Chem Proc Int Workshop — Ecological Physical Chemistry. Proceedings. International Workshop
Ecol Physiol Methods Cotton Fusarium Wilt Control — Ecologo-Physiological Methods of Cotton Fusarium Wilt Control
Ecol Publ Ecol Soc Am — Ecology. Publication. Ecological Society of America
Ecol Q — Ecologist Quarterly
Ecol Res — Ecological Research
Ecol Res Comm Bull — Ecological Research Committee. Bulletin
Ecol Resour Degrad Renewal Symp Br Ecol Soc — Ecology of Resource Degradation and Renewal. Symposium. British Ecological Society
Ecol Res Ser — Ecological Research Series
Ecol Rev — Ecological Review
Ecol Rev — Ecology Review
Ecol Rev (Sendai) — Ecological Review (Sendai)
Ecol Soc Am Spec Publ — Ecological Society of America. Special Publication
Ecol Soc Aust Mem — Ecological Society of Australia. Memoirs
Ecol Soc Aust Proc — Ecological Society of Australia. Proceedings
Ecol Stud — Ecological Studies
Ecol Stud Anal Synth — Ecological Studies, Analysis, and Synthesis
E Com — Echos du Commonwealth
ECOM — Economica
ECOM — Especialidades Consumidas por la Seguridad Social
ECOMA — Electrical Construction and Maintenance
ECOMINAS Bol Mens — ECOMINAS [Empresa Colombiana de Minas] Boletin Mensual
Econ — Econometrica
Econ — Economia
Econ — Economist
EconAb — Economic Abstracts
Econ Abstr — Economic Abstracts
Econ Act — Economic Activity
Econ Activity — Economic Activity in Western Australia
Econ Activity in WA — Economic Activity in Western Australia
Econ Activity WA — Economic Activity in Western Australia
Econ Act West Aust — Economic Activity in Western Australia
Econ Aff — Economic Affairs
Econ Afr — Economic Bulletin for Africa
Econ Agric — Economiste Agricole
Econ Agr (Paris) — Economie Agricole (Paris)
Econ Anal & Policy — Economic Analysis and Policy
Econ Analys — Economic Analysis
Econ Analysis and Policy (NS) — Economic Analysis and Policy (New Series)
Econ Analysis (Belgrade) — Economic Analysis and Workers' Management (Belgrade)
Econ & Financial Survey Aust — Economic and Financial Survey of Australia
Econ & Ind Democ — Economic and Industrial Democracy
Econ and Soc — Economy and Society
Econ and Social R (Dublin) — Economic and Social Review (Dublin)
Econ and Social Research Inst Q Econ Commentary — Economic and Research Institute. Quarterly Economic Commentary
Econ and Statis R (East Africa) — Economic and Statistical Review (East Africa)
Econ Ann — Economic Annalist
Econ Appl — Economie Appliquee
Econ Appliq — Economie Appliquee
Econ Appliquee — Economie Appliquee
ECONB — Electrical Contracting
Econ (BA) — Economica (Buenos Aires)
Econ B Afr — Economic Bulletin for Africa
Econ B Asia Far East — Economic Bulletin for Asia and the Far East [Later, Economic Bulletin for Asiaand the Pacific]
Econ B Asia Pacific — Economic Bulletin for Asia and the Pacific
Econ B (Athens) — Economic Bulletin. Commercial Bank of Greece (Athens)
Econ B (Cairo) — Economic Bulletin. National Bank of Egypt (Cairo)
Econ B Europe — Economic Bulletin for Europe

Econ B Latin Amer — Economic Bulletin for Latin America
Econ B (Oslo) — Economic Bulletin (Oslo)
Econ Bot — Economic Botany
Econ Botan — Economic Botany
Econ Bras Rio — Economia Brasileira (Rio de Janeiro)
Econ Bul A — Economic Bulletin for Asia and the Pacific
Econ Bul Asia and Far East — Economic Bulletin for Asia and the Far East [Later, Economic Bulletin for Asiaand the Pacific]
Econ Bul Asia and Pacific — Economic Bulletin for Asia and the Pacific
Econ Bul Europe — Economic Bulletin for Europe
Econ Bull — Economic Bulletin
Econ Bull Afr — Economic Bulletin for Africa
Econ Bull Eur — Economic Bulletin for Europe
Econ Bull for Europe — Economic Bulletin for Europe
Econ Bull Geol Surv West Malays — Economic Bulletin. Geological Survey of West Malaysia
Econ Bull Ghana — Economic Bulletin of Ghana
Econ Bull Lat Am — Economic Bulletin for Latin America
Econ Bull Sri Lanka Geol Surv Dep — Economic Bulletin. Sri Lanka Geological Survey Department
Econ Busin R KSU — Economic and Business Review KSU
Econ Bus Let — Economics and Business Letter
Econ Bus R — Economic and Business Review
Econ Bus Rev — Economics Business Review
Econ Can Sch — Economics in Canadian Schools
Econ Centre-Est — Economie du Centre-Est
Econ Cienc Soc — Economia y Ciencias Sociales
Econ Cien Soc Caracas — Economia y Ciencias Sociales (Caracas)
Econ Col Bogota — Economia Colombiana (Bogota)
Econ Colombiana 4a Epoca — Economia Colombiana. Cuarta Epoca
Econ Comp and Econ Cyb Stud and Res — Economic Computation and Economic Cybernetics Studies and Research
Econ Comput and Econ Cybern Stud and Res — Economic Computation and Economic Cybernetics Studies and Research
Econ Comput Econ Cybern Stud Res — Economic Computation and Economic Cybernetics Studies and Research
Econ Cont — Contents of Recent Economics Journals
Econ Counc Can Disc Pap — Economic Council of Canada. Discussion Papers
Econ Cr Proj A Rep — Economic Crime Project. Annual Report
ECOND — Energy Consumer
Econ Del Lav — Economia del Lavoro
Econ Dev & Cul Change — Economic Development and Cultural Change
Econ Dev Cu — Economic Development and Cultural Change
Econ Dev Cult Change — Economic Development and Cultural Change
Econ Dev Cult Chg — Economic Development and Cultural Change
Econ Devel and Cult Change — Economic Development and Cultural Change
Econ Devel Cult Ch — Economic Development and Cultural Change
Econ Devel Cult Change — Economic Development and Cultural Change
Econ Develop Cult Change — Economic Development and Cultural Change
Econ Development and Cultural Change — Economic Development and Cultural Change
Econ Dev Prog Rep S Afr — Economic Development Programme for the Republic of South Africa
Econ EC — Economia EC
Econ e Credito — Economia e Credito
Econ Educ Bul — Economic Education Bulletin
Econ e Gestao — Economia e Gestao
Econ El — Economie Electrique
Econ e Lav — Economia e Lavoro
Econ e Socialismo — Economia e Socialismo
Econ e Sociol — Economia e Sociologia
Econ Estad Bogota — Economia y Estadistica (Bogota)
Econ e Storia — Economia e Storia
Econ e Storia (2a Ser) — Economia e Storia (Seconda Serie)
Econ et Fins Agrics — Economie et Finances Agricoles
Econ et Human — Economie et Humanisme
Econ et Humanisme — Economie et Humanisme
Econ et Pol — Economie et Politique
Econ et Polit — Economie et Politique
Econ et Prevision — Economie et Prevision
Econ et Sante — Economie et Sante
Econ Et Soc — Economies et Societes. Cahiers de l'ISEA
Econ et Statist — Economie et Statistique
Econ Europ — Economie Europeenne
Econ Eye — Economic Eye
Econ Finances Agric — Economie et Finances Agricoles
Econ Financial Surv Aust — Economic and Financial Survey of Australia
Econ Financ R Central Bank Nigeria — Economic and Financial Review. Central Bank of Nigeria
Econ Finan Surv Aust — Economic and Financial Survey of Australia
Econ Fin Rep — Economist Financial Report
Econ Forum — Economic Forum
Econ Fruit Farm — Economics of Fruit Farming
Econ Geog — Economic Geography
Econ Geogr — Economic Geography
Econ-Geogr — Economic-Geographie
Econ Geography — Economic Geography
Econ Geogr Worcester — Economic Geography (Worcester)
Econ Geol — Economic Geology
Econ Geol — Economic Geology and the Bulletin of the Society of Economic Geologists
Econ Geol Bull Soc Econ Geol — Economic Geology and the Bulletin of the Society of Economic Geologists
Econ Geol Bull Thailand Dep Miner Resour Econ Geol Div — Economic Geology Bulletin. Thailand Department of Mineral Resources.Economic Geology Division

Econ Geol Monogr — Economic Geology Monograph
Econ Geology Mon — Economic Geology Monograph
Econ Geol Rep Alberta Res Counc — Economic Geology Report. Alberta Research Council
Econ Geol Rep Geol Surv Can — Economic Geology Report. Geological Survey of Canada
Econ Geol Rep Jam Geol Surv Dep — Economic Geology Report. Jamaica Geological Survey Department
Econ Geol Rep Jam Mines Geol Div — Economic Geology Report. Jamaica. Mines and Geology Division
Econ Geol Rep Miner Resour Div (Manitoba) — Economic Geology Report. Mineral Resources Division (Manitoba)
Econ Geol Rep Res Counc Alberta — Economic Geology Report. Research Council of Alberta
Econ Geol USSR (Engl Transl) — Economic Geology USSR (English Translation)
Econ Geol VT Geol Surv — Economic Geology. Vermont Geological Survey
Econ Grancol Bogota — Economia Grancolombiana (Bogota)
Econ Handb Wld — Economic Handbook of the World
Econ Hist — Economic History
Econ Hist — Economy and History
Econ Hist R — Economic History Review
Econ Hist Rev — Economic History Review
Econ Hist Rev Second Ser — Economic History Review. Second Series
EconHR — Economic History Review
Econ Idaho Agric Univ Idaho Coop Ext Serv — Economics for Idaho Agriculture. University of Idaho. Cooperative Extension Service
Econ Ind — Economia Industrial
Econ Indic — Economic Indicators
Econ Indicators — Economic Indicators
Econ Inf Argentina — Economic Information on Argentina
Econ Info Argentina — Economic Information on Argentina
Econ Inf Rep Food Resour Econ Dep Univ Fla Agric Exp Stns — Economic Information Report. University of Florida. Food and Resource EconomicsDepartment. Agricultural Experiment Stations
Econ Inf Rep Univ Fla Food Resour Econ Dep Agric Exp Stn — Economic Information Report. University of Florida. Food and Resource EconomicsDepartment. Agricultural Experiment Stations
Econ Inq — Economic Inquiry
Econ Inquiry — Economic Inquiry
Econ Int — Economia Internazionale. Revista. Istituto di Economia Internazionale
Econ Internaz — Economia Internazionale
Econ Internaz Fonti Energia — Economia Internazionale delle Fonti di Energia
Econ Int Fonti Energia — Economia Internazionale delle Fonti di Energia
Econ Int (Genova) — Economia Internazionale (Genova)
Econ Invest Fiji Geol Surv Dep — Economic Investigation. Fiji. Geological Survey Department
Econ Invest Fiji Miner Resour Dep — Economic Investigation. Fiji Mineral Resources Department
Econ Issues Dep Agric Econ Coll Agric Life Sci Univ Wis — Economic Issues. Department of Agricultural Economics. College of Agricultural and Life Sciences. University of Wisconsin
Econ Istruzione e Formazione Professionale — Economia. Istruzione e Formazione Professionale
Econ Italy — Economic News from Italy
Econ J — Economic Journal
Econ La Plata — Economica (La Plata, Argentina)
Econ Leaf — Economic Leaflets
Econ Leaflets — Economic Leaflets
Econ Lett — Economics Letters
Econ Letters — Economic Letters
Econ (Lisbon) — Economia (Lisbon)
Econ (London) — Economica (London)
Econ Marche — Economia Marche
Econ Mark Inf Mo Agric Univ Mo Coop Ext Serv — Economic and Marketing Information for Missouri Agriculture. University of Missouri. Cooperative Extension Service
Econ Med Anim — Economie et Medecine Animales
Econ Med Plant Res — Economic and Medicinal Plant Research
Econ Meridionale — Economie Meridionale
Econ Mex — Economista Mexicano
Econ Mex — Review of the Economic Situation of Mexico
Econ Microbiol — Economic Microbiology
Econ Monog — Economic Monographs
Econ Monographs — Economic Monographs
Econ Monograph (Vic) — Economic Monograph (Melbourne, Victoria)
Econ Mundial — Economia Mundial. Revista de Economia y Finanzas
Econ N — Economic News
Econ News — Economic News
Econ Newsl SD State Univ Coop Ext Serv Econ Dep — Economics Newsletter. South Dakota State University. Cooperative Extension Service. Economics Department
Econom Comp Econom Cybernet Stud Res — Economic Computation and Economic Cybernetics Studies and Research
Econom Comput Econom Cybernet Stud Res — Economic Computation and Economic Cybernetics Studies and Research
Econometric Rev — Econometric Reviews
Econometrics Oper Res — Econometrics and Operations Research
Economic Activity in WA — Economic Activity in Western Australia
Econom Lett — Economics Letters
Econom Oper Res — Econometrics and Operations Research
Econom Soc Monogr — Econometric Society Monographs
Econom Soc Monographs Pure Theory — Econometric Society Monographs in Pure Theory
Econom Soc Monographs Quantitative Econom — Econometric Society Monographs in Quantitative Economics

Econom Soc Tijdsch — Economisch en Sociaal Tijdschrift
Econom Theory — Economic Theory
Econom Theory Econometrics Math Econom — Economic Theory, Econometrics, and Mathematical Economics
Econom Twent Century — Economists of the Twentieth Century
Economy Soc — Economy and Society
Eco Not Ecol — Eco. Notiziario dell'Ecologia
Econ Out (CA) — Economic Outlook (California)
Econ Outlk — Economic Outlook
Econ Outlook — Economic Outlook USA
Econ Outlook (London) — Economic Outlook (London)
Econ Outlook USA — Economic Outlook USA
Econ Out US — Economic Outlook USA
Econ Out W — Economic Outlook World
Econ Pam SD Agric Exp Stn — Economics Pamphlet. South Dakota Agricultural Experiment Station
Econ Panorama (Bancomer) — Economic Panorama (Bancomer)
Econ Pap — Economic Papers
Econ Papers — Economic Papers
Econ Pap NC Dep Conserv Dev — Economic Paper. North Carolina Department of Conservation andDevelopment
Econ Pas (Australia and NZ) — Economic Papers (Australia and New Zealand)
Econ Pas (Warsaw) — Economic Papers (Warsaw)
Econ Pays Afr N — Economie des Pays d'Afrique Noire
Econ Pays Arabes — Economie des Pays Arabes
Econ Perspectives — Economic Perspectives
Econ Planning — Economics of Planning
Econ Planning (Helsinki) — Economic Planning (Helsinki)
Econ Plann J Agric Relat Ind — Economic Planning. Journal for Agriculture and Related Industries
Econ Pol 2a Epoca — Economia Politica. Segunda Epoca
Econ Policy Issues — Economic Policy Issues
Econ Polit Wkly — Economic and Political Weekly
Econ Pol W — Economic and Political Weekly
Econ Pres — Economic Report of the President
Econ Priorities Rep — Economic Priorities Report
Econ Proc R Dublin Soc — Economic Proceedings. Royal Dublin Society
Econ Progress Rep — Economic Progress Report
Econ Pubbl — Economia Pubblica
Econ Pubblica — Economia Pubblica
Econ Quito — Economia (Quito)
Econ R — Economic Review
Econ R Bank Israel — Economic Review. Bank of Israel
Econ R (Colombo) — Economic Review (Colombo)
Econ Rec — Economic Record
Econ Rep Banco Bilbao — Economic Report. Banco de Bilbao
Econ Rep Dep Agric Appl Econ Univ Minn — Economic Report. Department of Agricultural and Applied Economics. University of Minnesota
Econ Rep Edinburgh Sch Agr — Economic Report. Edinburgh School of Agriculture
Econ Rep Fiji Geol Surv Dep — Economic Report. Fiji. Geological Survey Department
Econ Rep Geol Surv Dep (Zambia) — Economic Report. Geological Survey Department (Zambia)
Econ Reporter — Economic Reporter
Econ Rep Univ Fla Agric Exp Stn Food Resour Econ Dep — Economics Report. University of Florida. Agricultural Experiment Stations. Foodand Resource Economics Department
Econ Rep Univ Fla Agric Exp Stns — Economics Report. University of Florida. Agricultural Experiment Stations
Econ Rep Zambia Geol Surv Dep — Economic Report. Zambia Geological Survey Department
Econ Res — Economic Research
Econ Rev — Economic Review
Econ Rev Bank Leumi — Economic Review. Bank Leumi
Econ Rev Fed Reserve Bank Atlanta — Economic Review. Federal Reserve Bank of Atlanta
Econ R Kansallis (Osake-Pankki) — Economic Review. Kansallis (Osake-Pankki)
Econ R (Karachi) — Economic Review (Karachi)
Econ Rur — Economie Rurale
Econ Rurale — Economie Rurale
Econ Sal S Salvador — Economia Salvadorena (San Salvador)
Econ Salvad — Economia Salvadorena
Econ Santiago — Economia (Santiago, Chile)
Econs et Socs — Economies et Societes
Econ Situation Rep — Economic Situation Report
Econ Soc — Economy and Society
Econ Soc Aust NZ NSW Br Econ Monog — Economic Society of Australia and New Zealand. New South Wales Branch. EconomicMonograph
Econ Soc Hist — Economic and Social History
Econ Sociaal Hist Jaarb — Economischen Sociaal-Historisch Jaarboek
Econ Societ — Economy and Society
Econ Soc Issues Calif Univ Berkeley Coop Ext Serv — Economic and Social Issues. University of California, Berkeley. Cooperative Extension Service
Econ Soc Issues Univ Calif Berkeley Coop Ext Serv — Economic and Social Issues. University of California, Berkeley. Cooperative Extension Service
Econ Soc R — Economic and Social Review
Econ Soc Rev — Economic and Social Review
Econ Soc Tijds — Economisch en Sociaal Tijdschrift
Econ-Sta Ber — Economisch-Statistische Berichten
Econ-Statist Ber — Economisch-Statistische Berichten
Econ Stor — Economia e Storia. Rivista Italiana di Storia Economica e Sociale
Econ Stud — Economic Studies
Econ Surv Jpn — Economic Survey of Japan
Econ Surv Lat Am — Economic Survey of Latin America

Econ Tech Int Mines — Economie et Technique Internationale des Mines
Econ Tech Rev Rep EPS (Can) — Economic and Technical Review. Report EPS [*Environmental Protection Service*] (Canada)
Econ Tecn Agric — Economia y Tecnica Agricola
Econ Tiers-Monde — Economiste du Tiers-Monde
Econ Trend — Tendances/Trends. Economie et Finances
Econ Trends — Economic Trends
Econ Trentina — Economia Trentina
Econ W — Economic World
Econ World — Economic World
Econ Y Adm — Economia y Administracion
Econ y Desarrollo — Economia y Desarrollo
Econ y Fin Esp — Economia y Finanzas Espanolas
ECOO N — Educational Computing Organization of Ontario. Newsletter
Eco Out (UK) — Economic Outlook (United Kingdom)
ECOPD — Engineering Conference. Proceedings
ECOQD — Electricity Conservation Quarterly
Eco Sur LA — Economic Survey of Latin America
Ecosystems World — Ecosystems of the World
Ecosyst Exp — Ecosystem Experiments
Ecosyst Struct Funct Proc Annu Biol Colloq — Ecosystem Structure and Function. Proceedings. Annual Biology Colloquium
Ecosyst World — Ecosystems of the World
Ecotoxicol Environ Qual — Ecotoxicology and Environmental Quality
Ecotoxicol Environ Saf — Ecotoxicology and Environmental Safety
Ecotoxicol Environ Safety — Ecotoxicology and Environmental Safety
Ecotoxicol Mar — Ecotoxicologie Marine
Ecotoxicol Monit — Ecotoxicology Monitoring
Ecotoxicol Proc Oikos Conf — Ecotoxicology. Proceedings. Oikos Conference
Eco Turkey — General Economic Conditions in Turkey
ECP — Economic Perspectives
ECP — (El) Comercio (Peru)
ECP — Engineering Costs and Production Economics
ECPED — Engineering Costs and Production Economics
EC Photovoltaic Sol Energy Conf Proc Int Conf — EC [*European Communities*] Photovoltaic Solar Energy Conference. Proceedings. International Conference
Ec Polytech Fed Lausanne Journ Electron — Ecole Polytechnique Federale de Lausanne. Journees d'Electronique
Ec Polytech Montreal CR Colloq Etud Annu — Ecole Polytechnique de Montreal. Comptes Rendus du Colloque EtudiantAnnuel
ECPRAG — Empire Cotton Growing Corporation. Progress Reports from Experiment Stations
Ec Prat Hautes Etud Inst Montp Mem Trav — Ecole Pratique des Hautes Etudes. Institut de Montpellier. Memoires et Travaux
ECP Rep — ECP [*Energy Conservation Project*] Report
EC Purdue Univ Coop Ext Serv — EC. Purdue University. Cooperative Extension Service
ECQ — Eastern Churches Quarterly
ECQUA — Engineering. Cornell Quarterly
ECQUDX — Ecletica Quimica
ECR — Eastern Churches Review
ECR — Economic Record
ECR — Economic Review. Federal Reserve Bank of Atlanta
Ecr — Ecritures
Ec R — Ecumenical Review
ECR — Environmental Control Report
ECr — Esprit Createur
ECr — Essays in Criticism
ECR — European Economic Review
ECR — Exchequer Court Reports
Ecran — Ecran 79
ECRCA — Echo des Recherches
ECRDA — Economic Record (Australia)
Ec Rev — Ecumenical Review
EcrN — Ecrits Nouveaux
ECRQDQ — Conseil de la Recherche et du Developpement Forestiers du Quebec. Etude
ECS — Economia y Ciencias Sociales
ECS — Educacao e Ciencias Socials [*Rio de Janeiro*]
ECS — Eighteenth-Century Studies
ECS — Tijdschrift voor Economie en Management
ECSBA — Economisch-Statistische Berichten
ECSDA — Electromechanical Components and Systems Design
ECSHAZ — Ecosphere
Ec Sit EEC — Economic Situation in the Community. European Economic Community
ECSMB — Environmental Control and Safety Management
ECSP — Enhanced Consumer Spending Patterns
ECSSD — Estuarine, Coastal, and Shelf Science
ECSSD3 — Estuarine, Coastal, and Shelf Science
ECSTA — Economist
ECSTC — Electrocomponent Science and Technology
ECSTD6 — Echinoderm Studies
Ec Stor — Economia e Storia; Rivista Italiana di Storia Economica e Sociale
Ec Super Agric Suede Ann — Ecole Superieure d'Agriculture de la Suede. Annales
Ec Svy Eur — Economic Survey of Europe
Ec Svy Fin — Economic Survey of Finland
Ec Svy Jpn — Economic Survey of Japan
ECT — Economist
ECT — Ecopress Italia
ECTAA — Electra
Ectr — Encounter
ECTTA — Economia Trentina
ECU — Economia Internazionale

Ecuador Dir Gen Geol Minas Publ — Ecuador. Direccion General de Geologia y Minas. Publication
Ecuador Dir Gen Geol Minas Rev — Ecuador. Direccion General Geologia y Minas. Revista
Ecumenical R — Ecumenical Review
Ecumenical Rev — Ecumenical Review
Ecumen Rev — Ecumenical Review
Ecum R — Ecumenical Review
Ecum St Hist — Ecumenical Studies in History
EC Univ Arkansas Coop Ext Serv — EC. University of Arkansas. Cooperative Extension Service
EC Univ SD Coop Ext Serv — EC. University of South Dakota. Cooperative Extension Service
EcuR — Ecumenical Review
ECV — Economic Review. Federal Reserve Bank of Cleveland
ECV — Eglise aus Cent Visages
Ec W — Economic Weekly
ECW — Essays on Canadian Writing
ECWODB — Ecosystems of the World
Ec World — Economic World
ECX — Echos. Le Quotidien de l'Economie
Ec Xaver — Ecclesiastica Xaveriana
Eczac Bul — Eczacilik Bulteni
Eczacilik Bul — Eczacilik Bulteni
Eczacilik Derg Marmara Univ — Eczacilik Dergisi. Marmara Universitesi
Eczacilik Fak Derg Hacettepe Univ — Eczacilik Fakultesi Dergisi. Hacettepe Universitesi
Ed — Edda
Ed — Edda. Revue de Litterature
ED — Educacion
Ed — Education
ED — El Derecho
ED — Ephemeris Dacoromana
ED — Etudes Dahomeennes
ED — Euntes Docete
ED — Explorations Archeologiques de Delos
EDA — Economic Development and Cultural Change
EDA — Educacion de Adultos
EdAb — Education Abstracts
EDA Bull — EDA [*British Electrical Development Association*] Bulletin
EdAd — Educational Administration Abstracts
Ed Adm & Sup — Educational Administration and Supervision
Ed Adm Q — Educational Administration Quarterly
Ed & Psychol M — Educational and Psychological Measurement
Ed & Psychol Rev — Education and Psychology Review
Ed & Pub — Editor and Publisher
Ed & Social Science — Education and Social Science
Ed & Training — Education and Training
Ed & Train Men Retard — Education and Training of the Mentally Retarded
Ed Arn — Editiones Arnamagnaenae
EDB — DOE [*Department of Energy*] Energy Data Base
EDB — Econometric Data Bank
EDB — Emily Dickinson Bulletin
EDB — Excise Duty Bulletin
EDBCA — Electricite de France. Bulletin de la Direction des Etudes et Recherches. SerieC. Mathematiques-Informatique
Ed Bell — Editions Bellarmin
Ed Bi-Mo — Educational Bi-Monthly
Ed B Int — Educational Broadcasting International
Ed Books and Equip — Educational Books and Equipment
EDC — Economic Development and Cultural Change
Ed Can — Education Canada
Ed Cat — Ediciones Catedra
EDCC — Economic Development and Cultural Change
EDCCA — Economic Development and Cultural Change
EDC Ch — Economic Development and Cultural Change
EDCHA — Education in Chemistry
Ed Circ WA — Education Circular. Education Department of Western Australia
E d D — Enciclopedia del Diritto
EDD — English Dialect Dictionary
EDD — Estudios de Derecho
EDDID — Energy and Development Digest
Ed Digest — Education Digest
EDEAC — EPRI [*Electric Power Research Institute*] Database for Environmentally Assisted Cracking
Edebiyat Fak Arastirma Derg — Edebiyat Fakultesi Arastirma Dergisi
EDENA — Educator
EDESA — Ediciones Espanolas Sociedad Anonima
EDETD — Energy Detente
E Deusto — Estudios de Deusto
Ed Exec Overview — Educational Executive's Overview
Ed Ex Feat — Educational Exchange Features
Ed Exp Res — Educational Experiments and Research
Ed Extraordinaires Inst Pharmacol Toxicol (Zagreb) — Editions Extraordinaires. Institut de Pharmacologie et de Toxicologie(Zagreb)
Ed F — Educational Forum
Ed Fac Agron Univ Agric Sci — Agrartudomanyi Egyetem Agronomiai Kar Kiadvanyai. Editions. Faculty of Agronomy. University of Agricultural Sciences
Ed for Dev — Education for Development
Ed for Teaching — Education for Teaching
Ed Forum — Educational Forum
Edfou — Tell Edfou
EDG — English Dialect Grammar
Edg All News — Edgar Allen News
Ed Gaz & Teach Aid (Vic) — Education Gazette and Teachers Aid (Victoria)

Ed Gaz NSW — Education Gazette. New South Wales Department of Education
Ed Gaz SA — Education Gazette. South Australia Department of Education
EDGEDA — Educational Gerontology
Edgerton Germeshausen & Grier Rept — Edgerton, Germeshausen, and Grier Report
EdH — Educational Horizons
EDH — Essays by Divers Hands
Ed Hd — Editiones Heidelbergenses
Ed Heidelb — Editiones Heidelbergenses
Ed Horiz — Educational Horizons
EDI — Educational Documentation and Information
EdI — Education Index
EDI — Endocrinology Index
Edic Bibliogr BA — Ediciones Bibliograficas (Buenos Aires)
EDICUDA — Editorial Cuadernos para el Dialogo
EDIGA — Engineering Digest
EDIGD — Energy Digest
Edilizia Mod — Edilizia Moderna
Edil Mod — Edilizia Moderna
Edinb Dent Hosp Gaz — Edinburgh Dental Hospital. Gazette
Edinb FC T — Transactions of the Edinburgh Naturalists' Field Club
Edinb Gl S T — Transactions of the Edinburgh Geological Society
Edinb G Soc Tr — Edinburgh Geological Society. Transactions
Edinb J Md Sc — Edinburgh Journal of Medical Science
Edinb J Nt Gg Sc — Edinburgh Journal of Natural and Geographical Science
Edinb J Sc — Edinburgh Journal of Science
Edinb J Sci Technol Photogr Art — Edinburgh Journal of Science, Technology, and Photographic Art
Edinb LJ — Edinburgh Law Journal
Edinb Math Notes — Edinburgh Mathematical Notes
Edinb Med and S J — Edinburgh Medical and Surgical Journal
Edinb Med J — Edinburgh Medical Journal
Edinb M J — Edinburgh Medical Journal
Edinb M J Md Sc — London and Edinburgh Monthly Journal of Medical Science
Edinb Mm Wern S — Memoirs of the Wernerian Natural History Society (Edinburgh)
Edinb Mth S P — Proceedings of the Edinburgh Mathematical Society
Edinb N Ph J — Edinburgh New Philosophical Journal
Edinb Ph J — Edinburgh Philosophical Journal
Edinb P Ps S — Proceedings of the Royal Physical Society of Edinburgh
Edinb P R S — Proceedings of the Royal Society of Edinburgh
Edinb R — Edinburgh Review
Edinb R S P — Proceedings of the Royal Society of Edinburgh
Edinb R S T — Transactions of the Royal Society of Edinburgh
Edinb Sch Agric Annu Rep — Edinburgh School of Agriculture. Annual Report
Edinb Sch Agric Exp Work — Edinburgh School of Agriculture. Experimental Work
Edinb Sc S Arts T — Transactions of the Royal Scottish Society of Arts (Edinburgh)
Edinb T R S — Transactions of the Royal Society of Edinburgh
Edinburgh Bibliogr Soc Trans — Edinburgh Bibliographical Society. Transactions
Edinburgh Bibliog Soc Pub — Edinburgh Bibliographical Society. Publications
Edinburgh Geol — Edinburgh Geologist
Edinburgh Geol Soc Trans — Edinburgh Geological Society. Transactions
Edinburgh J Sci — Edinburgh Journal of Science
Edinburgh Med J — Edinburgh Medical Journal
Edinburgh New Philos J — Edinburgh New Philosophical Journal
Edinburgh Philos J — Edinburgh Philosophical Journal
Edinburgh Rev — Edinburgh Review
Ed in Chem — Education in Chemistry
Ed in Japan — Education in Japan
Edin R — Edinburgh Review
Edin Rev — Edinburgh Review
Ed in Science — Education in Science
Ed in the North — Education in the North
Edirne Tip Fak Derg Istanbul Univ — Edirne Tip Fakultesi Dergisi. Istanbul Universitesi
EDISD — EDIS. Environmental Data and Information Service
Edison Electr Inst Bull — Edison Electric Institute. Bulletin
Edison Electr Inst Stat Yearb Electr Util Ind — Edison Electric Institute. Statistical Yearbook. Electric Utility Industry
Editorial Research Repts — Editorial Research Reports
Edit Publ — Editor and Publisher
Ed J — Educational Journal
Ed J Sci — Edinburgh Journal of Science, Technology, and Photographic Art
EDK — Handels Rundschau
EdL — Educational Leadership
EdL — Etudes de Lettres
EDLA — El Derecho. Legislacion Argentina
EDLA — Estudios de Linguistica Aplicada
Ed Lead — Educational Leadership
Ed Lib Bulletin — Education Libraries Bulletin
Ed LJ — Edinburgh Law Journal
EdM — Education Media
EDM — Erbe Deutscher Musik
Ed Mag — Educational Magazine
Ed Man — Education Manitoba
Ed Mat Fyz Lit — Edicia Matematicko-Fyzikalnej Literatury
Ed Med & Wiss — Edition Medizin und Wissenschaft
Ed Meth — Educational Method
ED MJ — Edinburgh Medical Journal
Ed Mo — Edinburgh Monthly Review
Ed Mod — Edilizia Moderna
Edmontn Jl — Edmonton Journal
Edmonton Geol Soc Q — Edmonton Geological Society. Quarterly
Edmonton Geol Soc Quart — Edmonton Geological Society. Quarterly

Edmonton J — Edmonton Journal
Edmonton P L News Notes — Edmonton Public Library. News Notes
Edmonton Rep — Edmonton Report
Edmonton Spring Symp — Edmonton Spring Symposium
EDMSAB — Educacion Medica y Salud
Ed Mus — Educazione Musicale
Ed Mus Mag — Education Music Magazine
EdN — Editors' Notes
EdNa — Education Nationale
Ed New Philos J — Edinburgh New Philosophical Journal
Ed News — Education News
Edn Hebd J Deb — Edition Hebdomadaire du Journal de Debats
Ednl Administration Bull — Educational Administration Bulletin
Ednl Broadcasting International — Educational Broadcasting International
Ednl Change and Dev — Educational Change and Development
Ednl Dev — Educational Development
Ednl Dev Centre R — Educational Development Centre Review
Ednl Dev International — Educational Development International
Ednl Documentation and Information — Educational Documentation and Information
Ednl R — Educational Review
Ednl Research — Educational Research
Ednl Sciences — Educational Sciences
Ednl Studies — Educational Studies
Ednl Studies in Maths — Educational Studies in Mathematics
Ed NS — Education Nova Scotia
Ed NSW — Education. New South Wales Teachers Federation
Ed Off Gaz Qld — Education Office Gazette. Queensland Department of Education
Ed Ont — Education Ontario
Ed Outl — Educational Outlook
EDP — EDP [*Electronic Data Processing*] Industry Report
EDP — Estudios de Poblacion
EDPAA — EDP [*Electronic Data Processing*] Analyzer
EDP A C S — EDP [*Electronic Data Processing*] Audit, Control, and Security Newsletter
EDP Anal — EDP [*Electronic Data Processing*] Analyzer
EDP Aud — EDP [*Electronic Data Processing*] Auditor
EDP Europa — EDP [*Electronic Data Processing*] Europa Report
Ed Philos J — Edinburgh Philosophical Journal
EDP In-Depth Rep — EDP [*Electronic Data Processing*] In-Depth Reports
EDP Indus Rep — EDP [*Electronic Data Processing*] Industry Report
EDP Japan — EDP [*Electronic Data Processing*] Japan Report
EDPKA2 — Endokrynologia Polska
EDP Performance Rev — EDP [*Electronic Data Processing*] Performance Review
EDP Perf Rev — EDP [*Electronic Data Processing*] Performance Review
EDPRICE — Energy Detente International Price/Tax Series
Ed Proc Int Cadmium Conf — Edited Proceedings. International Cadmium Conference
Ed Proc Int Conf Hot Dip Galvanizing — Edited Proceedings. International Conference on Hot Dip Galvanizing
Ed Proc Int Galvanizing Conf — Edited Proceedings. International Galvanizing Conference
Ed Prod Rep — Educational Product Report
EdPsy — Educational Psychologist
Ed Publ Fourth Estate — Editor and Publisher - the Fourth Estate
EDP Weekly — EDP [*Electronic Data Processing*] Weekly
Ed Q India — Education Quarterly (India)
Ed Q Nepal — Educational Quarterly (Nepal)
Ed Q Phil — Educational Quarterly (Philippines)
Ed Que — Education Quebec
EDR — Economic Development Review
Ed R — Edinburgh Review
EdR — Educational Record
Ed R — Educational Review
EDR — Educator's Desk Reference
EDR Anthrc — Energy Data Reports. Distribution of Pennsylvania Anthracite
EDR B Coal — Energy Data Reports. Bituminous Coal and Lignite Distribution
EDRCAM — Endocrine Research Communications
Ed R (China) — Educational Review (China)
EDR Coal B & L — Energy Data Reports. Coal, Bituminous and Lignite
Ed Rec — Educational Record. Tasmania Education Department
Ed Rec Bur Bul — Educational Records Bureau. Bulletins
Ed Res — Educational Research
Ed Res B — Educational Research Bulletin
Ed Res Record — Educational Research Record
Ed Res Rep (Wash DC) — Editorial Research Reports (Washington, DC)
EDR F Oils — Energy Data Reports. Fuel Oils by Sulphur Content
EDR Ker — Energy Data Reports. Sales of Fuel Oil and Kerosene
EDR LPS — Energy Data Reports. Liquefied Petroleum Sales
EDR N Gas — Energy Data Reports. Natural Gas
EDRO SARAP Res Tech Rep — EDRO [*Executive Director of Regional Operations*] SARAP Research TechnicalReports
EDR Pet St — Energy Data Reports. Petroleum Statement
EDRRA — Editorial Research Reports
EDRSA2 — Elma Dill Russell Spencer Foundation Series
EDS — Economic Digest
EdS — Ecrits des Saints
EDS — Elements de Doctrine Spirituelle
EDS — English Dance and Song
EDS — Etudes sur le Devenir Social
Ed San — Education Sanitaire
Ed Sci — Educational Sciences
Ed Screen — Educational Screen
Ed Screen AV G — Educational Screen and Audiovisual Guide [*Later, AV Guide: The Learning Media Magazine*]

Ed Ser Fla Dep Nat Resour Mar Res Lab — Educational Series. Florida Department of Natural Resources. Marine Research Laboratory
Ed Studies — Educational Studies
Ed Stud Math — Educational Studies in Mathematics
Ed Survey — Educational Survey
EdT — Educational Technology
ED T — Educational Times
EdT — Education Theory
E D Tch — Etudes et Documents Tchadiens
Ed Tech — Educational Technology
Ed Theatre J — Educational Theatre Journal
Ed Theory — Educational Theory
Ed Today — Education Today
EDTRED — Endodontics and Dental Traumatology
Ed TV Int — Educational Television International
Educ — Education
Educa — Education
EducacionH — Educacion (Havanna)
EducacionM — Educacion (Managua)
Educ Adm — Educational Administration
Educ Adm — Educational Administrator
Educ Adm Abstr — Educational Administration Abstracts
Educ Adm & Sup — Educational Administration and Supervision
Educ Admin — Educational Administration Quarterly
Educ Admin Abstr — Educational Administration Abstracts
Educ Admin Supervision — Educational Administration and Supervision
Educ Adm Q — Educational Administration Quarterly
Educ and Medicine — Education and Medicine
Educ & Psychol M — Educational and Psychological Measurement
Educ & Psychol Meas — Educational and Psychological Measurement
Educ and Train — Education and Training
Educ & Training — Education and Training
Educ & Train Men Retard — Education and Training of the Mentally Retarded
Educ & Train Mentally Retard — Education and Training of the Mentally Retarded
Educ & Urban Soc — Education and Urban Society
Educ and Urban Society — Education and Urban Society
Educa R — Educational Review
Educational Bldg Digest — Educational Building Digest
Educational Rec — Educational Record
Education Librs Bull — Education Libraries Bulletin
Education M — Education Musicale
Educatn 89 — Projections of Education Statistics to 1988-89
Educazione M — Educazione Musicale
Educ Botswana Lesotho & Swaziland — Education in Botswana, Lesotho, and Swaziland
Educ Brdcstng — Educational Broadcasting
Educ Broadcast Int — Educational Broadcasting International
Educ Broad Int — Educational Broadcasting International
Educ Bull — Education Bulletin
Educ Can — Education Canada
Educ Cap — Education Capital
Educ Caracas — Educacion (Caracas)
Educ Change Dev — Educational Change and Development
Educ Chem — Education in Chemistry
Educ Cien Humanas Lima — Educacion y Ciencias Humanas (Lima)
Educ Cien Soc Rio — Educacao e Ciencias Sociais. Boletim do Centro Brasileiro de Pesquisas Educacionais (Rio de Janeiro)
Educ Comm & Tech J — Educational Communication and Technology Journal
Educ Comput — Educational Computing
Educ Cult — Education and Culture
Educ Dent (Ica) — Educacion Dental (Ica, Peru)
Educ Dev Korea — Educational Development in Korea
Educ Dig — Education Digest
Educ Digest — Education Digest
Educ Dir Dent Aux — Educational Directions for Dental Auxiliaries
Educ Dir Dent Hyg — Educational Directions in Dental Hygiene
Educ Doc & Inf — Educational Documentation and Information
Educ East Afr — Education in Eastern Africa
Educ et Cult — Education and Culture
Educ et Develop — Education et Developpement
Educ Exec Overview — Educational Executives' Overview
EducF — Educational Forum
Educ Film Guide — Educational Film Guide
Educ Foc — Educational Focus
Educ Focus — Educational Focus
Educ For — Educational Forum
Educ Forum — Educational Forum
Educ Found Am Soc Plast Reconstr Surg Proc Symp — Educational Foundation. American Society of Plastic and Reconstructive Surgeons. Proceedings of the Symposium
Educ Gaz — Education Gazette
Educ Gazette — Education Gazette
Educ Gaz SA — Education Gazette. South Australia Department of Education
Educ Gerontol — Educational Gerontology
Educ Guard — Education Guardian
Educ Horiz — Educational Horizons
Educ Ind — Education Index
Educ Index — Education Index
Educ Ind Telev — Educational and Industrial Television
Educ Inf — Education for Information
Educ Innovations — Educational Innovations
Educ J — Education Journal
Educ Lead — Educational Leadership
Educ Leadersh — Educational Leadership
Educ Leg Serv Br — Educator's Legal Service Briefs

Educ Lg Cit — Education in Large Cities
Educ Libr Bull — Education Libraries Bulletin
Educ Libr Serv Bull — Education Library Service Bulletin
Educ Lima — Educacion (Lima)
Educ L Rep (West) — Education Law Reporter (West)
Educ Mag — Educational Magazine
Educ Manage Admin — Educational Management and Administration
Educ Media — Educational Media
Educ Media Int — Educational Media International
Educ Med Salud — Educacion Medica y Salud
Educ Mex — Educacion (Mexico)
Educ Microcomp Ann — Educational Microcomputing Annual
Educ Mus Mag — Educational Music Magazine
Educ N — Education News
Educ Nat — Education Nationale
Educ News — Education News
Educ NSW — Education. New South Wales Teachers Federation
EDUCOM — EDUCOM [*Educational Communications*] Bulletin
EDUCOM Bull — EDUCOM [*Educational Communications*] Bulletin
Educ Ont — Education Ontario
Educ Outl — Educational Outlook
Educ Perm — Education Permanente
Educ Philos Theory — Educational Philosophy and Theory
Educ Phil Theor — Educational Philosophy and Theory
Educ Plan — Educational Planning
Educ Policy Bull — Education Policy Bulletin
Educ Prod Rept — Educational Product Report
Educ Psychol — Educational Psychologist
Educ Psychol Measmt — Educational and Psychological Measurement
Educ Psychol Measure — Educational and Psychological Measurement
Educ Psyc M — Educational and Psychological Measurement
Educ Q — Education Quarterly
Educ Q Nepal — Education Quarterly. Katmandu, Nepal College of Education
Educ Quest — Educational Quest
Educ Quim — Educacion Quimica
Educ R — Educational Review
Educ Rec — Educational Record
Educ Rec Bur Bull — Educational Records Bureau. Bulletins
Educ Recd — Educational Record
Educ Record — Educational Record
Educ Res — Educational Research
Educ Res — Educational Researcher
Educ Res Bul — Educational Research Bulletin
Educ Researcher — Educational Researcher
Educ Res News — Educational Research News
Educ Resour Inf Cent Clgh — Educational Resources Information Center Clearinghouse
Educ Res Perspect — Education Research and Perspectives
Educ Res Q — Educational Research Quarterly
Educ Res Quart — Educational Research Quarterly
Educ Rev — Education Review
Educ Rural Rubio — Educacion Rural. Organizacion de los Estados Americanos (Rubio, Tachira, Venezuela)
Educ Safe Handl Pestic Appl Proc Int Workshop — Education and Safe Handling in Pesticide Application. Proceedings.International Workshop
Educ Sanit — Educazione Sanitaria
Educ Sci — Education in Science
Educ Screen — Educational Screen
Educ Ser Fl Dep Nat Resour Mar Res Lab — Educational Series. Florida. Department of Natural Resources. Marine Research Laboratory
Educ Ser Miner Resour Div (Manitoba) — Educational Series. Mineral Resources Division (Manitoba)
Educ Ser NC Miner Resour Sect — Educational Series. North Carolina Mineral Resources Section
Educ S Jose — Educacion (San Jose, Costa Rica)
Educ Software Rep — Educational Software Report
Educ Sordomuti — Educazione dei Sordomuti
Educ Stat — Projections of Education Statistics to 1992-93
Educ Stud — Educational Studies
Educ Stud Math — Educational Studies in Mathematics
Educ Sup Des — Educacion Superior y Desarrollo
Educ Suppl Yorks Beekprs Ass — Educational Supplement. Yorkshire Beekeepers Association
Educ Tech — Educational Technology
Educ Techn — Educational Technology
Educ Technol — Educational Technology
Educ Theatre J — Educational Theatre Journal
Educ Theor — Educational Theory
Educ Theory — Educational Theory
Educ Through Technol — Education through Technology
Educ Train Eng Des Int Conf — Education and Training of Engineering Designers. InternationalConference
Educ TV — Educational and Industrial Television
Educ Urban — Education and Urban Society
Educ Urb Soc — Education and Urban Society
Educ Vict — Education for Victory
Educ Visual — Education of the Visually Handicapped
Educ (WA) — Education (Perth, Western Australia)
Educ Wash — La Educacion (Washington, DC)
Edu D — Educational Digest
Ed USA — Education USA
EDV — Economic Development Review
EDVBD8 — EDV [*Elektronische Datenverarbeitung*] in Medizin und Biologie
Ed Vis Hand — Education of the Visually Handicapped
EDV Med Biol — EDV [*Elektronische Datenverarbeitung*] in Medizin und Biologie

Ed (WA) — Education (Western Australia)
Ed World — Education Around the World
EE — Eastern Economist
EE — East Europe
EE — Economia Instituto de Investigaciones Economicas y Financieras
EE — Electronic Editions
EE — Elementary English
EE — Enlightenment Essays
EE — Ensaios Ethnographicos
EE — Ensayos y Estudios
EE — Ephemeris Epigraphica
EE — Erasmus in English
EE — Estudios Eclesiasticos
EE — Estudios Eruditos en Memoriam de Bonilla y San Martin
Ee — Ethnographie
EE — Evreiskaia Entsiklopediia
EE — Journal of Environmental Engineering
EEA — Educational Administration Abstracts
EEA — Electrical and Electronics Abstracts
EEA — Electrical Engineering Abstracts
EEA — Epigrafia Ebraica Antica
EEAm — Enciclopedia Universal Ilustrada Europeo-Americana
EEAm S — Enciclopedia Universal Ilustrada Europeo-Americana. Suplement Anual
EE Ath — Epistemonike Epeteris tes Philosophikes Scholes tou Panepistemiou Athenon
EEAVA — Elektroenergetika i Avtomatika
EEB — European Trends
EEBD — Eastern European Business Directory
EEBS — Epeteris Hetaireias Byzantinon Spudon
EEC — Enfoques Educacionales (Chile)
EEC — Engineering Economist
EeC — Etudes et Commentaires
EEC Bull — European Economic Community. Bulletin of the European Communities
EEC Bull S — European Economic Community. Bulletin of the European Communities. Supplement
EECDNG — EEC Dangerous Chemicals Online
EECILS — Ephemeris Epigraphica. Corpus Inscriptionum Latinarum Supplementum
EECIT — Estudios Escenicos. Cuadernos del Instituto del Teatro
E Ecl — Estudios Eclesiasticos
EECSB3 — Electroencephalography and Clinical Neurophysiology. Supplement
EED — Eastern Economist
EEd — English Education
EEDID — Energy Executive Directory
EEDND — Energy Educator Newsletter
EEE — Eastern European Economics
EEE — Epeteris Epistemonikon Ereunon. Panepistemion Athenon
EEEVAL — East End Environment
EE Eval Engin — EE. Evaluation Engineering
EEF — Egypt Exploration Fund
EEFHRA — Estudos e Ensaios Folcloricos em Homenagem a Renato Almeida
EEFM — Egypt Exploration Fund Memoirs
EEG Cl Neur — Electroencephalography and Clinical Neurophysiology
EEGEA — EEG/EMG; Zeitschrift fuer Elektroenzephalographie, Elektromyographie, und Verwandte Gebiete
EEH — European Economic Review
EEH — Explorations in Economic History
EEHA/AEA — Anuario de Estudios Americanos. Consejo Superior de Investigaciones Cientificasy Universidad de Sevilla, Escuela de Estudios Hispano-Americanos
EEHA/HBA — Historiografia y Bibliografia Americanistas. Escuela de Estudios Hispano-Americanos de Sevilla
EEI — Edison Electric Institute. Bulletin
EEIBA — EEI [*Edison Electric Institute*] Bulletin
EEI Bul — Edison Electric Institute. Bulletin
EEI Elec P — Edison Electric Institute. Electric Perspectives
EEIND — Energy and the Environment: Interactions
EEISD — EIS. Environmental Impact Statements
EEJ — Eastern Economic Journal
EEK — Economisch en Sociaal Instituut voor de Middenstand. Informatieblad
EEL — Energy Policy
EELFS — Eunomia. Ephemeridis Listy Filiologicke. Supplementum
EELMA — Electricite-Electronique Moderne
EELOAZ — Eesti Loodus
EEM — Estudios Eclesiasticos (Madrid)
EEMA — Eglise et l'Etat au Moyen Age
EEMB — Emanu-El Men's Bulletin
EEMB — Estudios Eruditos en Memoriam de Bonilla y San Martin
EEMCA — Estudios de Edad Media de la Corona de Aragon
EEMF — Early English Manuscripts in facsimile
EEN — Environment
E End News — East End News
EENMA — Electrical Engineer and Merchandiser
EENTA — Eye, Ear, Nose, and Throat Journal
EENTDT — Ecological Entomology
EEOC Compl Man BNA — EEOC [*Equal Employment Opportunity Commission*] Compliance Manual. Bureau of National Affairs
EEOC Compl Man CCH — EEOC [*Equal Employment Opportunity Commission*] Compliance Manual. Commerce Clearing House
EEO Spotl — EEO [*Equal Employment Opportunity*] Spotlight
EeP — L'Eglise en Priere
E Epigr — Ephemeris Epigraphica
EEPMD — Energy Economics, Policy, and Management
EEPS — European Economic and Political Survey
EEPSAP — Epistemonike Epeteris tes Philosophikes Scholes tou Aristoteleiou Panepistemiou

EEPSAPT — Epistemonike Epeteris tes Philosophikes Scholes tou Aristoteleiou PanepistemiouThessalonikes
EEPSPA — Epistemonike Epeteris tes Philosophikes Scholes tou Panepistemiou Athenon
EEPSTh — Epistemonike Epeteris tes Philosophikes Scholes tou Panepistemiou Thessalonikes
EEQ — East European Quarterly
EEQEA — Electronic Equipment Engineering
EEQNA — Electronic Equipment News
EER — European Economic Review
EERGD — Energy (Ottawa)
EEROA — Elektro
EeS — Eglise et Societe
EESADV — Ecotoxicology and Environmental Safety
EESB — Expression. Journal of the English Society
EEsc — Estudis Escenics. Quaderns de l'Institut del Teatre de la Diputacio de Barcelona
EESE — Etudes d'Ethnographie, de Sociologie, et d'Ethnologie
EESGRM — Egypt Exploration Society. Graeco-Roman Memoirs
EESM — Egypt Exploration Society Memoirs
EESR — Egypt Exploration Society. Report
EES Rep Univ Wis Madison Eng Exp Stn — EES [*Engineering Experiment Station*] Report. University of Wisconsin-Madison. Engineering Experiment Station
Eesti Loodustead Arh 1 Ser — Eesti Loodusteaduse Arhiiv. 1 Ser. Geologica, Chemica, et Physica
Eesti Loodustead Arh 2 Ser — Eesti Loodusteaduse Arhiiv. 2 Ser. Biologica
Eesti Loodustead Arh Seer 2 — Eesti Loodusteaduse Arhiiv. 2 Seeria. Acta ad res Naturae Estonicae Perscrutandas Edita a Societate Rebus Naturae Investigandis in Universitate Tartuensi Constituta. Serie 2
Eesti Loomakasvatuse Vet Tead Uurim Inst Tead Toode Kogumik — Eesti Loomakasvatuse ja Veterinaaria Teadusliku Uurimise Instituut.Teaduslike Toode Kogumik
Eesti NSV Tead Akad — Eesti NSV Teaduste Akadeemia. Toimetised
Eesti NSV Tead Akad Fuus Astronoom Inst Uurim — Eesti NSV Teaduste Akadeemia. Fuusika ja Astronoomia Instituudi Uurimused
Eesti NSV Tead Akad Fuus Inst Uurim — Eesti NSV Teaduste Akadeemia. Fuusika Instituudi Uurimused
Eesti NSV Tead Akad Geol Inst Uurim — Eesti NSV Teaduste Akadeemia. Geoloogia Instituudi Uurimused
Eesti NSV Tead Akad Tartu Astronoom Observ Publ — Eesti NSV Teaduste Akadeemia. Tartu Astronoomia Observatooriumi Publikatsioonik
Eesti NSV Tead Akad Toim — Eesti NSV Teaduste Akadeemia. Toimetised
Eesti NSV Tead Akad Toim Biol — Eesti NSV Teaduste Akadeemia. Toimetised. Bioloogia
Eesti NSV Tead Akad Toim Biol Ser — Eesti NSV Teaduste Akadeemia. Toimetised. Bioloogiline Seeria
Eesti NSV Tead Akad Toim Fuus Mat — Eesti NSV Teaduste Akadeemia. Toimetised. Fuusika. Matemaatika
Eesti NSV Tead Akad Toim Fuus Mat Tehnikatead Seer — Eesti NSV Teaduste Akadeemia. Toimetised. Fuusika. Matemaatika ja Tehnikateaduste Seeria
Eesti NSV Tead Akad Toim Geol — Eesti NSV Teaduste Akadeemia. Toimetised. Geoloogia
Eesti NSV Tead Akad Toim Geol Izv Akad Nauk Est SSR Geol — Eesti NSV Teaduste Akadeemia. Toimetised. Geoloog Izvestiia Akademii Nauk Estonskoi SSR Geologiia
Eesti NSV Tead Akad Toim Izv Ser Geol — Eesti NSV Teaduste Akadeemia. Toimetised. Izvestiya. Seria Geoloogia
Eesti NSV Tead Akad Toim Izv Ser Keem — Eesti NSV Teaduste Akadeemia. Toimetised. Izvestiya. Seria Keemia
Eesti NSV Tead Akad Toim Keem — Eesti NSV Teaduste Akadeemia. Toimetised. Keemia
Eesti NSV Tead Akad Toim Keem Geol — Eesti NSV Teaduste Akadeemia. Toimetised. Keemia. Geoloogia
Eesti NSV Tead Akad Toim Keem Izv Akad Nauk Est SSR Khim — Eesti NSV Teaduste Akadeemia. Toimetised. Keemia. Izvestiia Akademii Nauk Estonskoi SSR Khimiia
Eesti NSV Tead Akad Toim Teh Fuus Mat Tead Seer — Eesti NSV Teaduste Akadeemia. Toimetised. Tehniliste jaFuusikalis-Matemaatiliste Teaduste Seeria
Eesti Pollumajanduse Akad Tead Toode Kogumik — Eesti Pollumajanduse Akadeemia Teaduslike Toode Kogumik
Eesti Statist — Eesti Statistika
Eesti Tead Akad Toim Biol — Eesti Teaduste Akadeemia Toimetised. Bioloogia
Eesti Tead Akad Toim Fuus Mat — Eesti Teaduste Akadeemia Toimetised, Fuusika, Matemaatika
Eesti Tead Akad Toim Keemia — Eesti Teaduste Akadeemia Toimetised. Keemia
Eesti Tead Akad Toim Ohisk Tead — Eesti Teaduste Akadeemia Toimetised. Uhiskonnateadused
Eesti Vabariigi Tartu Ulik Toim A — Eesti Vabariigi Tartu Ulikooli Toimetised A. Mathematica, Physica, Medica
Eesti Vabariigi Tartu Ulik Toim C — Eesti Vabariigi Tartu Ulikooli Toimetised C. Annales
EE/Systems Eng — EE/Systems Engineering Today
E/E Syst Eng Today — E/E Systems Engineering Today
Ee T — Eglise et Theologie
EETAD — ETA. Elektrowaerme im Technischen Ausbau
EETED — Elektrische Energie-Technik
EETh — Einfuehrung in die Evangelische Theologie
EEThS — Epistemonike Epeteris tes Theologikes Scholes tou Panepistemiou Thessalonikes
EETS — Early English Text Society
EETSES — Early English Text Society. Extra Series
EEU — East European Markets
EEU — Essais et Etudes Universitaires
E Eur — East Europe

E Eur Econ — Eastern European Economics
E Eur Mkts — East European Markets
E Europe Q — East European Quarterly
E Eur Q — East European Quarterly
EeV — Esprit et Vie. Langres
EF — Enciclopedia Filosofica
EF — Encyclopedie Francaise. Societe de Gestion de l'Encyclopedie Francaise
EF — Erlanger Forschungen
EF — Estudios Filosoficos
EF — Estudis Franciscans
EF — Etudes Foreziennes
EF — Etudes Francaises
EF — Etudes Franciscaines
EF — Experiments in Fluids
EFA — Etudes Francaises
EFAID — Energie Fluide, l'Air Industriel
EFAPA — Electronica y Fisica Aplicada
EFATD — Energia del Fuego al Atomo
EFB — EFTA [*European Free Trade Association*] Bulletin
EFBI — Etudes Francaises de Bar-Ilan
EFBSA — Bulletin. Direction des Etudes et Recherches. Serie A. Supplement (France)
EFCE Publ Ser — ERCE [*European Federation of Chemical Engineers*] Publication Series
EFCPA — Electric Furnace Conference Proceedings
EFD — Education for Development
EFD — European Energy Report
EFDBA — Bulletin. Direction des Etudes et Recherches. Serie B (France)
EFDNA — Bulletin. Direction des Etudes et Recherches. Serie A (France)
EFE — EFTA [*European Free Trade Association*] Bulletin
Efes Muz Yillik — Efes Muzesi Yillik
EFF — European Taxation
Eff Aging Regul Cereb Blood Flow Metab Abstr Satell Symp — Effects of Aging on Regulation of Cerebral Blood Flow and Metabolism.Abstracts. Satellite Symposium
Eff Chem Environ Fract Processes Tewksbury Symp — Effects of Chemical Environment on Fracture Processes. Tewksbury Symposium on Fracture
Eff Environ Cells Tissues Proc World Congr Anat Clin Pathol — Effects of Environment on Cells and Tissues. Proceedings. World Congress of Anatomic and Clinical Pathology
Eff Health Care — Effective Health Care
Effic Text — Efficience Textile
Eff Ind Membr Processes Benefits Oppor Proc Int Conf — Effective Industrial Membrane Processes. Benefits and Opportunities. Proceedings. International Conference
Effi Text — Efficience Textile
Effluent Water Treat J — Effluent and Water Treatment Journal
Eff Nicotine Biol Syst Satell Symp — Effects of Nicotine on Biological Systems. Satellite Symposium
Eff Ocean Environ Microb Act Proc US Jpn Conf — Effect of the Ocean Environment on Microbial Activities. Proceedings. United States-Japan Conference on Marine Microbiology
Eff Radiat Mater Int Symp — Effects of Radiation on Materials. International Symposium
Eff Rayonnem Semicond Congr Int Phys Semicond — Effets des Rayonnements sur les Semiconducteurs. Congres Internationalde Physique des Semiconducteurs
Eff Udobr — Effectivnost Udobrenii
Eff Wat Tre — Effluent and Water Treatment Journal
Eff Zashch Introd Rast Vrednykh Org Mater Koord Soveshch — Effektivnost Zashchity Introdutsirovannykh Rastenii ot VrednykhOrganizmov. Materialy Koordinatsionnogo Soveshchaniya
EFGRAQ — Eastern Fruit Grower
EFGUAZ — Escuela de Farmacia Guatemala
EFI — Enrico Fermi International Summer School of Physics
EFI — Estadisticas Financieras Internacionales
EFI — Euromarkt Nieuws
EFil — Estudios Filologicos
EFL — Epochen der Franzoesischen Literatur
EFL — Essays in French Literature
EFLL — Essays in Foreign Languages and Literature
EFMBB9 — Einfuehrungen zur Molekularbiologie
EFMEA — Engineering Fracture Mechanics
EFNED — Energy Forum in New England
EFOC Fiber Opt Commun Proc — EFOC [*European Fiber Optics and Communications*] Fiber Optics and Communications. Proceedings
EFOC Proc — EFOC [*European Fiber Optics and Communications Exposition*] Proceedings
EFP — Economiste Arabe. L'Economie et les Finances des Pays Arabes
EFPOD — Electric Farm Power
EFPRA3 — Estudos sobre a Fauna Portuguesa
EFPS — Elsevier Series in Forensic and Police Science
EFPSD9 — Annual Research Reviews. Effects of Psychotherapy
EFR — Editeurs Francais Reunis
EFR — Empire Forestry Review
Efr — Etudes Francaises
EFran — Etudes Franciscaines
EFreu — Etudes Freudiennes
E Fs — Estudios Filosoficos
EFSPA — L'Economie et la Finance de la Syrie et de Pays Arabes
EFT — English Fiction in Transition, 1880-1920 [*Later, English Literature in Transition, 1880-1920*]
EFTA — European Free Trade Association. Bulletin
EFTA Bull — EFTA [*European Free Trade Association*] Bulletin
EFT Report — EFT Report. The Newsletter of Electronic Funds Transfer

EFV — Enchiridion Fontium Valdensium
EFW — Executive Financial Woman
EFWSI — Explorations and Field-Work of the Smithsonian Institution
EFZo — Ergebnisse und Fortschritte der Zoologie
EG — Economic Geography
Eg — Egoist
EG — Employment Gazette
EG — English and Germanic Studies
EG — Epigrafia Greca
EG — Estate Gazette
EG — Estudios Geograficos
EG — Etudes Germaniques
EG — Europaeische Gesprache
EG — Evangelisches Gemeindeblatt fuer Galizien
EGA — Early Greek Armour and Weapons
EGAABL — Eley Game Advisory Station. Annual Review
EGAPBW — Egyptian Journal of Animal Production
EGASA6 — Eley Game Advisory Service. Booklet
EgC — Egypte Contemporaine
EGC — Egyptian Gazette (Cairo)
Eg Cont — Egypte Contemporaine
EGD — Economic News of Bulgaria
EGDJAS — Egyptian Dental Journal
EGE — Estudios Geograficos (Espana)
EGE Actual — EGE [*Eau-Gaz-Electricite et Applications*] Actualites
EGERDQ — Entomologica Germanica
EGerm — Etudes Germaniques
Egerton Coll Agric Bull — Egerton College. Agricultural Bulletin
EGESA — Egeszsegtudomany
Egesz — Egeszsegtudomany
Ege Univ Fen Fak Derg Seri B — Ege Universitesi Fen Fakultesi Dergisi. Seri B
Ege Univ Fen Fak Ilmi Rap Ser — Ege Universitesi Fen Fakultesi Ilmi Raporlar Serisi
Ege Univ Ziraat Fak Derg — Ege Universitesi Ziraat. Fakultesi Dergisi
Ege Univ Ziraat Fak Derg Seri A — Ege Universitesi Ziraat. Fakultesi Dergisi. Seri A
Ege Univ Ziraat Fak Yayin — Ege Universitesi Ziraat. Fakultesi Yayinlari
EGF — Epicorum Graecorum Fragmenta
EGF ESIS Publ — EGF/ESIS (European Group on Fracture/European Structural Integrity Society) Publication
EGF Publ — EGF (European Group on Fracture) Publication
EGG — Egyptian Gazette
EGGOA — Engineering Geology (Amsterdam)
Eg Gov School Med Rec — Egyptian Government School of Medicine. Records
Egg Prod — Egg Producer
EGGVG — Einfuehrungsgesetz zum Gerichtsverfassungsgesetz
EGH — Eclogae Geologicae Helvetiae
EGH — Essays in Greek History
EGH — Everton's Genealogical Helper
EGHVA — Eclogae Geologicae Helvetiae
EGHVAG — Eclogae Geologicae Helvetiae
EGI — Industrial Egypt
EGIM — Ezhegodnik Gosudarstvennogo Istoricheskogo Muzeia
EGIND — Energinfo
Egitto & Vic Oriente — Egitto e Vicino Oriente
EGJBAY — Egyptian Journal of Botany
EGJCA3 — Egyptian Journal of Chemistry
EGJGAF — Egyptian Journal of Geology
EGK — Epigrammata Graeca ex Lapidibus Conlecta
EGKAA — Energetika
EGKO — Einfuehrungsgesetz zur Konkursordnung
EGKZA — Engei Gakkai Zasshi
EGKZA9 — Engei Gakkai Zasshi
EGL — Economic Geology (Lancaster, Pennsylvania)
Egl Can — Eglise Canadienne
EGLI — Essay and General Literature Index
Eglise Th — Eglise et Theologie
EGLMA9 — Estudios Geologicos
Egl Th — Eglise et Theologie
Egl Viv — Eglise Vivante
Egm — Egmondiana
EGM — Egyptian Mail
EGN — Ellen Glasgow Newsletter
EGOPA — Engineering Optimization
EGP — Economic Geography
EGP — Energy Policy
EGPBAU — Egyptian Pharmaceutical Bulletin
EGPJBL — Egyptian Pharmaceutical Journal
EgR — Egyptian Religion
EGREAF — Egretta
Egri ME — Egri Muzeum Evkoenyve
Egri Muz E — Egri Muzeum Evkoenyve
Egri Muz Ev — Az Egri Muzeum Evkoenyve
Egri Tanarkepzoe Foeisk Tud Koezlem — Egri Tanarkepzoe Foeiskola Tudomanyos Koezlemenyei. Acta Academiae PaedagogicaeAgriensis
EGRTA — Energy Report (Alton, England)
EGS — English and Germanic Studies
EGSHEA — Etudes Generales. Societe d'Histoire de l'Eglise d'Alsace
EGSMA — Energomashinostroenie
EGT — Estates, Gifts, and Trusts Journal
EGTKA — Energetik
Eg Vic Or — Egitto e Vicino Oriente
EGWA — Enzyklopaedie der Geisteswissenschaftlichen Arbeitsmethoden
EGY — Economic Geography
EGYAA — Energetyka

EGYDA — Energy Digest
Egyp Astron Texts — Egyptian Astronomical Texts
Egy Phil Koez — Egyetemes Philologiai Koezloeny
Egypt Agric Organ Bahtim Exp Stn Tech Bull — Egyptian Agricultural Organization. Bahtim Experiment Station. Technical Bulletin
Egypt Agric Rev — Egyptian Agricultural Review
Egypt Comput J — Egyptian Computer Journal
Egypt Cott Gaz — Egyptian Cotton Gazette
Egypt Cotton Gaz — Egyptian Cotton Gazette
Egypt Dent J — Egyptian Dental Journal
Egypte Contemp — Egypte Contemporaine
Egypte Contemp Soc Khed — Egypte Contemporaine. Societe Khediviale d'Economie Politique, de Statistique et de Legislation
Egypt Explor Fund Mem — Egypt Exploration Fund Memoirs
Egypt Geol Surv Ann — Egypt Geological Survey. Annals
Egypt Geol Surv Min Auth Pap — Egyptian Geological Survey and Mining Authority. Paper
Egypt Geol Surv Pap — Egypt Geological Survey. Paper
Egyptian M Assn J — Egyptian Medical Association. Journal
Egyptian Statist J — Egyptian Statistical Journal
Egypt J Agron — Egyptian Journal of Agronomy
Egypt J Anal Chem — Egyptian Journal of Analytical Chemistry
Egypt J Anim Prod — Egyptian Journal of Animal Production
Egypt J Bilharz — Egyptian Journal of Bilharziasis
Egypt J Bilharziasis — Egyptian Journal of Bilharziasis
Egypt J Biochem — Egyptian Journal of Biochemistry
Egypt J Biomed Eng — Egyptian Journal of Biomedical Engineering
Egypt J Biotechnol — Egyptian Journal of Biotechnology
Egypt J Bot — Egyptian Journal of Botany
Egypt J Ch — Egyptian Journal of Chemistry
Egypt J Chem — Egyptian Journal of Chemistry
Egypt J Chest Dis Tuberc — Egyptian Journal of Chest Diseases and Tuberculosis
Egypt J Dairy Sci — Egyptian Journal of Dairy Science
Egypt J Food Sci — Egyptian Journal of Food Science
Egypt J Genet Cytol — Egyptian Journal of Genetics and Cytology
Egypt J Geol — Egyptian Journal of Geology
Egypt J Hortic — Egyptian Journal of Horticulture
Egypt J Immunol — Egyptian Journal of Immunology
Egypt J Microbiol — Egyptian Journal of Microbiology
Egypt J Neurol Psychiat Neurosurg — Egyptian Journal of Neurology, Psychiatry, and Neurosurgery
Egypt Jnl Vet Sci — Egyptian Journal of Veterinary Science
Egypt J Occup Med — Egyptian Journal of Occupational Medicine
Egypt J Pharm Sci — Egyptian Journal of Pharmaceutical Sciences
Egypt J Phyopathol — Egyptian Journal of Phytopathology
Egypt J Phys — Egyptian Journal of Physics
Egypt J Physiol Sci — Egyptian Journal of Physiological Sciences
Egypt J Phytopathol — Egyptian Journal of Phytopathology
Egypt J Psychiatry — Egyptian Journal of Psychiatry
Egypt J Psychol — Egyptian Journal of Psychology
Egypt J Soc Med — Egyptian Journal of Social Medicine
Egypt J Soil Sci — Egyptian Journal of Soil Science
Egypt J Vet Sci — Egyptian Journal of Veterinary Science
Egypt Minist Agric Tech Bull — Egypt. Ministry of Agriculture. Technical Bulletin
Egypt Natl Cancer Inst J — Egyptian National Cancer Institute. Journal
Egypt Orthop J — Egyptian Orthopaedic Journal
Egypt Pharm Bull — Egyptian Pharmaceutical Bulletin
Egypt Pharm J — Egyptian Pharmaceutical Journal
Egypt Pharm Rep — Egyptian Pharmaceutical Reports. Pharmaceutical Society of Egypt and the Syndicate of Pharmacists
Egypt Popul Fam Plann Rev — Egyptian Population and Family Planning Review
Egypt Revs Sci — Egyptian Reviews of Science
Egypt Soc Obstet Gynecol J — Egyptian Society of Obstetrics and Gynecology. Journal
Egypt Sugar Distill Co Sugar Cane Dep Res Bull — Egyptian Sugar and Distillation Company. Sugar Cane Department. Research Bulletin
Egypt Sugar Distill Co Sugar Cane Dep Tech Bull — Egyptian Sugar and Distillation Company. Sugar Cane Department. Technical Bulletin
Egypt Vet Med Assoc J — Egyptian Veterinary Medical Association. Journal
Egypt Vet Med J — Egyptian Veterinary Medical Journal
EGYSA — Energy Sources
EGYSAO — Energy Sources
Egyt Trav Mag — Egypt Travel Magazine
EH — Eastern Horizon
EH — Economic History
EH — Editiones Heidelbergenses
EH — Environmental Health
EH — Epeiroetike Hestia
EH — Ethiopian Herald
EH — Ethno History
EH — Etudes Haguenoviennes
EH — Europaeische Hochschulschriften
EH — Evolution de l'Humanite
EHA — Einzelhandelsberater
EHAF — Employee Health and Fitness
E Handel — Elektro-Handel
EHAT — Exegetisches Handbuch zum Alten Testament
EHB — Modern Power Systems
EHBS — Epeteris tes Hetaireias Byzantinon Spoudon
EHC — Educacao Hoy (Colombia)
EHD — English Historical Documents
EHD Can Environ Health Dir — EHD. Canada Environmental Health Directorate
EHDEDN — Early Human Development
Ehe Ges G — Ehegesundheitsgesetz
E Hest — Epeiroetike Hestia

EHGI — English-Hittite Glossary
EHHD — Epeteris tou Kentrou Ereunes tes Historias tou Hellenikou Dikaiou
Ehime Daigaku Nogaku Kiyo Mem Coll Agric Ehime Univ — Ehime Daigaku Nogakubu Kiyo. Memoirs of the College of Agriculture. Ehime University
Ehime J Med Technol — Ehime Journal of Medical Technology
EHJ — Economisch-Historisch Jaarboek
EHJ — Encyclopedia Hebraica (Jerusalem)
EHJIA — Ehara Jiho
EHJODF — European Heart Journal
E H K — Eine Heilige Kirche
EHK — Ermlaendischer Hauskalender
EHKM — Epeteris Hetaireias Kykladikon Meleton
Ehkon Neft Prom-St — Ehkonomika Neftyanoj Promyshlennosti
EHKS — Epeteris tes Hetaireias Kretikon Spoudon
Ehksp Khir Anesteziol — Ehksperimental'naya Khirurgiya i Anesteziologiya
Ehksp Onkol — Ehksperimental'naya Onkologiya
Ehkspress-Inf Lab Tekhnol Issled Obogashch Miner Syr'ya — Ehkspress-Informatsiya. Laboratornye Tekhnologicheskie Issledovaniya i Obogashchenie Mineral'nogo Syr'ya
Ehkspress-Inf Montazh Oborudovaniya Tepl Ehlektrostn — Ehkspress-Informatsiya. Montazh Oborudovaniya na Teplovykh Ehlektrostantsiyakh
Ehkspress-Inf Neftegazov Geol Geofiz — Ehkspress-Informatsiya. Neftegazovaya Geologiya i Geofizika
Ehkspress-Inf Ser Reg Razved Promysl Geofiz — Ehkspress-Informatsiya. Seriya. Regional'naya. Razvedochnaya i Promyslovaya Geofizika
Ehkspress-Inf Stroit Tepl Ehlektrostn — Ehkspress-Informatsiya. Stroitel'stvo Teplovykh Ehlektrostantsij
Ehkspress-Inf Svar Rab — Ehkspress-Informatsiya. Svarochnye Raboty
EHL — Essex Hall Lectures
EHLD — Etudes d'Histoire Litteraire et Doctrinale
Ehlektrofiz Appar — Ehlektrofizicheskaya Apparatura
Ehlektrokhim — Ehlektrokhimiya. Akademiya Nauk SSSR. Ezhemesyachnyj Zhurnal
Ehlektron Ionnye Protessy Tverd Telakh — Ehlektronnye i Ionnye Protessy v Tverdykh Telakh
Ehlektron Obrab Mater — Ehlektronnaya Obrabotka Materialov
Ehlektrosvyaz' Radiotekh — Ehlektrosvyaz' i Radiotekhnika
Ehlektr Stn — Ehlektricheskie Stantsii
EHN — Environmental Health News
Ehnerg Ehlektrif — Ehnergetika i Ehlektrifikatsiya
Ehnerg Stroit — Ehnergeticheskoe Stroitel'stvo
Ehnerg Stroit Rubezhom — Ehnergeticheskoe Stroitel'stvo za Rubezhom
Ehntomol Obozr — Ehntomologicheskoe Obozrenie
E Horizon — Eastern Horizon
EHP — Encyklopaedisches Handbuch der Paedagogik
EHP (Environ Health Perspect) — EHP (Environmental Health Perspectives)
EHPh R — Etudes d'Histoire et de Philosophie Religieuses
EHPR — Etudes d'Histoire et de Philosophie Religieuses
EHPRUS — Etudes d'Histoire et de Philosophie Religieuses. Universite de Strasbourg
EHR — Economic History Review
EHR — English Historical Review
EHR — Europese Documentatie
EH Rel — Etudes sur l'Histoire des Religions
EHRR — European Human Rights Reports
EHRS — English Historical Review. Supplement
EHSE — Estudios de Historia Social de Espana
EHSer — Elmore Harris Series
EHSM — Epeteris Hetaireias Stereoelladikon Meleton
EHSQ — Emergency Health Services Quarterly
EHSRE2 — Emergency Health Services Review
EHTED — Energie Alternative
EHU — Economie et Humanisme
E Hy — Weichardts Ergebnisse der Hygiene, Bakterien-, Immunitaetsforschung, und Experimentellen Therapie
EI — Economia Internazionale
EI — Education Index
EI — Elet es Irodalom
EI — Enciclopedia Italiana
EI — Enciclopedia Italiana di Scienze, Lettere, ed Arti
EI — Encyclopaedia of Islam
EI — Encyclopedie de l'Islam
EI — Engineering Index
EI — English Illustrated Magazine
EI — Epigraphia Indica
EI — Eretz - Israel
EI — Estudios Ibericos
EI — Estudios Italianos
EI — Etudes Irlandaises
EI — Etudes Italiennes
EI — Excerpta Indonesica
EI — Journal of Professional Issues in Engineering
EI — L'Educatore Israelita
EI — L'Egypte Industrielle
EI1 — Encyclopaedia of Islam [*Leiden, 1913-1942*]
EI2 — Encyclopaedia of Islam [*2nd Ed. Leiden, 1954*]
EIA — Environment Information Abstracts
EIA — Estudos Ibero-Americanos
EIAEA — Equipement Industriel. Achats et Entretien
EIA/EPUB — National Energy Information Center Electronic Publication System
EIA Publ New Releases — EIA [*Electronics Industries Association*] Publications. New Releases
EIB — Earthquake Information Bulletin
EIB — Educational/Instructional Broadcasting

EIB — Eigen Huis en Interieur
Elb — Ha-Ensiqlopedija Ha-Ibrit
Ei C — Einheit in Christus
EIC — Ephemerides Iuris Canonici
EIC — Essays in Criticism
EIC — Estudios Internacionales de Chile
Eichendorff Kal — Eichendorff-Kalender
Eich O — Eichordnung
Eichsfelder Heimath — Eichsfelder Heimathefte
Eichstaedter Bienenztg — Eichstaedter Bienenzeitung
Eickhogg-Mitt — Eickhogg-Mitteilungen
EIC Ne — EIC [*Engineering Institute of Canada*] News
EIC Trans — EIC [*Engineering Institute of Canada*] Transactions
EID — Economic and Industrial Democracy
Eid — Eidos. A Journal of Painting, Sculpture, and Design
EID — Electronic Instrument Digest
EID — Enzyklopaedie des Islam
EIDAA — Electrical India
Eidg Anst Forstl Versuchswes Mitt — Eidgenoessische Anstalt fuer das Forstliche Versuchswesen. Mitteilungen
Eidge Tech Hochsch Versuchsans Wasserbau Erdbau Mitt Zurich — Eidgenoessische Technische Hochschule. Versuchsanstalt fuer Wasserbau und Erdbau. Mitteilungen Zurich
Eidg Inst Reaktorforsch EIR Ber — Eidgenoessisches Institut fuer Reaktorforschung. EIR Bericht
Eidg Materialpruefungsanst ETH (Zurich) Ber — Eidgenoessische Materialpruefungsanstalt an der ETH (Zurich). Bericht
Eidg Materialpruef Versuchsanst — Eidgenoessische Materialpruefungs- und Versuchsanstalt
Eidg Tech Hochsch Inst Reaktortech Ber AF NST — Eidgenoessische Technische Hochschule. Institut fuer Reaktortechnik.Bericht AF-NST
Eidg Tech Hochsch Versuchsanst Wasserbau Erdbau Mitt — Eidgenoessische Technische Hochschule. Versuchsanstalt fuer Wasserbau und Erdbau. Mitteilungen
EI Dig — EI Digest. Industrial and Hazardous Waste Management
Eidikai Meletai Geol Ellados — Eidikai Meletai Edi tes Geologias tes Ellados
EIE — Economia Industrial
EIE — English Institute. Essays
EIEAD — Elektrowaerme International. Edition A. Elektrowaerme im Technischen Ausbau
EIEBD — Elektrowaerme International. Edition B. Industrielle Elektrowaerme
EIFAC Occas Pap — EIFAC [*European Inland Fisheries Advisory Commission*] Occasional Paper
EIFAC Tech Pap — EIFAC [*European Inland Fisheries Advisory Commission*] Technical Paper
EIFEB — Economia Internazionale delle Fonti di Energia
EIFPA2 — EIFAC [*European Inland Fisheries Advisory Commission*] Technical Paper
Eig — Eigse
Eigen Schoon & Braband — Eigen Schoon en de Brabander
Eight Century Curr Bibliogr — Eighteenth Century: a Current Bibliography
Eight Ct — Eighteenth Century Theory and Interpretation
Eight-Ct L — Eighteenth-Century Life
Eight-Ct St — Eighteenth-Century Studies
Eighteenth Cent — Eighteenth Century
Eighteenth Cent Life — Eighteenth-Century Life
Eighteenth-Cent Stud — Eighteenth-Century Studies
Eighteenth Cent Theory Interpr — Eighteenth Century Theory and Interpretation
Eigo S — Eigo Seinen
EIHC — Essex Institute. Historical Collections
EIHCA7 — Essex Institute. Historical Collections
Eih Pbl — Eichstaetter Pastoralblatt
EiJ — Einst und Jetzt
EIJID — Ebara Infiruko Jiho
EIK — Elektronische Informationsverarbeitung und Kybernetik
EIL — Echo de l'Industrie. Revue Luxembourgeoise de la Vie Economique et Sociale
EIL — Essays in Literature
EIL — Essays on International Law
EIL — Ezik i Literatura
EILS — Essays. Institute of Liturgical Studies
EIM — Epigraphia Indo-Moslemica
EIMC — Epigraphia Indo-Moslemica (Calcutta)
EIMKH — Ergebnisse der Inneren Medizin und Kinderheilkunde
EIMOB — Ekspress-Informatsiya. Montazh Oborudovaniya na Teplovykh Elektrostantsiyakh
EIN — Europa Informatie, Buitenlandse Betrekkingen
E in A — English in Africa
Einblicke Wiss — Einblicke in die Wissenschaft
EINDA — Electrified Industry
Einfuehr Molekularbiol — Einfuehrungen zur Molekularbiologie
Einfuehrungen Molekularbiol — Einfuehrungen zur Molekularbiologie
Einfuehrung Molekularbiol — Einfuehrungen zur Molekularbiologie
Einh — Einheit. Theoretische Zeitschrift des Wissenschaftlichen Sozialismus
Einheit Gesellschaftswiss — Einheit der Gesellschaftswissenschaften
Eins — Einsicht
EINS — Etudes/Inuit/Studies
EINSD — Eau et l'Industrie
Einstein QJ Biol Med — Einstein Quarterly Journal of Biology and Medicine
Einstein Stud — Einstein Studies
Einzeldarst Theor Klin Med — Einzeldarstellungen aus Theorie und Klinik der Medizin
Einzelv — Einzelveroeffentlichungen des Seewetteramtes
EIOPAD — EIFAC [*European Inland Fisheries Advisory Commission*] Occasional Paper

EIP — Estudos Italianos em Portugal
EIP — Excavations in Palestine during the years 1898-1900
EIPGA — Ekspress-Informatsiya. Seriya: Regional'naya, Razvedochnaya, i Promyslovaya Geofizika
Eir — Eirene. Studia Graeca et Latina
EIr — Encyclopaedia Iranica
EIR — European Industrial Relations Review
EIR-Ber — Eidgenoessisches Institut fuer Reaktorforschung. Bericht
EIR-Ber (Wuerenlingen) — EIR-[*Eidgenoessisches Institut fuer Reaktorforschung*] Bericht (Wuerenlingen)
EIRC — Exploration in Renaissance Culture
Eire — Ireland. A Journal of Irish Studies
Eire Dep Agric J — Eire. Department of Agriculture. Journal
Eire Ir — Eire-Ireland
EIRI — Energy Information Resources Inventory
EIRJa — Etimologiceskie Issledovanija po Russkomu Jazyku
EIRR — European Industrial Relations Review
EIS — Digest of Environmental Impact Statements
EIS — Epidemiology Information System
EIS — Essentials of Islam Series
EISD — Engineering and Industrial Software Directory
Eisei Dobutsu/Jap J Sanit Zool — Eisei Dobutsu/Japanese Journal of Sanitary Zoology
Eisei Shikenjo Hokoku/Bull Nat Inst Hyg Sci — Eisei Shikenjo Hokoku/Bulletin. National Institute of Hygienic Sciences
Eisenbahn-Ing — Eisenbahn-Ingenieur
Eisenbahnrechtl Entsch Abh — Eisenbahnrechtliche Entscheidungen und Abhandlungen
Eisenbahntech Rundsch — Eisenbahntechnische Rundschau
Eisenhower Consortium Bull — Eisenhower Consortium. Bulletin
Eisenhower Consortium Bull Rocky Mt For Range Exp — Eisenhower Consortium. Bulletin. United States Rocky Mountain Forest and Range Experiment Station
Eisen Ztg — Eisen-Zeitung
Eisen Ztg Beil — Eisen-Zeitung. Beilage
Eis Kaelte Ind — Eis- und Kaelte-Industrie
E Isl — Encyclopedie de l'Islam
EISOAU — Eiyo To Shokuryo
EISRA — Ekspress-Informatsiya. Svarochnye Raboty
Eis Shik Hok — Eisei Shikenjo Hokoku
Eisz — Eiszeit
Eiszeitalter Gegenw — Eiszeitalter und Gegenwart
Eiszeit & Urgesch — Eiszeit und Urgeschichte. Jahrbuch fuer Erforschung des Vorgeschichtlichen Menschen und Seines Zeitalters
Eisz Geg — Eiszeitalter und Gegenwart
EIT — Ezhegodnik Imperatorskikh Teatrov
EITBA — Engelhard Industries. Technical Bulletin
EITEA — Ekspress-Informatsiya. Stroitel'stvo Teplovykh Elektrostantsii
EIUES — English Institute of the University of Uppsala. Essays and Studies on English Language and Literature
EIVKA — Elektronische Informationsverarbeitung und Kybernetik
Eiweiss Forsch — Eiweiss-Forschung
EIY — Economic Inquiry
Eiyogaku Zasshi Jap J Nutr — Eiyogaku Zasshi/Japanese Journal of Nutrition
Eiyo Syok Gak — Eiyo Syokuryo Gakkai
EJ — Economic Journal
EJ — Edoth (Jerusalem)
EJ — Einbecker Jahrbuch
EJ — Encyclopaedia Judaica
EJ — English Journal
EJ — Eranos-Jahrbuch
EJ — Estudios Josefinos
EJ — European Judaism
EJ — Eusko-Jakintza. Revue des Etudes Basques
EJABDD — Applied Microbiology and Biotechnology
EJAGDS — Egyptian Journal of Agronomy
EJAMA — European Journal of Applied Microbiology
EJAPC — European Journal of Applied Physiology and Occupational Physiology
EJAPCK — European Journal of Applied Physiology and Occupational Physiology
EJASA — Engineering Journal
EJB — Encyclopaedia Judaica. Berlin
EJB — Engineering Industries of Japan
EJb — Eranos-Jahrbuch
EJBC — Egyptian Journal of Botany (Cairo)
EJBCAI — European Journal of Biochemistry
EJB Electron J Biotechnol — EJB Electronic Journal of Biotechnology
EJBLAD — Egyptian Journal of Bilharziasis
EJC — Egyptian Journal of Chemistry
EJC — Encyclopedia Judaica Castellana
EJC — Ephemerides Juris Canonici
EJCAAH — European Journal of Cancer
EJCBDN — European Journal of Cell Biology
EJCDAQ — Egyptian Journal of Chest Diseases and Tuberculosis
EJCDBR — European Journal of Cardiology
EJCIB8 — European Journal of Clinical Investigation
EJCOD — European Journal of Cancer and Clinical Oncology
EJCODS — European Journal of Cancer and Clinical Oncology
EJCPA — European Journal of Clinical Pharmacology
EJCPAS — European Journal of Clinical Pharmacology
EJDPD — European Journal of Drug Metabolism and Pharmacokinetics
EJDPD2 — European Journal of Drug Metabolism and Pharmacokinetics
EJEAAR — Empire Journal of Experimental Agriculture
EJER — Epigrafia Juridica de la Espana Romana
EJEV — Eusko-Jakintza. Revista de Estudios Vascos
EJFPA — European Journal of Forest Pathology

EJFPA9 — European Journal of Forest Pathology
EJFSAI — Egyptian Journal of Food Science
EJG — Egyptian Journal of Geology
EJGCA9 — Egyptian Journal of Genetics and Cytology
EJHCAE — Egyptian Journal of Horticulture
EJIMAF — European Journal of Immunology
EJM — Economist Journal
EJM — European Journal of Marketing
EJMBA2 — Egyptian Journal of Microbiology
EJMCA5 — European Journal of Medicinal Chemistry. Chimie Therapeutique
EJMED — Eizo Joho. Medíkaru
EJN — Directory of Educational Journal and Newsletters
EJNMD9 — European Journal of Nuclear Medicine
EJOODK — European Journal of Orthodontics
EJOR — European Journal of Operational Research
E Jos — Estudios Josefinos
EJP — European Journal of Parapsychology
EJPC — Egyptian Journal of Psychology (Cairo)
EJPEDT — European Journal of Pediatrics
EJPHAZ — European Journal of Pharmacology
EJPLAD — Egyptian Journal of Physiological Science
EJPN — European Journal of Paediatric Neurology. EJPN
EJPSBZ — Egyptian Journal of Pharmaceutical Sciences
EJRDD2 — European Journal of Respiratory Diseases
EJRSDD — European Journal of Respiratory Diseases. Supplement
EJSEDA — European Journal of Science Education
EJSSAF — Egyptian Journal of Soil Science
EJV — Estudios Josefinos (Valladolid)
EJVSAU — Egyptian Journal of Veterinary Science
EJW Gibb Mem Ser — Elias John Wilkinson Gibb Memorial Series
EK — Erdoel und Kohle
EK — Evangelische Kirchenzeitung
EK — Evangelische Kommentare
EKANA — Elektro-Anzeiger
Ekat S Our BII — Bulletin de la Societe Ouralienne d'Amateurs des Sciences Naturelles (Ekaterinburg)
EKBRD5 — Ekologia-CSSR
EKC — Economic Review. Federal Reserve Bank of Kansas City
EKD — Economic Titles/Abstracts
EKEEK — Epeteris tou Kentrou Epistemonikon Ereunon Kyprou
EKEHHD — Epeteris tou Kentrou Ereunes tes Historias tou Hellenikou Dikaiou
EKEHL — Epeteris tou Kentrou Ereunes tes Hellenikes Laographias
EKGB — Einzelarbeiten aus der Kirchengeschichte Bayerns
EKHAA — Eksperimental'naya Khirurgiya i Anesteziologiya
EKHAAF — Eksperimental'naya Khirurgiya i Anesteziologiya
EKI — Ekistic Index
EKI — Ekonomi dan Keuangan Indonesia
EKIAAK — Ekologiya
EKISA — Ekistics
Ekist — Ekistics
Ekistics Probl Sci Hum Settl — Ekistics; the Problems and Science of Human Settlements
Ekist Ind — Ekistic Index
EKK — Evangelisch-Katholischer Kommentar zum Neuen Testament
Ekkl AI — Ekklesiatike Aletheia
EKKV — Evangelisch-Katholischer Kommentar zum Neuen Testament. Vorarbeiten
EKL — Evangelisches Kirchenlexikon. Kirchlichtheologisches Handwoerterbuch
EKMMA8 — Eksperimentalna Meditsina i Morfologiya
EKMZAD — Conference Europeenne sur la Microcirculation/Conferenza Europea di Microcirculazione
EKMZAD — European Conference on Microcirculation
EKNPA — Ekonomika Neftianoi Promyshlennosti
EKNTB — Elektronika
EKOLDI — Ekologiya
Ekol Fiziol Korennogo Rosta Mezhdunar Simp — Ekologiya i Fiziologiya Korennogo Rosta. Mezhdunarodnyi Simpozion
Ekol Fiziol Metody Borbe Fuzarioznym Viltom Khlop — Ekologo-Fiziologicheskie Metody v Bor'be s Fuzarioznym ViltomKhlopchatnika
Ekol Fiziol Osob Rast Yuzhn Urala Ikh Resur — Ekologicheskie i Fiziologicheskie Osobennosti Rastenii Yuzhnogo Urala i Ikh Resursy
Ekol Khim — Ekologicheskaya Khimiya
Ekol Morya — Ekologiya Morya
Ekol Pol — Ekologia Polska
Ekol Pol Pol J Ecol — Ekologia Polska/Polish Journal of Ecology
Ekol Pol Ser A — Ekologia Polska. Seria A
Ekol Pol Ser B — Ekologia Polska. Seria B
Ekol Polska — Ekologia Polska
Ekol Tech — Ekologia i Technika
Ekol Zashch Lesa — Ekologiya i Zashchita Lesa
Ekon Cas — Ekonomicky Casopis
Ekon Forsknstift Skogsarb — Ekonomi. Forskningsstiftelsen Skogsarbeten
Ekon Gaz — Ekonomicheskaya Gazeta
Ekon Keuangan — Ekonomi dan Keuangan Indonesia
Ekon Matemat Met — Ekonomika i Matematiceske Metody
Ekon Matem Metody — Ekonomika i Matematiceske Metody
Ekon-Mate O — Ekonomicko-Matematicky Obzor
Ekon Mater Za — Ekonomiyu Materialov. Za
Ekon-Mat Obz — Ekonomicko-Matematicky Obzor
Ekon Nauki — Ekonomiceske Nauki
Ekon Neft Prom-Sti — Ekonomika Neftianoi Promyshlennosti
Ekonom i Mat Metody — Ekonomika i Matematiceske Metody
Ekonom-Mat Obzor — Ceskoslovenska Akademie Ved. Ekonomicko-Matematicky Obzor
Ekon Org Promysl Proizvodstva — Ekonomika i Organiztsiya Promyslennogo Proizvodstva

Ekon Poljopr — Ekonomika Poljoprivrede
Ekon Poljopriv — Ekonomika Poljoprivrede
Ekon Probl Effekt — Ekonomiceskie Problemy Effektivnosti Proizvodstva
Ekon Revy — Ekonomisk Revy
Ekon R (Ljubljana) — Ekonomska Revija (Ljubljana)
Ekon R (Stockholm) — Ekonomisk Revy (Stockholm)
Ekon Samf T — Ekonomiska Samfundets Tidskrift
Ekon Samfund Ts — Ekonomiska Samfundets Tidskrift
Ekon Sel' Khoz — Ekonomika Sel'skogo Khozyaistva
Ekon Sel'sk Choz — Ekonomika Sel'skogo Chozjajstva
Ekon Selsk Hoz — Ekonomika Sel'skogo Hozjajstva
Ekon Sel'sk Khoz — Ekonomika Sel'skogo Khozyaistva
Ekon Sov Ukr — Ekonomika Sovetskoi Ukrainy
Ekon Stavebnictva — Ekonomika Stavebnictva
Ekon Stroit — Ekonomika Stroitel'stva
Ekon Topl Za — Ekonomiya Topliva. Za
Ekon Zemed — Ekonomika Zemedelstvi
EKOSB — Ekonomika Stavebnictva
Ekotekhnol Resursosberezhenie — Ekotekhnologii i Resursosberezhenie
EKPOAT — Ekologia Polska. Seria A
Ekr — Ekran
EKRKA — Elektronik
EKSODD — Eksperimental'naya Onkologiya
Eksp Biol — Eksperimentine Biologija
Eksp Biol Vilnius — Eksperimental'naya Biologiya (Vilnius)
Eksp Bot — Eksperimental'naja Botanika
Eksp Chir — Eksperimental'naja Chirurgija
Eksp Chir Anest — Eksperimental'naja Chirurgija i Anesteziologija
Eksp Fiz Reakt Mater Vses Semin Probl Fiz Reakt — Eksperiment v Fizike Reaktorov. Materialy Vsesoyuznogo Seminara poProblemam Fiziki Raktorov
Eksp Infarkt Miokarda Usloviyakh Gipotermii — Eksperimental'nyi Infarkt Miokarda v Usloviyakh Gipotermii
Eksp Issled Fiziol Biofiz Farmakol — Eksperimental'nye Issledovaniya po Fiziologii, Biofizike, i Farmakologii
Eksp Khir — Eksperimental'naya Khirurgiya
Eksp Khir Anesteziol — Eksperimental'naya Khirurgiya i Anesteziologiya
Eksp Kliin Onkol — Eksperimentaalne ja Kliiniline Onkoloogia
Eksp Klin Farmakol — Eksperimentalnaia i Klinicheskaia Farmakologiia
Eksp Klin Farmakoter — Eksperimental'naya i Klinicheskaya Farmakoterapiya
Eksp Klin Issled Antibiot — Eksperimental'nye i Klinicheskie Issledovaniya po Antibiotikam
Eksp Klin Med — Eksperimental'naya i Klinicheskaya Meditsina
Eksp Klin Onkol — Eksperimental'naya i Klinicheskaya Onkologiya
Eksp Klin Radiol — Eksperimental'naya i Klinicheskaya a Radiologiya
Eksp Klin Stomatol — Eksperimentalnaia Klinicheskaia Stomatologiia
Eksp Med — Eksperimentalna Meditsina
Eksp Med (Kharkov) — Eksperimentalna Meditsina (Kharkov)
Eksp Med Morfol — Eksperimentalna Meditsina i Morfologiya
Eksp Med (Riga) — Eksperimental'naya Meditsina (Riga)
Eksp Metody Appar Issled Turbul Tr Vses Soveshch — Eksperimental'nye Metody i Apparatura dlya IssledovaniyaTurbulentnosti. Trudy Vsesoyuznogo Soveshchaniya
Eksp Mutagen Rast — Eksperimental'nyi Mutagenez Rastenii
Eksp Nauchno Issled Inst Kuznechno Pressovogo Mashinostr Sb — Eksperimental'nyi Nauchno-Issledovatel'skii InstitutKuznechno-Pressovogo Mashinostroeniya. Sbornik
Eksp Nauchno Issled Inst Metallorezhushchikh Stankov Tr — Eksperimental'nyi Nauchno-Issledovatel'skii InstitutMetallorezhushchikh Stankov. Trudy
Eksp Onkol — Eksperimental'naya Onkologiya
Ekspress-Inf Lab Tekhnol Issled Obogashch Miner Syr'ya — Ekspress-Informatsiya Laboratornye Tekhnologicheskie Issledovaniya i Obogashchenie Mineral'nogo Syr'ya
Ekspress-Inf Montazh Oborudovaniya Teplovykh Elektrosn — Ekspress-Informatsiya. Montazh Oborudovaniya na Teplovykh Elektrostantsiyakh
Ekspress Inf Morsk Gidrofiz Inst Akad Nauk Ukr SSR — Ekspress-Informatsiya. Morskoi Gidrofizicheskii Institut Akademiya Nauk Ukrainskoi SSR
Ekspress-Inf Nauchno-Issled Inst Sel Khoz Severn Zaural'ya — Ekspress-Informatsiya Nauchno-Issledovatel'skii Institut Sel'skogo Khozyaistva Severnogo Zaural'ya
Ekspress-Inf Neftegazov Geol Geofiz — Ekspress-Informatsiya. Neftegazovaya Geologiya i Geofizika
Ekspress-Inf Ser Reg Razved Prom Geofiz — Ekspress-Informatsiya. Seriya: Regional'naya, Razvedochnaya, i Promyslovaya Geofizika
Ekspress-Inf Stroit Tepl Elektrostn — Ekspress-Informatsiya. Stroitel'stvo Teplovykh Elektrostantsii
Ekspress-Inf Svar Rab — Ekspress-Informatsiya. Svarochnye Raboty
Eksp Tekh Metody Vysokotemp Izmer Sb Tr Soveshch — Eksperimental'naya Tekhnika i Metody Vysokotemperaturnykh Izmerenii.Sbornik Trudov Soveshchaniya
Eksp Tekh Mineral Petrogr Mater Soveshch — Eksperiment v Tekhnicheskoi Mineralogii i Petrografii, po MaterialamSoveshchaniya po Eksperimental'noi i Tekhnicheskoi Mineralogii i Petrografi
Eksp Tekh Svoistva Primen Avtomob Top Smaz Mater Sperszhidk — Ekspluatatsionno Tekhnicheskie Svoistva i Primenenie Avtomobil'nykh Topliv. Smazochnykh Materialov i Sperszhidkostei
Eksp Vodn Toksikol — Eksperimental'naya Vodnaya Toksikologiya
Eksp Vodn Toksikol Mater Vses Simp — Eksperimental'naya Vodnaya Toksikologiya. Materialy VsesoyuznogoSimpoziuma po Eksperimental'noi Vodnoi Toksikologii
Eksp Vozrastn Kardiol Mater Mezhvuz Konf — Eksperimental'naya i Vozrastnaya Kardiologiya. Materialy MezhvuzovskoiKonferentsii
Eksp Vozrastn Kardiol Tr Nauchn Konf — Eksperimental'naya i Vozrastnaya Kardiologiya. Trudy NauchnoiKonferentsii
EKSTA — Electricheskie Stantsii

EKSTB — Ekonomiska Samfundets Tidskrift
EKTCB — Elektrotechnik
EKT Electroizolacna Kablova Tech — EKT. Elektroizolacna a Kablova Technika
EKTKA — Elektrotechnik
EKTMA — Elektroteknikeren
EKTRA — Elektrie
EKTRB — Elektrotechnik
EKZ — Evangelische Kirchenzeitung
EKZgOe — Evangelische Kirchenzeitung fuer Oesterreich
EKZVA — Elektrizitaetsverwertung
EKZVA — Elktrosvyaz
EKZWA — Elektrizitaetswirtschaft
EL — Educational Leadership
EI — Electronics
EI — Electrotechnics
EI — Elektricestvo
EL — Elsevier Lexica
EL — Emergency Librarian
EL — Ephemerides Liturgicae
EL — Etudes de Lettres
EL — Europaeische Literatur
EL — Europa Letteraria
EL — Ezik i Literatura
EI A — Ephemerides Liturgicae. Analecta Historico-Ascetica
ELA — Espiral Letras y Arte
ELA — Etudes de Linguistique Appliquee
ELABB — Electroanalytical Abstracts
EI a BI — Ellis and Blackburn Queen's Bench Cases
Elabuz Gos Ped Inst Ucen Zap — Elabuzskii Gosudarstvennyi Pedagogiceskii Institut. Ucenye Zapiski
EI and Energi Elektrotek — EI and Energi Elektroteknikeren
E Lang T — English Language Teaching [*Later, English Language Teaching Journal*]
EI Anz — Elektro-Anzeiger
EI App Bull — Electronic Applications Bulletin
Elast — Elastomerics
Elastic Plast Fract Symp — Elastic-Plastic Fracture. Symposium
Elast Xtra — Elastomerics Extra
ELB — Environmental Law Bulletin
ELB — Evangelischer Literaturbeobachter
ELBAA — Elektrische Bahnen
Elbing Jb — Elbinger Jahrbuch
EI (Bruessel) — Electricite (Bruessel)
ELBUA — Electrical Business
ELC — (EI) Ciervo
ELC — Encyclopedia of the Lutheran Church
ELC — Europe's Largest Companies
ELCAA — Electrochimica Acta
ELCCA — Electronic Components
ELCFR — English Linguistics, 1500-1800: A Collection of Facsimile Reprints
EI Chim — Elektrochimija
EI Chim Acta — Electrochimica Acta
ELCIA — Electronics and Instrumentation
ELCMA — Electrical Communication
ELCNC4 — Electron
EI Commun — Electrical Communication
EI Commun Lab Rep — Electrical Communication Laboratory Reports
EI Comp — Electronic Components
EI Constr — Electrical Construction and Maintenance
EI Contract — Electrical Contracting
ELCRD — Electro Conference Record
ELCTDN — Electrophoresis
ELCWA — Electronics World
ELDATA Int Electron J Phys Chem Data — ELDATA. International Electronic Journal of Physico-Chemical Data
ELDDA — Electricidade
Elders W — Elders Weekly
EI Distrib — Electrical Distribution
ELDNB — Elektrodienst
ELDO/ESRO Bull — ELDO/ESRO [*European Launcher Development Organization/European Space Research Organization*] Bulletin
ELDO/ESRO Sci Tech Rev — ELDO/ESRO [*European Launcher Development Organization/European Space Research Organization*] Scientific and Technical Review
ELE — Elementi di Lingua Etrusca
ELE — European Electronics
Elec — Electra. Organ for Elektroinstallatorforeningen for Kobenhavn og Elektroinstallatorforeningen for Provinsen
Elec — [*The*] Electrician
ELEC — English Language Education Council. Bulletin
ELEC — Etudes de Litterature Etrangere et Comparee
ELECA — Electronics
ELECAD — Electronics
Elec & Electron Abstr — Electrical and Electronic Abstracts
Elec Aust — Electronics Australia
Elec Austr — Electronic Australia
Elec Bldg — Electricity in Building
Elec Busns — Electronic Business
Elec Can — Electricity Canada
Elec Com — Electrical Communication
Elec Comft — Electric Comfort Conditioning News
Elec Comm — Electrical Communication
Elec Commun — Electrical Communication
Elec Constr Maint — Electrical Construction and Maintenance
Elec Contacts — Electrical Contacts

Elec Contractor — Electrical Contractor
Elec Data — Advance Release of Data for the Statistical Year Book of the Electric Utility Industry
Elec Des — Electronic Design
Elec Desgn — Electronic Design
Elec Ed — Electronic Education
Elec Eng — Electrical Engineer
Elec Eng — Electrical Engineering
Elec Eng — Electronic Engineering
Elec Eng Abstr — Electrical Engineering Abstracts
Elec Eng & Merchandiser — Electrical Engineer and Merchandiser
Elec Eng Japan — Electrical Engineering in Japan
Elec Eng (Melbourne) — Electrical Engineer (Melbourne)
Elec Engr — Electrical Engineer
Elec Eng Rev — Electrical Engineering Review
Elec Engrg and Electronics — Electrical Engineering and Electronics
Elec Engrg Electron — Electrical Engineering and Electronics
Elec Eng T — Electronic Engineering Times
Elec En Jap — Electrical Engineering in Japan
Elec Fact — Electronic News Financial Fact Book and Directory
Elec Farm Mag — Electricity on the Farm Magazine
Elec Fr Bull Dir Etud Rech Ser A Nucl Hydraul Therm — Electricite de France. Bulletin de la Direction des Etudes et Recherches. SerieA. Nucleaire, Hydraulique, Thermique
Elec Fr Bull Dir Etud Rech Ser B Reseaux Elec Mater Elec — Electricite de France. Bulletin de la Direction des Etudes et Recherches. SerieB. Reseaux Electriques, Materiels Electriques
Elec Furnace Conf Proc AIME — Electric Furnace Conference Proceedings. Metallurgical Society of AIME. Iron and Steel Division
Elec Ind — Electronics Industry, Incorporating Electronic Components
Elec J — Electrical Journal
Elec M & M Sys — Electronic Mail and Message Systems
Elec Manuf — Electrical Manufacturing
Elec Merch — Electrical Merchandising
Elec Merch W — Electrical Merchandising Week
Elec Mkt — Electronic Market Data Book
Elec Mkt T — Electronic Market Trends
Elec Mus R — Electronic Music Review
Elec News — Electronic News
Elec News Eng — Electrical News and Engineering
Elec Opt Rep — Electro-Optics Report
Elec Outlk — US Electric Utility Industry Outlook to the Year 2000
Elec Powr A — Electric Power Annual
Elec Powr M — Electric Power Monthly
Elec Prod — Electronic Products
Elec Prog — Electronic Progress
Elec Publ Rev — Electronic Publishing Review
Elec Pub Rv — Electronic Publishing Review
Elec R — Electrical Review
Elec Res Ass ERA Rep — Electrical Research Association. ERA Report
Elec Retail — Electronics Retailing
Elec Rev — Electrical Review
Elec Revw — Electrical Review
Elec Ry J — Electric Railway Journal
Elect — Electrician
Elect Contractor — Electrical Contractor
Elec Technol (USSR) — Electric Technology (USSR)
Elect Electron Mfr — Electrical and Electronics Manufacturer
Elect Electron Trader — Electrical and Electronic Trader
Elect Engng Trans Instn Engrs Aust — Electrical Engineering Transactions. Institution of Engineers of Australia
Elect Engr (Melb) — Electrical Engineer (Melbourne)
Elec Equip — Electrical Equipment
Elec Times — Electric Times
Elec T Intnl — Electronics Today International
Elect J — Electric Journal
Electl Engr — Electrical Engineer
Elect Mech Engng Trans — Institution of Engineers of Australia. Electrical and Mechanical Engineering Transactions
Elec Tod — Electronics Today International
Elect Pwr — Electrical Power Engineer
Elect Pwr Engr — Electrical Power Engineer
Electr Act — Electrochimica Acta
Elec Traction — Electric Traction
Elec Trade — Electrical Trader
Electr and Electron — Electrical and Electronics Technician Engineer
Electr and Mech Executive Eng — Electrical and Mechanical Executive Engineer
Electr App — Electrical Apparatus
Electr Automob — Electricite Automobile
Electr Calculation — Electrical Calculation
Electr Club J — Electric Club Journal
Electr Co J — Electronics and Communications in Japan
Electr Comf Cond J — Electric Comfort Conditioning Journal
Electr Comf Cond News — Electric Comfort Conditioning News
Electr Commun — Electrical Communication
Electr Commun Lab Tech J — Electrical Communication Laboratories. Technical Journal
Electr Conserv Q — Electricity Conservation Quarterly
Electr Constr and Maint — Electrical Construction and Maintenance
Electr Consult — Electrical Consultant
Electr Contacts — Electrical Contacts
Electr Contacts Proc Annu Holm Conf Electr Contacts — Electrical Contacts. Proceedings of the Annual Holm Conference on Electrical Contacts
Electr Contract — Electrical Contracting
Electr Contract — Electrical Contractor

Electr Dig — Electrical Digest
Electr Distrib — Electrical Distribution
Electr Electron Abstr — Electrical and Electronics Abstracts
Electr Electron Insul — Electrical and Electronic Insulation
Electr Electron Insul Conf Proc — Electrical/Electronics Insulation Conference. Proceedings
Electr Electron Insul Relat Non Met — Electrical and Electronic Insulation and Related Non-Metallics
Electr-Electron Mod — Electricite-Electronique Moderne
Electr Energ Electron — Electricidade, Energia, Electronica
Electr Eng — Electrical Engineer
Electr Eng — Electronic Engineering
Electr Eng Abstr — Electrical Engineering Abstracts
Electr Eng Am Inst Electr Eng — Electrical Engineering. American Institute of Electrical Engineers
Electr Eng Aust NZ — Electrical Engineer of Australia and New Zealand
Electr Eng Jap — Electrical Engineering in Japan
Electr Eng (Johannesburg) — Electrical Engineer (Johannesburg)
Electr Eng Jpn — Electrical Engineering in Japan
Electr Eng (Melb) — Electrical Engineer (Melbourne)
Electr Eng Merch — Electrical Engineer and Merchandiser
Electr Eng Rev — Electrical Engineering Review
Electr Engrg Commun Signal Process Ser — Electrical Engineering, Communications, and Signal Processing Series
Electr Eng Trans — Electrical Engineering Transactions
Electr Eng Trans Inst Eng Aust — Electrical Engineering Transactions. Institution of Engineers of Australia
Electr Equip — Electrical Equipment
Elect Rev — Electrical Review
Electr Farm Power — Electric Farm Power
Electr Forum — Electric Forum
Electr Fr Bull Dir Etud et Rech Ser A Nucl Hydraul Therm — Electricite de France. Bulletin de la Direction des Etudes et Recherches. SerieA. Nucleaire, Hydraulique, Thermique
Electr Fr Bull Dir Etud Rech Ser A Nucl Hydraul Therm — Electricite de France. Bulletin de la Direction des Etudes et Recherches. SerieA. Nucleaire, Hydraulique, Thermique
Electr Fr Dir Etud Rech Bull Ser A — Electricite de France. Direction des Etudes et Recherches. Bulletin.Serie A. Nucleaire, Hydraulique, Thermique
Electr Fr Dir Etud Rech Bull Ser B — Electricite de France. Direction des Etudes et Recherches. Bulletin.Serie B. Reseaux Electriques, Materiels Electriques
Electr Furn Conf Proc — Electric Furnace Conference Proceedings
Electr Furn Proc Metall Soc AIME — Electric Furnace Conference Proceedings. Metallurgical Society of AIME. Iron and Steel Division
Electr Furn Steel — Electric Furnace Steel
Electr Furn Steel Proc — Electric Furnace. Steel Proceedings
Electr Heat J — Electric Heating Journal
Electric — Electrician and Electrical Engineer
Electric Bus — Electrical Business
Electric Comp — Electric Company Magazine
Electrich — Electricheskii
Electricte — Revue Generale de l'Electricite
Electrified Ind — Electrified Industry
Electrified Interfaces Phys Chem Biol — Electrified Interfaces in Physics, Chemistry, and Biology
Electr Ind — Electricien Industriel
Electr India — Electrical India
Electr Inf — Electrical Information
Electr Insul Conf Mater Appl — Electrical Insulation Conference. Materials and Applications
Electrique — Industries Electriques et Electroniques
Electr Ironmelt Conf Proc — Electric Ironmelting Conference. Proceedings
Electr J — Electrical Journal
Electr J — Electric Journal
Electr J (London) — Electrical Journal (London)
Electr Lett — Electronics Letters
Electr Light & Power — Electric Light and Power
Electr Light Power (Boston) — Electric Light and Power (Boston)
Electr Light Power Energy/Gener — Electric Light and Power. Energy/Generation
Electr Light Power Transm/Distrib — Electric Light and Power. Transmission/Distribution
Electr Mach and Electromech — Electric Machines and Electromechanics
Electr Mach and Power Syst — Electric Machines and Power Systems
Electr Mach Des Appl Int Conf — Electrical Machines. Design and Applications. International Conference
Electr Mach Electromech — Electric Machines and Electromechanics
Electr Mach Power Syst — Electric Machines and Power Systems
Electr Magn Giant Reson Nucl — Electric and Magnetic Giant Resonances in Nuclei
Electr Mag Ohm — Electrical Magazine Ohm
Electr Manuf — Electrical Manufacturing
Electr Mech Eng Trans Inst Eng Aust — Electrical and Mechanical Engineering Transactions. Institution of Engineers of Australia
Electrnc Wk — Electronics Week [*Later, Electronics*]
Electr News Eng — Electrical News and Engineering
Electr Nucl Technol — Electrical and Nuclear Technology
Electroact Polym Electrochem — Electroactive Polymer Electrochemistry
Electroanal — Electroanalysis
Electroanal Abstr — Electroanalytical Abstracts
Electroanal Chem — Electroanalytical Chemistry
Electrochem — Electrochemistry
Electrochem Cell Des Optim Proc Pap Conf — Electrochemical Cell Design and Optimization Procedures. Papers. Conference

Electrochem Eng Energy Proc Eur Symp Electr Eng — Electrochemical Engineering and Energy. Proceedings of the European Symposis onElectrical Engineering
Electrochem Ind Phys Chem — Electrochemistry and Industrial Physical Chemistry
Electrochem Ind Process and Biol — Electrochemistry in Industrial Processing and Biology
Electrochem Ind Process Biol (Engl Transl) — Electrochemistry in Industrial Processing and Biology (English Translation)
Electrochem Metall Ind — Electrochemical and Metallurgical Industry
Electrochem Methods Corros Res Proc Int Symp — Electrochemical Methods in Corrosion Research. Proceedings.International Symposium
Electrochem Molten and Solid Electrolytes — Electrochemistry of Molten and Solid Electrolytes
Electrochem Opt Tech Study Monit Met Corros — Electrochemical and Optical Techniques for the Study and Monitoring of MetallicCorrosion
Electrochem Sci Technol Polym — Electrochemical Science and Technology of Polymers
Electrochem Soc J — Electrochemical Society. Journal
Electrochem Soc Proc — Electrochemical Society. Proceedings
Electrochem Soc Symp Met Plast — Electrochemical Society Symposium on Metallized Plastics
Electrochem Solid State Lett — Electrochemical and Solid-State Letters
Electrochem Tech — Electrochemical Technology
Electrochem Technol — Electrochemical Technology
Electrochim Acta — Electrochimica Acta
Electrochim Met — Electrochimica Metallorum
Electrochim Metal — Electrochimica Metallorum
Electrocomponent Sci Technol — Electrocomponent Science and Technology
Electrocompon Sci and Technol — Electrocomponent Science and Technology
Electrocompon Sci Technol — Electrocomponent Science and Technology
Electrodeposition and Surf Treat — Electrodeposition and Surface Treatment
Electroencephalogr and Clin Neurophysiol — Electroencephalography and Clinical Neurophysiology
Electroencephalogr Clin Neurophysiol — Electroencephalography and Clinical Neurophysiology
Electroencephalogr Clin Neurophysiol Suppl — Electroencephalography and Clinical Neurophysiology. Supplement
Electroenceph Clin Neurophysiol — Electroencephalography and Clinical Neurophysiology
Electrolytic Condens Rev — Electrolytic Condenser Review
Electromagn Compat Int Conf — Electromagnetic Compatibility. International Conference
Electro Magnetobiol — Electro- and Magnetobiology
Electromagn Waves — Electromagnetic Waves
Electromech Compon Syst Des — Electromechanical Components and Systems Design
Electromech Des — Electromechanical Design
Electromed — Electromedica
Electromet Met Alloys Rev — Electromet Metals and Alloys Review
Electromet Rev — Electromet Review
Electromyography and Clin Neurophysiol — Electromyography and Clinical Neurophysiology
Electromyogr Clin Neurophysiol — Electromyography and Clinical Neurophysiology
Electron — Electronics
Electron Abstr J — Electronics Abstracts Journal
Electron & Communic Abstr J — Electronics and Communications Abstracts Journal
Electron and Commun Jpn — Electronics and Communications in Japan
Electron and Comput Mon — Electronics and Computing Monthly
Electron & Power — Electronics and Power
Electron and Power — Electronics and Power. Journal of the Institution of Electrical Engineers
Electron and Radio Tech — Electronic and Radio Technician
Electron Appl — Electronic Applications
Electron Appl Bull — Electronic Applications Bulletin
Electron Appl Components Mater — Electronic Applications. Components and Materials
Electron Appl Ind — Electronique et Applications Industrielles
Electron Aust — Electronics Australia
Electron Biotechnol Adv ELBA Forum Ser — Electronics and Biotechnology Advanced ELBA Forum Series
Electron Bus — Electronic Business
Electron Ceram — Electronic Ceramics
Electron Ceram Mater — Electronic Ceramic Materials
Electron Comm Japan — Electronics and Communications in Japan
Electron Comm Probab — Electronic Communications in Probability
Electron Commun — Electronic Communicator
Electron Commun Abstr J — Electronics and Communications Abstracts Journal
Electron Commun Eng J — Electronics and Communication Engineering Journal
Electron Commun Japan — Electronics and Communications in Japan
Electron Commun Jpn — Electronics and Communications in Japan
Electron Commun Jpn Part I — Electronics and Communications in Japan. Part I. Communications
Electron Commun Jpn Part II Electron — Electronics and Communications in Japan. Part II. Electronics
Electron Commun Jpn Part III Fundam Electron Sci — Electronics and Communications in Japan. Part III. Fundamental Electronic Science
Electron Compon — Electronic Components
Electron Compon Conf Proc — Electronic Components Conference. Proceedings
Electron Components — Electronic Components
Electron Components and Appl — Electronic Components and Applications
Electron Components Appl — Electronic Components and Applications
Electron Compon Technol Conf Proc — Electronic Components and Technology Conference. Proceedings

Electron Connector Stud Group Annu Connector Symp Proc — Electronic Connector Study Group. Annual Connector Symposium Proceedings
Electron Des — Electronic Design
Electron Device Lett — Electron Device Letters
Electron Dig — Electronics Digest
Electron Electr Eng Res Stud Electron Mater Ser — Electronic and Electrical Engineering Research Studies. Electronic Materials Series
Electron Electric Engrg Res Stud Appl Engrg Math Ser — Electronic and Electrical Engineering Research Studies. Applied and Engineering
Electron Electro-Optic Infrared Countermeas — Electronic, Electro-Optic, and Infrared Countermeasures
Electron Electro-Opt Infrared Countermeas — Electronic, Electro-Optic, and Infrared Countermeasures
Electron Eng — Electronic Engineering
Electron Eng (Lond) — Electronic Engineering (London)
Electron Eng Man — Electronic Engineering Manager
Electron Eng (Phila) — Electronic Engineering (Philadelphia)
Electron Eng (Tokyo) — Electronic Engineering (Tokyo)
Electron Equip Eng — Electronic Equipment Engineering
Electron Equip News — Electronic Equipment News
Electron et Microelectron Ind — Electronique et Microelectronique Industrielles
Electron Fis Apl — Electronica y Fisica Aplicada
Electron Hologr Proc Int Workshop — Electron Holography. Proceedings of the International Workshop
Electronic — Electronics
Electronic & Radio Eng — Electronic and Radio Engineer
Electronic Ind & Tele-Tech — Electronic Industries and Tele-Tech
Electronic Libr — Electronic Library
Electronic N — Electronic News
Electronic Prod — Electronic Products
Electronics Aust — Electronics Australia
Electronics Today — Electronics Today International
Electron Ind — Electronic Industries
Electron Ind — Electronics Industry
Electron Ind — Electronique Industrielle
Electron Ind Electron Instrum — Electronic Industries and Electronic Instrumentation
Electron Ind Tele Tech — Electronic Industries and Tele-Tech
Electron Inf and Plann — Electronics Information and Planning
Electron Inf Plann — Electronics Information and Planning
Electron Instrum — Electronics and Instrumentation
Electron Ion Beam Sci Technol — Electron and Ion Beam Science and Technology
Electron Ion Beam Sci Technol Int Conf — Electron and Ion Beam Science and Technology. International Conference
Electron J Combin — Electronic Journal of Combinatorics
Electron J Differential Equations — Electronic Journal of Differential Equations
Electron J Geotech Eng — Electronic Journal of Geotechnical Engineering
Electron J Linear Algebra — Electronic Journal of Linear Algebra
Electron J Probab — Electronic Journal of Probability
Electron J Theor Chem — Electronic Journal of Theoretical Chemistry
Electron Learn — Electronic Learning
Electron Lett — Electronics Letters
Electron Libr — Electronic Library
Electron Library — Electronic Library
Electron Mag — Electronics Magazine
Electron Mater Process Congr — Electronic Materials and Processing Congress
Electron Mater Ser — Electronic Materials Series
Electron Meas — Electronic Measuring
Electron Med — Electronique Medicale
Electron Meten — Electronisch Meten
Electron Mfr — Electronics Manufacturer
Electron Mi — Electron Microscopy Reviews
Electron Microanal Its Appl Proc Meet — Electron Microanalyser and Its Applications. Proceedings of the Meeting
Electron Microelectron Ind — Electronique et Microelectronique Industrielles
Electron Microsc — Electron-Microscopy
Electron Microsc Anal Proc Anniv Meet — Electron Microscopy and Analysis. Proceedings. Anniversary Meeting
Electron Microsc Biol — Electron Microscopy in Biology
Electron Microsc Cytochem Proc Int Symp — Electron Microscopy and Cytochemistry. Proceedings. International Symposium
Electron Microsc Hum Med — Electron Microscopy in Human Medicine
Electron Microsc Immunocytochem — Electron Microscopic Immunocytochemistry
Electron Microsc Proc Eur Congr — Electron Microscopy. Proceedings. European Congress on Electron Microscopy
Electron Microsc Proc Eur Reg Conf — Electron Microscopy. Proceedings. European Regional Conference
Electron Microsc Proc Int Cong — Electron Microscopy. Proceedings of the International Congress for Electron Microscopy
Electron Microsc Proc Reg Conf Asia Oceania — Electron-Microscopy. Proceedings of the Regional Conference in Asia and Oceania
Electron Microsc Proc Stockholm Conf — Electron Microscopy. Proceedings. Stockholm Conference
Electron Microsc Soc Am Annu Meet Proc — Electron Microscopy Society of America. Annual Meeting. Proceedings
Electron Microsc Soc Am Proc — Electron Microscopy Society of America. Proceedings
Electron Microsc Soc South Afr Proc — Electron Microscopy Society of Southern Africa. Proceedings
Electron Micros Soc Southern Afr Proc — Electron Microscopy Society of Southern Africa. Proceedings
Electron News — Electronic News
Electron Nouv — Electronique Nouvelle
Electron Packag and Prod — Electronic Packaging and Production

Electron Packag Prod — Electronic Packaging and Production
Electron Power — Electronics and Power
Electron Prod — Electronic Products Magazine
Electron Prod Des — Electronic Product Design
Electron Prod Methods & Equip — Electronic Production Methods and Equipment
Electron Prog — Electronic Progress
Electron Prop Mech High Tc Supercond Proc Int Workshop — Electronic Properties and Mechanisms of High Tc Superconductors. Proceedings. International Workshop
Electron Publ Abstr — Electronic Publishing Abstracts
Electron Publishing Rev — Electronic Publishing Review
Electron Publ Rev — Electronic Publishing Review
Electron Pwr — Electronics and Power
Electron Reliab Microminiaturization — Electronics Reliability and Microminiaturization
Electron Rep — Electronics Report
Electron Res Announc Amer Math Soc — Electronic Research Announcements of the American Mathematical Society
Electron Rev (Tokyo) — Electronics Review (Tokyo)
Electron Sound and RTE — Electronic Sound and RTE
Electron Spectrosc Theory Tech Appl — Electron Spectroscopy Theory, Techniques, and Applications
Electron Spin Reson — Electron Spin Resonance
Electron Struct Magnet Inorg Comp — Electronic Structure and Magnetism of Inorganic Compounds
Electron Struct Magn Inorg Compd — Electronic Structure and Magnetism of Inorganic Compounds
Electron Struct Prop Semicond — Electronic Structure and Properties of Semiconductors
Electron Surv Comput — Electronic Survey Computing
Electron Surv Computing — Electronic Survey Computing
Electron Technol — Electron Technology
Electron Technol Q — Electron Technology. Quarterly
Electron Technol Rep — Electronic Technology Reports
Electron Test — Electronics Test
Electron Times — Electronic Times
Electron Today — Electronics Today
Electron Today Int — Electronics Today International
Electron Trans Numer Anal — Electronic Transactions on Numerical Analysis
Electron Warf Def Electron — Electronic Warfare Defense Electronics
Electron Wkly — Electronics Weekly
Electron World — Electronics World
Electron World Wireless World — Electronics World and Wireless World
Electro-Opt — Electro-Optics
Electrooptics Rep — Electro-optics Report
Electro Opt Ser — Electro-Optics Series
Electro-Opt Syst Des — Electro-Optical Systems Design
Electro-Opt Systems — Electro-Optical Systems Design
Electrophoresis (Weinheim Fed Repub Ger) — Electrophoresis (Weinheim, Federal Republic of Germany)
Electrophotogr — Electrophotography
Electrophotogr Int Conf — Electrophotography. International Conference
Electroplat and Met Finish — Electroplating and Metal Finishing
Electroplat Eng Handb — Electroplating Engineering Handbook
Electroplat Finish Guangzhou Peoples Repub China — Electroplating and Finishing (Guangzhou, People's Republic of China)
Electroplat Met Finish — Electroplating and Metal Finishing
Electroplat Met Spraying — Electroplating and Metal Spraying
Electroplat Pollut Control — Electroplating and Pollution Control
Electroquim Corrasao — Electroquimica e Corrasao
Electroquim Corros — Electroquimica e Corrosao
Electroresponsive Mol Polym Syst — Electroresponsive Molecular and Polymeric Systems
Electro-Rev — Electro-Revue
Electrost Invited Contrib Pap Int Conf — Electrostatics. Invited and Contributed Papers. International Conference
Electro-Tech — Electro-Techniek
Electro-Tech — Electro-Technology
Electrotech J — Electrotechnical Journal
Electrotech J Jpn — Electrotechnical Journal of Japan
Electro Techn (Beverly Shores, Indiana) — Electro-Technology (Beverly Shores, Indiana)
Electro-Technol — Electro-Technology
Electro-Technol (Bangalore India) — Electro-Technology (Bangalore, India)
Electro Technol Newsl — Electro-Technology Newsletter
Electro-Technol (NY) — Electro-Technology (New York)
Electroteh Electron Autom Electroteh — Electrotehnica, Electronica, si Automatica. Serie Electrotehnica
Electrothermie Int Ed A — Electrothermie International. Edition A. l'Electrothermie dans l'Equipement Technique
Electrothermie Int Ed B — Electrothermie International. Edition B. Applications Industrielles de l'Electrothermie
Electr Overstress Electrost Discharge Symp Proc — Electrical Overstress/ Electrostatic Discharge Symposium Proceedings
Electr Perspect — Electric Perspectives
Electr Pow — Electronics and Power
Electr Power Commun — Electric Power Communicator
Electr Power Energy Syst — Electrical Power and Energy Systems
Electr Power Mon — Electric Power Monthly
Electr Power Res Inst J — Electric Power Research Institute. Journal
Electr Power Res Inst (Rep) EPRI AF — Electric Power Research Institute (Report) EPRI AF
Electr Power Res Inst Rep EPRI AP Palo Alto Calif — Electric Power Research Institute. Report EPRI AP (Palo Alto, California)

Electr Power Res Inst Rep EPRI CS (Palo Alto Calif) — Electric Power Research Institute. Report EPRI CS (Palo Alto, California)

Electr Power Res Inst (Rep) EPRI EA — Electric Power Research Institute (Report) EPRI EA

Electr Power Res Inst (Rep) EPRI EL — Electric Power Research Institute (Report) EPRI EL

Electr Power Res Inst (Rep) EPRI EM — Electric Power Research Institute (Report) EPRI EM

Electr Power Res Inst (Rep) EPRI ER — Electric Power Research Institute (Report) EPRI ER

Electr Power Res Inst (Rep) EPRI ER (Palo Alto Calif) — Electric Power Research Institute (Report) EPRI ER (Palo Alto, California)

Electr Power Res Inst (Rep) EPRI FP — Electric Power Research Institute (Report) EPRI FP

Electr Power Res Inst (Rep) EPRI FP (Palo Alto Calif) — Electric Power Research Institute (Report) EPRI FP (Palo Alto, California)

Electr Power Res Inst (Rep) EPRI NP — Electric Power Research Institute (Report) EPRI NP

Electr Power Res Inst (Rep) EPRI SR (Palo Alto Calif) — Electric Power Research Institute (Report) EPRI SR (Palo Alto, California)

Electr Power Res Inst Workshop Proc — Electric Power Research Institute. Workshop Proceedings

Electr Power Syst Res — Electric Power Systems Research

Electr Processes Atmos Proc Int Conf Atmos Electr — Electrical Processes in Atmospheres. Proceedings. International Conference on Atmospheric Electricity

Electr Prod — Electronic Products Magazine

Electr Rev — Electrical Review

Electr Rev Int — Electrical Review International

Electr Rev Int London — Electrical Review International (London)

Electr Rev London — Electrical Review (London)

Electr Sol — Electricite Solaire

Electr S P — Transactions and Proceedings of the London Electrical Society

Electr S T — Transactions and Proceedings of the London Electrical Society

Electr Superv — Electrical Supervisor

Electr Technol (USSR) — Electric Technology (USSR)

Electr Technol USSR Eng Transl — Electric Technology USSR (English Translation)

Electr Times — Electrical Times

Electr Util & Energy Abs — Electrical Utilization and Energy Abstracts

Elect Rv — Electrical Review

Electr Veh — Electric Vehicles

Electr Veh Batteries — Electric Vehicles and Batteries

Electr Veh Dev — Electric Vehicle Developments

Electr Veh News — Electric Vehicle News

Electr Week — Electrical Week

Electr Weld — Electric Welding

Electr West — Electrical West

Electr World — Electrical World

Elect Supervis — Electrical Supervisor

Elect Times — Electrical Times

Elect Tract — Electric Traction

Elect World — Electrical World

Elec Veh — Electric Vehicle News

Elec W — Electrical Weekly

Elec War D — Electronic Warfare Digest

Elec Week — Electronics Weekly

Elec West — Electrical West

Elec World — Electrical World

ELEGA — Electronic Engineering

ELEGC — Electric Light and Power. Energy/Generation

ELEKA — Elektrichestvo

Elek App — Elektronik Applikation

Elek Bahnen — Elektrische Bahnen

Elek Tech — Elektrotechniek

Elekt Ind — Elektronik Industrie

Elektr — Elektrichestvo

Elektr & Teplovoznaya Tyaga — Elektricheskaya i Teplovoznaya Tyaga

Elektr Ausruestung — Elektrische Ausruestung

Elektr Bahnen — Elektrische Bahnen

Elektr Energ-Tech — Elektrische Energie-Technik

Elektr Kontakty Tr Soveshch — Elektricheskie Kontakty. Trudy Soveshchaniya po Elektricheskim Kontaktam i Kontaktnym Materialam

Elektr Masch — Elektrische Maschinen

Elektr Muhendisligi — Elektrik Muhendisligi

Elektr Nachrichtenwes — Elektrisches Nachrichtenwesen

Elektr Nachr Tech — Elektrische Nachrichten Technik

Elektro-Anz — Elektro-Anzeiger

Elektrochem Z — Elektrochemische Zeitschrift

Elektrochem Zs — Elektrochemische Zeitschrift

Elektrodin Fiz SVCh — Elektrodinamika i Fizika SVCh (Sverkhvysokaya Chastota)

Elektroenerget i Avtomat — Elektroenergetika i Avtomatika

Elektrofiz Appar — Elektrofizicheskaya Apparatura

Elektrofiz App Sb Statei — Electrofizicheskaya Apparatura Sbornik Statei

Elektroiskrovaya Obrab Met — Elektroiskrovaya Obrabotka Metallov

Elektroizolacna Kablova Tech — Elektroizolacna a Kablova Technika

Elektroizol Kablova Tech — Elektroizolacna a Kablova Technika

Elektro-Jahrb — Elektro-Jahrbuch

Elektrokhim Margantsa — Elektrokhimiya Margantsa

Elektrok Tidsskr — Elektroteknisk Tidsskrift

Elektromagn Strukt Defekoskopiya — Elektromagnitnaya Strukturo- i Defektoskopiya

Elektromagn Vzaimodeistviya Yader Malykh Sredn Energ — Elektromagnitnye Vzaimodeistviya Yader pri Malykh i Srednikh Energiyakh. Trudy Seminara

Elektro Med — Elektro-Medizin

Elektro Med Biomed und Tech — Elektro Medizin, Biomedizin, und Technik

Elektromeister & Dtsch Elektrohandwerk — Elektromeister und Deutsches Elektrohandwerk

Elektron Anz — Elektronik-Anzeiger

Elektron Appl — Elektronik Applikation

Elektron Bol'shikh Moshch — Elektronika Bol'shikh Moshchnostei

Elektron Datenverarb — Elektronische Datenverarbeitung

Elektron Elektrotech — Elektronika ir Elektrotechnika

Elektron Entwickl — Elektronik Entwicklung

Elektron Heute — Elektronik Heute

Elektronik — Elektronik - Technologie - Anwendungen - Marketing

Elektronik — Elektronik-Zeitung

Elektronik Inf — Elektronik Information

Elektron Ind — Elektronik Industrie

Elektron Inf — Elektronik Informationen

Elektron Informationsverarbeit Kybernetik — Elektronische Informationsverarbeitung und Kybernetik

Elektron Informationsverarb Kybern — Elektronische Informationsverarbeitung und Kybernetik

Elektron Informationsverarb Kybernet — Elektronische Informationsverarbeitung und Kybernetik

Elektron Int — Elektron International

Elektron Ionnye Protsessy Ionnykh Krist — Elektronnye i Ionnye Protsessy u Ionnykh Kristallakh

Elektron Ionnye Protsessy Tverd Telakh — Elektronnye i Ionnye Protsessy v Tverdykh Telakh

Elektron J — Elektronik Journal

Elektron Khim Kardiol — Elektronika i Khimiya v Kardiologii

Elektronmikroskopiever Suidelike Afr Verrig — Elektronmikroskopievereniging van Suidelike Afrika. Verrigtings

Elektronmikroskopiever Suidelike Afr Verrigt — Elektronmikroskopievereniging van Suidelike Afrika. Verrigtings

Elektron Model — Elektronnoe Modelirovanie

Elektron (Muenchen) — Elektronik (Muenchen)

Elektronnaya Obrab Mater — Elektronnaya Obrabotka Materialov

Elektron Obrab Mater — Elektronnaya Obrabotka Materialov

Elektron Prax — Elektronik Praxis

Elektron Radio Telev — Elektroniikka Radio Televisio

Elektron Rechenanlagen — Elektronische Rechenanlagen

Elektron Rechenanlagen Comput Prax — Elektronische Rechenanlagen mit Computer Praxis

Elektron Rechnen Regeln Sonderband — Elektronisches Rechnen und Regeln. Sonderband

Elektron Rechnen und Regeln — Elektronisches Rechnen und Regeln

Elektron Rechnen und Regeln Sonderband — Elektronisches Rechnen und Regeln. Sonderband

Elektron Rech Regeln — Elektronisches Rechnen und Regeln

Elektron Rundsch — Elektronische Rundschau

Elektron Tekh Ser 1 Elektron — Elektronnaya Tekhnika. Seriya 1. Elektronika

Elektron Tekh Ser 12 — Elektronnaya Tekhnika. Seriya 12

Elektron Tekh Ser 12 Upr Kach Stand — Elektronaya Tekhnika. Seriya 12. Upravlenie Kachestvom i Standartizatsiya

Elektron Wiss Tech — Elektron in Wissenschaft und Technik

Elektron-Ztg — Elektronik-Zeitung

Elektro-Prakt — Elektro-Praktiker

Elektro Prom-St i Priborostroene — Elektro Promishlenost i Priborostroene

Elektroprom-St Priborostr — Elektropromishlenost i Priborostroene

Elektrosint Elektrodnye Reakts Uchastiem Org Soedin — Elektrosintez. Elektrodnye Reaktsii s Uchastiem Organicheskikh Soedinenii

Elektrotec — Elektrotechniek Elektronica

Elektro Tech — Elektro-Techniek

Elektrotech Cas — Elektrotechniky Casopis

Elektrotech Maschinenbau — Elektrotechnik und Maschinenbau

Elektrotechniek Meppel Neth — Elektrotechniek (Meppel, Netherlands)

Elektrotech Obz — Elektrotechnicky Obzor

Elektrotech und Maschinenbau — Elektrotechnik und Maschinenbau

Elektrotech Z A — Elektrotechnische Zeitschrift. Ausgabe A

Elektrotech Z Ausg A — Elektrotechnische Zeitschrift. Ausgabe A

Elektrotech Z Ausg B — Elektrotechnische Zeitschrift. Ausgabe B

Elektrotech Z B — Elektrotechnische Zeitschrift. Ausgabe B

Elektrotech Zeit — Elektrotechnische Zeitschrift

Elektrotech Zeitsch — Elektrotechnische Zeitschrift

Elektrotech Z Elektrotech Maschinenbau — Elektrotechnische Zeitschrift und Elektrotechnik und Maschinenbau

Elektrotech Z ETZ — Elektrotechnische Zeitschrift. ETZ

Elektrotech Z ETZ A — Elektrotechnische Zeitschrift. ETZ A

Elektrotech Z ETZ B — Elektrotechnische Zeitschrift. ETZ B

Elektroteh Ind Pogonu — Elektrotehnika u Industriji Pogonu

Elektroteh Vestn — Elektrotehniski Vestnik

Elektrotek — Elektroteknikeren

Elektrotekh — Elektrotekhnika

Elektrotekh Mater Elektr Kondens Provoda Kabeli — Elektrotekhnicheskie Materialy. Elektricheskie Kondensatory. Provoda i Kabeli

Elektrotekh Promst Elektrotekh Mater — Elektrotekhnicheskaya Promyshlennost. Elektrotekhnicheskie Materialy

Elektrotekh Promst Elektrotermiya — Elektrotekhnicheskaya Promyshlennost. Elektrotermiya

Elektrotekh Promst Khim Fiz Istochniki Toka — Elektrotekhnicheskaya Promyshlennost. Khimicheskie i Fizicheskie Istochniki Toka

Elektrotek Tidsskr — Elektroteknisk Tidsskrift

Elektrowaerme A — Elektrowaerme im Technischen-Ausbau

Elektrowaerme Int — Elektrowaerme International

Elektrowaerme Int A — Elektrowaerme International. Edition A. Elektrowaerme im Technischen Ausbau

Elektrowaerme Int A Elektrowaerme Tech Ausbau — Elektrowaerme International. Edition A. Elektrowaerme im Technischen Ausbau

Elektrowaerme Int B — Elektrowaerme International. Edition B. Industrielle Electrowaerme

Elektrowaerme Int B Elektrowaerme — Elektrowaerme International. Edition B. Industrielle Elektrowaerme

Elektrowaerme Int Ed A — Elektrowaerme International. Edition A. Elektrowaerme im Technischen Ausbau

Elektrowaerme Int Ed B — Elektrowaerme International. Edition B. Industrielle Elektrowaerme

Elektrowrm Tech-Ausbau — Elektrowaerme im Technischen-Ausbau

Elektr Stahlherstell — Elektrische Stahlherstellung

Elektr Stantsii — Elektricheskie Stantsii

Elektr Stn — Elektricheskie Stantsii

Elektr Stn Prilozh — Elektricheskie Stantsii. Prilozhenie

Elektr Svetsningsaktiebolaget Rev Dtsch Ausg — Elektriska Svetsningsaktiebolaget. Revue. Deutsche Ausgabe

Elektr Svetsningsaktiebolaget Rev Ed Fr — Elektriska Svetsningsaktiebolaget. Revue. Edition Francaise

Elektr Teplovoz Tyaga — Elektricheskaya i Teplovoznaya Tyaga

Elektr Therm Leitfaehigkeit Metalltag DDR — Elektrische und Thermische Leitfaehigkeit. Metalltagung in der DDR

Elektr Z B — Elektrotechnische Zeitschrift. Ausgabe B

Elekttech Z — Elektrotechnische Zeitschrift

Elek Zeit — Elektrotechnische Zeitschrift

Elelmez Ip — Elelmezesi Ipar

Elelmez Ipar — Elelmezesi Ipar

Elelm Ipar — Elelmezesi Ipar

Elelmiszervizgalati Kozl — Elelmiszervizgalati Kozlemenyek

Elelmiszervizgalati Kozlem — Elelmiszervizgalati Kozlemenyek

Elelmiszervizgalati Kozl — Elelmiszervizgalati Kozlemenyek

Elelmiszerv Kozl — Elelmiszervizgalati Kozlemenyek

ELEMA — Electrical Engineer (Melbourne)

Elem Anal Coal Its By Prod Int Conf Proc — Elemental Analysis of Coal and its By-Products. International Conference Proceedings

Elem Chastitsy — Elementarnye Chastitsy

Elem Chastitsy Kosm Luchi — Elementarnye Chastitsy i Kosmicheskie Luchi

ElemE — Elementary English

Elem Energy Cold Fusion — Elemental Energy (Cold Fusion)

Elem Engl — Elementary English

Element School Jour — Elementary School Journal. School of Education. University of Chicago

Elem Fontium Ed — Elementa ad Fontium Editiones

Elem Math — Elemente der Mathematik

Elem Math — Elements of Mathematics

Elem Math Suppl — Elemente der Mathematik. Supplement

Elem Met Clim — Elementos Meteorologicos e Climatologicos

Elem Part Theory Proc Nobel Symp — Elementary Particle Theory. Relativistic Groups and Analyticity. Proceedings. Nobel Symposium

Elem Sch J — Elementary School Journal

Elem School J — Elementary School Journal

Elem Teor Tekh Avtom Upr — Elementy Teorii i Tekhniki Avtomaticheskogo Upravleniya

ELENA — Electrical Engineering. American Institute of Electrical Engineers

El Enc Clin Neurophys — Electroencephalography and Clinical Neurophysiology

Elenchus Bibliogr Biblicus — Elenchus Bibliographicus Biblicus

Elenchus Bibliogr Biblicus Biblica — Elenchus Bibliographicus Biblicus of Biblica

ELEND — Electrical Engineer

El Energ — Electrical Energy

El Eng — Electrical Engineer

El Eng — Electrical Engineering. American Institute of Electrical Engineers

El Engl — Elementary English

El Engl R — Elementary English Review

ELEQB — Electric Equipment

ELet — Esperienze Letterarie. Rivista Trimestrale di Critica e Cultura

ELet — Etudes de Lettres

ELet — Europa Letteraria

ELETB — Electrical Engineering Transactions

Elettron & Telecomun — Elettronica e Telecomunicazioni

Elettron Oggi — Elettronica Oggi

Elettrotecn — Elettrotecnica

Elettrotecnica Suppl — Elettrotecnica. Supplemento

Elet Tud — Elet es Tudomany

Elev Aliment — Elevage et Alimentation

Elev Insemination — Elevage Insemination

Elev Kosmos — Elevtheros Kosmos

Elev Porcin — Elevage Porcin

ELEWA — Electrical West

Eley Game Advis Serv Annu Rep — Eley Game Advisory Service. Annual Report

Eley Game Advis Serv Bookl — Eley Game Advisory Service. Booklet

Eley Game Advis Stn Annu Rep — Eley Game Advisory Station. Annual Report

ELF — Etude de la Langue Francaise

ELFIS — Information System on Food, Agriculture, and Forestry

ELFOD — Electric Forum

Elga Prog — Elga Progress

Elgin Pap — Elgin Papers

Elgin State Hosp Collect Contrib Pap — Elgin State Hospital. Collected and Contributed Papers

ELH — Enciclopedia Linguistica Hispanica

ELH — Journal of English Literary History

ELH Engl L — ELH. English Literary History

ELI — Economic Literature Index

ELIAS — Environment Libraries Automated System

ELic — Entregas de la Licorne

ELIDA — Electronic Industries

El Ind — Electrical Industry

ELIND — Electricien Industriel

ELing — Etudes Linguistiques

Elin-Z — Elin- Zeitschrift

ELIPA — Experienced Librarians and Informational Personnel in the Developing Countries of Asia and Oceania

Elisha Mitchell Sci Soc J — Elisha Mitchell Scientific Society. Journal

ELiT — English Literature in Transition, 1880-1920

ELit — Estafeta Literaria

ELit — Etudes Litteraires

ElizS — Elizabethan Studies

ELJ — Elsass-Lothringisches Jahrbuch

El J — Ephemerides Liturgicae. Jus et Praxis Liturgica

ELJAA — Elektro-Jahrbuch

ELKCA — Elektrotechnicky Casopis

ELKHA — Elektro-Handel

ELKOA — Elektronik

ELKRD — Elektronik-Centralen. Report. ECR

Elkt — Elektroteknikeren. Elektroteknisk Todsskrift for Lys og Kraft, Telefoni og Telegrafi

ELkT — Epitheorese Logou Kai Technes

ELKTA — Elektrotekhnika

ELKTD — Elektronikk

ELKWA — Elektrowirtschaft

ELKZ — Evangelisch-Lutherische Kirchenzeitung

ELL — English Language and Literature

Ell B & Ell — Ellis, Blackburn, and Ellis' English Queen's Bench Reports

Ell Dig — Eller's Minnesota Digest

ELLEA — Electronics Letters

ELLF — Etudes de Langue et de Litterature Francaises

Elli — Ellipse

Elliott Soc N H Charleston Pr — Elliott Society of Natural History of Charleston. Proceedings

Ellipsom Metod Issled Poverkhn Rab Uchastnikov Vses Konf — Ellipsometriya. Metod Issledovaniya Poverkhnosti. Raboty Uchastnikov Vsesoyuznoi Konferentsii

Ellis — Stephen Ellis

Ellis Horwood Ser Anal Chem — Ellis Horwood Series in Analytical Chemistry

Ellis Horwood Ser Artificial Intelligence — Ellis Horwood Series in Artificial Intelligence

Ellis Horwood Ser Artificial Intelligence Found Concepts — Ellis Horwood Series in Artificial Intelligence Foundations and Concepts

Ellis Horwood Ser Civ Engrg — Ellis Horwood Series in Civil Engineering

Ellis Horwood Ser Comput Appl — Ellis Horwood Series. Computers and Their Applications

Ellis Horwood Ser Engrg Sci — Ellis Horwood Series in Engineering Science

Ellis Horwood Ser Math Appl — Ellis Horwood Series. Mathematics and Its Applications

Ellis Horwood Ser Math Appl Statist Oper Res — Ellis Horwood Series in Mathematics and its Applications. Statistics and Operational Research

Ellis Horwood Ser Math Appl Statist Oper Res Comput Math — Ellis Horwood Series in Mathematics and its Applications. Statistics, Operational Research, and Computational Mathematics

Ellis Horwood Ser Mech Engrg — Ellis Horwood Series in Mechanical Engineering

Ellis Horwood Ser Pure Appl Phys — Ellis Horwood Series in Pure and Applied Physics

Ell Jb — Ellwanger Jahrbuch. Ein Volksbuch fuer Heimatpflege in Virngau und Ries

ELLPA — Electric Light and Power

ELLS — English Literature and Language

Ellwanger Jb — Ellwanger Jahrbuch: Ein Volksbuch fuer Heimatpflege in Virngau und Ries

ELM — El Urogallo (Madrid)

ELMAA — Electrical Manufacturing

Elma Dill Russell Spencer Found Ser — Elma Dill Russell Spencer Foundation Series

ELMCBK — Electromedica

ELMMA — Elemente der Mathematik

ELMOD — Elektronnoe Modelirovanie

ELMYA — Electromyography [*Later, Electromyography and Clinical Neurophysiology*]

ELMYAH — Electromyography [*Later, Electromyography and Clinical Neurophysiology*]

ELMZA — Elelmiszertudomany

ELN — English Language Notes

ELN — Environmental Law Newsletter

ELODA — Electronic Design

E London Pap — East London Papers

ELOSA9 — Elsevier Oceanography Series

ELOWA — Electro-Technology

El Pal — El Palacio

El Paso Econ R — El Paso Economic Review

El Paso Geol Soc Annu Field Trip (Guideb) — El Paso Geological Society. Annual Field Trip (Guidebook)

ELPBA — Elektropromishlenost i Priborostroene

ELPLBS — Ekologia Polska

ELPLD — Electronics Information and Planning

ELPOA — Electronic Products

ELPPA — Electronic Packaging and Production

ELPVA — Elektroprivreda

ELPWA — Electronics and Power

ELR — English Literary Renaissance

ELR — Environmental Law Reporter

ELR — Environmental Law Reporter of New South Wales

ELR — European Law Review

ELRAA — Elektronische Rechenanlagen

ELREA — Electrical Review

ELRen — English Literary Renaissance

EL Rev — European Law Review
ELRMD — Electric Ratemaking
ELRPA — Environmental Law Reporter
ELRPD — ELCON [*Electricity Consumers Resource Council*] Report
Els — Elsinore
ELS — English Literary Studies
ELSA — Electronic Selective Archives
El Salvador Servicio Geol Nac Anales Bol Bol Sismol — El Salvador. Servicio Geologico Nacional. Anales. Boletin. Boletin Sismologico
El Salvador Univ Inst Tropical Inv Cient Anuario Comun — El Salvador. Universidad. Instituto Tropical de Investigaciones Cientificas. Anuario Comunicaciones
El Salv Dir Gen Invest Agron Secc Agron Bol Tec — El Salvador. Direccion General de Investigaciones Agronomicas. Seccion de Agronomia. Boletin Tecnico
El Salv Dir Gen Invest Agron Secc Entomol Bol Tec — El Salvador. Direccion General de Investigaciones Agronomicas. Seccion de Entomologia. Boletin Tecnico
El Salv M — Banco Central de Reserra de El Salvador. Revista Mensual
Elsass Lotharing Jb — Elsass-Lotharingisches Jahrbuch
El Sch Guid & Counsel — Elementary School Guidance and Counseling
El Sch J — Elementary School Journal
El School T — Elementary School Teacher
Elsevier Bus Intel Ser — Elsevier Business Intelligence Series
Elsevier Oceanogr Ser — Elsevier Oceanography Series
Elsevier Oceanogr Ser (Amsterdam) — Elsevier Oceanography Series (Amsterdam)
Elsevier Stud Appl Electromagn Mater — Elsevier Studies in Applied Electromagnetics in Materials
ELSM — Els Marges
ELSPA — Elektricheskie Seti i Sistemy
ELSRB — Electrotechnical Laboratory. Summaries of Reports
ELSS — Electronic Legislative Search System
ELSUA — Electrical Supervisor
ELT — Eagle's Law of Tithes
ELT — Electra
ELT — English Language Teaching [*Later, English Language Teaching Journal*]
ELT — English Literature in Transition, 1880-1920
ELTCA — Electricite
ELTEA — Electro-Technology
El Techn — Elektrotechnika
El Techn Cas — Elektrotechnicky Casopis
El Technol (USSR) — Electric Technology (USSR)
El Techn Zs — Elektrotechnische Zeitschrift
Eltek Aktuell Elektron — Elteknik med Aktuell Elektronik
Eltek Aktuell Elektron A — Elteknik med Aktuell Elektronik. Edition A
Elteknik med Aktuel Elektron — Elteknik med Aktuell Elektronik
ELTGA — Electric Technology
ELTHB — Elektrotehnika
ELTIA — Electrical Times
ELTJ — English Language Teaching Journal
ELTKA — Elektrotechniek
ELTPA — Electronic Progress
ELTRD — Elektronikschau
ELTSA — Elettrotecnica. Supplemento
ELTTA — Electrotehnica
Elt Z — Elektrotechnische Zeitschrift
ELTZA — Elettrificazione
ELu — Estudios Lulianos
ELul — Estudios Lulianos
EL Univ Arkansas Coop Ext Serv — EL. University of Arkansas. Cooperative Extension Service
ELVEA — Elektrontehniski Vestnik
El Verw — Elektrizitaetsverwertung
El Wi — Elektrizitaetswirtschaft
El Wiss Techn — Elektron in Wissenschaft und Technik
ELWIU — Essays in Literature. Western Illinois University
ELWLA — Elektrowelt
ELWOA — Electrical World
ELWYA — Electronics Weekly
El Z — Elektrotechnische Zeitschrift
EM — Dictionnaire Etymologique de la Langue Latine
EM — Early Music
EM — Ebony Man
EM — Eclectic Magazine
EM — Ecological Monographs
EM — Econometrica
EM — Ehrverskonomiske Meddelelser
EM — Elektrotechnik und Maschinenbau
EM — (El) Mundo
Em — Emerita
EM — Empirical Studies of the Arts
Em — Emuna
EM — Endocrinology and Metabolism
EM — English Miscellany
EM — Espana Misionera
EM — Ethnikon Mouseion
Em — Ethnomusicology
EM — Etymologicum Magnum
EM — Excavation Memoirs
EM — Excerpta Medica
EM — Journal of Engineering Mechanics
EM/A — Arstryck. Etnografiska Museum
EMA — Engineered Materials Abstracts
EMA — Environmental Monitoring and Assessment

EMA — Epeteris tou Mesaionikou Archeiou
EMA — Europe in the Middle Ages. Selected Studies
EMA — Ezegodnik Muzeja Architektury
EMA — MMS Equity Market Analysis
EMAAA — Epeteris Mesaionikou Archeiou Akademias Athenon
EMAB — EMA (Early Music Association) Bulletin
EmAb — Employment Relations Abstracts
Emailletech Mon Bl — Emailletechnische Monats Blaetter
Emailwaren Ind — Emailwaren-Industrie
Emajl Keram Staklo — Emajl - Keramika - Staklo
EM & D J Eng Mater Compon Des — EM and D [*Engineering Materials and Design*] Journal of Engineering Materials, Components, and Design
EM & D Prod Data — EM and D [*Engineering Materials and Design*] Product Data
EMA P — Epeteris tu Mesaioniku Archeiu. Paratema
E Maria — Estudios Marianos
EMASD — Environmental Monitoring and Assessment
EMB — Emballages Magazine
EMB — Engineering Manpower Bulletin
Emballage Dig — Emballage Digest
Em Benefit — Employee Benefit Plan Review
Emberiza Vogelschutz Vogelkd Rheinl Pfalz — Emberiza Vogelschutz und Vogelkunde in Rheinland Pfalz
EMBO (Eur Mol Biol Organ) J — EMBO (European Molecular Biology Organization) Journal
EMBO J — EMBO [*European Molecular Biology Organization*] Journal
Embo Rep — Embo Reports
Embouteillage Cond — Embouteillage Conditionnement
Embr — Embryologia
EMBRAPA Cen Pesqui Agropecu Trop Umido Comun Tec — EMBRAPA. (Empresa Brasileira de Pesquisa Agropecuaria) Centro de Pesquisa Agropecuaria do Tropico Umido. Comunicado Tecnico
EMBRAPA Empresa Bras Pesqui Agropecu — EMBRAPA. Empresa Brasileira de Pesquisa Agropecuaria
EMBZA6 — Emberiza
EMC — El Monte Carmelo
EMC — El Museo Canario
EMCAE8 — Environmental Mutagens and Carcinogens
EMCNA9 — Electromyography and Clinical Neurophysiology
EMC SD State Univ Coop Ext Serv — EMC. South Dakota State University. Cooperative Extension Service
EMC Test Des — EMC Test and Design
EMD — English Miscellany. St. Stephen's College (Delhi)
EMD — Export Market Digest
Emden Nf Gs Jbr — Jahresbericht der Naturforschende Gesellschaft in Emden
Emder Jb — Emder Jahrbuch
EMDJA2 — Ethiopian Medical Journal
EM D J Mater Components Des — EM and D [*Engineering Materials and Design*] Journal of Engineering Materials, Components, and Design
EME — Egri Muzeum Evkoenyve
EME — Euromoney
EMEA — Employment and Earnings
EM Econ Mocambique — EM. Economia de Mocambique
EMEDDQ — Ecologia Mediterranea
EMEED — Electrical and Mechanical Executive Engineer
EMELD — Electric Machines and Electromechanics
Emer — Emerita
E Mercks Jahresber — E Merck's Jahresberichte
Emerg Dep News — Emergency Department News
Emergency Lib — Emergency Librarian
Emergency Libn — Emergency Librarian
Emerg Health Serv Q — Emergency Health Services Quarterly
Emerg Health Serv Rev — Emergency Health Services Review
Emerg Infect Dis — Emerging Infectious Diseases
Emerging Infect Dis — Emerging Infectious Diseases
Emerging Pharm — Emerging Pharmaceuticals
Emerg Lib — Emergency Librarian
Emerg Med — Emergency Medicine
Emerg Med Annu — Emergency Medicine Annual
Emerg Med Care Dig — Emergency Medical Care Digest
Emerg Med Clin North Am — Emergency Medicine Clinics of North America
Emerg Med J — Emergency Medicine Journal
Emerg Med Serv — Emergency Medical Services
Emerg Med Tech Legal Bull — Emergency Medical Technician Legal Bulletin
Emerg Nurse Legal Bull — Emergency Nurse Legal Bulletin
Emerg Plann Dig — Emergency Planning Digest
Emerg Serv News — Emergency Services News
Emer Libr — Emergency Librarian
EMETD — Energy Meetings
EMFIA — Electroplating and Metal Finishing
EMFRA2 — Empire Forestry Review
E Mg — Entomological Magazine
EMH — Entomologische Mitteilungen. Zoologisches Staatinstitut und Zoologisches Museum. Hamburg University
EMI — Engineering Management International
EMIDD — Environment Midwest
E Midl Geogr — East Midland Geographer
Emilia Pr Rom — Emilia Preromana
EMIPA — Elelmezesi Ipar
EMIRA — Ezhegodnik Muzei Istorii Religii i Ateizma
EMIS — Electronic Materials Information Service
EMIS Datarev Ser — EMIS (Electronic Materials Information Service) Datareviews Series
EMJ — Engineering and Mining Journal
EMJ Eng Manage J — EMJ. Engineering Management Journal

E MJ Met Miner Mark — E and MJ (Engineering and Mining Journal) Metal and Mineral Markets
EMJODG — EMBO [*European Molecular Biology Organization*] Journal
Emlekbeszedek Magyar Tud Akad Tagjai Felett — Emlekbeszedek a Magyar Tudomanyos Akademia Tagjai Felett
Emlekbeszedek Magyar Tud Akad Tagjairol — Emlekbeszedek a Magyar Tudomanyos Akademia Tagjairol
Em LJ — Emory Law Journal
EMM — Entomologist's Monthly Magazine
EMM — Etudes de Metaphysique et de Morale
EMMSQP — Edinburgh Medical Missionary Society's Quarterly Paper
EMN — Early Music News
EMNED — Energy Management News
EMNGD — Environmental Management
EMODA — EMO [*Emergency Measures Organization*] Digest
EMO (Emerg Meas Organ) Dig — EMO (Emergency Measures Organization) Digest (Canada)
Emon — Elliott Monographs in Romance Languages and Literatures
E Mong — Etudes Mongoles
Emory L J — Emory Law Journal
Emory Univ J Med — Emory University Journal of Medicine
Emory Univ Quart — Emory University Quarterly
Emotion Reprod Int Cong Psychosom Obstet Gynecol — Emotion and Reproduction. International Congress of Psychosomatic Obstetrics and Gynecology
Emp — Empedocle
Emp — Employer
Emp — Empreintes
EMP — Etudes Musulmanes (Paris)
EMP — Experimental and Molecular Pathology
EMPA — Etudes Mensuelles sur l'Economie et les Finances de la Syrie et des Pays Arabes
Emp Club Canada — Empire Club of Canada
Emp Cott Grow Corp R — Empire Cotton Growing Corporation. Review
Emp Cott Grow Rev — Empire Cotton Growing Corporation. Review
Emp Cotton Grow Corp Conf Cotton Grow Probl Rep Summ Proc — Empire Cotton Growing Corporation. Conference on Cotton Growing Problems. Report and Summary of Proceedings
Emp Cotton Grow Corp Prog Rep Exp Stn — Empire Cotton Growing Corporation. Progress Reports from Experiment Stations
Emp Cotton Growing R — Empire Cotton Growing Review
Emp Cotton Grow Rev — Empire Cotton Growing Corporation. Review
Emp Dig — Empire Digest
Empe — Empedocle. Revue Litteraire Mensuelle
Emp For Handb — Empire Forestry Handbook
Emp For J — Empire Forestry Journal
Emp For Rev — Empire Forestry Review
Emphasis Nurs — Emphasis. Nursing
Empire Forest — Empire Forestry. Empire Forestry Association
Empire For J — Empire Forestry Journal
Empire J Exp Agr — Empire Journal of Experimental Agriculture
Empire J Exp Agric — Empire Journal of Experimental Agriculture
Empire Prod — Empire Producer
Empire R — Empire Review [*London*]
EMPIRES — Excerpta Medica Physicians Information Retrieval and Education Service
Empire State Rept — Empire State Report
Empire Sur Rev — Empire Survey Review
Empirical Econ — Empirical Economics
Empiric Stud Arts — Empirical Studies of the Arts
Empir Res T — Empirical Research in Theatre
Empir Res T Ann — Empirical Research in Theatre Annual
Empir Stud Psychoanal Theor — Empirical Studies of Psychoanalytic Theories
Emp J Exp Ag — Empire Journal of Experimental Agriculture
Emp J Exp Agric — Empire Journal of Experimental Agriculture
Emp J Expl Agric — Empire Journal of Experimental Agriculture
Empl & Training Rep BNA — Employment and Training Reporter. Bureau of National Affairs
Empl Benefit Plan Rev — Employee Benefit Plan Review
Empl Benefits J — Employee Benefits Journal
Empl B Jrl — Employee Benefits Journal
Empl Coordinator Research Inst Am — Employment Coordinator. Research Institute of America
Empl Gaz — Employment Gazette
Empl News — Employment News
Employ Benefit Plan Rev — Employee Benefit Plan Review
Employ Benefits J — Employee Benefits Journal
Employ Earn Hours — Employment Earnings and Hours
Employee Benefits Cas BNA — Employee Benefits Cases. Bureau of National Affairs
Employee Health Fitness Newsl — Employee Health and Fitness Newsletter
Employee Rel — Employee Relations
Employers R — Employers' Review
Employ Gaz — Employment Gazette
Employ Iss — Employment Issues
Employment — Employment and Earnings
Employ Rel Abstr — Employment Relations Abstracts
Employ Relat Abstr — Employment Relations Abstracts
Employ Relat Law J — Employee Relations Law Journal
Employ Rep — Employment Report
Empl Prac Dec CCH — Employment Practices Decisions. Commerce Clearing House
Empl Prac Guide CCH — Employment Practices Guide. Commerce Clearing House
Empl R — Employers' Review
Empl RA — Employment Relations Abstracts

Empl Relat Law J — Employee Relations Law Journal
Empl Rel LJ — Employee Relations Law Journal
Empl Rep — Employment Report
Empl Safety & Health Guide CCH — Employment Safety and Health Guide. Commerce Clearing House
Empl Secur Rev — Employment Security Review
Empl Serv R — Employment Service Review
Emplymnt S — Employment and Earnings. Supplement
Emp Min Metall Congr Proc — Empire Mining and Metallurgical Congress. Proceedings
Emporia State Res Stud — Emporia State Research Studies
Emporia St Res Stud — Emporia State Research Studies
Emp Prod — Empire Producer
Emp Prod Exp — Empire Production and Export
Emp R — Empire Review
Empr — Empreintes
Emp Rel — Employee Relations
Emp Rel LJ — Employee Relations Law Journal
Empresa Bras Pesqui Agropecu Cent Tecnol Agri — Empresa Brasiliera de Pesquisa Agropecuaria. Centro de Tecnologia Agricola e Alimentar
Emp Rev — Empire Review
EMPSA — Experimental and Molecular Pathology. Supplement
Emp St Rep — Empire State Report
Emp St Rep W — Empire State Report Weekly
Emp Surv Rev — Empire Survey Review
EMQ — Evangelical Missions Quarterly
EMR — Employee Relations
EMRIWTB — Canada. Department of Energy, Mines, and Resources. Inland Waters Branch. Technical Bulletin
EMROD — Ekspluatatsiya, Modernizatsiya i Remont Oborudovaniya v Neftepererabatyvayushchei i Neftekhimicheskoi Promyshlennosti
EMRSAV — East Malling Research Station. Annual Report
EMS — Encyclopedie des Musiques Sacrees
EmSA — Emakeele Seltsi Aastaraamat
EMSCD — English Miscellany. St. Stephen's College (Delhi)
EMSM — Employee Services Management
EMS Newsl — EMS [*Environmental Mutagen Society*] Newsletter
EMT — Econometrica
EMTDA — Engineering Materials and Design
EMTED2 — Enzyme and Microbial Technology
EMT J — EMT [*Emergency Medical Technician*] Journal
EMT Legal Bull — Emergency Medical Technician Legal Bulletin
EMTRA — Eastern Metals Review
Em Univ Q — Emory University Quarterly
EMVW — Enquetes du Musee de la Vie Wallonne
EMW — Enquetes. Musee de la Vie Wallonne
EMW — Evangelical Magazine of Wales
EM Wash State Univ Coop Ext Serv — EM. Washington State University. Cooperative Extension Service
EMZ — Evangelische Missionszeitschrift
EMZ — Evangelische Musikzeitung
EMZMAJ — Entomologische Mitteilungen. Zoologischen Museum
EMZSA3 — Entomologische Mitteilungen. Zoologischen Staatsinstitut und Zoologischen Museum
EN — Economic News
EN — Education Nationale
EN — Electronic News
En — Encounter
EN — Encuentro (Nicaragua)
En — Enquiry
EN — Ere Nouvelle
EN — Etudes Numismatiques
EN — Euromarkt Nieuws
EN — European Numismatics
EN — Europe Nouvelle
EN — Experimental Neurology
EN — Export Network
ENAAD — Energetika (Alma-Ata)
ENACD — Environmental Action
ENAEA — Electrical News and Engineering
ENAGDM — Energia Nuclear e Agricultura
ENALD — Energy and Alternatives Magazine
ENAMA3 — Entomologica Americana
Enamelist Bull — Enamelist Bulletin
Enat — Education Nationale
ENATA — Energia es Atomtechnika
ENB — Energiebesparing in Bedrijf en Instelling
ENB — Ethnologisches Notizblatt
ENC — Els Nostres Classics
ENC — Encounter
Enc — Encyclopedie ou Dictionnaire Raisonne des Sciences, des Arts, et des Metiers
EnC — Enseignement Chretien
Enc Am — Encyclopedia Americana
Enc Ass — Encyclopedia of Associations
Enc Biblia — Enciclopedia de la Biblia
Enc Brit — Encyclopaedia Britannica
Enc Bud — Encyclopaedia of Buddhism
Enc Buddh — Encyclopaedia of Buddhism
Enc Catt — Enciclopedia Cattolica
ENCEA — Encephale
ENCEAN — Encephale
Enc Ec V — Enciclopedia Ecclesiastica. Venezia
Enceph — Encephale
Enc Fr — Encyclopedie Francaise

Ench B — Enchiridion Biblicum
ENCHDZ — Specialist Periodical Reports. Environmental Chemistry
Ench Symb — Enchiridion Symbolorum
Encl — Encounter (Indianapolis)
Enc I — Encyclopedie de l'Islam
Encic Educ Monte — Enciclopedia de Educacion (Montevideo)
Enc Is — Encyclopaedia of Islam
Enc It — Enciclopedia Italiana di Scienze, Lettere, ed Arti
Enc Ital — Enciclopedia Italiana di Scienze, Lettere, ed Arti
EncL — Encounter (London)
ENCLD — Energy Clearinghouse
Enc Lik Umj — Enciklopedija Likovnik Umjetnosti
ENCMD — Energy Dollars and Sense of Conservation
Enc Mens O Mer — Encyclopedie Mensuelle d'Outre-Mer
Enc Mis — Encyclopedia of Missions
Enc Mus — Encyclopedie de la Musique
ENCO — Environmental Conservation
En Conserv — Energy Conservation News
Encont Civ Bras — Encontros com a Civilizacao Brasileira
Encontro Nac Fis Reatores Termoidraulica — Encontro Nacional de Fisica de Reatores e Termoidraulica
Encore — Encore American and Worldwide News
Encore Aust — Encore Australia
Encount — Encounter
Encounter (Chr Theol Sem) — Encounter (Christian Theological Seminary)
Enc Pamphl Ser — Encounter Pamphlet Series
Enc Phot — Encyclopedie Photographique de l'Art
Enc Psych — Encyclopedia of Psychology
ENCR — Environmental Carcinogenesis Reviews
Enc Rel — Encyclopedia of Religion
Enc SEI — Enciclopedia SEI
Enc Spett — Enciclopedia dello Spettacolo
Enc Th — Encyclopedie Theologique
Encuentro Nac Electroquim — Encuentro Nacional de Electroquimica
Enc Unif Sci — Encyclopedia of Unified Science
ENCYA — Engineering Cybernetics
Ency Amer — Encyclopaedia Americana
Ency Brit — Encyclopaedia Britannica
Encyc Buy G — Encyclopedia Buying Guide
Encycl Biol (Paris) — Encyclopedie Biologique (Paris)
Encycl Chem Technol — Encyclopedia of Chemical Technology
Encycl Chem Technol — Kirk-Othmer Encyclopedia of Chemical Technology
Encycl Earth Sci Ser — Encyclopedia of Earth Sciences Series
Encycl Entomol — Encyclopedie Entomologique
Encycl J — Encyclopaedisches Journal
Encycl Med-Chir — Encyclopedie Medico-Chirurgicale
Encycl Mycol — Encyclopedie Mycologique
Encyclopaedia Math Sci — Encyclopaedia of Mathematical Sciences
Encyclopedia Math Appl — Encyclopedia of Mathematics and Its Applications
Encycl Ornithol (Paris) — Encyclopedie Ornithologique (Paris)
Encycl Period Sci Med Biol Sect Biol Pathol — Encyclopedie Periodique des Sciences Medico-Biologiques. Section. Biologie and Pathologie
Encycl Period Sci Med Biol Sect Microbiol Appl Biol — Encyclopedie Periodique des Sciences Medico-Biologiques. Section. Microbiologieet Applications a la Biologie
Encycl Period Sci Med Biol Sect Neurol — Encyclopedie Periodique des Sciences Medico-Biologiques. Section. Neurologie
Encycl Plant Anat — Encyclopedia of Plant Anatomy
Encycl Plant Physiol New Ser — Encyclopedia of Plant Physiology. New Series
Encycl Rel Ethics — Encyclopaedia of Religion and Ethics
Encycl Urol — Encyclopedia of Urology
Encycl Vet Med Surg and Obst — Encyclopaedia of Veterinary Medicine, Surgery, and Obstetrics
ENCYDI — Encyclia
Ency Mens OM — Encyclopedie Mensuelle d'Outre-Mer
Ency Soc Sci — Encyclopedia of the Social Sciences
END — (El) Nuevo Dia
End — Endeavour
END — Environment News Digest
Endangered Species Tech Bull — Endangered Species Technical Bulletin
ENDCA — Endoscopy
ENDCAM — Endoscopy
ENDE — Endeavour
ENDEA — Endeavour
ENDEAS — Endeavour
Endeavour New Ser — Endeavour. New Series
ENDED — Energy Development
Endem Dis Bull Nagasaki Univ — Endemic Diseases Bulletin. Nagasaki University
ENDF — Evaluated Nuclear Data File
ENDGA — Engineers' Digest
ENDGD — Energy Digest
Endicott 86 — Northwestern Endicott Report, 1986. Employment Trends for College Graduates in Business
ENDID — Energy Dialog
End Interp Stat — Endlich's Commentaries on the Interpretation of Statutes
ENDKA — Endokrinologie
ENDKAC — Endokrinologie
Endl Vac — Endless Vacation
ENDOA — Endocrinology
ENDOAO — Endocrinology
ENDOC — Environmental Information and Documentation Centres
Endocr Bioassay Data — Endocrine Bioassay Data. United States Department of Health, Education, and Welfare
Endocr Exp — Endocrinologia Experimentalis

Endocr Genet Genet Growth Proc Int Clin Genet Semin — Endocrine Genetics and Genetics of Growth. Proceedings. International Clinical Genetics Seminar
Endocrinol — Endocrinology
Endocrinol Calcium Metab Proc Parathyroid Conf — Endocrinology of Calcium Metabolism. Proceedings. Parathyroid Conference
Endocrinol Exp — Endocrinologia Experimentalis
Endocrinol Ind — Endocrinology Index
Endocrinol Jpn — Endocrinologia Japonica
Endocrinol Jpn Suppl — Endocrinologia Japonica. Supplement
Endocrinol Metab — Endocrinology and Metabolism
Endocrinol Metab Clin N Am — Endocrinology and Metabolism Clinics of North America
Endocrinol Metab Clin North Am — Endocrinology and Metabolism Clinics of North America
Endocrinol Metab London — Endocrinology and Metabolism (London)
Endocrinol Metab NY — Endocrinology and Metabolism (New York)
Endocrinol Metab Ser — Endocrinology and Metabolism Series
Endocrinol Neuroendocrinol Neuropept — Endocrinology, Neuroendocrinology, Neuropeptides
Endocrinol Proc Int Cong — Endocrinology. Proceedings. International Congress of Endocrinology
Endocrinol Sci Cost — Endocrinologia e Scienza della Costituzione
Endocr J — Endocrine Journal
Endocr Jap — Endocrinologia Japonica
Endocr J Basingstoke UK — Endocrin Journal (Basingstoke, United Kingdom)
Endocr Pathol — Endocrine Pathology
Endocr Pract — Endocrine Practice
Endocr Regul — Endocrine Regulations
Endocr Relat Cancer — Endocrine-Related Cancer
Endocr Res — Endocrine Research
Endocr Res — Endocrine Research Communications
Endocr Res Commun — Endocrine Research Communications
Endocr Rev — Endocrine Reviews
Endocr Rev Monogr — Endocrine Reviews Monographs
Endocr Soc Aust Proc — Endocrine Society of Australia. Proceedings
Endod & Dent Traumatol — Endodontics and Dental Traumatology
Endod Dent Traumatol — Endodontics and Dental Traumatology
Endod Pr — Endodontic Practice
Endok Mekh Regul Prisposobleniya Org Myshechnoi Deyat — Endokrinnye Mekhanizmy Regulyatsii Prisposobleniya Organizma k Myshechnoi Deyatel'nosti
Endokr — Endokrinologie
Endokrinol — Endokrinologie
Endokr Pol — Endokrynologia Polska
Endokr Sist Org Toksicheskie Fakroty Vneshn Sredy Mater Konf — Endokrinnaya Sistema Organizma i Toksicheskie Faktory Vneshnei Sredy. MaterialyKonferentsii
Endokrynol Pol — Endokrynologia Polska
Endosc Surg Allied Technol — Endoscopic Surgery and Allied Technologies
Endothelial Cell Res Ser — Endothelial Cell Research Series
ENDRD — Energy Directory
ENE — Energy Economics
ENEAD — Energy in Agriculture
ENEC — Energy and Economics Data Bank
ENECA — Engineering Economist
ENEDD — Energy and Education
ENEGA — Energies
ENEIB — Energy International
ENELA — Energia Elettrica
ENERA — Energie
ENERB — Energy Conversion
ENERD — Energy
Energa Atom — Energia es Atomtechnika
Energ Alternative — Energie Alternative
Energa Nu — Energia Nucleare
Energa Nucl — Energia Nucleare
Energ Atomtech — Energia es Atomtechnika
Energ At Tekh — Energiya i Atomnaya Tekhnika
Energ Avtom — Energetika i Avtomatika
Energ-Brief — Energie-Brief
Energ Byull — Energeticheskii Byulleten
Energ Commun — Energy Communications
Energ El — Energia Elettrica
Energ Elektrif — Energetika i Elektrifikatsiya
Energ Elektrif (Kiev) — Energetika i Elektrifikatsiya (Kiev)
Energ Elektrotekh Prom — Energetika i Elektrotekhnicheskaya Promyshlennost
Energ Elektrotekh Promst — Energetika i Elektrotekhnicheskaya Promyshlennost
Energ Elet — Energia Elettrica
Energ Elettr — Energia Elettrica
Energ Elettr A — Energia Elettrica. A
Energ Elettr B — Energia Elettrica. B
Energ es Atomtech — Energia es Atomtechnika
Energeteknol Ispol'z Topl — Energetekhnologicheskow Ispol'zovanie Toplova
Energ Fluide — Energie Fluide
Energ Fluide et Lubr Hydraul Pneum Asservissements — Energie Fluide et Lubrification et Hydraulique Pneumatique Asservissements
Energ Fontes Altern — Energia. Fontes Alternativas
Energ Fuego At — Energia del Fuego al Atomo
Energ Hidroteh — Energetica si Hidrotehnica
Energia — Publicacion sobre Energia
Energieanwend Energietech — Energieanwendung und Energietechnik
Energieanwend Energ Umwelttech — Energieanwendung, Energie- und Umwelttechnik
Energie Mag — Energie Magazine
Energieonder Cent Ned Rep — Energieonderzoek Centrum Nederland Report
Energietech — Energietechnik

Energietech Ferienkurs Energieforsch — Energietechnik - Fereinkurs Energieforschung

Energietech Ges Fachber — Energietechnische Gesellschaft. Fachberichte

Energiewirtsch Tagesfr — Energiewirtschaftliche Tagesfragen

Energiewirtsch Tagesfragen — Energiewirtschaftliche Tagesfragen

Energ Ind — Energia e Industria

Energ Inst Im G M Krzhizhanovskogo Sb Tr — Energeticheskii Institut Imeni G. M. Krzhizhanovskogo. Sbornik Trudov

Energ Kerntech — Energie- und Kerntechnik

Energ Manage — Energy Management

Energ Manage Can — Energy Management Canada

Energ Mashinostr — Energeticheskoe Mashinostroenie

Energ Mater — Energetic Materials

Energ Metall Phenom — Energetics in Metallurgical Phenomena

Energ Mon — Energy Monitor

Energ Nucl — Energia Nuclear

Energ Nucl Agric — Energia Nuclear e Agricultura

Energ Nucl Agric Cong Nucl — Energia Nucleare in Agricoltura. Simposio. Congresso Nucleare

Energ Nucl Eng — Energetics and Nuclear Engineering

Energ Nucl (Lisbon) — Energia Nuclear. Boletim Informativo do Forum Atomico Portugues (Lisbon)

Energ Nucl (Madrid) — Energia Nuclear (Madrid)

Energ Nucl Mag — Energie Nucleaire Magazine [*Later, Energie Magazine*]

Energ Nucl (Milan) — Energia Nucleare (Milan)

Energ Nucl (Paris) — Energie Nucleaire (Paris)

Energ Nutz Abfallst Muelltech Semin — Energetische Nutzung von Abfallstoffen. Muelltechnisches Seminar

Energokhoz Rubezhom — Energokhozyaistvo za Rubezhom

Energotekhnol Ispol'z Topl — Energotekhnologicheskoe Ispol'zovante Topliva

Energ Pol Con Rep — Energy Policy and Conservation Report

Energ Polic — Energy Policy

Energ Reg Dig — Energy Regulation Digest

Energ Stroit — Energeticheskoe Stroitel'stvo

Energ Stroit Rubezhom — Energeticheskoe Stroitel'stvo za Rubezhom

Energ Stud Cent Rapp ESC (Petten Neth) — Energie Studie Centrum. Rapport ESC (Petten, Netherlands)

Energ Szakirod Tajek — Energiaipari Szakirodalmi Tajekoztato

Energ Tech — Energie und Technik

Energ Techn — Energietechnik

Energ Technik — Energie und Technik

Energ Technol Biol Elimination Wastes Proc Int Colloq — Energetics and Technology of Biological Elimination of Wastes. Proceedings of the International Colloquium

Energ Term — Energia Termica

Energ Trans — Energetika i Transport

Energ Transp — Energetika i Transport

Energ Wasser Prax — Energie und Wasser Praxis

Energy — Energy User News

Energy Abstr Policy Anal — Energy Abstracts for Policy Analysis

Energy Advis Bull Tex Manuf — Energy Advisory Bulletin for Texas Manufacturers

Energy Agri — Energy in Agriculture

Energy Agric — Energy in Agriculture

Energy Agri Waste Manage Proc Cornell Agri Waste Manage Conf — Energy, Agriculture and Waste Management. Proceedings. Cornell Agricultural Waste Management Conference

Energy Alternatives Mag — Energy and Alternatives Magazine

Energy and Build — Energy and Buildings

Energy Biomass 1 Proc Contract Meet — Energy from Biomass 1. Proceedings. Contractors' Meeting

Energy Biomass EC Conf — Energy from Biomass. EC Conference

Energy Biomass Wastes — Energy from Biomass and Wastes. Symposium Papers

Energy Bldgs — Energy and Buildings

Energy Bldgs — Energy in Buildings

Energy Build — Energy and Buildings

Energy Bus — Energy Business. The Future of Coal, 1981 and Beyond

Energy Ceram Proc Int Meet Mod Ceram Technol — Energy and Ceramics. Proceedings. International Meeting on Modern Ceramics Technologies

Energy Chem Outlook Pract Solutions Symp — Energy for Chemicals. Outlook and Practical Solutions. Symposium

Energy Clgh — Energy Clearinghouse

Energy Cnvers & Manage — Energy Conversion and Management

Energy Combust Environ — Energy, Combustion and the Environment

Energy Comm — Energy Communications

Energy Commun — Energy Communications

Energy Community Plann Prairies Proc Symp — Energy and Community Planning on the Prairies. Proceedings. Symposium

Energy Conserv Dig — Energy Conservation Digest

Energy Conserv Environ Fed Energy Adm Conserv Pap (US) — Energy Conservation and Environment. Federal Energy Administration. Conservation Paper (United States)

Energy Conserv Rep — Energy Conservation Report

Energy Conserv (Tokyo) — Energy Conservation (Tokyo)

Energy Conserv Update — Energy Conservation Update

Energy Conserv Workshop — Energy Conservation Workshop

Energy Consum — Energy Consumer

Energy Conv — Energy Conversion

Energy Convers — Energy Conversion

Energy Convers and Manage — Energy Conversion and Management

Energy Convers Intl J — Energy Conversion. An International Journal

Energy Convers Manage — Energy Conversion and Management

Energy Convers Tech Rep Aust Natl Univ Dep Eng Phys — Australian National University. Department of Engineering Physics. Energy Conversion Technical Report

Energy Coupling Photosynth Proc Harry Steenbock Symp — Energy Coupling in Photosynthesis. Proceedings. Harry Steenbock Symposium

Energy Data Rep Asphalt Sales — Energy Data Report. Asphalt Sales

Energy Data Rep Carbon Black — Energy Data Reports. Carbon Black

Energy Data Rep Coke Coal Chem Mon — Energy Data Report. Coke and Coal Chemicals Monthly

Energy Data Rep Coke Plant Rep — Energy Data Report. Coke Plant Report

Energy Data Rep Crude Pet Pet Prod Nat Gas Liq — Energy Data Reports. Crude Petroleum, Petroleum Products, and Natural Gas Liquids

Energy Data Rep Fuel Oils Sulfur Content — Energy Data Reports. Fuel Oils by Sulfur Content

Energy Data Rep Liquefied Pet Gas Sales — Energy Data Reports. Liquefied Petroleum Gas Sales

Energy Data Rep Nat Gas — Energy Data Reports. Natural Gas

Energy Data Rep Nat Gas Liq — Energy Data Reports. Natural Gas Liquids

Energy Data Rep Nat Gas Mon Rep — Energy Data Report. Natural Gas Monthly Report

Energy Data Rep Nat Synth Gas — Energy Data Report. Natural and Synthetic Gas

Energy Data Rep PAD Dist Supply Demand — Energy Data Reports. PAD (Petroleum Administration for Defense) Districts Supply/Demand

Energy Data Rep Pet Refin US US Territ — Energy Data Report. Petroleum Refineries in the United States and US Territories

Energy Data Rep Pet Statement — Energy Data Reports. Petroleum Statement

Energy Data Rep Sales Asphalt — Energy Data Report. Sales of Asphalt

Energy Data Rep US Imports Exports Nat Gas — Energy Data Reports. United States Imports and Exports of Natural Gas

Energy Data Rep Wkly Coal Rep — Energy Data Report. Weekly Coal Report

Energy Data Rep World Crude Oil Prod — Energy Data Report. World Crude Oil Production

Energy Dev — Energy and Development Journal

Energy Dev — Energy Developments

Energy Dev Jpn — Energy Developments in Japan

Energy Dev (New York) — Energy Development (New York). IEEE Power Engineering Society Papers

Energy Dig — Energy Digest

Energy Dig (Colo Spring Colo) — Energy Digest (Colorado Springs, Colorado)

Energy Dig (London) — Energy Digest (London)

Energy Dig (Wash DC) — Energy Digest (Washington, DC)

Energy Dig Watford UK — Energy Digest (Watford, United Kingdom)

Energy Dly — Energy Daily

Energy Dollars Sense Conserv — Energy Dollars and Sense of Conservation

Energy Ecol Modell Proc Symp — Energy and Ecological Modelling. Proceedings. Symposium

Energy Econ — Energy Economics

Energy Econ Policy Manage — Energy Economics, Policy, and Management

Energy Educ — Energy and Education

Energy Educ Newsl — Energy Educator Newsletter

Energy Eng — Energy Engineering

Energy Enging — Energy Engineering

Energy Environ — Energy and Environment

Energy Environ — Energy and the Environment. Proceedings. National Conference

Energy Environ Annu Tech Meet — Energy and the Environment. Annual Technical Meeting

Energy Environ Chem — Energy and Environmental Chemistry [*monograph*]

Energy Environ Dordrecht Neth — Energy and Environment (Dordrecht, Netherlands)

Energy Environ Eng — Energy, Environment. Engineering

Energy Environ Interact — Energy and the Environment. Interactions

Energy Environ (NY) — Energy and the Environment (New York)

Energy Environ (Oak Ridge Tenn) — Energy and the Environment (Oak Ridge, Tennessee)

Energy Environ Proc Nat Conf — Energy and the Environment. Proceedings of the National Conference

Energy Exec Dir — Energy Executive Directory

Energy Explor Exploit — Energy Exploration and Exploitation

Energy F & F — World Energy. The Facts and the Future

Energy Forum N Engl — Energy Forum in New England

Energy Fuels — Energy and Fuels

Energy in Bldgs — Energy in Buildings

Energy Ind — Energy Index

Energy Ind Commerce Q Bull — Energy for Industry and Commerce. Quarterly Bulletin

Energy Inf Abstr — Energy Information Abstracts

Energy Inf Adm Mon Pet Statement US — Energy Information Administration. Monthly Petroleum Statement (US)

Energy Inf Adm Pet Supply Mon US — Energy Information Administration. Petroleum Supply Monthly (United States)

Energy Inf Adm Wkly Coal Prod (US) — Energy Information Administration. Weekly Coal Production (United States)

Energy Int — Energy International

Energy Intake Act — Energy Intake and Activity

Energy Int J — Energy. The International Journal

Energy J — Energy Journal

Energy Lab Ser — Energy Laboratory Series

Energy Law J — Energy Law Journal

Energy LJ — Energy Law Journal

Energyl Newsl — Energylab Newsletter

Energy M — Energy Magazine

Energy Manage — Energy Management

Energy Manage (Cleveland Ohio) — Energy Management (Cleveland, Ohio)

Energy Manage (India) — Energy Management (India)

Energy Manage News — Energy Management News

Energy Mater Natl State of the Art Symp — Energy and Materials. National State-of-the-Art Symposium

Energy Meet — Energy Meetings
Energy Metab Farm Anim Proc Symp — Energy Metabolism of Farm Animals. Proceedings of the Symposium
Energy Metab Regul Metab Processes Mitochondria Proc Symp — Energy Metabolism and the Regulation of Metabolic Processes in Mitochondria. Proceedings. Symposium
Energy Mgr — Energy Manager
Energy Miner Resour — Energy and Minerals Resources
Energy Newsl — Energy Newsletter
Energy Perspect — Energy Perspectives
Energy Phys Proc Gen Conf Eur Phys Soc — Energy and Physics. Proceedings. General Conference. European Physical Society
Energy Pipelines Syst — Energy Pipelines and Systems
Energy Plann Network — Energy Planning Network
Energy Pol — Energy Policy
Energy Pollut Control — Energy and Pollution Control
Energy Probl Impacts Mil Res Dev AGARD Annu Meet — Energy Problem. Impacts on Military Research and Development. AGARD [*Advisory Group for Aerospace Research and Development*] Annual Meeting
Energy Process (Can) — Energy Processing (Canada)
Energy Process Ind — Energy and the Process Industries
Energy Prog — Energy Progress
Energy Purch Rep — Energy Purchasing Report
Energy Q — Energy Quarterly
Energy Rep (Alton Engl) — Energy Report (Alton, England)
Energy Rep States — Energy Report to the States
Energy Res — Energy Research
Energy Res Abstr — Energy Research Abstracts
Energy Res Bur — Energy Research Bureau
Energy Res Dev Adm ERDA Energy Res Abstr — Energy Research and Development Administration. ERDA Energy Research Abstracts
Energy Res Dev Adm Res Abstr — Energy Research and Development Administration. Research Abstracts
Energy Res Dev Adm Symp Ser — Energy Research and Development Administration. Symposium Series
Energy Res Dig — Energy Research Digest
Energy Resourc Technol — Energy Resources and Technology
Energy Resour (Osaka) — Energy and Resources (Osaka)
Energy Resour Res — Energy and Resources Research
Energy Res Rep — Energy Research Reports
Energy Rev — Energy Review
Energy Sci Technol — Energy Science and Technology
Energy Sources — Energy Sources
Energy Syst and Policy — Energy Systems and Policy
Energy Systems Pol — Energy Systems and Policy
Energy Syst Policy — Energy Systems and Policy
Energy Technol — Energy Technology
Energy Technol — Energy Technology. Proceedings. Energy Technology Conference
Energy Technol Conf Proc — Energy Technology Conference. Proceedings
Energy Technol Rev — Energy Technology Review
Energy Technol (Wash DC) — Energy Technology (Washington, DC)
Energy Top — Energy Topics
Energy Wld — Energy World
Energy World Agric — Energy in World Agriculture
ENETD — Environmental Ethics
ENEXA — Endocrinologia Experimentalis
ENEXAM — Endocrinologia Experimentalis
EnF — Encontro com o Folclore
ENFAD — Fusion Power Associates. Executive Newsletter
Enfant Milieu Trop — Enfant en Milieu Tropical
Enferm Infecc Microbiol Clin — Enfermedades Infecciosas y Microbiologia Clinica
Enferm Torax — Enfermedades del Torax
Enferm Torax Tuberc — Enfermedades del Torax y Tuberculosis
ENFL — Energy File
ENFLA — Energie Fluide
ENFTAF — Enfermedades del Torax
ENFUEM — Energy & Fuels
Eng — [*The*] Engineer
Eng — Engineering
Eng — English
Engage/Soc Act — Engage/Social Action
Eng Agric — Engenharia Agricola
Eng Anal Boundary Elem — Engineering Analysis with Boundary Elements</PHR>%
Eng & Bu Rec — Engineering and Building Record
Eng & Instrumentation — Engineering and Instrumentation
Eng & Min J — Engineering and Mining Journal
Eng and Sci — Engineering and Science
Eng and Technol — Engineering and Technology
Eng Appl Artif Intell — Engineering Applications of Artificial Intelligence
Eng Appl Fract Anal Proc Natl Conf Fract — Engineering Applications of Fracture Analysis. Proceedings. National Conferenceon Fracture
Eng Appl Fract Mech — Engineering Application of Fracture Mechanics
Eng Appl Hologr Symp Proc — Engineering Applications of Holography Symposium. Proceedings
Eng Apprent — Engineer Apprentice
Eng Aspects Magnetohydrodyn — Engineering Aspects of Magnetohydrodynamics
Eng Aspects Therm Pollut Proc Natl Symp Thermal Pollut — Engineering Aspects of Thermal Pollution. Proceedings. National Symposium on Thermal Pollution
Eng As South Tr — Engineering Association of the South. Transactions
Eng Aust — Engineers Australia
Eng Autom — Engineering and Automation

Eng Boilerhouse Rev — Engineering and Boilerhouse Review
Eng Boil H Rev — Engineering and Boiler House Review
Eng Build — Engineer and Builder
Eng Bull — Engineering Bulletin
Eng Bull Purdue Univ — Engineering Bulletin. Purdue University
Eng Bull Purdue Univ Eng Ext Ser — Engineering Bulletin. Purdue University. Engineering Extension Series
Eng Buy Guide — Engineer Buyers Guide
Eng Cem World — Engineering and Cement World
Eng Chem Dig — Engineering and Chemical Digest
Eng Chem Metall — Engineering Chemistry and Metallurgy
Eng Civ (Sao Paulo) — Engenharia Civil (Sao Paulo)
Eng Club Phila Pr — Engineers' Club of Philadelphia. Proceedings
Eng Comput — Engineering Computers
Eng Comput Swansea Wales — Engineering Computations (Swansea, Wales)
Eng Conf — Engineering Conference
Eng Conf Proc — Engineering Conference. Proceedings
Eng Constr World — Engineering Construction World
Eng Contract — Engineering and Contracting
Eng Contract Rec — Engineering and Contract Record
Eng Cornell Q — Engineering. Cornell Quarterly
Eng Costs Prod Econ — Engineering Costs and Production Economics
Eng Cybern — Engineering Cybernetics
Eng Cyc — English Cyclopaedia
Eng Dance — English Dance and Song
Eng Des Guides — Engineering Design Guides
Eng Design — Engineering Materials and Design
Eng Dig — Engineers' Digest
Eng Dig (London) — Engineers' Digest (London)
Eng Dig (NY) — Engineering Digest (New York)
Eng Dig (Toronto) — Engineering Digest (Toronto)
Eng Dom M — Englishwoman's Domestic Magazine
EngDS — English Dance and Song
Eng Econ — Engineering Economist
Eng Economist — Engineering Economist
Eng Educ — Engineering Education
Eng Educ — English Education
Eng Educ (Lancaster PA) — Engineering Education (Lancaster, Pennsylvania)
Engei Gakkai Zasshi J Jap Soc Hortic Sci — Engei Gakkai Zasshi/Journal of the Japanese Society for Horticultural Science
Engei Kogii Shihiryo Sakumotsu Bunken Shorokushu — Abstracts of Literature of Horticultural Crops, Special Crops, and Feed Crops
Engei Shikenjo Hokoku A — Engei Shikenjo Hokoku. A. Hiratsuka
Engei Shikenjo Hokoku B — Engei Shikenjo Hokoku. B. Okitsu
Engelhard Ind Tech Bull — Engelhard Industries. Technical Bulletin
Eng Eng — Engineers and Engineering
Engenh Min Met — Engenharia, Mineracao, Metalurgia
Engenh Quim — Engenharia e Quimica
Engen Miner Metal Rio — Engenharia, Mineracao, e Metalurgia (Rio de Janeiro)
Eng Exp Stat News — Engineering Experiment Station News
Eng Exp Stn Bull WVU — Engineering Experiment Station Bulletin. West Virginia University
Eng Exp Stn Bull WVU WVU — Engineering Experiment Station Bulletin WVU. West Virginia University
Eng Exp Stn Oreg State Coll Bull — Engineering Experiment Station. Oregon State College. Bulletin
Eng Exp Stn Oreg State Coll Repr — Engineering Experiment Station. Oregon State College. Reprint
Eng Exp Stn Publ WVU — Engineering Experiment Station Publication. West Virginia University
Eng Ext Ser Purdue Univ — Engineering Extension Series. Purdue University
Eng Failure Anal — Engineering Failure Analysis. Materials, Structures, Components, Reliability, Design
Eng FD & S Soc Jl — English Folk Dance and Song Society. Journal
Eng Field Notes US Dep Agric For Serv Eng Staff — Engineering Field Notes. US Department of Agriculture. Forest Service. Engineering Staff
Eng Finance — Engineering and Finance
Eng Food Proc Int Congr — Engineering and Food. Proceedings. International Congress on Engineering and Food
Eng Found — Engineering Foundation
Eng Found Conf — Engineering Foundation Conference
Eng Found Conf Cem Prod Use — Engineering Foundation Conference on Cement Production and Use
Eng Found Conf Enzyme Eng — Engineering Foundation Conference on Enzyme Engineering
Eng Found Conf Fluid — Engineering Foundation Conference on Fluidization
Eng Found Conf Fundam Adsorpt — Engineering Foundation Conference on Fundamentals of Adsorption
Eng Found Conf Waste Heat Util — Engineering Foundation Conference. Waste Heat Utilization
Eng Found Int Conf Sep Technol — Engineering Foundation's International Conference on Separation Technology
Eng Found Int Conf Workshop Small Fatigue Cracks — Engineering Foundation International Conference/Workshop on Small Fatigue Cracks
Eng Foundryman — Engineer and Foundryman
Eng Fract Mech — Engineering Fracture Mechanics
ENGGD — Ekspress-Informatsiya. Neftegazovaya Geologiya i Geofizika
Eng Geol — Engineering Geology
Eng Geol (Amsterdam) — Engineering Geology (Amsterdam)
Eng Geol Case Hist — Engineering Geology Case Histories
Eng Geol Krefeld Ger — Engineering Geology (Krefeld, Germany)
Eng Geol (Sacramento) — Engineering Geology (Sacramento)
Eng Geol Soils Eng Symp Proc — Engineering Geology and Soils Engineering Symposium. Proceedings
Eng Geol Symp Proc — Engineering Geology Symposium. Proceedings

Eng Graphics — Engineering Graphics
Eng Health Hot Countries Proc WEDC Conf — Engineering for Health in Hot Countries. Proceedings. WEDC (Water and Waste Engineering for Developing Countries) Conference
Eng His R — English Historical Review
Eng Hist Bul — English History Bulletin for Teachers in Secondary Schools
Eng Hist R — English Historical Review
Eng Hist Rev — English Historical Review
Engl — Engineering Index
ENGIA — [The] Engineer
Eng Illust — English Illustrated Magazine
Eng in Aust — English in Australia
Eng Ind — Engenharia na Industria
Eng Ind — Engineering Index
Eng Index — Engineering Index
Eng Index Annu — Engineering Index Annual
Eng Index Bioeng Abstr — Engineering Index. Bioengineering Abstracts
Eng Index Energy Abstr — Engineering Index. Energy Abstracts
Eng Index Mon — Engineering Index Monthly
Eng Index Mon Author Index — Engineering Index Monthly and Author Index
Eng Index Monthly Author Index — Engineering Index Monthly and Author Index
Eng Ind India — Engineering Index of India
Eng Ind (Iraq) — Engineering Industries (Iraq)
ENGINE — Australian Engineering Database
Engineers' Bull — Engineers' Bulletin,
Engineers Gaz — Engineers' Gazette
Engin M — Engineering Magazine
Engin Medic — Engineering in Medicine
Engin N — Engineering News-Record
Eng Insp — Engineering Inspection
Eng Inst Can — Engineering Institute of Canada
Eng Inst Canada Trans — Engineering Institute of Canada. Transactions
Eng Issues — Engineering Issues
Eng J — Engineering Journal
Eng J — English Journal
Eng J Am Inst Steel Constr — Engineering Journal. American Institute of Steel Construction
Eng J (Montreal) — Engineering Journal (Montreal)
Eng J (NY) — Engineering Journal (New York)
Eng Jour — English Journal. University of Chicago Press
Eng J Singapore — Engineering Journal of Singapore
Eng J Taipei — Engineering Journal (Taipei)
Engl Abstr Sel Art Sov Bloc Mainland China Tech J Ser 1 — English Abstracts of Selected Articles from Soviet Bloc and Mainland China Technical Journals. Series 1. Physics and Mathematics
Engl Abstr Sel Art Sov Bloc Mainland China Tech J Ser 2 — English Abstracts of Selected Articles from Soviet Bloc and Mainland China Technical Journals. Series 2. Chemistry
Engl Abstr Sel Art Sov Bloc Mainland China Tech J Ser 3 — English Abstracts of Selected Articles from Soviet Bloc and Mainland China Technical Journals. Series 3. Metals
Engl Abstr Sel Art Sov Bloc Mainland China Tech J Ser 5 — English Abstracts of Selected Articles from Soviet Bloc and Mainland China Technical Journals. Series 5. Electronics and Electrical Engineering
Engl Abstr Sel Art Sov Bloc Mainland China Tech J Ser 6 — English Abstracts of Selected Articles from Soviet Bloc and Mainland China Technical Journals. Series 6. Bio-Sciences
Engl Afr — English in Africa
Engl Alive — English Alive
Eng Lang Notes — English Language Notes
Eng Lang Teach J — English Language Teaching Journal
Eng Lasers — Engineering Lasers
Engl Aust — English in Australia
Engl Blaett — Englische Blaetter
Engl Bul — English Bulletin
Engl Educ — English in Education
Engl Elec J — English Electric Journal
Engl El J — English Electric Journal
Engl Heritage Monit — English Heritage Monitor
Engl Hist R — English Historical Review
Engl Hist Rev — English Historical Review
Engl Hist Rev — English History Review
Engl Hist Revw — English Historical Review
Engl Inst Ann — English Institute. Annual
Engl Inst N — English Institute. New Series
English Church M — English Church Music
English His — English Historical Review
English History Bul — English History Bulletin for Teachers in Secondary Schools
English Hist Rev — English Historical Review
English in Ed — English in Education
English J — English Journal
English Language Teaching J — English Language Teaching Journal
English MJ — English Music Journal
English R — English Review
English Stud Afr — English Studies in Africa
Eng Lit in Trans — English Literature in Transition, 1880-1920
Eng LJ — Energy Law Journal
Engl J — English Journal
Engl J (Col Ed) — English Journal (College Edition)
Engl J (HS Ed) — English Journal (High School Edition)
Engl Lang Lit — English Language and Literature
Engl Lang N — English Language Notes
Engl Lang Not — English Language Notes
Engl Lang Notes — English Language Notes
Engl Lang Tch — English Language Teaching

Engl Lang Teach — English Language Teaching [Later, English Language Teaching Journal]
Engl Lit Lang — English Literature and Language
Engl Lit Re — English Literary Renaissance
Engl Lit Renaiss — English Literary Renaissance
Engl Lit Renaissance — English Literary Renaissance
Engl Lit Tr — English Literature in Transition, 1880-1920
Engl Lit Transition — English Literature in Transition, 1880-1920
Engl Misc — English Miscellany. A Symposium of History
Engl NZ — English in New Zealand
Engl Place-Name Soc — English Place-Name Society. Annual Volume
Engl Q — English Quarterly
Engl R — English Review
Engl Rec — English Record
Engl Rev — English Review
Engl St — English Studies. A Journal of English Letters and Philology
Engl St Afr — English Studies in Africa
Engl St Can — English Studies in Canada
Engl Stud — Englische Studien
Engl Stud — English Studies
Engl Stud Afr — English Studies in Africa
Eng L T — English Language Teaching [Later, English Language Teaching Journal]
Engl Teach Assoc NSW Newsl — English Teachers Association of New South Wales. Newsletter
Engl Teach For — English Teaching Forum
Engl Usage Sthn Afr — English Usage in Southern Africa
Eng M — Engineering Magazine
Eng Mag — Engineering Magazine
Eng Man — Engineering Management and Equipment Digest
Eng Mat — Engineering Materials
Eng Mat Des — Engineering Materials and Design
Eng Mater — Engineering Materials
Eng Mater & Des — Engineering Materials and Design
Eng Mater Des — Engineering Materials and Design
Eng Mater Process Methods — Engineering Materials and Processing Methods
Eng Mater (Tokyo) — Engineering Materials (Tokyo)
Eng Med — Engineering in Medicine
Eng Med (Berlin) — Engineering in Medicine (Berlin)
Eng Mineracao Met — Engenharia, Mineracao, Metalurgia
Eng Mining J — Engineering and Mining Journal
Eng Min J — Engineering and Mining Journal
Eng Min J Press — Engineering and Mining Journal Press
Eng Min J Stat Suppl — Engineering and Mining Journal. Statistical Supplement
Eng Min Metal — Engenharia, Mineracao, Metalurgia
Eng Min World — Engineering and Mining World
Eng N — Engineering News-Record
ENGNA — Engineering
ENGND5 — Entomologia Generalis
Eng New-Rc — Engineering News-Record
Eng News — Engineering News
Eng News London — Engineering News (London)
Eng News (NY) — Engineering News (New York)
Eng News-Rec — Engineering News-Record
Eng News (Tokyo) — Engineering News (Tokyo)
Engng — Engineering
Engng Des — Engineering Designer
Engng Des Int — Engineering Design International
Engng Educ — Engineering Education
Engng Geol — Engineering Geology
Engng Index Mthlys — Engineering Index Monthlies
Engng J — Engineering Journal
Engng J (Can) — Engineering Journal (Canada)
Engng Mat Des — Engineering Materials and Design
Engng Mater Des — Engineering Materials and Design
Engng Med — Engineering in Medicine
Engng Min J — Engineering and Mining Journal
Engng Outlook — Engineering Outlook
Engng Prod — Engineering Production
Engng Struct — Engineering Structures
Engng Thermophys China — Engineering Thermophysics in China
Engng Today — Engineering Today
Eng (NY) — Engineer (New York)
Eng Optim — Engineering Optimization
Eng Optimization — Engineering Optimization
Eng Outlook Univ Ill — Engineering Outlook. University of Illinois
Eng Plast — Engineering Plastics
Eng Process Econ — Engineering and Process Economics
Eng Prod — Engineering Production
Eng Progr Univ Fla Bull — Engineering Progress. University of Florida. Bulletin
Eng Progr Univ Fla Tech Progr Rep — Engineering Progress. University of Florida. Technical Progress Report
Eng Prog Univ Fla Leafl Ser — Engineering Progress at the University of Florida. Leaflet Series
Eng Prog Univ Fla Tech Pap Ser — Engineering Progress at the University of Florida. Technical Paper Series
Eng Publ Univ NH Eng Exp Stn — Engineering Publication. University of New Hampshire. Engineering Experiment Station
Eng Quim — Engenharia e Quimica
Eng Quim (Sao Paulo) — Engenharia Quimica (Sao Paulo)
Engr — [The] Engineer
EngR — English Record
EngR — English Review
Eng Rec — Engineering Record
Eng Rep Iowa Eng Exp Stn Iowa State Univ — Engineering Report. Iowa Engineering Experiment Station. Iowa State University

Eng Rep Iowa State Coll Iowa Eng Exp Stn — Engineering Report. Iowa State College. Iowa Engineering Experiment Station

Eng Rep Natl Tsing Hua Univ — Engineering Reports. National Tsing Hua University

Eng Repr Div Eng Res Dev Univ RI — Engineering Reprint. Division of Engineering Research and Development. University of Rhode Island

Eng Repr Eng Exp Stn Univ RI — Engineering Reprint. Engineering Experiment Station. University of Rhode Island

Eng Rep Seoul Natl Univ — Engineering Report. Seoul National University

Eng Res Bull — Engineering Research Bulletin

Eng Res Bull Div Eng Res La State Univ — Engineering Research Bulletin. Division of Engineering Research. Louisiana State University

Eng Res Bull La State Univ Div Eng Res — Engineering Research Bulletin. Louisiana State University. Division of Engineering Research

Eng Res Bull Pa State Univ Coll Eng — Engineering Research Bulletin. Pennsylvania State University. College of Engineering

Eng Res Bull Rutgers Univ Coll Eng — Engineering Research Bulletin. Rutgers University. College of Engineering

Eng Res N — Engineering Research News

Eng Res News — Engineering Research News

Eng Rev — Engineering Review

EngRev — English Review/Eigo Hyoron [*Tokyo*]

Eng Rev — English Review. Salem State College

Engrg Comput — Engineering Computations. International Journal for Computer-aided Engineering and Software

Engrg Computers — Engineering with Computers

Engrg Cybernetics — Engineering Cybernetics

Engrg Dynamics Ser — Engineering Dynamics Series

Engrg Struc — Engineering Structures

Engrg Trans — Engineering Transactions. Polish Academy of Sciences. Institute of Fundamental Technological Research

Engrs Dig — Engineers' Digest

Engrs' Digest — Engineers' Digest

EngS — English Studies

Eng Sci — Engineering and Science

Eng Sci Data Item — Engineering Sciences Data Item

Eng Sci Educ J — Engineering Science and Education Journal

Eng Sci Mon — Engineering and Science Monthly

Eng-Sci News — Engineering-Science News

Eng Sci Rep Kyushu Univ — Engineering Sciences Reports. Kyushu University

Eng Ser Bull Univ Mo Eng Exp Stn — Engineering Series Bulletin. University of Missouri. Engineering Experiment Station

Eng Serv Lab Tech Rep ESL TR US Air Force Eng Serv Cent — Engineering and Services Laboratory. Technical Report. ESL-TR. United States Air Force Engineering and Services Center

Eng Soc Libr ESL Bibliogr — Engineering Societies Library. ESL Bibliography

Eng Soc W Pa — Engineers' Society of Western Pennsylvania. Proceedings

Eng Soc York Pr — Engineering Society of York. Proceedings

Eng Solids Pressure Pap Int Conf High Pressure — Engineering Solids under Pressure. Papers Presented at the International Conference on High Pressure

Eng St — English Studies

Eng S T — Transactions of the Society of Engineers

Eng Stn Doc Purdue Univ — Engineering Station Document. Purdue University

Eng Struct — Engineering Structures

Eng Stud — English Studies

Eng Syst — Engineered Systems

Eng T — Engineering Times

EngT — English Today

ENGTB — Energetika (Sofia, Bulgaria)

Eng Teach — English Teacher

Eng Teach Assn NSW News — English Teachers Association of New South Wales. Newsletter

Eng Teach Assoc NSW Newsl — English Teachers Association of New South Wales. Newsletter

Eng Technol (Osaka) — Engineering and Technology (Osaka)

Eng Tech Rev — Engineers' and Technicians' Review

Eng Times — Engineering Times

Eng Times (Calcutta) — Engineering Times (Calcutta)

Eng Today — Engineering Today

Eng Week — Engineering Week

Eng World — Engineering World

Eng WR — Englishwomen's Review

Engy (Austl) — Forecasts of Energy Demand and Supply (Australia). 1982-83 to 1991-92

Engy Bsns — Energy Business

Engy Insidr — Energy Insider

Engy Supply — Energy Supply to the Year 2000

ENH — Carrosserie

EnH — English Historical Review

Enhanced Oil-Recovery Field Rep — Enhanced Oil-Recovery Field Reports

ENHBA5 — Ehime Daigaku Nogakubu Enshurin Hokoku

ENHEA — Environmental Health

ENHID — Energy Highlights

ENI — Engineering Index

En Jnl — Energy Journal

ENJOA — Engineering Journal

ENJOD — Energy Journal

EnJuYB — Encyclopaedia Judaica Year Book

Enka Breda Rayon Rev — Enka en Breda Rayon Revue

EnLA — Entretiens sur les Lettres et les Arts

ENLB — Emergency Nurse Legal Bulletin

Enl E — Enlightenment Essays

ENLIBD — Entomologicke Listy

Enlightenment Diss — Enlightenment and Dissent

ENM — Economie

ENMAA — Enseignement Mathematique

En Manag — Energy Management

ENMGD — Energy Management

ENMJA — Engineering and Mining Journal

ENMR — Environmental Management Review

ENMS — Environments. Journal of Interdisciplinary Studies

ENN — Export News (New Zealand)

ENNCA — Energia Nuclear

ENNE — Environment News. Alberta Department of the Environment

ENNEDD — Essays in Neurochemistry and Neuropharmacology

ENNLA — Energia Nucleare

ENNLAV — Energia Nuclear

ENNOD — Energy News Notes. CERI

ENNSD — Energy News

ENNUA — Energie Nucleaire

En Nucl — Energie Nucleaire

ENNWD — Energy News

ENO — Econotities

ENORAK — Encyclopedie Ornithologique

ENP — Entomological News. Academy of Natural Sciences (Philadelphia)

ENP — Nouvel Economiste (Paris)

En Pas — En Passant

ENPBB — Environmental Physiology and Biochemistry

ENPED — Energy Perspectives

ENPGD — Energy Progress

En Profile — Energy in Profile

Enquete Mens Conjonct — Enquete Mensuelle de Conjoncture

Enquetes et Docum Hist Afr — Enquetes et Documents d'Histoire Africaine

Enquetes Mus Vie Wallonne — Enquetes. Musee de la Vie Wallonne

Enqu Musee Vie Wall — Enquetes. Musee de la Vie Wallonne

ENR — Engineering News-Record

EnR — English Review

ENRE — Energy Report. Community Information Center. Fairbanks North Star Borough

ENREA — Engineering News-Record

ENREB — Entomological Review

ENREP — Environmental Research Projects

ENRGD — Energies

ENRMC — Era Nova. Revista do Movimento Contemporaneo

ENRPD — Energy Report (Denver, Colorado)

ENRSD — Energy Research

ENRSE8 — Endocrine Research

ENRYD — Energy

ENS — Energy Nova Scotia

ENS — Evans Electronic News Service

ENSABO — Anais. Escola Nacional de Saude Publica e de Medicina Tropical

Ensaios FEE — Ensaios FEE. Fundacao de Economia e Estatistica

Ensay Estud — Ensayos y Estudios

Ensayos Econs — Ensayos Economicos

Ensayos Invest — Ensayos e Investigacion

Ensayos Pol Econ — Ensayos sobre Politica Economica

Ens Chr — Enseignement Chretien

ENSDF — Evaluated Nuclear Structure Data File

ENSDF-MEDLIST — Evaluated Nuclear Structure Data File - MEDLIST

Enseignement Math — Enseignement Mathematique

Enseign Math — Enseignement Mathematique

Enseign Math 2 — Enseignement Mathematique. Revue Internationale. 2e Serie

Enseign Phys Math Phys — Enseignement de la Physique. Mathematiques pour la Physique

Enseign Sci — Enseignement des Sciences

Enseign Sci — Enseignement Scientifique

Enseign Techn — Enseignement Technique

Ensenanza Invest Psicol — Ensenanza e Investigacion en Psicologia

ENSHBB — Engei Shikenjo Hokoku. C. Morioka

Enshurin Shuho/Rep Kyushu Univ Forests — Enshurin Shuho/Reports. Kyushu University Forests

Ens Mth — Enseignement Mathematique. Revue Internationale

ENSOD — Energy Sources

Ent — Entomologist

Ent — Entomologiste

Ent — Entschluss

ENT — Environmental Science and Technology

ENTAD — Energy News

Ent Arb — Entomologische Arbeiten aus dem Museum G Frey

Ent Arb Mus GF — Entomologische Arbeiten. Museum Georg Frey

ENTBAV — Entomologische Berichten

Ent Ber — Entomologische Berichten

Ent Ber (Amst) — Entomologische Berichten (Amsterdam)

Ent Ber (Berlin) — Entomologische Berichten (Berlin)

Ent Beri — Entomologische Berichten

Ent Circ Dep Agric (Br Columb) — Entomological Circular. Department of Agriculture (British Columbia)

Ent Circ Div Pl Ind Fla Dep Agric Consumer Serv — Entomology Circular. Division of Plant Industry. Florida Department of Agriculture and Consumer Services

ENTEA — Energie und Technik

En Techn — Energietechnik

Entente Afr — Entente Africaine

Enterp Western Aust — Enterprise Western Australia

Entertain Law Report — Entertainment Law Reporter

Ent Exp App — Entomologia Experimentalis et Applicata

Ent Exper Appl — Entomologia Experimentalis et Applicata

Ent Fact Sheet Univ Minn — Entomology Fact Sheet. University of Minnesota

Ent Gaz — Entomologist's Gazette

Ent Germ — Entomologica Germanica

ENT J — Ear, Nose, and Throat Journal
EntJ — Entomologisches Jahrbuch
Ent Jber — Entomologischer Jahresbericht
ENTJDO — Ear, Nose, and Throat Journal
Ent Leafl Univ MD — Entomology Leaflet. University of Maryland
Ent Listy — Entomologicke Listy
Ent M — Entomologiske Meddelelser
Ent Med — Entomologiske Meddelelser
Ent Medd — Entomologiske Meddelelser
Ent Meddr — Entomologiske Meddelelser
Ent Meded Ned Indiee — Entomologische Mededeelingen van Nederlandsch-Indiee
ENTMEY — Entomography
Ent Mitt — Entomologische Mitteilungen
Ent Mitt Zool Mus (Hamburg) — Entomologische Mitteilungen. Zoologischen Museum (Hamburg)
Ent Mitt Zool St Inst — Entomologische Mitteilungen. Zoologischen Staatsinstitut und Zoologischen Museum
Ent Mon Mag — Entomologist's Monthly Magazine
Ent Nachr — Entomologische Nachrichten
ENTND2 — ISSCT [International Society of Sugarcane Technologists] Entomology Newsletter
Ent News — Entomological News
Ent Obozr — Entomologicheskoe Obozrenie
Entom Month Mag — Entomologist's Monthly Magazine
Entom N — Entomological News
Entom News — Entomological News
Entomol — Entomologist
Entomol Abh (Dres) — Entomologische Abhandlungen (Dresden)
Entomol Abstr — Entomology Abstracts
Entomol Am — Entomologica Americana
Entomol Arb Mus G Frey (Tutzing-bei Muench) — Entomologische Arbeiten. Museum Georg Frey (Tutzing-bei Muenchen)
Entomol Arb Mus G Frey (Tutzing Muenchen) — Entomologische Arbeiten. Museum Georg Frey (Tutzing-bei Muenchen)
Entomol Ber (Amst) — Entomologische Berichten (Amsterdam)
Entomol Ber (Berl) — Entomologische Berichten (Berlin)
Entomol Bl — Entomologische Blaetter
Entomol Bl Biol Syst Kaefer — Entomologische Blaetter fuer Biologie und Systematik der Kaefer
Entomol Bull Brit Mus (Natur Hist) — Entomology Bulletin. British Museum (Natural History)
Entomol Exp Appl — Entomologia Experimentalis et Applicata
Entomol Gaz — Entomologist's Gazette
Entomol Gen — Entomologia Generalis
Entomol Ger — Entomologica Germanica
Entomol Hefte — Entomologische Hefte
Entomol Hell — Entomologia Hellenica
Entomol Listy — Entomologicke Listy
Entomol Mag Kyoto — Entomological Magazine. Entomological Society of Japan (Kyoto)
Entomol Medd — Entomologiske Meddelelser
Entomol Mem Dep Agric Fish Repub S Afr — Entomology Memoir. Department of Agriculture and Fisheries. Republic of South Africa
Entomol Mem S Afr Dep Agric — Entomology Memoir. South Africa. Department of Agriculture
Entomol Mimeo Ser Utah State Univ Agr Ext Serv — Entomology Mimeo Series. Utah State University. Agricultural Extension Service
Entomol Mitt Zool Mus (Hamb) — Entomologische Mitteilungen. Zoologischen Museum (Hamburg)
Entomol Mitt Zool Staatsinst Zool Mus (Hamb) — Entomologische Mitteilungen. Zoologischen Staatsinstitut und Zoologischen Museum (Hamburg)
Entomol Mon Mag — Entomologist's Monthly Magazine
Entomol Nachr — Entomologische Nachrichten
Entomol Nachr Ber — Entomologische Nachrichten und Berichte
Entomol News — Entomological News
Entomol Newsl — Entomologists' Newsletter
Entomol Obozr — Entomologicheskoe Obozrenie
Entomologia Exp Appl — Entomologia Experimentalis et Applicata
Entomologia Gen — Entomologia Generalis
Entomologie Phytopath Appl — Entomologie et Phytopathologie Appliquees
Entomologist's Gaz — Entomologist's Gazette
Entomologist's Mon Mag — Entomologist's Monthly Magazine
Entomologists Newsl — Entomologists' Newsletter
Entomologist's Rep Dep Agric Tanganyika — Entomologist's Report. Department of Agriculture. Tanganyika
Entomol Phytopathol — Entomology and Phytopathology/K'un Ch'ung Yue Chih Ping
Entomol Phytopathol Appl — Entomologie et Phytopathologie Appliquees
Entomol Probl — Entomologicke Problemy
Entomol Rec — Entomologist's Record
Entomol Rec J Var — Entomologist's Record and Journal of Variation
Entomol Rev — Entomological Review
Entomol Rev (Engl Transl Entomol Obozr) — Entomological Review (English Translation of Entomologicheskoye Obozreniye)
Entomol Scand — Entomologica Scandinavica
Entomol Scand Suppl — Entomologica Scandinavica. Supplementum
Entomol Ser — Entomological Series
Entomol Sin — Entomologia Sinica
Entomol Soc Amer N Cent State Br Proc — Entomological Society of America. North Central State Branch. Proceedings
Entomol Soc Am Spec Publ — Entomological Society of America. Special Publication
Entomol Soc BC J — Entomological Society of British Columbia. Journal
Entomol Soc Egypt Bull Econ Ser — Entomological Society of Egypt. Bulletin. Economic Series

Entomol Soc Nig Bull — Entomological Society of Nigeria. Bulletin
Entomol Soc Nigeria Occas Publ — Entomological Society of Nigeria. Occasional Publication
Entomol Soc NZ Bull — Entomological Society of New Zealand. Bulletin
Entomol Soc Ont Annu Rep — Entomological Society of Ontario. Annual Report
Entomol Soc Ont Proc — Entomological Society of Ontario. Proceedings
Entomol Soc Que Ann — Entomological Society of Quebec. Annals
Entomol Soc South Afr J — Entomological Society of Southern Africa. Journal
Entomol Soc Wash Proc — Entomological Society of Washington. Proceedings
Entomol Tidskr — Entomologisk Tidskrift
Entomol World — Entomological World. Organ. Insect Lovers Association
Entomol Z — Entomologische Zeitschrift
Entomol Zs — Entomologische Zeitschrift
Entomoph — Entomophaga
Entomophaga Mem Hors Ser — Entomophaga. Memoire Hors Serie
Entom Soc Am Ann — Entomological Society of America. Annals
Entom Ztg Stettin — Entomologische Zeitung (Stettin)
ENTPA — Entropie
Ent Problemy — Entomologicke Problemy
Entr — Entr'acte
En Trends — Energy Trends
Entrep — Entrepreneur
Entrepteneur — Entrepreneur Magazine
Entret Bichat Chir Spec — Entretiens de Bichat Chirurgie Specialites
Entret Bichat Med Biol — Entretiens de Bichat Medecine et Biologie
Entret Bichat Ther — Entretiens de Bichat Therapeutique
Entretiens Ant Cl — Entretiens sur l'Antiquite Classique
Entretiens Bichat Chir Spec — Entretiens de Bichat Chirurgie Specialites
Entretiens Bichat Med Biol — Entretiens de Bichat Medecine et Biologie
Entretiens Bichat Stomatol — Entretiens de Bichat Stomatologie
Entretiens Bichat Ther — Entretiens de Bichat Therapeutique
Entretiens Chize Ser Ecol Ethol — Entretiens de Chize. Serie Ecologie et Ethologie
Entretiens Chize Ser Physiol — Entretiens de Chize. Serie Physiologie
Entr Psych — Entretiens Psychiatriques
Ent Scand — Entomologica Scandinavica
Entsch Gerichte Verwbehoerden — Entscheidungen der Gerichte und Verwaltungsbehoerden
Entsch Preuss Oberverwaltger — Entscheidungen des Preussischen Oberverwaltungsgerichtes
Entsch Reichsger Strafs — Entscheidungen des Reichsgerichts in Strafsachen
Entsch Reichsoberhdlsger — Entscheidungen des Reichsoberhandelsgerichtes
ENTSD — Energy Times
Entsikl Izmer Kontrolya Avtom — Entsiklopediya Izmerenii. Kontrolya i Avtomatizatsii
Ent Soc — Entomological Society
Ent Tidskr — Entomologisk Tidskrift
ENT Univ Ky Coll Agric Coop Ext Serv — ENT. University of Kentucky. College of Agriculture. Cooperative Extension Service
Entw Ber Siemens — Entwicklungsberichte der Siemens
Entwicklungsber Siemens und Halske — Entwicklungsberichte der Siemens und Halske Aktiengesellschaft
Entwicklungsgesch Syst Pflanz — Entwicklungsgeschichte und Systematik der Pflanzen
Entwicklungsgesch Syst Pflanz Suppl — Entwicklungsgeschichte und Systematik der Pflanzen. Supplementum
Ent Z — Entomologische Zeitschrift
Ent Z (Frankf A M) — Entomologische Zeitschrift (Frankfurt Am Main)
ENUP — Environment Update. Environment Canada
ENUSA — Experimental Neurology. Supplement
ENV — (El) Nacional (Venezuela)
Env — Environment
Env — Environment/Ecology
Env — Environment Information Access
ENVA — Environmental Affairs
Env Action — Environment Action Bulletin
Env Aff — Environmental Affairs
Env Biol F — Environmental Biology of Fishes
Env Data Serv — Environmental Data Service
Env Entomol — Environmental Entomology
Env Exp Bot — Environmental and Experimental Botany
ENVG — Environment and Planning. A
ENVHA — Environmental Health
Env Health Persp — Environmental Health Perspectives
Envl — Environment Index
Envir — Environment
Envir Action — Environmental Action
Envir & Exper Bot — Environmental and Experimental Botany
Envir Behav — Environment and Behavior
Envir Child Health — Environmental Child Health
Envir Conserv — Environmental Conservation
Envir Ent — Environmental Entomology
Envir Geol — Environmental Geology
Envir Hlth Persp — Environmental Health Perspectives
Envir Lett — Environmental Letters
Envir L Rep — Environmental Law Reporter
Envirn Sci — Environmental Science and Technology
ENVIROFATE — Environmental Fate
Environ — Environnement
Environ Abstr — Environmental Abstracts
Environ Action — Environmental Action
Environ Aff — Environmental Affairs
Environ & Behavior — Environment and Behavior
Environ and Exp Bot — Environmental and Experimental Botany
Environ & Exper Bot — Environmental and Experimental Botany

Environ & Nutr Interact — Environmental and Nutritional Interactions

Environ and Planning — Environment and Planning

Environ Awareness — Environmental Awareness

Environ Behav — Environment and Behavior

Environ Biogeochem Geomicrobiol Proc Int Symp — Environmental Biogeochemistry and Geomicrobiology. Proceedings. International Symposium on Environmental Biogeochemistry

Environ Biol — Environmental Biology

Environ Biol Fish — Environmental Biology of Fishes

Environ Biol Fishes — Environmental Biology of Fishes

Environ Biol Med — Environmental Biology and Medicine

Environ Can Annu Rep — Environment Canada. Annual Report

Environ Can For Pest Manage Inst Rep FPM-X — Environment Canada. Forest Pest Management Institute. Report FPM-X

Environ Can Rapp Annu — Environnement Canada. Rapport Annuel

Environ Can Surveill Rep EP — Environment Canada. Surveillance Report EP

Environ Carcinog Ecotoxicol Rev — Environmental Carcinogenesis and Ecotoxicology Reviews. Part C. Journal of Environmental Science and Health

Environ Carcinog Rev — Environmental Carcinogenesis Reviews. Part C. Journal of Environmental Science and Health

Environ Carcinog Rev Part C J Environ Sci Health — Environmental Carcinogenesis Review. Part C. Journal of Environmental Science and Health

Environ Carcinog Sel Methods Anal — Environmental Carcinogens Selected Methods of Analysis

Environ Change — Environment and Change

Environ Change Marit Symp — Environmental Change in the Maritimes. Symposium

Environ Chem — Environmental Chemistry

Environ Chem Beijing — Environmental Chemistry (Beijing)

Environ Chem Dordrecht Neth — Environment and Chemistry (Dordrecht, Netherlands)

Environ Chem Hum Anim Health — Environmental Chemicals. Human and Animal Health. Proceedings of Annual Conference

Environ Comment — Environmental Comment

Environ Concern Tissue Inj — Environmental Concern and Tissue Injury

Environ Conf Proc — Environmental Conference. Proceedings

Environ Cons — Environmental Conservation

Environ Conser — Environmental Conservation

Environ Conserv — Environmental Conservation

Environ Conserv Eng — Environmental Conservation Engineering

Environ Conserv Eng Osaka — Environmental Conservation Engineering (Osaka)

Environ Contam Hyg — Environmental Contamination and Hygiene

Environ Contr Manage — Environmental Control Management

Environ Control Biol — Environment Control in Biology

Environ Control Manage — Environmental Control Management

Environ Control Proc Symp — Environmental Control. Proceedings. Symposium

Environ Control Saf Manage — Environmental Control and Safety Management

Environ Controls Coal Min Proc Natl Sem — Environmental Controls for Coal Mining. Proceedings. National Seminar

Environ Control Symp — Environmental Control Symposium

Environ Contr Safety Manage — Environmental Control and Safety Management

Environ Creat — Environmental Creation

Environ Creation — Environmental Creation

Environ Data Serv — Environmental Data Service

Environ Data Serv Rep — Environmental Data Services Report

Environ Degrad Eng Mater Aggressive Environ Proc Int Conf — Environmental Degradation of Engineering Materials in Aggressive Environments. Proceedings. International Conference on Environmental Degradation of Engineering Materials

Environ Degrad Eng Mater Hydrogen Proc Int Conf — Environmental Degradation of Engineering Materials in Hydrogen. Proceedings. International Conference on Environmental Degradation of Engineering Materials

Environ Des Ser — Environmental Design Series

Environ Ecol — Environment and Ecology

Environ Ecol Biochem — Environmental and Ecological Biochemistry

Environ Econ Consid Energy Util Proc Natl Conf Energy Environ — Environmental and Economic Considerations in Energy Utilization. Proceedings. National Conference on Energy and the Environment

Environ Educ — Environmental Education

Environ Eff Adv Mater — Environmental Effects on Advanced Materials

Environ Eng — Environmental Engineering

Environ Eng Beijing — Environmental Engineering (Beijing)

Environ Eng Pollut Control — Environmental Engineering and Pollution Control

Environ Engrg — Environmental Engineering

Environ Eng Sci — Environmental Engineering Science

Environ Eng Sci Conf Proc — Environmental Engineering and Science Conference. Proceedings

Environ Eng World — Environmental Engineering World

Environ Entomol — Environmental Entomology

Environ Ethics — Environmental Ethics

Environ Ethics Sci Policy Ser — Environmental Ethics and Science Policy Series

Environ Exp Bot — Environmental and Experimental Botany

Environ Fate Pestic — Environmental Fate of Pesticides

Environ Fluid Mech — Environmental Fluid Mechanics

Environ Forum — Environmental Forum

Environ Geochem Health — Environmental Geochemistry and Health

Environ Geol — Environmental Geology

Environ Geol Bul — Environmental Geology Bulletin

Environ Geol Bull WV Geol Econ Surv — Environmental Geology Bulletin. West Virginia Geological and Economic Survey

Environ Geol Colorado Geol Surv — Environmental Geology. Colorado Geological Survey

Environ Geol Notes III State Geol Surv — Environmental Geology Notes. Illinois State Geological Survey

Environ Geol NY — Environmental Geology (New York)

Environ Geol Water Sci — Environmental Geology and Water Sciences

Environ Geol Wat Sci — Environmental Geology and Water Science

Environ Health — Environmental Health

Environ Health Criter — Environmental Health Criteria

Environ Health Dir Rep EHD (Can) — Environmental Health Directorate. Report. EHD (Canada)

Environ Health (Lond) — Environmental Health (London)

Environ Health (Nagpur) — Environmental Health (Nagpur)

Environ Health Perspect — Environmental Health Perspectives

Environ Health Perspect Suppl — Environmental Health Perspectives Supplements

Environ Health Prev Med — Environmental Health and Preventive Medicine

Environ Health Ser Radiol Health — Environmental Health Series. Radiological Health

Environ Hist Newslett — Environmental History Newsletter

Environ Hlth — Environmental Health

Environ Hlth Perspectives — Environmental Health Perspectives

Environ Impact Assess Rev — Environmental Impact Assessment Review

Environ Impact News — Environmental Impact News

Environ Index — Environment Index

Environ India — Environment India

Environ Inf Dig — Environmental Information Digest

Environ Inf Sci — Environmental Information Science

Environ Int — Environment International

Environ Issues — Environmental Issues

Environ L — Environmental Law

Environ Law — Environmental Law

Environ Law Rep — Environmental Law Reporter

Environ Law Rev — Environment Law Review

Environ Lett — Environmental Letters

Environ L Rev — Environment Law Review

Environ Man — Environment and Man

Environ Manage — Environmental Management

Environ Manage NY — Environmental Management (New York)

Environ Meas Lab Environ Q US Dep Energy — Environmental Measurements Laboratory Environmental Quarterly. US Department of Energy

Environ Meas Lab Environ Rep US Dep of Energy — Environmental Measurements Laboratory. Environmental Report. United States Department of Energy

Environ Meas Lab Rep EML US Dep Energy — Environmental Measurements Laboratory. Report EML. US Department of Energy

Environ Med — Environmental Medicine. Annual Report of the Research Institute of Environmental Medicine. Nagoya University

Environ Med (Nagoya) — Environmental Medicine (Nagoya)

Environment Afr — Environment in Africa. Environment and Regional Planning Research Bulletin

Environ Microbiol — Environmental Microbiology

Environ Midwest — Environment Midwest

Environm L — Environmental Law

Environ Models Emiss Consequences Risoe Int Conf — Environmental Models. Emissions and Consequences. Risoe International Conference

Environ Mol Mutagen — Environmental and Molecular Mutagenesis

Environm Monit Assess — Environmental Monitoring and Assessment

Environm Policy & L — Environmental Policy and Law

Environmt — Environmental Action

Environ Mutagen — Environmental Mutagenesis

Environ Mutagen Carcinog — Environmental Mutagens and Carcinogens

Environ Mutagenesis — Environmental Mutagenesis

Environ Mutagen Res Commun — Environmental Mutagen Research Communications

Environ News — Environment News

Environ News Karachi — Environmental News (Karachi)

Environ Newsl — Environmental Newsletter

Environ Nutr — Environmental Nutrition

Environ Nutr Newsl — Environmental Nutrition Newsletter

Environ Per Bibl — Environmental Periodicals Bibliography

Environ Percep Res Work Pap — Environmental Perception Research. Working Paper

Environ Period Bibliogr — Environmental Periodicals Bibliography

Environ Phys — Environmental Physics

Environ Physiol — Environmental Physiology

Environ Physiol — Environmental Physiology. Nutrition, Pollution, and Toxicology

Environ Physiol Biochem — Environmental Physiology and Biochemistry

Environ Plann A — Environment and Planning. A

Environ Policy Law — Environmental Policy and Law

Environ Pol Law — Environmental Policy and Law

Environ Pollut — Environmental Pollution

Environ Pollut — Environment and Pollution

Environ Pollut — Environnement et Pollution

Environ Pollut (Barking) — Environmental Pollution (Barking)

Environ Pollut Health Hazards — Environmental Pollution and Health Hazards

Environ Pollut Manage — Environmental Pollution Management

Environ Pollut Mgmt — Environmental Pollution Management

Environ Pollut Pest — Environmental Pollution by Pesticides

Environ Pollut Proc Symp — Environmental Pollution. Proceedings. Symposium

Environ Pollut Ser A — Environmental Pollution. Series A. Ecological and Biological

Environ Pollut Ser A Ecol Biol — Environmental Pollution. Series A. Ecological and Biological

Environ Pollut Ser B — Environmental Pollution. Series B. Chemical and Physical

Environ Pollut Ser B Chem Phys — Environmental Pollution. Series B. Chemical and Physical

Environ Process Monit Technol — Environmental and Process Monitoring Technologies

Environ Prof — Environmental Professional

Environ Prog — Environmental Progress

Environ Prot Agency APTD US — Environmental Protection Agency. APTD [*Air Pollution Technical Data*] (United States)

Environ Prot Agency AP US — Environmental Protection Agency. AP (United States)

Environ Prot Agency Off Pestic Programs Rep EPA (US) — Environmental Protection Agency. Office of Pesticide Programs. Report EPA (United States)

Environ Prot Agency Off Pestic Toxic Subst Rep EPA US — Environmental Protection Agency. Office of Pesticide and Toxic Substances. Report EPA (United States)

Environ Prot Agency Off Radiat Programs Tech Rep EPA (US) — Environmental Protection Agency. Office of Radiation Programs. Technical ReportEPA (United States)

Environ Prot Agency Off Res Dev Rep EPA — Environmental Protection Agency. Office of Research and Development. Report EPA (US)

Environ Prot Agency Off Solid Waste Manage Programs Tech Rep — Environmental Protection Agency. Office of Solid Waste Management Programs. Technical Report SW (US)

Environ Prot Agency Off Toxic Subst Rep EPA US — Environmental Protection Agency. Office of Toxic Substances. Report EPA (United States)

Environ Prot Agency Reg 10 Rep EPA (US) — Environmental Protection Agency. Region 10. Report EPA (United States)

Environ Prot Agency (US) Publ AP Ser — Environmental Protection Agency (US). Publication. AP [*Air Pollution*] Series

Environ Prot Agency (US) Publ APTD Ser — Environmental Protection Agency (US). Publication. APTD [*Air Pollution Technical Data*] Series

Environ Prot Beijing — Environmental Protection (Beijing)

Environ Prot Bull — Environmental Protection Bulletin

Environ Prot Conf — Environmental Protection Conference

Environ Prot Eng — Environment Protection Engineering

Environ Prot Surv — Environmental Protection Survey

Environ Prot (Taipei) — Environmental Protection (Taipei)

Environ Prot Technol Ser — Environmental Protection Technology Series

Environ Prot Technol Ser EPA — Environmental Protection Technology Series. EPA

Environ Psychol Nonverbal Behav — Environmental Psychology and Nonverbal Behavior

Environ Q — Environmental Quarterly

Environ Qual — Environmental Quality

Environ Qual Abstr — Environmental Quality Abstracts

Environ Qual Res Dev Unit Tech Pap (NY) — Environmental Quality Research and Development Unit. Technical Paper (New York)

Environ Qual Res Unit Tech Pap NY — Environmental Quality Research Unit. Technical Paper (New York)

Environ Qual Saf — Environmental Quality and Safety

Environ Qual Saf Suppl — Environmental Quality and Safety. Supplement

Environ Quart — Environmental Quarterly

Environ Q US Dep Energy Environ Meas Lab — Environmental Quarterly. United States Department of Energy. Environmental Measurements Laboratory

Environ Q US Energy Res Dev Adm Health Saf Lab — Environmental Quarterly. United States Energy Research and Development Administration. Health and Safety Laboratory

Environ Radiat Bull — Environmental Radiation Bulletin

Environ Radiat Surveill Wash State — Environmental Radiation Surveillance in Washington State. Annual Report

Environ Radioact — Environmental Radioactivity

Environ Region — Environment and Region

Environ Regul Microb Metab — Environmental Regulation of Microbial Metabolism

Environ Rep Environ Meas Lab US Dep Energy — Environmental Report. Environmental Measurements Laboratory. United States Department of Energy

Environ Res — Environmental Research

Environ Res Cent Saga Prefect — Environmental Research Center of Saga Prefecture

Environ Res Forum — Environmental Research Forum

Environ Res Inst Mich Annu Rep — Environmental Research Institute of Michigan. Annual Report

Environ Resour — Environmental Resource

Environ Resour Manage Can Chem Eng Conf — Environment and Resource Management. Canadian Chemical Engineering Conference

Environ Rev — Environmental Review

Environ Risk Anal Chem — Environmental Risk Analysis for Chemicals

Environ Sanit Abstr — Environmental Sanitation Abstract

Environ Sanit Eng Res — Environmental and Sanitary Engineering Research

Environ Sanit Rev — Environmental Sanitation Review

Environ Sci — Environmental Sciences

Environ Sci & Tech — Environmental Science and Technology

Environ Sci and Technol — Environmental Science and Technology

Environ Sci Appl — Environmental Sciences and Applications

Environ Sci Beijing — Environmental Science (Beijing)

Environ Sci Eng — Environmental Science and Engineering

Environ Sci Eng Notes — Environmental Sciences and Engineering Notes

Environ Sci Policy — Environmental Science and Policy

Environ Sci Pollut Res Int — Environmental Science and Pollution Research International

Environ Sci Res — Environmental Science Research

Environ Sci Res Rep — Environmental Sciences Research Report

Environ Sci Technol — Environmental Science and Technology

Environ Sci Technol Dordrecht Neth — Environmental Science and Technology (Dordrecht, Netherlands)

Environ Sci Technol Libr — Environmental Science and Technology Library

Environ Sci Tokyo — Environmental Sciences (Tokyo)

Environ Sc Tech — Environmental Science and Technology

Environ Ser — Environmental Series

Environ Southwest — Environment Southwest

Environ Space Sci — Environmental Space Sciences

Environ Space Sci (Engl Transl Kosm Biol Med) — Environmental Space Sciences (English Translation of Kosmicheskaya Biologiya i Meditsina)

Environ Stud Can Dep Indian Aff North Dev — Environmental Studies. Canada. Department of Indian Affairs and Northern Development

Environ Stud Can Indian North Aff — Environmental Studies. Canada. Indian and Northern Affairs

Environ Symp Proc — Environmental Symposium. Proceedings

Environ Syst Plann Des Control Proc IFAC Symp — Environmental Systems Planning, Design, and Control. Proceedings. IFAC [*International Federation of Automatic Control*] Symposium

Environ Technol — Environmental Technology

Environ Technol Econ — Environmental Technology and Economics

Environ Technol Lett — Environmental Technology Letters

Environ Technol Proc Eur Conf — Environmental Technology. Proceedings. European Conference on Environmental Technology

Environ Test Anal — Environmental Testing and Analysis

Environ This Mon — Environment This Month

Environ Top — Environmental Topics

Environ Toxicol — Environmental Toxicology

Environ Toxicol Chem — Environmental Toxicology and Chemistry

Environ Toxicol Pharmacol — Environmental Toxicology and Pharmacology

Environ Toxicol Water Qual — Environmental Toxicology and Water Quality

Environ Toxin Ser — Environmental Toxin Series

Environ Views — Environment Views

Envir Plann — Environment and Planning

Envir Poll Control — Environmental Pollution Control

Envir Pollu — Environmental Pollution

Envir Qual — Environmental Quality. Annual Report of the Council of Environmental Quality

Envir Res — Environmental Research

Envir Sci & Tech — Environmental Science and Technology

Envir Sci Techn — Environmental Science and Technology

Envir Sc Technol — Environmental Science and Technology

Env L — Environmental Law

Env L Rev — Environmental Law Review

Env L Rptr — Environmental Law Reporter

ENVPA — Environmental Pollution

ENVPD — Environmental Progress

Env Phys Bi — Environmental Physiology and Biochemistry

Env Plann — Environment and Planning

ENVPSYCH — Environmental Psychology

ENVQA — Environmental Quarterly

ENVRA — Environmental Research

ENVRB — Environment Report

ENVS — Environment Views. Alberta Department of the Environment

Env Sci Tec — Environmental Science and Technology

ENVTA — Environment

ENVTAR — Environment

Envtl L — Environmental Law

Envtl LQ Newsl — Environmental Law Quarterly Newsletter

Envtl L Rep — Environmental Law Reporter

Envtl L Rep Envtl L Inst — Environmental Law Reporter. Environmental Law Institute

Envt Reg Handbook Envt Information Center — Environment Regulation Handbook. Environment Information Center

Envt Rep Cas BNA — Environment Reporter Cases. Bureau of National Affairs

ENW — Economic News

En Watch — Energy Watch

ENWSD — Energy Newsletter

ENY — Energy

Enz Rechtswiss — Birkmeyer. Enzyklopaedie der Rechtswissenschaft

ENZYA — Enzymologia

Enzym Biol Clin — Enzymologia Biologica et Clinica

Enzyme Eng — Enzyme Engineering

Enzyme Eng Pap Eng Found Conf — Enzyme Engineering. Papers. Engineering Foundation Conference on Enzyme Engineering

Enzyme Microb Technol — Enzyme and Microbial Technology

Enzyme Physiol Pathol — Enzyme Physiology and Pathology

Enzymes Anim Evol — Enzymes in Animal Evolution

Enzymes Biol Membr (2nd Ed) — Enzymes of Biological Membranes (2nd Edition)

Enzymes Gen Consid Compr Biochem — Enzymes-General Considerations. Comprehensive Biochemistry

Enzymes Med — Enzymes in Medicine

Enzymes Ther Congr Int Ther Rapp Commun — Enzymes en Therapeutique. Congres International de Therapeutique. Rapports et Communications

Enzyme Technol Rotenburg Ferment Symp — Enzyme Technology. Rotenburg Fermentation Symposium

Enzymol Biol Clin — Enzymologia Biologica et Clinica

Enzymol Klin Wyd — Enzymologia Kliniczna, Wydanie

Enzymol Mol Biol Carbonyl Metab — Enzymology and Molecular Biology of Carbonyl Metabolism

Enzymol Mol Biol Carbonyl Metab 2 Proc Int Workshop — Enzymology and Molecular Biology of Carbonyl Metabolism 2. Aldehyde Dehydrogenase, Alcohol Dehydrogenase, and Aldo-Keto Reductase. Proceedings. International Workshop

Enzymologia — Enzymologia Acta Biocatalytica

Enzymol Post Transl Modif Proteins — Enzymology of Post-Translational Modification of Proteins

Enzym Release Vasoact Pept Workshop Conf Hoechst — Enzymatic Release of Vasoactive Peptides. Workshop Conference Hoechst

EO — Echos d'Orient

E/O — Engineering Opportunities

EO — Entomologischeskoe Obozrenie

EO — Est et Ouest

EO — Europaeische Osten

EO — Europe and Oil
EO — Europe Orientale
EOA — Ethiopia Observer (Addis Ababa)
EOATD — Earth-Oriented Applications of Space Technology [*Formerly, Advances in Earth-Oriented Applications of Space Technology*]
EOBMA — Elektronnaya Obrabotka Materialov
EOBMAF — Elektronnaya Obrabotka Materialov
EOC Jnl — EOC [*Equal Opportunities Commission*] Journal
EOC Res Bul — EOC [*Equal Opportunities Commission*] Research Bulletin
EOD — Oriente Dominicano [*Quito*]
EOGRAL — European Journal of Obstetrics, Gynecology, and Reproductive Biology
EOM — Estudios-Padres de la Orden de la Merced
EOMC — Estudios Orientales (Mexico City)
EOMJA — Ecclesiae Occidentalis Monumenta Juris Antiquissima
EON — Eugene O'Neill Newsletter
EONE — Eastern Offshore News. Eastcoast Petroleum Operators' Association
EOO — Erasmi Opera Omnia
EOP — Economics of Planning
EOPPA — Ekonomika i Organizatsiya Promyshlennogo Proizvodstva
E Or — Echos d'Orient
EORTC Cancer Chemother Annu — EORTC [*European Organization for Research on Treatment of Cancer*] Cancer Chemotherapy Annual
EOS — Elsevier Oceanography Series
EOS — EOS. Revista Espanola de Entomologia
EOS J Immunol Immunopharmacol — EOS. Journal of Immunology and Immunopharmacology
EOS Rev Esp Entomol — EOS. Revista Espanola de Entomologia
EOS Riv Immunol Immunofarmacol — EOS. Rivista di Immunologia ed Immunofarmacologia
Eos Trans Am Geophys Union — Eos. Transactions of the American Geophysical Union
EOT — Economic Impact. A Quarterly Review of World Economics
Eotvoes Lorand Tudomanyegyet Evk — Eotvoes Lorand Tudomanyegyetem Evkoenyve
EOUPD — Ekonomika, Organizatsiya,i Upravlenie v Nefteprererabatyvayushchei i Neftekhimicheskoi Promyshlennosti
EOUSD — Economic Outlook USA
EP — Economic Papers
EP — Economic Planning. Journal for Agriculture and Related Industries
EP — Editor and Publisher
EP — El Pais
EP — El Palacio [*Santa Fe*]
EP — Epilogoe
Ep — Epoque
EP — Estate Planning
EP — Etnografia Portuguesa
EP — Etudes de Papyrologie
EP — Etudes Papyrologiques
EP — Etudes Peloponnesiennes
EP — Etudes Philosophiques
EPA — Entomologie et Phytopathologie Appliquees. Departement General de la Protection des Plantes. Ministere de l'Agriculture [*Teheran*]
EPA — Estudios Paraguayos (Asuncion)
EPA Cit Bul — EPA [*Environmental Protection Agency*] Citizens' Bulletin
EPA (Environ Prot Agency) Environ Prot Technol Ser — EPA (Environmental Protection Agency) Environmental Protection Technology Series
EPAHA — Etudes de Philologie, d'Archeologie, et d'Histoire Anciennes
EPA J — EPA [*Environmental Protection Agency*] Journal
EP & T — Electronic Products & Technology
EPA Newsl — EPA (European Photochemistry Association) Newsletter
EPap — Etudes de Papyrologie
EPAPS — Early Proceedings. American Philosophical Society
EPar — Ecrits de Paris. Revue des Questions Actuelles
EPB — Electronic Publishing and Bookselling
EPB — Employee Benefit Plan Review
EPB — Etudes Portugaises et Bresiliennes
EPBC — Egyptian Pharmaceutical Bulletin (Cairo)
EPBCA — Ergebnisse der Physiologie, Biologischen Chemie, und Experimentellen Pharmakologie
EPBCAQ — Ergebnisse der Physiologie, Biologischen Chemie, und Experimentellen Pharmakologie
EPBGPN — Environment Protection Board. Gas Pipeline Newsletter
EPD — Electric Power Database
EPDIC Proc Eur Powder Diffr Conf — EPDIC Proceedings. European Powder Diffraction Conference
EPE — Enzyklopaedie der Psychologie in Einzeldarstellungen
EPE — Export Direction
EPEBD7 — Environmental Pollution. Series A. Ecological and Biological
EPE Eur Prod Eng — EPE (European Production Engineering)
EP Electron Prod — EP. Electronic Production
EP Electron Prod London — EP Electronic Production (London)
EP Elektropromst Priborostr — EP. Elektropromishlenost i Priborostroene
EPEOD — Energy People
EPESA — Ediciones y Publicaciones Espanolas Sociedad Anonima
Epet — Epeteris tes Hetaireias Byzantinon Spoudon
Ep Etr — Epigrafia Etrusca
EPFBA — Florida. University. Engineering and Industrial Experiment Station. Bulletin Series
Ep Gr — Epigrafia Greca
Ep Graec Frag — Epicorum Graecorum Fragmenta
Ep Gr Frag — Epicorum Graecorum Fragmenta
Eph — Archaiologike Ephemeris
EPh — Ecclesiasticos Pharos
EpH — Epeirotike Hestia
EPh — Etudes Philosophiques

E Ph AHA — Etudes de Philologie, d'Archeologie et d'Histoire Anciennes
Eph Arch — Ephemeris Archaiologike
Ep HB Sp — Epeteris Hetaireias Byzantinon Spoudon
EphC — Ephemerides Carmeliticae
EphCarm — Ephemerides Carmeliticae. Cura Pontificiae Facultatis Theologicae S. Teresiae aJesu et Ionnis a Cruce
Eph Dac — Ephemeris Dacoromana
Eph DR — Ephemeris Dacoromana. Annuario. Scuola Romena di Roma
EPHE — Ecole Pratique des Hautes Etudes
EPHE/H — Homme. Revue Francaise d'Anthropologie. La Sorbonne, l'Ecole Pratique des Hautes Etudes
Ephem — Archaiologike Ephemeris
Ephemer Theologicae Lovanienses — Ephemerides Theologicae Lovanienses
Ephem Theol Lovanienses — Ephemerides Theologicae Lovanienses
Eph Ep — Ephemeris Epigraphica
Eph Epgr — Ephemeris Epigraphica. Corpus Inscriptionum Latinarum Supplementum
EPHESHPhA — Ecole Pratique des Hautes Etudes. IVe Section. Sciences Historiques et Philologiques. Annuaire
EPHESRA — Ecole Pratique des Hautes Etudes. Ve Section. Sciences Religieuses. Annuaire
EPhK — Egyetemes Philologiai Koezloeny
EphL — Ephemerides Liturgicae
Eph Lit — Ephemerides Liturgicae
EphLitg — Ephemerides Liturgicae
E Ph M — Etudes de Philosophie Medievale
EphMar — Ephemerides Mariologicae
Eph Th L — Ephemerides Theologicae Lovanienses
EPIA — Electric Power Industry Abstracts
Epidemiol Bull — Epidemiological Bulletin
Epidemiol Community Health — Epidemiology and Community Health
Epidemiol Exp Clin Stud Gastric Cancer Proc Int Conf — Epidemiological, Experimental, and Clinical Studies on Gastric Cancer. Proceedings. International Conference on Gastric Cancer
Epidemiol Infect — Epidemiology and Infection
Epidemiol Mikrobiol Immunol — Epidemiologie, Mikrobiologie, Immunologie
Epidemiol Mikrobiol Infekts Boles — Epidemiologiya Mikrobiologiya i Infektsiozni Bolesti
Epidemiol Prev — Epidemiologia e Prevenzione
Epidemiol Psichiatr Soc — Epidemiologia e Psichiatria Sociale
Epidemiol Rev — Epidemiologic Reviews
Epidemiol Rev (Engl Transl Przegl Epidemiol) — Epidemiological Review (English Translation of Przeglad Epidemiologiczny)
Epidem Mikrobiol — Epidemiologiya Mikrobiologiya i Infektsiozni Bolesti
Epig — Epigraphica
Epig Anek — Epigraphai Anekdotoi Anakalyphtheisai kai Ekdotheisai Hypo tou Archaiologikou Syllogou
Epig Indica — Epigraphia Indica
Epigraph Stud — Epigraphische Studies
Epigr Ast — Epigrafia Romana de Asturias
Epigr Gr — Epigrammata Graeca ex Lapidibus Conlecta
Epigr Stud — Epigraphische Studien
Epigr Vostok — Epigrafika Vostoka. Sbornik Statei
Epig Stud — Epigraphische Studien
Epi Ind A — Epigraphia Indica. Arabic and Persian Supplement
EPILA — Epilepsia
Epileps — Epilepsia. Revue Internationale a l'Etude de l'Epilepsie
Epilepsy Int Symp — Epilepsy. International Symposium
Epilepsy Pregnancy Child Proc Conf — Epilepsy, Pregnancy, and the Child. Proceedings. Conference
Epilepsy Res — Epilepsy Research
Epilepsy Res Suppl — Epilepsy Research. Supplement
Epileptic Disord — Epileptic Disorders
Epileptic Syndr Infancy Child Adolesc — Epileptic Syndromes in Infancy, Childhood, and Adolescence
Epimethee Essais Philos — Epimethee. Essais Philosophiques
Epist — Epistemonike Epeteris. Ethnikon kai Kapodistriakon Panepistemion
Epist — Epistemonike Epeteris tes Philosophikes Scholes tou Panepistemiou Athenon
Epistemata Wuerzburg Wissensch Schrift Reihe Philos — Epistemata. Wuerzburger Wissenschaftliche Schriften, Reihe Philosophie
Epistem Hist Didact Mat — Epistemologia, Historia, y Didactica de la Matematica
Epistemon Epeteris Kteniatr Sch — Epistemonike Epeteris Kteniatrikes Scholes
Epist Gr — Epistolographi Graeci
Epist Graec — Epistolographi Graeci
Epithelial Cell Biol — Epithelial Cell Biology
Epithelial Mesenchymal Interact Hahnemann Symp — Epithelial-Mesenchymal Interactions. Hahnemann Symposium
Epitheor Klin Farmakol Farmakokinet — Epitheorese Klinikes Farmakologias kai Farmakokinetikes
Epizootol Profil Prirodnoochagovykh Infekts — Epizootologiya i Profilaktika Prirodnoochagovykh Infektsii
EPJ — Essay-Proof Journal
EPK — Egyetemes Philologiai Koezloeny
EPKE — Epitheoresis Koinonikon Ereunon
EPL — Etudes Philosophiques et Litteraires
EPLAC — Enoch Pond Lectures on Applied Christianity
EPLL — Edinburgh University Publications. Language and Literature
EPM — Educational and Psychological Measurement
EPM — Environmental Pollution Management
EPM — Etudes de Philosophie Medievale
EPMEA — Educational and Psychological Measurement
Ep Mes Arch — Epeteris tou Messaionikou Archeiou
EPMSR — Environment Canada. Pacific Marine Science Reports
Ep Myc — Initiation a l'Epigraphie Mycenienne

EPN — European Plastics News
EPN — Expansion
EPNED — Energy Planning Network
EPN Eur Plast News — EPN. European Plastics News
EPNY — Editor and Publisher (New York)
EPo — Esperienza Poetica
EPOBAK — EPPO [European and Mediterranean Plant Protection Organization] Publications. Series C
Epochen d Franz Liter — Epochen der Franzoesische Literatur
EPOM — Estudios. Revista. Padres de la Orden de la Merced
Epoxy Resins Chem Technol — Epoxy Resins. Chemistry and Technology
Epoxy Resins Compos — Epoxy Resins and Composites
EPP — Estonian Papers in Phonetics
EPPO Bull — EPPO [European and Mediterranean Plant Protection Organization] Bulletin
EPPO (Eur Mediterr Plant Prot Organ) Publ Ser C — EPPO (European and Mediterranean Plant Protection Organization) Publications. Series C
EPPO Plant Health Newsl Publ Ser B — EPPO [European and Mediterranean Plant Protection Organization] Plant Health Newsletter Publications. Series B
EPPO Publ Ser C — EPPO [European and Mediterranean Plant Protection Organization] Publications. Series C
EPR — Earthquake Prediction Research
EPR — Economische Politierechter
EPR — Electronic Publishing Review
EPr — Etudes de Presse
EPRAD — Elektro-Praktiker
EPRCD — Electric Power Research Institute (Report) EPRI CS
EPRDA7 — Economic Proceedings. Royal Dublin Society
EPRDB8 — Ekologia Polska. Seria B
EPRI J — EPRI [Electric Power Research Institute] Journal
EPRI Rep NP — EPRI [Electric Power Research Institute] Report. NP
EPRI Workshop Proc — EPRI [Electric Power Research Institute] Workshop Proceedings
EPRJD — EPRI [Electric Power Research Institute] Journal
EPRO — Etudes Preliminaires aux Religions Orientales dans l'Empire Romain
EPRODER — Etudes Preliminaires aux Religions Orientales dans l'Empire Romain
EPROER — Etudes Preliminaires aux Religions Orientales dans l'Empire Romain
EprR — Schinz, Albert. Etat Present des Etudes sur Jean-Jacques Rousseau [monograph]
EPS — English Philological Studies
EPS3AP — Environment Protection Service. Air Pollution Report
EPS3WP — Environment Protection Service. Water Pollution Report
EPS4NW — Environment Protection Service. Northwest Region. Technology Development Report
EPS Gen Conf Energy Phys — EPS General Conference. Energy and Physics
Epsilon Let — Epsilon Letter
Epsilon Market Let — Epsilon Marketing Letter
EPSLA — Earth and Planetary Science Letters
EPsM — Educational and Psychological Measurement
EPSMD — Elektrotekhnicheskaya Promyshlennost. Seriya. Elektrotekhnicheskie Materialy
EPSNA — Sbornik Nauchnykh Trudov Estonskoi Sel'skokhozyaistvennoi Akademii
EPSnEC — Environment Protection Service. Environmental Impact Control Directorate. Surveillance Report
EPSnES — Environment Protection Service. Environmental Strategies Directorate. Economic and Technical Review
EPSnNW — Environment Protection Service. Northwest Region. Department of the Environment. Reports
EPS NR — Environmental Protection Service. Report Series. Northern Regions
EPSPDH — Environmental Pollution. Series B. Chemical and Physical
EPSRD — Electric Power Systems Research
EPST — Electric Power Statistics
Epst Cat — Catalogue of the Epstean Collection
Epstein Barr Virus Assoc Dis Proc Int Symp — Epstein-Barr Virus and Associated Diseases. Proceedings. International Symposium
EPTDA — Electric Light and Power. Transmission/Distribution
EPTQAM — Etudes Psychotherapiques
EPTSB — Environmental Protection Technology Series
EPubl — Enseignement Public
EPUBS — Electronic Publishing Abstracts
E Purdue Univ Coop Ext Serv — E. Purdue University. Cooperative Extension Service
EPW — Economic and Political Weekly
EQ — Education Quarterly
EQ — English Quarterly
EQ — European Quarterly
EQ — Evangelical Quarterly
EQA — Environmental Quality Abstracts
EQA — Eurodoc
Eq Empl Compl Man — Equal Employment Compliance Manual
EQL Memo Calif Inst Technol Environ Qual Lab — EQL Memorandum. California Institute of Technology. Environmental Quality Laboratory
EQM — Environmental Quality Magazine
EQMM — Ellery Queen's Mystery Magazine
EQND — Education Quarterly (New Delhi)
EQNX — Equinox
EQPRDF — Equine Practice
EQS Environ Qual Saf — EQS. Environmental Quality and Safety
EQS Environ Qual Saf Suppl — EQS. Environmental Quality and Safety. Supplement
Equal Now — Equality Now
Equal Opp — Equal Opportunity
Equal Opportunities Int — Equal Opportunities International
Equilib Res — Equilibrium Research
Equine Pharmacol Symp Proc — Equine Pharmacology Symposium. Proceedings

Equine Pract — Equine Practice
Equine Reprod Proc Int Symp — Equine Reproduction. Proceedings. International Symposium on Equine Reproduction
Equine Res Inst Bull — Equine Research Institute. Bulletin
Equine Vet J — Equine Veterinary Journal
Equip Dev Test Rep US For Serv Equip Dev Ctr San Dimas Calif — Equipment Development and Test Report. United States Forest Service. Equipment Center (San Dimas, California)
Equipement — Equipement - Logement - Transports
Equipe Pedol Fertil Solo Bol Tec — Equipe de Pedologia e Fertilidade do Solo. Boletim Tecnico
Equip Ind Achats & Entretien — Equipement Industriel. Achats et Entretien
Equip Mec — Equipement Mecanique
Equip Preview Chem Process Ind — Equipment Preview of Chemical Process Industries
Equip Tips US Dep Agric For Serv Equip Dev Cent — Equip Tips. United States Department of Agriculture. Forest Service Equipment Development Center
Equit Distr Rep — Equitable Distribution Reporter
ER — Ecclesiastical Review
ER — Economic Record
ER — Ecumenical Review
ER — Edinburgh Review
ER — Educational Review
ER — Eisenbahntechnische Rundschau
ER — Elektronische Rechenanlagen
ER — Energy Research
ER — Energy Review
ER — Englische Rundschau
ER — English Review
ER — Episcopal Recorder
Er — Eranos
Er — Erasme
Er — Erasmus
Er — Erevna
Er — Eriu
ER — Estudis Romanics
ER — Eternelle Revue
ER — Etudes Rabelaisiennes
ER — Etudes Rhodaniennes
ER — European Report
ER — Evergreen Review
ERA — Economic Record (Australia)
ERA — Egypt Research Account
ERA — Energy Research Abstracts
ERA — Epigrafia Romana de Asturias
ERA — ERA. Education Research Abstracts
ERA Abstr — ERA [British Electrical and Allied Industries Research Association] Abstracts
ERab — Etudes Rabelaisiennes
ERA Foeren Elektr Ration Anvaendning — ERA. Foerening foer Elektricitetens Rationella Anvaendning
Era M — Era Magazine
EranJb — Eranos-Jahrbuch
Eranos — Eranos-Jahrbuch
Eranos Jahrb — Eranos-Jahrbuch
Eranos-Jb — Eranos-Jahrbuch
Eranos Jhb — Eranos Jahrbuch
Eras — Erasmus. Speculum Scientiarum. Basel
Eras B — Erasmus Bibliothek
Erasmus E — Erasmus in English
ErasmusR — Erasmus Review
Erasmus Rev — Erasmus Review
Era Social — Era Socialista
ErasR — Erasmus Review
ERB — Educational Research Bulletin
ERB — Etudes Romanes de Brno
ERB — Key to Economic Science
ErbAuf — Erbe und Auftrag
Erbe der V — Erbe der Vergangenheit
Erbe U Auftrag — Erbe und Auftrag
ERBr — Etudes Romanes de Brno
Erb St G — Erbschaftssteuergesetz
ERC — Economic Review. Federal Reserve Bank of Cleveland
ERC — (El) Espectador. Magazin Dominical (Colombia)
ERC — Enciclopedia de la Religion Catolica
ERCBA8 — Ecological Research Committee. Bulletin
ERCDO — Etudes et Recherches. College Dominicain d'Ottawa
ERCEW — Ethical and Religious Classics of East and West
ERCHD — Energy Report from Chase
ERCOFTAC Ser — ERCOFTAC [European Research Community on Flow, Turbulence, and Combustion] Series
ERD — Economic Review. Federal Reserve Bank of Dallas
ERD — Erdkunde
ERD — Erdoel und Kohle, Erdgas, Petrochemie
ERDA Energy Res Abstr — ERDA (Energy Research and Development Administration) Energy Research Abstracts
ERDA (Energy Res Dev Adm) Symp Ser — ERDA (Energy Research and Development Administration) Symposium Series
ERDA Rep — ERDA (Energy Research and Development Administration). Report
ERDA Symp Ser — ERDA [Energy Research and Development Administration] Symposium Series
ERdB — Etudes Romanes de Brno
Erdelyi Muz Egyes Evk — Az Erdelyi Muzeum-Egyesulet Evkoenyve
Erdelyi Muzeum — Erdelyi Muzeum
Erdesz Ertes — Erdeszeti Ertesitoe

Erdeszeti Faipari Egy Tud Kozl — Erdeszeti es Faipari Egyetem Tudomanyos Kozlemenyei
Erdeszeti Faipari Tud Kozl — Erdeszeti es Faipari Tudomanyos Kozlemenyek
Erdeszeti Kiserl — Erdeszeti Kiserletek
Erdeszeti Kut — Erdeszeti Kutatasok
Erdeszettud Kozl — Erdeszettudomanyi Kozlemenyek
Erdesz Faipari Egyetem Kiad — Erdeszeti es Faipari Egyetem Kiadvanyai
Erdesz Faipari Egyetem Tud Kozl — Erdeszeti es Faipari Egyetem Tudomanyos Kozlemenyei
Erdesz Faip Egyet Tud Koezlem — Az Erdeszeti es Faipari Egyetem Tudomanyos Koezlemenyei. Wissenschaftliche Mitteilungen der Universitaet fuer Forst- und Holzwirtschaf
Erdesz Kut — Erdeszeti Kutatasok
Erdesz Kutat — Erdeszeti Kutatasok
Erdesz Kutatas — Erdeszeti Kutatasok
Erdesz Ujs — Erdeszeti Ujsag
Erdk — Erdkunde
Erd Kh — Erdoel und Kohle
Erd Koh EPB — Erdoel und Kohle, Erdgas, Petrochemie Vereinigt mit Brennstoff-Chemie
Erd M — Erdelyi Muzeum
Erdmagn Ber — Erdmagnetische Berichte
Erdm J Pr C — Journal fuer Praktische Chemie. Erdman
Erdm J Tech C — Journal fuer Technische und Oekonomische Chemie. Erdman
Erd Muz — Erdelyi Muzeum
Erd Muz — Erdelyi Muzeum-Egylet Evkoenyvei
Erd Muz Evk — Erdelyi Muzeum-Egylet Evkoenyvei
Erdoel Chem (Sofia) — Erdoel und Chemie (Sofia)
Erdoel Erdgas Budapest — Erdoel und Erdgas (Budapest)
Erdoel-Erdgas Z — Erdoel-Erdgas Zeitschrift
Erdoel Erdgas Z Int Ed — Erdoel-Erdgas Zeitschrift. International Edition
Erdoel Kohle — Erdoel und Kohle, Erdgas, Petrochemie
Erdoel Kohle Erdgas Petrochem — Erdoel und Kohle, Erdgas, Petrochemie
Erdoel Kohle Erdgas Petrochem Brennst-Chem — Erdoel und Kohle, Erdgas, Petrochemie Vereinigt mit Brennstoff-Chemie
Erdoel Kohle Erdgas Petrochem Ver Brennst Chem — Erdoel und Kohle, Erdgas, Petrochemie Vereinigt mit Brennstoff-Chemie
Erdoel-Z — Erdoel-Zeitschrift
Erdoel Z Bohr Foerdertech — Erdoel-Zeitschrift fuer Bohr- und Foerdertechnik
Erdoemern Foeisk Evk — Erdoemernoeki Foeiskola Evkoenyve
Erdoe Temesvar — Az Erdoe (Temesvar)
Erdol & Kohl — Erdoel und Kohle, Erdgas, Petrochemie
ERDSDX — ERDA [*Energy Research and Development Administration*] Symposium Series
ERE — Encyclopaedia of Religion and Ethics
ERec — English Record
EREND — Energy and the Environment
ERes — Education Research
Eretz Is — Eretz Israel. Archaeological, Historical, and Geographical Studies
Erevan Fiz Inst Nauchn Soobshch — Erevanskii Fizicheskii Institut. Nauchnoe Soobshchenie
Erevan Gos Inst Usoversh Vrachei Tr — Erevanskii Gosudarstvennyi Institut Usovershenstvovaniya Vrachei. Trudy
Erevan Gos Univ Ucen Zap Estesv Nauki — Erevanskii Gosudarstvennyi Universitet. Ucenye Zapiski. Estestvennye Nauki
Erevan Med Inst Tr — Erevanskii Meditsinskii Institut. Trudy
Er F — Erlanger Forschungen
Erfahr Denk — Erfahrung und Denken
Erfahrungswiss Bl — Erfahrungswissenschaftliche Blaetter
Erfelijkheid Prakt — Erfelijkheid in Praktijk. Orgaan van de Nederlandsche Genetische Vereeniging
Erf Hlkd — Erfahrungsheilkunde
Erfurt Ak Jb — Jahrbuecher der Koeniglichen Akademie Gemeinnuetziger Wissenschaften zu Erfurt
Erfurt Gel Zeitungen — Erfurtische Gelehrte Zeitungen
Erg Allg Path — Ergebnisse der Allgemeinen Pathologie und Pathologischen Anatomie
Erg Ang Math — Ergebnisse der Angewandten Mathematik
Erg Bl AZ — Ergaenzungsblaetter zur Allgemeinen Zeitung
Erg Blut Transf Forsch — Ergebnisse der Bluttransfusionsforschung
Erg Chir Orthop — Ergebnisse der Chirurgie und Orthopaedie
Erg D Inn Med u Kinderh — Ergebnisse der Inneren Medizin und Kinderheilkunde
Ergeb Agrikulturchem — Ergebnisse der Agrikulturchemie
Ergeb Allgem Pathol Pathol Anat — Ergebnisse der Allgemeinen Pathologie und Pathologischen Anatomie
Ergeb Allg Pathol Pathol Anat — Ergebnisse der Allgemeinen Pathologie und Pathologischen Anatomie
Ergeb Aminosaeuren Saeulenchromatogr — Ergebnisse der Aminosaeuren-Saeulenchromatographie
Ergeb Anat Entwicklungsgesch — Ergebnisse der Anatomie und Entwicklungsgeschichte
Ergeb Angew Phys Chem — Ergebnisse der Angewandten Physikalischen Chemie
Ergeb Angiol — Ergebnisse der Angiologie
Ergeb Biol — Ergebnisse der Biologie
Ergeb Bluttransfusionsforsch — Ergebnisse der Bluttransfusionsforschung
Ergeb Enzymforsch — Ergebnisse der Enzymforschung
Ergeb Exakten Naturwiss — Ergebnisse der Exakten Naturwissenschaften
Ergeb Exp Med — Ergebnisse der Experimentellen Medizin
Ergeb Gesamten Tuberk Lungenforsch — Ergebnisse der Gesamten Tuberkulose- und Lungenforschung
Ergeb Gesamten Zahnheilkd — Ergebnisse der Gesamten Zahnheilkunde
Ergeb Hochvakuumtech Phys Duenner Schichten — Ergebnisse der Hochvakuumtechnik und der Physik Duenner Schichten
Ergeb Hyg Bakteriol Immunitaetsforsch Exp Ther — Ergebnisse der Hygiene, Bakteriologie, Immunitaetsforschung und ExperimentellenTherapie

Ergeb Immunitaetsforsch Exp Ther Bakteriol Hyg — Ergebnisse der Immunitaetsforschung, Experimentellen Therapie, Bakteriologie und Hygiene
Ergeb Inn Med Kinderheilkd — Ergebnisse der Inneren Medizin und Kinderheilkunde
Ergeb Klin Nuklearmed Ges Nuklearmed Jahrestag — Ergebnisse der Klinischen Nuklearmedizin, Diagnostik, Therapie, Forschung, Gesellschaft fuer Nuklearmedizin. Jahrestagung
Ergeb Kosm Phys — Ergebnisse der Kosmischen Physik
Ergeb Landwirtsch Forsch Justus Liebig Univ — Ergebnisse Landwirtschaftlicher Forschung an der Justus Liebig-Universitaet
Ergeb Limnol — Ergebnisse der Limnologie
Ergeb Math Grenzgeb — Ergebnisse der Mathematik und Ihrer Grenzgebiete
Ergeb Med Grundlagenforsch — Ergebnisse der Medizinischen Grundlagenforschung
Ergeb Mikrobiol Immunitaetsforsch — Ergebnisse der Mikrobiologie und Immunitaetsforschung
Ergeb Mikrobiol Immunitatsforsch Exp Ther — Ergebnisse der Mikrobiologie, Immunitaetsforschung, und Experimentellen Therapie
Ergebn Allg Path u Path Anat — Ergebnisse der Allgemeinen Pathologie und Pathologischen Anatomie des Menschen und der Tiere
Ergebn Biol — Ergebnisse der Biologie
Ergebn D Ges Med — Ergebnisse der Gesamte Medizin
Ergebn Exakt Natwiss — Ergebnisse der Exakten Naturwissenschaft
Ergebn Hyg — Ergebnisse der Hygiene, Bakterien-, Immunitaetsforschung, und Experimentellen Therapie
Ergebn Pflanzengeogr Durchforsch Wuerttemberg — Ergebnisse der Pflanzengeographischen Durchforschung von Wuerttemberg, Baden, und Hohenzollern
Ergebn Physiol — Ergebnisse der Physiologie, Biologischen Chemie, und Experimentellen Pharmakologie
Ergebn Wiss Untersuch Schweiz Nationalparkes — Ergebnisse der Wissenschaftlichen Untersuchung des Schweizerischen Nationalparkes/ Resultats des Recherches Scientifiques Entreprises au Parc National Suisse
Ergeb Pathol — Ergebnisse der Pathologie
Ergeb Physiol Biol Chem Exp Pharmakol — Ergebnisse der Physiologie, Biologischen Chemie, und Experimentellen Pharmakologie
Ergeb Plasmaphys Gaselektron — Ergebnisse der Plasmaphysik und der Gaselektronik
Ergeb Plasmaphysik Gaselektronik — Ergebnisse der Plasmaphysik und der Gaselektronik
Ergeb Tech Roentgenkd — Ergebnisse der Technischen Roentgenkunde
Ergeb Vitam Hormonforsch — Ergebnisse der Vitamin und Hormonforschung
Erg Exakt Naturw — Ergebnisse der Exakten Naturwissenschaften
Ergnzngsbde Ztschr Veterinaerk — Ergaenzungsbaende zur Zeitschrift fuer Veterinaerkunde
ERGOA — Ergonomics
ERGOAX — Ergonomics
ERGODATA — Banque de Donnees Internationales de Biometrie Humaine et d'Ergonomie
Ergon — Ergon tes Archaiologikes Hetaireias
Ergon Abstr — Ergonomics Abstracts
Ergonomics Abstr — Ergonomics Abstracts
Ergot — Ergoterapeuten
ERGS — ETC: A Review of General Semantics
ERGStrafs — Entscheidungen des Reichsgerichts in Strafsachen
ERGTB — Engineering Times
ERGWD — Energiewesen
ERGYA — Energy
ERGYD — Energyline
ERH — Euronet News
ERHAD — Elektro Radio Handel
Erhvervsh A — Erhvervshistorisk Arbog
Erhvo T — Erhvervsokonomisk Tidsskrift
Erhvsl — Erhvervsliv
ERI — Employee Benefit Research Institute. Policy Forum
ERIAD — Electric Power Research Institute (Report) EPRI AP
ERIC Abstr — ERIC [*Educational Resources Information Center*] Abstracts
ERIC Curr Index J Educ — ERIC [*Educational Resources Information Center*] Current Index to Journals in Education
Ericsson Rev — Ericsson Review
Ericsson Te — Ericsson Technics
Ericsson Tech — Ericsson Technics
E Riding Archaeol — East Riding Archaeologist
Erie — Erie County Legal Journal
Erie Co Leg J — Erie County Legal Journal
Erie Co L J (PA) — Erie County Law Journal (Pennsylvania)
ERIND — Electrical Review International
Er Is — Eretz - Israel
Er Isr — Eretz Israel. Archaeological, Historical, and Geographical Studies
ERJ — Economic Research Journal
Er J — Eranos Jahrbuch
Er Jb — Eranos Jahrbuch
Erjedesipari Kut Intez Kozl — Erjedesipari Kutato Intezet Koslemenyei
ERK — Maandschrift Economie
Erkr Zootiere Verhandlungsber Int Symp — Erkrankungen der Zootiere. Verhandlungsbericht des Internationalen Symposium ueber die Erkrankungen des Zootiere
ERKUA3 — Erdeszeti Kutatasok
Erkundung Bewertung Altlasten Wassertech Semin — Erkundung und Bewertung von Altlasten. Kriterien und Untersuchungsprogramme. Wassertechnisches Seminar
ERKZ — Evangelisch-Reformierte Kirchenzeitung
ERL — Employee Relations Law Journal
ERL — English Recusant Literature
ERL — Epigrafia Romana de Lerida

ERL — Etudes Romanes de Lund
Erlang Ab — Abhandlungen der Physikalisch-Medicinischen Societaet in Erlangen
Erlanger Baust Fraenk Heimatforsch — Erlanger Bausteine zur Fraenkischen Heimatforschung
Erlanger Forsch Reihe B — Erlanger Forschungen. Reihe B. Naturwissenschaften
Erlanger Geol Abh — Erlanger Geologische Abhandlungen
Erlanger Jb Bienenk — Erlanger Jahrbuch fuer Bienenkunde
Erlangische Gel Anmerk Nachr — Erlangische Gelehrte Anmerkungen und Nachrichten
Erlang Ps Md S Sb — Sitzungsberichte der Physikalisch-Medicinischen Societaet zu Erlangen
Erlang Sb Ps Md S — Sitzungsberichte der Physikalisch-Medicinischen Societaet zu Erlangen
Erlenmeyer Z — Zeitschrift fuer Chemie und Pharmacie. Erlenmeyer
ErlHb — Erlanger Heimatbuch
ERLIA6 — Ergebnisse der Limnologie
Erm — Ermitage
ERM — Euromoney
Erman Arch Rs — Archiv fuer Wissenschaftliche Kunde von Russland. Erman
ERN — Economic Review (New Delhi)
ERN — Installatie Journaal
Ernaehr Med — Ernaehrung in der Medizin
Ernaehr Pflanze — Ernaehrung der Pflanze
Ernaehr Umsch — Ernaehrungs-Umschau
Ernaehrungsforsch Inst Ernaehr (Potsdam) — Ernaehrungsforschung. Institut fuer Ernaehrung (Potsdam)
Ernaehrungsl Ernaehrungsprax — Ernaehrungslehre und Ernaehrungspraxis
Ernaehrungsl Prax — Ernaehrungslehre und- Praxis
Ernaehrungsprobl Arbeitsschutz — Ernaehrungsprobleme und Arbeitsschutz
Ernaehrungswirtsch Lebensmitteltech (Hamburg) — Ernaehrungswirtschaft. Lebensmitteltechnik (Hamburg)
Ernahrungsforsch Wiss Prax — Ernaehrungsforschung Wissenschaft und Praxis
Ernest Orlando Lawrence Berkeley Natl Lab Rep LBNL — Ernest Orlando Lawrence Berkeley National Laboratory. Report. LBNL
ERNFA7 — Ernaehrungsforschung
ERNSDF — Ernstia
Ernst Moritz Arndt Univ Greifsw Wiss Z Math Naturwiss Reihe — Ernst-Moritz-Arndt-Universitaet Greifswald. Wissenschaftliche Zeitschrift. Mathematisch-Naturwissenschaftliche Reihe
Ernst Moritz Arndt Univ Greifsw Wiss Z Med Reihe — Ernst-Moritz-Arndt-Universitaet Greifswald. Wissenschaftliche Zeitschrift. Medizinische Reihe
Ernst Rodenwaldt Arch — Ernst-Rodenwaldt-Archiv
Ernst Schering Res Found Workshop — Ernst Schering Research Foundation Workshop
E Rodenwaldt Arch — Ernst Rodenwaldt Archiv
Eroeterv Koezl — Eroeterv Koezlemenyek
Erosion Ceram Mater — Erosion of Ceramic Materials
ERPH — Etudes Religiouses, Philosophiques, Historiques, et Litteraire
ERPL — Elucidario Regionalista de Ponte do Lima
ERR — Economic Review. Federal Reserve Bank of Richmond
ERR — Editorial Research Reports
ERRC Publ US Agric Res Serv East Reg Res Cent — ERRC Publication. United States. Agricultural Research Service. Eastern Regional Research Center
ERRL Publ US Agric Res Serv East Reg Res Lab — ERRL Publication. United States. Agricultural Research Service. Eastern Regional Research Laboratory
ERS — Economic Research Service. Reports
ERS — Electronic Rig Stats
ERS — English Reprint Series
ERS — En Route Supplement
ErS — Erwin von Steinbach-Stift Studien
ERS — Ethnic and Racial Studies
ERS — European Research
ERS Staff Rep US Dep Agric Econ Res Serv — ERS Staff Report. United States Department of Agriculture. Economic Research Service
ERSTD — Energy Report to the States
Erste Verh Freyen Landw Ges Niederrhein Dept Strasburg — Erste Verhandlungen der Freyen Landwirthschafts-Gesellschaft des Niederrheinischen Departements zu Strasburg
ERT — Elektroniikka Radio Televisio
ERT — Evangelical Review of Theology
ERT (Energy Resour Technol) — ERT (Energy Resources and Technology) [Formerly, Energy Resources Report]
ERTLA7 — Elektroniikka Radio Televisio
ERTR — Egyptian Religious Texts and Representations
ERUMAT — Ernaehrungs-Umschau
Eruptive Sol Flares Proc Colloq No 133 Int Astron Union — Eruptive Solar Flares. Proceedings. Colloquium No. 133. International Astronomical Union
ERV — Electrical Review
ERVC — Etruscan Red-Figured Vase Painting at Caere
ERW — Economic Review
ERW — Entomological Review (Washington, D.C.)
ERW — European Research. Marketing, Opinion, Advertising
Erythrocyte Mech Blood Flow — Erythrocyte Mechanics and Blood Flow
Erythrocyte Membr Recent Clin Exp Adv — Erythrocyte Membranes. Recent Clinical and Experimental Advances
Erythrocyte Struct Funct Proc Int Conf Red Cell Metab Funct — Erythrocyte Structure and Function. Proceedings. International Conference on Red Cell Metabolism and Function
Erythropoiesis Proc Int Conf — Erythropoiesis. Proceedings. International Conference on Erythropoiesis
Erzeug Krankheitszustaenden Exp — Erzeugung von Krankheitszustaenden durch das Experiment
ES — Economia e Storia
ES — Economisch-Statistische Berichten

ES — Educadores
ES — Educational Studies
ES — Englisches Seminar
ES — Englische Studien
ES — English Studies
ES — Entsiklopedicheskii Slovar
Es — Escorial
ES — Espana Sagrada
Es — Esprit
Es — Essais
ES — Essays and Studies
ES — Esslinger Studien
ES — ESSO Magazine
ES — Estudios Segovianos
ES — Etnologiska Studier
ES — Etruskische Spiegel
ES — Journal of Environmental Systems
ESA — Educational Studies (Ames, Iowa)
ESA — Emakeele Seltsi Aastaraamat
ESA — English Studies in Africa
E/SA — ESA. Engage/Social Action
ESA — Etudes Sud-Arabiques
ESA — Eurasia Septentrionalis Antiqua
ESAB Rev Dtsch Ausg — ESAB [*Elektriska Svetsningsaktiebolaget*] Revue. Deutsche Ausgabe
ESAB Svetsaren — ESAB [*Elektriska Svetsningsaktiebolaget*] Svetsaren
ESAB Svetsaren Engl — ESAB (Elektriska Svetsningsaktiebolaget) Svetsaren in English
ESAB Tidn Svetsaren — ESAB [*Elektriska Svetsningsaktiebolaget*] Tidning Svetsaren
ESA Bull — ESA [*European Space Agency*] Bulletin
ESAfr — English Studies in Africa
ESAIM Controle Optim Calc Var — European Series in Applied and Industrial Mathematics. Controle, Optimisation, et Calcul des Variations
ESA J — ESA [*European Space Agency*] Journal
ESAJD — ESA [*European Space Agency*] Journal
Esakia Occas Pap Hikosan Biol Lab Entomol — Esakia Occasional Papers of the Hikosan Biological Laboratory in Entomology
ES & T — Environmental Science and Technology
ESAPDG — Environmental Sciences and Applications
ESAR — Economic Survey of Ancient Rome
ESARCL — Edinburgh School of Agriculture. Annual Report
ESASAM — Ecological Studies, Analysis, and Synthesis
ESA Sci and Tech Rev — ESA [*European Space Agency*] Scientific and Technical Review
ESA Spec Publ — ESA (European Space Agency) Special Publication
ESAUAS — Endocrine Society of Australia. Proceedings
ESB — Economisch-Statistische Berichten
ESB — Eigen Schoon en de Brabander
ESB — Encyclopedia of Southern Baptists
ESBGA — Eisenbahn-Ingenieur
ESBIAV — Essays in Biochemistry
ESBP — Ezik i Stil na Balgarskite Pisateli
ESBr — Eigen Schoon en de Brabander
ESBUAX — Estuarine Bulletin
ESC — Eastern Snow Conference Annual Meetings. Proceedings
ESC — English Studies in Canada
Esc — Escorial
EsC — Esprit Createur
ESC — Estudios Sociales Centroamericanos
ESC — Exuviae Sacrae Constantinopolitanae
Esc Agric — Escuela de Agricultura. Revista Mensual
Esc Agron Amazonia Bol — Escola de Agronomia da Amazonia. Boletim
Esc Agron Vet An Univ Fed Goias — Escola de Agronomia e Veterinaria. Anais. Universidade Federal de Goias
Esc Agron Vet Univ Fed Parana Rev — Escola de Agronomia e Veterinaria. Universidade Federal do Parana. Revista
ESCBA — Earth Science Bulletin
ESCC — Explorations. Studies in Culture and Communication
ESC Energ Stud Cent Rapp — ESC [*Energy Studie Centrum*]. Rapport
Esc Eng Univ Minas Gerais Inst Pesqui Radioat Publ — Escola de Engenharia. Universidade de Minas Gerais. Instituto de Pesquisas Radioativas. Publicacao
Esc Farm — Escuela de Farmacia
Esc Farm Guatem — Escuela de Farmacia Guatemala
EsCl — Estudios Clasicos
ESCLBC — Estomatologia e Cultura
Esc Minas Rev (Ouro Preto Braz) — Escola de Minas. Revista (Ouro Preto, Brazil)
Esc Nac Agric (Chapingo) Monogr — Escuela Nacional de Agricultura (Chapingo). Monografias
Esc Nac Agric (Chapingo) Rev — Escuela Nacional de Agricultura (Chapingo). Revista
Esc Nac Agric (Chapingo) Ser Apuntes — Escuela Nacional de Agricultura (Chapingo). Serie de Apuntes
Esc Nac Agric (Chapingo) Ser Invest — Escuela Nacional de Agricultura (Chapingo). Serie de Investigaciones
Esc Nac Ing Bol Lima — Escuela Nacional de Ingenieros. Boletin (Lima)
Escola Secund Rio — Escola Secundaria (Rio de Janeiro)
Esc Opt Cuantica Curso — Escuela de Optica Cuantica. Curso
Esc Super Agric Luiz De Queiroz (Sao Paulo) Bol — Escola Superior de Agricultura "Luiz De Queiroz" (Sao Paulo). Boletin
Esc Veran Espectrosc — Escuela de Verano sobre Espectroscopia
ESD — Energy Systems and Policy
ESD — Estudios Sociales
ESDBAK — Eisei Dobutsu
ESDCA — Endocrinologia e Scienze della Costituzione

ESDU Data Items — Engineering Sciences Data Unit. Data Items
EsDXX — Espaces. Documents XXe Seicle
ESE — Encyclopedie des Sciences Ecclesiastiques
ESE — Review of the Economic Situation of Mexico
E Sec — L'Enseignement Secondaire
ESEE — Etudes Slaves et Est-Europeenes. Slavic and East European Studies
E Sef — Estudios Sefardies
E Seg — Estudios Segovianos
ESELL — Essays and Studies in English Language and Literature
ES Etude Spec Minist Richesses Nat Que — ES [*Etude Speciale*]. Ministere des Richesses Naturelles du Quebec
ESFM — Estudios, Notas, y Trabelhos de Servico de Fomento Mineiro
ESGM — Eta Sigma Gamma
ESH — Ecumenical Studies in History
ESHAA3 — Engei Shikenjo Hokoku. A. Hiratsuka
ESHBA6 — Engei Shikenjo Hokoku. B. Okitsu
ESHDAC — Engei Shikenjo Hokoku. D. Kurume
ESHDM — Etudes et Documents. Societe d'Histoire et d'Art du Diocese de Meaux
ESHG — Etudes Suisses d'Histoire Generale
ESI — Edizioni Scientifiche Italiane
EsI — Essex Institute Historical Collections
Esic-Market Estud Gestion Com Empr — Esic-Market, Estudios de Gestion Comercial y Empresa
ESISD — ESIS Newsletter
ESIS Newsl — ESIS [*European Shielding Information Service*] Newsletter
Esitelmat Poytak Suom Tiedeakat — Esitelmat ja Poytakirjat. Suomalainen Tiedeakatemia
ESJ — Elgar Society Journal
ESKGA — Eisei Kagaku
ESKGA2 — Eisei Kagaku
ESKHA — Eisei Shikenjo Hokoku
ESKHA5 — Eisei Shikenjo Hokoku
ESKI — Eskimo
ESKTD — Elektrotekhnicheskaya Promyshlennost. Seriya. Khimicheskie i Fizicheskie Istochniki Toka
ESL — (El) Sol
ESI — Etudes Slaves et Est-Europeennes
ESI — Etudes Slaves et Est-Europeennes. Slavic and East-European Studies
ESL — European Studies in Law
ESL — Evangelisches Soziallexikon
ESLR — Etudes Slaves et Roumaines
ESM — Escritos (Medillin)
ESMED9 — Ethics in Science and Medicine
ESMS — Eta Sigma Gamma. Monograph Series
ESMSLCC — Edward Sapir Monograph Series in Language, Culture, and Cognition
ESn — Englische Studien
ESNAAX — Essex Naturalist
ESNA Work Group Waste Irradiat Proc Int Conf — ESNA Working Group on Waste Irradiation. Proceedings. International Conference
ESO SRC CERN Conf Res Programmes New Large Telesc — ESO/SRC/CERN Conference on Research Programmes for the New Large Telescopes
ESOUA — Ekonomika Sovetskoi Ukrainy
ESov — Etudes Sovietiques
ESP — Energy Systems and Policy
ESP — English for Specific Purposes
ESP — English Symposium Papers
Esp — Esprit. Revue Internationale
EsP — Espuela de Plata
ESP — Estate Planning
EspA — Espanol Actual
Espace Geogr — Espace Geographique
Espaces et Soc — Espaces et Societes
ESPAHA — Estudios. Seminario de Prehistoria Arqueologia et Historia Antigua. Facultad deFilosofia y Letras de Zaragoza
Espana Mod — Espana Moderna
EspCr — Esprit Createur
Esp Dig — Espinasse's Digest of the Law of Actions at Nisi Prius
Esper Ricer Ist Agr Gen Colt Erbacee Univ Pisa — Esperienza e Ricerche. Istituto di Agronomia Generale e Coltivazioni Erbacee. Universita di Pisa
ESPES — Especialidades Farmaceuticas Espanolas
Esp Ganad — Espana Ganadera
Espionage Mag — Espionage Magazine
EspL — Esprit des Lettres. Revue Internationale d'Echange et de Culture
EspN — Espana Nueva
EspP — Esprit Public
Espr — Esprit
Esprit Cr — Esprit Createur
Esp Sag — Espana Sagrada
ESPSL — O Estado de Sao Paulo. Suplemento Literario
ESQ — Emerson Society. Quarterly
Esq — Esquire
Esquisses Math — Esquisses Mathematiques
ESR — Economic and Social Review
ESR — Emory Sources and Reprints
ESR — [*The*] Ethnic Studies Report
ESR — Etudes de Science Religieuse
ESR — Etudes Slaves et Roumaines
ESR — European Studies Review
ESR — Extension Service Review
ESR Appl Polym Res Proc Nobel Symp — ESR Applications to Polymer Research. Proceedings. Nobel Symposium
ESRBB — Energeticheskoe Stroitel'stvo za Rubezhom
ESREA — Earth Science Reviews
ESREAV — Earth-Science Reviews
ESREDY — Estuarine Research

ESRFR — Environmental Studies Revolving Funds Report
ESRLA — Estudios Socio-Religiosos Latino-Americanos
ESRN — ESSO [*Standard Oil*] Resources News
ESRNBP — Specialist Periodical Reports. Electron Spin Resonance
ESRO/ELDO Bull — ESRO/ELDO [*European Space Research Organization/ European Launcher Development Organization*] Bulletin
ESRS — Emporia State Research Studies
ESS — Encyclopaedia of the Social Sciences
ESs — English Studies
ESS — Environmental Science Series
ESS — Erasmus Speculum Scientiarum
Ess — Essai
Ess — Essence
EssAF — Essays. Albert Feuillerat
Essais Critiques — Essais Critiques, Artistiques, Philosophiques, et Litteraires
Essay Gen Lit Index — Essay and General Literature Index
Essay Phys — Essays in Physics
Essays Appl Microbiol — Essays in Applied Microbiology [*monograph*]
Essays Arts Sci — Essays in Arts and Sciences
Essays Biochem — Essays in Biochemistry
Essays Can Wri — Essays on Canadian Writing
Essays Chem — Essays in Chemistry
Essays Crit — Essays in Criticism
Essays Fr L — Essays in French Literature
Essays Fundam Immunol — Essays in Fundamental Immunology
Essays Geol Azerb — Essays on Geology of the Azerbaijan
Essays Lit — Essays in Literature
Essays Med Biochem — Essays in Medical Biochemistry
Essays Mod Mus — Essays on Modern Music
Essays Neurochem Neuropharmacol — Essays in Neurochemistry and Neuropharmacology
Essays Observ Phys Lit Soc Edinburgh — Essays and Observations. Physical and Literary. Read Before a Society in Edinburgh and Published by Them.
Essays Pap — Essays and Papers. Soong Jun University
Essays Pap Soong Jun Univ — Essays and Papers. Soong Jun University
Essays Phys — Essays in Physics
Essays Poet — Essays in Poetics
Essays Publ Works Hist — Essays in Public Works History
Essays Stud — Essays and Studies
Essays Stud Fac Hiroshima Jogakuin Coll — Essays and Studies by the Faculty of Hiroshima Jogakuin College
Essays Toxicol — Essays in Toxicology
Essay Toxico — Essays in Toxicology
EssB — Essays and Studies in Honor of Carleton Brown
Ess C — Essais Catholiques
EssCr — Essais Critiques, Artistiques, Philosophiques et Litteraires
Ess Crit — Essays in Criticism
Essent Pharmacol — Essentials of Pharmacology
Essent Student Algebra — Essential Student Algebra
Essenze Deriv Agrum — Essenze e Derivati Agrumari
Essex Archaeol Hist — Essex Archaeology and History
Essex Arch Hist — Essex Archaeology and History
Essex Co N H Soc J — Essex County Natural History Society. Journal
Essex I Bll — Bulletin of the Essex Institute
Essex I His — Essex Institute. Historical Collections
Essex Inst Annual Rep — Essex Institute. Annual Report
Essex Inst B — Essex Institute. Bulletin
Essex Inst Coll — Essex Institute. Historical Collections
Essex Inst Hist Coll — Essex Institute. Historical Collections
Essex Inst Hist Collect — Essex Institute. Historical Collections
Essex Inst Pr — Essex Institute. Proceedings
Essex I P — Proceedings of the Essex Institute
Essex J — Essex Journal
Essex Nat (Lond) — Essex Naturalist (London)
Essex Natur — Essex Naturalist
Essex Ntlist — Essex Naturalist. Being the Journal of the Essex Field Club
EssM — Jesuit Thinkers of the Renaissance. Essays Presented to John F. McCormick, S.J.
ESSN — ESSO North
Esso Agr — Esso Agricola
Esso Ant — Esso in the Antilles
ESSO Mag — ESSO Magazine
ESSO Oilways Int — ESSO [*Standard Oil*] Oilways International
Essor Frigorif Fr — Essor Frigorifique Francais
Ess R — Essex Review
ESSSD — Ekonomicheskoe Sotrudnichestvo Stran-Chlenov SEV
EST — Economisch en Sociaal Tijdschrift
E St — Eichstaetter Studien
ESt — Englische Studien
ESt — English Studies
ESt — Erlanger Studien
Est — Estudios
EstA — Estudios Americanos
Est A Alava — Estudios de Arqueologia Alavesa
Est Abulenses — Estudios Abulenses
Estac Cent Ecol Bol (Spain) — Estacion Central de Ecologia. Boletin (Spain)
Estac Exp Agric La Molina Bol — Estacion Experimental Agricola de La Molina. Boletin
Estac Exp Agric Tucuman Bol — Estacion Experimental Agricola de Tucuman. Boletin
Estac Exp Agric Tucuman Circ — Estacion Experimental Agricola de Tucuman. Circular
Estac Exp Agric Tucuman Publ — Estacion Experimental Agricola de Tucuman. Publicacion

Estac Exp Agric Tucuman Publ Misc — Estacion Experimental Agricola de Tucuman. Publicacion Miscelanea

Estac Exp Agropecu Pergamino Bol Divulg — Estacion Experimental Agropecuaria Pergamino. Boletin de Divulgacion

Estac Exp Agropecu Pergamino Publ Tec — Estacion Experimental Agropecuaria Pergamino. Publicacion Tecnico

Estac Exp Aula dei Zaragoza Bol — Estacion Experimental de Aula dei Zaragoza. Boletin

Estac Exp Aula dei Zaragoza Dep Mejora Ens — Estacion Experimental de Aula dei Zaragoza. Departamento de Mejora Ensayos

Estac Exp Reg Agropecu Parana Ser Notas Tec — Estacion Experimental Regional Agropecuaria Parana. Serie Notas Tecnicas

Estadist Espanola — Estadistica Espanola

Estadistica Esp — Estadistica Espanola

Estad Mex Wash — Estadistica. Journal. Inter-American Statistical Institute (Mexico, DF; Washington, DC)

Estad Peru Lima — Estadistica Peruana (Lima)

Est Ag — Estudio Agustiniano

Est Am — Estudios Americanos. Revista. Escuela de Estudios Hispano Americanos de Sevilla

Est and Tr Q — Estates and Trusts Quarterly

Est and Tr Rep — Estates and Trusts Reports

Estates Gaz — Estates Gazette

Estates Q — Estates and Trusts Quarterly

Estates Times Rev — Estates Times Review

EstB — Estudios Biblicos

EstBib — Estudios Biblicos

Est Biblicos — Estudios Biblicos. Organo de la Asociacion para el Fomento de Estudios Biblicosen Espana. CSIC (Consejo Superior de Investigaciones Cientificas)

ESTCC — Eighteenth-Century Short Title Catalogue

Est Cl — Estudios Clasicos

Est Clas — Estudios Clasicos

Est Clasicos — Estudios Clasicos. Anejo de Bordon. Sociedad Espanola de Pedagogia

Est Coas M — Estuarine and Coastal Marine Science

Est Contrib Int Biol Programme Prog Rep — Estonian Contributions to the International Biological Programme. Progress Report

Est Cult Maya — Estudios de Cultura Maya

EstD — Estudios. Duquesne University

Est de Arq Alavesa — Estudios de Arqueologia Alavesa

Est Demograficos — Estudios Demograficos

Est Deusto — Estudios de Deusto. Revista Dirigida. Profesores de las Facultades de Derecho yEconomia. Universidad de Deusto

EstdH — Estudios de Hispanofila

EstE — Estudios Eclesiasticos

EstE — Estudios Escenicos

EstEcl — Estudios Eclesiasticos

Est Ecles — Estudios Eclesiasticos. Revista Trimestral de Investigacion e Informacion Teologica. Publicada. Facultad de Teologia de la Compania de Jesus en Espana

Est Edad Media Corona Aragon — Estudios de Edad Media de la Corona de Aragon CSIC (Consejo Superior de Investigaciones Cientificas)

Estel-Ber Forsch Entwickl Unserer Werke — Estel-Berichte aus Forschung und Entwicklung Unserer Werke

Estestv Proizv Sily Rossii — Estestvennye Proizvoditel'nye Sily Rossii

Est Europ — Est Europeen

EstF — Estudios Franciscanos

Est Fil — Estudios Filosoficos

EstFilRelOr — Estudios de Filosofia y Religion Orientales

EstFr — Estudios Franciscanos

EstFranc — Estudios Franciscanos

Est Francisc — Estudios Franciscanos. Revista Cuatrimestral de Ciencias Eclesiasticas Publicada por los P.P. Capuchinos de Espana y America

Est Gaz — Estates Gazette

Est Gaz Dig — Estates Gazette Digest of Land and Property Cases

Est Geogr — Estudios Geograficos. CSIC (Consejo Superior de Investigaciones Cientificas)

Est Geologicos — Estudios Geologicos. CSIC (Consejo Superior de Investigaciones Cientificas)

ESTHA — Environmental Science and Technology

Est Hist Mod — Estudios de Historia Moderna. Centro de Estudios Historicos Internacionales. Universidad de Barcelona

Est Hist Social Esp — Estudios de Historia Social de Espana. CSIC (Consejo Superior de Investigaciones Cientificas)

EstHM — Estudios de Historia Moderna

Esti Loodus Tartu — Esti Loodus. Tartu Ulikooli Juures Oleva Loodusuurijate Seltsi Teataja. Esti Loodus Estonian Nature/Periodical. Society of Nature Investigators. University of Tartu

Estilo S Luis Potosi — Estilo. Revista de Cultura (San Luis Potosi, Mexico)

Esti Vabariigi Tartu Ulik Toimet — Acta et Commentationes Universitatis Tartuensis. A. Mathematica, Physica, Medica/Esti Vabariigi Tartu Ulikooli Toimetused

Est Jos — Estudios Josefinos

Est Learned Soc Am Yearb — Estonian Learned Society in America. Yearbook

EstLit — Estafeta Literaria

Est Lul — Estudios Lulioanos

EstMar — Estudios Marianos

Est Medievales — Estudios Medievales

Est Miss — Estudios Missionaries

EStn — Englische Studien

Est Nauchn Issled Inst Zemled Melior Sb Nauchn Tr — Estonskii Nauchno-Issledovatel'skii Institut Zemledeliya i Melioratsii. SbornikNauchnykh Trudov

Estomatol Cult — Estomatologia e Cultura

Est On — Estudios Onienses

EstOr — Estudios Orientales

Est-Ouest — Est et Ouest. Bulletin de l'Association d'Etudes et d'Informations Politiques Internationales

Est Pedag — Estudios Pedagogicos. Instituto San Jose de Calasanz de la Excma. Diputacion deZaragoza

Est Plan — Estate Planning

Est Polit — Estudios Politicos

Estr — Estreno. Cuadernos del Teatro Espanol Contemporaneo

Est Rom — Estudis Romanics

Est Romanics — Estudis Romanics

ESTS — Early Scottish Text Society

Est Seg — Estudios Segovianos

Est Segovianos — Estudios Segovianos. Revista Historica del Centro de Estudios Segovianos

Estuar Coast Shelf Sci — Estuarine Coastal and Shelf Science

Estuaries Pac Northwest Proc Tech Conf — Estuaries of the Pacific Northwest. Proceedings. Technical Conference

Estuarine Bull — Estuarine Bulletin

Estuarine Coastal Mar Sci — Estuarine and Coastal Marine Science

Estuarine Coastal Shelf Sci — Estuarine, Coastal, and Shelf Science

Estuarine Res — Estuarine Research

EStud — English Studies

Estud Agrar — Estudios Agrarios. Centro de Investigaciones Agrarias

Estud Agron — Estudos Agronomicos

Estud Agron Missao Estud Agron Ultramar — Estudos Agronomicos. Missao de Estudos Agronomicos do Ultramar

Estud Am Sevilla — Estudios Americanos (Sevilla)

Estud Andin — Estudios Andinos

Estud Arqueol Antofagasta — Estudios Arqueologicos. Publicacion Cientifica. Universidad de Chile (Antofagasta, Chile)

Estud As Afr — Estudios de Asia y Africa

Estud BA — Estudios. Academia Literaria del Plata (Buenos Aires)

Estud Bras Rio — Estudos Brasileiros. Instituto de Estudos Brasileiros (Rio de Janeiro)

Estud Bucaramanga — Estudio (Bucaramanga, Colombia)

Estud CEBRAP — Estudios CEBRAP

Estud Cl — Estudios Clasicos

Estud Clas — Estudios Clasicos

Estud Comunismo Santiago — Estudios Sobre el Comunismo (Santiago)

Estud Coop — Estudios Cooperativos

Estud Cult Maya — Estudios de Cultura Maya

Estud Cult Nahuatl — Estudios de Cultura Nahuatl

Estud Derecho 2a Epoca — Estudios de Derecho. Segunda Epoca

Estud Der Medellin — Estudios de Derecho. Facultad de Derecho y Ciencias Politicas. Universidad de Antioquia (Medellin, Colombia)

Estud Econ — Estudios de Economia

Estud Econ (Argentina) — Estudios sobre la Economia (Argentina)

Estud Econs — Estudios Economicos

Estud Empresar — Estudios Empresariales

Estud Empresariales — Estudios Empresariales

Estud Ensaios Doc Junta Invest Cient Ultramar (Port) — Estudos, Ensaios, e Documentos. Junta de Investigacoes Cientificas do Ultramar (Portugal)

Estud Espec Serv Geol Min (Peru) — Estudios Especiales. Servicio de Geologia y Mineria (Peru)

Estud Esteril — Estudios sobre Esterilidad

Estud Extremenos — Estudios Extremenos; Revista Historica, Literaria, y Artistica

Estud Fauna Port — Estudos sobre a Fauna Portuguesa

Estud Filol Valdivia — Estudios Filologicos (Valdivia, Chile)

Estud Filosof — Estudios Filosoficos

Estud Geogr — Estudios Geograficos

Estud Geogr Inst Juan Sebastian Elcano — Estudios Geograficos. Instituto "Juan Sebastian Elcano"

Estud Geol Inst Invest Geol "Lucas Mallada" — Estudios Geologicos. Instituto de Investigaciones Geologicas "Lucas Mallada"

Estud Geol Inst Invest Geol Lucas Mallada (Madrid) — Estudios Geologicos. Instituto de Investigaciones Geologicos Lucas Mallada (Madrid)

Estud Geol (Madr) — Estudios Geologicos (Madrid)

Estud Hist Agrar — Estudis d'Historia Agraria

Estud Hist Guadalajara — Estudios Historicos (Guadalajara, Mexico)

Estud Hist Marilia — Estudos Historicos (Marilia, Brazil)

Estud Ib-Am — Estudos Ibero-Americanos

E Studies — English Studies

Estud Inform Serv Flor Aquic (Portugal) — Estudos e Informacao. Servicos Florestais e Aquicolas (Portugal)

Estud Int — Estudios Internacionales

Estud Internac — Estudios Internacionales

EstudiosD — Estudios. Revista de Cultura Hispanica

Estudios Geol — Estudios Geologicos

Estudios Teol (Guatemala) — Estudios Teologicos (Guatemala)

Estud Legis — Estudos Legislativos

Estud Leopold — Estudos Leopoldenses

Estud Notas Trab Inst Geol Min — Estudos, Notas e Trabalhos do Instituto Geologico e Mineiro

Estud Notas Trab Serv Fom Min Lab DGGM Portugal — Estudos, Notas, e Trabathos. Servico de Fomento Mineiro e Laboratorio da DGGM [Direccao-Geral de Geologia e Minas] (Portugal)

Estud Notas Trab Serv Fom Min (Port) — Estudos. Notas e Trabalhos do Servico de Fomento Mineiro (Portugal)

ESTUDO — Estuaries

Estudos Agron — Estudos Agronomicos

Estudos Mat Inform — Estudos Matematica e Informatica

Estudos Teol (Brazil) — Estudos Teologicos (Brazil)

Estud Panama — Estudios. Instituto Nacional de Panama (Panama)

Estud Parag — Estudios Paraguayos

Estud Poblac — Estudios de Poblacion

Estud Quim Inst Nac Invest Ind (Port) — Estudos de Quimica. Instituto Nacional de Investigacao Industrial (Portugal)
Estud Sedimentol — Estudos Sedimentologicos
Estud Segov — Estudios Segovianos
Estud Sindic — Estudios Sindicales
Estud Sindicales — Estudios Sindicales
Estud Sindicales y Coops — Estudios Sindicales y Cooperativos
Estud Soc — Estudios Sociales. Revista de Ciencias Sociales
Estud Soc C — Estudios Sociales Centroamericanos
Estud Soc Centroam — Estudios Sociales Centroamericanos
Estud Soc Centroamer — Estudios Sociales Centroamericanos
Estud Social — Estudios Sociales
Estud Soc Rio — Estudos Sociais (Rio de Janeiro)
Estud Tecnol — Estudos Tecnologicos. Acta Geologica Leopoldensia
Estud Tec Serv Inf Agric Braz — Estudos Tecnicos. Servico de Informacao Agricola (Brazil)
Est Zaragoza — Estudios. Seminario de Prehistoria, Arqueologia, e Historia Antigua. Facultad de Filosofia y Letras de Zaragoza
ESU — Educacion Superior
ESU Bus Rev — Emporia State University. Business Review
ESY — Economisch en Sociaal Tijdschrift
ET — Economist
ET — Educational and Industrial Television
ET — Educational Television
ET — Eildon Tree
ET — Ekonomisk Tidskrift
ET — Epitheorese Technes
Et — Ethics
ET — Ethnomusicology
Et — Etoiles
Et — Etudes
ET — Etudes et Travaux. Travaux du Centre d'Archeologie Mediterraneenne de l'Academie Polonaise de Sciences
ET — Etudes Traditionnelles
ET — European Taxation
ET — European Trends
ET — Evangelische Theologie
ET — Expository Times
ET — Foreign Economic Trends and Their Implications for the United States
ET — Journal of Educational Technology
ETA — Etudes Administratives
EtA — Etudes Anglaises
ETAb — English Teaching Abstracts
ETAC — Etudes d'Archeologie Classique
ETA Elektrowaerme Tech Ausbau Ed A — ETA. Elektrowaerme im Technischen Ausbau. Edition A
E Tal — Ha-Ensiqlopedija Ha-Talmudit
ETAM — Etudes et Travaux d'Archeologie Marocaine
Et Ang — Etudes Anglaises
Et Angl — Etudes Anglaises
ETANSW News — English Teachers Association of New South Wales. Newsletter
Et Ar — Etudes Arabes
ETARAQ — Entomologische Arbeiten. Museum G. Frey (Tutzing-bei Muenchen)
ETAT — Eesti NSV Teaduste Akadeemia Toimetised. Uhiskonnateaduste Seeria
ETATA — Eesti NSV Teaduste Akadeemia. Toimetised. Bioloogia
ETATAW — Eesti NSV Teaduste Akadeemia. Toimetised. Bioloogia
Etat San Animaux Belgique — Etat Sanitaire des Animaux de la Belgique
Etat Solide Rapp Discuss Cons Phys Inst Int Phys Solvay — Etat Solide, Rapports et Discussions. Conseil de Physique. Institut International de Physique. Solvay
Et B — Etudes Bibliques
EtBalk — Etudes Balkaniques
Et Balkan — Etudes Balkaniques
EtBer — Etudes Bergsoniennes
ETBKAV — Entomologische Berichten
ETB TUG — ETB - TUG. Equipement Technique du Batiment - Technische Uitrusting van het Gebouw
EtByz — Etudes Byzantines
ETC — Environmental Toxicology and Chemistry
EtC — Et Caetera
Et Camer — Etudes Camerounaises
Et Carm — Etudes Carmelitaines
EtCCS — Etudes Canadiennes/Canadian Studies
Et Celt — Etudes Celtiques
Et Celtiques — Etudes Celtiques
Et Chypr — Etudes Chypriotes
EtCi — Etudes Cinematographiques
ETCJ — Etudes Theologiques de la Compagnie de Jesus
EtCl — Etudes Classiques
Et Cl Aix — Etudes Classiques. Faculte des Lettres et Sciences Humaines d'Aix
Et Class — Etudes Classiques
Et Cong — Etudes Congolaises
Et Congol — Etudes Congolaises
Et Conj — Etudes et Conjoncture
ETC Quart Index — European Translations Centre. Quarterly Index
EtCr — Etudes Creoles
Et Cret — Etudes Cretoises
ETC Rev Gen — ETC: A Review of General Semantics
Et Dahom — Etudes Dahomeennes
Et de Philos Mediev — Etudes de Philosophie Medievale
Et Doc Cons d'Etat — Etudes et Documents. Conseil d'Etat
ETEAA — Entomologia Experimentalis et Applicata
ETEAAT — Entomologia Experimentalis et Applicata
Et Eburn — Etudes Eburneennes
Et Ec — Etudes Economiques

Et Econ (Mons) — Etudes Economiques (Mons, Belgium)
Et Ec Rur — Etudes d'Economie Rurale
E Tenn Hist Soc Pub — East Tennessee Historical Society. Publications
Et Epigr et Philol — Etudes Epigraphiques et Philologiques
Eter — Eternity Magazine
ETERD — Energy Technology Review
Et et Conj — Etudes et Conjoncture
Et et Doc (Educ Nat) — Etudes et Documents (Education Nationale)
Et Et Expans — Etudes et Expansion
ETF — Estudios Teologicos y Filosoficos
EtF — Etudes Franciscaines
Et Fr — Etudes Francaises
Et Franc — Etudes Francaises
EtFranc — Etudes Franciscaines
Et Francisc — Etudes Franciscaines. Revue Mensuelle
ETGAA5 — Entomologist's Gazette
Et Gaul — Etudes Gaulliennes
Et Germ — Etudes Germaniques
ETG Fachber — ETG [*Energietechnische Gesellschaft Im Vde*] Fachberichte
Et Gr — Etudes Gregoriennes
Et Greg — Etudes Gregoriennes
Et Guin — Etudes Guineennes
E Th — Elizabethan Theatre
Eth — Ethics. An International Journal of Social, Political, and Legal Philosophy
ETH — Ethnologica [*Koeln*]
Eth — Ethnomusicology
Eth — Ethnos
ETH — Etudes de Theologie et d'Histoire de la Spiritualite
EthF — Ethnie Francaise
EthF — Ethnologia Fennica
Ethics Animals — Ethics and Animals
Ethics Sci Med — Ethics in Science and Medicine
Ethiop Geogr J — Ethiopian Geographical Journal
Ethiop Geol Surv Annu Rep — Ethiopia Geological Survey. Annual Report
Ethiop Geol Surv Bull — Ethiopia Geological Survey. Bulletin
Ethiopian J Dev Res — Ethiopian Journal of Development Research
Ethiopian Libr Ass Bull — Ethiopian Library Association Bulletin
Ethiopia Obs — Ethiopia Observer
Ethiop Inst Agric Res Rep — Ethiopian Institute of Agricultural Research. Report
Ethiop Med J — Ethiopian Medical Journal
Ethiop Pharm J — Ethopian Pharmaceutical Journal
Et Hist — Etudes Historiques
Et Hist — Etudes Historiques. Nouvelle Serie
Et Hist Mod — Etudes d'Histoire Moderne et Contemporaine
Et Hist Mod Contemp — Etudes d'Histoire Moderne et Contemporaine
EThL — Ephemerides Theologicae Lovanienses
E Th L B — Ephemerides Theologicae Lovanienses. Bibliotheca
Eth Mus — Ethno-Musicologica
Ethmus — Ethnomusicology
Ethmus Sel Repts — Ethnomusicology. Selected Reports
Ethn — Ethnographia
Ethn — Ethnohistory
Ethn Arch Z — Ethnographisch-Archaeologische Zeitschrift
Ethn Arch Zeitschr — Ethnographisch-Archaeologische Zeitschrift
Ethn Bud — Ethnographia (Budapest)
Ethn Dis — Ethnicity and Disease
Ethn Health — Ethnicity and Health
Ethnic & Racial Stud — Ethnic and Racial Studies
Ethnic Racial Stud — Ethnic and Racial Studies
Ethnic Stud — Ethnic Studies
Ethnic Stud Bibliogr — Ethnic Studies Bibliography
Ethno — Ethnohistory
EthnoE — Ethnologia Europaea
EthnoF — Ethnologie Francaise
Ethnog — Ethnographie. Paris
Ethnogr Arch — Ethnographisches Archiv
Ethnogr Archaeol Forsch — Ethnographisch-Archaeologische Forschungen
Ethnogr Archaeologische Z — Ethnographisch-Archaeologische Zeitschrift
Ethnogr Archaeol Z — Ethnographisch-Archaeologische Zeitschrift
Ethnogr AZ — Ethnographisch-Archaeologische Zeitschrift
Ethnogr Mus Univ Oslo Yb — Ethnographic Museum. University of Oslo. Yearbook
Ethnohist — Ethnohistory
Ethnol — Ethnologica. Koeln
Ethnol Amer — Ethnologia Americana
Ethnol Anz — Ethnologischer Anzeiger
Ethnol Eur — Ethnologia Europaea
Ethnol Europ — Ethnologia Europaea
Ethnol Fenn — Ethnologia Fennica
Ethnol Fennica — Ethnologia Fennica
Ethnol Fr — Ethnologie Francaise
Ethnol Franc — Ethnologie Francaise
Ethnol Pol — Ethnologia Polona
Ethnol Scand — Ethnologia Scandinavica
Ethnol Slav — Ethnologia Slavica
Ethnol Soc Lond Trans — Ethnological Society of London. Transactions
Ethnol Z — Ethnologische Zeitschrift
Ethnol Z Zuerich — Ethnologische Zeitschrift Zuerich
Ethnomedizin — Ethnomedizin. Ethnomedicine Zeitschrift fuer Interdisziplinare Forschung
Ethnomusic — Ethnomusicology
Ethnomusicol — Ethnomusicology
Ethno-Psych — Ethno-Psychologie
Ethno-Psychol — Ethno-Psychologie
Ethno Z — Ethnologisch Zeitschrift
Ethn Racial Stud — Ethnic and Racial Studies

Ethn Stud — Ethnic Studies
Ethol Ecol Evol — Ethology, Ecology, and Evolution
Et Hong — Etudes Hongroises
Ethp — Ethnopsychologie
EThR — Etudes Theologiques et Religieuses
Eth Rec — Ethical Record
E Th S — Erfurter Theologische Schriften
Eth S — Ethnologia Slavica
ETHS — Etudes de Theologie et d'Histoire de la Spiritualite
Eth Sc — Ethnologia Scandinavica
ETI — Electronics Today International
ETI — En Terre d'Islam
ETI — Foreign Economic Trends and Their Implications for the United States
EtIE — Etudes Indo-Europeennes
ETiM — Echo Teatrolne i Muzyczne
ETINA — Electronique Industrielle
Et Int — Etudes Internationales
ETIS — Environmental Technical Information System
Et It — Etudes Italiennes
ETITA — Energetekhnologicheskow Ispol'zovanie Toplova
Et Ital — Etudes Italiennes
ETJ — Educational Theatre Journal
ET J — ET [*Enterostomal Therapy*] Journal
Et J — Etudes Juives
EtK — Epeteris tou Kalabryton
ETKKA — Elteknik
ETL — Ephemerides Theologicae Lovanienses
EtL — Etudes de Lettres
ETL — Explicacion de Textos Literarios
ETLA — Epeteris tou Laographikov Arkheiov
EtLA — Etudes de Linguistique Appliquee
Et Lettres — Etudes des Lettres
Et Loire — Etudes Prehistoriques et Protohistoriques des Pays de la Loire
EtM — Etudes Mediterraneennes
ETM — Excise Tax Memoranda
ETM — Export Turkey Magazine
Et Mal — Etudes Maliennes
EtMar — Etudes Mariales
ETMDAA — Entomologiske Meddelelser
ETMNA — Entomological News
ETMR — Education and Training in Mental Retardation
ETMR — Education and Training of the Mentally Retarded
ETMSB — Ethnomusicology
Et Mu — Etudes Musulmanes
ETN — Elektrotechniek; Technisch-Economisch Tijdschrift
Etn — Etnografija. Moskva
ETNKA — Energietechnik
ETNLB6 — Ethnology
Etnoantrop Probl — Etnoantropoloski Problemi. Casopis
Etnogr Juz Slav Madar — Etnografija Juznih Slavena u Madarskoj
EtnogrMuus Aastar — EtnograafiaMuuseumi Aastaraamat
Etnogr Polska — Etnografia Polska
Etnogr Shqipt — Etnografia Shqiptare
Etnol Antropol Cult — Etnologia Antropologia Culturale
Etnol Istraz — Etnoloska Istrazivanja
Etnol Pregl — Etnoloski Pregled
Etnol Stud — Etnologiska Studier
Etnol Trib — Etnoloska Tribina
Et Normandes — Etudes Normandes
Et Notes Inform Batiment — Etudes et Notes d'Information. Direction du Batiment et des Travaux Publics et de la Conjoncture
ETNSAQ — Etnologiska Studier
Etn St — Etnologiska Studier
ETO — (El) Tiempo
Et O — Etudes Orientales. Institut Francaise d'Archeologie de Stamboul
ETOCDK — Environmental Toxicology and Chemistry
ETO Multicent Mol Integr Proc Int Conf — ETO (Exponential-Type Atomic Orbitals) Multicenter Molecular Integrals. Proceedings. International Conference
ETOPBN — Etizenia
ETOPD — Energy Topics
Et Or — Etudes Orientales
ETOXAC — Essays in Toxicology
EtP — Etnoloski Pregled
Et P — Etudes de Papyrologie
ETP — Excise Tariff Proposals
Et Pap — Etudes de Papyrologie
EtPapyr — Etudes de Papyrologie
Et Pelop — Etudes Peloponnesiennes
Et Pezenas — Etudes sur Pezenas et l'Herault
ETPH — Etudes de Theologie, de Philosophie, et d'Histoire
EtPL — Etudes Philosophiques et Litteraires
Et Planning Familial — Etudes de Planning Familial
EtPol — Etnografia Polska
Et Polemol — Etudes Polemologiques
Et Pr Hist — Etudes Prehistoriques
ETQ — Estates and Trusts Quarterly
ETR — East Timor Report
ETR — East Turkic Review
ETR — Employment Review
ETR — Estates and Trusts Reports
Etr — Eternity
ETR — ETR
ETR — Etudes Theologiques et Religieuses
ETR — European Trends
Et Region Paris — Etudes de la Region Parisienne

E T Rel — Etudes Theologiques et Religieuses
ETRMD — Electromagnetics
Et Rom — Etudes Romaines
Et Rou — Etudes Roussillonnaises
ETRSD — Electronic Technology Reports
ETRTA — Elettrotecnica
ETRUA — Eisenbahntechnische Rundschau
Et Rur — Etudes Rurales
ETS — Entomologisk Tidskrift (Stockholm)
EtS — Etudes Sociales
ETs — Etudes Tsiganes
ETS — Journal. Evangelical Theological Society
ETS — Scandinavian Journal of Economics
Et Sal — Etudes Salesiennes
Et Seneg — Etudes Senegalaises
Et Slav Est Eur — Etudes Slaves et Est-Europeennes/Slavic and East-European Studies
Et Soc (Paris) — Etudes Sociales (Paris)
ETSSD — Elektronnaya Tekhnika. Seriya 1. Elektronika
Et Statist Banque Etats Afr Centr — Etudes et Statistiques. Banque des Etats de l'Afrique Centrale. Bulletin Mensuel
Et Suisses Hist Gen — Etudes Suisses d'Histoire Generale
ETTCA — Elektrotechniker
ETTCB — Elettronica e Telecomunicazioni
Et Thas — Etudes Thasiennes
Et ThH — Etudes de Theologie Historique
Et Th HS — Etudes de Theologie et d'Histoire de la Spiritualite
Ettore Majorana Internat Sci Ser Phys Sci — Ettore Majorana International Science Series. Physical Sciences
Ettore Majorana Int Sci Ser Life Sci — Ettore Majorana International Science Series. Life Sciences
Ettore Majorana Int Sci Ser Phys Sci — Ettore Majorana International Science Series. Physical Sciences
EtTr — Etudes Traditionelles
Et Trav — Etudes et Travaux [*Studia i Prace*]. Travaux du Centre d'Archeologie Mediterraneenne de l'Academie Polonaise de Sciences
Et Tsi — Etudes Tsiganes
ETU — Economie et Statistique
Etu — Etudes
EtuB — Etudes Balkaniques
EtuC — Etudes Classiques
Etud Afr CRISP — Etudes Africaines du CRISP (Centre de Recherche et d'Information Socio-Politique)
Etud Ang — Etudes Anglaises
Etud Angl — Etudes Anglaises
Etud Anglaises — Etudes Anglaises
Etud Balk — Etudes Balkaniques
Etud Cinema — Etudes Cinematographiques
Etud Cl — Etudes Classiques
Etud Class — Etudes Classiques
Etud Classiq — Etudes Classiques
Etud Docum Balkan Medit — Etudes et Documents Balkaniques et Mediterraneens
Etude CEE Ser Agr — Etudes CEE [*Communaute Economique Europeenne*]. Serie Agriculture
Etude Cent Nat Etude Experim Machin Agr — Etude. Centre National d'Etudes et d'Experimentation de Machinisme Agricole
Etud Ecol — Etudes Ecologiques
Etud Econs et Fins — Etudes Economiques et Financieres
Etud Econs (Mons) — Etudes Economiques (Mons, Belgium)
Etud Econs (Paris) — Etudes Economiques (Paris)
Etude Exp Anti Inflammatoires Confront Pharmacol — Etude Experimentale des Anti-Inflammatoires, Confrontations Pharmacologiques
Etudes Celt — Etudes Celtiques
Etudes Cin — Etudes Cinematographiques
Etudes Cret — Etudes Cretoises
Etudes Crimin — Etudes Criminologiques
Etudes Entomol — Etudes Entomologiques
Etudes Franc — Etudes Francaises
Etude Spec Minist Richesses Nat Que — Etude Speciale. Ministere des Richesses Naturelles du Quebec
Etudes Philos Medievale — Etudes de Philosophie Medievale
Etudes Rech Inform — Etudes et Recherches en Informatique
Etude Stat Inst Nat Stat — Etudes Statistiques. Institut National de la Statistique et des Etudes Economiques
Etud et Expansion — Etudes et Expansion
Etude Trav — Etude du Travail
Etud Fr — Etudes Francais
Etud Fran — Etudes Francaises
Etud Franc — Etudes Francaises
Etud Freud — Etudes Freudiennes
Etud Ger — Etudes Germaniques
Etud Germaniques — Etudes Germaniques
Etud Hist Afr — Etudes d'Histoire Africaine
Etud Hist Droit Canon — Etudes Historiques de Droit Canonique
Etud Int — Etudes Internationales
Etud Internat — Etudes Internationales
Etud Inuit — Etudes Inuit
Etud Irland — Etudes Irlandaises
Etud Ital — Etudes Italiennes
Etud Limousines — Etudes Limousines
Etud Lit — Etudes Litteraires
Etud Malien — Etudes Maliennes
Etud Maliennes — Etudes Maliennes
Etud Mar — Etudes Mariales
Etud Mongol Siberien — Etudes Mongoles et Siberiennes

Etud OM — Etudes d'Outre-Mer
Etud Phil — Etudes Philosophiques
Etud Philos — Etudes Philosophiques
Etud Prot Epur Eaux — Etudes de Protection et Epuration des Eaux
Etud Psychother — Etudes Psychotherapiques
Etud Rech Inst Meteorol Part 2 — Etudes et Recherches. Institut de Meteorologie. Part 2. Hydrologie
Etud Reg Paris — Etudes de la Region Parisienne
Etud Rur — Etudes Rurales
Etud Rurales — Etudes Rurales
Etud Sci — Etudes Scientifiques
Etud Slav E — Etudes Slaves et Est-Europeennes
Etud Socs — Etudes Sociales
Etud Soins Serv Infirm — Etudes sur les Soins et le Service Infirmier
Etud Statis (Brussels) — Etudes Statistiques (Brussels)
Etud Tech Econ Ser E (Inst Geol Geophys) — Etudes Techniques et Economiques. Seria E. Hydrogeologie (Institut de Geologie et Geophysique)
Etud Theol — Etudes Theologiques et Religieuses
Etud Trad — Etudes Traditionnelles
Etud Trav Ec Maroc Agric Publ — Etudes et Travaux. Ecole Marocaine d'Agriculture. Publication
Etud Tsig — Etudes Tsiganes
Etud XVIIIe Siecle — Etudes sur le XVIIIe Siecle
Etud Zairoises — Etudes Zairoises
Et Volt — Etudes Voltaiques
Et W — Lateinisches Etymologisches Woerterbuch
Ety — Eternity
Etym Mag — Etymologicum Magnum
Etyudy Biogeokhim Agrokhim Elem Biofilov — Etyudy po Biogeokhimii i Agrokhimii Elementov-Biofilov
ETZ — Elektrotechnische Zeitschrift
ETZ A Elektrotech Z — ETZ-A. Elektrotechnische Zeitschrift. Zeitschrift fuer Elektrische Energietechnik
Et Zair — Etudes Zairoises
ETZ Arch — ETZ. Elektrotechnische Zeitschrift. Archiv
ETZ B Elektrotech Z — ETZ-B. Elektrotechnische Zeitschrift
ETZ Elektrotech Z — ETZ. Elektrotechnische Zeitschrift
ETZ Elektrotech Z Ausg A — ETZ. Elektrotechnische Zeitschrift. Ausgabe A
Eu — East Europe
EU — Estudos Ultramarinos
EU — Estudos Universitarios
Eu — Euclides
Eu — Euphorion
EU — Euromoney
Eu — Europe
EUA — Enciclopedia Universale dell'Arte
Eu A — Erbe und Auftrag
EUC — Estudis Universitaris Catalans
EUCADT — Euphoria et Cacophoria
EUCARPIA Congr Assoc Eur Amelior Plant — EUCARPIA [*European Association for Research on Plant Breeding*] Congres. Association Europeenne pour l'Amelioration des Plantes
Euch Tijd — Eucharistisch Tijdschrift
EUCLB — Euroclay
EUCRA9 — EUCARPIA [*European Association for Research on Plant Breeding*] Congres. Association Europeenne pour l'Amelioration des Plantes
EUDEBA — Editorial Universitaria de Buenos Aires
EUE — Europeen, Europaer. Magazine de l'Economie et de la Culture
E u F — Ehe und Familie im Privaten und Oeffentlichen Recht
EUF — Euromoney Trade Finance Report
EUFID — European File
EUFSAR — Ege Universitesi Fen Fakultesi Ilmi Raporlar Serisi
E u G — Eiszeitalter und Gegenwart
Eu G — Erkenntnis und Glaube
Eu G — Europaeisches Gespraech
EUG — European Industrial Relations Review
Eugen — Eugenics
Eugenics R — Eugenics Review
Eugenics Rev — Eugenics Review
Eugen Lab Lect Ser — Eugenics Laboratory. Lecture Series
Eugen Lab Mem — Eugenics Laboratory. Memoirs
Eugen News — Eugenical News
Eugen Q — Eugenics Quarterly
Eugen Rev — Eugenics Review
Eugen Soc Symp — Eugenics Society Symposia
Eug Q — Eugenics Quarterly
EUGQAQ — Eugenics Quarterly
Eug R — Eugenics Review
Euh — Euhemer
Euh F — Euhemer. Zeszyty Filozoficzne
Euh H — Euhemer. Zeszyty Historyczne
E u J — Einst und Jetzt
Eukleides A Agymnasio NS — Eukleides. Ekdose tes Ellenikes Mathemates Etairias. A. Agymnasio. Nea Seira
EUL — Europa van Morgen
Eu L — Europe Letteraria
Eulenburg Enz Jbb Heilkde — Eulenburgs Encyclopaedische Jahrbuecher der Gesamten Heilkunde
EULEP Newsl — EULEP [*European Late Effects Project Group*] Newsletter
Eul J — Eulenspiegel-Jahrbuch
Eul Ji Med J — Eul Ji Medical Journal
E u M — Elektrotechnik und Maschinenbau
EUM — (El) Universal (Mexico)
EUN — European Plastics News
E und M — Elektrotechnik und Maschinenbau

EuntDoc — Euntes Docete
EUP — Edinburgh University Publications
Eup — Euphorion
EUP — Europe
EUP — Extension [*O Intercambio*] Universitaria de la Plata
EUP G — Edinburgh University Publications. Geography and Sociology
EUP H — Edinburgh University Publications. History, Philosophy, and Economics
Euph — Euphorion
EUPHAA — Euphytica
Euphoria Cacophoria (Int Ed) — Euphoria et Cacophoria (International Edition)
Euphyt — Euphytica. Netherlands Journal of Plant Breeding
EUPJA — European Polymer Journal
EUP L — Edinburgh University Publications. Language and Literature
EUPNA — Europhysics News
EUPNB — European Plastics News
EUP T — Edinburgh University Publications. Theology
EUQ — Emory University Quarterly
EUR — Erlanger Universitaetsreden
EUR — Euromoney
Eur — Europe
Eur — Europe [*Paris*]
Eur A — Europa-Archiv
Eur Abwasser Abfallsymp — Europaeisches Abwasser- und Abfallsymposium
Eur Abwasser Abfall Symp EAS — Europaeisches Abwasser- und Abfall-Symposium EAS
Eur Acad Surf Technol Kongr — European Academy of Surface Technology Kongress
Eurafr Trib Tiers-Monde — Eurafrica et Tribune de Tiers-Monde
Eur Amyloidosis Res Symp — European Amyloidosis Research Symposium
Eur Antiproton Symp — European Antiproton Symposium
Eur Appl Res Rep — European Applied Research Reports
Eur Appl Res Rep Environ Nat Resour Sect — European Applied Research Reports. Environment and Natural Resources Section
Eur Appl Res Rep-Nucl Sci Technol Sect — European Applied Research Reports. Nuclear Science and Technology Section
Eur Arch — Europa-Archiv
Eur Arch Otorhinolaryngol — European Archives of Oto-Rhino-Laryngology
Eur Arch Otorhinolaryngol Suppl — European Archives of Oto-Rhino-Laryngology. Supplement
Eur Arch Psychiatry Clin Neurosci — European Archives of Psychiatry and Clinical Neuroscience
Eur Arch Psychiatry Neurol Sci — European Archives of Psychiatry and Neurological Sciences
Eur Assoc Anim Prod Publ — European Association for Animal Production. Publication
Eur Assoc Cancer Res Meet — European Association for Cancer Research. Meeting
Eur Assoc Cancer Res Proc Meet — European Association for Cancer Research. Proceedings. Meeting
Eur Assoc Poison Control Cent Int Congr — European Association of Poison Control Centres. International Congress
Eur Assoc Res Plant Breed Proc Congr — European Association for Research on Plant Breeding. Proceedings. Congress
Eur Assoc Vet Pharmacol Toxicol Congr — European Association for Veterinary Pharmacology and Toxicology Congress
Eur Astron Meet — European Astronomical Meeting
Eur At Energy Community EURATOM Rep — European Atomic Energy Community. EURATOM Report
EURATOM Bull — EURATOM [*European Atomic Energy Community*] Bulletin
EURATOM Bull Eur At Energy Community — EURATOM. Bulletin of the European Atomic Energy Community
Euratom Rev — Euratom Review
EURATOM Rev Eur At Energy Community — EURATOM Review. European Atomic Energy Community
Eur Aviat Space Med Congr — European Aviation and Space Medicine Congress
Eur Bienn Workshop Nucl Phys — European Biennial Workshop on Nuclear Physics
Eur Bioenerg Conf — European Bioenergetics Conference
Eur Biomass Conf — European Biomass Conference
Eur Biophys Congr Proc — European Biophysics Congress. Proceedings
Eur Biophys J — European Biophysics Journal
Eur Biotechnol Newsl — European Biotechnology Newsletter
Eur Brew Conv Monogr — European Brewery Convention. Monograph
Eur Brew Conv Proc Congr — European Brewery Convention. Proceedings of the Congress
Eur Ceram Soc J — European Ceramic Society. Journal
Eur Chem — Europa Chemie
Eur Chem Ind Ecol Toxicol Cent Tech Rep — European Chemical Industry Ecology and Toxicology Centre. Technical Report
Eur Chem N — European Chemical News
Eur Chem Ne — European Chemical News
Eur Chem News — European Chemical News
Eur Child Adolesc Psychiatry — European Child and Adolescent Psychiaty
Eur Chir Forsch — Europaeische Chirurgische Forschung
Eur Clin Sect Int Assoc Gerontol Congr Proc — European Clinical Section. International Association of Gerontology. Congress. Proceedings
Eur Coal Util Conf Proc — European Coal Utilisation Conference. Proceedings
Eur Coat J — European Coatings Journal
Eur Coat Symp — European Coating Symposium
Eur Co Chem Process Irradiat Fuels Eurochemic Tech Rep ETR — European Company for the Chemical Processing of Irradiated Fuels. Eurochemic Technical Report ETR
Eur Colloq Curr Trends Quantum Chem Final Rep — European Colloquium on Current Trends in Quantum Chemistry. Final Report
Eur Colloq Echinoderms — European Colloquium on Echinoderms

Eur Comm Rep EUR — European Commission. Report. EUR
Eur Commun Bull — European Communities Bulletin
Eur Commun Econ Soc Comm Bull — European Communities Economic and Social Committee. Bulletin
Eur Community — European Community
Eur Community Conf Radioact Waste Manage Disposal — European Community Conference on Radioactive Waste Management and Disposal
Eur Community (Engl Ed) — European Community (English Edition)
Eur Community Meet Labour Insp Trainers — European Community Meeting of Labour Inspector Trainers
Eur Conf Adv Mater Processes — European Conference on Advanced Materials and Processes
Eur Conf Anal Chem — European Conference on Analytical Chemistry
Eur Conf Anim Blood Groups Biochem Polymorph — European Conference on Animal Blood Groups and Biochemical Polymorphism
Eur Conf Anim Blood Groups Biochem Polymorphism — European Conference on Animal Blood Groups and Biochemical Polymorphism
Eur Conf Astron — European Conference on Astronomy
Eur Conf Biomass Energy Ind Environ — European Conference on Biomass for Energy, Industry, and Environment
Eur Conf Chem Environ — European Conference on Chemistry and the Environment
Eur Conf Chem Vap Deposition — European Conference on Chemical Vapour Deposition
Eur Conf Coal Liq Mixtures — European Conference on Coal Liquid Mixtures
Eur Conf Compos Mater — European Conference on Composite Materials
Eur Conf Controlled Fusion Plasma Phys Contrib — European Conference on Controlled Fusion and Plasma Physics.Contributions
Eur Conf Controlled Fusion Plasma Phys Proc — European Conference on Controlled Fusion and Plasma Physics. Proceedings
Eur Conf Electron Des Autom — European Conference on Electronic Design Automation
Eur Conf Flammability Fire Retard — European Conference on Flammability and Fire Retardants
Eur Conf Integr Opt — European Conference on Integrated Optics
Eur Conf Intern Frict Ultrason Attenuation Solids Proc — European Conference on Internal Friction and Ultrasonic Attenuation in Solids. Proceedings
Eur Conf Martensitic Transform Sci Technol — European Conference on Martensitic Transformation in Science and Technology
Eur Conf Microcirc — European Conference on Microcirculation
Eur Conf Mixing Proc — European Conference on Mixing. Proceedings
Eur Conf Opt Commun — European Conference on Optical Communication
Eur Conf Opt Fibre Commun — European Conference on Optical Fibre Communication
Eur Conf Opt Opt Syst Appl — European Conference on Optics, Optical Systems, and Applications
Eur Conf Organ Org Thin Films — European Conference on Organized Organic Thin Films
Eur Conf Part Phys Proc — European Conference on Particle Physics. Proceedings
Eur Conf Prenatal Diagn Genet Disord Proc — European Conference on Prenatal Diagnosis of Genetic Disorders. Proceedings
Eur Conf Prog X-Ray Synchrotron Radiat Res — European Conference on Progress in X-Ray Synchrotron Radiation Research
Eur Conf Smart Struct Mater — European Conference on Smart Structures and Materials
Eur Conf Spectrosc Biol Mol — European Conference on Spectroscopy of Biological Molecules
Eur Congr Allergol Clin Immunol — European Congress of Allergology and Clinical Immunology. Proceedings
Eur Congr Biopharm Pharmacokinet — European Congress of Biopharmaceutics and Pharmacokinetics
Eur Congr Biotechnol — European Congress of Biotechnology
Eur Congr Biotechnol Prepr — European Congress of Biotechnology. Preprints
Eur Congr Electron Microsc — European Congress of Electron Microscopy
Eur Congr Magnesium — European Congress on Magnesium
Eur Congr Perinat Med — European Congress of Perinatal Medicine
Eur Congr Sleep Res — European Congress on Sleep Research
Eur Cos Mkt — European Cosmetic Markets
Eur Cot Ind Stat — European Cotton Industry Statistics
EURCUP — Estudos Universitarios: Revista de Cultura da Universidade de Pernambuco
Eur Cytokine Netw — European Cytokine Network
Eur Demographic Info Bul — European Demographic Information Bulletin
Eur Demographic Info Bul (Hague) — European Demographic Information Bulletin (The Hague)
Eur Dial Transplant Assoc Eur Renal Assoc Proc — European Dialysis and Transplant Association - European Renal Association. Proceedings
Eur Dial Transplant Assoc Proc — European Dialysis and Transplant Association. Proceedings
Eur Dial Transplant Assoc Proc Congr — European Dialysis and Transplant Association. Proceedings of theCongress
Eur Dig — European Digest
Eur Domani — Europa Domani
Eur Drag Reduct Meet — European Drag Reduction Meeting
Eur Drosophila Res Conf — European Drosophila Research Conference
Eur Drug Metab Workshop — European Drug Metabolism Workshop
EUREA — Eugenics Review
EUREAB — Eugenics Review
Eur Economy — European Economy
Eur Econ R — European Economic Review
Eur Electro Opt Conf — European Electro-Optics Conference
Eur Electro Opt Mark Technol Conf — European Electro-Optics Markets and Technology Conference

Eur Electro Opt Mark Technol Conf Proc — European Electro-Optics Markets and Technology Conference. Proceedings
Eur Electr Propul Conf — European Electric Propulsion Conference
Eur Energy — European Energy Prospects to 1990
Eur en Formation — Europe en Formation
Eur Est — Europe de l'Est
Eur Est Union Soviet — Europe de l'Est et Union Sovietique
Eur Ethn — Europa Ethnica
Eur Ethnica — Europa Ethnica
Eur Fed Chem Eng Publ Ser — European Federation of Chemical Engineering. Publication Series
Eur File — European File
Eur Food Symp — European Food Symposium
Eur France OM — Europe France Outremer
Eur Fr Outremer — Europe France Outremer
Eur Gefluegelkonf Vortr — Europaeische Gefluegelkonferenz. Vortraege
Eur Geophys Soc Meet Abstr — European Geophysical Society. Meeting. Abstracts
Eur Great Proj Int Semin Proc — European Great Projects. International Seminar. Proceedings
Eur Group Fract Publ — European Group on Fracture Publication
Eur Grundrechte — Europaeische Grundrechte
EurH — Europaeische Hochschulschriften
Eur Heart J — European Heart Journal
Eur Hochschulschr Reihe 8 Chem Abt A — Europaeische Hochschulschriften. Reihe 8. Chemie. Abteilung A.Pharmazie
Eur Hochschulschr Reihe 8 Chem Abt B — Europaeische Hochschulschriften. Reihe 8. Chemie. Abteilung B.Biochemie
Euriam Bul — Euriam Bulteni
Eur Ind Rel R — European Industrial Relations Review
Eur Ind Res Manage Assoc EIRMA Conf Pap — European Industrial Research Management Association. EIRMA ConferencePapers
Eur Inland Fish Advis Comm Tech Pap — European Inland Fisheries Advisory Commission. Technical Paper
Eur Intellectual Property Rev — European Intellectual Property Review
Eur Intell Prop R — European Intellectual Property Review
Eur Int Pr R — European Intellectual Property Review
Euristop Off Inf Bookl — Eurisotop Office Information Booklet
EurJ — European Judaism
EURJA — European Rubber Journal
Eur J Agron — European Journal of Agronomy
Eur J Anaesthesiol — European Journal of Anaesthesiology
Eur J Anaesthesiol Suppl — European Journal of Anaesthesiology. Supplement
Eur J A Phy — European Journal of Applied Physiology and Occupational Physiology
Eur J Appl Microbiol — European Journal of Applied Microbiology
Eur J Appl Microbiol Biotechnol — European Journal of Applied Microbiology and Biotechnology
Eur J Appl Physiol — European Journal of Applied Physiology and Occupational Physiology
Eur J Appl Physiol Occup Physiol — European Journal of Applied Physiology and Occupational Physiology
Eur J App M — European Journal of Applied Microbiology
Eur J Basic Appl Histochem — European Journal of Basic and Applied Histochemistry
Eur J Bioch — European Journal of Biochemistry
Eur J Biochem — European Journal of Biochemistry
Eur J Canc — European Journal of Cancer
Eur J Cancer — European Journal of Cancer
Eur J Cancer B Oral Oncol — European Journal of Cancer. Part B. Oral Oncology
Eur J Cancer Clin Oncol — European Journal of Cancer and Clinical Oncology
Eur J Cancer Part A — European Journal of Cancer. Part A
Eur J Cancer Part B — European Journal of Cancer. Part B. Oral Oncology
Eur J Cancer Prev — European Journal of Cancer Prevention
Eur J Cardiol — European Journal of Cardiology
Eur J Cardiothorac Surg — European Journal of Cardio-Thoracic Surgery
Eur J Cell Biol — European Journal of Cell Biology
Eur J Cell Biol Suppl — European Journal of Cell Biology. Supplement
Eur J Cell Plast — European Journal of Cellular Plastics
Eur J Chiro — European Journal of Chiropractic
Eur J Cl In — European Journal of Clinical Investigation
Eur J Clin Biol Res — European Journal of Clinical and Biological Research
Eur J Clin Chem Clin Biochem — European Journal of Clinical Chemistry and Clinical Biochemistry
Eur J Clin Invest — European Journal of Clinical Investigation
Eur J Clin Microbiol — European Journal of Clinical Microbiology
Eur J Clin Microbiol Infect Dis — European Journal of Clinical Microbiology and Infectious Diseases
Eur J Clin Nutr — European Journal of Clinical Nutrition
Eur J Clin Pharmacol — European Journal of Clinical Pharmacology
Eur J Cl Ph — European Journal of Clinical Pharmacology
Eur J Comb — European Journal of Combinatorics
Eur J Contracept & Reprod Health Care — European Journal of Contraception and Reproductive Health Care
Eur J Dermatol — European Journal of Dermatology
Eur J Disord Commun — European Journal of Disorders of Communication
Eur J Drug Metab Pharmacokinet — European Journal of Drug Metabolism and Pharmacokinetics
Eur J Educ — European Journal of Education
Eur J Emerg Med — European Journal of Emergency Medicine
Eur J Endocrinol — European Journal of Endocrinology
Eur J Endocrinol Suppl — European Journal of Endocrinology. Supplement
Eur J Eng Educ — European Journal of Engineering Education
Eur J Epidemiol — European Journal of Epidemiology

Eur J Exp Musculoskeletal Res — European Journal of Experimental Musculoskeletal Research
Eur J Fertil Steril — European Journal of Fertility and Sterility
Eur J For Pathol — European Journal of Forest Pathology
Eur J Gastroenterol Hepatol — European Journal of Gastroenterology and Hepatology
Eur J Gynaecol Oncol — European Journal of Gynaecological Oncology
Eur J Haematol — European Journal of Haematology
Eur J Haematol Suppl — European Journal of Haematology. Supplementum
Eur J Heart Fail — European Journal of Heart Failure
Eur J Histochem — European Journal of Histochemistry
Eur J Hosp Pharm — European Journal of Hospital Pharmacy
Eur J Hum Genet — European Journal of Human Genetics
Eur J I Car — European Journal of Intensive Care Medicine
Eur J Imm — European Journal of Immunogenetics
Eur J Immun — European Journal of Immunology
Eur J Immunogenet — European Journal of Immunogenetics
Eur J Immunol — European Journal of Immunology
Eur J Inorg Chem — European Journal of Inorganic Chemistry
Eur J Intensive Care Med — European Journal of Intensive Care Medicine
Eur J Lab Med — European Journal of Laboratory Medicine
Eur J Mass Spectrom Biochem Med Environ Res — European Journal of Mass Spectrometry in Biochemistry, Medicine, and Environmental Research
Eur J Mech B Fluids — European Journal of Mechanics. B/Fluids
Eur J Mech Eng — European Journal of Mechanical Engineering
Eur J Med Chem — European Journal of Medicinal Chemistry
Eur J Med Chem Chim Ther — European Journal of Medicinal Chemistry. Chimica Therapeutica
Eur J Med Res — European Journal of Medical Research
Eur J Mineral — European Journal of Mineralogy
Eur J Mktg — European Journal of Marketing
Eur J Morphol — European Journal of Morphology
Eur J Neurol — European Journal of Neurology
Eur J Neurosci — European Journal of Neuroscience
Eur J Nucl Med — European Journal of Nuclear Medicine
Eur J Obstet Gynecol — European Journal of Obstetrics and Gynecology [Later, European Journal of Obstetrics, Gynecology, and Reproductive Biology]
Eur J Obstet Gynecol Reprod Biol — European Journal of Obstetrics, Gynecology, and Reproductive Biology
Eur J Oper Res — European Journal of Operational Research
Eur J Ophthalmol — European Journal of Ophthalmology
Eur J Oral Sci — European Journal of Oral Sciences
Eur J Org Chem — European Journal of Organic Chemistry
Eur J Orthod — European Journal of Orthodontics
Eur J Pain — European Journal of Pain
Eur J Pain London — European Journal of Pain (London)
Eur J Ped — European Journal of Pediatrics
Eur J Pediatr — European Journal of Pediatrics
Eur J Pediatr Surg — European Journal of Pediatric Surgery
Eur J Ped S — European Journal of Pediatric Surgery
Eur J Pharm — European Journal of Pharmacology
Eur J Pharmacol — European Journal of Pharmacology
Eur J Pharmacol Environ Toxicol Pharmacol Sect — European Journal of Pharmacology. Environmental Toxicology and Pharmacology Section
Eur J Pharmacol Mol Pharmacol Sect — European Journal of Pharmacology. Molecular Pharmacology Section
Eur J Pharm Biopharm — European Journal of Pharmaceutics and Biopharmaceutics
Eur J Ph-Mo — European Journal of Pharmacology. Molecular Pharmacology Section
Eur J Phys — European Journal of Physics
Eur J Physiol — European Journal of Physiology
Eur J Plant Pathol — European Journal of Plant Pathology
Eur J Popul — European Journal of Population
Eur J Public Health — European Journal of Public Health
Eur J Radiol — European Journal of Radiology
Eur J Respir Dis — European Journal of Respiratory Diseases
Eur J Respir Dis Suppl — European Journal of Respiratory Diseases. Supplement
Eur J Rheumatol Inflamm — European Journal of Rheumatology and Inflammation
Eur J Rheumatol Inflammation — European Journal of Rheumatology and Inflammation
Eur J Sci Educ — European Journal of Science Education
Eur J Sociol — European Journal of Sociology
Eur J Soc P — European Journal of Social Psychology
Eur J Soil Sci — European Journal of Soil Science
Eur J Solid State Inorg Chem — European Journal of Solid State and Inorganic Chemistry
Eur J Steroids — European Journal of Steroids
Eur J Surg — European Journal of Surgery
Eur J Surg Oncol — European Journal of Surgical Oncology
Eur J Surg Suppl — European Journal of Surgery. Supplement
Eur J Toxicol — European Journal of Toxicology
Eur J Toxicol Environ Hyg — European Journal of Toxicology and Environmental Hygiene
Eur Jud — European Judaism
Eur J Vasc Endovasc Surg — European Journal of Vascular and Endovascular Surgery
Eur J Water Pollut Control — European Water Pollution Control
Eur Konf Mikrozirk — Europaeische Konferenz ueber Mikrozirkulation
EurL — Europa Letteraria
Eur L Facs — European Linguistics. A Collection of Facsimile Reprints
Eur Mar Biol Symp Proc — European Marine Biology Symposium. Proceedings
Eur Mater Res Soc Meet Symp — European Materials Research Society Meeting. Symposium
Eur Mater Res Soc Monogr — European Materials Research Society Monographs

Eur Med Colloq DPHM INSERM — Europe du Medicament. Realities et Ambitions. Colloque DPHM-INSERM
Eur Med (Fr Ed) — Europa Medica (French Edition)
Eur Med (Ital Ed) — Europa Medica (Italian Edition)
Eur Mediterr Plant Prot Organ Publ Ser A — European and Mediterranean Plant Protection Organization. Publications. Series A
Eur Mediterr Plant Prot Organ Publ Ser D — European and Mediterranean Plant Protection Organization. Publications. Series D
Eur Med (Span Ed) — Europa Medica (Spanish Edition)
Eur Meet Wildfowl Conserv Proc — European Meeting on Wildfowl Conservation. Proceedings
Eur Monogr Hlth Educ Res — European Monographs in Health Education Research
Eur Neurol — European Neurology
Eur Neuropsychopharmacol — European Neuropsychopharmacology
Eur Nouv — Europe Nouvelle
Eur Nucl — Europa Nucleare
Euro Abstr Sec 1 — Research
Euro Abstr Sect 2 — Euro Abstracts. Section 2. Coal and Steel
EuroAsia Bus Rev — Euro-Asia Business Review
Euro Coop — Euro Cooperation
Euro Courses Adv Sci Tech — Euro Courses. Advanced Scientific Techniques
Euro Courses Chem Environ Sci — Euro Courses. Chemical and Environmental Science
Euro Courses Environ Manage — Euro Courses. Environmental Management
Euro Courses Nucl Sci Technol — Euro Courses. Nuclear Science and Technology
Euro Courses Reliab Risk Anal — Euro Courses. Reliability and Risk Analysis
Euro Courses Technol Innovation — Euro Courses. Technological Innovation
EUROGAS Proc Eur Appl Res Conf Nat Gas — EUROGAS. Proceedings. European Applied Research Conference on Natural Gas
Eur Oil — Europe and Oil
Eur Oil Gas Mag — European Oil and Gas Magazine
EUROLOC — Locate in Europe Information Retrieval System
Euromath Bull — Euromath Bulletin
Euromech Colloq — Euromech-Colloquium
Euromicro J — Euromicro Journal
Euromicro Newsl — Euromicro Newsletters
Euro Mon — EuroMonitor Review
Eurom Surveys Aust NZ Series — Euromarket Surveys. Australian/New Zealand Series
Europ — European
Europa Arch — Europe Archiv. Zeitschrift fuer Internationale Politik
Europ Busin — European Business
Europ Chem — Europa Chemie
Europ Demogr Inform B — European Demographic Information Bulletin
European Assocn for Archtl Education Newsheet — European Association for Architectural Education. Newsheet
European Consort Math Indust — European Consortium for Mathematics in Industry
European Ind Relations Rev — European Industrial Relations Review
European Inf Serv — European Information Service
European J Appl Math — European Journal of Applied Mathematics
European J Combin — European Journal of Combinatorics
European J Ed — European Journal of Education
European J Engineering Ed — European Journal of Engineering Education
European J Mech A Solids — European Journal of Mechanics. A. Solids
European J Mech B Fluids — European Journal of Mechanics. B. Fluids
European J of Science Ed — European Journal of Science Education
European J Oper Res — European Journal of Operational Research
European J Phys — European Journal of Physics
European L Rev — European Law Review
European Photogr — European Photography
European Rubber J — European Rubber Journal
European Sm Bus J — European Small Business Journal
Europe Com — European Community
Europe Communities Comm — European Communities Commission
Europ Econ and Pol Survey — European Economic and Political Survey
Europ Econ R — European Economic Review
Europe Daily Bull — Europe Daily Bulletin
Europe O Mer — Europe Outremer
Europhys Conf Abstr — Europhysics Conference Abstracts
Europhys Conf Macromol Phys Proc — Europhysics Conference on Macromolecular Physics. Proceedings
Europhys Conf Nucl Phys — Europhysics Conference on Nuclear Physics
Europhys Ind Workshop — Europhysics Industrial Workshop
Europhys Lett — Europhysics Letters
Europhys News — Europhysics News
Europ Intell Prop Rev — European Intellectual Property Review
Europ J Paediatr Neurol — European Journal of Paediatric Neurology. EJPN
Europ J Polit Res — European Journal of Political Research
Europ J Soc Psychol — European Journal of Social Psychology
Europlas Mon — Europlastics Monthly
Europlast Mon — Europlastics Monthly
Europ Law R — European Law Review
Europ R Agric Econ — European Review of Agricultural Economics
Europ Rdsch — Europaeische Rundschau
Europ Rev — Europaeische Revue
Europ Stud Newsl — European Studies Newsletter
Europ Stud R — European Studies Review
Europ Wehrkunde — Europaeische Wehrkunde
Europ YB — European Yearbook
Euro Rep Stud — Euro Reports and Studies
Euro Res — European Research
Euro Rev — Eurostat Review

Eur Organ Nucl Res High Energy React Anal Group Rep — European Organization for Nuclear Research. High-Energy Reaction Analysis Group. Report

Eur Organ Nucl Res Rep — European Organization for Nuclear Research. Report

Eur Organ Nucl Res Symp High Energy Accel Pion Phys Proc — European Organization for Nuclear Research. Symposium on High-Energy Accelerators and Pion Physics. Proceedings

Eur Organ Res Fluorine Dent Caries Prev Proc Congr — European Organization for Research on Fluorine and Dental Caries Prevention. Proceedings of the Congress

Eur Organ Res Treat Cancer (EORTC) Monogr Ser — European Organization for Research on Treatment of Cancer (EORTC). Monograph Series

Eur Organ Res Treat Cancer Monog Ser — European Organization for Research on the Treatment of Cancer. Monograph Series

Eur Organ Treat Cancer Monogr Ser — European Organization for Research on the Treatment of Cancer. Monograph Series

Eur Orient — Europa Orientale

Euro Space Agency (Spec Publ) ESA SP — European Space Agency (Special Publication). ESA SP

Euro Spectr — Euro-Spectra

Eur Osten — Europaeische Osten

Euro Surveill — Euro Surveillance

Eurotest Tech Bull — Eurotest Technical Bulletin

Eur Outremer — Europe Outremer

Eur Paed H — European Paediatric Haematology and Oncology

Eur Paediatr Haematol Oncol — European Paediatric Haematology and Oncology

Eur Pat Appl — European Patent Application

Eur Patentanmeld — Europaeische Patentanmeldung

Eur Patentbl — Europaeisches Patentblatt

Eur Pat Off Eur Pat Appl — European Patent Office. European Patent Application

Eur Pept Symp Proc — European Peptide Symposium. Proceedings

Eur Photochem Assoc Newsl — European Photochemistry Association. Newsletter

Eur Photovoltaic Sol Energy Conf — European Photovoltaic Solar Energy Conference

Eur Plas N — European Plastics News

Eur Plast News — European Plastics News

Eur Pol Data Newsl — European Political Data Newsletter

Eur Polym J — European Polymer Journal

Eur Polym Paint Colour J — European Polymers Paint Colour Journal

Eur Potato J — European Potato Journal

Eur Pot J — European Potato Journal

Eur Poult Sci — European Poultry Science

Eur Powder Metall Symp — European Powder Metallurgy Symposium

Eur Psychiatry — European Psychiatry

EurR — Europaische Revue

Eur Radiol — European Radiology

Eur Rdsch — Europaeische Rundschau

Eur Reg Tech Conf Plast Process — European Regional Technical Conference. Plastics and Processing

Eur Res — European Research

Eur Research — European Research

Eur Respir J — European Respiratory Journal

Eur Respir J Suppl — European Respiratory Journal. Supplement

Eur Rev — Europaeische Revue

Eur Rev — Europe Review

Eur Rev Agric Econ — European Review of Agricultural Economics

Eur Rev Endocrinol — European Review of Endocrinology

Eur Rev Endocrinol Suppl — European Review of Endocrinology. Supplement

Eur Rev Lit — Europe. Revue Litteraire Mensuelle

Eur Rev Med Pharmacol Sci — European Review for Medical and Pharmacological Sciences

Eur Rubber J — European Rubber Journal

Eur Rubb J — European Rubber Journal

Eur Rub Jl — European Rubber Journal

Eur Semicond — European Semiconductor

Eur Semicond Prod — European Semiconductor Production

Eur Semin Sanit Eng Rep — European Seminar for Sanitary Engineers. Report of the Seminar

Eur Shielding Inf Serv Newsl — European Shielding Information Service Newsletter

Eur Shipbldg — European Shipbuilding

Eur Shipbuild — European Shipbuilding

Eur Sicherh — Europaeische Sicherheit

Eur Soc Toxicol Proc — European Society of Toxicology. Proceedings

Eur Solid State Device Res Conf — European Solid State Device. Research Conference

Eur South Obs Bull — European Southern Observatory. Bulletin

Eur Space Agency Bull — European Space Agency. Bulletin

Eur Space Agency Sci Tech Rev — European Space Agency. Scientific and Technical Review

Eur Space Agency Spec Publ ESA SP — European Space Agency. Special Publication ESA SP

Eur Space Res Organ Contract Rep — European Space Research Organization. Contractor Report

Eur Space Res Organ Tech Memo — European Space Research Organization. Technical Memorandum

Eur Spectrosc News — European Spectroscopy News

Eur Spine J — European Spine Journal

Eur Struct Integr Soc Publ — European Structural Integrity Society Publication

Eur Stud R — European Studies Review

Eur Stud Rev — European Studies Review

Eur Sud-Est 5e Ser — Europe Sud-Est. Cinquieme Serie

Eur Surg Re — European Surgical Research

Eur Surg Res — European Surgical Research

Eur Symp Basic Res Gerontol Lect — European Symposium on Basic Research in Gerontology. Lectures

Eur Symp Calcif Tissues Proc — European Symposium on Calcified Tissues. Proceedings

Eur Symp Chem React Eng — European Symposium on Chemical Reaction Engineering

Eur Symp Eng Ceram Proc — European Symposium on Engineering Ceramics. Proceedings

Eur Symp Enhanced Oil Recovery — European Symposium on Enhanced Oil Recovery

Eur Symp Horm Cell Regul — European Symposium on Hormones and Cell Regulation

Eur Symp Lindane — European Symposium on Lindane

Eur Symp Mar Biol Proc — European Symposium on Marine Biology. Proceedings

Eur Symp Martensitic Transform Shape Mem Prop — European Symposium on Martensitic Transformation and Shape Memory Properties

Eur Symp Med Enzymol Proc — European Symposium on Medical Enzymology. Proceedings

Eur Symp Org Micropollut Aquat Environ — European Symposium on Organic Micropollutants in the Aquatic Environment

Eur Symp Polym Spectrosc — European Symposium on Polymer Spectroscopy

Eur Symp Powder Metall Prepr — European Symposium for Powder Metallurgy. Preprints

Eur Symp Pulvermetall Vorabdrucke — Europaeisches Symposium fuer Pulvermetallurgie. Vorabdrucke

Eur Tax — European Taxation

Eur Taxation — European Taxation

Eur Teach — European Teacher

Eur Team Workshop Int Semin Electromagn Field Anal — European Team Workshop and International Seminar in Electromagnetic Field Analysis

Eur Tech Dig — European Technical Digests

Eur Tech Symp Polyimides High Temp Polym — European Technical Symposium on Polyimides and High-Temperature Polymers

Eur Text Eng Rev — European Textile Engineering Review

Eur Textilind — Europaeische Textilindustrie

Eur Trans Electr Power Eng — European Transactions on Electrical Power Engineering/ETEP

Eur Transp L — European Transport Law

Eur Trans Telecommun Relat Technol — European Transactions on Telecommunications and Related Technologies

Eur Tribol Congr Proc — European Tribology Congress. Proceedings

Eur Univ Pap Ser 8 Chem Div A — European University Papers. Series 8. Chemistry. Division A. Pharmacy

Eur Urol — European Urology

Eur Water Manage — European Water Management

Eur Water Pollut Cont — European Water Pollution Control

Eur Wehrkunde — Europaeische Wehrkunde

Eur Z Cancerol — Europaeische Zeitschrift fuer Cancerologie

Eur Z Forstpathologie — Europaeische Zeitschrift fuer Forstpathologie

Eur Z Kartoffelforsch — Europaeische Zeitschrift fuer Kartoffelforschung

Eur Z Krankenhauspharm — Europaeische Zeitschrift der Krankenhauspharmazie

EUS — Economic Outlook USA

EUS — Market Research Europe

EUSND — Energy User News

EUSRBM — Europaeische Chirurgische Forschung

EUSSBP — Eugenics Society Symposia

EUV — (El) Universal (Venezuela)

EUV — Europa-Archiv

Eu W N — Eudora Welty Newsletter

EUZ — European Chemical News

EV — Economische Voorlichting

EV — Ecos de Valvanera

EV — El Vidente [*Villa Angela, Argentina*]

EV — (El) Visitante

EV — Encres Vivies

EV — Epegrafika Vostika

Ev — Evenement

EV — Evergreen Review

EVA — European Review of Agricultural Economics

Eval & Exper — Evaluation and Experiment. Some Critical Issues in Assessing Social Programs

Eval Educ — Evaluation in Education

Eval Eng — Evaluation Engineering

Eval Health Prof — Evaluation and the Health Professions

Eval Newsletter — Evaluation Newsletter

Eval Program Plann — Evaluation and Program Planning

Eval Q — Evaluation Quarterly

Eval Rev — Evaluation Review

Eval Stud Rev Ann — Evaluation Studies Review Annual

Evaluation Health Professions — Evaluation and the Health Professions

Evaluation in Ed — Evaluation in Education

Evaluation Q — Evaluation Quarterly

Evaluation R — Evaluation Review

Evaluatn — Evaluation: A Forum for Human Services Decision-Makers

Evalu Stu — Evaluation Studies. Review Annual

EVAN — Epigrafika Vostoka. Akademiia Nauk SSSR

Evang — Evangelical Quarterly

Evang Diaspora — Evangelische Diaspora

Evang Komment — Evangelische Kommentare

Evang Mis Mag — Evangelisches Missions-Magazin

Evang Q — Evangelical Quarterly

Evang R — Evangelical Review

Evang Th — Evangelische Theologie

Evang T Verd — Evangeliet til Verden

Evan Kirchor — Evangelische Kirchenchor

EVBAA — Electric Vehicles and Batteries
EVBHA — Environment and Behavior
EVBMA — Environmental Biology and Medicine
EVD — Exportmededelingen
Ev Dt B — Evangelische Deutschland. Beilage
Ev Enz — Evangelische Enzyklopaedie
Everday Sci — Everyday Science
Everglades Nat Hist — Everglades Natural History. A Magazine of Natural History of South Florida
Everglades Nat History — Everglades Natural History
Everybodys M — Everybody's Magazine
Everyman's Sci — Everyman's Science
EVETB — Environmental Entomology
EVF — Tendance des Ventes du Vetement Masculin pour Hommes et Juniors
Ev Fo — Evanglisches Forum
Evgl Musikztg — Evangelische Musikzeitung
EVH — Wereldmarkt
Ev Hum — L'Evolution de l'Humanite
Evid — Evidences
Evid Based Ment Health — Evidence-Based Mental Health
Ev J — Evangelische Jahresbriefe
Evk — A Magyar Tudos Tarasag Evkonyvei
EvK — Evangelische Kommentare
Evk Debrecen — Debreceni Deri Muzeum Evkoenyve
EVKOD — Evangelische Kommentare
EvKom — Evangelische Kommentare
EVLTA — Environmental Letters
EVLWA — Environmental Law
EVM — Evangelie en Maatschappij
Ev MQ — Evangelical Missions Quarterly
EVNSA — Electric Vehicle News
EVOC — Excerpta Medica Vocabulary
Evol — Evolution
Evol Biol — Evolutionary Biology
Evol Comput — Evolutionary Computation
Evol Concepts Methodes Eval Pollut Masses Eau Sediments — Evolution des Concepts et des Methodes d'Evaluation des Pollutions dans les Masses d'Eau et les Sediments
Evol Dev — Evolution & Development
Evol Genet Res Rep — Evolutionary Genetics Research Reports
Evol Med — Evolution Medicale
Evol Psychiatr — Evolution Psychiatrique
Evol Theory — Evolutionary Theory
Evolution Int J Org Evolution — Evolution. International Journal of Organic Evolution
EVP — Etruscan Vase-Painting
EVPHB — Environmental Physiology
EVPSA — Evolution Psychiatrique
EVPTD — Energy Viewpoint
Ev Q — Evangelical Quarterly
EVQMA — Environmental Quality
EvR — Evergreen Review
EVS — Economische Voorlichting Suriname
Ev Sat — Every Saturday
EVSCB — Everyman's Science
Ev Soz B — Evangelisch-Sozial. Beilage. Soziale Korrespondenz
EVSSAV — Environmental Space Sciences
EvT — Evangelische Theologie
EvTC — Evangelizing Today's Child
Ev Th — Evangelische Theologie
EvThB — Evangelische Theologie (Beiheft)
Ev W — Evangelische Welt
EvWelt — Evangelische Welt. Bethel bei Bielefeld
EW — East and West
EW — Eastern World
EW — Eco/Log Week
EW — Economic Week
EW — Economic Weekly
EW — Ecosystems of the World
EWB — Economic Weekly (Bombay)
EWB — Ernaehrungswirtschaft
EWCR — East-West Center Review
EWD — Elseviers Weekblad
EWD — Europaeischer Wissenschaftsdienst
EWe — East and West
EWHA Med J Coll Med EWHA Womans — EWHA Medical Journal. College of Medicine. EWHA Womans University
EWI — Ecologist
EWIP — Edinburgh University. Department of Linguistics. Work in Progress
EWM — Elseviers Magazine
EWN — Evelyn Waugh Newsletter
E World — Eastern World
EW Outl — East-West Outlook
EW Perspect — East-West Perspectives
EWR — East and West. Istituto Italiano per il Medio ed Estremo Oriente (Rome)
EWR — East-West Review
EWRSI Newsl — EWRSI [*East-West Resource Systems Institute*] Newsletter
EWTFA — Energiewirtschaftliche Tagesfragen
EWTJA — Effluent and Water Treatment Journal
EWTJAG — Effluent and Water Treatment Journal
EX — Ecclesiastica Xaveriana
Ex — Examiner
Ex — Exegetica. Delft
EX — Experiment
Ex — Explicator

EX — Export
Ex — Express
Exam — Examiner
Examples Math Structures — Examples of Mathematical Structures
Exam Sit Econ Mexico — Examen de la Situacion Economica de Mexico
EXav — Ecclesiastica Xaveriana
EXBRA — Experimental Brain Research
Exc — Excelsior [*Paris daily*]
Ex C — Expert Comptable
Exc Arq en Espana — Excavaciones Arqueologicas en Espana
EXCCA — Exceptional Children
Excel Com — Excellence in Communication
Excep Child — Exceptional Children
Except Chil — Exceptional Children
Except Child — Exceptional Child
Except Child Educ Abstr — Exceptional Child Education Abstracts [*Later, ECER*]
Except Child Educ Resour — Exceptional Child Education Resources
Except Infant — Exceptional Infant
Except Parent — Exceptional Parent
Excerp Bot — Excerpta Botanica
Excerp Criminol — Excerpta Criminologica
Excerpta Bot Sect A Taxon Chorol — Excerpta Botanica. Sectio A. Taxonomica et Chorologica
Excerpta Bot Sect B Sociol — Excerpta Botanica. Sectio B. Sociologica
Excerpta Criminol — Excerpta Criminologica
Excerpta Med — Excerpta Medica
Excerpta Med (Amst) — Excerpta Medica (Amsterdam)
Excerpta Med Biochem — Excerpta Medica. Section 2B. Biochemistry
Excerpta Med Int Congr Ser — Excerpta Medica. International Congress Series
Excerpta Med Pharmacol Toxicol — Excerpta Medica. Section 2C. Pharmacology and Toxicology
Excerpta Med Physiol — Excerpta Medica. Physiology
Excerpta Med Sect 1 — Excerpta Medica. Section 1. Anatomy, Anthropology, Embryology, and Histology
Excerpta Med Sect 2 — Excerpta Medica. Section 2. Physiology
Excerpta Med Sect 2A — Excerpta Medica. Section 2A. Physiology
Excerpta Med Sect 2B — Excerpta Medica. Section 2B. Biochemistry
Excerpta Med Sect 2C — Excerpta Medica. Section 2C. Pharmacology and Toxicology
Excerpta Med Sect 2 Physiol Biochem Pharmacol — Excerpta Medica. Section 2. Physiology, Biochemistry, and Pharmacology
Excerpta Med Sect 3 — Excerpta Medica. Section 3. Endocrinology
Excerpta Med Sect 4 — Excerpta Medica. Section 4. Medical Microbiology and Hygiene
Excerpta Med Sect 4 Med Microbiol Immunol Serol — Excerpta Medica. Section 4. Medical Microbiology, Immunology, and Serology
Excerpta Med Sect 5 — Excerpta Medica. Section 5. General Pathology and Pathological Anatomy
Excerpta Med Sect 6 — Excerpta Medica. Section 6. Internal Medicine
Excerpta Med Sect 7 — Excerpta Medica. Section 7. Pediatrics
Excerpta Med Sect 8 — Excerpta Medica. Section 8. Neurology and Psychiatry
Excerpta Med Sect 9 — Excerpta Medica. Section 9. Surgery
Excerpta Med Sect 10 — Excerpta Medica. Section 10. Obstetrics and Gynecology
Excerpta Med Sect 11 — Excerpta Medica. Section 11. Oto-Rhino-Laryngology
Excerpta Med Sect 12 — Excerpta Medica. Section 12. Ophthalmology
Excerpta Med Sect 13 — Excerpta Medica. Section 13. Dermatology and Venereology
Excerpta Med Sect 14 — Excerpta Medica. Section 14. Radiology
Excerpta Med Sect 15 — Excerpta Medica. Section 15. Chest Diseases, Thoracic Surgery, and Tuberculosis
Excerpta Med Sect 16 — Excerpta Medica. Section 16. Cancer
Excerpta Med Sect 17 — Excerpta Medica. Section 17. Public Health, Social Medicine, and Hygiene
Excerpta Med Sect 23 — Excerpta Medica. Section 23. Nuclear Medicine
Excerpta Med Sect 29 — Excerpta Medica. Section 29. Clinical Biochemistry
Excerpta Med Sect 30 — Excerpta Medica. Section 30. Pharmacology and Toxicology
ExChAb — Exceptional Child Education Abstracts [*Later, ECER*]
Exch Flower Nursery Gard Cent Trade — Exchange for the Flower, Nursery, and Garden Center Trade
Ex Child — Exceptional Children
Ex Chr — Experiment Christentum
Ex C R — Exchequer Court Reports
Excursions Rec Math Ser — Excursions in Recreational Mathematics Series
EXE — Executive
ExE — Explorations in Entrepreneurial History
Exec — Executive
Exec Admin — Executive Administrator
Exec Com — Executive Communications
Exec Disclosure Guide CCH — Executive Disclosure Guide. Commerce Clearing House
Exec Female — Executive Female
Exec Fit Newsl — Executive Fitness Newsletter
Exec Housekeeper — Executive Housekeeper
Exec Housekeeping Today — Executive Housekeeping Today
Exec Mem Jogger — Executive's Memory Jogger
Exec News — Executive News
Exec Prod — Executive Productivity
Exec Reading — Executive Reading
Exec Reprt — Executive Report
Exec Sci Inst — Executive Sciences Institute
Exec Skills — Executive Skills
Executive Eng — Executive Engineer
Exempt Org Rep CCH — Exempt Organizations Reports. Commerce Clearing House

Exerc Immunol Rev — Exercise Immunology Review
Exercise Sport Sci Rev — Exercise and Sport Sciences Reviews
Exerc Sport Sci Rev — Exercise and Sport Sciences Reviews
Exer Pat — Exercices de la Patience
Exeter Papers Econ Hist — Exeter Papers on Economic History
ExEx — Exercise Exchange
EXF — Executive Female
EXG — Exhibition Bulletin
EXGEA — Experimental Gerontology
Exhaust Gas Air Pollut Abs — Exhaust Gas and Air Pollution Abstracts
EXHE — Executive Health
EXHEB — Experimental Hematology
Exhib & Conf Gaz — Exhibitions and Conferences Gazette
Exhibition Bull — Exhibition Bulletin
Ex H Lec — Exeter Hall Lectures
Ex Il — Express Ilustrowany
Ex Immunology Rev — Exercise Immunology Review
Exist Psychiat — Existential Psychiatry
EXJO — Explorers Journal
EXKTA — Exaktn
EXM — Export Markt
EX Mag — EX Magazine
EXMDA — International Congress Series. Excerpta Medica
EXNEA — Experimental Neurology
Exner Rpm — Repertorium der Physik. Exner
Ex Nuzi — Excavation at Nuzi
EXON — Exxon USA
Exp — Experientia
Exp — Experiment
Exp — Explicator
EXP — Export
Exp — Expositor
Exp — Express
Exp Ag — Experimental Agriculture
Exp Aging Res — Experimental Aging Research
Exp Agri — Experimental Agriculture
Exp Agric — Experimental Agriculture
Exp An — Experimental Animals
Exp & Appl Acarol — Experimental and Applied Acarology
Exp Anim — Experimentation Animale
Exp Anim (Tokyo) — Experimental Animals (Jikken Dobutsu) (Tokyo)
Expansion Reg — Expansion Regionale
Expans Region — Expansion Regionale
Expans Region (Paris) — Expansion Regionale (Paris)
Ex Paras — Experimental Parasitology
Exp Biol — Experimental Biology
Exp Biol (Berl) — Experimental Biology (Berlin)
Exp Biol Med — Experimental Biology and Medicine
Exp Biol Med (Maywood) — Experimental Biology and Medicine. Maywood, NJ
Exp Biol Med Totowa NJ — Experimental Biology and Medicine (Totowa, New Jersey)
Exp Biol Online — Experimental Biology Online [*Electronic Publication*]
Exp Biol Vilnius — Experimental Biology (Vilnius)
Exp Bot — Experimental Botany
Exp Bot Int Ser Monogr — Experimental Botany: An International Series of Monographs
Exp Brain R — Experimental Brain Research
Exp Brain Res — Experimental Brain Research
Exp Brain Res Suppl — Experimental Brain Research. Supplementum
Exp Cell Biol — Experimental Cell Biology
Exp Cell Re — Experimental Cell Research
Exp Cell Res — Experimental Cell Research
Exp Cell Res Suppl — Experimental Cell Research. Supplement
Exp Cereb — Experimentation Cerebrale
Exp Chaos Conf — Experimental Chaos Conference
Exp Chem Thermodyn — Experimental Chemical Thermodynamics
Exp Clin Endocrinol — Experimental and Clinical Endocrinology
Exp Clin Endocrinol Diabetes — Experimental and Clinical Endocrinology and Diabetes
Exp Clin Gastroenterol — Experimental and Clinical Gastroenterology
Exp Clin Im — Experimental and Clinical Immunogenetics
Exp Clin Immunogenet — Experimental and Clinical Immunogenetics
Exp Clin Med Yerevan — Experimental and Clinical Medicine (Yerevan)
Exp Clin Oncol (Tallinn) — Experimental and Clinical Oncology (Tallinn)
Exp Clin Pharmacol — Experimental and Clinical Pharmacology
Exp Clin Psychiatry — Experimental and Clinical Psychiatry
Exp Clin Psychopharmacol — Experimental and Clinical Psychopharmacology
Exp CR — Experimental Cell Research
Exp Dermatol — Experimental Dermatology
EXPEA — Experientia
Exped — Expedition
Expedition — Expedition Bulletin. University Museum. University of Pennsylvania
Exp Embryol Teratol — Experimental Embryology and Teratology
Exper — Experientia
Exper Agric — Experimental Agriculture
Experien — Experiences. Bulletin. Section Belgoluxembourgeoise du CentreInternational de Recherches et d'Information sur l'Economie Collective
Experientiae Vicosa — Experientiae. Universidade Rural do Estado de Minas Gerais (Vicosa)
Experientia Suppl — Experientia. Supplementum
Experiment Math — Experimental Mathematics
Experiment Tech Phys — Experimentelle Technik der Physik
Exper Mech — Experimental Mechanics
Exper Med Surg — Experimental Medicine and Surgery
Exper Neurol — Experimental Neurology

Exper Parasitol — Experimental Parasitology
Exper Suppl — Experientia. Supplementum
Exper Suppl (Basel) — Experientia. Supplementum (Basel)
Exper Therm Fluid Sci — Experimental Thermal and Fluid Science
Expert Opin Invest Drugs — Expert Opinion on Investigational Drugs
Expert Opin Investig Drugs — Expert Opinion on Investigational Drugs
Expert Opin Pharmacother — Expert Opinion on Pharmacotherapy
Expert Opin Ther Pat — Expert Opinion on Therapeutic Patents
Expert Sys Appl — Expert Systems with Applications
Expert Syst — Expert Systems
Exp Eye Res — Experimental Eye Research
Exp Fluids — Experiments in Fluids
Exp Geront — Experimental Gerontology
Exp Gerontol — Experimental Gerontology
Exp Heat Transfer — Experimental Heat Transfer
Exp Hemat — Experimental Hematology
Exp Hematol — Experimental Hematology
Exp Hematol (Copenh) — Experimental Hematology (Copenhagen)
Exp Hematol (NY) — Experimental Hematology (New York)
Exp Hematol (Oak Ridge Tenn) — Experimental Hematology (Oak Ridge, Tennessee)
Exp Hematol Today — Experimental Hematology Today. Annual Meeting of the InternationalSociety for Experimental Hematology
Exp Hirnforsch — Experimentelle Hirnforschung
Exp Hort — Experimental Horticulture
Exp Hortic — Experimental Horticulture
Exp H R — Expositor and Homiletic Review
Exp Husb — Experimental Husbandry
Exp Immunotoxicol — Experimental Immunotoxicology [*monograph*]
Expl — Explicator
Expl — Explorations (London)
EXPL — Explore. Alberta's Outdoor Magazine
Expl Agric — Experimental Agriculture
Explan Leafl Intervention Bd Agric Prod — Explanatory Leaflet. Intervention Board for Agricultural Produce
Expl Brain Res — Experimental Brain Research
Expl Cell Res — Experimental Cell Research
Expl Delos — Explorations Archeologiques de Delos
Expl Ec His — Explorations in Economic History
Expl Gerontol — Experimental Gerontology
Expl Hort — Experimental Horticulture
Expl Husb — Experimental Husbandry
Explo Econ Hist — Explorations in Economic History
Explor — Explorations
Explorat Entrepreneurial Hist — Explorations in Entrepreneurial History
Explorations Econ Hist — Explorations in Economic History
Explorations Econ Research — Explorations in Economic Research
Explor Econ Hist — Explorations in Economic History
Explor Econ Pet Ind — Exploration and Economics of the Petroleum Industry
Explor Econ Petrol Ind — Exploration and Economics of the Petroleum Industry
Explor Econ Res — Explorations in Economic Research
Explor Entrep Hist — Explorations in Entrepreneurial History
Explor Geophys — Exploration Geophysics
Explor Geophys (Sydney) — Exploration Geophysics (Sydney)
Explor Geophys (USSR) — Exploration Geophysics (USSR)
Explor J — Explorers Journal
Explor Jour NY — Explorers Journal (New York)
Explor Parc Nat A — Exploration du Parc National Albert
Explor Rev — Exploration Review
Explor Sci Res — Exploration and Scientific Research. Pan-American Society of Tropical Research
Explos Eng — Explosives Engineer
Explos Explos — Explosion and Explosives
Explosives Eng — Explosives Engineer
Explosivst — Explosivstoffe
Explos Mater — Explosive Materials
Explos Res Dev Establ (GB) Tech Note — Explosives Research and Development Establishment (Great Britain). Technical Note
Expl Parasit — Experimental Parasitology
Expl Path — Experimental Pathology
Expl Rec Dep Agric S Aust — Experimental Record. Department of Agriculture. South Australia
Expl Text L — Explicacion de Textos Literarios
Exp Lung Res — Experimental Lung Research
Exp Magn — Experimental Magnetism
Exp Mech — Experimental Mechanics
Exp Med — Experimental Medicine
Exp Med Microbiol — Experimental Medicine and Microbiology
Exp Med Microbiol (Engl Transl) — Experimental Medicine and Microbiology (English Translation of Medycyna Doswiadczalna i Mikrobiologia)
Exp Med Microbiol (Engl Transl Med Dosw Mikrobiol) — Experimental Medicine and Microbiology (English Translation of Medycyna Doswiadczalna i Mikrobiologia)
Exp Med Pathol Klin — Experimentelle Medizin, Pathologie, und Klinik
Exp Med Surg — Experimental Medicine and Surgery
Exp Methods Microgravity Mater Sci Res — Experimental Methods for Microgravity Materials Science Research
Exp Methods Phys Sci — Experimental Methods in the Physical Sciences
Exp Molec Path — Experimental and Molecular Pathology
Exp Molec Pathol — Experimental and Molecular Pathology
Exp Molecul Pathol — Experimental and Molecular Pathology
Exp Mol Med — Experimental and Molecular Medicine
Exp Mol Pat — Experimental and Molecular Pathology
Exp Mol Pathol — Experimental and Molecular Pathology
Exp Mol Pathol Suppl — Experimental and Molecular Pathology. Supplement

Exp Mycol — Experimental Mycology
Exp Nephrol — Experimental Nephrology
Exp Neurol — Experimental Neurology
Exp Neurol Suppl — Experimental Neurology. Supplement
Exp Nucl Phys — Experimental Nuclear Physics
Exp (NY) — Export (New York)
Expo Annu Biochim Med — Exposes Annuels de Biochimie Medicale
Expo Congr Int Technol Pharm — Exposes. Congres International de Technologie Pharmaceutique
Export Dir — Export Direction
Export Nws — Export News
Export Rev Br Drug Chem Ind — Export Review of the British Drug and Chemical Industries
Exports of Aust — Exports of Australia
Exports of Aust & NZ — Exports of Australia and New Zealand
Expos — Expositor
Expos Ann Biochim Med — Exposes Annuels de Biochimie Medicale
Expos Annu Biochim Med — Exposes Annuels de Biochimie Medicale
Exposition Math — Expositiones Mathematicae. International Journal for Pure and Applied Mathematics
Exposit Tim — Expository Times
Exposit Times — Expository Times
Expos T — Expository Times
Exp Parasit — Experimental Parasitology
Exp Parasitol — Experimental Parasitology
Exp Path — Experimentelle Pathologie
Exp Pathol — Experimentelle Pathologie
Exp Pathol (Jena) — Experimental Pathology (Jena)
Exp Pathol Suppl — Experimental Pathology. Supplement
Exp Physiol — Experimental Physiology
Exp Physiol Biochem — Experiments in Physiology and Biochemistry
Exp Progr Grassland Res Inst (Hurley) — Experiments in Progress. Grassland Research Institute (Hurley)
Exp R — Expatriate Review
Exp Rec Dep Agric S Aust — Experimental Record. Department of Agriculture. South Australia
Exp Rec Grassland Husb Dept — Experimental Record. Grassland Husbandry Department. West of Scotland Agricultural College
Exp Rep Equine Health Lab — Experimental Reports of Equine Health Laboratory
Exp Rep Min Agr Natur Resour (Nigeria) Midwest Reg — Experiment Report. Ministry of Agriculture and Natural Resources (Nigeria). Midwest Region
Expression Syst Processes rDNA Prod — Expression Systems and Processes for rDNA Products
Express-Ne — Express-News
Express Transl Serv List — Express Translation Service List
Exp Results Phase Equilib Pure Compon Prop — Experimental Results for Phase Equilibria and Pure Component Properties
Exp Scr — Exempla Scripturarum
Exp Ship Guide — Export Shipping Guide
Exp Sta Rec — Experiment Station Record. Office of Experiment Station. US Department of Agriculture
Exp Sta Record — Experiment Station Record
Exp Stn Rec — Experiment Station Record. United States Department of Agriculture
Exp St Rec — Experiment Station Record
Exp Stress Anal Proc — Experimental Stress Analysis. Proceedings
ExpT — Expository Times
Exp Tech — Experimental Techniques
Exp Tech Phys — Experimentelle Technik der Physik
Exp Tech Phys Berlin — Experimentelle Technik der Physik (Berlin)
Exp Tech Phys Lemgo Ger — Experimental Technique of Physics (Lemgo, Germany)
Exp Therm Fluid Sci — Experimental Thermal and Fluid Science
Exp Thermodyn — Experimental Thermodynamics
Exp Ther (Osaka) — Experiment and Therapy (Osaka)
ExpTim — Expository Times
Exptl Mech — Experimental Mechanics
Exptl Tech — Experimental Techniques
Exp Toxicol Pathol — Experimental and Toxicologic Pathology
Exp USA — Expositor (Cleveland, Ohio, USA)
Exp Veterinaermed — Experimentelle Veterinaermedizin
Exp Water Toxicol — Experimental Water Toxicology
Exp Work Inst Pomol Skierniewice Pol — Experimental Work. Institute of Pomology. Skierniewice. Poland
EXS — Executive Skills
EXS — Exegesis
EXSP — Extracts from the Soviet Press on the Soviet North and Antarctic
Ex T — Expository Times
Ext — Extrapolation
Ext Abstr Conf Solid State Devices Mater — Extended Abstracts. Conference on Solid State Devices and Materials
Ext Abstr Meet Int Soc Electrochem — Extended Abstracts. Meeting. International Society of Electrochemistry
Ext Abstr Program Bienn Conf Carbon — Extended Abstracts and Program. Biennial Conference on Carbon
Ext Affairs — External Affairs
Ext Amer — Extension en las Americas
Ext Bull Agric Ext Serv Purdue Univ — Extension Bulletin. Agricultural Extension Service. Purdue University
Ext Bull Agric Ext Serv Univ Minn — Extension Bulletin. Agriculture Extension Service. University of Minnesota
Ext Bull ASPAC Food Fert Technol Cent — Extension Bulletin. ASPAC [*Asian and Pacific Council*]. Food and Fertilizer Technology Center
Ext Bull Coop Ext Serv Univ Md — Extension Bulletin. Cooperative Extension Service. University of Maryland

Ext Bull Cornell Agric Exp Stn — Extension Bulletin. Cornell Agricultural Experiment Station
Ext Bull Del Univ Agr Ext Serv — Extension Bulletin. Delaware University. Agricultural Extension Service
Ext Bull Dep Agric S Aust — Extension Bulletin. Department of Agriculture. South Australia
Ext Bull Dept Agric South Aust — Extension Bulletin. Department of Agriculture and Fisheries. South Australia
Ext Bull E Coop Ext Serv Mich State Univ — Extension Bulletin E. Cooperative Extension Service. Michigan State University
Ext Bull E Rutgers State Univ NJ Coop Ext Serv — Extension Bulletin E. Rutgers. The State University of New Jersey. Cooperative Extension Service
Ext Bull Flor Agric Exp St — Extension Bulletin. Florida Agricultural Experiment Station
Ext Bull Ind Agric Exp Stn — Extension Bulletin. Indiana Agricultural Experiment Station
Ext Bull Iowa State Univ — Extension Bulletin. Iowa State University
Ext Bull MD Univ Coop Ext Serv — Extension Bulletin. Maryland University. Cooperative Extension Service
Ext Bull Mich State Univ Coop Ext Serv — Extension Bulletin. Michigan State University. Cooperative Extension Service
Ext Bull Mich St Coll — Extension Bulletin. Michigan State College
Ext Bull ND State Univ Agric Appl Sci Coop Ext Serv — Extension Bulletin. North Dakota State University of Agriculture and Applied Science. Cooperative Extension Service
Ext Bull Ohio State Univ Coll Agr Coop Ext Serv — Extension Bulletin. Ohio State University. College of Agriculture. Cooperative Extension Service
Ext Bull Ohio St Univ — Extension Bulletin. Ohio State University
Ext Bull Oreg State Univ Coop Ext Serv — Extension Bulletin. Oregon State University. Cooperative Extension Service
Ext Bull Purdue Univ Agric Ext Serv — Extension Bulletin. Purdue University. Agricultural Extension Service
Ext Bull Purdue Univ Dep Agric Ext — Extension Bulletin. Purdue University. Department of Agricultural Extension
Ext Bull Univ Del Coop Ext Serv — Extension Bulletin. University of Delaware. Cooperative Extension Service
Ext Bull Univ MD Coop Ext Serv — Extension Bulletin. University of Maryland. Cooperative Extension Service
Ext Bull Univ Minn Agr Ext Serv — Extension Bulletin. University of Minnesota. Agricultural Extension Service
Ext Bull Univ Minn Agric Ext Serv — Extension Bulletin. University of Minnesota. Agricultural Extension Service
Ext Bull US Dep Agric — Extension Bulletin. United States Department of Agriculture
Ext Bull Wash State Univ Coll Agr Ext Serv — Extension Bulletin. Washington State University. College of Agriculture. Extension Service
Ext Bull Wash State Univ Coop Ext Serv — Extension Bulletin. Washington State University. Cooperative Extension Service
Ext Bull Wash St Coll — Extension Bulletin. Washington State College
Ext Circ Ark Coll Agric — Extension Circular. Arkansas College of Agriculture
Ext Circ EC Coop Ext Serv Utah State Univ — Extension Circular EC. Cooperative Extension Service. Utah State University
Ext Circ Ill Univ — Extension Circular. Illinois University
Ext Circ N Carol Agric Exp Stn — Extension Circular. North Carolina Agricultural Experiment Station
Ext Circ NC State Coll Agric Eng Agric Ext Serv — Extension Circular. North Carolina State College of Agriculture and Engineering. Agricultural Extension Service
Ext Circ NC State Univ Agr Ext Serv — Extension Circular. North Carolina State University. Agricultural Extension Service
Ext Circ Oreg State Univ Ext Serv — Extension Circular. Oregon State University. Extension Service
Ext Circ Pa State Univ Agric Ext Serv — Extension Circular. Pennsylvania State University. Agricultural Extension Service
Ext Circ PA St Coll Agric — Extension Circular. Pennsylvania State College. School of Agriculture
Ext Circ P Auburn Univ Agr Ext Serv — Extension Circular P. Auburn University. Agricultural Extension Service
Ext Circ Purdue Univ Coop Ext Serv — Extension Circular. Purdue University. Cooperative Extension Service
Ext Circ Purdue Univ Dept Agr Ext — Extension Circular. Purdue University. Department of Agricultural Extension
Ext Circ S Dak Coll Agric — Extension Circular. South Dakota College of Agriculture
Ext Circ S Dak State Univ Coop Ext Serv — Extension Circular. South Dakota State University. Cooperative Extension Service
Ext Circ Utah Agric Coll — Extension Circular. Utah Agricultural College
Ext Circ Wash State Univ Coll Agr Ext Serv — Extension Circular. Washington State University. College of Agriculture. Extension Service
Ext Circ Wash State Univ Coop Ext Serv — Extension Circular. Washington State University. Cooperative Extension Service
Ext Course Lect Ak Prim Assoc — Extension Course Lectures. Auckland Primary Principals Association
Ext Dev Unit Rep — Extension Development Unit Report
Extel Handbook Mark Leaders — Extel Handbook of Market Leaders
Extended Abstr Program Bienn Conf Carbon — Extended Abstracts and Program. Biennial Conference on Carbon
Extensn — Extension
Exterm Log — Exterminators' Log
External Stud Gaz — External Studies Gazette
External Studies Gaz — External Studies Gazette
Externer Ber Kernforschungszent Karlsruhe — Externer Bericht. Kernforschungszentrum Karlsruhe
Externer Ber Kernforschungszentr Karlsruhe — Externer Bericht. Kernforschungszentrum Karlsruhe

Externer Ber Kernforschungszentrum Karlsruhe — Externer Bericht. Kernforschungszentrum Karlsruhe

Ext Extra ExEx SD Coop Ext Serv — Extension Extra ExEx. South Dakota Cooperative Extension Service

Ext Facts Coop Ext Serv Oklahoma State Univ — Oklahoma State University. Cooperative Extension Service. Extension Facts

Ext Folder Agric Ext Serv Univ Minn — Extension Folder. Agricultural Extension Service. University of Minnesota

Ext Folder Mich State Univ Agr Appl Sci Coop Ext Serv — Extension Folder. Michigan State University of Agriculture and Applied Science.Cooperative Extension Service

Ext Folder Mich St Univ — Extension Folder. Michigan State University

Ext Folder NC Agric Ext Serv — Extension Folder. North Carolina Agricultural Extension Service

Ext Folder NC State Univ Agr Ext Serv — Extension Folder. North Carolina State University. Agricultural Extension Service

Ext Folder Univ Minn Agr Ext Serv — Extension Folder. University of Minnesota. Agricultural Extension Service

Ext Folder Univ Minn Agric Ext Serv — Extension Folder. University of Minnesota. Agricultural Extension Service

Ext Folder Univ NH Coll Agr Ext Serv — Extension Folder. University of New Hampshire. College of Agriculture. Extension Service

Ext Home Econ Fam Econ Resour Manage EHE Univ Arkansas Coop — Extension Home Economics. Family Economics Resource Management. EHE. Universityof Arkansas Cooperative Extension Service

ExTL — Explicacion de Textos Literarios

Ext Leafl Agric Ext Serv Purdue Univ — Extension Leaflet. Agricultural Extension Service. Purdue University

Ext Leafl Ohio State Univ Coll Agr Coop Ext Serv — Extension Leaflet. Ohio State University. College of Agriculture. Cooperative Extension Service

Ext Leafl Purdue Univ Agric Ext Serv — Extension Leaflet. Purdue University. Agricultural Extension Service

Ext Leafl Univ Md Coop Ext Serv — Extension Leaflet. University of Maryland. Cooperative Extension Service

Ext Leafl Utah State Univ Agr Ext Serv — Extension Leaflet. Utah State University. Agricultural Extension Service

Ext Leafl Utah State Univ Coop Ext Serv — Extension Leaflet. Utah State University. Cooperative Extension Service

Ext Leafl Utah St Univ — Extension Leaflet. Utah State University

Ext Mimeogr Circ S Dak State Univ Coop Ext Serv — Extension Mimeographed Circular. South Dakota State University. Cooperative Extension Service

Ext Mimeo Wash State Univ Coll Agr Ext Serv — Extension Mimeo. Washington State University. College of Agriculture. ExtensionService

Ext Misc Publ Agric Ext Serv Univ Minn — Extension Miscellaneous Publication. Agricultural Extension Service. Universityof Minnesota

Ext Publ Coop Ext Serv Univ NH — Extension Publication. Cooperative Extension Service. University of New Hampshire

Ext Publ Ill Univ N Cent Reg — Extension Publication. Illinois University. North Central Region

Ext Publ LA State Univ Agr Ext Serv — Extension Publication. Louisiana State University. Agricultural Extension Service

Ext Publ Wash St Coll — Extension Publication. Washington State College

Extracta Math — Extracta Mathematicae

Extra Mural Reptr — Extra-Mural Reporter

Extrap — Extrapolation

Extrapolat — Extrapolation

Ext Rev Fr — (Extrait de) La Revue Francaise

Ext Rev US Dep Agric — Extension Review. US Department of Agriculture

Extr Gynaecol — Extracta Gynaecologica

Extr Or Med — Extreme-Orient Medical

Extr Proces Verbaux Seances Acad Sci Montpellier — Extraits des Proces-Verbaux des Seances. Academie des Sciences et Lettres de Montpellier

Ext Serv Bull IA St Coll Agric — Extension Service Bulletin. Iowa State College of Agriculture

Ext Service R — Extension Service Review

Ext Serv Leafl Coll Agric Rutgers Univ — Extension Service Leaflet. College of Agriculture. Rutgers University

Ext Serv R — Extension Service Review

Ext Serv Rev — Extension Service Review

Ext Stud PA State Univ Ext Serv — Extension Studies. Pennsylvania State University. Extension Service

EXW — Europa Chemie

Ex W — Express Wieczorny

EXX — Expo Data

Exxon Monogr Ser — Exxon Monograph Series

EXY — Excerpta Indonesica

EY — European Yearbook

EY — Eye

EY — Journal of Energy Engineering

EYA — Etnologia y Arqueologia [Lima]

EYBIA5 — Encyclopedie Biologique

EyD — Economia y Desarrollo

EYDIDI — Ecology of Disease

Eye Ear Nos — Eye, Ear, Nose, and Throat Monthly

Eye Ear Nose Throat Mon — Eye, Ear, Nose, and Throat Monthly

Eye Ear Nose Throat Month — Eye, Ear, Nose, and Throat Monthly

EYENAZ — Encyclopedie Entomologique

Eye Sci — Eye Science

EYETD — Energy Economist

Eyewit — Eyewitness

EyF — Etnologia y Folklore

EYGZAD — Eiyogaku Zasshi

EY Loc Hist Ser — East Yorkshire Local History Series

EYMYA6 — Encyclopedie Mycologique

EYP — Dun's Electronic Yellow Pages

EYPSB — Energy Pipelines and Systems

EZ — Ehuzu

EZ — Elektronik-Zeitung fuer Industrie, Wirtschaft, Wissenschaft, und Verwaltung

EZ — Epigraphia Zeylanica

EZ — Ethnologische Zeitschrift

EZDK — Enchoria. Zeitschrift fuer Demotistik und Koptologie

Ezeg Imp Russk Geogr Obsc — Ezegodnik Imperatorskago Russkago Graficeskago Obscestva

Ezeg Muz Ist Rel At Ak N SSSR — Ezhegodnik Muzeja Istorii Religii i Ateizma Akademii Nauk SSSR

Ezheg Geol Mineral Ross — Ezhegodnik po Geologii i Mineralogii Rossii

Ezheg Gos Issled Inst Myasn Promsti — Ezhegodnik Gosudarstvennogo Issledovatel'skogo Instituta MyasnoiPromyshlennosti

Ezheg Inst Eksp Med Akad Med Nauk SSSR — Ezhegodnik Instituta Eksperimental'noi Meditsiny Akademii Meditsinskikh Nauk SSSR

Ezheg Inst Geokhim Sib Otd Akad Nauk SSSR — Ezhegodnik Instituta Geokhimii Sibirskogo Otdeleniya Akademii Nauk SSSR

Ezheg Inst Geol Geokhim Akad Nauk SSSR Ural Fil — Ezhegodnik. Institut Geologii i Geokhimii. Akademiya Nauk SSSR Ural'skii Filial

Ezheg Inst Geol Geokhim Akad Nauk SSSR Ural Nauchn Tsentr — Ezhegodnik. Institut Geologii i Geokhimii. Akademiya Nauk SSSR Ural'skii Nauchnyi Tsentr

Ezheg Inst Geol Komi Fil Akad Nauk SSSR — Ezhegodnik Instituta Geologii Komi Filiala Akademii Nauk SSSR

Ezheg Inst Tsvetn Metall (Plovdiv) — Ezhegodnik. Institut Tsvetnoi Metallurgii (Plovdiv)

Ezheg Nauchno Issled Inst Metall Obogashch — Ezhegodnik Nauchno-Issledovatel'skogo Instituta Metallurgii iObogashcheniya

Ezheg Nauchno Issled Inst Tsvetn Metall (Plovdiv) — Ezhegodnik Nauchno-Issledovatel'skogo Instituta Tsvetnoi Metallurgii(Plovdiv)

Ezheg Nauchn Rab Alma-At Inst Usoversh Vrachei — Ezhegodnik Nauchnykh Rabot Alma-Atinskii Institut Usovershenstvovaniya Vrachei

Ezheg Nauchn Rab Inst Usoversh Vrachei Kaz SSR — Ezhegodnik Nauchnykh Rabot Instituta Usovershenstvovaniya Vrachei Kazakhskoi SSR

Ezheg Nauchn Tr Medska Akad (Varna) — Ezhegodnik Nauchnykh Trudov. Meditsinskaya Akademiya (Varna)

Ezhegodnik GIM — Ezhegodnik Gosudarstvennyi Istoricheskii Muzei

Ezhegodnik Zool Muz Akad Nauk SSSR — Ezhegodnik Zoologicheskogo Muzeia Akademii Nauk Sofuza Sovetskikh Sotsialisticheskikh Respublik

Ezhegodnik Zool Muz Ross Akad Nauk — Ezhegodnik Zoologicheskogo Muzeia Rossiiskoi Akademii Nauk

Ezheg Ova Estestvoispyt — Ezhegodnik Obshchestva Estestvoispytatelei

Ezheg O-Va Estestvoispyt Akad Nauk Est SSR — Ezhegodnik Obshchestva Estestvoispytatelei Akademiya Nauk. Estonskoi SSR

Ezheg Pochvoved — Ezhegodnik Pochvovedeniya

Ezheg Pol Geol Ova — Ezhegodnik Pol'skogo Geologicheskogo Obshchestva

Ezheg Sib Inst Geokhim — Ezhegodnik Sibirskogo Instituta Geokhimii

Ezhe Inst Geokhim Sib Otd Akad Nauk SSSR — Ezhegodnik Instituta Geokhimii Sibirskogo Otdeleniya Akademii Nauk SSSR

EZI — Encyclopedia of Zionism and Israel

Ez Lit — Ezik i Literatura

EZS — Entomologische Zeitschrift (Stuttgart)

EZV — Erlanger Zeitschriften-Verzeichnis

EZZ — Ethnologische Zeitschrift (Zurich)

F

F — Farrago
F — February
F — Federal Reporter
F — Fennia
F — Filosofia
F — Flora oder Allgemeine Botanische Zeitung
F — Folio
F — Folklore
F — Fontaine
F — Fortnightly
F — Fortune
F — Forum
F — F. Revue Trimestrielle
F — Indian Folklore
F 3d — Federal Reporter, Third Series
Fa — Fabula
FA — Fantastic Adventures
FA — Fasti Archaeologici
FA — Filologiskt Arkiv
FA — [*The*] Financial Australian
FA — Finanzarchiv
FA — Folia Archaeologica
FA — Folklore Americano
FA — Foreign Affairs
FA — Foreign Agriculture. United States Department of Agriculture
FA — Forstarchiv
FA — France-Amerique
FA — Fronteras Argentinas
FAA — Functional Analysis and Its Applications
FAA — Office of Aviation Medicine. Report
FAA Aviat Ne — FAA [*Federal Aviation Administration*] Aviation News
FAA Aviat News — FAA (Federation Aviator Agency) Aviation News
FAA Gen Av N — FAA [*Federal Aviation Administration*] General Aviation News
FAATD — Fundamental and Applied Toxicology
Fab — Fabula
FAB — Festschrift fuer Alfred Bertholet
FAB — Foreign Affairs Bulletin
F Ab — Forestry Abstracts
FAB — Fuer Arbeit und Besinnung
Faba — Faba. Federation National du Legume Sec
FABAD Farm Bilimler Derg — FABAD [*Farmasotik Bilimler Ankara Dernegi*] Farmasotik Bilimler Dergisi
Faberg Mitt — Faberg-Mitteilungen
Faberg Tag — Faberg-Tagung. Fachnormenausschuss Bergbau
FABIS Newsl Faba Bean Inf Serv — FABIS Newsletter. Faba Bean Information Service
Fabric Rev — Fabric Review
Fabr Prog — Fabrication Progress
FABSAE — FAO [*Food and Agriculture Organization of the United Nations*] Fisheries Biology Synopsis
Fab Tr — Fabian Tract
FA (Bud) — Folia Archaeologica (Budapest)
FABZAZ — Flora oder Allgemeine Botanische Zeitung
FAC — Folia Antropologica [*Caracas*]
FAC — France au Combat
Fac Agron Montevideo Publ Misc — Facultad de Agronomia de Montevideo. Publicacion Miscelanea
Fac Cienc Agrar Para Bol — Faculdade de Ciencias Agrarias do Para. Boletim
Fac Cienc Agrar Univ Austral Chile Bol — Facultad de Ciencias Agrarias. Universidad Austral de Chile. Boletin
FAC Cocoa — Foreign Agriculture Circular. Cocoa
FAC Coffee — Foreign Agriculture Circular. Coffee
FAC Cotton — Foreign Agriculture Circular. Cotton
FAC Dairy — Foreign Agriculture Circular. Dairy Products
Fac Derecho R Univ Zulia — Facultad de Derecho. Revista. Universidad de Zulia
FAC DLP — Foreign Agriculture Circular. Livestock and Poultry Export Trade
Fac Farm Coimbra Bol — Faculdade de Farmacia de Coimbra. Boletim
Fac Farm Odontol Araraquara Rev — Faculdade de Farmacia e Odontologia de Araraquara. Revista
FAC GrainS — Foreign Agriculture Circular. World Grain Situation
FACH — Family and Community Health
Fa Ch — Fathers of the Church
Fachaerztl Winke — Fachaerztliche Winke
FachausschBer Dt Glastech Ges — Fachausschussbericht. Deutsche Glastechnische Gesellschaft

FachausschBer Dt Keram Ges — Fachausschussbericht. Deutsche Keramische Gesellschaft
Fachausschussber Dtsch Glastech Ges — Fachausschussbericht der Deutschen Glastechnischen. Gesellschaft
Fachber Huettenpraxis Metallweiterverarb — Fachberichte Huettenpraxis Metallweiterverarbeitung
Fachber Huettenprax Metallweiterverarb — Fachberichte Huettenpraxis Metallweiterverarbeitung
Fachber Metallbearb — Fachberichte fuer Metallbearbeitung
Fachber Metall Werkstofftech Umwelt Verfahrenstech — Fachberichte Metallurgie and Werkstofftechnik. Umwelt-Verfahrenstechnik
Fachber Oberflaechentech — Fachberichte fuer Oberflaechentechnik
Fachber Standis — Fachbereich Standisierung
Fachber Standis Glas — Fachbereich Standisierung Glas
Fachbl Holzarb — Fachblatt fuer Holzarbeiter
Fachbl Sudetendt Tieraerzte — Fachblatt der Sudetendeutschen Tieraerzte
Fachbuchreihe Schweisstech — Fachbuchreihe Schweisstechnik
Fachbuchr Schweisstech — Fachbuchreihe Schweisstechnik
Fachh Chemigr — Fachhefte fuer Chemigraphie, Lithographie, und Tiefdruck
Fachh Chemigr Lithogr Tiefdruck — Fachhefte fuer Chemigraphie, Lithographie, und Tiefdruck
Fachhft Chemiegr Lithogr Tiefdr — Fachhefte fuer die Chemiegraphie, Lithographie, und den Tiefdruck
Fach Inf Energ-Versorg Schwaben AG — Fach-Informationen. Energie-Versorgung Schwaben AG
Fachliche Mitt Austria Tabakwerke — Fachliche Mitteilungen der Austria Tabakwerke
Fachliche Mitt Oesterr Tabakregie — Fachliche Mitteilungen der Oesterreichischen Tabakregie
Fachl Mitt Oest Tabakregie — Fachliche Mitteilungen der Oesterreichischen Tabakregie
Fachl Publn Technol Gewerbemus Wien — Fachliche Publikationen des Technologischen Gewerbemuseums in Wien
FAC Hort — Foreign Agriculture Circular. Horticultural Products
Fac Humanid Cienc Rev (Montevideo) — Facultad de Humanidades y Ciencias. Revista (Montevideo)
Fachverb Strahlenschutz Ber FS — Fachverband fuer Strahlenschutz. Bericht FS
Fachztg Auto — Fachzeitung fuer Automobilismus
Fachztg Blechbearb U Install — Fachzeitung fuer Blechbearbeitung und Installation
FACI — Folklore Americano; Organo del Comite Interamericano de Folklore
Facial Orthop Temporomandibular Arthrol — Facial Orthopedics and Temporomandibular Arthrology
Facial Plast Surg — Facial Plastic Surgery
Facial Plast Surg Clin North Am — Facial Plastic Surgery Clinics of North America
Fac Ingen Agrimens (Montevideo) Publ Didact Inst Mat Estadis — Facultad de Ingenieria y Agrimensura (Montevideo). Publicaciones Didacticas delInstituto de Matematica y Estadistica
Fack — Fackel
Fac Lett Sc NS — Faculte des Lettres et Sciences Humaines. Universite de Clermont-Ferrand. Nouvelle Serie
Fac L Rev — Faculty of Law Review
Fac Med Madrid Arch — Facultad de Medicina de Madrid. Archivos
Fac Med Montevideo An — Facultad de Medicina de Montevideo. Anales
Fac Odontol Aracatuba Rev — Facultad de Odontologia de Aracatuba. Revista
Fac Odontol Ribeirao Preto Rev — Facultad de Odontologia de Ribeirao Preto. Revista
FACOEB — Food Additives and Contaminants
Fac of LR — Faculty of Law Review. University of Toronto
FAC Oil — Foreign Agriculture Circular. Oilseeds and Products
Fac Quim Farm Univ Cent Ecuador Rev — Facultad de Quimica y Farmacia. Universidad Central del Ecuador.Revista
Fac Res Lect Univ Calif Los Ang — Faculty Research Lectures. University of California at Los Angeles
Fac Res Pap — Faculty Research Papers
Fac Res Pap Hanyang Women's Jr Coll — Faculty Research Papers. Hanyang Women's Junior College
Fac Sci Agron Lab Biochim Nutr Publ — Faculte des Sciences Agronomiques. Laboratoire de Biochimie de la Nutrition. Publication
Fac Sci Agron Lab Biochim Nutr Publ Univ Cathol Louvain — Faculte des Sciences Agronomiques. Laboratoire de Biochimie de laNutrition. Publication. Universite Catholique de Louvain
Fac Sci Tunis Rev — Faculte des Sciences de Tunis. Revue
Facsimile Repr Herpetol — Facsimile Reprints in Herpetology
Facsimile Repr Soc Study Amphibians Reptiles — Facsimile Reprint. Society for the Study of Amphibians and Reptiles

Facsim Repr Herpetol — Facsimile Reprints in Herpetology
Facsim Repr Soc Study Amphibians Reptiles — Facsimile Reprint. Society for the Study of Amphibians and Reptiles
Facs Pubis Doct Theses Chem Chem Engng US Univ — Faculties, Publications, and Doctoral Theses in Chemistry and Chemical Engineering in US Universities
FAC Sugar — Foreign Agriculture Circular. Sugar, Molasses, and Honey
FACT — Facility for the Analysis of Chemical Thermodynamics
FACT — Fuel Abstracts and Current Titles
FACT Am Soc Mech Eng — FACT (Fuels and Combustion Technologies Division. ASME) American Society of Mechanical Engineers
Facta Univ Ser Math Inform — Facta Universitatis. Series. Mathematics and Informatics
Facta Univ Ser Mech Automat Control Robot — Facta Universitatis. Series. Mechanics, Automatic Control, and Robotics
Fact Bldg Stud — Factory Building Studies
FAC Tea — Foreign Agriculture Circular. Tea and Spices
Fact Equip Mater — Factory Equipment and Materials
Fact Equip News — Factory Equipment News
Facteurs Biol Chim Aliment Anim — Facteurs Biologiques et Chimiques dans l'Alimentation des Animaux
Fact Ind Manage — Factory and Industrial Management
Fact Ind Mgmt — Factory and Industrial Management
Fact Lab — Factory Laboratory
Fact Mag — Fact Magazine
Fact Manage Maint — Factory Management and Maintenance
Fact Manage (NY) — Factory Management (New York)
Fact Man Maint — Factory Management and Maintenance
Fact Mgmt Maint — Factory Management and Maintenance
Fact Mut Bull Loss Prev — Factory Mutual Bulletin of Loss Prevention
Fact Mut Rec — Factory Mutual Record
FAC Tobac — Foreign Agriculture Circular. Tobacco
Factores Biol Quim Nutr Anim — Factores Biologicos y Quimicos de la Nutricion Animal
Factor Odontol — Factor Odontologico
Factors Mag — Factor's Magazine
Factors Regul Blood Press Trans Confs Josiah Macy Jr Fdn — Factors Regulating Blood Pressure. Transactions of Conferences. Josiah Macy Jr. Foundation
Factors Regul Blood Pressure Trans Conf — Factors Regulating Blood Pressure. Transactions of the Conference
Factory and Ind Management — Factory and Industrial Management
Factory Mgt — Factory Management and Maintenance
Fact Pl — Factory and Plant
Fact Plant — Factory and Plant
Facts & Figures — Australian in Facts and Figures
Facts Fig — Facts and Figures
Facts (Finl) — Facts about Film (Finland)
Facts Fish — Facts on Fish. Fisheries Association of British Columbia
Fact Sheet Coll Agric Univ Nev-Reno Nev Coop Ext — Fact Sheet. College of Agriculture. University of Nevada-Reno. Nevada Cooperative Extension
Fact Sheet Coop Ext Serv Univ MD — Fact Sheet. Cooperative Extension Service. University of Maryland
Fact Sheet Oreg State Univ Coop Ext Serv — Fact Sheet. Oregon State University. Cooperative Extension Service
Fact Sheet S Dak State Univ Coop Ext Serv — Fact Sheet. South Dakota State University. Cooperative Extension Service
Fact Sheets Swed — Fact Sheets on Sweden
Fact Sheet Univ Arkansas Coop Ext Serv — Fact Sheet. University of Arkansas. Cooperative Extension Service
Fact Sheet Univ MD Coop Ext Serv — Fact Sheet. University of Maryland. Cooperative Extension Service
Fact Sheet USDA — Fact Sheet. United States Department of Agriculture
Fact Sh Univ Wis Ext — Fact Sheet. University of Wisconsin - Extension
Facts Hypalon Engrs Des — Facts about Hypalon for Engineers and Designers
Facts Ind — Facts for Industry
Facts Ind Plast Synth Resins — Facts for Industry. Plastics and Synthetic Resins
Facts Ind Tire Cord — Facts for Industry. Tire Cord and Tire Cord Fabrics
Facts Methods Sci Res — Facts and Methods for Scientific Research
Facts Sug — Facts about Sugar
Fac Vet Leon An — Facultad de Veterinaria de Leon. Anales
FAC WCP — Foreign Agriculture Circular. World Crop Production
Fac Wkshop Acts — Factory and Workshop Acts. Illustrated Series of Abstracts from Reports of Industrial Accidents. Industrial Accidents
FAD — Fantastic Adventures
F a D — Film a Divadlo
F Addit Contr Ser FAO — Food Additive Control Series. Food and Agriculture Organization of the United Nations
FADOA — Family Coordinator
FADR — Foreign Animal Disease Report
Fa Econ — Farm Economics
Fa Econ — Farm Economist
Faellesudvalget Statens Mejeri-Husdyrbrugsfors Beret — Faellesudvalget foer Statens Mejeri-og Husdyrbrugsforsog Beretning
Faerb Appretur — Faerberei und Appretur
Faerber Chemischrein — Faerber und Chemischreiniger
Faerbereiztg — Faerberei-Zeitung
Faerber Ztg — Faerber-Zeitung
Faerg Lack Scand — Faerg och Lack Scandinavia
Fa F — Faith and Freedom
FAF — Foreign Affairs
FAF — Philippine Development
FAFBAH — FAO [*Food and Agriculture Organization of the United Nations*] Fisheries Biology Technical Paper
FAFCAK — FAO [*Food and Agriculture Organization of the United Nations*] Fisheries Circular

F Affairs — Foreign Affairs
FAFLBE — Fauna and Flora
FAFN — Fauna Fennica
FAFRAV — Faune de France
FAFSBZ — FAO [*Food and Agriculture Organization of the United Nations*] Fisheries Synopsis
FAG — Foreign Agriculture
FAGAAS — Frankfurter Arbeiten aus dem Gebiete der Anglistik und der Amerika-Studien
Fagbl Norsk Skog Og Jordarb Forb — Fagblad for Norsk Skog- og Jordarbeider-Forbund
Fagbl Norsk TraearbForb — Fagblad for Norsk Traearbeiderforbund
FAGLAI — Farmaceutski Glasnik
Fagl Forum — Fagligt Forum
F Agric — Food and Agriculture
FAHAA — Family Handyman
FAH Rev — FAH [*Federation of American Hospitals*] Review
FAI — Fairplay International Shipping Weekly
FAICAZ — Folia Allergologica et Immunologica Clinica
Failure Anal Tech Appl Proc Int Conf — Failure Analysis. Techniques and Applications. Proceedings. International Conference on Failure Analysis
Failure Modes Compos — Failure Modes in Composites. Proceedings of the Symposium
Faim-Develop — Faim-Developpement
FAIPA — Faipar
Faip Kutatas — Faipari Kutatasok
Fairchild Trop Gard Bull — Fairchild Tropical Garden Bulletin
FAIREC — Fruits Agro-Industrie Regions Chaudes
Fair Empl Prac Cas BNA — Fair Employment Practice Cases. Bureau of National Affairs
Fairfax Mon — Fairfax Monthly
FAIR Newsl — Fast Access Information Retrieval. Newsletter
Faisneis — Faisneis Raithiuil Quarterly Bulletin
FAJ — Financial Analysts Journal
FAJAAY — Folia Anatomica Japonica
Fak Derg — Dil ve Tarih-Cografya Fakueltesi Dergisi
Fak Mat Univ Kiril Metodij Skopje Godisen — Skopje Univezitetot Kiril i Metodij Fakultet na Matematicka Godisen Zbornik (Skopje)
Faktory Vneshn Sredy Ikh Znach Zdorov'ya Naseleniya — Faktory Vneshykh Sredy i Ikh Znachenie dlya Zdorov'ya Naseleniya
Fakt Vneshn Sred Znach Zdor Nasel Resp Mezhved Sb — Faktory Vneshnykh Sredy i Ikh Znachenie dlya Zdorov'ya Naseleniya Respublikanskii Mezhvedomstvennyi i Sbornik
F a L — Field and Laboratory. Contributions from the Science Departments
FALAA — Farbe und Lack
FALau — Feuille d'Avis de Lausanne
Falke Monatsschr Ornithol — Falke Monatsschrift fuer Ornithologie und Vivarienkunde
Falke Monatsschr Ornithol Vivarienkd Ausg A — Falke Monatsschrift fuer Ornithologie und Vivarienkunde. Ausgabe A
Falkl Isl Depend Surv Sci Rep — Falkland Islands Dependencies Survey. Scientific Reports
Falk Symp — Falk Symposium
Fall Jt Comp Conf Proc — Fall Joint Computer Conference Proceedings
Fall Meet Miner Met Mater Soc Extr Process Div — Fall Meeting. Minerals, Metals, and Materials Society. Extractive and Processing Division
Fallos — Fallos de la Corte Suprema de Justicia de la Nacion
Fall Tech Meet Combust Inst East Sect — Fall Technical Meeting. Combustion Institute. Eastern Section
FAm — Folklore Americano
FAm — Folklore Americas
FAM — Fontes Artis Musicae
Fam Adv — Family Advocate
Fam Advocate — Family Advocate
Fa Man — Farm Management
FAMA Surv Rep Malays Fed Agric Mark Auth — FAMA Survey Report. Republic of Malaysia Federal Agricultural Marketing Authority
Fam Bibl — Familiengeschichtliche Bibliographie
Fam Com Hlth — Family and Community Health
Fam Community Health — Family and Community Health
Fam Coord — Family Coordinator
Fam Ct Act — New York Family Court Act
Fam Dev — Famille et Developpement
Fa Mechan — Farm Mechanization
Fam Econ Rev US Dep Agric Agric Res Serv — Family Economics Review. US Department of Agriculture. Agricultural Research Service
Fam Ec Rev — Family Economics Review
Fam Handy — Family Handyman
Fam Health — Family Health
Family Econ R — Family Economics Review
Family Hlth — Family Health
Family LQ — Family Law Quarterly
Family Plann Digest — Family Planning Digest
Family Pract — Family Practice
Fam L — Family Law
Fam Law — Family Law
Fam Law Fin Rep — Family Law Finance Report
Fam Law Q — Family Law Quarterly
Fam L Coord — Family Life Coordinator
FAMLI — Family Medicine Literature Index
FAMLI Fam Med Lit Index — FAMLI. Family Medicine Literature Index
Fam Life Educ — Family Life Educator
Fam Living Top T Okla State Univ Coop Ext Serv — Family Living Topics T. Oklahoma State University. Cooperative Extension Service
Fam LN — Family Law Notes

Fam L Newsl — Family Law Newsletter
Fam LQ — Family Law Quarterly
Fam LR — Family Law Reports
Fam LR — Family Law Review
Fam L Rep — Family Law Reporter
Fam L Rep BNA — Family Law Reporter. Bureau of National Affairs
Fam L Rev — Family Law Review
Fam L Tax Guide CCH — Family Law Tax Guide. Commerce Clearing House
Fam Med — Family Medicine
FAMN — Fogg Art Museum Notes
Fam Ped — Familles et Pedagogues
Fam Physician — Family Physician
Fam Plan N — Family Planning News
Fam Plann Inf Serv — Family Planning Information Service
Fam Plann (Lond) — Family Planning (London)
Fam Plann Perspect — Family Planning Perspectives
Fam Plann Popul Rep — Family Planning/Population Report
Fam Plann Resume — Family Planning Resume
Fam Plann Today — Family Planning Today
Fam Plan Pe — Family Planning Perspectives
Fam Plan Persp — Family Planning Perspectives
Fam Prac Surv — Family Practice Survey
Fam Pract — Family Practice
Fam Pract News — Family Practice News
Fam Pract Res J — Family Practice Research Journal
Fam Proc — Family Process
Fam Process — Family Process
FAMR — Family Relations
Fam Relat — Family Relations
Fam RZ — Zeitschrift fuer das Gesamte Familienrecht
Fam Strengths — Family Strengths
Fam Tebt — Family Archive from Tebtunis
Fan — Fanfare
FAN — Fantasy Fiction
FAN — Foreign Acquisitions Newsletter
FAN — Foreign Affairs (New York)
Fa N — Francais au Nigeria
FANA — Fantasiae
F Anal Jrl — Financial Analysts Journal
F & A Feed — Journal of Flour and Animal Feed Milling
F and D — Finance and Development
F & D — Fonetica si Dialectologie
F & Doba — Film a Doba
F & D Pkg — Food and Drug Packaging
F & F — Films and Filming
F & F — Forschungen und Fortschritte
F & Fernsehen — Film und Fernsehen
F&G Rdsch — F. & G. (Felten und Guilleaume) Rundschau
F & G Rundsch — F und G [*Felten und Guilleaume*] Rundschau
F & K — Film and Kino
F & Kino — Film and Kino
F & M Feinwerktech Messtech — F und M, Feinwerktechnik und Messtechnik
F&M Feinwerktech Mikrotechnik Messtechnik — F&M. Feinwerktechnik, Mikrotechnik, Messtechnik
F & O — Financial and Operating Data for Investor-Owned Water Companies
F and R — Faith and Reason
F&S Filtr Sep — F&S Filtrieren und Separieren
F & Televisie — Film et Televisie
F & Ton — Film und Ton
F & TV — Film et Televisie
F & TV Kam — Film und TV Kameramann
F & TV Tech — Film and Television Technician
F & W — Funk and Wagnalls Standard Dictionary
FanF — Fantasy Fiction
FANO — Fauna Norrlandica. Department of Ecological Zoology. Umea University
FanS — Fantasy Stories
Fans — Fantasy: The Magazine of Science Fiction
Fant — Fantasy
Fant & Sci Fict — Fantasy and Science Fiction
FAOADP — Food and Agriculture Organization. Agricultural Development Paper
FAO Ag Bul — Food and Agriculture Organization of the United Nations. Monthly Bulletin of Agriculture
FAO Agric Dev Pap — FAO [*Food and Agriculture Organization of the United Nations*] Agricultural Development Papers
FAO Agric Ser — FAO Agricultural Series
FAO Agric Serv Bull — FAO [*Food and Agriculture Organization of the United Nations*] Agricultural Services Bulletin
FAO Agric Stud — FAO [*Food and Agriculture Organization of the United Nations*] Agricultural Studies
FAO Aquacult Bull — FAO (Food and Agriculture Organization) Aquaculture Bulletin
FAO At Energy Ser — FAO [*Food and Agriculture Organization of the United Nations*] Atomic Energy Series
FAO Atom Energy Ser — FAO Atomic Energy Series
FAO Atom En Ser — FAO [*Food and Agriculture Organization of the United Nations*] Atomic Energy Series
FAOBA — Farmaceuticky Obzor
FAOBA — Food and Agriculture Organization. Monthly Bulletin of Agricultural Economics and Statistics
FAOBAS — Farmaceuticky Obzor
FAO Bull — FAO Bulletin
FAO Comm Inland Fish Afr CIFA Tech Pap — Food and Agriculture Organization of the United Nations. Committee for Inland Fisheries of Africa. CIFA Technical Paper
FAO Commod Rev — FAO Commodity Review

FAO Dev Program — FAO [*Food and Agriculture Organization of the United Nations*] DevelopmentProgram
FAO Doc — FAO [*Food and Agriculture Organization of the United Nations*] Documentation
FAO Econ Soc Dev Ser — FAO [*Food and Agriculture Organization of the United Nations*] Economicand Social Development Series
FAO Econ Soc Dev Series — FAO Economic and Social Development Series
FAOETAP — Food and Agriculture Organization. Expanded Technical Assistance Program
FAOFB — Food and Agriculture Organization. Fisheries Bulletin
FAOFDP — Food and Agriculture Organization. Forestry Development Paper
FAO Fish Biol Synop — FAO [*Food and Agriculture Organization of the United Nations*] Fisheries Biology Synopsis
FAO Fish Biol Tech Pap — FAO [*Food and Agriculture Organization of the United Nations*] Fisheries Biology Technical Paper
FAO Fish Bull — FAO [*Food and Agriculture Organization of the United Nations*] Fisheries Bulletin
FAO Fish Circ — FAO [*Food and Agriculture Organization of the United Nations*] Fisheries Circular
FAO Fish Rep — FAO [*Food and Agriculture Organization of the United Nations*] Fisheries Reports
FAO Fish Ser — FAO [*Food and Agriculture Organization of the United Nations*] Fisheries Series
FAO Fish Synop — FAO [*Food and Agriculture Organization of the United Nations*] Fisheries Synopsis
FAO Fish Tech Pap — FAO [*Food and Agriculture Organization of the United Nations*] Fisheries Technical Paper
FAO Food Nutr Pap — FAO [*Food and Agriculture Organization of the United Nations*] Food and Nutrition Paper
FAO Food Nutr Ser — FAO [*Food and Agriculture Organization of the United Nations*] Food and Nutrition Series
FAO For & For Prod Stud — FAO [*Food and Agriculture Organization of the United Nations*] Forestry and Forest Products Studies
FAO For Developm Pap — FAO [*Food and Agriculture Organization of the United Nations*] Forestry Development Papers
FAO For Dev Pap — FAO [*Food and Agriculture Organization of the United Nations*] Forestry Development Paper
FAO Gen Fish Counc Mediterr Circ — FAO [*Food and Agriculture Organization of the United Nations*] General Fisheries Council for the Mediterranean. Circular
FAO Gen Fish Counc Mediterr Stud Rev — FAO [*Food and Agriculture Organization of the United Nations*] General Fisheries Council for the Mediterranean. Studies and Reviews
FAOGFCMP — Food and Agriculture Organization. General Fisheries Council for Mediterranean. Proceedings
FAO Indo-Pac Fish Comm Proc — FAO [*Food and Agriculture Organization of the United Nations*] Indo-Pacific Fishery Commission. Proceedings
FAO Inf Pesca — FAO [*Food and Agriculture Organization of the United Nations*] Informes dePesca
FAO Inf Serv Bull — FAO [*Food and Agriculture Organization of the United Nations*] InformationService Bulletin
FAO Irrig Drain Pap — Food and Agriculture Organization of the United Nations. Irrigation and Drainage Paper
FAO Man Fish Sci — FAO [*Food and Agriculture Organization of the United Nations*] Manuals in Fisheries Science
FAO Mo Bul Ag Econ & Stat — FAO [*Food and Agriculture Organization of the United Nations*] Monthly Bulletin of Agricultural Economics and Statistics
FAO Nutr Meet Rep Ser — FAO [*Food and Agriculture Organization of the United Nations*] Nutrition Meetings. Report Series
FAO Nutr Stud — FAO [*Food and Agriculture Organization of the United Nations*] NutritionalStudies
FAOPA2 — FAO [*Food and Agriculture Organization of the United Nations*] Plant Protection Bulletin
FAO Pasture Fodder Crop Stud — FAO [*Food and Agriculture Organization of the United Nations*] Pasture andFodder Crop Studies
FAO Paturages Cult Fourrageres — FAO [*Food and Agriculture Organization of the United Nations*] Paturages et Cultures Fourrageres
FAOPIN — Food and Agriculture Organization. Plant Introduction Newsletter
FAO Plant — FAO [*Food and Agriculture Organization of the United Nations*] Plant Protection Bulletin
FAO Plant Prod Prot Ser — FAO [*Food and Agriculture Organization of the United Nations*] Plant Production and Protection Series
FAO Plant Prot Bull — FAO [*Food and Agriculture Organization of the United Nations*] Plant Protection Bulletin
FAO Pl Prot Bull — FAO [*Food and Agriculture Organization of the United Nations*] Plant Protection Bulletin
FAOPPB — Food and Agriculture Organization. Plant Protection Bulletin
FAO Prod Yb — FAO [*Food and Agriculture Organization of the United Nations*] Production Yearbook
FAO Rep — FAO [*Food and Agriculture Organization of the United Nations*] Report
FAO Rev — FAO Review
FAO Soils Bull — FAO [*Food and Agriculture Organization of the United Nations*] Soils Bulletin
FAO Tech Rep TF-RAS — Food and Agriculture Organization of the United Nations. TechnicalReport TF-RAS
FAO Timber — Food and Agriculture Organization of the United Nations. Timber Bulletin for Europe
FAO Timb Statist — FAO Timber Statistics
FAP — Fiscale en Administratieve Praktijkvragen
FAP — Fontes Archaeologici Posnanienses
FAP — Fontes Archaeologici Pragenses
FAPBBY — Fortschritte im Acker- und Pflanzenbau
FAPCES — Fundamental Aspects of Pollution Control and Environmental Science
FA Peguy — Feuillets Mensuels d'Information de l'Amitie Charles Peguy
FAPFAB — FAO [*Food and Agriculture Organization of the United Nations*] Pasture andFodder Crop Studies

FAPOA — Farmacja Polska
FAPRS — Federal Assistance Program Retrieval System
FAPSEK — Fundamental Aspects of Pollution Control and Environmental Science
F Ar — Fasti Archaeologici
FAR — Foreign Affairs Reports
FAR — Franco-American Review
FAR — French American Review
Faraday Dis — Faraday Discussions of the Chemical Society
Faraday Discuss — Faraday Discussions of the Chemical Society
Faraday Discuss Chem Soc — Faraday Discussions of the Chemical Society
Faraday House J — Faraday House Journal
Faraday Soc Symp — Faraday Society. Symposia
Faraday Soc Trans — Faraday Society. Transactions
Faraday Spec Discuss Chem Soc — Faraday Special Discussions of the Chemical Society
Faraday Symp Chem Soc — Faraday Symposia of the Chemical Society
Faraday Symp R Soc Chem — Faraday Symposia of the Royal Society of Chemistry
Farbe & Lack — Farbe und Lack
Farben Chem — Farben-Chemiker
Farben Chem Beil — Farben-Chemiker. Beilage
Farben Lacke Anstrichst — Farben, Lacke, Anstrichstoffe
Farben Rev Spec Ed (USA) — Farben Revue. Special Edition (USA)
Farben Ztg — Farben Zeitung
FARCA — Farm Chemicals
FARCAC — Farm Chemicals
FAREAI — Farmaceutisk Revy
Far East Ass Trop Med — Far Eastern Association of Tropical Medicine
Far East Ceram Bull — Far Eastern Ceramic Bulletin
Far East Econ R — Far Eastern Economic Review
Far Eastern Econ Rev — Far Eastern Economic Review
Far East J Anesth — Far East Journal of Anesthesia
Far East J Math Sci — Far East Journal of Mathematical Sciences
Far East LR — Far Eastern Law Review
Far East Med J — Far East Medical Journal
Far East Q — Far Eastern Quarterly
Far East Quart — Far Eastern Quarterly
Far East R — Far Eastern Review
Far East Rev — Far Eastern Review
Far East S — Far Eastern Survey
Far East Sci Bull — Far Eastern Science Bulletin
Far East Surv — Far Eastern Survey
Far East Univ Fac J — Far Eastern University. Faculty Journal
Far E Econ R — Far Eastern Economic Review
Far E Engr — Far East Engineer
Far E J Anesth — Far East Journal of Anesthesia
Far E Med J — Far Eastern Medical Journal/Tung Fong Hsueeh Tsa Chih
Far E Rev — Far Eastern Review. Engineering, Commerce, Finance
Far From Equilib Dyn Chem Syst Proc Int Symp — Far-From-Equilibrium Dynamics of Chemical Systems. Proceedings. International Symposium
Farg Fern — Farg och Fernissa
Farg Lack — Farg och Lack
FAR Horiz — Foreign Area Research Horizons
Farm — Farmacia
Farm — Farmacija
Farm — Farmaco
Farm — Farmalecta
Farmac — Farmacognosia
Farmaceuta Pol — Farmaceuta Polski
Farmaceuticky Obz — Farmaceuticky Obzor
Farmaceutisk Saertryksaml — Farmaceutisk Saertryksamling
Farmaceutisk Tid — Farmaceutisk Tidende
Farmaceutisk Tidsskr — Farmaceutisk Tidsskrift
Farmaceutiskt Notisbl — Farmaceutiskt Notisblad
Farmaceutski Glasn — Farmaceutski Glasnik
Farmaceutski Vest — Farmaceutski Vestnik
Farmacia Bratisl — Farmacia (Bratislava)
Farmacia Buc — Farmacia (Bucuresti)
Farmacia Mex — Farmacia (Mexico)
Farmacia Paris — Farmacia (Paris)
Farmacia S Jose — Farmacia (San Jose)
Farmacihist Ars — Farmacihistoriska Saellskapets Arsskrift
Farmacja Pol — Farmacja Polska
Farmaco Ed Prat — Farmaco. Edizione Pratica
Farmaco Ed Sci — Farmaco. Edizione Scientifica
Farmaco Ed Scient — Farmaco. Edizione Scientifica
Farmacog — Farmacognosia. Anales del Instituto Jose Celestino Mutis
Farmaco Pra — Farmaco. Edizione Pratica
Farmaco Sci — Farmaco. Edizione Scientifica
Farmacoter Act — Farmacoterapia Actual
Farmac Terap — Farmacologia y Terapeutica
Farm Aikak — Farmaseuttinen Aikakauslehti
Farmakol Alkaloidov — Farmakologiya Alkaloidov
Farmakol Khimioter Sredstva — Farmakologiya. Khimioterapevticheski Sredstva
Farmakol Khimioter Sredstva Toksikol Probl Farmakol — Farmakologiya. Khimioterapevticheski Sredstva. Toksikologiya. ProblemyFarmakologii
Farmakol Khimioter Sredstva Toksikol Probl Toksikol — Farmakologiya. Khimioterapevticheski Sredstva. Toksikologiya. ProblemyToksikologii
Farmakol T — Farmakologiya i Toksikologiya
Farmakol Toksikol — Farmakologiya i Toksikologiya
Farmakol Toksikol (Kiev) — Farmakologiya i Toksikologiya (Kiev)
Farmakol Toksikol (Mosc) — Farmakologiya i Toksikologiya (Moscow)
Farmakol Toksikol (Moscow) — Farmakologiya i Toksikologiya (Moscow)
Farmakol Toksikol Resp Mezhved Sb — Farmakologiya i Toksikologiya Respublikanskii Mezhvedomstvennyi Sbornik

Farmakoter Zpr — Farmakoterapeuticke Zpravy
Farmak Toks — Farmakologiya i Toksikologiya
Farm & Garden Ind — Farm and Garden Index
Farm & Home Sci — Farm and Home Science
Farmatsevt Prakt — Farmatsevt-Praktik
Farmatsevt Pregl — Farmatsevticheski Pregled
Farmatsevt Zh (Kiev) — Farmatsevtychnyi Zhurnal (Kiev)
Farm Bilimler Derg — Farmasotik Bilimler Dergisi
Farm Bldg Progress — Farm Building Progress
Farm Bldg R & D Studies — Farm Building R and D Studies
Farm Bldgs Digest — Farm Buildings Digest
Farm Bldgs Topics — Farm Buildings Topics
Farm Bras — Farmaceutico Brasileiro
Farm Bull US Dep Agric — Farmers' Bulletin. United States Department of Agriculture
Farm Bus — Farm Business
Farm Bus Summ East Cent Iowa Iowa State Univ Coop Ext Serv — Farm Business Summary for East Central Iowa. Iowa State University. CooperativeExtension Service
Farm Bus Summ Southwest Iowa Iowa State Univ Coop Ext Serv — Farm Business Summary for Southwest Iowa. Iowa State University. Cooperative Extension Service
Farm Chem — Farm Chemicals
Farm Chem Croplife — Farm Chemicals and Croplife
Farm Chemurg J — Farm Chemurgic Journal
Farm Clin — Farmacia Clinica
Farm Coop — Farmer Cooperatives
Farm Delt Ed Sci — Farmakevtikon Dheltion. Edition Scientifique
Farm Dhelt Epistim Ekdosis — Farmakevtikon Dheltion. Epistimoniki Ekdosis
Farm Econ — Farm Economics
Farm Econ — Farm Economist
Farm Econ Facts Opin Ill Univ Coop Ext Serv — Farm Economics. Facts and Opinions. Illinois University. Cooperative Extension Service
Farm Econ Facts Opin Univ Ill Dep Agric Econ Coop Ext Serv — Farm Economics Facts and Opinions. University of Illinois. Department of Agricultural Economics. Cooperative Extension Service
Farm Econ PA State Univ Coop Ext Serv — Farm Economics. Pennsylvania State University. Cooperative Extension Service
Farm Ed Prat — Farmaco. Edizione Pratica
Farm Ed Sci — Farmaco. Edizione Scientifica
Farm Eng — Farm Engineering
Farm Eq — Farm Equipment News
Farm Equip Dealer — Farm Equipment Dealer
Farmer Coop US Dep Agric Agric Coop Serv — Farmer Cooperatives. US Department of Agriculture. Agricultural Cooperative Service
Farmer Coop US Dep Agric Econ Stat Coop Serv — Farmer Cooperatives. United States Department of Agriculture. Economics Statistics and Cooperatives Service
Farmer's Advocate Can Countryman — Farmer's Advocate and Canadian Countryman
Farmers' B — Farmers' Bulletin
Farmers Bull — Farmers' Bulletin
Farmers Bull Dep Agric Can — Farmers' Bulletin. Department of Agriculture. Canada
Farmers Bull USDA — Farmers' Bulletin. United States Department of Agriculture
Farmers Leafl Natl Inst Agric Bot — Farmers Leaflet. National Institute of Agricultural Botany
Farmers Mag London — Farmers' Magazine (London)
Farmers Mag Useful Family Companion — Farmer's Magazine and Useful Family Companion
Farmers Newsl — Farmers' Newsletter
Farmers Rep Leeds Univ Dept Agr Econ Sect — Farmers' Report. Leeds University. Department of Agriculture. Economics Section
Farmers' Sci Joint Conf — Farmers' and Scientists' Joint Conference
Farmer Stockbr — Farmer and Stockbreeder
Farmers Wkly — Farmers Weekly
Farmers Wkly (Bloemfontein S Afr) — Farmers Weekly (Bloemfontein, South Africa)
Farm Esp — Farmacia Espanola
Farm Farmakol — Farmatsiya i Farmakologiya
Farm Food Res — Farm and Food Research
Farm For — Farm Forestry
Farm Gard Index — Farm and Garden Index
Farm Glas — Farmaceutski Glasnik
Farm Glasn — Farmaceutski Glasnik
Farm Home Res — Farm and Home Research
Farm Home Sci — Farm and Home Science
Farm Home Sci Utah Resources Ser — Farm and Home Science. Utah Resources Series. Utah State University. College ofAgriculture. Agricultural Experiment Station
Farm In — Farm Index
Farming Bus — Farming Business
Farming Dig — Farming Digest
Farming Mech — Farming Mechanization
Farming Progr — Farming Progress
Farming Rev — Farming Review
Farming SA — Farming in SA and Woman and Her Home
Farming S Afr — Farming in South Africa
Farming South Africa — Farming in South Africa. South Africa Department of Agriculture
Farm Ital — Farmacista Italiano
Farm Ital Deriv Ind Affi Res Ser — Farmaceutici Italiani Derivati Industriali ed Affi Research Series
Farm Ital Suppl — Farmacista Italiano. Supplement
Farm i Toksik — Farmakologija i Toksikologija

Farm J — Farm Journal
Farm J Brit Guiana — Farm Journal of British Guiana
Farm J (Calcutta) — Farm Journal (Calcutta)
Farm J (E Ed) — Farm Journal (Eastern Edition)
Farmkoter Zpr — Farmakoterapeuticke Zpravy
Farmkoter Zpr Suppl — Farmakoterapeuticke Zpravy. Supplementum
Farmline US Dep Agric Econ Res Serv — Farmline. United States Department of Agriculture. Economic Research Service
Farmline US Dep Agric Econ Stat Coop Serv — Farmline. United States Department of Agriculture. Economics Statistics and Cooperatives Service
Farm Lt Pwr — Farm-Light and Power [*New York*]
Farm Mach — Farm Machinery
Farm Manage — Farm Management
Farm Manage Newsl Mo Coop Ext Serv Univ Mo Lincoln Univ — Farm Management Newsletter. Missouri Cooperative Extension Service. University of Missouri and Lincoln University
Farm Manage Notes — Farm Management Notes
Farm Manage Rep Univ Hawaii Coop Ext Serv — Farm Management Report. University of Hawaii. Cooperative Extension Service
Farm Manage Rep USDA Coop Ext Serv — Farm Management Report. United States Department of Agriculture. Cooperative Extension Service
Farm Manage Rev — Farm Management Review
Farm Mech — Farm Mechanization
Farm Mech Stud — Farm Mechanization Studies
Farm Mod — Farmacia Moderna in Rapporto al Progresso delle Scienze Mediche [*Napoli*]
Farm Nac Santiago — Farmacia Nacional (Santiago de Chile)
Farm Ne — Farming News and North British Agriculturist
Farmnote West Aust Dep Agric — Farmnote. Western Australian Department of Agriculture
Farm Notisbl — Farmaceutiskt Notisblad
Farm Nova — Farmacia Nova
Farm Nueva — Farmacia Nueva
Farm Nuova — Farmacia Nuova
Farm Obz — Farmaceuticky Obzor
Farmos Med News — Farmos Medical News
Farm Peru — Farmacia Peruana
Farm Pol — Farmacja Polska
Farm Pol — Farm Policy
Farm Pol (1902-1914) — Farmaceuta Polski (1902-1914)
Farm Policy Rev Conf — Farm Policy Review Conference
Farm Power Equip — Farm and Power Equipment
Farm Q — Farmacia y Quimica
Farm Q — Farm Quarterly
Farm Quart — Farm Quarterly
Farm Quim — Farmacia y Quimica
Farm R — Farmacevtisk Revy
Farm Ranch Home Q — Farm, Ranch, and Home Quarterly
Farm Ranch Home Q Nebr Agric Exp Stn — Farm, Ranch, and Home Quarterly. Nebraska Agricultural Experiment Station
Farm Res — Farm Research
Farm Res News — Farm Research News
Farm Revy — Farmacevtisk Revy
FARMS — Farm Audience Readership Measurement Service
Farm Safety Rev — Farm Safety Review
Farm S Afr — Farming in South Africa
Farm Sci Ed — Farmaci. Scientific Edition
Farm Sci e Tec — Farmaco Scienza e Tecnica
Farm Surveys Rep — Farm Surveys Report
Farm T — Farmaceutisk Tidende
Farm Technol — Farm Technology
Farm Tid — Farmaceutisk Tidende
Farm Tid Copenhagen — Farmaceutisk Tidende (Copenhagen)
Farm Tidskr — Farmaceutisk Tidskrift
Farm Tijdschr Belg — Farmaceutisch Tijdschrift voor Belgie
Farm Today — Farming Today
Farm Toks — Farmakologija i Toksikologija
Farm Vestn — Farmacevtski Vestnik
Farm Vestn Ljubljana — Farmaceutski Vestnik (Ljubljana)
Farm Week — Farmers Weekly
Farm Wspolczesna — Farmacja Wspolczesna
Farm y Quim — Farmacia y Quimica
Farm Z — Farmatsevtychnyi Zhurnal
Farm Zh — Farmatsevtychnyi Zhurnal
Farm Zh (Kharkov) — Farmatsevtychnyi Zhurnal (Kharkov)
Farm Zh (Kiev) — Farmatsevtychnyi Zhurnal (Kiev)
Farm Zh (Leningrad) — Farmatsevtychnyi Zhurnal (Leningrad)
Farm Zh St Petersburg — Farmatsevticheskii Zhurnal (St. Petersburg)
Farm Zpr — Farmakoterapeuticke Zpravy
Faro Colon C Trujillo — El Faro a Colon (Ciudad Trujillo)
FARRA — Farm Research
FARRAN — Farm Research
Far Seas Fish Res Lab S Ser — Far Seas Fisheries Research Laboratory. S Series
Farthest N Colleg — Farthest North Collegian
F Artil J — Field Artillery Journal
F Arts Q — Fine Arts Quarterly
FARUA — Farumashia
Farve Lak — Farve og Lak
Far Wide — Far and Wide. Guest, Keen, and Nettlefolds, Ltd.
FAS — Fantastic Stories
FAS — Far Eastern Series
FAS — Frankfurter Althistorische Studien
FASBB — Soils Bulletin

FASBDH — FAO [*Food and Agriculture Organization of the United Nations*] Agricultural Services Bulletin
Fasc Brev Switz — Fascicule du Brevet (Switzerland)
Fasc Demande (Switz) — Fascicule de la Demande (Switzerland)
Fasc Math — Fasciculi Mathematici
Fasc Q — Fascist Quarterly
Fasc Technol Mecn Aviat — Fascicules Technologiques du Mecanicien d'Aviation
FASEB J — FASEB (Federation of American Societies for Experimental Biology) Journal
FASEB J Off Publ Fed Am Soc Exp Biol — FASEB Journal. Official Publication. Federation of American Societies for Experimental Biology
FASEB Monogr — FASEB [*Federation of American Societies for Experimental Biology*] Monographs
Faserforsch Textiltech — Faserforschung und Textiltechnik
Faserforsch TextTech — Faserforschung und Textiltechnik
Faserf T — Faserforschung und Textiltechnik
Faserstoffe Spinnpfl — Faserstoffe und Spinnpflanzen
Faserstoff PatSchau — Faserstoff-Patentschau
Faserst Spinnpflanzen — Faserstoffe und Spinnpflanzen
FASF — Fantastic Science Fiction
FAS/FA — Florida Anthropologist. Florida Anthropological Society
FASMDG — FASEB [*Federation of American Societies for Experimental Biology*] Monographs
Fa St — Faulkner Studies
Fast Cap — Fasti Capitolini
Fast Cons Imp — Fasti Consolari dell'Impero Romano
Fasti A — Fasti Archaeologici
FAST J — FAST (Florida Association of Science Teachers) Journal
FAST J — FAST Journal
Fast Protein Polypept Polynucleotide Liq Chromatogr Symp — Fast Protein, Polypeptide, and Polynucleotide Liquid Chromatography-Symposium
Fast React Power Stn Proc Int Conf — Fast Reactor Power Stations. Proceedings. International Conference
Fast React Technol Plant Des — Fast Reactor Technology. Plant Design
FAT — Fischer Athenaeum Taschenbuecher
Fatab — Fataburen
Fataburen — Fataburen. Nordiska Museets och Skansens Arsbok
FATD — Federal Applied Technology Database
Fatigue Adv Mater Proc Eng Found Int Conf — Fatigue of Advanced Materials. Proceedings. Engineering Foundation International Conference
Fatigue Des — Fatigue Design
Fatigue Eng Mater and Struct — Fatigue of Engineering Materials and Structures
Fatigue Eng Mater Struct — Fatigue of Engineering Materials and Structures
Fatigue Eng Mat Struct — Fatigue of Engineering Materials and Structures
Fatigue Environ Temp Eff — Fatigue. Environment and Temperature Effects
Fatigue Fract Eng Mater Struct — Fatigue and Fracture of Engineering Materials and Structures
Fatigue Strength Met Pap Conf — Fatigue Strength of Metals. Papers Presented at the Conference on the Fatigue of Metals
FATIPEC Congr — FATIPEC (Federation d'Associations de Techniciens des Industries des Peiintures, Vernis, Emaux et Encre d'Imprimerie de l'Europe Continentale) Congress
FATIS — FATIS [*Food and Agriculture Technical Information Service*] Publications
FATIS Rev — FATIS [*Food and Agriculture Technical Information Service*] Review
FATOA — Farmakologiya i Toksikologiya
FATOAO — Farmakologiya i Toksikologiya
FATOBP — Farmakologiya i Toksikologiya Respublikanskii Mezhvedomstvennyi Sbornik
Fat Oil Chem Scand Symp — Fat and Oil Chemistry, Composition, Oxidation, Processing. Scandinavian Symposium on Fats and Oils
Fat Rev — Fatis Review
FAT Schriftenr — FAT [*Forschungsvereinigung Automobiltechnik*] Schriftenreihe
Fat Sci Technol — Fat Science Technology
Fats Oils Deterg Yb — Fats, Oils, Detergents Yearbook
Fats Oils Oilseed Crushings Curr Ind Rep — Fats and Oils-Oilseed Crushings (Current Industrlal Reports)
Fats Oils Prod Consumption Stocks Curr Ind Rep — Fats and Oils-Production, Consumption, and Stocks (Current Industrial Reports)
Fats Oils Situ — Fats and Oils Situation
Fats Oils Stud — Fats and Oils Studies
F Att Com — Fragments of Attic Comedy after Meineke
FAU — Fantastic Universe Science Fiction
FAUCAR — Folia Anatomica Universitatis Conimbrigensis
Faug Szle — Faugyi Szemle
Fauldings Med J — Faulding's Medical Journal
Faulkner St — Faulkner Studies
Fauna Arct — Fauna Arctica
Fauna Argent — Fauna Argentina [*Berlin*]
Faun Abh (Dres) — Faunistische Abhandlungen (Dresden)
Faun Abh Staatl Mus Tierk Dresden — Faunistische Abhandlungen. Staatliches Museum fuer Tierkunde in Dresden
Fauna Bras — Fauna Brasiliense
Fauna Br East Cent Afr — Fauna of British Eastern and Central Africa
Fauna Bulg — Fauna na Bulgariya
Fauna Bull Fish Dep West Aust — Fauna Bulletin of the Fisheries Department. Western Australia
Fauna Contr Fish Game Dep Vict — Fauna Contributions to the Fish and Game Department. Victoria
Fauna Dt Kolon — Fauna der Deutschen Kolonien
Fauna Entomol Scand — Fauna Entomologica Scandinavica
Fauna Exot — Fauna Exotica
Fauna Fenn — Fauna Fennica
Fauna Fl — Fauna och Flora. Populaer Tidskrift foer Biologi
Fauna Fl Laurent — Fauna et Flora Laurentianae
Fauna Flora Csl — Fauna et Flora Cechoslovenica

Fauna Flora Golf Neapel — Fauna und Flora des Golfes von Neapel und der Angrenzenden Meeresabschnitte

Fauna Flora (Stockh) — Fauna och Flora (Stockholm)

Fauna Flora (Transvaal) — Fauna and Flora (Transvaal)

Fauna Hung — Fauna Hungariae

Fauna Ital — Fauna d'Italia

Fauna Natn Pks US — Fauna of the National Parks of the United States. Fauna Series

Fauna Ned — Fauna van Nederland

Fauna Norv Ser A — Fauna Norvegica. Series A

Fauna Norv Ser B — Fauna Norvegica. Series B

Fauna Norv Ser C — Fauna Norvegica. Series C

Fauna NZ — Fauna of New Zealand

Fauna Pol — Fauna Polski

Faune Fr — Faune de France

Faune Que — Faune du Quebec

Faune Que Rapp Spec — Faune du Quebec. Rapport Special

Faune Terr Eau Douce — Faune Terrestriale et d'Eau Douce

Faune Un Fr — Faune de l'Union Francais

Faunistische Abh — Faunistische Abhandlungen

Faun Maerkm — Faunistilisi Maerkmeid

Faun-Oekol Mitt — Faunistisch-Oekologische Mitteilungen

Faun Oekol Mitt Suppl — Faunistisch-Oekologische Mitteilungen. Supplement

Faun Rec Univ Qu — Faunistic Records. University of Queensland Papers

Faust B — Faust Blaetter

FaV — Fauilles au Vent

FAVUA — Fiziologicheski Aktivnye Veshchestva

Fawcett — Fawcett on Landlord and Tenant

FAWEA — Farmers Weekly

FAWEB — Farmers Weekly (Bloemfontein, South Africa)

Fawley Fdn Lect — Fawley Foundation Lecture. University of Southampton

FAY — Fantastic Adventures Yearbook

Fayette Leg J (PA) — Fayette Legal Journal

Fay LJ — Fayette Legal Journal

FAZ — Frankfurter Allgemeine Zeitung

Fazovye Prevrashch Neravnovesnye Protsessy — Fazovye Prevrashcheniya i Neravnovesnye Protsessy

Fazovye Ravnovesiya Met Splavakh — Fazovye Ravnovesiya v Metallicheskikh Splavakh

Fazovyi Khim Anal Rud Mineral — Fazovyi Khimicheskii Analiz Rud i Mineralov

FB — Fabula

FB — Fantasy Book

FB — First Break

FB — Folklore Brabancon

FB — Fonatana Books

FB — Fontane Blaetter

FB — Fords and Bridges

FB — Forschungen und Berichte

FB — Fraenkische Blaetter fuer Geschichtsforschung und Heimatpflege

FB — Franse Boek

FB — Fresno Bee

FBAA — Frankfurter Beitraege zur Anglistik und Amerikanistik

FBARAD — Freshwater Biological Association. Annual Report

FBASDJ — Fundacion Bariloche Series

FBB — Fabrimetal

FBB — Facet Books. Biblical Series

FBBGAJ — Folia Biochimica et Biologica Graeca

FBCICSR — Fairbanks North Star Borough. Community Information Center. Special Report

FBCN — Federation of British Columbia Naturalists. Newsletter

FBDLR — Forschungsbericht. Deutsche Luft und Raumfahrt

FBE — Fortschrittliche Betriebsfuehrung und Industrial Engineering

FBE Not — Noticiario das Actividades Sociais da Federacao Brasileira de Engenheiros

F Ber Bad Wuert — Forschungen und Berichte zur Vor- und Fruehgeschichte in Baden-Wuerttemberg

Fber Bad Wuert — Fundberichte aus Baden-Wuerttemberg

FBG — Frankfurter Beitraege zur Germanistik

FBH — Facet Books. Historical Series

FBH — Fichero Bibliografico Hispano-Americano

FBH — Fishermen's Bulletin (Haifa, Israel)

FBI Engr — FBI (Federation of British Industries) Engineer

FBIICR — Fairbanks North Star Borough. Impact Information Center. Report

FBIICSR — Fairbanks North Star Borough. Impact Information Center. Special Reports

FBI Law Enf Bul — FBI [*Federal Bureau of Investigation*] Law Enforcement Bulletin

FBILEB — FBI [*Federal Bureau of Investigation*] Law Enforcement Bulletin

FBI L Enforcement Bul — FBI. Law Enforcement Bulletin

FBIOAA — Feuillets de Biologie

FBIS — Foreign Broadcast Information Service

FBK — Fantasy Book

FBK — Flugblaetter der Bekennenden Kirche

FBKG — Forschung zur Bremischen Kirchengeschichte

FBKRA — Fiziologiya i Biokhimiya Kul'turnykh Rastenii

FBL — Farbe und Lack. Zentralblatt der Farbenindustrie und Lackindustrie und des Handels

FbLm — Forschungsberichte ueber Lebensmittel

FBM Fertigungs Technol — FBM Fertigungs-Technologie. Werkzeuge, Maschinen, Systeme

FBMIDF — Folia Botanica Miscellanea

FBPG — Forschungen zur Brandenburgisch-Preussischen Geschichte

FBR — Forbes

F Brab — Folklore Brabancon

FBRH — Fliegende Blatter aus dem Rauhen Hause zu Horn bei Hamburg

FBS — Facet Books. Social Ethics Series

F B Schwaben — Fundberichte aus Schwaben

FBSM — Forschungen und Berichte. Staatliche Museen

FBSSD — Fushoku Boshoku Shinpojumu Shiryo

F (Buc) — Forschungen zur Volks- und Landeskunde (Bucuresti)

F Bul — Film Bulletin

FBVBA — Fortschritt-Berichte. VDI [*Verein Deutscher Ingenieure*] Zeitschriften. Reihe 4. Bauingenieurwesen

FC — Family Circle

FC — Fasti Consolari dell'Impero Romano

FC — Fathers of the Church

FC — Federal Court Reports

FC — Film Comment

FC — Filosoficky Casopis

FC — Flying (Chicago)

FCA — Feiten en Cijfers. Economisch, Financieel, Sociaal, Fiscaal, Juridisch

FCAIM — Fundamental and Clinical Aspects of Internal Medicine

F Cap — Fasti Capitolini

FCAP (Fac Cienc Agrar Para) Inf Tec — FCAP (Faculdade de Ciencias Agrarias do Para) Informe Tecnico

F Cas — Federal Cases

FC Assoc Finish Processes SME — FC [*Series*]. Association for Finishing Processes of SME (Society of Manufacturing Engineers)

FCB — Federal Council Bulletin

FCB — Fenedexpress

FCCADG — Focus on Critical Care

FCCO — Fonti. Sacra Congregazione per la Chiesa Orientale. Codificazione Canonica Orientale

FCD — Fine Chemicals Directory Data Base

FCdZ — Feuille Centrale de Zofingue

FCE — Fondo de Cultura Economica

FCE/TE — Trimestre Economico. Fondo de Cultura Economica

FCGM — Fragmenta Comicorum Graecorum

FChPhphCh — Fortschritte der Chemie, Physik, und Physikalischen Chemie

FCHQ — Filson Club History Quarterly

FChrLDG — Forschungen zur Christlichen Literatur- und Dogmengeschichte

FCIQ — Fairbanks North Star Borough. Community Information Center. Quarterly

FCJ — Federal Court Judgments

FCKW Ausstieg Wohin Beitr Dechema Fachgespraechs Umweltschutz — FCKW (Fluorchlorkohlenwasserstoffe) - Ausstieg Wohin? Beitraege des Dechema-Fachgespraechs Umweltschutz

FCL — Federal Communications Law Journal

FCLBAR — Folia Clinica et Biologica

FCNEEG — Frontiers of Clinical Neuroscience

FCO — Federal Career Opportunities

F Com — Film Comment

F Comment — Film Comment

FCPJA3 — Fragmenta Coleopterologica Japonica

FCR — Federal Court Reporter

FCR — Federal Court Reports

FCR — Federal Court Rules

FCR — Filmcritica

FCR — Food and Cookery Review

FCR — Free China Review

F Criticism — Film Criticism

FCS — Fifteenth-Century Studies

FCS — Fiscal Studies

FC Soc Manuf Eng — FC [*Series*]. Society of Manufacturing Engineers

FCS Publ — FCS (Fish Culture Section) American Fisheries Society Publication

FCTF — Flue-Cured Tobacco Farmer

FCTOD7 — Food and Chemical Toxicology

FCTXAV — Food and Cosmetics Toxicology

FCTYA — Factory

F CUL — Film Culture

F Cultura — Filme Cultura

F Culture — Film Culture

FCW — Foreign Commerce Weekly. US Bureau of Foreign and Domestic Commerce

FD — Fanfulla della Domenica

FD — Filosofska Dumka

FD — Financieel Dagblad

FD — Finanzas y Desarrollo

FD — Fonetica si Dialectologie

FD — Fouilles de Delphes

FDA — Federal Drug Administration. Publications

FDA — Freiburger Diozesanarchiv

FDA — Fremdenverkehr + das Reiseburo. Tourismus und Kongress

FDACB — FDA [*Food and Drug Administration*] Consumer

FDA Clin Exp Abstr — FDA [*Food and Drug Administration*] Clinical Experience Abstracts

FDA Consum — FDA [*Food and Drug Administration*] Consumer

FDA Consum Food Drug Adm — FDA (Food and Drug Administration) Consumer

FDADA — FDA [*Food and Drug Administration*] Drug Bulletin

Fd Addit Control Ser FAO — Food Additive Control Series. FAO

FDA Drug Bull — FDA [*Food and Drug Administration*] Drug Bulletin

Fd Agric — Food and Agriculture. The FAO European Bulletin

Fd Agric Legisl — Food and Agricultural Legislation. FAO

FDA Pap — FDA [*Food and Drug Administration*] Papers

Fd Brief — Food in Brief

Fd Can — Food in Canada

Fd Cann Preserv Pckg — Food Canning, Preserving, and Packing

FDC Cont Newsl — FDC [*Food, Drug, and Cosmetics*] Control Newsletter

Fd Chem News Guide — Food Chemical News Guide

Fd Chem Toxic — Food and Chemical Toxicology

FDC Newsl — FDC (Furniture Development Council) Newsletter

FDCOA — Fundicao

Fd Cosmet Toxicol — Food and Cosmetics Toxicology
FDCSB7 — Faraday Discussions of the Chemical Society
FdD — Fouilles de Delphes
FDDL F Rep (Tex Agric Ext Serv Fish Dis Diagn Lab) — FDDL-F Report (Texas Agricultural Extension Service. Fish Disease Diagnostic Laboratory)
FDDL S Tex Agric Ext Serv Fish Dis Diagn Lab — FDDL-S (Texas Agricultural Extension Service. Fish Disease Diagnostic Laboratory)
Fd Drug News — Food and Drug News
Fd Drug Res — Food and Drug Research
Fd Drug Rev — Food and Drug Review
Fd Drug Tech Bull — Food and Drug Technical Bulletin
FDE — Fouilles de Doura-Europos
FDEC — Forum for Death Education and Counseling. Newsletter
F Delphes — Fouilles de Delphes
Fd Engng — Food Engineering
Fd Equip Preview — Food Equipment Preview
FDEVDS — Food Development
Fd Flavs Ingredients Process Packag — Food: Flavouring Ingredients Processing and Packaging
Fd Fld Reptr — Food Field Reporter
Fd Flow — Food and Flowers
Fd Fmg — Food and Farming
Fd Freez — Food Freezing
FDG — Folk Dance Guide
FDG — Forschungen zur Deutschen Geschichte
Fdg Gil — Fra det Gamle Gilleleje
FDGK — Fukui Daigaku Gakugeigakubu Kiyo
FDHRS — Freies Deutsches Hochstift: Reihe der Schriften
Fd Hyg Codes Pract — Food Hygiene Codes of Practice. Ministry of Health and Ministry of Agriculture, Fisheries, and Food
FDI — Food Engineering
FDIADJ — Frontiers in Diabetes
FDIIA6 — Food Irradiation Information
Fd Inds — Food Industries
Fd Inds Man — Food Industries Manual
Fd Inds Rev — Food Industries Review
Fd Inds S Afr — Food Industries of South Africa
Fd Inds Wkly — Food Industries Weekly
Fd Insp Decis US Bd Fd Drug Insp — Food Inspection Decisions. US Board of Food and Drug Inspection
Fd Invest — Food Investigation. Reports of the Superintendents of the Low Temperature Research Station and the Ditton Laboratory
Fd Invest Leafl — Food Investigation Leaflet
F Directions — Film Directions
Fd Irrad — Food Irradiation
FDKNEF — Bulletin. Fukuoka University of Education. Part 3. Mathematics, Natural Sciences, and Technology
FdL — Forum der Letteren
FDLJAO — Food, Drug, Cosmetic Law Journal
FDLVK — Forschung zur Deutschen Landes und Volkskunde
FDM — Francais dans le Monde
FDM — Furniture Design and Manufacturing
Fd Mater Equip — Food Materials and Equipment
Fd Mf — Food Manufacture
Fd Mf News Edn — Food Manufacture. News Edition
Fd Mf Wkly — Food Manufacture Weekly
Fdn Lect Albert Howard Fdn Org Husb — Foundation Lectures. Albert Howard Foundation of Organic Husbandry
Fd Nutr — Food and Nutrition
Fd Nutr Bull — Food and Nutrition Bulletin
Fd Nutr Notes Rev — Food and Nutrition. Notes and Reviews
Fd Nutr Notes Revs — Food and Nutrition. Notes and Reviews
F Doba — Film a Doba
F Dope — Film Dope
FDP — Foodpress, Economisch, en Technisch Weekblad voor de Voedingsmiddelenindustrie en Genotmiddelenindustrie en Groothandel in de Benelux
FDP — Four Decades of Poetry 1890-1930
Fd Pckr — Food Packer
FDPRBZ — FAO [*Food and Agriculture Organization of the United Nations*] DevelopmentProgram
Fd Preserv — Food Preservation
Fd Preserv Q — Food Preservation Quarterly
Fd Preview — Food Preview
Fd Process — Food Processing
Fd Process Ind — Food Processing Industry
Fd Process Market — Food Processing and Marketing
Fd Process Packag — Food Processing and Packaging
Fd Prod Dev — Food Product Development
FDQ — Florida Designers Quarterly
FDQTA — Fields and Quanta
Fd Res — Food Research
FDS — Fountainwell Drama Series
FDSD — Forschungen zur Deutschen Sprache und Dichtung
FDSTA — Feedstuffs
FDSUDR — Folia Dendrologica. Supplementum
FDT — Fountainwell Drama Texts
Fd Technol — Food Technology
Fd Technol Aust — Food Technology in Australia
Fd Technol Champaign — Food Technology (Champaign)
Fd Technol Lond — Food Technology (London)
Fd Th — Fouilles de Thorikos
Fd Trade Rev — Food Trade Review
FDTSC — Folger Documents of Tudor and Stuart Civilization
FDU — Flying Dutchman

FDV — Franz-Delitzsch-Vorlesungen
FDWG — Forschungen zur Deutschen Weltanschauungsskunde und Glaubensgeschichte
Fd X — Fouilles de Xanthos
FE — Far East
FE — Filosofskaia Entsiklopediia
FE — Forschungen in Ephesos
FE — France-Eurafrique
FE — Organo de Falange Espanola
Fe A — Fede e Arte
FEA — Financieel Economisch Magazine (Amsterdam)
FEA — St. Anthony's College. Far Eastern Affairs
FEAKA — Fel'dsher i Akusherka
FEAKAD — Fel'dsher i Akusherka
FEARTR — Federal Environmental Assessment Review Office. Technical Report
FEAST — Food Equipment and Additives Suppliers and Traders
F East Ship — Far East Shipping
Feath Wld — Feathered World and Poultry Farmer [*London*]
FEB — FABS Electronic Bible
FEB — Flugschriften des Evangelischen Bundes
FEBJA — Federal Bar Journal [*Later, Federal Bar News and Journal*]
FEBLAL — FEBS [*Federation of European Biochemical Societies*] Letters
FEBPBY — FEBS [*Federation of European Biochemical Societies*] Proceedings of the Meeting
FEBS Congr — FEBS (Federation of European Biochemical Scoieties) Congress
FEBS Fed Eur Biochem Soc Meet — FEBS (Federation of European Biochemical Societies) Meeting
FEBS Lett — FEBS [*Federation of European Biochemical Societies*] Letters
FEBS Proc Meet — FEBS [*Federation of European Biochemical Societies*] Proceedings of the Meeting
FEBS Symp — FEBS [*Federation of European Biochemical Societies*] Symposium
FEC — Far Eastern Economic Review
FeC — Formes et Couleurs
FECB — Far Eastern Ceramic Bulletin
Fechner Gb — Centralblatt fuer Naturwissenschaften und Anthropologie. Fechner
Fechners Repert — Repertorium der Experimental-Physik (Von Gustav Theodor Fechner) [*Leipzig*]
FECMDW — Forest Ecology and Management
Fecond Artif Anim Dom — Fecondazione Artificiale degli Animali Domestici
FECS Int Conf Chem Biotechnol Biol Act Nat Prod Proc — FECS (Federation of European Chemical Societies) International Conference on Chemistry and Biotechnology of Biologically Active Natural Products. Proceedings
FECS Int Conf Circ Dichroism — FECS (Federation of European Chemical Societies) International Conference on Circular Dichroism
FED — Federal Reserve Bulletin
FED — Losbladig Fiscaal Weekblad FED [*Formerly, Fiscaal Economische Documentatie*]
Fed Accountant — Federal Accountant
Fed Amer Soc Exp Biol Fed Proc — Federation of American Societies for Experimental Biology. Federation Proceedings
Fed Amer Soc Exp Biol Monogr — Federation of American Societies for Experimental Biology Monographs
Fed Am Hosp Rev — Federation of American Hospitals. Review
Fed Asian Oceanian Biochem Symp — Federation of Asian and Oceanian Biochemists Symposium
Fed Atlant — Federal Reserve Bank of Atlanta. Economic Review
Fed Audit Guide CCH — Federal Audit Guide. Commerce Clearing House
Fed Aust Music Teach Assoc Q Mag — Federation of Australian Music Teachers' Associations. Quarterly Magazine
Fed Aviat Adm Off Environ Energy Tech Rep FAA EE (US) — Federal Aviation Administration. Office of Environment and Energy. Technical Report FAA-EE (United States)
Fed BAJ — Federal Bar Association. Journal
Fed BA Jo — Federal Bar Association. Journal
Fed Bar J — Federal Bar News and Journal
Fed B Assn J — Federal Bar Association. Journal
Fed B J — Federal Bar Journal [*Later, Federal Bar News and Journal*]
Fed BN — Federal Bar News [*Later, Federal Bar News and Journal*]
Fed Bull — Federation Bulletin
Fed Can M Inst J — Federated Canadian Mining Institute. Journal
Fedcao Agric Torres Vedras — Federacao Agricola (Torres Vedras)
Fed Carr Cas CCH — Federal Carriers Cases. Commerce Clearing House
Fed Carr Rep CCH — Federal Carriers Reports. Commerce Clearing House
Fedcn Agr Extrem — Federacion Agraria Extremena [*Badajoz*]
Fedcn Sanit — Federacion Sanitaria [*Sevilla*]
Fed Com B J — Federal Communications Bar Journal [*Later, Federal Communications Law Journal*]
Fed Com LJ — Federal Communications Law Journal
Fed Comm BJ — Federal Communications Bar Journal [*Later, Federal Communications Law Journal*]
Fed Conf Great Lakes Proc — Federal Conference on the Great Lakes. Proceedings
Fed Conv Aust Water Wastewater Assoc — Federal Convention. Australian Water and Wastewater Association
Fed Counc Sci Technol ICAS Rep US — Federal Council for Science and Technology. ICAS (US Interdepartmental Committee for Atmospheric Sciences) Report
Fed Dallas — Federal Reserve Bank of Dallas. Farm and Ranch Bulletin
Feddes Repert — Feddes Repertorium
Feddes Repert Specierum Nov Regni Veg — Feddes Repertorium. Specierum Novarum Regni Vegetabilis
Feddes Repert Specierum Nov Regni Veg Beih — Feddes Repertorium. Specierum Novarum Regni Vegetabilis. Beihefte
Feddes Repert Z Bot Taxon Geobot — Feddes Repertorium. Zeitschrift fuer Botanische Taxonomie und Geobotanik

Feddes Reprium Z Bot Taxon Geobot — Feddes Repertorium. Zeitschrift fuer Botanische Taxonomie und Geobotanik

Fed Dev Ind Educ — Federal Development in Indian Education

FedE — Federado Escolar

Fed Emp — Federal Employee

Fed Employ Relat Man — Federal Employment Relations Manual

Fed Energy Adm Conserv Pap (US) — Federal Energy Administration. Conservation Paper (United States)

Fed Energy Reg Commn Rep CCH — Federal Energy Regulatory Commission Reports. Commerce Clearing House

Federacion Latinoam Bancos R — Federacion Latinoamericana de Bancos. Revista

Federal Home Loan Bank Bd J — Federal Home Loan Bank Board. Journal

Federal Law Rev — Federal Law Review

Federal L Rev — Federal Law Review

Federal Reserve Mo Chart Bk — Federal Reserve Monthly Chart Book

Federation Ins Couns Q — Federation of Insurance Counsel. Quarterly

Federation Proc — Federation Proceedings

Feder Rep — Federal Reporter

Fed Est & Gift Tax Rep — Federal Estate and Gift Tax Reports

Fed Est & Gift Tax Rep CCH — Federal Estate and Gift Tax Reports. Commerce Clearing House

Fed Eur Biochem Soc Congr — Federation of European Biochemical Societies Congress

Fed Eur Biochem Soc Lect Course — Federation of European Biochemical Societies Lecture Course

Fed Eur Biochem Soc Lett — Federation of European Biochemical Societies. Letters

Fed Eur Biochem Soc Meet Proc — Federation of European Biochemical Societies. Meeting Proceedings

Fed Eur Biochem Soc Symp — Federation of European Biochemical Societies Symposium

Fed Eur Biochem Soc Symp (Berl) — Federation of European Biochemical Societies. Symposium (Berlin)

Fed Eur Genie Chim EFCE Publ Ser — Federation Europeenne du Genie Chimique. EFCE Publication Series

Fed Eur Microbiol Soc FEMS Symp — Federation of European Microbiological Societies. FEMS Symposium

Fed Eur Microbiol Soc Microbiology Lett — Federation of European Microbiological Societies Microbiology Letters

Fed Eur Prot Eaux Bull Inf — Federation Europeenne pour la Protection des Eaux. Bulletin d'Information

FEDEX — Federal Energy Data Index

Fed Ex Tax Rep CCH — Federal Excise Tax Reports. Commerce Clearing House

Fed Fr Soc Sci Nat Bull Trimest — Federation Francaise des Societes de Sciences Naturelles. Bulletin Trimestriel

Fed Home Loan Bank Bd J — Federal Home Loan Bank Board. Journal

Fed Home Loan Bank Board J — Federal Home Loan Bank Board. Journal

Fed Home Loan Bk Bd J — Federal Home Loan Bank Board. Journal

Fed I Mn E T — Transactions of the Federated Institution of Mining Engineers

Fed Inc Gift & Est Taxn MB — Federal Income Gift and Estate Taxation. Matthew Bender

Fed Ins Counsel Q — Federal Insurance Counsel Quarterly

Fed Inst Ind Res Niger Res Rep — Federal Institute of Industrial Research. Nigeria. Research Report

Fed Inst Ind Res Tech Memo (Niger) — Federal Institute of Industrial Research. Technical Memorandum (Nigeria)

Fed Inst M Eng Tr — Federated Institution of Mining Engineers. Transactions

Fed Inter-Agency Sediment Conf Proc — Federal Inter-Agency Sedimentation Conference. Proceedings

Fed Int Lait Bull — Federation Internationale de Laiterie. Bulletin

Fed Int Lait Bull Annu — Federation Internationale de Laiterie. Bulletin Annuel

Fed Int Precontrainte Proc Congr — Federation Internationale de la Precontrainte. Proceedings. Congress

Fed Int Prod Jus Fruits Comm Sci Tech Rapp — Federation Internationale des Producteurs de Jus de Fruits. Commission Scientific et Technique. Rapports

Fed Int Soc Ing Tech Automob Congr Int Rapp — Federation Internationale des Societes d'Ingenieurs des Techniques de l'Automobile. Congres International. Rapport

Fed KC — Federal Reserve Bank of Kansas City. Monthly Review

Fedl Aid Fish Wildl Restor — Federal Aid in Fish and Wildlife Restoration. Annual Reports of the Dingell-Johnson and Pittman-Robertson Programs [*Washington*]

Fedl Aid Wildl Restor — Federal Aid in Wildlife Restoration. Annual Report of the Pittman-Robertson Program [*Washington*]

Fedl Archit — Federal Architect [*Washington*]

Fed LJ — Federal Law Journal of India

Fed LJ Ind — Federal Law Journal of India

Fed LQ — Federal Law Quarterly

Fed LR — Federal Law Reports

Fed LR — Federal Law Review

Fedl Register — Federal Register

Fed L Rep — Federal Law Reports

Fed L Rev — Federal Law Review

Fedl Vet — Federal Veterinarian [*Kansas City*]

Fed Malaya Dep Agric Bull — Federation of Malaya. Department of Agriculture. Bulletin

Fed Malaya Dep Agric Econ Ser — Federation of Malaya. Department of Agriculture. Economic Series

Fed Malaya Dep Agric Gen Ser — Federation of Malaya. Department of Agriculture. General Series

Fed Malaya Dep Agric Sci Ser — Federation of Malaya. Department of Agriculture. Scientific Series

Fed Malaya Div Agric Bull — Federation of Malaya. Division of Agriculture. Bulletin

Fedn Bull Fedn St Med Bds US — Federation Bulletin. Federation of State Medical Boards of the United States

Fedn Bull Scot Photogr Fedn — Federation Bulletin. Scottish Photographic Federation [*Glasgow*]

Fed'n Ins Counsel Q — Federation of Insurance Counsel. Quarterly

Fedn Mus J — Federation Museums Journal [*Perak*]

Fedn Pharm — Federation Pharmaceutique

Fedn Proc Fedn Am Socs Exp Biol — Federation Proceedings. Federation of American Societies for Experimental Biology

Fed Oper Dent — Federation of Operative Dentistry

Fed P — Federation Proceedings

Fed Phila — Federal Reserve Bank of Philadelphia. Business Review

Fed Power Serv MB — Federal Power Service. Matthew Bender

Fed Prob — Federal Probation

Fed Probat — Federal Probation

Fed Probation — Federal Probation

Fed Prob NL — Federal Probation Newsletter

Fed Proc — Federation Proceedings

Fed Proc — Proceedings. Federation of American Societies for Experimental Biology

Fed Proc Fed Am Soc Exp Biol — Federation Proceedings. Federation of American Societies for Experimental Biology

Fed Proc Transl Suppl — Federation Proceedings. Translation Supplement

FED Publ Am Soc Mech Eng Fluids Eng Div — FED Publication. American Society of Mechanical Engineers. Fluids Engineering Division

Fed Pub Serv J — Federal Public Service Journal

Fed R D — Federal Rules Decisions

Fed Reg — Federal Register

Fed Reg Empl Serv — Federal Regulation of Employment Service

Fed Regist — Federal Register

Fed Regist (Wash DC) — Federal Register (Washington, DC)

Fed Repub Ger Pat Doc Auslegeschr — Federal Republic of Germany. Patent Document. Ausleegeschrift

Fed Repub Ger Pat Doc Offenlegungsschr — Federal Republic of Germany. Patent Document. Offenlegungsschrift

Fed Repub Ger Pat Doc Patentschr — Federal Republic of Germany. Patent Document. Patentschrift

Fed Res Bank NY — Federal Reserve Bank of New York. Quarterly Review

Fed Res Bull — Federal Reserve Bulletin

Fed Reserve B — Federal Reserve Bulletin

Fed Reserve Bank New York — Federal Reserve Bank of New York

Fed Reserve Bank NYQ Rev — Federal Reserve Bank of New York. Quarterly Review

Fed Reserve Bank St Louis — Federal Reserve Bank of St Louis

Fed Reserve Bank St Louis Rev — Federal Reserve Bank of St. Louis. Review

Fed Reserve Bull — Federal Reserve Bulletin

Fed Richmd — Federal Reserve Bank of Richmond. Monthly Review

FEDRIP — Federal Research in Progress

Fed Rules Dec — Federal Rules Decisions

Fed Sci Prog — Federal Science Progress

Fed Ser Coat Technol — Federation Series on Coating Technology

Fed SF BFL — Federal Reserve Bank of San Francisco. Business and Financial Letter

FED-STAN — Standards Referenced in Federal Legislation

Fed Stat — Federal Reserve Statistical Release. Industrial Production

Fed Stat R — Federal Reserve Statistical Release. Industrial Production

Fed St L — Federal Reserve Bank of St. Louis. Monthly Review [*Later, Federal Reserve Bankof St. Louis. Review*]

Fed Tax Artic — Federal Tax Articles

Fed Tax Coordinator 2d Res Inst Am — Federal Tax Coordinator Second. Research Institute of America

Fed Tax Guide Rep CCH — Federal Tax Guide Reports. Commerce Clearing House

Fed Times — Federal Times

Fed Yellow Book — Federal Yellow Book

Fedzne Med — Federazione Medica

FEE — Far Eastern Economic Review

Feed Addit Compend — Feed Additive Compendium

Feed Bag Mag — Feed Bag Magazine

Feed Energy Sources Livest Pap Nutr Conf Feed Manuf — Feed Energy Sources for Livestock. Papers. Nutrition Conference for Feed Manufacturers

Feed Feed Dig — Feed and Feeding Digest

Feed Illus — Feeds Illustrated

Feed Ind — Feed Industry

Feed Ind Rev — Feed Industry Review

Feedlot Manage — Feedlot Management

Feed Manage — Feed Management

Feed Manage E Ed — Feed Management. Eastern Edition

Feed Mill Rev — Feed Milling Review

Feed Nutr Nonhum Primates Proc Symp — Feeding and Nutrition of Nonhuman Primates. Proceedings of a Symposium

Feed Protein Conf — Feed Protein Conference

Feed Situation USDA Econ Res Serv — Feed Situation. US Department of Agriculture. Economic Research Service

Feedst Feed Addit Compend — Feedstuffs Feed Additive Compendium

Feed Stuffs Rep La Agric Exp Stn — Feed Stuffs Report. Louisiana Agricultural Experiment Station

FEER — Far Eastern Economic Review

FEGADG — Fern Gazette

FEHP — Facsimiles of Egyptian Hieratic Papyri in the British Museum

FEHTA7 — Florists' Exchange

FEI — Foreign Investment Review

Feildens Mag — Feilden's Magazine

Feingeraete Tech — Feingeraete Technik

Feinmech Praezis — Feinmechanik und Praezision

Feinwerktech & Micronic — Feinwerktechnik und Micronic

Feinwerktech Messtech — Feinwerktechnik und Messtechnik

Feinwerktech und Messtech — Feinwerktechnik und Messtechnik
Feinwk Tech — Feinwerk-Technik
FEJ — Far East Journal
FEJR — Flugschriften aus den Ersten Jahren der Reformation
FEKTA — Forum foer Ekonomi och Teknik
FeL — Filologia e Letteratura
Feldsh Drug — Feldsherski Drugar'
Fel'dsher Akush — Fel'dsher i Akusherka
Feldsh Pregl — Feldsherski Pregled
Feldsh Vest — Feldsherskii Vestnik
Feldspars Proc NATO Adv Study Inst — Feldspars. Proceedings of a NATO Advanced Study Institute
Feld Wald Wasser — Feld, Wald, und Wasser
Feld Wald Wasser Schweiz Jagdztg — Feld, Wald, Wasser. Schweizerische Jagdzeitung
Feline Leuk — Feline Leukemia
Feline Pract — Feline Practice
Fell — Fellowship
Fellow Newsl Am Anthrop Ass — Fellow Newsletter. American Anthropological Association
FELPBG — Feline Practice
FELR — Far Eastern Law Review
Fel Rav — Felix Ravenna
Felsmech Ingenieurgeol — Felsmechanik und Ingenieurgeologie
Feltor — Feltornithologen
Feluletvedelem Klim — Feluletvedelem es Klimatizacio
FEMAA — Feed Management
FE Magazin — FE. The Magazine for Financial Executives
FEMED — Feinwerktechnik und Messtechnik
FEM (Fact Equip Mater) — FEM (Factory Equipment and Materials)
Feminist — Feminist Studies
Feministische Stud — Feministische Studies
Feminist Rev — Feminist Review
Feminist Stud — Feminist Studies
Femip Kut Intez Kozl — Femipari Kutato Intezet Kozlemenyei
Femip Kut Intez Kozlem — Femipari Kutato Intezet Kozlemenyei
Fem Issues — Feminist Issues
Fem R — Feminist Review
Fem Rview — Feminist Review
FEMS (Fed Eur Microbiol Soc) Microbiol Ecol — FEMS (Federation of European Microbiological Societies) Microbiology-Ecology
FEMS (Fed Eur Microbiol Soc) Microbiol Rev — FEMS [Federation of European Microbiological Societies] Microbiology Reviews
FEMS (Fed Eur Microbiol Soc) Symp — FEMS (Federation of European Microbiological Societies) Symposium
FEMS Immunol Med Microbiol — FEMS [Federation of European Microbiological Societies] Immunology and Medical Microbiological Societies
FEMS Mic Ec — FEMS [Federation of European Microbiological Societies] Microbiology-Ecology
FEMS Microbiol Immunol — FEMS (Federation of European Microbiological Societies) Microbiology Immunology
FEMS Microbiol Lett — FEMS [Federation of European Microbiological Societies] Microbiology Letters
FEMS Microbiol Lett Fed Eur Microbiol Soc — FEMS Microbiology Letters. Federation of European Microbiological Societies
FEMS Microbiol Rev — FEMS [Federation of European Microbiological Societies] Microbiology Reviews
FEMS Symp Fed Eur Microbiol Soc — FEMS Symposium. Federation of European Microbiological Societies
Fem Stud — Feminist Studies
FEMXAA — Folia Entomologica Mexicana
FEN — Antara Financial and Economic News
FEN — FEN. Factory Equipment News
FEN — Freshman English News
Fenarete — Fenarete-Letture d'Italia
Fen Bilimleri Derg Ataturk Univ — Fen Bilimleri Dergisi (Ataturk Universitesi)
Fen Bilimleri Derg Marmara Univ — Fen Bilimleri Dergisi (Marmara Universitesi)
Fen Bilimleri Derg Marmara Univ Ataturk Egitim Fak — Fen Bilimleri Dergisi (Marmara Universitesi Ataturk Egitim Fakultesi)
FENEA — Fertiliser News
Fen Fak Derg (Ataturk Univ) — Fen Fakultesi Dergisi (Ataturk Universitesi)
Fen Fak Derg Seri A Ege Univ — Fen Fakultesi Dergisi. Seri A (Ege Universitesi)
Fen Fak Derg Seri B Ege Univ — Fen Fakultesi Dergisi. Seri B (Ege Universitesi)
FEN Finite Elem News — FEN. Finite Element News
FENN — Fennia
FENNAJ — Fennia
Fenner V Belt J — Fenner V-Belt Journal
Fenno Chem — Fenno-Chemica
Fenno Chem Fin Kemistsamf Medd — Fenno-Chemica och Finska Kemistsamfundets Meddelanden
Fenol Roc Csl Repub — Fenologicki Rocenka Ceskoslovenske Republiky
FENUD — Fusion Energy Update
Fenway C — Fenway Court
Fenykep Het — Fenykepeszeti Hetilap
FEORA2 — Fertilite Orthogenie
FEPNDW — Forest Environmental Protection. United States Forest Service. Northern Region
FEPRA — Federation Proceedings
FEPRA7 — Federation Proceedings
FEPRB8 — Feuillets du Praticien
FEPXA — Fernmelde-Praxis
FEQ — Far Eastern Quarterly
FER — Far Eastern Economic Review
FER — Fear
FER — Federal Economic Review

FERIC (For Eng Res Inst Can) Tech Rep — FERIC (Forest Engineering Research Institute of Canada) Technical Report
FERMA2 — Fermentatio
Ferme Exter Grignon — Ferme Exterieure de Grignon
Fermente Wirk — Fermente und ihre Wirkungen
Ferment Ind — Fermentation and Industry
Ferment Ind Moscow — Fermentation Industry (Moscow)
Ferment Ind Tokyo — Fermentation and Industry (Tokyo)
Fermentn Spirt Promst — Fermentnaya i Spirtovaya Promyshlennost'
Ferment Process Dev Ind Org — Fermentation Process Development of Industrial Organisms
Ferment Technol Today Proc Int Ferment Symp — Fermentation Technology Today. Proceedings. International Fermentation Symposium
Ferment Vinifications Symp Int Oenol — Fermentations et Vinifications. Symposium International d'Oenologie
Fermenty Evol Zhivotn — Fermenty v Evolyutsii Zhivotnykh
Fermenty Gribov Ikh Primen Nar Khoz — Fermenty Gribov i Ikh Primenenie v Narodnom Khozyaistve
Fermenty Lab Diagn Mater Vses Sezda Vrachei Laborantov — Fermenty v Laboratornoi Diagnostike. Materialy Vsesoyuznogo S'ezda Vrachei-Laborantov
Fermenty Med Naznacheniya — Fermenty Meditsinskogo Naznacheniya
Fermenty Med Pishch Promsti Selsk Khoz — Fermenty v Meditsine. Pishchevoi Promyshlennosti i Sel'skom Khozyaistve
Fermenty Nar Khoz Med — Fermenty v Narodnom Khozyaistve i Meditsine
Fermes Mod — Fermes Modernes
Fermi Surf Proc Int Conf — Fermi Surface. Proceedings. International Conference
FERN — Federal Employee/Retiree Newsletter
Fern Bull — Fern Bulletin. A Quarterly Devoted to Ferns
Fern Gaz — Fern Gazette
Fernhurst Bull — Fernhurst Bulletin
Fern Internat — Fernwaerme International
Fernmelde-Ing — Fernmelde-Ingenieur
Fernmelde-Prax — Fernmelde-Praxis
Fernmeldetech Z — Fernmeldetechnische Zeitschrift
Fernmeldetech Zentralamt Forschungsinst Tech Ber Ger — Fernmeldetechnisches Zentralamt. Forschungsinstitut. Technischer Bericht (Germany)
Fernsch Holzwirt — Fernschule fuer die Holzwirtschaft
Fernseh- & Kino- Tech — Fernseh- und Kino- Technik
Fernsehen & B — Fernsehen und Bildung
Fernstroem Found Ser — Fernstroem Foundation Series
Fernwaerme Int — Fernwaerme International
Fernwaerme Int (Frankfurt Main) — Fernwaerme International (Frankfurt/Main)
FEROA — Ferroelectrics
Ferodo Int Tech News — Ferodo International Technical News
Ferranti Computer Wld — Ferranti Computer World
Ferrara Univ Ann Sez 9 — Ferrara. Universita. Annali. Sezione 9. Scienze Geologiche e Paleontologiche
Ferrity Dokl Vses Soveshch — Ferrity. Doklady. Prochitannye na Vsesoyuznom Soveshchanii po Fizicheskim i Fiziko-Khimicheskim Svoistvam Ferritov
Ferrocarr Tranv — Ferrocarriles y Tranvias
Ferro Concr — Ferro-Concrete
Ferroelectr — Ferroelectrics
Ferroelectr Lett — Ferroelectrics Letters
Ferroelectr Lett Sect — Ferroelectrics Letters Section
Ferroelectr Phys Proc Sch — Ferroelectrics Physics. Proceedings. School of Ferroelectrics Physics
Ferroelectr Proc Int Meet — Ferroelectricity. Proceedings. International Meeting
Ferroelectr Proc Symp — Ferroelectricity. Proceedings. Symposium on Ferroelectricity
Ferroelectr Relat Mater — Ferroelectrics and Related Materials
Ferroelectr Relat Phenom — Ferroelectricity and Related Phenomena
Ferrous Non Ferrous Alloy Processes Proc Int Symp — Ferrous and Non-Ferrous Alloy Processes. Proceedings. International Symposium
Fert Abstr — Fertilizer Abstracts
Fert Agric — Fertilizers and Agriculture
Fert Assoc India Proc — Fertiliser Association of India. Proceedings
Fert Assoc India Proc No R D — Fertiliser Association of India. Proceedings No. R and D
Fert Assoc India Proc No Tech — Fertiliser Association of India. Proceedings No. Tech
Fert Contracept — Fertility and Contraception
Fert Crops — Fertilizers and Crops
Fert Data — Fertilizer Summary Data
Fert Embryog Ovulated Plants Proc Int Cytoembryol Symp — Fertilization and Embryogenesis in Ovulated Plants. Proceedings. International Cytoembryological Symposium
Fert Farming Food — Fertiliser, Farming, and Food
Fert Feed Stuff Farm Supplies J — Fertiliser, Feedings Stuffs, and Farm Supplies Journal
Fert Feed Stuffs J — Fertilizer and Feeding Stuffs Journal
Fert Focus — Fertilizer Focus
Fert Green Bk — Fertilizer Green Book
Fert Green Book — Fertilizer Green Book
Fert Higher Plants Proc Int Symp — Fertilization in Higher Plants. Proceedings. International Symposium
Fertig Tech Betr — Fertigungstechnik und Betrieb
Fertigungstech Betr — Fertigungstechnik und Betrieb
Fertigungs Technol — Fertigungs-Technologie
Fertil Contracept — Fertility and Contraception
Fertile Fields Coop State Res Serv State Agric Exp Stn Syst — Fertile Fields. Cooperative State Research Service. State Agricultural Experiment Station System
Fertil Feed Stuffs J — Fertilizer and Feeding Stuffs Journal
Fertil Inf — Fertiliser Information

Fertil News — Fertiliser News
Fertil Orthogenie — Fertilite Orthogenie
Fertil Regul Hum Lactation Proc IPPF Biomed Workshop — Fertility Regulation during Human Lactation. Proceedings. IPPF [*International Planned Parenthood Federation*] Biomedical Workshop
Fertil Rep La Agric Exp Stn — Fertiliser Report. Louisiana Agricultural Experiment Station
Fertil Rep Statist — Fertiliser Report and Statistics
Fertil Rev — Fertilizer Review. National Fertilizer Association
Fertil Steril — Fertility and Sterility
Fertil Steril Proc World Congr — Fertility and Sterility. Proceedings. World Congress on Fertility and Sterility
Fertil Technol — Fertilizer Technology
Fert Ind Round Table Proc Annu Meet — Fertilizer Industry Round Table. Proceedings. Annual Meeting
Fert Inst (Delhi) Proc — Fertiliser Institute (Delhi). Proceedings
Fert Inst Environ Symp — Fertilizer Institute. Environmental Symposium
Fert Int — Fertilizer International
Fert Intnl — Fertilizer International
Fert Issues — Journal of Fertilizer Issues
Fert Mark News — Fertilizer Marketing News
Fert News — Fertilizer News
Fert Prog — Fertilizer Progress
Fert R — Fertilizer Review
Fert Res — Fertilizer Research
Fert Res Int J Fert Use Technol — Fertilizer Research. An International Journal on Fertilizer Use and Technology
Fert Rev — Fertilizer Review
Fert Sci Technol Ser — Fertilizer Science and Technology Series
Fert Soc Proc — Fertiliser Society. Proceedings
Fert Soc S Afr J — Fertilizer Society of South Africa. Journal
Fert Soc S Afr Publ — Fertilizer Society of South Africa Publication
Fert Soc (Tokyo) — Fertilizer Science (Tokyo)
Fert Solutions — Fertilizer Solutions
Fert Ster — Fertility and Sterility
Fert Steril — Fertility and Sterility
Fert Technol — Fertilizer Technology
Fert Technol Use — Fertilizer Technology and Use [*monograph*]
FES — Asian Survey
FES — Far Eastern Survey
FESTA — Fertility and Sterility
FESTAS — Fertility and Sterility
FestEH — Eumusia. Festgabe fuer Ernst Howald. Erlenbach-Zuerich, Rentsch
FestET — Festschrift fuer Ernst Tappolet. Basel, Schwabe
FestFN — Formen der Selbstdarstellung. Festgabe fuer Fritz Neubert
Festigkeitsprobl Materialverhalten Tag Festkoerpermech — Festigkeitsprobleme und Materialverhalten. Vorgelegt aus Anlass der Tagung Festkoerpermechanik
Festigkeit Verform Hoher Temp — Festigkeit und Verformung bei Hoher Temperatur
Festkoerperanal Tag — Festkoerperanalytik. Tagung
Festkoerperanal Tag Plenar Hauptvortr — Festkoerperanalytik, Tagung, Plenar- und Hauptvortraege
Festkoerperprobl — Festkoerperprobleme
FestOW — Festschrift Oskar Walzel. Wildpark-Potsdam, Athenaion M.B.H.
FestPB — Hauptfragen der Romanistik. Festschrift fuer Philipp August Becker
Festschr Kongr Ausstellung Wasser — Festschrift zu Kongress und Ausstellung Wasser
FET — Financieel Ekonomische Tijd
FET — Foreign Economic Trends
FET — Milling Feed and Fertilizer
Fetal Diagn Ther — Fetal Diagnosis and Therapy
Fetal Dosim Workshop — Fetal Dosimetry Workshop
Fetal Growth Retard Proc Symp — Fetal Growth Retardation. Proceedings of a Symposium
Fetal Postnatal Cell Growth — Fetal and Postnatal Cellular Growth [*monograph*]
FETEDP — Fertilizer Technology
F et H — Fides et Historia
FETID — Federal Times
Fet Sei Ans — Fette - Seifen - Anstrichmittel. Verbunden mit der Zeitschrift die Ernaehrungs Industrie
Fettchem Umsch — Fettchemische Umschau
Fette Seife — Fette - Seifen - Anstrichmittel
Fette Seifen Anstrichm — Fette - Seifen - Anstrichmittel
Fette Seifen Anstrmittel — Fette - Seifen - Anstrichmittel
Fett Parenter Ernaehr — Fett in der Parenteralen Ernaehrung. Symposium in Rottach-Egern
Fett Wiss Technol — Fett Wissenschaft Technologie
FEUBAI — Annali. Universita di Ferrara. Sezione IV. Botanica
FEUC — Forschungen zur Entstehung des Urchristentums, des Neuen Testaments, und der Kirche
Feuerfeste Werkst Konverter Stahlerzeug Int Feuerfest Kolloq — Feuerfeste Werkstoffe fuer Konverter zur Stahlerzeugung. Internationales Feuerfest-Kolloquium
Feuerungstech Ber — Feuerungstechnische Berichte
Feuer Wass — Feuer und Wasser
Feuerwehrtech Z — Feuerwehrtechnische Zeitschrift
FEUFJ — Far Eastern University. Faculty Journal
Feuill Biblphiq Ass Tech Ind Pap — Feuillets Bibliographiques. Association Technique de l'Industrie Papetiere
Feuill Biol — Feuillets de Biologie
Feuille Canton Vaud — Feuille du Canton de Vaud, ou Journal d'Agriculture Pratique, des Sciences Naturelles et d'Economie Publique
Feuille Infs Minist Agric — Feuille d'Informations du Ministere de l'Agriculture
Feuille Jeun Nat — Feuille des Jeunes Naturalistes
Feuille Nat — Feuille des Naturalistes

Feuille Not Explic Carte Geol Detaillee Fr Dep Guyane — Feuille et Notice Explicative. Carte Geologique Detaillee de la France. Departement de la Guyane
Feuilles Agric Econ Gen — Feuilles d'Agriculture et d'Economie Generale. Publiees par la Societe d'Agriculture et d'Economie du Canton de Vaud
Feuilles Hyg Med Nat — Feuilles d'Hygiene et de Medecine Naturelle
Feuilles Infs Oleic Int — Feuilles d'Informations Oleicoles Internationales
Feuilles Inst Fr Afr Noire — Feuilles. Institut Francais d'Afrique Noire
Feuille Suisse Brev Dessins Marques — Feuille Suisse des Brevets, Dessins, et Marques
Feuille Tech Cent Tech Bois — Feuille Technique. Centre Technique du Bois
Feuill Prat — Feuillets du Praticien
Feuill Radiol — Feuillets de Radiologie
Feversham Cttee — Committee on Human Artificial Insemination. Report
Few Body Probl — Few-Body Problems
Few Body Probl Proc Colloq Int Astron Union — Few Body Problem. Proceedings. Colloquium. International Astronomical Union
Few Body Syst — Few-Body Systems
Few Body Syst Suppl — Few-Body Systems. Supplementum
FEX — Financial Executive
Fe Zn Engl Edn — Fe+Zn. English Edition. Zinc Development Association
FF — Faith and Form
FF — Fanfare
FF — Faser-Forschung
FF — Fast Food
FF — Feuille Federale
FF — Filmfacts
FF — Films and Filming
FF — Foglio Federale Svizzero
FF — Folklore
FF — Folklore Forum
FF — FonoForum
FF — Forgotten Fantasy
FF — Forschungen und Fortschritte
FF — Fraenkische Forschungen
FF — France Franciscaine
FF — Frate Francesco
FFA — Frankfurter Allgemeine Zeitung fuer Deutschland
F Faero — Fra Faeroerne. Ur Foroyum
FFB — Fertilizer International
F Fbr A — Fra Frederiksborg Amt
FFC — Fibres, Fabrics, and Cordage
FFC — Folklore Fellows Communications
FFC Abstr — Forest Fire Control Abstracts
FFCLUSP Bol Bot — FFCLUSP (Faculdade de Filosofia, Ciencias, e Letras. Universidade de Sao Paulo) Boletim Botanica
FFCLUSP Bol Quim — FFCLUSP (Faculdade de Filosofia, Ciencias, e Letras. Universidade de Sao Paulo)Boletim Quimica
F F Commun — F F Communications
FFE — Blick durch die Wirtschaft
FFF — Faith for the Family
FFHAET — Flora and Fauna Handbook
FFHC Basic Stud — FFHC [*Freedom from Hunger Campaign*] Basic Studies
FFI (Forsvarets Forskningsints) Mikrosk — FFI (Forsvarets Forskningsinstitutt) Mikroskopet
FFI Mikrosk — FFI [*Forsvarets Forskningsinstitutt*] Mikroskopet
FFKL — Freiburger Forschungen zur Kunst und Literaturgeschichte
FFLR — Florida Foreign Language Reporter
FFM — Famous Fantastic Mysteries
FFM — Fast Food Management
FFM — Fan Fan Monthly
FFMA — Folklore and Folk Music Archivist
FFMDAP — Folia Facultatis Medicae Universitatis Comenianae Bratislaviensis
FFN — Fantasy Stories
FFNPE2 — FAO [*Food and Agriculture Organization of the United Nations*] Food and Nutrition Paper
FFODAZ — Forstlige Forsogsvaesen i Danmark
F Form — Film Form
FForum — Folklore Forum
FForumB — Folklore Forum. Bibliographic and Special Series
FFP — Fouilles Franco-Polonaises
FFP — France Franciscaine
FFPBAY — Folia Forestalia Polonica. Seria B (Drzewnictwo)
FFPOA5 — Folia Forestalia Polonica. Seria A (Lesnictwo)
FFR — Film Forum Review
FFRED — Farm and Food Research
F Fro — Tidsskrift for Froavlerforening
FFS — Fast Foodservice
FFS — Forhandlingar Fysiografiska Sallskab
FFS — Fouiles Franco-Suisses
FFSCDL — Folia Facultatis Scientiarum Naturalium Universitatis Purkynianae Brunensis: Chemia
FFSEDR — FAO [*Food and Agriculture Organization of the United Nations*] Fisheries Series
FFSJA5 — Fertilizer and Feeding Stuffs Journal
FFTC Book Ser — FFTC (Food and Fertilizer Technology Center) Book Series
FFTPAS — Forests Commission Victoria. Forestry Technical Papers
FFTPBT — FAO [*Food and Agriculture Organization of the United Nations*] Fisheries Technical Paper
FFUBAP — Folia Facultatis Naturalium Universitatis Purkynianae Brunensis: Biologia
FG — Financial Gazette
FG — Form und Geist
FG — Freiburger Geschichtsblaetter
FGADL — Forschungen zur Geschichte der Aelteren Deutschen Literatur

FgBl — Familiengeschichtliche Blaetter
FGGHA — Fukushima Daigaku Gakugei Gakubu Rika Hokoku
FGGM — Festschrift der Geographischen Gesellschaft in Muenchen
FGGYA — Fortschritte der Geburtshilfe und Gynaekologie
FGGYAV — Advances in Obstetrics and Gynaecology
FGH — Fragmente der Griechischen Historiker
FGIL — Forschungen zur Geschichte des Innerkirchlichen Lebens
FGLOA — Figyelo
FGLP — Forschungen zur Geschichte und Lehre des Protestantismus
FGNK — Forschungen zur Geschichte des Neutestamentlichen Kanons und der Altchristlichen Literatur
FGO — Forschungen zur Geschichte Oberoesterreichs
FGPBA7 — Folia Geobotanica et Phytotaxonomica
FGPP — Forschungen zur Geschichte der Philosophie und der Paedagogik
FGPS — Forschungen zur Geschichte des Paepstlichen Staatssekretariats
FGR — Filmograph
F Gr H — Fragmente der Griechischen Historiker
FGrHist — Fragmente der Griechischen Historiker
FGRNA — Fortschritte auf dem Gebiete der Roentgenstrahlen und der Nuklearmedizin
FGRP — Frankfurter Quellen und Forschungen zur Germanischen und Romanischen Philologie
FGRTA — Feingeraete Technik
FH — Fasti Hispanienses
FH — Feuilles d'Histoire
FH — Fides et Historia
FH — Folia Humanistica
FH — Foodservice and Hospitality
FH — Frankfurter Hefte
FH — Fundberichte aus Hessen
FHA — Fitzgerald-Hemingway Annual
FHA — Fontes Hispaniae Antiquae
FHB — Fine Homebuilding
F Hb A — Fra Holbaek Amt
FHC — Franciscan Historical Classics
FHCP — Fontes Historicae Congregationis Passionis
FHCYAI — Folia Histochemica et Cytochemica [*Later, Folia Histochemica et Cytobiologica*]
FHCYEM — Folia Histochemica et Cytobiologica
FHDR — Fontes Historiae Dacoromanae
F Her — Film Heritage
FHG — Fragmenta Historicorum Graecorum
FHG — Mueller. Fragmenta Historicorum Graecorum
FhG Ber — FhG [*Fraunhofer-Gesellschaft*] Berichte
FHist — Fides et Historia
FHL — Federal Home Loan Bank Board. Journal
FHLBA — Family Health Bulletin
FHLBB Jrl — Federal Home Loan Bank Board. Journal
F Hml — Fra Himmerland og Kjaer Herred
FHP — Fort Hare Papers
FHPAD — Fort Hare Papers
FHQ — Florida Historical Quarterly
FHR — Fontes Historiae Religionum
FHS — Freiburger Historische Studien
FHS — French Historical Studies
FHSCAW — Farm and Home Science
FHSM — Fontes Historici Societatis Mariae
FHUR — Fontes Historiae Ukraino-Russicae
FI — Farm Index
Fi — File di Istorie. Muzeul de Istoria
Fi — Filologia
FI — Folklore Italiano
FI — Foro Internacional
FI — Forsttechnische Informationen
FI — Forum Italicum
FI — Friends Intelligencer
FIA — Financial Analysts Journal
Fiamme Reaz Flusso Simp Int Din Reaz Chim — Fiamme quali Reazioni in Flusso. Simposio Internazionale di Dinamica delle Reazioni Chimiche
FIAS — Frontiers in Aging Series
FIAT Rev Germ Sci — F.I.A.T. (Field Information Agency Technical) Review of German Science
FIAT Tech Bull — F.I.A.T. (Field Information Agency Technical) Technical Bulletin
FIB — Bulletin. Federation des Industries Belges
FIB — Fiches Bibliographiques
FIB — Fish Industry Board. Bulletin
FIBBD — F + I Bau
Fiber and Integrated Opt — Fiber and Integrated Optics
Fiber Hum Nutr — Fiber in Human Nutrition
Fiber Integr Opt — Fiber and Integrated Optics
Fiber Laser — Fiber Laser News
Fiber Laser Sources Amplifiers — Fiber Laser Sources and Amplifiers
Fiber Opt — Fiber Optics News
Fiber Opt Adverse Environ — Fiber Optics in Adverse Environments
Fiber Opt Chem Sens Biosens — Fiber Optic Chemical Sensors and Biosensors
Fiber Opt Commun — Fiber Optics and Communications
Fiber Opt Commun Technol — Fiber Optic Communication Technology
Fiber Opt Compon Reliab — Fiber Optic Components and Reliability
Fiber Opt Couplers Connectors Splice Technol — Fiber Optic Couplers, Connectors, and Splice Technology
Fiberoptcs — Fiberoptics Report
Fiber Opt Datacom Comput Networks — Fiber Optic Datacom and Computer Networks
Fiber Opt Gyros — Fiber Optic Gyros
Fiber Opt Gyros Anniv Conf — Fiber Optic Gyros. Anniversary Conference

Fiber Opt Laser Sens — Fiber Optic and Laser Sensors
Fiber Opt Local Area Networks — Fiber Optics in Local Area Networks
Fiber Opt Med Fluoresc Sens Appl — Fiber Optic Medical and Fluorescent Sensors and Applications
Fiber Opt Mult Modulation — Fiber Optics Multiplexing and Modulation
Fiber Opt Networks Coherent Technol Fiber Opt Syst — Fiber Optic Networks and Coherent Technology in Fiber Optic Systems
Fiber Opt Reliab Benign Adverse Environ — Fiber Optics Reliability. Benign and Adverse Environments
Fiber Opt Sens — Fiber Optic Sensors
Fiber Opt Short Haul Long Haul Meas Appl — Fiber Optics. Short-Haul and Long-Haul Measurements and Applications
Fiber Opt Smart Struct Skins — Fiber Optic Smart Structures and Skins
Fiber Opt Syst Mobile Platforms — Fiber Optic Systems for Mobile Platforms
Fiber Prod — Fiber Producer
Fiber Sci Ind — Fiber Science and Industry
Fiber Sci Ser — Fiber Science Series
FIBID9 — Freshwater Invertebrate Biology
Fibonacci Q — Fibonacci Quarterly
Fibonacci Quart — Fibonacci Quarterly
FIBQA — Fibonacci Quarterly
FIBRC Proc — FIBRC (International Bat Research Conference) Proceedings
Fibrebd Pap Case — Fibre-Board and Paper Case, Carton, and Container
Fibre Chem — Fibre Chemistry
Fibre Chem (Engl Transl) — Fibre Chemistry (English Translation)
Fibre Containers — Fibre Containers and Paperboard Mills
Fibre Contain PapBd Mills — Fibre Containers and Paperboard Mills
Fibre Fabr — Fibre and Fabric
Fibre Inds Cord Wld — Fibre Industries and Cordage World
Fibre Reinf Compos Mater — Fibre Reinforcements for Composite Materials
Fibres & Polym — Fibres and Polymers
Fibre Sci Technol — Fibre Science and Technology
Fibres Eng Chem — Fibres, Engineering, and Chemistry
Fibres Fabr Cordage — Fibres, Fabrics, and Cordage
Fibres Fabrics Cord — Fibres, Fabrics, and Cordage
Fibres Fabrics J — Fibres and Fabrics Journal
Fibres Fabrics Mon — Fibres and Fabrics Monthly
Fibres Fabr J — Fibres and Fabrics Journal
Fibres Fabr Mon — Fibres Fabrics Monthly
Fibres Incorporating Fairfax Mon — Fibres. Incorporating Fairfax Monthly
Fibres Int — Fibres International
Fibres Nat Synth — Fibres, Natural and Synthetic
Fibres Plast — Fibres and Plastics
Fibres Text East Eur — Fibres and Textiles in Eastern Europe
Fibres Text Inds — Fibres and Textile Industries
Fibre Struct — Fibre Structure
Fibre Vetro — Fibre di Vetro
Fibrinkleber Orthop Traumatol Heidelb Orthop Symp — Fibrinkleber in Orthopaedie und Traumatologie. Heidelberger Orthopaedie-Symposium
Fibrinolys — Fibrinolysis
Fibrin Sealing Surg Nonsurg Fields — Fibrin Sealing in Surgical and Nonsurgical Fields
Fibr Text Ind — Fibres and Textile Industries
Fic — Ficcion
FiC — Filson Club History Quarterly
FICAAL — Flore Illustree des Champignons d'Afrique Centrale
Fich Aeronaut — Fiches Aeronautiques
Fichas Bibliogr Potos S Louis Potosi — Fichas de Bibliografia Potosina. Biblioteca, Universidad Autonoma de San Luis Potosi (San Luis Potosi)
Fichas Tec Inst Nac Carb Oviedo — Fichas Tecnicas. Instituto Nacional del Carbon (Oviedo)
Fichero Bibliogr Hispanoamer — Fichero Bibliografico Hispanoamericano
Fichero Med Terap Puriss — Fichero Medico-Terapeutico Purissismus
Fichero Med Ter Purissimus — Fichero Medico Terapeutico Purissimus
Fiches Identif Zooplancton — Fiches d'Identification du Zooplancton
Fiches Phytopathol Trop — Fiches de Phytopathologie Tropicale
Fich Ident Zooplancton — Fiches d'Identification du Zooplancton
Fichier Ent Chin — Fichier Entomologique Chinois
Fichier Mens Docum Tech Fabrimetal — Fichier Mensuel de Documentation Technique Fabrimetal
Fichier Micropaleontol Gen — Fichier Micropaleontologique General
Fich Ind — Fiches Industrielles
Fich Infs Pedog Tech — Fiches d'Informations Pedogogiques et Techniques
Fich Med — Fiches Medicales
Fich Phytopath Trop — Fiches de Phytopathologie Tropicale
Fic Int — Fiction International
FICO — Fireweed Country. Magazine of the Yukon
FICQ — Federation of Insurance Counsel. Quarterly
FICU — Folklore. Boletin del Departamento de Folklore del Instituto de Cooperacion Universitaria
FID — Finance and Development
FIDADT — US Forest Service. Forest Insect and Disease Leaflet
FID Commun — FID (Federation Internationale de Documentation) Communications
Fides H — Fides et Historia
FIDF — Financial Institutions Data File
Fidia Res Found Symp Ser — Fidia Research Foundation Symposium Series
FIDIA Res Ser — FIDIA [*Farmaceutici Italiani Derivati Industriali ed Affi*] Research Series
Fi Dis — Fight Against Disease
FIDMDV — US Forest Service. Forest Insect and Disease Management. Northern Region Report
FID News Bull — Federation Internationale de Documentation. News Bulletin
FID Publ — Federation Internationale de Documentation. Publication
FID R Doc — Federation Internationale de Documentation. Revue de la Documentation

Fi E — Forschungen in Ephesos
Fie Cr Abstr — Field Crop Abstracts
Field — Fieldiana
Field Anal Chem Technol — Field Analytical Chemistry and Technology
Field & Lab — Field and Laboratory
Field & S — Field and Stream
Field Artillery Jour — Field Artillery Journal. US Field Artillery Association
Field Col Mus Pub G S Zool S — Field Columbian Museum. Publications. Geological Series. Zoological Series
Field Columbian Mus Publ Geol Ser — Field Columbian Museum. Publications. Geological Series
Field Conf Guideb NM Geol Soc — Field Conference Guidebook. New Mexico Geological Society
Field Crop Abstr — Field Crop Abstracts
Field Crops Res — Field Crops Research
Field Dev N — Field Development Newsletter
Field Drain — Field Drainage
Field Facts Soils Insects Dis Weeds Crops SD State Univ Coop — Field Facts. Soils, Insects, Diseases, Weeds, Crops. South Dakota State University. Cooperative Extension Service. Plant Science Department
Fieldiana Anthrop — Fieldiana. Anthropology
Fieldiana Anthropol — Fieldiana Anthropology
Fieldiana Anthropol Ser — Fieldiana. Anthropological Series. Natural History Museum
Fieldiana Bot — Fieldiana Botany
Fieldiana Geol — Fieldiana Geology
Fieldiana Geol Mem — Fieldiana Geology. Memoirs
Fieldiana Geology Mem — Fieldiana Geology. Memoirs
Fieldiana Tech — Fieldiana Technique
Fieldiana Zool — Fieldiana Zoology
Fieldiana Zool Mem — Fieldiana Zoology. Memoirs
Fieldiana Zoology Mem — Fieldiana Zoology. Memoirs
Field II — Field Illustrated
Field Lab — Field and Laboratory
Field Meas Dinitrogen Fixation Denitrif Proc Symp — Field Measurement of Dinitrogen Fixation and Denitrification. Proceedings of a Symposium
Field Mus Bull — Field Museum of Natural History Bulletin
Field Mus Nat Hist Fieldiana Bot — Field Museum of Natural History. Fieldiana. Botany
Field Mus Nat Hist Fieldiana Geol — Field Museum of Natural History. Fieldiana. Geology
Field Mus Nat Hist Fieldiana Tech — Field Museum of Natural History. Fieldiana. Technique
Field Mus Nat Hist Fieldiana Zool — Field Museum of Natural History. Fieldiana. Zoology
Field Mus Nat Hist Publ Bot Ser — Field Museum of Natural History Publications. Botanical Series
Field Mus Nat Hist Publ Geol Ser — Field Museum of Natural History Publications. Geological Series
Field Mus Nat Hist Publ Zool Ser — Field Museum of Natural History Publications. Zoological Series
Field Nat — Field Naturalist
Field Naturalists Quart — Field Naturalists' Quarterly
Fieldnotes Arizona Bur Geol Miner Technol — Fieldnotes. Arizona Bureau of Geology and Mineral Technology
Field Notes US For Serv — Field Notes. United States Forest Service
Field Rep — Field Reporter
Field Res Proj Man Nat Ser — Field Research Projects. Man and Nature Series
Field Res Proj Nat Area Stud — Field Research Projects. Natural Area Studies
Field Seed Certif Guide III Crop Impr Ass — Field Seed Certification Guide. Illinois Crop Improvement Association
Fields Inst Commun — Fields Institute Communications
Fields Inst Monogr — Fields Institute Monographs
Field Stat Rec Div Plant Ind CSIRO — Field Station Record. Division of Plant Industry. Commonwealth Scientific and Industrial Research Organisation
Field Stn Rec — Field Station Record. Division of Plant Industry. Commonwealth Scientific and Industrial Research Organisation
Field Stn Rec Aust CSIRO Div Plant Ind — Australia. Commonwealth Scientific and Industrial Research Organisation. Division of Plant Industry. Field Station Record
Field Stn Rec Div Plant Ind CSIRO — Field Station Record. Division of Plant Industry. Commonwealth Scientific and Industrial Research Organisation
Field Stud — Field Studies
Field Study Initial Eval Urban Diffus Model Carbon Monoxide — Field Study for Initial Evaluation of an Urban Diffusion Model for Carbon Monoxide [*monograph*]
Field Test Instrum Rock Symp — Field Testing and Instrumentation of Rock. Symposium
Field Theory Many Body Probl Lect — Field Theory and the Many-Body Problem. Lectures
Field w Fie — Fields within Fields within Fields
FIENA — Fire Engineering
FIEP Bull — FIEP [*Federation Internationale d'Education Physique*] Bulletin
Fie Sci Abs — Fire Science Abstracts
FIFAO — Fouilles. Institut Francais d'Archeologie Orientale
FI (For Ital) — FI (Forum Italicum)
Fifth Est — Fifth Estate
FIG — Figaro
FIGCAD — Flore Iconographique des Champignons du Congo
Fig Can — Figures Canadiennes
FigH — Figaro Hebdomadaire
FigL — Figaro Litteraire
Fig Lit — Figaro Litteraire
Fig Litt — Figaro Litteraire
FIGWA — Forschung im Ingenieurwesen
FIHUL — Filmihullu

FII — Fussboden Zeitung
FIITA6 — Fauna d'Italia
Fiji Agric J — Fiji Agricultural Journal
Fiji Archt — Fiji Architect
Fiji Dep Agric Bull — Fiji. Department of Agriculture. Bulletin
Fiji Geol Surv Dep Bull — Fiji. Geological Survey Department. Bulletin
Fiji Geol Surv Dep Econ Invest — Fiji. Geological Survey Department. Economic Investigation
Fiji Geol Surv Dep Econ Rep — Fiji. Geological Survey Department. Economic Report
Fiji Geol Surv Dep Mem — Fiji. Geological Survey Department. Memoir
Fiji Miner Resour Div Bull — Fiji. Mineral Resources Division. Bulletin
Fiji Miner Resour Div Econ Invest — Fiji. Mineral Resources Division. Economic Investigation
Fiji Minist Lands Miner Resour Miner Resour Div Econ Invest — Fiji. Ministry of Lands and Mineral Resources. Mineral Resources Division. Economic Investigation
Fiji Timb — Fiji Timbers and Their Uses
FIK — Financiele Koerier
F II — Films Illustrated
Fil — Filologia
Fil — Filologia. Zeszyty Universytetu im Adama Mickiewiczu
Fil — Filologija
Fil — Filomata
Fil — Filosofia
Fi L — Forschungen in Lauriacum
Filam Fungi — Filamentous Fungi
Fil (BA) — Filologia (Buenos Aires)
FIL-IDF (Fed Int Lait Int Dairy Fed) Bull — FIL-IDF (Federation Internationale de Laiterie - International Dairy Federation) Bulletin
FIL-IDF (Fed Int Lait Int Dairy Fed) Stand — FIL-IDF (Federation Internationale de Laiterie - International Dairy Federation) Standards
Filip Farmer — Filipino Farmer
Filip For — Filipino Forester
Filip Forester — Filipino Forester. Society of Filipino Foresters
Fil Ist — File de Istorie. Culegere de Studii, Articole si Comunicari
Fil Koezl — Filologiai Koezloeny
Fil Let — Filologia e Letteratura
Film Appreciation News — Film Appreciation Newsletter
Film C — Film Criticism
Film Comm — Film Comment
Film Crit — Film Criticism
Film Cult — Film Culture
Filmf — Filmfacts
Film J — Film Journal
Film Lib Q — Film Library Quarterly
Film Libr Q — Film Library Quarterly
Film Lit Ind — Film Literature Index
Film Lit Index — Film Literature Index
Filmmakers M — Filmmakers' Monthly
Film Mus — Film Music
Film Mus Notes — Film Music Notes
Fil Mod — Filologia Moderna
Film Psych — Film Psychology Review
Film Q — Film Quarterly
Film Rech — Film de Recherche
Film Rev — Film Review
Films & F — Films and Filming
Films in R — Films in Review
Film u Ton Mag — Film und Ton Magazin
Filo — Filologica
Filol BA — Filologia. Facultad de Filosofia y Letras. Universidad Nacional de Buenos Aires(Buenos Aires)
Filol Vesti — Filologiceskie Vesti
Filo Met — Filo Metallico
Filos — Filosofia
Filos Letr Cien Educ Quito — Filosofia, Letras, y Ciencias de la Educacion. Facultad de Filosofia, Letras y Ciencias de la Educacion. Universidad Central del Educador (Quito)
Filos Letr Mex — Filosofia y Letras. Facultad de Filosofia y Letras. Universidad Nacional Autonoma de Mexico (Mexico)
Filos Nauc Kommunizm — Filosofija i Naucnyj Kommunizm
Filos Nauki — Filosofskie Nauki
Filosof Cas CSAV — Filosoficky Casopis CSAV
Filos Probl Obsc Soznanija — Filosofskie Problemy Obscestvennogo Soznanija
Filos Probl Suchasnoho Pryrodozn — Filosofski Problemy Suchasnoho Pryrodoznavstva
Filos Probl Suchasnoho Przyr Mizhvid Nauk Zb — Filosofichnii Problemy Suchasnoho Przyrodoznavstva Mizhvidomchyi Naukovyi Zbirnyk
Filos Vopr Fiz — Filosofskie Voprosy Fiziki
Filos Vopr Fiz Khim — Filosofskie Voprosy Fiziki i Khimii
Filos Vopr Kvantovoi Fiz — Filosofskie Voprosy Kvantovoi Fiziki
Filos Vopr Medicin Biol — Filosofskie Voprosy Mediciny i Biologii
Filoz Cas — Filozoficky Casopis
Filoz Figy — Filozofiai Figyelo
Fil Pregl — Filoloski Pregled
Fil Ro — Filologia Romanza
Fil Rom — Filologia Romanza
FILS — Filologicke Studie
FilSbAlm — Filologiceskij Sbornik [*Stat'i Aspirantov i Soiskatelej*]. Alma-Ata
Filson Club Hist Q — Filson Club History Quarterly
Filson Club Hist Quart — Filson Club History Quarterly
Filson C Q — Filson Club Quarterly
FILSUA — Forest Industry Lecture Series. University of Alberta Forestry Program
Fil Teach — Filipino Teacher

Filtration — Filtration and Separation
Filtr Congr — Filtration Congress
Filtr Eng — Filtration Engineering
Filtr Sep — Filtration and Separation
Filtr Sep Oil Gas Drill Prod Oper — Filtration and Separation in Oil and Gas Drilling and Production Operations
Filtr Soc Conf Liq Solid Sep Multi Ind Technol — Filtration Society's Conference on Liquid-Solid Separation. The Multi-Industry Technology
Filtr Tech Sep — Filtration et Techniques Separatives
Filtr Tech Separatives — Filtration et Techniques Separatives
Fil Vit — Filosofia e Vita
FilZ — Filologija (Zagreb)
FiM — Filologia Moderna
FIM — Financial Market Trends
F Imp — Fasti Consolari dell'Impero Romano
FIMR — Finnish Marine Research
FIMS — Folklore Institute. Monograph Series
FIN — Financieel Dagblad voor Handel, Industrie, Scheepvaart, en Cultures
Fin — Finanse
Fin — Finansije
Fin — Finlay
Fin Agr — Financing Agriculture
Final Control Elem — Final Control Elements
Final Rep Congr Wld Met Org — Final Report. Congress of the World Meteorological Organisation
Final Rep Electr Power Res Inst EPRI EL Palo Alto Calif — Final Report. Electric Power Research Institute EPRI EL (Palo Alto, California)
Finan Agri — Financing Agriculture
Fin Anal J — Financial Analysts Journal
Fin Analyst — Financial Analysts Journal
Fin Analysts J — Financial Analysts Journal
Financ Agric — Financing Agriculture
Financ Anal J — Financial Analysts Journal
Financ Analysts J — Financial Analysts Journal
Financ Dag — Financieel Dagblad
Finance & Dev — Finance and Development
Finance Dev — Finance and Development
Finances et Develop — Finances et Developpement
Finance Trade R — Finance and Trade Review
Financ Exec — Financial Executive
Financ Executive — Financial Executive
Financial E — Financial Executive
Financial M — Financial Management
Financial W — Financial Weekly
Financ Mail — Financial Mail
Financ Manage — Financial Management
Financ Times — Financial Times
Financ Times Europ Energy Rep — Financial Times. European Energy Report
Financ Times North Am Ed — Financial Times (North American Edition)
Financ Trade Rev — Finance and Trade Review
Financ Week — Finance Week
Financ World — Financial World
Fin & Devel — Finance and Development
Fin and Development — Finance and Development
Fin and Trade R (South Africa) — Finance and Trade Review (South Africa)
Finan Manag — Financial Management
Finanstid — Finanstidende
Finan World — Financial World
Finanzarch — Finanzarchiv
Finanzj — Finanzjournal
Finanz Rdsch — Finanz Rundschau
Fin Budget — National Budget for Finland
Fincl Mail — Financial Mail
F Ind — Food Industries
Fin Dev — Finance and Development
F Ind Man — Food Industries Manual
F Ind SA — Food Industries of South Africa
Fine Arts J — Fine Arts Journal
Fine Chem — Fine Chemicals
Fine Chem Tech Bull — Fine Chemicals Technical Bulletin
Fine Chem Tech Bull Am Cyanamid Co — Fine Chemical Technical Bulletin. American Cyanamid Co.
Fine Gard — Fine Gardening
Fine Part Filtr Sep — Fine Particle Filtration and Separation
Fine Part Soc Symp Part Technol Surf Phenom Miner Pet — Fine Particle Society Symposium on Particle Technology and Surface Phenomena in Minerals and Petroleum
Fine Pt — Fine Print
Fine Wood — Fine Woodworking
Fin Exec — Financial Executive
Finfish Nutr Fishfeed Technol Proc World Symp — Finfish Nutrition and Fishfeed Technology. Proceedings of a World Symposium
Fin Fisk — Finlands Fiskerier
FINF-Text — Firmeninformationen-Text
FINGA — Fernmelde-Ingenieur
Fin Gaz — Financial Gazette
Fin Ind — Financial Industry
Finish Handb Dir — Finishing Handbook and Directory
Finish Ind — Finishing Industries
Finishing Ind — Finishing Industries
Finish News — Finishing News
Finis Terr Santiago — Finis Terrae. Universidad Catolica de Chile (Santiago)
Finist S Sc BII — Bulletin de la Societe d'Etudes Scientifiques du Finistere
Finite Elem Anal Des — Finite Elements in Analysis and Design
Finite Elements Analysis Des — Finite Elements in Analysis and Design

Finite Elem News — Finite Element News
Finite Fields Appl — Finite Fields and their Applications
Fin Kemistsamf Medd — Finska Kemistsamfundet. Meddelanden
Fin Lakaresallsk Handl — Finska Lakaresallskapets Handlingar
Finlande Comm Geol Bull — Finlande. Commission Geologique. Bulletin
Finlay Rev Med-Hist Cubana — Finlay Revista Medico-Historica Cubana
Finl Djurskydd — Finlands Djurskydd
Finl Fisk — Finlands Fiskerier
Finl FlottFor Arsb — Finlands Flottareforeningens Arsbok
Finl Geodeettinen Laitos Julk — Finland Geodeettinen Laitos. Julkaisuja
Finl Geol Tutkimuslaitos Opas — Finland Geologinen Tutkimuslaitos. Opas
Finl Geol Tutkimuslaitos Bull — Finland Geologinen Tutkimuslaitos. Bulletin
Finl Geol Unders — Finlands Geologiska Undersokning
Finl Med Biblfi — Finlands Mediciniska Bibliografi
Finl MedForfatt — Finlands Medicinal-Forfattningar
Finl Mejeritidn — Finlands Mejeritidning
Finl Pat Doc — Finland. Patent Document
Finl SjofTidn — Finlands Sjofartstidning
Finl Utsadesfor ForedrSer — Finlands Utsadesforenings Foredragsserie
Finl Utsadesfor Smaskr — Finlands Utsadesforenings Smaskrifter
Finl Vesitutkimuslaitos Julk — Finland Vesitutkimuslaitos. Julkaisuja
Fin Mail (South Africa) — Financial Mail (South Africa)
Fin Mgt — Financial Management
Fin Mosskulturforen Arsb — Finska Mosskulturforeningens Arsbok
Finn — Finnish. Patent Document
Finn Acad Sci Lett Sodankyla Geophys Obs Rep — Finnish Academy of Science and Letters. Sodankyla Geophysical Observatory. Report
Finn Cent Radiat Nucl Saf Rep STUK A — Finnish Centre for Radiation and Nuclear Safety. Report STUK-A
Finn Chem L — Finnish Chemical Letters
Finn Chem Lett — Finnish Chemical Letters
Finn Dent Soc Proc — Finnish Dental Society. Proceedings
Finn Fish Res — Finnish Fisheries Research
Finn Found Alcohol Stud — Finnish Foundation for Alcohol Studies
Finn Fr Symp Water Supply Sewerage — Finnish-French Symposium on Water Supply and Sewerage
Finn Game Res — Finnish Game Research
Finn Ger Semin Nucl Waste Manage — Finnish-German Seminar on Nuclear Waste Management
Finnish Pap Timber — Finnish Paper and Timber Journal
Finnish Trade R — Finnish Trade Review
Finn J Dairy Sci — Finnish Journal of Dairy Science
Finnl Hydrogr Biol Unters — Finnlaendische Hydrographisch-Biologische Untersuchungen
Finn Mar Res — Finnish Marine Research
Finnmecc News — Finnmeccanica News
Finn Mus Q — Finnish Music Quarterly
Finn Pap Timb — Finnish Paper and Timber Journal
Finn Pap Timber — Finnish Paper and Timber Journal
Finn Pap Timber J — Finnish Paper and Timber Journal
Finn Psychiatry — Finnish Psychiatry
Finommech-Mikrotech — Finommechanika-Mikrotechnika
FINP — Finnish Periodicals Index in Economics and Business
FInP — France-Inde (Pierrefitte-sur-Seine)
Fin Paper — Finnish Paper and Timber Journal
Fin Planner — Financial Planner
Fin Planning Today — Financial Planning Today
Fin Plan Strat — Financial Planning Strategist
Fin Plan Today — Financial Planning Today
Fin Post — Financial Post
Fin Post M — Financial Post Magazine
Fin Post Mag — Financial Post Magazine
Fin R — Financial Review
FINRA — Fishery Industrial Research
Fin Rep IANEC — Final Report. Meeting. Inter-American Nuclear Energy Commission
FINS — Fishing Industry News Science
Finshng Ind — Finishing Industries
Finska ApotekFor Tidskr — Finska Apotekareforeningens Tidskrift
Finska ByggmForb Dir Publ — Finska Byggmastareforbundets Direktions Publikation
Finska Laekaresaellsk Handl — Finska Laekaresaellsk Handlinger
Finska MosskultForen Flygskr — Finska Mosskulturforeningens Flygskrifter
Finska Sagverskeg LantbrFor Meddn — Finska Sagverskegarnes Lantbruksforeningens Meddelanden
Finska SkogFor Tapios Skr Handb — Finska Skogsvardsforeningens Tapios Skrifter (Handbocker)
Finska TradgOdl — Finska Tradgarsodlaren
Fins Kem Med — Finska Kemistsamfundet Meddelanden
Finsk Mil Tidskr — Finsk Militaer Tidskrift
Finskt Mus — Finskt Museum
Finskt T — Finskt Tidskrift
Finsk Veterinaerts — Finsk Veterinaertidskrift
Finsk Veterinartidskr — Finsk Veterinaertidskrift
Finsk Vet Tidskr — Finsk Veterinaertidskrift
Fin SSSR — Finansy SSSR
Fin Strat Con — Financial Strategies and Concepts
FInt — Fiction International
FinT — Financial Times
Fin Ter — Finis Terrae
Fin Tid — Finsk Tidskrift
Fin Times — Financial Times
Fin Trade — Finnish Trade Review
Fin Veterinaertidskr — Finsk Veterinaertidskrift
Fin Wkly — Financial Weekly

Fin World — Financial World
FIO — Financieel Overheidsbeheer
FI O Hav — Fisk og Hav
Fiord Stud Caswell Nancy Sounds NZ — Fiord Studies. Caswell and Nancy Sounds. New Zealand
Fiore — Scrittori Stranieri. Il Fiore delle Varie Letterature in Traduzioni Italiane
FIPA Nouv — FIPA [*Federation Internationale des Producteurs Agricoles*] Nouvelles
FIP Congr Proc — FIP (Federation Internationale de la Precontrainte) Congress. Proceedings
FIPEDX — FAO [*Food and Agriculture Organization of the United Nations*] Informes dePesca
FIPRD — Fiber Producer
FIR — Films in Review
FIR — Filologia Romanza
FIR — Fontes Iuris Romani Antiqui
FIRA — Fontes Iuris Romani Antejustiniani
FIRA — Fontes Iuris Romani Antiqui
FIRA Bull — FIRA [*Furniture Industry Research Association*] Bulletin
FIRA Bull (Furn Ind Res Ass) — FIRA (Furniture Industry Research Association) Bulletin
FIRAD — Fiziologiya Rastenii
FIRA Tech Rep (Furn Ind Res Ass) — FIRA (Furniture Industry Research Association) Technical Report
FIRA Trans (Furn Ind Res Ass) — FIRA (Furniture Industry Research Association) Transaction
Firat Univ Vet Fak Derg — Firat Universitesi Veteriner Fakultesi Dergisi
Fire & Casualty Cas CCH — Fire and Casualty Cases. Commerce Clearing House
Fire Control Exp — Fire Control Experiments
Fire Control Exp Calif Div For — Fire Control Experiments. California Division of Forestry
Fire Dyn Heat Transfer Natl Heat Transfer Conf — Fire Dynamics and Heat Transfer. National Heat Transfer Conference
Fire Eng — Fire Engineering
Fire Eng J — Fire Engineers Journal
Fire Engnrs J — Fire Engineers Journal
Fire Engr — Fire Engineer
Fire Haz Inds — Fire Hazards in Industries
Fire J — Fire Journal
Fire J (Boston) — Fire Journal (Boston)
Fire Manage Notes USDA For Serv — Fire Management Notes. United States Department of Agriculture. Forest Service
Fire Manage Notes US Dep Agric For Serv — Fire Management Notes. US Department of Agriculture. Forest Service
Fire Mater — Fire and Materials
Firenze Ac Georg At — Atti della Reale Accademia Economico-Agraria dei Georgofili. Firenze
Firenze Agric — Firenze Agricola
Firenze A Ms Fis — Annali del Reale Museo di Fisica e Storia Naturale. Firenze
Firenze A Ms Imp — Annali del Museo Imperiale di Fisica e Storia Naturale di Firenze
Firenze At Ac Georg — Atti della Reale Accademia Economico-Agraria dei Georgofili. Firenze
Firenze R I Pb — Pubblicazioni del Reale Istituto di Studi Superiori Pratici e di Perfezionamento in Firenze. Sezione di Scienze Fisiche e Naturali
Firenze S Georg At — Atti della (Real) Societa Economica di Firenze Ossia de' Georgofili
Fire Prev — Fire Prevention
Fire Prev N — Fire Prevention News
Fire Prev Sci Tech — Fire Prevention Science and Technology
Fire Prev Sci Technol — Fire Prevention Science and Technology
Fire Prev Suppl — Fire Prevention. Supplement
Fire Prot — Fire Protection
Fire Prot Air Raid Precaut Rev — Fire Protection and Air Raid Precautions Review
Fire Prot Bull — Fire Protection Bulletin
Fire Protect — Fire Protection
Fire Prot Rev — Fire Protection Review
Fire Prot Yb — Fire Protection Yearbook
Fire Prot Yearb — Fire Protection Yearbook
Fire Res — Fire Research
Fire Res Abstr & Rev — Fire Research Abstracts and Reviews
Fire Res Bull — Fire Research Bulletin
Fire Res (Lausanne) — Fire Research (Lausanne)
Fire Res Leafl Div Forest Res Can — Fire Research Leaflet. Division of Forest Research. Canada
Fire Res Spec Rep — Fire Research Special Report
Fire Res Tech Pap UK Jt Fire Res Organ — Fire Research Technical Paper (United Kingdom. Joint Fire Research Organization)
Fire Retard Chem — Fire Retardant Chemistry
Fire Retard Chem Assoc Semi Annu Meet — Fire Retardant Chemicals Association. Semi-Annual Meeting
Fire Retard Proc Eur Conf Flammability Fire Retard — Fire Retardants. Proceedings of European Conference on Flammability and Fire Retardants
Fire Retard Proc Int Symp Flammability Fire Retard — Fire Retardants. Proceedings of International Symposium on Flammability and Fire
Fire Saf J — Fire Safety Journal
Fire Sci Abs — Fire Science Abstracts
Fire Sci Technol Noda Jpn — Fire Science and Technology (Noda, Japan)
Fire Sci Technol NY — Fire Science and Technology (New York)
Fire Sci Technol (Tokyo) — Fire Science and Technology (Tokyo)
Fire Study Natl Res Counc Can Div Build Res — Fire Study. National Research Council of Canada. Division of Building Research
Fire Surv — Fire Surveyor
Fire Tech — Fire Technology
Fire Technol — Fire Technology
Fire Technol Abs — Fire Technology Abstracts

Fire Toxicol Methods Eval Toxic Pyrolysis Combust Prod Rep — Fire Toxicology. Methods for Evaluation of Toxicity of Pyrolysis and Combustion Products. Report
Fire Wat — Fire and Water
Fire Wat Engng — Fire and Water Engineering
Fire Water Eng — Fire and Water Engineering
First Chi — First Chicago Report
First Internat Econ Hist — First International Conference of Economic History
First Nat City Bank — First National City Bank [*Later, Citibank*] of New York. Monthly Economic Letter
FIS — First Stage
FISC — Fisheries of Canada
Fiscal Europ — Fiscalite Europeenne
Fiscalite Eur — Fiscalite Europeenne
Fisc Europ — Fiscalite Europeenne
Fische Fischwar — Fische und Fischwaren
Fischereiforsch Inf Prax — Fischereiforschung. Informationen fuer der Praxis
FischersZ — Fischers Zeitschrift fuer Praxis und Gesetzgebung der Verwaltung, Zunaechst fuer das Koenigreich Sachsen
Fischer Taschenb — Fischer Taschenbuecher
Fischer Tropsch Synth — Fischer-Tropsch Synthesen
Fisch-Forsch — Fischerei-Forschung
Fischwaren Feinkost Ind — Fischwaren und Feinkost Industrie
Fischwirtsch Fischind Fischereiwelt — Fischwirtschaft mit die Fischindustrie und Fischereiwelt
FischZtg Weser u Ems Geb — Fischereizeitung fuer das Weser- und Ems-Gebiet
Fis e Tecnol — Fisica e Tecnologia
Fish B — Fishery Bulletin
Fish Board Swed Inst Freshwater Res (Drottningholm) Rep — Fishery Board of Sweden. Institute of Freshwater Research (Drottningholm). Report
Fish Board Swed Inst Mar Res Rep — Fishery Board of Sweden. Institute of Marine Research. Report
Fish Board Swed Ser Hydrogr Rep — Fishery Board of Sweden. Series Hydrography. Report
Fish Boat Wld — Fishing Boats of the World
Fish Bull — Fishery Bulletin
Fish Bull Calif — Fish Bulletin. California Fish and Game Commission
Fish Bull (Dublin) — Fisheries Bulletin (Dublin)
Fish Bull FAO — Fisheries Bulletin. Food and Agriculture Organization
Fish Bull Mass — Fisheries Bulletin. Massachusetts Division of Fisheries and Game
Fish Bull NZ — Fisheries Bulletin. New Zealand Marine Department
Fish Bull Papua — Fisheries Bulletin. Department of Agriculture, Stock, and Fisheries. Papua and New Guinea
Fish Bull S Afr — Fisheries Bulletin. South Africa
Fish Bull Singapore — Fisheries Bulletin. Fisheries Department. Colony of Singapore
Fish Bull Un S Afr — Fisheries Bulletin. Fisheries and Marine Biological Survey Division. Union of South Africa
Fish Bull West Aust — Fisheries Bulletin. Fisheries Department. Western Australia
Fish Circ Aust — Fisheries Circular. Council for Scientific and Industrial Research. Australia
Fish Circ Fish Lab Boothbay Harb — Fisheries Circular. Fisheries Laboratory. Boothbay Harbour, Maine
Fish Circ Me — Fisheries Circular. Department of Sea and Shore Fisheries of Maine
Fish Circ Vict — Fisheries Circular. Fisheries and Game Department. Victoria
Fish Commn Res Briefs Portland — Fish Commission Research Briefs (Portland, Oregon)
Fish Conserv Highlights — Fish Conservation Highlights
Fish Contr Vict — Victoria. Fisheries and Wildlife Department. Fisheries Contribution
Fish Cult Rep Taiwan — Fish Culture Report. Taiwan Fisheries Research Institute
Fish Cult Sect Publ Am Fish Soc — Fish Culture Section Publication (American Fisheries Society)
Fish Cultst — Fish Culturist
FISHD — Fisheries
Fish Dis Diagn Lab Rep FDDL F Tex Agric Ext Serv — Fish Disease Diagnostic Laboratory. Report FDDL-F. Texas Agricultural ExtensionService
Fish Dis Diagn Lab Tex Agric Ext Serv Rep FDDL-S — Fish Disease Diagnostic Laboratory. Texas Agricultural Extension Service. Report FDDL-S
Fish Environ — Fish and Environment
Fisheries — Fisheries of the US
Fisheries Nletter — Fisheries Newsletter
Fishermens Bull Haifa — Fishermens' Bulletin (Haifa)
Fishermens Naut Alm — Fishermen's Nautical Almanac
Fishery Bull Fish Wildl Serv US — Fishery Bulletin. Fish and Wildlife Service. United States Department of Interior
Fishery Bull Ill — Fishery Bulletin. Division of Fisheries. Illinois
Fishery Bull Un S Afr — Fishery Bulletin. Union of South Africa
Fishery Circ Bur Fish US — Fishery Circular. Bureau of Fisheries. US
Fishery Ind Res — Fishery Industrial Research
Fishery Invest Imp Fishery Exp Stn Tokyo — Fishery Investigation. Imperial Fishery Experimental Station. Tokyo
Fishery Invest Lond — Fishery Investigations. Ministry of Agriculture, Food, and Fisheries (London)
Fishery Invest Surv Dingell Johnson Div Tex — Fishery Investigations and Surveys. Dingell-Johnson Division. Texas Game and Fish Division
Fishery Leafl Fish Wildl Serv US — Fishery Leaflet. Fish and Wildlife Service. United States Department of the Interior
Fishery Leafl Manila — Fishery Leaflet (Manila)
Fishery Prod Rep Fish Wildl Serv US — Fishery Products Report. Fish and Wildlife Service. United States Department of the Interior
Fishery Rep Dep Oceanogr Wash St Univ — Fishery Report. Department of Oceanography. Washington State University

Fishery Res Mgmt Div Bull Me — Fishery Research and Management Division Bulletin (Maine)

Fishery Ser Chin Am Jt Comm Rur Reconstr — Fishery Series. Chinese-American Joint Committee on Rural Reconstruction

Fishery Serv Bull Wash — Fishery Service Bulletin. Bureau of Fisheries. U.S. (Washington)

Fishery Statist Can — Fishery Statistics of Canada

Fishery Statist Lond — Fishery Statistics. Board of Agriculture and Fisheries (London)

Fish Farmers Miss State Univ Coop Ext Serv — For Fish Farmers. Mississippi State University. Cooperative Extension Service

Fish Farming Int — Fish Farming International

Fish Farm Int — Fish Farming International

Fish Gaz — Fishing Gazette

Fishg Gaz Lond — Fishing Gazette (London)

Fishg Gaz NY — Fishing Gazette (New York)

Fishg News Aberd — Fishing News (Aberdeen)

Fishg News Int — Fishing News International

Fish Gt War — Fisheries in the Great War

Fish Hlth N — Fish Health News

Fish Ind — Fish Industry

Fish Ind Res — Fishery Industrial Research

Fish Instrum Lab Newsl — Fisheries Instrumentation Laboratory Newsletter

Fish Invest Minist Agric Fish Food (GB) Ser — Fishery Investigations. Ministry of Agriculture, Fisheries, and Food (Great Britain). Series II. Salmon and Freshwater Fisheries

Fish Invest Minist Agric Fish Food (GB) Ser IV — Fishery Investigations. Ministry of Agriculture, Fisheries, and Food (Great Britain). Series IV

Fish Invest Ser II Mar Fish GB Minist Agric Fish Food — Fishery Investigations. Series II. Marine Fisheries. Great Britain Ministry of Agriculture, Fisheries, and Food

Fishkeep Wat Life — Fishkeeping and Water Life

Fish Lab Publs NZ Mar Dep — Fisheries Laboratory Publications. New Zealand Marine Department

Fish Leafl Ill — Fisheries Leaflet. Illinois Division of Fisheries

Fish Manage — Fisheries Management

Fish Mark News — Fishery Market News

Fish Mar Serv (Can) Misc Spec Publ — Fisheries and Marine Service (Canada). Miscellaneous Special Publication

Fish Mar Serv (Can) Tech Rep — Fisheries and Marine Service (Canada). Technical Report

Fish Mar Serv Fish Oper Dir Cent Reg Tech Rep Ser Can — Fisheries and Marine Service. Fisheries Operations Directorate. Central Region.Technical Report Series (Canada)

Fish Mar Serv Manuscr Rep Can — Fisheries and Marine Service Manuscript Report (Canada)

Fish Meal Oil Ind — Fish Meal and Oil Industry

Fish Mgmt Bull Fla — Fish Management Bulletin (Florida)

Fish News — Fisheries Newsletter

Fish News Bangkok — Fisheries News (Bangkok)

Fish News Bull Can — Fisheries News Bulletin. Department of Fisheries. Canada

Fish News Int — Fishing News International

Fish Newsl — Fisheries Newsletter

Fish N Intnl — Fishing News International

Fish Notes — Queensland. Department of Harbours and Marine. Fisheries Notes

Fish Notes Dep Prim Ind Qd — Fisheries Notes. Department of Primary Industries. Queensland

Fish Notes Dep Prim Ind Queensl — Fisheries Notes. Department of Primary Industries. Queensland

Fish Not Lond — Fisheries Notices. Ministry of Agriculture and Fisheries (London)

Fish Nutr — Fish Nutrition

Fish Nutr Conf Work Pap — Fish in Nutrition. Conference Working Papers

Fish Nutr Diet Dev Int Semin — Fish Nutrition and Diet Development. International Seminar

Fish Oil Blood Vessel Wall Interact Proc Int Symp — Fish Oil and Blood-Vessel Wall Interactions. Proceedings. International Symposium

Fish Pamph Vict — Fisheries Pamphlets. Fisheries and Game Department. Victoria [*Melbourne*]

Fish Pap Dep Prim Ind — Australia. Department of Primary Industry. Fisheries Paper

Fish Pap FAO — Fisheries Papers. FAO

Fish Pathol — Fish Pathology

Fish Physiol — Fish Physiology

Fish Physiol Biochem — Fish Physiology and Biochemistry

Fish Plg Rec — Fish Planting Record

Fish Publs Del — Fisheries Publications. Delaware Board of Game and Fish Commissioners

Fish Publs Rhode Isl — Fisheries Publications. Rhode Island Division of Fish and Game

Fish Radiobiol Lab Tech Rep FRL (UK) — Fisheries Radiobiological Laboratory Technical Report FRL (United Kingdom)

Fish Rep Dep Agric — Fisheries Report. Department of Agriculture

Fish Rep Dep Prim Ind — Australia. Department of Primary Industry. Fisheries Report

Fish Rep Sask — Fisheries Report. Saskatchewan Department of Natural Resources

Fish Res (Amst) — Fisheries Research (Amsterdam)

Fish Res Board Can Annu Rep — Fisheries Research Board of Canada. Annual Report

Fish Res Board Can ARO Circ — Fisheries Research Board of Canada. ARO [*Atlantic Regional Office*] Circular

Fish Res Board Can Biol Stn St Andrews NB Gen Ser Circ — Fisheries Research Board of Canada. Biological Station. St. Andrews, New Brunswick. General Serie Circular

Fish Res Board Can Bull — Fisheries Research Board of Canada. Bulletin

Fish Res Board Can Gen Ser Circ — Fisheries Research Board of Canada. General Series Circular

Fish Res Board Can Misc Spec Publ — Fisheries Research Board of Canada. Miscellaneous Special Publication

Fish Res Board Can Prog Rep Atl Coast Stn — Fisheries Research Board of Canada. Progress Reports of the Atlantic Coast Stations

Fish Res Board Can Prog Rep Pac Coast Stn — Fisheries Research Board of Canada. Progress Reports of the Pacific Coast Station

Fish Res Board Can Rev — Fisheries Research Board of Canada. Review

Fish Res Board Can Tech Pap — Fisheries Research Board of Canada. Technical Paper

Fish Res Board Can Tech Rep — Fisheries Research Board of Canada. Technical Report

Fish Res Bull — Fisheries Research Bulletin

Fish Res Bull NY Conserv Dep — Fisheries Research Bulletin. New York Conservation Department

Fish Res Bull St Wash — Fisheries Research Bulletin. Department of Fisheries. State of Washington

Fish Res Bull (West Aust Mar Res Lab) — Fisheries Research Bulletin (Western Australia Marine Research Laboratories)

Fish Res Div Occas Publ (NZ) — Fisheries Research Division. Occasional Publication (New Zealand)

Fish Res J Phil — Fisheries Research Journal of the Philippines

Fish Res Pap St Wash — Fisheries Research Papers. Department of Fisheries. State of Washington

Fish Res Stn Sri Lanka Ceylon Bull — Fisheries Research Station. Sri Lanka (Ceylon). Bulletin

Fish Res Tech Rep (UK Dir Fish Res) — Fisheries Research Technical Report (United Kingdom. Directorate of Fisheries Research)

Fish Res Ves Kapala Cruise Rep — Cruise Report. Fisheries Research Vessel Kapala

Fish Sci — Fisheries Science

Fish Ser Caribb Res Coun — Fisheries Series. Caribbean Research Council

Fish Shellfish Immunol — Fish & Shellfish Immunology

Fish Stat BC — Fisheries Statistics of British Columbia

Fish Statist Philipp — Fisheries Statistics of the Philippines

Fish Statist Rep Wash St — Fisheries Statistical Report. Washington State Department of Fisheries

FISHSTATS — Fishery Statistics Data Base

Fish Stk Rec — Fish Stock Record. Ministry of Agriculture, Fisheries, and Food

Fish Stud FAO — Fisheries Studies. F.A.O.(Food and Agricultural Organization of the United Nations)

Fish Surv Rep Me — Fish Survey Report. Maine Department of Inland Fisheries and Game

Fish Surv Rep Singapore — Fisheries Survey Report (Singapore)

Fish Synopsis Div Fish Oceanogr CSIRO — Fisheries Synopsis. Division of Fisheries and Oceanography. Commonwealth Scientific and Industrial Research Organisation

Fish Technol — Fishery Technology

Fish Tech Rep NZ Mar Dep — Fisheries Technical Report. New Zealand Marine Department

Fish Tech Rep Wyo Game Fish Commn — Fisheries Technical Report. Wyoming Game and Fish Commission

Fish Trades Gaz — Fish Trades Gazette

Fish Util Contrib Res Int Symp — Fish Utilization. Contributions from Research. International Symposium

Fish Wildl Pap (Victoria) — Fisheries and Wildlife Paper (Victoria)

Fish Wildl Serv (US) Res Rep — Fish and Wildlife Service (United States). Research Report

Fish Yb Dir — Fisheries Yearbook and Directory

Fish Yb Nova Scotia — Fisheries Yearbook of Nova Scotia

Fisiol e Med — Fisiologia e Medicina

Fisiol Med (Rome) — Fisiologia e Medicina (Rome)

FISITA Congr — FISITA Congress

FISK — Fiskeridirektoratets Skrifter. Serie Havundersokelser

Fisk Dir Skr — Fiskeridirektoratets Skrifter

Fisk Dir Smaskr — Fiskeridirektoratets Smaskrifter

Fisken Hav — Fisken og Havet

Fiskeridir Skr Ser Ernaer — Fiskeridirektoratets Skrifter. Serie Ernaering

Fiskeridir Skr Ser Fisk — Fiskeridirektoratets Skrifter. Serie Fiskeri

Fiskeridir Skr Ser Havunders — Fiskeridirektoratets Skrifter. Serie Havundersokelser

Fiskeridir Skr Ser Teknol Unders — Fiskeridirektoratets Skrifter. Serie Teknologiske Undersokelser

Fisk For Finl — Fiskeriforeningen i Finland

Fisk Gang — Fiskets Gang

Fisk Univ News — Fisk University News

Fis Med — Fisiologia e Medicina

FISTB — Field and Stream

Fis Tecnol (Bologna) — Fisica e Tecnologia (Bologna)

FISZA — Fizikai Szemle

FITA — From Imperium to Autoritas

Fit & Sports Rev Int — Fitness & Sports Review International

FITCA — Fire Technology

FITEA — Fishery Technology

Fitness Inst Bull — Fitness Institute. Bulletin

Fitontsidy Ikh Biol Rol Znach Med Nar Khoz Rab Vses Soveshch — Fitontsidy. Ikh Biologicheskaya Rol i Znachenie dlya Meditsiny i Narodnogo Khozyaistva, Raboty, Dolozhennye na Vsesoyuznom Soveshchanii po Probleme Fitontsidov

Fitontsidy Ikh Rol Prir Izbr Dokl Soveshch Probl Fitontsidov — Fitontsidy. Ikh Rol v Prirode, Izbrannye Doklady Soveshchaniya po Probleme Fitontsidov

Fitontsidy Med — Fitontsidy v Meditsine

Fitontsidy Med Selsk Khoz Pishch Promsti — Fitontsidy v Meditsine. Sel'skom Khozyaistve i Pishchevoi Promyshlennosti

Fitontsidy Rol Biogeotsenozakh Znach Med Mater Soveshch — Fitontsidy. Rol v Biogeotsenozakh, Znachenie dlya Meditsiny, Materialy Soveshchaniya

Fitonutrizione Oligominerale Atti Simp Int Agrochim — Fitonutrizione Oligominerale. Atti del Simposio Internazionale di Agrochimica

Fitopat Bras — Fitopatologia Brasileira

Fitopatog Bakt Mater Vses Konf Bakt Bolezn Rast — Fitopatogennye Bakterii. Materialy Vsesoyuznoi Konferentsii po Bakterial'nym Boleznyam Rastenii

Fitopatol — Fitopatologia

Fitopatol Bras — Fitopatologia Brasileira

Fitopatol Colomb — Fitopatologia Colombiana

Fitopatol Mex — Fitopatologia Mexicana

Fitotec Latinoam — Fitotecnia Latinoamericana

Fitotecnia Latinoam — Fitotecnia Latinoamericana

FiTs — Finsk Tidskrift

FitzN — Fitzgerald Newsletter

FIU/CR — Caribbean Review. Florida International University. Office of Academic Affairs

Fi Vet Tidskr — Finsk Veterinaertidskrift

FIW — Forschungsinstitut fuer Wirtschaftsverfassung und Wettbewerb

FIW Dok — FIW [Forschungsinstitut fuer Wirtschaftsverfassung und Wettbewerb] Dokumentation

FIWOA — Financial World

FIW Schr — FIW [Forschungsinstitut fuer Wirtschaftsverfassung und Wettbewerb] Schriftenreihe

FIX — FID [Federation Internationale de Documentation] News Bulletin

FIZ — Farhang-E Iran-Zamin

Fiz Aerodispersnykh Sist — Fizika Aerodispersnykh Sistem

Fiz Aspekty Zagryaz Atmos Tezisy Dokl Mezhdunar Konf — Fizicheskie Aspekty Zagryazneniya Atmosfery. Tezisy Dokladov. Mezhdunarodnaya Konferentsiya

Fiz Atmos — Fizika Atmosfery

Fiz Atmos Okeana — Fizika Atmosfery i Okeana

Fiz At Yadra — Fizika Atomnogo Yadra. Materialy Zimnei Shkoly LIYaF (Leningradskii Institut Yadernoi Fiziki)

Fiz At Yadra Elem Chastits — Fizika Atomnogo Yadra I Elementarnykh Chastits. Materialy Zimnei Shkoly

Fiz At Yadra Elem Chastits Mater Zimnei Shk LIYaF — Fizika Atomnogo Yadra i Elementarnykh Chastits. Materialy Zimnei Shkoly LIYaF

Fiz At Yadra Kosm Luchei — Fizika Atomnogo Yadra i Kosmicheskikh Luchei

Fiz Chastits Vys Energ — Fizika Chastits Vysokikh Energii

Fiz Chastits Vys Energ Akad Nauk Gruz SSR Inst Fiz — Fizika Chastits Vysokikh Energii. Akademiya Nauk Gruzinskoi SSR. Institut Fiziki

Fiz Chem Ciala Stalego Przejscia Fazowe Zjawiska Kryt — Fizyka i Chemia Ciala Stalego. Przejscia Fazowe i Zjawiska Krytyczne

Fiz Chem Met (Katowice) — Fizyka i Chemia Metali (Katowice)

Fiz Chim Mech Mat — Fiziko-Chimiceskaja Mechanika Materialov

Fiz Chim Stekla — Fizika i Khimiya Stekla

Fiz Deform Uprochn Monokrist Dokl Soveshch — Fizika Deformatsionnogo Uprochneniya Monokristallov. Doklady Soveshchaniya po Fizike Deformatsionnogo Uprochneniya Monokristallov. Khark

Fiz Deform Uprochn Splavov Stalei Dokl Semin — Fizika Deformatsionnogo Uprochneniya Splavov i Stalei. Doklady prochitannye na Seminare po Problem Fizika Deformatsionnogo Uprochneniya Splavov i Stalei

Fiz Deleniya At Yader — Fizika Deleniya Atomnykh Yader

Fiz Dielektr Radiospektrosk — Fizyka Dielektrykow i Radiospektroskopia

Fiz Dielektr Tr Vses Konf — Fizika Dielektrikov. Trudy Vsesoyuznoi Konferentsii

Fiz Dokl Nauchn Konf Leningr Inzh Stroit Inst — Fizika. Doklady na Nauchnoi Konferentsii. Leningradskii Inzhenerno-Stroitel'nyiInstitut

Fiz Ehlem Chastits At Yad — Fizika Elementarnykh Chastits i Atomnogo Yadra

Fiz Elektron — Fizine Elektronika

Fiz Elektron At Stolknovenii Mater Simp V Vses Shk — Fizika Elektronnykh i Atomnykh Stolknovenii. Materialy Simpoziumov V Vsesoyuznoi Shkoly po Fizike Elektronnykh i Atomnykh Stolknovenii

Fiz Elektron (Lvov) — Fizichna Elektronika (Lvov)

Fiz Elektron (Moscow) — Fizicheskaya Elektronika (Moscow)

Fiz Elektron Nauchn Dokl Gertsenovskie Chteniya — Fizicheskaya Elektronika. Nauchnye Doklady. Gertsenovskie Chteniya

Fiz Elektron Tverd Tela — Fizika i Elektronika Tverdogo Tela

Fiz Elem Chastits — Fizika Elementarnykh Chastits. Materialy Zimnei Shkoly LIYaF (Leningradskii Institut Yadernoi Fiziki)

Fiz Elem Chastits At Yadra — Fizika Elementarnykh Chastits i Atomnogo Yadra

Fiz Elementar Castic i Atom Jadra — Fizika Elementarnyh Castic i Atomnogo Jadra

Fiz Elementar Chastits i Atom Yadra — Fizika Elementarnykh Chastits i Atomnogo Yadra. Obedinennyi Institut Yadernykh Issledovanii Dubna

Fiz Energ Inst Rap FEI — Fiziko-Energeticheskii Institut. Raport FEI

Fiz Faktory Proizvod Sredy Nek Vopr Fiziol Tr — Fizicheskie Faktory Proizvodstvennoi Sredy i Nekotorye Voprosy Fiziologii Truda

Fiz Fiz Khim Metody Eksp Klin — Fizicheskie i Fiziko-Khimicheskie Metody v Eksperimenta i Klinike

Fiz Fiz Khim Protsessy Din Rudoobraz Sist — Fizicheskie i Fiziko-Khimicheskie Protsessy v Dinamicheskikh Rudoobrazuyushchikh Sistemakh

Fiz Fiz Khim Rudoobraz Protsessov — Fizika i Fiziko-Khimiya Rudoobrazuyushchikh Protsessov

Fiz Fiz Khim Svoistva Ferritov — Fizicheskie i Fiziko-Khimicheskie Svoistva Ferritov

Fiz Fiz Khim Svoistva Ferritov Mater Dokl Vses Soveshch — Fizicheskie i Fiziko-Khimicheskie Svoistva Ferritov. Materialy Dokladov Vsesoyuznogo Soveshchaniya po Ferritam

Fiz Fiz-Khim Zhidk — Fizika i Fiziko-Khimiya Zhidkostei

Fiz Gazodin Ballist Issled — Fiziko-Gazodinamicheskie Ballisticheskie Issledovaniya

Fiz Gazodin Eksp Model Diagn — Fizicheskaya Gazodinamika. Eksperimental'noe Modelirovanie i Diagnostika

Fiz Gazodin Ioniz Khim Reagiruyushchikh Gazov — Fizicheskaya Gazodinamika Ionizirovannykh i Khimicheski Reagiruyushchikh Gazov

Fiz Gazodin Svoistva Gazov Vys Temp — Fizicheskaya Gazodinamika i Svoistva Gazov pri Vysokikh Temperaturakh

Fiz Gazodin Teploobmen — Fizicheskaya Gazodinamika i Teploobmen

Fiz Gazodin Teploobmen Termodin Gazov Vys Temp — Fizicheskaya Gazodinamika, Teploobmen, i Termodinamika Gazov Vysokikh Temperatur

Fiz Gazorazryadnoi Plazmy — Fizika Gazorazryadnoi Plazmy

Fiz Gazov Lazerov — Fizika Gazovykh Lazerov

Fiz Geogr — Fizicheskaya Geografiya

Fiz Geogr Geomorfol — Fizichna Geografiya ta Geomorfologiya

Fiz Geol Faktory Razrab Neft Neftegazokondens Mestorozhd — Fiziko-Geologicheskie Faktory pri Razrabotke Neftyanykh i Neftegazokondensatnykh Mestorozhdenii

Fiz Gidrodin Kinet Zhidk — Fizicheskaya Gidrodinamika i Kinetika Zhidkosti

Fiz Goreniya & Vzryva — Fizika Goreniya i Vzryva

Fiz Goreniya Metody Ed Issled — Fizika Goreniya i Metody. Ed. Issledovaniya

Fiz Gorn Porod Protsessov — Fizika Gornykh Porod i Protsessov

Fiz Gor Vzryva — Fizika Goreniya i Vzryva

FIZHD — Fiziologicheskii Zhurnal

Fiz Heohr Heomorfol Mizhvid Nauk Zb — Fizycheskaya Heohrafiya ta Heomorfolohiya Mizhvidomchyi Naukovyi Zbirnykh

Fizic Kult — Fizicheskaja Kul'tura v Skole

Fizic Z — Fiziceskij Zurnal

Fizika Khim Mat Tekh Sov Shk — Fizika, Khimiya, Matematika, Tekhnika v Sovetskoi Shkole

Fizika Metall — Fizika Metallov i Metallovedenie

Fizika Shk — Fizika v Shkole

Fizika Tverd Tela — Fizika Tverdogo Tela

Fizika (Zagreb) Suppl — Fizika (Zagreb). Supplement

Fiz i Khim Obrab Mater — Fizika i Khimiya Obrabotki Materialov

Fiz i Khim Stekla — Fizika i Khimiya Stekla

Fizikokhim Metall Maragantsa — Fizikokhimiya i Metallurgiya Margantsa

Fizikokhim Modelnykh Kletochnykh Membr — Fizikokhimiya Model'nykh Kletochnykh Membran

Fiz Inst Rak — Fizikas Instituta Raksti

Fiziol Aktiv Veshchestva — Fiziologicheski Aktivnye Veshchestva

Fiziol Akt Veshchestva — Fiziologicheski Aktivnye Veshchestva

Fiziol Biokhim Aspekty Ustoich Rast — Fiziologo-Biokhimicheskie Aspekty Ustoichivosti Rastenii

Fiziol Biokhim Kul't Rast — Fiziologiya i Biokhimiya Kul'turnykh Rastenii

Fiziol Biokhim Mekh Deistviya Pestits — Fiziologo-Biokhimicheskii Mekhanizm Deistviya Pestitsidov [monograph]

Fiziol Biokhim Osn Pitan Rast — Fiziologo-Biokhimicheskie Osnovy Pitaniya Rastenii

Fiziol Biokhim Osn Vzaimodeistviya Rast Fitotsenozakh — Fiziologo-Biokhimicheskie Osnovy Vzaimodeistviya Rastenii e Fitotsenozakh

Fiziol Biokhim Patol Endokr Sist — Fiziologiya, Biokhimiya, i Patologiya Endokrinnoi Sistemy

Fiziol Biokhim Sil's'kogospod Tvarin — Fiziologiya i Biokhimiya Sil's'kogospodars'kikh Tvarin

Fiziol Chel — Fiziologiya Cheloveka

Fiziol Cheloveka — Fiziologiia Cheloveka

Fiziol Chel Zhivotn — Fiziologiya Cheloveka i Zhivotnykh

Fiziol Drev Rast — Fiziologiya Drevesnykh Rastenii

Fiziol Fiz-Khim Mekh Regul Obmennykh Protsessov Org — Fiziologicheskie i Fiziko-Khimicheskie Mekhanizmy Regulyatsii Obmennykh Protsessov Organizma

Fiziol Norm Patol — Fiziologiya Normala si Patologica

Fiziologia Norm Patol — Fiziologia Normala si Patologica. Revista a Societatii Stiintelor Medicale din Republica Populara Romine

Fiziologiya Rast — Fiziologiya Rastenii

Fiziol Opt Akt Polim Veshchestva Tr Vses Simp — Fiziologicheski i Opticheski Aktivnye Polimernye Veshchestva. Trudy Vsesoyuznogo Simpoziuma po Khimii i Fiziko-Khimii Fiziologicheski i Opticheski Aktivnykh Polimernykh Veshchestv

Fiziol Patol Gisto Gematicheskikh Barerov Mater Soveshch — Fiziologiya i Patologiya Gisto-Gematicheskikh Bar'erov. Materialy Soveshchaniyapo Probleme Gisto-Gematicheskikh Bar'erov

Fiziol Patol Obmena Porfirinov Gema Mater Simp — Fiziologiya i Patologiya Obmena Porfirinov i Gema. Materialy Simpoziuma po Voprosam Obmena Porfirinov

Fiziol Patol Vyssh Nervn Deyat — Fiziologiya i Patologiya Vysshei Nervnoi Deyatel'nosti

Fiziol Rast — Fiziologiya Rastenii

Fiziol Rast (Engl Transl Plant Physiol) — Fiziologiya Rastenii (English Translation of Plant Physiology)

Fiziol Rast Itogi Nauki Tekh — Fiziologiya Rastenii. Itogi Nauki i Tekhniki

Fiziol Rast (Mosc) — Fiziologiya Rastenii (Moscow)

Fiziol Rast (Moscow) — Fiziologiya Rastenii (Moscow)

Fiziol Rast (Sofia) — Fiziologiya na Rasteniyata (Sofia)

Fiziol Vodoobmena Ustoich Rast — Fiziologiya Vodoobmena i Ustoichivosti Rastenii

Fiziol Z — Fiziologicheskii Zhurnal

Fiziol Z — Fiziolohicnyi Zurnal

Fiziol Zh — Fiziologichnyi Zhurnal

Fiziol Zh Akad Nauk Ukr RSR — Fiziologichnij Zhurnal. Akademiya Nauk Ukrainskoj RSR

Fiziol Zh Im I M Sechenova — Fiziologicheskii Zhurnal Imeni I. M. Sechenova

Fiziol Zh (Kiev) — Fiziolohichnyi Zhurnal (Kiev)

Fiziol Zh SSSR — Fiziologicheskii Zhurnal SSSR Imeni I. M. Sechenova

Fiziol Zh SSSR Im I M Sechenova — Fiziologicheskii Zhurnal SSSR Imeni I. M. Sechenova

Fizioter Vest — Fizioterapevticheskii Vestnik

Fiz Issled — Fizicheskie Issledovaniya

Fiz i Tekh Poluprovodn — Fizika i Tekhnika Poluprovodnikov

Fiz Khim — Fizicheskaya Khimiya

Focus — Focus/Midwest
Focus — Focus on Indiana Libraries
Focus AACN — Focus on American Association of Critical Care Nurses [*Later, Focus on Critical Care*]
Focus Amersfoort Neth — Focus (Amersfoort, Netherlands)
Focus Crit Care — Focus on Critical Care
Focus Excep Child — Focus on Exceptional Children
Focus Floric Purdue Univ Coop Ext Serv — Focus on Floriculture. Purdue University. Cooperative Extension Service
Focus Indiana Libr — Focus on Indiana Libraries
Focus Indo — Focus on Indonesia
Focus Int Comp Lib — Focus on International Comparative Librarianship
Focus Int Comp Librarianship — Focus on International and Comparative Librarianship
Focus Jpn — Focus Japan
Focus Ohio Dent — Focus on Ohio Dentistry
Focus on F — Focus on Film
Focus Renewable Nat Resour — Focus on Renewable Natural Resources
Focus Renew Nat Resour Univ Idaho For Wildl Range Exp Stn — Focus on Renewable Natural Resources. University of Idaho. Forest, Wildlife, and Range Experiment Station
FODEDF — Folia Dendrologica
FODN — Foothills Dempster Newsletter
Foed Eur Gewaesserschutz Informationsbl — Foederation Europaeischer Gewaesserschutz. Informationsblatt
FOEG — Forschungen zur Ost Europaeischen Geschichte
FOEGAN — Food Engineering
Foeld Ember — Foeld es Ember
Foeldmuevel Min Allami Gazd Foeigazgatosaga (Budapest) — Foeldmuevelesuegyi Miniszterium. Allami Gazdasagok Foeigazgatosaga (Budapest)
Foeldr Ert — Foeldrajzi Ertesitoe
Foeldr Koezlem — Foeldrajzi Koezlemenyek. Mitteilungen der Ungarischen Geographischen Gesellschaft. Bulletin de la Societe Hongroise de Geographie
Foeldt Szemle — Foeldtani Szemle
FOEMA7 — Faunistisch-Oekologische Mitteilungen
FOENAA — Folia Endocrinologica
Foerdern Heben — Foerdern und Heben
Foerdertech Rdsch — Foerdertechnische Rundschau
Foeredr Pyroteknikdagen — Foeredrag vid Pyroteknikdagen
Foerh Geol Foeren Stockholm — Foerhandlingar. Geologiska Foereningen i Stockholm
Foerh Kungl Fysiogr Saellsk — Foerhandlingar. Kungliga Fysiografiska Saellskapet
Foerster Al Bauztg — Allgemeine Bauzeitung. Forster
Foersvarets Forskningsanst Rep — Foersvarets Forskningsanstalt. Reports
FOFL — Fauna och Flora
FOFRAR — FAO [*Food and Agriculture Organization of the United Nations*] Fisheries Reports
FOFUA — Funtai Oyobi Funmatsuyakin
FOG — Forschungen zur Ost Europaeischen Geschichte
Fogasz Lapja — Fogaszok Lapja
FOGGA — Fuel-, Orr-, Gegegyogyaszat
Fogg Art Mus Acqu — Fogg Art Museum. Acquisitions
Fogg Mus Bul — Fogg Art Museum. Bulletin
Fogl Istruz R Oss Fitopatol Torino — Foglio d'Istruzione. Reale Osservatorio di Fitopatologia di Torino
Fogorv Sz — Fogorvosi Szemle
FOGRA (Dtsche Forschungsges Druck Reproduktionstech) Mitt — FOGRA (Deutsche Forschungsgesellschaft fuer Druck und Reproduktionstechnik) Mitteilungen
FOGRA Forschungsber — FOGRA (Deutsche Forschungsgesellschaft Fuer Druckund Reproduktionstechnik) Forschungsbericht
FOH — Focus on Holland
FOHEAW — Folia Haematologica
FOHPAV — Folia Hereditaria et Pathologica
FOHWA — Forst- und Holzwirt
Fol — Forum Italicum
Foi Cath — Foi Catholique
FOIJA — Food Industries Journal
FOIRA — Food Irradiation
FOIRA8 — Irradiation des Aliments
F o K — Folk og Kultur
FoK — Folk og Kultur. Arbog for Dansk Etnologi og Folkemindevidenskab
FOKOA9 — Foldtani Kozlony
FOL — Folia Linguistica. Acta Societatis Linguisticae Europaeae
Fol — Folium
FoL — Folk Life
FoL — Foundations of Language
Fol A — Folia Archaeologica. A Magyar Nemzeti Muzeum. Toerteneti Muzeum Evkoenyve
Fol Amb — Folia Ambrosiana
Fol Arch — Folia Archaeologica
Fol Biol — Folia Biologica
Fol Civ — Folia Civitatis
FolcL — Folclor Leterar
Fold Des — Folding and Design (London)
Folder Mont State Coll Coop Ext — Folder. Montana State College. Cooperative Extension Service
Folder Mont State Univ Coop Ext Serv — Folder. Montana State University. Cooperative Extension Service
Folder Univ Ariz Agric Exp Stn — Folder. University of Arizona. Agricultural Experiment Station
Folder Univ MO Coll Agr Ext Serv — Folder. University of Missouri. College of Agriculture. Extension Service

Folding Des — Folding and Design
Foldrajzi Ert — Foldrajzi Ertesito
Foldrajzi Ertes — Foldrajzi Ertesito
Foldrajzi Koezl — Foldrajzi Koezlemenyek
Foldr Ert — Foldrajzi Ertesito
Foldr Kozl — Foldrajzi Kozlemenyek. Kiadja a Magyar Foldrajzi Tarsasag
Foldt Evk — Foldtani Evkonyvei
Foldt Koezl — Foldtani Koezlony
Foldt Kozl — Foldtani Kozlony
Foldt Kut — Foldtani Kutatas
Foldt Szle — Foldtani Szemle
Fol Endocr — Folia Endocrinologica
Fol Endocr Jap — Folia Endocrinologica Japonica
Fol Ent Hung — Folia Entomologica Hungarica
Fol Ent Mex — Folia Entomologica Mexicana
Fol For — Folia Forestalia
Fol Geobot Phytotax — Folia Geobotanica et Phytotaxonomica
Fol Geogr — Folia Geographica
Fol Ggr Dan — Folia Geographica Danica
Fol Haemat — Folia Haematologica
Folha Med — Folha Medica
Folha Med (Rio De Janeiro) — Folha Medica (Rio De Janeiro)
Folha Vet — Folha Veterinaria
Folh Divulg Dir Ger Servs Flor Aquic — Folhetos de Divulgacao. Direccao Geral dos Servicos Florestais e Aquicolas
Folh Divulg Serv Flor Aquic (Portugal) — Folhetas de Divulgacao. Servicos Florestais e Aquicolas (Portugal)
Fol Hered Path — Folia Hereditaria et Pathologica
Fol Hist Art — Folia Historiae Artium
Fol Hist Cy — Folia Histochemica et Cytochemica [*Later, Folia Histochemica et Cytobiologica*]
Fol Hist Cytochem — Folia Histochemica et Cytochemica [*Later, Folia Histochemica et Cytobiologica*]
Fol Hum — Folia Humanistica. Ciencias, Artes, Letras
Fol Humanis — Folia Humanistica
Fo Li — Folia Linguistica
Folia Allergol — Folia Allergologica [*Later, Folia Allergologica et Immunologica Clinica*]
Folia Allergol Immunol Clin — Folia Allergologica et Immunologica Clinica
Folia Anat Jap — Folia Anatomica Japonica
Folia Anat Jpn — Folia Anatomica Japonica
Folia Anat Univ Conimbr — Folia Anatomica Universitatis Conimbrigensis
Folia Anat Univ Conimbrigensis (Coimbra) — Folia Anatomica Universitatis Conimbrigensis (Coimbra)
Folia Angiol — Folia Angiologica [*Milano*]
Folia Angiol (Pisa) — Folia Angiologica (Pisa)
Folia Arch — Folia Archeologica
Folia Archaeol — Folia Archaeologica
Folia Balc — Folia Balcanica
Folia Biochim Biol Graeca — Folia Biochimica et Biologica Graeca
Folia Biol — Folia Biologica
Folia Biol Buenos Aires — Folia Biologica (Buenos Aires)
Folia Biol (Cracow) — Folia Biologica (Cracow)
Folia Biol (Krakow) — Folia Biologica (Krakow)
Folia Biol (Prague) — Folia Biologica (Prague)
Folia Biol (Praha) — Folia Biologica (Praha)
Folia Biol Warsaw — Folia Biologica (Warsaw)
Folia Biotheor — Folia Biotheoretica
Folia Bot Misc — Folia Botanica Miscellanea
Folia Cardiol — Folia Cardiologica
Folia Cardiol Suppl — Folia Cardiologia. Supplemento
Folia Chim Sin — Folia Chimica Sinica
Folia Chim Theor Lat — Folia Chimica Theoretica Latina
Folia Clin Biol — Folia Clinica et Biologica
Folia Clin Biol Nova Ser — Folia Clinica et Biologica. Nova Serie
Folia Clin Chim Microsc — Folia Clinica. Chimica et Microscopica
Folia Clin Chim Microsc Bologna — Folia Clinica Chimica et Microscopica (Bologna)
Folia Clin Chim Microsc Salsomaggiore — Folia Clinica Chimica et Microscopica (Salsomaggiore)
Folia Clin Int — Folia Clinica Internacional
Folia Clin Int (Barc) — Folia Clinica Internacional (Barcelona)
Folia Clin Orient — Folia Clinica Orientalia
Folia Cryptog — Folia Cryptogamica
Folia Demogr Gynaec — Folia Demografica-Gynaecologica
Folia Dendrol — Folia Dendrologica
Folia Dendrol Suppl — Folia Dendrologica. Supplementum
Folia Dermatol Pisa — Folia Dermatologica (Pisa)
Folia Endocr — Folia Endocrinologica
Folia Endocrinol — Folia Endocrinologica
Folia Endocrinol Jpn — Folia Endocrinologica Japonica
Folia Endocrinol (Pisa) — Folia Endocrinologica (Pisa)
Folia Endocrinol (Rome) — Folia Endocrinologica (Rome)
Folia Endocr Jap — Folia Endocrinologica Japonica
Folia Ent Hung — Folia Entomologica Hungarica
Folia Ent Mex — Folia Entomologica Mexicana
Folia Entomol Hung — Folia Entomologica Hungarica
Folia Entomol Hung Rovartani Kozl — Folia Entomologica Hungarica. Rovartani Kozlemenyek
Folia Entomol Mex — Folia Entomologica Mexicana
Folia Ethnogr — Folia Ethnographica
Folia Ethnogr Bpest — Folia Ethnographica (Budapestini)
Folia Fac Med — Folia Facultatis Medicae
Folia Fac Med Univ Comenianae Bratisl — Folia Facultatis Medicae Universitatis Comenianae Bratislaviensis

Folia Fac Sci Nat Univ Purkynianae Brun Biol — Folia Facultatis Scientiarum Naturalium Universitatis Purkynianae Brunensis: Biologia
Folia Fac Sci Nat Univ Purkynianae Brun Chem — Folia Facultatis Scientiarum Naturalium Universitatis Purkynianae Brunensis: Chemia
Folia Fac Sci Nat Univ Purkynianae Brunensis Phys — Folia Facultatis Scientiarum Naturalium Universitatis Purkynianae Brunensis: Physica
Folia Fac Sci Nat Univ Purkynianae Brun Phys — Folia Facultatis Scientiarum Naturalium Universitatis Purkynianae Brunensis. Physica
Folia Fac Sci Natur Univ Masaryk Brun Math — Folia Facultatis Scientiarium Naturalium Universitatis Masarykiana Brunensis. Mathematica
Folia For — Folia Forestalia
Folia Forest — Folia Forestalia
Folia For (Helsinki) — Folia Forestalia (Helsinki)
Folia For Inst For Fenn — Folia Forestalia Instituti Forestalis Fenniae
Folia For Polon (Drzewn) — Folia Forestalia Polonica. Seria B (Drzewnictwo)
Folia For Polon (Lesn) — Folia Forestalia Polonica. Seria A (Lesnictwo)
Folia For Pol Ser A (Lesn) — Folia Forestalia Polonica. Seria A (Lesnictwo)
Folia For Pol Ser B — Folia Forestalia Polonica. Seria B. Drzewnictwo
Folia For Pol Ser B (Drzewnictwo) — Folia Forestalia Polonica. Seria B (Drzewnictwo)
Foliage Dig — Foliage Digest
Folia Geobot Phytotaxon — Folia Geobotanica et Phytotaxonomica
Folia Geogr Dan — Folia Geographica Danica
Folia Geogr Ser Geogr Phys — Folia Geographica. Series Geographica-Physica
Folia Gynaec Demogr — Folia Gynaecologica-Demografica
Folia Gynaec (Pavia) — Folia Gynaecologica (Pavia)
Folia Haemat Frankf — Folia Haematologica. Internationaler Magazin fuer Blutforschung (Frankfurt a.M.)
Folia Haemat Lpz — Folia Haematologica (Leipzig)
Folia Haematol Abt — Folia Haematologica. Abteilung 1. Archiv
Folia Haematol Abt 2 — Folia Haematologica. Abteilung 2. Zentral-Organ
Folia Haematol (Frankfurt Am Main) — Folia Haematologica (Frankfurt Am Main)
Folia Haematol (Leipz) — Folia Haematologica (Leipzig)
Folia Haematol (Leipzig) Arch — Folia Haematologica (Leipzig). Archiv
Folia Haematol (Leipzig) Zentralorgan — Folia Haematologica (Leipzig). Zentralorgan
Folia Hered Pathol — Folia Hereditaria et Pathologica
Folia Hered Patol — Folia Hereditaria et Patologica
Folia Histochem Cytobiol — Folia Histochemica et Cytobiologica
Folia Histochem Cytochem — Folia Histochemica et Cytochemica [*Later, Folia Histochemica et Cytobiologica*]
Folia Histochem Cytochem (Krakow) — Folia Histochemica et Cytochemica (Krakow) [*Later, Folia Histochemica et Cytobiologica*]
Folia Histochem Cytochem Suppl — Folia Histochemica et Cytochemica. Supplement
Folia Hortic Sin — Folia Horticulturea Sinica
Folia Hum — Folia Humanistica. Ciencias, Artes, Letras
Folia Jap Pharmac — Folia Japonica Pharmacologica
Folia Limnol Scand — Folia Limnologica Scandinavica
Folia Med — Folia Medico
Folia Med Bialostoc — Folia Medica Bialostocensia
Folia Med Bialostocensia — Folia Medica Bialostocensia
Folia Med Cracov — Folia Medica Cracoviensia
Folia Med Fac Med Univ Saraev — Folia Medica Facultatis. Medicinae Universitatis Saraeviensis
Folia Med Fac Med Univ Saraeviensis — Folia Medica Facultatis Medicinae Universitatis Saraeviensis
Folia Med Intern Orient — Folia Medicinae Internae Orientalia
Folia Med Lodz — Folia Medica Lodziensia
Folia Med (Naples) — Folia Medica (Naples)
Folia Med Neerl — Folia Medica Neerlandica
Folia Med Orient Sect 1 — Folia Medica Orientalia. Sectio 1. Folia Medicinae Internae Orientalia
Folia Med (Plovdiv) — Folia Medica (Plovdiv)
Folia Med Sof — Folia Medica (Sofia)
Folia Mendel — Folia Mendeliana Musei Moravia
Folia Microbiol — Folia Microbiologica
Folia Microbiol Delft — Folia Microbiologica (Delft)
Folia Microbiol (Prague) — Folia Microbiologica (Prague)
Folia Morph — Folia Morphologica
Folia Morphol (Prague) — Folia Morphologica (Prague)
Folia Morphol (Praha) — Folia Morphologica (Praha)
Folia Morphol (Warsaw) — Folia Morphologica (Warsaw)
Folia Morphol (Warsaw) (Engl Transl) — Folia Morphologica (Warsaw) (English translation)
Folia Morphol Warsz — Folia Morphologiica (Warszawa)
Folia Mus Rerum Nat Bohemiae Occident Geol — Folia Musei Rerum Naturalium Bohemiae Occidentalis. Geologica
Folia Myrmec Termit — Folia Myrmecologica et Termitologica
Folia Neuro Biol — Folia Neuro-Biologica
Folia Neuropath Eston — Folia Neuropathologica Estoniana
Folia Neuropathol — Folia Neuropathologica
Folia Neuropsiquiatr Sur Este Esp — Folia Neuropsiquiatrica del Sur y Este de Espana
Folia O — Folia Orientalia
Folia Odontol Pract — Folia Odontologica Practica
Folia Ophthal Jap — Folia Ophthalmologica Japonica
Folia Ophthalmol — Folia Ophthalmologica
Folia Ophthalmol Jpn — Folia Ophthalmologica Japonica
Folia Ophthalmol (Leipz) — Folia Ophthalmologica (Leipzig)
Folia Ophthal Orient — Folia Ophthalmologica Orientalia
Folia Orient — Folia Orientalia
Folia Oto Lar Orient — Folia Oto-Laryngologica Orientalia
Folia Parasit — Folia Parasitologica
Folia Parasitol (Prague) — Folia Parasitologica (Prague)

Folia Pharm — Folia Pharmaceutica
Folia Pharmacol Jpn — Folia Pharmacologica Japonica
Folia Pharm (Istanbul) — Folia Pharmaceutica (Istanbul)
Folia Pharm Prague — Folia Pharmaceutica (Prague)
Folia Phoniatr — Folia Phoniatrica
Folia Phoniatr (Basel) — Folia Phoniatrica (Basel)
Folia Phoniatr Logop — Folia Phoniatrica et Logopedica
Folia Praehist Posnan — Folia Praehistorica Posnaniensia
Folia Prima — Folia Primatologica
Folia Primat — Folia Primatologica
Folia Primatol — Folia Primatologica
Folia Psychiatr Neurol Jpn — Folia Psychiatrica et Neurologica Japonica
Folia Quat — Folia Quaternaria
Folia Sci Afr Cent — Folia Scientifica Africae Centralis
Folia Serol — Folia Serologica
Folia Soc Sci Lublinensis — Folia Societatis Scientiarum Lublinensis
Folia Soc Sci Lublinensis Biol — Folia Societatis Scientiarum Lublinensis. Biologia
Folia Soc Sci Lublinensis Geogr — Folia Societatis Scientiarum Lublinensis. Geografia
Folia Soc Sci Lublinensis Mat Fiz Chem — Folia Societatis Scientiarum Lublinensis. Matematyka-Fizyka-Chemia
Folia Soc Sci Lublinensis Sect A D Suppl — Folia Societatis Scientiarum Lublinensis. Sectio A-D. Supplementum
Folia Univ — Folia Universitaria
Folia Univ Agric Stetin — Folia Universitatis Agriculturae Stetinensis
Folia Univ Cochabamba — Folia Universitaria Cochabamba
Folia Vet — Folia Veterinaria
Folia Vet Lat — Folia Veterinaria Latina
Folia Vet (Prague) — Folia Veterinaria (Prague)
Folia Zool — Folia Zoologica
Folia Zool Hydrobiol — Folia Zoologica et Hydrobiologica
Folio Ser Geol Surv La — Folio Series. Geological Survey. Louisiana
Folio Supp — Folio. Guide to Magazine Suppliers
FOLK — Folk. Dansk Ethnografisk Tidsskrift
Folk — Folklore
Folk Am Coral Gables — Folklore Americas (Coral Gables, Florida)
Folk Am Lima — Folklore Americano. Comite Interamericano de Folklore. Instituto Panamericano de Geografia e Historia (Lima)
Folk Harp J — Folk Harp Journal
Folk Inst — Folklore Institute. Journal
Folkkult — Folkkultur
Folkl — Folklore
Folkl Am — Folklore Americano
Folkl Amer — Folklore Americano
Folkl Arch — Folklor Archivum
Folkl Arch — Folklore Archives
Folkl Brabancon — Folklore Brabancon
Folkl (Calcutta) — Folklore (Calcutta)
Folkl Champagne — Folklore de Champagne
Folklore Am — Folklore Americano
Folklore C — Folklore (Calcutta)
Folk-Lore J — Folk-Lore Journal
Folk Lore Rec — Folk-lore Record
Folklore Soc Pub — Folklore Society Publications
Folkl Rec — Folklore Record
Folkl St (P) — Folklore Studies (Peking)
Folkl Stud — Folklore Studies
Folkl Suisse — Folklore Suisse
Folkm — Folkminner och Folktankar
Folk Mus Arch — Folklore and Folk Music Archivist
Folk Music — Folk Music Journal
Folk Mus J — Folk Music Journal
Folk O Kult — Folk og Kultur
Folk O Min Nordsj — Folk og Minder fra Nordsjaelland
Folk Res — Journal of Folklore Research
FolkS — Folklore Studies
Foll Divulg Inst For (Chile) — Folleto de Divulgacion. Instituto Forestal (Santiago De Chile)
Folletos Divulg Ci Inst Biol — Folletos de Divulgacion Cientifica del Instituto de Biologia
Follicular Maturation Ovul Proc Reinier de Graaf Symp — Follicular Maturation and Ovulation. Proceedings of the Reinier de Graaf Symposium
Fol Limnol Scand — Folia Limnologica Scandinavica
Fol Ling — Folia Linguistica
Fol Lov — Folia Lovaniensia
Foll Tec For — Folletos Tecnicos Forestales
Foll Tec For Adm Nac Bosques (Argent) — Folletos Tecnicos Forestales. Administracion Nacional de Bosques (Argentina)
Foll Tec Univ Auton San Luis Potosi Inst Geol Metal — Folleto Tecnico. Universidad Autonoma de San Luis Potosi Instituto de Geologia y Metalurgia
FOLMA8 — Folia Medica
Fol Med — Folha Medica
Fol Med — Folia Medica
Fol Med Cracov — Folia Medica Cracoviensia
Fol Med Lodz — Folia Medica Lodziensia
Fol Med (Napoli) — Folia Medica (Napoli)
Fol Med Neerl — Folia Medica Neerlandica
Fol Mend — Folia Mendeliana
Fol Microb — Folia Microbiologica
Fol Microbiol — Folia Microbiologica
Fol Morph — Folia Morphologica
Fol Oecon Cracov — Folia Oeconomica Cracoviensia
Fol Or — Folia Orientalia
Fol Pharm J — Folia Pharmacologica Japonica
Fol Phoniat — Folia Phoniatrica

Fol Primat — Folia Primatologica
Fo LR — Fordham Law Review
Fol Serol — Folia Serologica
Fol Tec Secr Agr Ganad Inst Nac Invest Agr (Mexico) — Folleto Tecnico. Secretaria de Agricultura y Ganaderia. Instituto Nacional de Investigaciones Agricolas (Mexico)
Folya Farm — Folya Farmasotika
FOMAAB — Food Manufacture
FOMAD — Food Market Awareness Databank
FOMDA — Folia Medica
FOMDAK — Folia Medica
FOMEAN — Folha Medica
Fomento Agric — Fomento Agricola. Ministerio de Agricultura. Servico de Divulgacao Agricola
FOMIAZ — Folia Microbiologica
FOMIE5 — Food Microbiology
FOMNAG — Folia Medica Neerlandica
FOMOAJ — Folia Morphologica
Fom PR — Fomento de Puerto Rico
Fon — Fontes Artis Musicae
FoN — Fortid og Nutid
Fonaments — Fonaments Prehistoria i Mon Antic als Paisos Catalans
Fon Art Mus — Fontes Artis Musicae
Fonderia Ital — Fonderia Italiana
Fonderie Mod — Fonderie Moderne
Fonderie Suppl — Fonderie. Supplement
Fondeur — Fondeur d'Aujourd'hui
Fond Giorgio Ronchi Att — Fondazione Giorgio Ronchi. Atti
Fond Iniziative Zooprofil Zootec Collana — Fondazione Iniziative Zooprofilattiche e Zootecniche. Collana
Fond Merieux Symp — Fondation Merieux. Symposia
Fond Mod — Fonderie Moderne
Fond Politec Mezzogiorno Ital Quad — Fondazione Politecnica per il Mezzogiorno d'Italia. Quaderno
Fondren Sci Ser — Fondren Science Series
Fonds Rech For Univ Laval Bull — Fonds de Recherches Forestieres. Universite Laval. Bulletin
Fonds Rech For Univ Laval Contrib — Fonds de Recherches Forestieres. Universite Laval. Contribution
Fonds Rech For Univ Laval Note Tech — Fonds de Recherches Forestieres. Universite Laval. Note Technique
Fond Univ Luxemb Notes Rech — Fondation Universitaire Luxembourgeoise. Notes de Recherche
Fond Univ Luxemb Ser Notes Rech — Fondation Universitaire Luxembourgeoise. Serie Notes de Recherche
F on F — Facts on File
Fon Iur Rom Ant — Fontes Iuris Romani Antejustiniani
FONN — Federation of Ontario Naturalists. Newsletter
FONOBP — Forest Notes. New Hampshire's Conservation Magazine
Font — Fontaine
Font — Fontes Iuris Romani Antejustiniani
Font Amb — Fontes Ambrosiani
Fontane Bl — Fontane Blaetter
Font A Pos — Fontes Archaeologici Posnanienses
Font Archaeol Morav — Fontes Archeologiae Moravicae
Font Archaeol Posnan — Fontes Archaeologici Posnanienses
Fonte Nucl Futuro Energ Atti Giornate Energ Nucl — Fonte Nucleare nel Futuro Energetico. Atti Delle Giornate dell'Energia Nucleare
Fontes — Fontes Artis Musicae
Fontes A H — Fontes Archaeologici Hungariae
Fontes Arch — Fontes Archaeologici Hungariae
Fontes Arch Hung — Fontes Archaeologici Hungariae
Fontes Arch Posnan — Fontes Archaeologici Posnanienses
Fontes Arch Prag — Fontes Archaeologici Pragenses
FontesArtisM — Fontes Artis Musicae
Fontes Nick — Fontes au Nickel
Fonti Studi Storia Univ Pavia — Fonti e Studi per la Storia dell'Universita di Pavia
Font Iur Rom — Fontes Iuris Romani Antejustiniani
Font Iur Rom Antej — Fontes Iuris Romani Antejustiniani
Font Top Vet Urb Pert — Fontes ad Topographiam Veteris Urbis Romae Pertinentes
FONYA — Forskningsnytt
FOO — Food Processing
Food Addit Contam — Food Additives and Contaminants
Food Addit Contam Anal Surveillance Eval Control — Food Additives and Contaminants. Analysis, Surveillance, Evaluation, Control
Food Agric Immunol — Food and Agricultural Immunology
Food Agric Leg — Food and Agricultural Legislation
Food Agric Tech Inf Serv Bull — Food and Agriculture Technical Information Service. Bulletin
Food Agric Tech Inf Serv Rev — Food and Agriculture Technical Information Service. Review
Food & Bev — Food and Beverage Marketing
Food & Nutr — Food and Nutrition
Food and Nutr Notes and Rev — Food and Nutrition. Notes and Reviews
Food & Nutr Notes Revs — Food and Nutrition. Notes and Reviews
Food Aust — Food Australia
Food Biotechnol — Food Biotechnology
Food Biotechnol London — Food Biotechnology (London)
Food Biotechnol NY — Food Biotechnology (New York)
Food Bus — Food Business
Food Can — Food in Canada
Food Canad — Food in Canada
Food Chem — Food Chemistry
Food Chem Microbiol Technol — Food Chemistry, Microbiology, Technology

Food Chem Toxicol — Food and Chemical Toxicology
Food Chem Toxicol Int J Publ Br Ind Biol Res Organ — Food and Chemical Toxicology. An International Journal Published for the British Industrial Biological Research Organization
Food Cosmet — Food and Cosmetics Toxicology
Food Cosmetics Toxicol — Food and Cosmetics Toxicology
Food Cosmet Toxicol — Food and Cosmetics Toxicology
Food Dev — Food Development
Food Devel — Food Development
Food Drug Adm Bur Vet Med Tech Rep FDA BVM (US) — Food and Drug Administration. Bureau of Veterinary Medicine. Technical Report FDA/BVM (United States)
Food Drug Adm Publ FDA — Food and Drug Administration. Publication FDA
Food Drug C — Food, Drug, Cosmetic Law Journal
Food Drug Cosmet Law J — Food, Drug, Cosmetic Law Journal
Food Drug Cosmet Law Q — Food, Drug, Cosmetic Law Quarterly
Food Drug Cosm LJ — Food, Drug, Cosmetic Law Journal
Food Drug Cosm LQ — Food, Drug, Cosmetic Law Quarterly
Food Drug Cosm L Rep CCH — Food, Drug, Cosmetic Law Reports. Commerce Clearing House
Food Drugs Ind Bull — Food and Drugs Industry Bulletin
Food Eng — Food Engineering
Food Engin — Chilton's Food Engineering
Food Eng Int — Food Engineering International
Food Eng (NY) — Food Engineering (New York)
Food Eng (Philadelphia) — Food Engineering (Philadelphia)
Food Eng Syst — Food Engineering Systems
Food Extrusion Sci Technol — Food Extrusion Science and Technology
Food Facts Diet — Food Facts for Dietitians
Food Farming Agric — Food Farming and Agriculture. Journal for the Development of Food and Agriculture
Food Ferment Ind — Food and Fermentation Industries
Food Fert Technol Cent Book Ser — Food and Fertilizer Technology Center. Book Series
Food Fiber Econ Tex Agric Ext Serv Tex A & M Univ Syst — Food and Fiber Economics. Texas Agricultural Extension Service. The Texas A & M University System
Food Fish Mark Rev & Outl — Food Fish Market Review and Outlook
Food Fl — Food and Flowers. Hong Kong Agricultural Department
Food Flavour Ingredients Processing and Packaging — Food: Flavouring Ingredients Processing and Packaging
Food Hyg Stud — Food Hygiene Study
Food Ind — Food Industry
Food Ind (Budapest) — Food Industry (Budapest)
Food Ind J — Food Industries Journal
Food Ind (Moscow) — Food Industry (Moscow)
Food Ind Res Dev Inst Res Rep Taiwan — Food Industry Research and Development Institute. Research Report (Taiwan)
Food Ind S Afr — Food Industries of South Africa
Food Ind Sci — Food Industry Science
Food Ind (Tokyo) — Food Industry (Tokyo)
Food Ind USSR — Food Industry of the USSR
Food Ind Wkly — Food Industries Weekly
Food Irradiat — Food Irradiation
Food Irradiat Inf — Food Irradiation Information
Food Irradiat (Jpn) — Food Irradiation (Japan)
Food Manage — Food Management
Food Manuf — Food Manufacture
Food Manuf Wkly — Food Manufacture Weekly
Food Mater Equip — Food Materials and Equipment
Food Mfr — Food Manufacture
Food Microbiol (Lond) — Food Microbiology (London)
Food Microstruct — Food Microstructure
Food Mon — Food Monitor
FoodMonit — Food Monitor
Food News Consum — Food News for Consumers
Food Nutr — Food and Nutrition
Food Nutr Bull — Food and Nutrition Bulletin
Food Nutr Bull Suppl — Food and Nutrition Bulletin. Supplement
Food Nutr Hist Anthropol — Food and Nutrition in History and Anthropology
Food Nutrition Afr — Food and Nutrition in Africa
Food Nutr News — Food and Nutrition News
Food Nutr Notes Rev — Food and Nutrition. Notes and Reviews
Food Nutr (Rome) — Food and Nutrition (Rome)
Food Packag Technol — Food Packaging Technology
Food Packer Cann Age — Food Packer and Canning Age
Food PM — Food Production/Management
Food Pol — Food from Poland
Food Pol — Food Policy
Food Preservation Q — Food Preservation Quarterly
Food Preserv Q — Food Preservation Quarterly
Food Proc — Food Processing Industry
Food Proc — Food Processing News
Food Process — Food Processing
Food Process (Chic) — Food Processing (Chicago)
Food Process Chicago — Food Processing (Chicago)
Food Process Eng Proc Int Congr — Food Process Engineering. Proceedings. International Congress on Engineering and Food and the Eighth European Food Symposium
Food Process Ind — Food Processing Industry
Food Processing Mktg — Food Processing and Marketing
Food Process Mark (Chic) — Food Processing and Marketing (Chicago)
Food Process Mark (London) — Food Processing and Marketing (London)
Food Process Packag — Food Processing and Packaging

Food Process Waste Manage Proc Cornell Agric Waste Manage Con — Food Processing Waste Management. Proceedings of the Cornell Agricultural Waste Management Conference
Food Prod — Food Product Development
Food Prod Dev — Food Product Development
Food Prod Devel — Food Product Development
Food Prod/Manage — Food Production/Management
Food Res — Food Research
Food Res (Chicago) — Food Research (Chicago)
Food Res Dep Div Food Res CSIRO — Food Research Report. Division of Food Research. Commonwealth Scientific and Industrial Research Organisation
Food Research Inst Studies — Food Research Institute. Studies
Food Res Inst Stud — Food Research Institute. Studies
Food Res Inst Stud Agric Econ Trade Dev (Stanford) — Food Research Institute. Studies in Agricultural Economics, Trade, and Development (Stanford)
Food Res Inst Stud (Stanford) — Food Research Institute. Studies (Stanford)
Food Res Int — Food Research International
Food Rev — Food Review
Food Rev Int — Food Reviews International
Food Saf Assess — Food Safety Assessment
Food Saf Qual Assur Appl Immunoassay Syst Proc — Food Safety and Quality Assurance. Applications of Immunoassay Systems. Proceedings
Food Sci — Food Science
Food Sci Abstr — Food Science Abstracts
Food Sci & Tech Abstr — Food Science and Technology Abstracts
Food Sci & Technol (Zur) — Food Science and Technology (Zurich)
Food Sci (Beijing) — Food Science (Beijing)
Food Sci Hum Nutr — Food Science and Human Nutrition
Food Sci London — Food Science (London)
Food Sci Nutr — Food Sciences and Nutrition
Food Sci (NY) — Food Science (New York)
Food Sci Osaka — Food Science (Osaka)
Food Sci Rev — Food Science Reviews
Food Sci (Taipei) — Food Science (Taipei)
Food Sci Technol — Food Science and Technology
Food Sci Technol Abstr — Food Science and Technology Abstracts
Food Sci Technol Bucharest — Food Sciences and Technologies (Bucharest)
Food Sci Technol Int — Food Science and Technology International
Food Sci Technol Int Frederick Md — Food Science and Technology International (Frederick, Maryland)
Food Sci Technol Int London — Food Science and Technology International (London)
Food Sci Technol Int NY — Food Science and Technology International (New York)
Food Sci Technol Int Tsukuba Jpn — Food Science and Technology, International (Tsukuba, Japan)
Food Sci Technol London — Food Science and Technology (London)
Food Sci Technol Poznan — Food Science and Technology (Poznan)
Food Sci Technol Proc Int Congr — Food Science and Technology. Present Status and Future Direction. Proceedings of the International Congress of Food Science and Technology
Food Sci Technol Ser Monogr — Food Science and Technology. A Series of Monographs
Food Serv For — Food Service Forum
Food Serv Mark — Food Service Marketing
Food Serv Mkt — Food Service Marketing
Foods Food Ingredients J — Foods and Food Ingredients Journal
Foods Food Ingredients J Jpn — Foods and Food Ingredients Journal of Japan
Food S Mkt — Food Service Marketing
Foods Nutr Dent Health — Foods, Nutrition, and Dental Health
Food Struct — Food Structure
Foodstuffs Wld — Foodstuffs Round the World
Food Surveill Pap — Food Surveillance Paper
Food Tech — Food Technology
Food Tech Aust — Food Technology in Australia
Food Tech in Aust — Food Technology in Australia
Food Technol — Food Technology
Food Technol Aust — Food Technology in Australia
Food Technol Biotechnol — Food Technology and Biotechnology
Food Technol Chicago — Food Technology (Chicago)
Food Technol Dunedin NZ — Food Technologist (Dunedin, New Zealand)
Food Technol London — Food Technology (London)
Food Technol (Milan) — Food Technology (Milan)
Food Technol NZ — Food Technology in New Zealand
Food Technology in Aust — Food Technology in Australia
Food Technol Rev — Food Technology Review
Food Tech NZ — Food Technology in New Zealand
Food Trade R — Food Trade Review
Food Trade Rev — Food Trade Review
Food Wld N — Food World News
FOOHA — Fueloil and Oil Heat
FOOPDZ — Folia Ophthalmologica
Foot Ankle Clin — Foot and Ankle Clinics
Foot Ankle Int — Foot and Ankle International
Foote Prints Chem Met Alloys Ores — Foote Prints on Chemicals, Metals, Alloys, and Ores
Foot Mouth Dis Bull — Foot and Mouth Disease Bulletin
FPAAQ — Food Packer
FPE — Forgotten People
FPHA — Folia Phoniatrica
FPHAD — Aktuelle Probleme der Phoniatrie und Logopaedie
FPHAD — Folia Phoniatrica
FPMAS — Folia Pharmaceutica
FPMBT — Food Processing and Marketing
FP — Focal Points

FOPOD3 — Food Policy
FOPRA9 — Food Processing
FOPRB — Foret Privee
FOQUAN — Folia Quaternaria
For — Code Forestier
FOR — Foreign Affairs
Fo R — Fortnightly Review
FOR — Fortune
For Abstr — Forestry Abstracts
For Advis Newsl — Forestry Adviser's Newsletter
For Aff — Foreign Affairs
For Affairs — Foreign Affairs
For Aff Rep — Foreign Affairs Reports
Forage Res — Forage Research
For Agri — Foreign Agriculture
For Agric — Foreign Agriculture
For Agr Wash — Foreign Agriculture (Washington, DC)
For and Bird — Forest and Bird
For & Outdoors — Forest and Outdoors
For and Timb — Forest and Timber
For Anim Dis Rep — Foreign Animal Disease Report
For Bull Br Columb Univ — Forestry Bulletin. Faculty of Forestry. British Columbia University
For Bull Br Guiana — Forestry Bulletin. Forest Department. British Guiana
For Bull Dep For Clemson Univ — Forestry Bulletin. Department of Forestry. Clemson University
For Bull Duke Univ — Forestry Bulletin. Duke University
For Bull Jamaica — Forestry Bulletin. Forest Department. Jamaica
For Bull Palest — Forestry Bulletin. Department of Agriculture and Forestry. Palestine
For Bull Qd — Forestry Bulletin. Department of Public Lands. Queensland
For Bull R8 FB U US Dep Agric For Serv South Reg — Forestry Bulletin R8-FB/U. US Department of Agriculture. Forest Service. Southern Region
For Bull TVA — Forestry Bulletin. Tennessee Valley Authority
For Bull Univ Toronto — Forestry Bulletin. Faculty of Forestry. University of Toronto
For Bur Aust For Res Notes — Australia. Commonwealth Forestry and Timber Bureau. Forestry Research Notes
For Bur Aust Leaf — Australia. Commonwealth Forestry and Timber Bureau. Leaflet
For Bur Aust Timber Supp Rev — Australia. Commonwealth Forestry and Timber Bureau. Timber Supply Review
FORC — Forces. Hydro Quebec
For Can Gt Lakes For Cent Inf Rep O-X — Forestry Canada. Great Lakes Forestry Centre. Information Report O-X
For Chron — Forestry Chronicle
For Circ Ill — Forestry Circular. Illinois Natural History Survey
For Comm — Foreign Commerce Weekly
For Comm NSW Res Note — Forestry Commission of New South Wales. Research Note
For Comm Victoria Bull — Forests Commission Victoria. Bulletin
For Comm Victoria For Tech Pap — Forests Commission Victoria. Forestry Technical Papers
For Com Wkly — Foreign Commerce Weekly
Forc Sous M — Forces Sous-Marines
For Curr Lit — Forestry Current Literature. US Forest Service
For Def — For the Defense
For Dep Bull For Dep (Zambia) — Forest Department Bulletin. Forest Department (Zambia)
For Dep West Aust Res Pap — Forests Department of Western Australia. Research Paper
Fordertech Frachtverk — Foerdertechnik und Frachtverkehr
For Dev S Afr — Forestry Development in South Africa and Annual Report of the Department of Forestry. Union of South Africa
Ford For Cent Mich Technol Univ Bull — Ford Forestry Center. Michigan Technological University. Bulletin
Ford For Cent Mich Technol Univ Res Notes — Ford Forestry Center. Michigan Technological University. Research Notes
Fordham Corp Inst — Proceedings. Fordham Corporate Law Institute
Fordham Intl LF — Fordham International Law Forum
Fordham Int'l LJ — Fordham International Law Journal
Fordham Law Rev — Fordham Law Review
Fordham L R — Fordham Law Review
Fordham L Rev — Fordham Law Review
Fordham Urban L J — Fordham Urban Law Journal
Fordham Urb LJ — Fordham Urban Law Journal
For Dig — Forestry Digest. American Forest Products Industries [*Washington*]
For Dig (Philippines) — Forestry Digest (Philippines)
For Div Tech Note For Div (Tanz) — Forest Division Technical Note. Forest Division. (Dar Es Salaam, Tanzania)
Ford L Rev — Fordham Law Review
Ford Urban LJ — Fordham Urban Law Journal
FOREAE — Food Research
Forecast Guide US Weath Bur — Forecasting Guide. US Weather Bureau
Forecast Home Econ — Forecast for Home Economics
Forecast Home Econ — Forecast for the Home Economist
For Ecol & Mgt — Forest Ecology and Management
For Ecol Manage — Forest Ecology and Management
For Econ NY St Coll For — Forestry Economics. New York State University. College of Forestry at Syracuse University
For Econ Trd — Foreign Economic Trends and Their Implications for the United States
Foredr Nord ElektrotekMote — Foredrag. Nordisk Elektroteknikermote
FOREGE — Food Regulation Enquiries
Foreign Aff — Foreign Affairs

Foreign Aff Rep — Foreign Affairs Reports
Foreign Agr — Foreign Agriculture. US Foreign Agricultural Service
Foreign Agric — Foreign Agriculture
Foreign Agric Canned Fruits FCAN US Foreign Agric Serv — Foreign Agriculture Circular. Canned Fruits. FCAN. United States Foreign Agricultural Service
Foreign Agric Circ — Foreign Agriculture Circular. United States Department of Agriculture. Foreign Agriculture Service
Foreign Agric Circ Dried Fruit FDF USDA Foreign Agric Serv — Foreign Agriculture Circular. Dried Fruits. FDF. United States Department of Agriculture. Foreign Agricultural Service
Foreign Agric Circ Grains FG US Dep Agric Foreign Agric Serv — Foreign Agriculture Circular. Grains. FG. United States Department of Agriculture. Foreign Agricultural Service
Foreign Agric Circ US Dep Agric — Foreign Agriculture Circular. United States Department of Agriculture
Foreign Agric Circ US Dep Agric Serv Spices FTEA — Foreign Agricultural Circular. United States Department of Agriculture. ForeignAgricultural Services. Spices. FTEA
Foreign Agric Econ Rep US Dep Agric Econ Res Serv — Foreign Agricultural Economic Report. US Department of Agriculture. Economic Research Service
Foreign Agric Rep — Foreign Agricultural Report
Foreign Agric US Dep Agric Foreign Agric Serv — Foreign Agriculture. US Department of Agriculture. Foreign Agricultural Service
Foreign Agr Incl Foreign Crops Markets — Foreign Agriculture. Including Foreign Crops and Markets. US Foreign Agricultural Service
Foreign Agr Trade US — Foreign Agriculture Trade of the United States
Foreign Commer Wkly — Foreign Commerce Weekly
Foreign Compd Metab Mamm — Foreign Compound Metabolism in Mammals
Foreign Econ Trends Their Implic US — Foreign Economic Trends and Their Implications for the United States
Foreign Lan — Foreign Language Annals
Foreign Lang Index — Foreign Language Index
Foreign Language — Foreign Language Information Service Interpreter Release
Foreign Leg Per — Foreign Legal Periodicals Index
Foreign Miner Q — Foreign Minerals Quarterly. US Bureau of Mines
Foreign Monthly Rev Continental Lit J — Foreign Monthly Review and Continental Literary Journal
Foreign Pet Technol — Foreign Petroleum Technology
Foreign Pol — Foreign Policy
Foreign Sci Publ Natn Cent Sci Tech Econ Inf (Warsaw) — Foreign Scientific Publication. National Center for Scientific, Technical, and Economic Information (Warsaw)
Foreign Tr — Foreign Trade
Foren Dansk Samv Dansk Atlha — Foreningen Dansk Samvirke de Dansk Atlanterhavsoer
Foren Sci I — Forensic Science International
Forensic Sci — Forensic Science [Later, Forensic Science International]
Forensic Sci Circ — Forensic Science Circulars
Forensic Sci Gaz — Forensic Science Gazette
Forensic Sci Int — Forensic Science International
Forensic Sci Soc J — Forensic Science Society Journal
For Environ Prot US For Serv North Reg — Forest Environmental Protection. United States Forest Service. Northern Region
For Equipm Note FAO — Forestry Equipment Notes. FAO
For Equip Notes — Forestry Equipment Notes. FAO
Forest Abstr — Forestry Abstracts
Forest Adm A Rep Fed Nigeria — Forest Administration Annual Report. Federation of Nigeria
Forest Air Surv Publs — Forest Air Survey Publications
Forest Biblphy — Forest Bibliography. Department of Forestry. University of Oxford
Forest Bird — Forest and Bird
Forest Bull Taipei — Forestry Bulletin. Lin Yeh Chon K'an. Forestry Experiment Station. College of Agriculture. National Taiwan University (Taipei)
Forest Chro — Forestry Chronicle
Forest Chron — Forestry Chronicle. Canadian Society of Forest Engineers
Forest Ent — Forest Entomology. Forest Protection Service
Forester N Ire — Forester. Ministry of Agriculture of Northern Ireland
Forest Fire Haz Pap — Forest-Fire Hazard Paper
Forest Fire Losses Can — Forest Fire Losses in Canada
Forest Fire Prot Abstr — Forest Fire Protection Abstracts
Forest Fire Prot Notes — Forest Fire Protection Notes
Forest Fire Rep Calif — Forest Fire Report. Division of Forestry (California)
Forest Fire Res Leafl — Forest Fire Research Leaflets
Forest Fire Res Notes — Forest-Fire Research Notes
Forest Hist — Forest History
Forest Ind — Forest Industries
Forest Industr Monthly — Forestry Industry Monthly/Lin Ch'an Yueeh K'an
Forest Inf Bull Sun Yat Sen Univ — Forest Information Bulletin. College of Agriculture. Sun-Yat-Sen University
Forest Insect Invest — Forest Insect Investigations. Bimonthly Progress Report
Forest Inventory Ser Prince Albert — Forest Inventory Series (Prince Albert)
Forest Inventory Summ Br Columb — Forest Inventory Summaries. Forest Service. British Columbia
Forest Invest — Forestry Investigation. Lin-Hsun. China. Department of Agriculture and Forestry. Central Forestry Bureau
Forest Leafl Dehra Dun — Forest Leaflets. Forest Research Institute. Dehra Dun
Forest Leafl Un Prov Agra Oudh — Forest Leaflets. Forest Department. United Provinces of Agra and Oudh
Forest Leafl Uttar Pradesh — Forest Leaflets. Forest Department. Uttar Pradesh
Forest Log Ore — Forest Log. Oregon State Board of Forestry
Forest Log TVA — Forest Log. Tennessee Valley Authority
Forest Mem Pakistan — Forest Memoir. Pakistan Forest Department
Forest Mgmt Note — Forest Management Note. Northeastern Forest Experiment Station

Forest Mgmt Pap — Forest Management Paper. Northeastern Forest Experiment Station
Forest Ops Ser — Forest Operations Series. Forestry Commission
Forest Outdoors — Forest and Outdoors
Forest Path Spec Release — Forest Pathology Special Release. US Forest Products Laboratory
Forest Pest Leafl — Forest Pest Leaflet. Forest Service
Forest Pest Obsr — Forest Pest Observer
Forest PMT — Forest Products Market Trends
Forest Prod Bull — Forest Products Bulletin
Forest Prod J — Forest Products Journal
Forest Prod News — Forest Products News
Forest Prod News Lett — Forest Products News Letter
Forest Prod Note — Forest Products Note. Northeastern Forest Experiment Station
Forest Prod Pap — Forest Products Paper. Northeastern Forest Experiment Station
Forest Prod Res — Forest Products Research. Department of Scientific and Industrial Research
Forest Prod Res Bull — Forest Products Research Bulletin. Department of Scientific and Industrial Research
Forest Products R — Forest Products Review
Forest Quart — Forestry Quarterly
Forest Res News Midsouth — Forest Research News for the Midsouth
Forestry Abstr — Forestry Abstracts
Forestry Chron — Forestry Chronicle
Forestry Oxford — Forestry. Journal. Society of Foresters of Great Britain (Oxford)
Forestry Res Newsl — Forestry Research Newsletter
Forestry Res Rept Agr Expt Sta Univ Ill — Forestry Research Report. Agricultural Experiment Station. University of Illinois
Forestry Shanghai — Forestry/Hsueeh Lin (Shanghai)
Forestry Tech Paper — Forestry Technical Papers
Forests Bull Sudan — Forests Bulletin. Forests Department. Sudan
Forest Sci — Forest Science
Forest Sci Monogr — Forest Science Monographs
Forest South Africa — Forestry in South Africa
Forest Surv Release Calif — Forest Survey Release. California Forest and Range Experiment Station
Forest Surv Release Cent Sts Forest Exp Stn — Forest Survey Release. Central States Forest Experiment Station
Forest Surv Release Intermtn Forest Range Exp Stn — Forest Survey Release. Intermountain Forest and Range Experiment Station
Forest Surv Release Nth Rocky Mtn Forest Range Exp Stn — Forest Survey Release. Northern Rocky Mountain Forest and Range Experiment Station
Forest Surv Release Rocky Mtn Forest Range Exp Stn — Forest Survey Release. Rocky Mountain Forest and Range Experiment Station
Forest Surv Release SEast Forest Exp Stn — Forest Survey Release. Southeastern Forest Experiment Station
Forest Surv Release Sth Forest Exp Stn — Forest Survey Release. Southern Forest Experiment Station
Forest Surv Rep Pacif NW Forest Range Exp Stn — Forest Survey Report. Pacific Northwest Forest and Range Experiment Station
Forest Timb — Forest and Timber
Forest Treas Cyprus — Forest Treasures of Cyprus
Forest Trees Timb Br Emp — Forest Trees and Timbers of the British Empire
Forest Trees Timbers Brit Empire — Forest Trees and Timbers of the British Empire
Forest Tre Ser For Timb Bur — Forest Tree Series. Forestry and Timber Bureau
Forest Wkr — Forest Worker. US Department of Agriculture
Foret-Conserv — Foret-Conservation
Foret Fr — Foret Francaise, le Bois Francais et les Industries du Bois
Foret Gascogne — Foret de Gascogne. Journal Technique et Scientifique
Foret Queb — Foret Quebecoise
Forets Fr — Forets de France et Action Forestiere
For Exch Bull — Foreign Exchange Bulletin
For Farmer — Forest Farmer
Forfattn MedVas — Forfattningar Angaende Medicinalvasendet
Forfattn Tillv Brannvin — Forfattningar Angaende Tillverkning af Brannvin
For Fire Control Abstr — Forest Fire Control Abstracts
For Fire News For Fire Atmos Sci Res For Serv USDA — Forest Fire News. Forest Fire and Atmospheric Sciences Research. Forest Service. US Department of Agriculture
For Focus — Forest Focus
For For — Forschungen und Fortschritte. Korrenspondenzblatt der Deutschen Wissenschaft und Technik
FORGA — Forages
For Geol Rev Ga — Forestry-Geological Review. Department of Forestry and Geological Development. Georgia
Forg Heat Treat — Forging and Heat Treating
Forg Ind NR — Forging Industry Association's News Release
Forgn Agr — Foreign Agriculture
Forg Stamp Heat Treat — Forging, Stamping, Heat-Treating
Forg Stamping Heat Treat — Forging, Stamping, Heat Treating
Forg Top — Forging Topics
Forh Allm Svenska LakMot — Forhandlingar vid Allmanna Svenska Lakarmotet
Forh Finl Allm LakForb Allm Mote — Forhandlingar vid Finlands Allmanna Lakareforbunds Allmanna Mote
Forh Finska LakSallsk Allm Mote — Forhandlingar vid Finska Lakaresallskapets Allmanna Mote
Forh HalsovFor Stockh Sammank — Forhandlingar vid Halsovardsforeningens i Stockholm Sammankomster
Forh Kirurg Foren Krist Oslo — Forhandlinger i den Kirurgiske Forening Kristiania (Oslo)
Forh K Nor Vidensk Selsk — Forhandlinger det Kongelige Norske Videnskabers Selskab
Forh Med Selsk Krist — Forhandlinger i det Medicinske Selskab i Kristiania

Forh Skanska IngKlubb Kristidsmote — Forhandlingar vid Skanska Ingeniorsklubbens Kristidsmote

Forh Svenska Tek VetenskAkad Finl — Forhandlingar. Svenska Tekniska Vetenskapsakademien i Finland

Forh VidenskSelsk Krist — Forhandlinger i Videnskabsselskabet i Kristiania

FORIAQ — Forest Research in India

For Ind — Forest Industries

For Ind R — Forest Industries Review [*Later, Forest Industries*]

For Ind Rev — Forest Industries Equipment Review

For Ind Sci Technol — Forest Industry Science and Technology

For Indus Rev — Forest Industries Review [*Later, Forest Industries*]

For Inf Nanking — Forestry Information. Forest Research Institute (Nanking)

For Insect Dis Cond US — Forest Insect and Disease Conditions in the United States

For Insect Dis Leafl USDA For Serv — Forest Insect and Disease Leaflet. United States Department of Agriculture. Forest Service

For Inst For GB — Forestry. Institute of Foresters of Great Britain

Forintek Can Corp East For Prod Lab Rev Rep — Forintek Canada Corporation. Eastern Forest Products Laboratory. Review Report

Forintek Can Corp East For Prod Lab Tech Rep — Forintek Canada Corporation. Eastern Forest Products Laboratory. Technical Report

Forintek Can Corp East Lab Spec Publ — Forintek Canada Corporation. Eastern Laboratory. Special Publication

Forintek Can Corp Lab Prod For Est Rap Tech — Forintek Canada Corporation. Laboratoire des Produits Forestiers de l'Est. Rapport Technique

Forintek Can Corp Lab Prod For Est Rev Rep — Forintek Canada Corporation. Laboratoire des Produits Forestiers de l'Est. Review Report

For Int LJ — Fordham International Law Journal

For Investment R — Foreign Investment Review

For Invest Tech Note TVA — Forestry Investigations Technical Note. Tennessee Valley Authority

For Iowas Hlth — For Iowa's Health

For Irrig — Forestry and Irrigation

For J Inst Chart For — Forestry. Journal. Institute of Chartered Foresters

FOR KY Univ Coop Ext Serv — FOR. Kentucky University Cooperative Extension Service

For L — Forum Linguisticum

For Leaves — Forest Leaves

FORLG — Forschungen zur Oberrheinischen Landesgeschichte

For Ling — Forum Linguisticum

For Log — Forestry Log

For LR — Fordham Law Review

Formac Docum Prof — Formacion y Documentacion Profesional. Boletin Oficial de la Direccion General de Ensenanza Profesional y Tecnica

Forma Functio — Forma et Function

Formage Trait Metaux — Formage et Traitements des Metaux

Formage Trait Met Parachevement Assem — Formage et Traitements des Metaux. Parachevement. Assemblage

Form Aggiorn Mat Insegn — Formazione e Aggiornamento in Matematica degli Insegnanti

Formaldehyde Toxicol Epidemiol Mech Pap Meet — Formaldehyde. Toxicology, Epidemiology, Mechanisms. Papers of a Meeting

Formal Methods Syst Des — Formal Methods in System Design

For Manage Bull US Dep Agric For Serv — Forest Management Bulletin. US Department of Agriculture. Forest Service

Format Continue — Formation Continue

Formation Agric Develop Rur — Formation pour l'Agriculture et le Developpement Rural

Formazione Dom — Formazione Domani

For Mgmt Note BC For Serv — Forest Management Note. British Columbia Forest Service

Formica Wld — Formica World

Formirov Celov Kom Obsc — Formirovanie Celovska Kommunisticeskogo Obscestva

Form Kontrol Kach Poverkhn Vod — Formirovanie i Knotrol Kachestva Poverkhnostnykh Vod

Form Math — Forum Mathematicum

Formosan Agric Rev — Formosan Agricultural Review

Formosan Agr Rev — Formosan Agricultural Review

Formosan Sci — Formosan Science

Form Prop Gas Bubbles Conf — Formation and Properties of Gas Bubbles Conference

Forms Ind — Present and Future of the Forms Industry

Form Struct Pap Trans Symp — Formation and Structure of Paper. Transactions. Symposium

Form Tech — Form und Technik

Form Tech Rev — Form Tech Review

Formul A Nouv Remed — Formulaire Annuel des Nouveaux Remedes

Formulario Mat — Formulario Metematico

Formul Electn Mecn — Formulaire de l'Electricien et du Mecanicien

Formul Math — Formulaire de Mathematiques

Formul Medic Nouv — Formulaire des Medicaments Nouveaux

Formul Mens Ther — Formulaire Mensuel de Therapeutique

Formul Spec Pharm — Formulaire des Specialites Pharmaceutiques

Form Wood For Trees Symp — Formation of Wood in Forest Trees. Symposium

Forn — Fornvaennen

Forno Elett — Forno Elettrico

Forno Elettr — Forno Elettrico

For Note Ill Agric Exp Sta — Forestry Note. University of Illinois. Agricultural Experiment Station

For Note Ill Agric Exp Stn Dep For — Forestry Note. Illinois. Agricultural Experiment Station. Department of Forestry

For Notes — Forest Notes. New Hampshire's Conservation Magazine

For Notes Simla — Forestry Notes (Simla)

Fornv — Fornvaennen

Foro Amm — Foro Amministrativo

For Occas Pap — Forestry Occasional Paper

For Occ Pap FAO — Forestry Occasional Paper. FAO

FORODD — Fortschritte der Ophthalmologie

For of Educ — Forum of Education

Foro Int — Foro Internacional

Foro Internac — Foro Internacional

Foro Intern Mex — Foro Internacional (Mexico)

Foro It — Foro Italiano

Foro Nap — Foro Napoletano

Foro Pad — Foro Padano

Foro Pen — Foro Penale

FORP — Forestry Report. Northern Forest Research Centre. Canadian Forestry Service

For Pamph Trin — Forestry Pamphlet. Trinidad and Tobago

For People — Forests and People

For Pest Leafl — Forest Pest Leaflet

For Pest Leafl US For Serv — Forest Pest Leaflet. United States Forest Service

For Pest Manage Inst Rep FPMX Can — Forest Pest Management Institute. Report FPM-X (Canada)

For Plan — Forest Planning

For Pol — Foreign Policy

For Pol Ankara — Foreign Policy (Ankara)

For Policy — Foreign Policy

For Policy Bul — Foreign Policy Bulletin

For Policy Rep — Foreign Policy Reports

For Pol New York — Foreign Policy (New York)

FORPRIDE Dig — FORPRIDE [*Forest Products Research and Industries Development*] Digest

For Prod J — Forest Products Journal

For Prod Lab Bull Oreg — Forest Products Laboratory. Bulletin (Oregon)

For Prod Lab Gen Tech Rep FPL — Forest Products Laboratory. General Technical Report FPL

For Prod Lab Inf Cir — Forest Products Laboratory. Information Circular

For Prod Lab Res Leafl — Forest Products Laboratory. Research Leaflet

For Prod Ne Lett — Forest Products News Letter

For Prod Newsl — Forest Products Newsletter. Commonwealth Scientific and Industrial Research Organisation. Division of Forest Products

For Prod Res — Forest Products Research

For Prod Res Bull (GB) — Forest Products Research Bulletin (Great Britain)

For Prod Res Cent Bull (Oreg) — Forest Products Research Center. Bulletin (Oregon)

For Prod Res Cent Inf Circ (Oreg) — Forest Products Research Center. Information Circular (Oregon)

For Prod Res Dev Inst J — Forest Products Research and Development Institute. Journal

For Prod Residuals Pap Natl Meet AIChE — Forest Products Residuals. Papers. National Meeting. AIChE

For Prod Res Ind Dev Comm Tech Note Philipp — Forest Products Research and Industries Development Commission. Technical Note (Philippines)

For Prod Res Ind Dev Dig — Forest Products Research and Industries Development Digest

For Prod Res Inst Rep (Bogor Indones) — Forest Products Research Institute. Report (Bogor, Indonesia)

For Prod Res No — Forest Products Research Notes. Forest Research Institute

For Prod Res Rec Div For Prod (Zambia) — Forest Products Research Record. Division of Forest Products (Zambia)

For Prod Res Rep Dep For Res (Nigeria) — Forest Products Research Reports. Department of Forest Research (Nigeria)

For Prod Util Tech Rep US For Serv Coop For Div — Forest Products Utilization Technical Report. United States Forest Service. Cooperative Forestry Division

For Publ Civ Conserv Cps — Forestry Publication. Civilian Conservation Corps

For Publ Ohio — Forestry Publication. Ohio Agricultural Experiment Station

For Q — Foreign Quarterly Review

FOR Q — Forestry Quarterly

For Quar — Forest Quarterly

For R — Foreign Review

FORRAJ — Forest Record

For Rec For Comm (Lond) — Forest Record. Forestry Commission (London)

For Rec (Lond) — Forest Record (London)

For Recreat Res — Forest Recreation Research

For Rep R8-FR US Dep Agric For Serv South Reg — Forestry Report R8-FR. US Department of Agriculture. Forest Service. Southern Region

For Repr Un S Afr — Forestry Reprint. Department of Forestry. Union of South Africa

For Res Bull For Dep (Zambia) — Forest Research Bulletin. Forest Department (Zambia)

For Res India — Forest Research in India

For Res Inf Pap Minist Natl Res (Ont) — Forest Research Information Paper. Ministry of Natural Resources (Ontario)

For Res Inst (Bogor) Commun — Forest Research Institute (Bogor). Communication

For Res Note Ont For Res Cent — Forest Research Note. Ontario Forest Research Centre

For Res Notes — Forestry Research Notes

For Res Notes NZ — Forestry Research Notes. Forest Research Institute. New Zealand

For Res Notes Weyerhaeuser Timber Co — Forestry Research Notes. Weyerhaeuser Timber Company

For Res Notes Wis — Forestry Research Notes. Wisconsin University College of Agriculture and Conservation Department

For Res Note Wis Coll Agric — Forestry Research Notes. University of Wisconsin. College of Agriculture

For Resour Environ — Forest Resources and Environment

For Resour Newslett — Forest Resources Newsletter

For Resour Rep US For Serv — Forest Resource Report. United States Forest Service

For Res Pamphl Div For Res (Zambia) — Forest Research Pamphlet. Division of Forest Research (Zambia)

For Res Rep — Forest Resource Report. United States Forest Service

For Res Rep Agric Exp Stn Univ Ill — Forestry Research Report. Agricultural Experiment Station. University of Illinois

For Res Rep Ont Minist Nat Resour — Forest Research Report. Ontario Ministry of Natural Resources

For Res Rev — Forest Research Review. British Columbia Forest Service

For Res Ser SC Agric Exp Stn — Forest Research Series. South Carolina Agricultural Experiment Station

For Res Southeast US Southern For Exp Stn — Forest Research in the Southeast. United States Southeastern Forest Experiment Station

For Res West US Dep Agric For Serv — Forestry Research West. US Department of Agriculture. Forest Service

For Res West US For Serv — Forestry Research West. United States Forest Service

For Res What's New West — Forestry Research. What's New in the West

FORS — Forensic Science Database

Fors — Forsikring

For S Afr — Forestry in South Africa

Forsch Ag Ps — Forschungen auf dem Gebiete der Agrikultur-Physik

ForschArb Geb AzetSchweiss — Forschungsarbeiten auf dem Gebiet der Azetylenschweissung

ForschArb Geb IngWes — Forschungsarbeiten auf dem Gebiet des Ingenieurwesens

ForschArb Geb Schleif Polier — Forschungsarbeiten aus dem Gebiet Schleifen und Polieren

ForschArb Geb Schweiss Schneid Sauerstoff Azet — Forschungsarbeiten auf dem Gebiet des Schweissens und Schneidensmittels Sauerstoff und Azetylen

ForschArb KalzKarb Azet Sauerstoff — Forschungsarbeiten ueber Kalziumkarbid, Azetylen, Sauerstoff und Verwandte Gebiete

Forscharb Ver Dt Ingen — Forschungsarbeiten des Vereins Deutscher Ingenieure

Forsch Berat Forstw — Forschung und Beratung. Forstwirtschaft

Forsch Berat Reihe C — Forschung und Beratung. Reihe C. Wissenschaftliche Berichte und Diskussionsbeitraege

Forsch Ber Evangel Studiengemeinsch — Forschungen und Berichte. Evangelische Studiengemeinschaft

Forsch Ber Staatl Mus Berlin — Forschungen und Berichte. Staatliche Museen zu Berlin

Forsch Brandenburg Preuss Gesch — Forschungen zur Brandenburgischen und Preussischen Geschichte

Forsch D Ld u Volksk — Forschungen zur Deutschen Landes- und Volkskunde

Forsch Dt Landeskde — Forschungen zur Deutschen Landes- und Volkskunde

ForschErgebn Geb Gartenb Eidg VersAnst — Forschungsergebnisse aus dem Gebiet des Gartenbaues Ermittelt von den Eidgenoessischen Versuchsanstalten

ForschErgebn VerkWiss Inst Luftf Stuttg — Forschungsergebnisse. Verkehrswissenschaftliches Institut fuer Luftfahrt. Technische Hochschule

Forsch F — Forschungen und Fortschritte

Forsch Fortschr — Forschungen und Fortschritte

Forsch Fortschr Dtsch Wiss — Forschungen und Fortschritte. Nachrichtenblatt der Deutschen Wissenschaft und Technik

Forsch Fortschritte — Forschungen und Fortschritte

Forsch Geb Ingenieurwes — Forschung auf dem Gebiete des Ingenieurwesens

Forsch Geb Ingenieurwes Ausg B Beil — Forschung auf dem Gebiete des Ingenieurwesens. Ausgabe B. Beilage

Forsch Geb IngWes — Forschung auf dem Gebiet des Ingenieurwesens

Forsch Geb Pflanzenkrankh — Forschungen auf dem Gebiet der Pflanzenkrankheiten

Forsch Geogr Ges — Forschungen. Geographische Gesellschaft in Luebeck

Forsch Gesch Opt — Forschungen zur Geschichte der Optik

Forschgg Dt Geod — Forschungen zur Deutschen Geodaesie

Forschgg Lds u Volkskde — Forschungen der Landes- und Volkskunde

ForschHft Dt ForschInst TextInd Dresd — Forschungshefte des Deutschen Forschungsinstituts fuer Textilindustrie in Dresden

ForschHft ForschInst StrBahnw — Forschungshefte. Forschungsinstitut fuer Strassenbahnwesen

ForschHft Geb Stahlb — Forschungshefte aus dem Gebiet des Stahlbaues

ForschHft Schiffstech — Forschungshefte fuer Schiffstechnik

ForschHft StudGes HoechstspannAnl — Forschungshefte der Studiengesellschaft fuer Hoechstspannungsanlagen

ForschHft Ver Dt Ing — Forschungshefte. Verein Deutscher Ingenieure

Forsch H Schiffst — Forschungshefte fuer Schiffstechnik, Schiffbau, und Schiffsmaschinenbau

Forsch H Stahlbau — Forschungshefte aus dem Gebiete des Stahlbaues

Forschin Ephesos — Forschungen in Ephesos

Forsch Inf — Forschung und Information

Forsch Ing — Forschung auf dem Gebiete des Ingenieurwesens

Forsch Ingenieurw — Forschung im Ingenieurwesen

Forsch Ingenieurwes — Forschung im Ingenieurwesen

Forsch Ingenieurwesen — Forschung in Ingenieurwesen

Forsch Ing Wes — Forschung im Ingenieurwesen

Forsch KA — Forschungen zur Kunstgeschichte und Christlichen Archaeologie

Forsch Klin Lab — Forschung in der Klinik und im Labor

Forsch Komplementarmed Klass Naturheilkd — Forschende Komplementarmedizin und Klassische Naturheilkunde

Forsch Kraftwerkstech Vortr VGB Konf — Forschung in der Kraftwerkstechnik 1990, Vortraege, VGB-Konferenz

Forsch Lauriacum — Forschungen in Lauriacum

Forsch Mater Deutsch Aufklaer Abt III Indices — Forschungen und Materialien zur Deutschen Aufklarung. Abteilung III. Indices

Forsch Mittelalterl Gesch — Forschungen zur Mittelalterlichen Geschichte

Forschn Alkoholfrage — Forschungen zur Alkoholfrage

Forschn Bayer Landesk — Forschungen zur Bayerischen Landeskunde

Forschn Dt Kunstgesch — Forschungen zur Deutschen Kungstgeschichte

Forschn Dt Landes U Volksk — Forschungen zur Deutschen Landes- und Volkskunde

Forschn Forscher Tiroler Aerztesch — Forschungen und Forscher der Tiroler Aerzteschule

Forschn Fortschr — Forschungen und Fortschritte

Forschn Fortschr Lichttech — Forschungen und Fortschritte der Lichttechnik

Forschn Geb AgrikChem Bodenk — Forschungen auf dem Gebiet der Agrikulturchemie und Bodenkunde

Forschn Geb Dt Landw PflSchutzforsch — Forschungen auf dem Gebiet der Deutschen Landwirtschaftlichen Pflanzenschutzforschung

Forschn Geb PflKrankh Berl — Forschungen auf dem Gebiet der Pflanzenkrankheiten (Berlin)

Forschn Geb PflKrankh Tokyo — Forschungen aus dem Gebiet der Pflanzenkrankheiten (Tokyo)

Forschn Geogr Ges Luebeck — Forschungen der Geographischen Gesellschaft in Luebeck

Forschn Gesch Opt — Forschungen zur Geschichte der Optik

Forschn Kristallk — Forschungen zur Kristallkunde

Forschn Metallk — Forschungen zur Metallkunde

Forschn Sozialpsychol Ethnol — Forschungen zur Sozialpsychologie und Ethnologie

Forschn Vor U Fruehgesch — Forschungen zur Vor- und Fruehgeschichte. Karl Marx Universitaet

Forsch Ost Eur G — Forschungen zur Ost Europaeischen Geschichte

Forsch Osteur Gesch — Forschungen zur Osteuropaeischen Geschichte

Forsch Pflanzenkrankh — Forschungen auf dem Gebiet der Pflanzenkrankheiten/ Shokubutsu Byogai Kenkyu

Forsch Pflanzenkrankh Immunitaet Pflanzenr — Forschungen auf dem Gebiet der Pflanzenkrankheiten und der Immunitaet im Pflanzenreich

Forsch Planen Bauen — Forschen, Planen, Bauen

Forsch Stud — Forschung und Studium. Eine Sammlung Mathematischer Monographien

Forsch Tech Innovation — Forschung, Technik, und Innovation

Forsch u Berat — Forschung und Beratung. Forstwirtschaft

Forsch U ErfahrBer Reichsamt WettDienst — Forschungs- und Erfahrungsberichte. Reichsamt fuer Wetterdienst

Forsch u Fortschr — Forschungen und Fortschritte

Forschu Fortschr — Forschungen und Fortschritte. Korrespondenzblatt der Deutschen Wissenschaft und Technik

Forschungsarb Inst Pflanzenoele Proteine Waschmittel Sofia — Forschungsarbeiten. Institut fuer Pflanzenoele, Proteine, und Waschmittel. Sofia

Forschungsarb Pap Zellstoffach — Forschungsarbeiten aus dem Papier und Zellstoffach

Forschungsber Arbeitsgem Innenminist Bundeslaender Arbeitskre — Forschungsbericht. Arbeitsgemeinschaft der Innenministerien der Bundeslaender. Arbeitskreis 5. Unterausschuss Feuerwehrangelegenheiten

Forschungsber Bundesanst Arbeitsschutz Unfallforsch Dortmund — Forschungsbericht. Bundesanstalt fuer Arbeitsschutz und Unfallforschung. Dortmund

Forschungsber Bundesanst Materialpruef — Forschungsbericht. Bundesanstalt fuer Materialpruefung

Forschungsber Bundesminist Bild Wiss Kernforsch — Forschungsbericht. Bundesministerium fuer Bildung und Wissenschaft. Kernforschung

Forschungsber Bundesminist Bild Wiss Weltraumforsch — Forschungsbericht. Bundesministerium fuer Bildung und Wissenschaft. Weltraumforschung

Forschungsber Bundesminist Forsch Technol Hum Arbeitslebens — Forschungsbericht. Bundesministerium fuer Forschung und Technologie. Humanisierung des Arbeitslebens

Forschungsber Bundesminist Forsch Technol Inf Dok — Forschungsbericht. Bundesministerium fuer Forschung und Technologie. Information und Dokumentation

Forschungsber Bundesminist Forsch Technol Kernforsch — Forschungsbericht. Bundesministerium fuer Forschung und Technologie. Kernforschung

Forschungsber Bundesminist Forsch Technol Meeresforsch — Forschungsbericht. Bundesministerium fuer Forschung und Technologie. Meeresforschung

Forschungsber Bundesminist Forsch Technol Weltraumforsch Wel — Forschungsbericht. Bundesministerium fuer Forschung und Technologie. Weltraumforschung/Weltraumtechnologie

Forschungsber Dtsch Forsch Versuchsant Luft-Raumfahrt — Forschungsbericht. Deutsche Forschungs- und Versuchsanstalt fuer Luft- und Raumfahrt

Forschungsber Dtsch Ges Mineraloelwiss Kohlechem — Forschungsbericht. Deutsche Gesellschaft fuer Mineraloelwissenschaft und Kohlechemie

Forschungsber Fachbereich Bauwesen — Forschungsbericht aus dem Fachbereich Bauwesen

Forschungsber Forstl Forschungsanst Muenchen — Forschungsberichte. Forstliche Forschungsanstalt Muenchen

Forschungsber Holz — Forschungsberichte Holz

Forschungsber Inst Zuckerind Berlin — Forschungsbericht. Institut fuer Zuckerindustrie Berlin

Forschungsber Landes Nordrhein-Westfalen — Forschungsberichte des Landes Nordrhein-Westfalen

Forschungsber Wehrmed Bundesminist Verteidigung — Forschungsbericht aus der Wehrmedizin. Bundesministerium der Verteidigung

Forschungsber Wehrtech Bundesminist Verteidigung — Forschungsbericht aus der Wehrtechnik. Bundesministerium der Verteidigung

Forschungsber Wirtsch Verkehrminist Nordrhein-Westfalen — Forschungsberichte des Wirtschafts- und Verkehrsministeriums Nordrhein-Westfalen

Forschungsber Wirtsch Verkehrsminist Nordrhein-Westfalen — Forschungsberichte des Wirtschafts- und Verkehrsministeriums Nordrhein-Westfalen

Forschungsdienst Sonderhft — Forschungsdienst. Sonderhefte

Forschungsges Blechverarb Mitt — Forschungsgesellschaft Blechverarbeitung. Mitteilungen

Forschungsh Dtsch Forsch Inst Textilind Dresden — Forschungsheft des Deutschen Forschungs-Instituts fuer Textilindustrie in Dresden

Forschungsh Geb Stahlbaues — Forschungshefte aus dem Gebiete des Stahlbaues

Forschungsh Studienges Hoechstspannungsanlagen — Forschungshefte. Studiengesellschaft fuer Hoechstspannungsanlagen

Forschungsinst Edelmet Staatl Hoeheren Fachsch Schwaeb Gmuen — Forschungsinstitut fuer Edelmetalle an der Staatlichen Hoeheren Fachschule Schwaebisch Gmuend. Mitteilungen

Forschungsinst FTZ Tech Ber Ger — Forschungsinstitut beim FTZ. Technischer Bericht (Germany)

Forschungskolloq Dtsch Ausschusses Stahlbeton Ber — Forschungskolloquium des Deutschen Ausschusses fuer Stahlbeton. Berichte

Forschungstexte BUFZ — Forschungstexte des BUFZ (Brandenburgisches Umweltforschungszentrum)

Forschungsver Automobiltech Schriftenr — Forschungsvereinigung Automobiltechnik Schriftenreihe

Forschungszent Juelich Spez Ber — Forschungszentrum Juelich. Spezielle Berichte

Forschungszent Karlsruhe Nachr — Forschungszentrum Karlsruhe. Nachrichten

Forschungszent Karlsruhe Wiss Ber — Forschungszentrum Karlsruhe. Wissenschaftliche Berichte

Forschungszent Rossendorf Ber FZR — Forschungszentrum Rossendorf. Bericht FZR

Forsch U Sber Akad Raumforsch Landesplan — Forschungs- und Sitzungsberichte der Akademie fuer Raumforschung und Landesplanung

Forsch Volks Land — Forschungen zur Volks- und Landeskunde

Forsch Vor und Fruehgesch — Forschungen zur Vor- und Fruehgeschichte

Forsch Wiss — Forschung und Wissen

For Sci — Forestry Sciences

For Sci — Forest Science

For Sci Beijing — Forestry Science (Beijing)

For Sci Dordrecht Neth — Forestry Sciences (Dordrecht, Netherlands)

For Sci Intl — Forensic Science International

For Sci Monogr — Forest Science Monographs

For Sci (Sofia) — Forest Science (Sofia)

For Sci Suppl — Forest Science. Supplement

For Ser Chin Am Jt Comm Rur Reconstr — Forestry Series. Chinese-American Joint Committee on Rural Reconstruction

For Ser Pan Am Un — Forestry Series. Pan American Union

For Ser Un S Afr — Forestry Series. Union of South Africa

For Serv Res Note NE Northeast For Exp Stn US Dep Agric — Forest Service Research Note NE. Northeastern Forest Experiment Station. Forest Service. Department of Agriculture

For Serv Res Note NE US — Forest Service Research Note NE (United States)

For Serv Res Pap NE (US) — Forest Service Research Paper NE (United States)

Fors Forsk — Forsog och Forskning

Forsk Fors Landbr — Forskning og Forsok i Landbruket

Forsk Fors Landbruket — Forskning og Forsok i Landbruket

Forsk Framsteg — Forskning och Framsteg

Forsk Groenl — Forskning i Groenland

Forskningsrapp Statens Tek Forskningscent — Forskningsrapporter. Statens Tekniska Forskningscentral

Forsk O ForsResult — Forsknings- och Forsogsresultat

Forsk Samf — Forskningen og Samfundet

Forsk Tek Helsinki — Forskning och Teknik (Helskini)

Forsk Udvikling Uddannelse — Forskning Udvikling Uddannelse

ForsMeld Landbrtek Inst Vollebekk — Forsoksmelding. Landbruksteknisk Instituut. Vollebekk

For Social Agric Sci — For Socialist Agricultural Science

For Soil Relat North Am Pap North Am For Soils Conf — Forest-Soil Relationships in North America. Papers Presented at the North American Forest Soils Conference

For Soils For Land Manage Proc North Am For Soils Conf — Forest Soils and Forest Land Management. Proceedings. North American Forest Soils Conference

For Soils Jpn — Forest Soils of Japan

For Soils Land Use Proc North Am For Soils Conf — Forest Soils and Land Use. Proceedings. North American Forest Soils Conference

Forsokmeld Landbrukstek Inst — Forsoksmelding. Landbruksteknisk Institutt

Forst Arch Erweit Forst Jagd Wiss — Forst-Archiv zur Erweiterung der Forst- und Jagd-Wissenschaft und der Forst- und Jagd-Literatur

Forst Bl — Forstliche Blaetter

Forst Flugbl — Forstliche Flugblaetter

Forst Forsogvaes Dan — Forstlige Forsogsvaesen i Danmark

Forst ForsVaes Danm — Forstlige Forsoksvaesen i Danmark

Forst Fv — Det Forstlige Forsogsvaesen i Danmark

Forst Holz — Forst und Holz

Forst Holzwirt — Forst- und Holzwirt

Forst J — Forst-Journal

Forst Jagd — Forst und Jagd

Forst Jber — Forstlicher Jahresbericht

Forstl Bundesversuchsanst — Forstliche Bundesversuchsanstalt

Forstl Bundesversuchsanst Mariabrunn Mitt — Forstliche Bundesversuchsanstalt Mariabrunn. Mitteilungen

Forstl Bundesversuchsanst Wein Mitt — Forstliche Bundesversuchsanstalt Wein. Mitteilungen

Forstl Bundesversuchsanst (Wien) Jahresber — Forstliche Bundesversuchsanstalt (Wien). Jahresbericht

Forstl Forschungsanst Muenchen Forschungsber — Forstliche Forschungsanstalt Muenchen. Forschungsberichte

Forstl Forschungsberichte Muenchen — Forstliche Forschungsberichte Muenchen

Forstl Forsogsvaes Dan — Forstlige Forsogsvaesen i Danmark

Forstl Forsogsv Danm — Forstlige Forsogsvaesen i Danmark

Forstl Mitt — Forstliche Mitteilungen

Forstl Naturwiss Z — Forstlich-Naturwissenschaftliche Zeitschrift

Forst Rdsch — Forstliche Rundschau der Zeitschrift fuer Weltforstwirtschaft

Forstschutz-Merkbl — Forstschutz-Merkblaetter

Forsttech Inf — Forsttechnische Informationen

Forsttech Inform — Forsttechnische Informationen

Forst Tidskr — Forstlig Tidskrift

Forst Tidsskr — Forstligt Tidsskrift

Forst- u Holzw — Forst- und Holzwirt

Forst Umsch — Forstliche Umschau

Forstw Centbl — Forstwirtschaftliches Centralblatt

Forstw Holzw — Forstwirtschaft, Holzwirtschaft

Forstwirtsch Holzwirtsch — Forstwirtschaft Holzwirtschaft

Forstwiss Cbl — Forstwissenschaftliches Centralblatt

Forstwiss Centralbl (Hamb) — Forstwissenschaftliches Centralblatt (Hamburg)

Forstwiss Forsch — Forstwissenschaftliche Forschungen

Forstwiss Forsch Beih Forstwiss Centralbl — Forstwissenschaftliche Forschungen. Beihefte zum Forstwissenschaftlichen Centralblatt

Forstwiss Mitt — Forstwissenschaftliche Mitteilungen

Forstwiss Zbl — Forstwissenschaftliches Centralblatt

Forstwiss Zentbl — Forstwissenschaftliches Zentralblatt

Forstwiss Zentralbl — Forstwissenschaftliches Zentralblatt

Forstw Prax — Forstwirtschaftliche Praxis

Forst Wschr Silva — Forstliche Wochenschrift Silva

Fors u Fort — Forschungen und Fortschritte

For Surv Note BC For Serv — Forest Survey Notes. British Columbia Forest Service

Forsv ForsknInsts Arb — Forsvarets Forskningsinstitutts Arbok

FORTA — Fortune

For Tax L S-W Bull — Foreign Tax Law Semi-Weekly Bulletin

For Tax LS Weekly Bull — Foreign Tax Law Semi-Weekly Bulletin

For Tax LW Bull — Foreign Tax Law Weekly Bulletin

Fortbildungskurse Rheumatol — Fortbildungskurse fuer Rheumatologie

Fortbildungskurse Schweiz Ges Psychiatr — Fortbildungskurse. Schweizerische Gesellschaft fuer Psychiatrie

Fort Collins Int Hydrol Symp Proc — Fort Collins International Hydrology Symposium. Proceedings

Fort Dodge Bio-Chem Rev — Fort Dodge Bio-Chemic Review

Fort Dunlop News Lett — Fort Dunlop News Letter

For Tech Note NH Agric Exp Sta — Forestry Technical Notes. University of New Hampshire. Agricultural Experiment Station

For Tech Notes — Forestry Technical Notes. East African Forestry Department

For Tech Pap — Forestry Technical Papers

For Tech Pap For Comm Vict — Forestry Technical Papers. Forests Commission of Victoria

For Tech Publ Can For Serv — Forestry Technical Publication (Canadian Forestry Service)

For Tech Rep (Can For Serv) — Forestry Technical Report (Canadian Forestry Service)

Forteckn Chalmers Tek Hogsk Biblthk — Forteckning over Chalmers Tekniska Hogskolans Bibliothek

Forteckn Finl Pat — Forteckning ofver i Finland gallande Patent

Forteckn Svenska Lak Vet Tandlak — Forteckning pa Svenska Lakare, Veterinarer och Tandlakare

Forteckn Svenska VattkraftFor Ledamot — Forteckning over Svenska Vattenkraftforeningens Ledamoter

Forteckn Sver VattFall — Forteckning over Sveriges Vatterfall

Fortgesetzte Nachr Wiss Kuenste Koenigl Daen Reichen Laendern — Fortgesetzte Nachrichten von dem Zustande der Wissenschaften und Kuenste in denKoeniglich Daenischen Reichen und Laendern

Fort Hare Pap — Fort Hare Papers

Fort Hays Stud New Ser Sci Ser — Fort Hays Studies. New Series. Science Series

Forthcoming Int Sci & Tech Conf — Forthcoming International Scientific and Technical Conference

For the Riverina Teach — For the Riverina Teacher

Forth Nat Hist — Forth Naturalist and Historian

For Timb — Forest and Timber

For Timber — Forest and Timber

Fort LJ — Fortnightly Law Journal

Fortn — Fortnightly Review

Fortnightly LJ — Fortnightly Law Journal

Fortn LJ — Fortnightly Law Journal

Fortn L J — Fortnightly Law Journal [*Toronto*]

FortnR — Fortnightly Review

Fortn Rev — Fortnightly Review

Fortn Rev Chicago Dent Soc — Fortnightly Review of the Chicago Dental Society

Fortn Rev Chic Dent Soc — Fortnightly Review of the Chicago Dental Society

Fortn Rev St Louis — Fortnightly Review (St. Louis, Missouri)

Fortn R London — Fortnightly Review (London)

For Topic Ser — Forestry Topic Series. Forest Service. Canada

Fortpflanz Besamung Aufzucht Haustiere — Fortpflanzung Besamung und Aufzucht der Haustiere

Fortpflanz Zuchthyg Haustierbesamung — Fortpflanzung, Zuchthygiene, und Haustierbesamung

Fortpfl Besam Haustiere — Fortpflanzung und Besamung der Haustiere

Fortpfl Zuchthyg Haustierbesam — Fortpflanzung, Zuchthygiene und Haustierbesamung

Fort Pierce ARC Res Rep FTP Univ Fla Agric Res Cent — Fort Pierce ARC Research Report FTP. University of Florida. Agricultural Research Center

Fort Pierce ARC Res Rep R1 Univ Fla Agric Res Cent — Fort Pierce ARC Research Report R1. University of Florida. Agricultural Research Center

FortR — Fortnightly Review

For Trade Rev — Foreign Trade Review

For Tree Improv — Forest Tree Improvement

For Tree Ser Div For Res CSIRO — Forest Tree Series. Division of Forest Research. Commonwealth Scientific and Industrial Research Organisation

Fort Rev — Fortnightly Review

Fortsch-Ber VDI Z Reihe — Fortschritt-Berichte. VDI [*Verein Deutscher Ingenieure*] Zeitschriften. Reihe

Fortsch Klin Pharmakol — Fortschritte der Klinischen Pharmakologie

Fortsch Min — Fortschritte der Mineralogie

Fortsch Ophthalmol — Fortschritte der Ophthalmologie

Fortschr Abfallwirtsch Abfalltech Kolloq — Fortschritte in der Abfallwirtschaft. Abfalltechnisches Kolloquium

Fortschr Acker Pflanzenb — Fortschritte im Acker- und Pflanzenbau

Fortschr Acker- Pflanzenbau — Fortschritte im Acker- und Pflanzenbau

Fortschr Akus Plenarvortr Kurzref Tag Dtsch Arbeitsgem Akust — Fortschritte der Akustik. Plenarvortraege und Kurzreferate der Tagung der Deutschen Arbeitsgemeinschaft fuer Akustik

Fortschr Allergiel — Fortschritte der Allergielehre

Fortschr Androl — Fortschritte der Andrologie

Fortschr Angew Radioisotopie — Fortschritte der Angewandten Radioisotopie und Grenzgebiete

Fortschr Anorg Chem Ind — Fortschritte in der Anorganisch Chemischen Industrie

Fortschr Antimikrob Antineoplast Chemother — Fortschritte der Antimikrobiellen und Antineoplastischen Chemotherapie

Fortschr Anwend Flockungsverfahren Abwassertechnol Verfahren — Fortschritte bei der Anwendung von Flockungsverfahren in der Abwassertechnologie. Verfahrenstechnisches Seminar

Fortschr Arzneimittelforsch — Fortschritte der Arzneimittelforschung

Fortschr ArzneimittForsch — Fortschritte der Arzneimittelforschung

Fortschr Arzneimittelforsch Gesamtkongr Dtsch Pharm Wiss — Fortschritte in der Arznelmittelforschung. Gesamtkongress der Deutschen Pharmazeutischen Wissenschaften

Fortschr Astr — Fortschritte der Astronomie

Fortschr Atomspektrom Spurenanal — Fortschritte in der Atomspektrometrischen Spurenanalytik

Fortschr Augenheilk — Fortschritte der Augenheilkunde

Fortschr Augenheilkd — Fortschritte der Augenheilkunde

Fortschr BeleuchtWes Gasind — Fortschritte des Beleuchtungswesens und der Gasindustrie

FortschrBer ChemZtg — Fortschrittsberichte der Chemiker-Zeitung

Fortschrber Landw — Fortschrittsberichte fuer die Landwirtschaft

Fortschr Ber VDI Reihe 3 — Fortschritt-Berichte VDI. Reihe 3. Verfahrenstechnik

Fortschr Ber VDI Reihe 6 — Fortschritt - Berichte VDI. Reihe 6. Energietechnik

Fortschr Ber VDI Reihe 7 — Fortschritt - Berichte VDI. Reihe 7. Stroemungstechnik

Fortschr Ber VDI Reihe 8 — Fortschritt - Berichte VDI. Reihe 8. Mess-, Steuerungs-, und Regelungstechnik

Fortschr Ber VDI Reihe 9 — Fortschritt - Berichte VDI. Reihe 9. Elektronik

Fortschr Ber VDI Reihe 15 — Fortschritt-Berichte VDI. Reihe 15. Umwelttechnik

Fortschr Ber VDI Reihe 17 — Fortschritt-Berichte VDI. Reihe 17. Biotechnik

Fortschr Ber VDI Reihe 19 — Fortschritt-Berichte VDI. Reihe 19. Waermetechnik/ Kaeltetechnik

Fortschr Ber VDI Reihe 21 — Fortschritt-Berichte VDI. Reihe 21. Elektrotechnik

Fortschr Ber VDI Z — Fortschritt-Berichte. VDI [*Verein Deutscher Ingenieure*] Zeitschriften

Fortschr Ber VDI Zeitschr Reihe 2 — Fortschritt-Berichte. VDI [*Verein Deutscher Ingenieure*] Zeitschriften. Reihe 2

Fortschr-Ber VDI Z Reihe 4 — Fortschritt-Berichte. VDI [*Verein Deutscher Ingenieure*] Zeitschriften. Reihe 4. Bauingenieurwesen

Fortschr Ber VDI Z Reihe 5 — Fortschritt-Berichte der VDI Zeitschriften. Reihe 5. Grund- und Werkstoffe

Fortschr Betriebsfuehr Industr Engin — Fortschrittliche Betriebsfuehrung und Industrial Engineering

Fortschr Bot — Fortschritte der Botanik

Fortschr Bot Berl — Fortschritte der Botanik (Berlin)

Fortschr Chem Forsch — Fortschritte der Chemischen Forschung

Fortschr Chem Moscow — Fortschritte der Chemie (Moscow)

Fortschr Chem Org Natr — Fortschrltte der Chemie Organischer Naturstoffe

Fortschr Chem Org Natstoffe — Fortschritte der Chemie Organischer Naturstoffe

Fortschr Chem Org Naturst — Fortschritte der Chemie Organischer Naturstoffe

Fortschr Chem Org Naturst Prog Chem Org Nat Prod — Fortschritte der Chemie Organischer Naturstoffe (Progress in the Chemistry of Organic Natural Products)

Fortschr Chem Phys Phys Chem — Fortschritte der Chemie, Physik, und Physikalischen Chemie

Fortschr Chromatogr Methoden Ihre Anwend Klin Biochem — Fortschritte Chromatografischer Methoden und Ihre Anwendung in der Klinischen Biochemie Symposion Chromatografie in der Klinischen Biochemie

Fortschr Diabetesforsch Symp — Fortschritte der Diabetesforschung. Symposion

Fortschr Diagn Ther Urol Tumoren Onkol Semin — Fortschritte in Diagnostik und Therapie Urologischer Tumoren. Onkologisches Seminar

Fortschr Diag Ther Primaeren Glaukoms Hauptref Essener Fortb — Fortschritte in der Diagnostik und Therapie des Primaeren Glaukoms. Hauptreferate der Essener Fortbildung fuer Augenaerzte

Fortschr D Med — Fortschritte der Medizin

Fortschr D Neurol Psychiat — Fortschritte der Neurologie, Psychiatrie, und ihrer Grenzgebiete

Fortschr D Zahnh — Fortschritte der Zahnheilkunde

Fortschr Elektrotech — Fortschritte der Elektrotechnik

Fortschr Erbpath Rassenhyg — Fortschritte der Erbpathologie, Rassenhygiene, und ihrer Grenzgebiete

Fortschr Evolutionsforsch — Fortschritte der Evolutionsforschung

Fortschr Exp Theor Biophys — Fortschritte der Experimentellen und Theoretischen Biophysik

Fortschr Exp Tumorforsch — Fortschritte der Experimentellen Tumorforschung

Fortschr FernsprTech — Fortschritte der Fernsprech-Technik

Fortschr Funktech — Fortschritte der Funktechnik und ihrer Grenzgebiete

Fortschr Geb Roentgenstr — Fortschritte auf dem Gebiete der Roentgenstrahlen

Fortschr Geb Roentgenstrahlen — Fortschritte auf dem Gebiete der Roentgenstrahlen

Fortschr Geb Roentgenstr Nuklearmed — Fortschritte auf dem Gebiete der Roentgenstrahlen und der Nuklearmedizin

Fortschr Geb Roentgenstr Ver Roentgenprax — Fortschritte auf dem Gebiete der Roentgenstrahlen Vereinigt mit Roentgenpraxis

Fortschr Geb RoentgStrahl — Fortschritte auf dem Gebiete der Roentgenstrahlen

Fortschr Geb Roentgstrahl NuklMed — Fortschritte auf dem Gebiete der Roentgenstrahlen und der Nuklearmedizin

Fortschr Geburtshilfe Gynaekol — Fortschritte der Geburtshilfe und Gynaekologie

Fortschr Geol Palaeont — Fortschritte der Geologie und Palaeontologie

Fortschr Geol Rheinland Westfalen — Fortschritte in der Geologie von Rheinland und Westfalen

Fortschr Geol Rheinld Westf — Fortschritte in der Geologie von Rheinland und Westfalen

Fortschr Geol Rheinl Westfalen — Fortschritte in der Geologie von Rheinland und Westfalen

Fortschr GesundhFuers — Fortschritte der Gesundheitsfuersorge

Fortschr Haematol — Fortschritte der Haematologie

Fortschr Hals- Nasen Ohrenheilkd — Fortschritte der Hals- Nasen- Ohrenheilkunde

Fortschr Heilstoffchem — Fortschritte der Heilstoffchemie

Fortschr HochfreqTech — Fortschritte der Hochfrequenztechnik

Fortschr Hochpolym-Forsch — Fortschritte der Hochpolymeren-Forschung

Fortschr HochspannTech — Fortschritte der Hochspannungstechnik

Fortschr ImmunForsch — Fortschritte der Immunitaetsforschung

Fortschr Immunitaetsforsch — Fortschritte der Immunitaetsforschung

Fortschr IngWiss — Fortschritte der Ingenieurwissenschaften

Fortschritt Ber VDI Zeitschrift Reihe 11 — Fortschritt-Berichte. VDI [*Verein Deutscher Ingenieure*] Zeitschriften. Reihe 11

Fortschritt Ber VDI Zeitschr Reihe 8 — Fortschritt-Berichte. VDI [*Verein Deutscher Ingenieure*] Zeitschriften. Reihe 8

Fortschrittl Landw — Fortschrittliche Landwirt

Fortschrittsber Chem Ztg — Fortschrittsberichte der Chemiker-Zeitung

Fortschrittsber Dtsch Keram Ges — Fortschrittsberichte der Deutschen Keramischen Gesellschaft

Fortschrittsber Kolloide Polym — Fortschrittsberichte ueber Kolloide und Polymere

Fortschrittsber Landwirtsch — Fortschrittsberichte fuer die Landwirtschaft

Fortschrittsber Landwirtsch Nahrungsgueterwirtsch — Fortschrittsberichte fuer die Landwirtschaft und Nahrungsgueterwirtschaft

Fortschrittsber Lebensmitteltechnol — Fortschrittsberichte Lebensmitteltechnologie

Fortschr Kardiol — Fortschritte der Kardiologie

Fortschr Kiefer Gesichtschir — Fortschritte der Kiefer und Geschichts Chirurgie

Fortschr Kieferorthop — Fortschritte der Kieferorthopaedie

Fortschr Kiefer U Gesichts Chir — Fortschritte der Kiefer- und Gesichts-Chirurgie

Fortschr Klin Pharmakol — Fortschritte der Klinischen Pharmakologie

Fortschr Krebsforsch — Fortschritte der Krebsforschung

Fortschr Landw Berl — Fortschritte der Landwirtschaft (Berlin)

Fortschr Landwirtsch — Fortschritte der Landwirtschaft

Fortschr Landw Wien — Fortschritte der Landwirtschaft (Wien)

Fortschr Luftf — Fortschritte der Luftfahrt

Fortschr Luftf Flugtech — Fortschritte in Luftfahrt und Flugtechnik

Fortschr Math — Fortschritte der Mathematik

Fortschr Math Wiss Monogr — Fortschritte der Mathematischen Wissenschaften in Monographien

Fortschr Med — Fortschritte der Medizin

Fortschr Med Mikrobiol — Fortschritte der Medizinischen Mikrobiologie

Fortschr Med Monogr — Fortschritte der Medizin. Monographie

Fortschr Med Suppl — Fortschritte der Medizin. Supplement

Fortschr Med Virusforsch — Fortschritte der Medizinischen Virusforschung

Fortschr Metallogr Ber Int Metallogr Tag — Fortschritte in der Metallographie. Berichte der Internationalen Metallographie-Tagung

Fortschr Miner — Fortschritto der Mineralogie

Fortschr Mineral — Fortschritte der Mineralogie

Fortschr Mineral Beihe — Fortschritte der Mineralogie. Beiheft

Fortschr Mineral Kristallogr Petrogr — Fortschritte der Mineralogie, Kristallographie, und Petrographie

Fortschr Miner Beih — Fortschritte der Mineralogie. Beiheft

Fortschr Miner Kristallogr Petrogr — Fortschritte der Mineralogie, Kristallographie, und Petrographie

Fortschr Naturw Forsch — Fortschritte der Naturwissenschaftlichen Forschung

Fortschr Neurol Psychiat — Fortschritte der Neurologie und Psychiatrie und ihrer Grenzgebiete

Fortschr Neurol Psychiatr — Fortschritte der Neurologie-Psychiatrie

Fortschr Neurol Psychiatr — Fortschritte der Neurologie, Psychiatrie, und Ihrer Grenzgebiete

Fortschr Neurol Psychiatr Grenzgeb — Fortschritte der Neurologie, Psychiatrie, und Ihrer Grenzgebiete

Fortschr Neurol Psychiatr Ihrer Grenzgeb — Fortschritte der Neurologie, Psychiatrie, und Ihrer Grenzgebiete

Fortschr Onkol — Fortschritte der Onkologie

Fortschr Ophthalmol — Fortschritte der Ophthalmologie

Fortschr Organother — Fortschritte der Organotherapie

Fortschr Orthod — Fortschritte der Orthodontik

Fortschr Palaeont — Fortschritte der Palaeontologie

Fortschr Pflanzenzucht — Fortschritte der Pflanzenzuechtung

Fortschr Ph — Fortschritte der Physik

Fortschr Photokop — Fortschritte der Photokopie

Fortschr Phys — Fortschritte der Physik

Fortschr Phys Chem — Fortschritte der Physikalischen Chemie

Fortschr Phys Dtsche Phys Ges — Fortschritte der Physik. Deutsche Physikalische Gesellschaft

Fortschr Physik — Fortschritte der Physik
Fortschr Phys Sonderb — Fortschritte det Physik. Sonderband
Fortschr Phys Wiss Moscow — Fortschritte der Physikalischen Wissenschaften (Moscow)
Fortschr Prakt Geol Bergw — Fortschritte der Praktischen Geologie und Bergwirtschaft
Fortschr Psychosom Med — Fortschritte der Psychosomatischen Medizin
Fortschr Rheumatol Kongressband Tag Dtsch Ges Rheumatol — Fortschritte der Rheumatologie. Kongressband der Tagung der Deutschen Gesellschaft fuer Rheumatologie Gemeinsam mit der Schweizerischen Gesellschaft fuer Rheumatologie
Fortschr Roentgenstrahlen — Fortschritte auf dem Gebiet der Roentgenstrahlen
Fortschr Strahlenschutz — Fortschritte im Strahlenschutz
Fortschr Strukturforsch Beugungsmethoden — Fortschritte der Strukturforschung mit Beugungsmethoden
Fortschr Teerfarbenfabr Verw Industriezweige — Fortschritte der Teerfarbenfabrikation und Verwandter Industriezweige
Fortschr Ther — Fortschritte der Therapie
Fortschr Tierphysiol Tierernaehr — Fortschritte in der Tierphysiologie und Tierernaehrung
Fortschr Tuberkuloseforsch — Fortschritte der Tuberkuloseforschung
Fortschr Verfahrenstech — Fortschritte der Verfahrenstechnik
Fortschr Verfahrenstech Abt A — Fortschritte der Verfahrenstechnik Abteilung A. Grundlagen der Verfahrenstechnik
Fortschr Verfahrenstech Abt B — Fortschritte der Verfahrenstechnik Abteilung B. Mechanische Verfahrenstechnik
Fortschr Verfahrenstech Abt C — Fortschritte der Verfahrenstechnik. Abteilung C. Thermische Verfahrenstechnik
Fortschr Verfahrenstech Abt D — Fortschritte der Verfahrenstechnik. Abteilung D. Reaktionstechnik
Fortschr Verfahrenstech Abt E — Fortschritte der Verfahrenstechnik. Abteilung E. Planung und Betreib von Anlagen
Fortschr Verhaltensforsch — Fortschritte der Verhaltensforschung
Fortschr Veterinaermed — Fortschritte der Veterinaermedizin
Fortschr Wasserchem Ihrer Grenzgeb — Fortschritte der Wasserchemie und Ihrer Grenzgebiete
Fortschr Wasserchem Ihrer Grenzgebie — Fortschritte der Wasserchemie und Ihrer Grenzgebiete
Fortschr Zool — Fortschritte der Zoologie
Fortschr Zool Syst Evolutionsforsch — Fortschritte in der Zoologischen Systematik und Evolutionsforschung
Fortuna Ital — Fortuna Italiana
Fortune Sp — Fortune Special Issue. Investor's Guide
Fort Wayne Med J Mag — Fort Wayne Medical Journal-Magazine
Forum — Forum: Bench and Bar Review
Forum — Forum for the Discussion of New Trends in Education
Forum — Forum Law Review
Forum — International Trade Forum
Forum Appl Biotechnol — Forum for Applied Biotechnology
Forum Archit — Forum voor Architectuur
Forum Archit & Daarme Verbond Kst — Forum voor Architectuur en Daarme Verbonden Kunsten
Forum Brau Beil — Forum der Brauerei. Beilage
Forum Disc New Trends Educ — Forum for the Discussion of New Trends in Education
Forum Ed — Forum of Education
Forum Educ — Forum of Education
Forum Ekon Tek — Forum foer Ekonomi och Teknik
Forum Geol Ind Miner Proc — Forum on Geology of Industrial Minerals. Proceedings
ForumH — Forum (Houston)
Forum It — Forum Italicum
Forum Lett — Forum der Letteren
Forum LR — Forum Law Review
Forum M — Forum Musicum
Forum Med — Forum on Medicine
Forum Med Engl Ed — Forum Medicum (English Edition)
Forum Med Istanb — Forum Medicum (Istanbul)
Forum Microbiol — Forum Microbiologicum
Forum Mikrobiol — Forum Mikrobiologie
Forum Mod L — Forum for Modern Language Studies
Forum Nav — Forum Navale
Forum Pept — Forum on Peptides
Forum Pub Aff — Forum on Public Affairs
Forum Rep Atom Ind Forum — Forum Reports. Atomic Industrial Forum, Inc.
Forum Rep Sci Ind Forum Aust Acad Sci — Australian Academy of Science. Science and Industry Forum. Forum Report
Forum Rep Sci Ind Forum Aust Acad Sci — Forum Report. Science and Industry Forum. Australian Academy of Science
Forum Rev — Forum Law Review
ForumS — Forum: A Ukrainian Review (Scranton, Pennsylvania)
Forum Sekolah Pasca Sarjana Inst Pertanian Bogor — Forum Sekolah Pasca Sarjana Institut Pertanian Bogor
Forum Sol Int — Forum Solaire International
Forum Staedte Hyg — Forum Staedte Hygiene
Forum Stress Schlafforsch — Forum Stress- und Schlafforschung
Forum Theol — Forum Theologicum
Forum Umwelt Hyg — Forum Umwelt Hygiene
Forum Umw Hyg — Forum Umwelt Hygiene
ForumZ — Forum (Zagreb)
For Urb LJ — Fordham Urban Law Journal
ForV — Forces Vives
For V — Fortids Veje
Forw L — Forwood Lectures
Forze Sanit — Forze Sanitarie

FOSCAD — Forest Science
FOSCAN — Food News Scanning Database
FOSCDG — Food Science
Foseco Dev — Foseco Developments
Foseco Fndry Dev — Foseco Foundry Developments
Foseco Fndry Pract — Foseco Foundry Practice
Fosfornaya Promst — Fosfornaya Promyshlennost
Fosfororg Soedin Polim — Fosfororganicheskie Soedineniya i Polimery
FOSMA9 — Forest Science Monographs
Fossil Mammals Afr — Fossil Mammals of Africa
Foster Mo Ref — Foster's Monthly Reference Lists
FOSZAE — Fogorvosi Szemle
FOT — Fortune
Fotcent Bildtidn — Fotograficentrums Bildtidning
FOTEAO — Food Technology
Fot Film — Foto-Film
FOTIB3 — Forest and Timber
Fot It — Fotografia Italiana
Fot Lyubitel — Fotograf Lyubitel
Foto — Foto Smalfilm
Fot Obzor — Fotograficky Obzor
Fotoelektr Opt Yavleniya Poluprovodn Tr Vses Soveshch — Fotoelektricheskie i Opticheskie Yavleniya v Poluprovodnikakh. Trudy Vsesoyuznogo Soveshchaniya po Fotoelektricheskim i Opticheskim Yavleniyam v Poluprovodnikakh
Fotogr Ind — Fotographische Industrie
Fotogr Italiana — Fotografia Italiana
Fotogr Obz — Fotograficky Obzor
Fotogr Pol — Fotograf Polski
Fotogr Rdsch Mitt — Fotografische Rundschau und Mitteilungen
Fotokem Ind — Fotokemijska Industrija
Fotokhim Prom — Fotokhimicheskaya Promyshlennost
Fotokhim Protsessy Regist Gologramm Mater Vses Semin — Fotokhimicheskie Protsessy Registratsii Gologramm. Materialy Vsesoyuznogo Seminara Fotokhimicheskie Protsessy Registatsii Gologramm
Foto Kino Khim Prom — Foto-kino-khimicheskaya Promyshlennost'
Fotokinokhim Promst — Fotokinokhimicheskaya Promyshlennost
Foto Kino Tech — Foto-Kino-Technik
Foto Mag — Foto Magazin
Fototech Rdsch Wiss Prax — Fototechnische Rundschau in Wissenschaft und Praxis
FOTS — Foreign Office Treaty Series
FOU — Foundation
Fou — Foundations
Fouling Enhancement Interact Natl Heat Transfer Conf — Fouling and Enhancement Interactions. National Heat Transfer Conference
Foun — Foundations
FOUNA — Foundry
Foundations Semiotics — Foundations of Semiotics
Found Biotech Ind Ferment Res — Foundation for Biotechnical and Industrial Fermentation Research
Found Biotech Ind Ferment Res Publ — Foundation for Biotechnical and Industrial Fermentation Research. Publication
Found Comm — Foundations of Communications
Found Comput Decision Sci — Foundations of Computing and Decision Sciences
Found Comput Sci — Foundations of Computer Science
Found Comput Ser — Foundations of Computing Series
Found Control Eng — Foundations of Control Engineering
Founder Meml Lect — Founder Memorial Lecture
Found Facts — Foundation Facts
Found Fundam Res Matter Yearb — Foundation for Fundamental Research on Matter. Yearbook
Found Inst Nucl Res Yearb — Foundation Institute for Nuclear Research. Yearbook
Found Lang — Foundations of Language
Found Language — International Journal of Language and Philosophy. Foundations of Language
Found Lib Inform Sci — Foundations in Library and Information Science
Found Life Sci Symp — Foundation for Life Sciences. Symposium
Found Mater Res Sea Rep — Foundation for Materials Research in the Sea. Report
Found News — Foundation News
Found Philos Sci Tech Ser — Foundations and Philosophy of Science and Technology Series
Found Phys — Foundations of Physics
Found Phys Lett — Foundations of Physics Letters
Foundry Ind — Foundry Industry
Foundry Int — Foundry International
Foundry Manage Technol — Foundry Management and Technology
Foundry Met Treat — Foundry and Metal Treating
Foundry Pract — Foundry Practice
Foundry Processes Moulding Mater Proc Annu Conf Br Steel Cas — Foundry Processes and Moulding Materials. Proceedings. Annual Conference. British Steel Castings Research Association
Foundry Shenyang Peoples Repub China — Foundry (Shenyang, People's Republic of China)
Foundry Trade J — Foundry Trade Journal
Foundry Weld Prod Eng J — Foundry. Welding. Production Engineering Journal
Found Sci Research Surinam and Netherlands Antilles Pub — Foundation for Scientific Research in Surinam and the Netherlands Antilles. Publication
Found Space Biol Med — Foundations of Space Biology and Medicine
Found Trade J — Foundry Trade Journal
Four Corners Geol Soc Bull — Four Corners Geological Society. Bulletin
Four Corners Geol Soc Field Conf Guideb — Four Corners Geological Society. Field Conference. Guidebook

Four Qt — Four Quarters
Four Quart — Four Quarters
Fourrages Actual — Fourrages Actualites
FOUVAC — Folia Universitaria Cochabamba
F o V — Folk og Vaern
FOV — Visserijnieuws
FOWJ — Foothills Wilderness Journal
Fowlers Elect Engrs Pock Bk — Fowler's Electrical Engineers' Pocket Book
Fowlers Mech Engrs Pock Bk — Fowler's Mechanical Engineer's Pocket Book
Fowlers Mech Mach Pock Bk — Fowler's Mechanics' and Machinists' Pocket Book
FOX — Focus
Fox Breeders Gaz — Fox Breeders Gazette
Fox Chase Cancer Cent Sci Rep — Fox Chase Cancer Center. Scientific Report
FOYB — Foothills Yukon Bulletin
Foyer Agric Bel Abbes — Foyer Agricole Bel-Abbesien
Foyer Med — Foyer Medical
Foyer Med N — Foyer Medical du Nord
FOZODJ — Folia Zoologica
FP — Filoil Pipeline
FP — Filoloski Pregled
FP — Financial Post Magazine
FPA Jl — F.P.A. (Fire Protection Association) Journal
FP & E — Food Products and Equipment
FPARA9 — Folia Parasitologica
FPB — Foreign Policy Bulletin
FPE — Financial Practice and Education
FPEL — Fragmenta Poetarum Latinorum Epicorum et Lyricorum Praeter Ennium et Lucilium post A. Baehrens
FPG — Fragmenta Philosophorum Graecorum
FPGPAX — Family Planning Perspectives
F Phon — Folia Phoniatrica
FPJOAB — Forest Products Journal
FPK — Processed Prepared Food
FPL — Financial Planning
FPL — Fragmenta Poetarum Latinorum Epicorum et Lyricorum Praeter Ennium et Lucilium post A. Baehrens
FPLAAD — Flowering Plants of Africa
FPL Tech Notes — F.P.L. (Forest Products Laboratories) Technical Notes
FPLY — Foothills Pipe Lines (Yukon) Limited. News Releases
FPMADL — US Forest Service. Forest Pest Management. Nothern Region Report
FPMMA — Fortschritte der Psychosomatischen Medizin
FPMMAK — Advances in Psychosomatic Medicine
FPN — Financial Planning
FPn — Fryske Plaknammen
FPNJAG — Folia Psychiatrica et Neurologica Japonica
FPO — Financial Post
FPORD — Fusion Power Report
FPR — Foreign Policy Report
FPR — Foreign Projects Newsletter
FPR — Fragmenta Poetarum Romanorum
FPRDAI — Food Product Development
FPRDI J — FPRDI [*Forest Products Research and Development Institute*] Journal
FPRI/O — Orbis. Foreign Policy Research Institute
FPRMAB — Folia Primatologica
FPRS News Dig — FPRS (Forest Products Research Society) News Digest
FPSTB — Fire Prevention Science and Technology
FPSUEA — Facial Plastic Surgery
FPt — Far Point
FPTED — Fuel Processing Technology
FPW — Fenelon. Personlichkeit und Werk
FPYKA — Fortschritte der Physik
FPZ — Forum for the Problems of Zionism
FQ — Faerie Queene
FQ — Film Quarterly
FQ — Florida Quarterly
FQ — Four Quarters
FQ — French Quarterly
FQKGO — Forschungen und Quellen zur Kirchen- und Kulturgeschichte Ostdeutschlands
FQNZA — Frequenz
FQRSD5 — Faune du Quebec. Rapport Special
FQS — Franziskanische Quellenschriften
F Quarterly — Film Quarterly
FR — Australian Financial Review
FR — Fasti Romani
FR — Felix Ravenna
FR — Financial Review
FR — Fordham Law Review
FR — Fortnightly Review
Fr — France
Fr — Franciscana. Sint-Truiden
FR — French Review
Fr — Frontsoldat Erzaehlt
FR — Furtwaengler und Reichhold, Griechische Vasenmalerei
FRA — Fontes Rerum Austriacarum
Fr A — Fraenkische Alb
FrA — France-Asie
FRA — Fra Randers Amt
Frac — Fracastoro
FRACA — Fracastoro
Fractal Geom Biol Syst — Fractal Geometry in Biological Systems. An Analytical Approach [*monograph*]
Fractal Rev Nat Appl Sci Proc IFIP Work Conf — Fractal Reviews in the Natural and Applied Sciences. Proceedings of the IFIP Working Conference on Fractals in the Natural and Applied Sciences

Fractals Eng Proc Conf — Fractals in Engineering. Proceedings of the Conference
Fract Anal Proc Natl Symp Fract Mech — Fracture Analysis. Proceedings. National Symposium on Fracture Mechanics
Fract Compos Mater Proc USA USSR Symp — Fracture of Composite Materials. Proceedings. USA-USSR Symposium
Fract Fatigue Elasto Plast Thin Sheet Micromech Probl Proc C — Fracture and Fatigue. Elasto-Plasticity, Thin Sheet, and Micromechanisms Problems. Proceedings. Colloquium on Fracture
Fract Mech Ceram — Fracture Mechanics of Ceramics
Fract Mech Natl Symp Fract Mech — Fracture Mechanics. National Symposium on Fracture Mechanics
Fract Mech Proc Natl Symp — Fracture Mechanics. Proceedings. National Symposium on Fracture Mechanics
Fract Mech Symp — Fracture Mechanics. Symposium
Fract Mech Symp Natl Symp Fract Mech — Fracture Mechanics. Symposium. National Symposium on Fracture Mechanics
Fractogr Glasses Ceram — Fractography of Glasses and Ceramics
Fract Proc Int Conf — Fracture. Proceedings. International Conference on Fracture
Fract Toughness Slow Stable Cracking Proc Natl Symp Fract Mec — Fracture Toughness and Slow-Stable Cracking. Proceedings. National Symposium on Fracture Mechanics
Fr Actuelle — France Actuelle
FRAD — Fontes Rerum Austriacarum. Diplomataria et Acta
Fraenk Kourier — Fraenkischer Kourier
Fraenk Lebensbild — Fraenkische Lebensbilder
Fraenk Mag Statist — Fraenkisches Magazin fuer Statistik, Naturkunde, und Geschichte
FRAF — Fontes Rerum Austriacarum. Fontes Juris
Fra Fys Verd — Fra Fysikkens Verden
Fra Fys Verden — Fra Fysikkens Verden
Frag Com Graec — Fragmenta Comicorum Graecorum
Fragen Ernaehr — Fragen der Ernaehrung
Frag Hist Graec — Fragmenta Historicorum Graecorum
Fragipans Their Occurrence Classif Genesis Proc Symp — Fragipans. Their Occurrence, Classification, and Genesis. Proceedings. Symposium
Fragm Balcan — Fragmenta Balcanica. Musei Macedonici Scientiarum Naturalium
Fragm Balcan Prir Muz (Skopje) — Fragmenta Balcanica. Prirodonaucen Muzej (Skopje)
Fragm Balc Mus Macedonici Sci Nat — Fragmenta Balcanica. Musei Macedonici Scientiarum Naturalium
Fragm Bot — Fragmenta Botanica
Fragm Bot Mus Hist Nat Hung — Fragmenta Botanica Musei Historico-Naturalis Hungarici
Fragm Coleopterol — Fragmenta Coleopterologica
Fragm Coleopterol Jpn — Fragmenta Coleopterologica Japonica
Fragm Ent — Fragmenta Entomologica
Fragm Entomol — Fragmenta Entomologica
Fragm Faun — Fragmenta Faunistica
Fragm Faun Hung — Fragmenta Faunistica Hungarica
Fragm Faun Pol Akad Nauk Inst Zool — Fragmenta Faunistica. Polska Akademia Nauk Instytut Zoologii
Fragm Faun (Warsaw) — Fragmenta Faunistica (Warsaw)
Fragm Flor Geobot — Fragmenta Floristica et Geobotanica
Fragm Florist Geobot (Cracow) — Fragmenta Floristica et Geobotanica (Cracow)
Fragm Herbol Jugosl — Fragmenta Herbologica Jugoslavica
Fragm Mineral Palaeontol — Fragmenta Mineralogica et Palaeontologica
Fragm Nachr Abh Befoerd Finanz Naturk — Fragmente, Nachrichten und Abhandlungen zur Befoerderung der Finanz-, Polizey-, Oekonomie- und Naturkunde
Frag Poet Rom — Fragmenta Poetarum Romanorum
Fragrance J — Fragrance Journal
Fragrance Mag — Fragrance Magazine
Fr Agric — France Agricole
FrAm — France-Amerique
Fr Am Commer — French American Commerce
FRAME — Fund for the Replacement of Animals in Medical Experiments. Technical News
Framingham Monogr — Framingham Monograph. Community Health Station
FrAmL — France-Amerique de la Louisiane
Fr Am Rev — French American Review
FranA — Francais Aujourd'hui
Fra Natnmus Arbsm — Fra Nationalmuseets Arbejdsmark
Fra Nat Vaerkst — Fra Naturens Vaerksted
Franc — Franciscana
France Apic — La France Apicole
France As — France-Asie; Revue de Culture et de Synthese Franco-Asiatique
France Illus — France Illustration
France Illus Litt & Theat — France Illustration, Litteraire, et Theatrale
France Illus Sup — France Illustration. Supplement
France Indust — France Industrielle
France Litt — France Litteraire
Franchis'g — Franchising in the Economy, 1983-1985
Franciscan Stud — Franciscan Studies
FrancLA — Studii Biblici Franciscani. Liber Annuus
Franc Lev — Franciscaans Leven
Franc Mod — Francais Moderne
Franco Br Med Rev — Franco-British Medical Review
Franc S — Franciscan Studies
FrancSt — Franciscan Studies. Annual
Fran Djurvld — Fran Djurvarlden
Frank Connock Publ — Frank Connock Publication
Frankf Aerztekorr — Frankfurter Aerztekorrespondenz
FrankfAllg — Frankfurter Allgemeine
Frankf Geogr Hft — Frankfurter Geographische Hefte
Frankf Hefte — Frankfurter Hefte. Zeitschrift fuer Kultur und Politik

Frankf Hist Forsch — Frankfurter Historische Forschungen
Frankf Kakteen-Freund — Frankfurter Kakteen-Freund
Frankf Muenzztg — Frankfurter Muenzzeitung
Frankfurter Hft — Frankfurter Hefte
Frankfurter Med Ann Aerzte — Frankfurter Medizinische Annalen fuer Aerzte, Wundaerzte, Apotheker, und Denkende Leser aus Allen Staenden
Frankfurter Ver Geog Jber — Frankfurter Verein fuer Geographie und Statistik. Jahresbericht
Frankfurter Z Pathol — Frankfurter Zeitschrift fuer Pathologie
Frankfurt Forsch — Frankfurt Forschungen
Frankfurt H — Frankfurter Hefte
Frankfurt Illus — Frankfurter Illustrierte
Frankfurt Muenzztg — Frankfurter Muenzzeitung
Frankfurt Quellen u Forsch z German u Roman Philol — Frankfurter Quellen und Forschungen zur Germanischen und Romanischen Philologie
Frankfurt Ztg — Frankfurter Zeitung
Frankf Wohlfahrtsbl — Frankfurter Wohlfahrtsblaetter
Frankf Z Path — Frankfurter Zeitschrift fuer Pathologie
Frankf Z Pathol — Frankfurter Zeitschrift fuer Pathologie
Frankf Zt — Frankfurter Allgemeine Zeitung fuer Deutschland
Frank Leslies Illus Newspap — Frank Leslies' Illustrated Newspaper
Franklin I J — Journal of the Franklin Institute of the State of Pennsylvania
Frank Lloyd Wright Newslett — Frank Lloyd Wright Newsletter
Fran LA — Studii Biblici Franciscani. Liber Annus
Fr An Met — Annuaire Meteorologique de la France
Fran Mod — Francais Moderne
Fra Nmus Arbejdsmk — Fra Nationalmuseets Arbejdsmark
FranS — Franciscan Studies
Fran Stds — Franciscan Studies
Fran Stud — Franciscan Studies
FranT — Franc-Tireur
Franz Forsch — Franziskanische Forschungen
Franziskanische Stud — Franziskanische Studien
Franzisk St — Franziskanische Studien
Franzisk Stud — Franziskanische Studien
FranzS — Franziskanische Studien
Franz St — Franziskanische Studien
FRAR — Fire Research Abstracts and Reviews
FrAR — French-American Review
FRARA — Fire Research Abstracts and Reviews
FRAS — Fontes Rerum Austriacarum. Scriptores
Fraser — Fraser's Magazine
Fraser of Allander Inst Q Econ Commentary — Fraser of Allander Institute. Quarterly Economic Commentary
Frasers M — Fraser's Magazine
Frasers Mag — Fraser's Magazine
Fr Asie — France-Asie
Fra Sundhedsstyr — Fra Sundhedsstyrelsen
Fra Sundhedsstyr (Copenhagen) — Fra Sundhedsstyrelsen (Copenhagen)
Frat Order Police J — Fraternal Order of Police Journal [*Pittsburgh*]
Fratres Scholarum Christ — Fratres Scholarum Christianarum
Frauen & F — Frauen und Film
Fraunhofer Ges Foerd Angew Forsch Beispiele Angew Forsch — Fraunhofer-Gesellschaft zur Foerderung der Angewandten Forschung. Beispiele Angewandte Forschung
Fraunhofer Ges Foerd Angew Forsch Inst Chem Treib Explosivst — Fraunhofer-Gesellschaft zur Foerderung der Angewandte Forschung. Institut fuer Chemie der Treib- und Explosivstoffe. Jahrestagung
Fraunhofer-Inst Betriebsfestigkeit Ber — Fraunhofer-Institut fuer Betriebsfestigkeit. Bericht
Fraunhofer-Inst Chem Technol Int Jahrestag — Fraunhofer-Institut fuer Chemische Technologie. Internationale Jahrestagung
Fraunhofer Inst Treib Explosivst Int Jahrestag — Fraunhofer-Institut fuer Treib- und Explosivstoffe. Internationale Jahrestagung
FRB — Business Review. Federal Reserve Bank of Philadelphia
FRB — FABS Reference Bible
FRB — Federal Reserve Bulletin
FrB — Franse Boek
F Rb A — Fra Ribe Amt
FRB Annu Rep — FRB [*Fisheries Research Board, Canada*] Annual Report
FRBCB — Fisheries Research Board of Canada. Bulletin
FRBCTR — Fisheries Research Board of Canada. Technical Report
Fr Belg — France-Belgique
Frb GT — Frederiksberg Gennem Tiderne
FrBl — Freds-Bladet
FRBMRS — Fisheries Research Board of Canada. Manuscript Report Series
Fr Br — Front og Bro
FRBRD — Federal Reserve Bank of St. Louis. Review
Fr Bul Stat — Bulletin Mensuel de Statistique (France)
Fr Bur Rech Geol Min Bull Sect 2 Geol Gites Miner — France. Bureau de Recherches Geologiques et Minieres. Bulletin. Section 2. Geologie des Gites Mineraux
Fr Bur Rech Geol Minieres Bull Ser 2 Sect 1 — France. Bureau de Recherches Geologiques et Minieres. Bulletin. Serie 2. Section 1. Geologie de la France
Fr Bur Rech Geol Minieres Bull Ser 2 Sect 4 — France. Bureau de Recherches Geologiques et Minieres. Bulletin. Serie 2. Section 4
Fr Bur Rech Geol Minieres Mem — France. Bureau de Recherches Geologiques et Minieres. Memoires
Fr Bur Rech Geol Min Mem — France. Bureau de Recherches Geologiques et Minieres. Memoires
FrCa — France Catholique
Fr CAM — French CAM [*Certificat d'Addition a un Brevet Special Medicament*]. PatentDocument

Fr Cent Natl Exploit Oceans Publ Result Compagnes Mer — France. Centre National pour l'Exploitation des Oceans. Publications. Resultatsdes Compagnes a la Mer Brest
Fr Cent Natl Exploit Oceans Rapp Annu — France. Centre National pour l'Exploitation des Oceans. Rapport Annuel
Fr Cent Natl Rech Sci Colloq Int — France. Centre National de la Recherche Scientifique. Colloques Internationaux
Fr Cent Rech Zones Arides Publ Ser Geol — France. Centre de Recherches sur les Zones Arides. Publications. Serie Geologie
Fr Cg Sc — Sessions des Congres Scientifiques de France
FrChr — Freier Christentum
Fr Commis Energ At Note CEA N — France. Commissariat a l'Energie Atomique. Note CEA-N
Fr Commis Energ At Rap CEA CONF — France. Commissariat a l'Energie Atomique. Rapport. CEA-CONF
Fr Commis Energ At Rapp — France. Commissariat a l'Energie Atomique. Rapport
FRCRAX — Forestry Chronicle
FRD — Federal Rules Decisions
FrD — Freiburger Dioezesan Archiv
FRDC — Fishery Research Directorate (Cairo)
FRDCA — Fridericiana
Fr Demande — French Demande. Patent Document
F Reader — Film Reader
FREDA — Freddo
Freddo Artif Ind — Freddo Artificiale Industriale
Frederic W H Myers Lect — Frederic W. H. Myers Lectures. Society for Psychical Research
Free Assoc — Free Association
Free CC — Freeman's English Chancery Reports
Free China R — Free China Review
Freedom Soc — Freedom Socialist
Free Inq — Free Inquiry
Free Issue — Freedom at Issue
Free L — Free Lance
Free Lab Wld — Free Labour World
Free Lbr Wld — Free Labour World
Free Living Symbiotic Plathelminthes Proc Int Symp Biol Turb — Free-living and Symbiotic Plathelminthes. Proceedings. International Symposium.Biology of Turbellarians
Free News — Freedom News
Free Radical Biochem Radiat Inj Proc L H Gray Conf — Free Radical Biochemistry and Radiation Injury. Proceedings. L.H. Gray Conference
Free Radical Copolim Dispersions Glassy State Relax — Free Radical Copolimerization, Dispersions, Glassy State Relaxation
Free Radical Mech Tissue Inj — Free Radical Mechanisms of Tissue Injury
Free Radical Res Commun — Free Radical Research Communications
Free Radicals Biol — Free Radicals in Biology
Free Radicals Biol Syst Proc Symp — Free Radicals in Biological Systems. Proceedings. Symposium
Free Radicals Dig Dis Proc Int Symp — Free Radicals in Digestive Diseases. Proceedings. International Symposium. FreeRadicals in Digestive Diseases
Free Radicals Lipid Peroxidation Cancer Proc NFCR Cancer Symp — Free Radicals, Lipid Peroxidation, and Cancer. Proceedings. NFCR Cancer Symposium
Free Radicals Liver Inj Proc Int Meet — Free Radicals in Liver Injury. Proceedings. International Meeting
Free Radicals Med Biol Proc Pharm Symp — Free Radicals in Medicine and Biology. Proceedings. Pharmacia Symposium
Free Radic Biol Med — Free Radical Biology and Medicine
Free Radic Res — Free Radical Research
Free Soc — Freedom Socialist
Free Spir — Freeing the Spirit
Free St Fmr — Free State Farmer
Freiberg B — Berichte ueber die Verhandlungen der Naturforschenden Gesellschaft zu Freiburg i. B
Freiberger Forsch H — Freiberger Forschungshefte
Freiberger Forsch Ser C — Freiberger Forschungshefte. Series C. Geologie. Geophysik. Mineralogie-Lagerstaettenlehre und Paleontologie
Freiberger Forschungsh B Metall — Freiberger Forschungshefte. Reihe B. Metallurgie
Freiberg Forschungsh A — Freiberger Forschungshefte A
Freiberg Forschungsh B — Freiberger Forschungshefte. Reihe B
Freiberg Forschungsh C — Freiberger Forschungshefte. Reihe C
Freiberg Forschungsh D — Freiberger Forschungshefte. Reihe D
Freiberg Forschungsh Reihe A — Freiberger Forschungshefte. Reihe A
Freiberg Forschungsh Reihe C — Freiberger Forschungshefte. Reihe C
Freiberg Jb Berg Hm — Jahrbuch fuer den Berg- und Huettenmann. Herausg. von der Koenigl. Berg-Akademie zu Freiberg
Freib FH — Freiberger Forschungshefte
Freib Fortbildungstag Nephrol — Freiburger Fortbildungstagung ueber Nephrologie
FreibRu — Freiburger Rundbrief
Freib Symp Med Univ Klin — Freiburger Symposion an der Medizinischen Universitaets-Klinik
Freib Tag Nephrol — Freiburger Tagung ueber Nephrologie
FreibThSt — Freiburger Theologische Studien
Freiburg Archaeol — Freiburger Archaeologie
Freiburg Colloq Reprod Med — Freiburg Colloquium on Reproductive Medicine
Freiburg Congr Nephrol — Freiburg Congress on Nephrology
Freiburg Dioez Archv — Freiburger Dioezesan-Archiv
Freiburger Geog Mitt — Freiburger Geographische Mitteilungen
Freiburger Universitaetsbl — Freiburger Universitaetsblaetter
Freiburger Wiss Ges — Freiburger Wissenschaftliche Gesellschaft
Freiburg Geschbl — Freiburger Geschichtsblaetter
Freiburg Muensterbl — Freiburger Muensterblaetter

FreibZ — Freiburger Zeitschrift fuer Philosophie und Theologie
Freie Hft Naturw Mitt — Freie Hefte fuer Naturwissenschaftliche Mitteilungen, herausgegeben von Dr. Haas
Freie Wirtsch — Freie Wirtschaft
Freie Wohlfahrtspfl — Freie Wohlfahrtspflege
Freight & Container Transp — Freight and Container Transportation
Freight Handl Term Engng — Freight Handling and Terminal Engineering
Freight Mgmt — Freight Management
Frei Z Phil Theol — Freiburger Zeitschrift fuer Philosophie und Theologie
Fremt — Fremtiden
French Am Com — French-American Commerce
French Am Rev — French American Review
French Biblphical Dig Sci — French Bibliographical Digest Science
French Doct Theses — French Doctoral Theses
French Geneal — French Genealogist
French Hist St — French Historical Studies
French Hist Stud — French Historical Studies
French Pat Abstr — French Patent Abstracts
French Pln — Ninth Plan for Economic and Social Development, 1984-1988 (France)
French R — French Review
French Rev — French Review
French Rly Tech — French Railway Techniques
French Sci News — French Science News
French St — French Studies
French Stud — French Studies
French Tech Building Civ Engng & Town Planning — French Techniques. Building, Civil Engineering, and Town Planning
French Tech Electr Engn & Electron Ind — French Techniques. Electrical Engineering and Electronics Industries
French Tech Mech Hydraul & Consult Engng Ind — French Techniques. Mechanical, Hydraulic, and Consultant Engineering Industries
French Tech Metal Ind — French Techniques. Metal Industries
French Tech Misc Ind & Consum Goods — French Techniques. Miscellaneous Industries and Consumer Goods
French Tech Tranp Stud & Res — French Techniques. Transportation Studies and Research
Fr Energ — France Energetique
Freq — Frequenz
Freq Control Symp Proc — Frequency Control Symposium. Proceedings
Freq Distrib Total Amounts Rainf K Day Periods Stns Neth — Frequency Distribution of Total Amounts of Rainfall in K-Day Periods at Stations in the Netherlands
Freq Modul — Frequency Modulation. RCA Reviews
Freq Tabl Anemogr Analysis Singapore — Frequency Tables and Anemogram Analysis. Malayan Meteorological Service
Freq Tabl Bermuda — Frequency Tables, Visibility, Cloud Height, Surface and Upper Winds. Bermuda [Singapore]
Freq Wind Direct Speed Zurich Airp — Frequence of Wind Direction and Speed. Zurich Airport
Freq Zicht Hoog Laag Wolk — Frequentie van Zicht en Hoogte de Laagste Wolken
FRERDC — Forest Recreation Research
F Res — Food Research
Fresenius J Anal Chem — Fresenius Journal of Analytical Chemistry
Fresenius Z — Zeitschrift fuer Analytische Chemie. Fresenius
Fresenius Z Anal Chem — Fresenius' Zeitschrift fuer Analytische Chemie
Freshwater Biol — Freshwater Biology
Freshwater Biol Assoc Annu Rep — Freshwater Biology Association. Annual Report
Freshwater Biol Assoc Sci Publ — Freshwater Biology Association. Scientific Publication
Freshwater Fish Newsl — Freshwater Fisheries Newsletter
Freshwater Invertebr Biol — Freshwater Invertebrate Biology
Fresh Water Sea Proc Int Symp — Fresh Water from the Sea. Proceedings. International Symposium
Freshwat Fish Newsl — Freshwater Fisheries Newsletter
Freshwat Salm Fish Res — Freshwater and Salmon Fisheries Research
Freshw Biol — Freshwater Biology
Freshw Biol Assoc Annu Rep — Freshwater Biological Association. Annual Report
Freshw Biol Assoc Sci Publ — Freshwater Biological Association. Scientific Publication
Frets Mag — Frets Magazine
Freude Leben — Freude am Leben
Freunde Koeln Zoo — Freunde des Koelner Zoo
Freunde Naturw Ber (Haidinger) — Freunde der Naturwissenschaften in Wien. Berichte ueber die Mittheilungen (W. Haidinger)
Fr Eurafr — France-Eurafrique
Freyn Des — Freyn Design
Freywillige Beytr Hamburg Nachr Gelehrsamk — Freywillige Beytraege zu den Hamburgischen Nachrichten aus dem Reiche der Gelehrsamkeit
FrF — France-Forum [Paris]
Fr F — French Forum
FrFM — French Forum Monographs
FrFo — French Forum [Lexington, Ky.]
Fr For — Franziskanische Forschungen
Fr For NW Dt Zahn Ae — Freies Forum. Nordwestdeutscher Zahnaerzte
Fr Forum — French Forum
Fr Fr — France Franciscaine
FRG — Focus on Robert Graves
FRG — Forschungen zur Reformationsgeschichte
FRG — Revista de Filologie Romanica si Germanica
Fr Graph — France Graphique
Fr H — Frankfurter Hefte
FrH — Franzoesisch Heute
FrH — French Historical Studies

FrHe — Frankfurter Hefte
FRHEAJ — Facsimile Reprints in Herpetology
FRHED — Frankfurter Hefte
Fr Hist Stu — French Historical Studies
Fr Hist Stud — French Historical Studies
FRI Bull For Res Inst NZ For Serv — FRI Bulletin. Forest Research Institute. New Zealand Forest Service
Frict Wear Mach — Friction and Wear in Machinery
Frict Wear Mach (USSR) — Friction and Wear in Machinery (USSR)
Fridericiana Z Unlv Karlsruhe — Fridericiana. Zeitschrift der Universitaet Karlsruhe
Fried G Bl — Friedberger Geschichtsblaetter
FriedreichsBl — Friedrichs Blaetter fuer Gerichtliche Medizin und Sanitaetspolizei
Friedrichs Bl Gerichtl Med SanitPoliz — Friedrichs Blaetter fuer Gerichtliche Medizin und Sanitaetspolizei
Friedrich Schiller Univ Jena Wiss Z Naturwiss Reihe — Friedrich-Schiller-Universitaet Jena. Wissenschaftliche Zeitschrift. Naturwissenschaftliche Reihe
Friedrichswerther Mber — Friedrichswerther Monatsbericht. Blaetter fuer Tier- und Pflanzenzucht
Friend Ph — Friend. Philadelphia, Pennsylvania
Friends Forest — Friends of the Forest. Rinyu
Friends Hist Assoc Bul — Friends' Historical Association. Bulletin
Friends Hist Assoc Bull — Friends' Historical Association. Bulletin
Friends Hist Soc Jour — Friends' Historical Society. Journal
Friends Pl Nixon Med Hist Libr — Friends of the P. I. Nixon Medical Historical Library
Friends S Afr N Gal Newslett — Friends of the South African National Gallery Newsletter
Friends Wells Cathedral Rep — Friends of Wells Cathedral Reports
Fries LandBl — Fries Landbouwblad
Fries Landbouwbl — Fries Landbouwblad
Fries TuinbBl — Fries Tuinbouwblad
FRIJ — Frost i Jord/Frost Action in Soils
FRILAB — Indian Forest Leaflets
Fr Ill — France Illustration
Fri Memo — Friday Memo
FRIN — FRI [Fuel Research Institute] News
Fr Ind — Annuaire de Statistique Industrielle (France)
Fr Ind — France-Inde
Fr Ind — France-Indochine
Fr Ind M — Bulletin Mensuel de Statistique Industrielle (France)
Fr Inds — France-Industries
FRINEL — Food Reviews International
FRI News — FRI (Fuel Research Institute) News
Fr Inst Natl Propr Ind Bull Off Propr Ind Abr — France. Institut National de la Propriete Industrielle. Bulletin Officiel de laPropriete Industrielle. Abreges
Fr Inst Natl Propr Ind Bull Off Propr Ind Abr Descr — France. Institut National de la Propriete Industrielle. Bulletin Officiel de laPropriete Industrielle. Abreges Descriptifs
Fr Inst Natl Propr Ind Bull Off Propr Ind Brev Invent Abr Lis — France. Institut National de la Propriete Industrielle. Bulletin Officiel de la Propriete Industrielle. Brevets d'Invention. Abreges et Listes
Fri Report — Friday Report
Fris — Frigisinga
FRIS — Stanford University Food Research Institute Studies
Frit D — Frit Danmark. Udgivet af en Kreds af Danske
Frit Kobmandssk — Frit Kobmandsskab
Fritzsche Libr Bull — Fritzsche Library Bulletin
Friuli Med — Friuli Medico
Friul Med — Friuli Medico
Fr J Clin Biol Res — French Journal of Clinical and Biological Research
Fr Jpn Semin Compos Mater — France-Japan Seminar on Composite Materials
Fr J Water Sci — French Journal of Water Science
Fr K — Foeldrajzi Koezlemenyek
Frkf A M Ps Vr Jbr — Jahresbericht des Physikalischen Vereins zu Frankfurt am Main
Frkf Jbr Ps Vr — Jahresbericht des Physikalischen Vereins am Frankfurt am Main
Frkf Ps Vr Jb — Jahrbuch zur Verbreitung Naturwissenschaftlicher Kenntnisse, Veranstaltet vom Physikalischen Vereine zu Frankfurt
FRL — Forschungen zur Religion und Literatur des Alten und Neuen Testaments
FrL — France Latine
FrL — France Libre
Fr L — Frank Leslie's Popular Monthly
FRLANT — Forschungen zur Religion und Literatur des Alten und Neuen Testaments
FrLat — France Latine
Frld — Frankenland
Fr Lev — Franciscaans Leven
Fr Libre — France Libre
Fr Lit Ser — French Literature Series
Fr LM — French Literature on Microfiche
Fr M — Francais Moderne
FRM — France Alimentaire
Fr M — French Medicament. Patent Document
FRM — Fund Raising Management
FRMBA — Farmacia (Bucharest)
FRM Bericht — Forschungsreaktor Muenchen. Bericht
Fr Med — France Medicale
Fr Med Edn Etud — France Medicale. Edition des Etudiantes
Fr Med Revue Etud Hist Med — France Medicale. Revue d'Etudes d'Histoire de la Medecine
Fr Med Therm Clim — France Medico-Thermale et Climaterique
Fr Minist Agric Bull Tech Inf — France. Ministere de l'Agriculture. Bulletin Technique d'Information

Fr Minist Ind Mem Servir Explication Carte Geol Detaill Fr — France. Ministere de l'Industrie. Memoires pour Servir a l'Explication de la Carte Geologique. Detaillee de la France
Fr Miss — Franziskaner-Missionen
Fr Mo — Francais dans le Monde
Fr Mod — Francais Moderne
FrN — France Nouvelle
FRNM Bull — FRNM [*Foundation for Research on the Nature of Man*] Bulletin
FRNTA — Frontiers
Fro — Fronimo
FrOb — France Observateur
Fro Bot — Frohe Botschaft
Frodskaparrit Suppl — Frodskaparrit. Supplementum
Froebel J — Froebel Journal
F Roent Nuk — Fortschritte auf dem Gebiete der Roentgenstrahlen und der Nuklearmedizin
Fr Off Rech Sci Tech Outre-Mer Cah Ser Geol — France. Office de la Recherche Scientifique et Technique d'Outre-Mer. Cahiers. Serie Geologie
Fr Off Rech Sci Tech Outre-Mer Cah Ser Pedol — France. Office de la Recherche Scientifique et Technique d'Outre-Mer. Cahiers. Serie Pedologie
Fr Off Rech Sci Tech Outre-Mer Initiations Doc — France. Office de la Recherche Scientifique et Technique d'Outre-Mer. Initiations-Documentations-Techniques
Fr Off Rech Sci Tech Outre-Mer Monogr Hydrol — France. Office de la Recherche Scientifique et Technique d'Outre-Mer. Monographies Hydrologiques
Froid Clim — Froid et la Climatisation
Froid Glace Refrig — Froid, la Glace et la Refrigeration
Frokontrollanst Beratt Hernosand — Frokontrollanstaltens Berattelse (Hernosand)
Frokontrollanst Verks Lund — Frokontrollanstaltens Verksamhet (Lund)
FRom — Filologia Romanza
Fr O-Mer — France d'Outre-Mer
Frommanns Klassiker — Frommann's Klassiker der Philosophie
Frommels Jber Fortschr Geb Geburtsh Gynaek — Frommels Jahresbericht ueber die Fortschritte auf dem Gebiete der Geburtschilfe und Gynaekologie
From Metab Metab Metabolon — From Metabolite, to Metabolism, to Metabolon
From Theor Phys Biol Proc Int Conf — From Theoretical Physics to Biology. Proceedings. International Conference
Fron Matrix Biol — Frontiers of Matrix Biology
Front — Frontespizio
Front — Frontier
Front Aging Ser — Frontiers in Aging Series
Front Biol — Frontiers of Biology
Front Biomed Biotechnol — Frontiers in Biomedicine and Biotechnology
Front Bioprocess Proc — Frontiers in Bioprocessing. Proceedings
Front Biosci — Frontiers in Bioscience
Front Biotransform — Frontiers in Biotransformation
Front Carbohydr Res — Frontiers in Carbohydrate Research
Front Catecholamine Res Proc Int Catecholamine Symp — Frontiers in Catecholamine Research. Proceedings. International Catecholamine Symposium
Front Cell Surf Res Boehringer Ingelheim Ltd Symp — Frontiers in Cellular Surface Research. Boehringer Ingelheim Ltd. Symposium
Front Chem — Frontiers in Chemistry
Front Clin Neurosci — Frontiers of Clinical Neuroscience
Front Diabetes — Frontiers in Diabetes
Front Endocrinol — Frontiers in Endocrinology
Front Flavor Proc Int Flavor Conf — Frontiers of Flavor. Proceedings. International Flavor Conference
Front Foods Food Ingredients — Frontiers in Foods and Food Ingredients
Front Gastroenterol — Frontiers in Gastroenterology
Front Gastrointest Horm Res Proc Nobel Symp — Frontiers in Gastrointestinal Hormone Research. Proceedings. Nobel Symposium
Front Gastrointest Res — Frontiers of Gastrointestinal Research
Front Headache Res — Frontiers in Headache Research
Front Health Serv Manage — Frontiers of Health Services Management
Front Horm Res — Frontiers of Hormone Research
Frontiers Appl Math — Frontiers in Applied Mathematics
Frontiers Artificial Intelligence Appl — Frontiers in Artificial Intelligence and Applications
Frontiers Comput Sci — Frontiers in Computer Science
Frontiers in Phys — Frontiers in Physics
Frontiers in Systems Res — Frontiers in Systems Research
Frontiers Plant Sci — Frontiers of Plant Science
Frontiers Pl Sci — Frontiers of Plant Science. Connecticut Agricultural Experiment Station
Front Intern Med Int Congr — Frontiers of Internal Medicine. International Congress of Internal Medicine
Front Macromol Sci Proc IUPAC Int Symp Macromol — Frontiers of Macromolecular Science. Proceedings. IUPAC International Symposium on Macromolecules
Front Matrix Biol — Frontiers of Matrix Biology
Front Med Biol Eng — Frontiers of Medical and Biological Engineering
Front Mol Biol — Frontiers in Molecular Biology
Front Nat Prod Res — Frontiers in Natural Product Research
Front Nauki Tekh — Front Nauki i Tekhniki
F Ront Neue — Fortschritte auf dem Gebiete der Rontgenstrahlen und der Neuen Bildgebenden Verfahren
Front Neurobiol — Frontiers in Neurobiology
Front Neuroendocrinol — Frontiers in Neuroendocrinology
Front Nonequilib Stat Phys — Frontiers of Nonequilibrium Statistical Physics
Front Nucl Dyn — Frontiers in Nuclear Dynamics
Front Nucl Med — Frontiers of Nuclear Medicine
Front Nurs Serv Q Bull — Frontier Nursing Service. Quarterly Bulletin
Front Oral Biol — Frontiers of Oral Biology
Front Oral Physiol — Frontiers of Oral Physiology

Front Organosilicon Chem Proc Int Symp Organosilicon Chem — Frontiers of Organosilicon Chemistry. Proceedings. International Symposium on Organosilicon Chemistry
Front Part Phys — Frontiers in Particle Physics
Front Phys — Frontiers in Physics
Front Plant Sci — Frontiers of Plant Science
Front Plant Sci Conn Agric Exp Stn (New Haven) — Frontiers of Plant Science. Connecticut Agricultural Experiment Station (New Haven)
Front Pl Sci — Frontier of Plant Sciences
Front Polym Res Proc Int Conf — Frontiers of Polymer Research. Proceedings. International Conference
Front Power Conf Proc — Frontiers of Power Conference. Proceedings
Front Power Technol Conf Proc — Frontiers of Power Technology Conference. Proceedings
Front Radiat Ther Oncol — Frontiers of Radiation Therapy and Oncology
Front Sci (Tokyo) — Frontier Science (Tokyo)
Front Sl — Front Slobode
Front Wiss Tech — Front der Wissenschaft und Technik
Frooskap — Frooskaparrit
Froriep Not — Notizen aus dem Gebiete der Natur- und Heilkunde. Froriep
Fr ORSTOM Cah Ser Geophys — France. Office de la Recherche Scientifique et Technique d'Outre-Mer. Cahiers. Serie Geophysique
Fr ORSTOM Cah Ser Hydrol — France. Office de la Recherche Scientifique et Technique d'Outre-Mer. Cahiers. Serie Hydrologie
Fr ORSTOM Cah Ser Pedol — France. Office de la Recherche Scientifique et Technique d'Outre-Mer. Cahiers. Serie Pedologie
Fr ORSTOM Monogr Hydrol — France. Office de la Recherche Scientifique et Technique d'Outre-Mer. Monographies Hydrologiques
Frost — Frost and Sullivan News. American Market
FROSTI — Food RA [*Research Association*] Online Scientific and Technical Information
Frozen and Chilled Fds — Frozen and Chilled Foods
Frozen Fd Di — Frozen Food Digest
Frozen Fds — Frozen Foods
Frozen Food — Frozen Foods
FRP — Foreign Report
Fr P — France-Pologne
Fr Parf — France et ses Parfums
Fr Pat Doc Brev Invent — France. Patent Document. Brevet d'Invention
Fr Pat Doc Brev Spec Med — France. Patent Document. Brevet Special de Medicament
Fr Pat Doc Certif Addit — France. Patent Document. Certificat d'Addition
Fr Pat Doc Certif Addit Brev Spec Med — France. Patent Document. Certificat d'Addition a un Brevet Special Medicament
Fr Pat Doc Certif Util — France. Patent Document. Certificat d'Utilite
Fr Pat Doc Demande — France. Patent Document. Demande
Fr Peche — France Peche
FR Ph — Forschungen zur Romanischen Philologie
Fr Pharm — France-Pharmacie
Fr Plast — France Plastiques
FRPPAO — Farmaco. Edizione Pratica
FRPSAX — Farmaco. Edizione Scientifica
FrQ — French Quarterly
FRR — Federal Research Report
Fr Railw Tech — French Railway Techniques
Fr Repub Bur Rech Geol Min Bull — France. Republique. Bureau de Recherches Geologiques et Minieres. Bulletin
Fr Repub Bur Rech Geol Min Mem — France. Republique. Bureau de Recherches Geologiques et Minieres. Memoires
Fr Repub Dir Mines Publ Bur Rech Geol Geophys Min — France. Republique. Direction des Mines. Publications. Bureau de Recherches Geologiques et Geophysiques et Minieres
Fr Rev — French Review
Fr Ru — Freiburger Rundbrief
FRS — Federal Reserve Bulletin
FRS — Felix Ravenna. Supplement
FRS — Fontana Religious Series
FrS — France-Soir [*Paris daily*]
FRS — Frozen Foods
Fr SA — Franciscan Studies Annual
FRSABT — Food Research Institute. Studies in Agricultural Economics, Trade, and Development
Fr S Ag Bll — Bulletin des Seances de la Societe (Centrale) d'Agriculture de France
Fr S Ag Mm — Memoires d'Agriculture, d'Economie Rurale et Domestique Publies par la Societe d'Agriculture
Fr S Bt Bll — Bulletin de la Societe Botanique de France
Fr Sci N — French Science News
Fr Serv Carte Geol Bull — France. Service de la Carte Geologique. Bulletin
Fr Serv Exploit Ind Tab Allumettes Mem Ser B — France. Service d'Exploitation Industrielle des tabacs et des Allumettes. Memorial. Serie B. Publications. Institut Experimental des Tabacs de Bergerac
Fr Ses Parfums — France et Ses Parfums
Frsh Wat Biol — Freshwater Biology
FrSM — Franziskanische Studien (Munster)
Fr S Met An — Annuaire de la Societe Meteorologique de France
Fr S Met N Met — Nouvelles Meteorologiques Publiees sous les Auspices de la Societe Meteorologique de France
Fr S Mn Bll — Bulletin de la Societe Mineralogique de France
FRSS — Federal Register Search System
Fr St — Franciscan Studies
FrSt — Franziskanische Studien
Fr St — French Studies
FRSTAH — Forestry
Fr Stat A — Annuaire Statistique de la France

Fr Stud — French Studies. A Quarterly Review
FRSUB — Fra Sundhedsstyrelsen
Fr S Z BII — Bulletin de la Societe Zoologique de France
FRT — Fontes Rerum Transylvanicarum
Frt — Fraternite-Matin
FRT — Fruitteelt
FRTAA — Forstarchiv
Fr Tech — French Techniques
Fr Telephn — Industries Francaises du Telephone, du Telegraphe, et de Leurs Applications Telematiques
Fr Textil — Statistique Generale de l'Industrie Textile Francaise
Fr Therm — France Thermale. Organe Medical, Hydrologique, Scientifique
FRTRDJ — Great Britain. Ministry of Agriculture, Fisheries, and Food. Directorate of Fisheries Research. Fisheries Research Technical Report
FRu — Freiburger Rundbrief
Fru — Fruits
Fruchtfolgeforsch Fruchtfolgegestaltung Int Symp — Fruchtfolgeforschung und Fruchtfolgegestaltung. Internationales Symposium
Fruchtsaft Ind — Fruchtsaft Industrie
Fruehjahrskolloq Univ Bremen — Fruehjahrskolloquium der Universitaet Bremen
Fruehjahrstag Online Benutzergruppe DGD — Fruehjahrstagung der Online-Benutzergruppe der DGD
Fruehma St — Fruehmittelalterliche Studien
Frueh Mit Alt St — Fruehmittelalterliche Studien. Jahrbuch des Instituts fuer Fruehmittelalterforschung der Universitaet Muenster
Frueh Mittelalterl Stud — Fruehmittelalterliche Studien. Jahrbuch des Instituts fuer Fruehmittelalterforschung der Universitaet Muenster
Fruehmittelalt Stud — Fruehmittelalterliche Studien
FRUIA — Fruits
Fruit & Veg R — Fruit and Vegetable Review
Fruit Grow — Fruit Grower
Fruit Grower Hort — Fruit Grower and Horticulturist. A Monthly Magazine of Practical Horticulture
Fruit Notes Coop Ext Serv Univ Mass — Fruit Notes. Cooperative Extension Service. University of Massachusetts
Fruit Process — Fruit Processing
Fruit Prod J Am Food Manuf — Fruit Products Journal and American Food Manufacturer
Fruit Prod J Am Vinegar Ind — Fruit Products Journal and American Vinegar Industry
Fruit Sci Rep — Fruit Science Reports
Fruit Sci Rep (Skierniewice) — Fruit Science Reports (Skierniewice)
Fruit Situat US Dep Agric Econ Res Serv — Fruit Situation TFS. United States Department of Agriculture. Economic ResearchService
Fruits Prim Afr Nord — Fruits et Primeurs de l'Afrique du Nord
Fruit Trees — Fruit Trees/Kwaju
Fruit Var Hortic Dig — Fruit Varieties and Horticultural Digest
Fruit Var J — Fruit Varieties Journal
Fruit Veg Digest — Fruit and Vegetable Digest
Fruit Veg Honey Crop Mkt Rep — Fruit, Vegetable, and Honey Crop and Market Report
Fruit Veg Juice Process Technol — Fruit and Vegetable Juice Processing Technology
Fruit World Ann — Fruit World Annual
Fruit World Annu Orchardists' Guide — Fruit World Annual and Orchardists' Guide
Fruit World Market Grower — Fruit World and Market Grower
Fruit World Mark Grow — Fruit World and Market Grower
Fruit Yb — Fruit Yearbook
Frunz Politekh Inst Tr — Frunzenskii Politekhnicheskii Institut. Trudy
Fru O-Mer — Fruits d'Outre-Mer
FRUS — Foreign Relations of the United States
Frust Entomol Ist Entomol — Frustula Entomologica. Istituto di Entomologia
Frustula Entomol — Frustula Entomologica
F Rutan — Filmrutan
FRV — Financial Review
FrV — Freds-Varden
Fr Warte — Die Friedenswarte
Fr West Afr Insp Agric Bull Prot Veg — French West Africa. Inspection de l'Agriculture. Bulletin de la Protection Vegetaux
FRWMA — Fernwaerme International
FRXAAJ — Archivos. Fundacion Roux-Ocefa
FRXZZ — Archivos. Fundacion Roux-Ocefa
FryskJb — Frysk Jierboek
FRZ — Flugschriften aus der Reformationszeit in Facsimile Drucken
FRZ — Zeitschrift fuer Familienrecht
FRZBAW — Feddes Repertorium
Frz F — Franziskanische Forschungen
FRZKAP — Farmatsevtychnyi Zhurnal
FS — Faces
FS — Feminist Studies
FS — Folklore Studies
FS — Forest Science
FS — Fort Simpson Journal
FS — Franciscan Studies
FS — Franziskanische Studien
FS — French Studies
FS — Fruehgriechische Sagenbilder
FS — Funbericht aus Schwaben
FS — Furman Studies
FSA — Florecillas de San Antonio [Lima]
FSAC — Folia Scientifica Africae Centralis
FSAFA — Farming in South Africa
FSARAU — Facsimile Reprint. Society for the Study of Amphibians and Reptiles
FSASA — Fette - Seifen - Anstrichmittel

FSASAX — Fette - Seifen - Anstrichmittel
FSATS — Fortgesetzte Sammlung von Alten und Neuen Theologischen Sachen
FSB — Franziskanische Studien. Beiheft
FSBA — Federal and State Business Assistance Database
FS Ber — FS-Berichte
FSBUDD — FAO [Food and Agriculture Organization of the United Nations] Soils Bulletin
Fsch PG — Forschungen zur Neueren Philosophie und Ihrer Geschichte
Fschr Md — Fortschritte der Medicin
Fschr Mth — Jahrbuch ueber die Fortschritte der Mathematik
Fschr Ps — Fortschritte der Physik
Fschr Roentgenstr — Fortschritte auf dem Gebiete der Roentgenstrahlen
F Sci Abstr — Food Science Abstracts
FSCN/A — Antropologica. Fundacion La Salle de Ciencias Naturales. Instituto Caribe de Antropologia y Sociologia
FSC Ne — FSC [Friends Service Council] News
FS Coop Ext Serv Cook Coll — FS. Cooperative Extension Service. Cook College
FSCS — Fundamental Studies in Computer Science
FsD — Fonetica si Dialectologie
FsDGZ — Flugschriften der Deutschen Gesellschaft fuer Zuechtungskunde
FSE — Federal Reserve Bank of San Francisco. Economic Review
FSE — Fundamental Studies in Engineering
FSEPA — Filtration and Separation
FSF — Magazine of Fantasy and Science Fiction
FS Fact Sheet Oreg State Univ Ext Serv — FS. Fact Sheet. Oregon State University. Extension Service
FSFMA — Forskning och Framsteg
FSFRAL — Far Seas Fisheries Research Laboratory. S Series
FSHEB Coop Ext Serv Univ Arkansas Div Agric US Dep Agric Cty — FSHEB. Cooperative Extension Service. University of Arkansas. Division of Agriculture. US Department of Agriculture, and County Governments Cooperating
FSHED Coop Ext Serv Univ Arkansas — FSHED. Cooperative Extension Service. University of Arkansas
FSHEE Coop Ext Serv Univ Arkansas Div Agric US Dep Agric Cty — FSHEE. Cooperative Extension Service. University of Arkansas. Division of Agriculture. US Department of Agriculture, and County Governments Cooperating
FSHEF Univ Arkansas Coop Ext Serv — FSHEF. University of Arkansas. Cooperative Extension Service
FSHEH Univ Arkansas Div Coop Ext Serv — FSHEH. University of Arkansas. Division of Cooperative Extension Service
FSHEI Univ Arkansas Coop Ext Serv — FSHEI. University of Arkansas. Cooperative Extension Service
FSHEL Univ Arkansas Coop Ext Serv — FSHEL. University of Arkansas. Cooperative Extension Service
FSI — Fish and Shellfish Immunology
FSIND — Forensic Science International
FSINDR — Forensic Science International
FSIS Facts Food Safety Insp Serv US Dep Agric — FSIS Facts. Food Safety and Inspection Service. US Department of Agriculture
FSIZA — Fukushima Igaku Zasshi
FSJOD — Fire Safety Journal
FSL — Federal Reserve Bank of St. Louis. Review
FSL — Fleet Street Letter
FSl — Folia Slavica
F S Lbt — Fyns Stifts Landburgstidende
FSLPAB — Flora Slodkowodna Polski
FSM — Fairly Serious Monthly Magazine
FSM — Fantastic Story Magazine
FSM — Fine Scale Modeler
FSMNA — Fishermen's News
FSO — Flying Saucers from Other Worlds
F Soc Rev — Film Society Review
FS Oe Th — Forschungen zur Systematischen und Oekumenischen Theologie
FSPMAM — Fermentnaya i Spirtovaya Promyshlennost'
FSQ — Fantastic Story Quarterly
FSQS US Dep Agric Food Saf Qual Serve — FSQS. United States Department of Agriculture. Food Safety and Quality Service
FSR — Financial Services Review
FSR — Flying Saucer Review
FSRKA — Frankfurter Studien zur Religion und Kultur der Antike
FSRTS — Fyra Svenska Reformationskrifter Tryckta i Stockholm Ar 1562
FSS — Filosofia come Scienza dello Spirito
FSSA — French Studies in Southern Africa
FSSA J — FSSA [Fertilizer Society of South Africa] Journal
FSSA Publ — FSSA (Fertilizer Society of South Africa) Publication
FSSE — Fonti e Studi di Storia Ecclesiastica
FSt — Feminist Studies
FSt — Franciscan Studies
F St — Franziskanische Studien
FSt — Franzoesische Studien
F St — French Studies
FSTA — Food Science and Technology Abstracts
FSTEB — Fibre Science and Technology
FS Th R — Forschungen zur Systematischen Theologie und Religionsphilosophie
F St I — Fonti per la Storia d'Italia
F Stud — Franziskanische Studien
FSTXA — Faserforschung und Textiltechnik
F Supp — Federal Supplement
FSUS — Florida State University. Studies
FSUSP — Florida State University. Slavic Papers
FSYCA3 — Faraday Symposia of the Chemical Society
FSz — Folks-Sztyme
FT — Faserforschung und Textiltechnik
FT — Filipino Teacher
FT — Financial Times

FT — Finsk Tidskrift
FT — Finsk Tidskrift foer Vitterhet, Vetenskap, Konst, och Politik
FT — Fortean Times
FT — Fort McMurray Today
FT — Forum Theologicum
FT — Funk-Technik
FT135 — US Foreign Trade. FT 135. General Imports. Schedule A. Commodity by Country
FT410 — US Foreign Trade. FT 410. Exports. Schedule E. Commodity by Country
FT610 — US Foreign Trade. FT 610. Exports SIC Based Products by World Areas
FTA — Food Technology in Australia
FTA — Food Trade Review
FTAUAC — Food Technology in Australia
FTBR — Fort McMurray Today. Oil Sands Business Report
F Techn — Food Technology
FTF — Financial Times (Frankfurt)
FTF — Forhandlingar. Teologiska Foreningen
FT Farm Tid — FT. Farmaceutisk Tidende
Ft f B — Fagskrift for Bankvaaesen
FT (Fft) — Financial Times (Frankfurt Edition)
FTGBA — Fertigungstechnik und Betrieb
FThL — Forum Theologiae Linguisticae
FThought — Faith and Thought. Journal of the Victoria Institute
F Th St — Freiburger Theologische Studien
FTI — Foreign Traders Index
FTIPA3 — Forest Tree Improvement
Ftiziol — Ftiziologia
Ft Laud Nw — Fort Lauderdale News
FT (London) — Financial Times (London Edition)
Ft McMurray News — Fort McMurray News
FTMEA — Formage et Traitements des Metaux
FTP — Fruit and Tropical Products
FTP — Fuer Theologie und Philosophie
FTPP — Folklore. Tribuna del Pensamiento Peruano
FTPPA — Fizika i Tekhnika Poluprovodnikov
FTPTAG — Advances in Animal Physiology and Animal Nutrition
FTR — Australian Federal Tax Reporter
FTR — Federal Trial Reports
FTR — Finnish Trade Review
FT Rep — Foreign Trade Report
FTRIA — Fiziko-Tekhnicheskie Problemy Razrabotki Poleznykh Iskopaemykh
FTS — Financial Times
FTS — Financial Times. Supplements
FTS — Frankfurter Theologische Studien
FTSED — Filtration et Techniques Separatives
FTST — Futurist
FTT — Fanciful Tales of Time and Space
FTT — Finsk Teologisk Tidskrift
FTT — Fizika Tverdogo Tela
FTVURP — Fontes ad Topographiam Veteris Urbis Romae Pertinentes
FTW — Foreign Trade Review
Ftwr File — Men's, Women's, and Childrens' Footwear Fact File
Ftwr News — Footwear News
FTY — Fookien Times Yearbook
FTZ — Fernmeldetechnische Zeitschrift
FU — Forstliche Umschau
Fu — Furche. Freie Kulturpolitische Wochenschrift
FUABBV — Annali. Universita di Ferrara. Sezione III. Biologia Animale
Fu Abstr — Fuel Abstracts
Fu Abstr Curr Titl — Fuel Abstracts and Current Titles. Institute of Fuel
FUAFA8 — Annali. Universita di Ferrara. Sezione VI. Fisiologia e Chimica Biologica
FU (Amst) — Free University Quarterly. A Quarterly of Christian Knowledge and Life (Amsterdam)
FUB — Finance and Development
Fu B — Forschungen und Berichte. Staatliche Museen zu Berlin
FUB — Furman University. Bulletin
FUBA — Filologia. Instituto de Filologia Romancia Facultad de Filosofia y Letras. Universidad de Buenos Aires
Fu Ber Bad Wuert — Fundberichte aus Baden-Wuerttemberg
Fu Ber Hessen — Fundberichte aus Hessen
Fu Ber Oe — Fundberichte aus Oesterreich
Fudan J — Fudan Journal
Fudan J (Nat Sci) — Fudan Journal (Natural Science)
Fu Econ Rev — Fuel Economy Review
F Ue I — Friede ueber Israel
Fuel Abstr — Fuel Abstracts
Fuel Abstr Curr Titles — Fuel Abstracts and Current Titles
Fuel & Energy Abstr — Fuel and Energy Abstracts
Fuel Combust — Fuel and Combustion
Fuel Combust Eng — Fuel and Combustion Engineering
Fuel Econ — Fuel Economy
Fuel Econ 1925-1936 — Fuel Economist (1925-1936)
Fuel Econ Rev — Fuel Economy Review
Fuel Econ (Watford Engl) — Fuel Economist (Watford, England)
Fuel Eff Bull — Fuel Efficiency Bulletin
Fuel Effic — Fuel Efficiency
Fueloil & Oil Heat — Fueloil and Oil Heat and Solar Systems
Fuel Oil J — Fuel Oil Journal
Fuel Oil J Houston — Fuel Oil Journal (Houston)
Fueloil Oil Heat Sol Syst — Fueloil and Oil Heat and Solar Systems
Fuel Oils Sulfur Content — Fuel Oils by Sulfur Content
Fuel Oil Temp J — Fuel Oil and Temperature Journal
Fuel- Orr- Gegegyogy — Fuel-, Orr-, Gegegyogyaszat
Fuel Processing Tech — Fuel Processing Technology
Fuel Process Technol — Fuel Processing Technology

Fuel Res Dep Sci Ind Res GB — Fuel Research. Department of Scientific and Industrial Research (Great Britain)
Fuel Res Inst News — Fuel Research Institute. News
Fuel Res Inst (Pretoria) Bull — Fuel Research Institute (Pretoria). Bulletin
Fuel Res Inst S Afr Bull — Fuel Research Institute of South Africa. Bulletin
Fuel Sci Prac — Fuel in Science and Practice
Fuel Sci Pract — Fuel in Science and Practice
Fuel Sci Technol — Fuel Science and Technology
Fuel Sci Technol Int — Fuel Science and Technology International
Fuels Furn — Fuels and Furnaces
Fuel Soc J — Fuel Society Journal
Fuel Technol Manage — Fuel Technology and Management
Fuentes Hist Medieval — Fuentes de Historia Medieval
FUF — Finnisch-Ugrische Forschungen
FuF — Forschungen und Fortschritte
FUFAB — Funk-Fachhaendler
FUFOD — Fusion Forefront
Fu FS — Forschungen und Fortschritte. Sonderheft
F u G — Form und Geist
Fugg Magyar — Fuggetlen Magyarorszag
Fu H — Fuldaer Hefte
Fuhe Cailiao Xuebao — Fuhe Cailiao Xuebao/Acta Materiae Compositae Sinica
FUHYD — Forum Umwelt Hygiene
FUI — Foro
FUJ — Fuji Bank Bulletin
Fu Jen Stud — Fu Jen Studies
Fuji Bank — Fuji Bank Bulletin
Fuji Bank Bul — Fuji Bank Bulletin
Fuji Denki Rev — Fuji Denki Review
Fuji Electr J — Fuji Electric Journal
Fuji Electr Rev — Fuji Electric Review
Fujikura Tech Rev — Fujikura Technical Review
Fujikura Tech Rev Jpn — Fujikura Technical Review (in Japanese)
Fujitsu Gen — Fujitsu General
Fujitsu Sci Tech J — Fujitsu Scientific and Technical Journal
FUJTA — Fujitsu
Fukien Acad Res Bull — Fukien Academy. Research Bulletin
Fukien Agric — Fukien Agriculture/Fu-Chien Nung Yeh
Fukien Agric J — Fukien Agricultural Journal
Fukien Christ Univ Sci J — Fukien Christian University. Science Journal
Fukien Cult — Fukien Culture/Fukien Wen Hua
FUKOB — Funtai Kogaku
Fukuoka Acta Med — Fukuoka Acta Medica
Fukuoka Univ Sci Rep — Fukuoka University Science Reports
Fukushima J Med Sci — Fukushima Journal of Medical Science
Fukushima Med J — Fukushima Medical Journal
Fukush J Med Sci — Fukushima Journal of Medical Science
F u L — Farbe und Lack
Fulbright Educ Dev Program Grantee Rep — Fulbright Educational Development Program Grantee Reports
Fulbright Univ Adm Program Grantee Rep — Fulbright University Administrator Program Grantee Reports
Fulda Geschbl — Fuldaer Geschichtsblaetter
Fulda Geschbll — Fuldaer Geschichtsblaetter
Fulmer Res Inst Newsl — Fulmer Research Institute. Newsletter
Fulmer Res Inst Spec Rep — Fulmer Research Institute. Special Report
FulN — Fulbright Newsletter
FUMRA2 — FAO [Food and Agriculture Organization of the United Nations] General Fisheries Council for the Mediterranean. Studies and Reviews
FUN — From Unknown Worlds
FUNAAO — Fauna
Func — Functions
Funct Approx Comment Math — Functiones et Approximatio Commentarii Mathematici
Funct Approximatio Comment Math — Functiones et Approximatio Commentarii Mathematici
Funct Aspects Parasite Surf Symp Br Soc Parasitol — Functional Aspects of Parasite Surfaces. Symposium. British Society for Parasitology
Funct Biol Med — Functional Biology and Medicine
Funct Dev Morphol — Functional and Developmental Morphology
Funct Differential Equations Israel Sem — Functional Differential Equations. Israel Seminar
Funct Foods Dis Prev II Med Plants Other Foods — Functional Foods for Disease Prevention II. Medicinal Plants and Other Foods
Functional Anal Appl — Functional Analysis and Its Applications
Funct Mater Tokyo — Function and Materials (Tokyo)
Funct Morphol Vertebr Proc Int Symp Vertebr Morphol — Functional Morphology in Vertebrates. Proceedings. International Symposium on Vertebrate Morphology
Funct Neurol — Functional Neurology
Funct Organ Nucl Lab Guide — Functional Organization of the Nucleus. A Laboratory Guide
Funct Orthod — Functional Orthodontist
Funct Photgr — Functional Photography
Funct Photogr — Functional Photography
Funct Polym — Functional Polymer
Funct Struct Immune Syst — Function and Structure of the Immune System
Funct Units Protein Biosynth Fed Eur Biochem Soc Meet — Functional Units in Protein Biosynthesis. Federation of European Biochemical Societies Meeting
Fundam Aerosp Instrum — Fundamentals of Aerospace Instrumentation
Fundam Appl Entomol — Fundamentals of Applied Entomology
Fundam Appl Nematol — Fundamental and Applied Nematology
Fundam Appl Ternary Diffus Proc Int Symp — Fundamentals and Applications of Ternary Diffusion. Proceedings. International Symposium
Fundam Appl Toxicol — Fundamental and Applied Toxicology

Fundam Appl Toxicol Off J Soc Toxicol — Fundamental and Applied Toxicology. Official Journal. Society of Toxicology

Fundam Aspects Heterog Catal Stud Part Beams — Fundamental Aspects of Heterogeneous Catalysis Studied by Particle Beams

Fundam Aspects Inert Gases Solids — Fundamental Aspects of Inert Gases in Solids

Fundam Aspects Pollut Control Environ Sci — Fundamental Aspects of Pollution Control and Environmental Science

Fundam Balneo Bioclimatol — Fundamenta Balneo Bioclimatologica

Fundam Clin Pharmacol — Fundamental and Clinical Pharmacology

Fundam Cosmic Phys — Fundamentals of Cosmic Physics

Fundam Cosm Phys — Fundamentals of Cosmic Physics

Fundamentals Proc Design Dev — Fundamentals, Process Design, and Development

Fundamental Stud in Comput Sci — Fundamental Studies in Computer Science

Fundam Gas Phase Ion Chem — Fundamentals of Gas Phase Ion Chemistry

Fundam Inf — Fumdamenta Informaticae

Fundam Interact Phys Astrophys Lect Coral Gables Conf Fundam — Fundamental Interactions in Physics and Astrophysics. Lectures. Coral Gables Conference on Fundamental Interactions at High Energy

Fundam Interact Phys Proc Coral Gables Conf Fundam Interact — Fundamental Interactions in Physics. Proceedings. Coral Gables Conference on Fundamental Interactions

Fundam Osn Opt Pamyati Sredy — Fundamental'nye Osnovy Opticheskoi Pamyati i Sredy

Fundam Phenom Mater Sci — Fundamental Phenomena in the Material Sciences

Fundam Probl Metrol Mater Vses Semin — Fundamental'nye Problemy Metrologii. Materialy Vsesoyuznogo Seminara

Fundam Probl Stat Mech — Fundamental Problems in Statistical Mechanics. Proceedings. International Summer School on Fundamental Problems in Statistical Mechanics

Fundam Radiat Heat Transfer Natl Heat Transfer Conf — Fundamentals of Radiation Heat Transfer. National Heat Transfer Conference

Fundam Radiol — Fundamental Radiologica

Fundam Res Homogenous Catal — Fundamental Research in Homogenous Catalysis

Fundam Respir Dis — Fundamentals in Respiratory Diseases

Fundam Sci — Fundamenta Scientiae

Fundam Theor Phys — Fundamental Theories of Physics

Fund & Forsk — Fund og Forskning

Fund Bariloche Dep Recur Nat Energ Publ (Argent) — Fundacion Bariloche. Departamento de Recursos Naturales y Energia. Publicacion (San Carlos De Bariloche, Argentina)

Fund Bariloche Ser — Fundacion Bariloche Series

Fundber Baden-Wuerttemberg — Fundberichte aus Baden-Wuerttemberg

Fundber Hessen — Fundberichte aus Hessen

Fundber Oesterreich — Fundberichte aus Oesterreich

Fundber Schwaben — Fundberichte aus Schwaben

Fund Bras Conserv Nat Bol Inf — Fundacao Brasileira para a Conservacao da Natureza Boletim Informativo

Fundb Schwaben — Fundberichte aus Schwaben

Fund Cienc Apl Fac Eng Ind Rev Pesqui Tecnol FEI — Fundacao de Ciencias Aplicadas. Faculdade de Engenharia Industrial. Revista Pesquisa e Tecnologia FEI

F und E — Finanzierung und Entwicklung

Fundicao Mater Primas — Fundicao e Materias-Primas

Fund Inform — Fundamenta Informaticae

Fund Informat — Fundamenta Informaticae

Fund Inst Agron Parana Bol Tec — Fundacao Instituto Agronomico do Parana. Boletim Tecnico

Fund Juan March Ser Univ — Fundacion Juan March. Serie Universitaria

Fund Man Int — Fund Management International

Fund Math — Fundamenta Mathematicae

Fund Miguel Lillo Misc — Fundacion Miguel Lillo Miscelanea

Fund Raising Manage — Fund Raising Management

Fund Raising Mgt — Fund Raising Management

Fund Roux Ocefa Arch — Fundacion Roux-Ocefa. Archivos

Fund Sci — Fundamenta Scientiae

Fund Serv Saude Publica Rev (Braz) — Fundacao Servicos de Saude Publica. Revista (Brazil)

Fund Theories Phys — Fundamental Theories of Physics

Fund Zoobot Rio Grande Do Sul Publ Avulsas — Fundacao Zoobotanica do Rio Grande Do Sul. Publicacoes Avulsas

Fungal Genet Biol — Fungal Genetics and Biology

Fungal Spore Morphogenet Control Proc Int Fungal Spore Symp — Fungal Spore Morphogenetic Controls. Proceedings. International Fungal Spore Symposium

Fungal Viruses Int Congr Microbiol Mycol Sect — Fungal Viruses. International Congress of Microbiology. Mycology Section

Fung Herb Insect — Fungicides, Herbicides, Insecticides

Fungi Can — Fungi Canadenses

Funkc Anal — Funkcional'nyj Analiz i Ego Prilozenija

Funkcial Ekvac — Fako de l'Funkcialaj Ekvacioj Japana Matematika Societo

Funkcial Ekvac — Funkcialaj Ekvaciog

Funk Scott Annu Ind — Funk and Scott Annual Index of Corporations and Industries

Funk Scott Index Corp Ind — Funk and Scott Index of Corporations and Industries

Funk T — Funk-Technik

Funkt Biol Med — Funktionelle Biologie und Medizin

Funk-Tech — Funk-Technik

Funktionsanal Biol Syst — Funktionsanalyse Biologischer Systeme

Funkt Morphol Organ Zelle — Funktionelle und Morphologische Organisation der Zelle

Funktsional Anal i Prilozhen — Akademiya Nauk SSSR. Funktsional'nyi Analiz i ego Prilozheniya

Funktsional Anal i Prilozhen — Funktsional'nyi Analiz i ego Prilozheniya. Nauka. Moscow

Funkts Neirokhim Tsentr Nervn Sist Mater Vses Simp — Funktsional'naya Neirokhimiya Tsentral'noi Nervnoi Sistemy. Materialy Vsesoyuznogo Simpoziuma

Funkts Org Usloviyakh Izmen Gazov Sredy — Funktsii Organizma v Usloviyakh Izmenennoi Gazovoi Sredy

FUOFAA — Fauna och Flora

Fu O Fo — Fund og Forskning i Det Kongelige Biblioteks Samlinger

FUQ — Free University Quarterly. A Quarterly of Christian Knowledge and Life

F u R — Film und Recht

FUR — Forma Urbis Romae

FUR — Freiburger Universitaetsreden

Fur — Fureteur

Fur — Furioso

FUR — Futures

Furhner Wielands Samml Vergiftungsfaellen — Fuehner-Wieland's Sammlung von Vergiftungsfaellen

FurmS — Furman Studies

Furnas C C Meml Conf — Furnas (C. C.) Memorial Conference

Furn Des Struct Mater Fuels Ind Process Heat Symp Proc — Furnaces. Design, Structural Materials, and Fuels. Industrial Process Heating Symposium. Proceedings

Furn Hist — Furniture History

Furnit Manuf — Furniture Manufacturer

Furnit Prod — Furniture Production

Furnit Ret — Furniture Retailer

Furniture Wkrs P — Furniture Workers Press

Furn Mfr — Furniture Manufacturer

Fur St — Furche-Studien

Fur Trade J Can — Fur Trade Journal of Canada

Furukawa Electr Rev — Furukawa Electric Review

Furukawa Rev — Furukawa Review

FURWA — Furrow

FUS — Futurist

FUSHA — Funkschau

Fusion Energy Found Newsl — Fusion Energy Foundation. Newsletter

Fusion Eng Des — Fusion Engineering and Design

Fusion Fisssion Energy Syst Rev Meet Proc — Fusion/Fission Energy Systems Review Meeting. Proceedings

Fusion Nucl — Fusion Nucleaire

Fusion Power Assoc Exec Newsl — Fusion Power Associates. Executive Newsletter

Fusion Power Rep — Fusion Power Report

Fusion Technol — Fusion Technology

Fusion Technol Proc Symp — Fusion Technology. Proceedings. Symposium

Fuso Met — Fuso Metals

Fussboden Ztg — Fussboden Zeitung

FUSTA — Fujitsu Scientific and Technical Journal

Fut — Future Fiction

Fut — Futures

Fut — Futurist

Fut Abstr — Future Abstracts

FUTB — Futbol Internacional

Fut Comp Sys — Future Computing Systems

FUTEA — Funk-Technik

FUTF — Future Science Fiction

FUTJA — Foundry Trade Journal

Fut L — Future Life

FUTS — Futuristic Stories

FUTU — Futures

FUTU — Futures Information Service

FUTUA — Futurist

FUTUB — Futures

FUTUD — Futuribles

Future Child — Future of Children

Future Eur Jpn Remote Sens Sens Programs — Future European and Japanese Remote-Sensing Sensors and Programs

Future Gener Comput Syst — Future Generation Computer Systems

Futures Mich State Univ Agric Exp Stn — Futures. Michigan State University. Agricultural Experiment Station

Future Sur — Future Survey

Future Trends Biomed Appl Lasers — Future Trends in Biomedical Applications of Lasers

FUZED — Fussboden Zeitung

FUZg — Frankfurter Universitaets-Zeitung

Fuzzy Math — Fuzzy Mathematics

Fuzzy Sets and Syst — Fuzzy Sets and Systems

FV — Foi et Vie

FV — Fragmente der Vorsokratiker

FV — Fragmentos (Venezuela)

FVAS — Forschungen und Vorarbeiten zur Austria Sacra

F Vb A — Fra Viborg Amt. Aarbog Udgivet af Historisk Samfund for Viborg Amt

Fvfb — Ferskvandsfiskeribladet

FVFSA — Fortschritte der Verfahrenstechnik

FVK — Forschungen zur Volkskunde

FVKS — Freiburger Veroeffentlichungen aus dem Geebiete von Kirche und Staat

FVL — Forschungen zur Volks- und Landeskunde

FVL — Forschungsprobleme der Vergleichenden Literaturgeschichte [monograph]

FVLK — Forschungen zur Volks- und Landeskunde

FVMUDL — Flora et Vegetatio Mundi

FVPD — Film/Video Producers and Distributors

FVS — Fragmente der Vorsokratiker

FVTLAQ — Folia Veterinaria Latina

FW — Financial World

FW — Folktales of the World

FW — Free World
FW — Freie Wirtschaft
FWBLA — Freshwater Biology
FWD — Furniture World and Furniture Buyer and Decorator
F Weinberg Int Symp Solidif Process Proc — F. Weinberg International Symposium on Solidification Processing. Proceedings
FWF — Far Western Forum
F Wiss Beit — Filmwissenschaftliche Beitraege
F Wld Energy — Free World Energy Survey
FWLEEA — US Fish and Wildlife Service. Fish and Wildlife Leaflet
FWN — Footwear News
FWN — Futures World News
FWP J — FWP [*Founding, Welding, Production Engineering*] Journal
FWPJA — FWP [*Founding, Welding, Production Engineering*] Journal
FWPPAP — US Department of the Interior. Federal Water Pollution Control Administration. Water Pollution Control Research Series
FWSCA — Forstwissenschaftliches Centralblatt
FWSFAA — Feldwirtschaft
FWS/OBS US Fish Wildl Serv Off Biol Serv — FWS/OBS. United States Fish and Wildlife Service. Office of Biological Services
FWS Va Polytech Inst State Univ Sch For Wildl Resour — FWS. Viriginia Polytechnic Institute and State University. School of Forestry and Wildlife Resources
FX — Foreign Exchange
FX — Foreign Exchange Rate Service
FXBASE — International Interest and Exchange Rate Database
Fy Aa — Fynske Aarboger
FYCAB — Fyzikalny Casopis. Vydavatel'stvo Slovenskej Akademie Vied
FyD — Finanzas y Desarollo

FYI — News/Retrieval For Your Information
Fyiz Tverd Tyila — Fyizika Tverdogo Tyila
Fy J — Fynsk Jul
FYJKA — Fysiokjemikeren
FyL — Filosofia y Letras
Fyn Mind — Fynske Minder
Fyr — Fyring
Fysiatr Reumatol Vestn — Fysiatricky a Reumatologicky Vestnik
Fysiatr Vestn — Fysiatricky Vestnik
Fys T — Fysisk Tidsskrift
Fys Tidsskr — Fysisk Tidsskrift
FYTIA — Fysisk Tidsskrift
FYVDA — Fra Fysikkens Verden
Fyz Cas — Fyzikalny Casopis
FZ — Fieldiana. Zoology
FZ — Frankfurter Allgemeine Zeitung
FzB — Forschung zur Bibel
FzG — Forschungsberichte zur Germanistik
FZH — Folia Zoologica et Hydrobiologica
FZKAA — Fizika
FZKSA — Fizika [*Zagreb*]. Supplement
FZLZA — Fiziologicheskii Zhurnal SSSR Imeni I. M. Sechenova
FZNPA — Fiziologia Normala si Patologica
FZP — Frankfurter Zeitschrift fuer Pathologie
FZ Ph Th — Freiburger Zeitschrift fuer Philosophie und Theologie
FZPT — Freiburger Zeitschrift fuer Philosophie und Theologie
FZRSA — Fiziologiya na Rasteniyata
FZSEDV — Fortschritte in der Zoologischen Systematik und Evolutionsforschung
FZUKA — Fiziologichnii Zhurnal (Kiev)

G

G — Gemeentebestuur Tijdschrift van de Vereniging van NederlandseGemeenten
G — Geography
G — Germano-Slavica
G — Gids
G — Girl About Town
G — Globus [*Braunschweig*]
G — Guardian
G — Gymnasium. Zeitschrift fuer Kultur der Antike und Humanistische Bildung
GA — Gazeta das Aldeias
GA — Gazette Archeologique
GA — Geistige Arbeit
GA — Geografiska Annaler</PHR> %
GA — Geographical Abstracts
GA — Geographischer Anzeiger
GA — Georgia Reports
GA — Geotechnical Abstracts
GA — Germanistische Abhandlungen
GA — Germanistische Arbeitshefte
G A — Giornale dell'Arte
GA — Glos Anglii
GA — Graezistische Abhandlungen
GA — Graphic Arts Monthly
Ga 4H Cloverleaf News Views Ga Future Leaders — Georgia 4H Cloverleaf. News and Views of Georgia's Future Leaders
GAA — Gene Amplification and Analysis Series
GAA — Graphic Arts Abstracts
GAA — Skrifter Utgivna av Kungliga. Gustav Adolfs Akademien
GAABA — Gas Abstracts
GAAC — Gastroenterology. Abstracts and Citations
GAAG — Age and Ageing
GAAGA — Gas Age
GA Ag Coll — Georgia State College of Agriculture. Publications
GA Ag Exp — Georgia. Agricultural Experiment Station. Publications
GA Agric Exp Stn Annu Rep — Georgia. Agricultural Experiment Station. Annual Report
GA Agric Exp Stn Bienn Rep — Georgia. Agricultural Experiment Stations. Biennial Report
GA Agric Exp Stn Bull — Georgia. Agricultural Experiment Station. Bulletin
GA Agric Exp Stn Circ — Georgia. Agricultural Experiment Station. Circular
GA Agric Exp Stn Field Crops Variety Trials — Georgia. Agricultural Experiment Stations. Field Crops Variety Trials
GA Agric Exp Stn Field Crops Var Trials — Georgia. Agricultural Experiment Stations. Field Crops Variety Trials
GA Agric Exp Stn Leafl — Georgia. Agricultural Experiment Station. Leaflet
GA Agric Exp Stn Mimeogr Ser — Georgia. Agricultural Experiment Station. Mimeograph Series
GA Agric Exp Stn Res Bull — Georgia. Agricultural Experiment Station. Research Bulletin
GA Agric Exp Stn Res Rep — Georgia. Agricultural Experiment Station. Research Report
GA Agric Exp Stn Tech Bull — Georgia. Agricultural Experiment Station. Technical Bulletin
GA Agric Res — Georgia Agricultural Research
GA Agric Res GA Exp Stn — Georgia Agricultural Research. Georgia Experiment Stations
GA Agr Res — Georgia Agricultural Research. University of Georgia
GAAN — American Anthropologist
Ga App — Georgia Appeals Reports
GAAR — American Artist
GAAS — Gesammelte Abhandlungen zur Amerikanischen Sprach- und Alterthumskunde. Eduard Seler [*Berlin*]
GAB — Geoppinger Akademische Beitraege
GAB — Gifts and Decorative Accessories
GABA — ABA [*American Banking Association*] Journal
GABA CNS Proc Int Symp Peripher GABAergic Mech — GABA (Gamma-Aminobutyric Acid) outside the CNS. Proceedings. International Symposium on Peripheral GABAergic Mechanisms
Ga Bar Assn — Georgia Bar Association
GA Bar J — Georgia Bar Journal
GABAW — Gelehrte Anzeigen der Baierischen Akademie der Wissenschaften
Gabb Stat L — Gabbett. Abridgment of Statute Law
GABJ — Art Journal
GA B J — Georgia Bar Journal
GABP — Journal of Abnormal Psychology
GABPAG — Annales Geologiques de la Peninsule Balkanique
GABU — Art Bulletin

GA Bus — Georgia Business
GAC — Government Accountants Journal
GAC — Growth and Change
Gac A — Gaceta de Arte
Gac Algodonera — Gaceta Algodonera. Publicacion Defensora de Plantadores e Industriales del Algodon
Gac Arqueol Andina — Gaceta Arqueologica Andina
Gac Artes Graficas Libro Ind Pap — Gaceta de las Artes Graficas del Libro y de la Industria del Papel
Ga Cattleman — Georgia Cattleman
Gac AVDA — Gaceta de AVDA
G Accad Med Torino — Giornale. Accademia di Medicina di Torino
Gac Callejeia — Gaceta Callejeia
Gac Colmen — Gaceta del Colmenar
Gaceta Mat — Gaceta Matematica
Gaceta Mat I — Gaceta Matematica. Primera Serie
Gaceta Of Caracas — Gaceta Oficial (Caracas)
Gac Farm — Gaceta Farmaceutica
Gac Granja — Gaceta de Granja. Asociacion Argentina Criadores de Aves, Conejos, y Abejas
GACH — Antiques and Collecting Hobbies
Gac Lit — Gaceta de Literatura
GACM — Communications. ACM
Gac Mat (Madrid) — Gaceta Matematica (Madrid)
Gac Med — Gaceta Medica
Gac Med Bilbao — Gaceta Medica de Bilbao
Gac Med Bol — Gaceta Medica Boliviana
Gac Med Car — Gaceta Medica de Caracas
Gac Med Caracas — Gaceta Medica de Caracas
Gac Med Catalana — Gaceta Medica Catalana
Gac Med Del Sur — Gaceta Medica del Sur
Gac Med Esp — Gaceta Medica Espanola
Gac Med (Guayaquil) — Gaceta Medica (Guayaquil) Ecuador
Gac Medica Espan — Gaceta Medica Espanola
Gac Med Lima — Gaceta Medica de Lima
Gac Med Mex — Gaceta Medica de Mexico
Gac Med Norte Bilbao — Gaceta Medica del Norte Bilbao
Gac Med Quir Bol — Gaceta Medico-Quirurgica de Bolivia
Gac Med Urug — Gaceta Medica del Uruguay
Gac Med Zool — Gaceta de Medicina Zoologica
Gac Num — Gaceta Numismatica
GACOD — Graefe's Archive for Clinical and Experimental Ophthalmology
GA Code Ann (Harrison) — Code of Georgia, Annotated (Harrison)
GA Code Ann (Michie) — Official Code of Georgia, Annotated (Michie)
GA Comp R & Regs — Official Compilation of the Rules and Regulations of the State of Georgia
Gac Per Med Cirug — Gaceta Peruana de Medicina y Cirugia
Gac Propr Ind — Gaceta de la Propriedad Industrial
GACR — American Craft
Gac Sanit — Gaceta Sanitaria
Gac San Mil — Gaceta de Sanidad Militar
GACTD2 — Glossary of Acarological Terminology/Glossaire de la Terminologie Acarologique
Gac Vet (B Aires) — Gaceta Veterinaria (Buenos Aires)
GACY — American City and County
GADA — Journal. American Dietetic Association
GA Dep Mines Min Geol Geol Surv Bull — Georgia. Department of Mines, Mining, and Geology. Geological Survey. Bulletin
GA Dep Mines Min Geol Geol Surv Circ — Georgia. Department of Mines, Mining, and Geology. Geological Survey. Circular
GA Dep Mines Mining Geol Geol Surv Bull — Georgia. Department of Mines, Mining, and Geology. Geological Survey. Bulletin
Ga Dep Nat Resour Geol Surv Inf Circ — Georgia. Department of Natural Resources. Geological Survey. Information Circular
GA Dep Nat Resour Geol Water Resour Div Inf Circ — Georgia. Department of Natural Resources. Geologic and Water Resources Division. Information Circular
Gadja Mada J Med Sci — Gadja Mada Journal of the Medical Sciences
GADL — Adolescence
GADS — Ad Astra
Gads Dan Mag — Gads Danske-Magasin
Gaea Norveg — Gaea Norvegica
Gael J — Gaelic Journal
GAENA — Gas Engineer
GA Engineer — Georgia Engineer
Ga Entomol Soc J — Georgia Entomological Society. Journal

Gaertn Bot Briefe — Gaertnerisch-Botanische Briefe
Gaerungslose Fruechteverwert — Gaerungslose Fruechteverwertung
GAf — Geneve-Afrique
Ga Farm Bur News — Georgia Farm Bureau News
GAFI — American Film
Ga For — Georgia Forestry
GA For Res Counc Annu Rep — Georgia. Forest Research Council. Annual Report
GA For Res Counc Rep — Georgia. Forest Research Council. Report
GA For Res Pap — Georgia Forest Research Paper
GA For Res Pap GA For Res Counc — Georgia Forest Research Paper. Georgia Forest Research Council
GAFR — Africa Report
GAG — Geo Abstracts. G
GAG — Giornale d'Artiglieria e Genio
GAG — Goeppinger Arbeiten zur Germanistik
GAG — Grundriss der Akkadischen Grammatik
GAGE — Aging
GAGE — Gerontology and Geriatrics Education
GAGEA — Gakujutsu Geppo
GA Geol Surv Bull — Georgia. Geological Survey. Bulletin
GA Geol Surv Circ — Georgia. Geological Survey. Circular
GA Geol Survey Bull Circ — Georgia Geological Survey. Bulletin. Circular
GA Geol Surv Inf Circ — Georgia. Geological Survey. Information Circular
GA Geol Water Resour Div Inf Circ — Georgia. Geologic and Water Resources Division. Information Circular
GAGR — Agricultural Research
G Agr — Giornale di Agricoltura
G Agr Domen — Giornale di Agricoltura Domenica
GAGS — Goettingische Anzeigen von Gelehrten Sachen
GA GSB — Georgia. Geological Survey. Bulletin
GAHAD — Genshiryoku Anzen Hakusho
GAHE — American Heritage
GAHEDG — Geologische Abhandlungen Hessen
GAHGAJ — Geografiska Annaler. Series B. Human Geography
GAHI — American History Illustrated
GA His Q — Georgia Historical Quarterly
Ga His S — Georgia Historical Society. Collections
GA Hist Q — Georgia Historical Quarterly
Ga Hist Quar — Georgia Historical Quarterly. Georgia Historical Society
GA Hist Quart — Georgia Historical Quarterly
Ga Hist Soc Annals — Georgia Historical Society Annals
GA Hist Soc Coll — Georgia Historical Society. Collections
GAHQ — Georgia Historical Quarterly
GAHR — Alcohol Health and Research World
GAHU — American Hunter
GAI — Gli Archivi Italiani
GAI — Grotius Annuaire Internationle
GAIGD — Genshiryoku Anzen Iinkai Geppo
GA Inst Technol Eng Exp Sta Bull — Georgia Institute of Technology. Engineering Experiment Station. Bulletin
GA Inst Technol Eng Exp Stn Circ — Georgia Institute of Technology. Engineering Experiment Station. Circular
GA Inst Technol Eng Exp Stn Rep — Georgia Institute of Technology. Engineering Experiment Station. Report
GA Inst Technol Eng Exp Stn Repr — Georgia Institute of Technology. Engineering Experiment Station. Reprints
Ga Inst Technol Eng Exp Stn Res Eng — Georgia Institute of Technology. Engineering Experiment Station. The Research Engineer
GA Inst Technol Eng Exp Stn Spec Rep — Georgia Institute of Technology. Engineering Experiment Station. Special Reports
GA Inst Technol Environ Resour Cent ERC (Rep) — Georgia Institute of Technology. Environmental Resources Center. ERC (Report)
GA Inst Technol Ser Nucl Eng — Georgia Institute of Technology. Series in Nuclear Engineering
GAIQ — American Indian Quarterly
Gai S — Gai Saber. Revista de l'Escola Occitana
GAJ — General-Anzeiger fuer die Gesamten Interessen des Judentums
GA J Int & Comp L — Georgia Journal of International and Comparative Law
GA J Internat and Comparative Law — Georgia Journal of International and Comparative Law
GA J Int'l & Comp L — Georgia Journal of International and Comparative Law
GAJS — American Journal of Sociology
GA J Sci — Georgia Journal of Science
Ga J Sci Off Publ Ga Acad Sci — Georgia Journal of Science. Official Publication. Georgia Academy of Science
GAKGS — Gesammelte Aufsaetze zur Kulturgeschichte Spaniens
GAK Gummi Asbest Kunstst — GAK. Gummi, Asbest, Kunststoffe
GAKS — Gesammelte Aufsaetze zur Kulturgeschichte Spaniens
Gakujutsu Hokoku Bull Fac Agric Kagoshima Univ — Gakujutsu Hokoku. Bulletin. Faculty of Agriculture. Kagoshima University
Gakujutsu Hokoku Bull Utsunomiya Univ — Gakujutsu Hokoku. Bulletin of the College of Agriculture. Utsunomiya University
Gakujutsu Hokoku Tokushu Spec Bull — Gakujutsu Hokoku Tokushu. Special Bulletin
Gakujutsu Kenkyu Hokoku Res Bull Obihiro Univ — Gakujutsu Kenkyu Hokoku. Research Bulletin. Obihiro University
Gakujutsu Kenkyu Hokoku Res Rep Kochi Univ Nogaku — Gakujutsu Kenkyu Hokoku. Research Reports. Kochi University Nogaku
GAL — Galaxy
Gal — Galleria. Rassegna Bimestrale di Cultura
GA L — Georgia Law Review
GAL — Geschichte der Arabischen Literatur
Gal A — Galerie des Arts
Gal Act — Galenica Acta

GA Law R — Georgia Law Review
GA Laws — Georgia Laws
Ga Lawyer — Georgia Lawyer
GAlb — Gjurmime Albanologjike
Gal Bo — Galaxy Book
Gal Clin — Galicia Clinica
Gal Contemp Litt A — Galerie Contemporaine, Litteraire, Artistique
GALE — American Legion Magazine
GALE — Galerias de Arte y Salas de Exposiciones
Gale & Wh Eas — Gale and Whatley [later, Gale] on Easements
Gale Eas — Gale on Easements
Gali — Galileo
GA Libn — Georgia Librarian
GA Librn — Georgia Librarian
Galicia Clin — Galicia Clinica
Galicia Hist — Galicia Historica. Revista Bimestral
Galicia Hist Col Dip — Galicia Historica. Coleccion Diplomatica
GA LJ — Georgia Law Journal
Gal Jard A — Galerie Jardin des Arts
Gallagher — Gallagher Report
Gall Biol Act — Gallica Biologica Acta
Galleon — Galleon. Bulletin of the Society for Colonial History
Gallerie Grandi Opere Sotter — Gallerie e Grandi Opere Sotterranee
G Allevatori — Giornale degli Allevatori
Gallia F — Gallia. Fouilles et Monuments Archeologiques en France Metropolitaine
Gallia Prehist — Gallia Prehistoire
Gallia Pr Hist — Gallia Prehistoire
Gallia Suppl — Gallia-Supplement
Gallium Arsenide Relat Compd 1991 Proc Int Symp — Gallium Arsenide and Related Compounds 1991. Proceedings. International Symposium on Gallium Arsenide and Related Compounds
Gall Preh — Gallia Prehistoire
Gallup Rep — Gallup Report
Gallup Rept — Gallup Report
Gallup Rpt — Gallup Report
Gal Modes & Cost Fr — Galerie des Modes et Costumes Francais
Gal N It — Gallerie Nazionali Italiane
GALPBX — Geologie Alpine
Galpin S J — Galpin Society. Journal
Galpin Soc — Galpin Society. Journal
Galpin Soc J — Galpin Society. Journal
Galp Soc J — Galpin Society. Journal
GA LR — Georgia Law Review
GA L Rev — Georgia Law Review
GALS — Geschichte der Arabischen Litteratur. Supplement
Gal Stuker Bl — Galerie Stuker Blaetter
GALVA — Galvano
Galvano Organo Trait Surf — Galvano-Organo-Traitements de Surface
Galvano Tec — Galvano Tecnica [Later, Galvanotecnica & Processi al Plasma]
Galvanotech Kolloq — Galvanotechnisches Kolloquium
Galvanotech Oberflaechenschutz — Galvanotechnik und Oberflaechenschutz
Galvanotech Symp Kurzfassungen Vortr — Galvanotechnisches Symposium. Kurzfassungen der Vortraege
Galvanotec Nuove Finiture — Galvanotecnica and Nuove Finiture
Galvanotec Processi Plasma — Galvanotecnica e Processi al Plasma
Gal'vanotekh Obrab Poverkhn — Gal'vanotekhnika i Obrabotka Poverkhnosti
Galvano Tek Tidsskr — Galvano-Teknisk Tidsskrift
Galway Arch Hist Soc J — Galway Archaeological and Historical Society. Journal
Gam — Gambit
GAM — GAM. Bulletin du Groupe d'Acoustique Musicale
GAM — Gamma
GAME — America
Game Conservancy Annu Rev — Game Conservancy Annual Review
Game Res Assoc Annu Rep — Game Research Association. Annual Report
Game Res Rep Colo Div Wildl — Game Research Report. Colorado Division of Wildlife
Games Econom Behav — Games and Economic Behavior
Gamete Qual Fertil Regul Proc Reinier de Graaf Symp — Gamete Quality and Fertility Regulation. Proceedings. Renier de Graaf Symposium
Gamete Res — Gamete Research
GAMH — American Health
GA Mineral Newsletter — Georgia Mineral Newsletter
GA Miner Newsl — Georgia Mineral Newsletter
GAML — American Literature
GAMM — American Music
Gamma Field Symp — Gamma Field Symposia
GAMP — American Psychologist
GAMR — Americana
GAMS — Americas (English Edition)
GAMV — American Visions
Ganciclovir Ther Cytomegalovirus Infect — Ganciclovir Therapy for Cytomegalovirus Infection
Gand A — Gand Artistique
Gand A Ac — Annales Academiae Gandavensis
G & BS — Greek and Byzantine Studies
G & G — Gems & Gemology
G & G — Gyandoh and Griffiths. Sourcebook of the Constitutional Law of Ghana
G&L — Gitarre & Laute
G & N Coop — G & N Cooperator (Gippsland and Northern Cooperative)
G & PA — Girls and Physical Activity National Newsletter
G & R — Greece and Rome
G & S — Grai si Suflet
G & S J — Gilbert and Sullivan Journal
G & Wh Eas — Gale and Whatley [later, Gale] on Easements
G Anest Stomatol — Giornale di Anestesia Stomatologica

Ganita — Ganita Bharat Ganita Parisad
GANMA — Gann Monographs
Gann — Gann Japanese Journal of Cancer Research
Gann Mon — Gann Monographs
Gann Monogr — Gann Monographs
Gann Monogr Cancer Res — Gann Monograph on Cancer Research
Gannon Coll Chem J — Gannon College. Chemistry Journal
GANP — Annals. American Academy of Political and Social Science
GANQ — Antiquity
GANS — Animals
GANT — Magazine Antiques
GA Nurse — Georgia Nursing
Ga Nutr Conf Feed Ind Proc — Georgia Nutrition Conference for the Feed Industry. Proceedings
Gan Vanof IGA — Gan Vanof. Garden and Landscape. Israeli Gardeners' Association
GAnz — Geographischer Anzeiger
Ganz MAVAG Koezl — Ganz-MAVAG Koezlemenyek
GAO — Government and Opposition
GAO (Gen Accounting Office) R — GAO (General Accounting Office) Review
GA Oper — Georgia Operator
GAOR — General Assembly Including the Reports of the Meetings, the Annexes to Those Records, and the Supplements. Official Reports
GAO Rev — GAO [General Accounting Office] Review
Ga OS — Ganga Oriental Series
GAP — GAP [Group for the Advancement of Psychiatry] Report
GAP — Government of Alberta Publications
GAp — Guillaume Apollinaire
GAPH — American Journal of Public Health
GAPHYOR — Gaz-Physique-Orsay Database
GAPP — Academy of Political Science. Proceedings
Ga Practician — Georgia Practician
Ga Prob Offic Assn Conf Yrbk — Georgia Probation Officers Association Conference. Yearbook
GAPS — American Political Science Review
GAQT — Anthropological Quarterly
GAR — Galling Report on Italy
GA R — Georgia Review
G a R — Greece and Rome
GaR — Greece and Rome
GARA — Art in America
GARAD — Gastrointestinal Radiology
GArb — Geistige Arbeit
GARC — Archaeology
G Arcad Sci Lett & A — Giornale Arcadico di Scienze, Lettere, ed Arti
Garcia de Orta Geogr — Garcia de Orta. Serie de Geografia
Garcia de Orta Geol — Garcia de Orta. Serie de Geologia
Garcia de Orta (Lisb) — Garcia de Orta. (Lisbon)
Garcia de Orta Ser Bot — Garcia de Orta. Serie de Botanica
Garcia de Orta Ser Estud Agron — Garcia de Orta. Serie de Estudos Agronomicos
Garcia de Orta Ser Farmacogn — Garcia de Orta. Serie de Farmacognosia
Garcia de Orta Ser Geol — Garcia de Orta. Serie de Geologia
Garcia de Orta Ser Zool — Garcia de Orta. Serie de Zoologia
Garcia Lorca Rev — Garcia Lorca Review
Garcia Orta Ser Antropobiol — Garcia de Orta. Serie de Antropobiologia
GARC Newsl — GARC [Graphic Arts Research Center] Newsletter
Garc Orta — Garcia de Orta
GARD — Architectural Digest
Gard Abstr — Gardener's Abstracts
Gard & Home B — Garden and Home Builder
Gard Apercu Tr — Notice ou Apercu Analytique des Travaux de l'Academie Royale du Gard
Gard Beautiful — Garden Beautiful
Gard Bull (Singapore) — Gardens Bulletin (Singapore)
Gard Chron — Gardeners' Chronicle and Gardening Illustrated
Gard Chron Am — Gardeners' Chronicle of America
Gard Chron Amer — Gardener's Chronicle of America
Gard Chron (Lond) — Gardeners' Chronicle (London)
Gard Companion Florists Guide — Garden Companion and Florists' Guide
Gard Digest — Garden Digest
Garden & F — Garden and Forest
Gardener Edinburgh — Gardener. A Magazine of Horticulture and Floriculture (Edinburgh)
Garden Hist — Garden History. Journal. Garden History Society
Garden History Soc Newsletter — Garden History Society. Newsletter
Garden Is — Garden Island
Garden J — Garden Journal
Garden J R Hortic Soc — Garden. Journal of the Royal Horticultural Society
Garden New York — Garden. New York Botanical Garden
Gard Farmers J — Gardeners' and Farmers' Journal
Gard Foresters Rec — Gardener's and Forester's Record
Gard Fruit Flower Guide Miss Coop Ext Serv Ext Hortic Dep — Gardens, Fruit, and Flower Guide. Mississippi Cooperative Extension Service. Extension Horticulture Department
Gard Gardening — Gardens and Gardening. The Studio Gardening Annual
Gard Illustr — Gardening Illustrated
Gard J — Garden Journal
Gard J New York Bot Gard — Garden Journal. New York Botanical Garden
Gard J NY Bot Gard — Garden Journal. New York Botanical Garden
Gard Life London — Garden Life (London)
Gard M — Garden Magazine
Gard Mag Calcium — Gardening Magazine (Calcium)
Gard Mag London — Gardeners' Magazine (London)
Gard Monthly Hort — Gardener's Monthly and Horticulturist

Gard Not Tr Ac — Notice ou Apercu Analytique des Travaux de l'Academie Royale du Gard
Gard Pacific — Gardens of the Pacific
Gard Pract Florist — Gardener and Practical Florist
Gard Tr Ac — Notice ou Apercu Analytique des Travaux de l'Academie Royale du Gard
Gard Work Villa Gard — Garden-Work for Villa, Suburban, Town, and Cottage Gardens
Gard World — Gardening World
GA Rev — Georgia Review
GARI — American Rifleman
GARIA7 — Ghana. Animal Research Institute. Annual Report
Garland Ref Lib Humanities — Garland Reference Library of the Humanities
GARM — Armed Forces and Society
GARN — ARTnews
GARP Publ Ser — GARP [Global Atmospheric Research Programme] Publications Series
GARR — Architectural Record
Gartenbau Forsch — Gartenbau-Forschung
Gartenbau Reich — Gartenbau im Reich
Gartenbauwiss — Gartenbauwissenschaft
Garten u Kleintierz C (Imker) — Garten und Kleintierzucht. C (Imker)
Gartenzeitung Oesterr Gartenbauges Wien — Gartenzeitung der Oesterreichischen Gartenbaugesellschaft in Wien
Gartenz III Fl — Gartenzeitschrift Illustrierte Flora
G Arteriosclr — Giornale della Arteriosclerosi
G Artistico — Giornale Artistico
Gart Landschaft Landscape Archit Plann — Garten Landschaft. Landscape Architecture Planning
Gar TS — Garrett Theological Studies
Gart Schoenheit — Garten-Schoenheit. Illustrierte Schrift fuer den Garten- und Blumenfreund, Liebhaber und Fachmann
Gart Z Gaertn III Fl — Garten-Zeitschrift fuer Gaertner und Gartenfreunde, Siedler, und Kleingaertner.Illustrierte Flora
Garyounis Sci Bull — Garyounis Scientific Bulletin
GAS — Gas. Maandblad voor de Gasindustrie
GAS — German-American Studies
GAS — Geschichte des Arabischen Schrifttums
Gas A — Gaseta de les Arts
GASAA — Gazzetta Sanitaria
Gas Abstr — Gas Abstracts
Gas Age — Gas Age-Record
Gas Age Rec — Gas Age-Record
Gas Age Rec Nat Gas — Gas Age Record and Natural Gas
GA SBJ — Georgia State Bar Journal
Gas Can — Gas in Canada
Gas Chromat Abstr — Gas Chromatography Abstracts
Gas Chromatogr Int Sym — Gas Chromatography. International Symposium
Gas Chromatogr Proc Int Symp (Eur) — Gas Chromatography. Proceedings of the International Symposium (Europe)
Ga Sch Technol State Eng Exp Stn Circ — Georgia. School of Technology. State Engineering Experiment Station.Circular
GA Sch Technol State Eng Exp Stn Repr — Georgia. School of Technology. State Engineering Experiment Station. Reprint
Ga Sch Technol State Eng Exp Stn Res Eng — Georgia School of Technology. State Engineering Experiment Station. Research Engineer
Ga Sch Technol State Eng Exp Stn Spec Rep — Georgia. School of Technology. State Engineering Experiment Station.Special Report
Gas Cond Conf Proc — Gas Conditioning Conference. Proceedings
Gas Consum — Future Gas Consumption of the US
Gas Counc (GB) Res Commun — Gas Council (Great Britain). Research Communications
Gas Counc (Gt Brit) Res Commun — Gas Council (Great Britain). Research Communication
Gas Dig — Gas Digest
Gas Discharges Int Conf — Gas Discharges. International Conference
Gas Eng — Gas Engineer
Gas Eng — Gas Engineering
Gas Engine Manage — Gas Engineering and Management
Gas Eng Mag — Gas Engineering Magazine
Gas Eng Manage — Gas Engineering and Management
Gas Engng Mgmt — Gas Engineering and Management
Gas Engng Mgmt — Gas Engineering and Management
Gaseous Air Pollut Plant Metab Proc Int Symp — Gaseous Air Pollutants and Plant Metabolism. Proceedings. International Symposium on Gaseous Air Pollutants and Plant Metabolism
Gaseous Dielectr Proc Int Symp — Gaseous Dielectrics. Proceedings. International Symposium on Gaseous Dielectrics
Gaseous Electron Its Appl Pap Aust Jpn Workshop — Gaseous Electronics and its Applications. Papers. Australia-Japan Workshop on Gaseous Electronics and its Applications
Gases Res Ind — Gases in Research and Industry
Gases Res Ind Gas Div CIG — Gases in Research and Industry. Commonwealth Industrial Gases Ltd.
G As F — Goettinger Asiatische Forschungen
GASGB — Gasgemeinschaft
GASHD — Gazo Shindan
Gas Heat Ind — Gas Heat in Industry
Gas Heat Int — Gas Heat International
Gas Ind — Gas Industries
Gas Ind (Leipzig) — Gas Industrie (Leipzig)
Gas Ind (London) — Gas Industry (London)
Gas Ind Manuf Gas Ed — Gas Industry. Manufactured Gas Edition
Gas Ind Nat Gas Ed — Gas Industry. Natural Gas Edition
Gas Ind Park Ridge IL — Gas Industries (Park Ridge, Illinois)

Gas Inst News — Gas Institute News
Gas J — Gas Journal
Gas Kinet Energy Transfer — Gas Kinetics and Energy Transfer
G As (London) Pr — Geologists' Association (London). Proceedings
Gas Mag — Gas Magazine
Gas Meas Inst — Gas Measurement Institute
Gas Oil Pwr — Gas and Oil Power
GASP — American Spectator
GASPBY — Geological Association of Canada. Special Paper
Gas (Phila) — Gas (Philadelphia)
Gas Process Assoc Annu Conv Proc — Gas Processors Association. Annual Convention. Proceedings
Gas Process Assoc Proc — Gas Processors Association. Proceedings
GASR — American Sociological Review
Gas Rec — Gas Record
Gas Res Board Commun — Gas Research Board. Communication
Gas Res Inst Dig — Gas Research Institute Digest
Gas Rev — Gas Review
Gasschutz Luftschutz Ausg B — Gasschutz und Luftschutz. Ausgabe B
Gas Sep Purif — Gas Separation and Purification
Gas Supply Rev — Gas Supply Review
GAST — Astronomy
GAST — Gastronomia Espanola
GA St BJ — Georgia State Bar Journal
GASTDE — Butterworths International Medical Reviews. Gastroenterology
Gastech Proc — Gastech Proceedings
Gastroent — Gastroenterologia
Gastroent — Gastroenterology
Gastroenterol — Gastroenterologia
Gastroenterol Abstr & Cit — Gastroenterology. Abstracts and Citations
Gastroenterol Abstr Citations — Gastroenterology. Abstracts and Citations
Gastroenterol Acta Conv Med Intern Hung — Gastroenterologia Acta. Conventus Medicinae Internae Hungarici
Gastroenterol Annu — Gastroenterology Annual
Gastroenterol Clin Biol — Gastroenterologie Clinique et Biologique
Gastroenterol Clin North Am — Gastroenterology Clinics of North America
Gastroenterol Endosc — Gastroenterological Endoscopy
Gastroenterol Fortbildungskurse Prax — Gastroenterologische Fortbildungskurse fuer die Praxis
Gastroenterol Hepatol — Gastroenterologia y Hepatologia
Gastroenterol Jpn — Gastroenterologia Japonica
Gastroenterol Nurs — Gastroenterology Nursing
Gastroenterologia Suppl — Gastroenterologia. Supplementum
Gastroenterol Stoffwechsel — Gastroenterologie und Stoffwechsel
Gastroenty — Gastroenterology
Gastroin En — Gastrointestinal Endoscopy
Gastroint Endosc — Gastrointestinal Endoscopy
Gastrointest Endosc — Gastrointestinal Endoscopy
Gastrointest Endosc Clin N Am — Gastrointestinal Endoscopy Clinics of North America
Gastrointest Motil Int Symp — Gastrointestinal Motility. International Symposium
Gastrointest Motil Proc Int Symp — Gastrointestinal Motility. Proceedings. International Symposium onGastrointestinal Motility
Gastrointest Radiol — Gastrointestinal Radiology
Gastrointest Radiol Rev — Gastrointestinal Radiology Reviews
G Astron — Giornale di Astronomia
Gas Turb — Turbomachinery International
Gas Turb H — Turbomachinery International. Handbook
Gas Turbine Int — Gas Turbine International
GASU — Journal of Asian Studies
Gas Waerme Int — Gas Waerme International
Gas Wld — Gas World
Gas World Gas J — Gas World and Gas Journal
Gas World Int — Gas World International
Gas Z Ration Energieanwend — Gas. Zeitschrift fuer Rationelle Energieanwendung
Gateway Med — Gateway to Medicine
GATF Bull — GATF [Graphic Arts Technical Foundation] Bulletin
GATF Educ Rep — GATF [Graphic Arts Technical Foundation] Education Report
GATF Envir Control Rept — GATF [Graphic Arts Technical Foundation] Environmental Control Report
GATF Res Progr — GATF [Graphic Arts Technical Foundation] Research Progress
GATF Res Prog Rep — GATF [Graphic Arts Technical Foundation] Research Progress Report
GATF Res Proj Rep — GATF [Graphic Arts Technical Foundation] Research Project Report
GATF Tech Serv Inform — GATF [Graphic Arts Technical Foundation] Technical Service Information
Gath — [The] Gathering
GATN (German-Am Trade News) — GATN (German-American Trade News)
GATO — Africa Today
Gatooma Res Stn Annu Rep — Gatooma Research Station. Annual Report
GATT — General Agreement on Tariffs and Trade
GATT — General Agreement on Tariffs and Trade Bibliography
Gattefosse Bull Tech — Gattefosse. Bulletin Technique
Gattefosse Rep — Gattefosse. Report
Gau — Gaulois [Paris daily]
GAUD — Audubon
GAUSD — Gasohol USA
Gauss Ges (Goettingen) Mitt — Gauss Gesellschaft eV. (Goettingen). Mitteilungen
Gauss Resultate — Resultate aus den Beobachtungen des Magnetischen Vereins. Gauss und Weber
Gav — Gavroche
GAVC — Audio-Visual Communications
GAVC — AVC Delivery and Development [Formerly, Audio-Visual Communications]

GAVEA — Galpin Society. Journal
Gavel — Milwaukee Bar Association. Gavel
GA Vet — Georgia Veterinarian
Gavr — Gavroche
GA Water Qual Control Board Tech Rep — Georgia. Water Quality Control Board. Technical Report
Gay — Gay Liberation
Gayana Bot — Gayana Botanica
Gayana Bot Misc — Gayana Botanica Miscelanea
Gayana Misc — Gayana Miscelanea
Gayana Zool — Gayana Zoologia
Gay Insrg — Gay Insurgent
Gay L — Gay Literature
Gay News — Gay Community News
Gay Sun — Gay Sunshine
GAZ — Gesamtverzeichnis
Gaz — Weekly Law Gazette
Gaz A Diseg — Gazzettino dell'Arte del Disegno
Gaz Agr (Angola) — Gazeta do Agricultor (Angola)
Gaz Antiqua — Gazzetta Antiquaria
Gaz Apic — Gazette Apicole
Gaz Apicole — Gazette Apicole
Gaz Arch — Gazette Archeologique
Gaz Archeol — Gazette Archeologique
Gaz Architectes & Bat — Gazette des Architectes et du Batiment
Gaz Artisti — Gazzetta degli Artisti
Gaz Aujourd — Gaz d'Aujourd'hui
Gaz BA — Gazette des Beaux-Arts
Gaz Bea-Art — Gazette des Beaux-Arts
Gaz Beaux-Arts — Gazette des Beaux-Arts
Gaz Bergamo — Gazzetta di Bergamo
Gaz Bon Ton — Gazette du Bon Ton
Gaz Bur Brev — Gazette. Bureau des Brevets
Gaz Chal Int — Gaz Chaleur International
Gaz Chim It — Gazzetta Chimica Italiana
Gaz Chim Ital — Gazzetta Chimica Italiana
Gaz Clin — Gazeta Clinica
Gaz Clin (S Paulo) — Gazeta Clinica (Sao Paulo)
Gaz Com — Gazzetta Commerciale
Gaz Cukrow — Gazeta Cukrownicza
Gazdasag es Jogtud — Gazdasag es Jogtudomany
Gaz Des Trib Libano Syriens — Gazette des Tribunaux Libano-Syriens
Gaz D Hop — Gazette des Hopitaux Civils et Militaires
Gazd Koezl — Gazdaszati Koezloeny
Gazd Lapok — Gazdasagi Lapok
Gaz Econ — Gazette Economique
Gaz Egypt Paediatr Assoc — Gazette. Egyptian Paediatric Association
Gaz Egypt Soc Gynaecol Obstet — Gazette. Egyptian Society of Gynaecology and Obstetrics
Gazelle Rev Lit ME — Gazelle Review of Literature on the Middle East
Gazeta Agric Angola — Gazeta Agricola de Angola
Gazeta Cukrown — Gazeta Cukrownicza
Gazette — Law Society. Gazette
Gazette — Rhode Island Foreign Language Gazette
Gazette BA — Gazette des Beaux Arts
Gazette Univ WA — Gazette. University of Western Australia
Gaz Eur Inf — Gaz Europe Information
Gaz Fis — Gazeta di Fisica
Gaz Hebd Sci Med Bordeaux — Gazette Hebdomadaire des Sciences Medicales de Bordeaux
Gaz Hebd Sc Med Bordeaux — Gazette Hebdomadaire des Sciences Medicales de Bordeaux
Gaz Hop Civ Mil — Gazette des Hopitaux Civils et Militaires
Gaz Hopit Civ — Gazette des Hopitaux Civils et Militaires
Gazi Med J — Gazi Medical Journal
Gaz India — Gazette India
Gaz Inst Med Lab Sci — Gazette. Institute of Medical Laboratory Science
Gazi Univ Eczacilik Fak Derg — Gazi Universitesi Eczacilik Fakultesi Dergisi
Gazi Univ Fac Pharm J — Gazi University. Faculty of Pharmacy. Journal
Gaz Kasr El Aini Fac Med — Gazette. Kasr El Aini Faculty of Medicine
GazL — Gazette de Lausanne [Lausanne daily]
Gaz Laus — Gazette de Lausanne
GazLe — Gazette des Lettres
Gaz Lettres — Gazette des Lettres
Gaz Lett Torino — Gazzetta Letteraria di Torino
GazLit — Gazette Litteraire
Gaz Livre Md — Gazette du Livre Medieval
Gaz L Soc of Upper Can — Gazette. Law Society of Upper Canada
Gaz Mat — Gazeta de Matematica
Gaz Math — Gazette des Mathematiciens
Gaz Mat Mat Inform — Gazeta Matematica Perfectionare Metodica si Metodologica in Matematica si Informatica
Gaz Mat Publ Lunara pentru Tineret — Gazeta Matematica Publicatie Lunara pentru Tineret
Gaz Mat Ser A — Societatea de Stiinte Matematice din RPR. Gazeta Matematica Publicatie pentru Studiul si Raspindirea Stiintelor Matematice. Seria A
Gaz Med — Gazettes Medicales
Gaz Med Algerie — Gazette Medicale de l'Algerie
Gaz Med Bahia — Gazeta Medica da Bahia
Gaz Med De Paris — Gazette Medicale de Paris
Gaz Med Fr — Gazette Medicale de France
Gaz Med Nantes — Gazette Medicale de Nantes
Gaz Med Orient — Gazette Medicale d'Orient
Gaz Med Paris — Gazette Medicale de Paris
Gaz Med Picardie — Gazette Medicale de Picardie

Gaz Med Port — Gazeta Medica Portuguesa
Gaz Milano — Gazzetta di Milano
Gaz (Montrl) — Gazette (Montreal)
Gaz Mus — Gazeta Musical e de Todas las Artes
Gaz Num — Gazzettino Numismatico
Gaz Numi Fr — Gazette Numismatique Francaise
Gaz Obst — Gazette Obstetricale
Gazodin Teploobmen — Gazodinamika i Teploobmen
Gazov Delo — Gazovoe Delo
Gazov Khromatogr — Gazovaya Khromatografiya
Gazov Khromatogr Tr Vses Konf — Gazovaya Khromatografiya. Trudy Vsesoyuznoi Konferentsii
Gazov Promst — Gazovaya Promyshlennost
Gazov Promst Ser Ispolz Gaza Nar Khoz Obz Inf — Gazovaya Promyshlennost. Seriya. Ispol'zovanie Gaza v NarodnomKhozyaistve. Obzornaya Informatsiya
Gazov Promst Ser Ispolz Gaza Nar Khoz Ref Inf — Gazovaya Promyshlennost. Seriya. Ispol'zovanie Gaza v NarodnomKhozyaistve. Referativnaya Informatsiya
Gazov Promst Ser Podgot Pererab Gaza Gazov Kondens Obz Inf — Gazovaya Promyshlennost. Seriya. Podgotovka i Pererabotka Gaza iGazovogo Kondensata. Obzornaya Informatsiya
Gazov Promst Ser Podgot Pererab Gaza Gazov Kondens Ref Inf — Gazovaya Promyshlennost. Seriya. Podgotovka i Pererabotka Gaza iGazovogo Kondensata. Referativnaya Informatsiya
Gazov Promst Ser Transp Khranenie Gaza Obz Inf — Gazovaya Promyshlennost. Seriya. Transport i Khranenie Gaza. ObzornayaInformatsiya
Gazov Promst Ser Transp Khranenie Gaza Ref Inf — Gazovaya Promyshlennost. Seriya. Transport i Khranenie Gaza.Referativnaya Informatsiya
Gaz Paris — Gazette de Paris
Gaz Parma — Gazzetta di Parma
Gaz Pharm — Gazeta da Pharmacia
Gaz Privileg Milano — Gazzetta Privilegiata di Milano
Gaz Privileg Venezia — Gazzetta Privilegiata di Venezia
GAZS — Gesamtverzeichnis Auslaendischer Zeitschriften und Serien
Gaz Trav — Gazette du Travail
Gaz Uff — Gazzetta Ufficiale della Repubblica Italiana
Gaz Univ Newcastle — Gazette. University of Newcastle
Gaz Univ Syd — Gazette. University of Sydney
Gaz Univ WA — Gazette. University of Western Australia
Gaz Univ Wits — Gazette. University of the Witwatersrand
Gaz Ven — Gazzetta Veneta
Gaz Venezia — Gazzetta di Venezia
Gaz WA Inst Tech — Gazette: Official Journal of the Western Australian Institute of Technology
Gaz Woda Tech Sanit — Gaz Woda i Technika Sanitarna
Gazy Litom Met Dokl Soveshch Teor Liteinykh Protsessov — Gazy v Litom Metalle. Doklady Soveshchaniya po Teorii LiteinykhProtsessov
Gaz Zan EA — Gazette for Zanzibar and East Africa
Gazz Chim Ital — Gazzetta Chimica Italiana
Gazz Clin Sped Civ Palermo — Gazzetta Clinica dello Spedale Civico di Palermo
Gazz Internaz Med — Gazzetta Internazionale di Medicina
Gazz Internaz Med Chir — Gazzetta Internazionale di Medicina e Chirurgia
Gazz Int Med Chir — Gazzetta Internazionale di Medicina e Chirurgia
Gazz Med Ital — Gazzetta Medica Italiana
Gazz Med Ital Arch Sci Med — Gazzetta Medica Italiana. Archivio per le Scienze Mediche
Gazz Med Italo Argent — Gazzetta Medica Italo-Argentina
Gazz Med Ital Prov Venete — Gazzetta Medica Italiana. Provincie Venete
Gazz Med Napol — Gazzetta Medica Napolitana
Gazz Med Sicil — Gazzetta Medica Siciliana
Gazz Osped Clin — Gazzetta degli Ospedali e delle Cliniche
Gazz Osp Milano — Gazzetta degli Ospedali Milano
Gazz Sanit — Gazzetta Sanitaria
Gazz Sanit Edn Francaise — Gazzetta Sanitaria. Edition Francaise
Gazz Sanit (Engl Issue) — Gazzetta Sanitaria (English Issue)
Gazz Sicil Med e Chir — Gazzetta Siciliana di Medicina e Chirurgia d'Igiene e d'Interessi Professionali
Gazz Uff Repub Ital — Gazzetta Ufficiale della Repubblica Italiana
GB — Geschiedkundige Bladen
Gb — Gildeboek
GB — Golden Bough
GB — Gouvernementsblad van Suriname
GB — Grain Bulletin
GB — Grazer Beitraege
GB — Weekblad voor Gemeentebelangen
GBA — Gazette des Beaux-Arts
GBA & Tec — Giornale di Belle Arti e Technologia
GBAC — Backpacker
GB Aeronaut Res Counc Curr Pap — Great Britain. Aeronautical Research Council. Current Papers
GB Agric Res Counc Letcombe Lab Annu Rep — Great Britain. Agricultural Research Council. Letcombe Laboratory. Annual Report
GB Agric Res Counc Radiobiol Lab ARCRL — Great Britain. Agricultural Research Council. Radiobiological Laboratory. ARCRL
GBAM — Business America
GBAP — Gazette des Beaux Arts (Paris)
G Batteriol Immunol — Giornale di Batteriologia e Immunologia
G Batteriol Virol Immunol — Giornale di Batteriologia, Virologia, ed Immunologia
G Batteriol Virol Immunol Ann Osp Maria Vittoria Torino — Giornale di Batteriologia, Virologia, ed Immunologia. Annali dell'Ospedale Maria Vittoria di Torino
G Batteriol Virol Immunol Clin — Giornale di Batteriologia, Virologia, ed Immunologia. Annali dell'Ospedale Maria Vittoria di Torino. Parte 2. Sezione Clinica

G Batteriol Virol Immunol Microbiol — Giornale di Batteriologia, Virologia, ed Immunologia. Annali dell'Ospedale Maria Vittoria di Torino. Parte 1. Sezione Microbiologica
GBB — Gay Books Bulletin
GB Cent Unit Environ Pollut Pollut Pap — Great Britain. Central Unit on Environmental Pollution. Pollution Paper
GBCO — Great Britain. Colonial Office
GB Dep Health Soc Secur Rep Public Health Med Subj — Great Britain. Department of Health and Social Security. Reports on Public Health and Medical Subjects
GB Dep Sci Ind Res Chem Res Spec Rep — Great Britain. Department of Scientific and Industrial Research. Chemical Research. Special Report
GB Dep Sci Ind Res Food Invest Board Spec Rep — Great Britain. Department of Scientific and Industrial Research. Food Investigation Board. Special Report
GB Dep Sci Ind Res Food Invest Food Sci Abstr — Great Britain. Department of Scientific and Industrial Research. FoodInvestigation. Food Science Abstracts
GB Dep Sci Ind Res Food Invest Tech Pap — Great Britain. Department of Scientific and Industrial Research. Food Investigation Board. Technical Paper
GB Dep Sci Ind Res For Comm Rep For Res — Great Britain. Department of Scientific and Industrial Research.Forestry Commission. Reports on Forest Research
GB Dep Sci Ind Res For Prod Res — Great Britain. Department of Scientific and Industrial Research.Forest Products Research
GB Dep Sci Ind Res For Prod Res Bull — Great Britain. Department of Scientific and Industrial Research. Forest Products Research Bulletin
GB Dep Sci Ind Res For Prod Res Spec Rep — Great Britain. Department of Scientific and Industrial Research. Forest Products Research Special Report
GB Dep Sci Ind Res Fuel Res — Great Britain. Department of Scientific and Industrial Research. Fuel Research.Publication
GB Dep Sci Ind Res Fuel Res Fuel Abstr — Great Britain. Department of Scientific and Industrial Research. Fuel Research.Fuel Abstracts
GB Dep Sci Ind Res Fuel Res Surv Pap — Great Britain. Department of Scientific and Industrial Research. Fuel Research.Survey Paper
GB Dep Sci Ind Res Fuel Res Tech Pap — Great Britain. Department of Scientific and Industrial Research. Fuel Research.Technical Paper
GB Dep Sci Ind Res Index Lit Food Invest — Great Britain. Department of Scientific and Industrial Research. Indexto the Literature of Food Investigation
GB Dep Sci Ind Res Natl Build Stud Res Pap — Great Britain. Department of Scientific and Industrial Research. National Building Studies Research Paper
GB Dep Sci Ind Res Overseas Tech Rep — Great Britain. Department of Scientific and Industrial Research. Overseas Technical Report
GB Dep Sci Ind Res Pest Infest Res Board Rep — Great Britain. Department of Scientific and Industrial Research. Pest Infestation Research Board. Report
GB Dep Sci Ind Res Rep Warren Spring Lab — Great Britain. Department of Scientific and Industrial Research.Report. Warren Spring Laboratory
GB Dep Sci Ind Res Road Note — Great Britain. Department of Scientific and Industrial Research. Road Note
GB Dep Sci Ind Res Road Res Lab Rep RRL — Great Britain. Department of Scientific and Industrial Research. Road Research Laboratory. Report RRL
GB Dep Sci Ind Res Road Res Lab Road Res Tech Pap — Great Britain. Department of Scientific and Industrial Research. Road Research Laboratory. Road Research Technical Paper
GB Dep Sci Ind Res Road Res Road Abstr — Great Britain. Department of Scientific and Industrial Research.Road Research. Road Research Abstracts
GB Dep Sci Ind Res Torry Res Stn Annu Rep — Great Britain. Department of Scientific and Industrial Research. Torry ResearchStation. Annual Report
GB Dep Sci Ind Res Torry Tech Pap — Great Britain. Department of Scientific and Industrial Research. Torry Technical Paper
GB Dep Trade Ind Lab Gov Chem Misc Rep — Great Britain. Department of Trade and Industry. Laboratory of the GovernmentChemist. Miscellaneous Report
GB Dep Trade Ind Warren Spring Lab Rev — Great Britain. Department of Trade and Industry. Warren Spring Laboratory. Review
GBDHV — Geschichtsblaetter des Deutschen Hugenottenvereins
GB Digest — GB Digest (Girls' Brigade)
GBDP — Giessener Beitraege zur Deutschen Philologie
GBE — Great Britain and the East
GBEM — Journal of Broadcasting and Electronic Media
GB Explos Res Dev Establ Tech Note — Great Britain. Explosives Research and Development Establishment. Technical Note
GB Explos Res Dev Establ Tech Rep — Great Britain. Explosives Research and Development Establishment.Technical Report
GBF Monogr Ser — GBF [*Gesellschaft fuer Biotechnologische Forschung*] Monograph Series
GB For Comm Annu Rep For Comm — Great Britain. Forestry Commission. Annual Report of the Forestry Commissioners
GB For Comm Bookl — Great Britain. Forestry Commission. Booklet
GB For Comm Bull — Great Britain. Forestry Commission. Bulletin
GB For Comm For Rec — Great Britain. Forestry Commission. Forest Record
GB For Comm Leafl — Great Britain. Forestry Commission. Leaflet
GB For Comm Occas Pap — Great Britain. Forestry Commission. Occasional Paper
GB For Comm Rep For Res — Great Britain. Forestry Commission. Report on Forest Research
GB For Comm Res Branch Pap — Great Britain. Forestry Commission. Research Branch Paper
GB For Comm Res Dev Pap — Great Britain. Forestry Commission. Research and Development Paper
GB For Prod Res Board Bull — Great Britain. Forest Products Research Board. Bulletin
GB For Prod Res Bull — Great Britain. Forest Products Research Bulletin
GB For Prod Res Spec Rep — Great Britain. Forest Products Research Special Report
GBG — Good Book Guide
GBHG — Better Homes and Gardens

GBI — Guides Bleues Illustres
GBIK — Bicycling
GBIL — Billboard
GB Inst Geol Sci Annu Rep — Great Britain. Institute of Geological Sciences. Annual Report
GB Inst Geol Sci Geomagn Bull — Great Britain. Institute of Geological Sciences. Geomagnetic Bulletin
GB Inst Geol Sci Miner Assess Rep — Great Britain. Institute of Geological Sciences. Mineral Assessment Report
GB Inst Geol Sci Miner Resour Consult Comm Miner Dossier — Great Britain. Institute of Geological Sciences. Mineral Resources ConsultativeCommittee. Mineral Dossier
GB Inst Geol Sci Overseas Mem — Great Britain. Institute of Geological Sciences. Overseas Memoir
GB Inst Geol Sci Rep — Great Britain. Institute of Geological Sciences. Report
G Biochim — Giornale di Biochimica
G Biol Appl Ind Chim — Giornale di Biologia Applicata alla Industria Chimica
G Biol Appl Ind Chim Aliment — Giornale di Biologia Applicata alla Industria Chimica ed Alimentare
G Biol Ind Agrar Aliment — Giornale di Biologia Industriale Agraria ed Alimentare
G Biol Med Sper — Giornale di Biologia e Medicina Sperimentale
GBISAX — Godisnik na Bioloskog Instituta Univerziteta u Sarajevu
GBJ — Georgia Bar Journal
GB Jt Fire Res Organ Fire Res Tech Pap — Great Britain. Joint Fire Research Organization. Fire ResearchTechnical Paper
GBK — Gentse Bijdragen tot de Kunstgeschiedenis en de Ouheidkunde
GBKA — Gentsche Bijdragen tot de Kunstgeschiedenis (Antwerp)
GBKG — Gentsche Bijdragen tot de Kunstgeschiedenis
GBKMA — Gesellschaft zur Bekampfung der Krebskrankheiten im Nordrhein-Westfalen. Mitteilungsdienst
GBKO — Gentse Bijdragen tot de Kunstgeschiedenis en de Ouheidkunde
GBL — Brandstoffen Visie. Vakblad voor de Mandel in Aardolieprodukten en Vaste Brandstoffen
GBL — Geschichte des Byzantinischen Literatur
GBI — Gregoriusblatt. Organ fuer Katholische Kirchenmusik
GB Lab Gov Chem Occas Pap — Great Britain. Laboratory of the Government Chemist. Occasional Paper
GB Land Resour Dev Cent Land Resour Study — Great Britain. Land Resources Development Centre. Land Resource Study
GB Land Resour Div Land Resour Bibliogr — Great Britain. Land Resources Division. Land Resource Bibliography
GB Land Resour Div Land Resour Study — Great Britain. Land Resources Division. Land Resource Study
GBLC — Black Collegian
GBI I — Gesetzblatt der DDR. Teil I
GBI II — Gesetzblatt der DDR. Teil II
GBLS — Black Scholar
GBLS — Greifswalder Beitraege zur Literatur und Stilforschung
GBM — Gelre. Bijdragen en Mededeelingen
GBM — Golden Book Magazine
GB Miner Resour Consult Comm Miner Dossier — Great Britain. Mineral Resources Consultative Committee. Mineral Dossier
GB Minist Agric Fish Food Bull — Great Britain. Ministry of Agriculture, Fisheries, and Food. Bulletin
GB Minist Agric Fish Food Dir Fish Res Fish Res Tech Rep — Great Britain. Ministry of Agriculture, Fisheries, and Food. Directorate of Fisheries Research. Fisheries Research Technical Report
GB Minist Agric Fish Food Dir Fish Res Lab Leafl — Great Britain. Ministry of Agriculture, Fisheries, and Food. Directorate of Fisheries Research. Laboratory Leaflet
GB Minist Agric Fish Food Fish Radiobiol Lab Tech Rep — Great Britain. Ministry of Agriculture, Fisheries, and Food. FisheriesRadiobiological Laboratory. Technical Report
GB Minist Agric Fish Food Ref Book — Great Britain. Ministry of Agriculture, Fisheries, and Food. Reference Book
GB Minist Agric Fish Food Tech Bull — Great Britain. Ministry of Agriculture, Fisheries, and Food. Technical Bulletin
GB Minist Aviat Aeronaut Res Counc Curr Pap — Great Britain. Ministry of Aviation. Aeronautic Research Council. Current Papers
GB Minist Overseas Dev Land Resour Div Land Resour Bibliogr — Great Britain. Ministry of Overseas Development. Land Resources Division. Land Resource Bibliography
GB Minist Overseas Dev Land Resour Div Prog Rep — Great Britain. Ministry of Overseas Development. Land Resources Division. Progress Report
GB Minist Power Saf Mines Res Establ Res Rep — Great Britain. Ministry of Power. Safety in Mines Research Establishment. Research Report
GB Ministry Agric Fish Food Fish Lab Leafl New Ser — Great Britain. Ministry of Agriculture, Fisheries, and Food. Fisheries Laboratory Leaflet. New Series
GB Minist Technol For Prod Res Bull — Great Britain. Ministry of Technology. Forest Products Research. Bulletin
GB Minist Technol For Prod Res Spec Rep — Great Britain. Ministry of Technology. Forest Products Research. Special Report
GB Minist Technol Warren Spring Lab Rep — Great Britain. Ministry of Technology. Warren Spring Laboratory. Report
GBMRB — Geschichtsblaetter fuer Mittelrheinische Bistuemer
GB Nat Build Stud Res Pap — Great Britain. National Building Studies. Research Paper
GB Nat Build Stud Tech Pap — Great Britain. National Building Studies. Technical Paper
GB Nat Environ Res Counc News J — Great Britain. Natural Environment Research Council. News Journal
GB Nat Environ Res Counc Publ Ser D — Great Britain. Natural Environment Research Council. Publications. Series D
GB Nat Environ Res Counc Rep — Great Britain. Natural Environment Research Council. Report

GB Natl Eng Lab NEL Rep — Great Britain. National Engineering Laboratory. NEL Report
GBNBA7 — Geologische Blaetter fuer Nordost-Bayern und Angrenzende Gebiete
GBNTL — Goettingische Bibliothek der Neuesten Theologischen Literatur
GBOIA — Giornale Botanico Italiano
GBON — Bon Appetit
G Bordo — Giornale di Bordo
GBOSBU — Geobios
GBOT — Boating
G Bot Ital — Giornale Botanico Italiano
GB Pest Infest Res Board Rep — Great Britain. Pest Infestation Research Board. Report
GBPUA6 — Geological Bulletin. Punjab University
GBQMAL — Genie Biologique et Medical
GBR — Gemengde Branche. Vakblad voor de Huishoudelijke en Luxe Artikelen, Glas, Porselein, Aardewerk, en Kunstnijverheid
GB R Aircr Establ Tech Rep — Great Britain. Royal Aircraft Establishment. Technical Report
GB R Armament Res Dev Establ RARDE Memo — Great Britain. Royal Armament Research and Development Establishment. RARDE Memorandum
GBRD — Broadcasting
G Brescia — Giornale di Brescia
GB Road Res Lab Road Note — Great Britain. Road Research Laboratory. Road Note
GB Road Res Lab Road Tech Pap — Great Britain. Road Research Laboratory. Road Research Technical Paper
GBRP — Giessener Beitraege zur Romanischen Philologie
GBS — Glasgow Bibliographical Society
GB Saf Mines Res Establ Rep — Great Britain. Safety in Mines Research Establishment. Report
GB Saf Mines Res Establ Res Rep — Great Britain. Safety in Mines Research Establishment. Research Report
GBSC — Bioscience
GBSLM — Geschichtsblaetter fuer Stadt und Land Magdeburg
GB Soil Surv Engl Wales Annu Rep — Great Britain. Soil Survey of England and Wales. Annual Report
GB Soil Surv Spec Surv — Great Britain. Soil Survey. Special Survey
GBT — Ghana Bulletin of Theology
GBT — Guzarishhayi Bastanshinasi (Tehran)
GB Th — Gegenwartsfragen Biblischer Theologie
GB Torry Res Stn Torry Tech Pap — Great Britain. Torry Research Station. Torry Technical Paper
GB Trop Prod Inst Rep L — Great Britain. Tropical Products Institute. Report L
GBVCAG — Giornale di Batteriologia, Virologia, ed Immunologia. Annali dell'Ospedale Maria Vittoria di Torino. Parte II. Sezione Clinica
GBVID — Giornale di Batteriologia, Virologia, ed Immunologia
GBVMAC — Giornale di Batteriologia, Virologia, ed Immunologia. Annali dell'Ospedale Maria Vittoria di Torino. Parte I. Sezione Microbiologia
GB Warren Spring Lab LR — Great Britain. Warren Spring Laboratory. Report LR
GB Warren Spring Lab Miner Process Inf Note — Great Britain. Warren Spring Laboratory. Mineral Processing InformationNote
GB Warren Spring Lab Rep — Great Britain. Warren Spring Laboratory. Report
GB Warren Spring Lab Rev — Great Britain. Warren Spring Laboratory. Review
GB Water Resour Board Publ — Great Britain. Water Resource Board. Publication
GBZKA — Grazer Beitraege. Zeitschrift fuer die Klassische Altertumswissenschaft
GBZUA — Gidrobiologicheskii Zhurnal
GBZUAM — Gidrobiologicheskii Zhurnal
GC — Gaceta de Cuba
GC — Gallia Cristiana
GC — Glaneur Chatelleraudais
GC — Graphic Communications Weekly
GCACAK — Geochimica et Cosmochimica Acta
GCAF — Canadian Forum
GCAJS — Gratz College. Annual of Jewish Studies
GCAL — Callaloo
GCAR — Car and Driver
GCASD — Geochimica et Cosmochimica Acta. Supplement
GCAT — Cats Magazine
G Cat — Grandi del Cattolicesimo
GCAY — Current Anthropology
GCB — Gas. Zeitschrift fuer Rationale Energieanwendung
GCBI — Current Biography
GCBI — Godisnjak Centra za Balkanoloska Ispitivanja
GCCA Newsletter — GCCA [*Graduate Careers Council of Australia*] Newsletter
GCCI — Goucher College Cuneiform Inscriptions
GCCL — Classroom Computer Learning
GCCL — Technology and Learning [*Formerly, Classroom Computer Learning*]
GCCM — Common Cause Magazine
GCCP — Journal of Consulting and Clinical Psychology
GCCU — Grand Council of the Cree (of Quebec) Update
GCDC — Current
GCDI — Conservative Digest
GCDL — Crime and Delinquency
GCDQ — Career Development Quarterly
GCED — Childhood Education
GCEN — Chemical and Engineering News
G Centen Dante Alighieri — Giornale del Centenario di Dante Alighieri
GCFI — Giornale Critico della Filosofia Italiana
GCFP — Gerarchia Cattolica e la Famiglia Pontificia
GCGGA — Gulf Coast Association of Geological Societies. Field Trip Guidebook
GCHA — Change
GCHD — Child Development
GCHE — Chronicle of Higher Education
GCHI — Current History
G Chim Appl — Giornale di Chimica Applicata

G Chim Ind — Giornale di Chimica Industriale
G Chim Ind Appl — Giornale di Chimica Industriale ed Applicata
G Chir — Giornale di Chirurgia
GCHQ — China Quarterly
GCHS — Channels
GCHT — Changing Times
GCHT — Kiplinger's Personal Finance Magazine [Formerly, Changing Times]
GCHW — Child Welfare
GCIE — Computers in Education
GCIQ — Critical Inquiry
GCJB — Criminal Justice and Behavior
GCJR — Columbia Journalism Review
GCLA — Classical [Later, Classic CD]
GCLA — Classic CD [Formerly, Classical]
G Clin Med — Giornale di Clinica Medica
G Clin Med (Bologna) — Giornale di Clinica Medica (Bologna)
GCLT — Comparative Literature
GCMM — Communication Monographs
GCN — Gallia Christiana Novissima
GCN — Gay Community News
GCN — Government Computer News
GCNA — Guild of Carillonneurs in North America. Bulletin
GCNAC — Greek Coins in North American Collections
GCND — Journal of Counseling and Development. JCD
GCNED — Government Computer News
GCO — Gavault, Paul, ed. Conferences de l'Odeon
GCOD — Consumer's Digest
GCOE — Compute
GCOH — Journal of Community Health
GCOJ — Country Journal
GCOL — College English
GCOM — Commentary
GCON — Congressional Digest
GCOR — Consumer Reports
GCOR — Gulf Coast Oil Reporter
GCOS — Cosmopolitan
GCOS — Great Canadian Sands News
GCOU — Country Living
GCOW — Commonweal
GCP — Graecitas Christianorum Primaeva
GCPS — Journal of Counseling Psychology
GCQBD — Geo-Heat Center. Quarterly Bulletin
GCQW — Congressional Quarterly Weekly Report
GCR — German Canadian Review
G Crit Filosof Ital — Giornale Critico della Filosofia Italiana
GCRM — Consumers' Research Magazine
GCRRAE — Glasshouse Crops Research Institute. Annual Report
GCS — Die Griechische Christliche Schriftsteller der Ersten Drei Jahrhunderten
GCT — Gifted Child Today
GCTO — Christianity Today
GCTW — Canada and the World
GCTY — Children Today
GCUH — Current Health 2
GCUN — Courier [Formerly, UNESCO Courier]
GCUN — UNESCO Courier
GCW — Graphic Communications Weekly
GCWOD — Graphic Communications World
GCY — German-Canadian Yearbook
GCYC — Cycle
GD — Die Grossen Deutschen
GD — Giornale Dantesco
GD — Global Digest
GD — Guardian
GdA — Geschichte des Altertums
GDA — Godisnik na Duchovnata Akademija Sveti Kliment Ochridski
GDA — Greek Dark Ages
GDAD — Daedalus
GDAE — Design for Arts in Education
GDAJA — Journal. Georgia Dental Association
GDAM — Dance Magazine
Gdansk Tow Nauk Rozpr Wydz — Gdanskie Towarzystwo Naukowe Rozprawy Wydzialu
Gdansk Tow Nauk Rozpr Wydz 3 — Gdanskie Towarzystwo Naukowe. Rozprawy Wydzialu 3. NaukMatematyczno-Przyrodniczych
GdB — Giornale di Bordo. Mensile di Storia, Letteratura, ed Arte
GdC — Gaceta de Cuba
GdC — Gants du Ciel
GdD — Gegenwart der Dichtung
GDDTD — Gesetzblatt der Deutschen Demokratischen Republik. Teil 1
GDF — Geographic Data File
GDF — Gesta Dei per Francos
GdG — Grundlagen der Germanistik
Gd G — Grundriss der Geschichtswissenschaft
Gd House — Good Housekeeping
GdI — Giornale d'Italia
GDIKAN — Gifu Daigaku Igakubu Kiyo
GdiM — Giornale di Metafisica
GDIS — Discover
GDIY — Discovery
GDK — Geschichte der Kirche. Einsiedeln
GDKKD2 — Annual Report. Faculty of Education. Gunma University. Art, Technology, Health,and Physical Education and Science of Human Living Series
GDKTA — Genshi Doryoku Kenkyukai Teirei Kenkyukai Nenkai Hokokusho

GDKYA7 — Annual Report. Faculty of Education. Gunma University. Art and Technology Series
GDM — Gads Danske Magasin
GdM — Gazzetta del Mezzogiorno
G d Mg — Gads Danske Magasin
Gdn & Foo Nero — Garden and Foo Nero
Gdn & Forest — Garden and Forest
Gdng Ill — Gardening Illustrated
Gdn Hist — Garden History
Gdn J NY Bot Gdn — Garden Journal. New York Botanical Garden
Gdnrs Mag — Gardeners Magazine
Gdns Bull — Gardens Bulletin
Gdns Bull (Singapore) — Gardens Bulletin (Singapore)
GDOB — Down Beat
GDOG — Dog World
GDPS — Developmental Psychology
GDROA — Gidroaeromehanika
GDS — Going Down Swinging
Gd S — Gundriss der Sozialoekonomik
GDS — Overheidsdocumentatie. Orgaan voor Documentatie en Administratieve Organisatie der Overheid
GDSB — Department of State Bulletin
GDSS — Dissent
Gd Times — Good Times
GDU — Grand Dictionnaire Universel du XIX Siecle
GDV — Geschichtsschreiber der Deutschen Vorzeit
GDVMA — Gidravlicheskie Mashiny
GDWDA — Glaciological Data. World Data Center A
GDWDCA — Glaciological Data. World Data Center A
Ge — Gegenwart
GE — Giornale degli Economisti e Annali di Economia
Ge — Gli Ebrei nell'Alto Medioevo
GE — Grande Enciclopedia Portuguesa e Brasiliera
GE — Grande Encyclopedie
GeA — Geneve-Afrique
GEAEA — Geomagnetizm i Aeronomiya
GeAn — Geographical Analysis
GEARA — Georgia Agricultural Research
GEASA — Geofizika i Astronomiya Informatsionnyi Byulleten
GEB — Chefmagazin fuer Kleinbetriebe und Mittelbetriebe
GEBAAX — Geologica Bavarica
GEBAD2 — Geologica Balcanica
GEBO — Ebony
Gebrauchs — Gebrauchsgraphik
Gebrauchs Novum — Gebrauchsgraphik Novum
GEBSAJ — Geobios
Geburtsh Fr — Geburtshilfe und Frauenheilkunde
Geburtsh Frauenheilkd — Geburtshilfe und Frauenheilkunde
Geburtshilfe Frauenheilkd — Geburtshilfe und Frauenheilkunde
Geburtshilfe Frauenheilkd — Geburtshilfe und Frauenheilkunde
Geburtshilflich Gynaekol Prax Int Muensteraner Gespraech — Geburtshilflich-Gynaekologische Praxis. Internationales MuensteranerGespraech ueber Geburtshilflich-Gynaekologische Praxis
GEC At Energy Rev — GEC [General Electric Company] Atomic Energy Review
GEC Bibliogr — GEC [General Electric Company] Bibliography
GEC Eng — GEC Engineering
GECHB — Geochemistry
GECHD — Geochronique
GEC J — GEC [General Electric Company] Journal
GEC J Res — GEC Journal of Research
GEC J Sci & Technol — GEC [General Electric Company] Journal of Science and Technology
GEC J Technol — GEC [General Electric Company] Journal of Technology
GECO — Ecology
G Economisti — Giornale degli Economisti e Annali di Economia
GEC Telecommun — GEC [General Electric Company] Telecommunications
GEDEAL — Gesundheitswesen und Desinfektion
GEDED — General Dentistry
GEDID2 — Gerbil Digest
GEDL — Educational Leadership
GEDMAB — Geoderma
GEDP — Editor and Publisher
GEDR — Educational Record
Gedrag & Gezond — Gedrag und Gezondheid
Gedrag T P — Gedrag-Tijdschrift voor Psychologie
GEDW — Education Week
GEE/NA — Nova Americana. Giulio Einaudi Editore
GEF — Grands Ecrivains Francais
Gefaengnisgesellsch F D Prov Sachsen & Anhalt Jahr — Gefaengnisgesellschaft fuer die Provinz Sachsen und Anhalt. Jahrbuch
Gefahrstoffe Reinhalt Luft — Gefahrstoffe. Reinhaltung der Luft. Air Quality Control
GEFO — Geoforum
GEFR — George Eliot Fellowship Review
Geg — Gegenwart. Zeitschrift fuer Literatur, Wirtschaftsleben, und Kunst
GEG — Geluid en Omgeving
Gegenbaurs Morph Jb — Gegenbaurs Morphologisches Jahrbuch
Gegenbaurs Morphol Jahrb — Gegenbaurs Morphologisches Jahrbuch
Geg G S Erz — Gegenwartskunde Gesellschaft Staat Erziehung
GEGIA — Geneeskundige Gids
GegJ — Geographical Journal
GegR — Geographical Review
GeH — Georgia Historical Quarterly
GEHAD — Gekkan Haikibutsu
GEHEA7 — Gentes Herbarum

GEHIA — Gencho Hiroshima Igaku
Gehlen J — Journal fuer die Chemie und Physik. Gehlen
Geill Tuinbouwbl — Geillustreerd Tuinbouwblad
GEINA — Gesundheits-Ingenieur
GEIRD — Gendai Iryo
Geisinger Med Cent Bull — Geisinger Medical Center. Bulletin
Geist Arb — Geistige Arbeit
GeistLeb — Geist und Leben
GEJAA — Geologisches Jahrbuch
GEJAA5 — Geologisches Jahrbuch
GEJBA8 — Geologisches Jahrbuch. Beihefte
GEJO — Geographical Journal
GEJOBE — Geochemical Journal
GEJODG — Geomicrobiology Journal
Ge Ke — Gemeenschap der Kerken
GEKYA — Gensen-Kyo
GEL — Grands Evenements Litteraires
GEL — Greek-English Lexikon
Gel and Glue Res Assoc — Gelatin and Glue Research Association
Gel Anz — Gelehrte Anzeiger der Bayerischen Akademie der Wissenschaften
Gelatine Leim Klebst — Gelatine, Leim, Klebstoffe
Gelbe H — Gelbe Hefte
Gelbe Hh — Gelbe Hefte
Gel Ergoetzlichk Nachr — Gelehrte Ergoetzlichkeiten und Nachrichten
GELF — Grands Ecrivains de la France
Gelfand Math Sem — Gelfand Mathematical Seminars
GELL — Electronic Learning
GELS — Electronics
GELT — Studies in English Literature, 1500-1900
Gel Vrij — Geloof en Vrijheid
Gel Zeitung Kiel — Gelehrte Zeitung. Herausgegeben zu Kiel
Gem — Gemeente
GeM — Geographical Magazine
GEMA — Geographical Magazine
Gematol Pereliv Krovi — Gematologiya i Perelivanie Krovi
Gematol Pereliv Krovi Resp Mezhved Sb — Gematologiya i Perelivanie Krovi Respublikanskoi Mezhvedomstvennyi Sbornik
Gematol Transfuziol — Gematologiya i Transfuziologiya
GEMBAN — Getreide Mehl und Brot
GEMEE2 — Genitourinary Medicine
Gemeinnuetz Alman — Gemeinnuetziger Almanach
Gemeinnuetz Natur Kunstmag — Gemeinnuetziges Natur und Kunstmagazin oder Abhandlungen zur Befoerderung der Naturkunde, der Kuenste, Manufacturen und Fabriken
Gemeinnuetz Pesther J — Gemeinnuetziges Pesther Journal. Zeitung fuer Landwirthschaft, Gartenbau, Handel, Industrie, und Gewerbe
Gemeinsames Amtsbl A — Gemeinsames Amtsblatt. Ausgabe A
Gemeinsames Amtsbl Landes Baden-Wuerttemb A — Gemeinsames Amtsblatt des Landes Baden-Wuerttemberg. Ausgabe A
Gemeinsames Ministerialbl A — Gemeinsames Ministerialblatt A
GEMGA4 — Geological Magazine
GEMIA — Geologie en Mijnbouw
GEMIAA — Geologie en Mijnbouw
Gemmol Soc Jap J — Gemmological Society of Japan Journal
Gemol (Sao Paulo) — Gemologia. Associacao Brasileira de Gemologia e Mineralogia (Sao Paulo)
Gems Gemol — Gems and Gemology. Gemological Institute of America
Gems Miner — Gems and Minerals
Gem State News Lett — Gem State News Letter
Gem State RN News Lett — Gem State RN News Letter
Gen — Genava
GEN — GEN. Government Equipment News
Gen Appl Entomol — General and Applied Entomology
Gen Arm — Generals of the Army and the Air Force and Admirals of the Navy
Genave Afr — Genave-Afrique
Gen Bll I Nt — Bulletin de l'Institut National Genevois
Gen C Endoc — General and Comparative Endocrinology
Gen Chim — Genie Chimique
Gen Chr — Genie du Christianisme
Gen Chron & Lit Mag — General Chronicle and Literary Magazine
Gen Civ — Genie Civil. Revue Generale des Industries Francaises et Etrangeres
Gen Comp Endocr — General and Comparative Endocrinology
Gen Comp Endocrinol — General and Comparative Endocrinology
Gen Comp Endocrinol Suppl — General and Comparative Endocrinology. Supplement
Gen Conf Eur Phys Soc — General Conference. European Physical Society
Gen Contract — General Contracting
Gen Cytochem Methods — General Cytochemical Methods
Gen Dent — General Dentistry
Gen Diagn Pathol — General and Diagnostic Pathology
GENEA3 — Genetica
GENEAL MAG — Genealogical Magazine
Genealogical Period Annu Index — Genealogical Periodical Annual Index
Genealog Mag — Genealogists' Magazine
Geneal Per Ind — Genealogical Periodical Annual Index
Geneal Samf Finl Arsskr — Genealogiska Samfundets i Finland Arsskrift
Gene Amplif Anal — Gene Amplification and Analysis
Gene Anal T — Gene Analysis Techniques
Gene Anal Tech — Gene Analysis Techniques
Gen Ed Rev Coll Agric Vet Med Nihon Univ — General Education Review. College of Agriculture and Veterinary Medicine. Nihon University
Gen Ed Rev Toho Univ — General Education Review. Toho University
Geneesk — Geneeskunde
Geneesk Courant — Geneeskundige Courant voor het Koningrijk der Nederlanden
Geneeskd — Geneeskunde

Geneeskd Bl — Geneeskundige Bladen uit Kliniek en Laboratorium voor de Praktijk
Geneeskd Doc — Geneeskundige Documentatie
Geneeskd Gids — Geneeskundige Gids
Geneeskd Sport — Geneeskunde en Sport
Geneesk Tijdschr Nederl-Indiee — Geneeskundig Tijdschrift voor Nederlandsch-Indiee
Geneesk Tijdschr Ned Indie — Geneeskundig Tijdschrift voor Nederlandsch-Indie
Geneesk Verh Kon Sweedsche Akad — Geneeskundige Verhandelingen, aan de Kon. Sweedsche Akademie Medegedeelt en Door Dezelve Van Het Jaar 1739 Tot op Deezen Tijd Bekent Gamaakt
Genees Natuur Huishoudk Kab — Genees-, Natuur- en Huishoudkundig Kabinet
Gene Expr — Gene Expression
Gene Expression Dev Proc Int Congr Isozymes — Gene Expression and Development. Proceedings. International Congress onIsozymes
Gene Expression Its Regul Proc Int Lat Am Symp — Gene Expression and Its Regulation. Proceedings. International LatinAmerican Symposium
Gene Geogr — Gene Geography
Gen Elec R — General Electrical Review
Gen Electr Co Ltd At Rev — General Electric Company Limited. Atomic Review
Gen Electr Co Ltd J — General Electric Company Limited. Journal
Gen Electr Co Ltd J Sci Technol — General Electric Company Limited. Journal of Science and Technology
Gen Electr Co Power Eng Ltd Bibliogr — General Electric Company. Power Engineering Limited Bibliography
Gen Electr Rev — General Electric Review
Gen El Rev — General Electric Review
Gen Eng — General Engineer
Gen Eng Trans — General Engineering Transactions
General Ed — General Education
General Mag And Hist Chron — General Magazine and Historical Chronicle. University of Pennsylvania
General Topology and Appl — General Topology and Its Applications
Genes Cells — Genes to Cells
Genes Chromosomes Cancer — Genes, Chromosomes, and Cancer
Genes Dev — Genes and Development
Genes Funct — Genes and Function
Genes Genet Syst — Genes and Genetic Systems
Genes Immun — Genes and Immunity
Genesis Precambrian Iron Manganese Deposits Proc Kiev Symp — Genesis of Precambrian Iron and Manganese Deposits. Proceedings. Kiev Symposium
Genes Tumor Genes Workshop Conf Hoechst — Genes and Tumor Genes. Workshop Conference Hoechst
Genet — Genetics
Genet Abstr — Genetics Abstracts
Genet Agr — Genetica Agraria
Genet Agrar — Genetica Agraria
Genet Anal — Genetic Analysis
Genet Anal Biomol Eng — Genetic Analysis. Biomolecular Engineering
Genet Anal Tech Appl — Genetic Analysis, Techniques, and Applications
Genet Biokhim Immunokhim Osobo Opasnykh Infekts — Genetika Biokhimiya i Immunokhimiya Osobo Opasnykh Infektsii
Genet Biokhim Immunokhim Osobo Opasnykh Infektsii — Genetika Biokhimiya i Immunokhimiya Osobo Opasnykh Infektsii
Genet Biol Alcohol — Genetics and Biology of Alcoholism
Genet Biol Drosophila — Genetics and Biology of Drosophila
Genet Biotechnol Bacilli Proc Int Conf Bacilli — Genetics and Biotechnology of Bacilli. Proceedings. International Conference on Bacilli
Genet Breed (Sofia) — Genetics and Breeding (Sofia)
Genet Cell Technol — Genetic and Cellular Technology
Genet Chel — Genetika Cheloveka
Genet Colloq — Genetica. Colloqui
Genet Couns — Genetic Counseling
Genet Dev Evol Stadler Genet Symp — Genetics, Development, and Evolution. Stadler Genetics Symposium
Genet Eng Anim Proc Symp — Genetic Engineering of Animals. Proceedings. Symposium on Genetic Engineering of Animals
Genet Eng Biotechnol Yearb — Genetic Engineering and Biotechnology Yearbook
Genet Eng Lett — Genetic Engineering Letter
Genet Eng (London) — Genetic Engineering (London)
Genet Eng News — Genetic Engineering News
Genet Eng (NY) — Genetic Engineering (New York). Principles and Methods
Genet Eng Princ Methods — Genetic Engineering. Principles and Methods
Genet Eng Toxins — Genetically Engineered Toxins
Genet Epidemiol — Genetic Epidemiology
Genet Epidemiol Suppl — Genetic Epidemiology. Supplement
Genet Hear Impairment — Genetics of Hearing Impairment
Genet Hematol Disord Sel Pap Int Clin Genet Semin — Genetics of Hematological Disorders. Selected Papers. International Clinical Genetics Seminar
Gene Ther — Gene Therapy
Genet Hum — Genetique Humaine
Genet Hum Nutr Int Symp — Genetics and Human Nutrition. International Symposium
Genet Hypertens Proc Int Symp SHR Relat Stud — Genetic Hypertension. Proceedings. International Symposium on SHR and Related Studies
Genet Iber — Genetica Iberica
Genetic Psychol Monog — Genetic Psychology Monographs
Genetics Suppl — Genetics. Supplement
Genet Ind Microorg Proc Int Symp — Genetics of Industrial Microorganisms. Proceedings. InternationalSymposium on Genetics of Industrial Microorganisms
Genet Kidney Disord Proc Int Clin Genet Semin — Genetics of Kidney Disorders. Proceedings. International Clinical Genetics Seminar
Genet Lect — Genetics Lectures
Genet Maps — Genetic Maps
Genet Med — Genetics in Medicine

Genet Mol Biol — Genetics and Molecular Biology
GENETOX — Genetic Toxicity
Genet Pattern Form Growth Control — Genetics of Pattern Formation and Growth Control
Genet Physiol Note Inst Paper Chem — Genetics and Physiology Notes. Institute of Paper Chemistry
Genet Physiol Notes — Genetics and Physiology Notes
Genet Phys Mapp — Genetic and Physical Mapping
Genet Plant Breed — Genetics and Plant Breeding
Genet Pol — Genetica Polonica
Genet Princ Perspect — Genetics; Principles and Perspectives
Genet Prod Form Streptomyces — Genetics and Product Formation in Streptomyces
Genet Psych — Genetic Psychology Monographs
Genet Psychol Mon — Genetic Psychology Monographs
Genet Psychol Monog — Genetic Psychology Monographs
Genet Psychol Monogr — Genetic Psychology Monographs
Gene Transfer Expression Protoc — Gene Transfer and Expression Protocols
Genet Res — Genetical Research
Genet Resour Commun — Genetic Resources Communication
Genet Sel — Genetika i Selektsiya
Genet Sel Azerb — Genetika i Selektsiia v Azerbaidzhan
Genet Selektsiya — Genetika i Selektsiya
Genet Sel Evol — Genetics, Selection, Evolution
Genet Sel Evol — Genetique, Selection, Evolution
Genet Sel Genet Plant Breed — Genetika i Selektsiia. Genetics and Plant Breeding
Genet Sex Determ — Genetics of Sex Determination
Genet Sinica — Genetica Sinica
Genet Slecht — Genetika a Slechteni
Genet Slechteni — Genetika a Slechteni
Genet Soc Gen Psychol Monogr — Genetic, Social, and General Psychology Monographs
Genet Technol News — Genetic Technology News
Genet Test — Genetic Testing
Genet Zhivotn Evol Izbr Tr Mezhdunar Genet Kongr — Genetika Zhivotnykh i Evolyutsiya. Izbrannye Trudy MezhdunarodnogoGeneticheskogo Kongressa
Geneve-Afr — Geneve-Afrique
Genezis Boksitov Tr Soveshch — Genezis Boksitov. Trudy Soveshchaniya
Gen Fish Counc Mediterr Proc Tech Pap — General Fisheries Council for the Mediterranean. Proceedings andTechnical Papers
Gen Fish Counc Mediterr Sess Rep — General Fisheries Council for the Mediterranean. Session Report
GENGA — Geologiya Nefti i Gaza
GEN (Gastroenterol Endocrinol Nutr) (Caracas) — GEN (Gastroenterologia, Endocrinologia, Nutricion) (Caracas)
Geng Kenk — Gengo Kenkyu
Gen Gouv — Generalgouvernement
Gen Het Cycl Chem Ser — General Heterocyclic Chemistry Series
Gen Heterocycl Chem Ser — General Heterocyclic Chemistry Series
Gen Hosp Psychiatry — General Hospital Psychiatry
Gen Iber — Genetica Iberica
Genie Biol Med — Genie Biologique et Medical
Genie Chim — Genie Chimique
Genie Civ — Genie Civil
Genie Ind — Genie Industrial
Genie React React — Genie des Reacteurs et des Reactions
Gen Index — General Index
Gen Index Publ Reports — General Index to Published Reports. Mineral Resources Group
Gen I Nt Bll — Bulletin de l'Institut National Genevois
Gen I Nt Mm — Memoires de l'Institut National Genevois
Genitourin Med — Genitourinary Medicine
Genius Zeit — Genius der Zeit. Ein Journal
GENJ — English Journal
Gen Ling — General Linguistics
Gen Linguis — General Linguistics
Gen M As Que J — General Mining Association of the Province of Quebec. Journal
Gen Mm S Ps — Memoires de la Societe de Physique et d'Histoire Naturelle de Geneve
Gen Mot Corp Res Lab Res Publ — General Motors Corporation. Research Laboratories. Research Publication
Gen Mot Eng J — General Motors Engineering Journal
Gen Mot Res Lab Symp Ser — General Motors Research Laboratories Symposia Series
Gen Newsl Natl Res Counc (Can) Div Mech Eng — General Newsletter. National Research Council (Canada). Division of Mechanical Engineering
Genome Anal — Genome Analysis
Genome Anal Sequence Funct Eur Meet Hum Genome Organ — Genome Analysis. From Sequence to Function. European Meeting. Human Genome Organisation
Genome Evol — Genome Evolution
Genome Inform Ser Workshop Genome Inform — Genome Informatics Series
Genome Inf Ser — Genome Informatics Series
Genome Res — Genome Research
Genome Sci — Genome Science and Technology
Genome Sci & Technol — Genome Science and Technology
Genomic Responses Environ Stress — Genomic Responses to Environmental Stress
Genova Mm I Ligure — Memorie dell' Istituto Ligure. Genova
Genova Mm S Md — Memorie della Societa Medica di Emulazione di Genova
Genova S Lig At — Atti della Societa Ligustica di Scienze Naturali e Geografiche. Genova
Gen Pathol Pathol Anat — General Pathology and Pathological Anatomy
Gen Pharm — General Pharmacology

Gen Pharmacol — General Pharmacology
Gen Physiol Biophys — General Physiology and Biophysics
Gen Prac Adv — General Practice Adviser
Gen Pract Clin — General Practice Clinics
Gen Practnr (Lond) — General Practitioner (London)
Gen Psych Mon — Genetic Psychology Monographs
Gen Pub — General Publication
GENRA8 — Genetical Research
Gen Rad Exp — General Radio Experimenter
GENRB — Genie Rural
Gen Relat G — General Relativity and Gravitation
Gen Relativ and Gravitation — General Relativity and Gravitation
Gen Relativ Gravitation — General Relativity and Gravitation
Gen Relativity Gravitation — General Relativity and Gravitation
Gen Rep Dep Archit Sci Syd Univ — General Report. Department of Architectural Science. University of Sydney
Gen Rep Minist Mines Prov Que — General Report. Minister of Mines. Province of Quebec
Gen Repos — General Repository
Gen Rep R8 GR US Dep Agric For Serv South Reg — General Report R8-GR. US Department of Agriculture. Forest Service. Southern Region
Gen Res — Genetical Research
Gen Rur — Genio Rurale
GENSA — Journal. Georgia Entomological Society
Gen Sci Index — General Science Index
Gen Sci Q — General Science Quarterly
Gen Ser Colo State Agr Exp Sta — General Series. Colorado State University. Agricultural Experiment Station
Gen Ser Colo State Univ Exp Stn — General Series. Colorado State University. Experiment Station
Gen S Ps Mm — Memoires de la Societe de Physique et d'Histoire Naturelle de Geneve
Gen Synth Methods — General and Synthetic Methods
Gen Syst — General Systems
Gen Syst — General Systems Bulletin
GENTAE — Genetics
Gent Bijdr Kstgesch — Gentsche Bijdragen tot de Kunstgeschiedenis
Gent Bijdr Kstgesch & Oudhdknd — Gentse Bijdragen tot de Kunstgeschiedenis en de Oudheidkunde
Gent Bog — Gentofte-Bogen
Gen Tech Rep FPL US Dep Agric For Serv For Prod Lab — General Technical Report FPL. United States Department of Agriculture. Forest Service. Forest Products Laboratory
Gen Tech Rep FPL US For Prod Lab (Madison Wis) — General Technical Report FPL. United States. Forest Products Laboratory (Madison, Wisconsin)
Gen Tech Rep NE US Dep Agric For Serv Northeast For Exp Stn — General Technical Report NE. US Department of Agriculture. Forest Service. Northeastern Forest Experiment Station
Gen Tech Rep PSW Pac Southwest For Range Exp Stn — General Technical Report PSW. Pacific Southwest Forest and Range Experiment Stat
Gen Tech Rep PSW US For Serv — General Technical Report PSW. United States Forest Service
Gen Tech Rep RM Rocky Mt For Range Exp Stn US For Serv — General Technical Report. RM. Rocky Mountain Forest and Range Experiment Station. United States Forest Service
Gen Tech Rep SE US Dep Agric For Serv Southeast For Exp Stn — General Technical Report SE. US Department of Agriculture. Forest Service. Southeastern Forest Experiment Station
Gen Tech Rep SO US Dep Agric For Serv South For Exp Stn — General Technical Report SO. US Department of Agriculture. Forest Service. Southern Forest Experiment Station
Gen Tech Rep US Dep Agric For Serv Intermt Res Stn — General Technical Report. US Department of Agriculture. Forest Service. Intermountain Research Station
Gen Tech Rep WO US For Ser — General Technical Report WO. United States Forest Service
Gen Teleph Electron Corp Res Dev J — General Telephone and Electronics Corporation. Research and Development Journal
Gentes Herb — Gentes Herbarum
Gent Herb — Gentes Herbarum
Gentile da Fabriano Boll Mens Celeb Centen — Gentile da Fabriano. Bollettino Mensile per la Celebrazione Centenaria
Gent M — Gentleman's Magazine
Gent Mag — Gentleman's Magazine
Gent M NS — Gentleman's Magazine. New Series
GENV — Environment
Geo — Geography
Geo — Georgetown Law Journal
Ge O — Graecolatina et Orientalia
GeoAb — Geographical Abstracts
Geo Abs & Indexes — Geo Abstracts and Indexes
Geo Abstr — Geographical Abstracts
Geo Abstr B Climatol Hydrol — Geo Abstracts. B. Climatology and Hydrology
Geo Abstr C Econ Geog — Geo Abstracts. C. Economic Geography
Geo Abstr D Soc Hist Geog — Geo Abstracts. D. Social and Historical Geography
Geo Abstr E Sedimentology — Geo Abstracts. E. Sedimentology
Geo Abstr F Reg Com Plan — Geo Abstracts. F. Regional and Community Planning
Geo Abstr G Remote Sensing Photogram Cartogr — Geo Abstracts. G. Remote Sensing, Photogrammetry, and Cartography
Geoarchaeol — Geoarchaeology. An International Journal
Geo-Archeologia — Geo-Archeologia. Periodico dell'Associazione Geo-Archeologica Italiana
GeoOb — Geographical Observer
GEOBASE — Geographic Cross-Reference Data

GEOBD2 — Geobotany
Geobot Inst Rubel Veroeff — Geobotanisches Institut Rubel Veroeffentlichungen
Geobot Zbirn — Geobotanicnyj Zbirnyk. Recueil Geobotanique
GEOCD — Geochimica
Geoch Cos A — Geochimica et Cosmochimica Acta
Geoch Cosm A — Geochimica et Cosmochimica Acta
Geochem Environ — Geochemistry and the Environment
Geochem Explor Proc Int Geochem Explor Symp — Geochemical Exploration. Proceedings. International Geochemical Exploration Symposium
Geochem Geochem Methods Data — Geochemie. Geochemical Methods and Data
Geochem Int — Geochemistry International
Geochem Invest Field Higher Pressures Temp — Geochemical Investigation in the Field of Higher Pressures and Temperatures
Geochem J — Geochemical Journal
Geochem J (Geochem Soc Jap) — Geochemical Journal (Geochemical Society of Japan)
Geochem J (Nagoya) — Geochemical Journal (Nagoya)
Geochem J (Tokyo) — Geochemical Journal (Tokyo)
Geochem Mineral Petrol Sofia — Geochemistry, Mineralogy, and Petrology (Sofia)
Geochem News — Geochemical News
Geochem Rep Alaska Div Geol Geophys Surv — Geochemical Report. Alaska. Division of Geological and Geophysical Surveys
Geochem Soc India Bull — Geochemical Society of India. Bulletin
Geochem Soc Spec Publ — Geochemical Society. Special Publication
Geochim Bras — Geochimica Brasiliensis
Geochim Cosmochim Acta — Geochimica et Cosmochimica Acta
Geochim Cosmochim Acta Suppl — Geochimica et Cosmochimica Acta. Supplement
Geochim et Cosmochim Acta — Geochimica et Cosmochimica Acta
Geochim Org Sediments Mar Profonds — Geochimie Organique des Sediments Marins Profonds
GEOCOME Geol Congr Middle East Pap — GEOCOME. Geological Congress of the Middle East. Papers
Geod Aerophotogr Engl Transl — Geodesy and Aerophotography (English Translation)
Geod Aerophotogr (USSR) — Geodesy and Aerophotography [*Later, Geodesy, Mapping, and Photogrammetry*] (USSR)
Geodaet Geophys Veroeffentlichungen Reihe III — Geodaetische und Geophysikalische Veroeffentlichungen. Reihe III
Geodaet Inst Medd — Geodaetisk Institut. Meddelelse
Geodaet Inst Skrf — Geodaetisk Instituts Skrifter
Geod Darb — Geodezijos Darbai
Geodes Mapp Photogramm — Geodesy, Mapping, and Photogrammetry
GEODIAL — Geoscience Data Index for Alberta
Geodin Issled — Geodinamicheskie Issledovaniya
Geod Inst (Den) Medd — Geodaetisk Institut (Denmark). Meddelelse
Geod Inst Medd — Geodaetisk Institut. Meddelelse
Geod Inst Skr — Geodaetisk Institut. Skrifter
Geod Kartogr — Geodezia es Kartografia
Geod Kartogr Aerofotos — Geodeziia, Kartografiia, i Aerofotos'emka
Geod Kartogr (Budap) — Geodezia es Kartografia (Budapest)
Geod Kartogr Obzor — Geodeticky a Kartograficky Obzor
Geod List (Zagreb) — Geodetski List. Glasilo Saveza Geodeyskih Inzenjera i Geometara SFR Jugoslavija(Zagreb)
Geod Mapp Photogramm — Geodesy, Mapping, and Photogrammetry
Geod Mapp Photogramm Engl Transl — Geodesy, Mapping, and Photogrammetry. English Translation
Geod Soc Jap J — Geodetic Society of Japan. Journal
Geodyn Res — Geodynamic Researches
Geoexplor — Geoexploration
Geoexplor Monogr — Geoexploration Monographs
GEOF — Geoforum
Geofis Int — Geofisica International
Geofis Met — Geofisica e Meteorologia
Geofis Meteorol — Geofisica e Meteorologia
Geofis Pura Appl — Geofisica Pura e Applicata
Geofis Pur Appl — Geofisica Pura e Applicata
Geofiz App — Geofizicheskaya Apparatura
Geofiz Appar — Geofizicheskaya Apparatura
Geofiz Astron Inf Byull — Geofizika i Astronomiya Informatsionnyi Byulleten
Geofiz Byull — Geofizicheskii Byulleten
Geofiz Byull (Budapest) — Geofizicheskii Byulleten (Budapest)
Geofiz Geol Naft — Geofizyka i Geologia Naftowa
Geofiz Issled — Geofizicheskie Issledovaniya
Geofiz Issled Reshenii Geol Zadach Vost Sib — Geofizicheskie Issledovaniya pri Reshenii Geologicheskikh Zadach v Vostochnoi Sibri
Geofiz Koeslemenyek — Geofizikai Koeslemenyek
Geofiz Kozl — Geofizikai Koezlemenyek
Geofiz Kozlemenyek — Geofizikai Koezlemenyek
Geofiz Metody Poiskov Razved Rudn Nerudn Mestorozhd — Geofizicheskie Metody Poiskov i Razvedki Rudnykh i Nerudnykh Mestorozhdenii
Geofiz Metody Razved Arkt — Geofizicheskie Metody Razvedki v Arktike
Geofiz Priborostr — Geofizicheskoe Priborostroenie
Geofiz Razved — Geofizicheskaya Razvedka
Geofiz Sb — Geofizicheskii Sbornik
Geofiz Sb Akad Nauk Ukr SSR Inst Geofiz — Geofizicheskii Sbornik. Akademiya Nauk Ukrainskoi SSR. Institut Geofiziki
Geofiz Sb (Kiev) — Geofizicheskii Sbornik (Kiev)
Geofiz Sb Prague — Geofizicheskii Sbornik (Prague)
Geofiz Sb (Sverdlovsk) — Geofizicheskii Sbornik (Sverdlovsk)
Geofiz Zh — Geofizicheskii Zhurnal
Geof Koezl — Geofizikai Koezlemenyek
Geof Publ — Geofysiske Publikasjoner
Geofys Publ — Geofysiske Publikasjoner

Geofys Sb — Geofysikalni Sbornik
GEOG — Geografia
Geog Annaler — Geografiska Annaler
Geog Bul — Geographical Bulletin
Geog Gesell Hamburg Mitt — Geographische Gesellschaft in Hamburg. Mitteilungen
Geog Gesell In Wien Mitt — Geographische Gesellschaft in Wien
Geog Ges Muenchen Jber — Geographische Gesellschaft in Muenchen. Jahresbericht
Geog Graec Min — Geographi Graeci Minores
Geog Gr Min — Geographi Graeci Minores
Geog J — Geographical Journal
GeogJh — Geognostische Jahreshefte
Geog Jnl — Geographical Journal
Geog Jour — Geographical Journal. Royal Geographic Society
Geog Lat Min — Geographi Latini Minores
Geog M — Geographical Magazine
Geog Mag — Geographical Magazine
Geog Map Div Bull — Geography and Map Division Bulletin
Geog Phys et Quat — Geographie Physique et Quaternaire
Geogr — Geographia
Geogr — Geographica
Geogr R — Geographical Review
Geogr — Geography
Geogr A — Geografiska Annaler
Geogr Abstr — Geographical Abstracts
Geogr Anal — Geographical Analysis
Geogr Ann — Geografiska Annaler
Geogr Ann B — Geografiska Annaler. Series B. Human Geography
Geogr Ann Hum Geogr — Geografiska Annaler. B. Human Geography
Geogr Annlr — Geografiska Annaler
Geogr Ann Phys Geogr — Geografiska Annaler. A. Physical Geography
Geogr Ann Ser B Hum Geogr — Geografiska Annaler. Series B. Human Geography
Geogr Anz — Geographischer Anzeiger
Geogr B — Geographical Bulletin
Geogr Ber — Geographische Berichte
Geogr Bull Budapest — Geographical Bulletin (Budapest)
Geogr Can — Geographe Canadien
Geogr Cas — Geografiske Casopis
Geog Rdsch — Geographische Rundschau
Geogr Educ — Geographical Education
Geogr Et Rech — Geographie et Recherche
Geog Rev — Geographical Review
Geogr Ezheg — Geograficheskii Ezhegodnik
Geogr Ezheg Geogr Ova Lit SSR — Geografiya Ezhegodnogo Geograficheskogo Obshchestva Litovskoi SSR
Geogr Fis Din Quat — Geografia Fisica e Dinamica Quaternaria
Geogr Geol — Geografija ir Geologija
Geogr Geol Meded Physiogr Geol Reeks Geogr Inst (Utrecht) — Geographische en Geologische Mededelingen, Physiographisch Geologische Reeks, Geographisch Instituut (Utrecht)
Geogr Ges Hamb Mitt — Geographische Gesellschaft in Hamburg. Mitteilungen
Geogr Glas — Geografski Glasnik
Geogr Glasn — Geografski Glasnik
Geogr Helv — Geographica Helvetica
Geog R Ind — Geographical Review of India
Geogr Inf — Geographische Informationen
Geogr J — Geographical Journal
Geogr Jahrb — Geographisches Jahrbuch
Geogr Jb — Geographisches Jahrbuch
Geogr Jber Oesterr — Geographischer Jahresbericht aus Oesterreich
Geogr Jb Oester — Geographisches Jahrbuch aus Oesterreich
Geogr J (Lond) — Geographical Journal (London)
Geogr J London — Geographical Journal. Royal Geographical Society of London
Geogr Jour — Geographical Journal (London)
Geogr Journ — Geographical Journal
Geogr Knowl (Peking) — Geographical Knowledge (Peking)
Geogrl Abstr — Geographical Abstracts
Geogrl J — Geographical Journal
Geogrl Rev — Geographical Review
Geogr Mag (Lond) — Geographical Magazine (London)
Geogr Med — Geographia Medica
Geogr Metrastis — Geografinis Metrastis
Geogr Ovo SSSR Dokl — Geograficheskoe Obshchestvo SSSR Doklady
Geogr Pol — Geography Polonica
Geogr Pregl — Geografski Pregled
Geogr R — Geographical Review
Geogr Raka Turkm — Geografiya Raka v Turkmenii
Geogr Rdsch — Geographische Rundschau
Geogr Rev — Geographical Review
Geogr Rev Jap — Geographical Review of Japan
Geogr Rev (New York) — Geographical Review (New York)
Geogr Rev NY — Geographical Review (New York)
Geogr RI — Geographical Review of India
Geogr Rundsch — Geographische Rundschau
Geogr Sb — Geograficeskij Sbornik
Geogr Sborn — Geograficeskij Sbornik
Geogr Sb Penz Otd Geogr Ova SSSR — Geograficheskii Sbornik Penzenskogo Otdeleniya Geograficheskogo Obshchestva SSSR
Geogr Schriften — Geographische Schriften
Geogr Shk — Geografiya v Shkole
Geogr Stud — Geographical Studies
Geogr T — Geografisk Tidsskrift
Geogr TB — Geographisches Taschenbuch

Geogr Tchr — Geographical Teacher
Geogr Teach — Geography Teacher
Geogr Tidsskrift — Geografisk Tidsskrift
Geogr Tijdschr — Geografisch Tijdschrift
Geogr Tjds — Geografisch Tijdschrift
Geog Rund — Geographische Rundschau
Geogr Vestn — Geografski Vestnik
Geogr Z — Geographische Zeitschrift
Geogr Ztschr — Geographische Zeitschrift
Geog Soc Chicago B — Geographic Society of Chicago. Bulletin
Geog Soc Phila — Geographical Society of Philadelphia. Bulletin
Geog Soc Phila B — Geographical Society of Philadelphia. Bulletin
Geog Tidsskr — Geografisk Tidsskrift
Geog Z — Geographische Zeitschrift
Geog Zeits — Geographische Zeitschrift
GEOHAH — Geologi
Geo Heat Cent Q Bull — Geo-Heat Center. Quarterly Bulletin
Geo-Heat Util Center Q Bull — Geo-Heat Utilization Center. Quarterly Bulletin
Geo-Heat Util Cent Q Bull — Geo-Heat Utilization Center. Quarterly Bulletin
GEOIM — Geodaetisk Institut. Meddelelse
GEOIS — Geodaetisk Institut. Skrifter
Geo J — Geo Journal
GEOJA — Geophysical Journal. Royal Astronomical Society
GEOJDQ — Geojournal
Geokhim — Geokhimiya
Geokhim Akad Nauk (SSSR) — Geokhimiya Akademiya Nauk (SSSR)
Geokhim Chekh Tr Geokhim Konf — Geokhimiya v Chekhoslovakii. Trudy Geokhimicheskoi Konferentsii
Geokhim Elem Soedin Pochvakh — Geokhimiya Elementov i Soedinenii v Pochvakh
Geokhim Issled — Geokhimicheskie Issledovaniya
Geokhim Metody Poiskakh Razved Rudn Mestorozhd — Geokhimicheskie Metody pri Poiskakh i Razvedke Rudnykh Mestorozhdenii
Geokhim Metody Poiskov Nefti Gaza — Geokhimicheskie Metody Poiskov. Nefti i Gaza
Geokhim Mineral Petrogr — Geokhimiya, Mineralogiya, Petrografiya
Geokhim Mineral Petrol — Geokhimiya, Mineralogiya, i Petrologiya
Geokhim Nefti Neft Mestorozhd — Geokhimiya Nefti i Neftyanykh Mestorozhdenii
Geokhim Osad Porod Rud Mater Vses Litol Konf — Geokhimiya Osadochnykh Porod i Rud. Materialy Vsesoyuznoi Litologicheskoi Konferentsii
Geokhim Rudoobraz — Geokhimiya i Rudoobrazovanie
Geokhim Sb — Geokhimicheskii Sbornik
GeoL — Geographica (Lisbon)
Geol — Geologie
Geol — Geologija
Geol Abh Hessen — Geologische Abhandlungen Hessen
Geol Abstr — Geological Abstracts
Geol Alp — Geologie Alpine
Geol Anagoriseis Ekthesis — Geologikai Anagnoriseis Ekthesis
Geol An Balk Poluostrva — Geolshki Anali Balkanskoga Poluostrva
Geol Appl Idrogeol — Geologia Applicata e Idrogeologia
Geol Appl Prospect Miniere — Geologie Appliquee et Prospection Miniere
Geol Arch — Geologisches Archiv
Geol Assoc Can — Geological Association of Canada
Geol Assoc Canada Proc — Geological Association of Canada. Proceedings
Geol Assoc Can Cordilleran Sect Programme Abstr — Geological Association of Canada. Cordilleran Section. Programme and Abstracts
Geol Assoc Can Proc — Geological Association of Canada. Proceedings
Geol Assoc Can Spec Pap — Geological Association of Canada. Special Paper
Geol Assoc (Lond) Proc — Geologists' Association (London). Proceedings
Geol Atlas PA — Geologic Atlas of Pennsylvania
GEOLB — Geologues
Geol Balc — Geologica Balcanica
Geol Balc (Sofia) — Geologica Balcanica. Bulgarska Akademiya ne Naukite (Sofia)
Geol Bauwes — Geologie und Bauwesen
Geol Bav — Geologica Bavarica
Geol Bavar — Geologica Bavarica
Geol Bavarica — Geologica Bavarica
Geol Beih — Geologie. Beihefte
Geol Bl — Geologische Blaetter fuer Nordost-Bayern und Angrenzende Gebiete
Geol Blaett Nordost Bayern — Geologische Blaetter fuer Nordost-Bayern und Angrenzende Gebiete
Geol Bl Nordost-Bayern — Geologische Blaetter fuer Nordost-Bayern und Angrenzende Gebiete
Geol Bl Nordost-Bayern Angrenzende Geb — Geologische Blaetter fuer Nordost-Bayern und Angrenzende Gebiete
Geol Bull Fla Bur Geol — Geological Bulletin. Florida. Bureau of Geology
Geol Bull Geol Surv China — Geological Bulletin. Geological Survey of China
Geol Bull Natl Geol Surv China — Geological Bulletin. National Geological Survey of China
Geol Bull Punjab Univ — Geological Bulletin. Punjab University
Geol Bull Soc Belge Geol — Geologie. Bulletin de la Societe Belge de Geologie
Geol Bull Univ Peshawar — Geological Bulletin. University of Peshawar
Geol Bundesanst Abh Austria — Geologische Bundesanstalt. Abhandlungen (Austria)
Geol Carpathica — Geologica Carpathica
Geol Center Research Ser — Geological Center. Research Series
Geol Circ Ont Dep Mines — Geological Circular. Ontario. Department of Mines
Geol Circ Univ Tex Austin Bur Econ Geol — Geological Circular. University of Texas at Austin. Bureau of Economic Geology
Geol Coal Meas Stratigr Carboniferous USSR — Geology of Coal Measures and Stratigraphy of the Carboniferous in the USSR
Geol Colomb — Geologia Colombiana
Geol Correl — Geological Correlation
Geol Explor Min BC — Geology. Exploration and Mining in British Columbia

Geol Foeren St Foerh — Geologiska Foereningens i Stockholm. Foerhandlingar
Geol Foeren Stockh Foerh — Geologiska Foereningens i Stockholm. Foerhandlingar
Geol Foeren Stockholm Foerh — Geologiska Foereningens i Stockholm Foerhandlingar
Geol Foer Stockh Foerh — Geologiska Foereningens i Stockholm. Foerhandlingar
Geol Fr — Geologie de la France
Geol Geofiz — Geologiya i Geofizika
Geol Geofiz Meletai — Geologikai kai Geofizikai Meletai
Geol Geokhim — Geologiya i Geokhimiya
Geol Geokhim Goryuchikh Kopalin — Geologiya i Geokhimiya Goryuchikh Kopalin
Geol Geokhim Goryuch Iskop — Geologiya i Geokhimiya Goryuchikh Iskopaemykh
Geol Geokhim Goryuch Iskop Akad Nauk Ukr SSR — Geologiya i Geokhimiya Goryuchikh Iskopaemykh Akademiya Nauk Ukrain'skoi SSR
Geol Geokhim Goryuch Kopalin Akad Nauk Ukr RSR — Geologiya i Geokhimiya Goryuchikh Kopalin Akademiya Nauk Ukrain'skoi RSR
Geol Geokhim Mestorozhd Tverd Goryuch Iskop — Geologiya i Geokhimiya Mestorozhdenii Tverdykh Goryuchikh Iskopaemykh
Geol Geokhim Neft Gazov Mestorozhd — Geologiya i Geokhimiya Neftyanskh i Gazovykh Mestorozhdenii
Geol Geokhim Vses Neft Nauchno Issled Geologorazved Inst — Geologiya i Geokhimiya. Vsesoyuznyi Neftyanoi Nauchno-Issledovatel'skii Geologorazvedochnyi Institut
Geol Geophys (Novosibirsk) — Geology and Geophysics (Novosibirsk)
Geol Gidrogeol Polezn Iskop Beloruss Metody Ikh Issled Mater — Geologiya, Gidrogeologiya, Poleznye Iskopaemye Belorussii i Metody Ikh Issledovaniya. Materialy Dokladov Nauchnoi Konferentsii Molodykh Geologov Belorussii
Geol Gites Miner — Geologie des Gites Mineraux
Geol Glas — Geoloski Glasnik
Geol Glas Posebna Izd — Geoloski Glasnik. Posebna Izdanja
Geol Glas Sarajevo — Geoloski Glasnik (Sarajevo)
Geol Glas Sarajevo Posebna Izd — Geoloski Glasnik (Sarajevo). Posebna Izdanja
Geol Glas (Titograd Yugosl) — Geoloski Glasnik (Titograd, Yugoslavia)
Geol Ground Water Resour — Geology and Ground-Water Resources
Geol Hung — Geologica Hungarica
Geol Hung Ser Palaeontol — Geologica Hungarica. Series Palaeontologica
Geol i Geofiz — Geologiya i Geofizika
Geol Ind — Geologic Index
Geol Ing — Geologie de l'Ingenieur
Geol Inst Bucharest Guideb Ser — Geological Institute. Bucharest. Guidebook Series
Geol Inst Uurim Eesti NSV Tead Akad — Geoloogia Instituudi Uurimused. Eesti NSV Teaduste Akadeemia
Geol Inst (Vilnius) Darb — Geologijos Institutas (Vilnius). Darbai
Geol Invest Ser Geol Surv Pak Interim Geol Rep — Geological Investigation Series. Geological Survey of Pakistan. Interim Geological Report
Geol Izuch SSR — Geologicheskaya Izuchennost SSR
Geol J — Geological Journal
Geo LJ — Georgetown Law Journal
Geol Jahrb — Geologisches Jahrbuch
Geol Jahrb Beih — Geologisches Jahrbuch. Beihefte
Geol Jahrb Hessen — Geologisches Jahrbuch Hessen
Geol Jahrb Reihe A — Geologisches Jahrbuch. Reihe A. Allgemeine und Regionale Geologie BR Deutschland und Nachbargebiete, Tektonik, Stratigraphie, Palaeontologie
Geol Jahrb Reihe B — Geologisches Jahrbuch. Reihe B. Regionale Geologie Ausland
Geol Jahrb Reihe C — Geologisches Jahrbuch. Reihe C. Hydrogeologie, Ingenieurgeologie
Geol Jahrb Reihe D — Geologisches Jahrbuch. Reihe D. Mineralogie, Petrographie, Geochemie, Lagerstaettenkunde
Geol Jahrb Reihe E — Geologisches Jahrbuch. Reihe E. Geophysik
Geol Jahrb Reihe E Geophys — Geologisches Jahrbuch. Reihe E. Geophysik
Geol Jahrb Reihe F Bodenk — Geologisches Jahrbuch. Reihe F. Bodenkunde
Geol Jahrbuch Ser A — Geologisches Jahrbuch. Series A
Geol Jahrbuch Ser B — Geologisches Jahrbuch. Series B
Geol Jahrbuch Ser C — Geologisches Jahrbuch. Series C
Geol Jahrbuch Ser D — Geologisches Jahrbuch. Series D
Geol Jahrbuch Ser E — Geologisches Jarhbuch. Series E
Geol Jahr Reihe F — Geologisches Jahrbuch. Reihe F. Bodenkunde
Geol Jb — Geologisches Jahrbuch
Geol J Kiev — Geological Journal (Kiev)
Geol J (Liverpool) — Geological Journal (Liverpool)
Geol J Queen Mary Coll — Geological Journal of Queen Mary College
Geol J Univ — Geological Journal of Universities
Geol Kaz — Geologiya Kazakhstana
Geol Kaz — Geology of Kazakhstan
Geol Libya Symp — Geology of Libya. Symposium on the Geology of Libya
Geol Lit SSSR Bibliogr Yezhegodnik — Geologicheskaya Literatura SSSR Bibliograficheskiy Yezhegodnik
Geol M — Geological Magazine
Geol Maced — Geologica Macedonica
Geol Mag — Geological Magazine
Geol Map Deputy Minist Miner Resour (Saudi Arabia) — Geologic Map. Deputy Ministry for Mineral Resources (Kingdom of Saudi Arabia)
Geol Map GM Saudi Arabia Dir Gen Miner Resour — Geologic Map GM. Saudi Arabia. Directorate General of Mineral Resources
Geol Map Miner Resour Summ North Carolina Geol Surv — Geology Map and Mineral Resources Summary. North Carolina Geological Survey
Geol Map Miner Resour Summ (State Tennessee) — Geologic Map and Mineral Resources. Summary (State of Tennessee)
Geol Map Montana Bur Mines Geol — Geologic Map. Montana Bureau of Mines and Geology

Geol Mediter — Geologie Mediterraneenne

Geol Mem Geol Surv China Ser A — Geological Memoirs. Geological Survey of China. Series A

Geol Mem Geol Surv China Ser B — Geological Memoirs. Geological Survey of China. Series B

Geol Mestorozhd Redk Elem — Geologiya Mestorozhdenii Redkikh Elementov

Geol Metal — Geologia y Metalurgia

Geol Metal Bol — Geologia e Metalurgia. Boletim

Geol Metallog Copper Deposits Proc Copper Symp Int Geol Congr — Geology and Metallogeny of Copper Deposits. Proceedings. Copper Symposium. Inter

Geol Metal (San Luis Potosi) — Geologia y Metalurgia (San Luis Potosi)

Geol Metal (Sao Paulo) — Geologia e Metalurgia (Sao Paulo)

Geol Metamorf Kompleksov — Geologiya Metamorficheskikh Kompleksov

Geol Met Bol — Geologia e Metalurgia. Boletim. Escola Politecnica. Universidade de Sao Paulo

Geol Metod Tekh Razved Lab Rab — Geologiya. Metodika i Tekhnika Razvedki. Laboratornye Raboty

Geol Mijnb — Geologie en Mijnbouw

Geol Mijnbouw — Geologie en Mijnbouw

Geol Mijnbouwkd Dienst Suriname Meded — Geologisch Mijnbouwkundige Dienst van Suriname. Mededeling

Geol Mineral — Geologiya i Mineralogiya

Geol Miner Resour Far East — Geology and Mineral Resources of the Far East

Geol Miner Resur — Geologiya i Mineralni Resursi

Geol Miner Syre Dalnego Vostoka — Geologiya i Mineral'noe Syr'e Dal'nego Vostoka

Geol Min Metall Soc India Q J — Geological, Mining, and Metallurgical Society of India. Quarterly Journal

Geol Min Metall Soc Liberia Bull — Geological, Mining, and Metallurgical Society of Liberia. Bulletin

Geol Min Met Soc Liberia Bull — Geological, Mining, and Metallurgical Society of Liberia. Bulletin

Geol Min Surv Iran Rep — Geological and Mining Survey of Iran. Report

Geol Mitt — Geologische Mitteilungen

Geol Mon — Geology Monthly

Geol Morya — Geologiya Morya

Geol Nauchn Dokl Gertsenovskie Chteniya — Geologiya, Nauchnye Doklady, Gertsenovskie Chteniya

Geol Neftegazonosn Turkm — Geologiya i Neftegazonosnost Turkmenistana

Geol Nefti — Geologiya Nefti

Geol Nefti Gaza — Geologiya Nefti i Gaza

Geol Nefti Gaza Sev Vostoka Evr Chasti SSSR — Geologiya Nefti i Gaza Severo-Vostoka Evropeiskoi Chasti SSSR

Geol Nefti i Gaza — Geologiya Nefti i Gaza

Geol Notes Local Details 1:10000 Sheets Inst Geol Sci — Geological Notes and Local Details for 1:10,000 Sheets. Institute of GeologicalSciences

Geol Notes SC Geol Surv — Geologic Notes. South Carolina Geological Survey

Geol Offshore Miner Resour Cent Pac Basin — Geology and Offshore Mineral Resources of the Central Pacific Basin

Geologie Beih — Geologie. Beihefte

Geologie Mijnb — Geologie en Mijnbouw

Geologists' Assoc (London) Proc — Geologists' Association (London). Proceedings

Geology Club Puerto Rico Bull — Geology Club of Puerto Rico. Bulletin

Geol Ore Deposits Transl of Geol Rudn Mestorozhd — Geology of Ore Deposits (Translation of Geologiya Rudnykh Mestorozhdenii)

Geol Palaeontol — Geologica et Palaeontologica

Geol Palaeontol Southeast Asia — Geology and Palaeontology of Southeast Asia

Geol Paleontol Hydrol Brussels — Geologie, Paleontologie, Hydrologie (Brussels)

Geol Pap Carleton Univ Dep Geol — Geological Paper. Carleton University. Department of Geology

Geol Pap Geol Surv Malaysia — Geological Papers. Geological Survey of Malaysia

Geol Pap Miner Resour Div (Manitoba) — Geological Paper. Mineral Resources Division (Manitoba)

Geol Poberezh'ya Dna Chern Azovskogo Morei Predelakh Ukr SSR — Geologiya Poberezh'ya i Dna Chernogo i Azovskogo Morei v Predelakh Ukrainskoi SSR

Geol Poberezhya Dna Chern Azovskogo Morei Predelakh USSR — Geologiya Poberezh'ya i Dna Chernogo i Azovskogo Morei v Predelakh USSR

Geol Poiski Razved Nerudn Polezn Iskop — Geologiya, Poiski, i Razvedka Nerudnykh Poleznykh Iskopaemykh

Geol Poiski Razved Rudn Mestorozhd — Geologiya. Poiski i Razvedka Rudnykh Mestorozhdenii

Geol Pol — Geology of Poland

Geol Polezn Iskop Kalmytskoi ASSR — Geologiya i Polezne Iskopaemye Kalmytskoi ASSR

Geol Polezn Iskop Urala — Geologiya i Poleznye Iskopaemye Urala

Geol Polezn Iskop Zapadn Kaz — Geologiya i Poleznye Iskopaemye Zapadnogo Kazakhstana

Geol Polezn Iskop Zarub Stran — Geologiya i Poleznye Iskopaemye Zarubezhnykh Stran

Geol Polezn Isk Turkm — Geologiya i Poleznye Iskopaemye Turkmenii

Geol Pr — Geologicke Prace

Geol Prace Zpr — Geologicke Prace. Zpravy

Geol Pr (Bratisl) — Geologicke Prace (Bratislava)

Geol Precambrian — Geology of Precambrian

Geol Prieskum — Geologicky Prieskum

Geol Prospect — Geology and Prospecting

Geol Prov Buenos Aires Relat Congr Geol Argent — Geologia de la Provincia de Buenos Aires. Relatorio. Congreso Geologico Argentino

Geol Pruzkum — Geologicky Pruzkum

Geol Pruzkum np Ostrava Sb — Geologicky Pruzkum n.p. Ostrava. Sbornik

GeolR — Geologische Rundschau

Geol Razpr Porocila — Geologija. Razprave in Porocila

Geol Razrab Gazov Gazokondens Mestorozhd Ukr — Geologiya i Razrabotka Gazovykh i Gazokondensatnykh Mestorozhdenii Ukrainy

Geol Razrab Gazov Mestorozhd Ispolz Gaza Sredn Azii — Geologiya. Razrabotka Gazovykh Mestorozhdenii i Ispol'zovanie Gaza v Srednei Azii

Geol Razrab Neft Gazov Mestorozhd Dokl Vses Konf Molodykh Uch — Geologiya i Razrabotka Neftyanykh i Gazovykh Mestorozhdenii. Doklady na Vsesoyuznoi Konferentsii Molodykh Uchenykh

Geol Razved — Geologiya i Razvedka

Geol Razved Gazov Gazokondens Mestorozhd — Geologiya i Razvedka Gazovykh i Gazokondensatnykh Mestorozhdenii

Geol Razved Gazov Gazokondens Mestorozhd Nauchno Tekh Obz — Geologiya i Razvedka Gazovykh i Gazokondensatnykh Mestorozhdenii. Nauchno-Tekhnicheskii Obzor

Geol Razved Nedr — Geologiya i Razvedka Nedr

Geol Razved Razrab Gazov Gazokondens Mestorozhd Sev Kavk — Geologiya. Razvedka i Razrabotka Gazovykh i Gazokondensatnykh Mestorozhdenii Severnogo Kavkaza

Geol Rdsch — Geologische Rundschau

Geol Reconnaissance Rep — Geological Reconnaissance Report

Geol Recur Nat Neuquen Relat Congr Geol Argent — Geologia y Recursos Naturales del Neuquen, Relatorio. Congreso Geologico Argentino

Geol Rep Alaska — Geologic Report. Alaska

Geol Rep Coal Fields Korea — Geological Report on Coal Fields of Korea

Geol Rep Dep Nat Resour (Queb) — Geological Reports. Department of Natural Resources (Quebec)

Geol Rep Hiroshima Univ — Geological Report. Hiroshima University

Geol Rep Miner Resour Div (Manitoba) — Geological Report. Mineral Resources Division (Manitoba)

Geol Rep Ont Div Mines — Geological Report. Ontario Division of Mines

Geol Rep Que Dep Nat Resour — Geological Report. Quebec. Department of Natural Resources

Geol Rep Shimane Univ — Geological Reports. Shimane University

Geol Rep State Alaska Dep Nat Resour — Geologic Report. State of Alaska Department of Natural Resources

Geol Res Dev Cent Bull Bandung Indones — Geological Research and Development Centre. Bulletin (Bandung, Indonesia)

Geol Rev (Beijing) — Geological Review (Beijing)

Geol Rom — Geologica Romana

Geol Roman — Geologica Romana

Geol Rossypei Dokl Soveshch — Geologiya Rossypei. Doklady Soveshchaniya

Geol Rud Mestorozhd — Geologiya Rudnykh Mestorozhdenii

Geol Rudn Mestorozhd — Geologiya Rudnykh Mestorozhdenii

Geol Rudonosn Pritashk Raiona Zap Uzb Otd Vses Mineral Ova — Geologiya i Rudonosnost Pritashkentskogo Raiona. Zapiski Uzbekistanskogo Otdeleniya Vsesoyuznogo Mineralogicheskogo Obshchestva

Geol Rudonosn Yuga Ukr — Geologiya i Rudonosnost Yuga Ukrainy

Geol Rundsch — Geologische Rundschau

Geol Rundschau — Geologische Rundschau

Geol S Am B — Geological Society of America. Bulletin

Geol Sb Bratislava — Geologicky Sbornik (Bratislava)

Geol Sb Kavk Inst Miner Syrya — Geologicheskii Sbornik. Kavkazskii Institut Mineral'nogo Syr'ya

Geol Sb (Lvov) — Geologicheskii Sbornik (Lvov)

Geol Sb Moscow — Geologicheskii Sbornik (Moscow)

Geol Sbornik — Geologicheskii Sbornik

Geol Sb (Tiflis) — Geologicheskii Sbornik (Tiflis)

Geol Sb Vses Inst Nauchno Tekhnol Inf — Geologicheskii Sbornik Vsesoyuznogo Instituta Nauchno Tekhnologicheskoi Informatsii

Geol Sci (Beijing) — Geological Science (Beijing)

Geol Sci Technol Inf — Geological Science and Technology Information

Geol Sect Bull Libya Minist Ind — Geological Section. Bulletin. Libya Ministry of Industry

Geol Soc Am — Geological Society of America Bulletin

Geol Soc Am Abstr Programs — Geological Society of America. Abstracts with Programs

Geol Soc Am Annu Meet Field Trip Guideb — Geological Society of America. Annual Meeting. Field Trip Guidebook

Geol Soc Am Bull — Geological Society of America. Bulletin

Geol Soc Am Cordilleran Sect Annu Meet Guideb — Geological Society of America. Cordilleran Section. Annual Meeting Guidebook

Geol Soc Amer — Geological Society of America

Geol Soc Amer Bull — Geological Society of America. Bulletin

Geol Soc Amer Eng Geol Case Hist — Geological Society of America. Engineering Geology Case Histories

Geol Soc America Abs with Programs — Geological Society of America. Abstracts with Programs

Geol Soc America Spec Paper — Geological Society of America. Special Papers

Geol Soc Amer Mem — Geological Society of America. Memoir

Geol Soc Amer Spec Pap — Geological Society of America. Special Paper

Geol Soc Am Map Chart Ser — Geological Society of America. Map and Chart Series

Geol Soc Am Mem — Geological Society of America. Memoir

Geol Soc Am Meml — Geological Society of America. Memorials

Geol Soc Am Microform Publ — Geological Society of America. Microform Publication

Geol Soc Am Proc — Geological Society of America. Proceedings

Geol Soc Am Southeast Sect Guideb — Geological Society of America. Southeastern Section Guidebook

Geol Soc Am Spec Pap — Geological Society of America. Special Paper

Geol Soc Am Spec Pap (Reg Stud) — Geological Society of America. Special Paper (Regional Studies)

Geol Soc Australia J — Geological Society of Australia. Journal

Geol Soc Aust Spec Publ — Geological Society of Australia. Special Publication

Geol Soc Bull — Geological Society of America. Bulletin

Geol Soc China Proc — Geological Society of China. Proceedings

Geol Soc Dublin J — Geological Society of Dublin. Journal
Geol Soc Egypt Annu Meet Abstr — Geological Society of Egypt. Annual Meeting. Abstracts
Geol Soc Finl Bull — Geological Society of Finland. Bulletin
Geol Soc Greece Bull — Geological Society of Greece. Bulletin
Geol Soc India Bull — Geological Society of India. Bulletin
Geol Soc India J — Geological Society of India. Journal
Geol Soc India Jour — Geological Society of India. Journal
Geol Soc India Mem — Geological Society of India. Memoir
Geol Soc Iraq J — Geological Society of Iraq. Journal
Geol Soc J — Journal. Geological Society
Geol Soc Jam J — Geological Society of Jamaica. Journal
Geol Soc Jap J — Geological Society of Japan. Journal
Geol Soc Jpn Mem — Geological Society of Japan. Memoir
Geol Soc Korea J — Geological Society of Korea. Journal
Geol Soc Lond J — Geological Society of London. Journal
Geol Soc Lond Misc Pap — Geological Society of London. Miscellaneous Paper
Geol Soc (Lond) Newsl — Geological Society. Newsletter (London)
Geol Soc London Mem — Geological Society of London. Memoirs
Geol Soc London Spec Publ — Geological Society of London. Special Publication
Geol Soc Lond Q J — Geological Society of London. Quarterly Journal
Geol Soc Lond Spec Rep — Geological Society of London. Special Report
Geol Soc Malays Bull — Geological Society of Malaysia. Bulletin
Geol Soc Malays Newsl — Geological Society of Malaysia. Newsletter
Geol Soc Misc Pap London — Geological Society Miscellaneous Paper (London)
Geol Soc NJ Rept — Geological Society of New Jersey. Report
Geol Soc Norfolk Bull — Geological Society of Norfolk. Bulletin
Geol Soc NZ Newsl — Geological Society of New Zealand. Newsletter
Geol Soc Oregon Country News Letter — Geological Society of the Oregon Country. News Letter
Geol Soc Philipp J — Geological Society of the Philippines. Journal
Geol Soc Proc — Geological Society of America. Proceedings
Geol Soc S Afr Congr Abstr — Geological Society of South Africa. Congress Abstracts
Geol Soc S Afr Q News Bull — Geological Society of South Africa. Quarterly News Bulletin
Geol Soc S Afr Spec Publ — Geological Society of South Africa. Special Publication
Geol Soc S Afr Trans — Geological Society of South Africa. Transactions
Geol Soc So Africa Trans — Geological Society of South Africa. Transactions and Proceedings
Geol Soc Spec Publ — Geological Society Special Publication
Geol Soc Spec Publ London — Geological Society Special Publication (London)
Geol Soc Zimbabwe Spec Publ — Geological Society of Zimbabwe. Special Publication
Geol Space — Geology from Space
Geol SSSR — Geologiya SSSR
Geol Sticht Meded Nieuwe Ser Neth — Geologische Stichting. Mededelingen. Nieuwe Serie (Netherlands)
Geol Str Polezn Iskop Nizhnego Povolzhya — Geologicheskoe Stroenie i Poleznye Iskopaemye Nizhnego Povolzh'ya
Geol Str Polezn Iskop Kalmytskoi ASSR — Geologicheskoe Stroenie i Poleznye Iskopaemye Kalmytskoi ASSR
Geol Stud Dep Mines Geol Mysore — Geological Studies. Department of Mines and Geology. Mysore
Geol Sudetica — Geologia Sudetica
Geol Sudetica (Warsaw) — Geologia Sudetica (Warsaw)
Geol Surv Ala Circ — Geological Survey of Alabama. Circular
Geol Surv Ala Spec Rep — Geological Survey of Alabama. Special Report
Geol Surv Borneo Reg Malays Mem — Geological Survey. Borneo Region. Malaysia. Memoir
Geol Surv Borneo Reg Malays Rep — Geological Survey. Borneo Region. Malaysia. Report
Geol Surv Botswana Dist Mem — Geological Survey of Botswana. District Memoir
Geol Surv Br Guiana Bull — Geological Survey of British Guiana. Bulletin
Geol Surv Bull Indiana — Geological Survey Bulletin (Indiana)
Geol Surv Bull Tasmania — Tasmania. Geological Survey. Bulletin
Geol Surv Bull (US) — Geological Survey Bulletin (United States)
Geol Surv Can Bull — Geological Survey of Canada. Bulletin
Geol Surv Can Ec Geol Rep — Geological Survey of Canada. Economic Geology Report
Geol Surv Can Econ Geol Rep — Geological Survey of Canada. Economic Geology Report
Geol Surv Can Econ Geol Ser — Geological Survey of Canada. Economic Geology Series
Geol Surv Can Mem — Geological Survey of Canada. Memoir
Geol Surv Can Pap — Geological Survey of Canada. Paper
Geol Surv Ceylon Mem — Geological Survey of Ceylon. Memoir
Geol Surv Circ — Geological Survey Circular
Geol Surv Circ US — Geological Survey Circular (United States)
Geol Surv Den III Ser — Geological Survey of Denmark. III Series
Geol Surv Den II Ser — Geological Survey of Denmark. II Series
Geol Surv Den Rep — Geological Survey of Denmark. Report
Geol Surv Den Ser A — Geological Survey of Denmark. Serie A
Geol Surv Den Ser B — Geological Survey of Denmark. Serie B
Geol Surv Den Yearb — Geological Survey of Denmark. Yearbook
Geol Surv Dep Br Territ Borneo Rep — Geological Survey Department. British Territories in Borneo. Report
Geol Surv Dep Econ Rep (Zambia) — Geological Survey Department. Economic Report (Zambia)
Geol Surv Dep Fed Malaya Mem — Geological Survey Department. Federation of Malaya. Memoir
Geol Surv Dep (Jam) Bull — Geological Survey Department (Jamaica, West Indies). Bulletin

Geol Surv Dep (Jam West Indies) Occas Pap — Geological Survey Department (Jamaica, West Indies). Occasional Paper
Geol Surv Div Annu Rep Niger — Geological Survey Division. Annual Report (Nigeria)
Geol Surv East Malays Rep — Geological Survey. East Malaysia. Report
Geol Surv Egypt Ann — Geological Survey of Egypt. Annals
Geol Surv Fiji Bull — Geological Survey of Fiji. Bulletin
Geol Surv Fiji Mem — Geological Survey of Fiji. Memoir
Geol Surv Finl Bull — Geological Survey of Finland. Bulletin
Geol Surv GA Bull — Geological Survey of Georgia. Bulletin
Geol Surv Ga Inf Circ — Geological Survey of Georgia. Information Circular
Geol Surv GB Bull — Geological Survey of Great Britain Bulletin
Geol Surv GB Handb B Reg Geol — Geological Survey of Great Britain. Handbooks. British Regional Geology
Geol Surv GB Mem Geol Surv GB Engl Wales — Geological Survey of Great Britain. Memoirs. Geological Survey of Great Britain, England, and Wales
Geol Surv GB Mem Geol Surv (Scotl) — Geological Survey of Great Britain. Memoirs of the Geological Survey (Scotland)
Geol Surv Greenland Rep — Geological Survey of Greenland. Report
Geol Surv Greenl Bull — Geological Survey of Greenland. Bulletin
Geol Surv Greenl Rep — Geological Survey of Greenland. Report
Geol Surv Guyana Bull — Geological Survey of Guyana. Bulletin
Geol Surv India Bull Ser B — Geological Survey of India. Bulletins. Series B. Engineering Geology and Ground-Water
Geol Surv India Mem — Geological Survey of India. Memoirs
Geol Surv India Misc Publ — Geological Survey of India. Miscellaneous Publication
Geol Surv India News — Geological Survey of India. News
Geol Surv India Rec — Geological Survey of India. Records
Geol Surv India Spec Publ Ser — Geological Survey of India. Special Publication Series
Geol Surv Indones Publ Tek Seri Geol Ekon — Geological Survey of Indonesia. Publikasi Teknik. Seri Geologi Ekonomi
Geol Surv Indones Spec Publ — Geological Survey of Indonesia. Special Publication
Geol Surv Iowa Water Supply Bull — Geological Survey of Iowa. Water-Supply Bulletin
Geol Surv Iran Rep — Geological Survey of Iran. Report
Geol Surv Ir Bull — Geological Survey of Ireland. Bulletin
Geol Surv Irel Bull — Geological Survey of Ireland. Bulletin
Geol Surv Ir Info Circular — Geological Survey of Ireland. Information Circular
Geol Surv Isr Bull — Geological Survey of Israel. Bulletin
Geol Surv Jap Hydrogeol Maps Jap — Geological Survey of Japan. Hydrogeological Maps of Japan
Geol Surv Jap Rep — Geological Survey of Japan. Report
Geol Surv Jpn Cruise Rep — Geological Survey of Japan. Cruise Report
Geol Surv Jpn Rep — Geological Survey of Japan. Report
Geol Surv Jpn Spec Rep — Geological Survey of Japan. Special Report
Geol Surv Kenya Bull — Geological Survey of Kenya. Bulletin
Geol Surv Kenya Rep — Geological Survey of Kenya. Report
Geol Surv Korea Bull — Geological Survey of Korea. Bulletin
Geol Surv Korea Geol Rep Coal Fields Korea — Geological Survey of Korea. Geological Reports on Coal Fields of Korea
Geol Surv Korea Rep Geophys Geochem Explor — Geological Survey of Korea. Report of Geophysical and Geochemical Exploration
Geol Surv Korea Tech Pap — Geological Survey of Korea. Technical Paper
Geol Surv Malays Annu Rep — Geological Survey of Malaysia. Annual Report
Geol Surv Malays Dist Mem — Geological Survey of Malaysia. District Memoir
Geol Surv Malays Geol Pap — Geological Survey of Malaysia. Geological Papers
Geol Surv Nigeria Bull — Geological Survey of Nigeria. Bulletin
Geol Surv NSW Bull — Geological Survey of New South Wales. Bulletin
Geol Surv NSW Geol Surv Rep — Geological Survey of New South Wales. Geological Survey Report
Geol Surv NSW Miner Ind NSW — New South Wales. Geological Survey. Mineral Industry of New South Wales
Geol Surv NSW Miner Resour — Geological Survey of New South Wales. Mineral Resources
Geol Surv NSW Rec — Geological Survey of New South Wales. Records
Geol Surv NSW Rep — Geological Survey of New South Wales. Geological Survey Report
Geol Surv of NSW Miner Ind NSW — Geological Survey of New South Wales. Department of Mines. The Mineral Industryof New South Wales
Geol Surv Ohio Inf Circ — Geological Survey of Ohio. Information Circular
Geol Surv Ohio Rep Invest — Geological Survey of Ohio. Report of Investigations
Geol Surv Open File Rep (US) — Geological Survey Open-File Report (United States)
Geol Surv Pak Interim Geol Rep — Geological Survey of Pakistan. Interim Geological Report
Geol Surv Pap Geol Surv Can — Geological Survey Paper. Geological Survey of Canada
Geol Surv Pap Tas Dep Mines — Geological Survey Paper. Department of Mines. Tasmania
Geol Surv Papua New Guinea Rep — Geological Survey of Papua New Guinea. Report
Geol Surv Prof Pap (US) — Geological Survey Professional Paper (United States)
Geol Surv Queensl Pub — Geological Survey of Queensland. Publication
Geol Surv Queensl Publ — Geological Survey of Queensland. Publication
Geol Surv Queensl Rep — Geological Survey of Queensland. Report
Geol Surv Rec Tasmania — Geological Survey Record. Tasmania
Geol Surv Rep Dep Mines (NSW) — Geological Survey Report. Department of Mines (New South Wales)
Geol Surv Sierra Leone Bull — Geological Survey of Sierra Leone. Bulletin
Geol Surv South Aust Bull — Geological Survey of South Australia. Bulletin
Geol Surv South Aust Q Geol Notes — Geological Survey of South Australia. Quarterly Geological Notes

Geol Surv South Aust Rep Invest — Geological Survey of South Australia. Report of Investigations
Geol Surv Tanzania Bull — Geological Survey of Tanzania. Bulletin
Geol Surv Uganda Mem — Geological Survey of Uganda. Memoir
Geol Surv Uganda Rep — Geological Survey of Uganda. Report
Geol Surv Victoria Bull — Geological Survey of Victoria. Bulletin
Geol Surv Victoria Mem — Geological Survey of Victoria. Memoir
Geol Surv Water Supply Pap — Geological Survey. Water-Supply Paper
Geol Surv W Aust Bull — Geological Survey of Western Australia. Bulletin
Geol Surv West Aust Annu Rep — Geological Survey of Western Australia. Annual Report
Geol Surv West Aust Bull — Western Australia. Geological Survey. Bulletin
Geol Surv West Aust Miner Resour Bull — Geological Survey of Western Australia. Mineral Resources Bulletin
Geol Surv West Aust Rep — Geological Survey of Western Australia. Report
Geol Surv West Malays Econ Bull — Geological Survey of West Malaysia. Economic Bulletin
Geol Surv West Malaysia Dist Mem — Geological Survey of West Malaysia. District Memoir
Geol Surv Wyo Bull — Geological Survey of Wyoming. Bulletin
Geol Surv Wyo C Resour Ser — Geological Survey of Wyoming. County Resource Series
Geol Surv Wyo Mem — Geological Survey of Wyoming. Memoir
Geol Surv Wyo Prelim Rep — Geological Survey of Wyoming. Preliminary Report
Geol Surv Wyo Public Inf Circ — Geological Survey of Wyoming. Public Information Circular
Geol Surv Wyo Rep Invest — Geological Survey of Wyoming. Report of Investigations
Geol Syrevye Resur Redk Elem SSSR Tezisy Dokl Vses Soveshch — Geologiya i Syr'evye Resursy Redkikh Elementov v SSSR. Tezisy Dokladov na Vsesoyuznom Soveshchanii
Geol Tec — Geologia Tecnica
Geol Trans Rep — Geological Transactions and Reports
Geol Tsentr Kaz — Geologiya Tsentral'nogo Kazakhstana
Geol Tungsten — Geology of Tungsten
Geol Tutkimuslaitos Geotek Julk — Geologinen Tutkimuslaitos. Geoteknillisia Julkaisuja
Geol Tutkimuslaitos Tutkimusrap — Geologinen Tutkimuslaitos. Tutkimusraportti
Geol Ultriectina — Geologica Ultriectina
Geol Uzberezhzhya Dna Chorn Azovskogo Moriv Mezhakh URSR — Geologiya Uzberezhzhya i Dna Chornogo ta Azovs'kogo Moriv u Mezhakh URSR
Geol Ver S-Afr Kwart Nuusbull — Geologiese Vereniging van Suid-Afrika. Kwartaallikse Nuusbulletin
Geol Vjesn (Zagreb) — Geoloski Vjesnik (Zagreb)
Geol Zakaspiya — Geologiya Zakaspiya
Geol Zb — Geologicky Zbornik
Geol Zb Geol Carpathica — Geologicky Zbornik - Geologica Carpathica
Geol Zb Slov Akad Vied — Geologicky Zbornik - Geologica Carpathica. Slovenska Akademia Vied
Geol Zentralbl — Geologisches Zentralblatt. Anzeiger fuer Geologie, Petrographie, Palaeontologie, und Verwandte Wissenschaften. Revue Geologique/Geological Review/Rassegna Geologica
Geol Zh — Geologicheskii Zhurnal
Geol Zh (Russ Ed) — Geologicheskii Zhurnal (Russian Edition)
Geol Zh (Ukr Ed) — Geologichnii Zhurnal (Ukrainian Edition)
Geol Zurn — Geologicnyj Zurnal/Journal of Geology
GEOMA — Geophysical Magazine
Geo Mag — Geographical Magazine
Geomag Aer — Geomagnetizm i Aeronomiya
Geomagn Aeron — Geomagnetizm i Aeronomiya
Geomagn Aeron (Engl Transl) — Geomagnetism and Aeronomy (English Translation)
Geomagn Aeron (USSR) — Geomagnetism and Aeronomy (USSR)
Geomagn and Aeron — Geomagnetism and Aeronomy
Geomagn Bull Inst Geol Sci — Geomagnetic Bulletin. Institute of Geological Sciences
Geomagn Ser Earth Phys Branch — Geomagnetic Series. Earth Physics Branch
Geo-Mar Let — Geo-Marine Letters
Geo Mar Technol — Geo Marine Technology
Geo Mason UL Rev — George Mason University. Law Review
GEOMD — Geomimet
Geom Dedicata — Geometriae Dedicata
Geom Des Publ — Geometric Design Publications
Geomech Comput Progm — Geomechanics Computing Programme
Geom Funct Anal — Geometric and Functional Analysis
Geomicrobiol J — Geomicrobiology Journal
Geomicrobiology J — Geomicrobiology Journal
Geomorph Abstr — Geomorphological Abstracts
Geonomia Banyasz — Geonomia es Banyaszat
GEOPA7 — Geologicke Prace
Geophys — Geophysics
Geophys Abstr — Geophysical Abstracts
Geophys and Astrophys Fluid Dyn — Geophysical and Astrophysical Fluid Dynamics
Geophys Arb Mitt Meteorol Astrophys — Geophysikalische Arbeiten sowie Mitteilungen aus Meteorologie und Astrophysik
Geophys Aspects Energy Probl Proc Course — Geophysical Aspects of the Energy Problem. Proceedings. Course
Geophys Astrophys Fluid Dyn — Geophysical and Astrophysical Fluid Dynamics
Geophys Astrophys Fluid Dynamics — Geophysical and Astrophysical Fluid Dynamics
Geophys Astrophys Monogr — Geophysics and Astrophysics Monographs
Geophys Bull Moscow — Geophysical Bulletin (Moscow)
Geophys Case Histories — Geophysical Case Histories
Geophys Commun (Kiev) — Geophysical Communications (Kiev)

Geophys Explor — Geophysical Exploration
Geophys Fluid Dyn — Geophysical Fluid Dynamics
Geophys Geochem Explor — Geophysical and Geochemical Exploration
Geophys Geol — Geophysik und Geologie
Geophys Geol (Leipz) Karl-Marx-Univ Ser 3 — Geophysik und Geologie (Leipzig). Karl-Marx-Universitaet. Geophysikalische Veroeffentlichungen. Serie 3
Geophys Inst Fac Sci Tokyo Univ Geophys Notes Suppl — Geophysical Institute. Faculty of Science. Tokyo University. Geophysical Notes. Supplement
Geophys J — Geophysical Journal
Geophys J I — Geophysical Journal International
Geophys J (Moscow) — Geophysical Journal (Moscow)
Geophys Jour — Geophysical Journal
Geophys J Oxford — Geophysical Journal (Oxford)
Geophys J R — Geophysical Journal. Royal Astronomical Society
Geophys J R Astronom Soc — Geophysical Journal. Royal Astronomical Society
Geophys J R Astron Soc — Geophysical Journal. Royal Astronomical Society
Geophys J R Astr Soc — Geophysical Journal. Royal Astronomical Society
Geophys Lead Edge Explor — Geophysics. The Leading Edge of Exploration
Geophys Mag — Geophysical Magazine
Geophys Mag (Tokyo) — Geophysical Magazine (Tokyo)
Geophys Mem (Lond) — Geophysical Memoirs (London)
Geophys Monogr — Geophysical Monograph
Geophys Monogr Am Geophys Union — Geophysical Monograph. American Geophysical Union
Geophys Norv — Geophysica Norvegica
Geophys Note (Tokyo) — Geophysical Note (Tokyo)
Geophys Prospect — Geophysical Prospecting
Geophys Prospecting — Geophysical Prospecting
Geophys Prospect (The Hague) — Geophysical Prospecting (The Hague)
Geophys Pure Appl — Geophysique Pure et Applique
Geophys R B — Geophysical Research Bulletin
Geophys Res Bull — Geophysical Research Bulletin
Geophys Res Lett — Geophysical Research Letters
Geophys Res Norw — Geophysical Research in Norway
Geophys Res Pap — Geophysical Research Papers
Geophys R L — Geophysical Research Letters
Geophys Soc Tulsa Proc — Geophysical Society of Tulsa. Proceedings
Geophys Space Data Bull — Geophysics and Space Data Bulletin
Geophys Surv — Geophysical Surveys
Geophys Tecton Abstr — Geophysics and Tectonics Abstracts
Geophys Trans (Budapest) — Geophysical Transactions (Budapest)
Geo-Process — Geo-Processing
GEOQ — Geos. Canada Department of Energy, Mines, and Resources
GeoR — Geographical Review
Geo R — Georgia Review
GEORAD — Geographical Review
Geo Rev — Georgia Law Review
Georg Brandes Arb — Georg Brandes Arbog
George Peabody Coll Teach Contrib Educ — George Peabody College for Teachers. Contributions to Education
Georget Law — Georgetown Law Journal
Georget LJ — Georgetown Law Journal
Georgetown Dent J — Georgetown Dental Journal
Georgetown Immigr Law Q — Georgetown Immigration Law Quarterly
Georgetown Law J — Georgetown Law Journal
Georgetown Law Jour — Georgetown Law Journal. Georgetown University
Georgetown LJ — Georgetown Law Journal
Georgetown Med Bull — Georgetown Medical Bulletin
Georgetown Univ Law Cent Immigr Law Rep — Georgetown University Law Center Immigration Law Reporter
Georgetown Univ Sch Dent Mirror — Georgetown University. School of Dentistry. Mirror
George Wash — George Washington Law Review
George Washington J Internat Law and Econ — George Washington Journal of International Law and Economics
George Washington Law R — George Washington Law Review
George Washington Univ Bull — George Washington University. Bulletin
George Wash L Rev — George Washington Law Review
George Wash Univ Bull — George Washington University. Bulletin
Georg Group J — Georgian Group Journal
Georgia BJ — Georgia Bar Journal
Georgia Bot J Coll Sentinel — Georgia Botanic Journal and College Sentinel
Georgia Bus — Georgia Business
Georgia Dep Educ Stat Rep — Georgia Department of Education. Statistical Report
Georgia Geneal — Georgia Genealogist
Georgia Geneal Surv — Georgia Genealogical Survey
Georgia Hist Quart — Georgia Historical Quarterly
Georgia J Int Comp L — Georgia Journal of International and Comparative Law
Georgia Law Rep — Georgia Law Reporter
Georgia L Rev — Georgia Law Review
Georgia Mus Art Bull — Georgia Museum of Art Bulletin
Georgian Math J — Georgian Mathematical Journal
Georgia R — Georgia Review
Georgia Rev — Georgia Review
Georgia St BJ — Georgia State Bar Journal
Georgikon Delt — Georgikon Deltion
Georgr et Rech — Geographie et Recherche
GEOS — Geoscope
Geosci Abstr — Geoscience Abstracts
Geosci Can — Geoscience Canada
Geosci Doc — Geoscience Documentation
Geoscience Abs — Geoscience Abstracts
Geoscience Inf Soc Proc — Geoscience Information Society. Proceedings
Geosci J — Geoscience Journal

Geosci Mag — Geoscience Magazine
Geosci Man — Geoscience and Man
Geosci Rep Ont Div Mines — Geoscience Report. Ontario Division of Mines
Geosci Rep Shizuoka Univ — Geoscience Reports of Shizuoka University
Geosci Res Grant Program Summ Res — Geoscience Research Grant Program. Summary of Research
Geosci Stud — Geoscience Studies
Geosci Study Ont Div Mines — Geoscience Study. Ontario. Division of Mines
Geosci Wis — Geoscience Wisconsin
Geo Soc Am Bul — Geological Society of America Bulletin
Geostandards Newsl — Geostandards Newsletter
Geostand Newsl — Geostandards Newsletter
Geostat Appl Earth Sci Pap Int Geostat Congr — Geostatistics Applied to Earth Sciences. Papers. International Geostatistics Congress
Geosynth Int — Geosynthetics International
Geosynth Test Waste Containment Appl — Geosynthetic Testing for Waste Containment Applications
Geot — Geotimes
GEOTA — Geotimes
GEOTAJ — Geotimes
Geotech Abstr — Geotechnical Abstracts
Geotech Eng — Geotechnical Engineering
Geotech Environ Aspects Geopressure Energy Pap — Geotechnical and Environmental Aspects of Geopressure Energy. Papers
Geotechniq — Geotechnique
Geotech Spec Publ — Geotechnical Special Publication
Geotech Test J — Geotechnical Testing Journal
Geotecton — Geotectonics
Geotek Julk — Geoteknillisia Julkaisuja
Geoteknisk Inst Bull — Geoteknisk Institut. Bulletin
Geotekton — Geotektonika
Geotekton Forsch — Geotektonische Forschungen
Geotektonika Tektonofiz Geodinamika — Geotektonika, Tektonofizika, i Geodinamika
Geotektonische Forsch — Geotektonische Forschungen
Geotekton Tektonofiz Geodin — Geotektonika, Tektonofizika, i Geodinamika
Geoterm Issled Ispolz Tepla Zemli Tr Soveshch — Geotermicheskie Issledovaniya i Ispol'zovanie Tepla Zemli. Trudy Soveshchaniya po Geotermicheskim Issledovaniyam v SSSR
Geotext Geomembr — Geotextiles and Geomembranes
Geotherm — Geothermics
Geotherm Energy — Geothermal Energy
Geotherm Energy Mag — Geothermal Energy Magazine
Geotherm Energy Update — Geothermal Energy Update
Geotherm Hot Line — Geothermal Hot Line
Geotherm Rep — Geothermal Report
Geotherm Rep Miner Resour Dep (Fiji) — Geothermal Report. Mineral Resources Department (Fiji)
Geotherm Resour Counc Bull — Geothermal Resources Council Bulletin
Geotherm Resour Counc Spec Rep — Geothermal Resources Council. Special Report
Geotherm Resour Counc Trans — Geothermal Resources Council. Transactions
Geotherm Technol — Geothermal Technology
Geo Wash J Int L — George Washington Journal of International Law and Economics
Geo Wash J Intl L and Econ — George Washington Journal of International Law and Economics
Geo Wash L Rev — George Washington Law Review
Geowiss Unserer Zeit — Geowissenschaften in Unserer Zeit
GEP — Graduate English Papers
GEPA — EPA [*Environmental Protection Agency*] Journal
GEPACDE — Geographical Paper. Canada Department of Environment
GEPB — Grande Enciclopedia Portuguesa e Brasileira
GEPCA — GP. Journal of the American Academy of General Practice
GEPGA — Gepgyartastechnologia
GeR — Gengogaku Ronso
GeR — Georgia Review
GER — German Economic Review
Ger — Germania
Ger — Germanistik
Ger Am Brew J — German and American Brewers' Journal
Geraniums Around Wld — Geraniums Around the World. International Geranium Society
Gerber Cour — Gerber-Courier
Gerber Ztg — Gerber-Zeitung
Gerbil Dig — Gerbil Digest
Ger Bundesanst Bodenforsch Geol Jahrb Beih — Germany. Bundesanstalt fuer Bodenforschung und Geologische Landesaemter. Geologisches Jahrbuch. Beiheft
Ger Chem Eng — German Chemical Engineering
Ger Chem Engng — German Chemical Engineering
Gercke Norden — Gercke und Norden. Einleitung in die Altertumswissenschaft
Ger Democr Repub Pat Doc — German Democratic Republic. Patent Document
GEREA — General Electric Review
Ger Ec Bul — Economic Bulletin (Germany)
Ger Econ Re — German Economic Review
GERED — Geothermal Report
GerefTTS — Gereformeerd Theologisch Tijdschrift
Ge Rel — Gespraech der Religionen
Gerfaut Rev Sci Belge Ornithol — Gerfaut. Revue Scientifique Belge d'Ornithologie
Gergonne A Mth — Annales de Mathematiques Pures et Appliquees. Gergonne
Ger Hydrogr J — German Hydrographic Journal
GERIA — Geriatrics
Geriat Clin Pharmacol — Geriatric Clinical Pharmacology

Geriatric Nurs — Geriatric Nursing
Geriatr Med — Geriatric Medicine
Geriatr Nephrol Urol — Geriatric Nephrology and Urology
Geriatr Nurs — Geriatric Nursing
Geriatr Nurs (Lond) — Geriatric Nursing (London)
Geriatr Surv — Geriatrics Survey
GERIAZ — Geriatrics
Gerichts Zeit — Gerichts-Zeitung
Gerichtsztg — Gerichts-Zeitung
Ger J Cardiol — German Journal of Cardiology
Ger J Gastroenterol — German Journal of Gastroenterology
Ger J Ophthalmol — German Journal of Ophthalmology
Ger L & L — German Life and Letters
Gerlands Beitr Geophys — Gerlands Beitraege zur Geophysik
Ger Life L — German Life and Letters
Ger Life Lett — German Life and Letters
Germ — Germania
German Chem Engng — German Chemical Engineering
German Econ R — German Economic Review
German Fct — Facts and Figures (Germany)
Germania Korrbl — Germania. Korrespondenzblatt der Roemisch-Germanischen Kommission des DeutschenArchaeologischen Instituts
German Int — German International
German Internat — German International
German Med Monthly — German Medical Monthly
German Q — German Quarterly
German TN — German American Trade News
German Yb Int Law — German Yearbook of International Law
German Yb Int'l L — German Yearbook of International Law
Germ Ben — Germania Benedictina
GERMD — German Mining
Ger Med — German Medicine
Ger Med Mon — German Medical Monthly
Ger Med Res — German Medical Research
Germ Foreign Policy — German Foreign Policy
Germ Jud — Germania Judaica
Germ Jud S — Germania Judaica. Schriftenreihe
GermL — Germanistische Linguistik
Germ Mon — Germania Monastica
Germn Tb Q — German Tribune Quarterly Review
Germ R — Germanic Review
Germ Rev — Germanic Review
Germ-Rom Monat — Germanisch-Romanische Monatsschrift
Germ Sac — Germania Sacra
Germ Stud Newsl — German Studies Newsletter
Germ Tr Dir — German Trade Directory
GERNDJ — Gerontology
Ger Nmus [*Nuernberg*] Jber — Germanisches Nationalmuseum [*Nuernberg*]. Jahresbericht
Ger Note — Germanic Notes
GEROA — Gerontologia
GEROAJ — Gerontologia
Gerodontolo — Gerodontology
Ger Offen — German Offenlegungschrift. Patent Document
Gerontol — Gerontologist
Gerontol Abstr — Gerontological Abstracts
Gerontol Clin — Gerontologia Clinica [*Later, Gerontology*]
Gerontol Ext Lect — Gerontology Extension Lectures
Gerontol Geriatr — Gerontologiya i Geriatriya
Gerontol Geriatr Educ — Gerontology and Geriatrics Education
Gerontol Geriatr Kiev — Gerontology and Geriatrics (Kiev)
Ger Plast — German Plastics
Ger Q — German Quarterly
Ger Quart — German Quarterly
GERR — CQ Researcher [*Formerly, Editorial Research Reports*]
GERR — Editorial Research Reports
GERR — Government Employee Relations Report
Ger Rev — Germanic Review
Ger Roman Monatsschr — Germanisch-Romanische Monatsschrift
Ger Rom Mon — Germanisch-Romanische Monatsschrift
Ger Slav — Germano-Slavica
Ger Sol Energy Forum — German Solar Energy Forum
Ger S R — German Studies Review
Ger St Rev — German Studies Review
Ger Symp Laser Angioplasty — German Symposium on Laser Angioplasty
Ger Tekh — Germanskaya Tekhnika
Gertsinskie Magmat Kompleksy Vost Kaz — Gertsinskie Magmaticheskie Kompleksy Vostochnogo Kazakhstana
GERUA — Geologische Rundschau
G Erud A — Giornale di Erudizione Artistica
Ger Umweltbundesamt Ber — Germany. Umweltbundesamt. Berichte
Ger (West) Pat Doc Auslegeschr — Germany (West). Patent Document. Auslegeschrift
Ger West Pat Doc Offen — Germany (West). Patent Document. Offenlegungschrift
Ger Yugosl Meet Mater Sci Dev — German-Yugoslav Meeting on Materials Science and Development
Ger Zent Geol Inst Abh — Germany. Zentrales Geologisches Institut. Abhandlungen
Ger Zent Geol Inst Jahrb Geol — Germany. Zentrales Geologisches Institut. Jahrbuch fuer Geologie
Ger Zentrales Geol Inst Wiss-Tech Informationsdienst — Germany. Zentrales Geologisches Institut. Wissenschaftlich-Technischer Informationsdienst
Ges Aerosolforsch Conf — Gesellschaft fuer Aerosolforschung. Conference
Ges Aerosolforsch Jahrestag — Gesellschaft fuer Aerosolforschung. Jahrestagung

Gesammelte Abh Dtsch Lederinst (Freiberg) — Gesammelte Abhandlungen. Deutsches Lederinstitut (Freiberg)

Gesammelte Abh Kenn Kohle — Gesammelte Abhandlungen zur Kenntnis der Kohle

Gesammelte Arb Weissruss Landwirtsch Inst — Gesammelte Arbeiten des Weissrussischen Landwirtschaftlichen Instituts

Gesammelte Beitr Naturwiss Fak Palacky Univ Olomouc — Gesammelte Beitraege der Naturwissenschaftlichen Fakultaet der Palacky Universitaet in Olomouc

Gesammelte Ber Betr Forsch Ruhrgas Ag — Gesammelte Berichte aus Betrieb und Forschung der Ruhrgas Aktiengesellschaft

GESAMP Rep Stud — GESAMP (Joint Group of Experts on the Scientific Aspects of Marine Pollution) Reports and Studies

Gesamtber Weltkraftkonf — Gesamtbericht Weltkraftkonferenz

Gesamtkong Dtsch Pharm Wiss — Gesamtkongress der Deutschen Pharmazeutischen Wissenschaften

Gesamttag Ges Exp Med DDR — Gesamttagung der Gesellschaft fuer Experimentelle Medizin der DDR

Gesamtverzeichnis Oesterreichischer Diss — Gesamtverzeichnis Oesterreichischer Dissertationen

GESBA — Geologicky Zbornik

GESBAJ — Geologicky Zbornik

Ges Bekaempf Krebskrankh Nordrhein Westfalen Symp — Gesellschaft zur Bekaempfung der Krebskrankheiten Nordrhein-Westfalen. Symposium

Ges Bekampf Krebskr Nordrhein-Westfalen Mitteilungdienst — Gesellschaft zur Bekampfung der Krebskrankheiten im Nordrhein-Westfalen. Mitteilungsdienst

Ges Biol Chem Colloq — Gesellschaft fuer Biologische Chemie. Colloquium

Ges Biol Chem Konf — Gesellschaft fuer Biologische Chemie. Konferenz

Ges Biotechnol Forsch Monogr Ser — Gesellschaft fuer Biotechnologische Forschung. Monograph Series

GESC — Earth Science

Gesch Arab Lit — Geschichte der Arabischen Literatur

Geschbll Magdebg — Geschichtsblaetter fuer Stadt und Land Magdeburg

Gesch Darstellung Naturf Ges Emden — Geschichtliche Darstellung der Naturforschenden Gesellschaft in Emden

Gesch Darstellung Verh Naturf Ges Emden — Geschichtliche Darstellung der Verhandlungen der Naturforschenden Gesellschaft in Emden

Gesch Ges — Geschichte und Gesellschaft

Gesch Koeln — Geschichte in Koeln

Gesch Oberrheins — Geschichte des Oberrheins

Geschrift — Geschriften van de Vereniging voor Belastingswetenschap

Gesch Samml — Geschichte der Sammlungen

Gesch Schule — Geschichte in der Schule

Gesch U Ges — Geschichte und Gesellschaft

Gesch Wiss Unterr — Geschichte in Wissenschaft und Unterricht

Gesch Wiss Unterricht — Geschichte in Wissenschaft und Unterricht

Ges Dtsch Chem Fachgruppe Anal Chem Mitteilungsbl — Gesellschaft Deutscher Chemiker. Fachgruppe Analytische Chemie. Mitteilungsblatt

Ges Dtsch Chem Fachgruppe Chem Inf Comput Mitteilungsbl — Gesellschaft Deutscher Chemiker, Fachgruppe Chemie - Information - Commputer, Mitteilungsblatt

Ges Dtsch Chem Fachgruppe Chem Inf Vortragstag Tagungsber — Gesellschaft Deutscher Chemiker. Fachgruppe Chemie-Information. Vortragstagung.Tagungsbericht

Ges Dtsch Metallhuetten Bergleute Schriftenr — Gesellschaft Deutscher Metallhuetten- und Bergleute. Schriftenreihe

Ges Dtsch Metallhuetten- und Bergleute Schr — Gesellschaft Deutscher Metallhuetten- und Bergleute. Schriften

Ges Dtsch Naturforsch Aerzte Verh — Gesellschaft Deutscher Naturforscher und Aerzte. Verhandlungen

Ges Dtsch Naturforsch Aerzte Wiss Konf — Gesellschaft Deutscher Naturforscher und Aerzte. Wissenschaftliche Konferenz

Gesell Erdk Leipz Mitt — Gesellschaft fuer Erdkunde zu Leipzig. Mitteilungen

Gesell F Erdk Berlin Verhandl — Gesellschaft fuer Erdkunde. Verhandlungen (Berlin)

Gesell F Erdk Berlin Zeits — Gesellschaft fuer Erdkunde. Zeitschrift (Berlin)

Gesell f Kieler Stadtgesch Mitt — Gesellschaft fuer Kieler Stadtgeschichte. Mitteilungen

Gesell Kieler Stadtgesch Mitt — Gesellschaft fuer Kieler Stadtgeschichte. Mitteilungen

Gesellsch F Phys Anthrop Verh — Gesellschaft fuer Physische Anthropologie. Verhandlungen

Gesells Erdkunde Berlin Zeits — Zeitschrift der Gesellschaft fuer Erdkunde zu Berlin

Ges Erdk Berlin Verh Zs — Gesellschaft fuer Erdkunde zu Berlin. Verhandlungen. Zeitschrift

Gesetzblatt Dtsch Demokr Repub — Gesetzblatt der Deutschen Demokratischen Republik

Gesetzbl Baden-Wuerttemb — Gesetzblatt fuer Baden-Wuerttemberg

Gesetzbl DDR Teil I — Gesetzblatt der Deutschen Demokratischen Republik. Teil 1

Gesetz- Verordnungsbl Land Hessen Teil 1 — Gesetz- und Verordnungsblatt fuer das Land Hessen. Teil 1

Ges Fortschr Geb Inn Med Symp — Gesellschaft fuer Fortschritte auf dem Gebiet der Inneren Medizin. Symposion

Ges Geol Bergbaustud Oesterr Mitt — Gesellschaft der Geologie- und Bergbaustudenten in Oesterreich. Mitteilungen

Ges Geol Bergbaustud Wien Mitt — Gesellschaft der Geologie- und Bergbaustudenten in Wien. Mitteilungen

Ges Gesch & Bibliog Brauwes Jahrb — Gesellschaft fuer die Geschichte und Bibliographie des Brauwesens. Jahrbuch

GESHA — Genden Shiryo

Ges-Ing — Gesundheits-Ingenieur

GESKAC — Genetika i Selektsiya

Ges Kernenergieverwert Schiffbau Schiffahrt Ber — Gesellschaft fuer Kernenergieverwertung in Schiffbau und Schiffahrt. Bericht

GESLB — Genetika a Slechteni

GESLBG — Genetika a Slechteni

Gesn — Gesnerus

Ges Naturf Freund Berlin Szb — Gesellschaft Naturforschender Freunde zu Berlin. Sitzungsberichte

Ges Naturkd Wuerttemb Jahresh — Gesellschaft fuer Naturkunde in Wuerttemberg. Jahreshefte

Ges Naturw Marburg Schrift — Gesellschaft zur Befoerderung der Gesammten Naturwissenschaften zu Marburg. Schriften

Gesneriad J — Gesneriad Journal

Gesnerus Suppl — Gesnerus Supplement

Ges Neuropaediatr Jahrestag — Gesellschaft fuer Neuropaediatrie. Jahrestagung

Ges Oekol Jahresversamml — Gesellschaft fuer Oekologie. Jahresversammlung

Ges Oekol Verh — Gesellschaft fuer Oekologie. Verhandlungen

GESQ — Esquire

Ges Reaktorsicherh Ber — Gesellschaft fuer Reaktorsicherheit. Bericht

Ges Reaktorsicherh Ber GRS-S — Gesellschaft fuer Reaktorsicherheit. Bericht GRS-S

Ges Reaktorsicherh Ber GRS S Stellungnahmen Kernenergiefragen — Gesellschaft fuer Reaktorsicherheit. Bericht. GRS-S. Stellungnahmen zu Kernenergiefragen

GESS — Essence

Ges Schwerionenforsch Ber — Gesellschaft fuer Schwerionenforschung. Bericht

Ges Schwerionenforsch Rep — Gesellschaft fuer Schwerionenforschung. Report

Ges Strahlen Umweltforsch Bereich Projekttraegerschaften BPT — Gesellschaft fuer Strahlen- und Umweltforschung. Bereich Projekttraegerschaften. BPT-Bericht

Ges Strahlen Umweltforsch Ber P — Gesellschaft fuer Strahlen- und Umweltforschung. Bericht P

Ges Strahlen Umweltforsch GSF Ber BT — Gesellschaft fuer Strahlen- und Umweltforschung. GSF-Bericht BT

Ges Strahlen Umweltforsch Inst Oekol Chem Ber O — Gesellschaft fuer Strahlen- und Umweltforschung. Institut fuer Oekologische Chemie. Bericht O

Ges Strahlen Umweltforsch Inst Strahlenschutz GSF Ber S — Gesellschaft fuer Strahlen- und Umweltforschung. Institut fuer Strahlenschutz. GSF-Bericht S

Ges Strahlen Umweltforsch Inst Toxikol Biochem Abt Toxikol Be — Gesellschaft fuer Strahlen- und Umweltforschung. Institut fuer Toxikologie und bericht TOX

Gest — Gestion

GESTA — Gezetzgebungsstand

Gestion Dechets Solides C R Congr Int — Gestion des Dechets Solides. Comptes-Rendus du Congres International

Gest Lib J — Gest Library Journal

GESU — Journal of Ethnic Studies

Gesunde Pfl — Gesunde Pflanzen

Gesunde Pflanz — Gesunde Pflanzen

Gesundhd — Gesundheitsdienst

Gesundheitsfuehr Dtsch Volkes — Gesundheitsfuehrung des Deutschen Volkes

Gesundheits-Ing — Gesundheits-Ingenieur

Gesundheitswes Desinfekt — Gesundheitswesen und Desinfektion

Gesundh Fuers — Gesundheitsfuersorge

Gesundh-Ing — Gesundheits-Ingenieur

Gesundhtsingenieur — Gesundheits-Ingenieur

Gesundh U Erziehg — Gesundheit und Erziehung

Gesundh Wohlf — Gesundheit und Wohlfahrt

Gesund-Ing — Gesundheits-Ingenieur

Gesund-Ing Haustech-Bauphys-Umwelttech — Gesundheits-Ingenieur. Haustechnik-Bauphysik-Umwelttechnik

Gesund Umwelttechnik — Gesundheits- und Umwelttechnik

Gesun Wohlfahrt — Gesundheit und Wohlfahrt

Ges Wiss Goettingen Math Phys Kl Abh — Gesellschaft der Wissenschaften zu Goettingen. Mathematisch-Physikalische Klasse. Abhandlungen

Ges Wiss Goettingen Nachr Geschaeftliche Mitt — Gesellschaft der Wissenschaften zu Goettingen, Nachrichten. Geschaeftliche Mitteilungen

GESY — Journal of Educational Psychology

GET — Geografisch Tijdschrift. Nieuwe Reeks

Get — Getuigenis (Utrecht)

GETD — Geografisk Tidsskrift

Geterog Katal — Geterogennyi Kataliz. Trudy Mezhdunarodnogo Simpoziuma po Geterogennomu Katalizu

Geterog Katal Mater Vses Konf Mekh Katal Reakts — Geterogennyi Kataliz. Materialy Vsesoyuznoi Konferentsii po Mekhanizmu Kataliticheskikh Reaktsii

GETMA — Getreide und Mehl

Getreide Mehl — Getreide und Mehl

Getreide Mehl Brot — Getreide Mehl und Brot

Getriebe Mot Antriebselem — Getriebe Motoren Antriebselemente

Getty Conserv Inst Newslett — Getty Conservation Institute Newsletter

Getty Mus — J. Paul Getty Museum Journal

Getty Mus J — J. Paul Getty Museum. Journal

GEu — Geistiges Europa

GEVJA — Geoloski Vjesnik

GEVJAO — Geoloski Vjesnik

GeW — Germanica Wratislaviensia

GEW — Griechisches Etymologisches Woerterbuch

Gew A — Gewerbearchiv

GEWAD5 — Gewasbescherming

GEWED — Gewerbearchiv

Gewerbliche Rdsch — Gewerbliche Rundschau

Gewerbl Rechtsschutz — Gewerblicher Rechtsschutz

Gewerbl Rechtsschutz Urheberrecht — Gewerblicher Rechtsschutz und Urheberrecht

Gewerbl Rechtsschutz U Urheberr — Gewerblicher Rechtsschutz und Urheberrecht

Gewerk MH — Gewerkschaftliche Monatshefte

Gewerk Prax — Gewerkschaftliche Praxis

Gewerk Rd — Gewerkschaftliche Rundschau
Gewerkschaftliche Mhefte — Gewerkschaftliche Monatshefte
Gewerkschaftl Mh — Gewerkschaftliche Monatshefte
Gewerksch Monatsh — Gewerkschaftliche Monatshefte
Gewerksch Rundsch — Gewerkschaftliche Rundschau
Ge Wiss — Geschichte der Wissenschaften
Gew MH — Gewerkschaftliche Monatshefte
Gew Mon H — Gewerkschaftliche Monatshefte
Gew Rundsch — Gewerkschaftliche Rundschau
Gew St G — Gewerbesteuergesetz
GEXC — Exceptional Children
GEXP — Expedition
GEXR — Explicator
Geyer DT — Geyer's Dealer Topics
Geyer OD — Geyer's Office Dealer
GEYPA — Geologicky Pruzkum
GEYSD — Geyser
GEZHD — Geofizicheskii Zhurnal
Gezira Res Stn Substn Annu Rep — Gezira Research Station and Substations. Annual Report
Gezondheidsorgan TNO Afd Gezondheidstech Rapp — Gezondheidsorganisatie TNO [*Nederlands Centrale Organisatie voor Toegepast-Natuurwetenschappelijk Onderzoek*]. Afdeling Gezondheidstechniek. Rapport
Gf — Gitarrefreund
GF — Governmental Finance
GF — Grafiskt Forum
GF — Griechische Feste
GFAC — Family Circle
GFAM — Family Relations
GFAR — Farm Journal
G Farm Chim — Giornale di Farmacia Chimica e Scienze Affini
G Farm Chim Sci Affini — Giornale di Farmacia Chimica e Scienze Affini
GFB — Gustav Freytag Blaetter
GFCCAH — FAO [*Food and Agriculture Organization of the United Nations*] General Fisheries Council for the Mediterranean. Circular
GFCO — Film Comment
GFCR — Free China Review
Gfd — Geschichtsfreund
GFDA — FDA [*Food and Drug Administration*] Consumer
G Fd B — Geschichtsfreund. Beiheft
GFEM — Feminist Studies
GFF — Geologiska Foereningens i Stockholm. Foerhandlingar
GFF — Giornale Filologico Ferrarese
GFF — Grillparzer Forum Forchtenstein
GFF (Geol Foren Stockholm Forhandl) — GFF (Geologiska Foreningen i Stockholm Forhandlingar)
GFF Mitt — Mitteilungen der Gesellschaft zur Foerderung der Forschung an der Eidgenoessischen Technischen Hochschule
GFFNS — Godisnjak Filozofskog Fakulteta u Novom Sadu
GFHC — Family and Home-Office Computing
GFHC — Home-Office Computing [*Formerly, Family and Home-Office Computing*]
GFI — Giornale Critico della Filosofia Italiana
GFI — Gmelin Formula Index
GFIF — New Choices for the Best Years
GFIQ — Film Quarterly
G Fis — Giornale di Fisica
G Fis Quad — Giornale di Fisica. Quaderni
G Fis Sanit — Giornale di Fisica Sanitaria e Protezione Contro le Radiazioni
G Fis Sanit Protez Contro Radiaz — Giornale di Fisica Sanitaria e Protezione Contro le Radiazioni
G Fis Sanit Prot Radiaz — Giornale di Fisica Sanitaria e Protezione Contro le Radiazioni
G Fis Soc Ital Fis — Giornale di Fisica. Societa Italiana di Fisica
GFJ — Global Finance Journal
G f K — Gesellschaft fuer Konsumforschung
GFLY — Flying
GFM — Marktforschung
GFNG — Flower and Garden
GFNS — Field and Stream
GFOC — Focus
G Foeren Stockholm Foerh — Geologiska Foereningens i Stockholm. Foerhandlingar
GFOK — Journal of American Folklore
GFOR — Foreign Policy
GFP — Grenzfragen der Psychologie
GFPIAW — Ghana. Council for Scientific and Industrial Research. Forest Products ResearchInstitute. Annual Report
GFPP — Family Planning Perspectives
GFR — Geotechnical Fabrics Report
GFR — Groenten en Fruit
GFRRA — Georgia. Forest Research Council. Report
GFS — Government Finance Statistics Yearbook
GFS — Gower Federal Service
GFSFA — Geologiska Foereningens i Stockholm. Foerhandlingar
GFSFA4 — Geologiska Foereningens i Stockholm. Foerhandlingar
GFSRA — Giornale di Fisica Sanitaria e Protezione Contro le Radiazioni
GFSY — Government Finance Statistics
GFTNAX — Ghana. Council for Scientific and Industrial Research. Forest Products ResearchInstitute. Technical Newsletter
GFTP — Grenzfragen Zwischen Theologie und Philosophie
GFW — Druk en Werk
GFWJ — Gesellschaft zur Foerderung der Wissenschaft des Judentums
GFZ-CA Mitt — GFZ-CA [*Grossforschungszentrum Chemieanlagen*] Mitteilungen
GFZSA — Geofizicheskii Sbornik. Akademiya Nauk Ukrainskoi SSR. Institut Geofiziki

GG — Geist und Gestalt
GG — Gestalt und Gedanke
GG — Goedekes Grundriss zur Geschichte der Deutschen Dichtung
GG — Golden Goose
GG — Le Globe (Geneva)
GGA — Goettingische Gelehrte Anzeiger
GG Anz — Goettingische Gelehrte Anzeigen
GGASA — Geologiya i Geofizika
GGB — Giornale di Geologia (Bologna)
G Genio Civ — Giornale del Genio Civile
G Geol — Giornale di Geologia
G Geol (Bologna) — Giornale di Geologia (Bologna)
G Geol Mus Geol Bologna Ann — Giornale di Geologia. Museo Geologico di Bologna. Annali
G Gerontol — Giornale di Gerontologia
G Gerontol Suppl — Giornale di Gerontologia. Supplemento
GGF — Goeteborger Germanistische Forschungen
GGFA — Geografiska Annaler. Series A
GGGJ — Geographical Journal
GGGT — Gerontologist
GGGY — Geology
GG Hb — Grafschaft Glatzer Heimatblaetter
GgHv — Geographica Helvetica
GGHVA4 — Geographica Helvetica
GGHY-A — Geography
GGHYAD — Geography
Gg J — Geographical Journal. Including the Proceedings of the Royal Geographical Society
GGJ — Grundriss der Gesamtwissenschaft des Judentums
Gg Jb — Geographisches Jahrbuch
GGJO-A — Geographical Journal
GGK — Gaigokugo Gaigoku Bungaku Kenkyu
GGKGA — Godishnik na Sofiiskiya Universitet. Geologo-Geografski Fakultet. Kniga 1. Geologiya
GGL — Geschichte der Griechischen Literatur
GGLA — Glamour
GGM — Geographi Graeci Minores
GgMa — Geographical Magazine
GGMA-A — Geographical Magazine
GGNTAS — Glasgow Naturalist
GGOD — Golf Digest
GGOH — Good Housekeeping
GGOM — Golf Magazine
GGOU — Gourmet
GGP — Greek Geometric Pottery
GGP — Grundriss der Germanischen Philologie
GGPI — Pedagogical Institute in Gorki. Transactions
GGQQ — GQ. Gentlemens Quarterly
GGR — Geology and Geophysics. Academy of Sciences (USSR)
GGR — Geschichte der Griechischen Religion
GGR — Goed Geraakt
G Gr L — Geschichte der Griechischen Literatur
Ggr T — Geografisk Tidsskrift
GgRu — Geographische Rundschau
Ggr Z — Geographische Zeitschrift
GGS — Giessener Geographische Schriften
Gg S J — Journal of the Royal Geographical Society of London
Gg S P — Proceedings of the Royal Geographical Society of London
GGTI-A — Geografisk Tidskrift
GGUB — Groenlands Geologiske Undersoegelse. Bulletin
GGUMP — Groenlands Geologiske Undersoegelse. Miscellaneous Papers
GGUR — Groenlands Geologiske Undersoegelse. Rapport
Ggw Zukunft Abfallverwert Abfalltech Kolloq — Gegenwart und Zukunft der Abfallverwertung. Abfalltechnisches Kolloquium
GH — Gelbe Hefte
GH — Geographica Helvetica
GH — Glasgow Herald
GH — Gmelin's Handbuch der Anorganischen Chemie
GH — Good Housekeeping
GH — Grammaire Homerique
GH — Grosse Herder
GH — Gure Herria
GHA — Acta Universitatis Gothoburgensis / Goeteborgs Universitets Arsskrift
GHA — Gas, Wasser, Abwasser. Schweizerische Monatzeitschrift fuer Gasfoerderung und Siedlungswasserwirtschaft
GHA — Goeteborgs Hogskolas Arsskrift
GHAA Jnl — GHAA [*Group Health Association of America*] Journal
GHAB — Harper's Bazaar
Ghana Anim Res Inst Annu Rep — Ghana. Animal Research Institute. Annual Report
Ghana B Theol — Ghana Bulletin of Theology
Ghana Bull Theol — Ghana Bulletin of Theology
Ghana Counc Sci Ind Res For Prod Res Inst Tech Newsl — Ghana. Council for Scientific and Industrial Research. Forest Products ResearchInstitute. Technical Newsletter
Ghana CSIR For Prod Res Inst Annu Rep — Ghana. Council for Scientific and Industrial Research. Forest Products ResearchInstitute. Annual Report
Ghana CSIR For Prod Res Inst Tech Newsl — Ghana. Council for Scientific and Industrial Research. Forest Products ResearchInstitute. Technical Newsletter
Ghana Fish Res Unit Inf Rep — Ghana. Fishery Research Unit. Information Report
Ghana Fish Res Unit Mar Fish Res Rep — Ghana. Fishery Research Unit. Marine Fishery Research Reports
Ghana Fmr — Ghana Farmer
Ghana For J — Ghana Forestry Journal
Ghana J Agric Sci — Ghana Journal of Agricultural Science

Ghana J Sci — Ghana Journal of Science
Ghana J Sociol — Ghana Journal of Sociology
Ghana Library J — Ghana Library Journal
Ghana Libr J — Ghana Library Journal
Ghana Med J — Ghana Medical Journal
Ghana Notes — Ghana Notes and Queries
Ghana Nurse — Ghanaian Nurse
Ghana Soc S — Ghana Social Science Journal
Ghana Soc Sci J — Ghana Social Science Journal
GHAR — Harper's
GHAT — Goettinger Handkommentar zum Alten Testament (1917-1922)
GhB — Ghana Bulletin of Theology
GHBE — House Beautiful
GHBUD — Gl. Haustechnik, Bauphysik, Umwelttechnik
GHCR — Hastings Center Report
GH d A — Genealogisches Handbuch des Adels
GHDBAX — Glasnik Khemijskog Drushtva
GHE — Geography of the Hittite Empire
GHEA — Health
GHER — Harvard Educational Review
GHI — Selection of Greek Historical Inscriptions to the End of the Fifth Century B.C.
GHIF — High Fidelity
GHII — Journal of the History of Ideas
GHIR — Hispanic Review
GHIS — History Today
GHJ — George Herbert Journal
GHJSA — Ghana Journal of Science
GHJSAC — Ghana Journal of Science
GHLID — Geothermal Hot Line
GHMJA — Ghana Medical Journal
GHMJAY — Ghana Medical Journal
GHMR — Homeowner
GHMX — Home Mechanix
GHNG — House and Garden
GHNR — Horse and Rider
GHOJ — Horsemen's Journal
GHOM — Home
GHOR — Horizon
GHPADP — Geologica Hungarica. Series Palaeontologica
GHQ — Georgia Historical Quarterly
GHREA — Guy's Hospital Reports
GHRKA — Genshiryoku Heiwa Riyo Kenkyu Seika Hokokusho
GHRL — History of Religions
GHRS — Horseman
GHRV — American Historical Review
GHSP — Hispanic
GHT — Gas World
GHT — Goeteborgs Handelstidning
GHTC — Horticulture
GHZ — Geographica Helvetica (Zuerich and Berne)
GI — Gaceta Indigenista [*Caracas*]
GI — Gazette d'Israel
GI — Gesundheits-Ingenieur
GI — Glossaria Interpretum
GI — Guatemala Indigena
GIABS — Gastrointestinal Absorption Database
Giannini Found Res Rep — Giannini Foundation Research Report
Giannini Inf Ser Giannini Found Agric Econ — Giannini Information Series. Giannini Foundation of Agricultural Economics
Giant Mol Clouds Galaxy Gregynog Astrophys Workshop — Giant Molecular Clouds in the Galaxy. Gregynog Astrophysics Workshop
Giardini Soc Orticola — Giardini. Giornale della Societa Orticola di Lombardia
Giardino Colon Palermo Lav — Giardino Coloniale di Palermo. Lavori
Gi Biochim — Giornale di Biochimica
Gibridnye Vycisl Masiny i Kompleksy — Gibridnye Vychislitel'nye Mashiny i Kompleksy
GIC — Gids
GICCD7 — Giornale Italiano di Chimica Clinica
GICLDY — Ginecologia Clinica
GICQA — Gifted Child Quarterly
GIDAD — Gijutsu Daijesuto
GIDEP — Government-Industry Data Exchange Program
Gidratatsiya Tverd Tsem — Gidratatsiya i Tverdenie Tsementov
Gidravl Gidrotekh — Gidravlika i Gidrotekhnika
Gidravl Mash Gidroprivod — Gidravlicheskie Mashiny i Gidroprivod
Gidroaeromeh i Teor Uprogosti — Gidroaeromehanika i Teorija Uprugosti
Gidrobiol Issled — Gidrobiologicheskie Issledovaniya
Gidrobiol Issled Dukshtasskikh Ozer — Gidrobiologicheskie Issledovaniya Dukshtasskikh Ozer
Gidrobiol Zh — Gidrobiologicheskii Zhurnal
Gidrobiol Zh Akad Nauk Ukr SSR — Gidrobiologicheskii Zhurnal Akademiya Nauk Ukrainskoi SSR
Gidrobiol Zh Hydrobiol J — Gidrobiologicheskii Zhurnal/Hydrobiological Journal
Gidrobiol Zurn SSSR — Gidrobiologiceskij Zurnal SSSR
Gidrodin Bol'shikh Skorostei — Gidrodinamika Bol'shikh Skorostei
Gidrodin Teploobmen — Gidrodinamika i Teploobmen
Gidrogeol Gidrogeokhim — Gidrogeologiya i Gidrogeokhimiya
Gidrogeol Inzh Geol — Gidrogeologiya. Inzhenernaya Geologiya
Gidrogeol Inzh Geol Aridnoi Zony SSSR — Gidrogeologiya i Inzhenernaya Geologiya Aridnoi Zony SSSR
Gidrogeol Inzh Geol Urala — Gidrogeologiya i Inzhenernaya Geologiya Urala
Gidrogeol Karstoved — Gidrogeologiya i Karstovedenie
Gidrogeol Sb — Gidrogeologicheskii Sbornik
Gidrokhim Mater — Gidrokhimicheskiye Materialy
Gidrokhim Urala — Gidrokhimiya Urala

Gidroliz Lesokhim Promysh — Gidroliznaya i Lesokhimicheskaya Promyshlennost
Gidrol Lesohim Prom — Gidroliznaja i Lesohimiceskaja Promyshlennost
Gidromekh — Akademiya Nauk Ukrainskoi SSR. Institut Gidromekhaniki. Gidromekhanika
Gidromet Azerb Kasp Morya — Gidrometeorologiya Azerbaidzhana i Kaspiiskogo Morya
Gidroprivod Gidropnevmoavtomatika — Gidroprivod Gidropnevmoavtomatika
Gidrotekh Melior — Gidrotekhnika i Melioratsiya
Gidrotekh Melior Lat SSR — Gidrotekhnika i Melioratsiya v Latviiskoi SSR
Gidrotekh Stroit — Gidrotekhnicheskoe Stroitel'stvo
Gids — De Gids
GIE — Constructeur. Vaktijdschrift voor het Werktuigbouwkundig Construeren naar Functie, Vorm, en Kostprijs
GIENDG — Giornale Italiano di Entomologia
GIERB — Giesserei-Rundschau
GIESA — Giesserei
Giess — Giesserei
Giessen Beitr Kstgesch — Giessener Beitraege zur Kunstgeschichte
Giessener Abh Agr WirtForsch Eur Ostens — Giessener Abhandlungen zur Agrar- und Wirtschaftsforschung des Europaeischen Ostens
Giessener Beitr Entwicklungsforsch Reihe 1 — Giessener Beitraege zur Entwicklungsforschung. Reihe 1
Giessener Geol Schr — Giessener Geologische Schriften
Giessener Naturwiss Vortraege — Giessener Naturwissenschaftliche Vortraege
Giessener Schriftenr Tierz Haustiergenet — Giessener Schriftenreihe Tierzucht und Haustiergenetik
Giessen Oberh Gs B — Berichte der Oberhessischen Gesellschaft fuer Natur- und Heilkunde. Giessen
Giesserei-Erfah — Giesserei-Erfahrungsaustausch
Giesserei Maschinenbau Ztg — Giesserei und Maschinenbau Zeitung
Giesserei Prak — Giesserei-Praktiker
Giesserei Prax — Giesserei-Praxis
Giesserei-Rundsch — Giesserei-Rundschau
Giesserei Tech Wiss Belh — Giesserei. Technisch-Wissenschaftliche Beihefte, Giessereiwesen, und Metallkunde
Giessereiztg — Giesserei-Zeitung
GIF — Giornale Italiano di Filologia
GIF — Giornale Italiano di Filosofia
GIFB — Giornale Italiano di Filologia. Biblioteca
Giff L — Gifford Lectures
Gifford Soc Trop Bot Bull — Gifford Society of Tropical Botany. Bulletin
Gift Child — Gifted Child Quarterly
Gift Ch Q — Gifted Child Quarterly
Gifted Child Q — Gifted Child Quarterly
GIFT Int Semin Theor Phys — GIFT (Grupo Interuniversitario de Fisica Teorica) International Seminar on Theoretical Physics
Gifu Coll Agric Res Bull — Gifu College of Agriculture. Research Bulletin
Gig Aspekty Okhr Okruzh Sredy — Gigienicheskie Aspekty Okhrany Okruzhayushchei Sredy
GI Gesund Ing Haustech Bauphys Umwelttech — Gl. Gesundheits-Ingenieur-Haustechnik, Bauphysik, Umwelttechnik
Gigien — Gigienicheskii
Gig i Epidemiol — Gigiena i Epidemiologiia
G Ig Med Prev — Giornale di Igiene e Medicina Preventiva
Gig Naselennykh Mest — Gigiena Naselennykh Mest
Gig Nasel Mest Resp Mezhved Sb — Gigiena Naselennykh Mest Respublikanskoi Mezhvedomstvennyi Sbornik
Gig Primen Polim Mater Izdelii Nikh — Gigiena Primeneniya Polimernykh Materialov i Izdelii iz Nikh
Gig Primen Polim Mater Stroit Mater Vses Soveshch — Gigiena Primeneiya Polimernykh Materialov v Stroitel'stve. Materialy Vsesoyuznogo Soveshchaniya po Voprosam Sanitarno-Gigienicheskogo Kontrolya Primeneniem Polimernykh Materialov v Stroitel'stve
Gig Primen Toksikol Pestits Klin Otravlenii — Gigiena Primeneniya. Toksikologiya, Pestitsidov, i Klinika Otravlenii
Gig Prof Zabol — Gigiena i Professional'nye Zabolevaniya
Gig San — Gigiena i Sanitariya
Gig Sanit — Gigiena i Sanitariya
GIGTA7 — Gigiena Truda Respublikanskii Mezhvedomstvennyi Sbornik
Gig Toksikol Klin Nov Insektofungits Tr Vses Nauchn Konf — Gigiena. Toksikologiya i Klinika Novykh Insektofungitsidov. Trudy Vsesoyuznoi Nauchnoi Konferentsii po Gigiene i Toksikologii Insektofungitsidov
Gig Toksikol Nov Pestits Klin Otravlenii Dokl Vses Nauchn Ko — Gigiena i Toksikologiya Novykh Pestitsidov i Klinika Otravlenii. Doklady Vsesoyuznoi Nauchnoi Konferentsii
Gig Toksikol Pestitsi Klin Otravlenii — Gigiena i Toksikologiya Pestitsidov i Klinika Otravlenii
Gig Toksikol Polim Stroit Mater — Gigiena i Toksikologiya Polimernykh Stroitel'nykh Materialov
Gig Toksikol Polim Stroit Mater Nek Khim Veshchestv — Gigiena i Toksikologiya Polimernykh Stroitel'nykh Materialov i Nekotorykh Khimicheskikh Veshchestv
Gig Tr — Gigiena Truda
Gig Tr Prof Patol Est SSR — Gigiena Truda i Professional'naya Patologiya v Estonskoi SSR
Gig Tr Prof Zabol — Gigiena Truda i Professional'nye Zabolevaniya
Gig Tr Resp Mezhved Sb — Gigiena Truda Respublikanskii Mezhvedomstvennyi Sbornik
Giho Res Dev Headquarters Jpn Defense Agency — Giho. Research and Development Headquarters. Japan Defense Agency
GIJUA — Gijutsu
Gila Rev — Gila Review
Gilbert A — Annalen der Physik. Gilbert
Gilbrid Vychisl Mashiny Kompleksy — Gibridnye Vychislitel'nye Mashiny i Kompleksy
Gildebk — Gildeboek. Tijdschrift voor Kerkelijke Kunst en Oudheidkunde

H

H — Haolam
H — Harper's Magazine
H — Hermes. Zeitschrift fuer Klassische Philologie
H — Hesperia
H — Hispania
H — History
H — Homo [*Stuttgart*]
HA — Hadashot Arke'ologiyot
HA — Handes Amsorya
Ha — Harpers
HA — Heidelberger Abhandlungen
HA — Helvetia Archaeologica
Ha — Hermathena
HA — Herrigs Archiv fuer das Studium der Neueren Sprachen und Literaturen
HA — Hispanoamericano
HA — Historical Abstracts
HAA — Hispanic American Arts
HAA — Hitotsubashi University. Hitotsubashi Academy. Annals
Haa Fr — Haandarbejdets Fremme
Haagsch Maandbl — Haagsch Maandblad
HAA J — HAA [*Herpetological Association of Africa*] Journal
HAAN — Histoire Ancienne de l'Afrique du Nord
H Aa R — Historisk Aarbog fra Randers Amt
Haarl B — Haarlemsche Bijdragen
Haarl Ms Teyl Arch — Archives du Musee Teyler (Haarlem)
Haarl Ntk Vh — Natuurkundige Verhandelingen van de Bataafsche Hollandsche Maatschappij der Wetenschappen te Haarlem
Haarl Ntk Vh Mtsch — Natuurkundige Verhandelingen van de Bataafsche Hollandsche Maatschappij der Wetenschappen te Haarlem
Haarl Vh — Natuurkundige Verhandelingen van de Bataafsche Hollandsche Maatschappij der Wetenschappen te Haarlem
Haases Z Lueft Heiz — Haases Zeitschrift fuer Lueftung und Heizung
H Aa Th — Historisk Aarbog for Thisted Amt
HAB — Harper's Annotated Bible
HAB — Hethitisch-Akkadische Bilinguie des Hattusili I. Abhandlungen. Bayerische Akademie der Wissenschaften. Philosophisch-Historische Abteilung
HAB — Humanities Association. Bulletin
HAB — Humanities Association of Canada Bulletin
HAb — Koelner Historische Abhandlungen
Habana Ac A — Anales de la Real Academia de Ciencias Medicas, Fisicas y Naturales de la Habana. Revista Cientifica
Habana Med — Habana Medica
Habana Mus y Biblioteca Malacologia Circ — Habana Museo y Biblioteca de Malacologia. Circulares
Habana Mus y Biblioteca Zoologia Circ — Habana Museo y Biblioteca de Zoologia. Circulares
HABI — Habitat
Habitat Aust — Habitat Australia
Habitat Int — Habitat International
Habitat Vie Soc — Habitat et Vie Sociale
HABRA — Harvard Business Review
HABT-A — Habitat
HAC — Heating and Air Conditioning Journal
HAC — Historia-Augusta-Colloquium
Hac — La Hacienda
HACCA — Heating and Air Conditioning Contractor
Hacett B SS — Hacettepe Bulletin of Social Sciences and Humanities
Hacettepe Bull Med-Surg — Hacettepe Bulletin of Medicine-Surgery
Hacettepe Bull Nat Sci Eng — Hacettepe Bulletin of Natural Sciences and Engineering
Hacettepe Fen Muhendislik Bilimleri Derg — Hacettepe Fen ve Muhendislik Bilimleri Dergisi
Hacettepe Med J — Hacettepe Medical Journal
Hacettepe Muhendislik Bilimleri Derg — Hacettepe Fen ve Muhendislik Bilimleri Dergisi
Hachmeisters Lit Mber Bau U IngWiss — Hachmeister's Literarischer Monatsbericht fuer Bau- und Ingenieurwissenschaften, Elektrotechnik und Verwandte Gebiete
Hacienda Publica Esp — Hacienda Publica Espanola
Hackethal Nachr — Hackethal Nachrichten. Hackethal-Draht-und-Kabet-Werke A.G
Hac Publ Asuncion — Hacienda Publica (Asuncion)
Had Ark — Hadashot Arke'ologiyot
Hadashot Arch — Hadashot Archaeologioth
Hadassah Mag — Hadassah Magazine
Hadersl Samf Aa — Haderslev Samfundets Aarsskrift
Haders St — Haderslev Stiftsbog

Hadronic J — Hadronic Journal
Hadronic J Suppl — Hadronic Journal Supplement
Hadronic Press Collect Orig Artic — Hadronic Press Collection of Original Articles
Hadronic Press Monographs Math — Hadronic Press Monographs in Mathematics
Hadronic Press Monographs Theoret Phys — Hadronic Press Monographs in Theoretical Physics
Hadronic Press Monogr Appl Math — Hadronic Press Monographs in Applied Mathematics
Hadronic Press New Ser Reprints Hist Value — Hadronic Press New Series of Reprints of Historical Value
Hadronic Press Reprint Ser Math — Hadronic Press Reprint Series in Mathematics
HAE — Handbuch der Altchristlichen Epigraphik
HAE — Hispania Antiqua Epigraphica
HAEC — Holarctic Ecology
Haeders Z MaschBau Betr — Haeders Zeitschrift fuer Maschinenbau und Betrieb
HAEK — Historische. Archiv fuer die Erzbistum Koeln
HAEMA — Haematologica
Haemat Cracov — Haematologica Cracoviensia
Haemat Lat — Haematologica Latina
Haematol Blood Transfus — Haematology and Blood Transfusion
Haematol Bluttransfus — Haematologie und Bluttransfusion
Haematol Hung — Haematologia Hungarica
Haematol Lat — Haematologica Latina
Haematologia Suppl — Haematologia. Supplement
Haemat Pol — Haematologica Polonica
HAENE6 — Handbook of Endotoxin
HA Ep — Hispania Antiqua Epigraphica
HA Epigr — Hispania Antiqua Epigraphica
Haer — Haeren
Haerterei-Tech Mitt — Haerterei-Technische Mitteilungen
Haerterei-Tech Waermebehandl — Haerterei-Technik und Waermebehandlung
Haert-Tech Mitt — Haerterei-Technische Mitteilungen
Haert Tech Waermebehand — Haerterei-Technik und Waermebehandlung
HAFFB — Health Affairs
Haffkine Inst Annu Rep — Haffkine Institute. Annual Report
Haffkine Inst Bull — Haffkine Institute. Bulletin
Ha G — Hannoversche Geschichtsblaetter
Hagskyrs Isl — Hagskyrslur Islands
HAHGG — Historiche Avonden. Uitgegeven door het Historiche Genootschap te Groningen terGelegenheid van Zijn Twintigjarig Bestaan
Ha Hinnuk Ham M — Ha-Hinnuk Ham-Musiquali
Hahnemannian Advoc — Hahnemannian Advocate
Hahnemannian Inst — Hahnemannian Institute
Hahnemannian Mon — Hahnemannian Monthly
Hahnemann Int Symp Hypertens — Hahnemann International Symposium on Hypertension
Hahnemann Med Coll Circ — Hahnemann Medical College Circular
Hahnemann Med Coll Hosp Bull — Hahnemann Medical College and Hospital Bulletin
Hahnemann Symp — Hahnemann Symposium
Hahnemann Symp Hypertens Dis — Hahnemann Symposium on Hypertensive Disease
Hahnemann Symp Salt Water Retention — Hahnemann Symposium on Salt and Water Retention
Hahnenklee Symp — Hahnenklee-Symposion
Hahn Meitner Inst Kernforsch Berlin Ber — Hahn-Meitner-Institut fuer Kernforschung Berlin. Berichte
HAHR — Hispanic American Historical Review
HAID — Hispanic Americans Information Directory
Haidinger Ab — Naturwissenschaftliche Abhandlungen. Haidinger
Haidinger B — Berichte ueber die Mittheilungen von Freunden der Naturwissenschaften in Wien. Haidinger
Haidingers Abh — Naturwissenschaftliche Abhandlungen (Wilhelm Haidinger, Editor)
HAIL — Hague. Academy of International Law. Recueil des Cours
Haile Selassie I Univ Dep Geol Annu Rep — Haile Selassie I University. Department of Geology. Annual Report
Hain Mm S — Memoires et Publications de la Societe des Sciences, des Arts, et des Lettres du Hainaut
Hain S Mm — Memoires et Publications de la Societe des Sciences, des Arts, et des Lettres du Hainaut
Hair Res Proc Int Congr — Hair Research. Status and Future Aspects. Proceedings of the International Congress on Hair Research
Hair Trace Elem Hum Illness Hum Hair Symp — Hair, Trace Elements, and Human Illness. Human Hair Symposium

Haiti Med — Haiti Medicale
Hajdus Mehesz — Hajdusagi Mehesz
Hak — Collection of Early Voyages, Travels, and Discoveries. Richard Hakluyt
Hakata Symp — Hakata Symposium
Hakluyt Soc J — Hakluyt Society Journal
HAKOD4 — Bioscience and Industry
Hakodate Tech Coll Res Rep — Hakodate Technical College. Research Reports
Hakone Symp Proc — Hakone Symposium. Proceedings
Halbmon Literaturverz Fortschr Phys — Halbmonatliches Literaturverzeichnis der Fortschrifte der Physik
Halbmon LitVerz Fortschr Phys — Halbmonatliches Literaturverzeichniss der Fortschritte der Physik
Halbmschr Frauen U Kinderkrankh — Halbmonatsschrift fuer Frauen- und Kinderkrankheiten
Halbmschr Haut U Harnkrankh — Halbmonatsschrift fuer Haut- und Harnkrankheiten
Halbmschr Soz Hyg Prakt Med — Halbmonatsschrift fuer Soziale Hygiene und Praktische Medizin
HALEA — Harvey Lectures
Hale L — Hale Lectures
Half A Clim Rep Kuwait — Half-Annual Climatological Report. Kuwait
Half Yrly J Mysore Univ — Half-Yearly Journal. Mysore University
Half-Yrly J Mysore Univ Sect B Sci Incl Med Eng — Half-Yearly Journal. Mysore University. Section B. Science Including Medicine and Engineering
Halide Glasses Proc Int Symp — Halide Glasses. Proceedings of the International Symposium on Halide Glasses
Halifax Nat — Halifax Naturalist and Record of the Scientific Society
Hall ALJ — Hall's American Law Journal
Hall Am LJ — Hall's American Law Journal
Hall Bij — Bijdragen tot de Natuurkundige Wetenschappen. Hall
Halle Ab Nf Gs — Abhandlungen der Naturforschenden Gesellschaft zu Halle
(Halle) Beitr — Beitraege zur Geschichte der Deutschen Sprache und Literatur (Halle)
Halle Cuirs — Halle auz Cuirs
Halle Cuirs Part Tech — Halle aux Cuirs. Partie Technique
Halle Cuirs Suppl Tech Mens — Halle aux Cuirs. Supplement Technique Mensuel
Halle Jbr Nf Gs — Jahresbericht der Naturforschenden Gesellschaft zu Halle
Halle Jbr NW Vr — Jahresbericht des Naturwissenschaftlichen Vereins fuer Sachsen und Thueringen in Halle
Halle Nf Gs Ab — Abhandlungen der Naturforschenden Gesellschaft zu Halle
Halle Nf Gs B — Bericht ueber die Sitzungen der Naturforschenden Gesellschaft zu Halle
Halle Nf Gs Festschr — Festschrift der Naturforschenden Gesellschaft zu Halle
Haller Mb — Haller Muenzblaetter
Halle Sb Nf Gs — Bericht ueber die Sitzungen der Naturforschenden Gesellschaft zu Halle
Hallesches Jahrb Geowiss — Hallesches Jahrbuch fuer Geowissenschaften
Hallesches Jahrb Mitteldtsh Erdgesch — Hallesches Jahrbuch fuer Mitteldeutsche Erdgeschichte
Hallesches Jb Mitteldt Erdgesch — Hallesches Jahrbuch fuer Mitteldeutsche Erdgeschichte
Halle Univ Wiss Z Gesellsch & Sprachw Reihe — Halle Universitaet. Wissenschaftliche Zeitschrift Gesellschafts und Sprachwissenschaftliche Reihe
Halley Lect — Halley Lectures
Halle Z — Zeitschrift fuer die Gesammten Naturwissenschaften. Herausgegeben von dem Naturwissenschaftlichen Vereine fuer Sachsen und Thueringen in Halle
Halle Z Nw — Zeitschrift fuer die Gesammten Naturwissenschaften. Herausgegeben von dem Naturwissenschaftlichen Vereine fuer Sachsen und Thueringen in Halle
Hallische Monogr — Hallische Monographien
Hall Jour Jur — Journal of Jurisprudence (Hall's)
Hall LJ — Hall's American Law Journal
Hall's Am LJ — Hall's American Law Journal
Hall's J Jur — Journal of Jurisprudence (Hall's)
Hall W Pr — Hallisches Winckelmannsprogramme
HalM — Halve Maen
Halogen Chem — Halogen Chemistry
HALRA — Harvard Law Review
Halsbury — Halsbury's Law of England
Halsbury L Eng — Halsbury's Law of England
Halsbury's Laws — Halsbury's Law of England
Hals Nas U Ohrenheilk — Hals-, Nasen-, und Ohrenheilkunde
Halsovann Flygskr — Halsovannens Flygskrifter
HalsovFor Flygskr Helsingf — Halsovardsforeningens Flygskrifter (Helsingfors)
HalsovFor Stock Forh — Halsovardsforeningens i Stockholm Forhandlingar
HalsovNamnd Gamla Karleby Arsberatt — Halsovardsnamndens i Gamla Karleby Arsberattelse
HalsovNamnd Helsingf Arsberatt — Halsovardsnamndens i Helsingfors Arsberattelse om Halsotillstander i Staden
HalsovNamnds Arsberatt Goteborg — Halsovardsnamnds Arsberattelse (Goteborg)
Halton Bus Jnl — Halton Business Journal
HAm — Hispano-Americano. Seminario de la Vida y la Verdad
HAMAA — Harper's Magazine
HAMAD — Harvard Magazine
Hamb Beitr A — Hamburger Beitraege zur Archaeologie
Hamb Beitr Angew Mineral Kristallphys Petrog — Hamburger Beitraege zur Angewandten Mineralogie, Kristallphysik, und Petrogenese
Hamb Beitr Num — Hamburger Beitraege zur Numismatik
Hamb Ber — Hamburger Berichte
Hamb Ber Siedlungswasserwirtsch — Hamburger Berichte zur Siedlungswasserwirtschaft
Hamb Geophys Einzelschriften — Hamburger Geophysikalische Einzelschriften
Hambg Nachrr — Hamburger Nachrichten

Hamb Kuestenforsch — Hamburger Kuestenforschung
Hamb Mth Gs Mt — Mitteilungen der Mathematischen Gesellschaft in Hamburg
Hamb Nt Vr Vh — Verhandlungen des Naturwissenschaftlichen Vereins von Hamburg-Altona
Hamb St u Z Nachr — Hamburger Steuer und Zoll-Nachrichten
Hamb Symp Blutgerinnung — Hamburger Symposion ueber Blutgerinnung
Hamb Symp Tumormarker — Hamburger Symposium ueber Tumormarker
Hamburg Beitr Archaeol — Hamburger Beitraege zur Archaeologie
Hamburg Ber Neuen Gel Sachen — Hamburgische Berichte von Neuen Gelehrten Sachen
Hamburg Bietr Bknd — Hamburger Beitraege zur Buchkunde
Hamburg Bietr Numis — Hamburger Beitraege zur Numismatik
Hamburger Aerztekorr — Hamburger Aerztekorrespondenz
Hamburger Akad Rdsch — Hamburger Akademische Rundschau
Hamburger Beitr Angew Miner — Hamburger Beitraege zur Angewandten Mineralogie, Kristallphysik, und Petrogenese
Hamburger Geogr Stud — Hamburger Geographische Studien
Hamburger Jahrb Wirt Gesellschaftspol — Hamburger Jahrbuch fuer Wirtschafts- und Gesellschaftspolitik
Hamburger Kolon U FettwarZtg — Hamburger Kolonial- und Fettwarenzeitung
Hamburger Math Einzelschr — Hamburger Mathematische Einzelschriften
Hamburg Gart Alman — Hamburgischer Garten-Almanach
Hamburg Geol Staatsinstitut Mitt — Hamburg Geologischen Staatsinstitut. Mitteilungen
Hamburgische Med Ueberseehft — Hamburgische Medizinische Ueberseehefte
Hamburg Jb Wirtsch- u Ges-Polit — Hamburger Jahrbuch fuer Wirtschafts- und Gesellschaftspolitik
Hamburg Kstfreunde — Hamburgische Kunstfreunde
Hamburg Lehrer Verein Naturk Ber — Hamburgischer Lehrer-Verein fuer Naturkunde. Bericht
Hamburg Mag — Hamburgisches Magazin, oder Gesammlete Schriften, zum Unterricht und Vergnuegenaus der Naturforschung und den Angenehmen Wissenschaften Ueberhaupt
Hamburg Mittel & Ostdt Forsch — Hamburger Mittel- und Ostdeutsche Forschungen
Hamburg Schr Z Ges Strafrechtswiss — Hamburgische Schriften zur Gesamten Strafrechtswissenschaft
Hamb Wirtsch — Hamburger Wirtschaft
Hamb Ws Anst Jb — Jahrbuch der Hamburgischen Wissenschaftlichen Anstalten
Hamb Wschr Ae Zahn Ae — Hamburger Wochenschrift fuer Aerzte und Zahnaerzte
Hamb Zool Staatsinst u Zool Mus Mitt — Hamburg. Zoologisches Staatsinstitut und Zoologisches Museum. Mitteilungen
Hamdard Islam — Hamdard Islamicus
Hamdard Med — Hamdard Medicus
Hamdard Med Dig — Hamdard Medical Digest
Hameen Laan Maanviljelyss Vuosik — Hameen Laanin Maanviljelysseuran Vuosikirja
Hameen Satak Maanviljelyss Kert — Hameen-Satakunnan Maanviljelysseuran Kertomus
HAMIA — Hasler-Mitteilungen
Hamilton As J Pr — Hamilton Association. Journal and Proceedings
Hamilton Sc As J Pr — Hamilton Scientific Association. Journal and Proceedings
HamletR — Hamlet Review
Hamline LR — Hamline Law Review
Hamline L Rev — Hamline Law Review
Hammersmith Cardiol Workshop Ser — Hammersmith Cardiology Workshop Series
Ham Mo Bul — Ham (Walter P.) and Company. Monthly Bulletin
HAMNG — Heidelberger Abhandlungen zur Mittleren und Neueren Geschichte
HAMPBF — Hawaii. Agricultural Experiment Station. Miscellaneous Publication
Hamps Agric J — Hampshire Agricultural Journal
Hamps Beekpr — Hampshire Beekeeper
Hampstead Annu — Hampstead Annual
Hampton — Hampton's Magazine
Hampton Bul — Hampton Bulletin
Hampton Leafl — Hampton Leaflets. Hampton Normal and Agricultural Institute
Hamptons M — Hampton's Magazine
Ham Rad Horiz — Ham Radio Horizons
HAMSB — Heidelberger Akademie der Wissenschaften. Mathematisch-Naturwissenschaftliche Klasse. Sitzungsberichte
Hanauisches Mag — Hanauisches Magazin
Hancock Mus Bull — Hancock Museum Bulletin
Hancock Mus Newcastle upon Tyne Bull — Hancock Museum. Newcastle upon Tyne. Bulletin
Hand — Hand Book
Hand Am — Handes Amsoreaj/Handes Amsorya
Hand & Levensber Maatsch Ned Lettknd Leiden — Handelingen en Levensberichten van de Maatschappij der Nederlandse Letterkunde te Leiden
Handassa We Adrikh — Handassa We-Adrikhalut
Handb Adhes Bonding — Handbook of Adhesive Bonding
Handb Adv Mater Test — Handbook of Advanced Materials Testing
Handb Air Pollut Anal — Handbook of Air Pollution Analysis
Handb Allg Pathol — Handbuch der Allgemeinen Pathologie
Handball Mag — Handball Magazine
Handb Alt — Handbuch der Altertumswissenschaft
Handb Amyotrophic Lateral Scler — Handbook of Amyotrophic Lateral Sclerosis
Handb Anal Synth Polym Plast — Handbook of Analysis of Synthetic Polymers and Plastics
Handb Antioxid — Handbook of Antioxidants
Handb Anxiety — Handbook of Anxiety
Handb Appl Polym Process Technol — Handbook of Applied Polymer Processing Technology
Handb Astron Astrophys Geophys — Handbook of Astronomy, Astrophysics, and Geophysics

Handb Aud Vestibular Res Methods — Handbook of Auditory and Vestibular Research Methods

Handb Bakt Infekt Tieren — Handbuch der Bakteriellen Infektionen bei Tieren

Handb Bauw — Handbuch des Bauwesens

Handb Binnenfisch Mitteleur — Handbuch der Binnenfischerei Mitteleuropas

Handb Biochem ArbMeth — Handbuch der Biochemischen Arbeitsmethoden

Handb Biochem Mensch Tiere — Handbuch der Biochemie des Menschen und der Tiere

Handb Biochem Mol Biol — Handbook of Biochemistry and Molecular Biology

Handb Biochim — Handbuch der Biochimie

Handb Bioethanol — Handbook on Bioethanol. Production and Utilization

Handb Biol Aging — Handbook of the Biology of Aging

Handb Biol ArbMeth — Handbuch der Biologischen Arbeitsmethoden

Handb Biol Phys — Handbook of Biological Physics

Handb Brew — Handbook of Brewing

Handb Bur Econ Geol Univ Tex Austin — Handbook. Bureau of Economic Geology. University of Texas at Austin

Handb Chem Ind Ausserdt Laender — Handbuch der Chemischen Industrie der Ausserdeutschen Laender

Handb Chem Lasers — Handbook of Chemical Lasers

Handb Chem Neuroanat — Handbook of Chemical Neuroanatomy

Handb Chromatog Lipids — Handbook of Chromatography. Lipids

Handb Clin Neurol — Handbook of Clinical Neurology

Handb Compd Semicond — Handbook of Compound Semiconductors. Growth, Processing, Characterization, and Devices

Handb Compos — Handbook of Composites

Handb Contin Fiber Reinf Ceram Matrix Compos — Handbook on Continuous Fiber-Reinforced Ceramic Matrix Composites

Handb Cryosurg — Handbook of Cryosurgery

Handb Cryst Growth — Handbook of Crystal Growth

Handb Deposition Technol Films Coat — Handbook of Deposition Technologies for Films and Coatings. Science, Technology, and Applications

Handb Deriv Chromatogr — Handbook of Derivatives for Chromatography

Handb der Or — Handbuch der Orientalistik

Handb Deutsch Militaerges — Handbuch zur Deutschen Militaergeschichte

Handb Discontin Reinf Ceram Matrix Compos — Handbook on Discontinuously Reinforced Ceramic Matrix Composites

Handb Disinfect Antiseptics — Handbook of Disinfectants and Antiseptics

Handb Drug Abuse — Handbook on Drug Abuse

Handb Ecotoxicol — Handbook of Ecotoxicology

Handb Electr Mat — Handbook of Electronic Materials

Handb Elem Abundances Meteorites — Handbook of Elemental Abundances in Meteorites

Handb Endocrinol — Handbook of Endocrinology

Handb Endotoxin — Handbook of Endotoxin

Handb Ent — Handbuch der Entomologie

Handb Environ Chem — Handbook of Environmental Chemistry

Handb Enzyme Biotechnol — Handbook of Enzyme Biotechnology

Handb Ernaehr Stoffwechs Landw Nutztiere — Handbuch der Ernaehrung und des Stoffwechsels der Landwirtschaftlichen Nutztiere

Handb Exp Immunol — Handbook of Experimental Immunology

Handb Explor Geochem — Handbook of Exploration Geochemistry

Handb Exp Pharmacol — Handbook of Experimental Pharmacology

Handb Exp Pharmak — Handbuch der Experimentellen

Handb Exp Pharmakol — Handbuch der Experimentellen Pharmakologie

Handb ExpPhys — Handbuch der Experimentalphysik

Handb Fiberglass Adv Plast Compos — Handbook of Fiberglass and Advanced Plastics Composites

Handb Fillers Reinf Plast — Handbook of Fillers and Reinforcements for Plastics

Handb Flyvevab — Handbog for Flyvevabnet

Handb Food Allerg — Handbook of Food Allergies

Handb Food Anal — Handbook of Food Analysis

Handb Food Eng — Handbook of Food Engineering

Handb Food Prep — Handbook of Food Preparation

Handb Fuel Cell Technol — Handbook of Fuel Cell Technology

Handb Funct Gastrointest Disord — Handbook of Functional Gastrointestinal Disorders

Handb Genotoxic Eff Fish Chromosomes — Handbook of Genotoxic Effects and Fish Chromosomes

Handb Geophys — Handbuch der Geophysik

Handb Ges Dt Schriftt Landw — Handbuch fuer das Gesamte Deutsche Schrifttum der Landwirtschaft, Forstwirtschaft

Handb Glass Manuf — Handbook of Glass Manufacture

Handb Grignard Reagents — Handbook of Grignard Reagents

Handb Heat Transfer — Handbook of Heat Transfer

Handb High Toxic Mater Handl Manage — Handbook of Highly Toxic Materials Handling and Management

Handb Histochem — Handbuch der Histochemie

Handb Hypertens — Handbook of Hypertension

Handb Hypothal — Handbook of the Hypothalamus

Handb Ind Chem — Handbook of Industrial Chemistry

Handb Inflammation — Handbook of Inflammation

Handb Inflammatology — Handbook of Inflammatology

Handb Infrared Opt Mater — Handbook of Infrared Optical Materials

Handb Infusionsther Klin Ernaehr — Handbuch der Infusionstherapie und Klinischen Ernaehrung

Handb Ion Sources — Handbook of Ion Sources

Handb Kalibergwerke — Handbuch der Kalibergwerke, Salinen und Tiefbohrunternehmungen

Handbk A Rep Br Postgrad Med Fed — Handbook and Annual Report. British Postgraduate Medical Federation

Handbk A Rep Soc Promot Nat Reserves — Handbook and Annual Report of the Society for the Promotion of Nature Reserves

Handbk Astr Soc S Afr — Handbook. Astronomical Society of South Africa

Handb Kathod Korrosionsschutzes — Handbuch des Kathodischen Korrosionsschutzes

Handbk Br Astr Ass — Handbook. British Astronomical Association

Handbk Br Columb Prov Mus — Handbook. British Columbia Provincial Museum

Handbk Br Med Ass — Handbook of the British Medical Association

Handbk Br Refrig Mater — Handbook of British Refrigeration Material and Refrigeration Catalogue

Handbk Br Stand Instn — Handbook. British Standards Institution

Handbk Br W Indies Sug Ass — Handbook. British West Indies Sugar Association

Handbk Def Res Bd Can — Handbook. Defence Research Board. Canada

Handb Keram — Handbuch der Keramik

Handbk Ident Br Insects — Handbook for the Identification of British Insects. Royal Entomological Society

Handbk Inst Orthop — Handbook. Institute of Orthopaedics

Handbk Int Congr Docum Appl Chem — Handbook. International Congress on Documentation of Applied Chemistry

Handbk Iron Steel Inst — Handbook. Iron and Steel Institute

Handbk Life Sci Div R Ont Mus — Handbook. Life Science Division. Royal Ontario Museum

Handbk Lipids Hum Nutr — Handbood of Lipids in Human Nutrition

Handbk Miner Resour Ga — Handbook. Mineral Resources of Georgia

Handbk New Hamps Acad Sci — Handbook of the New Hampshire Academy of Science

Handbk NY St Mus — Handbook. New York State Museum

Handb Kolloidwiss Einzeldarst — Handbuch der Kolloidwissenschaft in Einzeldarstellungen

Handbk Reg Conf Electron Microsc Asia Oceania — Handbook. Regional Conference on Electron Microscopy in Asia and Oceania

Handbk R Ontario Mus Zool — Handbook of the Royal Ontario Museum of Zoology

Handbk S Aust Inst Technol — Handbook. South Australian Institute of Technology

Handbk Scient Instrum Appar — Handbook of Scientific Instruments and Apparatus

Handbk Ser Am Mus Nat Hist — Handbook Series. American Museum of Natural History

Handbk Ser Bur Stand — Handbook Series of the Bureau of Standards

Handbk Soc Automot Engrs — Handbook. Society of Automotive Engineers

Handbk Soc Nat Hist Peking — Handbook. Society of Natural History (Peking)

Handbk Statist Agric For Fish Tokyo — Handbook of Statistics of Agriculture, Forestry, and Fisheries (Tokyo)

Handbk Text Technol — Handbook of Textile Technology. Textile Institute

Handbk Tolson Meml Mus — Handbook. Tolson Memorial Museum

Handbk West Aust Nat Club — Handbook. Western Australian Naturalists' Club

Handb Landw PflZuecht — Handbuch der Landwirtschaftlichen Pflanzenzuechtung

Handb Lasers Sel Data Opt Technol — Handbook of Lasers with Selected Data on Optical Technology

Handb Lebensmittelchemie — Handbuch der Lebensmittelchemie

Handb Lipid Res — Handbook of Lipid Research

Handb Magn Mater — Handbook of Magnetic Materials

Handb Mater Processes Electron — Handbook of Materials and Processes for Electronics

Handb Med Radiol — Handbuch der Medizinschen Radiologie

Handb Med U VetWes Sachsen — Handbuch des Medizinal- und Veterinaerwesens im Koenigreich Sachsen

Handb Messtech Betriebskontrolle — Handbuch der Messtechnik in der Betriebskontrolle

Handb Methodol Assess Air Pollut Eff Veg — Handbook of Methodology for the Assessment of Air Pollution Effects on Vegetation

Handb Methods Gastrointest Pharmacol — Handbook of Methods in Gastrointestinal Pharmacology

Handb Met Ligand Interact Biol Fluids Bioinorg Chem — Handbook of Metal-Ligand Interactions in Biological Fluids. Bioinorganic Chemistry

Handb Micro Nano Tribol — Handbook of Micro/Nano Tribology

Handb Mikrosk Tech — Handbuch der Mikroskopie in der Technik

Handb Milk Compos — Handbook of Milk Composition

Handb Mineral — Handbuch der Mineralogie

Handb Mol Cytol — Handbook of Molecular Cytology

Handb Morph Wirbellosen Tiere — Handbuch der Morphologie der Wirbellosen Tiere

Handb Nat Occuring Food Toxicants — Handbook of Naturally Occuring Food Toxicants

Handb Nat Pestic Methods — Handbook of Natural Pesticides. Methods

Handb Nat Toxins — Handbook of Natural Toxins

Handb Neurochem — Handbook of Neurochemistry

Handb Neurohypophyseal Hor Analogs — Handbook of Neurohypophyseal Hormone Analogs

Handb Nonmed Appl Liposomes — Handbook of Nonmedical Applications of Liposomes

Handb Norg ByggforskInst — Handbok. Norges Byggforskningsinstitutt

Handb Norsk IngForen — Handbok. Norsk Ingeniorforening

Handb Nutr Suppl — Handbook of Nutritional Supplements

Handbook Appl Math Guidebook — Handbook of Applicable Mathematics Guidebook

Handbooks in Econom — Handbooks in Economics

Handbooks Sci Tech — Handbooks in Science and Technology

Handb Opt Prop — Handbook of Optical Properties

Handb Oral Contracept — Handbook on Oral Contraception

Handb Org Chem — Handbuch der Organischen Chemie

Handb Org Waste Convers — Handbook of Organic Waste Conversion

Handb Ozone Technol Appl — Handbook of Ozone Technology and Applications

Handb Palaeozool — Handbuch der Palaeozoologie

Handb PflAnat — Handbuch der Pflanzenanatomie

Handb Pflanzenanat — Handbuch der Pflanzenanatomie

Handb Pflernahr Dueng — Handbuch der Pflanzenernahrung und Duengung

Handb PflKrankh — Handbuch der Pflanzenkrankheiten
Handb PflPhysiol — Handbuch der Pflanzenphysiologie
Handb Pharmacokinet Pharmacodyn Correl — Handbook of Pharmacokinetic/Pharmacodynamic Correlation
Handb Pharmacol Methodol Study Neuroendocr Syst — Handbook of Pharmacologic Methodologies for the Study of the Neuroendocrine System
Handb Phycol Methods Physiol Biochem Methods — Handbook of Phycological Methods. Physiological and Biochemical Methods
Handb Phys — Handbuch der Physik
Handb Phys Chem Rare Earths — Handbook on the Physics and Chemistry of Rare Earths
Handb Physiol — Handbook of Physiology
Handb Physiol Meth — Handbuch der Physiologischen Methodik
Handb Physiol Sect 1 Nerv Syst — Handbook of Physiology. Section 1. The Nervous System
Handb Physiol Sect 2 Cardiovasc Syst — Handbook of Physiology. Section 2. The Cardiovascular System
Handb Physiol Sect 4 Adapt Environ — Handbook of Physiology. Section 4. Adaptation to the Environment
Handb Physiol Sect 5 Adipose Tissue — Handbook of Physiology. Section 5. Adipose Tissue
Handb Physiol Sect 6 Aliment Canal — Handbook of Physiology. Section 6. Alimentary Canal
Handb Physiol Sect 7 Endocrinol — Handbook of Physiology. Section 7. Endocrinology
Handb Physiol Sect 8 Renal Physiol — Handbook of Physiology. Section 8. Renal Physiology
Handb Physiol Sect 9 React Environ Agents — Handbook of Physiology. Section 9. Reactions to Environmental Agents
Handb Plant Cell Cult — Handbook of Plant Cell Culture
Handb Plast Elastomers — Handbook of Plastics and Elastomers
Handb Polym Compos Eng — Handbook of Polymer Composites for Engineers
Handb Polym Fibre Compos — Handbook of Polymer-Fibre Composites
Handb Powder Technol — Handbook of Powder Technology
Handb Precis Eng — Handbook of Precision Engineering
Handb Pressure Sensitive Adhes Technol — Handbook of Pressure-Sensitive Adhesive Technology
Handb Psychiatry Endocrinol — Handbook of Psychiatry and Endocrinology
Handb Psychopharmacol — Handbook of Psychopharmacology
Handb Psychophysiol — Handbook of Psychophysiology
Handb Radioimmunoassay — Handbook of Radioimmunoassay
Handb S Afr Geol Surv — Handbook. South Africa. Geological Survey
Handb Seefisch Nordeur — Handbuch der Seefischerei Nordeuropas
Handb Semicond — Handbook on Semiconductors
Handb Semicond Lasers Photonic Integr Circuits — Handbook of Semiconductor Lasers and Photonic Integrated Circuits
Handb Sens Actuators — Handbook of Sensors and Actuators
Handb Sens Physiol — Handbook of Sensory Physiology
Handb Sep Tech Chem Eng — Handbook of Separation Techniques for Chemical Engineers
Handb Shock Trauma — Handbook of Shock Trauma
Handb South Aust Dep Mines Energy — Handbook. South Australia Department of Mines and Energy
Handb South Pac Comm — Handbook. South Pacific Commission
Handb Soy Oil Process Util — Handbook of Soy Oil Processing and Utilization
Handb Spez Path Anat Haustiere (Ernst Joest) — Handbuch der Speziellen Pathologischen Anatomie der Haustiere (Ernst Joest)
Handb Staerke Einzeldarst — Handbuch der Staerke in Einzeldarstellungen
Handb Stainless Steels — Handbook of Stainless Steels
Handb Starch Hydrolysis Prod and their Deriv — Handbook of Starch Hydrolysis Products and their Derivatives
Handb Stereoisomers Drugs Psychopharmacol — Handbook of Stereoisomers. Drugs in Psychopharmacology
Handb Strata Bound Stratiform Ore Depostis — Handbook of Strata-Bound and Stratiform Ore Deposits
Handb Sulphur Aust Agric — Handbook on Sulphur in Australian Agriculture
Handb Surf Interfaces — Handbook of Surfaces and Interfaces
Handb Teratol — Handbook of Teratology
Handb Textilhilfsm — Handbuch der Textilhilfsmitte
Handb Thermoplas Elastomers — Handbook of Thermoplastic Elastomers
Handb Thick Film Technol — Handbook of Thick Film Technology
Handb Tierernaehr — Handbuch der Tierernaehrung
Handb Toxicol Met — Handbook on the Toxicology of Metals
Handb Trop Foods — Handbook of Tropical Foods
Handbuch Philos — Handbuch Philosophie
Handb Univ Tex Austin Bur Econ Geol — Handbook. University of Texas at Austin. Bureau of Economic Geology
Handb Urol — Handbuch der Urologie
Handb US Natn Bur Stand — Handbook. United States National Bureau of Standards
Handb Vac Arc Sci Technol — Handbook of Vacuum Arc Science and Technology. Fundamentals and Applications
Handb VererbWiss — Handbuch der Vererbungswissenschaft
Handb Vergl Physiol — Handbuch der Vergleichenden Physiologie
Handb Virusinfekt Tieren — Handbuch der Virusinfektionen bei Tieren
Handb Vitam — Handbook of Vitamins. Nutritional, Biochemical, and Clinical Aspects
Handb Water Soluble Gums Resins — Handbook of Water-Soluble Gums and Resins
Handb Werften — Handbuch der Werften
Handb X Ray Ultraviolet Photoelectron Spectrosc — Handbook of X-Ray and Ultraviolet Photoelectron Spectroscopy
Handb Zool — Handbuch der Zoologie
Handchir Mikrochir Plast Chir — Handchirurgie, Mikrochirurgie, Plastische Chirurgie

Hand Clin — Hand Clinics
Hand Congr Alg Synd SuikFabr Ned Indie — Handelingen van het Congres van het Algemeen Syndicaat van Suikerfabrikanten in Nederlandsch-Indie
H and CP — Hospital and Community Psychiatry
Hand d Arch — Handbuch der Archaeologie
Handel Ind — Handel en Industrie
Handelingen Commissie Toponymie & Dialectologie — Handelingen. Koninklijke Commissie voor Toponymie en Dialectologie
Handelingen Ned Phonol Werkgemeenschap — Handelingen. Nederlandse Phonologische Werkgemeenschap
Handel Jb — Handel Jahrbuch
Handel Koll Geneeskd S-Afr — Handelinge. Kollege van Geneeskunde van Suid-Afrika
Handel Kongr Weidingsvereniging Suidelike Afr — Handelinge van die Kongres van die Weidingsvereniging van Suidelike Afrika
Handel Ned Belg Ver Graanonderz — Handelingen. Nederlands-Belgische Vereniging van Graanonderzoekers
Handel Ned Belg Ver Graanonderz — Handelingen van de Nederlands-Belgische Vereeniging van Graanonderzoekers
Handel Ned Nat Geneeskd Congr — Handelingen. Nederlands Natuur- en Geneeskundig Congres
Handeln Entscheid Komplexen Oekon Situat — Handeln und Entscheiden in Komplexen Oekonomischen Situationen
Handel Oudheidkunde Mechelen — Handelingen. Koninklijke Kring voor Oudheidkunde. Letteren en Kunst van Mechelen Malines
Handel Oudheid Mechelen — Handelingen. Koninklijke Kring voor Oudheidkunde Letteren en Kunst van Mechelen
Handel Prov Genootsch Kunsten N Brabant — Handelingen. Provinciaal Genootschap van Kunsten en Wetenschappen in Noord Brabant
Handel S Afr Inst Electr Ing — Handelinge van die Suid-Afrikaanse Instituut van Elektriese Ingenieurs
Handel S Afr Ver Diereproduksie — Handelinge van die Suid-Afrikaanse Vereniging vir Diereproduksie
Handelsblt — Handelsblatt
Handelsbl Tuinb — Handelsblad voor den Tuinbouw
Handelsv T — Handelsvidenskabeligt Tidsskrift
Handel Voedingsver Suidelike Afr — Handelinge Voedingsvereniging van Suidelike Afrika
Handel Voeding Ver Suidel — Handelinge. Voedingvereeniging van Suidelike Afrika
Handel Weidingsvereniging Suidelike Afr — Handelinge. Weidingsvereniging van Suidelike Afrika
Handel Wewn — Handel Wewnetrzny
Handel Zagran — Handel Zagraniczy
Handes Amsorya — Handes Amsorya. Monatschrift fuer Armenische Philologie
H & G — House and Garden
Hand Genoot Gesch Soc Emul Brugge — Handelingen van het Genootschap voor Geschiedenis Gesticht Onder de Benaming Societe d'Emulation te Brugge
Hand Gent — Handelingen der Maatschappij voor Geschiedenis en Oudheidkunde te Gent
Hand Groningen Maatsch Landb — Handelingen van de Groningen Maatschappij van Landbouw
H & H — Hoofs and Horns
H & Home — House and Home
Hand Hydrobiol Club — Handelingen van de Hydrobiologische Club
Hand Hydrobiol Veren — Handelingen van de Hydrobiologische Vereniging
HandKonCommTop-Dial — Handelingen. Koninklijke Commissie voor Toponymie en Dialectologie
Hand Kon Gesch & Oudhdknd Kring Kortrijk — Handelingen van de Koninklijke Geschied- en Oudheidkundige Kring van Kortrijk
Hand Kon Kring Oudhdknd Lett & Kst Mechelen Bull Cerc Archeol — Handelingen van de Koninklijke Kring voor Oudheidkunde, Letteren, en Kunst van Mechelen/Bulletin du Cercle Archeologique, Litteraire, et Artistique de Malines
H & L & H — HLH. Zeitschrift fuer Heizung, Lueftung, Klimatechnik, Haustechnik
Handl & Shipp — Handling and Shipping [Later, Handling and Shipping Management]
Handl & Shipp Mgt — Handling and Shipping Management
Handl Chem Carcinog Lab Probl Saf — Handling Chemical Carcinogens in the Laboratory. Problems of Safety
Handl C Johans Foerb — Handlingar. Carl Johans Foerbundet
Handl Conveying Autom — Handling, Conveying, Automation
Handley Page Bull — Handley Page Bulletin
Handling Convey Automn — Handling, Conveying, and Automation
Handling Int — Handling International
Handl LandtbrVeck — Handlingar till Landtbruksveckan
Handl Nucl Inf Proc Symp — Handling of Nuclear Information. Proceedings of the Symposium
Handl Radiat Accid Proc Symp — Handling of Radiation Accidents. Proceedings of a Symposium
Handl Shipp Manage — Handling and Shipping Management
Handl St Namnd ByggnForsk — Handlingar. Statens Namnd for Byggnadsforskning
Handl Sven Forskningsinst Cem Betong K Tek Hoegsk Stockholm — Handlingar. Svenska Forskningsinstitutet foer Cement och Betong vid Kungliga Tekniska Hoegskolan i Stockholm
Handl Svenska ForskInst Cem Betong — Handlingar. Svenska Forskningsinstitutet for Cement och Betong
Handl T Kungl Krigsvet Akad — Handlingar och Tidskrift. Kungliga Krigsvetenskaps-Akademien
H & M — Hommes et Mondes
Hand Maatsch Gesch & Oudhdknd Gent — Handelingen der Maatschappij voor Geschiedenis en Oudheidkunde te Gent
H & M Mgmt — Hotel and Motel Management
H & N — Here and Now

Hand Ned Anthrop Vereen — Handelingen van de Nederlandsche Anthropologische Vereeniging
Hand Ned Indisch Natuurw Congr — Handelingen. Nederlandsch-Indisch Natuurwetenschappelijk Congres
Hand Ned Jur V — Handelingen. Nederlandse Juristen-Vereeniging
Hand Ned Nat En Geneesk Congr — Handelingen van het Nederlandsch Natuur- en Geneeskundig Congres
Hand Ned Tandheelk Genoot — Handelingen van het Nederlandsch Tandheelkundig Genootschap
Hand Ned TuinbRaad — Handelingen. Nederlandsche Tuinbouwraad
HandNFc — Handelingen. Nederlands Filologencongres
H & R — Humanisme et Renaissance
H & RI — Hotels and Restaurants International
H & S — Health and Safety
H & S — Health and Strength
H & S Mgmt — Handling and Shipping Management
Hand Surg — Hand Surgery
H & T — History and Theory
Hand Vereen Homoeop Geneesh Ned — Handelingen van de Vereeniging van Homoeopathische Geneesheeren in Nederland
Hand Vlaam Nat En Geneesk Congr — Handelingen van het Vlaamsch Natuur- en Geneeskundig Congres
Hand Vl Fc — Handelingen. Vlaamse Filologencongres
Hand VoedVeren Suid Afr — Handelinge van die Voedingvereniging van Suidelike Afrika
Handweaver — Handweaver and Craftsman
Hand Wewn — Handel Wewnetrzny
Handwk Zonder Grenzen — Handwerken Zonder Grenzen
Handw O — Handwerksordnung
Handyman — Family Handyman
Hanford Eng Dev Lab Rep HEDL TME — Hanford Engineering Development Laboratory. Report HEDL-TME
Han G — Hanauer Geschichtsblaetter
Hang L — Hanging Loose
Han Guk J Genet Eng — Han Guk Journal of Genetic Engineering
Han'guk Sikp'un Kwhak Hoechi Korea J Food Sci Technol — Han'guk Sikp'un Kwahak Hoechi. Korean Journal of Food Science and Technology
Hanji — Hanrei Jiho
Hann A — Hannoeverische Annalen fuer die Gesammte Heilkunde
Hannah Dairy Res Inst Rep — Hannah Dairy Research Institute. Report
Hannah Res — Hannah Research
Hannah Res Inst Rep — Hannah Research Institute. Report
Hann Archt Vr Z — Zeitschrift des Architekten- und Ingenieur-Vereins zu Hannover
Hannover Beytr Nutzen Vergnuegen — Hannoverische Beytraege zum Nutzen und Vergnuegen
Hannover Geschbl — Hannoversche Geschichtsblaetter
Hannover Mag — Hannoverisches Magazin worin kleine Abhandlungen, Gesamlet (Gesammelt) und Aufbewahret Sind
Hannover Partikushalle Niedersaechs Landtag — Hannover Partikushalle. Niedersaechsischer Landtag
Hannov FeuerwZtg — Hannoversche Feuerwehrzeitung
Hannov Geschbll — Hannoversche Geschichtsblaetter
Hann Rpfl — Hannoversche Rechtspflege
Hann Z Archt Vr — Zeitschrift des Architekten- und Ingenieur-Vereins zu Hannover
Hanomag Nachr — Hanomag-Nachrichten
Hanomag Trakt — Hanomag-Traktor
Hansard (C) — Hansard (Commons)
Hansard House Commons Off Rep — Hansard. House of Commons. Official Report
Hansard (L) — Hansard (Lords)
HANSB — Hanseniase
Hanseat Rechts U Gerichts Zeitsch — Hanseatische Rechts- und Gerichts-Zeitschrift
Hanseniase Resumos Not — Hanseniase. Resumos e Noticias
Hansenol Int — Hansenologia Internationalis
Hans G Bl — Hansische Geschichtsblaetter
Hans Gesch — Hansische Geschichtsblaetter
Hans Geschbl — Hansische Geschichtsblaetter
Hans Geschbll — Hansische Geschichtsblaetter
HansGZ — Hanseatische Gerichtszeitung
Hansische Gesch Bl — Hansische Geschichtsblaetter
Hans JV Bl — Hanseatisches Justizverwaltungsblatt
Hans Selye Symp Neuroendocrinol Stress — Hans Selye Symposia on Neuroendocrinology and Stress
HAnt — Hispania Antiqua
Hanta — Hanrei Taimuzu
Hant Ams — Hantes Amsoriay
Hanzaigaku Zasshi (Acta Criminol Med Leg Jpn) — Hanzaigaku Zasshi (Acta Criminologiae et Medicinae Legalis Japonica)
HAPG — Heidelberger Abhandlungen zur Philosophie und Ihrer Geschichte
HAPR — Homenaje al Profesor Paul Rivet [*Bogota*]
HAR — Hamburger Akademische Rundschau
Har — Harmonie
HAR — Harvard Journal on Legislation
HAR — Hebrew Annual Review
HAR — Humanities Association. Review
HarA — Harvard Advocate
Har Alum Bull — Harvard Alumni Bulletin
H Arb G — Heimarbeitsgesetz
Harbor Dent Log — Harbor Dental Log
Harbour — Australian Coal, Shipping, Steel, and the Harbour
Harbour & Shipp — Harbour and Shipping
Harburger Jahrb — Harburger Jahrbuch
Har Bus R — Harvard Business Review
Har Civ Ri LR — Harvard Civil Rights - Civil Liberties Law Review

Hardsyssels Aarb — Hardsyssels Aarbog
Hardware J — Hardware Journal
Hardware R — Hardware Retailing
Hardware Trade J — Hardware Trade Journal
Hardwood Rec — Hardwood Record
HAREA — Harefuah
Haref — Harefuah
Har Int LJ — Harvard International Law Journal
Har J Leg — Harvard Journal on Legislation
Harker Geol Soc J — Harker Geological Society. Journal
HarL — Harvard Library Bulletin
HARL — Hispamerica
Harl Arch Ms Teyl — Archives du Musee Teyler (Haarlem)
Harlem Hosp Bull (NY) — Harlem Hospital Bulletin (New York)
Harl Hosp Bull — Harlem Hospital Bulletin
Har LR — Harvard Law Review
Harmonika Jb — Harmonika-Jahrbuch
H A Ro A — Historisk Arbog for Roskilde Amt
Harokeach Haivri Heb Pharm (Sci Ed) — Harokeach Haivri. The Hebrew Pharmacist (Science Edition)
Harold L Lyon Arbor Lect — Harold L. Lyon Arboretum. Lecture
Harp — Harper's Magazine
Harp Ad Util Poult J — Harper Adams Utility Poultry Journal
Harp B — Harper's Bazaar
Harp Baz — Harper's Bazaar
Harper — Harper's Magazine
Harper Hosp Bull — Harper Hospital. Bulletin
Harpers — Harper's Magazine
Harper's Mag — Harper's New Monthly Magazine
Harpers Mon Mag — Harper's Monthly Magazine
Harpers Mthly — Harper's Monthly
Harpers New Mthly Mag — Harper's New Monthly Magazine
Harp MM — Harper's Monthly Magazine
Harp N — Harp News
Harp W — Harper's Weekly
Harris County Physician — Harris County Physician Newsletter
Harry G Armstrong Aerosp Med Res Lab Tech Rep AAMRL TR — Harry G. Armstrong Aerospace Medical Research Laboratory. Technical Report AAMRL-TR
Harry Steenbock Symp — Harry Steenbock Symposium
HarSemSer — Harvard Semitic Series
HarT — Harvard Theological Review
Hartfd Cou — Hartford Courant
Hartf Hosp Bull — Hartford Hospital. Bulletin
Hartford Hosp Bull — Hartford Hospital. Bulletin
Hartford Sem Rec — Hartford Seminary Record
Hartf Sem Rec — Hartford Seminary Record
Hartf Stud Ling — Hartford Studies in Linguistics
Har Theol Rev — Harvard Theological Review
Hartm Tds — Hartman's Tijdschrift ter Beoefening van het Administratieve Recht
Hart Q — Hartford Quarterly
Hart R — Hartwick Review
Harts Fuel Technol Manage — Hart's Fuel Technology and Management
Hart-Tech Mitt — Harterei-Technische Mitteilungen
HARU — Handbuch fuer Rundfunk und Fernsehen
Harv Ad — Harvard Advocate
Harv AIDS Inst Ser Gene Regul Hum Retroviruses — Harvard AIDS Institute Series on Gene Regulation of Human Retroviruses
Harvard A — Harvard Advocate
Harvard Archre Review — Harvard Architecture Review
Harvard BR — Harvard Business Review
Harvard Bsns R — Harvard Business Review
Harvard Busin R — Harvard Business Review
Harvard Bus R — Harvard Business Review
Harvard.Bus Rev — Harvard Business Review
Harvard Civil Rights - Civil Liberties Law R — Harvard Civil Rights - Civil Liberties Law Review
Harvard Civil Rights L Rev — Harvard Civil Rights - Civil Liberties Law Review
Harvard Coll Mus Comp Zoology Bull — Harvard College. Museum of Comparative Zoology. Bulletin
Harvard Coll Mus CZ An Rp — Harvard College. Museum of Comparative Zoology. Annual Report
Harvard Coll Mus C Z B — Harvard College. Museum of Comparative Zoology. Bulletin
Harvard Coll Mus C Z Mem — Harvard College. Museum of Comparative Zoology. Memoirs
Harvard Ed R — Harvard Educational Review
Harvard Educ R — Harvard Educational Review
Harvard Engl Stud — Harvard English Studies
Harvard Environ Law Rev — Harvard Environmental Law Review
Harvard Environmental Law R — Harvard Environmental Law Review
Harvard Forest Bull — Harvard Forest. Bulletin
Harvard Forest Pap — Harvard Forest Papers
Harvard Hist Stud — Harvard Historical Studies
Harvard Internat Law J — Harvard International Law Journal
Harvard Int LJ — Harvard International Law Journal
Harvard J Asiat Stud — Harvard Journal of Asiatic Studies
Harvard J Law and Public Policy — Harvard Journal of Law and Public Policy
Harvard J Legislation — Harvard Journal on Legislation
Harvard J on Legis — Harvard Journal on Legislation
Harvard Landscape Architect Monogr — Harvard Landscape Architecture Monographs
Harvard Law R — Harvard Law Review
Harvard Law Rev — Harvard Law Review
Harvard Lib Bul — Harvard Library Bulletin

Harvard Lib Bull — Harvard Library Bulletin
Harvard Libr Bull — Harvard Library Bulletin
Harvard L Rev — Harvard Law Review
Harvard Mag — Harvard Magazine
Harvard Med Alumni Bull — Harvard Medical Alumni Bulletin
Harvard Med Sch Health Let — Harvard Medical School. Health Letter
Harvard Mon Applied Sci — Harvard Monographs in Applied Science
Harvard Mthly — Harvard Monthly
Harvard Public Health Alumni Bull — Harvard Public Health Alumni Bulletin
Harvard Rev — Harvard Review
Harvard Slav Stud — Harvard Slavic Studies
Harvard Stud Class Philol — Harvard Studies in Classical Philology
Harvard Stud Cl Philol — Harvard Studies in Classical Philology
Harvard Stud Comp Lit — Harvard Studies in Comparative Literature
Harvard Theol R — Harvard Theological Review
Harvard Theol Rev — Harvard Theological Review
Harvard Th R — Harvard Theological Review
Harvard Univ B — Harvard University. Bulletin
Harvard Univ Bot Mus Leaflets — Harvard University. Botanical Museum Leaflets
Harvard Univ Dep Eng Publ — Harvard University. Department of Engineering. Publications
Harvard Univ Gray Herbarium Contr — Harvard University. Gray Herbarium. Contributions
Harvard Univ Harvard Soil Mech Ser — Harvard University. Harvard Soil Mechanics Series
Harvard Univ Mus Comp Zoology Bull — Harvard University. Museum of Comparative Zoology. Bulletin
Harvard Women's Law J — Harvard Women's Law Journal
Harv Asia — Harvard Journal of Asiatic Studies
Harv As Obs A — Annals of the Astronomical Observatory of Harvard College
Harv Books Biophys — Harvard Books in Biophysics
Harv Bus Re — Harvard Business Review
Harv Bus Rev — Harvard Business Review
Harv Bus Sch Alumni Assn Bul — Harvard Business School Alumni Association. Bulletin
Harv Civil Rights L Rev — Harvard Civil Rights - Civil Liberties Law Review
Harv Civ Rights - Civ Liberties Law Rev — Harvard Civil Rights - Civil Liberties Law Review
Harv Class Phil — Harvard Studies in Classical Philology
Harv CR-CLL — Harvard Civil Rights - Civil Liberties Law Review
Harv CR CL Law Rev — Harvard Civil Rights - Civil Liberties Law Review
Harv CR-CLL Rev — Harvard Civil Rights - Civil Liberties Law Review
HarvDBull — Harvard Divinity School. Bulletin
Harv Dent Alumni Bull — Harvard Dental Alumni Bulletin
Harv Div B — Harvard Divinity Bulletin
Harv East As Ser — Harvard East Asian Series
Harv Educ Rev — Harvard Educational Review
Harv Edu Re — Harvard Educational Review
Harv Environ Law Rev — Harvard Environmental Law Review
Harv Envtl L Rev — Harvard Environmental Law Review
Harvester in Aust — Harvester in Australia
Harvester Readings Hist Sci Philos — Harvester Readings in the History of Science and Philosophy
Harvest Q — Harvest Quarterly
Harvey Lect — Harvey Lectures
Harvey Lecture Ser — Harvey Lecture Series
Harv For Annu Rep — Harvard Forest. Annual Report
Harv For Bull — Harvard Forest. Bulletin
Harv For Pap — Harvard Forest. Papers
Harv Grad M — Harvard Graduates' Magazine
Harv Grad Mag — Harvard Graduates Magazine
Harv Int Law Rev — Harvard International Law Review
Harv Int L J — Harvard International Law Journal
Harv Int'l L Club Bull — Harvard International Law Club. Bulletin
Harv Int'l L Club J — Harvard International Law Club. Journal
Harv Int'l LJ — Harvard International Law Journal
Harv J Asia — Harvard Journal of Asiatic Studies
Harv J Asiatic Stud — Harvard Journal of Asiatic Studies
Harv JL and Pub Poly — Harvard Journal of Law and Public Policy
Harv J Leg — Harvard Journal on Legislation
Harv J Legis — Harvard Journal on Legislation
Harv J on Legis — Harvard Journal on Legislation
Harv Law R — Harvard Law Review
Harv Law Rev — Harvard Law Review
HarvLB — Harvard Library Bulletin
Harv Lib Bull — Harvard Library Bulletin
Harv Libr B — Harvard Library Bulletin
Harv Libr Bull — Harvard Library Bulletin
Harv L Lib Inf Bull — Harvard Law Library. Information Bulletin
Harv L R — Harvard Law Review
Harv L Rev — Harvard Law Review
Harv LS Bull — Harvard Law School Bulletin
Harv LS Rec — Harvard Law School. Record
Harv Mag — Harvard Magazine
Harv Med Alumni Bull — Harvard Medical Alumni Bulletin
Harv Med Sch Health Lett — Harvard Medical School. Health Letter
Harv Mem — Harvard Memoirs
Harv Mo — Harvard Monthly
Harv Pap Theoret Geogr — Harvard Papers in Theoretical Geography
Harv Pathophysiol Ser — Harvard Pathophysiology Series
Harv Public Health Alumni Bull — Harvard Public Health Alumni Bulletin
Harv R — Harvard Review
Harv Rev Psychiatry — Harvard Review of Psychiatry
Harv Sem Mon — Harvard Semitic Monographs
Harv Sem Ser — Harvard Semitic Series

Harv Ser Ukrain Stud — Harvard Series in Ukrainian Studies
Harv St — Harvard Studies in Classical Philology
Harv St Cla — Harvard Studies in Classical Philology
Harv St Cl Phil — Harvard Studies in Classical Philology
Harv Stud — Harvard Studies in Classical Philology
Harv Stud Class Philol — Harvard Studies in Classical Philology
Harv Teach Rec — Harvard Teachers Record
Harv Theol — Harvard Theological Review
Harv Theol R — Harvard Theological Review
Harv Theol Rev — Harvard Theological Review
Harv Th R — Harvard Theological Review
Harv Th Rev — Harvard Theological Review
HarvTR — Harvard Theological Review
Harv Univ Arnold Arbor J — Harvard University. Arnold Arboretum. Journal
Harv Univ Mus Comp Zool Bull — Harvard University. Museum of Comparative Zoology. Bulletin
Harv Univ Mus Comp Zool Spec Occas Publ — Harvard University. Museum of Comparative Zoology. Special Occasional Publication
Harv Univ Sch Public Health Dean's Rep — Harvard University. School of Public Health. Dean's Report
Harv Women LJ — Harvard Women's Law Journal
Har Women LR — Harvard Women's Law Review
Haryana Agric Univ J Res — Haryana Agricultural University. Journal of Research
Haryana J Agron — Haryana Journal of Agronomy
Haryana J Hort Sci — Haryana Journal of Horticulture Sciences
Harz Z — Harz Zeitschrift
HASB — Hefte des Archaeologischen Seminars der Universitaet Bern
Has Con LQ — Hastings Constitutional Law Quarterly
Has Int and Comp LR — Hastings International and Comparative Law Review
Hasler Mitt — Hasler-Mitteilungen
Hasler Rev — Hasler Review
Has LJ — Hastings Law Journal
HASSA — Hassadeh
Hast Cen St — Hastings Center. Studies
Hast Cent Rpt — Hastings Center. Report
Hast Cent St — Hastings Center. Studies
Hast Const LQ — Hastings Constitutional Law Quarterly
Hast Deering News — Hastings Deering News
Hastings Area Archaeol Pap — Hastings Area Archaeological Papers
Hastings Cent Rep — Hastings Center. Report
Hastings Cent Stud — Hastings Center. Studies
Hastings Const LQ — Hastings Constitutional Law Quarterly
Hastings Ctr Rept — Hastings Center. Report
Hastings E Suss Nat — Hastings and East Sussex Naturalist
Hastings Intl and Comp L Rev — Hastings International and Comparative Law Review
Hastings L J — Hastings Law Journal
Hast Law J — Hastings Law Journal
Hast LJ — Hastings Law Journal
HAT — Handbuch zum Alten Testament
HAT — Handelsblatt. Wirtschaftzeitung und Finanzzeitung
HATAA4 — Amino Acid and Nucleic Acid
Hatano Tob Exp Stn Jpn Monop Corp Spec Bull — Hatano Tobacco Experiment Station. Japan Monopoly Corporation. Special Bulletin
Hatcher Rev — Hatcher Review
H A Th — Historisk Arbog for Thy og Mors
HATS — Harvard Armenian Texts and Studies
HAUID — Han'guk Uikwahak
HAU J Res — HAU [*Haryana Agricultural University*] Journal of Research
HAUND — Hannover Uni
Hauptvortr Jahrestag Verb Dtsch Phys Ges — Hauptvortraege der Jahrestagung des Verbandes Deutscher Physikalischer Gesellschaften
Hauptvortr Tag Dtsch Physiol Ges — Hauptvortraege der Tagung der Deutschen Physiologische Gesellschaft
Hauptvortr Tag Phys Electron — Hauptvortraege. Tagung Physik und Elektronik
HAURBR — Encyclopedia of Urology
Hausm — Hausmusik
Hausmitt Jos Schneider — Hausmitteilungen Jos Schneider
Hausmus — Hausmusik
Haus Tech — Haus Technik
Haustech Bauphys Umwelttech — Haustechnik, Bauphysik, Umwelttechnik
Haustech Bauphys Umwelttech Gesund Ing — Haustechnik, Bauphysik, Umwelttechnik-Gesundheits-Ingenieur
Haus Tech Essen Vortragsveroeff — Haus der Technik-Essen-Vortragsveroeffentlichungen
Haustech Rundsch — Haustechnische Rundschau
Haus Tech-Vortrag-Veroeff — Haus der Technik-Vortrags-Veroeffentlichungen
Hauswirtsch U Wiss — Hauswirtschaft und Wissenschaft
Hausz VAW Erftwerk AG Alum — Hauszeitschrift der VAW und der Erftwerk AG fuer Aluminium
HAUTA — Hautarzt
Havana Bibl Nac R — Havana Biblioteca Nacional. Revista
Havana Univ Cienc Ser 4 Clenc Biol — Havana Universidad. Ciencias. Serie 4. Ciencias Biologicas
Havana Univ Cienc Ser 7 Geogr — Havana Universidad. Ciencias. Serie 7. Geografia
Havana Univ Cienc Ser 8 Invest Mar — Havana Universidad. Ciencias. Serie 8. Investigaciones Marinas
Havana Univ Tecnol Ser 10 Ing Hidraul — Havana Universidad. Tecnologia. Serie 10. Ingenieria Hidraulica
HAVC — Health Audiovisual On-line Catalog
Havforskningsinst Skr — Havsforskningsinstituets Skrift
HavL — Havre Libre [*Le Havre daily*]
Havsforskningsinst Skr Helsinki — Havsforskningsinstitutets Skrift (Helsinki)
HAW — Handbuch der Altertumswissenschaft

Haw — Hawaii Reports
Hawaii Ag Exp — Hawaii. Agricultural Experiment Station. Publications
Hawaii Agric Exp Sta Annual Rep — Hawaii Agricultural Experiment Station. Annual Report
Hawaii Agric Exp Sta Press Bull — Hawaii Agricultural Experiment Station. Press Bulletin
Hawaii Agric Exp Stn Agric Econ Bull — Hawaii. Agricultural Experiment Station. Agricultural Economics Bulletin
Hawaii Agric Exp Stn Bienn Rep — Hawaii. Agricultural Experiment Station. Biennial Report
Hawaii Agric Exp Stn Bull — Hawaii. Agricultural Experiment Station. Bulletin
Hawaii Agric Exp Stn Circ — Hawaii. Agricultural Experiment Station. Circular
Hawaii Agric Exp Stn Dep Pap — Hawaii Agricultural Experiment Station. Departmental Paper
Hawaii Agric Exp Stn Misc Pub — Hawaii. Agricultural Experiment Station. Miscellaneous Publication
Hawaii Agric Exp Stn Misc Publ — Hawaii. Agricultural Experiment Station. Miscellaneous Publication
Hawaii Agric Exp Stn Prog Notes — Hawaii. Agricultural Experiment Station. Progress Notes
Hawaii Agric Exp Stn Res Bull — Hawaii. Agricultural Experiment Station. Research Bulletin
Hawaii Agric Exp Stn Res Rep — Hawaii. Agricultural Experiment Station. Research Report
Hawaii Agric Exp Stn Spec Publ — Hawaii. Agricultural Experiment Station. Special Publication
Hawaii Agric Exp Stn Stn Prog Notes — Hawaii. Agricultural Experiment Station. Station Progress Notes
Hawaii Agric Exp Stn Tech Bull — Hawaii. Agricultural Experiment Station. Technical Bulletin
Hawaii Agric Exp Stn Tech Prog Rep — Hawaii. Agricultural Experiment Station. Technical Progress Report
Hawaii Agric Exp Stn Univ Hawaii Coll Agric Bull — Hawaii Agricultural Experiment Station. University of Hawaii College of Agriculture. Bulletin
Hawaii Agric Exp Stn Univ Hawaii Coll Agric Circ — Hawaii Agricultural Experiment Station. University of Hawaii College of Agriculture. Circular
Hawaii Agric Exp Stn Univ Hawaii Coll Agric Spec Publ — Hawaii Agricultural Experiment Station. University of Hawaii College of Agriculture. Special Publication
Hawaii Agric Exp Stn Univ Hawaii Coll Agric Stn Prog Notes — Hawaii Agricultural Experiment Station. University of Hawaii College of Agriculture. Station Progress Notes
Hawaii Agric Exp Stn Univ Hawaii Tech Prog Rep — Hawaii Agricultural Experiment Station. University of Hawaii. Technical Progress Report
Hawaiian For — Hawaiian Forester and Agriculturist
Hawaiian Forester Agric — Hawaiian Forester and Agriculturist
Hawaiian Hist Soc Pub — Hawaiian Historical Society. Papers
Hawaiian Hist Soc Rep — Hawaiian Historical Society. Annual Report
Hawaiian J Hist — Hawaiian Journal of History
Hawaiian Vol Obs — Hawaiian Volcano Observatory
Hawaii Archives Pub — Publications of the Archives of Hawaii
Hawaii B J — Hawaii Bar Journal
Hawaii BN — Hawaii Bar News
Hawaii Bsn — Hawaii Business
Hawaii Bus — Hawaii Business
Hawaii Dairy Newsl Hawaii Coop Ext Serv US Dep Agric — Hawaii Dairy Newsletter. Hawaii Cooperative Extension Service. US Department ofAgriculture
Hawaii Dent J — Hawaii Dental Journal
Hawaii Dep Land Nat Resour Div Water Land Dev Circ — Hawaii. Department of Land and Natural Resources. Division of Water and Land Development. Circular
Hawaii Dep Land Nat Resour Div Water Land Dev Rep — Hawaii. Department of Land and Natural Resources. Division of Water and Land Development. Report
Hawaii Div Hydrogr Bull — Hawaii. Division of Hydrography. Bulletin
Hawaii Div Water Land Dev Circ — Hawaii. Division of Water and Land Development. Circular
Hawaii Div Water Land Dev Rep — Hawaii. Division of Water and Land Development. Report
Hawaii Farm Sci — Hawaii Farm Science
Hawaii Food Process Hawaii Univ Coop Ext Serv — Hawaii Food Processor. Hawaii University. Cooperative Extension Service
Hawaii Food Technol News Hawaii Coop Ext Serv — Hawaii Food Technology News. Hawaii Cooperative Extension Service
Hawaii Inst Geophys Bienn Rep — Hawaii Institute of Geophysics. Biennial Report
Hawaii Inst Geophys Publ — Hawaii Institute of Geophysics. Publication
Hawaii Inst Geophys Rep HIG — Hawaii Institute of Geophysics. Report HIG
Hawaii Inst Trop Agric Hum Resour Res Ext Ser — Hawaii Institute of Tropical Agriculture and Human Resources. Research Extension Series
Hawaii J Hist — Hawaii Journal of History
Hawaii Lib Assn J — Hawaii Library Association. Journal
Hawaii Libr Assoc Newsl — Hawaii Library Association Newsletter
Hawaii Med J — Hawaii Medical Journal
Hawaii Med J Inter Isl Nurses Bull — Hawaii Medical Journal and Inter-Island Nurses' Bulletin
Hawaii Orchid J — Hawaii Orchid Journal
Hawaii Plant Mon — Hawaiian Planters' Monthly
Hawaii Plant Rec — Hawaiian Planters' Record
Hawaii Plrs' Rec — Hawaiian Planters' Record
Hawaii Shell News — Hawaiian Shell News
Hawaii Shell News (Honolulu) — Hawaiian Shell News (Honolulu)
Hawaii Sugar Plant Assoc Exp Stn Annu Rep — Hawaiian Sugar Planters' Association. Experiment Station. Annual Report
Hawaii Sugar Technol Rep — Hawaiian Sugar Technologists Reports
Hawaii Top Conf Part Phys Proc — Hawaii Topical Conference in Particle Physics. Proceedings

Hawaii Univ Coop Ext Serv Circ — Hawaii University. Cooperative Extension Service. Circular
Hawaii Univ Inst Geophys — Hawaii University. Institute of Geophysics. Report
Hawaii Univ Inst Geophys Contrib — Hawaii University. Institute of Geophysics. Contributions
Hawaii Univ Look Lab Oceanogr Eng Tech Rep — Hawaii University. Look Laboratory of Oceanographic Engineering. Technical Report
Hawaii Univ Sea Grant Prog Rep — Hawaii University. Sea Grant Program. Reports
Hawaii Unlv Water Resour Res Cent Annu Rep — Hawaii University. Water Resources Research Center. Annual Report
Hawaii Univ Water Resour Res Cent Tech Rep — Hawaii University. Water Resources Research Center. Technical Report
Hawaii Uni Water Resour Cent Tech Rep — Hawaii University. Water Resources Research Center. Technical Report
Hawai J Hist — Hawaiian Journal of History
Haw App — Hawaii Appellate Reports
HAWAT — Hebraeisches und Aramaeisches Woerterbuch zum Alten Testament
HAWFA — Hawaii Farm Science
HAWIA — Hauswirtschaft und Wissenschaft
Hawker Siddeley Tech Rev — Hawker Siddeley Technical Review
Ha Wpr — Hallisches Winckelmannsprogramme
Haw Rev Stat — Hawaii Revised Statutes
Haw Sess Laws — Session Laws. Hawaii
Haydn-Stud — Haydn-Studien
Haydn Yb — Haydn Yearbook
Haygaz Hayag Handes — Haygazean Hayagitagan Handes
HAYOE7 — Ocean Research
Hazard Assess Chem — Hazard Assessment of Chemicals
Hazard Cargo Bull — Hazardous Cargo Bulletin
Hazard Ind Solid Waste Test Symp — Hazardous and Industrial Solid Waste Testing. Symposium
Hazard Ind Waste Manage Test Symp — Hazardous and Industrial Waste Management and Testing. Symposium
Hazard Ind Wastes Proc Mid Atl Ind Waste Conf — Hazardous and Industrial Wastes. Proceedings of the Mid-Atlantic Industrial Waste Conference
Hazard Mater Control — Hazardous Materials Control
Hazard Mater Manage J — Hazardous Materials Management Journal
Hazardous Cargo Bull — Hazardous Cargo Bulletin
Hazards Bull — Hazards Bulletin
Hazards Chem Lab — Hazards in the Chemical Laboratory
Hazard Toxic Subst — Hazardous and Toxic Substances
Hazard Toxic Wastes Technol Manage Health Eff — Hazardous and Toxic Wastes. Technology, Management, and Health Effects
Hazard Waste — Hazardous Waste
Hazard Waste Hazard Mater — Hazardous Waste and Hazardous Materials
Hazard Waste Train Bul Sup — Hazard Waste Training Bulletin for Supervisors
Haz Bull — Hazards Bulletin
HAZINF — Hazardous Chemicals Information and Disposal
Haz P Reg — Hazard's Pennsylvania Register
Haz Rev — Hazards Review
HB — Handelsblatt
HB — Handelsblatt Databank
HB — Hebraeische Bibliographie
HB — Het Boek
HB — Historical Bulletin
HB — Historische Bibliothek
HB — Hojskolebladet
HB — Horn Book
HB — Hub. Hay River
HB — Human Behavior
HB — Human Biology
HBA — Hamburger Beitraege zur Archaeologie
HBA — Historiografia y Bibliografia Americanistas
HBalt — Hispania (Baltimore)
HB Arch — Handbuch der Archaeologie
HbAT — Handbuch zum Alten Testament
Hb AW — Handbuch der Altertumswissenschaft
HBBIAD — Harvard Books in Biophysics
Hb Colon Soc MA — Handbook of the Colonial Society of Massachusetts
HBD — Detailhandel Magazine
HBd — Haarlemsch Bijdragen
HBD — Harper's Bible Dictionary
HBD — Human Biology (Detroit)
Hb d G — Handbuch der Deutschen Gegenwartsliteratur
Hb d G A — Handbuch der Gesamten Arbeitsmedizin
Hb d Ps — Handbuch der Psychologie
Hb d W — Handbuch der Wirtschaftswissenschaften
HBG — Hospital Buyer's Guide
HBGDJ — Hamburger Beitraege zur Geschichte der Deutschen Juden
Hb Hist St — Handbuch der Historischen Staetten Deutschlands
Hb Inst Orth — Handbook. Institute of Orthopaedics
HBITDG — Handbuch der Bakteriellen Infektionen bei Tieren
HBJ Mth — HBJ [*Hypothec Bank of Japan*] Monthly
HBK — Herders Bibelkommentar
Hb KG — Handbuch der Kirchengeschichte
HB Kr I — Hamburger Beitraege zur Philosophie des Kritischen Idealismus
H Bl — Historische Blaetter
HBL — Hofmannsthal Blaetter
H Bl HVB — Heimatblaetter des Historischen Vereins Bamberg
HBLS — Historisch-Biographisches Lexikon der Schweiz
HBM — Die Haghe. Bijdragen en Mededeelingen
HBMB — Holy Blossom Men's Bulletin
Hb Mid Amer Ind — Handbook of Middle American Indians
Hb Miet R — Handbuch des Gesamten Miet und Raumrechts

HBN — Hamburger Beitraege zur Numismatik
Hb N Amer Ind — Handbook of North American Indians
Hb Norg Byggforsk Inst — Handbok. Norges Byggforskningsinstitut
Hb NT — Handbuch zum Neuen Testament
H Bo — Hethitische Keilschrifttexte aus Boghazkoei in Umschrift
Hb Palaeozool — Handbuch der Palaeozoologie
Hb Psych — Handbuch der Psychologie
HBR — Harvard Business Review
HBR — Harvard Business Review Online
HBR — Heidelberger Beitraege zur Romanistik
HBR — New York Herald Tribune Book Review
HBS — Henry Bradshaw Society
HBSA — Hjalmar Bergman Samfundet Arsbok
Hb SAE — Society of Automotive Engineers. Handbook
Hb S Amer Ind — Handbook of South American Indians
HBSN — Historic Brass Society Newsletter
HBSt — Hefte zum Bibelstudium
HBTF-A — Habiter
H Bull — Heart Bulletin
HBV — Hessische Blaetter fuer Volkskunde
HBVk — Hessische Blaetter fuer Volkskunde
HBZ — Hamburger Beitraege zur Zeitgeschichte
HbzAT — Handbuch zum Alten Testament
HC — Hand-Commentar zum Neuen Testament
HC — Hellenisme Contemporain
HC — Hessische Chronik
HC — Historicky Casopis
HC — Hollins Critic
HC — Hombre y Cultura
HC — Horn Call
HC — Hristianskoe Ctenie
HCA — Helvetica Chirurgica Acta
HCACA — Helvetica Chimica Acta
HCAIEJ — Health Care Instrumentation
HCal — Hispania (Stanford, California)
HCATA — Helvetica Chirurgica Acta
HCAUA — Handling, Conveying, Automation
HCF — Healthcare Financing Review
HCFA Rev — Health Care Financing Review
HCH — Handbook of Church History
HChA — Helvetica Chimica Acta
H Ch A — Helvetica Chirurgica Acta
HCHED7 — Specialist Periodical Reports. Heterocyclic Chemistry
H Ch I — Handbuch der Chaldischen Inschriften. Archiv fuer Orientforschung.
　Beiheft
Hchl — Hochland
HCHY — Hovering Craft and Hydrofoil
HCI — Human Cancer Immunology
HCIND5 — Health Communications and Informatics
H Ci W — Handbuecherei des Christen in der Welt
HCM — Health Care Management Review
HCMR — Health Care Management Review
HCN — Hart Crane Newsletter
HCO — Histoire des Cinciles Oecumeniques
HCompL — Hebrew Computational Linguistics
H Con — Histoire de Constantinople Depuis le Regne de l'Ancien Justin Jusqua la
　fin del'Empire
HCP — History in Christian Perspective
HCPB — Hodder Christian Paperbacks
HCR — Hoja (Costa Rica)
HCR — Horeca Info
HCR — Hotel and Catering Review
HCR — Human Communication Research
HCRCA — Harvard Civil Rights - Civil Liberties Law Journal
HCRE — Human Communications Research
HCS — Health Care Supervisor
HCS — Herald of Christian Science
HCSM — Histoire. Congregation de Saint-Maur
HCSTA — Hastings Center. Studies
HCT — Health Care Strategic Management
HCT — Historical Commentary on Thucydides
HCW — Hefte zur Christlichen Welt
HCWe — Heraut van de Christelijke Wetenschap
HC Wkly Inf Bull — House of Commons Weekly Information Bulletin
HCWSEN — Hammersmith Cardiology Workshop Series
HD — Harpsichord
HD — Hechos y Dichos
HD — Homo Dei
HD — Human Development
HdA — Handbuch der Altertumswissenschaft
HdA — Handbuch der Archaeologie
HDA Bull — H.D.A. (High Duty Alloys, Ltd.) Bulletin
HDAC — Homenaje al Doctor Alfonso Gaso [Mexico]
Hd Arch — Handbuch der Archaeologie
Hd AW — Handbuch der Altertumswissenschaft
HDB — Harvard Divinity Bulletin
Hdb Archaeol — Handbuch der Archaeologie
Hdb It Dial — Handbuch der Italischen Dialekte
HDBLA2 — Hidrobiologia
HDC — Histoire de la Democratie Chretienne
HDEG — Union List of Higher Degree Theses in Australian Libraries
HDEKM — Handbuch der Deutschen Evangelischen Kirchenmusik
H Dem — Hier et Demain
HDF — Histoire des Dioceses de France
HDG — Handbuch der Dogmengeschichte

HDGDD6 — Bulletin. Faculty of School Education. Hiroshima University. Part II
HDGHA — Hiroshima Daigaku Genbaku Hoshano Igaku Kenkyusho Nenpo
HDGKDR — Bulletin. Faculty of School Education. Hiroshima University. Part I
HDIEO — Histoire du Droit et des Institutions de l'Eglise en Occident
HDIZA — Medical Journal. Hiroshima University
Hd Jb — Heidelberger Jahrbuecher
HDKKA — Hokkaido Daigaku Kogakubu Kenkyu Hokoku
HDL — Handbuch der Deutschen Literaturgeschichte
HDLYDQ — Annual Research Reviews. Hodgkin's Disease and the Lymphomas
HDM — Handwoerterbuch des Deutschen Maerchens
HdO — Handbuch der Orientalistik
HdP — Hora de Poesia
Hdr A — Hardsyssels Arbog
HDREDU — HLA and Disease Registry
HDSA — Harvard Divinity School. Annual
Hds Aa — Hardsyssels Aarbog
HDSB — Harvard Divinity School. Bulletin
HDStW — Handwoerterbuch der Sozialwissenschaften
HDTYA — Heredity
Hdwd Rec — Hardwood Record
HDWSG — Handbuch der Deutschen Wirtschafts- und Sozialgeschichte
HDW Werkztg — Howaldtswerke Deutsche Werft. Aktiengesellschaft. Hamburg und
　Kiel. Werkzeitung
HDZ — Hrvatski Dijalektoloski Zbornik
HDZb — Hrvatski Dijalektoloski Zbornik
HE — Greek Anthology. Hellenistic Epigrams
HE — Handbooks in Economics
HE — Hare Express. Fort Good Hope
He — Hellweg. Wochenschrift fuer Deutsche Kunst
He — Henceforth
HE — Hethitisches Elementarbuch
HE — Histoire de l'Eglise
HE — Historia de Espana
HE — Human Events
HEADA — Headache
Headache Meet Ital Headache Soc — Headache. Meeting of the Italian Headache
　Society
Headline Ser — Headline Series
Head Neck — Head and Neck. Journal for the Sciences and Specialties of the
　Head and Neck
Head Neck Surg — Head and Neck Surgery
Head Nec Surg — Head and Neck Surgery
Head Teachers' R — Head Teachers' Review
HEAHB — Health
Heal Commun — Health Communication
Heal Ed Mon — Health Education Monographs
Heal Light — Healing Light
Health — Health Law in Canada
Health Aff — Health Affairs
Health Aff (Millwood) — Health Affairs (Millwood, Virginia)
Health Aff (Pa) — Health Affairs (Philadelphia)
Health & Med — Health and Medicine
Health Aspects Chem Saf Interim Doc — Health Aspects of Chemical Safety.
　Interim Document
Health Bul — Health Bulletin
Health Bull — Health Bulletin
Health Bull (Edinb) — Health Bulletin (Edinburgh)
Healthcare — Healthcare Marketing Report
Health Care Can — Health Care in Canada
Health Care Dimen — Health Care Dimensions
Health Care Educ — Health Care Education
Health Care Financing R — Health Care Financing Review
Healthcare Financ Manage — Healthcare Financial Management
Health Care Financ Rev — Health Care Financing Review
Health Care Financ Trends — Health Care Financing Trends
Health Care Instrum — Health Care Instrumentation
Health Care Law Newsl — Health Care Law Newsletter
Health Care Manag — Hli Health Care Manager
Health Care Manage Rev — Health Care Management Review
Health Care Manag Sci — Health Care Management Science
Health Care Mark Target Market — Health Care Marketer and Target Market
Health Care Newsl — Health Care Newsletter
Health Care Plan & Mkt — Health Care Planning and Marketing
Health Care Plann Market — Health Care Planning and Marketing
Health Care Secur Saf Manage — Health Care Security and Safety Management
Health Care Strateg Manage — Health Care Strategic Management
Health Care Superv — Health Care Supervisor
Health Care Syst — Health Care Systems
Health Care Wk — Health Care Week
Health Care Women Int — Health Care for Women, International
Healthc Comput Commun — Healthcare Computing and Communications
Healthc Executive — Healthcare Executive
Healthc Forum — Healthcare Forum Journal
Health Commun Inf — Health Communications and Informatics
Health Commun Informatics — Health Communications and Informatics
Health Congr R Soc Health Pap — Health Congress. Royal Society for the
　Promotion of Health. Papers
Health Congr R Soc Health Pap Discuss — Health Congress. Royal Society of
　Health. Papers for Discussion
Healthc Online — Healthcare Online
Health Cost Manage — Health Cost Management
Healthc Prot Manage — Healthcare Protection Management
Health Econ — Health Economics
Health Ed — Health Education
Health Ed J — Health Education Journal

Health Educ — Health Education
Health Educ — Health Education Journal
Health Educ Assoc NSW Newsl — Health Education Association of New South Wales. Newsletter
Health Educ Bull — Health Education Bulletin
Health Educ J — Health Education Journal
Health Educ Monogr — Health Education Monographs
Health Educ Q — Health Education Quarterly
Health Educ Q Suppl — Health Education Quarterly. Supplement
Health Educ Rep — Health Education Reports
Health Educ Welfare Publ Natl Inst Occup Saf Health US — Health, Education, and Welfare Publication. National Institute for Occupational Safety and Health (United States)
Health Expect — Health Expectations
Health Foods Bus — Health Foods Business
Health Hum Rights — Health and Human Rights
Health Hyg — Health and Hygiene
Health Ind — Health Industry Today
Health Inspectors Conf — Annual Conference of Health Inspectors of New South Wales
Health Insur Stat — Health Insurance Statistics
Health Lab — Health Laboratory Science
Health Lab Sc — Health Laboratory Science
Health Lab Sci — Health Laboratory Science
Health Law Proj Libr Bull — Health Law Project Library Bulletin
Health L Can — Health Law in Canada
Health Libr Rev — Health Libraries Review
Health Manage Forum — Health Management Forum
Health Manage Q — Health Management Quarterly
Health Manpow Lit — Health Manpower Literature
Health Manpow Rep — Health Manpower Report [*Later, Health Planning and Manpower Report*]
Health Mark Q — Health Marketing Quarterly
Health Med Care Serv Rev — Health and Medical Care Services Review
Health Mkt Q — Health Marketing Quarterly
Health NSW — Health in New South Wales
Health Officers J — Health Officers' Journal
Health-PAC Bull — Health-PAC [*Policy Advisory Center*] Bulletin
Health Perspect — Health Perspectives [*Later, Consumer Health Perspectives*]
Health Perspect Issues — Health Perspectives and Issues
Health Phys — Health Physics
Health Phys (Tokyo) — Health Physics (Tokyo)
Health Plann Manpower Rep — Health Planning and Manpower Report
Health Plann Manpow Rep — Health Planning and Manpower Report
Health Policy Educ — Health Policy and Education
Health Policy Q — Health Policy Quarterly
Health Popul Perspect Issues — Health and Population Perspectives and Issues
Health Pract Physician Assist — Health Practitioner. Physician Assistant
Health Prog — Health Progress
Health Promot Internation — Health Promotion International
Health Psychol — Health Psychology
Health Rep — Health Reports
Health Risk Anal Proc Life Sci Symp — Health Risk Analysis. Proceedings. Life Sciences Symposium
Health Saf Bull — Health and Safety Bulletin
Health Saf Ind Commer — Health and Safety in Industry and Commerce
Health Saf Lab Tech Pap (UK) — Health and Safety Laboratories. Technical Paper (United Kingdom)
Health Saf Work — Health and Safety at Work
Health Sci Rev — Health Science Review
Health Serv — Health Services Report
Health Serv J — Health Service Journal
Health Serv Manager — Health Services Manager
Health Serv Manpow Rev — Health Services Manpower Review
Health Serv Ment Health Adm US Health Rep — Health Services and Mental Health Administration (United States). Health Reports
Health Serv Rep — Health Service Reports
Health Serv Res — Health Services Research
Health Serv Res Notes — Health Services Research Notes
Health Social Serv J — Health and Social Service Journal
Health Soc Serv J — Health and Social Service Journal
Health Soc Work — Health and Social Work
Health Technol — Health Technology
Health Technol Assess — Health Technology Assessment
Health Technol Assess Rep — Health Technology Assessment Reports
Health (US) — Health Crisis 2000 (United States)
Health Values — Health Values. Health Behavior, Education and Promotion
Health Visit — Health Visitor
Health Welfare Stat — Health and Welfare Statistics
Hear Aid J — Hearing Aid Journal
Hear Aid Jnl — Hearing Aid Journal
Hearing N — Hearing News
Hear Instrum — Hearing Instruments
Hear Rehab Quart — Hearing Rehabilitation Quarterly
Hear Res — Hearing Research
Hearsts Int Cosmopol — Hearst's International. Cosmopolitan
Hearst's M — Hearst's Magazine
Heart Am Annu Gas Meas Inst — Heart of America Annual Gas Measurement Institute
Heart and Lung — Heart and Lung. Journal of Critical Care
Heart Br Card Soc Online — Heart. British Cardiac Society. Online [*electronic publication*]
Heart Bull — Heart Bulletin
Heart Cent Bull St Francis Hosp (Roslyn NY) — Heart Center Bulletin. St. Francis Hospital (Roslyn, New York)

Heart Dis — Heart Disease
Heart Fail Rev — Heart Failure Reviews
Heart Funct Metab Proc Int Meet Int Study Group Res Card Meta — Heart Function and Metabolism. Proceedings of the International Meeting of the International Study Group for Research in Cardiac Metabolism
Heart Lung — Heart and Lung. Journal of Critical Care
Heart Muscle Pump Proc Workshop Contract Behav Heart — Heart. Muscle and Pump. Proceedings. Workshop on Contractile Behavior of the Heart
Hearts Heart Like Organs — Hearts and Heart-Like Organs
Heart Surg Forum — Heart Surgery Forum
Heart Vessels Suppl — Heart and Vessels. Supplement
HEAS — Harvard East Asian Series
Heat — Heating and Ventilating Engineer
Heat Air Cond Contr — Heating and Air Conditioning Contractor
Heat Air Condit — Heating and Air Conditioning
Heat Air Condit Contractor — Heating and Air Conditioning Contractor
Heat Air Condit J — Heating and Air Conditioning Journal
Heat Air Condit Refrig — Heating, Air Conditioning, and Refrigeration
Heat Air Condit Sh Metal Contractor — Heating, Air Conditioning, Sheet Metal Contractor
Heat Air Cond J — Heating and Air Conditioning Journal
Heat Air Cond Refrig — Heating, Air Conditioning, and Refrigeration
Heat Air Treatm Engr — Heating and Air Treatment Engineer
Heat and Air Cond J — Heating and Air Conditioning Journal
Heat & Ven — Heating and Ventilating Magazine
Heat & Vent — Heating and Ventilating
Heat and Vent Eng — Heating and Ventilating Engineer
Heat & Vent Engr — Heating and Ventilating Engineer
Heat Biblphy — Heat Bibliography. Heat Division (Mechanical Engineering Research Laboratory) National Engineering Laboratory [*Edinburgh*]
Heat Combust Equip News — Heating/Combustion Equipment News
Heat Cool Pip — Heating, Cooling, and Piping
Heat Eng — Heat Engineering
Heat Engng — Heat Engineering
Heat Exch Journ Int Inst Fr Combust Energ — Heat Exchangers. Journees Internationales de l'Institut Francais des Combustibles et de l'Energie
Heating & Air Conditioning Jnl — Heating and Air Conditioning Journal
Heating Piping — Heating, Piping, and Air Conditioning
Heating Piping Air Cond — Heating/Piping/Air Conditioning
Heat Manage — Heat and Management
Heat Manage Pollut Control — Heat Management and Pollution Control
Heat Mass Transfer Australas Conf — Heat and Mass Transfer. Australasian Conference
Heaton Wks J — Heaton Works Journal
Heat Pip Air Condit — Heating, Piping, and Air Conditioning
Heat Piping Air Cond — Heating, Piping, and Air Conditioning
Heat Piping Air Cond (Tokyo) — Heating Piping and Air Conditioning (Tokyo)
Heat Pipng — Heating, Piping, and Air Conditioning
Heat Pumps Energy Savers Process Ind — Heat Pumps. Energy Savers for the Process Industries
Heat Pwr Engng Toronto — Heat and Power Engineering (Toronto)
Heat Pwr Engng Wash — Heat and Power Engineering (Washington)
Heat Recovery Syst — Heat Recovery Systems
Heat Recovery Syst CHP — Heat Recovery Systems and CHP. Combined Heat and Power
Heat Resist Mater Proc Int Conf — Heat-Resistant Materials. Proceedings. International Conference
Heat Sanit Age — Heating and Sanitary Age
Heat Technol — Heat Technology
Heat Technol (Bologna) — Heat and Technology (Bologna)
Heat Technol (Dresher Pa) — Heat Technology (Dresher, Pennsylvania)
Heat Technol Pisa — Heat and Technology (Pisa)
Heat Top — Heating Topics
Heat Transfer & Fluid Flow Dig — Heat Transfer and Fluid Flow Digest
Heat Transfer Electron Equip — Heat Transfer in Electronic Equipment
Heat Transfer Eng — Heat Transfer Engineering
Heat Transfer Engng — Heat Transfer Engineering
Heat Transfer Fluid Flow Nucl Syst — Heat Transfer and Fluid Flow in Nuclear Systems
Heat Transfer Fluid Flow Rotating Mach Int Symp Transp Phenom — Heat Transfer and Fluid Flow in Rotating Machinery. International Symposium on Transport Phenomena
Heat Transfer Fluid Mech Inst Prepr Pap — Heat Transfer and Fluid Mechanics Institute. Preprints of Papers
Heat Transfer Fluid Mech Inst Proc — Heat Transfer and Fluid Mechanics Institute. Proceedings
Heat Transfer Geophys Media Natl Heat Transfer Conf — Heat Transfer in Geophysical Media. National Heat Transfer Conference
Heat Transfer High Technol Power Eng Proc Semin — Heat Transfer in High Technology and Power Engineering. Proceedings of the Seminar
Heat Transfer Int Heat Transfer Conf — Heat Transfer. International Heat Transfer Conference
Heat Transfer - Japan Res — Heat Transfer. Japanese Research
Heat Transfer Jap Res — Heat Transfer. Japanese Research
Heat Transfer Jpn Res — Heat Transfer. Japanese Research
Heat Transfer Res — Heat Transfer Research
Heat Transfer Sov Res — Heat Transfer. Soviet Research
Heat Transfer Surv — Heat Transfer Survey
Heat Transfer Unsteady Flows Natl Heat Transfer Conf — Heat Transfer in Unsteady Flows. National Heat Transfer Conference
Heat Treat — Heat Treating
Heat Treat Forg — Heat Treating and Forging
Heat Treat J — Heat Treatment Journal
Heat Treatm — Heat Treatment
Heat Treatm Bull — Heat Treatment Bulletin

Heat Treat Met — Heat Treatment of Metals
Heat Treat Met (Beijing) — Heat Treatment of Metals (Beijing)
Heat Treat Met (China) — Heat Treatment of Metals (China)
Heat Treatm J — Heat Treatment Journal
Heat Treat Proc Int Heat Treat Conf — Heat Treatment. Proceedings of the International Heat Treatment Conference
Heat Treat Rev — Heat Treat Review
Heat Vent — Heating and Ventilating
Heat Vent Air Condit Guide — Heating, Ventilating, Air Conditioning Guide
Heat Vent Eng — Heating and Ventilating Engineer
Heat Vent Eng J Air Cond — Heating and Ventilating Engineer and Journal of Air Conditioning
Heat Vent Engr — Heating and Ventilating Engineer
Heat Vent Engr J Air Condit — Heating and Ventilating Engineer and Journal of Air Conditioning
Heat Vent Equip Dig — Heating and Ventilating Equipment Digest
Heat Vent Mag — Heating and Ventilating Magazine
Heat Ventn — Heating and Ventilation
Heat Vent News — Heating and Ventilating News
Heat Vent Res — Heating and Ventilating Research
Heat Vent Rev — Heating and Ventilating Review
Heaven B — Heaven Bone
Heavy Flavor Electroweak Theory Proc Int Symp — Heavy Flavor and Electroweak Theory. Proceedings of the International Symposium
Heavy Ion Collisions Energ Coulomb Barrier Proc Workshop — Heavy Ion Collisions at Energies near the Coulomb Barrier. Proceedings. Workshop
Heavy Ion Inertial Fusion Proc Int Symp — Heavy Ion Inertial Fusion. Proceedings. International Symposium
Heavy Ion Phys Today Tomorrow Proc Adriat Int Conf Nucl Phys — Heavy-Ion Physics Today and Tomorrow. Proceedings. Adriatic International Conference on Nuclear Physics
Heavy Ions Nucl At Phys Proc Mikolajki Summer Sch Nucl Phys — Heavy Ions in Nuclear and Atomic Physics. Proceedings. Mikolajki Summer School on Nuclear Physics
Heavy Met Environ — Heavy Metals in the Environment
Heavy Met Environ Int Conf 4th — Heavy Metals in the Environment. International Conference. 4th
Heavy Truck Equip N — Heavy Truck Equipment News
HEA Yb — H.E.A. (Horticultural Education Association) Year Book
HEA Yearb — HEA [Horticultural Education Association] Yearbook
He B — Homilectica et Biblica
Hebbel-Jahrb — Hebbel-Jahrbuch
Hebd Chim — Hebdomadaire de la Chimie
HEBIS-BIB — Hessische Bibliographie
Heb Med J — Hebrew Medical Journal
Heb Pharm — Hebrew Pharmacist
Heb Physn — Hebrew Physician
Hebr — Hebraica (Chicago)
Hebrew Union Coll Annu — Hebrew Union College Annual
Hebrew Univ (Jerusalem) — Hebrew University (Jerusalem)
Hebrew U St — Hebrew University. Studies in Literature
Hebridean Nat — Hebridean Naturalist
HebrUCA — Hebrew Union College. Annual
Heb St — Hebrew Student
Heb Tech Coll (Haifa) Sci Publ — Hebrew Technical College (Haifa). Scientific Publications
HEBUA — Heart Bulletin
Heb Un Coll Annu — Hebrew Union College Annual
Hec — Hecate
HEC — History of the English Church
HECL — Histoire Ecclesiastique et Civile de Lorraine
HECLINET — Health Care Literature Information Network
Hector Obs Bull — Hector Observatory Bulletin
HED — Health Devices
HeD — Hier et Demain
Hedend Letteroefen — Hedendaagsche Letteroefeningen
Hedeselsk Tidsskr — Hedeselskabets Tidsskrift
HEDJ — Health Education Journal
HEDO — Health Education
HEDQ — Health Education Quarterly
HEdR — Harvard Educational Review
HEDU — Health Education. Newsletter
HEDW — Health Education (Washington)
Hedw — Hedwigia. Notizblatt fuer Kryptogamische Studien, Nebst Repertorium fuer Kryptog. Literatur
HEE — Healthcare Executive
Hee — Historia Ecclesiastica de Espana
HEEMA — Health Education Monographs
HEENA — Heat Engineering
HEFOA — Hebezeuge und Foerdermittel
Hefte A Bern — Hefte des Archaeologischen Seminars der Universitaet Bern
Hefte Inst Wasser Boden Lufthy Bundesgesundheitsamtes — Hefte. Institut fuer Wasser-, Boden-, und Lufthygiene des Bundesgesundheitsamtes
Hefte Unfallheilkd — Hefte zur Unfallheilkunde
Heft Unfallheilk — Hefte zur Unfallheilkunde
HEG — Handbook of Exploration Geochemistry
HEG — Handbuch der Europaeischen Geschichte
Hegel-Jrbh — Hegel-Jahrbuch
Hegel-Stud — Hegel-Studien
HEH — Hvem er Hvem
HEHUA — Herba Hungarica
HEHYDD — Health and Hygiene
HEI — Handelsreiziger
Heid Ak Abh — Abhandlungen der Heidelberger Akademie der Wissenschaften. Philosophisch-Historische Klasse

Heid Ak Sb — Sitzungsberichte der Heidelberger Akademie der Wissenschaften. Philosophisch-Historische Klasse
Heidelb Betr Mineral Petrogr — Heidelberger Beitraege zur Mineralogie und Petrographie
Heidelb Colloq Spin Glasses Proc Colloq — Heidelberger Colloquium on Spin Glasses. Proceedings of a Colloquium
Heidelberg Akad Wiss Math Naturwiss Kl Sitzungsber — Heidelberger Akademie der Wissenschaften. Mathematisch-Naturwissenschaftliche Klasse. Sitzungsberichte
Heidelberger Beitr Mineralogie u Petrographie — Heidelberger Beitrage zur Mineralogie und Petrographie
Heidelberger Jahrb — Heidelberger Jahrbuecher
Heidelberger Klin Ann — Heldelberger Klinische Annalen
Heidelberg Fremdenbl — Heidelberger Fremdenblatt
Heidelberg Jb — Heidelberger Jahrbuecher
Heidelberg Jb Philol Hist Lit & Kst — Heidelbergische Jahrbuecher fuer Philologie, Historie, Literatur, und Kunst
Heidelb Geogr Arb — Heidelberger Geographische Arbeiten
Heidelb Gespraeche — Heidelberger Gespraeche
Heidelb Jahrb — Heidelberger Jahrbuecher
Heidelb News — Heidelberg News
Heidelb News Br Edn — Heidelberg News. British Edition
Heidelb Sci Libr — Heidelberg Science Library
Heidelb Taschenb — Heidelberger Taschenbuecher
HeidJb — Heidelberger Jahrbuecher
Heidl Nt Md Vh — Verhandlungen des Naturhistorisch-Medicinischen Vereins zu Heidelberg
Heidl Vh Nt Md — Verhandlungen des Naturhistorisch-Medicinischen Vereins zu Heidelberg
Heid Sitzb — Heidelberger Akademie der Wissenschaften. Sitzungsberichte
HEIG — Handbook of Environmental Isotope Geochemistry
Heil Gewuerz-Pflanz — Heil Gewuerz-Pflanzen
Heilige Kst — Heilige Kunst. Mitgliedsgabe des Kunstvereins der Dioezese Rottenburg
HeilL — Heilige Land
Heilpaedagog Forsch — Heilpaedagogische Forschung
Heilpaed For — Heilpaedagogische Forschung
Heil St — Heiligenkreuzer Studien
Heimatb Dt Russl — Heimatbund der Deutschen aus Russland
Heimatbl Siegkreises — Heimatblaetter des Siegkreisis
Heimatb Ostumsiedler — Heimatbuch der Ostumsiedler
Heimatfreund Erzgebirge — Heimatfreund fuer das Erzgebirge
Heimatknd Bl Kreis Tuebingen — Heimatkundliche Blaetter fuer den Kreis Tuebingen
Heimatkund Arbeitsgemein Nordschles — Schriften der Heimatkundlichen Arbeitsgemeinschaft fuer Nordschleswig
Heimatver Weil Stadt Ber & Mitt — Heimatverein Weil der Stadt, Berichte, und Mitteilungen
HeineJ — Heine-Jahrbuch
Heine-Jahrb — Heine-Jahrbuch
Heinkel Werkztg — Heinkel Werkzeitung
Heinolan Kaupunginmus Julkaisuja — Heinolan Kaupunginmuseon Julkaisuja
Heintz Vulcan — Heintz Vulcanizer
Heiz Lueft — Heizung und Lueftung
Heiz Lueft Haustech — Heizung, Lueftung, Haustechnik [Later, HLH. Zeitschrift fuer Heizung, Lueftung, Klimatechnik, Haustechnik]
Heiz Raumlufttech Ind Fertigungsstaetten Tag — Heiz- und Raumlufttechnik in Industriellen Fertigungsstaetten. Tagung
Heiztech Rdsch — Heizungstechnische Rundschau
Heizung-Lueftung Haustech — Heizung, Lueftung, Haustechnik
HEJ — Health Education Journal
HeJ — Heidelberger Jahrbuch
HEJ — History of Education Journal
He Jb — Heidelberger Jahrbuecher
HeJL — Hessisches Jahrbuch fuer Landesgeschichte
Hej Mar — Hejnal Mariacki
HEKG — Handbuch zum Evangelischen Kirchengesangbuch
HEKOD — Herder Korrespondenz
Hel — Helicon
Hel — Hellas-Jahrbuch
Helgolander Wiss Meeresunters Mar Invest — Helgolaender Wissenschaftliche Meeresuntersuchungen/Marine Investigations
Helgol Meeresunters — Helgolaender Meeresuntersuchungen
Helgol Wiss Meeresunters — Helgolaender Wissenschaftliche Meeresuntersuchungen
Helg W Meer — Helgolaender Wissenschaftliche Meeresuntersuchungen
Helicopter VTO Wld — Helicopter and VTO World
Helicop Wld — Helicopter World
Heli Intnl — Helicopter International
Helikon — Helikon. Revista di Tradizione e Cultura Classica dell'Universita di Messina
Helinium — Helinium. Revue Consacree a l'Archeologie des Pays-Bas de la Belgique et du Grand Duche de Luxembourg
Heliogr Kart Photosph — Heliographische Karten der Photosphaere
Helios Elektroprakt — Helios oder Elektropraktiker
Helium At Scattering Surf — Helium Atom Scattering from Surfaces
Heli World — Helicopter World
Hell — Hellenika. Philogikon, Hisstorikon kai Leographikon Periodikon Syngramma
Hell Adelphe — Hellenis Adelphe
Hell Anaisthesiol — Hellenike Anaisthesiologia
Hell Armed Forces Med Rev — Hellenic Armed Forces Medical Review
HellasJB — Hellas-Jahrbuch
Hellen — Hellenika
Hellenika Jb — Hellenika. Jahrbuch fuer die Freunde Griechenlands
Hellenika (S) — Hellenika (Salonika)

Hellenisme Contemp — Hellenisme Contemporain
Hellers Arch — Archiv fuer Physiologische und Pathologische Chemie und Mikroskopie (Von J. F. Heller)
Hell Kteniatr — Hellenike Kteniatrike
Hell Med J — Hellenic Medical Journal
Hell Mikrobiol Hygieinol Hetaireia Delt — Hellenike Mikrobiologike kai Hygieinologike Hetaireia Deltion
Hell P — Hellenica. Paris
Hell Period Stomat Gnathopathoprosopike Cheir — Helleniko Periodiko Gia Stomatike & Gnathoprosopike Cheirourgike
Hell Phil Syll — Hellenikos Philologikos Syllogos
Hell Stomatol Chron — Hellenika Stomatologika Chronika
Hell Vet Med — Hellenic Veterinary Medicine
Helm — Helmantica. Revista de Humanidades Clasicas
Helm — Helmantica. Salamanca
Helminth Abstr — Helminthological Abstracts
Helminthol — Helminthologia
Helminthol Soc Wash Proc — Helminthological Society of Washington. Proceedings
HELOA — Helgolaender Wissenschaftliche Meeresuntersuchungen
Help Person Group — Helping Person in the Group
Helsingen Kaupungin Hist — Helsingen Kaupungin Historia
Helsingf Acta — Acta Societatis Scientiarum Fennicae (Helsingfors)
Helsingf Ofv — Ofversigt af Finska Vetenskaps-Societetens Forhandlingar (Helsingfors)
Helsingin Tek Korkeakoulu Radiolaboratorio Intern Rep — Helsingin Teknillinen Korkeakoulu. Radiolaboratorio. Internal Report
Helsingin Tek Korkeakoulu Tiet Julk — Helsingin Teknillinen Korkeakoulu Tieteellisia Julkaisuja
Helsinki Univ Tech Inst Math Syst Res Rep — Helsinki University of Technology Institute of Mathematics Systems Research Reports
Helsinki Univ Technol Inst Process Metall Rep — Helsinki University of Technology. Institution of Process Metallurgy. Report
Helsinki Univ Technol Lab For Prod Chem Rep Ser C — Helsinki University of Technology. Laboratory of Forest Products Chemistry. Reports. Series C
Helsinki Univ Technol Lab Mater Process Powder Metall Rep TK — Helsinki University of Technology. Laboratory of Materials Processing and Powder Metallurgy. Report TKK-V-B
Helsinki Univ Technol Lab Phys Res Rep — Helsinki University of Technology. Laboratory of Physics. Research Report
Helsinki Univ Technol Res Pap — Helsinki University of Technology. Research Papers
Helv A — Helvetia Archaeologica
Helv Arch — Helvetica Archaeologica
Helv Biol Acta — Helvetica Biologica Acta
Helv Chim A — Helvetica Chimica Acta
Helv Chim Acta — Helvetica Chimica Acta
Helv Chir Acta — Helvetica Chirurgica Acta
Helv Chir Acta Suppl — Helvetica Chirurgica Acta. Supplementum
Helvet Arch — Helvetia Archaeologica
Helvetia Archaeol — Helvetia Archaeologica
Helvetica Odontol Acta Suppl — Helvetica Odontologica Acta. Supplementum
Helv Med Acta — Helvetica Medica Acta
Helv Med Acta Ser B — Helvetica Medica Acta. Series B. Helvetica Chirurgica Acta
Helv Med Acta Ser C — Helvetica Medica Acta. Series C. Helvetica Paediatrica Acta
Helv Med Acta Ser C Suppl — Helvetica Medica Acta. Series C. Helvetica Paediatrica Acta. Supplementum
Helv Med Acta Ser D — Helvetica Medica Acta. Series D. Helvetica Paediatrica Acta
Helv Med Acta Ser D Suppl — Helvetica Medica Acta. Series D. Helvetica Paediatrica Acta. Supplementum
Helv Med Acta Suppl — Helvetica Medica Acta. Supplementum
Helv Odon A — Helvetica Odontologica Acta
Helv Odont Acta — Helvetica Odontologica Acta
Helv Odontol Acta — Helvetica Odontologica Acta
Helv Odontol Acta Suppl — Helvetica Odontologica Acta. Supplementum
Helv Paed A — Helvetica Paediatrica Acta
Helv Paediat Acta — Helvetica Paediatrica Acta
Helv Paediatr Acta — Helvetica Paediatrica Acta
Helv Paediatr Acta Suppl — Helvetica Paediatrica Acta. Supplementum
Helv Phys A — Helvetica Physica Acta
Helv Phys Acta — Helvetica Physica Acta
Helv Phys Acta Suppl — Helvetica Physica Acta. Supplementum
Helv Physiol Pharmac Acta — Helvetica Physiologica et Pharmacologica Acta
Helv Physiol Pharmacol Acta — Helvetica Physiologica et Pharmacologica Acta
Helv Physiol Pharmacol Acta Suppl — Helvetica Physiologica et Pharmacologica Acta. Supplementum
Hem — Hemispheres
HEM — History of the Ecumenical Movement
HeM — Hommes et Mondes
Hem — Ons Hemecht
HEMAEZ — Hematology
Hematol — Hematology
Hematol Cell Ther — Hematology and Cell Therapy
Hematol Onc — Hematological Oncology
Hematol Oncol — Hematological Oncology
Hematol Oncol Clin North Am — Hematology/Oncology Clinics of North America
Hematol Pathol — Hematologic Pathology
Hematol Plenary Sess Sci Contrib Int Congr Hematol — Hematology. Plenary Sessions. Scientific Contributions. International Congress of Hematology
Hematol Rev — Hematologic Reviews
Hematopathol Mol Hematol — Hematopathology and Molecular Hematology
HEMEA — Hemel en Dampkring
HEMEDC — Helgolaender Meeresuntersuchungen

Hemerocallis J — Hemerocallis Journal
Hem Hron — Hemika Hronika
Hemijska Ind — Hemijska Industrija
Hem Ind — Hemijska Industrija
Hem Ind Ind Secera — Hemijska Industrija - Industrija Secera
Hemingway N — Hemingway Notes
Hemis — Hemisphere
Hemis — Hemispheres. French-American Quarterly of Poetry
HEMLOC — Health and Medical Libraries Catalogue
HEMOA — Hemostase
HEMOD — Hemoglobin
Hemorrh Fever Renal Synd Tick Mosq Born Viruses — Hemorrhagic Fever with Renal Syndrome. Tick- and Mosquito-Born Viruses
Hem Pregl — Hemiski Pregled
HemR — Hemingway Review
Hem Sver — Hem I Sverige
Hem Vlakna — Hemijska Vlakna
HEN — Harris Electronic News
HENA — Hemeroteca Nacional
Henderson Meml Lect — Henderson Memorial Lecture [*London*]
Henderson Trust Rep — Henderson Trust Reports [*Edinburgh*]
Henle U Pfeufer Z — Zeitschrift fuer Rationelle Medicin. Henle und Pfeufer
Henley Telegr — Henley Telegraph
Hennepin Law — Hennepin Lawyer
Hennepin Rep — Hennepin Reporter
Henning Symp Publ — Henning Symposium Publikation
Henry Beckman Conserv Bull — Henry Beckman Conservation Bulletin
Henry E Sigerist Suppl Bull Hist Med — Henry E. Sigerist Supplements. Bulletin of the History of Medicine
Henry Ford Hosp Int Symp — Henry Ford Hospital. International Symposium
Henry Ford Hosp Med Bull — Henry Ford Hospital. Medical Bulletin
Henry Ford Hosp Med J — Henry Ford Hospital. Medical Journal
Henry Myers Lect — Henry Myers Lecture
Henschel Rev — Henschel-Review
Heofyz Kharakt Ukr — Heofyzychna Kharakterystyka Ukrayny
Heohr Zb Lviv Vida Heohr Tov Ukr SSR — Heohragicheskyi Zbirnyk L'vivs'koho Vida Heohraficheskoho Tovarystva Ukrains'koho SSR
Heol Zh — Heolohychnyi Zhurnal
Heom Zbirn — Heometrychnyi Zbirnik
Heopolite Bull — Heopolite Bulletin
HEP — HEP [*Higher Education Publications*] Higher Education Directory
HEP — Hong Kong Economic Papers
HEPADF — Hepatology Research and Clinical Issues
Hepatic Metab Dispos Endo Xenobiot Proc Falk Symp — Hepatic Metabolism and Disposition of Endo- and Xenobiotics. Proceedings. Falk Symposium
Hepato-Gastroenterol — Hepato-Gastroenterology
Hepatol (Amst) — Journal of Hepatology (Amsterdam)
Hepatol Res Clin Issues — Hepatology. Research and Clinical Issues
Hepatotoxic Med — Hepatotoxicite Medicamenteuse
HEPIA — High Energy Physics Index
HE Purdue Univ Coop Ext Serv — HE. Purdue University. Cooperative Extension Service
HER — Harvard Educational Review
Her — Hermanthena
He R — Humanisme et Renaissance
HERA — Heritage Australia Information System
Her Acad Sci Kazakh SSR — Herald of the Academy of Sciences of the Kazakh SSR
Her Acad Sci USSR — Herald of the Academy of Sciences of the USSR
Heraklith Inf Sh — Heraklith Information Sheet
Heraklith Rdsch Radenthein — Heraklith Rundschau (Radenthein)
Heraklith Rdsch Simbach — Heraklith Rundschau (Simbach)
Heraklith Tech Bl — Heraklith Technisches Blatt
Heraklith Waermetech Merkbl — Heraklith Waermetechnisches Merkblatt
Herald Lib Sci — Herald of Library Science
Herald Research Bul — Herald Research Bulletin
Her Australia — Heritage Australia
Herb Abstr — Herbage Abstracts
Herbage Abstr — Herbage Abstracts
Herba Hung — Herba Hungarica
Herbal Practnr — Herbal Practitioner
Herba Pol — Herba Polonica
Herb Gen Amateur — Herbier General de l'Amateur, Contenant la Description, l'Histoire, Proprietes et la Culture des Vegetaux Utiles et Agreables
Herb Grower Mag — Herb Grower Magazine
Herbic Physiol Biochem Ecol — Herbicides. Physiology, Biochemistry, Ecology
Herb Nachr — Herbal Nachrichten
Herbnes Upsal — Herbationes Upsalienses
Herb Res Circ — Herbage Research Circular
Herb Resist Weeds Crops Long Ashton Int Symp — Herbicide Resistance in Weeds and Crops. Long Ashton International Symposium
Herb Rev — Herbage Reviews
Herb Seed Grow Leafl — Herbage Seed Growers' Leaflet
Herb Spice Med Plant Dig — Herb, Spice, and Medicinal Plant Digest
Herbs Spices Med Plants Recent Adv Bot Hortic Pharmacol — Herbs, Spices, and Medicinal Plants. Recent Advances in Botany, Horticulture, and Pharmacology
Her Bue — Herder Buecherei
Her Bue D — Herder Buecherei. Duenndruckausgaben
HERCA — Hercynia
Her Chr — Herbergen der Christenheit
Her Communs — Herald of Communications
Hercules Chem — Hercules Chemist
Hercules Plast Hi Lites — Hercules Plastics Hi-Lites

Hercynia Fachgeb Bot-Geogr-Geol Palaeontol-Zool — Hercynia fuer die Fachgebiete Botanik-Geographie-Geologie Palaeontologie-Zoologie
Herd Bldr — Herd Builder
Her Dent — Heraldo Dental
Herder Korresp — Herder Korrespondenz
HEREA — Hereditas
Hered — Hereditas
Hered — Heredity
Hereditas Lund Swed — Hereditas (Lund, Sweden)
Hereford Breed A — Hereford Breed Annual and Breeders' Guide
Hereford Breed J — Hereford Breed Journal
Hereford J Sthn Afr — Hereford Journal of Southern Africa
Hereford Q — Hereford Quarterly
Herefordsh Agric J — Herefordshire Agricultural Journal
Herefordsh Cty Coun Agric Q J — Herefordshire County Council Agricultural Quarterly Journal
Her Elect Ind — Herald of the Electrical Industry
HE Rev — HE Revista. Orgao Oficial do Centro de Estudos do Hospital-Escola da Universidade Federal de Juiz de Fora
Her Ferro Carr — Heraldo de Ferrocarriles
Her Geol — Herald Geological
Her Hig Soc — Heraldo de Higiene Social
HERI — Heavy Oil/Enhanced Recovery Index
HERI — Heritage. Monthly Newsletter. Alaska Office of History and Archaeology
Herion Inf — Herion Informationen
Heritage Enc Malt Cult & Civilis — Heritage. Encyclopedia of Maltese Culture and Civilisation
Heritage W — Heritage West
HERJ — Home Economics Research Journal
HerK — Herder Korrespondenz
Her Korr — Herder Korrespondenz
Her Korr B — Herder Korrespondenz. Beiheft
Herl — Herlovianeren
Her Leningr Univ — Herald of Leningrad University
Her Libr Sci — Herald of Library Science
Her Lib Sci — Herald of Library Science
Herm — Hermaea. Halle
Herm — Hermathena
Herm — Hermes. Collana di Testi Antichi
Herm — Hermes. Zeitschrift fuer Klassische Philologie
Her Mach Bldg — Herald of Machine Building
Hermbstaedt Bll — Bulletin des Neuesten und Wissenwuerdigsten aus der Naturwissenschaft.Von S.F. Hermbstaedt
Hermbstaedts Bull — Bulletin des Neuesten und Wissenswuerdigsten aus der Naturwissenschaft. Von S. F. Hermbstaedt
Her Med — Heraldo Medico
Hermes E — Hermes [Wiesbaden] Einzelschriften
Hermes Z Kl — Hermes. Zeitschrift fuer Klassische Philologie
Her Mosc Univ — Herald of Moscow University
Hermsdorfer Tech Mitt — Hermsdorfer Technische Mitteilungen
Hermstdt Vh — Verhandlungen und Mittheilungen des Siebenbuergischen Vereins fuer Naturwissenschaften. Hermannstadt
Her Nat — Heraldo Naturista
Herold — Der Herold. Vierteljahrsschrift fuer Heraldik, Genealogie, und Verwandte Wissenschaften
Herold Geschlechter Wappen & Siegelknd — Herold fuer Geschlechter-, Wappen-, und Siegelkunde
Heron (Engl Ed) — Heron (English Edition)
Her O Nu — Her og Nu
HERP — Health Education Reports
Herpetol Newsl — Herpetologica Newsletter
Herpetologi — Herpetologica
Herpetol Rev — Herpetological Review
Her Russ Acad Sci Transl of Vestn Ross Akad Nauk — Herald of the Russian Academy of Sciences (Translation of Vestnik Rossiiskoi Akademii Nauk)
Her T — Heraldisk Tidsskrift
Hertford A — Hertfordshire Archaeology
Hertfordshire Arch — Hertfordshire Archaeology
Hertfordshire Archaeol — Hertfordshire Archaeology
Hertfordshire Archaeol Rev — Hertfordshire Archaeological Review
Herts Cty Coun Agric Q Chron — Hertfordshire County Council Agricultural Quarterly Chronicle
Herts Fmr — Hertfordshire Farmer
Herts NH S T — Transactions of the Hertfordshire Natural History Society and Field Club
Her Vet — Heraldo de la Veterinaria
Herz Kreisl — Herz Kreislauf
Herzl YB — Herzl Year Book
HES — Harvard English Studies
HeS — Headline Series
HES — Healthcare Evaluation System
Hes — Hesperis. Paris
HeS — Homme et la Societe
HES — Humanidades
Hescho Mitt — Hescho-Mitteilungen
HESD — Hospital Equipment and Supplies Directory
Hesdoerffers Monatsh Blumen Gartenfreunde — Hesdoerffers Monatshefte fuer Blumen- und Gartenfreunde
HESEA — Health Services Research
HESOD — Heizen mit Sonne
Hesp — Hesperia
Hesp — Hesperis. Archives Berberes et Bulletin. Institut des Hautes Etudes Marocaines
Hess Aerztebl — Hessisches Aerzteblatt
Hess Biene — Hessische Biene

Hesse Landesamt Bodenforsch Notizblatt — Hesse Landesamt fuer Bodenforschung Notizblatt
Hess Feuerw Ztg — Hessische Feuerwehrzeitung
Hess Florist Briefe — Hessische Floristische Briefe
Hess Foersterztg — Hessische Foersterzeitung
Hess Heimat — Hessische Heimat
Hess Jb Landesgesch — Hessisches Jahrbuch fuer Landesgeschichte
Hess Lagerstaett Arch — Hessisches Lagerstaettenarchiv
Hess Lagerstaettenarch — Hessisches Lagerstaettenarchiv
Hess Landw Z — Hessische Landwirtschaftliche Zeitschrift
Hess Landw Ztg — Hessisches Landwirtschaftliche Zeitung
Hess Mus — [Aus] Hessischen Museen
Hess Quart Bl — Quartalblaetter des Historischen Vereins fuer das Grossherzogtum Hessen
Hes Ta — Hesperis. Tamuda
Het — Herterofonia
Heteroat Chem — Heteroatom Chemistry
Heterocycl Chem — Heterocyclic Chemistry
Heterocycl Commun — Heterocyclic Communications
Heterocycl Compd — Heterocyclic Compounds
Heterog Catal — Heterogeneous Catalysis
Heterog Catal Proc Int Symp — Heterogeneous Catalysis. Proceedings. International Symposium
Heterog Chem Rev — Heterogeneous Chemistry Reviews
He Tr — Helps for Translators Series
Het Voice — Heterodoxical Voice
Heubner Foundation Monograph Ser — Heubner Foundation Monograph Series
Heurtey Bull Inform — Heurtey Bulletin d'Informations. English Edition
Heusingers Zschr — Zeitschrift fuer die Organische Physik (Von C. F. Heusinger)
HEVEA — Heating and Ventilating
Heves Megyei Muesz Elet — Heves Megyei Mueszaki Elet
HEW — Department of Health, Education, and Welfare. Publication
HEWE — Heritage West. British Columbia's Leading Heritage Magazine
Hewitt Mag — Hewitt Magazine
Hewitt Top — Hewitt Topics
Hew L — Hewett Lectures
Hewlett — Hewlett-Packard Journal
Hewlett-Packard J — Hewlett-Packard Journal
HEX — Handicapped Educational Exchange
Hexag Dig — Hexagon Digest
Hey J — Heythrop Journal
HeythJ — Heythrop Journal. A Quarterly Review of Philosophy and Theology
Heythrop — Heythrop Journal
Heythrop J — Heythrop Journal
HF — Hamburger Fremdenblatt
HF — Harvest Field
HF — Heidelberger Forschungen
HF — High Fidelity
HF — Hoosier Folklore
HF — Husky Fever (The Musher's Monthly News. Insert in Northern News Report)
HfA — Hilfe fuers Amt
HFB — Bouwhandel
HFB — Hoosier Folklore Bulletin
HFBT — Helps for Bible Translators
HFC — Hants Field Club and Archaeological Society
HF Commun Syst Tech Int Conf — HF Communication Systems and Techniques. International Conference
HFE — Housing Finance Review
HFF — Health Affairs
HFH — Hsien-Tai Fo-Hsueh
HFHJA — Henry Ford Hospital. Medical Journal
HFK — Holland Quarterly
HFK — Homenagem a Fritz Krueger
HFM — Healthcare Financial Management
HFM — Historisk-Filosofiske Meddelelser Udgivet af det Kongelinge Danske Videnskabernes Selskab
HFM — History of the Freedom Movement
HF/MA — High Fidelity/Musical America
HFMKDVS — Historisk-Filosofiske Meddelelser Udgivet af det Kongelinge Danske Videnskabernes Selskab
HFN — Hi-Fi News and Record Review
HFPC — Historia Fisica y Politica de Chile, Documentos. Claudio Gay [Santiago]
HFrL — Horizon France Libre
HFSBG — Hi-Fi/Stereo Buyers' Guide
Hft Ksthist Semin U Muenchen — Hefte des Kunsthistorischen Seminars der Universitaet Muenchen
Hft Landw Marktforsch — Hefte fuer Landwirtschaftliche Marktforschung
Hft Unfallheilk — Hefte zur Unfallheilkunde
HG — Hammurabi's Gesetz
HG — Hannoversche Geschichtsblaetter
HG — Humanistisches Gymnasium
HG — Yr Haul a'r Gengell
HGA — Handbuecherei fuer Gemeindearbeit
HGAMA — Hidrotehnica Gospodarirea Apelor. Meteorologia
HGB — Hansische Geschichtsblaetter
HGB — Het Gildeboek. Tijdschrift voor Kerkelijke Kunst en Oudheidkunde
HGC — Hanes Gweithwyr Cymru
HGC — Histoire Generale des Civilisations
HGD — Handbuch der Griechischen Dialekte
HGG — Hotelgewerbe und Gastgewerbe Rundschau. Unabhangiges Fachorgan fuer Gastronomie, Betriebstechnische, und Kuhltechnische Praxis und Gemeinschaftsverpflegung
HGGSEB — Handelingen. Genootschap voor Geschiedenis Gesticht Onder de Benaming. Societe d'Emulation de Bruges
HGH — Hansische Geschichtsblaetter

HGJ — Hagiographischer Jahresberichte
HGKV — Hefte fuer Geschichte, Kunst, und Volkskunde
HGM — Harvard Graduates' Magazine
HGM — Historici Graeci Minores
HGR — Histoire Generale des Religions
HGRT — History of the Greek and Roman Theater
HGS — Harvard Germanic Studies
HGSD News — Harvard Graduate School of Design. News
H Gym — Humanistische Gymnasium
HH — Hapeol Hatzair
HH — Harofe Haivri
HH — Hierglyphes Hittites
HH — Hittite Hieroglyphs
HH — Hueso Humero
HH — Human Heredity
HHBLA — Harper Hospital. Bulletin
HHFA Tech Bull — HHFA (Housing and Home Finance Agency). Technical Bulletin
Hh GI — Hieroglyphisch-Hethitisches Glossar
HHHCA — Journal. Oceanological Society of Korea
HHHHD — Heh Hua Hsueh Yu Fang She Hua Hsueh
HHHPA — Hua Hsueh Pao
HHI Geophys Data — Heinrich Hertz Institut Geophysical Data
HHI Sol Data — Heinrich Hertz Institut Solar Data
HHM — Harvard Historical Monographs
HHM — Hittite Hieroglyphic Monuments
HHMHDB — Hispanic Health and Mental Health Data Base
HHN — Houthandel en Houtnijverheid. Algemeen Vakblad voor de Houthandel en de Houtnijverheid
HHO — Hessisches Hebopfer Theologischer und Philologischer Anmerkungen
H Hol — Herald of Holiness
HHRV — Holistic Health Review
HHS — Harvard Historical Studies
HHS — Hospital and Health Services Administration
HHTPA — Hua Hsueh Tung Pao
Hi — Hid
Hi — Hispania
HI — Historica Iberica
HI — Humanities Index
Hia — Hispania
HiAH — Hispanic American Historical Review
HIA J Mod Watchmaking — HIA [*Horological Institute of America*] Journal of Modern Watchmaking
HIAR — Hamburger Ibero-Amerikanische Reihe
HIAS — Heritage of Indian Art Series
Hibbert J — Hibbert Journal
HibbJ — Hibbert Journal
Hibernation Torpor Mamm Birds — Hibernation and Torpor in Mammals and Birds
HibJ — Hibbert Journal
Hib L — Hibbert Lectures
Hibridni Kukuruz Jugoslav — Hibridni Kukuruz Jugoslavie
HIC — Higher Education and Research in the Netherlands
HIC — History of Irish Catholicism
Hickenia (Bol Darwinion) — Hickenia (Boletin del Darwinion)
Hickory Task Force Rep Stheast For Exp Sta — Hickory Task Force Report. Southeastern Forest Experiment Station
HICL — Histoire des Idees et Critique Litteraire
HICLR — Hastings International and Comparative Law Review
HICW — History of the Canadian West
HID — Handbuch der Italischen Dialekte
Hide Leath — Hide and Leather
Hide Leather — Hide and Leather
Hide Leather Shoe Fact — Hide and Leather with Shoe Factory
HIDKA — Hiroshima Daigaku Kogakubu Kenkyu Hokoku
HIDRA — Hidrologiai Koezloeny
Hidrogr Godisn — Hidrografiski Godisnjak
Hidrol Biblfia — Hidrologiai Bibliografia
Hidrol Godisn — Hidroloski Godisnjak
Hidrol Koezl — Hidrologiai Koezloeny
Hidromet Glasn — Hidrometeoroloski Glasnik
Hidrometr Metrastis — Hidrometrinis Metrastis
Hidroteh Gospod Apelor Meteorol — Hidrotehnica Gospodarirea Apelor. Meteorologia
Hidroteh Melior Latv PSR — Hidrotehnika un Melioracija Latvijas PSR
Hiduminium Abstr Bull — Hiduminium Abstract Bulletin
HIE — Express. Daily Financial Newspaper
HIECA — High Energy Chemistry
Hiei Int Symp Teratocarcinoma Cell Surf — Hiei International Symposium on Teratocarcinoma and the Cell Surface
Hiero — Hierophant
HieS — Histoire Sociale/Social History
Hiet — Historia
Hif — Historia (France)
HiFi — Hi-Fi News and Record Reviews
Hi Fi — High Fidelity
Hi Fi — High Fidelity/Musical America
Hi Fi A — Hi-Fi Annual & Audio Handbook
Hi Fi Guide Yb — Hi-Fi Guide and Yearbook
Hi Fi/Mus Am — High Fidelity/Musical America
Hi-Fi News Rec Rev — Hi-Fi News and Record Review
Hi Fi Tape Record — Hi-Fi Tape Recording
Hi Fi Yb — Hi-Fi Year Book
Higashi Nippon Dent J — Higashi Nippon Dental Journal
Hig Cas Hig Mikrobiol Epidemiol Sanit — Higijena. Casopis za Higijenu, Mikrobiologiju, Epidemiologiju, i Sanitarnu Tehniku
Hig Epidemiol Mikrobiol — Higiena, Epidemiologiya, i Mikrobiologiya

Hig Escol — Higiene Escolar
Higg J Poet — Higginson Journal of Poetry
High Alt Med Biol — High Altitude Medicine & Biology
High Brightness Beams Adv Accel Appl — High Brightness Beams for Advanced Accelerator Applications
High Educ — Higher Education
High Educ Abstr — Higher Education Abstracts
High Educ Col Barg — Higher Education Collective Bargaining
High Educ Ex — Higher Education Exchange
High Educ R — Higher Education Review
High Educ R & D — Higher Education Research and Development
High Educ Rev — Higher Education Review
High Energy Chem — High Energy Chemistry
High Energy Chem (Engl Transl) — High Energy Chemistry (English Translation)
High Energy Chem Transl of Khim Vys Energ — High Energy Chemistry (Translation of Khimiya Vysokikh Energii)
High Energy Collisions Int Conf — High Energy Collisions. International Conference
High Energy Electromagn Interact Field Theory Sess — High Energy Electromagnetic Interactions and Field Theory. Session
High Energy Nucl Collisions Quark Gluon Plasma Int Symp — High Energy Nuclear Collisions and Quark Gluon Plasma. International Symposium
High Energy Nucl Phys Univ Rochester — High Energy Nuclear Physics (University of Rochester)
High Energy Phys Nuclear Phys — High Energy Physics and Nuclear Physics
High Energy Phys Nucl Phys — High Energy Physics and Nuclear Physics
High Energy Phys Nucl Struct Proc Int Conf — High Energy Physics and Nuclear Structure. Proceedings of theInternational Conference on High Energy Physics and Nuclear Structure
Higher Ed — Higher Education
Higher Ed J — Higher Education Journal
Higher Ed R — Higher Education Review
Higher Educ — Higher Education
Higher Math — Higher Mathematics
Higher Prod — Higher Productivity
High Freq Heat Rev — High Frequency Heating Review
Highlights Agric Res Ala Agric Exp Stn — Highlights of Agricultural Research. Alabama Agricultural Experiment Station
Highlights Agr Res — Highlights of Agricultural Research. Alabama Agricultural Experiment Station
Highlights Astron — Highlights of Astronomy
Highlights Mod Biochem Proc Int Congr Biochem — Highlights of Modern Biochemistry. Proceedings. International Congress of Biochemistry
Highlts Ophthal — Highlights of Ophthalmology
HIG (Honolulu) HI — Hawaii Institute of Geophysics (Honolulu). University of Hawaii
High Perform Cars — High Performance Cars
High Perform Compos 1990s Proc TMS Northeast Reg Symp — High Performance Composites for the 1990's. Proceedings. TMS Northeast Regional Symposium
High Perform Comput RIKEN — High Performance Computing in RIKEN
High Perform Fiber Reinf Cem Compos Proc Int Workshop — High Performance Fiber Reinforced Cement Composites. Proceedings. InternationalWorkshop
High Perform Liq Chromatogr — High-Performance Liquid Chromatography. Advances and Perspectives
High Per T — High Performance Textiles
High Polym — High Polymers
High Polym (Jpn) — High Polymers (Japan)
High Power Laser Part Beams — High Power Laser and Particle Beams
High Power Microwave Gener Appl Proc Course Workshop — High Power Microwave Generation and Applications. Proceedings. Course and Workshop
High Press — High Pressure
High Pressure Biotechnol Proc Eur Semin — High Pressure and Biotechnology. Proceedings. European Seminar
High Pressure Eng Int Conf — High Pressure Engineering. International Conference
High Pressure Res — High Pressure Research
High Pressure Sci Technol AIRAPT Conf — High-Pressure Science and Technology. AIRAPT [*International Association for the Advancement of High Pressure Science and Technology*] Conference
High Purity Mater Sci Technol Int Symp — High-Purity Materials in Science and Technology. InternationalSymposium
High Purity Mater Sci Technol Int Symp Proc — High Purity Materials in Science and Technology. International Symposium. Proceedings
High Resolut Disp Proj Syst — High-Resolution Displays and Projection Systems
High Resolut Sens Hybrid Syst — High-Resolution Sensors and Hybrid Systems
High Sch Chem Teach Mag — High School Chemistry Teachers' Magazine
High Sch J — High School Journal
High Solids Coat — High Solids Coatings
High Speed Flight Propuls Syst — High-Speed Flight Propulsion Systems
High Speed Ground Transp J — High Speed Ground Transportation Journal
High Speed Gr Transpn J — High Speed Ground Transportation Journal
High-Speed Surf Craft — High-Speed Surface Craft
High Speed Test — High Speed Testing
High Strain Rate Behav Refract Met Alloys Proc Symp — High Strain Rate Behavior of Refractory Metals and Alloys. Proceedings. Symposium
High Strength Concr Int Symp — High-Strength Concrete. International Symposium
High Abrength Mater Proc Berkeley Int Mater Conf — High-Strength Materials. Proceedings of the Berkeley InternationalMaterials Conference
High Tech — High Technology
High Technol — High Technology
High Technol Bus — High Technology Business
High Technol Lett — High Technology Letters
High Temp — High Temperature

High Temp Chem Processes — High Temperature Chemical Processes
High Temp (Engl Transl) — High Temperature (English Translation)
High Temp High Pressures — High Temperatures-High Pressures
High Temp Liq Met Heat Transfer Technol Meet Proc — High Temperature Liquid-Metal Heat Transfer Technology Meeting. Proceedings
High Temp Mater Processes — High Temperature Materials and Processes
High Temp Mater Processes NY — High Temperature Material Processes (New York)
High Temp Mater Sci — High Temperature and Materials Science
High Temp Oxid Sulphidation Processes Proc Int Symp — High-Temperature Oxidation and Sulphidation Processes. Proceedings. International Symposium
High Temp R — High Temperature USSR
High Temp React Rate Data — High Temperature Reaction Rate Data
High Temp S — High Temperature Science
High Temp Sci — High Temperature Science
High Temp Supercond — High Temperature Superconductivity
High Temp Supercond Compd III Proc Symp — High Temperature Superconducting Compounds III. Processing and Microstructure Property Relationships. Proceedings. Symposium
High Temp Supercond Localization Phenom Proc Int Conf — High Temperature Superconductivity and Localization Phenomena. Proceedings. International Conference
High Temp Supercond Proc LT 19 Satell Conf — High Temperature Superconductivity. Proceedings. LT-19 Satellite Conference
High Temp Technol — High Temperature Technology
High Temp Transl of Teplofiz Vys Temp — High Temperature (Translation of Teplofizika Vysokikh Temperatur)
High Voltage Electron Microsc Proc Int Conf — High Voltage Electron Microscopy. Proceedings of the International Conference
Highw — Highway
Highway Engr — Highway Engineer
Highway Geol Symp Proc — Highway Geology Symposium Proceedings
Highway Tr Fd Ann Rep — Highway Trust Fund. Annual Report
Highway User Q — Highway User Quarterly
Highw Bldr — Highway Builder
Highw Bridges — Highways and Bridges
Highw Bull Purdue Univ — Highway Bulletin. Purdue University
Highw Des Constr — Highways Design and Construction
Highw Eng — Highway Engineer
Highw Eng Aust — Highway Engineering in Australia
Highw Engng Aust — Highway Engineering in Australia
Highw Engr — Highway Engineer
Highw Engr Contract — Highway Engineer and Contractor
Highw Engr Loc Govt Surv — Highway Engineer and Local Government Surveyor
Highw Engrs Yb — Highway Engineer's Year Book
Highw Heavy Constr — Highway and Heavy Construction
Highw Mag Chicago — Highway Magazine (Chicago)
Highw Mag Middletown — Highway Magazine (Middletown)
Highw Maint — Highway Maintenance
Highw Plann Des Ser — Highway Planning and Design Series
Highw Prog — Highway Progress
Highw Public Wks — Highways and Public Works
Highw Public Works — Highways and Public Works
Highw Publ Wks — Highways and Public Works
Highw Rd Constr — Highways and Road Construction
Highw Res Abstr — Highway Research Abstracts
Highw Res Bd Nat Coop Highw Res Program Rep — Highway Research Board. National Cooperative Highway Research Program. Report
Highw Res Board Bull — Highway Research Board. Bulletin
Highw Res Board Bull Spec Rep — Highway Research Board. Bulletin. Special Reports
Highw Res Board Highw Res Abstr — Highway Research Board. Highway Research Abstracts
Highw Res Board Natl Coop Highw Res Program — Highway Research Board. National Cooperative Highway Research Program. Report
Highw Res Board Proc Annu Meet — Highway Research Board. Proceedings of the Annual Meeting
Highw Res Board Spec Rep — Highway Research Board. Special Report
Highw Res Bull — Highway Research Bulletin
Highw Res Bull (New Delhi) — Highway Research Bulletin (New Delhi)
Highw Res Circ — Highway Research Circular
Highw Res News — Highway Research News
Highw Res Rec — Highway Research Record
Highw Res Rev — Highway Research Review
Highw Road Const — Highways and Road Construction
Highw Road Constr Int — Highways and Road Construction International
Highws Bridges Aerodr — Highways, Bridges, and Aerodromes
Highws Bridges Engng Wks — Highways, Bridges, and Engineering Works
Highws Curr Lit — Highways Current Literature
Highws Inf Bull — Highways Information Bulletin
Highws Transpn — Highways and Transportation
Highw Times — Highway Times
Highw Top — Highway Topics
Highw Traff Engng — Highways of Traffic Engineering
Highw Transp — Highway Transport
Highw Urban Mass Transp — Highway and Urban Mass Transportation
Highw Veh Syst Contract Coord Meet Proc — Highway Vehicle Systems Contractors' Coordination Meeting. Proceedings
Hig Mod — Higiene Moderna
Hig Salub — Higiene y Salubridad
Hig Sanit — Higiena i Sanitariya
Hig Zdraveopaz — Higiena i Zdraveopazvane
HIH — Historia
HIHAD — Hanyang Idae Haksuljip
HIISAP — Industrija Secera

HIJMA — Hiroshima Journal of Medical Sciences
HIKAA — Hikaku Kagaku
Hikaku Kagaku Chem — Hikaku Kagaku (Chemistry)
Hikaku Kagaku Sci — Hikaku Kagaku (Science)
HIKEEV — Handbuch der Infusionstherapie und Klinischen Ernaehrung
HIKI Koezl — Hiradastechnikai Ipari Kutato Intezet Koezlemenyei
Hikobia J Hiroshima Bot Club — Hikobia Journal of the Hiroshima Botanical Club
HIKYA — Hinyokika Kiyo
HIKYAJ — Acta Urologica Japonica
Hilandarski Zborn — Hilandarski Zbornik
Hildebrandts Zentbl Pumpenind — Hildebrandts Zentralblatt der Pumpenindustrie
Hildesheim Allg Anz — Hildesheimer Allgemeiner Anzeiger
HILGA — Hilgardia
Hilgardia Calif Agric Exp Stn — Hilgardia. California Agricultural Experiment Station
Hilgardia J Agric Sci — Hilgardia. A Journal of Agricultural Science
Hilger J — Hilger Journal
Hilleshog Pamph — Hilleshog Pamphlet
Hill Fm Res — Hill Farm Research
Hillsdale Rev — Hillsdale Review
Hillside J Clin Psychiatry — Hillside Journal of Clinical Psychiatry
Hi Lo — High/Low Report
HIM — Handbuch der Inneren Mission
HiM — Hispania (Madrid)
HiM — Historia Mexicana
Himachal J Agric Res — Himachal Journal of Agricultural Research
Himalayan Chem Pharm Bull — Himalayan Chemical and Pharmaceutical Bulletin
Himalayan Geol — Himalayan Geology
Himalayan J — Himalayan Journal. Records. Himalayan Club
Himalay Cult — Himalayan Culture
Himal R — Himalayan Review
HIMDD3 — Hileia Medica
HiMe — Histoire de la Medecine
Himmel u Erde — Himmel und Erde
HINAA — Hindustan Antibiotics Bulletin
Hind Antibiot Bull — Hindustan Antibiotics Bulletin
Hindemith Jb — Hindemith-Jahrbuch
Hindi R — Hindi Review
Hind LJ — Hindu Law Journal
Hind LQ — Hindu Law Quarterly
Hindu Astronom Math Text Ser — Hindu Astronomical and Mathematical Text Series
Hindu R — Hindustan Review
Hindustan Antibiot Bull — Hindustan Antibiotics Bulletin
Hindustan R — Hindustan Review
HINL — History of Ideas Newsletter
HINT — Housewares Industry News and Topics
HINTD — Habitat International
HIPC — Historians of India, Pakistan, and Ceylon
HIPOA — High Polymers
HIPPA — Hippokrates
Hip T — Hippologisk Tidsskrift
HIR — Harvard International Review
HiR — Hispanic Review
HiR — History of Religions
HiR — Hititsubashi Review
HiR — Hitotsubashi Ronso
HIRAA — Hiradastechnika
Hiradas-Tech — Hiradastechnika. Hiradastechnikai Tudomanyos Egyesulet Lapja
Hiradastech Ipari Kutatointez Kozl — Hiradastechnikai Ipari Kutatointezet Koezlemenyei
Hiradastech Ipari Kut Intez Koezl — Hiradastechnikai Ipari Kutato Intezet Koezlemenyei
Hiram Po R — Hiram Poetry Review
HIRDAP — Geological Report. Hiroshima University
HIRIA — Hirosaki Igaku
HIRIB — Hifuka No Rinsho
HIROA — Hirosaki Daigaku Nogakubu Gakujutsu Hokoku
HiroBK — Hiroshima Daigaku Bungakubu Kiyo
Hirosaki Med J — Hirosaki Medical Journal
Hiroshima Chem Lab Rep — Hiroshima Chemical Laboratory Report
Hiroshima J Anesth — Hiroshima Journal of Anesthesia
Hiroshima J Med Sci — Hiroshima Journal of Medical Sciences
Hiroshima J M Sc — Hiroshima Journal of Medical Sciences
Hiroshima Math J — Hiroshima Mathematical Journal
Hiroshima Med J — Hiroshima Medical Journal
Hiroshima Univ Geol Rep — Hiroshima University Geological Report
Hiroshima Univ J Sci Ser C — Hiroshima University Journal of Science. Series C. Geology and Mineralogy
Hiros J Med — Hiroshima Journal of Medical Sciences
HIRRA — Highway Research Record
His — Hispania
His — Historia
HIS — History of Ideas Series
HIS — Humanities in Society
HisA — Historiallinen Aikakauskirja
His Am Hist Rev — Hispanic American Historical Review
Hisinger Afh — Afhandlingar i Fysik, Kemi, och Mineralogie. Hisinger och Berzelius
Hisinger Afh Fys — Afhandlingar i Fysik, Kemi, och Mineralogie. Hisinger och Berzelius
HisJ — Hispanic Journal
HisK — Hispania (University of Kansas. Lawrence)
H Isl — Handwoerterbuch des Islam
HisL — Hispania (University of Kansas. Lawrence)
HISLA — Revista Latinoamericana de Historia Economica y Social

H Isl S — Heroes of Islam Series
His Med Ser — History of Medicine Series
Hisn — Historian
His Outlook — Historical Outlook
Hisp — Hispania
Hisp — Hispania [*American Association of Teachers Spanish, Amherst, Mass.*]
HisP — Historia (Paris)
Hispam — Hispamerica. Revista de Literatura
Hisp Amer Hist Rev — Hispanic American Historical Review
Hisp Am Hist R — Hispanic American Historical Review
Hisp Am Hist Rev Durham — Hispanic American Historical Review (Durham, North Carolina)
Hisp Am Rept Stanford — Hispanic American Report (Stanford, California)
Hispan Am H — Hispanic American Historical Review
Hispan Am Hist R — Hispanic American Historical Review
Hispan Am Hist Rev — Hispanic American Historical Review
Hispan Am Rep — Hispanic American Report
Hispania Ant Epigr — Hispania Antiqua Epigraphica. Suplemento Anual de Archivo Espanol de Arqueologia
Hispanic Amer Hist Rev — Hispanic American Historical Review
Hispanic Am His R — Hispanic American Historical Review
Hispanic B — Hispanic Business
Hispanic Bus — Hispanic Business
Hispan Mon — Hispanic Monitor
Hispano — Hispanofila
Hispano Amer Hist Rev — Hispano-American Historical Review
Hispan R — Hispanic Review
Hispan Rev — Hispanic Review
Hispan T — Hispanic Times
Hisp Ant Epigr — Hispania Antiqua Epigraphica
HispCal — Hispania (Stanford, California)
Hispl — Hispanofila
HispM — Hispania (Madrid)
Hisp Med — Hispalis Medica
Hisp Press Ind — Hispanic Press Index
Hisp Rev — Hispanic Review
Hisp Sac — Hispania Sacra
Hisp Sacra — Hispania Sacra
His Q — History Quarterly
HISS News-J — HISS [*Herpetological Information Search Systems*] News-Journal
Hist — Historian
Hist — Historia. Revue d'Histoire Ancienne
Hist — Historia. Wiesbaden
Hist — Historica
Hist — Historie. Jyske Samlinger
Hist — History
HisT — History and Theory
HISTA — Historia Argentina
HistAb — Historical Abstracts
Hist Abstr — Historical Abstracts
Hist Abstr Part A Mod Hist Abstr — Historical Abstracts. Part A. Modern History Abstracts
Hist Abstr Part B Twent Century Abstr — Historical Abstracts. Part B. Twentieth Century Abstracts
Hist Acad Roy Sc — Histoire de l'Academie Royale des Sciences
Hist Acad Roy Sci Berlin — Histoire. Academie Royale des Sciences et Belles Lettres (Berlin)
Hist Acad Roy Sci Mem Math Phys Paris 12 — Histoire de l'Academie Royale des Sciences. Avec les Memoires de Mathematique and de Physique. In Duodecimo (Paris)
Hist Acad Roy Sci Mem Phys — Histoire. Academie Royale des Sciences. Avec les Memoires de Physique Tires desRegistres de Cette Academie
Hist Afr — History in Africa
Hist Africa — History in Africa
Hist Ag — Historia Agriculturae
Hist Aik — Historiallinen Aikakauskirja/Historische Zeitschrift
Hist A Mex — Historia del Arte Mexicano
Hist & Archeol — Histoire et Archeologie
Hist & Crit A — Histoire et Critique des Arts
Hist & Mem Inst Royal France Acad Inscr & B Lett — Histoire et Memoires de l'Institut Royal de France. Academie des Inscriptions et Belles-Lettres
Hist & Soc — Historia e Sociedade
Hist & T — History and Theory
Hist and Technol — History and Technology
Hist and Theory — History and Theory
Hist Anthropol Newslett — History of Anthropology Newsletter
Hist Archaeol — Historical Archaeology. The Annual Publication of the Society for Historical Archaeology
Hist Ark — Historiallinen Arkisto/Historisches Archiv
Hist Arkisto — Historiallinen Arkisto
Hist Arkv — Historiskt Arkiv
Hist B — Historia. Bratislava
Hist BA — Historia (Buenos Aires)
Hist Beiochem Compr Biochem — History of Biochemistry. Comprehensive Biochemistry
Hist Berwickshire Naturalists Club — History. Berwickshire Naturalists' Club
Hist Berwickshire Natur Club — History. Berwickshire Naturalists' Club
Hist Biblioth — Historiska Biblioteket
Hist Bogota — Historia (Bogota)
Hist Boliv — Historia Boliviana
Hist Bull — Historical Bulletin
Hist Can W — History of the Canadian West
Hist Cas — Historicky Casopis
Hist Casopis — Historicky Casopis
Hist Childhood Quart — History of Childhood Quarterly

Hist Child Q — History of Childhood Quarterly
Hist Cult — Historia y Cultura
HISTDD — Histopathology
Hist Doc — Historic Documents
Hist Dog — Histoire des Dogmes
His Teach M — History Teacher's Magazine
Hist Econ Soc — Histoire, Economie et Societe
Hist Educ — History of Education
Hist Educ J — History of Education Journal
Hist Educ Jour — History of Education Journal
Hist Educ Paris — Histoire de l'Education (Paris)
Hist Educ Q — History of Education Quarterly
Hist Educ Quart — History of Education Quarterly
Hist Educ Soc Bull — History of Education Society Bulletin
Hist Einzelschr — Historia Einzelschriften
Hist Envmt — Historic Environment
Hist Esp — Historia de Espana
Hist Eur Id — History of European Ideas
Hist Eur Ideas — History of European Ideas
Hist Euro Ideas — History of European Ideas
Hist Filol Meddel — Historisk-Filologiske Meddelelser
Hist Genootschap Utrecht Bijdragen — Bijdragen en Mededeelingen van het Historisch Genootschap (Gevestigd te Utrecht)
Hist Handl — Historiska Handlingar
Hist High Educ Annu — History of Higher Education Annual
Hist Hosp — Historia Hospitalium. Mitteilungen der Deutschen Gesellschaft fuer Kranken-Hausgeschichte
Hist Human Sci — History of the Human Sciences
Hist J — Historical Journal
Hist J — Historisches Jahrbuch
Hist Jahrb — Historisches Jahrbuch
Hist Jahrb Stadt Linz — Historisches Jahrbuch der Stadt Linz
Hist Jahrbuch — Historisches Jahrbuch
Hist J Auckland Waikato — Historical Journal Auckland-Waikato
Hist Jb — Historisches Jahrbuch
HistJb — Historisches Jahrbuch der Goerresgesellschaft
Hist Jb Goerres Ges — Historisches Jahrbuch der Goerres-Gesellschaft
Hist Jb Graz — Historisches Jahrbuch der Stadt Graz
Hist J Film — Historical Journal of Film, Radio, and Television
Hist J FR & TV — Historical Journal of Film, Radio, and Television
Hist Jnl F R & TV — Historical Journal of Film, Radio, and Television
Hist Ju (Birmingham) — Historical Journal (Birmingham)
Hist Jud — Historia Judaica
Hist J West Mass — Historical Journal of Western Massachusetts
Hist Kingston — Historic Kingston
Hist Kl Koen Bayer Akad Wiss — Historische Klasse der Koeniglichen Bayerischen Akademie der Wissenschaften
HistL — Historiographia Linguistica
Hist L — History (London)
Hist-Laerar Foeren Arsskr — Historielaerarnas Foerenings Aarsskrift
Hist Learn Sci Finland — History of Learning and Science in Finland
Hist Ling — Historiographia Linguistica
Hist Linguist — Historiographia Linguistica
Hist Litt Franc — Histoire Litteraire de la France
Hist Litt Hist Stud — Historiska och Litteraturhistoriska Studier
Hist Logic — History of Logic
Hist Lor — Histoire de Lorraine
Hist M — Historia. Milano
Hist M — Historical Magazine
HistM — Historical Magazine. Protestant Episcopal Church
Hist Mag — Historical Magazine of the Protestant Episcopal Church
Hist Mag PE Ch — Historical Magazine of the Protestant Episcopal Church
Hist Mag Prot Epsc Ch — Historical Magazine. Protestant Episcopal Church
Hist Mag Protest Episc Church — Historical Magazine of the Protestant Episcopal Church
Hist Math — Historia Mathematica
Hist Med — History of Medicine
Hist Meddel Kobenhavn — Historiska Meddelelser om Kobenhavn
Hist Medd Kobenhavn — Historiske Meddelelser om Staden Kobenhavn og dens Borgere
Hist Med Ser — History of Medicine Series
Hist Med Vet — Historia Medicinae Veterinariae
Hist Mem Acad Roy Sci Toulouse — Histoire et Memoires. Academie Royale des Sciences, Inscriptions, et Belles Lettres de Toulouse
Hist Mem Soc Sci Phys Lausanne — Histoire et Memoires de la Societe des Sciences Physiques de Lausanne
Hist Metall — Historical Metallurgy
Hist Metall Group Bull — Historical Metallurgical Group. Bulletin
Hist Meth — Historical Methods
Hist Methods Newsl — Historical Methods Newsletter
Hist Mex — Historia Mexicana
Hist Mexicana — Historia Mexicana. Colegio de Mexico
Hist Modern Phys Astronom — History of Modern Physics and Astronomy
Hist Mongol — Historium Mongolorum
Hist MSS Comm Rpts — Royal Commission on Historical Manuscripts. Reports
Hist Mus Basel Jber & Rechn — Historisches Museum Basel. Jahresberichte und Rechnungen
HistN — Historical New Hampshire
Hist Nat — Histoire et Nature. Cahiers de l'Association pour l'Histoire des Sciences de laNature
Hist News — Historical News
Hist NH — Historical New Hampshire
Histo — Historia
Histochem Cell Biol — Histochemistry and Cell Biology
Histochemis — Histochemistry

Histochem J — Histochemical Journal
Histocompat Test — Histocompatibility Testing
Hist of Photogr — History of Photography
Hist of Sci — History of Science
HistoJ — Historisches Jahrbuch
Histol Histopathol — Histology and Histopathology
Historia Math — Historia Mathematica
Historia Sci — Historia Scientiarum
Historia Sci 2 — Historia Scientiarum. Second Series
Historia Z — Historia. Zeitschrift fuer Alte Geschichte
Historia Z Alt Gesch — Historia. Zeitschrift fuer Alte Geschichte
Historical J — Historical Journal
Historical Jnl — Historical Journal
Historical Per — Historical Performance
Historic Brass J — Historic Brass Society Journal
Historievidensk — Historievidenskab
Historisk Tidskr — Historisk Tidskrift
HistorTd — Historisk Tidsskrift (Denmark)
HistorTf — Historisk Tidskrift
HistorTs — Historisk Tidsskrift
History — History Workshop
History of Ed Soc Bull — History of Education Society. Bulletin
HistoryP — History of Political Economy
History Rev — History. Reviews of New Books
HistoT — History Today
Hist Outl — Historical Outlook
Hist Outlook — Historical Outlook
Hist P — Historica. Praha
Hist Pap — Historical Papers
Hist Papers — Historical Papers
Hist Paraguaya Asuncion — Historia Paraguaya (Asuncion)
Hist Phil Life Sci — History and Philosophy of the Life Sciences
Hist Phil Logic — History and Philosophy of Logic
Hist Philol Meddel — Historiske-Philologiske Meddelelser
Hist Philos Life Sci (Pubbl Stn Zool Napoli Sect II) — History and Philosophy of the Life Sciences (Pubblicazioni della Stazione Zoologica di Napoli. Section II)
Hist Philos Logic — History and Philosophy of Logic
Hist Philos Soc Ohio Q Publ — Historical and Philosophical Society of Ohio. Quarterly Publications
Hist Phot — History of Photography
Hist Photo — History of Photography
Hist Photog — History of Photography
Hist Photogr — History of Photography
Hist Pisaurensia — Historica Pisaurensia
Hist Places NZ — Historic Places in New Zealand
Hist Pol Ec — History of Political Economy
Hist Pol Econ — History of Political Economy
Hist Pol Economy — History of Political Economy
Hist Polit — History of Political Economy
Hist Polit Econ — History of Political Economy
Hist Polit Thought — History of Political Thought
Hist Pol Th — History of Political Thought
Hist Portugal — Historia de Portugal
Hist Pres — Historic Preservation
Hist Preser — Historic Preservation
Hist Preserv — Historic Preservation
Hist Preservation — Historic Preservation
Hist Preserv Q Rep — Historic Preservation Quarterly Report
HistRB — Historical Review of Berks County
Hist Rec Aust Sci — Historical Records of Australian Science
Hist Refl D — Historical Reflections. Directions Series
Hist Reflec — Historical Reflections/Reflexions Historiques
Hist Reflect — Historical Reflections/Reflexions Historiques
Hist Rel — History of Religions
Hist Relig — History of Religions
Hist Religions — History of Religions
Hist Rev — Historical Review (New Zealand)
Histria A — Histria Archaeologica
Histria Arch — Histria Archaeologica
Hist Rio Piedras — Historia (Rio Piedras, Puerto Rico)
Hist R New Bk — History. Reviews of New Books
Hist Rom Rel — Historicorum Romanorum Reliquiae
Hist Rom Reliquiae — Historicorum Romanorum Reliquiae
HistS — Historical Studies
Hist Santiago — Historia. Instituto de Historia (Santiago, Chile)
Hist Sci — History of Science
Hist Sci Amer News Views — History of Science in America. News and Views
Hist Scientiarum — Historia Scientiarum. International Journal. History of Science Society of Japan
Hist Sci Med — Histoire des Sciences Medicales
Hist Sci Ser — History of Science Series
Hist Sci Textes Etudes — Histoire des Sciences. Textes et Etudes
Hist Sc Soc Manit Tr — Historical and Scientific Society of Manitoba. Transactions
Hist Ser Can Dep Agric — Historical Series. Canada Department of Agriculture
Hist Shqiperise — Historia e Shqiperise
Hist Soc — Histoire Sociale/Social History
Hist Soc Mont Contr — Historical Society of Montana. Contributions
Hist Soc Pa Archives — Historical Society of Pennsylvania. Archives
Hist Soc Q J — Historical Society of Queensland. Journal
Hist Soc Qld J — Historical Society of Queensland. Journal
Hist Soc Qld News — Historical Society of Queensland. News Bulletin
Hist Soc S CA Q — Historical Sociey of Southern California Quarterly
Hist Soc Sci Teach — History and Social Science Teacher
Hist St — Historicke Studie
Hist St Prob — On the History of Statistics and Probability

Hist Stud — Historical Studies
Hist Stud — Historical Studies-Australia and New Zealand
Hist Stud Aust NZ — Historical Studies-Australia and New Zealand
Hist Stud Austral — Historical Studies-Australia and New Zealand
Hist Studies — Historical Studies-Australia and New Zealand
Hist Stud Phys Biol Sci — Historical Studies in the Physical and Biological Sciences
Hist Stud Phys Sci — Historical Studies in the Physical Sciences
Histt — Historielaerarnas Foerenings Aarskrift
Hist Taschenb — Historisches Taschenbuch
Hist Tchr — History Teacher
Hist Tchr Mag — History Teacher's Magazine
Hist Teach — History Teacher
Hist Teach Assoc NSW Newsl — History Teachers Association of New South Wales. Newsletter
Hist Technol — History of Technology
Hist T Finl — Historisk Tidskrift foer Finland
Hist Theat — Histoire du Theatre
Hist Theor — History and Theory
Hist Theory — History and Theory
Hist Tidskr — Historisk Tidskrift
Hist Tidskr Finl — Historisk Tidskrift foer Finland
Hist Tidskr Skaneland — Historisk Tidskrift foer Skaneland
Hist Tidssk — Historisk Tidsskrift
Hist Tidsskr — Historisk Tidsskrift
Hist Tidsskr Kobenh — Historisk Tidsskrift udgivet af det Danske Historiske Forening (Kobenhaven)
Hist T Kopenhagen — Historisk Tidsskrift (Kopenhagen)
Hist Today — History Today
Hist T Oslo — Historisk Tidsskrift (Oslo)
Hist T Stockholm — Historisk Tidskrift (Stockholm)
Hist Tutk — Historiallisia Tutkimuksia/Historische Untersuchungen
Hist Tutkimuksia — Historiallisia Tutkimuksia. Suomen Historiallinen Seura
Hist Univ — History of Universities
Hist Ver Alt Dinkelsbuehl Jb — Historischer Verein Alt Dinkelsbuehl Jahrbuch
Hist Verein Oberpfalz & Regensburg Verh — Historischer Verein fuer Oberpfalz und Regensburg. Verhandlungen
Hist Ver f d Grafsch Ravensberg Jahresber — Historischer Verein fuer die Grafschaft Ravensberg zu Bielefeld. Jahresberichte
Hist Ver f Mittelfranken Jahresber — Historischer Verein fuer Mittelfranken. Jahresberichte
Hist Ver Straubing — Historischer Verein fuer Straubing und Umgebung
Hist Viertel — Historische Vierteljahrschrift
HistVjhrschr — Historische Vierteljahrsschrift
Hist Woonstede — Historische Woonstede
Hist Work S — History Workshop Series
Hist Worksh — History Workshop
Hist Workshop — History Workshop
Hist Workshop J — History Workshop Journal
Hist/WWII — History of the Second World War
Hist Z — Historische Zeitschrift
Hist Zbor — Historijski Zbornik
Hist Zeit — Historische Zeitschrift
Hist Zeitschr — Historische Zeitschrift
Hist Ztsch — Historische Zeitschrift
HIT — History of Political Economy
Hitachi Met Tech Rev — Hitachi Metals Technical Review
Hitachi Rev — Hitachi Review
Hitachi Technol — Hitachi Technology
Hitachi Zosen Tech Rev — Hitachi Zosen Technical Review
HITEA — High Temperature
HitK — Hitotsubashi Kenkyu
HITK — Hungarologiai Intezet Tudomanyos Kozlemenyei
Hitots J Econ — Hitotsubashi Journal of Economics
Hitotsubashi J Arts Sc — Hitotsubashi Journal of Arts and Sciences
Hitotsubashi J Arts Sci — Hitotsubashi Journal of Arts and Sciences
Hitotsubashi J Com Manag — Hitotsubashi Journal of Commerce and Management
Hitotsubashi J Commer and Mgt — Hitotsubashi Journal of Commerce and Management
Hitotsubashi J Commer Manage — Hitotsubashi Journal of Commerce and Management
Hitotsubashi J Econ — Hitotsubashi Journal of Economics
Hitotsubashi JL & Pol — Hitotsubashi Journal of Law and Politics
Hitotsubashi J Law and Politics — Hitotsubashi Journal of Law and Politics
Hitotsubashi J Social Studies — Hitotsubashi Journal of Social Studies
Hitotsubashi J Soc Stud — Hitotsubashi Journal of Social Studies
Hi Tr S — Historic Trials Series
HITSA — High Temperature Science
Hi Urb Mass Tran — Highway and Urban Mass Transportation
HiUS — Hispania (USA)
Hiyoshi Rev Natur Sci — Hiyoshi Review of Natural Science
HiZ — Historische Zeitschrift
HJ — Hibbert Journal
HJ — Historia Judaica
HJ — Historical Journal
HJ — Historisches Jahrbuch
HJ — Il Hagalgal (Jerusalem)
Hjaelp — Hjaelpskolan
HJAS — Harvard Journal of Asiatic Studies
HJAS — Hitotsubashi Journal of Arts and Sciences
H Jb — Handel Jahrbuch
HJb — Hebbel-Jahrbuch
HJB — Historisches Jahrbuch
HJB — Hojas Universitarias (Bogota)

HJC — Himalayan Journal (Calcutta)
HJC — Hitotsubashi Journal of Commerce and Management
HJCPDU — Hillside Journal of Clinical Psychiatry
HJDRB5 — Essays and Studies. Faculty of Hiroshima Jogakuin College
HJE — Hitotsubashi Journal of Economics
HJ Graz — Historisches Jahrbuch der Stadt Graz
HJH — Journal of History
HJIL — Houston Journal of International Law
Hj Kreis Hofgeismar — Heimatjahrbuch fuer den Kreis Hofgeismar
HJL — Heidelberger Jahrbuecher fuer Literatur
HJI — Hibbert Journal
HJLG — Hessisches Jahrbuch fuer Landesgeschichte
HJ Linz — Historisches Jahrbuch der Stadt Linz
HJMSA — Journal. Mysore University. Section B. Science
HJP — Hispanic Journal (Pennsylvania)
HJR — Henry James Review
HJS — Hungarian Jewish Studies
HJSS — Hitotsubashi Journal of Social Studies
HJud — Historia Judaica
HK — Hadtoertenelmi Koezlemenyek
HK — Hannoverscher Kourier
HK — Heritage of Kansas
HK — Hrvatsko Kolo
HKA — Handbuch des Kirchlichen Archivwesens
HKAW — Handbuch der Klassischen Altertumswissenschaft
HKCHDD — Korean Journal of Mycology
HKCSA — Hang K'ung Chih Shih
HKCTD — Handelingen. Koninklijke Commissie voor Toponymie en Dialectologie
HKDBK — Hokkaido Daigaku Bungakubu Kiyo
HK Econ Pap — Hong Kong Economic Papers
HKG — Handbuch der Kirchengeschichte fuer Studierende
HKGOKK — Handelingen. Koninklijke Gescheiden Oudheidkundige Kring van Kortrijk
HKGR — Hamburgische Kirche und Ihre Geistlichen seit der Reformation
H Ki — Hochkirche
HKKG — Heimatliche Kirchenkunst und Kirchengeschichte
HKL — Herder's Konservationslexikon
HKL — Hethitisches Keilschrift-Lesebuch
HK Law R — Hong Kong Law Review
HKLJ — Hong Kong Law Journal
HKN — Hogen Kenkyu Nenpo
HKOKD — Hakko Kogaku Kaishi
HKOM — Handelingen van de Kring voor Oudheidkunde, Letteren, en Kunst van Mechelen
HKROD — Bulletin of Environmental Sciences
HKSL — Handbuch der Katholischen Sittenlehre
HKT — Hethitische Keilschrifttexte aus Boghazkoei in Umschrift
HKTSA — Haikan To Sochi
HKU — Hilfsbuecher fuer den Kirchlichen Unterricht
H Ku G — Handbuch der Kulturgeschichte
H Ku G GD — Handbuch der Kulturgeschichte. Abteilung 1. Geschichte des Deutschen Lebens
H Ku G GV — Handbuch der Kulturgeschichte. Abteilung 2. Geschichte des Voelkerlebens
H Ku G KV — Handbuch der Kulturgeschichte. Neue Abteilung. Abteilung 2. Kulturen der Voelker
H Ku G ZD — Handbuch der Kulturgeschichte. Neue Abteilung. Abteilung 1. Zeitalter DeutscherKultur
HKW — Handbuch der Kunstwissenschaft
HKYSDK — Bulletin. Korea Ocean Research and Development Institute
HKZM — Handelingen. Koninklijke Zuidnederlandse Maatschappij voor Taal en Letterkunde en Geschiedenis
HL — Hanging Loose
HL — Harvard Library Bulletin
HL — Heilige Land
HL — Historiographia Linguistica
HI — Hochland
HL — Humanistica Lovaniensia
HLA Dis Regist — HLA and Disease Registry
HLA J — Hawaii Library Association. Journal
H Land — Heilig Land
HLB — Harvard Library Bulletin
HLB — Historisches Literaturblatt
HLB — Huntington Library. Bulletin
HLBFA — Heilberufe
HI D — Heiliger Dienst
HLE — Hispanofila
HLEKT — Handbuch der Literaturgeschichte in Einzeldarstellungen. Kroeners Taschenausgabe
HLF — Histoire de la Litterature Francaise. Publiee sous la Direction de Jean Calvet
HLF — Histoire Litteraire de la France
HLH Heiz Lueft Klimatech Haustech — HLH. Zeitschrift fuer Heizung, Lueftung, Klimatechnik, Haustechnik
HLH (Heiz Luftung Klimatech Haustech) — HLH. Zeitschrift fuer Heizung, Lueftung, Klimatechnik, Haustechnik
HLHR — Haskell Lectures on History of Religions
HLHS — Homenagem a D. Luis de Hoyos Sainz
HLHZA — HLH. Heizung, Lueftung, Klimatechnik, Haustechnik
HLH Zeit Heizung Lueftung Klim Haustech — HLH. Zeitschrift fuer Heizung, Lueftung, Klimatechnik, Haustechnik
HLH Z Heiz Lueft Klimatech Haustech — HLH. Zeitschrift fuer Heizung, Lueftung, Klimatechnik, Haustechnik
HLI — Hospital Literature Index
HLit — Hojas Litararias
HLJ — Hastings Law Journal

HLJ — Hindu Law Journal
HLK — Hanser Literatur-Kommentare
HLK — Hefte fuer Literatur und Kritik
HIK — Helikon. Rivista di Tradizione e Cultura Classica
HI L — Das Heilige Land. Koeln
HLPH — Holy Land Postal History
HLQ — Huntington Library. Quarterly
HLR — Haifa Law Reports
HLR — Harvard Law Review
HLR — Houston Law Review
HLS — Herald of Library Science
HLS — Historiska och Litteraturhistoriska Studier
HLS — Leather and Shoes
HISAN — Helsingin Sanomat
HLSCA — Health Laboratory Science
HLT — Hawaii's Labor Trends
Hlth — Health
Hlth Bull Br Columb — Health Bulletin of the British Columbia Department of Health and Welfare
Hlth Bull Dep Hlth Br Columb — Health Bulletin. Department of Health and Welfare. British Columbia
Hlth Bull Dep Hlth Scotl — Health Bulletin. Department of Health for Scotland
Hlth Bull Dep Hlth Vict — Health Bulletin. Department of Health. Victoria
Hlth Bull Malar Inst India — Health Bulletin. Malaria Institute of India
Hlth Bull Raleigh NC — Health Bulletin (Raleigh, N.C.)
Hlth Bull Salford — Health Bulletin (Salford)
Hlth Bull Simla — Health Bulletin (Simla, Calcutta)
Hlth Cent J Columbus — Health Center Journal (Columbus)
Hlth Educ Inf Bull — Health Education and Information Bulletin
Hlth Educ J — Health Education Journal
Hlth Educ Yb — Health Education Year Book
Hlth Emp — Health and Empire
Hlth Examr — Health Examiner [New York]
Hlth Forum — Health Forum
Hlth Homeop — Health through Homeopathy
Hlth Horiz — Health Horizon
Hlth Hyg Ho — Health and Hygiene in the Home
Hlth Hyg Home — Health and Hygiene in the Home
Hlth Inf Dig — Health Information Digest
Hlth Inf Dig Hot Count — Health Information Digest for Hot Countries
Hlth Instruct Yb — Health Instruction Yearbook
Hlth Instr Yb — Health Instruction Yearbook
Hlth Lab Sci — Health Laboratory Science
Hlth Ne — Health News
Hlth New — Health News
Hlth News Albany — Health News (Albany)
Hlth News Colombo — Health News (Colombo)
Hlth News Lond — Health News (London)
Hlth News Wash — Health News (Washington)
Hlth Notes S Aust — Health Notes for South Australia
Hlth Notes Springfield Mass — Health Notes (Springfield, Mass)
Hlth Offrs News Dig — Health Officers News-Digest
Hlth PAC — Health-PAC [Policy Advisory Center] Bulletin
Hlth Phys — Health Physics
Hlth Practnrs J — Health Practitioners' Journal
Hlth Pract Pamph — Health Practices Pamphlet
Hlth Rec — Health Record
Hlth Rght — Health Rights News
Hlth Saf at Work — Health and Safety at Work
Hlth Saf Code UK Atom Energy Auth — Health and Safety Code. United Kingdom Atomic Energy Authority
Hlth Saf Exec Direct Inf and Advisory Services Transl — Health and Safety Executive Directorate of Information and Advisory Services. Translations
Hlth Saf Monitor — Health and Safety Monitor
Hlth Sch Ch — Health of the School Child
Hlth Sch Child Allahabad — Health of the School Child (Allahabad)
Hlth Sch Child Lond — Health of the School Child (London)
Hlth Serv — Health Services
Hlth Serv Res — Health Services Research
Hlth Soc Serv J — Health and Social Service Journal
Hlth Soc Welf — Health and Social Welfare
Hlth Soc Wrk — Health and Social Work
Hlth Soil — Health and the Soil
Hlth Top — Health Topics
Hlth Torch — Health Torch. Libyan-American Joint Public Health Service
Hlth Transit Rev — Health Transition Review
Hlth Transit Ser — Health Transition Series
Hlth Yb — Health Yearbook
HLTPA — Health Physics
HLVG — Das Heilige Land in Vergangenheit und Gegenwart
HLW — Handbuch der Literaturwissenschaft
HLW — Landbode; Hollands Landbouwweekblad
HL Wkly Inf Bull — House of Lords Weekly Information Bulletin
HLWM — Handbuch der Literaturwissenschaft (Herausgegeben von Martimort)
HM — Haagsch Maandblad
HM — Hadasah Monthly
HM — Hallische Monographien
HM — Harper's Magazine
HM — Hejnat Mariacki
Hm — Hermes
HM — Historia Mathematica
HM — Historia Mexicana
HM — Hommes et Mondes
HM — Hortus Musicus
HM — Hospitality Management

HMA — Helvetica Medica Acta
HMACA — Helvetica Medica Acta
HMad — Hispania (Madrid)
HMANG — Handbuch der Mittelalterlichen und Neueren Geschichte
HMANGA — Handbuch der Mittelalterlichen und Neueren Geschichte. Abteilung 1. Allgemeines
HMANGH — Handbuch der Mittelalterlichen und Neueren Geschichte. Abteilung 4. Hilfswissenschaften und Altertuemer
HMANGP — Handbuch der Mittelalterlichen und Neueren Geschichte. Abteilung 2. Politische Geschichte
HMANGV — Handbuch der Mittelalterlichen und Neueren Geschichte. Abteilung 3. Verfassung,Recht, Wirtschaft
HMB — Hermannsburger Missionsblatt
HMCSR — Health and Medical Care Services Review
HMD — Hamdard Medical Digest
HMD — Handbuch der Modernen Datenverarbeitung
HMDDAH — Hamdard Medicus
HME — Hajkusagi Muzeum Evkoenyve
HME — Historical Magazine of the Protestant Episcopal Church
HMENR — High Mountain Ecology Research Station (Finse, Norway) Reports
H Mex — Historia Mexicana
HMFP — Historia de las Misiones Franciscanas y Narracion de los Progresos de la Geografia en el Oriente del Peru. B. Izaguirre [Lima]
HMGOG — Handelingen der Maatschappij voor Geschiedenis en Oudheidkunde te Gent
HMI — Hadashot Muzeon Israel
HMIF — Histoire et Memoires. Institute de France
HMJ — Hebrew Medical Journal
HmJ — Himalayan Journal
HMK — Hefte zur Missionskunde
HMK — Historiske Meddelelser om Staden Kobenhavn og dens Borgere
HM Kbh — Historiske Meddelelser om Staden Kobenhavn og dens Borgere
HML — Hale Memorial Lectures
HMM — Harper's Monthly Magazine
HMM — Hotel and Motel Management
HMMNL — Handelingen en Mededeelingen. Maatschappij der Nederlandsche Letterkunde te Leiden
HMN — Hemmings Motor News
HMOMC — Monumenta Historica Ordinis Minorum Capuccinorum
HMP — Homenaje a Menendez Pidal
HMPCD9 — Handchirurgie, Mikrochirurgie, Plastische Chirurgie
HMPEC — Historical Magazine of the Protestant Episcopal Church
HMQ — Hungarian Music Quarterly
HMR — Hungry Mind Review
HMS — Hazardous Materials Systems
HMS — Homenagem a Martins Sarmento
HMSCDO — Human Movement Science
HMSEDU — History of Medicine Series
HMSK — Historiske Meddelelser om Staden Kobenhavn
HMSO — Her Majesty's Stationary Office
HMSO Daily Lists — Her Majesty's Stationery Office Daily Lists
HMT — Handbuch der Moraltheologie
HMT — Handwoerterbuch der Musikalischen Terminologie
HMTGA4 — Helminthologia
HMW Jb — HMW [Heilmittelwerke] Jahrbuch
HMYB — Hinrichsen's Musical Year Book
HMZ — Helvetische Muenzen-Zeitung
HMZA — Hamburg in Zahlen
HN — Hadassah Newsletter
HN — Hamann Newsletter
HN — Hemingway Notes
HN — Here and Now
Hn — Historian
HN — Historia Numorum
Hn — Hochschulnachrichten
HN — Homme Nouveau
HNAND8 — Human Nutrition. Applied Nutrition
HNCNDI — Human Nutrition. Clinical Nutrition
HND — Handwierk
Hnd — Hunden
HNDKB — Hyogo Noka Daigaku Kiyo
HNews — Hemingway Newsletter
HNH — Historical New Hampshire
HNK — Ho Neos Koubaras
HNL — Hadassah Newsletter
HNL — HUD [Department of Housing and Urban Development] Newsletter
HNO — HNO. Hals-, Nasen-, Ohren-Heilkunde
HNorv — Humaniora Norvegica
HNO Weg Fac — HNO: Wegweiser fuer die Fachaerztliche Praxis [Later, HNO. Hals-, Nasen-, Ohren-Heilkunde]
HNR — Hikone Ronso
HNR — Historia Naturalis (Rome)
HNSWA — Health in New South Wales
HNT — Handbuch zum Neuen Testament
HNTA — Handbuch zu den Neutestamentlichen Apokryphen
HNTSup — Handbuch zum Neuen Testament. Supplement
HO — Handbuch der Orientalistik
Ho — Hochland
HO — Human Organization
HOAGDS — Annual Research Reviews. Hormones and Aggression
Ho & For R — Home and Foreign Review
Hoard's D — Hoard's Dairyman
Hoards Dairym — Hoard's Dairyman
HOASAR — Helvetica Odontologica Acta. Supplementum
Hob — Hobbies

Hobbybl — Hobby Bladet
Hobby Electron — Hobby Electronics
Hoch — Hochland. Monatsschrift fuer alle Gebiete des Wissens der Literatur und Kunst
Hochfrequenztech Elektroakust — Hochfrequenztechnik und Elektroakustik
Hochl — Hochland
Hochsch Archit Bauwes Weimar Wiss Z — Hochschule fuer Architektur und Bauwesen Weimar. WissenschaftlicheZeitschrift
Hochsch Archit Bauwes Weimar Wiss Z Reihe B — Hochschule fuer Architektur und Bauwesen Weimar. WissenschaftlicheZeitschrift. Reihe B
Hochschulb Math — Hochschulbuecher fuer Mathematik
Hochschulb Phys — Hochschulbuecher fuer Physik
Hochschulbuecher fuer Phys — Hochschulbuecher fuer Physik
Hochschuldidaktik Naturwiss — Hochschuldidaktik der Naturwissenschaften
Hochschullehrb Biol — Hochschullehrbuecher fuer Biologie
HochschulSammlung Ingenieurwiss Datenverarbeitung — HochschulSammlung Ingenieurwissenschaft Datenverarbeitung
HochschulSammlung Naturwiss Informat — HochschulSammlung Naturwissenschaft Informatik
HochschulSammlung Naturwiss Math — HochschulSammlung Naturwissenschaft Mathematik
Hoch u Tiefbau — Hoch- und Tiefbau
HOD — Holz-Zentralblatt. Unabhangiges Organ fuer die Forstwirtschaft und Holzwirtschaft
Hodowla Rosl — Hodowla Roslin
Hodowla Rosl Aklim Nasienn — Hodowla Roslin Aklimatyzacja i Nasiennictwo
HoE — Ho Eranistes
HOECD2 — Holarctic Ecology
Hoefchenbr Wiss Prax — Hoefchen-Briefe fuer Wissenschaft und Praxis
Hoehenklima Sein Einfluss Menschen Gedenkvorlesung — Hoehenklima und Sein Einfluss auf den Menschen. Gedenkvorlesung
Hoehle Wiss Beih — Hoehlankunde Wissenschaftliche Beihefte
Hoehle Z Karst Hoehlenkunde — Hoehle Zeitschrift fuer Karst- und Hoehlenkunde
Hoe Jb — Hoelderlin-Jahrbuch
Hoesch Ber Forsch Entwickl Unserer Werke — Hoesch. Berichte aus Forschung und Entwicklung Unserer Werke
Hoesch Ber Forsch Entwickl Werke — Hoesch. Arbeitskreis Forschung und Entwicklung, Berichte aus Forschung und Entwicklung Unserer Werke
Hoeven en Vriese Ts — Tijdschrift voor Natuurlijke Geschiedenis en Physiologie. Hoeven en Vriese
Hoffys Orchardists Companion — Hoffy's Orchardist's Companion. Or, Fruits of the United States
Hof LR — Hofstra Law Review
Hofstra L Rev — Hofstra Law Review
Hofstra Univ Yrbk Bus — Hofstra University. Yearbook of Business
Hogar & Archit — Hogar y Architectura
Hogarth Ess — Hogarth Essays
Hog Farm Manage — Hog Farm Management
Hogg — Hogg's Instructor
Hog Kenk — Hogaku Kenkyu
Hog Prod — Hog Production
HOH — Haunt of Horror
HOH — Houtwereld Vakblad Gewijd aan de Belangen van de Houthandel en van de Houtverwerkende Industrie
Hohenheimer Arb — Hohenheimer Arbeiten
Hohenheimer Umwelttag — Hohenheimer Umwelttagung
Hohenzoll Jb — Hohenzollern-Jahrbuch. Forschungen und Abbildungen zur Geschichte der Hohenzollern in Brandenburg-Preussen
Hohenzoll Jhft — Hohenzollerische Jahreshefte
HOI — Handbook of Inflammation
Hoja Divulgativa Campo Agric Exp (Valle Fuerte) — Hoja Divulgativa. Campo Agricola Experimental (Valle del Fuerte)
Hoja Tec INIA — Hoja Tecnica INIA
Hoja Tec (Inst Nac Invest Agrar) (Spain) — Hoja Tecnica. INIA (Instituto Nacional de Investigaciones Agrarias) (Spain)
Hoja Tisiol — Hoja Tisiologica
HoJb — Hoelderlin-Jahrbuch
Hojskolebl — Hojskolebladet
Hoj Tisiol — Hoja Tisiologica
HOK — Handbuch der Ostkirchenkunde
HOKBA — Hoken Butsuri
HOKDA — Hokkaido Daigaku Nogakubu Enshurin Kenkyu Hokoku
Hokkaido Forest Prod Res Inst Rept — Hokkaido Forest Products Research Institute. Reports
Hokkaido For Prod Res Inst Mon Rep — Hokkaido Forest Products Research Institute. Monthly Reports
Hokkaido Geol Surv Rep — Hokkaido Geological Survey. Report
Hokkaido J Med Sci — Hokkaido Journal of Medical Science
Hokkaido J Orthop & Trauma Surg — Hokkaido Journal of Orthopedic and Traumatic Surgery
Hokkaido J Public Health — Hokkaido Journal of Public Health
Hokkaido Math J — Hokkaido Mathematical Journal
Hokkaido Natl Agric Exp Stn Data — Hokkaido National Agricultural Experiment Station. Data
Hokkaido Natl Agric Exp Stn Rep — Hokkaido National Agricultural Experiment Station. Report
Hokkaido Natl Agric Exp Stn Soil Surv Rep — Hokkaido National Agricultural Experiment Station. Soil Survey Report
Hokkaido Univ Fac Sci J Ser 4 — Hokkaido University. Faculty of Science. Journal. Series 4. Geology and Mineralogy
Hokkaido Univ Inst Low Temp Sci Low Temp Sci Ser A Phys Sci — Hokkaido University. Institute of Low Temperature Science. Low Temperature Science. Series A. Physical Sciences
Hokkaido Univ Med Libr Ser — Hokkaido University. Medical Library Series
Hokk Daig Juig Bu — Hokkaido Daigaku Juigaku Bu

Hokoku Aichi-Ken Ringyo Shikenjo — Hokoku. Aichi-ken Ringyo Shikenjo
Hokoku Bull Akita Fruit Tree Exp Stn/Akita Kaju Shikenjo — Hokoku. Bulletin. Akita Fruit-Tree Experiment Station/Akita Kaju Shikenjo
Hokoku Bull Chugoku Natl Agric Exp Stn Ser E Environ Div — Hokoku. Bulletin. Chugoku National Agricultural Experiment Station. Series E. Environment Division
Hokoku Bull Kagoshima Tob Exp Stn/Kagoshima Tabako Shikenjo — Hokoku. Bulletin. Kagoshima Tobacco Experiment Station/Kagoshima Tabako Shikenjo
Hokoku Bull Natl Inst Agric Sci Ser A Phys and Stat — Hokoku. Bulletin. National Institute of Agricultural Sciences. Series A. Physics and Statistics
Hokoku Bull Tohoku Daigaku Nogaku Kenkyujo — Hokoku. Bulletin. Tohoku Daigaku Nogaku Kenkyujo
Hokoku Jap Tab Shikenjo Okayama/Bull Okayama Tob Exp Stn — Hokoku, Japan. Tabako Shikenjo Okayama/Bulletin. Okayama Tobacco Experiment Station
HOKSA — Hokkaido-Ritsu Kogyo Shikenjo Hokoku
Hokuriku J Anesthesiol — Hokuriku Journal of Anesthesiology
Hokuriku J Public Health — Hokuriku Journal of Public Health
HOL — Handbuch der Orientalistik (Leiden)
Holarct Ecol — Holarctic Ecology
Holarctic Ecol — Holarctic Ecology
Holbert H — Holbert Herald
Holb Rev — Holborn Review
Hol Crit — Hollins Critic
Holderlin-Jahrb — Hoelderlin-Jahrbuch
HoldhM — Holdheims Monatsschrift fuer Handelsrecht und Bankwesen. Steuerund Stempelfragen
Hollaend Mg — Hollaendisches Magazin der Naturkunde
Holland Reg Hist Tijdschr — Holland. Regional-Historisch Tijdschrift
Holland Shipbuild — Holland Shipbuilding
Holland Shipbuild — Holland Shipbuilding and Marine Engineering [Later, Holland Shipbuilding]
Hollands Maandbl — Hollands Maandblad
Holld Info — Holland Info
Holl Landbouwweekbl — Hollandsch Landbouwweekblad. Officieel Orgaan van de Hollandsche Maatschappij van Landbouw
Holloman Symp Primate Immunol Mol Genet — Holloman Symposium on Primate Immunology and Molecular Genetics
Hollow Sec — Hollow Section
Holl Rev — Hollandsche Revue
Holly Newslett — Holly Newsletter. Holly Society of America
Holly Soc J — Holly Society Journal
Hollywood Q — Hollywood Quarterly
Hologr Opt Secur Syst — Holographic Optical Security Systems
Holstein World — Holstein-Friesian World
Holy Name Mo — Holy Name Monthly
Holzchem Ind — Holzchemische Industrie
Holzf Holzv — Holzforschung und Holzverwertung
Holzf Holzverwert — Holzforschung und Holzverwertung
Holzforsch — Holzforschung
Holzforsch Holzverwert — Holzforschung und Holzverwertung
Holz Kur — Holz-Kurier
Holz Roh We — Holz als Roh- und Werkstoff
Holz Roh- Werkst — Holz als Roh- und Werkstoff
Holztechnol — Holztechnologie
Holz Zbl — Holz-Zentralblatt
Holz Zentralbl — Holz-Zentralblatt
Hom — Homiletics
Hom — Hommes et Mondes
Hombres Ci Tec — Hombres de la Ciencia y Tecnica
Hombre y Cult — Hombre y Cultura
HOME — Herman Otto Muzeum Evkoenyve
Home Auto — Home and Auto Buyer Guide
Home Build Jnl — Home Builders Journal
Home Com N — Home Computer News
Home Ec Bul — Home Economics Bulletin
Home Econ Guide GH Univ Mo Columbia Coop Ext Serv — Home Economics Guide GH. University of Missouri-Columbia. Cooperative ExtensionService
Home Econ Inf Kern Cty Coop Ext Univ Calif — Home Economics Information. Kern County. Cooperative Extension. University of California
Home Econ NC Agric Ext Serv — Home Economics. North Carolina Agricultural Extension Service
Home Econ News — Home Economics News
Home Econ Newsl — Home Economics Newsletter
Home Econ Res J — Home Economics Research Journal
Home Energy Dig Wood Burn Q — Home Energy Digest and Wood Burning Quarterly
Home Finan — Savings and Home Financing Source Book 1984
Home Fit Equip — Home Fitness and Equipment
Home For Fields — Home and Foreign Fields
Home Gard — Home Garden [Later, Family Handyman]
Home Gard Bull US Dep Agric — Home and Garden Bulletin. US Department of Agriculture
Home Gdn Bull — Home and Garden Bulletins
Home Geog Mo — Home Geographic Monthly
Home Geogr Mon — Home Geographic Monthly
Home Health Care Serv Q — Home Health Care Services Quarterly
Home Healthc Nurse — Home Healthcare Nurse
Home Health J — Home Health Journal
Home Health Rev — Home Health Review
Home Improvements Jnl — Home Improvements Journal
Home Mag — Homemakers' Magazine
Home Off Lib Bull — Home Office Library Bulletin
Home Off Res Bull — Home Office Research Bulletin
Home Prog — Home Progress

Homes & Gdns — Homes and Gardens
Home Sat Newsl — Home Satellite Newsletter
Home Sci — Home Science
Homes Int — Homes International
Home Tech — Home Techniques
Home Video — Home Video Publisher
Homicide Stat — Homicide Statistcs
Homiletic R — Homiletic Review
Homiletic Rev — Homiletic Review
Homme & Archit — Homme et l'Architecture
Homme et Soc — Homme et Societe
Homme Oiseau — Homme et l'Oiseau
Homme Preh — Homme Prehistorique
Hommes Aujourd Hui — Hommes d'Aujourd'Hui
Hommes et Migr — Hommes et Migrations
Hommes et Migr Doc — Hommes et Migrations. Documents
Hommes et Techn — Hommes et Techniques
Homme Soc — Homme et Societe
Hommes Tech — Hommes et Techniques
Homm O-Mer — Hommes d'Outre-Mer
Homm Techn — Hommes et Techniques
Homoeopath — Homoeopathic Digest
Homogeneous Catal Org Inorg Chem — Homogeneous Catalysis in Organic and Inorganic Chemistry
Hom Past Rev — Homiletic and Pastoral Review
Hom R — Homiletic Review
HON — Revue Commerciale
HONAA — Helvetica Odontologica Acta
Honam Math J — Honam Mathematical Journal
Honda Meml Ser Mater Sci — Honda Memorial Series on Materials Science
Hond Lit Tegucigalpa — Honduras Literaria (Tegucigalpa)
Hond Rotar Tegucigalpa — Honduras Rotaria (Tegucigalpa)
Honeybee Sci — Honeybee Science
Honeywell Comput J — Honeywell Computer Journal
Hongik Univ J — Hongik University. Journal
Hong Kong Anthrop — Hong Kong Anthropology
Hong Kong Eng — Hong Kong Engineer
Hong Kong Engr — Hong Kong Engineer
Hong Kong LJ — Hong Kong Law Journal
Hong Kong Med J — Hong Kong Medical Journal. Hong Kong Academy of Medicine
Hong Kong Nurs J — Hong Kong Nursing Journal
Hong Kong UL Jo — Hong Kong University. Law Journal
Hong Kong Univ Fish J — Hong Kong University. Fisheries Journal
HONKAY — Hokkaido National Agricultural Experiment Station. Soil Survey Report
Honolulu Acad A J — Honolulu Academy of Arts Journal
Honolulu Ad — Honolulu Advertiser
Hon Ulst — Honest Ulsterman
Hookers Icon Pl — Hooker's Icones Plantarum. Or Figures, with Brief Descriptive Characters and Remarks of New or Rare Plants
Hook J Bot — Journal of Botany (W. J. Hooker, Editor)
Hoosier Munic — Hoosier Municipalities
Hoosier Sch Lib — Hoosier School Libraries
Hop — Hopital
Hop Aide Soc Par — Hopital et l'Aide Sociale a Paris
Hop Aujourd — Hopital d'Aujourd'hui
Hop Belge — Hopital Belge
HOPE — History of Political Economy
Hopei Agric Forest J — Hopei Agricultural and Forestry Journal/Hopei Nung-Lin Hsueeh-K'an
Hope Rep Q — Hope Reports Quarterly
Hopf Rdsch — Hopfen Rundschau
Hopkins Q — Hopkins Quarterly
Hoppe-Seyler's Z Physiol Chem — Hoppe-Seyler's Zeitschrift fuer Physiologische Chemie
Hoppe-Seylers Zs — Hoppe-Seyler's Zeitschrift fuer Physiologische Chemie
Hoppe-Seyler's Ztschr Physiol Chem — Hoppe-Seyler's Zeitschrift fuer Physiologische Chemie
HopQ — Hopkins Quarterly
Hop R — Hopkins Review
HOPT — Handbook of Powder Technology
HO Publ — Hydrographic Office. Publication
HO Purdue Univ Coop Ext Serv — HO-Purdue University. Cooperative Extension Service
Hop U Stud — Johns Hopkins University. Studies in Historical and Political Science
HOQ — Hansard Oral Questions
H Or — Handbuch der Orientalistik
Hor — Horizon
Hor — Horizonte. Emuna
Hor — Horyzonty
Hora Med — Hora Medica
Hori — Horisont [Vasa, Finland]
HORI — Horizons
Horiz — Horizons
Horiz — Horizontes. Revista de la Universidad Catolica de Puerto Rico
Horiz Biochem Biophys — Horizons in Biochemistry and Biophysics
Horiz Endocrinol — Horizons in Endocrinology
Horizon Econ BA — Horizontes Economicos (Buenos Aires)
Horizon Ponce — Horizontes (Ponce, Puerto Rico)
Horizons Bib Th — Horizons in Biblical Theology
Horiz Unltd — Horizons Unlimited
HORM — Horizontes. Mexico
Hormayrs Taschenb — Taschenbuch fuer Vaterlaendische Geschichte (Von Hormayr)
Horm Behav — Hormones and Behavior

Horm Cancer Sel Pap Discuss Clin Cancer Semin — Hormones and Cancer. Selected Papers and Discussion from the ClinicalCancer Seminar
Horm Cell Regul — Hormones and Cell Regulation
Hormel Inst Univ Minn Annu Rep — Hormel Institute. University of Minnesota. Annual Report
Horm Factors Fertil Infertil Contracept Proc Meet — Hormonal Factors in Fertility, Infertility, and Contraception. Proceedings. Meeting. International Study Group for Steroid Hormones
Horm Front Gynecol — Hormone Frontier in Gynecology
Horm Immun Proc Int Conf — Hormones and Immunity. Proceedings of the International Conference onHormones and Immunity
Horm Metab — Hormones et Metabolisme
Horm Metab Res — Hormone and Metabolic Research
Horm Metab Res Horm Stoffwechselforsch Horm Metab — Hormone and Metabolic Research/Hormon- und Stoffwechselforschung/ Hormones et Metabolisme
Horm Metab Res (Suppl) — Hormone and Metabolic Research (Supplement)
Horm Metab Res Suppl Ser — Hormone and Metabolic Research. Supplement Series
Hormone Beh — Hormones and Behavior
Hormone Met — Hormone and Metabolic Research
Hormone Res — Hormone Research
Horm Percept Signal Transduction Anim Plants — Hormone Perception and Signal Transduction in Animals and Plants
Horm Recept — Hormone Receptors
Horm Res — Hormone Research
Horm Res (Basel) — Hormone Research (Basel)
Horm Signaling — Hormones and Signaling
Horm Steroids Proc Int Congr — Hormonal Steroids. Proceedings of the International Congress onHormonal Steroids
Horm Stoffwechselforsch — Hormon- und Stoffwechselforschung
Horn Afr — Horn of Africa
Horn Bk — Horn Book Magazine
Horn Hutn — Hornik a Hutnik
Horn Vestn — Hornicky Vestnik
Horn Vestn a Hornicke a Hutnicke Listy — Hornicky Vestnik a Hornicke a Hutnicke Listy
Horol Inst Am J — Horological Institute of America. Journal
Horol J — Horological Journal
HorsAb — Horseman's Abstracts
Hort — Horticultura
Hort — Horticulture
Hort — Horticulture News
Hort Abstr — Horticultural Abstracts
Hort Alsac — Horticulture Alsacienne
Hort Chalonnais — Horticulteur Chalonnais
Hort Genev — Horticulture Genevoise. Societe d'Horticulture de Geneve
Hortic Abstr — Horticultural Abstracts
Hortic Adv — Horticultural Advance
Hortic Adv (Sahranpur) — Horticultural Advance (Sahranpur)
Hortic Bull — Horticultural Bulletin
Hortic Cent Loughgall Annu Rep — Horticultural Centre Loughgall. Annual Report
Hortic Dig Univ Hawaii Coop Ext Serv — Horticulture Digest. University of Hawaii. Cooperative Extension Service
Hortic Div Tokai Kinki Agric Exp Stn Rep — Horticultural Division of Tokai Kinki Agricultural Experiment Station.Reports
Hortic Educ Assoc Yearb — Horticultural Education Association. Yearbook
Hortic Fr — Horticulture Francaise
Hortic Ind — Horticulture Industry
Hortic News NJ State Hortic Soc — Horticultural News. New Jersey State Horticultural Society
Hortic NZ — Horticulture in New Zealand
Hortic Prod Rev FHORT US Dep Agric Foreign Agric Serv — Horticultural Products Review FHORT. US Department of Agriculture. Foreign Agricultural Service
Hortic Res — Horticultural Research
Hortic Res Inst Ont Rep — Horticultural Research Institute of Ontario. Report
Hortic Rev — Horticultural Reviews
Hortic Sci (Calcutta) — Horticultural Science (Calcutta)
Hortic Sci (Stuttg) — Horticultural Science (Stuttgart)
Hortic Spec Crops — Horticulture and Special Crops
Horticulteur Franc — Horticulteur Francais. Journal des Amateurs et des Interets Horticoles
Horticulture Ind — Horticulture Industry
Hortic Vitic Sci (Sofia) — Horticultural and Viticultural Sciences (Sofia)
Hort J Florists Reg — Horticultural Journal, and Florists' Register, of Useful Information Connected with Floriculture
Hort J Roy Ladys Mag — Horticultural Journal and Royal Lady's Magazine
Hort J Rural Art Rural Taste — Horticulturist and Journal of Rural Art and Rural Taste
Hort Mach Leafl — Horticultural Machinery Leaflet
Hort N — Horticultural News
Hort Pl Breed — Horticultural Plan Breeding
Hort Praticien — Horticulteur Praticien
Hort Provencal — Horticulteur Provencal
Hort Reg Gen Mag — Horticultural Register, and General Magazine
Hort Res — Horticultural Research
Hort Res (Edinb) — Horticultural Research (Edinburgh)
Hort Res Rec — Horticultural Research Record. New South Wales Department of Agriculture. Division of Horticulture
Hort Rev Bot Mag — Horticultural Review and Botanical Magazine
HortSci — HortScience
Hort Times Kanagawa — Horticultural Times/Engei Tsushin (Kanagawa)
Hort Trop — Horticulture Tropicale. Taiwan Horticultural Society
HOS — Harvard Oriental Series

HOS — Holland Shipbuilding
Hos — Hospitality
Hos Ec — Hospitium Ecclesiae
Ho Sey Zs — Hoppe-Seyler's Zeitschrift fuer Physiologische Chemie
Hoshasen Kagaku Append — Hoshasen Kagaku. Appendix
HOSIA — Hospitals
Hosiery St — Hosiery Statistics
Hosiery Trade J — Hosiery Trade Journal
H o S Mus — Handels- og Sofartsmuseet paa Kronborg
Hosp — Hospital
Hosp — Hospitalia
Hosp — Hospitalis
Hosp — Hospitality
Hosp — Hospitals
HospAb — Hospital Abstracts
Hosp Abstr Serv — Hospital Abstract Service
Hosp Adm Can — Hospital Administration in Canada
Hosp Adm (Chicago) — Hospital Administration (Chicago)
Hosp Admin Curr — Hospital Administration Currents
Hosp Admitting Mon — Hospital Admitting Monthly
Hosp Adm (New Delhi) — Hospital Administration (New Delhi)
Hosp and Health — Hospital and Health Services Administration
Hosp Assoc J — Hospitals' Association. Journal
Hosp Bond Rev — Hospital Bond Review
Hosp Build Bull — Hospital Building Bulletin
Hosp Buyer — Hospital Buyer
Hosp Buyers Guide — Hospital Buyer's Guide
Hosp Cap Finance (Chicago) — Hospital Capital Finance (Chicago)
Hosp Care — Hospital Care
Hosp Cent Mil (Lomas De Sotelo Mex) Publ Trimest — Hospital Central Militar (Lomas De Sotelo, Mexico). Publicacion Trimestral
Hosp Colon Rev Med — Hospital Colonia. Revista Medica
Hosp Comm Psych — Hospital and Community Psychiatry
Hosp Commun — Hospital and Community Psychiatry
Hosp Community Psychiat — Hospital and Community Psychiatry
Hosp Community Psychiatr — Hospital and Community Psychiatry
Hosp Community Psychiatry — Hospital and Community Psychiatry
Hosp Dev — Hospital Development
Hosp Develop — Hospital Development
Hosp Dig Buyer — Hospital Digest and Buyer
Hosp Employee Health — Hospital Employee Health
Hosp Eng — Hospital Engineering
Hosp Equip Supplies — Hospital Equipment and Supplies
Hosp Financ Manage — Hospital Financial Management
Hosp Finan Manage — Hospital Financial Management
Hosp Fin Mgt — Hospital Financial Management
Hosp Food Nutr Focus — Hospital Food and Nutrition Focus
Hosp Formul — Hospital Formulary
Hosp Formul Manage — Hospital Formulary Management
Hosp Forum — Hospital Forum
Hosp Gen — Hospital General. Revista de Medicina y Cirugia
Hosp Gen (Madr) — Hospital General (Madrid)
Hosp Geral Santo Antonio Porto Bol — Hospital Geral de Santo Antonio-Porto. Boletim
Hosp Gift Shop Manage — Hospital Gift Shop Management
Hosp Health Care Newsl — Hospital Health Care Newsletter
Hosp Health Netw — Hospitals and Health Networks
Hosp Health Serv Adm — Hospital and Health Services Administration
Hosp Health Serv Admin — Hospital and Health Services Administration
Hosp Health Serv Rev — Hospital and Health Services Review
Hosp High — Hospital Highlights
Hosp Hlth Man — Hospital and Health Management
Hosp Hoje — Hospital de Hoje
Hosp-Hyg — Hospital-Hygiene
Hosp Hyg Gesundheitswes Desinfekt — Hospital-Hygiene, Gesundheitswesen, und Desinfektion
Hospice J — Hospice Journal
Hosp Infect Control — Hospital Infection Control
Hosp Inpat Stat West Aust — Hospital In-Patient Statistics. Western Australia
Hosp Int — Hospital International
Hospit Abstr — Hospital Abstracts
Hospital Admin — Hospital Administration
Hospitality Educ — Hospitality Educator
Hosp Ital La Plata Rev Med — Hospital Italiano de La Plata. Revista Medica
Hospital Mag — Hospital Magazine
Hospital Mus News — Hospital Music Newsletter
Hospital (Rio De J) — Hospital (Rio De Janeiro)
Hospit Lit Index — Hospital Literature Index
Hospit Manage Rev — Hospital Management Review
Hosp J — Hospice Journal
Hosp Jt Dis Bull — Hospital for Joint Diseases. Bulletin
Hosp Law Newsletter — Hospital Law Newsletter
Hosp Libr — Hospital Libraries
Hosp Lit Ind — Hospital Literature Index
Hosp Manag — Hospital Management
Hosp Manage Commun — Hospital Management Communications
Hosp Manage Q — Hospital Management Quarterly
Hosp Manager — Hospital Manager
Hosp Mater Manage — Hospital Materials Management
Hosp Mater Manage Q — Hospital Materiel Management Quarterly
Hosp Med — Hospital Medicine
Hosp Med Staff — Hospital Medical Staff
Hosp Med Staff Advocate — Hospital Medical Staff Advocate
Hospos Zpr — Hospodarsky Zpravodaj
Hosp Peer Rev — Hospital Peer Review

Hosp Pharm — Hospital Pharmacist
Hosp Pharm — Hospital Pharmacy
Hosp Pharm (Saskatoon Sask) — Hospital Pharmacist (Saskatoon, Saskatchewan)
Hosp Physician — Hospital Physician
Hosp Plan — Hospital Planning
Hosp Port — Hospitais Portugueses
Hosp Prac — Hospital Practice
Hosp Pract — Hospital Practice
Hosp Practice — Hospital Practice
Hosp Pract Off Ed — Hospital Practice. Office Edition
Hosp Prog — Hospital Progress
Hosp Progr — Hospital Progress
Hosp Purch Manage — Hospital Purchasing Management
Hosp Risk Manage — Hospital Risk Management
Hosp Secur Saf Manage — Hospital Security and Safety Management
Hosp Servidores Estado Rev Med — Hospital dos Servidores do Estado. Revista Medica
Hosp Social Serv — Hospital Social Service
Hosp Superv — Hospital Supervision
Hosp Superv Bull — Hospital Supervisors Bulletin
Hosp Technol Ser — Hospital Technology Series
Hosp Ther — Hospital Therapeutics
Hosp Top — Hospital Topics
Hosp Top Buyer — Hospital Topics and Buyer
Hosp Trib — Hospital Tribune
Hosp Trustee — Hospital Trustee
Hosp Vina Del Mar Bol Trimest — Hospital del Vina Del Mar. Boletin Trimestral
Hosp Vina Del Mar Publ Trimest — Hospital del Vina Del Mar. Publicacion Trimestral
Hosp Week — Hospital Week
Host Def — Host Defense
Hot Deform Alum Alloys Proc Symp — Hot Deformation of Aluminum Alloys. Proceedings. Symposium
Hotel & Motel Mgt — Hotel and Motel Management
Hotel Gaz SA — Hotel Gazette of South Australia
Hotel Motel Manage — Hotel and Motel Management
Hotel Rest — Hotels and Restaurants International
Hot Isostatic Pressing Theory Appl Proc Int Conf — Hot Isostatic Pressing. Theory and Applications. Proceedings. International Conference
Hot Lab Equip Conf Proc — Hot Laboratories and Equipment Conference. Proceedings
HOTOA — Hospital Topics
Houches Ec Ete Phys Theor — Houches. Ecole d'Ete de Physique Theoretique
Houil Blanc — Houille Blanche
Houille Bl — Houille Blanche
Hou J Int Law — Houston Journal of International Law
Hou J Intl L — Houston Journal of International Law
Hou LR — Houston Law Review
HO Univ KY Coll Agr Coop Ext Serv — HO-University of Kentucky. College of Agriculture. Cooperative Extension Service
Hous & Dev Rep BNA — Housing and Development Reporter. Bureau of National Affairs
Hous Build Pl — Housing, Building, and Planning
Hous Com — Householder Commentaries
House & G — House and Garden
House & Gard — House and Garden
House & Gdn — House and Garden
House B — House Beautiful
House Beautiful's Gard Outdoor Living — House Beautiful's Gardening and Outdoor Living
House Bldr — House Builder
House Garden Build Guide — House and Garden Building Guide
Household — Household and Personal Products Industry
Household Pers Prod Ind — Household and Personal Products Industry
Housesmith Jnl — Housesmiths Journal
House Words — Household Words
Housing 80 — Housing Industry, 1980-2000
Housing Abs — Housing Abstracts
Housing & Constr Tech Bull — Housing and Construction Technical Bulletin
Housing and Planning Refs — Housing and Planning References
Housing Eur — Housing Europe
Housing Fin R — Housing Finance Review
Housing Fin Rev — Housing Finance Review
Housing Mag — Housing Magazine
Housing Mo — Housing Monthly
Housing Mthly — Housing Monthly
Housing Plann Refs — Housing and Planning References
Housing Plann Rev — Housing and Planning Review
Housing Rev — Housing Review
Housing Soc — Housing and Society
Hous J Intl L — Houston Journal of International Law
Hous L Rev — Houston Law Review
HousP — Housing and Planning References
Hous Res Pap — Housing Research Papers
Houst L Rev — Houston Law Review
Houstn Chr — Houston Chronicle
Houstn Mag — Houston Magazine
Houston BJ — Houston Business Journal
Houston Geol Soc Bull — Houston Geological Society. Bulletin
Houston Ger Stud — Houston German Studies
Houston J Int'l L — Houston Journal of International Law
Houston J M — Houston Journal of Mathematics
Houston J Math — Houston Journal of Mathematics
Houston Law — Houston Law Review

Houston Liv — Houston Living
Houston L Rev — Houston Law Review
Houston Mag — Houston Magazine
Houston Sym — Houston Symphony. Program Notes
Hous Urb Dev Tr — Housing and Urban Development Trends
Houtinst TNO Circ — Houtinstituut TNO. Circulaire
Hov Craft Hydrof — Hovering Craft and Hydrofoil
Hovercr Wld — Hovercraft World
HO Voice — Hartford's Other Voice
Howard J — Howard Journal
Howard Journal — Howard Journal of Penology and Crime Prevention
Howard J Penology Crime Prev — Howard Journal of Penology and Crime Prevention
Howard Law J — Howard Law Journal
Howard L J — Howard Law Journal
Howard R — Howard Review
Howard Univ Rec — Howard University Record
Howard Univ Rev Sci — Howard University Reviews of Science
Howard Univ Stud Hist — Howard University Studies in History
How Eval Health Programs — How to Evaluate Health Programs
Howitt — Howitt's Journal
How J — Howard Journal
How J Pen — Howard Journal of Penology and Crime Prevention
How Law J — Howard Law Journal
How LJ — Howard Law Journal
How L Rev — Howard Law Review
HOY — Holland Schweiz
HOYU — Hospitality Yukon. Yukon Visitors Association
HP — Hazard Prevention
HP — Hijo Prodigo
HP — Historia Paraguaya
HP — Historical Performance
HPA — Helvetica Paediatrica Acta
HPAAA — Helvetica Paediatrica Acta
HPA Bull — HPA [*Hospital Physicists Association*] Bulletin
HPACA — Helvetica Physica Acta
H Paed — Handbuch der Paedagogik
HPANAJ — Handbuch der Pflanzenanatomie
HPAOA — Heating, Piping, and Air Conditioning
HPASA — Helvetica Physiologica et Pharmacologica Acta. Supplementum
HPB — Historisch-Politische Blaetter fuer das Katholische Deutschland
HPB — Historisch-Politisches Buch
HPBKD — Historisch-Politische Blaetter fuer das Katholische Deutschland
HPBL — Historisch-Politische Blaetter fuer das Katholische Deutschland
HPB Surg — HPB Surgery
HPCCEY — Handbook of Plant Cell Culture
HPCQA — Human Pathology
HPD — Harpsichord
HPE — History of Political Economy
HPEN — PEN Hongroie
HP Fachztg Auto Flugtech — H.P.-Fachzeitung fuer Automobilismus und Flugtechnik
HPG — Historischen Personennamen des Griechischen bis zur Kaiserzeit
H Ph — Handbuch der Philosophie
HPHAD — Han'guk Pusik Hakhoechi
HPHBA — Harvard Public Health Alumni Bulletin
H Phys Pharm A — Helvetica Physiologica et Pharmacologica Acta
HPI — Hochschulpolitische Informationen
HPI — Holland in South East Asia
HPJ — HP [*Heilpraktiker*] Journal
HPJ — HP [*Hewlett-Packard*] Journal
HP JI — HP (Hewlett Packard) Journal
HP Kurier — HP [*Heilpraktiker*] Kurier
HPKYA — Harbin Gongye Daxue Xuebao
HPLC Pharm Ind — HPLC (High Performance Liquid Chromatography) in the Pharmaceutical Industry
HPLC Proteins Pept Polynucleotides — HPLC (High Performance Liquid Chromatography) of Proteins, Peptides, and Polynucleotides. Contemporary Topics and Applications
HPLSDO — History and Philosophy of the Life Sciences. Pubblicazioni della Stazione Zoologica di Napoli. Section II
HPN — Historischen Personennamen des Griechischen bis zur Kaiserzeit
HPN — Richard Hakluyt's Principal Navigations and Voyages
HPN Hosp Purch News — HPN. Hospital Purchasing News
H Points — High Points
HPOQ — Health Policy Quarterly
HPPAA — Helvetica Physiologica et Pharmacologica Acta
HPPIDE — Health and Population Perspectives and Issues
HPPRA — Hydrocarbon Processing and Petroleum Refiner [*Later, Hydrocarbon Processing*]
HPR — Homiletic and Pastoral Review
HPR — Horizontes (Puerto Rico)
HPRM — Health Promotion Monographs
HPS — Hamburger Philologische Studien
HPS — Handbook of Paper Science
H Ps — Handbuch der Psychologie
H Ps K — Handbuch der Psychologie (Herausgegeben von Katz)
HPSO — Historical and Philosophical Society of Ohio. Bulletin
HPSY — Health Psychology
HPTC — Edward H. Spicer. Human Problems in Technological Change [*New York*]
HPTCHS — Historical Papers. Trinity College Historical Society
HPTGA — Herpetologica
HP Th — Handbuch der Pastoraltheologie
HPU — Humanidades Publicacion Universitaria
HPWBA — Heilpaedagogische Werkblaetter

HQ — Hartford Quarterly
HQ — Hopkins Quarterly
HR — Hamburger Rundschau
HR — Heaton Review
HR — Hermes. Messager Scientifique et Populaire de l'Antiquite Classique en Russie
HR — Hindustan Review
HR — Hispanic Review
HR — History of Religions
HR — Hlas Revoluce
HR — Hopkins Review
HR — Hrvatska Revija
H R — Hudebni Revue
HR — Hudson Review
HR — Humanisme et Renaissance
HR — Human Relations
HRA — Historical Records of Australia
HRA — Human Resources Abstracts
HRA — Human Resources Administration
HRAF — Human Relations Area Files
HRAF/BSR — Behavior Science Research. Journal of Comparative Studies. Human Relations AreaFiles
HRAF Newsl — HRAF [*Human Relations Area Files*] Newsletter
Hrana Ishr — Hrana i Ishrana
HRB — Hopkins Research Bulletin
HRBC — Historical Review of Berks County
HRC — Histoire Religieuse du Canada
HRC — Horeca
HRC CC J High Resolut Chromatogr Chromatogr Commun — Journal of High Resolution Chromatography and Chromatography Communications
HRC J High — HRC. Journal of High Resolution Chromatography
HRC J High Resolut Chromatogr — HRC. Journal of High Resolution Chromatography
HRD — Hamburger Romanistische Dissertationen
H Rel — History of Religions
HRen — Humanisme et Renaissance
HRFADM — Annual Research Reviews. Hypothalamic Releasing Factors
HRF Bull — HRF [*National College for Heating, Ventilating, Refrigeration, and Fan Engineering*] Bulletin
HRG — Handbuch der Regionalen Geologie
HRG — Handbuch der Relgionsgeschichte
HRG — Handwoerterbuch zur Deutschen Rechtsgeschichte
HRH — TextielVisie
HRI — Histoire des Relations Internationales
HRIPA — Publications. Hungarian Mining Research Institute
HRIS — Highway Research Information Service
HRISAK — Food and Nutrition
HRJ — Human Rights Journal
HRL — Human Relations
HRLSD J — HRLSD [*Health and Rehabilitative Library Services Division*] Journal
HRM — Human Reproductive Medicine
HRM — Human Resource Management
HRN — History Review of New Books
HRNB — History. Reviews of New Books
HRNSW — Historical Records of New South Wales
HRO — Gastvrij
H Ro — Hudebni Rozhledy
HRP — Handbuch der Rechtspraxis
HRP — Human Resource Planning
HRPV — Hermes. Revista del Pais Vasco
HRR — Handicapped Rights and Regulations
HRR — Historicorum Romanorum Reliquiae
HR Rel — Historicorum Romanorum Reliquiae
HRS — Historical Records and Studies
HRS — Historical Records Survey
HRTG — Heritage. Alberta Department of Culture, Youth, and Recreation
HR U — Historia Religionum. Uppsala
HRV — Historical Records of Victoria
Hrvatska Rev — Hrvatska Revija
Hrv Geogr Glasn — Hrvatski Geografski Glasnik
Hrv Kolo — Hrvatsko Kolo
HRW — Holz als Roh- und Werkstoff
HRWA — Heidelberger Rechtswissenschaftliche Abhandlungen
HRW L — Handbuch der Religionswissenschaft (Herausgegeben von Leipoldt)
HRZ — Hanseatische Rechts-Zeitschrift
Hrzn — Horizon
HS — Handbook of Statistics
HS — Hebrew Studies
Hs — Hemisphere
HS — Hippologische Sammlung
HS — Hispania
HS — Hispania Sacra
HS — Historical Studies
HS — Historical Studies, Australia and New Zealand
HS — Humanities in the South
HS — International Journal of Health Services
HS — Works Issued by the Hakluyt Society. First Series
HSA — Health Services Administration. Publications
HS A — Historische Studien (Herausgegeben von Arndt)
HSAI — Handbook of South American Indians
H Sal — Historia Salutis
H Sal T — Historia Salutis. Napoli. Serie Teologica
HSan — Helsingin Sanomat
HSAT — Die Heilige Schrift des Alten Testaments
HSC — Histoire de la Spiritualite Chretienne

H Sch — High School
H Sch J — High School Journal
H Sch Q — High School Quarterly
H Sch Teach — High School Teacher
HschW — Hochschulwissen
HSCL — Harvard Studies in Comparative Literature
HS Cl Ph — Harvard Studies in Classical Philology
HSCP — Harvard Studies in Classical Philology
HSCPA — Hospital and Community Psychiatry
HSCPS — Harvard Studies in Classical Philology. Supplemental Volume
HSCRA — Hastings Center. Report
HSCSBW — History of Science Series
HSDB — Hazardous Substances Data Bank
HSE — Histoire et Sociologie de l'Eglise
HSE — Hungarian Studies in English
Hse and Garden — House and Garden
Hse Builder — House Builder
HSELL — Hiroshima Studies in English Language and Literature
H Sem — Horae Semiticae
Hse of Lords Select Commit Eur Commun Rep — House of Lords. Select Committee on the European Communities. Reports
H S Glads — Historisk-Topografisk Selskab for Gladsaxe Kommune. Arsskrift
HSGTA — High Speed Ground Transportation Journal
HSGTJ — High Speed Ground Transportation Journal
HSGZA4 — Hokkaido Journal of Orthopedic and Traumatic Surgery
HSHCA — Han'guk Sikmul Poho Hakhoe Chi
HSHKA — Bulletin. Korean Fisheries Society
HSHRA — HSMHA [*Health Services and Mental Health Administration*] Health Report
HSHS — Johns Hopkins University Studies in Historical and Political Science
HSHTDS — Handbook of Shock Trauma
HSI Hung Sci Instrum — HSI. Hungarian Scientific Instruments
HSJ — High School Journal
HSJ — Historia Societatis Jesu
HSJ — Housman Society. Journal
Hskbl — Hojskolebladet. Tidende for Folkeoplysning
HSKCA — Han'guk Sikp'un Kwahakhoe Chi
HSKEA — Hoshasen Seibutsu Kenkyu
HSL — Hartford Studies in Literature
HSL — Highway Safety Literature Service
HSL Abs — HSL [*Health and Safety Executive Library*] Abstract
HSLNT — Historical and Linguistic Studies in Literature Related to the New Testament
HSLS — Harvard Slavic Studies
HSM — Handbook of Soil Mechanics
HSM — Handling and Shipping Management
HSM — Harvard Semitic Monographs
HSM — Health Services and Mental Health Administration. Publications
HSM — Human Systems Management
HSMHA Health Rep — HSMHA [*Health Services and Mental Health Administration*] Health Report
HSMPE8 — Herbs, Spices, and Medicinal Plants
HSN — Hawthorne Society. Newsletter
HSNPL — Harvard Studies and Notes in Philology and Literature
HSNT — Die Heilige Schrift des Neuen Testaments. Bonn
H Soed — Horae Soederblomianae
HSP — Hospitals
HSPh — Harvard Studies in Classical Philology
HSPhS — Historical Studies in the Physical Sciences
HSPL — Harvard Studies and Notes in Philology and Literature
HSR — Health Services Research
HSR — Hungarian Studies Review
HSRCA — Historical Series. Reformed Church in America
HSRC Newsletter — Human Sciences Research Council Newsletter
HSRI (High Saf Res Inst) Res Rev — HSRI (Highway Safety Research Institute) Research Review
HSRI Rep — HSRI [*Highway Safety Research Institute*] Report
HSRI Res Rev — HSRI [*Highway Safety Research Institute*] Research Review
HSRL — Harvard Studies in Romance Languages
HSRPA — Health Services Report
HSS — British Library Catalogue. Humanities and Social Sciences
HSS — Harvard Semitic Series
HSS — Harvard Slavic Studies
HSS — Works Issued by the Hakluyt Society. Second Series
HSSA — Health and Safety Science Abstracts
HSSC — High-Speed Surface Craft, Incorporating Hovering Craft and Hydrofoil
HSSC — Historical Society of Southern California. Quarterly
HSSCQ — Historical Society of Southern California. Quarterly
HSSJB — Health and Social Service Journal
HS St — Harvard Slavic Studies
H St — Hamlet Studies
HSt — Hebrew Studies
Hs T — Hedeselskabets Tidsskrift
H St — Historical Studies
HST — Holland's Export Magazine. Holland Shipping and Trading
H St B — Historical Studies. Biographies
HSTC Bull — HSTC [*History of Canadian Sciences, Technology, and Medicine*] Bulletin
H St Cl Ph — Harvard Studies in Classical Philology
Hst Kreise Olpe — Heimatstimmen aus dem Kreise Olpe
H St M — Historical Studies. Monasteries and Convents
H Studien — Hispanistische Studien
HSWR — Harvard Studies in World Religions
HSY — Health and Society
H-S Z Physl — Hoppe-Seyler's Zeitschrift fuer Physiologische Chemie

HT — Hartman's Tijdschrift ter Beoefening van het Administratieve Recht
HT — Hataassiya (Tel Aviv)
HT — Herald Tribune
H-T — Hesperis-Tamuda
HT — High Times
HT — Historisches Taschenbuch
HT — Historisk Tidskrift
HT — History Teacher
HT — History Today
HT — Horological Times
HT — Human Toxicology
HT — Humboldt-Taschenbuecher
HT — Iscrizioni Preeleniche di Hagia Triada in Creta e della Grecia Peninsulare
HTaL — Historisches Taschenbuch (Leipzig)
HTB — Harper Torchbook
HTB — Hoch- und Tiefbau
HTB — New York Herald Tribune Books
HTBHA — Han'guk T'oyang Bilyo Hakhoe Chi
HTCJ — Hebrew Theological College Journal
HTD — Dansk Historisk Tidskrift
HTF — Historisk Tidskrift foer Finland
HTFFA — Heat and Fluid Flow
HTG — Historisk Tidskrift
Htg — Holztechnologie
H Th — History and Theory
H Therm Envelope Build Sci — Journal of Thermal Envelope and Building Science
H Th G — Handbuch Theologischer Grundbegriffe
H Th K — Herders Theologischer Kommentar zum Neuen Testament
HTHPA — High Temperatures-High Pressures
HThR — Harvard Theological Review
H Th S — Harvard Theological Studies
HThSt — Harvard Theological Studies
HTI — Hindu Text Information
HTJ — Hardware Trade Journal
HTJPA — Heat Transfer. Japanese Research
HTK — Historisk Tidskrift
HTKNT — Herders Theologischer Kommentar zum Neuen Testament
HTL — Herders Theologische Lehrbuecher
HTL — History Today (London)
HTL — Hotel Revue. Beroepstijdschrift op Managementniveau
HTLStu — Historia i Teoria Literatury-Studia
HTM — History Teacher's Magazine
HTM-DB — High Temperature Materials Data Bank
HTM Haerterei-Tech Mitt — Haerterei-Technische Mitteilungen (HTM)
HTN — High Technology Business
HTN — Historisk Tidsskrift. Norske Historiske Forening
HTO — Historisk Tidskrift (Oslo)
HTQ — Hsueh Tsung Quarterly
HTQ — Revue Francaise de Gestion. Hommes et Techniques
HTR — Harvard Theological Review
Ht R — Haustechnische Rundschau
H Tr — Hethitischen Totenritual. Deutsches Akademie der Wissenschaften. Institut fuer Orientforschung. Veroeffentlichungen
HTRMB — Heat Treatment of Metals
HTS — Harvard Theological Studies
HTS — Hervormde Teologiese Studies
HTS — Historisk Tidskrift foer Skaneland
HTS — Historisk Tidskrift (Stockholm)
HTS — Historisk Tidsskrift. Svenska Historiska Foerening
HTS — Humanitas [Quito]
HTsFi — Historisk Tidskrift foer Finland
Ht TR — Hethitischen Totenritual. Deutsches Akademie der Wissenschaften. Institut fuer Orientforschung. Veroeffentlichungen
HTW — H2O. Tijdschrift voor Watervoorziening en Afvalwaterbehandeling
Hu — Humanist
HUAG — Hamburg. Universitaet. Arbeit aus dem Gebiete fuer Auslandskunde
HUAKA — Hua Hsueh Shih Chieh
Hua Tung Norm Univ J Nat Sci Ser — Hua-T'ung Normal University Journal. Natural Science Series/Hua-T'ung Shih ta Hsueeh Pao. Tzu Jan K'o Hsueeh
Huber Law Surv — Huber Law Survey
HUBIA — Human Biology
HUCA — Hebrew Union College. Annual
HUD — Handicapped Users' Database
HUD — Hungarian Digest
HUD Chal — HUD [Department of Housing and Urban Development] Challenge
Huddersfield Chamber Comm J — Huddersfield Chamber of Commerce Journal
HUDEA — Human Development
Hudeiba Res Stn Annu Rep — Hudeiba Research Station. Annual Report
HUD Intl Bull — HUD [Department of Housing and Urban Development] International Bulletin
HUD Intl Information Series — HUD [Department of Housing and Urban Development] International Information Series
Hud Nastroje — Hudebni Nastroje
HUD News — HUD [Department of Housing and Urban Development] Newsletter
HUD Newsl — HUD [US Department of Housing and Urban Development] Newsletter
Hud R — Hudebni Rozhledy
Hud R — Hudson Review
Hudrobiol Uurim — Hudrobiloogilised Uurimused
Hud Rozhl — Hudebni Rozhledy
Hudson — Hudson Review
Hudson R — Hudson Review
Hudson Rev — Hudson Review
Hud Veda — Hudebni Veda
Hud Zivot — Hudobny Zivot

HUE — New Hungarian Exporter
Huebner Internat Ser Risk Insur Econom Secur — Huebner International Series on Risk, Insurance, and Economic Security
Huelva A — Huelva Arqueologica
Huenefeld Rep — Huenefeld Report
HUF — Hungarian Foreign Trade
HUFAA — Human Factors
HUFB — Hungarofilm Bulletin
Hufeland J Arzn — Journal der Practischen Arzneykunde und Wundarzneykunst. Hufeland
HUG — Hungarian Economy
Hug Soc SC Trans — Huguenot Society of South Carolina. Transactions
Huguenot Soc Proc — Huguenot Society Proceedings
Huguenot Soc S Afr Bull — Huguenot Society of South Africa. Bulletin
HuH — Hethiter und Hethitisch
H u H — Holzforschung und Holzverwertung
HUHEA — Human Heredity
HUI — Homines
Huisarts Wet — Huisarts en Wetenschap
Huis Hof — Huis en Hof. Maandblad voor Liefhebbers van Bloem en Plant
Huit Colloq Biol Clin — Huit Colloques de Biologie Clinique
HUJ — Hebrew University (Jerusalem)
HUJGD — Hebrew University. Geological Department (Jerusalem)
HUJGDB — Hebrew University. Jerusalem. Geology Department. Bulletin
HUL — Houston Law Review
Hule Mex Plast — Hule Mexicano y Plasticos
Hul L — Hulsean Lectures
Hull Univ Occas Pap Geogr — Hull University. Occasional Papers in Geography
HULMK — Home University Library of Modern Knowledge
Hum — Humanidades
Hum — Humanist
Hum — Humanitas
HUM — Human Systems Management
Hum — Humus
Human — Humangenetik
Human — Humanite [Paris daily]
Human & Ren — Humanisme et Renaissance
Human Biol — Human Biology
Human Chr — Humanites Chretiennes
Human Comm Res — Human Communications Research
Human Cont — Human Context
HumanD — Humanite-Dimanche
Human Dev — Human Development
Human Ecol — Human Ecology
Humane Educ — Humane Education
Humane R — Humane Review
Human et Entr — Humanisme et Entreprise
Human Fact — Human Factors
Humangenet — Humangenetik
Human Guat — Humanidades (Guatemala)
Human Gym — Humanistische Gymnasium. Zeitschrift des Deutschen Gymnasialvereins
Human Hered — Human Heredity
Humanidades Ser 4 Logica Mat — Humanidades. Serie 4. Logica Matematica
Human Intel Int Newsl — Human Intelligence International Newsletter
Human Islam — Humaniora Islamica
Humanisme Renaiss — Humanisme et Renaissance
Humanit Index — Humanities Index
Human Life R — Human Life Review
Human Lovan — Humanistica Lovanensia
Human Merida — Humanidades. Facultad de Humanidades. Universidad de los Andes (Merida, Venezuela)
Human Mex — Humanidades (Mexico)
Human Org — Human Organization
Human Organ — Human Organization
Human Path — Human Pathology
Human Pracy — Humanizacja Pracy
Human Rel — Human Relations
Human Relat — Human Relations
Human Reprod Med — Human Reproductive Medicine
Human Reproduction & L Rep — Reporter on Human Reproduction and the Law
Human Resour Abstr — Human Resources Abstracts
Human Resource Dev — Human Resource Development
Human Resource Mgt — Human Resource Management
Human Rights J — Human Rights Journal
Human Rights Q — Human Rights Quarterly
Human Rights Rev — Human Rights Review
Human Rts J — Human Rights Journal
Human Rts Rev — Human Rights Review
Human S — Human Studies
Human Ser 4 Logica Mat — Humanidades. Serie 4. Logica Matematica
Human Soc — Humanities in Society
Hum Antibodies — Human Antibodies
Hum Antibodies Hybridomas — Human Antibodies and Hybridomas
Hum Ass Bull — Humanities Association of Canada. Bulletin
Hum Assoc R — Humanities Association. Review/Revue. Association des Humanites
Hum Assoc Rev — Humanities Association Review
HumB — Humanitas (Brescia)
Humb — Humboldt. Monatschrift fuer die Gesammten Naturwissenschaften
Hum(BA) — Humanidades (Buenos Aires)
Hum Behav — Human Behavior
Hum Biol — Human Biology
Hum Biol Oceania — Human Biology in Oceania
Humboldt Univ Ber — Humboldt Universitaet Berichte

Hum (Br) — Humanitas (Brescia)
HUMC — Histoire Universelle des Missions Catholiques
Hum C — Humanidades. Comillas
HumC — Humanisme Contemporain
Hum C — Humanitas Christiana
Hum Cancer Immunol — Human Cancer Immunology
Hum Cell — Human Cell
Hum Chr — Humanites Chretiennes
Hum Chrom Newsl — Human Chromosome Newsletter
HumCL — Humanites. Classes de Lettres. Sections Classiques
Hum C L — Humantias Christiana. Lateinische Reihe
HumCLm — Humanites. Classes de Lettres. Sections Modernes
Hum Commun — Human Communications
Hum Commun Res — Human Communication Research
Hum Comput Interact — Human-Computer Interaction
Hum Contemp — Humanisme Contemporain
Hum Context — Human Context
Hum Dev — Human Development
Hum Eco — Human Ecology
Hum Ecol — Human Ecology
Hum Ecol Forum — Human Ecology Forum
Hum Ecology — Human Ecology
Hum Ecol Race Hyg — Human Ecology and Race Hygiene
Hum Ecol Risk Assess — Human and Ecological Risk Assessment
Hum Environ Swed — Human Environment in Sweden
Hume Stud — Hume Studies
Hum et Ren — Humanisme et Renaissance
Hum Ev — Human Events
Hum Evol — Human Evolution
Hum Exp Toxicol — Human and Experimental Toxicology
Hum Fact — Human Factors
Hum Factors — Human Factors
Hum Factors Comput Syst — Conference Proceedings on Human Factors in Computing Systems
Hum Fertil — Human Fertility
Hum Genet — Human Genetics
Hum Gene Ther — Human Gene Therapy
Hum Genet Suppl — Human Genetics. Supplement
Hum Gymn — Humanistische Gymnasium
Hum Hair Symp Pap — Human Hair Symposium. Papers
Hum Hered — Human Heredity
Hum Heredity — Human Heredity
Hum Immunol — Human Immunology
Hum Ind — Humanities Index
Hum Lov — Humanistica Lovaniensia
Hum Lymphocyte Differ — Human Lymphocyte Differentiation
HumM — Humanitas (Monterrey)
Hum Mind Discuss Nobel Conf — Human Mind; a Discussion at the Nobel Conference
Hum Mol Genet — Human Molecular Genetics
Hum Mov Sci — Human Movement Science
Hum Mutat — Human Mutation
Hum Mutat Online — Human Mutation (Online) [*electronic publication*]
Hum Needs — Human Needs
Hum Neurob — Human Neurobiology
Hum Neurobiol — Human Neurobiology
HumNL — Humanitas (Nuevo Leon)
Hum(NRH) — Humanitas: La Nouvelle Revue des Humanites
Hum Nutr Appl Nutr — Human Nutrition. Applied Nutrition
Hum Nutr Appl Nutr Clin Pract — Human Nutrition. Applied Nutrition and Clinical Practice
Hum Nutr Cl — Human Nutrition. Clinical Nutrition
Hum Nutr Clin Nutr — Human Nutrition. Clinical Nutrition
Hum Nutr Compr Treatise — Human Nutrition. A Comprehensive Treatise
Hum Nutr Food Sci Nutr — Human Nutrition. Food Sciences and Nutrition
Hum Org — Human Organization
Hum Organ — Human Organization
Hum Organ Clgh Bull — Human Organization Clearinghouse Bulletin
Humorist Bl — Humoristische Blaetter. Woechentliches Illustriertes Wizblatt der Pariser-Zeitung
Hu Move Sci — Human Movement Science
Hum Path — Human Pathology
Hum Pathol — Human Pathology
Hum Pharmacol Drug Res — Human Pharmacology and Drug Research
Humph Dist Reg — Humphreys. District Registry Practice and Procedure
Hum Physiol — Human Physiology
Hum Physiol (Engl Transl Fiziol Chel) — Human Physiology (English Translation of Fiziologiya Cheloveka)
Hum Potential — Human Potential
Hum Psychop — Human Psychopharmacology. Clinical and Experimental
Hum Psychopharmacol — Human Psychopharmacology
Humpty D — Humpty Dumpty's Magazine
Hum (Q) — Humanitas. Boletin Ecuatoriano de Antropologia (Quito)
Hum Rel — Human Relations
Hum Relat — Human Relations
Hum Relations — Human Relations
Hum Reprod — Human Reproduction
Hum Reprod Med — Human Reproductive Medicine
Hum Reprod (Oxford) — Human Reproduction (Oxford)
Hum Reprod Proc World Congr — Human Reproduction. Proceedings of World Congress
Hum Reprod Update — Human Reproduction Update
Hum (RES) — Humanites. Revue d'Enseignement Secondaire et d'Education
Hum Resour Abstr — Human Resources Abstracts
Hum Resource Mgt — Human Resource Management

Hum Resour Forum — Human Resources Forum
Hum Resour Manage — Human Resource Management
Hum Resour Manage (Aust) — Human Resource Management (Australia)
Hum Resour Plann — Human Resource Planning
Hum Res Rep — Human Resource Report
Hum Rev — Humanities Review
Hum Rights — Human Rights
Hum Rights J — Human Rights Journal
Hum Rights Q — Human Rights Quarterly
Hum Rights Rev — Human Rights Review
Hum (RIPh) — Humanitas. Revue Internationale de Philologie Classique et Humanites
Hum Sci — Human Science
Hum Sci (Seoul) — Human Science (Seoul)
Hum Settlements — Human Settlements
Hum Soc — Humanities in Society
Hum Stud — Humana Studia
Hum Stud — Human Studies
Hum Syst Manage — Human Systems Management
HumT — Humanitas (Tucuman, Argentina)
Hum Tech — Humanismus und Technik
Hum Toxicol — Human Toxicology
Hum Vetensk Samf i Lund Arsberatt — Humanistiska Vetenskaps-Samfundet i Lund Arsberattelse
Hum Vision Visual Process Digital Disp — Human Vision, Visual Processing, and Digital Display
Hum Wld — Human World
HUN — Hungaropress
Hunan Ann Math — Hunan Annals of Mathematics
HUNEDR — Human Neurobiology
Hung — Hungarian Patent Document
Hung A Biol — Hungarica Acta Biologica
Hung Acad Sci Cent Res Inst Phys KFKI — Hungarian Academy of Sciences. Central Research Institute for Physics. Report KFKI
Hung A Chim — Hungarica Acta Chimica
Hung Acta Biol — Hungarica Acta Biologica
Hung Acta Chim — Hungarica Acta Chimica
Hung Acta Med — Hungarica Acta Medica
Hung Acta Phys — Hungarica Acta Physica
Hung Acta Physiol — Hungarica Acta Physiologica
Hung Agric Rev — Hungarian Agricultural Review
Hung Agr Rev — Hungarian Agricultural Review
Hung A Math — Hungarica Acta Mathematica
Hung A Med — Hungarica Acta Medica
Hung Annu Meet Biochem Proc — Hungarian Annual Meeting for Biochemistry. Proceedings
Hung A Phys — Hungarica Acta Physica
Hung A Physiol — Hungarica Acta Physiologica
Hungarian J Indust Chem (Vesprem) — Hungarian Journal of Industrial Chemistry (Vesprem)
Hungarian Q — Hungarian Quarterly
Hungarofilm Bull — Hungarofilm Bulletin
Hungar Quart — Hungarian Quarterly
Hung Build Bull — Hungarian Building Bulletin
Hung Econ — Hungarian Economy
Hung Foeldt Intez Evk — Hungary. Foeldtani Intezet. Evkoenyve
Hung For Sci Rev — Hungarian Forest Scientifical Review
Hung For Tr — Hungarian Foreign Trade
Hung Halasztott — Hungarian Halasztott
Hung Heavy Ind — Hungarian Heavy Industries
Hung J Chem — Hungarian Journal of Chemistry
Hung J Ind Chem — Hungarian Journal of Industrial Chemistry
Hung J Indus Chem — Hungarian Journal of Industrial Chemistry
Hung J Metall — Hungarian Journal of Metallurgy
Hung J Min Metall — Hungarian Journal of Mining and Metallurgy
Hung J Min Metall Min — Hungarian Journal of Mining and Metallurgy. Mining
Hung L Rev — Hungarian Law Review
Hung Mach — Hungarian Machinery
Hung Magy Allami Foeldt Intez Evk — Hungary. Magyar Allami Foeldtani Intezet. Evkoenyve
Hung Med Arch — Hungarian Medical Archives
Hung Med Biblio — Hungarian Medical Bibliography
Hung Med J — Hungarian Medical Journal
Hung Min J — Hungarian Mining Journal
Hung Mus G — Hungarian Musical Guide
Hung Notes World Hung Educ Serv — Hunger Notes. World Hunger Education Service
Hung Orsz Talalmanyi Hivatal Szabad Kozl Vedjegyert — Hungary. Orszagos Talalmanyi Hivatal. Szabadalmi Kozlony esVedjegyertesito
Hung Pat Doc Szabad Leiras — Hungary. Patent Document. Szabadalmi Leiras
Hung Pharmacol Soc Congr — Hungarian Pharmacological Society. Congress
Hung Press — Hungaropress
Hung R — Hungarian Review
Hung Rev Agric Sci — Hungarian Review of Agricultural Sciences
Hung S — Hungarian Survey
Hung Sci Instrum — Hungarian Scientific Instruments
Hung St Engl — Hungarian Studies in English
Hung Tanner — Hungarian Tanner
Hung Tech Abstr — Hungarian Technical Abstracts
Hung Teljes — Hungarian Teljes (Patent Document)
Hung Vet J — Hungarian Veterinary Journal
HunQ — Hungarian Quarterly
HUN/RU — Revista de la Universidad. Universidad Nacional Autonoma de Honduras
Hunt — Hunt's Merchants' Magazine

Hunter Nat Hist — Hunter Natural History
Hunter Res Found J — Hunter Valley Research Foundation. Journal
Hunter Valley Res Fdn Monograph — Hunter Valley Research Foundation. Monograph
Hunter Valley Res Found Spec Rep — Hunter Valley Research Foundation. Special Report
Hunt Gr Rev — Hunting Group Review
Hunting Group Rev — Hunting Group Review
Huntington Hist Soc Quart — Huntington Historical Society. Quarterly
Huntington Lib Q — Huntington Library Quarterly
Huntington Libr Q — Huntington Library. Quarterly
Hunt Lib Bull — Huntington Library. Bulletin
Hunt Lib Q — Huntington Library. Quarterly
Hunt Libr Q — Huntington Library. Quarterly
Huntsville Let — Huntsville Letter
HUORAY — Human Organization
HUPHD — Human Physiology
HUPPAE — Harvard University. Papers of the Peabody Museum of Archaeology and Ethnology
HUR — Hallische Universitaetsreden
HuR — Hudson Review
HuR — Humanisme et Renaissance
HUR — Human Relations
HuRe — Hudson Review
HUREEE — Human Reproduction
Huron Hist N — Huron Historical Notes
Huron Inst Pap — Huron Institute. Papers
HUS — Harvard Ukrainian Studies
HUSHA — Hua Hsueh
Hushall Sallsk Tidskr — Hushallnings Sallskapens Tidskrift
Husholdn Tek Medd — Husholdningsradets Tekniske Meddelelser
HUSIA — Hungarian Scientific Instruments
HUSL — Hebrew University. Studies in Literature
HUSRA — Science Reports. Hirosaki University
HussJ — Husserls Jahrbuch fuer Philosophie und Phaenomenologische Forschung
HussR — Husson Review
H u T — Hoch- und Tiefbau
HU Th — Hermeneutische Untersuchungen zur Theologie
HUTMA — Houtim
Hutn Aktual — Hutnicke Aktuality
Hutni Proj Praha Tech Ekon Zpr — Hutni Projekt Praha. Technicko-Ekonomicky Zpravodaj
Hutn (Katowice) — Hutnik (Katowice)
Hutn Listy — Hutnicke Listy
H u W — Haus und Wohnung
Huyck Felt Bull — Huyck Felt Bulletin
Hv — Haven. Medlemsblad for de Samvirkende Danske Haveselskaber
HV — Historische Vierteljahrschrift
HV — Hudebni Veda
HV — HudebXXX Veda
Hvalradets Skr — Hvalradets Skrifter
HV Bl — Hamburgisches Verordnungsblatt
HVECA — Heating and Ventilating Engineer and Journal of Air Conditioning
H V Eng — H and V Engineer
HVHAA — Handlingar. Vitterhets- Historie- och Antikvitets-Akademien
HVHAA FF — Handlingar. Vitterhets- Historie- och Antikvitets-Akademien. Filologisk-Filosofiska Serien
HVHW — Health Values. Achieving High Level Wellness
HVJ — Historische Vierteljahrschrift
HVJS — Historische Vierteljahrschrift
Hvk — Havekunst
HvM — Honar va Mardom
HVREA — Heating and Ventilating Review
HVSchr — Historische Vierteljahrschrift
HVU — Horizons
HVV — Vrije Volk
HW — Hatteva Wehaaretz
HW — Haus und Wohnung
HW — Hethitisches Woerterbuch
HW — Historical Wyoming
Hw — Hochschulwissen in Einzeldarstelungen
HW — Hollandsch Weekblad
Hware — Hardware Today
HWAY — Humble Way
Hwb d B — Handwoerterbuch der Betriebswirtschaft
Hwb d Sw — Handwoerterbuch der Sozialwissenschaften
Hwb Dt RG — Handwoerterbuch zur Deutschen Rechtsgeschichte
HWBW — Handwoerterbuch der Betriebswirtschaft
H W Gillett Meml Lect — H. W. Gillett Memorial Lecture
HWM — Helgolaender Wissenschaftliche Meeresuntersuchungen
HWMJA — Hawaii Medical Journal
HWP — Historisches Woerterbuch der Philosophie
HWPCG — Hazardous Waste and Pollution Compliance Guidelines
HWPr — Hallisches Winckelmannsprogramme
HWQ — Hansard Written Questions
HWR — Hindu Weekly Review
HWRCB — Highways and Road Construction
HWRW — Handwoerterbuch der Rechtswissenschaft
HWS — Handwoerterbuch der Soziologie
HWSNAM — Hawaiian Shell News
HwyResAb — Highway Research Abstracts
Hy — Hymn
HY — Journal of Hydraulic Engineering
Hyacinth Control J — Hyacinth Control Journal
Hyatt's PC — Hyatt's PC News Report

HYB — Herzl Year Book
Hy B — Hymnologische Beitraege
HYCYD — Haksul Yonguchi - Chungnam Taehakkyo. Chayon Kwahak Yonguso
Hy D — Hechos y Dichos
HYDCA — Hydrocarbure
HYDIDH — Scientific Works. Poultry Science. Poultry Research Institute
HYDKAK — Proceedings. Hoshi College of Pharmacy
Hydra Pneum — Hydraulics and Pneumatics
Hydraul & Air Engng — Hydraulic and Air Engineering
Hydraul & Pneum — Hydraulics and Pneumatics
Hydraul Eng — Hydraulic Engineering
Hydraul Eng (Budapest) — Hydraulic Engineering (Budapest)
Hydraul Pneum — Hydraulics and Pneumatics
Hydraul Pneumat — Hydraulics and Pneumatics
Hydraul Pneum Mech Power — Hydraulic Pneumatic Mechanical Power
Hydraul Pneum Power — Hydraulic Pneumatic Power [Later, Hydraulic Pneumatic Mechanical Power]
Hydraul Pneum Power Controls — Hydraulic Pneumatic Power and Controls
Hydraul Pneum Pwr — Hydraulic Pneumatic Power [Later, Hydraulic Pneumatic Mechanical Power]
Hydrazine Water Treat Proc Int Conf — Hydrazine and Water Treatment. Proceedings of the InternationalConference
Hydride Symp — Hydride Symposium
Hydrobiol — Hydrobiologia
Hydrobiol Bull — Hydrobiological Bulletin
Hydrobiol J — Hydrobiological Journal
Hydrobiol J (Engl Transl Gidrobiol Zh) — Hydrobiological Journal (English Translation of Gidrobiologicheskii Zhurnal)
Hydrobiol Stud — Hydrobiological Studies
Hydrocarbn — Hydrocarbon Processing
Hydrocarbon Contam Soils — Hydrocarbon Contaminated Soils
Hydrocarbon Contam Soils Groundwater — Hydrocarbon Contaminated Soils and Groundwater
Hydrocarbon Process — Hydrocarbon Processing
Hydrocarbon Process Int Ed — Hydrocarbon Processing. International Edition
Hydrocarbon Process Pet Refiner — Hydrocarbon Processing and Petroleum Refiner [Later, Hydrocarbon Processing]
Hydrochem Hydrogeol Mitt — Hydrochemische und Hydrogeologische Mitteilungen
Hydrochem Mater — Hydrochemische Materialien
Hydroc Proc — Hydrocarbon Processing
Hydrocyclones Pap Int Conf — Hydrocyclones. Papers Presented at the International Conference
Hydro Electr Power — Hydro Electric Power
Hydroelectr Power — Hydroelectric Power
Hydrog Bull — Hydrographic Bulletin
Hydrogen E — Hydrogen Energy
Hydrogene Mater Congr Int — Hydrogene et Materiaux. Congres International
Hydrogen Energy Prog 8 Proc World Hydrogen Energy Conf — Hydrogen Energy Progress 8. Proceedings. World Hydrogen Energy Conference
Hydrogen Met — Hydrogen in Metals
Hydrogen Prog — Hydrogen Progress
Hydrogeol Inf (Czech) — Hydrogeologicke Informace (Czechoslovakia. Ustav Geologickeho Inzenyrstvi)
Hydrog Rev — Hydrographic Review
Hydro Lab J — Hydro-Lab Journal
Hydrol Abt Dortm Stadtwerke Veroeff — Hydrologische Abteilung der Dortmunder Stadtwerke. Veroeffentlichungen
Hydrol Basis Water Resour Manage Proc Int Symp — Hydrological Basis for Water Resources Management. Proceedings. International Symposium
Hydrol Bibl — Hydrologische Bibliographie
Hydrol Bull RI Water Resour Board — Hydrologic Bulletin. Rhode Island. Water Resources Board
Hydrol J — Hydrological Journal
Hydrol Pap — Hydrology Papers
Hydrol Rep NM Bur Mines Miner Resour — Hydrologic Report. New Mexico. Bureau of Mines and Mineral Resources
Hydrol Rep St Bur Mines Miner Resour (New Mexico) — Hydrologic Reports. State Bureau of Mines and Mineral Resources (New Mexico)
Hydrol Sci Bull — Hydrological Sciences Bulletin
Hydrol Sci Bull Int Assoc Hydrol Sci — Hydrological Sciences Bulletin. International Association of Hydrological Sciences
Hydrol Sci Bull Sci Hydrol — Hydrological Sciences. Bulletin des Sciences Hydrologiques
Hydrol Sci J — Hydrological Sciences Journal
Hydrol Ser Aust Water Resour Counc — Hydrological Series. Australian Water Resources Council
Hydrol Ser Aust Wat Resour Coun — Hydrological Series. Australian Water Resources Council
Hydrol Symp — Hydrology Symposium
Hydrol Symp Proc (Ottawa) — Hydrology Symposium. Proceedings (Ottawa)
Hydrol Vuosik — Hydrologinen Vuosikirja
Hydrol Water Manage Large River Basins Proc Int Symp — Hydrology for the Water Management of Large River Basins. Proceedings. International Symposium
Hydrol Water Resour Ariz Southwest — Hydrology and Water Resources in Arizona and the Southwest
Hydrolysis Wood Chem USSR — Hydrolysis and Wood Chemistry USSR
Hydromech & Hydraul Engng Abstr — Hydromechanics and Hydraulic Engineering Abstracts
Hydro Res News — Hydro Research News
Hydro Sci J — Hydrological Sciences Journal
Hydrotech Constr — Hydrotechnical Construction
Hydrotech Constr (Engl Transl) — Hydrotechnical Construction (English Translation)
Hydrotech Trans — Hydrotechnical Transactions

Hydr Pneum — Hydraulics and Pneumatics
Hydr Pow Transm — Hydraulic Power Transmission
Hydr Res — Hydraulics Research
HYDWD — Hejubian Yu Dengliziti Wuli
Hyg — Hygiene
Hygiea Suppl — Hygiea. Supplement
Hyg Med — Hygiene und Medizin
Hyg Ment — Hygiene Mentale
Hyg Ment Suppl Encephale — Hygiene Mentale. Supplement de l'Encephale
HYGNA — Hyogo-Ken Gan Senta Nenpo
HygR — Hygienische Rundschau
Hyg Revy — Hygienisk Revy
Hyg Rundschau — Hygienische Rundschau
Hyg Sanit — Hygiene and Sanitation
Hyg Sanit (USSR) — Hygiene and Sanitation (USSR)
Hyg Viande Lait — Hygiene de la Viande et du Lait
Hyg Zentralbl — Hygienisches Zentralblatt
HYHN — Hsin-Ya Shu-Yuan Hsueh-Shy Nien-K'an
HYIS — Harvard-Yenching Institute Studies
HYJMUA — Mysore University. Half Yearly Journal. Series A. Arts
HYKMA — Hyogo-Kenritsu Nogyo Shikenjo Kenkyu Hokoku
HYKOE3 — Han Guk Journal of Genetic Engineering
HYMEA — Hygiene Mentale
HYMNB — Hyomen
Hymn M — Hymnologiske Meddelelser. Vaerkstedsblad om Salmer
Hymnol Med — Hymnologiske Meddelelser
Hyogo J Med Sci — Hyogo Journal of Medical Sciences
Hyogo Ken J Nat Hist — Hyogo-Ken Journal of Natural History/Hyogo-Ken Chuto Kyoiku Hakubutsugaku Zasshi
Hyogo Nat Hist — Hyogo Natural History/Hyogo Hakubutsugakkai Kaiho

Hyogo Univ J — Hyogo University Journal
Hyogo Univ Teach Educ J Ser 3 — Hyogo University of Teacher Education. Journal. Series 3. Natural Sciences,Practical Life Studies
Hyp — Hypomnemata. Geottingen
Hyperbaric Oxy Rev — Hyperbaric Oxygen Review
Hyperfine Interact — Hyperfine Interactions
Hypersonic Flow Res — Hypersonic Flow Research
Hypertens Atheroscler Lipids Proc Workshop — Hypertension, Atherosclerosis, and Lipids. Proceedings. Workshop
Hypertens Pregnancy — Hypertension in Pregnancy
Hypertens Res — Hypertension Research
Hypertens Res — Hypertension Research. Clinical and Experimental
Hypertens Suppl — Hypertension Supplement
Hyperthermia Oncol — Hyperthermia and Oncology
HYSAA — Hygiene and Sanitation
HYUC — Hundred Years of the University of Calcutta
HZ — Historijski Zbornik
HZ — Historische Zeitschrift
HZB — Historische Zeitschrift. Beiheft
HZBBA — Horizons in Biochemistry and Biophysics
HzK — Heimkehr zur Kirche
HZKLA — Herz Kreislauf
HZKP — Hermes. Zeitschrift fuer Klassische Philologie
HZM — Handelingen. Zuidnederlandse Maatschappij voor Taal-En Letterkunde en Geschiedenis
HZMTLG — Handelingen. Zuidnederlandse Maatschappij voor Taal-En Letterkunde en Geschiedenis
HZnMTL — Handelingen. Zuidnederlandse Maatschappij voor Taal-En Letterkunde en Geschiedenis
HZOO — Hunick Zoo. Monthly Publication of Tanana Chiefs Conference
HZS — Historische Zeitschrift. Sonderheft

I

I — Idler
I — Iqbal
I — Isis
I — Island
I — Italica
IA — Ibero-Americana
IA — Ibsen-Aarboken
IA — Indian Antiquary
IA — Inscriptiones Graecae Antiquissimae Praeter Atticas in Attica Repertas
IA — Insel-Almanach
IA — Insurance Advocate
IA — Insurance Asia
IA — International Affairs
IA — Iranica Antiqua
IA — Islam Ansiklopedisi
IA — Italia Antichissima
IAA — Ibero-Amerikanisches Archiv
IAA — Inter-American Economic Affairs
IAA — International Aerospace Abstracts
IAA — Izvestiia Nauk Azerbaidzhanskoi SSR
IAAA — Argumentation and Advocacy
IAAAAM — International Archives of Allergy and Applied Immunology
Ia Acad Sci Proc — Iowa Academy of Science. Proceedings
IAAEJ — Institution of Automotive and Aeronautical Engineers, Australia and New Zealand. Journal
IAAE Journal — Institution of Automotive and Aeronautical Engineers, Australia and New Zealand. Journal
IAAG — Animals Agenda
IA Ag Exp — Iowa State College of Agriculture and Mechanical Arts. Agricultural Experiment Station. Publications
IAAHA9 — Indian Council of Agricultural Research. Animal Husbandry Series
IAALD Q Bull — International Association of Agricultural Librarians and Documentalists. Quarterly Bulletin
IAANBS — Internationales Archiv fuer Arbeitsmedizin
IAARA5 — Indian Council of Agricultural Research. Annual Technical Report
IAAROP — Institute of Arctic and Alpine Research. Occasional Papers
IAB — Institut fuer Auslandsbeziehungen
IABLA — Izvestiya Akademii Nauk Azerbaidzhanskoi SSR Seriya Biologicheskikh Nauk
IABNA — Izvestiya Akademii Nauk Armyanskoi SSR Biologicheskie Nauki
IABO — American Journal of Botany
Ia B R — Iowa Bar Review
IABS — International Abstracts of Biological Sciences
IABY — American Baby
IAC — Imprimerie Artistique en Couleurs
IAC — Indo-Asian Culture
Ia Cath Hist Soc Coll — Iowa Catholic Historical Society. Collections
IACEAA — Indian Council of Agricultural Research. Cereal Crop Series
IACL — American Criminal Law Review
IACLAV — International Anesthesiology Clinics
IACP — Journal of Abnormal Child Psychology
IACPA — Proceedings. International Astronautical Congress
IACP Law Enforce Leg Rev — IACP [*International Association of Chiefs of Police*] Law Enforcement Legal Review
IACP Leg Pt — IACP [*International Association of Chiefs of Police*] Legal Points
IADC Newsl — IADC [*International Association of Dredging Companies*] Newsletter
IADD — Index to American Doctoral Dissertations
IADL — Adult Learning
IADL — Journal of Adolescence
IADS Newsl — International Association of Dental Students. Newsletter
IADV — Advocate. The National Gay and Lesbian News Magazine
IAE — India Economic Bulletin
IAE — Internationales Archiv fuer Ethnographie
IAEA Bibliogr Ser — International Atomic Energy Agency. Bibliographical Series
IAEA Bull — International Atomic Energy Agency. Bulletin
IAEA NPPCI Spec Meet New Instrum Water Cooled React Proc — IAEA-NPPCI Specialists' Meeting on New Instrumentation of Water Cooled Reactors. Proceedings
IAEA Proc Ser — International Atomic Energy Agency. Proceedings Series
IAEA Saf Ser — International Atomic Energy Agency. Safety Series
IAEA Symp Neutron Inelastic Scattering Proc Symp — IAEA (International Atomic Energy Agency) Symposium on Neutron Inelastic Scattering. Proceedings. Symposium
IAEA Tech Rep Ser — International Atomic Energy Agency. Technical Report Series
IAEH — India. Articles in Economic History

IAEHD — International Archives of Occupational and Environmental Health
IAEHDW — International Archives of Occupational and Environmental Health
IAE J — IAE (Institute of Atomic Engineers) Journal
IAEMAA — Indian Council of Agricultural Research. Entomological Monographs
IAEN — American Enterprise
IAEN — Department of Indian and Northern Affairs. Education Section. Northern ServicesDivision. Newsletter
IAFBAG — International Commission for the Northwest Atlantic Fisheries. Research Bulletin
IAFO — Artforum
IAFP — American Family Physician
IAFPAO — International Commission for the Northwest Atlantic Fisheries. Special Publication
IAG — Informatique et Gestion
IAG Bull — IAG [*Institute of Applied Geology*] Bulletin
IAGCBP — Contributi. Istituto di Ricerche Agrarie Milano
IAGFA — Izvestiya Akademii Nauk SSSR Seriya Geofizicheskaya
IAGGA — Izvestiya Akademii Nauk Armyanskoi SSR Geologicheskie i Geograficheskie Nauki
IAG J — IAG [*International Federation for Information Processing. Administrative Data Processing Group*] Journal
IAG Lit Auto — IAG [*International Federation for Information Processing. Administrative Data Processing Group*] Literature on Automation
IAGOD Symp — IAGOD (International Association of the Genesis of Ore Deposits) Symposium
IAGPBU — Investigaciones Agropecuarias
IAGRD4 — Investigacion Agricola
IAGYA — Izvestiya Akademii Nauk SSSR Seriya Geograficheskaya i Geofizicheskaya
IAHD — International Journal of Aging and Human Development
IAHI — International Archives of the History of Ideas
IAHS AISH Publ — IAHS-AISH (Association International des Sciences Hydrologiques) Publication
IAHS Publ — IAHS (International Association of Hydrological Sciences) Publication
IAI — International Affairs
IAI — Izvestija na Bulgarskija Archeologiceski Institut
IAIBAN — Izvestiia na Arkheologicheskiia Institut. Bulgarska Akademiia na Naukite
IAI Bull — IAI (International African Institute) Bulletin. African Studies Notes and News
IAI/I — Indiana. Beitraege zur Voelker- und Sprachenkunde, Archaeologie, und Anthropologie des Indianischen Amerika. Ibero-Amerikanisches Institut
IAIM — American Imago
IAIOI — Izvestija na Archeoogiceskija Institut. Otdelenie za Istorija, Archeologija i Filosofija
IAIR — Air Progress
IAIS — Indian and Inuit Supporter. A Newsletter of the Indian and Inuit Support Group of Newfoundland and Labrador
IA J — Iowa Journal of History and Politics
IAJE Res — IAJE (International Association of Jazz in Education) Jazz Research Papers
Ia J Hist Pol — Iowa Journal of History and Politics
Ia Jour Hist — Iowa Journal of History and Politics. State Historical Society of Iowa
IAJP — American Journal of Physics
IAJRC — IAJRC [*International Association of Jazz Record Collectors*] Journal
IAJS — American Journal of Science
IAJS — Index of Articles on Jewish Studies
IA J Soc Indust Archaeol — IA. Journal of the Society for Industrial Archaeology
IAK — Information Economique Africaine
IAK — Inschriften der Altassyrischen Koenige
IAK — Izvestiia Gosudarstvennoi Rossiiskoi Arkheologicheskoi Kommissii
IAKFA — Izvestiya Akademii Nauk Kazakhskoi SSR Seriya Fiziko-Matematicheskikh Nauk
IAKSA — Izvestiya Akademii Nauk SSSR
IAL — Arts and Letters. India and Pakistan
IAL — ERIC Identifier Authority List
IAL — Indian Art and Letters
IAL — Indice de Artes y Letras
IAL — Industries Alimentaires et Agricoles
IAL — International Affairs (London)
IALAA — Industries Alimentaires et Agricoles
IALAB — Lucrari Stiintifice. Institutul Agronomic "Dr. Petru Groza" (Cluj). Seria Agricultura
Ia Law Bul — Iowa Law Bulletin
Ia Law R — Iowa Law Review
IA Law Rev — Iowa Law Review
IAL Bol Inst Adolfo Lutz — IAL Boletim. Instituto Adolfo Lutz

IALBull — Institut Archeologique Liegeois. Bulletin
IA L Bull — Iowa Law Bulletin
IALI — American Libraries
IALK — Alaska
IALL Bull — Bulletin. International Association of Law Libraries
IALMAB — Institutul Agronomic "Dr. Petru Groza" (Cluj). Lucrari Stiintifice. Seria Medicina Veterinara si Zootehnie
IALR — Administrative Law Review
IALR — International Anthropological and Linguistic Review
IA LR — Iowa Law Review
IALRB — Indian Journal of Animal Research
IALRBR — Indian Journal of Animal Research
IA L Rev — Iowa Law Review
IALT — Alternatives
IAM — International Affairs (Moscow)
IAM — International Art Market
IAM — Istanbul Arkeolji Muezeleri Yiligi
IAM — Istanbul Asariatika Muzeleri Nesriyati
IAMEA — Inter-American Economic Affairs
IAMI — Iron Age Metalworking International [*Later, Chilton's IAMI Iron Age Metalworking International*]
IAMM — American Mathematical Monthly
IAMNA — Izvestiya Akademii Nauk Armyanskoi SSR Seriya Fiziko-Matematicheskikh Nauk
IAMOAM — Indian Council of Agricultural Research. Monograph
IAMP News Bull — IAMP [*International Association of Meteorology and Atmospheric Physics*] News Bulletin
IAMS Monogr — IAMS (International Association of Microbiolobical Societies) Monograph
IAMY — Istanbul Arkeolji Muezeleri Yiligi
IAn — Indian Antiquary
IAN — Izvestiia Academii Nauk SSSR
IAN — Izvestija Akademii Nauk SSSR Seriga Literatury i Jazuka
IAN — Izvestiya Akademii Nauk SSSR Seriya Literatury i Jazyka
IANA — American Naturalist
IANA — Izvestiia Akademii Nauk Azerbaidzhanskoi SSR
IANA — Izvestiia. Vestnik Obshchestvennykh Nauk. Akademia Nauk Armianskoi SSR
IANAB — Izvestiya Akademii Nauk Azerbaidzhanskoi SSR
IANB — Animal Behaviour
I and C — Ideology and Consciousness
I & CLQ — International and Comparative Law Quarterly
I & EC — Industrial and Engineering Chemistry
I & FR — Indian and Foreign Review
I & L — Iazyk i Literatura
I & L — Ideologies and Literature
I & O — Issues & Observations
I & R Mgmt — Information and Records Management
I & S I J — Journal of the Iron and Steel Institute
I & SM — Iron & Steelmaker
I & V — Ideas y Valores
IANE — Interconnections in the Ancient Near-East
IANFA — Izvestiya Akademii Nauk Seriya Fizicheskaya
IANKSA — Izvestiia Akademiia Nauk Kazakhskoi. Seriia Arkheologicheskaia
IANMA — Izvestiya Akademii Nauk SSSR Otdelenie Tekhnicheskikh Nauk Metallurgiya i Toplivo
IAN-OGN — Izvestiya Akademii Nauk SSSR Otdeleniya Gumanitarnykh Nauk
IAN-OLJa — Izvestiya Akademii Nauk SSSR Otdeleniya Literatury i Jazyka
IAN OON — Izvestiya Akademii Nauk SSSR Otdeleniya Obscestvennykh Nauk
IAN ORJaSL — Izvestiya Akademii Nauk SSSR Otdeleniya Russkogo Jazyka i Slavesnosti AkademiiNauk
IANQ — ANQ
IANR (Inst Agric Nat Resour) Q — IANR (Institute of Agriculture and Natural Resources) Quarterly
IANSA — Izvestiya Akademii Nauk SSSR Otdelenie Tekhnicheskikh Nauk Mekhanika i Mashinostroenie
IAN SSS Bio — Izvestiya Akademii Nauk SSSR Seriya Biologicheskaya
IAN SSS FAO — Izvestiya Akademii Nauk SSSR Seriya Fizika Atmosfery i Okeana
IAN SSS Fiz — Izvestiya Akademii Nauk SSSR Seriya Fizicheskaya
IANT — Izvestiia Akademii Nauk Tadzhikskoi SSR
IANTA — Izvestiya Akademii Nauk SSSR Otdelenie Tekhnicheskikh Nauk
IANUz — Izvestiya Akademii Nauk Uzbekistanskoj SSSR
IANZA — Industrie-Anzeiger
IAOHD — International Archives of Allergy and Applied Immunology
IAOP — International Abstracts in Operations Research
IAOR — International Abstracts in Operations Research
IAP — Ibero-American Pragensia. Anuario. Centro de Estudios de la Universidad Carolina
IAP — Inscrizioni Antico-Ebraiche Palestinesi
IAP — Islamic Academy Patrika
IAPAR (Fund Inst Agron Parana) Bol Tec — IAPAR (Fundacao Instituto Agronomico do Parana) Boletim Tecnico
IAPAR (Fund Inst Agron Parana) Circ — IAPAR (Fundacao Instituto Agronomico do Parana) Circular
IAPH — American Photo
IAPhgr — Internationales Archiv fuer Photogrammetrie
IAPL Newsl — IAPL (Indian Association for Programmed Learning) Newsletter
IAPMA — Monographs in Pathology
IAPMAV — International Academy of Pathology. Monograph
IAPO — American Poetry
I App — Law Reports, Privy Council, Indian Appeals
IAP/P — Pesquisas. Anuario do Instituto Anchietano de Pesquisas
IAPSB — Antennas and Propagation Society. International Symposium
IAPVA — Industria Alimentara. Produse Vegetale
IAPWA — International Journal of Air and Water Pollution

I Aq — Indian Antiquary
IAQ — Internationales Asienforum
IAQR — Imperial and Asiatic Quarterly Review
IAQSB — Industries Atomiques et Spatiales
IAR — Indian Affairs Record
IAR — Interavia Aerospace Review
IAR — International Automotive Review
IAR — Ivor's Art Review
IARB — Inter-American Review of Bibliography
IARCC — IARC [*International Agency for Research on Cancer*] Scientific Publications
IARC (Int Agency Res Cancer) Publ — IARC (International Agency for Research on Cancer) Publications
IARC Monogr — IARC [*International Agency for Research on Cancer*] Monographs
IARC Monogr Eval Carcinog Risk Chem Hum — IARC [*International Agency for Research on Cancer*] Monographs. Evaluation of the Carcinogenic Risk of Chemicals to Humans
IARC Monogr Eval Carcinog Risk Chem Hum Suppl — IARC [*International Agency for Research on Cancer*] Monographs. Evaluation of the Carcinogenic Risk of Chemicals to Humans. Supplement
IARC Monogr Eval Carcinog Risk Chem Man — IARC (International Agency for Research on Cancer) Monographs on the Evaluationof Carcinogenic Risk of Chemicals to Man
IARC Monogr Suppl — IARC (International Agency for Research on Cancer) Monographs. Supplement
IARC Publ — IARC [*International Agency for Research on Cancer*] Publications
IARC Sci Publ — IARC [*International Agency for Research on Cancer*] Scientific Publications
IARG — American Record Guide
IARKA — Izvestiya Akademii Nauk Armyanskoi SSR Khimicheskie Nauki
IARTAS — Indian Council of Agricultural Research. Report Series
IAS — Iberoamerikanische Studien
IAS — Industrial Arbitration Service
IAS — International Review of Administrative Sciences
IASA — Annual Survey of American Law
IAS Annu Meet Conf Rec — Industry Applications Society. Annual Meeting. Conference Record
IASB — Indian Art Sketch Book
IASC — American Scientist
IAS Current Review — Industrial Arbitration Service. Current Review
IASF — Analog Science Fiction-Science Fact
IASF — Isaac Asimov's Science Fiction Magazine
IASFAP — International Atlantic Salmon Foundation. Special Publication Series
Iasi Univ An Stiint Sect 2 B Ser Noua — Iasi Universitatea. Analele Stiintifice. Sectiunea 2-B. Geologie. Serie Noua
IASL — Internationales Archiv fuer Sozialgeschichte der Deutschen Literatur
IASLIC Bull — IASLIC [*Indian Association of Special Libraries and Information Centres*]Bulletin
IASODL — International Advances in Surgical Oncology
IASOP — Institute of African Studies. Occasional Publications
IASP — Journal of Applied Social Psychology
IASRR — Institute of African Studies. Research Review
IASS — Asian Survey
Ia St B Assn Proc — Iowa State Bar Association. Proceedings
Ia St Conf Soc Wk Proc — Iowa State Conference of Social Work. Proceedings
IA Stud Afr A — Iowa Studies in African Art
IASU — American School and University
IASUAB — Institute of Agricultural Sciences. University of Alaska. Bulletin
IASURR — Institute of Agricultural Sciences. University of Alaska. Research Reports
IAT — Izvestiya Akademii Nauk Turkmenskoi SSSR Seriya Obshchestvennych Nauk
IATE — Arithmetic Teacher
IATHA — Informations Aerauliques et Thermiques
Iatr Ath — Iatrikai Athenai
Iatr Epitheor Enoplon Dyn — Iatrike Epitheoresis Enoplon Dynameon
IATUL Proc — International Association of Technological University Libraries. Proceedings
IAU — Internal Auditor
IAU Circ — International Astronomical Union. Circular
IAUD — Audio
IAUE — Automotive Engineering
IAUN — Automotive News
IAUSA — International Astronomical Union. Symposium
IAUTA — Ingenieurs de l'Automobile
IAVCEI Proc Volcanol — IAVCEI (International Association of Volcanology and Chemistry of the Earth's Interior) Proceediings in Volcanology
Iav Skh Nauki Minist Selsk Khoz Arm SSR — Izvestiya. Sel'skokhozyaistvennye Nauki. Ministerstvo Sel'skogoKhozyaistva Armyanskoi SSR
IAWA Bull — IAWA [*International Association of Wood Anatomists*] Bulletin
IAWABV — International Association of Wood Anatomists. Bulletin
IAWPRC Wrkshp — IAWPRC (International Association on Water Pollution Research and Control) Workshop
IAY — International Atomic Energy Agency. Bulletin
IAZ — Industrie-Anzeiger
Ib — Ibero-Romania
Ib — Ibis
IB — Indogermanische Bibliothek
IB — Information Bulletin
IB — Instrumentenbau-Zeitschrift. Music International
IB — International Bibliography
IB — Introduction a la Bible
IB — Irish Book
IB — RAB [*Radio Advertising Bureau*] Instant Background
IBA — Idische (Buenos Aires)
IBA — Independent Banker

IBAC — Information Bulletin of Australian Criminology
IBAD — Izvestija na Bulgarskoto Archeologicesko Druzestvo
Ibadan — Ibadan Review
Ibadan Rev — Ibadan Review
Ibadan Soc Sci Ser — Ibadan Social Sciences Series
Ibadan Univ Dep For Bull — Ibadan University. Department of Forestry. Bulletin
IBAI — Izvestija na Bulgarskija Archeologiceski Institut
IBA of A — Investment Bankers Association of America. Bulletin
IBASB — Izvestiya na Sektsiyata po Astronomiya. Bulgarska Akademiya na Naukite
IBA Tech Rev — IBA [*Independent Broadcasting Authority*] Technical Review
IBAZA — Proceedings of the Convention. Institute of Brewing (Australia and New Zealand Section)
IBB — International Bottler and Packer
IBBD Bol Inf — IBBD [*Instituto Brasileiro de Bibliografia e Documentacao*] Boletim Informativo
IBBD Not Diversas — IBBD [*Instituto Brasileiro de Bibliografia e Documentacao*] Noticias Diversas
IBBNA5 — International Bulletin of Bacteriological Nomenclature and Taxonomy
IBC — Inscriptiones Britanniae Christianae
IBCOEH — Indian Botanical Contactor
IBCPAG — Atti. Istituto Botanico e Laboratorio Crittogamico. Universita di Pavia
IBD — Infant Behavior and Development
IBD — Internationaal Opereren
IBD — International Business Database
IBD — Internationale Bildungs- und Informations-Datenbank
IBD — Investor's Business Daily
IBDBAD — International Biodeterioration Bulletin
IBDEDP — Infant Behavior and Development
IBE — International Bibliography of Economics
IBEA — Beaver. Exploring Canada's History
IBEA Reports — Illinois Business Education Association. Reports
IBEC Res Inst Bull — IBEC Research Institute. Bulletin
IBEDH — International Bio-Energy Directory and Handbook
IBEE — Illustrated Broadcast Equipment Encyclopedia
IBEI — Beijing Review
IBEJA8 — Indian Bee Journal
IBE/RBE — Revista Brasileira de Economia. Fundacao Getulia Vargas. Instituto Brasileiro de Economia
Ibero — Ibero-Romania
Ibero Am — Ibero-Americana
Ibero Am Arch Berlin — Ibero-Amerikanische Archiv (Berlin)
Ibero Am Archiv — Ibero-Amerikanisches Archiv. Zeitschrift des Ibero-Americanischen. Forschungs-Insitut der Universitaet Bonn
Iberoamer Archiv — Ibero-Amerikanisches Archiv
Ibero Amer Archv — Ibero-Amerikanisches Archiv. Zeitschrift des Ibero-Amerikanischen Forschungs-Instituts der Universitaet Bonn
IBG — International Beverage News
IBGE/R — Revista Brasileira de Geografia. Conselho Nacional de Geografia. Instituto Brasileiro de Geografia e Estatistica
IBGE/RBE — Revista Brasileira de Estatistica. Ministerio do Planejamento e Coordenacao Geral. Instituto Brasileiro de Geografia e Estatistica
IBG/T — Transactions. Institute of British Geographers
IBHR — International Bibliography of the History of Relgions
IBHS — International Bibliography of Historical Sciences
IBi — Illustrazione Biellese
IBI — International Boat Industry
IBID — International Bibliography, Information, and Documentation
IBID — Izvestija na Balgarskoto Istoricesko Druzestvo
IBIFAG — Instituto Nacional de Pesca [*Ecuador*]. Boletin Informativo
IBIGB — Information Bulletin on Isotopic Generators
IBIODC — Specialist Periodical Reports. Inorganic Biochemistry
IBIRDL — Irish Birds
IBIS — ICAO [*International Civil Aviation Organization*] Bird Strike Information System
IBJ — Illinois Bar Journal
IBK — Illinois Banker
IBk — Index to Book Reviews in the Humanities
IBK — Indogaku Bukkuogaku Kenkyu
IBK — Innsbrucker Beitraege zur Kulturwissenschaft
IBKW — Innsbrucker Beitraege zur Kulturwissenschaft
IBKWS — Innsbrucker Beitraege zur Kulturwissenschaft. Sonderheft
IBL — Instytut Badan Literackick Polskiej Akademii Nauk
IBLA — Institut Belles-Lettres Arabes. Revue
IBLB — Independent Biological Laboratory Bulletin
IBM J — IBM [*International Business Machines Corp.*] Journal of Research and Development
IBM J R D — IBM [*International Business Machines Corp.*] Journal of Research and Development
IBM J Res — IBM [*International Business Machines Corp.*] Journal of Research and Development
IBM J Res and Dev — IBM [*International Business Machines Corp.*] Journal of Research and Development
IBM J Res Dev — IBM [*International Business Machines Corp.*] Journal of Research and Development
IBM J Res Develop — IBM [*International Business Machines Corp.*] Journal of Research and Development
IBM Jrl — IBM [*International Business Machines Corp.*] Journal of Research and Development
IBMM — International Business Men's Magazine
IBM Nachr — IBM [*International Business Machines Corp.*] Nachrichten
IBMOEX — International Bioscience Monographs
IBM Systems J — IBM [*International Business Machines Corp.*] Systems Journal
IBM Syst J — IBM [*International Business Machines Corp.*] Systems Journal
IBM Tech Discl Bull — IBM [*International Business Machines Corp.*] Technical Disclosure Bulletin

IBM Tech Disclosure Bull — IBM [*International Business Machines Corp.*] Technical Disclosure Bulletin
IBM User — IBM [*International Business Machines Corp.*] System User
IBNE — Behavioral Neuroscience
IBNF — International Buddhist News Forum
IBNS — International Bank Note Society. Quarterly Magazine
IbNY — Iberica (New York)
IBOJ — Informacni Bulletin pro Otazky Jazykovedne
IBOLB — Informatore Botanico Italiano
IBOS — Boston Magazine
IBOY — Boy's Life
IBP — Internationale Bibliothek fuer Psychologie und Soziologie
IBP — Italian Books and Periodicals
IBPE — Business and Professional Ethics Journal
IBP (Int Biol Programme) Handb — IBP (International Biological Programme) Handbook
IBP (Int Biol Programme) Norden — IBP (International Biological Programme) i Norden
IBPP — International Bulletin of Plant Protection
IBPRDM — International Biological Programme Series
IBPS — International Bibliography of Political Science
IBR — Inscriptiones Bavariae Romanae
IBR — Issues in Bank Regulation
IBREDR — Indian Botanical Reporter
IBRI/R — Revista Brasileira de Politica Internacional. Instituto Brasileiro de Relacoes Internacionais
IBRO Bull — International Brain Research Organization. Bulletin
IBRO Handb Ser — IBRO Handbook Series
IBRO (Int Brain Res Org) Handb Ser Methods Neurosci — IBRO (International Brain Research Organisation) Handbook Series. Methods in the Neurosciences
IBRO Monogr Ser — IBRO (International Brain Research Organization) Monograph Series
IBRSDZ — International Brain Research Organization. Monograph Series
IBRU — Ichthyological Bulletin. Department of Ichthyology. Rhodes University
IBS — Informacion Comercial Espanola
IBS — Innsbrucker Beitraege zur Sprachwissenschaft
IBS — International Bibliography of Sociology
IBS — International Bibliography of the Social Sciences, Economics, and Sociology
IBSA — Indian Behavioural Sciences Abstracts
IBSA — Institutiones Biblicae Scholis Accomodatae
IBSAI — Iraq. British School of Archaeology in Iraq
IBSCA — International Bibliography of Social and Cultural Anthropology
Ibsen Yearb — Ibsen Yearbook
IBSJ — Index Bibliographicus Societatis Jesu
IBSJBB — Instituut voor Biologisch en Scheikundig Onderzoek van Landbouwgewassen (Wageningen). Jaarverslag
IBSS — International Bibliography of the Social Sciences
IBU — Indice Bibliografico. UNAM (Universidad Nacional Autonoma de Mexico)
IBU — Journal of Business
IBW — Indien und die Buddhistische Welt
IBZ — Internationale Bibliographie der Zeitschriftenliteratur
IC — Icelandic Canadian
IC — Iconclass
IC — Imagination, Cognition, and Personality
IC — Indian Culture
IC — Industrial Arbitration Cases
IC — Inscriptiones Creticae Opera et Consilio Friderici Halbherr Collectae
IC — Instituto Coimbra
IC — Interfaces in Computing [*Later, Computer Standards and Interfaces*]
IC — Investors Chronicle
IC — Islamic Culture
IC — Istoriski Casopis
IC — Revue de Droit Intellectuel "l'Ingenieur Conseil"
ICA — Proceedings. International Congress of Americanists [*Paris*]
ICACH Tuxtla Gutierrez — ICACH. Organo del Instituto de Ciencias y Artes de Chiapas. Tuxtla Gutierrez (Chiapas, Mexico)
ICA Inf — ICA [*Instituto Colombiano Agropecuario*] Informa
ICA Informa Inst Colomb Agropecu — ICA Informa. Instituto Colombiano Agropecuario
ICA (Inst Colomb Agropecu) Bol Tec — ICA (Instituto Colombiano Agropecuario) Boletin Tecnico
ICAITI Bol Inform — ICAITI [*Instituto Centro Americano de Investigacion y Tecnologia Industrial*] Boletin Informativo
ICAITI (Inst Centroam Invest Tecnol Ind) Inf Tec — ICAITI (Instituto Centroamericano de Investigacion y Tecnologia Industrial) Informe Tecnico
ICAL — California
ICALEO Proc — ICALEO (International Conress oon Applications of Lasers and Electro-Optics) Proceedings
ICAM — Camping Magazine
ICAMA — Industria della Carta
ICAM J — Institute of Corn and Agricultural Merchants. Journal
ICAO Bull — ICAO [*International Civil Aviation Organization*] Bulletin
ICAP — Journal. American Academy of Child and Adolescent Psychiatry
ICAPDG — Indian Journal of Comparative Animal Physiology
ICAR — Imperial Indian Council of Agricultural Research
ICAR — Inventory of Canadian Agri-Food Research
ICARAJ — Indian Council of Agricultural Research. Miscellaneous Bulletin
IC Arb Q — Indian Council of Arbitration. Quarterly
ICARND — Indian Council of Agricultural Research (New Delhi)
ICATAP — Indian Council of Agricultural Research. Technical Bulletin
ICB — ICP [*International Computer Programs, Inc.*] Business Software Review
ICB — Index of Catholic Biographies
ICB — Institut Royal Colonial Belge. Compte Rendu des Seances
ICBCBE — International Congress of Biochemistry. Abstracts
ICBEA — Industrie Chimique Belge

ICBR — Iceberg Research. Scott Polar Research Institute
ICBRAO — India. Coffee Board. Annual Report
ICC — Information des Cours Complementaires
ICC — Instituto Caro y Cuervo
ICC — Intermediaire des Chercheurs et des Curieux
ICC — International Critical Commentary
ICC — International Critical Commentary of the Holy Scriptures
IC Card Syst Des — IC Card Systems and Design
ICC Bull — ICC (International Computation Centre) Bulletin
ICC Bus World — ICC [*International Chamber of Commerce*] Business World
ICCC — Christianity and Crisis
ICCE — Boletin Bibliografico ICCE
ICCP — Journal of Clinical Child Psychology
ICCPDQ — International Journal of Cancer Control and Prevention
ICC Prac J — ICC [*Interstate Commerce Commission*] Practitioners' Journal
ICC Pract J — ICC [*Interstate Commerce Commission*] Practitioners' Journal
ICDI — Canadian Dimension
ICD Sci Educ J — ICD [*International College of Dentists*] Scientific and Educational Journal
ICDSD6 — Indian Journal of Chest Diseases and Allied Sciences
ICE — Indice Cultural Espanol
ICE — Informacion Comercial Espanola
Ice Abs — Ice Abstracts
ICEA Cah — ICEA [*Institut Canadien d'Education des Adultes*] Cahiers
ICE Am Soc Mech Eng — ICE (Internal Combustion Engine Division, ASME) American Society of Mechanical Engineers
Ice Cream Field Ice Cream Trade J — Ice Cream Field and Ice Cream Trade Journal
Ice Cream R — Ice Cream Review
Ice Cream Rev — Ice Cream Review
Ice Cream Trade J — Ice Cream Trade Journal
ICED — Communication Education
ICEL — Ice (London)
Iceland Rev — Iceland Review
Icel Fish Lab Annu Rep — Icelandic Fisheries Laboratories. Annual Report
ICEN — ICEA [*International Childbirth Education Association*] News
ICEN — Ice News. Artec, Inc.
I CE P — Minutes of Proceedings of the Institution of Civil Engineers, containing Abstracts of the Papers and of the Discussions
ICEPAX — International Congress of Entomology. Proceedings
ICER — ICEA [*International Childbirth Education Association*] Review
Ice Refrig — Ice and Refrigeration
ICERV — Inscripciones Cristianas de la Espana Romana y Visigoda
ICEXBO — International Council for the Exploration of the Sea. Cooperative Research Report
ICFB — Integrative Control Functions of the Brain
ICFTU Econ & Social Bul — ICFTU [*International Confederation of Free Trade Unions*] Economic and Social Bulletin
ICGAD — IEEE. Computer Graphics and Applications
ICGM — Consumer Guide Magazine
ICGRAF — Indian Cotton Growing Review
ICH — Islamic Culture (Hyderabad, India)
ICHA — Chatelaine
ICHAA — Inorganica Chimica Acta
ICHCA J — ICHCA [*International Cargo Handling Coordination Association*] Journal
ICHCA Mon J — ICHCA [*International Cargo Handling Coordination Association*] Monthly Journal
ICHE — Journal of Chemical Education
ICHH — Christian Herald
ICHI — Chicago
ICHIA — Ingegneria Chimica
IChildMag — Subject Index to Children's Magazines
ICHPCG — Acta Genetica Sinica
ICHR — Illinois Catholic Historical Review
ICHR — Indian Church History Review
Ichthyol Aquarium J — Ichthyologica: The Aquarium Journal
Ichthyol Bull JLB Smith Inst Ichthyol — Ichthyological Bulletin. J. L. B. Smith Institute of Ichthyology
Ichthyol Ser Dep Biol Coll Sci Tunghai Univ — Ichthyological Series. Department of Biology. College of Science. Tunghai University
Ichtyophysiol Acta — Ichtyophysiologica Acta
I Ch'uan Hsueh Pao Acta Genet Sin — I Ch'uan Hsueh Pao. Acta Genetica Sinica
ICI — Index to Current Information
ICI — Informations Catholiques Internationales
ICIA — Cinema Canada
ICIA Inf Bull — ICIA [*International Center of Information on Antibiotics*] Information Bulletin
ICIASF Rec Int Congr Instrum Aerosp Simul Facil — ICIASF Record. Internaitonal Congress on Instrumentation in Aerospace Simulation Facilities
ICID Bull — ICID [*International Commission on Irrigation and Drainage*] Bulletin
ICID Bull Int Comm Irrig Drain — ICID Bulletin. International Commission on Irrigation and Drainage
ICIDCA Bol — ICIDCA [*Instituto Cubano de Investigaciones de los Derivados de la Cana de Azucar*] Boletin
ICI Engng Plast — ICI [*Imperial Chemical Industries Ltd.*] Engineering Plastics
ICI Mag — ICI [*Imperial Chemical Industries Ltd.*] Magazine
IC Infect Control — IC. Infection Control
ICI Rev — Imperial Chemical Industries Review
ICITA — Instituto Cubano de Investigaciones Tecnologicas. Serie de Estudios sobre Trabajos de Investigacion
ICJ — Insurance Counsel Journal
ICJE — Cambridge Journal of Economics
ICJRAU — Indian Central Jute Committee. Annual Report of the Jute Agricultural Research Institute
ICJ Rev — Review. International Commission of Jurists

ICJYB — International Court of Justice. Yearbook
ICK — Inscriptiones Cuneiformes du Kultepe
ICL — International Congress of Linguists. Proceedings
ICLH — Clearing House
ICLI — Inter-City Cost of Living Indicators
ICLIAD — Investigacion Clinica
ICLM — Index to Commonwealth Little Magazines
ICL Publ — ICL [*International Combustion Limited*] Publications
ICLQ — International and Comparative Law Quarterly
ICLQS — International and Comparative Law Quarterly. Supplement
ICLR — California Law Review
ICL Tech J — ICL [*International Computers Limited*] Technical Journal
ICLV — Columbia Law Review
ICLV — Inscriptiones Christianae Latinae Veteres
ICM — Imperial and Colonial Magazine
ICM — In the Company of Man. Joseph B. Casagrande [*New York*]
ICM — Iscrizioni delle Chiese e Degli Altri Edifici di Milano
ICM 90 Satell Conf Proc — ICM-90 Satellite Conference Proceedings
ICMC — International Catholic Migration
ICMC Ne — ICMC [*International Catholic Migration Commission*] News
ICME N — ICME [*International Committee for Museum of Ethnography*] News
ICMFA — Indian Chemical Manufacturer
ICMJD — International Cast Metals Journal
ICMO — Ceramics Monthly
ICMP — Canadian Composer
ICMR Ann — ICMR (International Center for Medical Research) Annals
ICMR (Int Cent Med Res) Ann — ICMR (International Center for Medical Research) Annals
ICMR Semin Proc — ICMR (International Center for Medical Research) Seminar. Proceedings
ICMU — Country Music
ICN — Indonesian Commercial Newsletter
ICNABY — International Commission for the Northwest Atlantic Fisheries. Statistical Bulletin
ICNAF — International Commission for the Northwest Atlantic Fisheries. Research Bulletin
ICNAFSP — International Commission for the Northwest Atlantic Fisheries. Special Publication
ICNFAE — International Commission for the Northwest Atlantic Fisheries. Annual Proceedings
ICNS — Canadian Consumer
ICNS — Ice Cap News. American Society of Polar Philatelists
ICNSAJ — Iowa Conservationist
ICNT — Crafts'n Things
ICN UCLA Symp Mol Biol — ICN-UCLA (International Chemical and Nuclear Corp. - University of California at Los Angeles) Symposium on Molecular Biology
ICN-UCLA Symp Mol Cell Biol — ICN-UCLA [*International Chemical and Nuclear Corp. - University of California at Los Angeles*] Symposia on Molecular and Cellular Biology
ICNWAV — International Commission for the Northwest Atlantic Fisheries. Redbook. Part III
ICOAB5 — India. Coffee Board. Research Department. Annual Detailed Technical Report
ICOFAJ — Indian Coffee
ICOG — Cognitive Psychology
ICOH — Colonial Homes
ICOJ — ICO [*Institute of Chemist-Opticians*] Journal
ICOJAV — Indian Coconut Journal
ICOL Meet — ICOL Meeting
ICOMOS Bull — ICOMOS [*International Council of Monuments and Sites*] Bulletin
ICON — Connoisseur
ICONDC — Annual Research Reviews. Intrauterine Contraception
Icon Fau Fl Medit — Iconographie de la Faune et de la Flore Mediterraneennes
Icon Fl Alpinae Pl — Icones Florae Alpinae Plantarum
Icon Fungorum Malayensium — Icones Fungorum Malayensium
Icon Med — Iconographia Medica
Icon Med Prat — Iconographie Medicale du Praticien
Iconog Post — Iconographiske Post. En Nordisk Blad om Billeder
Iconogr Dermatol — Iconographia Dermatologica, Syphilidologica, et Urologica
Iconog Relig — Iconography of Religions
Iconogr Mycol — Iconographia Mycologica
Icon Pl Afr — Icones Plantarum Africanarum
Icon Pl As Or — Iconographia Plantarum Asiae Orientalis
Icon Pl Formosan — Icones Plantarum Formosanarum nec non et Contributiones ad Floram Formosanam
Icon Pl Sin — Icones Plantarum Sinicarum
ICOPA — Industria Conserve
ICOPAF — Industria Conserve
ICOS — Communication Studies
I Cos — Inscriptions of Cos
ICOTA — International Review of Connective Tissue Research
ICP — ICP (Industria Chimica e Petrolifera). Rivista dell'Industria Chimica
ICP — Index to Chinese Periodicals
ICP — Informacao Cultural Portugues
ICP — International Currency Review
ICP — Irish Company Profiles
ICPADC — Investigative and Cell Pathology
ICP Admin — ICP [*International Computer Programs, Inc.*] Interface Administrative and Accounting
ICP Bank Indus — ICP [*International Computer Programs, Inc.*] Interface Banking Industry
ICPDATA — Commodity Production Statistics
ICP Dir — ICP [*International Computer Programs*] Directory
ICP DP Mgmt — ICP [*International Computer Programs, Inc.*] Interface Data Processing Management

ICPH — Contemporary Physics

ICPHS/D — Diogenes. International Council for Philosophy and Humanistic Studies

ICP Inf Newsl — ICP (Inductively Coupled Plasma) Information Newsletter

ICP J Inf Prod and Serv — ICP [*International Computer Programs, Inc.*] Journal of Information Products and Services

ICP J Software Prod and Serv — ICP [*International Computer Programs, Inc.*] Journal of Software Products and Services

ICPR — International Clinical Products Review

ICP/R — Revista. Instituto de Cultura Puertorriquena

ICPS — Journal of Clinical Psychology

ICP Soft Bus Rev — ICP [*International Computer Programs, Inc.*] Software Business Review

ICP Software J — ICP [*International Computer Programs, Inc.*] Software Journal

IC Publ — IC [*International Combustion Products Limited*] Publications

ICQ — Indian Cultures Quarterly

ICr — Inscriptiones Creticae

ICR — Intercollegiate Review

ICR — International Consumer Reports

ICR — International Currency Report

ICR — Iscrizioni delle Chiese e d'Altri Edifici di Roma

ICR Annu Rep — ICR (Institute for Chemical Research) Annual Report

ICRE — Iceland Review

ICret — Inscriptiones Creticae Opera et Consilio Friderici Halbherr Collectae

I Creticae — Inscriptiones Creticae Opera et Consilio Friderici Halbherr Collectae

ICRISAT Annu Rep — ICRISAT [*International Crops Research Institute for the Semi-Arid Tropics*] Annual Report

ICRISAT (Int Crops Res Inst Semi-Arid Trop) Res Bull — ICRISAT (International Crops Research Institute for the Semi-Arid Tropics) Research Bulletin

ICRP Ann — ICRP (International Commission on Radiological Protection) Annals

ICRP Publ — ICRP [*International Commission on Radiological Protection*] Publication

ICRRA2 — Indian Council of Agricultural Research. Research Series

ICR Rep Univ Tokyo Inst Cosmic Ray Res — ICR Report. University of Tokyo. Institute for Cosmic Ray Research

ICRS — Index Chemicus Registry System

ICRS Med Rep Monogr Sov Med Sci — ICRS [*Institute of Contemporary Russian Studies*] Medical Reports. Monographs in Soviet Medical Science

ICRU — Cruising World

ICRU Rep — ICRU [*International Commission on Radiological Units*] Report

ICRV — Contemporary Review

ICS — Ideas en Ciencias Sociales

ICS — Illinois Classical Studies

ICS — International Congress Series

ICS — Italia Che Scrive

ICSC — Index to Canadian Securities Cases

ICSD — Inorganic Crystal Structure Database

ICS/JCCP — Journal of Commonwealth and Comparative Politics. University of London. Institute of Commonwealth Studies

ICSMAQ — International Clearinghouse on Science and Mathematics. Curricular DevelopmentsReport

ICSP — Issues in Canadian Science Policy

ICSPD4 — Immunologia Clinica e Sperimentale

ICSSR Newsl — ICSSR (Indian Council of Social Science Research) Newsletter

ICSSR Res Abstr Q — ICSSR [*Indian Council of Social Science Research*] Research Abstracts Quarterly

ICST — Christopher Street

ICSU Comm Data Sci Technol CODATA Spec Rep — International Council of Scientific Unions. Committee on Data for Science and Technology. CODATA Special Report

ICSU Comm Data Sci Technol Proc Int CODATA Conf — International Council of Scientific Unions. Committee on Data for Science and Technology. Proceedings. International CODATA Conference

ICSU Inter Union Comm Geodyn Sci Rep — International Council of Scientific Unions. Inter-Union Commission on Geodynamics Scientific Report

ICSU Press Symp — ICSU (International Council of Scientific Unions) Press Symposium

ICSU Rev — International Council of Scientific Unions. Review

ICSU Rev World Sci — ICSU [*International Council of Scientific Unions*] Review of World Science

ICSU Sci Comm Probl Environ SCOPE Rep — International Council of Scientific Unions. Scientific Committee on Problems ofthe Environment. SCOPE Report

ICSU Short Rep — ICSU [*International Council of Scientific Unions*] Short Reports

ICSY — Contemporary Sociology

ICT — Industrial and Commercial Training

ICT — International Coal Trade

ICTD Pr — ICT [*International Computers and Tabulators Limited*] Data Processing Journal

ICTK — CHEMTECH

ICTP Coll Theor Comput Plasma Phys Sel Lect — ICTP College on Theoretical and Computational Plasma Physics. Selected Lectures(International Center for Theoretical Physics)

ICTPDF — Isozymes. Current Topics in Biological and Medical Research

ICTRA — Iron and Coal Trades Review

ICTSDI — IMLS [*Institute of Medical Laboratory Sciences*] Current Topics in MedicalLaboratory Sciences

ICTY — Countryside and Small Stock Journal

ICU — Hebdomadaire de la Production a la Distribution

ICUAER/B — Bulletin. International Committee on Urgent Anthropological and EthnologicalResearch

ICub — Ilustracion Cubana

ICUIS Abstr Service — ICUIS [*Institute on the Church in Urban-Industrial Society*] Abstract Service

ICUIS Bibliog — Institute on the Church in Urban-Industrial Society. Bibliography Series

ICUIS Occasional Paper — Institute on the Church in Urban-Industrial Society. Occasional Papers

ICUIS Occ Paper — Institute on the Church in Urban-Industrial Society. Occasional Papers

ICUNA5 — Improving College and University Teaching

ICUR — Inscriptiones Christianae Urbis Romae. Nova Series

ICURNS — Insriptiones Christianae Urbis Romae. Nova Series

ICUT — Improving College and University Teaching

ICWO — Catholic World

ICWRBS — International Commission on Whaling. Report

ICYSB — International Review of Cytology. Supplement

ICYW — Cycle World

Id — Idea. Mensile di Cultura Politica e Sociale

ID — Innovator's Digest

ID — Inscriptions de Delos

ID — Institutional Distribution

ID — Ionospheric Data

ID — Irish Digest

ID — Italia Dialettale

IDA — Industrial Development Abstracts

IDAADC — Infectious Diseases and Antimicrobial Agents

IDABA — Annual Bulletin. International Dairy Federation

IDABAC — International Dairy Federation. Annual Bulletin

Idaho — Idaho Reports

Idaho Ag Exp — Idaho. Agricultural Experiment Station. Publications

Idaho Agric Exp Stn Res Bull — Idaho. Agricultural Experiment Station. Research Bulletin

Idaho Agr Res Progr Rep — Idaho Agricultural Research Progress Report. University of Idaho. College of Agriculture

Idaho Agr Sci — Idaho Agricultural Science. University of Idaho. College of Agriculture

Idaho Bur Mines and Geology Earth Sci Ser — Idaho. Bureau of Mines and Geology. Earth Sciences Series

Idaho Bur Mines Geol Bull — Idaho. Bureau of Mines and Geology. Bulletin

Idaho Bur Mines Geol County Rep — Idaho. Bureau of Mines and Geology. County Report

Idaho Bur Mines Geol Inf Circ — Idaho. Bureau of Mines and Geology. Information Circular

Idaho Bur Mines Geol Miner Resour Rep — Idaho. Bureau of Mines and Geology. Mineral Resources Report

Idaho Bur Mines Geol Pam — Idaho. Bureau of Mines and Geology. Pamphlet

Idaho Cit — Idaho Citizen

Idaho Dep Fish Game Wildl Bull — Idaho. Department of Fish and Game. Wildlife Bulletin

Idaho Dep Reclam Water Inf Bull — Idaho. Department of Reclamation. Water Information Bulletin

Idaho Dept Reclamation Water Inf Bull — Idaho. Department of Reclamation. Water Information Bulletin

Idaho Dep Water Adm Water Inf Bull — Idaho. Department of Water Administration. Water Information Bulletin

Idaho Dep Water Resour Basic Data Release — Idaho. Department of Water Resources. Basic Data Release

Idaho Dep Water Resour Water Inf Bull — Idaho. Department of Water Resources. Water Information Bulletin

Idaho Div Environ Dep Health Welfare Water Qual Ser — Idaho. Division of Environment. Department of Health and Welfare. Water QualitySeries

Idaho For Wildl Range Exp Stn Bull — Idaho. Forest, Wildlife, and Range Experiment Station. Bulletin

Idaho For Wildl Range Exp Stn Inf Ser — Idaho. Forest, Wildlife, and Range Experiment Station. Information Series

Idaho For Wildl Range Exp Stn Note — Idaho. Forest, Wildlife, and Range Experiment Station. Note

Idaho For Wildl Range Exp Stn Pap — Idaho. Forest, Wildlife, and Range Experiment Station. Paper

Idaho For Wildl Range Exp Stn Stn Note — Idaho. Forest, Wildlife, and Range Experiment Station. Station Note

Idaho For Wildl Range Exp Stn Tech Rep — Idaho. Forest, Wildlife, and Range Experiment Station. Technical Report

Idaho Libn — Idaho Librarian

Idaho Librn — Idaho Librarian

Idaho LJ — Idaho Law Journal

Idaho L Rev — Idaho Law Review

Idaho Min Industry Ann Rept — Idaho Mining Industry. Annual Report

Idaho Power Co Bull — Idaho Power Company. Bulletin

Idaho Sess Laws — Session Laws. Idaho

Idaho Stat — Idaho Statesman

Idaho State Hortic Assoc Proc Annu Conv — Idaho. State Horticultural Association. Proceedings of the Annual Convention

Idaho Univ Agric Exp Stn Curr Inf Ser — Idaho University. Agricultural Experiment Station. Current Information Series

Idaho Univ Curr Inf Ser — Idaho University. Current Information Series

Idaho Univ Eng Exp Sta Bull — Idaho University. Engineering Experiment Station. Bulletin

Idaho Univ For Range Wildl Exp Stn Res Note — Idaho University. Forest, Range, and Wildlife Experiment Station. Research Note

Idaho Univ Water Resour Res Inst Res Tech Completion Rep — Idaho University. Water Resources Research Institute. Research Technical Completion Report

Idaho Yest — Idaho Yesterdays

IDA Jnl — IDA [*International Desalination Association*] Journal

IDAL — Dallas

Ida LR — Idaho Law Review

IDA Mag — IDA [*International Desalination Association*] Magazine

IDA Pap — IDA (Institute for Defense Analyses) Paper

I d B — Industries du Bois en Europe

IDB — INPADOC [*International Patent Documentation Center*] Data Base
IDB — Interpreter's Dictionary of the Bible
IDBu — Informatie- en Documentatiebulletin. Sociaal-Economische Raad
I d CC — Intermediaire des Chercheurs et des Curieux
IDCIDC — International Development Research Centre. Publication IDRC
IDCQA — Industrie Ceramique
IDD — Iowa State University of Science and Technology. Doctoral Dissertations. Abstracts and References
IDE — Idea. The Journal of Law and Technology
IDEA — Ideas/Idees. Department of Indian and Northern Affairs
Idea — Idea. The Journal of Law and Technology
Idea — Patent, Trademark, and Copyright Journal of Research and Education
Idea Jb Hamburg Ksthalle — Idea. Jahrbuch der Hamburger Kunsthalle
Idealist Neuphilol — Idealistische Neuphilologie
Ideal Stud — Idealistic Studies
Idea Personal Train — Idea Personal Trainer
Ideas for Mgmt — Ideas for Management
Ideas Manage — Ideas for Management
Ideas Mod Biol Proc Int Congr Zool — Ideas in Modern Biology. Proceedings. International Congress of Zoology
Ideggyogy Sz — Ideggyogyaszati Szemle
Ideggyogy Szle — Ideggyogyaszati Szemle
I Delos — Inscriptions de Delos
Idemitsu Pet J — Idemitsu Petroleum Journal
Iden — Identite
Idengaku Zasshi Suppl — Idengaku Zasshi. Supplement
Identif Anal Org Pollut Water Chem Congr North Am Cont — Identification and Analysis of Organic Pollutants in Water. Chemical Congress. North American Continent
Identif Syst Parameter Estim Proc IFAC Symp — Identification and System Parameter Estimation. Proceedings. IFAC (International Federation of Automatic Control) Symposium
IDEQ — Design Quarterly
IDES/DE — Desarrollo Economico. Instituto de Desarrollo Economico y Social
IDEU — Education
IDF Bul — IDF [*International Diabetes Federation*] Bulletin
IDF Bull — IDF (International Diabetes Federation) Bulletin
IDF Bull Brussels — IDF Bulletin (Brussels) (International Diabetes Federation)
Idg B — Indogermanische Bibliothek
IDGEAH — Industrial Gerontology
Idg Forsch — Indogermanische Forschungen
Idg Gr — Indogermanische Grammatik
Idg Jb — Indogermanisches Jahrbuch
IDHAA — Industrie und Handel
IDHLA9 — International Digest of Health Legislation
IDHOA — Proceedings. International District Heating Association
IDI — International Defense Intelligence
IDI — Management Today
IDIA — Informativo de Investigaciones Agricolas
IDIA Supl — IDIA [*Informativo de Investigaciones Agricolas*]. Suplemento
IDJOAS — International Dental Journal
IDKKB — Iwate Daigaku Kyoikugakubu Kenkyu Nenpo
IDKKBM — Annual Report. Faculty of Education. University of Iwate
IDKSA — Ibaraki Daigaku Kogakubu Kenkyu Shuho
IDL — Index to Dental Literature
IDLEB — Industrial Engineering
ID LJ — Idaho Law Journal
Id L J — Idaho Law Journal
ID LR — Idaho Law Review
IDMA Bull — IDMA [*Indian Drug Manufacturers' Association*] Bulletin
IDMGB — Industrial Management
IDMI — International Dun's Market Identifiers
IDNE — Design News
IDNGA — Ibaraki Daigaku Nogakubu Gakujutsu Hokoku
IDNHA — Iwate Daigaku Nogakubu Hokoku
IDOC Bul — IDOC [*International Documentation*] Bulletin
Idoj — Idojaras
IDOJA — Idojaras
IDPGA — Industrial and Commercial Photography
IDP Rep — IDP [*Information and Data Base Publishing*] Report
IDQT — Drama. The Quarterly Theatre Review
IDR — Industrial Relations
IDR — Industrie Diamanten Rundschau
IDR — Inscriptiile Daciei Romane
IDR — International Defense Review
IDR — Japan Letter
IDRCE2 — International Development Research Centre. Technical Studies IDRC-TS
IDRC (Int Dev Res Cent) TS — IDRC (International Development Research Centre) TS
IDRC Rep — IDRC [*International Development Research Centre*] Reports
IDR Ind Diamond Rev — IDR Industrial Diamond Review
IDRSA — Industrial Research
IDRSJ — Journal. International Double Reed Society
IDS — Industrial Development
IDS — Industry Data Sources
IDS — Izvestiya na Druzestvoto na Filolozite-Slavisti v Balgarija (Sofija)
IDSA J — IDSA [*Institute for Defense Studies and Analyses*] Journal
IDSB — International Dostoevsky Society. Bulletin
IDS Bulletin — IDS [*Institute of Development Studies*] Bulletin
IDSFA — Institute for Defence Studies and Analyses. Journal
IDS Report — Incomes Data Services Ltd. International Report
Id St B Proc — Idaho State Bar. Proceedings
ID Syst — ID Systems
IDT — Integracion Latinoamericana
IDTAA — Industrie Agrarie

IDTKA — Industriell Teknik
ID Univ Ky Coop Ext Serv — ID. University of Kentucky. Cooperative Extension Service
IDUPA — Issledovaniya po Uprugosti i Plastichnosti
IDV — International Trade Documentation
IDW — Industriemagazin. Management, Marketing, Technologie
IDW — Industry Week
IE — Illuminating Engineering [*Later, Illuminating Engineering Society. Journal*]
IE — Indice
IE — Industrieel Eigendom
IE — Informations Economiques
IE — Interdisciplinary Essays
IEA Coal Res Rep ICTIS ER — IEA (International Energy Agency) Coal Research. Report ICTIS/ER
IEA Coal Res Rep ICTIS TR — IEA (International Energy Agency) Coal Research. Report ICTIS/TR
IEAG — Instituto Ecuatoriano de Antropologia y Geografia. Informe
IEAL — Early American Life
IEAP — Instituto de Etnologia y Arqueologia, Universidad de San Marcos. Publicaciones [*Lima*]
IEAS — International Economic Appraisal
IEAS/R — Revista de Estudios Agro-Sociales. Instituto de Estudios Agro-Sociales
IEBEA — IEEE. Transactions on Biomedical Engineering
IEBY — Iowa English Bulletin. Yearbook
IEc — Index of Economic Articles
IEC — Industrial and Engineering Chemistry
IEC — Institut d'Estudis Catalans
IEC — International Economic Review
IEC Bull — IEC [*International Electrotechnical Commission*] Bulletin
IECE — International Educational and Cultural Exchange
IECFA — Industrial and Engineering Chemistry. Fundamentals
IECHA — Industrial and Engineering Chemistry
IECI — Economic Indicators
IECI Annu Conf Proc — IECI [*Industrial Electronics and Control Instrumentation Group*] Annual Conference Proceedings
IEcJ — Israel Economist (Jerusalem)
IECMB — IEEE. Transactions on Communications
I Econ J — Indian Economic Journal
IECON Proc — IECON (Industrual Electronics Conference) Proceedings
IECP — Journal of Experimental Child Psychology
IEC Process Des Dev — Industrial and Engineering Chemistry. Process Design and Development
IEC Prod Res Dev — Industrial and Engineering Chemistry. Product Research and Development
IEDP — Educational and Psychological Measurement
IEE — Indian Economic Journal
IEECA — IEEE. Transactions on Electronic Computers
IEE Colloq Dig — IEE Colloquium (Digest)
IEE Conf Publ (Lond) — IEE [*Institution of Electrical Engineers*] Conference Publication (London)
IEE Conf Telecommun — IEE Conference on Telecommunications
IEE Control Engrg Ser — IEE [*Institution of Electrical Engineers*] Control Engineering Series
IEEE ACM Trans Networking — IEEE/ACM Transactions on Networking
IEEE Acoust — IEEE. Transactions on Acoustics, Speech, and Signal Processing
IEEE Aer El — IEEE. Transactions on Aerospace and Electronic Systems
IEEE Aerosp Electron Syst Mag — IEEE Aerospace and Electronic Systems Magazine
IEEE Ann Hist Comput — IEEE Annals of the History of Computing
IEEE Annu Text Ind Tech Conf — IEEE. Annual Textile Industry Technical Conference
IEEE Annu Text Ind Tech Conf Proc — IEEE. Annual Textile Industry Technical Conference. Proceedings
IEEE Antenn — IEEE. Transactions on Antennas and Propagation
IEEE Antennas Propag Mag — IEEE Antennas and Propagation Magazine
IEEE Auto C — IEEE. Transactions on Automatic Control
IEEE Biomed — IEEE. Transactions on Biomedical Engineering
IEEE Broadc — IEEE. Transactions on Broadcasting
IEEE Cem Ind — IEEE [*Institute of Electrical and Electronics Engineers*] Cement Industry
IEEE Cem Ind Tech Conf Pap — IEEE. Cement Industry Technical Conference Paper
IEEE CHMT Eur Int Electron Manuf Technol Symp — IEEE/CHMT European International Electronic Manufacturing Technology Symposium
IEEE Circ S — IEEE. Transactions on Circuits and Systems
IEEE Circuits Devices Mag — IEEE Circuits and Devices Magazine
IEEE Circuits Syst Mag — IEEE. Circuits and Systems Magazine
IEEE CIT Conf — IEEE CIT Conference
IEEE Commun — IEEE. Transactions on Communications
IEEE Commun Mag — IEEE. Communications Magazine
IEEE Commun Soc Mag — IEEE. Communications Society. Magazine [*Later, IEEE. Communications Magazine*]
IEEE Comput — IEEE. Transactions on Computers
IEEE Comput Appl Power — IEEE Computer Applications in Power
IEEE Comput Graphics and Appl — IEEE. Computer Graphics and Applications
IEEE Comput Group News — IEEE. Computer Group News
IEEE Comput Sci Eng — IEEE Computational Science and Engineering
IEEE Comput Soc Press Reprint Collect — IEEE Computer Society Press Reprint Collections
IEEE Comput Soc Press Tech Ser — IEEE Computer Society Press Technology Series
IEEE Comput Soc Press Tutor — IEEE Computer Society Press Tutorial
IEEE Conf Hum Factors Power Plants — IEEE Conference on Human Factors and Power Plants

IGJ — Indogermanisches Jahrbuch
IGL — Israel Goldstein Lectures
IGLB — Index Generaux du Lineaire
Igles Puebl Cult — Iglesia, Pueblos y Culturas
IGLMP — Iscrizioni Greche Lapidarie del Museo di Palermo
IGLQ — Igalaaq. Nortext
IGLR — Inscriptiile Grecesti si Latine din Secolele IV-XII Descoperite in Romania
IGLS — Inscriptions Grecques et Latines de la Syrie
I GI Sv Mm — Memoirs of the Geological Survey of India
IGLSyr — Inscriptions Grecques et Latines de la Syrie
IGMA — Geographical Magazine
IGMEA — Ingegneria Meccanica
IGME/RG — Revista Geografica. Instituto Geografico Militar del Ecuador. Departamento Geografico
Ig Microb Epidem — Igiena, Microbiologie, si Epidemiologie
Ig Microbiol Epidemiol — Igiena, Microbiologie, si Epidemiologie
Ig Mod — Igiene Moderna
IGMS — International Guide to Medieval Studies
IGND — Indian Geographer (New Delhi)
IGNKB — Ispol'zovanie Gaza v Narodnom Khozyaistve
IGNTA — Ingenieurs et Techniciens
IGNTB — Ingenioer-Nytt
IGNVB — Izvestiya na Geologicheskiya Institut. Bulgarska Akademiya na Naukite. Seriya Neftena i Vuglishtna Geologiya
IGOPA — Izvestiya Glavnoi Astronomicheskoi Observatorii v Pulkove
IGOV — Governing
IGPIA — Public Information Circular. Iowa Geological Survey
I Gr B — Inscriptiones Graecae in Bulgaria Repertae
IGREB — Report. Institute of Geological Sciences
IGROM — Inscriptiones Graecae ad Res Romanas Pertinentes
IGRR — Inscriptiones Graecae ad Res Romanas Pertinentes
IGRV — Germanic Review
IGS — Inscriptiones Graecae Septentrionalis
IGS — Inscriptiones Graecae Siciliae et Infimae ad Ius Pertinentes
IGSA — Geological Society of America. Bulletin
Ig Sanita Pubblica — Igiene e Sanita Pubblica
Ig San Pubbl — Igiene e Sanita Pubblica
IGSBDO — Proceedings. Academy of Sciences of the Georgian SSR. Biological Series
IG Sept — Inscriptiones Graecae Septentrionalis
IGSI — Inscriptiones Graecae Siciliae et Infimae Italiae
IGSKD — Izvestiya Akademii Nauk Gruzinskoi SSR Seriya Khimicheskaya
IGSSA — Illinois State Geological Survey. Guidebook Series
IGTAAN — Institutul de Cercetari pentru Cereale si Plante Tehnice Fundulea Probleme de Genetica Teoretica si Aplicata
IGTJA — Indian Geotechnical Journal
IGT Nie — IGT [*Instituut voor Grafische Techniek*] Nieuws
IGU Newsl — IGU [*International Geographical Union*] Newsletter
IGUP — Guitar Player
IGUR — Inscriptiones Graecae Urbls Romae
IG Urbis Romae — Inscriptiones Graecae Urbis Romae
IGUTP — Instituti Geographici Universitatis Turkuensis. Publications
IGW — Internationales Gewerbearchiv der Kleinbetrieb und Mittelbetrieb in der Modernen Wirtschaft
IGW Inf — IGW [*Institut fuer Gesellschaft und Wissenschaft*] Informationen zur Wissenschaftsentwicklung
IGY Bull — IGY [*International Geophysical Year*] Bulletin
IGY Gen Rep Ser — IGY [*International Geophysical Year*] General Report Series
IGY Oc Rep — IGY [*International Geophysical Year*] Oceanography Report
IGY Rocket Rep — IGY [*International Geophysical Year*] Rocket Report
IGY Sat Rep Ser — IGY [*International Geophysical Year*] Satellite Report Series
IGY World Data Center A Gen Rept Ser — International Geophysical Year. World Data Center. A. General Report Series
IGY World Data Center A Glaciolog Rept Ser — International Geophysical Year. World Data Center. A. Glaciological Report Series
IH — Information Historique
IH — Information Hotline
IH — Internationaler Holzmarkt
IH — International Humanism Magazine
IH — Israel Horizon
IH — Ita Humanidades
IHA — Industrie Hoteliere
IHA — Information d'Histoire de l'Art
IHA — Islam d'Hier et Aujourd'hui
IH & HU — Industrial Health and Hazards Update
IHB — Indiana History Bulletin
IHB — International Journal of Social Economics (Bradford)
IHBO — Horn Book
IHC — Inscriptiones Hispaniae Christianae
IHCP — Indian History Congress. Proceedings
IHCR — Human Communication Research
IHCS — Inscriptiones Hispaniae Christianae
IHCTA2 — International Histological Classification of Tumors
IHE — Indice Historico Espanol
IHE — International Hospital Equipment
IHEJAG — Indian Heart Journal
Iheringia Bot — Iheringia. Botanica. Museo Rio-Grandense de Ciencias Naturais
Iheringia Ser Antropol — Iheringia. Serie Antropologia
Iheringia Ser Bot — Iheringia. Serie Botanica
Iheringia Ser Divulg — Iheringia. Serie Divulgacao
Iheringia Ser Geol — Iheringia. Serie Geologia
Iheringia Ser Misc — Iheringia. Serie Miscelanea
Iheringia Ser Zool — Iheringia. Serie Zoologia
IHFLBS — Institutt foer Husdyrernaering og Foringslaere Norges Landbrukshogskole Beretning

IHG — Investitionshilfegesetz
IHG — Irish Banking Review
IHH — Inscriptions Hittites Hieroglyphiques
IHHL — Harvard Health Letter
IHI Eng Rev — IHI [*Ishikawajima-Harima Heavy Industries*] Engineering Review
IHI Eng Rev Engl Ed — IHI Engineering Review (English Edition)
I Hist — Indian Historian
IHK — Industrie und Handelskammer
IHML — International Henry Miller Letter
IHN — Israel Horizons (New York)
I Horizons — Indian Horizons
IHPAB — Health Physics Research Abstracts
IHPD — International Health Physics Data
IHQ — Indian Historical Quarterly
IHR — International Hotel Review
IHRB — Institute of Historical Research. Bulletin
IHRC — Indian Historical Records Commission. Proceedings
IHRC — Proceedings. Indian Historical Records Commission
IH Rev — IH Review
IHRL — Revista. Instituto de Historia del Derecho
IHRO — Hot Rod
IHS — Irish Historical Studies
IHSN — International Horn Society Newsletter
IHSP — Indiana Historical Society. Publications
IHSPRS — Indiana Historical Society. Prehistory Research Series
IHT — International Herald Tribune
IHUOA9 — Institut de Recherches pour les Huiles et Oleagineux [*IRHO*]. Rapport Annuel
IHV — Inscripciones Hispanias en Verso
IHVE J — IHVE [*Institution of Heating and Ventilating Engineers*] Journal
IHW — Internationale Hefte der Widerstandsbewegung
IHW Ber — IHW [*Institut fuer Handwerkswirtschaft*] Berichte
IHYHA — Industrial Hygiene Highlights
IHYP — Hypatia
IHYRB — Industrial Hygiene Review
II — Illustrazione Italiana
II — Indo-Iranica
II — Inscriptiones Italiae
II — Institutional Investor
II — Irish Independent
II — Italia Intellettuale
IIASA Collab Proc Ser — IIASA Collaborative Proceedings Series (International Institute for Applied Systems Analysis)
IIASA Collab Publ — International Institute for Applied Systems Analysis. Collaborative Publications
IIASA Conf Energy Resour — IIASA Conference on Energy Resources (International Institute for Applied Systems Analysis)
IIASA Conf Energy Resour Proc — IIASA Conference on Energy Resources. Proceedings (International Institute for Applied Systems Analysis)
IIASA (Int Inst Appl Syst Anal) Collab Proc Ser — IIASA (International Institute for Applied Systems Analysis) Collaborative Proceedings Series
IIASA (Int Inst Appl Syst Anal) Exec Rep — IIASA (International Institute for Applied Systems Analysis) Executive Report
IIASA Proc Ser — IIASA [*International Institute for Applied Systems Analysis*] ProceedingsSeries
IIASA Prof Pap — International Institute for Applied Systems Analysis. Professional Paper
IIASA Rep — IIASA [*International Institute for Applied Systems Analysis*] Reports
IIASA Research Reports — International Institute for Applied Systems Analysis. Research Reports
IIASA Res Memo — International Institute for Applied Systems Analysis. Research Memorandum
IIASA Res Rep — International Institute for Applied Systems Analysis. Research Reports
IIAS/IRAS — International Review of Administrative Sciences. International Institute of Administrative Sciences
IIB — Industrial Information Bulletin
IIBDA — Izvestiya Vuzov Mashinostroenie
IIBE — Izvestiya na Instituta za Belgarski Ezik
IIBL — Izvestiya na Instituta za Belgarska Literatura
IIC — Indo-Iranica. Iran Society (Calcutta)
IIC — International Review of Industrial Property and Copyright Law
IIC Abstr — IIC [*International Institute for the Conservation of Museum Objects*] Abstracts
IIC Abstracts — Art and Archaeology Technical Abstracts
IICA (Inst Interam Cienc Agric) Ser Publ Misc — IICA (Instituto Interamericano de Ciencias Agricolas) Serie Publicaciones Miscelaneas
IICC — Inuit. Inuit Circumpolar Conference
IICEA — Industria Italiana del Cemento
IICEW — Industria Italiana del Cemento
IIC Int R Ind Prop Cop Law — IIC. International Review of Industrial Property and Copyright Law
IICODV — Infection Control
IID — Information Industry Directory
IID — Izvestiya na Istoriceskoto Druzestvo
IIDC/C — Civilizations. International Institute of Differing Civilizations
IID Comm — IID [*Institut International de Documentation*] Communications
IIDS — Izvestiya na Istoriceskoto Druzestvo
IIDWA — Informatik
IIE/A — Anales. Instituto de Investigaciones Esteticas
IIEB — Institute of International Education News Bulletin (Buffalo, New York)
IIEBB — Izvestiya na Instituta po Elektronika. Bulgarska Akademiya na Naukite
IIEH — Institut Indochinois pour l'Etude de l'Homme. Bulletin et Travaux
IIENB — Institute of International Education. News Bulletin
IIE Trans — IIE [*Institute of Industrial Engineers, Inc.*] Transactions

IIF — Independent Investors Forum
IIF IIR Comm Proc — IIF-IIR (Institut International du Froid - International Institute of Refrigeration) Commissions. Proceedings
IIFP — International Index to Film Periodicals
IIFPAC — Publicacion Especial. Instituto Nacional de Investigaciones Forestales
IIHR Rep — IIHR [*Iowa Institute of Hydraulic Research*] Report
IIHR Report — Iowa Institute of Hydraulic Research. Report
III — Industrial Marketing Digest
III — Institutional Investor. International Edition
III — International Intertrade Index
III/AI — America Indigena. Instituto Indigenista Interamericano
IIID — Inscriptiones Italiae Inferioris Dialecticae
IIIE — Ediciones Especiales del Instituto Indigenista Interamericano [*Mexico*]
IIIR — Integrated Instructional Information Resource
III Vs Rev — III-Vs Review
IIJ — Indo-Iranian Journal
IIKMA — Izvestiya na Instituta po Khidrologiya i Meteorologiya. Bulgarska Akademiya na Naukite
IILSAH — Investigations of Indiana Lakes and Streams
IIM — Indo-Iranian Monographs
IIM — International Insurance Monitor
IIM — International Investment Monitor
IIM — Izvestiya na Instituta za Muzika
IIMK — Institut Istorii Materialnoi Kultury
IIMMI — International Index to Multi-Media Information
IIMP — Information Industry Market Place
IIn — Index India
IIN — Institutional Investor
IINCEH — Intercellular and Intracellular Communication
IINS — Insight
IINT — Instructor
IIOOD — IO Management-Zeitschrift
IIP — Industrial and Intellectual Property in Australia
IIPA — Industrial and Intellectual Property in Australia
IIPTA — Izvestiya Nauchno-Issledovatel'skogo Instituta Postoyannogo Toka
IIQF — Indoiranische Quellen und Forschungen
IIRB Rev Inst Int Rech Better — IIRB. Revue de l'Institut International de Recherches Betteravieres
IIS — Index to International Statistics
IIS — Inscriptiones Italiae et Siciliae
IISSA — Ionosfernye Issledovaniya
I Ist Kul't Narod Uzbek — Iz Istorii Kul'tury Narodov Uzbekistana
IIT — Information der Internationalen Treuhand AG
IIt — Inscriptiones Italiae
I Iug — Inscriptiones Latinae quae in Iugoslavia Inter Annos MCMXL et MCMLX Repertae etEdita Sunt
IJ — Indogermanische Jahrbuch
IJ — International Journal
IJ — Irish Jurist
IJA — Institute of Jewish Affairs. Publication
IJA — International Journal of Advertising
IJA — International Journal of Andrology
IJACB — Indian Journal of Agricultural Chemistry
IJACBO — Indian Journal of Agricultural Chemistry
IJACDQ — Indian Journal of Acarology
I Ja DS — Institut Jazykoznanija. Doklady i Soobscenija
IJAE — Indian Journal of Agricultural Economics
IJAGAZ — Indian Journal of Agronomy
IJAGC3 — Iranian Journal of Agricultural Research
I J Agr Sci — Indian Journal of Agricultural Science
IJAHA4 — Indian Journal of Animal Health
IJAHE8 — International Journal of Adolescent Medicine and Health
I Jahrb — Indogermanische Jahrbuch
IJAHS — International Journal of African Historical Studies
IJAIDA — International Journal. Academy of Ichthyology
IJAL — International Journal of American Linguistics
IJALAG — Irish Journal of Agricultural Research
IJALM — International Journal of American Linguistics. Memoir
IJALS — International Journal of American Linguistics. Supplement
IJAM — International Journal of Arts Medicine
IJANBN — Indian Journal of Anaesthesia
IJANDP — International Journal of Andrology
IJAOD — International Journal of Artificial Organs
IJAODS — International Journal of Artificial Organs
IJAPA — International Journal of Air Pollution
IJAPBT — Indian Journal of Applied Psychology
IJAR — Israel Journal of Agricultural Research
IJARAY — International Journal of Applied Radiation and Isotopes
IJARC — Indian Journal of Agricultural Research
IJARC2 — Indian Journal of Agricultural Research
IJA Res Rep — Institute of Jewish Affairs Research Report
IJAS — Indian Journal of Agricultural Science
IJAS — Indian Journal of American Studies
IJaS — Inostrannye Jazyki v Skole
IJAS — Italian Journal of Animal Science
IJASA3 — Indian Journal of Agricultural Science
IJb — Indogermanische Jahrbuch
IJB — International Journal of Bank Marketing
IJB — Israel Journal of Botany
IJBCAS — Indian Journal of Biochemistry [*Later, Indian Journal of Biochemistry and Biophysics*]
IJBCB — International Journal of Biomedical Computing
IJBCBT — International Journal of Bio-medical Computing
IJBDDY — International Journal of Behavioral Development
IJBEAY — International Journal of Biomedical Engineering

I J Bioch B — Indian Journal of Biochemistry and Biophysics
IJBMAO — International Journal of Biometeorology
IJBMDR — International Journal of Biological Macromolecules
IJBOAU — Israel Journal of Botany
IJBOBV — International Journal of Biochemistry
IJBODX — Indian Journal of Botany
IJBPD2 — International Journal of Biological Research in Pregnancy
I Jb Pol — Internationales Jahrbuch der Politik
IJC — Indian Journal of Commerce
IJC — International Journal of Computer and Information Sciences
IJCAAR — Indian Journal of Cancer
IJCADU — Indian Journal of Chemistry. Section A. Inorganic, Physical, Theoretical, and Analytical
IJCBA — International Journal of Chronobiology
IJCBAU — International Journal of Chronobiology
IJCBD — International Journal of Clinical Pharmacology and Biopharmacy
IJCBDX — International Journal of Clinical Pharmacology and Biopharmacy
IJCCE3 — International Journal of Cell Cloning
IJCDA2 — Indian Journal of Chest Diseases [*Later, Indian Journal of Chest Diseases and Allied Sciences*]
IJCDD5 — International Journal of Cardiology
IJCEA — Indian Journal of Chemical Education
IJCGD — International Journal of Coal Geology
IJCHA — Indian Journal of Child Health
I J Chem — Indian Journal of Chemistry
IJCIS — International Journal of Computer and Information Sciences
IJCKBO — International Journal of Chemical Kinetics
IJCMDW — International Journal of Cosmetic Science
IJCNAW — International Journal of Cancer
IJCNF2 — International Journal of Clinical Neuropsychology
IJCP — American Journal of Community Psychology
IJCPB5 — International Journal of Clinical Pharmacology, Therapy, and Toxicology
IJCRD — Indian Journal of Cryogenics
IJCREE — International Journal of Crude Drug Research
IJCS — International Journal of Comparative Sociology
IJCSEH — Indonesian Journal of Crop Science
IJDEAA — Indian Journal of Dermatology [*Later, Indian Journal of Dermatology, Venereology, and Leprology*]
IJDEBB — International Journal of Dermatology
IJDL — International Journal of Dravidian Linguistics
IJDLDY — Indian Journal of Dermatology, Venereology, and Leprology
IJDMAY — Israel Journal of Dental Medicine
IJDN — International Journal of Developmental Neuroscience
IJDND6 — International Journal of Developmental Neuroscience
IJDSAI — Indian Journal of Dairy Science
IJDVAR — Indian Journal of Dermatology and Venereology [*Later, Indian Journal of Dermatology, Venereology, and Leprology*]
IJE — Indian Journal of Economics
IJE — Indian Journal of Entomology
IJE — International Journal of Ethics
IJEA — Indian Journal of Economics (Allahabad)
IJEAA3 — International Journal of Environmental Analytical Chemistry
IJEAB — Indian Journal of Earth Sciences
IJEAB4 — Indian Journal of Earth Sciences
IJEAD — Electric Power Applications. IEE Journal
IJEBA6 — Indian Journal of Experimental Biology
IJECDC — Indian Journal of Ecology
IJED — Journal of Education
IJEHA — International Journal of Clinical and Experimental Hypnosis
IJEHAO — International Journal of Clinical and Experimental Hypnosis
IJEHB — Indian Journal of Environmental Health
IJEHBP — Indian Journal of Environmental Health
IJEMA5 — Israel Journal of Experimental Medicine
IJENA8 — Indian Journal of Entomology
IJENB9 — Israel Journal of Entomology
IJENEC — International Journal of Entomology
IJEPAE — Indian Journal of Experimental Psychology
IJEPBF — International Journal of Epidemiology
IJERAK — Israel Journal of Earth-Sciences
IJERD — International Journal of Energy Research
IJES — Indian Journal of English Studies
IJES — International Journal of Environmental Studies
IJES — Israel Journal of Earth-Sciences
IJESDQ — International Journal of Ecology and Environmental Sciences
IJEVAW — International Journal of Environmental Studies
IJewAr — Index of Articles on Jewish Studies
IJewPer — Index to Jewish Periodicals
I J Ex Biol — Indian Journal of Experimental Biology
IJFIAW — Indian Journal of Fisheries
IJFMDD — International Journal of Food Microbiology
IJFODJ — Indian Journal of Forestry
IJFPDM — International Journal of Family Psychiatry
IJFSBT — Indian Journal of Farm Sciences
IJG — Recueil des Inscriptions Juridiques Grecques
IJGBAG — Indian Journal of Genetics and Plant Breeding
I J Genet P — Indian Journal of Genetics and Plant Breeding
IJGOAL — International Journal of Gynaecology and Obstetrics
IJGPA — International Journal of Group Psychotherapy
IJGPAO — International Journal of Group Psychotherapy
IJGPDR — International Journal of Gynecological Pathology
IJGSAX — International Journal of General Systems
IJGU — Internationales Jahrbuch fuer Geschichtsunterricht
IJH — Iowa Journal of History
IJHE — International Journal of Health Education
IJHE — Journal of Higher Education

IJHEAU — Indian Journal of Helminthology
IJHL — Indian Journal of Helminthology (Lucknow)
IJHM — Indian Journal of the History of Medicine
IJHMA — International Journal of Heat and Mass Transfer
IJHOAQ — Indian Journal of Horticulture
IJHP — Iowa Journal of History and Politics
IJHPBU — Indian Journal of Hospital Pharmacy
IJHS — International Journal of Health Services
IJHYEQ — International Journal of Hyperthermia
IJI — International Journal of Industrial Organization
IJIAA — Indian Journal of Science and Industry. Section A. Agricultural Sciences [Later, Indian Journal of Agricultural Research]
IJIDAW — Indian Journal of Industrial Medicine
IJIDE2 — International Journal of Invertebrate Reproduction and Development
IJIL — Indian Journal of International Law
IJIMBQ — International Journal of Insect Morphology and Embryology
IJIMDS — International Journal of Immunopharmacology
IJIMET — International Journal of Immunotherapy
I J Ind Rel — Indian Journal of Industrial Relations
IJIR — International Journal of Intercultural Relations
IJIRD9 — International Journal of Invertebrate Reproduction
IJ/JJ — Jamaica Journal. Institute of Jamaica
IJL — Indian Journal of Linguistics/Praci-Bhasha-Vijnan
IJL — International Journal of Leprosy
IJLAA4 — Indian Journal of Animal Sciences
IJLEAG — International Journal of Leprosy [Later, International Journal of Leprosy and Other Mycobacterial Diseases]
IJLL — International Journal of Law Libraries
IJM — Indian Journal of Malariology
IJM — International Journal of Manpower
IJMAA9 — Indian Journal of Malariology
IJMBA — Indian Journal of Microbiology
IJMCEJ — International Journal of Clinical Monitoring and Computing
IJMDAI — Israel Journal of Medical Sciences
I J Med R A — Indian Journal of Medical Research. Section A. Infectious Diseases
I J Med Res — Indian Journal of Medical Research
IJMEEP — Italian Journal of Medicine
IJMES — International Journal of Middle East Studies
IJMLEC — International Journal of Mycology and Lichenology
IJMNB — Indian Journal of Marine Sciences
IJMR — Indian Journal of Medical Research
IJMS — Israel Journal of Medical Sciences
IJMSAT — Irish Journal of Medical Science
IJN — International Journal of Neuroscience
IJNA — International Journal of Nautical Archaeology and Underwater Exploration
IJNGD — International Journal for Numerical and Analytical Methods in Geomechanics
IJNMC — International Journal of Nuclear Medicine and Biology
IJNSD3 — Italian Journal of Neurological Sciences
IJNUB — International Journal of Neuroscience
I J Nutr D — Indian Journal of Nutrition and Dietetics
IJO — International Journal of Operations and Production Management
IJO — International Journal of Osteoarchaeology
IJOA — International Journal of the Addictions
IJOAAJ — Israel Journal of Agricultural Research
IJOADM — International Journal of Acarology
IJOAR — International Journal of Opinion and Attitude Research
IJOCAP — Indian Journal of Chemistry
IJOF — International Journal of Finance
IJOH — International Journal of Oral History
IJOPM — International Journal of Operations and Production Management
IJP — Indian Journal of Philosophy
IJP — International Journal of Parapsychology
IJP — International Journal of Physical Distribution and Materials Management
IJP — International Journal of Psychiatry
IJP — International Journal of Psychoanalysis
IJP — International Journal of Public Administration
IJPA — Indian Journal of Public Administration
I J PA Phys — Indian Journal of Pure and Applied Physics
IJPDMM — International Journal of Physical Distribution and Materials Management
IJPE — International Journal of Political Education
IJPH — Journal of Philosophy
IJPHC — Iran Journal of Public Health
IJPHCD — Iranian Journal of Public Health
I J Physics — Indian Journal of Physics
IJPLBO — Iranian Journal of Plant Pathology
IJPP — Interpretation. A Journal of Political Philosophy
IJPPC — International Journal of Peptide and Protein Research
IJPR — International Journal of Production Research
IJPR — Israel Journal of Psychiatry and Related Sciences
IJPS — Indian Journal of Political Science
IJPsa — International Journal of Psychoanalysis
I J Psychol — Indian Journal of Psychology
IJR — International Journal of Research in Marketing
IJRE — International Journal of Religious Education
IJRED — International Journal of Radiation Engineering
IJ Rel Soz — Internationales Jahrbuch fuer Religionssoziologie
IJRR — [The] International Journal of Robotics Research
IJRRDK — Internationale Zeitschrift fuer Rehabilitationsforschung
IJRS — Internationales Jahrbuch fuer Religionssoziologie
IJRS — International Journal of Rumanian Studies
IJRSA — Indian Journal of Radio and Space Physics
IJRSD — International Journal of Radiation Sterilization
IJS — Inostrannye Jazyki v Skole
IJS — Internationales Jahrbuch der Sozialpolitik

IJS — International Journal of Sexology
IJS — International Journal of Social Economics
IJSBDB — Indian Journal of Chemistry. Section B. Organic Chemistry, Including Medicinal Chemistry
IJSCC — International Journal of Sulfur Chemistry
IJSCDE — Islamabad Journal of Sciences
IJSE — International Journal of Social Economics
IJSEA — Indian Journal of Sericulture
IJSH — Journal of School Health
IJSL — International Journal of the Sociology of Language
IJSLP — International Journal of Slavic Linguistics and Poetics
I J Soc Res — Indian Journal of Social Research
IJSoz — Internationales Jahrbuch fuer Soziologie
IJSPA — International Journal of Social Psychiatry
IJSPDJ — International Journal of Andrology. Supplement
IJS Rep R — IJS [Institut "Jozef Stefan"] Report R
IJSS — International Journal of Slavic Studies
IJSSET — Italian Journal of Surgical Sciences
IJSTBT — Iranian Journal of Science and Technology
IJSTDV — Italian Journal of Sports Traumatology
IJSW — Indian Journal of Social Work
IJSym — International Journal of Symbology
IJT — Indian Journal of Theology
IJT — International Journal of Transport Economics
IJT — International Journal. Toronto
IJTBAD — Indian Journal of Tuberculosis
I J Techn — Indian Journal of Technology
IJTEDP — Tissue Reactions
I J Theor P — Indian Journal of Theoretical Physics
IJTS — International Journal of Turkish Studies
I Jug Os I K — Izvestija Jugo-Osetinskogo Instituta Kraevedenija
IJUSC3 — International Journal of Health Services
IJVEAW — Indian Journal of Agricultural and Veterinary Education
IJVIEE — Indian Journal of Virology
IJVMDP — Indian Journal of Veterinary Medicine
IJVMEQ — Israel Journal of Veterinary Medicine
IJVSD9 — Indian Journal of Veterinary Surgery
IJVSH — Indian Journal of Veterinary Science and Animal Husbandry
IJWS — International Journal of Women's Studies
IJZ — Israel Journal of Zoology
IJZOAE — Israel Journal of Zoology
Ik — Ikon
IK — Inukshuk. Frobisher Bay
IK — Irodalomtorteneti Kozlemenyek
IK — Iskusstvo Kino
IKAOA — Izvestiya Krymskoi Astrofizicheskoi Observatorii
IKA Z fuer Int Kulturaustausch — IKA. Zeitschrift fuer Internationalen Kulturaustausch
IKBKA — Izvestiya na Khimicheskiya Institut. Bulgarska Akademiya na Naukite
IKBS — Internationaler Kongress fuer Byzantinische Studien
IKE — Iberiul-K'avk'asiuri Enatmecniereba
IKEND — Iwate-Ken Eisei Kenkyusho Nenpo
IKF — Institut fuer Kernphysik der Johann-Wolfgang-Goethe-Universitaet (Frankfurt)
IKK — Internationale Kamer van Koophandel
IKKF — Izvestija Karel'skogo i Kol'skogo Filialov Akademii Nauk
IKLF — Internationaler Kongress fuer Lutherforschung
IKMK — Istvan Kiraly Muzeum Koezlemenyei
IKM Koezl — Istvan Kiraly Muzeum Koezlemenyei
IKMLA — Ikonomicheska Mis'l
IKO — Internationaler Kongress fuer Orientalisten
IKO Inn Kolonisation Land Gemeinde — IKO. Innere Kolonisation Land und Gemeinde
Ikon Mekh Selsk Stop — Ikonomika i Mekhanizatsiya na Selskoto Stopanstvo
Ikon Selskoto Stop Rural Econ — Ikonomika na Selskoto Stopanstvo. Rural Economics
I Kourion — Inscriptions of Kourion
IKP — Internationaler Kongress fuer Papyrologie
IKPL — Internationaler Kongress fuer Pastoralliturgie
IKRG — Internationaler Kongress fuer Religionsgeschichte
IKRS — Internationaler Kongress fuer Religionssoziologie
IKSIA2 — Trudy Samarskogo Sel'skokhozyaistvennogo Instituta
Ikushugaku Zasshi/Jap J Breed — Ikushugaku Zasshi/Japanese Journal of Breeding
IKV — International Kongress der Volkserzaehlungsforscher
IKw — Inmun Kwahak
IKZ — Internationale Kirchliche Zeitschrift
IKZKA — Itogi Nauki i Tekhniki Korroziya i Zashchita ot Korrozii
IL — Illinois Music Educator
IL — Index Library
IL — Indian Librarian
IL — Indian Linguistics
IL — Indian Literature
IL — Information Litteraire
IL — Integracion Latinoamericana
IL — International Literature
IL — Investigaciones Linguisticas
IL — Islamic Literature
ILA — Indian Library Association. Journal
ILA — Inscriptions in the Minoan Linear Script of Class A
ILA — Inscriptions Latines d'Algerie
ILA — International Literary Annual
ILAB — India Library Association Bulletin
ILABAY — Instruments et Laboratoires
ILAf — Inscriptions Latines d'Afrique

ILAFA Congr Latinoam Sider Mem Tec — ILAFA. Congreso Latinoamericano de Siderurgia. Memoria Tecnica (Instituto Latinoamericano del Fierro y el Acero)

IL Afr — Inscriptions Latines d'Afrique

IL Al — Inscriptions Latines d'Algerie

IL Alg — Inscriptions Latines d'Algerie

Il Am — Illustrated American

ILAM — Los Angeles Magazine

ILAP — Lapidary Journal

ILAR — Language Arts

ILA Rec — Illinois Library Association. Record

ILAR J — ILAR Journal. National Research Council. Institute of Laboratory Animal Resources

IIATos — Ilmij Asarlari. V. I. Lenin Monidagi Toskent Davlat Universiteti

ILB — Illinois Business Review

ILBEA — Industrie Lackier-Betrieb

Il Boll — Il Bolletino

ILCA (Int Livest Centr Afr) Res Rep — ILCA (International Livestock Centre for Africa) Research Report

IL Ch V — Inscriptiones Latinae Christianae Veteres

Il Cim — Il Cimento, Rivista di Scienze, Lettere, ed Arti

IL Class Stud — Illinois Classical Studies

ILCV — Inscriptiones Latinae Christianae Veteres

ILD — International Labour Documentation

IL de Gaule — Inscriptions Latines des Trois Gaules

Ile — Ilerda

ILE — International Logo Exchange

IIEB — Illinois English Bulletin

ILENDP — Industrial Engineering

ILER — Inscripciones Latinas de la Espana Romana

ILEUA — Izvestiya Leningradskogo Elektrotekhnicheskogo Instituta

ILF — Studii si Cercetari de Istorie Literara si Folclor

ILG — Indian Labour Gazette

I Lg — Indian Linguistics

ILG — Inscriptions Latines de la Gaule

ILGCA — Illinois State Geological Survey. Circular

ILGIA — Report of Investigations. Illinois State Geological Survey

ILG (Narb) — Inscriptions Latines de la Gaule (Narbonnaise)

ILGPA — Illinois State Geological Survey. Illinois Petroleum

ILGU — Izvestiya Leningradskogo Gosudarstvennogo Universiteta

ILHP — Illinois Journal of Health, Physical Education, and Recreation

ILI — Indian Law Institute. Journal

I Lib — Indian Librarian

I L Ideol L — I and L. Ideologies and Literature

Iliff R — Iliff Review

ILin — Indian Linguistics

ILing — Incontri Linguistici

I Ling — Initiation a la Linguistique

ILIQ — Library Quarterly

I Lis M — Izvestija Lisicanskogo Muzeja

I Lit — Iasul Literar

I Lit — Indian Literature

ILIT — Library Trends

ILJ — Indiana Law Journal

ILJ — Insurance Law Journal

ILJM — Illinois Journal of Mathematics

Ill — Illinois Reports

Ill — Illiterati

ILL — Illustration

ILL — International Labour Documentation

ILL — Islamic Literature (Lahore)

Ill Admin Code — Illinois Administrative Code

Ill Ag Exp — Illinois. Agricultural Experiment Station. Publications

Ill Agr Econ — Illinois Agricultural Economics

Ill Agric Econ — Illinois Agricultural Economics

Ill Agric Econ Dep Agric Econ Ill Univ Agric Exp Stn — Illinois Agricultural Economics. Department of Agricultural Economics. IllinoisUniversity. Agricultural Experiment Station

Ill Agric Exp Stn Bull — Illinois. Agricultural Experiment Station. Bulletin

Ill Agric Exp Stn Circ — Illinois. Agricultural Experiment Station. Circular

Ill Agric Exp Stn Dep For For Note — Illinois. Agricultural Experiment Station. Department of Forestry. Forestry Note

Ill Agric Exp Stn Dep For For Res Rep — Illinois. Agricultural Experiment Station. Department of Forestry. Forestry Research Report

Ill Agric Exp Stn For Note — Illinois. Agricultural Experiment Station. Forestry Note

Ill Air Qual Rep — Illinois Air Quality Report

Ill Ann Conf Prev Juv Del Rep — Illinois Annual Conference on Prevention of Juvenile Delinquency. Report

Ill Ann Stat (Smith-Hurd) — Smith-Hurd's Illinois Annotated Statutes

Ill App — Illinois Appellate Court Reports

Illawarra Hist Soc Newsletter — Illawarra Historical Society. Newsletter

Illaw Hist Soc M Notice — Illawarra Historical Society. Monthly Notice

Ill BA Bull — Illinois State Bar Association. Quarterly Bulletin

Ill Bar J — Illinois Bar Journal

Ill Biol Mon — Illinois Biological Monographs

Ill Biol Monogr — Illinois Biological Monographs

Ill B J — Illinois Bar Journal

Ill Bus — Illinois Business

Ill Bus R — Illinois Business Review

Ill Cath His R — Illinois Catholic Historical Review

Ill Classic Stud — Illinois Classical Studies

Ill Class Stud — Illinois Classical Studies

Ill CLE — Illinois Continuing Legal Education

Ill Coal M Investigations B — Illinois Coal Mining Investigations. Cooperative Agreement. Bulletin

Ill Coal Proc Annu Ill Energy Conf — Illinois Coal. Proceedings. Annual Illinois Energy Conference

Ill Conf Pub Welf Proc — Illinois Conference on Public Welfare. Proceedings

Ill Cont Legal Ed — Illinois Continuing Legal Education

Ill Ct Cl — Illinois Court of Claims Reports

Ill Dent J — Illinois Dental Journal

Ill Dep Conserv Tech Bull — Illinois. Department of Conservation. Technical Bulletin

Ill Dep Energy Nat Resour Doc — Illinois Department of Energy and Natural Resources. Document

Ill Div Fish Spec Fish Rep — Illinois. Division of Fisheries. Special Fisheries Report

Ill Div Indus Plan and Devel Atlas Ill Res — Illinois. Division of Industrial Planning and Development. Atlas of Illinois Resources

Ill Educ — Illinois Education

Ill Energy Conf — Illinois Energy Conference

Ill Energy Notes — Illinois Energy Notes

Ill Eng — Illuminating Engineering [*Later, Illuminating Engineering Society. Journal*]

Ill Environ Prot Agency Lake Mich Water Qual Rep — Illinois. Environmental Protection Agency. Lake Michigan Water Quality Report

Ill Fl — Illustrierte Flora

Ill Geogr Soc Bull — Illinois Geographical Society. Bulletin

Ill Geol Surv Guide Leafl — Illinois State Geological Survey. Guide Leaflet

Ill Geol Surv Oil Gas Drill Ill Mon Rep — Illinois. Geological Survey. Oil and Gas Drilling in Illinois. Monthly Report

Ill Geol Surv Rev Act — Illinois State Geological Survey. Review of Activities

Ill Gov Res — Illinois Government Research

Ill G S B — Illinois State Geological Survey. Bulletin

Ill His Col — Illinois State Historical Library. Collections

Ill His J — Illinois State Historical Society. Journal

Ill His L — Illinois State Historical Library. Publications

Ill His S Trans — Illinois State Historical Society. Transactions

Ill Hist Coll — Illinois State Historical Library. Collections

Ill His Trans — Illinois State Historical Society. Transactions

Ill Hlth Ne — Illinois Health News

Ill Horiz — Illinois Horizons

Ill Hort — Illustration Horticole

Ill Ind Miner Notes — Illinois Industrial Minerals Notes

Illini Hort — Illini Horticulture. Illinois State Horticultural Society

Illinois Acad Sci Trans — Illinois State Academy of Science. Transactions

Illinois F — Illinois Farmer

Illinois Geol Survey Circ — Illinois State Geological Survey. Circular

Illinois J Math — Illinois Journal of Mathematics

Illinois Law Rev — Illinois Law Review

Illinois Med J — Illinois Medical Journal

Illinois Miner Notes — Illinois Mineral Notes

Illinois MJ — Illinois Medical Journal

Illinois Res — Illinois Research. University of Illinois Agricultural Experiment Station

Illinois Veg Growers Bull — Illinois Vegetable Growers' Bulletin. Illinois State Vegetable Growers' Association

Illinois Water Survey Rept Inv — Illinois State Water Survey. Reports of Investigations

Ill Inst Environ Qual Doc — Illinois Institute for Environmental Quality Document

Ill Inst Nat Resour Doc — Illinois Institute of Natural Resources Document

Ill Inst Nat Resour Ill State Water Surv Bull — Illinois Institute of Natural Resources. Illinois State Water Survey. Bulletin

Ill Inst Technol Res Publ — Illinois Institute of Technology. Research Publications

Ill Issues — Illinois Issues

Ill Jahrb Naturk — Illustriertes Jahrbuch der Naturkunde

Ill J Comm — Illinois Journal of Commerce

Ill J Math — Illinois Journal of Mathematics

Ill Labor Bull — Illinois Labor Bulletin

Ill Law R — Illinois Law Review

Ill Law Rev — Illinois Law Review

Ill Laws — Laws of Illinois

Ill LB — Illinois Law Bulletin

Ill Legis Serv (West) — Illinois Legislative Service (West)

Ill Leg N — Illustrated Legal News

Ill Lib — Illinois Libraries

Ill Libr — Illinois Libraries

Ill London News — Illustrated London News

Ill LQ — Illinois Law Quarterly

Ill L R — Illinois Law Review

Ill L Rev — Illinois Law Review

Ill Med Bull — Illinois Medical Bulletin

Ill Med Dent Monogr — Illinois Medical and Dental Monographs

Ill Med J — Illinois Medical Journal

Ill Miner Notes — Illinois Mineral Notes

Ill M J — Illinois Medical Journal

Ill Mo — Illinois Monthly Magazine

Ill Monogr Med Sci — Illinois Monographs in Medical Sciences

Ill Mschr Aerztl Polytechn — Illustrierte Monatsschrift der Aerztlichen Polytechnik

Ill Munic R — Illinois Municipal Review

Ill Nat Hist Surv Biol Notes — Illinois Natural History Survey. Biological Notes

Ill Nat Hist Surv Bull — Illinois Natural History Survey. Bulletin

Ill Nat Hist Surv Circ — Illinois Natural History Survey. Circular

Illne Scient — Illustrazione Scientifica

Ill N H Soc Tr — Illinois Natural History Society. Transactions

ILLP — Iscrizioni Latine Lapidarie del Museo di Palermo

Ill Pet — Illinois Petroleum

Ill Pet Mon — Illinois Petroleum Monitor

Ill Q — Illinois Quarterly

ILLR — Inscriptiones Latinae Liberae Rei Publicae

Ill Reg — Illinois Register

Ill Res — Illinois Research

Ill Res Agric Exp Stn — Illinois Research. Illinois Agricultural Experiment Station
Ill Res Ill Agric Exp Stn — Illinois Research. Illinois Agricultural Experiment Station
Ill Rev Stat — Illinois Revised Statutes
Ill Rosengart — Illustrirter Rosengarten
Ill SBAQB — Illinois State Bar Association. Quarterly Bulletin
Ill Sch J — Illinois Schools Journal
Ill Soc Eng — Illinois Society of Engineers and Surveyors
Ill St Ac Sc Tr — Illinois State Academy of Science. Transactions
Ill State Acad Sci Trans — Illinois State Academy of Science. Transactions
Ill State Florists Assoc Bull — Illinois State Florists Association. Bulletin
Ill State Geol Surv Bull — Illinois State Geological Survey. Bulletin
Ill State Geol Surv Circ — Illinois State Geological Survey. Circular
Ill State Geol Surv Coop Ground Water Rep — Illinois. State Geological Survey. Cooperative Ground-Water Report
Ill State Geol Surv Coop Resour Rep — Illinois. State Geological Survey. Cooperative Resources Report
Ill State Geol Surv Environ Geol Notes — Illinois State Geological Survey. Environmental Geology Notes
Ill State Geol Surv Guideb Ser — Illinois State Geological Survey. Guidebook Series
Ill State Geol Surv Ill Miner Note — Illinois State Geological Survey. Illinois Minerals Note
Ill State Geol Surv Ill Petrol — Illinois State Geological Survey. Illinois Petroleum
Ill State Geol Surv Ind Miner Notes — Illinois State Geological Survey. Industrial Minerals Notes
Ill State Geol Surv Rep Invest — Illinois. State Geological Survey. Report of Investigations
Ill State Hist Lib Pub — Illinois State Historical Library. Publication
Ill State Hist Soc Jour — Illinois State Historical Society. Journal
Ill State Hist Soc Trans — Illinois State Historical Society. Transactions
Ill State Hort Soc N L — Illinois State Horticultural Society. Newsletter
Ill State Mus Pop Sci Ser Sci Paper Story Ill Ser — Illinois State Museum. Popular Science Series. Scientific Papers. Story of Illinois Series
Ill State Mus Rep Invest — Illinois State Museum. Reports of Investigations
Ill State Univ Jour — Illinois State University. Journal
Ill State Water Surv Bull — Illinois State Water Survey. Bulletin
Ill State Water Surv Circ — Illinois State Water Survey. Circular
Ill State Water Survey Cooperative Ground-Water Rept — Illinois State Water Survey. Cooperative Ground-Water Report
Ill State Water Survey Div Bull Circ Rept Inv — Illinois State Water Survey. Division Bulletin. Circular. Reports of Investigations
Ill State Water Surv Ill State Geol Surv Coop Resour Rep — Illinois. State Water Survey. Illinois. State Geological Survey. Cooperative Resources Report
Ill State Water Surv Rep Invest — Illinois State Water Survey. Reports of Investigations
Ill State Water Surv State Geol Surv Coop Ground Water Rep — Illinois. State Water Survey and State Geological Survey. Cooperative Ground-Water Report
Ill State Water Surv State Geol Surv Coop Resour Rep — Illinois State Water Survey and State Geological Survey. Cooperative Resources Report
Ill St B Assn Proc — Illinois State Bar Association. Proceedings
Ill St Lab N H B — Illinois State Laboratory of Natural History. Bulletin
Ill St Mus N H B — Illinois State Museum of Natural History. Bulletin
Ill Stud Anthropol — Illinois Studies in Anthropology
Ill Stud Law — Illinois Student Lawyer
Ill Teach — Illinois Teacher
Ill Teach Home Econ — Illinois Teacher of Home Economics
Ill Tech Eng — Illinois Tech Engineer
Ill U Eng Exp Sta Bul — Illinois University. Engineering Experiment Station. Bulletin
Ill U Eng Exp Sta Circ — Illinois University. Engineering Experiment Station. Circular
Illum Eng — Illuminating Engineering [*Later, Illuminating Engineering Society. Journal*]
Illum Eng (London) — Illuminating Engineer (London)
Illum Eng (NY) — Illuminating Engineering (New York)
Illum Eng Soc J — Illuminating Engineering Society. Journal
Illum Eng Soc Trans — Illuminating Engineering Society. Transactions
Ill Univ Agric Exp Stn Bull — Illinois. University. Agricultural Experiment Station. Bulletin
Ill Univ Agric Exp Stn For Note — Illinois. University Agricultural Experiment Station. Forestry Note
Ill Univ B Univ Studies — Illinois University. Bulletin. University Studies
Ill Univ (Chicago Circle) Dep Geol Sci Tech Rep — Illinois University (Chicago Circle). Department of Geological Sciences. Technical Report
Ill Univ Civ Eng Stud Constr Res Ser — Illinois University. Civil Engineering Studies. Construction Research Series
Ill Univ Civ Eng Stud Hydraul Eng Ser — Illinois University. Civil Engineering Studies. Hydraulic Engineering Series
Ill Univ Civ Eng Stud Soil Mech Ser — Illinois University. Civil Engineering Studies. Soil Mechnanics Series
Ill Univ Civ Eng Stud Struct Res Ser — Illinois University. Civil Engineering Studies. Structural Research Series
Ill Univ Coll Agric Coop Ext Serv Circ — Illinois. University. College of Agriculture. Cooperative Extension Service. Circular
Ill Univ Coop Ext Serv Circ — Illinois University. Cooperative Extension Service. Circular
Ill Univ Dep Civ Eng Struct Res Ser — Illinois University. Department of Civil Engineering. Structural Research Series
Ill Univ Dep Electr Eng Aeron Lab Aeron Rep — Illinois University. Department of Electrical Engineering. Aeronomy Laboratory. Aeronomy Report
Ill Univ Dep Theor Appl Mech TAM Rep — Illinois University. Department of Theoretical and Applied Mechanics. TAM Report
Ill Univ Eng Exp Sta Bull — Illinois University. Engineering Experiment Station. Bulletin
Ill Univ Eng Exp Stn Bull — Illinois. University. Engineering Experiment Station. Bulletin

Ill Univ Eng Exp Stn Circ — Illinois. University. Engineering Experiment Station. Circular
Ill Univ Eng Exp Stn Repr Ser — Illinois. University. Engineering Experiment Station. Reprint Series
Ill Univ Eng Exp Stn Tech Rep — Illinois University. Engineering Experiment Station. Technical Report
Ill Univ Eng Expt Sta Bull Circ — Illinois University. Engineering Experiment Station. Bulletin. Circulars
Ill Univ Ext Serv Agric Home Econ Circ — Illinois. University. Extension Service in Agriculture and Home Economics. Circular
Ill Univ Proc Sanit Eng Conf — Illinois University. Proceedings of the Sanitary Engineering Conference
Ill Univ TAM Rep — Illinois University. Department of Theoretical and Applied Mechanics. TAM Report
Ill Univ Water Resour Cent Res Rep — Illinois University. Water Resources Center. Research Report
Illus A — Illustrated Arts
Illus Archaeol — Illustrated Archaeologist
Illus Archaeologist — Illustrated Archaeologist
Illus Austral News — Illustrated Australian News
Illus Bresc — Illustrazione Bresciana
Illus Fiorentino — Illustratore Fiorentino
Illus Kstgew Z Innendek — Illustrierte Kunstgewerbliche Zeitschrift fuer Innendekoration
Illus Landwirtsch Ztg — Illustrierte Landwirtschaftlichte Zeitung
Illus Lond N — Illustrated London News
Illus Lond News — Illustrated London News
Illus London News — Illustrated London News
Illus Motor Sp — Illustrerad Motor Sport
Illus Tek Tidn — Illustrerad Teknisk Tidning
Illus Tidn — Illustrerad Tidning
Illus Times — Illustrated Times
Illust Libri Rag — Illustratori di Libri per Ragazzi
Illust Pubb — Illustrazione Pubblicitaria
Illust Tosc — Illustrazione Toscana
Illus Vatic — Illustrazione Vaticana
Illus W Ind — Illustrated Weekly of India
Illus W Ind A — Illustrated Weekly of India. Annual
Illus Ztg — Illustrierte Zeitung
Ill Vat — Illustrazione Vaticana
Ill Vet — Illinois Veterinarian
Ill Wkly Ind — Illustrated Weekly of India
Ill Zs Tierfrde — Illustrierte Zeitschrift fuer Tierfreunde. Organ des Oesterreichischen Bundes der Vogelfreunde in Graz
ILM — Illustrated London Magazine
ILM — Indian Linguistics (Madras)
ILM — Industrial Minerals
ILM — Inscriptions Latines du Maroc
ILM — International Legal Materials
IL Mar — Inscriptions Latines du Maroc
IL Maroc — Inscriptions Latines du Maroc
Ilmenau Tech Hochsch Wiss Z — Ilmenau, Technische Hochschule, Wissenschaftliche Zeitschrift
Ilmenskii Zapov Tr — Il'menskii Zapovednik. Trudy
ILMH — Law, Medicine, and Health Care
ILML — Istituto Lombardo. Accademia di Scienze e Lettere. Memorie della Classe di Lettere
ILMM — Learning and Motivation
ILMN — Il Mondo
ILN — Illustrated London News
ILn — Indian Librarian
ILN — Indonesia Letter
ILNM — American Journal of Law and Medicine
Ilocos Fish J — Ilocos Fisheries Journal
Ilocos R — Ilocos Review
ILO Yb — ILO [*International Labour Organisation*] Yearbook
ILP — Il Ponte
ILP — Index Librorum Prohibitorum
ILP — Index to Legal Periodicals
ILPEAG — Agricultural Science
ILPO — Il Polo. Istituto Geografico Polare
Il Polit — Il Politecnico
ILPP — International Library of Psychology, Philosophy, and Scientific Method
Il Progresso — Il Progresso delle Scienze, Lettere, ed Arti
ILQ — Indian Law Quarterly
ILQ — International Law Quarterly
ILQR — Indian Law Quarterly Review
ILR — Indian Law Review
ILR — Industrial and Labor Relations Review
ILR — Industrial Law Review
ILR — International Labour Review
ILR — International Language Reporter
ILR — Iowa Law Review
ILR — Israel Business and Investors' Report
ILR — Israel Law Review
ILRBBI — Istituto Lombardo. Accademia di Scienze e Lettere. Rendiconti. B. Scienze Biologiche e Mediche
ILR Ber — ILR (Institut fuer Luft- und Raumfahrt) Bericht
ILRI Publ — ILRI [*International Institute for Land Reclamation and Improvement*] Publication
ILRI Publ Int Inst Land Reclam Improv — ILRI Publication. International Institute for Land Reclamation and Improvement
ILRL — Istituto Lombardo. Accademia di Scienze e Lettere. Rendiconti. Classe de Lettere
ILRM — Irish Law Reports Monthly

ILRR — Industrial and Labor Relations Review
ILRSS — International Labour Review. Statistical Supplement
ILS — Inscriptiones Latinae Selectae
ILS — Inventory Locator Service
Il Sac — Illyrici Sacri
IL Sard — Iscrizioni Latine della Sardegna
IL Soc Archit Mthly Bull — Illinois Society of Architects Monthly Bulletin
ILT — Il Tesaur
ILT — Irish Law Times
ILT & SJ — Irish Law Times and Solicitors' Journal
ILTG — Inscriptions Latines des Trois Gaules
ILT Jo — Irish Law Times Journal
ILTO — Labor Today
ILTR — Irish Law Times Reports
ILTR — Library Technology Reports
ILTSJ — Institute of Low Temperature Science. Contributions (Japan)
Ilu Cle — Ilustracion del Clero
ILUO — Inaugural Lectures. University of Oxford
Ilus Esp & Amer — Ilustracion Espanola y Americana
Ilus Mod — Ilustracao Moderna
Ilus Peru — Ilustracion Peruana
Ilus Port — Ilustracao Portuguesa
Ilus Potosina — Ilustracion Potosina
ILWCJ — International League of Women Composers Journal
ILZRO Ann Rev — ILZRO [*International Lead Zinc Research Organization*] Annual Review
Im — Illuminare
IM — Ilustracao Moderna
Im — Imagination
Im — Imago
IM — Imago Mundi
IM — Incontri Musicali
IM — Index Medicus
IM — Industrial Management
IM — Industrial Minerals
IM — Informes y Memorias de la Comisaria General de Excavaciones Arqueologicas
IM — Informes y Memorias. Servicio Nacional de Excavaciones Arqueologicas
IM — Insurance Magazine
IM — Internationale Monatsschrift fuer Wissenschaft, Kunst, und Technik
IM — International Journal of Instructional Media
IM — International Management
IM — International Musician
IMA — Instituts Mitteilungen
IMAC — International Marine and Air Catering
Imag — Imagines Inscriptionum Atticarum
IMAg — Islam and the Modern Age
Image & S — Image et Son
Image Dyn Sci Med — Image Dynamics in Science and Medicine
Image J Nurs Sch — Image. Journal of Nursing Scholarship
Image Process Algorithms Tech — Image Processing Algorithms and Techniques
Image Process Interchange Implementation Syst — Image Processing and Interchange. Implementation and Systems
Images Marquette Univ Dent Reflections — Images. Marquette University Dental Reflections
Image Storage Retr Syst — Image Storage and Retrieval Systems
Image Technol — Image Technology
Image Technol London — Image Technology (London)
Image Vis C — Image and Vision Computing
Image Vision Comput — Image and Vision Computing
Imag IGA — Imagines Inscriptionum Graecarum Antiquissimarum
Imaging Sci J — Imaging Science Journal
Imag Inscr Attic — Imagines Inscriptionum Atticarum
I Magn — Inschriften von Magnesia am Maeander
I Magnesia — Inschriften von Magnesia am Maeander
Imago Mundi Rev Early Cartography — Imago Mundi. A Review of Early Cartography
IMAI — Model Airplane News
IMA (Inst Math Appl) J Math Appl Med Biol — IMA (Institute of Mathematics and Its Applications) Journal of Mathematics Applied in Medicine and Biology
IMA J Appl Math — IMA [*Institute of Mathematics and Its Applications*] Journal of Applied Mathematics
IMA J Math Appl Bus Indust — IMA Journal of Mathematics Applied in Business and Industry
IMA J Math Appl Med Biol — IMA Journal of Mathematics Applied in Medicine and Biology
IMA J Math Control Inf — IMA [*Institute for Mathmatics and Its Applications*] Journal of Mathematical Control and Information
IMA J Math Control Inform — IMA Journal of Mathematical Control and Information
IMA J Math Management — IMA Journal of Mathematics in Management
IMA J Numer Anal — IMA [*Institute of Mathematics and Its Applications*] Journal of Numerical Analysis
IMA Monograph Ser — Institute of Mathematics and its Applications Monograph Series
IMA Monogr Ser — Institute of Mathematics and its Applications Monograph Series
IMARD — Industrial Marketing [*Later, Business Marketing*]
I Maroc — Inscriptions Latines du Maroc
IMASDR — Mississippi. Agricultural and Forestry Experiment Station. Information Sheet
IMA Spec Rep — International Management Association. Special Report
IMA Symp — IMA (Institute of Mathematics and Its Applications) Symposia
IMA Vol Math Appl — IMA Volumes in Mathematics and its Applications
IMA Vol Math Its Appl — IMA [*Institute for Mathematics and Its Applications*] Volumes in Mathematics and Its Applications

IMB — International Medieval Bibliography
IMBMA — Izvestiya na Instituta po Morfologiya. Bulgarska Akademiya na Naukite
IMCH — Mayo Clinic Health Letter
IMCHAZ — Immunochemistry
IMC J — IMC [*International Micrographic Congress*] Journal
IMC Jrnl — IMC [*International Information Management Congress*] Journal
IMCM — Indian Museum. Calcutta. Memoirs
IMCR — Indian Museum. Calcutta. Records
IMCU — Macuser
IMCVA9 — Investigaciones Marinas. Universidad Catolica de Valparaiso
IMCW — Macworld
IMD — Industrial Marketing Management
IMDAI — Istanbuler Mitteilungen. Deutsches Archaeologisches Institut
IMDJBD — Irish Medical Journal
IMD Spec Rep Ser — IMD [*Institute of Metal Division. American Institute of Mining, Metallurgical, and Petroleum Engineers*] Special Report Series
IME — Illinois Music Educator
IME — Insurance, Mathematics, and Economics
IME — Iparmueveszeti Muzeum Evkoenyvei
IMechE Conf Proc Inst Mech Eng — IMechE Conference. Proceedings. Institution of Mechanical Engineers
I Mech E Conf Publ — I Mech E Conference Publications
IMechE Conf Trans — IMechE Conference Transactions
IMechE Proc Part C Mech Engrg Sci — Institution of Mechanical Engineers. Proceedings. Part C. Mechanical Engineering Science
IMechE Semin — IMechE Seminar
IMed — Index Medicus
IMED — Innere Mission im Evangelischen Deutschland
IMEIDH — Investigacion Medica Internacional
IMEKO Symp Photon Detect — IMEKO Symposium on Photon Detectors (Internationale Messtechnische Konfoderation)
IMEKO Tech Comm Metrol TC8 Symp — IMEKO Technical Committee on Metrology-TC8. Symposium (Internationale Messtechische Konfoderation)
I ME P — Institution of Mechanical Engineers. Proceedings
IMF — Informatienieuws
IMF — International Monetary Fund. Staff Papers
IMF F & D — International Monetary Fund. Finance and Development
IMFL — Inventory of Marriage and Family Literature
IMFS — Magazine of Fantasy and Science Fiction
IMF/SP — Staff Papers. International Monetary Fund
IMF Staff Pa — International Monetary Fund. Staff Papers
IMF Svy — IMF [*International Monetary Fund*] Survey
IMF Symp Publ — IMF [*Institute of Metal Finishing*] Symposium. Publication
IMG — Indian Medical Gazette
IMG — International Management
IMG — International Music Guide
IMGA — Inventaire des Mosaiques de la Gaule et de l'Afrique
IMGIA — Itogi Nauki i Tekhniki Mestorozhdeniya Goryuchikh Poleznykh Iskopaemykh
IMH — Indiana Magazine of History
IMH — Itim Mizrah News Agency Hadashot. Current Comment
IMI — International Management Information
IMIDB — Instrumentation in the Mining and Metallurgy Industries
IMIL — Michigan Law Review
IMIND — Immunitaet und Infektion
IMINDI — Immunitaet und Infektion
IM Ind Miner — IM. Industrial Minerals
IMINEJ — Immunological Investigations
I Mis — Innere Mission
I Miss T — Den Indre Missions Tidende
IMIT — Izraelita Magyar Irodalmi Tarsulat Evkonyv
I Mitt — Istanbuler Mitteilungen
IMJ — Illinois Medical Journal
IMJ — Illustrierte Monatshefte fuer die Gesammten Interessen des Judentums
IMK — Incentive Marketing
IMK — Industrial Marketing [*Later, Business Marketing*]
Imker Prag — Deutsche Imker aus Boehmen. Organ des Deutschen Bienenwirtschaftlichen Landeszentralvereines fuer Boehmen (Prag)
IMKRA3 — Imkerfreund
IML — Information
IMLCA — Immunological Communications
IMLCAV — Immunological Communications
IMLED — Immunology Letters
IMLED6 — Immunology Letters
IMLS Gaz — Institute of Medical Laboratory Sciences. Gazette
IMLS (Inst Med Lab Sci) Curr Top Med Lab Sci — IMLS (Institute of Medical Laboratory Sciences) Current Topics in Medical Laboratory Sciences
Im M — Imago Mundi
Imm — Immagine. Rivista di Arte, di Critica, e di Letteratura
IMM — Industrial Marketing Management
IMM Abstr — IMM [*Institute of Mining and Metallurgy*] Abstracts
Immergrune Bl — Immergruene Blaetter
IMMI — Itinerari dei Musei e Monumenti d'Italia
Immig & Naturalization Serv Mo Rev — United States Immigration and Naturalization Service, Monthly Review
Immig B Bull — Immigration Bar Bulletin
Imm J — Immigration Journal
IMMLC — Industrie Minerale. Serie Mineralurgie
IMMLDW — Immunologiya
IMMM — M Inc
IMMNB — Industrie Minerale. Serie Mine
IMMND4 — Immunobiology
Immobilized Enzyme Eng Proc Natl Semin — Immobilized Enzyme Engineering. Proceedings. National Seminar
IMMUAM — Immunology

IMMUDP — Immunopharmacology

Immun — Immunology

Immun Atheroscler — Immunity and Atherosclerosis

Immun Bull — Immunity Bulletin

Immun Cancer Chemother Symp — Immunity, Cancer, and Chemotherapy. Basic Relationships on the Cellular Level. Symposium

Immun Cancer Proc Conf — Immunity to Cancer. Proceedings. Conference on Immunity to Cancer

Immun Commun — Immunological Communications

Immune Defic Anim Int Workshop Immune Defic Anim Exp Res — Immune-Deficient Animals. International Workshop on Immune-Deficient Animals in Experimental Research

Immune Mech Cutaneous Dis — Immune Mechanisms in Cutaneous Disease

Immun Environ — Immunity and Environment

Immune Regul Transfer Factor Proc Int Symp — Immune Regulators in Transfer Factor. Proceedings. International Symposium on Transfer Factor

Immune Syst Funct Ther Dysfunct — Immune System. Functions and Therapy of Dysfunction

Immune Syst Genes Recept Signals ICN UCLA Symp Mol Biol — Immune System. Genes, Receptors, Signals. ICN-UCLA Symposium on Molecular Biology

Immune Syst Infect Dis Int Convoc Immunol — Immune System and Infectious Diseases. International Convocation on Immunology

Immun Infekt — Immunitaet und Infektion

Immun Jpn Encephalitis Conf — Immunization for Japanese Encephalitis. Conference

Immunoassays Food Anal Proc Symp — Immunoassays in Food Analysis. Proceedings of a Symposium

Immunoassay Suppl — Immunoassay. Supplement

Immunoassay Technol — Immunoassay Technology

Immunobiol Immunother Cancer — Immunobiology and Immunotherapy of Cancer

Immunobiol Proteins Pept — Immunobiology of Proteins and Peptides

Immunobiol Suppl — Immunobiology Supplement

Immunobiol Transfer Factor Proc Int Workshop Transfer Factor — Immunobiology of Transfer Factor. Proceedings. International Workshop on Transfer Factor

Immunochem — Immunochemistry

Immunochem Assays Biosens Technol 1990s — Immunochemical Assays and Biosensor Technology for the 1990s

Immunochem Extracell Matrix — Immunochemistry of the Extracellular Matrix

Immunochem Proteins — Immunochemistry of Proteins

Immunochem Protoc — Immunochemical Protocols

Immunochem Tech — Immunochemical Techniques

Immunodiagn Cancer — Immunodiagnosis of Cancer

Immunoenzym Tech Proc Int Symp — Immunoenzymatic Techniques. Proceedings. International Symposium on Immunoenzymatic Techniques

Immunofluoresc Relat Staining Tech Proc Int Conf — Immunofluorescence and Related Staining Techniques. Proceedings. International Conference in Immunoflourescence and Related Staining Techniques

Immunogenet — Immunogenetics

Immunol Aging — Immunology and Aging

Immunol Allerg — Immunologiya i Allergiya

Immunol Allergy Clin North Am — Immunology and Allergy Clinics of North America

Immunol Aspekty Biol Razvit Mater Rab Soveshch — Immunologicheskie Aspekty Biologii Razvitiya. Materialy Rabochego SoveshchaniyaImmunologicheskie Aspekty Biologii Razvitiya

Immunol Bact Cell Envelope — Immunology of the Bacterial Cell Envelope

Immunol Bakteriol Khronicheskogo Infekts Protsessa — Immunologiya i Bakteriologiya Khronicheskogo Infektsionnogo Protsessa

Immunol Basis Connect Tissue Disord Proc Lepetit Colloq — Immunological Basis of Connective Tissue Disorders. Proceedings. Lepetit Colloquium

Immunol Cardiovasc Dis — Immunology of Cardiovascular Disease

Immunol Cell Biol — Immunology and Cell Biology

Immunol Clin — Immunologia Clinica

Immunol Clin Exp Diabetes — Immunology of Clinical and Experimental Diabetes

Immunol Clin Sper — Immunologia Clinica e Sperimentale

Immunol Com — Immunological Communications

Immunol Commun — Immunological Communications

Immunol Front — Immunology Frontier

Immunol Hematol Res Monogr — Immunology and Hematology Research. Monograph

Immunol Infect Dis — Immunology and Infectious Diseases

Immunol Invest — Immunological Investigations

Immunol Lett — Immunology Letters

Immunol Med Pract — Immunology in Medical Practice

Immunol Methods — Immunological Methods

Immunol Milk Neonate — Immunology of Milk and the Neonate

Immunology Ser — Immunology Series

Immunol Pol — Immunologia Polska

Immunol Razmnozheniya Tr Mezhdunar Simp — Immunologiya Razmnozheniya. Trudy Mezhdunarodnogo Simpoziuma

Immunol Reprod — Immunology of Reproduction [*monograph*]

Immunol Reprod Proc Int Symp — Immunology of Reproduction. Proceedings. International Symposium

Immunol Res — Immunologic Research

Immunol Rev — Immunological Reviews

Immunol Ser — Immunology Series

Immunol Today — Immunology Today

Immunopathol Int Convoc Immunol — Immunopathology. International Convocation on Immunology

Immunopharmacol Immunotoxicol — Immunopharmacology and Immunotoxicology

Immunop Tod — Immunoparasitology Today. A Combined Issue of Immunology Today and ParasitologyToday

Immunotoxicol Immunopharmacol — Immunotoxicology and Immunopharmacology

Immunotoxicol Proc Int Symp — Immunotoxicology. Proceedings. International Symposium on Immunotoxicology

Immun Parasites Symp Br Soc Parasitol — Immunity to Parasites. Symposium. British Society for Parasitology

Immun Pokoi Rast — Immunitet i Pokoi Rastenii

Immun Skh Rast Bolezn Vred — Immunitet Sel'skokhozyaistvennykh Rastenii k Boleznyam i Vreditelyam

Immun Tolerance Oncog — Immunity and Tolerance in Oncogenesis

Immun Virus Infect Symp — Immunity and Virus Infection. Symposium

IMMYB — International Monetary Market Year Book

IMN — Irisleabhar Mha Nuad

I Mn E T — Transactions of the Institution of Mining Engineers

IMNGA — Immunologiya

IMNGBK — Immunogenetics

IMNSA — Izvestiya na Mikrobiologicheskiya Institut. Bulgarska Akademiya na Naukite

IMO — International Insurance Monitor

IMO — Itim Mizrah News Agency. Bulletin on Palestinian Organizations

IMOL — Modern Language Review

Imono J Japan Foundrymen's Soc — Imono. Journal of the Japan Foundrymen's Society

IMOR — Imperial Oil Review

IMP — Illustrated Melbourne Post

ImP — Images de Paris

Imp — Impact

Imp — Impetus

Imp — Impulse

IMP — Industrial Models and Patterns

IMP — Iscrizioni Greche Lapidarie del Museo di Palermo

Impact Acid Rain Deposition Aquat Biol Syst Symp — Impact of Acid Rain and Deposition on Aquatic Biological Systems. Symposium

Impact Agric Res Tex Annu Rep — Impact. Agricultural Research in Texas. Annual Report

Impact Biol Mod Psychiatry Proc Symp — Impact of Biology on Modern Psychiatry. Proceedings. Symposium

Impact Comput Phys Proc Eur Conf Comput Phys — Impact of Computers on Physics. Proceedings. European Conference on Computational Physics

Impact Electrotechnol Ind Froid Pompe Chal — Impact de l'Electrotechnologie dans les Industries du Froid et de la Pompe a Chaleur

Impact Monit Agric Pestic Pap FAO UNEP Expert Consult — Impact Monitoring of Agricultural Pesticides. Papers. FAO/UNEP (Food and Agriculture Organization/United Nations Environmental Programme) Expert Consultation

Impact Proj Environ Congr AQTE — Impact des Projets sur l'Environnement. Congres AQTE

Impact Sci — Impact of Science on Society

Impact Sci Soc — Impact of Science on Society

Impact Sci Soc (Engl Ed) — Impact of Science on Society (English Edition)

Impacts Nucl Releases Aquat Environ Proc Int Symp — Impacts of Nuclear Releases into the Aquatic Environment. Proceedings. International Symposium

Impact Soc — Impacto Socialista

Impacts Radionuclide Releases Mar Environ Proc Int Symp — Impacts of Radionuclide Releases into the Marine Environment. Proceedings. International Symposium

Impacts Struct Paysages Agric Prot Cult Colloq Fr Pol — Impacts de la Structure des Paysages Agricoles sur la Protection des Cultures. Colloque France-Pologne

Impact Toxicol Food Process Symp — Impact of Toxicology on Food Processing. Symposium

Impact VLBI Astrophys Geophys Proc Symp Int Astron Union — Impact of VLBI (Viking Lander Biological Instrument) on Astrophysics and Geophysics. Proceedings. Symposium. International Astronomical Union

Imp & Trac RB — Implement and Tractor Red Book

Imp & Tractr — Implement and Tractor

Imp Asiat Q Rev — Imperial and Asiatic Quarterly Review

Imp Bur Anim Health Rev Ser — Imperial Bureau of Animal Health. Review Series

Imp Bur Dairy Sci Tech Commun — Imperial Bureau of Dairy Science. Technical Communication

Imp Bur Fruit Prod GB Tech Commun — Imperial Bureau of Fruit Production (Great Britain). Technical Communication

Imp Bur Hortic Plant Corps GB Tech Commun — Imperial Bureau of Horticulture and Plantation Corps (Great Britain). Technical Communication

Imp Bur Soil Sci Soils Fert — Imperial Bureau of Soil Science, Soils, and Fertilizers

Imp Bur Soil Sci Tech Commun — Imperial Bureau of Soil Science. Technical Communication

Imp Coll Sci Technol Appl Geochem Res Group Tech Commun — Imperial College of Science and Technology. Applied Geochemistry Research Group. Technical Communication

Imp Coll Sci Technol Geochem Prospect Res Cent Tech Commun — Imperial College of Science and Technology. Geochemical Prospecting Research Centre. Technical Communication

Imp Coll Sci Technol Rock Mech Res Rep — Imperial College of Science and Technology. Rock Mechanics Research Report

Imp Coll Trop Agric (Trinidad) Circ — Imperial College of Tropical Agriculture (Trinidad). Circular

Imp Coll Trop Agric (Trinidad) Low Temp Res Stn Mem — Imperial College of Tropical Agriculture (Trinidad). Low Temperature Research Station. Memoirs

Imp Coll Trop Agric (Trinidad) Mem Mycol Ser — Imperial College of Tropical Agriculture (Trinidad). Memoirs. Mycological Series

IMPE — Impetus. Magazine Supplement of the Financial Post

Imp Earthquake Investigation Com B — Imperial Earthquake Investigation Committee. Bulletin

Imperial Oil R — Imperial Oil Review

Imp Ethiop Gov Inst Agric Res Rep — Imperial Ethiopian Government Institute of Agricultural Research. Report
Imp Exp — Import/Export News
IMPID — Impianti
Imp Inst Agric Res (Pusa) Bull — Imperial Institute of Agricultural Research (Pusa). Bulletin
Imp Inst B — Imperial Institute Bulletin
IMPL — MPLS-St. Paul Magazine
Implant Hum Embryo Proc Bourn Hall Meet — Implantation of the Human Embryo. Proceedings. Bourn Hall Meeting
Implant Ovum Pap — Implantation of the Ovum. Papers
IMPODM — Immunologia Polska
Imp Oil R — Imperial Oil Review
Importance Fundam Princ Drug Eval Proc — Importance of Fundamental Principles in Drug Evaluation. Proceedings
Importance Vitam Hum Health Proc Kellogg Nutr Symp — Importance of Vitamins to Human Health. Proceedings. Kellogg Nutrition Symposium
Important Adv Oncol — Important Advances in Oncology
Imp Rev — Imperial Review
Impr Hum P — Improving Human Performance
Imprim Ind Graphiques — Imprimerie et Industries Graphiques
Impr Med — Imprensa Medica
Impr Nat — Imprimerie Nationale
Improv Catheter Site Care Proc Symp — Improving Catheter Site Care. Proceedings. Symposium
Improv Coll & Univ Teach — Improving College and University Teaching
Improv Coll Univ Teach — Improving College and University Teaching
Improv Coll Univ Teach Ybk — Improving College and University Teaching Yearbook
Improving Coll & Univ Teach — Improving College and University Teaching
Impr Pubbl — Impresa Pubblica
Imp Rus Ist Obshchestv Sborn — Imperatorskoye Russkoye Istoricheskoye Obshchestvo. Sbornik
Imp Sci Soc — Impact of Science on Society
IMPTU — Institute of Malariology and Parasitology. Tehran University
Impulse Entwickl Metall Verfahren Vortr Metall Semin — Impulse zur Entwicklung Metallurgischer Verfahren. Vortraege beim Metallurgischen Seminar
Impul'snaya Fotom — Impul'snaya Fotometriya
Impulstech — Impulstechniken
Imp Univ Tokyo Fac Sci J — Tokyo. Imperial University. Faculty of Science. Journal
Imp Zootech Exp Stn Bull — Imperial Zootechnical Experiment Station. Bulletin
IMR — Internationale Maschinenrundschau
IMR — International Migration Review
IMRA — Model Railroader
IMRE — Monthly Review
IMRED2 — Immunological Reviews
Imre Nagy Inst Rev — Imre Nagy Institute Review
IMR Ind Manage Rev — IMR. Industrial Management Review
IMRSB8 — Indian Council of Medical Research. Technical Report Series
IMRSEB — Immunologic Research
IMRVB — International Metallurgical Reviews
IMS — Impact of Science on Society
IMS — Industrial Medicine and Surgery
IMS — Inscriptions de la Mesie Superieure
IMS — Internationale Monatsschrift
IMS — International Marine Science
IMS — International Musicological Society. Report of the Congress
IMSCE2 — IRCS [*International Research Communications System*] Medical Science
IMS Clin Proc — IMS [*Industrial Management Society*] Clinical Proceedings
IMSED7 — Immunology Series
IMSF — Institut fuer Marxistische Studien und Forschungen
IMS Lecture Notes Monograph Ser — Institute of Mathematical Statistics Lecture Notes. Monograph Series
IMSN — Institute of Marine Science. Notes. University of Alaska
ImSS — Impact of Science on Society
IMSS — Institute of Mennonite Studies Series
IMSUA — Industrial Medicine and Surgery
IMSUAI — Industrial Medicine and Surgery
ImT — Imagen del Tiempo
IMT — Industrial Management
IMTCE7 — Immunoassay Technology
IMTOA — Itogi Nauki i Tekhniki Metallovedenie i Termicheskaya Obrabotka
IMTOD8 — Immunology Today
IMTP — Meet the Press
IMU — Italia Medioevale e Umanistica
IMUS — Inventario Musical
IMW — Internationale Monatsschrift fuer Wissenschaft, Kunst, und Technik
IMW — Sloan Management Review
IMWKT — Internationale Monatsschrift fuer Wissenschaft, Kunst, und Technik
IMZ Bul — IMZ [*Internationales Musikzentrum*] Bulletin
IN — Imagen
IN — Indiana Musicator
IN — Indiana Names
IN — Indian Notes [*New York*]
IN — Indonesie
IN — Industrial Marketing [*Later, Business Marketing*]
IN — Instrumentalist
In — Insula
IN — International NOTAMS
In — Interpretation
IN — Interpreter
IN — Italia Nostra
IN — Italia Numismatica
In A — Insel-Almanach

INA — Interface Age/Computing for Business
INA — International Affairs
INA — International Nannoplankton Association. Newsletter
INAB — Indian and Northern Affairs Backgrounder
INAC — Indian and Northern Affairs Communique
INAC — Nature Canada
Inadvertent Modif Immune Response Proc FDA Sci Symp — Inadvertent Modification of the Immune Response. Proceedings. FDA [*US Food and Drug Administration*] Science Symposium
InAf — Indian Affairs
INAGAT — Indian Agriculturist
INAJA4 — Irish Naturalists' Journal
INALA — Industria Alimentara
INALB — Industrie Alimentari
INAM — Indian America
INAQ — Inuit Art Quarterly
INARA — Ingenieur-Archiv. Gesellschaft fuer Angewandte Mathematik und Mechanik
INATA — Industries Atomiques
INAUA — Instrumentenbau Musik International
INAUA3 — Instruments and Automation
INB — In Business
InB — International Bulletin of Missionary Research
INB — Israel Numismatic Bulletin
INBID9 — Indian Biologist
INBIEA — International Biodeterioration Bulletin
INBL — National Black Law Journal
INBLA — Ingenieursblad
In Bus — In Business
Inc — Incidences
Inc — Incunable. Salamanca
INC — Indian Numismatic Chronicle
InC — Informaciones Culturales
InC — International Conciliation
Inc Aust Insurance Inst J — Incorporated Australian Insurance Institute. Journal
INCIBC — Instituto de Nutricion de Centro America y Panama. Informe Anual
IncL — Incorporated Linguist
INCLD — International Classification
Inc Linguist — Incorporated Linguist
Inclusion Compd — Inclusion Compounds
Inclusion Phenom Mol Recognit Proc Int Symp — Inclusion Phenomena and Molecular Recognition. Proceedings. International Symposium on Inclusion Phenomena and Molecular Recognition
Incntv Mkt — Incentive Marketing
Income Tax Rep — Income Tax Reporter
Incompat Newsl — Incompatibility Newsletter
Incontro Stud Possibilita Colt Allevamenti Territ Alp — Incontro di Studio su le Possibilita delle Colture e degli Allevamenti nei Territori Alpini
Incorp Bus — Incorporating Your Business
Incorp Ling — Incorporated Linguist
INCPA — Instrumentation in the Chemical and Petroleum Industries
INCR — National Catholic Reporter
INCRA Res Rep — INCRA [*International Copper Research Association, Inc.*] Research Report
Increasing Understanding Public Probl Policies — Increasing Understanding of Public Problems and Policies
Incremental Motion Control Syst Devices Newsl — Incremental Motion Control Systems and Devices. Newsletter
Inc Tax LJ — Income Tax Law Journal
INCW — Nation's Cities Weekly
Ind — Indagine. Quaderni di Critica e Filosofia
IND — Independent
Ind — Indiana Reports
Ind — Indice de Arte y Letras
IND — Industrial Distribution
Ind — Industrie
Ind 2000 — Industry 2000. New Perspectives
IndA — Independent Agent
Ind A & Lett — Indian Art and Letters
Ind Acad Sci Proc — Indiana Academy of Science. Proceedings
Ind Accid Law Bul — Industrial Accident Law Bulletin
Ind Acts — Acts. Indiana
Ind Admin Code — Indiana Administrative Code
Ind Adv — Indian Advocate
Ind Advoc — Indian Advocate
Ind Aeron — Index Aeronauticus
Ind Aeron Com Ann Rep — Indiana Aeronautics Commission. Annual Report
Ind Ag Exp — Purdue University. Indiana Agricultural Experiment Station. Publications
Indag Math — Indagationes Mathematicae
Indag Math NS — Indagationes Mathematicae. New Series
Ind Agr — Industrie Agrarie
Ind Agr — Revue Internationale des Industries Agricoles
Ind Agri Am Lat Caribe — Indice Agricole de America Latina y el Caribe
Ind A Ind — Industrial Arts Index
Ind Air Pollut — Industrial Air Pollution. Assessment and Control
INDAL — Indice de Artes y Letras
Ind Aliment — Industria Alimentaria
Ind Aliment Agr — Industries Alimentaires et Agricoles
Ind Aliment Agric (Paris) — Industries Alimentaires et Agricoles (Paris)
Ind Aliment Anim — Industries de l'Alimentation Animale
Ind Aliment (Bucharest) — Industria Alimentara (Bucharest)
Ind Aliment (Havana) — Industria Alimenticia (Havana)
Ind Aliment (Mexico City) — Industrias de la Alimentacion (Mexico City)
Ind Aliment (Pinerolo Italy) — Industrie Alimentari (Pinerolo, Italy)

Ind Aliment Prod Anim — Industria Alimentara. Produse Animale
Ind Aliment Prod Veg — Industria Alimentara. Produse Vegetale
Ind Aliment Veget — Industria Alimentara. Produse Vegetale
Ind Amer Per Verse — Index of American Periodical Verse
Ind Analyt Canc — Index Analyticus Cancerologiae
Ind & Coml Training — Industrial and Commercial Training
Ind & Eng Chem — Industrial and Engineering Chemistry
Ind & Eng Chem Fundamentals — Industrial and Engineering Chemistry. Fundamentals
Ind and Eng Chem Process Des and Dev — Industrial and Engineering Chemistry. Process Design and Development
Ind & Eng Chem Process Design — Industrial and Engineering Chemistry. Process Design and Development
Ind and Eng Chem Prod Res and Dev — Industrial and Engineering Chemistry. Product Research and Development
Ind & Engng Chem Fundam — Industrial and Engineering Chemistry. Fundamentals
Ind & Engng Chem Process Des & Dev — Industrial and Engineering Chemistry. Process Design and Development
Ind & Int Prop Aus — Industrial and Intellectual Property in Australia
Ind and Labor Relations Forum — Industrial and Labor Relations Forum
Ind and Labor Relations R — Industrial and Labor Relations Review
Ind and Labor Relations Rept — Industrial and Labor Relations Report
Ind & Labor Rel R — Industrial and Labor Relations Review
Ind and Labor Rels Rev — Industrial and Labor Relations Review
Ind & Lab Rel Rev — Industrial and Labor Relations Review
Ind & Lbr Rel R — Industrial and Labor Relations Review
Ind & L Rel Rev — Industrial and Labor Relations Review
Ind & Min R — Industrial and Mining Review
Ind & Min S — Industrial and Mining Standard
Ind & Min Standard — Industrial and Mining Standard
Ind Ant — Indian Antiquary
Ind Anthro — Indian Anthropologist
Ind Antiqua — Indian Antiquary
Ind-Anz — Industrie-Anzeiger
Ind App — Indiana Court of Appeals Reports
Ind Appl Hologr Speckle Meas Tech — Industrial Applications of Holographic and Speckle Measuring Techniques
Ind Appl Isot Power Gener Jt UKAEA ENEA Int Symp — Industrial Applications for Isotopic Power Generators. Joint UKAEA-ENEA International Symposium
Ind Appl Surfactants — Industrial Applications of Surfactants
Ind Ar — Indian Archaeology
Ind Arch — Indian Archives
Ind Arch — Industrial Architecture
Ind Archaeol — Industrial Archaeology
Ind Archaeol Rev — Industrial Archaeology Review
Ind Architect — Indian Architect
Ind Arts & Voc Ed — Industrial Arts and Vocational Education/Technical Education
Ind Arts & Voc Educ — Industrial Arts and Vocational Education
Ind Arts Index — Industrial Arts Index
Ind-Arts M — Industrial-Arts Magazine
Ind As Cult — Indo-Asian Culture
Ind At — Industries Atomiques
Ind At & Spat — Industries Atomiques et Spatiales
Ind At Spatiales — Industries Atomiques et Spatiales
Ind Aurel — Index Aureliensis
Ind Aust & Min Standard — Industrial Australian and Mining Standard
Ind Austr Min Stand — Industrial Australian and Mining Standard
Ind Azucar — Industria Azucarera
Ind Bcasting — Independent Broadcasting
Ind Bevande — Industrie delle Bevande
Ind Bibl — Index Bibliographicus
Ind Bl — Industrieblatt
Ind Bldg — Industrialised Building
Ind Bouwknd Tijdschr — Indische Bouwkunst Tijdschrift
Ind Bouwknd Tijdschr Locale Tech — Indisch Bouwkundig Tijdschrift Locale Techniek
Ind Buk Kenk — Indogaku Bukkyogaku Kenkyu
Ind Bul Char & Correc — Indiana Bulletin of Charities and Correction
Ind Bull — Industrial Bulletin
Ind Bull Arthur D Little Inc — Industrial Bulletin of Arthur D. Little, Incorporated
Ind Bull Bombay — Industrial Bulletin (Bombay)
Ind Bull NY State Dep Labor — Industrial Bulletin. New York State Department of Labor
Ind Bygn O Bo — Industrialismens Bygninger og Boliger
INDCA — Industrial Chemist
Ind Can — Industrial Canada
Ind Carta — Industria della Carta
Ind Carta Arti Grafiche — Industria della Carta e delle Arti Grafiche
Ind Catal News — Industrial Catalysis News
Ind CC — Indian Church Commentaries
Ind Ceram — Industrie Ceramique
Ind Ceram Silicat — Industria della Ceramica e Silicati
Ind Cereales — Industries des Cereales
Ind Chem — Industrial Chemist
Ind Chem Bull — Industrial Chemistry Bulletin
Ind Chem Libr — Industrial Chemistry Library
Ind Chem N — Industrial Chemical News
Ind Ch HR — Indian Church History Review
Ind Child Mag — Subject Index to Children's Magazines
Ind Chim — Industrie Chimique
Ind Chim Belge — Industrie Chimique Belge
Ind Chim Min Metall — Industria Chimica, Mineraria, e Metallurgica
Ind Chim (Paris) — Industrie Chimique (Paris)
Ind Chim Phosph — Industrie Chimique, le Phosphate

Ind Chim (Rome) — Industria Chimica (Rome)
Ind Chim Turin — Industria Chimica (Turin)
Ind Chur Hist R — Indian Church History Review
Ind Code — Indiana Code
Ind Code Ann (Burns) — Burns' Indiana Statutes, Annotated Code Edition
Ind Code Ann (West) — West's Annotated Indiana Code
Ind Comm Dev — Industry, Commerce, Development
Ind Commercial Photographer — Industrial and Commercial Photographer
Ind Commerc Train — Industrial and Commercial Training
Ind Commer Photogr — Industrial and Commercial Photographer
Ind Comm Gas — Industrial and Commercial Gas
Ind Comput — Industrial Computing
Ind Conserve — Industria Conserve
Ind Conserve (Parma) — Industria Conserve (Parma)
Ind Constr Mater Constr — Industria Constructiilor si a Materialelor de Constructii
Ind Coop R — Indian Cooperative Review
Ind Corps Gras — Industries des Corps Gras
Ind Cott Grow Rev — Indian Cotton Growing Review
Ind Cott Text Ind — Indian Cotton Textile Industry
Ind Cult — Indian Culture
Ind Cult Esp — Indice Cultural Espanol
Ind Cult Q — India Cultures Quarterly
Ind Curr Urb Doc — Index to Current Urban Documents
Ind Datatek — Industriell Datateknik
Ind Dent J — Indian Dental Journal
Ind Dent Rev — Indian Dental Review
Ind Des — Industrial Design
Ind Design — Industrial Design
Ind de Transformacao — Industrias de Transformacao
Ind Dev — Industrial Development
Ind Dev — Industrial Development and Manufacturers Record [*Later, Industrial Development*]
Ind Dev Abstr — Industrial Development Abstracts
Ind Devel — Industrial Development
Ind Develop Abstr — Industrial Development Abstracts
Ind Development of WA — Industrial Development of Western Australia
Ind Dev Manuf Rec — Industrial Development and Manufacturers Record [*Later, Industrial Development*]
Ind Dev N Asia Pac — Industrial Development News Asia and the Pacific
Ind Dev Officers — Industrial Development Officers
Ind d Gomma — Industria della Gomma
Ind Diamanten Rundsch — Industrie Diamanten Rundschau
Ind Diam Dev — Industrial Diamond Development
Ind Diamond Abstr — Industrial Diamond Abstracts
Ind Diamond Rev — Industrial Diamond Review
Ind Diam Re — Industrial Diamond Review
Ind Diam Rev — Industrial Diamond Review
Ind Dig — India Digest
Ind Distr — Industrial Distribution
Ind Distrib — Industrial Distribution
Ind Div Water Res Bull — Indiana. Division of Water Resources. Bulletin
IndE — Indian Economic and Social History Review
INDEA — Information Dentaire
Ind East Eng — Indian and Eastern Engineer
Ind Eccl St — Indian Ecclesiastical Studies
Ind Econ J — Index of Economic Journals
Ind Econ J — Indian Economic Journal
Ind Econ R — Indian Economic Review
Ind Econ Soc Hist R — Indian Economic and Social History Review
Ind Ec Rev — Industrial Economics Review
IndEcSt — Indian Ecclesiastical Studies
Ind Ed M — Industrial Education Magazine
Ind Ed News — Industrial Education Council. Newsletter
Ind Educ — Industrial Education Magazine
Ind Educ M — Industrial Education Magazine
Ind Educ R — Indian Educational Review
Ind Educ Vid — Index to Educational Videotapes
Ind Eigendom — Industriele Eigendom
Ind EJ — Indian Economic Journal
In Del — Inscriptions de Delos
Ind Elect — Industrial Electronics
Ind Electr Electron — Industries Electriques et Electroniques
Ind Electron — Industrial Electronics
Ind Electron — Industries Electroniques
Ind Electr (Osaka) — Industry and Electricity (Osaka)
Ind-Elektr Elektron — Industrie-Elektrik und Elektronik
Ind-Elektron Forsch Fertigung — Industrie-Elektronik in Forschung und Fertigung
Ind Eng — Industrial Engineer
Ind Eng — Industrial Engineering
Ind Eng 1922-1931 (NY) — Industrial Engineering 1922-1931 (New York)
Ind Eng Chem — Industrial and Engineering Chemistry
Ind Eng Chem Anal Ed — Industrial and Engineering Chemistry. Analytical Edition
Ind Eng Chem Analyt Ed — Industrial and Engineering Chemistry. Analytical Edition
Ind Eng Chem Fundam — Industrial and Engineering Chemistry. Fundamentals
Ind Eng Chem Fundamentals — Industrial and Engineering Chemistry. Fundamentals
Ind Eng Chem News Ed — Industrial and Engineering Chemistry. News Edition
Ind Eng Chem Process Design Develop — Industrial and Engineering Chemistry. Process Design and Development
Ind Eng Chem Prod Res Dev — Industrial and Engineering Chemistry. Product Research and Development
Ind Eng Chem Res — Industrial and Engineering Chemistry Research
Ind Eng F — Industrial and Engineering Chemistry. Fundamentals
Ind Engng — Industrial Engineering

Ind Engng Chem Analyt Edn — Industrial and Engineering Chemistry. Analytical Edition
Ind Eng Norcross GA — Industrial Engineering (Norcross, Georgia)
Ind Eng PDD — Industrial and Engineering Chemistry. Process Design and Development
Ind Eng PRD — Industrial and Engineering Chemistry. Product Research and Development
Indent Engl — Indent. Journal of International Dentistry. English Edition
Ind Environ — Industry and Environment
Ind Environ Res Lab (Research Triangle Park) Annu Rep — Industrial Environmental Research Laboratory (Research Triangle Park). Annual Report
INDEP — Independent
Indep Bap Mis Mess — Independent Baptist Missionary Messenger
Indep Broadcast — Independent Broadcasting
Indep Coal Oper — Independent Coal Operator
Indep Ed — Independent Education
Indep Educ — Independent Education
Independent Petroleum Assoc America Monthly — Independent Petroleum Association of America. Monthly
Independ J Phil — Independent Journal of Philosophy
Indep Energy — Independent Energy
Indep F J — Independent Film Journal
Indep Invest — Independent Investor
Indep J Philos — Independent Journal of Philosophy
Indep Pet Assoc Am Mon — Independent Petroleum Association of America. Monthly
Indep Voice — Independent Voice
Indep Woman — Independent Woman
Ind Equip Mater & Serv — Industrial Equipment Materials and Services
Ind Equip News — Industrial Equipment News
Ind Equip Sel — Industrial Equipment Selector
Inde Rest — Independent Restaurants
Ind ES — Indian Ecclesiastical Studies
Ind E St — Indian Ecclesiastical Studies
Ind Ethn — Index Ethnographicus
INDEX — Index on Censorship. Writers and Scholars International
Index 81 Eighty One Congr Pap — Index 81 [*Eighty-One*] Congress Papers
Index Am Period Verse — Index of American Periodical Verse
Index Anal Cancerol — Index Analyticus Cancerologiae
Index Book Rev Humanit — Index to Book Reviews in the Humanities
Index Can Leg Period Lit — Index to Canadian Legal Periodical Literature
Index Cat Med Vet Zool — Index Catalog of Medical and Veterinary Zoology
Index Censor — Index on Censorship
Index Chem — Index Chemicus
Index Commonw Leg Period — Index to Commonwealth Legal Periodicals
Index Conf Proc Received by BLLD — Index of Conference Proceedings Received by the British Library Lending Division
Index Current Urban Docs — Index to Current Urban Documents
Index Curr Urban Doc — Index to Current Urban Documents
Index Dent Lit — Index to Dental Literature
Index Econ Artic J Collect Vols — Index of Economic Articles in Journals and Collective Volumes
Index Econ J — Index of Economic Journals
Index Fed Tax Artic Supp — Index to Federal Tax Articles. Supplement
Index Foreign Leg Per — Index to Foreign Legal Periodicals
Index Foreign Leg Per Collect Essays — Index to Foreign Legal Periodicals and Collections of Essays
Index Free Period — Index to Free Periodicals
Index Gov Orders — Index to Government Orders
Index Horti Bot Univ Budapest — Index Horti Botanici Universitatis Budapestinensis
Index IEEE Publ — Index to IEEE [*Institute of Electrical and Electronic Engineers*] Publications
Index Indian Period Lit — Index to Indian Periodical Literature
Index Islam — Index Islamicus
Index Jew Period — Index to Jewish Periodicals
Index JSMPE — Index of Transactions and Journal. Society of Motion Picture Engineers
Index JSMPTE — Index to the Journal of the Society of Motion Picture and Television Engineers
Index Legal Period — Index to Legal Periodicals
Index Leg Period — Index to Legal Periodicals
Index Lit Am Indian — Index to Literature on the American Indian
Index Lit Food Invest — Index to the Literature of Food Investigation
Index Math Pap — Index of Mathematical Papers
Index Med — Index Medicus
Index New Engl Period — Index to New England Periodicals
Index New Z Period — Index to New Zealand Periodicals
Index Park Pract — Index to Park Practice
Index Park Pract Prog — Index. Park Practice Program
Index Period Artic Blacks — Index to Periodical Articles by and about Blacks
Index Period Artic Negroes — Index to Periodical Articles by and about Negroes [*Later, Index to Periodical Articles by and about Blacks*]
Index Period Artic Relat Law — Index to Periodical Articles Related to Law
Index Period Lit Aging — Index to Periodical Articles on Aging
Index Philip Period — Index to Philippine Periodicals
Index PI Chromosome Numbers — Index to Plant Chromosome Numbers
Ind Explos — Industrial Explosives
Ind Express — Indian Express
Index Psychoanal Wr — Index of Psychoanalytic Writings
Index Publ Am Soc Mech Eng — Index to Publications. American Society of Mechanical Engineers
Index Quad — Index Quaderni Camerti di Studi Romanistici
Index Sci Rev — Index to Scientific Reviews
Index Soc Pub — Index Society Publications

Index Soc Sci Humanit Proc — Index to Social Sciences and Humanities Proceedings
Index South Afr Period — Index to South African Periodicals
Index Specif Stand — Index Specifications and Standards
Index To Leg Per & L Lib J — Index to Legal Periodicals and Law Library Journal
Index to Relig Period Lit — Index to Religious Periodical Literature
Index US Gov Period — Index to United States Government Periodicals
Index Vet — Index Veterinarius
IndF — Indiana Folklore
Ind F — Indian Farming
Ind Farm — Indian Farming
Ind Farm — Industria dei Farmaci
Ind Farm Bioquim — Industria Farmaceutica y Bioquimica
Ind Fin — Industrial Finishing
Ind Finish — Industrial Finishing
Ind Finish & Surf Coatings — Industrial Finishing and Surface Coatings
Ind Finish Surf Coat — Industrial Finishing and Surface Coatings
Ind Finish (Wheaton III) — Industrial Finishing (Wheaton, Illinois)
Ind Finish Yearb — Industrial Finishing Yearbook
Ind For — Indian Forester
Ind For Leafl — Indian Forest Leaflets
Ind For R — Indian and Foreign Review
Ind For Rec — Indian Forest Records
Ind Forsch — Indogermanische Forschungen
Ind Fr Equip — Industries Francaises d'Equipement
Ind Gas — Industrial Gas
Ind Gas Acquedotti — Industria del Gas e degli Acquedotti
Ind Gas (Duluth) — Industrial Gas (Duluth)
Ind Gas Energy — Industrial Gas and Energy
Ind Geog J — Indian Geographical Journal
Ind Geogr — Indian Geographer
Ind Geogr J — Indian Geographical Journal
Ind Geo J — Indian Geographical Journal
Ind Geront — Industrial Gerontology
Ind Gerontol — Industrial Gerontology
Ind Gids — Indische Gids
Ind Gomma — Industria della Gomma. Minsiledi Economia e Tenica Degil Elastomeri
IndH — Indian Historian
IndH — Indian Horizons
Ind Handel — Industrie und Handel
Ind Health — Industrial Health
Ind Health Care — Industry and Health Care
Ind Health Care (Cambridge MA) — Industry and Health Care (Cambridge, Massachusetts)
Ind Health Found Symp — Industrial Health Foundation Symposia
Ind Health (Kawasaki) — Industrial Health (Kawasaki)
Ind Health Rev — Industrial Health Review
Ind Heart J — Indian Heart Journal
Ind Heat — Industrial Heating
Ind Heat Eng — Industrial Heating Engineer
Ind Heat (Pittsburg) — Industrial Heating (Pittsburg)
Ind Heat (Tokyo) — Industrial Heating (Tokyo)
Ind Heat Xian Peoples Repub China — Industrial Heating (Xi'an, People's Republic of China)
Ind His Col — Indiana Historical Commission. Collections
Ind His S — Indiana Historical Society. Publications
Ind Hist Bul — Indiana History Bulletin. Indiana Historical Commission
Ind Hist Bull — Indiana History Bulletin
Ind Hist Esp — Indice Historico Espanol
Ind Hist Q — Indian Historical Quarterly
Ind Hist Rec Comm Proc — Indian Historical Records Commission. Proceedings
Ind Hist Soc Publ — Indiana Historical Society. Publications
Ind Hlth Saf Educ — Index to Health and Safety Education
Ind Hom Rev — Indian Homoeopathic Review
Ind Hor — Indian Horizons
Ind Horizons — Indian Horizons
Ind Hyg Bull — Industrial Hygiene Bulletin
Ind Hyg Dig — Industrial Hygiene Digest
Ind Hyg Found Am Leg Ser Bull — Industrial Hygiene Foundation of America. Legal Series. Bulletin
Ind Hyg Found Am Med Ser Bull — Industrial Hygiene Foundation of America. Medical Series. Bulletin
Ind Hyg Found Am Trans Bull — Industrial Hygiene Foundation of America. Transactions. Bulletin
Ind Hyg Highlights — Industrial Hygiene Highlights
Ind Hygiene — Industrial Hygiene
Ind Hyg Ne — Industrial Hygiene News
Ind Hyg Rev — Industrial Hygiene Review
India AEC Bhabha At Res Cent Rep — India. Atomic Energy Commission. Bhabha Atomic Research Centre. Report
(India) Code Civ Proc — Code of Civil Procedure (India)
(India) Code Crim Proc — Code of Criminal Procedure (India)
India Coffee Bd Res Dep Annu Detailed Tech Rep — India. Coffee Board. Research Department. Annual Detailed Technical Report
India Coffee Board Annu Rep — India. Coffee Board. Annual Report
India Coffee Board Res Dep Annu Detailed Tech Rep — India. Coffee Board. Research Department. Annual Detailed Technical Report
India Coffee Board Res Dep Annu Rep — India. Coffee Board. Research Department. Annual Report
India Coffee Board Res Dep Bull — India. Coffee Board. Research Department. Bulletin
India CSIR Zool Mem — India. CSIR [*Council of Scientific and Industrial Research*] Zoological Memoir
(India) Curr Cen Leg — Current Central Legislation (India)

India Dir Plant Prot Quar Storage Plant Prot Bull — India. Directorate of Plant Protection, Quarantine, and Storage. Plant Protection Bulletin
India Econ Soc Hist R — Indian Economic and Social History Review
India Geol Surv Bull Ser A — India. Geological Survey. Bulletins. Series A. Economic Geology
India Geol Surv Bull Ser B — India. Geological Survey. Bulletins. Series B. Engineering Geology and Ground-Water
India Geol Surv Mem — India. Geological Survey. Memoirs
India Geol Surv Mem Palaeontol Indica New Ser — India. Geological Survey. Memoirs. Palaeontologia Indica. New Series
India Geol Surv Misc Publ — India. Geological Survey. Miscellaneous Publication
India Geol Surv News — India. Geological Survey. News
India Int Cent Q — India International Centre Quarterly
India Int Centre Quart — India International Centre Quarterly
India J Pol Sci — Indian Journal of Political Science
India Mag — India Magazine
Indiana Acad Sci Monogr — Indiana Academy of Science. Monograph
Indiana Agric Exp Stn Insp Rep — Indiana. Agricultural Experiment Station. Inspection Report
Indiana Agric Exp Stn Res Prog Rep — Indiana. Agricultural Experiment Station. Research Progress Report
Indiana Bs — Indiana Business
Indiana Busin R — Indiana Business Review
Indiana Bus R — Indiana Business Review
Indian Acad Geosci J — Indian Academy of Geoscience. Journal
Indian Acad Med Sci Ann — Indian Academy of Medical Sciences. Annual
Indian Acad Sci Pro — Indian Academy of Sciences. Proceedings
Indian Acad Sci Proc Plant Sci — Indian Academy of Sciences. Proceedings. Plant Sciences
Indian Acad Sci Proc Sect A — Indian Academy of Sciences. Proceedings. Section A. Earth and Planetary Sciences
Indian Acad Sci Proc Sect B — Indian Academy of Sciences. Proceedings. Section B
Indiana Dep Conserv Geol Surv Bull — Indiana. Department of Conservation. Geological Survey. Bulletin
Indiana Div Water Bull — Indiana. Division of Water. Bulletin
Indiana Geol Surv Bull — Indiana. Geological Survey. Bulletin
Indiana Geol Survey Mineral Economics Ser — Indiana. Geological Survey. Mineral Economics Series
Indiana Geol Surv Mineral Econ Ser — Indiana. Geological Survey. Mineral Economics Series
Indiana Geol Surv Miner Econ Ser — Indiana. Geological Survey. Mineral Economics Series
Indiana Geol Surv Misc Map — Indiana. Geological Survey. Miscellaneous Map
Indiana Geol Surv Occas Pap — Indiana. Geological Survey. Occasional Paper
Indiana Geol Surv Rep Prog — Indiana. Geological Survey. Report of Progress
Indiana Geol Surv Spec Rep — Indiana. Geological Survey. Special Report
Indian Agr — Indian Agriculturist
Indian Agric — Indian Agriculturist
Indian Agric Res Inst (New Delhi) Annu Rep — Indian Agricultural Research Institute (New Delhi). Annual Report
Indian Agric Res Inst (New Delhi) Annu Sci Rep — Indian Agricultural Research Institute (New Delhi). Annual Scientific Report
Indiana Hist Bull — Indiana History Bulletin
Indiana Hist Soc Publ — Indiana Historical Society. Publications
Indiana Law — Indiana Law Journal
Indiana Leg Forum — Indiana Legal Forum
Indiana LJ — Indiana Law Journal
Indiana L Rev — Indiana Law Review
Indiana Mag Hist — Indiana Magazine of History
Indiana Med — Indiana Medicine
Indiana Med J Evansville — Indiana Medical Journal. A Quarterly Record. Medical Sciences of the South and West (Evansville)
Indiana M Hist — Indiana Magazine of History
Indiana Mil Hist Jnl — Indiana Military History Journal
Indian Ant — Indian Antiquary
Indianapolis M J — Indianapolis Medical Journal
Indian Archt — Indian Architect
Indiana Slav Stud — Indiana Slavic Studies
Indiana Sp J — Indiana Speech Journal
Indian Assoc Cultiv Sci Proc — Indian Association for the Cultivation of Science. Proceedings
Indiana State Bar Assn — Indiana State Bar Association
Indiana State Univ Dep Geogr Geol Prof Pap — Indiana State University. Department of Geography and Geology. Professional Paper
Indiana Theory R — Indiana Theory Review
India Natl Acad Sci Proc Sect B — India. National Academy of Science. Proceedings. Section B
Indiana Univ Art Mus Publ — Indiana University Art Museum. Publications
Indiana Univ Ed Bul — Indiana University. School of Education. Bulletin
Indiana Univ Hum Ser — Indiana University Humanities Series
Indiana Univ Math J — Indiana University. Mathematics Journal
Indiana Univ Publ Afr Ser — Indiana University Publications. African Series
Indian Bee J — Indian Bee Journal
Indian Behav Sci Abstr — Indian Behavioural Sciences Abstracts
Indian Biol — Indian Biologist
Indian Bot Contactor — Indian Botanical Contactor
Indian Bot Rep — Indian Botanical Reporter
Indian Bur Mines Miner Econ Div Mark Surv Ser — Indian Bureau of Mines. Mineral Economics Division. Market Survey Series
Indian Cas — Indian Cases
Indian Cent Jute Comm Annu Rep Jute Agric Res Inst — Indian Central Jute Committee. Annual Report of the Jute Agricultural Research Institute
Indian Ceram — Indian Ceramics
Indian Ceramic Soc Trans — Indian Ceramic Society. Transactions

Indian Ceram Soc Trans — Indian Ceramic Society. Transactions
Indian Chem Eng — Indian Chemical Engineer
Indian Chem Engr — Indian Chemical Engineer
Indian Chem Eng Sect A — Indian Chemical Engineer. Section A. Journal of Indian Institute of Chemical Engineers
Indian Chem Eng Sect B — Indian Chemical Engineer. Section B. Industry and News
Indian Chem J — Indian Chemical Journal
Indian Chem J Ann Number — Indian Chemical Journal. Annual Number
Indian Chem Manuf — Indian Chemical Manufacturer
Indian Chem Manuf Annu Number — Indian Chemical Manufacturer. Annual Number
Indian Church Hist R — Indian Church History Review
Indian Coconut J — Indian Coconut Journal
Indian Cof — Indian Coffee
Indian Concr J — Indian Concrete Journal
Indian Cott Grow Rev — Indian Cotton Growing Review
Indian Cott J — Indian Cotton Journal
Indian Cotton Growing Rev — Indian Cotton Growing Review. Indian Central Cotton Committee
Indian Cotton Grow Rev — Indian Cotton Growing Review
Indian Counc Agric Res Anim Husb Ser — Indian Council of Agricultural Research. Animal Husbandry Series
Indian Counc Agric Res Annu Tech Rep — Indian Council of Agricultural Research. Annual Technical Report
Indian Counc Agric Res Cereal Crop Ser — Indian Council of Agricultural Research. Cereal Crop Series
Indian Counc Agric Res Entomol Monogr — Indian Council of Agricultural Research. Entomological Monographs
Indian Counc Agric Res Misc Bull — Indian Council of Agricultural Research. Miscellaneous Bulletin
Indian Counc Agric Res Monogr — Indian Council of Agricultural Research. Monograph
Indian Counc Agric Res Rep Ser — Indian Council of Agricultural Research. Report Series
Indian Counc Agric Res Res Ser — Indian Council of Agricultural Research. Research Series
Indian Counc Agric Res Rev Ser — Indian Council of Agricultural Research. Review Series
Indian Counc Agric Res Tech Bull — Indian Council of Agricultural Research. Technical Bulletin
Indian Counc Med Res Annu Rep — Indian Council of Medical Research. Annual Report
Indian Counc Med Res Tech Rep Ser — Indian Council of Medical Research. Technical Report Series
Indian East Eng — Indian and Eastern Engineer
Indian Ecol — Indian Ecologist
Indian Econ R — Indian Economic Review
Indian Econ Soc Hist Rev — Indian Economic and Social History Review
Indian Ed Rev — Indian Educational Review
Indian Educ — Indian Educator
Indian Eng — Indian Engineer
Indian Export Trade J — Indian Export Trade Journal
Indian Farm Mech — Indian Farm Mechanization
Indian Fmg — Indian Farming
Indian Food Pack — Indian Food Packer
Indian For — Indian Forester
Indian For Bull — Indian Forest Bulletin
Indian For Bull For Res Inst (Dehra) — Indian Forest Bulletin. Entomology. Forest Research Institute (Dehra)
Indian Forest Rec Bot — Indian Forest Records. Botany. Forest Research Institute
Indian For Leafl — Indian Forest Leaflets
Indian For Pol Ann Surv — Indian Foreign Policy Annual Survey
Indian For Rec — Indian Forest Records
Indian For Rec Bot — Indian Forest Records. Botany
Indian For Rec Entomol — Indian Forest Records. Entomology
Indian For Rec For Manage & Mensuration — Indian Forest Records. Forest Management and Mensuration
Indian For Rec For Pathol — Indian Forest Records. Forest Pathology
Indian For Rec Mycol — Indian Forest Records. Mycology
Indian For Rec Silvic — Indian Forest Records. Silviculture
Indian For Rec Silvics — Indian Forest Records. Silvics
Indian For Rec Stat — Indian Forest Records. Statistical
Indian For Rec Timber Mech — Indian Forest Records. Timber Mechanics
Indian For Rec Wild Life Recreat — Indian Forest Records. Wild Life and Recreation
Indian For Rec Wild Life Recreation — Indian Forest Records. Wild Life and Recreation
Indian For Rec Wood Anat — Indian Forest Records. Wood Anatomy
Indian For Rec Wood Preserv — Indian Forest Records. Wood Preservation
Indian For Rec Wood Seas — Indian Forest Records. Wood Seasoning
Indian For Rec Wood Technol — Indian Forest Records. Wood Technology
Indian Foundry J — Indian Foundry Journal
Indian Geohydrol — Indian Geohydrology
Indian Geol Assoc Bull — Indian Geologists Association. Bulletin
Indian Geol Index — Indian Geological Index
Indian Geotech J — Indian Geotechnical Journal
Indian Heart J — Indian Heart Journal
Indian Heart J Teach Ser — Indian Heart Journal. Teaching Series
Indian Highw — Indian Highways
Indian Hist — Indian Historian
Indian Hist Q — Indian Historical Quarterly
Indian Hort — Indian Horticulture
Indian Hortic — Indian Horticulture
Indian Ind — Indian Industries

Indian Inst Bankers J — Journal. Indian Institute of Bankers
Indian Inst Met Trans — Indian Institute of Metals. Transactions
Indian Inst of Archts Jnl — Indian Institute of Architects. Journal
Indian Inst Technol Bombay Ser — Indian Institute of Technology. Bombay Series
Indian J Acarol — Indian Journal of Acarology
Indian J Adult Ed — Indian Journal of Adult Education
Indian J Agr Econ — Indian Journal of Agricultural Economics
Indian J Agric Chem — Indian Journal of Agricultural Chemistry
Indian J Agric Econ — Indian Journal of Agricultural Economics
Indian J Agric Res — Indian Journal of Agricultural Research
Indian J Agric Sci — Indian Journal of Agricultural Science
Indian J Agric Vet Educ — Indian Journal of Agricultural and Veterinary Education
Indian J Agron — Indian Journal of Agronomy
Indian J Agr Sci — Indian Journal of Agricultural Science
Indian J Air Pollut Control — Indian Journal of Air Pollution Control
Indian J Anaesth — Indian Journal of Anaesthesia
Indian J Animal Health — Indian Journal of Animal Health
Indian J Anim Health — Indian Journal of Animal Health
Indian J Anim Res — Indian Journal of Animal Research
Indian J Anim Sci — Indian Journal of Animal Sciences
Indian J Appl Chem — Indian Journal of Applied Chemistry
Indian J Appl Psychol — Indian Journal of Applied Psychology
Indian J Biochem — Indian Journal of Biochemistry [*Later, Indian Journal of Biochemistry and Biophysics*]
Indian J Biochem Biophys — Indian Journal of Biochemistry and Biophysics
Indian J Bot — Indian Journal of Botany
Indian J Cancer — Indian Journal of Cancer
Indian J Cancer Chemother — Indian Journal of Cancer Chemotherapy
Indian J Chem — Indian Journal of Chemistry
Indian J Chem A — Indian Journal of Chemistry. Section A. Inorganic, Physical, Theoretical, and Analytical
Indian J Chem B — Indian Journal of Chemistry. Section B. Organic Chemistry, Including MedicinalChemistry
Indian J Chem Educ — Indian Journal of Chemical Education
Indian J Chem Sci — Indian Journal of Chemical Sciences
Indian J Chem Sect A — Indian Journal of Chemistry. Section A. Inorganic, Physical, Theoretical, and Analytical
Indian J Chem Sect A Inorg Bio Inorg Phys Theor Anal Chem — Indian Journal of Chemistry. Section A. Inorganic, Bio-inorganic, Physical, Theoretical, and Analytical Chemistry
Indian J Chem Sect A Inorg Phys Theor Anal — Indian Journal of Chemistry. Section A. Inorganic, Physical, Theoretical, and Analytical
Indian J Chem Sect B — Indian Journal of Chemistry. Section B. Organic Chemistry, Including Medicinal Chemistry
Indian J Chem Sect B Org Chem Incl Med Chem — Indian Journal of Chemistry. Section B. Organic Chemistry, Including MedicinalChemistry
Indian J Chem Technol — Indian Journal of Chemical Technology
Indian J Chest Dis — Indian Journal of Chest Diseases [*Later, Indian Journal of Chest Diseases and Allied Sciences*]
Indian J Chest Dis Allied Sci — Indian Journal of Chest Diseases and Allied Sciences
Indian J Child Health — Indian Journal of Child Health
Indian J Comp Anim Physiol — Indian Journal of Comparative Animal Physiology
Indian J Criminol — Indian Journal of Criminology
Indian J Cryog — Indian Journal of Cryogenics
Indian J Dairy Sci — Indian Journal of Dairy Science
Indian J Dermatol — Indian Journal of Dermatology [*Later, Indian Journal of Dermatology, Venereology, and Leprology*]
Indian J Dermatol Venereol — Indian Journal of Dermatology and Venereology [*Later, Indian Journal of Dermatology, Venereology, and Leprology*]
Indian J Dermatol Venereol Leprol — Indian Journal of Dermatology, Venereology, and Leprology
Indian J Earth Sci — Indian Journal of Earth Sciences
Indian J Ecol — Indian Journal of Ecology
Indian J Ed Adm & Res — Indian Journal of Educational Administration and Research
Indian J Eng Mater Sci — Indian Journal of Engineering and Materials Sciences
Indian J Engrg Math — Indian Journal of Engineering Mathematics
Indian J Ent — Indian Journal of Entomology
Indian J Entomol — Indian Journal of Entomology
Indian J Environ Health — Indian Journal of Environmental Health
Indian J Environ Prot — Indian Journal of Environmental Protection
Indian J Exp Biol — Indian Journal of Experimental Biology
Indian J Expl Biol — Indian Journal of Experimental Biology
Indian J Exp Psychol — Indian Journal of Experimental Psychology
Indian J Ext Educ — Indian Journal of Extension Education
Indian J Farm Chem — Indian Journal of Farm Chemicals
Indian J Farm Sci — Indian Journal of Farm Sciences
Indian J Fish — Indian Journal of Fisheries
Indian J For — Indian Journal of Forestry
Indian J Gastroenterol — Indian Journal of Gastroenterology
Indian J Genet Plant Breed — Indian Journal of Genetics and Plant Breeding
Indian J Genet Pl Breed — Indian Journal of Genetics and Plant Breeding
Indian J Helminthol — Indian Journal of Helminthology
Indian J Hered — Indian Journal of Heredity
Indian J Heterocycl Chem — Indian Journal of Heterocyclic Chemistry
Indian J Hist Med — Indian Journal of History of Medicine
Indian J History Sci — Indian Journal of History of Science. National Institute of Sciences of India
Indian J Hist Sci — Indian Journal of History of Science
Indian J Hort — Indian Journal of Horticulture
Indian J Hortic — Indian Journal of Horticulture
Indian J Hosp Pharm — Indian Journal of Hospital Pharmacy
Indian J Ind Med — Indian Journal of Industrial Medicine
Indian J Ind Rel — Indian Journal of Industrial Relations

Indian J Int Law — Indian Journal of International Law
Indian J Int'l L — Indian Journal of International Law
Indian J Lepr — Indian Journal of Leprosy
Indian J Malariol — Indian Journal of Malariology
Indian J Mar Sci — Indian Journal of Marine Sciences
Indian J Math — Indian Journal of Mathematics
Indian J Mech Math — Indian Journal of Mechanics and Mathematics
Indian J Med Res — Indian Journal of Medical Research
Indian J Med Research — Indian Journal of Medical Research
Indian J Med Res Sect A — Indian Journal of Medical Research. Section A
Indian J Med Res Sect B — Indian Journal of Medical Research. Section B
Indian J Med Sci — Indian Journal of Medical Sciences
Indian J Med Surg — Indian Journal of Medicine and Surgery
Indian J Meteorol and Geophys — Indian Journal of Meteorology and Geophysics [*Later, Mausam*]
Indian J Meteorol Geophys — Indian Journal of Meteorology and Geophysics [*Later, Mausam*]
Indian J Meteorol Hydrol and Geophys — Indian Journal of Meteorology, Hydrology, and Geophysics [*Later, Mausam*]
Indian J Meteorol Hydrol Geophys — Indian Journal of Meteorology, Hydrology, and Geophysics [*Later, Mausam*]
Indian J Microbiol — Indian Journal of Microbiology
Indian J M Res — Indian Journal of Medical Research
Indian J Mycol Plant Pathol — Indian Journal of Mycology and Plant Pathology
Indian J Mycol Res — Indian Journal of Mycological Research
Indian J Nat Prod — Indian Journal of Natural Products
Indian J Nat Rubber Res — Indian Journal of Natural Rubber Research
Indian J Nematol — Indian Journal of Nematology
Indian J Nutr Diet — Indian Journal of Nutrition and Dietetics
Indian J Occup Health — Indian Journal of Occupational Health
Indian J of Internat L — Indian Journal of International Law
Indian J of Publ Adm — Indian Journal of Public Administration
Indian J Ophthalmol — Indian Journal of Ophthalmology
Indian J Orthop — Indian Journal of Orthopaedics
Indian J Otolaryngol — Indian Journal of Otolaryngology
Indian J Parasitol — Indian Journal of Parasitology
Indian J Pathol Bacteriol — Indian Journal of Pathology and Bacteriology [*Later, Indian Journal of Pathology and Microbiology*]
Indian J Pathol Microbiol — Indian Journal of Pathology and Microbiology
Indian J Pediatr — Indian Journal of Pediatrics
Indian J Pharm — Indian Journal of Pharmacy
Indian J Pharmacol — Indian Journal of Pharmacology
Indian J Pharm Educ — Indian Journal of Pharmaceutical Education
Indian J Pharm Sci — Indian Journal of Pharmaceutical Sciences
Indian J Phys — Indian Journal of Physics
Indian J Phys Anthrop Hum Genet — Indian Journal of Physical Anthropology and Human Genetics
Indian J Phys Anthropol Hum Genet — Indian Journal of Physical Anthropology and Human Genetics
Indian J Phys B — Indian Journal of Physics. B
Indian J Physiol Allied Sci — Indian Journal of Physiology and Allied Sciences
Indian J Physiol Pharmacol — Indian Journal of Physiology and Pharmacology
Indian J Phys Nat Sci — Indian Journal of Physical and Natural Sciences
Indian J Phys Part A — Indian Journal of Physics. Part A
Indian J Phys Part B — Indian Journal of Physics. Part B
Indian J Plant Pathol — Indian Journal of Plant Pathology
Indian J Plant Physiol — Indian Journal of Plant Physiology
Indian J Plant Prot — Indian Journal of Plant Protection
Indian J Poult Sci — Indian Journal of Poultry Science
Indian J Poult Sci Off J Indian Poult Sci Assoc — Indian Journal of Poultry Science. Official Journal. Indian Poultry Science Association
Indian J Power and River Val Dev — Indian Journal of Power and River Valley Development
Indian J Power River Val Dev — Indian Journal of Power and River Valley Development
Indian J Power River Val Develop — Indian Journal of Power and River Valley Development
Indian J Psychiatry — Indian Journal of Psychiatry
Indian J Psychol — Indian Journal of Psychology
Indian J Psychol Med — Indian Journal of Psychological Medicine
Indian J Pub Admin — Indian Journal of Public Administration
Indian J Publ Health — Indian Journal of Public Health
Indian J Public Health — Indian Journal of Public Health
Indian J Pure and Appl Math — Indian Journal of Pure and Applied Mathematics
Indian J Pure and Appl Phys — Indian Journal of Pure and Applied Physics
Indian J Pure Appl Math — Indian Journal of Pure and Applied Mathematics
Indian J Pure Appl Phys — Indian Journal of Pure and Applied Physics
Indian J Pure Appl Sci — Indian Journal of Pure and Applied Science
Indian J Radio and Space Phys — Indian Journal of Radio and Space Physics
Indian J Radiol — Indian Journal of Radiology
Indian J Radiol Imag — Indian Journal of Radiology and Imaging
Indian J Radio Space Phys — Indian Journal of Radio and Space Physics
Indian J Reg Sci — Indian Journal of Regional Science
Indian J Sci Ind — Indian Journal of Science and Industry
Indian J Sci Ind Sect A — Indian Journal of Science and Industry. Section A. Agricultural Sciences [*Later, Indian Journal of Agricultural Research*]
Indian J Sci Ind Sect A Agric Anim Sci — Indian Journal of Science and Industry. Section A. Agricultural and Animal Sciences
Indian J Sci Ind Sect B Anim Sci — Indian Journal of Science and Industry. Section B. Animal Sciences [*Later, Indian Journal of Animal Research*]
Indian J Seric — Indian Journal of Sericulture
Indian J Social Work — Indian Journal of Social Work
Indian J Soil Conser — Indian Journal of Soil Conservation
Indian J Sugar Cane Res Dev — Indian Journal of Sugar Cane Research and Development

Indian J Surg — Indian Journal of Surgery
Indian J Tech — Indian Journal of Technology
Indian J Technol — Indian Journal of Technology
Indian J Text Res — Indian Journal of Textile Research
Indian J Theor Phys — Indian Journal of Theoretical Physics
Indian J Tuberc — Indian Journal of Tuberculosis
Indian J Tuberculosis — Indian Journal of Tuberculosis
Indian J Ven Dis — Indian Journal of Venereal Diseases
Indian J Vet Med — Indian Journal of Veterinary Medicine
Indian J Vet Pathol — Indian Journal of Veterinary Pathology
Indian J Vet Sci — Indian Journal of Veterinary Science and Animal Husbandry
Indian J Vet Sci Anim Husb — Indian Journal of Veterinary Science and Animal Husbandry
Indian J Vet Surg — Indian Journal of Veterinary Surgery
Indian J Virol — Indian Journal of Virology
Indian J Weed Sci — Indian Journal of Weed Science
Indian J Zool — Indian Journal of Zoology
Indian J Zootomy — Indian Journal of Zootomy
Indian Lac Res Inst Annu Rep — Indian Lac Research Institute. Annual Report
Indian Lac Res Inst Bull — Indian Lac Research Institute. Bulletin
Indian Lac Res Inst Res Notes — Indian Lac Research Institute. Research Notes
Indian Lac Res Inst Tech Note — Indian Lac Research Institute. Technical Notes
Indian Lib Assn J — Indian Library Association. Journal
Indian Libr Ass Bull — Indian Library Association. Bulletin
Indian Librn — Indian Librarian
Indian Libr Sci Abstr — Indian Library Science Abstracts
Indian Lib Sci Abstr — Indian Library Science Abstracts
Indian LJ — Indian Law Journal
Indian L Rep Am Indian Law Training Program — Indian Law Reporter. American Indian Lawyers Training Program
Indian L Rev — Indian Law Review
Indian Med Forum — Indian Medical Forum
Indian Med Gaz — Indian Medical Gazette
Indian Med J (Calcutta) — Indian Medical Journal (Calcutta)
Indian Med R — Indian Medical Review
Indian Med Res Mem — Indian Medical Research Memoirs
Indian M Gaz — Indian Medical Gazette
Indian Min Engng J — Indian Mining and Engineering Journal
Indian Miner — Indian Minerals
Indian Mineral — Indian Mineralogist
Indian Miner Yearb — Indian Minerals Yearbook
Indian MJ — Indian Music Journal
Indian M Rec — Indian Medical Record
Indian M S — Indian Musicological Society. Journal
Indian Mus Bull — Indian Museum. Bulletin
Indian Mus Q — Indian Music Quarterly
Indian Mus Rec — Indian Museum. Records
Indian Natl Sci Acad Monogr — Indian National Science Academy. Monographs
Indian Natl Sci Acad Proc Part A — Indian National Science Academy. Proceedings. Part A. Physical Sciences
Indian Natl Sci Acad Trans — Indian National Science Academy. Transactions
Indian Nat Resour — Indian Natural Resources
Indian Nat Sci Acad Bull — Indian National Science Academy. Bulletin
Indian Paediatr — Indian Paediatrics
Indian Pediatr — Indian Pediatrics
Indian Perfum — Indian Perfumer
Indian Phil Cult — Indian Philosophy and Culture
Indian Phil Quart — Indian Philosophical Quarterly
Indian Phys Math J — Indian Physico-Mathematical Journal
Indian Phytopathol — Indian Phytopathology
Indianpl B — Indianapolis Business Journal
Indian Pl Gard — Indian Planting and Gardening
Indianpl S — Indianapolis Star
Indian Potash J — Indian Potash Journal
Indian Potato J — Indian Potato Journal
Indian Poult Gaz — Indian Poultry Gazette
Indian Poult Rev — Indian Poultry Review
Indian Pract — Indian Practitioner
Indian Psychol Abstr — Indian Psychological Abstracts
Indian Psychol R — Indian Psychological Review
Indian Pulp Pap — Indian Pulp and Paper
Indian R — Indian Review
Indian Rec — Indian Record
Indian Refract Makers Assoc J — Indian Refractory Makers Association. Journal
Indian Rev Life Sci — Indian Review of Life Sciences
Indian Rubber Manuf Res Assoc Tech Semin Proc — Indian Rubber Manufacturers Research Association. Technical Seminar. Proceedings
Indian Sci Abstr — Indian Science Abstracts
Indian Sci Abstracts — Indian Science Abstracts
Indian Sci Abstr New Delhi — Indian Science Abstracts (New Delhi)
Indian Sci Cong Assoc Proc — Indian Science Congress Association. Proceedings
Indian Sci Congr Assoc Proc — Indian Science Congress Association. Proceedings
Indian Sci Cruiser — Indian Science Cruiser
Indian Sci Ind — Indian Science Index
Indian Sci Index — Indian Science Index
Indian Soc Desert Technol Univ Cent Desert Stud Trans — Indian Society of Desert Technology and University Centre of Desert Studies. Transactions
Indian Soc Nuclear Tech Agric Biol Newsl — Indian Society for Nuclear Techniques in Agriculture and Biology. Newsletter
Indian Soc Nucl Tech Agric Biol Newsl — Indian Society for Nuclear Techniques in Agriculture and Biology. Newsletter
Indian Soc Soil Sci Bull — Indian Society of Soil Science. Bulletin
Indian Soc Soil Sci J — Indian Society of Soil Science. Journal
Indian Sug — Indian Sugar

Indian Tea Assoc Proc Annu Conf — Indian Tea Association. Proceedings of the Annual Conference
Indian Tea Assoc Sci Dep Tocklai Exp Stn Annu Rep — Indian Tea Association. Scientific Department. Tocklai Experimental Station. Annual Report
Indian Tea Assoc Sci Dep Tocklai Exp Stn Memo — Indian Tea Association. Scientific Department. Tocklai Experimental Station. Memorandum
Indian Tea Assoc Tocklai Exp Stn Annu Rep — Indian Tea Association. Tocklai Experimental Station. Annual Report
Indian Tea Assoc Tocklai Exp Stn Memo — Indian Tea Association. Tocklai Experimental Station. Memorandum
Indian Tea Assoc Tocklai Exp Stn Memor — Indian Tea Association. Tocklai Experimental Station. Memorandum
Indian Terr — Indian Territory Reports
Indian Text J — Indian Textile Journal
Indian Tob J — Indian Tobacco Journal
Indian Vet J — Indian Veterinary Journal
Indian Vet Med J — Indian Veterinary Medical Journal
Indian Weld J — Indian Welding Journal
Indian Yb of Internat Aff — Indian Yearbook of International Affairs
Indian Zool — Indian Zoologist
Indian Zool Mem — Indian Zoological Memoirs
India Oil Nat Gas Comm Bull — India. Oil and Natural Gas Commission. Bulletin
India Pol Sci R — Indian Political Science Review
India Q — India Quarterly
India Quar — India Quarterly
India Quart — India Quarterly
India Rubb R — India Rubber Review
India Rubb Wld — India Rubber World
India Rub World NY — India Rubber World (New York)
India Soc Stud Q — Indian Social Studies Quarterly
Indicadores Econs (Mexico) — Indicadores Economicos (Mexico)
Indicadores Econs (RS) — Indicadores Economicos (Rio Grande Do Sul)
Indicateur Ant Suisses — Indicateur d'Antiquites Suisses
Indicateurs Econ Centre — Indicateurs de l'Economie du Centre
Indic Cartotec — Indicatore Cartotecnico
Indice Agricola Am Lat Caribe — Indice Agricola de America Latina y el Caribe
Indice Bibliogr Lepra — Indice Bibliografico de Lepra
Indice Cult Espan — Indice Cultural Espanol
IndiceH — Indice (Havanna)
Indice Lit Dent Castellano — Indice de la Literatura Dental en Castellano
Indice Lit Dent Period Castellano — Indice de la Literatura Dental Periodica en Castellano
Indice Med Esp — Indice Medico Espanol
Indice Rev Bibliotecol — IREBI. Indices de Revista de Bibliotecologia
Indices Altdeutsch Schrift — Indices zum Altdeutschen Schrifttum
Indices Monographs Philos Logic Formal Linguistics — Indices. Monographs in Philosophical Logic and Formal Linguistics
Indice Taxon — Indice Taxonomico. Asociacion Sudamericana de Fitotaxonomistos
Indic Grafico — Indicatore Grafico
INDIDJ — International Journal of Eating Disorders
Indi Math J — Indiana University. Mathematics Journal
Ind India — Index India
Ind India — Industrial India
Ind Ind Med Per — Index of Indian Medical Periodicals
Ind Information Bul — Industrial Information Bulletin
Ind Inst Adv Stud — Indian Institute of Advanced Studies
Ind Inst Pub Admin — Indian Institute of Public Administration
Ind Inst Pub Opin — Indian Institute of Public Opinion
Ind Int — Industry International
Indirect — Indirections
Indirect Liquefaction Proc Contract Rev Meet — Indirect Liquefaction. Proceedings. Contractors' Review Meeting
Indische Cult — De Indische Culturen
Indisch Genoot — Indisch Genootschap
Ind Isl — Index Islamicus
Ind Islam — Index Islamicus
Ind Ital Cem — Industria Italiana del Cemento
Ind Ital Conserve — Industria Italiana delle Conserve
Ind Ital Conserve Aliment — Industria Italiana delle Conserve Alimentari
Ind Ital Elettrotec — Industria Italiana Elettrotecnica
Ind Ital Elettrotec & Elettron — Industria Italiana Elettrotecnica ed Elettronica
Ind Ital Freddo — Industria Italiana del Freddo
Ind Ital Laterizi — Industria Italiana dei Laterizi
Indium Phosphide Relat Mater Int Conf — Indium Phosphide and Related Materials. International Conference
Indium Phosphide Relat Mater Process Technol Devices — Indium Phosphide and Related Materials. Processing, Technology, and Devices
Individ Onsite Wastewater Syst — Individual Onsite Wastewater Systems
Indiv Inst — Individual Instruction
Indiv Psych — Individual Psychologist
Ind J Ad Ed — Indian Journal of Adult Education
Ind J Adult Ed — Indian Journal of Adult Education
Ind J Agr Econ — Indian Journal of Agricultural Economics
Ind J Agric Chem — Indian Journal of Agricultural Chemistry
Ind J Agric Econ — Indian Journal of Agricultural Economics
Ind J Agric Sci — Indian Journal of Agricultural Science
Ind J Agric Vet Educ — Indian Journal of Agricultural and Veterinary Education
Ind J Agri Econ — Indian Journal of Agricultural Economics
Ind J Agri Sci — Indian Journal of Agricultural Science
Ind J Ag Sci — Indian Journal of Agricultural Science
Ind J Anesth — Indian Journal of Anaesthesia
Ind J Anim Sci — Indian Journal of Animal Sciences
Ind J Chest Dis — Indian Journal of Chest Disease
Ind J Commer — Indian Journal of Commerce
Ind J Econ — Indian Journal of Economics

Ind J Ent — Indian Journal of Entomology
Ind Jew Per — Index to Jewish Periodicals
Ind J Forest — Indian Journal of Forestry
Ind J Indus Rel — Indian Journal of Industrial Relations
Ind J Industr Relat — Indian Journal of Industrial Relations
Ind J Int L — Indian Journal of International Law
Ind J Int Law — Indian Journal of International Law
Ind J Med Res — Indian Journal of Medical Research
Ind J Occup Hlth — Indian Journal of Occupational Health
Ind J Otol — Indian Journal of Otolaryngology
Ind J Para — Indian Journal of Parasitology
Ind J Ped — Indian Journal of Pediatrics
Ind J Phys — Indian Journal of Physics
Ind J Polit — Indian Journal of Politics
Ind J Polit Sci — Indian Journal of Political Science
Ind J Pol Sci — Indian Journal of Political Science
Ind J Power Riv Val Dev — Indian Journal of Power and River Valley Development
Ind J Psych — Indian Journal of Psychiatry
Ind J Pub Health — Indian Journal of Public Health
Ind J Publ Adm — Indian Journal of Public Administration
Ind J Reg Sci — Indian Journal of Regional Science
Ind J Soc Res — Indian Journal of Social Research
Ind J Soc Wk — Indian Journal of Social Work
Ind J Stat — Indian Journal of Statistics
IndJT — Indian Journal of Theology
Ind J Th — Indian Journal of Theology
Ind J Trop Agri — Indian Journal of Tropical Agriculture
Ind J Vet Med — Indian Journal of Veterinary Medicine
Ind J Vet Sci — Indian Journal of Veterinary Science
Ind J Vet Sci An Hus — Indian Journal of Veterinary Science and Animal Husbandry
Ind L — Indian Literature
INDLA — Industrial Laboratory
Ind Lab — Industrial Laboratories
Ind Lab — Industrial Laboratory
Ind Lab Diagn Mater — Industrial Laboratory (Diagnostics of Materials)
Ind Lab J — Indian Labour Journal
Ind Labor Relat Rev — Industrial and Labor Relations Review
Ind Lab Rel — Industrial and Labor Relations Review
Ind Lab Rel Rep — Industrial and Labor Relations Report
Ind Lab (US) — Industrial Laboratory (United States)
Ind Lab (USSR) — Industrial Laboratory (USSR)
Ind Lackier-Betr — Industrie Lackier-Betrieb
Ind Lackier-Betrb — Industrie Lackier-Betrieb
Ind Latt Zootee — Industria Lattiera e Zooteenia
Ind Law J — Industrial Law Journal
Ind Law Jour — Indiana Law Journal
Ind Leche — Industria Lechera
Ind Left Rev — Indian Left Review
Ind Legal F — Indiana Legal Forum
Ind Leg Per — Index to Legal Periodicals
Ind Lemnului — Industria Lemnului
Ind Lemnului Celul Hirtiei — Industria Lemnului Celulozei si Hirtiei
Ind LH — Indian Law Herald
Ind Lib — Indian Librarian
Ind Lib Assoc Bul — Indian Library Association Bulletin
Ind Ling — Indian Linguistics
Ind Linguist — Indian Linguistics
IndLit — Indian Literature
Ind Lit Amer Indian — Index to Literature on the American Indian
Ind Lit Dent — Indice de la Literatura Dental en Castellano
Ind Little Mag — Index to Little Magazines
Ind L J — Indiana Law Journal
Ind L Mag — Indian Law Magazine
Ind LQ — Indian Law Quarterly
Ind LR — Indiana Law Review
Ind LR — Indian Law Review
Ind LR — Industrial Law Review
Ind L Rev — Indiana Law Review
Ind LT — Indian Law Times
Ind Lubr & Technol — Industrial Lubrication and Technology
Ind Lubric — Industrial Lubrication
Ind Lubric Tribology — Industrial Lubrication and Tribology
Ind Lubr Tribol — Industrial Lubrication and Tribology
Ind M — Indiana Magazine of History
Ind Mach — Industrial Machinery
Ind Mag Hist — Indiana Magazine of History
Ind Main Pl Op — Industrial Maintenance and Plant Operation
Ind Manage — Industrial Management
Ind Manage and Data Syst — Industrial Management and Data Systems
Ind Management — Industrial Management
Ind Management (London) — Industrial Management (London)
Ind Management R — Industrial Management Review
Ind Mark — Industrial Marketing [*Later, Business Marketing*]
Ind Market — Industrial Marketing [*Later, Business Marketing*]
Ind Market Dig — Industrial Marketing Digest
Ind Mark Manage — Industrial Marketing Management
Ind Math — Industrial Mathematics
Ind Med — Index Medicus
Ind Med — Industrial Medicine
Ind Med — Industrial Medicine and Surgery
Ind Med & Surg — Industrial Medicine and Surgery
Ind Med Esp — Indice Medico Espanol
Ind Med For — Indian Medical Forum
Ind Med Gaz — Indian Medical Gazette

Ind Med J — Indian Medical Journal
Ind Med Rec — Indian Medical Record
Ind Med Res Mem — Indian Medical Research Memoirs
Ind Med Serv — Indian Medical Service
Ind Med Serv N — Indian Medical Service News
Ind Med Surg — Industrial Medicine and Surgery
Ind Med Wld — Indian Medical World
Ind Mgt — Industrial Management
Ind Mgt & Data Syst — Industrial Management and Data Systems
Ind Mgt R — Industrial Management Review
Ind Miljoe — Industri og Miljoe
Ind Min — Industrial Minerals
Ind Miner — Industrial Minerals
Ind Miner — Industrie Minerale
Ind Miner (London) — Industrial Minerals (London)
Ind Miner Mine — Industrie Minerale. Mine
Ind Miner Mineralurgie — Industrie Minerale. Mineralurgie
Ind Miner Mines Carr — Industrie Minerale. Mines et Carrieres
Ind Miner Mines Carr Tech — Industrie Minerale. Mines et Carrieres. Les Techniques
Ind Miner (Paris) — Industrie Minerale (Paris)
Ind Miner Rocks — Industrial Minerals and Rocks
Ind Miner Ser Mineralurgie — Industrie Minerale. Serie Mineralurgie
Ind Miner Ser Tech — Industrie Minerale. Serie Techniques
Ind Miner (St Etienne) — Industrie Minerale (St. Etienne)
Ind Miner (St Etienne Fr) — Industrie Minerale (St. Etienne, France)
Ind Miner Suppl Techniques (St Etienne) — Industrie Minerale. Supplement. Les Techniques (St. Etienne)
Ind Miner Tech — Industrie Minerale. Serie Techniques
Ind Min J — Indian Mining Journal
Ind Min (Madrid) — Industria Minera (Madrid)
Ind Min Quebec — Industrie Miniere du Quebec
Ind Min (Rome) — Industria Mineraria (Rome)
Ind Mkt — Industrial Marketing [*Later, Business Marketing*]
Ind Mktg — Industrial Marketing [*Later, Business Marketing*]
Ind Mkt Man — Industrial Marketing Management
Ind Mkt Mgt — Industrial Marketing Management
Ind Mktng — Industrial Marketing [*Later, Business Marketing*]
Ind Mus Bull — Indian Museum Bulletin
Ind Mus Not — Indian Museum Notes
Indn — Indiana Social Studies Quarterly
INDN — Indian News
Ind Natl Sci Acad Math Table — Indian National Science Academy. Mathematical Tables
Indn Notes — Indian Notes
Indn Notes Monogr — Indian Notes and Monographs
Ind Norte Port — Industria do Norte de Portugal
Ind Notes — Indian Notes
Ind NZ Per — Index to New Zealand Periodicals
Indo — Indonesia
Indo-As — Indo-Asia
Indo Asian Cult — Indo-Asian Culture
Ind Obst- Gemueseverwert — Industrial Obst- und Gemueseverwertung
Indochina — Indochina Chronicle
Ind Odont — Index Odontologicus
Indogerm Etymol Woert — Indogermanisches Etymologisches Woerterbuch
Indogerm F — Indogermanische Forschungen
Indo Germ Forsch — Indogermanische Forschungen
Indogerm Forschgg — Indogermanische Forschungen
Indogerm Jb — Indogermanisches Jahrbuch
Indog Forsch — Indogermanische Forschungen
Ind Oggi — Industria Oggi
Indo Iran J — Indo-Iranian Journal
Indo J Geog — Indonesian Journal of Geography
Ind Olii Miner Grassi — Industria degli Olii Minerali i dei Grassi
Indol Tagung — Indologen-Tagung
Indon Dir Higher Educ Res J — Indonesia. Directorate of Higher Education. Research Journal
Indones Abstr — Indonesian Abstracts
Indones Circ — Indonesia Circle
Indones Dev News — Indonesia Development News
Indones Dir Geol Publ Chusus — Indonesia. Direktorat Geologi. Publikasi Chusus
Indones Dir Geol Publ Tek Ser Geofis — Indonesia. Direktorat Geologi. Publikasi Teknik. Seri Geofisika
Indones Dir Geol Publ Tek Ser Geol Ekon — Indonesia. Direktorat Geologi. Publikasi Teknik. Serie Geologi Ekonomi
Indones Dir Geol Publ Tek Ser Paleontol — Indonesia. Direktorat Geologi. Publikasi Teknik. Seri Paleontologi
Indonesia Circ — Indonesia Circle
Indonesia New — Indonesia. News and Views
Indonesian J G — Indonesian Journal of Geography
Indonesia Tour Stat — Indonesia Tourist Statistics
Indones Inst Mar Res Oceanogr Cruise Rep — Indonesian Institute of Marine Research. Oceanographical Cruise Report
Indones J Crop Sci — Indonesian Journal of Crop Science
Indones J Geogr — Indonesian Journal of Geography
Indones J Pharm — Indonesian Journal of Pharmacy
Indones Pet Assoc Annu Conv Proc — Indonesian Petroleum Association. Annual Convention. Proceedings
Indones Quart — Indonesian Quarterly
Indoor Environ — Indoor + Built Environment
Indoor Environ — Indoor Environment
Indo-Pac Fish Counc Occas Pap — Indo-Pacific Fisheries Council. Occasional Papers
Indo-Pac Fish Counc Proc — Indo-Pacific Fisheries Council. Proceedings

Indo-Pac Fish Counc Reg Stud — Indo-Pacific Fisheries Council. Regional Studies
Indo-Pac Fish Counc Spec Publ — Indo-Pacific Fisheries Council. Special Publications
Indo Pacific Prehist Assoc Bull — Indo-Pacific Prehistory Association Bulletin
Indo-Pac Mollusca — Indo-Pacific Mollusca
Indo Q — Indonesian Quarterly
Ind Org — Industrielle Organisation
Ind Org Hlth — Industrial Organisation and Health
Indo Soviet Symp Cryst Growth — Indo-Soviet Symposium on Crystal Growth
Indo Sov Symp Organomet Chem — Indo-Soviet Symposium on Organometallic Chemistry
Ind Parf — Industrie de la Parfumerie
Ind Parf Cosm — Industries de la Parfumerie et de la Cosmetique
Ind Parfum Cosmet — Industries de la Parfumerie et de la Cosmetique
Ind Ped — Indian Pediatrics
Ind Per Art Relat Law — Index to Periodical Articles Related to Law
Ind Per Blacks — Index to Periodical Articles by and about Blacks
Ind Per Lit — Indian Periodical Literature
Ind Per Negroes — Index to Periodical Articles by and about Negroes [*Later, Index to Periodical Articles by and about Blacks*]
Ind Pet — Industrie du Petrole
Ind Pet Energ Ind — Industrie du Petrole et Energies Industrielles
Ind Pet Eur Gaz Chim — Industrie du Petrole en Europe. Gaz-Chimie
Ind Pet Gaz Chim — Industrie du Petrole. Gaz-Chimie
Ind Pet Monde Gaz-Chim — Industrie du Petrole dans le Monde. Gaz-Chimie
Ind Petr — Industrie du Petrole
Ind Petrol Gaz-Chim — Industrie du Petrole. Gaz-Chimie
Ind Pharm — Indian Pharmacist
Ind Pharmacol — Industrial Pharmacology
Ind Philippines — Industrial Philippines
Ind Philo A — Indian Philosophical Annual
Ind Phot — Industrial Photography
Ind Photogr — Industrial Photography
Ind Phyc — Indian Physician
Ind Phys — Indian Physiologist
Ind Phys — Industrial Physicist
Ind Phys Math J — Indian Physico-Mathematical Journal
Ind Phyto — Indian Phytopathology
Ind Plann Dev — Industrial Planning and Development
Ind Plast — Industrie des Plastiques
Ind Plast Mod — Industrie des Plastiques Modernes
Ind Plast Mod Elastomeres — Industrie des Plastiques Modernes et Elastomeres [*Later, Plastiques Modernes et Elastomeres*]
Ind Plast (Paris) — Industries des Plastiques (Paris)
Ind Police N — Indiana Police News
Ind Polit Sci R — Indian Political Science Review
Ind Pol J — Indian Police Journal
Ind Pol Sci R — Indian Political Science Review
Ind Pol Sci Rev — Indian Political Science Review
Ind Port — Industria Portuguesa
Ind Power — Industry and Power
Ind Power Mass Prod — Industrial Power and Mass Production
Ind Power Steam Heat Light Air Fuel Econ — Industrial Power, Steam Heat, Light, and Air and the Fuel Economist
Ind Probl — Indagini e Problemi
Ind Process Des Pollut Control — Industrial Process Design for Pollution Control. Proceedings. Workshop
Ind Process Heat — Industrial and Process Heating
Ind Prod Eng — Industrial and Production Engineering
Ind Prod Mag — Industrial Products Magazine
Ind Prog Dev — Industrial Progress and Development
Ind Progress — Industrial Progress and Development
Ind Progress and Development — Industrial Progress and Development
Ind Prop Q — Industrial Property Quarterly
Ind Prop Quart — Industrial Property Quarterly
Ind Prop Sem — Industrial Property Seminar (Monash University, 1972)
Ind Psychotechn — Industrielle Psychotechnik
Ind Psych R — Indian Psychological Review
Ind Publ Hlth Munic J — Indian Public Health and Municipal Journal
Ind Q — India Quarterly
Ind Q J Int Aff — Indian Quarterly Journal of International Affairs
Ind Quality Control — Industrial Quality Control
Ind Quart — India Quarterly
Ind Quim (Buenos Aires) — Industria y Quimica (Buenos Aires)
Ind R — Indian Review
INDRA — Industrial Diamond Review
Ind Radiogr — Industrial Radiography and Non-Destructive Testing
Ind Radiogr Non Destr Test — Industrial Radiography and Non-Destructive Testing
Ind R & Mining Yrbk — Industrial Review and Mining Year Book
Ind Rare Met — Industrial Rare Metals
INDRBA — Indian Drugs
Ind Reg — Indiana Register
Ind Rel — Industrial Relations
Ind Relat — Industrial Relations
Ind Relations — Industrial Relations
Ind Relations (Berkeley) — Industrial Relations (Berkeley)
Ind Relations (Quebec) — Industrial Relations (Quebec)
Ind Relat J S Afr — Industrial Relations Journal of South Africa
Ind Relat Rev Rep — Industrial Relations Review and Report
Ind Rel Briefing — Industrial Relations Briefing
Ind Rel J — Industrial Relations Journal
Ind Rel J Econ & Soc — Industrial Relations: Journal of Economy and Society
Ind Rel Law J — Industrial Relations Law Journal
Ind Rel LJ — Industrial Relations Law Journal
Ind Rel News — Industrial Relations News

Ind Rel Rev Rep — Industrial Relations Review and Report
Ind Rel Soc Proc — Industrial Relations Society. Proceedings of Convention
Ind Rept Chemicals — Industry Report. Chemicals
Ind Rept Containers Pkg — Industry Report. Containers and Packaging
Ind Rept Pulp Pbd — Industry Report. Pulp, Paper, and Board
Ind Res — Industrial Research
Ind Res — Industrial Research and Development
Ind Res & Devel — Industrial Research and Development
Ind Res/Dev — Industrial Research and Development
Ind Res (Lond) — Industrial Research (London)
Ind Res News — Industrial Research News
Ind Res News CSIRO — Industrial Research News. Commonwealth Scientific and Industrial Research Organisation
Ind Review Jap — Industrial Review of Japan
Ind Robot — Industrial Robot
Ind Rom — Index Romanus
Ind Rub J — India Rubber Journal
Ind Rub Wd — India Rubber World
IndS — Independent Shavian
Ind S — Indian Studies: Past and Present
Ind S — Staatsblad van Indonesie
Ind Saccarif Ital — Industria Saccarifera Italiana
Ind Sacc Ital — Industria Saccarifera Italiana
Ind Saf — Industrial Safety
Ind Saf Chron — Industrial Safety Chronicle
Ind Saf Data File — Industrial Safety Data File
Ind Safety — Industrial Safety
Ind Saf Hlth Bull — Industrial Safety and Health Bulletin
Ind Saf Surv — Industrial Safety Survey
Ind SA Per — Index to South African Periodicals
Ind Sapon Olii Stearin Profum — Industria Saponiera e degli Olii. Steariniera. Profumiera
Ind Sch Bull — Independent School Bulletin
Ind Sci Abstr — Indian Science Abstracts
Ind Sci Agric — Indian Scientific Agriculturist
Ind Sci Eng — Industrial Science and Engineering
Ind Sci Instrum — Industrial and Scientific Instruments
Ind Sci Rev — Index to Scientific Reviews
Ind Sci Technol — Industrial Science and Technology
Ind Secera — Industrija Secera
Ind Sel Per — Index to Selected Periodicals
Inds et Trav Outremer — Industries et Travaux d'Outre-Mer
Inds Habillement — Industries de l'Habillement
Ind Short-Term Trends — Industrial Short-Term Trends
Ind Sid Eur — Industrie Siderurgique en Europe
Ind Silic — Industrie dei Silicati
Ind Slav St — Indiana Slavic Studies
Ind Soap J — Indian Soap Journal
Ind Soc — Indian Sociologist
Ind Soc B — Indian Sociological Bulletin
Ind Soc Rev — Indian Sociological Review
Ind Spec — Industrial Specification
Ind St — Indische Studien
Ind Stand — Industrial Standardization
Ind Stand Commer Stand Mon — Industrial Standardization and Commercial Standards. Monthly
Ind State Rlwys Mag — Indian State Railways Magazine
Ind Stbl — Staatsblad van Nederlandsch Indie
Ind St M Assn J — Indiana State Medical Association. Journal
Ind Stud — Indian Studies
Ind Sup — Industrial Supervisor
INDTA — Industries et Techniques
Ind Teacher — Indiana Teacher
Ind Tech — Industries et Techniques
Ind Technol Res Inst Chungnam Univ — Industrial Technology Research Institute. Chungnam University
Ind Tek — Industriell Teknik
Ind Text — Industrie Textile
Ind Text Bucharest — Industria Textila (Bucharest)
Ind Text Eur — Industrie Textile en Europe
Ind Textil — Industrie Textile
Ind Therm — Industries Thermiques
Ind Therm Aerauliques — Industries Thermiques et Aerauliques
Ind Today — Industry Today
Ind Trav O-Mer — Industries et Travaux d'Outre-Mer
Ind TvhR — Indisch Tijdschrift van het Recht
INDUA — Industria
Induct Flowering — Induction of Flowering. Some Case Histories
Ind Umwelt — Industrie und Umwelt
Ind Umwelt Massnahmen Plan Umweltschutz Oesterr Vortragsr — Industrie und Umwelt. Massnahmen und Planungen zum Umweltschutz in Oesterreich. Vortragsreihen
Ind Un Art B — Indiana University. Art Museum. Bulletin
Ind Univ Adv Mater Conf 2 Proc Conf — Industry-University Advanced Materials Conference 2. Proceedings. Conference
Ind Univ Coop Chem Program — Industry-University Cooperative Chemistry Program
Ind Univ Extension Division Bull — Indiana University. Extension Division Bulletin
Ind Univ Sch Ed B — Indiana University. School of Education. Bulletin
Indus and Eng Chemistry — Industrial and Engineering Chemistry
Indus & Lab Rel F — Industrial and Labor Relations Forum
Indus & Lab Rel Rev — Industrial and Labor Relations Review
Indus Diamond Rev — Industrial Diamond Review
Indus Eng — Industrial Engineering

Indus Fish Prod Mark Rev & Outl — Industrial Fishery Products Market Review and Outlook
Indus Free China — Industry of Free China
Ind US Gov Per — Index to United States Government Periodicals
Indus Libric Trib — Industrial Lubrication and Tribology
Indus LJ — Industrial Law Journal
Indus L Rev — Industrial Law Review
Indus Minerals — Industrial Minerals
Ind Usoara — Industria Usoara
Ind Usoara Piel — Industria Usoara Pielarie
Ind Usoara Text Tricotaje Confectii Text — Industria Usoara. Textile, Tricotaje, Confectii Textile
Indus Rel — Industrial Relations
Indus Rel Guide P-H — Industrial Relations Guide. Prentice-Hall
Indus Rel LJ — Industrial Relations Law Journal
Indus Sit Ind — Industrial Situation in India
Indust A — Industrial Arts
Indust & Engin Chem — Industrial and Engineering Chemistry
Indust & L Rel Rev — Industrial and Labor Relations Review
Indust Archaeol Rev — Industrial Archaeology Review
Indust Bull — Industrial Bulletin
Indust Corrosion — Industrial Corrosion
Indust Des — Industrial Design
Indust Engineering — Industrial Engineering
Indust Engr — Industrial Engineer
Indust Forum — Industrial Forum
Indust It Cemento — Industria Italiana del Cemento
Indust Labour Information — Industrial and Labour Information
Indust Law Rev — Industrial Law Review
Indust LJ — Industrial Law Journal
Indust L Rev — Industrial Law Review
Indust L Rev Q — Industrial Law Review Quarterly
Indust L Soc Bull — Bulletin. Industrial Law Society
Indust Man — Industrial Management
Indust Management — Industrial Management
Indust Math — Industrial Mathematics
Indust Med — Industrial Medicine and Surgery
Indust Progress — Industrial Progress and Development
Indust Prop Law Ann — Industrial Property Law Annual
Indust Prop Q — Industrial Property Quarterly
Indust Prop'y Yb — Industrial Property Yearbook
Indust Psychol — Industrial Psychology
Indust Rel LJ — Industrial Relations Law Journal
Industr Engng Chem (Int Ed) — Industrial and Engineering Chemistry (International Edition)
Industr Franc Coton Fibres Alliees — Industrie Francaise du Coton et des Fibres Alliees
Industr Gerontol — Industrial Gerontology
Industrial & Labor Rel Rev — Industrial and Labor Relations Review
Industrial et Productiv — Industrialisation et Productivite
Industrial L Rev Q — Industrial Law Review Quarterly
Industrial Phot — Industrial Photography
Industrieabwasser Vermeiden Vermindern Behandeln Symp — Industrieabwasser Vermeiden, Vermindern, Behandeln. Symposium
Industrie Agr — Industrie Agrarie
Industrie Aliment — Industrie Alimentari
Industrie Anz — Industrie-Anzeiger
Industr Lab Relat R — Industrial and Labor Relations Review
Industr Lemn — Industria Lemnului
Industr Petrole — Industrie du Petrole
Industr Progr — Industrial Progress and Development
Industr Prop'y Q — Industrial Property Quarterly
Industr Relat — Industrial Relations
Industr Relat Berkeley — Industrial Relations (Berkeley)
Industr Relat Calcutta — Industrial Relations (Calcutta)
Industr Relat J — Industrial Relations Journal
Industr Res — Industrial Research/Kung Yeh Chung Hsin
Industr Res Study Timb Res Developm Ass — Industrial Research Study. Timber Research and Development Association
Industr Trav O-Mer — Industries et Travaux d'Outre-Mer
Industry Free China — Industry of Free China
Indus Week — Industry Week
Ind Util Sugar Mill By-Prod — Industrial Utilisation of Sugar and Mill By-Products
Ind Veg Turf Pest Manage — Industrial Vegetation Turf and Pest Management
Ind Vernice — Industria della Vernice
Ind Vet — Index Veterinarius
Ind Vet J — Indian Veterinary Journal
Ind Vic — Industrial Victoria
Ind W — Industry Week
Ind Waste Adv Water Solid Waste Conf Proc — Industrial Waste. Advanced Water and Solid Waste Conference. Proceedings
Ind Waste Conf Proc — Industrial Waste Conference Proceedings
Ind Wastes — Industrial Wastes
Ind Wastes (Chicago) — Industrial Wastes (Chicago)
Ind Water Eng — Industrial Water Engineering
Ind Water Treat — Industrial Water Treatment
Ind Water Wastes — Industrial Water and Wastes
Ind Week — Industry Week
Ind Weld — Industry and Welding
Ind Welf — Indiana Welfare
Ind Woman — Independent Woman
Ind Wrkr — Industrial Worker
Ind YBIA — Indian Yearbook of International Affairs
Ind Yb Int Aff — Indian Yearbook of International Affairs
INE — Industrieel Eigendom

INEA — NEA [National Education Association] Today
INED — Indian-Ed. University of Alberta
INED/P — Population. Institut National d'Etudes Demographiques
INeg — Index to Periodical Articles by and about Negroes [Later, Index to PeriodicalArticles by and about Blacks]
INEN — Indian Education Newsletter
INENE6 — Invertebrate Endocrinology
INEP — Index to New England Periodicals
Inequal Educ — Inequality in Education
INER — International Environment Reporter
INEUB — Izvestiya Nauchno-Issledovatel'skogo Instituta Nefte- i Uglekhimicheskogo Sinteza pri Irkutskom Universitete
InF — Indogermanische Forschungen
Inf — Infinity Science Fiction
INF — Information and Management
INF — Information Services and Use
Inf — Information ueber Steuer und Wirtschaft
InF — Inozemna Filologiya
INF — Interface. Data Processing Management
Inf A — Informacion Arqueologica
INFAA2 — Indian Farming
INFAC — Interfaces
Inf Aerauliques Therm — Informations Aerauliques et Thermiques
Inf Age — Information Age
Inf Age Perspect — Information Age in Perspective
Inf Agric — Informacion Agricola
Inf Agric Chem — Information on Agricultural Chemicals
Inf Agric (Paris) — Information Agricole (Paris)
Inf Agropecu Empresa Pesqui Agropecu Minas Gerais — Informe Agropecuario [Agricultural Report]. Empresa de Pesquisa Agropecuaria de Minas Gerais
Infan Adol Caracas — Infancia y Adolescencia (Caracas)
Inf and Control — Information and Control
Inf & Doc — Information et Documentation
Inf & Gestion — Informatique et Gestion
Inf and Manage — Information and Management
Inf and Referral J Alliance Inf Referral Syst — Information and Referral. Journal of the Alliance of Information and Referral Systems
Inf Anorm — Infanzia Anormale
Infant Behav & Dev — Infant Behavior and Development
Infant Nutr Dev Dis Symp — Infant Nutrition, Development, and Disease. Symposium
Inf Antrop — Informes Antropologicos
Infantry — Infantry Magazine
Infantry Jour — Infantry Journal. United States Infantry Association
Inf Arqu — Informacion Arqueologica
Inf Astr Soc Astr Bordeaux — Information Astronomique. Societe Astronomique de Bordeaux
Inf Battelle Frankfurt — Information Battelle Frankfurt
Inf Bienenw — Information Bienenwirtschaft
Inf Bienenzucht — Information Bienenzucht
Inf Bild Wiss — Informationen Bildung Wissenschaft
Infbl — Informatieblad van het Economisch en Sociaal Instituut voor deMiddenstand
InfBl — Informationsblatt fuer die Gemeinden in den Niederdeutschen Lutherischen Landeskirchen
Inf Bot Ital — Informatore Botanico Italiano
Inf B Scient Res Coun — Information. Bulletin. Scientific Research Council
Inf Bull AGARD Struct Mater Panel — Information Bulletin. Advisory Group for Aeronautical Research and Development. Structures and Materials Panel
Inf Bull Alumin Dev Ass — Information Bulletin of the Aluminium Development Association
Inf Bull: Append Provis Nomencl Symb Terminol Conv (IUPAC) — Information Bulletin: Appendices on Provisional Nomenclature, Symbols, Terminology, and Conventions (International Union of Pure and Applied Chemistry)
Inf Bull Append Provis Nomencl Symb Units Stand (IUPAC) — Information Bulletin: Appendices on Provisional Nomenclature, Symbols, Units, and Standards (International Union of Pure and Applied Chemistry)
Inf Bull Append Prov Nomencl Symb Terminol Conv (IUPAC) — Information Bulletin: Appendices on Provisional Nomenclature, Symbols, Terminology, and Conventions (International Union of Pure and Applied Chemistry)
Inf Bull Ass Isl Mar Labs — Information Bulletin. Association of Island Marine Laboratories
Inf Bull Ass Plann Reg Reconstr — Information Bulletin of the Association for Planning and Regional Reconstruction
Inf Bull Bitum Coal Res — Information Bulletin. Bituminous Coal Research
Inf Bull Coop Ext NY St Coll Agric Life Sci — Information Bulletin. Cooperative Extension. New York State College of Agriculture and Life Sciences
Inf Bull Crane Pckg — Information Bulletin. Crane Packing Ltd
Inf Bull Czech Archaeol Inst — Information Bulletin of the Czechoslovak Archaeological Institute
Inf Bull Div Anim Prodn CSIRO — Information Bulletin. Division of Animal Production. Commonwealth Scientific and Industrial Research Organisation
Inf Bull Gen Fish Coun Mediterr — Information Bulletin. General Fisheries Council for the Mediterranean
Inf Bull Hung Natn FAO Comm — Information Bulletin of the Hungarian National F.A.O. Committee
Inf Bull Int Assoc Stud Cult Cent Asia — Information Bulletin of the International Association for the Study of the Cultures of Central Asia
Inf Bull Int Cent Inf Antibiot — Information Bulletin. International Center of Information on Antibiotics
Inf Bull Inter Am Inst Agric Sci — Information Bulletin. Inter-American Institute of Agricultural Sciences
Inf Bull Int Scient Radio Un — Information Bulletin of the International Scientific Radio Union
Inf Bull Int Scient Rad Un — Information Bulletin. International Scientific Radio Union

Inf Bull Int Un Pure Appl Chem — Information Bulletin. International Union of Pure and Applied Chemistry
Inf Bull Isot Generators — Information Bulletin on Isotopic Generators
Inf Bull ISWA (Int Solid Wastes Public Clean Assoc) — Information Bulletin. ISWA (International Solid Wastes Public Cleansing Association)
Inf Bull IUPAC Append Provis Nomencl Symb Units Stand — Information Bulletin. International Union of Pure and Applied Chemistry. Appendices on Provisional Nomenclature, Symbols, Units, and Standards
Inf Bull IUPAC Tech Rep — Information Bulletin. International Union of Pure and Applied Chemistry. Technical Reports
Inf Bull Libr Autom Syst Inf Exch — Information Bulletin. Library Automated Systems Information Exchange
Inf Bull Mysore St Dep Agric — Information Bulletin. Mysore State Department of Agriculture
Inf Bull Nigerian Forests — Information Bulletin. Nigerian Forests
Inf Bull NY State Coll Agric Coop Ext Serv — Information Bulletin. New York State College of Agriculture. Cooperative Extension Service
Inf Bull NY St Coll Agric — Information Bulletin. New York State College of Agriculture
Inf Bull Pacif Sci Ass — Information Bulletin. Pacific Science Association
Inf Bull Planktol Japan — Information Bulletin on Planktology in Japan
Inf Bull Prod Dep Natn Coal Bd — Information Bulletin. Production Department. National Coal Board
Inf Bull Refrig Res Fdn — Information Bulletin. Refrigeration Research Foundation
Inf Bull Scient Res Comm Jamaica — Information Bulletin of the Scientific Research Committee. Jamaica
Inf Bull SE Asia Sci Coop Off — Information Bulletin. South East Asia Science Cooperation Office. United National Educational, Scientific, and Cultural Organization
Inf Bull Statist Res Bur Dep Ment Hyg Calif — Information Bulletin. Statistical Research Bureau. Department of Mental Hygiene. California
Inf Bull Timb Dev Ass — Information Bulletin. Timber Development Association
Inf Bull Variable Stars — Information Bulletin on Variable Stars
Inf Bull Wrought It Alloys Dev Ass — Information Bulletin of the Wrought Light Alloys Development Association
Inf Byull Inst Geol Arkt — Informatsionnyi Byulleten' Instituta Geologii Arktiki
Inf Byull Inst Geol Arktiki — Informatsionnyi Byulleten' Instituta Geologii Arktiki
Inf Byull Mezhdun Assot Izecheniyu Kult Tsent Azii — Informationnyy Byulleten' Mezhdunarodnoy Assotsiatsii po Izucheniyu Kul'tur Tsentral'noy Azii
Inf Byull Mezhved Geofiz Kom Prezidiume Akad Nauk Ukr SSR — Informatsionnyi Byulleten' Mezhvedomstvennyi Geofizicheskii Komitet pri Prezidiume Akademii Nauk Ukrainskoi SSR
Inf Byull Mikroelem Sib — Informatsionnyi Byulleten' Mikroelementy Sibirii
Inf Byull Mosk Nauchno Issled Inst Sanit Gig — Informatsionnyi Byulleten' Moskovskogo Nauchno Issledovatel'skogo Instituta Sanitarii i Gigieny
Inf Byull Nauchn Sov Probl Radiobiol Akad Nauk SSSR — Informatsionnyi Byulleten' Nauchnyi Sovet po Problemam Radiobiologii Akademiya Nauk SSSR
Inf Byull Orgenergostroi — Informatsionnyi Byulleten Orgenergostroi
Inf Byull Sib Inst Fiziol Biokhim Rast — Informatsionnyi Byulleten' Sibirskii Institut Fiziologii i Biokhimii Rastenii
Inf Byull Sov Antarkt Eksped — Informatsionnyi Byulleten' Sovetskoi Antarkticheskoi Ekspeditsii
Inf Byull Vses Inst Proekt Organ Energ Stroit — Informatsionnyi Byulleten' Vsesoyuznyi Institut po Proektirovaniyu OrganizatsiiEnergeticheskogo Stroitel'stva
Inf Byull Vses Nauchno Issled Inst Mash Promsti Stroit Mater — Informatsionnyi Byulleten' Vsesoyuznyi Nauchno Issledovatel'skii Institut po Mashinam dlya Promyshlennosti Stroitel'nykh Materialov
Inf C — Information and Control
INFCA — Informations-Chimie
Inf Card Clemson Univ Coop Ext Serv — Information Card. Clemson University. Cooperative Extension Service
Inf Cath Int — Informations Catholiques Internationales
Inf Cent Chem Ind Bull — Information Centre on the Chemical Industry. Bulletin
Inf Chem Pharmacol Pat — Information in Chemistry, Pharmacology, and Patents
Inf Chil Nitrate Agric Serv — Information. Chilean Nitrate Agricultural Service
Inf-Chim — Informations-Chimie
Inf Cient — Informaciones Cientificas
Inf Circ Air Hyg Fdn Am — Information Circular. Air Hygiene Foundation of America
Inf Circ Am Refract Inst — Information Circular. American Refractories Institute
Inf Circ Arkans Geol Comm — Information Circular. Arkansas Geological Commission
Inf Circ Ark Geol Conserv Commn — Information Circular. Arkansas Geological and Conservation Commission
Inf Circ Ark Geol Surv — Information Circular. Arkansas Geological Survey
Inf Circ BHP Central Res Lab — Information Circular. BHP [*Broken Hill Proprietary Ltd.*] Central ResearchLaboratories
Inf Circ Br Whiting Fed Res Coun — Information Circular. British Whiting Federation Research Council
Inf Circ Bur Mines Geosci (Philipp) — Information Circular. Bureau of Mines and Geo-Sciences (Philippines)
Inf Circ Calif St Div Mines — Information Circular. California State Division of Mines
Inf Circ Def Stand Labs Maribyrnong — Information Circular. Defence Standards Laboratories. Maribyrnong
Inf Circ Div Fish Oceanogr CSIRO — Information Circular. Division of Fisheries and Oceanography. Commonwealth Scientific and Industrial Research Organisation
Inf Circ Div Geol Surv Ohio — Information Circular. Division of Geological Survey. Ohio
Inf Circ Div Geol Tenn — Information Circular. Division of Geology. Department of Conservation. Tennessee
Inf Circ Div Miner Resour Va — Information Circular. Division of Mineral Resources. Virginia

Inf Circ Econ Geol Res Unit Univ Witwaters — Information Circular. Economic Geology Research Unit. University of the Witwatersrand
Inf Circ Forest Prod Lab Ore St Coll — Information Circular. Forest Products Laboratory. Oregon State College
Inf Circ Forest Prod Res Cent Ore — Information Circular. Forest Products Research Center. Oregon
Inf Circ Forest Prod Res Ore — Information Circular. Forest Products Research. Oregon Forest Research Center
Inf Circ Ga Div Mines Min Geol — Information Circular. Georgia Division of Mines, Mining, and Geology
Inf Circ GA Geol Water Resour Div — Information Circular. Georgia Geologic and Water Resources Division
Inf Circ Geol Physiogr Sect Nat Conserv Counc — Information Circular. Geology and Physiography Section. Nature Conservancy Council
Inf Circ Geol Sect Dep Nat Resour Newfoundl — Information Circular. Geological Section. Department of Natural Resources. Newfoundland
Inf Circ Geol Surv Can — Information Circular. Geological Survey. Canada
Inf Circ Heat Vent Res Coun — Information Circular. Heating and Ventilating Research Council
Inf Circ Inst Transpn Traff Engng Univ Calif — Information Circular. Institute of Transportation and Traffic Engineering. University of California
Inf Circ Int Atom Energy Ag — Information Circular. International Atomic Energy Agency
Inf Circ Kentucky Geol Surv — Information Circular. Kentucky Geological Survey
Inf Circ Mines Inf Bur St Coll Wash — Information Circular. Mines Information Bureau. State College of Washington
Inf Circ Minn Geol Surv — Information Circular. Minnesota Geological Survey
Inf Circ Mo Geol Surv — Information Circular. Missouri Geological Survey and Water Resources
Inf Circ Munit Supply Labs Maribyrnong — Information Circular. Munitions Supply Laboratories. Maribyrnong
Inf Circ Newfoundland Labrador Miner Resour Div — Information Circular. Newfoundland and Labrador Mineral Resources Division
Inf Circ Newfoundland Miner Resour Div — Information Circular. Newfoundland Mineral Resources Division
Inf Circ Newfoundl Geol Surv — Information Circular. Newfoundland Geological Survey
Inf Circ Philipp Bur Mines — Information Circular. Philippines Bureau of Mines
Inf Circ Philipp Isl Bur Mines — Information Circular. Philippine Islands Bureau of Mines
Inf Circ South Pac Comm — Information Circular. South Pacific Commission
Inf Circ St Metall Res Lab St Coll Wash — Information Circular. State Metallurgical Research Laboratory. State College of Washington
Inf Circ Tenn Div Geol — Information Circular. Tennessee Division of Geology
Inf Circ Topogr Geol Surv Pa — Information Circular. Topographic and Geologic Survey. Pennsylvania
Inf Circ US Bur Mines — Information Circular. United States Bureau of Mines
Inf Circ Vict Fish Game Dep — Information Circular. Victoria Fisheries and Game Department
Inf Circ Wash St Div Mines Min — Information Circular. Washington State Division of Mines and Mining
Inf Circ Wis Geol Nat Hist Surv — Information Circular. Wisconsin Geological and Natural History Survey
Inf Community Alliance Prog — Information Community. An Alliance for Progress
Inf Constr — Informes de la Construccion
Inf Contr — Information and Control
Inf Control — Information and Control
Inf Cuttings Serv World Min Ind — Information Cuttings Service on World Mining Industry
Inf Decis Technol — Information and Decision Technologies
Inf Dent — Informacion Dental
Inf Dent — Information Dentaire
Inf Digest — Information Digest
Inf Disp — Information Display
Inf Display — Information Display
Inf Doc Sel Teh Nucl — Informare si Documentare Selectiva. Tehnica Nucleara
Inf Dyn — Information Dynamics
INFEA — Ingegneria Ferroviaria
Infec Immun — Infection and Immunity
Inf Econ Inst Econ Agric — Informacoes Economicas. Instituto de Economia Agricola
Inf Econ Policy — Information Economics and Policy
Infect Agents Dis — Infectious Agents and Disease
Infect Cont — Infection Control
Infect Control — Infection Control
Infect Control Dig — Infection Control Digest
Infect Control Hosp Epidemiol — Infection Control and Hospital Epidemiology
Infect Control Rounds — Infection Control Rounds
Infect Control (Thorofare) — Infection Control (Thorofare)
Infect Control Urol Care — Infection Control and Urological Care
Infect Dis Antimicrob Agents — Infectious Diseases and Antimicrobial Agents
Infect Dis Clin North Am — Infectious Disease Clinics of North America
Infect Dis Rev — Infectious Disease Reviews
Infect Dis Ther — Infectious Disease and Therapy
Infect Immun — Infection and Immunity
Infect Inflammation & Immun — Infection, Inflammation, and Immunity
Inf e Diritto — Informatica e Diritto
Infekt Blutgerinnung Haemostase Hamb Symp Blutgerinnung — Infektion, Blutgerinnung und Haemostase. Hamburger Symposion ueber Blutgerinnung
Infektionskr Ihre Erreger — Infektionskrankheiten und Ihre Erreger
Infektionsprophyl Intensivmed Sel Darmdekontam SDD — Infektionsprophylaxe in der Intensivmedizin. Die Selektive Darmdekontamination (SDD)
Infekts Gepatit — Infektsionnyi Gepatit
Infekts Gepatit Resp Mezhved Sb — Infektsionnye Gepatit Respublikanskoi Mezhvedomstvennyi Sbornik

Infekts Kult Rast Mold — Infektsionnye Zabolevaniya Kul'turnykh Rastenii Moldavii
Inf-Elektron — Informacio-Elektronika
Inf Elettron — Informazione Elettronica
Inf Estac Exp Agric La Molina (Lima) — Informe. Estacion Experimental Agricola de "La Molina" (Lima)
Inf-Fachber — Informatik-Fachberichte
Inf Fischwirtsch — Informationen fuer die Fischwirtschaft
Inf Fitopatol — Informatore Fitopatologico
Inf Gas — Information Gas
Inf Geogr — Information Geographique
Inf Geol Sci Terre — Informatique Geologique. Sciences de la Terre
Inf Giovane Entomol — Informatore del Giovane Entomologo
Inf Grasas Aceites — Informaciones sobre Grasas y Aceites
InfH — Information Historique
Inf Hist — Information Historique
Inf Hist A — Information d'Histoire de l'Art
Inf Hotline — Information Hotline
INFIB — Infection and Immunity
INFID — Information fuer die Fischwirtschaft
In Fil — Inozemna Filologiia
INF Inf Tec — INF [*Inventario Nacional Forestal*] Informacion Tecnica
Inf INT — Informativo do INT
Inf Intell Online Newsl — Information Intelligence Online Newsletter
Inf Int Online Newsletter — Information Intelligence Online Newsletter
INF (Inventario Nac For) Nota — INF (Inventario Nacional Forestal) Nota
Inf Invest Agric (Mexico) — Informe de Investigacion Agricola (Mexico)
Inf Invest Cent Invest Tecnol (Pando Urug) — Informe de Investigacion. Centro de Investigaciones Tecnologicas (Pando, Uruguay)
Infirm Aux — Infirmiere Auxiliaire
Infirm Can — Infirmiere Canadienne
Infirm Fr — Infirmiere Francaise
Infirm Haiti — Infirmiere Haitienne
Inf Irradiat Denrees — Informations sur l'Irradiation des Denrees
Inf Ist Beni A Cult Nat Reg Emilia Romagna — Informazioni. Istituto per i Beni Artistici Culturali Naturali della Regione Emilia-Romagna
InfJ — Information Juive
Inf Jou — Information Jouets
Inf Juridica — Informacion Juridica. Comision de Legislacion Extranjera del Ministerio de Justicia
Inf Kerntech Normung — Informationen Kerntechnische Normung
Inflammation Drug Ther Ser — Inflammation and Drug Therapy Series
Inflammation Res — Inflammation Research
Inflammatory Dis Ther — Inflammatory Disease and Therapy
Inflamm Res — Inflammation Research
Inf Leafl Fed Br Aquat Socs — Information Leaflets. Federation of British Aquatic Societies
Inf Leafl Interafr Bur Anim Hlth — Information Leaflets. Interafrican Bureau for Animal Health
Inf Leafl Mar Labs Univ Delaware — Information Leaflets. Marine Laboratories. University of Delaware
Inf Leafl Westingho Brake Signal Co — Information Leaflets. Westinghouse Brake and Signal Company
Inf Lett Asph Ass — Information Letter. Asphalt Association
Inf Liaison Bull Ass Afr Geol Surv — Information and Liaison Bulletin. Association of African Geological Surveys
Inf Litt — Information Litteraire
Infl Ser Gulf St Mar Fish Commn — Informational Series. Gulf States Marine Fisheries Commission
Influence Polym Addit Velocity Temp Fields Symp Proc — Influence of Polymer Additives on Velocity and Temperature Fields. Symposium. Proceedings
Inf Manage — Information and Management
Inf Marmista — Informatore del Marmista
Inf Med — Information Medicale [*Lille*]
Inf Med — Informatore Medico
Inf Med (Genoa) — Informatore Medico (Genoa)
Inf Med (Havana) — Informaciones Medicas (Havana)
Inf Med Roum — Information Medicale Roumaine
Infme Mens Estac Exp Agric La Molina — Informe Mensual. Estacion Experimental Agricola de "La Molina"
Inf Memor Am Silv Prod Res Proj — Information Memoranda. American Silver Producers Research Project
Inf Memor EMI Engng Dev — Information Memorandum. E.M.I. Engineering Development
Inf Mem Soc Ing Peru — Informaciones y Memorias. Sociedad de Ingenieros del Peru
Inf Mens Estac Exp Agric La Molina (Lima) — Informe Mensual. Estacion Experimental Agricola de "La Molina" (Lima)
Infmes Cient Tec Univ Nac Cuyo — Informes Cientificos y Tecnicos. Universidad Nacional de Cuyo
Infme Tec Estac Exp Agropec — Informe Tecnico. Estacion Experimental Regional Agropecuaria [*Pergamino*].Instituto Nacional de Tecnologia Agropecuaria
Infme Tec Minst Asuntos Agrarios (Buenos Aires) — Informe Tecnico (Provincia de Buenos Aires). Ministerio de Asuntos Agrarios. Direccion de Agricultura
INFN — Information North. AINA [*Arctic Institute of North America*] Newsletter
Inf Naturschutz Landschaftspflege Nordwestdeutschl — Informationen zu Naturschutz und Landschaftspflege in Nordwestdeutschland
Inf Nauchno Issled Rab Fil VIN i TI — Informatsiya o Nauchno-Issledovatel'skikh Rabotakh Filial Vsesoyuznogo Instituta Nauchnoi i Tekhnicheskoi Informatsii
Inf Nauchno Issled Rab Inst Tekh Ekon Inf — Informatsiya o Nauchno-Issledovatel'skikh Rabotakh Institut Tekhniko-Ekonomicheskoi Informatsii
Inf News — Information News
Inf News & Sources — Information News and Sources
Inf Nitrate Corp Chile Chil Nitrate Agric Serv — Information. Nitrate Corporation of Chile. Chilean Nitrate Agricultural Service
Inf Nitr Corp Chile — Information. Nitrate Corporation of Chile Limited

Inf Note Natn Res Coun Can — Information Note. National Research Council. Canada
Inf Note Warren Spring Lab — Information Note. Warren Spring Laboratory
Inf Num — Information Numismatique
Info — Information
Info Age — Information Age
Info & Mgmt — Information and Management
Info and Record Managem — Information and Records Management
Info and Referral — Information and Referral
Infobrief Res Technol — Infobrief Research and Technology
Info Chimie — Information Chimie
Info Comer Esp — Informacion Comercial Espanola
Infodoc — Infodoc Aerospace and Military Equipment
Inf Odontostomatol — Informatore Odonto-Stomatologico
Info Econ — Informe Economico
Info Econ Afr — Information Economique Africaine
Info Econ Argentina — Informacion Economica de la Argentina
Info Econ Synd — Informations Economiques et Syndicales
Info et Docs — Informations et Documents
Info Exec — Information Executive
Info Manager — Information Manager
Info Mgmt — Information Management
Info Mgr — Information Manager
INFORBW — Information on Research in Baden-Wuerttemberg
INFOR Canad J Operational Res and Information Processing — INFOR. Canadian Journal of Operational Research and Information Processing
INFOR Canad J Oper Res Inform Process — INFOR. Canadian Journal of Operational Research and Information Processing
Info Rec Mgmt — Information and Records Management
Info Relaciones Mex-Estados Unidos — Informe Relaciones Mexico-Estados Unidos
Info Rep EX Can For Serv Policy Anal Program Dev Branch — Information Report E-X. Canadian Forestry Service. Policy, Analysis, and Program Development Branch
Info Rep M-X Mar For Res Cent — Information Report M-X. Maritimes Forest Research Centre. Canadian Forestry Service
Info Rep NOR X North For Res Cen Can For Serv — Information Report NOR-X. Northern Forest Research Centre. Canadian Forestry Service
INFOR J — INFOR. Canadian Journal of Operational Research and Information Processing
Inform Access Ser — Information Access Series
Informac-Elektron — Informacio-Elektronika
Informac Quim Analit — Informacion de Quimica Analitica
Inform Agr — Informatore Agrario
Inform Agric Algiers — Informations Agricoles (Algiers)
Inform Am — Information America
Inform and Comput — Information and Computation
Inform and Control — Information and Control
Inform and Control Shenyang — Information and Control. Xinxi yu Kongzhi (Shenyang)
Inform Apic — Informador Apicola
Informat et Gestion — Informatique et Gestion
Informateur Batim — Informateur du Batiment
Informateur Med — Informateur Medical
Informatik-Ber (Bonn) — Informatik-Berichte (Bonn)
Informatik-Fachber — Informatik-Fachberichte
Information Bulletin IGCP Project No 61 Sealevel — Information Bulletin. International Geological Correlation Programme. Project Number 61. Sealevel
Information Commun Europ — Information. Commission des Communautes Europeennes
Information Processing Lett — Information Processing Letters
Informationsber Bayer Landesamtes Wasserwirtsch — Informationsberichte des Bayerischen Landesamtes fuer Wasserwirtschaft
Information Sci — Information Sciences
Informationsdienst Arbeitsgem Pharm Verfahrenstech — Informationsdienst. Arbeitsgemeinschaft fuer Pharmazeutische Verfahrenstechnik
Informationsteknol Samhaellsplanering Nord Forskarsemin — Informationsteknologi och Samhaellsplanering. Nordiskt Forskarseminarium
Information Syst — Information Systems
Informativo Bibliogr Rosario — Informativo Bibliografico (Rosario, Argentina)
Inform Ber — Informatik Berichte
Inform Bezoekers — Informatieblad voor Bezoekers
Inform Bibliogr BA — Informacion Bibliografica. Caja Nacional de Ahorro Postal (Buenos Aires)
Inform Bull Timb Res Developm Ass — Information Bulletin. Timber Research and Development Association
Inform Card Clemson Agr Coll Ext Serv — Information Card. Clemson Agricultural College. Extension Service
Inform Cathol Int — Informations Catholiques Internationales
INFORM Champaign Ill — INFORM (Champaign, Illinois)
Inform Ci Franc — Informaciones Cientificas Francesas. Association pour la Diffusion de la PenseeFrancaise
Inform Com Esp — Informacion Comercial Espanola
Inform Constit Parl — Informations Constitutionnelles et Parlementaires
Inform Contr — Information and Control
Inform Coop — Informations Cooperatives
Inform Doc — Informations and Documents
Inform Doc Agr — Informations et Documentation Agricoles
Informe Anu Labores Costa Rica Min Agr Ganad — Informe Anual de Labores. Costa Rica. Ministerio de Agricultura y Ganaderia
Inform Econ Mund — Informacion Economica Mundial
Inform Educ — Information on Education
Informe Est Exper La Molina Lima — Informe. Estacion Experimental Agricola La Molina (Lima)
Inform-Elektron — Informacio-Elektronika

Informe Mens Estac Exp Agr "La Molina" (Lima) — Informe Mensual. Estacion Experimental Agricola de "La Molina" (Lima)

Inform Erzieh Bildungshist Forsch — Informationen zur Erziehungs- und Bildungshistorischen Forschung

Informes PMV Am Lat — Informes de Pro Mundi Vita America Latina

Informes y Mem — Informes y Memorias. Servicio Nacional de Excavaciones Arqueologicas

Inform et Doc — Informations et Documents

Informe Tec — Informe Tecnico. Instituto Forestal

Informe Tec Estac Exp Agropecuar (Pergamino) — Informe Tecnico. Estacion Experimental Agropecuaria (Pergamino)

Inform Fitopatol — Informatore Fitopatologico

Inform Geogr — Information Geographique

Inform Grasas Aceites — Informaciones sobre Grasas y Aceites

Inform Haut — Informationzentrum Haut

Inform Hist — Information Historique

Inform Imperialist Ostforsch — Informationen der Abteilung fuer Geschichte der Imperialistischen Ostforschung an der Humboldt-Universitaet

Inform Ind Cinemat Bras — Informacoes sobre a Industria Cinematografica Brasileira. Anuario

Inform Intelligence Artificielle — Informatique/Intelligence Artificielle

Inform Kybernet Rechentech — Informatik - Kybernetik - Rechentechnik

Inform Pathol — Informatics in Pathology

Inform Process Japan — Information Processing in Japan

Inform Process Lett — Information Processing Letters

Inform Process Mach — Information Processing Machines

Inform Raumentwicklung — Informationen zur Raumentwicklung

Inform Recht — Informatik und Recht

Inform Rep For Fire Res Inst (Ottawa) — Information Report. Forest Fire Research Institute (Ottawa)

Inform Rep For Mgmt Inst (Ottawa) — Information Report. Forest Management Institute (Ottawa)

Inform Rep For Prod Lab (Vancouver) — Information Report. Forest Products Laboratory (Vancouver)

Inform Rep For Res Lab (Calgary) — Information Report. Forest Research Laboratory (Calgary)

Inform Rep For Res Lab (Quebec) — Information Report. Forest Research Laboratory (Quebec)

Inform Rep For Res Lab (Victoria BC) — Information Report. Forest Research Laboratory (Victoria, British Columbia)

Inform Res — Information Resources Annual

Inform Sci — Information Science Abstracts

Inform Sci — Information Sciences

Inform Sci Hum — Informatique et Sciences Humaines

Inform Sci Humaines — Informatique et Sciences Humaines

Inform Senal Ser Pecu — Informacion Senal Serie. Pecuaria

Inform Ser Agr Econ Univ Calif Agr Ext Serv — Information Series in Agricultural Economics. University of California. Agricultural Extension Service

Inform Seriche — Informazioni Seriche. Rivista dell' Industria Bacologica e Serica

Inform Ser NZ For Serv — Information Series. New Zealand Forest Service

Inform Sheet Miss Agr Exp Sta — Information Sheet. Mississippi Agricultural Experiment Station

Inform Soc Lima — Informaciones Sociales (Lima)

Inform Soc (Paris) — Informations Sociales (Paris)

Inform Steuer Wirtsch — Information ueber Steuer und Wirtschaft

Inform Stor Retrieval — Information Storage and Retrieval

Inform (Swed) — Information (Swedish Pulp and Paper Association)

Inform Technol Train — Information Technology Training

Inform Tech Ser — Information Technology Series

Inform Univ Profes Int — Informations Universitaires et Professionnelles Internationales

Inform Yugoslav — Informatologia Yugoslavica

Inform Zootec — Informatore Zootecnico

Inf Orthod Kieferorthop — Informationen aus Orthodontie und Kieferorthopaedie mit Beitraegen aus der Internationalen Literatur

Inf Ortoflorofruttic — Informatore di Ortoflorofrutticoltura

Infort Traum Lav — Infortunistica e Traumatologia del Lavoro

InfoS — Information Sciences

Info Serv Leafl Div Mech Eng CSIRO — Information Service Leaflet. Division of Mechanical Engineering. Commonwealth Scientific and Industrial Research Organisation

Info Soc — Informacao Social

Info Stud Vivaldiani — Informazioni e Studi Vivaldiani

Infosys — Infosystems

Info Sys New — Information Systems News

Info Systems — Information Systems

Info Tech — Information Technology and Libraries

Info Technol — Information Technology

Info Times — Information Times

Info Univ Rel Inter Etud Etran — Informations Universitaires en Relations Internationales et Etudes Etrangeres

Info Wash — Information Washington

Info Wld Rv — InfoWorld in Review. Special Report from InfoWorld

Info WP Rep — Information and Word Processing Report

InfP — Information Processing Journal

INFPA — Infrared Physics

Inf Pamph Mysore St Dep Agric — Information Pamphlet. Mysore State Department of Agriculture

Inf Pap Aust AEC — Information Paper. Australian Atomic Energy Commission

Inf Privacy — Information Privacy

Inf Pr Man — Information Processing and Management

Inf Process and Manage — Information Processing and Management

Inf Processing & Mgt — Information Processing and Management

Inf Process Lett — Information Processing Letters

Inf Process Mach — Information Processing Machines

Inf Process Manage — Information Processing and Management

Inf Process Soc Jpn (Joho Shori) — Information Processing Society of Japan (Joho Shori)

Inf Proc Man — Information Processing and Management

Inf Prov Buenos Aires Com Invest Cient — Informes. Provincia de Buenos Aires. Comision de Investigaciones Cientificas

Inf Psiquiat — Informaciones Psiquiatricas

Inf Psych — Information Psychiatrique

Inf Psychiat — Information Psychiatrique

Inf Psychiatr — Information Psychiatrique

Inf: Pt 1 — Information: Part 1: News/Sources/Profiles

Inf: Pt 2 — Information: Part 2: Reports/Bibliographies

Inf Publ Stredisko Tech Inf Potravin Prum — Informacni Publikace. Stredisko Technickych Informacni Potravinarskeho Prumyslu

Inf Quadrature Cercle — Information. La Quadrature du Cercle

Inf Quim Anal — Informacion de Quimica Analitica

Inf Quim Anal (Madrid) — Informacion de Quimica Analitica (Madrid)

Inf Quim Anal Pura Apl Ind — Informacion de Quimica Analitica, Pura, y Aplicada a la Industria

Inf Rade Koncar — Informacije Rade Koncar

Infrared Fiber Opt — Infrared Fiber Optics

Infrared Focal Plane Array Prod Relat Mater — Infrared Focal Plane Array Producibility and Related Materials

Infrared Imaging Syst Des Anal Model Test — Infrared Imaging Systems. Design, Analysis, Modeling, and Testing

Infrared Phys — Infrared Physics

Infrared Phys Technol — Infrared Physics and Technology

Infrared Sens Detect Electron Signal Process — Infrared Sensors. Detectors, Electronics, and Signal Processing

Infrar Phys — Infrared Physics

Inf Raumentwickl — Informationen zur Raumentwicklung

In Freight — International Freighting Weekly

Inf Release Geol Surv Pak — Information Release. Geological Survey of Pakistan

Inf Rep Air Intell Brch USAAF — Information Report. Air Intelligence Branch. US A.A.F

Inf Rep Atom Energy Res Estab — Information Report. Atomic Energy Research Establishment

Inf Rep BC X Can For Serv Pac For Cent — Information Report BC-X. Canadian Forestry Service. Pacific Forestry Centre

Inf Rep Bibliogr — Information Reports and Bibliographies

Inf Rep Chem Control Res Inst (Can) — Information Report. Chemical Control Research Institute (Canada)

Inf Rep Chem Control Res Inst Envir Can For Serv — Information Report. Chemical Control Research Institute. Environment Canada Forestry Service

Inf Rep DPC X — Information Report DPC-X

Inf Rep FMR-X For Manage Inst — Information Report FMR-X. Forest Management Institute

Inf Rep FPM-X For Pest Manage Inst — Information Report FPM-X. Forest Pest Management Institute

Inf Rep Furn Dev Coun — Information Report. Furniture Development Council</PHR> %

Inf Rep M X Marit For Res Cent Can For Serv — Information Report M-X. Maritimes Forest Research Centre. Canadian Forestry Service

Inf Rep NOR-X North For Res Cent — Information Report NOR-X. Northern Forest Research Centre

Inf Rep N X Can For Serv Newfoundland For Res Cent — Information Report N-X. Canadian Forestry Service. Newfoundland Forest ResearchCentre

Inf Rep O X Can For Serv Great Lakes For Cent — Information Report O-X. Canadian Forestry Service. Great Lakes Forestry Centre

Inf Rep Ser Fish — Information Report Series. Fisheries

Inf Rept Bibliog — Information Reports and Bibliographies

Inf Rep Washington Res — Information Report. Washington Researches

Inf Retr Libr Automn — Information Retrieval and Library Automation Letter

Inf Sb Inst Zemnoi Kory Sib Otd Akad Nauk SSSR — Informatsionnyi Sbornik Institut Zemnoi Kory Sibirskoe Otdelenie Akademiya NaukSSSR

Inf Sb Tr Vychisl Tsentra Irkutsk Gos Univ — Informatsionnyi Sbornik Trudov Vychislitel'nogo Tsentra Irkutskii Gosudarstvennyi Universitet

Inf Sb Vses Nauchno Issled Geol Inst — Informatsionnyi Sbornik Vsesoyuznyi Nauchno-Issledovatel'skii Geologicheskii Institut

Inf Sci — Information Sciences

Inf Sci — Informations Scientifiques

InfSciAb — Information Science Abstracts

Inf Sciences — Information Sciences

Inf Scient — Information Scientist

Inf Scientist — Information Scientist

Inf Ser Asph Inst — Information Series. Asphalt Institute

Inf Ser Colorado Geol Surv — Information Series. Colorado Geological Survey

Inf Ser Colo State Univ Environ Resour Cent — Information Series. Colorado State University. Environmental Resources Center

Inf Ser Dep Scient Ind Res NZ — Information Series. New Zealand Department of Scientific and Industrial Research

Inf Ser Geogr Bur Can — Information Series. Geographical Bureau. Department of Mines and Resources. Canada

Inf Ser Mar Labs Univ Delaware — Information Series. Marine Laboratories. University of Delaware

Inf Ser NZ Dep Sci Ind Res — Information Series. New Zealand Department of Scientific and Industrial Research

Inf Ser NZ Forest Serv — Information Series. New Zealand Forest Service

Inf Ser NZ For Serv — Information Series. New Zealand Forest Service

Inf Ser St Forest Serv NZ — Information Series. State Forest Service. New Zealand

Inf Ser Univ Idaho For Wildl Range Exp Stn — Information Series. University of Idaho. Forest Wildlife and Range Experiment Station

Inf Serv — National Council of Churches of Christ in the USA. Information Service

Inf Serv Leafl CILES CSIRO — Information Service Leaflet. Central Information, Library, and Editorial Section. Commonwealth Scientific and Industrial Research Organisation
Inf Serv Sheet Div Build Res CSIRO — Information Service Sheet. Division of Building Research. Commonwealth Scientific and Industrial Research Organisation
Inf Serv Sheet Div Mech Eng CSIRO — Information Service Sheet. Division of Mechanical Engineering. Commonwealth Scientific and Industrial Research Organisation
Inf Serv Use — Information Services and Use
Inf Sh Br Claywkr — Information Sheet. British Clayworker
Inf Sh Br Resin Prod — Information Sheet. British Resin Products Ltd
Inf Sheet Miss State Univ Coop Ext Serv — Information Sheet. Mississippi State University. Cooperative Extension Service
Inf Sh Inst Ind Res Stand Dubl — Information Sheet. Institute for Industrial Research and Standards (Dublin)
Inf Sh Miss Agric Exp Stn — Information Sheet. Agricultural Experiment Station. Mississippi State University
Inf Sh Natn Bldg Res Inst Un S Afr — Information Sheet. National Building Research Institute. Union of South Africa
Inf Sh Sir John Burnet Tait & Lorne — Information Sheet. Sir John Burnet, Tait, and Lorne
Inf So — Informazioni Soimet
Inf Soc — Information Society
Inf Soc — Informations Sociales
Inf Soc Franc Photogr — Informations. Societe Francaise de Photographie
Inf Soc (L) — Informaciones Sociales (Lima)
Inf Soc (P) — Informations Sociales (Paris)
Inf Softw Technol — Information and Software Technolgy
Inf-Spektrum — Informatik-Spektrum
Infs Tech Serv Vet — Informations Techniques des Services Veterinaires
Inf Storage — Information Storage and Retrieval
Inf Storage & Retr — Information Storage and Retrieval
Inf Storage Retr — Information Storage and Retrieval
Inf Stor Retr — Information Storage and Retrieval
Inf Studi Vivaldiani — Informazioni e Studi Vivaldiani
Inf Syst — Information Systems
INFTD — Informant
Inf Tec Argent Repub Estac Exp Agropecu Manfredi — Informacion Tecnica. Argentine Republic. Estacion Experimental Agropecuaria Manfredi
Inf Tec Estac Exp Reg Agropecu (Pergamino) — Informe Tecnico. Estacion Experimental Regional Agropecuaria (Pergamino)
Inf Tech — Informations Techniques
Inf Tech Cent Tech Interprof Ol Metrop — Informations Techniques. Centre Technique Interprofessionnel des Oleagineux Metropolitains
Inf Techn CETIOM — Informations Techniques. Centre Technique Interprofessionnel des Oleagineux Metropolitains
Inf Technol and Libr — Information Technology and Libraries
Inf Technol Libr — Information Technology and Libraries
Inf Technol Res and Dev — Information Technology. Research and Development
Inf Tech People — Information Technology and People
Inf Tec ICAITI — Informe Tecnico. Instituto Centroamericano de Investigacion y Tecnologia Industrial
Inf Tec Inst Centroam Invest Tecnol Ind — Informe Tecnico. Instituto Centroamericano de Investigacion y Tecnologia Industrial
Inf Tec Inst For (Santiago Chile) — Informe Tecnico. Instituto Forestal (Santiago, Chile)
Inf Tec Inst Invest Pesq — Informes Tecnicos. Instituto de Investigaciones Pesqueras
Inf Tecnol — Informacion Tecnologica
INFTET — Infectologia
Inf Text Ser Coll Trop Agric Hum Resour Univ Hawaii Coop Ext — Information Text Series. College of Tropical Agriculture and Human Resources. University of Hawaii. Cooperative Extension Service
Inftore Agr — Informatore Agrario
Inftore Fitopatol — Informatore Fitopatologico
Inf UFOD — Informations UFOD
Infusionsther Klin Ernaehr — Infusionstherapie und Klinische Ernaehrung
Infusionsther Klin Ernaehr Sonderh — Infusionstherapie und Klinische Ernaehrung. Sonderheft
Infusionsther Klin Ernaer Forsch Prax — Infusionstherapie und Klinische Ernaehrung. Forschung und Praxis
Infusionsther Transfusionsmed — Infusionstherapie und Transfusionsmedizin
Inf World (Abingdon) — Information World (Abingdon)
Inf World Rev — Information World Review
Inf World (Washington DC) — Information World (Washington, DC)
Inf Zootec — Informatore Zootecnico
Inf Zp VLIS — Informacni Zpravodaj VLIS
Inf Zukunfts-Friedensforsch — Information Zukunfts- und Friedensforschung
Ing — Ingenieur
Ing — Ingenioren
INGAB8 — Ingenieria Agronomica
Ing Aeronaut Astronaut — Ingenieria Aeronautica y Astronautica
Ing Agron — Ingenieria Agronomica
Ing Agron (Caracas) — Ingenieria Agronomica (Caracas)
Ing Ambientale — Ingegneria Ambientale
Ing & Tech — Ingenieurs et Techniciens
Ing-Arch — Ingenieur-Archiv. Gesellschaft fuer Angewandte Mathematik und Mechanik
Ing Arquit — Ingenieria y Arquitectura
Ing Arquitec Bogota — Ingenieria y Arquitectura (Bogota)
Ing Arts Metiers — Ingenieurs. Arts et Metiers
Ingauna et Intemelia NS — Rivista Ingauna et Intemelia N.S.
Ing Auto — Ingenieurs de l'Automobile
Ing Bygningsvaes — Ingenioer- og Bygningsvaesen

Ing Bygningsv Ugeovers — Ingenioer- og Bygningsvaesen Ugeoversigt
Ing Chim (Brussels) — Ingenieur Chimiste (Brussels)
Ing Chim It — Quaderni dell'Ingegnere Chimico Italiano
Ing Chim Ital — Ingegneria Chimica Italiana
Ing Chim (Milan) — Ingegneria Chimica (Milan)
Ing Civ (Havana) — Ingenieria Civil (Havana)
Ing Civil — Ingenieria Civil
Ing-Dig — Ingenieur-Digest
Ing Dt Bu Po — Ingenieur der Deutschen Bundespost
INGEA — Ingenioeren (1892-1966)
Ing Ec Super Phys Chim Ind — Ingenieurs de l'Ecole Superieure de Physique et de Chimie Industrielles
Ing Electr & Mec — Ingenieria Electrica y Mecanica
Ingen For — Ingenieria Forestal
Ingenieria Hidraul Mex — Ingenieria Hidraulica en Mexico
Ingenioersvetenskapsakad Handl — Ingenioersvetenskapsakademien. Handlingar
Ingenioervidensk Skr — Ingenioervidenskabelige Skrifter
Ingenioervidensk Skr Ser A — Ingenioervidenskabelige Skrifter. Series A
Ingenioervidensk Skr Ser B — Ingenioervidenskabelige Skrifter. Series B
Ingen Villes France — Ingenieurs des Villes de France
Ing EPCI — Ingenieurs de l'Ecole Superieure de Physique et de Chimie Industrielles
InGerar — In Gerardagum
Ing Ferrov — Ingegneria Ferroviaria
Ing-Forsk — Ingenioeren-Forskning
Ing Hidraul Mex — Ingenieria Hidraulica en Mexico (Mexico)
Ing Hidraul Mexico — Ingenieria Hidraulica en Mexico
Inghirami Opusc — Nuova Collezione di Opuscoli e Notizie di Scienze. Inghirami
Ing Journ — Ingenieur-Journal
Ing-Mag — Ingenioer-Magasinet
Ing Mecc — Ingegneria Meccanica
Ing Mec y Electr — Ingenieria Mecanica y Electrica
Ing Mex — Ingenieria. Escuela Nacional de Ingenieros (Mexico)
INGNA — Industrial Gas
Ing Nav (Madrid) — Ingenieria Naval (Madrid)
Ing Ned Indie — Ingenieur in Nederlandsch Indie
Ing Nucl — Ingegneria Nucleare
Ing o B — Ingenior- og Bygningsvaesen
Ing Pet — Ingenieria Petrolera
Ing Quim Ind — Ingenieria Quimica e Industrias
Ing Quim Madrid — Ingenieria Quimica (Madrid)
Ing Quim (Medellin Colombia) — Ingenieria Quimica (Medellin, Colombia)
Ing Quim (Mexico City) — Ingenieria Quimica (Mexico City)
INGRA — Ingenieur
In Grade Sch — In the Grade School
Ing Sanit — Ingegneria Sanitaria
Ing Text (Barcelona) — Ingenieria Textil (Barcelona)
Ing Ugebl — Ingenioerens Ugeblad
Ing Ves — Vesey, Junior's, English Chancery Reports, Edited by Ingraham
Ing Vetenskaps Akad Medd — Ingeniors Vetenskaps Akademien. Meddelande
IngZg — Ingenieur-Zeitung
Inhaled Part — Inhaled Particles
Inhal Ther — Inhalation Therapy
Inhal Toxicol — Inhalation Toxicology
Inha Univ IIR — Inha University IIR
INHB — Negro History Bulletin
INHBA — Bulletin. Illinois Natural History Survey
INHEA — Industrial Health
INHEAO — Industrial Health
Inheemsche Nijverh Java — Inheemsche Nijverheid op Java, Madoera, Bali en Lombok
INHEES — Index Hepaticarum
INHMP — Iraq Natural History Museum. Publications
INHOAK — Indian Horticulture
INHP — Indiana Journal. Indiana Association for Health, Physical Education, and Recreation
INHTA — Industrial Heating
INI — International Nursing Index
Iniciacao Mat — Iniciacao a Matematica
INIE — Nieman Reports
Ini Isl — Initiation a l'Islam
ININA — Industrial India
INIREB Informa Inst Invest Recur Bioticos — INIREB Informa. Instituto de Investigaciones sobre Recursos Bioticos
INIS — INIS [*International Nuclear Information System*] Atomindex
INIS — International Nuclear Information System
INITB — Installatore Italiano
Initiative — Industrial Arts Initiative
Initiatives Popul — Inititatives in Population
Iniz — Iniziative
INJ — Internationales Verkehrswesen; Fachzeitschrift fuer Information und Kommunikation in Verkehr
INJ — Israel Numismatic Journal
INJABN — International Journal of the Addictions
Injectable Contraceptives Newsl — Injectable Contraceptives Newsletter
INJFA3 — International Journal of Fertility
INJHA — Indian Journal of Heredity
INJHA9 — Indian Journal of Heredity
INJPA — Indian Journal of Psychology
Inj Prev — Injury Prevention
INKACORP — Inka Corporate Authorities
INKYD — Rihaknonjip. Research Institute of Applied Science. Kon-Kuk University
InL — Indian Literature
InL — Inostrannaya Literatura
Inland Architect & News Rec — Inland Architect and News Record
Inland Archt — Inland Architect

Inland P — Inland Printer/American Lithographer
Inland Printer Am Lithogr — Inland Printer/American Lithographer
Inland Ptr — Inland Printer
Inland Waters Dir Rep Ser Can — Inland Waters Directorate. Report Series (Canada)
Inl Bird-Banding News — Inland Bird-Banding News
IN LF — Indiana Legal Forum
InLi — Incontri Linguistici
Inlichitingsblad CCMB — Inlichitingsblad van de Christelijke Centrale der Metaalbewerkers vanBelgie
IN LJ — Indiana Law Journal
INLJ — National Law Journal
INLL — Informationsblatt fuer de Gemeinden in den Niederdeutschen Lutherischen Landeskirchen
INLND6 — Informationen zu Naturschutz und Landschaftspflege in Nordwestdeutschland
IN LR — Indiana Law Review
INLR-A — International Labour Review
INM — Indian Notes and Monographs. Museum of the American Indian. Heye Foundation [*New York*]
INM — Industrial Management
INM — Industrie Textile. Revue Mensuelle Internationale Technique et Economique Textile
INMAD — Invention Management
Inmersion Cienc — Inmersion y Ciencia
INMI — International Migration
INMID — Industria Minera
INMOA — Ingenieur (Montreal)
INMR — Izvestiia na Narodniia Muzei Ruse
INMRA — Industria Mineraria
INMV — Izvestiia na Narodniia Muzei Varna
INNDDK — Investigational New Drugs
Innere Med — Innere Medizin
Innere Mission Im Evang Deut — Innere Mission im Evangelischen Deutschland
Innes — Innes' Registration of Title
Innes Rev — Innes Review
INNLA — INIS [*International Nuclear Information System*] Newsletter
INNO — Inter-Nord
Innovations Mater Res — Innovations in Materials Research
Innov High Educ — Innovative Higher Education
InnR — Innes Review
INNS — International Nuclear News Service
Innsb Ferd Z — Zeitschrift des Ferdinandeums fuer Tirol und Vorarlberg
Innsb Nt Md B — Berichte des Naturwissenschaftlich-Medizinischen Vereins in Innsbruck
Innsbruck Hist Stud — Innsbrucker Historische Studien
Innsbruck Nachr — Innsbrucker Nachrichten
INNUA — Ingegneria Nucleare
INO — Inc.
INO — Indonesia
INOCA — Inorganic Chemistry
INOGA — Industrielle Obst- und Gemueseverwertung
INOGAV — Industrielle Obst- und Gemueseverwertung
INOK — Inuit Okakheet. Kitikmeot Inuit Association
INOM — New Orleans Magazine
INOMA — Inorganic Materials
INOPA — Investigations in Ophthalmology and Visual Science
INOPAO — Investigative Ophthalmology [*Later, Investigative Ophthalmology and Visual Science*]
INOPD — International Ophthalmology
Inorg and Nucl Chem Lett — Inorganic and Nuclear Chemistry Letters
Inorg Chem — Inorganic Chemistry
Inorg Chem Commun — Inorganic Chemistry Communications
Inorg Chem Main Group Elem — Inorganic Chemistry of the Main Group Elements
Inorg Chem Transition Elem — Inorganic Chemistry of the Transition Elements
Inorg Chim — Inorganica Chimica Acta
Inorg Chim Acta — Inorganica Chimica Acta
Inorg Chim Acta Rev — Inorganica Chimica Acta. Reviews
Inorg Ion Exch Chem Anal — Inorganic Ion Exchangers in Chemical Analysis
Inorg Macromol Rev — Inorganic Macromolecules Reviews
Inorg Mater — Inorganic Materials
Inorg Mater Tokyo — Inorganic Materials (Tokyo)
Inorg Mater Transl of Neorg Mater — Inorganic Materials (Translation of Neorganicheskie Materialy)
Inorg Mater (USSR) — Inorganic Materials (USSR)
Inorg Nucl — Inorganic and Nuclear Chemistry Letters
Inorg Nucl Chem Lett — Inorganic and Nuclear Chemistry Letters
Inorg Organomet Oligomers Polym Proc IUPAC Symp Macromol — Inorganic and Organometallic Oligomers and Polymers. Proceedings. IUPAC Symposium on Macromolecules
Inorg Perspect Biol Med — Inorganic Perspectives in Biology and Medicine
Inorg React Mech — Inorganic Reaction Mechanisms
Inorg Synth — Inorganic Syntheses
InostrJazyki — Inostrannye Jazyki v Skole
Inostr Tekh Org Sel Khoz — Inostrannaya Tekhnika i Organizatsiya Sel'skogo Khozyaistva
InozF — Inozemna Filolohiji
INPAA — Instrument Practice
InPEN — Indian PEN
INPFCB — International North Pacific Fisheries Commission. Bulletin
INPh — Idealistische Neuphilologie
INPHA — Industrial Photography
INPI — Information Pipeline. Norman Wells Project Review
In-Plant Reprod — In-Plant Reproductions
INPO Impact — INPO [*Institute of Nuclear Power Operations*] Impact

INPO Rev — INPO [*Institute of Nuclear Power Operations*] Review
In Pract — In Practice
INPS — Individual Psychology
INPXAJ — Internistische Praxis
INQ — Innovatie Informatiebulletin ter Bevordering van de Industriele Vernieuwing in Ons Land
Inq — Inquiry
INQB — Information North Quebec. Bulletin de Liaison des Centres de Recherches Nordique de Quebec
INQU — Indians of Quebec. Confederation of Indians of Quebec
Inqueritos Nac de Precos (Capitais) — Inqueritos Nacional de Precos (Capitais)
Inqueritos Nac de Precos (Unidades da Federacao) — Inqueritos Nacional de Precos (Unidades da Federacao)
Inquiry Mag — Inquiry Magazine
INQYA — Inquiry
INR — Industrial Relations
INR — Informatie
In R — Innes Review
INRE — Indian Record
In Rev — In Review. Canadian Books for Young People
INRFDC — Interferon
INROADS — Information on Roads
INRSDH — International Goat and Sheep Research
INS — Industrial Society
InS — Inland Seas
INS — Insight
Ins — Instrumentalist
Ins — Insula
INS — Insurance
INSAA — Ingegneria Sanitaria
INSA Bull — Indian National Science Academy. Bulletin
Ins Coun J — Insurance Counsel Journal
Ins Counsel J — Insurance Counsel Journal
Insc Pont Euxini — Inscriptiones Antiquae Orae Septentrionalis Ponti Euxini
Inscr Brit Christ — Inscriptiones Britanniae Christianae
Inscr Bulg — Inscriptiones Graecae in Bulgaria Repertae
Inscr Christ — Inscriptions Chretiennes de la Gaule Anterieures au VIIIe Siecle
Inscr Cos — Inscriptions of Cos
Inscr de Delos — Inscriptions de Delos
Inscr Gr — Inscriptiones Graecae
Inscr Graec — Inscriptiones Graecae
Inscr Graec ad Res Rompert — Inscriptiones Graecae ad Res Romanas Pertinentes
Inscr Gr Antiq — Inscriptiones Graecae Antiquissimae Praeter Atticas in Attica Repertas
Inscr Grec Lat la Syrie — Inscriptions Grecques et Latines de la Syrie
Inscr Gr Lat Syrie — Inscriptions Grecques et Latines de la Syrie
Inscript Cret — Inscriptiones Creticae Opera et Consilio Friderici Halbherr Collectae
Inscr Ital — Inscriptiones Italiae
Inscr Iug — Inscriptiones Latinae quae in Iugoslavia Inter Annos MCMXL et MCMLX Repertae etEdita Sunt
Inscr Jurid — Recueil des Inscriptions Juridiques Grecques
Inscr Kourion — Inscriptions of Kourion
Inscr Lat Afr — Inscriptions Latines d'Afrique
Inscr Lat Alg — Inscriptions Latines d'Algerie
Inscr Lat Christ Vet — Inscriptiones Latinae Christianae Veteres
Inscr Lat Gaule — Inscriptions Latines de la Gaule (Narbonnaise)
Inscr Lat Librei Publicae — Inscriptiones Latinae Liberae Rei Publicae
Inscr Lat Sel — Inscriptiones Latinae Selectae
Inscr Mus Alex — Iscrizioni Greche e Latine. Catalogue General des Antiquites d'Egyptiennes du Musee d'Alexandrie
Inscr Olymp — Inschriften von Olympia
Inscr Or Sept Pon Eux — Inscriptiones Antiquae Orae Septentrionalis Ponti Euxini
Inscr Perg — Inschriften von Pergamon
Inscr Philae — Inscriptions Grecques de Philae
Inscr Pyliae Mycen Aet Pert — Inscriptiones Pyliae ad Mycenaeum Aetatem Pertinentes
Inscr Rom Gal — Inscripciones Romanas de Galicia
Inscr Sardegna — Iscrizioni Latine della Sardegna
Inscr Tunisie — Inscriptions Latins de la Tunisie
In Search — In Search/En Quete
Ins Econ Surv — Insurance Economics Surveys
Insecta Matsum — Insecta Matsumurana
Insecta Matsumurana Suppl — Insecta Matsumurana. Supplement
Insect Answers Coop Ext Serv Wash St Univ — Insect Answers. Cooperative Extension Service. Washington State University
Insecta Sin — Insecta Sinensia
Insect Bioc — Insect Biochemistry
Insect Biochem — Insect Biochemistry
Insect Biochem Mol Biol — Insect Biochemistry and Molecular Biology
Insect Bol Biol — Insect Molecular Biology
Insect Dis Rep US For Serv North Reg — Insect Disease Report. United States Forest Service. Northern Region
Insect Ecol — Insect Ecology
Insectes Soc — Insectes Sociaux
Insectic Abstr News Summ — Insecticides Abstracts and News Summary
Insectic Acaricide Tests — Insecticide and Acaricide Tests
Insectic Newsl — Insecticide Newsletter
Insect Inf — Insect Information
Insect Neurochem Neurophysiol Proc Int Conf — Insect Neurochemistry and Neurophysiology. Proceedings. International Conference
Insect Pest Leafl NSW — Insect Pest Leaflets. Department of Agriculture. New South Wales
Insect Pest Surv Bull US — Insect Pest Survey Bulletin. US Department of Agriculture

Insect Pest Surv NSW — Insect Pest Survey. Entomological Branch. Division of Science. New South Wales
Insect Pest Surv Spec Suppl US — Insect Pest Survey. Special Supplements. US Department of Agriculture
Insect Plant Interact — Insect-Plant Interactions
Insect Sci Appl — Insect Science and Its Application
Insect Sci Its Applica — Insect Science and Its Application
Insects Micronesia — Insects of Micronesia
Insect Soc — Insectes Sociaux
Insects Soc Soc Insects — Insectes Sociaux/Social Insects
Insect Wld — Insect World
Insect Wld Dig — Insect World Digest
Insecutor Inscit Menstr — Insecutor Inscitiae Menstruus
INSERM Colloq — INSERM [*Institut National de la Sante et de la Recherche Medicale*] Colloque
INSERM Symp — INSERM [*Institut National de la Sante et de la Recherche Medicale*] Symposia
Ins Field (Fire Ed) — Insurance Field (Fire and Casualty Edition)
Ins Field (Life Ed) — Insurance Field (Life Edition)
Ins Geog Geol Estado Sao Paulo Bol — Instituto Geografico e Geologico. Estado de Sao Paulo. Boletim
INSI — Insight
INSIA — Industria Saccarifera Italiana
Inside Canb — Inside Canberra
Inside Educ — Inside Education
Inside Prt — Inside Print. The Voice of Print Advertising
Insiders' Chr — Insiders' Chronicle
In Silico Biol — In Silico Biology
In Situ Oil Coal Shale Miner — In Situ. Oil-Coal-Shale-Minerals
Ins Law J — Insurance Law Journal
Ins L J — Insurance Law Journal
Ins LR — Insurance Litigation Reporter
Ins L Rep CCH — Insurance Law Reports. Commerce Clearing House
INSMD4 — Intersectum
INSOA7 — Insectes Sociaux
INSP — NASSP [*National Association Secondary School Principals*] Bulletin
Insp Adv — Inspection and Advice
Insp Bouch — Inspection de la Boucherie
Insp Bull Natn Cann Ass — Inspection Bulletin. National Canners' Association
Insp Circ Kans Agric Exp Stn — Inspection Circular. Kansas Agricultural Experiment Station
INSPEL — INSPEL. International Journal of Special Libraries
Insp Engr — Inspection Engineer
Insp Equip News — Inspection Equipment News
Insp Rep Agric Exp Stn Purdue Univ — Inspection Report. Agricultural Experiment Station. Purdue University
Insp Rep Purdue Univ Agric Exp Stn — Inspection Report. Purdue University. Agricultural Experiment Station
INSRAG — Instrumentation
Insrg Soc — Insurgent Sociologist
Inst — Institutions
Inst — Instructor
INST — Revenue Canada. Customs and Excise Institutions List
Inst Actuaries J — Journal. Institute of Actuaries
Inst Aeronaut Sci Sherman M Fairchild Publ Fund Prepr — Institute of the Aeronautical Sciences. Sherman M. Fairchild Publication Fund. Preprint
Inst Afr Stud — Institute of African Studies
Inst Agric Cat San Isidro Rev — Instituto Agricola Catalan de San Isidro. Revista
Inst Agric Res Annu Rep (Addis Ababa) — Institute of Agricultural Research. Annual Report (Addis Ababa)
Inst Agric Res Annu Res Semin Proc (Addis Ababa) — Institute of Agricultural Research. Annual Research Seminar. Proceedings (AddisAbaba)
Inst Agric Res Prog Rep (Addis Ababa) — Institute of Agricultural Research. Progress Report (Addis Ababa)
Inst Agric Res Samaru Annu Rep — Institute of Agricultural Research. Samaru. Annual Report
Inst Agron Dr Petru Groza (Cluj) Lucr Stiint Ser Agric — Institutul Agronomic "Dr. Petru Groza" (Cluj). Lucrari Stiintifice. Seria Agricultura
Inst Agron Dr Petru Groza (Cluj) Lucr Stiint Ser Med Vet — Institutul Agronomic "Dr. Petru Groza" (Cluj). Lucrari Stiintifice. Seria Medicina Veterinara
Inst Agron Dr Petru Groza (Cluj) Lucr Stiint Ser Zooteh — Institutul Agronomic "Dr. Petru Groza" (Cluj). Lucrari Stiintifice. Seria Zootehnie
Inst Agron Ion Ionescu de la Brad (Iasi) Lucr Stiint — Institutul Agronomic "Ion Ionescu de la Brad" (Iasi). Lucrari Stiintifice
Inst Agron Ion Ionescu de la Brad Iasi Lucr Stiint Ser Agron — Institutul Agronomic "Ion Ionescu de la Brad" (Iasi). Lucrari Stiintifice. Seria Agronomie
Inst Agron Nicolae Balcescu Bucuresti Lucr Stiint Ser B — Institutul Agronomic Nicolae Balcescu. Bucuresti. Lucrari Stiintifice. Seria B.Horticultura
Inst Agron Timisoara Lucr Stiint Ser Agron — Institutul Agronomic Timisoara Lucrari Stiintifice. Seria Agronomie
Inst Agron Timisoara Lucr Stiint Ser Med Vet — Institutul Agronomic Timisoara Lucrari Stiintifice. Seria Medicina Veterinara
Inst Agron Timisoara Lucr Stiint Ser Zooteh — Institutul Agronomic Timisoara Lucrari Stiintifice. Seria Zootehnie
Inst Alatne Masine Alate Monogr — Institut za Alatne Masine i Alate. Monografije
Inst Alatne Masine Alate Saopstanja — Institut za Alatne Masine i Alate. Saopstenja
Installatore Ital — Installatore Italiano
Installatoren Elektrotek Tidskr — Installatoren. Elektroteknisk Tidskrift
Install Bl — Installateur-Blatter
Install Ital — Installatore Italiano
Install Klempn — Installation und Klempnerei
Inst Anim Physiol Rep — Institute of Animal Physiology. Report
Inst Antart Argent Contrib — Instituto Antartico Argentino. Contribuciones
Inst Antart Chileno Bol — Instituto Antartico Chileno. Boletin

Instant Med — Instantanes Medicaux
Instant Res — Instant Research on Peace and Violence
Instant Res Peace Violence — Instant Research on Peace and Violence
Inst Appl Res Nat Resour (Abu Ghraib Iraq) Tech Rep — Institute for Applied Research on Natural Resources (Abu-Ghraib, Iraq). Technical Report
Inst Appl Res Nat Resour Tech Rep (Bull) — Institute for Applied Research on Natural Resources. Technical Report (Bulletin)
Inst Archeol E Geog Pernamb R — Instituto Archeologico e Geographico Pernambucano. Revista
Inst Arch Ethnog — Internationales Archiv fuer Ethnographie
Inst Arct Alp Res Univ Colo Occas Pap — Institute of Arctic and Alpine Research. University of Colorado. Occasional Paper
Inst Astr Geod Univ Liege — Institut d'Astronomie et de Geodesie. Universite de Liege
Inst At Energ I V Kurchatova Rap IAE — Institut Atomnoi Energii Imeni I. V. Kurchatova. Raport IAE
Inst Auslandsbezieh Mitt — Institut fuer Auslandsbeziehungen. Mitteilungen
Inst Aust Foundrymen Annu Proc — Institute of Australian Foundrymen. Annual Proceedings
Inst Aust Foundrymen NSW Div Annu Proc — Institute of Australian Foundrymen. New South Wales Division. Annual Proceedings
Inst Bankers J — Institute of Bankers. Journal
Inst Bauwissenschaftliche Forsch Publ — Institut fuer Bauwissenschaftliche Forschung. Publikation
Inst Bauwissensch Forsch Publ — Institut fuer Bauwissenschaftliche Forschung. Publikation
Inst Belge Amelior Betterave Publ — Institut Belge pour l'Amelioration de la Betterave. Publication
Inst Belge Amelior Betterave Publ Trimest — Institut Belge pour l'Amelioration de la Betterave. Publication Trimestrielle
Inst Biol Apl Publ (Barcelona) — Instituto de Biologia Aplicada. Publicaciones (Barcelona)
Inst Biol Bahia Bol — Instituto Biologico da Bahia. Boletim
Inst Biol J — Institute of Biology [*London*]. Journal
Inst Biol (Lond) Symp — Institute of Biology (London). Symposium
Inst Biol Mar (Mar Del Plata) Contrib — Instituto de Biologia Marina (Mar Del Plata). Contribucion
Inst Biol Mar (Mar Del Plata) Mem Anu — Instituto de Biologia Marina (Mar Del Plata). Memoria Anual
Inst Biol Mar (Mar Del Plata) Ser Contrib — Instituto de Biologia Marina (Mar Del Plata). Serie Contribuciones
Inst Biol Pesqui Tecnol (Curitiba) Bol — Instituto de Biologia e Pesquisas Tecnologicas (Curitiba). Boletim
Inst Biol Scheikd Onderz Landbouwgewassen (Wageningen) Jaarb — Instituut voor Biologisch en Scheikundig Onderzoek van Landbouwgewassen (Wageningen). Jaarboek
Inst Biol Scheikd Onderz Landbouwgewassen (Wageningen) Meded — Instituut voor Biologisch en Scheikundig Onderzoek van Landbouwgewassen (Wageningen). Mededeling
Inst Biol Stud Biol — Institute of Biology's Studies in Biology
Inst Biol Symp (Lond) — Institute of Biology. Symposia (London)
Inst Bodemvruchtbaarheid Haren-Gr Jaarversl — Instituut voor Bodemvruchtbaarheid Haren-Groningen. Jaarverslag
Inst Bodemvruchtbaarheid Haren-Gr Rapp — Instituut voor Bodemvruchtbaarheid Haren-Groningen. Rapport
Inst Bodemvruchtbaarheid Jaarversl — Instituut voor Bodemvruchtbaarheid. Jaarverslag
Inst Bodemvruchtbaarheid Rapp — Instituut voor Bodemvruchtbaarheid. Rapport
Inst Bot Acad Sin Monogr Ser — Institute of Botany. Academia Sinica Monograph Series
Inst Bot "Dr Goncalo Sampaio" Fac Cien Univ Porto Publ — Instituto de Botanica "Dr. Goncalo Sampaio." Faculdade de Ciencias. Universidade do Porto. Publicacoes
Inst Bot Univ Geneve — Institut de Botanique. Universite de Geneve
Inst Brew (Aust NZ Sect) Proc Conv — Institute of Brewing (Australia and New Zealand Section). Proceedings of the Convention
Inst Br Geographers Trans — Institute of British Geographers. Transactions
Inst Br Geogr Trans — Institute of British Geographers. Transactions
Inst Bull Inst Br Carr Auto Mfrs — Institute Bulletin. Institute of British Carriage and Automobile Manufacturers
Inst Cancer Res (Phila) Sci Rep — Institute for Cancer Research (Philadelphia). Scientific Report
Inst Celul Papier Pr — Instytut Celulozowo-Papierniczego. Prace
Inst Cent Am Investig Tecnol Ind Publ Geol — Instituto Centro Americano de Investigacion y Tecnologia Industrial. Publicaciones Geologicas
Inst Cercet Ind Chim Aliment Lucr Cercet — Institutul de Cercetari pentru Industrie si Chimie Alimentara. Lucrari de Cercetare
Inst Cercet Vet Bioprep Pasteur Lucr — Institutul de Cercetari Veterinare si Biopreparate Pasteur. Lucrarile
Inst Certif Mech Electr Eng S Afr Arthur Hallet Mem Lect — Institution of Certificated Mechanical and Electrical Engineers. South Africa. Arthur Hallet Memorial Lectures
Inst Chem Eng Q Bull — Institution of Chemical Engineers. Quarterly Bulletin
Inst Chem Eng Symp Ser — Institution of Chemical Engineers. Symposium Series
Inst Chem Eng Trans — Institution of Chemical Engineers. Transactions
Inst Chem Irel J — Institute of Chemistry of Ireland. Journal
Inst Chim Aliment Lucr Cercet — Institutul de Chimie Alimentara. Lucrari de Cercetare
Inst Ciencias Socs R — Revista. Instituto de Ciencias Sociales
Inst Cienc Nat Mat Univ El Salvador Comun — Instituto de Ciencias Naturales y Matematicas. Universidad de El Salvador. Comunicaciones
Inst Civ Eng Ir Trans — Transactions. Institution of Civil Engineers of Ireland
Inst Civ Engr Proc — Institution of Civil Engineers. Proceedings
Inst Civ Engrs Proc Part 1 — Institution of Civil Engineers. Proceedings. Part 1. Design and Construction

Inst Civ Engrs Proc Part 2 — Institution of Civil Engineers. Proceedings. Part 2. Research and Theory

Inst Col Int — Institut Colonial International

Inst Colomb Agropecu Bol Tec — Instituto Colombiano Agropecuario. Boletin Tecnico

Inst Control Engrg — Technical University of Poznan. Institute of Control Engineering

Inst Cubano Invest Tecnol Ser Estud Trab Invest — Instituto Cubano de Investigaciones Tecnologicas. Serie de Estudios sobre Trabajos de Investigacion

Inst Def Anal Pap — Institute for Defense Analyses. Paper

Inst Def Stud Anal J — Institute for Defence Studies and Analyses. Journal

Inst d'Egypte Bull — Institut d'Egypte Bulletin

Inst Dent Res Bienn Rep (Syd) — Institute of Dental Research. Biennial Report (Sydney)

Inst Dent Res United Dent Hosp Sydney Annu Rep — Institute of Dental Research. United Dental Hospital of Sydney. Annual Report

Inst Dev Stud Bull — Institute of Development Studies. Bulletin

Inst Distrib — Institutional Distribution

InstDokAB — Institutionendokumentation zur Arbeitsmarkt- und Berufsforschung

Inst E B — Instituto de Estudos Brasileiros

Inst Econ Prod Ganad Ebro Comun — Instituto de Economia y Producciones Ganaderas del Ebro. Comunicaciones

Inst Ecuat Cienc Nat Contrib — Instituto Ecuatoriano de Ciencias Naturales. Contribucion

Inst Eduardo Torroja Constr Cem Monogr — Instituto Eduardo Torroja de la Construccion y del Cemento. Monografias

Inst E E J — Institution of Electrical Engineers. Journal

Inst E E Proc — Institution of Electrical Engineers. Proceedings

Inst Elec Eng Conf Publ — Institution of Electrical Engineers. Conference Publication

Inst Elec Eng J — Institution of Electrical Engineers. Journal

Inst Elect & Electronics Eng Proc — Institute of Electrical and Electronics Engineers. Proceedings

Inst Elect & Electronics Eng Trans IA — Institute of Electrical and Electronics Engineers. Transactions on Industry Application

Inst Elect & Electronics Eng Trans PAS — Institute of Electrical and Electronics Engineers. Transactions on Power Apparatus and Systems

Inst Electr Eng Proc A Sci Meas Technol — Institution of Electrical Engineers Proceedings. A. Science, Measurement, and Technology

Inst Electr Eng Proc Part A Phys Sci Meas Instrum Manage Educ — Institution of Electrical Engineers Proceedings. Part A. Physical Science, Measurement and Instrumentation, Management and Education

Inst Electr Eng Proc Part I Solid State Electron Devices — Institution of Electrical Engineers Proceedings. Part I. Solid-State and Electron Devices

Inst Electron Commun Eng Jpn Trans Sect E — Institute of Electronics and Communication Engineers of Japan. Transactions. Section E. English

Inst Electron Inf Commun Eng Trans Sect E — Institute of Electronics, Information, and Communication Engineers. Transactions. Section E. English

Inst Electron Radio Eng Conf Proc — Institution of Electronic and Radio Engineers. Conference Proceedings

Inst Electron Telecommun Eng J — Institution of Electronics and Telecommunication Engineers. Journal

Inst Elev Med Vet Pays Trop Rapp Act — Institut d'Elevage et de Medecine Veterinaire des Pays Tropicaux. Rapport d'Activite

Inst Elie Cartan — Institut Elie Cartan

Inst Energ Biul — Instytut Energetyki. Biuletyn

Inst Eng Aust Chem Eng Aust — Institution of Engineers of Australia. Chemical Engineering in Australia

Inst Eng Aust Chem Eng Trans — Institution of Engineers of Australia. Chemical Engineering Transactions

Inst Eng Aust Civ Eng Trans — Institution of Engineers of Australia. Civil Engineering Transactions

Inst Eng (Aust) Elec Eng Trans — Institution of Engineers of Australia. Electrical Engineering Transactions

Inst Eng Aust Electr Eng Trans — Institution of Engineers of Australia. Electrical Engineering Transactions

Inst Eng (Aust) Gen Eng Trans — Institution of Engineers of Australia. General Engineering Transactions

Inst Eng Aust J — Institution of Engineers of Australia. Journal

Inst Eng Aust Mech and Chem Eng Trans — Institution of Engineers of Australia. Mechanical and Chemical Engineering Transactions

Inst Eng Aust Mech & Chem Trans — Institution of Engineers of Australia. Mechanical and Chemical Engineering Transactions

Inst Eng Aust Mech Chem Eng — Institution of Engineers. Australia. Mechanical and Chemical Engineering. Transactions

Inst Eng (Aust) Mech Chem Eng Trans — Institution of Engineers of Australia. Mechanical and Chemical Engineering Transactions

Inst Eng (Aust) Mech Eng Trans — Institution of Engineers of Australia. Mechanical Engineering Transactions

Inst Eng Aust Queensland Div Tech Pap — Institution of Engineers of Australia. Queensland Division. Technical Papers

Inst Eng Aust South Aust Div Bull — Institution of Engineers of Australia. South Australia Division. Bulletin

Inst Eng Aust Trans Electr Eng — Institution of Engineers. Australia. Transactions. Electrical Engineering

Inst Eng (Ceylon) Trans — Institution of Engineers (Ceylon). Transactions

Inst Engineers Aust J — Institution of Engineers of Australia. Journal

Inst Engrs Tas Bul — Institution of Engineers of Australia. Tasmania Division. Bulletin

Inst Environ Sci — Institute of Environmental Sciences Proceedings

Inst Environ Sci Annu Tech Meet Proc — Institute of Environmental Sciences. Annual Technical Meeting. Proceedings

Inst Environ Sci Proc — Institute of Environmental Sciences. Proceedings

Inst Environ Sci Tech Meet Proc — Institute of Environmental Sciences. Technical Meeting. Proceedings

Inst Environ Sci Technol Proc — Institute of Environmental Sciences and Technology. Proceedings

Inst Ernaehrungsforsch (Rueschlikon-Zuerich) Schriftenr — Institut fuer Ernaehrungsforschung (Rueschlikon-Zuerich). Schriftenreihe

Inst Esp Oceanogr Notas Resumenes — Instituto Espanol de Oceanografia. Notas y Resumenes

Inst Estate Plan — Institute on Estate Planning

Inst Est Catalanes — Institut d'Estudis Catalans

Inst Estud Alicantinos Rev — Instituto de Estudios Alicantinos. Revista

Inst Ethmus Sel Repts — Institute of Ethnomusicology. Selected Reports

Inst Exp Invest Fom Agric Ganad (St Fe) Publ Tec — Instituto Experimental de Investigacion y Fomento Agricola-Ganadero (Santa Fe).Publicacion Tecnica

Inst Farb Lakierow Biul Inf — Instytut Farb i Lakierow. Biuletyn Informacyjny

Inst Fed Rech For Mem — Institut Federal de Recherches Forestieres. Memoires

Inst Ferment Res Commun (Osaka) — Institute for Fermentation Research Communications (Osaka)

Inst Fire Eng Q — Institution of Fire Engineers. Quarterly

Inst Fisico-Geog Nac Costa Rica An — Instituto Fisico-Geografico Nacional de Costa Rica. Anales

Inst Fiz At Rep (Rom) — Institutul de Fizica Atomica. Report (Romania)

Inst Fiz Ing Nucl Rep (Rom) — Institutul de Fizica si Inginerie Nucleara. Report (Romania)

Inst Flor Bol Tecn — Instituto Florestal Boletim Tecnico

Inst Florest Bol Tec (Sao Paulo) — Instituto Florestal. Boletim Tecnico (Sao Paulo)

Inst Florest Publ (Sao Paulo) — Instituto Florestal. Publicacao (Sao Paulo)

Inst Folk — Boletin. Instituto de Folklore

Inst Fom Algod (Bogota) — Instituto de Fomento Algodonero (Bogota)

Inst Fom Pesq Bol Cient — Instituto de Fomento Pesquero. Boletin Cientifico

Inst Fom Pesq Publ — Instituto de Fomento Pesquero. Publicacion

Inst Fondam Afr Noire Bull Ser A — Institut Fondamental d'Afrique Noire. Bulletin. Serie A. Sciences Naturelles

Inst For Aust Newslett — Institute of Foresters of Australia. Newsletter

Inst Foresters Aust Newsl — Institute of Foresters of Australia. Newsletter

Inst Foresters Aust Newslett — Institute of Foresters of Australia. Newsletter

Inst For Invest Exp Comun — Instituto Forestal de Investigaciones y Experiencias [Madrid]. Comunicacion

Inst For Invest Exper (Madrid) An — Instituto Forestal de Investigaciones y Experiencias (Madrid). Anales

Inst For Invest Exper (Madrid) Bol — Instituto Forestal de Investigaciones y Experiencias (Madrid). Boletin

Inst For Invest Exper (Madrid) Comun — Instituto Forestal de Investigaciones y Experiencias (Madrid). Comunicacion

Inst For Invest Exper (Madrid) Trab — Instituto Forestal de Investigaciones y Experiencias (Madrid). Trabajos

Inst For Nac Foll Tec For — Instituto Forestal Nacional. Folleto Tecnico Forestal

Inst For Prod Colleg For Resour Univ Wash Contrib — Institute of Forest Products. College of Forest Resources. University of Washington. Contribution

Inst Forum — Institute Forum

Inst For Zool Res Notes — Institute of Forest Zoology. Research Notes

Inst Francais d'Haiti Mem — Institut Francais d'Haiti. Memoires

Inst Francais Petrole Rev — Institut Francais du Petrole. Revue et Annales des Combustible Liquides [Later, Institut Francais du Petrole. Revue]

Inst Franc Washington Hist Doc — Institut Francais de Washington. Historical Documents

Inst Fr Cafe Cacao Bull — Institut Francais du Cafe et du Cacao. Bulletin

Inst Freshwater Res (Drottningholm) Rep — Institute of Freshwater Research (Drottningholm). Report

Inst Freshw Res (Drottningholm) Rep — Institute of Freshwater Research (Drottningholm). Report

Inst Fr Etud Andines — Institut Francais d'Etudes Andines. Bulletin

Inst Fr Pet Rev — Institut Francais du Petrole. Revue et Annales des Combustible Liquides [Later, Institut Francais du Petrole. Revue]

Inst Fr Rech Exploit Mer Actes Colloq — Institut Francais de Recherche pour l'Exploitation de la Mer. Actes de Colloques

Inst Fuel (London) Bull — Institute of Fuel (London). Bulletin

Inst Fuel (London) Wartime Bull — Institute of Fuel (London). Wartime Bulletin

Inst Fuel Symp Ser (London) — Institute of Fuel. Symposium Series (London)

Inst Fuel Wartime Bull — Institute of Fuel Wartime Bulletin

Inst Gas Eng — Institution of Gas Engineers. Communications

Inst Gas Eng Commun — Institution of Gas Engineers. Communications

Inst Gas Eng J — Institution of Gas Engineers. Journal

Inst Gas Technol — Institute of Gas Technology

Inst Gas Technol (Chicago) Res Bull — Institute of Gas Technology (Chicago). Research Bulletin

Inst Gas Technol (Chicago) Tech Rep — Institute of Gas Technology (Chicago). Technical Report

Inst Gemol Esp Bol — Instituto Gemologico Espanol. Boletin

Inst Gen Psychol Bul — Institut General Psychologique. Bulletin General

Inst Geofis Andes Colomb Publ Ser A — Instituto Geofisico de los Andes Colombianos. Publicacion. Serie A. Sismologia

Inst Geog E Hist Da Bahia R — Instituto Geographico e Historico da Bahia. Revista

Inst Geog Nac Bol Geol (Guatemala) — Instituto Geografico Nacional. Boletin Geologico (Guatemala)

Inst Geogr Geol Estado Sao Paulo Bol — Instituto Geografico e Geologico. Estado de Sao Paulo. Boletim

Inst Geogr Na (Guatem) Bol Geol — Instituto Geografico Nacional (Guatemala). Boletin Geologico

Inst Geol Bassin Aquitaine Bull — Institut de Geologie du Bassin d'Aquitaine. Bulletin

Inst Geol Bassin Aquitaine Mem — Institut de Geologie du Bassin d'Aquitaine. Memoires

Inst Geol Geofiz Bucharest Stud Teh Econ Ser E — Institutul de Geologie si Geofizica. Bucharest. Studii Tehnice si Economice. Seria E. Hidrogeologie

Inst Geol Geofiz Stud Teh Econ Ser E — Institutul de Geologie si Geofizica. Studii Tehnice si Economice. Seria E. Hidrogeologie

Inst Geol Geofiz Stud Teh Econ Ser I — Institutul de Geologie si Geofizica. Studii Tehnice si Economice. Seria I. Mineralogie-Petrografie

Inst Geol Min Esp Mapa Geol Esp — Instituto Geologico y Minero de Espana. Mapa Geologico de Espana

Inst Geol Min Rev Univ Nac Tucuman — Instituto de Geologia y Mineria. Revista. Universidad Nacional de Tucuman

Inst Geol Rom Anu — Institutul Geologic al Romaniei. Anuarul

Inst Geol Sci Charles Univ Rep Res — Institute of Geological Science. Charles University. Report on Research

Inst Geol Sci (London) Rep — Institute of Geological Sciences (London). Report

Inst Geol Sci Overseas Mem — Institute of Geological Sciences. Overseas Memoir

Inst Geol Sci Rep — Institute of Geological Sciences. Report

Inst Geol Stud Teh Econ Ser E — Institutul Geologic. Studii Tehnice si Economice. Seria E. Hidrogeologie

Inst Geol Stud Teh Econ Ser I — Institutul Geologic. Studii Tehnice si Economice. Seria I. Mineralogie-Petrografie

Inst Geol Urug Bol — Instituto Geologico del Uruguay. Boletin

Inst Geol (Warsaw) Pr — Instytut Geolgiczny (Warsaw). Prace

Inst Gerontol Ser — Institute of Gerontology Series

Inst Gezondheidstech TNO Rapp — Instituut voor Gezondheidstechniek TNO [*Toegepast-Natuurwetenschappelijk Onderzoek*]. Rapport

Inst Goryuch Iskop Tr — Institut Goryuchikh Iskopaemykh Trudy

Inst Grand Ducal Luxemb Sect Sci Nat Phys Math Arch — Institut Grand-Ducal de Luxembourg. Section des Sciences Naturelles. Physiques et Mathematiques. Archives

Inst Hautes Etudes Sci Publ Math — Institut des Hautes Etudes Scientifiques. Publications Mathematiques

Inst Hierro Acero (Madrid) Publ — Instituto del Hierro y del Acero (Madrid). Publicaciones

Inst Highw Engrs J — Institution of Highway Engineers. Journal

Inst Hist E Geog Bras R — Instituto Historico e Geographico Brasileiro. Revista

Inst Hist Res Bul — Institute of Historical Research. Bulletin

Inst Hist Res Bull — Institute of Historical Research. Bulletin

Inst Husdyrernaer Foringslaere Nor Landbrukshogsk Beret — Institutt foer Husdyrernaering og Foringslaere Norges Landbrukshogskole Beretning

Inst Husdyrernaering Foringslaere Nor Landbrukshogsk Beret — Institutt foer Husdyrernaering og Foringslaere Norges Landbrukshogskole Beretning

Inst Hutn Pr — Instytutow Hutniczych. Prace

Inst Hydromech Wasserwirtsch Eidg Tech Hochsch Zuerich — Institut fuer Hydromechanik und Wasserwirtschaft. Eidgenoessische Technische Hochschule Zuerich

Inst Indochin Etud Homme Bull & Trav — Institut Indochinois pour l'Etude de l'Homme. Bulletins et Travaux

Inst Int Am De Protec A La Infancia Bol — Instituto Internacional Americano de Proteccion a la Infancia. Boletin

Inst Int De Statist Bul — Institut International de Statistique. Bulletein

Inst Int Educ N Bul — Institute of International Education. News Bulletin

Inst Interam Nino Bol — Instituto Interamericano del Nino. Boletin

Inst Intermed Int De La Haye Bul — Institut Intermediaire International de la Haye. Bulletin

Inst Interm Int Bul — Institut Intermediare International. Bulletin

Inst Internat Admin Publique Bul — Bulletin. Institut International d'Administration Publique

Inst Internat Pedagog Report — Institutionen foer Internationell Pedagogik. Report

Inst Interuniv Sci Nucl Monogr — Institut Interuniversitaire des Sciences Nucleaires. Monographie

Inst Interuniv Sci Nucl Rapp Annu — Institut Interuniversitaire des Sciences Nucleaires. Rapport Annuel

Inst Int Rech Better Congr Hiver CR — Institut International de Recherches Betteravieres. Congres d'Hiver. Compte Rendu

Inst Int Rech Better CR Definitif Assem — Institut International de Recherches Betteravieres. Compte Rendu Definitif de l'Assemblee

Inst Int Rech Better Rev — Institut International de Recherches Betteravieres. Revue

Inst Int Rel Proc — Institute of International Relations. Proceedings

Inst Int Stat R — Institut International de Statistique. Revue

Inst Invest — Institutional Investor

Inst Invest Agron (Angola) Ser Cient — Instituto de Investigacao Agronomica (Angola). Serie Cientifica

Inst Invest Agron (Angola) Ser Tec — Instituto de Investigacao Agronomica (Angola). Serie Tecnica

Inst Invest Agron (Mocambique) Ser Mem — Instituto de Investigacao Agronomica (Mocambique). Serie Memorias

Inst Invest Biomed Univ Nac Auton Mex Inf — Instituto de Investigaciones Biomedicas. Universidad Nacional Autonoma de Mexico. Informe

Inst Invest Cient (Angola) Relat Comun — Instituto de Investigacao Cientifica (Angola). Relatorios e Comunicacoes

Inst Invest Geol Bol Chile — Instituto de Investigaciones Geologicas. Boletin (Chile)

Inst Investor — Institutional Investor

Inst Invest Recur Mar (Callao) Inf — Instituto de Investigacion de los Recursos Marinos (Callao). Informe

Inst Invst — Institutional Investor

Instit Psiquiat Bol — Instituto Psiquiatrico. Boletin

Institutiones Math — Institutiones Mathematicae

Instituto Nac Previs Soc Boln Mens — Instituto Nacional de Prevision Social Boletin Mensual

Inst J Inst Ophthal Optns — Institute Journal. Institute of Ophthalmic Opticians

Inst Jozef Stefan IJS Porocilo — Institut Jozef Stefan. IJS Porocilo

Inst Jozef Stefan IJS Rep — Institut Jozef Stefan. IJS Report

Inst Kerntech Tech Univ (Berlin) Ber — Institut fuer Kerntechnik der Technischen Universitaet (Berlin). Bericht

Inst Khim Akad Nauk Tadzh SSR Tr — Institut Khimii Akademiya Nauk Tadzhikskoi SSR Trudy

Inst Krajowych Wlok Nat Pr — Instytut Krajowych Wlokien Naturalnych. Prace

Inst Lake Super Geol Tech Sess Abstr Field Guides — Institute on Lake Superior Geology. Technical Sessions, Abstracts, and Field Guides

Inst Lekow Biul — Instytut Lekow. Biuletyn

Inst Lekow Biul Inf — Instytut Lekow. Biuletyn Informacyjny

Inst Locomotive Eng J — Institution of Locomotive Engineers. Journal

Inst Mar Eng Annu Rep — Institute of Marine Engineers. Annual Report

Inst Mar Eng Annu Vol — Institute of Marine Engineers. Annual Volume

Inst Mar Eng Trans — Institute of Marine Engineers. Transactions

Inst Mar Eng Trans Ser C — Institute of Marine Engineers. Transactions. Series C

Inst Mar Environ Res Rep — Institute for Marine Environmental Research. Report

Inst Marine Sci Pub — Institute of Marine Science. Publications

Inst Mar Peru (Callao) Inf — Instituto del Mar del Peru (Callao). Informe

Inst Mar Res Lysekil Ser Biol Rep — Institute of Marine Research. Lysekil Series Biology Report

Inst Mar Sci Rep Univ Alaska — Institute of Marine Science. Report. University of Alaska

Inst Mater Modelos Estruct Bol Tec Univ Cent Venez — Instituto de Materiales y Modelos Estructurales. Boletin Tecnico. Universidad Central de Venezuela

Inst Mater Ogniotrwalych Biul Inf — Instytut Materialow Ogniotrwalych. Biuletyn Informacyjny

Inst Mat Estestv Severo Kavkazsk Gosud Univ — Institut Matematiki i Estestvoznanija pri Severo-Kavkazskom Gosudarstvennom Universitete/Institute of Mathematics and Natural Sciences to the North Caucasus State University/Institut des Mathematiques et des Science Naturelles

Inst Math Appl Conf Ser New Ser — Institute of Mathematics and its Applications Conference Series. New Series

Inst Math Its Appl Bull — Institute of Mathematics and Its Applications. Bulletin

Inst Math Its Appl Conf Ser — Institute of Mathematics and Its Applications Conference Series

Inst Math Statist Bull — Institute of Mathematical Statistics. Bulletin

Inst Maurice Thorez Cah Hist — Cahiers d'Histoire. Institut Maurice Thorez

Inst Maurice Thorez Confs — Conferences. Institut Maurice Thorez

Inst Meat Bull — Institute of Meat Bulletin

Inst Mech Eng Conf Trans — Institution of Mechanical Engineers Conference Transactions

Inst Mech Eng J & Proc — Institution of Mechanical Engineers. Journal and Proceedings

Inst Mech Eng (Lond) Proc — Institution of Mechanical Engineers (London). Proceedings

Inst Mech Eng Proc — Institution of Mechanical Engineers. Proceedings

Inst Mech Eng Proc Part 3 — Institution of Mechanical Engineers. Proceedings. Part 3

Inst Mech Eng Ry Div J — Institution of Mechanical Engineers. Railway Division. Journal

Inst Mech Eng Semin — Institution of Mechanical Engineers. Seminar

Inst Mech Eng War Emerg Proc — Institution of Mechanical Engineers. War Emergency Proceedings

Inst Med Leg Med Soc Arch — Institut de Medecine Legale et de Medecine Sociale. Archives

Inst Med Proc — Institute of Medicine. Chicago. Proceedings

Inst Meh Moskov Gos Univ Naucn Trudy — Institut Mehaniki Moskovskogo Gosudarstvennogo Universiteta Naucnye Trudy

Inst M Eng Tr — Institution of Mining Engineers. Transactions

Inst Metall Autumn Rev Course Ser 3 (London) — Institution of Metallurgists. Autumn Review Course. Series 3 (London)

Inst Metall Course Vol Ser 3 (London) — Institution of Metallurgists. Course Volume. Series 3 (London)

Inst Metall Ser 3 (London) — Institution of Metallurgists. Series 3 (London)

Inst Metall Spring Resid Course Ser 3 (London) — Institution of Metallurgists. Spring Residential Course. Series 3 (London)

Inst Metall Tech Conf Pap (London) — Institute of Metallurgical Technicians. Conference Papers (London)

Inst Metals J — Institute of Metals. Journal

Inst Metal Zelaza Pr — Instytut Metalurgii Zelaza. Prace

Inst Meteorol Hidrol Culegere Lucr Meteorol — Institutul de Meteorologie si Hidrologie. Culegere de Lucrari de Meteorologie

Inst Meteorol Hidrol Stud Cercet Partea 1 — Institutul de Meteorologie si Hidrologie. Studii si Cercetari. Partea 1. Meteorologie

Inst Meteorol Hidrol Stud Cercet Partea 2 — Institutul de Meteorologie si Hidrologie. Studii si Cercetari. Partea 2. Hidrologie

Inst Met Monogr Rep Ser — Institute of Metals. Monograph and Report Series

Inst Met Niezelazn Biul — Instytut Metali Niezelaznych. Biuletyn

Inst Mex Minas Met Inf — Instituto Mexicano de Minas y Metalurgia. Informes y Memorias

Inst Mex Pet Publ — Instituto Mexicano del Petroleo. Publicacion

Inst Mex Petrol Rev — Instituto Mexicano del Petroleo. Revista

Inst Mex Recur Nat Renov Ser Mesas Redondas — Instituto Mexicano de Recursos Naturales Renovables. Serie de Mesas Redondas

Inst Michel Pacha Ann — Institut Michel Pacha. Annales

Inst Microbiol Rutgers Univ Annu Rep — Institute of Microbiology. Rutgers University. Annual Report

Inst Min & Met Trans — Institution of Mining and Metallurgy. Transactions

Inst Mine Petrosani Lucr Stiint — Institutul de Mine Petrosani. Lucrarile Stiintifice

Inst Mining Met Trans Sect B — Institution of Mining and Metallurgy. Transactions. Section B. Applied Earth Science

Inst Min L — Institute on Mineral Law

Inst Min Metall Bull — Institution of Mining and Metallurgy. Bulletin

Inst Min Metall Trans Sect A — Institution of Mining and Metallurgy. Transactions. Section A. Mining Industry

Inst Min Metall Trans Sect A Min Ind — Institution of Mining and Metallurgy. Transactions. Section A. Mining Industry

Inst Min Metall Trans Sect B — Institution of Mining and Metallurgy. Transactions. Section B. Applied Earth Science

Inst Min Metall Trans Sect C — Institution of Mining and Metallurgy. Transactions. Section C. Mineral Processing and Extractive Metallurgy

Inst Min Miner Res Univ K Tech Rep — Institute for Mining and Mineral Research. University of Kentucky. Technical Report

Inst Munic Cienc Nat Misc Zool — Instituto Municipal de Ciencias Naturales Miscelanea. Zoologica

Inst Munic Engrs J — Institution of Municipal Engineers. Journal

Inst Munic Eng S Afr Dist Annu J — Institution of Municipal Engineers. South African District. Annual Journal

Inst Nac Carbon (Oviedo Spain) Bol Inf — Instituto Nacional del Carbon (Oviedo, Spain). Boletin Informativo

Inst Nac Carbon Sus Deriv "Francisco Pintado Fe" Publ INCAR — Instituto Nacional del Carbon y Sus Derivados "Francisco Pintado Fe." Publicacion INCAR

Inst Nac Conserv Nat Estac Cent Ecol Bol (Spain) — Instituto Nacional para la Conservacion de la Natureleza. Estacion Central de Ecologia. Boletin (Spain)

Inst Nac Conserv Nat Nat Hisp — Instituto Nacional para la Conservacion de la Naturaleza. Naturalia Hispanica

Inst Nac Invest Agrar An Ser Technol Agrar Spain — Instituto Nacional de Investigaciones Agrarias. Anales. Serie. Tecnologia Agraria (Spain)

Inst Nac Invest Agrar Comun Ser Prot Veg (Spain) — Instituto Nacional de Investigaciones Agrarias. Comunicaciones. Serie: Proteccion Vegetal (Spain)

Inst Nac Invest Agric SAG (Mex) Foll Tec — Instituto Nacional de Investigaciones Agricolas. Secretaria de Agricultura y Ganaderia (Mexico). Folleto Tecnico

Inst Nac Invest Agric Secr Agric Ganad (Mex) Foll Tec — Instituto Nacional de Investigaciones Agricolas. Secretaria de Agricultura y Ganaderia (Mexico). Folleto Tecnico

Inst Nac Invest Agron Bol — Instituto Nacional de Investigaciones Agronomicas. Boletin

Inst Nac Invest Agron (Madr) Conf — Instituto Nacional de Investigaciones Agronomicas (Madrid). Conferencias

Inst Nac Invest Agron (Spain) Cuad — Instituto Nacional de Investigaciones Agronomicas (Spain). Cuaderno

Inst Nac Invest Fom Min (Peru) Ser Memo — Instituto Nacional de Investigacion y Fomento Mineros (Peru). Serie Memorandum

Inst Nac Invest For Bol Tec — Instituto Nacional de Investigaciones Forestales. Boletin Tecnico

Inst Nac Invest For Cat — Instituto Nacional de Investigaciones Forestales. Catalogo

Inst Nac Invest For Publ Esp — Instituto Nacional de Investigaciones Forestales. Publicacion Especial

Inst Nac Inv For Bol Divulg — Instituto Nacional de Investigaciones Forestales. Boletin Divulgativo

Inst Nac Med Leg Colomb Rev — Instituto Nacional de Medicina Legal de Colombia. Revista

Inst Nac Nutr Caracas Publ — Instituto Nacional de Nutricion. Caracas. Publicacion

Inst Nac Pesca Bol Cient Tec — Instituto Nacional de Pesca. Boletin Cientifico y Tecnico

Inst Nac Pesca Bol Inf (Guayaquil) — Instituto Nacional de Pesca. Boletin Informativo (Guayaquil)

Inst Nac Pesca (Cuba) Cent Invest Pesq Bol Divulg Tec — Instituto Nacional de la Pesca (Cuba). Centro de Investigaciones Pesqueras. Boletin de Divulgacion Tecnica

Inst Nac Pesca (Cuba) Cent Invest Pesq Contrib — Instituto Nacional de la Pesca (Cuba). Centro de Investigaciones Pesqueras. Contribucion

Inst Nac Pesca (Ecuador) Bol Inf — Instituto Nacional de Pesca (Ecuador). Boletin Informativo

Inst Nac Pesca Inf Espec — Instituto Nacional de Pesca. Informativo Especial

Inst Nac Pesca Ser Inf Pesq — Instituto Nacional de Pesca. Serie Informes Pesqueros

Inst Nac Pesqui Amazonia Publ Quim — Instituto Nacional de Pesqui Amazonia. Publicacao Quimica

Inst Nac Tecnol Agropecu Bol Inf — Instituto Nacional de Tecnologia Agropecuaria. Boletin Informativo

Inst Nac Tecnol Agropecu Suelos Publ — Instituto Nacional de Tecnologia Agropecuaria. Suelos Publicacion

Inst Nac Tecnol Bol — Instituto Nacional de Tecnologia. Boletim

Inst Nac Tecnol Ind Bol Tec (Argentina) — Instituto Nacional de Tecnologia Industrial. Boletin Tecnico (Argentina)

Instn Amelior Bett — Institution pour l'Amelioration de la Betterave

Inst Napoleon R — Institut Napoleon. Revue

Inst Nat Amelior Conserves Legumes Bull Trimest (Belg) — Institut National pour l'Amelioration des Conserves de Legumes. Bulletin Trimestriel (Belgium)

Inst Nat Ind Charbonniere Bull Tech-Mines — Institut National de l'Industrie Charbonniere. Bulletin Technique - Mines

Inst Nat Ind Extr Bull Tech-Mines Carrieres — Institut National des Industries Extractives. Bulletin Technique. Mineset Carrieres

Inst Natl Amelior Conserves Legumes Bull Bimest (Belg) — Institut National pour l'Amelioration des Conserves de Legumes. Bulletin Bimestriel (Belgium)

Inst Nat Lang Lect Ser — Institute of National Language. Lecture Series

Inst Natl Genevois Bull — Institut National Genevois. Bulletin

Inst Natl Genevois Bull NS — Institut National Genevois. Bulletin. New Series

Inst Natl Ind Extr (Liege) Bull Tech Mines Carrieres — Institut National des Industries Extractives (Liege). Bulletin Technique. Mineset Carrieres

Inst Natl Radioelem (Belg) Rapp — Institut National des Radioelements (Belgium). Rapport

Inst Natl Rech Agron Serv Ind Agric Aliment — Institut National de la Recherche Agronomique au Service des Industries Agricoles et Alimentaires

Inst Natl Rech Agron Tunis Ann — Institut National de la Recherche Agronomique de Tunisie. Annales

Inst Natl Rech Agron Tunis Doc Tech — Institut National de la Recherche Agronomique de Tunisie. Documents Techniques

Inst Natl Rech Agron Tunisie Doc Tech — Institut National de la Recherche Agronomique de Tunisie. Documents Techniques

Inst Natl Rech Agron Tunisie Lab Arboric Fruit Rapp Act — Institut National de la Recherche Agronomique de Tunisie. Laboratoire d'Arboriculture Fruitiere. Rapport d'Activite

Inst Natl Rech Agron Tunis Lab Aboriculture Fruit Rapp Act — Institut National de la Recherche Agronomique de Tunisie. Laboratoire d'Arboriculture Fruitiere. Rapport d'Activite

Inst Natl Sante Rech Med Colloq — Institut National de la Sante et de la Recherche Medicale. Colloque

Inst Nat Rech Agron (Paris) — Institut National de la Recherche Agronomique (Paris)

Inst Nat Rech Agron Tunisie — Institut National de la Recherche Agronomique de Tunisie

Inst Nat Sci Nanyang Univ Tech Rep — Institute of Natural Sciences. Nanyang University. Technical Report

Inst Neorg Khim Elektrokhim Akad Nauk Gruz SSR Sb — Institut Neorganicheskoi Khimii i Elektrokhimii Akademiya Nauk Gruzinskoi SSR Sbornik

Instn Fire Engrs Q — Institution of Fire Engineers Quarterly

Inst Niezel Pr — Instytut Metali Niezelaznych Prace

Inst Nisk Temp Badan Strukt PAN Pr Ser Pr Kom Krystalogr — Instytut Niskich Temperatur i Badan Strukturalnych PAN Prace. Seria. Prace Komitetu Krystalografii

Inst N L — Instituto Nacional do Livro

Instn Lect Stud Instn Civ Engrs — Institution Lectures to Students. Institution of Civil Engineers

Inst Nomads Pet Expo Symp — Institute of Nomads. Petroleum Exposition Symposium

Inst Nonlinear Sci — Institute for Nonlinear Science

Inst Notes Inst Transp — Institute Notes. Institute of Transport

Instn Prod Engrs J — Institution of Production Engineers Journal

Instn Publ Hlth Engrs J — Institution of Public Health Engineers Journal

Instn Publ Ltg Engrs Supts Pap — Institution of Public Lighting Engineers and Superintendents. Papers

Inst Nucl Chem Technol Rep INCT — Institute of Nuclear Chemistry and Technology. Report INCT

Inst Nucl Phys (Cracow) Rep — Institute of Nuclear Physics (Cracow). Report

Inst Nucl Res (Warsaw) Rep — Institute of Nuclear Research (Warsaw). Report

Inst Nucl Study Univ Tokyo INS Rep — Institute for Nuclear Study. University of Tokyo. INS-Report

Inst Nucl Study Univ Tokyo Rep — Institute for Nuclear Study. University of Tokyo. Reports

Inst Nutr Cent Am Panama Inf Anu — Instituto de Nutricion de Centro America y Panama. Informe Anual

Inst Oceanogr Ann — Institut Oceanographique. Annales

Inst Oceanogr Nha Trang — Institut Oceanographique de Nha Trang

Inst Oceanogr Ribar (Split) Biljeske — Institut za Oceanograflju i Ribarstvo (Split). Biljeske

Inst Oceanogr Sci Annu Rep — Institute of Oceanographic Sciences. Annual Report

Inst Oceanogr Sci Col Repr — Institute of Oceanographic Sciences. Collected Reprints

Inst Ochr Rosl Mater Ses Nauk — Instytut Ochrony Roslin. Materialy Sesji Naukowej

Inst of Clerks of Works Jnl — Institute of Clerks of Works. Journal

Inst Oil & Gas L & Taxation — Institute on Oil and Gas Law and Taxation

Inst on Plan Zon and Eminent Domain Proc — Institute on Planning, Zoning, and Eminent Domain. Proceedings

Inst on Priv Inv & Inv Abroad — Institute on Private Investments and Investors Abroad. Proceedings

Inst on Priv Invest and Investors Abroad Proc — Institute on Private Investments and Investors Abroad. Proceedings

Inst on Sec Reg — Institute on Securities Regulation

Inst Ophthal Monogr — Instutute of Ophthalmology Monographs

Inst Orientac Asist Tec Oeste Anu — Instituto de Orientacion y Asistencia Tecnica del Oeste. Anuario

Inst Pap Commonw For Inst — Institute Paper. Commonwealth Forestry Institute

Inst Pap Inst Forest Genet — Institute Papers. Institute of Forest Genetics

Inst Parcs Nationaux Congo Belge Explor Parc Natl Albert — Institut des Parcs Nationaux du Congo Belge. Exploration du Parc National Albert

Inst Parcs Nationaux Congo Explor Parc Natl Albert — Institut des Parcs Nationaux du Congo Belge. Exploration du Parc National Albert

Inst Pasteur Bangui Rapp Annu — Institut Pasteur Bangui. Rapport Annuel

Inst Pasteur Repub Unie Cameroun Rapp Fonct Tech — Institut Pasteur de la Republique Unie du Cameroun. Rapport sur le Fonctionnement Technique

Inst Past Guy Ter L In — Institut Pasteur de la Guyane et du Territoire de l'Inini. Publications

Inst Pathol Ig Anim Colect Indrumari (Buchar) — Institutul de Pathologie si Igiena Animala. Colectia Indrumari (Bucharest)

Inst Pathol Ig Anim Probl Epizootol Vet (Buchar) — Institutul de Pathologie si Igiena Animala. Probleme de Epizootologie Veterinara (Bucharest)

Inst Peches Mar Bul — Institut des Peches Maritimes. Bulletin

Inst Peches Marit Rev Trav — Institut des Peches Maritimes. Revue des Travaux

Inst Personnel Mgmt Dig — Institute of Personnel Management. Digest

Inst Pesqui Agron Bol Tec — Instituto de Pesquisas Agronomicas. Boletim Tecnico

Inst Pesqui Agron Pernambuco Bol Tec — Instituto de Pesquisas Agronomicas de Pernambuco. Boletim Tecnico

Inst Pesqui Agron Pernambuco Circ — Instituto de Pesquisas Agronomicas de Pernambuco. Circular

Inst Pesqui Agron Pernambuco Publ — Instituto de Pesquisas Agronomicas de Pernambuco. Publicacao

Inst Pesqui Agron (Recife) Bol Tec — Instituto de Pesquisas Agronimicas (Recife). Boletim Tecnico

Inst Pesqui Agropecu Norte Bol Tec — Instituto de Pesquisas Agropecuarias do Norte. Boletim Tecnico

Inst Pesqui Agropecu Norte (IPEAN) Bol Tec — Instituto de Pesquisa Agropecuaria do Norte (IPEAN). Boletim Tecnico

Inst Pesqui Agropecu Norte (IPEAN) Ser Fitotec — Instituto de Pesquisas e Experimentacao Agropecuarias do Norte (IPEAN). Serie Fitotecnia

Inst Pesqui Agropecu Sul Bol Tec — Instituto de Pesquisas Agropecuarias do Sul. Boletim Tecnico

Inst Pesqui Exp Agropecu Norte (Belem) Bol Tec — Instituto de Pesquisas e Experimentacao Agropecuarias do Norte (Belem). BoletimTecnico

Inst Pesqui Exp Agropecu Norte (IPEAN) (Belem) Bol Tec — Instituto de Pesquisas e Experimentacao Agropecuarias do Norte (IPEAN) (Belem).Boletim Tecnico

Inst Pesqui Exp Agropecu Norte (IPEAN) Ser Bot Fisiol Veg — Instituto de Pesquisas e Experimentacao Agropecuarias do Norte (IPEAN). Serie Botanica e Fisiologia Vegetal

Inst Pesqui Exp Agropecu Norte (IPEAN) Ser Cult Amazonia — Instituto de Pesquisas e Experimentacao Agropecuarias do Norte (IPEAN). Serie Culturas da Amazonia

Inst Pesqui Exp Agropecu Norte (IPEAN) Ser Estud Bovinos — Instituto de Pesquisas e Experimentacao Agropecuarias do Norte (IPEAN). Serie Estudos sobre Bovinos

Inst Pesqui Exp Agropecu Norte (IPEAN) Ser Estud Bubalinos — Instituto de Pesquisas e Experimentacao Agropecuarias do Norte (IPEAN). Serie Estudos sobre Bubalinos

Inst Pesqui Exp Agropecu Norte (IPEAN) Ser Estud Ens — Instituto de Pesquisas e Experimentacao Agropecuarias do Norte (IPEAN). Serie Estudos e Ensaios

Inst Pesqui Exp Agropecu Norte (IPEAN) Ser Estud Ensaios — Instituto de Pesquisas e Experimentacao Agropecuarias do Norte (IPEAN). Serie Estudos e Ensaios

Inst Pesqui Exp Agropecu Norte (IPEAN) Ser Fertil Solos — Instituto de Pesquisas e Experimentacao Agropecuarias do Norte (IPEAN). Serie Fertilidade de Solos

Inst Pesqui Exp Agropecu Norte (IPEAN) Ser Fitotec — Instituto de Pesquisas e Experimentacao Agropecuarias do Norte (IPEAN). Serie Fitotecnia

Inst Pesqui Exp Agropecu Norte (IPEAN) Ser Quim Solos — Instituto de Pesquisas e Experimentacao Agropecuarias do Norte (IPEAN). Serie Quimica de Solos

Inst Pesqui Exp Agropecu Norte (IPEAN) Ser Solos Amazonia — Instituto de Pesquisas e Experimentacao Agropecuarias do Norte (IPEAN). Serie Solos da Amazonia

Inst Pesqui Exp Agropecu Norte (IPEAN) Ser Tecnol — Instituto de Pesquisas e Experimentacao Agropecuarias do Norte (IPEAN). Serie Tecnologia

Inst Pesqui Exp Agropecu Norte Ser Bot Fisiol Veg — Instituto de Pesquisas e Experimentacao Agropecuarias do Norte (IPEAN). Serie Botanica e Fisiologia Vegetal

Inst Pesqui Exp Agropecu Norte Ser Cult Amazonia — Instituto de Pesquisas e Experimentacao Agropecuarias do Norte (IPEAN). Serie Culturas da Amazonia

Inst Pesqui Exp Agropecu Norte Ser Estud Bovinos — Instituto de Pesquisas e Experimentacao Agropecuarias do Norte (IPEAN). Serie Estudos sobre Bovinos

Inst Pesqui Exp Agropecu Norte Ser Estud Bubalinos — Instituto de Pesquisas e Experimentacao Agropecuarias do Norte (IPEAN). Serie Estudos sobre Bubalinos

Inst Pesqui Exp Agropecu Norte Ser Estud Ens — Instituto de Pesquisas e Experimentacao Agropecuarias do Norte (IPEAN). Serie Estudos e Ensaios

Inst Pesqui Exp Agropecu Norte Ser Fertil Solos — Instituto de Pesquisas e Experimentacao Agropecuarias do Norte (IPEAN). Serie Fertilidade de Solos

Inst Pesqui Exp Agropecu Norte Ser Fitotec — Instituto de Pesquisas e Experimentacao Agropecuarias do Norte (IPEAN). Serie Fitotecnia

Inst Pesqui Exp Agropecu Norte Ser Quim Solos — Instituto de Pesquisas e Experimentacao Agropecuarias do Norte (IPEAN). Serie Quimica de Solos

Inst Pesqui Exp Agropecu Norte Ser Solos Amazonia — Instituto de Pesquisas e Experimentacao Agropecuarias do Norte (IPEAN). Serie Solos da Amazonia

Inst Pesqui Exp Agropecu Norte Ser Tecnol — Instituto de Pesquisas e Experimentacao Agropecuarias do Norte (IPEAN). Serie Tecnologia

Inst Pesqui Exp Agropecu Sul Circ — Instituto de Pesquisas e Experimentacao Agropecuarias do Sul. Circular

Inst Pesqui Tecnol (Sao Paulo) Boletim — Instituto de Pesquisas Tecnologicas (Sao Paulo). Boletim

Inst Pesqui Tecnol (Sao Paulo) Publ — Instituto de Pesquisas Tecnologicas (Sao Paulo). Publicacao

Inst Pesqui Vet Desiderio Finamor Arq — Instituto de Pesquisas Veterinarias Desiderio Finamor. Arquivos

Inst Pet Abstr — Institute of Petroleum. Abstracts

Inst Pet Gaze Bucuresti Stud — Institutul de Petrol si Gaze din Bucuresti. Studii

Inst Pet J — Institute of Petroleum. Journal

Inst Pet (Lond) Pap — Institute of Petroleum (London). Papers

Inst Petroleum Rev — Institute of Petroleum. Review

Inst Petroleum Tech J — Institution of Petroleum Technologists. Journal

Inst Petrol Rev — Institute of Petroleum Review

Inst Petrol Tech Pap — Institute of Petroleum. Technical Papers

Inst Pet Tech Pap IP — Institute of Petroleum. Technical Paper IP

Inst Phonet Rep — Institute of Phonetics. Report

Inst Phys Chem Res Rikagaku Kenkyusho Sci Pap — Institute of Physical and Chemical Research. Rikagaku Kenkyusho. Scientific Papers

Inst Phys Conf Dig — Institute of Physics. Conference Digest

Inst Phys Conf Ser — Institute of Physics. Conference Series

Inst Phys Nucl Eng Rep (Rom) — Institute for Physics and Nuclear Engineering Report (Romania)

Inst Phys Short Meet Ser — Institute of Physics Short Meetings Series

Inst Phytopathol Res Annu Rep — Institute of Phytopathology Research. Annual Report

Inst Plant Eng J — Institution of Plant Engineers. Journal

Inst Plasma Phys Nagoya Univ Rep IPPJ REV — Institute of Plasma Physics. Nagoya University. Report IPPJ-REV

Inst Pluimveeonderz "Het Spelderholt" Jaarversl — Instituut voor Pluimveeonderzoek "Het Spelderholt." Jaarverslag

Inst Pluimveeonderz "Het Spelderholt" Meded — Instituut voor Pluimveeonderzoek "Het Spelderholt." Mededeling

Inst Pluimveeteelt "Het Spelderholt" Meded — Instituut voor de Pluimveeteelt "Het Spelderholt." Mededeling

Inst Police Adm Proc — Institute of Police Administration. Proceedings

Inst Politeh Bucuresti Bul Ser Chim — Institutul Politehnic Bucuresti. Buletinul. Seria Chimie

Inst Politeh Bucuresti Bul Ser Metal — Institutul Politehnic Bucuresti. Buletinul. Seria Metalurgie

Inst Politeh Gheorghe Gheorghiu Dej Bucuresti Bul Ser Chim — Institutul Politehnic "Gheorghe Gheorghiu-Dej" Bucuresti. Buletinul. Seria Chimie

Inst Politeh Gheorghe Gheorghiu Dej Bucuresti Bul Ser Mec — Institutul Politehnic "Gheorghe Gheorghiu-Dej" Bucuresti. Buletinul. Seria Mecanica

Inst Politeh Iasi Bul Sect 1 — Institutul Politehnic din Iasi. Buletinul. Sectia 1. Matematica, Mecanica Teoretica, Fizica

Inst Politeh Iasi Bul Sect 5 — Institutul Politehnic din Iasi. Buletinul. Sectia 5. Constructii-Arhitectura

Inst Politeh Iasi Bul Sect 7 — Institutul Politehnic din Iasi. Buletinul. Sectia 7. Textile, Pielarie

Inst Politehn Traian Vuia Timisoara Lucrar Sem Mat Fiz — Institutului Politehnic Traian Vuia Timisoara. Lucrarile Seminarului de Matematica si Fizica

Inst Politeh Traian Vuia Semin Mat Fiz Lucr — Institutul Politehnic "Traian Vuia." Seminarul di Matematica si Fizica. Lucrarile

Inst Post Office Elec Eng Paper — Institution of Post Office Electrical Engineers. Paper

Inst Printed Circuits Tech Rep — Institute of Printed Circuits. Technical Report

Inst Private Investments — Institute on Private Investments Abroad and Foreign Trade

Inst Prof Librn Ont Newsl — Institute of Professional Librarians of Ontario. Newsletter

Inst Prov Agropecuar (Mendoza) Bol Tec — Instituto Provincial Agropecuario (Mendoza). Boletin Tecnica

Inst Prov Paleontol Sabadell Bol Inf — Instituto Provincial de Paleontologia de Sabadell. Boletin Informativo

Inst Przem Org Pr — Instytut Przemyslu Organicznego. Prace

Inst Przem Tworzyw Farb Biul Inf — Instytut Przemyslu Tworzyw i Farb. Biuletyn Informacyjny

Inst Przem Wiazacych Mater Budow Krakow Biul Inf — Instytut Przemyslu Wiazacych Materialow Budowlanych. Krakow. Biuletyn Informacyjny

Inst Psychiatry Maudsley Monogr — Institute of Psychiatry. Maudsley Monographs

Inst Pub Hlth Eng Yearb — Institution of Public Health Engineers Yearbook

Inst Public Health Eng J — Institution of Public Health Engineers. Journal

Inst Public Serv Vocat Train Bull — Institute for Public Service and Vocational Training. Bulletin

Inst Quim Agric (Rio De Janeiro) Mem — Instituto de Quimica Agricola (Rio De Janeiro). Memoria

Inst Quim Apl Farm (Lima) Bol Inf — Instituto de Quimica Aplicada a la Farmacia (Lima). Boletim Informativo

Instr — Instructor

Inst Radio & Electron Engrs Aust Proc — Institution of Radio and Electronics Engineers of Australia. Proceedings

Inst Radio Electron Eng Aust Proc — Institution of Radio and Electronics Engineers of Australia. Proceedings

Inst Radio Eng Proc — Institute of Radio Engineers. Proceedings

Instr & Autom — Instruments and Automation

Inst Rasteniev — Institut Rastenievodstva

Inst R Colon Belge Bull Seances — Institut Royal Colonial Belge. Bulletin des Seances

Inst R Colon Belge Sect Sci Nat Med Mem Collect 4o — Institut Royal Colonial Belge. Section des Sciences Naturelles et Medicales. Memoires. Collection in Quarto

Inst R Colon Belge Sect Sci Nat Med Mem Collect 8 — Institut Royal Colonial Belge. Section des Sciences Naturelles Medicales. Memoires. Collection in Octavo

Instr Contr — Instruments and Control Systems

Instr Course Lect — Instructional Course Lectures

Instr Eccles — Instrumenta Ecclesiastica

Inst Rech Caoutch Viet Nam Arch — Institut des Recherches sur le Caoutchouc au Viet-Nam. Archive

Inst Rech Caoutch Viet Nam Laikhe Rapp Annu — Institut des Recherches sur le Caoutchouc au Viet-Nam Laikhe. Rapports Annuels

Inst Rech Entomol Phytopathol Evine Dep Bot — Institut de Recherches Entomologiques et Phytopathologiques d'Evine. Departement de Botanique

Inst Rech Huiles Oleagineux (IRHO) Rapp Annu — Institut de Recherches pour les Huiles et Oleagineux (IRHO). Rapport Annuel

Inst Rech Huiles Ol Rapp Annu — Institut de Recherches pour les Huiles et Oleagineux [*IRHO*]. Rapport Annuel

Inst Rech Ressour Hydraul (Budapest) Commun Lang Etrang — Institut de Recherches des Ressources Hydrauliques (Budapest). Communications en Langues Etrangeres

Inst Refrig London Proc — Institute of Refrigeration London. Proceedings

Inst Rep Natn Inst Ind Psychol — Institute Report. National Institute of Industrial Psychology

Inst Res Ment Retard Monogr (Oxford) — Institute for Research into Mental Retardation. Monograph (Oxford)

Inst Res Ment Retard (Oxford) Symp — Institute for Research into Mental Retardation (Oxford). Symposium

Instr Exp Techn — Instruments and Experimental Techniques

Inst Ribna Prom Fil Sladkovodno Ribar (Plovdiv) Izv — Institut po Ribna Promishlenost. Filial po Sladkovodno Ribarstvo (Plovdiv). Izvestiya

Inst Ribni Resur (Varna) Izv — Institut po Ribni Resursi (Varna). Izvestiya

Instr Innov — Instructional Innovator

Instr Innovator — Instructional Innovator

Inst R Meteorol Belg Bull Trimest Obs Ozone — Institut Royal Meteorologique de Belgique. Bulletin Trimestriel. Observations d'Ozone

Instr Naut — Instructions Nautiques

Instrn Technol — Instrumentation Technology

Inst Roy Sci Natur Belgique Bul — Institut Royal des Sciences Naturelles de Belgique. Bulletin

Instr Res — Instructional Resources

Instr Sci — Instructional Science

Inst R Sci Nat Belg Bull — Institut Royal des Sciences Naturelles de Belgique. Bulletin

Inst R Sci Nat Belg Bull Sci Terre — Institut Royal des Sciences Naturelles de Belgique. Bulletin. Sciences de la Terre

Inst R Sci Nat Belg Doc Trav — Institut Royal des Sciences Naturelles de Belgique. Documents de Travail

Inst R Sci Nat Belg Mem — Institut Royal des Sciences Naturelles de Belgique. Memoires

Inst R Sci Nat Belg Mem Deuxieme Ser — Institut Royal des Sciences Naturelles de Belgique. Memoires. Deuxieme Serie

Instr Sh Cent Exp Fm (Ottawa) — Instruction Sheet. Central Experimental Farm (Ottawa)

Instr Teach — Instructor and Teacher

Instr Tech — Instrumentation Technology

Instruct Bull Instn Radio Engrs Aust — Instructional Bulletin. Institution of Radio Engineers. Australia

Instruct Course Lect Am Acad Orthop Surg — Instructional Course Lectures. American Academy of Orthopedic Surgeons

Instructive Pap Br Acet Weld Ass — Instructive Papers. British Acetylene and Welding Association

Instruct Naut — Instructions Nautiques

Instruct Somm Inst Fr Afr Noire — Instructions Sommaires. Institut Francais d'Afrique Noire

Instrukcje Podreczn Panst Inst Hydrol Met — Instrukcje i Podreczniki. Panstwowy Instytut Hydrologiczno-Meteorologiczny

Instruktsii Otd Plankt Vses Nauchno Issled Inst Ryb Khoz Okeanogr — Instruktsii-Otdel Planktona. Vsesoyuznyi Nauchno-Issledovatel'skii Institut Rybnogo Khozyaistva i Okeanografii

Instruktsii Progrm Izuch Promysl Fauny Promyslov — Instruktsii i Programmy po Izucheniyu Promyslovoi Fauny i Promyslov

Instrum Abstr — Instrument Abstracts

Instrum Aerosp Ind — Instrumentation in the Aerospace Industry

Instrum and Control Syst — Instruments and Control Systems

Instrum and Exp Tech — Instruments and Experimental Techniques

Instrum Appar News — Instrument and Apparatus News

Instrum Autom — Instrumentation and Automation

Instrum Automat — Instruments and Automation

InstrumBau Z — Instrumentenbau-Zeitschrift

Instrum Bull — Instrumentation Bulletin

Instrum Chem Pet Ind — Instrumentation in the Chemical and Petroleum Industries

Instrum Constr — Instrument Construction [London]

Instrum Constr (USSR) — Instrument Construction (USSR)

Instrum Control Engng — Instrument and Control Engineering

Instrum Control Syst — Instruments and Control Systems

Instrum Contr Syst — Instruments and Control Systems

Instrum Cryog Ind — Instrumentation in the Cryogenic Industry

Instrum Electr Dev — Instruments and Electronics Developments

Instrum Eng — Instrument Engineer

Instrum Engr — Instrument Engineer

Instrument — Instrumentalist

Instrumentation Tech — Instrumentation Technology

Instrumentenbau Z — Instrumentenbau-Zeitschrift

Instrum Exp Tech — Instruments and Experimental Techniques

Instrum Food Beverage Ind — Instrumentation in the Food and Beverage Industry

Instrum Forsch — Instrument und Forschung

Instrum Geophys Res — Instrumentation for Geophysical Research. Air Force Cambridge Research Center

Instrum India — Instruments India

Instrum Iron Steel Ind — Instrumentation in the Iron and Steel Industry

Instrum Lab — Instruments et Laboratoires

Instruml Bull Seism Obs Fordham Univ — Instrumental Bulletin of the Seismic Observatory. Fordham University

Instrum Maint Manage — Instrument Maintenance Management

Instrum Maker — Instrument Maker

Instrum Manuf — Instrument Manufacturing

Instrum Med — Instrumentation in Medicine

Instrum Met Ind — Instrumentation in the Metals Industries

Instrum Metody Anal Ekol — Instrumental'nye Metody Analiza v Ekologii

Instrum Mf — Instrument Manufacture

Instrum Mfg — Instrument Manufacturing

Instrum Min Metall Ind — Instrumentation in the Mining and Metallurgy Industries

Instrum Mkr — Instrument Maker

Instrum News — Instrument News

Instrumn Geophys Astrophys — Instrumentation for Geophysics and Astrophysics. Air Force Cambridge Research Center

Instrumn Syst Engng — Instrumentation and Systems Engineering

Instrum Nucl — Instrumentation Nucleaire

Instrum Planet Terr Atmos Remote Sens — Instrumentation for Planetary and Terrestrial Atmospheric Remote Sensing

Instrum Power Ind — Instrumentation in the Power Industry

Instrum Power Ind Proc — Instrumentation in the Power Industry. Proceedings

Instrum Pract — Instrument Practice

Instrum Pulp Pap Ind — Instrumentation in the Pulp and Paper Industry

Instrum Pulp Pap Ind Proc — Instrumentation in the Pulp and Paper Industry. Proceedings

Instrum Rationis Sources Hist Logic Modern Age — Instrumenta Rationis. Sources for the History of Logic in the Modern Age

Instrum Rev — Instrument Review

Instrum Rev (Leiden) — Instrument Revue (Leiden)

Instrums Automn — Instruments and Automation

Instrum Sci Technol — Instrumentation Science and Technology

Instrums Control Syst — Instruments and Control Systems

Instrums Exp Tech Pittsburgh — Instruments and Experimental Techniques (Pittsburgh)

Instrums Exp Tech Wash — Instruments and Experimental Techniques (Washington)

Instrums Ind — Instruments in Industry

Instrums Labs — Instruments et Laboratoires

Instrums Note Aeronaut Res Labs Aust — Instruments Note. Aeronautical Research Laboratories. Australia

Instrums Note Div Aero Naut Aust — Instruments Note. Division of Aeronautics. C.S.I.R. (afterwards Department of Supply and Development). Australia

Instrum Soc Amer Conf Preprint — Instrument Society of America. Conference Preprint

Instrum Soc Am Instrum Index — Instrument Society of America. Instrumentation Index

Instrum Soc India J — Instrument Society of India. Journal

Instrums Prod Dent — Instruments et Prodiuts Dentaires

Instrum Tech — Instrumentation Technology

Instrum Technol — Instrumentation Technology

Instrum Test Rep Bur Meteor — Instrumentation Test Report. Bureau of Meteorology

Instrum Trace Org Monit — Instrumentation for Trace Organic Monitoring

Instrum Wld — Instrument World

Instrum Zeit — Instrumentenbau Zeitschrift

Inst Sci Agron Burundi (ISABU) Rapp Annu Notes Annexes — Institut des Sciences Agronomiques du Burundi (ISABU). Rapport Annuel et Notes Annexes

Inst Sci Cherifien Trav Ser Gen — Institut Scientifique Cherifien. Travaux. Serie Generale

Inst Sci Cherifien Trav Ser Sci Phys — Institut Scientifique Cherifien. Travaux. Serie Sciences Physiques

Inst Sci Mag — Institute of Science Magazine

Inst Sect 1 — Institut. Journal des Sciences et des Societes Savantes en France et a l'Etranger. Section 1

Inst Securities Reg — Institute on Securities Regulation

Inst Sewage Purif J Proc — Institute of Sewage Purification. Journal and Proceedings

Inst Siedlungswasserwirtsch Univ Karlsruhe Schriftenr — Institut fuer Siedlungswasserwirtschaft. Universitaet Karlsruhe. Schriftenreihe

Inst Skoglig Mat Stat Rapp Uppsatser — Institutionen foer Skoglig Matematisk Statistik Rapporter och Uppsatser

Inst Skogsforyngring Rapp Uppsatser — Institutionen foer Skogsforyngring Rapporter och Uppsatser

Inst Skogszool Rapp Uppsatser — Institutionen foer Skogszoologi Rapporter och Uppsatser

Inst Social Science (Tokyo) Annals — Annals. Institute of Social Sciences (Tokyo)

Inst Socioeconomic Studies J — Institute for Socioeconomic Studies. Journal

Inst Sociol R — Revue. Institut de Sociologie

Inst Soc Stud Hague Res Rep Ser — Institute of Social Studies. The Hague Research Report Series

Inst Soil Sci Acad Sin Soil Res Rep — Institute of Soil Science. Academia Sinica. Soil Research Report

Inst Sound Vib — Institute of Sound and Vibration

Inst Space Aeronaut Sci Univ Tokyo Rep — Institute of Space and Aeronautical Science. University of Tokyo. Report

Inst Spokesm Natn Lubric Grease Inst — Institute Spokesman. National Lubricating Grease Institute

Inst Strahlenhyg Ber — Institut fuer Strahlenhygiene Berichte

Inst Strahlenhyg Bundesundheitsamtes Heft — Institut fuer Strahlenhygiene des Bundesundheitsamtes. Heft

Inst Stud Proiect Energ Bul — Institutul de Studii si Proiectari Energetice. Buletinul

Inst Suisse Rech For Mem — Institut Suisse de Recherches Forestieres. Memoires

Inst Tech — Instrumentation Technology

Inst Tech Batim Trav Pub Ann — Institut Technique du Batiment et des Travaux Publics. Annales

Inst Tech Budow Pr — Instytut Techniki Budowlanej. Prace

Inst Technol Mater Elektron Pr — Instytut Technologii Materialow Elektronicznych. Prace

Inst Tec Monterrey Div Cienc Agropecu Marit Inf Invest — Instituto Tecnologico de Monterrey. Division de Ciencias Agropecuarias y Maritimas. Informe de Investigacion

Inst Tecnol Alimentos Bol — Instituto de Tecnologia de Alimentos. Boletin

Inst Tecnol Estud Super Monterrey Dep Quim Bol — Instituto Tecnologico y de Estudios Superiores de Monterrey. Departamento de Quimica. Boletin

Inst Tecnol Ind Estado Minas Gerais Avulso — Instituto de Tecnologia Industrial. Estado de Minas Gerais. Avulso

Inst Tecnol Ind Estado Minas Gerais Boletim — Instituto de Tecnologia Industrial. Estado de Minas Gerais. Boletim

Inst Tecnol Monterrey Div Cien Agropecu Marit Inf Invest — Instituto Tecnologico de Monterrey. Division de Ciencias Agropecuarias y Maritimas. Informe de Investigacion

Inst Tecnol Rio Grande Sul Bol — Instituto Tecnologico do Rio Grande Do Sul. Boletim

Inst Text Faserforsch Stuttgart Ber — Institut fuer Textil- und Faserforschung. Stuttgart. Berichte

Inst Text Fr Nord Bull Inf — Institut Textile de France-Nord. Bulletin d'Information

Inst Textile Fr Bul — Institut Textile de France. Bulletin

Inst Toegepast Biol Onderz Nat Meded — Instituut voor Toegepast Biologisch Onderzoek in de Natuur [*Institute for Biological Field Research*]. Medeling

Inst Toegepast Biol Onderzoek Meded — Instituut voor Toegepast Biologisch Onderzoek in de Natuur [*Institute for Biological Field Research*]. Mededeling

Inst Tsvetna Metal (Plovdiv) God — Institut po Tsvetna Metalurgiya (Plovdiv). Godishnik

Inst Univ Pedagog Caracas Monogr Cient Augusto Pi Suner — Instituto Universitario Pedagogico de Caracas. Monografias Cientificas "AugustoPi Suner"

Inst Vatten Luftvaardsforsk Publ B — Institutet foer Vatten- och Luftvaardsforskning. Publikation B

Inst Verkstadstek Forsk IVF Resultat — Institutet fuer Verkstadsteknisk Forskning. IVF Resultat

Inst Vitreous Enamellers Bull — Institute of Vitreous Enamellers. Bulletin

Inst Vol Feed — Institutions/Volume Feeding

Inst/Vol Feeding Mgt — Institutions/Volume Feeding Management [*Later, Institutions/Volume Feeding*]

Inst Wasserforsch Dortmund Veroeff — Institut fuer Wasserforschung Dortmund. Veroeffentlichungen

Inst Wassergefaehrdende Stoffe Schriftenr — Institut fuer Wassergefaehrdende Stoffe. Schriftenreihe

Inst Water Eng J — Institution of Water Engineers. Journal [*Later, Institution of Water Engineersand Scientists. Journal*]

Inst Water Eng Sci J — Institution of Water Engineers and Scientists. Journal

Inst Water Environ Manage J — Institution of Water and Environmental Management. Journal

Inst Wlok Pr — Instytut Wlokiennictwa. Prace

Inst World Affairs Proc — Institute of World Affairs. Proceedings

Instytut Met Niezel Biul — Instytut Metali Niezelaznych Biuletyn

Inst Zast Bilja Posebna Izd — Institut za Zastitu Bilja. Posebna Izdanja

Inst Zool Parazitol Akad Nauk Tadzh SSR Tr — Institut Zoologii i Parazitologii Akademiya Nauk Tadzhikskoi SSR Trudy

Inst Zootec Bol Tec (Sao Paulo) — Instituto de Zootecnia. Boletim Tecnico (Sao Paulo)

Inst Zootech Biul Inf — Instytut Zootechniki. Biuletyn Informacyjny

Inst Zootech Pol Wydawn Wlasne — Instytut Zootechniki w Polsce Wydawnictwa Wlasne

Inst Zootech Pol Wyniki Oceny Wartosci Hodowlanej Buhajow — Instytut Zootechniki w Polsce Wyniki Oceny Wartosci Hodowlanej Buhajow

Insul — Insulana

Insul — Insulation

InsulaH — Insula (Havanna)

Insulation J — Insulation Journal

Insulatn — Insulation

Insulatn — Insulation Journal

Insul/Circuits — Insulation/Circuits

Insulin Recept Part A Methods Study Struct Funct — Insulin Receptors. Part A. Methods for the Study of Structure and Function

Insul Mater Test Appl — Insulation Materials. Testing and Applications

Insul Rev — Insulation Review

Insurance D — Insurance Decisions

Insurance F — Insurance Facts

Insurance Math Econom — Insurance, Mathematics, and Economics

Insur Couns J — Insurance Counsel Journal

Insur Engng — Insurance Engineering

Insur Engng Rep — Insurance Engineering Reports. Boston Mfrs' Mutual Fire Insurance Co.

Insur Field — Insurance Field

Insurg Soc — Insurgent Sociologist

Insur Law J — Insurance Law Journal

Insur Lines — Insurance Lines

Insur LJ — Insurance Law Journal

Insv Priene — Inschriften von Priene

Ins Wkr — Insurance Worker

Int — Intentions

INT — Interfaces

INT — International Science Fiction

INT — International Textiles

Int — Interpretation. A Journal of Bible and Theology

Int — Interpreter

INTA — Interaction

IntA — Inter-American Review of Bibliography

Int A Aller — International Archives of Allergy and Applied Immunology

Int A Am Process Yb — International Annual and American Process Yearbook

Int Abstr Biol Sci — International Abstracts of Biological Sciences

Int Abstr Oper Res — International Abstracts in Operations Research

Int Abstr Ops Res — International Abstracts in Operations Research

Int Abstr Surg — International Abstracts of Surgery

Int Acad Biomed Drug Res — International Academy for Biomedical and Drug Research

Int Acad Pathol Monogr — International Academy of Pathology. Monograph

INTA/CONIE Inf Aeroesp — INTA/CONIE [*Instituto Nacional de Tecnica Aeroespacial/Comision Nacional de Investigacion del Espacio*] Informacion Aeroespacial

Int Act Congr Trans — International Actuarial Congress Transactions

Int Advertiser — International Advertiser

Int Adv Nondestr Test — International Advances in Nondestructive Testing

Int Adv Surg Oncol — International Advances in Surgical Oncology

IntAe — International Aerospace Abstracts

Int Aeronaut Abstr — International Aeronautical Abstracts

Int Aerosp Abstr — International Aerospace Abstracts

INTA Estac Exp Manfredi Inf Tec — INTA [*Instituto Nacional de Tecnologia Agropecuaria*]. Estacion Experimental Manfredi. Informacion Tecnica

INTA Estac Exp Reg Agropecu (Parana) Ser Tec — INTA [*Instituto Nacional de Tecnologia Agropecuaria*]. Estacion Experimental Regional Agropecuaria (Parana). Serie Tecnica

INTA Estac Exp Reg Agropecu Pergamino Inf Tec — INTA [*Instituto Nacional de Tecnologia Agropecuaria*]. Estacion Experimental Regional Agropecuaria (Pergamino). Informe Tecnico

INTA Estac Exp Reg Agropecu Pergamino Publ Tec — INTA [*Instituto Nacional de Tecnologia Agropecuaria*]. Estacion Experimental Regional Agropecuaria (Pergamino). Publicacion Tecnica

Int Aff — International Affairs

Int Affairs — International Affairs

Int Aff Bull — International Affairs. Bulletin

Int Aff (London) — International Affairs (London)

Int Aff Moscow — International Affairs (Moscow)

Int Aff Stud — International Affairs. Studies

Int Afr Bibliogr — International African Bibliography

Int Afr Forum — Internationales Afrikaforum

Int Afrikaforum — Internationales Afrikaforum

Int Agency Res Cancer Monogr Eval Carcinog Risk Chem Man — International Agency for Research on Cancer. Monographs on the Evaluation of Carcinogenic Risk of Chemicals to Man

Int Agric Collab Ser — International Agricultural Collaboration Series. US Department of Agriculture

Int Agric Eng J — International Agricultural Engineering Journal

Int Agric Publ Gen Ser — International Agriculture Publications. General Series

Int Agri Dev — International Agricultural Development

Int Agro Clim Ser Am Inst Crop Ecol — International Agro-Climatological Series. American Institute of Crop Ecology

INTA (Inst Nac Tecnol Agropecu) Colecc Cient — INTA (Instituto Nacional de Tecnologia Agropecuaria) Coleccion Cientifica

INTA (Inst Nac Tecnol Agropecu) Divulg Tec — INTA (Instituto Nacional de Tecnologia Agropecuaria) Divulgacion Tecnica

INTA (Inst Nac Tecnol Agropecu) Man Agropecu — INTA (Instituto Nacional de Tecnologia Agropecuaria) Manual Agropecuario

INTA (Inst Nac Tecnol Agropecu) Ser Tec — INTA (Instituto Nacional de Tecnologia Agropecuaria). Serie Tecnia

INTAL/IL — Integracion Latinoamericana. Instituto para la Integracion de America Latina

Intam Inst Mus Res — Inter-American Institute for Musical Research. Yearbook

Int-Am L Rev — Inter-American Law Review

Intam Mus B — Boletin Interamericano de Musica/Inter-American Music Bulletin

Intam Mus B (Eng Ed) — Inter-American Music Bulletin (English Edition)

Intam Mus R — Inter-American Music Review

Intam Mus Res Yrbk — Inter-American Musical Research. Yearbook

Int Anal — International Analyst

Int & Comp — International and Comparative Law Quarterly

Int & Comp L Q — International and Comparative Law Quarterly

Int Anesthesiol Clin — International Anesthesiology Clinics

Int Angiol — International Angiology

Int Annu Pezcoller Symp — International Annual Pezcoller Symposium

Int Anthrop Ling Rev — International Anthropological and Linguistic Review

Int A Occup — International Archives of Occupational and Environmental Health

Int Arb J — International Arbitration Journal

Int Arch Allergy Appl Immunol — International Archives of Allergy and Applied Immunology

Int Arch Allergy Immunol — International Archives of Allergy and Immunology

Int Arch Arbeitsmed — Internationales Archiv fuer Arbeitsmedizin

Int Arch Arbeits-Umweltmed — Internationales Archiv fuer Arbeits- und Umweltmedizin

Int Arch Arb Umweltmed — Internationales Archiv fuer Arbeits- und Umweltmedizin

Int Arch Gewerbepathol Gewerbehyg — Internationales Archiv fuer Gewerbepathologie und Gewerbehygiene

Int Archit — International Architect

Int Archiv Ethnog — Internationales Archiv fuer Ethnographie

Int Archiv Ethnogr — Internationales Archiv fuer Ethnographie

Int Arch Occup Env Health — International Archives of Occupational and Environmental Health

Int Arch Occup Environ Health — International Archives of Occupational and Environmental Health

Int Arch Occup Health — International Archives of Occupational Health [*Later, International Archives of Occupational and Environmental Health*]

Int Arch Photogramm — International Archives of Photogrammetry

Int Archs Allergy Appl Immun — International Archives of Allergy and Applied Immunology

Int Archs Ethnogr — International Archives of Ethnography

Int Archvs Ethnog — International Archives of Ethnography

Int Archv Vlkerknd — Internationales Archiv fuer Voelkerkunde

Int As For — Internationales Asienforum

Int Asienf — Internationales Asienforum

Int Asien Forum — Internationales Asienforum

Int Ass — International Association

Int Assn Bridge Struct Eng Publ — International Association for Bridge and Structural Engineering. Publications

Int Assn Chiefs Police Proc — International Association of Chiefs of Police. Proceedings

Int Assn Chiefs Police Yrbk — International Association of Chiefs of Police. Yearbook

Int Assn Identif Calif Div Proc — International Association for Identification. California Division. Proceedings

Int Assn Identif Proc — International Association for Identification. Proceedings

Int Assn Identif Tex Div Proc — International Association for Identification. Texas Division. Proceedings

Int Assoc/Assoc Int — International Associations/Associations Internationales

Int Assoc Dairy Milk Insp Annu Rep — International Association of Dairy and Milk Inspectors. Annual Report
Int Assoc Dent Child J — International Association of Dentistry for Children. Journal
Int Assoc Eng Geol Bull — International Association of Engineering Geology. Bulletin
Int Assoc Engng Geol Bull — International Association of Engineering Geology. Bulletin
Int Assoc Hydraul Res Congr Proc — International Association for Hydraulic Research. Congress. Proceedings
Int Assoc Hydrogeol Mem — International Association of Hydrogeologists. Memoirs
Int Assoc Hydrol Sci Assoc Int Sci Hydrol Publ — International Association of Hydrological Sciences - Association Internationaledes Sciences Hydrologiques. Publication
Int Assoc Hydrol Sci Hydrol Sci Bull — International Association of Hydrological Sciences. Hydrological Sciences Bulletin
Int Assoc Hydrol Sci Publ — International Association of Hydrological Sciences. Publication
Int Assoc Hydrol Sci Spec Publ — International Association of Hydrological Sciences Special Publication
Int Assoc Math Geol J — International Association for Mathematical Geology. Journal
Int Assoc Sci Hydrol Bull — International Association of Scientific Hydrology. Bulletin
Int Assoc Sedimentol Spec Publ — International Association of Sedimentologists. Special Publication
Int Assoc Theor Appl Limnol Commun — International Association of Theoretical and Applied Limnology. Communication
Int Assoc Theor Appl Limnol Proc — International Association of Theoretical and Applied Limnology. Proceedings
Int Assoc Univ Pap Rep — International Association of Universities. Papers and Reports
Int Assoc Volcanol Chem Earth's Inter Spe Ser — International Association of Volcanology and Chemistry of the Earth's Interior.Special Series
Int Assoc Wood Anat Bull — International Association of Wood Anatomists. Bulletin
Int Astronaut Congr Proc — International Astronautical Congress. Proceedings
Int Astron Union Colloq — International Astronomical Union Colloquium
Int Astron Union Symp — International Astronomical Union. Symposium
Int At Energy Ag Bibliogr Ser — International Atomic Energy Agency. Bibliographical Series
Int At Energy Agency Bull — International Atomic Energy Agency. Bulletin
Int At Energy Agency Saf Ser — International Atomic Energy Agency. Safety Series
Int At Energy Agency Tech Rep Ser — International Atomic Energy Agency. Technical Report Series
Int At Energy Ag Proc Ser — International Atomic Energy Agency. Proceedings Series
Int Atl Salmon Found Spec Publ Ser — International Atlantic Salmon Foundation. Special Publication Series
Int Atom Ener Agen Bul — International Atomic Energy Agency Bulletin
Int Atom Energy Ag Bull — International Atomic Energy Agency Bulletin
Int Aud — Internal Auditor
Int Auditor — Internal Auditor
Intava Wld — Intava World
Int B — Interpreter's Bible
Int Bank Fin Law Bul — International Banking and Financial Law Bulletin
Int Bar J — International Bar Journal
Int Bauxite Assoc Q Rev — International Bauxite Association. Quarterly Review
INTBEB — Interferon y Biotecnologia
Int Beekeep Congr Prelim Sci Meet — International Beekeeping Congress. Preliminary Scientific Meeting
Int Beekeep Congr Summ — International Beekeeping Congress. Summaries of Papers
Int Beekeep Congr Summ Suppl — International Beekeeping Congress. Summaries Supplement
Int Behav Scientist — International Behavioural Scientist
Int Bergwirtsch Bergtech — Internationale Bergwirtschaft und Bergtechnik
Int Bibliogr — International Bibliography
Int Bibliogr Book Rev — International Bibliography of Book Reviews
Int Bibliogr Book Rev Schol Lit — International Bibliography of Book Reviews of Scholarly Literature
Int Bibliogr Hist Relig — International Bibliography of the History of Religions
Int Bibliogr Period Lit — International Bibliography of Periodical Literature
Int Bibliogr Zeitschriftenliteratur Allen Gebieten Wissens — Internationale Bibliographie der Zeitschriftenliteratur aus AllenGebieten des Wissens
Int Bibllphy For — International Bibliography of Forestry. Norwegian Forest Research Institute
Int Biblphy Agric Econ — International Bibliography of Agricultural Economics
Int Biblphy Atom Energy — International Bibliography on Atomic Energy
Int Biblphy Autom Control — International Bibliography of Automatic Control
Int Biblphy Electron Microsc — International Bibliography of Electron Microscopy
Int Biblphy Photogramm — International Bibliography of Photogrammetry
Int Biblphy Soc Cult Anthrop — International Bibliography of Social and Cultural Anthropology
Int Bibl Rezen — Internationale Bibliographie der Rezensionen
Int Bibl Rezen Wiss Lit — Internationale Bibliographie der Rezensionen Wissenschaftlicher Literatur
Int Bibl Soc Sci — International Bibliography of the Social Sciences
Int Biod B — International Biodeterioration Bulletin
Int Biodeterior — International Biodeterioration Bulletin
Int Biodeterior Biodegrad — International Biodeterioration and Biodegradation
Int Biodeterior Biodegrad Symp — International Biodeterioration and Biodegradation Symposium

Int Biodeterior Bull — International Biodeterioration Bulletin
Int Bioindic Symp — International Bioindicators Symposium
Int Biol Programme — International Biological Programme Series
Int Biol Programme Handb — International Biological Programme. Handbook
Int Biosci Monogr — International Bioscience Monographs
Int B Miss R — International Bulletin of Missionary Research
Int Bot Congr — International Botanical Congress. Papers
Int Bot Congr Recent Advan Bot — International Botanical Congress. Recent Advances in Botany
Int Bottler Pckr — International Bottler and Packer
Int Brain Res Organ Monogr Ser — International Brain Research Organization. Monograph Series
Int Broadcast Eng — International Broadcast Engineer
Int Broadcast Syst and Oper — International Broadcasting Systems and Operation
Int Broadc Engr — International Broadcast Engineer
Int Build Serv Abstr — International Building Services Abstracts
Int Bull Bacteriol Nomencl Taxon — International Bulletin of Bacteriological Nomenclature and Taxonomy
Int Bull Bact Nomencl Taxon — International Bulletin of Bacteriological Nomenclature and Taxonomy
Int Bull Bibliogr Educ — International Bulletin of Bibliography on Education
Int Bull Ind Prop — International Bulletin of Industrial Property
Int Bull Indust Prop — International Bulletin of Industrial Property
Int Bull Inf Refrig — International Bulletin on Information on Refrigeration
Int Bull Metal Engng Wkrs — International Bulletin of Metal and Engineering Workers
Int Bull Pl Prot — International Bulletin of Plant Protection
Int Bull Pl Protect — International Bulletin of Plant Protection
Int Bull Print All Trades — International Bulletin for the Printing and Allied Trades
Int Bull Res E Eur — International Bulletin for Research on Law in Eastern Europe
Int Bull Wkrs Metal Engng Inds — International Bulletin of Workers in the Metal and Engineering Industries
Int Bul Miss R — International Bulletin of Missionary Research
Int Bur Ed B — International Bureau of Education. Bulletin
Int Bur Educ Bul — International Bureau of Education. Bulletin
Int Bus Equip — International Business Equipment
Int Bus Opp Egy — International Business Opportunities. Egypt
Int Bus Opp Oil Gas Afr — International Business Opportunities. Oil and Gas in Africa
Int Bus Res Ser — International Business Research Series
Int Cadmium Conf — International Cadmium Conference
Int Can — International Canada
Int Cancer Congr Abstr — International Cancer Congress. Abstracts
Int Cancer Res Found Rep Act — International Cancer Research Foundation. Report of Activities
Int Can Stud N — International Canadian Studies News
Int Cast Met J — International Cast Metals Journal
Int Cataloguing — International Cataloguing
Int Cat Scient Lit — International Catalogue of Scientific Literature
Int Cell Plast Conf Proc — International Cellular Plastics Conference. Proceedings
Int Cem J — International Cement Journal
Int Cem Semin Proc — International Cement Seminar Proceedings
Int Cent Arid Semi-Arid Land Stud Publ — International Center for Arid and Semi-Arid Land Studies. Publication
Int Cent Mech Sci Courses Lect — International Centre for Mechanical Sciences. Courses and Lectures
Int Cent Med Res Semin Proc — International Center for Medical Research. Seminar Proceedings
Int Ceram Monogr — International Ceramic Monographs
Int Chem En — International Chemical Engineering
Int Chem Eng — International Chemical Engineering
Int Chem Engng — International Chemical Engineering
Int Chem Engng Process Inds — International Chemical Engineering and Process Industries
Int Chem Eng Process Ind — International Chemical Engineering and Processing Industries
Int Chem Export Ind — International Chemical and Export Industry
Int Chem Inf Conf — International Chemical Information Conference
Int Chick News — International Chickpea Newsletter
Int Child Cent Cour — International Children's Center. Courrier
Int Child Welfare Rev — International Child Welfare Review
Int Child Welf Rev — International Child Welfare Review
Int Choc Rev — International Chocolate Review
Int Civ Eng Mon — International Civil Engineering Monthly
Int Civ Engr Contractor — International Civil Engineer and Contractor
Int Classif — International Classification
Int Classification — International Classification
Int Clgh Sci Math Curricular Dev Rep — International Clearinghouse on Science and Mathematics. Curricular DevelopmentsReport
Int Clin — International Clinics
Int Clin Genet Semin — International Clinical Genetics Seminar
Int Clin Inf Bul — Inter-Clinic Information Bulletin
Int Clin Psychopharmacol — International Clinical Psychopharmacology
Int Coal Rep — International Coal Report
Int CODATA Conf Proc — International CODATA (Committee on Data for Science and Technology) Conference Proceedings
Int Colloq Anc Mosaics — International Colloquium on Ancient Mosaics
Int Colloq Diffr Opt Elem — International Colloquium on Diffractive Optical Elements
Int Colloq Durability Polym Based Compos Syst Struct Appl — International Colloquium on Durability of Polymer Based Composite Systems for Structural Applications
Int Colloq Lecithin Phospholipids — International Colloquium on Lecithin. Phospholipids. Biochemical, Pharmaceutical, and Analytical Considerations

Int Colloq Role Chem Archaeol — International Colloquium on Role of Chemistry in Archaeology

Int Com — International Commerce

Int Comet Q — International Comet Quarterly

Int Comm — International Commerce

Int Comm Bird Preserv Pan Am Sect Res Rep — International Committee for Bird Preservation. Pan American Section. Research Report

Int Commer — International Commerce

Int Comm Hist Geol Sci Newsl — International Committee on the History of Geological Sciences. Newsletter

Int Comm Illum Proc — International Commission on Illumination. Proceedings

Int Comm Irr Drain Bul — International Commission on Irrigation and Drainage Bulletin

Int Comm Northwest Atl Fish Annu Proc — International Commission for the Northwest Atlantic Fisheries. Annual Proceedings

Int Comm Northwest Atl Fish Annu Rep — International Commission for the Northwest Atlantic Fisheries. Annual Report

Int Comm Northwest Atl Fish Redb Part III — International Commission for the Northwest Atlantic Fisheries. Redbook. Part III

Int Comm Northwest Atl Fish Res Bull — International Commission for the Northwest Atlantic Fisheries. Research Bulletin

Int Comm Northwest Atl Fish Sel Pap — International Commission for the Northwest Atlantic Fisheries. Selected Papers

Int Comm Northwest Atl Fish Spec Publ — International Commission for the Northwest Atlantic Fisheries. Special Publication

Int Comm Northwest Atl Fish Stat Bull — International Commission for the Northwest Atlantic Fisheries. Statistical Bulletin

Int Comm Radiol Prot Ann — International Commission on Radiological Protection. Annals

Int Comm Radiol Prot Publ — International Commission on Radiological Protection. Publication

Int Commun Heat and Mass Transfer — International Communications in Heat and Mass Transfer

Int Commun Rev — International Communications Review

Int Comm Whaling Rep — International Commission on Whaling. Report

Int Com News — International Communications News

Int Comp — Interactive Computing

Int Comp Law Q — International and Comparative Law Quarterly

Int Comp Law Quart — International and Comparative Law Quarterly

Int Comp Pub Pol — International and Comparative Public Policy

Int Concil — International Conciliation

Int Conf AC DC Power Transm — International Conference on AC and DC Power Transmission

Int Conf Adv Compos Mater — International Conference on Advances in Composite Materials

Int Conf Adv Mater Symp A1 — International Conference on Advanced Materials. Symposium A1

Int Conf Adv Struct Test Anal Des — International Conference on Advances in Structural Testing, Analysis, and Design

Int Conf Alum Health — International Conference on Aluminum and Health

Int Conf Antennas Propag — International Conference on Antennas and Propagation

Int Conf Antifungal Chemother — International Conference on Antifungal Chemotherapy

Int Conf Appl Theory Period Struct — International Conference. Application and Theory of Periodic Structures

Int Conf Archit Support Program Lang Oper Syst ASPLOS — International Conference on Architectural Support for Programming Languages and Operating Systems. ASPLOS

Int Conf Artif Neural Networks — International Conference on Artificial Neural Networks

Int Conf At Spectrosc — International Conference on Atomic Spectroscopy

Int Conf Automot Electron — International Conference on Automotive Electronics

Int Conf Bacilli — International Conference on Bacilli

Int Conf Biomass Energy Ind Environ — International Conference on Biomass for Energy, Industry, and Environment

Int Conf Biotechnol Microb Prod — International Conference on the Biotechnology of Microbial Products

Int Conf Calorim High Energy Phys — International Conference on Calorimetry in High Energy Physics

Int Conf Cell Polym — International Conference on Cellular Polymers

Int Conf Cent High Energy Form Proc — International Conference. Center for High Energy Forming. Proceedings

Int Conf Ceram Powder Process Sci — International Conference on Ceramic Powder Processing Science

Int Conf Circ Fluid Beds — International Conference on Circulating Fluidized Beds

Int Conf Compos Mater — International Conference on Composite Materials

Int Conf Compos Mater Proc — International Conference on Composite Materials. Proceedings

Int Conf Compos Struct — International Conference on Composite Structures

Int Conf Comput Aided Des Compos Mater Technol — International Conference on Computer Aided Design in Composite Material Technology

Int Conf Comput Chem Res Educ Technol — International Conference on Computers in Chemical Research, Education, and Technology

Int Conf Comput Electromagn — International Conference on Computation in Electromagnetics

Int Conf Conduct Breakdown Dielectr Liq — International Conference on Conduction and Breakdown in Dielectric Liquids

Int Conf Creep Mater — International Conference on Creep of Materials

Int Conf Cyclotrons Their Appl — International Conference on Cyclotrons and Their Applications

Int Conf Dev Power Syst Prot — International Conference on Developments in Power System Protection

Int Conf Die Cast — International Conference on Die Casting

Int Conf Educ Optics — International Conference on Education in Optics

Int Conf Eff Hydrogen Behav Mater — International Conference on the Effect of Hydrogen on the Behavior of Materials

Int Conf Eff Ind Membr Processes Benefits Oppor — International Conference on Effective Industrial Membrane Processes. Benefits and Opportunities

Int Conf Electr Mach Drives — International Conference on Electrical Machines and Drives

Int Conf Electron Mater — International Conference on Electronic Materials

Int Conf Electrophor Supercomput Hum Genome — International Conference on Electrophoresis, Supercomputing, and the Human Genome

Int Conf Electrophotogr — International Conference on Electrophotography

Int Conf Electrorheol Fluids — International Conference on Electrorheological Fluids

Int Conf Elem Anal Coal Its By Prod — International Conference on Elemental Analysis of Coal and Its By-Products

Int Conf Environ Pollut — International Conference on Environmental Pollution

Int Conf Exp Methods Microgravity Mater Sci Res — International Conference on Experimental Methods for Microgravity Materials Science Research

Int Conf Facil Oper Safeguards Interface — International Conference on Facility Operations-Safeguards Interface

Int Conf Failure Anal — International Conference on Failure Analysis

Int Conf Fire Saf Proc — International Conference on Fire Safety. Proceedings

Int Conf Fluid Bed Combust Proc — International Conference on Fluidized Bed Combustion. Proceedings

Int Conf Fluid Sealing Proc — International Conference on Fluid Sealing. Proceedings

Int Conf Food Saf Qual Assur Appl Immunoassay Syst — International Conference on Food Safety and Quality Assurance. Applications of Immunoassay Systems

Int Conf Food Sci Refrig Air Cond — International Conference on Food Science. Refrigeration and Air Conditioning

Int Conf Fourier Transform Spectrosc — International Conference on Fourier Transform Spectroscopy

Int Conf Freq Control Synth — International Conference on Frequency Control and Synthesis

Int Conf Front Polym Res — International Conference on Frontiers of Polymer Research

Int Conf Fundam Adsorpt — International Conference on Fundamentals of Adsorption

Int Conf Genet — International Conference on Genetics

Int Conf Heat Resist Mater — International Conference on Heat-Resistant Materials

Int Conf Heavy Crude Tar Sands — International Conference on Heavy Crude and Tar Sands

Int Conf High Energy Phys Proc — International Conference on High Energy Physics. Proceedings

Int Conf High Energy Rate Fabr Proc — International Conference on High Energy Rate Fabrication. Proceedings

Int Conf Hologr Syst Compon Appl — International Conference on Holographic Systems, Components, and Applications

Int Conf Hyperbaric Med Proc — International Conference on Hyperbaric Medicine. Proceedings

Int Conf Image Process Its Appl — International Conference on Image Processing and its Applications

Int Conf Indium Phosphide Relat Mater — International Conference on Indium Phosphide and Related Materials

Int Conf Inf Decis Action Syst Complex Organ — International Conference on Information-Decision-Action Systems in Complex Organisations

Int Conf Insect Neurochem Neurophysiol — International Conference on Insect Neurochemistry and Neurophysiology

Int Conf Insect Path Biol Control — International Conference on Insect Pathology and Biological Control

Int Conf Intell Syst Eng — International Conference on Intelligent Systems Engineering

Int Conf Interfacial Phenom Compos Mater — International Conference on Interfacial Phenomena in Composite Materials

Int Conf Intern Frict Ultrason Attenuation Solids — International Conference on Internal Friction and Ultrasonic Attenuation in Solids

Int Conf In Vivo Methods — International Conference on In Vivo Methods

Int Conf Ion Exch — International Conference on Ion Exchange

Int Conf Ion Exch Processes — International Conference on Ion Exchange Processes

Int Conf Large Electr Syst Proc — International Conference on Large Electric Systems. Proceedings

Int Conf Laser Anemom Adv Appl — International Conference on Laser Anemometry, Advances, and Applications

Int Conf Laser M2P — International Conference Laser M2P

Int Conf Laser Spectrosc — International Conference on Laser Spectroscopy

Int Conf Lattice Dyn Proc — International Conference on Lattice Dynamics. Proceedings

Int Conf Lymphatic Tissues Germinal Cent Immune React — International Conference on Lymphatic Tissues and Germinal Centres in Immune Reactions

Int Conf Mech Fatigue Adv Mater — International Conference on Mechanical Fatigue in Advanced Materials

Int Conf Mech Phys Behav Mater Dyn Loading — International Conference on Mechanical and Physical Behaviour of Materials under Dynamic Loading

Int Conf Metall Weld Qualif Microalloyed HSLA Steel Weldments — International Conference on the Metallurgy, Welding, and Qualification of Microalloyed (HSLA) Steel Weldments

Int Conf Methods Protein Sequence Anal — International Conference on Methods in Protein Sequence Analysis

Int Conf Microelectron — International Conference of Microelectronics. Microelectronics

Int Conf Microsc Oxid — International Conference on the Microscopy of Oxidation

Int Conf Millimeter Wave Far Infrared Sci Technol Proc — International Conference on Millimeter Wave and Far Infrared Science and Technology Proceedings

Int Conf Miner Met Environ — International Conference. Minerals, Metals, and the Environment

Int Conf Mobile Radio Pers Commun — International Conference on Mobile Radio and Personal Communications

Int Conf Model Cast Weld Processes — International Conference on Modeling of Casting and Welding Processes

Int Conf Nat Glasses — International Conference on Natural Glasses

Int Conf New Diamond Sci Technol — International Conference on the New Diamond Science and Technology

Int Conf New Nucl Phys Adv Tech — International Conference on New Nuclear Physics with Advanced Techniques

Int Conf Noise Control Eng Proc — International Conference on Noise Control Engineering. Proceedings

Int Conf Nucl At Clusters — International Conference on Nuclear and Atomic Clusters

Int Conf Nucl Struct High Angular Momentum — International Conference on Nuclear Structure at High Angular Momentum

Int Conf Org Coat Sci Technol Proc (Technomic Publ) — International Conference in Organic Coatings Science and Technology. Proceedings (Technomic Publication)

Int Conf Pervaporation Processes Chem Ind — International Conference on Pervaporation Processes in the Chemical Industry

Int Conf Pet Refin Petrochem Process — International Conference on Petroleum Refining and Petrochemical Processing

Int Conf Photochem Convers Storage Sol Energy — International Conference on Photochemical Conversion and Storage of Solar Energy

Int Conf Photochem Processes Organ Mol Syst — International Conference on Photochemical Processes in Organized Molecular Systems

Int Conf Photosynth — International Conference on Photosynthesis

Int Conf Phys Electron At Collisions — International Conference on the Physics of Electronic and Atomic Collisions

Int Conf Phys Non Cryst Solids — International Conference on the Physics of Non-Crystalline Solids

Int Conf Phys Semicond — International Conference on the Physics of Semiconductors

Int Conf Phys Semicond Proc — International Conference on the Physics of Semiconductors. Proceedings

Int Conf Plant Growth Subst — International Conference on Plant Growth Substances

Int Conf Plant Pathog Bact — International Conference on Plant Pathogenic Bacteria

Int Conf Plasma Source Mass Spectrom — International Conference on Plasma Source Mass Spectrometry

Int Conf Plasma Surf Eng — International Conference on Plasma Surface Engineering

Int Conf PM Aerosp Mater — International Conference on PM Aerospace Materials

Int Conf Polariz Phenom Nucl Phys — International Conference on Polarization Phenomena in Nuclear Physics

Int Conf Powder Metall — International Conference on Powder Metallurgy

Int Conf Probab Methods Appl Electr Power Syst — International Conference on Probabilistic Methods Applied to Electric Power Systems

Int Conf Protein Eng — International Conference on Protein Engineering

Int Conf Quar Plant Prot Pests Dis Rep Soviet Deleg — International Conference on Quarantine and Plant Protection Against Pests and Diseases. Report of the Soviet Delegation

Int Conf Radar Meteorol — International Conference on Radar Meteorology

Int Conf Radiat Mater Sci — International Conference on Radiation Materials Science

Int Conf Radioact Nucl Beams — International Conference on Radioactive Nuclear Beams

Int Conf Res Thermochem Biomass Convers — International Conference on Research in Thermochemical Biomass Conversion

Int Conf Reyes Syndr Proc — International Conference on Reye's Syndrome. Proceedings

Int Conf Rheol Fresh Cem Concr — International Conference on Rheology of Fresh Cement and Concrete

Int Conf Saf Eval Reg Chem — International Conference on Safety Evaluation and Regulation of Chemicals

Int Conf Sarcoidosis Other Granulomatous Dis Proc — International Conference on Sarcoidosis and Other Granulomatous Diseases. Proceedings

Int Conf Sarcoidosis Proc — International Conference on Sarcoidosis. Proceedings

Int Conf Sci Opt Imaging — International Conference on Scientific Optical Imaging

Int Conf Second Ion Mass Spectrom — International Conference on Secondary Ion Mass Spectrometry

Int Conf Sep Sci Technol — International Conference on Separations Science and Technology

Int Conf Silicon Carbide — International Conference on Silicon Carbide

Int Conf Simul Methods Nucl Eng — International Conference on Simulation Methods in Nuclear Engineering

Int Conf Software Eng Telecommun Switching Syst — International Conference on Software Engineering for Telecommunication Switching Systems

Int Conf Software Eng Telecommun Syst Serv — International Conference on Software Engineering for Telecommunication Systems and Services

Int Conf Soil Mech Found Eng Proc — International Conference on Soil Mechanics and Foundation Engineering. Proceedings

Int Conf Solidif Proc — International Conference on Solidification. Proceedings

Int Conf Solid Solid Phase Transform — International Conference on Solid-Solid Phase Transformations

Int Conf Solid State Nucl Track Detect — International Conference on Solid State Nuclear Track Detectors

Int Conf Solid Surf — International Conference on Solid Surfaces

Int Conf Spectral Line Shapes — International Conference on Spectral Line Shapes

Int Conf Spectrosc Proc — International Conference on Spectroscopy. Proceedings

Int Conf Spectrosc Spectrum — International Conference on Spectroscopy across the Spectrum

Int Conf Spin Isospin Nucl Interact — International Conference on Spin and Isospin in Nuclear Interactions

Int Conf Sputtering Its Appl — International Conference on Sputtering and Its Applications

Int Conf Stable Isot Proc — International Conference on Stable Isotopes. Proceedings

Int Conf Strength Met Alloys — International Conference on Strength of Metals and Alloys

Int Conf Strength Met Alloys Conf Proc — International Conference on the Strength of Metals and Alloys. Conference. Proceedings

Int Conf Strontium Metab Pap — International Conference on Strontium Metabolism. Papers

Int Conf Struct Mech React Technol — International Conference on Structural Mechanics in Reactor Technology

Int Conf Sulphur Constr — International Conference on Sulphur in Construction

Int Conf Supercond Quantum Devices Proc — International Conference on Superconducting Quantum Devices. Proceedings

Int Conf Superlattices Microstruct Microdevices — International Conference on Superlattices, Microstructures, and Microdevices

Int Conf Superoxide Superoxide Dismutase — International Conference on Superoxide and Superoxide Dismutase

Int Conf Surf Eng — International Conference on Surface Engineering

Int Conf Surf Modif Technol — International Conference on Surface Modification Technology

Int Conf Surf Waves Plasmas Solids — International Conference on Surface Waves in Plasmas and Solids

Int Conf Telecommun Transm Digital Era — International Conference on Telecommunication Transmission. Into the Digital Era

Int Conf Tetanus — International Conference on Tetanus

Int Conf Tetanus Proc — International Conference on Tetanus. Proceedings

Int Conf Texture Proc — International Conference on Texture. Proceedings

Int Conf Textures Mater Proc — International Conference on Textures of Materials. Proceedings

Int Conf Theor Phys Biol — International Conference on Theoretical Physics and Biology

Int Conf Therm Anal — International Conference on Thermal Analysis

Int Conf Therm Anal Proc — International Conference on Thermal Analysis. Proceedings

Int Conf Therm Conduct Proc — International Conference on Thermal Conductivity. Proceedings

Int Conf Therm Insul Proc — International Conference on Thermal Insulation. Proceedings

Int Conf Thermion Electr Power Gener — International Conference on Thermionic Electrical Power Generation

Int Conf Thermoelectr Energy Convers Proc — International Conference on Thermoelectric Energy Conversion. Proceedings

Int Conf Thermoelectr Proc — International Conference on Thermoelectrics. Proceedings

Int Conf Thermoelectr Prop Met Conduct Proc — International Conference on Thermoelectric Properties of Metallic Conductors. Proceedings

Int Conf Thermoplast Elastomer Markets Prod — International Conference on Thermoplastic Elastomer Markets and Products

Int Conf Thermoplast Elastomers — International Conference on Thermoplastic Elastomers

Int Conf Therm Stable Polym Invited Main Lect — International Conference on Thermally Stable Polymers. Invited and Main Lectures

Int Conf Thin Film Phys Appl — International Conference on Thin Film Physics and Applications

Int Conf Thromb Embolism Proc — International Conference on Thrombosis and Embolism. Proceedings

Int Conf Titanium — International Conference on Titanium

Int Conf Titanium Prod Appl — International Conference on Titanium Products and Applications

Int Conf Toxic Dinoflagellate Blooms — International Conference on Toxic Dinoflagellate Blooms

Int Conf Toxic Dinoflagellates — International Conference on Toxic Dinoflagellates

Int Conf Transfer Water Resour Knowl Proc — International Conference on Transfer of Water Resources Knowledge. Proceedings

Int Conf Transmutat Doping Semicond — International Conference on Transmutation Doping in Semiconductors

Int Conf Trends On Line Comput Control Syst — International Conference on Trends in On-Line Computer Control Systems

Int Conf Trends Quantum Electron — International Conference. Trends in Quantum Electronics

Int Conf Triazenes — International Conference on Triazenes. Chemical, Biological, and Clinical Aspects

Int Conf Trichinellosis — International Conference on Trichinellosis

Int Conf Trop Ozone Atmos Change — International Conference on Tropical Ozone and Atmospheric Change

Int Conf Tumor Necrosis Factor Relat Cytokines — International Conference on Tumor Necrosis Factor and Related Cytokines

Int Conf Ultrastruct Process Ceram Glasses Compos — International Conference on Ultrastructure Processing of Ceramics, Glasses, andComposites

Int Conf Unsteady State Processes Catal — International Conference on Unsteady State Processes in Catalysis

Int Conf Uranium Hexafluoride Handl — International Conference on Uranium Hexafluoride Handling

Int Conf Uranium Mine Waste Disposal Proc — International Conference on Uranium Mine Waste Disposal. Proceedings

Int Conf Vac Metall — International Conference on Vacuum Metallurgy

Int Conf Vac Metall Electroslag Remelting Processes Proc — International Conference on Vacuum Metallurgy and Electroslag Remelting Processes. Proceedings

Int Conf Vac Web Coat — International Conference on Vacuum Web Coating

Int Conf Vib Surf — International Conference on Vibrations at Surfaces

Int Conf Water Pollut Modell Meas Predict — International Conference on Water Pollution. Modelling, Measuring, and Prediction

Int Conf Water Pollut Res — International Conference on Water Pollution Research. Proceedings

Int Conf Wear Mater Proc — International Conference on Wear of Materials. Proceedings

Int Conf X Ray Opt Microanal Proc — International Conference on X-Ray Optics and Microanalysis. Proceedings

Int Conf Zeolites — International Conference on Zeolites

Int Conf Zinc Coated Steel Sheet — International Conference on Zinc Coated Steel Sheet

Int Cong Chem Cem Proc — International Congress on the Chemistry of Cement. Proceedings

Int Cong Ment Hyg Proc — International Congress on Mental Hygiene. Proceedings

Int Congr Acarol — International Congress of Acarology

Int Congr Allergol — International Congress of Allergology

Int Congr Amino Acid Res — International Congress on Amino Acid Research

Int Congr Anat — International Congress of Anatomy

Int Congr Angiol — International Congress of Angiology

Int Congr Anim Hyg — International Congress for Animal Hygiene

Int Congr Anim Prod Proc — International Congress of Animal Production. Proceedings

Int Congr Anim Reprod Artif Insemin — International Congress on Animal Reproduction and Artificial Insemination

Int Congr Appl Lasers Electro-Opt Proc — International Congress of Applications of Lasers and Electro-Optics. Proceedings

Int Congr Appl Mineral Miner Ind — International Congress on Applied Mineralogy in the Minerals Industry

Int Congr Astronaut Proc — International Congress on Astronautics. Proceedings

Int Congr Bioceram Hum Body — International Congress on Bioceramics and the Human Body

Int Congr Biochem — International Congress of Biochemistry

Int Congr Biochem Abstr — International Congress of Biochemistry. Abstracts

Int Congr Biochem Proc — International Congress of Biochemistry. Proceedings

Int Congr Biogenet — International Congress of Biogenetics

Int Congr Catal — International Congress on Catalysis

Int Congr Catal Prepr — International Congress on Catalysis. Preprints

Int Congr Catal Proc — International Congress on Catalysis. Proceedings

Int Congr Cataract Surg — International Congress on Cataract Surgery

Int Congr Cell Biol — International Congress on Cell Biology

Int Congr Chem Cem — International Congress on the Chemistry of Cement

Int Congr Chem Cem Proc — International Congress on the Chemistry of Cement. Proceedings

Int Congr Chem Eng Chem Equip Des Autom Proc — International Congress of Chemical Engineering, Chemical Equipment Design, and Automation. Proceedings

Int Congr Chemother — International Congress of Chemotherapy

Int Congr Chemother Proc — International Congress of Chemotherapy. Proceedings

Int Congr Child Neurol Proc — International Congress of Child Neurology. Proceedings

Int Congr Clin Enzymol — International Congress of Clinical Enzymology

Int Congr Clin Pathol Eight Colloq Pathol — International Congress of Clinical Pathology. Eight Colloquia on Pathology

Int Congr Combust Engines Proc — International Congress on Combustion Engines. Proceedings

Int Congr Compat React Polym Alloying — International Congress on Compatibilizers and Reactive Polymer Alloying

Int Congr Comp Physiol Biochem — International Congress of Comparative Physiology and Biochemistry

Int Congr Cybern Syst — International Congress of Cybernetics and Systems

Int Congr Deterior Conserv Stone — International Congress on Deterioration and Conservation of Stone

Int Congr Diet Nutr — International Congress on Diet and Nutrition

Int Congr Dis Cattle — International Congress on Diseases of Cattle

Int Congr Dis Chest — International Congress on Diseases of the Chest

Int Congr Ecol — International Congress of Ecology

Int Congr Electro Heat Proc — International Congress on Electro-Heat. Proceedings

Int Congr Electron Microsc — International Congress for Electron Microscopy

Int Congr Electron Micros Proc — International Congress on Electron Microscopy. Proceedings

Int Congr Endocrinol — International Congress of Endocrinology

Int Congr Eng Food — International Congress on Engineering and Food

Int Congr Entomol Proc — International Congress of Entomology. Proceedings

Int Congr Essent Oils Fragrances Flavours — International Congress of Essential Oils, Fragrances, and Flavours

Int Congr Essent Oils Pap — International Congress of Essential Oils. Papers

Int Congr Eur Assoc Poison Control Cent — International Congress. European Association of Poison Control Centers

Int Congr Food Sci Technol — International Congress of Food Science and Technology

Int Congr Fruit Juices — International Congress of Fruit Juices

Int Congr Game Biol Trans — International Congress of Game Biologists. Transactions

Int Congr Gastroenterol — International Congress of Gastroenterology

Int Congr Genet Sel Pap — International Congress of Genetics. Selected Papers

Int Congr Gerontol Condens Pap — International Congress of Gerontology. Condensations of Papers

Int Congr Gerontol Proc — International Congress of Gerontology. Proceedings

Int Congr Glass — International Congress on Glass

Int Congr Glass Fibre Reinf Cem Proc — International Congress on Glass Fibre Reinforced Cement. Proceedings

Int Congr Glass Pap — International Congress on Glass. Papers

Int Congr Glass Tech Pap — International Congress on Glass. Technical Papers

Int Congr Hair Res — International Congress on Hair Research

Int Congr Heat Treat Mater — International Congress on Heat Treatment of Materials

Int Congr Hematol Lect — International Congress of Hematology. Lectures

Int Congr Heterocycl Chem — International Congress of Heterocyclic Chemistry

Int Congr High Speed Photogr — International Congress on High-Speed Photography

Int Congr High Speed Photogr Photonics — International Congress on High-Speed Photography and Photonics

Int Congr Hist Oceanogr — International Congress on the History of Oceanography

Int Congr Histo Cytochem Proc — International Congress of Histo- and Cytochemistry. Proceedings

Int Congr Hydrogen Mater — International Congress on Hydrogen and Materials

Int Congr Hydrogen Met — International Congress on Hydrogen in Metals

Int Congr Hyg Prev Med Proc — International Congress for Hygiene and Preventive Medicine. Proceedings

Int Congr Hyperbaric Med Proc — International Congress on Hyperbaric Medicine. Proceedings

Int Congr Immunol — International Congress of Immunology

Int Congr Immunol Satell Workshop — International Congress of Immunology Satellite Workshop

Int Congr Industr Chem — International Congress of Industrial Chemistry

Int Congr Infect Dis Proc — International Congress for Infectious Diseases. Proceedings

Int Congr Infect Pathol Commun — International Congress of Infectious Pathology. Communications

Int Congr Inflammation — International Congress of Inflammation

Int Congr Instrum Aerosp Simul Facil — International Congress on Instrumentation in Aerospace Simulation Facilities

Int Congr Instrum Aerosp Simul Facil Rec — International Congress on Instrumentation in Aerospace Simulation Facilities. Record

Int Congr Intern Med — International Congress of Internal Medicine

Int Congr Intern Med Proc — International Congress of Internal Medicine. Proceedings

Int Congr Int Organ Study Hum Dev — International Congress. International Organization for the Study of Human Development

Int Congr Int Solid Wastes Public Clean Assoc Proc — International Congress. International Solid Wastes and Public Cleansing Association. Proceedings

Int Congr Int Union Study Soc Insects — International Congress. International Union for the Study of Social Insects

Int Congr IUSSI — International Congress. IUSSI

Int Congr Large Dams — International Congress on Large Dams

Int Congr Liver Dis — International Congress of Liver Diseases

Int Congr Lymphol Proc — International Congress of Lymphology. Proceedings

Int Congr Man Made Text Econ Technol Rep — International Congress of Man Made Textiles. Economic and Technological Reports

Int Congr Mar Corros Fouling — International Congress on Marine Corrosion and Fouling

Int Congr Meat Sci Technol — International Congress of Meat Science and Technology

Int Congr Med Plant Res — International Congress on Medicinal Plant Research

Int Congr Menopause — International Congress on the Menopause

Int Congr Met Corros Proc — International Congress on Metallic Corrosion. Proceedings

Int Congr Microbiol — International Congress of Microbiology

Int Congr Microbiol Rep Proc — International Congress for Microbiology. Report of Proceedings

Int Congr Microbiol Symp — International Congress for Microbiology. Symposia

Int Congr Mil Med Pharm — International Congress of Military Medicine and Pharmacy

Int Congr Nephrol Proc — International Congress of Nephrology. Proceedings

Int Congr Neuromuscular Dis — International Congress on Neuromuscular Diseases

Int Congr Neuropathol Rapp Discuss — International Congress of Neuropathology. Rapports et Discussions

Int Congr Nitrogen Fixation — International Congress on Nitrogen Fixation

Int Congr Nutr — International Congress of Nutrition

Int Congr Obes Proc — International Congress on Obesity. Proceedings

Int Congr Occup Health — International Congress on Occupational Health

Int Congr Occup Health Chem Ind — International Congress on Occupational Health in the Chemical Industry

Int Congr Ophthalmol — International Congress of Ophthalmology

Int Congr Parasitol — International Congress of Parasitology

Int Congr Pediatr — International Congress of Pediatrics

Int Congr Pest Chem — International Congress of Pesticide Chemistry

Int Congr Pharmacol Proc — International Congress of Pharmacology. Proceedings

Int Congr Pharm Sci FIP Proc — International Congress of Pharmaceutical Sciences of FIP [*Federation of Internationale Pharmacutique*]. Proceedings

Int Congr Phosphorus Compd Proc — International Congress on Phosphorus Compounds. Proceedings

Int Congr Photobiol — International Congress on Photobiology

Int Congr Photosynth Proc — International Congress on Photosynthesis. Proceedings

Int Congr Physiol Sci — International Congress of Physiological Sciences

Int Congr Physiol Sci Lect Symp — International Congress of Physiological Sciences. Lectures and Symposia
Int Congr Placental Proteins — International Congress on Placental Proteins
Int Congr Plant Pathol — International Congress of Plant Pathology
Int Congr Plant Prot Proc Conf — International Congress of Plant Protection. Proceedings. Conference
Int Congr Plant Tissue Cell Cult — International Congress of Plant Tissue and Cell Culture
Int Congr Plant Tissue Cell Cult Proc — International Congress of Plant Tissue and Cell Culture. Proceedings
Int Congr Pl Prot — International Congress of Plant Protection
Int Congr Polym Concr — International Congress on Polymer Concretes
Int Congr Precast Concr Ind Proc Main Suppl Pap — International Congress. Precast Concrete Industry. Proceedings. Main and Supplementary Papers
Int Congr Primatol — International Congress of Primatology
Int Congr Protozool — International Congress of Protozoology
Int Congr Protozool Proc Congr — International Congress of Protozoology. Proceedings. Congress
Int Congr Pteridines Handb — International Congress on Pteridines. Handbook
Int Congr Pure Appl Chem — International Congress of Pure and Applied Chemistry
Int Congr Pure Appl Chem Proc — International Congress of Pure and Applied Chemistry. Proceedings
Int Congr Quantum Chem — International Congress of Quantum Chemistry
Int Congr Quantum Chem Proc — International Congress of Quantum Chemistry. Proceedings
Int Congr Radiol Trans — International Congress of Radiology. Transactions
Int Congr Reprod Immunol — International Congress of Reproductive Immunology
Int Congr Reprogr Inf — International Congress on Reprography and Information
Int Congr Rheol — International Congress on Rheology
Int Congr Rock Mech — International Congress on Rock Mechanics
Int Congr Role Viruses Hum Cancer — International Congress. The Role of Viruses in Human Cancer
Int Congr Rural Med — International Congress of Rural Medicine
Int Congr Scand Chem Eng Proc — International Congress in Scandinavia on Chemical Engineering. Proceedings
Int Congr Sedimentology — International Congress on Sedimentology
Int Congr Ser Excerpta Med — International Congress Series. Excerpta Medica
Int Congr Sexol — International Congress of Sexology
Int Congr Soc Advanc Breed Res Asia Oceania — International Congress. Society for the Advancement of Breeding Researches in Asia and Oceania
Int Congr Soilless Cult Proc — International Congress on Soilless Culture. Proceedings
Int Congr Soil Sci — International Congress of Soil Science
Int Congr Speleol Abh — International Congress of Speleology. Abhandlungen
Int Congr Static Electr — International Congress on Static Electricity
Int Congr Stereol Proc — International Congress for Stereology. Proceedings
Int Congr Study Bauxites Alumina Alum Prepr — International Congress for the Study of Bauxites, Alumina, and Aluminum. Preprints
Int Congr Surf Act Subst — International Congress on Surface Active Substances
Int Congr Surf Technol — International Congress on Surface Technology
Int Congr Symp Semin Ser — International Congress, Symposium, and Seminar Series
Int Congr Symp Ser R Soc Med Serv Ltd — International Congress and Symposium Series. Royal Society of Medicine ServicesLimited
Int Congr Syst Evol Biol — International Congress of Systematic and Evolutionary Biology
Int Congr Theor Appl Mech — International Congress of Theoretical and Applied Mechanics
Int Congr Toxicol — International Congress on Toxicology
Int Congr Ultra Low Doses — International Congress on Ultra Low Doses
Int Congr Unitas Malacol Eur — International Congress of Unitas Malacologica Europaea
Int Congr Vasc Neuroeff Mech — International Congress on Vascular Neuroeffector Mechanisms
Int Congr Vitreous Enamelling Proc — International Congress in Vitreous Enamelling. Proceedings
Int Congr Waves Instab Plasmas — International Congress on Waves and Instabilities in Plasmas
Int Congr X Ray Opt Microanal Proc — International Congress on X-Ray Optics and Microanalysis. Proceedings
Int Cong Zool Pr — International Congress of Zoology. Proceedings
Int Constr — International Construction
Int Contact Sticht Ned Graan Cent — International Contact. Stichting Nederlands Graan-Centrum
Int Controlled Release Pest Symp Proc — International Controlled Release Pesticide Symposium. Proceedings
Int Convoc Immunol Proc — International Convocation on Immunology. Proceedings
Int Copper Inf Bull — International Copper Information Bulletin
Int Copper Res Assoc Res Rep — International Copper Research Association Research Report
Int Coral Reef Symp Proc — International Coral Reef Symposium. Proceedings
Int Corbicula Symp — International Corbicula Symposium
Int Coronelli Ges Inf — Internationale Coronelli-Gesellschaft. Information
Int Corros Conf Ser — International Corrosion Conference Series
Int Corros Congr Proc — International Corrosion Congress. Proceedings
Int Cosmic Ray Conf Conf Pap — International Cosmic Ray Conference. Conference Papers
Int Cott Bull — International Cotton Bulletin
Int Cott Ind Statist — International Cotton Industry Statistics
Int Cotton Bull — International Cotton Bulletin
Int Counc Explor Sea Coop Res Rep — International Council for the Exploration of the Sea. Cooperative Research Report

Int Counc Explor Sea Coop Res Rep Ser A — International Council for the Exploration of the Sea. Cooperative Research Report. Series A
Int Counc Explor Sea Coop Res Rep Ser B — International Council for the Exploration of the Sea. Cooperative Research Report. Series B
Int Counc Lab Anim Sci Symp — International Council for Laboratory Animal Science. Symposium
Int Counc Sci Unions — International Council of Scientific Unions
Int Counc Sci Unions Inter-Union Comm Geodynamics Rep — International Council of Scientific Unions. Inter-Union Commission on Geodynamics. Report
Int Course Mater Sci — International Course on Materials Science
Int Course New Methods Study Transp Cell Membr — International Course on New Methods in the Study of Transport across the Cell Membrane
Int Course Peritoneal Dial — International Course on Peritoneal Dialysis
Int Course Transplant Clin Immunol — International Course on Transplantation and Clinical Immunology
Int Crim Police Rev — International Criminal Police Review
Int Crit Tabl — International Critical Tables
Int Crop Rep — International Crop Report
Int Cryog Eng Conf — International Cryogenic Engineering Conferences
Int Currency R — International Currency Review
Int Curr Meter Group Rep — International Current Meter Group. Report
Int Curr Rev — International Currency Review
Int Cystic Fibrosis Congr — International Cystic Fibrosis Congress
Int Cytoembryol Symp — International Cytoembryological Symposium
Int Dairy Congr Congr Rep — International Dairy Congress. Congress Report
Int Dairy Congr Proc — International Dairy Congress. Proceedings
Int Dairy Fed Annu Bull — International Dairy Federation. Annual Bulletin
Int Dairy Fed Bull — International Dairy Federation. Bulletin
Int Dairy Fed Spec Issue — International Dairy Federation Special Issue
Int Dairy J — International Dairy Journal
Int DATA Ser Ser A — International DATA Series. Series A
Int Deep Drawing Res Group Bienn Congr — International Deep Drawing Research Group. Biennial Congress
Int Def Intell — International Defense Intelligence
Int Demogr — International Demographics
Int Dent — International Dentistry
Int Dent J — International Dental Journal
Int Dent J Lond — International Dental Journal (London)
Int Dent J Philad — International Dental Journal (Philadelphia)
Int Dent Rev — International Dental Review
Int Des — Interior Design
Int Desalin Water Reuse Q — International Desalination and Water Reuse Quarterly
Int Des Equip — International Design and Equipment
Int Dev Abstr — International Development Abstracts
Int Develop R — International Development Review
Int Dev Res Cent Publ IDRC — International Development Research Centre. Publication IDRC
Int Dev Res Cent Tech Rep IDRC — International Development Research Centre. Technical Report. IDRC
Int Dev Res Cent Tech Stud IDRC-TS — International Development Research Centre. Technical Studies IDRC-TS
Int Dev Rev — International Development Review
Int Diabetes Fed Bull — International Diabetes Federation. Bulletin
Int Dialog Z — Internationale Dialog Zeitschrift
Int Dichtungstag — Internationale Dichtungstagung
Int Die Cast Expos Congr Trans — International Die Casting Exposition and Congress. Transactions
Int Dig — International Digest
Int Dig Health Legis — International Digest of Health Legislation
Int Dig Hlth Legisl — International Digest of Health Legislation. World Health Organisation
Int Dig Organother — International Digest of Organotherapy
Int Dir Exec Recruit — International Directory of Executive Recruiters
Int Dissolving Pulps Conf Conf Pap — International Dissolving Pulps Conference. Conference Papers
Int Dissolving Pulps Conf Prepr — International Dissolving Pulps Conference. Preprints
Int Dist Heat Assoc Off Proc — International District Heating Association. Official Proceedings
Int Dredg Abstr — International Dredging Abstracts
Int Dredging Rev — International Dredging Review
Int Drug Regul Monit — International Drug Regulatory Monitor
Int Drying Symp — International Drying Symposium
Int Dyer — International Dyer, Textile Printer, Bleacher, and Finisher
Int Dyer Text Printer Bleacher Finish — International Dyer, Textile Printer, Bleacher, and Finisher
Int Dyke Conf — International Dyke Conference
INTEAG — Internist
InTech (Instrum Technol) — InTech (Instrumentation Technology)
Int Econ R — International Economic Review
Int Ec R — International Economic Review
Int Ed — International Education
Int Ed & Cul Exch — International Educational and Cultural Exchange
Integ Ed — Integrated Education: Race and Schools
Integ Educ — Integrated Education
Integral Transform Spec Funct — Integral Transformations and Special Functions. An International Journal
Integrated Circuits Int — Integrated Circuits International
Integrated Educ — Integrated Education
Integr Circuit Metrol Insp Process Control — Integrated Circuit Metrology, Inspection, and Process Control
Integr Control Weeds Proc — Integrated Control of Weeds. Proceedings
Integr Crop Livest Fish Farming — Integrated Crop-Livestock-Fish Farming
Integr Ferroelectr — Integrated Ferroelectrics

Integr Ind — Integral Industrial
Integr Intern Med Proc Int Congr Intern Med — Integration in Internal Medicine. Proceedings. International Congress of Internal Medicine
Integr Konzepte Abfallentsorgung Muelltech Semin — Integrierte Konzepte der Abfallentsorgung. Muelltechnisches Seminar
Integr Latinoamer — Integracion Latinoamericana
Integr Opt — Integrated Optics
Integr Opt Circuit Eng — Integrated Optical Circuit Engineering
Integr Opt Circuit Eng Int Conf — Integrated Optical Circuit Engineering. International Conference
Integr Opt Circuits — Integrated Optical Circuits
Integr Optoelectron Commun Process — Integrated Optoelectronics for Communication and Processing
Integr Physiol Behav Sci — Integrative Physiological and Behavioral Science
Integr Pollut Control Clean Technol — Integrated Pollution Control through Clean Technology
Integr Virusy — Integratsionnye Virusy
Integr VLSI J — Integration, the VLSI Journal
Int El Dep Conf — International Electrodeposition Conference
INTELEC Int Telecommun Energy Conf Proc — INTELEC. International Telecommunications Energy Conference. Proceedings
Int Electron — International Electronics
Int Electron Devices Meet Tech Dig — International Electron Devices Meeting. Technical Digest
Int Electron Packag Conf — International Electronics Packaging Conference
Int Electrophor Soc Meet — International Electrophoresis Society. Meeting
Int Electrotech Comm Publ — International Electrotechnical Commission. Publications
Int Electr Veh Symp — International Electric Vehicle Symposium
Int Elektr — Internationale Elektronische Rundschau
Int Elektron Rundsch — Internationale Elektronische Rundschau
Intell — Intelligence
Intellbl Jen Allg Lit Zt — Intelligenzblatt der Jenaischen Allgemeinen Literatur-Zeitung
Intell Bull Commonw Econ Comm — Intelligence Bulletin. Commonwealth Economic Committee
Intell Dig — Intelligence Digest
Intell Instrum Comput — Intelligent Instruments and Computers
Intell Memor Br Alumin Co — Intelligence Memorandum. British Aluminium Company
Intell Process Mater State of the Art Implementation Symp — Intelligent Processing of Materials. State of the Art and Implementation Symposium
Intell Prop L Rev — Intellectual Property Law Review
Intell Rob Comput Vision — Intelligent Robots and Computer Vision
Intell Syst Eng — Intelligent Systems Engineering
Intell Veh Highw Syst — Intelligent Vehicle Highway Systems
Intel Obs — Intellectual Observer
Int Emailkongr — Internationaler Emailkongress
In Tema Med Cult — In Tema di Medicina e Cultura
Inten Agric — Intensive Agriculture
Int Enamelist — International Enamelist
Int Encycl Food Nutr — International Encyclopedia of Food and Nutrition
Int Endod J — International Endodontic Journal
Int Endothelial Cell Symp — International Endothelial Cell Symposium
Int Energie Forum — Internationales Energie-Forum
Int Engr — International Engineer
Intensive Agr — Intensive Agriculture
Intensive Care Med — Intensive Care Medicine
Intensive Care Nurs — Intensive Care Nursing
Intensivmed Diagn — Intensivmedizin und Diagnostik
Intensivmed Notfallmed — Intensivmedizin und Notfallmedizin
Intensivmed Notfallmed Anaesthesiol — Intensivmedizin, Notfallmedizin, Anaesthesiologie
Intensivmed Prax — Intensivmedizinische Praxis
Intensivpflege Neugeborenen Int Symp — Intensivpflege bei Neugeborenen. Internationales Symposion
Int Environ Saf — International Environment and Safety
Int Env Saf — International Environment and Safety
Inter — Interiors
IntER — International Economic Review
Interact Cell Signalling Syst — Interactions Among Cell Signalling Systems
Interaction Mech Math Ser — Interaction of Mechanics and Mathematics Series
Interact Mech Math Ser — Interaction of Mechanics and Mathematics Series
Inter Afr Soils Conf — Inter-African Soils Conference
Interagency Workshop In Situ Water Qual Sens Biol Sens — Interagency Workshop on In-Situ Water Quality Sensing. Biological Sensors
Inter-Am — Inter-American
Inter Am Bibliogr Rev Wash — Inter-American Bibliographical Review (Washington, DC)
Inter Am Cacao Conf Proc — Inter-American Cacao Conference. Proceedings
Inter Am Conf Congenital Defects Pap Discuss — Inter-American Conference on Congenital Defects. Papers and Discussions
Interam Conf Mater Technol Proc — Interamerican Conference on Materials Technology. Proceedings
Inter Am Conf Radiochem Proc — Inter-American Conference on Radiochemistry. Proceedings
Inter Am Congr Brucell Pap — Inter-American Congress on Brucellosis. Papers
Inter-Am Econ Affairs — Inter-American Economic Affairs
Inter-Amer Econ Aff — Inter-American Economic Affairs
Inter-Amer M Bul — Inter-American Music Bulletin
Inter-Amer M R — Inter-American Music Review
Inter Amer Q — Inter-American Quarterly
Inter Amer Symp Peaceful Appl Nucl Energy Proc — Inter-American Symposium on the Peaceful Application of Nuclear Energy. Proceedings

Inter Am Inst Agric Sci OAS Trop Cent Res Grad Train Rep — Inter-American Institute of Agricultural Sciences of the OAS. Tropical Center for Research and Graduate Training. Report
Interam J P — Interamerican Journal of Psychology
Inter-Am L Rev — Inter-American Law Review
Inter Am M — Inter-American Music Review
Inter Am Meet Foot Mouth Dis Zoonoses Control — Inter-American Meeting on Foot-and-Mouth Disease and Zoonoses Control
Inter Am Music Bull Wash — Inter-American Music Bulletin (Washington, DC)
Inter-Am Q — Inter-American Quarterly
Inter Am Quart Wash — Inter-American Quarterly (Washington, DC)
Interam Rev Bibliogr — Inter-American Review of Bibliography
Interam Symp Isot Hydrol Pap — Interamerican Symposium on Isotope Hydrology. Papers
Inter Am Symp Peaceful Applic Nucl Energy — Inter-American Symposium on the Peaceful Application of Nuclear Energy
Inter Am Symp Peaceful Appl Nucl Energy Pap — Inter-American Symposium on the Peaceful Application of Nuclear Energy. Papers
Inter-Am Trop Tuna Comm Bull — Inter-American Tropical Tuna Commission. Bulletin
Inter-Am Trop Tuna Comm Spec Rep — Inter-American Tropical Tuna Commission. Special Report
Interavia Air Lett — Interavia Air Letter
Interavia (Engl Ed) — Interavia (English Edition)
Inter Ballist Guns — Interior Ballistics of Guns
Inter B C — Interracial Books for Children. Bulletin
Intercalation Compd Proc Int Conf — Intercalation Compounds. Proceedings. International Conference on Intercalation Compounds
Intercell Intracell Commun — Intercellular and Intracellular Communication
Interchem Rev — Interchemical Review
Interchurch N — Interchurch News
Intercol Law J — Intercollegiate Law Journal
Intercoll Rev — Intercollegiate Review
Intercolon Gas J Can — Intercolonial Gas Journal of Canada
Intercolon Med Congr Australasia — Intercolonial Medical Congress of Australasia
Intercolon Med J Australas — Intercolonial Medical Journal of Australasia
Intercolon Med J Australasia — Intercolonial Medical Journal of Australasia
Intercol Socialist — Intercollegiate Socialist
Intercont — Intercontinental Press
Intercontinental Pr — Intercontinental Press
Intercontinental Text — Inter-Continental Textilian
Interdep Comm Atmos Sci ICAS Rep US — Interdepartmental Committee for Atmospheric Sciences. ICAS. Report. (US)
Interdep Comm Atmos Sci Rep US — Interdepartmental Committee for Atmospheric Sciences. Report. United States
Inter Depend — Inter Dependent
Inter Des — Interior Design
Interdis Center Eur Stud Newslett — Interdisciplinary Center for European Studies. Newsletter
Interdiscip Appl Math — Interdisciplinary Applied Mathematics
Interdiscip Conf Electromagn Scattering — Interdisciplinary Conference on Electromagnetic Scattering
Interdiscip Inform Sci — Interdisciplinary Information Sciences
Interdisciplinary Math — Interdisciplinary Mathematics
Interdisciplinary Sci Rev — Interdisciplinary Science Reviews
Interdisciplinary Systems Res — Interdisciplinary Systems Research
Interdiscip Math — Interdisciplinary Mathematics
Interdiscip Neuroendocrinol Int Meet — Interdisciplinary Neuroendocrinology. International Meeting
Interdiscip Sci Rev — Interdisciplinary Science Reviews
Interdiscip Statist — Interdisciplinary Statistics
Interdiscip Top Gerontol — Interdisciplinary Topics in Gerontology
Interdisc Semin Tachyons Relat Top Proc — Interdisciplinary Seminars on Tachyons and Related Topics. Proceedings
Interdis Sci Rev — Interdisciplinary Science Reviews
Interdiszip Gerontol — Interdisziplinaere Gerontologie
Interecon — Intereconomics
Inter Econ Indic & Comp Tr — International Economic Indicators and Competitive Trends
Inter Ed & Cul Ex — International Educational and Cultural Exchange
Inter Electron — Inter Electronique
Interface Comput Educ Q — Interface. The Computer Education Quarterly
Interfaces Comput — Interfaces in Computing [*Later, Computer Standards and Interfaces*]
Interfaces Consens Syst — Interfaces in Condensed Systems
Interfaces New Mater Proc Workshop — Interfaces in New Materials. Proceedings. Workshop
Interfacial Phenom Biol Syst — Interfacial Phenomena in Biological Systems
Interfacial Phenom Compos Mater Proc Int Conf — Interfacial Phenomena in Composite Materials. Proceedings. International Conference
Interferon Biotecnol — Interferon y Biotecnologia
Intergov Oceanogr Comm Tech Ser — Intergovernmental Oceanographic Commission. Technical Series
Intergov Oceanogr Comm Workshop Rep — Intergovernmental Oceanographic Commission. Workshop Report
Intergov Persp — Intergovernmental Perspective
Interim Biblphy Int Geophys Yr — Interim Bibliography on the International Geophysical year
Interim Doc Health Aspects Chem Saf — Interim Document. Health Aspects of Chemical Safety
Interim Proc Geol Soc Am — Interim Proceedings of the Geological Society of America
Interim Rep Advis Comm Aeronaut — Interim Report. Advisory Committee for Aeronautics

Interim Rep Aust Natn Antarct Res Exped — Interim Report. Australian National Antarctic Research Expedition
Interim Tech Rep MIT — Interim Technical Report. Massachusetts Institute of Technology
Interior Des — Interior Design
Interior Des Contract Furnish — Interior Design and Contract Furnishing
Interior Finish Floor — Interior Finishing and Flooring
Interior Landscape Intl — Interior Landscape International
Interiors Ind Des — Interiors and Industrial Design
Int Erlangen Nuremberg Symp Exp Gerontol — International Erlangen-Nuremberg Symposium on Experimental Gerontology
Interlend and Doc Supply — Interlending and Document Supply
Interlending Rev — Interlending Review
Inter M — International Monthly
Intermag Conf Dig — Intermag Conference. Digests
Interm des Cherch et Curieux — Intermediaire des Chercheurs et Curieux
Intermed Afas — Intermediaire de l'Afas
Intermed Bombycult Ent — Intermediaire des Bombyculteurs et Entomologistes
Intermed Chercheurs — Intermediaire des Chercheurs et des Curieux
Intermed Chercheurs & Curieux — Intermediaire des Chercheurs et des Curieux
Intermed Int Quinc — Intermediaire International de la Quincaillerie, des Metaux
Intermed Math — Intermediaire des Mathematiciens
Intermed Rech Math — Intermediaire des Recherches Mathematiques
Intermed Sci Curric Study Newsl — Intermediate Science Curriculum Study. Newsletter
Intermountain Econ R — Intermountain Economic Review
Intermount Ind — Intermountain Industry
Intermt Assoc Geol Annu Field Conf Guideb — Intermountain Association of Geologists. Annual Field Conference. Guidebook
Intermt Assoc Pet Geol Annu Field Conf Guideb — Intermountain Association of Petroleum Geologists. Annual Field Conference. Guidebook
Intermt Econ Rev — Intermountain Economic Review
Internacia Med Revuo — Internacia Medicina Revuo
Internacia Sci Revuo — Internacia Scienca Revuo
Internal Combust Engng — Internal Combustion Engineering
Internal Combust Engr — Internal Combustion Engineer
Internal J Adapt Control Signal Process — International Journal of Adaptive Control and Signal Processing
Internal J Algebra Comput — International Journal of Algebra and Computation
Internal Rep Irrig Res Stn Griffith — Internal Report. Irrigation Research Station. Griffith, N.S.W.
Internasjonal Polit — Internasjonal Politikk
Internas Polit — Internasjonal Politikk
Internat — International Quarterly
Internat Abstr Surg — International Abstracts of Surgery
Internat Aff — International Affairs
Internat Affairs (London) — International Affairs (London)
Internat Affairs (Moscow) — International Affairs (Moscow)
Internat Afrikaforum — Internationales Afrikaforum
Internat and Comparative Law Q 4th Ser — International and Comparative Law Quarterly. Fourth Series
Internat Anesth Clin — International Anesthesiology Clinics
Internat Annals Criminology — International Annals of Criminology
Internat Appl Mech — International Applied Mechanics
Internat Arch Allergy — International Archives of Allergy and Applied Immunology
Internat Archiv Ethnog — Internationales Archiv fuer Ethnographie
Internat Archiv f Ethno — Internationales Archiv fuer Ethnologie
Internat Asienforum — Internationales Asienforum
Internat Ass Med Mus Bull — International Association of Medical Museums. Bulletin and Journal of TechnicalMethods
Internat Assoc Sci Hydrology Bull — International Association of Scientific Hydrology. Bulletin
Internat Assoc Sci Hydrology Bull Pub — International Association of Scientific Hydrology. Bulletin. Publication
Internat Assoc Sci Hydrology Pub — International Association of Scientific Hydrology. Publications
Internat Betriebswirt Zeitschriftenreport — Internationaler Betriebswirtschaftlicher Zeitschriftenreport
Internat Bus — International Business
Internat Chem Engng — International Chemical Engineering
Internat Clin — International Clinics
Internat Com Hist Sci Bul — International Committee of Historical Sciences. Bulletin
Internat Comm Coal Petrology Proc — International Committee for Coal Petrology. Proceedings
Internat Commer Bank China Econ R — International Commercial Bank of China. Economic Review
Internat Comm Jurists R — International Commission of Jurists. Review
Internat Comp LQ — International and Comparative Law Quarterly
Internat Comput Sci Ser — International Computer Science Series
Internat Conciliation — International Conciliation
Internat Contract — International Contract
Internat Correspondence Schools Serial — International Correspondence Schools. Serial
Internat Currency R — International Currency Review
Internat Development R — International Development Review
Internat Econ Indicators — International Economic Indicators
Internat Econom Rev — International Economic Review
Internat Econ R — International Economic Review
Internat Entwicklung — Internationale Entwicklung
Internat Family Planning Perspectives — International Family Planning Perspectives
Internat Family Planning Perspectives and Dig — International Family Planning Perspectives and Digest
Internat Fin Chase — International Finance. Chase Manhattan Bank

Internat Geology Rev — International Geology Review
International R Ed — International Review of Education
Internat J — International Journal
Internat J Accounting — International Journal of Accounting
Internat J Appl Sci Comput — International Journal of Applied Science and Computations
Internat J Approx Reason — International Journal of Approximate Reasoning
Internat Jb Gesch Unterricht — Internationales Jahrbuch fuer Geschichtsunterricht
Internat J Bifur Chaos Appl Sci Engrg — International Journal of Bifurcation and Chaos in Applied Sciences and Engineering
Internat J Bio-Med Comput — International Journal of Bio-Medical Computing
Internat J Circuit Theory Appl — International Journal of Circuit Theory and Applications
Internat J Comp Sociol — International Journal of Comparative Sociology
Internat J Comput and Fluids — International Journal. Computers and Fluids
Internat J Comput Geom Appl — International Journal of Computational Geometry and Applications
Internat J Comput Information Sci — International Journal of Computer and Information Sciences
Internat J Comput Inform Sci — International Journal of Computer and Information Sciences
Internat J Comput Math — International Journal of Computer Mathematics. Section A. Programming Languages. Theory and Methods
Internat J Control — International Journal of Control
Internat J Electron — International Journal of Electronics
Internat J Engng Science — International Journal of Engineering Science
Internat J Engrg Sci — International Journal of Engineering Science
Internat J Environmental Studies — International Journal of Environmental Studies
Internat J Fertil — International Journal of Fertility
Internat J Found Comput Sci — International Journal of Foundations of Computer Science
Internat J Fracture — International Journal of Fracture
Internat J Game Theory — International Journal of Game Theory
Internat J Gen Syst — International Journal of General Systems
Internat J Gen Systems — International Journal of General Systems
Internat J Heat Fluid Flow — International Journal of Heat and Fluid Flow
Internat J Heat Mass Transfer — International Journal of Heat and Mass Transfer
Internat J Inform Management Sci — International Journal of Information and Management Sciences
Internat J Leprosy — International Journal of Leprosy [Later, International Journal of Leprosy and Other Mycobacterial Diseases]
Internat J Man-Machine Studies — International Journal of Man-Machine Studies
Internat J Man-Mach Stud — International Journal of Man-Machine Studies
Internat J Math — International Journal of Mathematics
Internat J Math Ed Sci Tech — International Journal of Mathematical Education in Science and Technology
Internat J Math Math Sci — International Journal of Mathematics and Mathematical Sciences
Internat J Math Statist Sci — International Journal of Mathematical and Statistical Sciences
Internat J Mental Health — International Journal of Mental Health
Internat J Middle East Studies — International Journal of Middle East Studies
Internat J Mineral Proc — International Journal of Mineral Processing
Internat J Modern Phys A — International Journal of Modern Physics. A
Internat J Modern Phys B — International Journal of Modern Physics. B
Internat J Modern Phys C — International Journal of Modern Physics C. Computational Physics. Physical Computation
Internat J Modern Phys D — International Journal of Modern Physics. D. Gravitation, Astrophysics, Cosmology
Internat J Modern Phys E — International Journal of Modern Physics. E. Nuclear Physics
Internat J Multiphase Flow — International Journal of Multiphase Flow
Internat J Neuropsychiat — International Journal of Neuropsychiatry
Internat J Non-Linear Mech — International Journal of Non-Linear Mechanics
Internat J Numer Analyt Methods Geomech — International Journal for Numerical and Analytical Methods in Geomechanics
Internat J Numer Methods Engrg — International Journal for Numerical Methods in Engineering
Internat J Numer Methods Fluids — International Journal for Numerical Methods in Fluids
Internat J Numer Methods Heat Fluid Flow — International Journal of Numerical Methods for Heat and Fluid Flow
Internat J Numer Modelling — International Journal of Numerical Modelling. Electronic Networks, Devices, andFields
Internat J of Leg Res — International Journal of Legal Research
Internat Jour Ethics — International Journal of Ethics. University of Chicago Press
Internat Jour Rock Mechanics and Mining Sci — International Journal of Rock Mechanics and Mining Sciences [Later, International Journal of Rock Mechanics and Mining Sciences and Geomechanics Abstracts]
Internat J Parallel Programming — International Journal of Parallel Programming
Internat J Physical Distribution and Materials Mgt — International Journal of Physical Distribution and Materials Management
Internat J Policy Anal Inform Systems — International Journal of Policy Analysis and Information Systems
Internat J Robust Nonlinear Control — International Journal of Robust and Nonlinear Control
Internat J Social Econ — International Journal of Social Economics
Internat J Sociol — International Journal of Sociology
Internat J Solids and Structures — International Journal of Solids and Structures
Internat J Systems Sci — International Journal of Systems Science
Internat J Theoret Phys — International Journal of Theoretical Physics
Internat J Uncertain Fuzziness Knowledge Based Systems — International Journal of Uncertainty, Fuzziness, and Knowledge-Based Systems

Internat J Urban and Regional Research — International Journal of Urban and Regional Research

Internat Kirchl Z — Internationale Kirchliche Zeitschrift

Internat Labour R — International Labour Review

Internat Lawyer — International Lawyer. Quarterly Publication of the Section of International andComparative Law of the American Bar Association

Internatl Cong Hist Sci Proc — International Congress of Historical Sciences. Proceedings

Internat Lecture Ser Comput Sci — International Lecture Series in Computer Science

Internat Legal Materials — International Legal Materials

Internatl Goat Sheep Res — International Goat and Sheep Research

Internat Lib Anthropol — International Library of Anthropology

Internat Lib Econom — International Library of Economics

Internatl Jour — International Journal

Internat Logic Rev — International Logic Review

Internatl Organ — International Organization

Internat LQ — International Law Quarterly

Internat M — International Magazine

Internat Math News — International Mathematical News

Internat Math Res Notices — International Mathematics Research Notices

Internat Mgt — International Management

Internat Migration — International Migration

Internat Migration R — International Migration Review

Internat Mo — International Monthly

Internat Monetary Fund Staff Pas — International Monetary Fund. Staff Papers

Internat Oceanog Found Bull — International Oceanographic Foundation. Bulletin

Internat Org — International Organization

Internat Perspectives (Can) — International Perspectives (Canada)

Internat Problems — International Problems

Internat Problems (Tel-Aviv) — International Problems (Tel-Aviv)

Internat R — International Review

Internat R Admin Science (Brussels) — International Review of Administrative Sciences (Brussels)

Internat R Admin Sciences — International Review of Administrative Sciences

Internat R Criminal Policy — International Review of Criminal Policy

Internat Recht und Diplomatie — Internationales Recht und Diplomatie

Internat Rec Med — International Record of Medicine

Internat Relations — Relations Internationales/International Relations

Internat Rev Missions — International Review of Missions

Internat Rev Soc Hist — International Review of Social History

Internat Rev Trop Med — International Review of Tropical Medicine

Internat Schools Comput Sci — International Schools for Computer Scientists

Internat Schriftenreihe Numer Math — Internationale Schriftenreihe zur Numerischen Mathematik

Internat Security — International Security

Internat Security R — International Security Review

Internat Ser Appl Systems Anal — International Series on Applied Systems Analysis

Internat Ser Comput Engrg — International Series on Computational Engineering

Internat Ser Management Sci Oper Res — International Series in Management Science/Operations Research

Internat Ser Mod Appl Math Comput Sci — International Series in Modern Applied Mathematics and Computer Science

Internat Ser Monographs Comput Sci — International Series of Monographs on Computer Science

Internat Ser Monographs in Natural Philos — International Series of Monographs in Natural Philosophy

Internat Ser Monographs Phys — International Series of Monographs on Physics

Internat Ser Monographs Pure Appl Math — International Series of Monographs in Pure and Applied Mathematics

Internat Ser Monogr Chem — International Series of Monographs on Chemistry

Internat Ser Natural Philos — International Series in Natural Philosophy

Internat Ser Nonlinear Math Theory Methods Appl — International Series in Nonlinear Mathematics. Theory, Methods, and Application

Internat Ser Numer Math — International Series of Numerical Mathematics

Internat Ser Oper Res Management Sci — International Series in Operations Research and Management Science

Internat Ser Pure Appl Math — International Series in Pure and Applied Mathematics

Internat Social Science J — International Social Science Journal

Internat Soc Sci Bull — International Social Sciences Bulletin

Internat Soc Sci J — International Social Sciences Journal

Internat Spectator — Internationale Spectator

Internat Statist Rev — International Statistical Review

Internat Stud Econom Econometrics — International Studies in Economics and Econometrics

Internat Studies (New Delhi) — International Studies (New Delhi)

Internat Studio — International Studio

Internat Stud Philos Sci — International Studies in the Philosophy of Science

Internat Sympos Econom Theory Econometrics — International Symposia in Economic Theory and Econometrics

Internat Tax J — International Tax Journal

Internat Trade Forum — International Trade Forum

Internat Trade Law and Practice — International Trade Law and Practice

Internat Union Cryst Cryst Sympos — International Union of Crystallography Crystallographic Symposia

Internat Year Book Game Theory Appl — International Year-Book of Game Theory and Applications

Internat Z Landw — Internationale Zeitschrift der Landwirtschaft

Intern Audit — Internal Auditor

Intern Beitr Ernaehrgsstoer — Internationale Beitraege zur Pathologie und Therapie der Ernaehrungsstoerungen,Stoffwechsel- und Verdauungskrankheiten

Intern Biodet Bull — International Biodeterioration Bulletin. Reference Index

Intern Combust Eng — Internal Combustion Engine

Internet J Chem — Internet Journal of Chemistry

Internet J Sci Biol Chem — Internet Journal of Science. Biological Chemistry

Internetworking Res Exper — Internetworking. Research and Experience

Internist Prax — Internistische Praxis

Internist Welt — Internistische Welt

Intern J System Bacteriol — International Journal of Systematic Bacteriology

Internl Photogr — International Photographer

Intern Med — Internal Medicine

Intern Med Adv — Internal Medicine Adviser

Intern Med (Amsterdam) — Internal Medicine (Amsterdam)

Intern Med J — Internal Medicine Journal

Intern Med News — Internal Medicine News

Intern Med Ser Tokyo — Internal Medicine Series (Tokyo)

Intern Med (Tokyo) — Internal Medicine (Tokyo)

Intern Mitt Bodenkde — Internationale Mitteilungen fuer Bodenkunde

Intern Mod Language Series — International Modern Language Series

Inter Noise — Inter-Noise Proceedings. International Conference on Noise Control Engineering

Intern Organ Boston — International Organization (Boston)

Intern Pbd Ind — International Paper Board Industry

Intern Phot — International Photography

Intern Phot Tech — International Photography Techniques

Intern Rep Miner Policy Sector Dep Energy Mines Resour (Can) — Internal Report. Mineral Policy Sector. Department of Energy, Mines, and Resources (Canada)

Intern Rep Tech Univ Helsinki Radio Lab — Internal Report. Technical University of Helsinki. Radio Laboratory

Intern Rep Univ Oxford Dep Eng Sci — Internal Report. University of Oxford. Department of Engineering Science

Intern Rev Ges Hydrobiol — Internationale Revue der Gesamten Hydrobiologie und Hydrographie

Intern Sci Technol — International Science and Technology

Intern Soc Sc Bull Paris — International Social Science Bulletin (Paris)

Intern Soc Sc Jour Paris — International Social Science Journal (Paris)

Intern Spin Struct Nucleon Symp — Internal Spin Structure of the Nucleon. Symposium

Interntl F G — International Film Guide

Intern Vjschr Dt Ges Phot — Intern. Vierteljahresschrift der Deutschen Gesellschaft fuer Photographie

Intern Zs Aerztl Psychoanal — Internationale Zeitschrift fuer Aerztliche Psychoanalyse

Interp — Interpretation

Inter-Parliamentary Bul — Inter-Parliamentary Bulletin

Inter Parliamentary Bull — Inter-Parliamentary Bulletin

Interpers D — Interpersonal Development

Interpr — Interpretation. A Journal of Bible and Theology

Interpretat — Interpretation

Interracial Bks Child Bull — Interracial Books for Children. Bulletin

Interracial Rev — Interracial Review

Inter Reg — Inter Regions

Interreg Symp Iron Steel Ind Pap — Interregional Symposium on the Iron and Steel Industry. Papers

Inter Res Counc Comm Pollut Res IRCCOPR Semin Rep — Inter-Research Council Committee on Pollution Research. IRCCOPR Seminar Report

Inter Rev for Bus Ed — International Review for Business Education

Intersch Ath Adm — Interscholastic Athletic Administration

Intersch Athl Adm — Interscholastic Athletic Administration

Intersci Conf Antimicrob Agents Chemother — Interscience Conference on Antimicrobial Agents and Chemotherapy

Intersci Conf Antimicrob Agents Chemother Proc — Interscience Conference on Antimicrobial Agents and Chemotherapy. Proceedings

Interscience Libr Chem Eng Process — Interscience Library of Chemical Engineering and Processing

Intersci Monogr Phys Astron — Interscience Monographs in Physics and Astronomy

Intersci Monogr Texts Phys Astron — Interscience Monographs and Texts in Physics and Astronomy

Intersci Publ — Interscience Publication

Inter Sci Techn — International Science and Technology

Intersekc Sestanek Med Biokem SR Slov SR Hrvat Clanki — Intersekcijski Sestanek Medicinskih Biokemikov SR Slovenije in SR Hrvatske. Clanki

Inter Ser Monogr Chem — International Series of Monographs on Chemistry

Intersoc Cryog Symp — Intersociety Cryogenics Symposium

Intersoc Energy Convers Eng Conf Proc — Intersociety Energy Conversion Engineering Conference. Proceedings

Intersoc Plast Semin Ser Managing Corros Plast — Intersociety Plastics Seminar Series. Managing Corrosion with Plastics

INTERSOL 85 Proc Bienn Congr Int Sol Energy Soc — INTERSOL 85. Proceedings. Biennial Congress. International Solar Energy Society

Interstate — Forecast. First Interstate Bank. Annual Report

Interstate Conf of Headmistresses — Interstate Conference of Headmistresses of Australian Girls' Schools. Report

Interstate Oil Compact Comm Comm Bull — Interstate Oil Compact Commission. Committee Bulletin

Interstate Oil Compact Quart Bull — Interstate Oil Compact. Quarterly Bulletin

Interstitial Nephropathies Symp Nephrol — Interstitial Nephropathies. Symposium on Nephrology

Inter-Union Comm Geodyn Sci Rep — Inter-Union Commission on Geodynamics. Scientific Report

Inter-Univ Electron Ser — Inter-University Electronics Series

Interuniv Fac Work Conf — Inter-University Faculty Work Conference

Interuniv Inst Kernwet Monogr — Interuniversitair Instituut voor Kernwetenschappen. Monografie

Interv — Interview

Intervirolo — Intervirology

Interv Rest G N Pal Spinola — Interventi di Restauro. Galleria Nazionale del Palazzo Spinola

Intest Horm Lebertag Sozialmed — Intestinale Hormone, Maldigestion-Malabsorption, Lebertagung der Sozialmediziner

Intest Toxicol — Intestinal Toxicology

Int Estuarine Res Conf — International Estuarine Research Conference

Int Estuarine Res Conf Proc — International Estuarine Research Conference. Proceedings

Int Exec — International Executive

Int Exec Trans — International Executive Transfers

Int Exhib Conf Power Gener Ind Power Gen — International Exhibition and Conference for the Power Generation Industries. Power-Gen

Int Export Chem — International Export Chemist

Int Fabr Altern Forum Proc — International Fabric Alternatives Forum. Proceedings

Int Fachmesse Fachtag Kerntech Ind Vortr — Internationale Fachmesse und Fachtagungen fuer die Kerntechnische Industrie. Vortraege

Int Fachschr Schok Ind — Internationale Fachschrift fuer die Schokoladen-Industrie

Int Fair Tech Meet Nucl Ind — International Fair and Technical Meetings of Nuclear Industries

Int Fam Plann Dig — International Family Planning Digest

Int Fam Plann Perspect — International Family Planning Perspectives

Int Farbensymp — Internationales Farbensymposium

Int Fed Autom Control Proc Ser — International Federation of Automatic Control. Proceedings Series

Int Fed Autom Control Symp Ser — International Federation of Automatic Control Symposia Series

Int Fed Autom Control Workshop — International Federation of Automatic Control Workshop

Int Fed Autom Control Workshop Modell Control Biotech Process — International Federation of Automatic Control Workshop on Modelling and Controlof Biotechnical Processes

Int Fed Fruit Juice Prod Sci Tech Comm Rep — International Federation of Fruit Juice Producers. Scientific-Technical Commission. Reports

Int Fed Soc Cosmet Chem Congr — International Federation of Societies of Cosmetic Chemists Congress

Int Ferment Symp — International Fermentation Symposium

Int Ferro Alloys Congr — International Ferro-Alloys Congress

Int Fert Congr Pap Foreign Participants — International Fertilizer Congress. Papers of Foreign Participants

Int Fert Dev Cent Spec Publ — International Fertilizer Development Center. Special Publication

Int Fertil Corresp — International Fertilizer Correspondent

Int Feuerfest Kolloq — Internationales Feuerfest-Kolloquium

Int Fiber Opt Commun Expos US Pap — International Fiber Optics and Communications Exposition in the US Papers

Int Fict R — International Fiction Review

Int Field Emiss Symp — International Field Emission Symposium

Int Field Year Great Lakes Tech Man Ser — International Field Year for the Great Lakes. Technical Manual Series

Int Fire Chief — International Fire Chief

Int Fire Fighter — International Fire Fighter

Int Fish Other Fd J — International Fish and Other Food Journal

Int Flame Res Found Members Conf — International Flame Research Foundation. Members Conference

Int Flavor Conf — International Flavor Conference

Int Flavours Food Addit — International Flavours and Food Additives

Int Flklore Rev — International Folklore Review

Int Fluid Bed Combust Appl Technol Symp — International Fluidized-Bed-Combustion and Applied-Technology Symposium

Int Fluid Conf Proc — International Fluidization Conference. Proceedings

Int Folk Bibliogr — International Folklore Bibliography

Int Folk Mus Council Jl — International Folk Music Council. Journal

Int Food Ind Congr Proc — International Food Industries Congress. Proceedings

Int Food Ingredients — International Food Ingredients

Int Forg Conf — International Forging Conference

Int Forum — International Forum

Int Forum Inf and Doc — International Forum on Information and Documentation

Int Forum Inf Docu — International Forum on Information and Documentation

Int Forum Inf Docum — International Forum on Information and Documentation

Int Forum Logotherapy — International Forum for Logotherapy

Int Foundry Conf Pap — International Foundry Conference. Papers

Int Foundry Cong Congr Pap — International Foundry Congress. Congress Papers

Int Free Trade Un — International Free Trade Union News

Int Freight — International Freighting Weekly

Int Fruchtsaft Kongr Kongr Hauptber — Internationaler Fruchtsaft-Kongress. Kongress-Hauptbericht

Int Fruchtsaftunion Wiss-Tech Komm Ber — Internationale Fruchtsaftunion. Wissenschaftlich-Technische Kommission. Berichte

Int Fruit Wld — International Fruit World

Int Fruit World — International Fruit World

Int Fund Res Symp — International Fundamental Research Symposium

Int Fungal Spore Symp — International Fungal Spore Symposium

INTGA — In Theory Only

Int GABA B Symp — International GABA B Symposium

Int Galvanizing Conf Ed Proc — International Galvanizing Conference. Edited Proceedings

Int Gas Conf Trans Pap — International Gas Conference. Transactions and Papers

Int Gas Res Conf — International Gas Research Conference

Int Gas Technol Highlights — International Gas Technology Highlights

Int G Class Stud — International Guide to Classical Studies

Int Geochem Explor Symp — International Geochemical Exploration Symposium

Int Geochem Explor Symp Proc — International Geochemical Exploration Symposium. Proceedings

Int Geog Cong Rp Verh — International Geographical Congress. Report. Verhandlungen

Int Geogr Congr — International Geographical Congress

Int Geogr Congr Pap - Congr Int Geogr Commun — International Geographical Congress. Papers - Congres International de Geographie. Communications

Int Geol Congr — International Geological Congress

Int Geol Congr Abstr Congr Geol Int Resumes — International Geological Congress. Abstracts. Congres Geologique International.Resumes

Int Geol Congr Rep Sess — International Geological Congress. Report of the Session

Int Geol Rev — International Geology Review

Int Geophys Ser — International Geophysics Series: A Series of Monographs

Int Geophys Year Rocket Rep — International Geophysical Year. Rocket Report

Int Geosci Remote Sens Symp IGARSS — International Geoscience and Remote Sensing Symposium (IGARSS)

Int Ges Gesch Pharm Veroeff — Internationale Gesellschaft fuer Geschichte der Pharmazie. Veroeffentlichungen

Int Ges Getreidechem Ber — Internationale Gesellschaft fuer Getreidechemie. Berichte

Int Gewerbearchiv — Internationales Gewerbearchiv

Int Giessener Symp Exp Gerontol — International Giessener Symposium on Experimental Gerontology

Int Giessereikongr — Internationaler Giessereikongress

Int Glaciospeleological Surv Bull — International Glaciospeleological Survey. Bulletin

Int Glaskongr — International Glaskongress

Int Glaskongr Fachvortr — Internationaler Glaskongress. Fachvortraege

Int Glass Rev — International Glass Review

Int Goat Sheep Res — International Goat and Sheep Research

Int Gothenburg Symp Chem Treat — International Gothenburg Symposium on Chemical Treatment

Int Gothenburg Symp Chem Water Wastewater Treat — International Gothenburg Symposium on Chemical Water and Wastewater Treatment

Int Grafik — International Grafik

Int Grassl Congr — International Grassland Congress

Int Grassl Congr Proc — International Grassland Congress. Proceedings

Int Grassl Congr Rep — International Grassland Congress. Report

Int Green Crop Drying Congr — International Green Crop Drying Congress

Int Gruenlandkongr Verhandlungsber — Internationaler Gruenlandkongress. Verhandlungsbericht

Int Gstaad Symp Proc — International Gstaad Symposium. Proceedings

Int GST Conf — International GST (Glutathione S-Transferases) Conference

IntGuC — International Guide to Classical Studies

Int Guide Classical Stud — International Guide to Classical Studies

Int Gym — International Gymnast

Int Haarmann Reimer Symp Fragrance Flavor Subst — International Haarmann and Reimer Symposium on Fragrance and Flavor Substances

Int Handb Child Care Prot — International Handbook of Child Care and Protection

Int Health News — International Health News

Int Heat Pipe Conf Pap — International Heat Pipe Conference. Papers

Int Heat Transfer Conf — International Heat Transfer Conference

Int Heat Treat Conf Proc — International Heat Treatment Conference. Proceedings

Int Hist Nurs J — International History of Nursing Journal

Int Histol Classif Tumors — International Histological Classification of Tumors

Int Hist R — International History Review

Int Hlth Bull — International Health Bulletin of the League of Red Cross Societies

Int Hlth Yb — International Health Year Book

Int Holzmarkt — Internationaler Holzmarkt

Int Hort Congr — International Horticulture Congress

Int Hortic Congr — International Horticultural Congress

Int Hous Tn Plann Bull — International Housing and Town Planning Bulletin

Int Humic Subst Soc Volunteered Pap Int Conf — International Humic Substances Society. Volunteered Papers. International Conference

Int Hyd Rev — International Hydrographic Review

Int Hydrocarbon Process — International Hydrocarbon Processing

Int Hydrogr Bull — International Hydrographic Bulletin

Int Hydrogr Conf — International Hydrographic Conference

Int Hydrogr Rev — International Hydrographic Review

Int Hydrol Decade Newsl — International Hydrological Decade. Newsletter

Int Hydrol Symp — International Hydrology Symposium

Int Hydromikrobiol Symp Verh — Internationales Hydromikrobiologisches Symposium. Verhandlungen

Int Hyperbaric Congr Proc — International Hyperbaric Congress Proceedings

Int Hypersonics Conf — International Hypersonics Conference

Int IEEE VLSI Multilevel Interconnect Conf — International IEEE VLSI [*Very-Large-Scale Integration*] Multilevel Interconnection Conference

Int IFAC Conf Instrum Autom Pap Rubber Plast Ind Proc — International IFAC (International Federation of Automatic Control) Conference on Instrumentation and Automation in the Paper, Rubber, and Plastics Industries. Proceedings

Int IGT Symp Gas Oil Coal Environ Biotechnol — International IGT Symposium on Gas, Oil, Coal, and Environmental Biotechnolgoy

Int Immunobiol Symp Proc — International Immunobiological Symposium. Proceedings

Int Immunol — International Immunology

Int Ind — International Index

Int Ind — International Industry

Int Ind Biotechnol — International Industrial Biotechnology

Int Ind Diamond Symp — International Industrial Diamond Symposium

Int Ind Eng Conf Proc — International Industrial Engineering Conference Proceedings

Int Index — International Index

Int Index Aeronaut Tech Rep — International Index to Aeronautical Technical Reports

Int Index Annu Cumu — International Index. Annual Cumulation

Int Index Film Period — International Index to Film Periodicals

Int Index Multi Media Inf — International Index to Multi-Media Information
Int Index Period — International Index to Periodicals
Int Ind Film — International Index to Film Periodicals
Int Indoor Clim Symp — International Indoor Climate Symposium
Int Inst Ammonia Refrig Annu Meet — International Institute of Ammonia Refrigeration. Annual Meeting
Int Inst Appl Syst Anal Collab Proc Ser — International Institute for Applied Systems Analysis. Collaborative ProceedingsSeries
Int Inst Appl Syst Anal Proc Ser — International Institute for Applied Systems Analysis. Proceedings Series
Int Inst Appl Syst Anal Prof Pap — International Institute for Applied Systems Analysis. Professional Paper
Int Inst Appl Syst Anal Res Mem — International Institute for Applied Systems Analysis. Research Memorandum
Int Inst Appl Syst Anal Res Rep RR — International Institute for Applied Systems Analysis. Research Report RR
Int Inst Conserv Hist Artistic Works Abstr — International Institute for Conservation of Historic and Artistic Works. Abstracts
Int Inst Labour Stud Bull — International Institute for Labour Studies Bulletin
Int Inst Land Reclam Impr (Netherlands) Bibliogr — International Institute for Land Reclamation and Improvement (Netherlands). Bibliography
Int Inst Land Reclam Impr (Netherlands) Bull — International Institute for Land Reclamation and Improvement (Netherlands). Bulletin
Int Inst Land Reclam Impr (Netherlands) Publ — International Institute for Land Reclamation and Improvement (Netherlands). Publication
Int Inst Land Reclam Improv Annu Rep — International Institute for Land Reclamation and Improvement. Annual Report
Int Inst Land Reclam Improv Bull — International Institute for Land Reclamation and Improvement. Bulletin
Int Inst Land Reclam Improv ILRI Publ — International Institute for Land Reclamation and Improvement. ILRI Publication
Int Inst Land Reclam Improv (Neth) Pub — International Institute for Land Reclamation and Improvement (Netherlands). Publication
Int Inst Land Reclam Improv Publ — International Institute for Land Reclamation and Improvement. Publication
Int Inst Ld Reclam Improv — International Institute for Land Reclamation and Improvement. Publication
Int Inst Ph — International Institute of Philosophy. Symposia
Int Inst Prev Treat Alcohol Pap — International Institute on the Prevention and Treatment of Alcoholism. Papers
Int Inst Prev Treat Drug Depend Pap — International Institute on the Prevention and Treatment of Drug Dependence. Papers
Int Inst Prod Eng Res Ann — International Institution for Production Engineering Research Annals
Int Inst Refrig Bull — International Institute of Refrigeration. Bulletin
Int Inst Refrig Bull Annexe — International Institute of Refrigeration. Bulletin. Annexe
Int Instrum Rev — International Instrument Review
Int Instrum Symp Proc — International Instrumentation Symposium. Proceedings
Int Inst Seismol Earthquake Eng Bull — International Institute of Seismology and Earthquake Engineering. Bulletin
Int Inst Seismol Earthquake Eng Individ Stud — International Institute of Seismology and Earthquake Engineering. Individual Studies by Participants
Int Inst Sugar Beet Res J — International Institute for Sugar Beet Research. Journal
Int Inst Synth Rubber Prod Annu Meet Proc — International Institute of Synthetic Rubber Producers. Annual Meeting Proceedings
Int Insulin Symp — International Insulin Symposium
Int Interp — International Interpreter
Int Iron Steel Congr Proc — International Iron and Steel Congress. Proceedings
Int Iron Steel Inst Annu Conf Rep Proc — International Iron and Steel Institute. Annual Conference. Report of Proceedings
Int Iron Steel Inst Annu Meet Conf Panel Discuss Speeches — International Iron and Steel Institute. Annual Meeting and Conference. Panel Discussion Speeches
Int IUPAP Conf Few Body Probl Phys — International IUPAP [*International Union of Pure and Applied Physics*] Conference on Few Body Problems in Physics
Int J — International Journal
IntJA — International Journal of African Historical Studies
Int J A Aff — International Journal of Agrarian Affairs
Int J Abstr Statist Meth Ind — International Journal of Abstracts on Statistical Methods in Industry
Int J Abstr Statist Theory Meth — International Journal of Abstracts. Statistical Theory and Method
Int J Acad Ichthyol — International Journal. Academy of Ichthyology
Int J Acarol — International Journal of Acarology
Int J Adapt Control Signal Process — International Journal of Adaptive Control and Signal Processing
Int J Addic — International Journal of the Addictions
Int J Addict — International Journal of the Addictions
Int J Adhes Adhes — International Journal of Adhesion and Adhesives
Int J Adhesion & Adhesives — International Journal of Adhesion and Adhesives
Int J Adolesc Med Health — International Journal of Adolescent Medicine and Health
Int J Adult Orthodon Orthognath Surg — International Journal of Adult Orthodontics and Orthognathic Surgery
Int J Adult Youth Ed — International Journal of Adult and Youth Education
Int J Adv Couns — International Journal for the Advancement of Counselling
Int J Adv Manuf Technol — International Journal of Advanced Manufacturing Technology
Int J Afr H — International Journal of African Historical Studies
Int J Afr Hist Stud — International Journal of African Historical Studies
Int J Afric Hist Stud — International Journal of African Historical Studies
Int J Afr Stud — International Journal of African Historical Studies
Int J Ag Affairs — International Journal of Agrarian Affairs

Int J Aging — International Journal of Aging and Human Development
Int J Aging Hum Dev — International Journal of Aging and Human Development
Int J Agr Aff — International Journal of Agrarian Affairs
Int Jahrb Tribol — Internationales Jahrbuch der Tribologie
Int Jahrestag Inst Chem Treib Explosivst — Internationale Jahrestagung. Institut fuer Chemie der Treib- und Explosivstoffe
Int J Air Pollut — International Journal of Air Pollution
Int J Air Water Pollut — International Journal of Air and Water Pollution
Int J Air Wat Pollut — International Journal of Air and Water Pollution
Int J Alcohol — International Journal of Alcohol and Alcoholism
Int J Amb Energy — International Journal of Ambient Energy
Int J Ambient Energy — International Journal of Ambient Energy
Int J Amer — International Journal of American Linguistics
Int J Amer Ling — International Journal of American Linguistics
Int J Am Ling — International Journal of American Linguistics
Int J Anaesth — International Journal of Anaesthesia
Int J Androl — International Journal of Andrology
Int J Andrology — International Journal of Andrology
Int J Androl Suppl — International Journal of Andrology. Supplement
Int J Anesth — International Journal of Anesthesia
Int J Anim Sci — International Journal of Animal Sciences
Int J Anthrop — International Journal of Anthropology
Int J Antimicrob Agents — International Journal of Antimicrobial Agents
Int J Appl Electromagn Mater — International Journal of Applied Electromagnetics in Materials
Int J Appl Radiat — International Journal of Applied Radiation and Isotopes
Int J Appl Radiat and Isot — International Journal of Applied Radiation and Isotopes
Int J Appl Radiat Isot — International Journal of Applied Radiation and Isotopes
Int J Appl Radiat Isotopes — International Journal of Applied Radiation and Isotopes
Int J A Rad — International Journal of Applied Radiation and Isotopes
Int J Artif Organs — International Journal of Artificial Organs
Int J Behav Dev — International Journal of Behavioral Development
Int J Behav Geriatrics — International Journal of Behavioral Geriatrics
Int Jb Gesch und Geogr Unterr — Internationales Jahrbuch fuer Geschichts- und Geographie-Unterricht
Int J Bioch — International Journal of Biochemistry
Int J Biochem — International Journal of Biochemistry
Int J Biochem Cell Biol — International Journal of Biochemistry and Cell Biology
Int J BioChemiPhysics — International Journal of BioChemiPhysics
Int J Bio Chromatogr — International Journal of Bio-Chromatography
Int J Bioclim — International Journal of Bioclimatology and Biometeorology
Int J Bioclimatol Biometeorol — International Journal of Bioclimatology and Biometeorology
Int J Bioclim Biomet — International Journal of Bioclimatology and Biometeorology
Int J Biol Macromol — International Journal of Biological Macromolecules
Int J Biol Markers — International Journal of Biological Markers
Int J Biol Res Pregnancy — International Journal of Biological Research in Pregnancy
Int J Bio-M — International Journal of Bio-Medical Computing
Int J Biom — International Journal of Biometeorology
Int J Biomed Comp — International Journal of Biomedical Computing
Int J Bio-Med Comput — International Journal of Bio-Medical Computing
Int J Biomed Eng — International Journal of Biomedical Engineering
Int J Biometeorol — International Journal of Biometeorology
Int Jb Pol — Internationales Jahrbuch der Politik
Int Jb Relig Soziol — Internationales Jahrbuch fuer Religionssoziologie
Int J Canc — International Journal of Cancer
Int J Cancer — International Journal of Cancer
Int J Cancer Control Prev — International Journal of Cancer Control and Prevention
Int J Cancer Suppl — International Journal of Cancer. Supplement
Int J Card Imaging — International Journal of Cardiac Imaging
Int J Cardiol — International Journal of Cardiology
Int J Cast Met Res — International Journal of Cast Metals Research
Int J C E Hy — International Journal of Clinical and Experimental Hypnosis
Int J Cell Cloning — International Journal of Cell Cloning
Int J Cem Compos — International Journal of Cement Composites
Int J Cem Compos Lightweight Concr — International Journal of Cement Composites and Lightweight Concrete
Int J Cement Composites — International Journal of Cement Composites
Int J Chem Kinet — International Journal of Chemical Kinetics
Int J Child — International Journal of Child Psychotherapy
Int J Ch K — International Journal of Chemical Kinetics
Int J Chronobiol — International Journal of Chronobiology
Int J C Inf — International Journal of Computer and Information Sciences
Int J Circuit Theory and Appl — International Journal of Circuit Theory and Applications
Int J Circuit Theory Appl — International Journal of Circuit Theory and Applications
Int J Clim — International Journal of Climatology
Int J Clin — International Journal of Clinical Pharmacology and Biopharmacy
Int J Clin & Exp Hypnosis — International Journal of Clinical and Experimental Hypnosis
Int J Clin Exp Hypn — International Journal of Clinical and Experimental Hypnosis
Int J Clin Exp Hypnos — International Journal of Clinical and Experimental Hypnosis
Int J Clin Lab Res — International Journal of Clinical and Laboratory Research
Int J Clin Monit Comput — International Journal of Clinical Monitoring and Computing
Int J Clin Neuropsychol — International Journal of Clinical Neuropsychology
Int J Clin Pharm — International Journal of Clinical Pharmacology, Therapy, and Toxicology

Int J Clin Pharmacol Biopharm — International Journal of Clinical Pharmacology and Biopharmacy

Int J Clin Pharmacol Res — International Journal of Clinical Pharmacology Research

Int J Clin Pharmacol Ther — International Journal of Clinical Pharmacology and Therapeutics

Int J Clin Pharmacol Ther Toxicol — International Journal of Clinical Pharmacology, Therapy, and Toxicology

Int J Clin Pharm Res — International Journal of Clinical Pharmacology Research

Int J Clin Pract — International Journal of Clinical Practice

Int J Clin Pract Suppl — International Journal of Clinical Practice. Supplement

Int J Coal Geol — International Journal of Coal Geology

Int J Colorectal Dis — International Journal of Colorectal Disease

Int J Com M — International Journal of Computer Mathematics

Int J Com P — International Journal of Community Psychiatry and Experimental Psychotherapy

Int J Comp — International Journal of Comparative Sociology

Int J Compar Sociol — International Journal of Comparative Sociology

Int J Comp Soc — International Journal of Comparative Sociology

Int J Comp Sociol — International Journal of Comparative Sociology

Int J Comp Sociology — International Journal of Comparative Sociology

Int J Comput & Inf Sci — International Journal of Computer and Information Sciences

Int J Comput Appl Technol — International Journal of Computer Applications in Technology

Int J Comput Math — International Journal of Computer Mathematics

Int J Comput Math Sect A — International Journal of Computer Mathematics. Section A. Programming Languages. Theory and Methods

Int J Comput Math Sect B — International Journal of Computer Mathematics. Section B. Computational Methods

Int J Comput Vision — International Journal of Computer Vision

Int J Con S — International Journal of Contemporary Sociology

Int J Contemporary Sociol — International Journal of Contemporary Sociology

Int J Contemp Sociol — International Journal of Contemporary Sociology

Int J Contin Eng Educ — International Journal of Continuing Engineering Education

Int J Contr — International Journal of Control

Int J Control — International Journal of Control

Int J Cosmet Sci — International Journal of Cosmetic Science

Int J Criminol — International Journal of Criminology and Penology

Int J Criminology Penology — International Journal of Criminology and Penology

Int J Crude Drug Res — International Journal of Crude Drug Research

Int J Dairy Technol — International Journal of Dairy Technology

Int J Damage Mech — International Journal of Damage Mechanics

Int J Dent Symp — International Journal of Dental Symposia

Int J Dermatol — International Journal of Dermatology

Int J Dev Biol — International Journal of Developmental Biology

Int J Dev Neurosci — International Journal of Developmental Neuroscience

Int J Dev Tech — International Journal for Development Technology

Int J Dev Technol — International Journal for Development Technology

Int J Dravid Ling — International Journal of Dravidian Linguistics

Int J Earthquake Eng Struct Dyn — International Journal of Earthquake Engineering and Structural Dynamics

Int J Eat Disor — International Journal of Eating Disorders

Int J Eating Disord — International Journal of Eating Disorders

Int J Ecol Environ Sci — International Journal of Ecology and Environmental Sciences

Int J Elec Eng Educ — International Journal of Electrical Engineering Education

Int J Elec Engng Educ — International Journal of Electrical Engineering Education

Int J Elect — International Journal of Electronics

Int J Electr Eng Educ — International Journal of Electrical Engineering Education

Int J Electron — International Journal of Electronics

Int J Electr Power Energy Syst — International Journal of Electrical Power Amp Energy Systems

Int J El En — International Journal of Electrical Engineering Education

Int J Emerg Ment Health — International Journal of Emergency Mental Health

Int J Energy Res — International Journal of Energy Research

Int J Energy Syst — International Journal of Energy Systems

Int J Eng — International Journal of Engineering

Int J Eng Fluid Mech — International Journal of Engineering Fluid Mechanics

Int J Eng Modell — International Journal for Engineering Modelling

Int J Engng Sci — International Journal of Engineering Science

Int J Eng S — International Journal of Engineering Science

Int J Eng Sci — International Journal of Engineering Science

Int J Entomol — International Journal of Entomology

Int J Environ Anal Chem — International Journal of Environmental Analytical Chemistry

Int J Environ Health Res — International Journal of Environmental Health Research

Int J Environ Pollut — International Journal of Environmental Pollution

Int J Environ Stud — International Journal of Environmental Studies

Int J Environ Studies — International Journal of Environmental Studies

Int J Env S — International Journal of Environmental Studies

Int J Epid — International Journal of Epidemiology

Int J Epidemiol — International Journal of Epidemiology

Int J Equilib Res — International Journal of Equilibrium Research

Int J Ethics — International Journal of Ethics

Int J Exp Clin Chemother — International Journal of Experimental and Clinical Chemotherapy. Basic and Clinical Research. Clinical Experience

Int J Exp Diabetes Res — International Journal of Experimental Diabetes Research

Int J Expert Syst — International Journal of Expert Systems

Int J Exp Med — International Journal of Experimental Medicine

Int J Exp Pathol — International Journal of Experimental Pathology

Int J Fam Psychiatry — International Journal of Family Psychiatry

Int J Fatigue — International Journal of Fatigue

Int J Fert — International Journal of Fertility

Int J Fertil — International Journal of Fertility

Int J Fertil Menopausal Stud — International Journal of Fertility and Menopausal Studies

Int J Fertil Womens Med — International Journal of Fertility and Women's Medicine

Int J F Mic — International Journal of Food Microbiology

Int J Food Microbiol — International Journal of Food Microbiology

Int J Food Prop — International Journal of Food Properties

Int J Food Sci Nutr — International Journal of Food Sciences and Nutrition

Int J Food Sci Technol — International Journal of Food Science and Technology

Int J Food Technol Food Process Eng — International Journal of Food Technology and Food Process Engineering

Int J Forensic Dent — International Journal of Forensic Dentistry

Int J Forensic Doc Exam — International Journal of Forensic Document Examiners

Int J Fract — International Journal of Fracture

Int J Fract Mech — International Journal of Fracture Mechanics

Int J Fusion Energy — International Journal of Fusion Energy

Int J Game Theory — International Journal of Game Theory

Int J Gastroent — International Journal of Gastro-Enterology

Int J Gas Util — International Journal on Gas Utilization

Int J Genome Res — International Journal of Genome Research

Int J Gen S — International Journal of General Systems

Int J Gen Syst — International Journal of General Systems

Int J Geriatr Psychiatry — International Journal of Geriatric Psychiatry

Int J Geriatr Psychopharmacol — International Journal of Geriatric Psychopharmacology

Int J Global Energy Issues — International Journal of Global Energy Issues

Int J Group Psychother — International Journal of Group Psychotherapy

Int J Group Tensions — International Journal of Group Tensions

Int J Grp P — International Journal of Group Psychotherapy

Int J Grp Psychother — International Journal of Group Psychotherapy

Int J Grp T — International Journal of Group Tensions

Int J Gynaecol Obstet — International Journal of Gynaecology and Obstetrics

Int J Gynecol Cancer — International Journal of Gynecological Cancer

Int J Gynecol Pathol — International Journal of Gynecological Pathology

Int J Healt — International Journal of Health Education

Int J Health Educ — International Journal of Health Education

Int J Health Plann Manage — International Journal of Health Planning and Management

Int J Health Serv — International Journal of Health Services

Int J Heat — International Journal of Heat and Mass Transfer

Int J Heat & Mass Transfer — International Journal of Heat and Mass Transfer

Int J Heat Fluid Flow — International Journal of Heat and Fluid Flow

Int J Heat Mass Transfer — International Journal of Heat and Mass Transfer

Int J Heat Technol — International Journal of Heat and Technology

Int J Hematol — International Journal of Hematology

Int J He Se — International Journal of Health Services

Int J High Speed Electron Syst — International Journal of High Speed Electronics and Systems

Int J High Technol Ceram — International Journal of High Technology Ceramics

Int J Hist Sport — International Journal of the History of Sport

Int J Hlth Educ — International Journal of Health Education

Int J Hlth Serv — International Journal of Health Services

Int J Hosp Manage — International Journal of Hospitality Management

Int J Housing Sc Applications — International Journal for Housing Science and Its Applications

Int J Hous Sci Appl — International Journal for Housing Science and Its Applications

Int J Hum Factors Manuf — International Journal of Human Factors in Manufacturing

Int J Hybrid Microelectron — International Journal for Hybrid Microelectronics

Int J Hydrogen Energy — International Journal of Hydrogen Energy

Int J Hyg Environ Med — International Journal of Hygiene and Environmental Medicine

Int J Hyperthermia — International Journal of Hyperthermia

Int J Imaging Syst Technol — International Journal of Imaging Systems and Technology

Int J Immunochem — International Journal of Immunochemistry

Int J Immunopathol Pharmacol — International Journal of Immunopathology and Pharmacology

Int J Immunopharmacol — International Journal of Immunopharmacology

Int J Immunother — International Journal of Immunotherapy

Int J Impot Res — International Journal of Impotence Research

Int J Ind Ergon — International Journal of Industrial Ergonomics

Int J Individ Psychol — International Journal of Individual Psychology

Int J Indiv Psychol — International Journal of Individual Psychology

Int J Ind Med Surg — International Journal of Industrial Medicine and Surgery

Int J Infrared Millimeter Waves — International Journal of Infrared and Millimeter Waves

Int J Infrared Millim Waves — International Journal of Infrared and Millimeter Waves

Int J Insect Morph Embryol — International Journal of Insect Morphology and Embryology

Int J Insect Morphol Embryol — International Journal of Insect Morphology and Embryology

Int J Inst Mangt in Higher Educ — International Journal of Institutional Management in Higher Education

Int J Instr Media — International Journal of Instructional Media

Int J Intell Syst — International Journal of Intelligent Systems

Int J Invertebr Reprod — International Journal of Invertebrate Reproduction

Int J Invertebr Reprod Dev — International Journal of Invertebrate Reproduction and Development

Int J Joining Mater — International Journal for the Joining of Materials

Int J Jpn Soc Precis Eng — International Journal. Japan Society for Precision Engineering

Int J Law Legisl Fd Agric — International Journal of Law and Legislation Relating to Food and Agriculture
Int J Law Lib — International Journal of Law Libraries
Int J Law Libr — International Journal of Law Libraries
Int J Law Librs — International Journal of Law Libraries
Int J Law Psychiatry — International Journal of Law and Psychiatry
Int J Law Sci — International Journal of Law and Science
Int J Legal — International Journal of Legal Medicine
Int J Legal Med — International Journal of Legal Medicine
Int J Lepr — International Journal of Leprosy [*Later, International Journal of Leprosy and Other Mycobacterial Diseases*]
Int J Lepr Other Mycobact Dis — International Journal of Leprosy and Other Mycobacterial Diseases
Int J Life Cycle Assess — International Journal of Life Cycle Assessment
Int J Life Educ — International Journal of Lifelong Education
Int J Lightweight Concr — International Journal of Lightweight Concrete
IntJM — International Journal of Middle East Studies
Int J Mach — International Journal of Machine Tool Design and Research
Int J Mach Tool Des Res — International Journal of Machine Tool Design and Research
Int J Mach Tools Manuf — International Journal of Machine Tools and Manufacture
Int J Magn — International Journal of Magnetism
Int J Mamm Biol — International Journal of Mammalian Biology
Int J Man-M — International Journal of Man-Machine Studies
Int J Man-Mach Stud — International Journal of Man-Machine Studies
Int J Manpower — International Journal of Manpower
Int J Manuf Sci & Prod — International Journal for Manufacturing Science and Production
Int J Masonry Constr — International Journal of Masonry Construction
Int J Mass — International Journal of Mass Spectrometry and Ion Physics [*Later, International Journal of Mass Spectrometry and Ion Processes*]
Int J Mass Spectrom — International Journal of Mass Spectrometry
Int J Mass Spectrom and Ion Phys — International Journal of Mass Spectrometry and Ion Physics [*Later, International Journal of Mass Spectrometry and Ion Processes*]
Int J Mass Spectrom Ion Phys — International Journal of Mass Spectrometry and Ion Physics [*Later, International Journal of Mass Spectrometry and Ion Processes*]
Int J Mass Spectrom Ion Processes — International Journal of Mass Spectrometry and Ion Processes
Int J Mater Eng Appl — International Journal of Materials in Engineering Applications
Int J Mater Eng Res — International Journal of Materials Engineering Research
Int J Mater Prod Technol — International Journal of Materials and Product Technology
Int J Math Educ Sci and Technol — International Journal of Mathematical Education in Science and Technology
Int J Math Educ Sci Technol — International Journal of Mathematical Education in Science and Technology
Int J Mech — International Journal of Mechanical Sciences
Int J Mechanochem Mech Alloying — International Journal of Mechanochemistry and Mechanical Alloying
Int J Mech Engng Educ — International Journal of Mechanical Engineering Education
Int J Mech Sci — International Journal of Mechanical Sciences
Int J Med Microbiol — International Journal of Medical Microbiology
Int J Med Microbiol Virol Parasitol Infect Dis — International Journal of Medical Microbiology, Virology, Parasitology, and Infectious Diseases
Int J Med Surg — International Journal of Medicine and Surgery and the Surgical Journal
Int J Ment — International Journal of Mental Health
Int J Ment Health — International Journal of Mental Health
Int J M E St — International Journal of Middle East Studies
Int J Microbiol Hyg Abt 1 Orig A — International Journal of Microbiology and Hygiene. Abt. 1. Originale A. MedicalMicrobiology, Infectious Diseases, Parasitology
Int J Microbiol Hyg Abt 1 Orig B — International Journal of Microbiology and Hygiene. Abteilung 1. Originale B. Environmental Hygiene, Hospital Hygiene, Industrial Hygiene, Preventive Medicine
Int J Microbiol Hyg Gen Appl Ecol Microbiol — International Journal of Microbiology and Hygiene. General, Applied, and Ecological Microbiology
Int J Microbiol Hyg Ser A — International Journal of Microbiology and Hygiene. Series A. Medical Microbiology, Infectious Diseases, Virology, Parasitology
Int J Microbiol Hyg Ser B — International Journal of Microbiology and Hygiene. Series B. Environmental Hygiene, Hospital Hygiene, Industrial Hygiene, Preventive Med
Int J Microcirc Clin Exp — International Journal of Microcirculation. Clinical and Experimental
Int J Microcircuits Electron Packag — International Journal of Microcircuits and Electronic Packaging
Int J Microelectron Packag — International Journal of Microelectronic Packaging
Int J Microgr and Video Technol — International Journal of Micrographics and Video Technology
Int J Micrograph Opt Technol — International Journal of Micrographics and Optical Technology
Int J Microwave Millimeter Wave Comput Aided Eng — International Journal of Microwave and Millimeter-Wave Computer-Aided Engineering
Int J Middle East Stud — International Journal of Middle East Studies
Int J Mid East Stud — International Journal of Middle East Studies
Int J Mid E Stud — International Journal of Middle East Studies
Int J Min Eng — International Journal of Mining Engineering
Int J Miner Process — International Journal of Mineral Processing
Int J Mine Water — International Journal of Mine Water
Int J Mini and Microcomput — International Journal of Mini and Microcomputers
Int J Mini Microcomput — International Journal of Mini and Microcomputers

Int J Mol Med — International Journal of Molecular Medicine
Int J Multiphase Flow — International Journal of Multiphase Flow
Int J Multiph Flow — International Journal of Multiphase Flow
Int J Mus Ed — International Journal of Music Education
Int J Mushroom Sci — International Journal of Mushroom Sciences
Int J Mus Mgmt & Cur — International Journal of Museum Management and Curatorship
Int J Mycol Lichenol — International Journal of Mycology and Lichenology
Int JNA — International Journal of Nautical Archaeology and Underwater Exploration
Int J Naut — International Journal of Nautical Archaeology and Underwater Exploration
Int J Naut Archaeol Underwater Explor — International Journal of Nautical Archaeology and Underwater Exploration
Int J Nephrol Urol Androl — International Journal of Nephrology, Urology, Andrology
Int J Network Manage — International Journal of Network Management
Int J Neural Syst — International Journal of Neural Systems
Int J Neuro — International Journal of Neurology
Int J Neurol — International Journal of Neurology
Int J Neuropharmacol — International Journal of Neuropharmacology
Int J Neuropsychiatr — International Journal of Neuropsychiatry
Int J Neuropsychiatry — International Journal of Neuropsychiatry
Int J Neuropsychiatry Suppl — International Journal of Neuropsychiatry. Supplement
Int J Neurosci — International Journal of Neuroscience
Int J Neurs — International Journal of Neuroscience
Int Jnl Adv — International Journal of Advertising
Int J Nondestr Test — International Journal of Nondestructive Testing
Int J Nondestruct Test — International Journal of Nondestructive Testing
Int J Non Equilib Process — International Journal of Non-Equilibrium Processing
Int J Non-Linear Mech — International Journal of Non-Linear Mechanics
Int J Nonlinear Opt Phys — International Journal of Nonlinear Optical Physics
Int J Nucl Med & Biol — International Journal of Nuclear Medicine and Biology
Int J Nucl Med Biol — International Journal of Nuclear Medicine and Biology
Int J Nuc M — International Journal of Nuclear Medicine and Biology
Int J Num Anal Meth Geomech — International Journal for Numerical and Analytical Methods in Geomechanics
Int J Numer Anal Methods Geomech — International Journal for Numerical and Analytical Methods in Geomechanics
Int J Numer and Anal Methods Geomech — International Journal for Numerical and Analytical Methods in Geomechanics
Int J Numer Methods Eng — International Journal for Numerical Methods in Engineering
Int J Numer Methods Engng — International Journal for Numerical Methods in Engineering
Int J Numer Methods Fluids — International Journal for Numerical Methods in Fluids
Int J Numer Methods Heat Fluid Flow — International Journal of Numerical Methods for Heat and Fluid Flow
Int J Numer Modell Electron Networks Devices Fields — International Journal of Numerical Modelling. Electronic Networks, Devices, and Fields
Int J Num Meth Eng — International Journal for Numerical Methods in Engineering
Int J Num Meth Engng — International Journal for Numerical Methods in Engineering
Int J Nurs — International Journal of Nursing Studies
Int J Nurs Stud — International Journal of Nursing Studies
Int J Obes — International Journal of Obesity
Int J Obesity — International Journal of Obesity
Int J Obes Relat Metab Disord — International Journal of Obesity and Related Metabolic Disorders
Int J Occ H — International Journal of Occupational Health and Safety
Int J Occup Environ Health — International Journal of Occupational and Environmental Health
Int J Occup Health and Saf — International Journal of Occupational Health and Safety
Int J Occup Health Saf — International Journal of Occupational Health and Safety
Int J Occup Med Environ Health — International Journal of Occupational Medicine and Environmental Health
Int J Occup Med Toxicol — International Journal of Occupational Medicine and Toxicology
Int J Occup Saf Ergon — International Journal of Occupational Safety and Ergonomics
Int J Occup Saf Ergon — International Journal of Occupational Safety and Ergonomics. JOSE
Int J Oceanol Limnol — International Journal of Oceanology and Limnology
Int J Offen — International Journal of Offender Therapy [*Later, International Journal of Offender Therapy and Comparative Criminology*]
Int J Offend Therapy — International Journal of Offender Therapy and Comparative Criminology
Int J Offshore Polar Eng — International Journal of Offshore and Polar Engineering
Int J Oncol — International Journal of Oncology
Int J Oper and Prod Manage — International Journal of Operations and Production Management
Int J Optoelectron — International Journal of Optoelectronics
Int J Oral — International Journal of Oral History
Int J Oral Maxillofac Implants — International Journal of Oral and Maxillofacial Implants
Int J Oral Maxillofac Surg — International Journal of Oral and Maxillofacial Surgery
Int J Oral Myol — International Journal of Oral Myology
Int J Oral Surg — International Journal of Oral Surgery
Int J Orofacial Myology — International Journal of Orofacial Myology
Int J Or Su — International Journal of Oral Surgery
Int J Orthod — International Journal of Orthodontics

Int J Orthod Dent Child — International Journal of Orthodontia and Dentistry for Children

Int J Orthodont — International Journal of Orthodontics

Int J Orthodontia — International Journal of Orthodontia

Int J Pancreatol — International Journal of Pancreatology

Int J Parallel Program — International Journal of Parallel Programming

Int J Parapsychol — International Journal of Parapsychology

Int J Paras — International Journal for Parasitology

Int J Parasitol — International Journal for Parasitology

Int J Partial Hosp — International Journal of Partial Hospitalization

Int J PE — International Journal of Physical Education

Int J Pediatr Nephrol — International Journal of Pediatric Nephrology

Int J Pediatr Otorhinolaryngol — International Journal of Pediatric Otorhinolaryngology

Int J Pept — International Journal of Peptide and Protein Research

Int J Peptide Protein Res — International Journal of Peptide and Protein Research

Int J Peptide Prot Res — International Journal of Peptide and Protein Research

Int J Pept Protein Res — International Journal of Peptide and Protein Research

Int J Periodontics Restorative Dent — International Journal of Periodontics and Restorative Dentistry

Int J Pharm — International Journal of Pharmaceutics

Int J Pharmacogn — International Journal of Pharmacognosy

Int J Pharm Adv — International Journal of Pharmaceutical Advances

Int J Pharm (Amst) — International Journal of Pharmaceutics (Amsterdam)

Int J Pharm Technol Prod Manuf — International Journal of Pharmaceutical Technology and Product Manufacture

Int J Phil — International Journal for Philosophy of Religion

Int J Philos Relig — International Journal for Philosophy of Religion

IntJPhilRel — International Journal for Philosophy of Religion

Int J Phil Relig — International Journal for Philosophy of Religion

Int J Ph Rel — International Journal for Philosophy of Religion

Int J Phys Distrib J Ser — International Journal of Physical Distribution [*Later, International Journal of Physical Distribution and Materials Management*]. Journal Series

Int J Phys Distrib Monogr Ser — International Journal of Physical Distribution [*Later, International Journal of Physical Distribution and Materials Management*]. Monograph Series

Int J Phys Educ — International Journal of Physical Education

Int J Phys Med — International Journal of Physical Medicine

Int J PIXE — International Journal of PIXE

Int J Plant Physiol — International Journal of Plant Physiology

Int J Plant Physiol (Stuttgart) — International Journal of Plant Physiology (Stuttgart)

Int J Plant Sci — International Journal of Plant Sciences

Int J Plast — International Journal of Plasticity

Int J Policy Anal Inf Syst — International Journal of Policy Analysis and Information Systems

Int J Policy and Inf — International Journal on Policy and Information

Int J Polit — International Journal of Politics

Int J Polym Anal Charact — International Journal of Polymer Analysis and Characterization

Int J Polym Mat — International Journal of Polymeric Materials

Int J Polym Mater — International Journal of Polymeric Materials

Int J Powd — International Journal of Powder Metallurgy

Int J Powder Metall — International Journal of Powder Metallurgy

Int J Powder Metall & Powder Tech — International Journal of Powder Metallurgy and Powder Technology

Int J Powder Metall Powder Technol — International Journal of Powder Metallurgy and Powder Technology

Int J Powder Metall Technol — International Journal of Powder Metallurgy and Powder Technology

Int J Pressure Vessels Piping — International Journal of Pressure Vessels and Piping

Int J Primatol — International Journal of Primatology

Int J Prod Res — International Journal of Production Research

Int J Prophyl Med Sozialhyg — Internationales Journal fuer Prophylaktische Medizin und Sozialhygiene

Int J Prosthod — International Journal of Prosthodontics

Int J Protein Res — International Journal of Protein Research

Int J Ps Ps — International Journal of Psychoanalytic Psychotherapy

Int J Psych — International Journal of Psychoanalysis

Int J Psychiat — International Journal of Psychiatry

Int J Psychiatry — International Journal of Psychiatry

Int J Psychiatry Clin Pract — International Journal of Psychiatry in Clinical Practice

Int J Psychiatry Med — International Journal of Psychiatry in Medicine

Int J Psychoanal — International Journal of Psychoanalysis

Int J Psychoanal Psychother — International Journal of Psychoanalytic Psychotherapy

Int J Psycho Analysis — International Journal of Psycho-Analysis

Int J Psychobiol — International Journal of Psychobiology

Int J Psychol — International Journal of Psychology

Int J Psychophysiol — International Journal of Psychophysiology

Int J Psychosom — International Journal of Psychosomatics

Int J Psyci — International Journal of Psychiatry

Int J Psyco — International Journal of Psychology

Int J Psy M — International Journal of Psychiatry in Medicine

Int J Publ Hlth — International Journal of Public Health

Int J Pure Appl Biophys — International Journal of Pure and Applied Bio-Physics

Int J Qual Health Care — International Journal for Quality in Health Caree

Int J Quant — International Journal of Quantum Chemistry

Int J Quant Chem — International Journal of Quantum Chemistry

Int J Quant Chem Quant Biol Symp — International Journal of Quantum Chemistry. Quantum Biology Symposium

Int J Quant Chem Symp — International Journal of Quantum Chemistry. Symposium

Int J Quantum Chem — International Journal of Quantum Chemistry

Int J Quantum Chem Quantum Biol Symp — International Journal of Quantum Chemistry. Quantum Biology Symposium

Int J Quantum Chem Quantum Chem Symp — International Journal of Quantum Chemistry. Quantum Chemistry Symposia

Int J Quantum Chem Sym — International Journal of Quantum Chemistry. Symposium

Int J Quantum Chem Symp — International Journal of Quantum Chemistry. Symposium

Int J Rad Appl Instrum A — International Journal of Radiation Applications and Instrumentation. Part A. Applied Radiation and Isotopes

Int J Rad Appl Instrum B — International Journal of Radiation Applications and Instrumentation. Part B. Nuclear Medicine and Biology

Int J Rad B — International Journal of Radiation Biology

Int J Radiat Appl Instrum Part A Appl Radiat Isot — International Journal of Radiation Applications and Instrumentation. Part A. Applied Radiation and Isotopes

Int J Radiat Appl Instrum Part C — International Journal of Radiation Applications and Instrumentation. Part C

Int J Radiat Appl Instrum Part E — International Journal of Radiation Applications and Instrumentation. Part E

Int J Radiat Biol — International Journal of Radiation Biology

Int J Radiat Biol — International Journal of Radiation Biology and Related Studies in Physics, Chemistry, and Medicine

Int J Radiat Biol Relat Stud Phys Chem Med — International Journal of Radiation Biology and Related Studies in Physics, Chemistry, and Medicine

Int J Radiat Eng — International Journal of Radiation Engineering

Int J Radiat Oncol-Biol-Phys — International Journal of Radiation: Oncology-Biology-Physics

Int J Radiat Oncology Biol Phys — International Journal of Radiation: Oncology-Biology-Physics

Int J Radiat Phys and Chem — International Journal for Radiation Physics and Chemistry [*Later, Radiation Physics and Chemistry*]

Int J Radiat Phys Chem — International Journal for Radiation Physics and Chemistry [*Later, Radiation Physics and Chemistry*]

Int J Radiat Steril — International Journal of Radiation Sterilization

Int J Radioact Mater Transp — International Journal of Radioactive Materials Tansport

Int J Rad O — International Journal of Radiation: Oncology-Biology-Physics

Int J Rad P — International Journal for Radiation Physics and Chemistry [*Later, Radiation Physics and Chemistry*]

Int J Rapid Solidif — International Journal of Rapid Solidification

Int J Rap S — International Journal of Rapid Solidification

Int J Refract and Hard Met — International Journal of Refractory and Hard Metals

Int J Refract Hard Met — International Journal of Refractory and Hard Metals

Int J Refract Met Hard Mater — International Journal of Refractory Metals and Hard Materials

Int J Refrig — International Journal of Refrigeration

Int J Rehabil Res — International Journal of Rehabilitation Research

Int J Reliab Qual Saf Eng — International Journal of Reliability, Quality, and Safety Engineering

Int J Relig Ed — International Journal of Religious Education

Int J Relig Educ — International Journal of Religious Education

Int J Remot — International Journal of Remote Sensing

Int J Remote Sens — International Journal of Remote Sensing

Int J Res Manage — International Journal of Research Management

Int J Res Phys Chem Chem Phys — International Journal of Research in Physical Chemistry and Chemical Physics

Int J Robot Res — International Journal of Robotics Research

Int J Rob Res — International Journal of Robotics Research

Int J Robust Nonlinear Control — International Journal of Robust and Nonlinear Control

Int J Rock — International Journal of Rock Mechanics

Int J Rock Mech and Min Sci and Geomech Abstr — International Journal of Rock Mechanics and Mining Sciences and Geomechanics Abstracts

Int J Rock Mech Mining Sci — International Journal of Rock Mechanics and Mining Sciences [*Later, International Journal of Rock Mechanics and Mining Sciences and Geomechanics Abstracts*]

Int J Rock Mech Mining Sci Geomech Abstr — International Journal of Rock Mechanics and Mining Sciences and Geomechanics Abstracts

Int J Rock Mech Min Sci — International Journal of Rock Mechanics and Mining Sciences [*Later, International Journal of Rock Mechanics and Mining Sciences and Geomechanics Abstracts*]

Int J Rock Mech Min Sci Geomech Abstr — International Journal of Rock Mechanics and Mining Sciences and Geomechanics Abstracts

Int J Self Propag High Temp Synth — International Journal of Self-Propagating High-Temperature Synthesis

Int J Sex — International Journal of Sexology

Int J Sex Econ Orgone Res — International Journal of Sex-Economy and Orgone Research

Int J Soc Econ — International Journal of Social Economics

Int J Soc F — International Journal of Sociology of the Family

Int J Social Psych — International Journal of Social Psychiatry

Int J Social Psychiat — International Journal of Social Psychiatry

Int J Sociol — International Journal of Sociology

Int J Sociol Family — International Journal of Sociology of the Family

Int J Sociol Lang — International Journal of the Sociology of Language

Int J Sociol Law — International Journal of the Sociology of Law

Int J Sociol Soc Policy — International Journal of Sociology and Social Policy

Int J Soc L — International Journal of the Sociology of Language

Int J Soc Lang — International Journal of the Sociology of Language

Int J Soc P — International Journal of Social Psychiatry

Int J Soc Psych — International Journal of Social Psychiatry

Int J Soc Psychiat — International Journal of Social Psychiatry

Int J Soc Psychiatr — International Journal of Social Psychiatry

Int J Soc Psychiatry — International Journal of Social Psychiatry
Int J Soil Dyn and Earthquake Eng — International Journal of Soil Dynamics and Earthquake Engineering
Int J Solar Energy — International Journal of Solar Energy
Int J Sol Energy — International Journal of Solar Energy
Int J Solids and Struct — International Journal of Solids and Structures
Int J Solids & Structures — International Journal of Solids and Structures
Int J Solids Struct — International Journal of Solids and Structures
Int J Speleol — International Journal of Speleology
Int J Sport Nutr — International Journal of Sport Nutrition
Int J Sport Nutr Exerc Metab — International Journal of Sport Nutrition and Exercise Metabolism
Int J Sport Nutrition — International Journal of Sport Nutrition
Int J Sport Psy — International Journal of Sport Psychology
Int J Sport Psychol — International Journal of Sport Psychology
Int J Sports Med — International Journal of Sports Medicine
Int J Sp Ps — International Journal of Sport Psychology
Int J STD AIDS — International Journal of STD and AIDS
Int J Stud Anim Probl — International Journal for the Study of Animal Problems
Int J Study Anim Probl — International Journal for the Study of Animal Problems
Int J Sulfur Chem — International Journal of Sulfur Chemistry
Int J Sulfur Chem Part A — International Journal of Sulfur Chemistry. Part A. Original Experimental
Int J Sulfur Chem Part B — International Journal of Sulfur Chemistry. Part B. Quarterly Reports on Sulfur Chemistry
Int J Sulfur Chem Part C — International Journal of Sulfur Chemistry. Part C. Mechanisms of Reactions of Sulfur Compounds
Int J Surf Min Reclam Environ — International Journal of Surface Mining, Reclamation, and Environment
Int J Surg — International Journal of Surgery
Int J Surg Investig — International Journal of Surgical Investigation
Int J Surg Pathol — International Journal of Surgical Pathology
Int J Sy B — International Journal of Systematic Bacteriology
Int J Symb — International Journal of Symbology
Int J Syst — International Journal of Systems Science
Int J Syst Bacteriol — International Journal of Systematic Bacteriology
Int J Syst Evol Microbiol — International Journal of Systematic and Evolutionary Microbiology
Int J Syst Sci — International Journal of Systems Science
Int J Technol Adv — International Journal of Technology Advances
Int J Technol Assess Health Care — International Journal of Technology Assessment in Health Care
Int J Theor — International Journal of Theoretical Physics
Int J Theor Phys — International Journal of Theoretical Physics
Int J Therm — International Journal of Thermophysics
Int J Thermophys — International Journal of Thermophysics
Int J Thymol — International Journal of Thymology
Int J Tissue React — International Journal on Tissue Reactions
Int J Toxicol — International Journal of Toxicology
Int J Toxicol Occup Environ Health — International Journal of Toxicology, Occupational, and Environmental Health
Int J Transp Econ — International Journal of Transport Economics
Int J Trop Agric — International Journal of Tropical Agriculture
Int J Trop Plant Dis — International Journal of Tropical Plant Diseases
Int J Tuberc Lung Dis — International Journal of Tuberculosis and Lung Diseaase
Int J Turk Stud — International Journal of Turkish Studies
Int J Urban Reg Res — International Journal of Urban and Regional Research
Int Jurid Assn Bull — International Juridical Association. Bulletin
Int J Urol — International Journal of Urology
Int J Veh Des — International Journal of Vehicle Design
Int J Vitam Nutr Res — International Journal for Vitamin and Nutrition Research
Int J Vitam Nutr Res Suppl — International Journal for Vitamin and Nutrition Research. Supplement
Int J Vit N — International Journal for Vitamin and Nutrition Research
Int J Water Resour Dev — International Journal of Water Resources Development
Int J Womens Stud — International Journal of Women's Studies
Int J Wood Preserv — International Journal of Wood Preservation
Int J Zoonoses — International Journal of Zoonoses
Int Kath Z — Internationale Katholische Zeitschrift
Int KfK TNO Conf Contam Soil — International KfK/TNO Conference on Contaminated Soil
Int KfK TNO Kongr Atlastensanierung — Internationaler KfK/TNO Kongress ueber Atlastensanierung
Int Kimberlite Conf Proc — International Kimberlite Conference. Proceedings
IntKiZ — Internationale Kirchliche Zeitschrift
Int Kongr Elektronenmikrosk Verh — Internationaler Kongress fuer Elektronenmikroskopie. Verhandlungen
Int Kongr Roentgenoptik Mikroanal — Internationaler Kongress fuer Roentgenoptik und Mikroanalyse
Int Kongr Tier Fortpflanz Kuenstliche Besamung — Internationaler Kongress ueber die Tierische Fortpflanzung und die Kuenstliche Besamung
Int Krimin Verein Mitt — Internationale Kriminalistische Vereinigung. Mitteilungen
Int Kupffer Cell Symp — International Kupffer Cell Symposium
Int Lab — International Laboratory
Int Labmate — International Labmate
Int Labor Organ Occup Saf Health Ser — International Labor Organization. Occupational Safety and Health Series
Int Labor W — International Labor and Working Class History
Int Labour Doc — International Labour Documentation
Int Labour Off Occup Saf Health Ser — International Labour Office. Occupational Safety and Health Series
Int Labour R — International Labour Review
Int Labour Rev — International Labour Review
Int Labour R Stat Sup — International Labour Review. Statistical Supplement
Int Lab R — International Labour Review

Int Lab Rev — International Labour Review
Int'l & Comp LQ — International and Comparative Law Quarterly
Int'l Arb J — International Arbitration Journal
Intl Archt — International Architect
Intl Asbestos Cement Review — International Asbestos-Cement Review
Int'l Assoc L Lib Bull — International Association of Law Libraries. Bulletin
Int Law — International Lawyer
Int Law J Int Inst Agric — International Law Journal. International Institute of Agriculture
Int Lawyer — International Lawyer
Int'l BA Bull — International Bar Association. Bulletin
Int'l Bar J — International Bar Journal
Int'l BJ — International Bar Journal
Int Lbr R — International Labour Review
Int L Bull — International Law Bulletin
Int'l Bull Research E Eur — International Bulletin for Research on Law in Eastern Europe
Intl Bus Law — International Business Lawyer
Intl Comm Jurists Rev — International Commission of Jurists. Review
Intl Comp Symp — International Computer Symposium Proceedings
Int'l Dig — International Digest
Int Lib Ph — International Library of Philosophy
Int Lib R — International Library Review
Int Libr Re — International Library Review
Int Libr Rev — International Library Review
Int Lichenol Newslett — International Lichenological Newsletter
Int Lighting Rev — International Lighting Review
IntLit — International Literature
Int'l J — International Journal
Intl J Analyt Exptl Model Analysis — International Journal of Analytical and Experimental Modal Analysis
Intl J Comp and App Crim Just — International Journal of Comparative and Applied Criminal Justice
Int'l J Crimin & Penol — International Journal of Criminology and Penology
Int'l J Engrg Sci — International Journal of Engineering Science
Intl J Envir Stud — International Journal of Environmental Studies
Intl J Fatigue — International Journal of Fatigue
Intl J Impact Engrg — International Journal of Impact Engineering
Intl J L and Psych — International Journal of Law and Psychiatry
Intl J Legal Info — International Journal of Legal Information
Int'l J Legal Infor — International Journal of Legal Information
Intl JL Lib — International Journal of Law Libraries
Intl J Mach Tools Manufact — International Journal of Machine Tools Manufacture
Intl J Materials Prod Tech — International Journal of Materials and Product Technology
Intl J Mech Sci — International Journal of Mechanical Sciences
Intl Jnl of Ambient Energy — International Journal of Ambient Energy
Intl Jnl Rel Ed — International Journal of Religious Education
Intl J Nonlin Mech — International Journal of Nonlinear Mechanics
Intl J Numer Anal Methods Geomech — International Journal for Numerical and Analytical Methods in Geomechanics
Intl J Numer Methods Engrg — International Journal for Numerical Methods in Engineering
Intl J Offend Ther and Comp Criminology — International Journal of Offender Therapy and Comparative Criminology
Int'l J of PRD — International Journal of Periodontics and Restorative Dentistry
Int'l J Pol — International Journal of Politics
Intl J Soc L — International Journal of the Sociology of Law
Intl J Solids Struc — International Journal of Solids and Structures
Intl J Vehicle Des — International Journal of Vehicle Design
Int'l Lab Off Leg S — International Labour Office. Legislative Series
Int'l Lab Rev — International Labour Review
Int'l L Ass'n Bull — Bulletin. International Law Association
Intl Law — International Lawyer
Int'l Lawyer — International Lawyer
Intl Legal Mat — International Legal Materials
Int'l Legal Materials — International Legal Materials
Intl Lighting Review — International Lighting Review
Intl L News — International Law News
Int'l LQ — International Law Quarterly
Intl Modal Anal Conf — International Modal Analysis Conference
Int L News — International Law News
Int Log Rev — International Logic Review
Intl Org — International Organization
Int Loss Prev Symp — International Loss Prevention Symposium
Int LQ — International Law Quarterly
Int LR — International Labour Review
Int'l Rev Ind Prop & C'right L — International Review of Industrial Property and Copyright Law
Int'l Rev Ind Prop'y & Copyr — International Review of Industrial Property and Copyright Law
Intl Rev L and Econ — International Review of Law and Economics
Intl Tax J — International Tax Journal
Int Ltg Rev — International Lighting Review
Int'l Trade L & Prac — International Trade Law and Practice
Intl Trade LJ — International Trade Law Journal
Intl Trade Rep BNA — International Trade Reporter. Bureau of National Affairs
Intm — International Musician
Int Mag Steel Met Mater — International Magazine for Steel, Metals, and Materials
Int Manag — International Management
Int Manage — International Management
Int Manage Afr — International Management Africa
Int Manage Asia Pac — International Management. Asia/Pacific
Int Man Dig — International Management Digest
Int Man Inf — International Management Information

Int Man Ser — International Management Series
Int Mar Engng — International Marine Engineering
Int Marit Health — International Maritime Health
Int Mater Rev — International Materials Review
Int Med Abstr Rev — International Medical Abstracts and Reviews
Int Med Cong Trans — International Medical Congress. Transactions
Int Med Dig — International Medical Digest
Int Medieval Bibliogr — International Medieval Bibliography
Int Med M — International Medical Magazine
Int Med Mag — International Medical Magazine
Int Med Newsl — International Medical Newsletter
Int Med Surg Surv — International Medical and Surgical Survey
Int Meet Anaesthesiol Resusc — International Meeting of Anaesthesiology and Resuscitation
Int Meet Cholinesterases — International Meeting on Cholinesterases
Int Meet Ital Soc Endocrinol — International Meeting. Italian Society of Endocrinology
Int Meet Polym Sci Technol Rolduc Polym Meet — International Meeting on Polymer Science and Technology. Rolduc Polymer Meeting
Int Ment Heal Res Newsl — International Mental Health Research Newsletter
Int Metall Rev — International Metallurgical Reviews
Int Metall Revs — International Metallurgical Reviews
Int Met Rev — International Metals Reviews
Int Mgmt — International Management
Int Mgt — International Management
Int Microchem Symp — International Microchemical Symposium
Int Microelectron Symp Proc — International Microelectronic Symposium. Proceedings
Int Migration R — International Migration Review
Int Migration Rev — International Migration Review
Int Migr Re — International Migration Review
Int Migr Rev — International Migration Review
Int Min — International Mining
Int Min Equip — International Mining Equipment
Int Miner Process Congr Tech Pap — International Mineral Processing Congress. Technical Papers
Int Miner Scene — International Minerals Scene
Int Min Man — International Mining Manual
Int Min News — International Mining News
Int Mis Council — International Missionary Council
IntMitt — Mitteilungen des Reichsverbandes der Deutschen Industrie
Int Mitt Bodenkd — Internationale Mitteilungen fuer Bodenkunde
Int Mo — International Monthly
Int Mod Foundry — International Modern Foundry
Int Molders J — International Molders' Journal
Int Monetar — International Monetary Fund. Staff Papers
Int Monetary Fund Staff Pa — International Monetary Fund. Staff Papers
Int Monetary Fund Staff Paps — International Monetary Fund Staff Papers
Int Monet Fund Staff Pap — International Monetary Fund. Staff Papers
Int Monogr Obesity Ser — International Monographs on Obesity Series
Int Mould J — International Moulders' Journal
Int Movmt Fertil — International Movement in Fertilizers
Int Mus — International Musician
Int Mus Ed — International Music Educator
INTN — Inuit Today Newsletter. Inuit Ublumi Tusagatsangit
Int Nematol Network Newsl — International Nematology Network Newsletter
Int News Fats Oils Relat Mater — International News on Fats, Oils, and Related Materials
Int Newsl Chem Educ — International Newsletter on Chemical Education
Int Nickel — International Nickel
Intnl Advt — International Advertiser
Intnl Def R — International Defense Review
Intnl Demo — International Demographics
Intnl Info — International Info
Intnl Sec — International Security
Int Nonwoven Fabr Conf — International Nonwoven Fabrics Conference
Int Nonwovens Bull — International Nonwovens Bulletin
Int North Pac Fish Comm Annu Rep — International North Pacific Fisheries Commission. Annual Report
Int North Pac Fish Comm Bull — International North Pacific Fisheries Commission. Bulletin
IntNurl — International Nursing Index
Int Nurs Bull — International Nursing Bulletin
Int Nurs Index — International Nursing Index
Int Nursing R — International Nursing Review
Int Nurs Re — International Nursing Review
Int Nurs Rev — International Nursing Review
Int Nurs Revue — International Nursing Revue
Int Nutr Policy Ser — International Nutrition Policy Series
Int Off Cocoa Choc Period Bull — International Office of Cocoa and Chocolate. Periodic Bulletin
Int Oil — International Oil. Equipment and Methods
Int Oilman — International Oilman
Int Oil Scouts Assoc Yearb — International Oil Scouts Association. Yearbook
Int Opg Engr — International Operating Engineer
Int Ophthalmol — International Ophthalmology
Int Ophthalmol Clin — International Ophthalmology Clinics
Int Opt Comp Conf Proc — International Optical Computing Conference Proceedings
Int Org — International Organization
Int Organ — International Organization
Int Organ Study Hum Dev Int Congr — International Organization for the Study of Human Development. International Congress
Int Orthop — International Orthopaedics

Int Pac Halibut Comm Annu Rep — International Pacific Halibut Commission. Annual Report
Int Pac Halibut Comm Sci Rep — International Pacific Halibut Commission. Scientific Report
Int Pac Halibut Comm Tech Rep — International Pacific Halibut Commission. Technical Report
Int Packag Abs — International Packaging Abstracts
Int Packag Abstr — International Packaging Abstracts
Int Pac Salmon Fish Comm Annu Rep — International Pacific Salmon Fisheries Commission. Annual Report
Int Pac Salmon Fish Comm Bull — International Pacific Salmon Fisheries Commission. Bulletin
Int Pac Salmon Fish Comm Prog Rep — International Pacific Salmon Fisheries Commission. Progress Report
Int Pap Bd Ind — International Paper Board Industry
Int Pat J — International Patents Journal
Int Peat Congr Proc — International Peat Congress. Proceedings
Int Peat Soc Bull — International Peat Society. Bulletin
Int Pediatr Assoc Bull — International Pediatric Association. Bulletin
Int Perfumer — International Perfumer
Int Perspect — International Perspectives
Int Perspectives — International Perspectives
Int Perspect Urol — International Perspectives in Urology
Int Pest Contr — International Pest Control
Int Pest Control — International Pest Control
Int Pet Abstr — International Petroleum Abstracts
Int Petrol Annu — International Petroleum Annual
Int Petrol Technol — International Petroleum Technology
Int Petrol Times — International Petroleum Times
Int Petrol Trade — International Petroleum Trade. US Bureau of Mines
Int Petr Tms — International Petroleum Times
Int Pet Technol — International Petroleum Technology
Int Pet Times — International Petroleum Times
Int Pharm Abstr — International Pharmaceutical Abstracts
Int Pharmac — International Pharmacopsychiatry
Int Pharmacopsychiatry — International Pharmacopsychiatry
Int Pharm Technol Prod Manuf Abstr — International Pharmaceutical Technology and Product Manufacture
Int Pharm Technol Symp — International Pharmaceutical Technology Symposium
Int Philo Q — International Philosophical Quarterly
Int Philos Q — International Philosophical Quarterly
Int Phil Q — International Philosophical Quarterly
Int Phil Quart — International Philosophical Quarterly
Int Photobiol Congr — International Photobiological Congress
Int Photogr — International Photographer
Int Photo Ind — International Photography Index
Int Photo Tech — International Photo-Technik
Int Phys Workshop Ser — International Physics Workshop Series
Int Pict Police J — International Pictorial Police Journal
Int Pipeline Technol Conv — International Pipeline Technology Convention
Int Pipe Ln — International Pipe Line Industry
Int Pipes Pipelines — International Pipes and Pipelines
Int Plann Parent Fed Med Bull — International Planned Parenthood Federation. Medical Bulletin
Int Plansee Semin — International Plansee Seminar
Int Plast Engng — International Plastics Engineering
Int Polit (Bergen) — Internasjonal Politikk (Bergen)
Int Politikk (Oslo) — Internasjonal Politikk (Oslo)
Int Polit (O) — Internasjonal Politikk (Oslo)
Int Polit Sci Abstr — International Political Science Abstracts
IntPolSc — International Political Science Abstracts
Int Polym Sci & Technol — International Polymer Science and Technology
Int Potash Inst Bull — International Potash Institute. Bulletin
Int Potash Inst Colloq Proc — International Potash Institute. Colloquium. Proceedings
Int Potash Inst Res Top — International Potash Institute. Research Topics
Int Power Generation — International Power Generation
Int Power Sources Symp London — International Power Sources Symposium (London)
Int Power Sources Symp Proc — International Power Sources Symposium. Proceedings
Intpr — Interpretation. A Journal of Bible and Theology
Int Presidents Bul — International President's Bulletin
Int Pressure Die Cast Conf Conf Pap — International Pressure Die Casting Conference. Conference Papers
Int Print — International Printing
Int Probl (Belgrade) — International Problems (Belgrade)
Int Problems — International Problems
Int Probl (Tel-Aviv) — International Problems (Tel-Aviv)
Int Prog Urethanes — International Progress in Urethanes
Int Proj — International Projectionist
Int Project — International Projectionist
Int Prop Invest Jnl — International Property Investment Journal
Int Prop Rev — International Property Review
Int Psoriasis Bull — International Psoriasis Bulletin
Int Psych — Integrative Psychiatry
Int Psychiatry Clin — International Psychiatry Clinics
Int Psycho Anal Assoc Mono — International Psycho-Analytical Association. Monograph
Int Psycho-Anal Assoc Monogr Ser — International Psycho-Analytical Association. Monograph Series
Int Psychogeriatr — International Psychogeriatrics
Int Pwr Fuel Bibliphy — International Power and Fuel Bibliography
Int Pwr Rev — International Power Review
Int Q — International Quarterly

INTQ — International Tourism Quarterly
Int Q Anal Chem — International Quarterly of Analytical Chemistry
Int Q Entomol — International Quarterly of Entomology
Int R — International Review
IntR — International Review of Social History
Int (R) — Interpretation (Richmond)
INTR — Interpreter
Intr — Intransigeant
Intracell Calcium Depend Proteolysis — Intracellular Calcium-Dependent Proteolysis
Intracell Messengers — Intracellular Messengers
Intracell Regul Ion Channels — Intracellular Regulation of Ion Channels
Intracell Transfer Lipid Mol — Intracellular Transfer of Lipid Molecules
Int R Admin Sci — International Review of Administrative Sciences
Int R Adm Sci — International Review of Administrative Sciences
Int R Aesthestics Sociology M — International Review of the Aesthetics and Sociology of Music
Int R Aesthetics & Soc — International Review of the Aesthetics and Sociology of Music
Int R Aesthetics & Soc Mus — International Review of the Aesthetics and Sociology of Music
Int R Ag — International Review of Agriculture
Int R Ag Econ — International Review of Agricultural Economics
Int R Agric Econ — International Review of Agricultural Economics
Int Railw Gaz — International Railway Gazette
Int Railw J — International Railway Journal
Intra L Rev (Am U) — Intramural Law Review of American University
Intra L Rev (NYU) — Intramural Law Review of New York University
Intra L Rev (St LU) — Intramural Law Review (St. Louis University)
Intra L Rev UCLA — Intramural Law Review of University of California at Los Angeles
Intramol Nonlinear Dyn — Intramolecular and Nonlinear Dynamics
Intramural LJ — Intramural Law Journal
Intramural L Rev — Intramural Law Review
Intran — Intransigeant
Intra-Sci Chem Rep — Intra-Science Chemistry Reports
Int R Com Dev — International Review of Community Development
Int R Comm Dev — International Review of Community Development
Int R Community Develop — International Review of Community Development
Int Rd Saf Traff Rev — International Road Safety and Traffic Review
Int Read Assn Conf Pa — International Reading Association Conference. Papers
Int Read Assn Conv Pa — International Reading Association Convention. Papers
Int Rec Child Welf Wk — International Record of Child Welfare Work
Int Recht u Diplom — Internationales Recht und Diplomatie
Int Rec Med — International Record of Medicine
Int Rec Med Gen Pract Clin — International Record. Medicine and General Practice Clinics
Int R Ed — International Review of Education
Int R Ed Cinemat — International Review of Educational Cinematography
Int R Educ — International Review of Education
Int R Educ Cinematog — International Review of Educational Cinematography
Int Ref Serv — International Reference Service
Int Reg Sci Rev — International Regional Science Review
Int Rehabil Med — International Rehabilitation Medicine
Int Rehab Rev — International Rehabilitation Review
Int Reinf Plast Conf Pap — International Reinforced Plastics Conference. Papers
Int Rel — International Relations
Int Relations — International Relations. Journal. David Davies Memorial Institute of International Studies
Int Relat (London) — International Relations (London)
Int Relat (Prague) — International Relations (Prague)
Int Relat (Teheran) — International Relations (Teheran)
Int Rep Div Mech Eng CSIRO — Internal Report. Division of Mechanical Engineering. Commonwealth Scientific and Industrial Research Organisation
Int Res Commun Syst Med Sci Libr Compend — International Research Communications System Medical Science. Library Compendium
Int Rescuer — International Rescuer
Int Res Group Refuse Disposal Inf Bull — International Research Group on Refuse Disposal Information. Bulletin
Int Rev Aerosol Phys Chem — International Reviews in Aerosol Physics and Chemistry
Int Rev Aes — International Review of the Aesthetics and Sociology of Music
Int Rev Agric — International Review of Agriculture
Int Rev Agric Econ — International Review of Agricultural Economics
Int Rev Army Navy Air Force Med Serv — International Review of the Army, Navy, and Air Force Medical Services
Int Rev Biochem — International Review of Biochemistry
Int Rev Bull — Internal Revenue Bulletin
Int Rev Chiro — International Review of Chiropractic
Int Rev Connect Tissue Res — International Review of Connective Tissue Research
Int Rev Cott All Text Inds — International Review of Cotton and Allied Textile Industries
Int Rev Cyt — International Review of Cytology
Int Rev Cytol — International Review of Cytology
Int Rev Cytol Suppl — International Review of Cytology. Supplement
Int Rev Edu — International Review of Education
Int Rev Educ — International Review of Education
Int Rev Educ Cinemat — International Review of Educational Cinematography
Int Rev Exp Pathol — International Review of Experimental Pathology
Int Rev Forest Res — International Review of Forestry Research
Int Rev For Res — International Review of Forestry Research
Int Rev Gen Exp Zool — International Review of General and Experimental Zoology
Int Rev Gesamten Hydrobiol — Internationale Revue der Gesamten Hydrobiologie

Int Rev Gesamten Hydrobiol Hydrogr — Internationale Revue der Gesamten Hydrobiologie und Hydrographie
Int Rev Gesamten Hydrobiol Syst Beih — Internationale Revue der Gesamten Hydrobiologie. Systematische Beihefte
Int Rev His — International Review of History and Political Science
Int Rev Hydrobiol — International Review of Hydrobiology
Int Rev I 10 — International Revue i 10
Int Rev Immunol — International Reviews of Immunology
Int Rev Med Surg — International Review of Medicine and Surgery
Int Rev Miss — International Review of Missions
Int Rev Mission — International Review of Mission
Int Rev Missions — International Review of Missions
Int Rev Mod — International Review of Modern Sociology
Int Rev Neurobiol — International Review of Neurobiology
Int Rev Neurobiol Suppl — International Review of Neurobiology. Supplement
Int Rev Phys Chem — International Reviews in Physical Chemistry
Int Rev Physiol — International Review of Physiology
Int Rev Phys Med — International Review of Physical Medicine
Int Rev Poult Sci — International Review of Poultry Science
Int Rev Psychoanal — International Review of Psychoanalysis
Int Rev Sci Pract Agric — International Review of the Science and Practice of Agriculture
Int Rev Serv — International Review Service
Int Rev S H — International Review of Social History
Int Rev Soc Hist — International Review of Social History
Int Rev Soc Sport — International Review for the Sociology of Sport
Int Rev Sport Soc — International Review of Sport Sociology
Int Rev Timb Util — International Review on Timber Utilization
Int Rev Trach — International Review of Trachoma
Int Rev Trop Med — International Review of Tropical Medicine
Int Rev Wood Util — International Review on Wood Utilization
Int R Gesam — Internationale Revue der Gesamten Hydrobiologie
Int R Hist Polit Sci — International Review of History and Political Science
Int R Hist Pol Sci — International Review of History and Political Science
Int Rice Comm Newsl — International Rice Commission. Newsletter
Int Rice Res Inst (Los Banos) Annu Rep — International Rice Research Institute (Los Banos). Annual Report
Int Rice Res Inst (Los Banos) Tech Bull — International Rice Research Institute (Los Banos). Technical Bulletin
Int Rice Res Inst Res Pap Ser — International Rice Research Institute. Research Paper Series
Int Rice Res Inst Techn Bull — International Rice Research Institute. Technical Bulletin
Int Rice Res Newsl — International Rice Research Newsletter
Int Rice Yb — International Rice Yearbook
Int Rly J NY — International Railway Journal (New York)
Int Rly J Philad — International Railway Journal (Philadelphia)
Int R Miss — International Review of Missions
Int R Missions — International Review of Missions
Int R Mod Sociol — International Review of Modern Sociology
Introd Aklim Rosl Ukr — Introduktsiya ta Aklimatizatsiya Roslin na Ukraini
Introd Eksp Ekol Rosl — Introduktsiya ta Eksperimental'na Ekologiya Roslin
Introd Genet Modif Org Environ — Introduction of Genetically Modified Organisms into the Environment
Introd Glass Integr Opt — Introduction to Glass Integrated Optics
Introd Mol Genet Cancer — Introduction to the Molecular Genetics of Cancer
Int Roehrenind — Internationale Roehrenindustrie
Int Ropeway Rev — International Ropeway Review
Intrpub NR — Interpublic Group of Companies, Incorporated. News Release
Int R Sci & Prac Ag — International Review of the Science and Practice of Agriculture
Int R Scl Hist — International Review of Social History
Int R Soc Hist — International Review of Social History
Int R Sport Sociol — International Review of Sport Sociology
Int Rubb Dig — International Rubber Digest
Int Rv — International Review
Int Salzburg Conf — International Salzburg Conference
Int SAMPE Electron Conf — International SAMPE Electronics Conference
Int SAMPE Environ Conf — International SAMPE (Society for the Advancement of Material and Process Engineering) Environmental Conference
Int SAMPE Symp Exhib — International SAMPE Symposium and Exhibition
Int SAMPE Tech Conf — International SAMPE Technical Conference
Int Sch Atmos Phys Proc Course — International School of Atmospheric Physics. Proceedings. Course
Int Sch Biol Lumin — International School on Biological Luminescence
Int Sch Laser Surf Microprocess — International School on Laser Surface Microprocessing
Int Sch Neurosci — International School of Neuroscience
Int Sch Phys Probl Microelectron — International School on Physical Problems in Microelectronics
Int Sci — International Science
Int Sci Counc Trypanosomiasis Res Control Publ — International Scientific Council for Trypanosomiasis Research and Control. Publication
Int Sci Counc Trypanosomiasis Res Publ — International Scientific Council for Trypanosomiasis. Research Publication
Int Sci Res News — International Science Research News
Int Sci Rev Ser — International Science Review Series
Int Sci Technol — International Science and Technology
Int Sculp — International Sculpture
Int Sec — International Security
Int Secur — International Security
Int Secur Rev — International Security Review
Int Sedim Petrogr Ser — International Sedimentary Petrographical Series
Int Sed Petrograph Ser — International Sedimentary Petrographical Series
Int Seismol Cent Bull — International Seismological Centre. Bulletin

Int Seism Summ — International Seismological Summary

Int Sem — International Seminars

Int Semin Elastomers Pap — International Seminar on Elastomers. Papers

Int Semin High Energy Phys Probl — International Seminar on High Energy Physics Problems

Int Semin Magn — International Seminar on Magnetism

Int Semin Non Destr Exam Relat Struct Integr — International Seminar on Non-Destructive Examination in Relation to Structural Integrity

Int Semin Reprod Physiol Sex Endocrinol — International Seminar on Reproductive Physiology and Sexual Endocrinology

Int Ser Biomech — International Series on Biomechanics

Int Ser Exp Psychol — International Series in Experimental Psychology

Int Ser Mater Sci Technol — International Series on Materials Science and Technology

Int Ser Monogr Anal Chem — International Series of Monographs in Analytical Chemistry

Int Ser Monogr Exp Psychol — International Series of Monographs in Experimental Psychology

Int Ser Monogr Nat Philos — International Series of Monographs in Natural Philosophy

Int Ser Monogr Nucl Energy — International Series of Monographs on Nuclear Energy

Int Ser Monogr Nucl Energy Div 7 — International Series of Monographs on Nuclear Energy. Division 7. Reactor Engineering

Int Ser Monogr Oral Biol — International Series of Monographs in Oral Biology

Int Ser Monogr Pure Appl Biol Div Biochem — International Series of Monographs on Pure and Applied Biology. Division Biochemistry

Int Ser Monogr Pure Appl Biol Div Bot — International Series of Monographs on Pure and Applied Biology. Division Botany

Int Ser Monogr Pure Appl Biol Mod Trends Physiol Sci — International Series of Monographs on Pure and Applied Biology. Modern Trends in Physiological Sciences

Int Ser Monogr Sci Solid State — International Series of Monographs in the Science of the Solid State

Int Ser Pure Appl Biol Zool Div — International Series of Monographs on Pure and Applied Biology. Zoology Division

Int Ser Sci Solid State — International Series of Monographs in the Science of the Solid State

Int Ser Sport Sci — International Series on Sport Sciences

Int Shade Tree Conf Proc — International Shade Tree Conference. Proceedings

Int Shipbldg Prog — International Shipbuilding Progress

Int Shipbldg Progr — International Shipbuilding Progress

Int Shipbuild Prog — International Shipbuilding Progress

Int Shipbuild Progress — International Shipbuilding Progress

Int Ship Painting Corros Conf Proc — International Ship Painting and Corrosion Conference. Proceedings

Int Ship Shipbuild Dir — International Shipping and Shipbuilding Directory

Int Soc Biochem Endocrinol Meet — International Society for Biochemical Endocrinology. Meeting

Int Soc Dev — International Social Development Review

Int Soc Dev Rev — International Social Development Review

Int Soc Free Radical Res Bienn Meet — International Society for Free Radical Research. Biennial Meeting

Int Soc Heart Res Annu Meet — International Society for Heart Research. Annual Meeting

Int Social R — International Socialist Review

Int Social Sci J — International Social Science Journal

Int Soc Pet Ind Biol Annu Meet — International Society of Petroleum Industry Biologists. Annual Meeting

Int Soc Rock Mech Congr Proc — International Society for Rock Mechanics. Congress Proceedings

Int Soc Sc Bull — International Social Science Bulletin

Int Soc Sci — International Social Science Journal

Int Soc Sci J — International Social Science Journal

Int Soc Sc J — International Social Science Journal

Int Soc Security Rev — International Social Security Review

Int Soc Secur R — International Social Security Review

Int Soc Secur Rev — International Social Security Review

Int Soc Work — International Social Work

Int Sol Energy Soc Am Sect Proc Annu Meet — International Solar Energy Society. American Section. Proceedings of the AnnualMeeting

Int Sol Energy Soc Congr — International Solar Energy Society Congress

Int Solid Wastes Public Clean Assoc Inf Bull — International Solid Wastes and Public Cleansing Association. Information Bulletin

Int Sourceb Corros Mar Environ — International Sourcebook. Corrosion in Marine Environment

INTSOY Ser — INTSOY [*International Soybean Program*] Series

INTSOY Ser Univ Ill Coll Agric — INTSOY [*International Soybean Program*] Series. University of Illinois. College of Agriculture

Int Sp — Internationale Spectator

Int Spec Conf Cold Formed Steel Struct — International Specialty Conference on Cold-Formed Steel Structures

Int Spect — Internationale Spectator

Int Spectator — International Spectator

Int Spektrochem Colloq Ber — Internationales Spektrochemisches Colloquium. Berichte

Int St — International Studies

Int Stat R — International Statistical Review

Int Stat Rev — International Statistical Review

Int Steam Engr — International Steam Engineer

Int St E As — International Studies. East Asian Series Research Publication

Int Steel Met Mag — International Steel and Metals Magazine

Int St Rvw — International Statistical Review

Int Stud — International Studies

Int Studio — International Studio

Int Stud Manage Org — International Studies of Management and Organization

Int Stud (New Delhi) — International Studies (New Delhi)

Int Stud Phil — International Studies in Philosophy

Int Stud Q — International Studies Quarterly

Int Stud Quart — International Studies Quarterly

Int Stud Sparrows — International Studies on Sparrows

Int Stud (Stockholm) — Internationelle Studier (Stockholm)

Int Sugar Confect Manuf Assoc Period Bull — International Sugar Confectionery Manufacturers' Association. Periodic Bulletin

Int Sugar J — International Sugar Journal

Int Sug J — International Sugar Journal

Int Summer Sch Fundam Probl Stat Mech — International Summer School on Fundamental Problems in Statistical Mechanics

Int Summer Sch Low Level Meas Man Made Radionuclides Environ — International Summer School on Low-Level Measurements of Man-Made Radionuclidesin the Environment

Int Supercond Technol Cent J — International Superconductivity Technology Center. Journal

Int Surg — International Surgery

Int Surg Dig — International Surgical Digest

Int Swarm Semin — International Swarm Seminar

Int Symp Adenosine Adenine Nucleotides — International Symposium on Adenosine and Adenine Nucleotides

Int Symp Adjuvants Agrochem — International Symposium on Adjuvants for Agrochemicals

Int Symp Adv Struct Mat — International Symposium on Advanced Structural Materials

Int Symp Agric Food Process Wastes Proc — International Symposium on Agricultural and Food Processing Wastes. Proceedings

Int Symp Alcohol Fuels — International Symposium on Alcohol Fuels

Int Symp Amyloidosis — International Symposium on Amyloidosis

Int Symp Antibiot Resist — International Symposium on Antibiotic Resistance

Int Symp Appl Laser Tech Fluid Mech — International Symposium on Applications of Laser Techniques to Fluid Mechanics

Int Symp Batteries Proc — International Symposium on Batteries. Proceedings

Int Symp Biochem Eng — International Symposium on Biochemical Engineering

Int Symp Biolumin Chemilumin — International Symposium on Bioluminescence and Chemiluminescence

Int Symp Biosens Fundam Appl — International Symposium on Biosensors. Fundamentals and Applications

Int Symp Biotechnol Growth Factors Vasc Nerv Syst — International Symposium on Biotechnology of Growth Factors. Vascular and Nervous Systems

Int Symp Biotechnol Nutr — International Symposium on Biotechnology and Nutrition

Int Symp Boron Steels — International Symposium on Boron Steels

Int Symp Can Soc Immunol — International Symposium. Canadian Society for Immunology

Int Symp Carotenoids — International Symposium on Carotenoids

Int Symp Carotenoids Other than Vitam A Abstr Commun — International Symposium on Carotenoids Other than Vitamin A. Abstracts of Communications

Int Symp Cationic Polym — International Symposium on Cationic Polymerization

Int Symp Cationic Polym Relat Ionic Processes — International Symposium on Cationic Polymerizations and Related Ionic Processes

Int Symp Cells Hepatic Sinusoid — International Symposium on Cells of the Hepatic Sinusoid

Int Symp Ceram Mater Compon Engines — International Symposium on Ceramic Materials and Components for Engines

Int Symp Charge Field Eff Biosyst — International Symposium on Charge and Field Effects in Biosystems

Int Symp Chemother — International Symposium on Chemotherapy

Int Symp Chem Oxid — International Symposium Chemical Oxidation. Technologies for the Nineties

Int Symp Chiral Sep — International Symposium on Chiral Separations

Int Symp Chromatogr Isol Insect Horm Pheromones Relat Compd — International Symposium on Chromatography and Isolation of Insect Hormones, Pheromones, and Related Compounds

Int Symp Clin Enzymol — International Symposium on Clinical Enzymology

Int Symp Colloid Surf Eng — International Symposium on Colloid and Surface Engineering

Int Symp Comb Ther — International Symposium on Combination Therapies

Int Symp Combust Pap — International Symposium on Combustion. Papers

Int Symp Contam Control Proc — International Symposium on Contamination Control. Proceedings

Int Symp Controlled Release Bioact Mater — International Symposium on Controlled Release of Bioactive Materials

Int Symp Corals Coral Reefs Proc — International Symposium on Corals and Coral Reefs. Proceedings

Int Symp Crop Prot Pap — International Symposium on Crop Protection. Papers

Int Symp Cyclodextrins — International Symposium on Cyclodextrins

Int Symp Decontam Nucl Install — International Symposium on the Decontamination of Nuclear Installations

Int Symp Disp Hologr — International Symposium on Display Holography

Int Symp Electrets — International Symposium on Electrets

Int Symp Electrometall Plant Pract — International Symposium on Electrometallurgical Plant Practice

Int Symp Electron Beam Ion Sources Their Appl — International Symposium on Electron Beam Ion Sources and their Applications

Int Symp Endothelium Deriv Vasoact Factors — International Symposium on Endothelium-Derived Vasoactive Factors

Int Symp Environ Aspects Pestic Microbiol — International Symposium on Environmental Aspects of Pesticide Microbiology

Int Symp Equine Med Control — International Symposium on Equine Medication Control

Int Symp Extr Refin Fabr Light Met — International Symposium on Extraction, Refining, and Fabrication of Light Metals

Int Symp Far From Equilib Dyn Chem Syst — International Symposium on Far-From-Equilibrium Dynamics of Chemical Systems

Int Symp Ferrous Non Ferrous Alloy Processes — International Symposium on Ferrous and Non-Ferrous Alloy Processes

Int Symp Fire Saf Sci — International Symposium on Fire Safety Science

Int Symp Fish Oil Blood Vessel Wall Interact — International Symposium on Fish Oil and Blood-Vessel Wall Interactions

Int Symp Flammability Fire Retard Proc — International Symposium on Flammability and Fire Retardants. Proceedings

Int Symp Flavins Flavoproteins — International Symposium on Flavins and Flavoproteins

Int Symp Forest Hydrol (Pennsylvania) — International Symposium on Forest Hydrology (Pennsylvania)

Int Symp Found Plast — International Symposium on Foundations of Plasticity

Int Symp Fresh Water Sea Proc — International Symposium on Fresh Water from the Sea. Proceedings

Int Symp Fundam Appl Ternary Diffus — International Symposium on Fundamentals and Applications of Ternary Diffusion

Int Symp Gaseous Dielectr — International Symposium on Gaseous Dielectrics

Int Symp Gas Flow Chem Lasers — International Symposium on Gas Flow and Chemical Lasers

Int Symp Gas Oil Coal Environ Biotechnol — International Symposium on Gas, Oil, Coal, and Environmental Biotechnology

Int Symp Gas Transfer Water Surf — International Symposium on Gas Transfer at Water Surfaces

Int Symp Gonorrhea Proc — International Symposium on Gonorrhea. Proceedings

Int Symp Heterog Catal Proc — International Symposium on Heterogeneous Catalysis. Proceedings

Int Symp High Energy Nucl Collisions Quark Gluon Plasma — International Symposium on High Energy Nuclear Collisions and Quark Gluon Plasma

Int Symp High Temp Oxid Sulphidation Processes — International Symposium on High-Temperature Oxidation and Sulphidation Processes

Int Symp Hosei Univ — International Symposium. Hosei University

Int Symp Humidity and Moisture — International Symposium on Humidity and Moisture

Int Symp Immunopathol — International Symposium on Immunopathology

Int Symp Inclusion Phenom Mol Recognit — International Symposium on Inclusion Phenomena and Molecular Recognition

Int Symp Injection Process Metall — International Symposium on Injection in Process Metallurgy

Int Symp Interface Microbiol Anal Chem — International Symposium on the Interface between Microbiology and Analytical Chemistry

Int Symp Isol Charact Use Hepatocytes — International Symposium on Isolation, Characterization, and Use of Hepatocytes

Int Symp Lab Autom Rob — International Symposium on Laboratory Automation and Robotics

Int Symp Landslide Control Proc — International Symposium on Landslide Control. Proceedings

Int Symp Lymphol — International Symposium on Lymphology

Int Symp Macromol — International Symposium on Macromolecules

Int Symp Macromol Met Complexes — International Symposium on Macromolecule-Metal Complexes

Int Symp Mass Spectrom Biochem Med — International Symposium of Mass Spectrometry in Biochemistry and Medicine

Int Symp Mass Spectrom Health Life Sci — International Symposium on Mass Spectrometry in the Health and Life Sciences

Int Symp Mater Handl Pyrometall — International Symposium on Materials Handling in Pyrometallurgy

Int Symp Mater Perform Maint — International Symposium on Materials Performance Maintenance

Int Symp Metall Appl Superalloys 718 625 Var Deriv — International Symposium on the Metallurgy and Applications of Superalloys 718, 625, and Various Derivatives

Int Symp Metalwork Lubr — International Symposium on Metalworking Lubrication

Int Symp Microb Drug Resist — International Symposium on Microbial Drug Resistance

Int Symp Mol Beams Proc — International Symposium on Molecular Beams. Proceedings

Int Symp Multipart Dyn — International Symposium on Multiparticle Dynamics

Int Symp Nanostruct Mesosc Syst — International Symposium on Nanostructures and Mesoscopic Systems

Int Symp Nephrotoxic — International Symposium on Nephrotoxicity

Int Symp Nerves Gut — International Symposium on Nerves and the Gut

Int Symp Neutron Capture Ther Cancer — International Symposium on Neutron Capture Therapy for Cancer

Int Symp New Polym React React Mech — International Symposium on New Polymerization Reactions and Reaction Mechanisms

Int Symp New Trends Allergy — International Symposium New Trends in Allergy

Int Symp Nondestr Charact Mater — International Symposium on Nondestructive Characterization of Materials

Int Symp Nucl Induced Plasmas Nucl Pumped Lasers Pap — International Symposium on Nuclear Induced Plasmas and Nuclear Pumped Lasers. Papers

Int Symp Organosilicon Chem — International Symposium on Organosilicon Chemistry

Int Symp Passivity — International Symposium on Passivity

Int Symp Peripher GABAergic Mech — International Symposium on Peripheral GABAergic Mechanisms

Int Symp Pharmacol Cereb Ischemia — International Symposium on Pharmacology of Cerebral Ischemia

Int Symp Pharmacol Thermoregul — International Symposium on the Pharmacology of Thermoregulation

Int Symp Phylog T B Cells Proc — International Symposium on the Phylogeny of T and B Cells. Proceedings

Int Symp Phys Chem Ecol Seas Frozen Soils Proc — International Symposium on Physics, Chemistry, and Ecology of Seasonally Frozen Soils. Proceedings

Int Symp Plant Lipids — International Symposium on Plant Lipids

Int Symp Plast Its Curr Appl — International Symposium on Plasticity and Its Current Applications

Int Symp Platinum Other Met Coord Compd Cancer Chemother — International Symposium on Platinum and Other Metal Coordination Compounds in Cancer Chemotherapy

Int Symp Pollen Physiol Fert — International Symposium Pollen Physiology and Fertilization

Int Symp Polym Microelectron Sci Technol — International Symposium on Polymers for Microelectronics. Science and Technology

Int Symp Polynucl Aromat Hydrocarbons — International Symposium on Polynuclear Aromatic Hydrocarbons

Int Symp Positive Strand RNA Viruses — International Symposium on Positive-Strand RNA Viruses

Int Symp Princess Takamatsu Cancer Res Fund — International Symposium. Princess Takamatsu Cancer Research Fund

Int Symp Prod Refin Fabr Recycl Light Met — International Symposium on Production, Refining, Fabrication, and Recycling of Light Metals

Int Symp Protein Struct Funct — International Symposium on Protein Structure-Function

Int Symp Pteridines Folic Acid Deriv — International Symposium on Pteridines and Folic Acid Derivatives. Chemical, Biological, and Clinical Aspects

Int Symp Qual Control — International Symposium on Quality Control

Int Symp Radiosensitizers Radioprot Drugs — International Symposium on Radiosensitizers and Radioprotective Drugs

Int Symp Rarefied Gas Dyn — International Symposium on Rarefied Gas Dynamics

Int Symp Recycl Polym Sci Technol — International Symposium on Recycling of Polymers. Science and Technology

Int Symp Regul Streams — International Symposium on Regulated Streams

Int Symp Remote Sensing Environ Proc — International Symposium on Remote Sensing of Environment. Proceedings

Int Symp Reprod Physiol Fish — International Symposium on the Reproductive Physiology of Fish

Int Symp Ring Opening Cyclopolym — International Symposium on Ring-Opening and Cyclopolymerization

Int Symp Sol Terr Phys Proc — International Symposium on Solar-Terrestrial Physics. Proceedings

Int Symp Spec Polym — International Symposium on Specialty Polymers

Int Symp Spec Top Chem Propul — International Symposium on Special Topics in Chemical Propulsion

Int Symp Struct Dyn Nucleic Acids Proteins — International Symposium on Structure and Dynamics of Nucleic Acids and Proteins

Int Symp Struct Eye — International Symposium on the Structure of the Eye

Int Symp Struct Funct Plant Popul — International Symposium on the Structure and Functioning of Plant Populations

Int Symp Strukt Funkt Erythrozyten — Internationales Symposium ueber Struktur und Funktion der Erythrozyten

Int Symp Stud Brandstofcellen Versl — International Symposium over de Studie der Brandstofcellen. Verslaggevingen

Int Symp Subscriber Loops Serv — International Symposium on Subscriber Loops and Services

Int Symp Sub Trop Trop Hortic — International Symposium on Sub-Tropical and Tropical Horticulture

Int Symp Sulphur Agric Proc — International Symposium on Sulphur in Agriculture. Proceedings

Int Symp Sulphur Emiss Environ — International Symposium. Sulphur Emissions and the Environment

Int Symp Supercond — International Symposium on Superconductivity

Int Symp Superheavy Elem Proc — International Symposium on Superheavy Metals. Proceedings

Int Symp Surfactants Solution — International Symposium on Surfactants in Solution

Int Symp Surf Phenom Addit Water Based Coat Print Technol — International Symposium on Surface Phenomena and Additives in Water-Based Coatings and Printing Technology

Int Symp Survival Cold — International Symposium for Survival in the Cold

Int Symp Sweet Potato — International Symposium. Sweet Potato

Int Symp Synergetics Coop Phenom Solids Macromol — International Symposium Synergetics and Cooperative Phenomena in Solids and Macromolecules

Int Symp Synth Appl Isot Labeled Compd — International Symposium on the Synthesis and Applications of Isotopically Labeled Compounds

Int Symp Systemfungiz — Internationales Symposium ueber Systemfungizide

Int Symp Tardigrades — International Symposium on Tardigrades

Int Symp Taurine — International Symposium on Taurine

Int Symp Tech Comm Photon Detect Int Meas Confed Proc — International Symposium. Technical Committee on Photon-Detectors. InternationalMeasurement Confederation. Proceedings

Int Symp Tech Comm Photonic Meas Photon Detect Proc — International Symposium. Technical Committee on Photonic Measurement (Photon-Detectors). Proceedings

Int Symp Tech Diagn — International Symposium on Technical Diagnostics

Int Symp Test Failure Anal — International Symposium for Testing and Failure Analysis

Int Symp Test In Situ Concr Struct Prelim Rep — International Symposium on Testing In Situ of Concrete Structures. Preliminary Reports

Int Symp Tests Bitumens Bitum Mater — International Symposium devoted to Tests on Bitumens and Bituminous Materials

Int Symp Theory Pract Affinity Tech — International Symposium on Theory and Practice in Affinity Techniques

Int Symp Thermodyn Nucl Mater — International Symposium on Thermodynamics of Nuclear Materials

Int Symp Tocopherol Oxygen Biomembr — International Symposium on Tocopherol, Oxygen, and Biomembranes

Int Symp Top Probl Orthop Surg — International Symposium on Topical Problems in Orthopedic Surgery

Int Symp Top Surf Chem Proc — International Symposium on Topics in Surface Chemistry. Proceedings

Int Symp Toxicol Carbon Disulphide Proc — International Symposium on Toxicology of Carbon Disulphide. Proceedings

Int Symp Toxicol Trop — International Symposium on Toxicology in the Tropics

Int Symp Trace Anal Technol Dev — International Symposium on Trace Analysis and Technological Development

Int Symp Trace Elem Man Anim — International Symposium on Trace Elements in Man and Animals

Int Symp Trace Elem Metab Anim — International Symposium on Trace Element Metabolism in Animals

Int Symp Transfer Factor — International Symposium on Transfer Factor

Int Symp Transition Met Catal Polym — International Symposium on Transition Metal Catalyzed Polymerizations

Int Symp Transition Radiat High Energy Part — International Symposium on Transition Radiation of High Energy Particles

Int Symp Transp Phenom — International Symposium on Transport Phenomena

Int Symp Tumor Pharmacother — International Symposium on Tumor Pharmacotherapy

Int Symp Tumor Viruses — International Symposium on Tumor Viruses

Int Symp Turbul Shear Flows — International Symposium on Turbulent Shear Flows

Int Symp Turbul Shear Flows Sel Pap — International Symposium on Turbulent Shear Flows. Selected Papers

Int Symp Uranium Eval Min Tech — International Symposium on Uranium Evaluation and Mining Techniques

Int Symp Uranium Supply Demand Proc — International Symposium on Uranium Supply and Demand. Proceedings

Int Symp Urolithiasis Relat Clin Res — International Symposium on Urolithiasis and Related Clinical Research

Int Symp Urolithiasis Res — International Symposium on Urolithiasis Research

Int Symp Use Isot Radiat Res Soil Plant Relat — International Symposium on the Use of Isotopes and Radiation in Research on Soil-Plant Relationships

Int Symp Vasc Neuroeff Mech — International Symposium on Vascular Neuroeffector Mechanisms

Int Symp Viral Hepatitis — International Symposium on Viral Hepatitis

Int Symp Viruses Wastewater Treat — International Symposium on Viruses and Wastewater Treatment

Int Symp Visual Processes Vertebr — International Symposium on Visual Processes in Vertebrates

Int Symp Vitam B6 Carbonyl Catal — International Symposium on Vitamin B6 and Carbonyl Catalysis

Int Symp Warmfeste Metallwerkstoffe — Internationales Symposium ueber Warmfeste Metallwerkstoffe

Int Symp Wasserunkraeuter — Internationales Symposium ueber Wasserunkraeuter

Int Symp Water Chem Corros Probl Nucl React Syst Compon — International Symposium on Water Chemistry and Corrosion Problems of Nuclear Reactor Systems and Components

Int Symp Water Rock Interact — International Symposium on Water-Rock Interaction

Int Symp Water Rock Interact Proc — International Symposium on Water-Rock Interaction. Proceedings

Int Symp Weak Electromagn Interact Nucl — International Symposium on Weak and Electromagnetic Interactions in Nuclei

Int Symp Weak Supercond — International Symposium on Weak Superconductivity

Int Symp Weathering Plast Rubbers — International Symposium. Weathering of Plastics and Rubbers

Int Symp Winter Concreting — International Symposium on Winter Concreting

Int Symp Wood Pulping Chem — International Symposium on Wood and Pulping Chemistry

Int Symp Workshop Part Multiphase Processes — International Symposium Workshop on Particulate and Multiphase Processes

Int Symp Wound Healing — International Symposium on Wound Healing

Int Symp Yeast Other Protoplasts — International Symposium on Yeast and Other Protoplasts

Int Symp Yeasts — International Symposium on Yeasts

Int Synth Rubber Symp Lect — International Synthetic Rubber Symposium. Lectures

Int Tag Elektr Kontakte — Internationale Tagung ueber Elektrische Kontakte

Int Tag Elektr Kontakte Vortr — Internationale Tagung ueber Elektrische Kontakte. Vortraege

Int Tag Grenzflaechenakt Stoffe Originalbeitr — Internationale Tagung ueber Grenzflaechenaktive Stoffe. Originalbeitraege

Int Tag Restlose Vergasung Gefoerderter Kohle — Internationale Tagung ueber die Restlose Vergasung von Gefoerderter Kohle

Int Tag Stud Brennstoffzellenbatterien Tagungsber — Internationale Tagung fuer das Studium der Brennstoffzellenbatterien. Tagungsbericht

Int Tailing Symp Proc — International Tailing Symposium. Proceedings

Int Tax J — International Tax Journal

Int Teach — Intermediate Teacher

Int Teamster — International Teamster

Int Tech Conf Slurry Transp — International Technical Conference on Slurry Transportation

Int Tech Conf Toxic Air Contam — International Technical Conference on Toxic Air Contaminants

Int Tech Coop Cent Rev — International Technical Cooperation Centre Review

Int Tech Titles — International Technical Titles

Int Telem Conf Proc — International Telemetering Conference. Proceedings

Int Telemetering Conf Proc — International Telemetering Conference. Proceedings

Int Teleph Rev — International Telephone Review

Int Text — Interior Textiles

Int Text Bull Dyeing Print Finish — International Textile Bulletin. Dyeing/Printing/ Finishing

Int Text Bull Nonwovens Ind Text — International Textile Bulletin. Nonwovens Industrial Textiles

Int Text Mach — International Textile Machinery

Int Text Rev — International Textile Review

Int Theor Sch High Energy Phys Exp — International Theoretical School on High Energy Physics for Experimentalists

Int Ther — International Therapeutics

Int Therm Expans Symp — International Thermal Expansion Symposium

Int Therm Spraying Conf — International Thermal Spraying Conference

Int Therm Spraying Conf Proc — International Thermal Spraying Conference. Proceedings

Int Thyroid Conf Proc — International Thyroid Conference. Proceedings

Int Thyroid Conf Trans — International Thyroid Conference. Transactions

Int Thyroid Symp — International Thyroid Symposium

Int Tierzuchtkongr — Internationale Tierzuchtkongress

Int Tijdschr Brouw Mout — Internationaal Tijdschrift voor Brouwertj en Mouterij

Int Timber Mag — International Timber Magazine

Int Tinnitus J — International Tinnitus Journal

Int Tinplate Conf — International Tinplate Conference

Int Tin Res Counc Rep — International Tin Research Council. Reports

Int Tin Res Dev Counc Bull — International Tin Research and Development Council. Bulletin

Int Tin Res Dev Counc Gen Rep — International Tin Research and Development Council. General Report

Int Tin Res Dev Counc Inf Circ — International Tin Research and Development Council. Information Circular

Int Tin Res Dev Counc Misc Publ — International Tin Research and Development Council. Miscellaneous Publications

Int Tin Res Dev Counc Publ — International Tin Research and Development Council. Publication

Int Tin Res Dev Counc Stat Bull — International Tin Research and Development Council. Statistical Bulletin

Int Tin Res Dev Counc Tech Publ Ser A — International Tin Research and Development Council. Technical Publication. Series A

Int Tin Res Dev Counc Tech Publ Ser B — International Tin Research and Development Council. Technical Publication. Series B

Int Tin Res Dev Counc Tech Publ Ser D — International Tin Research and Development Council. Technical Publication. Series D

Int Tin Res Inst Publ — International Tin Research Institute Publication

Int Titanium Cast Semin — International Titanium Casting Seminar

Int TNO Conf Contam Soil — International TNO Conference on Contaminated Soil

Int TNO Conf Proc — International TNO Conference on Biotechnology. Proceedings

Int TNO Meet Biol Interferon Syst — International TNO Meeting on the Biology of the Interferon System

Int Top Conf Electron Beam Res Technol Proc — International Topical Conference on Electron Beam Research and Technology. Proceedings

Int Top Conf High Power Electron Ion Beam Res Technol Proc — International Topical Conference on High Power Electron and Ion Beam Research and Technology. Proceedings

Int Top Conf Kinet Aggregation Gelation — International Topical Conference on Kinetics of Aggregation and Gelation

Int Top Conf Meson Nucl Phys — International Topical Conference on Meson-Nuclear Physics

Int Top Conf Phys MOS Insul — International Topical Conference on the Physics of MOS Insulators

Int Top Conf Phys SiO2 Its Interfaces Proc — International Topical Conference on the Physics of SiO2 and Its Interfaces. Proceedings

Int Top Meet Fast React Saf — International Topical Meeting on Fast Reactor Safety

Int Top Meet React Therm Hydraul — International Topical Meeting on Reactor Thermal Hydraulics

Int Tracts Comput Sci Technol Their Appl — International Tracts in Computer Science and Technology and Their Application

Int Trade Forum — International Trade Forum

Int Trade LJ — International Trade Law Journal

Int Trade Rep US Exp W — International Trade Reporter's US Export Weekly

Int Trade Union N — International Trade Union News

Int Transp Commun — International Transport and Communications

Int Transplutonium Elem Symp — International Transplutonium Element Symposium

Int Tree Crops J — International Tree Crops Journal

Int Tribol Congr Proc — International Tribology Congress EUROTRIB. Proceedings

Int Tug Conv (Proc) — International Tug Convention (Proceedings)

Int Tungsten Symp — International Tungsten Symposium

Int Turfgrass Res Conf — International Turfgrass Research Conference

Int Turtle Tortoise Soc J — International Turtle and Tortoise Society. Journal

Int TV Tech Rev — International TV Technical Review

INTU — Indian Truth

Int Union Air Pollut Prev Assoc Int Clean Air Congr Pap — International Union of Air Pollution Prevention Associations. International Clean Air Congress. Papers

Int Union Biochem Symp — International Union of Biochemistry Symposium

Int Union Biochem Symp Ser — International Union of Biochemistry Symposium Series

Int Union Biol Sci Ser B — International Union of Biological Sciences. Series B

Int Union Biol Sci Ser B — International Union of Biological Sciences. Series B. Colloquia

Int Union Biol Sci Ser D Newsl — International Union of Biological Sciences. Series D. Newsletter

Int Union Cancer Monogr Ser — International Union Against Cancer. Monograph Series

Int Union Cancer Tech Rep Ser — International Union Against Cancer. Technical Report Series

Int Union Cancer UICC Tech Rep Ser — International Union Against Cancer. UICC [*Union Internationale Contre le Cancer*] Technical Report Series

Int Union Conserv Nat Nat Resour Annu Rep — International Union for Conservation of Nature and Natural Resources. Annual Report

Int Union Conserv Nat Nat Resour Proc Pap — International Union for the Conservation of Nature and Natural Resources. Proceedings and Papers. Technical Meeting

Int Union Crystallogr Comm Crystallogr Appar Bibliogr — International Union of Crystallography. Commission on Crystallographic Apparatus. Bibliography

Int Union Crystallogr Crystallogr Symp — International Union of Crystallography. Crystallographic Symposia

Int Union For Res Organ Conf Wood Qual Util Trop Spec — International Union of Forestry Research Organizations Conference on Wood Quality and Utilization of Tropical Species

Int Union Geol Sci Int Subcomm Stratigr Cl Circ — International Union of Geological Sciences. International Subcommission on Stratigraphic Classification. Circular

Int Union Geol Sci Ser A — International Union of Geological Sciences. Series A

Int Union Geol Sci Ser B — International Union of Geological Sciences. Series B

Int Union Pure Appl Chem — International Union of Pure and Applied Chemistry

Int Union Quat Res — International Union for Quaternary Research

Int Union Study Soc Insects Int Congr — International Union for the Study of Social Insects. International Congress

Int Urinary Stone Conf — International Urinary Stone Conference

Int Urogynecol J Pelvic Floor Dysfunct — International Urogynecology Journal and Pelvic Floor Dysfunction

Int Urol Nephrol — International Urology and Nephrology

Int Vac Congr — International Vacuum Congress

Int Vac Microelectron Conf Tech Dig — International Vacuum Microelectronics Conference. Technical Digest

Int Velsicol Symp Proc — International Velsicol Symposium. Proceedings

Int Verb Materialpruef Kongr — Internationaler Verband fuer Materialpruefung. Kongress

Int Verbrennungskraftmasch Kongr — Internationaler Verbrennungskraftmaschinen-Kongress

Int Veredler Jahrb — Internationales Veredler-Jahrbuch

Int Verkehrswesen — Internationales Verkehrswesen

Int Ver Theor Angew Limnol Mitt — International Vereinigung fuer Theoretische und Angewandte Limnologie. Mitteilungen

Int Ver Theor Angew Limnol Verh — Internationale Vereinigung fuer Theoretische und Angewandte Limnologie und Verhandlungen

Int Vet Bull — International Veterinary Bulletin

Int Vet News — International Veterinary News

Int Vet Rev — International Veterinary Review

Int Virol — International Virology

Int Visual Field Symp — International Visual Field Symposium

Int Warsaw Meet Elem Part Phys — International Warsaw Meeting on Elementary Particle Physics

Int Wash Spring Symp — International Washington Spring Symposium

Int Wasserversorgungskongr Int Water Supply Assoc — Internationaler Wasserversorgungskongress der International Water Supply Association

Int Wasserversorgungskongr Int Water Supply Assoc IWSA — Internationaler Wasserversorgungskongress der International Water Supply Association. IWSA

Int Wasserversorgungskongr IWSA — Internationaler Wasserversorgungskongress der IWSA (International Water Supply Association)

Int Water Conf Annu Meet Eng Soc West Pa — International Water Conference. Annual Meeting. Engineers' Society of Western Pennsylvania

Int Water Conf Off Proc — International Water Conference. Official Proceedings

Int Water Conservancy Exhib — International Water Conservancy Exhibition

Int Waterfowl Res Bur Bull — International Waterfowl Research Bureau Bulletin

Int Water Pollut Res Conf Pap — International Water Pollution Research Conference. Papers

Int Water Power & Dam Constr — International Water Power and Dam Construction

Int Water Power Dam — International Water Power and Dam Construction

Int Water Supply Assoc Congr — International Water Supply Association. Congress

Int Water Supply Congr Exhib — International Water Supply Congress and Exhibition

Int Water Supply Congr Proc — International Water Supply Congress. Proceedings

Int Whaling Comm Rep — International Whaling Commission. Reports

Int Whaling Comm Rep Comm — International Whaling Commission. Report of the Commission

Int Whal Statist — International Whaling Statistics

Int Wheat Genet Symp — International Wheat Genetics Symposium

Int Wildfowl Inq — International Wildfowl Inquiry

Int Wildl — International Wildlife

Int Wildlife — International Wildlife

Int Williston Basin Symp Pap — International Williston Basin Symposium. Papers

Int Williston Basin Symp Proc — International Williston Basin Symposium. Proceedings

Int Winter Meet Fundam Phys — International Winter Meeting on Fundamental Physics

Int Winter Sch Crystallogr Comput — International Winter School on Crystallographic Computing

Int Winter Sch Curr Trends Biomol Struct — International Winter School on Current Trends in Biomolecular Structure

Int Wire Cable Symp Proc — International Wire and Cable Symposium. Proceedings

Int Wire Mach Assoc Int Conf — International Wire and Machinery Association. International Conference

Int Wiss Kolloq Kaffee — Internationales Wissenschaftliches Kolloquium ueber Kaffee

Int Wiss Kolloq Tech Hochsch Ilmenau — Internationales Wissenschaftliches Kolloquium. Technische Hochschule Ilmenau

Int Wiss Korresp Gesch Dtsch Arb-Bew — Internazionale Wissenschaftliche Korrespondenz zur Geschichte der Deutschen Arbeiterbewegung

Int Wolltext Forschungskonf Proc — Internationale Wolltextil-Forschungskonferenz. Proceedings

Int Woodworker — International Woodworker

Int Wool Text Res Conf Proc — International Wool Textile Research Conference. Proceedings

Int Work Conf Stored Prod Entomol — International Working Conference on Stored-Product Entomology

Int Workshop Adenosine Xanthine Deriv — International Workshop on Adenosine and Xanthine Derivatives

Int Workshop Appl Adapt Control Pap — International Workshop on Applications of Adaptive Control. Papers

Int Workshop Articular Cartilage Osteoarthritis — International Workshop on Articular Cartilage and Osteoarthritis

Int Workshop Ascorbic Acid Domest Anim — International Workshop on Ascorbic Acid in Domestic Animals

Int Workshop Basic Prop Clin Appl Transfer Factor — International Workshop on Basic Properties and Clinical Applications of Transfer Factor

Int Workshop Behav Eff Nicotine — International Workshop on Behavioral Effects of Nicotine

Int Workshop Bicarbonate Use Photosynth — International Workshop on Bicarbonate Use in Photosynthesis

Int Workshop Biol Prop Peptidoglycan — International Workshop on the Biological Properties of Peptidoglycan

Int Workshop Bone Histomorphom — International Workshop on Bone Histomorphometry

Int Workshop Carbonic Anhydrase — International Workshop on Carbonic Anhydrase

Int Workshop Cold Neutron Sources — International Workshop on Cold Neutron Sources

Int Workshop Condens Matter Phys — International Workshop on Condensed Matter Physics

Int Workshop Coord Regul Gene Expression — International Workshop on Coordinated Regulation of Gene Expression

Int Workshop Cysticercosis — International Workshop on Cysticercosis

Int Workshop Determ Antiepileptic Drugs Body Fluids — International Workshop on the Determination of Antiepileptic Drugs on Body Fluids

Int Workshop Dev Renal Physiol — International Workshop on Development Renal Physiology

Int Workshop Ecol Phys Chem — International Workshop on Ecological Physical Chemistry

Int Workshop Electron Prop Mech High Tc Supercond — International Workshop on Electronic Properties and Mechanisms of High Tc Superconductors

Int Workshop Electroweak Phys Stand Model — International Workshop on Electroweak Physics beyond the Standard Model

Int Workshop Environ Probl Extr Ind — International Workshop on Environmental Problems of the Extractive Industries

Int Workshop Fetal Brain Dev — International Workshop on Fetal Brain Development

Int Workshop Fundam Res Homogeneous Catal — International Workshop on Fundamental Research in Homogeneous Catalysis

Int Workshop Geom Interfaces — International Workshop on Geometry and Interfaces

Int Workshop Gluten Proteins — International Workshop on Gluten Proteins

Int Workshop Hemopoiesis Cult — International Workshop on Hemopoiesis in Culture

Int Workshop High Perform Fiber Reinf Cem Compos — International Workshop High Performance Fiber Reinforced Cement Composites

Int Workshop Hum Gene Mapp — International Workshop on Human Gene Mapping

Int Workshop Hum Leukocyte Differ Antigens — International Workshop on Human Leukocyte Differentiation Antigens

Int Workshop Iloprost — International Workshop on Iloprost

Int Workshop Immune Defic Anim — International Workshop on Immune-Deficient Animals

Int Workshop Immune Defic Anim Exp Res — International Workshop on Immune-Deficient Animals in Experimental Research

Int Workshop Ind Biofouling Biocorros — International Workshop on Industrial Biofouling and Biocorrosion

Int Workshop Inelastic Ion Surf Collisions — International Workshop on Inelastic Ion-Surface Collisions

Int Workshop Intrauterine Contracept Adv Future Prospects — International Workshop on Intrauterine Contraception. Advances and Future Prospects

Int Workshop Lantibiotics — International Workshop on Lantibiotics

Int Workshop Lessons Anim Diabetes — International Workshop. Lessons from Animal Diabetes

Int Workshop Light Absorpt Aerosol Part — International Workshop on Light Absorption by Aerosol Particles

Int Workshop Low Temp Detect Neutrinos Dark Matter — International Workshop on Low Temperature Detectors for Neutrinos and Dark Matter

Int Workshop Male Contracept Adv Future Prospects — International Workshop on Male Contraception. Advances and Future Prospects

Int Workshop Membr Bioenerg — International Workshop on Membrane Bioenergetics

Int Workshop Membr Tumour Growth — International Workshop on Membranes in Tumour Growth

Int Workshop Methods Struct Anal Modulated Struct Quasicryst — International Workshop on Methods of Structural Analysis of Modulated Structures and Quasicrystals

Int Workshop MeV keV Ions Cluster Interact Surf Met — International Workshop on MeV and keV Ions and Cluster Interactions with Surfaces and Metals

Int Workshop Mol Solids Pressure — International Workshop on Molecular Solids under Pressure

Int Workshop NK Cells — International Workshop on NK Cells

Int Workshop Nude Mice Proc — International Workshop on Nude Mice. Proceedings

Int Workshop Oxygen Free Radicals Shock — International Workshop on Oxygen Free Radicals in Shock

Int Workshop Photoinduced Self Organ Eff Opt Fiber — International Workshop on Photoinduced Self-Organization Effects in Optical Fiber. Quebec

Int Workshop Phys Eng Comput Multidimens Imaging Process — International Workshop on Physics and Engineering of Computerized Multidimensional Imaging and Processing

Int Workshop Phys Eng Med Imaging — International Workshop on Physics and Engineering in Medical Imaging

Int Workshop Physiol Biochem Stressed Plants — International Workshop on Physiology and Biochemistry of Stressed Plants

Int Workshop Phys Semicond Devices — International Workshop on the Physics of Semiconductor Devices

Int Workshop Positron Positronium Chem — International Workshop on Positron and Positronium Chemistry

Int Workshop QSAR Environ Toxicol — International Workshop on QSAR [*Quantitative Structure-Activity Relationship*] in Environmental Toxicology

Int Workshop Quark Gluon Struct Hadrons Nucl — International Workshop on Quark-Gluon Structure of Hadrons and Nuclei

Int Workshop Rare Earth Cobalt Perm Magnets Their Appl — International Workshop on Rare Earth-Cobalt Permanent Magnets and Their Applications

Int Workshop Rare Earth Magnets Their Appl — International Workshop on Rare-Earth Magnets and Their Applications

Int Workshop Relativ Aspects Nucl Phys — International Workshop on Relativistic Aspects of Nuclear Physics

Int Workshop Res Front Fertil Regul — International Workshop on Research Frontiers in Fertility Regulation

Int Workshop Scale Up Water Wastewater Treat Processes — International Workshop on Scale-Up of Water and Wastewater Treatment Processes

Int Workshop Solvent Substitution — International Workshop on Solvent Substitution

Int Workshop Take All Cereals — International Workshop on Take-All of Cereals

Int Workshop Trace Elem Anal Chem Med Biol — International Workshop on Trace Element Analytical Chemistry in Medicine and Biology

Int Workshop Transfer Factor — International Workshop on Transfer Factor

Int Workshop Weak Interact Neutrinos — International Workshop on Weak Interactions and Neutrinos

Int Yb Agric Statist — International Yearbook of Agricultural Statistics

Int Yb Child Care Prot — International Yearbook of Child Care and Protection

Int Yb Neph — International Yearbook of Nephrology

Int Yearb Cartogr — International Yearbook of Cartography

Int Yearbook Ag Leg — International Yearbook of Agricultural Legislation

Int Yearbook of Ed — International Yearbook of Education

Int Yeast Symp — International Yeast Symposium

Int Yrbk Ed — International Yearbook of Education

Int Z Angew Phsyiol Einschl Arbeitsphysiol — Internationale Zeitschrift fuer Angewandte Physiologie Einschliesslich Arbeitsphysiologie

Int Z Angew Physiol — Internationale Zeitschrift fuer Angewandte Physiologie Einschliesslich Arbeitsphysiologie

Int Z Bibelwiss — Internationale Zeitschriftenschau fuer Bibelwissenschaft und Grenzgebiete

Int Z Bohrtech Erdoelbergbau Geol — Internationale Zeitschrift fuer Bohrtechnik, Erdoelbergbau, und Geologie

Int Zeitsch F Individualpsychol — Internationale Zeitschrift fuer Individualpsychologie

Int Zeitschriftenschau Bibelwissenschaft Grenzgeb — Internationale Zeitschriftenschau fuer Bibelwissenschaft undGrenzgebiete

Int Z Elektrowaerme — Internationale Zeitschrift fuer Elektrowaerme

Int Zeolite Conf — International Zeolite Conference

Int Z Erzieh — Internationale Zeitschrift fuer Erziehungswissenschaft

Int Z Exp Med — Internationale Zeitschrift fuer Experimentelle Medizin

Int Z Gas Waerme — Internationale Zeitschrift fuer Gas Waerme

Int Z Haematol — Internationale Zeitschrift fuer Haematologie

Int Z Kernenerg — Internationale Zeitschrift fuer Kernenergie

Int Z Klin Pharmakol Ther Toxicol — Internationale Zeitschrift fuer Klinische Pharmakologie, Therapie, und Toxicologie

Int Z Landwirtsch — Internationale Zeitschrift der Landwirtschaft

Int Z Lebensm Technol Verfahrenstech — Internationale Zeitschrift fuer Lebensmittel-Technologie und -Verfahrenstechnik

Int Z Metallogr — Internationale Zeitschrift fuer Metallographie

Int Zool Cong — International Zoological Congress

Int Zoo Yearb — International Zoo Yearbook

Int Z Phys Chem Biol — Internationale Zeitschrift fuer Physikalisch Chemische Biologie

Int Z Rehabilitationsforsch — Internationale Zeitschrift fuer Rehabilitationsforschung

Int Z Theor Angew Genet — Internationale Zeitschrift fuer Theoretische und Angewandte Genetik

Int Z Theorie U Praxis Statist — Internationale Zeitschrift fuer Theorie und Praxis. Statistische Hefte

Int Zurich Semin Digital Commun — International Zurich Seminar on Digital Communications

Int Z Vitam-Ernaehrungsforsch — Internationale Zeitschrift fuer Vitamin und Ernaehrungsforschung

Int Z Vitam Ernaehrungsforsch Beih — Internationale Zeitschrift fuer Vitamin- und Ernaehrungsforschung. Beiheft

Int Z Vitamforsch — Internationale Zeitschrift fuer Vitaminforschung

Int Z Vitaminforsch — Internationale Zeitschrift fuer Vitaminforschung

Int Z Vitaminforsch Beih — Internationale Zeitschrift fuer Vitaminforschung. Beiheft

Int Z Wasser Versorg — Internationale Zeitschrift fuer Wasser-Versorgung

INUCA — Inorganic and Nuclear Chemistry Letters

INUI — Inuit Today

Inuit Art Q — Inuit Art Quarterly

INUL — Inulirijut. Department of Indian and Northern Affairs. Education Section. Social Development Division

INUM — Inummarit

INUN — Inuit North

In Univ Fol — Indiana University. Folklore Institute. Monograph Series

INUR — Nursing

INURAQ — Investigative Urology

INUSA — Industria Usoara

INUT — Inuttitut

INUT — Nutrition Reviews

INUV — Inuvialuit

INV — Inventaire des Inscriptions de Palmyre

Inv — Inventario

INV — Investment Review

Inv Banking — Investment Banking

Inv Chron — Investors Chronicle and Stock Exchange Gazette

Inv DD — Investment Dealers' Digest

Inventaire Mal Plantes Can — Inventaire des Maladies des Plantes au Canada

Inventaire Mineral Fr — Inventaire Mineralogique de la France

Inventaria — Inventaria Archaeologica

Invent Intell — Invention Intelligence

Invention — Invention Intelligence

Invent Manage — Invention Management

Invent Math — Inventiones Mathematicae

Inverse Ill posed Probl Ser — Inverse and Ill-posed Problems Series

Inverse Pr — Inverse Problems

Inverse Probl Eng — Inverse Problems in Engineering

Invertebr Endocrinol — Invertebrate Endocrinology

Invertebr Models Biomed Res — Invertebrate Models for Biomedical Research

Invertebr Neurosci — Invertebrate Neuroscience

Invertebr R — Invertebrate Reproduction and Development

Invertebr Reprod Dev — Invertebrate Reproduction and Development

Invertebr Syst Vitro Proc Int Conf — Invertebrate Systems in Vitro. Proceedings. International Conference on Invertebrate Tissue Culture

Invertebr Taxon — Invertebrate Taxonomy

Invertebr Tissue Cult Appl Med Biol Agric Proc Int Conf — Invertebrate Tissue Culture. Applications in Medicine, Biology, and Agriculture. Proceedings. International Conference on Invertebrate Tissue Culture

Invertebr Tissue Cult Res Appl Ext Proc US Jpn Semin — Invertebrate Tissue Cultures. Research Applications. Extended Proceedings. United States-Japan Seminar

Invert Neurosci — Invertebrate Neuroscience

Invest Agrar Prod Prot Veg — Investigacion Agraria. Produccion y Proteccion Vegetales

Invest Agric — Investigacion Agricola. Consejo Nacional de Investigaciones Agricolos

Invest Agric (Santiago) — Investigacion Agricola (Santiago)

Invest Agropecu (Lima) — Investigaciones Agropecuarias (Lima, Peru)

Invest Agropecu (Peru) — Investigaciones Agropecuarias (Lima, Peru)

Invest Anal J — Investment Analysts Journal

Invest Apl Latinoam — Investigacion Aplicada Latinoamericana

Invest Campo — Investigaciones de Campo

Invest Cell Pathol — Investigative and Cell Pathology

Invest Cetacea — Investigations on Cetacea

Invest Clin — Investigacion Clinica

Invest Clin Lab — Investigacion en la Clinica y en el Laboratorio

Invest Clin (Maracaibo) — Investigacion Clinica (Maracaibo)

Invest Clin Supl — Investigacion Clinica. Suplemento

Invest Dec — Investment Decisions

Invest Econ — Investigacion Economica

Invest Ext Appl Melanoma Boron Neutron Capture Ther — Investigation for the Extended Application of Melanoma Boron Neutron Capture Therapy

Invest Fish Control — Investigations in Fish Control

Invest For — Investment Forum

Invest Geotherm Potential UK Br Geol Surv — Investigation of the Geothermal Potential of the UK. British Geological Survey

Invest Geotherm Potential UK Inst Geol Sci — Investigation of the Geothermal Potential of the UK. Institute of Geological Sciences

Invest Hist Mex — Investigaciones Historicas (Mexico)

Investigacion Agric — Investigacion Agricola

Investigacion Econ — Investigacion Economica

Investigacion Oper — Investigacion Operacional

Investigacion Pesq — Investigacion Pesquera

Investigation Air Pollut-Deposit Gauge Lead Diox Candle — Investigation of Air Pollution - Deposit Gauge and Lead Dioxide Candle

Investigation Air Pollut Smoke Sulph Diox Surv — Investigation of Air Pollution - Smoke and Sulphur Dioxide Survey

Investigation Report-CSIRO Institute of Earth Resources — Investigation Report. Commonwealth Scientific and Industrial Research Organization. Institute of Earth Resources

Invest INAH — Investigaciones del Instituto Nacional de Antropologia e Historia

Invest Indiana Lakes Streams — Investigations of Indiana Lakes and Streams

Invest Inf Text — Investigacion e Informacion Textil

Invest Inf Text Tens — Investigacion e Informacion Textil y de Tensioactivos

Invest Inf Text Tensioactivos — Investigacion e Informacion Textil y de Tensioactivos

Invest Lab Quim Biol Univ Nac Cordoba — Investigaciones. Laboratorio de Quimica Biologica. Universidad Nacional de Cordoba

Invest Let — Investment Letter

Invest Man Wld — Investment Management World

Invest Mar CICIMAR — Investigaciones Marinas CICIMAR (Centro Interdisciplinario de Ciencias Marinas)
Invest Mar Univ Catol Valparaiso — Investigaciones Marinas. Universidad Catolica de Valparaiso
Invest Med Int — Investigacion Medica Internacional
Investment Appraisals Chem Eng — Investment Appraisals for Chemical Engineers
Investment Dealers Dig — Investment Dealers' Digest
Invest Microtech Med Biol — Investigative Microtechniques in Medicine and Biology
Invest Mon — Investment Monthly
Invest New Drugs — Investigational New Drugs
Invest Ophth — Investigative Ophthalmology [Later, Investigative Ophthalmology and Visual Science]
Invest Ophthalmol — Investigative Ophthalmology [Later, Investigative Ophthalmology and Visual Science]
Invest Ophthalmol Vis Sci — Investigative Ophthalmology and Visual Science
Invest Ophthalmol Visual Sci — Investigative Ophthalmology and Visual Science
Invest Ophthal Visual Sci — Investigative Ophthalmology and Visual Science
Investor Owned Hosp Rev — Investor-Owned Hospital Review
Investors Chron — Investors Chronicle
Investors Chronicle — Investors Chronicle and Financial World
Invest Pediatr — Investigacion Pediatrica
Invest Pesq — Investigacion Pesquera
Invest Pesq Supl Result Exped Cient — Investigacion Pesquera. Suplemento. Resultados Expediciones Cientificas
Invest Pestic Residues — Investigations on Pesticide Residues
Invest Prog Agric — Investigacion y Progreso Agricola
Invest Radiol — Investigative Radiology
Invest Rates Mech React — Investigation of Rates and Mechanisms of Reactions
Invest Rep CSIRO (Aust) — Investigation Reports. Commonwealth Scientific and Industrial Research Organisation (Australia)
Invest Rep CSIRO Inst Earth Resour — CSIRO [Commonwealth Scientific and Industrial Research Organisation] Institute of Earth Resources. Investigation Report
Invest Rep CSIRO Miner Res Lab — CSIRO [Commonwealth Scientific and Industrial Research Organisation] Minerals Research Laboratories. Investigation Report
Invest Rep Div Miner Chem CSIRO — Investigation Report. Division of Mineral Chemistry. Commonwealth Scientific and Industrial Research Organisation
Invest Rep Div Miner CSIRO — Investigation Report. Division of Mineralogy. Commonwealth Scientific and Industrial Research Organisation
Invest Rep Div Miner Phys CSIRO — Investigation Report. Division of Mineral Physics. Commonwealth Scientific and Industrial Research Organisation
Invest Rep Miner Res Lab CSIRO — Investigation Report. Minerals Research Laboratories. Commonwealth Scientific and Industrial Research Organisation
Invest Rep Mines Branch Can — Investigation Report. Mines Branch. Canada
Invest S Paulo — Investigacoes (Sao Paulo)
Invest Stats — Investment Statistics
Invest Tech Oncol Pap Annu Multidiscip Symp Clin Oncol — Investigational Techniques in Oncology. Papers. Annual Multidisciplinary Symposium on Clinical Oncology
Invest Tec Papel — Investigacion y Tecnica del Papel
Invest Urol — Investigative Urology
Invest Util Clays Clay Miner Proc Symp — Investigation and Utilization of Clays and Clay Minerals. Proceedings. Symposium
Invest Zool Chil — Investigaciones Zoologicas Chilenas
Inv Ind Lakes and Streams — Investigations of Indiana Lakes and Streams
Invited Lect Contrib Pap Int Conf Clustering Phenom Nucl — Invited Lectures and Contributed Papers. International Conference on ClusteringPhenomena
Invited Lect Contrib Pap Int Symp Polym Amines Ammonium Salts — Invited Lectures and Contributed Papers presented at the International Symposium on Polymeric Amines and Ammonium Salts
Invited Pap Eur Conf Controlled Fusion Plasma Phys — Invited Papers. European Conference on Controlled Fusion and Plasma Physics
Invited Pap Eur Solid State Circuits Conf — Invited Papers presented at the European Solid State Circuits Conference
Invited Pap Int Conf Multiphoton Processes — Invited Papers. International Conference on Multiphoton Processes
Invited Pap Int Conf Phenom Ioniz Gases — Invited Papers. International Conference on Phenomena in Ionized Gases
Invited Pap Int Conf Phys Electron At Collisions — Invited Papers. International Conference on the Physics of Electronic and Atomic Collisions
Invited Pap Int Symp Discharges Electr Insul Vac — Invited Papers. International Symposium on Discharges and Electrical Insulationin Vacuum
Invited Pap Natl Conf At Spectrosc — Invited Papers. National Conference on Atomic Spectroscopy
Invited Rapp Pap Int Conf Cosmic Rays — Invited and Rapporteur Papers. International Conference on Cosmic Rays
In Vitr Mol Toxicol — In Vitro & Molecular Toxicology
In Vitro Cell Dev Biol — In Vitro Cellular and Developmental Biology
In Vitro Cell Dev Biol Anim — In Vitro Cellular and Developmental Biology. Animal
In Vitro Cell Dev Biol J Tissue Cult Assoc — In Vitro Cellular and Developmental Biology. Journal. Tissue Cultural Association
In Vitro Cell Dev Biol Plant — In Vitro Cellular and Developmental Biology. Plant
In Vitro Eff Miner Dusts Int Workshop — In Vitro Effects of Mineral Dusts. International Workshop
In Vitro Immunol — In Vitro Immunology
In Vitro J Tissue Cult Assoc — In Vitro. Journal of the Tissue Culture Association
In Vitro Mol Toxicol — In Vitro and Molecular Toxicology
In Vitro Monogr — In Vitro Monograph
In Vitro Toxicol — In Vitro Toxicology
In Vitro Toxicol Mech New Technol — In Vitro Toxicology. Mechanisms and New Technology
In Vivo Bus Med Rep — In Vivo. The Business and Medicine Report

INVL — Inuvialuit
INVMDJ — Invasion and Metastasis
Inv Mos — Inventaire des Mosaiques de la Gaule et de l'Afrique
Inv Mos Afrique — Inventaire des Mosaiques de la Gaule et de l'Afrique
Inv Mosaiques — Inventaire des Mosaiques de la Gaule et de l'Afrique
INVO — Indian Voice
Inv Ophth — Investigative Ophthalmology [Later, Investigative Ophthalmology and Visual Science]
Inv Pesq — Investigacion Pesquera
Inv Radiol — Investigative Radiology
INVRAV — Investigative Radiology
Invt Arch — Inventaria Archaeologica
Inv Urol — Investigative Urology
Inv Waddington — Inventaire Sommaire de la Collection Waddington
Inv Zool Chilenas — Investigaciones Zoologicas Chilenas
INWAB — Industrial Wastes
Inwest i Budown — Inwestycje i Budownictwo
INWI — International Wildlife
INWO — Indian World
INWWAH — Industrial Water and Wastes
INX — Eigen Vervoer. Magazine voor Eigen Vervoerders en Verladers
INYL — New York University Law Review
INZAA — Insatsu Zasshi
Inz Apar Chem — Inzynieria i Aparatura Chemiczna
Inz Budownictwo — Inzynieria i Budownictwo
Inz Chem — Inzynieria Chemiczna
Inz Chem i Proc — Inzynieria Chemiczny i Procesowa
Inz-Fiz Z — Inzenerno-Fiziceskii Zurnal
Inzhenerno Fizicheskii Zh — Inzhenerno Fizicheskii Zhurnal
Inzh-Fiz Zh — Inzhenerno-Fizicheskii Zhurnal
Inzh-Fiz Zh Akad Nauk Belorus SSR — Inzhenerno-Fizicheskii Zhurnal Akademiya Nauk Beloruskoi SSR
Inzh Geol — Inzhenernaya Geologiya
Inzh Geol Khidrogeol — Inzhenerna Geologiya i Khidrogeologiya
Inzh Sb — Inzhenernyi Sbornik
Inzh Zh — Inzhenernyi Zhurnal
Inzh Zh Mekh Tverd Tela — Inzhenernyi Zhurnal. Mekhanika Tverdogo Tela
Inz i Aparat Chem — Inzynieria i Aparatura Chemiczna
Inz Materialowa — Inzynieria Materialowa
Inz Powierzchni — Inzynieria Powierzchni
INZSA — Inzhenernyi Sbornik
Inz Stavby — Inzenyrske Stavby
Inz-Stroitel Inst Kuibysev Sb Trudov — Moskovskii Ordena Trudovogo Krasnogo Znameni Inzenerno-Stroitel'nyi Institut Imeni V. V. Kuibyseva Sbornik Trudov
Inz Z Meh Tverd Tela — Inzenernyi Zurnal Mehanika Tverdogo Tela
IO — Iowa Music Educator
IO — Itinerario
IOB — Internationale Oekumenische Bibliographie
IOBKA — Izvestiya na Instituta po Obshta i Neorganichna Khimiya. Bulgarska Akademiya naNaukite
IOBLAM — Iowa Bird Life
IOC — Isotopes in Organic Chemistry
IOCC Bull — Interstate Oil Compact Commission. Bulletin
IOCEB7 — Specialist Periodical Reports. Inorganic Chemistry of the Transition Elements
IOC/M — Memorias. Instituto Oswaldo Cruz
IOCTAH — Intergovernmental Oceanographic Commission. Technical Series
Iodine Abstr Rev — Iodine Abstracts and Reviews
IOE — Industry and Development
IOENT — Izvestiia. Otdelenie Eztestvennykh Nauk. Akademiia Nauk Tadzhikskoi SSR
IOFF — Off Road
IOG — International Organization
IOHSA — International Journal of Occupational Health and Safety
IOK — Informationen aus der Orthodoxen Kirche
IOKKA — Izvestiya na Instituta po Organichna Khimiya. Bulgarska Akademiya na Naukite
IOKNA — Izvestiya na Otdelenieto za Khimicheski Nauki. Bulgarska Akademiya na Naukite
IOLRAM — Israel Oceanographic and Limnological Research. Annual Report
I Olympia — Inschriften von Olympia
I on C — Index on Censorship
Ion Channels Vasc Smooth Muscle Cells Endothelial Cells Proc — Ion Channels of Vascular Smooth Muscle Cells and Endothelial Cells. Proceedings. International Society for Heart Research
Ion Exch — Ion Exchange and Membranes
Ion Exch Adsorpt — Ion Exchange and Adsorption
Ion Exch and Membranes — Ion Exchange and Membranes
Ion Exch Membr — Ion Exchange and Membranes
Ion Exch Prog — Ion Exchange Progress
Ion Exch Solvent Extr — Ion Exchange and Solvent Extraction
Ion Exch Symp Proc — Ion-Exchange Symposium. Proceedings
Ion Form Org Solids Proc Int Conf — Ion Formation from Organic Solids. Proceedings. International Conference
Ion Implant Proc Int Conf — Ion Implantation. Proceedings. International Conference on Ion Implantation in Semiconductors
Ion Implant Semicond Other Mater Proc Int Conf — Ion Implantation in Semiconductors and Other Materials. Proceedings. International Conference
Ioniz Phenom Gases Proc Int Conf — Ionization Phenomena in Gases. Proceedings. International Conference
Ioniz Radiat (Tokyo) — Ionizing Radiation (Tokyo)
Ionos Issled — Ionosfernye Issledovaniya
Ionos Res — Ionospheric Researches
Ion Plasma Assisted Tech Int Conf — Ion and Plasma Assisted Techniques. International Conference

Ion-Selective Electrode Rev — Ion-Selective Electrode Reviews
Ion-Sel Electrode Rev — Ion-Selective Electrode Reviews
Ion Sel Electrodes Anal Chem — Ion-Selective Electrodes in Analytical Chemistry
Ion Sel Electrodes Symp — Ion-Selective Electrodes. Symposium
IOONT — Izvestiia. Otdelenie Obshchestvennykh Nauk. Akademiia Nauk Tadzhikskoi SSR
IOP — International Journal of Operations and Production Management
IOPCA — International Ophthalmology Clinics
IOPIA — Itogi Nauki i Tekhniki Obogashchenie Poleznykh Iskopaemykh
IOP Short Meet Ser — IOP (Institute of Physics) Short Meetings Series
IOR — Management Zeitschrift
IORMA3 — Specialist Periodical Reports. Inorganic Reaction Mechanisms
IORMJ — India Office Records. Marine Journal
IOSCR — Institute of Ocean Sciences. Patricia Bay. Contractor Report
IOS Data Report — Institute of Oceanographic Sciences. Data Report
IOSPE — Inscriptiones Antiquae Orae Septentrionalis Ponti Euxini
IOS Report — Institute of Oceanographic Sciences. Report
IOUT — OUT-LOOK
IOVSDA — Investigative Ophthalmology and Visual Science
Iowa — Iowa Reports
Iowa Acad Sci J — Iowa Academy of Science. Journal
Iowa Acad Sci Proc — Iowa Academy of Science. Proceedings
Iowa Ac Sc P — Proceedings of the Iowa Academy of Sciences
Iowa Ac Sc Pr — Iowa Academy of Science. Proceedings
Iowa Acts — Acts and Joint Resolutions of the State of Iowa
Iowa Admin Bull — Iowa Administrative Bulletin
Iowa Admin Code — Iowa Administrative Code
Iowa Agric Exp Sta Res Bull — Iowa Agricultural Experiment Station. Research Bulletin
Iowa Agric Exp Sta Special Rep — Iowa Agricultural Experiment Station. Special Report
Iowa Agric Exp Stn Res Bull — Iowa. Agricultural Experiment Station. Research Bulletin
Iowa Agric Home Econ Exp Stn Res Bull — Iowa. Agriculture and Home Economics Experiment Station. Research Bulletin
Iowa Agric Home Econ Exp Stn Soil Surv Rep — Iowa. Agriculture and Home Economics Experiment Station. Soil Survey Reports
Iowa Agric Home Econ Exp Stn Spec Rep — Iowa. Agriculture and Home Economics Experiment Station. Special Report
Iowa Bur Lab Bien Rep — Iowa Bureau of Labor. Biennial Report
Iowa Code Ann (West) — Iowa Code, Annotated (West)
Iowa Conserv — Iowa Conservationist
Iowa Corn Res Inst Publ Contrib — Iowa Corn Research Institute Publications. Contributions
Iowa Dent Bull — Iowa Dental Bulletin
Iowa Dent J — Iowa Dental Journal
Iowa Drug Inf Serv — Iowa Drug Information Service
Iowa Eng Exp Stn Eng Rep — Iowa Engineering Experiment Station. Engineering Report
Iowa Farm Sci — Iowa Farm Science
Iowa Geol Surv Annu Rep — Iowa Geological Survey. Annual Report
Iowa Geol Survey Water Atlas — Iowa. Geological Survey. Water Atlas
Iowa Geol Survey Water-Supply Bull — Iowa. Geological Survey. Water-Supply Bulletin
Iowa Geol Surv Rep Invest — Iowa. Geological Survey. Report of Investigations
Iowa Geol Surv Tech Pap — Iowa. Geological Survey. Technical Paper
Iowa Geol Surv Water Atlas — Iowa Geological Survey Water Atlas
Iowa Hist Rec — Iowa Historical Record
Iowa Institutions B — Iowa State Institutions. Bulletin
Iowa Jour Hist and Pol — Iowa Journal of History and Politics
Iowa Law R — Iowa Law Review
Iowa LB — Iowa Law Bulletin
Iowa L Bull — Iowa Law Bulletin
Iowa Legis Serv (West) — Iowa Legislative Service (West)
Iowa Lib Q — Iowa Library Quarterly
Iowa L Rev — Iowa Law Review
Iowa Med — Iowa Medicine
Iowa Med J — Iowa Medical Journal
Iowa Nat — Iowa Naturalist
Iowa Orthop J — Iowa Orthopaedic Journal
IowaR — Iowa Review
Iowa SBA — Iowa State Bar Association. Proceedings
Iowa State Coll Agric Mech Arts Eng Exp Stn Bull — Iowa State College of Agriculture and Mechanical Arts. Engineering Experiment Station. Bulletin
Iowa State Coll Agric Mech Arts Eng Exp Stn Eng Rep — Iowa State College of Agriculture and Mechanical Arts. Engineering Experiment Station. Engineering Report
Iowa State Coll Eng Expt Sta Eng Rept Proj — Iowa State College. Engineering Experiment Station. Engineering Report. Project
Iowa State Coll Iowa Eng Exp Stn Eng Rep — Iowa State College. Iowa Engineering Experiment Station. Engineering Report
Iowa State Coll J Sci — Iowa State College. Journal of Science
Iowa State Coll Vet — Iowa State College Veterinarian
Iowa State J Res — Iowa State Journal of Research
Iowa State J Sci — Iowa State Journal of Science
Iowa State Univ (Ames) Eng Res Inst Rep — Iowa State University (Ames). Engineering Research Institute. Report
Iowa State Univ Bull Eng Rep Iowa Eng Exp Stn — Iowa State University Bulletin. Engineering Report. Iowa Engineering Experiment Station
Iowa State Univ Dept Earth Sci Pub — Iowa State University. Department of Earth Sciences. Publication
Iowa State Univ Eng Exp Sta Bull — Iowa State University of Science and Technology. Engineering Experiment Station. Bulletin
Iowa State Univ Eng Res Inst Rep — Iowa State University. Engineering Research Institute. Report

Iowa State Univ Eng Res Inst Tech Rep ISU-ERI-AMES — Iowa State University. Engineering Research Institute. Technical Report ISU-ERI-AMES
Iowa State Univ Press Ser Hist Tech Sci — Iowa State University Press Series in the History of Technology and Science
Iowa State Univ Sci and Technology Eng Expt Sta Bull — Iowa State University of Science and Technology. Engineering Experiment Station. Bulletin
Iowa State Univ Sci Technol Agric Home Econ Exp Stn Res Bull — Iowa State University of Science and Technology. Agriculture and Home Economics Experiment Station. Research Bulletin
Iowa State Univ Sci Technol Eng Exp Stn Bull — Iowa State University of Science and Technology. Engineering Experiment Station. Bulletin
Iowa State Univ Sci Technol Eng Exp Stn Eng Rep — Iowa State University of Science and Technology. Engineering Experiment Station. Engineering Report
Iowa State Univ Stat Lab Annu Rep — Iowa State University. Statistical Laboratory. Annual Report
Iowa State Univ Vet — Iowa State University Veterinarian
Iowa State Water Resour Res Inst Annu Rep — Iowa State Water Resources Research Institute. Annual Report
Iowa St BA News Bull — Iowa State Bar Association. News Bulletin
Iowa St BAQ — Iowa State Bar Association. Quarterly
Iowa St J Sci — Iowa State Journal of Science
Iowa Symp Toxic Mech Proc — Iowa Symposium on Toxic Mechanisms. Proceedings
Iowa Univ Lab N H B — Iowa State University. Laboratories of Natural History. Bulletin
Iowa Univ L Bull — Iowa University. Law Bulletin
IP — Indische Post
IP — Inscriptiones Pyliae ad Mycenaeum Aetatem Pertinentes
IP — Inside Palestine
IP — Instrumenta Patristica
IP — International Post
IP — Inuit Nipingat. Baker Lane. Northwest Territory
IP — Investigacion y Progreso
IP — Israel Philatelist
IP — Istoricheski Pregled
IP — L'Illustration (Paris)
IPA — Institute of Public Affairs. Review
IPA — International Journal of Public Administration
IPA — International Petroleum Annual
IPA — International Pharmaceutical Abstracts
IPA/A — Allpanchis. Instituto de Pastoral Andina
IPAA — Inventario del Patrimonio Arquitectonico Espanol
IPA Bol Tec — IPA [*Instituto Provincial Agropecuario Mendoza, Argentina*] Boletin Tecnico
IPAC — Performing Arts and Entertainment in Canada
IPAC — Performing Arts in Canada
IPAGBA — Investigacion y Progreso Agricola
IPAJ — International Phonetic Association Journal
IPAR — IPA [*Institute of Public Affairs*] Review
IPA Rev — IPA [*Institute of Public Affairs*] Review
IPA Rev — IPA [*International Pharmaceutical Abstracts*] Review
Ipargazd Szle — Ipargazdasagi Szemle
Ipari Energiagazd — Ipari Energiagazdalkodas
IPARL — Index to Periodical Articles Related to Law
Ipar ME — Iparmueveszeti Muzeum es a Hopp Ferenc Keletazssiai Mueveszeti Muzeum Evkoenyve
Iparmuveszeti Muz Ev — Iparmueveszeti Muzeum Evkoenyvei
IPAT — Inventario del Patrimonio Historico-Artistico Espanol
IPA (VIC) R — Institute of Public Affairs (Victoria). Review
IPB Bul Stiint Chem Mater Sci — IPB Buletin Stiintific, Chemistry, and Materials Science
IPBKA — Izvestiya Sektora Platiny i Drugikh Blagorodnykh Metallov Institut Obshchei i Neorganicheskoi Khimii Akademiya Nauk SSSR
IPC — Indian Philosophy and Culture. Quarterly
IPCBA — Bibliographic Series. Institute of Paper Chemistry
IP(Ch) — Israel Philatelist (Chur)
IPCH — Police Chief
IPCM — PC Magazine
IPC Mg — IPC [*Institute of Philippine Culture*] Monographs
IPC Pap — IPC [*Institute of Philippine Culture*] Papers
IPCR Cyclotron Prog Rep — IPCR (Institute of Physical and Chemical Research) Cyclotron Progress Report
IPCTAO — Impact. Agricultural Research in Texas. Annual Report
IPCW — PC Week
IPD — International Journal of Physical Distribution and Materials Management
IPE — Inscriptiones Antiquae Orae Septentrionalis Ponti Euxini
IPE — International Paper Board Industry. Corrugated Manufacture and Conversion
IPE/EE — Estudos Economicos. Universidade de Sao Paulo. Instituto de Pesquisas Economicas
IPEF Inst Pesqui Estud Florest — IPEF. Instituto de Pesquisas e Estudos Florestais
IPEF Inst Pesqui Estud Florestais — IPEF. Instituto de Pesquisas e Estudos Florestais
IPEF Publ Semest — IPEF [*Instituto de Pesquisas e Estudos Florestais*] Publicacao Semestral
IPE Ind Prod Eng — IPE. Industrial and Production Engineering
IPE Int — IPE [*Industrial and Production Engineering*] International
IPE Int Ind Prod Eng — IPE International Industrial and Production Engineering
IPEK — Jahrbuch fuer Praehistorische und Ethnographische Kunst
IPEN — Indian PEN
Ip Energiagazd — Ipari Energiagazdalkodas
IPERAS — Indian Perfumer
I Pergamon — Inschriften von Pergamon
IPESAV — Investigacion Pesquera
I Pest Cntrl — International Pest Control

IPETA — Industrie du Petrole
IPEUB — Industrie du Petrole en Europe. Gaz-Chimie
IPF — Intellectual Property Forum
IPF — Japan Pulp and Paper
IPFABH — Instituto de Pesquisas e Experimentacao Agropecuarias do Norte (IPEAN). Serie Estudos sobre Forrageiras na Amazonia
IPG — International Planning Glossaries
IPGH/RHI — Revista de Historia de las Ideas. Instituto Panamericano de Geografia e Historia
IPHA — American Journal of Physical Anthropology
IPHCSR — International Pacific Halibut Commission. Scientific Report
IPHCTR — International Pacific Halibut Commission. Technical Report
I Philae — Inscriptions Grecques de Philae
IPHJAJ — Israel Pharmaceutical Journal
IPHL — Philadelphia Magazine
IPHS — Industrial Production. Historical Statistics
IPHSA — Institute of Physics. Conference Series
IPHTCGP — Iscrizioni Preeleniche di Hagia Triada in Creta e della Grecia Peninsulare
IPHYA — Indian Phytopathology
IPI — Insurance Periodicals Index
IPIBD3 — IPI [*International Potash Institute*] Bulletin
IPI Bull — IPI [*International Potash Institute*] Bulletin
IPI Res Top — IPI [*International Potash Institute*] Research Topics
IPK — Petroleum Economist
IPL — Iraq Petroleum (London)
IPLL — Illinois Publications in Language and Literature
IPLMAE — Instituut voor de Pluimveeteelt "Het Spelderholt." Mededeling
IPLO Q — IPLO [*Institute of Professional Librarians of Ontario*] Quarterly
IPLRB — Revue. Institut Pasteur de Lyon
IPM — Industrial Products Magazine
IPM — Information Processing and Management
IPMCD — Industrie du Petrole dans le Monde. Gaz-Chimie
IPMPC — International Journal of Powder Metallurgy and Powder Technology
IPMS — Perceptual and Motor Skills
IPN — Indian Phytopathology (New Delhi)
IPNA — Instituto Peruano-Norte Americano
IPNR — Parks and Recreation
IPOE — Poetry
IPOGA — Indian Musician
I Polit Sci — Indian Political Science Review
IPOTA — Izobreteniya Promyshlennye Obraztsy Tovarnye Znaki
IPP Ber — IPP (Max Planck Institut fuer Plasmaphysik) Bericht
IPPF Med Bull — IPPF [*International Planned Parenthood Federation*] Medical Bulletin
IPPF Med Bull (Engl Ed) — IPPF [*International Planned Parenthood Federation*] Medical Bulletin (English Edition)
IPPIC — Instrumentation in the Pulp and Paper Industry
IPP Presseinf — IPP [*Max Planck Institut fuer Plasmaphysik*] Presseinformationen
IPPTA — Indian Pulp and Paper Technical Association. Journal
IPQ — International Petroleum Quarterly
IPQ — International Philosophical Quarterly
IPR — Institute of Pacific Relations
IPR — Intellectual Property Reports
IPR — Internacia Pedagogia Recuo
IPRAA — Indian Practitioner
IPRADB — Intensivmedizinische Praxis
IPRCDH — In Practice
IPRDA — Israeli Annals of Psychiatry
IPRDAH — Israel Annals of Psychiatry and Related Disciplines
IPRE — Premiere
IPREA — Institute of Petroleum. Review
IPRHA — Industrial and Process Heating
I Priene — Inschriften von Priene
IPRSDV — Israel Journal of Psychiatry and Related Sciences
IPS — Institutiones Philosophicae Scholasticae
IPS — Inventors' and Patenting Sourcebook
IPSA — PSA Journal
IPSFCPR — International Pacific Salmon Fisheries Commission. Progress Report
IPSM — Physician and Sportsmedicine
IPSOCS — Institute of Polar Studies (Ohio). Contribution Series
IPSR — Psychological Reports
IPST — American Journal of Psychotherapy
IPSTS — Index of Potters' Stamps on Terra Sigillata
IPSY — Journal of Psychology
IPSYA — Individual Psychologist
I Psychol R — Indian Psychological Review
IPTCB — Collection. Colloques et Seminaires. Institut Francais du Petrole
IPTHA5 — International Congress on Pteridines. Handbook
IPW Ber — IPW [*Institut fuer Internationale Politik und Wirtschaft der Deutschen Demokratischen Republik*] Berichte
IPW Forsch-H — IPW [*Institut fuer Internationale Politik und Wirtschaft der Deutschen Demokratischen Republik*] Forschungshefte
IPW Forschungshefte — IPW (Institut fuer Internationale Politik und Wirtschaft der Deutschen Demokratischen Republik) Forschungshefte
IPWIA — Instrumentation in the Power Industry
IQ — India Quarterly
IQ — International Quarterly of Community Health Education
IQ — Investment Quality Trends
IQ — Islamic Quarterly
IQ — Italian Quarterly
IQAPA — Informacion de Quimica Analitica, Pura, y Aplicada a la Industria
Iqbal R — Iqbal Review
IQCH — International Quarterly of Community Health Education
IQE — Israel Quarterly of Economics

IQLL — Quill
IQND — India Quarterly (New Delhi)
IqR — Iqbal Review
IQRL — Quarterly Review of Literature
IQ Soc Manuf Eng — IQ [*Series*] Society of Manufacturing Engineers
IQT — International Tourism Quarterly
IQY — Inquiry
IR — Iliff Review
IR — Index Romanus
IR — Indian Review
IR — Industrial Relations
IR — Industrial Relations Review and Report
IR — Inlandsch Reglement
IR — Innere Reich
IR — International Relations
IR — International Revue
IR — Iowa Journal of Research in Music Education
IR — Irish Reports
IR — Israelitische Rundschau
IR — Iton Rishmi
IR — Journal of Irrigation and Drainage
IR — South Australian Industrial Reports
IRA — Information Resources Annual
IRA — Inscriptions Romaines d'Algerie
IRA — Internationale Rundschau der Arbeit
IRA — International Review of Administrative Sciences
IRA — Iron Age
IRAA — Railway Age
Ir Ac P — Proceedings of the Royal Irish Academy. Science
Ir Ac T — Transactions of the Royal Irish Academy. Science
Ir Age Int — Iron Age Metalworking International [*Later, Chilton's IAMI Iron Age Metalworking International*]
IRAL — International Review of American Linguistics
IRAL — International Review of Applied Linguistics in Language Teaching
IRAM — Islamic Research Asociation Miscellany
IRAMD — International Review of the Aesthetics and Sociology of Music
Iran — Iran Journal. British Institute of Persian Studies
IRAN — Izvestiia Rossiiskoi Akademii Nauk
Iran Ant — Iranica Antiqua
Iran Antiq — Iranica Antiqua
Ir Ancest — Irish Ancestor
Iran Dep Bot Minist Agric Dev Rural — Iran. Departement de Botanique. Ministere de l'Agriculture et du Developpement Rural
Iran Dkml — Iranische Denkmaeler
Iran Geol Surv Rep — Iran Geological Survey. Report
Iranian J Sci Tech — Iranian Journal of Science and Technology
Iranian R Internat Relations — Iranian Review of International Relations
Iranica Ant — Iranica Antiqua
Iranica Ant Suppl — Iranica Antique. Supplements
Iran J Agric Res — Iranian Journal of Agricultural Research
Iran J Agric Sci — Iranian Journal of Agricultural Sciences
Iran J Brit Inst Persian Stud — Iran. Journal of the British Institute of Persian Studies
Iran J Chem Chem Eng — Iranian Journal of Chemistry and Chemical Engineering
Iran J Med Sci — Iranian Journal of Medical Sciences
Iran J Plant Pathol — Iranian Journal of Plant Pathology
Iran J Polym Sci Technol Engl Ed — Iranian Journal of Polymer Science and Technology (English Edition)
Iran J Polym Sci Technol Persian Ed — Iranian Journal of Polymer Science and Technology (Persian Edition)
Iran J Public Health — Iranian Journal of Public Health
Iran J Sci and Technol — Iranian Journal of Science and Technology
Iran J Sci Technol — Iranian Journal of Science and Technology
Iran Plant Pests Dis Res Inst Dep Bot Publ — Iran Plant Pests and Diseases Research Institute. Department of Botany. Publication
Iran Polym J — Iranian Polymer Journal
Iran R Int Relat — Iranian Review of International Relations
IranS — Iranian Studies
Iran Stud — Iranian Studies
IrAnt — Iranica Antiqua
IRAO — Izvestiia Gosudarstvennoi Rossiiskoi Arkheologicheskoi Kommissii
Iraqi Acad J — Iraqi Academy. Journal
Iraqi Chem Soc J — Iraqi Chemical Society. Journal
Iraqi Dent J — Iraqi Dental Journal
Iraqi Geogr J — Iraqi Geographical Journal
Iraqi J Sci — Iraqi Journal of Science
Iraq Nat Hist Mus Publ — Iraq Natural History Museum. Publication
Iraq Nat Hist Mus Rep — Iraq Natural History Museum. Report
Ir Archaeol Res Forum — Irish Archaeological Research Forum
Ir Arch Bull — Irish Archival Bulletin
IRAS — Iranica Antiqua. Supplements
IRAS — Islamic Research Association Series
IRASM — International Review of the Aesthetics and Sociology of Music
Ira Stud — Iranian Studies
IRAT Bull Agron — IRAT (Institut de Recherches Agronomiques Tropicales et Cultures Vivrieres) Bulletin Agronomique
IRB — International Reformed Bulletin
IRBAA — Bulletin. Institut International du Froid. Annexe
Ir Bibliog Pamph — Irish Bibliographical Pamphlets
Ir Birds — Irish Birds
Ir Bld — Irish Builder
Ir Bld Engineer — Irish Builder and Engineer
Ir Book — Irish Book
Ir Booklore — Irish Booklore
Ir Book Lov — Irish Book Lover

IRC — Steel Times (Redhill)
Ir Cath Hist Comm Proc — Irish Catholic Historical Committee Proceedings
IRC Bull — IRC [Indian Roads Congress] Bulletin
IRCCOPR Semin Rep — IRCCOPR (Inter-Research Council Committee on Pollution Research) Seminar Report
IRCD — International Research Centers Directory
IRCD-A — International Review of Community Development
IRCD Bul — Yeshiva University. Information Retrieval Center on the Disadvantaged. Bulletin
Ir Chem Assoc J — Irish Chemical Association Journal
IRC Highw Res Board Highw Res Bull — IRC [Indian Roads Congress] Highway Research Board. Highway Research Bulletin
Ir Coll Phys Surg J — Journal. Irish Colleges of Physicians and Surgeons
Ir Comm Hist Sci Bull — Irish Committee of Historical Sciences. Bulletin
Ir Comput — Irish Computer
IRCPA — IRE [Institute of Radio Engineers] Transactions on Component Parts
IRCPUBS — Institute for Research in Construction. Publications
IRCS (Int Res Commun Syst) Med Sci — IRCS (International Research Communications System) Medical Science
IRCS Libr Compend — IRCS (International Research Communications System) Library Compendium
IRCS Med Sci — IRCS [International Research Communications System] Medical Science
IRCS Med Sci-Libr Compend — IRCS [International Research Communications System] Medical Science. Library Compendium
IRCTD — IRCS [International Research Communications System] Research on Clinical Pharmacology and Therapeutics
IRCYA — International Review of Cytology
IRDC — Reader's Digest (Canadian English Edition)
Ir Def J — Irish Defence Journal
Ir Dent J — Irish Dental Journal
Ir Dept Agric Fish Fish Leaflet — Ireland. Department of Agriculture and Fisheries. Fishery Leaflet
Ir Dept Agric J — Ireland. Department of Agriculture. Journal
IRDN — Industrial Research and Development News
IRD News — News from International Resource Development, Incorporated
IRE — International Review of Education
IREBI — Indices de Revista de Bibliotecologia
Ir Eccles Gaz — Irish Ecclesiastical Gazette
Ir Eccles Rec — Irish Ecclesiastical Record
IrEccRec — Irish Ecclesiastical Record
Ir Econ Soc Hist — Irish Economic and Social History
IRED — Journal of Reading
IRE Int Conv Rec — IRE [Institute of Radio Engineers] International Convention Record
IRE-ITTD — International Research and Evaluation-Information and Technology Transfer Database
IREL — Australian Industrial Relations Database
Ireland Welcomes — Ireland of the Welcomes
Irel Dep Agric Fish J — Ireland. Department of Agriculture and Fisheries. Journal
Irel Dep Agric J — Ireland. Department of Agriculture. Journal
Irel Dep Fish For Trade Inf Sect Fish Leafl — Ireland. Department of Fisheries and Forestry. Trade and Information Section. Fishery Leaflet
Ireld Yrbk — Ireland Administration. Yearbook and Diary
Irel Geol Surv Bull — Ireland. Geological Survey. Bulletin
Irel Natl Soil Surv Soil Surv Bull — Ireland. National Soil Survey. Soil Survey Bulletin
Iren — Irenikon
IRE Natl Conv Rec — IRE [Institute of Radio Engineers] National Convention Record
Ir Eng — Irish Engineers
IRE Rapp Inst Natl Radioelem Belg — IRE [Institute of Radio Engineers] Rapport. Institut National des Radioelements. Belgium
IrERec — Irish Ecclesiastical Record
IRE Rev — IRE (Institute of Radio Engineers) Revue
IRE Trans Aeronaut Navig Electron — IRE [Institute of Radio Engineers] Transactions on Aeronautical and Navigational Electronics
IRE Trans Aerosp Navig Electron — IRE [Institute of Radio Engineers] Transactions on Aerospace and Navigational Electronics
IRE Trans Antennas Propag — IRE (Institute of Radio Engineers) Transactions on Antennas and Propagation
IRE Trans Audio — IRE [Institute of Radio Engineers] Transactions on Audio
IRE Trans Autom Control — IRE [Institute of Radio Engineers] Transactions on Automatic Control
IRE Trans Bio Med Electron — IRE [Institute of Radio Engineers] Transactions on Bio-Medical Electronics
IRE Trans Broadcast — IRE [Institute of Radio Engineers] Transactions on Broadcasting
IRE Trans Broadcast Telev Receivers — IRE [Institute of Radio Engineers] Transactions on Broadcast and Television Receivers
IRE Trans Broadcast Transm Syst — IRE [Institute of Radio Engineers] Transactions on Broadcast TransmissionSystems
IRE Trans Circuit Theory — IRE [Institute of Radio Engineers] Transactions on Circuit Theory
IRE Trans Commun Syst — IRE [Institute of Radio Engineers] Transactions on Communications Systems
IRE Trans Component Parts — IRE [Institute of Radio Engineers] Transactions on Component Parts
IRE Trans Electron Comput — IRE [Institute of Radio Engineers] Transactions on Electronic Computers
IRE Trans Electron Devices — IRE (Institute of Radio Engineers) Transactions on Electron Devices
IRE Trans Eng Manage — IRE [Institute of Radio Engineers] Transactions on Engineering Management

IRE Trans Hum Factors Electron — IRE (Institute of Radio Engineers) Transactions on Human Factors in Electronics
IRE Trans Ind Electron — IRE [Institute of Radio Engineers] Transactions on Industrial Electronics
IRE Trans Inform Theory — Institute of Radio Engineers. Transactions on Information Theory
IRE Trans Instrum — IRE [Institute of Radio Engineers] Transactions on Instrumentation
IRE Trans Med Electron — IRE [Institute of Radio Engineers] Transactions on Medical Electronics
IRE Trans Microwave Theory Tech — IRE [Institute of Radio Engineers] Transactions on Microwave Theory and Techniques
IRE Trans Mil Electron — IRE [Institute of Radio Engineers] Transactions on Military Electronics
IRE Trans Nucl Sci — IRE [Institute of Radio Engineers] Transactions on Nuclear Science
IRE Trans Prod Eng Prod — IRE (Institute of Radio Engineers) Transactions on Product Engineering and Production
IRE Trans Prod Tech — IRE [Institute of Radio Engineers] Transactions on Production Techniques
IRE Trans Radio Freq Interference — IRE (Institute of Radio Engineers) Transactions on Radio Frequency Interference
IRE Trans Reliab Qual Control — IRE [Institute of Radio Engineers] Transactions on Reliability and Quality Control
IRE Trans Space Electron Telem — IRE (Institute of Radio Engineers) Transactions on Space Electronics and Telemetry
IRE Trans Telem Remote Control — IRE [Institute of Radio Engineers] Transactions on Telemetry and Remote Control
IRE Trans Ultrason Eng — IRE [Institute of Radio Engineers] Transactions on Ultrasonics Engineering
IRE Trans Veh Commun — IRE [Institute of Radio Engineers] Transactions on Vehicular Communications
IRE WESCON Conv Rec — IRE [Institute of Radio Engineers] WESCON Convention Record
IRE West Electron Show Conv Conv Rec — IRE [Institute of Radio Engineers] Western Electronic Show and Convention. Convention Record
IRF — Acta Instituti Romani Finlandiae
Ir Fish Invest Ser A Freshwater — Irish Fisheries Investigations. Series A. Freshwater
Ir Fish Invest Ser B Mar — Irish Fisheries Investigations. Series B. Marine
IRFOA4 — Irish Forestry
Ir Folk Song Soc J — Irish Folk Song Society Journal
Ir For — Irish Forestry
IRG — Inscripciones Romanas de Galicia
IRG — Issues in Bank Regulation
Ir Geneal — Irish Genealogist
Ir Genes Ia Antigens Proc Ir Gene Workshop — Ir Genes and Ia Antigens. Proceedings. Ir Gene Workshop
Ir Geog — Irish Geography
Ir Geogr B — Irish Geographical Bulletin
Ir Georg Soc Qtr Bull — Irish Georgian Society. Quarterly Bulletin
IRGGA — Internationales Archiv fuer Gewerbepathologie und Gewerbehygiene
IRGGAJ — Internationales Archiv fuer Gewerbepathologie und Gewerbehygiene
Ir GI S J — Journal of the Royal Geological Society of Ireland
IrH — Irish Historical Studies
IRHH — Internationale Revue der Gesammten Hydrobiologie und Hydrographie</PHR> %
Ir Hib — Iris Hibernia
Ir Hist St — Irish Historical Studies
Ir Hist Stud — Irish Historical Studies
IRIABC — Indian Agricultural Research Institute [New Delhi]. Annual Report
Ir Int Fibres Fabr J — Irish and International Fibres and Fabrics Journal
IRIS — Instructional Resources Information System
IRISAV — Indian Agricultural Research Institute [New Delhi]. Annual Scientific Report
Irish Agr Creamery Rev — Irish Agricultural and Creamery Review
Irish Agric Mag — Irish Agricultural Magazine
Irish Am Geneal — Irish-American Genealogist
Irish Arch Res For — Irish Archaeological Research Forum
Irish A Rev — Irish Arts Review
Irish A Rev Yb — Irish Arts Review Yearbook
Irish Astr — Irish Astronomical Journal
Irish Astron J — Irish Astronomical Journal
Irish Banking R — Irish Banking Review
Irish Bcasting R — Irish Broadcasting Review
Irish Beekpr — Irish Beekeeper
Irish Bldr — Irish Builder
Irish Bldr & Engin — Irish Builder and Engineer
Irish Bldr & Engineer — Irish Builder and Engineer
Irish Bus — Business and Finance (Ireland)
Irish Cath Mag — Irish Catholic Magazine
Irish Eccles Rec — Irish Ecclesiastical Record
Irish Econ — Irish Economist
Irish Econ Soc Hist — Irish Economic and Social History
Irish Farmers J Weekly Intelligencer — Irish Farmers' Journal and Weekly Intelligencer
Irish Folk M Stud — Irish Folk Music Studies
Irish For — Irish Forestry
Irish Georgian Soc Bull — Irish Georgian Society. Bulletin
Irish Georgian Soc Qly Bull — Irish Georgian Society. Quarterly Bulletin
Irish Georg Soc Bull — Irish Georgian Society Bulletin
Irish Hist — Irish Historical Studies
Irish Hist Stud — Irish Historical Studies
Irish J Agr — Irish Journal of Agricultural Research

Irish J Agric Econ and Rural Sociol — Irish Journal of Agricultural Economics and Rural Sociology

Irish J Agric Res — Irish Journal of Agricultural Research

Irish J Agr Res — Irish Journal of Agricultural Research

Irish J Ed — Irish Journal of Education

Irish J Environ Sci — Irish Journal of Environmental Science

Irish J Food Sci Technol — Irish Journal of Food Science and Technology

Irish J Med — Irish Journal of Medical Science

Irish Jnl Psych Nurs — Irish Journal of Psychiatric Nursing

Irish J Psy — Irish Journal of Psychology

Irish Jur — Irish Jurist

Irish Lib Bul — Irish Library Bulletin

Irish Lit S — Irish Literary Studies

Irish LT — Irish Law Times

Irish Math Soc Bull — Irish Mathematical Society Bulletin

Irish Med J — Irish Medical Journal

Irish Med Times — Irish Medical Times

Irish Mo — Irish Monthly

Irish Num — Irish Numismatics

Irish Q — Irish Quarterly Review

Irish Q Rev — Irish Quarterly Review

Irish S — Irish Sword

Irish Stat — Irish Statistical Bulletin

Irish Statis Bul — Irish Statistical Bulletin

Irish Theol Quart — Irish Theological Quarterly

IrishThQ — Irish Theological Quarterly

Irish U Rev — Irish University Review

Irish Wildfowl Comm Publ — Irish Wildfowl Committee. Publication

IR Izobret Ratsion — IR. Izobretatelstvo i Ratsionalizatorstvo

IRJ — European Rubber Journal

IRJ — Industrial Relations Journal

IRJ — Industrial Relations Law Journal

IRJADJ — Iranian Journal of Agricultural Sciences

Ir J Agric Econ Rural Sociol — Irish Journal of Agricultural Economics and Rural Sociology

Ir J Agric Food Res — Irish Journal of Agricultural and Food Research

Ir J Agric Res — Irish Journal of Agricultural Research

Ir J Agr Res — Irish Journal of Agricultural Research

IRJaSl — Institut Russkogo Jazyka i Slovesnosti pri Akademii Nauk SSSR

Ir J Earth Sci — Irish Journal of Earth Sciences

Ir J Ed — Irish Journal of Education

Ir J Environ Sci — Irish Journal of Environmental Science

Ir J Food Sci Technol — Irish Journal of Food Science and Technology

Ir J Med Sci — Irish Journal of Medical Science

IR Jour — Indian Rulings, Journal Section

IRJPAR — Irish Journal of Psychology

IRJPDU — Irish Journal of Psychotherapy

Ir J Psychol — Irish Journal of Psychology

Ir J Psychol Med — Irish Journal of Psychological Medicine

Ir J Psychother — Irish Journal of Psychotherapy

Ir J Psychother Psychosom Med — Irish Journal of Psychotherapy and Psychosomatic Medicine

IRJSD5 — Iraqi Journal of Science

Ir Jur — Irish Jurist

Ir Jurist — Irish Jurist

Ir Jur NS — Irish Jurist. New Series

Ir Jur R — Irish Jurist Reports

Irkutsk Gos Nauchno Issled Inst Redk Tsvetn Met Nauchn Tr — Irkutskii Gosudarstvennyi Nauchno-Issledovatel'skii Institut Redkikh i Tsvetnykh Metallov. Nauchnye Trudy

Irkutsk Nauchno Issled Inst Epidemiol Mikrobiol Tr — Irkutskii Nauchno-Issledovatel'skii Institut Epidemiologii i Mikrobiologii. Trudy

Irkutsk Nauchno Issled Vet Stn Tr — Irkutskaya Nauchno-Issledovatel'skaya Veterinarnaya Stantsiya. Trudy

Irkutsk Politehn Inst Trudy — Irkutskii Politehniceskii Institut Trudy

IRL — Industrial Relations Law Journal

IRLA — Information Retrieval and Library Automation

Ir Law T — Irish Law Times

IRLCAW — IRCS [*International Research Communications System*] Medical Science. Library Compendium

IRLCD — IRCS [*International Research Communications System*] Medical Science. Library Compendium

IRLI — Italianistica. Revista di Letteratura Italiana

IRLIB — Industrial Relations Legal Information Bulletin

Ir Lib Bull — Irish Library Bulletin

Ir Lit Inquirer — Irish Literary Inquirer

Ir LJ — Irish Law Journal

Ir L T — Irish Law Times

Ir L Times and Solicitors' J — Irish Law Times and Solicitors' Journal. A Weekly Gazette of Legal News and Information

Ir LTJ — Irish Law Times and Solicitors' Journal

Ir LTJ — Irish Law Times Journal

Ir LT Jour — Irish Law Times Journal

Ir LT Journal — Irish Law Times and Solicitors' Journal

Ir LTR — Irish Law Times Reports

Ir LT Rep — Irish Law Times Reports

IRM — Information and Records Management

IRM — Information Management

IRM — International Review of Missions

IrM — Irish Monthly

Ir Mag — Irish Magazine

IRMA J — IRMA [*Indian Refractory Makers Association*] Journal

IRMAS — International Review of Music Aesthetics and Sociology [*Later, International Review of the Aesthetics and Sociology of Music*]

Ir Med J — Irish Medical Journal

IRMLA — IRE [*Institute of Radio Engineers*] Transactions on Military Electronics

IRMMD2 — IRMMH [*Institute for Research into Mental and Multiple Handicap*] Monograph

IRMMH Monogr — IRMMH [*Institute for Research into Mental and Multiple Handicap*] Monograph

IRMNA2 — Institute for Research into Mental Retardation. Monograph

Ir Mon — Irish Monthly

IRMRA Rubber Conf Programme Pap — IRMRA (India Rubber Manufacturers Research Association) Rubber Conference. Programme and Papers

IRMR Study Group — IRMR [*Institute for Research into Mental Retardation*] Study Group

Ir Mthl — Irish Monthly

IRN — Illinois Resource Network

IRN — Inscriptiones Regni Neopolitani

Ir Nat — Irish Naturalist

Ir Nat J — Irish Naturalists' Journal

IRNC — Intellectual Repository for the New Church

IRNGA — Itogi Nauki i Tekhniki Razrabotka Neftyanykh i Gazovykh Mestorozhdenii

IRNJM — Intellectual Repository and New Jerusalem Magazine

IRNRAJ — Iraq Natural History Museum. Report

IRNSA — IRE [*Institute of Radio Engineers*] Transactions on Nuclear Science

Ir Ntlist — Irish Naturalist. A Monthly Journal of General Irish Natural History

Ir Num — Irish Numismatist

Ir Nurse J — Irish Nurses' Journal

Ir Nurs Hosp W — Irish Nursing and Hospital World

Ir Nurs Hosp World — Irish Nursing and Hospital World

Ir Nurs News — Irish Nursing News

Irodal F — Irodalomtorteneti Fuzetek

Irod Szle — Irodalmi Szemle

Ir Offshore Rev — Irish Offshore Review

Iron — Ironwood

Iron Age — Iron Age. Metal Producing Management Edition

Iron Age Emerg Mark Bull — Iron Age Emergency Market Bulletin

Iron Age Metalwork Int — Iron Age Metalworking International [*Later, Chilton's IAMI Iron Age Metalworking International*]

Iron and Steel Eng — Iron and Steel Engineer

Iron and Steel Int — Iron and Steel International

Iron Biochem Med — Iron in Biochemistry and Medicine [*monograph*]

Iron Coal Trades Rev — Iron and Coal Trades Review

Ironmaking Conf Proc — Ironmaking Conference Proceedings

Ironmaking Proc — Ironmaking Proceedings

Ironmaking Proc AIME — Ironmaking Proceedings. Metallurgical Society of AIME. Iron and Steel Division

Iron Metab Its Disord Proc Workshop Conf Hoechst — Iron Metabolism and Its Disorders. Proceedings. Workshop Conference Hoechst

Ironmkg Steelmkg — Ironmaking and Steelmaking

Iron Nutr Interact Plants Proc Int Symp — Iron Nutrition and Interactions in Plants. Proceedings. International Symposium

Iron St — Iron and Steel

Iron Steel — Iron and Steel

Iron Steel Can — Iron and Steel of Canada

Iron Steel Cast Curr Ind Rep — Iron and Steel Castings. Current Industrial Reports

Iron Steel Eng — Iron and Steel Engineer

Iron Steel Ind — Iron and Steel Industry

Iron Steel Ind China — Iron and Steel Industry in China

Iron Steel Inst Carnegie Scholarship Mem — Iron and Steel Institute. Carnegie Scholarship Memoirs

Iron Steel Inst Jpn Spec Rep — Iron and Steel Institute of Japan. Special Report

Iron Steel Inst (London) Bibliogr Ser — Iron and Steel Institute (London). Bibliographical Series

Iron Steel Inst London Carnegie Scholarship Mem — Iron and Steel Institute. London. Carnegie Scholarship Memoirs

Iron Steel Inst London Corros Comm Rep — Iron and Steel Institute. London. Corrosion Committee. Report

Iron Steel Inst (London) Publ — Iron and Steel Institute (London). Publication

Iron Steel Inst (London) Spec Rep — Iron and Steel Institute (London). Special Report

Iron Steel Int — Iron and Steel International

Iron Steelmaker I & SM — Iron & Steelmaker (I & SM)

Iron Steel Rev (Kao hsiung Taiwan) — Iron and Steel Review (Kao-hsiung, Taiwan)

Iron Steel Soc AIME Trans — Iron and Steel Society of AIME. Transactions

Iron Steel Soc Trans — Iron and Steel Society. Transactions

Iron St Int — Iron and Steel International

Iron Trade R — Iron Trade Review

Iron Trade Rev — Iron Trade Review

Iron Tr R — Iron Trade Review

IRPA Eur Congr Radiat Prot — IRPA European Congress on Radiation Protection

IRPHD — International Review of Physiology

IRPL — Index to Religious Periodical Literature

IRPRD — In-Plant Reproductions

IRPS — International Review of Publications in Sociology

IRPSDZ — IRRI [*International Rice Research Institute*] Research

IRPTC — International Register of Potentially Toxic Chemicals

IRPWA — Irrigation and Power

IRQQ — RQ

Ir Qtr Rev — Irish Quarterly Review

IRR — Industrial Relations Research Association. Proceedings

Ir R — Irish Review

IRRA — Industrial Relations Research Association. Proceedings

Irradiat Aliments — Irradiation des Aliments

Irradiat Aliments (Engl Ed) — Irradiation des Aliments (English Edition)

Irr Age — Irrigation Age

Ir Rail Rec Soc J — Irish Railway Record Society Journal

IRRD — International Road Research Documentation

IR Research Repts — IR Research Reports
Irreversible Processes Selforgan Proc Int Conf — Irreversible Processes and Selforganization. Proceedings. International Conference on Irreversible Processes and Selforganization
IRRI — Interagency Rehabilitation Research Information System
Irrig Age — Irrigation Age
Irrig & Power Abstr — Irrigation and Power Abstracts
Irrig Assoc Tech Conf Proc — Irrigation Association. Technical Conference Proceedings
Irrig Drain Pap — Irrigation and Drainage Paper
Irrig Drain Pap (FAO) — Irrigation and Drainage Paper (Food and Agriculture Organization of the United Nations)
Irrig Drain Syst Int J — Irrigation and Drainage Systems. An International Journal
Irrig Eng Maint — Irrigation Engineering and Maintenance
Irrig Farmer — Irrigation Farmer
Irrig Fmr — Irrigation Farmer
Irrig J — Irrigation Journal
Irrig Mexico — Irrigacion en Mexico. Mexico. Comicion Nacional de Irrigacion
Irrig Power — Irrigation and Power
Irrig Power J — Irrigation and Power Journal
Irrig Sci — Irrigation Science
Irrig Ser Kans Geol Surv — Irrigation Series (Kansas Geological Survey)
Irrig Winter Wheat Tech Publ — Irrigated Winter Wheat. Technical Publication
IRRI Res Pap Ser — IRRI [*International Rice Research Institute*] Research Paper Series
IRRI Res Pap Ser Int Rice Res Inst — IRRI Research Paper Series. International Rice Research Institute
IRRI/SD — Studia Diplomatica. Institut Royal des Relations Internationales
IRRP — Review of Radical Political Economics
IRRSA8 — Indian Council of Agricultural Research. Review Series
IRS — Indian Research Series
IRS — Insurance Sales
IrS — Iranian Studies
IRS — Iran Service
IRS Alcohl — Alcohol, Tobacco, and Firearms Summary Statistics. US Internal Revenue Service
IRSCD2 — Irrigation Science
IRSH — International Review of Social History
IRSIA CR Rech — IRSIA. [*Institute pour l'Encouragement de la Recherche Scientifique dans l'Industrie et l'Agriculture*] Comptes Rendus de Recherches
IRSID Inst Rech Sider Fr Rapp — IRSID. Institut de Recherches de la Siderurgie Francaise. Rapport
IRS Kurz-Inf Reihe A — IRS [*Institut fuer Reaktorischerheit der Technischen Ueberwachungs-Vereine*] Kurz-Information. Reihe A
IRS Kurz-Inf Reihe B — IRS [*Institut fuer Reaktorischerheit der Technischen Ueberwachungs-Vereine*] Kurz-Information. Reihe B
IRS Kurz-Inf Reihe C — IRS [*Institut fuer Reaktorischerheit der Technischen Ueberwachungs-Vereine*] Kurz-Information. Reihe C
IRS Kurz-Inf Reihe D — IRS [*Institut fuer Reaktorischerheit der Technischen Ueberwachungs-Vereine*] Kurz-Information. Reihe D
IRSL — International Review of Slavic Linguistics
IRS Mitt — IRS [*Institut fuer Reaktorischerheit der Technischen Ueberwachungs-Vereine*] Mitteilungen
IRSNAW — Koninklijk Belgisch Instituut voor Natuurwetenschappen. Studiedocumenten
IRSPAU — Illinois Rail System Plan. Annual Update
Ir Spel — Irish Speleology
Ir Spelaeol — Irish Spelaeology
IRSS — Infrared Search System
Ir Sword — Irish Sword
IRT — Irish Times
IRTCA4 — Instrumentation Technology
Ir Text J — Irish Textile Journal
Ir Theol Qtr — Irish Theological Quarterly
Ir Times — Irish Times
IRT Nucl J — IR and T Nuclear Journal
IRTO — Real Estate Today
IRTOD9 — IPI [*International Potash Institute*] Research Topics
Ir Today — Ireland Today
Irtoert — Irodalomtoertenet
IrTQ — Irish Theological Quarterly
Ir Univ Rev — Irish University Review
IRV — Istituto Tecnico Statale Commerciale e per Geometri Roberto Valturio
Ir Vet J — Irish Veterinary Journal
Irving View — Irving Trust Company. Economic View from One Wall Street
IRW — Islamic Review (Woking, England)
IRW — Rubber World
Ir Wel — Ireland of the Welcomes
Irwin Strasburger Meml Semin Immunol Proc — Irwin Strasburger Memorial Seminar on Immunology. Proceedings
Ir WLR — Irish Weekly Law Reports
Ir Writing — Irish Writing
IS — Industrial Society
IS — Inland South America [*Edinburgh, New York*]
IS — INSERM [*Institut National de la Sante et de la Recherche Medicale*] Symposia
IS — Insurance Salesman
IS — Inter American Scene
IS — International Socialist
IS — International Studies
IS — Irish Statesman
Is — Isis
IS — Islamic Studies
IS — Italian Studies
IS — Italia Sacra
IS — Italienische Studien

IS — Staatsblad van Indonesie
ISA — Illinois Studies in Anthropology
ISA — Information Science Abstracts
ISA — Institute of Social Anthropology. Publications [*Washington*]
Isaac Newton Inst Ser Lectures — Isaac Newton Institute Series of Lectures
ISAC — Issues and Commentary
ISAFA — Industrial Safety
ISA J — ISA [*Instrument Society of America*] Journal
ISAJA — ISA [*Instrument Society of America*] Journal
ISAL — Inland South America Leaflets [*New York*]
IS & TP — Index to Scientific and Technical Proceedings
ISA Prepr — ISA [*Instrument Society of America*] Conference Preprint
ISA Proc Annu Instrum Autom Conf Exhib — ISA (Instrument Society of America) Proceedings. Annual Instrument-Automation Conference and Exhibit
ISA Proc Int Power Instrum Symp — ISA [*Instrument Society of America*] Proceedings. International Power Instrumentation Symposium
ISA Proc Natl Aerosp Instrum Symp — ISA [*Instrument Society of America*] Proceedings. National Aerospace Instrumentation Symposium
ISA Proc Natl Conf Instrum Iron Steel Ind — ISA (Instrument Society of America) Proceedings. National Conference. Instrumentation for the Iron andd Steel Industry
ISA Proc Natl Power Instrum Symp — ISA [*Instrument Society of America*] Proceedings. National Power Instrumentation Symposium
I Sardegna — Iscrizioni Latine della Sardegna
ISATA — ISA [*Instrument Society of America*] Transactions
ISATA Proc — ISATA [*International Symposium on Autommotive Technology and Automation*] Proceedings
ISATAZ — ISA [*Instrument Society of America*] Transactions
ISA Trans — ISA [*Instrument Society of America*] Transactions
ISAU — Illinois Studies in Anthropology. Urbana
ISB — Independent School Bulletin
ISB — Internationale Spectator
ISB — International Society of Bassists. Newsletter
ISBE — International Standard Bible Encyclopedia
ISBN — International Society of Bassists Newsletter
ISCA — School Arts
ISCA Quart — ISCA [*International Society of Copier Artists*] Quarterly
ISCC — Scholastic Coach
ISCC Newsl — Inter-Society Color Council Newsletter
ISCJ — Southern Communication Journal
ISCL — School Library Journal
ISCP — Iowa Studies in Clasical Philology
ISCT — Science Teacher
ISCV — Supreme Court Review
ISCW — Inventaire Sommaire de la Collection Waddington
ISCW — Science World
ISD Ber — ISD (Institut fuer Statik und Dynamik) -Bericht
ISDO Bul — ISDO [*Industrial Services Centre. Documentation and Publication Branch*] Bulletin
ISE — Ibadan Studies in English
ISE — Information in Science Extension
ISE — International Journal of Social Economics
ISEBD4 — International Series on Biomechanics
ISED — Social Education
ISEGRN — Institute of Social, Economic, and Government Research. University of Alaska. Research Notes
ISEGROP — Institute of Social, Economic, and Government Research. University of Alaska. Occasional Papers
ISEGRR — Institute of Social, Economic, and Government Research. University of Alaska. Report
ISEGRS — Institute of Social, Economic, and Government Research. University of Alaska. Research Summary
ISEPDC — International Series in Experimental Psychology
Isere S Bll — Bulletin de la Societe de Statistique, des Sciences Naturelles, et des Arts Industriels du Departement de l'Isere
ISF — Imagination Science Fiction
ISFAM — Israelitisches Familienblatt
ISFM — San Francisco Magazine
ISFT — Istituto di Studi Filosofici Classici. Sezione di Torino
ISGBBC — Israel. Geological Survey. Bulletin
ISGEA — Issledovaniya po Genetike
Is Geol Univ Milano Pubbl Ser G — Istituto di Geologia. Universita di Milano. Pubblicazione. Serie G
ISGE Trans Geotherm J — ISGE [*International Society for Geothermal Engineering*] Transactions and the Geothermal Journal
ISGE Trans Geotherm World J — ISGE [*International Society for Geothermal Engineering*] Transactions and Geothermal World Journal
I Sh — Independent Shavian
I Shaw — Independent Shavian
ISH Ber — ISH (Institut fuer Strahlenhygiene) Berichte
ISHD — Journal of Speech and Hearing Disorders
ISHGA — Ishikawajima-Harima Giho
Ishikawajima-Harima Eng Rev — Ishikawajima-Harima Engineering Review
Ishikawajima Harima Heavy Ind Co Eng Rev — Ishikawajima-Harima Heavy Industries Company. Engineering Review
ISHM J — ISHM [*International Society for Hybrid Microelectronics*] Journal
ISHM Proc — ISHM [*International Society for Hybrid Microelectronics*] Proceedings
ISHOW — Information System for Hazardous Organics in Water
ISHS — Illinois State Historical Society. Journal
ISHSJ — Illinois State Historical Society. Journal
ISHTCP — Inventory of Sources for History of Twentieth Century Physics
ISIADL — Insect Science and Its Application
ISI Atlas Sci Anim Plant Sci — ISI [*Institute for Scientific Information*] Atlas of Science. Animal and Plant Sciences

ISI Atlas Sci Biochem — ISI [*Institute for Scientific Information*] Atlas of Science. Biochemistry
ISI Atlas Sci Immunol — ISI [*Institute for Scientific Information*] Atlas of Science. Immunology
ISI Atlas Sci Pharmacol — ISI (Institute for Scientific Information) Atlas of Science. Pharmacology
ISI Bull — ISI [*Indian Standards Institution*] Bulletin
ISIDB — Instruments India
ISI/ISTP & B — ISI [*Institute for Scientific Information*] Index to Scientific and Technical Proceedings and Books
ISIJ Int — ISIJ (Iron and Steel Institute of Japan) International
ISIP — Iron and Steel Industry Profiles
ISIS — Integriertes Statistisches Informationssystem
ISJ — Israel Export and Trade Journal
ISJCAT — Israel Journal of Chemistry
ISJM — Israeli Journal of Mathematics
ISJR — Iowa State Journal of Research
ISJRA — Iowa State Journal of Research
ISJRA6 — Iowa State Journal of Research
ISJSA9 — Iowa State Journal of Science
ISJTAC — Israel Journal of Technology
Isk & Rabochiy Kl — Iskusstvo i Rabochiy Klass
Isk Azerbaydzhana — Iskusstvo Azerbaydzhana. Akademiya nauk Azerbaydzhanskoy SSR. Institut Arkhitektury i Iskusstva
ISKHDI — Ishikawa-Ken Nogyo Shikenjo Kenkyu Hokoku
Isk Knigi — Iskusstvo Knigi
Isk Komm — Iskusstvo Kommuny
Isk Krit — Iskusstvo i Kritika
Iskop Rify Metod Ikh Izuch Tr Paleoekol Litol Sess — Iskopaemye Rify i Metodika Ikh Izucheniya. Trudy Paleoekologo-Litologicheskoi Sessii
Isk Tadz Narodna — Iskusstvo Tadzhikskogo Naroda
Iskus K — Iskusstvo Kino
Iskusstv Mater — Iskusstvennye Materialy
Iskusstvo K — Iskusstvo Kino
Iskusstv Sputniki Zemli — Iskusstvennye Sputniki Zemli
Iskusstv Sputniki Zemli Akad Nauk SSSR — Iskusstvennye Sputniki Zemli Akademiya Nauk SSSR
Iskusstv Volokno — Iskusstvennoe Volokno
Isk Zapadnoy Evropy & Vizatii — Isskustvo Zapadnoy Evropy i Vizatii
Isk Zodchikh Uzbekistana — Iskusstvo Zodchikh Uzbekistana
ISL — Industrie Lackier-Betrieb. Zentralblatt fuer Lackiertechnik und Beschichtungstechnik
Isl — Islam
Isl — Islamica
Islam — Der Islam. Zeitschrift fuer Geschichte und Kultur des Islamischen Orients
Islam A — Islamic Art
Islamabad J Sci — Islamabad Journal of Sciences. Journal of Mathematics and Sciences
Islam Archaeol Stud — Islamic Archaeological Studies
Islam Cult — Islamic Culture
Islamic Quart — Islamic Quarterly
Islam Mod Age — Islam and the Modern Age
Islam Rev — Islamic Review
Islam S — Al-Islam. Singapore
Islam Soc S Sahara — Islam et Societes au Sud du Sahara
Islam Stud — Islamic Studies
Islam Tetkikleri Enst Derg — Islam Tetkikleri Enstitusu Dergisi
Islam Z — Islam (Zuerich)
Isl Ans — Islam Ansiklopedisi
Isl Arc — Island Arc
Islas S Clara — Islas (Santa Clara, Cuba)
IslC — Islamic Culture
ISLIC Bull — Israel Society of Special Libraries and Information Centers. Bulletin
ISLIC Int Conf Inf Sci Proc — ISLIC International Conference on Information Science. Proceedings
Is Lit — Islamic Literature
ISLL — Illinois Studies in Language and Literature
Isl Landbunadarrannsoknir — Islenzkar Landbunadarrannsoknir
Islm Wld D — Islamic World Defence
IslQ — Islamic Quarterly
Isl R — Islamic Review
Is LR — Israel Law Review
ISLRBH — Islenzkar Landbunadarrannsoknir
ISLS — Information System Language Studies
Isl S — Islamic Surveys
Isl St — Islamic Studies
ISLV — Stanford Law Review
ISM — Interavia Space Markets
ISM — International Studies of Management and Organization
ISM — Mitteilungen. Internationale Stiftung Mozarteum
ISMCEE — International Series of Monographs on Chemistry
ISMD — Social Science and Medicine
ISMEC Bull — ISMEC [*Information Service in Mechanical Engineering*] Bulletin
Ismert Oesszmuev Gazd Keresk — Ismertetoe Oesszmueveszetben, Gazdasagban es Kereskedesben
ISME Yb — ISME [*International Society for Music Education*] Yearbook
ISMJAV — Israel Medical Journal
ISMTB — Instrumentalist
ISNTAW — Indian Society for Nuclear Techniques in Agriculture and Biology. Newsletter
ISO — Oxford Bulletin of Economics and Statistics
ISOBA — Izotopy v SSSR
ISOKD — Izvestiya Sibirskogo Otdeleniya Geologicheskogo Komiteta
Isokinetics & Ex Sci — Isokinetics and Exercise Science
Isol Clim — Isolation, Climatisation

Isol Purif — Isolation and Purification
Isol Revetements Archit Evol — Isolation. Revetements et Architecture Evolutive
I Solvay Tr — Institut Solvay. Travaux de Laboratoire
ISOOA — Izvestiya Sibirskogo Otdeleniya Akademii Nauk SSSR Seriya Obshchestvennykh Nauk
Isot Environ Health Stud — Isotopes in Environmental and Health Studies
Isot Generator Inf Cent (Gif Sur Yvette) Newsl — Isotopic Generator Information Centre (Gif-Sur-Yvette). Newsletter
Isot Gener Inf Cent Gif sur Yvette News — Isotopic Generator Information Centre. Gif-sur-Yvette. Newsletter
Isot Geosci — Isotope Geoscience
Isot Ind Landwirtsch — Isotope in Industrie und Landwirtschaft
Isot News — Isotope News
Isotopenprax — Isotopenpraxis
Isotopes Radiat — Isotopes Radiation
Isotop Radiat Technol — Isotopes and Radiation Technology
Isot Org Chem — Isotopes in Organic Chemistry
Isot Oxygene — Isotopes de l'Oxygene
Isot Phys Biomed Sci — Isotopes in the Physical and Biomedical Sciences
Isot Radiat — Isotopes and Radiation
Isot Radiat Parasitol — Isotopes and Radiation in Parasitology
Isot Radiat Res — Isotope and Radiation Research
Isot Radiat Res Anim Dis Vec — Isotope and Radiation Research on Animal Diseases and Their Vectors. Proceedings
Isot Radiat Technol — Isotopes and Radiation Technology
Isot Tech — Isotopen Technik
Isozymes Curr Top Biol Med Res — Isozymes. Current Topics in Biological and Medical Research
ISPA — Sports Afield
ISPBA — Buletinul. Institutului de Studii si Projectari Energetice
IS Ph — International Studies in Philosophy
Ispol'z Gaza Nar Khoz — Ispol'zovanie Gaza v Narodnom Khozyaistve
Ispolz Mikroorg Nar Khoz — Ispol'zovanie Mikroorganizmov v Narodnom Khozyaistve
Ispol'z Neorg Resur Okeanicheskoi Vody — Ispol'zovanie Neorganicheskikh Resursov Okeanicheskoi Vody
Ispol'z Tverd Topl Sernistykh Mazutov Gaza — Ispol'zovanie Tverdykh Topliv Sernistykh Mazutov i Gaza
ISPOR — Institute of Polar Studies (Ohio). Reports
ISPP — Indian Studies Past and Present
ISPS — Journal of Social Psychology
ISPY — International Journal of Social Psychiatry
ISQ — Informatie. Maandblad voor Informatieverwerking
ISQ — Information Standards Quarterly
IsQ — Islamic Quarterly
ISR — Index to Scientific Reviews
ISR — Information Processing and Management
ISR — Interdisciplinary Science Reviews
Isr Acad Sci Humanit Proc Sect Sci — Israel Academy of Sciences and Humanities. Proceedings. Section of Sciences
Isr AEC IA Rep — Israel. Atomic Energy Commission. IA Report
Isr AEC LS Rep — Israel. Atomic Energy Commission. LS Report
Israel & Mid E Econ Rev — Israel and Middle East Economic Review
Israel Ann Psychiat — Israel Annals of Psychiatry
Israel Bus — Israel Business
Israel E — Israel Economist
Israel Explor J — Israel Exploration Journal
Israel Explor Journal — Israel Exploration Journal. Jerusalem
Israel Inv — Israel Business and Investors' Report
Israel J Agric Res — Israel Journal of Agricultural Research
Israel J Agr Res — Israel Journal of Agricultural Research
Israel J Bot — Israel Journal of Botany
Israel J Chem — Israel Journal of Chemistry
Israel J Earth Sci — Israel Journal of Earth-Sciences
Israel J Ent — Israel Journal of Entomology
Israel J Math — Israel Journal of Mathematics
Israel J Med Sc — Israel Journal of Medical Sciences
Israel J Tech — Israel Journal of Technology
Israel J Technol — Israel Journal of Technology
Israel J Zool — Israel Journal of Zoology
Israel Law R — Israel Law Review
Israel L Rev — Israel Law Review
Israel Math Conf Proc — Israel Mathematical Conference Proceedings
Israel Mus J — Israel Museum Journal
Israel Mus News — Israel Museum News
Israel Orient Stud — Israel Oriental Studies
Israel Yb on Human Rights — Israel Yearbook on Human Rights
Isr Agric Res Organ Spec Publ — Israel. Agricultural Research Organization. Special Publication
Isr Agric Res Organ Volcani Cent Bet Dagan Spec Publ — Israel. Agricultural Research Organization. Volcani Center. Bet Dagan. Special Publication
Isr Agric Res Organ Volcani Cent Pam — Israel. Agricultural Research Organization. Volcani Center. Pamphlet
Isr Agric Res Organ Volcani Cent Prelim Rep — Israel. Agricultural Research Organization. Volcani Center. Preliminary Report
Isr Agric Res Org Div For Trienn Rep Res — Israel. Agricultural Research Organization. Division of Forestry. Triennial Report of Research
Isr Agric Res Stn Rehovot Rec — Israel Agricultural Research Station. Rehovot. Records
Isr Altern En Rev — Israel Alternative Energy Review
Isr Ann Psy — Israel Annals of Psychiatry and Related Disciplines
Isr Ann Psychiatry — Israel Annals of Psychiatry and Related Disciplines
Isr Ann Psychiatry Relat Discip — Israel Annals of Psychiatry and Related Disciplines
Isr Aquacult Bamidgeh — Israeli Journal of Aquaculture Bamidgeh

Isr Chem — Israeli Chemist
Isr Ecol Soc Sci Conf — Israel Ecological Society. Scientific Conference
IsrEJ — Israel Exploration Journal
I S Revw — International Socialist Review
Isr Ex J — Israel Exploration Journal
Isr Expl J — Israel Exploration Journal
Isr Geol Soc Annu Meet — Israel Geological Society. Annual Meeting
Isr Geol Surv Bull — Israel. Geological Survey. Bulletin
Isr Geol Surv Geol Data Process Unit Rep — Israel. Geological Survey. Geological Data Processing Unit. Report
Isr Geol Surv Rep — Israel. Geological Survey. Report
Isr Hydrol Serv Rep — Israel. Hydrological Service. Report
Isr Inst Agric Eng Sci Act — Israel. Institute of Agricultural Engineering. Scientific Activities
Isr Inst Anim Sci Sci Act — Israel. Institute of Animal Science. Scientific Activities
Isr Inst Field Gard Crops Sci Act — Israel. Institute of Field and Garden Crops. Scientific Activities
Isr Inst Hortic Sci Act — Israel. Institute of Horticulture. Scientific Activities
Isr Inst Plant Prot Sci Act — Israel. Institute of Plant Protection. Scientific Activities
Isr Inst Soils Water Sci Act — Israel. Institute of Soils and Water. Scientific Activities
Isr Inst Technol Storage Agric Prod Sci Act — Israel. Institute for Technology and Storage of Agricultural Products. Scientific Activities
ISR Interdisciplinary Systems Res — ISR Interdisciplinary Systems Research
ISR Interdiscip Sci Rev — ISR. Interdisciplinary Science Reviews
Isr J Agric Res — Israel Journal of Agricultural Research
Isr J Bot — Israel Journal of Botany
Isr J Chem — Israel Journal of Chemistry
Isr J Dent Med — Israel Journal of Dental Medicine
Isr J Earth — Israel Journal of Earth-Sciences
Isr J Earth-Sci — Israel Journal of Earth-Sciences
Isr J Entomol — Israel Journal of Entomology
Isr J Exp Med — Israel Journal of Experimental Medicine
Isr J Math — Israel Journal of Mathematics
Isr J Med S — Israel Journal of Medical Sciences
Isr J Med Sci — Israel Journal of Medical Sciences
Isr J Plant Sci — Israel Journal of Plant Sciences
Isr J Psychiatr Relat Sci — Israel Journal of Psychiatry and Related Sciences
Isr J Psychiatry Relat Sci — Israel Journal of Psychiatry and Related Sciences
Isr J Tech — Israel Journal of Technology
Isr J Technol — Israel Journal of Technology
Isr J Vet Med — Israel Journal of Veterinary Medicine
Isr J Zool — Israel Journal of Zoology
Isr Law Rev — Israel Law Review
IsrLLetters — Israel Life and Letters
Isr Med Assoc J — Israel Medical Association Journal
Isr Med J — Israel Medical Journal
Isr Min Agr Water Comm Hydrol Serv Hydrol Paper — Israel. Ministry of Agriculture. Water Commission. Hydrological Service. Hydrological Paper
Isr Minhal Ha Mechkar Ha Chaklai Merkaz Volkani Bul — Israel. Mlnhal Ha-Mechkar Ha-Chaklai. Merkaz Volkani. Buletin
Isr Mschr — Israelitische Monatsschrift
Isr Mus N — Israel Museum News
Isr Natl Counc Res Dev Rep — Israel. National Council for Research and Development. Report
Isr Natl Counc Res Dev Rep NCRD — Israel. National Council for Research and Development. Report NCRD
Isr Nucl Soc Trans Annu Meet — Israel Nuclear Society. Transactions. Annual Meeting
Isr Num J — Israel Numismatic Journal
ISRO — Socialist Review
Isr Oceanogr Limnol Res Annu Rep — Israel Oceanographic and Limnological Research. Annual Report
Isr Orient Stud — Israel Oriental Studies
Isr Pat Doc — Israel. Patent Document
Isr Pat Off Pat Des J — Israel. Patent Office. Patents and Designs Journal
Isr Pharm J — Israel Pharmaceutical Journal
Isr Phys Soc Ann — Israel Physical Society. Annals
Isr Rd — Israelitische Rundschau
ISRRT Newsl — ISRRT [*International Society of Radiographers and Radiological Technicians*] Newsletter
Isr Sci Technol Dig — Israel Science and Technology Digest
Isr Sec Rev — Israel Securities Review
Isr Soc Spec Libr Inf Cent Bull — Israel Society of Special Libraries and Information Centers. Bulletin
Isr Soc Spec Libr Inf Cent Int Conf Inf Sci Proc — Israel Society of Special Libraries and Information Centres. International Conference on Information Science. Proceedings
Isr State Rec Pat Des J — Israel State Records. Patents and Designs Journal
Isr Symp Desalin — Israel Symposium on Desalination
ISRTAI — Isotopes and Radiation Technology
Isr Tax Law Let — Israel Tax Law Letter
ISS — Indiana Slavic Studies
ISS — Ismaili Society Series
IsS — Istorya SSSR
ISS — NTIAC [*Nondestructive Testing Information Analysis Center*] Information Support System
ISSB — International Social Science Bulletin
ISSCT (Int Soc Sugarcane Technol) Entomol Newsl — ISSCT (International Society of Sugarcane Technologists) Entomology Newsletter
ISSF — Izvestija na Seminara po Slavjanska Filologija
ISSJ — International Social Science Journal
Issled Betonu Zhelezobetonu — Issledovaniya po Betonu i Zhelezobetonu
Issled Bionike — Issledovaniya po Bionike
Issled Dalnevost Morei SSSR — Issledovaniya Dal'nevostochnykh Morei SSSR

Issled Din Protsessov Verkhn Atmos — Issledovanie Dinamicheskikh Protsessov v Verkhnei Atmosfere
Issled Ekosist Balt Morya — Issledovanie Ekosistemy Baltiiskogo Morya. Sovetsko-Shvedskaya Kompleksnaya Ekspeditsiya v Baltiiskom More
Issled Elektrokhim Magnetokhim Elektrokhim Metodam Anal — Issledovaniya po Elektrokhimii Magnetokhimii i Elektrokhimicheskim Metodam Analiza
Issled Fauny Morei — Issledovaniya Fauny Morei
Issled Fiz Atmos Akad Nauk Est SSR — Issledovaniya po Fizike Atmosfery Akademiya Nauk Estonskoi SSR
Issled Fiz Kipeniya — Issledovaniya po Fizike Kipeniya
Issled Genet — Issledovaniya po Genetike
Issled Geomagn Aeron Fiz Solntsa — Issledovaniya po Geomagnetizmii, Aeronomii, i Fizike Solntsa
Issled Ispolz Soln Energ — Issledovaniya po Ispol'zovaniyu Solnechnoi Energii
Issled Khim Pererab Rud — Issledovaniya po Khimicheskoi Pererabotke Rud
Issled Konstr Primen Plastmass — Issledovanie Konstruktsii s Primeneniem Plastmass
Issled Kosm Prostranstva — Issledovanie Kosmicheskogo Prostranstva
Issled Kvantovoi Teor Sist Mnogikh Chastits — Issledovaniya po Kvantovoi Teorii Sistem Mnogikh Chastits
Issled Mekh Stroit Mater Konstr — Issledovaniya po Mekhanike Stroitel'nykh Materialov i Konstruktsii
Issled Melior Fiz Pochv Mold — Issledovaniya po Melioratsii i Fizike Pochv Moldavii
Issled Mikrobiol — Issledovaniya po Mikrobiologii
Issled Nekotoryh Voprosov Mat Kibernet — Issledovanija Nekotoryh Voprosov Matematiceskoi Kibernetiki
Issled Obl Fiz Khim Kauch Rezin — Issledovaniya v Oblasti Fiziki i Khimii Kauchukov i Rezin
Issled Obl Fiz Khim Rezin — Issledovaniya v Oblasti Fiziki i Khimii Rezin
Issled Obl Fiz Khim Tverd Tela — Issledovaniya v Oblasti Fiziki i Khimii Tverdogo Tela
Issled Obl Fiz Tverd Tela — Issledovaniya v Oblasti Fiziki Tverdogo Tela
Issled Obl Genezisa Pochv — Issledovaniya v Oblasti Genezisa Pochv
Issled Obl Khim Drev Tezisy Dokl Konf Molodykh Uch — Issledovaniya v Oblasti Khimii Drevesiny. Tezisy Dokladov. Konferentsiya Molodykh Uchenykh
Issled Obl Khim Fiz Metodov Anal Miner Syrya — Issledovaniya v Oblasti Khimicheskikh i Fizicheskikh Metodov Analiza Mineral'nogo Syr'ya
Issled Obl Khim Istochnikov Toka — Issledovaniya v Oblasti Khimicheskikh Istochnikov Toka
Issled Obl Khim Khim Tekhnol Drev — Issledovaniya v Oblasti Khimii i Khimicheskoi Tekhnologii Drevesiny
Issled Obl Khim Redkozem Elem — Issledovaniya v Oblasti Khimii Redkozemel'nykh Elementov
Issled Obl Khim Silik Okislov — Issledovaniya v Oblasti Khimii Silikatov i Okislov
Issled Obl Khim Tekhnol Prod Pererab Goryuch Iskop — Issledovaniya v Oblasti Khimii i Tekhnologii Produktov Pererabotki Goryuchikh Iskopaemykh
Issled Obl Kinet Model Optim Khim Protsessov — Issledovaniya v Oblasti Kinetiki Modelirovaniya i Optimizatsii Khimicheskikh Protsessov
Issled Obl Kompleksn Ispol'z Topl — Issledovaniya v Oblasti Kompleksnogo Ispol'zovaniya Topliv
Issled Obl Neorg Fiz Khim — Issledovaniya v Oblasti Neorganicheskoi i Fizicheskoi Khimii
Issled Obl Plast Obrab Met Davleniem — Issledovaniya v Oblasti Plastichnosti i Obrabotki Metallov Davleniem
Issled Obl Sint Katal Org Soedin — Issledovaniya v Oblasti Sinteza i Kataliza Organicheskikh Soedinenii
Issled Obl Tekhnol Miner Udobr — Issledovaniya v Oblasti Tekhnologii Mineral'nykh Udobrenii
Issled Obl Tekh Tekhnol Lakokras Pokrytii — Issledovaniya v Oblasti Tekhniki i Tekhnologii Lakokrasochnykh Pokrytii
Issled Operacii i Statist — Issledovanie Operacii i Statisticeskoe Modelirovanie
Issled Optim Protsessov Tekst Tekhnol — Issledovanie i Optimizatsiya Protsessov Tekstil'noi Tekhnologii
Issledovaniya Istor Arkhit — Issledovaniya po Istorii Arkhitektury
Issled Plazmennykh Sgustkov — Issledovanie Plazmennykh Sgustkov
Issled Prikl Mat — Kazanskii Universitet Issledovanija po Prikladnoi Matematike
Issled Protsessov Obrab Met Davleniem — Issledovanie Protsessov Obrabotki Metallov Davleniem
Issled Sist — Issledovanie Sistem
Issled Solntsa Krasnykh Zvezd — Issledovanie Solntsa i Krasnykh Zvezd
Issled Splavov Tsvetn Met — Issledovanie Splavov Tsvetnykh Metallov
Issled Stroit — Issledovaniya po Stroitel'stvu
Issled Stroit Tekhnol Dolgovechnost Avtoklavn Betonov — Issledovaniya po Stroitel'stvu. Tekhnologiya i DolgovechnostAvtoklavnykh Betonov
Issled Strukt Sostoyaniya Neorg Veshchestv — Issledovaniya Strukturnogo Sostoyaniya Neorganicheskikh Veshchestv
Issled Tekhnol Rybn Prod — Issledovaniya po Tekhnologii Rybnykh Produktov
Issled Tekhnol Stroit Mater — Issledovaniia po Tekhnologii Stroitel'nykh Materialov
Issled Teor Plastin i Obolochek — Kazanskii Universitet Issledovaniya po Teorii Plastin i Obolochek
Issled Teor Plastin Obolochek — Issledovaniya po Teorii Plastin i Obolochek
Issled Tsentr Am Morei — Issledovaniya Tsentral'no-Amerikanskikh Morei
Issled Uprugosti Plast — Issledovaniya po Uprugosti i Plastichnosti
Issled Uprug Plast — Issledovaniya po Uprugosti i Plastichnosti
Issled Vodopodgot — Issledovaniya po Vodopodgotovke
Issled Vyazhushchikh Veshchestv Izdelii Ikh Osn — Issledovaniya Vyazhushchikh Veshchestv i Izdelii na Ikh Osnove
Issled Zashch Met Korroz Khim Prom — Issledovaniya po Zashchite Metallov ot Korrozii v KhimicheskoiPromyshlennosti
Issled Zemli Kosmosa — Issledovanie Zemli iz Kosmosa
Issled Zharoprochn Splavam — Issledovaniya po Zharoprochnym Splavam
Issled Zharoproch Splavam — Issledovaniya po Zharoprochnym Splavam
Issl Kafedra Bot — Issledovatel'skaja Kafedra Botaniki. Cabinet Botanique
ISSM — Ismaili Society Series. Monographs and Collections of Articles

ISSM — School Science and Mathematics
ISSOA8 — Impact of Science on Society
Iss Stud — Issues and Studies
ISST — Ismaili Society Series. Texts and Translations
Issue Briefing Pap USDA Off Gov Pub Aff — Issue Briefing Paper. United States Department of Agriculture. Office of Governmental and Public Affairs
Issues — Issues in Writing
Issues Account Educ — Issues in Accounting Education
Issues Anc Philos — Issues in Ancient Philosophy
Issues and Stud — Issues and Studies
Issues Bank Regul — Issues in Bank Regulation
Issues Bul — Issues Bulletin
Issues Compr Pediatr Nurs — Issues in Comprehensive Pediatric Nursing
Issues Crim — Issues in Criminology
Issues Eng — Issues in Engineering
Issues Engng J Prof Activities Proc ASCE — Issues in Engineering. Journal of Professional Activities. Proceedings of the American Society of Civil Engineers
Issues Environ Sci Technol — Issues in Environmental Science and Technology
Issues Health Care Women — Issues in Health Care of Women
Issues Hlth Care Tech — Issues in Health Care Technology
Issues Law Med — Issues in Law and Medicine
Issues Ment Health Nurs — Issues in Mental Health Nursing
Issues Policy Summ — Issues and Policy Summaries
Issues Rev Teratol — Issues and Reviews in Teratology
Issues Sci Technol — Issues in Science and Technology
Issues Stud — Issues and Studies
Issues Stud Natl Res Counc (US) — Issues and Studies. National Research Council (United States)
ISt — Insemnari Stiintifice
Ist — Israelite
Ist — Istina
ISt — Italian Studies
Ist Agron Esper Ric — Istituto di Agronomia e Coltivazioni Erbacee. Esperienzi e Ricerche. Universitadi Pisa
Istamb A Muez Yil — Istanbul Arkeolji Muezeleri Yiligi
Istanb Forsch — Istanbuler Forschungen
Istanbul Ark Muz Yilligi — Istanbul Arkeologi Muzeleri Yilligi
Istanbul Contrib Clin Sci — Istanbul Contribution to Clinical Science
Istanbuler Beitr Klin Wiss — Istanbuler Beitrage zur Klinischen Wissenschaft
Istanbuler Mitt — Istanbuler Mitteilungen. Deutsches Archaeologisches Institut
Istanbul Goz Klin Bul — Istanbul Goz Klinigi Bulteni
Istanbul Med Fac Med Bull Istanbul Univ — Istanbul Medical Faculty. Medical Bulletin. Istanbul University
Istanbul Mitt — Istanbuler Mitteilungen
Istanbul Tek Univ Bul — Istanbul Teknik Universitesi Bulteni
Istanbul Tek Univ Derg — Istanbul Teknik Universitesi Dergisi
Istanbul Tek Univ Nukl Enerji Enst Bul — Istanbul Teknik Universitesi Nukleer Enerji Enstitusu. Bulten
Istanbul Tip Fak Mecm — Istanbul Tip Fakultesi Mecmuasi
Istanbul U Hukuk Fak Mecmuasi — Istanbul Universitesi. Hukuk Fakultesi Mecmuasi
Istanbul U Iktisat Fak Mecmuasi — Istanbul Universitesi. Iktisat Fakultesi Mecmuasi
Istanbul Univ Dishekim Fak Derg — Istanbul Universitesi Dishekimligi Fakultesi Dergisi
Istanbul Univ Eczacilik Fak Mecm — Istanbul Universitesi Eczacilik Fakultesi Mecmuasi
Istanbul Univ Edebiyat Fak Turk ve Edebiyat Dergisi — Istanbul Universitesi Edebiyat Fakultesi Turk ve Edebiyat Dergisi
Istanbul Univ Fen Fak Hidrobiol Arastirma Enst Yayin — Istanbul Universitesi Fen Fakultesi Hidrobiologi Arastirma Enstitusu Yayinlari
Istanbul Univ Fen Fak Mat Derg — Istanbul Universitesi. Fen Fakultesi. Matematik Dergisi
Istanbul Univ Fen Fak Mecm — Istanbul Universitesi Fen Fakultesi Mecmuasi
Istanbul Univ Fen Fak Mecm Ser A — Istanbul Universitesi Fen Fakultesi Mecmuasi. Seri A
Istanbul Univ Fen Fak Mecm Ser B — Istanbul Universitesi Fen Fakultesi Mecmuasi. Seri B. Tabii Ilimler
Istanbul Univ Fen Fak Mecm Ser C — Istanbul Universitesi Fen Fakultesi Mecmuasi. Seri C. Astronomi-Fizik-Kimya
Istanbul Univ Fen Fak Mecm Seri B Tabii Ilimler — Istanbul Universitesi Fen Fakultesi Mecmuasi. Seri B. Tabii Ilimler
Istanbul Univ Med Bull — Istanbul University. Medical Bulletin
Istanbul Univ Med Fac Med Bull — Istanbul University. Medical Faculty. Medical Bulletin
Istanbul Univ Obs Yazilari — Istanbul Universitesi Observatuari Yazilari
Istanbul Univ Orman Fak Derg Seri A — Istanbul Universitesi Orman Fakultesi Dergisi. Seri A
Istanbul Univ Rev Geog Inst Internat Ed — Istanbul University. Review of the Geographical Institute. International Edition
Istanbul Univ Tip Fak Mecm — Istanbul Universitesi Tip Fakultesi Mecmuasi
Istanbul Univ Vet Fak Derg — Istanbul Universitesi Veteriner Fakultesi Dergisi
Istanbul Univ Vet Fak Derg J Fac Vet Med Univ Istanbul — Istanbul Universitesi Veteriner Fakultesi Dergisi/Journal of the Faculty of Veterinary Medicine. University of Istanbul
Istanbul Univ Yay (Orm Fak) — Istanbul Universitesi Yaymlam (Orman Fakultesi)
Istanb Univ fen Fak Mecm — Istanbul Universitesi fen Fakueltesi Mecmuasi
Istanb Univ Orman Fak Derg — Istanbul Universitesi Orman Fakultesi Dergisi
Ist Ark Etnog Sred Azii — Istoriia, Arkheologiia, i Etnografiia Srednei Azii
Ist Autom Univ Roma Not — Istituto di Automatica. Universita di Roma Notiziario
Ist Bologna R Ac Sc Cl Sc Fis Mem — Istituto de Bologna. Reale Accademia delle Scienze. Classe di Scienze Fisiche. Memorie
Ist Bot Palermo Lav — Istituto Botanico di Palermo. Lavori
Ist Bot Univ Lab Crittogam (Pavia) Atti — Istituto Botanico dell' Universita. Laboratorio Crittogamico (Pavia). Atti

ISTC — Incunable Short Title Catalogue
Ist Carlo Erba Ric Ter Racc Pubbl Chim Biol Med — Istituto Carlo Erba per Ricerche Terapeutiche. Raccolta diPublicazioni Chimiche, Biologiche, e Mediche
Ist Cas — Istoriski Casopis
Ist Cent Patol Libro Alfonso Gallo Boll — Istituto Centrale per la Patologia del Libro Alfonso Gallo. Bollettino
Ist Chim Agrar Sper Gorizia Nuovi Anna Pubbl — Istituto Chimico Agrario Sperimentale di Gorizia. Nuovi Annali.Pubblicazione
Ist Chim Agrar Sper Gorizia Nuovi Ann Pubbl — Istituto Chimico Agrario Sperimentale di Gorizia. Nuovi Annali. Pubblicazione
Ist Col Ital Mem E Mon Ser Pol — Istituto Coloniale Italiano. Memorie e Monografie. Serie Politica
Ist Dzerela Vykorystannja — Istorycni Dzerela ta ich Vykorystannja
ISTEC J — ISTEC (International Superconductivity Technology Center) Journal
Ist Elem Archit & Rilievo Mnmt Quad [Genova] — Istituto di Elementi di Architettura e Rilievo dei Monumenti. Quaderno [Genova]
Ist Elem Archit & Rilievo Mnmt Quad [Palermo] — Istituto di Elementi di Architettura e Rilievo dei Monumenti. Quaderno [Palermo]
ISTFA Proc Int Symp Test Failure Anal — ISTFA (International Symposium for Testing and Failure Analysis) Proceedings. International Symposium for Testing and Failure Analysis
Ist Fed Ric For Mem — Istituto Federale di Ricerche Forestali. Memorie
Ist-Filol Z — Istoriko-Filologiceskij Zurnal
Ist Filol Zh — Istoriko-Filologicheskii Zhurnal
Ist Fil Zhur A N Armian — Istoriko-Filologicheskii Zhurnal. Akademia Nauk Armianskoi
Ist Fis Tec Impianti Termotec Univ Genova Relaz FTR — Istituto di Fisica Tecnica e Impianti Termotecnici dell'Universita di Genova. Relazione FTR
Ist Forsch — Istanbuler Forschungen
IstG — Istorijski Glasnik
Ist Geof (Trieste) Pubbl — Istituto Geofisico (Trieste). Pubblicazione
Ist Geol Paleontol Geogr Fis Univ Milano Pubbl Ser G — Istituto di Geologia, Paleontologia, e Geografia Fisica. Universitadi Milano. Pubblicazione. Serie G
Ist Geol Univ Milano Pubbl Ser G — Istituto di Geologia. Universita di Milano. Pubblicazione. Serie G
Ist GI — Istoriski Glasnik
Ist Incoraggiamento Napoli Atti — Istituto d'Incoraggiamento di Napoli. Atti
Ist Ital D Attuari Gior — Istituto Italiano degli Attuari. Giornale
Ist Ital Idrobiol Dott Marco de Marchi Mem — Istituto Italiano di Idrobiologia Dottore Marco de Marchi. Memorie
Ist Ital Lat Am Pubbl — Istituto Italo-Latino Americano. Pubblicazione
Ist It Lat Am Not — Istituto Italo-Latino Americano. Noticiero
Istit Lombardo Accad Sci Lett Rend A — Istituto Lombardo. Accademia di Scienze e Lettere. Rendiconti. A. Scienze Matematiche, Fisiche, Chimiche, e Geologiche
Ist It Medio & Estrem Orient Rep & Mem — Istituto Italiano per il Medio ed Estremo Oriente. Rapporti e Memorie
Istit Ric Base Ser Monogr Adv Math — Istituto per la Ricerca di Base. Series of Monographs in Advanced Mathematics
Istit Veneto Sci Lett Arti Atti Cl Sci Mat Natur — Istituto Veneto di Scienze, Lettere, ed Arti. Venezia. Atti. Classe di Scienze Matematiche e Naturali
Ist Lomb Accad Sci Lett Rend A Sci Mat Fis Chim Geol — Istituto Lombardo. Accademia di Scienze e Lettere. Rendiconti. A. Scienze Matematiche, Fisiche, Chimiche, e Geologiche
Ist Lomb Accad Sci Lett Rend B — Istituto Lombardo. Accademia di Scienze e Lettere. Rendiconti. B.Scienze Biologiche e Mediche
Ist Lomb Accad Sci Lett Rend Parte Gen Atti Uffic — Istituto Lombardo. Accademia di Scienze e Lettere. Rendiconti. ParteGenerale e Atti Ufficiali
Ist Lombardo Accad Sci e Lettere Rend — Istituto Lombardo. Accademia di Scienze e Lettere. Rendiconti
Ist Lombardo Accad Sci Lett Rend A — Istituto Lombardo. Accademia di Scienze e Lettere. Rendiconti. Scienze Matematiche, Fisiche, Chimiche, e Geologiche. A
Ist Lombardo Accad Sci Lett Rend Sci Biol Med B — Istituto Lombardo. Accademia di Scienze e Lettere. Rendiconti. Scienze Biologiche e Mediche. B
Ist Lombard Sci & Lett Rendi — Istituto Lombardo di Scienze e Lettere. Rendiconti
Ist Mat Kul't Uzbek — Istoriia Material-noj Kul'tury Uzbekistana
Ist Mit — Istanbuler Mitteilungen
Ist Mitt — Istanbuler Mitteilungen
Ist Mitt — Istanbuler Mitteilungen. Deutsches Archaeologisches Institut
Ist Mitt — Mitteilungen. Deutsches Archaeologische Institut. Abteilung Istanbul
Ist Mitt Bh — Istanbuler Mitteilungen. Beiheft
Ist Naz Genet Cerealicolt Nazareno Strampelli — Istituto Nazionale di Genetica per la Cerealicoltura Nazareno Strampelli
Istochniki Rudn Veshchestva Endog Mestorozhd — Istochniki Rudnogo Veshchestva Endogonnykh Mestorozhdenii
Istor Astron Issled — Isotriko-Astronomicheskie Issledovaniia
Istor-Astronom Issled — Istoriko-Astronomiceskie Issledovanija
Istor Estestvoznan Tehn Armen — Akademija Nauk Armjanskoi SSR. Istorija Estest'voznanija i Tehniki v Armenii
Istor Filol Zhurnal Akad Nauk Arm SSR — Istoriko-Filologicheskiy Zhurnal Akademii Nauk Arm SSR
Istoria Artei — Studii si Cercetari de Istoria Artei
Istor-Mat Issled — Istoriko-Matematiceskie Issledovanija
Istor Mat Kult Uzbekistana — Istoriya Material'noy Kul'tury Uzbekistana
Istor Metodol Estestv Nauk — Istoriya i Metodologiya Estestvennykh Nauk
Istor SSSR — Istorija SSSR
IstP — Istoricheski Prehled
Ist Patologia Libro Boll — Istituto di Patologia del Libro. Bollettino
Ist Pr — Istoriceski Pregled
Ist Preg — Istoricheski Pregled
Ist Prog Archit [Genova] Quad — Istituto di Progettazione d'Architettura [Genova]. Quaderno
Ist Ric Acque Quad — Istituto di Ricerca sulle Acque. Quaderni
Ist Ric Acque Rapp Tec — Istituto di Ricerca sulle Acque. Rapporti Tecnici

Ist Sanita Pubblica Rend — Istituto di Sanita Pubblica. Rendiconti
Ist Sb Inst Ist Arheol Etnogr — Istoriceskij Sbornik Instituta Istorii, Arheologii, i Etnografii
Ist Schr — Istanbuler Schriften
Ist Sper Cerealic Ann — Istituto Sperimentale per la Cerealicoltura. Annali
Ist Sper Met Leggeri Mem Rapp — Istituto Sperimentale dei Metalli Leggeri. Memorie e Rapport
Ist Sper Nutr Piante Ann — Istituto Sperimentale per la Nutrizione delle Piante. Annali
Ist Sper Olivic Ann Numero Spec — Istituto Sperimentale per l'Olivicoltura. Annali. Numero Speciale
Ist Sper Tab Ann — Istituto Sperimentale per il Tabacco. Annali
Ist Sper Talassogr (Trieste) Pubbl — Istituto Sperimentale Talassografico (Trieste). Pubblicazione
Ist Sper Valorizzazione Tecnol Prod Agric (Milano) Ann — Istituto Sperimentale per la Valorizzazione Tecnologica dei ProdottiAgricoli (Milano). Annali
Ist Sper Vitic (Conegliano Italy) Ann — Istituto Sperimentale per la Viticoltura (Conegliano, Italy). Annali
Ist Sper Zootec Ann — Istituto Sperimentale per la Zootecnia. Annali
Ist SSSR — Istorija SSSR
Ist Super Sanita Lab Fis Lect ISS L (Rome) — Istituto Superiore di Sanita. Laboratori di Fisica. Lectures ISS L(Rome)
Ist Super Sanita Lab Fis Prepr ISS P (Rome) — Istituto Superiore di Sanita. Laboratori di Fisica. Preprints ISS P(Rome)
Ist Super Sanita Lab Fis Rapp — Istituto Superiore di Sanita. Laboritori di Fisica. Rapporti
Ist Super Sanita Lab Fis Rep Rev ISS R (Rome) — Istituto Superiore di Sanita. Laboratori di Fisica. Reports and ReviewsISS R (Rome)
Ist Super Sanita Lab Fis Tech Notes ISS T (Rome) — Istituto Superiore di Sanita. Laboratori di Fisica. Technical Notes ISST (Rome)
Ist Super Sanita Lab Radiaz Prepr ISS P (Rome) — Istituto Superiore di Sanita. Laboratorio delle Radiazioni. Preprints.ISS P (Rome)
Ist Super Sanita Lab Radiaz Rep Rev ISS R (Rome) — Istituto Superiore di Sanita. Laboratorio delle Radiazioni. Reports andReviews ISS R (Rome)
Ist Super Sanita Lab Radiaz Tech Notes ISS T (Rome) — Istituto Superiore di Sanita. Laboratorio delle Radiazioni. TechnicalNotes ISS T (Rome)
Ist Super Sanita Rapp — Istituto Superiore di Sanita. Rapporti
Ist Svizz Ric For Mem — Istituto Svizzero di Ricerche Forestali. Memorie
Ist Talassogr (Trieste) Pubbl — Istituto Talassografico (Trieste). Pubblicazione
Ist Tec Agr Stat (Macerata) — Istituto Tecnico Agrario Statale (Macerata)
Ist Univ Bergamo Studi Arch — Istituto Universitario di Bergamo. Studi Archeologici
Ist Univ Nav (Napoli) Ann — Istituto Universitario Navale (Napoli). Annali
Ist Univ Orient Nap Ann Sez Ger — Istituto Universitario Orientale di Napoli. Annali. Sezione Germanica
Ist Veneto Sci Lett Arti Atti Cl Sci Fis Mat Nat — Istituto Veneto di Scienze, Lettere, ed Arti. Atti. Classe di ScienzeFisiche, Matematiche, e Naturali
Ist Veneto Sci Lett Arti Atti Cl Sci Mat Nat — Istituto Veneto di Scienze, Lettere, ed Arti. Atti. Classe di ScienzeMatematiche e Naturali
Ist Veneto Sci Lett Arti Atti Cl Sci Mat Natur — Istituto Veneto di Scienze, Lettere, ed Arti. Venezia. Atti. Classe di Scienze Matematiche e Naturali
IstZap — Istoriceskii Zapiski
Ist Zhurn — Istoricheskii Zhurnal
Ist Zurn — Istoriceskij Zurnal
ISU — Information Services and Use
ISU — International Sugar Journal
ISUDX — Information Services and Use
ISU Mitt — Interdisziplinarer Sonderbereich Umweltschutz. Mitteilungen
ISU/PS — Politics and Society. Iowa State University
ISV — Informations-Chimie
ISVG — Soviet Geography
ISVY — Survey
ISWA Inf Bull — ISWA [*International Solid Wastes and Public Cleansing Association*] Information Bulletin
ISWOS — Israelitische Wochenschrift
ISWS Bull Ill Water Surv — ISWS Bulletin. Illinois Water Survey
ISXR — Sex Roles. A Journal of Research
ISY — IBM [*International Business Machines Corp.*] Systems Journal
I Sz — Irodalmi Szemle
IT — Ilustracao Trasmontana
IT — Indisch Tijdschrift van het Recht
IT — Information Today
IT — International Trumpet Guild. Newsletter
IT — Iraq Times
It — Irodalomtoertenet
IT — Islenzk Tunga
It — Italia Che Scrive
It — Italica
ITA — Income Tax Act Regulations
ITA — Interavia. Revue Internationale Aeronautique, Astronautique, Electronique
ITA — International Television Almanac
ITA — International Trade Administration Report
It Agr — Italia Agricola
ITA J — International Trombone Association. Journal
Ital — Italianistica. Revista di Letteratura Italiana
Ital — Italian. Patent Document
Ital — Italica
Ital A — Italian Americana
Ital Agr — Italia Agricola
Ital Agric — Italia Agricola
Ital Am — Italian Americana
Italamer — Italamerican
Ital Aust Bul Commerce — Italian-Australian Bulletin of Commerce
Ital Cereali — Italia e i Cereali

Ital Exped Karakorum Hindu Kush Sci Rep — Italian Expeditions to the Karakorum [K^2] and Hindu Kush. Scientific Reports
Ital For Mont — Italia Forestale e Montana
Ital Gen Rev Derm — Italian General Review of Dermatology
Ital Gen Rev Dermatol — Italian General Review of Dermatology
Ital Gen Rev Oto-Rhino-Laryng — Italian General Review of Oto-Rhino-Laryngology
Italia A — Italia Artistica
Italia Agric — Italia Agricola
Italia Am Lat Napoli — Italia-America Latina (Naples)
Italia Futur — Italia Futurista
Italia Lett — Italia Letteraria
Italia Med & Uman — Italia Medioevale e Umanistica
Italia Medioevale Uman — Italia Medioevale e Umanistica
Italian-Am Bus — Italian-American Business
Italian Yb of Int'l L — Italian Yearbook of International Law
Italia R Comitato G B — Italia Real Comitato Geologico. Bollettino
Itali Heart J — Italian Heart Journal
Ital J Anim Sci — Italian Journal of Animal Science
Ital J Bioc — Italian Journal of Biochemistry
Ital J Biochem — Italian Journal of Biochemistry
Ital J Biochem (Engl Ed) — Italian Journal of Biochemistry (English Edition)
Ital J Chest Dis — Italian Journal of Chest Diseases
Ital J Food Sci — Italian Journal of Food Science
Ital J Gastroenterol — Italian Journal of Gastroenterology
Ital J Gastroenterol Hepatol — Italian Journal of Gastroenterology and Hepatology
Ital J Med — Italian Journal of Medicine
Ital J Miner Electrolyte Metab — Italian Journal of Mineral and Electrolyte Metabolism
Ital J Neurol Sci — Italian Journal of Neurological Sciences
Ital J Ophthalmol — Italian Journal of Ophthalmology
Ital J Orthop Traumatol — Italian Journal of Orthopaedics and Traumatology
Ital J Orthop Traumatol Suppl — Italian Journal of Orthopaedics and Traumatology. Supplementum
Ital J Sports Traumatol — Italian Journal of Sports Traumatology
Ital J Surg Sci — Italian Journal of Surgical Sciences
Ital J Zool — Italian Journal of Zoology
Ital L — Italian Linguistics
Ital Med — Italia Medica
Ital Milit — Italia Militare
Ital Phys Soc Conf Proc — Italian Physical Society. Conference Proceedings
Ital Q — Italian Quarterly
Ital Quart — Italian Quarterly
Ital Rev Orthop Traumatol — Italian Review of Orthopaedics and Traumatology
Ital Vinic Agrar — Italia Vinicola ed Agraria
Ital Weine — Italienische Weine
(Italy) Agr — Annuario di Statistica Agraria (Italy)
Italy Ann — Annuario Statistico Italiano
Italy Com Naz Energ Nucl CNEN RT CHI — Italy. Comitato Nazionale per l' Energia Nucleare. CNEN-RT/CHI
Italy Com Naz Energ Nucl CNEN RT FIMA — Italy. Comitato Nazionale per l' Energia Nucleare. CNEN-RT/FIMA
Italy Com Naz Energ Nucl CNEN RT ING — Italy. Comitato Nazionale per l'Energia Nucleare. CNEN-RT/ING
Italy Com Naz Energ Nucl Rapp Tec CNEN RT BIO — Italy. Comitato Nazionale per l'Energia Nucleare. Rapporto Tecnico CNEN-RT/BIO
Italy Com Naz Energ Nucl Rapp Tec CNEN RT DISP — Italy. Comitato Nazionale per l'Energia Nucleare. Rapporto Tecnico CNEN-RT/DISP
Italy Com Naz Energ Nucl Rapp Tec CNEN RT FARE SDI — Italy. Comitato Nazionale per l'Energia Nucleare. Rapporto Tecnico CNEN-RT/FARE-SDI
Italy Com Naz Energ Nucl Rapp Tec CNEN RT FARE SIN — Italy. Comitato Nazionale per l'Energia Nucleare. Rapporto TecnicoCNEN-RT/FARE-SIN
Italy Com Naz Energ Nucl Rapp Tec CNEN RT FI — Italy. Comitato Nazionale per l'Energia Nucleare. Rapporto Tecnico CNEN-RT/FI
Italy Com Naz Energ Nucl Rapp Tec CNEN RT MET — Italy. Comitato Nazionale per l'Energia Nucleare. Rapporto Tecnico CNEN-RT/MET
Italy Com Naz Energ Nucl Rapp Tec CNEN RT PROT — Italy. Comitato Nazionale per l'Energia Nucleare. Rapporto Tecnico CNEN-RT/PROT
Italy Com Naz Energ Nucl Rapp Tec RT AI — Italy. Comitato Nazionale per l'Energia Nucleare. Rapporto Tecnico RT/AI
Italy Com Naz Energ Nucl Rapp Tec RT BIO — Italy. Comitato Nazionale per l'Energia Nucleare. Rapporto Tecnico RT/BIO
Italy Com Naz Energ Nucl Rapp Tec RT CHI — Italy. Comitato Nazionale per l'Energia Nucleare. Rapporto Tecnico RT/CHI
Italy Com Naz Energ Nucl Rapp Tec RT DISP — Italy. Comitato Nazionale per l'Energia Nucleare. Rapporto Tecnico RT/DISP
Italy Com Naz Energ Nucl Rapp Tec RT EC — Italy. Comitato Nazionale per l'Energia Nucleare. Rapporto Tecnico RT/EC
Italy Com Naz Energ Nucl Rapp Tec RT EL — Italy. Comitato Nazionale per l'Energia Nucleare. Rapporto Tecnico RT/EL
Italy Com Naz Energ Nucl Rapp Tec RT FI — Italy. Comitato Nazionale per l'Energia Nucleare. Rapporto Tecnico RT/FI
Italy Com Naz Energ Nucl Rapp Tec RT FIMA — Italy. Comitato Nazionale per l'Energia Nucleare. Rapporto Tecnico RT/FIMA
Italy Com Naz Energ Nucl Rapp Tec RT GEN — Italy. Comitato Nazionale per l'Energia Nucleare. Rapporto Tecnico RT/GEN
Italy Com Naz Energ Nucl Rapp Tec RT GEO — Italy. Comitato Nazionale per l'Energia Nucleare. Rapporto Tecnico RT/GEO
Italy Com Naz Energ Nucl Rapp Tec RT GIU — Italy. Comitato Nazionale per l'Energia Nucleare. Rapporto Tecnico RT/GIU
Italy Com Naz Energ Nucl Rapp Tec RT ING — Italy. Comitato Nazionale per l'Energia Nucleare. Rapporto Tecnico RT/ING
Italy Com Naz Energ Nucl Rapp Tec RT MET — Italy. Comitato Nazionale per l'Energia Nucleare. Rapporto Tecnico RT/MET

Italy Com Naz Energ Nucl Rapp Tec RT PROT — Italy. Comitato Nazionale per l'Energia Nucleare. Rapporto Tecnico RT/PROT
Italy Doc Notes — Italy. Documents and Notes
Italy Docs and Notes — Italy. Documents and Notes
Italy Ist Super Poste Telecomun Note Recens Not — Italy. Istituto Superiore delle Poste e delle Telecomunicazioni. Note Recensioni e Notizie
Italy Minist Agric For Collana Verde — Italy. Ministero dell'Agricoltura e delle Foreste Collana Verde
Italy Pat Doc — Italy. Patent Document
Italy Serv Geol Boll — Italy. Servizio Geologico. Bollettino
Italy Serv Geol Mem — Italy. Servizio Geologico. Memorie per Servire alla Descrizione della Carta Geologica d'Italia
Italy Uffic Cent Brev Boll Brev Invenz Modelli Marchi — Italy. Ufficio Centrale Brevetti. Bollettino dei Brevetti perInvenzioni, Modelli, e Marchi
ITA N — International Trombone Association. Newsletter
I Tatti Stud — I Tatti Studies
ItB — It Beaken
ITBO — Trailer Boats
ITC — Institute of Traditional Cultures. Bulletin
ITC — International Travel Catering
ItC — Italian Culture
ITC — Srinivasan's Reports of Income Tax Cases
ITCCC — ITCC [*International Technical Cooperation Centre*] Review
ITCC Rev — ITCC [*International Technical Cooperation Centre*] Review
ITC J — ITC [*International Training Centre for Aerial Survey*] Journal
ITCO — Technical Communication
ITCSA — In Vitro. Journal of the Tissue Culture Association
ITCSAF — In Vitro
It Cult — Italian Culture
ITDA — Income Tax Decisions of Australasia
It Dial — Italia Dialettale. Rivista di Dialettologia Italiana
ITD Izotoptech Diagn — ITD. Izotoptechnika, Diagnosztika
ITEA — Infraestructura Teatral
ITEAA5 — INTA [*Instituto Nacional de Tecnologia Agropecuaria*]. Estacion Experimental Regional Agropecuaria . Serie Tecnica
It Econ Surv — Italian Economic Survey
ITE J — ITE [*Institute of Transportation Engineers*] Journal
ITEME Newsl — ITEME [*Institution of Technician Engineers in Mechanical Engineering*] Newsletter
ITES — Times Educational Supplement
ITF — International Trade Forum
ItF — Italyan Filolojisi
ITF — Italy. Documents and Notes
It For Montan — Italia Forestale e Montana
It Forsch Kstgesch — Italienische Forschungen zur Kunstgeschichte
It Forsch Ksthist Inst Florenz — Italienische Forschungen des Kunsthistorischen Instituts in Florenz
It Fr — Italia Francescana
ITG — Australian Income Tax Guide
ITG — Inbound Traffic Guide
ITG — International Trumpet Guild. Journal
ITGEA — Interdisciplinary Topics in Gerontology
ITGEAR — Interdisciplinary Topics in Gerontology
ITG Fachber — ITG [*Informationstechnische Gesellschaft*] Fachberichte
ITG J — International Trumpet Guild. Journal
ITG N — International Trumpet Guild. Newsletter
ITH — Internationaler Holzmarkt
ITH — Iranische Texte und Hilfsbuecher
IThI — International Theatre Informations
I Th Q — Irish Theological Quarterly
ITI — Intermediair. Informatie voor Leidinggevende Functionarissen
ITIK — Tikkun
Itin — Itineraires. Chroniques et Documents
Itin — Itinerari
Itin — Itinerarium
ITIPD5 — Informes Tecnicos. Instituto de Investigaciones Pesqueras
ITJ — Indian Tax Journal
ITJ — International Tax Journal
ITKBA — Izvestiya na Tsentralnata Khelmintologichna Laboratoriya. Bulgarska Akademiya na Naukite
ITL — Information Technology and Libraries
ITLI — Trailer Life
ITLJ — Income Tax Law Journal
ITMIB2 — Instituto Tecnologico de Monterrey. Division de Ciencias Agropecuarias y Maritimas. Informe de Investigacion
ITMZBJ — Intensivmedizin
ITN — International Television News
ITNC — Town and Country Monthly
ITO — In Theory Only
ITOBAO — Akhboroti Akademiyai Fankhoi RSS Tochikiston Shu-Bai Fankhoi Biologi
Itogi Eksp Rab Molodykh Issled Vopr Sel'sk Khoz — Itogi Eksperimental'nykh Rabot Molodykh Issledovatelei po Voprosam Sel'skogo Khozyaistva
Itogi Nauk & Tekh Ser Issled Kosm Prostranstva — Itogi Nauki i Tekhniki Seriya Issledovanie Kosmicheskogo Prostranstva
Itogi Nauki Astron — Itogi Nauki Astronomiya
Itogi Nauki Biol Khim — Itogi Nauki Biologicheskaya Khimiya
Itogi Nauki Biol Nauki — Itogi Nauki Biologicheskie Nauki
Itogi Nauki Biol Osn Rastenievod — Itogi Nauki Biologicheski Osnovy Rastenievodstva
Itogi Nauki Biol Ultrastrukt — Itogi Nauki Biologicheskie Ul'trastruktury
Itogi Nauki Elektrokhim — Itogi Nauki Elektrokhimiya
Itogi Nauki Embriol — Itogi Nauki Embriologiya
Itogi Nauki Farmakol Khimioter Sredstva — Itogi Nauki Farmakologiya. Khimioterapevticheskie Sredstva
Itogi Nauki Farmakol Toksikol — Itogi Nauki Farmakologiya. Toksikologiya

Itogi Nauki Fiziol Chel Zhivotn — Itogi Nauki Fiziologiya, Cheloveka, i Zhivotnykh
Itogi Nauki Fiz Khim — Itogi Nauki Fizicheskaya Khimiya
Itogi Nauki Fiz Mat Nauki — Itogi Nauki Fiziko-Matematicheskie Nauki
Itogi Nauki Geofiz — Itogi Nauki Geofizika
Itogi Nauki Geokhim Mineral Petrogr — Itogi Nauki Geokhimiya Mineralogiya Petrografiya
Itogi Nauki Khim Nauki — Itogi Nauki Khimicheskie Nauki
Itogi Nauki Khim Tekhnol Vysokomol Soedin — Itogi Nauki Khimiya i Tekhnologiya Vysokomolekulyarnykh Soedinenii
Itogi Nauki Korroz Zashch Korroz — Itogi Nauki Korroziya i Zashchita ot Korrozii
Itogi Nauki Kristallokhim — Itogi Nauki Kristallokhimiya
Itogi Nauki Nemet Polezn Iskop — Itogi Nauki. Nemetallicheskie Poleznye Iskopaemye
Itogi Nauki Neorg Khim — Itogi Nauki Neorganicheskaya Khimiya
Itogi Nauki Obshch Genet — Itogi Nauki Obshchaya Genetika
Itogi Nauki Obshch Vopr Patol — Itogi Nauki Obshchie Voprosy Patologii
Itogi Nauki Onkol — Itogi Nauki Onkologiya
Itogi Nauki Rudn Mestorozhd — Itogi Nauki Rudnye Mestorozhdeniya
Itogi Nauki Tekh At Energ — Itogi Nauki i Tekhniki Atomnaya Energetika
Itogi Nauki Tekh Biofiz — Itogi Nauki i Tekhniki Biofizika
Itogi Nauki Tekh Elektrokhim — Itogi Nauki i Tekhniki Elektrokhimiya
Itogi Nauki Tekh Farmakol Khimioter Sredstva Toksikol — Itogi Nauki i Tekhniki Farmakologiya Khimioterapevticheski Sredstva Toksikolog iya
Itogi Nauki Tekh Fiziol Chel Zhivotn — Itogi Nauki i Tekhniki Fiziologiya Cheloveka i Zhivotnykh
Itogi Nauki Tekh Fiziol Rast — Itogi Nauki i Tekhniki Fiziologiya Rastenii
Itogi Nauki Tekh Fiz Khim Kinet — Itogi Nauki i Tekhniki Fizicheskaya Khimiya Kinetika
Itogi Nauki Tekh Genet Chel — Itogi Nauki i Tekhniki Genetika Cheloveka
Itogi Nauki Tekh Geokhim Mineral Petrogr — Itogi Nauki i Tekhniki Geokhimiya Mineralogiya Petrografiya
Itogi Nauki Tekh Gidrogeol Inzh Geol — Itogi Nauki i Tekhniki Gidrogeologiya, Inzhenernaya Geologiya
Itogi Nauki Tekh Gorn Delo — Itogi Nauki i Tekhniki Gornoe Delo
Itogi Nauki Tekh Issled Kosm Prostranstva — Itogi Nauki i Tekhniki Issledovanie Kosmicheskogo Prostranstva
Itogi Nauki Tekh Khim Tekhn Vysokimol Soedin — Itogi Nauki i Tekhniki Khimiya i Tekhnologiya Vysokimolekulyarnykh Soedininii
Itogi Nauki Tekh Khim Termodin Ravnovesiya — Itogi Nauki i Tekhniki Khimicheskaya Termodinamika i Ravnovesiya
Itogi Nauki Tekh Korroz Zashch Korroz — Itogi Nauki i Tekhniki Korroziya i Zashchita ot Korrozii
Itogi Nauki Tekh Kristallokhim — Itogi Nauki i Tekhniki Kristallokhimiya
Itogi Nauki Tekh Mestorozhd Goryuch Polezn Iskop — Itogi Nauki i Tekhniki Mestorozhdeniya Goryuchikh Poleznykh Iskopaemykh
Itogi Nauki Tekh Metalloved Term Obrab — Itogi Nauki i Tekhniki Metallovedenie i Termicheskaya Obrabotka
Itogi Nauki Tekh Metall Tsvetn Redk Met — Itogi Nauki i Tekhniki Metallurgiya Tsvetnykh i Redkikh Metallov
Itogi Nauki Tekh Mikrobiol — Itogi Nauki i Tekhniki Mikrobiologiya
Itogi Nauki Tekh Mol Biol — Itogi Nauki i Tekhniki Molekulyarnaya Biologiya
Itogi Nauki Tekh Nauki — Itogi Nauki Tekhnicheskie Nauki
Itogi Nauki Tekh Nemet Polezn Iskop — Itogi Nauki i Tekhniki Nemetallicheskie Poleznye Iskopaemye
Itogi Nauki Tekh Neorg Khim — Itogi Nauki i Tekhniki Neorganicheskaya Khimiya
Itogi Nauki Tekhnol Org Veshchestv — Itogi Nauki Tekhnologiya Organicheskikh Veshchestv
Itogi Nauki Tekh Obogashch Polezn Iskop — Itogi Nauki i Tekhniki Obogashchenie Poleznykh Iskopaemykh
Itogi Nauki Tekh Obshch Ekol Biotsenol — Itogi Nauki i Tekhniki Obshchaya Ekologiya, Biotsenologiya
Itogi Nauki Tekh Obshch Geol — Itogi Nauki i Tekhniki Obshchaya Geologiya
Itogi Nauki Tekh Onkol — Itogi Nauki i Tekhniki Onkologiya
Itogi Nauki Tekh Pozharnaya Okhr — Itogi Nauki i Tekhniki Pozharnaya Okhrana
Itogi Nauki Tekh Proizvod Chuguna Stali — Itogi Nauki i Tekhniki Proizvodstvo Chuguna i Stali
Itogi Nauki Tekh Rudn Mestorozhd — Itogi Nauki i Tekhniki Rudnye Mestorozhdeniya
Itogi Nauki Tekh Ser Astron — Itogi Nauki i Tekhniki Seriya Astronomiya
Itogi Nauki Tekh Ser At Energ — Itogi Nauki i Tekhniki Seriya Atomnaya Energetika
Itogi Nauki Tekh Ser Biofiz — Itogi Nauki i Tekhniki Seriya Biofizika
Itogi Nauki Tekh Ser Biol Khim — Itogi Nauki i Tekhniki Seriya Biologicheskaya Khimiya
Itogi Nauki Tekh Ser Biotekhnol — Itogi Nauki i Tekhniki Seriya Biotekhnologiya
Itogi Nauki Tekh Ser Diagrammy Sostoyaniya Nemet Sist — Itogi Nauki i Tekhniki Seriya Diagrammy Sostoyaniya NemetallicheskikhSistem
Itogi Nauki Tekh Ser Elektrokhim — Itogi Nauki i Tekhniki Seriya Elektrokhimiya
Itogi Nauki Tekh Ser Elektron Ee Primen — Itogi Nauki i Tekhniki Seriya Elektronika i Ee Primenenie
Itogi Nauki Tekh Ser Farmakol Khimioter Sredstva — Itogi Nauki i Tekhniki Seriya Farmakologiya, KhimioterapeuticheskieSredstva
Itogi Nauki Tekh Ser Fiziol Chel Zhivotn — Itogi Nauki i Tekhniki Seriya Fiziologiya Cheloveka i Zhivotnykh
Itogi Nauki Tekh Ser Fiziol Khim Kinet — Itogi Nauki i Tekhniki Seriya Fiziologiya, Khimiya, Kinetika
Itogi Nauki Tekh Ser Fiz Rast — Itogi Nauki i Tekhniki Seriya Fizicheskaya Rastenii
Itogi Nauki Tekh Ser Fiz Zemli — Itogi Nauki i Tekhniki Seriya Fiziki Zemli
Itogi Nauki Tekh Ser Genet Chel — Itogi Nauki i Tekhniki Seriya Genetika Cheloveka
Itogi Nauki Tekh Ser Geokhim Mineral Petrogr — Itogi Nauki i Tekhniki Seriya Geokhimiya, Mineralogiya, Petrografiya
Itogi Nauki Tekh Ser Gidrogeol Inzh Geol — Itogi Nauki i Tekhniki Seriya Gidrogeologiya, Inzhenernaya Geologiya

Itogi Nauki Tekh Ser Gidrol Sushi — Itogi Nauki i Tekhniki Seriya Gidrologiya Sushi
Itogi Nauki Tekh Ser Gorn Delo — Itogi Nauki i Tekhniki Seriya Gornoe Delo
Itogi Nauki Tekh Ser Immunolo — Itogi Nauki i Tekhniki Seriya Immunologiya
Itogi Nauki Tekh Ser Issled Kosm Prostranstva — Itogi Nauki i Tekhniki Seriya Issledovanie Kosmicheskogo Prostranstva
Itogi Nauki Tekh Ser Khim Neftepererab Polim Mashinostr — Itogi Nauki i Tekhniki Seriya Khimicheskoe, Neftepererabatyvayushcheei Polimernoe Mashinostroenie
Itogi Nauki Tekh Ser Khim Tekhnol Vysokomol Soedin — Itogi Nauki i Tekhniki Seriya Khimiya i TekhnologiyaVysokomolekulyarnykh Soedinenii
Itogi Nauki Tekh Ser Khim Termodin Ravnovesiya — Itogi Nauki i Tekhniki Seriya Khimicheskaya Termodinamika iRavnovesiya
Itogi Nauki Tekh Ser Khim Tverd Tela — Itogi Nauki i Tekhniki Seriya Khimiya Tverdogo Tela
Itogi Nauki Tekh Ser Khromatogr — Itogi Nauki i Tekhniki Seriya Khromatografiya
Itogi Nauki Tekh Ser Kinet Katal — Itogi Nauki i Tekhniki Seriya Kinetika i Kataliz
Itogi Nauki Tekh Ser Korroz Zashch Korroz — Itogi Nauki i Tekhniki Seriya Korroziya i Zashchita ot Korrozii
Itogi Nauki Tekh Ser Kristallokhim — Itogi Nauki i Tekhniki Seriya Kristallokhimiya
Itogi Nauki Tekh Ser Mekh Zhidk Gaza — Itogi Nauki i Tekhniki Seriya Mekhanika Zhidkosti i Gaza
Itogi Nauki Tekh Ser Mestorozhd Goryuch Polezn Iskop — Itogi Nauki i Tekhniki Seriya Mestorozhdeniya Goryuchikh PoleznykhIskopaemykh
Itogi Nauki Tekh Ser Metalloved Term Obrab — Itogi Nauki i Tekhniki Seriya Metallovedenie i TermicheskayaObrabotka
Itogi Nauki Tekh Ser Metall Tsvetn Redk Met — Itogi Nauki i Tekhniki Seriya Metallurgiya Tsvetnykh i RedkikhMetallov
Itogi Nauki Tekh Ser Mikrobiol — Itogi Nauki i Tekhniki Seriya Mikrobiologiya
Itogi Nauki Tekh Ser Mol Biol — Itogi Nauki i Tekhniki Seriya Molekulyarnaya Biologiya
Itogi Nauki Tekh Ser Morfol Chel Zhivotn — Itogi Nauki i Tekhniki Seriya Morfologiya Cheloveka i Zhivotnykh
Itogi Nauki Tekh Ser Nemet Polezn Iskop — Itogi Nauki i Tekhniki Seriya Nemetallicheskie Poleznye Iskopaemye
Itogi Nauki Tekh Ser Neorg Khim — Itogi Nauki i Tekhniki Seriya Neorganicheskaya Khimiya
Itogi Nauki Tekh Ser Obogashch Polezn Iskop — Itogi Nauki i Tekhníki Seriya Obogashchenie Poleznykh Iskopaemykh
Itogi Nauki Tekh Ser Obshch Ekol Biotsenol Gidrobiol — Itogi Nauki i Tekhniki Seriya Obshchaya Ekologiya, Biotsenologiya,Gidrobiologiya
Itogi Nauki Tekh Ser Obshch Genet — Itogi Nauki i Tekhniki Seriya Obshchaya Genetika
Itogi Nauki Tekh Ser Obshch Geol — Itogi Nauki i Tekhniki Seriya Obshchaya Geologiya
Itogi Nauki Tekh Ser Obshch Probl Fiz Khim Biol — Itogi Nauki i Tekhniki Seriya Obshchie Problemy Fiziko-KhimicheskoiBiologii
Itogi Nauki Tekh Ser Obshch Vopr Patol — Itogi Nauki i Tekhniki Seriya Obshchie Voprosy Patologii
Itogi Nauki Tekh Ser Okeanol — Itogi Nauki i Tekhniki Seriya Okeanologiya
Itogi Nauki Tekh Ser Onkol — Itogi Nauki i Tekhniki Seriya Onkologiya
Itogi Nauki Tekh Ser Org Khim — Itogi Nauki i Tekhniki Seriya Organicheskaya Khimiya
Itogi Nauki Tekh Ser Pochvoved Agrokhim — Itogi Nauki i Tekhniki Seriya Pochvovedenie i Agrokhimiya
Itogi Nauki Tekh Ser Pozharnaya Okhr — Itogi Nauki i Tekhniki Seriya Pozharnaya Okhrana
Itogi Nauki Tekh Ser Proizvod Chuguna Stali — Itogi Nauki i Tekhniki Seriya Proizvodstvo Chuguna i Stali
Itogi Nauki Tekh Ser Prokatnoe Volochil'noe Proizvod — Itogi Nauki i Tekhniki Seriya Prokatnoe i Volochil'noe Proizvodstvo
Itogi Nauki Tekh Ser Protsessy Appar Khim Tekhnol — Itogi Nauki i Tekhniki Seriya Protsessy i Apparaty KhimicheskoiTekhnologii
Itogi Nauki Tekh Ser Puchki Zaryazhennykh Chastits Tverd Telo — Itogi Nauki i Tekhniki. Seriya. Puchki Zaryazhennykh Chastits i Tverdoe Telo
Itogi Nauki Tekh Ser Radiats Biol — Itogi Nauki i Tekhniki Seriya Radiatsionnaya Biologiya
Itogi Nauki Tekh Ser Rastvory Rasplavy — Itogi Nauki i Tekhniki Seriya Rastvory, Rasplavy
Itogi Nauki Tekh Ser Razrab Mestorozhd Tverd Polezn Iskop — Itogi Nauki i Tekhniki Seriya Razrabotka Mestorozhdenii TverdykhPoleznykh Iskopaemykh
Itogi Nauki Tekh Ser Razrab Neft Gazov Mestorozhd — Itogi Nauki i Tekhniki Seriya Razrabotka Neftyanykh i GazovykhMestorozhdenii
Itogi Nauki Tekh Ser Rudn Mestorozhd — Itogi Nauki i Tekhniki Seriya Rudnye Mestorozhdeniya
Itogi Nauki Tekh Ser Str Mol Khim Svyaz — Itogi Nauki i Tekhniki Seriya Stroenie Molekul i Khimicheskaya Svyaz
Itogi Nauki Tekh Ser Svarka — Itogi Nauki i Tekhniki Seriya Svarka
Itogi Nauki Tekh Ser Svetotekh Infrakrasnaya Tekh — Itogi Nauki i Tekhniki Seriya Svetotekhnika i Infrakrasnaya Tekhnika
Itogi Nauki Tekh Ser Tekh Anal Metall — Itogi Nauki i Tekhniki Seriya Tekhnicheskii Analiz v Metallurgii
Itogi Nauki Tekh Ser Tekhnol Mashinostr — Itogi Nauki i Tekhniki. Seriya. Tekhnologiya Mashinostroeniya
Itogi Nauki Tekh Ser Tekhnol Org Veshchestv — Itogi Nauki i Tekhniki Seriya Tekhnologiya Organicheskikh Veshchestv
Itogi Nauki Tekh Ser Tekhnol Razrab Mestorozhd — Itogi Nauki i Tekhniki Seriya Tekhnologiya Razrabotki Mestorozhdenii
Itogi Nauki Tekh Ser Teor Metall Protsessov — Itogi Nauki i Tekhniki Seriya Teoriya Metallurgicheskikh Protsessov
Itogi Nauki Tekh Ser Toksikol — Itogi Nauki i Tekhniki Seriya Toksikologiya
Itogi Nauki Tekh Ser Virusol — Itogi Nauki i Tekhniki Seriya Virusologiya
Itogi Nauki Tekh Ser Zashch Rast — Itogi Nauki i Tekhniki Seriya Zashchita Rastenii

Itogi Nauki Tekh Ser Zhivotnovod Vet — Itogi Nauki i Tekhniki Seriya Zhivotnovodstvo i Veterinariya
Itogi Nauki Tekh Svarka — Itogi Nauki i Tekhniki Svarka
Itogi Nauki Tekh Svetotekh Infrakrasnaya Tekh — Itogi Nauki i Tekhniki Svetotekhnika i Infrakrasnaya Tekhniki
Itogi Nauki Tekh Tekhnol Mashinostr — Itogi Nauki i Tekhniki Tekhnologiya Mashinostroeniya
Itogi Nauki Tekh Teor Metall Protsessov — Itogi Nauki i Tekhniki Teoriya Metallurgicheskikh Protsessov
Itogi Nauki Tekh Toksikol — Itogi Nauki i Tekhniki Toksikologiya
Itogi Nauki Tekh Virusol — Itogi Nauki i Tekhniki Virusologiya
Itogi Nauki Tekh Zhivotnovod Vet — Itogi Nauki i Tekhniki Zhivotnovodstvo i Veterinariya
Itogi Nauki Tsitol Obshch Genet Genet Chel — Itogi Nauki Tsitologiya Obshchaya Genetika. Genetika Cheloveka
Itogi Nauki Vet — Itogi Nauki Veterinariya
Itogi Nauki Virusol Mikrobiol — Itogi Nauki Virusologiya i Mikrobiologiya
Itogi Nauki Vysokomol Soedin — Itogi Nauki Vysokomolekulyarnye Soedineniya
Itogi Nauki Zashch Rast — Itogi Nauki Zashchita Rastenii
Itogi Polev Rabot Inst Etnogr — Itogi Polevyh Rabot Instituta Etnografii
Itogi Voronezsk Stancii Zasc Rast — Itogi Voronezskaja Stancii Zascity Rastenij
ITOIAE — Izvestiia Tavricheskogo Obshchestva Istorii. Arkheologii i Ethografii
ITOIAE — Izvestija Tavreiceskogo Obscestva Istorii, Archeologii, Etnografii
ITOMA — Industries et Travaux d'Outre-Mer
ITORGO — Izvestija Turkestanskogo Otdela Russkogo Geograficeskogo Obscestva
ITPR — Inuit Tapirisat of Canada. Press Release
ITPSB — IEEE. Transactions on Plasma Science
ITPTBG — Interpretation
ITQ — Irish Theological Quarterly
ItQ — Italian Quarterly
ITR — Indian Tax Reports
ITR — Indisch Tijdschrift van het Recht
ITR — International Trade Reporter
It R — Itineraria Romana. Roemisiche Reisewege an der Hand der Tabula Peutingeriana
ITRCDB — Interciencia
ITRI — Trial
ITRID — Itogi Nauki i Tekhniki Razrabotka Mestorozhdenii Tverdykh Poleznykh Iskopaemykh
ITRIS — International Trade and Resource Information System
ITRJDW — International Tree Crops Journal
ITRM — Trains
ITRMB5 — Conseil Scientifique International de Recherches sur les Trypanosomiases
IT Rulings — Income Tax Rulings
It Sac — Italia Sacra
It S Gl BIl — Bollettino della Societa Geologica Italiana
ITSMA — Ispol'zovanie Tverdykh Topliv Sernistykh Mazutov i Gaza
It S Met An — Annuario Meteorologico Italiano Pubblicato per cura del Comitato Direttivo della Societa Meteorologica Italiana
ITSOD — Itogi Nauki i Tekhniki. Seriya. Okeanologiya
It St — Italian Studies
ITS Text Leader — ITS Textile Leader
It Stud — Italian Studies
ITT — In These Times
ITUAK — Izvestiia Tavricheskoi Uchenoi Arkhivnoi Kommissii
ITUFA — Izvestiya Akademii Nauk Turkmenskoi SSR Seriya Fiziko-Tekhnicheskikh, Khimicheskikh, i Geologicheskikh Nauk
ITvhR — Indisch Tijdschrift van het Recht
ITVQ — Television Quarterly
ITXM — Texas Monthly
ITXPA9 — Estacion Experimental Agropecuaria Pergamino. Publicacion Tecnico
ITXPA9 — INTA [*Instituto Nacional de Tecnologia Agropecuaria*]. Estacion Experimental Regional Agropecuaria . Publicacion Tecnica
ITYB — Investment Trust Year Book
IU — Informador Universitario
IU — Instant Update
IU/AL — Anthropological Linguistics; a Publication of the Archives of the Languages of the World. Indiana University. Anthropology Department
IUB — Indiana University Bookman
IUB (Int Union Biochem) Symp Ser — IUB (International Union of Biochemistry) Symposium Series
IUCC Bull — IUCC [*Inter-University Committee on Computing*] Bulletin
IUCC Newsl — IUCC [*Inter-University Committee on Computing*] Newsletter
IUCN — International Union for Conservation of Nature and Natural Resources. TechnicalMeeting
IUCN Ann Rep — IUCN [*International Union for Conservation of Nature and Natural Resources*] Annual Report
IUCN Bull — IUCN [*International Union for Conservation of Nature and Natural Resources*] Bulletin
IUCN OSG Bull — IUCN (International Union for Conservation of Nature and Natural Resources) Otter Specialist Group Bulletin
IUCN Publ New Ser — IUCN [*International Union for Conservation of Nature and Natural Resources*] Publications. New Series
IUCN Yearb — IUCN [*International Union for Conservation of Nature and Natural Resources*] Yearbook
IUCr Crystallogr Symp — IUCr (International Union of Crystallography) Crystallographic Symposia
IUF — India's Urban Future
IUFS — Indiana University. Folklore Series
IUGG Chron — IUGG [*International Union of Geodesy and Geophysics*] Chronicle
IUGG Newsl — International Union of Geodesy and Geophysics. Newsletter
Iugosl Physiol Pharmacol Acta — Iugoslavica Physiologica Pharmacologica Acta
IUH — In Touch with the Dutch
IUHS — Indiana University. Humanities Series

IUPA — University of Pennsylvania Law Review

IUPAC Chem Data Ser — IUPAC [*International Union of Pure and Applied Chemistry*] Chemical Data Series

IUPAC Inf Bull — International Union of Pure and Applied Chemistry. Information Bulletin

IUPAC Inf Bull Append Provis Nomencl Symb Terminol Conv — International Union of Pure and Applied Chemistry. Information Bulletin. Appendices on Provisional Nomenclature, Symbols, Terminology, and Conventions

IUPAC Inf Bull Append Tentative Nomencl Symb Units Stand — International Union of Pure and Applied Chemistry. Information Bulletin. Appendices on Tentative Nomenclature, Symbols, Units, and Standards

IUPAC Int Symp Macromol — IUPAC (International Union of Pure and Applied Chemistry) International Symposium on Macromolecules

IUPAC Symp Macromol — IUPAC (International Union of Pure and Applied Chemistry) Symposium on Macromolecules

IUPAL — Indiana University Publications. Anthropology and Linguistics

IUPFS — Indiana University Publications. Folklore Series

IUPH — Indiana University Publications. Humanities Series

IUPHAR Satell Meet Serotonin — IUPHAR Satellite Meeting on Serotonin

IUPHS — Indiana University Publications. Humanistic Series

IUPLSM — Indiana University Publications. Language Science Monographs

IUPSEES — Indiana University Publications. Slavic and East European Series

IUPUAS — Indiana University Publications. Uralic and Altaic Series

IUR — International UFO Reporter

IUR — Irish University Review

IURCAFL — Indiana University. Research Center in Anthropology, Folklore, and Linguistics

IUS — Industrie

IUSHTL — Indiana University Studies in the History and Theory of Linguistics

IUSRAV — Iowa State University. Statistical Laboratory. Annual Report

IUTFAY — Istanbul Universitesi Tip Fakultesi Mecmuasi

IV — Der Israelitische Volkslehrer

IV — Ideas y Valores

IV — Illustrazione Vaticana

IV — Istoritcheskii Viestnik

IVA — IVA [*Ingenjoersvetenskapsakademien*] och des Laboratorien

IVA — IVA [*Ingenjoersvetenskapsakademien*] Tidskrift foer Teknisk-Vetenskaplig Forskning

IVA — Jugobanka. Economic News

IVAAA — IVA [*Ingenjoersvetenskapsakademien*] Tidskrift foer Teknisk-Vetenskaplig Forskning

IVAD — Izvestiya na Varnenskoto Archeologicesko Druzestvo

IVA (Ingenjoersvetenskapsakad) Medd — IVA (Ingenjoersvetenskapsakademien) Meddelande

Ivano Frankivs'kii Derzh Med Inst Nauk Zap — Ivano-Frankivs'kii Derzhavnii Medichnii Institut Naukovi Zapiski

Ivanov Gos Ped Inst Ucen Zap — Ivanovskii Gosudarstvennyi Pedagogiceskii Institut Imeni D. A. Furmanova Ivanovskoe Matematiceskoe Obscestvo Ucenye Zapiski

Ivanov Gos Univ Ucen Zap — Ivanovskii Gosudarstvennyi Universitet Ucenye Zapiski

IVat — Illustrazione Vaticana

IVA Tidskr Tek-Vetenskaplig Forsk — IVA [*Ingenjoersvetenskapsakademien*] Tidskrift foer Teknisk-Vetenskaplig Forskning

IVA Tidskr Tek Vetensk Forsk — IVA [*Ingenjoersvetenskapsakademien*] Tidskrift foer Teknisk-Vetenskaplig Forskning

IVEJ — Vocational Education Journal

IVERC — Illustrated Video Equipment Reference Catalog

IVF J In Vitro Fert Embryo Transfer — IVF. Journal of In Vitro Fertilization and Embryo Transfer

IVGewRSchutz — Jahrbuch der Internationalen Vereinigung fuer Gewerblichen Rechtsschutz

IVGO — Izvestija Vsesojuznogo Geograficeskogo Obscestva

IVGOA — Izvestiya Vsesoyuznogo Geograficheskogo Obshchestva

IVGPI — Izvestiya Voronezskogo Gosudarstvennogo Pedagogiceskogo Instituta

IVI — Ikuska. Instituto Vasco de Investigaciones

IVIZ — Institutionenverzeichnis fuer Internationale Zusammenarbeit

IVL — Internationale Wirtschaft mit den Mitteilungen der Bundeswirtschaftskammer

IVL Bull — IVL [*Instituet foer Vatten och Luftvardsforskning*] Bulletin

IVL Publ B — IVL (Institutet foer Vatten och Luftvaardsforskning) Publikation B

IVL Rapp — IVL (Institutet foer Vatten och Luftvaardsforskning) Rapport

IVL Rep — IVL (Institutet foer Vatten och Luftvaardsforskning) Report

IVM — Incentive Marketing

IvM — Inschriften von Magnesia am Maeander

IVMJDL — Indian Veterinary Medical Journal

IVMOD2 — In Vitro Monograph

IVNCDN — Investigations on Cetacea

IvO — Inschriften von Olympia

Iv Ol — Inschriften von Olympia

IVONANA — Izvestiia. Vestnik Obshchestvennykh Nauk. Akademia Nauk Armianskoi SSR

Ivor's Art R — Ivor's Art Review

Ivory Coast Dir Mines Geol Bull — Ivory Coast. Direction des Mines et de la Geologie. Bulletin

IvP — Inschriften von Pergamon

Iv Pr — Inschriften von Priene

IVR — International Journal of Physical Distribution and Materials Management

IVRYA — Intervirology

IVRYAK — Intervirology

IVS — Index of Veterinary Specialities

IVSOIRGO — Izvestija Vostocno-Sibirskogo Otdela Imperatorskogo Russkogo Geograficeskogo Obscestva

IVSORGO — Izvestija Vostocno-Sibirskogo Otdela Russkogo Geograficeskogo Obscestva

IVTAN Rev — IVTAN [*Institut Vysokikh Temperatur Akademiya Nauk*] Reviews

IVTAN Rev High Temp Inst Acad Sci USSR — IVTAN [*Institut Vysokikh Temperatur Akademiya Nauk*] Reviews of the High Temperature Institute Academy of Sciences of the USSR

IVT Jaarversl — IVT [*Instituut voor de Veredeling van Tuinbouwgewassen*] Jaarverslag

IVTLAP — International Association of Theoretical and Applied Limnology. Proceedings

IVTMAS — Communications. International Association of Theoretical and Applied Limnology

IVT Mededel — IVT [*Instituut voor de Veredeling van Tuinbouwgewassen*] Mededeling

IVTRBA — In Vitro v CSSR

IVUAA — Izvestiya Vysshikh Uchebnykh Zavedenii Aviatsionnaya Tekhnika

IVUGA — Izvestiya Vysshikh Uchebnykh Zavedenii Geologiya i Razvedka

IVUKA — Izvestiya Vysshikh Uchebnykh Zavedenii Khimiya i Khimicheskaya Tekhnologiya

IVUMA — Izvestiya Vysshikh Uchebnykh Zavedenii Chernaya Metallurgiya

IVUNA — Izvestiya Vysshikh Uchebnykh Zavedenii Neft' i Gaz

IVUPA — Izvestiya Vysshikh Uchebnykh Zavedenii Pishchevaya Tekhnologiya

IVUPA8 — Izvestiya Vysshikh Uchebnykh Zavedenii Pishchevaya Tekhnologiya

IVUZ Fiz — Izvestiya Vysshikh Uchebnykh Zavedenii Fizika

IVZEA — Izvestiya Vysshikh Uchebnykh Zavedenii Energetika

IW — Illustrated World

IW — Industry Week

IW — Islamic World

IW — Israelitisches Wochenblatt

Iwan Mueller — Handbuch der Klassischen Altertumswissenschaft (Iwan von Mueller, Editor)

Iwata Inst Plant Biochem Publ — Iwata Institute of Plant Biochemistry. Publication

Iwata Tob Shikenjo Hokoku Bull Iwata Tob Exp Stn — Iwata Tob Shikenjo Hokoku/Bulletin. Iwata Tobacco Experimental Station

Iwate Univ Technol Rep — Iwate University. Faculty of Engineering. Technology Reports

IWB — Israelitisches Wochenblatt (Berlin)

IWB — Literatuurinformatie Wetenschapsbeleid

IWCR — International Whaling Commission. Reports

IWCRSI — International Whaling Commission. Reports. Special Issue

IWDV — World Development

IWEEA — Industry Week

IWEGA — Industrial Water Engineering

IWEGAA — Industrial Water Engineering

IWER — Whole Earth Review

IWGIAD — IWGIA [*International Work Group for Indigenous Affairs*] Document

IWGIAN — IWGIA [*International Work Group for Indigenous Affairs*] Newsletter

IWIN — Wine Spectator

IWK — Internationale Wissenschaftliche Korrespondenz zur Geschichte der Deutschen Arbeiterbewegung

IWK — Israelitische Wochenschrift (Klausner)

IWLB — Wilson Library Bulletin

IWLRAA — Indian Forest Records. Wild Life and Recreation

IWO — Informationsdienst West-Ost

IWOM — World Magazine

IWPCD — International Water Power and Dam Construction

IWR — Information World Review

IWR — Islamic World Review

IWRBBR — Iowa. Agriculture and Home Economics Experiment Station. Research Bulletin

IWRD — Writer's Digest

IWRUAR — Institute for Water Resources. University of Alaska. Report

IWSA Eur Spec Conf Atrazine Other Pestic — IWSA (International Water Supply Association) European Specialized Conference on Atrazine and Other Pesticides

IWSA Eur Spec Conf Managing Water Distrib Syst — IWSA (International Water Supply Association) European Specialized Conference on Managing Water Distribution Systems

IWSA Int Water Supply Conf Exhib — IWSA (International Water Supply Association) International Water Supply Conference and Exhibition

IWSRBC — Iowa. Agriculture and Home Economics Experiment Station. Special Report

IWS Schriftenr — IWS (Institut fuer Wassergefaehrdende Stoffe) Schriftenreihe

IWT — Indiana Writing Today

IWT — Indian Writing Today

IWTO — World Today

IWW — International Who's Who

IWWD — Information World

IWWM — Weight Watchers' Magazine

IWX — Aspekten van Internationale Samenwerking

IXAB — Journal of the Experimental Analysis of Behavior

IXEH — Explorations in Economic History

Ixo Int Rev — Ixo. Internationale Revue

IXS — International Social Science Journal

IXSAAZ — International Council for the Exploration of the Sea. Cooperative Research Report. Series A

IXSBB5 — International Council for the Exploration of the Sea. Cooperative Research Report. Series B

IXTP — Extrapolation

IY — Idaho Yesterdays

IYAC — Yachting

IYaSh — Inostrannye Jazyki v Skole

IYB — [*The*] Israel Year Book

IYBIA — Indian Year Book of International Affairs

IYH — Israel Youth Horizon

IYHR — Israel Yearbook on Human Rights

IYIA — Indian Yearbook of International Affairs

IYJC — Yale Journal of Criticism

IYJGDH — Italian Journal of Gastroenterology
IYPA — Yearbook of Physical Anthropology
IYV — Ideas y Valores
IYYYA8 — Immok Yukchong Yonku-So Yongu Pogo
IZ — Instrumentenbau-Zeitschrift
IZ — Istoriceskii Zapiski Akademii Nauk SSSR
IZ — Istoriceskij Zurnal
Iz — Izvestiya
IzANA — Izvestiia Akademii Nauk Armianskoi SSR
IzANAz — Izvestiia Akademii Nauk Azerbaidzhanskoi SSR
IzANK — Izvestiia Akademii Nauk Kazakhskoi SSR
IzANKi — Izvestiia Akademii Nauk Kirghizskoi SSR
IzANT — Izvestiia Akademii Nauk Turkmenskoi SSR
IzANTa — Izvestiia Akademii Nauk Tadzhikskoi SSR
IzANU — Izvestiia Akademiia Nauk Uzbekskoi SSR
IZAPA — Internationale Zeitschrift fuer Angewandte Physiologie
Iz Balg Muz — Izvestiia na Balgarskite Muzei
IZBG — Internationale Zeitschriftenschau fuer Bibelwissenschaft und Grenzgebiete
IzBID — Izvestiia na B'lgarskoto Istorichesko Druzestvo
IzBSI — Izvestiia Biologicheskogo i Sel'skokhoziaistvennogo Instituta Akademii Nauk Armianskoi SSR
IZBTBM — Instituto de Zootecnia. Boletim Tecnico
Izd Severo Kavkazsk Kraev Stancii Zasc Rast Ser A Naucn Organ — Izdanija Severo-Kavkazskoj Kraevoj Stancii Zascity Rastenij. Ser. A. Naucnye i Organizacionnye Raboty
Izd Zavod Hidroteh Gradevinskog Fak Sarajevu — Izdanja Zavod za Hidrotehniku Gradevinskog Fakulteta u Sarajevu
Izd Zavod Ribar SR Maked — Izdanija. Zavod za Ribarstvo na SR Makedonija
IZEnt — Illustrierte Zeitschrift fuer Entomologie
IZEW — Internationale Zeitschrift fuer Erziehungswissenschaft
IZFMB — Izvestiya Akademii Nauk Moldavskoi SSR Seriya Fiziko-Tekhnicheskikh i Matematicheskikh Nauk
Izhevsk Med Inst Tr — Izhevskii Meditsinskii Institut Trudy
Izhevsk Skh Inst Tr — Izhevskii Sel'skokhozyaistvennyi Institut. Trudy
Iz Ist Biol — Iz Istorii Biologii
Iz Ist Estestvozn TekhbPribaltiki — Iz Istorii Estestvoznaniia i Tekhniki i Pribaltiki
Iz Istor Biol — Iz Istorii Biologii
Izk — Izkustvo
IZKPAK — Internationale Zeitschrift fuer Klinische Pharmakologie, Therapie, und Toxikologie
IZM — Indian Zoological Memoirs on Indian Animal Types
Izmen Pochv Okyl't Klassif Diagnostika "Kolos" — Izmenenie Pochvy pri Okyl'turivanii Ikh Klassifikatsiya i Diagnostika "Kolos"
Izmer Techn — Izmeritel'naja Technika
Izmer Tekh — Izmeritel'naya Tekhnika
Izmer Tekh Proverochn Delo — Izmeritel'naya Tekhnika i Proverochnoe Delo
Iz Narod Muz (Rousse) — Izvestiia na Narodniia Muzei (Rousse)
Iz Narod Muz Sumen — Izvestiia Narodni Muzefa Sumen Bulgaria
Iz Narod Muz (Varna) — Izvestiia na Narodniia Muzei (Varna)
Iznos Zashch Konstr Prom Zdanii — Iznos i Zashchita Konstruktsu Promyshlennykh Zdanii
Izobrazitelnoye Isk — Izobrazitel'noye Iskusstvo
Izobret Prom Obraztsy Tovarnye Znaki — Izobreteniya Promyshlennye Obraztsy Tovarnye Znaki
Izobret Ratsion — Izobretatel i Ratsionalizator
IZOCAZ — Investigaciones Zoologicas Chilenas
Izol Elektr Mash — Izolyatsiya Elektricheskikh Mashin
Izotoptech Diagn — Izotoptechnika, Diagnosztika
Izot SSSR — Izotopy v SSSR
IZSch — Internationale Zeitschriftenschau fuer Bibelwissenschaft und Grenzgebiete
IZSEA — Izvestiya Akademii Nauk SSSR Seriya Ekonomicheskaia
Izsled Biol Borba Vred Rast — Izsledvaniya po Biologichnata Borba s Vreditelite na Rasteniyata
IzSO — Izvestiia Severo-Osetinskogo Nauchno-Issledovatelskogo Instituta
IZSORGO — Izvestija Zapadno-Sibirskogo Otdela Russkogo Graficeskogo Obscestva
Izuch Mirchinskoi Biol — Izuchenie Mirchinskoi Biologii
Izuch Prichin Avarii Povrezhdenii Stroit Konstr — Izuchenie Prichin Avarii i Povrezhdenii Stroitel'nykh Konstruktsii
Izv Abhaz Inst Jaz Lit Ist — Izvestija Abhazskogo Instituta Jazyka, Literatury, i Istorii
Izv Acad Sci USSR Atmos and Oceanic Phys — Izvestiya. Academy of Sciences USSR. Atmospheric and Oceanic Physics
Izv Acad Sci USSR Atmos Oceanic Phys — Izvestiya. Academy of Sciences USSR. Atmospheric and Oceanic Physics
Izv Acad Sci USSR Atmospher Ocean Phys — Izvestiya. Academy of Sciences USSR. Atmospheric and Oceanic Physics
Izv Acad Sci USSR Geol Ser — Izvestiya. Academy of Sciences USSR. Geologic Series
Izv Acad Sci USSR Phys Solid Earth — Izvestiya. Academy of Sciences USSR. Physics of the Solid Earth
Izv Akad Agrar Nauk Belarusi — Izvestiya Akademii Agrarnykh Nauk Belarusi
Izv Akad Krupnogo Sots Selsk Khoz — Izvestiya Akademii Krupnogo Sotsialisticheskogo Sel'skogo Khozyaistva
Izv Akad Latv SSR Ser Fiz Tekh Nauk — Izvestiya Akademii Latviiskoi SSR Seriya Fizicheskikh i Tekhnicheskikh Nauk
Izv Akad Nauk — Izvestiya Akademii Nauk
Izv Akad Nauk Arm Fiz — Izvestiya Akademii Nauk Armenii. Fizika
Izv Akad Nauk Armjan SSR Ser Fiz — Izvestija Akademii Nauk Armjanskoi SSR Serija Fizika
Izv Akad Nauk Armjan SSR Ser Mat — Izvestija Akademii Nauk Armjanskoi SSR Serija Matematika
Izv Akad Nauk Armjan SSR Ser Meh — Izvestija Akademii Nauk Armjanskoi SSR Serija Mehanika

Izv Akad Nauk Armjan SSR Ser Tehn Nauk — Izvestija Akademii Nauk Armjanskoi SSR Serija Tehniceskih Nauk
Izv Akad Nauk Arm Nauki Zemle — Izvestiya Akademii Nauk Armenii. Nauki o Zemle
Izv Akad Nauk Arm SSR — Izvestiya Akademii Nauk Armyanskoi SSR
Izv Akad Nauk Arm SSR Biol Nauki — Izvestiya Akademii Nauk Armyanskoi SSR Biologicheskie Nauki
Izv Akad Nauk Arm SSR Biol S-Kh Nauki — Izvestiya Akademii Nauk Armyanskoi SSR Biologicheskie i Sel'skokhozyaistvennyeNauki
Izv Akad Nauk Arm SSR Estestv Nauki — Izvestiya Akademii Nauk Armyanskoi SSR Estestvennye Nauki
Izv Akad Nauk Arm SSR Fiz — Izvestiya Akademii Nauk Armyanskoi SSR Fizika
Izv Akad Nauk Arm SSR Fiz Mat Estest Tekh Nauki — Izvestiya Akademii Nauk Armyanskoi SSR Fiziko Matematicheskie Estestvennye i T ekhnicheskie Nauki
Izv Akad Nauk Arm SSR Geol Geogr Nauki — Izvestiya Akademii Nauk Armyanskoi SSR Geologicheskie i Geograficheskie Nauki
Izv Akad Nauk Arm SSR Khim Nauki — Izvestiya Akademii Nauk Armyanskoi SSR Khimicheskie Nauki
Izv Akad Nauk Arm SSR Med Nauki — Izvestiya Akademii Nauk Armyanskoi SSR Meditsinskie Nauki
Izv Akad Nauk Arm SSR Mekh — Izvestiya Akademii Nauk Armyanskoi SSR Mekhanika
Izv Akad Nauk Arm SSR Nauki Zemle — Izvestiya Akademii Nauk Armyanskoi SSR Nauki po Zemle
Izv Akad Nauk Arm SSR Ser Fiz-Mat Nauk — Izvestiya Akademii Nauk Armyanskoi SSR Seriya Fiziko-Matematicheskikh Nauk
Izv Akad Nauk Arm SSR Ser Khim Nauk — Izvestiya Akademii Nauk Armyanskoi SSR Seriya Khimicheskikh Nauk
Izv Akad Nauk Arm SSR Ser Mat — Izvestiya Akademii Nauk Armyanskoi SSR Seriya Matematika
Izv Akad Nauk Arm SSR Ser Mekh — Izvestiya Akademii Nauk Armyanskoi SSR Seriya Mekhanika
Izv Akad Nauk Arm SSR Ser Tekh Nauk — Izvestiya Akademii Nauk Armyanskoi SSR Seriya Tekhnicheskikh Nauk
Izv Akad Nauk Armyan SSR Biol Nauk — Izvestiya Akademiya Nauk Armyanskoi SSR Biologicheskie Nauk
Izv Akad Nauk Armyan SSR Ser Mekh — Izvestiya Akademii Nauk Armyanskoi SSR Seriya Mekhanika
Izv Akad Nauk Armyan SSR Ser Tekhn Nauk — Izvestiya Akademii Nauk Armyanskoi SSR Seriya Tekhnicheskikh Nauk
Izv Akad Nauk Azerbaidzan SSR Ser Fiz Tehn Mat Nauk — Izvestija Akademii Nauk Azerbaidzanskoi SSR Serija Fiziko-Tehniceskih i Matematiceskih Nauk
Izv Akad Nauk Azerbajdzansk SSR Ser Biol Selskohoz Nauk — Izvestija Akademii Nauk Azerbajdzanskogo SSR. Serija Biologiceskih i Sel'skohozjajstvennyh Nauk. Azaerbajgan SSR Elmlaer Akademijasynn Haebaerlae
Izv Akad Nauk Azerb Ser Fiz Tekh Mat Nauk — Izvestiya Akademii Nauk Azerbaidzhana. Seriya Fiziko-Tekhnicheskikh i Matematicheskikh Nauk
Izv Akad Nauk Azerb SSR — Izvestiya Akademii Nauk Azerbaidzhanskoi SSR
Izv Akad Nauk Azerb SSR Ser Biol Nauk — Izvestiya Akademii Nauk Azerbaidzhanskoi SSR Seriya Biologicheskikh Nauk
Izv Akad Nauk Azerb SSR Ser Lit Jaz Isk — Izvestiya Akademii Nauk Azerbajdzanskogo SSR Serija Literatury, Jazyka, i Iskusstva
Izv Akad Nauk Azerb SSR Ser Nauk Zemle — Izvestiya Akademii Nauk Azerbajdzanskoi SSR Seriya Nauk i Zemle
Izv Akad Nauk Az SSR — Izvestiya Akademii Nauk Azerbaidzhanskoi SSR
Izv Akad Nauk Az SSR Ser Biol Med Nauk — Izvestiya Akademii Nauk Azerbaidzhanskoi SSR Seriya Biologicheskikh i Meditsinskikh Nauk
Izv Akad Nauk Az SSR Ser Biol Nauk — Izvestiya. Akademii Nauk Azerbaidzhanskoi SSR Seriya Biologicheskikh Nauk
Izv Akad Nauk Az SSR Ser Biol Skh Nauk — Izvestiya Akademii Nauk Azerbaidzhanskoi SSR Seriya Biologicheskikh iSel'skokhozyaistvennykh Nauk
Izv Akad Nauk Az SSR Ser Fiz Mat Tekh Nauk — Izvestiya Akademii Nauk Azerbaidzhanskoi SSR SeriyaFiziko-Matematicheskikh i Tekhnicheskikh Nauk
Izv Akad Nauk Az SSR Ser Fiz-Tekh i Mat Nauk — Izvestiya Akademii Nauk Azerbaidzhanskoi SSR Seriya Fiziko-Tekhnicheskikh i Matematicheskikh Nauk
Izv Akad Nauk Az SSR Ser Fiz Tekh Khim Nauk — Izvestiya Akademii Nauk Azerbaidzhanskoi SSR SeriyaFiziko-Tekhnicheskikh i Khimicheskikh Nauk
Izv Akad Nauk Az SSR Ser Fiz-Tekh Mat Nauk — Izvestiya Akademii Nauk Azerbaidzhanskoi SSR Seriya Fiziko-Tekhnicheskikh i Matematicheskikh Nauk
Izv Akad Nauk Az SSR Ser Geol Geogr Nauk — Izvestiya Akademii Nauk Azerbaidzhanskoi SSR SeriyaGeologo-Geograficheskikh Nauk
Izv Akad Nauk Az SSR Ser Nauk Zemle — Izvestiya Akademii Nauk Azerbaidzhanskoi SSR Seriya Nauki i Zemle
Izv Akad Nauk Belarusi Ser Biol Nauk — Izvestiya Akademii Nauk Belarusi. Seriya Biologicheskikh Nauk
Izv Akad Nauk Belarusi Ser Fiz Energ Nauk — Izvestiya Akademii Nauk Belarusi. Seriya Fiziko-Energeticheskikh Nauk
Izv Akad Nauk Belarusi Ser Fiz Mat Nauk — Izvestiya Akademii Nauk Belarusi. Seriya Fiziko-Matematicheskikh Nauk
Izv Akad Nauk Belarusi Ser Fiz Tekh Nauk — Izvestiya Akademii Nauk Belarusi. Seriya Fiziko-Tekhnicheskikh Nauk
Izv Akad Nauk Belarusi Ser Khim Nauk — Izvestiya Akademii Nauk Belarusi. Seriya Khimicheskikh Nauk
Izv Akad Nauk Beloruss SSR Ser Biol Nauk — Izvestiya Akademii Nauk Belorusskoi SSR. Seriya Biologicheskikh Nauk
Izv Akad Nauk Beloruss SSR Ser Skh Nauk — Izvestiya Akademii Nauk Belorusskoi SSR. Seriya Sel'skokhozyaistvennykh Nauk
Izv Akad Nauk B SSR — Izvestiya Akademii Nauk Belorusskoi SSR
Izv Akad Nauk B SSR Ser Biol Nauk — Izvestiya Akademii Nauk Belorusskoi SSR Seriya Biologicheskikh Nauk
Izv Akad Nauk BSSR Ser Fiz Energ Nauk — Izvestiya Akademii Nauk BSSR Seriya Fiziko-Energeticheskikh Nauk
Izv Akad Nauk BSSR Ser Fiz-Mat Nauk — Izvestiya Akademii Nauk BSSR Seriya Fiziko-Matematicheskikh Nauk

Izv Akad Nauk BSSR Ser Fiz Tekh Nauk — Izvestiya Akademii Nauk BSSR Seriya Fiziko-Tekhnicheskikh Nauk

Izv Akad Nauk BSSR Ser Khim Nauk — Izvestiya Akademii Nauk BSSR Seriya Khimicheskikh Nauk

Izv Akad Nauk B SSR Ser S Kh Nauk — Izvestiya Akademii Nauk Belorusskoi SSR Seriya Sel'skokhozyaistvennykh Nauk

Izv Akad Nauk BSSR Ser S-Kh Navuk — Izvestiia Akademii Nauk BSSR. Seriia Selskokhoziaistvennykh Navuk

Izv Akad Nauk Ehst SSR Geol — Izvestiya Akademii Nauk Ehstonskoj SSR Geologiya

Izv Akad Nauk Ehst SSR Khim Geol — Izvestiya Akademii Nauk Ehstonskoj SSR Khimiya i Geologiya

Izv Akad Nauk Energ — Izvestiya Akademii Nauk. Energetika

Izv Akad Nauk Est Biol — Izvestiya Akademii Nauk Estonii. Biologiya

Izv Akad Nauk Est Fiz Mat — Izvestiya Akademii Nauk Estonii. Fizika, Matematika

Izv Akad Nauk Est Khim — Izvestiya Akademii Nauk Estonii. Khimiya

Izv Akad Nauk Estonskoi SSR Fiz Mat — Izvestiya Akademii Nauk Estonskoi SSR Seriya Fizichesko. Matematicheskaya

Izv Akad Nauk Estonskoi SSR Khim — Izvestiya Akademii Nauk Estonskoi SSR Seriya Khimicheskaya

Izv Akad Nauk Estonsk SSR Ser Biol — Izvestija Akademii Nauk Estonskoj SSR. Serija Biologii, Sel'skohozjajstvennyh Nauk i Medicinskih Nauk

Izv Akad Nauk Eston SSR Obsc Nauki — Izvestija Akademii Nauk Estonskoj SSR Obscestvennye Nauki

Izv Akad Nauk Eston SSR Ser Biol — Izvestija Akademii Nauk Estonskoi SSR Seriya Biologicheskaya

Izv Akad Nauk Est SSR — Izvestiya Akademii Nauk Estonskoi SSR

Izv Akad Nauk Est SSR Biol — Izvestiia Akademii Nauk Estonskoi SSR. Biologiia

Izv Akad Nauk Est SSR Fiz Mat — Izvestiya Akademii Nauk Estonskoi SSR Fizika Matematika

Izv Akad Nauk Est SSR Geol — Izvestiya Akademii Nauk Estonskoi SSR. Geologiya

Izv Akad Nauk Est SSR Khim — Izvestiya Akademii Nauk Estonskoi SSR. Khimiya

Izv Akad Nauk Est SSR Khim Eesti NSV Tead Akad Toim Keem — Izvestiia Akademii Nauk Estonskoi SSR Khimiia Eesti NSV Teaduste Akadeemia Toimetised Keemia

Izv Akad Nauk Est SSR Ser Biol — Izvestiya Akademii Nauk Estonskoi SSR Seriya Biologicheskaya

Izv Akad Nauk Est SSR Ser Fiz Mat Tekh Nauk — Izvestiia Akademii Nauk Estonskoi SSR Seriia Fiziko-Matematicheskikh i Tekhnicheskikh Nauk

Izv Akad Nauk Est SSR Ser Tekh Fiz Mat Nauk — Izvestiya Akademii Nauk Estonskoi SSR Seriya Tekhnicheskikh iFiziko-Matematicheskikh Nauk

Izv Akad Nauk Fiz Atmos Okeana — Izvestiya Akademii Nauk. Fizika Atmosfery i Okeana

Izv Akad Nauk Gruz Ser Biol — Izvestiya Akademii Nauk Gruzii. Seriya Biologicheskaya

Izv Akad Nauk Gruz Ser Khim — Izvestiya Akademii Nauk Gruzii. Seriya Khimicheskaya

Izv Akad Nauk Gruz SSR Ser Biol — Izvestiya Akademii Nauk Gruzinskoi SSR Seriya Biologicheskaya

Izv Akad Nauk Gruz SSR Ser Khim — Izvestiya Akademii Nauk Gruzinskoi SSR Seriya Khimicheskaya

Izv Akad Nauk Kazahsk SSR Ser Bot — Izvestija Akademii Nauk Kazahskoj SSR. Serija Botaniceskaja. Kazak SSR Gylym Akademijasynyn Habarlary

Izv Akad Nauk Kazah SSR Ser Fiz-Mat — Izvestija Akademii Nauk Kazahskoj SSR Serija Fiziko-Matematiceskaja

Izv Akad Nauk Kazah SSR Ser Obsc Nauk — Izvestija Akademii Nauk Kazahskoj SSR Serija Obscestvennyh Nauk

Izv Akad Nauk Kazakh SSR — Izvestiya Akademii Nauk Kazakhskoi SSR

Izv Akad Nauk Kazakh SSR Ser Biol — Izvestiya Akademii Nauk Kazakhskoi SSR Seriya Biologicheskaya

Izv Akad Nauk Kazakh SSR Ser Bot Pochvoved — Izvestiya Akademii Nauk Kazakhskoi SSR Seriya Botaniki i Pochvovedeniya

Izv Akad Nauk Kazakh SSR Ser Obshch Nauk — Izvestiya Akademiya Nauk Kazakhskoy SSR Seriya. Obshchestvennykh Nauk

Izv Akad Nauk Kaz SSR Ser Astron Fiz — Izvestiya Akademii Nauk Kazakhskoi SSR Seriya Astronomicheskaya i Fizicheskaya

Izv Akad Nauk Kaz SSR Ser Astron Fiz Mat Mekh — Izvestiya Akademii Nauk Kazakhskoi SSR Seriya Astronomii, Fiziki, Matematiki, Mekhaniki

Izv Akad Nauk Kaz SSR Ser Biol — Izvestiya Akademii Nauk Kazakhskoi SSR Seriya Biologicheskaya

Izv Akad Nauk Kaz SSR Ser Biol Nauk — Izvestiya Akademii Nauk Kazakhskoi SSR Seriya Biologicheskikh Nauk

Izv Akad Nauk Kaz SSR Ser Bot — Izvestiya Akademii Nauk Kazakhskoi SSR Seriya Botanicheskaya

Izv Akad Nauk Kaz SSR Ser Bot Pochvoved — Izvestiya Akademii Nauk Kazakhskoi SSR Seriya Botaniki i Pochvovedeniya

Izv Akad Nauk Kaz SSR Ser Energ — Izvestiya Akademii Nauk Kazakhskoi SSR Seriya Energeticheskaya

Izv Akad Nauk Kaz SSR Ser Fiziol — Izvestiya Akademii Nauk Kazakhskoi SSR Seriya Fiziologicheskaya

Izv Akad Nauk Kaz SSR Ser Fiziol Biokhim Rast — Izvestiya Akademii Nauk Kazakhskoi SSR Seriya Fiziologii i Biokhimii Rastenii

Izv Akad Nauk Kaz SSR Ser Fiziol Med — Izvestiya Akademii Nauk Kazakhskoi SSR Seriya Fiziologii i Meditsiny

Izv Akad Nauk Kaz SSR Ser Fiz-Mat — Izvestiya Akademii Nauk Kazakhskoi SSR Seriya Fiziko-Matematicheskaya

Izv Akad Nauk Kaz SSR Ser Fiz-Mat Nauk — Izvestiya Akademii Nauk Kazakhskoi SSR Seriya Fiziko-Matematicheskikh Nauk

Izv Akad Nauk Kaz SSR Ser Geol — Izvestiya Akademii Nauk Kazakhskoi SSR Seriya Geologicheskaya

Izv Akad Nauk Kaz SSR Ser Gorn Dela — Izvestiya Akademii Nauk Kazakhskoi SSR Seriya Gornogo Dela

Izv Akad Nauk Kaz SSR Ser Gorn Dela Metall Stroit Stroimat — Izvestiya Akademii Nauk Kazakhskoi SSR Seriya Gornogo Dela Metallurgii Stroitel'stva i Stroimaterialov

Izv Akad Nauk Kaz SSR Ser Khim — Izvestiya Akademii Nauk Kazakhskoi SSR Seriya Khimicheskaya

Izv Akad Nauk Kaz SSR Ser Mat Mekh — Izvestiya Akademii Nauk Kazakhskoi SSR Seriya Matematiki i Mekhaniki

Izv Akad Nauk Kaz SSR Ser Med Fiziol — Izvestiya Akademii Nauk Kazakhskoi SSR Seriya Meditsiny i Fiziologii

Izv Akad Nauk Kaz SSR Ser Med Nauk — Izvestiya Akademii Nauk Kazakhskoi SSR Seriya Meditsinskikh Nauk

Izv Akad Nauk Kaz SSR Ser Metall Obogashch Ogneuporov — Izvestiya Akademii Nauk Kazakhskoi SSR Seriya Metallurgii. Obogashcheniya i Ogneuporov

Izv Akad Nauk Kaz SSR Ser Mikrobiol — Izvestiya Akademii Nauk Kazakhskoi SSR Seriya Mikrobiologicheskaya

Izv Akad Nauk Kaz SSR Ser Tekh Khim Nauk — Izvestiya Akademii Nauk Kazakhskoi SSR Seriya Tekhnicheskikh Khimicheskikh Nauk

Izv Akad Nauk Kaz SSR Ser Zool — Izvestiya Akademii Nauk Kazakhskoi SSR Seriya Zoologicheskaya

Izv Akad Nauk Kirgiz SSR — Izvestija Akademija Nauk Kirgizskoi SSR

Izv Akad Nauk Kirgiz SSR Ser Biol Nauk — Izvestiya Akademii Nauk Kirgizskoi SSR Seriya Biologicheskikh Nauk

Izv Akad Nauk Kirg SSR — Izvestiya Akademii Nauk Kirgizskoi SSR

Izv Akad Nauk Kirg SSR Fiz Tekh Mat Nauki — Izvestiya Akademii Nauk Kirgizskoi SSR Fiziko-Tekhnicheskie iMatematicheskie Nauki

Izv Akad Nauk Kirg SSR Khim Tekhnol Nauki — Izvestiya Akademii Nauk Kirgizskoi SSR Khimiko-Tekhnologicheskie Nauki

Izv Akad Nauk Kirg SSR Ser Biol Nauk — Izvestiya Akademii Nauk Kirgizskoi SSR Seriya Biologicheskikh Nauk

Izv Akad Nauk Kirg SSR Ser Estestv Tekh Nauk — Izvestiya Akademii Nauk Kirgizskoi SSR Seriya Estestvennykh i Tekhnicheskikh Nauk

Izv Akad Nauk Latvii SSR — Izvestiya Akademii Nauk Latviiskoi SSR

Izv Akad Nauk Latvijsk SSR — Izvestija Akademii Nauk Latvijskoj SSR. Latvijas PSR Zinatnu Akademijas Vestis

Izv Akad Nauk Latv SSR — Izvestiya Akademii Nauk Latviiskoi SSR

Izv Akad Nauk Latv SSR Khim — Izvestiya Akademii Nauk Latviiskoi SSR Seriya Khimicheskikh Nauk

Izv Akad Nauk Latv SSR Ser Fiz Tekh Nauk — Izvestiya Akademii Nauk Latviiskoi SSR Seriya Fizicheskikh i Tekhnicheskikh Nauk

Izv Akad Nauk Latv SSR Ser Khim — Izvestiya Akademii Nauk Latviiskoi SSR Seriya Khimicheskaya

Izv Akad Nauk Mekh Zhidk Gaza — Izvestiya Akademii Nauk. Mekhanika Zhidkosti i Gaza

Izv Akad Nauk Moldav SSR — Izvestiya Akademii Nauk Moldavskoi SSR

Izv Akad Nauk Moldav SSR Ser Fiz-Tehn Mat Nauk — Izvestija Akademii Nauk Moldavskoj SSR Serija Fiziko-Tehniceskih i Matematiceskih Nauk

Izv Akad Nauk Mold SSR — Izvestiya Akademii Nauk Moldavskoi SSR

Izv Akad Nauk Mold SSR Ser Biol — Izvestiya Akademii Nauk Moldavskoi SSR Seriya Biologicheskaya

Izv Akad Nauk Mold SSR Ser Biol Khim Nauk — Izvestiya Akademii Nauk Moldavskoi SSR Seriya Biologicheskikh i Khimicheskikh Nauk

Izv Akad Nauk Mold SSR Ser Biol S-Kh Nauk — Izvestiya Akademii Nauk Moldavskoi SSR Seriya Biologicheskikh i Sel'skokhozyaistvennykh Nauk

Izv Akad Nauk Mold SSR Ser Fiz-Tekh Mat Nauk — Izvestiya Akademii Nauk Moldavskoi SSR Seriya Fiziko-Tekhnicheskikh i Matematicheskikh Nauk

Izv Akad Nauk Mold SSR Ser Obsc Nauk — Izvestija Akademii Nauk Moldavskoj SSR Serija Obscestvennyh Nauk

Izv Akad Nauk Resp Kaz Ser Biol — Izvestiya Akademii Nauk Respubliki Kazakhstan. Seriya Biologicheskaya

Izv Akad Nauk Resp Kaz Ser Fiz Mat — Izvestiya Akademii Nauk Respubliki Kazakhstan. Seriya Fiziko-Matematicheskaya

Izv Akad Nauk Resp Kaz Ser Geol — Izvestiya Akademii Nauk Respubliki Kazakhstan. Seriya Geologicheskaya

Izv Akad Nauk Resp Kaz Ser Khim — Izvestiya Akademii Nauk Respubliki Kazakhstan. Seriya Khimicheskaya

Izv Akad Nauk Resp Kyrg Fiz Tekh Mat Gorno Geol Nauki — Izvestiya Akademii Nauk Respubliki Kyrgyzstan. Fiziko-Tekhnicheskie, Matematicheskie, i Gorno-Geologicheskie Nauki

Izv Akad Nauk Resp Kyrg Khim Tekhnol Biol Nauki — Izvestiya Akademii Nauk Respubliki Kyrgyzstan. Khimiko-Tekhnologicheskie i Biologicheskie Nauki

Izv Akad Nauk Resp Mold Biol Khim Nauki — Izvestiya Akademii Nauk Respubliki Moldova. Biologicheskie i Khimicheskie Nauki

Izv Akad Nauk Resp Tadzh Otd Biol Nauk — Izvestiya Akademii Nauk Respubliki Tadzhikistan. Otdelenie Biologicheskikh Nauk

Izv Akad Nauk Resp Tadzh Otd Fiz Mat Khim Nauk — Izvestiya Akademii Nauk Respubliki Tadzhikistan. Otdelenie Fiziko-Matematicheskikh i Khimicheskikh Nauk

Izv Akad Nauk Respub Armeniya Mekh — Akademiya Nauk Respubliki Armeniya. Izvestiya. Mekhanika

Izv Akad Nauk Respub Moldova Fiz Tekhn — Akademiya Nauk Respubliki Moldova. Izvestiya. Fizika i Tekhnika

Izv Akad Nauk Respub Moldova Mat — Akademiya Nauk Respubliki Moldova. Izvestiya. Matematika

Izv Akad Nauk Ser Biol — Izvestiia Akademii Nauk. Seriia Biologicheskaia

Izv Akad Nauk Ser Fiz — Izvestiya Akademii Nauk. Seriya Fizicheskaya

Izv Akad Nauk Ser Geol — Izvestiya Akademii Nauk. Seriya Geologicheskaya

Izv Akad Nauk Ser Khim — Izvestiya Akademii Nauk. Seriya Khimicheskaya

Izv Akad Nauk SSR Mekh Zhidk Gaza — Izvestiya Akademii Nauk SSSR Mekhanika Zhidkosti i Gaza

Izv Akad Nauk SSR Mold Biol Khim Nauki — Izvestiya Akademii Nauk SSR Moldova. Biologicheskie i Khimicheskie Nauki

Izv Akad Nauk SSSR — Izvestiya Akademii Nauk SSSR

Izv Akad Nauk SSSR Biol — Izvestiya Akademii Nauk SSSR Seriya Biologicheskaya

Izv Akad Nauk SSSR Energ Transp — Izvestiya Akademii Nauk SSSR Energetika i Transport

Izv Akad Nauk SSSR Fiz — Izvestiya Akademii Nauk SSSR Seriya Fizicheskaya

Izv Akad Nauk SSSR Fiz Atmos i Okeana — Izvestiya Akademii Nauk SSSR Fizika Atmosfery i Okeana

Izv Akad Nauk SSSR Fiz Atmos Okeana — Izvestiya Akademii Nauk SSSR Fizika Atmosfery i Okeana

Izv Akad Nauk SSSR Fiz Zemli — Izvestiya Akademii Nauk SSSR Fizika Zemli

Izv Akad Nauk SSSR Khim — Izvestiya Akademii Nauk SSSR Seriya Khimicheskaya

Izv Akad Nauk SSSR Meh Tverd Tela — Izvestija Akademii Nauk SSSR Mehanika Tverdogo Tela

Izv Akad Nauk SSSR Meh Zidk Gaza — Izvestija Akademii Nauk SSSR Mehanika Zidkosti i Gaza

Izv Akad Nauk SSSR Mekh — Izvestiya Akademii Nauk SSSR Mekhanika

Izv Akad Nauk SSSR Mekh Mashinostr — Izvestiya Akademii Nauk SSSR Mekhanika i Mashinostroenie

Izv Akad Nauk SSSR Mekh Tverd Tela — Izvestiya Akademii Nauk SSSR Mekhanika Tverdogo Tela

Izv Akad Nauk SSSR Mekh Zhidk Gaza — Izvestiya Akademii Nauk SSSR Mekhanika Zhidkosti i Gaza

Izv Akad Nauk SSSR Mekh Zhidk i Gaza — Izvestiya Akademii Nauk SSSR Mekhanika Zhidkosti i Gaza

Izv Akad Nauk SSSR Mekh Zhidkosti Gaza — Izvestiya Akademii Nauk SSSR Mekhanika Zhidkosti i Gaza

Izv Akad Nauk SSSR Met — Izvestiya Akademii Nauk SSSR Metally

Izv Akad Nauk SSSR Metall Gorn Delo — Izvestiya Akademii Nauk SSSR Metallurgiya i Gornoe Delo

Izv Akad Nauk SSSR Metally — Izvestiya Akademii Nauk SSSR Metally

Izv Akad Nauk SSSR Neorg Mater — Izvestiya Akademii Nauk SSSR Neorganicheskie Materialy

Izv Akad Nauk SSSR Otd Fiz Mat Nauk — Izvestiya Akademii Nauk SSSR Otdelenie Fiziko-Matematicheskikh Nauk

Izv Akad Nauk SSSR Otd Khim Nauk — Izvestiya Akademii Nauk SSSR Otdelenie Khimicheskikh Nauk

Izv Akad Nauk SSSR Otd Mat Estest Nauk Ser Biol — Izvestiya Akademii Nauk SSSR Otdelenie Matematicheskikh iEstestvennykh Nauk. Seriya Biologicheskaya

Izv Akad Nauk SSSR Otd Mat Estest Nauk Ser Fiz — Izvestiya Akademii Nauk SSSR Otdelenie Matematicheskikh iEstestvennykh Nauk. Seriya Fizicheskaya

Izv Akad Nauk SSSR Otd Mat Estest Nauk Ser Geogr Geofiz — Izvestiya Akademii Nauk SSSR Otdelenie Matematicheskikh iEstestvennykh Nauk. Seriya Geograficheskaya i Geofizicheskaya

Izv Akad Nauk SSSR Otd Mat Estest Nauk Ser Geol — Izvestiya Akademii Nauk SSSR Otdelenie Matematicheskikh iEstestvennykh Nauk. Seriya Geologicheskaya

Izv Akad Nauk SSSR Otd Mat Estest Nauk Ser Khim — Izvestiya Akademii Nauk SSSR Otdelenie Matematicheskikh iEstestvennykh Nauk. Seriya Khimicheskaya

Izv Akad Nauk SSSR Otd Mat Estestv Nauk — Izvestiya Akademii Nauk SSSR Otdelenie Matematicheskikh i Estestvennykh Nauk

Izv Akad Nauk SSSR Otd Mat Nauk Ser Biol — Izvestiya Akademii Nauk SSSR. Otdelenie Matematiceskih i Estestvennyh Nauk. Serija Biologiceskaja/Bulletin. Academie des Sciences de l'URSS. Classe des Sciences Mathematiques et Naturelles. Serie Biologique

Izv Akad Nauk SSSR Otd Tekh Nauk — Izvestiya Akademii Nauk SSSR Otdelenie Tekhnicheskikh Nauk

Izv Akad Nauk SSSR Otd Tekh Nauk Energ Avtom — Izvestiya Akademii Nauk SSSR Otdelenie Tekhnicheskikh Nauk Energetika i Avtomatika

Izv Akad Nauk SSSR Otd Tekh Nauk Energ Transp — Izvestiya Akademii Nauk SSSR Otdelenie Tekhnicheskikh Nauk Energetika i Transport

Izv Akad Nauk SSSR Otd Tekh Nauk Mekh Mashinstr — Izvestiya Akademii Nauk SSSR Otdelenie Tekhnicheskikh Nauk Mekhanika i Mashinostroenie

Izv Akad Nauk SSSR Otd Tekh Nauk Mekh Masinostr — Izvestiya Akademii Nauk SSSR Otdelenie Tekhnicheskikh Nauk Mekhanika i Mashinostroenie

Izv Akad Nauk SSSR Otd Tekh Nauk Metall Gorn Delo — Izvestiya Akademii Nauk SSSR Otdelenie Tekhnicheskikh NaukMetallurgiya i Gornoe Delo

Izv Akad Nauk SSSR Otd Tekh Nauk Metall Topl — Izvestiya Akademii Nauk SSSR Otdelenie Tekhnicheskikh Nauk Metallurgiya i Toplivo

Izv Akad Nauk SSSR Otd Tekh Nauk Tekh Kibern — Izvestiya Akademii Nauk SSSR Otdelenie Tekhnicheskikh NaukTekhnicheskaya Kibernetika

Izv Akad Nauk SSSR Ser Biol — Izvestiya Akademii Nauk SSSR Seriya Biologicheskaya

Izv Akad Nauk SSSR Ser Ekon — Izvestija Akademii Nauk SSSR Serija Ekonomiceskaja

Izv Akad Nauk SSSR Ser Fiz — Izvestiya Akademii Nauk SSSR Seriya Fizicheskaya

Izv Akad Nauk SSSR Ser Fiz Atmosfer i Okeana — Izvestija Akademii Nauk SSSR Serija Fizika Atmosfery i Okeana

Izv Akad Nauk SSSR Ser Fiz Zemli — Izvestija Akademii Nauk SSSR Serija Fizika Zemli

Izv Akad Nauk SSSR Ser Geofiz — Izvestiya Akademii Nauk SSSR Seriya Geofizicheskaya

Izv Akad Nauk SSSR Ser Geogr — Izvestiya Akademii Nauk SSSR Seriya Geograficheskaya

Izv Akad Nauk SSSR Ser Geogr Geofiz — Izvestiya Akademii Nauk SSSR Seriya Geograficheskaya i Geofizicheskaya

Izv Akad Nauk SSSR Ser Geol — Izvestiya Akademii Nauk SSSR Seriya Geologicheskaya

Izv Akad Nauk SSSR Ser Geol (Transl Abstr) — Izvestiya Akademii Nauk SSSR Seriya Geologicheskaya (Translated Abstracts)

Izv Akad Nauk SSSR Ser Khim — Izvestiya Akademii Nauk SSSR Seriya Khimicheskaya

Izv Akad Nauk SSSR Ser Mat — Izvestiya Akademii Nauk SSSR Seriya Matematicheskaya

Izv Akad Nauk SSSR Tehn Kibernet — Izvestija Akademii Nauk SSSR Tekhniceskaja Kibernetika

Izv Akad Nauk SSSR Tekh Kibern — Izvestiya Akademii Nauk SSSR Tekhnicheskaya Kibernetika

Izv Akad Nauk SSSR Tekhn Kibernet — Izvestiya Akademii Nauk SSSR Tekhnicheskaya Kibernetika

Izv Akad Nauk Tadzhik SSR Otd Biol Nauk — Izvestiya Akademii Nauk Tadzhikskoi SSR Otdelenie Biologicheskikh Nauk

Izv Akad Nauk Tadzhik SSR Otdel Fiz-Mat Khim i Geol Nauk — Izvestiya Akademii Nauk Tadzhikskol SSR Otdelenle Flzlko-Matematicheskikh, Khimicheskikh, i Geologicheskikh Nauk

Izv Akad Nauk Tadzhik SSR Otd Fiz-Tekh Khim Nauk — Izvestiya Akademii Nauk Tadzhikskoi SSR Otdelenie Fizichesko-Tekhnicheskikh i Khimicheskikh Nauk

Izv Akad Nauk Tadzhik SSR Ser Filos Ekon Pravoved — Izvestiya Akademiya Nauk Tadzhikskoy SSR Seriya. Filosofiya, Ekonomika, Pravovedeniye

Izv Akad Nauk Tadzhik SSR Ser Vostokoved Ist Filol — Izvestiya Akademiya Nauk Tadzhikskoy SSR Seriya. Vostokovedeniye Istoriya Filologiya

Izv Akad Nauk Tadzh SSR Otd Biol Nauk — Izvestiya Akademii Nauk Tadzhikskoi SSR Otdelenie Biologicheskikh Nauk

Izv Akad Nauk Tadzh SSR Otd Estestv Nauk — Izvestiya Akademii Nauk Tadzhikskoi SSR Otdelenie Estestvennykh Nauk

Izv Akad Nauk Tadzh SSR Otd Fiz-Mat Geol-Khim Nauk — Izvestiya Akademii Nauk Tadzhikskoi SSR Otdelenie Fiziko-Matematicheskikh i Geologo-Khimicheskikh Nauk [*Later, Izvestiya Akademi Nauk Tadzhikskoi SSR Otdelenie Fiziko-Matematicheskikh, Khimicheskikh, i Geologicheskikh Nauk*]

Izv Akad Nauk Tadzh SSR Otd Fiz Mat Khim Geol Nauk — Izvestiya Akademii Nauk Tadzhikskoi SSR Otdelenie Fiziko-Matematicheskikh, Khimicheskikh, i Geologicheskikh Nauk

Izv Akad Nauk Tadzh SSR Otd Fiz-Tekh Khim Nauk — Izvestiya Akademii Nauk Tadzhikskoi SSR Otdelenie Fiziko-Tekhnicheskikh i Khimicheskikh Nauk

Izv Akad Nauk Tadzh SSR Otd Geol Khim Tekh Nauk — Izvestiya Akademii Nauk Tadzhikskoi SSR OtdelenieGeologo-Khimicheskikh i Tekhnicheskikh Nauk

Izv Akad Nauk Tadzh SSR Otd S-Kh Biol Nauk — Izvestiya Akademii Nauk Tadzhikskoi SSR Otdelenie Sel'skokhozyaistvennykh i Biologicheskikh Nauk

Izv Akad Nauk Tadzik SSR Otdel Fiz-Mat i Geolog-Him Nauk — Izvestija Akademii Nauk Tadzikskoi SSR Otdelenie Fiziko-Matematiceskih i Geologo-Himicesikh Nauk

Izv Akad Nauk Tadz SSR Otdelenie Obsc Nauk — Izvestija Akademii Nauk Tadzikiskoj SSR Otdelenie Obscestvennyh Nauk

Izv Akad Nauk Teh Kibern — Izvestija Akademii Nauk. Tekhnicheskaia Kibernetika

Izv Akad Nauk Turkm — Izvestiya Akademii Nauk Turkmenistana

Izv Akad Nauk Turkmensk SSR — Izvestija Akademii Nauk Turkmenskoj SSR. Turkmenistan SSRnin Ylymlar Akademijasynyn Habarlary

Izv Akad Nauk Turkmen SSR Ser Biol Nauk — Izvestiya Akademii Nauk Turkmenskoi SSR Seriya Biologicheskikh Nauk

Izv Akad Nauk Turkmen SSR Ser Fiz-Tehn Him Geol Nauk — Izvestija Akademii Nauk Turkmenskoi SSR Serija Fiziko-Tehniceskih Himiceskih i Geologiceskih Nauk

Izv Akad Nauk Turkm Ser Biol Nauk — Izvestiya Akademii Nauk Turkmenistana. Seriya Biologicheskikh Nauk

Izv Akad Nauk Turkm Ser Fiz Mat Tekh Khim Geol Nauk — Izvestiya Akademii Nauk Turkmenistana. Seriya Fiziko-Matematicheskikh. Tekhnicheskikh. Khimicheskikh i Geologicheskikh Nauk

Izv Akad Nauk Turkm SSR — Izvestiya Akademii Nauk Turkmenskoi SSR

Izv Akad Nauk Turkm SSR Ser Biol Nauk — Izvestiya Akademii Nauk Turkmenskoi SSR Seriya Biologicheskikh Nauk

Izv Akad Nauk Turkm SSR Ser Fiz-Tekh Khim Geol Nauk — Izvestiya Akademii Nauk Turkmenskoi SSR Seriya Fiziko-Tekhnicheskikh, Khimicheskikh, i Geologicheskikh Nauk

Izv Akad Nauk Turkm SSR Ser Obsc Nauk — Izvestija Akademii Nauk Turkmenskoj SSR Serija Obscestvennyh Nauk

Izv Akad Nauk Turkm SSSR Ser Obshchestv Nauk — Izvestiya Akademii Nauk Turkmenskoi SSSR Seriya Obshchestvennykh Nauk

Izv Akad Nauk Uzbeksk SSR — Izvestija Akademi Nauk Uzbekskoj SSR. Uzbekiston SSR Fanlar Akademijasining Ahboroti

Izv Akad Nauk Uzb SSR — Izvestiya Akademii Nauk Uzbekskoi SSR

Izv Akad Nauk Uzb SSR Ser Biol — Izvestiya Akademii Nauk Uzbekskoi SSR Seriya Biologicheskaya

Izv Akad Nauk Uzb SSR Ser Fiz-Mat Nauk — Izvestiya Akademii Nauk Uzbekskoi SSR Seriya Fiziko-Matematicheskikh Nauk

Izv Akad Nauk Uzb SSR Ser Geol — Izvestiya Akademii Nauk Uzbekskoi SSR Seriya Geologicheskaya

Izv Akad Nauk Uzb SSR Ser Khim Nauk — Izvestiya Akademii Nauk Uzbekskoi SSR Seriya Khimicheskikh Nauk

Izv Akad Nauk Uzb SSR Ser Med — Izvestiya Akademii Nauk Uzbekskoi SSR Seriya Meditsinskaya

Izv Akad Nauk Uzb SSR Ser Tekh Nauk — Izvestiya Akademii Nauk Uzbekskoi SSR Seriya Tekhnicheskikh Nauk

Izv Akad Nauk UzSSR Ser Biol — Izvestiya Akademii Nauk UzSSR Seriya Biologicheskaya

Izv Akad Nauk UzSSR Ser Fiz-Mat Nauk — Izvestija Akademii Nauk UzSSR. Serija Fiziko-Matematiceskih Nauk

Izv Akad Nauk UzSSR Ser Geol — Izvestiya Akademii Nauk UzSSR Seriya Geologicheskaya

Izv Akad Nauk UzSSR Ser Khim Nauk — Izvestiya Akademii Nauk UzSSR Seriya Khimicheskikh Nauk

Izv Akad Nauk UzSSR Ser Med — Izvestiya Akademii Nauk UzSSR Seriya Meditsinskaya

Izv Akad Nauk UzSSR Ser Tekh Nauk — Izvestiya Akademii Nauk Uzbekskoi SSR Seriya Tekhnicheskikh Nauk

Izv Akad Nauk UzSSR Tekh Nauki — Izvestiya Akademii Nauk UzSSR, Tekhnicheskie Nauki

Izv Akad Pedagog Nauk RSFSR — Izvestiya Akademii Pedagogicheskikh Nauk RSFSR

Izv Akad Selskostop Nauki Gorskostop Nauka — Izvestiya na Akademiyata na Selskostopanskite Nauki. GorskostopanskiNauka

Izv Akad Selskostop Nauki Gradinar Lozar Nauka — Izvestiya na Akademiyata na Selskostopanskite Nauki. Gradinarska iLozarska Nauka

Izv Akad Selskostop Nauki Rastenievud Nauki — Izvestiya na Akademiyata na Selskostopanskite Nauki. RastenievudniNauki

Izv Akad Selskostop Nauki Vet Med Nauki — Izvestiya na Akademiyata na Selskostopanskite Nauki. VeterinarnoMeditsinski Nauki

Izv Akad Selskostop Nauki Zhivotnovud Nauki — Izvestiya na Akademiyata na Selskostopanskite Nauki. ZhivotnovudniNauki

Izv Akad Stroit Arkhit SSSR — Izvestiya Akademii Stroitel'stva i Arkhitektury SSSR

Izv Akad Uzb SSR — Izvestiya Akademii Nauk Uzbekskoi SSR

Izv Akad Uzb SSR Fiz-Mat — Izvestiya Akademii Nauk Uzbekskoi SSR Seriya Fiziko-Matematicheskikh Nauk

Izv Ak N Armj SSR — Izvestija Akademii Nauk Armjanskoj SSR

Izv Ak N Kaz — Izvestija Akademii Nauk Kazahskoj SSR

Izv Ak N Mold SSR — Izvestija Akademii Nauk Moldavskoj SSR

Izv Ak N SSSR — Izvestija Akademii Nauk SSSR

Izv Ak N SSSR Ser Geogr — Izvestija Akademii Nauk SSSR Serija Geograficeskaja 1 Geofiziceskaja

Izv Altai Otd Geogr O-Va SSSR — Izvestiya Altaiskogo Otdela Geograficheskogo Obscestva SSSR

IzvAN — Izvestiya Akademii Nauk SSSR Otdelenie Literatury i Jazyka

IzvANArm — Izvestiya Akademii Nauk Armjanskoj SSR Obscestvennyh Nauk

IzvANAzerb — Izvestiya Akademii Nauk Azerbajdzhanskoj SSR Seriya Obscestvennych Nauk

IzvANKaz — Izvestiya Akademii Nauk Kazakhskoi SSR Seriya Filologii i Iskusstvovedeniya

Izv ANO Ch N — Izvestiya Akademii Nauk Otdelenie Chimiceskich Nauk

Izvanredna Izd Farmakol Inst Zagrebu — Izvanredna Izdanja Farmakoloskog Instituta Zagrebu

Izvanredna Izd Inst Farmakol Toksikol Zagrebu — Izvanredna Izdanja Instituta za Farmakologiju i Toksikologiju u Zagrebu

Izvanredna Izd Zavoda Farmakol Toksikol Med Fak Zagrebu — Izvanredna Izdanja Zavoda za Farmakologiju i Toksikologiju MedicinskogFakulteta u Zagrebu

IzvANTadz — Izvestiya Akademii Nauk Tadzhikskoi SSR Otdelenie Obscestvennych Nauk

IzvANTurkm — Izvestiya Akademii Nauk Turkmenskoi SSSR Seriya Obshchestvennych Nauk

Izv Arch Comm — Izvestiia Gosudarstvennoi Rossiiskoi Arkheologicheskoi Kommissii

Izv Arch Inst — Izvestija na Archeologiceskija Institut

Izv Arm Fil Akad Nauk SSSR — Izvestiya Armyanskogo Filiala Akademii Nauk SSSR

Izv Arm Fil Akad Nauk SSSR Estestv Nauki — Izvestiya Armyanskogo Filiala Akademii Nauk SSSR Estestvennye Nauki

IzvArmZPI — Izvestiya Armyanskogo Gosudarstvennogo Zaocnogo Pedagogiceskogo Instituta

Izv Astrofiz Inst Akad Nauk Kaz SSR — Izvestiya Astrofizicheskogo Instituta Akademiya Nauk Kazakhskoi SSR

Izv Azerb — Izvestiia Akademii Nauk Azerbaidzhanskoi SSR

Izv Azerb Fil Akad Nauk SSSR — Izvestiya Azerbaidzhanskogo Filiala Akademii Nauk SSSR

IZVBA — Internationale Zeitschrift fuer Vitaminforschung. Beiheft

IzvBAI — Izvestiya na Balgarskiya Archeologiceski Institut

Izv Batum Bot Sada — Izvestiya Batumskogo Botanicheskogo Sada

Izv Batum Bot Sada Akad Nauk Gruz SSR — Izvestiya Batumskogo Botanicheskogo Sada Akademii Nauk Gruzinskoi SSR

Izv Batumsk Subtrop Bot Sada — Izvestiya Batumskogo Subtropiceskogo Botaniceskogo Sada

Izv Biol Geogr Nauchno Issled Inst Irkutsk Gos Univ — Izvestiya Biologo-Geograficeskogo Nauchno-Issledovatel'skogo Instituta pri Irkutskom Gosudarstvennom Universitete

Izv Biol Geogr Naucno Issl Inst Vost Sibirsk Gosud Univ — Izvestija Biologo-Geograficeskogo Naucno-Issledovatel'skogo Instituta pri Vostocno-Sibirskom Gosudarstvennom Universitete. Bulletin de l'Institut Scientifique de Biologie et de Geographie a l'Universite d'Irkutsk

Izv Biol Inst — Izvestija na Biologiceskija Institut. Bulgarska Akademija na Naukite, Otdelenieza Biologicne i Medicinski Nauki

Izv Biol Inst Bulg Akad Nauk — Izvestiya na Biologicheskiya Institut. Bulgarska Akademiya na Naukite

Izv Biol Nauchno-Issled Inst Biol Stn Permsk Gos Univ — Izvestiya Biologicheskogo Nauchno-Issledovatel'skogo Instituta i BiologicheskoiStantsii pri Permskom Gosudarstvennom Universitete

Izv Biol Nauchno Issled Inst Molotov Gos Univ — Izvestiya Biologicheskogo Nauchno-Issledovatel'skogo Instituta pri Molotovskom Gosudarstvennom Universitete

Izv Biol Nauchno Issled Inst Permsk Gos Univ — Izvestiya Biologicheskogo Nauchno-Issledovatel'skogo Instituta priPermskom Gosudarstvennom Universitete

Izv Biol Naucno Issl Inst Permsk Gosud Univ Gorkogo — Izvestija Biologiceskogo Naucno-Issledovatel'skogo Instituta pri Permskom Gosudarstvennom Universitete imeni A.M. Gor'kogo. Bulletin de l'Institut des Recherches Biologiques de Perm

Izv Biol Nauki — Izvestija. Biologiceskie Nauki. Telekagir. Biologiakan Gitouthjounner

Izv Bot Inst — Izvestija na Botaniceskija Institut

Izv Bot Inst B Akad Nauk Otd Biol Nauki — Izvestiya na Botanicheskiya Instituta B'lgarska Akademiya Naukite Otdelenie za Biologichni Nauki

Izv Bot Inst B'lg Akad Nauk — Izvestiya na Botanicheskiya Instituta B'lgarska Akademiya na Naukite

Izv Bot Inst Bulg Akad Nauk — Izvestiya na Botanicheskiya Institut. Bulgarska Akademiya na Naukite

Izv Bot Zavoda Kr Sveucilista U Zagrebu — Acta Botanica Instituti Botanici Universitatis Zagrebiensis. Izvesta BotanickogZavoda Kr Sveucilista u Zagrebu

Izv Bulg A — Izvestiia na Arkheologicheskiia Institut. Bulgarska Akademiia na Naukite

Izv Bulg Akad Nauk Otd Fiz Mat Tekh Nauki Ser Fiz — Izvestiya na Bulgarskata Akademiya na Naukite. Otdelenie za Fiziko-Matematicheski i Tekhnicheski Nauki Seriya Fizicheska

Izv Bulg Bot Druz — Izvestija na Bulgarskoto Botanicesko Druzestvo. Bulletin de la Societe Botanique de Bulgarie

Izv Bulg Ist Druz — Izvestiia na Bulgarskoto Istorichesko Druzhestvo

Izv Burgas — Izvestija na Narodnija Muzej Burgas

Izv Byuro Evgen Akad Nauk SSSR — Izvestiya Byuro po Evgenike. Akademiya Nauk SSSR

Izv Byuro Genet Akad Nauk SSSR — Izvestiya Byuro po Genetike. Akademiya Nauk SSSR

Izv Byuro Genet Evgen Akad Nauk SSSR — Izvestiya Byuro po Genetike i Evgenike. Akademiya Nauk SSSR

Izv Cent Chelmint Lab — Izvestija na Centralnata Chelmintologicna Laboratorija

IzvCIngNII — Izvestiya Ceceno-Ingusskogo Naucno-Issledovatel-Skogo Instituta Istorii, Jazyka, i Literatury

Izv Dnepropetr Gorn Inst — Izvestiya Dnepropetrovskogo Gornogo Instituta

Izv Dobruzhan Selskostop Nauchnoizsled Inst Tolbukhin — Izvestiya na Dobrudzhanskiya Selskostopanski Nauchnoizsledovatelski Institut Tolbukhin

IzvDS — Izvestiya na Druzestvoto na Filolozite-Slavisti v Balgaria (Sofija)

Izv Durzh Inst Kontrol Lek Sredstva — Izvestiya na Durzhavniya Institut za Kontrol na Lekarstvenite Sredstva

Izv Ekaterinosl Gorn Inst — Izvestiya Ekaterinoslavskogo Gornogo Instituta

Izv Ekaterinosl Vyssh Gorn Uchil — Izvestiya Ekaterinoslavskogo Vysshago Gornago Uchilishcha

Izv Elektrotekh Inst (Leningrad) — Izvestiya Elektrotekhnicheskogo Instituta (Leningrad)

Izv Energ Inst Akad Nauk SSSR — Izvestiya Energeticheskogo Instituta Akademiya Nauk SSSR

Izv Erevan Med Inst Med Ova Arm — Izvestiya Erevanskogo Meditsinskogo Instituta i MeditsinskogoObshchestva Armenii

Izv Estestvennonauchn Inst Molotov Gos Univ — Izvestiya Estestvennonauchnogo Instituta pri MolotovskomGosudarstvennom Universitete

Izv Estestvennonauchn Inst Permsk Gos Univ — Izvestiya Estestvennonauchnogo Instituta pri Permskom Gosudarstvennom Universitet

Izv Estestv Nauchn Inst Im P S Lesgafta — Izvestiya Estestvenno-Nauchnogo Instituta Imeni P. S. Lesgafta

Izv Estestv-Nauchn Inst Molotov Gos Univ Im M Gor'kogo — Izvestiya Estestvenno-Nauchnogo Instituta pri Molotovskom Gosudarstvennom Universiteta Imeni M. Gor'kogo

Izv Estestv Naucn Inst Molotovsk Univ Gorkogo — Izvestija Estestvenno-Naucnogo Instituta pri Molotovskom Universitete imeni A. A. Gor'kogo

Izv Estestv Nauki — Izvestija. Estestvennye Nauki. Telekagir. Bnakan Gitouthjounner/Bulletin. Academy of Sciences. Armenian SSR

Izvestia-Varna — Izvestiia na Narodniia Muzei Varna

Izvestiia-Institut — Izvestiia na Arkheologicheskiia Institut. Bulgarska Akademiia na Naukite

Izvestija Inst MBAN — Izvestija na Instituta za Muzyka pri Bulgarskata Akademija na Naukite

Izvestija Varna — Izvestiia na Narodniia Muzei Varna

Izvest Imp Akad Nauk (S Petersburg) — Izvestiya Imperatorskoi Akademii Nauk (St. Petersburg)

Izvestiya Akad Nauk Kazakh SSR Seriya Obshchestvennaya — Izvestiya Akademii Nauk Kazakhskoy SSR. Seriya Obshchestvennaya

Izvestiya Akad Nauk SSSR — Izvestiya Akademii Nauk SSSR Otdelenie Literatury i Jazyka

Izvestiya Akad Nauk Tadzhiks SSR Otdeleniye Obshchestvennykh — Izvestiya Akademii Nauk Tadzhikskoy SSR. Otdeleniye Obshchestvennykh Nauk

Izvestiya Azerbay Filiala Akad Nauk SSSR — Izvestiya Azerbaydzhanskogo Filiala Akademii Nauk SSSR

Izvestiya Balg Arkheol Inst — Izvestiya na Balgarski Arkheologicheski Institut

Izvestiya Etnog Muz — Izvestiya na Etnografskiya Muzey

Izvestiya Imp Rus Geog Obshchestva — Izvestiya Imperatorskogo Russkogo Geograficheskogo Obshchestva

Izvestiya Inst Istor Mat Kult — Izvestiya Instituta Istorii Material'noy Kul'tury

Izvestiya Inst Izobrazitelni Izk — Izvestiya na Instituta za Izobrazitelni Izkustva

Izvestiya Jugo-Oset Nauc-Issl — Izvestiya Jugo-Osetinskogo Naucno-Issledovatel'skogo Instituta Akademii Nauk-Gruzinskoj SSR

Izvestiya Kirgiz Filiala Akad Nauk SSSR — Izvestiya Kirgizskogo Filiala Akademii Nauk SSSR

Izvestiya Tavricheskogo Obshchestva Istor Arkheol & Etnog — Izvestiya Tavricheskogo Obshchestva Istorii, Arkheologii Etnografii

Izvestiya Turkestanksogo Otdeleniya Imp Geog — Izvestiya Turkestanskogo Otdeleniya Imperatorskogo Geograficheskogo

Izvestiya Turkm Filiala Akad Nauk SSSR — Izvestiya Turkmenskogo Filiala Akademii Nauk SSSR

Izvestiya Voronezskogo Gos Ped Inst — Izvestiya Voronezskogo Gosudarstvennego Pedagogiceskogo Instituta

Izvest Ross Akad Nauk — Izvestiia Rossiiskoi Akademii Nauk

Izv Fak S kh Nauk Moshonmad'yarovar Vengriya — Izvestiya Fakul'teta Sel'skokhozyaistvennykh Nauk Moshonmad'yarovar Vengriya

Izv Fil Sladkovodno Ribar (Plovdiv) Inst Ribna Promst — Izvestiya na Filiala po Sladkovodno Ribarstvo (Plovdiv). Institut poRibna Promishlenost

Izv Fiz Inst ANEB Bulg Akad Nauk — Izvestiya na Fizicheskiya Instituta ANEB. Bulgarska Akademiya naNaukite

Izv Fiz-Khim Nauchno-Issled Inst Irkutsk Gos Univ — Izvestiya Fiziko-Khimicheskogo Nauchno-Issledovatel'skogo Instituta pri Irkutskom Gosudarstvennom Universitete

Izv Geofiz Inst — Izvestiya na Geofizichniya Institut

Izv Geofiz Inst Bulg Akad Nauk — Izvestiya na Geofizichniya Institut. Bulgarska Akademiya na Naukite

Izv Geol Inst Bulg Akad Nauk — Izvestia na Geologicheskiya Institut. Bulgarska Akademiya na Naukite

Izv Geol Inst Bulg Akad Nauk Ser Geokhim Mineral Petrogr — Izvestiya na Geologicheskiya Institut. Bulgarska Akademiya na Naukite. Seriya Geokhimiya, Mineralogiya, i Petrografiya

Izv Geol Inst Bulg Akad Nauk Ser Geotekton — Izvestiya na Geologicheskiya Institut. Bulgarska Akademiya na Naukite. Seriya Geotektonika

Izv Geol Inst Bulg Akad Nauk Ser Geotektonika Stratig Litol — Izvestiya na Geologicheskiya Institut. Bulgarska Akademiya na Naukite. Seriya Geotektonika, Stratigrafiya, i Litologiya

Izv Geol Inst Bulg Akad Nauk Ser Geotekton Stratigr Litol — Izvestiya na Geologicheskiya Institut. Bulgarska Akademiya na Naukite.Seriya Geotektonika, Stratigrafiya, i Litologiya

Izv Geol Inst Bulg Akad Nauk Ser Inzh Geol Khidrogeol — Izvestiya na Geologicheskiya Institut. Bulgarska Akademiya na Naukite. Seriya Inzhenerna Geologiya i Khidrogeologiya

Izv Geol Inst Bulg Akad Nauk Ser Neftena Vuglishtna Geol — Izvestiya na Geologicheskiya Institut. Bulgarska Akademiya na Naukite. Seriya Neftena i Vuglishtna Geologiya

Izv Geol Inst Bulg Akad Nauk Ser Neft Vuglishtna Geol — Izvestiya na Geologicheskiya Institut. Bulgarska Akademiya na Naukite.Seriya Neftena i Vuglishtna Geologiya

Izv Geol Inst Bulg Akad Nauk Ser Paleontol — Izvestiya na Geologicheskiya Institut. Bulgarska Akademiya na Naukite. Seriya Paleontologiya

Izv Geol Inst Bulg Akad Nauk Ser Prilozh Geofiz — Izvestiya na Geologicheskiya Institut. Bulgarska Akademiya na Naukite.Seriya Prilozhna Geofizika

Izv Geol Inst Bulg Akad Nauk Ser Prilozhna Geof — Izvestiya na Geologicheskiya Institut. Bulgarska Akademiya na Naukite. Seriya Prilozhna Geofizika

Izv Geol Inst Bulg Akad Nauk Ser Stratigr Litol — Izvestiya na Geologicheskiya Institut. Bulgarska Akademiya na Naukite. Seriya Stratigrafiya i Litologiya

Izv Geol Inst Ser Paleontol (Sofia) — Izvestiya na Geologicheskiya Institut. Seriya Paleontologiya (Sofia)

Izv Geol Inst Ser Prilozh Geofiz — Izvestiya na Geologicheskiya Institut. Seriya Prilozhna Geofizika

Izv Geol Ova Gruz — Izvestiya Geologicheskogo Obshchestva Gruzii

Izv GI Astron Obs Pulkove — Izvestiya Glavnoi Astronomicheskoi Observatorii v Pulkove

Izv Glavn Bot Sada SSSR — Izvestija Glavnogo Botaniceskogo Sada SSSR. Bulletin du Jardin Botanique Principal de l'URSS

Izv GI Ross Astron Obs — Izvestiya Glavnoi Rossiiskoi Astronomicheskoi Observatorii

Izv Gorskogo S'kh Inst — Izvestiya Gorskogo Sel'skokhozyaistvennogo Instituta

Izv Gos Nauchno-Issled Inst Kolloidn Khim — Izvestiya Gosudarstvennogo Nauchno-Issledovatel'skogo Instituta Kolloidnoi Khimii

Izv Gos Nauchno-Issled Inst Ozern Rechn Rybn Khoz — Izvestiya Gosudarstvennogo Nauchno-Issledovatel'skogo Instituta Ozernogo i Rechnogo Rybnogo Khozyaistva

Izv Gosud Ross Arkh Kom — Izvestiia Gosudarstvennoi Rossiiskoi Arkheologicheskoi Kommissii

Izv Gruz Nauchno Issled Inst Gidrotekh Melior — Izvestiya Gruzinskogo Nauchno-Issledovatel'skogo InstitutaGidrotekhniki i Melioratsii

IzvIBE — Izvestiya na Instituta za Belgarski Ezik

Izv Imp Akad Nauk — Izvestiya Imperatorskoi Akademii Nauk

Izv Imp Bot Sada Petra Velikago — Izvestija Imperatorskago Botaniceskago Sada Petra Velikago

Izv Imp Kazansk Univ — Izvestija Imperatorskago Kazanskago Universiteta

Izv Imp Lesn Inst — Izvestiya Imperatorskago Lesnago Instituta

Izv Inst Arch Bulg — Izvestiia na Arkheologicheskiia Institut. Bulgarska Akademiia na Naukite

Izv Inst Biokhim Bulg Akad Nauk — Izvestiya na Instituta po Biokhimiya. Bulgarska Akademiya na Naukite

Izv Inst Biol Bulg Akad Nauk — Izvestiya na Instituta po Biologiya. Bulgarska Akademiya na Naukite

Izv Inst Biol Metodij Popov — Izvestija na Instituta po Biologi Metodij Popov/ Bulletin. Methodi Popoff Institute of Biology

Izv Inst Biol "Metod Popov" Bulg Akad Nauk — Izvestiya na Instituta po Biologiya "Metodii Popov." Bulgarskoi Akademii Nauk

Izv Inst Chist Khim Reakt — Izvestiya Instituta Chistykh Khimicheskikh Reaktivov

Izv Inst Eksp Med Bulg Akad Nauk — Izvestiya na Instituta po Eksperimentalna Meditsina. Bulgarska Akademiya na Naukite

Izv Inst Eksp Vet Med Bulg Akad Nauk — Izvestiya na Instituta po Eksperimentalna Veterinarna Meditsina. Bulgarska Akademiya na Naukite

Izv Inst Elektron — Izvestiya na Instituta po Elektronika

Izv Inst Elektron Bulg Akad Nauk — Izvestiya na Instituta po Elektronika. Bulgarska Akademiya na Naukite

Izv Inst Energ Bulg Akad Nauk — Izvestiya na Instituta po Energetika. Bulgarska Akademiya na Naukite

Izv Inst Fizikokhim Bulg Akad Nauk — Izvestiya na Instituta po Fizikokhimiya. Bulgarska Akademiya na Naukite

Izv Inst Fiziol B'lg Akad Nauk — Izvestiya na Instituta po Fiziologiya. B'lgarska Akademiya na Naukite

Izv Inst Fiziol Bulg Akad Nauk — Izvestiya na Instituta po Fiziologiya. Bulgarska Akademiya na Naukite

Izv Inst Fiziol Rast Bulg Akad Nauk — Izvestiya na Instituta po Fiziologiya na Rasteniyata. Bulgarska Akademiya na Naukite

Izv Inst Fiziol Rast "Metodii Popov" Bulg Akad Nauk — Izvestiya na Instituta po Fiziologiya na Rasteniyata "Metodii Popov." BulgarskaAkademiya na Naukite

Izv Inst Fiziol Rast "Metod Popov" Bulg Akad Nauk — Izvestiya na Instituta po Fiziologiya na Rasteniyata "Metodii Popov." Bulgarskoi Akademii Nauk

Izv Inst Fiziol (Sofia) — Izvestiia na Instituta po Fiziologiia (Sofia)

Izv Inst Fiz Khim Anal Akad Nauk SSSR — Izvestiya Instituta Fiziko-Khimicheskogo Analiza. Akademiya Nauk SSSR

Izv Inst Furazhite Pleven — Izvestiya. Institut po Furazhite. Pleven

Izv Inst Gorata Akad Selskostop Nauki Bulg — Izvestiya na Instituta za Gorata. Akademiya na Selskostopanskite Nauki v Bulgariya

Izv Izuch Platin Drugikh Blagorodn Met Akad Nauk SSSR — Izvestiya na Instituta po Izucheniya Platiny i Drugikh Blagorodnykh Metallov. Akademiya Nauk SSSR

Izv Inst Khidrol Meteor — Izvestiya na Instituta po Khidrologiya i Meteorologiya. Bulgarska Akademiya na Naukite

Izv Inst Khidrol Meteorol Bulg Akad Nauk — Izvestiya na Instituta po Khidrologiya i Meteorologiya. Bulgarska Akademiya na Naukite

Izv Inst Khidrotekh Melior Akad Selskostop Nauki Bulg — Izvestiya na Instituta Khidrotekhnika i Melioratsii. Akademiya Selskostopanskite Nauki v Bulgariya

Izv Inst Khranene Bulg Akad Nauk — Izvestiya na Instituta po Khranene. Bulgarska Akademiya na Naukite

Izv Inst Klin Obshchest Med Bulg Akad Nauk — Izvestiya na Instituta za Klinichna i Obshchestvena Meditsina. Bulgarska Akademiya na Naukite

Izv Inst Lozar Vinar (Pleven) Akad Selskostop Nauki Bulg — Izvestiya na Instituta po Lozarstvo i Vinarstvo (Pleven). Akademiya na Selskostopanskite Nauki v Bulgariya

Izv Inst Morfol B'lg Akad Nauk Med Nauki — Izvestiya na Instituta po Morfologiya. Bulgarska Akademiya na Naukite za Meditsinski Nauki

Izv Inst Morfol Bulg Akad Nauk — Izvestiya na Instituta po Morfologiya. Bulgarska Akademiya na Naukite

Izv Inst Nauk Iskusstv SSR Arm — Izvestiya Instituta Nauk i Iskusstv SSR Armenii

Izv Inst Obshcha Sravn Patol B'lg Akad Nauk — Izvestiya na Instituta po Obshcha i Sravnitelna Patologiya. Bulgarska Akademiyana Naukite

Izv Inst Obshcha Sravn Patol Bulg Akad Nauk — Izvestiya na Instituta po Obshcha i Sravnitelna Patologiya. Bulgarska Akademiyana Naukite

Izv Inst Obshch Sravn Patol Bulg Akad Nauk — Izvestiya na Instituta po Obshcha i Sravnitelna Patologiya. Bulgarska Akademiyana Naukite

Izv Inst Obshta Neorg Khim Bulg Akad Nauk — Izvestiya na Instituta po Obshta i Neorganichna Khimiya. Bulgarska Akademiya naNaukite

Izv Inst Obshta Neorg Khim Org Khim Bulg Akad Nauk — Izvestiya na Instituta po Obshta i Neorganichna Khimiya i po OrganichnaKhimiya. Bulgarska Akademiya na Naukite

Izv Inst Obshta Sravn Patol Bulg Akad Nauk — Izvestiya na Instituta po Obshta i Sravnitelna Patologiya. BulgarskaAkademiya na Naukite

Izv Inst Obshta Sravn Patol Bylg — Izvestiya na Instituta po Obshta i Sravnitelna Patologiya. Bylgarska Akademiya na Naukite

Izv Inst Okeanogr Ribno Stop Bulg Akad Nauk — Izvestiya na Instituta po Okeanografiya i Ribno Stopanstvo. Bulgarska Akademiyana Naukite

Izv Inst Org Khim Bulg Akad Nauk — Izvestiya na Instituta po Organichna Khimiya. Bulgarska Akademiya na Naukite

Izv Inst Ovoshcharstvo — Izvestiya na Instituta po Ovoshcharstvo. Gara Kostinbrod

Izv Inst Pamuka (Chirpan) — Izvestiya na Instituta po Pamuka (Chirpan)

Izv Inst Pochvozn Agrotekh Akad Selskostop Nauki Bulg — Izvestiya na Instituta za Pochvoznanie i Agrotekhnika. Akademiya naSelskostopanskite Nauki v Bulgariya

Izv Inst Pocvov Sredne Aziatsk Gosud Univ — Izvestija Instituta Pocvovedenija i Geobotaniki Sredne-Aziatskogo Gosudarstvennogo Universiteta. Bulletin. Institut de Pedologie et de Geobotanique. Universitede l'Asie Centrale

Izv Inst Pshenitsata Slunchogleda (Tolbukhin) — Izvestiya. Institut po Pshenitsata i Slunchogleda (Tolbukhin)

Izv Inst Rast Bulg Akad Nauk — Izvestiya na Instituta po Rastenievudstvo. Bulgarska Akademiya na Naukite

Izv Inst Rastenievud Akad Selskostop Nauki Bulg — Izvestiya na Instituta po Rastenievudstvo. Akademiya na Selskostopanskite Naukiv Bulgariya

Izv Inst Ribni Resur (Varna) — Izvestiya. Institut Ribni Resursov (Varna)

Izv Inst Ribovud Ribolov (Varna) Bulg Akad Nauk — Izvestiya na Instituta po Ribovudstvo i Ribolov (Varna). BulgarskaAkademiya na Naukite

Izv Inst Rybn Resur — Izvestiya. Institut Rybnykh Resursov (Varna)

Izv Inst Sladkovodno Ribovud (Plovdiv) — Izvestiya. Institut po Sladkovodno Ribovudstvo (Plovdiv)

Izv Inst Sravn Patol Zhivotn — Izvestiya na Instituta po Sravnitelna Patologiya na Zhivotnite

Izv Inst Sravn Patol Zhivotn B'lg Akad Nauk Otd Biol Nauki — Izvestiya na Instituta po Sravnitelna Patologiya na Zhivotnite. Bulgarska Akademiya na Naukite Otdelenie za Biologichni Nauki

Izv Inst Sravn Patol Zhivotn Bulg Akad Nauk — Izvestiya na Instituta po Sravnitelna Patologiya na Zhivotnite. Bulgarska Akademiya na Naukite

Izv Inst Sravn Patol Zhivotn Bylg — Izvestiya na Instituta po Sravnitelna Patologiya na Zhivotnite. Bylgarska Akademiya na Naukite

Izv Inst Srav Patol Zhivotn Bulg Akad Nauk — Izvestiya na Instituta po Sravnitelna Patologiya na Zhivotnite. Bulgarska Akademiya na Naukite

Izv Inst Tekh Kibern — Izvestiya na Instituta po Tekhnicheska Kibernetika

Izv Inst Tekh Kibern Bulg Akad Nauk — Izvestiya na Instituta po Tekhnicheska Kibernetika. Bulgarska Akademiyana Naukite

Izv Inst Tekh Mekh Bulg Akad Nauk — Izvestiya na Instituta po Tekhnicheska Mekhanika. Bulgarska Akademiya na Naukite

Izv Inst Tsarevitsata-Knezha — Izvestiya na Instituta po Tsarevitsata-Knezha

Izv Inst Tyutyuna (Plovdiv) Akad Selskostop Nauki Bulg — Izvestiya na Instituta po Tyutyuna (Plovdiv). Akademiya na Selskostopanskite Nauki v Bulgariya

Izv Inst Vodni Probl Bulg Akad Nauk — Izvestiya na Instituta po Vodni Problemi. Bulgarska Akademiya na Naukite

Izv Inst Vodno Stop Stroit Bulg Akad Nauk — Izvestiya na Instituta po Vodno Stopanstvo i Stroitelstvo. Bulgarska Akademiya na Naukite

Izv Inst Vodn Probl Bulg Akad Nauk — Izvestiya na Instituta po Vodni Problemi. Bulgarska Akademiya na Naukite. Otdelenie za Tekhnicheskij Nauki

Izv Inst Zhivotn Bulg Akad Nauk — Izvestiia. Institut za Zhivotnovudstvo Bulgarska Akademiya na Naukite

Izv Inst Zhivotnovud Bulg Akad Nauk — Izvestiya na Instituta po Zhivotnovudstvo. Bulgarska Akademiya naNaukite

Izv Inst Zhivotnovud (Kostinbrod) Akad Selskostop Nauki Bulg — Izvestiya na Instituta po Zhivotnovudstvo (Kostinbrod). Akademiya na Selskostopanskite Nauki v Bulgariya

IzvIRGruz — Izvestiya. Institut Rukopisej Akademii Nauk Gruzinskoj SSR

Izv Irkutsk Gos Pedagog Inst — Izvestiya Irkutskogo Gosudarstvennogo Pedagogicheskogo Instituta

Izv Irkutsk Nauchno-Issled Protivochumn Inst Sib Dal'n Vost — Izvestiya Irkutskogo Nauchno-Issledovatel'skogo Protivochumnogo Instituta Sibiri i Dal'nego Vostoka

Izv Irkutsk Skh Inst — Izvestiya Irkutskogo Sel'skokhozyaistvennogo Instituta

Izv Ivanovo Voznesensk Politekh Inst — Izvestiya Ivanovo-Voznesenskogo Politekhnicheskogo Instituta

Izv Ivanov Skh Inst — Izvestiya Ivanovskogo Sel'skokhozyaistvennogo Instituta

Izv Jakutsk Otd Imp Russk Geogr Obsc — Izvestija Jakutskago Otdela Imperatorskago Russkago Geograficeskago Obscestva

Izvjesca Inst Oceanogr Ribar Splitu — Izvjesca. Institut za Oceanografiju i Ribarstvo u Splitu

IzvJOsNII — Izvestiya Jugo-Osetinskogo Naucno-Issledovatel'skogo Instituta

Izv Jugo Oset Nauc-Issled Inst Akad Nauk Gruz SSR — Izvestija Jugo-Osetinskogo Naucno-Issledovatelskogo Instituta Akademii Nauk Gruzinskoj SSR

IzvJuOsI — Izvestiya Jugo-Osetinskogo Naucno-Issledovatel'skogo Instituta Akademii Nauk-Gruzinskoj SSR

Izv Juzno Ussurijsk Otd Gosud Russk Geogr Obsc — Izvestija Juzno-Ussurijskogo Otdela Gosudarstvennogo Russkogo Geograficeskogo Obscestva/ Bulletin. Southern Ussuri Branch. Russian Geographical Society

Izv Kalinin Gos Pedagog Inst — Izvestiya Kalininskogo Gosudarstvennogo Pedagogicheskogo Instituta

Izv Kamarata Nar Kult Ser Biol Zemed Lesovud — Izvestiya na Kamarata na Narodnata Kultura. Seriya Biologiya Zemedelie i Lesovudstvo

Izv Karel Kolsk Fil Akad Nauk SSSR — Izvestiya Karel'skogo i Kol'skogo Filialov Akademii Nauk SSSR

Izv Karelo Finsk Fil Akad Nauk SSSR — Izvestija Karelo-Finskogo Filiala Akademii Nauk SSSR

Izv Kaz — Izvestiia Akademiia Nauk Kazakhskoi. Seriia Arkheologicheskaia

Izv Kazahsk Fil Akad Nauk SSSR — Izvestiya Kazahskogo Filiala Akademii Nauk SSSR. KSRO Gylym Akademijasynyn Kazak Filialynyn Habarlary

Izv Kazan Fil Akad Nauk SSR — Izvestiya Kazanskogo Filiala Akademii Nauk SSR

Izv Kazan Fil Akad Nauk SSSR Ser Biol Nauk — Izvestiya Kazanskogo Filiala Akademii Nauk SSSR Seriya Biologicheskikh Nauk

Izv Kazan Fil Akad Nauk SSSR Ser Biol Skh Nauk — Izvestiya Kazanskogo Filiala Akademii Nauk SSSR Seriya Biologicheskikh i Sel's kokhozyaistvennykh Nauk

Izv Kazan Fil Akad Nauk SSSR Ser Fiz-Mat i Tehn Nauk — Izvestija Kazanskogo Filiala Akademii Nauk SSSR Serija Fiziko-Matematiceskih iTehniceskih Nauk

Izv Kazan Fil Akad Nauk SSSR Ser Fiz Mat Tekh Nauk — Izvestiya Kazanskogo Filiala Akademii Nauk SSSR Seriya Fiziko-Matematicheskikhi Tekhnicheskikh Nauk

Izv Kazan Fil Akad Nauk SSSR Ser Geol Nauk — Izvestiya Kazanskogo Filiala Akademii Nauk SSSR Seriya Geologicheskikh Nauk

Izv Kazan Fil Akad Nauk SSSR Ser Khim Nauk — Izvestiya Kazanskogo Filiala Akademii Nauk SSSR Seriya Khimicheskikh Nauk

Izv Kazan Lesotekh Inst — Izvestiya Kazanskogo Lesotekhnicheskogo Instituta

Izv Kaz Fil Akad Nauk SSSR Ser Biol — Izvestiya Kazakhskogo Filiala Akademii Nauk SSSR. SeriyaBiologicheskaya

Izv Kaz Fil Akad Nauk SSSR Ser Bot — Izvestiya Kazakhskogo Filiala Akademii Nauk SSSR. Seriya Botanicheskaya

Izv Kaz Fil Akad Nauk SSSR Ser Energ — Izvestiya Kazakhskogo Filiala Akademii Nauk SSSR. SeriyaEnergeticheskaya

Izv Kaz Fil Akad Nauk SSSR Ser Fiziol Biokhim Rast — Izvestiya Kazakhskogo Filiala Akademii Nauk SSSR. Seriya Fiziologii iBiokhimii Rastenii

Izv Kaz Fil Akad Nauk SSSR Ser Gorn Dela — Izvestiya Kazakhskogo Filiala Akademii Nauk SSSR. Seriya Gornogo Dela

Izv Kaz Fil Akad Nauk SSSR Ser Zool — Izvestiya Kazakhskogo Filiala Akademii Nauk SSSR. SeriyaZoologicheskaya

Izv Khidravl Lab Inzh Stroit Inst — Izvestiya na Khidravlicheskata Laboratoriya. Inzhenerno-StroitelenInstitut

Izv Khidravl Lab Vissh Inzh Stroit Inst — Izvestiya na Khidravlicheskata Laboratoriya Vissh Inzhenerno-Stroitelen Institut

Izv Khim — Izvestiya po Khimiya

Izv Khim Inst Bulg Akad Nauk — Izvestiya na Khimicheskiya Institut. Bulgarska Akademiya na Naukite

Izv Khlopchatobum Prom — Izvestiya Khlopchatobumazhnoi Promyshlennosti

Izv Khlopchatobum Promsti — Izvestiya Khlopchatobumazhnoi Promyshlennosti

Izv Kiev Politekh Inst — Izvestiya Kievskogo Politekhnicheskogo Instituta

Izv Kievsk Bot Sada — Izvestiya Kievskogo Botaniceskogo Sada. Visnyk Kyjivsk'kogo Botanicnogo Sadu. Bulletin de Jardin Botanique de Kieff

Izv Kirg Fil Akad Nauk SSSR — Izvestiya Kirgizskogo Filiala Akademii Nauk SSSR

Izv Kirg Fil Vses Ova Pochvovedov — Izvestiya Kirgizskogo Filiala Vsesoyuznogo Obshchestva Pochvovedov

Izv Kirg Geogr Ova — Izvestiya Kirgizskogo Geograficheskogo Obshchestva

Izv Kom Fiz Planet Akad Nauk SSSR — Izvestiya Komissii po Fizike Planet Akademiya Nauk SSSR

Izv Komi Fil Geogr Obsc SSSR — Izvestija Komi Filiala Geograficeskogo Obscestva SSSR

Izv Komi Fil Geogr Ova SSSR — Izvestiya Komi Filiala Geograficheskogo Obshchestva SSSR

Izv Komi Fil Vses Geogr Obshch — Izvestiya Komi Filiala Vsesoyuznogo Geograficheskogo Obshchestva

Izv Komi Fil Vses Geogr Ova — Izvestiya Komi Filiala Vsesoyuznogo Geograficheskogo Obshchestva

Izv Komi Fil Vses Geogr O-Va SSSR — Izvestiya Komi Filiala Vsesoyuznogo Geograficheskogo Obshchestva SSSR

Izv Kompleks Selskostop Nauchnoizsled Inst (Karnobat) — Izvestiya na Kompleksniya Selskostopanski Nauchnoizsledovatelski Institut (Karnobat)

Izv Krasnojarsk Otd Russk Geogr Obsc — Izvestiya Krasnojarskogo Otdela Russkogo Geograficeskogo Obscestva

Izv Krasnojarsk Podotd Vost Sibirsk Otd Imp Russk Geogr Obsc — Izvestija Krasnojarskago Podotdela Vostocno-Sibirskago Otdela Imperatorskago Russkago Geograficeskago Obscestva

Izv Krym Astrofiz Obs — Izvestiya Krymskoi Astrofizicheskoi Observatorii

Izv Krym Otd Geogr Ova SSSR — Izvestiya Krymskogo Otdela Geograficheskogo Obshchestva SSSR

Izv Krym Pedagog Inst — Izvestiya Krymskogo Pedagogicheskogo Instituta

Izv Krymsk Otd Geog Obshch Soyuza SSR — Izvestiya Krymskogo Otdela Geograficheskogo Obshchestva SSSR

Izv Kuban Pedagog Inst — Izvestiya Kubanskogo Pedagogicheskogo Instituta

Izv Kuibyshev Inzh Melior Inst — Izvestiya Kuibyshevskogo Inzhenerno-Meliorativnogo Instituta

Izv Kuibyshev Sel'khoz Inst — Izvestiya Kuibyshevskogo Sel'skokhozyaistvennogo Instituta

Izv Kuibyshev S-Kh Inst — Izvestiya Kuibyshevskogo Sel'skokhozyaistvennogo Instituta

Izv Kurgan Mashinostroit Inst — Izvestiya Kurganskogo Mashinostroitel'nogo Instituta

Izv Latv Akad Nauk — Izvestiya Latviiskoi Akademii Nauk

Izv Leningr Elektrotekh Inst — Izvestiya Leningradskogo Elektrotekhnicheskogo Instituta

Izv Leningr Elektrotekh Inst Im V I Ul'yanova — Izvestiya Leningradskogo Elektrotekhnicheskogo Instituta Imeni V. I.Ul'yanova

Izv Leningr Lesn Inst — Izvestiya Leningradskogo Lesnogo Instituta

Izv Lesotekh Akad — Izvestiya Lesotekhnicheskoi Akademii

Izv Med Inst Bulg Akad Nauk — Izvestiya na Meditsinskite Institut. Bulgarska Akademiya na Naukite

Izv Mikrobiol Inst Bulg Akad Nauk — Izvestiya na Mikrobiologicheskiya Institut. Bulgarska Akademiya na Naukite

Izv Mikrobiol Inst Sof — Izvestiya na Mikrobiologicheskiya Institut Sofiya

Izv Mikrobiol Inst (Sofia) — Izvestiya na Mikrobiologicheskiia Institut (Sofia)

Izv Minist Nauki Akad Nauk Resp Kaz Ser Biol — Izvestiya Ministerstva Nauki. Akademii Nauk Respubliki Kazakhstan. Seriya Biologicheskaya

Izv Minist Nauki Akad Nauk Resp Kaz Ser Biol Med — Izvestiya Ministerstva Nauki. Akademii Nauk Respubliki Kazakhstan. Seriya Biologicheskaya i Meditsinskaya

Izv Minist Nauki Akad Nauk Resp Kaz Ser Fiz Mat — Izvestiya Ministerstva Nauki-Akademii Nauk Respubliki Kazakhstan. Seriya Fiziko-Matematicheskaya

Izv Minist Nauki Akad Nauk Resp Kaz Ser Khim — Izvestiya Ministerstva Nauki-Akademii Nauk Respubliki Kazakhstan. Seriya Khimicheskaya

Izv Minist Proizvod Zagotovok S-Kh Prod Arm SSR — Izvestiya Ministerstva Proizvodstva i Zagotovok Sel'skokhozyaistvennykh Productov Armyanskoi SSR

Izv Minist Selsk Khoz Arm SSR — Izvestiya Ministerstvo Sel'skogo Khozyaistva Armyanskoi SSR

Izv Minist Sel'sk Khoz Arm SSR S-Kh Nauki — Izvestiya Ministerstvo Sel'skogo Khozyaistva Armyanskoi SSR Sel'skokhozyaistvennye Nauki

Izv Minist Skh Arm SSR — Izvestiya Ministerstvo Sel'skogo Khozyaistva Armyanskoi SSR

Izv Mold Fil Akad Nauk SSSR — Izvestiya Moldavskogo Filiala Akademii Nauk SSSR

Izv Mosk Skh Inst — Izvestiya Moskovskogo Selskokhozyaistvennogo Instituta

Izv Mosk Tekst Inst — Izvestiya Moskovskii Tekstil'nyi Institut

Izv Muz Juz Balg — Izvestija na Muzeite ot Juzna Balgarija

Izv Nachnoizsled Inst Okeanogr Ribno Stop (Varna) — Izvestiya na Nauchnoizsledovatelskiya Institut po Okeanografiya i Ribno Stopanstvo (Varna)

Izv Narod Muz Burgas — Izvestiia na Narodniia Muzei Burgas

Izv Nats Akad Nauk Armenii Mat — Natsional'naya Akademiya Nauk Armenii. Izvestiya. Matematika

Izv Nats Akad Nauk Resp Kaz Ser Biol — Izvestiya Natsional'noi Akademii Nauk Respubliki Kazakhstan. Seriya Biologicheskaya

Izv Nats Akad Nauk Resp Kaz Ser Fiz Mat — Izvestiya Natsional'noi Akademii Nauk Respubliki Kazakhstan. Seriya Fiziko-Matematicheskaya

Izv Nats Akad Nauk Resp Kaz Ser Geol — Izvestiya Natsional'noi Akademii Nauk Respubliki Kazakhstan. Seriya Geologicheskaya

Izv Nats Akad Nauk Resp Kaz Ser Khim — Izvestiya Natsional'noi Akademii Nauk Respubliki Kazakhstan. Seriya Khimicheskaya

Izv Nauchno Issled Geol Inst (Sofia) — Izvestiya Nauchno-Issledovatel'skogo Geologicheskogo Instituta (Sofia)

Izv Nauchno Issled Inst Gidrotekh — Izvestiya Nauchno-Issledovatel'skogo Instituta Gidrotekhniki

Izv Nauchno Issled Inst Mashinostr Metalloobrab — Izvestiya Nauchno-Issledovatel'skogo Instituta Mashinostroeniya iMetalloobrabotki

Izv Nauchno-Issled Inst Nefte Uglekhim Sint Irkutsk Univ — Izvestiya Nauchno-Issledovatel'skogo Instituta Nefte- i Uglekhimicheskogo Sinteza pri Irkutskom Universitete

Izv Nauchno Issled Inst Ozern Rechn Rybn Khoz — Izvestiya Nauchno-Issledovatel'skogo Instituta Ozernogo i Rechnogo Rybnogo Khozyaistva

Izv Nauchno-Issled Inst Postoyan Toka — Izvestiya Nauchno-Issledovatel'skogo Instituta Postoyannogo Toka

Izv Nauchno Issled Inst Uglya (Prague) — Izvestiya Nauchno-Issledovatel'skogo Instituta Uglya (Prague)

Izv Nauchnoizsled Geol Inst (Sofia) — Izvestiya na Nauchnoizsledovatelskiya Geolozhki Institut (Sofia)

Izv Nauchnoizsled Inst Gorata — Izvestiya na Nauchnoizsledovatelski Institut za Gorata

Izv Nauchnoizsled Inst Kinematogr Radio — Izvestiya na Nauchnoizsledovatelskiya Institut po Kinematografiya i Radio

Izv Nauchnoizsled Inst Lozar Vinar (Pleven) — Izvestiya na Nauchnoizsledovatelski Institut po Lozarstvo i Vinarstvo(Pleven)

Izv Nauchnoizsled Inst Ovoshtarstvo Gara Kostinbrod — Izvestiya na Nauchnoizsledovatelski Institut po Ovoshtarstvo. GaraKostinbrod

Izv Nauchnoizsled Inst Pochvozn Agrotekh — Izvestiya na Nauchnoizsledovatelskiya Institut po Pochvoznanie iAgrotekhnika

Izv Nauchnoizsled Inst Rastenievud — Izvestiya na Nauchnoizsledovatelskiya Institut po Rastenievudstvo

Izv **Nauchnoizsled Inst Ribno Stop Okeanogr (Varna)** — Izvestiya na Nauchnoizsledovatelskiya Institut za Ribno Stopanstvo i Okeanografiya (Varna)

Izv **Nauchnoizsled Inst Zasht Rast** — Izvestiya na Nauchnoizsledovatelskiya Institut za Zashtita naRasteniyata

Izv **Nauchnoizsled Inst Zhivotnovud Kostinbrod** — Izvestiya na Nauchnoizsledovatelskiya Institut po Zhivotnovudstvo.Kostinbrod

Izv **Naucn Inst Lesgafta** — Izvestija Naucnogo Instituta imeni P. F. Lesgafta. Bulletin. Institut Scientifique Lesshaft

Izv **Nikolaev GI Astron Obs** — Izvestiya Nikolaevskoi Glavnoi Astronomicheskoi Observatorii

Izv **Obsc Izuc Vost Sibirsk Kraja** — Izvestija Obscestva Izucenija Vostocno-Sibirskogo Kraja

Izv **Okra Istor Muz** — Izvestiia na Okrazhniia Istoricheski Muzei

Izv **Okraz Istor Muz** — Izvestiia na Okrazhniia Istoricheski Muzei

Izv **Omsk Otd Geogr O-Va SSR** — Izvestiya Omskogo Otdeleniya Geograficheskogo Obshchestva SSR

Izv **Oset Nauchno Issled Inst Kraeved** — Izvestiya Osetinskogo Nauchno-Issledovatel'skogo Instituta Kraevedeniya

Izv **Otd Biol Med Nauki Bulg Akad Nauk** — Izvestiya na Otdelenieto za Biologicheski i Meditsinski Nauki. Bulgarska Akademiya na Naukite

Izv **Otdel Obshchest Nauk A N Tadzh** — Izvestiia Otdeleniia Obshchestvennykh Nauk Akademii Nauk Tadzhikskoi SSR

Izv **Otd Estestv Nauk** — Izvestija Otdelenija Estestvennyh Nauk

Izv **Otd Estestv Nauk Akad Nauk Tadzh SSR** — Izvestiya Otdeleniya Estestvennyh Nauk. Akademiya Nauk Tadzhikskoi SSR

Izv **Otd Khim Nauki Bulg Akad** — Izvestiya na Otdelenieto za Khimicheski Nauki. Bulgarska Akademiya na Naukite

Izv **Otd Khim Nauki Bulg Akad Nauk** — Izvestiya na Otdelenieto za Khimicheski Nauki. Bulgarska Akademiya na Naukite

Izv **Permsk Biol Nauchno-Issled Inst** — Izvestiya Permskogo Biologicheskogo Nauchno-Issledovatel'skogo Instituta

Izv **Permsk Biol Naucno Issl Inst** — Izvestija Permskogo Biologiceskogo Naucno-Issledovatel'skogo Instituta. Bulletin de l'Institut des Recherches Biologiques de Perm

Izv **Petrograd Lesn Inst** — Izvestiya Petrogradskogo Lesnogo Instituta

Izv **Petrogradsk Obl Stancii Zasc Rast Vredit** — Izvestija Petrogradskoj Oblastnoj Stancii Zascity Rastenij ot Vreditelej. Bulletin. Station Regionale Protectrice des Plantes a Petrograd

Izv **Petrovskoi Skh Akad** — Izvestiya Petrovskoi Sel'skokhozyaistvennoi Akademii

Izv **Petrovskoi Zemled Lesn Akad** — Izvestiya Petrovskoi Zemledel'cheskoi i Lesnoi Akademii

Izv **Petrovsk Skh Akad** — Izvestiya Petrovskoi Sel'skokhozyaistvennoi Akademii

Izv **Petrovsk Zemled Lesn Akad** — Izvestiya Petrovskoi Zemledel'cheskoi i Lesnoi Akademii

Izv **Phys Solid Earth** — Izvestiya. Physics of the Solid Earth

Izv **Pochv Inst Bulg Akad Nauk** — Izvestiya na Pochveniya Institut. Bulgarska Akademiya na Naukite

Izv **Povolzh Lesotekh Inst** — Izvestiya Povolzhskogo Lesotekhnicheskogo Instituta

Izv **Razpr Mat Prir Razr Jugoslav Akad Znan** — Izvesca o Razpravama Matematicko-Prirodoslovnoga Razreda Jugoslavenska AkademijaZnanosti i Umjetnosti. Bulletin des Travaux. Classe des Sciences Mathematiques et Naturelles. Academie Jougoslave des Sciences et des Beaux-Arts

Izv **Ross Akad Nauk** — Izvestiya Rossiiskoi Akademii Nauk

Izv **Ross Akad Nauk Energ** — Izvestiya Rossiiskoi Akademii Nauk. Energetika

Izv **Ross Akad Nauk Fiz Zemli** — Izvestiya Rossiiskoi Akademii Nauk. Fizika Zemli

Izv **Ross Akad Nauk Mekh Zhidk Gaza** — Izvestiya Rossiiskoi Akademii Nauk. Mekhanika Zhidkosti i Gaza

Izv **Ross Akad Nauk Ser Biol** — Izvestiya Rossiiskoi Akademii Nauk. Seriya Biologicheskaya

Izv **Ross Akad Nauk Ser Fiz** — Izvestiya Rossiiskoi Akademii Nauk. Seriya Fizicheskaya

Izv **Ross Akad Nauk Ser Mat** — Rossiiskaya Akademiya Nauk. Izvestiya. Seriya Matematicheskaya

Izv **Ross Inst Prikl Khim** — Izvestiya Rossiiskogo Instituta Prikladnoi Khimii

Izv **Rostov Donu Nauchno-Issled Inst Epidemiol Mkroblol Glg** — Izvestiya Rostovskogo na Donu Nauchno-Issledovatel'skogo Instituta Epidemiologii Mikrobiologii i Gigieny

Izv **Rostovsk Stancii Zasc Rast** — Izvestiya Rostovskoj Stancii Zascity Rastenij

Izv **Russ Acad Sci Atmospher Ocean Phys** — Russian Academy of Sciences. Izvestiya. Atmospheric and Oceanic Physics

Izv **Sakhalin Otd Geogr Ova SSSR** — Izvestiya Sakhalinskogo Otdela Geograficheskogo Obshchestva SSSR

Izv **Samar Skh Inst** — Izvestiya Samarskogo Sel'skokhozyaistvennogo Instituta

Izv **Sapropel Komiteta** — Izvestija Sapropelevogo Komiteta. Bulletin du Comite pour l'Etude des Sapropelites

Izv **Sarat Ova Estestvoispyt** — Izvestiya Saratovskogo Obshchestva Estestvoispytatelei

Izv **Sekt Fiz-Khim Anal Inst Obshch Neorg Khim Akad Nauk SSSR** — Izvestiya Sektora Fiziko-Khimicheskogo Analiza Institut Obshchei i Neorganicheskoi Khimii Akademiya Nauk SSSR

Izv **Sekt Platiny Drugikh Obshch Neorg Khim Akad Nauk SSSR** — Izvestiya Sektora Platiny i Drugikh Blagorodnykh Metallov Institut Obshchei i Neorganicheskoi Khimii Akademiya Nauk SSSR

Izv **Sekts Astron Bulg Akad Nauk** — Izvestiya na Sektsiyata po Astronomiya. Bulgarska Akademiya na Naukite

Izv **Sel'khoz Nauk** — Izvestiya Sel'skokhozyaistvennykh Nauk

Izv **Sel'-Khoz Nauki Minist Sel' Khoz Armyan SSR** — Izvestiya Sel'skokhozyaistvennoi Nauki.Ministerstvo Sel'skogo Khozyaistva Armyanskoi SSR

Izv **Severo-Kavkaz Nauchn Tsentra Vyssh Shkoly Ser Tekhn Nauk** — Izvestiya Severo-Kavkazskogo Nauchnogo Tsentra Vysshei Shkoly Seriya Tekhnicheskie Nauki

Izv **Severo-Kavkaz Naucn Centra Vyss Skoly Ser Estestv Nauk** — Izvestiya Severo-Kavkazskogo Naucnogo Centra Vyssei Skoly Serija Estestvennye Nauki

Izv **Severo-Kavkaz Naucn Centra Vyss Skoly Ser Tehn Nauk** — Izvestija Severo-Kavkazskogo Naucnogo Centra Vyssei Skoly Serija Tehniceskie Nauki

Izv **Sev-Kavk Nauc Centra Vyss Skoly Ser Obsc Nauk** — Izvestiya Severo-Kavkazskogo Naucnogo Centra Vyssei Skoly Serija Obscestvennyh Nauk

Izv **Sev-Kavk Nauchn Tsentra Vyssh Shk Estestv Nauki** — Izvestiya Severo-Kavkazskogo Nauchnogo Tsentra Vysshei Shkoly Seriya Estestvennye Nauki

Izv **Sev-Kavk Nauchn Tsentra Vyssh Shk Ser Estestv Nauk** — Izvestiya Severo-Kavkazskogo Nauchnogo Tsentra Vysshei Shkoly Seriya Estestvennye Nauki

Izv **Sev Kavk Nauchn Tsentra Vyssh Shk Tekh Nauki** — Izvestiya Severo-Kavkazskogo Nauchnogo Tsentra Vysshei Shkoly.Tekhnicheskie Nauki

Izv **Sev Oset Nauchno Issled Inst** — Izvestiya Severo-Osetinskogo Nauchno-Issledovatel'skogo Instituta

Izv **Sibir Otd Akad Nauk SSSR** — Izvestiya Sibirskogo Otdeleniya Akademii Nauk SSSR

Izv **Sibir Otd Akad Nauk SSSR Khim** — Izvestiya Sibirskogo Otdeleniya Nauk SSSR Seriya Khimicheskikh Nauk

Izv **Sibir Otd Akad Nauk SSSR Ser Khim Nauk** — Izvestiya Sibirskogo Otdeleniya Akademii Nauk SSSR Seriya Khimicheskikh Nauk

Izv **Sibir Otd Akad Nauk SSSR Ser Tekh Nauk** — Izvestiya Sibirskogo Otdeleniya Akademii Nauk SSSR Seriya Tekhnicheskikh Nauk

Izv **Sibir Otd Akad Nauk SSSR Ser Tekh** — Izvestiya Sibirskogo Otdeleniya Akademii Nauk SSSR Seriya Tekhnicheskikh Nauk

Izv **Sibir Otdel Akad Nauk SSSR Ser Biol Nauk** — Izvestija Sibirskogo Otdelenija Akademii Nauk SSSR Serija Biologiceskih Nauk

Izv **Sibirsk Kraev Stancii Zasc Rast Vredit** — Izvestija Sibirskoj Kraevoj Stancii Zascity Rastenij ot Vreditelej

Izv **Sibirsk Otdel Akad Nauk SSSR** — Izvestija Sibirskogo Otdelenija Akademija Nauk SSSR

Izv **Sibirsk Otdel Akad Nauk SSSR Ser Tehn Nauk** — Izvestija Sibirskogo Otdelenija Akademija Nauk SSSR Serija Tehniceskih Nauk

Izv **Sibirsk Otd Imp Russk Geogr Obsc** — Izvestija Sibirskago Otdela Imperatorskago Russkago Geograficeskago Obscestva

Izv **Sib Mekh-Mashinostroit Inst** — Izvestiya Sibirskogo Mekhaniko-Mashinostroitel'nogo Instituta

Izv **Sib Otd Akad Nauk SSSR** — Izvestiya Sibirskogo Otdeleniya Akademii Nauk SSSR

Izv **Sib Otd Akad Nauk SSSR Geol Geofiz** — Izvestiya Sibirskogo Otdeleniya Akademii Nauk SSSR Geologiya i Geofizika

Izv **Sib Otd Akad Nauk SSSR Ser Biol-Med Nauk** — Izvestiya Sibirskogo Otdeleniya Akademii Nauk SSSR Seriya Biologo-Meditsinskikh Nauk

Izv **Sib Otd Akad Nauk SSSR Ser Biol Nauk** — Izvestiya Sibirskogo Otdeleniya Akademii Nauk SSSR Seriya Biologicheskikh Nauk

Izv **Sib Otd Akad Nauk SSSR Ser Khim Nauk** — Izvestiya Sibirskogo Otdeleniya Akademii Nauk SSSR Seriya Khimicheskikh Nauk

Izv **Sib Otd Akad Nauk SSSR Ser Obshchestv Nauk** — Izvestiya Sibirskogo Otdeleniya Akademii Nauk SSSR Seriya Obshchestvennykh Nauk

Izv **Sib Otd Akad Nauk SSSR Ser Tekh Nauk** — Izvestiya Sibirskogo Otdeleniya Akademii Nauk SSSR Seriya Tekhnicheskikh Nauk

Izv **Sib Otd Akad Nauk SSSR Sib Biol Zh** — Izvestiya Sibirskogo Otdeleniya Akademii Nauk SSSR. Sibirskii Biologicheskii Zhurnal

Izv **Sib Otd Akad Nauk SSSR Sib Fiz Tekh Zh** — Izvestiya Sibirskogo Otdeleniya Akademii Nauk SSSR. Sibirskii Fiziko-Technicheskii Zhurnal

Izv **Sib Otd Akad Nauk SSSR Sib Khim Zh** — Izvestiya Sibirskogo Otdeleniya Akademii Nauk SSSR. Sibirskii Khimicheskii Zhurnal

Izv **Sib Otdel Akad Nauk SSSR Ser Biol-Med Nauk** — Izvestiya Sibirskogo Otdeleniya Akademii Nauk SSSR Seriya Biologo-Meditsinskikh Nauk

Izv **Sib Otdel Akad Nauk SSSR Ser Biol Nauk** — Izvestiya Sibirskogo Otdeleniya Akademii Nauk SSSR Seriya Biologicheskikh Nauk

Izv **Sib Otdel Akad Nauk SSSR Ser Obsc Nauk** — Izvestiya Sibirskogo Otdeleniya Akademii Nauk SSSR Serija Obscestvennyh Nauk

Izv **Sib Otd Geol Kom** — Izvestiya Sibirskogo Otdeleniya Geologicheskogo Komiteta

Izv **Sib Tekhnol Inst** — Izvestiya Sibirskogo Tekhnologicheskogo Instituta

Izv **Skh Akad Im K A Timiryazeva** — Izvestiya Sel'skokhozyaistvennoi Akademii Imeni K. A. Timiryazeva

Izv **S-Kh Nauk** — Izvestiya Sel'skokhozyaistvennykh Nauk

Izv **Skh Nauki Minist Proizvod Zagotovok Skh Prod Arm SSR** — Izvestiya. Sel'skokhozyaistvennye Nauki. Ministerstva Proizvodstva iZagotovok Sel'skokhozyaistvennykh Produktov Armyanskoi SSR

Izv**SLF** — Izvestiya Seminara po Slavjanske Filologii

Izv**SOsNII** — Izvestiya Severo-Osetinskogo Nauchno-Issledovatel'skogo Instituta

Izv **S Peterburgsk Biol Lab** — Izvestija S.-Peterburgskoj Biologiceskoj Laboratorii. Bulletin du Laboratoire Biologique de Saint-Petersbourg

Izv **Sredne Aziatsk Otd Gosud Russk Geogr Obsc** — Izvestija Sredne-Aziatskogo Otdela Godusarstvennogo Russkogo Geograficeskogo Obscestva

Izv **St Peterb Lesn Inst** — Izvestiya Sankt-Peterburgskago Lesnago Instituta

Izv**TadzikAN** — Izvestiya Tadzikskogo Filiala Akademii Nauk

Izv **Tbilis Nauchno Issled Inst Sooruzh Gidroenerg** — Izvestiya Tbilisskogo Nauchno-Issledovatel'skogo Instituta Sooruzhenii i Gidroenergetiki

Izv **Tekh Inst Bulg Akad Nauk** — Izvestiya na Tekhnicheskiya Institut. Bulgarska Akademiya na Naukite

Izv **Tekh Univ Plovdiv Fund Nauk Prilozhen** — Tekhnicheskiya Universitet v Plovdiv. Izvestiya. Fundamentalni Nauki i Prilozheniya

Izv **Tekst Promsti Torg** — Izvestiya Tekstil'noi Promyshlennosti i Torgovli

Izv **Teplotekh Inst (Moscow)** — Izvestiya Teplotekhnicheskogo Instituta (Moscow)

Izv **Tihookeansk Naucn Inst Rybn Hoz** — Izvestiya Tihookeanskogo Nauchnogo Instituta Rybnogo Hozjajstva

Izv **Tihookeansk Naucno Promysl Stancii** — Izvestija Tihookeanskoj Naucno-Promyslovoj Stancii/Bulletin. Pacific ScientificResearch Station

Izv **Tikhookean Nauchn Inst Rybn Khoz** — Izvestiya Tikhookeanskogo Nauchnogo Instituta Rybnogo Khozyaistva

Izv **Tikhookean Nauchno-Issled Inst Rybn Khoz Okeanogr** — Izvestiya Tikhookeanskogo Nauchno-Issledovatel'skogo Instituta Rybnogo Khozyaistva i Okeanografii

Izv Tikhookean Nauchno Promysl Stn — Izvestiya Tikhookeanskoi Nauchno-Promyslovoi Stantsii

Izv Timiryazev Sel'-Khoz Akad — Izvestiya Timiryazevskoi Sel'skokhozyaistvennoi Akademii

Izv Timiryazev S-Kh Akad — Izvestiya Timiryazevskoi Sel'skokhozyaistvennoi Akademii

Izv Timiryazevsk Skh Akad — Izvestiya Timiryazevskoi Sel'skokhozyaistvennoi Akademii

Izv Tomsk Gos Univ — Izvestiya Tomskogo Gosudarstvennogo Universiteta

Izv Tomsk Ind Inst — Izvestiya Tomskogo Industrial'nogo Instituta

Izv Tomsk Otd Russ Bot Ova — Izvestiya Tomskogo Otdeleniya Russkogo Botanicheskogo Obshchestva

Izv Tomsk Otd Vses Bot Ova — Izvestiya Tomskogo Otdeleniya Vsesoyuznogo Botanicheskogo Obshchestva

Izv Tomsk Otd Vsesojuzn Bot Obsc — Izvestija Tomskogo Otdelenija Vsesojuznogo Botaniceskogo Obscestva

Izv Tomsk Politehn Inst — Izvestija Tomskogo Ordena Trudovogo Krasnogo Znameni Politehniceskogo Institutalmeni S. M. Kirova

Izv Tomsk Politekh Inst — Izvestiya Tomskogo Politekhnicheskogo Instituta Imeni S. M. Kirova

Izv Tomsk Politekh Inst Mekh Mashinostr — Izvestiya Tomskogo Politekhnicheskogo Instituta Mekhanika i Mashinostroenia

Izv Tomsk Univ — Izvestija Tomskago Universiteta

Izv Tr Kharb Politekh Inst — Izvestiya i Trudy Kharbinskogo Politekhnicheskogo Instituta

Izv Tr Russ Kitaiskogo Politekh Inst — Izvestiya i Trudy Russko-Kitaiskogo Politekhnicheskogo Instituta

Izv Tsent Nauchnoizsled Inst Zasht Rast — Izvestiya na Tsentralniya Nauchnoizsledovatelski Institut za Zashnita na Rasteniyata

Izv Tsent Nauchnoizsled Inst Zhivotnuvd "Georgi Dimitrov" — Izvestiya na Tsentralniya Nauchnoizsledovatelski Institut po Zhivotnovudstvo "Georgi Dimitrov"

Izv Tsentr Biokhim Lab Bulg Akad Nauk — Izvestiya na Tsentralnata Biokhimichna Laboratoriya. BulgarskaAkademiya na Naukite

Izv Tsentr Inst Razvit Gorn Promsti — Izvestiya Tsentral'nogo Instituta po Razvitiyu Gornoi Promyshlennosti

Izv Tsentr Khelmintol Lab B'lg Akad Nauk — Izvestiya na Tsentralnata Khelmintologichna Laboratoriya. Bulgarska Akademiya na Naukite

Izv Tsentr Lab Biokhim Bulg Akad Nauk — Izvestiya na Tsentralnata Laboratoriya po Biokhimiya. Bulgarska Akademiya na Naukite

Izv Tsentr Lab Energ Bulg Akad Nauk — Izvestiya na Tsentralnata Laboratoriya po Energetika. Bulgarska Akademiya na Naukite

Izv Tsentr Nauchno Issled Biokhim Inst Pishch Vkusovoi Proms — Izvestiya Tsentral'nogo Nauchno-Issledovatel'skogo Biokhimicheskogo Instituta Pishchevoi i Vkusovoi Promyshlennosti SSSR

Izv Tsentr Nauchno Issled Inst Kozh Promsti — Izvestiya Tsentral'nogo Nauchno-Issledovatel'skogo Instituta Kozhevennoi Promyshlennosti

Izv Tsentr Nauchno Issled Inst Pishch Vkusovoi Promsti — Izvestiya Tsentral'nogo Nauchno-Issledovatel'skogo Instituta Pishchevoi i Vkusovoi Promyshlennosti

Izv Tsentr Nauchnoizsled Inst Gorata — Izvestiya na Tsentralniya Nauchnoizsledovatelski Institut za Gorata

Izv Tsentr Nauchnoizsled Inst Lozar Vinar Pleven — Izvestiya na Tsentralniya Nauchnoizsledovatelski Institut po Lozarstvo i Vinarstro. Pleven

Izv Tsentr Nauchnoizsled Inst Nezarazni Boles Zookhig — Izvestiya na Tsentralniya Nauchnoizsledovatelski Institut po Nezarazni Bolesti i Zookhigiena

Izv Tsentr Nauchnoizsled Inst Ovoshtarstvo Gara Kostinbrod — Izvestiya na Tsentralniya Nauchnoizsledovatelski Institut za Ovoshtarstvo. Gara Kostinbrod

Izv Tsentr Nauchnoizsled Inst Pochvozn Agrotekh — Izvestiya na Tsentralniya Nauchnoizsledovatelski Institut po Pochvoznanie i Agrotekhnika

Izv Tsentr Nauchnoizsled Inst Rastenievudrotekh — Izvestiya na Tsentralniya Nauchnoizsledovatelski Institut po Rastenievudstvo

Izv Tsentr Nauchnoizsled Inst Ribovud Ribolov Varna Bulg Aka — Izvestiya na Tsentralniya Nauchnoizsledovatelski Institut po Ribovudstvo i Ribolov, Varna, Bulgarska Akademiya na Naukite

Izv Tsentr Nauchnoizsled Inst Tyutyuna Plovdiv — Izvestiya na Tsentralniya Nauchnoizsledovatelski Institut po Tyutyuna. Plovdiv

Izv Tsentr Nauchnoizsled Inst Zasht Rast — Izvestiya na Tsentralniya Nauchnoizsledovatelski Institut za Zashtita na Rasteniyata

Izv Tsentr Nauchnoizsled Inst Zhivotnovud Kostinbrod — Izvestiya na Tsentralniya Nauchnoizsledovatelski Institut po Zhivotnovudstvo. Kostinbrod

Izv Tsentr Nauchnoizsled Lab Khidravl Izsled — Izvestiya na Tsentralnata Nauchnoizsledovatelska Laboratoriya za Khidravlichni Izsledvaniya

Izv Tsentr Nauchnoizsled Veterinarnokhig Inst Zhivotin Prod — Izvestiya na Tsentralniya Nauchnoizsledovatelski Veterinarnokhigien Institut za Zhivotinski Produkti

Izv Tsentr Nauchnoizsled Vet Inst Virusol — Izvestiya na Tsentralniya Nauchnoizsledovatelski Veterinaren Institut po Virusologiya

Izv Tsentr Vet Inst Zarazni Parazit Boles — Izvestiya na Tsentralniya Veterinaren Institut za Zarazni i Parazitni Bolesti

Izv Tsentr Vet Nauchnoizsled Inst Nezarazni Boles Zookhig — Izvestiya na Tsentralniya Veterinarniya Nauchnoizsledovatelski Institut za Nezarazni Bolesti i Zookhigiena

Izv Turkm Fil Akad Nauk SSR — Izvestiya Turkmenskogo Filiala Akademii Nauk SSR

Izv Uch Zap Imp Kazan Univ — Izvestiya i Uchenyya Zapiski Imperatorskago Kazanskago Universiteta

Izv Ural Gorn Inst Ekaterinburge — Izvestiya Ural'skogo Gornogo Instituta v Ekaterinburge

Izv Ural Gos Univ — Izvestiya Ural'skogo Gosudarstvennogo Universiteta

Izv Ural Politekh Inst — Izvestiya Ural'skogo Politekhnicheskogo Instituta

Izv Uzbekistansk Fil Akad Nauk SSSR — Izvestija Uzbekistanskogo Filiala Akademii Nauk SSSR. Uzbekiston Filialining Ahboroti

Izv Uzb Fil Geogr Ova SSSR — Izvestiya Uzbekistanskogo Filiala Geograficheskogo Obshchestva SSSR

Izv Uzb Geogr Ova — Izvestiya Uzbekskogo Geograficheskogo Obshchestva

Izv Varna — Izvestija na Narodnija Muzej Varna

Izv Veng Gorno Issled Inst — Izvestiya Vengerskogo Gorno-Issledovatel'skogo Instituta

Izv Veng S'kh Nauchno-Issled Inst A — Izvestiya Vengerskikh Sel'skokhozyaistvennykh Nauchno-Issledovatel'skikh Institutow A. Rastenievodstvo

Izv Veng Skh Nauchno Issled Inst B — Izvestiya Vengerskikh Sel'skokhozyaistvennykh Nauchno-Issledovatel'skikh Institutov. B. Zhivotnovodstvo

Izv Veng S kh Nauchno-Issled Inst C — Izvestiya Vengerskikh Sel'skokhozyaistvennykh Nauchno-Issledovatel'skikh Institutow C. Sadovodstvo

Izv Veterinarnokhig Inst Zhivotin Prod Akad Selskostop Nauki — Izvestiya na Veterinarnokhigienniya Institut za Zhivotinski Produkti. Akademiyana Selskostopanskie Nauki v Bulgaria

Izv Vet Inst Virusol Akad Selskostop Nauki Bulg — Izvestiya na Veterinarniya Institut po Virusologiya. Akademiya na Selskostopanskite Nauki v Bulgaria

Izv Vet Inst Zarazni Parazit Boles Akad Selskostop Nauki Bulg — Izvestiya na Veterinarniya Institut po Zarazni i Parazitni Bolesti. Akademiya na Selskostopanskite Nauki v Bulgaria

Izv Vissh Mash-Elektrotekh Inst Lenin — Izvestiya na Visshiya Mashinno-Elektrotekhnicheski Institut Lenin

Izv Vmei "Lenin" — Izvestiya na Vmei "Lenin"

Izv VNIIG im BE Vedeneeva — Izvestiya VNIIG [*Vsesoiuznyi Nauchno-Issledovatel'ski Institut Gidrotekhniki*] imeni B.E. Vedeneeva

Izv Voronez Gos Ped Inst — Izvestija Voronezskogo Gosudarstvennogo Pedagogiceskogo Instituta

Izv Voronezh Gos Pedagog Inst — Izvestiya Voronezhskogo Gosudarstvennogo Pedagogicheskogo Instituta

Izv Voronezh Gos Ped Inst — Izvestiya Voronezhskogo Gosudarstvennogo Pedagogicheskogo Instituta

Izv Voronezh Otd Vses Bot Ova — Izvestiya Voronezhskogo Otdeleniya Vsesoyuznogo Botanicheskogo Obshchestva

Izv Voronez Pedag Inst — Izvestiya Voronezhskogo Pedagogiceskogo Instituta

Izv Voronezsk Stancii Borbe Vredit Rast — Izvestija Voronezskoj Stancii po Bor'be s Vrediteljami Rasteni

IzvVorPI — Izvestiya Voronezhskogo Gosudarstvennogo Pedagogiceskogo Instituta

Izv Vost Fil Akad Nauk SSSR — Izvestiya Vostochnykh Filialov Akademii Nauk SSSR

Izv Vost Filial Akad Nauk SSSR — Izvestiya Vostochnykh Filialov Akademii Nauk SSSR

Izv Vostochnosib Skh Inst — Izvestiya Vostochnosibirskogo Sel'skokhozyaistvennogo Instituta

Izv Vost Sibirsk Otd Imp Russk Geogr Obsc — Izvestija Vostocno-Sibirskago Otdela Imperatorskago Russkago Geograficeskago Obscestva. Isvestija der Ost-Sibirischen Abtheilung der Kaiserlich-Russischen Geographischen Gesellschaft

Izv Vost Sib Otd Geogr Ova SSSR — Izvestiya Vostochno-Sibirskogo Otdela Geograficheskogo Obshchestva SSSR

Izv Vses Geogr Obshch — Izvestiya Vsesoyuznogo Geograficheskogo Obshchestva

Izv Vses Geogr O-Va — Izvestiya Vsesoyuznogo Geograficheskogo Obshchestva

Izv Vses Nauchno-Issled Inst Gidrotekh — Izvestiya Vsesoyuznogo Nauchno-Issledovatel'skogo Instituta Gidrotekhniki

Izv Vses Nauchno Issled Inst Gidrotekh im BE Vedeneeva — Izvestiya Vsesoyuznogo Nauchno-Issledovatel'skogo Instituta Gidrotekhniki imeniB.E. Vedeneeva

Izv Vses Nauchno Issled Inst Ozern Rechn Rybn Khoz — Izvestiya Vsesoyuznogo Nauchno-Issledovatel'skogo Instituta Ozernogo i RechnogoRybnogo Khozyaistva

Izv Vsesojuz Geogr Obsc — Izvestija Vsesojuznogo Geograficeskogo Obscestva

Izv Vsesojuzn Geogr Obsc — Izvestija Vsesojuznogo Geograficeskogo Obscestva/Izvestia de la Societe de Geographie de l'URSS/Bulletin. USSR Geographical Society

Izv Vses Teplotekh Inst — Izvestiya Vsesoyuznogo Teplotekhnicheskogo Instituta

Izv VUZ Aviats Tekh — Izvestiya Vysshikh Uchebnykh Zavedenii Aviatsionnaya Tekhnika

Izv VUZ Chernaya Metall — Izvestiya Vysshikh Uchebnykh Zavedenii Chernaya Metallurgiya

Izv VUZ Elektromekh — Izvestiya Vysshikh Uchebnykh Zavedenii Elektromekhanika

Izv VUZ Energ — Izvestiya Vysshikh Uchebnykh Zavedenii Energetika

Izv VUZ Fiz — Izvestiya Vysshikh Uchebnykh Zavedenii Fizika

Izv VUZ Gornyi Zh — Izvestiya Vysshikh Uchebnykh Zavedenii Gornyi Zhurnal

Izv VUZ Kh i Kh Tekh — Izvestiya Vysshikh Uchebnykh Zavedenii Khimiya i Khimicheskaya Tekhnologiya

Izv VUZ Khim i Khim Tekhnol — Izvestiya Vysshikh Uchebnykh Zavedenii Khimiya i Khimicheskaya Tekhnologiya

Izv VUZ Lesnoi Zh — Izvestiya Vysshikh Uchebnykh Zavedenii Lesnoi Zhurnal

Izv VUZ Mashinostr — Izvestiya Vysshikh Uchebnykh Zavedenii Mashinostroenie

Izv VUZ Mat — Izvestiya Vysshikh Uchebnykh Zavedenii Matematika

Izv Vuzov Mashinostr — Izvestiya Vuzov Mashinostroenie

Izv VUZOV Stroit Arkhit — Izvestiya VUZOV Stroitel'stvo i Arkhitektura

Izv VUZ Pishch Tekhnol — Izvestiya Vysshikh Uchebnykh Zavedenii Pishchevaya Tekhnologiya

Izv VUZ Priborostr — Izvestiya Vysshikh Uchebnykh Zavedenii Priborostroenie

Izv VUZ Radioelektron — Izvestiya Vysshikh Uchebnykh Zavedenii Radioelektronika

Izv VUZ Radiofiz — Izvestiya Vysshikh Uchebnykh Zavedenii Radiofizika

Izv VUZ Tekh Leg Prom — Izvestiya Vysshikh Uchebnykh Zavedenii Tekhnologiya Legkoi Promyshlennosti

Izv VUZ Tekhnol Legkoi Prom-St — Izvestiya Vysshikh Uchebnykh Zavedenii Tekhnologiya Legkoi Promyshlennosti

Izv VUZ Tekhnol Tekstil Prom — Izvestiya Vysshikh Uchebnykh Zavedenii Tekhnologiya Tekstil'noi Promyshlennosti

Izv VUZ Tsvetn Metall — Izvestiya Vysshikh Uchebnykh Zavedenii Tsvetnaya Metallurgiya

Izv Vyssh Uchebn Zaved — Izvestiya Vysshikh Uchebnykh Zavednii

Izv Vyssh Uchebn Zaved Agrar Nauk Moshonmadyarovare Vengriya — Izvestiya Vysshego Uchebnogo Zavedeniya Agrarnykh Nauk v Moshonmadyarovare (Vengriya)

Izv Vyssh Uchebn Zaved Aviats Tekh — Izvestiya Vysshikh Uchebnykh Zavedenii Aviatsionnaya Tekhnika

Izv Vyssh Uchebn Zaved Chern Metall — Izvestiya Vysshikh Uchebnykh Zavedenii Chernaya Metallurgiya

Izv Vyssh Uchebn Zaved Ehlektromekh — Izvestiya Vysshikh Uchebnykh Zavedenii Ehlektromekhanika

Izv Vyssh Uchebn Zaved Ehnerg — Izvestiya Vysshikh Uchebnykh Zavedenii Ehnergetika

Izv Vyssh Uchebn Zaved Energ Obedin SNG Energ — Izvestiya Vysshikh Uchebnykh Zavedenii i Energeticheskikh Ob'edinenii SNG. Energetika

Izv Vyssh Uchebn Zaved Fiz — Izvestiya Vysshikh Uchebnykh Zavedenij Fizika

Izv Vyssh Uchebn Zaved Geod Aerofotos'emka — Izvestiya Vysshikh Uchebnykh Zavedenii Geodeziya i Aerofotos'emka

Izv Vyssh Uchebn Zaved Geol Razved — Izvestiya Vysshikh Uchebnykh Zavedenii Geologiya i Razvedka

Izv Vyssh Uchebn Zaved Gorn Zh — Izvestiya Vysshikh Uchebnykh Zavedenij Gornyj Zhurnal

Izv Vyssh Uchebn Zaved Khim Khim Tekhnol — Izvestiya Vysshikh Uchebnykh Zavedenii Khimiya i Khimicheskaya Tekhnologiya

Izv Vyssh Uchebn Zaved Lesn Zh — Izvestiya Vysshikh Uchebnykh Zavedenii Lesnoi Zhurnal

Izv Vyssh Uchebn Zaved Mashinostr — Izvestiya Vysshikh Uchebnykh Zavedenii Mashinostroenie

Izv Vyssh Uchebn Zaved Neft' Gaz — Izvestiya Vysshikh Uchebnykh Zavedenii Neft' i Gaz

Izv Vyssh Uchebn Zaved Pishch Tekhnol — Izvestiya Vysshikh Uchebnykh Zavedenii Pishchevaya Tekhnologiya

Izv Vyssh Uchebn Zaved Priborostr — Izvestiya Vysshikh Uchebnykh Zavedenii Priborostroenie

Izv Vyssh Uchebn Zaved Prikl Nelinein Dinamika — Izvestiya Vysshikh Uchebnykh Zavedenii. Prikladnaya Nelineinaya Dinamika

Izv Vyssh Uchebn Zaved Radioelektron — Izvestiya Vysshikh Uchebnykh Zavedenii Radioelektronika

Izv Vyssh Uchebn Zaved Radiofiz — Izvestiya Vysshikh Uchebnykh Zavedenij Radiofizika

Izv Vyssh Uchebn Zaved Radiotekh — Izvestiya Vysshikh Uchebnykh Zavedenii Radiotekhnika

Izv Vyssh Uchebn Zaved Ser Radiofiz — Izvestiya Vysshikh Uchebnykh Zavedenii. Seriya Radiofizika

Izv Vyssh Uchebn Zaved Severo Kavkaz Reg Estestv Nauk — Izvestiya Vysshikh Uchebnykh Zavedenii. Severo-Kavkazskii Region. Estestvennye Nauki

Izv Vyssh Uchebn Zaved Sev Kavk Reg Estestv Nauki — Izvestiya Vysshikh Uchebnykh Zavedenii. Severo-Kavkazskii Region. Estestvennye Nauki

Izv Vyssh Uchebn Zaved Sev Kavk Reg Tekh Nauki — Izvestiya Vysshikh Uchebnykh Zavedenii, Severo-Kavkazskii Region. Tekhnicheskie Nauki

Izv Vyssh Uchebn Zaved Stroit — Izvestiya Vysshikh Uchebnykh Zavedenii. Stroitel'stvo

Izv Vyssh Uchebn Zaved Stroit Arkhit — Izvestiya Vysshikh Uchebnykh Zavedenii Stroitel'stvo i Arkhitektura

Izv Vyssh Uchebn Zaved Tekhnol Legk Promsti — Izvestiya Vysshikh Uchebnykh Zavedenii Tekhnologiya Legkoi Promyshlennosti

Izv Vyssh Uchebn Zaved Tekhnol Tekst Promsti — Izvestiya Vysshikh Uchebnykh Zavedenii Tekhnologiya Tekstil'noi Promyshlennosti

Izv Vyssh Uchebn Zaved Tsvetn — Izvestiya Vysshikh Uchebnykh Zavedenij. Tsvetnaya Metallurgiya

Izv Vyssh Uchebn Zaved Tsvetn Metall — Izvestiya Vysshikh Uchebnykh Zavedenii Tsvetnaya Metallurgiya

Izv Vyssh Ucheb Zaved Chern Met — Izvestiya Vysshikh Uchebnykh Zavedenii Chernaya Metallurgiya

Izv Vyssh Ucheb Zaved Elektromekh — Izvestiya Vysshikh Uchebnykh Zavedenii Elektromekhanika

Izv Vyssh Ucheb Zaved Energ — Izvestiya Vysshikh Uchebnykh Zavedenii Energetika

Izv Vyssh Ucheb Zavedenii Geol Razvedka — Izvestiya Vysshikh Uchebnykh Zavedenii Geologiya i Razvedka

Izv Vyssh Ucheb Zaved Geol i Razved — Izvestiya Vysshikh Uchebnykh Zavedenii Geologiya i Razvedka

Izv Vyssh Ucheb Zaved Gorn Zh — Izvestiya Vysshikh Uchebnykh Zavedenii Gornyi Zhurnal

Izv Vyssh Ucheb Zaved Khim i Khim — Izvestiya Vysshikh Uchebnykh Zavedenii Khimiya i Khimicheskaya

Izv Vyssh Ucheb Zaved Neft i Gaz — Izvestiya Vysshikh Uchebnykh Zavedenii Neft' i Gaz

Izv Vyssh Ucheb Zaved Ser Pishch Tekhnol — Izvestiya Vysshikh Uchebnykh Zavedenii Seriya Pishchevaya Tekhnologiya

Izv Vyssh Ucheb Zaved Tekh Legk — Izvestiya Vysshikh Uchebnykh Zavedenii Tekhnologiya Legkoi Promyshlennosti

Izv Vyssh Ucheb Zaved Tsvet Met — Izvestiya Vysshikh Uchebnykh Zavedenii Tsvetnaya Metallurgiya

Izv Vyss Ucebn Zaved Aviacion Tehn — Izvestija Vyssih Ucebnyh Zavedenii Aviacionnaja Tehnika

Izv Vyss Ucebn Zaved Elektromehanika — Izvestija Vyssih Ucebnyh Zavedenii Elektromehanika

Izv Vyss Ucebn Zaved Fizika — Izvestija Vyssih Ucebnyh Zavedenii Fizika

Izv Vyss Ucebn Zaved Geod i Aerofot — Izvestija Vyssih Ucebnyh Zavedenii Geodezija i Aerofotos Emka

Izv Vyss Ucebn Zaved Matematika — Izvestija Vyssih Ucebnyh Zavedenii Matematika

Izv Vyss Ucebn Zaved Radiofizika — Izvestija Vyssih Ucebnyh Zavedenii Radiofizika

Izv Zabaik Fil Geogr O-Va SSSR — Izvestiya Zabaikal'skogo Filiala Geograficheskogo Obshchestva SSSR

Izv Zabaik Otd Vses Geogr Ova SSSR — Izvestiya Zabaikal'skogo Otdela Vsesoyuznogo Geograficheskogo Obshchestva SSSR

Izv Zapadno Sibirsk Kraev Stancii Zasc Rast — Izvestija Zapadno-Sibirskoj Kraevoj Stancii Zascity Rastenij

Izv Zool Inst Muz Bulg Akad Nauk — Izvestiya na Zoologicheskiya Institut s Muzei. Bulgarska Akademiya na Naukite

IZWWAX — Instytut Zootechniki w Polsce Wydawnictwa Wlasne

IZYM — Zymurgy

IzYONI — Izvestiia Yugo-Osetinskogo Nauchno-Issledovatelskogo Instituta

J

J — Australian Journalist
J — Het Jachtbedrijf
J — Janus
J — Jeunesse
J — Jezik
J — Judiciary
J — Justitia
J17 — Just Seventeen
JA — Jahrbuch fuer Amerikastudien
JA — January
JA — Japan Architect
JA — Jeune Afrique
JA — Jewish Advocate
JA — Jewish Affairs
JA — Journal. American Musicological Society
J A — Journal A. Presses Academiques Europeennes
JA — Journal Asiatique
JA — Journal of Advertising
JA — Journal of Aesthetics and Art Criticism
JA — Journal of Andrology
JA — Journal of Apocrypha
JA — Jurisprudence du Port D'Anvers
JA — Jurisprudencia Argentina
JaA — Jahrbuch der Albertus-Universitat zu Konigsberg
JAA — Journal. British Archaeological Association
JAA — Journal of Accounting Auditing and Finance
JAA — Journal of African Administration
JAA — Journal of Anthropological Archaeology
JAA — Journal of Asian Art
JAA — Journal of Astrophysics and Astronomy
JAA — Journal of the Architectural Association
JAAC — Journal of Aesthetics and Art Criticism
JAACP — Journal. American Chamber of Commerce of the Philippines
JAADDB — Journal. American Academy of Dermatology
JAAHBL — Journal. American Animal Hospital Association
JAAK — Jahrbuch fuer Aesthetik und Allgemeine Kunstwissenschaft
JAAMI J Assoc Adv Med Instrum — JAAMI. Journal. Association for the Advancement of Medical Instrumentation
JAAML — Journal. American Academy of Matrimonial Lawyers
JA & Des Educ — Journal of Art and Design Education
JA & FC — Journal of Agricultural and Food Chemistry
JA & Ideas — Journal of Arts and Ideas
Ja Ann Int Law — Japanese Annual of International Law
Ja Ann Law Pol — Japan Annual of Law and Politics
J AANNT — Journal. American Association of Nephrology Nurses and Technicians
JAAP — Journal. American Academy of Psychoanalysis
JAAPCC — Journal. American Academy of Psychoanalysis
JAAPD — Journal of Analytical and Applied Pyrolysis
JAAPDD — Journal of Analytical and Applied Pyrolysis
J AAPOS — Journal of AAPOS (American Association for Pediatric Ophthalmology and Strabismus)
JAAR — Journal. American Academy of Religion
Jaarb Ak Amst — Jaarboek. Akademie te Amsterdam
Jaarber Ex Oriente Lux — Jaarbeericht. Vooraziatisch - Egyptisch Genootschap Ex Oriente Lux
Jaarb Inst Biol Scheik Onderz LandbGewass — Jaarboek. Instituut voor Biologisch en Scheikundig Onderzoek van Landbouwgewassen
Jaarb K Acad Overzeese Wet (Brussels) — Jaarboek. Koninklijke Academie voor Overzeese Wetenschappen (Brussels)
Jaarb Kankeronderz Kankerbestrijding Ned — Jaarboek van Kankeronderzoek en Kankerbestrijding in Nederland
Jaarb Karakul Breeders Soc S Afr — Jaarboek. Karakul Breeders Society of South Africa
Jaarb Kon Akad Wetensch Amsterdam — Jaarboek van de Koninklijke Akademie van Wetenschappen, Gevestigd te Amsterdam
Jaarb Kon Alg Ver Bloembollencult — Jaarboekje van de Koninklijke Algemeene Vereeniging von Bloembollencultuur
Jaarb Kon Vlaamse Acad Wetensch Belgiee — Jaarboek. Koninklijke Vlaamse Academie voor Wetenschappen, Letteren en Schone Kunsten van Belgiee
Jaarb K Vlaam Acad Wet Lett Schone Kunsten Belg — Jaarboek. Koninklijke Vlaamse Academie voor Wetenschappen, Letteren en Schone Kunsten van Belgie
Jaarbl Bot Ver S-Afr — Jaarblad. Botaniese Vereniging van Suid-Afrika
Jaarb Natuurw Studiekring Suriname Curacao — Jaarboek van de Natuurwetenschappelijke Studiekring voor Suriname en Curacao
Jaarb Ned Natuurk Ver — Jaarboek. Nederlandse Natuurkundige Vereniging

Jaarboek BZ — Jaarboek van het Ministerie van Buitenlandse Zaken
Jaarb Proefstat Boomkwekerij Boskoop — Jaarboek. Proefstation voor de Boomkwekerij te Boskoop
Jaarb Rijksinst Onderz Zee — Jaarboek. Rijksinstituut voor het Onderzoek der Zee
Jaarb Rijksuniv Utrecht — Jaarboek. Rijksuniversiteit te Utrecht
Jaarb Sticht Fundam Onderz Mater Sticht Inst Kernphys Onderz — Jaarboek. Stichting voor Fundamenteel Onderzoek der Materie en Stichting Instituut voor Kernphysisch Onderzoek
Jaarb Suid Afr Buro Rasse Aangeleenthede — Jaarboek Suid-Afrikaanse Buro vir Rasse-Aangeleenthede
Jaarb VRG — Jaarboek van het Vlaams Rechtsgenootschap
Jaarl Semin Teor Fis — Jaarlikse Seminaar oor Teoretiese Fisika
Jaars Terpen Groningen — Jaarsverslag van de Vereeniging voor Terpenonderzoek over de Vereenigingsjaren Groningen
JAAR Thematic St — Journal. American Academy of Religion. Thematic Studies
Jaarversl Inst Bodemvruchtbaarheid — Jaarverslag. Instituut voor Bodemvruchtbaarheid
Jaarversl Inst Graan Meel Brood (Wageningen) — Jaarverslag. Institut voor Graan, Meel, en Brood (Wageningen)
Jaarversl Lab Bloembollenonderz Lisse — Jaarverslag. Laboratorium voor Bloembollenonderzoek Lisse
Jaarversl TNO — Jaarverslag. TNO
JAAS — Journal. Aberystwyth Agriculture Society
JAAS — Journal of Analytical Atomic Spectrometry [Formerly, ARAAS]
JAAS — Journal of Asian and African Studies
JaAS — Journal of Asian Studies
JAASAJ — Journal. Alabama Academy of Science
JAASD — Journal. American Audiology Society
JAB — Journal of Applied Behavioral Science
JAB — Journal of Applied Behavior Analysis
JAB — Journal of Applied Biochemistry
JABA — Journal of Applied Behavior Analysis
JABAA4 — Journal of Applied Bacteriology
JABAE8 — Journal of Animal Breeding and Genetics
JABCAA — Journal of Abnormal Child Psychology
J Abdom Surg — Journal of Abdominal Surgery
JABGDP — Journal. Adelaide Botanic Gardens
JABIDV — Journal of Applied Biochemistry
JABKG — Jahrbuch fuer Altbayerische Kirchengeschichte
J Abnorm Child Psychol — Journal of Abnormal Child Psychology
J Abnorm Psychol — Journal of Abnormal Psychology
J Abnorm Psychol Monogr — Journal of Abnormal Psychology. Monograph
J Abnorm Psychol Soc Psychol — Journal of Abnormal Psychology and Social Psychology
J Abnorm Soc Psychol — Journal of Abnormal and Social Psychology
J Abn Psych — Journal of Abnormal Psychology
JAbP — Journal of Abnormal Psychology
JABPAF — Journal of Abnormal Psychology. Monograph
JABS — Journal of Applied Behavioral Science
JABSBP — Journal of Abdominal Surgery
J Ab Social Psychol — Journal of Abnormal and Social Psychology
J Abstr Br Ship — Journal of Abstracts. British Ship Research Association
J Abstr Int Educ — Journal of Abstracts in International Education
J Abstr Proc Sydney Univ Engng Soc — Journal and Abstract of Proceedings of the Sydney University Engineering Society
JAC — Jahrbuch fuer Antike und Christentum
JAC — Journal of Accountancy
JAC — Journal of Advanced Composition
Ja C — Judaism and Christianity
J Acad A & Archit — Journal of the Academy of Art and Architecture
J Acad Gen Dent — Journal. Academy of General Dentistry
J Acad Hyg Paris — Journal de l'Academie d'Hygiene (Paris)
J Acad Libnship — Journal of Academic Librarianship
J Acad Libr — Journal of Academic Librarianship
J Acad Librarianship — Journal of Academic Librarianship
J Acad Nat Sci Phila — Journal. Academy of Natural Sciences of Philadelphia
J Acad Nat Sci Philadelphia — Journal. Academy of Natural Sciences of Philadelphia
J Acad Soc Agric Moscow — Journal. Academy of Socialist Agriculture. Moscow
JACBB — Journal of Applied Chemistry and Biotechnology
JACCDI — Journal. American College of Cardiology
J Accel Sci Technol — Journal of Accelerator Science and Technology
J Accid Emerg Med — Journal of Accident and Emergency Medicine
J Accidental Med — Journal of Accidental Medicine
JACC J Am Coll Cardiol — JACC. Journal. American College of Cardiology

J Accouch — Journal d'Accouchements et Revue de Medecine et de Chirurgie Pratiques
J Account — Journal of Accountancy
J Accountancy — Journal of Accountancy
J Account Audit Finance — Journal of Accounting Auditing and Finance
J Accountin — Journal of Accounting Research
J Accounting Res — Journal of Accounting Research
J Account Res — Journal of Accounting Research
J Acctcy — Journal of Accountancy
J Acct Res — Journal of Accounting Research
J Accy — Journal of Accountancy
JACDA — Journal. American College of Dentists
JACE — Jahrbuch fuer Antike und Christentum. Ergaenzungsband
JACEB — JACEP. Journal of the American College of Emergency Physicians
JACEP — Journal. American College of Emergency Physicians
JACEP — Journal. American College of Emergency Physicians and the University Association for Emergency Medical Services
J Acet Carb Calc — Journal de l'Acetylene, Carbure de Calcium, Acetylene et Derives
J Acet Gas Ltg — Journal of Acetylene Gas Lighting and Carbide of Calcium Review
J Acet Inds — Journal de l'Acetylene et des Industries qui s'y Rattachent
J Acet Ltg — Journal of Acetylene Lighting
J Acet Weld — Journal of Acetylene Welding
J Acetylene Carbure Calcium Acetylene Deriv — Journal de l'Acetylene, Carbure de Calcium, Acetylene et Derives
J Acetylene Light — Journal of Acetylene Lighting
JACF — Journal of Applied Corporate Finance
JACh — Jahrbuch fuer Antike und Christentum
JACH — Journal of American College Health
JACHD — Journal of Antimicrobial Chemotherapy
JACHDX — Journal of Antimicrobial Chemotherapy
JACHEY — Journal of American College Health
Ja Christ Q — Japan Christian Quarterly
JACHS — Australian Catholic Historical Society. Journal
JACI — Journal. American Concrete Institute
JACIA — Journal. American Concrete Institute
JACIBY — Journal of Allergy and Clinical Immunology
Jack Journl — Jackson Journal of Business
Jackson Meml Hosp Bull — Jackson Memorial Hospital Bulletin
Jacksonville M — Jacksonville Monthly
JACL — Journal of African and Comparative Literature
JACM — Journal. Association for Computing Machinery
JACM — Journal of Alternative and Complementary Medicine
JACODK — Journal of Altered States of Consciousness
J Acoust Emiss — Journal of Acoustic Emission
J Acoustical Soc Am — Journal. Acoustical Society of America
J Acoust So — Journal. Acoustical Society of America
J Acoust Soc Am — Journal. Acoustical Society of America
J Acoust Soc Amer — Journal. Acoustical Society of America
J Acoust Soc Am Suppl — Journal. Acoustical Society of America. Supplement
J Acoust Soc India — Journal. Acoustical Society of India
J Acoust Soc Jap — Journal. Acoustical Society of Japan
J Acoust Soc Jpn — Journal. Acoustical Society of Japan
J Acoust Soc Jpn E — Journal of the Acoustical Society of Japan. E. (English Translation of Nippon Onkyo Gakkaishi)
J Acoust Wash — Journal of Acoustics (Washington)
JACPA — Journal. American Academy of Child Psychiatry
J Acquired Immune Defic Syndr — Journal of Acquired Immune Deficiency Syndromes
J Acquired Immune Defic Syndr Hum Retrovirol — Journal of Acquired Immune Deficiency Syndromes and Human Retrovirology
J Acquir Immune Defic Syndr Hum Retrovirol — Journal of Acquired Immune Deficiency Syndromes and Human Retrovirology
JACRAQ — Journal of Apicultural Research
JAcS — Journal. Acoustical Society of America
JACS — Journal. American Chemical Society
JACS — Journal of Applied Communication Series
JACSA — Journal. American Chemical Society
JACSAT — Journal. American Chemical Society
JACT — Journal. American College of Toxicology
JACTA — Journal. American Ceramic Society
JACTA — Journal. Australasian Commercial Teachers' Association
JACTDZ — Journal. American College of Toxicology
JACT News — JACT (Japanese Association of Casting Technology) News
J Act Oxygens Free Radicals — Journal of Active Oxygens and Free Radicals
JAD — Journal of Advertising Research
JADA — Journal. American Dietetic Association
JADAA — Journal. American Dietetic Association
JADAAE — Journal. American Dietetic Association
Jadav J Comp Lit — Jadavpur Journal of Comparative Literature
J Addict Dis — Journal of Addictive Diseases
J Addict Res Found — Journal. Addiction Research Foundation
JADE — Journal of Alcohol and Drug Education
JADEA — Jaderna Energie
J Adelaide Bot Gard — Journal. Adelaide Botanic Gardens
Jad Energ — Jaderna Energie
JA Dept Hist A Diego Velazquez — Jornadas de Arte. Departamento de Historia del Arte Diego Velazquez
Jadernaja Fiz — Jadernaja Fizika
J Adhes — Journal of Adhesion
J Adhesion — Journal of Adhesion
J Adhes Sci — Journal of Adhesion Science and Technology
J Adhes Sci Technol — Journal of Adhesion Science and Technology
J Adhes Sealant Counc — Journal. Adhesive and Sealant Council

J Adhes Soc Jpn — Journal. Adhesion Society of Japan
JADID7 — Journal of Affective Disorders
J Admin Overseas — Journal of Administration Overseas
J Adm Overs — Journal of Administration Overseas
J Adm Overseas — Journal of Administration Overseas
JADO — Journal of Administration Overseas
J Adolesc — Journal of Adolescence
J Adolescence — Journal of Adolescence
J Adolescent Res — Journal of Adolescent Research
J Adolesc Health — Journal of Adolescent Health
J Adolesc Health Care — Journal of Adolescent Health Care
JADPDS — Journal of Applied Developmental Psychology
Jadranski Zborn — Jadranski Zbornik
Jadr Zbor — Jadranski Zbornik. Prolozi za Povijest Istre, Rijeke, i Hrvatskog Primorja
JADSA — Journal. American Dental Association
JADSAY — Journal. American Dental Association
J Adult Ed — Journal of Adult Education
J Adult Educ — Journal of Adult Education
J Adv — Journal of Advertising
J Advanced Transp — Journal of Advanced Transportation
J Adv Educ — Journal of Advanced Education
J Advert — Journal of Advertising
J Advertising — Journal of Advertising
J Advert Res — Journal of Advertising Research
J Adv Mater — Journal of Advanced Materials
J Adv Nurs — Journal of Advanced Nursing
J Adv Oxid Technol — Journal of Advanced Oxidation Technologies
J Adv Res — Journal of Advertising Research
J Adv Sci — Journal of Advanced Science
J Adv Ther — Journal of Advanced Therapeutics
J Adv Transp — Journal of Advanced Transportation
J Adv Zool — Journal of Advanced Zoology
Jad Zborn — Jadranski Zbornik. Prilozi za Povjest Istre, Rijeke i Hrvatskog Primorja
JAe — Jahrbuch fuer Aesthetik und Allgemeine Kunstwissenschaft
JAE — Jeune Afrique Economie
JAE — Journal of Accounting and Economics
JAE — Journal of Advanced Education
JAE — Journal of Aesthetic Education
JAE — Journal of Agricultural Economics
JAE — Journal of Animal Ecology
JAE — Training and Development Journal
JAEA — Journal of American Ethnology and Archaeology
JAeAK — Jahrbuch fuer Aesthetik und Allgemeine Kunstwissenschaft
JAECAP — Journal of Animal Ecology
Ja Echo — Japan Echo
Ja Econ Stud — Japanese Economic Studies
JAEDB — Journal of Aesthetic Education
JAEH — Journal of American Ethnic History
JAEMA — Journal. Albert Einstein Medical Center
JAEMAL — Journal. Albert Einstein Medical Center
JAENES — Journal of Agricultural Entomology
JAEPM — Jahresbericht des Allgemeinen Evngelisch-Protestantischen Missionsvereins
JAERA2 — Journal of Agricultural Engineering Research
JAERI Res — JAERI (Japan Atomic Energy Research Institute) Research
JAERI Rev — JAERI-Review
J Aerol Lab Tateno — Journal of the Aerological Laboratory at Tateno
J Aero Med Soc — Journal. Aero Medical Society
J Aero Med Soc India — Journal. Aero Medical Society of India
J Aeronaut Mater Beijing — Journal of Aeronautical Materials (Beijing)
J Aeronaut Met — Journal of Aeronautical Meteorology
J Aeronaut Res Inst Tokyo — Journal. Aeronautical Research Institute. Tokyo Imperial University
J Aeronaut Sci — Journal. Aeronautical Sciences
J Aeronaut Soc India — Journal. Aeronautical Society of India
J Aeronaut Soc S Afr — Journal. Aeronautical Society of South Africa
J Aero Sci — Journal of the Aeronautical Sciences
J Aerosol Res Jpn — Journal of Aerosol Research (Japan)
J Aerosol Sci — Journal of Aerosol Science
J Aerosol Science — Journal of Aerosol Science
J Aero/Space Sci — Journal of the Aero/Space Sciences [*Later, American Institute of Aeronautics and Astronautics. Journal*]
J Aerosp Eng — Journal of Aerospace Engineering
J Aerosp Sci — Journal. Aerospace Sciences
J Aerosp Transp Div Am Soc Civ Eng — Journal. Aerospace Transport Division. American Society of Civil Engineers
JAERT — Journal. Association for Education by Radio-Television
JAES — Journal. Audio Engineering Society
JAES — Journal of African Earth Sciences
J Aes Art C — Journal of Aesthetics and Art Criticism
J Aes Art Crit — Journal of Aesthetics and Art Criticism
JAesE — Journal of Aesthetic Education
J Aes Ed — Journal of Aesthetic Education
J Aes Educ — Journal of Aesthetic Education
J Aesth — Journal of Aesthetics and Art Criticism
J Aesth & A Crit — Journal of Aesthetics and Art Criticism
J Aesth & Art C — Journal of Aesthetics and Art Criticism
J Aesth Educ — Journal of Aesthetic Education
J Aesthet Art Crit — Journal of Aesthetics and Art Criticism
J Aesthet E — Journal of Aesthetic Education
J Aesthetic Educ — Journal of Aesthetic Education
J Aesthetics — Journal of Aesthetics and Art Criticism
JAf — Jewish Affairs
JAF — Journal of American Folklore

JAFCAU — Journal of Agricultural and Food Chemistry
JAff — Jewish Affairs
J Affairs — Jewish Affairs
J Affect Disord — Journal of Affective Disorders
J Affective Disord — Journal of Affective Disorders
JAf H — Journal of African History
JAf L — Journal of African Law
JAFL — Journal of American Folklore
Ja Found Newsl — Japan Foundation Newsletter
J Afr Adm — Journal of African Administration
J Afr Earth Sci — Journal of African Earth Sciences
J Afr Earth Sci Middle East — Journal of African Earth Sciences and the Middle East
JAfrH — Journal of African History
J Afr Hist — Journal of African History
J Afric — Journal des Africanistes
J African Hist — Journal of African History
Africanistes — Journal des Africanistes
J African Law — Journal of African Law
J African Soc — Journal. African Society
J African Studies — Journal of African Studies
J Afric Hist — Journal of African History
JAfrL — Journal of African Languages
J Afr L — Journal of African Law
J Afr Lang — Journal of African Languages
J Afr Langs — Journal of African Languages
J Afr Languages — Journal of African Languages
J Afr Law — Journal of African Law
J Afr Relig & Philos — Journal of African Religion and Philosophy
J Afr S — Journal. African Society
J Afr Sci Technol Ser A — Journal Africain de Science et Technologie. Serie A. Technologie
J Afr Sci Technol Ser B — Journal Africain de Science et Technologie. Serie B. Science
J Afr Soc — Journal. African Society
J Afr Stud — Journal of African Studies
JAFS — Journal of American Folklore. Supplement
JAf S — Journal. Royal African Society
JAG — JAG [*Judge Advocate General, US Air Force*] Bulletin
JaG — Jahrbuch der Gesellschaft fuer Niedersaechsische Kirchengeschichte
JAG — Journal. Alaska Geological Society
J Ag & Food Chem — Journal of Agricultural and Food Chemistry
JAG Bull — Judge Advocate General Bulletin
Jagd Forst Neuigk — Jagd- und Forst-Neuigkeiten
J Ag Econ — Journal of Agricultural Economics
JAGGAD — Journal des Agreges
Jagger J — Jagger Journal
J Aging & Phys Act — Journal of Aging and Physical Activity
JAG J — JAG [*Judge Advocate General, US Navy*] Journal
JAG Journal — Judge Advocate General of the Navy. Journal
JAG L Rev — United States. Air Force Judge Advocate General. Law Review
J Ag New Zealand — New Zealand Journal of Agriculture
J Ag Pratique — Journal d'Agriculture Pratique
JAGRA — Journal of Agricultural Research
J Agr Ass China — Journal. Agricultural Association of China
J Agr Che J — Journal. Agricultural Chemical Society of Japan
J Agr Chem Soc Jap — Journal. Agricultural Chemical Society of Japan
J Agr Econ — Journal of Agricultural Economics
J Agr Econ Dev — Journal of Agricultural Economics and Development
J Agreges — Journal des Agreges
J Agr Eng R — Journal of Agricultural Engineering Research
J Agr Eng Res — Journal of Agricultural Engineering Research
J Agr Eng Soc Jap — Journal. Agricultural Engineering Society of Japan
J Ag Res — Journal of Agricultural Research
J Agr Exp Sta Chosen — Journal. Agricultural Experiment Station of Chosen
J Agr Food — Journal of Agricultural and Food Chemistry
J Agr Food Chem — Journal of Agricultural and Food Chemistry
J Agric — Journal of Agriculture
J Agric Ass China — Journal. Agricultural Association of China
J Agric Assoc China — Journal. Agricultural Association of China
J Agric Assoc China New Ser — Journal. Agricultural Association of China. New Series
J Agric Assoc China Taipei — Journal. Agricultural Association of China (Taipei)
J Agric Chem Soc Japan — Journal. Agricultural Chemical Society of Japan
J Agric Chem Soc Jpn — Journal. Agricultural Chemical Society of Japan
J Agric Econ — Journal of Agricultural Economics
J Agric Econ Dev — Journal of Agricultural Economics and Development
J Agric Econ Res — Journal of Agricultural Economics Research
J Agric Edinburgh — Journal of Agriculture (Edinburgh)
J Agric Eng — Journal of Agricultural Engineering
J Agric Engin Res — Journal of Agricultural Engineering Research
J Agric Engng Res — Journal of Agricultural Engineering Research
J Agric Eng Res — Journal of Agricultural Engineering Research
J Agric Eng Soc Jpn — Journal. Agricultural Engineering Society. Japan
J Agric Entomol — Journal of Agricultural Entomology
J Agric Ethics — Journal of Agricultural Ethics
J Agric Exp — Journal de l'Agriculture Experimentale
J Agric Exp Sta Gov Gen Chosen — Journal. Agricultural Experiment Station. Government General Chosen/Noji Shikenjo Kenkyu Hokoku
J Agric Fac Ege Univ — Journal of Agricultural Faculty of Ege University
J Agric Fd Chem — Journal of Agricultural and Food Chemistry
J Agric Food Chem — Journal of Agricultural and Food Chemistry
J Agric For — Journal of Agriculture and Forestry
J Agric For Nanking — Journal of Agriculture and Forestry (Nanking)

J Agric For Natl Chung Hsing Univ — Journal of Agriculture and Forestry (National Chung Hsing University)
J Agric For Taichung — Journal of Agriculture and Forestry (Taichung)
J Agric Hort Montreal — Journal d'Agriculture et d'Horticulture (Montreal)
J Agric Hort Montreal — Journal of Agriculture and Horticulture (Montreal)
J Agric Hort Pract — Journal d'Agriculture et d'Horticulture Pratiques
J Agric Ind S Aust — Journal of Agriculture and Industry of South Australia
J Agric Ind South Aust — Journal of Agriculture and Industry of South Australia
J Agric Industr South Australia — Journal of Agriculture and Industry of South Australia. Agricultural Bureau
J Agric Lab (Chiba) — Journal. Agricultural Laboratory (Chiba)
J Agric Med — Journal d'Agriculture, de Medecine, et des Sciences Accessoires
J Agric Meteorol — Journal of Agricultural Meteorology
J Agric Meteorol Tokyo — Journal of Agricultural Meteorology (Tokyo)
J Agric Met (Tokyo) — Journal of Agricultural Meteorology (Tokyo)
J Agric Nord — Journal de l'Agriculture du Nord
J Agric NW Front Prov — Journal of Agriculture. Northwest Frontier Province
J Agric NZ Dep Agric — Journal of Agriculture. New Zealand Department of Agriculture
J Agric Pays Bas — Journal d'Agriculture, d'Economie Rurale, et des Manufactures du Royaume des Pays-Bas
J Agric Prat — Journal d'Agriculture Pratique
J Agric Prat Basses Pyren — Journal d'Agriculture Pratique des Basses-Pyrenees
J Agric Prat Vitic Econ Rur — Journal d'Agriculture Pratique, de Viticulture, et d'Economie Rurale
J Agric Res — Journal of Agricultural Research
J Agric Res (Alexandria) — Journal of Agricultural Research (Alexandria)
J Agric Res Cent (Vantaa Finl) — Journal. Agricultural Research Centre (Vantaa, Finland)
J Agric Res China — Journal of Agricultural Research of China
J Agric Res Icel — Journal of Agricultural Research in Iceland
J Agric Res Lahore — Journal of Agricultural Research (Lahore)
J Agric Res Punjab — Journal of Agricultural Research (Punjab)
J Agric Res Ranchi Univ — Journal of Agricultural Research. Ranchi University
J Agric Res (Riyadh Saudi Arabia) — Journal of Agricultural Research (Riyadh, Saudi Arabia)
J Agric Res Tokai Kinki Region — Journal. Agricultural Researches in Tokai-Kinki Region/Tokai Kinki Nogy Kenkyu
J Agric Saf Health — Journal of Agricultural Safety and Health
J Agric (S Aust) — Journal of Agriculture (South Australia)
J Agric Sci — Journal of Agricultural Science
J Agric Sci Beijing — Journal of Agricultural Science (Beijing)
J Agric Sci (Camb) — Journal of Agricultural Science (Cambridge)
J Agric Sci Finl — Journal of Agricultural Science in Finland
J Agric Sci Finl Maataloustieteellinen Aikak — Journal of Agricultural Science in Finland. Maataloustieteellinen Aikakauskjirja
J Agric Sci Helsinki — Journal of Agricultural Science (Helsinki)
J Agric Sci Inst Agric Sci Chungnam Natl Univ — Journal of Agricultural Science. Institute of Agricultural Science. (Chungnam National University)
J Agric Sci Peking — Journal of Agricultural Science (Peking)
J Agric Sci Res — Journal of Agricultural and Scientific Research
J Agric Sci Tokyo — Journal of Agricultural Science/Tokyo Nogyo Daigaku Nogyo Shuho (Tokyo)
J Agric Sci Tokyo Nogyo Daigaku — Journal of Agricultural Science. Tokyo Nogyo Daigaku
J Agric Sci Tokyo Nogyo Daigaku Suppl — Journal of Agricultural Science. Tokyo Nogyo Daigaku. Supplement
J Agric Soc Jpn — Journal. Agricultural Society of Japan
J Agric Soc Trin — Journal. Agricultural Society of Trinidad and Tobago
J Agric Soc Trin & Tobago — Journal. Agricultural Society of Trinidad and Tobago
J Agric Soc Trinidad Tobago — Journal. Agricultural Society of Trinidad and Tobago
J Agric Soc Trin Tob — Journal. Agricultural Society of Trinidad and Tobago
J Agric Soc Univ Coll Wales — Journal. Agricultural Society. University College of Wales
J Agric Soc Univ Coll Wales (Aberyst) — Journal. Agricultural Society. University College of Wales (Aberystwyth)
J Agric Soc Western Australia — Journal. Agricultural and Horticultural Society of Western Australia
J Agric (South Aust) — Journal of Agriculture (South Australia)
J Agric (South Perth Aust) — Journal of Agriculture (South Perth, Australia)
J Agric Sud Ouest — Journal d'Agriculture du Sud-Ouest/Societe d'Horticulture de la Haute-Garonne
J Agric Suisse — Journal d'Agriculture Suisse
J Agric Tradit Bot Appl Trav Ethnobot Ethnozool — Journal d'Agriculture Traditionnelle et de Botanique Appliquee. Travaux d'Ethnobotanique et d'Ethnozoologie
J Agric Trop — Journal d'Agriculture Tropicale
J Agric Trop Botan Appl — Journal d'Agriculture Tropicale et de Botanique Appliquee [*Later, Journal d'Agriculture Traditionnelle et de Botanique Appliquee*]
J Agric Trop Bot Appl — Journal d'Agriculture Tropicale et de Botanique Appliquee [*Later, Journal d'Agriculture Traditionnelle et de Botanique Appliquee*]
J Agricultural Food Chem — Journal of Agricultural and Food Chemistry
J Agric Univ PR — Journal of Agriculture. University of Puerto Rico
J Agric Univ Puerto Rico — Journal of Agriculture. University of Puerto Rico
J Agric (VIC) — Journal of Agriculture (Department of Agriculture. Victoria)
J Agric (Vict) — Journal of Agriculture (Victoria)
J Agric Vict Dep Agric — Journal of Agriculture. Victoria Department of Agriculture
J Agric (Victoria) — Journal of Agriculture (Victoria)
J Agric Victoria Aust — Journal of Agriculture (Victoria, Australia)
J Agric Water Resour Res — Journal of Agriculture and Water Resources Research
J Agric (West Aust) — Journal of Agriculture (Department of Agriculture. Western Australia)
J Agri Food Chem — Journal of Agricultural and Food Chemistry

J Agri Hort Soc Madras — Journal of the Agri-Horticultural Society of Madras
J Agri Hort Soc West India — Journal of the Agri-Horticultural Society of Western India
J Agr Ind SA — Journal of Agricultural Industry, South Australia
J Agr Lab — Journal. Agricultural Laboratory
J Agr (Melbourne) — Journal of Agriculture (Melbourne)
J Agr Meteorol (Japan) — Journal of Agricultural Meteorology (Japan)
J Agron Crop Sci — Journal of Agronomy and Crop Science
J Agron Educ — Journal of Agronomic Education
J Agr Prat — Journal d'Agriculture Pratique
J Agr Res — Journal of Agricultural Research
J Agr Res Tokai-Kinki Reg — Journal of Agricultural Research in the Tokai-Kinki Region
J Agr (S Aust) — Journal of Agriculture (South Australia)
J Agr Sci — Journal of Agricultural Science
J Agr Sci Tokyo Nogyo Daigaku — Journal of Agricultural Science. Tokyo Nogyo Daigaku
J Agr Soc Trinidad Tobago — Journal. Agricultural Society of Trinidad and Tobago
J Agr Soc Wales — Journal. Agricultural Society. University College of Wales
J Agr Trad Bot Appl — Journal d'Agriculture Traditionnelle et de Botanique Appliquee
J Agr Trop Bot Appl — Journal d'Agriculture Tropicale et de Botanique Appliquee
   [*Later, Journal d'Agriculture Traditionnelle et de Botanique Appliquee*]
J Agr Univ PR — Journal of Agriculture. University of Puerto Rico
J Agr W Aust — Journal of Agriculture of Western Australia
JAGS — Journal. American Geographical and Statistical Society
JAGS — Journal. American Geographical Society
JAGSA — Journal. American Geriatrics Society
J Ag (SA) — Journal of Agriculture (South Australia)
JAGSAF — Journal. American Geriatrics Society
J Ag T and L — Journal of Agricultural Taxation and Law
J Ag Univ Puerto Rico — Journal of Agriculture. University of Puerto Rico
JAGVAO — Journal of Agriculture
J Ag (VIC) — Journal of Agriculture (Department of Agriculture. Victoria)
JAGW — Jahrbuecher der Akademie Gemeinnuetziger Wissenschaften
J Ag (WA) — Journal of Agriculture (Department of Agriculture. Western Australia)
JAH — Journal of African History
JAH — Journal of American History
JAH — Journal of Asian History
JAHAA — Journal. American College Health Association
JAHAAY — Journal. American College Health Association
Jahangirnagar Rev Part A Sci — Jahangirnagar Review Part A. Science
Jahan Rev — Jahangirnagar Review
JahAs — Jahrbuch fuer Amerikastudien
JAHCD9 — Journal of Adolescent Health Care
JAHEDF — Journal of Allied Health
JaHK — Jahrbuch der Hessischen Kirchengeschichtliche Vereinigung
Jahrb Akad Wiss Gottingen — Jahrbuch. Akademie der Wissenschaften in Goettingen
Jahrb Akad Wiss Lit (Mainz) — Jahrbuch. Akademie der Wissenschaften und der Literatur (Mainz)
Jahrb Altkde — Jahrbuch fuer Altertumskunde
Jahrb Amerikastud — Jahrbuch fuer Amerikastudien
Jahrb Anz — Archaeologischer Anzeiger
Jahrb Arbeitsgemein Futterungsberat — Jahrbuch. Arbeitsgemeinschaft fuer Fuetterungsberatung
Jahrb Arbeitsgem Fuetterungsberat — Jahrbuch. Arbeitsgemeinschaft fuer Fuetterungsberatung
Jahrb Bayer Akad Wiss — Jahrbuch. Bayerische Akademie der Wissenschaften
Jahrb Bergbau Energ Mineraloel Chem — Jahrbuch fuer Bergbau Energie Mineraloel und Chemie
Jahrb Ber M — Jahrbuch. Berliner Museen
Jahrb Bodenden Meck — Jahrbuch. Bodendenkmalpflege in Mecklenburg
Jahrb Brandenburg Landesgesch — Jahrbuch fuer Brandenburgische Landesgeschichte
Jahrb Brennkrafttech Ges — Jahrbuch der Brennkrafttechnischen Gesellschaft
Jahrb Bundesanst Pflanzenbau Samenpruef (Wien) — Jahrbuch. Bundesanstalt fuer Pflanzenbau und Samenpruefung (Wien)
Jahrb Bundesanst Pflanzenbau Samenpruf — Jahrbuch. Bundesanstalt fuer Pflanzenbau und Samenpruefung
Jahrb Chem Ind — Jahrbuch Chemische Industrie
Jahrb Chem Technol Hochsch Prof Dr A Zlatarov Burgas — Jahrbuch der Chemisch-Technologischen Hochschule Prof. Dr. A. Zlatarov. Burgas
Jahrb Coburg Landesstift — Jahrbuch. Coburger Landesstiftung
Jahrb DAI — Jahrbuch des Deutschen Archaeologischen Instituts
Jahrbd Arch Inst — Jahrbuch des Deutschen Archaeologischen Instituts
Jahrb D Charakterol — Jahrbuch der Charakterologie
Jahrb der Ges fuer Lothring Geschichte — Jahrbuch der Gesellschaft fuer Lothringische Geschichte und Altertumskunde
Jahrb Deut Akad Landwirt Wiss (Berlin) — Jahrbuch. Deutsche Akademie der Landwirtschaftswissenschaften (Berlin)
Jahrb Deutsch Akad Wiss Berlin — Jahrbuch der Deutschen Akademie der Wissenschaften zu Berlin
Jahrb Deutsch Kakteen Ges — Jahrbuch der Deutschen Kakteen-Gesellschaft in der Deutschen Gesellschaft fuer Gartenkultur
Jahrb Deutsch Mikrol Ges — Jahrbuch der Deutschen Mikrologischen Gesellschaft
Jahrb D Koeln Geschichtsver — Jahrbuch des Koelnischen Geschichtsvereins
Jahrb d Kunsthist Samml d Kaiserhauses — Jahrbuch. Kunsthistorische Sammlungen des Allerhoechsten Kaiserhauses
Jahrbd Oesterreich Inst — Jahreshefte des Oesterreichischen Archaeologischen Institutes in Wien
Jahrb d Preuss Kunstsamml — Jahrbuch. Preussische Kunstsammlungen
Jahrb d Staatl Kunstsammlungen Bad Wuertt — Jahrbuch der Staatlichen Kunstsammlungen in Baden-Wuerttemberg
Jahrb Dtsch Ges Chronom — Jahrbuch. Deutsche Gesellschaft fuer Chronometrie

Jahrb Eisenbahnwes — Jahrbuch des Eisenbahnwesens
Jahr Berliner Mus — Jahrbuch. Berliner Museen
Jahrb F Kultur U Gesch D Slaven — Jahrbuecher fuer Kultur und Geschichte der Slaven
Jahrb F Nationaloekon U Statist — Jahrbuecher fuer Nationaloekonomie und Statistik
Jahrb Forschungsinst Erdoelverarb Petrochem — Jahrbuch des Forschungsinstituts fuer Erdoelverarbeitung und Petrochemie
Jahrb F Psychiat U Neurol — Jahrbuecher fuer Psychiatrie und Neurologie
Jahrb Fraenk Landesforsch — Jahrbuch fuer Fraenkische Landesforschung
Jahrb Freien Deut Hochstifts — Jahrbuch des Freien Deutschen Hochstifts
Jahrb FrG — Jahrbuch der Entscheidungen der Freiwilligen Gerichtsbarkeit und des Grundbuchwesens
Jahrb Geol Bundesanst — Jahrbuch. Geologische Bundesanstalt
Jahrb Geol Bundesanst Austria — Jahrbuch der Geologischen Bundesanstalt (Austria)
Jahrb Geol Bundesanst Sonderb — Jahrbuch. Geologische Bundesanstalt. Sonderband
Jahrb Geol Landesanst (Austria) — Jahrbuch der Geologischen Landesanstalt (Austria)
Jahrb Geol Reichsanst Austria — Jahrbuch der Geologischen Reichsanstalt (Austria)
Jahrb Geol Staatsanst — Jahrbuch der Geologischen Staatsanstalt
Jahrb Geol Staatsanst Austria — Jahrbuch der Geologischen Staatsanstalt (Austria)
Jahrb Gesch — Jahrbuecher fuer Geschichte Osteuropas
Jahrb Gesch & Kunst Mittelrheins & Nachbargeb — Jahrbuch fuer Geschichte und Kunst des Mittelrheins und Seiner Nachbargebiete
Jahrb Gesch Mittel Ostdeut — Jahrbuch fuer die Geschichte Mittel- und Ostdeutschlands
Jahrb Gesch Mittel Ostdtschl — Jahrbuch fuer die Geschichte Mittel- und Ostdeutschlands
Jahrb Gesch Osteur — Jahrbuecher fuer Geschichte Osteuropas
Jahrb Gesch Osteurop — Jahrbuecher fuer Geschichte Osteuropas
Jahrb Gesch Osteuropas — Jahrbuecher fuer Geschichte Osteuropas
Jahrb Gesch Soz Laender Eur — Jahrbuch fuer Geschichte der Socialistischen Laender Europas
Jahrb Gewaechsk — Jahrbuecher der Gewaechskunde
Jahrb Hafenbautech Ges — Jahrbuch. Hafenbautechnische Gesellschaft
Jahrb Hist Forsch Bundesrepub Deut — Jahrbuch der Historischen Forschung in der Bundesrepublik Deutschland
Jahrb Hist Mus Bern — Jahrbuch des Bernischen Historischen Museums
Jahrb Hist Ver Dilling — Jahrbuch des Historischen Vereins Dillingen
Jahrb Hist Ver Liechten — Jahrbuch des Historischen Vereins fuer das Fuerstentum Liechtenstein
Jahrb Hochsch Chem Technol Burgas Bulg — Jahrbuch der Hochschule fuer Chemische Technologie. Burgas, Bulgaria
Jahrb Inst Brennst Waermetech — Jahrbuch des Instituts fuer Brennstoffe und Waermetechnik
Jahrb Inst Deut Gesch — Jahrbuch des Instituts fuer Deutsche Geschichte
Jahrb Inst Ne-Metall (Plovdiv) — Jahrbuch. Institut fuer Ne-Metallurgie (Plovdiv)
Jahrb Kinderh — Jahrbuch fuer Kinderheilkunde und Physische Erziehung
Jahrb Kinderheilkd — Jahrbuch fuer Kinderheilkunde
Jahrb Kinderheilkd Phys Erzieh — Jahrbuch fuer Kinderheilkunde und Physische Erziehung
Jahrb KK Geol Reichsanst Austria — Jahrbuch der K. K. Geologischen Reichsanstalt (Austria)
Jahrb K K Polytechn Inst Wien — Jahrbuecher des Kaiserlich Koeniglichen Polytechnischen Instituts in Wien
Jahrb Koenigl Akad Gemeinnuetz Wiss Erfurt — Jahrbuecher der Koeniglichen Akademie Gemeinnuetziger Wissenschaften zu Erfurt
Jahrb Koenigl Saechs Akad Forst Landwirte Tharandt — Jahrbuch der Koeniglich Saechsischen Akademie fuer Forst- und Landwirte zu Tharandt
Jahrb K Tieraerzti Landwirtsch Univ (Copenhagen) — Jahrbuch. Koenigliche Tieraerztliche und Landwirtschaftliche Universitaet (Copenhagen)
Jahrb Kunsth Samml — Jahrbuch der Kunsthistorischen Sammlungen
Jahrb Kunsth Samml Kaiserh — Jahrbuch. Kunsthistorische Sammlungen des Allerhoechsten Kaiserhauses
Jahrb Lederwirtsch Oesterr — Jahrbuch. Lederwirtschaft Oesterreich
Jahrb Liturg & Hymnol — Jahrbuch fuer Liturgik und Hymnologie
Jahrb Max Planck Ges — Jahrbuch. Max-Planck-Gesellschaft
Jahrb Max Planck Ges Foerd Wiss — Jahrbuch der Max-Planck-Gesellschaft zur Foerderung der Wissenschaften
Jahrb Mikroskop — Jahrbuch fuer Mikroskopiker
Jahrb Milchwirtsch — Jahrbuch der Milchwirtschaft
Jahrb Morphol Mikrosk Anat Abt 2 — Jahrbuch fuer Morphologie und Mikroskopische Anatomie. Abteilung 2
Jahrb Nassauischen Vereins Naturk — Jahrbuecher des Nassauischen Vereins fuer Naturkunde
Jahrb Nassau Ver Naturkd — Jahrbuecher. Nassauischer Verein fuer Naturkunde
Jahrb Neuesten Wichtigsten Erfind Entdeck — Jahrbuch der Neuesten und Wichtigsten Erfindungen und Entdeckungen
Jahrb Nordrh Westfal Landesamt Forsch — Jahrbuch. Nordrhein Westfalen Landesamt fuer Forschung
Jahrb N St — Jahrbuecher fuer National-Oekonomie und Statistik
Jahrb Numism Geldgesch — Jahrbuch fuer Numismatik und Geldgeschichte
Jahrb Oberflaechentech — Jahrbuch Oberflaechentechnik
Jahrb Oberoesterr Musealver — Jahrbuch. Oberoesterreichischer Musealverein
Jahrb Oberoesterr Museavereins — Jahrbuch des Oberoesterreichischen Musealvereins
Jahrb Oesterr Byzantinistik — Jahrbuch der Oesterreichischen Byzantinistik
Jahrb Oesterreich Byzant Gesell — Jahrbuch der Oesterreichischen Byzantinistik Gesellschaft
Jahrb Oesterreich Byzantinistik — Jahrbuch der Oesterreichischen Byzantinistik
Jahrb Opt Feinmech — Jahrbuch fuer Optik und Feinmechanik

Jahrb Org Chem — Jahrbuch der Organischen Chemie

Jahrb Philos Fak 2 Univ Bern — Jahrbuch der Philosophischen Fakultaet. 2. Universitaet Bern

Jahrb Philos Fak 2 Zweite Univ Bern — Jahrbuch der Philosophischen Fakultaet 2. Zweite der Universitaet Bern

Jahrb Photogr Reproduktionstech — Jahrbuch fuer Photographie und Reproduktionstechnik

Jahrb Preuss Geol Landesanst — Jahrbuch. Preussische Geologische Landesanstalt

Jahrb Preuss Kunstsamml — Jahrbuch. Preussische Kunstsammlungen

Jahrb Psychiatr Neurol — Jahrbuecher fuer Psychiatrie und Neurologie

Jahrb Radioakt Elektron — Jahrbuch der Radioaktivitaet und Elektronik

Jahrb Reichsamts Bodenf — Jahrbuch des Reichsamts fuer Bodenforschung

Jahrb Reichsamts Bodenforsch — Jahrbuch des Reichsamts fuer Bodenforschung

Jahrb Reichsstelle Bodenforsch (Ger) — Jahrbuch der Reichsstelle fuer Bodenforschung (Germany)

Jahrb Reisen Neuesten Statist — Jahrbuch der Reisen und Neuesten Statistik

Jahrb Schiffbautech Ges — Jahrbuch. Schiffbautechnische Gesellschaft

Jahrb Schlesischen Friedrich Wilhelms Univ — Jahrbuch der Schlesischen Friedrich-Wilhelms-Universitaet zu Breslau

Jahrb Schweiz Gesell Urgesch — Jahrbuch der Schweizerischen Gesellschaft fuer Urgeschichte

Jahrb Schweiz Ges Urgesch — Jahrbuch der Schweizerischen Gesellschaft fuer Urgeschichte

Jahrb Schweiz Naturforsch Ges Wiss Teil — Jahrbuch der Schweizerischen Naturforschenden Gesellschaft. Wissenschaftlicher Teil

Jahrb Siebenbuerg Karpathen Vereins — Jahrbuch des Siebenbuergischen Karpathen-Vereins

Jahrb Sozia — Jahrbuch fuer Sozialwissenschaft

Jahrb Staatl Mus Mineral Geol Dresden — Jahrbuch. Staatliches Museum fuer Mineralogie und Geologie zu Dresden

Jahrb Staatl Mus Naturkd Stuttgart — Jahrbuch des Staatlichen Museums fuer Naturkunde in Stuttgart

Jahrb Staudenk — Jahrbuch fuer Staudenkunde

Jahrb Studienges Foerd Kernenergieverwert Schiffbau Schiffahr — Jahrbuch der Studiengesellschaft zur Foerderung der Kernenergieverwertung in Schiffbau und Schiffahrt e. V

Jahrb Tech Univ Muenchen — Jahrbuch. Technische Universitaet Muenchen

Jahrb Uberblicke Math — Jahrbuch Ueberlicke Mathematik

Jahrbuch d Diss d Philos Fak Berlin — Jahrbuch der Dissertationen der Philosophisches Fakultaet der Friedrich-WilhelmUniversitaet zu Berlin

Jahrbuch Deut Arch Inst — Jahrbuch des Deutschen Archaeologischen Instituts

Jahrbuch d Philos Fak Leipzig — Jahrbuch der Philosophischen Fakultaet zu Leipzig

Jahrbuch Hamburger Kunstsam — Jahrbuch. Hamburger Kunstsammlungen

Jahrbuch Niederdonau — Jahrbuch fuer Landeskunde von Niederdonau

Jahrb Ung Forschungsinst Fleischwirtsch — Jahrbuch des Ungarischen Forschungsinstituts fuer Fleischwirtschaft

Jahrb Ung Geol Anst — Jahrbuch der Ungarischen Geologischen Anstalt

Jahrb Ung Karpathen Vereines — Jahrbuch des Ungarischen Karpathen-Vereines

Jahrb Vereins Schutze Alpenpfl — Jahrbuch des Vereins zum Schutze der Alpenpflanzen

Jahrb Vereins Schutze Alpenpfl Alpentiere — Jahrbuch des Vereins zum Schutze der Alpenpflanzen und -tiere

Jahrb Ver Freunde Univ Mainz — Jahrbuch der Vereinigung Freunde der Universitaet Mainz

Jahrb Ver Gesch Stadt Wien — Jahrbuch des Vereins fuer Geschichte der Stadt Wien

Jahrb Ver Naturkd Herzogthum Nassau — Jahrbuecher des Vereins fuer Naturkunde im Herzogthum Nassau

Jahrb Ver Schutz Bergwelt — Jahrbuch des Vereins zum Schutz der Bergwelt

Jahrb Ver Schutze Alpenpflanz Tiere — Jahrbuch des Vereins zum Schutze der Alpenpflanzen und Tiere

Jahrb Vers Lehranst Brau Berlin — Jahrbuch. Versuch und Lehranstalt fuer Brauerei in Berlin

Jahrb Volks — Jahrbuch fuer Volksliedforschung

Jahrb Wiss Bot — Jahrbuecher fuer Wissenschaftliche Botanik

Jahrb Wiss Forsch Proekt Konstruktionsinst Ne Metall Plovdiv — Jahrbuch des Wissenschaftlichen Forschungs-, Proektierungs-, und Konstruktionsinstitut fuer Ne-Metallurgie (Plovdiv)

Jahrb Wiss Forsch Projektierungsinst Erzbergbau Aufbereit — Jahrbuch des Wissenschaftlichen Forschungs- und Projektierungsinstituts fuer Erzbergbau und Aufbereitung

Jahrb Wiss Forschungsinst Bergbau Stara Zagora Bulg — Jahrbuch des Wissenschaftlichen Forschungsinstituts fuer Bergbau. Stara Zagora, Bulgaria

Jahrb Wiss Forschungsinst Buntmetall (Plovdiv) — Jahrbuch. Wissenschaftliches Forschungsinstitut fuer Buntmetallurgie (Plovdiv)

Jahrb Wiss Forschungsinst Chem Ind Sofia — Jahrbuch des Wissenschaftlichen Forschungsinstitut fuer Chemische Industrie. (Sofia)

Jahrb Wiss Forschungsinst Metall Aufbereit — Jahrbuch des Wissenschaftlichen Forschungsinstituts fuer Metallurgie und Aufbereitung

Jahrb Wiss Krit — Jahrbuecher fuer Wissenschaftliche Kritik. Herausgegeben von der Societaet fuerWissenschaftliche Kritik zu Berlin

Jahrb Zuckerruebenbau — Jahrbuch fuer Zuckerruebenbau

Jahrb Zuerichsee — Jahrbuch vom Zuerichsee

Jahrb Zweigstelle Wien Reichsstelle Bodenforsch — Jahrbuch der Zweigstelle Wien der Reichsstelle fuer Bodenforschung

Jahr Deutsch Archaeol Inst — Jahrbuch. Deutsches Archaeologisches Institut

Jahresber Abh Naturwiss Vereins Magdeburg — Jahresbericht und Abhandlungen des Naturwissenschaftlichen Vereins in Magdeburg

Jahresber Bayer Bodendenkmal — Jahresbericht der Bayerischen Bodendenkmalpflege

Jahresber Bot Gart Bern — Jahresbericht ueber den Botanischen Garten in Bern

Jahresber Bot Vereines Mittel Niederrheine — Jahresbericht des Botanischen Vereines am Mittel- und Niederrheine

Jahresber Bot Verein Hamb EV — Jahresbericht. Botanischer Verein zu Hamburg EV

Jahresber Bundesanst Materialpruef — Jahresbericht der Bundesanstalt fuer Materialpruefung

Jahresber Chem Tech Reichsanst — Jahresbericht. Chemisch Technische Reichsanstalt

Jahresber der Schles Gesellschaft fuer Vaterland Kultur — Jahresbericht der Schlesischen Gesellschaft fuer Vaterlandische Kultur

Jahresber Deut Math Ver — Jahresberichte der Deutschen Mathematiker-Vereinigung

Jahresber DFVLR — Jahresbericht. Deutsche Forschungs- und Versuchsanstalt fuer Luftund Raumfahrt

Jahresber Dtsch Hydrogr Inst (Hamburg) — Jahresbericht. Deutsches Hydrographische Institut (Hamburg)

Jahresber Dtsch Pflanzenschutzdienstes — Jahresberichte des Deutschen Pflanzenschutzdienstes

Jahresber Fortschr Anim Physiol — Jahresbericht ueber die Fortschritte der Animalischen Physiologie

Jahresber Fortschr Chem Verw Theile Andrer Wiss — Jahresbericht ueber die Fortschritte der Chemie und Verwandter Theile Anderer Wissenschaften

Jahresber Fortschr Gesamtgeb Agrikulturchem — Jahresbericht ueber die Fortschritte auf dem Gesamtgebiete der Agrikulturchemie

Jahresber Fortschr Pharmakogn — Jahresbericht ueber die Fortschritte der Pharmakognosie, Pharmacie, und Toxicologie

Jahresber Fortschr Pharm in Allen Laendern — Jahresbericht ueber die Fortschritte in der Pharmacie in Allen Laendern

Jahresber Fortschr Physiol — Jahresbericht ueber die Fortschritte der Physiologie

Jahresber Fortschr Tierchm — Jahresbericht ueber die Fortschritte der Tierchemie

Jahresber Gartenbauvereins Mainz — Jahresbericht des Gartenbauvereins in Mainz

Jahresber Geogr Ges Hamburg — Jahresbericht der Geographischen Gesellschaft in Hamburg

Jahresber Geogr Vereins Frankfurt — Jahresbericht des Geographischen Vereins zu Frankfurt

Jahresber Ges Natur Heil Kunde Dresden — Jahresbericht von der Gesellschaft fuer Natur- und Heil-Kunde zu Dresden

Jahresber GPV — Jahresbericht. Gesellschaft pro Vindonissa. Basel

Jahresber Hist Mus Bern — Jahresbericht des Bernischen Historischen Museums in Bern

Jahresber Hist Ver Dillingen — Jahrbuch des Historischen Vereins Dillingen

Jahresber Hist Ver Straubing — Jahresbericht des Historischen Vereins fuer Straubing und Ungebung

Jahresbericht Grabunden — Jahresbericht. Historisch-Antiquarische Gesellschaft von Graubuenden

Jahresbericht (Zuerich) — Jahresbericht. Schweizerisches Landesmuseum (Zuerich)

Jahresber Inst Gesch Naturwiss — Jahresbericht der Instituts fuer Geschichte der Naturwissenschaft

Jahresber Inst Hydrol CSF Forschungszent Umwelt Gesund — Jahresbericht. Institut fuer Hydrologie. CSF-Forschungszentrum fuer Umwelt und Gesundheit

Jahresber Inst Strahlenphys Kernphys Univ Bonn — Jahresbericht. Institut fuer Strahlen- und Kernphysik. Universitaet Bonn

Jahresber Kernforschungsanlage Juelich — Jahresbericht. Kernforschungsanlage Juelich

Jahresber K Ung Geol Anst — Jahresberichte der Koeniglichen Ungarischen Geologischen Anstalt

Jahresber Kurashiki-Zentralhosp — Jahresbericht. Kurashiki-Zentralhospital

Jahresber Landesanst Immissions Bodennutzungsschutz Landes N — Jahresbericht der Landesanstalt fuer Immissions- und Bodennutzungsschutz des Landes Nordrhein-Westfalen

Jahresber Med Inst Lufthyg Silikoseforsch — Jahresbericht. Medizinisches Institut fuer Lufthygiene und Silikoseforschung

Jahresber Med Inst Umwelthyg — Jahresbericht. Medizinisches Institut fuer Umwelthygiene

Jahresber Mitth Gartenbau Vereins Grossherzogth Hessen — Jahresbericht und Mittheilungen des Gartenbau-Vereins im Grossherzogthum Hessen

Jahresber Mitth Gartenbau Vereins Neuvorpommern — Jahresbericht und Mittheilungen des Gartenbau-Vereins fuer Neuvorpommern und Rugen

Jahresber Mitt Oberrheinischen Geol Ver — Jahresberichte und Mitteilungen. Oberrheinischer Geologische Verein

Jahresber MPI Plasmaphys Garching — Jahresbericht. Max-Planck-Institut fuer Plasmaphysik. Garching bei Muenchen

Jahresber Naturf Ges Freiburg — Jahresbericht der Naturforschenden Gesellschaft zu Freiburg

Jahresber Naturf Ges Halle — Jahresbericht der Naturforschenden Gesellschaft zu Halle

Jahresber Naturhist Ges Hannover — Jahresberichte der Naturhistorischen Gesellschaft zu Hannover

Jahresber Naturhist Kantonal Ges Solothurn — Jahresbericht der Naturhistorischen Kantonal-Gesellschaft in Solothurn

Jahres Ber Naturhist Vereins Passau — Jahres-Bericht des Naturhistorischen Vereins in Passau

Jahresber Naturwiss Ges Elberfeld — Jahresbericht der Naturwissenschaftlichen Gesellschaft zu Elberfeld

Jahresber Naturwiss Verein Fuerstenth Lueneburg — Jahresbericht ueber den Naturwissenschaftlichen Verein des Fuerstenthums Lueneberg

Jahres Ber Naturwiss Vereins Elberfeld — Jahres-Berichte des Naturwissenschaftlichen Vereins in Elberfeld

Jahresber Naturwiss Vereins Halle — Jahresbericht des Naturwissenschaftlichen Vereins in Halle

Jahresber Naturwiss Vereins Magdeburg Sitzungsber — Jahresbericht des Naturwissenschaftlichen Vereins zu Magdeburg. Nebst den Sitzungsberichten

Jahresber Niedersaechs Bot Vereins — Jahresbericht des Niedersaechsischen Botanischen Vereins/Botanische Abteilung der Naturhistorischen Gesellschaft zu Hannover

Jahresber Nordoberfraenk Vereins Natur Familienk Hof — Jahresbericht des Nordoberfraenkischen Vereins fuer Natur-, Geschichts-, Landes-, und Familienkunde in Hof A.D.S

Jahresber Oberoesterr Musealver — Jahrbuch des Oberoesterreichischen Musealvereins

Jahresber Pharm — Jahresbericht der Pharmazie

Jahresber Phys Vereins Frankfurt — Jahresbericht des Physikalischen Vereins zu Frankfurt am Main

Jahresber Schicksale Vereins Kunde Natur Fuerstenth Hildeshei — Jahresbericht ueber die Schicksale des Vereins fuer Kunde der Natur und der Kunst im Fuerstenthum Hildesheim und der Stadt Goslar

Jahresber Schweiz Akad Med Wiss — Jahresbericht. Schweizerische Akademie der Medizinischen Wissenschaften

Jahresber Schweiz Ges Urgesch — Jahrbuch der Schweizerischen Gesellschaft fuer Urgeschichte

Jahresber Schweiz Ges Vererbungsforsch — Jahresbericht. Schweizerische Gesellschaft fuer Vererbungsforschung

Jahresber Schweiz Landesmus Zuerich — Jahresbericht. Schweizerisches Landesmuseum (Zuerich)

Jahresber Schweiz Urgesch — Jahresbericht der Schweizer Gesellschaft fuer Urgeschichte

Jahresber Sonnblick Vereins — Jahresbericht des Sonnblick-Vereins

Jahresber Thueringer Gartenbau Vereins Gotha — Jahresbericht des Thueringer Gartenbau Vereins zu Gotha

Jahresber Trier — Trier Jahresberichte

Jahresber Ung Geol Anst — Jahresbericht der Ungarischen Geologischen Anstalt

Jahresber Univ Wuerzb — Jahresbericht. Universitaet Wuerzburg

Jahresber Vereinigung Vertreter Angew Bot — Jahresbericht der Vereinigung der Vertreter der Angewandten Botanik

Jahres Ber Verein Kunde Natur Fuerstenth Hildesheim — Jahres-Bericht ueber den Verein fuer Kunde der Natur und der Kunst im Fuerstenthum Hildesheim und in der Stadt Goslar

Jahresber Vereins Naturk Unterweser — Jahresbericht des Vereins fuer Naturkunde an der Unterweser

Jahresber Vereins Naturk Zwickau — Jahresbericht des Vereins fuer Naturkunde zu Zwickau in Sachsen

Jahres Ber Westphael Ges Vaterl Cult — Jahres-Bericht der Westphaelischen Gesellschaft fuer Vaterlaendische Cultur

Jahresber Wetterauischen Ges Gesamte Naturkd Hanau — Jahresberichte der Wetterauischen Gesellschaft fuer die Gesamte Naturkunde zu Hanau

Jahresber Zuecherischen Bot Ges — Jahresbericht der Zuercherischen Botanischen Gesellschaft

Jahresb Fortschr Altertswiss — Bursians Jahresbericht ueber die Fortschritte der Klassischen Altertumswissenschaft

Jahresb Fortschr Lehre Path Mikroorganism — Jahresbericht ueber die Fortschritte in der Lehre von den Pathogenen Mikroorganismen Umfassend Bacterien, Pilze, und Protozoen

Jahresb Leistung Vet-Med — Jahresbericht ueber die Liestungen auf dem Gebiete der Veterinaer-Medizin

Jahresb Nàturhist Ges Nuernberg — Jahresbericht der Naturhistorischen Gesellschaft Nuernberg

Jahresb PVB — Jahresbericht. Philologischer Verein zu Berlin

Jahresb Schles Gesellsch Vaterl Kult — Jahresberichte. Schlesische Gesellschaft fuer Vaterlaendische Kultur

Jahresb Schweiz Urgesch — Jahrbuch der Schweizerischen Gesellschaft fuer Urgeschichte

Jahresb Vet Med — Jahresbericht Veterinaer-Medizin

Jahresh — Jahreshefte des Oesterreichischen Archaeologischen Institutes in Wien

Jahresh Geol Landesamtes Baden Wuerttemb — Jahresheft. Geologisches Landesamt in Baden Wuerttemberg

Jahresh Ges Naturkd Wuerttemb — Jahreshefte. Gesellschaft fuer Naturkunde in Wuerttemberg

Jahresh Oesterr Arch Inst — Jahreshefte des Oesterreichischen Archaeologischen Institutes in Wien

Jahresh Vereins Math Ulm — Jahreshefte des Vereins fuer Mathematik und Naturwissenschaften in Ulm

Jahresh Ver Vaterl Naturkd Wuerttemb — Jahreshefte. Verein fuer Vaterlaendische Naturkunde in Wuerttemberg

Jahreskat Wiener Bot Tauschvereins — Jahreskatalog der Wiener Botanischen Tauschvereins

Jahresk F Aerztl Fortbild — Jahreskurse fuer Aerztliche Fortbildung

Jahresk F Jurist Fortbild — Jahreskurse fuer Juristische Fortbildung

Jahreskolloq Sonderforschungsbereichs 270 Univ Stuttgart — Jahreskolloquium des Sonderforschungsbereichs 270 der Universitaet Stuttgart

Jahreskurse Aerztl Fortbild — Jahreskurse fuer Aerztliche Fortbildung

Jahrestag Fachverb Strahlenschutz — Jahrestagung des Fachverbandes fuer Strahlenschutz

Jahrestag Ges Erforsch Makromol Organo Immunother Kongressbe — Jahrestagung der Gesellschaft zur Erforschung der Makromolekularen Organo- und Immunotherapie. Kongressberichte

Jahrestag Inst Chem Treib Explosivst Fraunhofer Ges — Jahrestagung. Institut fuer Chemie der Treib- und Explosivstoffe der Fraunhofer-Gesellschaft

Jahrestag Kerntech Tagungsber — Jahrestagung Kerntechnik. Tagungsbericht

Jahrestreffen Katal DDR Programm Tagungsber — Jahrestreffen der Katalytiker der DDR. Programm und Tagungsbericht

Jahresversamml Dtsch Arbeitsgem Blutgerinnungsforsch — Jahresversammlung der Deutschen Arbeitsgemeinschaft fuer Blutgerinnungsforschung

Jahresversamml Ges Oekol — Jahresversammlung. Gesellschaft fuer Oekologie

Jahr Hamburger Kunstsam — Jahrbuch. Hamburger Kunstsammlungen

Jahr Kunsthist Sam (Wien) — Jahrbuch. Kunsthistorischen Sammlungen (Wien)

Jahrliche Z Physiatr Chemother Krebs — Jahrliche Zeitschrift fuer Physiatrie und Chemotherapie bei Krebs

Jahrliche Z Physiatr Prophyl — Jahrliche Zeitschrift fuer Physiatrie und Prophylaxie

JAHRS — Journal. Andhra Historical Research Society

Jahrs Ber Naturwiss Vereins Hamburg — Jahrs-Bericht des Naturwissenschaftlichen Vereins in Hamburg

JAHum — Journal of American Humor

JAHYA4 — Journal. American Dental Hygienists' Association

JAI — Jahrbuch des Deutschen Archaeologischen Instituts

JAI — Jahrbuch des Kaiserlichen Archaeologischen Instituts

JAI — Journal. Anthropological Institute

JAI — Journal of Advertising Research

JAI — Journal of American Insurance

JAI — Journal of the Anthropological Institute of Great Britain and Ireland

JAI — Journal. Royal Anthropological Institute of Great Britain and Ireland

JAI — Journal. Royal Archaeological Institute

JAIA — Journal. American Institute of Architects

JAIA — Journal. Archaeological Institute of America

JAIA — Journal. Australian Indonesian Association

JAIAS — Journal. Australian Institute of Agricultural Science

JAIB — Journal. Royal Anthropological Institute of Great Britain and Ireland

J Aichi Med Univ Assoc — Journal. Aichi Medical University Association

JAIH — Journal of Ancient Indian History

JAIHA — Journal. American Institute of Homeopathy

JAIHAQ — Journal. American Institute of Homeopathy

JAIL — Japanese Annual of International Law

JaiL — Jazyk i Literatura

JAIM — Janus. Archives Internationales pour l'Histoire de la Medecine

JAINAA — Journal. Anatomical Society of India

Jaina Antiq — Jaina Antiquary

Jain J — Jain Journal

Ja Interp — Japan Interpreter

JAIP — Journal. American Planning Association

Jaipur LJ — Jaipur Law Journal

J Aircr — Journal of Aircraft

J Aircraft — Journal of Aircraft

J Air L — Journal of Air Law and Commerce

J Air L and Com — Journal of Air Law and Commerce

J Air Pollu — Journal. Air Pollution Control Association

J Air Pollut — Journal of Air Pollution [*London*]

J Air Pollut Contr A — Air Pollution Control Association. Journal

J Air Pollut Contr Ass — Journal. Air Pollution Control Association

J Air Pollut Control Assoc — Journal. Air Pollution Control Association

J Air Pollution Control Assoc — Journal. Air Pollution Control Association

J Air Raid Prot Inst — Journal of the Air Raid Protection Institute [*London*]

J Air Traff Control — Journal of Air Traffic Control [*Washington*]

J Air Transp Div Am Soc Civ Eng — Journal. Air Transport Division. American Society of Civil Engineers

J Air Transp Div Am Soc Civ Engrs — Journal of the Air Transport Division. American Society of Civil Engineers

J Air Waste Manag Assoc — Journal. Air and Waste Management Association

J Air Waste Manage Assoc — Journal of the Air and Waste Management Association

JAISDS — Journal. All India Institute of Medical Sciences

JAJ — Jewish Affairs (Johannesburg)

Ja J — Judge Advocate Journal

JAJAAA — Journal of Antibiotics. Series A

JaJGL — Jahrbuecher fuer Juedische Geschichte und Literatur

JAJHS — Journal and Proceedings. Australian Jewish Historical Society

Ja J Rel Stud — Japanese Journal of Religious Studies

JAK — Jahrbuch der Asiatischen Kunst

JAK — Jahrbuch fuer Altertumskunde

JAk — Jazykovedny Aktuality

J Akita Min Coll — Journal of the Akita Mining College

JAL — Japan (London)

JAL — Jewish Affairs (London)

JAL — Jewish Apocryphal Literature

JAL — Journal of Academic Librarianship

JAL — Journal of African Languages

JAL — Journal of African Law

JAL — Journal of Arab Literature

JAL — Journal of Arts and Lettres

JAL — Jurisprudence de la Cour d'Appel de Liege

J Acad Sci — Journal. Alabama Academy of Science

J Alab Acad Sci — Journal. Alabama Academy of Science

J Alabama Acad Sci — Journal. Alabama Academy of Science

Ja Labor B — Japan Labor Bulletin

J Ala Dent Assoc — Journal. Alabama Dental Association

J Alagappa Chettiar Coll Technol — Journal. Alagappa Chettiar College of Technology

J Alberta Soc Pet Geol — Journal. Alberta Society of Petroleum Geologists

J Albert Einstein Med Cent — Journal. Albert Einstein Medical Center

J Albert Einstein Med Cent (Phila) — Journal. Albert Einstein Medical Center (Philadelphia)

J Alc — Journal of Alcoholism

JALCA — Journal. American Leather Chemists' Association

JALCAQ — Journal. American Leather Chemists' Association

JALCBR — Journal of Alcoholism

J Alc Drug — Journal of Alcohol and Drug Education

J Alchem Soc — Journal of the Alchemical Society [*London*]

J Alcohol — Journal of Alcoholism

J Alcohol & Drug Educ — Journal of Alcohol and Drug Education

J Algebra — Journal of Algebra

J Algebraic Combin — Journal of Algebraic Combinatorics

J Algebraic Geom — Journal of Algebraic Geometry
J Algorithms — Journal of Algorithms
Ja Lit Today — Japanese Literature Today
JALL — Journal of African Languages and Linguistics
J All — Journal of Allergy
J All Dent Socs — Journal of the Allied Dental Societies [New York]
J Allerg Cl — Journal of Allergy and Clinical Immunology
J Allergy — Journal of Allergy [Later, Journal of Allergy and Clinical Immunology]
J Allergy Clin Immun — Journal of Allergy and Clinical Immunology
J Allergy Clin Immunol — Journal of Allergy and Clinical Immunology
J Allergy Clin Immunol Off Publ Am Acad Allergy — Journal of Allergy and Clinical Immunology. Official Publication of American Academy of Allergy
J Allied Dent Soc — Journal. Allied Dental Societies
J Allied Health — Journal of Allied Health
J All India Dent Assoc — Journal. All India Dental Association
J All India Inst Med Sci — Journal. All India Institute of Medical Sciences
J All India Inst Ment Health — Journal. All India Institute of Mental Health
J All India Ophthalmol Soc — Journal. All India Ophthalmological Society
J All India Ophthal Soc — Journal of the All-India Ophthalmological Society
J All Ind Ophth Soc — Journal. All-India Ophthalmological Society
J All Japan Contact Lens Soc — Journal of the All-Japan Contact Lens Society
J Alloy Phase Diagrams — Journal of Alloy Phase Diagrams
J Alloys Compd — Journal of Alloys and Compounds
J All Socs — Journal of the Allied Societies [New York]
JALP — Japan Annual of Law and Politics
J ALS — Journal. American Liszt Society
JALT — Journal. Association of Law Teachers
J Altered States Conscious — Journal of Altered States of Consciousness
J Altern Complement Med — Journal of Alternative and Complementary Medicine
J Alumni Ass Coll Phys and Surg (Baltimore) — Journal. Alumni Association. College of Physicians and Surgeons (Baltimore)
J Alumni Ass Coll Physns Surg Baltimore — Journal of the Alumni Association of the College of Physicians and Surgeons (Baltimore)
JAM — Jamaica Exports. Complimentary Guide to Trade and Investment Opportunities
JAM — Journal. American Planning Association
JAM — Journal d'Analyse Mathematique
JAM — Journal of American Musicology
JAM — Journal of Applied Management
JAMA — Journal. American Medical Association
JAMAA — Journal. American Medical Association
JAMAAP — Journal. American Medical Association
J Am Acad Appl Nutr — Journal. American Academy of Applied Nutrition
J Am Acad Audiol — Journal. American Academy of Audiology
J Am Acad Child Adolesc Psychiatry — Journal. American Academy of Child and Adolescent Psychiatry
J Am Acad Child Psych — Journal. American Academy of Child Psychiatry
J Am Acad Child Psychiatry — Journal. American Academy of Child Psychiatry
J Am Acad Dermatol — Journal. American Academy of Dermatology
J Am Academy Child Psychiatry — Journal. American Academy of Child Psychiatry
J Am Acad Gnathol Orthop — Journal. American Academy of Gnathologic Orthopedics
J Am Acad Gold Foil Oper — Journal. American Academy of Gold Foil Operators
J Am Acad P — Journal. American Academy of Psychoanalysis
J Am Acad Psychoanal — Journal. American Academy of Psychoanalysis
J Am Acad Rel — Journal. American Academy of Religion
J Am Acad Relig — Journal. American Academy of Religion
J Am Acad Religion — Journal. American Academy of Religion
J Am A Chil — Journal. American Academy of Child Psychiatry
JAmAcRel — Journal. American Academy of Religion
JAMAET — Journal. American Mosquito Control Association
Jamaica Ag Soc J — Jamaica Agricultural Society. Journal
Jamaica Archt — Jamaica Architect
Jamaica Geol Survey Dept Ann Rept — Jamaica. Geological Survey Department. Annual Report
Jamaica Geol Survey Dept Bull — Jamaica. Geological Survey Department. Bulletin
Jamaica Geol Survey Dept Occ Pap — Jamaica. Geological Survey Department. Occasional Paper
Jamaica Geol Survey Dept Short Pap — Jamaica. Geological Survey Department. Short Paper
Jamaica Geol Survey Pub — Jamaica. Geological Survey Department. Publication
Jamaica Handb — Jamaica Handbook
Jamaica J — Jamaica Journal
Jamaica Phys J — Jamaica Physical Journal
JAMA J Am Med Assoc — JAMA. Journal. American Medical Association
J Am Analg Soc — Journal. American Analgesia Society
J Am Anim Hosp Assoc — Journal. American Animal Hospital Association
J Am A Rel — Journal. American Academy of Religion
J Am Asiat Ass — Journal of the American Asiatic Association
J Am Ass Cereal Chem — Journal of the American Association of Cereal Chemists
J Am Ass Hlth — Journal of the American Association for Health, Physical Education, and Recreation
J Am Ass Instruct Invest Poult Husb — Journal of the American Association of Instructors and Investigators in Poultry Husbandry
J Am Ass Med Phys Res — Journal of the American Association for Medico-Physical Research
J Am Ass Med Rec Libr — Journal. American Association of Medical Record Librarians
J Am Assoc — Journal. American Association for Hygiene and Baths
J Am Assoc Cereal Chem — Journal. American Association of Cereal Chemists
J Am Assoc Gynecol Laparosc — Journal of the American Association of Gynecologic Laparoscopists
J Am Assoc Hyg Baths — Journal. American Association for Hygiene and Baths

J Am Assoc Nephrol Nurses Tech — Journal. American Association of Nephrology Nurses and Technicians
J Am Assoc Nurse Anesth — Journal. American Association of Nurse Anesthetists
J Am Assoc Promot Hyg Public Baths — Journal. American Association for Promoting Hygiene and Public Baths
Jam Assoc Sugar Technol J — Jamaican Association of Sugar Technologists. Journal
Jam Assoc Sugar Technol Q — Jamaican Association of Sugar Technologists. Quarterly
J Am Assoc Teach Educ Agric — Journal. American Association of Teacher Educators in Agriculture
J Am Assoc Variable Star Obs — Journal. American Association of Variable Star Observers
J Am Ass Orif Surg — Journal of the American Association of Orificial Surgeons
J Am Ass Prog Med — Journal of the American Association of Progressive Medicine
J Am Ass Promot Hyg — Journal. American Association for Promoting Hygiene and Public Baths
J Amat Orchid Grow Soc — Journal of the Amateur Orchid Growers Society
J Am Audiol Soc — Journal. American Audiology Society
J Am Aud Soc — Journal. American Auditory Society
J Am Bak Ass — Journal. American Bakers Association and American Institute of Baking
J Am Bakers Assoc Am Inst Baking — Journal. American Bakers Association and American Institute of Baking
J Am Bankers' Assn — Journal. American Bankers Association
Jam Bauxite Inst Dig — Jamaica Bauxite Institute Digest
JAMBF — Jahrbuch des Akademischen Missionsbundes der Universitaet Freiburg
J Am Board Fam Pract — Journal. American Board of Family Practice
J Ambulatory Care Manage — Journal of Ambulatory Care Management
J Ambul Care Manage — Journal of Ambulatory Care Management
J Am Ceram — Journal. American Ceramic Society
J Am Ceram Soc — Journal. American Ceramic Society
J Am Ceram Soc Adv Ceram Mater Commun — Journal. American Ceramic Society Incorporating Advanced Ceramic Materials and Communications
J Am Ceram Soc Commun — Journal. American Ceramic Society with Communications
J Am Cer Soc — Journal. American Ceramic Society
J Am Chem S — Journal. American Chemical Society
J Am Chem Soc — Journal. American Chemical Society
J Am Coll Cardiol — Journal. American College of Cardiology
J Am Coll Dent — Journal. American College of Dentists
J Am Coll H — Journal. American College Health Association
J Am Coll Health — Journal of American College Health
J Am Coll Health Assn — Journal. American College Health Association
J Am Coll Health Assoc — Journal. American College Health Association
J Am Coll Nutr — Journal. American College of Nutrition
J Am Coll Surg — Journal. American College of Surgeons
J Am Coll Toxicol — Journal. American College of Toxicology
J Am Concr Inst — Journal. American Concrete Institute
J Am Cult — Journal of American Culture
JAMDAY — Journal. American Medical Technologists
J Am Den Ass Dent Cosmos — Journal of the American Dental Association and Dental Cosmos
J Am Dent A — Journal. American Dental Association
J Am Dent Ass — Journal of the American Dental Association
J Am Dent Assoc — Journal. American Dental Association
J Am Dent Assoc Dent Cosmos — Journal. American Dental Association and the Dental Cosmos
J Am Dent Assoc (Ed Ital) — Journal of the American Dental Association (Edizione Italiana)
J Am Dent Hyg Assoc — Journal. American Dental Hygienists' Association
J Am Dent Labs Ass — Journal. American Dental Laboratories Association
J Am Dent Soc Anesth — Journal of the American Dental Society of Anesthesiology
J Am Dent Soc Anesthesiol — Journal. American Dental Society of Anesthesiology
Jam Dep Agric Bull — Jamaica. Department of Agriculture. Bulletin
Jam Dep Sci Agric Bull — Jamaica. Department of Science and Agriculture. Bulletin
J Am Diet A — Journal. American Dietetic Association
J Am Diet Ass — Journal of the American Dietetic Association
J Am Diet Assoc — Journal. American Dietetic Association
J Am Dietet A — Journal. American Dietetic Association
JAME — Nyiregyhazi Josa Andras Muzeum Evkonyve
J Am Elect Rly Ass — Journal of the American Electric Railway Association
J Amer Acad Psychoanal — Journal. American Academy of Psychoanalysis
J Amer Assoc Promot Sci — Journal. American Association for the Promotion of Science, Literature, and the Arts
J Amer Ceram Soc — Journal. American Ceramic Society
J Amer Chem Soc — Journal. American Chemical Society
J Amer Coll Dent — Journal. American College of Dentists
J Amer Coll Toxicol Part B — Journal. American College of Toxicology. Part B
J Amer Cult — Journal of American Culture
J Amer Diet Ass — Journal. American Dietetic Association
J Amer Flklore — Journal of American Folklore
J Amer Folkl — Journal of American Folklore
J Amer Heli — Journal. American Helicopter Society
J Amer Hist — Journal of American History
J Amer Inst Architects — Journal of the American Institute of Architects
J Amer Inst Conserv — Journal of the American Institute for Conservation
J Amer Inst Planners — Journal. American Institute of Planners
J Amer Leather Chem Ass — Journal. American Leather Chemists' Association
J Amer Math Soc — Journal of the American Mathematical Society
J Amer Med Ass — Journal. American Medical Association

J Amer Musicol Soc — Journal. American Musicological Society
J Amer Oil — Journal. American Oil Chemists' Society
J Amer Oil Chem Soc — Journal. American Oil Chemists' Society
J Amer Orient Soc — Journal. American Oriental Society
J Amer Pharm Assoc — Journal. American Pharmaceutical Association
J Amer Pharm Ass Sci Ed — Journal. American Pharmaceutical Association. Scientific Edition
J Amer Plann Assoc — Journal. American Planning Association
J Amer Port Soc — Journal of the American Portuguese Society
J Amer Psychoanal Ass — Journal. American Psychoanalytic Association
J Amer Res Cent Egypt — Journal of the American Research Center in Egypt
J Amer Scient Affil — Journal. American Scientific Affiliation
J Amer Soc Agron — Journal. American Society of Agronomy
J Amer Soc Archit Hist — Journal of the American Society of Architectural Historians
J Amer Soc Farm Manage Rural Appraisers — Journal. American Society of Farm Managers and Rural Appraisers
J Amer Soc Hort Sci — Journal. American Society for Horticultural Science
J Amer Soc Inform Sci — Journal. American Society for Information Science
J Amer Soc Orient A — Journal of the American Society of Oriental Art
J Amer Soc Safety Eng — Journal. American Society of Safety Engineers
J Amer Soc Sugar Beet Tech — Journal. American Society of Sugar Beet Technologists
J Amer Soc Sugar Beet Technol — Journal. American Society of Sugar Beet Technologists
J Amer Statist Assoc — Journal. American Statistical Association
J Amer Stud — Journal of American Studies
J Amer Vet Med Ass — Journal. American Veterinary Medical Association
J Amer Water Works Ass — Journal. American Water Works Association
James Arthur Lect Evol Hum Brain — James Arthur Lecture on the Evolution of the Human Brain
James Bay Environ Symp Proc — James Bay-Environment Symposium. Proceedings
James Cook Univ North Queensl Dep Trop Vet Sci Vet Rev Monog — James Cook University of North Queensland. Department of Tropical Veterinary Science. Veterinary Reviews and Monographs
James Joyce Q — James Joyce Quarterly
James Joy Q — James Joyce Quarterly
James Madison J — James Madison Journal
James Sprunt Hist Publ — James Sprunt Historical Publications
James Sprunt Hist Stud — James Sprunt Historical Studies
J Am Ethnol Archaeol — Journal of American Ethnology and Archaeology
J Am F-Lore — Journal of American Folklore
J Am Folk — Journal of American Folklore
J Am Folkl — Journal of American Folklore
J Am Folklo — Journal of American Folklore
J Am Folklore — Journal of American Folklore
J Am Foundrym Ass — Journal of the American Foundrymen's Association
J Am Geogr Soc — Journal of the American Geographical Society of New York
Jam Geol Surv Dep Econ Geol Rep — Jamaica. Geological Survey Department. Economic Geology Report
J Am Geriatrics Soc — Journal. American Geriatrics Society
J Am Geriatr Soc — Journal. American Geriatrics Society
J Am Geriat Soc — Journal. American Geriatrics Society
J Am Ger So — Journal. American Geriatrics Society
J A Mgmt & Law — Journal of Arts Management and Law
J Am Health Care Assoc — Journal. American Health Care Association
J Am Helicopter Soc — Journal. American Helicopter Society
J Am His — Journal of American History
J Am Hist — Journal of American History
Jam Hist Rev — Jamaican Historical Review
Jamia Ed Q — Jamia Educational Quarterly
Jam I J — Journal of the Institute of Jamaica
J Am Ind Hyg Assoc — Journal. American Industrial Hygiene Association
J Am Indian Ed — Journal of American Indian Education
J Am Ins — Journal of American Insurance
J Am Inst Archit — Journal of the American Institute of Architects
J Am Inst Elect Engrs — Journal of the American Institute of Electrical Engineers
J Am Inst Electr Eng — Journal. American Institute of Electrical Engineers
J Am Inst Homeop — Journal. American Institute of Homeopathy
J Am Inst Homeopath — Journal. American Institute of Homeopathy
J Am Inst Homeopathy — Journal. American Institute of Homeopathy
J Am Inst Homoeop — Journal of the American Institute of Homoeopathy
J Am Inst Met — Journal. American Institute of Metals
J Am Inst Metals — Journal of the American Institute of Metals
J Am Inst P — Journal. American Institute of Planners
J Am Inst Plann — Journal. American Institute of Planners
J Am Insur — Journal of American Insurance
J Am Intraocul Implant Soc — Journal. American Intraocular Implant Society
Ja Mission B — Japan Missionary Bulletin
J Am Jud Soc — Journal. American Judicature Society
J Am Killifish Assoc — Journal. American Killifish Association
JAMLD — Journal of Applied Metalworking
J Am Leath — Journal. American Leather Chemists' Association
J Am Leath Chem Ass — Journal. American Leather Chemists' Association
J Am Leather Chem Assoc — Journal. American Leather Chemists' Association
J Am Leather Chem Assoc Suppl — Journal. American Leather Chemists' Association. Supplement
Jam LJ — Jamaica Law Journal
JAMM — JAMM. Journal for Australian Music and Musicians
JAMMD — Journal. Australian Mathematical Society. Series B. Applied Mathematics
J Am Med A — Journal. American Medical Association
J Am Med Ass — Journal. American Medical Association
J Am Med Assoc — Journal. American Medical Association
J Am Med Edit Ass — Journal of the American Medical Editors' Association

J Am Med Inform Assoc — Journal. American Medical Informatics Association
J Am Med Rec Assoc — Journal. American Medical Record Association
Jam Med Rev — Jamaica Medical Review
J Am Med Technol — Journal. American Medical Technologists
J Am Med Wom Ass — Journal. American Medical Women's Association
J Am Med Wom Assoc — Journal. American Medical Women's Association
J Am Med Women Assoc — Journal. American Medical Women's Association
J Am Med Women's Assoc — Journal. American Medical Women's Association
Jam Mines Geol Div Spec Publ — Jamaica. Mines and Geology Division. Special Publication
Jam Minist Agric Bull — Jamaica. Ministry of Agriculture. Bulletin
Jam Minist Agric Fish Bull — Jamaica. Ministry of Agriculture and Fisheries. Bulletin
Jam Minist Agric Lands Annu Rep — Jamaica. Ministry of Agriculture and Lands. Annual Report
Jam Minist Agric Lands Bull — Jamaica. Ministry of Agriculture and Lands. Bulletin
J Am Mosq Control Assoc — Journal. American Mosquito Control Association
J Am Mosq Control Assoc Suppl — Journal. American Mosquito Control Association. Supplement
J Am Mot Wks Ass — Journal. American Motor Works Association
J Am Music — Journal. American Musicological Society
J Am Mus In — Journal. American Musical Instrument Society
J Am Oil Ch — Journal. American Oil Chemists' Society
J Am Oil Chem Soc — Journal. American Oil Chemists' Society
J Am Optom Ass — Journal of the American Optometric Association
J Am Optom Assoc — Journal. American Optometric Association
J Am Orient — Journal. American Oriental Society
J Am Orient Soc — Journal. American Oriental Society
J Am Or Soc — Journal. American Oriental Society
J Am Osteop Ass — Journal of the American Osteopathic Association
J Am Osteopath A — Journal. American Osteopathic Association
J Am Osteopath Assoc — Journal. American Osteopathic Association
JAMP — Journal of Animal Morphology and Physiology
JAMPA2 — Journal of Animal Morphology and Physiology
J Am Paraplegia Soc — Journal. American Paraplegia Society
JAMPB3 — Journal. American Peanut Research and Education Association
J Am Peanut Res Educ Assoc — Journal. American Peanut Research and Education Association
J Am Peat Soc — Journal. American Peat Society
J Am Phar — Journal. American Pharmaceutical Association. Practical Pharmacy Edition
J Am Pharm — Journal. American Pharmaceutical Association
J Am Pharm Ass — Journal. American Pharmaceutical Association
J Am Pharm Assoc — Journal. American Pharmaceutical Association
J Am Pharm Assoc Pract Pharm Ed — Journal. American Pharmaceutical Association. Practical Pharmacy Edition
J Am Pharm Assoc Sci Ed — Journal. American Pharmaceutical Association. Scientific Edition
J Am Plann Assoc — Journal. American Planning Association
J Am Pl Fd Coun — Journal of the American Plant Food Council
J Am Podiatr Med Assoc — Journal. American Podiatric Medical Association
J Am Podiatry Assoc — Journal. American Podiatry Association
J Am Psycho — Journal. American Psychoanalytic Association
J Am Psychoanal Ass — Journal. American Psychoanalytic Association
J Am Psychonal Assoc — Journal. American Psychoanalytic Association
J Am Publ Hlth Ass — Journal of the American Public Health Association
J Am Real Estate Urban Econ Assoc — Journal. American Real Estate and Urban Economics Association
J Am Rocket Soc — Journal. American Rocket Society
JAMS — Journal. Academy of Marketing Science
JAMS — Journal. American Musical Society
JAMS — Journal. American Musicological Society
JAmS — Journal of American Studies
JAMSA — Journal. Arkansas Medical Society
J Am S Hort — Journal. American Society for Horticultural Science
J Am S Infor — Journal. American Society for Information Science
J Am Soc Agron — Journal. American Society of Agronomy
J Am Soc Brew Chem — Journal. American Society of Brewing Chemists
J Am Soc Brew Technol — Journal of the American Society of Brewing Technology
J Am Soc CLU — Journal. American Society of Chartered Life Underwriters
J Am Soc Echocardiogr — Journal. American Society of Echocardiography
J Am Soc Engng Contract — Journal of the American Society of Engineering Contractors
J Am Soc Engr Draftsm — Journal of the American Society of Engineer Draftsmen
J Am Soc Geriatr Dent — Journal. American Society for Geriatric Dentistry
J Am Soc Heat Vent Eng — Journal. American Society of Heating and Ventilating Engineers
J Am Soc Heat Vent Engrs — Journal of the American Society of Heating and Ventilating Engineers
J Am Soc Hortic Sci — Journal. American Society for Horticultural Science
J Am Soc Hort Sci — Journal. American Society for Horticultural Science
J Am Soc Inf Sci — Journal. American Society for Information Science
J Am Soc Mar Draftsm — Journal of the American Society of Marine Draftsmen
J Am Soc Mech Eng — Journal. American Society of Mechanical Engineers
J Am Soc Mech Engrs — Journal of the American Society of Mechanical Engineers
J Am Soc Nav Eng — Journal. American Society of Naval Engineers
J Am Soc Nav Engrs — Journal of the American Society of Naval Engineers
J Am Soc Nephrol — Journal. American Society of Nephrology
J Am Soc Prev Dent — Journal. American Society for Preventive Dentistry
J Am Soc Psychosom Dent — Journal. American Society of Psychosomatic Dentistry and Medicine

J Am Soc Psychosom Dent Med — Journal. American Society of Psychosomatic Dentistry and Medicine
J Am Soc Psych Res — Journal. American Society for Psychical Research
J Am Soc Saf Eng — Journal. American Society of Safety Engineers
J Am Soc Saf Engrs — Journal of the American Society of Safety Engineers
J Am Soc Study Orthod — Journal. American Society for the Study of Orthodontics
J Am Soc Sugar Beet Technol — Journal. American Society of Sugar Beet Technologists
J Am Soc Sug Beet Technol — Journal. American Society of Sugar Beet Technologists
J Am S Psyc — Journal. American Society for Psychical Research
J Am St — Jahrbuch fuer Amerikastudien
J Am St — Journal of American Studies
J Am Stat A — Journal. American Statistical Association
J Am Stat Assoc — Journal. American Statistical Association
J Am Statist Ass — Journal of the American Statistical Association
J Am Steel Treaters' Soc — Journal. American Steel Treaters' Society
J Am Steel Treat Soc — Journal of the American Steel Treaters' Society
J Am Stud — Journal of American Studies
J Am Studies — Journal of American Studies
JAMTD — Journal. Canadian Association for Music Therapy
J Amusant — Journal Amusant
J Am Vener Dis Assoc — Journal. American Venereal Disease Association
J Am Vet Me — Journal. American Veterinary Medical Association
J Am Vet Med Ass — Journal. American Veterinary Medical Association
J Am Vet Med Assoc — Journal. American Veterinary Medical Association
J Am Vet Ra — Journal. American Veterinary Radiology Society
J Am Vet Radiol Soc — Journal. American Veterinary Radiology Society
J Am Voila S — Journal. American Viola Society
JAMWA — Journal. American Medical Women's Association
JAMWAM — Journal. American Medical Women's Association
J Am Water — Journal. American Water Works Association
J Am Water Resour Assoc — Journal of the American Water Resources Association
J Am Water Works Assoc — Journal. American Water Works Association
J Am Wat Wks Ass — Journal of the American Water Works Association
J Am Weld Soc — Journal. American Welding Society
J Am Wine Soc — Journal. American Wine Society
J Am Zinc Inst — Journal. American Zinc Institute
Jan — Janus. Archives Internationales pour l'Histoire de la Medecine
JAN — Japan. The Economic and Trade Picture
JAN — Jewish Affairs (New York)
JAN — Journal International d'Archeologie Numismatique
JANAF — Joint Army-Navy-Air Force Thermochemical Tables
J Anal — Journal of Analysis
J Anal Appl Pyrolysis — Journal of Analytical and Applied Pyrolysis
J Anal At Spectrom — Journal of Analytical Atomic Spectrometry
J Anal C — Journal of Analytical and Applied Chemistry
J Anal Chem — Journal of Analytical Chemistry of the USSR
J Anal Chem Moscow — Journal of Analytical Chemistry (Moscow)
J Anal Chem Transl of Zh Anal Khim — Journal of Analytical Chemsitry (Translation of Zhurnal Analiticheskoi Khimii)
J Anal Chem USSR Engl Transl — Journal of Analytical Chemistry. USSR (English Translation)
J Anal Math — Journal d'Analyse Mathematique
J Anal Psych — Journal of Analytical Psychology
J Anal Psychol — Journal of Analytical Psychology
J Anal Sci — Journal of Analytical Science
J Anal Toxicol — Journal of Analytical Toxicology
J Analyse Math — Journal d'Analyse Mathematique
J Analyt Chem USSR — Journal of Analytical Chemistry of the USSR
J Analyt Chem Wash — Journal of Analytical Chemistry (Washington)
J Analyt Psychol — Journal of Analytical Psychology
J Anat — Journal of Anatomy
J Anat Phys — Journal of Anatomy and Physiology
J Anat Physiol — Journal of Anatomy and Physiology
J Anat Physiol Lond — Journal of Anatomy and Physiology (London)
J Anat Physiol Norm Pathol Homme Anim — Journal de l'Anatomie et de la Physiologie Normales et Pathologiques de l'Hommeet des Animaux
J Anat Physiol Paris — Journal de l'Anatomie et de la Physiologie Normales et Pathologiques de l'Homme et des Animaux (Paris)
J Anat Soc Ind — Journal. Anatomical Society of India
J Anat Soc India — Journal. Anatomical Society of India
J Anc Chron Forum — Journal of the Ancient Chronology Forum
J Anc Ind Hist — Journal of Ancient Indian History
J Anc Near East Soc — Journal. Ancient Near East Society of Columbia University
J Anc Near East Soc Columbia Univ — Journal. Ancient Near Eastern Society. Columbia University
J Anc Nr E Soc — Journal of the Ancient Near East Society
J Andhra Hist Res Soc — Journal. Andhra Historical Research Society
J and J Danz Lectures — Jessie and John Danz Lectures. University of Washington Press
J & Proc A & Crafts Soc Ireland — Journal and Proceedings of the Arts and Crafts Society of Ireland
J & Proc A'sian Methodist Historical Soc — Australasian Methodist Historical Society. Journal and Proceedings
J & Proc Asiat Soc Bengal — Journal and Proceedings of the Asiatic Society of Bengal
J & Proc Aust Methodist Hist Soc — Australasian Methodist Historical Society. Journal and Proceedings
J Androl — Journal of Andrology
JANES — Journal. Ancient Near Eastern Society
Janes Def W — Jane's Defence Weekly
J Anesth — Journal of Anesthesia

J Ang Chem — Journal fuer Angewandte Chemie
J Angew Chem — Journal fuer Angewandte Chemie
J Angew Math Mech — Journal fuer Angewandte Mathematik und Mechanik
J Anglo It Stud — Journal of Anglo-Italian Studies
J Anglo-Mongol Soc — Journal. Anglo-Mongolian Society
J Anhui Med Coll — Journal of Anhui Medical College
J Animal Ecol — Journal of Animal Ecology
J Animal Ecology — Journal of Animal Ecology
J Animal Sci — Journal of Animal Science
J Anim Behav — Journal of Animal Behavior
J Anim Breed Genet — Journal of Animal Breeding and Genetics
J Anim Ecol — Journal of Animal Ecology
J Anim Morphol Physiol — Journal of Animal Morphology and Physiology
J Anim Morph Physiol — Journal of Animal Morphology and Physiology
J Anim Physiol Anim Nutr — Journal of Animal Physiology and Animal Nutrition
J Anim Prod Res — Journal of Animal Production Research
J Anim Prod UAR — Journal of Animal Production of the United Arab Republic
J Anim Prod Un Arab Repub — Journal of Animal Production of the United Arab Republic
J Anim Sci — Journal of Animal Science
J Anim Tech Ass — Journal. Animal Technicians Association
J Anim Tech Assoc — Journal. Animal Technicians Association
J Anim Techns Ass — Journal of the Animal Technicians Association
JanL — Janua Linguarum
JANMA — Japanese Nuclear Medicine
J Annamalai Univ — Journal. Annamalai University
J Annamalai Univ Part B — Journal. Annamalai University. Part B
JANPA7 — Journal of Analytical Psychology
Jan Pan Evk — Janus Pannonius Muzeum Evkoenyve
J An Pl — Journal of Anatomy and Physiology, Normal and Pathological
JANSA — Journal of Animal Science
JANSAG — Journal of Animal Science
JAnSB — Journal of the Anthropological Society of Bombay
Janssen Chim Acta — Janssen Chimica Acta
Janssen Res Found Ser — Janssen Research Foundation Series
JANTA — Journal of the Australian Natural Therapists Association
JANTAJ — Journal of Antibiotics
J Anthr — Journal of Anthropology
JAnthrl — Journal. Royal Anthropological Institute of Great Britain and Ireland
J Anthr Inst — Journal. Royal Anthropological Institute of Great Britain and Ireland
J Anthrop — Journal des Anthropologues
J Anthrop — Journal of Anthropology
J Anthrop Archaeol — Journal of Anthropological Archaeology
J Anthropol Archaeol — Journal of Anthropological Archaeology
J Anthropol Inst — Journal. Anthropological Institute of Great Britain and Ireland
J Anthropol Inst GB & Ireland — Journal of the Anthropological Institute of Great Britain and Ireland
J Anthropol Res — Journal of Anthropological Research
J Anthropol Soc Nippon — Journal. Anthropological Society of Nippon
J Anthropol Soc Oxford — Journal. Anthropolglcal Soclety of Oxford
J Anthrop Res — Journal of Anthropological Research
J Anthrop Soc Bombay — Journal. Anthropological Society of Bombay
J Anthrop Soc Japan — Journal of the Anthropological Society of Japan
J Anthrop Soc Oxf — Journal of the Anthropological Society of Oxford
J Anthrop Soc Oxford — Journal. Anthropological Society of Oxford
J Anthrop Soc Tokyo — Journal. Anthropological Society of Nippon/Jinruigaku Zasshi (Tokyo)
J Anthrop Stud Hum Move — Journal for the Anthropological Study of Human Movement
J Anthrop Surv India — Journal of the Anthropological Survey of India
J Anthro Res — Journal of Anthropological Research
J Anthr Res — Journal of Anthropological Research
J Anthr S N — Journal. Anthropological Society of Nippon
J Anti Aging Med — Journal of Anti-Aging Medicine
J Antibact Antifungal Agents Jpn — Journal of Antibacterial and Antifungal Agents. Japan
J Antibiot — Journal of Antibiotics
J Antibiot Ser A — Journal of Antibiotics. Series A
J Antibiot Ser B — Journal of Antibiotics. Series B
J Antibiot Ser B (Japan) — Journal of Antibiotics. Series B (Japan)
J Antibiot (Tokyo) — Journal of Antibiotics (Tokyo)
J Antibiot (Tokyo) Ser A — Journal of Antibiotics (Tokyo). Series A
J Antimicrob Chemother — Journal of Antimicrobial Chemotherapy
J Ant Ire — Journal. Royal Society of Antiquaries of Ireland
J Antro Sos — Jernal Antropoloji dan Sosioloji
Janus Pannonius Muz Evkoenyve — Janus Pannonius Muzeum Evkoenyve
Janus Pannon Muz Evk — Janus Pannonius Muzeum Evkoenyve
J Anxiety Disord — Journal of Anxiety Disorders
JAOA — Journal. American Osteopathic Association
JAOAA — Journal. American Osteopathic Association
JAOAAZ — Journal. American Osteopathic Association
J AOAC — Journal. Association of Official Analytical Chemists
J AOAC Inst — Journal. AOAC [*Association of Official Analytical Chemists*] International
J AOAC Int — Journal of AOAC (Assoc. Off. Anal. Chem.) International
JAOCA — Journal. American Oil Chemists' Society
JAOCA7 — Journal. American Oil Chemists' Society
JAOCS — Journal. American Oil Chemists' Society
JAOCS J Am Oil Chem Soc — JAOCS. Journal. American Oil Chemists' Society
JAOPB — Journal. American Optometric Association
JAOPBD — Journal. American Optometric Association
JAOS — Journal. American Oriental Society
JAOSS — Journal. American Oriental Society. Supplement
J Aoyama Gakuin Woman's Jr Coll — Journal. Aoyama Gakuin Woman's Junior College

JAP — Journal of Abnormal Psychology
JAP — Journal of American Photography
JAP — Journal of Applied Physics
JAP — Journal of Applied Psychology
JAPA — Journal. American Planning Association
Jap Acad Proc — Japan Academy. Proceedings
JAPAEA — Journal. American Podiatric Medical Association
Jap Agric Res Q — Japanese Agricultural Research Quarterly
Jap Agr Res Q — Japan Agricultural Research Quarterly
Jap Am — Japan and America
Japan Annu Int Law — Japanese Annual of International Law
Japan Arch — Japan Architect
Japan Archt — Japan Architect
Japan A Soc Psychol — Japanese Annals of Social Psychology
Japan Chem — Japan Chemical Week
Japan Circ J — Japanese Circulation Journal
Japan Econ — White Paper of Japanese Economy
Japan Econ Stud — Japanese Economic Studies
Japanese An Internat Law — Japanese Annual of International Law
Japanese Econ Studies — Japanese Economic Studies
Japanese Fin and Industry — Japanese Finance and Industry
Japanese J Fuzzy Theory Systems — Japanese Journal of Fuzzy Theory and Systems
Japanese Jour Geology and Geography — Japanese Journal of Geology and Geography
Japanese MT — Japanese Military Technology. Procedures for Transfers to the United States
Japan Fertilizer News — Japan Fertilizer News/Nihon Hiryo Shinbun
Japan Inter — Japan Interpreter
Japan J Appl Math — Japan Journal of Applied Mathematics
Japan J Geol & Geog — Japanese Journal of Geology and Geography
Japan J Math — Japanese Journal of Mathematics
Japan J Math NS — Japanese Journal of Mathematics. New Series
Japan J Med Sc Pt 4 Pharmacol — Japanese Journal of Medical Sciences. Part 4. Pharmacology
Japan J Nurs Art — Japanese Journal of Nursing Art
Japan Lbr Bul — Japan Labor Bulletin
Japan Med Gaz — Japan Medical Gazette
Japan Med World — Japan Medical World
Jap Ann Bib Econ — Japanese Annual Bibliography of Economics
Jap Ann of Law & Pol — Japan Annual of Law and Politics
Japan Pestic Inf — Japan Pesticide Information
Japan Q — Japan Quarterly
Japan Quart — Japan Quarterly
Japan Soc B — Japan Society Bulletin
Japan Soc London Bull — Japan Society of London Bulletin
Japan Stat — Japan Statistical Yearbook
Japan Stud — Japanese Studies
Japan Stud Hist Sci — Japanese Studies in the History of Science
Jap Arch — Japan Architect
Jap Arch Int Med — Japanese Archives of Internal Medicine
JA [*Paris*] — Journal des Arts [*Paris*]
Jap Assoc Lang Teach Jnl — Japan Association of Language Teachers. Journal
Jap Assoc Mineral Petrol Econ Geol J — Japanese Association of Mineralogists, Petrologists, and Economic Geologists. Journal
Jap Assoc Pet Technol J — Japanese Association of Petroleum Technologists. Journal
Jap As S T — Transactions of the Asiatic Society of Japan
Jap Bee J — Japanese Bee Journal
J Ap Behav Sci — Journal of Applied Behavioral Science
Jap Bus — Japan Business
JAPCA — Journal. Air Pollution Control Association
JAPCA — Journal of Abnormal Psychology
JAPCAC — Journal of Abnormal Psychology
JAPCA J Air — JAPCA. The Journal of the Air and Waste Management Association
Jap Chem — Japan Chemistry
Jap Chem Week — Japan Chemical Week
Jap Chr Q — Japan Christian Quarterly
Jap Circ J — Japanese Circulation Journal
Jap Comp — Japan Computers
J APDSA (Tokyo) — Journal. Asian Pacific Dental Student Association (Tokyo)
Jap Dt Zs Wiss Techn — Japanisch-Deutsche Zeitschrift fuer Wissenschaft und Technik
JAPE — Journal of Australian Political Economy
JAPEAI — Journal of Applied Ecology
J Ap Ecol — Journal of Applied Ecology
Jap Econ St — Japanese Economic Studies
Jap Electron (Wash) — Japan Electronics (Washington)
Jap En — Japan Energy
Jap Ev — Japan Evangelist
Jap Fruits — Japanese Fruits/Kajitsu Nihon
Jap Geol Surv Bull — Japan Geological Survey. Bulletin
Jap Geol Surv Rep — Japan Geological Survey. Report
Jap Geotherm Energy Assoc J — Japan Geothermal Energy Association. Journal
Jap Heart J — Japanese Heart Journal
J Apic Res — Journal of Apicultural Research
J Apicult R — Journal of Apicultural Research
Jap Inst Nav J — Japan. Institute of Navigation. Journal
Jap Inter — Japan Interpreter
Jap J Allergy — Japanese Journal of Allergy
Jap J Anaesth — Japanese Journal of Anaesthesiology
Jap J A Phy — Japanese Journal of Applied Physics
Jap J Appl Entomol Zool — Japanese Journal of Applied Entomology and Zoology
Jap J Appl Ent Zool — Japanese Journal of Applied Entomology and Zoology
Jap J Appl Phys — Japanese Journal of Applied Physics

Jap J Appl Phys Suppl — Japanese Journal of Applied Physics. Supplement
Jap J Appl Zool — Japanese Journal of Applied Zoology
Jap J Astr — Japanese Journal of Astronomy
Jap J Astr Geophys — Japanese Journal of Astronomy and Geophysics
Jap J Bot — Japanese Journal of Botany
Jap J Botan — Japanese Journal of Botany
Jap J Breed — Japanese Journal of Breeding
Jap J Canc Res — Japanese Journal of Cancer Research
Jap J Child — Japanese Journal of Child Psychiatry
Jap J Clin Med — Japanese Journal of Clinical Medicine
Jap J Clin Path — Japanese Journal of Clinical Pathology
Jap J Ecol — Japanese Journal of Ecology
Jap J Edu P — Japanese Journal of Educational Psychology
Jap J Ethnol — Japanese Journal of Ethnology
Jap J Exp M — Japanese Journal of Experimental Medicine
Jap J Exp Med — Japanese Journal of Experimental Medicine
Jap J Gen — Japanese Journal of Genetics
Jap J Genet — Japanese Journal of Genetics
Jap J Geol Geogr — Japanese Journal of Geology and Geography
Jap J Geophys — Japanese Journal of Geophysics
Jap J Hum G — Japanese Journal of Human Genetics
Jap J Hum Gen — Japanese Journal of Human Genetics
Jap J Ichthyol — Japanese Journal of Ichthyology
Jap J Limnol — Japanese Journal of Limnology
Jap J Med — Japanese Journal of Medicine
Jap J Med Electron & Biol Eng — Japanese Journal of Medical Electronics and Biological Engineering
Jap J Med S — Japanese Journal of Medical Science and Biology
Jap J Med Sci Biol — Japanese Journal of Medical Science and Biology
Jap J Med Sci Pt 4 Pharmacol — Japanese Journal of Medical Sciences. Part 4. Pharmacology
Jap J Micro — Japanese Journal of Microbiology
Jap J Microb — Japanese Journal of Microbiology
Jap J Microbiol — Japanese Journal of Microbiology. Japan Bacteriological Society
Jap J Midwife — Japanese Journal for the Midwife
Jap J Nurs — Japanese Journal of Nursing
Jap J Nurses Educ — Japan Journal of Nurses' Education
Jap J Nurs Res — Japanese Journal of Nursing Research
Jap J Nutr — Japanese Journal of Nutrition
Jap J Ophthal — Japanese Journal of Ophthalmology
Jap J Palynol — Japanese Journal of Palynology
Jap J Parasit — Japanese Journal of Parasitology
Jap J Pharm — Japanese Journal of Pharmacology
Jap J Pharmac — Japanese Journal of Pharmacology
Jap J Pharmacogn — Japanese Journal of Pharmacognosy
Jap J Phys — Japanese Journal of Physiology
Jap J Physi — Japanese Journal of Physiology
Jap J Physiol — Japanese Journal of Physiology
Jap J Psych — Japanese Journal of Psychology
Jap J Psychol — Japanese Journal of Psychology
Jap J Relig Stud — Japanese Journal of Religious Studies
Jap J Sanit Zool — Japanese Journal of Sanitary Zoology
Jap J Trop Agr — Japanese Journal of Tropical Agriculture
Jap J Trop Agri — Japanese Journal of Tropical Agriculture-Netai Nogyo
Jap J Vet R — Japanese Journal of Veterinary Research
Jap J Vet Res — Japanese Journal of Veterinary Research
Jap J Vet S — Japanese Journal of Veterinary Science
Jap J Vet Sci — Japanese Journal of Veterinary Science
Jap J Vet Sci Nigon Juigaku Zasshi — Japanese Journal of Veterinary Science/ Nigon Juigaku Zasshi
Jap J Zool — Japanese Journal of Zoology
Jap J Zootech Sci — Japanese Journal of Zootechnical Science
JAPLA — Journal. Atlantic Provinces Linguistic Association/Revue. Association de Linguistique des Provinces Atlantiques
JAPLD — Japanese Journal of Applied Physics. Part 2. Letters
JAPMA8 — Journal. American Pharmaceutical Association. Scientific Edition
Jap Man — Japan Manufacturing
Jap Mat — Japan Materials
Jap Meteorol Agency Volcanol Bull — Japan Meteorological Agency. Volcanological Bulletin
J Ap Meterol — Journal of Applied Meteorology
Jap M World — Japan Medical World
Jap Nat Ry Ry Tech Res — Japanese National Railways. Railway Technical Research
JAPND — Japanese Journal of Applied Physics. Part 1. Regular Papers and Short Notes
JAPNEF — Journal of Animal Physiology and Animal Nutrition
J Ap Nutrition — Journal of Applied Nutrition
JAPOA — Journal. American Psychoanalytic Association
JAPOAE — Journal. American Psychoanalytic Association
JaPP — Jahrbuch fuer Psychologie und Psychotherapie
J App Bact — Journal of Applied Bacteriology
J App Bacteriol — Journal of Applied Bacteriology
J App Behav Anal — Journal of Applied Behavior Analysis
J App Behavioral Sci — Journal of Applied Behavioral Science
J App Behav Anal — Journal of Applied Behavior Analysis
J App Behav Sci — Journal of Applied Behavioral Science
J App Ecol — Journal of Applied Ecology
Jap Per Ind — Japanese Periodicals Index
Jap Pesi Inf — Japanese Pesticide Information
Jap Pestic Inf — Japan Pesticide Information
J Appl Anal — Journal of Applied Analysis
J Appl Anim Res — Journal of Applied Animal Research
Jap Plast Age — Japan Plastics Age
J Appl Bact — Journal of Applied Bacteriology

J Appl Bacteriol — Journal of Applied Bacteriology
J Appl Bacteriol Suppl — Journal of Applied Bacteriology. Supplement
J Appl Be A — Journal of Applied Behavior Analysis
J Appl Beh — Journal of Applied Behavioral Science
J Appl Behav Anal — Journal of Applied Behavior Analysis
J Appl Behav Sci — Journal of Applied Behavioral Science
J Appl Bio — Journal of Applied Biomechanics
J Appl Biochem — Journal of Applied Biochemistry
J Appl Biol — Journal of Applied Biology
J Appl Biomater — Journal of Applied Biomaterials
J Appl Bot — Journal of Applied Botany
J Appl Cardiol — Journal of Applied Cardiology
J Appl Ch B — Journal of Applied Chemistry and Biotechnology
J Appl Chem — Journal of Applied Chemistry
J Appl Chem — Journal of Applied Chemistry of the USSR
J Appl Chem Abstr — Journal of Applied Chemistry. Abstracts
J Appl Chem and Biotechnol — Journal of Applied Chemistry and Biotechnology
J Appl Chem Biotechnol — Journal of Applied Chemistry and Biotechnology
J Appl Chem Biotechnol Abstr — Journal of Applied Chemistry and Biotechnology. Abstracts
J Appl Chem Leningrad — Journal of Applied Chemistry (Leningrad)
J Appl Chem (London) — Journal of Applied Chemistry (London)
J Appl Chem USSR — Journal of Applied Chemistry of the USSR
J Appl Chem USSR Engl Transl — Journal of Applied Chemistry. USSR. English Translation
J Appl Clin Med Phys — Journal of Applied Clinical Medical Physics
J Appl Cosmetol — Journal of Applied Cosmetology
J Appl Crys — Journal of Applied Crystallography
J Appl Crystallogr — Journal of Applied Crystallography
J Appld Chem USSR — Journal of Applied Chemistry of the USSR
J Appl Dev Psychol — Journal of Applied Developmental Psychology
J Appld Math Mech — Journal of Applied Mathematics and Mechanics
J Appld Mech Tech Physics — Journal of Applied Mechanics and Technical Physics
J Appld Polymer Science — Journal of Applied Polymer Science
J Appl Ecol — Journal of Applied Ecology
J Appl Ecol Shenyang Peoples Repub China — Journal of Applied Ecology (Shenyang, People's Republic of China)
J Appl Educ Stud — Journal of Applied Educational Studies
J Appl Elec — Journal of Applied Electrochemistry
J Appl Electrochem — Journal of Applied Electrochemistry
J Appl Entomol — Journal of Applied Entomology
J Appl Fire Sci — Journal of Applied Fire Science
J Appl Geophys — Journal of Applied Geophysics
J Appl Gerontol — Journal of Applied Gerontology
J Appl Glycosci — Journal of Applied Glycoscience
J Appl Ichthyol — Journal of Applied Ichthyology
J Applied Ecology — Journal of Applied Ecology
J Applied Ednl Studies — Journal of Applied Educational Studies
J Applied Micr (Rochester NY) — Journal of Applied Microscopy (Rochester, New York)
J Applied Physics — Journal of Applied Physics
J Appl Mag Soc Jpn — Journal. Applied Magnetics Society of Japan
J Appl Manage — Journal of Applied Management
J Appl Manuf Sys — Journal of Applied Manufacturing Systems
J Appl Math Mech — Journal of Applied Mathematics and Mechanics
J Appl Math Mech (Engl Transl) — Journal of Applied Mathematics and Mechanics (English Translation)
J Appl Math Phys — Journal of Applied Mathematics and Physics
J Appl Math Simulation — Journal of Applied Mathematics and Simulation
J Appl Mech — Journal of Applied Mechanics. Transactions. ASME
J Appl Mech and Tech Phys — Journal of Applied Mechanics and Technical Physics
J Appl Mech Tech Phys — Journal of Applied Mechanics and Technical Physics
J Appl Mech Trans ASME — Journal of Applied Mechanics. Transactions. ASME
J Appl Med — Journal of Applied Medicine
J Appl Met — Journal of Applied Meteorology
J Appl Metalwork — Journal of Applied Metalworking
J Appl Meteorol — Journal of Applied Meteorology
J Appl Microbiol — Journal of Applied Microbiology
J Appl Microbiol Suppl — Journal of Applied Microbiology. Supplement
J Appl Microscop Lab Meth — Journal of Applied Microscopy and Laboratory Methods
J Appl Mycol — Journal of Applied Mycology
J Appl Non Classical Logics — Journal of Applied Non-Classical Logics
J Appl Nutr — Journal of Applied Nutrition
J Appl Photogr Eng — Journal of Applied Photographic Engineering
J Appl Phycol — Journal of Applied Phycology
J Appl Phys — Journal of Applied Physics
J Appl Physiol — Journal of Applied Physiology [Later, Journal of Applied Physiology: Respiratory, Environmental, and Exercise Physiology]
J Appl Physiol Respir Environ Exercise Physiol — Journal of Applied Physiology: Respiratory, Environmental, and Exercise Physiology
J Appl Physiol Respir Environ Exerc Physiol — Journal of Applied Physiology: Respiratory, Environmental, and Exercise Physiology
J Appl Phys Jpn — Journal of Applied Physics. Japan
J Appl Phys (Moscow) — Journal of Applied Physics (Moscow)
J Appl Pl Sociol — Journal of Applied Plant Sociology
J Appl Pneum — Journal of Applied Pneumatics
J Appl Poly — Journal of Applied Polymer Science
J Appl Polym Sci — Journal of Applied Polymer Science
J Appl Polym Sci Appl Polym Symp — Journal of Applied Polymer Science. Applied Polymer Symposium
J Appl Poult Res — Journal of Applied Poultry Research
J Appl Probab — Journal of Applied Probability

J Appl Probability — Journal of Applied Probability
J Appl Psyc — Journal of Applied Psychology
J Appl Psychol — Journal of Applied Psychology
J Appl Sci — Journal of Applied Sciences
J Appl Sci Comput — Journal of Applied Science and Computations
J Appl Sci Eng A — Journal of Applied Science and Engineering. Section A. Electrical Power and Information Systems
J Appl Sci Eng Sect A Electr — Journal of Applied Science and Engineering. Section A. Electrical Power and Information Systems
J Appl Sci Shanghai — Journal of Applied Sciences (Shanghai)
J Appl So P — Journal of Applied Social Psychology
J Appl Spectrosc — Journal of Applied Spectroscopy
J Appl Spectrosc Engl Transl — Journal of Applied Spectroscopy (English Translation)
J Appl Spectrosc (USSR) — Journal of Applied Spectroscopy (USSR)
J Appl Sport Psy — Journal of Applied Sport Psychology
J Appl Statist — Journal of Applied Statistics
J Appl Statist Sci — Journal of Applied Statistical Sciences
J Appl Syst Anal — Journal of Applied Systems Analysis
J Appl Systems Analysis — Journal of Applied Systems Analysis
J Appl Ther — Journal of Applied Therapeutics
J Appl Ther Res — Journal of Applied Therapeutic Research
J Appl Toxicol — Journal of Applied Toxicology
J Appl Toxicol JAT — Journal of Applied Toxicology. JAT
J App Mech — Journal of Applied Mechanics
J App Meteor — Journal of Applied Meteorology
J App Nutr — Journal of Applied Nutrition
Jap Poultry Sci — Japanese Poultry Science
Jap Poult Sci — Japanese Poultry Science
J App Physiol — Journal of Applied Physiology [Later, Journal of Applied Physiology: Respiratory, Environmental, and Exercise Physiology]
J App Prob — Journal of Applied Probability
J App Psy — Journal of Applied Psychology
J App Psychol — Journal of Applied Psychology
Jap Prog Climatol — Japanese Progress in Climatology
J Approximation Theory — Journal of Approximation Theory
J Approx Th — Journal of Approximation Theory
J Approx Theory — Journal of Approximation Theory
J App Soc Psychol — Journal of Applied Social Psychology
J Ap Psychol — Journal of Applied Psychology
Jap Psy Res — Japanese Psychological Research
Jap Public Works Res Inst Rep (Minist Constr) — Japan Public Works Research Institute. Report. Ministry of Construction
Jap Pulp Pap — Japan Pulp and Paper
Jap Q — Japan Quarterly
Jap Quart — Japan Quarterly
Jap R — Japanese Religions
JAPRCP — Journal of Anthropological Research
JAPRDQ — Journal of Animal Production Research
Jap Rel — Japanese Religions
JAP Respir Environ Exercise Physiol — JAP. Respiratory, Environmental, and Exercise Physiology
JAPS — Journal. American Portuguese Society
JAPs — Journal of Applied Psychology
JAPSA — Journal of Applied Psychology
Jap Seism S T — Transactions of the Seismological Society of Japan
Jap Semicond Tech N — Japanese Semiconductor Technology News
Jap Shipbldg Mar Eng — Japan Shipbuilding and Marine Engineering
Jap Shipbuild & Mar Engng — Japan Shipbuilding and Marine Engineering
Jap Soc Grassland Sci J — Japanese Society of Grassland Science Journal/Nihon Sochi Gakkai Shi
J Ap Sociol — Journal of Applied Sociology
Jap Soc Promot Sci Sub-Comm Phys Chem Steelmaking Spec Rep — Japan Society for the Promotion of Science. Sub-Committee for Physical Chemistry of Steelmaking. Special Report
Jap Soc Scien Fish Bul — Japanese Society of Scientific Fisheries Bulletin
Jap Stud Hist Sci — Japanese Studies in the History of Science
JAPT — Journal of Approximation Theory
JAPTB — Journal. American Physical Therapy Association
Jap Telecom — Japan Telecommunications Review
Jap Transport — Japan Transportation
Jap W Chron — Japan Weekly Chronicle
Jap Weld Soc Trans — Japan Welding Society. Transactions
JAPYA — Journal of Applied Physiology [Later, Journal of Applied Physiology: Respiratory, Environmental, and Exercise Physiology]
Ja Q — Japan Quarterly
JAQ — Journal of Buyouts and Acquisitions
J Aquaric — Journal of Aquaculture
J Aquaric & Aquat Sci — Journal of Aquaculture and Aquatic Sciences
JA Quart J Automat Control — Journal. A Quarterly Journal of Automatic Control
J Aquat Food Prod Technol — Journal of Aquatic Food Product Technology
J Aquatic Pl Management — Journal of Aquatic Plant Management
J Aquat Pl — Journal of Aquatic Plant Management
J Aquat Plant Manage — Journal of Aquatic Plant Management
JAR — Journal of Accounting Research
JAR — Journal of Advertising Research
JAR — Journal of Anthropological Research
JAR — Juedischer Altestenrat
J Arab Affairs — Journal of Arab Affairs
JArabL — Journal of Arabic Literature
J Arab Lit — Journal of Arabic Literature
J Arab Stud — Journal of Arabian Studies
J Arab Vet Med Assoc — Journal. Arab Veterinary Medical Association
J Arachnol — Journal of Arachnology
J Arboric — Journal of Arboriculture

JArC — Journal of Aesthetics and Art Criticism
JARCA — Journal of Aesthetics and Art Criticism
JARCE — Journal. American Research Center in Egypt
J Archaeol Chem — Journal of Archaeological Chemistry
J Archaeol Rep — Journal of Archaeological Reports
J Archaeol Sci — Journal of Archaeological Science
J Archit & Planning Res — Journal of Architectural and Planning Research
J Archit Educ — Journal of Architectural Education
J Archit Plann Res — Journal of Architectural and Planning Research
J Arch Num — Journal International d'Archeologie Numismatique
J Arch Sci — Journal of Archaeological Science
Jard A — Jardin des Arts
Jard Bot — Jardin Botanico/Secretaria de Agricultura y Fomento
Jard Fr — Jardins de France
Jard Modes — Jardin des Modes
Jard Portatif — Jardinier Portatif
JAREB — Japanese Railway Engineering
JARED — JASCO [*Japan Spectroscopic Company*] Report
JARE Data Rep — JARE [*Japanese Antarctic Research Expedition*] Data Reports
JARE (Jpn Antarct Res Exped) Data Rep — JARE (Japanese Antarctic Research Expedition) Data Reports
Ja Rel — Japanese Religions
JARE Sci Rep Ser C — JARE (Japanese Antarctic Research Expedition) Scientific Reports. Series C. Earth Sciences
JARE Sci Rep Ser D — JARE (Japanese Antarctic Research Expedition) Scientific Reports. Series D. Oceanography
JARE Sci Rep Ser E Biol — JARE [*Japanese Antarctic Research Expedition*] Scientific Reports. Series E. Biology
JARF — Journal. Addiction Research Foundation
JARGV — Jahrbuch. Arbeitsgemeinschaft der Rheinischen Geschichtsvereine
JARI — Journal of Agricultural Research in Iceland
J Arid Environ — Journal of Arid Environments
J Ariz Acad Sci — Journal. Arizona Academy of Science
JArizH — Journal of Arizona History
J Ariz Hist — Journal of Arizona History
J Ariz Nev Acad Sci — Journal. Arizona-Nevada Academy of Science
J Arizona Hist — Journal of Arizona History
J Arkansas Acad Sci — Journal of the Arkansas Academy of Science
J Arkansas Med Soc — Journal. Arkansas Medical Society
J Ark Med Soc — Journal. Arkansas Medical Society
Jar L — Jarrow Lecture
J Ar L — Journal of Arabic Literature
J Armament Stud — Journal of Armament Studies
JARMAN — Journal of the Association for Rapid Method and Automation in Microbiology
J Arms Armour Soc — Journal. Arms and Armour Society
Jarmuevek Mezoegazd Gepek — Jarmuevek, Mezoegazdasagi Gepek
J Arn Arb — Journal. Arnold Arboretum
J Arn Arbor — Journal. Arnold Arboretum
J Arnold Arbor — Journal. Arnold Arboretum. Harvard University
J Arnold Arboretum Harvard Univ — Journal. Arnold Arboretum (Harvard University)
J Arnold Arbor Harv Univ — Journal. Arnold Arboretum. Harvard University
J Arnold Schoenberg Inst — Journal. Arnold Schoenberg Institute
Jaroslav Gos Ped Inst Dokl Naucn Konfer — Jaroslavskii Gosudarstvennyi Pedagogiceskii Institut Doklady na Naucnyh Konferencijah
Jaroslav Gos Ped Inst Ucen Zap — Jaroslavskii Gosudarstvennyi Pedagogiceskii Institut Imeni K. D. Usinskogo Ucenye Zapiski
Jaroslav Tehn Inst Fiz-Mat Nauk Sb Naucn Trudov — Jaroslavskii Tehnologiceskii Institut Fiziko-Matematiceskie Nauki Sbornik Naucnyh Trudov
JARQ — JARQ. Japan Agricultural Research Quarterly
JARQ Jap Agric Res Q — JARQ. Japan Agricultural Research Quarterly
JARQ Jpn Agric Res Q — JARQ. Japan Agricultural Research Quarterly
J Arquitectos — Jornal dos Arquitectos
JARR — Journal of Architectural Research
JARS — Journal. Assam Research Society
J Arthroplasty — Journal of Arthroplasty
J Artificial Intelligence Res — Journal of Artificial Intelligence Research
J Artistes — Journal des Artistes
J Art Mgmt L — Journal of Arts Management and Law
J Arts Mgt and L — Journal of Arts Management and Law
JAS — Jahrbuch fuer Amerikastudien
JAS — Journal. Acoustical Society of America
JAS — Journal. American Society for Information Science
JAS — Journal. Asiatic Society of Great Britain and Ireland
JAs — Journal Asiatique
JAS — Journal des Associations Patronales
JAS — Journal of Aerospace Science
JAS — Journal of American Studies
JAS — Journal of Archaeological Science
JAS — Journal of Asian Studies
JAS — Journal of Atmospheric Sciences
JAS — Journal of Australian Studies
JAS — Journal of Austronesian Studies
JASA — Journal. Acoustical Society of America
JASA — Journal. American Scientific Affiliation
JASA — Journal. American Statistical Association
J As Aff — Journal of Asian Affairs
J As Afr Stud (T) — Journal of Asian and African Studies (Tokyo)
JASAH — Journal. Society of Architectural Historians
J Asahikawa Nat College Tech — Journal of the Asahikawa National College of Technology
J Asahikawa Natl Coll Technol — Journal. Asahikawa National College of Technology
J Asahikawa Tech Coll — Journal. Asahikawa Technical College

J Asahikawa Tech College — Journal. Asahikawa Technical College
JASAT — Journal. American Studies Association of Texas
JASB — Journal and Proceedings. Asiatic Society of Bengal
JASB — Journal. Anthropological Society of Bombay
JASB — Journal. Asiatic Society of Bengal
JAS B — Journal. Asiatic Society of Bombay
JASBA — Journal. American Society of Sugar Beet Technologists
JASBAO — Journal. American Society of Sugar Beet Technologists
JASBe — Journal. Royal Asiatic Society of Bengal
JASBeA — Journal. Royal Asiatic Society of Bengal. Part 3. Anthropology
JASBeH — Journal. Royal Asiatic Society of Bengal. Part 1. History, Antiquities
JASBeL — Journal. Royal Asiatic Society of Bengal. London Edition
JASBeN — Journal. Royal Asiatic Society of Bengal. Part 2. Natural History
JASBeP — Journal. Royal Asiatic Society of Bengal. Pirated Edition
JASB(L) — Journal. Asiatic Society. Bengal (Letters)
JASBo — Journal. Asiatic Society of Bombay
JASBoS — Journal. Asiatic Society of Bombay. Supplement
JASC — Journal. Asiatic Society of Calcutta
JAS Calcutta — Journal. Asiatic Society of Calcutta
JASCEV — Journal of Agronomy and Crop Science
J A Schoenb — Journal. Arnold Schoenberg Institute
J A Scien — Journal of Archaeological Science
JASCO Appl Notes — Japan Spectroscopic Company. Application Notes
JASCO Rep — JASCO [*Japan Spectroscopic Company*] Report
J As Cult — Journal of Asian Culture
JASFE6 — Journal of Agricultural Science in Finland
J As Hist — Journal of Asian History
JASI — Journal. Arnold Schoenberg Institute
JASIAB — Journal of Agricultural Science
J Asia Electron Union — Journal of Asia Electronics Union
J Asian Afr — Journal of Asian and African Studies
J Asian Afr Stud — Journal of Asian and African Studies
J Asian Afr Stud Tokyo — Journal of Asian and African Studies. Institute for the Study of Languages and Cultures of Asia and Africa (Tokyo)
J Asian & Afric Stud — Journal of Asian and African Studies
J Asian His — Journal of Asian History
J Asian Hist — Journal of Asian History
J Asian Martial Arts — Journal of Asian Martial Arts
J Asian Nat Prod Res — Journal of Asian Natural Products Research
J Asian St — Journal of Asian Studies
J Asian Stud — Journal of Asian Studies
J Asia Stud — Journal of Asian Studies
J Asiat — Journal Asiatique
J Asiatique — Journal Asiatique
J Asiat Soc — Journal. Asiatic Society
J Asiat Soc Bangla — Journal. Asiatic Society of Bangladesh
J Asiat Soc Bangladesh Sci — Journal. Asiatic Society of Bangladesh. Science
J Asiat Soc Bengal — Journal. Asiatic Society of Bengal
J Asiat Soc Bengal Lett — Journal. Asiatic Society of Bengal. Letters
J Asiat Soc Bengal Sci — Journal. Asiatic Society of Bengal. Science
J Asiat Soc Bombay — Journal. Asiatic Society of Bombay
J Asiat Soc Calcutta — Journal of the Asiatic Society of Calcutta
J Asiat Soc Pak — Journal of the Asiatic Society of Pakistan
J Asiat Soc Sci — Journal. Asiatic Society. Science
J Asiat Stud — Journal of Asiatic Studies
JASIS — Journal. American Society for Information Science
JASJ — Journal of the Anthropological Society of Japan
JASL — Journal. Asiatic Society. Letters
JASMA — Journal. Acoustical Society of America
JASMAN — Journal. Acoustical Society of America
JASMU — Journal pour l'Avancement des Soins Medicaux d'Urgence
Ja Socialist R — Japan Socialist Review
Ja Soc Lond B — Japan Society of London. Bulletin
JASP — Journal. Asiatic Society of Pakistan
JASP — Journal of Abnormal and Social Psychology
JASP — Journal of Applied Social Psychology
J As Pac World — Journal of Asian-Pacific and World Perspectives
JASPAW — Journal of Abnormal and Social Psychology
JASPD — Journal of the Asiatic Society of Pakistan (Dacca)
JASPR — Journal. American Society for Psychical Research
JASR — Jane Austen Society. Report
JASRE8 — Journal of Agricultural and Scientific Research
JaSRL — Japan Science Review. Literature, Philosophy, and History
JASSA — JASSA. Journal of the Australian Society of Security Analysts
J Ass Advan Med Instrum — Journal. Association for the Advancement of Medical Instrumentation
J Assam Res Soc — Journal. Assam Research Society
J Assam Sci Soc — Journal. Assam Science Society
J Ass Comput Mach — Journal. Association for Computing Machinery
J ASSE — Journal. ASSE (American Society of Safety Engineers)
J Assist Reprod Genet — Journal of Assisted Reproduction and Genetics
J Ass'n L Teachers — Journal. Association of Law Teachers
J Assn Mil Surg US — Journal. Association of Military Surgeons. United States
J Assoc Acad Minor Phys — Journal. Association for Academic Minority Physicians
J Assoc Adv Agric Sci Afr — Journal. Association for the Advancement of Agricultural Sciences in Africa
J Assoc Adv Med Instrum — Journal. Association for the Advancement of Medical Instrumentation
J Assoc Am Med Coll — Journal. Association of American Medical Colleges
J Assoc Av Afr Sci Agric — Journal de l'Association pour l'Avancement en Afrique des Sciences de l'Agriculture
J As Soc Beng — Journal. Asiatic Society of Bengal
J Assoc Can Radiol — Journal. Association Canadienne des Radiologistes

J Assoc Care Child Health — Journal. Association for the Care of Children's Health

J Assoc Care Child Hosp — Journal. Association for the Care of Children in Hospitals

J Assoc Comput Mach — Journal. Association for Computing Machinery

J Assoc Dent Can — Journal d l'Association Dentaire Canadienne

J Assoc Eng Archit Isr — Journal. Association of Engineers and Architects in Israel

J Assoc Eng Archit Palest — Journal. Association of Engineers and Architects in Palestine

J Assoc Eng (Calcutta) — Journal. Association of Engineers (Calcutta)

J Assoc Eng (India) — Journal. Association of Engineers (India)

J Assoc Eng Soc — Journal. Association of Engineering Societies

J Assoc Hosp Med Educ — Journal. Association for Hospital Medical Education

J Assoc L Teachers — Journal. Association of Law Teachers

J Assoc Lunar and Planet Obs Strolling Astron — Journal. Association of Lunar and Planetary Observers. Strolling Astronomer

J Assoc Med Can — Journal. Association Medicale Canadienne

J Assoc Med Illus — Journal. Association of Medical Illustrators

J Assoc Nurses AIDS Care — Journal. Association of Nurses in AIDS Care

J Assoc Off Agric Chem — Journal. Association of Official Agricultural Chemists

J Assoc Off Anal Chem — Journal. Association of Official Analytical Chemists

J Assoc Offic Anal Chem — Journal. Association of Official Analytical Chemists

J Assoc Pediatr Oncol Nurses — Journal. Association of Pediatric Oncology Nurses

J Assoc Pers Comput Chem — Journal. Association of Personal Computers for Chemists

J Assoc Physicians India — Journal. Association of Physicians of India

J Assoc Phys Ment Rehabil — Journal. Association for Physical and Mental Rehabilitation

J Assoc Public Anal — Journal. Association of Public Analysts

J Assoc Res Otolaryngol — Journal of the Association for Research in Otolaryngology

J Assoc Sci Ouest Afr — Journal. Association Scientifique de l'Ouest Africain

J Assoc Study Percept — Journal. Association for the Study of Perception

J Assoc Vet Anaesth — Journal. Association of Veterinary Anaesthetists

J Ass Off Agric Chem — Journal. Association of Official Agricultural Chemists

J Ass Off Analyt Chem — Journal. Association of Official Analytical Chemists

J Ass Offic Anal Chem — Journal. Association of Official Analytical Chemists

J Asso Teach Ja — Journal. Association of Teachers of Japanese

J Ass Public Analysts — Journal. Association of Public Analysts

J As Stud P — Journal. Association for the Study of Perception

JASt — Journal of Asian Studies

JASTAA — Journal. Agricultural Society of Trinidad and Tobago

J Asthma — Journal of Asthma

J Asthma Res — Journal of Asthma Research [*Later, Journal of Asthma*]

JAST J — JAST (Jamaican Association of Sugar Technologists) Journal

JAST Q — JAST (Jamaican Association of Sugar Technologists) Quarterly

J Astronaut — Journal of the Astronautical Sciences

J Astronaut Sci — Journal of the Astronautical Sciences

J Astronomical Soc VIC — Journal. Astronomical Society of Victoria

J Astron (Peiping) — Journal of Astronomy (Peiping)

J Astrophys and Astron — Journal of Astrophysics and Astronomy

J Astrophys Astron — Journal of Astrophysics and Astronomy

JAStud — Journal of American Studies

Ja Stud Hist Sci — Japanese Studies in the History of Science

JAT — Jaarboekje van J. A. Alberdingk-Thym

JAT — Journal of Accounting and Public Policy

JAT — Journal of Applied Toxicology

JATAAQ — Journal. Animal Technicians Association

JATADT — Journal d'Agriculture Traditionnelle et de Botanique Appliquee. Travaux d'Ethnobotanique et d'Ethnozoologie

JATBAT — Journal d'Agriculture Tropicale et de Botanique Appliquee [*Later, Journal d'Agriculture Traditionnelle et de Botanique Appliquee*]

JATC — Journal of Air Traffic Control

J At Energy Comm (Jpn) — Journal. Atomic Energy Commission (Japan)

J At Energy Soc Jap — Journal. Atomic Energy Society of Japan

J At Energy Soc Jpn — Journal. Atomic Energy Society of Japan

J Atherosclerosis Res — Journal of Atherosclerosis Research

J Atheroscler Res — Journal of Atherosclerosis Research

J Atheroscler Thromb — Journal of Atherosclerosis and Thrombosis

J Ath Train — Journal of Athletic Training

JATI — Journal. Association of Teachers of Italian

JATJ — Journal-Newsletter. Association of Teachers of Japanese

JAT J Appl Toxicol — JAT. Journal of Applied Toxicology

JATL — Journal fuer Auserlesene Theologische Literatur

JATLA — Journal. American Trial Lawyers Association

J At Miner Sci — Journal of Atomic Mineral Science

J Atmos and Terr Phys — Journal of Atmospheric and Terrestrial Physics

J Atmos Chem — Journal of Atmospheric Chemistry

J Atmospheric Sci — Journal of the Atmospheric Sciences

J Atmospher Terrestr Phys — Journal of Atmospheric and Terrestrial Physics

J Atmos Sci — Journal of the Atmospheric Sciences

J Atmos Sol Terr Phys — Journal of Atmospheric and Solar-Terrestrial Physics

J Atmos Terr Phys — Journal of Atmospheric and Terrestrial Physics

J Atmos Terr Phys Suppl — Journal of Atmospheric and Terrestrial Physics. Supplement

J Atm Ter P — Journal of Atmospheric and Terrestrial Physics

JATOD3 — Journal of Analytical Toxicology

JAUCB — Journal of Autism and Childhood Schizophrenia

J Auckland Waikato Hist Soc — Journal of the Auckland/Waikato Historical Society

J Aud Eng S — Journal. Audio Engineering Society

J Aud Eng Soc — Journal. Audio Engineering Society

J Audio Eng Soc — Journal. Audio Engineering Society

J Audiov Media Med — Journal of Audiovisual Media in Medicine

J Aud Res — Journal of Auditory Research

J Aud Res Suppl — Journal of Auditory Research. Supplement

JAUEA — Journal of Automotive Engineering

JAUK — Jahrbuch. Albertus Universitaet zu Koenigsberg

J Aukland Hist Soc — Journal of the Aukland Historical Society

JAUMA — Journal. Australian Mathematical Society

JAUMLA — Journal. Australasian Universities Modern Language Association

Jaunakais Mezsaimn — Jaunakais Mezsaimnieciba

Jaundice Proc Int Symp Can Hepatic Found — Jaundice. Proceedings. International Symposium. Canadian Hepatic Foundation

JAUPA — Journal of Agriculture. University of Puerto Rico

JAUPA8 — Journal of Agriculture. University of Puerto Rico

JAURA — Journal of Auditory Research

JA [*USA*] — Journal of Art [*USA*]

J Aus I Agr — Journal. Australian Institute of Agricultural Science

J Aus I Met — Journal. Australian Institute of Metals

J Aus Mat A — Journal. Australian Mathematical Society. Series A. Pure Mathematics andStatistics

J Aus Mat B — Journal. Australian Mathematical Society. Series B. Applied Mathematics

J Aust Cath Hist Soc — Journal. Australian Catholic Historical Society

J Aust Ceramic Soc — Journal. Australian Ceramic Society

J Aust Ceram Soc — Journal. Australian Ceramic Society

J Aust Coll Speech Ther — Journal. Australian College of Speech Therapists

J Aust Entomol Soc — Journal. Australian Entomological Society

J Aust Ent Soc — Journal. Australian Entomological Society

J Aust Inst Agric Sci — Journal. Australian Institute of Agricultural Science

J Aust Inst Agr Sci — Journal. Australian Institute of Agricultural Science

J Aust Inst Ag Science — Journal. Australian Institute of Agricultural Science

J Aust Inst Hort — Journal. Australian Institute of Horticulture

J Aust Inst Hortic — Journal. Australian Institute of Horticulture

J Aust Inst Met — Journal. Australian Institute of Metals

J Aust Inst Metals — Journal. Australian Institute of Metals

J Aust Inst Surg Dent Tech — Journal. Australian Institute of Surgical and Dental Technicians

J Aust Math Soc — Journal. Australian Mathematical Society

J Aust Planning Inst — Journal. Australian Planning Institute

J Aust Polit Econ — Journal of Australian Political Economy

J Australas Ceram Soc — Journal. Australasian Ceramic Society

J Australas Inst Met — Journal. Australasian Institute of Metals

J Australas Inst Metals — Australasian Institute of Metals. Journal

J Austral Inst Agric Sci — Journal. Australian Institute of Agricultural Science

J Austral Math Soc Ser A — Journal. Australian Mathematical Society. Series A

J Austral Math Soc Ser B — Journal. Australian Mathematical Society. Series B

J Austral Rhododendron Soc — Journal. Australian Rhododendron Society

J Austral Stud — Journal of Australian Studies

J Austronesian Stud — Journal of Austronesian Studies

J Aust Stud — Journal of Australian Studies

J Autism & Child Schizo — Journal of Autism and Childhood Schizophrenia

J Autism & Devel Dia — Journal of Autism and Developmental Disorders

J Autism Ch — Journal of Autism and Childhood Schizophrenia

J Autism Child Schizophr — Journal of Autism and Childhood Schizophrenia

J Autism Child Schizophrenia — Journal of Autism and Childhood Schizophrenia

J Autism Dev Disord — Journal of Autism and Developmental Disorders

J Autism Dev Disorders — Journal of Autism and Developmental Disorders

J Autoimmun — Journal of Autoimmunity

J Automat Inform Sci — Journal of Automation and Information Sciences

J Automat Reason — Journal of Automated Reasoning

J Autom Chem — Journal of Automatic Chemistry

J Automot Eng — Journal of Automotive Engineering

J Autom Reasoning — Journal of Automated Reasoning

J Auton Nerv Syst — Journal of the Autonomic Nervous System

J Auton Pharmacol — Journal of Autonomic Pharmacology

JAVAD5 — Journal. American Venereal Disease Association

J Aviat Hist Soc Aust — Aviation Historical Society of Australia. Journal

J Aviation Med — Journal of Aviation Medicine

J Aviat Med — Journal of Aviation Medicine

JAVMA — Journal. American Veterinary Medical Association

JAVMA4 — Journal. American Veterinary Medical Association

JAVR — Jewish Audio-Visual Review

JAVRAJ — Journal. American Veterinary Radiology Society

JAVTA — Journal. South African Veterinary Association

JAW — Jahresberichte ueber die Fortschritte der Klassischen Altertumswissenschaft

JAWAA7 — Journal of Agriculture of Western Australia

JAWG — Jahrbuch der Akademie der Wissenschaften. Goettingen

JAWL — Jahrbuch der Akademie der Wissenschaften und der Literatur in Mainz

JAWM — Jahrbuch. Akademie der Wissenschaften und der Literatur. Mainz

JAWRES — Journal of Agriculture and Water Resources Research

JAWWA — Journal. American Water Works Association

JAWWA5 — American Water Works Association. Journal

JAY — Journal of Applied Psychology

JAZ — Jahrbuch fuer Sozialwissenschaft. Zeitschrift fuer Wirtschaftswissenschaften

JazA — Jazykovedny Aktuality. Zpravodaj Jazykovedneho Sdruzeni pri Ceskoslovenske Akademii Ved

JAZODX — Journal of Advanced Zoology

JazS — Jazykovedny Studie

JazSb — Jazykovedny Sbornik

JAZU — Jugoslavenske Akademije Znanosti i Umjetnosti

JAZU — Radovi Instituta Jugoslavenske Akademiji Znanosti i Umjetnosti u Zadru

Jazz Ed J — Jazz Educators Journal

Jazzf — Jazzforschung

Jazz Ieri — Jazz di Ieri e di Oggi

Jazz J — Jazz Journal [*Later, Jazz Journal International*]

Jazz J Int — Jazz Journal International

Jazz JI — Jazz Journal [*Later, Jazz Journal International*]

Jazz Mag — Jazz Magazine
Jazz Mag (US) — Jazz Magazine (United States)
Jazz Mo — Jazz Monthly
Jazz R — Jazz Review
Jazz Rept — Jazz Report
Jazz Res — Jazz Research
Jazz Rytm — Jazz Rytm i Piosenka
Jazz Studies — Annual Review of Jazz Studies
Jazz T — Jazz Times
JB — Bursians Jahresbericht ueber die Fortschritte der Klassischen Altertumswissenschaft
JB — Journal of Band Research
JB — Journal of Broadcasting [*Later, Journal of Broadcasting and Electronic Media*]
JB — Journal of Business
JB — Judaica Bohemiae
JB — Junior Bookshelf
Jb — Juristenblad
JBA — Japan Baptist Annual
JBA — Jewish Book Annual
JBA — Journal. Board of Agriculture
JBA — Journal of Banking and Finance
JBA — Journal of Belizean Affairs
JBA — Journal of Business Administration
JBAA — Journal. British Archaeological Association
JBA & Lit — Journal des Beaux-Arts et de la Litterature
JBA & Sci — Journal des Beaux-Arts et des Sciences
Jb Absatz und Verbrauchsforsch — Jahrbuch der Absatz- und Verbrauchsforschung
JbAC — Jahrbuch fuer Antike und Christentum
J BAC — Journal. International Union of Bricklayers and Allied Craftsmen
JbAChr — Jahrbuch fuer Antike und Christentum
J Bact — Journal of Bacteriology
J Bacteriol — Journal of Bacteriology
Jb Adalbert Stift Ver — Jahrbuch des Adalbert Stifter Vereins in Muenchen
J BADC — Journal. Bar Association of the District of Columbia
JBA Dist Colum — Journal. Bar Association of the District of Columbia
Jb Aesth & Allg Kstwiss — Jahrbuch fuer Aesthetik und Allgemeine Kunstwissenschaft
J Bahamas Hist Soc — Journal of the Bahamas Historical Society
J BA Kan — Journal. Bar Association of the State of Kansas
Jb Albertus Univ Koenigsberg — Jahrbuch der Albertus-Universitaet zu Koenigsberg
Jb Albertus Univ Koenigsberg Beih — Beihefte zum Jahrbuch der Albertus-Universitaet zu Koenigsberg
J Ballist — Journal of Ballistics
JBalS — Journal of Baltic Studies
J Bal Stud — Journal of Baltic Studies
Jb Altbayer Kirchengesch — Jahrbuch fuer Altbayerische Kirchengeschichte
Jb Altertskde Wien — Jahrbuch fuer Altertumskunde
J Baltic St — Journal of Baltic Studies
J Baltimore Coll Dent Surg — Journal. Baltimore College of Dental Surgery
Jb Alt Kde — Jahrbuch fuer Altertumskunde
JBAM — Journal. British Association of Malaysia
J Band Res — Journal of Band Research
J Bangladesh Acad Sci — Journal. Bangladesh Academy of Sciences
J Bankers Inst Australas — Bankers' Institute of Australasia. Journal
J Bank Finance — Journal of Banking and Finance
J Banking and Fin — Journal of Banking and Finance
J Banking Finance — Journal of Banking and Finance
J Bank Res — Journal of Bank Research
J Bank Research — Journal of Bank Research
Jb Ant & Christ — Jahrbuch fuer Antike und Christentum
Jb Antwerpens Oudhdknd Kring — Jaarboek van Antwerpens Oudheidkundige Kring
J Baoji Coll Arts Sci Nat Sci — Journal of Baoji College of Arts and Science. Natural Science
J Baoji College Arts Sci Nat Sci — Journal. Baoji College of Arts and Science. Natural Science
J Barb Mus Hist Soc — Journal. Barbados Museum and Historical Society
Jb Arch I — Jahrbuch des Deutschen Archaeologischen Instituts
Jb Archit — Jahrbuch fuer Architektur
Jb AS — Jahrbuch fuer Amerikastudien
JBASB — Journal of Band Research
Jb Asiat Kst — Jahrbuch fuer Asiatische Kunst
Jb Asiat Kunst — Jahrbuch der Asiatischen Kunst
J Basic Clin Physiol Pharmacol — Journal of Basic and Clinical Physiology and Pharmacology
J Basic Eng — Journal of Basic Engineering
J Basic Eng Trans ASME — Journal of Basic Engineering. Transactions. ASME
J Basic Eng Trans ASME Ser D — Journal of Basic Engineering. Transactions. ASME [*American Society of Mechanical Engineers*]. Series D
J Basic Microbiol — Journal of Basic Microbiology
J Basic Sci Hanyang Inst Basic Sci — Journal of Basic Sciences. Hanyang Institute of Basic Science
J Bas S — Journal of Basque Studies
JB Assn St Kan — Journal. Bar Association of the State of Kansas
J Baukst — Journal fuer die Baukunst
Jb Ausw Politik — Jahrbuch fuer Auswaertige Politik
JBAW — Jahrbuch. Bayerische Akademie der Wissenschaften
JbAWG — Jahrbuch. Akademie der Wissenschaften in Goettingen
JbAWL — Jahrbuch. Akademie der Wissenschaften und der Literatur
JBB — Jahresbericht der Bayerischen Bodendenkmalpflege
Jb Balt Deutschtum — Jahrbuch des Baltischen Deutschtums
JBBAS — Journal. Bombay Branch. Royal Asiatic Society
JbBAW — Jahrbuch. Bayerische Akademie der Wissenschaften

Jb Bayer Akad Wiss — Jahrbuch der Bayerischen Akademie der Wissenschaften
Jb Bayer Dkmlpf — Jahrbuch der Bayerischen Denkmalpflege
Jbb Dogm Buergerl R — Jahrbuecher fuer die Dogmatik des Buergerlichen Rechts
Jbb Dt Armee — Jahrbuecher fuer die Deutsche Armee und Marine
Jb Belg Ned — Jaarboek. Vereniging voor de Vergelijkende Studie van het Recht van Belgie enNederland
Jb Berg Hw — Jahrbuch fuer das Berg- und Huettenwesen im Koenigreiche Sachsen
Jb Berlin — Jahrbuch der Deutschen Akademie der Wissenschaften zu Berlin
Jb Berliner Mus — Jahrbuch der Berliner Museen
Jb Berlin Mus — Jahrbuch der Berliner Museen
Jb Berl Mus — Jahrbuch. Berliner Museen
JB Bern Hist Mus — Jahrbuch. Bernisches Historisches Museum
Jb Bernischen Hist Mus — Jahrbuch des Bernischen Historischen Museums
Jb BHM — Jahrbuch des Bernischen Historischen Museums
Jb Bib Hertz — Jahrbuch der Bibliotheca Hertziana
Jb Bild Kst Ostseeprov — Jahrbuch fuer Bildende Kunst in den Ostseeprovinzen
Jbb In u Ausld Ges Med — Schmidts Jahrbuecher der In- und Auslaendischen Gesamten Medizin
Jb Bischof Gymnas Kolleg Petrinum — Jahresbericht. Bischoefliches Gymnasium und Dioezesanseminar. Kollegium Petrinum in Urfar
JBBKG — Jahrbuch fuer Berlin-Brandenburgische Kirchengeschichte
Jbb Lit Heidelbg — Jahrbuecher der Literatur. Verhandlungen des Naturhistorisch-Medicinischen Vereins zu Heidelberg
JbBM — Jahrbuch der Berliner Museen
JBBMD — Journal of Biochemical and Biophysical Methods
Jbb Nationaloek Statist — Jahrbuecher der Nationaloekonomie und Statistik
Jbb Philol — Jahrbuecher fuer Philologie
Jb Brandbg Kirchgesch — Jahrbuch fuer Brandenburgische Kirchengeschichte
Jb Brandenburg Gesch — Jahrbuch fuer Brandenburgische Geschichte
JBBRAS — Journal. Bombay Branch. Royal Asiatic Society
Jb Braunschweig Geschver — Jahrbuch des Braunschweigischen Geschichtsvereins
Jbb Saechs Oberverwaltgsger — Jahrbuecher des Saechsischen Oberverwaltungsgerichts
Jbb Wiss Bot — Jahrbuecher fuer Wissenschaftliche Botanik
JBC — Jerome Biblical Commentary
JBC — Journal of Business Communication
JBC — Journal. State Bar of California
Jb Centr Bureau Geneal — Jaarboek van het Centraal Bureau voor Genealogie
Jb Coburg Landesst — Jahrbuch. Coburger Landesstiftung
Jb Coburg Landesstift — Jahrbuch der Coburger Landesstiftung
JBCSA — Journal. British Ceramic Society
J Bd Ag — Journal. Board of Agriculture
J Bd Agric Br Gui — Journal. Board of Agriculture. British Guiana
J Bd Agric (London) — Journal. Board of Agriculture (London)
JbDAI — Jahrbuch. Deutsches Archaeologische Institut
JbDAI ArAnz — Jahrbuch. Deutsches Archaeologische Institut. Archaeologischer Anzeiger
JbDAW — Jahrbuch. Deutsche Akademie der Wissenschaften zu Berlin
Jb Deutschen Saengerbundes — Jahrbuch des Deutschen Saengerbundes
JbDG — Jahrbuch. Dante Gesellschaft
Jb Die Haghe — Jaarboek Die Haghe
Jb Diplom Akad (Wien) — Jahrbuch. Diplomatische Akademie (Wien)
Jb Drahtl Telegr — Jahrbuch der Drahtlosen Telegraphie
Jb Dt Akad Spr & Dicht — Jahrbuch der Deutschen Akademie fuer Sprache und Dichtung
Jb Dt Akad Wiss Berlin — Jahrbuch der Deutschen Akademie der Wissenschaften zu Berlin
Jb Dt Alpenver — Jahrbuch des Deutschen Alpenvereins
Jb Dt Archaeol Inst — Jahrbuch des Deutschen Archaeologischen Instituts
Jb Dt Buehnenspiele — Jahrbuch der Deutschen Buehnenspiele
Jb Dt Bulg Ges 1939 — Jahrbuch 1939 der Deutsch-Bulgarischen Gesellschaft e. V. Leipzig
Jb Dt Dante Ges — Jahrbuch der Deutschen Dante-Gesellschaft
Jb Dt Recht — Jahrbuch des Deutschen Rechtes
Jb Dt Schillerges — Jahrbuch der Deutschen Schillergesellschaft
JBE — Japan Biographical Encyclopedia
JBE — Journal of Behavioral Economics
JBE — Journal of Business Education
JBE — Journal of Business Ethics
J Beaux Arts Sci — Journal des Beaux-Arts et des Sciences
J Beckett S — Journal of Beckett Studies
J Beckett Stud — Journal of Beckett Studies
J Beck S — Journal of Beckett Studies
J Behav Assess — Journal of Behavioral Assessment
J Behav Exp — Journal of Behavior Therapy and Experimental Psychiatry
J Behavioural Sci — Journal of Behavioural Science
J Behav Med — Journal of Behavioral Medicine
J Behav Sci — Journal of Behavioural Science
J Behav Ther Exp Psychiatry — Journal of Behavior Therapy and Experimental Psychiatry
J Beijing For Coll — Journal of Beijing Forestry College
J Beijing For Univ — Journal of Beijing Forestry University
J Beijing Inst Chem Technol Nat Sci — Journal of Beijing Institute of Chemical Technology. Natural Science
J Beijing Inst Tech — Journal. Beijing Institute of Technology
J Beijing Inst Technol Engl Ed — Journal of Beijing Institute of Technology. English Edition
J Beijing Inst Technol Engl Lang Iss — Journal of Beijing Institute of Technology. English Language Issue
J Beijing Med Coll — Journal of Beijing Medical College
J Beijing Med Univ — Journal of Beijing Medical University
J Beijing Norm Univ Nat Sci — Journal of Beijing Normal University. Natural Science

J Beijing Polytech Univ — Journal of Beijing Polytechnic University

J Beijing Univ Aeronaut Astronaut — Journal of Beijing University of Aeronautics and Astronautics

J Beijing Univ Iron Steel Technol — Journal of Beijing University of Iron and Steel Technology

Jb Elektrochem — Jahrbuch der Elektrochemie

J Belge Med Phys — Journal Belge de Medecine Physique

J Belge Med Phys Rehabil — Journal Belge de Medecine Physique et de Rehabilitation

J Belge Med Phys Rhumatol — Journal Belge de Medecine Physique et de Rhumatologie

J Belge Neurol Psychiatr — Journal Belge de Neurologie et de Psychiatrie

J Belge Radiol — Journal Belge de Radiologie

J Belge Radiol Monogr — Journal Belge de Radiologie. Monographie

J Belge Rhumatol Med Phys — Journal Belge de Rhumatologie et de Medecine Physique

J Belg Rad — Journal Belge de Radiologie

JBeNHS — Journal of the Bengal Natural History Society

JbEOL — Jaarbericht. Vooraziatische-Egyptisch Genootschap "Ex Oriente Lux"

Jber Altertwiss — Jahresberichte fuer Altertumswissenschaft

Jber Anat — Jahresberichte ueber die Fortschritte der Anatomie und Entwicklungsgeschichte

Jber Augst & Kaiseraugst — Jahresberichte aus Augst und Kaiseraugst

Jber Basl Kstver — Jahresberichte. Basler Kunstverein

Jber Deutsch Math-Verein — Jahresbericht. Deutsche Mathematiker-Vereinigung

Jber Dt Gesch — Jahresbericht der Deutschen Geschichte

Jber EOL — Jaarbeericht. Vooraziatisch - Egyptisch Genootschap Ex Oriente Lux

Jber Fortschr Chir — Jahresbericht ueber die Fortschritte auf dem Gebiete der Chirurgie

Jber Fortschr Klass Altertswiss — Bursians Jahresbericht ueber die Fortschritte der Klassischen Altertumswissenschaft

Jber Fortschr Tierchem — Jahresbericht ueber die Fortschritte der Tierchemie

Jber Freies Dt Hochstift 1972-73 — Jahresbericht des Freien Deutschen Hochstifts, 1972-73

J Bergen Cty Dent Soc — Journal. Bergen County Dental Society

Jber Geog Ges Bern — Jahresberichte der Geographischen Gesellschaft von Bern

Jber Germ Philol — Jahresbericht ueber Germanische Philologie

Jber Ger Nmus — Jahresbericht des Germanischen Nationalmuseums

Jber Ger Nmus Nuernberg — Jahresbericht. Germanisches Nationalmuseum Nuernberg

Jber Ges Tuberkforsch — Jahresbericht ueber die Gesamte Tuberkulose-Forschung

Jber Heimatver Landkreis Augsburg — Jahresbericht des Heimatvereins fuer den Landkreis Augsburg

Jber Hist Ges Graub — Jahresbericht. Historisch-Antiquarische Gesellschaft von Graubuenden

Jber Hist Mus Basel — Jahresberichte des Historischen Museums Basel

Jber Hist Mus Bern — Jahresberichte des Historischen Museums in Bern

Jber Hist Ver Dillingen — Jahresbericht des Historischen Vereins Dillingen

Jber Hist Ver Mittelfranken — Jahresberichte des Historischen Vereins fuer Mittelfranken

Jber Hist Ver Oberbayern — Jahresbericht des Historischen Vereines von (und fuer) Oberbayern

Jber Hist Ver Straubing & Umgebung — Jahresbericht des Historischen Vereins fuer Straubing und Umgebung

Jber Inn M — Jahresbericht ueber die Fortschritte der Inneren Medizin im Inund Auslande

Jber Inst Vg Frankf — Jahresbericht des Instituts fuer Vorgeschichte der Universitaet Frankfurt

Jber Kant Lehranstalt Sarnen — Jahresbericht ueber die Kantonale Lehranstalt zu Sarnen

Jber Leistg Fortschr Anat — Jahresbericht ueber die Leistungen und Fortschritte in der Anatomie und Physiologie

Jber Leistg Fortschr Milsanitw — Roths Jahresbericht ueber die Leistungen und Fortschritte auf dem Gebiete des Militaersanitaetswesens

Jber Linz Musver Verm Schr — Jahresberlcht des Linzer Musealvereines. Vermischte Schriften

Jber Lit Zbl — Jahresbericht des Literarischen Zentralblatts

J Berl M — Jahrbuch. Berliner Museen

Jber Mus Francisco Carolinium — Jahresbericht des Museum Francisco-Carolinium

Jber Mus (Han) — Jahresbericht Kestner-Museum (Hannover)

Jber Naturf Ges Fraubuendens — Jahresbericht. Naturforschende Gesellschaft Fraubuendens

Jber Naturw Ver Wuppertal — Jahresbericht. Naturwissenschaftlicher Verein zu Wuppertal

Jber Neuer Dt Litgesch — Jahresbericht fuer Neuere Deutsche Literaturgeschichte

Jber Ophth — Jahresbericht ueber die Leistungen und Fortschritte im Gebiete der Ophthalmologie

Jber Physik Ver Frankf — Jahresbericht des Physikalischen Vereins zu Frankfurt

Jber Pro Vindon — Jahresbericht. Gesellschaft pro Vindonissa

Jber Roemerhaus & Mus Augst — Jahresbericht. Roemerhaus und Museum Augst

Jber Roemer Mus — Jahresbericht des Roemer-Museums

Jberr Ver Mecklenb Gesch — Jahresberichte des Vereins fuer Mecklenburgische Geschichte

Jber Schles Ges Vaterld Kult — Jahresbericht der Schlesischen Gesellschaft fuer Vaterlaendische Kultur

Jber Schweiz Landesmus Zuerich — Jahresbericht. Schweizerisches Landesmuseum in Zuerich

Jber Tierseuch — Jahresbericht ueber die Verbreitung von Tierseuchen im Deutschen Reiche

Jber Ver Alt Rothenburg — Jahresbericht des Vereins Alt-Rothenburg

Jber Vereing Angew Bot — Jahresbericht der Vereinigung fuer Angewandte Botanik

Jber Vooraziat Egyp Genoot Ex Oriente Lux — Jaarbericht van het Vooraziatisch-Egyptisch Genootschap ex Oriente Lux

Jber Vorarlbg Museum Ver — Jahresbericht des Vorarlberger Museum-Vereins

Jb Erziehgswiss Jugendkde — Jahrbuch fuer Erziehungswissenschaft und Jugendkunde

Jber (Zuerich) — Jahresbericht. Schweizerisches Landesmuseum (Zuerich)

J Bethune Med Univ — Journal of Bethune Medical University

J Bethune Univ Med Sci — Journal. Bethune University of Medical Sciences

J Beverly Hills Ba — Journal. Beverly Hills Bar Association

J Bev Hills BA — Journal. Beverly Hills Bar Association

JBF — Journal of Banking and Finance

JBF — Journal of Business Finance and Accounting

JBFA — Journal of Business Finance and Accounting

JbFL — Jahrbuch fuer Fraenkische Landesforschung

Jb f Niederdeut Spr — Jahrbuch fuer Niederdeutsche Sprachforschung

Jb f Niederdt Spr — Jahrbuch fuer Niederdeutsche Sprachforschung

Jb f Psych — Jahrbuecher fuer Psychiatrie und Neurologie

Jb Fraenk Landesforsch — Jahrbuch fuer Fraenkische Landesforschung

Jb Freien Dt Hochstifts — Jahrbuch des Freien Deutschen Hochstifts

Jb Friedens- u Konfliktforsch — Jahrbuch fuer Friedens- und Konfliktforschung

Jb Fuer Musikalische Volks und Voelkerkunde — Jahrbuch fuer Musikalische Volks- und Voelkerkunde

JBG — Brazil Journal

JBG — Jahrbuch. Barlach-Gesellschaft

JbG — Jahrbuch fuer die Geschichte Mittel- und Ostdeutschlands

JBG — Jahresbericht der Geschichtswissenschaft

JBG — Jinbungaku

JBG — Journal of Business Logistics

JBGA — Japan Bibliographical Annual

Jb Gehestiftg — Jahrbuch der Gehe-Stiftung

Jb Genoot Amstelodamum — Jaarboek van het Genootschap Amstelodamum

Jb Genootschap Amstelodamum — Jaarboek van het Genootschap Amstelodamum

Jb Geol Reichsanst Wien — Jahrbuch der Geologischen Reichsanstalt Wien

Jb Ger Zentmus Mainz — Jahrbuch des Germanischen Zentralmuseums (Mainz)

Jb Gesch & Oudhdknd Leiden & Omstreken — Jaarboekje voor Geschiedenis en Oudheidkunde van Leiden en Omstreken

Jb Gesch des Deutschen Ostens — Jahrbuch fuer die Geschichte Mittel- und Ostdeutschlands. Band 1. Jahrbuch fuerdie Geschichte des Deutschen Ostens

Jb Gesch Mittel U Ostdtl — Jahrbuch fuer die Geschichte Mittel- und Ostdeutschlands

Jb Gesch Oberdt Reichsstaedte — Jahrbuch fuer Geschichte der Oberdeutschen Reichsstaedte

Jb Gesch Osteur — Jahrbuecher fuer Geschichte Osteuropas

Jb Gesch Ost U Mitteleur — Jahrbuch fuer Geschichte der Deutsch-Slawischen Beziehungen und Geschichte Ost-und Mitteleuropas

Jb Gesch Oudhdknd Kring Leuven & Omgev — Jaarboek van de Geschied- en Oudheidkundige Kring voor Leuven en Omgeving

Jb Gesch Sozial Land Europas — Jahrbuch fuer Geschichte der Sozialistischen Lander Europas

Jb Gesch UdSSR — Jahrbuch fuer Geschichte der UdSSR und der Volksdemokratischen Laender Europas

Jb Gesetzg Verw — Jahrbuch fuer Gesetzgebung, Verwaltung und Rechtspflege des Deutschen Reichs

Jb Ges Gesch Protestantismus Oesterreich — Jahrbuch der Gesellschaft fuer die Geschichte des Protestantismus in Oesterreich

Jb Ges Hamburg Kstfreunde — Jahrbuch der Gesellschaft Hamburgischer Kunstfreunde

Jb Ges Oester Volkswirte — Jahrbuch der Gesellschaft Oesterreichischer Volkswirte

Jb Ges Schweiz Famforsch — Jahrbuch der Gesellschaft fuer Schweizerische Familienforschung

Jb Ges Wiener Theater F — Jahrbuch. Gesellschaft fuer Wiener Theater-Forschung

Jb Gewaesserkde Norddtld — Jahrbuch fuer die Gewaesserkunde Norddeutschlands

JbGFNG — Jahresbericht der Gesellschaft von Freunden der Naturwissenschaft zu Gera

JBGH — Jinbun Gakuho

JbGO — Jahrbuch fuer Geschichte Osteuropas

Jb Goethe Ges — Jahrbuch der Goethe-Gesellschaft

JB Goett — Jahrbuch. Akademie der Wissenschaften in Goettingen

Jb G Ost — Jahrbuch fuer die Geschichte Osteuropas

Jb GPV — Jahresbericht. Gesellschaft pro Vindonissa. Basel

JBGSA — Journal of the British Grassland Society (Aberystwyth)

JbGSI — Jahrbuch zur Geschichte der Slaven

Jb H — Jaarboekje van de Vergelijkende van Directeuren van Hypotheekbanken

Jb Haarlem — Jaarboek Haarlem

Jb Hafenbautechn Ges — Jahrbuch der Hafenbautechnischen Gesellschaft

Jb Hamb Ku Samml — Jahrbuch. Hamburger Kunstsammlungen

Jb Hamburg Kstsamml — Jahrbuch der Hamburger Kunstsammlungen

Jb Hamburg Wiss Anstalten — Jahrbuch der Hamburgischen Wissenschaftlichen Anstalten

J Bhandarkar Res Inst — Journal of the Bhandarkar Research Institute

Jb Hist Ver Dillingen — Jahrbuch des Historischen Vereins Dillingen

Jb Hist Ver Mittelfranken — Jahrbuch des Historischen Vereins fuer Mittelfranken

Jb Hist Ver Noerdlingen & Umgebung — Jahrbuch des Historischen Vereins fuer Noerdlingen und Umgebung

JBHM — Jahrbuch des Bernischen Historischen Museums

JBHS — Journal. Bombay Historical Society

Jb HVFL — Jahrbuch des Historischen Vereins fuer das Fuerstentum Liechtenstein

JBHVMF — Jahresbericht. Historischer Verein fuer Mittelfranken

J Bibliogr Bibl Zeitgesch — Jahresbibliographie. Bibliothek fuer Zeitgeschichte, Weltkriegsbuecherei

J Bib Lit — Journal of Biblical Literature

J Bibl Lit — Journal of Biblical Literature
JBIC — Journal of Biocommunication
JBIC J Biol Inorg Chem — JBIC. Journal of Biological Inorganic Chemistry
JBI Dig — JBI (Jamaica Bauxite Institute) Digest
J Bihar Agric Coll — Journal. Bihar Agricultural College
J Bihar & Orissa Res Soc — Journal of the Bihar and Orissa Research Society
J Bihar Math Soc — Journal of the Bihar Mathematical Society
J Bihar Puravid Parishad — Journal of the Bihar Puravid Parishad
J Bihar Pur Par — Journal. Bihar Puravid Parishad
J Bihar RS — Journal. Bihar Research Society
JBIIA — Journal. British Institute of International Affairs
Jb Imkers — Jahrbuch der Imkers
Jb Inst Dt Ostarbeit Krakau — Jahrbuch des Instituts fuer Deutsche Ostarbeit (Kraukau)
Jb Inst Grenz U Auslandsstud — Jahrbuch des Instituts fuer Grenz- und Auslandsstudien
Jb Intern Vereing Gewerbl Rschutz — Jahrbuch der Internationalen Vereinigung fuer Gewerblichen Rechtsschutz
Jb Int R — Jahrbuch fuer Internationales und Auslaendisches Oeffentliches Recht
Jb Int Recht — Jahrbuch fuer Internationales Recht
J Bioact Compat Polym — Journal of Bioactive and Compatible Polymers
J Biochem — Journal of Biochemistry
J Biochem and Biophys Methods — Journal of Biochemical and Biophysical Methods
J Biochem Microbiol Tech Eng — Journal of Biochemical and Microbiological Technology and Engineering
J Biochem Microbiol Technol Eng — Journal of Biochemical and Microbiological Technology and Engineering
J Biochem Mol Biol — Journal of Biochemistry and Molecular Biology
J Biochem Mol Biol Biophys — Journal of Biochemistry, Molecular Biology, and Biophysics
J Biochem Mol Toxicol — Journal of Biochemical and Molecular Toxicology
J Biochem Organ — Journal of Biochemical Organization
J Biochem (Tokyo) — Journal of Biochemistry (Tokyo)
J Biochem Toxicol — Journal of Biochemical Toxicology
J Biocommun — Journal of Biocommunication
J Bioelectr — Journal of Bioelectricity
J Bioenerg — Journal of Bioenergetics [Later, Journal of Bioenergetics and Biomembranes]
J Bioenerg Biomembr — Journal of Bioenergetics and Biomembranes
J Bioeng — Journal of Bioengineering
J Bioeth — Journal of Bioethics
J Biogeogr — Journal of Biogeography
J Biol Board Can — Journal. Biological Board of Canada
J Biol (Bronx NY) — Journal of Biology (Bronx, NY)
J Biol Bucc — Journal de Biologie Buccale
J Biol Buccale — Journal de Biologie Buccale
J Biol Bucharest — Journal of Biology (Bucharest)
J Biol Chem — Journal of Biological Chemistry
J Biol Educ — Journal of Biological Education
J Biol Inorg Chem — Journal of Biological Inorganic Chemistry
J Biol Inst — Journal. Biological Institute
J Biol Med Exp — Journal de Biologie et de Medecine Experimentales
J Biol Med Nucl — Journal de Biologie et de Medecine Nucleaires
J Biol Moscow — Journal de Biologie (Moscow)
J Biological Ed — Journal of Biological Education
J Biol Osaka City Univ — Journal of Biology. Osaka City University
J Biol Phot — Journal. Biological Photographic Association
J Biol Phot Assn — Journal. Biological Photographic Association
J Biol Photogr — Journal of Biological Photography
J Biol Photogr Ass — Journal. Biological Photographic Association
J Biol Photogr Assoc — Journal. Biological Photographic Association
J Biol Phys — Journal of Biological Physics
J Biol Psychol — Journal of Biological Psychology
J Biol Regul Homeost Agents — Journal of Biological Regulators and Homeostatic Agents
J Biol Regul Homeostatic Agents — Journal of Biological Regulators and Homeostatic Agents
J Biol Res — Journal of Biological Research
J Biol Res Naples — Journal of Biological Research (Naples)
J Biol Response Mod — Journal of Biological Response Modifiers
J Biol Response Modif — Journal of Biological Response Modifiers
J Biol Rhythms — Journal of Biological Rhythms
J Biol Sci — Journal of Biological Sciences
J Biol Sci (Baghdad) — Journal of Biological Sciences (Baghdad)
J Biol Sci (Bombay) — Journal of Biological Sciences (Bombay)
J Biol Sci Res — Journal of Biological Sciences Research
J Biol Sci Res Publ — Journal of Biological Sciences Research Publication
J Biol Stan — Journal of Biological Standardization
J Biol Stand — Journal of Biological Standardization
J Biol Systems — Journal of Biological Systems
J Biolumin Chemilumin — Journal of Bioluminescence and Chemiluminescence
J Biomat Appl — Journal of Biomaterials Applications
J Biomater Appl — Journal of Biomaterials Applications
J Biomater Dent — Journal de Biomateriaux Dentaires
J Biomater Sci Polym Ed — Journal of Biomaterials Science. Polymer Edition
J Biomath — Journal of Biomathematics
J Biomech — Journal of Biomechanics
J Biomechan — Journal of Biomechanics
J Biomech Eng — Journal of Biomechanical Engineering
J Biomech Eng Trans ASME — Journal of Biomechanical Engineering. Transactions. ASME
J Biomed Eng — Journal of Biomedical Engineering
J Biomed Inform — Journal of Biomedical Informatics
J Biomed Mater Res — Journal of Biomedical Materials Research

J Biomed Mater Res Biomed Mater Symp — Journal of Biomedical Materials Research. Biomedical Materials Symposium
J Biomed Mater Res Symp — Journal of Biomedical Materials Research Symposium
J Biomed Mat Res — Journal of Biomedical Materials Research
J Biomed MR — Journal of Biomedical Materials Research
J Biomed Opt — Journal of Biomedical Optics
J Biomed Sci Basel — Journal of Biomedical Science (Basel)
J Biomed Syst — Journal of Biomedical Systems
J Biomol NMR — Journal of Biomolecular NMR [Nuclear Magnetic Resonance]
J Biomol Screening — Journal of Biomolecular Screening
J Biomol Struct & Dyn — Journal of Biomolecular Structure and Dynamics
J Biomol Struct Dyn — Journal of Biomolecular Structure and Dynamics
J Biopharm Sci — Journal of Biopharmaceutical Sciences
J Biopharm Stat — Journal of Biopharmaceutical Statistics
J Biophys Biochem Cytol — Journal of Biophysical and Biochemical Cytology
J Biophys Biomec — Journal de Biophysique et de Biomecanique
J Biophys Med Nucl — Journal de Biophysique et de Medecine Nucleaire
J Biophys Soc Jpn — Journal. Biophysical Society of Japan
J Biophys (Tokyo) — Journal of Biophysics (Tokyo)
J Biosci — Journal of Biosciences
J Biosci (Bangalore) — Journal of Biosciences (Bangalore)
J Biosoc — Journal of Biosocial Science
J Biosocial Sci — Journal of Biosocial Science
J Biosocial Sci Suppl — Journal of Biosocial Science. Supplement
J Biosoc Sc — Journal of Biosocial Science
J Biosoc Sci — Journal of Biosocial Science
J Biosoc Sci Suppl — Journal of Biosocial Science. Supplement
J Biotech — Journal of Biotechnology
J Biotechnol — Journal of Biotechnology
JbIR — Jahrbuch fuer den Internationalen Rechtsverkehr
J Birla Inst Tech and Sci (Pilani) — Journal. Birla Institute of Technology and Science (Pilani)
J Birla Inst Technol and Sci — Journal. Birla Institute of Technology and Science
J Birla Inst Technol Sci — Journal. Birla Institute of Technology and Science
J Birmingham Metall Soc — Journal. Birmingham Metallurgical Society
JBIRS — Journal. Bihar Research Society
JBIS — Journal. British Interplanetary Society
JBITD4 — Journal of Biotechnology
JbJTS — Jahresberichte. Juedisch-Theologisches Seminar "Frankelsche Stiftung"
Jb Junge Kunst — Jahrbuch fuer Junge Kunst
Jb Jungen Kst — Jahrbuch der Jungen Kunst
JBK — Jahresbriefe des Berneuchener Kreises
JBK — Journal. Bar Association of the State of Kansas
JBK — Journal of Banking and Finance
JbKAF — Jahrbuch fuer Kleinasiatische Forschung
JBKG — Jahrbuch fuer Brandenburgische Kirchengeschichte
Jb Kgl Preuss Kunstsamml — Jahrbuch der Koeniglich Preussischen Kunstsammlungen
JBKK — Jinbun Kenkyu
Jb Klass Philol — Jahrbuch fuer Klassische Philologie
Jb Kl F — Jahrbuch fuer Kleinasiatische Forschung
Jb K Mus Schon Kunst Antwerp — Jaarboek. Koninklijke Museum voor Schone Kunsten Antwerpen
JbKNA — Jaarboek. Koninklijke Nederlandsche Academie van Wetenschappen
Jb Koeln Geschver — Jahrbuch des Koelner Geschichtsvereins
Jb Koen Preuss Kstsamml — Jahrbuch der Koeniglich-Preussischen Kunstsammlungen
Jb Kon Mus S Kst — Jaarboek. Koninklijk Museum voor Schone Kunsten
Jb Kon Ned Akad Wet — Jaarboek van de Koninklijke Nederlandse Akademie van Wetenschappen
Jb Kon Oudhdkd Kring Antwerpen — Jaarboek van de Koninklijke Oudheidkundige Kring van Antwerpen
Jb Kon Vl Acad Wet Lett & S Kst Belgie — Jaarboek. Koninklijke Vlaamse Academie voor Wetenschappen, Letteren, en Schone Kunsten van Belgie
Jb Kreis Trier Saarburg — Jahrbuch Kreis Trier-Saarburg
Jb Ksr Dt Archaeol Inst — Jahrbuch des Kaiserlichen Deutschen Archaeologischen Instituts
Jb Ksr Koen Zent Komm Erforsch & Erhaltung Kst & Hist Dkml — Jahrbuch der K.-K. [Kaiserlich-Koeniglichen] Zentral-Kommission fuer Erforschung und Erhaltung der Kunst- und Historischen Denkmale
Jb Kst & Kstpf Schweiz — Jahrbuch fuer Kunst und Kunstpflege der Schweiz
Jb Kstgesch — Jahrbuch fuer Kunstgeschichte
Jb Kstgesch Bundesdkmlamt — Jahrbuch der Kunstgeschichte des Bundesdenkmalamtes
Jb Ksthist Inst — Jahrbuch des Kunsthistorischen Institutes
Jb Ksthist Inst Graz — Jahrbuch des Kunsthistorischen Institutes der Universitaet Graz
Jb Ksthist Inst Ksr Koen Zent Komm Dkmlpf — Jahrbuch des Kunsthistorischen Institutes der K.-K. [Kaiserlich-Koeniglichen] Zentral-Kommission fuer Denkmalpflege
Jb Ksthist Inst Staatsdkmlamt — Jahrbuch des Kunsthistorischen Institutes des Staatsdenkmalamtes
Jb Ksthist Samml Allhoech Ksrhaus — Jahrbuch der Kunsthistorischen Sammlungen des Allerhoechsten Kaiserhauses
Jb Ksthist Samml Wien — Jahrbuch der Kunsthistorischen Sammlungen in Wien
Jb Kstsamml Allhoech Ksrhaus — Jahrbuch der Kunstsammlungen des Allerhoechsten Kaiserhauses
Jb Kstwiss — Jahrbuch fuer Kunstwissenschaft
Jb Kstwiss — Jahrbuecher fuer Kunstwissenschaft
Jb KS (Wien) — Jahrbuch. Kunsthistorische Sammlungen (Wien)
Jb Kult Gesch Slaven — Jahrbuecher fuer Kultur und Geschichte der Slaven
Jb Kunsthist Samml (Wien) — Jahrbuch. Kunsthistorische Sammlungen (Wien)
Jb Kunstwiss — Jahrbuch fuer Kunstwissenschaft

Jb Ku Samml Bad Wuert — Jahrbuch. Staatlichen Kunstsammlungen in Baden-Wuerttemberg

JbKVA — Jaarboek. Koninklijke Vlaamse Academie voor Taal-en Letterkunde

JbKVAW — Jaarboek. Koninklijke Vlaamse Academie voor Wetenschappen

JbKW — Jahrbuch fuer Kunstwissenschaft

JBL — Jahrbuch fuer Brandenburgische Landesgeschichte

JBL — Journal of Biblical Literature

JBL — Journal of Business Law

JBI — Juedische Blaetter

JBI — Juristische Blaetter

J Black Poetry — Journal of Black Poetry

JBlackS — Journal of Black Studies

J Black St — Journal of Black Studies

J Black Stud — Journal of Black Studies

J Black Studies — Journal of Black Studies

Jb Landeshptstadt Halle — Jahrbuch der Landeshauptstadt Halle

Jb Landesknd Niederoesterreich — Jahrbuch fuer Landeskunde von Niederoesterreich

Jb Leipzig Bienenztg — Jahrbuch. Leipziger Bienenzeitung

JBLG — Jahrbuch fuer Brandenburgische Landesgeschichte

JBLG — Jahresberichte. Berliner Literatur Gesellschaft

Jb Liechtenstein — Jahrbuch des Historischen Vereins fuer des Fuerstentum Liechtenstein

Jb Liechtenstein Kstges — Jahrbuch der Liechtensteinischen Kunstgesellschaft

JbLitHymn — Jahrbuch fuer Liturgik und Hymnologie

Jb Liturgik Hymnologie — Jahrbuch fuer Liturgik und Hymnologie

Jb Liturgwiss — Jahrbuch der Liturgiewissenschaft

Jb LKNOe — Jahrbuch fuer Landeskunde von Niederoesterreich

JBLMS — Journal of Biblical Literature. Monograph Series

JbLN — Jahrbuch fuer Landeskunde von Niederoesterreich

JbLW — Jahrbuch fuer Litergiewissenschaft

JBM — Jahrbuch. Berliner Museen

JBM — Jahrbuch. Bernisches Historische Museum

JBM — Jahrbuch fuer das Bistum (Mainz)

JBM — Journal Botanique de l'URSS (Moscow)

JBM — Journal of Organizational Behavior Management

Jb Maatsch Ned Lettknd Leiden — Jaarboek van de Maatschappij der Nederlandse Letterkunde te Leiden

Jb Maerkischen Mus — Jahrbuch des Maerkischen Museums

Jb (Mainz) — Jahrbuch. Akademie der Wissenschaften und der Literatur (Mainz)

Jb Max Planck Ges Foerderung Wiss — Jahrbuch der Max-Planck-Gesellschaft zur Foerderung der Wissenschaften

Jb Max Planck Ges Foerd Wiss — Jahrbuch. Max-Planck-Gesellschaft zur Foerderung der Wissenschaften

JB Meck — Jahrbuch. Bodendenkmalpflege in Mecklenburg

Jb Mij Nederl Letterkde — Jaarboek van de Maatschappij der Nederlandsche Letterkunde te Leiden

Jb Mijnw Ned Ind — Jaarboek van het Mijnwezen in Nederlandsch Oost-Indie

Jb Miner — Jahrbuch fuer Mineralogie, Geognosie, Geologie, und Petrefaktenkunde

Jb Miss — Jahrbuch fuer Mission

JBM J Bras Med — JBM. Jornal Brasileiro de Medicina

JBMK — Jahrbuch der Bayerischen Missionskonferenz

JBMNA — Journal de Biologie et de Medecine Nucleaires

JbMNL — Jaarboek. Maatschappij der Nederlandsche Letterkunde te Leiden

Jb M P — Jahrbuch der Musikbibliothek Peters

JbMu — Jahrbuch. Marburger Universitaetsbund

JB (Muenchen) — Jahrbuch. Bayerische Akademie der Wissenschaften (Muenchen)

Jb Munt & Penningknd — Jaarboek voor Munt-en Penningkunde

Jb Museum Voelkerkde Leipzig — Jahrbuch des Museums fuer Voelkerkunde zu Leipzig

Jb Musikbibl Peters — Jahrbuch der Musikbibliothek Peters

Jb Musik Volks-u Voelkerk — Jahrbuch fuer Musikalische Volks- und Voelkerkunde

Jb Mus Vlkerknd Leipzig — Jahrbuch des Museums fuer Voelkerkunde zu Leipzig

Jb Mus Voelkerkunde zu Leipzig — Jahrbuch des Museums fuer Voelkerkunde zu Leipzig

Jb Mus Volkerk Lpz — Jahrbuch des Museums fuer Volkerkunde zu Leipzig

Jb M Volks Volkerkunde — Jahrbuch fuer Musikalische Volks- und Voelkerkunde

JBMz — Jahrbuch fuer das Bistum Mainz

JBN — Judaica Book News

Jb Nationaloekon Statist — Jahrbuecher fuer Nationaloekonomie und Statistik

Jb Nationaloekon und Statis — Jahrbuecher fuer Nationaloekonomie und Statistik

Jb NG — Jahrbuch fuer Numismatik und Geldgeschichte

JBNHS — Journal. Bombay Natural History Society

Jb Niftarlake — Jaarboekje Niftarlake

JbNo — Jahrbuch fuer Landeskunde von Niederoesterreich

JBNSA — Journal. British Nuclear Energy Society

JbNsGV — Jahresbericht des Niedersaechsischen Geologischen Vereins

Jb Num — Jahrbuch fuer Numismatik und Geldgeschichte

Jb Numi & Geldgesch — Jahrbuch fuer Numismatik und Geldgeschichte

JBO — Journal of Buyouts and Acquisitions

JBO — Journal of Economic Behavior and Organization

J Board Agric (GB) — Journal. Board of Agriculture (Great Britain)

J Board Dir Am Soc Civ Eng — Journal. Board of Direction. American Society of Civil Engineers

J Board Greenkeeping Res — Journal. Board of Greenkeeping Research

Jb Oberoesterreich Musver — Jahrbuch des Oberoesterreichischen Musealvereines

Jb Oberoesterreich Musver Ges Landesknd — Jahrbuch des O[ber]-Oe[sterreichischen] Musealvereines. Gesellschaft fuer Landeskunde

JbOeBG — Jahrbuch der Oesterreichischen Byzantinistik Gesellschaft

Jb Oe Byz — Jahrbuch der Oesterreichischen Byzantinistik

Jb Oeffentl R — Jahrbuch des Oeffentlichen Rechts

Jb Oeff Recht — Jahrbuch des Oeffentlichen Rechts der Gegenwart

Jb Oeff Rechts — Jahrbuch des Oeffentlichen Rechts der Gegenwart

Jb Oesterr Byzant Ges — Jahrbuch der Oesterreichischen Byzantinischen Gesellschaft

Jb Oesterreich Bundesdkmlamt — Jahrbuch des Oesterreichischen Bundesdenkmalamtes

Jb Oesterreich Byz — Jahrbuch der Oesterreichischen Byzantinistik

Jb Oesterreich Byz Ges — Jahrbuch der Oesterreichischen Byzantinischen Gesellschaft

Jb Oesterreich Kstgesch — Jahrbuch fuer Oesterreichische Kunstgeschichte

Jb Oesterreich Kultgesch — Jahrbuch fuer Oesterreichische Kulturgeschichte

Jb Oldenburger Muensterland — Jahrbuch fuer das Oldenburger Muensterland

J Bombay Branch Royal Asiat Soc — Journal of the Bombay Branch of the Royal Asiatic Society

J Bombay Hist Soc — Journal of the Bombay Historical Society

J Bombay Nat Hist Soc — Journal. Bombay Natural History Society

J Bom Natur Hist Soc — Journal. Bombay Natural History Society

J Bone (Am V) — Journal of Bone and Joint Surgery (American Volume)

J Bone (Br V) — Journal of Bone and Joint Surgery (British Volume)

J Bone Joint Surg — Journal of Bone and Joint Surgery

J Bone Joint Surg (Am) — Journal of Bone and Joint Surgery (American Volume)

J Bone Joint Surg (Br) — Journal of Bone and Joint Surgery (British Volume)

J Bone Jt Surg — Journal of Bone and Joint Surgery

J Bone Jt Surg (Am Vol) — Journal of Bone and Joint Surgery (American Volume)

J Bone Jt Surg (Br Vol) — Journal of Bone and Joint Surgery (British Volume)

J Bone Miner Metab — Journal of Bone and Mineral Metabolism

J Bone Miner Metab Jpn Ed — Journal of Bone and Mineral Metabolism (Japanese Edition)

J Bone Miner Res — Journal of Bone and Mineral Research

Jb OOe MV — Jahrbuch des Oberoesterreichischen Musealvereins

Jb Oranjeboom — Jaarboek de Oranjeboom

Jb Oranjeboom — Jaarboek van de Geschieden Oudheidkundige Kring van stad en land van Breda de Oranjeboom

JBORS — Journal. Bihar and Orissa Research Society [Later, Journal. Bihar Research Society]

Jb Ostas Kunst — Jahrbuch der Ostasiatischen Kunst

Jb Ostdt Volkskde — Jahrbuch fuer Ostdeutsche Volkskunde

Jb Osterreich Kultur Gesch — Jahrbuch fuer Oesterreichische Kulturgeschichte

Jb Osteur Inst Breslau — Jahrbuch des Osteuropa-Instituts zu Breslau

J Boston Soc Civ Eng — Journal. Boston Society of Civil Engineers

J Boston Soc Civ Eng Sect ASCE — Journal. Boston Society of Civil Engineers Section. American Society of Civil Engineers

J Boston Soc Civil Engin — Journal of the Boston Society of Civil Engineers

Jb Ostrecht — Jahrbuch fuer Ostrecht

J Bot Acad Sci RSS Ukr — Journal Botanique. Academie des Sciences. RSS d'Ukraine

J Bot Agric — Journal de Botanique, Appliquee a l'Agriculture, a la Pharmacie, a la Medecine,et aux Arts

J Bot Br Foreign — Journal of Botany. British and Foreign

J Bot Hooker — Journal of Botany (W. J. Hooker, Editor)

J Bot Lond — Journal of Botany, British and Foreign (London)

J Bot Schrader — Journal fuer die Botanik (Goettingen) (Edited by H. A. Schrader)

J Bot Soc S Afr — Journal. Botanical Society of South Africa

J Bot Soc South Africa — Journal. Botanical Society of South Africa

J Bot UAR — Journal of Botany. United Arab Republic

J Bot URSS — Journal Botanique de l'URSS

Jb Oud Utrecht — Jaarboek Oud-Utrecht

J Bowman Gray Sch Med Wake For Coll — Journal. Bowman Gray School of Medicine. Wake Forest College

Jb P — Jahrbuch der Musik Bibliothek Peters

JBPAA — Journal. Biological Photographic Association

Jb Peters — Jahrbuch Peters

Jb Pf Kst — Jahrbuch zur Pflege der Kuenste

JBPHB — Journal of Biological Physics

Jb Philos Spekul Theol — Jahrbuch fuer Philosophie und Spekulative Theologie

Jb Politik Auslandskde — Jahrbuch der Weltpolitik. Band 1. Jahrbuch fuer Politik und Auslandskunde

Jb Praehist Ethnog Kst — Jahrbuch fuer Praehistorische und Ethnographische Kunst

Jb Preuss Geol Ldsanst — Jahrbuch der Preussischen Geologischen Landesanstalt

Jb Preuss Kstsamml — Jahrbuch der Preussischen Kunstsammlungen

Jb Preuss Kultbes — Jahrbuch Preussischer Kulturbesitz

Jb Pr Ks — Jahrbuch der Preussischen Kunstsammlung

JBPSA — Jornal Brasileiro de Psiquiatria

JbPsN — Jahrbuch fuer Psychiatrie und Neurologie

Jb Psychiatr Neurol — Jahrbuch fuer Psychiatrie und Neurologie

JBR — Journal of Bank Research

JBR — Journal of Bible and Religion

J Br A Ass — Journal. British Archaeological Association

J Brain Sci — Journal of Brain Science

JBRAS — Journal. Bombay Branch. Royal Asiatic Society

J Bras Doencas Torac — Jornal Brasileiro de Doencas Toracicas

J Bras Ginecol — Jornal Brasileiro de Ginecologia

J Brasil — Jornal do Brasil

J Bras Med — Jornal Brasileiro de Medicina

J Bras Nefrol — Jornal Brasileiro de Nefrologia

J Bras Neurol — Jornal Brasileiro de Neurologia

J Bras Patol — Jornal Brasileiro de Patologia

J Bras Psiquiatr — Jornal Brasileiro de Psiquiatria

J Br Astron Assoc — Journal. British Astronomical Association

J Bras Urol — Jornal Brasileiro de Urologia

J Br Boot Shoe Instn — Journal. British Boot and Shoe Institution

J Br Ceram Soc — Journal. British Ceramic Society

J Br Dent Assoc — Journal. British Dental Association

Jb Rechnung Hist Mus (Basel) — Jahresberichte und Rechnungen. Historisches Museum (Basel)

J Br Endod Soc — Journal. British Endodontic Society

J Brew — Journal of Brewing

J Brew Soc Jpn — Journal. Brewing Society of Japan

J Br Fire Serv Assoc — Journal. British Fire Services Association

J Br Grassl — Journal. British Grassland Society

J Br Grassld Soc — Journal. British Grassland Society

J Br Grassl Soc — Journal. British Grassland Society

Jb RGZ — Jahrbuch des Roemisch-Germanischen Zentral Museums Mainz

Jb Rhein Dkmlpf — Jahrbuch der Rheinischen Denkmalpflege

Jb Rhein Ver Dkmlpf & Landschaftsschutz — Jahrbuch des Rheinischen Vereins fuer Denkmalpflege und Landschaftsschutz

J Br Inst Radio Eng — Journal. British Institution of Radio Engineers

J Brit Archaeol Ass 3 Ser — Journal. British Archaeological Association. Series 3

J Brit Archaeol Assoc — Journal of the British Archaeological Association

J Brit Archaeol Soc — Journal of the British Archaeological Society

J Brit Arch Ass — Journal. British Archaeological Association

J Brit Astron Ass — Journal. British Astronomical Association

J Brit Ceram Soc — Journal. British Ceramic Society

J Brit Dental Assoc — Journal. British Dental Association

J Brit Guiana Mus & Zoo — Journal of the British Guiana Museum and Zoo

J Brit Inst Int Affairs — Journal. British Institute of International Affairs

J Brit Interplanet Soc — Journal. British Interplanetary Society

J Brit Nucl Energy Soc — Journal. British Nuclear Energy Society

J Brit Ship Res Ass — Journal. British Ship Research Association

J Brit Soc Master Glass Paint — Journal. British Society of Master Glass Painters

J Brit Soc Phenomenol — Journal. British Society for Phenomenology

J Brit Stud — Journal of British Studies

J Br KG — Jahrbuch fuer Brandenburgische Kirchengeschichte

JBRM — Journal of Biological Response Modifiers

JBRMA — Jornal Brasileiro de Medicina

JBRNA — Jornal Brasileiro de Neurologia

Jb'r Nat-Oekon Statist — Jahrbuecher fuer National-Oekonomie und Statistik

J Br Nucl E — Journal. British Nuclear Energy Society

J Br Nucl Energy Soc — Journal. British Nuclear Energy Society

J Broadcast — Journal of Broadcasting [*Later, Journal of Broadcasting and Electronic Media*]

J Broadcasting — Journal of Broadcasting [*Later, Journal of Broadcasting and Electronic Media*]

J Broadcst — Journal of Broadcasting and Electronic Media

Jb Roem Ger Zentmus — Jahrbuch des Roemisch-Germanischen Zentralmuseums

J Bromeliad Soc — Journal. Bromeliad Society

JBRS — Journal. Bihar Research Society

JBRS — Journal. Burma Research Society

J Br Soc Ph — Journal. British Society for Phenomenology

J Br Stud — Journal of British Studies

Jb Ruhr U Bochum — Jahrbuch der Ruhr-Universitaet Bochum

J Br Waterworks Assoc — Journal. British Waterworks Association

J Br Wood Preserv Assoc — Journal. British Wood Preserving Association

J Bryol — Journal of Bryology

JBS — Journal of Applied Behavioral Science

JBS — Journal of British Studies

JBS — Journal of Business Research

JBS — Journal of Byelorussian Studies

Jb Sal St — Jahrbuch fuer Salesianische Studien

Jb Salzburg Mus Carolino Augusteum — Jahrbuch des Salzburger Museums Carolino Augusteum

JbSAW — Jahrbuch. Saechsische Akademie der Wissenschaften zu Leipzig

Jb Schiffbautechn Ges — Jahrbuch der Schiffbautechnischen Gesellschaft

Jb Schles Kirche Kirchengesch — Jahrbuch fuer Schlesische Kirche und Kirchengeschichte

Jb Schles Univ Breslau — Jahrbuch der Schlesischen Friedrich-Wilhelms-Universitaet zu Breslau

Jb Schule Weisht — Jahrbuch der Schule der Weisheit

Jb Schweiz Ges Ur Fruehgesch — Jahrbuch. Schweizerische Gesellschaft fuer Ur- und Fruehgeschichte

Jb Schweiz Inst Kstwiss — Jahrbuch der Schweizerischen Instituts fuer Kunstwissenschaft

Jb Schw Ges Urgesch — Jahrbuch der Schweizerischen Gesellschaft fuer Urgeschichte

Jb Schw Ges Urgesch — Jahrbuch. Schweizerische Gesellschaft fuer Ur- und Fruehgeschichte

JBSDD6 — Journal of Biomolecular Structure and Dynamics

Jb SGU — Jahrbuch der Schweizerischen Gesellschaft fuer Urgeschichte

JbSh — Jahrbuch der Deutschen Shakespeare-Gesellschaft

JbShG — Jahrbuch. Shakespeare Gesellschaft

JbSL — Jahrbuch der Stadt Linz

JBSMGP — Journal. British Society of Master Glass-Painters

J Bsns — Journal of Business

J Bsns Ed — Journal of Business Education

J Bsns Educ — Journal of Business Education

Jb Sozialwiss — Jahrbuch fuer Sozialwissenschaft

Jb Soz -Wiss — Jahrbuch fuer Sozialwissenschaft

JBSP — Journal. British Society for Phenomenology

JBSPE9 — Journal of Biological Sciences Research Publication

J B Speed A Mus Bull — J. B. Speed Art Museum Bulletin

JBSQ — Jacob Boehme Society Quarterly

JBSREF — Journal of Biological Sciences Research

Jb Staatl Kstsamml Baden Wuerttemberg — Jahrbuch der Staatlichen Kunstsammlungen in Baden-Wuerttemberg

Jb Staatl Kstsamml Dresden — Jahrbuch der Staatlichen Kunstsammlungen Dresden

Jb Staatl Mus Mineral & Geol Dresden — Jahrbuch des Staatlichen Museums fuer Mineralogie und Geologie zu Dresden

Jb Stad Brugge Stedl Mus — Jaarboek. Stad Brugge Stedelijke Musea

Jb Staedt Mus Voelkerkde — Jahrbuch des Staedtischen Museums fuer Voelkerkunde

Jb Staedt Mus Volk Lpz — Jahrbuch des Staedtischen Museums fuer Voelkerkunde zu Leipzig

JBSTB — Journal of Biological Standardization

Jb Stift Klosterneuburg — Jahrbuch des Stiftes Klosterneuburg

Jb Stift Preuss Kul Bes — Jahrbuch der Stiftung Preussischer Kulturbesitz

Jb Stift Preuss Kultbesitz — Jahrbuch der Stiftung Preussischer Kulturbesitz

Jb St Kunstsamml (Dresden) — Jahrbuch. Staatliche Kunstsammlungen (Dresden)

J Bt — Journal of Botany, British and Foreign

JBT — Journal of Business Ethics

JBTC — Iowa Journal of Business and Technical Communication

JBTS — Journal. Buddhist Text and Anthropological Society

JBU — Journal of Business

JBU — Journal of Business Research

JBUA — Journal. Bombay University. Arts

Jbuch — Jahrbuch ueber die Fortschritte der Mathematik

Jbuch Heidelberger Akad Wiss — Jahrbuch. Heidelberger Akademie der Wissenschaften

Jb u Ersch Ger Lit — Jahresberichte ueber die Erscheinungem auf dem Gebiete der Germanischen Literaturgeschichte

J Build Mater Shanghai — Journal of Building Materials (Shanghai)

J Burma Res Soc — Journal of the Burma Research Society

J Burn Care Rehabil — Journal of Burn Care and Rehabilitation

J Bus — Journal of Business

J Busan Med Coll — Journal. Busan Medical College

J Bus Commun — Journal of Business Communication

J Bus Communic — Journal of Business Communication

J Bus Econom Statist — Journal of Business and Economic Statistics

J Bus Ed — Journal of Business Education

J Bus Ethics — Journal of Business Ethics

J Busin — Journal of Business

J Bus L — Journal of Business Law

J Bus Res — Journal of Business Research

J Bus Research — Journal of Business Research

J Bus Strategy — Journal of Business Strategy

J Butler Soc — Journal. Butler Society

JBV — Juedische Buch Vereinigung

Jb Ver Altertfreund Rheinlande — Jahrbuecher des Vereins von Altertumsfreunden im Rheinlande

Jb Ver Augsburg Bistumsgesch — Jahrbuch des Vereins fuer Augsburger Bistumsgeschichte

Jb Verband Dt Mus Tschech Repub — Jahrbuch des Verbandes der Deutschen Museen in der Tschechoslowakischen Republik

Jb Ver Christ Kst — Jahrbuch des Vereins fuer Christliche Kunst

Jb Ver Christ Kst Muenchen — Jahrbuch des Vereins fuer Christliche Kunst in Muenchen

Jb Ver Gesch Stadt Wien — Jahrbuch des Vereins fuer Geschichte der Stadt Wien

Jb Ver Gesch Wein — Jahrbuch des Vereins fuer Geschichte der Stadt Wien

Jb Ver Heimatknd Kreis Merzig — Jahrbuch des Vereins fuer Heimatkunde Kreis Merzig

Jb Verkehrswiss — Jahrbuch fuer Verkehrswissenschaft

Jb Ver Niederdt Sprachforsch — Jahrbuch des Vereins fuer Niederdeutsche Sprachforschung

Jb Ver Oranje Nassau Mus — Jaarboek. Vereniging Oranje-Nassau Museum

Jb Ver Oudhdknd & Hist (Geschknd) Kring Belgie — Jaarboeken. Vereniging van Oudheidkundige en Historische (Geschiedkundige) Kringen van Belgie

Jb Ver Vgl St R B Nedl — Jaarboek. Vereniging voor de Vergelijkende Studie van het Recht vanBelgie en Nederland

Jb V f Niederd Sprachf — Jahrbuch des Vereins fuer Niederdeutsche Sprachforschung

Jb VGSW — Jahrbuch des Vereins fuer Geschichte der Stadt Wien

JbVH — Jahrbuch fuer Volkskunde der Heimatvertriebenen

Jb Vlksknd — Jahrbuch fuer Volkskunde

Jb Volkskde Heimatvertriebenen — Jahrbuch fuer Volkskunde der Heimatvertriebenen

Jb Volksk Kulturgesch — Jahrbuch fuer Volkskunde und Kulturgeschichte

Jb Volksliedf — Jahrbuch fuer Volksliedforschung

Jb Vorarlberg — Jahrbuch des Vorarlberger Landesmuseumsvereins

Jb Vorarlberg Landesmusver — Jahrbuch des Vorarlberger Landesmuseumsvereines

JBW — Jahrbuch der Biblischen Wissenschaft

JbW — Jahrbuch fuer Wirtschaftsgeschichte

JBW — Journal of Basic Writing

Jb Weichsel Warthe — Jahrbuch Weichsel-Warthe

Jb Wels — Jahrbuch des Musealvereines Wels

Jb Weltpolit — Jahrbuch der Weltpolitik

JbWerkKaTNed — Jaarboek. Werkgenootschap van Katholieke Theologen in Nederland

Jb Wien Goethe Ver — Jahrbuch des Wiener Goethe-Vereins

Jb Wirtschaftsgesch — Jahrbuch fuer Wirtschaftsgeschichte

Jb Wirtsch -Gesch — Jahrbuch fuer Wirtschaftsgeschichte

Jb Wirtsch Osteuropas — Jahrbuch der Wirtschaft Osteuropas

Jb Wiss Prakt Tierzucht — Jahrbuch fuer Wissenschaftliche und Praktische Tierzucht

Jb Wiss Prakt Zuechtgskde — Jahrbuch fuer Wissenschaftliche und Praktische Zuechtungskunde

JbxO — Jahrbucher fuer Geschichte Osteuropas

J Byelorus Stud — Journal of Byelorussian Studies

JByelS — Journal of Byelorussian Studies

JBZ — Mid-Atlantic Journal of Business

Jb Zentinst Kstgesch — Jahrbuch des Zentralinstituts fuer Kunstgeschichte

Jb Z Mus (Mainz) — Jahrbuch. Roemisch-Germanisches Zentralmuseum (Mainz)

Jb Ztrkomm Erhaltg Dttums — Jahrbuch der Zentralkommission fuer Erhaltung des Deutschtums
JC — Jazykovedny Casopis
JC — Jewish Chronicle
JC — Journal de Conchyliologie
JC — Journal of Chromatography
JC — Journal of Church Music
JC — Journal of Communication
JC — Journal of Conchology
JC — Joven Cuba
JC — Jus Canonicum
JCA — Journal of Color and Appearance
JCA — Journal of Consumer Affairs
JCA — Journal of Contemporary Asia
J CA & Gt Basin Anthropol — Journal of California and Great Basin Anthropology
JCACDM — Journal of Carbohydrate Chemistry
J Cact Succ Soc Amer — Journal. Cactus and Succulent Society of America
J Caisses Epargne — Journal des Caisses d'Epargne
JCAL — Jurisprudence de la Cour d'Appel de Liege
J Calif Dent Assoc — Journal. California Dental Association
J Calif Gt Basin Anthrop — Journal of California and Great Basin Anthropology
J Calif Gt Basin Anthrop Pap Ling — Journal of California and Great Basin Anthropology Papers in Linguistics
J Calif Hortic Soc — Journal. California Horticultural Society
J Calif Hort Soc — Journal. California Horticultural Society
J Calif Rare Fruit Grow — Journal. California Rare Fruit Growers
J Calif State Dent Assoc — Journal. California State Dental Association
J Camborne Sch Mines — Journal. Camborne School of Mines
J Camera Club (London) — Journal. Camera Club (London)
J Canad Dent A — Journal. Canadian Dental Association
J Can A Hist — Journal of Canadian Art History
J Can Anaesth Soc — Journal. Canadian Anaesthetists' Society
J Can Anesth — Journal Canadien d'Anesthesie
J Can Art Hist — Journal of Canadian Art History
J Can Assoc Radiol — Journal. Canadian Association of Radiologists
J Can Ath Ther Assoc — Journal. Canadian Athletic Therapists Association
J Can Ba — Journal. Canadian Bar Association
J Can B Ass'n — Journal. Canadian Bar Association
J Can Biochim — Journal Canadien de Biochimie
J Can Bot — Journal Canadien de Botanique
J Can Ceram Soc — Journal. Canadian Ceramic Society
J Cancer Cent Niigata Hosp — Journal. Cancer Center. Niigata Hospital
J Cancer Educ — Journal of Cancer Education
J Cancer Res — Journal of Cancer Research
J Cancer Res Clin Oncol — Journal of Cancer Research and Clinical Oncology
J Cancer Res Comm Univ Sydney — Journal. Cancer Research Committee. University of Sydney
J Can Ch H — Journal. Canadian Church Historical Society
J Can Chim — Journal Canadien de Chimie
J Can Chir — Journal Canadien de Chirurgie
J Can Chiro Assoc — Journal. Canadian Chiropractic Association
JC & ED — Journal of Chemical and Engineering Data
J Can Dent Assoc — Journal. Canadian Dental Association
J Can Diet Ass — Journal. Canadian Dietetic Association
J Can Diet Assoc — Journal. Canadian Dietetic Association
JC and UL — Journal of College and University Law
J Can Fic — Journal of Canadian Fiction
J Can Fict — Journal of Canadian Fiction
J Can Genet Cytol — Journal Canadien de Genetique et de Cytologie
J Can Inst Food Sci Technol — Journal. Canadian Institute of Food Science and Technology
J Can Microbiol — Journal Canadien de Microbiologie
J Can Min Inst — Journal. Canadian Mining Institute
J Can Ophtalmol — Journal Canadien d'Ophtalmologie
J Can Otolaryngol — Journal Canadien d'Otolaryngologie
J Can Petrol Technol — Journal of Canadian Petroleum Technology
J Can Pet T — Journal of Canadian Petroleum Technology
J Can Pet Technol — Journal of Canadian Petroleum Technology
J Can Pharm Hosp — Journal Canadien de la Pharmacie Hospitaliere
J Can Phys — Journal Canadien de Physique
J Can Physiol Pharmacol — Journal Canadien de Physiologie et Pharmacologie
J Can Psychiatr Assoc — Journal. Canadian Psychiatric Association
J Can Rech For — Journal Canadien de la Recherche Forestiere
JCanS — Journal of Canadian Studies
J Can Sci Appl Sport — Journal Canadien des Sciences Appliquees au Sport
J Can Sci Halieutiques Aquat — Journal Canadien des Sciences Halieutiques et Aquatiques
J Can Sci Neurol — Journal Canadien des Sciences Neurologiques
J Can Sci Sport — Journal Canadien des Sciences du Sport
J Can Sci Terre — Journal Canadien des Sciences de la Terre
J Can Soc Forensic Sci — Journal. Canadian Society of Forensic Science
J Can Stud — Journal of Canadian Studies
J Can Studies — Journal of Canadian Studies
J Cant Bot Soc — Journal. Canterbury Botanical Society
J Can Zool — Journal Canadien de Zoologie
J Capillary Electrophor — Journal of Capillary Electrophoresis
J Cap Inst Med — Journal. Capital Institute of Medicine
J Cap Mgmt — Journal of Capacity Management
JCARA — Journal. Canadian Association of Radiologists
J Carb-Nucl — Journal of Carbohydrates-Nucleosides-Nucleotides
J Carbohyd-Nucl-Nucl — Journal of Carbohydrates-Nucleosides-Nucleotides
J Carbohydr Chem — Journal of Carbohydrate Chemistry
J Carbohydr-Nucleosides-Nucleotides — Journal of Carbohydrates-Nucleosides-Nucleotides
J Card Fail — Journal of Cardiac Failure

J Card Failure — Journal of Cardiac Failure
J Cardiac Rehab — Journal of Cardiac Rehabilitation
J Cardiogr — Journal of Cardiography
J Cardiol — Journal of Cardiology
J Cardiopul Rehab — Journal of Cardiopulmonary Rehabilitation
J Cardiothorac Vasc Anesth — Journal of Cardiothoracic and Vascular Anesthesia
J Cardiovasc Electrophysiol — Journal of Cardiovascular Electrophysiology
J Cardiovasc Magn Reson — Journal of Cardiovascular Magnetic Resonance
J Cardiovasc Med — Journal of Cardiovascular Medicine
J Cardiovasc Nurs — Journal of Cardiovascular Nursing
J Cardiovasc Pharmacol — Journal of Cardiovascular Pharmacology
J Cardiovasc Pharmacol Ther — Journal of Cardiovascular Pharmacology and Therapeutics
J Cardiovasc Risk — Journal of Cardiovascular Risk
J Cardiovasc Surg — Journal of Cardiovascular Surgery
J Cardiovasc Surg (Torino) — Journal of Cardiovascular Surgery (Torino)
J Cardiovasc Ultrason — Journal of Cardiovascular Ultrasonography
J Cardiovas Surg — Journal of Cardiovascular Surgery
J Cardpulm Rehabil — Journal of Cardiopulmonary Rehabilitation
J Card Surg — Journal of Cardiovascular Surgery
J Car Ed — Journal of Career Education
JCAS — Journal. Catgut Society
JCAS — Journal. Royal Central Asian Society
J Catal — Journal of Catalysis
J Catal (Dalian) — Journal of Catalysis (Dalian)
J Catalysis — Journal of Catalysis
J Cat & Class — Journal of Cataloging and Classification
J Cataract Refract Surg — Journal of Cataract and Refractive Surgery
J Cataract Refract Surg — Journal of Cataract and Refractive Surgery
JCATD — Journal of Computer-Assisted Tomography
J Cathol Med Coll — Journal. Catholic Medical College
J Cathol Nurses Guild Engl Wales — Journal. Catholic Nurses Guild of England and Wales
JCAUD8 — Journal of Cardiovascular Ultrasonography
J Cave Karst Stud — Journal of Cave and Karst Studies
J CAYC — Journal. Canadian Association for Young Children
JCB — Journal of Commercial Bank Lending
JCB — Journal of Contemporary Business
JCB — Journal of Creative Behavior
JCB — Jurisprudence Commerciale de Bruxelles
JCB — Kansas Judicial Council. Bulletin
JCBADL — Biomedical Applications
JCBAS — Journal. Ceylon Branch. Royal Asiatic Society
JCBF — Journal of Cerebral Blood Flow and Metabolism
JCBI — Journal of Computer-Based Instruction
JCBI — Juedisches Zentralblatt
JCBMDN — Journal of Cerebral Blood Flow and Metabolism
JCBSD7 — Journal of Cellular Biochemistry. Supplement
JCC — Journal of Carbohydrate Chemistry
JCC — Journal of Christian Camping
JCC — Journal of Computational Chemistry
JCCBD — Journal of Clinical Chemistry and Clinical Biochemistry
JCCHS — Journal. Canadian Church Historical Society
JCCMB — Journal of Coordination Chemistry
JCCP — Journal of Commonwealth and Comparative Politics
JCCP — Journal of Cross-Cultural Psychology
JCCS — Journal. Canadian Ceramic Society
JCCSA — Journal. Canadian Ceramic Society
JCDAA — Journal. Canadian Dental Association
JCDEA — Journal. California State Dental Association
JCDIA — Journal of Communication Disorders
JCDTBI — Journal. Chemical Society. Dalton Transactions
JCDVA — Journal of Child Development
JCE — Journal of Chemical Education
JCE — Journal of Christian Education
JCE — Journal of Comparative Economics
JCEA — Journal of Central European Affairs
JCEBD — Journal of Cellular Biochemistry
JCEG — Journal of Clinical and Experimental Gerontology
J Cell Biochem — Journal of Cellular Biochemistry
J Cell Biochem Suppl — Journal of Cellular Biochemistry. Supplement
J Cell Biol — Journal of Cell Biology
J Cell Comp Physiol — Journal of Cellular and Comparative Physiology [Later, Journal of Cellular Physiology]
J Cell Eng incorporating Mol Eng — Journal of Cellular Engineering incorporating Molecular Engineering
J Cell Pharmacol — Journal of Cellular Pharmacology
J Cell Phys — Journal of Cellular Physiology
J Cell Physiol — Journal of Cellular Physiology
J Cell Physiol Suppl — Journal of Cellular Physiology. Supplement
J Cell Plast — Journal of Cellular Plastics
J Cell Sci — Journal of Cell Science
J Cell Sci Suppl — Journal of Cell Science. Supplement
J Cellular Plastics — Journal of Cellular Plastics
J Cellul Inst (Tokyo) — Journal. Cellulose Institute (Tokyo)
J Cellul Sci Technol — Journal of Cellulose Science and Technology
JCeltS — Journal of Celtic Studies
JCEM — Journal of Clinical Endocrinology and Metabolism
JCEN — Journal of Continuing Education in Nursing
JCEND — Journal of Clinical Engineering
J Cent Agr Exp Sta — Journal. Central Agricultural Experiment Station
J Cent Agric Exp Stn — Journal. Central Agricultural Experiment Station
J Cent Asia — Journal of Central Asia
J Cent Bur Anim Husb Dairy India — Journal. Central Bureau for Animal Husbandry and Dairying in India

J Cent China Norm Univ Nat Sci — Journal. Central China Normal University. Natural Sciences

J Cent China Teach Coll Nat Sci Ed — Journal. Central China Teachers College. Natural Sciences Edition

J Cent Eur Aff — Journal of Central European Affairs

J Cent Eur Affairs — Journal of Central European Affairs

J Central China Normal Univ Natur Sci — Journal of Central China Normal University. Natural Sciences

J Centr Eur Aff — Journal of Central European Affairs

J Cent South Inst Min Metall — Journal. Central-South Institute of Mining and Metallurgy

J Cent South Univ Technol Chin Ed — Journal of Central South University of Technology (Chinese Edition)

J Cent South Univ Technol Engl Ed — Journal of Central South University of Technology (English Edition)

J Ceram Assoc Jpn — Journal. Ceramic Association of Japan

J Ceram Soc Japan Int Ed — Journal of the Ceramic Society of Japan. International Edition

J Ceram Soc Jpn — Journal. Ceramic Society of Japan

J Ceram Soc Jpn (Jpn Ed) — Journal. Ceramic Society of Japan (Japanese Edition)

J Cereal Sci — Journal of Cereal Science

J Cereb Blood Flow Metab — Journal of Cerebral Blood Flow and Metabolism

J Cer Hist — Journal of Ceramic History

J Cer Soc Jap — Journal. Ceramic Society of Japan

J Ceylon Branch Brit Med Assoc — Journal. Ceylon Branch. British Medical Association

J Ceylon Branch Royal Asiat Soc — Journal of the Ceylon Branch of the Royal Asiatic Society

J Ceylon Br Brit Med Ass — Journal. Ceylon Branch. British Medical Association

J Ceylon Inst Architects — Journal of the Ceylon Institute of Architects

J Ceylon Law — Journal of Ceylon Law

JCF — Journal of Canadian Fiction

JCF — Jurisprudence Commerciale des Flandres

JCFl — Jurisprudence Commerciale des Flandres

JCfR — Journal of Conflict Resolution

JCFRB — Journal of Coffee Research

JCFS — Journal of Comparative Family Studies

JCG — Journal of Commerce. European Edition

JCH — Journal of Caribbean History

JCH — Journal of Contemporary History

J Changchun Coll Geol — Journal. Changchun College of Geology

J Changchun Geol Inst — Journal. Changchun Geological Institute

J Changchun Univ Earth Sci — Journal. Changchun University of Earth Science

J Changchun Univ Sci Technol — Journal of Changchun University of Science and Technology

J Changsha Comm Inst — Journal of Changsha Communications Institute

J Changsha Comm Univ — Changsha Communications University. Journal

J Changsha Norm Univ Water Res Electr Power Nat Sci Ed — Journal. Changsha Normal University of Water Resources and Electric Power. Natural Sciences Edition

J Changsha Railway Inst — Journal of Changsha Railway Institute

J Changsha Univ Electr Power Nat Sci Ed — Journal of Changsha University of Electric Power. Natural Science Edition

J Charles H Tweed Int Found — Journal. Charles H. Tweed International Foundation

J Chart Inst Bld Serv — Journal. Chartered Institution of Building Services

J Chart Inst Build Serv — Journal. Chartered Institution of Building Services

J Chart Inst Transp — Journal. Chartered Institute of Transport

J Chart Inst Water Environ Manage — Journal of the Chartered Institution of Water and Environmental Management

JCHAS — Journal. Cork Historical and Archaeological Society

JCHE — Journal of Computing in Higher Education

J Chekiang Prov Libr — Journal. Chekiang Provincial Library/Che Chiang T'u Shu Kuan Pao

J Chekiang Univ — Journal. Chekiang University

J Chem An — Japan Chemical Annual

J Chem Biochem Kinet — Journal of Chemical and Biochemical Kinetics

J Chem Crystallogr — Journal of Chemical Crystallography

J Chem Doc — Journal of Chemical Documentation

J Chem Docum — Journal of Chemical Documentation

J Chem Ecol — Journal of Chemical Ecology

J Chem Ed — Journal of Chemical Education

J Chem Educ — Journal of Chemical Education

J Chem Educ Software — Journal of Chemical Education. Software

J Chem Educ Software Ser A — Journal of Chemical Education. Software. Series A

J Chem Educ Software Ser B — Journal of Chemical Education. Software. Series B

J Chem Educ Software Ser C — Journal of Chemical Education. Software. Series C

J Chem Educ Software Ser D — Journal of Chemical Education. Software. Series D

J Chem Educ Software Spec Issue — Journal of Chemical Education. Software. Special Issue

J Chem En D — Journal of Chemical and Engineering Data

J Chem Eng (Beijing) — Journal of Chemical Engineering (Beijing)

J Chem Eng Data — Journal of Chemical and Engineering Data

J Chem Eng Educ — Journal of Chemical Engineering Education

J Chem Eng Jap — Journal of Chemical Engineering of Japan

J Chem Eng Jpn — Journal of Chemical Engineering of Japan

J Chem Engng Data — Journal of Chemical Engineering Data

J Chem Engng Japan — Journal of Chemical Engineering of Japan

J Chem Eng Tianjin — Journal of Chemical Engineering (Tianjin)

J Chem Eng (Tientsin) — Journal of Chemical Engineering (Tientsin)

J Chem Fert Ind — Journal of the Chemical Fertilizer Industry

J Chem Ind (Budapest) — Journal of Chemical Industry (Budapest)

J Chem Ind Eng — Journal of Chemical Industry and Engineering

J Chem Ind Eng (China Chin Ed) — Journal of Chemical Industry and Engineering (China, Chinese Edition)

J Chem Ind Jpn — Journal of Chemical Industry (Japan)

J Chem Ind (Moscow) — Journal der Chemischen Industrie (Moscow)

J Chem Ind (Moscow) — Journal of Chemical Industry (Moscow)

J Chem Inf — Journal of Chemical Information and Computer Sciences

J Chem Inf and Comput Sci — Journal of Chemical Information and Computer Sciences

J Chem Inf Comp Sci — Journal of Chemical Information and Computer Sciences

J Chem Inf Comput Sci — Journal of Chemical Information and Computer Sciences

J Chem Inform Comput Sci — Journal of Chemical Information and Computer Science

J Chem Metall Min Soc S Afr — Journal. Chemical, Metallurgical, and Mining Society of South Africa

J Chem Metall Soc S Afr — Journal. Chemical and Metallurgical Society of South Africa

J Chem Neur — Journal of Chemical Neuroanatomy

J Chem Neuroanat — Journal of Chemical Neuroanatomy

J Chemom — Journal of Chemometrics

J Chemother — Journal of Chemotherapy

J Chemother Adv Ther — Journal of Chemotherapy and Advanced Therapeutics

J Chemother (Florence) — Journal of Chemotherapy (Florence)

J Chemother Infect Dis Malig — Journal of Chemotherapy of Infectious Diseases and Malignancies

J Chemother (Philadelphia) — Journal of Chemotherapy (Philadelphia)

J Chem PET — Plant Engineering and Technology. PET Japan. Chemical Week Supplement

J Chem Phys — Journal fuer Chemie und Physik

J Chem Phys — Journal of Chemical Physics

J Chem Physics — Journal of Chemical Physics

J Chem Res M — Journal of Chemical Research. Part M

J Chem Res Miniprint — Journal of Chemical Research. Miniprint

J Chem Res Part S — Journal of Chemical Research. Part S. Synopses

J Chem Res S — Journal of Chemical Research. Part S. Synopses

J Chem Res Synop — Journal of Chemical Research. Part S. Synopses

J Chem Rev — Japan Chemical Review. Japan Chemical Week Supplement

J Chem S — Japan Chemical Week. Supplement. Where Is Great Change in Chemical Industry's Scope Leading

J Chem S Ch — Journal. Chemical Society. Chemical Communications

J Chem Sci — Journal of Chemical Sciences

J Chem S Da — Journal. Chemical Society. Dalton Transactions

J Chem S F I — Journal. Chemical Society. Faraday Transactions. I

J Chem S F II — Journal. Chemical Society. Faraday Transactions. II

J Chem Soc — Journal. Chemical Society

J Chem Soc A — Journal. Chemical Society. A. Inorganic, Physical, Theoretical

J Chem Soc Abstr — Journal. Chemical Society. Abstracts

J Chem Soc A Inorg Phys Theor — Journal. Chemical Society. A. Inorganic, Physical, Theoretical

J Chem Soc B — Journal. Chemical Society. B. Physical, Organic

J Chem Soc B Phys Org — Journal. Chemical Society. B. Physical Organic

J Chem Soc C — Journal. Chemical Society. C. Organic

J Chem Soc Chem Commun — Journal. Chemical Society. Chemical Communications

J Chem Soc C Org — Journal. Chemical Society. C. Organic

J Chem Soc Dalton Trans — Journal. Chemical Society. Dalton Transactions

J Chem Soc D Chem Commun — Journal. Chemical Society. D. Chemical Communications

J Chem Soc Faraday Trans — Journal. Chemical Society. Faraday Transactions

J Chem Soc Faraday Trans I — Journal. Chemical Society. Faraday Transactions. I

J Chem Soc Faraday Trans II — Journal. Chemical Society. Faraday Transactions. II

J Chem Soc Jap Ind Chem Sect — Journal. Chemical Society of Japan. Industrial Chemistry Section

J Chem Soc Jpn — Journal. Chemical Society of Japan

J Chem Soc Jpn Chem Ind Chem — Journal. Chemical Society of Japan. Chemistry and Industrial Chemistry

J Chem Soc Jpn Pure Chem Sect — Journal. Chemical Society of Japan. Pure Chemistry Section

J Chem Soc (London) — Journal. Chemical Society (London)

J Chem Soc (London) A Inorg Phys Theor — Journal. Chemical Society (London). Section A. Inorganic, Physical, Theoretical

J Chem Soc (London) B Phys Org — Journal. Chemical Society (London). Section B. Physical, Organic

J Chem Soc (London) Chem Commun — Journal. Chemical Society (London). Section D. Chemical Communications

J Chem Soc (London) C Org — Journal. Chemical Society (London). Section C. Organic Chemistry

J Chem Soc (London) Dalton Trans — Journal. Chemical Society (London). Dalton Transactions

J Chem Soc (London) D Chem Commun — Journal. Chemical Society (London). Section D. Chemical Communications

J Chem Soc (London) Faraday Trans I — Journal. Chemical Society (London). Faraday Transactions. I

J Chem Soc (London) Faraday Trans II — Journal. Chemical Society (London). Faraday Transactions. II

J Chem Soc (London) Perkin Trans I — Journal. Chemical Society (London). Perkin Transactions. I

J Chem Soc (London) Perkin Trans II — Journal. Chemical Society (London). Perkin Transactions. II

J Chem Soc Pak — Journal. Chemical Society of Pakistan

J Chem Soc Perkin Trans — Journal. Chemical Society. Perkin Transactions. I
J Chem Soc Perkin Trans I — Journal. Chemical Society. Perkin Transactions. I
J Chem Soc Perkin Trans II — Journal. Chemical Society. Perkin Transactions. II
J Chem Soc Trans — Journal. Chemical Society. Transactions
J Chem Software — Journal of Chemical Software
J Chem S P I — Journal. Chemical Society. Perkin Transactions. I
J Chem S P II — Journal. Chemical Society. Perkin Transactions. II
J Chem Tech Biotech — Journal of Chemical Technology and Biotechnology
J Chem Tech Biotechnol — Journal of Chemical Technology and Biotechnology
J Chem Technol and Biotechnol — Journal of Chemical Technology and Biotechnology
J Chem Technol Biotechnol — Journal of Chemical Technology and Biotechnology
J Chem Technol Biotechnol A — Journal of Chemical Technology and Biotechnology. A. ChemicalTechnology
J Chem Technol Biotechnol A Chem Technol — Journal of Chemical Technology and Biotechnology. A. Chemical Technology
J Chem Technol Biotechnol B — Journal of Chemical Technology and Biotechnology. B. Biotechnology
J Chem Technol Biotechnol B Biotechnology — Journal of Chemical Technology and Biotechnology. B. Biotechnology
J Chem Technol Biotechnol Chem Technol — Journal of Chemical Technology and Biotechnology. A. Chemical Technology
J Chem Ther — Journal of Chemical Thermodynamics
J Chem Thermodyn — Journal of Chemical Thermodynamics
J Chem Thermodyn Thermochem — Journal of Chemical Thermodynamics and Thermochemistry
J Chem (UAR) — Journal of Chemistry (United Arab Republic)
J Chem Vap Deposition — Journal of Chemical Vapor Deposition
J Chengdu Inst Technol — Journal of Chengdu Institute of Technology
J Chengdu Univ Natur Sci — Journal of Chengdu University. Natural Sciences
J Chengdu Univ Sci Tech — Journal of Chengdu University of Science and Technology
J Chengdu Univ Sci Technol — Journal of Chengdu University of Science and Technology
J Cheng Kung Univ Sci Eng — Journal. Cheng Kung University. Science and Engineering
J Cheng Kung Univ Sci Eng Med — Journal. Cheng Kung University. Science, Engineering, and Medicine
J Cherokee Stud — Journal of Cherokee Studies
J Che Soc Sect C Org Chem — Journal. Chemical Society [London] Section C. Organic Chemistry
J Chester Archaeol Soc — Journal. Chester Archaeological Society
J Chester Arch Soc — Journal. Chester Archaeological Society
JCHi — Journal of Contemporary History
J Chiba Med Soc — Journal. Chiba Medical Society
J Child Adolesc Psychopharmacol — Journal of Child and Adolescent Psychopharmacology
J Child Contemp Soc — Journal of Children in Contemporary Society
J Child Lang — Journal of Child Language
J Child Language — Journal of Child Language
J Child Neurol — Journal of Child Neurology
J Child Psy — Journal of Child Psychology and Psychiatry
J Child Psych & Psychiatry — Journal of Child Psychology and Psychiatry
J Child Psychol — Journal of Child Psychology and Psychiatry
J Child Psychol & Psych — Journal of Child Psychology and Psychiatry and Allied Disciplines [Later, Journal of Child Psychology and Psychiatry]
J Child Psychol Psychiat — Journal of Child Psychology and Psychiatry
J Child Psychol Psychiatry — Journal of Child Psychology and Psychiatry and Allied Disciplines [Later, Journal of Child Psychology and Psychiatry]
J Child Psychol Psychiatry Allied Discipl — Journal of Child Psychology and Psychiatry and Allied Disciplines [Later, Journal of Child Psychology and Psychiatry]
J Child Psychol Psychiatry Book Suppl — Journal of Child Psychology and Psychiatry. Book Supplement
J Child Psychotherapy -– Journal of Child Psychotherapy
J Child Sex A — Journal of Child Sexual Abuse
J Chim Appl — Journal de Chimie Appliquee
J Chim Gen — Journal de Chimie Generale
J Chim Med Pharm Toxicol — Journal de Chimie Medicale, de Pharmacie, et de Toxicologie
J Chim Phys — Journal de Chimie Physique
J Chim Phys — Journal de Chimie Physique et de Physico-Chimie Biologique
J Chim Phys et Phys-Chim Biol — Journal de Chimie Physique et de Physico-Chimie Biologique
J Chim Phys Phys-Chim Biol — Journal de Chimie Physique et de Physico-Chimie Biologique
J Chim Phys Rev Gen Colloides — Journal de Chimie Physique et Revue Generale des Colloides
J Chim Ukr — Journal Chimique de l'Ukraine
J China Coal Soc — Journal. China Coal Society
J China Coal Soc (Beijing) — Journal. China Coal Society (Beijing)
J Chin Agri Chem Soc — Journal. Chinese Agricultural Chemical Society
J China Med Univ (Chin Ed) — Journal. China Medical University (Chinese Edition)
J Chin Amer Engin — Journal of Chinese and American Engineers
J China Pharm Univ — Journal. China Pharmaceutical University
J Chin Archaeol — Journal of Chinese Archaeology
J China Soc Chem Ind — Journal. China Society of Chemical Industry
J Chin Assoc Refrig — Journal. Chinese Association of Refrigeration
J China Text Eng Assoc — Journal. China Textile Engineering Association
J China Text Univ Engl Ed — Journal of China Textile University. English Edition
J China Univ Geosci — Journal of China University of Geosciences
J China Univ Geosci Chin Ed — Journal of China University of Geosciences (Chinese Edition)
J China Univ Sci Tech — Journal of China University of Science and Technology
J China Univ Sci Technol — Journal. China University of Science and Technology

J Chin Biochem Soc — Journal. Chinese Biochemical Society
J Chin Ceram Soc — Journal. Chinese Ceramic Society
J Chin Chem — Journal. Chinese Chemical Society
J Chin Chem Soc — Journal. Chinese Chemical Society
J Chin Chem Soc (Peking) — Journal. Chinese Chemical Society (Peking)
J Chin Chem Soc (Taipei) — Journal. Chinese Chemical Society (Taipei)
J Chin Colloid Interface Soc — Journal. Chinese Colloid and Interface Society
J Chin Electron Microsc Soc — Journal of Chinese Electron Microscopy Society
J Chin Environ Prot Soc — Journal. Chinese Environmental Protection Society
J Chinese Inst Chem Engrs — Journal. Chinese Institute of Chemical Engineers
J Chinese Inst Engrs — Journal. Chinese Institute of Engineers
J Chinese Inst Indust Engrs — Journal. Chinese Institute of Industrial Engineers
J Chinese Ling — Journal of Chinese Linguistics
J Chin Foundrymen's Assoc — Journal. Chinese Foundrymen's Association
J Ching Hua Univ — Journal. Ching Hua University
J Chin Inst Chem Eng — Journal. Chinese Institute of Chemical Engineers
J Chin Inst Eng — Journal. Chinese Institute of Engineers
J Chin Inst Eng Trans Chin Inst Eng Ser A — Journal of the Chinese Institute of Engineers. Transactions of the Chinese Institute of Engineers. Series A
J Chin Inst Environ Eng — Journal of the Chinese Institute of Environmental Engineering
JChinL — Journal of Chinese Linguistics
J Chin Lang Teach Asso — Journal. Chinese Language Teachers Association
J Chin Ling — Journal of Chinese Linguistics
J Chin Nutr Soc — Journal of the Chinese Nutrition Society
JChinP — Journal of Chinese Philosophy
J Chin Pharm Sci — Journal of Chinese Pharmaceutical Sciences
J Chin Phil — Journal of Chinese Philosophy
J Chin Philo — Journal of Chinese Philosophy
J Chin Rare Earth Soc — Journal. Chinese Rare Earth Society
J Chin Silicates Soc — Journal. Chinese Silicate Society
J Chin Silic Soc — Journal. Chinese Silicate Society
J Chin Soc Vet Sci — Journal. Chinese Society of Veterinary Science
J Chin Soc Vet Sci (Taipei) — Journal. Chinese Society of Veterinary Science (Taipei)
J Chin U HK — Journal. Chinese University of Hong Kong
J Chin Univ Hong Kong — Journal. Chinese University of Hong Kong
J Chir — Journal de Chirurgie
J Chiro — Journal of Chiropractic
J Ch L — Journal of Child Language
JChM — Journal of Church Music
J Ch Mnmts Soc — Journal of the Church Monuments Society
JCHOD — Journal of Clinical Hematology and Oncology
J Chongqing Univ — Journal. Chongqing University
J Chosen Agric Soc — Journal. Chosen Agricultural Society/Chosen Nokai Ho. Keijo
J Chosen Med Assoc — Journal. Chosen Medical Association
JCHQA — Japan Chemical Quarterly
JChr — Jewish Chronicle
J Chr Ed — Journal of Christian Education
J Christ Educ — Journal of Christian Education
J Christian Ed — Journal of Christian Education
J Christian Educ — Journal of Christian Education
J Christian Juris — Journal of Christian Jurisprudence
J Christ Juris — Journal of Christian Jurisprudence
J Christ Med Assoc India — Journal. Christian Medical Association of India
J Christ Nurs — Journal of Christian Nursing
J Christ Nurse — Journal of Christian Nursing
J Chromat — Journal of Chromatography
J Chromat Biomed Appl — Journal of Chromatography. Biomedical Applications
J Chromat Chromat Rev — Journal of Chromatography. Chromatographic Reviews
J Chromatogr — Journal of Chromatography
J Chromatogr A — Journal of Chromatography. A
J Chromatogr B Biomed Appl — Journal of Chromatography. B. Biomedical Applications
J Chromatogr Biomed Appl — Journal of Chromatography. Biomedical Applications
J Chromatogr Libr — Journal. Chromatography Library
J Chromatogr Libr (Amsterdam) — Journal. Chromatography Library (Amsterdam)
J Chromatogr Sci — Journal of Chromatographic Science
J Chromatogr Suppl Vol — Journal of Chromatography. Supplementary Volume
J Chromat Sci — Journal of Chromatographic Science
J Chrom Sci — Journal of Chromatographic Science
J Chron Dis — Journal of Chronic Diseases
J Chronic Dis — Journal of Chronic Diseases
J Chr Philos — Journal of Christian Philosophy
J Ch S — Journal of Church and State
J Ch St — Journal of Church and State
J Chulalongkorn Hosp Med Sch (Bangkok) — Journal. Chulalongkorn Hospital Medical School (Bangkok)
J Church & State — Journal of Church and State
J Church M — Journal of Church Music
J Church Mus — Journal of Church Music
J Church St — Journal of Church and State
J Church State — Journal of Church and State
JCICS — Journal of Chemical Information and Computer Sciences
JCIEM — Journal du Conseil International pour l'Exploration de la Mer
JCILS — Journal. Centre of Islamic Legal Studies
JCIMD — Journal of Clinical Immunology
J Cin BA — Journal. Cincinnati Bar Association
JCIRA — Japanese Circulation Journal
J Circuits Systems Comput — Journal of Circuits, Systems, and Computers
JCISD — Journal of Chemical Information and Computer Sciences
J City Plann Div Am Soc Civ Eng — Journal. City Planning Division. American Society of Civil Engineers

J Civ D — Journal of Civil Defense
J Civ Eng Des — Journal of Civil Engineering Design
J Civ Eng (Taipei) — Journal of Civil Engineering (Taipei)
J Civ Hydraul Eng (Taipei) — Journal of Civil and Hydraulic Engineering (Taipei)
JCK — Jahrbuch fuer Christliche Kunst
JCL — Jahrbuch. Coburger Landesstiftung
JCL — Journal. Chromatography Library
JCL — Journal of Commonwealth Literature
JCL — Journal of Comparative Legislation and International Law and the Review of Legislation
JCL — Journal of Conchology (London and Leeds)
JCL — Journal of Corporation Law
JCL — Journal of Criminal Law
JCLA — Journal. Canadian Linguistic Association
JCLa — Journal of Child Language
JCLA — Journal of Comparative Literature and Aesthetics
JCL & IL — Journal of Comparative Legislation and International Law
J Classif — Journal of Classification
J Classification — Journal of Classification
J Clay Prod Inst Am — Journal. Clay Products Institute of America
J Clay Res Group Jpn — Journal. Clay Research Group of Japan
J Clay Sci Soc Jpn — Journal. Clay Science Society of Japan
JCLCPS — Journal of Criminal Law, Criminology, and Police Science [*Later, Journal of Criminal Law and Criminology*]
J Clean Prod — Journal of Cleaner Production
J Clean Technol Environ Sci — Journal of Clean Technology and Environmental Sciences
J Clean Technol Environ Toxicol Occup Med — Journal of Clean Technology, Environmental Toxicology, and Occupational Medicine
J Clerks Works Assoc GB — Journal. Clerks of Works Association of Great Britain
J Cleveland Eng Soc — Journal. Cleveland Engineering Society
JCLIA — Jornal dos Clinicos
JCLIDR — Journal. Chromatography Library
J Clim — Journal of Climate
J Clim and Appl Meteorol — Journal of Climate and Applied Meteorology
J Clim App Meteorol — Journal of Climate and Applied Meteorology
J Climatol — Journal of Climatology
J Clin Anesth — Journal of Clinical Anesthesia
J Clin Apheresis — Journal of Clinical Apheresis
J Clin Biochem Nutr — Journal of Clinical Biochemistry and Nutrition
J Clin Chem Clin Biochem — Journal of Clinical Chemistry and Clinical Biochemistry
J Clin Chil — Journal of Clinical Child Psychology
J Clin Child Psychol — Journal of Clinical Child Psychology
J Clin Comput — Journal of Clinical Computing
J Clin Densitom — Journal of Clinical Densitometry
J Clin Dent — Journal of Clinical Dentistry
J Clin Dermatol — Journal of Clinical Dermatology
J Clin Dysmorphol — Journal of Clinical Dysmorphology
J Clin Electron Microsc — Journal of Clinical Electron Microscopy
J Clin Electron Microsc Soc Jpn — Journal. Clinical Electron Microscopy Society of Japan
J Clin Endocr — Journal of Clinical Endocrinology
J Clin Endocrinol — Journal of Clinical Endocrinology
J Clin Endocrinol — Journal of Clinical Endocrinology and Metabolism
J Clin Endocrinol Metab — Journal of Clinical Endocrinology and Metabolism
J Clin Eng — Journal of Clinical Engineering
J Clin Epidemiol — Journal of Clinical Epidemiology
J Clin Ethics — Journal of Clinical Ethics
J Clin Exp Gerontol — Journal of Clinical and Experimental Gerontology
J Clin Exp Hypn — Journal of Clinical and Experimental Hypnosis
J Clin Exp Med — Journal of Clinical and Experimental Medicine
J Clin Exp Med (Tokyo) — Journal of Clinical and Experimental Medicine (Tokyo)
J Clin Exp Neuropsychol — Journal of Clinical and Experimental Neuropsychology
J Clin Exp Psychopathol — Journal of Clinical and Experimental Psychopathology
J Clin Exp Psychopathol Q Rev Psychiatry Neurol — Journal of Clinical and Experimental Psychopathology and Quarterly Review of Psychiatry and Neurology
J Clin Gast — Journal of Clinical Gastroenterology
J Clin Gastroenterol — Journal of Clinical Gastroenterology
J Clin Hematol Oncol — Journal of Clinical Hematology and Oncology
J Clin Hosp Pharm — Journal of Clinical and Hospital Pharmacy
J Clin Hypertens — Journal of Clinical Hypertension
J Clin Immunoassay — Journal of Clinical Immunoassay
J Clin Immunol — Journal of Clinical Immunology
J Clin Inv — Journal of Clinical Investigation
J Clin Invest — Journal of Clinical Investigation
J Clin Lab Anal — Journal of Clinical Laboratory Analysis
J Clin Lab Autom — Journal of Clinical Laboratory Automation
J Clin Lab Immunol — Journal of Clinical and Laboratory Immunology
J Clin Lab Work (Peking) — Journal of Clinical Laboratory Work (Peking)
J Clin Laser Med Surg — Journal of Clinical Laser Medicine & Surgery
J Clin Med — Journal of Clinical Medicine
J Clin Micr — Journal of Clinical Microbiology
J Clin Microbiol — Journal of Clinical Microbiology
J Clin Monit — Journal of Clinical Monitoring
J Clin Neuro-Ophthalmol — Journal of Clinical Neuro-Ophthalmology
J Clin Neurophysiol — Journal of Clinical Neurophysiology
J Clin Neuropsychol — Journal of Clinical Neuropsychology
J Clin Neurosci — Journal of Clinical Neuroscience
J Clin Nutr — Journal of Clinical Nutrition
J Clin Nutr Gastroenterol — Journal of Clinical Nutrition and Gastroenterology
J Clin Nutr (Tokyo) — Journal of Clinical Nutrition (Tokyo)
J Clin Oncol — Journal of Clinical Oncology
J Clin Orthod — Journal of Clinical Orthodontics

J Clin Path — Journal of Clinical Pathology
J Clin Pathol — Journal of Clinical Pathology
J Clin Pathol Clin Mol Pathol — Journal of Clinical Pathology. Clinical Molecular Pathology
J Clin Pathol (Lond) — Journal of Clinical Pathology (London)
J Clin Pathol (Suppl) — Journal of Clinical Pathology (Supplement)
J Clin Pathol Suppl R Coll Pathol — Journal of Clinical Pathology. Supplement. Royal College of Pathologists
J Clin Pediatr (Sapporo) — Journal of Clinical Pediatrics (Sapporo)
J Clin Periodontol — Journal of Clinical Periodontology
J Clin Phar — Journal of Clinical Pharmacology
J Clin Pharm — Journal of Clinical Pharmacy
J Clin Pharmacol — Journal of Clinical Pharmacology
J Clin Pharmacol — Journal of Clinical Pharmacology and the Journal of New Drugs
J Clin Pharmacol J New Drugs — Journal of Clinical Pharmacology and the Journal of New Drugs
J Clin Pharmacol New Drugs — Journal of Clinical Pharmacology and the Journal of New Drugs
J Clin Pharm Ther — Journal of Clinical Pharmacy and Therapeutics
J Clin Psyc — Journal of Clinical Psychology
J Clin Psychiatry — Journal of Clinical Psychiatry
J Clin Psychol — Journal of Clinical Psychology
J Clin Psychopharmacol — Journal of Clinical Psychopharmacology
J Clin Sci — Journal of Clinical Science
J Clin Stomatol Conf — Journal of Clinical Stomatology Conferences
J Clin Surg — Journal of Clinical Surgery
J Clin Ultrasound — Journal of Clinical Ultrasound
JCLPB — Journal of Consulting and Clinical Psychology
JCIS — Journal of Classical Studies. Classical Society of Japan
JCLTA — Journal. Chinese Language Teachers Association
JCLTB — Journal of Clinical Ultrasound
J Clube Mineral — Jornal. Clube de Mineralogia
JCM — Journal of Church Music
JCM — Journal of Country Music
J C Med — Journal de Chimie Medicale, de Pharmacie, et de Toxicologie
JCMEDK — Journal of Cardiovascular Medicine
JCMHA — Journal. Cornish Methodist Historical Association
JCMID — Journal of Clinical Microbiology
JCML — John Coffin Memorial Lectures
JCMNA — Journal of Communication
JCMS — Journal of Crystal and Molecular Structure
JCMVASA — Journal. Central Mississippi Valley American Studies Association
JCN — Journal of Collective Negotiations in the Public Sector
JCNEA — Journal of Comparative Neurology
JCNOD — Journal of Clinical Neuro-Ophthalmology
JCNPS — Journal of Collective Negotiations in the Public Sector
JCNRD — Journal of Cyclic Nucleotide Research
J Coal Min Eng Assoc Kyushu — Journal. Coal Mining Engineers Association of Kyushu
J Coal Qual — Journal of Coal Quality
J Coal Res Inst (Tokyo) — Journal. Coal Research Institute (Tokyo)
J Coastal Res — Journal of Coastal Research
J Coated Fabr — Journal of Coated Fabrics
J Coated Fabrics — Journal of Coated Fabrics
J Coated Fibrous Mater — Journal of Coated Fibrous Materials
J Coatings Technol — Journal of Coatings Technology
J Coat Technol — Journal of Coatings Technology
J Coconut Ind — Journal of Coconut Industries
J Coconut Industr — Journal of Coconut Industries
J Coffee Res — Journal of Coffee Research
JCOI — Journal. Cama Oriental Institute
J Co Kildare Archaeol Soc — Journal. County Kildare Archaeological Society
J Cold Reg Eng — Journal of Cold Regions Engineering
J Coll Agric Hokkaido Imp Univ — Journal. College of Agriculture. Hokkaido Imperial University
J Coll Agric Tohoku Imp Univ — Journal. College of Agriculture. Tohoku Imperial University
J Coll Agric Tokyo Imp Univ — Journal. College of Agriculture. Tokyo Imperial University
J Coll Ag Tokyo — Journal. College of Agriculture. Tokyo Imperial University
J Coll and U L — Journal of College and University Law
J Coll & Univ L — Journal of College and University Law
J Coll & Univ Personnel Assn — Journal. College and University Personnel Association
J Coll Arts Chiba Univ — Journal. College of Arts and Sciences. Chiba University/ Chiba Daigaku Bunri Gakubu Kiyo. Shizen Kagaku
J Coll Arts Sci Chiba Univ — Journal. College of Arts and Sciences. Chiba University
J Coll Arts Sci Chiba Univ Nat Sci — Journal. College of Arts and Sciences. Chiba University. Natural Science
J Coll Ceram Technol Univ Calcutta — Journal. College of Ceramic Technology. University of Calcutta
J Coll Dairy Agr — Journal. College of Dairy Agriculture
J Coll Dairy Agric — Journal. College of Dairy Agriculture
J Coll Dairy Agric (Ebetsu Jpn) — Journal. College of Dairy Agriculture (Ebetsu, Japan)
J Coll Dairy Agric (Nopporo) — Journal. College of Dairy Agriculture (Nopporo)
J Coll Dairy Agri (Ebetsu Japan) — Journal. College of Dairy Agriculture (Ebetsu, Japan)
J Coll Dairy (Ebetsu Japan) — Journal. College of Dairying (Ebetsu, Japan)
J Coll Dairy Nat Sci (Ebetsu) — Journal. College of Dairying. Natural Science (Ebetsu)
J Coll Dairy (Nopporo) — Journal. College of Dairying (Nopporo)

J Collect Negotiations Public Sect — Journal of Collective Negotiations in the Public Sector

J Coll Educ Seoul Natl Univ — Journal. College of Education. Seoul National University

J College Place — Journal of College Placement

J College Sci Univ Riyadh — Journal. College of Science. University of Riyadh

J Coll Eng Nihon Univ — Journal. College of Engineering. Nihon University

J Coll Eng Technol Jadavpur Univ — Journal. College of Engineering and Technology. Jadavpur University

J Coll Eng Tokyo Imp Univ — Journal. College of Engineering. Tokyo Imperial University

J Coll Gen Pract — Journal. College of General Practitioners

J Col Lib Arts — Journal. College of Liberal Arts and Sciences. University of the East

J Coll Ind Technol Nihon Univ — Journal. College of Industrial Technology. Nihon University

J Coll Ind Technol Nihon Univ A — Journal. College of Industrial Technology. Nihon University. Series A

J Coll Ind Technol Nihon Univ B — Journal. College of Industrial Technology. Nihon University. Series B

J Coll I Sc — Journal of Colloid and Interface Science

J Coll Lib Arts Toyama Univ Nat Sci — Journal. College of Liberal Arts. Toyama University. Natural Sciences

J Coll Mar Sci Technol Tokai Univ — Journal. College of Marine Science and Technology. Tokai University

J Colloid and Interface Sci — Journal of Colloid and Interface Science

J Colloid Interface Sci — Journal of Colloid and Interface Science

J Colloid Interface Science — Journal of Colloid and Interface Science

J Colloid Sci — Journal of Colloid Science [*Later, Journal of Colloid and Interface Science*]

J Colloid Sci Suppl — Journal of Colloid Science. Supplement

J Coll Placement — Journal of College Placement

J Coll Radiol Aust — Journal. College of Radiologists of Australia

J Coll Radiol Australas — Journal. College of Radiologists of Australasia

J Coll Radiol Australasia — Journal. College of Radiologists of Australasia

J Coll Sci Eng Natl Chung Hsing Univ — Journal. College of Science and Engineering. National Chung HsingUniversity

J Coll Sci Imp Univ Tokyo — Journal. College of Science. Imperial University of Tokyo

J Coll Sci King Saud Univ — Journal. College of Science. King Saud University

J Coll Sci Teach — Journal of College Science Teaching

J Coll Sci Univ Riyadh — Journal. College of Science. University of Riyadh

J Coll Stud — Journal of College Student Personnel

J Coll Student Personnel — Journal of College Student Personnel

J Coll Stud Personnel — Journal of College Student Personnel

J Coll Surgeons Australasia — Journal. College of Surgeons of Australasia

J Coll Univ — Journal. College and University Personnel Association

J Col Negot — Journal of Collective Negotiations in the Public Sector

J Colo Dent Assoc — Journal. Colorado Dental Association

J Color — Journal of Color and Appearance

J Color Appearance — Journal of Color and Appearance

J Colour Soc — Journal. Colour Society

J Co Louth Archaeol Soc — Journal of the County Louth Archaeological Society

J Colo-Wyo Acad Sci — Journal. Colorado-Wyoming Academy of Science

J Col Placement — Journal of College Placement

J Col Stud Personnel — Journal of College Student Personnel

J Combat — Jewish Combatant

J Comb Chem — Journal of Combinational Chemistry

J Combinatorial Theory Ser A — Journal of Combinatorial Theory. Series A

J Combinatorial Theory Ser B — Journal of Combinatorial Theory. Series B

J Combinatorics Information Syst Sci — Journal of Combinatorics, Information, and System Sciences

J Combin Des — Journal of Combinatorial Designs

J Combin Inform System Sci — Journal of Combinatorics, Information, and System Sciences

J Combin Math Combin Comput — Journal of Combinatorial Mathematics and Combinatorial Computing

J Combin Theory Ser A — Journal of Combinatorial Theory. Series A

J Combin Theory Ser B — Journal of Combinatorial Theory. Series B

J Comb Th A — Journal of Combinatorial Theory. Series A

J Comb Th B — Journal of Combinatorial Theory. Series B

J Comb Theory — Journal of Combinatorial Theory

J Comb Theory Ser A — Journal of Combinatorial Theory. Series A

J Comb Theory Ser B — Journal of Combinatorial Theory. Series B

J Combustion Toxicol — Journal of Combustion Toxicology

J Combust Sci Technol — Journal of Combustion Science and Technology

J Combust Toxic — Journal of Combustion Toxicology

J Combust Toxicol — Journal of Combustion Toxicology

J Comerc — Jornal do Comercio

JComLit — Journal of Commonwealth Literature

J Comm — Journal of Communication

J Comm B — Jurisprudence Commerciale de Belgique

J Comm Bank Lending — Journal of Commercial Bank Lending

J Comm Dis — Journal of Communication Disorders

J Comment — Jewish Comment

J Commer — Journal of Commerce

J Commer Bank Lending — Journal of Commercial Bank Lending

J Commercio — Jornal do Commercio

J Com Mkt S — Journal of Common Market Studies

J Comm Market Studs — Journal of Common Market Studies

J Comm Mkt Stud — Journal of Common Market Studies

J Common Market Stud — Journal of Common Market Studies

J Common Market Studies — Journal of Common Market Studies

J Common Mark Stud — Journal of Common Market Studies

J Common Mkt Stud — Journal of Common Market Studies

J Commonw Comp Pol — Journal of Commonwealth and Comparative Politics

J Commonw Comp Polit — Journal of Commonwealth and Comparative Politics

J Commonwealth Comp Polit — Journal of Commonwealth and Comparative Politics

J Commonwealth Lit — Journal of Commonwealth Literature

J Commonw Lit — Journal of Commonwealth Literature

J Commonw Polit Stud — Journal of Commonwealth Political Studies

J Comm Pol Studs — Journal of Commonwealth Political Studies

J Comm Rural Reconstr China (US Repub China) Plant Ind Ser — Joint Commission on Rural Reconstruction in China (United States and Republic of China). Plant Industry Series

J Commun — Journal of Communication

J Commun Dis — Journal of Communicable Diseases

J Commun Disord — Journal of Communication Disorders

J Commun Health — Journal of Community Health

J Communication — Journal of Communication

J Community Action — Journal of Community Action

J Community Dev Soc — Journal. Community Development Society

J Community Educ — Journal of Community Education

J Community Health — Journal of Community Health

J Community Health Nurs — Journal of Community Health Nursing

J Community Psychol — Journal of Community Psychology

J Commun Res Lab — Journal of the Communications Research Laboratory

J Comp Adm — Journal of Comparative Administration

J Comp & Physiol Psychol — Journal of Comparative and Physiological Psychology

J Company Master Mar Aust — Company of Master Mariners of Australia. Journal

J Comparative Econ — Journal of Comparative Economics

J Compar PE & Sport — Journal of Comparative Physical Education and Sport

J Comp Corp L — Journal of Comparative Corporate Law and Securities Regulation

J Comp Corp L and Sec — Journal of Comparative Corporate Law and Securities Regulation

J Comp Corp L and Sec Reg — Journal of Comparative Corporate Law and Securities Regulation

J Comp Econ — Journal of Comparative Economics

J Comp Ethol — Journal of Comparative Ethology

J Comp Family Stud — Journal of Comparative Family Studies

J Comp Fam Stud — Journal of Comparative Family Studies

J Com Physl — Journal of Comparative and Physiological Psychology

J Comp Leg — Journal of Comparative Legislation and International Law

J Comp Leg — Journal. Society of Comparative Legislation

J Comp Leg & Int Law — Journal of Comparative Legislation and International Law

J Comp Legis — Journal of Comparative Legislation and International Law

J Comp Legis Int Law — Journal of Comparative Legislation and International Law

J Complem Dict Sci Med — Journal Complementaire du Dictionaire des Sciences Medicales

J Compliance Health Care — Journal of Compliance in Health Care

J Comp Med and Vet Arch — Journal of Comparative Medicine and Veterinary Archives

J Comp Med Surg — Journal of Comparative Medicine and Surgery

J Comp Neur — Journal of Comparative Neurology

J Comp Neurol — Journal of Comparative Neurology

J Comp Neurol Psychol — Journal of Comparative Neurology and Psychology

J Compos Constr — Journal of Composites for Construction

J Composite Mat — Journal of Composite Materials

J Compos Ma — Journal of Composite Materials

J Compos Mater — Journal of Composite Materials

J Compos Technol Res — Journal of Composites Technology and Research

J Comp Path — Journal of Comparative Pathology

J Comp Path and Therap — Journal of Comparative Pathology and Therapeutics

J Comp Pathol — Journal of Comparative Pathology

J Comp Pathol Ther — Journal of Comparative Pathology and Therapeutics

J Comp Phys — Journal of Comparative Physiology

J Comp Physiol — Journal of Comparative Physiology

J Comp Physiol A — Journal of Comparative Physiology. A. Sensory, Neural, and Behavioral Physiology

J Comp Physiol A Sens Neural Behav Physiol — Journal of Comparative Physiology. A. Sensory, Neural, and Behavioral Physiology

J Comp Physiol B — Journal of Comparative Physiology. B. Biochemical, Systemic, and Environmental Physiology

J Comp Physiol B Biochem Syst Environ Physiol — Journal of Comparative Physiology. B. Biochemical, Systemic, and Environmental Physiology

J Comp Physiol B Metab Transp Funct — Journal of Comparative Physiology. B. Metabolic and Transport Functions

J Comp Physiol Psychol — Journal of Comparative and Physiological Psychology

J Comp Psychol — Journal of Comparative Psychology

J Comp Tech Res — Journal of Composites and Technology Research

J Comput Acoust — Journal of Computational Acoustics

J Comput Aided Mater Des — Journal of Computer-Aided Materials Design

J Comput Aided Mol Des — Journal of Computer-Aided Molecular Design

J Comput and Syst Sci — Journal of Computer and System Sciences

J Comput Appl Math — Journal of Computational and Applied Mathematics

J Comput Assisted Microsc — Journal of Computer-Assisted Microscopy

J Comput Assisted Tomogr — Journal of Computer-Assisted Tomography

J Comput Assist Tomogr — Journal of Computer-Assisted Tomography

J Computational Phys — Journal of Computational Physics

J Comput Based Instr — Journal of Computer-Based Instruction

J Comput Biol — Journal of Computational Biology

J Comput Chem — Journal of Computational Chemistry

J Comput Civ Eng — Journal of Computing in Civil Engineering

J Comput Graph Statist — Journal of Computational and Graphical Statistics

J Comput Inform — Journal of Computing and Information

J Comput Math — Journal of Computational Mathematics

J Comput Math and Sci Teach — Journal of Computers in Mathematics and Science Teaching
J Comput Neurosci — Journal of Computational Neuroscience
J Comput Ph — Journal of Computational Physics
J Comput Phys — Journal of Computational Physics
J Comput Sci Tech English Ed — Journal of Computer Science and Technology (English Edition)
J Comput Sci Technol — Journal of Computer Science and Technology
J Comput Soc India — Journal. Computer Society of India
J Comput Sy — Journal of Computer and System Sciences
J Comput System Sci — Journal of Computer and System Sciences
J Comput Systems Sci Internat — Journal of Computer and Systems Sciences International
J Comput Syst Sci — Journal of Computer and System Sciences
J Comput Syst Sci Int — Journal of Computer and Systems Sciences International
J Comput Tomogr — Journal of Computed Tomography
J Con A — Journal of Consumer Affairs
J Conat Law — Journal of Conational Law
J Conchol — Journal of Conchology
J Conchyl — Journal de Conchyliologie
J Conchyliol — Journal de Conchyliologie
J Conf Chem Inst Can Am Chem Soc Abstr Pap — Joint Conference. Chemical Institute of Canada/American Chemical Society. Abstracts of Papers
J Conf CIC/ACS Abstr Pap — Joint Conference. Chemical Institute of Canada/American Chemical Society. Abstracts of Papers
J Conflict Resol — Journal of Conflict Resolution
J Conflict Resolu — Journal of Conflict Resolution
J Conflict Resolution — Journal of Conflict Resolution
J Confl Res — Journal of Conflict Resolution
J Conf Res — Journal of Conflict Resolution
J Conf Workshop — Journalism Conference and Workshop
J Connaissances Usuelles Prat — Journal des Connaissances Usuelles et Pratiques
J Conn Med Chir — Journal des Connaissances Medico-Chirurgicales
J Conn State Dent As — Journal. Connecticut State Dental Association
J Conn State Dent Assoc — Journal. Connecticut State Dental Association
J Conn State Med Soc — Journal. Connecticut State Medical Society
J Cons Affairs — Journal of Consumer Affairs
J Cons ASCE — Journal. Construction Division. Proceedings of the American Society of Civil Engineers
J Cons Clin — Journal of Consulting and Clinical Psychology
J Cons Cons Int Explor Mer — Journal du Conseil. Conseil International pour l'Exploration de la Mer
J Cons Cons Perm Int Explor Mer — Journal du Conseil. Conseil Permanent International pour l'Exploration de la Mer
J Conseil — Journal du Conseil
J Cons Int Explor Mer — Journal du Conseil. Conseil International pour l'Exploration de la Mer
J Const Div Proc ASCE — Journal. Construction Division. Proceedings of the American Society of Civil Engineers
J Const Parl Stud — Journal of Constitutional and Parliamentary Studies
J Constr Div Amer Soc Civil Eng Proc — Journal. Construction Division. Proceedings of the American Society of Civil Engineers
J Constr Div Am Soc Civ Eng — Journal. Construction Division. Proceedings of the American Society of Civil Engineers
J Constr Eng Manage — Journal of Construction Engineering and Management
J Constr Steel Res — Journal of Constructional Steel Research
J Consult & Clin Psychol — Journal of Consulting and Clinical Psychology
J Consult Clin Psychol — Journal of Consulting and Clinical Psychology
J Consulting Psychol — Journal of Consulting Psychology
J Consult Psychol — Journal of Consulting Psychology
J Consum Af — Journal of Consumer Affairs
J Consum Aff — Journal of Consumer Affairs
J Consumer Aff — Journal of Consumer Affairs
J Consumer Affairs — Journal of Consumer Affairs
J Consumer Policy — Journal of Consumer Policy
J Consumer Prod Flamm — Journal of Consumer Product Flammability
J Consumer Prod Flammability — Journal of Consumer Product Flammability
J Consumer Res — Journal of Consumer Research
J Consumer Studies and Home Econ — Journal of Consumer Studies and Home Economics
J Consum Policy — Journal of Consumer Policy
J Consum Prod Flamm — Journal of Consumer Product Flammability
J Consum Prod Flammability — Journal of Consumer Product Flammability
J Consum Res — Journal of Consumer Research
J Consum Stud Home Econ — Journal of Consumer Studies and Home Economics
J Contam Hydrol — Journal of Contaminant Hydrology
J Cont Asia — Journal of Contemporary Asia
J Cont Bus — Journal of Contemporary Business
J Cont Ed Nurs — Journal of Continuing Education in Nursing
J Contemp — Journal of Contemporary Asia
J Contemp A — Journal of Contemporary Art
J Contemp Afr Stud — Journal of Contemporary African Studies
J Contemp Asia — Journal of Contemporary Asia
J Contemp Bus — Journal of Contemporary Business
J Contemp Busin — Journal of Contemporary Business
J Contemp Health Law Policy — Journal of Contemporary Health Law and Policy
J Contemp Hist — Journal of Contemporary History
J Contemp L — Journal of Contemporary Law
J Contemp Math Anal — Journal of Contemporary Mathematical Analysis
J Contemp Neurol — Journal of Contemporary Neurology
J Contemporary Bus — Journal of Contemporary Business
J Contemporary Hist — Journal of Contemporary History
J Contemporary Studies — Journal of Contemporary Studies

J Contemp Stud — Journal of Contemporary Studies
J Cont Hist — Journal of Contemporary History
J Contin Educ Health Prof — Journal of Continuing Education in the Health Professions
J Contin Educ Nurs — Journal of Continuing Education in Nursing
J Contin Educ Obstet Gynecol — Journal of Continuing Education in Obstetrics and Gynecology
J Contin Educ Psychiatry — Journal of Continuing Education in Psychiatry
J Cont L — Journal of Contemporary Law
J Cont Psyt — Journal of Contemporary Psychotherapy
J Contracept — Journal of Contraception
J Controlled Release — Journal of Controlled Release
J Convex Anal — Journal of Convex Analysis
J Cooling Tower Inst — Journal. Cooling Tower Institute
J Coop Educ — Journal of Cooperative Education
J Cooperage Sci Tech — Journal of Cooperage Sciences and Techniques
J Coord Ch — Journal of Coordination Chemistry
J Coord Chem — Journal of Coordination Chemistry
J Copyright Socy USA — Journal. Copyright Society of the USA
J Cork Hist Archaeol Soc — Journal. Cork Historical and Archaeological Society
J Corp L — Journal of Corporation Law
J Corp Law — Journal of Corporation Law
J Corpn L — Journal of Corporation Law
J Corporate Taxation — Journal of Corporate Taxation
J Corp Tax — Journal of Corporate Taxation
J Corros Sci Eng Electronic Publication — Journal of Corrosion Science and Engineering [Electronic Publication]
J Corros Sci Soc Korea — Journal. Corrosion Science Society of Korea
J Cosmet Sci — Journal of Cosmetic Science
J Counc Sci Ind Res (Australia) — Journal. Council for Scientific and Industrial Research (Australia)
J Coun Psyc — Journal of Counseling Psychology
J Coun Scient Ind Res (Aust) — Journal. Council for Scientific and Industrial Research (Australia)
J Counsel & Devt — Journal of Counseling and Development
J Counsel Ply — Journal of Counseling Psychology
J Counsel Psychol — Journal of Counseling Psychology
J Couns Psych — Journal of Counseling Psychology
J Country M — Journal of Country Music
J Country Mus — Journal of Country Music
JCP — Jew's College Publications
JCP — Journal of Clinical Psychology
JCP — Journal of Communication
JCP — Journal of Comparative Psychology
JCP — Journal of Contemporary Psychotherapy
JCP — Journal of Counseling Psychology
JCP — La Semaine Juridique (Juris-Classeur Periodique)
JCPFD — Journal of Consumer Product Flammability
JCPGB — Journal of Cross-Cultural Psychology
JC Ph — Jahrbuecher fuer Classische Philologie
JCPHA — Journal of Consulting Psychology
JC Ph S — Jahrbuecher fuer Classische Philologie. Supplement
JCPP — Journal of Comparative and Physiological Psychology
JCPPA — Journal of Comparative and Physiological Psychology
JCPQA — Journal de Chimie Physique
JCPs — Journal of Clinical Psychology
JCPS — Journal of Commonwealth Political Studies
JCPS — Journal of Constitutional and Parliamentary Studies
JCPSA — Journal of Chemical Physics
JCPSB — Journal of Cellular Physiology. Supplement
JCPSD — Journal of Community Psychology
JCPT — Journal of Canadian Petroleum Technology
JCPT — Journal of Contemporary Puerto Rican Thought
JCPT J Can Pet Technol — JCPT. Journal of Canadian Petroleum Technology
JCPYA — Journal of Clinical Psychology
JCQ — Japan Christian Quarterly
JCR — Joint Center Report
JCR — Journal Citation Reports
JCR — Journal of Christian Reconstruction
JCR — Journal of Conflict Resolution
JCR — Journal of Consumer Research
J Craniofac Genet Dev Biol — Journal of Craniofacial Genetics and Developmental Biology
J Craniofac Genet Dev Biol Suppl — Journal of Craniofacial Genetics and Developmental Biology. Supplement
J Craniofacial Genet Dev Biol — Journal of Craniofacial Genetics and Developmental Biology
J Craniofacial Genet Dev Biol Suppl — Journal of Craniofacial Genetics and Developmental Biology. Supplement
J Craniomandibular Pract — Journal of Cranio-Mandibular Practice
J Craniomaxillofac Surg — Journal of Cranio-Maxillo-Facial Surgery
J Craniomaxillofac Trauma — Journal of Cranio-Maxillofacial Trauma
JCRAS — Journal. Ceylon Branch. Royal Asiatic Society
JCRDA — Proceedings. Japan Conference on Radioisotopes
J Creat Beh — Journal of Creative Behavior
J Creative Behavior — Journal of Creative Behavior
J Criminal Justice — Journal of Criminal Justice
J Criminal Law and Criminology — Journal of Criminal Law and Criminology
J Crim Jus — Journal of Criminal Justice
J Crim Just — Journal of Criminal Justice
J Crim L — Journal of Criminal Law
J Crim L — Journal of Criminal Law and Criminology
J Crim L & Crimin — Journal of Criminal Law and Criminology
J Crim L and Criminology — Journal of Criminal Law and Criminology
J Crim Law — Journal of Criminal Law and Criminology

J Crim Law & Criminol — Journal of Criminal Law and Criminology
J Crim Law Criminol Police Sci — Journal of Criminal Law, Criminology, and Police Science [*Later, Journal of Criminal Law and Criminology*]
J Crim LC & PS — Journal of Criminal Law, Criminology, and Police Science [*Later, Journal of Criminal Law and Criminology*]
J Crim L (Eng) — Journal of Criminal Law (English)
J Crim Sci — Journal of Criminal Science
J Crit Anal — Journal of Critical Analysis
J Crit Care — Journal of Critical Care
J Croatian Studies — Journal of Croatian Studies
J Croat Stud — Journal of Croatian Studies
J Crop Prod — Journal of Crop Production
J Cross-Cul — Journal of Cross-Cultural Psychology
J Cross-Cult Psych — Journal of Cross-Cultural Psychology
J Cross-Cult Psychol — Journal of Cross-Cultural Psychology
JCRS — Judaic-Christian Research Symposium
J Crustacean Biol — Journal of Crustacean Biology
J Crust Biol — Journal of Crustacean Biology
J Cryosurg — Journal of Cryosurgery
J Cryptol — Journal of Cryptology
J Cryptology — Journal of Cryptology
J Crystallogr and Spectrosc Res — Journal of Crystallographic and Spectroscopal Research
J Crystallogr Soc Jap — Journal. Crystallographic Society of Japan
J Cryst and Mol Struct — Journal of Crystal and Molecular Structure
J Cryst Gr — Journal of Crystal Growth
J Cryst Growth — Journal of Crystal Growth
J Cryst Mol — Journal of Crystal and Molecular Structure
J Cryst Mol Struct — Journal of Crystal and Molecular Structure
JCS — Journal. Chemical Society
JCS — Journal of Caribbean Studies
JCS — Journal of Celtic Studies
JCS — Journal of Cereal Science
JCS — Journal of Chromatographic Science
JCS — Journal of Church and State
JCS — Journal of Classical Studies
JCS — Journal of Common Market Studies
JCS — Journal of Croatian Studies
JCS — Journal of Cuneiform Studies
JCS — Journal of Curriculum Studies
JCS — Journal of Management Consulting
JCSA — Journal. Catch Society of America
JCSA — Journal. Chemical Society. Abstracts
JCSCA — Journal of Colloid Science [*Later, Journal of Colloid and Interface Science*]
JCSCDA — Journal of Cereal Science
JCS Chem Comm — Journal. Chemical Society. Chemical Communications
JCS Dalton — Journal. Chemical Society. Dalton Transactions. Inorganic Chemistry
JCSF — Journal of Caribbean Studies (Florida)
JCS Faraday I — Journal. Chemical Society. Faraday Transactions. I. Physical Chemistry
JCS Faraday II — Journal. Chemical Society. Faraday Transactions. II. Chemical Physics
JcSH — Jihocesky Sbornik Historicky
JCSP — Journal of Classical and Sacred Philology
JCS Perkin I — Journal. Chemical Society. Perkin Transactions. I. Organic and Bioorganic Chemistry
JCS Perkin II — Journal. Chemical Society. Perkin Transactions. II. Physical Organic Chemistry
JCSS — Journal of Computer and System Sciences
JCST — Journal. Chemical Society. Transactions
JC St — Journal of Caribbean Studies
JC St — Journal of Celtic Studies
J C St — Journal of Church and State
JCST — Journal of College Science Teaching
JCSTD — Journal of Contemporary Studies
JCSW — Jahrbuch fuer Christliche Sozialwissenschaften der Westfaelischen Wilhelms-Universitaet Muenster
JCT — Journal of Common Market Studies
JCT — Journal of Corporate Taxation
JCTED — Journal of Coatings Technology
JCTOD — Journal of Combustion Toxicology
J Ctry Mus — Journal of Country Music
JCTTDW — Journal of Chemical Technology and Biotechnology. A. Chemical Technology
JCU — Journal of Clinical Ultrasound
JCU J Clin Ultrasound — JCU. Journal of Clinical Ultrasound
J Cult & Ideas — Journal of Cultures and Ideas
J Cult Assoc Solomon Islands — Journal of the Cultural Association of the Solomon Islands
J Cuneiform St — Journal of Cuneiform Studies
J Cuneiform Stud — Journal of Cuneiform Studies
J Cun S — Journal of Cuneiform Studies
J Cun St — Journal of Cuneiform Studies
J Curr Biosci — Journal of Current Biosciences
J Currents — Jewish Currents
J Current Social Issues — Journal of Current Social Issues
J Curric St — Journal of Curriculum Studies
J Curr Laser Abstr — Journal of Current Laser Abstracts
J Curr Soc Issues — Journal of Current Social Issues
J Curr Stud — Journal of Curriculum Studies
J Cur Soc Issues — Journal of Current Social Issues
J Cutan Dis — Journal of Cutaneous Diseases including Syphilis
J Cutaneous Pathol — Journal of Cutaneous Pathology
J Cutan Laser Ther — Journal of Cutaneous Laser Therapy

J Cutan Pathol — Journal of Cutaneous Pathology
J Cutan Veneral Dis — Journal of Cutaneous and Veneral Diseases
J Cut Path — Journal of Cutaneous Pathology
JCV — Jahrbuch des Caritasverbandes
JCV — Jurisprudence Commerciale de Verviers
JCW — Jahrbuch fuer Caritaswissenschaft und Caritasarbeit
JCW — Japan Chemical Week
JCW — Journal of Comparative Business and Capital Market Law
JCWTS — Journal. Civil War Token Society
JCY — Japan Christian Year Book
J Cyb — Journal of Cybernetics
J Cyber Chem — Journal of Cyber Chemistry
J Cybern — Journal of Cybernetics
J Cybern and Inf Sci — Journal of Cybernetics and Information Science
J Cybernet — Journal of Cybernetics
J Cybern Inf Sci — Journal of Cybernetics and Information Science
J Cycle Phys Chim Acad Sci Ukr — Journal du Cycle de Physique et de Chimie. Academie des Sciencesd'Ukraine
J Cycle Res — Journal of Cycle Research
J Cyclic Nucleotide Protein Phosphor Res — Journal of Cyclic Nucleotide and Protein Phosphorylation Research
J Cyclic Nucleotide Protein Phosphorylation Res — Journal of Cyclic Nucleotide and Protein Phosphorylation Research
J Cyclic Nucleotide Res — Journal of Cyclic Nucleotide Research
J Cycl Nucl — Journal of Cyclic Nucleotide Research
J Cytol Genet — Journal of Cytology and Genetics
J Czech Geol Soc — Journal of the Czech Geological Society
JD — Journal des Debats
JD — Journal of Documentation
JD — Juris Doctor
JDA — Jahrbuch der Dioezese Augsburg
JDA — Journal of Developing Areas
JDA — Recueil de Jurisprudence du Droit Administratif et du Conseil d'Etat
JDAI — Jahrbuch. Deutsches Archaeologische Institut
JDAIE — Jahrbuch des Deutschen Archaeologischen Instituts. Ergaenzungsheft
J Dairy Res — Journal of Dairy Research
J Dairy Sci — Journal of Dairy Science
J Dalian Eng Inst — Journal. Dalian Engineering Institute
J Dalian Inst Tech — Journal of Dalian Institute of Technology
J Dalian Inst Technol — Journal. Dalian Institute of Technology
J Dalian Univ Tech — Journal of Dalian University of Technology
J Dalian Univ Technol — Journal of Dalian University of Technology
JdAM — Journal d'Analyse Mathematique
J Dames & Modes — Journal des Dames et des Modes
J Dan Archaeol — Journal of Danish Archaeology
JD Arch Inst — Jahrbuch des Deutschen Archaeologischen Instituts
JDASD — Jahrbuch. Deutsche Akademie fuer Sprache und Dichtung in Darmstadt
J Data Ed — Journal of Data Education
J Data Manage — Journal of Data Management
J Data Mgt — Journal of Data Management
JDAW — Jahrbuch der Deutschen Akademie der Wissenschaften
JDB — Jahrbuch Deutscher Bibliophilen
JDB — Jewish Daily Bulletin
JDBP — Journal of Developmental and Behavioral Pediatrics
Jdb T — Jordburgs-Teknik
JDCD — JDC Digest
J DC Dent Soc — Journal. District of Columbia Dental Society
JdCh — Jahrbuch der Charakterologie
JDCHA — Journal of Dentistry for Children
Jd Co — Journal des Communautes
JDCR — JDC Review
JdD — Journal des Debats. Paris and Clermont-Ferrand Daily
JDD — Journal of Developing Areas
JDDD — Judicial Discipline and Disability Digest
JDE — Journal of Development Economics
Jdeb — Journal des Debats, Politiques, et Litteraires
J Debats — Journal des Debats
J Debats — Journal des Debats Politiques et Litteraires
J Dec & Propaganda A — Journal of the Decorative and Propaganda Arts
J Dec A Soc — Journal of the Decorative Arts Society
JDECU — Journal. Department of English. Calcutta University
J De Geneve — Journal de Geneve
J De L Anat Et De La Physiol — Journal de l'Anatomie et de la Physiologie Normales et Pathologiques de l'Hommeet des Animaux
J Delin — Journal of Delinquency
J Delinq — Journal of Delinquency
J de Mecanique Theor Appl — Journal de Mecanique Theorique et Appliquee
J De Med De Lyon — Journal de Medecine de Lyon
J De Med De Paris — Journal de Medecine de Paris
J Dendrol — Journal of Dendrology
J De Neurol Et De Psychlat — Journal de Neurologie et de Psychiatrie
J Denning LS — Journal. Denning Law Society
J Dent — Journal of Dentistry
J Dent Assoc S Afr — Journal. Dental Association of South Africa
J Dent Assoc Thai — Journal. Dental Association of Thailand
J Dent Assoc Thailand — Journal. Dental Association of Thailand
J Dent Aux — Journal of the Dental Auxiliaries
J Dent Chil — Journal of Dentistry for Children
J Dent Child — Journal of Dentistry for Children
J Dent Educ — Journal of Dental Education
J Dent Eng — Journal of Dental Engineering
J Dent Guid Counc Handicap — Journal. Dental Guidance Council on the Handicapped
J Dent Handicap — Journal of Dentistry for the Handicapped
J Dent Health — Journal of Dental Health

J Dent Health (Tokyo) — Journal of Dental Health (Tokyo)
J Dent Med — Journal of Dental Medicine
J Dent Pract Adm — Journal of Dental Practice Administration
J Dent Que — Journal Dentaire du Quebec
J Dent Res — Journal of Dental Research
J Dent Sch Natl Univ Iran — Journal of the Dental School. National University of Iran
J Dent Tech — Journal of Dental Technics
J Dent Technol — Journal of Dental Technology
J Dep Agric Fish (Irel) — Journal. Department of Agriculture and Fisheries (Republic of Ireland)
J Dep Agric (Irel) — Journal. Department of Agriculture (Ireland)
J Dep Agric Kyushu Imp Univ — Journal. Department of Agriculture. Kyushu Imperial University
J Dep Agric (PR) — Journal. Department of Agriculture of (Puerto Rico)
J Dep Agric Repub Irel — Journal. Department of Agriculture. Republic of Ireland
J Dep Agric S Aust — Journal. Department of Agriculture. South Australia
J Dep Agric (Union S Afr) — Journal. Department of Agriculture (Union of South Africa)
J Dep Agric Un S Afr — Journal. Department of Agriculture. Union of South Africa
J Dep Agric Vict — Journal. Department of Agriculture. Victoria
J Dep Agric Victoria Aust — Journal. Department of Agriculture. Victoria, Australia
J Dep Agric W Aust — Journal. Department of Agriculture. Western Australia
J Dep Agric West Aust — Journal. Department of Agriculture. Western Australia
J Dep Geogr Natl Univ Malaysia — Journal. Department of Geography. National University of Malaysia
J Dep Lands Agric (Irel) — Journal. Department of Lands and Agriculture (Ireland)
J De Ps — Journal de Physique, de Chimie, et d'Histoire Naturelle
J De Ps — Journal de Physique Theorique et Appliquee
J Dept Ag Ireland — Journal. Irish Free State Department of Agriculture
J Dept Ag (Puerto Rico) — Journal. Department of Agriculture (Puerto Rico)
J Dept Agr Fish (Dublin) — Journal. Department of Agriculture and Fisheries (Dublin)
J Dept Agric Kyushu Imp Univ — Journal. Department of Agriculture. Kyushu Imperial University
J Dept Agric W Aust — Journal. Department of Agriculture. Western Australia
J Dept Agr S Aust — Journal. Department of Agriculture. South Australia
J Dept Agr Victoria — Journal. Department of Agriculture. Victoria
J Dept Agr W Aust — Journal. Department of Agriculture. Western Australia
J Dept Ag SA — Journal. Department of Agriculture. South Australia
J Dept Ag S Africa — Journal. Department of Agriculture. South Africa
J Dept Ag S Australia — Journal. Department of Agriculture. South Australia
J Dept Ag VIC — Journal. Department of Agriculture. Victoria
J Dept Ag Victoria — Journal. Department of Agriculture. Victoria
JDeR — Journal of Dental Research
J Dermatol — Journal of Dermatology
J Dermatol Sci — Journal of Dermatological Science
J Dermatol Surg — Journal of Dermatological Surgery
J Dermatol Surg Oncol — Journal of Dermatologic Surgery and Oncology
J Dermatol (Tokyo) — Journal of Dermatology (Tokyo)
J Dermatol Treat — Journal of Dermatological Treatment
J Des & Manuf — Journal of Design and Manufactures
J Des Autom and Fault-Tolerant Comput — Journal of Design Automation and Fault-Tolerant Computing
J Des Autom Fault Tolerant Comput — Journal of Design Automation and Fault-Tolerant Computing
J Design Automat Fault-Tolerant Comput — Journal of Design Automation and Fault-Tolerant Computing
J Des Juges De Paix Paris — Journal des Juges de Paix, Juges Suppleants et Greffiers de Paix (Paris)
J des Savants — Journal des Savants
J Deterg — Journal of Detergents
J Deterg Collect Chem — Journal of Detergents and Collective Chemistry
J Deuterium Sci — Journal of Deuterium Science
J Dev Areas — Journal of Developing Areas
J Dev Behav Pediatr — Journal of Developmental and Behavioral Pediatrics
J Dev Biol — Journal of Developmental Biology
J Dev Econ — Journal of Development Economics
J Devel Areas — Journal of Developing Areas
J Devel Econ — Journal of Development Economics
J Develop Areas — Journal of Developing Areas
J Develop Econ — Journal of Development Economics
J Developing Areas — Journal of Developing Areas
J Development Econ — Journal of Development Economics
J Development Planning — Journal of Development Planning
J Development Studies — Journal of Development Studies
J Development Studs — Journal of Development Studies
J Develop Plan — Journal of Development Planning
J Develop Read — Journal of Developmental Reading
J Develop Stud — Journal of Development Studies
J Devel Stud — Journal of Development Studies
J Devon Trust Nat Conserv — Journal. Devon Trust for Nature Conservation
J Dev Physiol — Journal of Developmental Physiology
J Dev Physiol (Oxf) — Journal of Developmental Physiology (Oxford)
J Dev Planning — Journal of Development Planning
J Dev Stud — Journal of Development Studies
J Dev Studies — Journal of Development Studies
JDF — Jewish Daily Forward
JDF — Journal Pratique de Droit Fiscal et Financier
JDFisc — Journal Pratique de Droit Fiscal et Financier
JDG — Jahrbuch. Droste-Gesellschaft
JdG — Journal de Geneve
JDGCK — Jahresmappe der Deutschen Gesellschaft fuer Christliche Kunst
J d g L A — Jahrbuch der Geologischen Landesanstalt
J Dharma — Journal of Dharma

Jdl — Jahrbuch. Deutsches Archaeologische Institut
J Diabet Complications — Journal of Diabetic Complications
J Diabetes Complications — Journal of Diabetes and Its Complications
J Diabetic Assoc India — Journal. Diabetic Association of India
JDIAD — Journal of Dialysis
J Dial — Journal of Dialysis
J Diar Dis Res — Journal of Diarrhoeal Disease Research
J Diarrhoeal Dis Res — Journal of Diarrhoeal Diseases Research
JDI-EH — Jahrbuch. Deutsches Archaeologische Institut. Ergaenzungsheft
J Diet Assoc (Victoria) — Journal. Dietetic Association (Victoria)
J Diet Home Econ — Journal of Dietetics and Home Economics
J Diff Equa — Journal of Differential Equations
J Differential Equations — Journal of Differential Equations
J Differential Geom — Journal of Differential Geometry
J Differential Geometry — Journal of Differential Geometry
J Differ Equations — Journal of Differential Equations
J Differ Equations Appl — Journal of Difference Equations and Applications
J Digest — Jewish Digest
J Digital Syst — Journal of Digital Systems
J Digital Systems — Journal of Digital Systems
J Digit Imaging — Journal of Digital Imaging
J Dispersion Sci Technol — Journal of Dispersion Science and Technology
J Distrib — Journal of Distribution
J Divorce — Journal of Divorce
JDJ — John Donne Journal. Studies in the Age of Donne
JDKG — Jahrbuch fuer Deutsche Kirchengeschichte
JdL — Jornal de Letras
JDLC — Journal. Department of Letters. Calcutta University
JdIT — Jahrbuch der Drahtlosen Telegraphie
JDM — Jahrbuch der Musikwelt
JDM — Journal of Data Management
Jdm — Judaism
J D Mis Evang — Journal des Missions Evangeliques
JDNB — Jewish Telegraphic Agency. Daily News Bulletin
J Doc — Journal of Documentation
J Do Comm — Jornal do Commercio
J Doc Reprod — Journal of Documentary Reproduction
J Docum — Journal of Documentation
J Document — Journal of Documentation
J Documentation — Journal of Documentation
JdOI — Jahreshefte. Oesterreichisches Archaeologische Institut in Wien
J Domest Wastewater Treat Res — Journal of Domestic Wastewater Treatment Research
JdP — Journal des Poetes
JDP — Journal of Development Studies
JDPA — Japan Directory of Professional Associations
JDPL — Journal des Debats Politiques et Litteraires
JDR — Journal of Defense Research
JDR — Juta's Daily Reporter, Cape Provincial Division
J Dr Int — Journal du Droit International
JDR J Drug Res — JDR. Journal of Drug Research
JDR J Drugther Res — JDR. Journal for Drugtherapy and Research
J Droit Afr — Journal de Droit Africain
J Droit Int — Journal du Droit International
J Droit Internat — Journal du Droit International
J Drug Dev — Journal of Drug Development
J Drug Dev Clin Pract — Journal of Drug Development and Clinical Practice
J Drug Dev Suppl — Journal of Drug Development. Supplement
J Drug Educ — Journal of Drug Education
J Drug Iss — Journal of Drug Issues
J Drug Issues — Journal of Drug Issues
J Drug Res (Cairo) — Journal of Drug Research (Cairo)
J Drug Res JDR — Journal of Drug Research. JDR
J Drug Target — Journal of Drug Targeting
J Drugther Res — Journal for Drugtherapy and Research
JDS — Jacobean Drama Studies
JdS — Journal des Savants
JDS — Journal of Development Studies
JDSEA — Jido Seigyo
JDSG — Jahrbuch der Deutschen Shakespeare-Gesellschaft
JDSG — Jahrbuch. Deutsche Schiller-Gesellschaft
JDSh — Jahrbuch. Deutsche Shakespeare-Gesellschaft
JDT — Jahrbuecher fuer Deutsche Theologie
JDTh — Jahrbuecher fuer Deutsche Theologie
JDTL — Jahrbuechlein der Detuschen Theologischen Literatur
JDU — Journal. Durham University
J Du Dr Int — Journal du Droit International
J du Droit Int'l — Journal du Droit International
J du MP — Journal du Ministere Public
JduP — Journal du Peuple
J Durham Sch Agr — Journal. Durham School of Agriculture
J Dynam Control Systems — Journal of Dynamical and Control Systems
J Dynam Differential Equations — Journal of Dynamics and Differential Equations
J Dynam Syst Meas Control Trans ASME — Journal of Dynamic Systems, Measurement, and Control. Transactions. American Society of Mechanical Engineers
J Dyn Syst Meas Control — Journal of Dynamic Systems, Measurement, and Control
J Dyn Syst Meas Control Trans ASME — Journal of Dynamic Systems, Measurement and Control. Transactions of the ASME
JDZ — Japanisch-Deutsche Zeitschrift
JE — Jewish Encyclopedia
JE — Journal of Ecology
JE — Journal of Education
JE — Juedisches Echo

JE — June
JEA — Journal des Etudes Anciennes
JEA — Journal of Egyptian Archaeology
J Ea Afr Nat Hist Soc — Journal. East Africa Natural History Society
JEAB — Journal of the Experimental Analysis of Behavior
JEAC — Journal of Electroanalytical Chemistry
JEAfrSC — Journal. East African Swahili Committee
Jealott's Hill Bull — Jealott's Hill Bulletin
Jean-Paul-Gesellsch Jahrb — Jean-Paul-Gesellschaft. Jahrbuch
JE Arch — Journal of Egyptian Archaeology
J Early Adolescence — Journal of Early Adolescence
J Early Repub — Journal of the Early Republic
J Early S Dec A — Journal of Early Southern Decorative Arts
J Earth Sci — Journal of Earth Sciences
J Earth Sci (Dublin) — Journal of Earth Sciences (Dublin)
J Earth Sci (Leeds Engl) — Journal of Earth Sciences (Leeds, England)
J Earth Sci Nagoya Univ — Journal of Earth Sciences. Nagoya University
J Earth Sci R Dublin Soc — Journal of Earth Sciences. Royal Dublin Society
J Earth Space Phys (Tehran) — Journal of the Earth and Space Physics (Tehran)
JEAS — Journal of East Asiatic Studies
J E Asia — Journal of Eastern Asia
J East Afr Nat Hist Soc Natl Mus — Journal. East Africa Natural History Society and National Museum
J East Afr Res Dev — Journal of Eastern African Research and Development
J East Afr Res Develop — Journal of Eastern African Research and Development
J East Asian Affairs — Journal of East Asian Affairs
J East China Inst Chem Technol — Journal. East China Institute of Chemical Technology
J East China Inst Metall — Journal of East China Institute of Metallurgy
J East China Inst Text Sci Technol — Journal. East China Institute of Textile Science and Technology
J East China Norm Univ Nat Sci — Journal of East China Normal University. Natural Science
J East China Norm Univ Natur Sci Ed — Journal of East China Normal University. Natural Science Edition
J East China Petrol Inst — Journal. East China Petroleum Institute
J East China Univ Sci Technol — Journal of East China University of Science and Technology
J East India Assn — Journal. East India Association
J East West Stud — Journal of East and West Studies
JEB — Jahrbuch des Evangelischen Bundes
JEB — Journal of Economic Behavior
JEB — Journal of Economic Literature
JEB — Journal of Economics and Business
JEB — Journal of Education (Boston University School of Education)
JEB — Journal of Experimental Botany
JEBH — Journal of Economic and Business History
Je C — Jewish Currents
J Ec — Journal des Economistes
JEC — Journal of Econometrics
JECAB — Journal of Electrocardiology
J Eccles Hist — Journal of Ecclesiastical History
J Ecclesiast Hist — Journal of Ecclesiastical History
J Eccl H — Journal of Ecclesiastical History
J Eccl Hist — Journal of Ecclesiastical History
JECEA — Journal. Institution of Engineers (India). Chemical Engineering Division
J Ec Ent — Journal of Economic Entomology
JEcH — Journal of Ecclesiastical History
Je Ci — Jewish Civilization
JECMA — Journal of Electronic Materials
JECMB — Journal of Econometrics
J Ecobiol — Journal of Ecobiology
J Ecol — Journal of Ecology
J Ecology — Journal of Ecology
J Econ — Journal des Economistes
J Econ Abstr — Journal of Economic Abstracts
J Econ Aff — Journal of Economic Affairs
J Econ and Bus — Journal of Economics and Business
J Econ & Soc Hist Orient — Journal of the Economic and Social History of the Orient
J Econ Biol — Journal of Economic Biology
J Econ Bus — Journal of Economics and Business
J Econ Bus Hist — Journal of Economic and Business History
J Econ Dynam Control — Journal of Economic Dynamics and Control
J Econ Dyn and Control — Journal of Economic Dynamics and Control
J Econ Ed — Journal of Economic Education
J Econ Educ — Journal of Economic Education
J Econ Ent — Journal of Economic Entomology
J Econ Entom — Journal of Economic Entomology
J Econ Entomol — Journal of Economic Entomology
J Econ H — Journal of Economic History
J Econ Hist — Journal of Economic History
J Econ Hist S — Journal of Economic History. Supplement
J Econ Iss — Journal of Economic Issues
J Econ Issues — Journal of Economics Issues
JEconLit — Journal of Economic Literature
J Econ Liter — Journal of Economic Literature
J Econom — Journal of Econometrics
J Econom Behavior Organization — Journal of Economic Behavior and Organization
J Econom Dynamics Control — Journal of Economic Dynamics and Control
J Economet — Journal of Econometrics
J Econometrics — Journal of Econometrics
J Economistes — Journal des Economistes
J Econom Theory — Journal of Economic Theory

J Econ Res — Journal of Economic Research
J Econ Soc Hist Or — Journal of the Economic and Social History of the Orient
J Econ Soc Hist Orient — Journal of the Economic and Social History of the Orient
J Econ Soc Meas — Journal of Economic and Social Measurement
J Econ Studies — Journal of Economic Studies
J Econ Taxon Bot — Journal of Economic and Taxonomic Botany
J Econ Theo — Journal of Economic Theory
J Econ Theory — Journal of Economic Theory
J Ecotoxicol Environ Monit — Journal of Ecotoxicology and Environmental Monitoring
JECPA — Journal of Experimental Child Psychology
J Ec Polytech — Journal. Ecole Polytechnique
J Ec Polytech (Paris) — Journal. Ecole Polytechnique (Paris)
J Ec St — Journal of Ecumenical Studies
J Ecumenical Stud — Journal of Ecumenical Studies
J Ecumen Stud — Journal of Ecumenical Studies
J Ecum Stud — Journal of Ecumenical Studies
JECVA — Journal. Institution of Engineers (India). Civil Engineering Division
JED — Jaarboek voor de Eredienst
J Ed — Jewish Education
JED — Journal of Economic Dynamics and Control
J Ed — Journal of Education
J Ed Admin — Journal of Educational Administration
J Ed & Psychol — Journal of Education and Psychology
Jeddah J Mar Res — Jeddah Journal of Marine Research
J Ed Data Process — Journal of Educational Data Processing
Jedermann Eigener Fussball — Jedermann sein Eigener Fussball
J Ed (London) — Journal of Education (London)
J Ed M — Journal of Educational Measurement
J Ednl Admin and History — Journal of Educational Administration and History
J Ednl Technology — Journal of Educational Technology
JEdP — Journal of Educational Psychology
J Ed Psychol — Journal of Educational Psychology
JEdR — Journal of Educational Research
J Ed Res — Journal of Educational Research
J Ed Soc — Journal of Educational Sociology
J Ed Stat — Journal of Educational Statisics
J Ed Thought — Journal of Educational Thought
J Educ — Journal of Education
J Educ Adm — Journal of Educational Administration
J Educ Adm Hist — Journal of Educational Administration and History
J Educ Admin Hist — Journal of Educational Administration and History
J Educ Data Proc — Journal of Educational Data Processing
J Educ Dept Niigata Univ — Journal. Education Department. Niigata University
J Educ D P — Journal of Educational Data Processing
J Educ Fin — Journal of Education Finance
J Educ for Teach — Journal of Education for Teaching
J Educ Libr — Journal of Education for Librarianship
J Educ Librarianship — Journal of Education for Librarianship
J Educ (Lond) — Journal of Education (London)
J Educ M — Journal of Educational Measurement
J Educ Media Science — Journal of Educational Media Science
J Educ Meth — Journal of Educational Method
J Educ Method — Journal of Educational Method
J Educ Modules Mater Sci Eng — Journal of Educational Modules for Materials Science and Engineering
J Educ Psyc — Journal of Educational Psychology
J Educ Psych — Journal of Education and Psychology
J Educ Psychol — Journal of Educational Psychology
J Educ Res — Journal of Educational Research
J Educ Research — Journal of Educational Research
J Educ Soc — Journal of Educational Sociology
J Educ Soc — Journal of Education for Social Work
J Educ Social — Journal of Educational Sociology
J Educ Sociol — Journal of Educational Sociology
J Educ Soc Work — Journal of Education for Social Work
J Educ Technol Syst — Journal of Educational Technology Systems
J Educ Tech Syst — Journal of Educational Technology Systems
J Educ Th — Journal of Educational Thought
J Educ Univ Natal — Journal of Education. Faculty of Education. University of Natal
J Ed Univ HK — Journal of Education. University of Hong Kong
JEE — Japan Electronic Engineering
JEE — JEE. Journal of Electronic Engineering
JEE — Journal of Economic Entomology
JEE — Journal of Engineering Education
JEE — Journal of Environmental Economics and Management
JEE — Journal of Experimental Education
JEED — Journal. Environmental Engineering Division. Proceedings of the American Society of Civil Engineers
JEEGA — Journal. Environmental Engineering Division. American Society of Civil Engineers
JEE J Electron Eng — JEE. Journal of Electronic Engineering
JEE Jpn Electron Eng — JEE [*Japan Electronic Engineering*] Japan Electronic Engineering
JEELA — Journal. Institution of Engineers (India). Electrical Engineering Division
JEEMD — Journal of Environmental Economics and Management
JEEND — JEE. Journal of Electronic Engineering
JEF — Japan Economic Journal
JEFDS — Journal. English Folk Dance and Song Society
JEFDSS — Journal. English Folk Dance and Song Society
Jeffrsn B — Jefferson Business
JEFS — Journal. English Folk Dance and Song Society
J Eg Arch — Journal of Egyptian Archaeology
JEGH — Juris Ecclesiastici Graecorum Hisoria et Monumenta

J Eg Or Soc — Journal. Egyptian and Oriental Society
JEGP — Journal of English and Germanic Philology
JEGPA — Journal. Egyptian Public Health Association
JEG Ph — Journal of English and Germanic Philology
JEG Phil — Journal of English and Germanic Philology
J Egypt Arch — Journal of Egyptian Archaeology
J Egypt Archaeol — Journal of Egyptian Archaeology
J Egyptian MA — Journal. Egyptian Medical Association
J Egyptian Math Soc — Journal of the Egyptian Mathematical Society
J Egypt Med Ass — Journal. Egyptian Medical Association
J Egypt Med Assoc — Journal. Egyptian Medical Association
J Egypt Med Soc — Journal. Egyptian Medical Society
J Egypt Pharm — Journal of Egyptian Pharmacy
J Egypt Public Health Assoc — Journal. Egyptian Public Health Association
J Egypt Soc Obstet Gynecol — Journal. Egyptian Society of Obstetrics and Gynecology
J Egypt Soc Parasitol — Journal. Egyptian Society of Parasitology
J Egypt Vet Med Ass — Journal. Egyptian Veterinary Medical Association
JEH — Journal of Ecclesiastical History
JEH — Journal of Economic History
JEH/S — Journal of Economic History/Supplement
JEHV — Jahrbuch des Emslaendischen Heimatvereins
JEI — Japan Electronics Industry
JEI — Journal. English Institute
JEI — Journal of Economic Issues
JEIA — Journal. East India Association
JEI J Electron Ind — JEI. Journal of the Electronics Industry
JEI Jpn Electron Ind — JEI. Japan Electronic Industry
JEIND — Journal of Endocrinological Investigation
J E India Assoc — Journal. East India Association
JEJ — Jahrbuch fuer Erziehungswissenschaft und Jugendkunde
JEJ — Japan Economic Journal
JEJ — Jazz Educators Journal
Jeju Univ J Nat Sci — Jeju University Journal. Natural Sciences
JEL — Journal of Economic Literature
JEL — Journal of English Linguistics
J El Ass J — Journal. Electrochemical Association of Japan
J Elast — Journal of Elasticity
J Elasticity — Journal of Elasticity
J Elastomers Plast — Journal of Elastomers and Plastics
J Elastoplast — Journal of Elastoplastics [Later, Journal of Elastomers and Plastics]
J Elcardiol — Journal of Electrocardiology
J Elchem So — Journal. Electrochemical Society
J El Chem Soc — Journal. Electrochemical Society
J Elec — Journal of Electricity
J Elec Buy — Japan Electronics Buyers' Guide
J Elec Chem — Journal of Electroanalytical Chemistry and Interfacial Electrochemistry
J Elec Def — Journal of Electronic Defense
J Elec E — Journal of Electronic Engineering
J Elec Mat — Journal of Electronic Materials
J Elec Micr — Journal of Electron Microscopy
J Elec Spec — Journal of Electron Spectroscopy and Related Phenomena
J Electr — Journal of Electricity
J Electr Commun Lab — Journal. Electrical Communications Laboratory
J Electr Electron Eng (Aust) — Journal of Electrical and Electronics Engineering (Australia)
J Electr Eng — Journal of Electrical Engineering
J Electr Eng Soc (Tokyo) — Journal. Electric Engineering Society (Tokyo)
J Electr Microsc — Journal of Electron Microscopy
J Electroanal Chem — Journal of Electroanalytical Chemistry
J Electroanal Chem Abstr Sect — Journal of Electroanalytical Chemistry. Abstract Section
J Electroanal Chem Interfacial Electrochem — Journal of Electroanalytical Chemistry and Interfacial Electrochemistry
J Electrocardiol — Journal of Electrocardiology
J Electrocardiol (San Diego) — Journal of Electrocardiology (San Diego)
J Electroceram — Journal of Electroceramics
J Electrochem Soc — Journal. Electrochemical Society
J Electrochem Soc India — Journal. Electrochemical Society of India
J Electrochem Soc Japan — Journal. Electrochemical Society of Japan
J Electrodepositors Tech Soc — Journal. Electrodepositors' Technical Society
J Electromyo & Kines — Journal of Electromyography and Kinesiology
J Electron — Journal of Electronics
J Electron (Beijing) — Journal of Electronics (Beijing)
J Electron Control — Journal of Electronics and Control
J Electron Devices — Journal of Electron Devices
J Electron Eng — Journal of Electronic Engineering
J Electron Imaging — Journal of Electronic Imaging
J Electron Manuf — Journal of Electronics Manufacturing
J Electron Mater — Journal of Electronic Materials
J Electron Microsc — Journal of Electron Microscopy
J Electron Microsc Tech — Journal of Electron Microscopy Technique
J Electron Microsc (Tokyo) — Journal of Electron Microscopy (Tokyo)
J Electron Micry — Journal of Electron Microscopy
J Electron Packag Trans ASME — Journal of Electronic Packaging. Transactions of the ASME
J Electron Spectrosc and Relat Phenom — Journal of Electron Spectroscopy and Related Phenomena
J Electron Spectrosc Relat Phenom — Journal of Electron Spectroscopy and Related Phenomena
J Electron Test Theory Appl JETTA — Journal of Electronic Testing, Theory, and Applications (JETTA)
J Electroph — Journal of Electrophysiological Techniques

J Electroplat Depositors Tech Soc — Journal. Electroplater's and Depositors' Technical Society
J Electrost — Journal of Electrostatics
J Electrostat — Journal of Electrostatics
J Electrostatics — Journal of Electrostatics
J Electr Power Gas — Journal of Electricity, Power, and Gas
J Electr Spectr — Journal of Electron Spectroscopy and Related Phenomena
J Electr West Ind — Journal of Electricity and Western Industry
J Elect Spectrosc — Journal of Electron Spectroscopy and Related Phenomena
Jelenkor — Jelenkor. Irodalmi es Muveszeti Folyoirat
JELIS — Journal of Education for Library and Information Science
J Elisha Mitchell Scient Soc — Journal. Elisha Mitchell Scientific Society
J Elisha Mitchell Sci Soc — Journal. Elisha Mitchell Scientific Society
J Elisha Mitch Sci Soc — Journal. Elisha Mitchell Scientific Society
J El Soc — Journal. Electrochemical Society
JEM — Journal of Enterprise Management
JEM — Journal of Environmental Economics and Management
JEMA — Journal of the (Royal) Egyptian Medical Association
JEMAA — Journal. Egyptian Medical Association
J Emb Exp M — Journal of Embryology and Experimental Morphology
J Embr Exp Morph — Journal of Embryology and Experimental Morphology
J Embryol Exp Morphol — Journal of Embryology and Experimental Morphology
Jemen Rep — Jemen-Report
J Emergency Nurs — Journal of Emergency Nursing
J Emerg Med — Journal of Emergency Medicine
J Emerg Med Serv JEMS — Journal of Emergency Medical Services. JEMS
J Emerg Nurs — Journal of Emergency Nursing
J Emerg Services — Journal of Emergency Services
JEMFA — JEMF [John Edwards Memorial Foundation] Quarterly
JEMFQ — JEMF [John Edwards Memorial Foundation] Quarterly
JEMF Quart — JEMF [John Edwards Memorial Foundation] Quarterly
JEMIC Tech Rep — JEMIC [Japan Electric Meters Inspection Corporation] Technical Report
Jemna Mech a Opt — Jemna Mechanika a Optika
Jemna Mech Opt — Jemna Mechanika a Optika
J Empl Coun — Journal of Employment Counseling
J Employ Counsel — Journal of Employment Counseling
JEMSA — Journal. Elisha Mitchell Scientific Society
JEN — Japan Economic Newswire
JEN — Journal de l'Enregistrement et du Notariat
JEN — Journal of Emergency Nursing
J En — Journal of English
JEN — Journal of Enterprise Management
Jenaer Harnsteinsymp — Jenaer Harnsteinsymposium
Jenaer Jahrb — Jenaer Jahrbuch
Jenaer Rundsch — Jenaer Rundschau
Jenaische Zeitschrift — Jenaische Zeitschrift fuer Medizin und Naturwissenschaft
Jenaische Z Med — Jenaische Zeitschrift fuer Medizin Herausgegeben von der Medicinisch-Naturwissenschaftlichen Gesellschaft zu Jena
Jenaische Z Naturwiss — Jenaische Zeitschrift fuer Naturwissenschaft Herausgegeben von der Medicinisch-Naturwissenschaftlichen Gesellschaft zu Jena
Jenaische Ztschr Med u Naturw — Jenaische Zeitschrift fuer Medizin und Naturwissenschaft
Jenaische Ztschr Naturw — Jenaische Zeitschrift fuer Naturwissenschaft
Jen Allg Lit Ztg — Jenaische Allgemeine Literatur-Zeitung
Jena Rev — Jena Review
Jena Rev Suppl — Jena Review. Supplement
Jena Rundsch — Jenaer Rundschau
Jena Sb — Sitzungsberichte der Jenaischen Gesellschaft fuer Medicin und Naturwissenschaft
Jena Z — Jenaische Zeitschrift fuer Naturwissenschaft Herausgegeben von der Medicinisch-Naturwissenschaftlichen Gesellschaft zu Jena
Jena Z Med Naturwiss — Jenaische Zeitschrift fuer Medizin und Naturwissenschaft
Jena Z Naturw — Jenaische Zeitschrift fuer Naturwissenschaft
Jena Z Naturwiss — Jenaische Zeitschrift fuer Naturwissenschaft
Jena Zs Med — Jenaische Zeitschrift fuer Medizin und Naturwissenschaft
Jena Zs Med Naturw — Jenaische Zeitschrift fuer Medizin und Naturwissenschaft
JENDD — Journal of Energy and Development
J Endocr — Journal of Endocrinology
J Endocrinol — Journal of Endocrinology
J Endocrinol Invest — Journal of Endocrinological Investigation
J Endocrinol Reprod — Journal of Endocrinology and Reproduction
J Endod — Journal of Endodontics
J Endodont — Journal of Endodontics
J Endotoxin Res — Journal of Endotoxin Research
J Endourol — Journal of Endourology
J Endovasc Surg — Journal of Endovascular Surgery
J Endovasc Ther — Journal of Endovascular Therapy
J Energ Mater — Journal of Energetic Materials
J Energy — Journal of Energy
J Energy and Development — Journal of Energy and Development
J Energy Dev — Journal of Energy and Development
J Energy Develop — Journal of Energy and Development
J Energy Div Am Soc Civ Eng — Journal. Energy Division. American Society of Civil Engineers
J Energy Div ASCE — Journal. Energy Division. American Society of Civil Engineers
J Energy Div Proc ASCE — Journal. Energy Division. American Society of Civil Engineers. Proceedings
J Energy Eng — Journal of Energy Engineering
J Energy Heat Mass Transfer — Journal of Energy, Heat, and Mass Transfer
J Energy L & Pol'y — Journal of Energy Law and Policy
J Energy Law and Policy — Journal of Energy Law and Policy
J Energy L P — Journal of Energy Law and Policy

J Energy Resources Technol — Journal of Energy Resources Technology

J Energy Resources Tech Trans ASME — Journal of Energy Resources Technology. Transactions. American Society of Mechanical Engineers

J Energy Resour Technol — Journal of Energy Resources Technology

J Energy Resour Technol Trans ASME — Journal of Energy Resources Technology. Transactions of the American Society ofMechanical Engineers

JENER Publ — JENER [*Joint Establishment for Nuclear Energy Research. Netherlands and Norway*] Publication

JENER Rep — JENER [*Joint Establishment for Nuclear Energy Research. Netherlands and Norway*] Report

J Eng and Germ Philol — Journal of English and Germanic Philology

J Eng Appl Sci Peshawar — Journal of Engineering and Applied Sciences (Peshawar)

J Eng Ed — Journal of Engineering Education

J Eng Educ — Journal of Engineering Education

J Eng Gas Turbines Power — Journal of Engineering for Gas Turbines and Power

J Eng Ger Philol — Journal of English and Germanic Philology

J Eng Ind — Journal of Engineering for Industry

J Eng Ind Tran ASME — Journal of Engineering for Industry. Transactions of the American Society of Mechanical Engineers

J Eng Ind Trans ASME — Journal of Engineering for Industry. Transactions of the American Society of Mechanical Engineers

J Eng L — Journal of English Linguistics

J Engl Agric Soc — Journal. English Agricultural Society

J Engl & Germ Philol — Journal of English and Germanic Philology

J Engl Ger — Journal of English and Germanic Philology

J Engl Ger Philol — Journal of English and German Philology

J Eng Lit Hist — Journal of English Literary History

J Engl Place-Name Soc — Journal. English Place-Name Society

J Eng Mat & Tech — Journal of Engineering Materials and Technology

J Eng Mater — Journal of Engineering Materials and Technology

J Eng Materials & Tech — Journal of Engineering Materials and Technology

J Eng Mater Technol — Journal of Engineering Materials and Technology

J Eng Mater Technol Trans ASME — Journal of Engineering Materials and Technology. Transactions of the American Society of Mechanical Engineers

J Eng Math — Journal of Engineering Mathematics

J Eng Mech — Journal of Engineering Mechanics

J Eng Mech Div Amer Soc Civil Eng Proc — Journal. Engineering Mechanics Division. Proceedings of the American Society ofCivil Engineers

J Eng Mech Div Am Soc Civ Eng — Journal. Engineering Mechanics Division. Proceedings of the American Society ofCivil Engineers

J Eng Natl Chung Hsing Univ — Journal of Engineering. National Chung-hsing Univeristy

J Engng Math — Journal of Engineering Mathematics

J Engng Mech Div Proc ASCE — Journal. Engineering Mechanics Division. Proceedings of the American Society ofCivil Engineers

J Engn Phys — Journal of Engineering Physics

J Eng Phys — Journal of Engineering Physics

J Eng Phys (Belgrade) — Journal of Engineering Physics (Belgrade)

J Eng Phys (Engl Transl) — Journal of Engineering Physics (English Translation of Inzhenerno-Fizicheskii Zhurnal)

J Eng Phys (Minsk) — Journal of Engineering Physics (Minsk)

J Eng Power — Journal of Engineering for Power

J Eng Power Trans ASME — Journal of Engineering for Power. Transactions of the American Society of Mechanical Engineers

J Eng Psychol — Journal of Engineering Psychology

J Engrg Gas Turbines Power Trans ASME — Journal of Engineering for Gas Turbines and Power. Transactions. American Society of Mechanical Engineers

J Engrg Indus Trans ASME — Journal of Engineering for Industry. Transactions. American Society of Mechanical Engineers

J Engrg Math — Journal of Engineering Mathematics

J Engrg Mech ASCE — Journal of Engineering Mechanics. American Society of Civil Engineers

J Engrg Phys — Journal of Engineering Physics

J Engrg Phys Thermophys — Journal of Engineering Physics and Thermophysics

J Eng S — Journal of English Studies

J Eng Sci — Journal of Engineering Sciences

J Eng Sci (Saudi Arabia) — Journal of Engineering Sciences (Saudi Arabia)

J Eng Sci Technol Seoul — Journal of Engineering Science and Technology (Seoul)

J Eng Technol Manage JET M — Journal of Engineering and Technology Management - JET-M

J Eng Thermophy — Journal of Engineering Thermophysics

J Enhanced Heat Transfer — Journal of Enhanced Heat Transfer

Jenner Symp — Jenner Symposium

Jennings Mag — Jennings Magazine

JENS — Journal. Eighteen Nineties Society

Jen-Sal J — Jen-Sal Journal

J Ent — Journal of Entomology

J Enteros Ther — Journal of Enterstomal Therapy

J Enterostom Ther — Journal of Enterostomal Therapy

Jentgens Artif Silk Rev — Jentgen's Artificial Silk Review

Jentgens Rayon Rev — Jentgen's Rayon Review

J Entomol A — Journal of Entomology. Series A. General Entomology

J Entomol B — Journal of Entomology. Series B. Taxonomy

J Entomol Res — Journal of Entomological Research

J Entomol Res (New Delhi) — Journal of Entomological Research (New Delhi)

J Entomol Sci — Journal of Entomological Science

J Entomol Ser A — Journal of Entomology. Series A. General Entomology

J Entomol Ser A Gen Entomol — Journal of Entomology. Series A. General Entomology

J Entomol Ser A Physiol Behav — Journal of Entomology. Series A. Physiology and Behaviour

J Entomol Ser B Taxon — Journal of Entomology. Series B. Taxonomy

J Entomol Ser B Taxon Syst — Journal of Entomology. Series B. Taxonomy and Systematics

J Entomol Soc Aust — Journal. Entomological Society of Australia

J Entomol Soc Aust (NSW) — Journal. Entomological Society of Australia (New South Wales)

J Entomol Soc BC — Journal. Entomological Society of British Columbia

J Entomol Soc S Afr — Journal. Entomological Society of Southern Africa

J Entomol Soc South Afr — Journal. Entomological Society of Southern Africa

J Entomol Soc Sthn Afr — Journal. Entomological Society of Southern Africa

J Entomol Zool — Journal of Entomology and Zoology

J Ent Soc Aust — Journal. Entomological Society of Australia

J Ent Soc Aust (NSW) — Journal. Entomological Society of Australia (New South Wales Branch)

J Ent Soc BC — Journal. Entomological Society of British Columbia

J Ent Soc Qd — Journal. Entomological Society of Queensland

J Ent Soc South Afr — Journal. Entomological Society of Southern Africa

J Ent Soc Sth Afr — Journal. Entomological Society of Southern Africa

J Ent Zool — Journal of Entomology and Zoology

J Env Educ — Journal of Environmental Education

J Envir Econ Man — Journal of Environmental Economics and Management

J Envir Eng — Journal. Environmental Engineering Division. American Society of Civil Engineers

J Envir Mgm — Journal of Environmental Management

J Environ Biol — Journal of Environmental Biology

J Environ Chem — Journal of Environmental Chemistry

J Environ Chem Technol — Journal of Environmental Chemistry and Technology

J Environ Conserv Technol — Journal of Environmental Conservation Technology

J Environ Econ Manage — Journal of Environmental Economics and Management

J Environ Educ — Journal of Environmental Education

J Environ Eng — Journal of Environmental Engineering

J Environ Eng Div Am Soc Civ Eng — Journal. Environmental Engineering Division. American Society of Civil Engineers

J Environ Eng Div ASCE — Journal. Environmental Engineering Division. American Society of Civil Engineers

J Environ Eng (Los Angeles) — Journal of Environmental Engineering (Los Angeles)

J Environ Engng Div Proc ASCE — Journal. Environmental Engineering Division. Proceedings of the American Society of Civil Engineers

J Environ Health — Journal of Environmental Health

J Environ Hortic — Journal of Environmental Horticulture

J Environ Lab Assoc — Journal. Environmental Laboratories Association

J Environ Manage — Journal of Environmental Management

J Environmental Econ and Mgt — Journal of Environmental Economics and Management

J Environ Pathol Toxicol — Journal of Environmental Pathology and Toxicology

J Environ Pathol Toxicol Oncol — Journal of Environmental Pathology, Toxicology, and Oncology

J Environ Plann Pollut Control — Journal of Environmental Planning and Pollution Control

J Environ Pollut Control (Tokyo) — Journal of Environmental Pollution Control (Tokyo)

J Environ Prot Soc (Repub China) — Journal. Environmental Protection Society (Republic of China)

J Environ Qual — Journal of Environmental Quality

J Environ Radioact — Journal of Environmental Radioactivity

J Environ Sci — Journal of Environmental Sciences

J Environ Sci (Beijing) — Journal of Environmental Sciences (Beijing, China)

J Environ Sci Health B — Journal of Environmental Science and Health. Part B. Pesticides, Food Contaminants, and Agricultural Wastes

J Environ Sci Health (C) — Journal of Environmental Science and Health. Part C. Environmental Health Sciences

J Environ Sci Health Part A — Journal of Environmental Science and Health. Part A. Environmental Science and Engineering

J Environ Sci Health Part A Environ Sci Eng — Journal of Environmental Science and Health. Part A. Environmental Science and Engineering

J Environ Sci Health Part A Environ Sci Eng Toxic Hazard — Journal of Environmental Science and Health. Part A. Environmental Science and Engineering and Toxic and Hazardous Substance Control

J Environ Sci Health Part A Environ Sci Eng Toxic Hazard Subst — Journal of Environmental Science and Health. Part A. Environmental Science and Engineering & Toxic and Hazardous Substance Control

J Environ Sci Health Part A Tox Hazard Subst Environ Eng — Journal of Environmental Science and Health. Part A. Toxic/Hazardous Substances & Environmental Engineering

J Environ Sci Health Part A Toxic Hazard Subst Environ Eng — Journal of Environmental Science and Health. Part A. Toxic/Hazardous Substances & Environmental Engineering

J Environ Sci Health Part B — Journal of Environmental Science and Health. Part B. Pesticides, Food Contaminants, and Agricultural Wastes

J Environ Sci Health Part B Pestic Food Contam Agric Wastes — Journal of Environmental Science and Health. Part B. Pesticides, Food Contaminants, and Agricultural Wastes

J Environ Sci Health Part C — Journal of Environmental Science and Health. Part C

J Environ Sci Health Part C Environ Carcinog Ecotoxicol Rev — Journal of Environmental Science and Health. Part C. Environmental Carcinogenesis and Ecotoxicolgy Reviews

J Environ Sci Health Part C Environ Carcinog Rev — Journal of Environmental Science and Health. Part C. Environmental Carcinogenesis Reviews

J Environ Sci Health Part C Environ Health Sci — Journal of Environmental Science and Health. Part C. Environmental Health Sciences

J Environ Syst — Journal of Environmental Systems

J Environ Systems — Journal of Environmental Systems

J Envir Q — Journal of Environmental Quality

J Envir Qual — Journal of Environmental Quality

J Envir Quality — Journal of Environmental Quality
J Envir Sci — Journal of Environmental Sciences
J Envir Sci Hlth — Journal of Environmental Science and Health
Jen Zeiss Jb — Jenaer Zeiss-Jahrbuch
J Enzyme Inhib — Journal of Enzyme Inhibition
JeO — Jeunesse et Orgue
JEOFD — Jeofizik
JEOL — Jaarbericht. Vooraziatisch-Egyptisch Genootschap "Ex Oriente Lux"
JEOL (Jpn Electron Opt Lab) News — JEOL (Japan Electron Optics Laboratory) News
JEOL News Ser Anal Instrum — JEOL [Japan Electron Optics Laboratory] News. Series Analytical Instrumentation
JeP — Jeune Philosophie
JEP — Journal of Economic Psychology
JEP — Journal of Educational Psychology
JEP — Journal of Evolutionary Psychology
JEP — Journal of General Management
JEPG — Journal of Experimental Psychology. General
JEPH — Journal of Experimental Psychology. Human Perception and Performance
JEPHA — Journal of the Egyptian Public Health Association
J Epid Com Health — Journal of Epidemiology in Community Health
J Epidemiol — Journal of Epidemiology
J Epidemiol Biostat — Journal of Epidemiology and Biostatistics
J Epidemiol Community Health — Journal of Epidemiology and Community Health
JEPL — Journal of Experimental Psychology. Learning, Memory, Cognition
JEPLA — Journal of Elastomers and Plastics
JEPP — Japan English Publications in Print
JEPs — Journal of Educational Psychology
JEPSA — Journal of Experimental Psychology
JEPSB — Journal Europeen des Steroides
JEPSBL — European Journal of Steroids
Je Q — Jerusalem Quarterly
J Equine Med Surg — Journal of Equine Medicine and Surgery
J Equine Vet Sci — Journal of Equine Veterinary Science
J Equip Electr et Electron — Journal de l'Equipement Electrique et Electronique
JER — Japan Economic Review
J e R — Jeta e Re
JER — Journal of Educational Research
J Erfind Natur Arzneiwiss — Journal der Erfindungen, Theorien, und Widerspueche in der Naturund Arzneiwissenschaft
Jernb — Jernbanen
Jernkon Ann — Jernkontorets Annaler
Jern Kont A — Jern-Kontoret's Annaler
Jernkontorets Ann — Jernkontorets Annaler
Jernkontorets Ann Ed A — Jernkontorets Annaler. Edition A
Jernkontorets Ann Ed B — Jernkontorets Annaler. Edition B
Jer Q — Jerusalem Quarterly
Jersey B — Jersey Bulletin and Dairy World
Jersey Bul — Jersey Bulletin
Jersey J — Jersey Journal
JERTD — Journal of Energy Resources Techology
Jerusalem J Int Relat — Jerusalem Journal of International Relations
Jerusalem Q — Jerusalem Quarterly
Jerusalem Rep — Jerusalem Report
Jerusalem Stud Jew Flklore — Jerusalem Studies in Jewish Folklore
Jerusalem Winter School Theoret Phys — Jerusalem Winter School for Theoretical Physics
Jerus J Int Rel — Jerusalem Journal of International Relations
Jerus Symp Quantum Chem Biochem — Jerusalem Symposia on Quantum Chemistry and Biochemistry
JES — Japanese Economic Studies. A Journal of Translations
JES — Journal of Economics and Sociology
JES — Journal of Economic Studies
JES — Journal of Ecumenical Studies
JES — Journal of English Studies
JES — Journal of Entomological Science
JES — Journal of European Studies
Jesch — Jeschurun (Berlin)
JESHO — Journal of the Economic and Social History of the Orient
JESIA — Journal. Electrochemical Society of India
JESL — Journal. Ethnological Society (London)
Jes Miss — Jesuites Missionnaires
JESOA — Journal. Electrochemical Society
JeSS — Jewish Social Studies
J Essent Oil Res — Journal of Essential Oil Research
J Essent Oil Res JEOR — Journal of Essential Oil Research. JEOR
JESt — Journal of Ethiopian Studies
JEST — Journees d'Etudes. Societe Thomiste
J Estomat — Jornal de Estomatologia
Jesu — Jesuiten
JET — Jahrbuch der Elektrotechnik
JET — Journal of Economic Theory
JET — Journal of Environmental Systems
JET — Journal of Real Estate Taxation
JETAA — Journal. Faculty of Engineering. University of Tokyo. Series A. Annual Report
JETAI — Journal of Experimental and Theoretical Artificial Intelligence
JETBA — Journal. Faculty of Engineering. University of Tokyo. Series B
JETCA — Journal of Ethnic Studies
J Ethiopian Law — Journal of Ethiopian Law
J Ethiopian Stud — Journal of Ethiopian Studies
J Ethiop Law — Journal of Ethiopian Law
JEthiopSt — Journal of Ethiopian Studies
J Ethiop Stud — Journal of Ethiopian Studies
J Ethiop Studs — Journal of Ethiopian Studies

J Ethnic Stud — Journal of Ethnic Studies
J Ethnobiol — Journal of Ethnobiology
J Ethnopharmacol — Journal of Ethnopharmacology
J Ethol — Journal of Ethology
JEthS — Journal of Ethiopian Studies
J Eth S — Journal of Ethnic Studies
JETI — JETI. Japan Energy and Technology Intelligence
JET J Educ Teach — JET. Journal of Education for Teaching
JETOAS — European Journal of Toxicology
JETP — Journal of Experimental and Theoretical Physics
JETPA — Jet Propulsion
JETP Lett — JETP Letters
Jet Propul — Jet Propulsion
Jet Propul Lab Publ — Jet Propulsion Laboratory. Publication
Jet Propul Lab Q Tech Rev — Jet Propulsion Laboratory. Quarterly Technical Review
Jet Propul Lab Spec Publ JPL SP — Jet Propulsion Laboratory. Special Publication JPL SP
Jet Propul Lab Tech Memo — Jet Propulsion Laboratory. Technical Memorandum
JETS — Journal. Evangelical Theological Society
J Et S — Journal of Ethiopian Studies
JETXA — Journal of Existentialism
JEU — Jeune Afrique
JEU — Journal of European Industrial Training
Jeugd En Beroep — Jeugd en Beroep. Tijdschrift voor Jeugdpsychologie Voorlichting bij Beroepskeuze en Beroepsvorming
J Eukaryot Microbiol — Journal of Eukaryotic Microbiology
JeuneA — Jeune Afrique
Jeune C — Jeune Cinema
Jeune Sci — Jeune Scientifique
Jeunesse — Jeunesse et Orgue
Jeunes Trav — Jeunes Travailleurs
J Eur Cancerol — Journal Europeen de Cancerologie
J Eur Ceram Soc — Journal. European Ceramic Society
J Eur Econ Hist — Journal of European Economic History
J Eur Hydrol — Journal Europeen d'Hydrologie
J Eur Ind Train — Journal of European Industrial Training
J Eur Ind Training — Journal of European Industrial Training
J Europ Econ Hist — Journal of European Economic History
J Europ Training — Journal of European Training
J Eur Opt Soc Part A — Journal. European Optical Society. Part A
J Eur Opt Soc Part B — Journal of the European Optical Society. Part B
J Eur Pathol For — Journal Europeen de Pathologie Forestiere
J Eur Pharm Hosp — Journal Europeen de la Pharmacie Hospitaliere
J Eur Radiother — Journal Europeen de Radiotherapie, Oncologie, Radiophysique, Radiobiologie
J Eur Steroides — Journal Europeen des Steroides
J Eur Stud — Journal of European Studies
J Eur Toxicol — Journal Europeen de Toxicologie
J Eur Toxicol Suppl — Journal Europeen de Toxicologie. Supplement
J Eur Train — Journal of European Training
J Ev — Journal de l'Evangelisation
J Eval Clin Pract — Journal of Evaluation in Clinical Practice
J Evang Th S — Journal. Evangelical Theological Society
JEVEB — Journal of Environmental Education
JEVMA — Journal of the Egyptian Veterinary Medical Association
J Ev Miss — Jahrbuch Evangelischer Mission
J Evol Bioc — Journal of Evolutionary Biochemistry and Physiology
J Evol Biochem Physiol (Engl Transl Zh Evol Biokhim Fiziol) — Journal of Evolutionary Biochemistry and Physiology (English Translation of Zhurnal Evolyutsionnoi Biokhimii i Fiziologii)
J Evol Biochem Physiol (USSR) — Journal of Evolutionary Biochemistry and Physiology (USSR)
J Evol Biol — Journal of Evolutionary Biology
J Evolut Biochem Physiol — Journal of Evolutionary Biochemistry and Physiology
JEVQA — Journal of Environmental Quality
JEVSB — Journal of Environmental Systems
J Ev Th S — Journal. Envangelical Theological Society
JEVWK — Jahrbuch. Evangelischer Verein fuer Westfaelische Kirchengeschichte
JEVWKG — Jahrbuch des Evangelischen Vereines fuer Westfaelische Kirchengeschichte
Jew A — Jewish Art
Jew Aff — Jewish Affairs
Jew Chr — Jewish Chronicle
JewChron — Jewish Chronicle
Jew Com — Jewish Commentary
Jewel Stud — Jewellery Studies
Jew Flklore & Ethnol Newslett — Jewish Folklore and Ethnology Newsletter
Jew For — Jewish Forum
Jew Fron — Jewish Frontier
J Ewha Med Assoc — Journal. Ewha Medical Association
Jew Hist Soc England Trans — Jewish Historical Society of England. Transactions
Jew Hist Soc Engl Trans — Jewish Historical Society of England. Transactions
Jewish Cu — Jewish Currents
Jewish Ed — Jewish Education
Jewish Educ — Jewish Education
Jewish Hist Soc of England Trans — Jewish Historical Society of England. Transactions
Jewish J Sociol — Jewish Journal of Sociology
Jewish J Sociology — Jewish Journal of Sociology
Jewish Mus & Lit — Journal of Jewish Music and Liturgy
Jewish Q Rev — Jewish Quarterly Review
Jewish Quar Rev — Jewish Quarterly Review
Jewish Soc Serv Q — Jewish Social Service Quarterly
Jewish Soc Stud — Jewish Social Studies

JewJSoc — Jewish Journal of Sociology
Jew J Socio — Jewish Journal of Sociology
JewL — Jewish Life
Jew Meml Hosp Bull — Jewish Memorial Hospital Bulletin
JewQ — Jewish Quarterly Review
Jew Q R — Jewish Quarterly Review
Jew Q Rev — Jewish Quarterly Review
Jew Quart R — Jewish Quarterly Review
JewRev — Jewish Review
JewSocSt — Jewish Social Studies
Jew Soc Stu — Jewish Social Studies
Jew Soc Stud — Jewish Social Studies
JEx — Journal of Existentialism
J Ex An Beh — Journal of the Experimental Analysis of Behavior
J Excep Child — Journal of Exceptional Children
J Existent — Journal of Existentialism
JExP — Journal of Experimental Psychology
J Exp Anal Behav — Journal of the Experimental Analysis of Behavior
J Exp Analysis Behav — Journal of the Experimental Analysis of Behavior
J Exp Anim — Journal of Experimental Animal Science
J Exp Anim Sci — Journal of Experimental Animal Science
J Exp Biol — Journal of Experimental Biology
J Exp Biol Med — Journal of Experimental Biology and Medicine
J Exp Bot — Journal of Experimental Botany
J Exp Child Psy — Journal of Experimental Child Psychology
J Exp Child Psychol — Journal of Experimental Child Psychology
J Exp Clin Cancer Res — Journal of Experimental and Clinical Cancer Research
J Exp C Psy — Journal of Experimental Child Psychology
J Exp Ed — Journal of Experimental Education
J Exp Educ — Journal of Experimental Education
J Exper Anal Behav — Journal of the Experimental Analysis of Behavior
J Exper Biol — Journal of Experimental Biology
J Exper Bot — Journal of Experimental Botany
J Exper Child Psychol — Journal of Experimental Child Psychology
J Exper Educ — Journal of Experimental Education
J Experiment Theoret Phys — Journal of Experimental and Theoretical Physics
J Exper Marine Biol & Ecol — Journal of Experimental Marine Biology and Ecology
J Exper Med — Journal of Experimental Medicine
J Expermntl Child Psychol — Journal of Experimental Child Psychology
J Expermntl Psychol — Journal of Experimental Psychology. Human Perception and Performance
J Exper Psychol Human Learn Mem — Journal of Experimental Psychology: Human Learning and Memory
J Exper Psychol Human Percept & Perf — Journal of Experimental Psychology: Human Perception and Performance
J Exper Social Psychol — Journal of Experimental Social Psychology
J Exper Soc Psychol — Journal of Experimental Social Psychology
J Exper Zool — Journal of Experimental Zoology
J Ex P H P — Journal of Experimental Psychology: Human Perception and Performance
J Ex P L — Journal of Experimental Psychology: Human Learning and Memory
J Exploit Corps Gras Ind — Journal de l'Exploitation des Corps Gras Industriels
J Explos Eng — Journal of Explosives Engineering
J Explos Propellants ROC — Journal of Explosives and Propellants. R.O.C.
J Exp M — Journal of Experimental Medicine
J Exp Mar B — Journal of Experimental Marine Biology and Ecology
J Exp Mar Biol Ecol — Journal of Experimental Marine Biology and Ecology
J Exp Med — Journal of Experimental Medicine
J Exp Med Sci — Journal of Experimental Medical Sciences
J Expo Anal Environ Epidemiol — Journal of Exposure Analysis and Environmental Epidemiology
J Exposure Anal Environ Epidemiol — Journal of Exposure Analysis and Environmental Epidemiology
J Exp Pathol — Journal of Experimental Pathology
J Exp Pathol NY — Journal of Experimental Pathology (New York)
J Exp Psy A — Journal of Experimental Psychology: Animal Behavior Processes
J Exp Psych — Journal of Experimental Psychology
J Exp Psychol — Journal of Experimental Psychology
J Exp Psychol Animal Behav Proc — Journal of Experimental Psychology: Animal Behavior Processes
J Exp Psychol Anim Behav Process — Journal of Experimental Psychology. Animal Behavior Processes
J Exp Psychol Anim Behav Processes — Journal of Experimental Psychology: Animal Behavior Processes
J Exp Psychol Appl — Journal of Experimental Psychology. Applied
J Exp Psychol Gen — Journal of Experimental Psychology: General
J Exp Psychol Hum Learn Mem — Journal of Experimental Psychology: Human Learning and Memory
J Exp Psychol Hum Percept Perform — Journal of Experimental Psychology: Human Perception and Performance
J Exp Psychol Hum Perc Perf — Journal of Experimental Psychology: Human Perception and Performance
J Exp Psychol Learn Mem Cogn — Journal of Experimental Psychology: Learning, Memory, and Cognition
J Exp Psychol Monogr — Journal of Experimental Psychology: Monograph
J Exp Psy G — Journal of Experimental Psychology: General
J Exp Psy H — Journal of Experimental Psychology: Human Learning and Memory
J Exp Psy P — Journal of Experimental Psychology: Human Perception and Performance
J Exp Res Pers — Journal of Experimental Research in Personality
J Exp Soc Psych — Journal of Experimental Social Psychology
J Exp Soc Psychol — Journal of Experimental Social Psychology
J Exp S Psy — Journal of Experimental Social Psychology
J Exp Ther — Journal of Experimental Therapeutics

J Exp Ther Oncol — Journal of Experimental Therapeutics and Oncology
J Exp Zool — Journal of Experimental Zoology
J Exp Zool Suppl — Journal of Experimental Zoology. Supplement
J Ext — Journal of Extension
J Extra Corporeal Technol — Journal of Extra-Corporeal Technology
J Extra Corpor Technol — Journal of Extra-Corporeal Technology
JEY — Journal of Employment Counseling
J Eye — Journal of the Eye
JF — Jewish Frontier
JF — Jornal de Filologia
JF — Journal of Finance
JF — Juznoslovenski Filolog
JFA — Jahresbericht ueber die Fortschritte der Klassischen Altertumswissenschaft
JFA — Journal of Field Archaeology
JfAaK — Jahrbuch fuer Aesthetik und Allgemeine Kunstwissenschaft
J Fabrik — Journal fuer Fabrik, Manufactur, und Handlungen
J Fabr Sucre — Journal des Fabricants de Sucre
J Fac Agric Hokkaido Imp Univ — Journal. Faculty of Agriculture. Hokkaido Imperial University
J Fac Agric Hokkaido Univ — Journal. Faculty of Agriculture. Hokkaido University
J Fac Agric Hokkaido Univ Ser Entomol — Journal. Faculty of Agriculture. Hokkaido University. Series Entomology
J Fac Agric Iwate Univ — Journal. Faculty of Agriculture. Iwate University
J Fac Agric Kyushu Univ — Journal. Faculty of Agriculture. Kyushu University
J Fac Agric Shinshu Univ — Journal. Faculty of Agriculture. Shinshu University
J Fac Agric Tottori Univ — Journal. Faculty of Agriculture. Tottori University
J Fac Agr Iwate Univ — Journal. Faculty of Agriculture. Iwate University
J Fac Agr Kyushu Univ — Journal. Faculty of Agriculture. Kyushu University
J Fac Agr Shinshu Univ — Journal. Faculty of Agriculture. Shinshu University
J Fac Agr Tottori Univ — Journal. Faculty of Agriculture. Tottori University
J Fac Appl Biol Sci Hiroshima Univ — Journal. Faculty of Applied Biological Science. Hiroshima University
J Fac Ed Saga Univ — Journal. Faculty of Education. Saga University
J Fac Ed Saga Univ Part 1 — Journal. Faculty of Education. Saga University. Part 1
J Fac Educ Nat Sci Tottori Univ — Journal. Faculty of Education. Natural Sciences. Tottori University
J Fac Educ Tottori Univ Nat Sci — Journal. Faculty of Education. Tottori University. Natural Science
J Fac Eng Chiba Univ — Journal. Faculty of Engineering. Chiba University
J Fac Eng Ibaraki Univ — Journal. Faculty of Engineering. Ibaraki University
J Fac Engng Univ Tokyo — Journal. Faculty of Engineering. University of Tokyo
J Fac Engrg Chiba Univ — Journal. Faculty of Engineering. Chiba University
J Fac Engrg Univ Tokyo Ser B — Journal. Faculty of Engineering. University of Tokyo. Series B
J Fac Eng Shinshu Univ — Journal. Faculty of Engineering. Shinshu University
J Fac Eng Tokyo Imp Univ — Journal. Faculty of Engineering. Tokyo Imperial University
J Fac Eng Univ Tokyo — Journal. Faculty of Engineering. University of Tokyo
J Fac Eng Univ Tokyo Ser A — Journal. Faculty of Engineering. University of Tokyo. Series A. Annual Report
J Fac Eng Univ Tokyo Ser B — Journal. Faculty of Engineering. University of Tokyo. Series B
J Fac Fish Anim Husb Hiroshima Univ — Journal. Faculty of Fisheries and Animal Husbandry. Hiroshima University
J Fac Fish Anim Husb Hir Univ — Journal. Faculty of Fisheries and Animal Husbandry. Hiroshima University
J Fac Fish Prefect Univ Mie — Journal. Faculty of Fisheries. Prefectural University of Mie
J Fac Hum Life Sci Prefect Univ Kumamoto — Journal of the Faculty of Human Life Sciences. Prefectural University of Kumamoto
J Fac Internat Stud Cult Kyushu Sangyo Univ — Journal. Faculty of International Studies of Culture. Kyushu Sangyo University
J Fac Lib Arts Sci Shinshu Univ — Journal. Faculty of Liberal Arts and Sciences. Shinshu University
J Fac Lib Arts Shinshu Univ Part II Nat Sci — Journal. Faculty of Liberal Arts. Shinshu University: Part II. Natural Sciences
J Fac Liberal Arts Yamaguchi Univ — Journal. Faculty of Liberal Arts. Yamaguchi University
J Fac Liberal Arts Yamaguchi Univ Natur Sci — Journal. Faculty of Liberal Arts. Yamaguchi University. Natural Sciences
J Fac Mar Sci King Abdulaziz Univ — Journal. Faculty of Marine Science. King Abdulaziz University
J Fac Mar Sci Technol Tokai Univ — Journal. Faculty of Marine Science and Technology. Tokai University
J Fac Med (Baghdad) — Journal. Faculty of Medicine (Baghdad)
J Fac Med Chulalongkorn Univ (Bangkok) — Journal. Faculty of Medicine. Chulalongkorn University (Bangkok)
J Fac Med Shin Univ — Journal. Faculty of Medicine. Shinshu University
J Fac Med Univ Ankara — Journal. Faculty of Medicine. University of Ankara
J Fac Med Univ Ankara Suppl — Journal. Faculty of Medicine. University of Ankara. Supplement
J Fac Oceanogr Tokai Univ — Journal. Faculty of Oceanography. Tokai University
J Fac Pharm Ankara Univ — Journal. Faculty of Pharmacy. Ankara University
J Fac Pharm Gazi Univ — Journal. Faculty of Pharmacy. Gazi University
J Fac Pharm Istanbul Univ — Journal. Faculty of Pharmacy. Istanbul University
J Fac Polit Sci Econ Tokai Univ — Journal. Faculty of Political Science and Economics. Tokai University
J Fac Rad — Journal. Faculty of Radiologists
J Fac Radiol (Lond) — Journal. Faculty of Radiologists (London)
J Fac Sci Ege Univ — Journal of the Faculty of Science. Ege University
J Fac Sci Ege Univ Ser A — Journal. Faculty of Science. Ege University. Series A
J Fac Sci Ege Univ Ser A B — Journal of the Faculty of Science. Ege University. Series A-B

J Fac Sci Hokkaido Imp Univ Ser 4 — Journal. Faculty of Science. Hokkaido Imperial University. Series 4.Geology and Mineralogy

J Fac Sci Hokkaido Imp Univ Ser 5 — Journal. Faculty of Science. Hokkaido Imperial University. Series 5.Botany

J Fac Sci Hokkaido Imp Univ Ser 5 Bot — Journal. Faculty of Science. Hokkaido Imperial University. Ser V. Botany/Rigaku-Bu Kiyo

J Fac Sci Hokkaido Univ — Journal. Faculty of Science. Hokkaido University

J Fac Sci Hokkaido Univ Ser I — Journal. Faculty of Science. Hokkaido University. Series I. Mathematics

J Fac Sci Hokkaido Univ Ser IV — Journal. Faculty of Science. Hokkaido University. Series IV. Geology andMineralogy

J Fac Sci Hokkaido Univ Ser IV Geol Mineral — Journal. Faculty of Science. Hokkaido University. Series IV. Geology and Mineralogy

J Fac Sci Hokkaido Univ Ser V Bot — Journal. Faculty of Science. Hokkaido University. Series V. Botany

J Fac Sci Hokkaido Univ Ser VI — Journal. Faculty of Science. Hokkaido University. Series VI. Zoology

J Fac Sci Hokkaido Univ Ser VII — Journal. Faculty of Science. Hokkaido University. Series VII. Geophysics

J Fac Sci Hokkaido Univ Ser VI Zool — Journal. Faculty of Science. Hokkaido University. Series VI. Zoology

J Fac Sci Hokkaido Univ VI — Journal. Faculty of Science. Hokkaido University. Series VI. Zoology

J Fac Sci Imp Univ Tokyo Sect II — Journal. Faculty of Science. Imperial University of Tokyo. Section II.Geology, Mineralogy, Geography, Seismology

J Fac Sci Imp Univ Tokyo Sect IV Zool — Journal. Faculty of Science. Imperial University of Tokyo. Section IV. Zoology

J Fac Sci Imp Univ Tokyo Sect V — Journal. Faculty of Science. Imperial University of Tokyo. Section V.Anthropology

J Fac Sci Nigata Univ — Journal. Faculty of Science. Nigata University

J Fac Sci Niigata Univ Ser II Biol Geol Mineral — Journal. Faculty of Science. Niigata University. Series II. Biology, Geology, and Mineralogy

J Fac Sci Riyad Univ — Riyad University. Faculty of Science. Journal

J Fac Sci Ser A Ege Univ — Journal. Faculty of Science. Series A. Ege University

J Fac Sci Ser B Ege Univ — Journal. Faculty of Science. Series B. Ege University

J Fac Sci Shinshu Univ — Journal. Faculty of Science. Shinshu University

J Fac Sci Tech Kinki Univ — Journal of the Faculty of Science and Technology. Kinki University

J Fac Sci Technol Kinki Univ — Journal. Faculty of Science and Technology. Kinki University

J Fac Sci Tokyo Anthrop — Journal of the Faculty of Science Section V. Anthropology

J Fac Sci Tokyo Univ — Journal. Faculty of Science. Tokyo University

J Fac Sci Univ Tokyo — Journal. Faculty of Science. University of Tokyo

J Fac Sci Univ Tokyo Sect 2 — Journal of the Faculty of Science. University of Tokyo. Section 2. Geology, Mineralogy, Geography, Geophysics

J Fac Sci Univ Tokyo Sect IA — Journal. Faculty of Science. University of Tokyo. Section IA. Mathematics

J Fac Sci Univ Tokyo Sect IA Math — Journal. Faculty of Science. University of Tokyo. Section IA. Mathematics

J Fac Sci Univ Tokyo Sect II Geol Mineral Geogr Geophys — Journal. Faculty of Science. University of Tokyo. Section II. Geology, Mineralogy, Geography, and Geophysics

J Fac Sci Univ Tokyo Sect III Bot — Journal. Faculty of Science. University of Tokyo. Section III. Botany

J Fac Sci Univ Tokyo Sect IV — Journal. Faculty of Science. University of Tokyo. Section IV. Zoology

J Fac Sci Univ Tokyo Sect IV Zool — Journal. Faculty of Science. University of Tokyo. Section IV. Zoology

J Fac Sci Univ Tokyo Sect V — Journal. Faculty of Science. University of Tokyo. Section V. Anthropology

J Fac Sci Univ Tokyo Sect V Anthropol — Journal. Faculty of Science. University of Tokyo. Section V. Anthropology

J Fac Text Sci Technol Shinshu Univ Ser A — Journal. Faculty of Textile Science and Technology. Shinshu University.Series A. Biology

J Fac Text Sci Technol Shinshu Univ Ser A Biol — Journal. Faculty of Textile Science and Technology. Shinshu University. Series A. Biology

J Fac Text Sci Technol Shinshu Univ Ser B — Journal. Faculty of Textile Science and Technology. Shinshu University. Series B. Textile Engineering

J Fac Text Sci Technol Shinshu Univ Ser C — Journal. Faculty of Textile Science and Technology. Shinshu University. Series C. Chemistry

J Fac Text Sci Technol Shinshu Univ Ser D — Journal. Faculty of Textile Science and Technology. Shinshu University. Series D. Arts

J Fac Text Sci Technol Shinshu Univ Ser E — Journal. Faculty of Textile Science and Technology. Shinshu University. Series E. Agriculture and Sericulture

J Fac Text Sci Technol Shinshu Univ Ser E Agric Seric — Journal. Faculty of Textile Science and Technology. Shinshu University. Series E. Agriculture and Sericulture

J Fac Text Sci Technol Shinshu Univ Ser F — Journal. Faculty of Textile Science and Technology. Shinshu University.Series F. Physics and Mathematics

J Fac Text Seric Shinshu Ser E Seric — Journal. Faculty of Textile Science and Sericulture. Shinshu University. SeriesE. Sericulture

J Fac Text Seric Shinshu Univ Ser A — Journal. Faculty of Textile Science and Sericulture. Shinshu University. SeriesA. Biology

J Fac Text Seric Shinshu Univ Ser B — Journal. Faculty of Textile Science and Sericulture. Shinshu University. SeriesB. Textile Engineering

J Fac Text Seric Shinshu Univ Ser C — Journal. Faculty of Textile Science and Sericulture. Shinshu University. SeriesC. Chemistry

J Fac Text Seric Shinshu Univ Ser D — Journal. Faculty of Textile Science and Sericulture. Shinshu University. SeriesD. Arts and Sciences

J Fac Text Seric Shinshu Univ Ser E — Journal. Faculty of Textile Science and Sericulture. Shinshu University. SeriesE. Sericulture

J Fac Text Sericu Shinshu Univ Ser A Biol — Journal. Faculty of Textile Science and Sericulture. Shinshu University. SeriesA. Biology

J Fac Tok I — Journal. Faculty of Science. University of Tokyo. Section I. Mathematics, Astronomy, Physics, and Chemistry

J Faculty Arts Roy Univ Malta — Journal. Faculty of Arts. Royal University of Malta

J Fac Vet Med Univ Ankara — Journal. Faculty of Veterinary Medicine. University of Ankara

J Fac Vet Med Univ Firat — Journal. Faculty of Veterinary Medicine. University of Firat

J Fac Vet Med Univ Istanbul — Journal. Faculty of Veterinary Medicine. University of Istanbul

J Faits — Journal des Faits

JFAKA — Journal. Faculty of Agriculture. Kyushu University

J Fam Couns — Journal of Family Counseling

J Fam Hist — Journal of Family History

J Family L — Journal of Family Law

J Fam Issues — Journal of Family Issues

J Fam L — Journal of Family Law

J Fam Law — Journal of Family Law

J Fam Plann Reprod Health Care — Journal of Family Planning and Reproductive Health Care

J Fam Pract — Journal of Family Practice

J Fam Psychol — Journal of Family Psychology

J Fam Wel — Journal of Family Welfare

J Fam Welf — Journal of Family Welfare

J Farm — Jornal dos Farmaceuticos

J Farm Anim Sci — Journal of Farm Animal Science

J Farm Econ — Journal of Farm Economics

J Farmers' Club — Journal. Farmers' Club

J Farnham Mus Soc — Journal. Farnham Museum Society

JFAW — Bursians Jahresbericht ueber die Fortschritte der Klassischen Altertumswissenschaft

JFBND — Journal Francais de Biophysique et Medecine Nucleaire

JFC — Journal of Business Forecasting

JFCC Rev — JFCC (Japan Fine Ceramics Center) Review

JFDH — Jahrbuch. Freies Deutsche Hochstift

J Fd Hyg Soc Jap — Journal. Food Hygienic Society of Japan

J Fd Sci — Journal of Food Science

J Fd Sci Technol — Journal of Food Science and Technology

J Fd Technol — Journal of Food Technology

JFE — Journal of Farm Economics

JFE — Journal of Financial Economics

JFE — Journal of Freshwater Ecology

JFE — Journal of Fusion Energy

JFEC — Journal of Financial Economics

JFED — Journal of Financial Education

JFE J Four Electr — JFE. Journal du Four Electrique

JFE J Four Electr Ind Electrochim — JFE. Journal du Four Electrique et desIndustries Electrochimiques

J Feline Med Surg — Journal of Feline Medicine and Surgery

JFEND — Journal of Fusion Energy

J Fengchia Coll Eng Bus — Journal. Fengchia College. of Engineering and Business

J Feng Chia Univ — Journal. Feng Chia University

J Ferm Bioe — Journal of Fermentation and Bioengineering

J Ferment Assoc Jpn — Journal. Fermentation Association of Japan

J Ferment Bioeng — Journal of Fermentation and Bioengineering

J Ferment Ind — Journal of Fermentation Industries

J Ferment Techn — Journal of Fermentation Technology

J Ferment Technol — Journal of Fermentation Technology

J Ferment Technol (1944-1976) — Journal of Fermentation Technology (1944-1976)

J Ferment Technol (Osaka) — Journal of Fermentation Technology (Osaka)

J Ferm Tech — Journal of Fermentation Technology

J Ferrocem — Journal of Ferrocement

J Ferrocement — Journal of Ferrocement

J Fert Issues — Journal of Fertilizer Issues

JFEU — Far Eastern University. Journal

JFF — Juedische Familien Forschung

JFF — Jugend Film Fernsehen

JFFJ — Japanese Fantasy Film Journal

JFG — Jahrbuch der Philosophischen Fakultaet. Universitaet zu Goettingen

JFHLA — Federal Home Loan Bank Board. Journal

JFHS — Journal. Flintshire Historical Society

JFHS — Journal. Friends' Historical Society

JFHSS — Journal. Friends' Historical Society. Supplement

JFI — Journal. Folklore Institute

JFI — Journal. Franklin Institute

JFI — Journal of Finance

JFI — Journal of Financial Intermediation

J Fibrinolysis — Journal of Fibrinolysis

J Field A — Journal of Field Archaeology

J Field Arch — Journal of Field Archaeology

J Field Archaeol — Journal of Field Archaeology

J Field Ornithol — Journal of Field Ornithology

J Fin — Journal of Finance

JFINA — Journal. Franklin Institute

J Finance — Journal of Finance

J Financ Econ — Journal of Financial Economics

J Financ Quant Anal — Journal of Financial and Quantitative Analysis

J Fin Planning — Journal of Financial Planning [Later, Journal of Financial Planning Today]

J Fin Qu An — Journal of Financial and Quantitative Analysis

J f IR — Jahrbuch fuer Internationales und Auslaendisches Oeffentliches Recht

J Fire Flamm — Journal of Fire and Flammability

J Fire Flammability — Journal of Fire and Flammability

J Fire Flammability Combust Toxicol Suppl — Journal of Fire and Flammability/ Combustion Toxicology. Supplement

J Fire Flammability Consum Prod Flammability Suppl — Journal of Fire and Flammability/Consumer Product Flammability. Supplement

J Fire Flammability Fire Retard Chem Suppl — Journal of Fire and Flammability/ Fire Retardant Chemistry. Supplement

J Fire Prot Eng — Journal of Fire Protection Engineering

J Fire Retardant Chem — Journal of Fire Retardant Chemistry

J Fire Retard Chem — Journal of Fire Retardant Chemistry

J Fire Sc — Journal of Fire Sciences

J Fire Sci — Journal of Fire Sciences

J Fish — Journal of Fisheries/Nippon Suisangaku Zasshi

J Fish Bio — Journal of Fish Biology

J Fish Biol — Journal of Fish Biology

J Fish Dis — Journal of Fish Diseases

J Fisheries Res Board Can — Journal. Fisheries Research Board of Canada

J Fish Res — Journal. Fisheries Research Board of Canada

J Fish Res Board Can — Journal. Fisheries Research Board of Canada

J Fish Res Board Canada — Journal. Fisheries Research Board of Canada

J Fish Sausage — Journal of Fish Sausage

J Fish Sci Technol — Journal of Fisheries Science and Technology

J Fish Soc Taiwan — Journal. Fisheries Society of Taiwan

J Fiz Malays — Jurnal Fizik Malaysia

JFKA — Jahresbericht ueber die Fortschritte der Klassischen Altertumswissenschaft

JFKAW — Jahresberichte ueber die Fortschritte der Klassischen Altertumswissenschaft

JfKs — Jahrbuch fuer Kunstsammler

JFL — Jahrbuch fuer Fraenkische Landesforschung

JFL — Jewish Family Living

J Fla Acad Gen Pract — Journal. Florida Academy of General Practice

J Fla Anti Mosq Assoc — Journal. Florida Anti-Mosquito Association

J Fla Eng Soc — Journal. Florida Engineering Society

J Fla Med Ass — Journal. Florida Medical Association

J Fla Med Assoc — Journal. Florida Medical Association

J Fla State Dent Soc — Journal. Florida State Dental Society

J Flemish Assoc Gastro Enterol — Journal. Flemish Association of Gastro-Enterology

J FL Eng Soc — Journal. Florida Engineering Society

JFLF — Jahrbuch fuer Fraenkische Landesforschung

JFLI — Journal. Folklore Institute

J Floresc Miner Soc — Journal. Fluorescent Mineral Society

J Florida MA — Journal. Florida Medical Association

J Flour Anim Feed Milling — Journal of Flour and Animal Feed Milling

J Flow Injection Anal — Journal of Flow Injection Analysis

J Fluency Dis — Journal of Fluency Disorders

J Fluency Disord — Journal of Fluency Disorders

J Fluid Control — Journal of Fluid Control

J Fluid Eng Trans ASME — Journal of Fluids Engineering. Transactions of the American Society of Mechanical Engineers

J Fluid Mec — Journal of Fluid Mechanics

J Fluid Mech — Journal of Fluid Mechanics

J Fluids Eng — Journal of Fluids Engineering. Transactions of the American Society of Mechanical Engineers

J Fluids Eng Trans ASME — Journal of Fluids Engineering, Transactions of the ASME [*American Society of Mechanical Engineers*]

J Fluoresc — Journal of Fluorescence

J Fluorine — Journal of Fluorine Chemistry

J Fluorine Chem — Journal of Fluorine Chemistry

JfLW — Jahrbuch fuer Litergiewissenschaft

JFM — Journal of Forms Management

JFM — Journal of Futures Markets

JFMA — Journal. Florida Medical Association

J f MG — Jahrbuch fuer Mineralogie und Geologie

JFMI — Journal of the Royal Faculty of Medicine of Iraq

JFNF — Jewish Family Name File

JfNG — Jahrbuch fuer Numismatik und Geldgeschichte

J f N St — Jahrbuecher fuer Nationaloekonomie und Statistik

J f Num — Jahrbuch fuer Numismatik und Geldgeschichte

J Fo — Jewish Forum

JFOAB — Journal Francais d'Oto-Rhino-Laryngologie, Audio-Phonologie, et Chirurgie Maxillo-Faciale

J Foetal Med — Journal of Foetal Medicine

J Folk Inst — Journal. Folklore Institute

J Folkl Inst — Journal. Folklore Institute

J Folklore Inst — Journal. Folklore Institute

J Folkl Res — Journal of Folklore Research

J Food Agric — Journal of Food and Agriculture

J Food Biochem — Journal of Food Biochemistry

J Food Compos Anal — Journal of Food Composition and Analysis

J Food Distrib Res — Journal of Food Distribution Research

J Food Eng — Journal of Food Engineering

J Food Hygienic Soc Jap — Journal. Food Hygienic Society of Japan

J Food Hyg Soc Jap — Journal. Food Hygienic Society of Japan

J Food Hyg Soc Jpn — Journal. Food Hygienic Society of Japan

J Food Nutr (Canberra) — Journal of Food and Nutrition (Canberra)

J Food Process Eng — Journal of Food Process Engineering

J Food Process Preserv — Journal of Food Processing and Preservation

J Food Prot — Journal of Food Protection

J Food Protect — Journal of Food Protection

J Food Qual — Journal of Food Quality

J Food Resour Dev — Journal of Food Resources Development

J Food Saf — Journal of Food Safety

J Food Safety — Journal of Food Safety

J Food Sci — Journal of Food Science

J Food Sci Kyoto Women's Univ — Journal of Food Science. Kyoto Women's University

J Food Sci Nutr — Journal of Food Science and Nutrition

J Food Sci Off Publ Inst Food Technol — Journal of Food Science. An Official Publication. Institute of Food Technologists

J Food Sci Tech — Journal of Food Science and Technology

J Food Sci Technol — Journal of Food Science and Technology

J Food Sci Technol (Mysore) — Journal of Food Science and Technology (Mysore)

J Food Sci Technol (Tokyo) — Journal of Food Science and Technology (Tokyo)

J Food Serv Syst — Journal of Food Service Systems

J Food Technol — Journal of Food Technology

J Foot Ankle Surg — Journal of Foot and Ankle Surgery

J Foot Surg — Journal of Foot Surgery

J For — Journal of Forestry

J Foraminiferal Res — Journal of Foraminiferal Research

J For (Budapest) — Journal of Forestry (Budapest)

J For Comm — Journal. Forestry Commission

J Forecasting — Journal of Forecasting

J Foren Sci — Journal of Forensic Sciences

J Forensic Med — Journal of Forensic Medicine

J Forensic Med Istanbul — Journal of Forensic Medicine (Istanbul)

J Forensic Med Toxicol — Journal of Forensic Medicine and Toxicology

J Forensic Odontostomatol — Journal of Forensic Odonto-Stomatology

J Forensic Sci — Journal of Forensic Sciences

J Forensic Sci Soc — Journal. Forensic Science Society

J Forensic Sci Soc India — Journal. Forensic Science Society of India

J Forest — Journal of Forestry

J Forest Hist — Journal of Forest History

J Forestry — Journal of Forestry

J Forest Washington — Journal of Forestry (Washington, DC)

J For Hist — Journal of Forest History

JFORL — Journal Francais d'Oto-Rhino-Laryngologie

J For Med — Journal of Forensic Medicine

J Formosan Forest — Journal of Formosan Forestry/Taiwan Sanrinkai Kaiho

J Formosan Med Assoc — Journal. Formosan Medical Association

J Forms Man — Journal of Forms Management

J For Prod Res Soc — Journal. Forest Products Research Society

J For Sci — Journal of Forest Sciences

J For Sci (Chittagong Bangladesh) — Journal of Forest Science (Chittagong, Bangladesh)

J For Sci Socy — Journal. Forensic Science Society

J For Suisse — Journal Forestier Suisse

J For Suisse Schweiz Z Forstwes — Journal Forestier Suisse/Schweizerische Zeitschrift fuer Forstwesen

J Four Elec — Journal du Four Electrique

J Four Electr — Journal du Four Electrique

J Four Electr Ind Electrochim — Journal du Four Electrique et des Industries Electrochimiques

J Fourier Anal Appl — Journal of Fourier Analysis and Applications

J Fourth Mil Med Univ — Journal of the Fourth Military Medical University

JFP — Journal of Financial Planning Today

JfPhil — Jahrbuch fuer Philologie

JFPRD — Journal of Food Protection

J F Psychol U Neurol — Journal fuer Psychologie und Neurologie

JFQ — Journal of Financial and Quantitative Analysis

JFQA — Journal of Financial and Quantitative Analysis

J Fr — Jewish Frontier

JFR — Journal of Financial Research

JFR — Journal of Folklore Research

J Fract Calc — Journal of Fractional Calculus

J Fr Agric — Journal de la France Agricole

J Frankl I — Journal. Franklin Institute

J Franklin Inst — Journal. Franklin Institute

J Franklin Inst B — Journal of the Franklin Institute. B. Engineering and Applied Mathematics

J Franklin Inst Monogr — Journal. Franklin Institute. Monograph

JFRB — Journal. Fisheries Research Board of Canada

JFRBA — Journal. Fisheries Research Board of Canada

J Fr Biophys Med Nucl — Journal Francais de Biophysique et Medecine Nucleaire

JFRCD — Journal of Fire Retardant Chemistry

JFRDD — Journal of Food Resources Development

J Free Radicals Biol Med — Journal of Free Radicals in Biology and Medicine

J Free Radic Biol Med — Journal of Free Radicals in Biology and Medicine

J Freshwater — Journal of Freshwater

J Freshwater Ecol — Journal of Freshwater Ecology

J Freshw Ec — Journal of Freshwater Ecology

J Fr Hydrol — Journal Francais d'Hydrologie

J Fr Med Chir Thorac — Journal Francais de Medecine et Chirurgie Thoraciques

JFrN — Jewish Frontier (New York)

J Fron — Jewish Frontier

J Fr Ophtalmol — Journal Francais d'Ophtalmologie

J Fr Oto-Rhino-Laryngol — Journal Francais d'Oto-Rhino-Laryngologie et Chirurgie Maxillo-Faciale [*Later,Journal Francais d'Oto-Rhino-Laryngologie*]

J Fr Oto Rhino Laryngol Audio Phonol Chir Maxillo Fac — Journal Francais d'Oto-Rhino-Laryngologie, Audio-Phonologie, et Chirurgie Maxillo-Faciale

J Fr Oto Rhino Laryngol Chir — Journal Francais d'Oto-Rhino-Laryngologie et Chirurgie Maxillo-Faciale

J Fr Oto Rhino Laryngol Chir Maxillo Fac — Journal Francais d'Oto-Rhino-Laryngologie et Chirurgie Maxillo-Faciale [*Later,Journal Francias d'Oto-Rhino-Laryngologie*]

J Frottement Ind — Journal du Frottement Industriel

J Fruit Ornamental Plant Res — Journal of Fruit and Ornamental Plant Research

JFS — Jane's Fighting Ships

JFSGW — Journal. Folklore Society of Greater Washington

JFSR — Journal of Financial Services Research
JFSS — Journal. Folk Song Society
JFSUB — Journal of Foot Surgery
JFTED — Journal of Fermentation Technology
JFU — Journal of Futures Markets
J Fudan Univ Nat Sci — Journal. Fudan University. Natural Science
J Fudan Univ Natur Sci — Journal of Fudan University. Natural Science
J Fuel Chem Technol (Taiyuan Peoples Repub China) — Journal of Fuel Chemistry and Technology (Taiyuan, People's Republic ofChina)
J Fuel Heat Technol — Journal of Fuel and Heat Technology
J Fuel Soc Jap — Journal. Fuel Society of Japan
J Fuel Soc Jpn — Journal. Fuel Society of Japan
J fuer Bot Schrader — Journal fuer die Botanik (Goettingen) (Edited by H. A. Schrader)
J Fujian Agric Coll — Journal. Fujian Agricultural College
J Fujian Teach Univ Nat Sci Ed — Journal. Fujian Teachers University. Natural Science Edition
J Fukuoka Dent Col — Journal. Fukuoka Dental College
J Funct Ana — Journal of Functional Analysis
J Funct Anal — Journal of Functional Analysis
J Functional Analysis — Journal of Functional Analysis
J Funct Logic Programming — Journal of Functional and Logic Programming
J Funct Mater — Journal of Functional Materials
J Funct Mater Devices — Journal of Functional Materials and Devices
J Funct Programming — Journal of Functional Programming
J Fur Higher Educ — Journal of Further and Higher Education
J Furn Hist Soc — Journal of the Furniture History Society
JFUS — Journal of Forestry (United States)
J Fushun Pet Inst — Journal of Fushun Petroleum Institute
J Fusion Energy — Journal of Fusion Energy
J Futures Markets — Journal of Futures Markets
J Fuzhou Univ Nat Sci Ed — Journal of Fuzhou University. Natural Science Edition
J Fuzzy Math — Journal of Fuzzy Mathematics
JfVw — Jahrbuch fuer Verkehrswissenschaft
J f Zahnhlk — Journal fuer Zahnheilkunde
JG — Jongleur
JG — Journal de Geneve
JG — Journal of Geography
JG — Journal of Geology
JG — Juedisches Gemeinde
JG — Schmollers Jahrbuch fuer Gesetzgebung, Verwaltung, und Volkwissenschaft im Deutschen Reich
J Ga — Jauna Gaita
Jgabe Altmaerk Mus Stendhal — Jahresgabe. Altmaerkisches Museum Stendhal
J GA Dent Assoc — Journal. Georgia Dental Association
J GA Entomol Soc — Journal. Georgia Entomological Society
J GA Ent Soc — Journal. Georgia Entomological Society
J Gakugei Tokushima Univ — Journal of Gakugei. Tokushima University
J Gakugei Tokushima Univ Nat Sci — Journal. Gakugei Tokushima University. Natural Science
J Galway Archaeol Hist Soc — Journal. Galway Archaeological and Historical Society
J Gan Jha Kend Sans Vid — Journal. Ganganatha Jha Kendriya Sanskrit Vidyapeetha
J Gansu Teach Univ Nat Sci Ed — Journal. Gansu Teachers' University. Natural Science Edition
J Garden Hist — Journal of Garden History
J Gard Hist — Journal of Garden History
J Gartenkunst — Journal fuer die Gartenkunst
J Gasbeleucht Verw Beleuchtungsarten Wasserversorg — Journal fuer Gasbeleuchtung und Verwandte Beleuchtungsarten sowie fuerWasserversorgung
J Gas Chromatogr — Journal of Gas Chromatography
J Gas Lighting — Journal of Gas Lighting
J Gas Light Water Supply Sanit Improv — Journal of Gas Lighting, Water Supply, and Sanitary Improvement
J Gastroenterol — Journal of Gastroenterology
J Gastroenterol Hepatol — Journal of Gastroenterology and Hepatology
J Gastrointest Res — Journal of Gastrointestinal Research
JGC — Journal of General Chemistry
JGC — Journal of Geology (Chicago)
JGCEA — Journal of Geochemical Exploration
JGCRA — Journal of Gas Chromatography
J Gdn Hist — Journal of Garden History
JGDO — Jahrbuch fuer Geschichte des Deutschen Ostens
JGE — Journal of General Education
J Gemmol — Journal of Gemmology and Proceedings of the Gemmological Associationof Great Britain
J Gemmol — Journal of Gemmology
J Gemmol Soc Jpn — Journal. Gemmological Society of Japan
J Gen — Journal de Geneve
J Gen A Mic — Journal of General and Applied Microbiology
J Gen Appl Microbiol — Journal of General and Applied Microbiology
J Gen Biol (Moscow) — Journal of General Biology (Moscow)
J Gen Chem — Journal of General Chemistry
J Gen Chem USSR — Journal of General Chemistry of the USSR
J Gen Chem USSR (Engl Transl) — Journal of General Chemistry of the USSR (English Translation)
J Gen Civ — Journal du Genie Civil des Scienes et des Arts
J Gend Specif Med — Journal of Gender-Specific Medicine
J Gen Ed — Journal of General Education
J Gen Ed Tokyo Nogyo Daigaku — Journal of General Education. Tokyo Nogyo Daigaku
J Gen Educ — Journal of General Education
J Gene Med — Journal of Gene Medicine

J Genet — Journal of Genetics
J Genet & Breed — Journal of Genetics and Breeding
J Genet Hum — Journal de Genetique Humaine
J Genet Psy — Journal of Genetic Psychology
J Genet Psychol — Journal of Genetic Psychology
J Geneve — Journal de Geneve
J Gen Intern Med — Journal of General Internal Medicine
J Gen Litt Etrangere — Journal General de la Litterature Etrangere, ou Indicateur Bibliographique et Raisonne des Livres Nouveaux
J Gen Manag — Journal of General Management
J Gen Med Chir et Pharm — Journal General de Medecine, de Chirurgie, et de Pharmacie
J Gen Med Franc Etrangeres — Journal General de Medecine, de Chirurgie, et de Pharmacie, Francaises et Etrangeres
J Gen Mgt — Journal of General Management
J Gen Micro — Journal of General Microbiology
J Gen Microbiol — Journal of General Microbiology
J Gen Philos Sci — Journal for General Philosophy of Science
J Gen Physiol — Journal of General Physiology
J Gen Physl — Journal of General Physiology
J Gen Ps — Journal of Genetic Psychology
J Gen Psych — Journal of General Psychology
J Gen Psychol — Journal of General Psychology
J Gen Soc Trav Sci France Etranger Sect 1 Sci Math — Journal General. Societes et Travaux Scientifiques de la France et de l'Etranger. Section 1. Sciences Mathematiques, Physiques, et Naturelles
J Gen Virol — Journal of General Virology
J Geo — Journal of Geology
J Geobot — Journal of Geobotany
J Geochem E — Journal of Geochemical Exploration
J Geochem Explor — Journal of Geochemical Exploration
J Geochem Soc India — Journal. Geochemical Society of India
JGEOD — Journal of Geophysics
J Geodyn — Journal of Geodynamics
J Geog — Journal Geographica
J Geog — Journal of Geography
J Geogr — Journal of Geography
J Geogr Higher Educ — Journal of Geography in Higher Education
J Geogr (Tokyo) — Journal of Geography (Tokyo)
J Geol — Journal of Geology
J Geol Educ — Journal of Geological Education
J Geol S — Journal. Geological Society
J Geol Sci Appl Geophys — Journal of Geological Sciences. Applied Geophysics
J Geol Sci Econ Geol Mineral — Journal of Geological Sciences. Economic Geology, Mineralogy
J Geol Sci Geol — Journal of Geological Sciences. Geology
J Geol Sci Palaeontol — Journal of Geological Sciences. Palaeontology
J Geol Sci Technol Geochem (Prague) — Journal of Geological Sciences. Technology, Geochemistry (Prague)
J Geol S In — Journal. Geological Society of India
J Geol Soc Aust — Journal. Geological Society of Australia
J Geol Soc Australia — Journal. Geological Society of Australia
J Geol Soc China — Journal. Geological Society of China
J Geol Soc India — Journal. Geological Society of India
J Geol Soc Iraq — Journal. Geological Society of Iraq
J Geol Soc Jam — Journal. Geological Society of Jamaica
J Geol Soc Jpn — Journal. Geological Society of Japan
J Geol Soc Korea — Journal. Geological Society of Korea
J Geol Soc London — Journal. Geological Society of London
J Geol Soc Philipp — Journal. Geological Society of the Philippines
J Geol Soc (Seoul) — Journal. Geological Society (Seoul)
J Geol Soc Thailand — Journal. Geological Society of Thailand
J Geol Soc Tokyo — Journal. Geological Society of Tokyo
J Geol UAR — Journal of Geology. United Arab Republic
J Geol Ukr Acad Sci Inst Geol — Journal of Geology. Ukrainian Academy of Sciences. Institute of Geology
J Geom — Journal of Geometry
J Geomagn & Geoelectr — Journal of Geomagnetism and Geoelectricity
J Geomagn G — Journal of Geomagnetism and Geoelectricity
J Geomagn Geoelec — Journal of Geomagnetism and Geoelectricity
J Geom Anal — Journal of Geometric Analysis. Mathematics
J Geomet Phys — Journal of Geometry and Physics
J Geometry — Journal of Geometry
J Geom Phy — Journal of Geometry and Physics
J Geoph Res — Journal of Geophysical Research
J Geophys — Journal of Geophysics
J Geophys (Kiev) — Journal of Geophysics (Kiev)
J Geophys (Moscow) — Journal of Geophysics (Moscow)
J Geophys Prospect — Journal of Geophysical Prospecting
J Geophys Res — Journal of Geophysical Research
J Geophys Res — Journal of Geophysical Research. Series D. Atmospheres
J Geophys Res A Space Phys — Journal of Geophysical Research. A. Space Physics
J Geophys Res Atmos — Journal of Geophysical Research. Atmospheres
J Geophys Res B — Journal of Geophysical Research. Series B
J Geophys Res C Oceans — Journal of Geophysical Research. Series C. Oceans
J Geophys Res C Oceans Atmos — Journal of Geophysical Research. Series C. Oceans and Atmospheres
J Geophys Res D Atmos — Journal of Geophysical Research. Series D. Atmospheres
J Geophys Res Oceans — Journal of Geophysical Research. Series C. Oceans
J Geophys Res Planets — Journal of Geophysical Research. Planets
J Geophys Res Solid Earth Planets — Journal of Geophysical Research. Solid Earth and Planets
J Geophys Res Space Phys — Journal of Geophysical Research. Space Physics

J Geophys Zeitschr Geophys — Journal of Geophysics/Zeitschrift fuer Geophysik

J Geo R-O A — Journal of Geophysical Research. Series C. Oceans and Atmospheres

J Geo R-S P — Journal of Geophysical Research. Space Physics

J Geosci Osaka City Univ — Journal of Geosciences. Osaka City University

J Geotech Eng — Journal of Geotechnical Engineering

J Geotech Eng Div Amer Soc Civil Eng Proc — Journal. Geotechnical Engineering Division. Proceedings of the American Societyof Civil Engineers

J Geotech Eng Div Am Soc Civ Eng — Journal. Geotechnical Engineering Division. Proceedings of the American Societyof Civil Engineers

J Geotech Engng Div ASCE — Journal. Geotechnical Engineering Division. American Society of Civil Engineers

J Geotech Engng Div Proc ASCE — Journal. Geotechnical Engineering Division. Proceedings of the American Societyof Civil Engineers

J Geotech Engrg ASCE — Journal of Geotechnical Engineering. American Society of Civil Engineers

J Geotech Geoenviron Eng — Journal of Geotechnical and Geoenvironmental Engineering

J Geotherm Energy Res Dev Co Ltd — Journal. Geothermal Energy Research and Development Company, Limited

JGEPs — Journal of Genetic Psychology

J Geriat Ps — Journal of Geriatric Psychiatry

J Geriatr Psychiatry — Journal of Geriatric Psychiatry

J Geriatr Psychiatry Neurol — Journal of Geriatric Psychiatry and Neurology

J Geront — Journal of Gerontology

J Gerontol — Journal of Gerontology

J Gerontol A Biol Sci Med Sci — Journals of Gerontology. Series A. Biological Sciences and Medical Sciences

J Gerontol B Psychol Sci Soc Sci — Journals of Gerontology. Series B. Psychological Sciences and Social Sciences

J Gerontol Nurs — Journal of Gerontological Nursing

J Gerontology — Journal of Gerontology

J Gerontol Ser A — Journals of Gerontology. Series A. Biological Sciences and Medical Sciences

J Gerontol Soc Work — Journal of Gerontological Social Work

J Gesamte Oberflaechentech — Journal of Gesamte Oberflaechentechnik

JGF — Jenaer Germanistische Forschungen

JGG — Goerres-Gesellschaft zur Pflege der Wissenschaft im Katholischen Deutschland. Literaturwissenschaftliches Jahrbuch

JGG — Jahrbuch. Goethe-Gesellschaft

JGG — Jahrbuch. Grillparzer-Gesellschaft

JGG — Jahresbericht der Goerresgesellschaft

JGGAS — Journal. Hongkong University. Geographical, Geological, and Archaeological Society

JGGJC — Jahrbuch. Gesellschaft fuer Geschichte der Juden in der Cechoslovakischen Republik

JGGM — Jahresbericht der Geographischen Gesellschaft in Muenchen

JGGPO — Jahrbuch. Gesellschaft fuer die Geschichte des Protestantismus in Oesterreich

JGGPOe — Jahrbuch der Gesellschaft fuer die Geschichte des Protestantismus in Oesterreich

JGGPOes — Jahrbuch. Gesellschaft fuer die Geschichte des Protestantismus in Oesterreich

JGHHG — Jahresberichte der Geschichtswissenschaft. Herausgegeben von der Historischen Gesellschaft

J Ginseng Res — Journal of Ginseng Research

JGIS — Journal. Greater India Society

JGJ — Jahrbuch fuer die Geschichte der Juden

JGJ — Java Gazette (Jakarta)

JGJC — Jahrbuch. Gesellschaft fuer Geschichte der Juden in der Cechoslovakischen Republik

JGJJ — Jahrbuch fuer die Geschichte der Juden und des Judentums

JGJRI — Journal. Ganganatha Jha Research Institute

JGKM — Jahrbuch fuer Geschichte und Kunst des Mittelrheins und Seiner Nachbargebiete

JGKMR — Jahrbuch fuer Geschichte und Kultur Kunst des Mittelrheins und Seiner Nachbargebiete

JGL — Jahrbuch fuer Juedische Geschichte und Literatur

JGL — Juedische Gemeinde Luzern

J Glaciol — Journal of Glaciology

J Glass Stud — Journal of Glass Studies

J Glaucoma — Journal of Glaucoma

JGLG — Jahrbuch der Gesellschaft fuer Lothringische Geschichte und Altertumskunde

JGLGA — Jahrbuch. Gesellschaft fuer Lothringische Geschichte und Altertumskunde

JGLGAK — Jahrbuch. Gesellschaft fuer Lothringische Geschichte und Altertumskunde

J Global Optim — Journal of Global Optimization

JGLRD — Journal of Great Lakes Research

JGLS — Journal. Gypsy Lore Society

JGM — Journal of General Management

JGMAA — Journal of General Management

JGMOD — Jahrbuch fuer die Geschichte Mittel- und Ostdeutschlands

J GMS OSU — Journal. Graduate Music Students. Ohio State University

J Gnathol — Journal of Gnathology

JGNKG — Jahrbuch der Gesellschaft fuer Niedersaechsische Kirchengeschichte

JGNKG B — Jahrbuch der Gesellschaft fuer Niedersaechsische Kirchengeschichte. Beiheft

JGNOAC — Jugoslovenska Ginekologija i Opstetricija

JGNSKG — Jahrbuch. Gesellschaft fuer Niedersaechsische Kirchengeschichte

JGO — Jahrbuch fuer die Geschichte des Herzogtums Oldenburg

JGO — Jahrbuecher fuer Geschichte Osteuropas

JGOBA — Journal de Gynecologie, Obstetrique, et Biologie de la Reproduction

JGOE — Jahrbuecher fuer Geschichte Osteuropas

JGOL — Jaarboekje voor Geschiedenis en Oudheidkunde van Leiden en Omstreken

JGOLR — Jaarboekje voor Geschiedenis en Oudheidkunde van Leiden en Rijnland

J Gov Mech Lab (Jpn) — Journal of Government Mechanical Laboratory (Japan)

JGP — Journal of General Psychology

JGP — Journal of Genetic Psychology

JGPr Oe — Jahrbuch der Gesellschaft fuer die Geschichte des Protestantismus in Oesterreich

JGPr Oe S — Jahrbuch der Gesellschaft fuer die Geschichte des Protestantismus in Oesterreich. Sonderheft

JGPs — Journal of General Psychology

JGPSA — Journal of General Psychology

JGPYA — Journal of Genetic Psychology

JGR — Journal of Geophysical Research

J Grad Res Cent — Journal. Graduate Research Center

J Grad Res Cent South Methodist Univ — Journal. Graduate Research Center. Southern Methodist University

J Grad Sch Fac Eng Univ Tokyo Ser B — Journal of the Graduate School and Faculty of Engineering. The University of Tokyo. Series B

J Graph Theory — Journal of Graph Theory

JGR C — Journal of Geophysical Research. Series C. Oceans and Atmospheres

J Great Lakes Res — Journal of Great Lakes Research

JGrG — Jahrbuch. Grillparzer-Gesellschaft

JGRI — Journal. Ganganatha Jha Research Institute

JGR J Geophys Res — JGR. Journal of Geophysical Research

JGR J Geophys Res A — JGR. Journal of Geophysical Research. Series A. Space Physics

JGR J Geophys Res C Oceans Atmos — JGR. Journal of Geophysical Research. Series C. Oceans and Atmospheres

JGR J Geophys Res D Atmos — JGR. Journal of Geophysical Research. Series D. Atmospheres

JGR J Geophys Res Planets — JGR. Journal of Geophysical Research. Planets

JGR J Geophys Res Solid Earth — JGR. Journal of Geophysical Research. Solid Earth

JGR J Geophys Res Solid Earth Planets — JGR. Journal of Geophysical Research. Solid Earth and Planets

J Group Experts Sci Aspects Mar Pollut — Joint Group of Experts on the Scientific Aspects of Marine Pollution

J Group Theory Phys — Journal of Group Theory in Physics. An International Journal Devoted to Applications of Group Theory to Physical Problems

J Growth — Journal of Growth

JGRS — Journal. Gujarat Research Society

JGS — Journal of Glass Studies

JGSC — Journal of Glass Studies (Corning, New York)

JGSI — Jahrbuecher fuer Geschichte der Slaven

JGSLA — Jahrbuch fuer die Geschichte von Staat, Wirtschaft, und Gesellschaft Lateinamerikas

JGSLA — Journal. Geological Society of London

JGSTD — Journal. Gyeongsang National University. Science and Technology

JGSV — Jahresheft. Gemeinschaft der Selbstverwirklichung

JGSW — Journal of Gerontological Social Work

JGSWGL — Jahrbuch fuer Geschichte von Staat, Wirtschaft, und Gesellschaft Lateinamerikas

J Gt Houst Dent Soc — Journal of the Greater Houston Dental Society

Jgt o Fsk — Jagt og Fiskeri

J Gtr India Soc — Journal of the Greater India Society

J Guangdong Inst Technol — Journal of Guangdong Institute of Technology

J Guangdong Non Ferrous Met — Journal of Guangdong Non-Ferrous Metals

J Guangdong Univ Technol — Journal of Guangdong University of Technology

J Guidance & Control — Journal of Guidance and Control

J Guidance Control — Journal of Guidance and Control

J Guid and Control — Journal of Guidance and Control

J Guid Control — Journal of Guidance and Control

J Guid Control and Dyn — Journal of Guidance, Control, and Dynamics

J Guid Control Dyn — Journal of Guidance, Control, and Dynamics

J Guilin Coll Geol — Journal of Guilin College of Geology

J Guilin Inst Technol — Journal of Guilin Institute of Technology

J Guizhou Inst Tech — Journal of Guizhou Institute of Technology

J Gujarat Res Soc — Journal. Gujarat Research Society

J Guj Res Soc — Journal. Gujarat Research Society

J Gunma Ken Nucl Med Forum — Journal of Gunma-ken Nuclear Medicine Forum

JGW — Jahresbericht fuer Geschichtswissenschaft

JGWT — Jahrbuch. Gesellschaft fuer Wiener Theater-Forschung

J Gyeongsang Natl Univ Nat Sci — Journal. Gyeongsang National University. Natural Sciences

J Gyeongsang Natl Univ Sci Technol — Journal. Gyeongsang National University. Science and Technology

JGyLS — Journal. Gypsy Lore Society

J Gynaecol Endocr — Journal of Gynaecological Endocrinology

J Gynaecol Endocrinol — Journal of Gynaecological Endocrinology

J Gynecol Obstet Biol Reprod — Journal de Gynecologie, Obstetrique, et Biologie de la Reproduction

J Gynecol Pract — Journal of Gynecological Practice

J Gynecol S — Journal of Gynecologic Surgery

J Gypsy Lore Soc — Journal of the Gypsy Lore Society

JH — Jazz-Hot

JH — Jewish Heritage

JH — Journal of History

JHAG — Jahresbericht. Historisch-Antiquarische Gesellschaft von Graubuenden

JHAGG — Jahresbericht der Historisch-Antiquarischen Gesellschaft von Graubuenden

J Hand Surg — Journal of Hand Surgery

J Hand Surg Am — Journal of Hand Surgery. American Volume

J Hand Surg Br — Journal of Hand Surgery. British Volume

J Hand Ther — Journal of Hand Therapy

J Hangzhou Univ Nat Sci Ed — Journal. Hangzhou University. Natural Science Edition
J Hanyang Med Coll — Journal. Hanyang Medical College
J Harbin Ind Coll — Journal. Harbin Industrial College
J Harbin Inst Tech — Journal of Harbin Institute of Technology
J Harbin Inst Technol — Journal. Harbin Institute of Technology
J Harbin Univ Sci Technol — Journal. Harbin University of Science and Technology
J Hard Mater — Journal of Hard Materials
J Hard Tissue Biol — Journal of Hard Tissue Biology
J Haryana Stud — Journal of Haryana Studies
JHAS — Journal. Hyderabad Archaeological Society
J Hattori Bot Lab — Journal. Hattori Botanical Laboratory
JHAW — Jahrbuch. Heidelberger Akademie der Wissenschaften
J Hawaii Dent Assoc — Journal. Hawaii Dental Association
J Hawaii Pac Agric — Journal for Hawaiian and Pacific Agriculture
J Hawaii State Dent Assoc — Journal. Hawaii State Dental Association
J Hazard Mater — Journal of Hazardous Materials
J Hazard Materials — Journal of Hazardous Materials
J Hazardous Mat — Journal of Hazardous Materials
JHbG — Jahrbuch der Hafenbautechnischen Gesellschaft
JHBLEM — Journal of Human Behavior and Learning
JHBSA — Journal of the History of the Behavioral Sciences
JhBW — Jahrbuch. Biblische Wissenschaften
J H Clearing House — Junior High Clearing House
JHCM — Journal of Health Care Marketing
JHD — Journal of the Hellenic Diaspora
JHDA — Journal. Hawaii Dental Association
JHE — Journal of Historical Geography (England)
JHE — Journal of Home Economics
J Health Adm Educ — Journal of Health Administration Education
J Health & Phys Educ — Journal of Health and Physical Education
J Health & Soc Behav — Journal of Health and Social Behavior
J Health & Social Behavior — Journal of Health and Social Behavior
J Health Care Finance — Journal of Health Care Finance
J Health Care Mark — Journal of Health Care Marketing
J Health Care Market — Journal of Health Care Marketing
J Health Care Mkt — Journal of Health Care Marketing
J Health Care Poor Underserved — Journal of Health Care for the Poor and Underserved
J Health Care Technol — Journal of Health Care Technology
J Healthc Educ Train — Journal of Healthcare Education and Training
J Healthc Mater Manage — Journal of Healthcare Materiel Management
J Healthc Prot Manage — Journal of Healthcare Protection Management
J Health Econ — Journal of Health Economics
J Health Ed — Journal of Health Education
J Health Hum Behav — Journal of Health and Human Behavior
J Health Hum Resour Adm — Journal of Health and Human Resources Administration
J Health Hum Resources Admin — Journal of Health and Human Resources Administration
J Health Phys Ed Rec — Journal of Health, Physical Education, Recreation
J Health Phys Radiat Prot — Journal of Health Physics and Radiation Protection
J Health Pol — Journal of Health Politics, Policy, and Law
J Health Polit Policy Law — Journal of Health Politics, Policy, and Law
J Health Pol Poly and L — Journal of Health Politics, Policy, and Law
J Health So — Journal of Health and Social Behavior
J Health Soc Behav — Journal of Health and Social Behavior
J Health Toxicol — Journal of Health Toxicology
J Heart Lung Transplant — Journal of Heart and Lung Transplantation
J Heart Valve Dis — Journal of Heart Valve Disease
J Heat Recovery Syst — Journal of Heat Recovery Systems
J Heat Recovery Systems — Journal of Heat Recovery Systems
J Heat Tech — Journal of Heating Technics
J Heat Tran — Journal of Heat Transfer. Transactions of the American Society of Mechanical Engineers
J Heat Transfer — Journal of Heat Transfer. Transactions of the American Society of Mechanical Engineers. Series C
J Heat Transfer Soc Jpn — Journal of the Heat Transfer Society of Japan
J Heat Transfer Trans ASME — Journal of Heat Transfer. Transactions of the American Society of Mechanical Engineers
J Heat Treat — Journal of Heat Treating
J Hebd Med — Journal Hebdomadaire de Medecine
J Hebd Progr Sci Med — Journal Hebdomadaire des Progres des Sciences Medicales
J Hebei Acad Sci — Journal. Hebei Academy of Sciences
J Hebei Coll Geol — Journal. Hebei College of Geology
J Hebei Inst Technol — Journal. Hebei Institute of Technology
J Hebei Norm Univ Nat Sci Ed — Journal. Hebei Normal University. Natural Science Edition
J Hebei Univ Nat Sci Ed — Journal. Hebei University. Natural Science Edition
J Hebei Univ Technol — Journal of Hebei University of Technology
JHebrSt — Journal of Hebraic Studies
JHEL — Journal of Hellenic Studies
J Hellenic Stud — Journal of Hellenic Studies
J Hellen St — Journal of Hellenic Studies
J Hellen Stud — Journal of Hellenic Studies
J Hell St — Journal of Hellenic Studies
J Hell Stud — Journal of Hellenic Studies
J Helm — Journal of Helminthology
J Helminth — Journal of Helminthology
J Helminthol — Journal of Helminthology
J Hel Stud — Journal of Hellenic Studies
J Helv — Journal Helvetique
J Hematother — Journal of Hematotherapy

J Hematother Stem Cell Res — Journal of Hematotherapy & Stem Cell Research
J Hepatol — Journal of Hepatology
J Hepatol (Amst) — Journal of Hepatology (Amsterdam)
J Hepatol Suppl — Journal of Hepatology. Supplement
J Herald Soc Scotland — Journal of the Heraldry Society of Scotland
J Hered — Journal of Heredity
J Heredity — Journal of Heredity
J Herpetol — Journal of Herpetology
J Herpetol Assoc Afr — Journal. Herpetological Association of Africa
JHeS — Journal of Hellenic Studies
J Hetero Ch — Journal of Heterocyclic Chemistry
J Heterocycl Chem — Journal of Heterocyclic Chemistry
JHEW — Journal of Home Economics (Washington, D.C.)
Jhft Oesterreich Archaeol Inst Wien — Jahreshefte des Oesterreichischen Archaeologischen Institutes in Wien
JHGA — Jahrbuch. K. K. Heraldische Gesellschaft, "Adler"
JHGSW — Journal. Heraldic and Genealogical Society of Wales
JHH — Journal of Health and Human Resources Administration
JHH — Journal of Holistic Health
Jhh Oester Archaeol Inst — Jahreshefte des Oesterreichischen Archaeologischen Instituts
JHI — Journal of the History of Ideas
JHId — Journal. History of Ideas
J Hi E — Journal of Higher Education
J High Educ — Journal of Higher Education
J Higher Educ — Journal of Higher Education
J High Polym (Shanghai) — Journal of High Polymers (Shanghai)
J High Pressure Gas Saf Inst Jpn — Journal. High Pressure Gas Safety Institute of Japan
J High Resolut Chromatogr — Journal of High Resolution Chromatography
J High Resolut Chromatogr Chromatogr Commun — Journal of High Resolution Chromatography and Chromatography Communications
J High Speed Networks — Journal of High Speed Networks
J High Temp Chem Processes — Journal of High Temperature Chemical Processes
J High Temp Soc — Journal. High Temperature Society
J High Temp Soc (Jpn) — Journal. High Temperature Society (Japan)
J High Temp Soc (Suita Jpn) — Journal. High Temperature Society (Suita, Japan)
J Highw Div Am Soc Civ Eng — Journal. Highway Division. American Society of Civil Engineers
J Hillside Hosp — Journal. Hillside Hospital
JHINDS — Journal of Hospital Infection
J Hirnforsch — Journal fuer Hirnforschung
J Hiroshima Bot Club — Journal. Hiroshima Botanical Club
J Hiroshima Med Assoc — Journal. Hiroshima Medical Association
J Hiroshima Univ Dent Soc — Journal. Hiroshima University. Dental Society
J His — Journal of History
J Hispan Ph — Journal of Hispanic Philology
J Hist & Litt — Journal Historique et Litteraire
J Hist Arabic Sci — Journal for the History of Arabic Science
J Hist Archit — Journal d'Histoire de l'Architecture
J Hist Astron — Journal for the History of Astronomy
J Hist Astronom — Journal for the History of Astronomy
J Hist Beh — Journal of the History of the Behavioral Sciences
J Hist Behav Sci — Journal of the History of the Behavioral Sciences
J Hist Beh Sci — Journal of the History of the Behavioral Sciences
J Hist Biol — Journal of the History of Biology
J Hist Col — Journal of the History of Collections
J Hist Collns — Journal of the History of Collections
J Hist Cyto — Journal of Histochemistry and Cytochemistry
J Hist Firearms Soc S Afr — Journal. Historical Firearms Society of South Africa
J Hist G — Journal of Historical Geography
J Hist Geog — Journal of Historical Geography
J Hist Geogr — Journal of Historical Geography
J Hist Id — Journal of the History of Ideas
J Hist Idea — Journal of the History of Ideas
J Hist Ideas — Journal of the History of Ideas
J Hist Med — Journal of the History of Medicine and Allied Sciences
J Hist Med Allied Sci — Journal of the History of Medicine and Allied Sciences
J Hist Medic & Allied Sci — Journal of the History of Medicine and Allied Sciences
J Hist Metall Soc — Journal. Historical Metallurgy Society
J Histochem Cytochem — Journal of Histochemistry and Cytochemistry
J Histotechnol — Journal of Histotechnology
J Hist Phil — Journal of the History of Philosophy
J Hist Philos — Journal of the History of Philosophy
J Hist Res — Journal of Historical Research
J Hist Sci (Jpn) — Journal of the History of Science (Japan)
J Hist Sexuality — Journal of the History of Sexuality
J Hist Soc Church Wales — Journal. Historical Society of the Church in Wales
J Hist Sociol — Journal of the History of Sociology
J Hist Soc Nig — Journal. Historical Society of Nigeria
J Hist Soc Nigeria — Journal. Historical Society of Nigeria
J Hist Soc QD — Historical Society of Queensland. Journal
J Hist Soc Qld — Historical Society of Queensland. Journal
J Hist Soc SA — Journal. Historical Society of South Australia
J Hist Soc Sierra Leone — Journal. Historical Society of Sierra Leone
J Hist Stud — Journal of Historical Studies
J HIV Ther — Journal of HIV Therapy
JHK — Jahrbuch der Hamburger Kunstsammlungen
J HK Br Roy Asiat Soc — Journal. Hong Kong Branch. Royal Asiatic Society
JHKGV — Jahrbuch der Hessischen Kirchengeschichtlichen Vereinigung
JHL — Journal of Helminthology. School of Hygiene and Tropical Medicine (London)
JHLB — Journal. Federal Home Loan Bank Board
JHM — Journal of the History of Medicine
JHM — Journal of the History of Medicine and Allied Sciences

JHMa — Johns Hopkins Magazine
JHMEDL — Journal of Holistic Medicine
JHMS — Journal. Historical Metallurgy Society
JHMSDT — Journal of Human Movement Studies
JHMT — Jahresbericht des Historischen Museums Schloss Thun
JHN — Jewish Horizon (New York)
JHO — Journal of Housing
JhOAI — Jahreshefte. Oesterreichisches Archaeologische Institut in Wien
J Ho E — Journal of Home Economics
JhOeArl — Jahreshefte des Oesterreichischen Archaeologischen Instituts
J Hohai Univ — Journal of Hohai University
J Hokkaido Dent Assoc — Journal. Hokkaido Dental Association
J Hokkaido Fish Exp Stn — Journal. Hokkaido Fisheries Experimental Station
J Hokkaido Fish Sci Inst — Journal. Hokkaido Fisheries Scientific Institution
J Hokkaido Forest Prod Res Inst — Journal. Hokkaido Forest Products Research Institute
J Hokkaido Gakugei Univ — Journal. Hokkaido Gakugei University
J Hokkaido Gakugei Univ Sect B — Journal. Hokkaido Gakugei University. Section B
J Hokkaido Gynecol Obstet Soc — Journal. Hokkaido Gynecology and Obstetrical Society
J Hokkaido Soc Grassl Sci — Journal of Hokkaido Society of Grassland Science
J Hokkaido Univ Ed Sect IIA — Journal. Hokkaido University of Education. Section II-A
J Hokkaido Univ Educ — Journal. Hokkaido University of Education
J Hokkaido Univ Educ IIB — Journal. Hokkaido University of Education. Section II-B
J Hokkaido Univ Educ Sect II A — Journal. Hokkaido University of Education. Section II-A
J Hokkaido Univ Educ Sect II-B — Journal. Hokkaido University of Education. Section II-B
J Hokkaido Univ Educ Sect II C — Journal. Hokkaido University of Education. Section II-C
J Hokuto Tech Jr Coll — Journal. Hokuto Technical Junior College
J Holistic Med — Journal of Holistic Medicine
J Holistic Nurs — Journal of Holistic Nursing
J Home Econ — Journal of Home Economics
J Home Econ Jpn — Journal of Home Economics of Japan
J Homosex — Journal of Homosexuality
J Homosexuality — Journal of Homosexuality
J Hong Kong Branch Royal Asiat Soc — Journal of the Hong Kong Branch of the Royal Asiatic Society
J Hong Kong Branch Roy Asiatic Soc — Journal. Hong Kong Branch. Royal Asiatic Society
J Hong Kong Brch R Asiat Soc — Journal of the Hong Kong Branch of the Royal Asiatic Society
J Hongkong Fish Res Sta — Journal. Hongkong Fisheries Research Station
J Hopeh Univ Nat Sci — Journal. Hopeh University. Natural Science
J Horizon — Jewish Horizon
J Horol Inst Jpn — Journal. Horological Institute of Japan
J Hort Assoc Japan — Journal. Horticultural Association of Japan/Engei Gakkai Zasshi
J Hortic — Journal of Horticulture
J Hortic Assoc Jpn — Journal. Horticulture Association of Japan
J Hortic Assoc London — Journal. Horticulture Association of London
J Hortic Sci — Journal of Horticultural Science
J Hortic Sci Biotechnol — Journal of Horticultural Science and Biotechnology
J Hort Pract Gard — Journal of Horticulture and Practical Gardening
J Hort Prat Jard — Journal d'Horticulture Pratique et de Jardinage
J Hort Sci — Journal of Horticultural Science
J Hort Suisse — Journal d'Horticulture Suisse
J Hosp & Leisure Market — Journal of Hospitality & Leisure Marketing
J Hosp Dent Pract — Journal of Hospital Dental Practice
J Hosp Infect — Journal of Hospital Infection
J Hospitality Educ — Journal of Hospitality Education
J Hosp Supply Process Distrib — Journal of Hospital Supply, Processing, and Distribution
J Hotel Dieu de Montreal — Journal. Hotel Dieu de Montreal
J Housing — Journal of Housing
J Housing Elderly — Journal of Housing for the Elderly
J Houston Dist Dent Soc — Journal. Houston [Texas] District Dental Society
JHP — Journal of Hispanic Philology
JHP — Journal of the History of Philosophy
JHPh — Journal of the History of Philosophy
JHPLD — Journal of Health Politics, Policy, and Law
JHPP — Journal of Health Politics, Policy, and Law
JHPS — Journal of History and Political Science
JHR — Journal of Historical Research
JHR — Journal of Human Relations
JHR — Journal of Human Resources
JHS — Jewish History Series
JHS — Johns Hopkins Studies in Romance Literatures and Languages
JHS — Journal of Hellenic Studies
JHS — Journal of Historical Studies
JHS-AR — Journal of Hellenic Studies. Archaeological Reports
JHSB — Journal of Health and Social Behavior
JHSch — Jahresberichte ueber das Hoehre Schulwesen
JHSCW — Journal. Historical Society of the Church in Wales
JHSEM — Jewish Historical Society of England. Miscellanies
JHSET — Jewish Historical Society of England. Transactions
JHSPCW — Journal. Historical Society of the Presbyterian Church of Wales
JHSRLL — Johns Hopkins Studies in Romance Language and Literature
JHSS — Journal of Hellenic Studies. Supplement
JHSS — Journal of History for Senior Students
JHSSA — Journal. Historical Society of South Australia

JH St — Journal of Hellenic Studies
JHSt — Journal of Historical Studies
JHStud — Journal of Historical Studies
JHSUD — Journal of Hand Surgery
J Huazhong Cent China Agric Univ — Journal of Huazhong (Central China) Agricultural University
J Huazhong (Cent China) Univ Sci Technol — Journal. Huazhong (Central China) University of Science and Technology
J Huazhong Inst Tech — Journal. Huazhong Institute of Technology. English Edition
J Huazhong Inst Technol — Journal. Huazhong Institute of Technology
J Huazhong Inst Technol Engl Ed — Journal. Huazhong Institute of Technology. English Edition
J Huazhong Univ Sci Tech — Journal. Huazhong [Central China] University of Science and Technology. English Edition
JHUC — Journal. Hebrew Union College
J Humanistic Psychol — Journal of Humanistic Psychology
J Humanist Psychol — Journal of Humanistic Psychology
J Human Resources — Journal of Human Resources
J Human Stress — Journal of Human Stress
J Hum Behav Learn — Journal of Human Behavior and Learning
J Hum Ecol — Journal of Human Ecology
J Hum Ecol Spec Issue — Journal of Human Ecology. Special Issue
J Hum Ergol — Journal of Human Ergology
J Hum Ergol (Tokyo) — Journal of Human Ergology (Tokyo)
J Hum Evol — Journal of Human Evolution
J Hum Evolution — Journal of Human Evolution
J Hum Genet — Journal of Human Genetics
J Hum Hypertens — Journal of Human Hypertension
J Hum Mov Stud — Journal of Human Movement Studies
J Hum Nutr — Journal of Human Nutrition
J Hum Nutr Diet — Journal of Human Nutrition and Dietetics
J Hu Move Stud — Journal of Human Movement Studies
J Hum Psy — Journal of Humanistic Psychology
J Hum Psychol — Journal of Humanistic Psychology
J Hum Relat — Journal of Human Relations
J Hum Relations — Journal of Human Relations
J Hum Resources — Journal of Human Resources
J Hum Serv Abstr — Journal of Human Services Abstracts
J Hum Stress — Journal of Human Stress
J Hum Technol — Journal for the Humanities and Technology
J Hum Virol — Journal of Human Virology
J Hunan Educ Inst — Journal of Hunan Educational Institute
J Hunan Norm Univ Nat Sci Ed — Journal. Hunan Normal University. Natural Science Edition
J Hunan Sci Technol Univ — Journal. Hunan Science and Technology University
J Hunan Univ — Journal. Hunan University
J H Un Cir — Johns Hopkins University Circulars
J Hung Chem Soc — Journal. Hungarian Chemical Society
J Hung Soc Eng Archit — Journal. Hungarian Society of Engineers and Architects
J Hung Vet Surg — Journal. Hungarian Veterinary Surgeons
J Hunter Valley Research Foundation — Journal. Hunter Valley Research Foundation
JHuR — Journal of Human Relations
J H U Studies — Johns Hopkins University. Studies in Historical and Political Science
JHVD — Jahrbuch. Historischer Verein Dillingen
JHVDill — Jahrbuch des Historischen Vereins Dillingen
JHVF — Jahrbuch des Historischen Vereins fuer Wuerttembergisch Franken
JHVFB — Jahrbuch. Historischer Verein fuer das Fuerstbistum Bamberg
JHVG — Jahrbuch des Historischen Vereins des Kantons Glarus
JHVGR — Jahresbericht des Historischen Vereins fuer die Grafschaft Ravensberg
JHVL — Jahrbuch des Historischen Vereins fuer das Fuerstentum Liechtenstein
JHVM — Jahrbuch des Historischen Vereins fuer Mittelfranken
JHVS — Jahresbericht des Historischen Vereins fuer Straubing und Ungebung
JHVSe — Jahresberichte der Historischen Vereinigung Seetal
JHWA — Jahrbuch der Hamburger Wissenschaftlichen Anstalten
JHYDA7 — Journal of Hydrology
J Hyderabad Geol Surv — Journal. Hyderabad Geological Survey
J Hydr-ASCE — Journal. Hydraulics Division. American Society of Civil Engineers
J Hydraul Div Amer Soc Civil Eng Proc — Journal. Hydraulics Division. Proceedings of the American Society of Civil Engineers
J Hydraul Div Am Soc Civ Eng — Journal. Hydraulics Division. American Society of Civil Engineers
J Hydraul Div Proc ASCE — Journal. Hydraulic Division. Proceedings of the American Society of Civil Engineers
J Hydraul Eng (Peking) — Journal of Hydraulic Engineering (Peking)
J Hydraul Res — Journal of Hydraulic Research
J Hydraul Res J Rech Hydraul — Journal of Hydraulic Research/Journal de Recherches Hydrauliques
J Hydrodyn — Journal of Hydrodynamics
J Hydrodyn Ser B English Ed — Journal of Hydrodynamics. Series B (English Edition)
J Hydrogen Energy Syst Soc Jpn — Journal of the Hydrogen Energy Systems Society of Japan
J Hydrogeol — Journal of Hydrogeology
J Hydrol — Journal of Hydrology
J Hydrol (Amst) — Journal of Hydrology (Amsterdam)
J Hydrol (Dunedin) — Journal of Hydrology (Dunedin)
J Hydrol Hydromech — Journal of Hydrology and Hydromechanics
J Hydrol (Neth) — Journal of Hydrology (Netherlands)
J Hydrol Sci — Journal of Hydrological Sciences
J Hydronaut — Journal of Hydronautics
J Hyg — Journal of Hygiene
J Hyg (Ankara) — Journal of Hygiene (Ankara)

J Hyg (Camb) — Journal of Hygiene (Cambridge)
J Hyg Chem — Journal of Hygienic Chemistry
J Hyg Chem Soc Japan — Journal. Hygienic Chemical Society of Japan
J Hyg Epidemiol Microbiol Immunol — Journal of Hygiene, Epidemiology, Microbiology, and Immunology
J Hyg Epidemiol Microbiol Immunol (Prague) — Journal of Hygiene, Epidemiology, Microbiology, and Immunology (Prague)
J Hyg Ep Mi — Journal of Hygiene, Epidemiology, Microbiology, and Immunology
J Hygiene — Journal of Hygiene
J Hyg (Lond) — Journal of Hygiene (London)
J Hyg (Paris) — Journal d'Hygiene Clintologie (Paris)
J Hyg Res — Journal of Hygiene Research
J Hyg Suppl — Journal of Hygiene. Supplement
J Hyogo Coll Med — Journal. Hyogo College of Medicine
J Hypertens — Journal of Hypertension
J Hypertens Suppl — Journal of Hypertension. Supplement
JI — Japan Interpreter
JI — Journal. American Musical Instrument Society
JI — Journal of Immunology
JI — Journal of Insurance
JIA — Journal of Indian Art and Industry
JIA — Journal of Industrial Archaeology
JIA — Journal of International Affairs
JIAI — Journal. Indian Anthropological Institute
JIAN — Journal International d'Archeologie Numismatique
Jiangsu J Tradit Chin Med — Jiangsu Journal of Traditional Chinese Medicine
Jiangsu Med J — Jiangsu Medical Journal
Jiangsu Mus & Jiangsu Archaeol Stud Confer — Jiangsu Museum and Jiangsu Archaeological Study Conference
JIAP — Journal. Indian Academy of Philosophy
J I Archip — Journal of the Indian Archipelago and Eastern Asia
J IARI Post-Grad Sch — Journal. IARI [*Indian Agricultural Research Institute*]. Post-Graduate School
JIAS — Journal. Indian Anthropological Society
JIAS — Journal of Interamerican Studies
JIASRA — Journal. International Arthur Schnitzler Research Association
JIB — Jobs Impact Bulletin
JIB — Journal. Institute of Bankers
JIB — Journal of International Business Studies
JIBHS — Journal. Irish Baptist Historical Society
J I Brewing — Journal. Institute of Brewing
JIBS — Journal of Indian and Buddhist Studies
JIBS — Journal of the Indian Botanical Society
JIC — Jugoslovenski Istoriski Casopis
JICH — Journal of Imperial and Commonwealth History
Jichi Med Sch J — Jichi Medical School Journal
J ICHPER-SD — Journal. International Council for Health, Physical Education, and Recreation
J Ichthyol — Journal of Ichthyology
J Ichthyol (Engl Trans Vopr Ikhtiol) — Journal of Ichthyology (English Translation of Voprosy Ikhtiologii)
J Ichthyol (USSR) — Journal of Ichthyology (USSR)
JICJ — Journal. International Commission of Jurists
JICST File CS — JICST [*Japan Information Center of Science and Technology*] File on Current Science and Technology Research in Japan
JICST File MS — JICST [*Japan Information Center of Science and Technology*] File on Medical Science in Japan
JICST File ST — JICST [*Japan Information Center of Science and Technology*] File on Science and Technology
JICST File STM — JICST [*Japan Information Center of Science and Technology*] File on Science, Technology, and Medicine in Japan
JICSW — Jahrbuch des Instituts fuer Christliche Sozialwissenschaften der WestfaelischenWilhelms-Universitaet
J Idaho Acad Sci — Journal. Idaho Academy of Science
JIDRS — Journal. International Double Reed Society
JIDSDP — Journal. Idaho Academy of Science
JIDXA — Journal. Indiana State Medical Association
JIE — Japan Information Exchange
JIE — Journal of Industrial Economics
JIE — Journal of International Economics
JIECA — Journal of Industrial and Engineering Chemistry
JIEE — Jews in Eastern Europe
JIEND — Jinetsu Enerugi
JIES — Journal of Indo-European Studies
J IES — Journal of the IES (Institute of Environmental Sciences)
J IEST — Journal of the IEST (Institute of Environmental Science and Technology)
J IETE — Journal of the IETE (Institution of Electronics and Telecommunication Engineers)
JIF — Journal of Information Systems Management
JIFC — Journal. International Folk Music Council
JIFM — Journal. International Folk Music Council
JIFMC — Journal. International Folk Music Council
JIFSA — Journal. Indian Academy of Forensic Sciences
JIFUA — Journal. Institute of Fuel
J I Fuel — Journal. Institute of Fuel
JIG — Jahrbuch fuer Internationale Germanistik
JIG — Journal of Irish Genealogy
J IGPL — Journal of the Interest Group in Pure and Applied Logics
JIH — Journal of Indian History
JIHA — Journal of Indian History (Allahabad University)
JI Hist — Journal de l'Institut Historique
JIHS — Journal. Illinois State Historical Society
JIHTA — Journal of Industrial Hygiene and Toxicology
JIHVE — Journal. Institution of Heating and Ventilating Engineers
JIIB — Journal. Indian Institute of Bankers

JIIM — Journal of Information and Image Management
JIIT — Journal of Industrial Irradiation Technology
JIKEA — Jikken Keitaigakushi
Jikeikai Med J — Jikeikai Medical Journal
JIL — George Washington Journal of International Law and Economics
JIL — Journal of Irish Literature
JILA Inf Cent Rep — Joint Institute for Laboratory Astrophysics. Information Center. Report
JILA Rep — Joint Institute for Laboratory Astrophysics. Report
JILEA — Journal. Institution of Locomotive Engineers
JILI — Journal. Indian Law Institute
J Ill Hist Soc — Journal. Illinois State Historical Society
JILLHS — Journal. Illinois State Historical Society
J Illinois State Hist Soc — Journal. Illinois State Historical Society
J Ill State Hist Soc — Journal. Illinois State Historical Society
J Illum Eng Inst Jap — Journal. Illuminating Engineering Institute of Japan
J Illum Engng Soc — Journal. Illuminating Engineering Society
J Illum Eng Soc — Journal. Illuminating Engineering Society
J Illus — Journal Illustre
JILTA — Journal. Indian Law Teachers Association
JIM — Journal of Industrial Microbiology
JIM — Journal of Information Management
JIM — Journal of Internal Medicine
J IMA — Journal. Islamic Medical Association of the United States and Canada
JIMA — Journal of the Indian Medical Association
J Image Guid Surg — Journal of Image Guided Surgery
J Imaging Sci — Journal of Imaging Science
J Imaging Sci Technol — Journal of Imaging Science and Technology
J Imaging Technol — Journal of Imaging Technology
J I Math Ap — Journal. Institute of Mathematics and Its Applications
JIMEA — Journal. Institute of Metals
JIMF — Journal of International Money and Finance
JIMGA — Journal of Immunogenetics
JIMMA — Journal. Institute of Metals. Metallurgical Abstracts
JIMMA — Journal. Institute of Muslim Minority Affairs
J Immun — Journal of Immunology
J Immunoassay — Journal of Immunoassay
J Immunoassay Immunochem — Journal of Immunoassay & Immunochemistry
J Immunogen — Journal of Immunogenetics
J Immunogenet — Journal of Immunogenetics
J Immunogenet (Oxf) — Journal of Immunogenetics (Oxford)
J Immunol — Journal of Immunology
J Immunol M — Journal of Immunological Methods
J Immunol Methods — Journal of Immunological Methods
J Immunology — Journal of Immunology
J Immunol Virus Res Exp Chemother — Journal of Immunology, Virus Research, and Experimental Chemotherapy
J Immunopharmacol — Journal of Immunopharmacology
J Immunother — Journal of Immunotherapy
J Immunother Emphasis Tumor immunol — Journal of Immunotherapy with Emphasis on Tumor Immunology
JIMP — Journal of the Iraqi Medical Professions
J Imp Agr Exp Sta (Tokyo) — Journal. Imperial Agricultural Experiment Station (Tokyo)
J Imp Agric Exp Sta Nishigahara Tokyo — Journal. Imperial Agricultural Experiment Station. Nishigahara, Tokyo/Noji Shikenjo Iho
J Imp Coll Chem Eng Soc — Journal. Imperial College. Chemical Engineering Society
J Imp Coll Chem Soc — Journal. Imperial College. Chemical Society
J Imp Com H — Journal of Imperial and Commonwealth History
J Imp Common Hist — Journal of Imperial and Commonwealth History
J Imp Commonw Hist — Journal of Imperial and Commonwealth History
J Imp Fish Inst (Jpn) — Journal. Imperial Fisheries Institute (Japan)
JIMS — Journal. Indian Mathematical Society
JIMSA — Journal. Irish Medical Association
JIMSD2 — Journal of Interdisciplinary Modeling and Simulation
JIN — Journal International d'Archeologie Numismatique
JIN — Journal of International Economics
JIN — Journal of Israel Numismatics
JINBA — Journal. Institute of Brewing
J Inc Aust Insurance Inst — Journal. Incorporated Australian Insurance Institute
J Inc Brew Guild — Journal. Incorporated Brewers' Guild
J Inc Clerks Works Assoc GB — Journal. Incorporated Clerks of Works Association of Great Britain
J Incl Phen — Journal of Inclusion Phenomena
J Inclusion Phenom — Journal of Inclusion Phenomena
J Inclusion Phenom Mol Recognit Chem — Journal of Inclusion Phenomena and Molecular Recognition in Chemistry
J Ind — Journal of Industry
J Ind A & Indust — Journal of Indian Art and Industry
J Ind Acad Philo — Journal. Indian Academy of Philosophy
J Ind Aero — Journal of Industrial Aerodynamics
J Ind Aerodyn — Journal of Industrial Aerodynamics
J Ind & Fin — Journal of Industry and Finance
J Ind Anthropol Soc — Journal. Indian Anthropological Society
J Ind Anthro Soc — Journal of the Indian Anthropological Society
J Ind Arts Ed — Journal of Industrial Arts Education
J Ind Bot Soc — Journal. Indian Botanical Society
J Ind Chem — Journal of Industrial Chemistry
J Ind Ch S — Journal. Indian Chemical Society
J Ind Color — Journal de l'Industrie des Colorants
J Ind Ecol — Journal of Industrial Ecology
J Ind Econ — Journal of Industrial Economics
J Ind Eng — Journal of Industrial Engineering
J Ind Eng Chem — Journal of Industrial and Engineering Chemistry

J Ind Eng Chem Seoul — Journal of Industrial and Engineering Chemistry (Seoul)

J Ind Engng Chem — Journal of Industrial and Engineering Chemistry

J Ind Explos Soc (Jap) — Journal. Industrial Explosives Society. Explosion and Explosives (Japan)

J Ind Explos Soc (Jpn) — Journal. Industrial Explosives Society (Japan)

J Ind Fabr — Journal of Industrial Fabrics

J Ind Gaz — Journal des Industries du Gaz

J Ind Hist — Journal of Indian History

J Ind Hyg — Journal of Industrial Hygiene

J Ind Hyg — Journal of Industrial Hygiene and Toxicology

J Ind Hyg Toxicol — Journal of Industrial Hygiene and Toxicology

J Indian Acad Dent — Journal. Indian Academy of Dentistry

J Indian Acad Forensic Sci — Journal. Indian Academy of Forensic Sciences

J Indian Acad Geosci — Journal. Indian Academy of Geoscience

J Indian Acad Phil — Journal. Indian Academy of Philosophy

J Indian Acad Sci — Journal. Indian Academy of Sciences

J Indian Acad Wood Sci — Journal. Indian Academy of Wood Science

J Indiana Dent Assoc — Journal. Indiana Dental Association

J Indiana MA — Journal. Indiana State Medical Association

J Indian Anthropol Soc — Journal. Indian Anthropological Society

J Indian Anthrop Soc — Journal of the Indian Anthropological Society

J Indianap Dist Dent Soc — Journal. Indianapolis District Dental Society

J Indian Assoc Commun Dis — Journal. Indian Association for Communicable Diseases

J Indiana State Dent Assoc — Journal. Indiana State Dental Association

J Indiana State Med Assoc — Journal. Indiana State Medical Association

J Indian Bot — Journal of Indian Botany

J Indian Bot Soc — Journal. Indian Botanical Society

J Indian Ceram Soc — Journal. Indian Ceramic Society

J Indian Chem Soc — Journal. Indian Chemical Society

J Indian Chem Soc Ind News Ed — Journal. Indian Chemical Society. Industrial and News Edition

J Indian Counc Chem — Journal. Indian Council of Chemists

J Indian Dent Assoc — Journal. Indian Dental Association

J Indian Geophys Union — Journal. Indian Geophysical Union

J Indian Geosci Assoc — Journal. Indian Geoscience Association

J Indian Hist — Journal of Indian History

J Indian I — Journal. Indian Institute of Science

J Indian Ind Labour — Journal of Indian Industries and Labour

J Indian Inst Sci — Journal. Indian Institute of Science

J Indian Inst Sci Sect A — Journal. Indian Institute of Science. Section A

J Indian Inst Sci Sect B — Journal. Indian Institute of Science. Section B

J Indian Inst Sci Sect C — Journal. Indian Institute of Science. Section C

J Indian Inst Sci Sect C Biol Sci — Journal. Indian Institute of Science. Section C. Biological Sciences

J Indian Law Inst — Journal. Indian Law Institute

J Indian Leather Technol Assoc — Journal. Indian Leather Technologists Association

J Indian Math Soc — Journal. Indian Mathematical Society

J Indian Med A — Journal. Indian Medical Association

J Indian Med Ass — Journal. Indian Medical Association

J Indian Med Assoc — Journal. Indian Medical Association

J Indian Med Prof — Journal of the Indian Medical Profession

J Indian Musicol Soc — Journal. Indian Musicological Society

J Indian Nat Soc Soil Mech Found Eng — Journal. Indian National Society of Soil Mechanics and Foundation Engineering

J Indian P — Journal of Indian Philosophy

J Indian Pediatr Soc — Journal. Indian Pediatric Society

J Indian Phil — Journal of Indian Philosophy

J Indian Plywood Ind Res Inst — Journal. Indian Plywood Industries Research Institute

J Indian Potato Assoc — Journal. Indian Potato Association

J Indian Refract Makers Assoc — Journal. Indian Refractory Makers Association

J Indian Roads Congr — Journal. Indian Roads Congress

J Indian Soc Agric Stat — Journal. Indian Society of Agricultural Statistics

J Indian Soc Agricultural Statist — Journal of the Indian Society of Agricultural Statistics

J Indian Soc Agr Statist — Journal. Indian Society of Agricultural Statistics

J Indian Soc Pedod Prev Dent — Journal. Indian Society of Pedodontics and Preventive Dentistry

J Indian Soc Soil Sci — Journal. Indian Society of Soil Science

J Indian Soc Statist Oper Res — Journal. Indian Society of Statistics and Operations Research

J Indian Statist Assoc — Journal. Indian Statistical Association

J India Soc Eng — Journal. India Society of Engineers

J Ind Irradiat Technol — Journal of Industrial Irradiation Technology

J Ind Irrad Tech — Journal of Industrial Irradiation Technology

J Individ Psychol — Journal of Individual Psychology

J Indiv Psy — Journal of Individual Psychology

J Ind Med Assoc — Journal of the Indian Medical Association

J Ind Microbiol — Journal of Industrial Microbiology

J Ind Microbiol & Biotechnol — Journal of Industrial Microbiology and Biotechnology

J Ind Microbiol Suppl — Journal of Industrial Microbiology. Supplement

J Ind Mus — Journal of Indian Museums

J Ind Musicol Soc — Journal. Indian Musicological Society

J Indn Acad Math — Indian Academy of Mathematics. Journal

J Indn Psychoan Inst — Samiska. Journal. Indian Psychoanalytic Institute

J Indn St A — Journal. Indian Statistical Association

J Indo-Eur — Journal of Indo-European Studies

J Indo-European Stud — Journal of Indo-European Studies

J Indo Eur Stud — Journal of Indo-European Studies

J Indones At Energy Agency — Journal. Indonesian Atomic Energy Agency

J Indoor Air Int — Journal of Indoor Air International

J Ind Philo — Journal of Indian Philosophy

J Ind Pollut Control — Journal of Industrial Pollution Control

J Ind Pot Assoc — Journal of the Indian Potato Association

J Ind Rel — Journal of Industrial Relations

J Ind Relations — Journal of Industrial Relations

J Ind Soc — Journal of Indian Sociology

J Ind Soc A — Journal of the Indian Society of Art

J Ind Soc Orient A — Journal of the Indian Society of Oriental Art

J Ind Soil Sci — Journal of the Indian Society for Soil Science

J Ind Teach Educ — Journal of Industrial Teacher Education

J Ind Technol — Journal of Industrial Technology

J Ind Technol Myong-Ji Univ — Journal of Industrial Technology. Myong-Ji University

J Ind Textile Hist — Journal of Indian Textile History

J Ind Trade — Journal of Industry and Trade

J Indus Rel — Journal of Industrial Relations

J Indust — Journal of Industry

J Indust Hyg — Journal of Industrial Hygiene

J Indust Hyg Toxicol — Journal of Industrial Hygiene and Toxicology

J Industr Econ — Journal of Industrial Economics

J Indust Relations — Journal of Industrial Relations

J Industr Relat — Journal of Industrial Relations

J Industr Teacher Educ — Journal of Industrial Teacher Education

J Industry — Journal of Industry

JINEA — Journal. Indian Chemical Society. Industrial and News Edition

J Inf and Optimiz Sci — Journal of Information and Optimization Sciences

J Infect — Journal of Infection

J Infect Chemother — Journal of Infection and Chemotherapy

J Infect Dis — Journal of Infectious Diseases

J Infect Dis Pharmacother — Journal of Infectious Disease Pharmacotherapy

J Inferential Deductive Biol — Journal of Inferential and Deductive Biology

J Inf Image Manage — Journal of Information and Image Management

J Inflamm — Journal of Inflammation

J Inflammation — Journal of Inflammation

J Info Mgmt — Journal of Information Management

J Info Process — Journal of Information Processing

J Information Processing — Journal of Information Processing

J Inform Optim Sci — Journal of Information and Optimization Sciences

J Inform Process — Journal of Information Processing

J Inform Process Cybernet — Journal of Information Processing and Cybernetics

J Info Sci — Journal of Information Science. Principles and Practice

J Info Sys Mgmt — Journal of Information Systems Management

J Inf Process Cybern — Journal of Information Processing and Cybernetics

J Inf Process Manage — Journal of Information Processing and Management

J Inf Process Soc Jap — Journal. Information Processing Society of Japan

J Inf Process Soc Jpn — Journal. Information Processing Society of Japan

J Infrared Millimeter Waves — Journal of Infrared and Millimeter Waves

J Inf Rec — Journal of Information Recording

J Inf Rec Mat — Journal of Information Recording Materials

J Inf Rec Mater — Journal of Information Recording Materials

J Inf Sci — Journal of Information Science

J Inf Sci Princ and Pract — Journal of Information Science. Principles and Practice

J Inf Sci Technol Assoc (Jpn) — Journal. Information Science and Technology Association (Japan)

J Inf Tech Ind Fonderie — Journal d'Informations Techniques des Industries de la Fonderie

J Infus Chemother — Journal of Infusional Chemotherapy

J Ing — Journal des Ingenieurs

J Ing URTB — Journal des Ingenieurs de l'URTB

J Inherited Metab Dis — Journal of Inherited Metabolic Disease

J Inherit Metab Dis — Journal of Inherited Metabolic Disease

J Injection Molding Technol — Journal of Injection Molding Technology

J Inland Fish Soc India — Journal. Inland Fisheries Society of India

J Inl Fish Soc India — Journal. Inland Fisheries Society of India

J Inorg and Nucl Chem — Journal of Inorganic and Nuclear Chemistry

J Inorg Biochem — Journal of Inorganic Biochemistry

J Inorg Chem (Nanjing Peoples Repub China) — Journal of Inorganic Chemistry (Nanjing, People's Republic of China)

J Inorg Chem (USSR) — Journal of Inorganic Chemistry (USSR)

J Inorg Mat — Journal of Inorganic Materials

J Inorg Mater — Journal of Inorganic Materials

J Inorg Nuc — Journal of Inorganic and Nuclear Chemistry

J Inorg Nucl Chem — Journal of Inorganic and Nuclear Chemistry

J Inorg Nucl Chem Suppl — Journal of Inorganic and Nuclear Chemistry. Supplement

J Inorg Organomet Polym — Journal of Inorganic and Organometallic Polymers

J INOR NUCL CHEM — Journal of Inorganic and Nuclear Chemistry

J Ins — Journal of Insurance

J Insect Behav — Journal of Insect Behavior

J Insect Path — Journal of Insect Pathology

J Insect Pathol — Journal of Insect Pathology

J Insect Ph — Journal of Insect Physiology

J Insect Physiol — Journal of Insect Physiology

Jinsen Med J — Jinsen Medical Journal

J Insp Sch — Journal of Inspectors of Schools of Australia and New Zealand

J Inst — Institutes of Justinian

J Inst A Educ — Journal of the Institute of Art Education

J Inst Agric Resour Utiliz Chinju Agric Coll — Journal. Institute for Agricultural Resources Utilization. Chinju Agricultural College

J Inst Anim Tech — Journal. Institute of Animal Technicians

J Inst Architects Malaya — Journal of the Institute of Architects. Malaya

J Inst Armament Stud (Poona India) — Journal. Institute of Armament Studies (Poona, India)

J Inst Armament Technol (Poona India) — Journal. Institute of Armament Technology (Poona, India)

J Inst Asian Stud Madras — Journal of the Institute of Asian Studies (Madras)

J Inst Auto & Aero Engrs — Journal. Institution of Automotive and Aeronautical Engineers

J Inst Automob Eng (London) — Journal. Institution of Automobile Engineers (London)

J Inst Automot Aeronaut Eng — Journal. Institution of Automotive and Aeronautical Engineers

J Inst Automotive & Aeronautical Eng — Journal. Institution of Automotive and Aeronautical Engineers

J Inst Automotive & Aeronautical Engrs — Journal. Institution of Automotive and Aeronautical Engineers

J Inst Bang Stud — Journal of the Institute of Bangladesh Studies

J Inst Bankers — Journal of the Institute of Bankers

J Inst Biol — Journal. Institute of Biology

J Inst Brew — Journal. Institute of Brewing

J Inst Brew Suppl — Journal. Institute of Brewing. Supplement

J Inst Br Foundrymen — Journal. Institute of British Foundrymen

J Inst Can Sci Technol Aliment — Journal. Institut Canadien de Science et Technologie Alimentaire

J Inst Can Technol Aliment — Journal. Institut Canadien de Technologie Alimentaire

J Inst Certif Eng (S Afr) — Journal. Institution of Certificated Engineers (South Africa)

J Inst Chem (India) — Journal. Institute of Chemistry (India)

J Inst Chem (India) — Journal. Institution of Chemists (India)

J Inst Chem Irel — Journal. Institute of Chemistry of Ireland

J Inst Chin Stud Hong Kong — Journal of the Institute of Chinese Studies (Hong Kong)

J Inst Civ Eng — Journal. Institution of Civil Engineers

J Inst Civ Engin — Journal of the Institution of Civil Engineers

J Inst Clerks Works GB — Journal. Institute of Clerks of Works of Great Britain

J Inst Clerks Works G Bt — Journal. Institute of Clerks of Works of Great Britain

J Inst Comput Sci — Journal. Institution of Computer Sciences

J Inst Def Stud Anal — Journal. Institute for Defence Studies and Analyses

J Inst Draftsmen — Journal. Institute of Draftsmen

J Inst Electr Commun Eng Jap — Journal. Institute of Electrical Communication Engineers of Japan [*Later, Journal. Institute of Electronics and Communication Engineers of Japan*]

J Inst Electr Eng — Journal. Institute of Electrical Engineers

J Inst Electr Eng — Journal. Institution of Electrical Engineers

J Inst Electr Eng (1949-63) — Journal. Institution of Electrical Engineers (1949-63)

J Inst Electr Eng (1889-1940) — Journal. Institution of Electrical Engineers (1889-1940)

J Inst Electr Eng Jpn — Journal. Institution of Electrical Engineers of Japan

J Inst Electr Eng Part 1 — Journal. Institution of Electrical Engineers. Part 1. General

J Inst Electr Eng Part 2 — Journal. Institution of Electrical Engineers. Part 2. Power Engineering

J Inst Electr Eng Part 3 — Journal. Institution of Electrical Engineers. Part 3. Radio and Communication Engineering

J Inst Electron and Commun Eng Jpn — Journal. Institute of Electronics and Communication Engineers of Japan

J Inst Electron Commun Eng Jap — Journal. Institute of Electronics and Communication Engineers of Japan

J Inst Electron Commun Eng Jpn — Journal. Institute of Electronics and Communication Engineers of Japan

J Inst Electron Telecommun Eng — Journal. Institution of Electronics and Telecommunication Engineers

J Inst Electron Telecommun Eng (New Delhi) — Journal. Institution of Electronics and Telecommunication Engineers(New Delhi)

J Inst En — Journal of the Institute of Engineers

J Inst Energy — Journal. Institute of Energy

J Inst Eng (Aust) — Journal. Institution of Engineers (Australia)

J Inst Eng (Bangladesh) — Journal. Institution of Engineers (Bangladesh)

J Inst Eng (India) — Journal. Institution of Engineers (India)

J Inst Eng India Aerosp Eng J — Journal of the Institution of Engineers (India). Aerospace Engineering Journal

J Inst Eng India Agric Eng Div — Journal of the Institution of Engineers (India). Agricultural Engineering Division

J Inst Eng India Archit Eng Div — Journal of the Institution of Engineers (India). Architectural Engineering Division

J Inst Eng (India) Chem Eng Div — Journal. Institution of Engineers (India). Chemical Engineering Division

J Inst Eng (India) Civ Eng Div — Journal. Institution of Engineers (India). Civil Engineering Division

J Inst Eng (India) Elec Eng Div — Journal. Institution of Engineers (India). Electrical Engineering Division

J Inst Eng India Electr Eng — Journal of the Institution of Engineers (India). Electrical Engineering

J Inst Eng (India) Electron and Telecommun Eng Div — Journal. Institution of Engineers (India). Electronics and Telecommunication Engineering Division

J Inst Eng India Electron & Telecommun Eng J — Journal of the Institution of Engineers (India). Electronics and Telecommunication Engineering Journal

J Inst Eng (India) Electron Telecommun Eng Div — Journal. Institution of Engineers (India). Electronics and Telecommunication Engineering Division

J Inst Eng India Environ Eng — Journal of the Institution of Engineers (India). Environmental Engineering

J Inst Eng (India) Environ Eng Div — Journal. Institution of Engineers (India). Environmental Engineering Division

J Inst Eng (India) Gen Eng Div — Journal. Institution of Engineers (India). General Engineering Division

J Inst Eng India Hindi Div — Journal. Institution of Engineers. (India) Hindi Division

J Inst Eng (India) Ind Dev Gen Eng Div — Journal. Institution of Engineers. (India). Industrial Development and General Engineering Division

J Inst Eng (India) Interdisciplinary and Gen Eng — Journal. Institution of Engineers (India). Interdisciplinary and General Engineering

J Inst Eng (India) Mech Eng Div — Journal. Institution of Engineers (India). Mechanical Engineering Division

J Inst Eng India Metall Mater Sci Div — Journal of the Institution of Engineers (India). Metallurgy and Material Science Division

J Inst Eng (India) Min and Metall Div — Journal. Institution of Engineers (India). Mining and Metallurgy Division

J Inst Eng (India) Mining Met Div — Journal. Institution of Engineers (India). Mining and Metallurgy Division

J Inst Eng (India) Min Metall Div — Journal. Institution of Engineers (India). Mining and Metallurgy Division

J Inst Eng (India) Part CH — Journal. Institution of Engineers (India). Part CH. ChemicalEngineering Division

J Inst Eng India Part CH Chem — Journal. Institution of Engineers. (India) Part CH. Chemical Engineering Division

J Inst Eng (India) Part GE — Journal. Institution of Engineers (India). Part GE. General Engineering

J Inst Eng (India) Part IDGE — Journal. Institution of Engineers (India). Part IDGE

J Inst Eng India Part MM Min — Journal. Institution of Engineers. (India) Part MM. Mining and Metallurgy Division

J Inst Eng (India) Part MM Min Metall Div — Journal. Institution of Engineers (India). Part MM. Mining andMetallurgy Division

J Inst Eng (India) Pub Health Eng Div — Journal. Institution of Engineers (India). Public Health Engineering Division

J Inst Eng (India) Public Health Eng Div — Journal. Institution of Engineers (India). Public Health Engineering Division

J Inst Eng (Malaysia) — Journal. Institution of Engineers (Malaysia)

J Inst Engrs (Aust) — Journal. Institution of Engineers (Australia)

J Inst Engrs (Australia) — Journal. Institution of Engineers (Australia)

J Inst Engrs (India) — Journal. Institution of Engineers (India)

J Inst Engrs (India) Part CI — Journal. Institution of Engineers (India). Part CI

J Inst Engrs (India) Part ME — Journal. Institution of Engineers (India). Part ME

J Inst Enol Viti Yamanashi Univ — Journal. Institute of Enology and Viticulture. Yamanashi University

J Inst Environ Sci — Journal of the Institute of Environmental Sciences

J Inst Fuel — Journal. Institute of Fuel

J Inst Fuel Suppl — Journal. Institute of Fuel. Supplement

J Inst Gas Eng — Journal. Institution of Gas Engineers

J Inst Geol Vikram Univ — Journal. Institute of Geology. Vikram University

J Inst Heat Vent Eng — Journal. Institution of Heating and Ventilating Engineers

J Inst Highw Eng — Journal. Institute of Highway Engineers

J Inst (India) Electron Telecommun Eng Div — Journal. Institution of Engineers (India). Electronics and Telecommunication Engineering Division

J Institute Socioecon Stud — Journal. Institute for Socioeconomic Studies

J Inst Jamaica — Journal. Institute of Jamaica

J Inst Math and Appl — Journal. Institute of Mathematics and Its Applications

J Inst Math Appl — Journal. Institute of Mathematics and Its Applications

J Inst Math Applic — Journal. Institute of Mathematics and Its Applications

J Inst Math Comput Sci Comput Sci Ser — Journal. Institute of Mathematics and Computer Sciences (Computer Science Series)

J Inst Math Comput Sci Math Ser — Journal. Institute of Mathematics and Computer Sciences (Mathematics Series)

J Inst Math Its Appl — Journal. Institute of Mathematics and Its Applications

J Inst Mech Eng (London) — Journal. Institution of Mechanical Engineers (London)

J Inst Metals — Journal of the Institute of Metals

J Inst Met (Lond) — Journal. Institute of Metals (London)

J Inst Met Suppl — Journal. Institute of Metals. Supplement

J Inst Mine Surv S Afr — Journal. Institute of Mine Surveyors of South Africa

J Inst Min Surv S Afr — Journal. Institute of Mine Surveyors of South Africa

J Inst Munic Eng — Journal. Institution of Municipal Engineers

J Inst Navig — Journal. Institute of Navigation

J Instn Engrs (Aust) — Journal. Institution of Engineers (Australia)

J Instn Gas Engrs — Journal. Institution of Gas Engineers

J Instn Heat Vent Engrs — Journal. Institution of Heating and Ventilating Engineers

J Instn Highw Engrs — Journal. Institution of Highway Engineers

J Instn Loco Engrs — Journal. Institution of Locomotive Engineers

J Instn Munic Engrs — Journal. Institution of Municipal Engineers

J Instn Nucl Engrs — Journal. Institution of Nuclear Engineers

J Instn Rubb Ind — Journal. Institution of the Rubber Industry

J Inst Nucl Eng — Journal. Institution of Nuclear Engineers

J Inst Nucl Mater Manage — Journal. Institute of Nuclear Materials Management

J Instn Wat Engrs — Journal. Institution of Water Engineers

J Instn Wat Engrs Scientists — Journal. Institution of Water Engineers and Scientists

J Instn Water Engnrs Sci — Journal. Institution of Water Engineers and Scientists

J Inst Pet — Journal. Institute of Petroleum

J Inst Pet Abstr — Journal. Institute of Petroleum. Abstracts

J Inst Pet Technol — Journal. Institution of Petroleum Technologists

J Inst Polytech Osaka City Univ Ser C — Journal. Institute of Polytechnics. Osaka City University. Series C. Chemistry

J Inst Polytech Osaka City Univ Ser D — Journal. Institute of Polytechnics. Osaka City University. Series D. Biology

J Inst Polytech Osaka City Univ Ser E — Journal. Institute of Polytechnics. Osaka City University. Series E. Engineering

J Inst Polytech Osaka City Univ Ser G — Journal. Institute of Polytechnics. Osaka City University. Series G. Geoscience

J Inst Polytech Osaka Cy Univ — Journal. Institute of Polytechnics. Osaka City University

J Inst Prod Eng — Journal. Institution of Production Engineers

J Inst Public Health Eng — Journal. Institution of Public Health Engineers

J Inst Renseign Sci Tech Acad Tchecoslovaque Agric — Journal de l'Institut des Renseignements Scientifiques et Techniques de l'Academie Tchecoslovaque de l'Agriculture

J Inst Renseign Tech Acad Tchecoslovaque Agric — Journal. Institut des Renseignements Scientifiques et Techniques.Academie Tchecoslovaque de l'Agriculture

J Instr Psychol — Journal of Instructional Psychology
J Inst Rubber Ind — Journal. Institution of the Rubber Industry
J Instrum Mater — Journal of Instrument Materials
J Instrum Soc Am — Journal. Instrument Society of America
J Instrum Soc India — Journal. Instrument Society of India
J Inst Saf High Pressure Gas Eng — Journal. Institute of Safety of High Pressure Gas Engineering
J Inst Sanit Eng — Journal. Institution of Sanitary Engineers
J Inst Sci Eng Chuo Univ — Journal of the Institute of Science and Engineering. Chuo University
J Inst Sci Tech Inf Czech Acad Agric — Journal. Institute for Scientific and Technical Information.Czechoslovak Academy of Agriculture
J Inst Sci Technol — Journal. Institute of Science Technology
J Inst Sewage Purif — Journal. Institute of Sewage Purification
J Inst Socioecon Stud — Journal. Institute for Socioeconomic Studies
J Inst Telecommun Eng — Journal. Institution of Telecommunication Engineers
J Inst Telecommun Eng (New Delhi) — Journal. Institution of Telecommunication Engineers (New Delhi)
J Inst Telev Eng Jpn — Journal. Institute of Television Engineers of Japan
J Inst Transp — Journal. Institute of Transport
J Inst Transport — Journal. Institute of Transport (Australian Section)
J Inst Water Eng — Journal. Institution of Water Engineers
J Inst Water Engrs & Sci — Journal. Institution of Water Engineers and Scientists
J Inst Water Eng Sci — Journal. Institution of Water Engineers and Scientists
J Inst Water Environ Manage — Journal. Institution of Water and Environmental Management
J Inst Water Environ Manage — Journal of the Institution of Water and Environmental Management
J Inst Wood Sci — Journal. Institute of Wood Science
J Int — Jewish Intelligencer
J Int Acad Prev Med — Journal. International Academy of Preventive Medicine
J Int Aff — Journal of International Affairs
J Int Affairs — Journal of International Affairs
J Int A Mat — Journal. International Association for Mathematical Geology
J Intam St — Journal of Interamerican Studies and World Affairs
J Int Ar Num — Journal International d'Archeologie Numismatique
J Int Arqueol & Etnog — Jornadas Internacionales de Arqueologia y Etnografia
J Int Ass Math Geol — Journal. International Association for Mathematical Geology
J Int Assoc Artif Prolongation Hum Specific Lifespan — Journal. International Association on the Artificial Prolongation of the Human Specific Lifespan
J Int Assoc Buddhist Stud — Journal of the International Association of Buddhist Studies
J Int Assoc Dent Child — Journal. International Association of Dentistry for Children
J Int Assoc Math Geol — Journal. International Association for Mathematical Geology
J Int Biomed Inf Data — Journal of International Biomedical Information and Data
J Int Bus Stud — Journal of International Business Studies
J Int Cancer — Journal International du Cancer
J Int Coll Dent Jpn — Journal. International College of Dentists. Japan Section
J Int Coll Surg — Journal. International College of Surgeons
J Int Comm Jurists — Journal. International Commission of Jurists
JINTD — Journal of Industrial Technology. Myong-Ji University
J Int Desalin Assoc — Journal. International Desalination Association
J Int Econ — Journal of International Economics
J Integral Equations — Journal of Integral Equations
J Integral Equations Appl — Journal of Integral Equations and Applications
J Integral Equations Math Phys — Journal of Integral Equations and Mathematical Physics
J Intellect Disabil Res — Journal of Intellectual Disability Research
J Intell Manuf — Journal of Intelligent Manufacturing
J Intell Mater Syst Struct — Journal of Intelligent Material Systems and Structures
J Intell Rob Syst Theor Appl — Journal of Intelligent and Robotic Systems. Theory and Applications
J Interamer Stud — Journal of Interamerican Studies and World Affairs
J Inter Amer Stud World Affairs — Journal of Inter American Studies and World Affairs
J Interam Stud — Journal of Interamerican Studies and World Affairs
J Interam Stud World Aff — Journal of Interamerican Studies and World Affairs
J Intercult Stud — Journal of Intercultural Studies
J Intercultural Stud — Journal of Intercultural Studies
J Interd Cy — Journal of Interdisciplinary Cycle Research
J Interd H — Journal of Interdisciplinary History
J Interdiscip Cycle Res — Journal of Interdisciplinary Cycle Research
J Interdiscip Hist — Journal of Interdisciplinary History
J Interdiscipl Cycle Res — Journal of Interdisciplinary Cycle Research
J Interdisciplinary Modeling Simulation — Journal of Interdisciplinary Modeling and Simulation
J Interdiscip Model Simul — Journal of Interdisciplinary Modeling and Simulation
J Interdis H — Journal of Interdisciplinary History
J Interdis Hist — Journal of Interdisciplinary History
J Interferon Cytokine Res — Journal of Interferon and Cytokine Research
J Interferon Res — Journal of Interferon Research
J Intergroup Rel — Journal of Intergroup Relations
J Internat Affairs — Journal of International Affairs
J Internat Assoc Mathematical Geol — Journal. International Association for Mathematical Geology
J Internat Assoc Math Geol — Journal. International Association for Mathematical Geology
J Internat Bus Studies — Journal of International Business Studies
J Internat Coll Surgeons — Journal. International College of Surgeons
J Internat Econ — Journal of International Economics
J Internat Law and Econ — Journal of International Law and Economics
J Internat Rel — Journal of International Relations
J Intern Med — Journal of Internal Medicine

J Intern Med Suppl — Journal of Internal Medicine. Supplement
J Intern Rel — Journal of International Relations
J Interv Card Electrophysiol — Journal of Interventional Cardiac Electrophysiology
J Int Fed Clin Chem — Journal of the International Federation of Clinical Chemistry
J Int Fed Clin Chem Lab Med — Journal of the International Federation of Clinical Chemistry and Laboratory Medicine
J Int Fed Gynaecol Obstet — Journal. International Federation of Gynaecology and Obstetrics
J Int Folk Mus Coun — Journal. International Folk Music Council
J Int Hematol — Journal International d'Hematologie
J Int Inst Aerial Surv Earth Sci — Journal. International Institute for Aerial Survey and Earth Sciences
J Int Inst Sugar Beet Res — Journal. International Institute for Sugar Beet Research
J Intl Aff — Journal of International Affairs
J Int L and Ec — Journal of International Law and Economics
J Int Law & Econ — Journal of International Law and Economics
J Int Law E — Journal of International Law and Economics
J Intl L and Econ — Journal of International Law and Economics
J Int'l L & Pol — Journal of International Law and Politics
J Int Med Exp — Journal International de Medecine Experimentale
J Int Med R — Journal of International Medical Research
J Int Med Res — Journal of International Medical Research
J Int Neuropsychol Soc — Journal of the International Neuropsychological Society
J Int Num — Journal International d'Archeologie Numismatique
J Int Num — Journal of International Numismatics
J Int Phonetic Assoc — Journal. International Phonetic Association
J Int Psychol — Journal International de Psychologie
J Int Relations — Journal of International Relations
J Int Res Commun — Journal of International Research Communications
J Int Sci Vigne Vin — Journal International des Sciences de la Vigne et du Vin
J Int Soc Leather Trades Chem — Journal. International Society of Leather Trades' Chemists
J Int Th C — Journal. Interdenominational Theological Center
J Int Vitaminol — Journal International de Vitaminologie
J Int Vitaminol Nutr — Journal International de Vitaminologie et de Nutrition
J Int Vitaminol Nutr Suppl — Journal International de Vitaminologie et de Nutrition. Supplement
J I Nucl En — Journal. Institution of Nuclear Engineers
J Invasive Cardiol — Journal of Invasive Cardiology
J Inver Pat — Journal of Invertebrate Pathology
J Inverse Ill Posed Probl — Journal of Inverse and Ill-Posed Problems
J Invertebr Pathol — Journal of Invertebrate Pathology
J Invert Path — Journal of Invertebrate Pathology
J Inves Der — Journal of Investigative Dermatology
J Invest Allergol Clin Immunol — Journal of Investigational Allergology and Clinical Immunology
J Invest Dermat — Journal of Investigative Dermatology
J Invest Dermatol — Journal of Investigative Dermatology
J Invest Dermatol Symp Proc — Journal of Investigative Dermatology Symposium Proceedings
J Investig Allergol Clin Immunol — Journal of Investigational Allergology and Clinical Immunology
J Investig Med — Journal of Investigative Medicine
J Invest Surg — Journal of Investigative Surgery
J In Vitro Fert Embryo Transfer — Journal of In Vitro Fertilization and Embryo Transfer
JIO — Journal of Industrial Economics (Oxford)
J Ion Exch — Journal of Ion Exchange
JIOS — Journal. Israel Oriental Society
JIOS — Journal of Information and Optimization Sciences
J Iowa Acad Sci — Journal. Iowa Academy of Science
J Iowa Acad Sci JIAS — Journal. Iowa Academy of Science. JIAS
J Iowa Med Soc — Journal. Iowa Medical Society
J Iowa State Med Soc — Journal. Iowa State Medical Society
JIP — Journal of Indian Philosophy
JIPA — Journal. Indian Potato Association
JIPA — Journal. International Phonetic Association
JIP/AMD — JIP/Areal Marketing Database
JIPEA — Journal. Institute of Petroleum
JIPHA — Journal of Insect Physiology
JIPL — Journal of the Institute of Petroleum (London)
JIPs — Journal of Individual Psychology
JIR — Journal of Industrial Relations
J Iraqi Acad — Journal. Iraqi Academy
J Iraqi Chem Soc — Journal. Iraqi Chemical Society
J Iraqi Med Prof — Journal of the Iraqi Medical Professions
JIRC — Journal. Indian Roads Congress
J Ir Coll Physicians Surg — Journal. Irish Colleges of Physicians and Surgeons
J Ir Dent Assoc — Journal. Irish Dental Association
JIREDJ — Journal of Interferon Research
JIRIA — Jibi To Rinsho
J Irish C P — Journal. Irish Colleges of Physicians and Surgeons
J Irish Lit — Journal of Irish Literature
J Irish MA — Journal. Irish Medical Association
J Irish Rlwy Rec Soc — Journal of the Irish Railway Record Society
J Ir Lit — Journal of Irish Literature
J Ir Med Assoc — Journal. Irish Medical Association
J Iron & Steel Eng — Journal of Iron and Steel Engineering
J Iron & Steel Inst — Journal of the Iron and Steel Institute
J Iron Steel Assoc — Journal. Iron and Steel Association
J Iron Steel Inst Jpn — Journal. Iron and Steel Institute of Japan
J Iron Steel Inst (London) — Journal. Iron and Steel Institute (London)
J Iron Steel Inst West Scotl — Journal. Iron and Steel Institute of West Scotland
J Iron Steel Res — Journal of Iron and Steel Research

J Iron St Inst — Journal. Iron and Steel Institute
J Irrig & Drain Div Proc ASCE — Journal. Irrigation and Drainage Division. Proceedings of the American Society of Civil Engineers
J Irrig Drain Div Am Soc Civ Eng — Journal. Irrigation and Drainage Division. Proceedings of the American Societyof Civil Engineers
J Irrig Drain Div ASCE — Journal. Irrigation and Drainage Division. Proceedings of the American Society of Civil Engineers
J Irrig Drain Eng — Journal of Irrigation and Drainage Engineering
JIRS — Jewish Information and Referral Service Directory
JIS — Japan Investment Service
JIS — Jezik in Slovstvo
JIS — Journal. Institute for Socioeconomic Studies
JIS — Journal of Insurance
JIS — Journal of Interamerican Studies and World Affairs
JIS — Journal of Iran Society
JISCD — Journal of Information Science
JISGA — Journal. Institution of Engineers (Australia)
JISHS — Journal. Illinois State Historical Society
J Islam & Comp L — Journal of Islamic and Comparative Law
J Islamic Comp Law — Journal of Islamic and Comparative Law
J'ism Quart — Journalism Quarterly
JISOA — Journal. Indian Society of Oriental Art
J Isot — Journal of Isotopes
J Israel Inst Architects — Journal of the Israel Institute of Architects
J Isr Med Assoc — Journal. Israel Medical Association
JISS — Journal. Indian Sociological Society
JISS — Journal of the Indian Society of Soil Science
JISSD — Journal. Institute for Socioeconomic Studies
J Ital Astron Soc — Journal. Italian Astronomical Society
J Ital Dairy Sci Assoc — Journal. Italian Dairy Science Association
JITE — Journal. Institution of Telecommunication Engineers
JITEBR — Oto-Rhino-Laryngology
JITH — Journal of Indian Textile History
JITHA — Journal of Ichthyology
JITL — Jahresbericht der Israelitisch-Theologischen Lehranstalt
JITUD — Journal of Industrial Technology. Daegu University
JIUEAV — Junta de Investigacoes do Ultramar. Estudos, Ensaios, e Documentos
JIVPAZ — Journal of Invertebrate Pathology
J Iwate Daigaku Nogaku — Journal. Iwate Daigaku Nogaku-Bu
J Iwate Med Assoc — Journal. Iwate Medical Association
JIWE — Journal of Indian Writing in English
J I Wood Sc — Journal. Institute of Wood Science
JIWSA — Journal. Institute of Wood Science
JIZAAA — Journal. Anthropological Society of Nippon
JJ — Jamaica Journal
JJ — Journal of Jazz Studies
J Jam Agric Soc — Journal. Jamaica Agricultural Society
J Jamaica Bauxite Inst — Journal. Jamaica Bauxite Institute
J Japan Assoc Cryst Growth — Journal. Japanese Association of Crystal Growth
J Japanese Soc Comput Statist — Journal of the Japanese Society of Computational Statistics
J Japanese Trade and Industry — Journal of Japanese Trade and Industry
J Japan Hydraul & Pneum Soc — Journal. Japan Hydraulic and Pneumatic Society
J Japan Soc Lubr Engrs — Journal. Japan Society of Lubrication Engineers
J Japan Soc Lubr Enrs Int Edn — Journal. Japan Society of Lubrication Engineers. International Edition
J Japan Soc Precis Engng — Journal. Japan Society of Precision Engineering
J Japan Soc Vet Sc — Journal. Japanese Society of Veterinary Science
J Japan Statist Soc — Journal. Japan Statistical Society
J Japan Wood Res Soc — Journal. Japan Wood Research Society
J Jap Ass Mineral Petrol Econ Geol — Journal. Japanese Association of Mineralogists, Petrologists, and Economic Geologists
J Jap Assoc Autom Control Eng — Journal. Japan Association of Automatic Control Engineers
J Jap Assoc Infect Dis — Journal. Japanese Association for Infectious Diseases
J Jap Assoc Philos Sci — Journal. Japan Association for Philosophy of Science
J Jap Biochem Soc — Journal. Japanese Biochemical Society
J Jap Bot — Journal of Japanese Botany
J Jap Chem — Journal of Japanese Chemistry
J Jap Forest Soc — Journal. Japanese Forestry Society/Nippon Ringaku Kaishi
J Jap For Soc — Journal. Japanese Forestry Society
J Jap Hort Soc — Journal. Japanese Horticultural Society/Journal. Societe d'Horticulture du Japon / Zeitschrift der Japanischen Gartenbau-Gesellschaft / Nippon Engeikai Zasshi
J Jap Inst Light Metals — Journal. Japan Institute of Light Metals
J Jap Inst Met — Journal. Japan Institute of Light Metals
J Jap S Lub — Journal. Japan Society of Lubrication Engineers
J Jap Soc Air Pol — Journal. Japan Society of Air Pollution
J Jap Soc Civ Eng — Journal. Japan Society of Civil Engineers
J Jap Soc Fd Nutr — Journal. Japanese Society of Food and Nutrition
J Jap Soc Food Nutr — Journal. Japanese Society of Food and Nutrition
J Jap Soc Grassland Sci — Journal. Japanese Society of Grassland Science
J Jap Soc Grassld Sci — Journal. Japanese Society of Grassland Science
J Jap Soc Mech Eng — Journal. Japanese Society of Mechanical Engineers
J Jap Soc Powder Met — Journal. Japan Society of Powder and Powder Metallurgy
J Jap Soc Precis Eng — Journal. Japan Society of Precision Engineering
J Jap Soc Technol Plast — Journal. Japan Society for Technology of Plasticity
J Jap Stud — Journal of Japanese Studies
J Jap Turfgrass Res Assoc — Journal. Japan Turfgrass Research Association
J Jap Vet Med Ass — Journal. Japan Veterinary Medical Association
J Jap Wood Res Soc — Journal. Japan Wood Research Society
J Ja Stud — Journal of Japanese Studies

JJATS J Jpn Assoc Thorac Surg — JJATS. Journal. Japanese Association for Thoracic Surgery
J Jazz Stud — Journal of Jazz Studies
J Jazz Studies — Journal of Jazz Studies
JJCL — Jadavpur Journal of Comparative Literature
JJCRA — Japanese Journal of Clinical Radiology
JJCS — Journal of Jewish Communal Service
JJE — Japanese Journal of Ethnology
JJE — Jaszberenyi Jaszmuseum Evkoenyve
JJeCoS — Journal of Jewish Communal Service
J Jew A — Journal of Jewish Art
J Jew Commun Serv — Journal of Jewish Communal Service
J Jewish Communal Service — Journal of Jewish Communal Service
J Jewish St — Journal of Jewish Studies
JJewLorePh — Journal of Jewish Lore and Philosophy
JJewS — Journal of Jewish Studies
J Jew Stud — Journal of Jewish Studies
JJFED — JFE. Journal du Four Electrique et des Industries Electrochimiques
JJGL — Jahrbuch fuer Juedische Geschichte und Literatur
JJI — Jazz Journal International
J Jianghan Pet Inst — Journal of Jianghan Petroleum Institute
J Jiangsu Inst Petrochem Technol — Journal of Jiangsu Institute of Petrochemical Technology
J Jinan Univ Nat Sci Med Ed — Journal. Jinan University. Natural Science and Medicine Edition
JJIND — JNCI. Journal of the National Cancer Institute
J Jinsen Med Sci — Journal of Jinsen Medical Sciences
J Jishou Univ Nat Sci Ed — Jishou University Journal. Natural Science Edition
J Jishou Univ Nat Sci Ed — Journal of Jishou University. Natural Science Edition
J Jiwaji Univ — Journal. Jiwaji University
J Jiwaji Univ Sci Technol Med — Journal. Jiwaji University. Science, Technology, and Medicine
J JJ Group Hosp Grant Med Coll — Journal. JJ Group of Hospitals and Grant Medical College
JJK — Josai Jinbun Kenkyu
JJLG — Jahrbuch. Juedisch-Literarische Gesellschaft
JJLP — Journal of Jewish Lore and Philosophy
JJOGA — Journal. Japanese Obstetrical and Gynecological Society
J Johannesburg Hist Found — Journal. Johannesburg Historical Foundation
J Joint Panel Nucl Mar Propul — Journal. Joint Panel on Nuclear Marine Propulsion
JJOMD — JOM. Journal of Occupational Medicine
JJOPA7 — Japanese Journal of Ophthalmology
JJoS — Jewish Journal of Sociology
JJP — Journal des Juges de Paix
JJP — Journal of Juristic Papyrology
JJPAA — Japanese Journal of Pharmacology
JJPAAZ — Japanese Journal of Pharmacology
JJPES — Journal. Jewish Palestine Exploration Society
JJPG — Jahrbuch. Jean-Paul-Gesellschaft
JJPHA — Japanese Journal of Physiology
JJPHAM — Japanese Journal of Physiology
JJPHDP — Japanese Journal of Phycology
J Jpn Acad Surg Metab Nutr — Journal. Japan Academy of Surgical Metabolism and Nutrition
J Jpn Accident Med Assoc — Journal. Japan Accident Medical Association
J Jpn Air Clean Assoc — Journal. Japan Air Cleaning Association
J Jpn Anodizing Assoc — Journal. Japanese Anodizing Association
J Jpn Aromat Ind Assoc — Journal. Japan Aromatic Industry Association
J Jpn Assoc Automat Control Eng — Journal. Japan Association of Automatic Control Engineers
J Jpn Assoc Dent Sci — Journal. Japanese Association for Dental Science
J Jpn Assoc Infect Dis — Journal. Japanese Association for Infectious Diseases
J Jpn Assoc Mineral Pet Econ Geol — Journal. Japanese Association of Mineralogists, Petrologists, and Economic Geologists
J Jpn Assoc Mineral Petrol Econ Geol — Journal. Japanese Association of Mineralogists, Petrologists, andEconomic Geologists
J Jpn Assoc Periodontol — Journal. Japanese Association of Periodontology
J Jpn Assoc Pet Technol — Journal. Japanese Association of Petroleum Technologists
J Jpn Assoc Phys Med Balneol Climatol — Journal. Japanese Association of Physical Medicine, Balneology, and Climatology
J Jpn Assoc Thorac Surg — Journal. Japanese Association for Thoracic Surgery
J Jpn Atherosclerosis Soc — Journal. Japan Atherosclerosis Society
J Jpn Balneo Climatol Assoc — Journal. Japanese Balneo-Climatological Association
J Jpn Biochem Soc — Journal. Japanese Biochemical Society
J Jpn Boiler Assoc — Journal. Japan Boiler Association
J Jpn Bot — Journal of Japanese Botany
J Jpn Broncho-Esophagol Soc — Journal. Japan Broncho-Esophagological Society
J Jpn Ceram Assoc — Journal. Japanese Ceramic Association
J Jpn Ceram Soc — Journal. Japanese Ceramic Society
J Jpn Chem — Journal of Japanese Chemistry
J Jpn Chem Suppl — Journal of Japanese Chemistry. Supplement
J Jpn Coll Angiol — Journal. Japanese College of Angiology
J Jpn Contact Lens Soc — Journal. Japan Contact Lens Society
J Jpn Copper Brass Res Assoc — Journal. Japan Copper and Brass Research Association
J Jpn Cosmet Sci Soc — Journal. Japanese Cosmetic Science Society
J Jpn Crystallogr Soc — Journal. Japanese Crystallographical Society
J Jpn Dent Anesth Soc — Journal. Japanese Dental Anesthesia Society
J Jpn Dent Assoc — Journal. Japan Dental Association
J Jpn Dent Soc Anesthesiol — Journal. Japan Dental Society of Anesthesiology
J Jpn Dermatol Assoc — Journal. Japanese Dermatological Association

J Jpn Diabetes Soc — Journal. Japan Diabetes Society
J Jpn Diabetic Soc — Journal. Japan Diabetic Society
J Jpn Electr Assoc — Journal. Japan Electric Association
J Jpn Epilepsy Soc — Journal. Japan Epilepsy Society
J Jpn Explos Soc — Journal of the Japan Explosives Society
J Jpn For Soc — Journal. Japanese Forestry Society
J Jpn Foundry Eng Soc — Journal of Japanese Foundry Engineering Society
J Jpn Foundry Eng Soc — Journal of Japan Foundry Engineering Society
J Jpn Foundrymens Soc — Journal. Japan Foundrymen's Society
J Jpn Gas Assoc — Journal. Japan Gas Association
J Jpn Gen Foundry Cent — Journal. Japan General Foundry Center
J Jpn Geotherm Energy Assoc — Journal. Japan Geothermal Energy Association
J Jpn Health Phys Soc — Journal. Japan Health Physics Society
J Jpn Hosp Assoc — Journal. Japan Hospital Association
J Jpn Inst Energ — Journal. Japan Institute of Energy
J Jpn Inst Landscape Archit — Journal. Japanese Institute of Landscape Architects
J Jpn Inst Light Met — Journal. Japan Institute of Light Metals
J Jpn Inst Met — Journal. Japan Institute of Metals
J Jpn Inst Met (Sendai) — Journal. Japan Institute of Metals (Sendai)
J Jpn Inst Navig — Journal. Japan Institute of Navigation
J Jpn Med Assoc — Journal. Japan Medical Association
J Jpn Med Coll — Journal. Japan Medical College
J Jpn Med Soc Biol Interface — Journal. Japanese Medical Society for Biological Interface
J Jpn Obstet Gynecol — Journal. Japanese Obstetrics and Gynecology
J Jpn Obstet Gynecol Soc (Engl Ed) — Journal. Japanese Obstetrical and Gynecological Society (English Edition)
J Jpn Obstet Gynecol Soc (Jpn Ed) — Journal. Japanese Obstetrical and Gynecological Society (Japanese Edition)
J Jpn Oil Chem Soc — Journal. Japan Oil Chemists Society
J Jpn Orthop Assoc — Journal. Japanese Orthopaedic Association
J Jpn Pancreas Soc — Journal. Japan Pancreas Society
J Jpn Pap Pulp Assoc — Journal. Japan Paper and Pulp Association
J Jpn Perfum Flavour Assoc — Journal. Japan Perfumery Flavouring Association
J Jpn Pet Inst — Journal. Japan Petroleum Institute
J Jpn Pharm Assoc — Journal. Japan Pharmaceutical Association
J Jpn Plat Soc — Journal. Japan Plating Society
J Jpn Psychosom Soc — Journal. Japanese Psychosomatic Society
J Jpn Res Assoc Text End-Uses — Journal. Japan Research Association for Textile End-Uses
J Jpn Sewage Works Assoc — Journal. Japan Sewage Works Association
J Jpn Soc Aeronaut and Space Sci — Journal. Japan Society for Aeronautical and Space Sciences
J Jpn Soc Air Pollut — Journal. Japan Society of Air Pollution
J Jpn Soc Atmos Environ — Journal of Japan Society for Atmospheric Environment
J Jpn Soc Biomater — Journal. Japanese Society for Biomaterials
J Jpn Soc Blood Transfus — Journal. Japan Society of Blood Transfusion
J Jpn Soc Cancer Ther — Journal. Japan Society for Cancer Therapy
J Jpn Soc Clin Microbiol — Journal of the Japanese Society for Clinical Microbiology
J Jpn Soc Clin Nutr — Journal. Japanese Society of Clinical Nutrition
J Jpn Soc Colo-Proctol — Journal. Japan Society of Colo-Proctology
J Jpn Soc Colour Mater — Journal. Japan Society of Colour Material
J Jpn Soc Compos Mater — Journal. Japan Society of Composite Materials
J Jpn Soc Cutaneous Health — Journal. Japanese Society for Cutaneous Health
J Jpn Soc Dent Appar Mater — Journal. Japan Society for Dental Apparatus and Materials
J Jpn Soc Dent Mater Devices — Journal. Japanese Society for Dental Materials and Devices
J Jpn Soc Dent Prod — Journal of Japanese Society for Dental Products
J Jpn Soc Fluid Mech — Journal. Japan Society of Fluid Mechanics
J Jpn Soc Food Nutr — Journal. Japanese Society of Food and Nutrition
J Jpn Soc Food Sci Technol — Journal. Japan Society for Food Science and Technology
J Jpn Soc Grassl Sci — Journal. Japanese Society of Grassland Science
J Jpn Soc Heat Treat — Journal. Japan Society for Heat-Treatment
J Jpn Soc Herb Crops Grassl Farming — Journal. Japanese Society of Herbage Crops and Grassland Farming
J Jpn Soc Hist Chem — Journal of the Japanese Society for the History of Chemistry
J Jpn Soc Hortic Sci — Journal. Japanese Society for Horticultural Science
J Jpn Soc Hosp Pharm — Journal. Japanese Society of Hospital Pharmacists
J Jpn Soc Hypothermia — Journal. Japanese Society for Hypothermia
J Jpn Soc Infrared Sci Technol — Journal. Japan Society of Infrared Science and Technology
J Jpn Soc Intern Med — Journal. Japanese Society of Internal Medicine
J Jpn Soc Irrig Drain Reclam Eng — Journal. Japanese Society of Irrigation, Drainage, and ReclamationEngineering
J Jpn Soc Lubr Eng — Journal. Japan Society of Lubrication Engineers
J Jpn Soc Magnesium Res — Journal. Japanese Society for Magnesium Research
J Jpn Soc Mech Eng — Journal. Japan Society of Mechanical Engineers
J Jpn Soc Nutr Food Sci — Journal. Japanese Society of Nutrition and Food Science
J Jpn Soc Polym Process — Journal of the Japan Society of Polymer Processing
J Jpn Soc Poult Dis — Journal. Japanese Society on Poultry Diseases
J Jpn Soc Powder Metall — Journal. Japan Society of Powder and Powder Metallurgy
J Jpn Soc Powder Powder Metall — Journal. Japan Society of Powder and Powder Metallurgy
J Jpn Soc Precis Eng — Journal. Japan Society of Precision Engineering
J Jpn Soc Reticuloendothel Syst — Journal. Japan Society of the Reticuloendothelial System
J Jpn Soc Saf Eng — Journal. Japan Society for Safety Engineering

J Jpn Soc Simulation Technol — Journal. Japan Society for Simulation Technology
J Jpn Soc Starch Sci — Journal. Japanese Society of Starch Science
J Jpn Soc Strength Fract Mater — Journal. Japanese Society for Strength and Fracture of Materials
J Jpn Soc Study Obes — Journal of Japan Society for the Study of Obesity
J Jpn Soc Technol Plast — Journal. Japan Society for Technology of Plasticity
J Jpn Soc Tribol — Journal. Japanese Society of Tribologists
J Jpn Soc Waste Manage Experts — Journal. Japan Society of Waste Management Experts
J Jpn Soc Water Environ — Journal of Japan Society on Water Environment
J Jpn Soc X-Ray Tech — Journal. Japanese Society of X-Ray Technicians
J Jpn Soy Sauce Res Inst — Journal. Japan Soy Sauce Research Institute
J Jpn Stomatol Soc — Journal. Japan Stomatological Society
J Jpn Stud — Journal of Japanese Studies
J Jpn Surg Soc — Journal. Japanese Surgical Society
J Jpn Tar Ind Assoc — Journal. Japan Tar Industry Association
J Jpn Tech Assoc Pulp Pap Ind — Journal. Japanese Technical Association of the Pulp and Paper Industry
J Jpn Therm Spraying Soc — Journal. Japan Thermal Spraying Society
J Jpn Turfgrass Res Assoc — Journal. Japan Turfgrass Research Association
J Jpn Vet Med Assoc — Journal. Japan Veterinary Medical Association
J Jpn Water Works Assoc — Journal. Japan Water Works Association
J Jpn Weld Soc — Journal. Japan Welding Society
J Jpn Womens Univ Fac Sci — Journal of Japan Women's University. Faculty of Science
J Jpn Wood Res Soc — Journal. Japan Wood Research Society
JJQ — James Joyce Quarterly
J J Qtr — James Joyce Quarterly
JJR — James Joyce Review
J Jr Inst Eng (London) — Journal. Junior Institution of Engineers (London)
JJS — Jewish Journal of Sociology
JJS — Journal of Japanese Studies
JJS — Journal of Jazz Studies
JJS — Journal of Jewish Studies
JJSAAG — Japanese Journal of Studies on Alcohol
JJSGA — Japanese Journal of Surgery
JJSGAY — Japanese Journal of Surgery
JJSL — Jewish Journal of Sociology (London)
J JSLE (Jpn Soc Lubr Eng) Int Ed — Journal. JSLE (Japan Society of Lubrication Engineers). International Edition
JJSO — Jewish Journal of Sociology
JJ Soc — Jewish Journal of Sociology
JJSt — Journal of Jewish Studies
JJTCAR — Japanese Journal of Tuberculosis and Chest Diseases
J Jt Panel Nucl Mar Propul — Journal. Joint Panel on Nuclear Marine Propulsion
J Jundi Shapur Med Sch — Journal. Jundi Shapur Medical School
J Jur — Journal of Jurisprudence
J Jur P — Journal of Juristic Papyrology
J Jur Pap — Journal of Juristic Papyrology
J Jur Papyrol — Journal of Juristic Papyrology
J Juvenile Res — Journal of Juvenile Research
J Juv L — Journal of Juvenile Law
J Juv Res — Journal of Juvenile Research
J Juzen Med Soc — Journal. Juzen Medical Society
JJV — Jahrbuch fuer Juedische Volkskunde
JJVK — Jahrbuch fuer Juedische Volkskunde
JJVRA — Japanese Journal of Veterinary Research
JJVRAE — Japanese Journal of Veterinary Research
JJWUA — Journal. Jiwaji University
JJZOAP — Japanese Journal of Zoology
JK — Junge Kirche
JKAF — Jahrbuch fuer Kleinasiatische Forschung. Internationale Orientalistische Zeitschrift
J Kagawa Nutr Coll — Journal. Kagawa Nutrition College
JKAHS — Journal. Kerry Archaeological and Historical Society
JkA Jernkontorets Ann — JkA. Jernkontorets Annaler
J Kajian Kejuruteraan — Journal Kajian Kejuruteraan
J Kanagawa Odontol Soc — Journal. Kanagawa Odontological Society
J Kanagawa Prefect J Coll Nutr — Journal. Kanagawa Prefectural Junior College of Nutrition
J Kanazawa Med Univ — Journal. Kanazawa Medical University
J Kan BA — Journal. Kansas Bar Association
J Kan Med Soc — Journal. Kansas Medical Society
J Kansai Med Sch — Journal. Kansai Medical School
J Kansai Med Univ — Journal. Kansai Medical University
J Kansas Geol Surv — Journal. Kansas Geological Survey
J Kansas Med Soc — Journal. Kansas Medical Society
J Kans Dent Assoc — Journal. Kansas Dental Association
J Kans Entomol Soc — Journal. Kansas Entomological Society
J Kans Ent Soc — Journal. Kansas Entomological Society
J Kans Med Soc — Journal. Kansas Medical Society
J Kans State Dent Assoc — Journal. Kansas State Dental Association
J Kanto-Tosan Agr Exp Sta — Journal. Kanto-Tosan Agricultural Experiment Station
J Kanto Tosan Agric Exp Sta — Journal. Kanto Tosan Agricultural Experiment Station/Kanto Tosan Nogyo ShikenjoKenkyu Hokoku
J Karadeniz Univ Fac Arts Sci Ser Math Phys — Journal Karadeniz University. Faculty of Arts and Sciences. Series of Mathematics-Physics
J Karnatak U Hum — Journal. Karnatak University. Humanities
J Karnatak Univ — Journal. Karnatak University
J Karnatak Univ Sci — Journal. Karnatak University. Science
J Karnatak U Soc Sci — Journal. Karnatak University. Social Sciences
J Karyopathol Espec Tumor Tumorvirus — Journal of Karyopathology; Especially Tumor and Tumorvirus

J Karyopathol Tumor Tumorvirus — Journal of Karyopathology; Especially Tumor and Tumorvirus
JKAUA — Journal. Karnatak University
JKAW — Jahresbericht ueber die Fortschritte der Klassischen Altertumswissenschaft
JKAWA — Jaarboek. Koninklijke Academie van Wetenschappen (Amsterdam)
JKBW — Jahrbuch der Staatlichen Kunstsammlungen in Baden-Wuerttemberg
JKD — Jahrbuch der Staatlichen Kunstsammlungen (Dresden)
JKE — Journal of Post Keynesian Economics
J Keio Med Soc — Journal. Keio Medical Society
J Kementerian Pelajaran Min Ed Malay — Journal. Ministry of Education. Malaysia
J Kerala Acad Biol — Journal. Kerala Academy of Biology
J Kerry Archaeol Hist Soc — Journal. Kerry Archaeological and Historical Society
JKF — Anadolu Arastirmalari. Jahrbuch fuer Kleinasiatische Forschung
JKF — Jahrbuch fuer Kleinasiatische Forschung
JKFSD — Journal. Korean Forestry Society
JKG — Jahrbuch. Kleist-Gesellschaft
JKG — Jidische Kultur Gezelschaft
JKG — Juedische Kulturgemeinschaft
JKGKA — Joho Kagaku Gijutsu Kenkyu Shukai Happyo Ronbunshu
JKGS — Jahrbuecher fuer Kultur und Geschichte der Slaven
JKGV — Jahrbuch. Koelnischer Geschichtsverein
JKGVH — Jahrbuch der Kirchengeschichtlichen Vereinigung in Hessen und Nassau
JKH — Jahresschrift des Kreismuseums Haldensleben
J Khediv Agric Soc — Journal. Khedivial Agricultural Society
JKHHA — Journal. Korea Institute of Electronics Engineers
JKIEA — Journal. Korean Institute of Electrical Engineers
J King Saud Univ Agric Sci — Journal of King Saud University. Agricultural Sciences
J King Saud Univ Eng Sci — Journal. King Saud University. Engineering Science
J King Saud Univ Sci — Journal. King Saud University. Science
J Kirin Univ Nat Sci — Journal. Kirin University. Natural Science
JKKNA — Jaarboek van Kankeronderzoek en Kankerbestrijding in Nederland
JKMAD — Journal. Korea Military Academy
JKMG — Jahrbuch. Karl-May-Gesellschaft
JKMSA — Journal. Kansas Medical Society
JKMSD — Journal. Korean Mathematical Society
JKNA — Jaarboek. Koninklijke Nederlandsche Academie
JKNCD — Journal. Kongju National Teacher's College
J Knot Theory Ramifications — Journal of Knot Theory and its Ramifications
J Kongju Natl Teach Coll — Journal. Kongju National Teacher's College
J Korea Electr Assoc — Journal. Korea Electric Association
J Korea For Energy — Journal of Korea Forestry Energy
J Korea Inf Sci Soc — Journal. Korea Information Science Society
J Korea Inst Electron Eng — Journal. Korea Institute of Electronics Engineers
J Korea Merch Mar Coll Nat Sci Ser — Journal. Korea Merchant Marine College. Natural Sciences Series
J Korea Mil Acad — Journal. Korea Military Academy
J Korean Acad Maxillofac Radiol — Journal. Korean Academy of Maxillofacial Radiology
J Korean Acad Periodontol — Journal. Korean Academy of Periodontology
J Korean Agric Chem Soc — Journal. Korean Agricultural Chemical Society
J Korean Assoc Radiat Prot — Journal. Korean Association for Radiation Protection
J Korean Astron Soc — Journal. Korean Astronomical Society
J Korean Cancer Res Assoc — Journal. Korean Cancer Research Association
J Korean Ceram Soc — Journal. Korean Ceramic Society
J Korean Chem Soc — Journal. Korean Chemical Society
J Korean Dent Assoc — Journal. Korean Dental Association
J Korean Fiber Soc — Journal. Korean Fiber Society
J Korean For Soc — Journal. Korean Forestry Society
J Korean Ind Eng Chem — Journal. Korean Industrial and Engineering Chemistry
J Korean Infect Dis — Journal. Korean Infectious Diseases
J Korean Inst Chem Eng — Journal. Korean Institute of Chemical Engineers
J Korean Inst Electr Eng — Journal. Korean Institute of Electrical Engineers
J Korean Inst Electron Eng — Journal. Korean Institute of Electronics Engineers
J Korean Inst Met — Journal. Korean Institute of Metals
J Korean Inst Min — Journal. Korean Institute of Mining
J Korean Inst Min Eng — Journal. Korean Institute of Mining Engineers
J Korean Inst Miner Mining Eng — Journal. Korean Institute of Mineral and Mining Engineers
J Korean Inst Min Geol — Journal. Korean Institute of Mining Geology
J Korean Inst Rubber Ind — Journal. Korean Institute of Rubber Industry
J Korean Inst Surf Eng — Journal. Korean Institute of Surface Engineering
J Korean Math Soc — Journal. Korean Mathematical Society
J Korean Med Assoc — Journal. Korean Medical Association
J Korean Med Sci — Journal of Korean Medical Science
J Korean Meteorol Soc — Journal. Korean Meteorological Society
J Korean Nucl Soc — Journal. Korean Nuclear Society
J Korean Ophthalmol Soc — Journal. Korean Ophthalmological Society
J Korean Orient Med Soc — Journal. Korean Oriental Medical Society
J Korean Pharm Sci — Journal of Korean Pharmaceutical Sciences
J Korean Phys Soc — Journal. Korean Physical Society
J Korean Prev Med Soc — Journal. Korean Preventive Medicine Society
J Korean Radiol Soc — Journal. Korean Radiological Society
J Korean Res Inst Better Living — Journal. Korean Research Institute for Better Living
J Korean Res Soc Dent Hypn — Journal. Korean Research Society for Dental Hypnosis
J Korean Res Soc Radiol Technol — Journal. Korean Research Society of Radiological Technology
J Korean Soc Agric Eng — Journal. Korean Society of Agricultural Engineers
J Korean Soc Agric Mach — Journal. Korean Society of Agricultural Machinery
J Korean Soc Civ Eng — Journal. Korean Society of Civil Engineers
J Korean Soc Crop Sci — Journal. Korean Society of Crop Science

J Korean Soc Food Nutr — Journal. Korean Society of Food and Nutrition
J Korean Soc Hortic Sci — Journal. Korean Society for Horticultural Science
J Korean Soc Hort Sci — Journal. Korean Society for Horticultural Science
J Korean Soc Mech Eng — Journal. Korean Society of Mechanical Engineers
J Korean Soc Microbiol — Journal. Korean Society for Microbiology
J Korean Soc Nutr Food — Journal. Korean Society of Nutrition and Food
J Korean Soc Soil Sci Fert — Journal. Korean Society of Soil Science and Fertilizer
J Korean Soc Text Eng Chem — Journal. Korean Society of Textile Engineers and Chemists
J Korean Statist Soc — Journal. Korean Statistical Society
J Korean Surg Soc — Journal. Korean Surgical Society
JKORS — Journal. Korean Operations Research Society
J Koyasan Univ — Journal. Koyasan University
JKS — Jahrbuch. Kunsthistorische Sammlungen
JKSW — Jahrbuch. Kunsthistorische Sammlungen (Wien)
JKSWB — Jahrbuch der Kunsthistorischen Sammlung in Wien. Beilage
JKU — Journal. Karnatak University
J Kukem — Journal of Kukem
J Kumamoto Med Soc — Journal. Kumamoto Medical Society
J Kumamoto Women's Univ — Journal. Kumamoto Women's University
J Kumasi Univ Sci Technol — Journal. Kumasi University of Science and Technology
JKUR — Jammu and Kashmir University Review
J Kurume Med Assoc — Journal. Kurume Medical Association
J Kuwait Med Assoc — Journal. Kuwait Medical Association
JKVA — Jaarboek. Koninklijke Vlaamse Academie voor Wetenschappen. Letteren en Schone Kunsten van Belgie
JKW — Jahrbuch fuer Kunstwissenschaft
J KY Med Assoc — Journal. Kentucky Medical Association
JKYND — Journal. Materials Science Research Institute. Dongguk University
J Kyorin Med Soc — Journal. Kyorin Medical Society
J Kyoto Med Assoc — Journal. Kyoto Medical Association
J Kyoto Prefect Med Univ — Journal. Kyoto Prefectural Medical University
J Kyoto Prefect Univ Med — Journal. Kyoto Prefectural University of Medicine
J Ky State Med Assoc — Journal. Kentucky State Medical Association
J Kyungpook Eng — Journal. Kyungpook Engineering
J Kyungpook Eng Kyungpook Natl Univ — Journal. Kyungpook Engineering. Kyungpook National University
J Kyushu Coal Min Tech Assoc — Journal. Kyushu Coal Mining Technicians Association
J Kyushu Dent Soc — Journal. Kyushu Dental Society
J Kyushu Hematol Soc — Journal. Kyushu Hematological Society
JL — Jornal de Letras
JL — Journal. American Liszt Society
JL — Journal of Linguistics
JL — Juedisches Lexikon
JL — July
JLA — Jornal de Letras e Artes
JLAB — Jamaica Library Association Bulletin
J Lab Clin Med — Journal of Laboratory and Clinical Medicine
J Label Com — Journal of Labelled Compounds [*Later, Journal of Labelled Compounds and Radiopharmaceuticals*]
J Label Compound Radiopharm — Journal of Labelled Compounds and Radiopharmaceuticals
J Labelled Compd — Journal of Labelled Compounds [*Later, Journal of Labelled Compounds and Radiopharmaceuticals*]
J Labelled Compd Radiopharm — Journal of Labelled Compounds and Radiopharmaceuticals
J Labor Research — Journal of Labor Research
J Labour Hyg Iron Steel Ind — Journal of Labour Hygiene in Iron and Steel Industry
JLACBF — Justus Liebigs Annalen der Chemie
J La Cl Med — Journal of Laboratory and Clinical Medicine
J LA Dent Assoc — Journal. Louisiana Dental Association
JLAEA — Journal. Language Association of Eastern Africa
Jl Aesthetics — Journal of Aesthetics and Art Criticism
JLAL — Journal of Latin American Lore
J LA Med Soc — Journal. Louisiana State Medical Society
J-Lancet — Journal-Lancet
J Lanchow Univ Nat Sci — Journal. Lanchow University. Natural Sciences
J Land & Pub Util Econ — Journal of Land and Public Utility Economics
J Land & Pub Utility Econ — Journal of Land and Public Utility Economics
J Land & PU Econ — Journal of Land and Public Utility Economics
J L and Com — Journal of Law and Commerce
JL & Com Soc — Journal. Law and Commerce Society
J L and Ec — Journal of Law and Economics
J L & Econ — Journal of Law and Economics
JL & Econ Dev — Journal of Law and Economic Development
J L & Econ Develop — Journal of Law and Economic Development
J L and Ed — Journal of Law and Education
J L & Educ — Journal of Law and Education
JL & Information Science — Journal of Law and Information Science
J Landw Gartenbau — Journal fuer Landwirtschaft und Gartenbau
J Landwirtsch — Journal fuer Landwirtschaft
J Landwirtsch Wiss — Journal fuer Landwirtschaftliche Wissenschaft
J Lang Teach — Journal for Language Teaching
J Language Ass East Afr — Journal. Language Association of Eastern Africa
J Lanzhou Railway College — Journal of Lanzhou Railway College
J Lanzhou Railway Inst — Journal of Lanzhou Railway Institute
J Lanzhou Univ Nat Sci — Journal. Lanzhou University. Natural Sciences
J Laparoendosc Surg — Journal of Laparoendoscopic Surgery
Jl Appl Photogr Engin — Journal of Applied Photographic Engineering
J Lar Otol — Journal of Laryngology and Otology
J Laryng — Journal of Laryngology and Otology

J Laryngol Otol — Journal of Laryngology and Otology
J Laryngol Otol Suppl — Journal of Laryngology and Otology. Supplement
J Laryng Ot — Journal of Laryngology and Otology
JLAS — Journal. Linguistic Association of the Southwest
JLAS — Journal of Latin American Studies
J Laser Appl — Journal of Laser Applications
J LA State Med Soc — Journal. Louisiana State Medical Society
J Lat Amer Lore — Journal of Latin American Lore
J Lat Amer Stud — Journal of Latin American Studies
J Lat Am L — Journal of Latin American Lore
J Lat Am St — Journal of Latin American Studies
J Lat Am Stud — Journal of Latin American Studies
J Latin Amer Lore — Journal of Latin American Lore
J Latin Amer Stud — Journal of Latin American Studies
J Law & Econ — Journal of Law and Economics
J Law & Econ Dev — Journal of Law and Economic Development
J Law & Educ — Journal of Law and Education
J Law Econ — Journal of Law and Economics
J Law Reform — Journal of Law Reform
J Law Soc — Journal of Law and Society
J Law Soc Sc — Journal. Law Society of Scotland
J Law Soc Scot — Journal. Law Society of Scotland
J Law Soc'y Scotland — Law Society of Scotland. Journal
J Layman — Jewish Layman
JLB — Journal of Labor Economics
JLB — Juedisches Litteratur-Blatt
Jl Belge Radiol — Journal Belge de Radiologie
JLBI — Juedisches Literaturblatt
J Lbr Res — Journal of Labor Research
JLB Smith Inst Ichthyol Spec Publ — J. L. B. Smith Institute of Ichthyology. Special Publication
Jl Bus Fin — Journal of Business Finance and Accounting
Jl Bus Strat — Journal of Business Strategy
Jl Commun — Journal of Communication
Jl Con Mkt — Journal of Consumer Marketing
Jl Consmr R — Journal of Consumer Research
Jl Cont B — Journal of Contemporary Business
JLCPA — Journal of Counseling Psychology
JLCR — Jordan Lectures in Comparative Religion
JLCRD — Journal of Labelled Compounds and Radiopharmaceuticals
JLCSA4 — Journal. American Leather Chemists' Association. Supplement
JLD — Journal of Learning Disabilities
J Ldb — Jydsk Landbrug
JLDIA — Journal of Learning Disabilities
JLDS — Journal. Lancashire Dialect Society
JLE — Journal of Law and Economics
J Lear Disabil — Journal of Learning Disabilities
J Learn Di — Journal of Learning Disabilities
J Learn Dis — Journal of Learning Disabilities
J Learn Disab — Journal of Learning Disabilities
J Learn Disabil — Journal of Learning Disabilities
Jl E Asiat Stud — Journal of East Asiatic Studies
J Leather Ind Res Inst S Afr — Journal. Leather Industries Research Institute of South Africa
J Leather Res — Journal of Leather Research
J Leeds Univ Text Assoc — Journal. Leeds University Textile Association
J Leeds Univ Text Stud Assoc — Journal. Leeds University Textile Students' Association
J Leeds Univ Union Chem Soc — Journal. Leeds University Union Chemical Society
J Legal Ed — Journal of Legal Education
J Legal Educ — Journal of Legal Education
J Legal Med — Journal of Legal Medicine
J Legal Plur — Journal of Legal Pluralism and Unofficial Law
J Legal Prof — Journal of the Legal Profession
J Legal Stud — Journal of Legal Studies
J Leg Ed — Journal of Legal Education
J Leg Educ — Journal of Legal Education
J Leg Hist — Journal of Legal History
J Legis — Journal of Legislation
J Legis Assembly Prov Canada — Journals of the Legislative Assembly of the Province of Canada
J Legislation — Journal of Legislation
J Leg Med — Journal of Legal Medicine
J Leg Plur — Journal of Legal Pluralism and Unofficial Law
J Leg Stud — Journal of Legal Studies
J Leis Res — Journal of Leisure Research
J Leisur — Journal of Leisurability
J Leisurability — Journal of Leisurability
J Leisure — Journal of Leisure Research
J Leisure Res — Journal of Leisure Research
JLEMA — Journal of Engineering Mathematics
J Lepidopt Soc — Journal. Lepidopterists Society
J Lepid Soc — Journal. Lepidopterists' Society
JLER — Journal of Leisure Research
J Less-C Met — Journal of the Less-Common Metals
J Less Common Met — Journal of the Less-Common Metals
J Leukoc Biol — Journal of Leukocyte Biology
J Leukoc Biol Suppl — Journal of Leukocyte Biology. Supplement
J Leukocyte Biol — Journal of Leukocyte Biology
JLFAA — Journal de la France Agricole
JLG — Jahrbuch. Juedisch-Literarische Gesellschaft
J Lg — Journal of Linguistics
JLH — Jahrbuch fuer Liturgik und Hymnologie

JLH — Journal of Library History [Later, Journal of Library History, Philosophy, andComparative Librarianship]
JLH — Journal of Library History, Philosophy, and Comparative Librarianship
JLHPA — Jan Liao Hsueh Pao
JLHYAD — Journal of Hydrology
JLi — Jewish Life
J Liaoning Norm Univ Nat Sci — Journal of Liaoning Normal University (Natural Science)
J Lib Admin — Journal of Library Administration
J Lib and Info Science — Journal of Library and Information Science
J Lib Arts Nat Sci Sapporo Med Coll — Journal of Liberal Arts and Natural Sciences. Sapporo Medical College
J Lib Arts Sci Kitasato Univ — Journal of Liberal Arts and Sciences. Kitasato University
J Lib Arts Sci Sapporo Med Coll — Journal of Liberal Arts and Sciences. Sapporo Medical College
J Lib Automation — Journal of Library Automation
J Liber Stud — Journal of Libertarian Studies
J Libertar Stud — Journal of Libertarian Studies
J Lib Hist — Journal of Library History [Later, Journal of Library History, Philosophy, andComparative Librarianship]
J Lib Hist — Journal of Library History, Philosophy, and Comparative Librarianship
J Lib Inf Sci — Journal of Library and Information Science
J Libnship — Journal of Librarianship
J Libr — Journal of Librarianship
J Librarianship — Journal of Librarianship
J Libr Aut — Journal of Library Automation
J Libr Auto — Journal of Library Automation
J Libr Autom — Journal of Library Automation
J Libr Automn — Journal of Library Automation
J Libr Hist — Journal of Library History [Later, Journal of Library History, Philosophy, andComparative Librarianship]
J Libr Hist — Journal of Library History, Philosophy, and Comparative Librarianship
J Libr Inf Sci — Journal of Library and Information Science
JLIEA — Journal of Industrial Engineering
J Lie Theory — Journal of Lie Theory
J Life — Jewish Life
J Life Sci — Journal of Life Sciences
J Life Sci R Dublin Soc — Journal of Life Sciences. Royal Dublin Society
J Light Met Weld Constr — Journal of Light Metal Welding and Construction
J Light Visual Environ — Journal of Light and Visual Environment
J Lightwave Technol — Journal of Lightwave Technology
J Limnol Soc South Afr — Journal. Limnological Society of South Africa
J Ling — Journal of Linguistics
J Ling Anthrop — Journal of Linguistic Anthropology
J Linguist — Journal of Linguistics
J Linguistics — Journal of Linguistics
J Linn Soc Lond Bot — Journal. Linnean Society of London. Botany
J Linn Soc Lond Zool — Journal. Linnean Society of London. Zoology
J Lipid M — Journal of Lipid Mediators
J Lipid Mediat Cell Signal — Journal of Lipid Mediators and Cell Signalling
J Lipid Mediators — Journal of Lipid Mediators
J Lipid Mediators Cell Signalling — Journal of Lipid Mediators and Cell Signalling
J Lipid Res — Journal of Lipid Research
J Lipid Research — Journal of Lipid Research
J Liposome Res — Journal of Liposome Research
J Liq Chromatogr — Journal of Liquid Chromatography
J Liq Chromatogr Relat Technol — Journal of Liquid Chromatography and Related Technologies
J Liquid Chromatogr — Journal of Liquid Chromatography
JLIS — Journal of Law and Information Science
J Lit Kunst Gesellliges Leben — Journal fuer Literatur, Kunst, und Gesellliges Leben
J Lit Sem — Journal of Literary Semantics
JLitt — Journal Litteraire
J Litt Theatern — Journal foer Litteraturen og Theatern
J Li W — Jahrbuch fuer Liturgiewissenschaft
JLKHS — Jahrbuecher fuer die Landeskunde der Herzogtuemer Schleswig, Holstein und Lauenburg
JLKNO — Jahrbuch fuer Landeskunde von Niederoesterreich
J L Med — Journal of Legal Medicine
JLMPA — Journal of Microwave Power
JLMS — Journal. London Mathematical Society
Jl Musicology — Journal of Musicology
JLN — Jack London Newsletter
JLN — Jahrbuch fuer Landeskunde von Niederoesterreich
J Lndw — Journal fuer Landwirthschaft
JLN Oe — Jahrbuch fuer Landeskunde von Nieder-Oesterreich
Jl NY Ent Soc — Journal. New York Entomological Society
Jl NZ Diet Ass — Journal. New Zealand Dietetic Association
JLO — Jurisprudence de Louage d'Ouvrage
J Local Adm Ov — Journal of Local Administration Overseas
Jl of Research — Journal of Research in Music Education
J Logic Comput — Journal of Logic and Computation
J Logic Lang Inform — Journal of Logic, Language, and Information
J Logic Program — Journal of Logic Programming
J Logic Programming — Journal of Logic Programming
J Lond Math — Journal. London Mathematical Society
J London Math Soc — Journal. London Mathematical Society
J London Math Soc (2) — Journal. London Mathematical Society. Second Series
J London School Trop Med — Journal. London School of Tropical Medicine
J London Soc — Journal of the London Society
J Lond Soc — Journal. London Society
J Long Term Care — Journal of Long-Term Care Administration
J Long Term Care Adm — Journal of Long-Term Care Administration

J Long Term Care Admin — Journal of Long-Term Care Administration
J Long Term Eff Med Implants — Journal of Long-Term Effects of Medical Implants
JLOTA — Journal of Laryngology and Otology
J Louis St Med Soc — Journal. Louisiana State Medical Society
J Low Freq Noise Vib — Journal of Low Frequency Noise and Vibration
J Low Temp Phys — Journal of Low Temperature Physics
JLR — Jewish Language Review
JLR — Journal of Labor Research
JLR — Journal of Linguistic Research
Jl R Agric Soc — Journal. Royal Agricultural Society of England
Jl R Anthrop Inst — Journal. Royal Anthropological Institute of Great Britain and Ireland
Jl R Aust Hist Soc — Royal Australian Historical Society. Journal
Jl R Hist Soc Qd — Royal Historical Society of Queensland. Journal
Jl R Hort Soc — Journal. Royal Horticulture Society
Jl R Microsc Soc — Journal. Royal Microscopical Society
Jl R Soc Arts — Journal. Royal Society of Arts
Jl R Soc NZ — Journal. Royal Society of New Zealand
JLRU — Journal. Library of Rutgers University
JLS — Journal. Law Society of Scotland
JLS — Journal of Literary Semantics
Jl S Afr Bot — Journal of South African Botany
Jl S-East Agric Coll (Wye) — Journal. South-Eastern Agricultural College (Wye)
JLSMA — Journal. Louisiana State Medical Society
Jl Small Bus — American Journal of Small Business
Jl Soc Mot Pict Telev Engin — Journal. Society of Motion Picture and Television Engineers
Jl Soc Photogr Sci — Journal. Society of Photographic Science and Technology of Japan
Jl Soc Photogr Sci Technol Japan — Journal. Society of Photographic Science and Technology of Japan
JL Soc Scotland — Journal. Law Society of Scotland
JL Soc'y — Journal. Law Society of Scotland
J L Socy Scot — Journal. Law Society of Scotland
J L Studies — Journal of Legal Studies
JLT — Journal du Textile
J L Temp Ph — Journal of Low Temperature Physics
Jl Test Eval — Journal of Testing and Evaluation
JLu — J'ai Lu
J Lubric Technol Trans ASME — Journal of Lubrication Technology. Transactions of the American Society of Mechanical Engineers
J Lubr Tech — Journal of Lubrication Technology
J Lubr Technol — Journal of Lubrication Technology
J Lubr Technol Trans ASME — Journal of Lubrication Technology. Transactions of the American Society of Mechanical Engineers
J Lub Tech — Journal of Lubrication Technology. Transactions of the American Society of Mechanical Engineers
J Lumin — Journal of Luminescence
J Luminesc — Journal of Luminescence
J Luoyang Univ — Journal. Luoyang University
J Lute — Journal. Lute Society of America
J Lute Soc Amer — Journal. Lute Society of America
J LUU Chem Soc — Journal. Leeds University Union Chemical Society
J Luxus & Mod — Journal des Luxus und der Moderne
JLW — Jahrbuch fuer Liturgiewissenschaft
J Lymphol — Journal of Lymphology
JLZ — Jahresberichte des Literarischen Zentralblattes
JM — Jesuit Missions
JM — Jewish Monthly
JM — Journal of Marketing
JM — Journal of Music Theory
JMA — Journal of Macroeconomics
J Macomb Dent Soc — Journal. Macomb Dental Society
J Macromol Chem — Journal of Macromolecular Chemistry
J Macromol Sci A — Journal of Macromolecular Science. Part A. Chemistry
J Macromol Sci B — Journal of Macromolecular Science. Part B. Physics
J Macromol Sci C — Journal of Macromolecular Science. Part C. Reviews in Macromolecular Chemistry
J Macromol Sci Chem — Journal of Macromolecular Science. Chemistry
J Macromol Sci Chem A — Journal of Macromolecular Science. Part A. Chemistry
J Macromol Sci Chem Suppl — Journal of Macromolecular Science. Chemistry. Supplement
J Macromol Sci Part A — Journal of Macromolecular Science. Part A. Chemistry
J Macromol Sci Part A Chem — Journal of Macromolecular Science. Part A. Chemistry
J Macromol Sci Part B — Journal of Macromolecular Science. Part B. Physics
J Macromol Sci Part C — Journal of Macromolecular Science. Part C. Reviews in MacromolecularChemistry
J Macromol Sci Part D — Journal of Macromolecular Science. Part D. Reviews in PolymerTechnology
J Macromol Sci Phys — Journal of Macromolecular Science. Part B. Physics
J Macromol Sci Pure Appl Chem — Journal of Macromolecular Science. Pure and Applied Chemistry
J Macromol Sci Rev Macromol Chem — Journal of Macromolecular Science. Part C. Reviews in Macromolecular Chemistry
J Macromol Sci Rev Macromol Chem Phys — Journal of Macromolecular Science. Reviews in Macromolecular Chemistry and Physics
J Macromol Sci Rev Polym Technol — Journal of Macromolecular Science. Part D. Reviews in Polymer Technology
J Macr S Ch — Journal of Macromolecular Science. Part A. Chemistry
J Macr S Ph — Journal of Macromolecular Science. Part B. Physics
J Macr S Rm — Journal of Macromolecular Science. Part C. Reviews in Macromolecular Chemistry
J MACT — Journal. Maulana Azad College of Technology

J Madhya Pradesh Itihasa Parishad — Journal of the Madhya Pradesh Itihasa Parishad
J Madras Agric Stud Union — Journal. Madras Agricultural Students' Union
J Madras Inst Technol — Journal. Madras Institute of Technology
J Madras Univ — Journal. Madras University
J Madras Univ B — Journal. Madras University. Section B. Contributions in Mathematics, Physical and Biological Science
J Madras Univ Sect B — Journal. Madras University. Section B. Contributions in Mathematics, Physical and Biological Science
J Madurai Kamaraj Univ — Journal. Madurai Kamaraj University
J Madurai Univ — Madurai University. Journal
JMAG — Journal of Molecular and Applied Genetics
J Magic Hist — Journal of Magic History
J Magn and Magn Mater — Journal of Magnetism and Magnetic Materials
J Magnetohydrodyn Plasma Res — Journal of Magnetohydrodynamics and Plasma Research
J Magn Magn Mater — Journal of Magnetism and Magnetic Materials
J Magn Res — Journal of Magnetic Resonance
J Magn Reson — Journal of Magnetic Resonance
J Magn Resonance — Journal of Magnetic Resonance
J Magn Reson B — Journal of Magnetic Resonance. Series B
J Magn Reson Imaging — Journal of Magnetic Resonance Imaging
J Magn Reson Ser A — Journal of Magnetic Resonance. Series A
J Magn Reson Ser B — Journal of Magnetic Resonance. Series B
J Magn Soc Jpn — Journal. Magnetics Society of Japan
J Maharaja Sayajirao U Baroda — Journal of the Maharaja Sayajirao University (Baroda)
J Maharaja Sayajirao Univ Baroda — Journal. Maharaja Sayajirao University of Baroda
J Maharashtra Agric Univ — Journal. Maharashtra Agricultural Universities
J Mahar Sayayira Univ Baroda — Journal. Maharaja Sayayira University of Baroda
J Maine Dent Assoc — Journal. Maine Dental Association
J Maine Med Assoc — Journal. Maine Medical Association
J Makromol Chem — Journal fuer Makromolekulare Chemie
J Mal — Journal of Malacology
J Malacol Soc Aust — Journal. Malacological Society of Australia
J Malac Soc Aust — Journal. Malacological Society of Australia
J Mal & Comp L — Journal of Malaysian and Comparative Law
J Malar Inst India — Journal. Malaria Institute of India
J Malaya Branch Br Med Assoc — Journal. Malayan Branch. British Medical Association
J Malay Branch Roy Asiatic Soc — Journal. Malaysian Branch. Royal Asiatic Society
J Malay Brch R Asiat Soc — Journal of the Malaysian Branch Royal Asiatic Society
J Malay Br Roy Asia — Journal. Malaysian Branch. Royal Asiatic Society
J Malays Branch R Asiat Soc — Journal. Malaysian Branch. Royal Asiatic Society
J Mal Br Brit Med Ass — Journal. Malayan Branch. British Medical Association
J Mal Br Roy Asiat Soc — Journal. Malaysian Branch. Royal Asiatic Society
J Mal Vasc — Journal des Maladies Vasculaires
J Mal Vet Med Ass — Journal. Malayan Veterinary Medical Association
JMAM — Journal. Music Academy (Madras)
JMAM — Journal of Mammalogy
J Mammal — Journal of Mammalogy
J Mammal Soc Jpn — Journal. Mammalogical Society of Japan
J Mammary Gland Biol Neoplasia — Journal of Mammary Gland Biology and Neoplasia
J Mammillaria Soc — Journal. Mammillaria Society
J Manage — Journal of Management
J Manage Eng — Journal of Management in Engineering
J Manage Stud — Journal of Management Studies
J Manag Stu — Journal of Management Studies
J Manch — Journal. Manchester University Egyptian and Oriental Scoiety
J Manchester Geogr Soc — Journal. Manchester Geographical Society
J Manch Geogr Soc — Journal. Manchester Geographical Society
J Manch Geol Ass — Journal. Manchester Geological Association
J Manip Physiol Ther — Journal of Manipulative and Physiological Therapeutics
J Manipulative Physiol Ther — Journal of Manipulative and Physiological Therapeutics
J Manuf Oper Management — Journal of Manufacturing and Operations Management
J Manx Mus — Journal. Manx Museum
J Manx Mus — Journal of the Manx Museum
JMAPD — Journal de Mecanique Appliquee
J Mar Biol Ass India — Journal. Marine Biological Association of India
J Mar Biol Assoc (India) — Journal. Marine Biological Association (India)
J Mar Biol Assoc (UK) — Journal. Marine Biological Association (United Kingdom)
J Mar Biol Ass (UK) — Journal. Marine Biological Association (United Kingdom)
J Mar Eng Soc Jpn — Journal. Marine Engineering Society in Japan
J Mar Environ Eng — Journal of Marine Environmental Engineering
J Mar Fam — Journal of Marriage and the Family
J Marine Bi — Journal. Marine Biological Association
J Marine Biol Ass (United Kingdom) — Journal. Marine Biological Association (United Kingdom)
J Marine Re — Journal of Marine Research
J Marine Res — Journal of Marine Research
J Marital Fam Ther — Journal of Marital and Family Therapy
J Maritime L — Journal of Maritime Law and Commerce
J Maritime Law and Commer — Journal of Maritime Law and Commerce
J Marit Law — Journal of Maritime Law and Commerce
J Marit Saf Acad Part 2 — Journal. Maritime Safety Academy. Part 2
J Mar J Prac & Proc — John Marshall Journal of Practice and Procedure
J Mark — Journal of Marketing
J Market — Journal of Marketing
J Marketing — Journal of Marketing

J Marketing Res — Journal of Marketing Research
J Market (L) — Journal. Market Research Society (London)
J Market R — Journal of Marketing Research
J Market Research Society Vic — Journal. Market Research Society of Victoria
J Market Res Soc — Journal. Market Research Society
J Mark Prof — Journal of Marketing for Professions
J Mark Res — Journal of Marketing Research
J Marktforsch — Journal fuer Marktforschung
J Mar L and Com — Journal of Maritime Law and Commerce
J Mar Law & Com — Journal of Maritime Law and Commerce
J Mar LR — John Marshall Law Review
J Mar L Rev — John Marshall Law Review
J Marmara Univ Dent Fac — Journal of Marmara University Dental Faculty
J Mar March — Journal de la Marine Marchande
J Marr & Fam — Journal of Marriage and the Family
J Mar Res — Journal of Marine Research
J Marriage — Journal of Marriage and the Family
J Marriage & Fam — Journal of Marriage and the Family
J Marriage Family — Journal of Marriage and the Family
J Mar Sci — Journal of Marine Science
J Marshall J — John Marshall Journal of Practice and Procedure
J Mar Technol Soc — Journal. Marine Technology Society
JMAS — Journal of Modern African Studies
J Mass Dent Soc — Journal. Massachusetts Dental Society
J Mass Spectrom — Journal of Mass Spectrometry and Ion Physics
J Mass Spectrom Ion Phys — Journal of Mass Spectrometry and Ion Physics
J Mass Sp Ion P — Journal of Mass Spectrometry and Ion Physics
J Mat Chem — Journal of Materials Chemistry
J Mater — Journal of Materials
J Mater Chem — Journal of Materials Chemistry
J Mater Civ Eng — Journal of Materials in Civil Engineering
J Mater Energy Syst — Journal of Materials for Energy Systems
J Mater Eng — Journal of Materials Engineering
J Mater Eng Perform — Journal of Materials Engineering and Performance
J Mater Enregistrement Signaux — Journal pour les Materiaux d'Enregistrement des Signaux
J Materials Sci — Journal of Materials Science
J Matern Fetal Med — Journal of Maternal-Fetal Medicine
J Mater Nucl — Journal des Materiaux Nucleaires
J Mater Process Manuf Sci — Journal of Materials Processing and Manufacturing Science
J Mater Process Technol — Journal of Materials Processing Technology
J Mater Res — Journal of Materials Research
J Mater Sci — Journal of Materials Science
J Mater Sci Lett — Journal of Materials Science. Letters
J Mater Sci Mater Electron — Journal of Materials Science. Materials in Electronics
J Mater Sci Mater Med — Journal of Materials Science. Materials in Medicine
J Mater Sci Res Inst Dongguk Univ — Journal. Materials Science Research Institute. Dongguk University
J Mater Sci Soc Jpn — Journal. Materials Science Society of Japan
J Mater Sci Technol — Journal of Materials Science and Technology
J Mater Sci Technol Sofia — Journal of Materials Science and Technology (Sofia)
J Mater Shaping Technol — Journal of Materials Shaping Technology
J Mater Technol — Journal of Materials Technology
J Mater Test Res Assoc — Journal. Material Testing Research Association
J Math Anal — Journal of Mathematical Analysis and Applications
J Math Anal and Appl — Journal of Mathematical Analysis and Applications
J Math Anal Appl — Journal of Mathematical Analysis and Applications
J Math & Phys — Journal of Mathematics and Physics
J Math and Phys Sci — Journal of Mathematical and Physical Sciences
J Math Biol — Journal of Mathematical Biology
J Math Chem — Journal of Mathematical Chemistry
J Math Econom — Journal of Mathematical Economics
J Mathematical and Physical Sci — Journal of Mathematical and Physical Sciences
J Mathematical Phys — Journal of Mathematical Physics
J Mathematical Psychology — Journal of Mathematical Psychology
J Mathematical Sociology — Journal of Mathematical Sociology
J Math Imaging Vision — Journal of Mathematical Imaging and Vision
J Math (Jabalpur) — Journal of Mathematics (Jabalpur)
J Math Jap — Journal. Mathematical Society of Japan
J Math Kyoto Univ — Journal of Mathematics. Kyoto University
J Math Mech — Journal of Mathematics and Mechanics
J Math Modelling Teach — Journal of Mathematical Modelling for Teachers
J Math NS — Journal of Mathematics. New Series
J Math P A — Journal de Mathematiques Pures et Appliquees
J Math Phys — Journal of Mathematical Physics
J Math Phys — Journal of Mathematics and Physics
J Math Phys Appl — Journal de Mathematiques et de Physique Appliquees
J Math Phys (Cambridge Mass) — Journal of Mathematics and Physics (Cambridge, Massachusetts)
J Math Phys (NY) — Journal of Mathematical Physics (New York)
J Math Psyc — Journal of Mathematical Psychology
J Math Psych — Journal of Mathematical Psychology
J Math Psychol — Journal of Mathematical Psychology
J Math Pures Appl — Journal de Mathematiques Pures et Appliquees
J Math Pures Appl 9 — Journal de Mathematiques Pures et Appliquees. Neuvieme Serie
J Math Res Exposition — Journal of Mathematical Research and Exposition
J Math Sci — Journal of Mathematical Sciences
J Math Sci — Journal of Mathematics and Sciences
J Math Sci Univ Tokyo — Journal of Mathematical Sciences. University of Tokyo
J Math Soci — Journal of Mathematical Sociology
J Math Sociol — Journal of Mathematical Sociology

J Math Soc Japan — Journal. Mathematical Society of Japan
J Math Soc Jpn — Journal. Mathematical Society of Japan
J Math Study — Journal of Mathematical Study
J Math Systems Estim Control — Journal of Mathematical Systems, Estimation, and Control
J Math Tokushima Univ — Journal of Mathematics. Tokushima University
J Mat Sci — Journal of Materials Science
J Mat Sci Lett — Journal of Materials Science. Letters
J Matsumoto Dent Coll Soc — Journal. Matsumoto Dental College Society
J Maulana Azad College Tech — Journal. Maulana Azad College of Technology
J Maxillofac Orthop — Journal of Maxillofacial Orthopedics
J Maxillofac Surg — Journal of Maxillofacial Surgery
J Mayan Ling — Journal of Mayan Linguistics
JMB — Japan Missionary Bulletin
JMB — Journal of Molecular Biology
JMB — Journal of Money, Credit, and Banking
JMBAS — Journal. Malayan Branch. Royal Asiatic Society
JMBCD — Journal de Microscopie et de Biologie Cellulaire
JMBM — Jewish Monuments in Bohemia and Moravia
JMBRAS — Journal. Malayan Branch. Royal Asiatic Society
JMBS — Journal. Maha-Bodhi Society
JMBXA — Journal de Medecine de Bordeaux
JMC — Japan Medical Congress
JMC — Journal Musical Canadien
JMC — Journal of Medicinal Chemistry
JMCAD — Journal of Molecular Catalysis
JMCB — Journal of Money, Credit, and Banking
JMCI — Journal of Molecular and Cellular Immunology
JMCI J Mol Cell Immunol — JMCI. Journal of Molecular and Cellular Immunology
J Mcrgr — Journal de Micrographie
J Mcr Sc — Quarterly Journal of Microscopical Science
JMD — Journal of Management Development
J MD Acad Sci — Journal. Maryland Academy of Sciences
JMDR — Journal of Missile Defense Research
J MD State Dent Assoc — Journal. Maryland State Dental Association
JME — Journal des Missions Evangeliques
JME — Journal of Mathematical Economics
JME — Journal of Monetary Economics
J Mec — Journal de Mecanique
J Mecanique — Journal de Mecanique
J Mecan Phys Atm — Journal de Mecanique et Physique de l'Atmosphere
J Mec Appl — Journal de Mecanique Appliquee
J Mech — Journal of Mechanisms
J Mechanochem & Cell Motility — Journal of Mechanochemistry and Cell Motility
J Mechanochem Cell Motil — Journal of Mechanochemistry and Cell Motility
J Mechanochem Cell Motility — Journal of Mechanochemistry and Cell Motility
J Mech Behav Mater — Journal. Mechanical Behavior of Materials
J Mech Des — Journal of Mechanical Design
J Mech Des Trans ASME — Journal of Mechanical Design. Transactions of the American Society of Mechanical Engineers
J Mech E — Journal of Mechanical Engineering Science
J Mech Eng — Journal of Mechanical Engineering Science
J Mech Eng Assoc Witwatersrand — Journal. Mechanical Engineers Association of Witwatersrand
J Mech Eng Lab — Journal. Mechanical Engineering Laboratory
J Mech Eng Lab (Tokyo) — Journal. Mechanical Engineering Laboratory (Tokyo)
J Mech Engng Lab — Journal. Mechanical Engineering Laboratory
J Mech Engng Sci — Journal of Mechanical Engineering Science
J Mech Eng Sci — Journal of Mechanical Engineering Science
J Mech Lab Jap — Journal. Mechanical Laboratory of Japan
J Mech Lab Jpn — Journal. Mechanical Laboratory of Japan
J Mech Lab (Tokyo) — Journal. Mechanical Laboratory (Tokyo)
J Mech Phys — Journal of the Mechanics and Physics of Solids
J Mech Phys Solids — Journal of the Mechanics and Physics of Solids
J Mech Transm Autom In Des Trans ASME — Journal of Mechanisms, Transmission, and Automation in Design. Transactions. American Society of Mechanical Engineers
J Mech Working Technol — Journal of Mechanical Working Technology
J Mech Work Technol — Journal of Mechanical Working Technology
J Mec Phys Atmos — Journal de Mecanique et Physique de l'Atmosphere
J Mec Theor Appl — Journal de Mecanique Theorique et Appliquee
J Mec Theor et Appl — Journal de Mecanique Theorique et Appliquee
J Med — Jornal do Medico
JMEd — Journal of Medical Education
J Med — Journal of Medicine
JMEDA — Journal of Medical Education
J Med A Alabama — Journal. Medical Association of the State of Alabama
J Med & Ren Stud — Journal of Medieval and Renaissance Studies
J Med Aromat Plant Sci — Journal of Medicinal and Aromatic Plant Sciences
J Med Ass Eire — Journal. Medical Association of Eire
J Med Ass Form — Journal. Medical Association of Formosa
J Med Assn GA — Journal. Medical Association of Georgia
J Med Assoc Croat — Journal. Medical Association of Croatia
J Med Assoc Eire — Journal. Medical Association of Eire
J Med Assoc GA — Journal. Medical Association of Georgia
J Med Assoc Isr — Journal. Medical Association of Israel
J Med Assoc Iwate Prefect Hosp — Journal. Medical Association of Iwate Prefectural Hospital
J Med Assoc Jam — Journal. Medical Association of Jamaica
J Med Assoc S Afr — Journal. Medical Association of South Africa
J Med Assoc State Ala — Journal. Medical Association of the State of Alabama
J Med Assoc State Alabama — Journal. Medical Association of the State of Alabama
J Med Assoc Taiwan — Journal. Medical Association of Taiwan
J Med Assoc Thai — Journal. Medical Association of Thailand

J Med Assoc Thail — Journal. Medical Association of Thailand
J Med Assoc Thailand — Journal. Medical Association of Thailand
J Med Ass Ok — Journal. Medical Association of Okayama
J Med Ass South Africa — Journal. Medical Association of South Africa
J Med Ass Thail — Journal. Medical Association of Thailand
J Med (Basel) — Journal of Medicine. Experimental and Clinical (Basel)
J Med Besancon — Journal de Medecine de Besancon
J Med Biochem — Journal of Medicine and Biochemistry
J Med Bord — Journal de Medecine de Bordeaux
J Med Bordeaux — Journal de Medecine de Bordeaux
J Med Bordeaux Sud Ouest — Journal de Medecine de Bordeaux et du Sud-Ouest
J Med Bord Sud-Ouest — Journal de Medecine de Bordeaux et du Sud-Ouest
J Med Brux — Journal Medical de Bruxelles
J Med Caen — Journal de Medecine de Caen
J Med Chem — Journal of Medicinal Chemistry
J Med Chir — Journal de Medecine et de Chirurgie
J Med Chir — Journal Medico-Chirurgical
J Med Chir Pharm Militaires — Journal de Medecine, de Chirurgie, et de Pharmacie Militaires
J Med Chir Pharm (Paris) — Journal de Medecine, Chirurgie, Pharmacie (Paris)
J Med Chir Phm — Journal de Medecine, Chirurgie, Pharmacie
J Med Chir Prat — Journal de Medecine et de Chirurgie Pratiques
J Med (Cincinnati) — Journal of Medicine (Cincinnati)
J Med Coll Keijo — Journal. Medical College in Keijo
J Med Coll PLA — Journal. Medical Colleges of PLA
J Med Dent Assoc Botswana — Journal. Medical and Dental Association of Botswana
J Med Ed — Journal of Medical Education
J Med Educ — Journal of Medical Education
J Med El — Journal of Medical Electronics
J Med Electron — Journal of Medical Electronics
J Med Eng and Technol — Journal of Medical Engineering and Technology
J Med Eng Technol — Journal of Medical Engineering and Technology
J Med Ent — Journal of Medical Entomology
J Med Ento — Journal of Medical Entomology
J Med Entomol — Journal of Medical Entomology
J Med Entomol Suppl — Journal of Medical Entomology. Supplement
J Med Enzymol — Journal of Medical Enzymology
J Med et Chir Prat — Journal de Medecine et de Chirurgie Pratiques
J Med Ethic — Journal of Medical Ethics
J Med Ethics — Journal of Medical Ethics
J Med Exp Clin — Journal of Medicine. Experimental and Clinical
J Med Food — Journal of Medicinal Food
J Med Fr — Journal Medical Francais
J Med Franc — Journal Medical Francais
J Med Genet — Journal of Medical Genetics
J Med Gironde — Journal Medical de la Gironde
J Med Hait — Journal Medical Haitien
J Med Hist — Journal of Medical History
J Med Humanit Bioethics — Journal of Medical Humanities and Bioethics
J Med Hum Bioeth — Journal of Medical Humanities and Bioethics
J Medicaid Manage — Journal for Medicaid Management
J Medicaid Mgt — Journal for Medicaid Management
J Medieval Hist — Journal of Medieval History
J Medieval Renaiss Stud — Journal of Medieval and Renaissance Studies
J Mediev Hi — Journal of Medieval History
J Mediev R — Journal of Medieval and Renaissance Studies
J Mediev Renaissance Stud — Journal of Medieval and Renaissance Studies
J Med Internet Res — Journal of Medical Internet Research
J Med Int Med Abstr Rev — Journal of Medicine and International Medical Abstracts and Reviews
J Medit Anthropol & Archaeol — Journal of Mediterranean Anthropology and Archaeology
J Mediterr Anthropol Archaeol — Journal of Mediterranean Anthropology and Archaeology
J Medit Stud — Journal of Mediterranean Studies
J Med Kosmet — Journal fuer Medizinische Kosmetik
J Med Lab Technol — Journal of Medical Laboratory Technology
J Med Leg Droit Med — Journal de Medecine Legale. Droit Medical
J Med Leg Psych Anthr — Journal de Medecine Legale Psychiatrique et d'Anthropologie Criminelle
J Med Liban — Journal Medical Libanais
J Med Lyon — Journal de Medecine de Lyon
J Med Micro — Journal of Medical Microbiology
J Med Microbiol — Journal of Medical Microbiology
J Med Mie Prefect Univ — Journal of Medicine. Mie Prefectural University
J Med Montp — Journal de Medecine de Montpellier
J Med Montpellier — Journal de Medecine de Montpellier
J Med Nucl Biophys — Journal de Medecine Nucleaire et Biophysique
J Med Pa — Journal de Medecine de Paris
J Med Pernambuco — Jornal de Medicina de Pernambuco
J Med Pharm Chem — Journal of Medicinal and Pharmaceutical Chemistry
J Med Pharm Sci — Journal of Medicine and Pharmaceutical Science
J Med Pharm Soc Wakan Yaku — Journal. Medical and Pharmaceutical Society for Wakan-Yaku
J Med Phil — Journal of Medicine and Philosophy
J Med Philos — Journal of Medicine and Philosophy
J Med Plant Res — Journal of Medicinal Plant Research. Planta Medica
J Med Poitiers — Journal de Medecine de Poitiers
J Med (Porto) — Jornal do Medico (Porto)
J Med Prim — Journal of Medical Primatology
J Med Primatol — Journal of Medical Primatology
J Med Prof Ass — Journal. Medical Professions Association
J Med Res — Journal of Medical Research
J Med Sch Jundi Shapur Univ — Journal. Medical School. Jundi Shapur University

J Med Sci — Journal of Medical Sciences
J Med Sci Banaras Hindu Univ — Journal of Medical Sciences. Banaras Hindu University
J Med Sci Taipei — Journal of Medical Sciences (Taipei)
J Med Screen — Journal of Medical Screening
J Med Soc New Jers — Journal. Medical Society of New Jersey
J Med Soc New Jersey — Journal. Medical Society of New Jersey
J Med Soc NJ — Journal. Medical Society of New Jersey
J Med Soc Toho Univ — Journal. Medical Society of Toho University
J Med Strasb — Journal de Medecine de Strasbourg
J Med Strasbourg — Journal de Medecine de Strasbourg
J Med Syst — Journal of Medical Systems
J Med Technol — Journal of Medical Technology
J Med Technol (Tokyo) — Journal of Medical Technology (Tokyo)
J M Educ — Journal of Medical Education
J Med (Ukr) — Journal Medicale (Ukraine)
J Med Vet et Comp — Journal de Medecine Veterinaire et Comparee
J Med Vet et Zootech (Lyon) — Journal de Medecine Veterinaire et de Zootechnie (Lyon)
J Med Vet (Lyon) — Journal de Medecine Veterinaire (Lyon)
J Med Vet Mil — Journal de Medecine Veterinaire Militaire
J Med Vet Mycol — Journal of Medical and Veterinary Mycology
J Med Virol — Journal of Medical Virology
J Med (Westbury NY) — Journal of Medicine (Westbury, New York)
J Med Wom Fed — Journal. Medical Women's Federation
JMeH — Journal of Medieval History
J Meikai Univ Sch Dent — Journal. Meikai University School of Dentistry
J Membrane Biol — Journal of Membrane Biology
J Membrane Sci — Journal of Membrane Science
J Membr Bio — Journal of Membrane Biology
J Membr Biol — Journal of Membrane Biology
J Membr Sci — Journal of Membrane Science
J Mens Psychiatr Neurol — Journal Mensuel de Psychiatrie et de Neurologie
J Mental Def Research — Journal of Mental Deficiency Research
J Ment Def — Journal of Mental Deficiency Research
J Ment Defic Res — Journal of Mental Deficiency Research
J Ment Health — Journal of Mental Health
J Ment Health Adm — Journal. Mental Health Administration
J Ment Sc — Journal of Mental Science
J Ment Sci — Journal of Mental Science
J Ment Subnorm — Journal of Mental Subnormality
J Menuiserie — Journal de la Menuiserie
JMEOS — Journal. Manchester Egyptian and Oriental Society
J Mercer Dent Soc — Journal. Mercer Dental Society
J Merioneth Hist Rec Soc — Journal. Merioneth Historical Record Society
JMES — Journal. Middle East Society
J Met — Journal of Metals
J Met — Journal of Meteorology
JMETA — Journal. Manitoba Elementary Teachers' Association
J Metab Res — Journal of Metabolic Research
J Metal Finish Soc Korea — Journal. Metal Finishing Society of Korea
J Metall — Journal of Metallurgy
J Metall Club R Coll Sci Technol — Journal. Metallurgical Club. Royal College of Science and Technology
J Metall Club Univ Strathclyde — Journal. Metallurgical Club. University of Strathclyde
J Metall Soc Jpn — Journal. Metallurgical Society of Japan
J Metals — Journal of Metals
J Metamorph Geol — Journal of Metamorphic Geology
J Meteorol — Journal of Meteorology
J Meteorol Res — Journal of Meteorological Research
J Meteorol Soc Jpn — Journal. Meteorological Society of Japan
J Met Finish — Journal of Metal Finishing
J Met Finish Soc Jap — Journal. Metal Finishing Society of Japan
J Met Finish Soc Jpn — Journal. Metal Finishing Society of Japan
J Met Finish Soc Korea — Journal. Metal Finishing Society of Korea
J Methodist Hist Soc of S Afr — Journal of the Methodist Historical Society of South Africa
J Met Phys Adv Technol — Journal of Metal Physics and Advanced Technologies
J Met Soc Jap — Journal. Meteorological Society of Japan
J Met (Tokyo) — Journal of Metals (Tokyo)
J Mex Am Hist — Journal of Mexican American History
JMF — Journal Musical Francais
JMF — Journal of International Money and Finance
JMF — Journal of Marriage and the Family
JMFT — Journal of Milk and Food Technology [*Later, Journal of Food Protection*]
JMG — Journal of Information and Image Management
JMG — Journal of Management Consulting
JMG — Journal of Metamorphic Geology
JMG — Journal of Micrographics
JMG — Journal of Molecular Graphics
JM Genet — Journal of Medical Genetics
JMGS — Journal. Manchester Geographical Society
JMGS — Journal of Modern Greek Studies
J Mgt — Journal of Management
J Mgt Stud — Journal of Management Studies
J Mgt Studies — Journal of Management Studies
JMH — Journal of Medieval History
JMH — Journal of Mississippi History
JMH — Journal of Modern History
J Mich Dent Assoc — Journal. Michigan Dental Association
J Mich Med Soc — Journal. Michigan State Medical Society
J Mich State Dent Assoc — Journal. Michigan State Dental Association
J Mich State Dent Soc — Journal. Michigan State Dental Society
J Mich State Med Soc — Journal. Michigan State Medical Society

J Mich St Med Soc — Journal. Michigan State Medical Society
J Micr and Nat Sc — Journal of Microscopy and Natural Science
J Microb Biotechnol — Journal of Microbial Biotechnology
J Microbiol — Journal of Microbiology
J Microbiol (Chaoyang Peoples Repub China) — Journal of Microbiology (Chaoyang, People's Republic of China)
J Microbiol Epidem Immunobiol — Journal of Microbiology, Epidemiology, and Immunobiology
J Microbiol Epidemiol Immunobiol Engl Transl — Journal of Microbiology, Epidemiology, and Immunobiology. EnglishTranslation
J Microbiol Epidemiol Immunobiol (USSR) — Journal of Microbiology, Epidemiology, and Immunobiology (USSR)
J Microbiol Immunol Infect — Journal of Microbiology, Immunology and Infection
J Microbiol Methods — Journal of Microbiological Methods
J Microbiol Seoul — Journal of Microbiology (Seoul)
J Microbiol Serol — Journal of Microbiology and Serology
J Microbiol UAR — Journal of Microbiology of the United Arab Republic
J Microcolumn Sep — Journal of Microcolumn Separations
J Microcomput Appl — Journal of Microcomputer Applications
J Microelectromech Syst — Journal of Microelectromechanical Systems
J Microencapsul — Journal of Microencapsulation
J Microencapsulation — Journal of Microencapsulation
J Microg — Journal de Micrographie
J Microgr — Journal of Micrographics
J Micrographics — Journal of Micrographics
J Micromech Microeng — Journal of Micromechanics and Microengineering. Structures, Devices, and Systems
J Micromech Microengineering — Journal of Micromechanics and Microengineering
J Micronutr Anal — Journal of Micronutrient Analysis
J Microorg Ferment — Journal of Microorganisms and Fermentation
J Microphotogr — Journal of Microphotography
J Microsc — Journal de Microscopie
J Microsc — Journal of Microscopy
J Microsc B — Journal de Microscopie et de Biologie Cellulaire
J Microsc Biol Cell — Journal de Microscopie et de Biologie Cellulaire
J Microsc et Spectrosc Electron — Journal de Microscopie et de Spectroscopie Electroniques
J Microsc (O) — Journal of Microscopy (Oxford)
J Microscop — Journal de Microscopie/Societe Francaise de Microscopie Electronique
J Microscopie — Journal de Microscopie
J Microscopy — Journal of Microscopy
J Microsc (Oxf) — Journal of Microscopy (Oxford)
J Microsc (Paris) — Journal de Microscopie (Paris)
J Microsc Soc — Journal. Royal Microscopical Society
J Microsc Soc Am — Journal of the Microscopy Society of America
J Microsc Spectrosc Electron — Journal de Microscopie et de Spectroscopie Electroniques
J Microsc Spectrosc Electron (France) — Journal de Microscopie et de Spectroscopie Electroniques (France)
J Microsurg — Journal of Microsurgery
J Microwave Power — Journal of Microwave Power
J Microwave Power Eltromagn Energy Publ Int Microwave Power — Journal of Microwave Power and Electromagnetic Energy. A Publication. International Microwave Power Institute
J Microwave Pwr — Journal of Microwave Power
J Microw Power Electromagn Energy — Journal of Microwave Power and Electromagnetic Energy
J Midwifery Womens Health — Journal of Midwifery & Womens Health
J Mie Med Coll — Journal. Mie Medical College
JMiH — Journal of Mississippi History
J Milk & Food Tech — Journal of Milk and Food Technology [*Later, Journal of Food Protection*]
J Milk Food — Journal of Milk and Food Technology [*Later, Journal of Food Protection*]
J Milk Food Technol — Journal of Milk and Food Technology [*Later, Journal of Food Protection*]
J Milk Tech — Journal of Milk Technology
J Milk Technol — Journal of Milk Technology
J Mil Serv Inst — Journal. Military Service Institution
J Mil Soc — Journal of Political and Military Sociology
J Minami Osaka Hosp — Journal. Minami Osaka Hospital
J Min Coll Akita Univ Ser A — Journal. Mining College. Akita University. Series A. Mining Geology
J Mineral — Jornal de Mineralogia
J Mineral Geol Prague — Journal of Mineralogy and Geology (Prague)
J Mineral Petrol — Journal of Mineralogy and Petrology
J Mineral Petrol Econ Geol — Journal of Mineralogy, Petrology, and Economic Geology
J Mineral Soc Jpn — Journal. Mineralogical Society of Japan
J Mines — Journal des Mines, ou Recueil de Memoires sur l'Exploitation des Mines, et sur les Sciences et les Arts qui s'y Rapportent
J Mines Metall — Journal des Mines et de la Metallurgie
J Mines Metals Fuels — Journal of Mines, Metals, and Fuels
J Mines Met Fuels — Journal of Mines, Metals, and Fuels
J Mines Met Fuels (Calcutta) — Journal of Mines, Metals, and Fuels (Calcutta)
J Mine Vent Soc S Afr — Journal. Mine Ventilation Society of South Africa
J Min Geol — Journal of Mining and Geology
J Mining Met Inst Jap — Journal. Mining and Metallurgical Institute of Japan
J Min Inst Jpn — Journal. Mining Institute of Japan
J Min Inst Kyushu — Journal. Mining Institute of Kyushu
J Minist Agric (GB) — Journal. Ministry of Agriculture (Great Britain)
J Minist Hlth — Journal. Ministry of Health
J Ministry Ag — Agriculture (Journal of the Ministry of Agriculture)

J Min Mat Process Inst Jpn — Journal. Mining and Materials Processing Institute of Japan
J Min Metall Foundry — Journal of Mining and Metallurgy. Foundry
J Min Metall Inst Jap — Journal. Mining and Metallurgical Institute of Japan
J Min Metall Metall — Journal of Mining and Metallurgy. Metallurgy
J Minn Acad Sci — Journal. Minnesota Academy of Science
JMIR — Journal. Ministere de l'Instruction Publique en Russie
J Mirror — Jewish Mirror
J Miss Acad Sci — Journal. Mississippi Academy of Sciences
JMissH — Journal of Mississippi History
J Miss Hist — Journal of Mississippi History
J Mississippi Med Ass — Journal. Mississippi State Medical Association
J Miss Med Ass — Journal. Mississippi State Medical Association
J Missouri Dent Assoc — Journal. Missouri Dental Association
J Miss State Med Assoc — Journal. Mississippi State Medical Association
J Miss St Med Ass — Journal. Mississippi State Medical Association
JMJ — John Marshall Journal of Practice and Procedure
JMK — Journal of Marketing
JMKNA2 — Annual Reports. Institute of Population Problems
JMKOA — Jemna Mechanika a Optika
J Mkt — Journal of Marketing
J Mktg — Journal of Marketing
J Mktg Res — Journal of Marketing Research
J Mkting — Journal of Marketing
J Mkting Res — Journal of Marketing Research
J Mkt Res — Journal of Marketing Research
JMKU — Journal of Mathematics. Kyoto University
JML — Journal Medical Libanais
JML — Journal of Memory and Language
JML — Journal of Modern Literature
JMLB — Jahrbuch des Martin-Luther-Bundes
JM Ling — Journal of Mayan Linguistics
JMLR — John Marshall Law Review
JMM — Jahrbuch der Maenner von Morgenstern, Heimatbund and Elb- und Wesermuendung
JMM — Journal de la Marine Marchande et de la Navigation Aerienne
JMM — Journal. Manx Museum
JMM — Journal of Macromarketing
JMM — Journal of Microbiological Methods
JMMAA — Journal. Maine Medical Association
JMMMD — Journal of Magnetism and Magnetic Materials
JMMNA — Journal de la Marine Marchande et de la Navigation Aerienne
JMMSD — Journal. Korea Merchant Marine College. Natural Sciences Series
JMN — Journal of Management Studies
J MO B — Journal. Missouri Bar
J MO Bar — Journal. Missouri Bar
J Mod Afric Stud — Journal of Modern African Studies
J Mod Afr S — Journal of Modern African Studies
J Mod Afr Stud — Journal of Modern African Studies
J Mod Afr Studs — Journal of Modern African Studies
J Mode & Gout — Journal de la Mode et du Gout
J Moden — Journal der Moden
J MO Dent Assoc — Journal. Missouri Dental Association
J Modern Opt — Journal of Modern Optics
J Mod Hist — Journal of Modern History
J Mod Lit — Journal of Modern Literature
J Mod Opt — Journal of Modern Optics
J Mod Watchmaking — Journal of Modern Watchmaking
J Mol Appl Genet — Journal of Molecular and Applied Genetics
J Mol Biol — Journal of Molecular Biology
J Mol Catal — Journal of Molecular Catalysis
J Mol Catal A Chem — Journal of Molecular Catalysis A. Chemical
J Mol Catal B Enzym — Journal of Molecular Catalysis B. Enzymatic
J Mol Catal (China) — Journal of Molecular Catalysis (China)
J Mol Cel C — Journal of Molecular and Cellular Cardiology
J Mol Cell Cardiol — Journal of Molecular and Cellular Cardiology
J Mol Cell Immunol — Journal of Molecular and Cellular Immunology
J Mol Diagn — Journal of Molecular Diagnostics
J Molec Biol — Journal of Molecular Biology
J Mol Electron — Journal of Molecular Electronics
J Mol Endoc — Journal of Molecular Endocrinology
J Mol Endocrinol — Journal of Molecular Endocrinology
J Mol Evol — Journal of Molecular Evolution
J Mol Graph — Journal of Molecular Graphics
J Mol Graphics — Journal of Molecular Graphics
J Mol Graphics & Modell — Journal of Molecular Graphics and Modelling
J Mol Liq — Journal of Molecular Liquids
J Molluscan Stud — Journal of Molluscan Studies
J Molluscan Stud Suppl — Journal of Molluscan Studies. Supplement
J Mol Med — Journal of Molecular Medicine
J Mol Med Berlin — Journal of Molecular Medicine (Berlin)
J Mol Microbiol Biotechnol — Journal of Molecular Microbiology and Biotechnology
J Mol Model — Journal of Molecular Modeling. Electronic Publication
J Mol Model Electronic Publication — Journal of Molecular Modeling [*Electronic Publication*]
J Mol Neuro — Journal of Molecular Neuroscience
J Mol Neurosci — Journal of Molecular Neuroscience
J Mol Recognit — Journal of Molecular Recognition
J Mol Sci — Journal of Molecular Science
J Mol Sci Int Ed — Journal of Molecular Science. International Edition
J Mol Spect — Journal of Molecular Spectroscopy
J Mol Spectrosc — Journal of Molecular Spectroscopy
J Mol Struct — Journal of Molecular Structure
J Mond Pharm — Journal Mondial de Pharmacie

J Monetary Econ — Journal of Monetary Economics
J Monet Econ — Journal of Monetary Economics
J Money Cred & Bank — Journal of Money, Credit, and Banking
J Money Cred Bank — Journal of Money, Credit, and Banking
J Money Credit & Banking — Journal of Money, Credit, and Banking
J Money Credit Bank — Journal of Money, Credit, and Banking
J Moral Ed — Journal of Moral Education
J Moral Educ — Journal of Moral Education
J Mormon Hist — Journal of Mormon History
J Morph — Journal of Morphology
J Morph and Physiol — Journal of Morphology and Physiology
J Morphol — Journal of Morphology
J Morphol Physiol — Journal of Morphology and Physiology
J Morphol Suppl — Journal of Morphology. Supplement
J Morris Soc — Journal of the William Morris Society
JMOS — Journal. Manchester Oriental Society
J Moscow Patr — Journal of the Moscow Patriarchate
J Moscow Phys Soc — Journal. Moscow Physical Society
J Mo State Med Assoc — Journal. Missouri State Medical Association
J Mot Behav — Journal of Motor Behavior
J Motion Pict Soc India — Journal. Motion Picture Society of India
J Motor Beh — Journal of Motor Behavior
J MO Water Sewage Conf — Journal. Missouri Water and Sewage Conference
J Mo Water Sewerage Conf — Journal. Missouri Water and Sewerage Conference
JMP — Journal of Morphology and Physiology (Philadelphia)
JMP — Journal of Moscow Patriarchate
JMP — Journal of Public Policy and Marketing
JMPMA — Journal of Medical Primatology
JMPO — Journal of Microwave Power
JMPPD — Journal of Marketing and Public Policy
JMPSB — Journal of Mathematical and Physical Sciences
JMPT — Journal of Manipulative and Physiological Therapeutics
JmQ — Journalism Quarterly
JMR — Journal of Marketing Research
JMR — Journal of Molecular Recognition
JMRAS — Journal. Malayan Branch. Royal Asiatic Society
JMRPDC — Japan Medical Research Foundation. Publication
JMRS — Journal. Market Research Society
JMRS — Journal of Medieval and Renaissance Studies
JMS — Journal of Maltese Studies
JMS — Journal of Management Studies
JMS — Journal of Mithraic Studies
JMS — Journal of Molecular Structure
JMSBA — Journal of Mental Subnormality
JMSCA — Journal of Mental Science
JMSED — Journal de Microscopie et de Spectroscopie Electroniques
JMSJ — Journal. Mathematical Society of Japan
JMSMD — Journal of Materials for Energy Systems
JMSNA — Journal. Medical Society of New Jersey
JMSUB — Journal. Maharaja Sayajirao University of Baroda
JMT — Journal of Music Therapy
JMTAA — Journal. Institute of Mathematics and Its Applications
JMTE — Journal. Michigan Teachers of English
JMTE — Journal of Music Teacher Education
JMTheory — Journal of Music Theory
JMTherapy — Journal of Music Therapy
J Mt Sinai Hosp — Journal. Mount Sinai Hospital
J Mt Sinai Hosp (NY) — Journal. Mount Sinai Hospital (New York)
JMUB — Jahrbuch des Marburger Universitaetsbundes
JMUEOS — Journal. Manchester University. Egyptian and Oriental Society
JMUES — Journal. Manchester University Egyptian and Oriental Society
JMultiAn — Journal of Multivariate Analysis
J Multivar Anal — Journal of Multivariate Analysis
J Multivariate Anal — Journal of Multivariate Analysis
JMus — Journal of Musicology
JMUSA — Journal. American Musicological Society
J Muscle Res Cell Motil — Journal of Muscle Research and Cell Motility
J Mus Ethnog — Journal of Museum Ethnography
J Mus Ethnogr — Journal of Museum Ethnography
J Mus F A Boston — Journal of the Museum of Fine Arts (Boston)
J Mus Francais — Journal Musical Francais
J Music Res — Journal of Musicological Research
J Music Theory — Journal of Music Theory
J Music Ther — Journal of Music Therapy
J Music Thr — Journal of Music Theory
J Mus Res — Journal of Musicological Research
J Mus Theory — Journal of Music Theory
J Mus Theory Pedagogy — Journal of Music Theory Pedagogy
J Mus Ther — Journal of Music Theory
J Mus Therapy — Journal of Music Therapy
JMUTA — Journal of Music Therapy
JMUTB — Journal of Music Theory
JMV — Jahresschrift fuer Mitteldeutsche Vorgeschichte
JMVK — Jahrbuch des Museums fuer Voelkerkunde zu Leipzig
JMVL — Jahrbuch des Staedtischen Museums fuer Voelkerkunde (Leipzig)
JMVL — Jahrbuch. Museum fuer Voelkerkunde zu Leipzig
JMW — Jahrbuch des Musealvereins Wels
J Mycol — Journal of Mycology
J Mycol Plant Pathol — Journal of Mycology and Plant Pathology
J Mysore Agr Exp Union — Journal. Mysore Agricultural and Experimental Union
J Mysore Med Assoc — Journal. Mysore Medical Association
J Mysore State Ed Fed — Journal. Mysore State Education Federation
J Mysore U Arts — Journal. Mysore University. Section A. Arts
J Mysore Univ Sect B — Journal. Mysore University. Section B. Science
J Mysore Univ Sect B Sci — Journal. Mysore University. Section B. Science

J My Th — Jahrbuch fuer Mystische Theologie
JMYUAP — Journal. Mysore University. Section B. Science
JN — Jewish Newsletter
JN — Johnsonian News Letter
JN — Jornal de Noticas
JN — Journal Numismatique
JN — Journal of Neuroscience
JN — Juilliard News Bulletin
JNAA — Journal. National Academy of Administration
JNABD — Journal of Nuclear Agriculture and Biology
JNABI — Journal. National Association of Biblical Instructors
JNAFS — Journal of Northwest Atlantic Fishery Science
J Nagano-ken Jr Coll — Journal of Nagano-ken Junior College
J Nagasaki Earth Sci Assoc — Journal. Nagasaki Earth Science Association
J Nagasaki Med Assoc — Journal of Nagasaki Medical Association
J Nagasaki Public Health Soc — Journal. Nagasaki Public Health Society
J Nagoya City Univ Med Assoc — Journal. Nagoya City University Medical Association
J Nagoya Med Assoc — Journal. Nagoya Medical Association
J Nakanihon Automot Jr Coll — Journal. Nakanihon Automotive Junior College
JNALA — Journal of the New African Literature and the Arts
J NAL Assoc — Journal of NAL Associates
J Nanjing Agric Coll — Journal. Nanjing Agricultural College
J Nanjing Agric Univ — Journal. Nanjing Agricultural University
J Nanjing Coll Pharm — Journal. Nanjing College of Pharmacy
J Nanjing For Univ — Journal. Nanjing Forestry University
J Nanjing Inst Chem Technol — Journal of Nanjing Institute of Chemical Technology
J Nanjing Inst For — Journal. Nanjing Institute of Forestry
J Nanjing Inst Tech — Journal of Nanjing Institute of Technology
J Nanjing Inst Tech English Ed — Journal of Nanjing Institute of Technology (English Edition)
J Nanjing Inst Technol — Journal. Nanjing Institute of Technology
J Nanjing Norm Univ Nat Sci Ed — Journal of Nanjing Normal University. Natural Science Edition
J Nanjing Technol Coll For Prod — Journal. Nanjing Technological College of Forest Products
J Nanjing Univ Aeronaut Astronaut — Journal of Nanjing University of Aeronautics and Astronautics
J Nanjing Univ Nat Sci Ed — Journal. Nanjing University. Natural Science Edition
J Nanjing Univ Sci Technol — Journal of Nanjing University of Science and Technology
J Nanking Eng Inst — Journal. Nanking Engineering Institute
JNAPPH — Journal. National Association of Private Psychiatric Hospitals
J Nara Gakugei Univ — Journal. Nara Gakugei University
J Nara Gakugei Univ Nat Sci — Journal. Nara Gakugei University. Natural Science
J Nara Med Ass — Journal. Nara Medical Association
J Nara Med Assoc — Journal. Nara Medical Association
JNA Referees Bank — Journal. National Association of Referees in Bankruptcy
J Narr Tech — Journal of Narrative Technique
J Nat Acad Math India — Journal of National Academy of Mathematics. India
J Nat Agric Soc Ceylon — Journal. National Agricultural Society of Ceylon
J Natal Zulu Hist — Journal of Natal and Zulu History
J Nat Assn Col Adm Counsel — Journal. National Association of College Admissions Counselors
J Nat Canc — Journal. National Cancer Institute
J Nat Cancer Inst — Journal. National Cancer Institute
J Nat Chem Lab Ind — Journal. National Chemical Laboratory for Industry
J Nat Chiao Tung Univ — National Chiao Tung University. Journal
J Nat Dent Assoc — Journal. National Dental Association
J Nat Ed Soc Ceylon — Journal. National Education Society of Ceylon
J Nat Gas Chem — Journal of Natural Gas Chemistry
J Nat Hist — Journal of Natural History
J Nat Hist Sci Soc Western Australia — Journal. Natural History and Science Society of Western Australia
J Nat Inst Agric Bot (UK) — Journal. National Institute of Agricultural Botany (United Kingdom)
J Nat Inst Hospital Adm — Journal. National Institute of Hospital Administration
J Nat Inst Soc Sci — Journal. National Institute of Social Sciences
J Natl Acad Sci — Journal. National Academy of Sciences
J Natl Acad Sci (Repub Korea) Nat Sci Ser — Journal. National Academy of Sciences (Republic of Korea). Natural Sciences Series
J Natl Agric Exp Sta Nishigahara Tokyo — Journal. National Agricultural Experiment Station. Nishigahara, Tokyo/Noji Shikenjo Iho
J Natl Agric Soc Ceylon — Journal. National Agricultural Society of Ceylon
J Natl Analg Soc — Journal. National Analgesia Society
J Natl Assn Coll Adm Counsel — Journal. National Association of College Admissions Counselors
J Natl Assn Women Deans Adm & Counsel — Journal. National Association for Women Deans, Administrators, and Counselors
J Natl Assoc Hosp Dev — Journal. National Association for Hospital Development
J Natl Assoc Priv Psychiatr Hosp — Journal. National Association of Private Psychiatric Hospitals
J Natl Cancer Inst — Journal. National Cancer Institute
J Natl Cancer Inst Monogr — Journal of the National Cancer Institute Monographs
J Natl Chem Lab Ind — Journal. National Chemical Laboratory for Industry
J Natl Chiao Tung Univ — Journal. National Chiao Tung University
J Natl Def Med Coll — Journal. National Defense Medical College
J Natl Inst Agric Bot — Journal. National Institute of Agricultural Botany
J Natl Inst Pers Res S Afr CSIR — Journal. National Institute for Personnel Research. South African Council for Scientific and Industrial Research
J Natl Med Assoc — Journal. [US] National Medical Association
J Natl Res Counc Thail — Journal. National Research Council of Thailand
J Natl Res Counc Thailand — Journal. National Research Council of Thailand
J Natl Sci Counc Sri Lanka — Journal. National Science Council of Sri Lanka

J Natl Tech Assoc — Journal. National Technical Association
J Natl Univ Def Technol — Journal. National University of Defense Technology
J Nat Malar Soc — Journal. National Malaria Society
J Natn Cancer Inst — Journal. National Cancer Institute
J Natn Inst Agric Bot — Journal. National Institute of Agricultural Botany
J Nat Philos — Journal of Natural Philosophy, Chemistry, and the Arts
J Nat Prod — Journal of Natural Products
J Nat Prod (Lloydia) — Journal of Natural Products (Lloydia)
J Nat Res Coun Thai — Journal. National Research Council of Thailand
J Nat Rubber Res — Journal of Natural Rubber Research
J Nat Sci — Journal of Natural Sciences
J Nat Sci and Math — Journal of National Science and Mathematics
J Nat Sci Beijing Norm Univ — Journal of Natural Science. Beijing Normal University
J Nat Sci Chonnam Natl Univ — Journal of Natural Science. Chonnam National University
J Nat Sci Coll Gen Stud Seoul Natl Univ — Journal of Natural Sciences. College of General Studies. Seoul NationalUniversity
J Nat Sci Coll Sci Korea Univ — Journal of Natural Science. College of Science. Korea University
J Nat Sci Counc Sri Lanka — Journal. National Science Council of Sri Lanka
J Nat Sci Math — Journal of Natural Sciences and Mathematics
J Nat Sci Math (Lahore) — Journal of Natural Sciences and Mathematics (Lahore)
J Nat Sci Res Inst — Journal. Natural Science Research Institute. Yonsei University
J Nat Sci Res Inst Yonsei Univ — Journal. Natural Science Research Institute. Yonsei University
J Nat Sci Seoul — Journal of Natural Sciences (Seoul)
J Nat Sci Soc Ichimura Gakuen J Coll — Journal. Natural Scientific Society. Ichimura Gakuen Junior College
J Nat Sci Soc Ichimura Gakuen Univ Ichimura Gakuen J Coll — Journal. Natural Scientific Society. Ichimura Gakuen University and Ichimura Gakuen Junior College
J Nat Sci Yeungnam Univ — Journal of Natural Sciences. Yeungnam University
J Nat Sun Yat-sen Univ — Journal. National Sun Yat-sen University
J Nat Tech Assoc — Journal. National Technical Association
J Natural Hist — Journal of Natural History
J Natur Geom — Journal of Natural Geometry
J Natur Hist — Journal of Natural History
J Natur Phys Sci — Journal of Natural Physical Sciences
J Natur Sci and Math — Journal of Natural Sciences and Mathematics
J Natur Sci Math — Journal of Natural Sciences and Mathematics
J Naut Arch — International Journal of Nautical Archaeology and Underwater Exploration
J Naut Soc Jpn — Journal. Nautical Society of Japan
J Navig — Journal of Navigation
J Navigation — Royal Institute of Navigation. Journal of Navigation
JNAW — Jaarboek der Nederlandse Akademie van Wetenschappen
J NAWDAC — Journal. National Association for Women Deans, Administrators, and Counselors
JNB — J. N. Banerjea Memorial Volume
JNB — Julliard News Bulletin
JNBIA — Journal. Newark Beth Israel Hospital
JNBMDW — Journal. New Brunswick Museum
J NB Mus — Journal. New Brunswick Museum
JNC — Journal. National Cancer Institute
JNCB — Journal. North China Branch. Royal Asiatic Society
JNCBRAS — Journal. North China Branch. Royal Asiatic Society
J NC Dent Soc — Journal. North Carolina Dental Society
J N Cer Soc — Journal of the Northern Ceramic Society
J N China Branch Royal Asiat Soc — Journal of the North China Branch of the Royal Asiatic Society
J N Ch R A S — Journal. North China Branch. Royal Asiatic Society
JNCI — JNCI. Journal of the National Cancer Institute
JNCI J Natl Cancer Inst — JNCI. Journal of the National Cancer Institute
JNCLA — Journal. National Chemical Laboratory for Industry
J NC Sect Am Water Works Assoc NC Water Pollut Control Assoc — Journal. North Carolina Section of the American Water Works Association and North Carolina Water Pollution Control Association
JNCUD — Journal of Natural Science. Chonnam National University
JNCYA — Journal of Neurocytology
J NDI — Journal of NDI
JNDRA — Journal of New Drugs
Jn D Rv — Jane's Defence Review
JNE — Journal of Near Eastern Studies
JNE — Journal of Negro Education
JNE — Journal of Nursing Education
JNE — Journal of Nutrition Education
J Near East — Journal of Near Eastern Studies
J Near Eastern Stud — Journal of Near Eastern Studies
J Near East St — Journal of Near Eastern Studies
J Near East Stud — Journal of Near Eastern Studies
J Near E St — Journal of Near Eastern Studies
J Near E Stud — Journal of Near Eastern Studies
J Nebr Dent Assoc — Journal. Nebraska Dental Association
J Ned Gen — Jaarboek van het Koninklijk Nederlandsch Genootschap voor Munt- en Penningkunde
JNEEA — Journal of Negro Education
J Ne Exp Ne — Journal of Neuropathology and Experimental Neurology
J Neg Hist — Journal of Negro History
J Negro Ed — Journal of Negro Education
J Negro Educ — Journal of Negro Education
J Negro His — Journal of Negro History
J Negro Hist — Journal of Negro History
JNELDA — Journal of Nutrition for the Elderly

J Nematol — Journal of Nematology
J Ne Ne Psy — Journal of Neurology, Neurosurgery, and Psychiatry
J N Engl Water Pollut Control Assoc — Journal. New England Water Pollution Control Association
J N Engl Water Works Assoc — Journal. New England Water Works Association
J Nepal Chem Soc — Journal. Nepal Chemical Society
J Nepal Pharm Assoc — Journal. Nepal Pharmaceutical Association
J Nephrol — Journal of Nephrology
J Nephrol Nurs — Journal of Nephrology Nursing
J Nerv Ment — Journal of Nervous and Mental Disease
J Nerv Ment Dis — Journal of Nervous and Mental Disease
JNES — Journal of Near Eastern Studies
JNETD — Journal of Non-Equilibrium Thermodynamics
J Network Syst Manage — Journal of Network and Systems Management
J Neueste Holl Med Naturhist Lit — Journal fuer die Neueste Hollaendische Medizinische und Naturhistorische Literatur
J Neuesten Land Seereisen — Journal fuer die Neuesten Land- und Seereisen und das Interessanteste aus der Voelker- und Laenderkunde
J Neural Tr — Journal of Neural Transmission
J Neural Transm — Journal of Neural Transmission
J Neural Transm Gen Sect — Journal of Neural Transmission. General Section
J Neural Transm Park Dis Dement Sect — Journal of Neural Transmission. Parkinsons Disease and Dementia Section
J Neural Transm Parkinson's Dis Dementia Sect — Journal of Neural Transmission Parkinson's Disease and Dementia Section
J Neural Transm Suppl — Journal of Neural Transmission. Supplementum
J Neural Transplant Plast — Journal of Neural Transplantation and Plasticity
J Neurobiol — Journal of Neurobiology
J Neurochem — Journal of Neurochemistry
J Neurocyt — Journal of Neurocytology
J Neurocytol — Journal of Neurocytology
J Neuroendo — Journal of Neuroendocrinology
J Neuroendocrinol — Journal of Neuroendocrinology
J Neurogen — Journal of Neurogenetics
J Neurogenet — Journal of Neurogenetics
J Neuroimaging — Journal of Neuroimaging
J Neuroimmunol — Journal of Neuroimmunology
J Neuroimmunol Suppl — Journal of Neuroimmunology. Supplement
J Neurol — Journal of Neurology
J Neurol & Psychopath — Journal of Neurology and Psychopathology
J Neurol (Berlin) — Journal of Neurology (Berlin)
J Neurol Neurosurg Psychiat — Journal of Neurology, Neurosurgery, and Psychiatry
J Neurol Neurosurg Psychiatry — Journal of Neurology, Neurosurgery, and Psychiatry
J Neurol Sci — Journal of the Neurological Sciences
J Neurol Soc India — Journal. Neurological Society of India
J Neuro-Oncol — Journal of Neuro-Oncology
J Neuroophthalmol — Journal of Neuro-Ophthalmology
J Neuropath Exper Neurol — Journal of Neuropathology and Experimental Neurology
J Neuropath Exp Neurol — Journal of Neuropathology and Experimental Neurology
J Neuropathol Exp Neurol — Journal of Neuropathology and Experimental Neurology
J Neurophysiol — Journal of Neurophysiology
J Neurophysiol (Bethesda) — Journal of Neurophysiology (Bethesda)
J Neuropsychiat — Journal of Neuropsychiatry
J Neuropsychiatr Suppl — Journal of Neuropsychiatry. Supplement
J Neuropsychiatry — Journal of Neuropsychiatry
J Neuropsychiatry Clin Neurosci — Journal of Neuropsychiatry and Clinical Neurosciences
J Neuroradiol — Journal of Neuroradiology
J Neurosci — Journal of Neuroscience
J Neurosci Methods — Journal of Neuroscience Methods
J Neurosci Nurs — Journal of Neuroscience Nursing
J Neurosci Res — Journal of Neuroscience Research
J Neurosurg — Journal of Neurosurgery
J Neurosurg Anesthesiol — Journal of Neurosurgical Anesthesiology
J Neurosurg Nurs — Journal of Neurosurgical Nursing
J Neurosurg Sci — Journal of Neurosurgical Sciences
J Neurotrauma — Journal of Neurotrauma
J Neurovirol — Journal of Neurovirology
J Neuro-Visc Relat — Journal of Neuro-Visceral Relations
J Neuro Visc Relat Suppl — Journal of Neuro-Visceral Relations. Supplementum
J Neurphysl — Journal of Neurophysiology
J Neur Sci — Journal of the Neurological Sciences
J Neur Tr-G — Journal of Neural Transmission. General Section
J Neur Tr-P — Journal of Neural Transmission. Parkinson's Disease and Dementia Section
J Neutron Res — Journal of Neutron Research
J Nevropat I Psikhiat — Jurnal Nevropatologii I Psikhiatrii Imeni
J New Afr Lit Arts — Journal. New African Literature and the Arts
J Newark Beth Israel Hosp — Journal. Newark Beth Israel Hospital
J Newark Beth Isr Hosp — Journal. Newark Beth Israel Hospital
J Newark Beth Isr Med Cent — Journal. Newark Beth Israel Medical Center
J Newcastle Sch Arts — Newcastle School of Arts. Journal
J New Drugs — Journal of New Drugs
J New Energy — Journal of New Energy
J New Engl Water Works Ass — Journal. New England Water Works Association
J New Engl Water Works Assoc — Journal. New England Water Works Association
J New Generation Comput Systems — Journal of New Generation Computer Systems

J New Haven Colony Hist Soc — Journal of the New Haven Colony Historical Society
J New Mater Electrochem Syst — Journal of New Materials for Electrochemical Systems
J New Mus Res — Journal of New Music Research
J New Rem Clin — Journal of New Remedies and Clinics
J Newsletter — Jewish Newsletter
J New World Archaeol — Journal of New World Archaeology
JNFA — Journal of Numismatic Fine Arts
JNFI — Jahrbuch des Nordfriesichen Instituts
JNFS — Journal of Northwest Atlantic Fishery Science
JNG — Jahrbuch fuer Numismatik und Geldgeschichte
JNGG — Jahrbuch fuer Numismatik und Geldgeschichte
JNH — Journal of Negro History
J NH Dent Soc — Journal. New Hampshire Dental Society
JNI — Jahrbuch. Nordfriesisches Institut
J Niger Assoc Dent Stud — Journal. Nigeria Association of Dental Students
J Nigerian Inst Oil Palm Res — Journal. Nigerian Institute for Oil Palm Research
J Nigerian Math Soc — Journal of the Nigerian Mathematical Society
J Nihon Univ Med Assoc — Journal. Nihon University Medical Association
J Nihon Univ Sch Dent — Journal. Nihon University School of Dentistry
J Niigata Agric Exp Stn — Journal. Niigata Agricultural Experiment Station
J Nippon Dent Assoc — Journal. Nippon Dental Association
J Nippon Dent Coll — Journal. Nippon Dental College
J Nippon Dent Univ — Journal of the Nippon Dental University
J Nippon Hosp Pharm Assoc Sci Ed — Journal. Nippon Hospital Pharmacists Association. Scientific Edition
J Nippon Med Sch — Journal. Nippon Medical School
J Nippon Univ Sch Dent — Journal. Nippon University School of Dentistry
JNIPRMSI — Japan. National Institute of Polar Research. Memoirs. Special Issue
J Nissei Hosp — Journal. Nissei Hospital
J NJ Dent Assoc — Journal. New Jersey Dental Association
J NJ Dent Hyg Assoc — Journal. New Jersey Dental Hygienists Association
J NJ State Dent Soc — Journal. New Jersey State Dental Society
JNKVV Res J — JNKVV [*Jawaharlal Nehru Krishi Vishwa Vidyalaya*] Research Journal
JNL — Johnsonian News Letter
JNL — Journalist. Orgaan van de Nederlandse Vereniging van Journalisten
JNL — Journal of Northern Luzon
Jnl Abstr Brit Ship Res Assoc — Journal of Abstracts. British Ship Research Association
Jnl Aesthetics — Journal of Aesthetics and Art Criticism
Jnl Aesthetics & Art Crit — Journal of Aesthetics and Art Criticism
Jnl Afr Afro Am Aff — Journal of African-Afro-American Affairs
Jnl Am Folklore — Journal of American Folklore
Jnl Am Hist — Journal of American History
Jnl Am Res Cent Egypt — Journal. American Research Center in Egypt
Jnl Area Stud — Journal of Area Studies
Jnl Asian Stu — Journal of Asian Studies
Jnl Bar Cound India — Journal. Bar Council of India
Jnl Basque Stud — Journal of Basque Studies
Jnl Behav Asses — Journal of Behavioral Assessment
Jnl Bharati Res Inst — Journal. Bharati Research Institute
Jnl Bus Adm — Journal of Business Administration
Jnl Business Ed — Journal of Business Education
Jnl Can Cult — Journal of Canadian Culture
Jnl Cardiac Rehab — Journal of Cardiac Rehabilitation
Jnl Cardiovasc Med — Journal of Cardiovascular Medicine
Jnl Com — Journal of Commerce
Jnl Com Import Bul — Journal of Commerce Import Bulletin
Jnl Constr Div Am Soc Civ Eng — Journal. Construction Division. American Society of Civil Engineers
Jnl Counsel Psych — Journal of Counseling Psychology
Jnl Cranio Mandib Pract — Journal of Cranio-Mandibular Practice
Jnl Crim Law Criminology — Journal of Criminal Law and Criminology
Jnl Crustacean Biol — Journal of Crustacean Biology
Jnl Diet Home Ec — Journal of Dietetics and Home Economics
Jnl Earth Sci R Dublin Soc — Journal of Earth Sciences. Royal Dublin Society
Jnl Econ Hist — Journal of Economic History
Jnl Ec Studies — Journal of Ecumenical Studies
Jnl Electrophysiol — Journal of Electrophysiology
Jnl Engl Ger Philol — Journal of English and Germanic Philology
Jnl Gen Ed — Journal of General Education
Jnl Ger Am Stud — Journal of German-American Studies
Jnl Health Care Tech — Journal of Health Care Technology
Jnl Hepatol — Journal of Hepatology
Jnl Higher Ed — Journal of Higher Education
Jnl Hisp Pol — Journal of Hispanic Politics
Jnl Hist Ideas — Journal of the History of Ideas
Jnl Home Econ — Journal of Home Economics
Jnl Indones Atom Energ Agency — Journal. Indonesian Atomic Energy Agency
Jnl Inorg Chem (Nanjing PRC) — Journal of Inorganic Chemistry (Nanjing, People's Republic of China)
Jnl Inst Armament Stud — Journal. Institute of Armament Studies
Jnl Inst Eng (Fed Malaysia) — Journal. Institution of Engineers (Federation of Malaysia)
Jnl Int Ass Dent Child — Journal. International Association of Dentistry for Children
Jnl Ital Ling — Journal of Italian Linguistics
Jnl KY Dent Assoc — Journal. Kentucky Dental Association
Jnl Lib Hist — Journal of Library History [*Later, Journal of Library History, Philosophy, andComparative Librarianship*]
Jnl Life Sci — Journal of Life Sciences
Jnl Low Temp Plas Chem — Journal of Low-Temperature Plasma Chemistry
Jnl Marketing — Journal of Marketing
Jnl Marr & Fam — Journal of Marriage and the Family

Jnl Med Caen — Journal de Medecine de Caen
Jnl Minn Pub Law — Journal of Minnesota Public Law
Jnl Mithraic Stud — Journal of Mithraic Studies
Jnl Mod Hist — Journal of Modern History
Jnl Mol Appl Genet — Journal of Molecular and Applied Genetics
Jnl Muscle Res Cell Motil — Journal of Muscle Research and Cell Motility
Jnl Negro Ed — Journal of Negro Education
Jnl Negro Hist — Journal of Negro History
Jnl Neuroimmunol — Journal of Neuroimmunology
Jnl New Wld Archaeol — Journal of New World Archaeology
JnlOBP — Journal of Black Poetry
Jnl Ocular Ther Surg — Journal of Ocular Therapy and Surgery
Jnl of Archtl Education — Journal of Architectural Education
Jnl of Archtl Research — Journal of Architectural Research
Jnl of Canadian Art History — Journal of Canadian Art History
Jnl of Environmental Psychology — Journal of Environmental Psychology
Jnl of Garden History — Journal of Garden History
Jnl of Planning & Environment Law — Journal of Planning and Environment Law
Jnl Oil Fat Ind — Journal of Oil and Fat Industries
JnlONJP — Journal of New Jersey Poets
JnlOPC — Journal of Popular Culture
Jnl Orthomol Psych — Journal of Orthomolecular Psychiatry
Jnl Philos — Journal of Philosophy
Jnl Photoacoust — Journal of Photoacoustics
Jnl Polit Econ — Journal of Political Economy
Jnl Politics — Journal of Politics
Jnl Relig — Journal of Religion
Jnl Sov Cardiovasc Res — Journal of Soviet Cardiovascular Research
Jnl Traf Med — Journal of Traffic Medicine
Jnl Vet Orthoped — Journal of Veterinary Orthopedics
JNM — JNM. Journal of Nuclear Medicine
JNMD — Journal of Nervous and Mental Disease
JNMDA — Journal of Nervous and Mental Disease
JNMED — Journal of Neuroscience Methods
JNMM — JNMM. Journal. Institute of Nuclear Materials Management
JNMM — Journal of the Institute of Nuclear Materials Management
J NMR Med — Journal of NMR [*Nuclear Magnetic Resonance*] Medicine
JNMSD — Journal of Nuclear Medicine and Allied Sciences
JNMTA — Journal of Nonmetals
J N Mus Ceylon — Journal of the National Museums of Ceylon
JNNPA — Journal of Neurology, Neurosurgery, and Psychiatry
JNNVA — Jaarboek. Nederlandse Natuurkundige Vereniging
J No Luzon — Journal of Northern Luzon
J Non Classical Logic — Journal of Non-Classical Logic
J Non-Cryst — Journal of Non-Crystalline Solids
J Non-Cryst Solids — Journal of Non-Crystalline Solids
J Nondestr Eval — Journal of Nondestructive Evaluation
J Non-Destr Insp — Journal of Non-Destructive Inspection
J Non-Equilib Thermodyn — Journal of Non-Equilibrium Thermodynamics
J Nonlinear Math Phys — Journal of Nonlinear Mathematical Physics
J Nonlinear Opt Phys Mater — Journal of Nonlinear Optical Physics and Materials
J Nonlinear Sci — Journal of Nonlinear Science
J Nonmet — Journal of Nonmetals [*Later, Semiconductors and Insulators*]
J Nonmet and Semicond — Journal of Nonmetals and Semiconductors [*Later, Semiconductors and Insulators*]
J Nonmet Semicond — Journal of Nonmetals and Semiconductors [*Later, Semiconductors and Insulators*]
J Non-Newtonian Fluid Mech — Journal of Non-Newtonian Fluid Mechanics
J Nonparametr Statist — Journal of Nonparametric Statistics
J Nonverbal Behav — Journal of Nonverbal Behavior
J Northampton Mus — Journal. Northampton Museum and Art Gallery
J Northampton Mus & A G — Journal of the Northampton Museums and Art Gallery
J Northamptonshire Natur Hist Soc Fld Club — Journal. Northamptonshire Natural History Society and Field Club
J North China Inst Technol — Journal of North China Institute of Technology
J Northeast Agric Univ Engl Ed — Journal of Northeast Agricultural University (English Edition)
J Northeast Asian Studies — Journal of Northeast Asian Studies
J Northeast Norm Univ Nat Sci Ed — Journal of Northeast Normal University. Natural Science Edition
J Northeast Univ Nat Sci — Journal of Northeastern University. Natural Science
J Northeast Univ Tech — Journal of Northeast University of Technology
J Northwest Atl Fish Sci — Journal of Northwest Atlantic Fishery Science
J Northwest Univ — Journal of Northwest University. Natural Sciences
J Northwest Univ Nat Sci Ed — Journal. Northwest University. Natural Science Edition
J Norw Med Assoc — Journal. Norwegian Medical Association
JNOS — Jahrbuecher fuer Nationaloekonomie und Statistik
J NPA — Journal. Nepal Pharmaceutical Association
JNPAB — Journal of Personality Assessment
JNPRD — Journal of Natural Products
JNPS — Journal. Nagari Pracarini Sabha
J Nr E Stud — Journal of Near Eastern Studies
JNRM — Journal of Natural Resources Management and Interdisciplinary Studies
JNRREQ — Journal of Natural Rubber Research
JNS — Jahrbuecher fuer National-Oekonomie und Statistik
JNSCA — Journal of the Neurological Sciences
JNSEL — Journal of the Northwest Semitic Languages
JNSI — Journal. Numismatic Society of India
JNSL — Journal of the Northwest Semitic Languages
JNSMP — Journal. Numismatic Society of Madhya Pradesh
JNSNA — Journal of Neurosurgical Nursing
JNSSB — Journal of Neurosurgical Sciences
JNSt — Jahrbuecher fuer Nationaloekonomie und Statistik

J NSW Council for Mentally Handicapped — Journal. New South Wales Council for the Mentally Handicapped
JNT — Journal of Narrative Technique
JNTAD — Journal. National Technical Association
JNUCA — Journal of Nuclear Energy
J Nucl Agri Bio — Journal of Nuclear Agriculture and Biology
J Nucl Agric Biol — Journal of Nuclear Agriculture and Biology
J Nucl Biol — Journal of Nuclear Biology and Medicine
J Nucl Biol Med — Journal of Nuclear Biology and Medicine
J Nucl Cardiol — Journal of Nuclear Cardiology
J Nuclear Med — Journal of Nuclear Medicine
J Nuclear Sci Tech — Journal of Nuclear Science and Technology
J Nucl Energ — Journal of Nuclear Energy
J Nucl Energy — Journal of Nuclear Energy
J Nucl Energy Part A — Journal of Nuclear Energy. Part A. Reactor Science
J Nucl Energy Part B — Journal of Nuclear Energy. Part B. Reactor Technology
J Nucl Energy Part C — Journal of Nuclear Energy. Part C. Plasma Physics, Accelerators, Thermonuclear Research
J Nucl Energy Parts A/B — Journal of Nuclear Energy. Parts A/B. Reactor Science and Technology
J Nucl Fuel Cycle Environ — Journal of Nuclear Fuel Cycle and Environment
J Nucl Mat — Journal of Nuclear Materials
J Nucl Mater — Journal of Nuclear Materials
J Nucl Mater Manage — Journal of Nuclear Materials Management
J Nucl Med — Journal of Nuclear Medicine
J Nucl Med Allied Sci — Journal of Nuclear Medicine and Allied Sciences
J Nucl Med Pam — Journal of Nuclear Medicine. Pamphlet
J Nucl Med Suppl — Journal of Nuclear Medicine. Supplement
J Nucl Med Technol — Journal of Nuclear Medicine Technology
J Nucl Phys (Moscow) — Journal of Nuclear Physics (Moscow)
J Nucl Radiochem (Peking) — Journal of Nuclear and Radiochemistry (Peking)
J Nucl Sci and Technol — Journal of Nuclear Science and Technology
J Nucl Sci (Seoul) — Journal of Nuclear Sciences (Seoul)
J Nucl Sci Technol — Journal of Nuclear Science and Technology
J Nuc Sci T — Journal of Nuclear Science and Technology
J Number Th — Journal of Number Theory
J Number Theory — Journal of Number Theory
J Numer Methods Comput Appl — Journal on Numerical Methods and Computer Applications
J Numi Soc India — Journal of the Numismatic Society of India
J Nurs Adm — Journal of Nursing Administration
J Nurs Admin — Journal of Nursing Administration
J Nurs Care — Journal of Nursing Care
J Nurs Care Qual — Journal of Nursing Care Quality
J Nurs Ed — Journal of Nursery Education
J Nurs Ed — Journal of Nursing Education
J Nurs Educ — Journal of Nursing Education
J Nurse Midwife — Journal of Nurse Midwifery
J Nurse Midwifery — Journal of Nurse-Midwifery
J Nurs Ethics — Journal of Nursing Ethics
J Nurs Hist — Journal of Nursing History
J Nurs Meas — Journal of Nursing Measurement
J Nurs Midwife — Journal of Nurse Midwifery
J Nurs Staff Dev — Journal of Nursing Staff Development
J Nurs (Taipei) — Journal of Nursing (Taipei)
J Nutr — Journal of Nutrition
J Nutr Assess — Journal of Nutritional Assessment
J Nutr Biochem — Journal of Nutritional Biochemistry
J Nutr Diet — Journal of Nutrition and Dietetics
J Nutr Educ — Journal of Nutrition Education
J Nutr Elderly — Journal of Nutrition for the Elderly
J Nutr Environ Med — Journal of Nutritional and Environmental Medicine
J Nutr Growth Cancer — Journal of Nutrition, Growth, and Cancer
J Nutr Health Aging — Journal of Nutrition, Health & Aging
J Nutr Immunol — Journal of Nutritional Immunology
J Nutrition — Journal of Nutrition
J Nutr Sci — Journal of Nutritional Sciences
J Nutr Sci Suppl — Journal of Nutritional Sciences. Supplementum
J Nutr Sci Vitaminol — Journal of Nutritional Science and Vitaminology
J Nutr Sc V — Journal of Nutritional Science and Vitaminology
J Nutr Suppl — Journal of Nutrition. Supplement
J Nutr (Tokyo) — Journal of Nutrition (Tokyo)
JNVBDV — Journal of Nonverbal Behavior
J NVCA — Journal. National Volleyball Coaches Association
JNWSemL — Journal of the Northwest Semitic Languages
J Nw SL — Journal of the Northwest Semitic Languages
J NY Bot Gdn — Journal. New York Botanical Garden
J NY Entomol Soc — Journal. New York Entomological Society
J NY Ent So — Journal. New York Entomological Society
J NY Med Coll Flower and Fifth Ave Hosp — Journal. New York Medical College. Flower and Fifth Avenue Hospitals
J NY Med Coll Flower Fifth Ave Hosp — Journal. New York Medical College. Flower and Fifth Avenue Hospitals
J NY State Nurses Assoc — Journal. New York State Nurses Association
J NY State Sch Nurse Teach Assoc — Journal. New York State School Nurse Teachers Association
J NZ Assoc Bacteriol — Journal. New Zealand Association of Bacteriologists
J NZ Diet Assoc — Journal. New Zealand Dietetic Association
J NZ Fed Hist Soc — Journal. New Zealand Federation of Historical Societies
J NZ Inst Chem — Journal. New Zealand Institute of Chemistry
J NZ Inst Med Lab Technol — Journal. New Zealand Institute of Medical Laboratory Technology
JNZKA — Jinko Zoki
J NZ Soc Periodontol — Journal. New Zealand Society of Periodontology
JO — Jewish Observer and Middle East Review

JO — Journal fuer Ornithologie
JO — Journal Officiel de la Republique Francaise. Recueil Dalloz
JO — Journal Officiel des Communautes Europeennes
JoA — Jewel of Africa
JOA — Journal of Advertising
JOABAW — Journal of Applied Behavior Analysis
JOAD — Journal. American Dietetic Association
JOADE8 — Journal of Adolescence
JOAEEB — Journal of Applied Entomology
JoAH — Journal of American History
JOAIW — Jahreshefte des Oesterreichischen Archaeologischen Institutes in Wien
JOALAS — Journal of Allergy [*Later, Journal of Allergy and Clinical Immunology*]
JOAM — Jahrbuch fuer Ostasienmission
JoAm — Journal of American Studies
JOAN — Journal of Applied Nutrition
JOANAY — Journal of Anatomy
JOAND3 — Journal of Andrology
JOAP — Journal of Applied Psychology
JOB — Jahrbuch der Oesterreichischen Byzantinistik Gesellschaft
JoB — Journal of British Studies
JOB — Journal of Broadcasting [*Later, Journal of Broadcasting and Electronic Media*]
JOB — Journal of Business
JOB — Journal of Business Administration
JOB — Journal of Occupational Behaviour
JOB — Judicial Officers Bulletin
J Obesity Weight Regul — Journal of Obesity and Weight Regulation
J Obes Weight Regul — Journal of Obesity and Weight Regulation
JOBG — Jahrbuch. Oesterreichische Byzantinische Gesellschaft
J Object Oriented Program — Journal of Object-Oriented Programming
Jobless Newsl — Jobless Newsletter
JOBM — Journal of Behavioral Medicine
Job Outlk — Job Outlook for College Graduates through 1990
J Obs — Journal des Observateurs
Job Safe & H — Job Safety and Health
JOBSDN — Journal of Biosciences
JOBSEO — Journal. Orissa Botanical Society
J Observer — Jewish Observer
Jobsons Invest Dig — Jobson's Investment Digest
Jobsons Investment D — Jobson's Investment Digest
Jobsons Min Yearb — Jobson's Mining Yearbook
J Obst and Gynaec Brit Emp — Journal of Obstetrics and Gynaecology of the British Empire
J Obstet Gynaec Br Commonw — Journal of Obstetrics and Gynaecology of the British Commonwealth
J Obstet Gynaec Brit Cmwlth — Journal of Obstetrics and Gynaecology of the British Commonwealth
J Obstet Gynaec Brit Common — Journal of Obstetrics and Gynaecology of the British Commonwealth
J Obstet Gynaec Brit Emp — Journal of Obstetrics and Gynaecology of the British Empire
J Obstet Gynaecol — Journal of Obstetrics and Gynaecology
J Obstet Gynaecol Br Commonw — Journal of Obstetrics and Gynaecology of the British Commonwealth
J Obstet Gynaecol Br Emp — Journal of Obstetrics and Gynaecology of the British Empire
J Obstet Gynaecol Brit Empire — Journal of Obstetrics and Gynaecology. British Empire
J Obstet Gynaecol India — Journal of Obstetrics and Gynaecology of India
J Obstet Gynaecol Res — Journal of Obstetrics and Gynaecology Research
J Obstet Gynaecol Tokyo — Journal of Obstetrics and Gynaecology (Tokyo)
J Obstet Gynecol Neonatal Nurs — Journal of Obstetric, Gynecologic, and Neonatal Nursing
JoC — Journal of Church and State
JOC — Journal of Communication
JOC — Journal of Communication Management
J OCCA — Journal. Oil and Colour Chemists' Association
J Occ Bhvr — Journal of Occupational Behaviour
J Occ Health Safety Aust — Journal of Occupational Health and Safety in Australia
J Occ Med — Journal of Occupational Medicine
J Occ Psy — Journal of Occupational Psychology
J Occup Accid — Journal of Occupational Accidents
J Occupa Med — Journal of Occupational Medicine
J Occupa Psychol — Journal of Occupational Psychology
J Occupational Accidents — Journal of Occupational Accidents
J Occupat Med — Journal of Occupational Medicine
J Occup Behav — Journal of Occupational Behaviour
J Occup Environ Med — Journal of Occupational and Environmental Medicine
J Occup Health — Journal of Occupational Health
J Occup Med — Journal of Occupational Medicine
J Occup Med Toxicol — Journal of Occupational Medicine and Toxicology
J Occup Psychol — Journal of Occupational Psychology
J Oceanogr — Journal of Oceanography
J Oceanogr Soc Jpn — Journal. Oceanographical Society of Japan
J Oceanol Soc Korea — Journal. Oceanological Society of Korea
J Ocean Technol — Journal of Ocean Technology
J Ocean Univ Qingdao — Journal. Ocean University of Qingdao
JOCECA — Journal Officiel. Communaute Europeenne du Charbon et de l'Acier
JOCH — Journal of Community Health
JoCH — Journal of Contemporary History
JOCMA — Journal of Occupational Medicine
JOCNEE — Journal of Child Neurology
JOCS — Journal of Offender Counseling, Services, and Rehabilitation
J Ocul Pharmacol — Journal of Ocular Pharmacology
J Ocul Pharmacol Ther — Journal of Ocular Pharmacolgy and Therapeutics

J Ocul Ther Surg — Journal of Ocular Therapy and Surgery
JoD — Journal of Developing Areas
JOD — Journal of Development
JOD — Journal of Documentation
JOD — Juedischer Ordnungsdienst
JODC — Journal of Dentistry for Children
JODE — Journal of Drug Education
JODI — Journal of Drug Issues
J Odontol Osaka Univ — Journal of Odontology. Osaka University
J Odor Control — Journal of Odor Control
JODV — Journal of Divorce
JoE — Journal of Ecclesiastical History
JOEAI — Jahreshefte. Oesterreichisches Archaeologische Institut in Wien
JOEB — Jahrbuch der Oesterreichischen Byzantinistik
JOEBG — Jahrbuch der Oesterreichischen Byzantinistik Gesellschaft
JOEByz — Jahrbuch der Oesterreichischen Byzantinistik
JOEEA — Journal of Emotional Education
JOEF — France. Journal Officiel de l'Empire Francais
JOeffR — Jahrbuch des Oeffentlichen Rechts
JoEH — Journal of Economic History
JOeLG — Jahrbuch der Oesterreichischen Leo-Gesellschaft
JOENA — Journal of Endocrinology
Joenkoepings Laens Hushallningssaellsk Tidskr — Joenkoepings Laens Hushallningssaellskaps. Tidskrift
Joensuun Korkeakoulun Julk Sar B1 — Joensuun Korkeakoulun Julkaisuja. Sarja B1
Joensuun Korkeakoulun Julk Sar B2 — Joensuun Korkeakoulun Julkaisuja. Sarja B2
Joensuun Korkeakoulun Julk Sar B11 — Joensuun Korkeakoulun Julkaisuja. Sarja B11
JOERA — Journal of Educational Research
JoES — Journal of European Studies
JOET — Journal of Education for Teaching
JoEtS — Journal of Ethnic Studies
JoEuE — Journal of European Economic History
JOF — Journal of Finance
JOF — Journal of Forecasting
J of Air L & Commerce — Journal of Air Law and Commerce
J of Bcasting — Journal of Broadcasting [*Later, Journal of Broadcasting and Electronic Media*]
J of Black Stud — Journal of Black Studies
J of Ceylon L — Journal of Ceylon Law
J of Ed (NS) — Journal of Education. Department of Education (Nova Scotia)
J of Ethiop L — Journal of Ethiopian Law
J Officiel — Journal Officiel
J Off Rech Pech Can — Journal. Office des Recherches sur les Pecheries du Canada
J Off Repub Alger Democr Pop — Journal Officiel. Republique Algerienne Democratique et Populaire
J Off Repub Fr — Journal Officiel de la Republique Francaise
J Offshore Mech Arct Eng Trans ASME — Journal of Offshore Mechanics and Arctic Engineering. Transactions of the ASME
J Offshore Mech Arctic Engrg Trans ASME — Journal of Offshore Mechanics and Arctic Engineering. Transactions. American Society of Mechanical Engineers
J of Gen Educ — Journal of General Education
JOFH — Journal of Family History. Studies in Family, Kinship, and Demography
J of H and SB — Journal of Health and Social Behavior
J of Home Ec Ed — Journal of Home Economics Education
J of Human Rela — Journal of Human Relations
J of Ins of Arbitrators — Journal. Institute of Arbitrators
J of Intergroup Rela — Journal of Intergroup Relations
J of Internat L and Econ — Journal of International Law and Economics
J of MACT — Journal. Maulana Azad College of Technology
J of Marit L and Commerce — Journal of Maritime Law and Commerce
J of Neg Ed — Journal of Negro Education
J of Negro Educ — Journal of Negro Education
J of Negro Hist — Journal of Negro History
J of Phys B At Mol Phys — Journal of Physics. B: Atomic and Molecular Physics
J of Prac App — Journal of Practical Approaches to Developmental Handicap
J of Relig Thought — Journal of Religious Thought
J of Rel Thought — Journal of Religious Thought
J of the L Soc of Scotl — Journal. Law Society of Scotland
JOGEA — Journal of Gerontology
JOGG A — Journal of Geography
JOGL — Journal of Glaciology
JOGM — Jord og Myr. Tidsskrift foer det Norske Jord og Myselskap
JOGNB — JOGN [*Journal of Obstetric, Gynecologic, and Neonatal Nursing*] Nursing
JOGNN — Journal of Obstetric, Gynecologic, and Neonatal Nursing
JOGN Nurs — JOGN [*Journal of Obstetric, Gynecologic, and Neonatal Nursing*] Nursing
Jogtud Koezl — Jogtudomanyi Koezloeny
JOH — Journal of Housing
JOHE — Journal of Health Economics
JOHEA — Journal of Heredity
JOHEEC — Journal of Hepatology
JOHH — Journal of Holistic Health
J Ohio Herpetol Soc — Journal. Ohio Herpetological Society
JOHJ — John O'Hara Journal
John Alexander Monogr Ser Var Phases Thorac Surg — John Alexander Monograph Series on Various Phases of Thoracic Surgery
John Dewey Soc Yrbk — John Dewey Society. Yearbook
John Donne J — John Donne Journal
John Herron Art Inst Bul — John Herron Art Institute. Bulletin
John Innes Bull — John Innes Bulletin

John Innes Hortic Inst Annu Rep — John Innes Horticultural Institution. Annual Report
John Innes Inst Annu Rep — John Innes Institute. Annual Report
John Innes Symp — John Innes Symposium
John Jacob Abel Symp Drug Dev Proc — John Jacob Abel Symposium on Drug Development. Proceedings
John Lawrence Interdiscip Symp Phys Biomed Sci — John Lawrence Interdisciplinary Symposium on the Physical andBiomedical Sciences
John Lee Pratt Int Symp Nutr Manage Food Anim Enhance Prot En — John Lee Pratt International Symposium on Nutrient Management of Food Animals toEmbrace and Protect the Environment
John Mar J Prac & Proc — John Marshall Journal of Practice and Procedure
John Marshall J — John Marshall Journal of Practice and Procedure
John Marshall Jr — John Marshall Journal of Practice and Procedure
John Marshall L Q — John Marshall Law Quarterly
John Marshall LQ — John Marshall Law Quarterly
John Marsh LJ — John Marshall Law Journal
John Marsh LQ — John Marshall Law Quarterly
John Marsh L Rev — John Marshall Law Review
John Mary J — John and Mary's Journal. Dickinson College Friends of the Library
John Rylands Lib Bul — John Rylands Library. Bulletin
Johns H Med — Johns Hopkins Medical Journal
Johns Hopkins Alumni Mag — Johns Hopkins Alumni Magazine
Johns Hopkins APL Tech Dig — Johns Hopkins University. Applied Physics Laboratory. Technical Digest
Johns Hopkins APL Technical Digest — Johns Hopkins University. Applied Physics Laboratory. Technical Digest
Johns Hopkins Appl Phys Lab Tech Dig — Johns Hopkins Applied Physics Laboratory. Technical Digest
Johns Hopkins Cent Alternatives Anim Test Newsl — Johns Hopkins Center for Alternatives to Animal Testing. Newsletter
Johns Hopkins Hosp Bul — Johns Hopkins Hospital Bulletin
Johns Hopkins Hosp Bull — Johns Hopkins Hospital. Bulletin
Johns Hopkins Hosp Rep — Johns Hopkins Hospital Reports
Johns Hopkins M — Johns Hopkins Magazine
Johns Hopkins Mag — Johns Hopkins Magazine
Johns Hopkins Med J — Johns Hopkins Medical Journal
Johns Hopkins Med J Suppl — Johns Hopkins Medical Journal. Supplement
Johns Hopkins Oceanogr Stud — Johns Hopkins Oceanographic Studies
Johns Hopkins Ser in Math Sci — Johns Hopkins Series in the Mathematical Sciences
Johns Hopkins Stud Math Sci — Johns Hopkins Studies in the Mathematical Sciences
Johns Hopkins Univ Appl Phys Lab Spec Rep — Johns Hopkins University. Applied Physics Laboratory. Special Report
Johns Hopkins Univ Appl Phys Lab Tech Dig — Johns Hopkins University. Applied Physics Laboratory. Technical Digest
Johns Hopkins Univ Chesapeake Bay Inst Tech Rept — Johns Hopkins University. Chesapeake Bay Institute. Technical Report
Johns Hopkins Univ Cir — Johns Hopkins University. Circular
Johns Hopkins Univ McCollum Pratt Inst Contrib — Johns Hopkins University. McCollum Pratt Institute. Contribution
Johns Hopkins Univ Stud — Johns Hopkins University. Studies in Historical and Political Science
Johns Hopkins Univ Studies — Johns Hopkins University Studies
Johns Hopkins Univ Studies in Geology — Johns Hopkins University. Studies in Geology
Johns Hopkins Workshop Curr Probl Part Theory Proc — Johns Hopkins Workshop on Current Problems in Particle Theory. Proceedings
Johns H U Stud — Johns Hopkins University. Studies in Historical and Political Science
John Tracy Clin Res Pap — John Tracy Clinic Research Papers
John Updike Newsl — John Updike Newsletter
JOHOA — Journal of Housing
JOHPER — Journal of Health, Physical Education, Recreation
JOHR — Journal of Orissa Historical Research
JoHS — Journal of Hellenic Studies
JOHS — Journal. Organ Historical Society
JOHX — Journal of Homosexuality
JOI — Journal. Oriental Institute
JOIB — Journal. Oriental Institute (Baroda)
JOICA — Journal. Institution of Chemists
Joides J — Joides Journal
JOIDES Journal — Joint Oceanographic Institutions for Deep Earth Sampling. Journal
JoIH — Journal of Indian History
J Oil Col C — Journal. Oil and Colour Chemists' Association
J Oil Colour Chem Ass — Journal. Oil and Colour Chemists' Association
J Oil Colour Chem Assoc — Journal. Oil and Colour Chemists' Association
J Oil Fat Ind — Journal of Oil and Fat Industries
J Oilseeds Res — Journal of Oilseeds Research
J Oil Technol Assoc India — Journal. Oil Technologists' Association of India
J Oil Technol Assoc India (Bombay) — Journal. Oil Technologists' Association of India (Bombay)
J Oil Technol Assoc India (Kanpur India) — Journal. Oil Technologists' Association of India (Kanpur, India)
Joinery Woodwkg Mfr — Joinery and Woodworking Manufacturer
Joining Mater — Joining and Materials
Joining Sci — Joining Sciences
Joint Automat Contr Conf Prepr Tech Pap — Joint Automatic Control Conference. Preprints of Technical Papers
Joint Publ Imp Agric Bur — Joint Publication. Imperial Agricultural Bureaux
JoIS — Journal of Inter-American Studies and World Affairs
Joly — Journal of Interdisciplinary History
JOJAA — Journal of Otolaryngology of Japan

Jo Je S — Journal of Jewish Studies
Jo Jur — Journal of Jurisprudence
JOK — Jahrbuch der Ostasiatischen Kunst
J Okayama Dent Soc — Journal. Okayama Dental Society
J Okayama Med Soc — Journal. Okayama Medical Society
J Okayama Med Soc Suppl — Journal. Okayama Medical Society. Supplement
J Okayama Prefect Agric Exp Sta — Journal of Okayama Prefectural Agricultural Experiment Station/Okayama-KenritsuNogyo Shikenjo Jiho
J Okla Dent Assoc — Journal. Oklahoma Dental Association
J Okla State Dent Assoc — Journal. Oklahoma State Dental Association
J Okla State Med Assoc — Journal. Oklahoma State Medical Association
JOKU — Jokull
JOKUA — Joekull (Reykjavik)
Jol — Journal of Law and Economics
JoL — Journal of Library History
JOL — Journal of Oriental Literature
JOLA — Journal of Library Automation
JOLAB — Journal-Lancet
J Old Athlone Soc — Journal. Old Athlone Society
J Old Wexford Soc — Journal. Old Wexford Society
JoLI — Journal of Long Island History
JOM — Jornal o Medico
JOM — Journal of Management
JOM — Journal of Metals
JoM — Journal of Mississippi History
JOM — Journal of Occupational Medicine
JoMa — Journal of Medieval and Renaissance Studies
JOMA — Journal of Military Assistance
J Oman Stud — Journal of Oman Studies
JoMAS — Journal of Modern African Studies
JOMER — Jewish Observer and Middle East Review
JOMF — Journal of Marriage and the Family
JoMH — Journal of Modern History
JOM J Min — JOM. Journal. Minerals, Metals, and Materials Society
JOM J Occup Med — JOM. Journal of Occupational Medicine
JOML — Journal. Organometallic Chemistry Library
JOMMA — Journal of Mathematics and Mechanics
JOMS — Journal of Oral and Maxillofacial Surgery
JOMSD — Journal of Oral and Maxillofacial Surgery
JOMV — Jahrbuch. Oberoesterreichischer Musealverein
JOMYA — Journal of Meteorology
JoN — Journal of Negro History
J Oncol Pharm Pract — Journal of Oncology Pharmacy Practice
J Oncol Tianjin Med J Suppl — Journal of Oncology. Tianjin Medical Journal. Supplement
JONE — Journal of Nutrition Education
JONEA — Journal of Neurophysiology
JONS — Journal of Northern Studies
J Ont Dent Assoc — Journal. Ontario Dental Association
JONUDL — Journal. American College of Nutrition
Jonxis Lect — Jonxis Lectures
Jony Met Przejsciowych Ukladach Biol Semin Inst Biol Mol UJ — Jony Metali Przejsciowych w Ukladach Biologicznych. SeminariumInstytutu Biologii Molekularnej UJ
Jo O — Jodisk Orientering
JOOEM — Jahrbuch des Oberoesterreichischen Musealvereins
JOOFA — Journal Officiel de la Republique Francaise
JOOM — Journal of Occupational Medicine
JOP — Journal of Occupational Psychology
JoP — Journal of Politics
JOPD — Journal of Psychoactive Drugs
JOPDA — Journal of Pediatrics
J Open Educ Assoc Qld — Journal. Open Education Association of Queensland
J Operational Psychiatr — Journal of Operational Psychiatry
J Operations Res Soc Japan — Journal. Operations Research Society of Japan
J Operator Theory — Journal of Operator Theory
J Oper Brew Guild — Journal. Operative Brewers' Guild
J Oper Res Soc — Journal. Operational Research Society
J Oper Res Soc Am — Journal. Operation Research Society of America
J Oper Res Soc Jap — Journal. Operations Research Society of Japan
JOPHA — Journal de Physiologie
J Ophthalmic Nurs Technol — Journal of Ophthalmic Nursing and Technology
JOPID — Journal of Pipelines
JOPKG — Jahrbuch fuer Ostpreussische Kirchengeschichte
JoPo — Journal of Politics
JoPop — Journal of Popular Culture
JOPP — Journal of Primary Prevention
JOPPA — Journal de Physiologie (Paris). Supplement
JoPr — Journal of Presbyterian History
J Op Res So — Journal. Operations Research Society of Japan
J Op Res Soc — Journal. Operational Research Society
JOPSA — Journal of Psychology
J Opt — Journal of Optics
J Opt Commun — Journal of Optical Communications
J Optical Soc America — Journal of the Optical Society of America
J Optimization Theory Appl — Journal of Optimization Theory and Applications
J Optimiz Theory and Appl — Journal of Optimization Theory and Applications
J Optim Nutr — Journal of Optimal Nutrition
J Optim Th — Journal of Optimization Theory and Applications
J Optim Theory Appl — Journal of Optimization Theory and Applications
J Opt Res — Journal of Optics Research
J Opt Soc — Journal. Optical Society of America
J Opt Soc Am — Journal. Optical Society of America
J Opt Soc Am A — Journal. Optical Society of America. A. Optics and Image Science

J Opt Soc Am B Opt Phys — Journal. Optical Society of America. B. Optical Physics
J Opt Soc Amer — Journal. Optical Society of America
J Opt Soc Am Rev Sci Instrum — Journal. Optical Society of America and Review of Scientific Instruments
J Opt Soc Cum Ind — Journal. Optical Society of America. Cumulative Index
J Opt Soc Korea — Journal of the Optical Society of Korea
J Opt Soc Korea Korean Ed — Journal of the Optical Society of Korea. Korean Edition
JoR — Jorden Runt
JOR — Journal of Organizational Behavior Management
JOR — Journal of Oriental Research
JoR — Journal of Religious History
JORADF — Journal de Radiologie
Jo Radio Law — Journal of Radio Law
J Oral Implantol — Journal of Oral Implantology
J Oral Implant Transplant Surg — Journal of Oral Implant and Transplant Surgery
J Oral Maxillofac Surg — Journal of Oral and Maxillofacial Surgery
J Oral Med — Journal of Oral Medicine
J Oral Pathol — Journal of Oral Pathology
J Oral Pathol Med — Journal of Oral Pathology and Medicine
J Oral Rehabil — Journal of Oral Rehabilitation
J Oral Sci — Journal of Oral Science
J Oral Sci — Journal of Oral Science [*Tokyo*]
J Oral Surg — Journal of Oral Surgery
J Oral Surg Anesth Hosp Dent Serv — Journal of Oral Surgery, Anesthesia, and Hospital Dental Service
J Oral Therap Pharmacol — Journal of Oral Therapeutics and Pharmacology
J Oral Ther Pharmacol — Journal of Oral Therapeutics and Pharmacology
Jordan Dent J — Jordan Dental Journal
Jordan Med J — Jordan Medical Journal
Jordan Minist Agric Annu Rep (Eng Ed) — Jordan. Ministry of Agriculture. Annual Report (English Edition)
Jordan Pln — Five-Year Plan for Economic and Social Development, 1981-85 (Jordan)
Jordbr Blad — Jordbrukerens Blad
Jordbr Ekon Uppg — Jordbruksekonomiska Uppgifter
Jordbr ForBl — Jordbrukarnas Foreningsblad
JordbrForsk — Jordbruks-Forskning
Jordbr J — Jordbruks-Journalen
Jordbr Och Mejeritidn — Jordbruks- och Mejeritidning
Jordbr Tek — Jordbrugs-Teknik
Jordbr Tidn — Jordbrukarens Tidning
Jordbruksekon Meddel — Jordbruksekonomiska Meddelanden
Jordbruksekon Medd Statens Jordbruksnamned — Jordbruksekonomiska Meddelanden. Statens Jordbruksnamned
Jordbrukstek Inst Cirk — Jordbrukstekniska Institutet. Cirkulaer
Jordbundsutv Smaaskr — Jordbundsutvalgets Smaaskrifter
Jord-Ekon Medd — Jordbruksekonomiska Meddelanden
Jord F — Jordens Folk
Jordmagn Publner K Sjokartevk — Jordmagnetiska Publikationer. Kungliga Sjokarteverk
Jord Skog — Jord och Skog
JOREA — Journal of Rehabilitation
JOREDR — Journal of Orthopaedic Research
JOREES — Journal of Oilseeds Research
J Oreg Dent Assoc — Journal. Oregon Dental Association
JORF — Journal Officiel de la Republique Francaise
J Organometal Chem — Journal of Organometallic Chemistry
J Organometallic Chem — Journal of Organometallic Chemistry
J Organomet Chem — Journal of Organometallic Chemistry
J Organomet Chem Libr — Journal. Organometallic Chemistry Library
J Org Chem — Journal of Organic Chemistry
J Org Chem USSR — Journal of Organic Chemistry of the USSR
J Orgl Bhvr Mgt — Journal of Organizational Behavior Management
J Orgl Com — Journal of Organizational Communication
J Orgmet Ch — Journal of Organometallic Chemistry
J Oriental Soc Aust — Journal. Oriental Society of Australia
J Orient Inst (Baroda) — Journal. Oriental Institute (Baroda)
J Orient Med — Journal of Oriental Medicine/Manshu Igaku Zasshi
J Orient Res — Journal of Oriental Research
J Orient Stud — Journal of Oriental Studies
J Or Inst — Journal. Oriental Institute
J Orissa Bot Soc — Journal. Orissa Botanical Society
J Orissa Math Soc — Journal. Orissa Mathematical Society
JORM — Journal of Oriental Research. Madras
Jornada Med — Jornada Medica
Jornadas Agron Trab — Jornadas Agronomicas. Trabajos
Jornadas Agron Vet Univ B Aires — Jornadas Agronomicas y Veterinarias. Universidad de Buenos Aires
Jornadas Agron Vet Univ Buenos Aires Fac Agron Vet — Jornadas Agronomicas y Veterinarias. Universidad de Buenos Aires. Facultad de Agronomia y Veterinaria
Jornadas Argent Kinesiol — Jornadas Argentinas de Kinesiologia
Jornadas Quir — Jornadas Quirurgicas
Jorn Agric Hort Prat — Jornal de Agricultura e Horticultura Pratica
Jorn Agron — Jornal de Agronomia
Jorn Ass Port Urol — Jornal da Associacao Portugueza da Urologia
Jorn Bras Med — Jornal Brasileiro de Medicina
Jorn Bras Neurol — Jornal Brasileiro de Neurologia
Jorn Bras Psicol — Jornal Brasileiro de Psicologia
Jorn Bras Psiquiat — Jornal Brasileiro de Psiquiatria
Jorn Cienc Vet — Jornal de Ciencias Veterinarias
Jorn Estomat — Jornal de Estomatologia
Jorn Farm — Jornal dos Farmaceuticos

Jorn Hort Agric — Jornal Horticolo-Agricola</PHR> %
J Ornithol — Journal fuer Ornithologie
Jorn Med — Jornada Medica
Jorn Med — Jornal do Medico
Jorn Med Cirurg — Jornal de Medicina e Cirurgia
Jorn Med Pernamb — Jornal de Medicina de Pernambuco
Jorn Med Pharm Port — Jornal dos Medicos e Pharmaceuticos Portuguezes
Jorn Metal Hisp Fr — Jornadas Metalurgicas Hispano-Francesas
Jorn Nac Farm Anal Clin Trab — Jornadas Nacionales de Farmaceuticos Analistas Clinicos. Trabajos
Jorn Pediat — Jornal de Pediatria
Jorn Pesc — Jornal de Pescador
Jorn Pharm Chim — Jornal de Pharmacia e Chimica
Jorn Sci Math Astr — Jornal de Sciencias Mathematicas e Astronomicas
Jorn Sci Math Phys Nat — Jornal de Sciencias Mathematicas, Physicas, e Naturaes
Jorn Sci Nat — Jornal de Sciencias Naturais
Jorn Soc Pharm Lusit — Jornal de Sociedade Pharmaceutica Lusitana
Jorn Soc Sci Med Lisb — Jornal da Sociedade das Sciencias Medicas de Lisboa
Jorn Tec Papeleras Trab — Jornadas Tecnicas Papeleras. Trabajos
JORRI — Journal. Operating Room Research Institute
JORS — Journal. Operational Research Society
JORSJ — Journal. Operations Research Society of Japan
J Or Soc Aust — Journal. Oriental Society of Australia
J Or Stud — Journal of Oriental Studies
J Ortho and Sports Phys Ther — Journal of Orthopaedic and Sports Physical Therapy
J Orthod — Journal of Orthodontics
J Orthomol Psychiatry — Journal of Orthomolecular Psychiatry
J Orthop R — Journal of Orthopaedic Research
J Orthop Res — Journal of Orthopaedic Research
J Orthop Sports Phys Ther — Journal of Orthopaedic and Sports Physical Therapy
J Orthop Trauma — Journal of Orthopaedic Trauma
JOS — Jezyki Obce w Szkole
JOS — Journal of Oriental Studies
JOSA — Journal. Optical Society of America
JOSA — Journal. Oriental Society of Australia
JOSAA — Journal. Optical Society of America
Josa Andras Muz Ev — Josa Andras Muzeum Evkoenyve
J Osaka City Med Cent — Journal. Osaka City Medical Center
J Osaka Dent Univ — Journal. Osaka Dental University
J Osaka Ind Univ Nat Sci — Journal. Osaka Industrial University. Natural Sciences
J Osaka Inst Sci Technol Part 1 — Journal. Osaka Institute of Science and Technology. Part 1
J Osaka Med Coll — Journal. Osaka Medical College
J Osaka Odontol Soc — Journal. Osaka Odontological Society
J Osaka Sangyo Univ Nat Sci — Journal. Osaka Sangyo University. Natural Ssciences
J Osaka Univ Dent Sch — Journal. Osaka University Dental School
J Osaka Univ Dent Soc — Journal. Osaka University Dental Society
Josan Zass — Josanpu Zasshi. Japanese Journal for Midwives
JOSH — Job Safety and Health
JOSH — Journal of School Health
JOSHA — Joho Shori
JOSHB — Journal. American Society for Horticultural Science
JOSHB5 — Journal. American Society for Horticultural Science
JOS J Off Stat — JOS. Journal of Official Statistics
J Oslo City Hosp — Journal. Oslo City Hospital
J Osmania Univ — Journal. Osmania University
JoSoc — Journal of Social History
JoSos — Journal of Southeast Asian Studies
JoSou — Journal of Southern History
Jos Shik Daig Kiyo — Josai Shika Daigaku Kiyo. Bulletin of the Josai
J Ost Arch Inst — Jahreshefte des Oesterreichischen Archaeologischen Institutes in Wien
JOstByzGes — Jahrbuch. Oesterreichische Byzantinische Gesellschaft
JOT — Journal of Coatings Technology
JOT — Journal of Taxation
JOT J Oberflaechentech — JOT. Journal fuer Oberflaechentechnik
JOTOD — Journal of Otolaryngology
JOTODX — Journal d'Oto-Rhino-Laryngologie
J Otolaryngol — Journal of Otolaryngology
J Otolaryngol Jpn — Journal of Otolaryngology of Japan
J Oto-Laryngol Soc Aust — Journal. Oto-Laryngological Society of Australia
J Otolaryngol Suppl — Journal of Otolaryngology. Supplement
J Oto-Rhino-Laryngol — Journal d'Oto-Rhino-Laryngologie
J Oto-Rhino-Laryngol Soc Jpn — Journal. Oto-Rhino-Laryngological Society of Japan
JOTPA — Journal of Oral Therapeutics and Pharmacology
J Otto Rank — Journal. Otto Rank Association
J Otto Rank Assoc — Journal. Otto Rank Association
JOU — Jaarboekje van Oud-Utrecht
J Ouest Afr Pharmacol Rech Med — Journal Ouest-Africain de Pharmacologie et de Recherche sur les Medicaments
Jour Acoust Soc — Journal. Acoustical Society of America
Jour Aesthetics and Art Crit — Journal of Aesthetics and Art Criticism
Jour Agr Univ P R Rio Piedras — Journal of Agriculture. University of Puerto Rico (Rio Piedras)
Jour Agr Univ Puerto Rico — Journal of Agriculture. University of Puerto Rico
Jour Am Folklore — Journal of American Folklore
Jour Am Hist — Journal of American History. National Historical Society
Jour Am Inst Archit — Journal. American Institute of Architecture
Jour Am Jud Soc — Journal. American Judicature Society
Jour Am Soc Agron — Journal. American Society of Agronomy

Jour Am Studies — Journal of American Studies
Jour Arnold Arboretum — Journal. Arnold Arboretum
Jour As Soc Nat Hist Bengal — Journal. Asiatic Society of Bengal
Jour Biol Chem — Journal of Biological Chemistry
Jour Bombay Nat Hist Soc — Journal. Bombay Natural History Society
Jour Bot Desvaux — Journal de Botanique, Redige par une Societe de Botanistes (Edited by Desvaux)
Jour Bot Hooker — Journal of Botany (W. J. Hooker, Editor)
Jour Bot Neerl — Journal de Botanique Neerlandaise
Jour Brit Studies — Journal of British Studies
Jour Chemical Educ — Journal of Chemical Education
Jour Chem Physics — Journal of Chemical Physics
Jour Church and State — Journal of Church and State
Jour Comp Leg — Journal. Society of Comparative Legislation
Jour Comp Legis And Internat Law — Journal of Comparative Legistlation and International Law. Society of Comparative Legislation
Jour Conat Law — Journal of Conational Law
Jour Conchyliologie — Journal de Conchyliologie
Jour Conflict Resolution — Journal of Conflict Resolution
Jour Conseil — Journal du Conseil
Jour Contemp Hist — Journal of Contemporary History
Jour Criminal Law — Journal of Criminal Law and Criminology
Jour Crim L — Journal of Criminal Law and Criminology
Jour Crim Law — Journal of Criminal Law, Criminology, and Police Science [*Later, Journal of Criminal Law and Criminology*]
Jour De Bot — Journal de Botanique
Jour de Bot — Journal de Botanique, Redige par une Societe de Botanistes (Edited by Desvaux)
Jour Devel Areas — Journal of Developmental Areas
JourE — Journal de l'Est
Jour Eccl Hist — Journal of Ecclesiastical History
Jour Ecology — Journal of Ecology
Jour Econ and Bus Hist — Journal of Economic and Business History
Jour Econ And Business Hist — Journal of Economic and Business History. Business Historical Society
Jour Econ Hist — Journal of Economic History
JourEd — Journalism Educator
Jour Educ Psychology — Journal of Educational Psychology
Jour Educ Research — Journal of Educational Research. Educational Research Association
Jour Educ Sociology — Journal of Educational Sociology
Jour Farm Hist — Journal of Farm History
Jour Folklore Inst — Journal. Folklore Institute
Jour f Psychol u Neurol — Journal fuer Psychologie und Neurologie
Jour Gemmology — Journal of Gemmology and Proceedings of the Gemmological Association of Great Britain
Jour Geog — Journal of Geography. National Council of Geography Teachers
Jour Geogr Chicago — Journal of Geography (Chicago)
Jour Geol Education — Journal of Geological Education
Jour Glaciology — Journal of Glaciology
Jour Hist Ideas — Journal of the History of Ideas
Jour Hist Med — Journal of the History of Medicine
Jour Hist Phil — Journal of the History of Philosophy
Jour Home Econ — Journal of Home Economics. American Home Economics Association
Jour Human Rel — Journal of Human Relations
Jour Inorganic and Nuclear Chemistry — Journal of Inorganic and Nuclear Chemistry
Jour Inter Am Stud Gainesville Coral Gables — Journal of Inter-American Studies (Gainesville, Florida; Coral Gables, Florida)
Jour Interam Studies — Journal of Interamerican Studies and World Affairs
Jour Jur — Journal of Jurisprudence
Jour Juris — Hall's Journal of Jurisprudence
Jour Jur Sc — Journal of Jurisprudence and Scottish Law Magazine
Jour Land Public Utility Econ — Journal of Land and Public Utility Economics
Jour Law — Journal of Law
Jour Law and Econ — Journal of Law and Economic Development
Jour Legal Ed — Journal of Legal Education
Jour Lib Hist — Journal of Library History [*Later, Journal of Library History, Philosophy, andComparative Librarianship*]
Jour Mammal — Journal of Mammalogy
Jour Miss Hist — Journal of Mississippi History
Jour Mod Hist — Journal of Modern History
Journ — Journalisten
Journ — Journal [*Paris daily*]
Journ Actual Biopharm Clermont Ferrand CR — Journee d'Actualites Biopharmaceutiques de Clermont-Ferrand. Compte Rendu
Journ Adm Com — Journal des Administrations Communales
Journ Afric Soc — Journal. African Society
Journ Agr Univ Puerto Rico — Journal of Agriculture. University of Puerto Rico
Journal Cork Hist Soc — Journal. Cork Historical and Archaeological Society
Journal Greater India Soc — Journal. Greater India Society
Journal Gujarat Research Soc — Journal. Gujarat Research Society
Journal Intern d'Archeol Numism — Journal International d'Archeologie Numismatique
Journalism Conf Workshop ADA — Journalism Conference and Workshop. American Dental Association Council on Journalism and American Association of Dental Editors
Journalism Educ — Journalism Educator
Journalism Q — Journalism Quarterly
Journalism Quar — Journalism Quarterly
Journalism Quart — Journalism Quarterly
Journal Near East Stud — Journal of Near Eastern Studies
Journal of Eg Arch — Journal of Egyptian Archaeology
Journal of RPS — Journal. Royal Photographic Society

Journal Q — Journalism Quarterly
Journal Sadul Rajasthani Research Inst — Journal. Sadul Rajasthani Research Institute
Journal Soc Antiq — Journal. Royal Society of Antiquaries of Ireland
Journal Soc Antiqu Ireland — Journal. Royal Society of Antiquaries of Ireland
Journal Soc Finno-Ougr — Journal. Societe Finno-Ougrienne
Journ Amer Pharm Assoc — Journal. American Pharmaceutical Association
Journ Angeiol Lang Fr — Journees Angeiologiques de Langue Francaise
Journ Annu Diabetol Hotel-Dieu — Journees Annuelles de Diabetologie Hotel-Dieu
Journ Anthr Inst — Journal. Anthropological Institute of Great Britain and Ireland
Journ Anthropology — Journal of Anthropology
Journ Appl Mycol Japan — Journal of Applied Mycology. Hokkaido University/Oyo Kinkagu (Japan)
Journ Arn Arb — Journal. Arnold Arboretum
Journ Asiat — Journal. Asiatic Society of Bengal
Journ Asiat Soc — Journal. Royal Asiatic Society of Great Britain and Ireland
Journ Ass Med Mut — Journal. Association Medicale Mutuelle
Journ Atmos Terr Phys — Journal of Atmospheric and Terrestrial Physics
Journ Be Neur Psych — Journal Belge de Neurologie et de Psychiatrie
Journ Be Radiol — Journal Belge de Radiologie
Journ Be Urol — Journal Belge d'Urologie
Journ Biblical Lit — Journal of Biblical Literature
Journ Bib Lit — Journal of Biblical Literature
Journ Biochem — Journal of Biochemistry
Journ Biochem Micr Tech Eng — Journal of Biochemical and Microbiological Technology and Engineering
Journ Biochim Lat Rapp — Journees Biochimiques Latines. Rapports
Journ Biol Chem — Journal of Biological Chemistry
Journ Biol Inst Univ Seoul Korea — Journal. Biological Institute (Seoul, Korea)
Journ Biophys Biochem Cytol — Journal of Biophysical and Biochemical Cytology
Journbl — Journalistbladet
Journ Bot — Journal of Botany
Journ Bot Appl Agric — Journal de Botanique, Appliquee a l'Agriculture, a la Pharmacie, a la Medecine,et aux Arts
Journ Bot Brit For — Journal of Botany. British and Foreign
Journ Bot Neerland — Journal de Botanique Neerlandaise
Journ Bot Paris — Journal de Botanique (Paris) (Edited by L. Morot)
Journ Br Astr Ass — Journal. British Astronomical Association
Journ Buddh Text Soc — Journal. Buddhist Text Society
Journ Calorim Anal Therm — Journees de Calorimetrie et d'Analyse Thermique
Journ Calorim Anal Therm Prepr — Journees de Calorimetrie et d'Analyse Thermique. Preprints
Journ Calorim Anal Therm Thermodyn Chim — Journees de Calorimetrie et d'Analyse Thermique et de Thermodynamique Chimique
Journ Ceyl Obstet Gyn Ass — Journal. Ceylon Obstetric and Gynaecological Association
Journ Chem Phys — Journal of Chemical Physics
Journ Chem Soc — Journal. Chemical Society
Journ Chim Phys Chim — Journal de Chimie Physique et de Physico-Chimie Biologique
Journ Chin Chem Soc — Journal. Chinese Chemical Society
Journ Chir — Journal de Chirurgie
Journ Clin Ophthal — Journal of Clinical Ophthalmology
Journ Clin Path — Journal of Clinical Pathology
Journ Clin Psychol — Journal of Clinical Psychology
Journ Cons — Conseil Permanent International pour l'Exploration de la Mer. Journal du Conseil
Journ Deb — Journal des Debats
Journ de Bot — Journal de Botanique, Appliquee a l'Agriculture, a la Pharmacie, a la Medecine,et aux Arts
Journ De Bot Desv — Journal de Botanique. Redige par une Societe de Botanistes (Desvaux, Editor)
Journ Depoussierage Fumees Gaz Ind CR — Journee du Depoussierage des Fumees et Gaz Industriels. Compte Rendu
Journ Diabetol Hotel Dieu — Journees de Diabetologie. Hotel-Dieu
Journ Diabetol Vals CR — Journees de Diabetologie de Vals. Comptes Rendus
Journ Eg Arch — Journal of Egyptian Archaeology
Jour Negro Hist — Journal of Negro History
Journ Egypt Arch — Journal of Egyptian Archaeology
Journ Electron — Journees d'Electronique
Journ Electron Microtech — Journees d'Electronique et de Microtechnique
Journ Engl Germ Philol Urbana — Journal of English and Germanic Philology (Urbana)
Journ Etud Flammes Rapp — Journee d'Etudes sur les Flammes. Rapports
Journ Etud Pllut Mar Mediterr — Journee d'Etudes sur les Pollutions Marines en Mediterranee
Journ Fisc — Journal Pratique de Droit Fiscal et Financier
Journ Hell St — Journal of Hellenic Studies
Journ Hell Stud — Journal of Hellenic Studies
Journ Hist Behavioral Sci — Journal of the History of the Behavioral Sciences
Journ Ind Art — Journal of Indian Art
Journ Inf Corps Gras Anim CR — Journees d'Information sur les Corps Gras Animaus. Compte Rendu
Journ Inf Inst Corps Gras — Journees d'Information. Institut des Corps Gras
Journ Int Arch Num — Journal International d'Archeologie Numismatique
Journ Int Etude Groupe Polyphenols Assem Gen — Journees Internationales d'Etude. Groupe Polyphenols et Assemblee Generale
Journ Int GABIM — Journees Internationales du G.A.B.I.M.
Journ Int Groupe Polyphenols — Journees Internationales. Groupe Polyphenols
Journ Int Huiles Essent — Journees Internationales Huiles Essentielles
Journ Int Sider — Journees Internationales de Siderurgie
Journ J Paix — Journal des Juges de Paix
Journ Jur — Journal de Jurisprudence
Journ Landwirtsch — Journal fuer Landwirtschaft

Journ Med Annu Broussais La Charite — Journees Medicales Annuelles de Broussais-La Charite
Journ Med Fr — Journees Medicales de France et de l'Union Francaise
Journ Med Hop Lille — Journees Medicales des Hopitaux de Lille
Journ Metall Hisp Fr — Journees Metallurgiques Hispano-Francaises
Journ Natl Biol CR — Journees Nationales de Biologie. Comptes-Rendus
Journ Natl Compos — Journees Nationales sur les Composites
Journ of Egypt Archaeol — Journal of Egyptian Archaeology
Journ of Exp Med — Journal of Experimental Medicine
Journ of Jur Pap — Journal of Juristic Papyrology
Journ of Phil — Journal of Philology
Journ of Rom Stud — Journal of Roman Studies
Journ of the Ant Inst — Journal. Royal Anthropological Institute of Great Britain and Ireland
Journ Ornithol — Journal fuer Ornithologie
Journ Paris Pediatr — Journees Parisiennes de Pediatrie
Journ Pharm Fr — Journees Pharmaceutiques Francaises
Journ Philology — Journal of Philology
Journ Prakt Chem — Journal fuer Praktische Chemie
Journ Prat Dr Fisc et Fin — Journal Pratique de Droit Fiscal et Financier
Journ Pr Chem — Journal fuer Praktische Chemie
Journ Printemps Mec Ind — Journees de Printemps de la Mecanique Industrielle
Journ Q — Journalism Quarterly
Journ Rech Ovine Caprine — Journees de la Recherche Ovine et Caprine
Journ Rech Porcine Fr — Journees de la Recherche Porcine en France
Journ Rech Porcine Fr CR — Journees de la Recherche Porcine en France. Compte Rendu
Journ Rom St — Journal of Roman Studies
Journ Rom Stud — Journal of Roman Studies
Journ Royal Artill — Journal. Royal Artillery
Journ Roy Geog Soc — Journal. Royal Geographical Society
Journ Sav — Journal des Savants
Journ Sci Cent Natl Coord Etud Rech Nutr Aliment — Journees Scientifiques. Centre National de Coordination des Etudes et Recherches sur la Nutrition et l'Alimentation
Journ Sciences Milit — Journal des Sciences Militaires
Journ Theol Stud — Journal of Theological Studies
Journ Trib — Journal des Tribunaux
Journ Trib Outr — Journal des Tribunaux d'Outre-Mer
Journ Vinic Export — Journee Vinicole Export
Journ Warburg Inst — Journal. Warburg and Courtauld Institutes
Jour of Indian Art and Ind — Journal of Indian Art and Industry
Jour of Int Affairs — Journal of International Affairs
Jour of Relig — Journal of Religion
Jour of Soc Issues — Journal of Social Issues
Jour of West — Journal of the West
Jour Pac Hist — Journal of Pacific History
Jour Palynology — Journal of Palynology
Jour Philos — Journal of Philosophy
Jour Pol Econ — Journal of Political Economy
Jour Politics — Journal of Politics
Jour Presby Hist — Journal of Presbyterian History
Jour Ps Med — Journal of Psychological Medicine and Medical Jurisprudence
Jour Pub Law — Journal of Public Law
Jour Relig Hist — Journal of Religious History
Jour Religion — Journal of Religion
Jour Royal Artillery — Journal of the Royal Artillery. Royal Artillery Institution
Jour Soc Am Paris — Journal. Societe des Americanistes (Paris)
Jour Soc Hist — Journal of Social History
Jour Society Archit Historians — Journal. Society of Architectural Historians
Jour Soc Philos — Journal of Social Philosophy
Jour Soc Sci — Journal of Social Sciences
Jour Speech Disorders — Journal of Speech Disorders
JOUSD — Journal of Science. Busan National University
J Outlook — Jewish Outlook
JOV — Jahrbuch des Oesterreichischen Volksliedwerkes
JOV — Jahrbuch fuer Ostdeutsche Volkskunde
JOWRDN — Journal of Obesity and Weight Regulation
JOYA — Journal of Youth and Adolescence
JOYS — Journal of Youth Services in Libraries
JP — Jahrbuch fuer Philologie
JP — Jerusalem Post
JP — Jet Publications
JP — Jezyk Polski
JP — Journal de Psychologie Normale et Pathologique
JP — Journal of Paleontology
JP — Journal of Parapsychology
JP — Journal of Philology
JP — Journal of Philosophy
JP — Journal of Politics
JP — Journal of Psychology
JP — Juristische Praxis
JP — Justice of the Peace and Local Government Review
JP — Justice of the Peace Reports
JP — Justice of the Peace. Weekly Notes of Cases
JPA — Journal of Policy Analysis and Management
JPA — Jurisprudence du Port D'Anvers
J PA Acad Sci — Journal. Pennsylvania Academy of Science
J Pac Hist — Journal of Pacific History
J Pacif Hist — Journal of Pacific History
J Pacific Hist — Journal of Pacific History
J Paediatr Child Health — Journal of Paediatrics and Child Health
J Paediatr Dent — Journal of Paediatric Dentistry
J Pain Symptom Manage — Journal of Pain and Symptom Management
J Paint Tec — Journal of Paint Technology

J Paint Technol — Journal of Paint Technology
J Paix — Journal de la Paix
JPaix — Journal des Juges de Paix
J Pak Hist Soc — Journal. Pakistan Historical Society
J Pak HS — Journal. Pakistan Historical Society
J Pak Med Ass — Journal. Pakistan Medical Association
J Pak Med Assoc — Journal. Pakistan Medical Association
J Palaegr Soc — Journal. Palaeographical Society
J Paleont — Journal of Paleontology
J Paleontol — Journal of Paleontology
J Pales Stu — Journal of Palestine Studies
J Palest Arab Med Ass — Journal. Palestine Arab Medical Association
J Palestine Stud — Journal of Palestine Studies
J Palestine Studies — Journal of Palestine Studies
J Palliat Care — Journal of Palliative Care
J Palliat Med — Journal of Palliative Medicine
J Palynol — Journal of Palynology
J Palynology — Journal of Palynology
J Palynol Palynol Soc India — Journal of Palynology. Palynological Society of India
JPAMD — Journal of Policy Analysis and Management
JPANDA — Journal of Psychoanalytic Anthropology
J P and L — Journal of Psychiatry and Law
J Pang Med Soc — Journal. Pangasinan Medical Society
J Pan HS — Journal. Panjab Historical Society
J Panjab Hist Soc — Journal of the Panjab Historical Society
JPaOrS — Journal. Palestine Oriental Society
JPAPD — Journal of Experimental Psychology: Animal Behavior Processes
J Papua NG Society — Journal. Papua and New Guinea Society
J Parapsych — Journal of Parapsychology
J Parapsychol — Journal of Parapsychology
J Paras — Journal of Parasitology
J Parasit — Journal of Parasitology
J Parasit Dis — Journal of Parasitic Diseases
J Parasitol — Journal of Parasitology
J Parasitol Appl Anim Biol — Journal of Parasitology and Applied Animal Biology
J Parasitology — Journal of Parasitology
J Par Distr — Journal of Parallel and Distributed Computing
J Parenter Drug Assoc — Journal. Parenteral Drug Association
J Parenter Enteral Nutr — Journal of Parenteral and Enteral Nutrition
J Parenter Sci Technol — Journal of Parenteral Science and Technology
J Paris — Journal de Paris
J Park Rec Adm — Journal of Park and Recreation Administration
J Parlia Info — Journal of Parliamentary Information
J Parodontol — Journal de Parodontologie
J Partial Differential Equations — Journal of Partial Differential Equations
J Partial Differential Equations Ser A — Journal of Partial Differential Equations. Series A
JPASB — Journal and Proceedings. Royal Asiatic Society of Bengal
J Past Care — Journal of Pastoral Care
J Past Coun — Journal of Pastoral Counseling
J Pastoral Care — Journal of Pastoral Care
J Path and Bacteriol — Journal of Pathology and Bacteriology
J Path Bact — Journal of Pathology and Bacteriology
J Pathol — Journal of Pathology
J Pathol Bacteriol — Journal of Pathology and Bacteriology
J Pathology — Journal of Pathology
J Patient Acc Manage — Journal of Patient Account Management
J Pat Off Soc — Journal. Patent Office Society
J Pat Off Soc'y — Journal. Patent Office Society
J Pat Of So — Journal. Patent Office Society
JPAW — Jahrbuch der Preussischen Akademie der Wissenschaften
J PA Water Works Oper Assoc — Journal. Pennsylvania Water Works Operators' Association
JPB — Journal des Poetes (Brussels)
JPBAEB — Journal of Psychopathology and Behavioral Assessment
JPBEA — Journal de Pharmacie de Belgique
JPBPB — Journal of Pharmacokinetics and Biopharmaceutics
JPC — Journal of Pastoral Care
JPC — Journal of Planar Chromatography
JPC — Journal of Popular Culture
JPCAAC — Journal. Air Pollution Control Association
J PCA Res Dev Lab — Journal. PCA (Portland Cement Association, Chicago) Research and Development Laboratories
JPCCA — Journal of Physical and Colloid Chemistry
JPCCC — Journal of the Pakistan Central Cotton Committee
JPCh — Journal fuer Praktische Chemie
JPCMA — Journal of Photochemistry
JPCRB — Journal of Physical and Chemical Reference Data
JPCRD — Journal of Physical and Chemical Reference Data
JPCSB — Journal of Physics and Chemistry of Solids. Supplement
JPCSC — Journal of Physical and Chemical Reference Data. Supplement
JPD — Japan Publishers Directory
JPDAAH — Journal. American Podiatry Association
JPDADK — Journal. Parenteral Drug Association
JPDEA — Journal of Prosthetic Dentistry
JPDF — Journal Pratique de Droit Fiscal et Financier
JPDMB — American Society of Psychosomatic Dentistry and Medicine. Journal
JPDMBK — Journal. American Society of Psychosomatic Dentistry and Medicine
JPDPA — Journal of Periodontology - Periodontics
J PE — Journal of Physical Education and Program
JPE — Journal of Political Economy
JPE — Journal of Politics and Economics
J Peace Res — Journal of Peace Research
J Peace Research — Journal of Peace Research

J Peace Sci — Journal of Peace Science
J PE and Sport Sci — Journal of Physical Education & Sport Sciences
J Peasant Stud — Journal of Peasant Studies
J Peasant Studies — Journal of Peasant Studies
J Peas Stud — Journal of Peasant Studies
J Ped — Jornal de Pediatria
J Ped — Journal of Pediatrics
JPEDD — Journal of Physics Education
J Pediat — Journal of Pediatrics
J Pediat Psychol — Journal of Pediatric Psychology
J Pediatr — Journal of Pediatrics
J Pediatr Adolesc Gynecol — Journal of Pediatric and Adolescent Gynecology
J Pediatr Berlin — Journal of Pediatrics (Berlin)
J Pediatr Encodrinol — Journal of Pediatric Endocrinology
J Pediatr Endocr — Journal of Pediatric Endocrinology
J Pediatr Endocrinol Metab — Journal of Pediatric Endocrinology and Metabolism
J Pediatr Gastroenterol Nutr — Journal of Pediatric Gastroenterology and Nutrition
J Pediatr Hematol Oncol — Journal of Pediatric Hematology/Oncology
J Pediatrics — Journal of Pediatrics
J Pediatr Nurs — Journal of Pediatric Nursing. Nursing Care of Children and Families
J Pediatr Oncol Nurs — Journal of Pediatric Oncology Nursing
J Pediatr Ophthalmol — Journal of Pediatric Ophthalmology
J Pediatr Ophthalmol Strabismus — Journal of Pediatric Ophthalmology and Strabismus
J Pediatr Orthop — Journal of Pediatric Orthopedics
J Pediatr Orthop B — Journal of Pediatric Orthopaedics. Part B
J Pediatr Perinat Nutr — Journal of Pediatric and Perinatal Nutrition
J Pediatr Psychol — Journal of Pediatric Psychology
J Pediatr (St Louis) — Journal of Pediatrics (St. Louis)
J Pediat Surg — Journal of Pediatric Surgery
J Pediat Surg — Journal of Pediatric Surgery
J Pedod — Journal of Pedodontics
J Ped Surg — Journal of Pediatric Surgery
JPEK — Jahrbuch fuer Praehistorische und Ethnographische Kunst
J Peking Natl Univ — Journal. Peking National University/Kuo Li Pei-p'ing Ta Hsueeh Hsueeh Pao
JPEL — Journal of Planning and Environment Law
JPEN — Journal of Parenteral and Enteral Nutrition
J Pendid UKM — Jurnal Pendidikan. Universiti Kebangsaan Malaysia
J Pendid UM — Jurnal Pendidikan. University of Malaya
J Penicillin — Journal of Penicillin
JPEN J Parent Enteral Nutr — JPEN. Journal of Parenteral and Enteral Nutrition
JPEN J Parenter Enteral Nutr — JPEN. Journal of Parenteral and Enteral Nutrition
J Pen Pl and Comp — Journal of Pension Planning and Compliance
J Pension Plan and Compliance — Journal of Pension Planning and Compliance
J Pension Planning and Compliance — Journal of Pension Planning and Compliance
J PE NZ — Journal of Physical Education New Zealand
J Pept Res — Journal of Peptide Research
J Pept Sci — Journal of Peptide Science
JPer — Journal of Personality
J PERD — Journal of Physical Education, Recreation, and Dance
J Perform Constr Facil — Journal of Performance of Constructed Facilities
J Perinat — Journal of Perinatology
J Perinat Med — Journal of Perinatal Medicine
J Perinatol — Journal of Perinatology
J Periodont — Journal of Periodontology
J Periodontal Res — Journal of Periodontal Research
J Periodontal Res Suppl — Journal of Periodontal Research. Supplement
J Periodontol — Journal of Periodontology
J Periodontol-Periodontics — Journal of Periodontology - Periodontics
J Period Re — Journal of Periodontal Research
J Peripher Nerv Syst — Journal of the Peripheral Nervous System
J Perm Way Instn — Permanent Way Institution. Journal
JPers — Journal of Personality
J Pers Asse — Journal of Personality Assessment
J Pers Assess — Journal of Personality Assessment
J Personal — Journal of Personality
J Personal Disord — Journal of Personality Disorders
J Personality & Social Psychol — Journal of Personality and Social Psychology
J Personnel Res — Journal of Personnel Research
J Person Soc Psychol — Journal of Personality and Social Psychology
J Pers Soc — Journal of Personality and Social Psychology
J Pers Soc Psychol — Journal of Personality and Social Psychology
J Perth Hosp — Journal. Perth Hospital
JPESB — Jewish Palestine Exploration Society. Bulletin
J Pestic Reform Publ Northwest Coalition Alternatives Pestic — Journal of Pesticide Reform. A Publication. Northwest Coalition for Alternatives to Pesticides
J Pestic Sci — Journal of Pesticide Science
J Pestic Sci Int Ed — Journal of Pesticide Science (International Edition)
J Pestic Sci (Nihon Noyakugaku Kaishi) — Journal of Pesticide Science (Nihon Noyakugaku Kaishi)
JPET — Journal of Petroleum Technology
J Pet Geol — Journal of Petroleum Geology
J Pet Res — Journal of Petroleum Research
J Petrol — Journal of Petrology
J Petrol Geol — Journal of Petroleum Geology
J Petrol Techn — Journal of Petroleum Technology
J Petrol Technol — Journal of Petroleum Technology
J Petro Tec — Journal of Petroleum Technology
J Pet Sci Eng — Journal of Petroleum Science and Engineering
J Pet Tech — Journal of Petroleum Technology
J Pet Technol — Journal of Petroleum Technology

JPF — Journal of Popular Film [*Later, Journal of Popular Film and Television*]
JPFAEV — Journal of Psychotherapy and the Family
JPFB — Jahrbuch der Philosophischen Fakultaet Bonn
JPFF — Journal Pratique de Droit Fiscal et Financier
JPFMA — Journal of Physics. F: Metal Physics
JPGED — Journal of Experimental Psychology: General
JPGR — Journal of Plant Growth Regulation
JPH — Journal of Pacific History
JPh — Journal of Philology
JPh — Journal of Philosophy
JPh — Journal of Phonetics
J Ph — Journal of Physiology
JPH — Journal of Presbyterian History
JPHAA — Journal. American Pharmaceutical Association
JPHAA3 — Journal. American Pharmaceutical Association
JPHAC — Journal of Physics. A: Mathematical and General
J Phar Biop — Journal of Pharmacokinetics and Biopharmaceutics
J Pharm — Journal de Pharmacie
J Pharmacobio-Dyn — Journal of Pharmacobio-Dynamics
J Pharmacokinet Biopharm — Journal of Pharmacokinetics and Biopharmaceutics
J Pharmacokinet Pharmacodyn — Journal of Pharmacokinetics and Pharmacodynamics
J Pharmacol — Journal de Pharmacologie
J Pharmacol Clin — Journal de Pharmacologie Clinique
J Pharmacol Exper Therap — Journal of Pharmacology and Experimental Therapeutics
J Pharmacol Exp Ther — Journal of Pharmacology and Experimental Therapeutics
J Pharmacol Methods — Journal of Pharmacological Methods
J Pharmacol (Paris) — Journal de Pharmacologie (Paris)
J Pharmacol Toxicol Methods — Journal of Pharmacological and Toxicological Methods
J Pharm (Antwerp) — Journal de Pharmacie (Antwerp)
J Pharm Assoc Hyogo — Journal of Pharmaceutical Association of Hyogo
J Pharm Assoc Siam — Journal. Pharmaceutical Association of Siam
J Pharm Assoc Thailand — Journal. Pharmaceutical Association of Thailand
J Pharm B — Journal of Pharmaceutical and Biomedical Analysis
J Pharm Belg — Journal de Pharmacie de Belgique
J Pharm Biomed Anal — Journal of Pharmaceutical and Biomedical Analysis
J Pharm Chim — Journal de Pharmacie et de Chimie
J Pharm Clin — Journal de Pharmacie Clinique
J Pharm Els Lothr — Journal der Pharmazie von Elsass-Lothringen
J Pharm Exp — Journal of Pharmacology and Experimental Therapeutics
J Pharm Exp Ther — Journal of Pharmacology and Experimental Therapeutics
J Pharm (Lahore) — Journal of Pharmacy (Lahore)
J Pharm (Paris) — Journal de Pharmacie et des Sciences Accessoires (Paris)
J Pharm Pha — Journal of Pharmacy and Pharmacology
J Pharm Pharmac — Journal of Pharmacy and Pharmacology
J Pharm Pharmacol — Journal of Pharmacy and Pharmacology
J Pharm Pharmacol Suppl — Journal of Pharmacy and Pharmacology. Supplement
J Pharm Pharm Sci — Journal of Pharmacy & Pharmaceutical Sciences
J Pharm Res Dev — Journal of Pharmaceutical Research and Development
J Pharm Sc — Journal of Pharmaceutical Sciences
J Pharm Sci — Journal of Pharmaceutical Sciences
J Pharm Sci Accessoires — Journal de Pharmacie et des Sciences Accessoires
J Pharm Sci (Ankara) — Journal of Pharmaceutical Sciences (Ankara)
J Pharm Sci Mahidol Univ — Journal of Pharmaceutical Sciences. Mahidol University
J Pharm Sci Technol — Journal of Pharmaceutical Science and Technology
J Pharm Sci Technol Jpn — Journal of Pharmaceutical Science and Technology (Japan)
J Pharm Sci UAR — Journal of Pharmaceutical Sciences of the United Arab Republic
J Pharm Soc Hyogo — Journal. Pharmaceutical Society of Hyogo
J Pharm Soc Jap — Journal. Pharmaceutical Society of Japan
J Pharm Soc Japan — Journal. Pharmaceutical Society of Japan
J Pharm Soc Jpn — Journal. Pharmaceutical Society of Japan
J Pharm Soc Korea — Journal. Pharmaceutical Society of Korea
J Pharm Soc Pilani — Journal of Pharmaceutical Society. Pilani
J Pharm Technol — Journal of Pharmacy Technology
J Pharm Univ Karachi — Journal of Pharmacy. University of Karachi
J Pharm Univ Marmara — Journal of Pharmacy of University of Marmara
J Pharm Yaba Niger — Journal of Pharmacy (Yaba, Nigeria)
J Phase Equilibr — Journal of Phase Equilibria
J Phase Equilibria — Journal of Phase Equilibria
J Ph Ch Ref Data — Journal of Physical and Chemical Reference Data
JPHD — Journal of Public Health Dentistry
J Phenomen — Journal of Phenomenological Psychology
JPHGB — Journal of Physics. G: Nuclear Physics
J Ph GUW — Jahrbuch der Philosophischen Gesellschaft an der Universitaet Wien
J Phil — Journal of Philosophy
J Phila Assoc Psychoanal — Journal. Philadelphia Association for Psychoanalysis
J Phila Cty Dent Soc — Journal. Philadelphia County Dental Society
J Philadelphia Coll Pharm — Journal. Philadelphia College of Pharmacy
J Philadelphia Gen Hosp — Journal. Philadelphia General Hospital
J Phil Dev — Journal of Philippine Development
J Phil Educ — Journal of Philosophy of Education
J Philipp Dent Assoc — Journal. Philippine Dental Association
J Philipp Fed Priv Med Pract — Journal. Philippine Federation of Private Medical Practitioners
J Philippine Development — Journal of Philippine Development
J Philippine MA — Journal. Philippine Medical Association
J Philippine Statis — Journal of Philippine Statistics
J Philipp Isl Med Assoc — Journal. Philippine Islands Medical Association
J Philipp Med Assoc — Journal. Philippine Medical Association

J Philipp Pharm Assoc — Journal. Philippine Pharmaceutical Association
J Philipp Vet Med Assoc — Journal. Philippine Veterinary Medical Association
J Phil Log — Journal of Philosophical Logic
J Phil Logic — Journal of Philosophical Logic
J Phil Med Assoc — Journal of the Philippine Medical Association
J Philos — Journal of Philosophy
J Philos Lo — Journal of Philosophical Logic
J Philos Logic — Journal of Philosophical Logic
J Philos Sport — Journal of the Philosophy of Sport
J Philos Stud — Journal of Philosophical Studies
J Phil Sport — Journal of the Philosophy of Sport
J Phil Stat — Journal of Philippine Statistics
J Phil Stud — Journal of Philosophical Studies
J Phm — Journal de Pharmacie et des Sciences Accessoires
JPHMD — Journal of Experimental Psychology: Human Learning and Memory
JPhon — Journal of Phonetics
J Photoacoust — Journal of Photoacoustics
J Photochem — Journal of Photochemistry
J Photochem Etching — Journal of Photochemical Etching
J Photochem Photobiol A — Journal of Photochemistry and Photobiology. A. Chemistry
J Photochem Photobiol B — Journal of Photochemistry and Photobiology. B. Biology
J Photogr Sci — Journal of Photographic Science
J Photogr Soc Am — Journal. Photographic Society of America
J Photomicrogr Soc — Journal. Photomicrographic Society
J Photopolym Sci Technol — Journal of Photopolymer Science and Technology
J Photosci — Journal of Photoscience
J Phot Sci — Journal of Photographic Science
J Phot Soc — Journal of the Photographic Society
J Phot Soc Amer — Journal. Photographic Society of America
J Ph P — Journal of Philosophy, Psychology, and Scientific Methods
JPHP — Journal of Public Health Policy
JPHPD — Journal of Experimental Psychology: Human Perception and Performance
JPHS — Journal of the Pakistan Historical Society
JPHS — Journal. Presbyterian Historical Society
JPHS — Pakistan Historical Society. Journal
JPHS — Punjab Historical Society. Journal
JPHSE — Journal of Presbyterian Historical Society of England
JPHSESP — Journal of Presbyterian Historical Society of England. Special Publication
J Ph ST — Jahrbuch fuer Philosophie und Spekulative Theologie
J Ph ST E — Jahrbuch fuer Philosophie und Spekulative Theologie. Ergaenungsheft
JPhV — Jahresbericht des Philologischen Vereins
JPhV — Jahresbericht. Philologischer Verein
J Phy — Journal de Physique, de Chimie, d'Histoire Naturelle, et des Arts
JPHYA — Journal of Physiology
J Phycol — Journal of Phycology
J Phycology — Journal of Phycology
J Phys — Journal de Physique
J Phys — Journal of Physics
J Phys — Journal of Physiology
J Phys 1 Phys Gen Phys Stat — Journal de Physique 1. Physique Generale, Physique Statistique, Matiere Condensee, Domaines Interdisciplinaires
J Phys 2 Phys At Mol Phys Chim — Journal de Physique 2. Physique Atomique et Moleculaire, Physico-Chimie, Mecanique et Hydrodynamique
J Phys 3 Phys Appl Sci Mater — Journal de Physique 3. Physique Applique, Science des Materiaux, Fluides, Plasmas et Instrumentation
J Phys A — Journal of Physics. A: Mathematical and General
J Phys A Gen Phys — Journal of Physics. A: General Physics
J Phys A (London) — Journal of Physics. A: General Physics (London)
J Phys A (London) Math Gen — Journal of Physics. A: Mathematical and General (London)
J Phys A (London) Proc Phys Soc Gen — Journal of Physics. A: Proceedings. Physical Society. General (London)
J Phys A Math Gen — Journal of Physics. A. Mathematical and General
J Phys A Math Nucl Gen — Journal of Physics. A: Mathematical, Nuclear, and General
J Phys & Chem Ref Data — Journal of Physical and Chemical Reference Data
J Phys and Chem Solids — Journal of Physics and Chemistry of Solids
J Phys & Colloid Chem — Journal of Physical and Colloid Chemistry
J Phys B — Journal of Physics. B: Atomic and Molecular Physics
J Phys Bangalore India — Journal of Physics (Bangalore, India)
J Phys B At Mol Opt Phys — Journal of Physics B. Atomic, Molecular, and Optical Physics
J Phys B (London) — Journal of Physics. B: Atomic and Molecular Physics (London)
J Phys B Proc Phys Soc At Mol — Journal of Physics. B. Proceedings. Physical Society. Atomic and Molecular Physics
J Phys C — Journal of Physics. C: Solid State Physics
J Phys Chem — Journal of Physical Chemistry
J Phys Chem A — Journal of Physical Chemistry A. Molecules, Spectroscopy, Kinetics, Environment, and General Theory
J Phys Chem B — Journal of Physical Chemistry B. Materials, Surfaces, Interfaces, and Biophysical
J Phys Chem Earth Sci — Journal of Physics, Chemistry, and Earth Science
J Phys Chem Moscow — Journal fuer Physikalische Chemie (Moscow)
J Phys Chem Moscow — Journal of Physical Chemistry (Moscow)
J Phys Chem Niigata — Journal of Physics and Chemistry of Niigata
J Phys Chem Ref Data — Journal of Physical and Chemical Reference Data
J Phys Chem Ref Data Monogr — Journal of Physical and Chemical Reference Data. Monograph
J Phys Chem Ref Data Suppl — Journal of Physical and Chemical Reference Data. Supplement
J Phys Chem Sol — Journal of Physics and Chemistry of Solids

J Phys Chem Solids — Journal of Physics and Chemistry of Solids
J Phys Chem Solids Lett Sect — Journal of Physics and Chemistry of Solids. Letters Section
J Phys Chem Solids Suppl — Journal of Physics and Chemistry of Solids. Supplement
J Phys Chem (Wash) — Journal of Physical Chemistry (Washington, DC)
J Phys Chim Hist Nat Arts — Journal de Physique, de Chimie, d'Histoire Naturelle, et des Arts
J Phys Ch S — Journal of Physics and Chemistry of Solids
J Phys C (London) — Journal of Physics. C: Solid State Physics (London)
J Phys Coll Chem — Journal of Physical and Colloid Chemistry
J Phys Colloq — Journal de Physique. Colloque
J Phys-Cond — Journal of Physics. Condensed Matter
J Phys Condens Matter — Journal of Physics. Condensed Matter
J Phys C Proc Phys Soc Solid — Journal of Physics. C. Proceedings. Physical Society. Solid State Physics
J Phys C Solid State Phys — Journal of Physics. C: Solid State Physics
J Phys C Suppl — Journal of Physics. C. Solid State Physics. Supplement
J Phys D Appl Phys — Journal of Physics. D: Applied Physics
J Phys D (London) — Journal of Physics. D: Applied Physics (London)
J Phys E — Journal of Physics. E: Scientific Instruments
J Phys Earth — Journal of Physics of the Earth
J Phys Ed — Journal of Physical Education
J Phys Educ — Journal of Physical Education
J Phys Educ & Rec — Journal of Physical Education and Recreation [*Later, Journal of Physical Education, Recreation, and Dance*]
J Phys Educ Rec & Dance — Journal of Physical Education, Recreation, and Dance
J Phys Educ Recr — Journal of Physical Education and Recreation [*Later, Journal of Physical Education, Recreation, and Dance*]
J Phys E (London) Sci Instrum — Journal of Physics. E: Scientific Instruments (London)
J Phys E Sci Instrum — Journal of Physics. E: Scientific Instruments
J Phys F — Journal of Physics. F: Metal Physics
J Phys Fitness Nutr Immunol — Journal of Physical Fitness, Nutrition, and Immunology
J Phys F Met Phys — Journal of Physics. F: Metal Physics
J Phys G — Journal of Physics. G: Nuclear Physics
J Phys G Nu — Journal of Physics. G: Nuclear Physics
J Phys G Nucl Part Phys — Journal of Physics. G. Nuclear and Particle Physics
J Phys G Nucl Phys — Journal of Physics. G. Nuclear Physics
J Phys I — Journal de Physique I. General Physics, Statistical Physics, Condensed Matter, Cross-Disciplinary Physics
J Physical Chem — Journal of Physical Chemistry
J Phys II — Journal de Physique II. Atomic, Molecular and Cluster Physics, Chemical Physics, Mechanics, and Hydrodynamics
J Phys III — Journal de Physique III. Applied Physics, Materials Science, Fluids, Plasma, and Instrumentation
J Physiol — Journal of Physiology
J Physiol Anthropol Appl Human Sci — Journal of Physiological Anthropology and Applied Human Science
J Physiol Biochem — Journal of Physiology and Biochemistry
J Physiol Cambridge UK — Journal of Physiology (Cambridge, United Kingdom)
J Physiol et Path Gen — Journal de Physiologie et de Pathologie Generale
J Physiol Exper — Journal de Physiologie Experimentale et Pathologique
J Physiol (Lond) — Journal of Physiology (London)
J Physiol (London) — Journal of Physiology (London)
J Physiol (Paris) — Journal de Physiologie (Paris)
J Physiol Paris — Journal of Physiology. Paris
J Physiol (Paris) Suppl — Journal de Physiologie (Paris). Supplement
J Physiol Pathol Gen — Journal de Physiologie et de Pathologie Generale
J Physiol Pharmacol — Journal of Physiology and Pharmacology
J Physiol Soc Jpn — Journal. Physiological Society of Japan
J Physique — Journal de Physique
J Physique I — Journal de Physique. I. Physique Generale, Physique Statistique, Matiere Condensee Domaines Interdisciplinaires
J Physique IV — Journal de Physique IV
J Phys IV — Journal de Physique IV
J Phys Jap — Journal. Physical Society of Japan
J Phys (Les Ulis Fr) — Journal de Physique (Les Ulis, France)
J Phys Lett — Journal de Physique. Lettres
J Physl (Lon) — Journal de Physiologie (London)
J Physl (Par) — Journal de Physiologie (Paris)
J Phys (Moscow) — Journal of Physics (Moscow)
J Phys Ocea — Journal of Physical Oceanography
J Phys Oceanogr — Journal of Physical Oceanography
J Phys Org Chem — Journal of Physical Organic Chemistry
J Phys (Orsay Fr) — Journal de Physique (Orsay, France)
J Phys (Paris) — Journal de Physique (Paris)
J Phys (Paris) Colloq — Journal de Physique (Paris). Colloque
J Phys (Paris) Lett — Journal de Physique. Lettres (Paris)
J Phys (Paris) Suppl — Journal de Physique (Paris). Supplement
J Phys Rad — Journal de Physique et le Radium
J Phys Radium — Journal de Physique et le Radium
J Phys Radium Phys Appl — Journal de Physique et le Radium. Physique Appliquee
J Phys Sci — Journal of Physical Science
J Phys (Soc Fr Phys) Colloq — Journal de Physique (Societe Francaise de Physique). Colloque
J Phys Soc Jap — Journal. Physical Society of Japan
J Phys Soc Jpn — Journal. Physical Society of Japan
J Phys Soc Jpn Suppl — Journal. Physical Society of Japan. Supplement
J Phys Stud — Journal of Physical Studies
J Phys Theor Appl — Journal de Physique Theorique et Appliquee
J Phys (USSR) — Journal of Physics (USSR)

J Phys Uzb — Journal of Physics of Uzbekistan
J Phytol Res — Journal of Phytological Research
J Phytopathol — Journal of Phytopathology
J Phytopathol (Berl) — Journal of Phytopathology (Berlin)
J Phytopathol (UAR) — Journal of Phytopathology (UAR)
JPI — Journal of Product Innovation Management
JPIFAN — Japan Pesticide Information
JPIM — Journal of Product Innovation Management
J Pineal Res — Journal of Pineal Research
J Pipeline Div Am Soc Civ Eng — Journal. Pipeline Division. American Society of Civil Engineers
J Pipelines — Journal of Pipelines
JP/J — Journal of Psychology and Judaism
JPJ — Justice of the Peace. Weekly Notes of Cases
JPJo — Justice of the Peace. Weekly Notes of Cases
JPJu — Journal of Psychology and Judaism
JPK — Jahrbuch der Preussischen Kunstsammlung
JPKS — Jahrbuch. Preussische Kunstsammlungen
JPL — Journal of Parasitology (Lancaster, Pennsylvania)
JPL — Journal of Philosophical Logic
J P L — Journal of Planning Law
JPL — Journal of Products Liability
J Plan & Environ L — Journal of Planning and Environment Law
J Plan & Prop L — Journal of Planning and Property Law
J Planar Chromatogr Mod TLC — Journal of Planar Chromatography-Modern TLC
J Plan Envir Law — Journal of Planning and Environment Law
J Planif Develop — Journal de la Planification du Developpement
J Plankton Res — Journal of Plankton Research
J Plann Environ Law — Journal of Planning and Environment Law
J Planning and Environment Law — Journal of Planning and Environment Law
J Plann Property Law — Journal of Planning and Property Law
J Plant Anat Morphol (Jodhpur) — Journal of Plant Anatomy and Morphology (Jodhpur)
J Plant Biochem Biotechnol — Journal of Plant Biochemistry and Biotechnology
J Plant Biol — Journal of Plant Biology
J Plant Breed — Journal of Plant Breeding
J Plant Crops — Journal of Plantation Crops
J Plant Dis Prot — Journal of Plant Diseases and Protection
J Plant Foods — Journal of Plant Foods
J Plant Growth Regul — Journal of Plant Growth Regulation
J Plantn Crops — Journal of Plantation Crops
J Plant Nut — Journal of Plant Nutrition
J Plant Nutr — Journal of Plant Nutrition
J Plant Nutr Soil Sci — Journal of Plant Nutrition and Soil Science
J Plant Pathol — Journal of Plant Pathology
J Plant Physiol — Journal of Plant Physiology
J Plant Prot — Journal of Plant Protection
J Plant Prot Res — Journal of Plant Protection Research
J Plant Prot Suwon Korea — Journal of Plant Protection (Suwon, Korea)
J Plant Prot Trop — Journal of Plant Protection in the Tropics
J Plant Resour Environ — Journal of Plant Resources and Environment
J Plas Age — Japan Plastics Age
J Plasma Ph — Journal of Plasma Physics
J Plasma Phys — Journal of Plasma Physics
J Plast An — Japan Plastics Industry Annual
J Plast Film Sheeting — Journal of Plastic Film and Sheeting
J Plast Reconstr Surg Nurs — Journal of Plastic and Reconstructive Surgical Nursing
J Platn Crops — Journal of Plantation Crops
J Playing Card Soc — Journal of the Playing Card Society
J Pl L — Journal of Planning Law
J Pl Pth Gen — Journal de Physiologie et de Pathologie Generale
JPL Publ — JPL (Jet Propulsion Laboratory) Publication
JPL Publ 78 — Jet Propulsion Laboratory. Publication 78
JPL Q Tech Rev — JPL [*Jet Propulsion Laboratory*] Quarterly Technical Review
JPLSA — Journal. Polarographic Society
JPL Space Programs Summ — Jet Propulsion Laboratory. Space Programs Summary
JPL Tech Memo — JPL [*Jet Propulsion Laboratory*] Technical Memorandum
JPL Tech Rep — JPL [*Jet Propulsion Laboratory*] Technical Report
JPM — Janus Pannonius Muezeum Evkoenyve
JPM — Jerusalem Post Magazine
JPM — Journal of Portfolio Management
JPM — Journal of Property Management
JPM — Journal of Purchasing and Materials Management
JPM — Personnel Management
JPMA — Journal of the Pakistan Medical Association
JPMA J Pak Med Assoc — JPMA. Journal. Pakistan Medical Association
JPME — Janus Pannonius Muezeum Evkoenyve
JPMEA — Journal. Philippine Medical Association
JPMSA — Journal of Pharmaceutical Sciences
JPN — Journal of Personal Selling and Sales Management
Jpn Agric Res Q — Japan Agricultural Research Quarterly
Jpn Anal Annu Rev — Japan Analyst. Annual Review
Jpn Analyst — Japan Analyst
Jpn Annu Rev Electron Comput Telecommun — Japan Annual Reviews in Electronics, Computers, and Telecommunications
Jpn Antarct Res Exped Data Rep — Japanese Antarctic Research Expedition. Data Reports
Jpn Antarct Res Exped Sci Rep Ser C — Japanese Antarctic Research Expedition. Scientific Reports. Series C. Geology
Jpn Antarct Res Exped Sci Rep Ser D — Japanese Antarctic Research Expedition. Scientific Reports. Series D. Oceanography
Jpn Arch Histol — Japanese Archives of Histology
Jpn Arch Intern Med — Japanese Archives of Internal Medicine

Jpn Archit — Japan Architect
Jpn Assoc Anim Cell Technol Annu Meet — Japanese Association for Animal Cell Technology. Annual Meeting
Jpn Assoc Fire Sci Eng J — Japanese Association of Fire Science and Engineering. Journal
Jpn Assoc Ion Exch J — Japan Association of Ion Exchange. Journal
Jpn At Energy Res Inst Annu Rep Acc — Japan. Atomic Energy Research Institute. Annual Report and Account
Jpn At Energy Res Inst Rep JAERI-M — Japan Atomic Energy Research Institute. Report JAERI-M
Jpn At Energy Res Inst Rep Res Rep — Japan. Atomic Energy Research Institute. Report. Research Report
Jpn Cancer Assoc Gann Monogr — Japanese Cancer Association. Gann Monograph
Jpn Chem Anal Cent Rep — Japan Chemical Analysis Center. Report
Jpn Chem Annu — Japan Chemical Annual
Jpn Chem Fibres Mon — Japan Chemical Fibres Monthly
Jpn Chem Ind — Japan Chemical Industry
Jpn Chem Ind Assoc Mon — Japan Chemical Industry Association Monthly
Jpn Chem Pharm J — Japanese Chemical Pharmaceutical Journal
Jpn Chem Q — Japan Chemical Quarterly
Jpn Chem Rev — Japan Chemical Review
Jpn Chem Week — Japan Chemical Week
Jpn Chin Symp Coagulation Fibrinolysis Platelets — Japanese-Chinese Symposium on Coagulation, Fibrinolysis, and Platelets
Jpn Circ J — Japanese Circulation Journal
Jpn Clin — Japanese Clinics
Jpn Conf Liq Atomisation Spray Syst — Japan Conference on Liquid Atomisation and Spray System
Jpn Dent J — Japanese Dental Journal
Jpn Dtsch Med Ber — Japanisch-Deutsche Medizinische Berichte
Jpn Eco A — Japan Economic Almanac
Jpn Econ J — Japan Economic Journal
Jpn Elec I — Japan Electronics Industry
Jpn Electron Eng — Japan Electronic Engineering
Jpn Electro Opt Lab JEOL News — Japan Electron Optics Laboratory. JEOL News
Jpn Energy Technol Intell — Japan Energy and Technology Intelligence
Jpn Export — Export Statistical Schedule (Japan)
Jpn Fine Ceram Cent Rev — Japan Fine Ceramics Center Review
Jpn Finish — Japan Finishing
Jpn Food Sci — Japan Food Science
Jpn Forcst — Five-Year Economic Forecast (Japan)
Jpn Foundrymens Soc Trans — Japan Foundrymen's Society. Transactions
Jpn Fr Semin Compos Mater — Japan-France Seminar on Composite Materials
Jpn Fudo Saiensu — Japan Fudo Saiensu
Jpn Gas Assoc J — Japan Gas Association. Journal
Jpn-Ger Med Rep — Japan-Germany Medical Reports
Jpn Heart J — Japanese Heart Journal
Jpn Hosp — Japan Hospitals
Jpn Import — Import Statistical Schedule (Japan)
Jpn Ind Technol Assoc Nyusu — Japan Industrial Technology Association Nyusu
Jpn Ind Technol Bull — Japan Industrial and Technological Bulletin
Jpn Italy Jt Symp Heavy Ion Phys — Japan-Italy Joint Symposium on Heavy Ion Physics
Jp Niv — Jurisprudence des Tribunaux de l'Arrondissement de Nivelles
Jpn J Aerosp Environ Med — Japanese Journal of Aerospace and Environmental Medicine
Jpn J Aerosp Med Psychol — Japanese Journal of Aerospace Medicine and Psychology
Jpn J Alcohol Stud & Drug Depend — Japanese Journal of Alcohol Studies and Drug Dependence
Jpn J Allergol — Japanese Journal of Allergology
Jpn J Allergy — Japanese Journal of Allergy
Jpn J Anesthesiol — Japanese Journal of Anesthesiology
Jpn J Anim Reprod — Japanese Journal of Animal Reproduction
Jpn J Antibiot — Japanese Journal of Antibiotics
Jpn J Appl Entomol Zool — Japanese Journal of Applied Entomology and Zoology
Jpn J Appl Phys — Japanese Journal of Applied Physics
Jpn J Appl Phys 1 — Japanese Journal of Applied Physics. Part 1
Jpn J Appl Phys 2 Lett — Japanese Journal of Applied Physics. Part 2. Letters
Jpn J Appl Phys Part 1 — Japanese Journal of Applied Physics. Part 1. Regular Papers and Short Notes
Jpn J Appl Phys Part 2 — Japanese Journal of Applied Physics. Part 2. Letters
Jpn J Appl Phys Part 2 Letter — Japanese Journal of Applied Physics. Part 2. Letters
Jpn J Appl Phys Suppl — Japanese Journal of Applied Physics. Supplement
Jpn J Artif Organs — Japanese Journal of Artificial Organs
Jpn J Astron — Japanese Journal of Astronomy
Jpn J Astron Geophys — Japanese Journal of Astronomy and Geophysics
Jpn J Bacteriol — Japanese Journal of Bacteriology
Jpn J Biochem Exercise — Japanese Journal of Biochemistry of Exercise
Jpn J Bot — Japanese Journal of Botany
Jpn J Brain Physiol — Japanese Journal of Brain Physiology
Jpn J Breed — Japanese Journal of Breeding
Jpn J Burn Inj — Japan Journal of Burn Injuries
Jpn J Cancer Clin — Japanese Journal of Cancer Clinics
Jpn J Cancer Res — Japanese Journal of Cancer Research
Jpn J Cancer Res (Gann) — Japanese Journal of Cancer Research (Gann)
Jpn J Chem — Japanese Journal of Chemistry
Jpn J Chemother — Japanese Journal of Chemotherapy
Jpn J Chest Dis — Japanese Journal of Chest Diseases
Jpn J Child Adoles Psychiatry — Japanese Journal of Child and Adolescent Psychiatry
Jpn J Clin Chem — Japanese Journal of Clinical Chemistry

Jpn J Clin Electron Microsc — Japanese Journal of Clinical Electron Microscopy
Jpn J Clin Exp Med — Japanese Journal of Clinical and Experimental Medicine
Jpn J Clin Hematol — Japanese Journal of Clinical Hematology
Jpn J Clin Med — Japanese Journal of Clinical Medicine
Jpn J Clin Oncol — Japanese Journal of Clinical Oncology
Jpn J Clin Ophthalmol — Japanese Journal of Clinical Ophthalmology
Jpn J Clin Pathol — Japanese Journal of Clinical Pathology
Jpn J Clin Pathol Suppl — Japanese Journal of Clinical Pathology. Supplement
Jpn J Clin Pharmacol — Japanese Journal of Clinical Pharmacology
Jpn J Clin Pharmacol Ther — Japanese Journal of Clinical Pharmacology and Therapeutics
Jpn J Clin Radiol — Japanese Journal of Clinical Radiology
Jpn J Clin Urol — Japanese Journal of Clinical Urology
Jpn J Const Med — Japanese Journal of Constitutional Medicine
Jpn J Crop Sci — Japanese Journal of Crop Science
Jpn J Dairy Food Sci — Japanese Journal of Dairy and Food Science
Jpn J Dairy Sci — Japanese Journal of Dairy Science
Jpn J Dent Health — Japanese Journal of Dental Health
Jpn J Dermatol — Japanese Journal of Dermatology
Jpn J Dermatol Ser B — Japanese Journal of Dermatology. Series B
Jpn J Dermatol Ser B (Engl Ed) — Japanese Journal of Dermatology. Series B (English Edition)
Jpn J Dermatol Urol — Japanese Journal of Dermatology and Urology
Jpn J Dermatol Venereol — Japanese Journal of Dermatology and Venereology
Jpn J Deuterium Sci — Japanese Journal of Deuterium Science
Jpn J Dev Pharmacol Ther — Japanese Journal of Developmental Pharmacology and Therapeutics
Jpn J Ecol — Japanese Journal of Ecology
Jpn J Endocrinology — Japanese Journal of Endocrinology
Jpn J Eng Abstr — Japanese Journal of Engineering. Abstracts
Jpn J Ergonomics — Japanese Journal of Ergonomics
Jpn J Ethnol — Japanese Journal of Ethnology
Jpn J Exp Med — Japanese Journal of Experimental Medicine
Jpn J Exp Morphol — Japanese Journal of Experimental Morphology
Jpn J Fertil Steril — Japanese Journal of Fertility and Sterility
Jpn J Food Chem — Japanese Journal of Food Chemistry
Jpn J Food Microbiol — Japanese Journal of Food Microbiology
Jpn J Forensic Toxicol — Japanese Journal of Forensic Toxicology
Jpn J Freezing Drying — Japanese Journal of Freezing and Drying
Jpn J Gastroenterol — Japanese Journal of Gastroenterology
Jpn J Genet — Japanese Journal of Genetics
Jpn J Genet Suppl — Japanese Journal of Genetics. Supplement
Jpn J Geol Geogr — Japanese Journal of Geology and Geography
Jpn J Geophys — Japanese Journal of Geophysics
Jpn J Geriatr — Japanese Journal of Geriatrics
Jpn J Herpetol — Japanese Journal of Herpetology
Jpn J Hosp Pharm — Japanese Journal of Hospital Pharmacy
Jpn J Hum Genet — Japanese Journal of Human Genetics
Jpn J Hyg — Japanese Journal of Hygiene
Jpn J Ichthyol — Japanese Journal of Ichthyology
Jpn J Ind Health — Japanese Journal of Industrial Health
Jpn J Infect Dis — Japanese Journal of Infectious Diseases
Jpn J Leg Med — Japanese Journal of Legal Medicine
Jpn J Lepr — Japanese Journal of Leprosy
Jpn J Limnol — Japanese Journal of Limnology
Jpn J Lymphol — Japanese Journal of Lymphology
Jpn J Magn Reson Med — Japanese Journal of Magnetic Resonance in Medicine
Jpn J Malacol — Japanese Journal of Malacology
Jpn J Math — Japanese Journal of Mathematics
Jpn J Med — Japanese Journal of Medicine
Jpn J Med Electron and Biol Eng — Japanese Journal of Medical Electronics and Biological Engineering
Jpn J Med Electron Biol — Japanese Journal of Medical Eelctronics and Biological Engineering
Jpn J Med Electron Biol Eng — Japanese Journal of Medical Electronics and Biological Engineering
Jpn J Med Mycol — Japanese Journal of Medical Mycology
Jpn J Med Prog — Japanese Journal of Medical Progress
Jpn J Med Sci 1 — Japanese Journal of Medical Sciences. Part 1. Anatomy
Jpn J Med Sci 2 — Japanese Journal of Medical Sciences. Part 2. Biochemistry
Jpn J Med Sci 3 — Japanese Journal of Medical Sciences. Part 3. Biophysics
Jpn J Med Sci 4 — Japanese Journal of Medical Sciences. Part 4. Pharmacology
Jpn J Med Sci 5 — Japanese Journal of Medical Sciences. Part 5. Pathology
Jpn J Med Sci 6 — Japanese Journal of Medical Sciences. Part 6. Bacteriology and Parasitology
Jpn J Med Sci 7 — Japanese Journal of Medical Sciences. Part 7. Social Medicine and Hygiene
Jpn J Med Sci 8 — Japanese Journal of Medical Sciences. Part 8. Internal Medicine, Pediatry, and Psychiatry
Jpn J Med Sci 9 — Japanese Journal of Medical Sciences. Part 9. Surgery, Orthopedy, and Odontology
Jpn J Med Sci 10 — Japanese Journal of Medical Sciences. Part 10. Ophthalmology
Jpn J Med Sci 11 — Japanese Journal of Medical Sciences. Part 11. Gynecology and Tocology
Jpn J Med Sci 12 — Japanese Journal of Medical Sciences. Part 12. Oto-Rhino-Laryngology
Jpn J Med Sci 13 — Japanese Journal of Medical Sciences. Part 13. Dermatology and Urology
Jpn J Med Sci Biol — Japanese Journal of Medical Science and Biology
Jpn J Med Technol — Japanese Journal of Medical Technology
Jpn J Michurin Biol — Japanese Journal of Michurin Biology
Jpn J Microbiol — Japanese Journal of Microbiology
Jpn J Midwife — Japanese Journal for the Midwife

Jpn J Mutagen Tests Chem — Japanese Journal of Mutagenicity Tests on Chemicals
Jpn J Nations Health — Japanese Journal of the Nation's Health
Jpn J Natl Med Serv — Japanese Journal of National Medical Services
Jpn J Nephrol — Japanese Journal of Nephrology
Jpn J Neurol Psychiatry — Japanese Journal of Neurology and Psychiatry
Jpn J Neurosci Res Assoc — Japanese Journal of the Neurosciences Research Association
Jpn J Neuroshychopharmcol — Japanese Journal of Neuropsychopharmacology
Jpn J Nucl Med — Japanese Journal of Nuclear Medicine
Jpn J Nucl Med Technol — Japanese Journal of Nuclear Medicine Technology
Jpn J Nurs — Japanese Journal of Nursing
Jpn J Nurs Res — Japanese Journal of Nursing Research
Jpn J Nutr — Japanese Journal of Nutrition
Jpn J Obstet Gynecol — Japanese Journal of Obstetrics and Gynecology
Jpn J Ophthalmol — Japanese Journal of Ophthalmology
Jpn J Opt — Japanese Journal of Optics
Jpn J Oral Biol — Japanese Journal of Oral Biology
Jpn J Palynol — Japanese Journal of Palynology
Jpn J Pap Technol — Japanese Journal of Paper Technology
Jpn J Parasitol — Japanese Journal of Parasitology
Jpn J Pediat — Japanese Journal of Pediatrics
Jpn J Pediatr — Japanese Journal of Pediatrics
Jpn J Pediat Surg Med — Japanese Journal of Pediatric Surgery and Medicine
Jpn J Pharm — Japanese Journal of Pharmacognosy
Jpn J Pharmacogn — Japanese Journal of Pharmacognosy
Jpn J Pharmacognosy — Japanese Journal of Pharmacognosy
Jpn J Pharmacol — Japanese Journal of Pharmacology
Jpn J Pharm Chem — Japanese Journal of Pharmacy and Chemistry
Jpn J Phycol — Japanese Journal of Phycology
Jpn J Phycol Jpn Ed — Japanese Journal of Phycology (Japanese Edition)
Jpn J Phys — Japanese Journal of Physics
Jpn J Phys Educ — Japanese Journal of Physical Education
Jpn J Phys Fitness Sports Med — Japanese Journal of Physical Fitness and Sports Medicine
Jpn J Physiol — Japanese Journal of Physiology
Jpn J Plast Reconstr Surg — Japanese Journal of Plastic and Reconstructive Surgery
Jpn J Proctol — Japanese Journal of Proctology
Jpn J Psychiatry Neurol — Japanese Journal of Psychiatry and Neurology
Jpn J Psychol — Japanese Journal of Psychology
Jpn J Psychopharmacol — Japanese Journal of Psychopharmacology
Jpn J Psychosom Med — Japanese Journal of Psychosomatic Medicine
Jpn J Public Health — Japanese Journal of Public Health
Jpn J Radiol Technol — Japanese Journal of Radiological Technology
Jpn J Relig — Japanese Journal of Religious Studies
Jpn J Sanit Zool — Japanese Journal of Sanitary Zoology
Jpn J Smooth Muscle Res — Japanese Journal of Smooth Muscle Research
Jpn J Soil Sci Plant Nutr — Japanese Journal of Soil Science and Plant Nutrition
Jpn J Stroke — Japanese Journal of Stroke
Jpn J Stud Alcohol — Japanese Journal of Studies on Alcohol
Jpn J Surg — Japanese Journal of Surgery
Jpn J Surg Metab Nutr — Japanese Journal of Surgical Metabolism and Nutrition
Jpn J Taste Smell Res — Japanese Journal of Taste and Smell Research
Jpn J Thermophys Prop — Japan Journal of Thermophysical Properties
Jpn J Thorac Dis — Japanese Journal of Thoracic Diseases
Jpn J Toxicol — Japanese Journal of Toxicology
Jpn J Toxicol Environ Health — Japanese Journal of Toxicology and Environmental Health
Jpn J Trop Agric — Japanese Journal of Tropical Agriculture
Jpn J Trop Med Hyg — Japanese Journal of Tropical Medicine and Hygiene
Jpn J Tuberc — Japanese Journal of Tuberculosis
Jpn J Tuberc Chest Dis — Japanese Journal of Tuberculosis and Chest Diseases
Jpn J Urol — Japanese Journal of Urology
Jpn J Vet R — Japanese Journal of Veterinary Research
Jpn J Vet Res — Japanese Journal of Veterinary Research
Jpn J Vet Sci — Japanese Journal of Veterinary Science
Jpn J Water Pollut Res — Japan Journal of Water Pollution Research
Jpn J Zool — Japanese Journal of Zoology
Jpn J Zootech Sci — Japanese Journal of Zootechnical Science
Jpn Light Met Weld — Japan Light Metal Welding
Jpn Market — Dentsu Japan Marketing/Advertising Yearbook
Jpn Med J — Japanese Medical Journal
Jpn Med Lit — Japanese Medical Literature
Jpn Med Res Found Publ — Japan Medical Research Foundation. Publication
Jpn Med World — Japan Medical World
Jpn Natl Conf Soi Mech Soil Eng — Japan National Conference on Soil Mechanics and Soil Engineering
Jpn Natl Congr Appl Mech — Japan National Congress for Applied Mechanics
Jpn Natl Lab High Energy Phys KEK — Japan National Laboratory for High Energy Physics. Report KEK
JPNNB — Journal of Psychiatric Nursing and Mental Health Services
Jpn Nickel Rev — Japan Nickel Review
Jpn Nucl Med — Japanese Nuclear Medicine
JPNP — Journal de Psychologie Normale et Pathologique
JPNPA — Journal de Psychologie Normale et Pathologique
Jpn Pat Doc Kokai Tokkyo Koho — Japan. Patent Document. Kokai Tokkyo Koho
Jpn P Comp — Japanese Invasion of America's Personal Computer Market
Jpn Pestic Inf — Japan Pesticide Information
Jpn Petrol — Japan Petroleum and Energy Weekly
Jpn Pharmacol Ther — Japanese Pharmacology and Therapeutics
Jpn P Indx — Japan Price Indexes Annual, 1984
Jpn Plast — Japan Plastics
Jpn Plast Age — Japan Plastics Age
Jpn Plast Age News — Japan Plastics Age News

Jpn Plast Q Issue — Japan Plastics. Quarterly Issue
Jpn Poult Sci — Japanese Poultry Science
Jpn Printer — Japan Printer
Jpn Psychol Res — Japanese Psychological Research
Jpn Quart — Japan Quarterly
Jpn Railw Eng — Japanese Railway Engineering
Jpn Res Soc Deterg Environ Sci J — Japanese Research Society of Detergents and Environmental Science. Journal
Jpn Rev Clin Ophthalmol — Japanese Review of Clinical Ophthalmology
Jpn Saf Forces Med J — Japanese Safety Forces Medical Journal
Jpn Sci Mon — Japanese Scientific Monthly
Jpn Sci Rev Biol Sci — Japan Science Review. Biological Sciences
Jpn Sci Rev Med Sci — Japan Science Review. Medical Sciences
Jpn Sci Rev Min Metall — Japanese Science Review. Mining and Metallurgy
Jpn Semicond Technol Rep — Japan Semiconductor Technology Reports
JPNS J Peripher Nerv Syst — JPNS. Journal of the Peripheral Nervous System
Jpn Soc Aeronaut Space Sci Trans — Japan Society for Aeronautical and Space Sciences. Transactions
Jpn Soc Cancer Ther J — Japan Society for Cancer Therapy. Journal
Jpn Soc Compos Mater Trans — Japan Society for Composite Materials. Transactions
Jpn Soc Lubr Eng Int Tribol Conf — Japan Society of Lubrication Engineers. International Tribology Conference
Jpn Soc Mech Eng Bull — Japan Society of Mechanical Engineers. Bulletin
Jpn Soc Mech Eng Int J — Japan Society of Mechanical Engineers. International Journal
Jpn Soc Mech Eng Int J Ser 1 — Japan Society of Mechanical Engineers. International Journal. Series 1. Solid Mechanics, Strength of Materials
Jpn Soc Mech Eng Int J Ser 2 — Japan Society of Mechanical Engineers. International Journal. Series 2. Fluids Engineering, Heat Transfer, Power, Combustion, Thermophysical Properties
Jpn Soc Precis Eng Bull — Japan Society of Precision Engineering. Bulletin
Jpn Soc Precis Eng Int J — Japan Society for Precision Engineering. International Journal
Jpn Soc Tuberc Annu Rep — Japanese Society for Tuberculosis. Annual Report
Jpn Sov Symp Mechanochem — Japan-Soviet Symposium on Mechanochemistry
Jpn Spectros Co Appl Notes — Japan Spectroscopic Company. Application Notes
Jpn Spinners Insp Found Rep — Japan Spinners' Inspecting Foundation. Report
Jpn Steel Bull — Japan Steel Bulletin
Jpn Steel Tube Tech Rev — Japan Steel and Tube Technical Review
Jpn Steel Works — Japan Steel Works
Jpn Steel Works Tech News — Japan Steel Works. Technical News
Jpn Steel Works Tech Rev — Japan Steel Works. Technical Review
Jpn Steel Works Tech Rev (Engl Ed) — Japan Steel Works. Technical Review (English Edition)
Jpn Stud Hist Sci — Japanese Studies in the History of Science
JP (NSW) — Justice of the Peace (New South Wales)
Jpn Symp Plasma Chem Proc — Japanese Symposium on Plasma Chemistry. Proceedings
Jpn Symp Thermophys Prop — Japan Symposium on Thermophysical Properties
Jpn TAPPI — Japan TAPPI
Jpn Telecommun Rev — Japan Telecommunications Review
Jpn Text News — Japan Textile News
Jpn Trade — Standard Trade Index of Japan
Jpn Urea Ammonium Sulphate Ind Assoc Rep — Japan Urea and Ammonium Sulphate Industry Association. Reports
Jpn US Conf Compos Mater — Japan-US Conference on Composite Materials
Jpn US Semin HTGR Saf Technol Proc — Japan-US Seminar on HTGR [High-Temperature Gas-Cooled Reactor] Safety Technology. Proceedings
Jpn US Semin Polym Synth — Japan-U.S. Seminar on Polymer Synthesis
Jpn USSR Jt Symp Phys Chem Metall Processes — Japan-USSR Joint Symposium on Physical Chemistry of Metallurgical Processes
Jpn USSR Polym Symp Proc — Japan-USSR Polymer Symposium. Proceedings
Jpn Weld Soc Int Symp — Japan Welding Society. International Symposium
JPO — Journal of Portfolio Management
JPOCB — Journal of Popular Culture
J Podiatr Med Educ — Journal of Podiatric Medical Education
JPOGDP — Journal of Psychosomatic Obstetrics and Gynaecology
JPO J Prac Orthod — JPO. Journal of Practical Orthodontics
JPol — Jezyk Polski
JPol — Journal of Politics
J Pol and Military Sociol — Journal of Political and Military Sociology
J Polarogr Soc — Journal. Polarographic Society
J Pol Econ — Journal of Political Economy
J Pol Economy — Journal of Political Economy
J Police Sci Adm — Journal of Police Science and Administration
J Police Sci and Ad — Journal of Police Science and Administration
J Police Sci & Adm — Journal of Police Science and Administration
J Polic Sci — Journal of Police Science and Administration
J Policy Anal Manage — Journal of Policy Analysis and Management
J Policy Analysis and Mgt — Journal of Policy Analysis and Management
J Policy Analysis Manage — Journal of Policy Analysis and Management
J Policy Model — Journal of Policy Modeling
J Polit — Journal of Politics
J Polit Ec — Journal of Political Economy
J Polit Econ — Journal of Political Economy
J Politics — Journal of Politics
J Polit Mil — Journal of Political and Military Sociology
J Polit Milit Sociol — Journal of Political and Military Sociology
J Polit Stud — Journal of Political Studies
J Pollut Control (Tokyo) — Journal of Pollution Control (Tokyo)
J Pol Mil Sociol — Journal of Political and Military Sociology
J Pol Modeling — Journal of Policy Modeling
J Pol Sci — Journal of Polymer Science

J Pol Sci C — Journal of Polymer Science. Part C: Polymer Symposia [*Later, Journal of Polymer Science. Polymer Symposia Edition*]
J Pol Sc PC — Journal of Polymer Science. Polymer Chemistry Edition
J Pol Sc PL — Journal of Polymer Science. Polymer Letters Edition
J Pol Sc PP — Journal of Polymer Science. Polymer Physics Edition
J Pol Soc — Journal. Polynesian Society
J Pol Stud — Journal of Political Studies
J Polym Eng — Journal of Polymer Engineering
J Polym Mater — Journal of Polymer Materials
J Polym Res — Journal of Polymer Research
J Polym Sci — Journal of Polymer Science
J Polym Sci A-1 — Journal of Polymer Science. Part A-1: Polymer Chemistry
J Polym Sci A-2 — Journal of Polymer Science. Part A-2: Polymer Physics
J Polym Sci B — Journal of Polymer Science. Part B: Polymer Letters
J Polym Sci Macromol Rev — Journal of Polymer Science. Macromolecular Reviews
J Polym Sci Part A — Journal of Polymer Science. Part A. Polymer Chemistry
J Polym Sci Part A1 — Journal of Polymer Science. Part A-1. Polymer Chemistry
J Polym Sci Part A-1: Polym Chem — Journal of Polymer Science. Part A-1: Polymer Chemistry
J Polym Sci Part A2 — Journal of Polymer Science. Part A-2. Polymer Physics
J Polym Sci Part A-2: Polym Phys — Journal of Polymer Science. Part A-2: Polymer Physics
J Polym Sci Part A Gen Pap — Journal of Polymer Science. Part A. General Papers
J Polym Sci Part A Polym Chem — Journal of Polymer Science. Part A. Polymer Chemistry
J Polym Sci Part B — Journal of Polymer Science. Part B. Polymer Physics
J Polym Sci Part B: Polym Lett — Journal of Polymer Science. Part B: Polymer Letters
J Polym Sci Part C — Journal of Polymer Science. Part C: Polymer Symposia [*Later, Journal of Polymer Science. Polymer Symposia Edition*]
J Polym Sci Part C Polym Lett — Journal of Polymer Science. Part B. Polymer Letters
J Polym Sci Part C: Polym Symp — Journal of Polymer Science. Part C: Polymer Symposia [*Later, Journal of Polymer Science. Polymer Symposia Edition*]
J Polym Sci Part D — Journal of Polymer Science. Part D: Macromolecular Reviews
J Polym Sci Part D: Macromol Rev — Journal of Polymer Science. Part D: Macromolecular Reviews
J Polym Sci Polym Chem — Journal of Polymer Science. Polymer Chemistry Edition
J Polym Sci Polym Chem Ed — Journal of Polymer Science. Polymer Chemistry Edition
J Polym Sci Polym Lett — Journal of Polymer Science. Polymer Letters Edition
J Polym Sci Polym Lett Ed — Journal of Polymer Science. Polymer Letters Edition
J Polym Sci Polym Phys — Journal of Polymer Science. Polymer Physics Edition
J Polym Sci Polym Phys Ed — Journal of Polymer Science. Polymer Physics Edition
J Polym Sci Polym Symp — Journal of Polymer Science. Polymer Symposia Edition
J Polynesia — Journal. Polynesian Society
J Polynesian Soc — Journal. Polynesian Society
J Polynes Soc — Journal of the Polynesian Society
J Polynes Soc — Journal. Polynesian Society
J Polyn Soc — Journal. Polynesian Society
J Polytech — Journal Polytechnique
J Pomol — Journal of Pomology
J Pomol Hortic Sci — Journal of Pomology and Horticultural Science
J Pomol Hort Sci — Journal of Pomology and Horticultural Science
J Pomology — Journal of Pomology and Horticultural Science
JPONED — Journal of Psychosocial Oncology
J Pop Cul — Journal of Popular Culture
J Pop Cult — Journal of Popular Culture
J Pop Culture — Journal of Popular Culture
J Pop F & TV — Journal of Popular Film and Television
J Pop Film & TV — Journal of Popular Film and Television
J Pop Fi TV — Journal of Popular Film and Television
J Pop Res — Journal of Population Research
J Popul — Journal of Population
J Popular F — Journal of Popular Film and Television
J Popul Behav Soc Environ Issues — Journal of Population. Behavioral, Social, and Environmental Issues
J Porous Mater — Journal of Porous Materials
J Porous Media — Journal of Porous Media
J Porphyrins Phthalocyanines — Journal of Porphyrins and Phthalocyanines
J Port Econ e Fins — Jornal Portugues de Economia e Financas
J Portf Manage — Journal of Portfolio Management
J Portfolio Mgt — Journal of Portfolio Management
J Portugal Med — Jornadas sobra Portugal Medieval
JPOS — Journal. Palestine Oriental Society
J POS — Journal. Patent Office Society
JPOS — Peking Oriental Society. Journal
J Post Anesth Nurs — Journal of Post Anesthesia Nursing
J Postgrad Med (Bombay) — Journal of Postgraduate Medicine (Bombay)
J Postgrad Pharm Hosp Ed — Journal of Postgraduate Pharmacy. Hospital Edition
J Post Grad Sch Indian Agric Res Inst — Journal. Post Graduate School. Indian Agricultural Research Institute
J Post Keynes Econ — Journal of Post Keynesian Economics
J Powder Bulk Solids Tech — Journal of Powder and Bulk Solids Technology
J Powder Bulk Solids Technol — Journal of Powder and Bulk Solids Technology
J Power Div Am Soc Civ Eng — Journal. Power Division. American Society of Civil Engineers
J Power Sources — Journal of Power Sources
JPP — Jahrbuecher fuer Philologie und Paedagogik

JPP — Journal of Pastoral Practice
JPPDA — Journal of Child Psychology and Psychiatry and Allied Disciplines [*Later, Journal of Child Psychology and Psychiatry*]
JPPF — Jahrbuch fuer Philosophie und Phaenomenologische Forschungen
JPPFE — Jahrbuch fuer Philosophie und Phaenomenologische Forschungen. Ergaenzungsband
JPPIAX — Jugoslovenska Pediajatrija
JPPL — Journal of Planning and Property Law
JPPMB — Jahrbuch fuer Psychologie, Psychotherapie, und Medizinische Anthropologie
JPPSA — Journal of Pharmacy and Pharmacology. Supplement
JPQCA — Journal de Physique. Colloque
JPQSA — Journal de Physique. Supplement
JPr — Die Juedische Presse
JPR — Journal of Peace Research
JPR — Journal of Psycholinguistic Research
JPR — Journal of Purchasing and Materials Management
JPR — Justice of the Peace and Local Government Review Reports
J Pract Nurs — Journal of Practical Nursing
J Pract Pharm — Journal of Practical Pharmacy
J Prag — Journal of Pragmatics
J Prak Chem — Journal fuer Praktische Chemie
J Prakt Chem — Journal fuer Praktische Chemie
J Prakt Chem Ztg — Journal fuer Praktische Chemie/Chemiker-Zeitung
J Prat de Droit Fiscal — Journal Pratique de Droit Fiscal et Financier
J PR Board Comm Agric — Journal. Porto Rico Board of Commissioners of Agriculture
J Pr C — Journal fuer Praktische Chemie
JPRe — Journal of Peace Research
JPREA — Japanese Psychological Research
JPREAV — Japanese Psychological Research
J Pre Concr — Journal. Prestressed Concrete Institute
J Predent Fac Gifu Coll Dent — Journal. Predental Faculty. Gifu College of Dentistry
J Pre-Med Course Sapporo Med Coll — Journal of Pre-Medical Course. Sapporo Medical College
J Pre-Raph — Journal of Pre-Raphaelite Studies
J Pre Raphaelite & Aesth Stud — Journal of Pre-Raphaelite and Aesthetic Studies
J Pre Raphaelite Stud — Journal of Pre-Raphaelite Studies
J Presby H — Journal of Presbyterian History
J Presby Hist Soc — Journal. Presbyterian Historical Society
J Pres H — Journal of Presbyterian History
J Press — Jewish Press
J Pressure Vessel Technol — Journal of Pressure Vessel Technology
J Pressure Vessel Technol Trans ASME — Journal of Pressure Vessel Technology. Transaction. ASME
J Pressure Vessel Tech Trans ASME — Journal of Pressure Vessel Technology. Transactions. American Society of Mechanical Engineers
J Prestressed Concr Inst — Journal. Prestressed Concrete Institute
J Prev — Journal of Prevention
J Prev Dent — Journal of Preventive Dentistry
J Prev Med — Journal of Preventive Medicine
J Prev Psychiatry — Journal of Preventive Psychiatry
JPRGA — Journal de Chimie Physique et Revue Generale des Colloides
JPRH — Journal of Prison Health
J Print Hist Soc — Journal. Printing Historical Society
J Prison Jail Health — Journal of Prison and Jail Health
JPrK — Jahrbuch der Preussischen Kunstsammlungen
JPrKS — Jahrbuch. Preussische Kunstsammlungen
JPRLB — Journal of Psycholinguistic Research
J Proc Am Hort Soc — Journal of Proceedings. American Horticultural Society
J Proc Arts Crafts Soc Ir — Journal and Proceedings. Arts and Crafts Society of Ireland
J Proc Asiat Soc Bengal — Journal and Proceedings. Asiatic Society of Bengal
J Proc Aust Hist Soc — Australian Historical Society. Journal and Proceedings
J Proc Aust Jewish Hist Soc — Australian Jewish Historical Society. Journal and Proceedings
J Proc Australas Meth Hist Soc — Australasian Methodist Historical Society. Journal and Proceedings
J Proc Broken Hill Hist Soc — Broken Hill Historical Society. Journal and Proceedings
J Process Control — Journal of Process Control
J Proc Inst Chem GB Irel — Journal and Proceedings. Institute of Chemistry of Great Britain and Ireland
J Proc Inst Chem (India) — Journal and Proceedings. Institution of Chemists (India)
J Proc Inst Mech Eng London — Journal and Proceedings. Institution of Mechanical Engineers. London
J Proc Instn Chem (India) — Journal and Proceedings. Institution of Chemists (India)
J Proc Inst Rd Transp Engrs — Journal and Proceedings. Institute of Road Transport Engineers
J Proc Inst Sewage Purif — Journal and Proceedings. Institute of Sewage Purification
J Proc Mueller Bot Soc Western Australia — Journal of Proceedings. Mueller Botanic Society of Western Australia
J Proc Newcastle Hunter Dist Hist Soc — Newcastle and Hunter District Historical Society. Journal and Proceedings
J Proc Oil Technol Assoc — Journal and Proceedings. Oil Technologists' Association
J Proc Parramatta Dist Hist Soc — Parramatta and District Historical Society. Journal and Proceedings
J Proc R Aust Hist Soc — Royal Australian Historical Society. Journal and Proceedings
J Proc R Inst Chem — Journal and Proceedings. Royal Institute of Chemistry

J Proc Royal Austral Hist Soc — Journal of the Proceedings of the Royal Australian Historical Society

J Proc Royal Inst Brit Architects — Journal of the Proceedings of the Royal Institute of British Architects

J Proc Roy Soc NSW — Journal and Proceedings. Royal Society of New South Wales

J Proc R Soc NSW — Journal and Proceedings. Royal Society of New South Wales

J Proc R Soc West Aust — Journal and Proceedings. Royal Society of Western Australia

J Proc Sydney Tech Coll Chem Soc — Journal and Proceedings. Sydney Technical College. Chemical Society

J Proc W Aust Hist Soc — Western Australian Historical Society. Journal and Proceedings

J Proc Winchester Hampshire Sci Soc — Journal. Proceedings. Winchester and Hampshire Scientific and Literary Society

J Prod Agric — Journal of Production Agriculture

J Prod Innovation Manage — Journal of Product Innovation Management

J Prod L — Journal of Products Law

J Prod Law — Journal of Products Law

J Prod Liab — Journal of Products Liability

J Prod Liability — Journal of Products Liability

J Prof Act Am Soc Civ Eng — Journal of Professional Activities. American Society of Civil Engineers

J Prof Issues Eng Educ Pract — Journal of Professional Issues in Engineering Education and Practice

J Prof Nurs — Journal of Professional Nursing

J Prof Serv Mark — Journal of Professional Services Marketing

J Proj Constr Chem Ind USSR — Journal of Projection and Construction of the Chemical Industry in USSR

J Project Techniques — Journal of Projective Techniques and Personality Assessment [Later, Journal ofPersonality Assessment]

J Proj Tech — Journal of Projective Techniques

J Property Mgt — Journal of Property Management

J Prop Manage — Journal of Property Management

J Prop Mgt — Journal of Property Management

J Propul P — Journal of Propulsion and Power

J Propul Power — Journal of Propulsion and Power

J Propul Technol — Journal of Propulsion Technology

J Pros Dent — Journal of Prosthetic Dentistry

J Prosthet Dent — Journal of Prosthetic Dentistry

J Protein Chem — Journal of Protein Chemistry

J Protozool — Journal of Protozoology

JPRS — Joint Publications Research Service

JPRSA — Journal and Proceedings. Royal Society of New South Wales

J Prsbyt Hist — Journal of Presbyterian History

J Prtg Hist Soc — Journal of the Printing Historical Society

JPS — Journal of Collective Negotiations in the Public Sector

JPS — Journal of Palestine Studies

JPS — Journal of Peasant Studies

JPS — Journal of Personal Selling and Sales Management

JPS — Journal of Polymer Science

J Ps — Journal of Psychology

JPs — Journal of Psychology

JPS — Journal. Polynesian Society

JPSA — Journal. Photographic Society of America

JPSBA — Journal of Psychology of the Blind

J Ps C — Journal of Physical Chemistry

JPSCD — Journal of Polymer Science. Part C. Polymer Symposia [Later, Journal of Polymer Science. Polymer Symposia Edition]

JPSI — Journal of the Palaeontological Society of India

JPsNP — Journal de Psychologie Normale et Pathologique

JPSO — Journal of Psychosocial Oncology

JPSP — Journal of Personality and Social Psychology

JPSPB — Journal of Personality and Social Psychology

JPSRB — Journal of Psychological Researches

JPSS — Journal of Personality and Social Systems

JPST — Jahrbuch fuer Philosophie und Spekulative Theologie

JPST — Journal of Parenteral Science and Technology

JPsy — Journal of Psychology

JPsych — Journal de Psychologie Normale et Pathologique

J Psych and L — Journal of Psychiatry and Law

J Psych & Law — Journal of Psychiatry and Law

J Psychedel Drugs — Journal of Psychedelic Drugs

J Psychedelic Drugs — Journal of Psychedelic Drugs

J Psychiatr Biol Ther — Journal de Psychiatrie Biologique et Therapeutique

J Psychiatr Infant — Journal de Psychiatrie Infantile

J Psychiatr Law — Journal of Psychiatry and Law

J Psychiatr Nurs — Journal of Psychiatric Nursing and Mental Health Services

J Psychiatr Res — Journal of Psychiatric Research

J Psychiatr Treat Eval — Journal of Psychiatric Treatment and Evaluation

J Psychiatry & L — Journal of Psychiatry and Law

J Psychiatry Neurosci — Journal of Psychiatry and Neuroscience

J Psych Law — Journal of Psychiatry and Law

J Psychoact Drugs — Journal of Psychoactive Drugs

J Psychoanal Anthropol — Journal of Psychoanalytic Anthropology

J Psycho Asthenics — Journal of Psycho-Asthenics

J Psychohist — Journal of Psychohistory

J Psychol — Journal of Psychology

J Psycholin — Journal of Psycholinguistic Research

J Psycholing Res — Journal of Psycholinguistic Research

J Psycholinguist Res — Journal of Psycholinguistic Research

J Psychol Neurol — Journal fuer Psychologie und Neurologie

J Psychol Norm Path — Journal de Psychologie Normale et Pathologique

J Psychol Norm Pathol (Paris) — Journal de Psychologie Normale et Pathologique (Paris)

J Psychological Medicine — Journal of Psychological Medicine and Medical Jurisprudence

J Psychol Res — Journal of Psychological Researches

J Psychol T — Journal of Psychology and Theology

J Psychol u Neurol — Journal fuer Psychologie und Neurologie

J Psychopathol Behav Assess — Journal of Psychopathology and Behavioral Assessment

J Psychopharmacol London — Journal of Psychopharmacology (London)

J Psychopharmacol (Margate NJ) — Journal of Psychopharmacology (Margate, New Jersey)

J Psychopharmacol (Oxford) — Journal of Psychopharmacology (Oxford)

J Psychosocial Nurs — Journal of Psychosocial Nursing and Mental Health Services

J Psychosoc Nurs — Journal of Psychosocial Nursing and Mental Health Services

J Psychosoc Nurs Ment Healt Serv — Journal of Psychosocial Nursing and Mental Health Services

J Psychosoc Oncol — Journal of Psychosocial Oncology

J Psychosom — Journal of Psychosomatic Research

J Psychosom Obstet Gynaecol — Journal of Psychosomatic Obstetrics and Gynaecology

J Psychosom Res — Journal of Psychosomatic Research

J Psychother & Fam — Journal of Psychotherapy and the Family

J Psychother Pract Res — Journal of Psychotherapy Practice and Research

J Psych Res — Journal of Psychiatric Research

J Psych Th — Journal of Psychology and Theology

JPsyR — Journal of Psycholinguistic Research

JPT — Jahrbuch fuer Philosophie und Spekulative Theologie

JPT — Jahrbuecher fuer Protestantische Theologie

JPT — Journal of Partnership Taxation

JPT — Journal of Petroleum Technology

JPT — Journal of Psychology and Theology

JPTEA — Journal of Projective Techniques [Later, Journal of Personality Assessment]

JP Th — Jahrbuecher fuer Protestantische Theologie

JPT J Pet Technol — JPT. Journal of Petroleum Technology

JPTS — Journal. Pali Text Society

JPTUAL — Japanese Journal of Tuberculosis

JPU — Journal of Public Economics

JPU — Journal. Poona University

J Pub L — Journal of Public Law

J Publ Econ — Journal of Public Economics

J Public and Internat Affairs — Journal of Public and International Affairs

J Public Econ — Journal of Public Economics

J Public Health — Journal of Public Health

J Public Health Dent — Journal of Public Health Dentistry

J Public Health Med — Journal of Public Health Medicine

J Public Health Med Technol Korea Univ — Journal of Public Health and Medical Technology. Korea University

J Public Health Policy — Journal of Public Health Policy

J Public Health Pract — Journal of Public Health Practice

J Public Nuisance Tokyo — Journal of Public Nuisance (Tokyo)

J Public Policy — Journal of Public Policy

J Public Service Papua & NG — Journal. Public Service of Papua and New Guinea

JPUHS — Journal. Panjab University Historical Society

J Pulp and Pap Sci — Journal of Pulp and Paper Science

J Punjab Hist Soc — Journal of the Punjab Historical Society

J Purch — Journal of Purchasing [Later, Journal of Purchasing and Materials Management]

J Purchasing & Materials Mgt — Journal of Purchasing and Materials Management

J Purch Mater Manage — Journal of Purchasing and Materials Management

J Pure Appl Algebra — Journal of Pure and Applied Algebra

J Pure Appl Sci — Journal of Pure and Applied Sciences

J Pure Appl Sci (Ankara) — Journal of Pure and Applied Sciences (Ankara)

J Pure Math — Journal of Pure Mathematics

J Pusan Med Coll — Journal. Pusan Medical College

JPVDA — Journal of Preventive Dentistry

JPVTA — Journal of Pressure Vessel Technology

JPW — Jerusalem Post Weekly

JP (WA) — Justice of the Peace (Western Australia)

JPY — Journal of Political Economy

JPYABL — Annals. Japan Association for Philosophy of Science

JPYBA — Journal of Polymer Science. Polymer Letters Edition

JPYCA — Journal of Polymer Science. Polymer Symposia Edition

J Pyrotech — Journal of Pyrotechnics

JQ — Japan Quarterly

JQ — Jerusalem Quarterly

JQ — Jewish Quarterly

JQ — Journalism Quarterly

JQE — Journal of Quantum Electronics

J Qingdao Inst Chem Technol — Journal of Qingdao Institute of Chemical Technology

J Qingdao Univ Eng Technol Ed — Journal of Qingdao University. Engineering and Technology Edition

J Qingdao Univ Nat Sci Ed — Journal of Qingdao University. Natural Science Edition

J Qing Hua Univ — Journal. Qing Hua University

JQR — Jewish Quarterly Review

JQT — Journal of Quality Technology

J Qual Clin Pract — Journal of Quality in Clinical Practice

J Quality Tech — Journal of Quality Technology

J Qual Tech — Journal of Quality Technology

J Qual Technol — Journal of Quality Technology
J Quan Spec — Journal of Quantitative Spectroscopy and Radiative Transfer
J Quant Anthrop — Journal of Quantitative Anthropology
J Quant Spectrosc and Radiat Transfer — Journal of Quantitative Spectroscopy and Radiative Transfer
J Quant Spectrosc Radiat Transfer — Journal of Quantitative Spectroscopy and Radiative Transfer
J Quant Trait Loci — Journal of Quantitative Trait Loci
J Quekett Microsc Club — Journal. Quekett Microscopical Club
J Quekett Microscop Club — Journal. Quekett Microscopical Club
JR — Jezyk Rosyjski
JR — Journal of Reading
JR — Journal of Religion
JR — Juedische Rundschau
JR — Juridical Review
Jr A — Journal of Arizona History
JRA — Journal of Religion in Africa
JRA — Journal. Society of Research Administrators
J Race Dev — Journal of Race Development
J Race Development — Journal of Race Development
J Racial Aff — Journal of Racial Affairs
J Racial Affairs — Journal of Racial Affairs
JRADA — Journal of Radiology
J Rad Chem — Journal of Radioanalytical Chemistry [*Later, Journal of Radioanalytical and Nuclear Chemistry*]
J Radiat Curing — Journal of Radiation Curing
J Radiat Curing Radiat Curing — Journal of Radiation Curing/Radiation Curing
J Radiat Res — Journal of Radiation Research
J Radiat Res Radiat Process — Journal of Radiation Research and Radiation Processing
J Radiat Res (Tokyo) — Journal of Radiation Research (Tokyo)
J Radioanal Chem — Journal of Radioanalytical Chemistry [*Later, Journal of Radioanalytical and Nuclear Chemistry*]
J Radioanal Nucl Chem — Journal of Radioanalytical and Nuclear Chemistry
J Radiol — Journal de Radiologie
J Radio L — Journal of Radio Law
J Radiol Brussels — Journal de Radiologie (Brussels)
J Radiol Electrol — Journal de Radiologie et d'Electrologie
J Radiol Electrol Arch Electr Med — Journal de Radiologie et d'Electrologie et Archives d'Electricite Medicale
J Radiol Electrol Med Nucl — Journal de Radiologie, d'Electrologie, et de Medecine Nucleaire [*Later, Journal de Radiologie*]
J Radiol (Paris) — Journal de Radiologie (Paris)
J Radiol Phys Med — Journal of Radiology and Physical Medicine
J Radiol Phys Ther Univ Kanazawa — Journal of Radiology and Physical Therapy. University of Kanazawa
J Radiol Prot — Journal of Radiological Protection
J Radio Nucl Chem — Journal of Radioanalytical and Nuclear Chemistry
J Radio Res Lab — Journal. Radio Research Laboratories
J Rad Res L — Journal. Radio Research Laboratories
J R Aeronaut Soc — Journal. Royal Aeronautical Society
J R Afr Soc — Journal. Royal African Society
JRAfS — Journal. Royal African Society
JRAGAY — Journal. Royal Agricultural Society of England
J R Agric Soc — Journal. Royal Agricultural Society
J R Agric Soc Engl — Journal. Royal Agricultural Society of England
JRAHS — Journal. Royal Australian Historical Society
JRAI — Journal. Royal Anthropological Institute of Great Britain and Ireland
J Raj Inst Hist Res — Journal. Rajasthan Institute of Historical Research
J Rakuno Gakuen Univ Nat Sci — Journal. Rakuno Gakuen University. Natural Science
JRAM — Journal fuer Reine und Angewandte Mathematik
JRAMA — Journal. Royal Army Medical Corps
J Raman Sp — Journal of Raman Spectroscopy
J Raman Spectrosc — Journal of Raman Spectroscopy
J Ramanujan Math Soc — Journal of the Ramanujan Mathematical Society
J Range Man — Journal of Range Management
J Range Manage — Journal of Range Management
J Range Mgt — Journal of Range Management
J R Anthropol Inst GB Irel — Journal. Royal Anthropological Institute of Great Britain and Ireland
JRAPDU — Journal of Research APAU
J Rapid Methods Autom Microbiol — Journal of Rapid Methods and Automation in Microbiology
JRARA — Journal of Radiation Research
J R Army Med Corps — Journal. Royal Army Medical Corps
J R Army Vet Corps — Journal. Royal Army Veterinary Corps
JRAS — Journal. Royal Asiatic Society of Great Britain and Ireland
JRASA — Journal. Royal Astronomical Society of Canada
JRASBB — Journal. Royal Asiatic Society. Bombay Branch
JRASBengal — Journal. Royal Asiatic Society of Bengal
JRAS Bombay — Journal. Bombay Branch. Royal Asiatic Society
JRASCB — Journal. Royal Asiatic Society. Ceylon Branch
JRASHKB — Journal. Royal Asiatic Society. Hong Kong Branch
J R Asiat Soc — Journal of the Royal Asiatic Society
J R Asiat Soc Bengal Sci — Journal. Royal Asiatic Society of Bengal. Science
JR Asiat Soc GB Irel — Journal. Royal Asiatic Society of Great Britain and Ireland
JRASM — Journal. Royal Asiatic Society. Malayan Branch
JRASMB — Journal. Royal Asiatic Society. Malayan Branch
J R Astron Soc Can — Journal. Royal Astronomical Society of Canada
J R Aust Hist Soc — Journal. Royal Australian Historical Society
JRB — Journal of Retail Banking
JRBA-A — Journal. Royal Institute of British Architects
JRBED2 — Journal of Reproductive Biology and Comparative Endocrinology
Jr Bkshelf — Junior Bookshelf

JRBM — Journal of Renaissance and Baroque Music
Jr Br Assoc Teach Deaf — Journal. British Association of Teachers of the Deaf
JRBSDA — British Columbia Forest Service-Canadian Forestry Service. Joint Report
JRCAS — Journal. Royal Central Asian Society
JRCE-A — Journal. Irrigation and Drainage Division. Proceedings of the American Society of Civil Engineers
JRCI — Journal. Regional Cultural Institute
J R Coll Gen Pract — Journal. Royal College of General Practitioners
J R Coll Gen Pract Occas Pap — Journal. Royal College of General Practitioners. Occasional Paper
Jr Coll J — Junior College Journal
Jr Coll Jnl — Junior College Journal
J R Coll Physicians — Journal. Royal College of Physicians of London
J R Coll Physicians Lond — Journal. Royal College of Physicians of London
J R Coll Surg Edinb — Journal. Royal College of Surgeons of Edinburgh
J R Coll Surg Edinburg — Journal. Royal College of Surgeons of Edinburg
J R Coll Surg Irel — Journal. Royal College of Surgeons in Ireland
Jr Com Fl — Jurisprudence Commerciale des Flandres
JRCSA — Journal. Royal College of Surgeons of Edinburgh
JRD — Jahrbuch der Rheinischen Denkmalpflege
JRd — Juedische Rundschau
JRDCA — Journal of Radiation Curing
JRDP — Jahrbuch der Rheinischen Denkmalpflege
JRE — Journal of Econometrics
JRE — Journal of Real Estate Taxation
JRe — Journal of Religion
JRE — Journal of Religious Ethics
J Read — Journal of Reading
J Read Beh — Journal of Reading Behavior
J Read Behav — Journal of Reading Behavior
J Read Behavior — Journal of Reading Behavior
J Read Writ Learn Disabil Int — Journal of Reading, Writing, and Learning Disabilities International
J Real Est Tax — Journal of Real Estate Taxation
J Recent Adv Appl Sci — Journal of Recent Advances in Applied Sciences
J Recept Res — Journal of Receptor Research
J Recept Signal Transduction Res — Journal of Receptor and Signal Transduction Research
J Recept Signal Transduct Res — Journal of Receptor and Signal Transduction Research
J Rech Atmos — Journal de Recherches Atmospheriques
J Rech Cent Natl Rech Sci Lab Bellevue (Paris) — Journal des Recherches. Centre National de la Recherche Scientifique. Laboratoires de Bellevue (Paris)
J Rech CNRS — Journal des Recherches. Centre National de la Recherche Scientifique
J Rech Oceanogr — Journal de Recherche Oceanographique
J Reconstr Diet Aliment — Journal of Reconstructive Dietics and Alimentation
J Reconstr Microsurg — Journal of Reconstructive Microsurgery
J Recreational Math — Journal of Recreational Mathematics
J Rec Trans Jr Inst Eng — Journal and Record of Transactions. Junior Institution of Engineers
JREE — Journal of Real Estate Education
JREFEC — Journal of Real Estate Finance and Economics
J Refract — Journal Refractories
J Refract Corneal Surg — Journal of Refractive and Corneal Surgery
J Refract Surg — Journal of Refractive Surgery
J Refrig — Journal of Refrigeration
J Reg Col Ed Bhopal — Journal. Regional College of Education (Bhopal)
J Reg Cult — Journal of Regional Cultures
J Reg Cult Inst — Journal of the Regional Cultural Institute
J Regional Science — Journal of Regional Science
J Region Sci — Journal of Regional Science
J Reg Sc — Journal of Regional Science
J Reg Sci — Journal of Regional Science
J R Egypt Med Assoc — Journal. Royal Egyptian Medical Association
J Rehab — Journal of Rehabilitation
J Rehabil — Journal of Rehabilitation
J Rehabil Asia — Journal of Rehabilitation in Asia
J Rehabil D — Journal of Rehabilitation of the Deaf
J Rehabil Med — Journal of Rehabilitation Medicine
J Rehabil R D — Journal of Rehabilitation R and D
J Rehabil Res Dev — Journal of Rehabilitation Research and Development
J Rehabil Res Dev Clin Suppl — Journal of Rehabilitation Research and Development. Clinical Supplement
J Reine Angew Math — Journal fuer die Reine und Angewandte Mathematik
J Reinf Plast Comp — Journal of Reinforced Plastics and Composites
J Reinf Plast Compos — Journal of Reinforced Plastics and Composites
J Rein Math — Journal fuer die Reine und Angewandte Mathematik
J Rel — Journal of Religion
J Rel Africa — Journal of Religion in Africa
JR Electr and Mech Eng — Journal. Royal Electrical and Mechanical Engineers
J R Electr Mech Eng — Journal. Royal Electrical and Mechanical Engineers
J Rel Ethics — Journal of Religious Ethics
J Rel H — Journal of Religious History
J Rel Health — Journal of Religion and Health
J Rel Hist — Journal of Religious History
J Relig — Journal of Religion
J Relig Afr — Journal of Religion in Africa
J Relig Africa — Journal of Religion in Africa
J Relig Educ — Journal of Religious Education
J Relig Ethics — Journal of Religious Ethics
J Relig H — Journal of Religion and Health
J Relig His — Journal of Religious History
J Relig Hist — Journal of Religious History

J Religion Health — Journal of Religion and Health
J Religious History — Journal of Religious History
J Rel Psych Res — Journal of Religion and Psychical Research
J Rel St — Journal of Religious Studies
J Rel Thot — Journal of Religious Thought
J Rel Thought — Journal of Religious Thought
J Remote Sensing — Journal of Remote Sensing
J Remount Vet Corps — Journal of the Remount and Veterinary Corps
J Ren & Bar Mus — Journal of Renaissance and Baroque Music
J Reprd & Fert — Journal of Reproduction and Fertility
J Repr Fert — Journal of Reproduction and Fertility
J Reprod Biol Comp Endocrinol — Journal of Reproductive Biology and Comparative Endocrinology
J Reprod Dev — Journal of Reproduction and Development
J Reprod Fert — Journal of Reproduction and Fertility
J Reprod Fertil — Journal of Reproduction and Fertility
J Reprod Fertil — Journal of Reproductive Fertility
J Reprod Fertil Abstr Ser — Journal of Reproduction and Fertility. Abstract Series
J Reprod Fertil Suppl — Journal of Reproduction and Fertility. Supplement
J Reprod Immunol — Journal of Reproductive Immunology
J Reprod Med — Journal of Reproductive Medicine
J Reprod Med Lying-In — Journal of Reproductive Medicine. Lying-In
JRER — Journal of Real Estate Research
JRERDM — Journal of Receptor Research
J Re S — Journal of Religious Studies
JRES-A — Journal of Regional Science
J Res & Devel Educ — Journal of Research and Development in Education
J Res APAU (Andhra Pradesh Agric Univ) — Journal of Research APAU (Andhra Pradesh Agricultural University)
J Res Asiatic — Journal. Society for Research in Asiatic Music
J Res Assam Agric Univ — Journal of Research. Assam Agricultural University
J Res Assoc Powder Technol (Jpn) — Journal. Research Association of Powder Technology (Japan)
J Res Chichibu Onoda Cem Corp — Journal of Research of the Chichibu Onoda Cement Corporation
J Res Commun Stud — Journal of Research Communication Studies
J Res Crime — Journal of Research in Crime and Delinquency
J Res Crime & Del — Journal of Research in Crime and Delinquency
J Res Crime & Delinq — Journal of Research in Crime and Delinquency
J Res Dev E — Journal of Research and Development in Education
J Res Develop Educ — Journal of Research and Development in Education
J Res Dev Lab Portland Cem Assoc — Journal. Research and Development Laboratories. Portland Cement Association
J Research M Education — Journal of Research in Music Education
J Res Haryana Agric Univ — Haryana Agricultural University. Journal of Research
J Res Indian Med — Journal of Research in Indian Medicine
J Res Indian Med Yoga Homoeopathy — Journal of Research in Indian Medicine, Yoga, and Homoeopathy
J Res Inst Catal Hokkaido Univ — Journal. Research Institute for Catalysis. Hokkaido University
J Res Inst Catalysis Hokkaido Univ — Journal. Research Institute for Catalysis. Hokkaido University
J Res Inst Med Sci Korea — Journal. Research Institute of Medical Science of Korea
J Res Inst Sci and Technol Nihon Univ — Journal. Research Institute of Science and Technology. Nihon University
J Res Inst Sci Technol Nihon Univ — Journal. Research Institute of Science and Technology. Nihon University
J Res (Jpn) — Journal of Research (Japan)
J Res Lab Med Milan — Journal of Research and Laboratory Medicine (Milan)
J Res Lepid — Journal of Research on the Lepidoptera
J Res (Ludhiana) — Journal of Research (Ludhiana)
J Res M & T — Journal of Resource Management and Technology
J Res Math Educ — Journal for Research in Mathematics Education
J Res Mus Ed — Journal of Research in Music Education
J Res Mus Educ — Journal of Research in Music Education
J Res Music — Journal of Research in Music Education
J Res Music Educ — Journal of Research in Music Education
J Res Nat Bur Stand — Journal of Research. [US] National Bureau of Standards
J Res Nat Bur Standards — Journal of Research. [US] National Bureau of Standards
J Res Nat Bur Stand Sect A Phys Chem — Journal of Research. [US] National Bureau of Standards. Section A. Physics and Chemistry
J Res Nat Bur Stand Sect B Math Sci — Journal of Research. [US] National Bureau of Standards. Section B. Mathematical Sciences
J Res Nat Bur Stand Sect C — Journal of Research. [US] National Bureau of Standards. Section C. Engineering and Instrumentation
J Res Nat Bur Stand Sect C Eng Instrum — Journal of Research. [US] National Bureau of Standards. Section C. Engineering and Instrumentation
J Res Nat Bur Stand Sect D — Journal of Research. [US] National Bureau of Standards. Section D. Radio Science
J Res Nat I — Journal of Research. National Institute of Standards and Technology
J Res Natl Bur Stand A — Journal of Research. [US] National Bureau of Standards. Section A. Physics and Chemistry
J Res Natl Bur Stand A Phys Chem — Journal of Research. National Bureau of Standards. A. Physics and Chemistry
J Res Natl Bur Stand B — Journal of Research. [US] National Bureau of Standards. Section B. Mathematics and Mathematical Physics
J Res Natl Bur Stand B Math Math — Journal of Research. National Bureau of Standards. B. Mathematics and Mathematical Physics
J Res Natl Bur Stand C — Journal of Research. [US] National Bureau of Standards. Section C. Engineering and Instrumentation
J Res Natl Bur Stand C Eng — Journal of Research. National Bureau of Standards. C. Engineering and Instrumentation

J Res Natl Bur Stand (US) — Journal of Research. National Bureau of Standards (United States)
J Res Natl Inst Stand Technol — Journal of Research. National Institute of Standards. C. Technology
J Res Natl Inst Stand Tehcnol — Journal of Research. National Institute of Standards and Technology
J Res NBS — Journal of Research. [US] National Bureau of Standards
J Res NBS A — Journal of Research. [US] National Bureau of Standards. Section A. Physics and Chemistry
J Res NBS B — Journal of Research. [US] National Bureau of Standards. Section B. Mathematical Sciences
J Res Onoda Cem Co — Journal of Research. Onoda Cement Co.
J Resour Environ — Journal of Resources and Environment
J Res Pers — Journal of Research in Personality
J Res Punjab Agric Univ — Journal of Research. Punjab Agricultural University
J Res Punjab Agr Univ — Journal of Research. Punjab Agricultural University
J Res Read — Journal of Research in Reading
J Res Sci Agra Univ — Journal of Research in Science. Agra University
J Res Sci Teach — Journal of Research in Science Teaching
J Res Singing — Journal of Research in Singing
J Res Singing — Journal of Research in Singing and Applied Vocal Pedagogy
J Res Soc Pak — Journal. Research Society of Pakistan
J Res Soc Pakistan — Journal of the Research Society of Pakistan
J Res US Geol Surv — Journal of Research. United States Geological Survey
J Res US G S — Journal of Research. United States Geological Survey
J Res Visva Bharati — Journal of Research. Visva-Bharati
J Retail — Journal of Retailing
J Retail Bank — Journal of Retail Banking
J Retail Banking — Journal of Retail Banking
J Retailing — Journal of Retailing
J Retail Traders Assn NSW — Journal of the Retail Traders' Association of New South Wales
J Retail Traders Assoc NSW — Journal of the Retail Traders' Association of New South Wales
J Retic Soc — Journal. Reticuloendothelial Society
J Reticuloendothel Soc — Journal. Reticuloendothelial Society
J Rev — Jewish Review
JRFS — Janssen Research Foundation Series
JRG — Jahrbuch. Raabe-Gesellschaft
JRG — Journal of Regional Science
JRGS — Journal. Royal Geographical Society
JRGZ — Jahrbuch. Roemisch-Germanisches Zentralmuseum
JRGZM — Jahrbuch des Roemisch-Germanischen Zentral Museums Mainz
JRGZMainz — Jahrbuch. Roemisch-Germanisches Zentralmuseum (Mainz)
JRH — Journal of Religious History
JRH — Journal of Rural Health
JR He — Journal of Religion and Health
J Rheol — Journal of Rheology
J Rheol Easton Pa — Journal of Rheology (Easton, Pennsylvania)
J Rheology — Journal of Rheology
J Rheumatol — Journal of Rheumatology
J Rheumatol Suppl — Journal of Rheumatology. Supplement
J R Hortic Soc — Journal. Royal Horticultural Society
JRI — Journal of Risk and Insurance
JRIBA — Journal. Royal Institute of British Architects
JRIHDC — Journal of Research in Indian Medicine, Yoga, and Homoeopathy
JRIIA — Journal. Royal Institute of International Affairs
JRIMD — Journal of Reproductive Immunology
JRINA — Journal. Research Institute for Catalysis. Hokkaido University
J R Inst Br Archit — Journal. Royal Institute of British Architects
J R Inst Chem — Journal. Royal Institute of Chemistry
J R Inst Public Health — Journal. Royal Institute of Public Health
J R Inst Public Health Hyg — Journal. Royal Institute of Public Health and Hygiene
J Rio Grande Val Hortic Soc — Journal. Rio Grande Valley Horticulture Society
J Rire — Journal pour Rire
J Risk & Insur — Journal of Risk and Insurance
J Risk Ins — Journal of Risk and Insurance
J Risk Insur — Journal of Risk and Insurance
J RI State Dent Soc — Journal. Rhode Island State Dental Society
J Ritual Stud — Journal of Ritual Studies
JRJ — Journal of Reform Judaism
JRKUN — Jaarboek der Roomisch-Katholieke Universiteit te Nijmegen
JRL — John Rylands Library. Bulletin
JRL — Journal of Retailing
Jrl Ad Res — Journal of Advertising Research
Jrl Advtg — Journal of Advertising
Jrl Audit — Journal of Accounting Auditing and Finance
JRLB — John Rylands Library. Bulletin
Jrl Bldg S — Journal. Chartered Institution of Building Services
Jrl Bus — Journal of Business
Jrl Coatng — Journal of Coatings Technology
Jrl Comm — Journal of Commerce
Jrl Def & D — Journal of Defense and Diplomacy
Jrl Elec I — Journal of the Electronics Industry
Jrl Eng Pwr — Journal of Engineering for Power
Jr Lib — Junior Libraries
Jrl Int B — Journal of International Business Studies
Jrl Irrep — Journal of Irreproducible Results
Jrl Market — Journal of Marketing
Jrl Metals — Journal of Metals
Jrl Mkt R — Journal of Marketing Research
Jrl P — Journal. Patent Office Society
Jrl Petro — Journal of Petroleum Technology
Jrl P Mgmt — Journal of Portfolio Management

Jrl Retail — Journal of Retailing
Jrl RE Tax — Journal of Real Estate Taxation
Jrl Solar — Journal of Solar Energy Engineering
J Rly Div Instn Mech Engrs — Institution of Mechanical Engineers. Railway Division. Journal
JRM — Jahresbericht der Rheinischen Mission
JRM — Journal of Range Management
JRM — Journal of Research in Music Education
JRME — Journal of Research in Music Education
JRMEA — Journal of Research in Music Education
J R Microsc Soc — Journal. Royal Microscopical Society
JRMIE2 — Journal of Reconstructive Microsurgery
JRMMRA — Journal. Rocky Mountain Medieval and Renaissance Association
JRMS — Journal. Royal Meteorological Society
J R Nav Med Serv — Journal. Royal Naval Medical Service
JRNBA — Journal of Research. [*US*] National Bureau of Standards
JRNCDM — Journal of Radioanalytical and Nuclear Chemistry
J R Neth Chem Soc — Journal. Royal Netherlands Chemical Society
Jr N H — Journal of Negro History
JRNMA — Journal. Royal Naval Medical Service
J Rob Syst — Journal of Robotic Systems
J ROK Nav Med Corps — Journal. ROK (Republic of Korea) Naval Medical Corps
J Roman Archaeol — Journal of Roman Archaeology
J Roman Stud — Journal of Roman Studies
J Rom S — Journal of Roman Studies
JRomSt — Journal of Roman Studies
J Rom Stud — Journal of Roman Studies
J Root Crops — Journal of Root Crops
J Rossica Soc — Journal. Rossica Society of Russian Philately
J Rouen — Journal de Rouen
J Roy Agric Soc England — Journal. Royal Agricultural Society of England
J Roy Agr S — Journal. Royal Agricultural Society of England
J Royal Anthropol Inst GB & Ireland — Journal of the Royal Anthropological Institute of Great Britain and Ireland
J Royal Archit Inst Canada — Journal of the Royal Architectural Institute of Canada
J Royal Asiat Soc GB & Ireland — Journal of the Royal Asiatic Society of Great Britain and Ireland
J Royal Asiat Soc Sri Lankan Branch — Journal of the Royal Asiatic Society. Sri Lankan Branch
J Royal Aust Hist Soc — Journal. Royal Australian Historical Society
J Royal Cent Asian Soc — Journal of the Royal Central Asian Society
J Royal Coll Phys — Journal of the Royal College of Physicians
J Royal Geog Soc — Journal of the Royal Geographical Society
J Royal Hist & Archaeol Assoc Ireland — Journal of the Royal Historical and Archaeological Association of Ireland
J Royal Hort Soc — Journal of the Royal Horticultural Society
J Royal Inst — Journal of the Royal Institution
J Royal Military College Aust — Journal. Royal Military College of Australia
J Royal Soc A — Journal of the Royal Society of Arts
J Royal Soc Antiqua Ireland — Journal of the Royal Society of Antiquaries of Ireland
J Royal Soc New Zeal — Journal. Royal Society of New Zealand
J Royal Soc WA — Journal. Royal Society of Western Australia
J Royal Soc W Australia — Journal of the Royal Society of Western Australia
J Royal Vict Inst Architects — Journal of the Royal Victorian Institute of Architects
J Roy Anthrop Inst Gt Br Ire — Journal. Royal Anthropological Institute of Great Britain and Ireland
J Roy Anthropol Inst — Journal. Royal Anthropological Institute
J Roy Anthropol Inst Gr Brit — Journal. Royal Anthropological Institute of Great Britain and Ireland
J Roy Artil — Journal of the Royal Artillery
J Roy Arty — Journal of the Royal Artillery
J Roy Asia — Journal. Royal Asiatic Society of Great Britain and Ireland
J Roy Asiatic Soc — Journal. Royal Asiatic Society
J Roy Asiat Soc — Journal. Royal Asiatic Society
J Roy Astro — Journal. Royal Astronomical Society of Canada
J Roy Astron Soc Can — Journal. Royal Astronomical Society of Canada
J Roy Aust — Journal. Royal Australian Historical Society
J Roy Centr Asian Soc — Journal. Royal Central Asian Society
J Roy Coll Gen Pract — Journal. Royal College of General Practitioners
J Roy Coll Phys London — Journal. Royal College of Physicians of London
J Roy Col P — Journal. Royal College of Physicians of London
J Roy Commonw Soc — Journal. Royal Commonwealth Society
J Roy Hort Soc — Journal. Royal Horticultural Society
J Roy Inst Br Archit — Journal. Royal Institute of British Architects
J Roy Inst Cornwall — Journal. Royal Institution of Cornwall
J Roy Inst Cornwall N Ser — Journal. Royal Institution of Cornwall. New Series
J Roy Microscop Soc — Journal. Royal Microscopical Society
J Roy Micr Soc — Journal. Royal Microscopical Society
J Roy New Zealand Inst Hort — Journal. Royal New Zealand Institute of Horticulture
J Roy Soc Antiq Ir — Journal. Royal Society of Antiquaries of Ireland
J Roy Soc Arts — Journal. Royal Society of Arts
J Roy Soc Med — Journal. Royal Society of Medicine
J Roy Soc NSW — Royal Society of New South Wales. Journal and Proceedings
J Roy Soc W Aust — Royal Society of Western Australia. Journal
J Roy Sta A — Journal. Royal Statistical Society. Series A. General
J Roy Sta B — Journal. Royal Statistical Society. Series B. Methodological
J Roy Sta C — Journal. Royal Statistical Society. Series C. Applied Statistics
J Roy Statis — Journal. Royal Statistical Society
J Roy Statist Soc — Journal. Royal Statistical Society
J Roy Statist Soc Ser A — Journal. Royal Statistical Society. Series A. General
J Roy Statist Soc Ser B — Journal. Royal Statistical Society. Series B. Methodological

J Roy Statist Soc Ser C — Journal. Royal Statistical Society. Series C. Applied Statistics
J Roy Statist Soc Ser C Appl Statist — Journal. Royal Statistical Society. Series C. Applied Statistics
J Roy Stat Soc A J Verb Learn Verb Beh — Journal. Royal Statistical Society. A Journal of Verbal Learning and Verbal Behavior
J Roy United Serv Instn — Journal. Royal United Service Institutions
J Roy Un Serv Instn — Journal. Royal United Services Institution
JRP — Journal of Religious Psychology
J RPF — Journal RPF
JRPFA — Journal of Reproduction and Fertility
Jr Philipp Sci — Junior Philippine Scientist
JRPUA — Journal of Research. Punjab Agricultural University
JRRIAN — Journal. Rubber Research Institute of Malaysia
J RRI Malaysia — Journal. Rubber Research Institute of Malaysia
J RRI Sri Lanka — Journal. Rubber Research Institute of Sri Lanka
JRRLA — Journal. Radio Research Laboratories
JRS — Journal. Market Research Society
JRS — Journal of Regional Science
JRS — Journal of Research in Singing
JRS — Journal of Roman Studies
JRS — Journal of Russian Studies
JRSA — Journal. Royal Society of Arts
JRSAA — Journal. Royal Society of Arts
JRSAI — Journal. Royal Society of Antiquaries of Ireland
J R Sanit Inst — Journal. Royal Sanitary Institute
J R Sanit Inst G B — Journal. Royal Sanitary Institute of Great Britain
JRSAntl — Journal. Royal Society of Antiquaries of Ireland
Jr Sch Mines — Journal. Royal School of Mines
Jr Schol — Junior Scholastic
JRSHDS — Journal. Royal Society of Health
JR Signals Inst — Journal. Royal Signals Institution
JRS J Raman Spectrosc — JRS. Journal of Raman Spectroscopy
JRSL — Journal of Roman Studies (London)
J RSNZ — Journal. Royal Society of New Zealand
J R Soc Arts — Journal. Royal Society of Arts
J R Soc Encour Arts Manuf Commer — Journal. Royal Society for the Encouragement of Arts, Manufactures, and Commerce
J R Soc Health — Journal. Royal Society of Health
J R Soc Hlth — Journal. Royal Society of Health
J R Soc Med — Journal. Royal Society of Medicine
J R Soc NZ — Journal. Royal Society of New Zealand
J R Soc W Aust — Journal. Royal Society of Western Australia. Journal
J R Soc West Aust — Journal. Royal Society of Western Australia
JRSOD — Journal. Reticuloendothelial Society
JRSP — Journal. Research Society of Pakistan
JRSS — Journal. Royal Statistical Society
J R Stat Soc — Journal. Royal Statistical Society
JRSUA — Journal. Royal Society of Western Australia
J R Swaziland Soc Sci Technol — Journal. Royal Swaziland Society of Science and Technology
J R Swed Acad Agric — Journal. Royal Swedish Academy of Agriculture
J R Swed Acad Agric For — Journal. Royal Swedish Academy of Agriculture and Forestry
J R Swed Acad Agric For Suppl — Journal. Royal Swedish Academy of Agriculture and Forestry. Supplement
J R Swed Acad For Agric — Journal. Royal Swedish Academy of Forestry and Agriculture
JRT — Journal of Religious Thought
JRT — Journal of Retailing
JR Telev Soc — Journal. Royal Television Society
J R Th — Journal of Religious Thought
JRU — Journal of Risk and Uncertainty
J Rubber Ind Jpn — Journal. Rubber Industry. (Japan)
J Rubber Ind Moscow — Journal. Rubber Industry (Moscow)
J Rubber Res Inst Malaya — Journal. Rubber Research Institute of Malaya
J Rubber Res Inst Malays — Journal. Rubber Research Institute of Malaysia
J Rubber Res Inst Sri Lanka — Journal. Rubber Research Institute of Sri Lanka
J Rubber Res Kuala Lumpur — Journal of Rubber Research (Kuala Lumpur)
J Rubb Res Inst Malaya — Journal. Rubber Research Institute of Malaya
JRUL — Journal. Rutgers University Library
J R United Serv Inst — Journal. Royal United Service Institution [*Later, Journal. Royal United Services Institute for Defence Studies*]
J Rural Coop Int Res Cent Rural Coop Communities — Journal of Rural Cooperation. International Research Center on Rural Cooperative Communities
J Rural Dev — Journal of Rural Development
J Rural Econ and Development — Journal of Rural Economics and Development
J Rural Educ — Journal of Rural Education
J Rural Eng Dev — Journal of Rural Engineering and Development
J Rural Health — Journal of Rural Health
J Rural Stud — Journal of Rural Studies
J Rur Coop — Journal of Rural Cooperation
J Rur Dev — Journal of Rural Development
J Rur Develop — Journal of Rural Development
J Rur Econ Dev — Journal of Rural Economics and Development
JRuS — Journal of Russian Studies
JRUSI — Journal. Royal United Service Institution
J Russe Physiol — Journal Russe de Physiologie
J Russ Laser Res — Journal of Russian Laser Research
J Russ Phys Chem Ges — Journal der Russischen Physikalisch-Chemischen Gesellschaft
J Russ Phys Chem Soc — Journal. Russian Physical-Chemical Society
J Rutgers Univ Libr — Journal. Rutgers University Library
JRVRI — Journal. Rama Varma Research Institute
JRVSB — Jena Review. Supplement

JRW — Nederlandsche Jaarboeken voor Rechts-Geleerdheid en Wetgeving

JRWL — Journal fuer Religion, Wahrheit, und Litteratur

JS — Janus. Supplements

JS — Jazykovedny Sbornik

JS — Jazykovedny Studie

JS — Journal. Arnold Schoenberg Institute

JS — Journal des Savants

JS — Journal des Societes

JS — Judaic Studies

JS — Junior Scholastic

JSA — Journal. Societe des Africanistes

JSA — Journal. Societe des Americanistes

JSA — Journal. Society of Archivists

JSAB — Journal of South African Botany

JSACA — Journal. South African Chemical Institute

J SA Chem I — Journal. South African Chemical Institute

JSAED — Journal of Strain Analysis for Engineering Design

JSAE Rev — JSAE (Society of Automotive Engineers of Japan) Review

JSAf — Journal. Societe des Africanistes

JSAFA4 — Journal. South African Forestry Association

JSAFE — Journal of South-East Asia and the Far East

J Safe Res — Journal of Safety Research

J SA For Assoc — Journal. South African Forestry Association

JSAfr — Journal. Societe des Africanistes

J S Afr Assoc Anal Chem — Journal. South African Association of Analytical Chemists

J S Afr Biol Soc — Journal. South African Biological Society

J S Afr Bot — Journal of South African Botany

J S Afr Bot Suppl Vol — Journal of South African Botany. Supplementary Volume

J S Afr Chem Inst — Joernaal van die Suid-Afrikaanse Chemiese Instituut

J S Afr Chem Inst — Journal. South African Chemical Institute

J Saf Res — Journal of Safety Research

J S Afr For Assoc — Journal. South African Forestry Association

J African Chem Inst — Journal. South African Chemical Institute

J S Afr Inst Civ Eng — Journal of the South African Institution of Civil Engineers

J S Afr Inst Eng — Journal. South African Institution of Engineers

J S Afr Inst Mining Met — Journal. South African Institute of Mining and Metallurgy

J S Afr Inst Min Metall — Journal. South African Institute of Mining and Metallurgy

J S Afr Speech Hear Assoc — Journal. South African Speech and Hearing Association

J S Afr Vet Assoc — Journal. South African Veterinary Association

J S Afr Vet Med Assoc — Journal. South African Veterinary Medical Association [*Later, South African Veterinary Association. Journal*]

J Sagami Womens Univ — Journal. Sagami Women's University

JSAH — Journal of Southeast Asian History

JSAH — Journal. Society of Architectural Historians

JSAI — Jerusalem Studies in Arabic and Islam

JSAI — Journal. Royal Society of Antiquaries of Ireland

J SA I Min — Journal. South African Institute of Mining and Metallurgy

J Sains Alam Semula Jadi — Jernal Sains Alam Semula Jadi

J Sains Fiz — Jurnal Sains Fizikal

J Sains Inst Penyelidikan Getah Malays — Jurnal Sains Institut Penyelidikan Getah Malaysia

J Sains Malays — Jernal Sains Malaysia

J Sains Malays Ser A — Jurnal Sains Malaysia. Series A. Life Sciences

J Sains Malays Ser B — Jurnal Sains Malaysia. Series B. Physical and Earth Sciences

J Sains Nukl — Jernal Sains Nuklear

J Sains Nukl Malays — Jurnal Sains Nuklear Malaysia

J Sains Pusat Penyelidikan Getah Malays — Jurnal Sains Pusat Penyelidikan Getah Malaysia

JSAIS — Journal. Royal Society of Antiquaries of Ireland. Supplement

J Saitama Inst Technol — Journal of Saitama Institute of Technology

J Saitama Med Sch — Journal of Saitama Medical School

J Saitama Med Soc — Journal. Saitama Medical Society

J Saitama U For Lang & Lit — Journal of Saitama University. Foreign Languages and Literature

J Saitama Univ Fac Ed Math Natur Sci — Journal. Saitama University. Faculty of Education. Mathematics and Natural Science

J Saitama Univ Math Nat Sci — Journal of Saitama University. Mathematics and Natural Science

J Saitama Univ Nat Sci — Journal. Saitama University. Natural Science

JSAKM — Jahrbuch der Staatlichen Akademie fuer Kirchen- und Schulmusik

JSAL — Journal of South African Law

JSAL — Journal of South Asian Languages

JSALO — Journal of Studies on Alcohol

JSAm — Journal. Societe des Americanistes de Paris

JSAMA — Journal. South African Institute of Mining and Metallurgy

JSAmP — Journal. Societe des Americanistes de Paris

J San Antonio Dent Soc — Journal. San Antonio District Dental Society

J San Diego Hist — Journal of San Diego History

J Sanit Eng Div Am Soc Civ Eng — Journal. Sanitary Engineering Division. American Society of Civil Engineers

J Sanit Eng Div Proc Am Soc Civ Eng — Journal. Sanitary Engineering Division. Proceedings. American Society of Civil Engineers

J Sanshi Norm Coll — Journal of Shansi Normal College/Shan Hsi Sze Fan Hsueeh Yuan Hsueeh Pao

J San'yo Assoc Adv Sci Technol — Journal. San'yo Association for Advancement of Science and Technology

J Saorstat Eireann Dep Agric — Journal. Saorstat Eireann Department of Agriculture

JSAP — Journal. Societe des Americanistes de Paris

J Sapporo Munic Gen Hosp — Journal. Sapporo Municipal General Hospital

J Sapporo Soc Agric — Journal. Sapporo Society of Agriculture and Forestry/ Sapporo Noringakkai-Ho

J Sapporo Soc Agric For — Journal. Sapporo Society of Agriculture and Forestry

J S Archit — Journal. Society of Architectural Historians

JSAS — Journal of Southeast Asian Studies

J S Asia L — Journal of South Asian Literature

J Saudi Chem Soc — Journal of Saudi Chemical Society

J Sav — Journal des Savants

JSav — Journal des Savants

J Savants — Journal des Savants

JSAW — Jahrbuch der Saechsischen Akademie der Wissenschaften

JSB — Journal of Small Business Management

JSBAS — Journal. Straits Branch. Royal Asiatic Society

JSBCD3 — Journal. American Society of Brewing Chemists

JSBL — Journal. Society of Biblical Literature

JSBRAS — Journal. Straits Branch. Royal Asiatic Society

JSc — Journal des Scavans

JSC — Journal. Institute for Socioeconomic Studies

J Sc — Journal of Science and Annals of Astronomy, Biology, Geology, Industrial Arts, Manufactures, and Technology

JSC — Journal of Structural Chemistry

J S CA A Mag — Journal. Southern California Arts Magazine

J Scavans Amsterdam — Journal des Scavans (Amsterdam)

J Scavans Leipzig — Le Journal des Scavans (Leipzig)

J SCCJ — Journal of SCCJ

J Sc Food Agriculture — Journal of the Science of Food and Agriculture

J Sch Healt — Journal of School Health

J Sch Health — Journal of School Health

J Sch Hlth — Journal of School Health

J Sc Hiroshima Univ S B Div 1 Zool — Journal of Science. Hiroshima University. Series B. Division 1. Zoology

J SC Hist Soc — Journal of the South Carolina History Society

J Sch Lib Assoc Qld — Journal. School Library Association of Queensland

J Sch Lib Ass Q — Journal. School Library Association of Queensland

J Sch Libr Assoc Qld — Journal. School Library Association of Queensland

J Schoenberg Inst — Journal of the Arnold Schoenberg Institute

J Sch Pharm Med Sci Univ Tehran — Journal of the School of Pharmacy. Medical Sciences University of Tehran

J Sch Pharm Univ Tehran — Journal. School of Pharmacy. University of Tehran

J Sch Psych — Journal of School Psychology

J Sch Psychol — Journal of School Psychology

Jschr Mitteldtsch Vorgesch — Jahresschrift fuer Mitteldeutsche Vorgeschichte

Jschr Mitteldt Vorgesch — Jahresschrift fuer Mitteldeutsche Vorgeschichte

Jschr Salzburg Mus Carolino Augusteum — Jahresschrift des Salzburger Museums Carolino Augusteum

J Schr Vg (Halle) — Jahresschrift fuer Mitteldeutsche Vorgeschichte (Halle)

Jschr Vorgesch Saechs-Thuering Laender — Jahresschrift fuer die Vorgeschichte der Saechsischen-Thueringischen Laender

Jschr Vorgesch Saechs Thuer Laender — Jahresschrift fuer die Vorgeschichte der Saechsisch-Thueringischen Laender

J Sci — Journal of Science

J Sci Agric — Journal of Scientific Agriculture

J Sci Agric Essays — Journal for Scientific Agricultural Essays

J Sci Agric Res — Journal for Scientific Agricultural Research

J Sci Agric Soc Finl — Journal. Scientific Agricultural Society of Finland

J Sci Agric Soc Tokyo — Journal of Scientific Agricultural Society (Tokyo)

J Sci Agr Res — Journal for Scientific Agricultural Research

J Sci & A — Journal of Science and the Arts

J Sci and Ind Res — Journal of Scientific and Industrial Research

J Sci and Technol — Journal of Science and Technology

J Sci Ann Astron — Journal of Science, and Annals of Astronomy, Biology, Geology, Industrial Arts, Manufactures, and Technology

J Sci Arts Metiers — Journal des Sciences, Arts, et Metiers. Par Une Societe de Gens de Lettres et d'Artistes

J Sci Assoc Maharajah's Coll — Journal. Science Association. Maharajah's College

J Sci Busan Natl Univ — Journal of Science. Busan National University

J Sci Club — Journal of the Science Club

J Sci Coll Gen Educ Univ Tokushima — Journal of Science. College of General Education. University of Tokushima

J Sci Comput — Journal of Scientific Computing

J Sci Educ Chonnam Natl Univ — Journal of Science Education. Chonnam National University

J Sci Educ Chungbuk Natl Univ — Journal of Science Education. Chungbuk National University

J Sci Educ Jeonbug Natl Univ — Journal of Science Education. Jeonbug National University

J Sci Educ (Jeonju) — Journal of Science Education (Jeonju)

J Sci Educ Sci Educ Res Inst Teach Coll Kyungpook Univ — Journal of Science Education. Science Education Research Institute Teacher's College. Kyungpook University

J Sci Educ Technol — Journal of Science Education and Technology

J Sci Eng Natl Chung Hsing Univ — Journal of Science and Engineering (National Chung Hsing University)

J Sci Eng Res — Journal of Science and Engineering Research

J Sci Engrg Res — Journal of Science and Engineering Research

J Scient Agric Soc Finl — Journal. Scientific Agricultural Society of Finland

J Scient Ind Res — Journal of Scientific and Industrial Research

J Scient Instrum — Journal of Scientific Instruments

J Scient Stud Relig — Journal for the Scientific Study of Religion

J Sci Explor — Journal of Scientific Exploration

J Sci Fac Chiangmai Univ — Journal. Science Faculty of Chiangmai University

J Sci Fd Agric — Journal of the Science of Food and Agriculture

J Sci Food — Journal of the Science of Food and Agriculture

J Sci Food Agr — Journal of the Science of Food and Agriculture

J Sci Food Agric — Journal of the Science of Food and Agriculture

J Sci Food Agric Abstr — Journal of the Science of Food and Agriculture. Abstracts
J Sci Gakugei Fac Tokushima Univ — Journal of Science. Gakugei Faculty. Tokushima University
J Sci Hiroshima Univ — Journal of Science. Hiroshima University
J Sci Hiroshima Univ A — Journal of Science. Hiroshima University. Series A. Physics and Chemistry
J Sci Hiroshima Univ Ser A — Journal of Science. Hiroshima University. Series A. Physics and Chemistry
J Sci Hiroshima Univ Ser A-II — Journal of Science. Hiroshima University. Series A-II
J Sci Hiroshima Univ Ser A Math Phys Chem — Journal of Science. Hiroshima University. Series A. Mathematics, Physics, Chemistry
J Sci Hiroshima Univ Ser A Phys — Journal of Science. Hiroshima University. Series A. Physics and Chemistry
J Sci Hiroshima Univ Ser A Phys Chem — Journal of Science. Hiroshima University. Series A. Physics and Chemistry
J Sci Hiroshima Univ Ser B Div 1 Zool — Journal of Science. Hiroshima University. Series B. Division 1. Zoology
J Sci Hiroshima Univ Ser B Div 2 Bot — Journal of Science. Hiroshima University. Series B. Division 2. Botany
J Sci Hiroshima Univ Ser C — Journal of Science. Hiroshima University. Series C. Geology and Mineralogy
J Sci Hiroshima Univ Ser C (Geol Mineral) — Journal of Science. Hiroshima University. Series C. Geology and Mineralogy
J Sci Hydrol — Journal des Sciences Hydrologiques
J Sci Ind R — Journal of Scientific and Industrial Research
J Sci Ind Res — Journal of Scientific and Industrial Research
J Sci Ind Res (India) — Journal of Scientific and Industrial Research (India)
J Sci Ind Res Sect A — Journal of Scientific and Industrial Research. Section A. General
J Sci Ind Res Sect B — Journal of Scientific and Industrial Research. Section B
J Sci Ind Res Sect C — Journal of Scientific and Industrial Research. Section C. Biological Sciences
J Sci Ind Res Sect D — Journal of Scientific and Industrial Research. Section D. Technology
J Sci Industr Res C Biol Sci — Journal of Scientific and Industrial Research. C. Biological Sciences
J Sci Instr — Journal of Scientific Instruments
J Sci Instrum — Journal of Scientific Instruments
J Sci Instrum Phys Ind — Journal of Scientific Instruments and Physics in Industry
J Sci Instrum Suppl — Journal of Scientific Instruments. Supplement
J Sci Islamic Repub Iran — Journal of Sciences. Islamic Republic of Iran
J Sci (Karachi) — Journal of Science (Karachi)
J Sci (Katmandu Nepal) — Journal of Science (Katmandu, Nepal)
J Sci Lab D — Journal. Scientific Laboratories. Denison University
J Sci Lab Denison Univ — Journal. Scientific Laboratories. Denison University
J Sci Labor — Journal of Science of Labor
J Sci Labour Part 1 (Jpn) — Journal of Science of Labour. Part 1 (in Japanese)
J Sci Labour Part 2 — Journal of Science of Labour. Part 2
J Sci Math Phys Nat — Jornal de Sciencias Mathematicas, Physicas, e Naturaes
J Sci Med Jinan Univ — Journal of Science and Medicine of Jinan University
J Sci Med Jundi Shapur Univ — Journal of Scientific Medicine of Jundi Shapur University
J Sci Med Lille — Journal des Sciences Medicales de Lille
J Sci Med Sport — Journal of Science and Medicine in Sport [Belconnen]
J Sci Meteorol — Journal Scientifique de la Meteorologie
J Sci Natl Univ Shantung — Journal of Science. National University of Shantung/Kuo-li Shantung ta Hsueeh K'o Hsueeh Ts'ung K'an
J Sci Nutr — Journal des Sciences de la Nutrition
J Sci Nutr Suppl — Journal des Sciences de la Nutrition. Supplementum
J Sci Res — Journal of Scientific Research
J Sci Res Banaras Hindu Univ — Journal of Scientific Research. Banaras Hindu University
J Sci Res (Bhopal) — Journal of Scientific Research (Bhopal)
J Sci Res Bhopal India — Journal of Scientific Research (Bhopal, India)
J Sci Res Counc Jam — Journal. Scientific Research Council of Jamaica
J Sci Res (Hardwar) — Journal of Scientific Research (Hardwar, India)
J Sci Res (Hardwar India) — Journal of Scientific Research (Hardwar, India)
J Sci Res (Indones) — Journal of Scientific Research (Indonesia)
J Sci Res Inst — Journal. Scientific Research Institute
J Sci Res Inst Han Nam Univ — Journal of Science Research Institute of Han Nam University
J Sci Res Inst Ministr Agric Bulg — Journal. Scientific Research Institutes. Ministry of Agriculture (Bulgaria)
J Sci Res Inst (Tokyo) — Journal. Scientific Research Institute (Tokyo)
J Sci Res (Lahore) — Journal of Scientific Research (Lahore)
J Sci Res Plants & Med — Journal of Scientific Research in Plants and Medicines
J Sci Soc Thailand — Journal. Science Society of Thailand
J Sci Soil Anim Fert (Jpn) — Journal of the Science of Soil and Animal Fertilizers (Japan)
J Sci Soil Manure (Jap) — Journal of the Science of Soil and Manure (Japan)
J Sci St Re — Journal for the Scientific Study of Religion
J Sci Stud Rel — Journal for the Scientific Study of Religion
J Sci Stud Relig — Journal for the Scientific Study of Religion
J Sci Tech — Journal of Science and Technology
J Sci Tech Agric Essays — Journal for Scientific and Technical Agricultural Essays
J Sci Technol — Journal of Science and Technology
J Sci Technol (Aberdeen Scotl) — Journal of Science Technology (Aberdeen, Scotland)
J Sci Technol (London) — Journal of Science and Technology (London)
J Sci Technol (Peshawar) — Journal of Science and Technology (Peshawar)
J Sci Tech Tonnellerie — Journal des Sciences et Techniques de la Tonnellerie
JSCJA — Journal. Society of Chemical Industry (Japan)
JSCL — Journal. Society of Comparative Legislation

JSCMA — Journal. South Carolina Medical Association
JS SC Med Assoc — Journal. South Carolina Medical Association
J SC Medic Assoc — Journal of the South Carolina Medical Association
JSCOD — Job Safety Consultant
JS Com Ind L — Journal. Society of Commercial and Industrial Law
J S Cosm Ch — Journal. Society of Cosmetic Chemists
J Scot Georg Soc — Journal of the Scottish Georgian Society
J Scott Assoc Geogr Teach — Journal. Scottish Association of Geography Teachers
JSCP — Journal of Sacred and Classical Philology
JSCPB — Proceedings. Japan Society of Civil Engineers
JSCSA — Journal of Statistical Computation and Simulation
JScStRel — Journal for the Scientific Study of Religion
JSCUD — Journal of Science Education. Chungbuk National University
J Scunthorpe Mus Soc — Journal. Scunthorpe Museum Society
JSD — JiJi Securities Data Service
JSDC — Journal. Society of Dyers and Colourists
J S Dye Col — Journal. Society of Dyers and Colourists
JSEAH — Journal of South-East Asian History
J Sea Res — Journal of Sea Research
J SE Asian Hist — Journal of Southeast Asian History
J SE Asian Stud — Journal of Southeast Asian Studies
J SE Asia S — Journal of Southeast Asian Studies
J Se As Stud — Journal of Southeast Asian Studies
J Seattle King Cty Dent Soc — Journal. Seattle-King County Dental Society
J Sec Ed — Journal of Secondary Education
J Sedimentol Soc Jpn — Journal of the Sedimentological Society of Japan
J Sediment Petrol — Journal of Sedimentary Petrology
J Sediment Petrology — Journal of Sedimentary Petrology
J Sediment Res — Journal of Sedimentary Research
J Sediment Res Sect A — Journal of Sedimentary Research. Section A. Sedimentary Petrology and Processes
J Sed Pet — Journal of Sedimentary Petrology
J Sed Petrol — Journal of Sedimentary Petrology
J Seed Technol — Journal of Seed Technology
J Seismol Soc Jpn — Journal. Seismological Society of Japan
J Sej — Jernal Sejarah
J Semitic S — Journal of Semitic Studies
J Semitic Stud — Journal of Semitic Studies
JSemS — Journal of Semitic Studies
J Sem St — Journal of Semitic Studies
J Sens Stud — Journal of Sensory Studies
J Seoul Woman's Coll — Journal. Seoul Woman's College
J Separ Proc Technol — Journal of Separation and Process Technology
J Sep Process Technol — Journal of Separation Process Technology
J Serb Chem Soc — Journal. Serbian Chemical Society
J Seric Sci Jpn — Journal of Sericultural Science of Japan
J Serotonin Res — Journal of Serotonin Research
JSeS — Journal of Semitic Studies
JSET — Journal of Sex Education and Therapy
J Severance Union Med Coll — Journal. Severance Union Medical College
JSExc — Memorias. Junta Superior de Excavaciones y Antiquedades
J Sex Marital Ther — Journal of Sex and Marital Therapy
J Sex Res — Journal of Sex Research
JSexZ — Jahrbuch fuer Sexuelle Zwischenstufen
J Seychelles Soc — Journal. Seychelles Society
JSFA — Journal of the Science of Food and Agriculture
JSFOu — Journal. Societe Finno-Ougrienne
JSFWUB — Jahrbuch der Schlesischen Friedrich-Wilhelms-Universitaet zu Breslau. Beiheft
JSFWUB — Jahrbuch. Schlesische Friedrich-Wilhelm Universitaet zu Breslau
JSG — Jahrbuch fuer Schweizerische Geschichte
JSG — Jahrbuch. Schiller-Gesellschaft
JSGLL — Japanese Studies in German Language and Literature
JSGU — Jahrbuch. Schweizerische Gesellschaft fuer Urgeschichte
JSGVK — Jahresbericht der Schlesischen Gesellschaft fuer Vaterlaendische Kultur
JSH — Jihocesky Sbornik Historicky
JSH — Journal of Social History
JSH — Journal of Southern History
J Shaanxi Norm Univ Nat Sci Ed — Journal of Shaanxi Normal University. Natural Science Edition
JSHABP — Journal. South African Speech and Hearing Association
J Shandong Coll Oceanol — Journal. Shandong College of Oceanology
J Shandong Univ Nat Sci Ed — Journal. Shandong University. Natural Science Edition
J Shanghai Chiao-tung Univ — Journal. Shanghai Chiao-tung University
J Shanghai Coll Text Technol — Journal. Shanghai College of Textile Technology
J Shanghai First Second Med Coll — Journal. Shanghai First and Second Medical College
J Shanghai Inst Chem Technol — Journal. Shanghai Institute of Chemical Technology
J Shanghai Inst Railway Tech — Journal. Shanghai Institute of Railway Technology
J Shanghai Jiaotong Univ — Journal of Shanghai Jiaotong University/Shanghai Jiaotong Daxue Xuebao
J Shanghai Sci Inst — Journal. Shanghai Science Institute
J Shanghai Sci Inst Sect 1 — Journal. Shanghai Science Institute. Section 1. Experimental Biology and Medicine
J Shanghai Sci Inst Sect 1 — Journal. Shanghai Science Institute. Section 1. Mathematics, Astronomy, Physics, Geophysics, Chemistry, and Allied Sciences
J Shanghai Sci Inst Sect 2 — Journal. Shanghai Science Institute. Section 2. Geology, Palaeontology, Mineralogy, and Petrology
J Shanghai Sci Inst Sect 3 — Journal. Shanghai Science Institute. Section 3. Systematic and Morphological Biology

J Shanghai Sci Inst Sect 4 — Journal. Shanghai Science Institute. Section 4. Experimental Biology and Medicine

J Shanghai Sci Inst Sect 5 — Journal. Shanghai Science Institute. Section 5. General

J Shanghai Second Med Univ — Journal of Shanghai Second Medical University

J Shanghai Univ Nat Sci — Journal of Shanghai University. Natural Science

J Shanghai Univ Sci Technol — Journal of Shanghai University of Science and Technology

J Shanghai Univ Technol — Journal of Shanghai University of Technology

J Shanxi Med Univ — Journal of Shanxi Medical University

J Shanxi Univ Nat Sci Ed — Journal. Shanxi University. Natural Science Edition

J Shanxi Univ Natur Sci Ed — Journal. Shanxi University. Natural Science Edition

J SHASE — Journal. Society of Heating, Air Conditioning, and Sanitary Engineers of Japan

JSHD — Journal of Speech and Hearing Disorders

JSHDA — Journal of Speech and Hearing Disorders

JSHEA — Journal of School Health

J Sheffield Univ Met Soc — Journal. Sheffield University Metallurgical Society

J Shellfish Res — Journal of Shellfish Research

J Shenyang Coll Pharm — Journal. Shenyang College of Pharmacy

J Shenyang Inst Chem Technol — Journal of Shenyang Institute of Chemical Technology

J Shenyang Pharm Univ — Journal of Shenyang Pharmaceutical University

J Shiga Prefect Jr Coll Ser A — Journal. Shiga Prefectural Junior College. Series A

J Shiga Univ Med Sci — Journal. Shiga University of Medical Science

J Shikoku Public Health Soc — Journal. Shikoku Public Health Society

J Shimane Med Assoc — Journal. Shimane Medical Association

J Shimonoseki Coll Fish — Journal. Shimonoseki College of Fisheries

J Shimonoseki Univ Fish — Journal. Shimonoseki University of Fisheries

J Ship Prod — Journal of Ship Production

J Ship Res — Journal of Ship Research

J S Hist — Journal of Southern History

J Shivaji Univ — Journal. Shivaji University

J Shivaji Univ Sci — Journal. Shivaji University (Science)

J Shoreline Manage — Journal of Shoreline Management

J Shoulder Elbow Surg — Journal of Shoulder and Elbow Surgery

J Showa Med Assoc — Journal. Showa Medical Association

J Showa Univ Dent Soc — Journal. Showa University Dental Society

JSHR — Journal of Speech and Hearing Research

J-S H Sch Clearing House — Junior-Senior High School Clearing House

JSHY — Journal of Social History

JSI — Journal. American Society for Information Science

JSI — Journal of Social Issues

JSI — Journal of Societal Issues

JSIAM — Journal. Society of Industrial and Applied Mathematics

J Siamese Vet Assoc — Journal. Siamese Veterinary Association

J Siam Soc — Journal. Siam Society

J Siam Soc Nat Hist Suppl — Journal. Siam Society. Natural History Supplement

J Sichuan Univ Nat Sci Ed — Journal. Sichuan University. Natural Science Edition

J Sigenkagaku Kenkyusyo — Journal. Sigenkagaku Kenkyusyo/Shigen Kagaku Kenkyusho Obun Hokoku

J Signalaufzeichnungsmater — Journal fuer Signalaufzeichnungsmaterialien

J Signalaufzeichnungsmaterialien — Journal fuer Signalaufzeichnungsmaterialien

J Signal Rec Mater — Journal of Signal Recording Materials

JSIN — Journal. Society for International Numismatics

J Sind Nac Farm Soc Farm Lusit — Jornal do Sindicato Nacional dos Farmaceuticos. Sociedade Farmaceutica Lusitana

J Singapore Nat Acad Sci — Journal. Singapore National Academy of Science

J Singapore Natl Acad Sci — Journal. Singapore National Academy of Science

J Singapore Paediatr Soc — Journal. Singapore Paediatric Society

JSISD — Journal of Current Social Issues

JSJ — Journal for the Study of Judaism [*Later, Journal for the Study of Judaism in thePersian, Hellenistic, and Roman Periods*]

JSJC — Je Sais, Je Crois

JSK — Jahrbuch des Stiftes Klosterneuburg

JSK — Jahrbuch. Sammlung Kippenberg Duesseldorf

JSKG — Jahrbuch fuer Schlesische Kirchengeschichte

JSL — Journal of Sacred Literature and Biblical Record

JSL — Journal of Symbolic Logic

JSL — Journal. School of Languages

JSLB — Japan Society of London. Bulletin

JSLCA — Journal of Solution Chemistry

J Sleep Res — Journal of Sleep Research

JslF — Juznoslovenski Filolog

JSLQ — Journal of Symbolic Logic. Quarterly

JSLS — Journal of the Society of Laparoendoscopic Surgeons. JSLS

JSM — Journal of Synagogue Music

JSM — Journal of Systems Management

J Small Anim Med — Journal of Small Animal Medicine

J Small Anim Pract — Journal of Small Animal Practice

J Small Bus Can — Journal of Small Business Canada

J Small Bus Manage — Journal of Small Business Management

J Small Bus Mgt — Journal of Small Business Management

J Sm Anim P — Journal of Small Animal Practice

JSMCA — Jahresschrift des Salzburger Museums Carolino-Augusteum

JSMCCA — Jahresschrift des Salzburger Museums Carolino-Augusteum

JSME Internat J — JSME (Japan Society of Mechanical Engineers) International Journal

JSME Int J — JSME [*Japan Society of Mechanical Engineers*] International Journal

JSME Int J Ser 2 — JSME (Japan Society of Mechanical Engineers) International Journal. Series 2. Fluids Engineering, Heat Transfer, Power, Combusion, and Thermophysical Properties

JSME Int J Ser A — JSME International Journal. Series A. Mechanics and Material Engineering

JSME Int J Ser B — JSME [*Japan Society of Mechanical Engineers*] International Journal. Series B. Fluids and Thermal Engineering

JSME Int J Ser C — JSME (Japan Society of Mechanical Engineers) International Journal. Series C. Dynamics, Control, Robotics, Design, and Manufacturing

JSME Int J Ser C — JSME [*Japan Society of Mechanical Engineers*] International Journal. Series C. Mechanical Systems, Machine Elements, and Manufacturing

JSME Intl J — JSME (Japan Society of Mechanical Engineers) International Journal

JSME Pap Jt JSME ASME Appl Mech West Conf — - ASME Appled Mechanics Western Conference

JSMK — Jahrbuch der Saechsischen Missionskonferenz

JSMMART — Journal. Society for Mass Media and Resource Technology

J Smooth Muscle Res — Journal of Smooth Muscle Research

J Smooth Muscle Res Jpn Sect — Journal of Smooth Muscle Research. Japanese Section

JSMPE — Journal. Society of Motion Picture Engineers

J SMPTE — Journal. SMPTE

JSMVK — Jahrbuch des Staedtischen Museums fuer Voelkerkunde zu Leipzig

JSNT — Journal for the Study of the New Testament

JSNTDC — Annuaire. Societe Helvetique des Sciences Naturelles. Partie Scientifique

JSO — Journal. Societe des Oceanistes

J So AL — Journal of South Asian Literature

J So Asia Mid East Stud — Journal of South Asian and Middle Eastern Studies

JSOc — Journal. Societe des Oceanistes

J Soc A — Journal of the Society of Arts

J Soc Afr — Journal. Societe des Africanistes

J Soc African — Journal. Societe des Africanistes

J Soc Africanistes — Journal. Societe des Africanistes

J Soc Air-Cond Refrig Eng Korea — Journal. Society of Air-Conditioning and Refrigerating Engineers of Korea

J Soc Am — Journal. Societe des Americanistes

J Soc Amer — Journal. Societe des Americanistes

J Soc American — Journal de la Societe des Americanistes

J Soc Americanistes — Journal de la Societe des Americanistes

J Soc Am Paris — Journal. Societe des Americanistes de Paris

J Soc Arch — Journal. Society of Archivists

J Soc Archer-Antiq — Journal. Society of Archer-Antiquaries

J Soc Arch H — Journal. Society of Architectural Historians

J Soc Arch Hist — Journal. Society of Architectural Historians

J Soc Architect Hist — Journal. Society of Architectural Historians

J Soc Archit Hist — Journal of the Society of Architectural Historians

J Soc Army Hist Res — Journal. Society for Army Historical Research

J Soc Arts — Journal. Society of Arts

J Soc Automot Eng — Journal. Society of Automotive Engineers

J Soc Automot Eng Jpn — Journal. Society of Automotive Engineers of Japan

J Soc Automot Eng Jpn Inc — Journal. Society of Automotive Engineers of Japan, Incorporated

J Soc Automot Engrs Australas — Society of Automotive Engineers of Australasia. Journal

J Soc Bibliog Nat Hist — Journal of the Society for the Bibliography of Natural History

J Soc Bibliogr Nat Hist — Journal. Society for the Bibliography of Natural History

J Soc Bibliogr Natur Hist — Journal. Society for the Bibliography of Natural History

J Soc Brew (Japan) — Journal. Society of Brewing (Japan)

J Soc Brew (Tokyo) — Journal. Society of Brewing (Tokyo)

J Soc Can Anesth — Journal. Societe Canadienne des Anesthesistes

J Soc Can Sci Judiciaires — Journal. Societe Canadienne des Sciences Judiciaires

J Soc Casework — Social Casework Journal

J Soc Chem Ind (Jpn) — Journal. Society of Chemical Industry (Japan)

J Soc Chem Ind (Lond) — Journal. Society of Chemical Industry (London)

J Soc Chem Ind (London) — Journal. Society of Chemical Industry (London)

J Soc Chem Ind (London) Abstr — Journal. Society of Chemical Industry (London). Abstracts

J Soc Chem Ind (London) Rev Sect — Journal. Society of Chemical Industry (London). Review Section

J Soc Chem Ind (London) Trans Commun — Journal. Society of Chemical Industry (London). Transactions and Communications

J Soc Chem Ind Vic — Journal. Society of Chemical Industry of Victoria

J Soc Chim Hong — Journal. Societe des Chimistes Hongrois

J Soc Cienc Med Lisb — Jornal. Sociedade das Ciencias Medicas de Lisboa

J Soc Comp Leg — Journal. Society of Comparative Legislation

J Soc Comp Legis — Journal. Society of Comparative Legislation

J Soc Cosmet Chem — Journal. Society of Cosmetic Chemists

J Soc Dairy Technol — Journal. Society of Dairy Technology

J Soc Domest Sanit Eng — Journal. Society of Domestic and Sanitary Engineering

J Soc Dy Colour — Journal. Society of Dyers and Colourists

J Soc Dyers — Journal. Society of Dyers and Colourists

J Soc Dyers Colour — Journal. Society of Dyers and Colourists

J Soc Dyers Colourists — Journal. Society of Dyers and Colourists

J Soc Earth Sci Amat Jpn — Journal. Society of Earth Scientists and Amateurs of Japan

J Soc Electr Mater Eng — Journal of the Society of Electrical Materials Engineering

J Soc Eng (Lond) — Journal. Society of Engineers (London)

J Soc Eng Miner Springs — Journal. Society of Engineers for Mineral Springs

J Soc Eng Miner Springs Jpn — Journal. Society of Engineers for Mineral Springs. Japan

J Soc Env Engrs — Journal. Society of Environmental Engineers

J Soc Environ Eng — Journal. Society of Environmental Engineers

J Soc Environ Engrs — Journal. Society of Environmental Engineers

J Soc Exp Agric — Journal. Society of Experimental Agriculturists

J Soc Fiber Sci Technol Jpn — Journal. Society of Fiber Science and Technology. Japan

J Soc Forest — Journal. Society of Forestry/Ringakukai Zasshi

J Soc Friends Dunblane Cathedral — Journal of the Society of Friends of Dunblane Cathedral

J Soc Friends Glasgow Cathedral — Journal of the Society of Friends of Glasgow Cathedral

J Soc Glass Tech — Journal of the Society of Glass Technology

J Soc Glass Technol — Journal. Society of Glass Technology

J Soc Gynecol Invest — Journal of the Society for Gynecologic Investigation

J Soc Gynecol Investig — Journal of the Society for Gynecologic Investigation

J Soc Health Syst — Journal. Society for Health Systems

J Soc High Polym Jpn — Journal. Society of High Polymers of Japan

J Soc High Pressure Gas Ind — Journal. Society of High Pressure Gas Industry

J Soc Hist — Journal of Social History

J Soc Hyg — Journal of Social Hygiene

J Soc Hygiene — Journal of Social Hygiene

J Social and Econ Studies — Journal of Social and Economic Studies

J Social and Pol Studies — Journal of Social and Political Studies

J Social Casework — Journal of Social Casework

J Social Forces — Journal of Social Forces

J Social Hyg — Journal of Social Hygiene

J Social Issues — Journal of Social Issues

J Social Pol and Econ Studies — Journal of Social, Political, and Economic Studies

J Social Policy — Journal of Social Policy

J Social Psychol — Journal of Social Psychology

J Social Sci — Journal of Social Science

J Soc Ind Appl Math — Journal. Society of Industrial and Applied Mathematics

J Soc Ind Appl Math Ser A — Journal. Society for Industrial and Applied Mathematics. Series A. Control

J Soc Inf Disp — Journal of the Society for Information Display

J Soc Ing Automob — Journal. Societe des Ingenieurs de l'Automobile

J Soc Instrum and Control — Journal. Society of Instrument and Control Engineers

J Soc Instrum Control Eng — Journal. Society of Instrument and Control Engineers

J Soc Int Chim Ind Cuir — Journal. Societe Internationale des Chimistes des Industries du Cuir

J Soc Int Odonatologica — Journal. Societas Internationalis Odonatologica

J Sociol Chengchi — Journal of Sociology. National Chengchi University

J Sociol Med — Journal of Sociologie Medicine

J Soc Iss — Journal of Social Issues

J Soc Issue — Journal of Social Issues

J Soc Issues — Journal of Societal Issues

J Soc Laparoendosc Surg — Journal of the Society of Laparoendoscopic Surgeons. JSLS

J Soc Leath Technol Chem — Journal. Society of Leather Technologists and Chemists

J Soc Leath Trades Chem — Journal. Society of Leather Trades Chemists

J Soc Maroc Chim — Journal de la Societe Marocaine de Chimie

J Soc Mater Eng Resour Jpn — Journal. Society of Materials Engineering for Resources of Japan

J Soc Mater Sci (Jpn) — Journal. Society of Materials Science (Japan)

J Soc Metall Russe — Journal. Societe Metallurgique Russe

J Soc Motion Pict and Telev Eng — Journal. Society of Motion Picture and Television Engineers

J Soc Motion Pict Eng — Journal. Society of Motion Picture Engineers

J Soc Motion Pict Telev Eng — Journal. Society of Motion Picture and Television Engineers

J Soc Mot Pict Eng — Journal. Society of Motion Picture Engineers

J Soc Mot Pict Tel Eng — Journal. Society of Motion Picture and Television Engineers

J Soc Nav Archit Jpn — Journal. Society of Naval Architects of Japan

J Soc Nav Arch Japan — Journal. Society of Naval Architects of Japan

J Soc Non-Destr Test — Journal. Society for Non-Destructive Testing

J Soc Occup Med — Journal. Society of Occupational Medicine

J Soc Ocean — Journal. Societe des Oceanistes

J Soc Oceanistes — Journal. Societe des Oceanistes

J Soc Org Syn Chem (Jpn) — Journal. Society of Organic Synthetic Chemistry (Japan)

J Soc Org Synth Chem — Journal. Society of Organic Synthetic Chemistry

J Soc Osteopaths (Lond) — Journal. Society of Osteopaths (London)

J Soc Ouest Afr Chim — Journal de la Societe Ouest-Africaine de Chimie

J Soc Pet Eng — Journal. Society of Petroleum Engineers

J Soc Phil — Journal of Social Philosophy

J Soc Photogr Sci and Technol Jpn — Journal. Society of Photographic Science and Technology of Japan

J Soc Photo Opt Instrum Eng — Journal. Society of Photo-Optical Instrumentation Engineers

J Soc Phys Chim Russe — Journal. Societe Physico-Chimique Russe

J Soc Pol — Journal of Social Policy

J Soc Polic — Journal of Social Policy

J Soc Policy — Journal of Social Policy

J Soc Polit Stud — Journal of Social and Political Studies

J Soc Pop & Repub A — Journal de la Societe Populaire et Republicaine des Arts

J Soc Powder Technol Jpn — Journal. Society of Powder Technology (Japan)

J Soc Psych — Journal of Social Psychology

J Soc Psychol — Journal of Social Psychology

J Soc Psych Res — Journal. Society for Psychical Research

J Soc Pub Teach Law N S — Journal. Society of Public Teachers of Law. New Series

J Soc Pub T L — Journal. Society of Public Teachers of Law

J Soc Pure Appl Nat Sci — Journal. Society for Pure and Applied Natural Sciences

J Soc Radiol Prot — Journal. Society for Radiological Protection

J Soc Regionale Hort N France — Journal. Societe Regionale d'Horticulture du Nord de la France

J Soc Res — Journal of Social Research

J Soc Resour Geol — Journal. Society of Resource Geology

J Soc Rheol Jpn — Journal. Society of Rheology. Japan

J Soc Rubber Ind (Jpn) — Journal. Society of Rubber Industry (Japan)

J Soc S — Jewish Social Studies

J Soc Sci — Journal of Social Sciences

J Soc Sci Hum — Journal of Social Sciences and Humanities

J Soc Sci Photogr Jpn — Journal. Society of Scientific Photography of Japan

J Soc Statist Paris — Journal. Societe Statistique de Paris

J Soc Stud — Journal of Social Studies

J Soc Stud Egyp Ant — Journal of the Society for the Study of Egyptian Antiquities

J Soc Ther — Journal of Social Therapy

J Soc Trop Agric — Journal. Society of Tropical Agriculture/Nettai Nogaku Kwaishi

J Soc Trop Agric Taihoku Imp Univ — Journal. Society of Tropical Agriculture. Taihoku Imperial Univerisity

J Soc Underwater Technol — Journal. Society for Underwater Technology

J Soc Water Treat Exam — Journal. Society for Water Treatment and Examination

J Soc Welfare L — Journal of Social Welfare Law

J Soc Work & Hum Sex — Journal of Social Work and Human Sexuality

J Socy Pub Tchrs L — Journal. Society of Public Teachers of Law

J Software Maint — Journal of Software Maintenance

JSoG — Jahrbuch fuer Solothurnische Geschichte

J So Hist — Journal of Southern History

J Soil & Water Conser — Journal of Soil and Water Conservation

J Soil Biol & Ecol — Journal of Soil Biology and Ecology

J Soil Conservation Serv NSW — Journal. Soil Conservation Service of New South Wales

J Soil Conserv NSW — Journal. Soil Conservation Service of New South Wales

J Soil Conserv Service NSW — Journal. Soil Conservation Service of New South Wales

J Soil Conserv Serv NSW — Journal. Soil Conservation Service of New South Wales

J Soil Contam — Journal of Soil Contamination

J Soil Mech Found Div Am Soc Civ Eng — Journal. Soil Mechanics and Foundations Division. American Society of Civil Engineers

J Soil Sci — Journal of Soil Science

J Soil Sci Shenyang Peoples Repub China — Journal of Soil Science (Shenyang, People's Republic of China)

J Soil Sci Soc Am — Journal. Soil Science Society of America

J Soil Sci Soc Philipp — Journal. Soil Science Society of the Philippines

J Soil Sci UAR — Journal of Soil Science of the United Arab Republic

J Soil Sci Un Arab Repub — Journal of Soil Science of the United Arab Republic

J Soil Wat — Journal of Soil and Water Conservation

J Soil Water Conserv — Journal of Soil and Water Conservation

J Soil Water Conserv India — Journal of Soil and Water Conservation in India

J Sol Chem — Journal of Solution Chemistry

J Sol Energy Eng — Journal of Solar Energy Engineering

J Sol Energy Eng Trans ASME — Journal of Solar Energy Engineering. Transactions of the ASME

J Sol Energy Res — Journal of Solar Energy Research

J Sol Energy Sci Eng — Journal of Solar Energy Science and Engineering

J Sol Energy Soc Korea — Journal. Solar Energy Society of Korea

J Sol En Sci — Journal of Solar Energy Science and Engineering

J Sol G — Jahrbuch fuer Solothurnische Geschichte

J Sol Gel Sci Technol — Journal of Sol-Gel Science and Technology

J Solid Lubr — Journal of Solid Lubrication

J Solid-Phase Biochem — Journal of Solid-Phase Biochemistry

J Solid State Chem — Journal of Solid State Chemistry

J Solid State Electrochem — Journal of Solid State Electrochemistry

J Solid Wastes — Journal of Solid Wastes

J Solid Wastes Manage — Journal of Solid Wastes Management

J Solid Waste Technol Manage — Journal of Solid Waste Technology and Management

J Soln Chem — Journal of Solution Chemistry

J Soloman Islands Mus Assoc — Journal of the Solomon Islands Museum Association

J Sol St Ch — Journal of Solid State Chemistry

J Solut Chem — Journal of Solution Chemistry

J Solution Chem — Journal of Solution Chemistry

J Somat Exp — Journal of Somatic Experience

J Somerset Mines Res Group — Journal. Somerset Mines Research Group

J Soochow Univ Coll Arts — Journal of Soochow University. College of Arts and Sciences/Tung-Wu Hsueeh-Pao

J Soonchunhyang Coll — Journal. Soonchunhyang College

JSOPK — Jahrbuch der Synodalkommission und des Vereins fuer Ostpreussische Kirchengeschichte

JSOR — Journal. Society of Oriental Research

JSOT — Journal for the Study of the Old Testament

J Soudure — Journal de la Soudure

J Sound and Vib — Journal of Sound and Vibration

J Sound Vib — Journal of Sound and Vibration

J Sound Vibration — Journal of Sound and Vibration

J South Afr Aff — Journal of Southern African Affairs

J South Afr Chem Inst — Journal. South African Chemical Institute

J South Afr Stud — Journal of Southern African Studies

J South Afr Vet Assoc — Journal. South African Veterinary Association

J South Afr Vet Med Ass — Journal. South African Veterinary Medical Association [Later, South African Veterinary Association. Journal]

J South Afr Wildl Manage Assoc — Journal. Southern African Wildlife Management Association

J South Asian Lit — Journal of South Asian Literature

J South As Lit — Journal of South Asian Literature

J South Calif Dent Assistants Assoc — Journal. Southern California Dental Assistants Association
J South Calif Dent Assoc — Journal. Southern California Dental Association
J South Calif Meter Assoc — Journal. Southern California Meter Association
J South California Dent A — Journal. Southern California Dental Association
J South Calif State Dent Assoc — Journal. Southern California State Dental Association
J South China Inst Technol — Journal. South China Institute of Technology
J South China Inst Technol Nat Sci — Journal. South China Institute of Technology. Natural Sciences
J South China Normal Univ Natur Sci Ed — Journal of South China Normal University. Natural Science Edition
J South China Norm Univ Nat Sci Ed — Journal of South China Normal Univesity. Natural Science Edition
J South China Univ Technol Nat Sci — Journal. South China University of Technology. Natural Science
J Southeast Agric Coll (Wye England) — Journal. Southeastern Agricultural College (Wye, England)
J Southeast Asian Stud — Journal of Southeast Asian Studies
J Southeast Res — Journal of Southeastern Research
J Southeast Sect Am Water Works Assoc — Journal. Southeastern Section. American Water Works Association
J Southeast Univ (China) — Journal. Southeast University (China)
J Southern Hist — Journal of Southern History
J South His — Journal of Southern History
J South Hist — Journal of Southern History
J South Orthop Assoc — Journal. Southern Orthopaedic Association
J South Res — Journal of Southern Research
J South West Afr Sci Soc — Journal. South West African Scientific Society
J Southwest China Teach Coll Ser B — Journal. Southwest-China Teachers College. Series B. Natural Science
J Southwest Pet Inst — Journal of Southwest Petroleum Institute
J Southw Scotland Grassland Soc — Journal. Southwest Scotland Grassland Society
J Sov Cardiovasc Res — Journal of Soviet Cardiovascular Research
J Soviet Math — Journal of Soviet Mathematics
J Sov Laser Res — Journal of Soviet Laser Research
J Sov Oncol — Journal of Soviet Oncology
J Sp — Jewish Spectator
JSP — Journal of Sedimentary Petrology
JSP — Journal of Social Psychology
JSP — Journal of Statistical Planning and Inference
J Spacecraft Rockets — Journal of Spacecraft and Rockets
J Spacecr and Rockets — Journal of Spacecraft and Rockets
J Spacecr Rockets — Journal of Spacecraft and Rockets
J Space Flight — Journal of Space Flight
J Space L — Journal of Space Law
J Space Law — Journal of Space Law
J Spac Rock — Journal of Spacecraft and Rockets
J Span Stud — Journal of Spanish Studies. Twentieth Century
JSPDA5 — Journal. American Society of Psychosomatic Dentistry
J Sp Disorders — Journal of Speech and Hearing Disorders
JSPEB — Journal of Special Education
J Spec — Jewish Spectator
J Spec Ed — Journal of Special Education
J Spec Ed Men Retard — Journal for Special Educators of the Mentally Retarded [Later, Journal for Special Educators]
J Spec Educ — Journal of Special Education
J Spec Philos — Journal of the Speculative Philosophy
J Spectrosc — Journal of Spectroscopy
J Spectros Soc Jpn — Journal. Spectroscopical Society of Japan
J Sp Educ — Journal of Special Education
J Sp Educators — Journal for Special Educators
J Sp Educ Men Retard — Journal for Special Educators of the Mentally Retarded [Later, Journal for Special Educators]
J Speech & Hear Dis — Journal of Speech and Hearing Disorders
J Speech & Hear Disord — Journal of Speech and Hearing Disorders
J Speech & Hear Res — Journal of Speech and Hearing Research
J Speech D — Journal of Speech and Hearing Disorders
J Speech He — Journal of Speech and Hearing Research
J Speech Hear Disord — Journal of Speech and Hearing Disorders
J Speech Hearing Dis — Journal of Speech and Hearing Disorders
J Speech Hear Res — Journal of Speech and Hearing Research
JSPFE — Journal of the Society for the Preservation of the Wild Fauna of the Empire
JSPG — Jahrbuch der Schweizerischen Philosophischen Gesellschaft
JSPH — Journal of Social Philosophy and Jurisprudence
JSPh — Journal of Speculative Philosophy
JSPHA — Journal of Speech and Hearing Research
JSPIJ — Journal of Social and Political Ideas in Japan
J Spinal Cord Med — Journal of Spinal Cord Medicine
J Spinal Disord — Journal of Spinal Disorders
JSPK — Jahrbuch. Stiftung Preussischer Kulturbesitz
JSPMA — Journal of Supramolecular Structure [Later, Journal of Cellular Biochemistry]
J Sport & Ex Psy — Journal of Sport & Exercise Psychology
J Sport and Soc Iss — Journal of Sport and Social Issues
J Sport Beh — Journal of Sport Behavior
J Sport Behav — Journal of Sport Behavior
J Sport Hist — Journal of Sport History
J Sport Management — Journal of Sport Management
J Sport Med — Journal of Sports Medicine and Physical Fitness
J Sport Psy — Journal of Sport Psychology
J Sport Psychol — Journal of Sport Psychology
J Sport Rehab — Journal of Sport Rehabilitation

J Sport Sci — Journal of Sports Sciences
J Sports Med — Journal of Sports Medicine
J Sports Med and P Fit — Journal of Sports Medicine and Physical Fitness
J Sports Med Phys Fit — Journal of Sports Medicine and Physical Fitness
J Sports Med Phys Fitness — Journal of Sports Medicine and Physical Fitness
J Sport Soc Iss — Journal of Sport and Social Issues
J Sports Sci — Journal of Sports Sciences
J Sports Trauma — Journal of Sports Traumatology
J Sports Turf Res Inst — Journal of the Sports Turf Research Institute
JSPR — Journal. Society for Psychical Research
J Spray Coat Soc Jpn — Journal. Spray Coating Society of Japan
JSPs — Journal of Social Psychology
JSPSA — Journal of Social Psychology
JSPSE — Journal. Society of Photographic Scientists and Engineers
JSPSR — Journal of Transactions. Society for Promoting the Study of Religions
JSPTL — Journal. Society of Public Teachers of Law
JSR — Japanese Sociological Review
JSR — Japan Socialist Review
JSR — Jewish Student Review
JSR — Journal of Ship Research
JSR — Journal of Social Research
JSR — Journal of Spacecraft and Rockets
JSRBA — Journal of Scientific Research. Banaras Hindu University
JSRHS — Japan Science Review. Humanistic Studies
JSR LPH — Japan Science Review. Literature, Philosophy, and History
JSRS — Jewish Social Research Series
JSRSA — JARE [Japanese Antarctic Research Expedition] Scientific Reports. SpecialIssue
JSs — Jahresbericht der Schlesichen Gesellschaft fuer Vaterlaendische Kultur
JSS — Jewish Social Studies
JSS — Journal of Semitic Studies
JSS — Journal of Social Sciences
JSS — Journal of Spanish Studies. Twentieth Century
JSS — Journal of Sports Sciences
JSS — Journal of Systems and Software
JSS — Journal. Siam Society
JSSB — Journal. Siam Society (Bangkok)
JSSC — Journal of Solid-State Circuits
JSSEA — Journal. American Society of Safety Engineers
JSSM — Journal of Semitic Studies (Manchester University)
JSSO — Journal of Soil Science (Oxford)
JSSP News — JSSP [Junior Secondary Science Project] Newsletter
JSS Proj Tech Rep — JSS [Japanese, Swiss, Swedish] Project. Technical Report
JSSQ — Jewish Social Service Quarterly
JSSR — Journal for the Scientific Study of Religion
JSSR — Journal of Social Services Research
JSSRel — Journal for the Scientific Study of Religion
JSSSG — Journal. Society for the Study of State Governments
JSSt — Journal of Semitic Studies
JSSTC — Journal of Spanish Studies. Twentieth Century
JS St M — Journal of Semitic Studies. Monograph
JST — Johnson Society. Transactions
JST — Journal of Business Strategy
JST — Journal of Science and Technology
JSTAA — Journal. Royal Statistical Society. Series A. General
J Stained Glass — Journal of Stained Glass
J Standard — Jewish Standard
J Starch Its Relat Carbohyd Enzymes — Journal for Starch and Its Related Carbohydrates and Enzymes
J Starch Sweet Technol Res Soc Japan — Journal. Starch Sweetener Technological Research Society of Japan
J Starch Technol Res Soc Jpn — Journal of Starch Technology. Research Society of Japan
J Stat Comput Simul — Journal of Statistical Computation and Simulation
J State Med — Journal of State Medicine
J Statis Soc — Journal. Statistical Society
J Statist Comp and Simulation — Journal of Statistical Computation and Simulation
J Statist Comput Simulation — Journal of Statistical Computation and Simulation
J Statist Phys — Journal of Statistical Physics
J Statist Plann Inference — Journal of Statistical Planning and Inference
J Statist Res — Journal of Statistical Research
J Stat Phys — Journal of Statistical Physics
J Stat Plann and Inference — Journal of Statistical Planning and Inference
J Stat Plann Inference — Journal of Statistical Planning and Inference
J Stat Rsr — Journal of Statistical Research
JSTBA — Journal. Royal Statistical Society. Series B. Methodological
J St Bar Calif — Journal. State Bar of California
J St Barnabas Med Cent — Journal. Saint Barnabas Medical Center
J Stefan Inst Phys Rep — J. Stefan Institute of Physics. Reports
J Stefan Inst Rep — J Stefan Institute. Reports
J Ster Biochem — Journal of Steroid Biochemistry
J Sterile Serv Manage — Journal of Sterile Services Management
J Steroid B — Journal of Steroid Biochemistry
J Steroid Biochem — Journal of Steroid Biochemistry
J Steroid Biochem Mol Biol — Journal of Steroid Biochemistry and Molecular Biology
J Steward Anthropol Soc — Journal. Steward Anthropological Society
J Steward Anthrop Soc — Journal of the Steward Anthropological Society
J Steward Anthro Soc — Journal. Steward Anthropological Society
J Sth Afr Stud — Journal of Southern African Studies
J Sth Afr Vet Med Ass — Journal. South African Veterinary Medical Association [Later, South African Veterinary Association. Journal]
JStJu — Journal for the Study of Judaism in the Persian, Hellenistic, and Roman Periods

J St Jud — Journal for the Study of Judaism [*Later, Journal for the Study of Judaism in the Persian, Hellenistic, and Roman Periods*]

J St Med — Journal of State Medicine

JSTNA — Journal. American Statistical Association

J St N T — Journal for the Study of the New Testament

J Stomat — Journal de Stomatologie

J Stomatol Belg — Journal de Stomatologie de Belgique

J Stomatol Soc (Jpn) — Journal. Stomatological Society (Japan)

J Stored Pr — Journal of Stored Products Research

J Stored Prod Res — Journal of Stored Products Research

J Stor Prod Res — Journal of Stored Product Research

J St OT — Journal for the Study of the Old Testament

JSTPD — Journal of Science and Technology (Peshawar, Pakistan)

J St Petersbourg — Journal de St Petersbourg

J Strain Anal — Journal of Strain Analysis

J Strain Anal Eng Des — Journal of Strain Analysis for Engineering Design

J Strain Anal Engng Des — Journal of Strain Analysis for Engineering Design

J Strain Analysis — Journal of Strain Analysis

J Straits Branch Royal Asiat Soc — Journal of the Straits Branch of the Royal Asiatic Society

J Straits Branch Roy Asiat Soc — Journal. Straits Branch. Royal Asiatic Society

J Streng & Con Res — Journal of Strength and Conditioning Research

JST Rep — JST [*Japan. Semiconductor Technology*] Reports

J Struc Engrg ASCE — Journal of Structural Engineering. American Society of Civil Engineers

J Struc Mec — Journal of Structural Mechanics

J Struct Biol — Journal of Structural Biology

J Struct Ch — Journal of Structural Chemistry

J Struct Chem — Journal of Structural Chemistry

J Struct Chem (Engl Transl) — Journal of Structural Chemistry (English Translation)

J Struct Di — Journal. Structural Division. Proceedings of the American Society of Civil Engineers

J Struct Div Amer Soc Civil Eng Proc — Journal. Structural Division. Proceedings of the American Society of Civil Engineers

J Struct Div Proc ASCE — Journal. Structural Division. Proceedings of the American Society of Civil Engineers

J Struct Eng — Journal of Structural Engineering

J Struct Geol — Journal of Structural Geology

J Struct Le — Journal of Structural Learning

J Struct Mech — Journal of Structural Mechanics

J Structural Learning — Journal of Structural Learning

J Structural Mech — Journal of Structural Mechanics

J St Tax'n — Journal of State Taxation

J Stud Alc — Journal of Studies on Alcohol

J Stud Alcohol — Journal of Studies on Alcohol

J Stud Alcohol (Suppl) — Journal of Studies on Alcohol (Supplement)

J Stud Amer Med Ass — Journal. Student American Medical Association

J Stud Econ Economet — Journal for Studies in Economics and Econometrics

J Studies Alcohol — Journal of Studies on Alcohol

J Studies Econ and Econometrics — Journal for Studies in Economics and Econometrics

J Study Iron Metall — Journal for Study of Iron Metallurgy

J Study Met Tokyo — Journal for Study of Metals. Tokyo

JSUB — Jahrbuch. Schlesische Friedrich-Wilhelm Universitaet zu Breslau

J Submic Cy — Journal of Submicroscopic Cytology

J Submicrosc Cytol — Journal of Submicroscopic Cytology

J Submicrosc Cytol Pathol — Journal of Submicroscopic Cytology and Pathology

J Subst Abuse — Journal of Substance Abuse

J Subst Abuse Treat — Journal of Substance Abuse Treatment

J Suffolk Acad L — Journal. Suffolk Academy of Law

J Sugarcane Res — Journal of Sugarcane Research

J Sugar Ind — Journal. Sugar Industry

J Sui Pharm — Journal Suisse de Pharmacie

J Suisse Apic — Journal Suisse d'Apiculture

J Suisse Chim Pharm — Journal Suisse de Chimie et Pharmacie

J Suisse Horlog — Journal Suisse d'Horlogerie

J Suisse Horlog Bijout — Journal Suisse d'Horlogerie et de Bijouterie

J Suisse Med — Journal Suisse de Medecine

J Suisse Pharm — Journal Suisse de Pharmacie

J Suisse Photogr — Journal Suisse de Photographie

J Sul-Am Biocienc — Jornal Sul-Americano de Biociencias

J Sul-Am Med — Jornal Sul-Americano de Medicina

J Sulfuric Acid Assoc Jpn — Journal. Sulfuric Acid Association of Japan

J Sun Yat Sen Univ Nat Sci Ed — Journal. Sun Yat-Sen University. Natural Science Edition

J Supercomput — Journal of Supercomputing

J Supercond — Journal of Superconductivity

J Supercrit Fluids — Journal of Supercritical Fluids

J Supervision — Journal of Supervision and Training in Ministry

J Supervision Tr Min — Journal of Supervision and Training in Ministry

J Supramolecular Struct — Journal of Supramolecular Structure [*Later, Journal of Cellular Biochemistry*]

J Supramol Struct — Journal of Supramolecular Structure [*Later, Journal of Cellular Biochemistry*]

J Supramol Struct Cell Biochem — Journal of Supramolecular Structure and Cellular Biochemistry [*Later, Journal of Cellular Biochemistry*]

J Supramol Struct (Suppl) — Journal of Supramolecular Structure (Supplement)

J Supram St — Journal of Supramolecular Structure [*Later, Journal of Cellular Biochemistry*]

J Surfactants Deterg — Journal of Surfactants and Detergents

J Surf Anal — Journal of Surface Analysis

J Surf Finish Soc Jpn — Journal. Surface Finishing Society of Japan

J Surf Sci Technol — Journal of Surface Science and Technology

J Surg Oncol — Journal of Surgical Oncology

J Surg Oncol Suppl — Journal of Surgical Oncology. Supppplement

J Surg Res — Journal of Surgical Research

J Surv & Mapp Div Proc ASCE — Journal. Surveying and Mapping Division. Proceedings of the American Society ofCivil Engineers

J Surv Eng — Journal of Surveying Engineering

J Survey — Jewish Survey

J Surv Mapp — Journal. Surveying and Mapping Division. Proceedings of the American Society ofCivil Engineers

J Surv Mapping Div Amer Soc Civil Eng Proc — Journal. Surveying and Mapping Division. Proceedings of the American Society ofCivil Engineers

JSVIA — Journal of Sound and Vibration

JSW — Jahrbuch fuer Sozialwissenschaft

J SWA Sci Soc — Journal. South West African Scientific Society

J SWA (South West Afr) Sci Soc — Journal. SWA (South West Africa) Scientific Society

J SWA Wiss Ges — Journal. SWA Wissenschaftliche Gesellschaft

JSWC — Journal of Soil and Water Conservation

J Swim Res — Journal of Swimming Research

JSWL — Journal of Social Welfare Law

JSWS — Journal of Social Work and Human Sexuality

JSW Tech Rev — JSW [*Japan Steel Works*] Technical Review

J Symb Anthropol — Journal of Symbolic Anthropology

J Symb Log — Journal of Symbolic Logic

J Symb Logic — Journal of Symbolic Logic

J Symbolic Logic — Journal of Symbolic Logic

J Symbol Logic — Journal of Symbolic Logic

J Sym Log — Journal of Symbolic Logic

J Synchrotron Radiat — Journal of Synchrotron Radiation

J Syn Org (J) — Journal of Synthetic Organic Chemistry (Japan)

J Synth Cryst — Journal of Synthetic Crystals

J Synth Lubr — Journal of Synthetic Lubrication

J Synth Org Chem (Jpn) — Journal of Synthetic Organic Chemistry (Japan)

J Synth Rubber Ind (Lanzhou People's Repub China) — Journal of Synthetic Rubber Industry (Lanzhou, People's Republic of China)

J Sys and Soft — Journal of Systems and Software

J Sys Mgmt — Journal of Systems Management

J Sys Mgt — Journal of Systems Management

J Syst and Software — Journal of Systems and Software

J System J — Justice System Journal

J Systems Engrg — Journal of Systems Engineering

J Systems Mgt — Journal of Systems Management

J Systems Sci Math Sci — Journal of Systems Science and Mathematical Sciences

J Systems Software — Journal of Systems and Software

J Syst Eng — Journal of Systems Engineering

J Syst Engng — Journal of Systems Engineering

J Syst Man — Journal of Systems Management

J Syst Manage — Journal of Systems Management

J Syst Mgt — Journal of Systems Management

J Syst Software — Journal of Systems and Software

JT — Jahrbuch der Technik

JT — Jewish Tribune

JT — Jornal de Turismo

JT — Journal des Tribunaux

JT — Journal de Trevoux. Memoires pour l'Histoire des Sciences et Beaux Arts

JT — Journal of Music Therapy

JT — Journal of Thought

JT — Juridisk Tidsskrift

JTA — Journal of Thermal Analysis

J Tachikawa Coll Tokyo — Journal. Tachikawa College of Tokyo

J Taiwan Agric Res — Journal of Taiwan Agricultural Research

J Taiwan Agr Res — Journal of Taiwan Agricultural Research

J Taiwan Mus — Journal. Taiwan Museum

J Taiwan Pharm Assoc — Journal. Taiwan Pharmaceutical Association

J Taiyuan Inst Technol — Journal. Taiyuan Institute of Technology

J Taiyuan Univ Technol — Journal. Taiyuan University of Technology

J Takeda Res Lab — Journal. Takeda Research Laboratories

J Takeda Res Labs — Journal. Takeda Research Laboratories

J Talien Eng Inst — Journal. Talien Engineering Institute

J Tamil Stud — Journal of Tamil Studies

J Tam S — Journal of Tamil Studies

JTASA — Journal. Tennessee Academy of Science

Jt Assess Commod Chem — Joint Assessment of Commodity Chemicals

J Tax — Journal of Taxation

J Taxation — Journal of Taxation

J Tax'n — Journal of Taxation

JTB — Journal of Theoretical Biology

JTBBD7 — Journal of Chemical Technology and Biotechnology. B. Biotechnology

Jt Bull Vt Bot Bird Club — Joint Bulletin. Vermont Botanical and Bird Club

JTC — Journal for Theology and the Church

JTCE — Journal of Transportation Engineering. Proceedings. American Society of Civil Engineers

JTCh — Journal for Theology and the Church

Jt China US Phycol Symp Proc — Joint China-US Phycology Symposium. Proceedings

JTCMD — Journal of Tissue Culture Methods

JTCMEC — Journal of Traditional Chinese Medicine

Jt Comm J Qual Improv — Joint Commission Journal on Quality Improvement

Jt Comm Rural Reconstr China US Repub China Plant Ind Ser — Joint Commission on Rural Reconstruction in China (United States and Republic of China). Plant Industry Series

Jt Conf Appl Air Pollut Meteorol Conf Pap — Joint Conference on Applications of Air Pollution Meteorology. Conference Papers

Jt Conf Chem Inst Can Am Chem Soc Abstr Pap — Joint Conference. Chemical Institute of Canada and the American Chemical Society. Abstracts of Papers

Jt Conf Cholera — Joint Conference on Cholera
Jt Conf Cholera Proc — Joint Conference on Cholera. Proceedings
Jt Conf CIC ACS Abstr Pap — Joint Conference CIC/ACS. Abstracts of Papers
Jt Conf Proc Ferrous Div Pac Coast Meet Wire Assoc Int — Joint Conference Proceedings. Ferrous Division/Pacific Coast Meeting. Wire Association International
Jt Conf Proc Wire Assoc Int Nonferrous Electr Div — Joint Conference Proceedings. Wire Association International. Nonfererous/Electrical Divisions
Jt Conf Sens Environ Pollut Collect Tech Pap — Joint Conference on Sensing of Environmental Pollutants. A Collection of Technical Papers
Jt Conf Sens Environ Pollut Proc — Joint Conference on Sensing of Environmental Pollutants. Proceedings
Jt Conf US Jpn Coop Med Sci Program Cholera Panel — Joint Conference. US-Japan Cooperative Medical Science Program. Cholera Panel
Jt Congr Eur Tissue Cult Soc Eur Reticuloendothel Soc — Joint Congress. European Tissue Culture Society and the European Reticuloendothelial Society
Jt Corros Conf — Joint Corrosion Conference
JTCP — Jahrbuecher fuer Theoogie und Christliche Philosophie
JTD — Japan Trade Directory
JTDAA — Journal. Tennessee Dental Association
JTE — Journal of Teacher Education
JTE — Journal of Transport Economics and Policy
J Teach Ed — Journal of Teacher Education
J Teach Educ — Journal of Teacher Education
J Teaching PE — Journal of Teaching in Physical Education
J Teach Learn — Journal of Teaching and Learning
J Teach Res Chem — Journal of Teaching and Research in Chemistry
J Tea Sci — Journal of Tea Science
J Tech Assoc Fur Ind — Journal. Technical Association of the Fur Industry
J Tech Assoc Pulp Pap Ind Korea — Journal. Technical Association of Pulp and Paper Industry of Korea
J Tech Bengal Engrg College — Journal of Technology. Bengal Engineering College
J Tech Councils ASCE Proc ASCE — Journal. Technical Councils of ASCE. Proceedings of the American Society of Civil Engineers
J Tech Lab (Tokyo) — Journal. Technical Laboratory (Tokyo)
J Tech Meth — Journal of Technical Methods and Bulletin of the International Association of Medical Museums
J Techn — Journal of Technology
J Techn Meth — Journal of Technical Methods and Bulletin. International Association of MedicalMuseums
J Technol — Journal of Technology
J Technol Bengal Eng Coll — Journal of Technology. Bengan Engineering College
J Technol Educ Electrochem Soc Jpn — Journal of Technology and Education. Electrochemical Society of Japan
J Technol Eng — Journal of Technology and Engineering
J Technol Res Coll Eng Kanto Gakuin Univ — Journal of Technological Researches. College of Engineering. Kanto Gakuin University
J Technol Res Fac Eng Kanto Gakuin Univ — Journal of Technological Researches. Faculty of Engineering. Kanto Gakuin University
J Technol Soc Starch — Journal. Technological Society of Starch
J Tech Phys — Journal of Technical Physics
J Tech Phys Warsaw — Journal of Technical Physics (Warsaw)
J Tech Sci — Journal of Technical Sciences
J Tech Vocat Educ S Afr — Journal for Technical and Vocational Education in South Africa
J Tech Writ Commun — Journal of Technical Writing and Communication
J Teflon — Journal of Teflon
J Tel — Journal Telegraphique Publie par le Bureau International des Administrations Telegraphiques
J Telecommun Networks — Journal of Telecommunication Networks
J Telecom Net — Journal of Telecommunication Networks
J Telemed Telecare — Journal of Telemedicine and Telecare
J Tenn Acad Sci — Journal. Tennessee Academy of Science
J Tenn Dent Assoc — Journal. Tennessee Dental Association
J Tennesee Med Assoc — Journal. Tennessee Medical Association
J Tennessee Acad Sci — Journal. Tennessee Academy of Science
J Tenn Med Ass — Journal. Tennessee Medical Association
J Tenn Med Assoc — Journal. Tennessee Medical Association
J Tenn State Dent Assoc — Journal. Tennessee State Dental Association
J Tenn State Med Assoc — Journal. Tennessee State Medical Association
JTEP — Journal of Transport Economics and Policy
J Terramech — Journal of Terramechanics
J Terramechanics — Journal of Terramechanics
J Tertiary Educ Adm — Journal of Tertiary Educational Administration
Jt Establ Nucl Energy Res Neth Norway Publ — Joint Establishment for Nuclear Energy Research (Netherlands and Norway). Publication
J Test and Eval — Journal of Testing and Evaluation
J Test Eval — Journal of Testing and Evaluation
Jt Eur Torus Rep JET R — Joint European Torus. Report. JET-R
JTEVA — Journal of Testing and Evaluation
J Texas Dent Hyg Assoc — Journal. Texas Dental Hygienists Association
J Text Assoc — Journal. Textile Association
J Text Eng Taichung Taiwan — Journal of Textile Engineering (Taichung, Taiwan)
J Textile Inst — Journal. Textile Institute
J Text Inst — Journal. Textile Institute
J Text Inst Abstr — Journal. Textile Institute. Abstracts
J Text Inst Part 1 — Journal of the Textile Institute. Part 1. Fibre Science and Textile Technology
J Text Inst Proc — Journal. Textile Institute. Proceedings
J Text Inst Proc Abstr — Journal. Textile Institute. Proceedings and Abstracts
J Text Inst Trans — Journal. Textile Institute. Transactions
J Text Mach Soc Jap — Journal. Textile Machinery Society of Japan
J Text Mach Soc Jpn Jpn Ed — Journal. Textile Machinery Society of Japan (Japanese Edition)

J Text Res Shanghai — Journal of Textile Research (Shanghai)
J Text Sci — Journal of Textile Science
J Text Stud — Journal of Texture Studies
J Texture Stud — Journal of Texture Studies
JTG — Journal of Tropical Geography
JTGG-A — Journal of Tropical Geography
JTGGAA — Journal of Tropical Geography
Jt Group Experts Sci Aspects Mar Pollut Rep Stud — Joint Group of Experts on the Scientific Aspects of Marine Pollution. Reports and Studies
JtH — Journal of the Historical Society of Nigeria
JTh — Journal of Thought
J Thai Vet Med Assoc — Journal. Thai Veterinary Medical Association
J Thanatol — Journal of Thanatology
JtHB — Journal of the History of the Behavioral Sciences
J Theol St — Journal of Theological Studies
J Theol Sthn Afr — Journal of Theology for Southern Africa
J Theol Stud — Journal of Theological Studies
J Theor Appl Mech — Journal of Theoretical and Applied Mechanics
J Theor Bio — Journal of Theoretical Biology
J Theor Biol — Journal of Theoretical Biology
J Theor Crit Vis Art — Journal of the Theory and Criticism of the Visual Arts
J Theoret Appl Mech — Journal of Theoretical and Applied Mechanics
J Theoret Biol — Journal of Theoretical Biology
J Theoret Probab — Journal of Theoretical Probability
J Theor N — Journal of Theoretical Neurobiology
J Theor Nombres Bordeaux — Journal de Theorie des Nombres de Bordeaux
J Theor Sci — Journal of Theoretical Science
J Theor Soc Behav — Journal for the Theory of Social Behavior
J Theory Soc Behav — Journal for the Theory of Social Behavior
J Ther — Journal of Therapy
J Thermal Anal — Journal of Thermal Analysis
J Thermal Insulation — Journal of Thermal Insulation
J Thermal Stresses — Journal of Thermal Stresses
J Therm Ana — Journal of Thermal Analysis
J Therm Anal — Journal of Thermal Analysis
J Therm Bio — Journal of Thermal Biology
J Therm Biol — Journal of Thermal Biology
J Therm Eng — Journal of Thermal Engineering
J Therm Engng — Journal of Thermal Engineering
J Therm Insul — Journal of Thermal Insulation
J Thermoelectr — Journal of Thermoelectricity
J Thermophys Heat Transfer — Journal of Thermophysics and Heat Transfer
J Thermoplast Compos Mater — Journal of Thermoplastic Composite Materials
J Thermosetting Plast (Jpn) — Journal of Thermosetting Plastics (Japan)
J Therm Spraying Soc Jpn — Journal. Thermal Spraying Society of Japan
J Therm Spray Technol — Journal of Thermal Spray Technology
J Therm Stresses — Journal of Thermal Stresses
JtHI — Journal of the History of Ideas
J Th KR — Jahrsschriften fuer Theologie und Kirchenrecht der Katholiken
JtHM — Journal of the History of Medicine and Allied Sciences
J Thora Cardiovasc Surg — Journal of Thoracic and Cardiovascular Surgery
J Thorac Cardiovasc Surg — Journal of Thoracic and Cardiovascular Surgery
J Thorac Cardiov Surg — Journal of Thoracic and Cardiovascular Surgery
J Thoracic Cardiovas Surg — Journal of Thoracic and Cardiovascular Surgery
J Thoracic Surg — Journal of Thoracic Surgery
J Thorac Imaging — Journal of Thoracic Imaging
J Thorac Surg — Journal of Thoracic Surgery
J Thor Surg — Journal of Thoracic and Cardiovascular Surgery
J Thought — Journal of Thought
J Thromb Thrombolysis — Journal of Thrombosis and Thrombolysis
JThS — Journal of Theological Studies
J Th SB — Jahrbuch der Theologischen Schule Bethel
J Th So Africa — Journal of Theology for Southern Africa
J Th St — Journal of Theological Studies
JTI — Journal of Taxation of Investments
JtI — Journal of the Illinois State Historical Society
J Tianjin Univ — Journal. Tianjin University
J-TIES — Japan Technology Information and Evaluation Service
J Tiles & Archit Cer Soc — Journal. Tiles and Architectural Ceramics Society
J Timber Dev Assoc India — Journal. Timber Development Association of India
J Timber Dryers Preserv Assoc India — Journal. Timber Dryers' and Preservers' Association of India
J Time Ser Anal — Journal of Time Series Analysis
Jt Inst Lab Astrophy Rep — Joint Institute for Laboratory Astrophysics. Report
Jt Inst Lab Astrophys Inf Cent Rep — Joint Institute for Laboratory Astrophysics. Information Center. Report
Jt Inst Nucl Invest Dubna USSR Rep JINR — Joint Institute for Nuclear Investigations. Dubna, USSR. Report JINR
Jt Inst Nucl Res CERN Sch Phys — Joint Institute for Nuclear Research-CERN School of Physics
Jt Inst Nucl Res Dubna USSR Prepr — Joint Institute for Nuclear Research. Dubna, USSR. Preprint
Jt Int Conf Creep Pap — Joint International Conference on Creep. Papers
J Tissue Cult Methods — Journal of Tissue Culture Methods
Jt Ital Pol Semin Multicompon Polym Syst — Joint Italian-Polish Seminar on Multicomponent Polymeric Systems
JTL — Journal fuer Theologische Literatur
JtL — Journal of the Lancaster County Historical Society
JtM — Journal of the Malaysian Branch. Royal Asiatic Society
JTM & H — Journal of Tropical Medicine and Hygiene
JTMH — Journal of Tropical Medicine and Hygiene
JTMMA — Journal. Tennessee Medical Association
JTMTDE — Journal of Trace and Microprobe Techniques
JTO — Journal des Tribunaux d'Outre-Mer
J Tohoku Dent Univ — Journal. Tohoku Dental University

J Tohoku Min Soc — Journal. Tohoku Mining Society
J Tokyo Agric Coll — Journal. Tokyo Agricultural College/Tokyo Nogyo Daigaku Kiyo
J Tokyo Chem Soc — Journal. Tokyo Chemical Society
J Tokyo Coll Fish — Journal. Tokyo College of Fisheries
J Tokyo Dent Coll Soc — Journal. Tokyo Dental College Society
J Tokyo Med Assoc — Journal. Tokyo Medical Association
J Tokyo Med Coll — Journal. Tokyo Medical College
J Tokyo Soc Vet Sci Anim Sci — Journal. Tokyo Society of Veterinary Science and Animal Science
J Tokyo Univ Fish — Journal. Tokyo University of Fisheries
J Tokyo Univ Fish Spec Ed — Journal. Tokyo University of Fisheries. Special Edition
J Tokyo Univ Merc Mar Nat Sci — Journal. Tokyo University of Mercantile Marine. Natural Sciences
J Tokyo Women's Med Coll — Journal. Tokyo Women's Medical College
JTOM — Journal des Tribunaux d'Outre-Mer
J Tongji Med Univ — Journal. Tongji Medical University
J Tosoh Res — Journal. Tosoh Research
J Tottori Daigaku Nogaku — Journal. Tottori Daigaku Nogaku-Buo
J Town Plan Inst — Journal of the Town Planning Institute
J Town Pl I — Journal of Town Planning Institute
J Town Reg Plann — Journal for Town and Regional Planning
J Tox Env H — Journal of Toxicology and Environmental Health
J Toxicol — Journal of Health Toxicology
J Toxicol Clin Exp — Journal de Toxicologie Clinique et Experimentale
J Toxicol Clin Toxicol — Journal of Toxicology. Clinical Toxicology
J Toxicol Cutaneous Ocul Toxicol — Journal of Toxicology. Cutaneous and Ocular Toxicology
J Toxicol Environ Health — Journal of Toxicology and Environmental Health
J Toxicol Environ Health Part A — Journal of Toxicology and Environmental Health. Part A
J Toxicol Environ Health Part B — Journal of Toxicology and Environmental Health. Part B. Critical Reviews
J Toxicol Med — Journal de Toxicologie Medicale
J Toxicol Public Health — Journal of Toxicology and Public Health
J Toxicol Sci — Journal of Toxicological Sciences
J Toxicol Toxin Rev — Journal of Toxicology. Toxin Reviews
J Toyota Natl Tech Coll — Journal. Toyota National Technical College
J Toyo Univ Gen Educ Nat Sci — Journal. Toyo University. General Education. Natural Science
JTP — Jeux, Treteaux, Personnages. Cahiers Mensuels d'Art Dramatique
JtP — Journal of the Pakistan Historical Society
JTP — Journal of Transport Economics and Policy
JT Ph — Jahrbuch fuer Technische Physik
JtPHS — Journal of the Presbyterian Historical Society of England
Jt Polytech Symp Manuf Eng — Joint Polytechnics Symposium on Manufacturing Engineering
Jt Publs Commonw Agric Bur — Joint Publications. Commonwealth Agricultural Bureaux
Jt Publs Pa Univ Mus Philad Anthrop Soc — Joint Publications of the Pennsylvania University Museum and the Philadelphia Anthropological Society
JTR — Journal of European Industrial Training
JtR — Journal of the Royal Australian Historical Society
JTR — Journal of Travel Research
JTR — Journal of Typographic Research
J Trace Elem Electrolytes Health Dis — Journal of Trace Elements and Electrolytes in Health and Disease
J Trace Elem Exp Med — Journal of Trace Elements in Experimental Medicine
J Trace Elem Med Biol — Journal of Trace Elements in Medicine and Biology
J Trace Microprobe Tech — Journal of Trace and Microprobe Techniques
J Tradit Chin Med — Journal of Traditional Chinese Medicine
J Tradit Med — Journal of Traditional Medicines
J Tradit Sino Jpn Med — Journal of Traditional Sino-Japanese Medicine
J Trans Harbin Polytech Inst Manchuria China — Journal and Transactions. Harbin Polytechnic Institute. Manchuria, China
J Transp Ec — Journal of Transport Economics and Policy
J Transp Econ Policy — Journal of Transport Economics and Policy
J Transp Eng — Journal of Transportation Engineering
J Transp Eng Div Amer Soc Civil Eng Proc — Journal. Transportation Engineering Division. American Society of Civil Engineers. Proceedings
J Transpersonal Psychol — Journal of Transpersonal Psychology
J Transpers Psych — Journal of Transpersonal Psychology
J Transp Hist — Journal of Transport History
J Transp Med — Journal of Transportation Medicine
J Transport Econ and Policy — Journal of Transport Economics and Policy
J Transport Econ Pol — Journal of Transport Economics and Policy
J Transport Hist — Journal of Transport History
J Trans Russ Chin Polytech Inst Harbin — Journal and Transactions. Russian-Chinese Polytechnic Institute of Harbin
J Trans Soc Eng (London) — Journal and Transactions. Society of Engineers (London)
J Transvaal Inst Mech Eng — Journal. Transvaal Institute of Mechanical Engineers
J Trauma — Journal of Trauma
J Trauma Inj Infect Crit Care — Journal of Trauma. Injury, Infection, and Critical Care
J Trauma Stress — Journal of Traumatic Stress
J Trav INSERM-DPHM — Journees de Travail INSERM [*Institut National de la Sante et de la RechercheMedicale*]-DPHM
J Travis County Med Soc — Journal. Travis County Medical Society
Jt Rep For Brch — Joint Report of the Forestry Branches. Ministry of Agriculture (London)
J Trevithick Soc — Journal. Trevithick Society
J Trib — Journal des Tribunaux
J Tribol — Journal of Tribology

J Tribol Trans ASME — Journal of Tribology. Transactions of the ASME
J Trib Trans ASME — Journal of Tribology. Transactions. American Society of Mechanical Engineers
J Trop Agric — Journal of Tropical Agriculture
J Trop Ecol — Journal of Tropical Ecology
J Trop For — Journal of Tropical Forestry
J Trop Geog — Journal of Tropical Geography
J Trop Geogr — Journal of Tropical Geography
J Tropical Geography — Journal of Tropical Geography
J Trop Med — Journal of Tropical Medicine and Hygiene
J Trop Med and Hyg (London) — Journal of Tropical Medicine and Hygiene (London)
J Trop Med Hyg — Journal of Tropical Medicine and Hygiene
J Trop Med (London) — Journal of Tropical Medicine (London)
J Trop Ped — Journal of Tropical Pediatrics
J Trop Pediat — Journal of Tropical Pediatrics
J Trop Pediatr — Journal of Tropical Pediatrics
J Trop Pediatr Afr Child Health — Journal of Tropical Pediatrics and African Child Health
J Trop Pediatr Environ Child Health — Journal of Tropical Pediatrics and Environmental Child Health
J Trop Pediatr Environ Child Health Monogr — Journal of Tropical Pediatrics and Environmental Child Health. Monograph
J Trop Subtrop Bot — Journal of Tropical and Subtropical Botany
J Trop Vet Sc — Journal of Tropical Veterinary Science
JTRS — Journal. Thailand Research Society
JtRSA — Journal of the Royal Society of Antiquaries of Ireland
JtRU — Journal of the Rutgers University Library
JTS — Journal of Tamil Studies
JTS — Journal of Theological Studies
JtSAH — Journal of the Society of Architectural Historians
J T S Behav — Journal for the Theory of Social Behavior
Jt Ser Publs Fac Agric Univ Alberta & Alberta Dep Agric — Joint Series Publications. Faculty of Agriculture University of Alberta and Alberta Department of Agriculture
J Tsing Hua Univ — Journal. Tsing Hua University
J Tsinghua Univ Peking Univ Sci Technol — Journal. Tsinghua University and Peking University. Science and Technology
J Tsinghua Univ Sci Technol — Journal. Tsinghua University. Science and Technology
J Tsuda College — Journal. Tsuda College
JTSV — Jahresbericht des Thueringisch-Saechsischen Vereins fuer Erforschung des Vaterlaendischen Altertums
Jt Symp Scaling Up Chem Plant Processes Proc — Joint Symposium. Scaling-Up of Chemical Plant and Processes. Proceedings
JTTN — Jahrbuecher der Theologie und Theologischer Nachrichten
JTTRD9 — Journal of Toxicology. Toxin Reviews
J Tuberc Lepr — Journal of Tuberculosis and Leprosy
JTUFA — Journal. Tokyo University of Fisheries
J Tung-Chi Univ — Journal. Tung-Chi University
J Turbomachinery Trans ASME — Journal of Turbomachinery. Transactions. American Society of Mechanical Engineers
J Turbomach Trans ASME — Journal of Turbomachinery. Transactions of the ASME
J Turfgrass Manage — Journal of Turfgrass Management
J Turk Med Soc — Journal. Turkish Medical Society
J Turk Phytopathol — Journal of Turkish Phytopathology
JTV — Journal. Transactions. Victoria Institute
JTVI — Journal of Transactions. Victoria Institute
JTW — Journal of Teaching Writing
JtW — Journal of the West
JTW — Journey-to-Work Database
JTWC — Journal of Technical Writing and Communication
JTWS — Journal of Third World Studies
JTX — Journal of Taxation
J Typograph Res — Journal of Typographic Research
J Typogr Bibliogr — Journal Typographique et Bibliographique
J Typogr Res — Journal of Typographic Research
Ju — Judaism
JU — Juilliard Review. Annual
JUAG — Jahrbuch. Ungarische Archaeologische Gesellschaft
JUB — Journal. Bombay University
JUB — Journal of the University of Bombay
Jub — Jubilee
Jubilee Geol Vol — Jubilee Geological Volume
Jubiliejines Mokslines Tech Konf Kauno Politech Inst Darb — Jubiliejines Mokslines-Technines Konferencijos. Kauno Politechnikos Institutas. Darbai
Ju Ch — Junyj Chudoznik
JUCO Rev — JUCO [*National Junior College Athletic Association*] Review
JUCS — JUCS. Journal of Universal Computer Science
JUD — Jahrbuch. Universitaet Duesseldorf
Jud — Judaica
Jud — Judaism
Jud Boh — Judaica Bohemiae
Jud Coun (NY) — Judicial Council (New York). Annual Reports
Judenfrage — Judenfrage in Politik, Recht, Kultur, und Wirtschaft
Judge Advo J — Judge Advocate Journal
Judges J — Judges' Journal
Judic — Judicature
Judicature — Journal. American Judicature Society
Judicature J Am Jud Soc'y — Judicature. Journal of the American Judicature Society
Jud J — Judges' Journal
Jud QR — Judicature Quarterly Review
JUE — Jewish Universal Encyclopedia

JUE — Journal of Urban Economics
Juedische Wohlfahrtspfl U Sozialpol — Juedische Wohlfahrtspflege und Sozialpolitik
Jued Litbl — Juedisches Literaturblatt
Jued Pr — Juedische Presse
Jued Pr L — Juedische Presse. Literaturblatt
Jued Rd — Juedische Rundschau
Jued Rd L — Juedische Rundschau. Literaturblatt
Jued Rd S — Juedische Rundschau. Schriftenreihe
Jued Zbl — Juedisches Zentralblatt
J U Film As — Journal. University Film Association
JUG — Journal. University of Gauhati
JUGA — Journal. University of Gauhati. Arts
Jug Ist Cas — Jugoslovenski Istorijski Casopis
Jugosl Drus Primjenu Goriva Maziva Strucna Izd — Jugoslavensko Drustvo za Primjenu Goriva i Maziva. Strucna Izdanja
Jugosl Drus Prouc Zemljista Posebne Publ — Jugoslovensko Drustvo za Proucavanje Zemljista. Posebne Publikacije
Jugosl Ginekol Opstet — Jugoslovenska Ginekologija i Opstetricija
Jugosl Ginekol Perinatol — Jugoslavenska Ginekologija i Perinatologija
Jugosl Med Biohem — Jugoslovenska Medicinska Biohemija
Jugosl Med Biokem — Jugoslavenska Medicinska Biokemija
Jugosl Mednar Simp Alum Clanki — Jugoslovanski Mednarodni Simpozij o Aluminiju. Clanki
Jugosl Pcelarstvo — Jugoslovensko Pcelarstvo
Jugosl Pedijatr — Jugoslovenska Pediajatrija
Jugosl Pregl — Jugoslovenski Pregled
Jugosl Pronalazastvo — Jugoslovensko Pronalazastvo
Jugosl Simp Elektrohem — Jugoslovenski Simpozijum o Elektrohemiji
Jugosl Simp Hmeljarstvo Ref — Jugoslovanski Simpozij za Hmeljarstvo Referati
Jugosl Vet Glasn — Jugoslovenski Veterinarski Glasnik
Jugosl Vinograd Vinar — Jugoslovensko Vinogradarstvo i Vinarstvo
Jugosl Vocarstvo — Jugoslovensko Vocarstvo
Jugos Medjunar Simp Alum — Jugoslovenski Medjunarodni Simpozij o Aluminiju
JUGS — Journal. University of Gauhati. Science
Juhasz Gyula Tanarkepzo Foiskola Tud Kozl — Juhasz Gyula Tanarkepzo Foiskola Tudomanyos Kozlemenyei
JUHS — Journal. Universalist Historical Society
Juilliard R — Juilliard Review
JUKGS — Journal of Ukrainian Graduate Studies
J Ukr Stud — Journal of Ukrainian Studies
JUL — Journal of Urban Law
Ju Lieb Ann Chem — Justus Liebigs Annalen der Chemie
Jul i Ka — Jul i Kalundborg og Omegn
Jul i Ro — Jul i Roskilde
Jul i Sk — Jul i Skive
Jul i Ve — Jul i Vejle
Jul i Vestj — Jul i Vestjylland
Julk Oulu Yliopisto Ydintek Laitos — Julkaisuja-Oulu Yliopisto. Ydintekniikkan Laitos
Jul p B — Jul paa Bornholm
J Ultra Res — Journal of Ultrastructure Research
J Ultrasound Med — Journal of Ultrasound in Medicine
J Ultrastruct Mol Struct Res — Journal of Ultrastructure and Molecular Structure Research
J Ultrastruct Res — Journal of Ultrastructure Research
J Ultrastruct Res Suppl — Journal of Ultrastructure Research. Supplement
JUM — Judaism
JUMP — Museum Journal. University Museum. University of Pennsylvania
JUNA — Juedische Nachrichten
Jun Col J — Junior College Journal
Junge Destill Brenner — Junge Destillateur und Brenner
Jung Wirt — Junge Wirtschaft
J Union Propr Appar Acetylene — Journal. Union des Proprietaires d'Appareils a Acetylene
Junior Coll J — Junior College Journal
Junior Inst Eng (London) J Rec Trans — Junior Institution of Engineers (London). Journal and Record of Transactions
J United Prov Hist Soc — Journal of the United Provinces Historical Society
J United Ser Inst Ind — Journal. United Service Institution of India
J United Serv Inst — Journal. United Service Institution
J United Serv Inst India — Journal. United Service Institution of India
J Univ Agric Prague Agron Ser A — Journal of University of Agriculture. Prague. Agronomy. Series A. Crop Production
J Univ Agric Prague Agron Ser B — Journal. University of Agriculture. Prague. Agronomy. Series B. Livestock Production
J Univ Bom Arts Hum & Soc Sci — Journal of the University of Bombay Arts Humanities and Social Sciences
J Univ Bombay — Journal. University of Bombay
J Univ Bombay NS — Journal. University of Bombay. New Series
J Univ Durban-Westville — Journal. University of Durban-Westville
J Univ F Assoc — Journal. University Film Association
J Univ Fish — Journal of University of Fisheries
J Univ Gauhati — Journal. University of Gauhati
J Univ Geol Soc (Nagpur) — Journal. University Geological Society (Nagpur)
J Univ Kuwait (Sci) — Journal. University of Kuwait (Science)
J Univ Merc Mar Nat Sci Tokyo — Journal. University of Mercantile Marine. Natural Science (Tokyo)
J Univ Occup Environ Health — Journal. University of Occupational and Environmental Health
J Univ Peshawar — Journal. University of Peshawar
J Univ Poona — Journal. University of Poona
J Univ Poona Sci Technol — Journal. University of Poona. Science and Technology
J Univ Saugar — Journal. University of Saugar

J Univ Saugar Part 2 Sect A — Journal. University of Saugar. Part 2. Section A. Physical Sciences
J Univ Sci Technol Beijing — Journal of University of Science and Technology Beijing
J Univ Sheffield Geol Soc — Journal. University of Sheffield. Geological Society
J Univ S Med Soc — Journal. University of Sydney. Medical Society
J Univ Stud — Journal of University Studies
JUNKA — Junkatsu
Junta Ci Nat — Junta de Ciencias Naturals
Junta Energ Nucl Rep JEN Spain — Junta de Energia Nuclear. Report. JEN (Spain)
Junta Energ Nucl Rep (Spain) — Junta de Energia Nuclear. Report (Spain)
Junta Invest Cient Ultramar Estud Ensaios Doc (Port) — Junta de Investigacoes Cientificas do Ultramar. Estudos, Ensaios, e Documentos (Portugal)
Junta Invest Ultramar Estud Ens Doc — Junta de Investigacoes do Ultramar. Estudos, Ensaios, e Documentos
Junta Invest Ultramar Port Estud Ensaios Doc — Junta de Investigacoes do Ultramar. Portugal. Estudos, Ensaios, e Documentos
Juntendo Med J — Juntendo Medical Journal
J UOEH — Journal of UOEH
JUP — Journal. University of Peshawar
JUP — Journal. University of Poona. Humanities Section
JUPD-A — Journal. Urban Planning and Development Proceedings. American Society of Civil Engineers
J U P Hist Soc — Journal of the U.P. Historical Society
JUPHS — Journal. United Provinces Historical Society
JUPOA — Journal of Undergraduate Psychological Research
JUPOA — Journal. University of Poona. Science and Technology
JUPSA — Journal. Physical Society of Japan
JUr — Journal of Urology
Jur — Jurisprudentie van het Hof van Justitie van de Europese Gemeenschappen
Jur — Juristen
Jur — Juristen & Okonomen
Jur — Jurist. Quarterly Journal of Jurisprudence
Jur A — Jurisprudence du Port D'Anvers
Jur Abh — Juristische Abhandlungen
Jur & Dr du Congo — Jurisprudence et Droit du Congo
Jur Anv — Jurisprudence du Port D'Anvers
Jura Riv — Jura. Rivista Internazionale di Diritto Romano e Antico
Jur B — Jurisprudence Commerciale de Bruxelles
J Urban — Journal of Urban Law
J Urban Affairs — Journal of Urban Affairs
J Urban Anal — Journal of Urban Analysis
J Urban Analysis — Journal of Urban Analysis
J Urban Ec — Journal of Urban Economics
J Urban Econ — Journal of Urban Economics
J Urban H — Journal of Urban History
J Urban Health — Journal of Urban Health [Cary, NC]
J Urban His — Journal of Urban History
J Urban Hist — Journal of Urban History
J Urban L — Journal of Urban Law
J Urban Law — Journal of Urban Law
J Urban Living Health Assoc — Journal. Urban Living and Health Association
J Urban Pla — Journal. Urban Planning and Development Division. Proceedings of the American Society of Civil Engineers
J Urban Plann Dev — Journal of Urban Planning and Development
J Urban Plann Dev Div Am Soc Civ Eng — Journal. Urban Planning and Development Division. American Society of Civil Engineers
J Urban Planning & Dev Div Proc ASCE — Journal. Urban Planning and Development Division. Proceedings of the American Society of Civil Engineers
Jur Bl — Juristische Blaetter
Jur Com Brux — Jurisprudence Commerciale de Bruxelles
Jur Comm Fl — Jurisprudence Commerciale des Flandres
Jur Comm Verviers — Jurisprudence du Tribunal de Commerce de Verviers
Jur Congo — Jurisprudence et Droit du Congo
Jur Div — Jurisprudence du Divorce et de la Separation de Corps
Jur Etat — Jurisprudence de l'Etat Independant du Congo
Jur Fl — Jurisprudence Commerciale de Flandres
Jur Foeren I Finl T — Juridiska Foereningen i Finland. Tidskrift
Juridical Rev — Juridical Review
Jurid R — Juridical Review
Jurid Rev — Juridical Review
Juri J — Jurimetrics Journal
Jurimetrics — Jurimetrics Journal
Jurimetrics J — Jurimetrics Journal
Jurist Bl — Juristische Blaetter
Juristen Zeit F D Geb D Tschecho Slowak — Juristen-Zeitung fuer das Gebiet der Tschechoslowakischen Republik
Jurist Rundsch — Juristische Rundschau
Jurist Sch — Juristische Schulung
Jurist Wchnschr — Juristische Wochenschrift
Jur L — Jurisprudence de la Cour d'Appel de Liege
Jur Litbl — Juristisches Literaturblatt
J Urol — Journal of Urology
J Urol (Baltimore) — Journal of Urology (Baltimore)
J Urol Med Chir — Journal d'Urologie Medicale et Chirurgicale
J Urol Neph — Journal d'Urologie et de Nephrologie
J Urol Nephrol — Journal d'Urologie et de Nephrologie
J Urol Nephrol Suppl — Journal d'Urologie et de Nephrologie. Supplement
J Urol Paris — Journal d'Urologie (Paris)
Jur Ouv — Jurisprudence de Louage d'Ouvrage
Jur Pap — Juristische Papyri
Jur Port Anv — Jurisprudence du Port D'Anvers
JUR R — Juridical Review
Jur R — Juristische Rundschau

Jur Rd — Juristische Rundschau
Jur Rev — Juridical Review
JURT — Juneau Report
J Urusvati Himalayan Res Inst Roerich Mus — Journal. Urusvati Himalayan Research Institute of Roerich Museum
Jur V — Jurisprudence Commerciale de Verviers
Jur Vjschr — Juristische Vierteljahresschrift
JurZ — Deutsche Juristenzeitung
Jur Zs Els Lothr — Juristische Zeitschrift fuer das Reichsland Elsass-Lothringen
Ju S — Juristische Schulung
Jus — Jus; Rivista di Scienze Giuridiche
J US Artillery — Journal. United States Artillery
Jus Doc Rio — Jus Documentacao (Rio de Janeiro)
Jus Ecc — Jus Ecclesiasticum
Jus Eccl — Jus Ecclesiasticum
JUSII — Journal. United Service Institution of India
J Usines Gaz — Journal des Usines a Gaz
JUSNC — Journal. United States National Committee
Jus Rom MA — Jus Romanum Medii Aevi
Just Econ — Just Economics
Justice System J — Justice System Journal
Just Intonation — Journal. Just Intonation Network
Justizminbl — Justizministerialblatt
Just Lieb Ann Chem — Justus Liebigs Annalen der Chemie
Just P — Justice of the Peace
Just P — Justice of the Peace and Local Government Review
Just Peace — Justice of the Peace and Local Government Review
Just Sys J — Justice System Journal
Just Syst J — Justice System Journal
Justus Liebigs Ann Chem — Justus Liebigs Annalen der Chemie
Juta — Juta's Daily Reporter
Jute — Jute and Jute Fabrics - Bangladesh Newsletter
Jute Abstr — Jute Abstracts
Jute Bull — Jute Bulletin
Jute Jute Fabr Bangladesh Newsl — Jute and Jute Fabrics. Bangladesh Newsletter
Jutendo Med — Jutendo Medicine
J Util Agric Prod — Journal. Utilization of Agricultural Products
J Utiliz Agr Prod — Journal of Utilization of Agricultural Products
J Uttar Pradesh Gov Colleges Acad Soc — Journal. Uttar Pradesh Government Colleges Academic Society
J Uttar Pradesh Hist Soc — Journal of the Uttar Pradesh Historical Society
Ju V — Justiz und Verwaltung
Juv and Fam Courts J — Juvenile and Family Court Journal
Juv & Fam Ct J — Juvenile and Family Court Journal
Juv Ct J — Juvenile Court Journal
Juv Ct JJ — Juvenile Court Judges Journal
Juv Ct Judges J — Juvenile Court Judges Journal
Juven Just — Juvenile Justice
Juv Ev — Juventude Evangelica
Juv Res Bul — Juvenile Research Bulletin
Juz Fil — Juznoslovenski Filolog. Povremeni Spis za Slovensku Filologiju i Lingvistiku
JUZIAG — Juzen Igakkai Zasshi
JV — Jahrbuch fuer Volksliedforschung
JV — Journal. Violin Society of America
JVA — Jaarboek. Vereeniging Amstelodanum
JVA — Jahrbuch. Verein von Altertumsfreunden im Rheinland
JVA — Journal of Volunteer Administration
JVABG — Jahrbuch des Vereins fuer Augsburger Bistumgeschichte
J Vac Sci and Technol — Journal of Vacuum Science and Technology
J Vac Sci and Technol A — Journal of Vacuum Science and Technology. A. Vacuum, Surfaces, and Films
J Vac Sci and Technol B — Journal of Vacuum Science and Technology. B. Micro-Electronics Processing and Phenomena
J Vac Sci T — Journal of Vacuum Science and Technology
J Vac Sci Tech — Journal of Vacuum Science and Technology
J Vac Sci Technol — Journal of Vacuum Science and Technology
J Vac Soc Jpn — Journal. Vacuum Society of Japan
JVAFR — Jahrbuecher des Vereins von Altertumsfreunden im Rheinlande
J Value Eng — Journal of Value Engineering
J Value Inq — Journal of Value Inquiry
J Varendra Res Mus — Journal of the Varendra Research Museum
JVARh — Jahrbuch. Verein von Altertumsfreunden im Rheinland
J Vasc Interv Radiol — Journal of Vascular and Interventional Radiology
J Vasc Res — Journal of Vascular Research
J Vasc Surg — Journal of Vascular Surgery
JV(B) — Juedisches Volksblatt (Breslau)
JV Bl — Justizverwaltungsblatt
JVCEW — Jahrbuch des Vereins fuer Christliche Erziehungswissenschaft
J Vector Ecol — Journal of Vector Ecology
JVEG — Jaarbericht. Vooraziatische-Egyptisch Genootschap "Ex Oriente Lux"
JVEKGM — Jahrbuch des Vereins fuer Evangelische Kirchengeschichte der Grafschaft Mark
JVEKGW — Jahrbuch des Vereins fuer die Evangelische Kirchengeschichte Westfalens
J Vener Dis Inf — Journal of Venereal Disease Information
JVER — Journal of Vocational Education Research
J Verbal Learn — Journal of Verbal Learning and Verbal Behavior
J Verb Learn — Journal of Verbal Learning and Verbal Behavior
J Verb Learn Verb Behav — Journal of Verbal Learning and Verbal Behavior
Jversl Fund Hondius — Jaarverslag Fundation Hondius
Jversl Oranje Nassau Mus — Jaarverslag Oranje-Nassau Museum
Jversl Rijksbureau Ksthist Doc s Gravenhage — Jaarverslag Rijksbureau voor Kunsthistorische Documentatie te 's-Gravenhage

Jversl Sticht Textielgesch — Jaarverslag Stichting Textielgeschiedenis
Jversl Ver Rembrandt — Jaarverslag Vereniging Rembrandt
J Vertebr Paleontol — Journal of Vertebrate Paleontology
J Ver Vaterl Naturk Wuertt — Jahresheft. Verein fuer Vaterlaendische Naturkunde in Wuerttemberg
J Vestib Res — Journal of Vestibular Research
J Vet Anaesth — Journal of Veterinary Anaesthesia
J Vet Anim Husb Res (India) — Journal of Veterinary and Animal Husbandry Research (India)
J Vet Assoc Thailand — Journal. Veterinary Association of Thailand
J Vet Diagn Invest — Journal of Veterinary Diagnostic Investigation
J Vet Fac Univ Tehran — Journal. Veterinary Faculty. University of Tehran
J Vet Intern Med — Journal of Veterinary Internal Medicine
J Vet Med — Journal of Veterinary Medicine
J Vet Med Educ — Journal of Veterinary Medical Education
J Vet Med Sci — Journal of Veterinary Medical Science
J Vet Med Ser A — Journal of Veterinary Medicine. Series A
J Vet Med Ser B — Journal of Veterinary Medicine. Series B
J Vet Med Teheran — Journal of Veterinary Medicine (Teheran)
J Vet Med Tokyo — Journal. Veterinary Medicine (Tokyo)
J Vet Midi — Journal des Veterinaires du Midi
J Vet Pharmacol Ther — Journal of Veterinary Pharmacology and Therapeutics
J Vet Pharm Ther — Journal of Veterinary Pharmacology and Therapeutics
J Vet Sci UAR — Journal of Veterinary Science of the United Arab Republic
JVevKW — Jahrbuch des Vereins fuer die Evangelische Kirchengeschichte Westfalens
JVF — Jahrbuch fuer Volksliedforschung
JV Gew R Schutz — Jahrbuch der Internationalen Vereinigung fuer Gewerblichen Rechtsschutz
JVGW — Jahrbuch des Vereins fuer Geschichte der Stadt Wien
JVH — Jahrbuch fuer Volkskunde der Heimatvertriebenen
JVH — Jahresbericht. Vereins fuer Heimatgeschichte
JVH — Jahresverzeichnis der Deutschen Hochschulschriften
J Vib Acoust Stress Rel Des Trans ASME — Journal of Vibration, Acoustics, Stress, and Reliability in Design. Transactions. American Society of Mechanical Engineers
J Vib Acoust Trans ASME — Journal of Vibration and Acoustics. Transactions of the ASME
J Vib Control — Journal of Vibration and Control
JVIBDM — Journal of Visual Impairment and Blindness
J Vic Teachers Union — Journal of the Victorian Teachers' Union
J Victoria Univ Manchester — Journal. Victoria University of Manchester
J Vinyl Addit Technol — Journal of Vinyl and Additive Technology
J Vinyl Technol — Journal of Vinyl Technology
J Viola da Gamba Soc Amer — Journal. Viola da Gamba Society of America
J Violin S — Journal. Violin Society of America
J Violin Soc Amer — Journal. Violin Society of America
J Viral Hepat — Journal of Viral Hepatitis
J Virol — Journal of Virology
J Virol Methods — Journal of Virological Methods
J Virology — Journal of Virology
J Virol (Tokyo) — Journal of Virology (Tokyo)
J Visual Commun Image Represent — Journal of Visual Communication and Image Representation
J Visual Impairment & Blind — Journal of Visual Impairment and Blindness
J Vitaminol — Journal of Vitaminology
J Vitaminol (Kyoto) — Journal of Vitaminology (Kyoto)
J Vitam Soc Jpn — Journal. Vitamin Society of Japan
JVJE — Jahrbuch. Vereinigung Juedischer Exportakademiker
JVJGL — Jahrbuch. Verein fuer Juedische Geschichte und Literatur
JVL — Jahrbuch. Vorarlberger Landesmuseums Vereins
JVLBA — Journal of Verbal Learning and Verbal Behavior
JVLHOD — Jahrbuch. Verein fuer Landeskunde und Heimatpflege im Gau Oberdonau
J VLSI Comput Systems — Journal of VLSI and Computer Systems
J VLSI Signal Process — Journal of VLSI Signal Processing
JVLV — Jahrbuch. Vorarlberger Landesmuseums Vereins
JVLVB — Journal of Verbal Learning and Verbal Behavior
JVMAE6 — Journal of Veterinary Medicine. Series A
JVMBE9 — Journal of Veterinary Medicine. Series B
JVMED — Journal of Virological Methods
JVMG — Jahrbuecher des Vereins fuer Mecklenburgische Geschichte und Altertumskunde
J V N M — Jaarboek. Vereeniging voor Nederlandsche Muziekgeschiedenis
JVNS — Jahrbuch. Verein fuer Niederdeutsche Sprachforschung
J Vocat Beh — Journal of Vocational Behavior
J Vocat Behav — Journal of Vocational Behavior
J Voc Behav — Journal of Vocational Behavior
J Voice — Journal of Voice
J Volcanol Geotherm Res — Journal of Volcanology and Geothermal Research
J Volun Act — Journal of Voluntary Action Research
J Volun Action Res — Journal of Voluntary Action Research
J Volunteer Adm — Journal of Volunteer Administration
JVP — Jewish Voice Pictorial
JVP — Journal of Vertebrate Paleontology
JVPADK — Journal of Vertebrate Paleontology
JVPTD9 — Journal of Veterinary Pharmacology and Therapeutics
JVQ — Japan Views Quarterly
JVR — Jaarboek van het Vlaams Rechtsgenootschap
JVRDG — Jahresbericht des Vereins zur Erforschung der Regensburger Domgeschichte
JVSC — Journal. Visva-Bharati Study Circle
JVSch — Jahrbuch. Verein Schweizerischer Gymnasial-Lehrer
JVSKG — Jahrbuch der Vereins fuer Schlesische Kirchengeschichte
JVSUES — Journal of Vascular Surgery

JVT — Jaarsverlag van de Vereeniging voor Terpenonderzoek over de Vereenigingsjaren

J Vulg Hort — Journal de Vulgarisation de l'Horticulture

JVUN — Jahresbericht des Vereins zur Unterstutzung der Armen Negerkinder

JVVKA — Jahrbuch des Verbandes der Vereine Katholischer Akademiker

JVVNW — Jahresheft des Vereins fuer Vaterlaendische Naturkunde in Wuerttemberg

JVVS — Jaarboek. Vereniging voor de Vergelijkende Studie van het Recht vanBelgie en Nederland

JVWK — Jahrbuch. Verein fuer Westfaelische Kirchengeschichte

JVWP — Jahrbuch des Vereins fuer Wissenschaftliche Paedagogik

JVZ — Juedische Volkszeitung

JW — Jahrbuch. Kunsthistorische Sammlungen (Wien)

JW — [The] Jewish Week

JW — Journal of the West

JWABAQ — Journal for Water and Wastewater Research

JWAfrL — Journal of West African Languages

J W Afr Langs — Journal of West African Languages

JW Afr Sci Ass — Journal. West African Science Association

JWAG — Journal. Walters Art Gallery

J Wagga Wagga Dist Hist Soc — Wagga Wagga and District Historical Society. Journal

J Wakayama Med Soc — Journal. Wakayama Medical Society

JWAL — Journal of West African Languages

JWalt — Journal. Walters Art Gallery

J Walters A G — Journal of the Walters Art Gallery

J Walters Art Gal — Journal. Walters Art Gallery

J WA Nurses — Journal. Western Australian Nurses Association

JWarb — Journal. Warburg and Courtauld Institute

J Warb & Court Inst — Journal of the Warburg and Courtauld Institutes

J Warb Inst — Journal of the Warburg Institute

J Warburg and Courtauld Inst — Journal. Warburg and Courtauld Institute

J Warburg C — Journal. Warburg and Courtauld Institute

J Warburg Courtauld Inst — Journal. Warburg and Courtauld Institute

JWAS — Journal. Washington Academy of Sciences

JWASA — Journal. Washington Academy of Sciences

J Wash Acad Sci — Journal. Washington Academy of Sciences

J Washington Acad Sci — Journal. Washington Academy of Sciences

J Water Borne Coat — Journal of Water Borne Coatings

J Water Electrolyte Metab — Journal of Water and Electrolyte Metabolism

J Water P C — Journal. Water Pollution Control Federation

J Water Pollut Contr Fed — Journal. Water Pollution Control Federation

J Water Pollut Control Fed — Journal. Water Pollution Control Federation

J Water Pollut Control Fed — Water Pollution Control Federation. Journal

J Water Resour — Journal of Water Resources

J Water Resour Planning & Manage Div Proc ASCE — Journal. Water Resources Planning and Management Division. Proceedings of the American Society of Civil Engineers

J Water Resour Plann Manage — Journal of Water Resources Planning and Management

J Water Resour Plann Manage Div Am Soc Civ Eng — Journal. Water Resources Planning and Management Division. Proceedings of the American Society of Civil Engineers

J Water Resour Plann Manage Div ASCE — Journal. Water Resources Planning and Management Division. Proceedings of the American Society of Civil Engineers

J Water Reuse Technol — Journal of Water Re-use Technology

J Water Sci — Journal of Water Science

J Water Solid Wastes Manage — Journal of Water and Solid Wastes Management

J Water Waste — Journal of Water and Waste

J Water Wastewater Res — Journal for Water and Wastewater Research

J Waterway — Journal. Waterways, Harbors, and Coastal Engineering Division. American Societyof Civil Engineers

J Waterway Port Coastal & Ocean Div Proc ASCE — Journal. Waterways, Port, Coastal, and Ocean Division. Proceedings. American Society of Civil Engineers

J Waterway Port Coastal Ocean Div Amer Soc Civil Eng Proc — Journal. Waterways, Port, Coastal, and Ocean Division. American Society of Civil Engineers. Proceedings

J Waterw Harbors Coastal Eng Div Am Soc Civ Eng — Journal. Waterways, Harbors, and Coastal Engineering Division. American Society of Civil Engineers

J Waterw Harbors Div Am Soc Civ Eng — Journal. Waterways and Harbors Division. American Society of Civil Engineers

J Water Works Assoc — Journal. Water Works Association

J Waterworks Sewerage Assoc — Journal. Waterworks and Sewerage Association

J Waterw Port Coastal Ocean Div ASCE — Journal. Waterways, Port, Coastal, and Ocean Division. American Society of Civil Engineers

J Waterw Port Coastal Ocean Eng — Journal of Waterway, Port, Coastal, and Ocean Engineering

JWB — Jahrbuch der Wittheit zu Bremen

JWBS — Journal. Welsh Bibliographic Society

JWCBRS — Journal. West China Border Research Society

J W China Border Res Soc — Journal. West China Border Research Society

JWCI — Journal. Warburg and Courtauld Institute

JWCTD — Journal of Wood Chemistry and Technology

JWCTDJ — Journal of Wood Chemistry and Technology

JWD — Journal of Workforce Diversity

J Weavers Spinners Dyers — Journal of Weavers, Spinners, and Dyers

J Wednesday Soc — Journal. Wednesday Society

J Weld Soc — Journal. Welding Society

J Well Perspect — Journal of Wellness Perspectives

J Welsh Bibliog Soc — Journal. Welsh Bibliographical Society

J West — Journal of the West

J West Afr Inst Oil Palm Res — Journal. West African Institute for Oil Palm Research

J West Afr Sci Assoc — Journal. West African Science Association

J West Aust Nurses — Journal. West Australian Nurses

J West China Univ Med Sci — Journal. West China University of Medical Sciences

J West Scot Iron Steel Inst — Journal. West of Scotland Iron and Steel Institute

J West Soc Eng — Journal. Western Society of Engineers

J West Soc Periodont — Journal. Western Society of Periodontology

J West Soc Periodontol — Journal. Western Society of Periodontology

JWG — Jahrbuch fuer Wirtschaftsgeschichte

JWGL — Jahrbuch der Wissenschaftlichen Gesellschaft fuer Luftfahrt

JWGV — Jahrbuch. Wiener Goethe-Verein

JWH — Journal of World History

JWI — Journal. Warburg and Courtauld Institute

JWIDA — Journal of Wildlife Diseases

J Wildl Dis — Journal of Wildlife Diseases

J Wildlife Manage Suppl — Journal of Wildlife Management. Supplement

J Wildlife Mgt — Journal of Wildlife Management

J Wildl Man — Journal of Wildlife Management

J Wildl Manage — Journal of Wildlife Management

J Wildl Mgmt — Journal of Wildlife Management

JWIM — Journal of Wildlife Management

J Wind Eng and Ind — Journal of Wind Engineering and Industrial Aerodynamics

J Wind Engng & Ind Aerodyn — Journal of Wind Engineering and Industrial Aerodynamics

J Wind Engng Ind Aerodynam — Journal of Wind Engineering and Industrial Aerodynamics

J Wisc Dent Assoc — Journal. Wisconsin Dental Association

J Wis Dent Assoc — Journal. Wisconsin Dental Association

J Wis State Dent Soc — Journal. Wisconsin State Dental Society

JWKTN — Jaarboek en Discussies. Voordrachten Werkgenootschap van Katholieke Theologen in Nederland

J Wld Hist — Cahiers d'Histoire Mondiale/Journal of World History

J Wld Hist — Journal of World History

J Wld Trade Law — Journal of World Trade Law

JWMS — Journal. William Morris Society

J Womens Health — Journal of Women's Health

J Won Kwang Public Health Jr Coll — Journal. Won Kwang Public Health Junior College

J Wood Chem Technol — Journal of Wood Chemistry and Technology

J Wood Sci — Journal of Wood Science

J World — Jewish World

J World For — Journal of World Forestry

J World For Resour Manage — Journal of World Forest Resource Management

J World Hist — Journal of World History

J World Maric Soc — Journal. World Mariculture Society

J World Maricult Soc — Journal. World Mariculture Society

J World Prehist — Journal of World Prehistory

J World Tr — Journal of World Trade Law

J World Trade L — Journal of World Trade Law

J World Trade Law — Journal of World Trade Law

J World Tr L — Journal of World Trade Law

JWPCF — Journal. Water Pollution Control Federation

JWPFA — Journal. Water Pollution Control Federation

JWPTZ — Jahrbuch der Wissenschaftlichen und Praktischen Tierzucht

JWPZK — Jahrbuch fuer Wissenschaftliche und Praktische Zuechtungskunde

JWR — Juedische Weltrundschau

JWREEG — Journal of Water Resources

JWS — Jahrbuch fuer Wirtschafts und Sozialpaedagogik

JWS — Journal of Western Speech

JWSL — Journal of Women's Studies in Literature

JWT — Journal of World Trade Law

JWTL — Journal of World Trade Law

J Wuhan Inst Tech — Journal of Wuhan Institute of Technology

J Wuhan Univ Nat Sci Ed — Journal. Wuhan University. Natural Sciences Edition

J Wuhan Univ Natur Sci Ed — Journal of Wuhan University. Natural Sciences Edition

J Wuhan Univ Technol — Journal. Wuhan University of Technology

J Wuhan Univ Technol Mater Sci Ed — Journal of Wuhan University of Technology. Materials Science Edition

JW u S — Jahrbuch fuer Wirtschafts und Sozialpaedagogik

J Wuxi Inst Light Ind — Journal of the Wuxi Institute of Light Industry

J Wuxi Univ Light Ind — Journal of the Wuxi University of Light Industry

J W Vir Phil Soc — Journal. West Virginia Philosophical Society

JWWJA — Journal. Japan Water Works Association

JWZ — Juedische Wochenzeitung

J Xiamen Univ Nat Sci — Journal. Xiamen University. Natural Science

J Xian Coll Geol — Journal of Xi'an College of Geology

J Xian Eng Univ — Journal of Xi'an Engineering University

J Xiangtan Min Inst — Journal of Xiangtan Mining Institute

J Xian Jiaotong Univ — Journal. Xi'an Jiaotong University

J Xian Med Univ — Journal of Xi'an Medical University

J Xian Pet Inst — Journal of Xi'an Petroleum Institute

J Xinjiang Univ Natur Sci — Journal Xinjiang University. Natural Science

J X Ray Sci Technol — Journal of X-Ray Science and Technology

J X-Ray Technol — Journal of X-Ray Technology

JY — Jewish Yearbook

JYADA6 — Journal of Youth and Adolescence

J Yamagata Agric For Soc — Journal. Yamagata Agriculture and Forestry Society

J Yamashina Inst Ornithol — Journal. Yamashina Institute for Ornithology

J Yangzhou Univ Nat Sci Ed — Journal of Yangzhou University. Natural Science Edition

JYB — Jewish Year Book

JYCE-A — Journal. Hydraulics Division. Proceedings of the American Society of Civil Engineers

J Yiyang Teachers College — Journal of Yiyang Teachers' College

JYM — Journal of Property Management

J Yokohama City Univ Chem Phys Ser — Journal. Yokohama City University. Chemical and Physical Series

J Yokohama City Univ Ser C — Journal. Yokohama City University. Series C. Natural Science

J Yokohama Med Assoc — Journal. Yokohama Medical Association

J Yokohama Munic Univ — Journal. Yokohama Municipal University

J Yokohama Munic Univ Ser C Nat Sci — Journal. Yokohama Municipal University. Series C. Natural Sciences/Yokohama Shiritsu Daigaku Kiyo

J Yonago Med Assoc — Journal. Yonago Medical Association

J Youth Ado — Journal of Youth and Adolescence

J Youth Adol — Journal of Youth and Adolescence

J Youth Adolesc — Journal of Youth and Adolescence

J Youth & Adolescence — Journal of Youth and Adolescence

Jy Saml — Jyske Samlinger

Jysk Hist — Jyske Historiker

J Yugosl Pomol — Journal of Yugoslav Pomology

J Yunnan Univ Ser A — Journal. Yunnan University. Series A/Yun Nan Ta Hsueeh Hsueeh Pao. Lui

Jyvaeskylaen Yliopiston Taidehist Laitoksen Julkaisuja — Jyvaeskylaen Yliopiston Taidehistorian Laitoksen Julkaisuja

JZ — Jazykovedny Zbornik

Jz — Jazz Magazine

Jz — Jezykoznawca

JZ — Jinruigaku Zasshi

JZ — Juedische Zeitung

JZ — Juristenzeitung

JZ Bl — Juedisches Zentralblatt

J Zhejiang Agric Univ — Journal of Zhejiang Agricultural University

J Zhejiang Eng Inst — Journal. Zhejiang Engineering Institute

J Zhejiang Inst Technol — Journal of Zhejiang Institute of Technology

J Zhejiang Med Univ — Journal. Zhejiang Medical University

J Zhejiang Univ — Journal. Zhejiang University

J Zhejiang Univ Nat Sci Ed — Journal. Zhejiang University. Natural Science Edition

JZKg — Jahrbuch der Zeit- und Kulturgeschichte

JZO — Juedische Zeitung fuer Ostdeutschland

JZOOAE — Journal of Zoology

J Zoo Anim Med — Journal of Zoo Animal Medicine

J Zool — Journal of Zoology

J Zool (Lond) — Journal of Zoology (London)

J Zool Proc Zool Soc Lond — Journal of Zoology. Proceedings. Zoological Society of London

J Zool Res — Journal of Zoological Research

J Zool Res (Aligarh) — Journal of Zoological Research (Aligarh)

J Zool Ser A — Journal of Zoology. Series A

J Zool Ser B — Journal of Zoology. Series B

J Zool Soc India — Journal. Zoological Society of India

J Zoo Soc Ind — Journal of the Zoological Society of India

J Zoo Wild — Journal of Zoo and Wildlife Medicine

J Zoo Wildl Med — Journal of Zoo and Wildlife Medicine

JZRED2 — Journal of Zoological Research

JZSAEU — Journal of Zoology. Series A

JZSBEX — Journal of Zoology. Series B

JZSI — Journal of the Zoological Society of India

J Zuckerind — Journal der Zuckerindustrie

J Zurita — Jeronimo Zurita. Cuadernos de Historia. Institucion Fernando el Catolico

JZWL — Juedische Zeitschrift fuer Wissenschaft und Leben

K

K — Kant-Studien
K — Keyboard
K — Kingdom Come
K — Klio. Beitraege zur Alten Geschichte
K — Knjizevnost
K — Knowledge
K — Kollasuyo [La Paz]
K — Kultur
K — Kunststoffe
KA — Kanina
KA — Kansas Music Review
KA — Korean Affairs
KA — Kultura
KA — Kulturarbeit
KA — Kunstmuseets Arsskrift
KA — Kyrkohistorisk Arsskrift
KAA — Koelner Anglistische Arbeiten
Kabard Balkar Gos Univ Sb Nauchn Rab Aspir — Kabardino-Balkarskii
 Gosudarstvennyi Universitet. Sbornik Nauchnykh Rabot Aspirantov
Kabard Balkar Opytn Stn Sadovod Tr — Kabardino-Balkarskaya Opytnaya
 Stantsiya Sadovodstva. Trudy
Kabardino-Balkarsk Gos Univ Ucen Zap — Kabardino-Balkarskii Gosudarstvennyi
 Universitet. Ucenyi Zapiski
Kabeln Tekh — Kabel'naya Tekhnika
Kabel Tekh — Kabel'naya Tekhnika
K Abg G — Kommunalabgabengesetz
Kab Natuurl Hist — Kabinet der Natuurlijke Historien, Wetenschappen, Konsten en
 Handwerken
Kab Seb — Kabar Sebarang. Sulating Maphilindo
Kabul Univ Fac Agric Res Note — Kabul University. Faculty of Agriculture.
 Research Notes
Kabul Univ Fac Agric Tech Bull — Kabul University. Faculty of Agriculture.
 Technical Bulletin
KAC   Kappor
K Acad Belg Jaarb — Koninklijk Academie van Belgie. Jaarboek
K Acad Belg Kl Wet Verh Verzamel 8 — Koninklijke Academie van Belgie. Klasse
 der Wetenschappen, Verhandelingen. Verzameling in 8
K Acad Geneeskd Belg Verh — Koninklijke Academie voor Geneeskunde van
 Belgie. Verhandelingen
K Acad Kolon Wet Meded Zittingen — Koninklijke Academie voor Koloniale
 Wetenschappen. Mededelingen der Zittingen
K Acad Overzeese Wet Kl Tech Wet Verh 8 Brussels — Koninklijke Academie
 voor Overzeese Wetenschappen. Klasse voor Technische Wetenschappen.
 Verhandelingen in 8 (Brussels)
K Acad Overzeese Wet Meded Zittingen — Koninklijke Academie voor Overzeese
 Wetenschappen. Mededelingen der Zittingen
Kachelofen Keram — Kachelofen und Keramik
Kachest Stal — Kachestvennaya Stal'
Kachestvo Poverkh Detal Mash — Kachestvo Poverkhnosti Detalei Mashin
Kach Mater Poluprovodn Tekh — Kachestvo Materialov dlya Poluprovodnikovoi
 Tekhniki
Kach Poverkhn Detalei Mash — Kachestvo Poverkhnosti Detalei Mashin
Kach Prom Zelenchukovu Sortove — Kachestva na Promishlenite Zelenchukovu
 Sortove
Kach Stal — Kachestvennaya Stal
Kach Stali Splavy — Kachestvennye Stali i Splavy
Kadel R — Kadelpian Review
KadmosS — Kadmos. Supplement
Kadry Selsk Khoz — Kadry Sel'sko Khoziaistva
Kaelte Ind — Kaelte-Industrie
Kaelte Ind Moscow — Kaelte-Industrie (Moscow)
Kaelte-Klima-Prakt — Kaelte-Klima-Praktiker
Kaelte Klimatech — Kaelte und Klimatechnik
Kaeltetech Anz — Kaeltetechnischer Anzeiger
Kaeltetech-Klim — Kaeltetechnik-Klimatisierung
Kaernbraenslesaekerhet Tek Rapp — Kaernbraenslesaekerhet. Teknisk Rapport
Kaernten Landms Jb — Jahrbuch des Naturhistorischen Landesmuseums von
 Kaernten
KAeT — Kleine Aegyptische Texte
KAF — Kleinasiatische Forschungen
Kaffee Tee Markt — Kaffee- und Tee-Markt
KAFPAC — Catalogus Faunae Poloniae
KAG — Keesings Archiv der Gegenwart
Kag Kog — Kagaku Kogaku
KagoBH — Kagoshima Daigaku Bunka Hokoku
KaH — Kansas Historical Quarterly

KAH — Keilschrifttexte aus Assur. Historischen Inhalts
Kahncrete Engng — Kahncrete Engineering
KAI — Kanaanaeische und Araemaische Inschriften
KAIGBZ — Japanese Journal of Nuclear Medicine
Kair — Kairos. Zeitschrift fuer Religionswissenschaft und Theologie
KairosSt — Kairos. Religionswissenschaftliche Studien
Kais Akad d Wiss Denksch Philos-Hist Kl — Kaiserliche Akademie der
 Wissenschaften in Wien. Philosophisch-Historische Klasse. Denkschriften
Kais Akad d Wissensch Sitzungsb Philos-Hist Klasse — Kaiserliche Akademie
 der Wissenschaften in Wien. Philosophisch-Historische Klasse. Sitzungsberichte
Kais-Deutsch Archaol Inst Jahrb — Kaiserlich-Deutsches Archaeologisches
 Institut. Jahrbuch
Kaiser Fdn Med Bull — Kaiser Foundation Medical Bulletin
Kaiser Found Med Bull — Kaiser Foundation Medical Bulletin
Kaiser Found Med Bull Abstr Issue — Kaiser Foundation Medical Bulletin.
 Abstract Issue
KAIZAN — Acta Anatomica Nipponica
KAJ — Keilschrifttexte aus Assur. Juristischen Inhalts
Kajaanin Maanviljelyss Vuosikert — Kajaanin Maanviljelysseuran Vuosikertomus
Kaj Ekon Mal — Kajian Ekonomi Malaysia
Kajian Vet — Kajian Veterinaire
KAJKA — Kagaku Kojo
Kaju Shikenjo Hokoku Bull Fruit Tree Res Stn Ser A Yatabe — Kaju Shikenjo
 Hokoku. Bulletin of the Fruit Tree Research Station. Series A. Yatabe
Kakao Zuck — Kakao und Zucker
Kakatiya J Eng Stud — Kakatiya Journal of English Studies
KAKEA — Kakuyugo Kenkyu
Kakeishu — Kakyu Saibansho Keiji Saibanreishu
KAKOA — Kagaku Kogyo
Kakteen Orchideen Rundsch — Kakteen und Orchideen Rundschau
Kakteen Sukk — Kakteen und Andere Sukkulenten. Organ der Deutschen Kakteen
Kakteen Sukkulenten — Kakteen und Andere Sukkulenten
Kakuriken Kenkyu Hokoku Suppl — Kakuriken Kenkyu Hokoku. Supplement
K Ak Wiss Mat-Nat Kl Szb — Kaiserliche Akademie der Wissenschaften.
 Mathematische-Naturwissenschaftliche Klasse. Sitzungsberichte
KAKYA — Kagaku (Kyoto)
KAKZA — Kagaku Keizai
KAL — Kyushu American Literature
Kala Azar Bull — Kala Azar Bulletin. Royal Society
Kalamazoo Med — Kalamazoo Medicine
Kalast Tarkast Julk — Kalastusten Tarkastajan Julkaisuja
Kalast Tarkast Tiedon — Kalastusten Tarkastajan Tiedonantoja
Kal Baumwollind — Kalender fuer die Baumwollindustrie
Kal Eisen Emailind — Kalender fuer die Eisen-Emailindustrie
Kal Elektrochem — Kalender fuer Elektrochemiker
Kal Elektrotech — Kalender fuer Elektrotechnik
Kal Elektrotechr — Kalender fuer Elektrotechniker
Kal Farm Pol — Kalendarz Farmaceutyczny Polski
Kal Gas U WassFach — Kalender fuer das Gas- und Wasserfach
Kal GesundhTech — Kalender fuer Gesundheitstechniker
Kal Handb Holz U Holzverarb Ind — Kalender und Handbuch fuer die Holz- und
 Holzverarbeitenden Industrien
Kali Erz Kohle — Kali, Erz, und Kohle
Kal Ing MaschBau — Kalender fuer Ingenieure des Maschinenbaues
Kalinin Gos Ped Inst Ucen Zap — Kalininskii Gosudarstvennyi Pedagogiceskii
 Institut Imeni M. I. Kalinina Ucenye Zapiski
Kaliningrad Gos Ped Inst Ucen Zap — Kaliningradskii Gosudarstvennyi
 Pedagogiceskii Institut Ucenye Zapiski
Kaliningrad Gos Univ Differencial'naja Geom Mnoobraz Figur —
 Kaliningradskogo Gosudarstvennogo Universitet Differencial'naja Geometrija
 Mnoobrazii Figur
Kaliningrad Gos Univ Trudy Kaf Teoret i Eksper Fiz — Kaliningradskii
 Gosudarstvennyi Universitet Trudy Kafedry Teoreticeskoi i Eksperimental'noi
 Fiziki
Kaliningrad Gos Univ Ucen Zap — Kaliningradskii Gosudarstvennyi Universitet
 Ucenye Zapiski
Kaliningr Gos Univ Kafedra Teor Eksp Fiz Tr — Kaliningradskii Gosudarstvennyi
 Universitet. Kafedra Teoreticeskoi i Eksperimental'noi Fiziki. Trudy
Kaliningr Tekh Inst Rybn Promsti Khoz Tr — Kaliningradskii Tekhnicheskii Institut
 Rybnoi Promyshlennosti i Khozyaistva. Trudy
Kalinin Politekh Inst Tr — Kalininskii Politekhnicheskii Institut. Trudy
Kal Inser — Kaleidoscope Insert
Kali Steinsalz — Kali und Steinsalz
Kalium Qual Landwirtsch Prod Ber Reg Kolloq Int Kali Inst — Kalium und die
 Qualitaet Landwirtschaftlicher Produkte. Bericht ueber Regional-Kolloquium des
 Internationalen Kali-Institutes

Kalium Symp — Kalium Symposium
Kali Verw Salze — Kali und Verwandte Salze
Kali Verw Salze Erdoel — Kali, Verwandte Salze, und Erdoel
Kal Kaeltetech — Kalender fuer Kaeltetechniker
Kalkbrenn Jb Forstbeamte — Kalkbrenners Jahrbuch fuer Forstbeamte
Kalk Gips Schamotteztg — Kalk-, Gips-, und Schamottezeitung
Kalksandstein Arch — Kalksandstein-Archiv
Kalk Zem — Kalk und Zement
Kalk Ziegel Stein U TonindZtg — Kalk-, Ziegel-, Stein-, u Tonindustriezeitung
Kal LandmessWes KultTech — Kalender fuer Landmessungswesen und Kulturtechnik
Kal-Mad — Kaleidoscope-Madison
Kalmartidn Barom — Kalmartidningen Barometern
Kal-Mil — Kaleidoscope-Milwaukee
Kalmytskii Nauchno-Issled Inst Myasn Skotovod Nauchn Tr — Kalmytskii Nauchno-Issledovatel'skii Institut Myasnogo Skotovodstva. Nauchnye Trudy
Kal Russk Sadov — Kalendar' Russkago Sadovoda
Kal Rysist Gosud Konnozav — Kalendar' Rysistyi Gosudarstvennago Konnozavodstva
Kal Schweiz Imkers — Kalender des Schweizer Imkers
Kal Spinn Web — Kalender fuer Spinnerei und Weberei
Kal Sver Bergh — Kalender foer Sveriges Berghandtering
Kal Sver Berghandt — Kalender foer Sveriges Berghandtering
Kal Text Ind — Kalender fuer die Textil-Industrie
Kal Ukrmet Ukr Met Hydrol Sluzhba — Kalendar Ukrmet. Ukrayins'ka Meteorolohychna ta Hydrolohychna Sluzba
Kaluzh Sanit Obz — Kaluzhskii Sanitarnyi Obzor
Kaluzh Vet Byull — Kaluzhskii Veterinarnyi Byulleten'
Kal VermessWes KultTech — Kalender fuer Vermessungswesen und Kulturtechnik
Kal ZentVer Dt Aerzte Boehm — Kalender des Zentralvereins Deutscher Aerzte in Boehmen
Kam — Kamena
Kamaishi Tech Rep — Kamaishi Technical Report
Kaminshu — Kakyu Saibansho Minji Saibanreishu
KAMJD — Kawasaki Medical Journal
Kamloops For Reg Newsl — Kamloops Forest Region Newsletter
Kammer Tech Suhl Tagungsband — Kammer der Technik Suhl. Tagungsband
Kamper Alm — Kamper Almanak
Kampf GeschlKrankh — Kampf Gegen die Geschlechtskrankheiten
Kampf Laerm — Kampf dem Laerm
Kamp's Paed Tb — Kamp's Paedagogische Taschenbuecher
Kamptal Stud — Kamptal-Studien
Kampuchea Bull — Kampuchea Bulletin
Kamyr Nachr — Kamyr Nachrichten
Kan — Kansas Reports
Kan Acad Sci Trans — Kansas Academy of Science. Transactions
Kan Ac Sc T — Transactions of the Kansas Academy of Science
Kan Admin Regs — Kansas Administrative Regulations
Kanagawa Prefect Mus Bull — Kanagawa Prefectural Museum. Bulletin
Kan Ag Exp — Kansas State Agricultural College. Agricultural Experiment Station. Publications
Kan App — Kansas Court of Appeals Reports
Kan App 2d — Kansas Court of Appeals Reports. Second Series
Kanazawa Univ Res Inst Tuberc Annu Rep — Kanazawa University. Research Institute of Tuberculosis. Annual Report
KanazHB — Kanazawa Daigaku Hobungakubu Ronshu. Bungakuhen
KanazJK — Kanazawa Daigaku Kyoyobu Ronshu. Jinbunkagakuhen
Kan BAJ — Kansas Bar Association. Journal
Kan B Ass'n J — Kansas Bar Association. Journal
Kan City L R — Kansas City Law Review
Kan City L Rev — Kansas City Law Review
Kan Civ Proc Code Ann (Vernon) — Vernon's Kansas Statutes, Annotated, Code of Civil Procedure
Kan Conf Soc Wk Handbk Kan Soc Resources — Kansas Conference of Social Work. Handbook on Kansas Social Resources
Kan Corp Code Ann (Vernon) — Vernon's Kansas Statutes, Annotated, Corporation Code
Kan Crim Code Ann (Vernon) — Vernon's Kansas Statutes, Annotated, Criminal Code
Kan Crim Proc Code Ann (Vernon) — Vernon's Kansas Statutes, Annotated, Code of Criminal Procedure
K & C — Kunst en Cultuur
Kandem Hausmitt — Kandem Hausmitteilungen
Kandem Mschr — Kandem Monatsschrift
Kandem Rev — Kandem Review
K & K — Kunst und Kuenstler
K & S — Kunst und Sprache
Kan Geol Surv Short Pap Res — Kansas Geological Survey. Short Papers in Research
Kan Govt J — Kansas Government Journal
Kan Hist Quar — Kansas Historical Quarterly
Kan Jud Council Bull — Kansas Judicial Council. Bulletin
Kan Law Rev — Kansas Law Review
Kan Lib Bull — Kansas Library Bulletin
Kan Libr Bull — Kansas Library Bulletin
Kan LJ — Kansas Law Journal
Kan L Rev — Kansas Law Review
Kan Ment Hyg Soc Bul — Kansas Mental Hygiene Society. Bulletin
Kan M Soc J — Kansas Medical Society. Journal
Kan Munic — Kansas Municipalities
Kan Offic — Kansas Official
Kano S — Kano Studies
Kano Stud — Kano Studies
Kan Prob Code Ann (Vernon) — Vernon's Kansas Statutes, Annotated, Probate Code

Kanpur Agric Coll J — Kanpur Agricultural College Journal
KanQ — Kansas Quarterly
Kan Reg — Kansas Register
Kans Acad Sci Trans — Kansas Academy of Science. Transactions
Kans Ac Sc Tr — Kansas Academy of Science. Transactions
Kans Agric Exp Stn Bienn Rep Dir — Kansas Agricultural Experiment Station. Biennial Report of the Director
Kans Agric Exp Stn Bull — Kansas Agricultural Experiment Station. Bulletin
Kans Agric Exp Stn Circ — Kansas Agricultural Experiment Station. Circular
Kans Agric Exp Stn Res Publ — Kansas Agricultural Experiment Station. Research Publication
Kans Agric Exp Stn Tech Bull — Kansas Agricultural Experiment Station. Technical Bulletin
Kans Agr Situation — Kansas Agricultural Situation. Kansas State University of Agriculture and Applied Science. Extension Service
Kansai Soc NA Jnl — Kansai Society of Naval Architects. Journal
Kansallis-Osake-Pankki Econ R — Kansallis-Osake-Pankki. Economic Review
Kansantal Aikakausk — Kansantaloudellinen Aikakauskirja
Kansas Acad Sci Trans — Kansas Academy of Science. Transactions
Kansas Agric Exp Sta Bull — Kansas State Agricultural College. Agricultural Experiment Station. Bulletin
Kansas Agric Exp Sta Circ — Kansas State Agricultural College. Agricultural Experiment Station Circular
Kansas Agric Exp Sta Progr Rep — Kansas State Agricultural College. Agricultural Experiment Station Progress Report
Kansas Agric Exp Sta Techn Bull — Kansas State Agricultural College. Agricultural Experiment Station Technical Bulletin
Kansas Bus Tchr — Kansas Business Teacher
Kansas City L Rev — University of Kansas City. Law Review
Kansas City Rv Sc — Kansas City Review of Science and Industry
Kansas Geol Survey Map — Kansas Geological Survey. Map
Kansas J Sociol — Kansas Journal of Sociology
Kansas Lib Bul — Kansas Library Bulletin
Kansas LJ — Kansas Law Journal
Kansas R — Kansas City Review
Kansas State Hist Soc Trans — Kansas State Historical Society. Transactions
Kansas Univ Lawyer — Kansas University Lawyer
Kansas Univ Mus Nat History Misc Pub — Kansas University. Museum of Natural History. Miscellaneous Publication
Kansas Univ Paleont Contr — Kansas University. Paleontological Contributions
Kansas Univ Sci Bull — Kansas University Science Bulletin
Kansas Water Resources Board Bull — Kansas State Water Resources Board. Bulletin
Kansatiet Kertom — Kansatieteellisia Kertomuksia
Kans BA — Kansas City Bar Journal
Kans Ci Med J — Kansas City Medical Journal
Kans Cy Archit Bldr — Kansas City Architect and Builder
Kans Cy Dent J — Kansas City Dental Journal
Kans Cy Med Index Lancet — Kansas City Medical Index-Lancet
Kans Cy Med J — Kansas City Medical Journal
Kans Cy Med Rec — Kansas City Medical Record
Kans Cy Sth Rly Agric Ind Bull — Kansas City Southern Railway Agricultural and Industrial Bulletin
Kans Eng Exp Stn Bull — Kansas Engineering Experiment Station. Bulletin
Kans Eng Exp Stn (Manhattan Kans) Spec Rep — Kansas. Engineering Experiment Station (Manhattan, Kansas). Special Report
Kans Environ Health Serv Bull — Kansas Environmental Health Services Bulletin
Kan Sess Laws — Session Laws. Kansas
Kans Fish Game — Kansas Fish and Game
Kans Fmr — Kansas Farmer
Kans Geol Surv Basic Data Ser Ground Water Release — Kansas Geological Survey. Basic Data Series. Ground-Water Release
Kans Geol Surv Bull — Kansas Geological Survey. Bulletin
Kans Geol Surv Chem Qual Ser — Kansas Geological Survey. Chemical Quality Series
Kans Geol Surv Ground Water Ser — Kansas Geological Survey. Ground-Water Series
Kans Geol Surv Irrig Ser — Kansas Geological Survey. Irrigation Series
Kans Geol Surv Ser Spat Anal — Kansas Geological Survey. Series on Spatial Analysis
Kans Ground Water Basic-Data Release — Kansas Ground Water. Basic-Data Release
Kans Highw — Kansas Highways
Kans Hist Q — Kansas Historical Quarterly
Kans Ind — Kansas Industrialist. Kansas State Agricultural College
Kans Med — Kansas Medicine
Kans Nurse — Kansas Nurse
Kans Sch Nat — Kansas School Naturalist
Kans State Board Agric Div Entomol Act — Kansas State Board of Agriculture. Division of Entomology. Activities
Kans State Dep Health Environ Health Serv Bull — Kansas State Department of Health. Environmental Health Services. Bulletin
Kans State Geol Surv Bull — Kansas State Geological Survey. Bulletin
Kans State Geol Surv Comput Contrib — Kansas State Geological Survey. Computer Contribution
Kans State Geol Surv Computer Contrib — Kansas State Geological Survey. Computer Contribution
Kans State Geol Surv Ground Water Ser — Kansas State Geological Survey. Ground-Water Series
Kans State Geol Surv Spec Distrib Publ — Kansas State Geological Survey. Special Distribution Publication
Kans State Geol Surv Spec Distribution Publication — Kansas State Geological Survey. Special Distribution Publication
Kans State Hortic Soc Trans — Kansas State Horticultural Society. Transactions

Kans State Univ Agric Appl Sci Agric Exp Stn Tech Bull — Kansas State University of Agriculture and Applied Science. Agricultural Experiment Station. Technical Bulletin

Kans State Univ Bull — Kansas State University. Bulletin

Kans State Univ Bull Kans Eng Exp Sta Bull — Kansas State University Bulletin. Kansas Engineering Experiment Station. Bulletin

Kans State Univ Cent Energy Stud Rep — Kansas State University. Center for Energy Studies. Report

Kans State Univ Eng Exp Stn Bull — Kansas State University. Engineering Experiment Station. Bulletin

Kans State Univ Eng Exp Stn Repr — Kansas State University. Engineering Experiment Station. Reprint

Kans State Univ Eng Exp Stn Spec Rep — Kansas State University. Engineering Experiment Station. Special Report

Kans State Univ Inst Syst Des Optim Rep — Kansas State University. Institute for Systems Design and Optimization. Report

Kans St Bd Agr Tr An Rp Bien Rp — Kansas State Board of Agriculture. Transactions. Annual Report. Biennial Report

Kans Stockm — Kansas Stockman

Kans Stockman — Kansas Stockman

Kan Stat Ann — Kansas Statutes Annotated

Kan State Hist Soc Coll — Kansas State Historical Society. Collections

Kan State Univ Inst Syst Des Optim Rep — Kansas State University. Institute for Systems Design and Optimization. Report

Kan St B Assn Proc — Kansas State Bar Association. Proceedings

Kans Teach — Kansas Teacher and Western School Journal

Kan St LJ — Kansas State Law Journal

Kans Univ B Ed — Kansas University. Bulletin of Education

Kans Univ Engng Bull — Kansas University Engineering Bulletin

Kans Univ Mus Nat History Pub Paleont Contr Sci Bull — Kansas University. Museum of Natural History. Publications. Paleontological Contributions. Science Bulletin

Kans Univ Paleontol Contrib Pap — Kansas University. Paleontology Contribution Paper

Kans Univ Q — Kansas University. Quarterly

Kans Univ Sc B — Kansas University. Science Bulletin

Kans Univ Sci Bull — Kansas University. Science Bulletin

Kansu Sci Educ J — Kansu Science Education Journal

Kans Water Res Board Bull — Kansas Water Resources Board. Bulletin

Kans Water Resour Res Inst Contrib — Kansas Water Resources Research Institute. Contribution

Kans Water Sewage Works Assoc Proc — Kansas Water and Sewage Works Association. Proceedings

Kans Water Sewage Works Assoc Rep — Kansas Water and Sewage Works Association. Report

Kans Wheat Qual Kans State Board Agr — Kansas Wheat Quality. Kansas State Board of Agriculture

Kan Teach & W Sch J — Kansas Teacher and Western School Journal

Kanto J Orthop Traumatol — Kanto Journal of Orthopedics and Traumatology

KantS — Kantstudien

Kant-Stud — Kant-Studien

Kantu Rev A — Kantu. Revista de Arte

Kan UCC Ann (Vernon) — Vernon's Kansas Statutes Annotated (Uniform Commercial Code)

Kan Univ Kan Studies Ed — Kansas University. Kansas Studies in Education

Kan Un Q — Kansas University Quarterly

KAnz — Kunstgeschichtliche Anzeigen

KAO — Im Kampf und den Alten Orient

Kaohsiung J Med Sci — Kaohsiung Journal of Medical Sciences

KAP — Kampioen

Kapala Cruise Rep — Kapala Cruise Report

Kapital — Kapitalistate

Kapital Erfind — Kapital und Erfindung

Kapitalis — Kapitalistate

KaQ — Kansas Quarterly

K Ar — Kansatieteellinen Arkisto

KAR — Keilschrifttexte aus Assur. Religioesen Inhalts

Karachi Math Assoc Riazi Souvenir — Riazi Souvenir. Karachi Mathematics Association

Karachi Univ Gaz — Karachi University Gazette

Karachi Univ J Sci — Karachi University. Journal of Science

Karakulevod Zverovod — Karakulevodstvo i Zverovodstvo

Karakulev Zverov — Karakulevodstvo i Zverovodstvo

Karb Azet — Karbid und Azetylen

Karbo Energochem Ekol — Karbo-Energochemia-Ekologia

Karcher Symp — Karcher Symposium

Kardiol Mater Konf Nauchn Ova Kardiol Lit SSR — Kardiologiya. Materialy Konferentsii Nauchnogo Obshchestva Kardiologov Litovskoi SSR

Kardiol Pol — Kardiologia Polska

Kardiol Pol Tow Internistow Pol Sek Kardiol — Kardiologia Polska. Towarzystwo Internistow Polskich. Sekeja Kardiologiczna

Karger Biobehav Med Ser — Karger Biobehavioral Medicine Series

Karger Contin Educ Ser — Karger Continuing Education Series

Kariba Stud — Kariba Studies

KARJA — Karjantuote

KARKA — Karada No Kagaku

Karl-August-Forster-Lect — Karl-August-Forster-Lectures

Kar LJ — Karachi Law Journal

Karlov Laz Cas — Karlovarsky Lazensky Casopis

Karlsbader Aerztl Vortr — Karlsbader Aerztliche Vortraege

Karlsburger Symp Diabetesfragen — Karlsburger Symposium ueber Diabetesfragen

Karlsburg Symp — Karlsburg Symposium

Karlsruhe Nt Vr Vh — Verhandlungen des Naturwissenschaftlichen Vereins in Karlsruhe

Karlsruher Akad Red — Karlsruher Akademische Reden

Karlsruher Beitr Entwicklungsphysiol Pflanz — Karlsruher Beitraege zur Entwicklungsphysiologie der Pflanzen

Karlsruher Ber Ingenieurbiol — Karlsruher Berichte zur Ingenieurbiologie

Karlsruher Geochem Hefte — Karlsruher Geochemische Hefte

Karlsruher Geogr Hefte — Karlsruher Geographische Hefte

Karnataka Med J — Karnataka Medical Journal

Karnatak Univ J Sci — Karnatak University. Journal of Science

Karolinska Foerb Arsb — Karolinska Foerbundets Arsbok

Karolinska Inst Lab Clin Stress Res Rep — Karolinska Institute. Laboratory for Clinical Stress Research. Reports

Karolinska Inst Nobel Conf — Karolinska Institute Nobel Conference

Karolinska Symp Res Methods Reprod Endocrinol — Karolinska Symposia on Research Methods in Reproductive Endocrinology

Kaross FahrzBau — Karosserie und Fahrzeugbau

Karpaten Jb — Karpatenjahrbuch

Karpato Balk Geol Assots Mater Kom Mineral Geokhim — Karpato-Balkanskaya Geologicheskaya Assotsiatsiya. Materialy Komissii Mineralogii i Geokhimii

KARRAA — Kenya. Department of Agriculture. Annual Report

Karsten Arch — Archiv fuer Mineralogie, Geognosie, Bergbau, und Huettenkunde. Karsten

Karsten Arch Bergbau — Archiv fuer Bergbau und Huettenwesen. Karsten

Karszt Barlangkut — Karszt- es Barlangkutatas

Kart — Karthago. Revue d'Archeologie Africaine

Karth — Karthago. Revue d'Archeologie Africaine

Kartinna Gal — Kartinna Galleriya

Kartoffel Tag — Kartoffel-Tagung

Kartoffel Tag Vortr Anlaesslich Fachtag Arbeitsgem Kartoffelf — Kartoffel-Tagung, Vortraege Anlaesslich der Fachtagung der Arbeitsgemeinschaft Kartoffelforschung e. V

Kartoffel u Furageztg — Kartoffel- und Furagezeitung</PHR> %

Kartogr Let — Kartograficeskaja Letopis

Kartogr Mitt — Kartographische Mitteilungen

Kartogr Nachr — Kartographische Nachrichten

Kartogr Nachr Bielefeld — Kartographische Nachrichten. Mitteilungen der Deutschen Gesellschaft fuer Kartographie e.V. Bielefeld

Kartogr Nachr (Stuttg) — Kartographische Nachrichten (Stuttgart)

Kartogr Pr — Kartograficky Prehled

Kartogr Prehl — Kartograficky Prehled

Kartogr SchrReihe — Kartographische Schriftenreihe

Kartogr Schulgeogr Z — Kartographische und Schulgeographische Zeitschrift

Kartogr Schulgeogr Zs — Kartographische und Schulgeographische Zeitschrift

Kartonagen Papierwaren-Ztg — Kartonagen und Papierwaren-Zeitung

Kartonn U PapWarenztg — Kartonnagen- und Papierwarenzeitung

Kartoplya Ovochevi Bashtanni Kult — Kartoplya Ovochevi ta Bashtanni Kul'turi

KARU — Klosterarchive, Tegesten, und Urkunden

Kasai Geppo — Katei Saiban Geppo

Kasan Med J — Kasaner Medizinisches Journal

KASEA — Kagaku To Seibutsu

Kaseigaku Zasshi J Home Econ Jap — Kaseigaku Zasshi. Journal of Home Economics of Japan

Kasetsart J — Kasetsart Journal

Kasetsart Univ Fish Res Bull — Kasetsart University. Fishery Research Bulletin

Kas His S — Kansas State Historical Society. Collections

Kashmir LJ — Kashmir Law Journal

Kashmir Sci — Kashmir Science

Kashmir Univ Fac Sci Res J — Kashmir University. Faculty of Science. Research Journal

Kask — Kaskelot

Kask Paed Saernr — Kaskelot. Paedagogiske Saernumre

KASL — Kasseler Arbeiten zur Sprache und Literatur. Anglistik-Germanistik-Romanistik

KASP — Kleine Allgemeine Schriften zur Philosophie, Theologie, und Geschichte

KASPG — Kleine Allgemeine Schriften zur Philosophie, Theologie, und Geschichte. Geschichtliche Reihe

KASPP — Kleine Allgemeine Schriften zur Philosophie, Theologie, und Geschichte. Philosophische Reihe

KASPT — Kleine Allgemeine Schriften zur Philosophie, Theologie, und Geschichte. Theologische Reihe

Kasr El-Aini J Surg — Kasr El-Aini Journal of Surgery

Kassel Vr Nt Ab U B — Abhandlungen und Bericht des Vereins fuer Naturkunde zu Kassel

Kassel Vr Nt B — Bericht des Vereines fuer Naturkunde zu Kassel

Kassel Vr Nt Festschr — Festschrift des Vereins fuer Naturkunde zu Cassel zur Feier Seines Fuenfzigjaehrigen Bestehens

Kassenzahnarzt Colloq Med Dent — Kassenzahnarzt. Colloquium Med Dent

Kastner Arch C — Archiv fuer Chemie und Meteorologie. Kastner

Kastner Arch Ntl — Archiv fuer die Gesammte Naturlehre. Kastner

Kat — Katholiek

Katal — Katallagete

Katal Katal — Kataliz i Katalizatory

Katal Konvers Uglevodorodov — Katalicheskaya Konversiya Uglevodorodov

Katal Pererab Uglevodorodnogo Syr'ya — Katalicheskaya Pererabotka Uglevodorodnogo Syr'ya

Katal Prevrashch Uglevodorodov — Katalicheskie Prevrashcheniya Uglevodorodov

Katal Reakts Zhidk Faze Mater Vses Konf — Katalicheskie Reaktsii v Zhidkoi Faze. Materialy Vsesoyuznoi Konferentsii po Katalicheskim Reaktsiyam v Zhidkoi Faze

Katal Reakts Zhidk Faze Tr Vses Konf — Katalicheskie Reaktsii v Zhidkoi Faze. Trudy Vsesoyuznoi Konferentsii

Katal Vyssh Shk Tr Mezhvuz Soveshch — Kataliz v Vysshei Shkole. Trudy Mezhvuzovskogo Soveshchaniya po Katalizu

Kat Bl — Katechetische Blaetter

Kat Datamater Nor Berggrunn — Katalog over Datamateriale for Norges Berggrunn
Kat Fauny Pol — Katalog Fauny Polski
Kat Fauny Polski — Katalog Fauny Polski
Kath — Katholiek
Kath — Katholik
Kath Ar — Katholiek Archief
Kath Cult Tijdsch — Katholiek Cultureel Tijdschrift
Kath Dig — Katholischer Digest
Kath Jb — Katholische Jahrbuch
KathL — De Katholiek (Leiden)
Kathmandu Summer Sch Lect Notes — Kathmandu Summer School Lecture Notes
Kath MJS — Katholisches Missionsjahrbuch der Schweiz
Kathol Schweizerbl — Katholische Schweizerblaetter
Kathol Univ Leuven Landbouwinst Verh — Katholieke Universiteit te Leuven. Landbouwinstituut. Verhandelingen
Katilolehti — Katilolehti. Tidskrift foer Barnmorskor
Katl Prevrashch Uglevodorodov — Kataliticheskie Prevrascheniya Uglevodorodov
Kat Mschr — Katechetische Monatsschrift
KATO — Kahtou: a Publication of the Native Communications Society of British Columbia
Katseasj Nouk Toim — Katseasjanduse Noukogu Toimetused
Kat Soln Deyat Glav Astr Obs Pulkove — Katalog Solnechnoi Deyatel'nosti. Glavnaya Astronomicheskaya Observatoriya v Pulkove
Kat Zs — Katechetische Zeitschrift
Kauch i Rezina — Kauchuk i Rezina
Kauno Politech Inst Darb — Kauno Politechnikos Instituto Darbai
Kauno Politech Inst Jubiliejines Mokslines Tech Konf Darb — Kauno Politechnikos Instituto Jubiliejines Mokslines-Technines Konferencijos. Darbai
Kauno Valstibinio Univ Tech Fak Darb — Kauno Valstibinio Universiteto Technikos Fakulteto Darbai
Kauno Valstybinio Med Inst Darb — Kauno Valstybinio Medicinos Instituto Darbai
KAUP — Kauppalehti
Kauri Gum Ind — Kauri-Gum Industry
Kausale Ther — Kausale Therapie
Kautch Gummi Kunstst Asbest — Kautschuk und Gummi. Kunststoffe. Asbest
Kaut Gum Ku — Kautschuk und Gummi. Kunststoffe
Kaut Gummi — Kautschuk und Gummi. Kunststoffe
Kautsch Gummi — Kautschuk und Gummi
Kautsch Gummi Kunstst — Kautschuk und Gummi. Kunststoffe
Kautsch Gummi Kunstst Asbest — Kautschuk und Gummi. Kunststoffe, Asbest
Kautsch Gummi Kunstst Plastomere Elastomere Duromere — Kautschuk und Gummi. Kunststoffe. Plastomere, Elastomere, Duromere
Kautsch Gummi Moscow — Kautschuk und Gummi (Moscow)
Kautschuk Anwend — Kautschuk Anwendungen
Kautschuk Infn — Kautschuk-Informationen
Kaut u Gummi Kunst — Kautschuk und Gummi. Kunststoffe
KAV — Keilschrifttexte aus Assur Vverschiedenen Inhalts
Kavkaz Etnogr Sborn Tbilisi — Kavkazskiy Etnograficheskiy Sbornik. Akademiya Nauk Gruzinskoy SSR (Tbilisi)
Kavk Etnogr Sb — Kavkazskij Etnograficeskij Sbornik
Kavk Inst Miner Syrya Tr — Kavkazskii Institut Mineral'nogo Syr'ya. Trudy
Kavk Sb — Kavkazskii Sbornik
Kavk Sel Khoz — Kavkazskoe Sel'skoe Khozyaistvo
Kawamata Chem Bull Leather Technol — Kawamata Chemical Bulletin of Leather Technology
Kawasaki J Med Welfare — Kawasaki Journal of Medical Welfare
Kawasaki Med J — Kawasaki Medical Journal
Kawasaki Rev — Kawasaki Review
Kawasaki Rozai Tech Rep — Kawasaki Rozai Technical Report
Kawasaki Steelmaking Tech Rep — Kawasaki Steelmaking Technical Report
Kawasaki Steel Tech Bull — Kawasaki Steel Technical Bulletin
Kawasaki Steel Tech Rep — Kawasaki Steel Technical Report
Kawasaki Tech Rev — Kawasaki Technical Review
KAZ — Konsument. Test Magazine der Konsumenteninformation
Kazah Gos Ped Inst Ucen Zap — Kazakhskii Gosudarstvennyi Pedagogiceskii Institut Imeni Abaja Ucenye Zapiski
Kazak Ak Habarlary — Kazak SSR Gylym Akademijasynyn Habarlary. Izvestija Akademii Nauk Kazachskoj SSR
Kazan Aviats Inst im AN Tupoleva Tr KAI — Kazanskii Aviatsionnyi Institut imeni A.N. Tupoleva. Trudy KAI
Kazan Gos Med Inst Nauchn Tr — Kazanskii Gosudarstvennyi Meditsinskii Institut. Nauchnye Trudy
Kazan Gos Pedagog Inst Uch Zap — Kazanskii Gosudarstvennyi Pedagogicheskii Institut. Uchenye Zapiski
Kazan Gos Univ Ucen Zap — Kazanskii Ordena Trudovogo Krasnogo Znameni Gosudarstvennyi Universitet Imeni V. I. Ul'janova-Lenina Ucenye Zapiski
Kazan Gos Vet Inst im NE Baumana Nauchn Tr — Kazanskii Gosudarstvennyi Veterinarnyi Institut imeni N.E. Baumana. Nauchnye Trudy
Kazan Khim Tekhnol Inst Tr — Kazanskii Khimiko-Tekhnologicheskii Institut. Trudy
Kazan Med Z — Kazanskii Meditsinskii Zhurnal
Kazan Med Zh — Kazanskii Meditsinskii Zhurnal
Kazan Med Zhurnal — Kazanskii Meditsinskii Zhurnal
Kazan Mm Un — Scientific Memoirs Published by the Imperial University of Kazan
Kazan Muz Vest — Kazanskii Muzeinyi Vestnik
Kazan Muz Vestnik — Kazansky Muzeyny Vestnik
Kazan S Nt Ps Mth P — Proceedings of the Physico-Mathematical Section of the Naturalists' Society of the Imperial University of Kazan
Kazan S Nt T — Transactions of the Naturalists' Society of the Imperial University of Kazan
Kazan S Ps Mth BII — Bulletin de la Societe Physico-Mathematique de Kazan
Kazan Un Mm — Scientific Memoirs published by the Imperial University of Kazan
Kaz Nauchn Issled Gidrometeorol Inst Tr — Kazakhskii Nauchno-Issledovatel'skii Gidrometeorologicheskii Institut. Trudy

Kaz Nauchno-Issled Inst Lesn Khoz Agrolesomelio Tr — Kazakhskii Nauchno-Issledovatel'skii Institut Lesnogo Khozyaistva i Agrolesomelioratsii Trudy
Kaz Nauchno-Issled Inst Lesn Khoz Tr — Kazakhskii Nauchno-Issledovatel'skii Institut Lesnogo Khozyaistva Trudy
Kaz Nauchn Issled Inst Zashch Rast Tr — Kazakhskii Nauchno-Issledovatel'skii Institut Zashchity Rastenii. Trudy
Kaz Petrogr Soveshch — Kazakhstanskoe Petrograficheskoe Soveshchanie
Kaz Reg Nauchno Issled Inst Tr — Kazakhskii Regional'nyi Nauchno-Issledovatel'skii Institut. Trudy
Kaz Skh Inst Tr — Kazakhskii Sel'skokhozyaistvennyi Institut. Trudy
K B — Deutsches Kolonialblatt
KB — Keilschriftliche Bibliothek
KB — Kew Bulletin
KB — Komunist (Belgrade)
KB — Kulturos Barai
KB — Kunstgeschichte in Bildern
KBA — Korte Berichten voor de Machinebranche en Apparatenbranche
KBAA — Kieler Beitraege zur Anglistik und Amerikanistik
KBAMA — Kosmicheskaya Biologiya i Aviakosmicheskaya Meditsina
KBANT — Kommentare und Beitraege zum Alten und Neuen Testament
K-Bayer Ak Wiss Muenchen Mat-Phys Kl Szb Abh — Koeniglich-Bayerische Akademie der Wissenschaften zu Muenchen. Mathematisch-Physikalische Klasse. Sitzungsberichte. Abhandlungen
KBB — Kentucky Bench and Bar
KBB — Kraks Blaa Bog
KBB — Kulturas Biroja Biletins
KBCJ — Koninklijke Belgische Commissie voor Volkskunde, Vlaamse Afdeling Jaarboek
KBDA — Korrespondenzblatt. Gesamtverein der Deutschen Geschichte und Altertumsvereine
KBDF — Kleine Beitraege zur Droste-Forschung
KBDGA — Korrespondenz-Blatt der Deutschen Gesellschaft fuer Anthropologie, Ethnologie, und Urgeschichte
KBE — Key British Enterprises
KBE — Kirche in Bewegung und Entscheidung
KBE — Korean Business Review
KBE — Kratka Bulgarska Enciklopedija
KBEA J — Kentucky Business Education Association. Journal
KBEBD — Kvartalsskrift. Bergen Bank
K Belg Inst Natuurwet Studiedoc — Koninklijk Belgisch Instituut voor Natuurwetenschappen. Studiedocumenten
K Belg Inst Natuurwet Verh — Koninklijk Belgisch Instituut voor Natuurwetenschappen. Verhandelingen
K Belg Inst Verbetering Biet Driemaand Publ — Koninklijk Belgisch Instituut tot Verbetering van de Biet. Driemaandelijkse Publicatie
K Belg Kolon Inst Afd Nat Geneeskd Wet Verh 4 — Koninklijk Belgisch Koloniaal Instituut. Afdeeling der Natuur- en GeneeskundigeWetenschappen. Verhandelingen in 4
K Belg Kolon Inst Afd Nat Geneeskd Wet Verh 8 — Koninklijk Belgisch Koloniaal Instituut. Afdeeling der Natuur- en Geneeskundige Wetenschappen. Verhandelingen 8
K Belg Kolon Inst Bull Zittingen — Koninklijk Belgisch Koloniaal Instituut. Bulletijn der Zittingen
K Belg Ver Electrotech Bull — Koninklijke Belgische Vereniging der Electrotechnici. Bulletin
KBEMD — Kultuurpatronen. Bulletin Etnografisch Museum (Delft)
Kbf T — Kobstadforeningens Tidsskrift
KBGL — Kopenhagener Beitraege zur Germanistischen Linguistik
KBGWAB — Koninklijk Museum voor Midden-Afrika [*Tervuren, Belgie*]. Annalen. Reeks in Octavo. Geologische Wetenschappen
Kbh H — Kobenhavns Havneblad
KBJ — Kentucky Bar Journal
KBJ — Kentucky State Bar Journal
KBK — Korte Berichten voor de Kledingbranche
KBKL — Kritische Berichte zur Kunstgeschichtlichen Literatur
KBKOD — Steinkohlenbergbauverein Kurznachrichten
KBL — Koehler, Ludwig und Walter Baumgartner. Lexicon in Veteris Testamenti Libros
Kbl — Korrespondenzblatt. Verein fuer Niederdeutsche Sprachforschung
KBIAnthr — Korrespondenzblatt der Deutschen Gesellschaft fuer Anthropologie
K BI BE — Koelner Blaetter fuer Berufserziehung
KBLG — Kritische Blaetter zur Literatur der Gegenwart
KBI Ref — Kirchenblatt fuer die Reformierte Schweiz
Kbl RS — Kirchenblatt fuer die Reformierte Schweiz
KBM — Korte Berichten voor de Meubelbranche en Stofferingsbranche
KBMEA — Kosmicheskaya Biologiya i Meditsina
KBMEDO — Karger Biobehavioral Medicine Series
KBN — Korpus Bosporskikh Nadpisei
KBO — Berichten uit het Buitenland
KBO — Keilschrifttexte aus Boghazkoei
K-Boehm Ges Wiss Mat-Nat Kl Szb — Koeniglich-Boehmische Gesellschaft der Wissenschaften in Prag. Mathematisch-Naturwissenschaftliche Klasse. Sitzungsberichte
KBP — Korte Berichten voor de Verpakkingsbranche
KBP Q — Kappa Beta Pi Quarterly
KBR — Keio Business Review
KBR — Rheinisch-Westfaelisches Institut fuer Wirtschaftsforschung. Konjunkturberichte
KBRS — Kirchenblatt fuer die Reformierte Schweiz
KBS — Kavkazsko-Blizhnevostochnyi Sbornik
KBSEA — Bulletin. Kyoto Educational University. Series B. Mathematics and Natural Science
KBS Tech Rep — KBS [*Kaernbraenslesaekerhet*] Technical Report
KBS Tek Rapp — KBS [*Kaernbraenslesaekerhet*] Teknisk Rapport
KBV — Korte Berichten voor de Verfbranche

KBW — Korrespondenzblatt fuer die Hoeheren Schulen Wuerttembergs
KC — Keyboard Classics
KC — Kratkie Soobshcheniia Instituta Arkheologii. Akademiia Nauk URSR
KC — Kritika Chronika
KC — Kunstchronik
KCA — Keesing's Contemporary Archives
KCBNAY — Annals. Kurashiki Central Hospital
KC Bsns Jl — Kansas City Business Journal
KCESDX — Karger Continuing Education Series
KCH — Korte Berichten voor de Chemiebranche
K Ch — Kritika Chronika
Kchfd — Kirchenfreund
K Chr — Kretika Chronika
KChron — Kretika Chronika
KC Phil — Kansas City Philharmonic Program Notes
KCR — Kansas City Law Review
KCR — University of Missouri at Kansas City. Law Review
KCRAB8 — Annual Report. Cancer Research Institute. Kanazawa University
KCREEN — Kapala Cruise Report
KCS — Knowing Christianity Series
KCsA — Koeroesi Csoma-Archivum
KCSN — Kralovska Ceska Spolecnost Nauk
KCS Sci J — K.C.S. Science Journal
KC Star — Kansas City Star
KCT — Katholiek Cultureel Tijdschrift
KC Times — Kansas City Times
KCTS — Katholiek Cultureel Tijdschrift Streven
KCWD — Kaleidoscope. Current World Data
K D — Kerygma und Dogma
KD — Kirchliche Dogmatik
KD — Kristeligt Dagblad
K d Abg Sten Ber — Verhandlungen. Kammer der Abgeordneten des Bayerischen Landtags. Stenographische Berichte
K Danske Vidensk Selsk Skr — Kongelige Danske Videnskabernes Selskab. Skrifter
K Dan Vidensk Selsk Biol Medd — Kongelige Danske Videnskabernes Selskab. Biologiske Meddelelser
K Dan Vidensk Selsk Biol Skr — Kongelige Danske Videnskabernes Selskab. Biologiske Skrifter
K Dan Vidensk Selsk Mat Fys Medd — Kongelige Danske Videnskabernes Selskab. Matematisk-Fysisk Meddelelser
K Dan Vidensk Selsk Mat Fys Skr — Kongelige Danske Videnskabernes Selskab. Matematisk-Fysisk Skrifter
K Dan Vidensk Selsk Over Selsk Virksomhed — Kongelige Danske Videnskabernes Selskab. Oversigt Selskabets Virksomhed
K Dan Vidensk Selsk Skr Naturvidensk Mat Afd — Kongelige Danske Videnskabernes Selskab. Skrifter. Naturvidenskabelig og Mathematisk Afdeling
KDB — Koelner Domblatt
KDDGAU — Deutsche Dendrologische Gesellschaft. Kurzmitteilungen
KDD Tech J — KDD Technical Journal
KDF — Koenigsberger Deutsche Forschungen
KDGA — Korrespondenzblatt der Deutschen Gesellschaft fuer Anthropologie, Ethnologie, und Urgeschichte
KDGK — Kuerchners Deutscher Gelehrtenkalender
KDGNB — Kinki Daigaku Genshiryoku Kenkyusho Nenpo
KDGNBX — Annual Report. Kinki University. Atomic Energy Research Institute
KDKHB — Kyoto Daigaku Kogyo Kyoin Yoseijo Kenkyu Hokoku
KDKIA — Kyoto Daigaku Kogaku Kenkyusho Iho
KDKKB — Kagoshima Daigaku Kogakubu Kenkyu Hokoku
KDKSB — Kyushu Daigaku Kogaku Shuho
KDNKDR — Proceedings. Faculty of Agriculture. Kyushu Tokai University
KdO — Kunst des Orients
K d Oe L — Kritik des Oeffentlichen Lebens
KDPM — Kleine Deutsche Prosadenkmaeler des Mittelalters
KDRNBK — Annual Report. Noto Marine Laboratory
KDSGA — Kagoshima Daigaku Suisangakubu Kiyo
KDSL — Konzepte der Sprack- und Literaturwissenschaft
KDSRA2 — Annals of Science. Kanazawa University. Part 2. Biology-Geology
KDTIA — Kumamoto Daigaku Taishitsu Igaku Kenkyusho Hokoku
KDV — Kalender der Detuschen Volksgemeinschaft fuer Rumaenien
KDVS — Kongelige Danske Videnskabernes Selskab. Historisk-Filosofiske Meddelelser
KDVSA — Kongelige Danske Videnskabernes Selskab. Matematisk-Fysisk Meddelelser
KDVSS — Kongelige Danske Videnskabernes-Selskabs Skrivter
KE — Katholieke Encyclopaedie
KE — Keewatin Echo
Ke — Kemi. Revue de Philologie et d'Archeologie Egyptiennes et Coptes
Keats-Shell — Keats-Shelley Journal
Keats-Shelley J — Keats-Shelley Journal
Keats-Shelley J Ann Bibl — Keats-Shelley Journal. Annual Bibliography
Keats Sh M — Keats-Shelley Memorial Association. Bulletin
KEBR — Kobe Economic and Business Review
Ke Do — Kerygma and Dogma
KEE — Kantoor en Efficiency
KEE — Kratkaia Evreiskaia Entsiklopediia
Keem Teated — Keemia Teated
Keep Abreast J — Keeping Abreast. Journal of Human Nurturing
Keep Abreast J Hum Nurt — Keeping Abreast. Journal of Human Nurturing
Keesings Med Dig — Keesing's Medical Digest
KEGEAC — Japanese Journal of Plastic and Reconstructive Surgery
KEH — Kurzgefasstes Exegetisches Handbuch
KEH — Kurzgefasstes Exegetisches Handbuch zum Alten Testament
Kehutanan Indones — Kehutanan Indonesia
KEI — Keidanren Review of Japanese Economy

Keighley Mus Notes — Keighley Museum Notes
Keighley Text Ass J — Keighley Textile Association Journal
Keijo J Med — Keijo Journal of Medicine
KEIKA — Keikinzoku
Keikinzoku J Jpn Inst Light Met — Keikinzoku/Journal of Japan Institute of Light Metals
Keilinschr Bibl — Keilinschriftliche Bibliothek
Keio Bus R — Keio Business Review
Keio Econ S — Keio Economic Studies
Keio Econ Stud — Keio Economic Studies
Keio Eng Rep — Keio Engineering Reports
Keio Engrg Rep — Keio Engineering Reports
Keio J Med — Keio Journal of Medicine
Keio J Polit — Keio Journal of Politics
Keio Math Sem Rep — Keio Mathematical Seminar. Reports
Keio Sci Tech Rep — Keio Science and Technology Reports
KEIS — Kentucky Economic Information System
Keisai Geppo — Keiji Saiban Geppo
Keishu — Saiko Saibansho Keiji Hanreishu
Keisoho — Keiji Soshoho
Keith Shipton Dev Spec Study — Keith Shipton Developments. Special Study
Keizyo J Med — Keizyo Journal of Medicine
Ke K — Keiryo Kokugogaku
KEK — Kritisch-Exegetischer Kommentar ueber das Neue Testament
KEK Annu Rep (Natl Lab High Energy Phys) — KEK Annual Report (National Laboratory for High Energy Physics)
KEKHA — Koshu Eiseiin Kenkyu Hokoku
KEK Proc — KEK Proceedings
Keleti Szle — Keleti Szemle
Kelle Retorte — Kelle und Retorte
Kellogg Found Int Food Res Symp — Kellogg Foundation International Food Research Symposium
Kellogg Nutr Symp — Kellogg Nutrition Symposium
Kellogg Nutr Symp Proc — Kellogg Nutrition Symposium. Proceedings
Kel Sz — Keleti Szemle
Kelvin Hughes Mar Rev — Kelvin Hughes Marine Review
KEMA Publ — KEMA [Keuring van Elektrotechnische Materialen Arnhem] Publikaties
Kem Arb Stockh Hogsk Biokem Lab — Kemiska Arbeten fran Stockholms Hogskolas Biokemiska Laboratorium
KEMA Sci Tech Rep — KEMA [Keuring van Elektrotechnische Materialen Arnhem] Scientific and Technical Reports
KEMEDB — Infection, Inflammation, and Immunity
Kemerov Gos Ped Inst Ucen Zap — Kemerovskii Gosudarstvennyi Pedagogiceskii Institut Ucenye Zapiski
Kemija Ind — Kemija u Industriji
Kem Ind — Kemija u Industriji
Kem Int — Kemio Internacia
Kemi Rev Philol & Archeol Egyp & Copt — Kemi. Revue de Philologie et d'Archeologie Egyptiennes et Coptes
Kemixon Reptr — Kemixon Reporter
Kem-Kemi — Kemia-Kemi
Kem Kesk Julk — Kemian Keskusliiton Julkaisuja
Kem Kesk Tied — Kemian Keskusliiton Tiedoituksia
Kem Keskus Erip — Kemian Keskusliiton Eripainoksia
KEM Konstr Elem Methoden — KEM. Konstruktion, Elemente, Methoden
Kem Kozl — Kemiai Kozlemenyek
Kem Kozlem — Kemiai Kozlemenyek
Kem Lap — Kemikusok Lapja
Kem Lapja — Kemikusok Lapja
Kem M — Kemisk Maanedsblad og Nordisk Handelsblad for Kemisk Industri
Kem Maanedsbl Nord Handelsbl Kem Ind — Kemisk Maanedsblad. Nordisk Handelsblad foer Kemisk Industri
Kem Maanedsbl — Kemisk Maanedsblad og Nordisk Handelsblad for Kemisk Industri
Kem Poljopr — Kemija u Poljoprivredi
Kem-Talajt — Kemia-Talajtani Tanszek
Kem Teollisuus — Kemian Teollisuus
Kem Tidskr — Kemisk Tidskrift
Kem Tidskr Kemivaerlden — Kemisk Tidskrift/Kemivaerlden
Kem Vaextskyddsmedel — Kemiska Vaextskyddsmedel
Kem Vjest — Kemijski Vjestnik
Kem Vjestn — Kemijski Vjestnik
KeN — Kenkyu Nempo Tokyo Daigaku Kyoiku-gabuku
KeN — Keynotes
Kenana Res Stn Annu Rep — Kenana Research Station. Annual Report
Kenchiku Bunka Archit Cult — Kenchiku Bunka/Architecture Culture
Kendalls Lib Statist — Kendall's Library of Statistics
Kenkyu Hokoku Bull Fac Agric Tamagawa Univ — Kenkyu Hokoku. Bulletin. Faculty of Agriculture. Tamagawa University
Kenkyu Hokoku J Niigata Agricultural Experiment Station — Kenkyu Hokoku. Journal. Niigata Agricultural Experiment Station
Kenkyu Hokoku J Tottori Univ Nat Sci — Kenkyu Hokoku. Journal. Faculty of Education. Tottori University. Natural Science
Kenkyu Hokoku Res Bull Hokkaido Natl Agric Exp Stn — Kenkyu Hokoku. Research Bulletin. Hokkaido National Agricultural Experiment Station
Kenkyu Hokoku Sci Pap Cent Res Inst Jap Tob Salt Public Corp — Kenkyu Hokoku. Scientific Papers. Central Research Institute. Japan Tobacco and Salt Public Corporation
Kenley Abstr — Kenley Abstracts
KENMER — Koezlemenyek az Erdelyi Nemzeti Muzeum Erem es Regisegtarabal
Kenneccot Lect — Kennecot Lectures
Kennedy Q — Kennedy Quarterly
KenR — Kenyon Review
Kent Agric Grow J — Kent Agricultural and Growers Journal

Kent A R — Kent Archaeological Review
Kent Archaeol Rev — Kent Archaeological Review
Kent Bird Rep — Kent Bird Report
Kent Fmr — Kent Farmer
Kent Fmrs J — Kent Farmers' Journal
Kent Rev — Kent Review
Kent Tech Rev — Kent Technical Review
Kentucky Acad Sci Trans — Kentucky Academy of Science. Transactions
Kentucky For Lang Jour Lexington — Kentucky Foreign Language Journal (Lexington)
Kentucky Geol Surv Bull — Kentucky. Geological Survey. Bulletin
Kentucky Geol Survey Bull — Kentucky. Geological Survey. Bulletin
Kentucky Geol Survey County Rept — Kentucky. Geological Survey. County Report
Kentucky Geol Survey Inf Circ — Kentucky. Geological Survey. Information Circular
Kentucky Geol Survey Rept Inv — Kentucky. Geological Survey. Report of Investigations
Kentucky Geol Survey Spec Pub — Kentucky. Geological Survey. Special Publication
Kentucky LJ — Kentucky Law Journal
Kentucky Med J — Kentucky Medical Journal
Kenya and East African Med J — Kenya and East African Medical Journal
Kenya Coff — Kenya Coffee
Kenya Colony Prot Dep Agric Bull — Kenya. Colony and Protectorate. Department of Agriculture. Bulletin
Kenya Colony Prot Geol Surv Mem — Kenya. Colony and Protectorate. Geological Survey. Memoir
Kenya Colony Prot Min Geol Dep Geol Surv Kenya Rep — Kenya. Colony and Protectorate. Mining and Geological Department. Geological Survey of Kenya. Report
Kenya Dairy Fmr — Kenya Dairy Farmer
Kenya Dep Agric Annu Rep — Kenya. Department of Agriculture. Annual Report
Kenya E Afr Med J — Kenya and East African Medical Journal
Kenya Fmr — Kenya Farmer
Kenya Geol Surv Kenya Bull — Kenya. Geological Survey of Kenya. Bulletin
Kenya Geol Surv Kenya Mem — Kenya. Geological Survey of Kenya. Memoir
Kenya Geol Surv Kenya Rep — Kenya. Geological Survey of Kenya. Report
Kenya Hist Rev — Kenya Historical Review
Kenya Inform Serv Bull — Kenya Information Services. Bulletin
Kenya Inst Admin — Kenya Institute of Administration
Kenya J Sci Technol Ser A — Kenya Journal of Science and Technology. Series A. Physical and Chemical Sciences
Kenya J Sci Technol Ser B Biol Sci — Kenya Journal of Science and Technology. Series B. Biological Sciences
Kenya Med J — Kenya Medical Journal
Kenya Mines Geol Dep Rep — Kenya. Mines and Geological Department. Report
Kenya Minist Nat Resour Mines Geol Dep Rep — Kenya. Ministry of Natural Resources. Mines and Geological Department. Report
Kenya Nurs J — Kenya Nursing Journal
Kenya Past Pres — Kenya Past and Present
Kenya R — Kenya Review
Kenya Reg Stud — Kenya Regional Studies
Kenya Sisal Bd Bull — Kenya Sisal Board Bulletin
Kenya Tuberc Invest Cent Annu Rep — Kenya. Tuberculosis Investigation Centre. Annual Report
Kenya Tuberc Respir Dis Res Cent Ann Rep — Kenya. Tuberculosis and Respiratory Diseases Research Centre. Annual Report
Kenyon Engng News — Kenyon Engineering News
Kenyon R — Kenyon Review
Kenyon Rev — Kenyon Review
Keokuk Med Coll Bull — Keokuk Medical College Bulletin
Kep es Hangtech — Kep- es Hangtechnika
KER — Kern
Kerala J Vet Sci — Kerala Journal of Veterinary Science
Kerala Soc Pap — Kerala Society Papers
Keram Glas (Moscow) — Keramik und Glas (Moscow)
Keram Inst TNO Meded — Keramisch Instituut TNO. Mededelingen
Keram Jb — Keramisches Jahrbuch
Keram Mag — Keramik Magazin
Keram Mh — Keramische Monatshefte
Keram Promst Promst Stroit Mater — Keramicheskaya Promyshlennost. Promyshlennost Stroitel'nykh Materialov
Keram Promst Ref Inf — Keramicheskaya Promyshlennost. Referativnaya Informatsiya
Keram Rundsch — Keramische Rundschau
Keram Rundsch Kunst-Keram — Keramische Rundschau und Kunst-Keramik
Keram Sb — Keramicheskii Sbornik
Keram Steklo — Keramika i Steklo
Keram Z — Keramische Zeitschrift
Keram Z Beil — Keramische Zeitschrift. Beilage
Ker & Steklo — Keramika i Steklo
KerC — Kerkyraika Chronika
KerDo — Kerygma und Dogma
Ker Freunde Schweiz — Keramik-Freunde der Schweiz
Ker Kuop Laan Maanviljelyss Toim — Kertomus Kuopion Laanin Maanviljelysseuran Toiminnasta
Ker LT — Kerala Law Times
Kern Citrus Coop Ext Univ Calif — Kern Citrus. Cooperative Axtension. University of California
Kern Cotton Univ Calif Coop Ext Serv — Kern Cotton. University of California. Cooperative Extension Service
Kernenerg — Kernenergie
Kernenerg Beil — Kernenergie. Beilage
Kernenergie Beil — Kernenergie. Beilage

Kernenerg Ing — Kernenergie-Ingenieur
Kernforschungsanlage Juelich Ber Juel — Kernforschungsanlage Juelich. Berichte Juel
Kernforschungsanlage Juelich Jahresber — Kernforschungsanlage Juelich. Jahresbericht
Kernforschungsanlage Juelich Spez Ber — Kernforschungsanlage Juelich. Spezielle Berichte
Kernforschungszent Karlsruhe Ber KfK — Kernforschungszentrum Karlsruhe. Bericht KfK
Kernforschungszent Karlsruhe Externer Ber — Kernforschungszentrum Karlsruhe. Externer Bericht
Kernforschungszent Karlsruhe Nachr — Kernforschungszentrum Karlsruhe. Nachrichten
Kernforschungsz Karlsruhe Ber — Kernforschungszentrum Karlsruhe. Bericht
Kern Irrig Coop Ext Univ Calif — Kern Irrigation. Cooperative Extension. University of California
Kernontwikkelingskorporasie S Afr Versl PEL — Kernontwikkelingskorporasie van Suid-Afrika. Verslag PEL
Kernontwikkelingskorporasie S Afr Versl PER — Kernontwikkelingskorporasie van Suid-Afrika. Verslag PER
Kerntech Atomprax — Kerntechnik Vereinigt mit Atompraxis
Kerntech Isotopentech — Kerntechnik und Isotopentechnik
Kerntech Isotopentech Chem — Kerntechnik, Isotopentechnik, und Chemie
Kerntechnik Isotpentech Chem — Kerntechnik, Isotopentechnik, und Chemie
Kerntech Normung Inf — Kerntechnische Normung Informationen
Ker Rundschau — Keramische Rundschau
Kerry Arch Hist Soc J — Kerry Archaeological and Historical Society. Journal
Kerry Arch Mag — Kerry Archaeological Magazine
Kert Egy Kozl — Kerteszeti Egyetem Kozlemenyei
Kertesz Egyet Kozl — Kerteszeti Egyetem Kozlemenyei
Kerteszgazda Nep Kert — Kerteszgazda Nep Kertesze
Kertesz Kozl — Kerteszeti Kozlony
Kertesz Kut Intez Evk — Kerteszeti Kutato Intezet Evkonyve
Kertesz Lap — Kerteszeti Lapok
Kertesz Szle — Kerteszeti Szemle
Kertesz Szolesz Foisk — Kerteszeti es Szoleszeti Foiskola Evkoryve
Kertesz Szolesz Foisk Kozl — Kerteszeti es Szoleszeti Foiskola Kozlemenyei
Kert Etela Pohjanm Maanviljelyss Toim — Kertomus Etela-Pohjanmaan Maanjelysseuran Toiminnasta
Kert Fuez — Kerteszeti Fuezetek
Kert Ilmaj Maamiess Toim — Kertomus Ilmajoen Maamiesseuran Toiminnasta
Kert Irod Tajekozt — Kerteszeti Irodalmi Tajekoztato
Kert Ita Ham Maanviljelyss Toim — Kertomus Ita-Hameen Maanviljelysseuran Toiminnasta
Kert Lounais Suom Maanviljelyss Toim — Kertomus Lounais-Suomen Maanjelysseuran Toiminnasta
Kert Oul Laan Meijeril Toim — Kertomus Oulun Laanin Meijeriliiton Toiminnasta
Kert Oul Piirin Hevossiitosl Toim — Kertomus Oulun Piirin Hevossiitosliiton Toiminnasta
Kert Pera Pohjolan Maamiess Toim — Kertomus Pera-Pohjolan Maamiesseuran Toiminnasta
Kert Pohjois Karj Hevosjalostusyhd Voiman Toim — Kertomus Pohjois-Karjalan Hevosjalostusyhdistystenliiton Voiman Toiminnasta
Kert Pohjois Karj Maanviljelyss Toim — Kertomus Pohjois-Karjalan Maanviljelysseuran Toiminnasta
Kert Pohjois Savon Hevossiitosyhd Toim — Kertomus Pohjois-Savon Hevossiitosyhdistystenliiton Toiminnasta
Kert Szoelesz — Kerteszet es Szoleszet
Kert Szoelesz Foeisk Evk — Kerteszeti es Szoeleszeti Foeiskola Evkoenyve. Annales Academiae Horti- et Viticulturae
Kert Szolesz Foiskola Evk — Kerteszeti es Szoleszeti Foiskola Evkoryve
Kert Szolesz Foiskola Kozl — Kerteszeti es Szoleszeti Foiskola Kozlemenyei
Kert Vaasan Laan Maanviljelyss Toim — Kertomus Vaasan Laanin Maanviljelysseuran Toiminnasta
Kert Varsinais Suom Hevossiitosl Toim — Kertomus Varsinais-Suomen Hevossiitosliitton Toiminnasta
Kert Viipurin Laan Maanviljelyss Toim — Kertomus Viipurin Laanin Maanviljelysseuran Toiminnasta
KES — Keio Economic Studies
Keski Suomen Maanviljelyss Julk — Keski-Suomen Maanviljelysseuran Julkaisuja
Keski Suomen Maanviljelyss Lentoleht — Keski-Suomen Maanviljelysseuran Lentolehtisia
Keski Suomen Maanviljelyss Vuosijulk — Keski-Suomen Maanviljelysseuran Vuosijulkaisu
KESS — Kartvelur Enata St'rukt'uris Sak'itxebi
Keszthelyi Mesogazd Akad Kozl — Keszthelyi Mesogazdasagi Akademia Kozlemenyei
Keston News — Keston News Service
Keszthelyi Mezoegazd Akad Koezlem — Keszthelyi Mezoegazdasagi Akademia Koezlemenyei
Keszthelyi Mezogazd Akad Kiad — Keszthelyi Mezogazdasagi Akademia Kiadvanyai
Keszthelyi Mezogazdasagtud Kar Kozl — Keszthelyi Mezogazdasagtudomanyi Kar Kozlemenyei
Ketavim Met — Ketavim Meteorologiim. Meteorological Service, Israel
Kettering Int Symp Nitrogen Fixation — Kettering International Symposium on Nitrogen Fixation
Keuring Elektrotech Mater Sci Tech Rep — Keuring van Elektrotechnische Materialen. Scientific and Technical Reports
KEVN — Kevo Notes
Kew Bull — Kew Bulletin
Kew Bull Addit Ser — Kew Bulletin. Additional Series
Kew Bull R Bot Gard — Kew Bulletin. Royal Botanic Gardens
Kew Mag — Kew Magazine
Kexue Tongbao (Chin Ed) — Kexue Tongbao (Chinese Edition)

Kexue Tongbao (Foreign Lang Ed) — Kexue Tongbao (Foreign Language Edition)
Key — Keyboard Magazine
Key — Key to Christian Education
Keybd Mag — Keyboard Magazine
Key Econ Sci — Key to Economic Science
Key Econ Sci Manage Sci — Key to Economic Science and Managerial Sciences
Key Eng Mat — Key Engineering Materials
Key Eng Mater — Key Engineering Materials
Keyhan Int — Keyhan International
Key Notes — Key Notes Donemus
Key Oceanogr Rec Doc — Key to Oceanographic Records Documentation
Key Potato Trials — Key to Potato Trials and Collections at East Crays and Philpstoun [*Edinburgh*]
KEYRA — Keyboard
Keys Regener Proc Eur Conf Tissue Post Trauma Regener — Keys for Regeneration. Proceedings. European Conference on Tissue and Post-Traumatic Regeneration
Keystone Fmr — Keystone Farmer [*Harrisburg*]
Keystone Mag Optom — Keystone Magazine of Optometry
Keystone News Bull — Keystone News Bulletin
Key Texts Classic Stud Hist Ideas — Key Texts. Classic Studies in the History of Ideas
Key Var Fld Veg Crops — Key to Varieties of Field and Vegetable Crops under Trial, Observation, and Propagation
Keyword Index Intern Med — Keyword Index in Internal Medicine
Keyword Index Med Lit — Keyword Index for the Medical Literature
Key Word Index Wildl Res — Key Word Index of Wildlife Research
KF — Kleinasiatische Forschungen
KF — Korean Frontier
KF — Kwartalnik Filosoficzny
KfA — Kunst fuer Alle
KFA Jahresber — KFA (Kernforschungsanlage) Jahresbericht
KFAS Proc Ser — KFAS [*Kuwait Foundation for the Advancement of Sciences*] Proceedings Series
KFFMA — Klepzig Fachberichte fuer die Fuehrungskraefte aus Maschinenbau und Huettenwesen
KFFUA — Kraftfutter
KFIZA — Kyoto Furitsu Ika Daigaku Zasshi
KFK Hausmitt — KFK [*Kernforschungszentrum Karlsruhe*] Hausmitteilungen
KFKI Kozl — KFKI [*Kozponti Fizikai Kutato Intezet*] Kozlemenyek
KFKI Rep — KFKI [*Kozponti Fizikai Kutato Intezet*] Report
KFK Nachr — KFK [*Kernforschungszentrum Karlsruhe*] Nachrichten
KFLQ — Kentucky Foreign Language Quarterly
KFQ — Keystone Folklore Quarterly
KFR — Kentucky Folklore Record
KFS — Kentucky Folklore Series
KFSAAX — Kungliga Fysiografiska Saellskapets i Lund. Arsbok
KFSLAW — Kungliga Fysiografiska Saelleskapets i Lund. Foerhandlingar
KFT — KFT. Kraftfahrzeugtechnik
KFT Kraftfahrztech — KFT. Kraftfahrzeugtechnik
KFTTA — Kao Fen Tzu T'ung Hsun
KfW — Kirche fuer die Welt
K Fysiogr Sallsk Lund Arsb — Kungliga Fysiografiska Saellskapets i Lund. Arsbok
K Fysiogr Sallsk Lund Forh — Kungliga Fysiografiska Saellskapets i Lund. Foerhandlingar
K Fysiogr Sallsk Lund Handl — Kungliga Fysiografiska Sallskapets i Lund. Handlingar
KFZ Fachbl — KFZ (Kraftfahrzeug)-Fachblatt
KFZTA — Kraftfahrzeugtechnik
KFZ Tech — KFZ (Kraftfahrzeug)-Technik
KG — Katholische Gedanken
KG — Kirchengeschichte
KGA — Kirchengeschichtliche Abhandlungen
KGA — Kunstgeschichtliche Anzeigen
KGAAM — Kungliga Gustav Adolfs Akademiens. Minnesbok
K Gad — Kritikas Gadagramata
K Ges Wiss Goettingen Abh — Koenigliche Gesellschaft der Wissenschaften zu Goettingen. Abhandlungen
KGF — Kulturgeschichtliche Forschungen
KGGB — Korrespondenzblatt. Geographisch-Ethnologische Gesellschaft (Basel)
KGGJ — Klaus-Groth-Gesellschaft. Jahresgabe
KGGP — Kurzer Grundriss der Germanischen Philologie
KGH — Kanbum Gakkai Kaiho
KGHKA — Kogyo Gijutsuin. Hakko Kenkyusho Kenkyu Hokoku
KGI — Komeet
KgJ — Kunstgeschichtliches Jahrbuch der Zentralkommission fuer Erforschung und Erhaltung der Kunst- und Historischen Denkmale
KGKK — Kangaku Kenkyu
KGKR — Kansai Gaidai Kenkyu Ronshu
KGKZA — Kogyo Kagaku Zasshi
Kgl Danske Vidensk Selsk Oversigt — Kongelige Danske Videnskabernes Selskab. Oversigt Selskabets Virksomhed
KGNBA — Kenritsu Gan Senta Niigata Byoin Ishi
KGR — Kobe Gaidai Ronso
KGS — Koelner Germanistische Studien
KGS NCIC Newsl — KGS-NCIC [*Kentucky Geological Survey. National Cartographic Information Center*] Newsletter
KG St — Kirchengeschichtliche Studien
KGU — Kwansei Gakuin University
KGUAS — Kwansei Gakuin University. Annual Studies
KGVDG — Korrespondenzblatt des Gesamtvereins der Deutschen Geschichts- und Altertumsvereine
KGWOe — Katholischer Glaube und Wissenschaft in Oesterreich
KH — Kirchliches Handbuch fuer das Katholliche Deutschland
KH — Kwartalnik Historyczny

KHA — Keesings Historisch Archief
KHA — Kyrkohistorisk Arsskrift
Khadi Gram — Khadi Gramodyong
KHAr — Kerkhistorisch Archief
Kharchova Promst — Kharchova Promyslovist
Kharchova Sil Hosp Prom — Karchova ta Sil'sko-Hospodars'ka Promyslovist'
Khar'k Inst Mekh Elektrif Sel'sk Khoz Nauchn Zap — Khar'kovskii Institut Mekhanizatsii i Elektrifikatsii Sel'skogo Khozyaistva Nauchnye Zapiski
Khar'k Med Inst Tr — Khar'kovskii Meditsinskii Institut Trudy
Kharkov Med Zh — Khar'kovskii Meditsinskii Zhurnal
Kharkov Mth S Com — Communications and Proceedings of the Mathematical Society of the Imperial University of Kharkov
KHAT — Kurzer Hand-Commentar zum Alten Testament
KHC — Kurzer Hand-Commentar zum Alten Testament
Kh Ch — Khristianskoe Chtenie
KHCK — Kuo-Hsueh Chi-K'an
KHCLA — K'o Hsueh Chi Lu
Kheberleri Izv — Kheberleri Izvestiya
Khematol Kruvoprelivane — Khematologiya i Kruvoprelivane
Kherson Sb — Khersonesskii Sbornik
KHF — Koenigsberger Historische Forschungen
Khidrol Met — Khidrologiya i Meteorologiya
Khidrol Meteorol — Khidrologiya i Meteorologiya
KHIGA — Khirurgiya
Khig Epidemiol Mikrobiol — Khigiena. Epidemiologiya i Mikrobiologiya
Khig Zdraveopaz — Khigiena i Zdraveopazvane
Khig Zdraveopazvane — Khigiena i Zdraveopazvane
Khim Belka — Khimiya Belka
Khim Dizain — Khimicheskii Dizain. Fiziko-Khimicheskie Modeli i Propedevtika v Estestvoznanii
Khim Drev — Khimiya Drevesiny
Khim Elementoorg Soedin — Khimiya Elementoorganicheskikh Soedinenii
Khim Farm Prom — Khimiko-Farmatsevticheskaya Promyshlennost'
Khim Farm Promst — Khimiko Farmatsevticheskaya Promyshlennost
Khim-Farm Zh — Khimiko-Farmatsevticheskii Zhurnal
Khim-Far Zh — Khimiko-Farmatsevticheskii Zhurnal
Khim Fiz-Khim Prir Sint Polim — Khimiya i Fiziko-Khimiya Prirodnykh i Sinteticheskikh Polimerov
Khim Geogr Gidrogeokhim — Khimicheskaya Geografiya i Gidrogeokhimiya
Khim Getero — Khimiya Geterotsiklicheskikh Soedineniya
Khim Geterotsiklich Soedin — Khimiya Geterotsiklicheskikh Soedinenii
Khim Geterotsikl Soedin — Khimiya Geterotsiklicheskikh Soedinenii
Khim Geterotsikl Soedin Akad Nauk Latv SSR — Khimiya Geterotsiklicheskikh Soedinenii Akademiya Nauk Latviiskoi SSR
Khim Geterotsikl Soedin Sb — Khimiya Geterotsiklicheskikh Soedinenii Sbornik
Khim Geterot Soed — Khimiya Geterotsiklicheskikh Soedinenii. Sbornik
Khimik Farm — Khimik i Farmatsevt
Khimik Proiz — Khimik na Proizvodstve
Khim Ind — Khimiya i Industriya
Khim Ind (Sofia) — Khimiya i Industriya (Sofia)
Khim i Neft Mashinostr — Khimicheskoe i Neftyanoe Mashinostroenie
Khim Interesakh Ustoich Razvit — Khimiya v Interesakh Ustoichivogo Razvitiya
Khim i Tekhnol Topliv i Masel — Khimiya i Tekhnologiya Topliv i Masel
Khimiya Ind — Khimiya i Industria
Khimiya Khoz — Khimiya i Khozyaistvo
Khimiya Obor — Khimiya i Oborona
Khimiya Redk Elem — Khimiya Redkikh Elementov
Khimiya Shk — Khimiya v Shkole
Khimiya Sots Khoz — Khimiya i Sotsialisticheskoe Khozyaistvo
Khimiya Tekhnol Polim — Khimiya i Tekhnologiya Polimerov
Khimiya Tekhnol Topl — Khimiya i Tekhnologiya Topliva
Khimiya Tekhnol Topl Masel — Khimiya i Tekhnologiya Topliva i Masel
Khimiya Trudyashch — Khimiya Trudyashchimsya
Khimiya Tverd Topl — Khimiya Tverdogo Topliva
Khimiya Zhizn — Khimiya i Zhizn'
Khimiz Sots Zeml — Khimizatsiya Sotsialisticheskogo Zemledeliya
Khim Khim Tekhnol (Alma-Ata) — Khimiya i Khimicheskaya Tekhnologiya (Alma-Ata)
Khim Khim Tekhnol (Drev) — Khimiya i Khimicheskaya Tekhnologiya (Drevesiny)
Khim Khim Tekhnol (Ivanovo USSR) — Khimiya i Khimicheskaya Tekhnologiya (Ivanovo, USSR)
Khim Khim Tekhnol (Lvov) — Khimiya i Khimicheskaya Tekhnologiya (Lvov)
Khim Khim Tekhnol (Minsk) — Khimiya i Khimicheskaya Tekhnologiya (Minsk)
Khim Khim Tekhnol (Tomsk) — Khimiya i Khimicheskaya Tekhnologiya (Tomsk)
Khim Khim Teknol (Cheboksary USSR) — Khimiya i Khimicheskaya Tekhnologiya (Cheboksary, USSR)
Khim Mashinost — Khimicheskoe Mashinostroenie
Khim Mashinostr (Kiev) — Khimicheskoe Mashinostroenie (Kiev)
Khim Mashinostr (Moscow) — Khimicheskoe Mashinostroenie (Moscow)
Khim Mashinostr Mosk Inst Khim Mashinostr — Khimicheskoe Mashinostroenie Moskovskii Institut Khimicheskogo Mashinostroeniya
Khim Mash Mosk Inst Khim Mash — Khimicheskoe Mashinostroenie. Moskovskii Institut KhimicheskogoMashinostroeniya
Khim Med — Khimiya i Meditsina
Khim Mekh Pererab Drev Drev Otkhodov — Khimicheskaya i Mekhanicheskaya Pererabotka Drevesiny i DrevesnykhOtkhodov
Khim Nauchn Dokl Gertsenovskie Chteniya — Khimiya, Nauchnye Doklady, Gertsenovskie Chteniya
Khim Nauka Prom — Khimicheskaya Nauka i Promyshlennost'
Khim Nauka Prom-St — Khimicheskaya Nauka i Promyshlennost
Khim Neftegazov Mashinostr — Khimicheskoe i Neftegazovoe Mashinostroenie
Khim Neftepererab Polim Mashinostr — Khimicheskoe, Neftepererabatyvayushchee i Polimernoe Mashinostroenie
Khim Neft Mashinostr — Khimicheskoe i Neftyanoe Mashinostroenie

Khim Neorg Gidridov Dokl Vses Soveshch — Khimiya Neorganicheskikh Gidridov. Doklady Vsesoyuznogo Soveshchaniya po Khimii Neorganicheskikh Gidridov

Khim Nepredelnykh Soedin — Khimiya Nepredel'nykh Soedinenii

Khim Oborona — Khimiya i Oborona

Khim Ochistki Teploenerg Oborud — Khimicheskie Ochistki Teploenergeticheskogo Oborudovaniya

Khim Okeanol Issled Mater Vses Konf Khim Morei Okeanov — Khimiko-Okeanologicheskie Issledovaniya. Materialy VsesoyuznoiKonferentsii po Khimii Morei i Okeanov

Khim Pererab Drev — Khimicheskaya Pererabotka Drevesiny

Khim Pererab Drev Nauchno-Tekh Sb — Khimicheskaya Pererabotka Drevesiny Nauchno-Tekhnicheskii Sbornik

Khim Pererab Topl — Khimiya i Pererabotka Topliv

Khim Plazmy — Khimiya Plazmy

Khim Plazmy — Khimiya Plazmy Sbornik Statej

Khim Prakt Primen Kremneorg Soedin Tr Konf — Khimiya i Prakticheskoe Primenenie Kremneorganicheskikh Soedinenii.Trudy Konferentsii

Khim Primen Elementoorg Soedin — Khimiya i Primenenie Elementoorganicheskikh Soedinenii

Khim Primen Fosfororg Soedin Tr Konf — Khimiya i Primenenie Fosfororganicheskikh Soedinenii. TrudyKonferentsii

Khim Primen Fosfororg Soedin Tr Yubileinoi Konf — Khimiya i Primenenie Fosfororganicheskikh Soedinenii. TrudyYubileinoi Konferentsii

Khim Prirod Soed — Khimiya Prirodnykh Soedinenii

Khim Prir S — Khimiya Prirodnykh Soedinenii

Khim Prir Soedin — Khimiya Prirodnykh Soedinenii

Khim Prir Soedin (Tashk) — Khimiya Prirodnykh Soedinenii (Tashkent)

Khim Prod Koksovaniya Uglei Vostoka SSSR — Khimicheskie Produkty Koksovaniya Uglei Vostoka SSSR

Khim Proizvod — Khimiya. Proizvodstvu

Khim Prom — Khimicheskaya Promyshlennost

Khim Promst (Kiev) — Khimichna Promislovist (Kiev)

Khim Promst (Moscow) — Khimicheskaya Promyshlennost (Moscow)

Khim Promst Nauk Tekh Zb — Khimichna Promislovist. Naukovo-Tekhnichnii Zbirnik

Khim Promst Rubezhom — Khimicheskaya Promyshlennost za Rubezhom

Khim Promst Ser Anilinokras Promst — Khimicheskaya Promyshlennost Seriya Anilinokrasochnaya Promyshlennost

Khim Promst Ser Avtom Khim Proizvod — Khimicheskaya Promyshlennost Seriya Avtomatizatsiya KhimicheskikhProizvodstv. Nauchno-Tekhnicheskii Referativnyi Sbornik

Khim Promst Ser Azotn Promst — Khimicheskaya Promyshlennost Seriya Azotnaya Promyshlennost.Nauchno-Tekhnicheskii Referativnyi Sbornik

Khim Promst Ser Fosfornaya Promst — Khimicheskaya Promyshlennost Seriya Fosfornaya Promyshlennost

Khim Promst Ser Kaliinaya Promst — Khimicheskaya Promyshlennost Seriya Kaliinaya Promyshlennost.Nauchno-Tekhnicheskii Referativnyi Sbornik

Khim Promst Ser Khim Tekhnol Izot Mechenykh Soedin — Khimicheskaya Promyshlennost Seriya Khimiya i Tekhnologiya Izotopov iMechenykh Soedinenii

Khim Promst Ser Khim Tekhnol Lyuminoforov Chist Neorg Mater — Khimicheskaya Promyshlennost Seriya Khimiya i TekhnologiyaLyuminoforov i Chistykh Neorganicheskikh Materialov. Nauchno-TekhnicheskiiReferativnyi Sbornik

Khim Promst Ser Khlornaya Promst — Khimicheskaya Promyshlennost Seriya Khlornaya Promyshlennost.Nauchno-Tekhnicheskii Referativnyi Sbornik

Khim Promst Ser Kislorodn Promst — Khimicheskaya Promyshlennost Seriya Kislorodnaya Promyshlennost.Nauchno-Tekhnicheskii Referativnyi Sbornik

Khim Promst Ser Okhr Okruzh Sredy Ratsion Ispol'z Prir Resur — Khimicheskaya Promyshlennost. Seriya. Okhrana Okruzhayushchei Sredy i Ratsional'noe Ispol'zovanie Prirodnykh Resursov

Khim Promst Ser Proizvod Pererab Plastmass Sint Smol — Khimicheskaya Promyshlennost Seriya Proizvodstvo i PererabotkaPlastmass i Sinteticheskikh Smol. Nauchno-Tekhnicheskii Referativnyi Sbornik

Khim Promst Ser Promst Gornokhim Syrya — Khimicheskaya Promyshlennost Seriya Promyshlennost GornokhimicheskogoSyr'ya. Nauchno-Tekhnicheskii Referativnyi Sbornik

Khim Promst Ser Promst Khim Volokon — Khimicheskaya Promyshlennost Seriya Promyshlennost KhimicheskikhVolokon. Nauchno-Tekhnicheskii Referativnyi Sbornik

Khim Promst Ser Promst Miner Udobr Sernoi Kosloty — Khimicheskaya Promyshlennost Seriya Promyshlennost Mineral'nykhUdobrenii i Sernoi Kosloty. Nauchno-Tekhnicheskii Referativnyi Sbornik

Khim Promst Ser Promst Tovarov Bytovoi Khim — Khimicheskaya Promyshlennost Seriya Promyshlennost Tovarov BytovoiKhimii. Nauchno-Tekhnicheskii Referativnyi Sbornik

Khim Promst Ser Reakt Osobo Chist Veshchestva — Khimicheskaya Promyshlennost Seriya Reaktivy i Osobo ChistyeVeshchestva. Nauchno-Tekhnicheskii Referativnyi Sbornik

Khim Promst Ser Sist Sredstva Avtom Khim Proizvod — Khimicheskaya Promyshlennost Seriya Sistemy i Sredstva AvtomatizatsiiKhimicheskikh Proizvodstv

Khim Promst Ser Stekloplast Steklovokno Obz Inf — Khimicheskaya Promyshlennost Seriya Stekloplastiki i Steklovokno,Obzornaya Informatsiya

Khim Promst Ser Toksikol Sanit Khim Plastmass — Khimicheskaya Promyshlennost Seriya Toksikologiya i SanitarnayaKhimiya Plastmass. Nauchno-Tekhnicheskii Referativnyi Sbornik

Khim Prom-St' Ukr — Khimicheskaya Promyshlennost' Ukrainy

Khim Promst Ukr — Khimichna Promislovist Ukraini

Khim Rastvorov — Khimiya Rastvorov

Khim Rastvorov Redkozem Elem — Khimiya Rastvorov Redkozemel'nykh Elementov

Khim Reakt Prep — Khimicheskie Reaktivy i Preparaty

Khim Redk Elem — Khimiya Redkikh Elementov

Khim Ref Zh — Khimicheskii Referativnyi Zhurnal

Khim Sel'Khoz — Khimiya v Sel'skom Khozyaistve

Khim Sel'sk Khoz — Khimiya v Sel'skom Khozyaistve

Khim Selsk Khoz — Khimizatsiya Sel'skogo Khozyaistva

Khim Sel'sk Khoz Bashk — Khimizatsiya Sel'skogo Khozyaistva Bashkirii

Khim Sera Azotorg Soedin Soderzh Neftyakh Nefteprod — Khimiya Sera- i Azotorganicheskikh Soedinenii Soderzhashchikhsiya v Neftyakh iNefteproduktakh

Khim Seraorg Soedin Soderzh Neftyakh Nefteprod — Khimiya Seraorganicheskikh Soedinenii, Soderzhashchikhsiya v Neftyakh i Nefteproduktakh

Khim Shk — Khimiya v Shkole

Khim Signal Zhivotn — Khimicheskie Signaly Zhivotnykh

Khim Sots Zemled — Khimizatsiya Sotsialisticheskogo Zemledeliya

Khim Sredstva Zashch Rast — Khimicheskie Sredstva Zashchity Rastenii

Khim Svyaz' Krist Fiz Svoj — Khimicheskaya Svyaz' v Kristallakh i Ikh Fizicheskie Svojstva

Khim Tekhnol — Khimicheskaia Tekhnologiia

Khim Tekhnol Biol Akt Soedin — Khimicheskaya Tekhnologiya Biologicheski Aktivnykh Soedinenii

Khim Tekhnol Bum — Khimiya i Tekhnologiya Bumagi

Khim Tekhnol Drev Tsellyul Bum — Khimiya i Tekhnologiya Drevesiny Tsellyulozy i Bumagi

Khim Tekhnol Elementoorg Soedin Polim — Khimiya i Tekhnologiya Elementoorganicheskikh Soedinenii i Polimerov

Khim Tekhnol Goryuch Slantsev Prod Ikh Pererab — Khimiya i Tekhnologiya Goryuchikh Slantsev i Produktov Ikh Pererabotki

Khim Tekhnol Izot Mechenykh Soedin — Khimiya i Tekhnologiya Izotopov i Mechenykh Soedinenii. R-ferativnyiSbornik

Khim Tekhnol (Kharkov) — Khimicheskaya Tekhnologiya (Kharkov)

Khim Tekhnol Khim — Khimicheskaya Tekhnologiya i Khimiya

Khim Tekhnol (Kiev) — Khimicheskaya Tekhnologiya (Kiev)

Khim Tekhnol Kondens Fosfatov Tr Vses Soveshch — Khimiya i Tekhnologiya Kondensirovannykh Fosfatov. Trudy VsesoyuznogoSoveshchaniya po Fosfatam (Kondensirovannym)

Khim Tekhnol Krasheniya Sint Krasitelei Polim Mater — Khimiya i Tekhnologiya Krasheniya, Sinteza Krasitelei, i PolimernykhMaterialov

Khim Tekhnol Molbdena Vol'frama — Khimiya i Tekhnologiya Molibdena i Vol'frama

Khim Tekhnol Nauchno Proizvod Sb — Khimicheskaya Tekhnologiya. Nauchno-Proizvodstvennyi Sbornik

Khim Tekhnol Neorg Proizvod — Khimiya i Tekhnologiya Neorganicheskikh Proizvodstv

Khim Tekhnol Oksidnykh Magn Mater — Khimiya i Tekhnologiya Oksidnykh Magnitnykh Materialov

Khim Tekhnol Org Proizvod — Khimiya i Tekhnologiya Organicheskikh Proizvodstv

Khim Tekhnol Pererab Nefti Gaza — Khimicheskaya Tekhnologiya Pererabotki Nefti i Gaza

Khim Tekhnol Prod Org Sint Poluprod Sint Poliamidov — Khimiya i Tekhnologiya Produktov Organicheskogo Sinteza, Poluproduktydlya Sinteza Poliamidov

Khim Tekhnol Resp Mezhved Nauchno Tekh Sb — Khimicheskaya Tekhnologiya. Respublikanskii MezhvedomstvennyiNauchno-Tekhnicheskii Sbornik

Khim Tekhnol Svoistva Primen Plastmass — Khimicheskaya Tekhnologiya Svoistva i Primenenie Plastmass

Khim Tekhnol Topl — Khimiya i Tekhnologiya Topliva

Khim Tekhnol Topl Masel — Khimiya i Tekhnologiya Topliv i Masel

Khim Tekhnol Topl Prod Ego Pererab — Khimiya i Tekhnologiya Topliva i Produktov Ego Pererabotki

Khim Tekhnol Top Masel — Khimiya i Tekhnologiya Topliv i Masel

Khim Tekhnol Tsellyul — Khimiya i Tekhnologiya Tsellyulozy

Khim Tekhnol Tsellyul Volokna — Khimiya i Tekhnologiya Tsellyulozy i Volokna

Khim Tekhnol Vody — Khimiya i Tekhnologiya Vody

Khim Tekhnol Voloknistykh Mater — Khimicheskaya Tekhnologiya Voloknistykh Materialov

Khim Tekhnol Vysokomol Soedin — Khimiya i Tekhnologiya Vysokomolekulyarnykh Soedinenii

Khim Tekh Rezult Kamp Sakharov — Khimiko-Tekhnicheskie Rezul'taty Kampanii Sakharovareniya

Khim Term Obrab Stali Splavov — Khimiko-Termicheskaya Obrabotka Stali i Splavov

Khim Termodin Rast — Khimiya i Termodinamika Rastvorov

Khim Termodin Rastvorov — Khimiya i Termodinamika Rastvorov

Khim Termodin Ravnovesiya — Khimicheskaya Termodinamika i Ravnovesiya

Khim Trudyashchimsya — Khimiya Trudyashchimsya

Khim Tverd Tela — Khimiya Tverdogo Tela

Khim Tverd Topl (Leningrad) — Khimiya Tverdogo Topliva (Leningrad)

Khim Tverd Topl (Moscow) — Khimiya Tverdogo Topliva (Moscow)

Khim Volokna — Khimicheskie Volokna

Khim Volokna Ser Monogr — Khimicheskie Volokna. Seriya Monografii

Khim Vys Ehnerg — Khimiya Vysokikh Ehnergij

Khim Vys Energ — Khimiya Vysokikh Energij

Khim Zb Lviv Derzh Univ — Khimichnii Zbirnik. L'vivs'kii Derzhavnii Universitet

Khim Zh Arm — Khimicheskii Zhurnal Armenii

Khim Zhizn — Khimiya i Zhizn

Khim Zh Ser A — Khimicheskii Zhurnal. Seriya A

Khim Zh Ser B — Khimicheskii Zhurnal. Seriya B

Khim Zh Ser G — Khimicheskii Zhurnal. Seriya G

Khim Zh Ser V — Khimicheskii Zhurnal. Seriya V

KHIRAE — Khirurgiya

Khir Arkh Velyaminova — Khirurgicheskii Arkhiv Velyaminova

Khir Lietop — Khirurgicheskaia Lietopis

Khirurgiya Ortop — Khirurgiya i Ortopediya

Khir Zhelchevyvodyashchikh Putei — Khirurgiya Zhelchevyvodyashchikh Putei

KHI Tech Rev — KHI [*Kawasaki Heavy Industries*] Technical Review

Khleb Delo — Khlebnoe Delo
Khleb List — Khlebnyi Listok
Khleb Mukom Elevat Delo SSSR — Khlebnoe, Mukomol'noe i Elevatornoe Delo
SSSR
Khlebopekar Konditer Prom — Khlebopekarnaya i Konditerskaya Promyshlennost
Khlebopek Konditer Promst — Khlebopekarnaya i Konditerskaya Promyshlennost
Khlebopek Kondit Prom — Khlebopekarnaya i Konditerskaya Promyshlennost
Khlebopek Kondter Promst — Khlebopekarnaya i Konditerskaya Promyshlennost
Khlebopek Promst — Khlebopekarnaya Promyshlennost
Khlopch Bum Prom — Khlopchato-Bumazhnaya Promyshlennost
Khlopehatobuma Promst — Khlopehatobumazhnaya Promyshlennost
Khlopk Delo — Khlopkovoe Delo
Khlopk Nezavisimost Za — Khlopkovuyu Nezavisimost, Za
Khlopkovod — Khlopkovodstvo
Khlopk Promst — Khlopkovaya Promyshlennost
KHM — Kunst in Hessen und am Mittelrhein
KHMEA — Khidrologiya i Meteorologiya
KHMR — Kunst in Hessen und am Mittelrhein
Kholod Boen Delo — Kholodil'noe i Boenskoe Delo
Kholod Delo — Kholodil'noe Delo
Kholod Prom — Kholodil'naya Promyshlennost
Kholod Promst — Kholodil'naya Promyshlennost
Kholod Tekh — Kholodil'naya Tekhnika
Kholod Tekhn — Kholodil'naya Tekhnika
Kholod Tekh Tekhnol — Kholodil'naya Tekhnika i Tekhnologiya
Khoz Donbassa — Khozyaistvo Donbassa
Khoz Donu — Khozyaistvo na Donu
Khoz Severa — Khozyaistvo Severa
Khoz Ukr — Khozyaistvo Ukrainy
Khoz Upravl — Khozyaistvo i Upravlenie
Khoz Urala — Khozyaistvo Urala
KHQ — Kansas Historical Quarterly
Khranitelna Prom-St — Khranitelna Promishlenost
Khranitelnoprom Nauka — Khranitelnopromishlena Nauka
Khranit Prom — Khranitelna Promishlenost
Khranit Prom-St — Khranitelna Promishlenost
Khron VOZ — Khronika VOZ
KHS — Kentucky Historical Society. Register
KHS — Kerkehistoriske Samlinger
KhSB — Khersonesskii Sbornik. Materialy po Arkheologii Khersonesa
Tavricheskogo
KHSK — Kirkehistoriske Studier (Kobenhavn)
KHSR — Kentucky Historical Society. Register
KH St — Kerkhistorische Studien
KHSYA — Kexue Shiyan
KHT — Konsthistorisk Tidskrift
KHTPBU — Kexue Tongbao
Khudozhestvennaya Gaz — Khudozhestvennaya Gazeta
Khutor Gaz — Khutorskaya Gazeta
KHVSU — Kungliga Humanistiska Vetenskapssamfundet i Uppsala
KHZ — Koenigsberger Hartungsche Zeitung
KHZAD — Kachiku Hanshokugaku Zasshi
Ki — Kierunki
KI — Kinatuinamot Illengajuk
KiA — Kirche im Angriff
KIAM — Kul'tura i Iskusstvo Antichnogo Mira i Vostoka
Kiangsi J Tradit Chin Med — Kiangsi Journal of Traditional Chinese Medicine
KIB — Kunstgeschichte in Bildern
KIBBA — Konstruktiver Ingenieurbau Berichte
Kiber i Sist Anal — Kibernetika i Sistemnyj Analis
Kibernet i Vychisl Tekhn — Akademiya Nauk Ukrainskoi SSR. Institut Kibernetiki.
Kibernetika i Vychislitelnaya Tekhnika
Kibernet i Vychisl Tekhn — Kibernetika i Vychislitel'naya Tekhnika
Kibernet i Vycisl Tehn — Kibernetika i Vycislitel'naya Tehnika
Kibernet Sistem Anal — Kibernetika i Sistemnyi Analiz
Kibern i Vychisl Tekh — Kibernetika i Vychislitel'naya Tekhnika
Kibern Vychisl Tekh — Kibernetika i Vychislitel'naya Tekhnika
Kidde Ind — Kidde Industry. Walter Kidde and Co. [New York]
KIDID6 — Kidney Disease
Kidma Isr J Dev — Kidma. Israel Journal of Development
Kidney Blood Pressure Res — Kidney and Blood Pressure Research
Kidney Dis — Kidney Disease
Kidney Int — Kidney International
Kidney Int Suppl — Kidney International. Supplement
KIDZD — Kanazawa Ika Daigaku Zasshi
Kie — Kierkegaardiana
Kieferchir — Kieferchirurgie
Kieler Beitr — Kieler Beitraege
Kieler Bl — Kieler Blaetter
Kieler Blaett — Kieler Blaetter
Kieler Meeresforsch — Kieler Meeresforschungen
Kieler Milchw ForschBer — Kieler Milchwirtschaftliche Forschungsberichte
Kieler Rechtswiss Abh — Kieler Rechtswissenschaftliche Abhandlungen
Kieler Studien — Kieler Studien zur Deutschen Literaturgeschichte
Kiel Meeresforsch — Kieler Meeresforschungen
Kiel Meeresforsch Sonderh — Kieler Meeresforschungen, Sonderheft
Kiel Milchwirtsch Forschungsber — Kieler Milchwirtschaftliche
Forschungsberichte
Kiel Not Pflanzenkd Schleswig Holstein — Kieler Notizen zur Pflanzenkunde in
Schleswig Holstein
Kiel Schr — Schriften der Universitaet zu Kiel
KIER Bulletin — Korea. Institute of Energy and Resources. Bulletin
Kierk — Kierkegaardiana

KIER Misc Rep — KIER [Korea Institute of Energy and Resources] Miscellaneous
Report
KIER Res Rep — KIER (Korean Institute of Energy and Resources) Research
Report
Kiev S Nt Mm — Memoirs of the Kiev Naturalists' Society
Kiev Univ Visn Ser Geogr — Kiev Universitet Visnik Seriya Geografi
Kiewsk Univers Izwestia — Kiewska Uniwersitetskia Izwestia
KIG — Kirche in Ihrer Geschichte
KIGAM Bull — KIGAM [Korea Research Institute of Geoscience and Mineral
Resources] Bulletin
KII — Kwartaalreeks over Informatie en Informatie Beleid
KIIGD — Kitasato Igaku
Kiito Kensajo Kenkyu Hokoku Res Rep Silk Cond — Kiito Kensajo Kenkyu
Hokoku. Research Reports of the Silk Conditioning Houses
Kiiv Derzh Univ Im T G Shevchenka Nauk Shchorichnik — Kiivs'kii Derzhavnii
Universitet Imeni T. G. Shevchenka Naukovi Shchorichnik
Kiiv Derzh Univ Nauk Zap — Kiivs'kii Derzhavnii Universitet. Naukovi Zapiski
Kiiv Derzh Univ Stud Nauk Pr — Kiivs'kii Derzhavnii Universitet Students'ki
Naukovi Pratsi
KiJ — Knjizevnost i Jezik
Ki Klima Kaelte Heiz — Ki, Klima, Kaelte, Heizung
Ki Klima Kaelte Ing — Ki, Klima, und Kaelte-Ingenieur
Kildare Arch Soc J — County Kildare Archaeological Society. Journal
Kilkenny SE Ir Arch Soc J — Kilkenny and South-East of Ireland Archaeological
Society. Journal
Kilobaud Microcomput — Kilobaud Microcomputing
Ki Luft Kaeltetech — Ku Luft- und Kaeltetechnik
Kim Ann — Kimya Annali
Kimballs Dairy Fmr — Kimball's Dairy Farmer
Kimball's D F — Kimball's Dairy Farmer
Kim Handasa Kim — Kimiya, Handasa Kimit
Kim Inst Zinat Rak — Kimijas Instituta Zinatniskie Raksti
Kim Muhendisligi — Kimya Muhendisligi
Kim Sanayi — Kimya ve Sanayi
Kin — Kinesis
Kind and First Grade — Kindergarten and First Grade
Kinderaerztl Prax — Kinderaerztliche Praxis
Kindler Tb — Kindler Taschenbuecher Geist und Psyche
Kindling Symp — Kindling Symposium
Kind M — Kindergarten Primary Magazine
Kinemat Fiz Nebesn Tel — Kinematika i Fizika Nebesnykh Tel
Kinematika Fiz Nebesnykh Tel — Kinematika i Fizika Nebesnykh Tel
Kinemat Lant Wkly — Kinematograph and Lantern Weekly [London]
Kinemat Telev Yb — Kinematograph and Television Year Book [London]
Kinemat Wkly — Kinematograph Weekly [London]
Kinesither Sci — Kinesitherapie Scientifique
Kinet Catal — Kinetics and Catalysis
Kinet Catal (Engl Transl) — Kinetics and Catalysis (English Translation)
Kinet Catal Microheterog Syst — Kinetics and Catalysis in Microheterogeneous
Systems
Kinet Catal Transl of Kinet Katal — Kinetics and Catalysis (Translation of Kinetika
i Kataliz)
Kinet Goreniya Iskop Topl — Kinetika Goreniya Iskopaemykh Topliv
Kinet Katal — Kinetika i Kataliz
Kinet Katal Itogi Nauki Tekh — Kinetika i Kataliz. Itogi Nauki i Tekhniki
Kinet Mech Polym — Kinetics and Mechanisms of Polymerization
Kinet Ordering Growth Surf — Kinetics of Ordering and Growth at Surfaces
King Abdulaziz Med J — King Abdulaziz Medical Journal
King Abdulaziz Univ Fac Earth Sci Bull — King Abdulaziz University. Faculty of
Earth Sciences. Bulletin
King Abdulaziz Univ Fac Mar Sci J — King Abdulaziz University. Faculty of Marine
Sciences. Journal
King Abdulaziz Univ Fac Sci Bull — King Abdulaziz University. Faculty of Science.
Bulletin
King Abdulaziz Univ Inst Appl Geol Bull — King Abdulaziz University. Institute of
Applied Geology. Bulletin
King Faisal Spec Hosp Med J — King Faisal Specialist Hospital. Medical Journal
King Saud Univ Coll Sci J — King Saud University. College of Science. Journal
King Saud Univ Eng Sci J — King Saud University. Engineering Science. Journal
King Saud Univ J Eng Sci — King Saud University. Journal. Engineering Science
King Saud Univ J Sci — King Saud University. Journal. Science
King Saud Univ Sci J — King Saud University. Science. Journal
Kings Coll Engng Soc J Newcastle — King's College Engineering Society Journal
(Newcastle-on-Tyne)
Kings Coll Hosp Gaz — King's College Hospital Gazette [London]
Kings Coll Hosp Rep — King's College Hospital Reports [London]
Kings Coll Min Bull Newcastle — King's College Mining Bulletin
[Newcastle-on-Tyne]
Kings Coll Min Soc J Newcastle — King's College Mining Society Journal
[Newcastle-on-Tyne]
Kings Engr — King's Engineer [London]
Kings Gaz — King's Gazette
Kings Highw — King's Highway [London]
Kingston Geol Rev — Kingston Geology Review
Kingston LR — Kingston Law Review
Kingston L Rev — Kingston Law Review
Kingston Med Q — Kingston Medical Quarterly
Kingston-On-Hull Mus Bull — Kingston-On-Hull Museums. Bulletin
Kingston Ont Hist Soc Proc — Kingston (Ontario) Historical Society. Proceedings
Kingston Upon Hull Mus Bull — Kingston-Upon-Hull Museums Bulletin
Kininy Kininovaya Sist Krovi — Kininy i Kininovaya Sistema Krovi. Biokhimiya,
Farmakologiya, Patfiziologiya, Metody Issledovaniya. Rol V. Patologii
Kin Kei — Kinyu Keizai
Kinki Chugoku Agric Res — Kinki Chugoku Agricultural Research
Kinko Amat — Kinko-Amateur

Kino Foto Khim Prom — Kino-Foto-Khimicheskaya Promyshlennost'
Kino Foto Khimpromst — Kino-Foto-Khimpromyshlennost
Kino Photo Ind — Kino-Photo Industry
Kinotech — Kinotechnik
Kino Tech (Berlin) — Kino-Technik (Berlin)
Kinotech Filmtech — Kinotechnik und Filmtechnik
Kinotech Filmtech Ausg A — Kinotechnik und Filmtechnik. Ausgabe A
Kinotech Filmtech Ausg B — Kinotechnik und Filmtechnik. Ausgabe B
Kinotech Jb — Kinotechnisches Jahrbuch
Kinotech Umsch — Kinotechnische Umschau
K Inst Trop Afd Trop Prod Meded — Koninklijk Instituut voor de Tropen. Afdeling Tropische Producten.Mededeling
K Inst Tropen Meded Afd Tropische Producten — Koninklijk Instituut voor de Tropen. Mededeling. Afdeling Tropische Producten
Kintyre Antiqu Nat Hist Soc Mag — Kintyre Antiquarian and Natural History Society. Magazine
K i O — Kirche im Osten
Ki o Ku — Kirke og Kultur
Kipenie Kondens — Kipenie i Kondensatsiya
KIPOB — Kompleksnye Issledovaniya Prirody Okeana
KIPR — Kwartalnik Institutu Polsko-Radzieckiego
Kir — Kirkus
KiR — Kniga i Revoljucija
KI Rapp — Korrosionsinstitutet. Rapport
Kirchenmusik Jb — Kirchenmusikalisches Jahrbuch
Kirchhoffs Tech Bl — Kirchhoffs Technische Blaetter
Kirchor — Kirchenchor
Kirch PA — Kirchner, Prosopographia Attica
Kirg Gos Med Inst Sb Nauchn Tr — Kirgizskii Gosudarstvennyi Meditsinskii Institut. Sbornik NauchnykhTrudov
Kirg Gos Med Inst Tr — Kirgizskii Gosudarstvennyi Meditsinskii Institut. Trudy
Kirg Gos Med Inst Tr Ser Khim Nauk — Kirgizskii Gosudarstvennyi Meditsinskii Institut. Trudy. SeriyaKhimicheskikh Nauk
Kirg Nauchno Issled Inst Pochvoved Tr — Kirgizskii Nauchno-Issledovatel'skii Institut Pochvovedeniya. Trudy
Kirg Nauchno Issled Inst Zhivotnovod Vet Tr — Kirgizkii Nauchno-Issledovatel'skii Institut Zhivotnovodstva i Veterinarii. Trudy
Kirin Univ J Nat Sci — Kirin University Journal. Natural Sciences
Kirk A — Kirkefondets Arbog
Kirke og Kult — Kirke og Kultur
Kirk F — Kirkens Front
Kirkh Saml — Kirkehistoriske Samlinger
Kirkia Jnl — Kirkia. Journal. Federal Herbarium
Kirk Saml — Kirkehistoriske Samlinger
Kirkus — Virginia Kirkus' Service. Bulletin
Kirkus R — Kirkus Reviews
Kirmus — Kirchenmusiker
Kirov Gos Pedagog Inst Uch Zap — Kirovskii Gosudarstvennyi Pedagogicheskii Institut. Uchenye Zapiski
Kirov Gos Ped Inst Ucen Zap — Kirovskii Gosudarstvennyi Pedagogiceskii Institut Imeni V. I. Lenina. Ucenye Zapiski
Kirton Agric J — Kirton Agricultural Journal
Kiruna Geophys Data Summ — Kiruna Geophysical Data Summary
KiS — Kultura i Spoleczenstwo
KISDA — Report. Institute for Systems Design and Optimization. Kansas State University
Kiserletugyi Koezlem — Kiserletugyi Koezlemenyek
Kiserletugyi Kozl A — Kiserletugyi Koezlemenyek. A Kotet. Novenytermesztes
Kiserletugyi Kozl B — Kiserletugyi Koezlemenyek. B Kotet. Allattenyesztes
Kiserletugyi Kozl C — Kiserletugyi Koezlemenyek. C Kotet. Kerteszet
Kiserletugyi Kozl Mellek — Kiserletugyi Koezlemenyek. Melleklet
Kiserl Gazd Evk — Kiserleti Gazdasagok Evkonyve
Kiserl Koezlem — Kiserletuegyi Koezlemenyek
Kiserl Koezl Erdogazdasag — Kiserletugyi Koezlemenyek. Erdogazdasag
Kiserl Kozl — Kiserletugyi Koezlemenyek
Kiserl Orvostud — Kiserletes Orvostudomany
Kishechnye Infekts — Kishechnye Infektsii
Kishinev Politekh Inst Tr — Kishinevskii Politekhnicheskii Institut. Trudy
Kishinev Skh Inst Im M V Frunze — Kishinevskii Sel'skokhozyaistvennyi Institut Imeni M. V. Frunze. Trudy
Kisinev Gos Univ Ucen Zap — Kisinevskii Gosudarstvennyi Universitet. Ucenye Zapiski
Kislorodn Promst — Kislorodnaya Promyshlennost
KISZAR — Japanese Journal of Parasitology
KIT — Koninklijk Instituut voor de Tropen. Centrale Bibliotheek. Aanwinstenlijst
Kitakanto Med J — Kitakanto Medical Journal
Kitano Hosp J Med — Kitano Hospital Journal of Medicine
Kit Arch Exp Med — Kitasato Archives of Experimental Medicine
Kitasato Arch Exp Med — Kitasato Archives of Experimental Medicine
Kitasato Med — Kitasato Medicine
Kit Jik Igaku — Kitasato Jikken Igaku
KITLVTS — Koninklijk Instituut voor Taals-Land- en Volkenkunde. Translation Series
Kitto — Kitto's Journal of Sacred Literature
K i W — Kirche in der Welt
KiW — Ksiazka i Wiedza
Kiyo J Fac Sci Hokkaido Univ Ser VI Zool — Kiyo. Journal of the Faculty of Science. Hokkaido University. Series VI. Zoology
KIZRA — Kinzoku Zairyo
KIZV — Kieler Zeitschriftenverzeichnis
KJ — Jahrbuch des Historischen Vereins fuer Wuerttembergisch Franken
KJ — Kipling Journal
KJ — Kirchenmusikalisches Jahrbuch
KJ — Kirchliches Jahrbuch fuer die Evangelischen Landeskirchen Deutschlands
KJ — Knjizevnost i Jezik

KJ — Koloniales Jahrbuch
KJ — Korea Journal
K Jb — Kirchenmusikalisches Jahrbuch
K Jb — Koelner Jahrbuch fuer Vor- und Fruehgeschichte
KJb — Kurtrierisches Jahrbuch
Kjeller Rep — Kjeller Report. Institutt for Atomenergi [*Lillestrom*]
KJG — Kunstwissenschaftliches Jahrbuch. Gorresgesellschaft
KJGEDG — Korean Journal of Genetics
KJHKD5 — Bulletin. Fruit Tree Research Station. Series D
KJIS — Korean Journal of International Studies
KjK — Keel ja Kirjandus
KJKD — Kritisches Journal fuer das Katholische Deutschland
KJMDA — Kobe Journal of Medical Sciences
KJNNA — Koku Igaku Jikkentai Hokoku
KJNTL — Kritisches Journal der Neuesten Theologischen Literatur
Kjob Bt F Mdd — Meddelelser fra den Botaniske Forening i Kjobenhavn
Kjob Carlsb Lb Mdd — Meddelelser fra Carlsberg Laboratoriet (Kjobenhavn)
Kjob Dn Vd Selsk Afh — Kongelige Danske Videnskabernes Sekskabs Naturvidenskabelige og Mathematiske Afhandlinger (Kiobenhavn)
Kjob Dn Vd Selsk Skr — Kongelige Danske Videnskabernes Selskabs Skrifter. Naturvidenskabelig og Mathematisk Afdeling (Kjobenhavn)
Kjob Dn Vd Selsk Skr — Kongelige Danske Videnskabernes Selskabs Skrivter (Kiobenhavn)
Kjobenhavn Danm Geol Unders — Danmarks Geologiske Undersoegelse
Kjobenhavns Univ J — Kjobenhavns Universitets Journal
Kjob Med Selsk Forh — Kjobenhavnske Mediciniske Selskabs Forhandlinger
Kjob Ov — Oversigt Over det Kongelige Danske Videnskabernes Selskabs Forhandlinger (Kjobenhavn)
Kjob Skr — Kongelige Danske Videnskabernes Selskabs Skrifter. Naturvidenskabelig og Mathematisk Afdeling (Kjobenhavn)
Kjoletek FrysNaer — Kjoleteknikk og Fryserinaering
KJS — Knjizevnost i Jezik u Skoli
KJSAA — Kumamoto Journal of Science. Series A. Mathematics, Physics, and Chemistry
KJSBA — Kumamoto Journal of Science. Series B. Section 2. Biology
KJVFG — Koelner Jahrbuch fuer Vor- und Fruehgeschichte
KJVSA — Kerala Journal of Veterinary Science
KK — Kirke og Kultur
KK — Kokugo To Kokubungaku
KK — Kunstchronik und Kunstmarkt
KK — Kurzgefasster Kommentr zu den Heiligen Schriften Alten und Neuen Testamentes
KK — Kwartalnik Klasyczny
KK — Welt der Bibel. Kleinkommentare zur Heiligen Schrift
KKA — Kamer van Koophandel en Fabrieken te Paramaribo. Bulletin
KKATD — Klima-Kaelte-Technik
KKDKA — Bulletin. Kyushu Institute of Technology
KKEB — Kirchliche Korrespondenz des Evangelischen Bundes zur Wahrung der Deutsch-Protestantischen Interessen
KKEHA — Kobayashi Rigaku Kenkyusho Hokoku
KKF — Kleiner Kirchenfuehrer
K-K Geog Ges Wien Mitt — Kaiserlich-Koenigliche Geographische Gesellschaft in Wien. Mitteilungen
K-Kg Reichsanstalt Verh Jb — Kaiserlich-Koenigliche Geologische Reichsanstalt. Verhandlungen. Jahrbuch
KKH — Kunst und Kultur der Hethiter
KKHKA — Kagaku Keisatsu Kenkyusho Hokoku, Hokagaku Hen
KKI — Kritika Burzhuaznykh Kontseptsii Vseobshchei Istorii
KKIU — Keele ja Kirjanduse Instituudi Uurimused
KKJHD — Koseisho Gan Kenkyu Joseikin Ni Yoru Kenkyu Hokoku
KKK — Kokugo Kokubun No Kenkyu
KKKDB — Kyushu Ketsueki Kenkyu Dokokaishi
KKKEA6 — Tuberculosis Research
KKK Mitt — KKK (Kuhnle, Kopp, & Kausch)-Mitteilungen
KKL — Kwartalnik Klasyczny
KKIE — Katholisches Kirchenblatt
K-K Naturh Hofmus An — Kaiserlich-Koenigliche Naturhistorische Hofmuseum. Annalen
KKOSB — Kagaku Kogyo. Supplement
K Krigsvetenskapakad Handlingar Tidskr — Kungliga Krigsvetenskapsakademiens. Handlingar och Tidskrift
KKRTD — KFT. Kraftfahrzeugtechnik
KKS — Konfessionskundliche Schriftenreihe
KKSANIA — Kratkie Soobshcheniia. Akademiia Nauk SSSR. Institut Arkheologii
KKSKA — Kanagawa-Ken Kogyo Shikenjo Kenkyu Hokoku
KKSMI — Konfessionskundliche Schriften des Johann Adam Moehler Instituts
KKTS — Konfessionskundliche und Kontroverstheologische Studien
KKWZ — Katholische Kirche im Wandel der Zeiten und Voelker
KKYHB — Kakuriken Kenkyu Hokoku
KKZ — Katholische Kirchenzeitung
KL — Kirchenlexikon
Kl — Kleio
Kl — Klerenomia
Kl — Klio. Beitraege zur Alten Geschichte
KL — Kultur in Literatur
Kl — Kunstliteratur
KL — Kunst und Literatur
KL — Kypriakos Logos
KLA Bul — KLA (Korean Library Association) Bulletin
K Landesanst Wasserhyg Berlin Dahlem Mitt — Koenigliche Landesanstalt fuer Wasserhygiene zu Berlin-Dahlem.Mitteilungen
K Landtbr Akad Handl Tidskr — Kungliga Landtbruksakademiens Handlingar och Tidskrift
K LandtbrStyr Underddn Beratt — Kungliga Landtbruksstyrelsens Underdaniga Berattelse

Klank — Klank en Weerklank
K LantbrAkad Tidskr — Kungliga Lantbruksacademiens Tidskrift
K Lantbrhogsk Annlr — Kungliga Lantbrukshoegskolans. Annaler
K Lantbruksakad Ekon Avd Medd — Kungliga Lantbruksakademien. Ekonomiska Avdelning. Meddelande
K Lantbruks Akad Handl Tidskr — Kungliga Lantbruks-Akademiens. Handlingar och Tidskrift
K Lantbruksakad Tek Avd Medd — Kungliga Lantbruksakademien. Tekniska Avdelning. Meddelande
K Lantbruksakad Tidskr — Kungliga Lantbruksakademiens. Tidskrift
K Lantbruksakad Traedgaardsavd Medd — Kungliga Lantbruksakademien. Traedgaardsavdelning. Meddelande
K Lantbruksakad Vetenskapsavd Medd — Kungliga Lantbruksakademien. Vetenskapsavdelning. Meddelande
K Lantbruks Hoegsk Ann — Kungliga Lantbruks-Hoegskolans Annaler
K Lantbrukshoegsk Statens Lantbruksfoers Jordbruksfoers Medd — Kungliga Lantbrukshoegskolan och Statens Lantbruksfoersoek. Statens Jordbruksfoersoek Meddelande
K Lantbrukshogsk Ann — Kungliga Lantbrukshoegskolans. Annaler
K Lantbruksstyr Medd — Kungliga Lantbruksstyrelsen. Meddelande
Klasicni Naucn Spisi Mat Inst (Beograd) — Klasicni Naucn. Spisi. Matematicki Institut (Beograd)
Klas Nauch Spisi Mat Inst Beogr — Klasicni Naucni Spisi. Matematicki Institut (Beograd)
Klassiker Med — Klassiker der Medizin
Klassiker Naturw — Klassiker der Naturwissenschaften
Klass Phil Stud — Klassisch-Philologische Studien
KLATA8 — Kungliga Lantbruksakademiens. Tidskrift
KLB — Kulturhistorische Liebhaberbibliothek
Kl Beitr Dresden — Kleine Beitraege. Staatliches Museum (Dresden)
Kl Bl — Klerusblatt
Kl Bl S — Klerus-Blatt (Salzburg)
KLE — Kratkaja Literaturnaja Enciklopedija
Kleberg Stud Nat Resour — Kleberg Studies in Natural Resources
Klei Glas Keram — Klei/Glas/Keramiek
Klei Keram — Klei en Keramiek
Kleine Beitr Staatl Mus Vlkerknd Dresden — Kleine Beitraege des Staatlichen Museums fuer Voelkerkunde Dresden
Kleine Ergaenzungsreihe Hochschulbuechern Math — Kleine Ergaenzungsreihe zu den Hochschulbuechern fuer Mathematik
Kleine Landw — Kleine Landwirtschaft
Kleine Mitt Mitgl Ver Wass Boden U Lufthyg — Kleine Mitteilungen fuer die Mitglieder des Vereins fuer Wasser-, Boden-, und Lufthygiene
Kleine Mitt Mitgl Ver WassVersorg — Kleine Mitteilungen fuer die Mitglieder des Vereins fuer Wasserversorgung und Abwaesserbeseitigung
Kleine Naturwiss Bibliothek — Kleine Naturwissenschaftliche Bibliothek
Kleinere Veroff Reichsanst Met Erdmagn Bpest — Kleinere Veroeffentlichungen der Reichsanstalt fuer Meteorologie und Erdmagnetismus (Budapest)
Kleinere Veroff Ung Astrophys Obs — Kleinere Veroeffentlichungen des Ungarischen Astrophysikalischen Observatoriums [Budapest]
Kleinere Veroff UnivSternw Berl Babelsberg — Kleinere Veroeffentlichungen der Universitaetssternwarte zu Berlin-Babelsberg
Kleinere Veroff UnivSternw Breslau — Kleinere Veroeffentlichungen der Universitaetssternwarte in Breslau
Kleinere Veroff ZentAnst Met Bpest — Kleinere Veroeffentlichungen der Zentralanstalt fuer Meteorologie (Budapest)
Kleine Schr Ges Bild Kst Mainz — Kleine Schriften der Gesellschaft fuer Bildende Kunst in Mainz
Kleine Schr Ges Theatgesch — Kleine Schriften der Gesellschaft fuer Theatergeschichte
Kleine Schriften Naturf Ges Emden — Kleine Schriften der Naturforshenden Gesellschaft in Emden
Kleine Schr Naturf Ges Emden — Kleine Schriften der Naturforschenden Gesellschaft in Emden
Kleine Veroff Remeis Sternw — Kleine Veroeffentlichungen der Remeis-Sternwarte
Kleinheubacher Ber — Kleinheubacher Berichte
Kleintier Prax — Kleintier-Praxis
Kleintierzucht Forsch Lehre — Kleintierzucht in Forschung und Lehre
Kleintierzucht Gartenb — Kleintierzucht und Gartenbau
KLEPA — Kleintier-Praxis
Klepzig Fachber — Klepzig Fachberichte fuer die Fuehrungskraefte aus Maschinenbau und Huettenwesen
Klepzig Fachber Fuehrungskraefte Ind Prax — Klepzig Fachberichte fuer die Fuehrungskraefte aus Industrie und Praxis
Klepzig Fachber Fuehrungskraefte Ind Tech — Klepzig Fachberichte fuer die Fuehrungskraefte aus Industrie und Technik
Klepzigs Fachber FuehrKraefte Ind Tech — Klepzigs Fachberichte fuer die Fuehrungskraefte aus Industrie und Technik
Klepzigs Textilz — Klepzigs Textilzeitschrift
Klepzigs Text Z — Klepzig's Textil-Zeitschrift
Klerksdorp Min Rec — Klerksdorp Mining Record [Klerksdorp, Transvaal]
Klett Studienbuecher Math — Klett Studienbuecher Mathematik
KLF — Kleinasiatische Forschungen
KLFO — Kleinasiatische Forschungen
KlForsch — Kleinasiatische Forschungen
KLHAAK — Kungliga Lantbrukshoegskolans. Annaler
KLI — Herrenjournal International. Fachzeitschrift fuer Herrenmode
Kliatt — Kliatt Paperback Book Guide
Klima Kaelte Heiz — Klima, Kaelte, Heizung
Klima Kaelte Ing — Klima und Kaelte Ingenieur
Klima Kaelteing — Klima und Kaelteingenieur
Klima-Kaelte-Tech — Klima-Kaelte-Technik
Klima Konigr Sachsen — Klima des Koenigreiches Sachsen
Klima Schn D — Klima-Schnellmeldedienst

Klima-Tech — Klima-Technik
Klim Grej Hlad — Klimatisacija Grejanje Hladenje
Klim Kaelte Ing — Klima und Kaelte-Ingenieur
Klim Konsult Split — Klimatoloski Konsultaciju (Split)
Klim Mubers Prov Nieder U Oberschles — Klimatographische Monatsuebersicht fuer die Provinzen Nieder- und Oberschlesien und den Kreis Fraustadt, Grenzmark
Klim Ost — Klimatographie von Oesterreich
Klin — Klinikus
Klin Anaesthesiol Intensivther — Klinische Anaesthesiologie und Intensivtherapie
Klin Biochem Metab — Klinicka Biochemie a Metabolismus
Kline Chem — Kline Guide to the Chemical Industry
Klin Eksp Med — Kliniska un Eksperimentala Medicina
Klin Ernaehr — Klinische Ernaehrung
Klin Exp Urol — Klinische und Experimentelle Urologie
Klinich — Klinicheskii
Klinik Prax — Klinik und Praxis
Klinik Psych Nerv Krankh — Klinik fuer Psychische und Nervoese Krankheiten
Klin Jahrb — Klinisches Jahrbuch
Klin Jb — Klinisches Jahrbuch
Klin Khir — Klinicheskaia Khirurgiia
Klin Khir — Klinicheskaya Khirurgiya
Klin Khir — Klinichna Khirurhiia
Klin Lab Diagn — Klinicheskaia Laboratornaia Diagnostika
Klin Lab Diagn — Klinicheskaya Laboratornaya Diagnostika
Klin Labor — Klinisches Labor. Zeitschrift fuer Klinische Laboratorien und Transfusionsserologische Diagnostik
Klin Lech Zlokach Novoobraz — Klinika i Lechenie Zlokachestvennykh Novoobrazovanii
Klin Lekts — Klinicheskiya Lektsii
Klin Mbl Augenheilk — Klinische Monatsblaetter fuer Augenheilkunde
Klin Med (Mosc) — Klinicheskaya Meditsina (Moscow)
Klin Med (Moscow) — Klinicheskaya Meditsina (Moscow)
Klin Med (Moscow) — Klinische Medizin (Moscow)
Klin Med Osterr Z Wiss Prakt Med — Klinische Medizin. Oesterreichische Zeitschrift fuer Wissenschaftliche und Praktische Medizin
Klin Med (Vienna) — Klinische Medizin (Vienna)
Klin Monats — Klinische Monatsblaetter fuer Augenheilkunde
Klin Monatsbl Augenheilkd — Klinische Monatsblaetter fuer Augenheilkunde
Klin Monatsbl Augenheilkd Beih — Klinische Monatsblaetter fuer Augenheilkunde. Beihefte
Klin Monogr S Peterb — Klinicheskiya Monografii (S. Peterburg)
Klin Oczna — Klinika Oczna
Klin Onkol — Klinicheskaya Onkologiya
Klin Padiatr — Klinische Padiatrie
Klin Paediat — Klinische Paediatrie
Klin Paediatr — Klinische Paediatrie
Klin Physiol — Klinische Physiologie
Klin Prax — Klinik und Praxis
Klin Pr Vdel — Klinicke Prace a Vdeleni
Klin Radiol Semin — Klinisch-Radiologisches Seminar
Klin Rentgenol Resp Mezhved Sb — Klinicheskoi Rentgenologii Respublikanskoi Mezhvedomstvennyi Sbornik
Klin Spisy Vys Sk Zverolek Brno — Klinicke Spisy Vysoke Skoly Zverolekarske (Brno)
Klin Therap Wchnschr — Klinisch-Therapeutische Wochenschrift
Klin Ther Forelaesn — Klinisk-Therapeutiske Forelaesninger
Klin Ther Wschr — Klinisch-Therapeutische Wochenschrift
Klin Unders Rigshosp Afd B — Kliniske Undersogelser fra Rigshospitalets Afd. B
Klin Vortr Geb Otol Pharyngo Rhinol — Klinische Vortraege aus dem Gebiet der Otologie und Pharyngo-Rhinologie
Klin Wchnschr — Klinische Wochenschrift
Klin Woch — Klinische Wochenschrift
Klin Wochenschr — Klinische Wochenschrift
Klin Ws — Klinische Wochenschrift
Klin Wschr — Klinische Wochenschrift
Klin Zh — Klinicheskii Zhurnal
Klio — Klio. Beitraege zur Alten Geschichte
KLJ — Kentucky Law Journal
KLK — Katholisches Leben und Kaempfen
Kl KF — Kleinen Kirchenfuehrer
KLKHA — Klinicheskaya Khirurgiya
KLKIA — Ki, Klima, und Kaelte-Ingenieur
KLL — Kindlers Literatur Lexikon
KIMb — Klinische Monatsblaetter fuer Augenheilkunde
KLMIA — Klinicheskaya Meditsina
KLM LitOverz — KLM (Koninklijke Luchtvaart Maatschappij) Literatuuroverzicht
KLN — Kirke-Leksikon for Norden
KLNMD — Kulturhistorisk Leksikon foer Nordisk Middelalder
KLNMN — Kulturhistorisk Leksikon foer Nordisk Middelalder
KLNMS — Kulturhistoriskt Lexsikon foer Nordisk Medeltid
KIP — Kleine Pauly. Lexikon der Antike
Kl Pauly — Kleine Pauly. Lexikon der Antike
Kl Prot — Klassiker des Protestantismus
KIRel — Klassiker der Religion
KLSSAR — Kungliga Lantbrukshoegskolan och Statens Lantbruksfoersoek. Statens Husdjursforsok Meddelande
KLT — Kerala Law Times
KIT — Kleine Texte fuer Vorlesungen und Uebungen
Klucze Oznaczania Bezkregowcow Pol — Klucze do Oznaczania Bezkregowcow Polski
Klucze Oznaczania Owadow Pol — Klucze do Oznaczania Owadow Polski
Klucze Oznacz Kreg Pol — Klucze do Oznaczania Kregowcow Polski
Klucze Oznacz Owad Pol — Klucze do Oznaczania Owadow Polski

Kluwer Internat Ser Engrg Comput Sci — Kluwer International Series in Engineering and Computer Science
Kluwer Internat Ser Engrg Comput Sci VLSI Comput Archit — Kluwer International Series in Engineering and Computer Science. VLSI, ComputerArchitecture and Digital Signal Processing
Kluwer Texts Math Sci — Kluwer Texts in the Mathematical Sciences
KLWOA — Klinische Wochenschrift
KI Ws — Klinische Wochenschrift
KLY — Klei en Keramiek
KM — Kansas Magazine
KM — Katholischen Missionen
KM — Kent Messenger
KM — Kieler Meeresforschungen
Km — Kirchenmusiker
KM — Kwartalnik Muzyczny
KMA — Koopman
KMAGA — Konstruktion im Maschinen-, Apparate-, und Geraetebau
KMAUA — Klinische Monatsblaetter fuer Augenheilkunde
KMB — Kleine Marianische Buecherei
KMBI — Amtsblatt des Bayerischen Staatsministeriums fuer Unterricht und Kultus
KMFB — Kieler Milchwirtschaftliche Forschungsberichte
KMHP — K'ung Meng Msueh-Pao
KMI — Commercium. Maandblad voor Economisch, Administratief, en Ondernemersonderwijs
Km J — Kirchenmusikalisches Jahrbuch
Km Jb — Kirchenmusikalisches Jahrbuch
KMJS — Katholisches Missionsjahrbuch der Schweiz
KMLWA — Kommunalwirtschaft
KMMRA — Khimicheskoe Mashinostroenie
KMNA — Kirchliche Mitteilungen aus und Ueber Nord-Amerika
Km Nachrichten — Kirchenmusikalische Nachrichten
K Ms — Kirchliche Monatsschrift
KMS Lecture Notes Math — KMS Lecture Notes in Mathematics. Korean Math
KMT — Krete, Mykene, Troy
K Mus Midden Afr (Tervuren Belg) Ann Reeks 8 Geol Wet — Koninklijk Museum voor Midden-Afrika (Tervuren, Belgie) Annalen. Reeksin Octavo. Geologische Wetenschappen
K Mus Midden-Afr (Tervuren Belg) Ann Reeks 8o Geol Wet — Koninklijk Museum voor Midden-Afrika (Tervuren, Belgie). Annalen. Reeks in Octavo. Geologische Wetenschappen
K Mus Midden-Afr (Tervuren Belg) Ann Reeks Octavo Geol Wet — Koninklijk Museum voor Midden-Afrika (Tervuren, Belgie). Annalen. Reeks in Octavo. Geologische Wetenschappen
K Mus Midden-Afr (Tervuren Belg) Ann Reeks Octavo Zool Wet — Koninklijk Museum voor Midden-Afrika (Tervuren, Belgie). Annalen. Reeks in Octavo. Zoologische Wetenschappen
K Mus Midden-Afr (Tervuren Belg) Rapp Annu Dep Geol Mineral — Koninklijk Museum voor Midden-Afrika (Tervuren, Belgie). Rapport Annuel. Departement de Geologie et de Mineralogie
K Mus Midden-Afr (Tervuren Belg) Zool Doc — Koninklijk Museum voor Midden-Afrika (Tervuren, Belgie). Zoologische Documentatie
KN — Kainai News
Kn — Knox's Supreme Court Reports
KN — Krasnaja Nov'
KN — Kunst der Nederlanden
KN — Kwartalnik Neofilologiczny
Knaur Tb — Knaur Taschenbuecher
Knaur Vis — Knaur Visuell
K Ned Akad Wet Afd Natuurkd Verh Tweede Reeks — Koninklijke Nederlandse Akademie van Wetenschappen, Afdeling Natuurkunde, Verhandelingen, Tweede Reeks
K Ned Akad Wet Afd Natuurk Verh Eerste Reeks — Koninklijke Nederlandse Akademie van Wetenschappen. Afdeling Natuurkunde. Verhandelingen. Eerste Reeks
K Ned Akad Wet Proc — Koninklijke Nederlandse Akademie van Wetenschappen. Proceedings
K Ned Akad Wet Proc Ser A — Koninklijke Nederlandse Akademie van Wetenschappen. Proceedings. Series A. Mathematical Sciences
K Ned Akad Wet Proc Ser A Math Sci — Koninklijke Nederlandse Akademie van Wetenschappen. Proceedings. Series A. Mathematical Sciences
K Ned Akad Wet Proc Ser B Palaeontol Geol Phys Chem — Koninklijke Nederlandse Akademie van Wetenschappen. Proceedings. Series B. Palaeontology, Geology, Physics, and Chemistry
K Ned Akad Wet Proc Ser B Phys Sci — Koninklijke Nederlandse Akademie van Wetenschappen. Proceedings. Series B. Physical Sciences
K Ned Akad Wet Proc Ser C — Koninklijke Nederlandse Akademie van Wetenschappen. Proceedings. Series C. Biological and Medical Sciences
K Ned Akad Wet Verh Afd Natuurkd Tweede Reeks — Koninklijke Nederlandse Akademie van Wetenschappen. Verhandelingen. Afdeling Natuurkunde. Tweede Reeks
K Ned Akad Wet Versl Gewone Vergad Afd Natuurkd — Koninklijke Nederlandse Akademie van Wetenschappen. Verslag van de Gewone Vergadering van de Afdeling Natuurkunde
K Nederlandsch Aardrijkskundig Genootschap Tijdschrift — Koninklijk Nederlandsch Aardrijkskundig Genootschap. Tijdschrift
K Nederlandsch Geol-Mijn Genootschap Verh Geol Ser — Koninklijk Nederlandsch Geologisch-Mijnbouwkundig Genootschap Verhandelingen. Geologische Serie
K Nederlandse Akad Wetensch Afd Natuurk Verh Proc — Koninklijke Nederlandse Akademie van Wetenschappen. Afdeling Natuurkunde. Verhandelingen. Proceedings
K Ned Geol Mijnbouwkd Genoot Verh — Koninklijk Nederlands Geologisch Mijnbouwkundig Genootschap. Verhandelingen
K Ned Heidemaatsch Tijdschr — Koninklijke Nederlandsche Heidemaatschappij. Tijdschrift

K Ned Natuurhist Ver Uitg — Koninklijke Nederlandse Natuurhistorische Vereniging. Uitgave
Knee Surg Sports Traumatol Arthrosc — Knee Surgery, Sports Traumatology, Arthroscopy
Kn Epsil — Kniznica Epsilon
KNf — Kwartalnik Neofilologiczny
KNGYA — K'uang Yeh
Knick — Knickerbocker Magazine
Knick Wkly — Knickerbocker Weekly
Knight's Local Govt R — Knight's Local Government Reports
Knih Geol Ustavu Cechy Moravu — Knihovna Geologickeho Ustavu pro Cechy a Moravu
Knih Statniho Geol Ustavu Cesk Repub — Knihovna Statniho Geologickeho Ustavu Ceskoslovenske Republiky
Knih Ustred Ustavu Geol — Knihovna Ustredniho Ustavu Geologickeho
Knih Ustred Ust Geol — Knihovna Ustredniho Ustavu Geologickeho
Knih UUG — Knihovna Ustredniho Ustavu Geologickeho
Knitters Circ Mon Rec — Knitter's Circular and Monthly Record
Knit Times — Knitting Times
Knitting Int — Knitting International
Knizhnaya Letopis Dopl Vyp — Knizhnaya Letopis. Dopolnitel'nyi Vypusk
Knizhnaya Letopis Ukazatel Ser Izdanii — Knizhnaya Letopis Ukazatel Seriinykh Izdanii
Kniznaja Letopis Dopl Vyp — Kniznaja Letopis Dopolnitelnyi Vypusk
Kniznice & Ved Inf — Kniznice a Vedecke Informacie
Kniznice Odborn Ved Spisu Vysoke Uceni Tech v Brne — Kniznice Odbornych a Vedeckych Spisu Vysokeho Uceni Technickeho v Brne
Kniznice Odb Ved Spisu Vys Uceni Tech Brne — Kniznice Odbornych a Vedeckych Spisu Vysokeho Uceni Technickeho v Brne
Kniznice Odb Ved Spisu Vys Uceni Tech Brne A — Kniznice Odbornych a Vedeckych Spisu Vysokeho Uceni Technickeho v Brne.Rada A
Kniznice Odb Ved Spisu Vys Uceni Tech Brne B — Kniznice Odbornych a Vedeckych Spisu Vysokeho Uceni Technickeho v Brne. Rada B
Kniz Sb Pr Tatransk Narod Parku — Kniznica Sbornika Prac. Sprava Tatranskeho Narodneho Parku
Knji — Knjizevnost
KnjiK — Knjizevna Kritika. Casopis za Estetiku Knjizevnosti
KnjiNov — Knjizevne Novine
Knjlst — Knjizevna Istorija
Knjiz — Knjizevnost
Knjizevna Repub — Knjizevna Republika
Knjiz Sigma — Knjizica Sigma
Knj J — Knjizevnost i Jezik
Knj Mat Srp — Knjige Matice Srpske
Knj Skop Nauc Drust — Knjige Skopskog Naucnog Drustva
Kn Let — Kniznaja Letopis
Kn Letopis Dop Vyp — Knizhnaya Letopis. Dopolnitel'nyi Vypusk
KNM — Ondernemersvisie
KNMB — Koninklijke Nederlandse Middenstandsbond
KNMI — Koninklijk Nederlandsch Meteorologisch Instituut
KnN — Knjizevne Novine
KNNOe — Kultur und Natur in Niederoesterreich
Kn (NSW) — Knox's Supreme Court Reports (New South Wales)
KNNUDP — Koninklijke Nederlandse Natuurhistorische Vereniging. Uitgave
KNO — Kwartalnik Naucyzciela Opolskiego
KNOB — Bulletin. Koninklijke Nederlandse Oudheidkundige Bond
Knobel Nachr — Knobel-Nachrichten
Knochenverarb Leim — Knochenverarbeitung und Leim
Knolls Mitt Artze — Knoll's Mitteilungen fuer Aerzte
K Norske Vidensk Selsk Forh — Kongelige Norske Videnskabernes Selskabs Forhandlinger
K Norske Vidensk Selsk Mus Aarsberetn Arb — Kongelige Norske Videnskabernes Selskabs Museets Aarsberetning
K Norske Vidensk Selsk Mus Oldsaksaml Tilv — Kongelige Norske Videnskabernes Selskabs Museets Oldsaksamlingens Tilvekst
K Norske Vidensk Selsk Skr — Kongelige Norske Videnskabernes Selskabs Skrifter
K Nor Vidensk Selsk Foerhandl — Kongelige Norske Videnskabers Selskab. Foerhandlinger
K Nor Vidensk Selsk Forh — Kongelige Norske Videnskabers Selskab. Foerhandlinger
K Nor Vidensk Selsk Mus Bot Avd Rapp — Kongelige Norske Videnskabers Selskab Museet. Botanisk Avdeling Rapport
K Nor Vidensk Selsk Mus Misc — Kongelige Norske Videnskabers Selskab. Museet. Miscellanea
K Nor Vidensk Selsk Mus Rapp Bot Ser — Kongelige Norske Videnskabers Selskab Museet. Rapport Botanisk Serie
K Nor Vidensk Selsk Skr — Kongelige Norske Videnskabers Selskab. Skrifter
Knowl — Knowledge
Knowl Based Control Solidif Processes Symp — Knowledge-Based Control of Solidification Processes' Symposium
Knowledge — Knowledge and Illustrated Scientific News [London]
Knowledge Practice Math — Knowledge and Practice of Mathematics
Knowl Org — Knowledge Organization
Knowl Plant Pathol (Peking) — Knowledge of Plant Pathology (Peking)
Knowl Soc — Knowledge and Society. Studies in the Sociology of Culture Past and Present
Knowl Strength — Knowledge is Strength [Washington]
Knox & Fitz — Knox and Fitzhardinge's Reports
Knox (NSW) — Knox's Supreme Court Reports (New South Wales)
Kn Pedag Psikhol — Knizhki Pedagogicheskoi Psikhologii
KNPJB — Konepajamies
KNR — Koninklijke Nederlandsche Reedersvereeniging
KNRV — Koninklijke Nederlandsche Reedersvereeniging
KNSFA2 — Kongelige Norske Videnskabers Selskab. Foerhandlinger

KNSJA — Journal. Korean Nuclear Society
KNSM — Koninklijke Nederlandsche Stoomboot Maatschappij
Knstm Aa — Kunstmuseets Aarskrift
KNT — Kommentar zum Neuen Testament
KNVS — Kongelige Norske Videnskabers Selskab
KNVTO — Koninklijke Nederlandse Vereniging van Transportondernemingen
KNWAA — Koninklijke Nederlandse Akademie van Wetenschappen. Proceedings. Series A. Mathematical Sciences
KNWBA — Proceedings. Koninklijke Nederlandse Akademie van Wetenschappen. Series B. Physical Sciences
KNWCA — Koninklijke Nederlandse Akademie van Wetenschappen. Proceedings. Series C. Biological and Medical Sciences
KO — Kirche im Osten
KO — Kolloidnyi Zhurnal
KO — Kongo-Overzee. Tijdschrift voor en Over Belgisch-Kongo en Andere Overzeese Gewesten
KO — Korea Observer
Ko — Kovcezic
KO — Kunst des Orients
KOA — Karate and Oriental Arts
Koala Mag — Koala Magazine [*Sydney*]
KOAOA — Klinika Oczna
KOARER — Korean Arachnology
KOB — Kirche im Osten. Beiheft
Kobe Econ Bus R — Kobe Economic and Business Review
Kobe J Math — Kobe Journal of Mathematics
Kobe J Med Sci — Kobe Journal of Medical Sciences
Kobe Kogyo Tech Rep — Kobe Kogyo Technical Report
Kobelco Tech Bull — Kobelco Technical Bulletin
KOBELCO Technol Rev — KOBELCO Technology Review
Kobe Res Dev — Kobe Research Development
Kobe Steel Rep — Kobe Steel Report
Kobe U Econ R — Kobe University. Economic Review
Kobe U Law R — Kobe University. Law Review
Kobe Univ Econ R — Kobe University. Economic Review
Kobe Univ Law R — Kobe University. Law Review
Kobe Univ L Rev — Kobe University. Law Review
Ko Bl A f A — Korrespondenzblaetter des Archivs fuer Anthropologie und Urgeschichte
Ko Bl DAG — Korrespondenzblatt der Deutschen Anthropologischen Gesellschaft
KoBlGV — Korrespondenzblaetter des Gesamtvereins der Deutschen Geschichts- und Altertumsvereine
Ko Bl VSL — Korrespondenzblatt des Vereins fuer Siebenbuergische Landeskunde
KOBPDP — Klucze do Oznaczania Bezkregowcow Polski
Kobunshi Ronbun — Kobunshi Ronbunshu
Kobunshi Ronbunshu Jpn J Polym Sci Technol — Kobunshi Ronbunshu/ Japanese Journal of Polymer Science and Technology
Kobunsh Ron — Kobunshi Ronbunshu
KOCMA — Koroze a Ochrana Materialu
Kocsigy Ipar — Kocsigyarto Ipar [*Budapest*]
Kodaikanal Obs Bull A — Kodaikanal Observatory Bulletin. Series A
Kodaikanal Obs Bull B — Kodaikanal Observatory Bulletin. Series B
Kodaikanal Obs Bull Ser A — Kodaikanal Observatory Bulletin. Series A
Kodai Math J — Kodai Mathematical Journal
Kodai Math Semin Rep — Kodai Mathematical Seminar Reports
Kodai Math Sem Rep — Kodai Mathematical Seminar Reports
Kodak Bull Curr Photogr Inf — Kodak Bulletin of Current Photographic Information
Kodak Bull Graph Arts — Kodak Bulletin for the Graphic Arts
Kodak Data Book of Applied Phot — Kodak Data Book of Applied Photography
Kodak Data Sh — Kodak Data Sheets
Kodak Dig — Kodak Digest of Current Photographic Information
Kodak Internat Fotogr — Kodak International Fotografie
Kodak Lab Chem Bull — Kodak Laboratory Chemicals Bulletin
Kodak Mag — Kodak Magazine
Kodak Publ G 47 — Kodak Publication. G-47
Kodak Publ G 49 — Kodak Publication. G-49
Kodak Publ G 102 — Kodak Publication. G-102
Kodak Rec — Kodak Recorder
Kodak Res Lab Mon Abstr Bull — Kodak Research Laboratories. Monthly Abstract Bulletin
Kodak Spec — Kodak Special
Kodak Tech Photogr Bull — Kodak Technical and Photographic Bulletin
Kodaly — Kodaly Envoy
Koe D Bl — Koelner Domblatt
Koedoe Monogr — Koedoe Monograph
Koe Geogr Arb — Koelner Geographische Arbeiten
Koeln — Koeln. Vierteljahreschrift fuer Freunde der Stadt
Koeln Dombl — Koelner Domblatt
Koeln Encycl J — Koelnisches Encyclopedisches Journal
Koelner Vjsh F Soz — Koelner Vierteljahrshefte fue Soziologie
Koelner Z — Koelner Zeitschrift fuer Soziologie und Sozial-Psychologie
Koelner Z fuer Soziologie und Sozialpsychol — Koelner Zeitschrift fuer Soziologie und Sozialpsychologie
Koelner Z Soz — Koelner Zeitschrift fuer Soziologie und Sozial-Psychologie
Koelner Z Soziol — Koelner Zeitschrift fuer Soziologie. N.F. der Koelner Vierteljahrshefte fuer Soziologie
Koelner Z Soziol Sozialpsych — Koelner Zeitschrift fuer Soziologie und Sozialpsychologie
Koelner Z Soziol Sozialpsychol — Koelner Zeitschrift fuer Soziologie und Sozialpsychologie
Koelner Z Soziol u Soz-Psychol — Koelner Zeitschrift fuer Soziologie und Sozial-Psychologie
Koeln Geogr Arb — Koelner Geographische Arbeiten
Koeln Geol H — Koelner Geologische Hefte
Koeln JB V Frueh Gesch — Koelner Jahrbuch fuer Vor- und Fruehgeschichte

Koeln Jb Vor & Fruehgesch — Koelner Jahrbuch fuer Vor- und Fruehgeschichte
Koeln Mus Bull — Koelner Museums Bulletin
Koeln RAST Symp — Koelner RAST [*Radio-Allergo-Sorbens-Tests*] Symposion
Koeln Sozialpolit Vjhh — Koelner Sozialpolitische Vierteljahrshefte
Koen Akad D Wiss Berlin Sitzungsb — Koenigliche Akademie der Wissenschaften (Berlin). Sitzungsberichte
Koenigl Akad Wiss Paris Phys Abh — Koeniglichen Akademie der Wissenschaften in Paris. Physische Abhandlungen
Koenigl Norweg Ges Wiss Schriften — Der Koeniglich Norwegischen Gesellschaft der Wissenschaften Schriften
Koenigsberger Arch Naturwiss Math — Koenigsberger Archiv fuer Naturwissenschaft und Mathematik
Koenigsberger Naturwiss Unterhalt — Koenigsberger Naturwissenschaftliche Unterhaltungen
Koenigsb Gelehrten Ges Naturwiss Kl Schr — Koenigsberger Gelehrten Gesellschaft. Naturwissenschaftliche Klasse.Schriften
Koenigsbg Hartung Ztg — Koenigsberger Hartungsche Zeitung
Koenigsb Nw Unterh — Koenigsberger Naturwissenschaftliche Unterhaltungen
Koenigsb SB — Schriften der Koeniglichen Physikalisch-Oekonomischen Gesellschaft zu Koenigsberg
Koenigsb Schr — Schriften der Koeniglichen Physikalisch-Oekonomischen Gesellschaft zu Koenigsberg
Koenigsteiner Bl — Koenigsteiner Blaetter
KOERA — Kolorisztikai Ertesito
Koerp St G — Koerperschaftssteuergesetz
Koe T — Koelner Tageblatt
Koetoim Kayt — Koetoiminta ja Kaytanto
Koezgazd Szle — Koezgazdasagi Szemle
Koezlekedes Tud Sz — Koezlekedes Tudomanyi Szemle
Koezlek Sz — Koezlekedestudomanyi Szemle
Koezlemenyek-MTA Szamitastechn Automat Kutato Int (Budapest) — Koezlemenyek-MTA Szamitastechnikai es Automatizalasi Kutato Intezet (Budapest)
Koezl Erdel Nem Muz Er Reg — Koezlemenyek az Erdelyi Nemzeti Muzeum Erem es Regisegtarabal
Koezl Magy Tud Akad Musz Fiz Kut Intez — Koezlemenyei Magyar Tudomanyos Akademia Muszaki Fizikai Kutato Intezetenek
Koezl-MTA Szamitastech Automat Kutato Int (Budapest) — Koezlemenyek-MTA Szamitastechnikai es Automatizalasi Kutato Intezet (Budapest)
Koezn — Koezneveles
Koe Z Soz Soz Psych — Koelner Zeitschrift fuer Soziologie und Sozial-Psychologie
KOF — Kultur og Folkeminder
KOGAA — Koatsu Gasu
Koge Mus A — Koge Museum. Arbog
KOGJA — Kogyo Gijutsu
KOH — Konjunkturpolitik. Zeitschrift fuer Angewandte Konjunkturforschung. Beihefte
Kohasz Lap — Kohaszati Lapok
Kohasz Lapok — Kohaszati Lapok
Kohasz Lapok Mellek — Kohaszati Lapok. Melleklete
KOHED — Kohle und Heizoel
Kohle Erz — Kohle und Erz
Kohle Kali — Kohle und Kali [*Halberstadt*]
Kohlenw Welt Zahl — Kohlenwirtschaft der Welt in Zahlen
Kohlevergasung Vortr VGB Konf — Kohlevergasung, Vortraege, VGB-Konferenz
K'o Hsueh T'Ung PAO (Foreign Lang Ed) — K'o Hsueh T'Ung PAO (Foreign Language Edition)
Koin — Koinonia
Koinonike Epitheor — Koinonike Epitheoresis
KOISA — Kosmicheskie Issledovaniya
KOJ — Konjunkturpolitik. Zeitschrift fuer Angewandte Konjunkturforschung
KoJ — Korea Journal
KOJAA — Konkurito Janaru
Ko Jis — Kostnicke Jiskry
KOJUA — Kokyu To Junkan
KOK — Keukenkompas. Vakblad voor Inbouwkeukens, Inbouwapparatuur, en Accessoires
KoK — Kirke og Kultur
KOKAA — Kobunshi Kagaku
KOKAB — Kobunshi Kako
Kokalos — Kokalos Studi Pubblicati. Istituto di Storia Antica. Universita di Palermo
Kokeishu — Koto Saibansho Keiji Hanreishu
Kok Gak Zas — Kokka Gakkai Zassi
KOKKA — Koks i Khimiya
Koks Chem — Koks und Chemie
Koks Khim — Koks i Khimiya
Koksnes Kim — Koksnes Kimija
Kol — Kolokon
Kol Abhandl — Koloniale Abhandlungen
Kolch Proizv — Kolchoznoe Proizvodstvo
Koleopterol Rundsch — Koleopterologische Rundschau
Koleopt Rdsch — Koleopterologische Rundschau
Koleopt Z — Koleopterologische Zeitschrift
Kolhospnyk Ukr — Kolhospnyk Ukrainy
Kolkhozno-Sovkhoznoe Proizod Turkm — Kolkhozno-Sovkhoznoe Proizvodstvo Turkmenistana
Kolkhoz Opyt — Kolkhoznoe Opytnichestvo
Kolkhoz Paseka — Kolkhoznaya Paseka
Kolkhoz Proizv — Kolkhoznoe Proizvodstvo
Kolkhoz Proizvod — Kolkhoznoe Proizvodstvo
Kolkhoz-Sovkhoz Proizvod — Kolkhozno-Sovkhoznoe Proizvodstvo
Kolkhoz-Sovkhoz Proizvod Kirgizii — Kolkhozno-Sovkhoznoe Proizvodstvo Kirgizii
Kolkhoz-Sovkhoz Proizvod Mold — Kolkhozno-Sovkhoznoe Proizvodstvo Moldavil
Kolkhoz-Sovkhoz Proizvod RSFSR — Kolkhozno-Sovkhoznoe Proizvodstvo RSFSR
Kollas La Paz — Kollasuyo (La Paz)

Koll Azerb — Kollektsioner Azerbaidzhana
Koll Bl Neuburg — Neuburger Kollektaneenblatt
Kollekt Kefti Gaza Bolshikh Glubinakh Mater Vses Konf — Kollektory Nefti i Gaza na Bol'shikh Glubinakh. Materialy Vsesoyuznoi Konferentsii
Koll Kavk Muz — Kollektsii Kavkazskago Muzeya
Koll Khoz — Kollektivnoe Khozyaistvo
Kolloid Beih — Kolloid-Beihefte
Kolloidchem Beih — Kolloidchemische Beihefte
Kolloidchem Beihh — Kolloidchemische Beihefte
Kolloidforsch Einzeldarst — Kolloidforschung in Einzeldarstellungen
Kolloidkem Konf — Kolloidkemiai Konferencia
Kolloidkem Konf Eloadasai — Kolloidkemiai Konferencia Eloadasai
Kolloidnyi Zh — Kolloidnyi Zhurnal
Kolloidn Zh — Kolloidnyi Zhurnal
Kolloid-Z — Kolloid-Zeitschrift
Kolloid-Z & Z Polym — Kolloid-Zeitschrift und Zeitschrift fuer Polymere
Kolloid Z Beih — Kolloid-Zeitschrift. Beihefte
Kolloid Zh — Kolloidnyi Zhurnal
Kolloid Z Z Polym Suppl — Kolloid-Zeitschrift und Zeitschrift fuer Polymere. Supplementum
Kolloq Klin Pharmakol Exp Ther — Kolloquium fuer Klinische Pharmakologie und Experimentelle Therapie
Kolloq Tech Anwend Verarbeitungstechnol Kunstst — Kolloquium ueber Technischen Anwendung und Verarbeitungstechnologien von Kunststoffen
Kolloq Tech Anwend Verarb Kunstst — Kolloquium ueber Technische Anwendung und Verarbeitung von Kunststoffen
Koll Pchelov Delo — Kollektivnoe Pchelovodnoe Delo
Koll Z — Kolloidnyi Zhurnal
Koll Zh — Kolloidnyi Zhurnal
Koln Geol Hft — Koelner Geologische Hefte
Koln Jb Vor Fruh Gesch — Koelner Jahrbuch fuer Vor- und Fruehgeschichte
Koln Tech Bl — Koelner Technische Blaetter
Koln Vierteljahr Freunde — Koeln. Vierteljahrsschrift fuer Freunde der Stadt
Kolok Nizk Radioakt Zb Ref — Kolokvium o Nizkych Radioaktivitach. Zbornik Referatov
Kolomen Ped Inst Ucen Zap — Kolomenskii Pedagogiceskii Institut Ucenye Zapiski
Kolonialdeutsche Wiss Beih — Der Kolonialdeutsche. Wissenschaftliche Beihefte
Koloniale Stud — Koloniale Studien
Kolonialforstl Merkbl — Kolonialforstliche Merkblaetter
Kolonialforstl Mitt — Kolonialforstliche Mitteilungen
Kolon Inst Amsterdam Afd Handelsmus Meded — Koloniaal Instituut te Amsterdam. Afdeeling Handelsmuseum. Mededeeling
Kolon Inst Amsterdam Afd Trop Hyg Meded — Koloniaal Instituut te Amsterdam. Afdeeling Tropische Hygiene. Mededeeling
Kolon Rdsch — Koloniale Rundschau
Kolorad Zhuk — Koloradskii Zhuk i Mery Bor'by s Nim
Kolor Ert — Kolorisztikai Ertesito
Kolorist — Koloristisch
Kolor Izv — Koloristicheskie Izvestiya
Kolor Rundsch — Koloristische Rundschau
Kolozsvari Ferenc Jozsef Tudomanyegyet Evk — Kolozsvari Ferenc Jozsef Tudomanyegyetem Evkoenyve
Kolozsvar Orv Term Tars Ets — Ertesito a Kolozsvari Orvos-Termeszettudomanyi Tarsulat -nak az Orvosi, Termeszettudomanyi Szakuleseirol
Kolozsv Orvos Termeszettud Ert — Kolozsvari Orvos-Termeszettudomanyi Ertesito
KolR — Koloniale Rundschau
Kol Rundschau — Koloniale Rundschau
Kol St — Koloniale Studien
Kol T — Koloniaal Tijdschrift
KOM — Kirche im Osten. Monographienreihe
KoM — Komunikaty Mazursko-Warminskie
KOM — Tijdschrift voor Effectief Directiebeleid
Kom Aa — Kommunal Aarbog
KOMAA — Kovove Materialy
KOMAB — Korean Medical Abstracts
Komarom Meg Muz Koz — Komarom Megyei Muzeumok Koezlemenei
Komarom MK — Komarom Megyei Muzeumok Koezlemenyei
Komarov Chten — Komarovskie Chteniya
Komarovskie Chteniya Bot Inst Akad Nauk SSSR — Komarovskie Chteniya Botanicheskogo Instituta Academii Nauk SSSR
Kombin Anal — Kombinatornyi Analiz
Kombinatornyi Anal — Kombinatornyi Analiz
Koml — Kommunisticeskij Internatsional
Kominshu — Koto Saibansho Minji Hanreishu
Kom Krystalogr PAN Biul Inf — Komisja Krystalogradfii PAN [*Polska Akademia Nauk*]. Biuletyn Informacyjny
Komm Abg G — Kommunalabgabengesetz
Kom Mazur-Warmin — Komunikaty Mazursko-Warminskie
Komment Arzneib DDR — Kommentare zum Arzneibuch der Deutschen Demokratischen Republik
Komm Erforsch Luftverunreinig Dtsch Forschungsgem Mitt — Kommission zur Erforschung der Luftverunreinigung. Deutsche Forschungsgemeinschaft. Mitteilung
Komm Eur Gem — Kommission der Europaeischen Gemeinschaften
Komm Eur Gem Ber EUR — Kommission der Europaeischen Gemeinschaften. Bericht. EUR
Komm Kass Z — Kommunal-Kassen-Zeitschrift
Komm Sov Latv — Kommunist Sovetskoj Latvii
Komm St Z — Kommunale Steuer-Zeitschrift
Kommulaarb — Kommunalarbejderen
Kommunal'n Khoz — Kommunal'nvoe Khozyaistvo
Kommunalwirtschaft Sonderh — Kommunalwirtschaft. Sonderheft
Kommunik SARP — Kommunikat Stowarzyszenia Architektow Polskich
Kommun Int — Kommunistische Internationale

Kommunist Azerbajd — Kommunist Azerbajdzana
Kommunist Sov Latvi — Kommunist Sovetskoj Latvii
Kommunist Tss — Kommunistisk Tidsskrift
Kommun u Klassenkampf — Kommunismus und Klassenkampf
Komm Wasserforsch Mitt Dtsch Forschungsgem — Kommission fuer Wasserforschung. Mitteilung. Deutsche Forschungsgemeinschaft
Kom Ochr Przyr PAU — Komitet Ochrony Przyrody PAU
KompH — Komparatistische Hefte
Kompleksn Globalnyi Monit Mirovogo Okeana Tr Mezhdunar Simp — Kompleksnyi Global'nyi Monitoring Mirovogo Okeana. Trudy Mezhdunarodnogo Simpoziuma
Kompleksn Ispol'z Miner Syr'ya — Kompleksnoe Ispol'zovanie Mineral'nogo Syr'ya
Kompleksn Ispolz Rud Chern Met — Kompleksnoe Ispol'zovanie Rud Chernykh Metallov
Kompleksn Issled Kasp Morya — Kompleksnye Issledovaniya Kaspiiskogo Morya
Kompleksn Issled Prir Okeana — Kompleksnye Issledovaniya Prirody Okeana
Kompleksn Issled Vodokhran — Kompleksnye Issledovaniya Vodokhranilishch
Kompleksn Razvit KMA — Kompleksnoe Razvitie KMA
Kompleksoobraz Okislitelno Vosstanov Sist — Kompleksoobrazovanie v Okislitel'no-Vosstanovitel'nykh Sistemakh
Kompoz Polim Mater — Kompozitsionnye Polimernye Materialy
Kom Ukr — Kommunist Ukrainy
Komun Inst Geofiz Met Univ Lwow — Komunikaty Instituta Geofizyki i Meteorologii Uniwersytetu Jana Kazimierza we Lwowie
Komun Zakl Konstr Mech Przem Wegl — Komunikaty. Zaklady Konstrukcyjno-Mechanizacyjne Przemyslu Weglowego
KoN — Konyv es Neveles
Konan Women's Coll Res — Konan Women's College. Researches
Koncar Strucne Inf — Koncar Strucne Informacije
Kon Chal — Konzil von Chalkedon
Konf Aktuel Probl Tabakforsch — Konferenz ueber Aktuelle Probleme der Tabakforschung
Konf Cesk Fyz Sb Prednasek — Konference Ceskoslovenskych Fyziku. Sbornik Prednasek
Konf Feuerbetone — Konferenz ueber Feuerbetone
Konf Forschungszent Juelich — Konferenzen des Forschungszentrums Juelich
Konf Genet Sel Zhivotn — Konferentsiya po Genetike i Selektsii Zhivotnykh
Konf Ges Biol Chem — Konferenz der Gesellschaft fuer Biologische Chemie
Konf Ges Biol Chem Pap — Konferenz der Gesellschaft fuer Biologische Chemie. Papers
Konf Int Ges Biol Rhythm Forsch — Konferenz der Internationalen Gesellschaft fuer Biologische Rhythmusforschung
Konf Keram Elektron — Konference o Keramice pro Elektroniku
Konf Keram Elektron Pr — Konference o Keramice pro Elektroniku. Prace
Konf Kom Biol Nowotworow Pol Akad Nauk — Konferencja Komisji Biologii Nowotworow Polskiej Akademii Nauk
Konf Lepeni Kovov Intermetalbond Pr — Konferencia o Lepeni Kovov Intermetalbond. Prace
Konf Mater Podzespoly Magn — Konferencja. Materialy i Podzespoly Magnetyczne
Konf Menschl Schilddruese — Konferenz ueber die Menschliche Schilddruese
Konf Metalozn Mater Konf — Konferencja Metaloznawcza. Materialy Konferencyjne
Konf Metal Proszkow Mater Konf — Konferencja Metalurgii Proszkow. Materialy Konferencyjne
Konf Metal Proszkow Pol Mater Konf — Konferencja Metalurgii Proszkow w Polsce. Materialy Konferencyjne
Konf Metal Proszkow Ref — Konferencja Metalurgii Proszkow. Referaty
Konf Metody Badan Odpornosci Mater Pekanie Zbior Pr — Konferencja na temat Metody Badan Odpornosci Materialow na Pekanie, Zbior Prac
Konf Mikrosk Elektron Ciala Stalego — Konferencja Mikroskopii Elektronowej Ciala Stalego
Konf Molodykh Fiziol Zakavk — Konferentsiya Molodykh Fiziologov Zakavkaz'ya
Konf Molodykh Nauchn Rab Inst Neorg Khim Akad Nauk Latv SSR — Konferentsiya Molodykh Nauchnykh Rabotnikov Instituta Neorganicheskoi Khimii. Akademiya Nauk Latviiskoi SSR
Konf Molodykh Spets Mekh Polim Tezisy Dokl — Konferentsiya Molodykh Spetsialistov po Mekhanike Polimerov. Tezisy Dokladov
Konf Molodykh Uch Dalnego Vostoka — Konferentsiya Molodykh Uchenykh Dal'nego Vostoka
Konf Molodykh Uch Eksp Sovrem Biol Med Mater — Konferentsiya Molodykh Uchenykh Eksperiment v Sovremennoi Biologii i Meditsine Materialy
Konf Molodykh Uch Inst Probl Kompleksn Osvoeniya Nedr — Konferentsiya Molodykh Uchenykh. Institut Problem Kompleksnogo Osvoeniya Nedr
Konf Molodykh Uch Lab Monit Prir Sredy Klim — Konferentsiya Molodykh Uchenykh Laboratorii Monitoringa Prirodnoi Sredy i Klimata
Konf Molodykh Uch Mold — Konferentsiya Molodykh Uchenykh Moldavii
Konf Molodykh Uch Onkol Tezisy Dokl — Konferentsiya Molodykh Uchenykh-Onkologov. Tezisy Dokladov
Konf Molodykh Uch Sint Issled Biol Akt Soedin Tezisy Dokl — Konferentsiya Molodykh Uchenykh po Sintezu i Issledovaniyu Biologicheski Aktivnykh Soedinenii. Tezisy Dokladov
Konf Molodykh Uch Spets Biol Med Biomed Tekh — Konferentsiya Molodykh Uchenykh i Spetsialistov po Biologii, Meditsine i Biomeditsinskoi Tekhnicke
Konf Molodykh Uch Uzb Selsk Khoz Vet — Konferentsiya Molodykh Uchenykh Uzbekistana po Sel'skomu Khozyaistvu Veterinariya
Konf Nauk Sekc Wenerol Pol Tow Dermatol — Konferencja Naukowa Sekcji Wenerologicznej Polskiego Towarzystwa Dermatologicznego
Konf Nauk Tech Electrost Przem ELSTAT 80 Osiemdziesiat — Konferencja Naukowo-Techniczna Elektrostatyka w Przemysle, ELSTAT-80 Osiemdziesiat
Konf Nauk Tech Rozwoj Stali Odpornych Koroz — Konferencja Naukowo-Techniczna. Rozwoj Stali Odpornych na Korozje
Konf Nauk Tech Spiekane Stale Szybkotnace — Konferencja Naukowo-Techniczna. Spiekane Stale Szybkotnace

Konf Nauk Tech Technol Rob Antykoroz — Konferencja Naukowo-Techniczna Technologia Robot Antykorozyjnych
Konf N Nitroso Verbind Lactone — Konferenz ueber N-Nitroso-Verbindungen und Lactone
Konf Oberflaechenschutz Org Ueberzeuge Vortr — Konferenz ueber Oberflaechenschutz durch Organische Ueberzuege. Vortraege
Konf Poverkhn Silam Sb Dokl — Konferentsiya po Poverkhnostnym Silam. Sbornik Dokladov
Konf Poverkhn Yavleniyam Zhidk Mater — Konferentsiya po Poverkhnostnym Yavleniyam v Zhidkostyakh. Materialy
Konf Radioelektron — Konferentsiya po Radioelektronike
Konf Schweisstech — Konferenz fuer Schweisstechnik
Konf Sicherheitstech Landwirtsch Chem Vortr — Konferenz ueber Sicherheitstechnik der Landwirtschaftlichen Chemisierung. Vortraege
Konf Silik Promsti Nauki Silik — Konferentsiya Silikatnoi Promyshlennosti i Nauki o Silikatakh
Konf Svarke Legk Tsvetn Tugoplavkikh Met Splavov — Konferentsiya po Svarke Legkikh, Tsvetnykh i Tugoplavkikh Metallov i Splavov
Konf Teor Chem Pol — Konferencja Teoretyczna Chemikow Polskich
Konf Teor Vopr Adsorbts — Konferentsiya po Teoreticheskim Voprosam Adsorbtsii
Konf Teplofiz Svoistvam Veshchestv — Konferentsiya po Teplofizicheskim Svoistvam Veshchestv
Konf Term Anal Zb — Konferencia o Termickej Analyze. Zbornik
Konf Tribol Vortr — Konferenz ueber Tribologie. Vortraege
Konf Vopr Ispolz Zoly — Konferentsiya po Voprosam Ispol'zovaniya Zoly
Konf Vopr Tsito Gistokhim Dokl — Konferentsiya po Voprosam Tsito- i Gistokhimii. Doklady
Konf Zahr Ucastou Celostatne Dni Tepelneho Spracovania — Konferencia so Zahranicnou Ucastou Celostatne Dni Tepelneho Spracovania
Konf Zharostoikim Betonam — Konferentsiya po Zharostoikim Betonam
Konf Ziarobetonoch Pr — Konferencia o Ziarobetonoch. Prace
Kongel Danske Vidensk Selsk Bekiendtg — Kongelige Danske Videnskabernes Selskabs Bekiendtgiorelse
Kongel Norske Vidensk Selsk Mus Arsbok — Kongelige Norske Videnskabers Selskabs Museet. Arsbok
Kongl Fysiogr Saellsk Handl — Acta Universitatis Lundensis. Lunds Universitets Arsskrift. Afdelningen foer Mathematik och Naturvetenskap. Kongliga Fysiografiska Saellskapets i Lund Handlingar
Kongl Fysiogr Saellsk Lund Handl NF — Acta Universitatis Lundensis. Lunds Universitets Arsskrift. Afdelningen foer Mathematik och Naturvetenskap. Kongl Fysiografiska Saellskapets i Lund Handlingar.Ny Foeljd
Kongl Vetensk Acad Nya Handl — Kongl. Vetenskaps Academiens Nya Handlingar
Kongr Ausstellung Wasser — Kongress und Ausstellung Wasser
Kongr Ber Int Fruchtsaft Kongr — Kongress-Bericht. Internationaler Fruchtsaft-Kongress
Kongr Bulg Mikrobiol Mater — Kongres na Bulgarskite Mikrobiolozi. Materiali
Kongr Chem Polnohospod Pr — Kongres Chemia v Pol'nohospodarstve. Prace
Kongr Dtsch Ges Allerg Immunitaetsforsch — Kongress der Deutschen Gesellschaft fuer Allergie- und Immunitaetsforschung
Kongr Dtsch Ges Biol Psychiatr — Kongress der Deutschen Gesellschaft fuer Biologische Psychiatrie
Kongr Dtsch Veterinaermed Ges — Kongress der Deutschen Veterinaermedizinischen Gesellschaft
Kongr Eur Fed Corros Voordrukken — Kongres van de Europese Federatie van de Corrosie. Voordrukken
Kongr Eur Foed Korros Vordrucke — Kongress der Europaeischen Foederation Korrosion. Vordrucke
Kongr Eur Ges Haematol Verh — Kongress der Europaeischen Gesellschaft fuer Haematologie. Verhandlungen
Kongr Eur Ges Zuechtungsforsch — Kongress der Europaeischen Gesellschaft fuer Zuechtungsforschung
Kongr Ilmu Penget Nas — Kongres Ilmu Pengetahuan Nasional
Kongr INQUA Nov Zelandii Itogi Mater — Kongress INQUA v Novoi Zelandii, Itogi, i Materialy
Kongr Khim Selsk Khoz — Kongress Khimiya v Sel'skom Khozyaistve
Kongr Lederind — Kongress der Lederindustrie
Kongr Mikrobiol Mater Kongr Mikrobiol Bulg — Kongres po Mikrobiologiya. Materiali ot Kongres na Mikrobiolozite v Bulgariya
Kongr Pharm Wiss Vortr Originalmitt — Kongress der Pharmazeutischen Wissenschaften, Vortraege und Originalmitteilungen
Kongr Tagungsber Martin Luther Univ Halle Wittenberg — Kongress- und Tagungsberichte der Martin-Luther-Universitaet Halle-Wittenberg
Kongr Thromb Blutstillung — Kongress fuer Thrombose und Blutstillung
Kongr Zbl Ges Inn Med — Kongresszentralblatt fuer die Gesamte Innere Medizin und Ihre Grenzgebiete
KongrZentbl Ges Inn Med — Kongresszentralblatt fuer die Gesamte Innere Medizin
Kongr ZentVerb Balneol Oest — Kongress des Zentralverbands der Balneologen Oesterreichs
Kong Zentralbl Ges Innere Med — Kongresszentralblatt fuer die Gesamte Innere Medizin und Ihre Grenzgebiete
Konigsberger Land U Forstw Ztg — Koenigsberger Land- und Forstwirtschaftliche Zeitung
Konigsberg Univ Jahrb — Koenigsberg Universitaet. Jahrbuch
Koninkl Nederlandse Akad Wetensch Proc — Koninklijke Nederlandse Akademie van Wetenschappen. Proceedings
Koninkl Nederlandse Akad Wetensch Verh Afd Natuurk — Koninklijke Nederlandse Akademie van Wetenschappen. Verhandelingen. Afdeling Natuurkunde
Konink Nederl Akad Wetensch Verh Afd Natuurk Eerste Reeks — Koninklijke Nederlandse Akademie van Wetenschappen. Verhandelingen. Afd Natuurkunde Eerste Reeks
KONJD — Konjunkturberichte
Konj Pol — Konjunkturpolitik

Konjunkturber — Konjunkturberichte
Konjunkturpol — Konjunkturpolitik
Kon Kuk J Genet Eng — Kon Kuk Journal of Genetic Engineering
Kon Ned Oudhdknd Bond Bull KNOB — Koninklijke Nederlandse Oudheidkundige Bond. Bulletin KNOB
KONPA — Konzerv- es Paprikaipar
Konserv Dybfrost — Konserves and Dybfrost
Konserv Ind Allg Dtsch Konserv Ztg — Konserven-Industrie. Allgemeine Deutsche Konserven-Zeitung
Konserv Ind Moscow — Konserven-Industrie (Moscow)
Konservn Ovoshchesush Prom-St — Konservnaya i Ovoshchesushil'naya Promyshlennost'
Konservn Plodoovoschchn Prom — Konservnaya i Plodoovoshchchnaya Promyshlennost
Konservn Plodoovoshchn Promst — Konservnaya i Plodoovoshchnaya Promyshlennost
Konserv Promst — Konservnaya Promyshlennost
Konserv Obst Gemueseind — Konserven-, Obst- und Gemueseindustrie
Konserv Ovoshchesush Prom — Konservnaya i Ovoshchesushil'naya Promyshlennost'
Konserv Ovoshch Prom — Konservnaya i Ovoshchesushil'naya Promyshlennost'
Konserv Plodoov Prom — Konservnaya i Plodoovoshchnaya Promyshlennost'
Konserv Prom — Konservnaya Promyshlennost'
Konserv U ReinigMittel — Konservierungs- und Reinigungsmittel
Konspekt Lektsii Mezhdunar Shk Spets Rostu Krist — Konspekt Lektsii. Mezhdunarodnaya Shkola Spetsialistov po Rostu Kristallov
Konstanz Bl Hochschulfr — Konstanzer Blaetter fuer Hochschulfragen
Konsthist T — Konsthistorisk Tidskrift
Konsthist Tid — Konsthistorisk Tidskrift
Konsthist Tidskrift — Konsthistorisk Tidskrift
Konsthist Ts — Konsthistorisk Tidskrift
Konstit Klin — Konstitution und Klinik. Zeitschrift fuer Gesundheitsforschung und Konstitutionsmedizin
Konstit Med — Konstitutionelle Medizin
Konstit Med Neur Ther — Konstitutionelle Medizin und Neuraltherapie
Konst Klin — Konstitution und Klinik
Konstr — Konstruktion. Organ der VDI Gesellschaft Konstruktion und Entwicklung
Konstr Bauausf — Konstruktion und Bauausfuehrung
Konstr Elem Methoden — Konstruktion, Elemente, Methoden
Konstr Giessen — Konstruieren und Giessen
Konstr Ingenieurbau Ber — Konstruktiver Ingenieurbau Berichte
Konstr Kunstst Vortr Konstr Symp DECHEMA — Konstruieren mit Kunststoffen. Vortraege vom Konstruktions-Symposion der DECHEMA
Konstr Masch-Appar- Geraetebau — Konstruktion im Maschinen-, Apparate-, und Geraetebau
Konstr Masch App Geraetebau — Konstruktion im Maschinen-, Apparate-, und Geraetebau
Konstr Mater Osn Grafita — Konstruktsionnye Materialy na Osnove Grafita
Konstr Mater Osn Ugleroda — Konstruktsionnye Materialy na Osnove Ugleroda
Konstr Uglegrafitovye Mater Sb Tr — Konstruktsionnye Uglegrafitovye Materialy Sbornik Trudov
Konstrukt — Konstruktorskii
Konstrukt — Konstruktsionnyi
Konst Svoistva Miner — Konstitutsiya i Svoistva Mineralov
Konst Svoj Miner — Konstitutsiya i Svoistva Mineralov
Konsult Mater Ukr Gos Inst Eksp Farm — Konsultatsionnye Materialy Ukrainskiï Gosudarstvennyi Institut Eksperimental'noi Farmatsii
Kont — Kontexte
Kontakt Med Nmus — Kontakt Med Nationalmuseum
Kontakt Stud — Kontakt und Studium
Kon Tiki Mus Occ Pap — Kon-Tiki Museum Occasional Papers
Kontinent Holzztg — Kontinentale Holzzeitung
Kontorbl — Kontorbladet
Kontr — Kontrol'nyi
Kontrollnamnd Redog Malmo — Kontrollnamndens Redogorelse (Malmo)
Kontrol'no Izmer Tekh — Kontrol'no Izmeritel'naya Tekhnika
Kontrol Tekhnol Protsessov Obogashch Polezn Iskop — Kontrol i Tekhnologiya Protsessov Obogashcheniya Poleznykh Iskopaemykh
Kon Veren Indische Inst — Koninklijke Vereeniging Indische Instituut
Kon Veren Kol Inst G — Koninklijke Vereeniging Koloniaal Instituut Gids in het Volkenkundig Museum
Konyvtari Figy — Konyvtari Figyelo
Konzepte Zeitgemaess Physikunterrichts — Konzepte eines Zeitgemaessen Physikunterrichts
Konzern Nachr H Fuld U Co — Konzern-Nachrichten. H. Fuld und Co. Telephon- und Telegraphenwerke
Konzervipari Hig Napok — Konzervipari Higieniai Napok
Konzerv-Paprikaip — Konzerv- es Paprikaipar
Koop — Kooperationen
KOOPA — Kozhevenno-Obuvnaya Promyshlennost
Kooper Zemed — Kooperativno Zemedelie
Koop Zemed Sof — Kooperativno Zemedelie. Sofiya
Koord Khim — Koordinatsionnaya Khimiya
Koord Soveshch Zashch Dekor Introd Rast Bot Sadakh Ukr SSR — Koordinatsionnoe Soveshchanie po Zashchite Dekorativnykh Introdutsirovannykh Rastenii v Botanicheskikh Sadakh Ukrainskoi SSR
KOP — Kansallis-Osake-Pankki. Economic Review
Kopalnictwo Naft Pol — Kopalnictwo Naftowe w Polsce
KOP Econ R — KOP Economic Review
KopGS — Kopenhagener Germanistische Studien
Kopparb Lans HushallnSallsk Handl — Kopparbergs Lans Hushallningssallskaps Handlingar
Koppers Mag — Koppers Magazine
Koppers Mitt — Koppers Mitteilungen
Koppers Rev — Koppers Review

Ko Pr — Komsomol'skaja Pravda
KOPRA — Konservnaya i Ovoshchesushil'naya Promyshlennost'
Kor — Khayats Oriental Reprints
KORADQ — Key to Oceanographic Records Documentation
Koranyi Sandor Tarsasag Tud Ulesei — Koranyi Sandor Tarsasag Tudomanyos Ulesei
Kora Vyvetriv — Kora Vyvetrivaniya. Institut Geologii Rudnykh Mestorozhdenii, Petrografii i Geokhimii
Kor Cult — Korean Culture
Korea Exchange Bank Mo R — Monthly Review. Korea Exchange Bank
Korea Geol and Miner Inst Rep of Geol Miner Explor — Korea. Geological and Mineral Institute. Report of Geological and Mineral Exploration
Korea Geol Surv Bull — Korea. Geological Survey. Bulletin
Korea Geol Surv Geol Ground Water Resour — Korea. Geological Survey. Geology and Ground-Water Resources
Korea Inst Energy Resour Rep Geosci Miner Resour — Korea Institute of Energy and Resources. Report on Geoscience and Mineral Resources
Korea Inst Forest Genet Res Rept — Korea. Institute of Forest Genetics. Research Reports
Korea J — Korea Journal
Korea Kultmag — Korea-Kulturmagazin
Korea Med J — Korea Medical Journal
Korean Appl Phys — Korean Applied Physics
Koreana Quart — Koreana Quarterly
Korean Arachnol — Korean Arachnology
Korean Bee J — Korean Bee Journal
Korean Biochem J — Korean Biochemical Journal
Korean Cent J Med — Korean Central Journal of Medicine
Korean Chem Soc Bull — Korean Chemical Society. Bulletin
Korean Choong Ang Med J — Korean Choong Ang Medical Journal
Korean Inst Miner Min Eng J — Korean Institute of Mineral and Mining Engineers. Journal
Korean J Agric Econ — Korean Journal of Agricultural Economics
Korean J Anim Sci — Korean Journal of Animal Sciences
Korean J Appl Entomol — Korean Journal of Applied Entomology
Korean J Appl Microbiol Bioeng — Korean Journal of Applied Microbiology and Bioengineering
Korean J Appl Statist — Korean Journal of Applied Statistics
Korean J Biochem — Korean Journal of Biochemistry
Korean J Biol — Korean Journal of Biology
Korean J Biol Sci — Korean Journal of Biological Sciences
Korean J Bot — Korean Journal of Botany
Korean J Breed — Korean Journal of Breeding
Korean J Ceram — Korean Journal of Ceramics
Korean J Chem Eng — Korean Journal of Chemical Engineering
Korean J Comp L — Korean Journal of Comparative Law
Korean J Comput Appl Math — Korean Journal of Computational and Applied Mathematics
Korean J Dairy Sci — Korean Journal of Dairy Science
Korean J Dermatol — Korean Journal of Dermatology
Korean J Entomol — Korean Journal of Entomology
Korean J Environ Health Soc — Korean Journal of Environmental Health Society
Korean J Fd Sci Technol — Korean Journal of Food Science and Technology
Korean J Food Sci Technol — Korean Journal of Food Science and Technology
Korean J Genet — Korean Journal of Genetics
Korean J Ginseng Sci — Korean Journal of Ginseng Science
Korean J Hematol — Korean Journal of Hematology
Korean J Hortic Sci — Korean Journal of Horticultural Science
Korean J Hort Sci — Korean Journal of Horticultural Science
Korean J Ind Stud — Korean Journal of International Studies
Korean J Infect Dis — Korean Journal of Infectious Diseases
Korean J Intern Med — Korean Journal of Internal Medicine
Korean J Mater Res — Korean Journal of Materials Research
Korean J Med Chem — Korean Journal of Medicinal Chemistry
Korean J Microbiol — Korean Journal of Microbiology
Korean J Mycol — Korean Journal of Mycology
Korean J Nucl Med — Korean Journal of Nuclear Medicine
Korean J Nutr — Korean Journal of Nutrition
Korean J Obstet Gynecol — Korean Journal of Obstetrics and Gynecology
Korean J of Internat L — Korean Journal of International Law
Korean J Ophthalmol — Korean Journal of Ophthalmology
Korean J Parasitol — Korean Journal of Parasitology
Korean J Pharmacogn — Korean Journal of Pharmacognosy
Korean J Pharmacol — Korean Journal of Pharmacology
Korean J Physiol — Korean Journal of Physiology
Korean J Physiol Pharmacol — Korean Journal of Physiology and Pharmacology
Korean J Plant Pathol — Korean Journal of Plant Pathology
Korean J Plant Prot — Korean Journal of Plant Protection
Korean J Prev Med — Korean Journal of Preventive Medicine
Korean J Public Health — Korean Journal of Public Health
Korean J Radiol — Korean Journal of Radiology
Korean J Seric Sci — Korean Journal of Sericultural Science
Korean J Toxicol — Korean Journal of Toxicology
Korean J Urol — Korean Journal of Urology
Korean J Vet Res — Korean Journal of Veterinary Research
Korean J Zool — Korean Journal of Zoology
Korean R — Korean Review
Korean Res Bull — Korean Research Bulletin
Korean Res Inst Geosci Miner Resour Rep Geosci Miner Resour — Korean Research Institute of Geoscience and Mineral Resources. Report on Geoscience and Mineral Resources
Korean Sci Abstr — Korean Scientific Abstracts
Korean Sci Abstracts — Korean Scientific Abstracts
Korean Soc Anim Nutr & Feedstuffs — Korean Society of Animal Nutrition and Feedstuffs

Korean Stud For — Korean Studies Forum
Korea Polym J — Korea Polymer Journal
Korea Res Inst Geosci Miner Resour KIGAM Bull — Korea Research Institute of Geoscience and Mineral Resources. KIGAM Bulletin
Korea Univ Med J — Korea University. Medical Journal
Korea Wld Aff — Korea World Affairs
Korh Orvostech — Korhaz- es Orvostechnika
Kor J — Korea Journal
Kor J Comp Law — Korea Journal of Comparative Law
Kor J Int Stud — Korea Journal of International Studies
Korma Korml Skh Zhivotn — Korma i Kormlenie Sel'skokhozyaitvennykh Zhivotnykh
Korma Prod Zhivotnovod — Korma i Produkty Zhivotnovodstva
Kor Med — Korean Medicine
Kormi Godivlya Sil's'kogospod Tvarin — Kormi ta Godivlya Sil's'kogospodars'kikh Tvarin
Korml Skh Zhivotn — Kormlenie Sel'skokhozyaistvennykh Zhivotnykh
Kormoproizvod Sb Nauchn Rab — Kormoproizvodstvo Sbornik Nauchnykh Rabot
Korm Rast Senok Pastb SSSR — Kormovye Rasteniya Senokosov i Pastbishch SSSR
Korngrenzen Met Werkst — Korngrenzen in Metallischen Werkstoffen
Korn Mag — Korn Magasinet
Kor Obs — Korea Observer
Koronarinsuffizienz Symp Dtsch Ges Fortschr Geb Inn Med — Koronarinsuffizienz. Symposium der Deutschen Gesellschaft fuer Fortschritte aufdem Gebiet der Inneren Medizin
Korose Ochr Mater — Korose a Ochrana Materialu
Koroze Ochr Mater — Koroze a Ochrana Materialu
Koroz Zast — Korozija i Zastita
Korpuskularphotogr Vortr Diskuss Int Kolloq — Korpuskularphotographie. Vortraege und Diskussionen auf dem Internationalen Kolloquium ueber Korpuskularphotographie
Korrbl Aerztl Kreisver Sachs — Korrespondenzblatt der Aerztlichen Kreis- und Bezirksvereine in Sachsen
Korrbl Arbeitkreises Siebenburg Landesknd — Korrespondenzblatt des Arbeitkreises fuer Siebenbuergische Landeskunde
Korr Blatt — Korrespondenzblatt der Deutschen Gesellschaft fuer Anthrolopogie, Ethnologie, und Urgeschichte
Korr Bl Bayr — Bayerisches Aerztliches Korrespondenzblatt
Korrbl Dt Ges Anthr Eth Urgesch — Korrespondenzblatt der Deutschen Gesellschaft fuer Anthrolopogie, Ethnologie, und Urgeschichte
Korrbl Dt Ges Anthropol — Korrespondenzblatt der Deutschen Gesellschaft fuer Anthropologie
Korrbl Gesamtver Dt Geschver — Korrespondenzblatt des Gesamt-Vereins der Deutschen Geschichtsund Altertumsvereine
Korrbll Arch Anthropol — Korrespondenzblaetter des Archivs fuer Anthropologie und Urgeschichte
Korrbl Natfver Riga — Correspondenzblatt des Naturforschervereins zu Riga
Korr Bl Nd S — Korrespondenzblatt des Vereins fuer Niederdeutsche Sprachforschung
Korr Bl Thuering — Korrespondenzblaetter des Allgemeinen Aerztlichen Vereins von Thueringen
Korrbl Ver Niederdt Sprachforsch — Korrespondenzblatt des Vereins fuer Niederdeutsche Sprachforschung
Korrbl Ver Siebenbuerg Landesknd — Korrespondenzblatt des Vereins fuer Siebenbuergische Landeskunde
Korrbl Westdn Zeitschr — Korrespondenzblatt der Westdeutschen Zeitschrift fuer Geschichte und Kunst
Korrbl Westdt Zs Gesch — Korrespondenzblatt der Westdeutschen Zeitschrift fuer Geschichte und Kunst
Korrel Endog Protsessov Dalnego Vostoka SSSR — Korrelyatsiya Endogennykh Protsessov Dal'nego Vostoka SSSR
Korrel Uravn Org Khim — Korrelyatsionnykh Uravnenii v Organicheskoi Khimii
Korresp Abt Trinkbranntwein U Likoerfabr Inst GaerGew Berl — Korrespondenz der Abteilung fuer Trankbranntwein- und Likoerfabrikation am Institut fuer Gaerungsgewerbe in Berlin
Korresp Abwasser — Korrespondenz Abwasser
KorrespBl Aerzte Prov Hessen Nassau — Korrespondenzblatt fuer die Aerzte der Aerztekammer der Provinz Hessen-Nassau
KorrespBl Aerztl Ver Hessen — Korrespondenzblatt der Aerztlichen Vereine in Hessen
KorrespBl Aerztl Ver Rheinprov — Korrespondenzblatt der Aerztlichen Vereine der Rheinprovinz
KorrespBl Allg Aerztl Ver Thueringen — Korrespondenzblatt des Allgemeinen Aerztlichen Vereins von Thueringen
KorrespBl Allg Mecklenb Aerztver — Korrespondenzblatt des Allgemeinen Mecklenburgischen Aerztevereins
KorrespBl Beil Iris — Korrespondenzblatt. Beilage zur Deutschen Entomologischen Zeitschrift Iris
KorrespBl Dt Ges Anthrop — Korrespondenzblatt der Deutschen Gesellschaft fuer Anthropologie, Ethnologie, und Urgeschichte
KorrespBl Fischzuechter — Korrespondenzblatt fuer Fischzuechter, Teichwirte, und Seenbesitzer
KorrespBl Geogr Ges Basel — Korrespondenzblatt der Geographischen Gesellschaft (Basel)
KorrespBl Mecklenb AerzteverBund — Korrespondenzblatt des Mecklenburgischen Aerztevereinsbundes
KorrespBl NaturfVer Riga — Korrespondenzblatt des Naturforschervereins zu Riga
KorrespBl Schweizer Aerzte — Korrespondenzblatt fuer Schweizer Aerzte
KorrespBl Ver Aerzte RegBezirk Merseburg — Korrespondenzblatt des Vereins der Aerzte im Regierungsbezirk Merseburg und in dem Herzogtum Anhalt
KorrespBl Ver Dt Aerzte Reichenberg — Korrespondenzblatt des Vereins Deutscher Aerzte in Reichenberg
KorrespBl Zahnaerzte — Korrespondenzblatt fuer Zahnaerzte
KorrespBr ZuckFabr — Korrespondenzbriefe fuer Zuckerfabriken

Korrespondenzbl Wuertt — Korrespondenzblatt fuer die Hoeheren Schulen Wuerttembergs

Korrespondenzbriefe Zuckerfabr — Korrespondenzbriefe fuer Zuckerfabriken

Korros Ihre Bekaempf — Korrosion und Ihre Bekaempfung

Korrosionsinst Bull — Korrosionsinstitutet. Bulletin

Korrosionsinst Rapp — Korrosionsinstitutet. Rapport

Korros Metallschutz — Korrosion und Metallschutz

Korros Nytt — Korrosjons-Nytt

Korros Ytskydd — Korrosion och Ytskydd

Korroz Borba Nei — Korroziya i Bor'ba s Nei

Korroz Figy — Korrozios Figyelo

Korroz Figyelo — Korrozios Figyelo

Korroz Khim Proizvod Sposoby Zashch — Korroziya v Khimicheskikh Proizvodstvakh i Sposoby Zashchity

Korroz Met Splavov — Korroziya Metallov i Splavov

Korroz Tsem Mery Borby Nei — Korroziya Tsementov i Mery Bor'by s Nei

Korroz Zashch — Korroziya i Zashchita v Neftegazovoi Promyshlennosti Nauchno-Tekhnicheskii Sbornik

Korroz Zashch Konstr Met Mater — Korroziya i Zashchita Konstruktsionnykh Metallicheskikh Materialov

Korroz Zashch Korroz — Korroziya i Zashchita ot Korrozii

Korroz Zashch Met — Korroziya i Zashchita Metallov

Korroz Zashch Neftegazov Prom-St — Korroziya i Zashchita v Neftegazovoi Promyshlennosti

Korsakov J Neurol Psychiat — Korsakov Journal of Neurology and Psychiatry [London]

Korsakov J Neurol Psychiatry — Korsakov Journal of Neurology and Psychiatry

Kors J Neur Psych — Korsakov Journal of Neurology and Psychiatry

Kor Stud Forum — Korea Studies Forum

Korsz Egeszsegv — Korszeru Egeszsegvedelem

Kort — Kortars, Irodalmi es Kritikai Folyoirat

Korte Ber Dep Landb Buitenz — Korte Berichten. Departemente van Landbouw, Nijverheid en Handel

Korte Ber Landb — Korte Berichten Voor Landbouw, Nijverheid en Handel

Korte Ber LandbVoorlichtDienst Buitenz — Korte Berichten Uitgaande van den Landbouwvoorlichtingsdienst. Selectie- en Zaadtuin te Buitenzorg

Korte Ber Proefstn Aardappelverwerk — Korte Berichten. Proefstation voor Aardappelverwerking

Korte Meded Afd Landb Buitenz — Korte Mededeelingen van de Afdeeling Landbouw, Departement van Landbouw (Buitenzorg)

Korte Meded Alg Proefstn Landb Buitenz — Korte Mededeelingen van het Algemeen Proefstation voor den Landbouw (Buitenzorg)

Korte Meded Bosbouwproefsta — Korte Mededeling Stichting Bosbouwproefstation "De Dorschkamp"

Korte Meded BosbProefstn TNO — Korte Mededeelingen. Bosbouwproefstation, T.N.O

Korte Meded Inst PlZiekt Buitenz — Korte Mededeelingen van het Instituut voor Plantenziekten (Buitenzorg)

Korte Meded Landbouwproefstat Suriname — Korte Mededeeling van het Landbouwproefstation in Suriname

Korte Meded Ned Indische Vereen NatBescherm — Korte Mededeelingen. Nederlandsch-Indische Vereeniging tot Natuurbescherming

Korte Meded Proefstn Boschw Buitenz — Korte Mededeelingen van het Proefstation voor het Boschwezen (Buitenzorg)

Korte Meded Proefstn Cacao Salatiga — Korte Mededeelingen. Proefstation voor Cacao (Salatiga)

Korte Meded Proefstn Java SuikInd — Korte Mededeelingen van het Proefstation voor de Java-Suikerindustrie te Pasoeroean

Korte Meded RijksboschbProefstn — Korte Mededeelingen van het Rijksboschbouwproefstation

Korte Meded Sticht Bosbproefstn Dorschkamp — Korte Mededelingen Stichting Bosbouwproefstation "De Dorschkamp"

Kort Versl Werkz Ned Proefstn Strooverwerk — Kort Verslag van de Werkzaamheden van het Nederlandsch Proefstation voor Strooverwerking te Groningen

Kor World Aff — Korea and World Affairs

KOS — Kansallis-Osake-Pankki. Economic Review

KOSAB — Korean Scientific Abstracts

KOSBA — Kosmos. Seria A. Biologia (Warsaw)

Kosm B Av M — Kosmicheskaya Biologiya i Aviakosmicheskaya Meditsina

Kosm Bd — Kosmos-Baendchen

Kosm Biol Aviakosm Med — Kosmicheskaya Biologiya i Aviakosmicheskaya Meditsina

Kosm Biol Med — Kosmicheskaya Biologiya i Meditsina

Kosmet Chem Kongr Int Foed Ges Kosmet Chem Vortr Diskuss — Kosmetische Chemie, Kongress der Internationalen Foederation der Gesellschaftender Kosmetik-Chemikev. Vortraege und Diskussionen

Kosmet Int — Kosmetik International

Kosmet J — Kosmetik Journal

Kosmetol — Kosmetologie. Zeitschrift fuer Kosmetik in Wissenschaft und Praxis

Kosmet Parfum Drogen Rundsch — Kosmetik-Parfum-Drogen Rundschau

Kosmices Issled — Kosmiceskie Issledovanija

Kosmich — Kosmicheskii

Kosmic Issled — Kosmiceskie Issledovanija

Kosm Issled — Kosmicheskie Issledovaniya

Kosz Issled Ukr — Kosmicheskie Issledovaniya na Ukraine

Kosm Issled Zemnykh Resur — Kosmicheskie Issledovaniya Zemnykh Resursov Metody i Sredstva Izmerenii i ObrAabotki Informatsii

Kosm Izsled Bulg — Kosmichni Izsledvaniya v Bulgariya

Kosm Luchi — Kosmicheskie Luchi

Kosm Luchi Probl Kosmofiz Tr Vses Soveshch — Kosmicheskie Luchi i Problemy Kosmofiziki. Trudy Vsesoyuznogo Soveshchaniya po Kosmofizicheskomu Napravleniyu Issledovanii Kosmicheskikh Luchei

Kosm Mineral Mater Sezda MMA — Kosmicheskaya Mineralogiya, Materialy S'ezda MMA

Kosmokhim Meteorit Mater Vses Simp — Kosmokhimiya i Meteoritika. Materialy Vsesoyuznogo Simpoziuma

Kosmos Bibl — Kosmos Bibliothek

Kosmos Ser A Biol (Warsaw) — Kosmos. Seria A. Biologia (Warsaw)

Kosmos Ser A (Warsaw) — Kosmos. Seria A. Biologia (Warsaw)

Kosmos (Warsaw) Ser B — Kosmos. Seria B. Przyroda Nieozywiona (Warsaw)

Kosm Veshchestvo Zemle Dokl Simp Probl Kosmokhim — Kosmicheskoe Veshchestvo na Zemle. Doklady Prochitannye na Simpoziume po Problemam Kosmokhimii

K Ost — Kirche im Osten

Kostrom Gos Ped Inst Ucen Zap — Kostromskoi Gosudarstvennyi Pedagogiceskii Institut Imeni N. A. Nekrasova UcenyEe Zapiski

KOT — Khayats Oriental Translations

Ko T — Kirken og Tiden

KoTi — Konsthistorisk Tidskrift

KOTN — Keep on Truckin' News

Kov — Kovcezic

KOV — Kriegsopferversorgung

Kovodelny Prum — Kovodelny Prumysl

Kovove Mater — Kovove Materialy

Koyl Fayd Bilg — Koyluye Faydali Bilgiler

KOZAA — Kozarstvi

Kozegeszseg Kalauz — Kozegeszsegugyi Kalauz

Kozel Listy — Kozeluzske Listy

Kozepisk Math Fiz Lap — Kozepiskolai Mathematikai es Fizikai Lapok

Kozgazd Statiszt Irod Tajek — Kozgazdasagi es Statisztikai Irodalmi Tajekoztato

Kozgazd Szle — Kozgazdasagi Szemle

KOZHA — Kolloidnyi Zhurnal

Kozhevobuv Prom — Kozhevenno-Obuvnaya Promyshlennost'

Kozh Obuvn Prom SSSR — Kozhevenno-Obuvnaya Promyshlennost SSSR

Kozh-Obuvn Promst — Kozhevenno-Obuvnaya Promyshlennost

Kozh Obuvn Promst SSSR — Kozhevenno-Obuvnaya Promyshlennost SSSR

Kozlekedestud Szle — Kozlekedestudomanyi Szemle

Kozlem Agrartud Oszt Magy Tud Akad — Koezlemenyei. Agrartudomanyok Osztalyanak. Magyar Tudomanyos Akademia

Kozlemenyek-MTA Szamitastechn Automat Kutato Int (Budapest) — Koezlemenyek-MTA Szamitastechnikai es Automatizalasi Kutato Intezet (Budapest)

Kozlem Mosonmagyoarovari Agrartud Foiskola — Koezlemenyei. Mosonmagyoarovari Agrartudomanyi Foiskola

Kozl Keskenyv Vasut Tererol — Kozlemenyek a Keskenyvaganyu Vasutak Tererol

Kozl Magy K Foldt Intez — Kozlemenyei. Magyar Kiralyi Foldtani Intezet

Kozp Elelmiszerip Kutatointez Kozl — Kozponti Elelmiszeripari Kutatointezet Kozlemenyei

Kozp Fiz Kut Intez Kozl — Kozponti Fizikai Kutato Intezet Kozlemenyek

Kozp Fiz Kut Intez Rep KFKI — Kozponti Fizikai Kutato Intezet. Report KFKI

KP — Keeping Posted

KP — Kleine Pauly. Lexikon der Antike

KP — Kolkhoznoye Proizvodstvo

KP — Kritika Phylla

KP — Kulturni Politika

KP — Kwartalnik Prasoznawczy

KPAB — Kentucky Philological Association. Bulletin

KPG — Kliatt Paperback Book Guide

KPG — Kurzberichte aus dem Papyrussammlungen. Universitaets Bibliothek. Giessen

KPK — Kampeer + Caravan Kampioen

K Pl B — Klein Placaatboek

KPN — Kleinasiatische Personennamen

KPR — Kniga i Proletarskaya Revolyutsiya

K Pruefungsanst Wasserversorg Abwaesserbeseit Berlin Mitt — Koenigliche Pruefungsanstalt fuer Wasserversorgung und Abwaesserbeseitigung zu Berlin. Mitteilungen

KPS — Klassich-Philologische Studien

KPSJA — Journal. Korean Physical Society

KPT — Keeping Posted for Teachers

KQ — Kansas Quarterly

KQ — Koreana Quarterly

KQT — Kondordanz zu den Qumrantexten

KQYK — Kalikaq Yugnek. Bethel Regional High School

KR — Kenyon Review

KR — Kirchenreform

KR — Kirkus Reviews

KR — Koleopterologische Rundschau

KR — Koloniale Rundschau

Kr — Kreis. Zeitschrift fuer Kunstlerische Kultur (Hamburg)

Kr — Krokodil

Kr — Kroniek

Kr — Kronika

KRA — Kirchenrechtliche Abhandlungen

KRA — Koelner Romanistische Arbeiten

KRA — Kroniek van het Ambacht/Kleinbedrijf en Middenbedrijf

Kraeved Zap Kamc Obl Kraeved Muzeja — Kraevedceskie Zapiski Kamcatskaja Oblastnajakraevedceskaja Muzeja

Kraeved Zap Obl Kraeved Muz Upr Magadan Oblispolkoma — Kraevedceskie Zapiski Oblastnoi Kraevedcheskoi Muzei Upravleniya Magadanskogo Oblispolkoma

Kraev Zadachi Differ Uravn — Kraevye Zadachi dlya Differentsial'nykh Uravnenij

Kraft Betr — Kraft und Betrieb

Kraft Drift — Kraft och Drift. Tidskrift for Maskinister

Kraftfahrtech ForschArb — Kraftfahrtechnische Forschungsarbeiten

Kraftfahrtech Forschungsarb — Kraftfahrtechnische Forschungsarbeiten

Kraftfahrz Anz — Kraftfahrzeug-Anzeiger

Kraft Licht Dusseld — Kraft und Licht. Zeitschrift fuer Maschinenbau (Dusseldorf)

Kraft Licht Zurich — Kraft und Licht. Zeitschrift fuer Fabrikbetrieb (Zurich)

Kraft Ljus — Kraft och Ljus
Kraftomnibus Lastkraftwagen — Kraftomnibus und Lastkraftwagen
Krajobr Rosl Pol — Krajobrazy Roslinne Polski
Krajowa Konf Kalorym Anal Term Pr — Krajowa Konferencja Kalorymetrii i Analizy Termicznej. Prace
Krajowa Szk Temat Mikrosk Elektron — Krajowa Szkola na Temat Mikroskopii Elektronowej
Krajowe Symp Badania Nieniszczace Budow — Krajowe Sympozjum Badania Nieniszczace w Budownictwie
Krajowe Symp Kryst Przem — Krajowe Sympozjum Krystalizacja Przemyslowa
Krajowe Symp Podstawy Teor Wyladowan Elektr Gazach Pr — Krajowe Sympozjum Podstawy Teorii Wyladowan Elektrycznych w Gazach. Prace
Krajowe Symp Zastosow Izot Tech Ref — Krajowe Sympozjum Zastosowan Izotopow w Technice. Referaty
Krajowy Zjazd Endokrynol Pol — Krajowy Zjazd Endokrynologow Polskich
Krakhmalo Patochn Promst Nauchno Tekh Ref Sb — Krakhmalo-Patochnaya Promyshlennost. Nauchno-Tekhnicheskii Referativnyi Sbornik
Kralupsky Vlastiv Sborn — Kralupsky Vlastivedny Sbornik
Krankenh Apoth — Krankenhaus-Apotheke
KrankenhArzt Wiss Recht Wirt — Krankenhausarzt und Wissenschaft, Recht, und Wirtschaft
Krankenhaus Apoth — Krankenhaus-Apotheke
Krankenh Umsch — Krankenhaus Umschau
Krankenpfl — Krankenpflege Journal
Krankenpfl Soins Infirm — Krankenpflege. Soins Infirmiers
Kranke Pfl — Kranke Pflanze
Krank Hs — Krankenhaus
K Rap TC At Enerj Kom — K (Rapor) TC Atom Enerjisi Komisyonu
Krasnodar Gos Pedagog Inst Tr — Krasnodarskii Gosudarstvennyi Pedagogicheskii Institut. Trudy
Krasnodar Nauchno Issled Inst Pishch Promsti Tr — Krasnodarskii Nauchno-Issledovatel'skii Institut Pishchevoi Promyshlennosti. Trudy
Krasnodar Politekh Inst Tr — Krasnodarskii Politekhnicheskii Institut. Trudy
Krasnojarsk Politehn Inst Sb Naucn Trudov Meh Fak — Krasnojarskii Politehniceski Institut. Sbornik Naucnyh Trudov Mehaniceskogo Fakul'teta
Krasnoyarsk Gos Med Inst Tr — Krasnoyarskii Gosudarstvennyi Meditsinskii Institut. Trudy
Krasnoyarsk Inst Tsvetn Met Sb Tr — Krasnoyarskii Institut Tsvetnykh Metallov. Sbornik Trudov
Krasn Put Zheleznod — Krasnyi put' Zheleznodorozhnika
Kra Soob — Kratkie Soobscenija o Doklakach i Polevych Issledovanijach Instituta Archeologii
Kra Soob — Kratkie Soobshcheniia. Akademiia Nauk SSSR. Institut Arkheologii
Kra Soob Inst A — Kratkie Soobshcheniia. Akademiia Nauk SSSR. Institut Arkheologii
Kra Soob Inst A — Kratkie Soobshcheniia Instituta Arkheologii. Akademiia Nauk URSR
Kratkije Soobscenija Inst Eth — Kratkije Soobscenija Instituta Ethnografiji Akademiji Nauk SSSR
Kratkiye Soobscheniya Inst Arkheol AN SSSR — Kratkiye Soobscheniya Instituta Arkheologii Akademii Nauk SSR
Kratkiye Soobscheniya Inst Istor Mat Kult — Kratkiye Soobscheniya Instituta Istorii Material'noy Kul'tury
Kratk Otch Deyat Don Byuro Borbe Vredit Sel Khoz Rast — Kratkii Otchet o Deyatel'nosti Donskogo Byuro po Bor'be s Vreditelyami Sel'sko-Khozyaistvennykh Rastenii
Kratk Otch Rab Lab Zemled Saratov — Kratkii Otchet o Rabotakh Laboratorii Zemledeliya (Saratov)
Kratk Soderzh Dokl Vses Konf Emiss Elektron — Kratkie Soderzhaniya Dokladov. Vsesoyuznaya Konferentsiya po Emissionnoi Elektronike
Kratk Soderzh Dokl Vses Simp Vtorichnoi Fotoelektron Emissii — Kratkie Soderzhaniya Dokladov. Vsesoyuznaya Simpozium po Vtorichnoi i Fotoelektronmoi Emissii
Kratk Soobshch Buryat Kompleksn Nauchno-Issled Inst — Kratkie Soobshcheniya Buryatskogo Kompleksnogo Nauchno-Issledovatel'skogo Instituta
Kratk Soobshch Fiz — Kratkie Soobshcheniya po Fizike
Kratk Soobshch Inst Arkheol Moscow — Kratkiye Soobshcheniya o Dokladakh i Polevykh Issledovaniyakh. Instituta Arkheologii. Akademiya Nauk SSR (Moscow)
Kratk Soobshch Inst Etnogr — Kratkie Soobshcheniya. Institut Etnografii. Akademiya Nauk SSSR
Krat Soob Akad Nauk Inst Arkh — Kratkie Soobshcheniia. Akademiia Nauk SSSR. Institut Arkheologii
Krat Soob Akad Nauk SSSR Inst Ark — Kratkie Soobshcheniia. Akademiia Nauk SSSR. Institut Arkheologii
Krat Soob Inst Ark A N SSSR — Kratkie Soobshcheniia Instituta Arkheologii Akademii Nauk SSSR
Krat Soob Inst Etnogr — Kratkie Soobshcheniia Institut Etnografii Akademiia Nauk SSSR
Krat Soob Inst Ist Mater Kul't — Kratkie Soobshcheniia Institut Istorii Material'noi Kul'tury Akademiia Nauk SSSR
Krat Soob OGAM — Kratkie Soobshcheniia o Polevykh Arkheologicheskikh Issledovaniiakh Odesskogo Gosudarstvennogo Arkheologicheskogo Muzeia
KRB — Kredietbank. Weekberichten
Kr Ch — Kretika Chronika
Kr Chron — Kritika Chronika
KRE — Korea Exchange Bank. Monthly Review
Krebs A — Krebsarzt
Krebsforsch — Krebsforschung
Krebsforsch Krebsbekaempf — Krebsforschung und Krebsbekaempfung
Kredietbank W Bul — Kredietbank. Weekly Bulletin
Kredietbnk — Weekly Bulletin. Kredietbank
Kredit U Kapital — Kredit und Kapital
Kresge Art Bull — Kresge Art Center. Bulletin

Kresge Eye Inst Bull — Kresge Eye Institute. Bulletin
Krestanska Rev — Krest'anska Revue
Krest Delo — Krest'yanskoe Delo
Krest Khoz — Krest'yanskoe Khozyaistvo
KrestR — Krestanska Revue
KrestRTPril — Krestanska Revue. Theologicka Priloha
Krest Zemled — Krest'yanskoe Zemledelie
Kret Chron — Kretika Chronika
KRev — Kentucky Review
KRFWU — Kriegsvortraege der Rheinischen Friedrich-Wilhelms-Universitaet Bonn am Rhein
Kr Ge — Kristen Gemenskap
Kr Hs A — Krankenhausarzt
Kr Hs Umsch — Krankenhaus-Umschau
Kriegschir Hft Beitr Klin Chir — Kriegschirurgische Hefte der Beitrage zur Klinischen Chirurgie
Kriegs Sanitaetswes — Kriegs-Sanitaetswesen
Kriegstech Z — Kriegstechnische Zeitschrift
Kriegst Zs Berlin — Kriegstechnische Zeitschrift (Berlin)
Krigsh T — Krigshistorisk Tidsskrift
Krim Forensische Wiss — Kriminalistik und Forensische Wissenschaften
Krimin Abh — Kriminalistische Abhandlungen
Kriminal Arch — Kriminal-Archiv
Kriminalfors — Kriminalforsorgen
Kriminalpolit — Kriminalpolitik
Krimin Monatsh — Kriminalistische Monatshefte. Zeitschrift fuer die Gesamte Kriminalistische Wissenschaft und Praxis
Kriminol Abh — Kriminologische Abhandlungen
Krimin Probl — Kriminalistische Probleme
Kriog Mash — Kriogennye Mashiny
Kriog Vak Tekh — Kriogennaya i Vakuumnaya Tekhnika
KRISA — Kristallografiya
Kris Study Group NY Psychoanal Inst Monogr — Kris Study Group of the New York Psychoanalytic Institute. Monograph
Kristallogr — Kristallografiya
Kristallogr Grundl Anwend — Kristallographie. Grundlagen und Anwendung
Kristallokhim Neorg Soedin — Kristallokhimiya Neorganicheskikh Soedinenii
Kristall Tech — Kristall und Technik
Kristiania Etnogr Mus Bull — Kristiania Etnografiska Museums Bulletin
Kristiania Etnogr Mus Skr — Kristiania Etnografiska Museums Skrifter
Krist Met Tr Soveshch Teor Liteinykh Protsessov — Kristallizatsiya Metallov. Trudy Soveshchaniya po Teorii Liteinykh Protsessov
Krist Svoistva Krist — Kristallizatsiya i Svoistva Kristallov
Krist Tech — Kristall und Technik
Krist und Tech — Kristall und Technik
Krist Zhidk — Kristallizatsiya Zhidkosti
Krit — Kriterion
Krit Ber — Kritische Berichte
Krit Blaett Boersenhalle — Kritische Blaetter der Boersenhalle
Krit Blaett Forst Jagdwiss — Kritische Blaetter der Forst- und Jagdwissenschaft
KritC — Kritik (Copenhagen)
Krit Chron — Kretika Chronika
Kriter Prognoznoi Otsenki Territ Tverd Polezn Iskop — Kriterii Prognoznoi Otsenki Territorii na Tverdye Polezne Iskopaemye
Kritika Chron — Kritika Chronica
Krit Justiz — Kritische Justiz
Krit Schnellber Wes Schriftt Schweisstech — Kritischer Schnellbericht ueber das Wesentliche Schrifttum der Schweisstechnik des In- und Auslandes
Krit Viertel Ges Recht — Kritische Vierteljahresschrift fuer Gesetzgebung und Rechtswissenschaft
KritVj — Kritische Vierteljahrsschrift fuer Gesetzgebung und Rechtswissenschaft
Krit Vjber Berg U Huettenm Lit — Kritischer Vierteljahrsbericht ueber die Berg- und Huettenmaennische und Verwandte Literatur
Krit VJSchr — Kritische Vierteljahrsschrift fuer Gesetzgebung und Rechtswissenschaft
KRJUD — Kritische Justiz
KrK — Krestanska Revue
Krk Ak Mt Prz Rz & Sp — Rozprawy. Wydzialu Matematyczno. Przyrodniczego Akademii Umiejetnosci
KRKHB — Krankenhaus-Umschau
Krk Roczn Tow Nauk — Rocznik Towarzystwa Naukowego z Uniwersytetem Krakowskiego Polaczonego. Krakowie
Krk Roczn Uniwers — Rocznik Towarzystwa Naukowego z Uniwersytetem Krakowskim Polaczonego. Krakowie
KrL — Kritikon Litterarum. International Book Review for American, English, Romance, and Slavic Studies
KRMJA — Kurme Medical Journal
KRMNA — Kriminalistik
KRN — Food Magazine
Kroc Found Ser — Kroc Foundation Series
Kroc Found Symp — Kroc Foundation Symposia
Kroeber Anthropol Soc Pap — Kroeber Anthropological Society Papers
Kroeber Anthro Soc Pap — Kroeber Anthropological Society Papers
Kroeber Anthro Soc Pap — Kroeber Anthropological Society. Papers
Krolikovod Zverovod — Krolikovodstvo i Zverovodstvo
Kron — Kronika
Kron Farm Warsaw — Kronika Farmaceutyczna (Warsaw)
Kron Hist Genoot Utrecht — Kroniek van het Historisch Genootschap te Utrecht
Kroniek van Afr — Kroniek van Afrika
Kron Kst Kult — Kroniek van Kunst en Kultur
Kron Nootdorp — Kroniek van Nootdorp
Kronobergsboken — Kronobergsboken Arsbok foer Hylten-Cavallius Foereningen
Kron Rembrandthuis — Kroniek van het Rembrandthuis
Kron Slov Mest — Kronika Slovenskych Mest
KROZP — Katalog Rekopisow Orientalnych ze Zbirorow Polskich

KRQ — Kentucky Romance Quarterly
Kr R — Krestanska Revue
KrRThPr — Krestanska Revue. Theologicka Priloha
KRSHB3 — Annals of Science. Kanazawa University
KRS Jugosl/Carsus Iugosl — KRS Jugoslavije/Carsus Iugoslaviae
KrSoob(Kiev) — Kratkije Soobscenija Breves Communications de l'Institute d'Archeologie (Kiev)
Kr Soobsc Inst Arheol — Kratkie Soobscenija Instituta Arheologii
KRTEA — Kristall und Technik
KRTRA — Krupp Technical Review
Kruppsche Monatsh — Kruppsche Monatsheft
Krupp Tech Rev (Engl Transl) — Krupp Technical Review (English Translation)
Krym Gos Med Inst Tr — Krymskii Gosudarstvennyi Meditsinskii Institut Trudy
Kryst Przem Krajowe Symp Mater Konf — Krystalizacja Przemyslowa. Krajowe Sympozjum. Materialy Konferencyjne
Krzepniecie Met Stopow — Krzepniecie Metali i Stopow
KS — Akademiia Nauk SSSR. Institut Narodov Azii. Kratkie Soobshcheniia
KS — Kant-Studien
KS — Keleti Szemle
KS — Kirjath Sepher
KS — Koloniale Studien
KS — Korean Survey
KS — Kratkie Soobshcheniia
KS — Kultura Slova
KS — Kyklos
KS — Kypriakai Spoudai
KSABD — Korean Scientific Abstracts
KSAC Engr — K.S.A.C. (Kansas State Agricultural College) Engineer
K-Saechs Ges Wiss Leipzig Mat-Phys Kl Ber — Koeniglich-Saechsische Gesellschaft der Wissenschaften zu Leipzig. Mathematisch-Physische Klasse. Berichte ueber die Verhandlungen
KSAN — Kratie Soobshcheniia. Akademiia Nauk SSSR. Institut Etnografii
KSB — Katolikus Szemle. Budapest
KSB Tech Ber — Klein, Schanzlin, und Becker Aktiengesellschaft. Technische Berichte
KSB Tech Ber — KSB [Klein, Schanzlin, Becker] Technische Berichte
KSBurNII — Kratkir Soobscenija Burjatskogo Kompleksnogo Naucnoissledovatel'skogo InstitutaSerija Storiko-Filologiceskaja
KSCGH — Kyushu Chugokugakkaiho
KSDB — Kommunal Statistisk DataBank
KSDKA — Kobe Shosen Daigaku Kiyo. Dai-2-Rui. Kokai, Kikan, Rigaku-Hen
KSDL — Kieler Studien zur Deutschen Literaturgeschichte
Ksenolity Gomeogennye Vklyucheniya Mater Simp Ksenolitam — Ksenolity i Gomeogennye Vklyucheniya. Materialy Simpoziuma po Ksenolitam
KSGT — Kleine Schriften. Gesellschaft fuer Theatergeschichte
KSHAB2 — Bulletin. Fruit Tree Research Station. Series A
KSHSR — Kentucky State Historical Society. Register
KSIA — Kratkie Soobshcheniia Instituta Arkheologii. Akademiia Nauk URSR
KSIA — Kratkie Soobshcheniya. Akademiya Nauk SSSR. Institut Arkheologii
KSI AAN USSR — Kratkie SoobshchenIia Instituta Arkheologii. Akademiia Nauk URSR
Ksia Kiev — Kratkie Soobshcheniia Instituta Arkheologii. Akademiia Nauk URSR (Kiev)
KSIE — Kratkie Soobshcheniya. Akademiya Nauk SSSR. Institut Etnografii imeni N. N. Miklucho-Maklaja
KSIIMK — Kratkie Soobshcheniia o Dokladah i Polevyh Issledovaniiah Instituta Istorii Materialnoi Kultury
KSINA — Kratkie Soobshcheniia Instituta Narodov Azii
KSISL — Kratkije Soobscenija Instituta Slajanovednija Akademija Nauk SSSR
KSIV — Kratkije Soobscenija Instituta Vostokovednija Akademija Nauk SSSR
KSJ — Keats-Shelley Journal
KS Kiev — Kratkie Soobshcheniia Instituta Arkheologii. Akademiia Nauk URSR (Kiev)
KSKK — Katolikus Szemle. Roma. Kis Koenyvtara
K Skogshogsk Skr — Kungliga Skogshogskolans Skrifter
K Skogs Lantbruksakad Tidskr — Kungl Skogs- och Lantbruksakademiens Tidskrift
K Skogs Lantbruksakad Tidskr Suppl — Kungl Skogs- och Lantbruksakademiens Tidskrift. Supplement
K Skogs o Lantbr Akad Tidskr — Kungliga Skogs- och Lantbruksakademiens. Tidskrift
KSl — Kultura Slova
KS LR — Kansas Law Review
KSLTA — Kungliga Skogs- och Lantbruksakademiens. Tidskrift
KSM — Katholiek Staatskundig Maandschrift
KSMB — Keats-Shelley Memorial Bulletin
KSMB(R) — Keats-Shelley Memorial Bulletin (Rome)
KSMGA — Koks, Smola, Gaz
KSMSA — Kosmos
KSN — Kokusai Shukyo Nyuzu
KS Odessa — Kratkie Soobshcheniia o Polevykh Arkheologicheskikh Issledovaniiakh Odesskogo Gosudarotvennogo Arkheologicheskogo Muzeia
KSOGAM — Kratkie Soobshcheniia o Polevykh Arkheologicheskikh Issledovaniiakh Odesskogo Gosudarotvennogo Arkheologicheskogo Muzeia
KSp — Kypriakai Spoudai
KSPRA — Kuznechno-Shtampovochnoe Proizvodstvo
KSPV — Koelner Sozialpolitische Vierteljahresschrift
KsQ — Kansas Quarterly
KSRNA — Kiso To Rinsho
KSRS — Kevo Subarctic Research Station. Reports
KSS — Kashi Sanskrit Series
KSSH — Kungl Skytteanska Samfundets Handlingar
KSt — Kant-Studien
KST — Katholiek Sociaal Tijdschrift
KST — Kleinere Sanskrit Texte

Kst Alle Mal Plast Graph Archit — Kunst fuer Alle. Malerei, Plastik, Graphik, Architektur
Kst & Altert — Kunst und Altertum
Kst & Ant — Kunst und Antiquitaeten
Kst & Gew — Kunst und Gewerbe
Kst & Handwk — Kunst und Handwerk
Kst & Kirche — Kunst und Kirche
Kst & Kstgew — Kunst und Kunstgewerbe
Kst & Ksthandwk — Kunst und Kunsthandwerk
Kst & Kstler — Kunst und Kuenstler
Kst & Kult Oslo — Kunst og Kultur [Oslo]
Kst & Kunstnere — Kunst og Kunstnere
Kst & Levensbeeld — Kunst- en Levensbeelden
Kst & Mus — Kunst og Museum
Kst & Sch — Kunst und Schule
Kst & S Heim — Kunst und das Schoene Heim
Kst & Stein — Kunst und Stein
Kst & Unterricht — Kunst und Unterricht
Kst Bedeuttr — Kunst als Bedeutungstraeger
Kst Bull Schweiz Kstver — Kunst-Bulletin des Schweizerischen Kunstvereins
Kstchron & Kstlit — Kunstchronik und Kunstliteratur
Kstchron & Kstmarkt — Kunstchronik und Kunstmarkt. Wochenschrift fuer Kenner und Sammler
Kstdkml Freistaat Hessen — Kunstdenkmaeler im Freistaat Hessen
Kst Dritten Reich — Kunst im Dritten Reich
Kst Dt Reich — Kunst im Deutschen Reich
Kstforum Int — Kunstforum International. Die Aktuelle Zeitschrift fuer alle Bereiche der Bildenden Kunst
Kstfuehrer Schweiz — Kunstfuehrer durch Die Schweiz
Kstgesch Auslandes — Zur Kunstgeschichte des Auslandes
Kstgesch Forsch Rhein Heimatbundes — Kunstgeschichtliche Forschungen des Rheinischen Heimatbundes
Kstgesch Geistesgesch — Kunstgeschichte als Geistesgeschichte
Kstgesch Ges — Kunstgeschichtliche Gesellschaft
Kstgesch Ges Berlin — Kunstgeschichtliche Gesellschaft zu Berlin
Kstgesch Jb Bib Hertz — Kunstgeshichtliches Jahrbuch der Bibliotheca Hertziana
Kstgesch Jb Ksr Koen Zent Komm Erforsch & Erhaltung Kst & His — Kunstgeschichtliches Jahrbuch der K.-K. [Kaiserlich-Koeniglichen] Zentral-Kommission fuer Erforschung und Erhaltung der Kunst- und Historischen Denkmale
Kstgesch Nederlanden — Kunstgeschiedenis der Nederlanden
Kst Gew — Kunst in Gewerbe
KSTh — Kleine Schriften zur Theologie
Ksthandwke Boehmen — Kunsthandwerke in Boehmen
Ksthaus Zuerich Ges Jber — Kunsthaus der Zuericher Gesellschaft. Jahresbericht
Kst Hessen & Mittelrhein — Kunst in Hessen und am Mittelrhein
Ksthist Inst Graz Jb Ksthist Inst U Graz — Kunsthistorisches Institut Graz. Jahrbuch des Kunsthistorischen Instituts der Universitaet Graz
Ksthist Jb Graz — Kunsthistorisches Jahrbuch Graz
Ksthist Meded Rijksbureau Ksthist Doc — Kunsthistorische Mededelingen van het Rijksbureau voor Kunsthistorische Documentatie
Ksthist Saellsk Pubn — Konsthistoriska Saellskapets Publikation
Ksthist Tidskr — Konsthistorisk Tidskrift
Kst Idag — Kunsten Idag
Kstinf — Kunstinformatie
Kstjb Stadt Linz — Kunstjahrbuch der Stadt Linz
KSTKBO — Clean Air. Special Edition
Kst Mhft Freie & Angewandte Kst — Kunst. Monatshefte fuer Freie und Angewandte Kunst
Kstmus Arsskr — Kunstmuseets Arsskrift
Kst Orients — Kunst des Orients
Kstrundschau — Kunstrundschau
Kst Schleswig Holstein — Kunst in Schleswig-Holstein
KSTSDG — Kenya Journal of Science and Technology. Series B. Biological Sciences
K St T — Kanonistische Studien und Texte
Kst Volke — Kunst dem Volke
Kstwiss Stud — Kunstwissenschaftliche Studien
Kstwk — Kunstwerk. Eine Zeitschrift ueber alle Gebiete der Bildenden Kunst
KSU (Kyoto Sangyo Univ) Econ and Bus R — KSU (Kyoto Sangyo University). Economic and Business Review
KSV — Kirjallisuudentutkijain Seuran Vuosikirja
K Svenska Vet-Ak Hdl Oefv — Kungliga Svenska Vetenskaps-Akademiens. Handlingar. Oefversigt til Handlingar
K Svenska VetensAkad Lefnadsteck — Kungliga Svenska Vetenskapsakademiens Lefnadsteckningar
K Svenska VetensAkad Skr Naturskydd — Kungliga Svenska Vetenskapsakademiens Skrifter i Naturskyddsarenden
K Svenska VetenskAkad Arsb — Kungliga Svenska Vetenskapsakademiens Arsbok
K Svenska VetenskAkad Avh Naturskydd — Kungliga Svenska Vetenskapsakademiens Avhandlingar i Naturskyddsarenden
K Svenska VetenskAkad Handl — Kungliga Svenska Vetenskapsakademiens Handlingar
K Sven Vetenskapsakad Avh Naturskyddsarenden — Kungliga Svenska Vetenskapsakademiens. Avhandlingar i Naturskyddsarenden
K Sven Vetenskapsakad Handl — Kungliga Svenska Vetenskapsakademiens. Handlingar
K Sven Vetenskapsakad Skr Naturskyddsarenden — Kungliga Svenska Vetenskapsakademiens. Skrifter i Naturskyddsarenden
KSVK — Kalevalaseuran Vuosikirja
KSz — Keleti Szemle
KT — Kaiser-Traktate
KT — Khaleej Times
KT — Khristianskoe Tchtenie

KT — Knossos Tablets
KT — Koloniaal Tijdschrift
KT — Kommunist Turkmenistana
KT — Konsthistorisk Tidskrift
KTA — Kroeners Taschenausgabe
Ktavim Rec Agric Res Stn — Ktavim Records of the Agricultural Research Station
K Tek Hoegsk Handl — Kungliga Tekniska Hoegskolans. Handlingar
K Tek Hogsk Avh — Kungliga Tekniska Hogskolans Avhandlingar
KTF — Kwartaalfacetten. Informatie over Krediet en Financiering
KTh — Kerk en Theologie
KTheol — Kerk en Theologie
K Tieraerztl Landwirtsch Univ Jahrb Copenhagen — Koenigliche Tieraerztliche und Landwirtschaftliche Universitaet. Jahrbuch. Copenhagen
KTL Ber Landtech — Kuratorium fuer Technik in der Landwirtschaft. Berichte ueber Landtechnik
KTMF Tud Koezl — KTMF. Tudomanyos Koezlemenyei
KTMK — Katimavik. Faculty of Physical Education. University of Alberta
KtoK — Kokugo To Kokubungaku
KTR — Korea Trade Report
KTU — Keilalphabetischen Texte aus Ugarit
KTVU — Kleine Texte fuer Vorlesungen und Uebungen
KU — Karnatak University. Journal
KUA — Kobe University. Economic Review
KuA — Kunst und Antiquariat
KUB — Keilschrifturkunden aus Boghazkoei
Kuban Gos Univ Naucn Trudy — Kubanskii Gosudarstvennyi Universitet Naucnyi Trudy
Kuban Otd Vses Ova Genet Sel Tr — Kubanskoe Otdelenie Vsesoyuznogo Obshchestva Genetikov i Selektsionerov. Trudy
KUBEA — Kunststoff-Berater
Kubota Tech Rep — Kubota Technical Reports
Kuchurganskii Liman Okhladitel Mold GRES — Kuchurganskii Liman - Okhladitel Moldavskoi GRES
KuD — Kerygma und Dogma
Ku D B — Kerygma und Dogma. Beiheft
KUDKA — Kumamoto Daigaku Kogakubu Kenkyu Hokoku
Kuehlungsborner Kolloq — Kuehlungsborner Kolloquium
Kuehn-Arch — Kuehn-Archiv
Kuelf Agrarirod Roevid Kivonatai Kert — Kuelfoeldi Agrarirodalmi Roevid Kivonatai. Kerteszet, Szoeleszet, Boraszat
Kuelf Agrarirod Roevid Kivonatai Noevenyved — Kuelfoeldi Agrarirodalmi Roevid Kivonatai. Noevenyvedelem
Kuelf Agrarirod Szemleje Kert Szoelesz — Kuelfoeldi Agrarirodalom Szemleje. Kerteszet es Szoeleszet
Kuelf Agrarirod Szemle Noevenyved — Kuelfoeldi Agrarirodalmi Szemle. Noevenyvedelem
Kuelf Hazai Agrarirod Szemle Erdesz — Kuelfoeldi es Hazai Agrarirodalmi Szemle. Erdeszet
Kuelf Hazai Agrarirod Szemle Noevenyved — Kuelfoeldi es Hazai Agrarirodalmi Szemle. Noevenyvedelem
Kuelfoeldi Mehesz Szemle — Kuelfoeldi Meheszeti Szemle
Kuelt Ve Sanat — Kueltuer ve Sanat
Kuenstlerische Gesch Vortr Int Glaskongr — Kuenstlerische und Geschichtliche Vortraege. Internationaler Glaskongress
KUER — Kobe University. Economic Review
KuFr — Kultur-Fronten
KuG — Kirche und Gesellschaft
Kugellager-Z — Kugellager-Zeitschrift
KUHCA — Journal. Korean Institute of Metals
KuhnsZ — Kuhns Zeitschrift fuer Vergleichende Sprachforschung
Kuibysev Gos Ped Inst Naucn Trudy — Kuibysevskii Gosudarstvennyi Pedagogiceskii Institut Naucnyi Trudy
Kuibysev Gos Ped Inst Ucen Zap — Ministerstvo Prosvescenija RSFSR Kuibysevskii Gosudarstvennyi Pedagogiceskii Institut Imeni V. V. Kuibyseva Ucenyi Zapiski
Kuibyshev Aviats Inst im Akad SP Koroleva Tr — Kuibyshevskii Aviatsionnyi Institut imeni Akademika S.P. Koroleva. Trudy
Kuibyshev Gos Pedagog Inst im VV Kuibysheva Nauchn Tr — Kuibyshevskii Gosudarstvennyi Pedagogicheskii Institut imeni V.V. Kuibysheva. Nauchnye Trudy
Kuibyshev Inzh Stroit Inst Tr — Kuibyshevskii Inzhenerno-Stroitel'nyi Institut Trudy
Kuibyshev Med Inst im DI Ulyanova Tr — Kuibyshevskii Meditsinskii Institut imeni D. I. Ul'yanova. Trudy
Kuibyshev Nauchno Issled Inst Neft Promsti Tr — Kuibyshevskii Nauchno-Issledovatel'skii Institut Neftyanoi Promyshlennosti. Trudy
Kuibyshev Nauchno Issled Vet Stn Sb Nauchn Tr — Kuibyshevskaya Nauchno-Issledovatel'skaya Veterinarnaya Stantsiya. Sbornik Nauchnykh Trudov
Kuibyshev Neft — Kuibyshevskaya Neft
KUISA — Japanese Journal of Aerospace Medicine and Psychology
KUK — Temperatur Technik. Zeitschrift fuer das Gesamte Temperaturgebiet Kaltetechnik,Klimatechnik, und Heizungstechnik Einschliesslich Isolierung Lueftung, Kuehltransport, und Tiefkuehltransport
Kukem Derg — Kukem Dergisi
KuKh — Kunst und Kunsthandwerk
KuKi — Kunst und Kirche
Ku Kl — Kultur og Klasse
KUKUA — Kukuruza
KuKv — Klassizismus und Kulturverfall
Kul — Kultura. Szkice, Opowladania, Sprawozdania
KuL — Kunst und Literatur
Kul Kath — Kultur und Katholizismus
Kulliyat Ulum Maj — Kulliyat al-Ulum, Majallah
Kulort S — Kulorte Sider
Kult & Zhizn — Kul'tura i Zhizn'
Kult Barai — Kulturos Barai

Kult es Jozosseg — Kultura es Jozosseg
Kultggr — Kulturgeografi
Kulthist Ab — Kulturhistorisk Arsbok
Kulthist Leks Nord Midald — Kulturhistorisk Leksikon foer Nordisk Middelalder
Kult i Spolecz — Kultura i Spoleczenstwo
Kultm — Kulturminder
Kult Mesicnik Litomerickeho Okresu — Kulturni Mesicnik Litomerickeho Okresu
Kult Naslestvo — Kulturno Naslestvo
Kult Pop — Kultura Populore
Kult u Leben — Kultur und Leben
KulturaW — Kultura (Warsaw)
Kulturen — Kulturen Arsbok till Medlemmerna av Kulturhistoriska Foerening foer Soedra Sverige
Kultur O Klasse — Kultur og Klasse
Kulturpflanze Beih — Kulturpflanze Beiheft
Kult Vaerld — Kulturens Vaerld
Kulu Bl — Kulu Bladet
Ku M — Kerygma und Mythos
Kumamoto J Math — Kumamoto Journal of Mathematics
Kumamoto Jour Sci Ser A Mathematics Physics and Chemistry — Kumamoto Journal of Science. Series A. Mathematics, Physics, and Chemistry
Kumamoto J Sci — Kumamoto Journal of Science
Kumamoto J Sci Biol — Kumamoto Journal of Science. Biology
Kumamoto J Sci Geol — Kumamoto Journal of Science. Geology
Kumamoto J Sci Math — Kumamoto Journal of Science. Mathematics
Kumamoto J Sci Sect 2 Biol — Kumamoto Journal of Science. Sect 2. Biology
Kumamoto J Sci Ser A — Kumamoto Journal of Science. Series A. Mathematics, Physics, and Chemistry
Kumamoto J Sci Ser B Sect 1 — Kumamoto Journal of Science. Series B. Section 1. Geology
Kumamoto J Sci Ser B Sect 2 Biol — Kumamoto Journal of Science. Series B. Section 2. Biology
Kumamoto Med J — Kumamoto Medical Journal
Kumamoto Pharm Bull — Kumamoto Pharmaceutical Bulletin
KUMJA — Kumamoto Medical Journal
KUMJB — Kyungpook University. Medical Journal
KUN — Kunststoffe
Kun Bib Hand — Kungliga Bibliotekets Handlingar
Kun Chung Hseuh Pao Acta Entomol Sin — Kun Chung Hseuh Pao. Acta Entomologica Sinica
Kungl Krigsvetenskapsakad T — Kungliga Krigsvetenskapsakademiens Tidskrift
Kun O Antik — Kunst- og Antikvitetsarbogen
KUNSA — Kunststoffe. Organ der Deutschen Kunststoff-Fachverbaende
Kunst-Ber — Kunststoff-Berater
Kunstbl Jugend — Kunstblatt der Jugend
Kunstchr — Kunstchronik
Kunstduenger Leim Ind — Kunstduenger- und Leim-Industrie
Kunstharze — Kunstharze und Andere Plastische Massen
Kunstharz Nachr — Kunstharz-Nachrichten
Kunst Mus — Kunst og Museum
Kunstof Rub — Kunststof en Rubber
Kunst Or — Kunst des Orients
Kunst Pressst — Kunst- und Pressstoffe
Kunstst — Kunststoffe
Kunstst Bau — Kunststoffe im Bau
Kunstst Ber — Kunststoff-Berichte
Kunstst-Berat — Kunststoff-Berater
Kunstst-Berat Rundsch Tech — Kunststoff-Berater Vereinigt mit Kunststoff-Rundschau und Kunststoff-Technik
Kunstst Fortschrittsber — Kunststoffe Fortschrittsberichte
Kunstst Ger Plast — Kunststoffe. German Plastics
Kunstst Gummi — Kunststoff und Gummi
Kunstst J — Kunststoff Journal
Kunstst Med — Kunststoffe in der Medizin
Kunstoff — Kunststoffe. German Plastics, Including Kunststoffe im Bau
Kunststoff Ber — Kunststoff-Berichte
Kunststoffberat Rundsch Tech — Kunststoffberater, Rundschau, und Technik
Kunststoffe Plast — Kunststoffe-Plastics
Kunststoff Prax — Kunststoff-Praxis
Kunststoff Rdsch — Kunststoff-Rundschau
Kunststoff Tech — Kunststoff-Technik
Kunststofftech Kolloq IKV Aachen Ber — Kunststofftechnisches Kolloquium des IKV (Institut fuer Kunststoffverarbeitung an der Rheinisch-Westfaelischen Technischen Hochschule Aachen) in Aachen. Berichte
Kunststofftech Kunststoffanwend — Kunststofftechnik und Kunststoffanwendung
Kunstst-Plast — Kunststoffe-Plastics
Kunst Plast Munich — Kunststoffe-Plasticos (Munich)
Kunstst Plast Solothurn Switz — Kunststoffe-Plastics (Solothurn, Switzerland)
Kunstst Rubber — Kunststof en Rubber
Kunstst-Rundsch — Kunststoff-Rundschau
Kunst Tech Kunstst Anwend — Kunststoff-Technik und Kunststoff-Anwendung
Kunstst Verarb — Kunststoff-Verarbeitung
Kunst u Antiq — Kunst und Antiquaria
Kunst u Lit — Kunst und Literatur. Sowjetwissenschaft Zeitschrift zur Verbreitung Sowjetischer Erfahrungen
Kun Vitt Hist & Ant Akad Hand — Kungliga Vitterhets. Historie och Antikvitets Akademins Handlingar
KUO — Keeping Up with Orff Schulwerk in the Clasroom
Ku O F — Kultur og Folkeminder
Kuopion Maanviljelys Vuosik — Kuopion Maanviljelysseuran Vuosikirja
Ku Or — Kunst des Orients
KUP — Kunststoffe-Plastics; Schweizerische Fachzeitschrift fuer Herstellung, Verarbeitung, und Anwendung von Kunststoffen
Kupfer Mitt — Kupfer-Mitteilungen
Kupf Spinne — Kupfer-Spinne

KUPLA — Kunststoffe-Plastics

KURAAV — Annual Reports. Research Reactor Institute. Kyoto University

Kurator Tech Landwirt Flugschr — Kuratorium fuer Technik in der Landwirtschaft. Flugschrift

Kurber Erfolge Phys Diat Heilfakt — Kurberichte ueber Erfolge der Physikalisch-diaetetischen Heilfaktoren

Kureha Text Rev — Kureha Textile Review

Kurgan Skh Inst Sb Nauchn Rab — Kurganskii Sel'skokhozyaistvennyi Institut. Sbornik Nauchnykh Rabot

KurhessMitt — Mitteilungen aus der Rechtspflege im Gebiete des Ehemaligen Kurfuerstentums Hessen

Kurme Med J — Kurme Medical Journal

Kurort Fizioter — Kurortologiya i Fizioterapiya

Kurortol Fizioter — Kurortologiya i Fizioterapiya

Kurortol Fizioter Tbilisi — Kurortologiya i Fizioterapiya (Tbilisi)

Kurortol Reumatol Klausimai — Kurortologijos ir Reumatologijos Klausimai

Kurortol Uurim — Kurortoloogilised Uurimused

Kuroshi 4 (Four) Proc Symp Coop Stud Kuroshio Adjacent Reg — Kuroshi 4 (Four). Proceedings. Symposium for the Co-operative Study of the Kuroshio and Adjacent Regions

Kursk Gos Med Inst Sb Tr — Kurskii Gosudarstvennyi Meditsinskii Institut. Sbornik Trudov

Kursk Gos Pedagog Inst Nauchn Tr — Kurskii Gosudarstvennyi Pedagogicheskii Institut. Nauchnye Trudy

Kursk Gos Ped Inst Ucen Zap — Kurskii Gosudarstvennyi Pedagogiceskii Institut. Ucenye Zapiski

Kursk Sadov Plodov Ogorod — Kurskoe Sadovodstvo i Plodovodstvo i Ogorodnichestvo

Kurtrie Jb — Kurtrierisches Jahrbuch

Kurtrier Jb — Kurtrierisches Jahrbuch

Kurt Weill N — Kurt Weill Newsletter

KURUA — Kunststoff-Rundschau

Kuruk Univ Res J — Kurukshetra University Research Journal. Aris and Humanities

Kurume Med J — Kurume Medical Journal

Kurume Univ J — Kurume University. Journal

Kurzausz Schriftt EisenbWes — Kurzauszuege aus dem Schrifttum fuer das Eisenbahnwesen

Kurzausz Schriftt WerkstDienst — Kurzauszuege aus dem Schrifttum fuer den Werkstattendienst

Kurze Mitt Fischbiol Abt Max Planck Inst Meeresbiol Wilhelmsh — Kurze Mitteilungen aus der Fischereibiologischen Abteilung des Max-Planck-Instituts fuer Meeresbiologie in Wilhelmshaven

Kurze Mitt Inst FischBiol Univ Hamb — Kurze Mitteilungen aus dem Institut fuer Fischereibiologie der Universitaet Hamburg

Kurze Uebers Verh Allg Schweiz Ges Gesammten Naturwiss — Kurze Uebersicht der Verhandlungen der Allgemeinen Schweizerischen Gesellschaftfuer die Gesammten Naturwissenschaften

Kurzfassungen Vortr Galvanotech Symp — Kurzfassungen der Vortraege des Galvanotechnischen Symposiums

Kurzfassung Vortr OGEW DGMK Gemeinschaftstag — Kurzfassung der Vortraege der OGEW/DGMK Gemeinschaftstagung

Kurz Mber Preuss Aeronaut Obs — Kurzer Monatsbericht des Preussischen Aeronautischen Observatoriums in Lindenberg

Kurzmitt Dtsch Dendrol Ges — Kurzmitteilungen Deutsche Dendrologische Gesellschaft

Kurzmitt Eidg Anst Forst VersWes — Kurzmitteilungen. Eidgenossische Anstalt fuer das Forstliche Versuchswesen

Kurznachr Akad Wiss Goettingen — Kurznachrichten. Akademie der Wissenschaften in Goettingen

Kurznachr Akad Wiss Goettingen Sammelh — Kurznachrichten. Akademie der Wissenschaften in Goettingen. Sammelheft

KUSEB — Kuki Seijo

KuSh — Kuo-li Taiwan Shih-fan Ta-hsueeh Li-shih Hsueeh-pao

Kut — Kurtrierisches Jahrbuch

Kutoma Ja Paperlteoll Julk — Kutoma- ja Paperiteollisuuden Julkaisuja

Kuw — Kunstwerke aus den Berlinersammlungen

Kuwait Bull Mar Sci — Kuwait Bulletin of Marine Science

Kuwait Found Adv Sci Proc Ser — Kuwait Foundation for the Advancement of Sciences Proceedings Series

Kuwait Inst Sci Res Annu Res Rep — Kuwait Institute for Scientific Research. Annual Research Report

Kuwait J Sci Eng — Kuwait Journal of Science and Engineering

Kuwait J Sci Engrg — Kuwait Journal of Science and Engineering. An International Journal of Kuwait University

Kuwait Med Assoc J — Kuwait Medical Association. Journal

Ku Welt Berl Mus — Kunst der Welt in den Berliner Museen

Kuz — Kuznica

Kuzbasskii Politekh Inst Sb Nauchn Tr — Kuzbasskii Politekhnicheskii Institut. Sbornik Nauchnykh Trudov

Kuznechno-Shtampov — Kuznechno-Shtampovochnoe Proizvodstvo

Kuznechno Shtampovochnoe Proizvod — Kuznechno-Shtampovochnoe Proizvodstvo

Kuznechno Shtamp Proizv — Kuznechno-Shtampovochnoe Proizvodstvo

KV — General History and Collection of Voyages and Travels, Arranged in Systematic Order. R. Kerr

KV — Kalevalaseuran Vuosikirja

KV — Kirkens Verden

KV — Koloniaal Verslag

KV — Korte Verklaring der Heilige Schrift

KV — Untersuchungen zu den Kertschen Vasen

Kvan Elektr — Kvantovaya Elektronika

Kvant — Akademija Nauk SSSR i Akademija Pedagogicesikh Nauk SSSR. Kvant

Kvantovaya Ehlektron — Kvantovaya Ehlektronika

Kvantovaya Elektron (Kiev) — Kvantovaya Elektronika (Kiev)

Kvantovaya Elektron (Moskva) — Kvantovaya Elektronika (Moskva)

Kvartalsskrift (Stockh) — Kvartalsskrift (Stockholm)

Kvart Byull Tbilis Seism Sta — Kvartal'nyi Byulleten' Tbilisskoi Seismicheskoi Stantsii

Kvart Zh Istor Nauki Tekh Warsaw — Kvartal'nyi Zhurnal Istorii Nauki i Tekhniki (Warsaw)

Kvasny Prum — Kvasny Prumysl

KVATL — Koninklijke Vlaamse Academie voor Taal- en Letterkunde

KVAWJ — Korrespondenzblatt des Vereins zur Gruendung und Erhaltung einer Akademie fuer die Wissenschaft des Judentums

KVBMAS — Biologiske Meddelelser Kongelige Danske Videnskabernes Selskab

KVCV Tijd — KVCV (Koninklijke Vlaamse Chemische Vereniging) Tijdingen. Tijdschrift voor Chemie-Informatie. Onderwijs, Onderzoek en Industrie

K Ver Indisch Inst Afd Trop Hyg Mededed — Koninklijke Vereniging Indisch Instituut, Afdeling Tropische Hygiene. Mededeling

K Ver Kolon Inst Afd Handelsmus Meded — Koninklijke Vereeniging Koloniaal Instituut, Afdeeling Handelsmuseum. Mededeling

K Ver Kolon Inst Afd Trop Hyg Meded — Koninklijke Vereeniging Koloniaal Instituut. Afdeeling Tropische Hygiene. Mededeeling

K Vetensk Akad Handl — Kungliga Vetenskaps-Akademiens. Handlingar

K Vetensk Akad N Handl (Stockholm) — Kungliga Vetenskaps-Akademiens. Nya Handlingar (Stockholm)

K Vetenskapsakad Nobelinst Medd — Kungliga Vetenskapsakademien. Nobelinstitut. Meddelanden

K Vetenskapssamh Uppsala Arsb — Kungliga Vetenskapssamhaellets i Uppsala. Arsbok

K VetenskSamh Upps Arsb — Kungliga Vetenskapssamhallets i Uppsala Arsbok

K VetenskSamh Upps Handl — Kungliga Vetenskapssamhallets i Uppsala Handlingar

K Vetensk-Soc Arsb — Kungliga Vetenskaps-Societetens. Arsbok

K VetHogsk Beratt — Kungliga Veterinarhogskolans Berattelse

K Vet-Landbohojsk Arsskr — Kongelige Veterinaer-og Landbohojskole Arsskrift

K Vet Landbohojsk Inst Sterilitetsforsk Arsberet — Kongelige Veterinaer og Landbohojskole Institut foer Sterilitetsforskning Arsberetning

K Vet Og Landbohoisk — Kongelige Veterinaer- og Landbohoiskoles Aarsskrift

KVG — Kritische Vierteljahresschrift fuer Gesetzgebung

KVGR — Kritische Vierteljahresschrift fuer Gesetzgebung und Rechtswissenschaft

KVHAAH — Kungliga Vitterhets Historie och Antikvitets Akademiens. Handlingar

KVHS — Korte Verklaring der Heilige Schrift

KVII — Koninklijke Vereeniging Indisch Instituut. Mededeling

KVjhS — Koelner Vierteljahrshefte fuer Sozialwissenschaft

KVJS — Kritische Vierteljahresschrift

KVKEK — Kroniek van Kunst en Kultur

KVL — Kirchliche Verwaltungslehre

K Vlaam Acad Wet Lett Schone Kunsten Belg Jaarb — Koninklijke Vlaamse Academie voor Wetenschappen. Letteren en Schone Kunsten vanBelgie. Jaarboek

K Vlaam Acad Wet Lett Schone Kunsten Belg Versl Meded — Koninklijke Vlaamsche Academie voor Wetenschappen. Letteren en Schone Kunsten van Belgie. Verslagen en Mededeelingen

K Vlaam Chem Ver Tijd — Koninklijke Vlaamse Chemische Vereniging Tijdingen

KVMFA — Kongelige Danske Videnskabernes Selskab. Matematisk-Fysisk Skrifter

KVMW — Kontakblad van de Historische Vereniging van het Land van Maas en Waal

KVNM — Tijdschrift van de Koninklijke Vereniging voor Nederlandse Muziekgeschiedenis

KVNS — Korrespondenzblatt. Verein fuer Niederdeutsche Sprachforschung

Kv o S — Kvinden og Samfundet

KVPRA — Kvasny Prumysl

KVR — Kleine Vandenhoeck-Reihe

KVS — Kabelvisie Onafhankelijk Tijdschrift voor Kabel en Lokale Televisie

KVS — Koelner Vierteljahrshefte fuer Sozioogie

KVSW — Koelner Vierteljahrshefte fuer Sozialwissenschaften

KVSWS — Koelner Vierteljahrshefte fuer Sozialwissenschaften. Soziologische Hefte

KVSWSP — Koelner Vierteljahrshefte fuer Sozialwissenschaften. Soziolpolitische Hefte

KW — Kirchen der Welt

KW — Koloniaal Weekblad

Kwang Chi Med J — Kwang Chi Medical Journal

Kwangju Teach Coll Sci Educ Cent Rev — Kwangju Teachers College. Science Education Center. Review

Kwangsi Agric — Kwangsi Agriculture/Kuang Hsi Nung Yeh

Kwansei Gakuin Sociol Dept Stud — Kwansei Gakuin University. Sociology Department Studies

Kwansei Gakuin U Ann Stud — Kwansei Gakuin University. Annual Studies

Kwansei Gakuin Univ Annu Stud — Kwansei Gakuin University. Annual Studies

Kwansei Gakuin Univ Annu Stud — Kwansei Gakuin University Annual Studies

Kwansei Gakuin Univ Nat Sci Rev — Kwansei Gakuin Univesity Natural Sciences Review

Kwar Hist Kul Mat — Kwartalnik Historii Kultury Materialnej

Kwartalnik Geol — Kwartalnik Geologiczny

Kwartalnik Hist — Kwartalnik Historyczny

Kwart Archit & Urb — Kwartalnik Architektury i Urbanistyk

Kwart Biul Inf Minist Osw Spraw Ochr Przyr — Kwartalny Biuletyn Informacyjny. Ministerstwo Oswiaty do Spraw Ochrony Przyrody

Kwart Geol — Kwartalnik Geologiczny

Kwart Geol (Pol Inst Geol) — Kwartalnik Geologiczny (Poland. Instytut Geologiczny)

Kwart Hist Kul Mater — Kwartalnik Historii Kultury Materialnej

Kwart Hist Kult — Kwartalnik Historii Kultury

Kwart Hist Kult Mat — Kwartalnik Historii Kultury Materialnej

Kwart Hist Kult Mater — Kwartalnik Historii Kultury Materialnej

Kwart Hist Nauki i Tech — Kwartalnik Historii Nauki i Techniki

Kwart Hist Nauki Tech — Kwartalnik Historii Nauki i Techniki

Kwart Hist Nauk Tech — Kwartalnik Historii Nauki i Techniki

Kwart Opolski — Kwartalnik Opolski
Kwart Stomat — Kwartalnik Stomatologiczny
KwartVersl RubbSticht — Kwartaalverslag. Rubberstichting
KWDR — Kwandur Newsletter. Council for Yukon Indians
KWGEA — Kwartalnik Geologiczny
KwH — Kwartalnik Historyczny
KWHCA — Kwangsan Hakhoe Chi
Kw Hist — Kwartalnik Historyczny
Kw Kl — Kwartalnik Klasyczny
KWN — Kurt Weill Newsletter
KwO — Kwartalnik Opolski
KWR — Kerk en Wereld Reeks
KWT — Kuwait Times
KWURA — KWU [*Kraftwerk Union AG, Muehlheim*] Report
KWU Rep — KWU [*Kraftwerk Union AG, Muehlheim*] Report
KWZ — Korrespondenzblatt der Westdeutschen Zeitschrift fuer Geschichte und Kunst
KY — Kentucky Reports
KY Acts — Kentucky Acts
KY Admin Reg — Kentucky Administrative Register
KY Admin Regs — Kentucky Administrative Regulations Service
KY Ag Exp — Kentucky. Agricultural Experiment Station. Publications
KY Agri-Bus Q — Kentucky Agri-Business Quarterly
KY AgriBus Spotlight — Kentucky Agri-Business Spotlight
KY Agric Exp Stn Annu Rep — Kentucky. Agricultural Experiment Station. Annual Report
KY Agric Exp Stn Bull — Kentucky. Agricultural Experiment Station. Bulletin
KY Agric Exp Stn Misc Pubs — Kentucky. Agricultural Experiment Station. Miscellaneous Publications
KY Agric Exp Stn Prog Rep — Kentucky. Agricultural Experiment Station. Progress Report
KY Agric Exp Stn Regul Bull — Kentucky. Agricultural Experiment Station. Regulatory Bulletin
Ky Agric Exp Stn Regul Ser Bull — Kentucky. Agricultural Experiment Station. Regulatory Series. Bulletin
KY Agric Exp Stn Results Res — Kentucky. Agricultural Experiment Station. Results of Research
KY Agric Ext Serv Leafl — Kentucky. Agricultural Extension Service. Leaflet
Kyb — Kybernetik
Kyb — Kybernetika
KY Bench and B — Kentucky Bench and Bar
Kybernetika Suppl — Kybernetika. Supplement
Kybernet Informationsverarbeitung — Kybernetik. Informationsverarbeitung
KY B J — Kentucky Bar Journal
KYBNA — Kybernetika
KY Bus Led — Kentucky Business Ledger
KyC — Kypriaka Chronika
Ky Coal J — Kentucky Coal Journal
KYCSA — K'uang Yeh Chi Shu
KY Dent J — Kentucky Dental Journal
KY Dep Fish Wildl Resour Fish Bull — Kentucky. Department of Fish and Wildlife Resources. Fisheries Bulletin
KY Dep Mines Miner Geol Div Bull — Kentucky. Department of Mines and Minerals. Geological Division. Bulletin
KY Dep Mines Miner Geol Div Ser 8 Bull — Kentucky. Department of Mines and Minerals. Geological Division. Series 8. Bulletin
KY Dep Mines Resour Geol Div Bull — Kentucky. Department of Mines and Resources. Geological Division. Bulletin
KYDKAJ — Annual Report. Kyoritsu College of Pharmacy
Ky Drugg — Kentucky Druggist
KY Economy — Kentucky Economy
Ky Engr — Kentucky Engineer
KY Farm Home Sci — Kentucky Farm and Home Science
Ky Fmg — Kentucky Farming
Ky Fm Home Sci — Kentucky Farm and Home Science
Ky Fmr Breed — Kentucky Farmer and Breeder
KY Folkl Rec — Kentucky Folklore Record
KY Folk Rec — Kentucky Folklore Record
KY Geol Surv Bull — Kentucky. Geological Survey. Bulletin
KY Geol Surv Cy Rep — Kentucky. Geological Survey. County Report
KY Geol Survey Bull Inf Circ Rept Inv Special Pub — Kentucky. Geological Survey. Bulletin. Information Circular. Report of Investigations. Special Publication
KY Geol Surv Inf Circ — Kentucky. Geological Survey. Information Circular
KY Geol Surv Rep Invest — Kentucky. Geological Survey. Report of Investigations
KY Geol Surv Ser 9 Bull — Kentucky. Geological Survey. Series 9. Bulletin
KY Geol Surv Ser 9 Rep Invest — Kentucky. Geological Survey. Series 9. Report of Investigation
KY Geol Surv Ser 9 Spec Publ — Kentucky. Geological Survey. Series 9. Special Publication
KY Geol Surv Ser 10 Cty Rep — Kentucky. Geological Survey. Series 10. County Report
KY Geol Surv Ser 10 Inf Circ — Kentucky. Geological Survey. Series 10. Information Circular
KY Geol Surv Ser 10 Rep Invest — Kentucky. Geological Survey. Series 10. Report of Investigation
Ky Geol Surv Spec Publ — Kentucky. Geological Survey. Special Publication
Ky Geol Surv Thesis Ser — Kentucky. Geological Survey. Thesis Series
KY G S Rp Prog B — Kentucky. Geological Survey. Report of Progress. Bulletin
Ky Highw — Kentucky Highways
KY Hist Soc Reg — Kentucky Historical Society. Register
KYHS — Kentucky Historical Society. Register

Kyk — Kyklos
Kyklos Int Z Sozialwiss Int Rev Soc Sci — Kyklos. Internationale Zeitschrift fuer Sozialwissenschaften. Revue International des Sciences Sociales. International Review for Social Sciences
KY Law J — Kentucky Law Journal
KY Lib Assn Bull — Kentucky Library Association. Bulletin
KY Libr Ass Bull — Kentucky Library Association. Bulletin
KY L J — Kentucky Law Journal
KY L Rev — Kentucky Law Review
KY L Rptr — Kentucky Law Reporter
Kyltek Tidskr — Kylteknisk Tidskrift
KY Med J — Kentucky Medical Journal
KY Nat Preserv Comm Tech Rep — Kentucky. Nature Preserves Commission. Technical Report
Kynoch J — Kynoch Journal
Kynoch J Tech Res — Kynoch Journal of Technical Research
Kynol Handb — Kyoto Med J
Kynol Rdsch — Kynologische Rundschau
Kynol Wschr — Kynologische Wochenschrift
KY Nurse — Kentucky Nurse
KY Nurses Assoc Newsl — Kentucky Nurses' Association. Newsletter
KY Nurses Assoc News Lett — Kentucky Nurses' Association. Newsletter
Kyo — Kyoto University. Economic Review
KY Op — Kentucky Opinions
Kyorin J Med Med Technol — Kyorin Journal of Medicine and Medical Technology
Kyoto Daigaku Nogaku-Bu Enshurin Hokoku Bull Kyoto Univ For — Kyoto Daigaku Nogaku-Bu Enshurin Hokoku/Bulletin. Kyoto University Forests
Kyoto N Mus Bull — Kyoto National Museum Bulletin
Kyoto Univ Afr Stud — Kyoto University. African Studies
Kyoto Univ Econ R — Kyoto University. Economic Review
Kyoto Univ Fac Sci Mem Ser Geol Mineral — Kyoto University. Faculty of Science. Memoirs. Series of Geology and Mineralogy
Kyoto Univ Geophys Res Stn Rep — Kyoto University. Geophysical Research Station. Reports
Kyoto Univ Inst Chem Res Annu Rep — Kyoto University. Institute for Chemical Research. Annual Report
Kypr Spud — Kypriakai Spoudai
Kyp Spoudai — Kypriakai Spoudai
KYR — Kentucky Review
KY Reg — Kentucky State Historical Society. Register
KY Rev — Kentucky Review
KY Rev Stat & R Serv (Baldwin) — Kentucky Revised Statutes and Rules Service (Baldwin)
KY Rev Stat Ann (Baldwin) — Baldwin's Official Edition. Kentucky Revised Statutes, Annotated
KY Rev Stat Ann (Michie/Bobbs-Merrill) — Kentucky Revised Statutes, Annotated. Official Edition(Michie/Bobbs-Merrill)
Kyrkohist Arsskr — Kyrkohistorisk Arsskrift
KY Roman Q — Kentucky Romance Quarterly
KyS — Kypriakai Spoudai
KY SBJ — Kentucky State Bar Journal
KY Sch J — Kentucky School Journal
Ky State Hist Soc Reg — Kentucky State Historical Society. Register
KY St BJ — Kentucky State Bar Journal
Kyung Hee Univ Orient Med J — Kyung Hee University. Oriental Medical Journal
Kyungpook Educ Forum — Kyungpook Education Forum
Kyungpook Math J — Kyungpook Mathematical Journal
Kyungpook Univ Med J — Kyungpook University. Medical Journal
KY Univ Coll Agric Coop Ext Serv Rep — Kentucky. University. College of Agriculture. Cooperative Extension Service. Report
KY Univ Office Res Eng Services Bull — Kentucky University. Office of Research and Engineering Services. Bulletin
KY Univ Off Res Eng Serv Bull — Kentucky University. Office of Research and Engineering Services. Bulletin
Kyush J Med Sci — Kyushu Journal of Medical Science
Kyushu Agric Res — Kyushu Agricultural Research
Kyushu Agr Res — Kyushu Agricultural Research
Kyushu J Math — Kyushu Journal of Mathematics
Kyushu J Med Sci — Kyushu Journal of Medical Science
Kyushu Mem Med Sci — Kyushu Memoirs of Medical Sciences
Kyushu Univ Coll Gen Educ Rep Earth Sci — Kyushu University. College of General Education. Reports on Earth Science
Kyushu Univ Dep Geol Sci Rep — Kyushu University. Department of Geology. Science Reports
Kyushu Univ Fac Agr Sci Bull — Kyushu University. Faculty of Agriculture. Science Bulletin
Kyushu Univ Fac Sci Mem Ser D — Kyushu University. Faculty of Science. Memoirs. Series D. Geology
Kyushu Univ Faculty Sci Mem — Kyushu University. Faculty of Science. Memoirs
Kyushu Univ Rep Res Inst Appl Mech — Kyushu University. Reports of Research Institute for Applied Mechanics
KY Warbler — Kentucky Warbler
KZ — Karakulevodstvo i Zverovodstvo
KZ — Kirchliche Zeitschrift
KZ — Kulturny Zivot
KZAIA — Kogyo Zairyo
KZATV — Kartellzeitung Akademisch-Theologischer Vereine
KZGKA — Kinzoku Zairyo Gijutsu Kenkyusho Kenkyu Hokoku
KZMTLG — Koninklijke Zuidnederlandse Maatschappij voor Taal- en Letterkunde en Geschiedenis
KZS — Koelner Zeitschrift fuer Soziologie
KZSS — Koelner Zeitschrift fuer Soziologie und Sozial-Psychologie
KZZPA — Kolloid-Zeitschrift und Zeitschrift fuer Polymere**

L

L — Lancet
L — Language
L — Latomus
L — Leodium
L — Leonardo
L — Listener
L — Lusa
LA — Language Arts
La — Laographia
La — Laos
LA — Lastenausgleich
LA — Le Arti
La — Letteratura
LA — Lexikon der Aegyptologie
LA — Lincoln Annex
LA — Linguistica Antverpiensia
LA — Linguistische Arbeiten
LA — Lisan Al-'Arabi
LA — Literarische Anzeiger
LA — Literaturanzeiger fuer das Allgemeine Wissenschaftliche Schrifttum
LA — Living Age
LA — Loteria
La — Louisiana Reports
La A — Landarzt
LaA — Latin American Research Review
LAA — Latinoamericana (Argentina)
La Aa — Ladelund Elevforenings Aarskrift
LAAA — Liverpool Annuals of Archaeology and Anthropology
La Acad Sci Proc — Louisiana Academy of Sciences. Proceedings
La Acts — State of Louisiana. Acts of the Legislature
La Admin Code — Louisiana Administrative Code
LA Ag Exp — Louisiana. Agricultural Experiment Station. Publications
La Agr — Louisiana Agriculture
LA Agric — Louisiana Agriculture
LA Agric Exp Stn Bull — Louisiana. Agricultural Experiment Station. Bulletin
La Agric La Agric Exp Stn — Louisiana Agriculture. Louisiana Agricultural Experiment Station
L Aalst — Land van Aalst
LAANAQ — Ecole Superieure d'Agriculture de la Suede. Annales
La Ann — Louisiana Annual Reports
LAAP — (La) Antigua (Panama)
La App — Louisiana Courts of Appeal Reports
LAA Univ & Coll Lib Sec News — Library Association of Australia. University and College Libraries Section. News Sheet
LAA Univ Lib Sec News — Library Association of Australia. University Libraries Section. News Sheet
LAA Univ Lib Sec News Sheet — Library Association of Australia. University Libraries Section. News Sheet
LAAW — Lotus. Afro-Asian Writings
La B — La Bas
Lab — Labeo. Rassegna di Diritto Romano
Lab — Laboratorio
Lab — Labyrinthe
LAB — Latin America in Books
LAB — Literaturny Azerbaidzhan (Baku)
LAB — Los Angeles Bar Bulletin
Lab 2000 Duemila — Laboratorio 2000 Duemila
Lab and Emp — Labour and Employment Gazette
Lab and Empl — Labour and Employment Gazette
Lab and Empl L — Labor and Employment Law
Lab Anim — Lab Animal
Lab Anim — Laboratory Animals
Lab Anim Care — Laboratory Animal Care
Lab Anim Drug Test Symp Int Comm Lab Anim — Laboratory Animal in Drug Testing. Symposium. International Committee on Laboratory Animals
Lab Anim Handb — Laboratory Animal Handbooks
Lab Anim Sc — Laboratory Animal Science
Lab Anim Sci — Laboratory Animal Science
Lab Anim Study Reprod Symp Int Comm Lab Anim — Laboratory Animal in the Study of Reproduction. Symposium. International Committee on Laboratory Animals
Lab Anim Symp — Laboratory Animal Symposia
Lab Arb BNA — Labor Arbitration Reports. Bureau of National Affairs
LA Bar J — Louisiana Bar Journal
Lab Autom Inf Manage — Laboratory Automation and Information Management

LABB — Los Angeles Bar Bulletin
Lab Biochim Nutr Publ Univ Cathol Louvain Fac Sci Agron — Laboratoire de Biochimie de la Nutrition. Publication. Universite Catholique deLouvain. Faculte des Sciences Agronomiques
Lab Biogeokhim Pustyn Tr — Laboratoriya Biogeokhimii Pustyn. Trudy
Lab-Bl — Laboratoriums-Blaetter
LAB Bull — Los Angeles Bar Bulletin
Lab Cent Fabr Peint Vernis Encres Impr Bull Lab Prof — Laboratoire Central des Fabricants de Peintures, Vernis, et Encresd'Imprimerie. Bulletin du Laboratoire Professionnel
Lab Cent Ponts Chaussees Bull Liaison Lab Ponts Chaussees — Laboratoire Central des Ponts et Chaussees. Bulletin de Liaison des Laboratoires des Ponts et Chaussees
Lab Cent Ponts Chaussees Note Inf Tech — Laboratoire Central des Ponts et Chaussees. Note d'Information Technique
Lab Cent Ponts Chaussees Rapp Rech — Laboratoire Central des Ponts et Chaussees. Rapport de Recherche
Lab Cent Ponts Chaussees Rapp Rech LPC — Laboratoire Central des Ponts et Chaussees. Rapport de Recherche LPC
Lab Central Ensayo Mater Constr Madrid Publ — Laboratorio Central de Ensayo de Materiales de Construccion. Madrid. Publicacion
Lab Clin — Laboratorio Clinico
Lab Clin Stress Res Karolinska Inst Rep — Laboratory for Clinical Stress Research. Karolinska Institute. Reports
Lab Clin Stress Res Karolinska Sjukhuset Rep — Laboratory for Clinical Stress Research. Karolinska Sjukhuset. Reports
LABDA — Laboratornoe Delo
Lab Del — Laboratornoe Delo
Lab Delo — Laboratornoe Delo
Labdev J Sci & Technol A — Labdev Journal of Science and Technology. Part A. Physical Sciences
Labdev J Sci & Technol B — Labdev Journal of Science and Technology. Part B. Life Sciences
Labdev J Sci Technol — Labdev Journal of Science and Technology
Labdev J Sci Technol Part B Life Sci — Labdev Journal of Science and Technology. Part B. Life Sciences
Labdev J Sci Tech Part A — Labdev Journal of Science and Technology. Part A. Physical Sciences
Labdev Part A — Labdev Journal of Science and Technology. Part A. Physical Sciences
Labdev Part B — Labdev Journal of Science and Technology. Part B. Life Sciences
Lab Diagn — Laboratoriumi Diagnosztika
Lab Diagn Med — Laboratorio nella Diagnosi Medica
Lab Dig — Laboratory Digest
Labelled Compd Part AB — Labelled Comppounds. Part A-B
Lab Ensayo Mater Invest Tecnol An — Laboratorio de Ensayo de Materiales e Investigaciones Tecnologicas. Anales
Lab Ensayo Mater Invest Tecnol Prov Buenos Aires Publ Ser 1 — Laboratorio de Ensayo de Materiales e Investigaciones Tecnologicas dela Provincia de Buenos Aires. Publicaciones. Serie 1. Memorias
Lab Ensayo Mater Invest Tecnol Prov Buenos Aires Publ Ser 2 — Laboratorio de Ensayo de Materiales e Investigaciones Tecnologicas dela Provincia de Buenos Aires. Publicaciones. Serie 2
Lab Ensayo Mater Invest Tecnol Prov Buenos Aires Publ Ser 4 — Laboratorio de Ensayo de Materiales e Investigaciones Tecnologicas dela Provincia de Buenos Aires. Publicaciones. Serie 4. Informes Generales
Lab Ens Mater Esc Polytech (Sao Paulo) Bol — Laboratorio de Ensaio de Materiales. Escola Polytechnica (Sao Paulo).Boletim
Lab Equip Dig — Laboratory Equipment Digest
Lab Etude Controle Environ Sider Publ P — Laboratoire d'Etude et de Controle de l'Environnement Siderurgique. Publication P
Lab Etude Controle Environ Sider Rapp Exter RE — Laboratoire d'Etude et de Controle de l'Environnement Siderurgique. Rapport Exterieur RE
Lab Fed Essai Mater Inst Rech Ind Genie Civ Arts Metiers — Laboratoire Federal d'Essai des Materiaux et Institut de Recherches.Industrie, Genie Civil, Arts et Metiers
Lab For Prod Chem Rep Ser C — Laboratory of Forest Products Chemistry. Reports. Series C
Lab Gaz — Labour Gazette
Lab Gov Chem (GB) Misc Rep — Laboratory of the Government Chemist (Great Britain). Miscellaneous Report
Lab Gov Chem (GB) Occas Pap — Laboratory of the Government Chemist (Great Britain). Occasional Paper
L Abh — Abhandlungen. Saechsische Gesellschaft der Wissenschaften zu Leipzig
Lab Hist — Labor History
Lab Hist — Labour History

Lab Ind — Labour and Industry
Lab Inf Rec — Labour Information Record
Lab Instrum — Lab Instrumenten
Lab Instrum Tech Ser — Laboratory Instrumentation and Techniques Series
Lab Inv — Laboratory Investigation
Lab Invest — Laboratory Investigation
LABJ — Los Angeles Bar Journal
LA B J — Louisiana Bar Journal
Lab J Australas — Laboratory Journal of Australasia
LABLD — Laboratoriums-Blaetter
Lab L J — Labor Law Journal
Lab L Rep CCH — Labor Law Reports. Commerce Clearing House
LabM — Labour Monthly
LABMA — Laboratory Management
Lab Manage — Laboratory Management
Lab Manage Today — Lab Management Today
Lab Marit Dinard Bull — Laboratoire Maritime de Dinard. Bulletin
Lab Marit Mus Natl Hist Nat Arsenal Saint Servan — Laboratoire Maritime de Museum National d'Histoire Naturelles a l'Arsenal de Saint Servan
Lab Med — Laboratory Medicine
Lab Med — Labor Medica
Lab Med (Mainz) — Laboratoriums Medizin (Mainz)
Lab Med (Stuttgart) — Laboratoire Medical (Stuttgart)
Lab Microcomput — Laboratory Microcomputer
Lab Mo — Labour Monthly
Lab N — Labor News
Lab Nac Eng Civ (Port) Mem — Laboratorio Nacional de Engenharia Civil (Portugal). Memoria
Lab Nac Fom Ind Tecnol LANFI — Laboratorios Nacionales de Fomento Industrial Tecnologia LANFI
Labo Pharma Probl Tech — Labo-Pharma. Problemes et Techniques
Laborat et Museum — Laboratorium et Museum et Clinicum
Laboratoriumsbl Med Diagn E Behring — Laboratoriumsblaetter fuer die Medizinische Diagnostik E. V. Behring
Labor His — Labor History
Labor Hist — Labor History
Labor Hyg Occup Dis (Engl Transl) — Labor Hygiene and Occupational Diseases (English Translation)
Labor Hyg Occup Dis (USSR) — Labor Hygiene and Occupational Diseases (USSR)
LABORINFO — Labour Information Database
Labor Law J — Labor Law Journal
Labor L J — Labor Law Journal
Labor Med — Labor-Medizin
Labor Nts — Labor Notes
LaborPraxis Med — LaborPraxis in der Medizin
Labor Tdy — Labor Today
Labour — Labour/Le Travailleur
Labour and Employment Gaz — Labour and Employment Gazette
Labour Gaz — Labour Gazette
Labour Hist — Labour History
Labour Mo — Labour Monthly
Labour Res — Labour Research
Labour Research Bul — Labour Research Bulletin
Labour Soc — Labour and Society
Labour Wkly — Labour Weekly
LABPA — Laboratory Practice
Lab Patol Clin — Laboratorio di Patologia Clinica
Lab Ponts Chaussees Bull Liaison — Laboratoire des Ponts et Chaussees. Bulletin de Liaison
Lab Ponts Chaussees Rapp Rech — Laboratoire des Ponts et Chaussees. Rapport de Recherche
Lab Pract — Laboratory Practice
Lab Practice — Laboratory Practice
Lab Prakt — Laboratornaya Praktika
Lab Prax — Laboratoriumspraxis
Lab Prod For Est (Can) Rapp — Laboratoire des Produits Forestiers de l'Est (Canada). Rapport
Lab Prod For Est Rapp Tech Forintek Can Corp — Laboratoire des Produits Forestiers de l'Est. Rapport Technique. Forintek Canada Corporation
Lab Prof Peint (Vitry Thiais Fr) Bull Liaison Lab — Laboratoire de la Profession des Peintures (Vitry-Thiais, France).Bulletin de Liaison du Laboratoire
Lab Psicol Sperim Un Roma — Contributi Psicologici del Laboratorio di Psicologia Sperimentale della Reale Universita di Roma
Lab Radiol Dozim Cesk Akad Ved Report — Laborator Radiologicke Dozimetrie. Ceskoslovenska Akademie Ved. Report
Lab Rech Controle Caoutch Rapp Tech — Laboratoire de Recherches et de Controle du Caoutchouc. RapportTechnique
Lab Rel and Empl News — Labor Relations and Employment News
Lab Rel Rep — Labor Relations Reporter
Lab Rel Rep BNA — Labor Relations Reporter. Bureau of National Affairs
Lab Rel Ybk — Labor Relations Yearbook
Lab Rep Franklin Inst — Laboratory Report. Franklin Institute
Lab Rep Transp Road Res Lab — Laboratory Report. Transport and Road Research Laboratory
Lab Res Methods Biol Med — Laboratory and Research Methods in Biology and Medicine
Labr Hist — Labour History
Lab Rob Autom — Latoratory Robotics and Automation
Lab Sci — Laboratorio Scientifico
Lab Sci Terre (St Jerome Marseille) Trav Ser B — Laboratoires des Sciences de la Terre (Saint Jerome, Marseille).Travaux. Serie B
LA Bsns Jl — Los Angeles Business Journal
Lab Soc — Labour and Society
LABSTAT — Labor Statistics

Lab Stat Bull — Labour Statistics Bulletin
Lab Tech — Laboratoire et Technique
Lab Tech Biochem Mol Biol — Laboratory Techniques in Biochemistry and Molecular Biology
Lab Tech Rep Div Mech Eng Natl Res Counc Can — Laboratory Technical Report. Division of Mechanical Engineering. National Research Council of Canada
Lab Tech Rep LTR UA Nat Res Counc Can Unsteady Aerodyn Lab — Laboratory Technical Report. LTR-UA National Research Council. Canada. UnsteadyAerodynamics Laboratory
Lab Tech Rep Nat Res Counc of Can Div Mech Eng — Laboratory Technical Report. National Research Council. Canada. Division of Mechanical Engineering
Lab Tuinbouwplantenteelt Landbouwhogesch Wageningen Publ — Laboratorium voor Tuinbouwplantenteelt Landbouwhogeschool Wageningen Publikatie
La Bur Sci Res Geol Bull — Louisiana. Bureau of Scientific Research. Geological Bulletin
La Bur Sci Res Stat Geol Bull — Louisiana. Bureau of Scientific Research and Statistics. GeologicalBulletin
LA Bus R — Louisiana Business Review
LA Bus Survey — Louisiana Business Survey
LA Bus Svy — Louisiana Business Survey
Lab Waste Treat Plant Bull — Laboratory Waste Treatment Plant Bulletin
Laby — Labyrinthe
LAC — Labour Appeal Cases
LAC — Labour Arbitration Cases
LAC — Letteratura ed Arte Contemporanea
LACB — Legal Aid Clearinghouse. Bulletin
LACHD — Liebigs Annalen der Chemie
LA Civ Code Ann (West) — West's Louisiana Civil Code, Annotated
Lac Jur — Lackawanna Jurist
Lacka Leg News — Lackawanna Legal News
Lackawanna Hist Soc Pub — Lackawanna Historical Society. Publications Series
Lackawanna Inst Pr — Lackawanna Institute of History and Science. Proceedings and Collections
Lack Farben Chem — Lack- und Farben-Chemie
Lack Farben Z — Lack- und Farben-Zeitschrift
Lack Jur — Lackawanna Jurist
Lack Jurist — Lackawanna Jurist
Lack Leg N — Lackawanna Legal News
Lack Leg News (PA) — Lackawanna Legal News
Lack LN — Lackawanna Legal News
LACM — Los Angeles County Museum. Bulletin of the Art Division
LA Code Civ Proc Ann (West) — West's Louisiana Code of Civil Procedure, Annotated
LA Code Crim Proc Ann (West) — West's Louisiana Code of Criminal Procedure, Annotated
LA Code Juv Proc Ann (West) — West's Louisiana Code of Juvenile Procedure, Annotated
La Conserv — Louisiana Conservationist
LACR — Latin America Commodities Report
La Cros Bsn — La Crosse City Business
LACSD — Los Angeles Council of Engineers and Scientists. Proceedings Series
LACT — Library of Anglo-Catholic Theology
Lactation Rev — Lactation Review
LACTW — Literarischer Anzeiger fuer Christliche Theologie und Wissenschaft Ueberhaupt
LACUNY J — LACUNY [*Library Association. City University of New York*] Journal
LA Daily J — Los Angeles Daily Journal
LADB — Laboratory Animal Data Bank
La Dep Conserv Bur Sci Res Miner Div Geol Bull — Louisiana. Department of Conservation. Bureau of Scientific Research.Minerals Division. Geological Bulletin
La Dep Conserv Bur Sci Res Stat Geol Bull — Louisiana. Department of Conservation. Bureau of Scientific Research and Statistics. Geological Bulletin
La Dep Conserv Geol Bull — Louisiana. Department of Conservation. Geological Bulletin
La Dep Conserv Geol Surv Dep Public Works Water Resour Pam — Louisiana. Department of Conservation. Geological Survey and Departmentof Public Works. Water Resources Pamphlet
LA Dep Conserv Geol Surv Miner Resour Bull — Louisiana. Department of Conservation. Geological Survey. Mineral Resources Bulletin
LA Dep Public Works Basic Rec Rep — Louisiana. Department of Public Works. Basic Records Report
LA Dep Public Works Tech Rep — Louisiana. Department of Public Works. Technical Report
LA Dep Public Works Water Resour Spec Rep — Louisiana. Department of Public Works. Water Resources Special Report
LA Dept Conserv Bienn Rept — Louisiana. Department of Conservation. Biennial Report
LA Dept Public Works Water Res Pamph — Louisiana. Department of Public Works. Water Resources Pamphlet
Ladewig Forschung Aktuell Reihe IV Inform Statist Math — Ladewig Forschung Aktuell. Reihe IV. Informatik, Statistik, Mathematik
Lad HJ — Ladies' Home Journal
Ladies' H J — Ladies' Home Journal
Ladies Home J — Ladies' Home Journal
Lad Schl G — Ladenschlussgesetz
LAe — Lexikon der Aegyptologie
LAEADA — Alabama. Agricultural Experiment Station. Leaflet (Auburn University)
LAECA — Land Economics
LA Economy — Louisiana Economy
LA Eng — Louisiana Engineer
LAER — Latin America Economic Report
LAeS — Leipziger Aegyptologische Studien

LAES Mimeo Ser La Agric Exp Stn — LAES Mimeo Series. Louisiana Agricultural Experiment Station
Laesn Allmogen Kronobergs Laen — Laesning foer Allmogen i Kronobergs Laen. Hushallssaellskapet
Laesp — Laesepaedagogen
LaF — Langue Francaise
LAF — Linzer Archaeologische Forschungen
LAFacTLima — Libro Anual. Facultad de Teologia. Universidad Pontificia y Civil
Lafayette Clin Stud Schizophr — Lafayette Clinic. Studies on Schizophrenia
LAFOA — Laser Focus
LA Free P — Los Angeles Free Press
LaG — La Giustizia
La G — Terre, Air, Mer. La Geographie
Lag Bull — Lag Bulletin
La Geog — La Geographie
LA Geol Surv Clay Resour Bull — Louisiana. Geological Survey. Clay Resources Bulletin
La Geol Surv Dep Public Works Water Resour Bull — Louisiana. Geological Survey and Department of Public Works. Water Reources Bulletin
LA Geol Surv Geol Bull — Louisiana. Geological Survey. Geological Bulletin
LA Geol Surv Miner Resour Bull — Louisiana. Geological Survey. Mineral Resources Bulletin
LA Geol Surv Water Resour Bull — Louisiana. Geological Survey and Department of Public Works. Water Resources Bulletin
LA Geol Surv Water Resour Pam — Louisiana. Geological Survey and Department of Public Works. Water Resources Pamphlet
Lagos Notes Rec — Lagos Notes and Records
Lagr L — Lagrange Lectures
LAGS — Linguistic Atlas of the Gulf States
La H — Labor History
LaH — Louisiana History
Lahey Clin Found Bull — Lahey Clinic Foundation. Bulletin
LA His Q — Louisiana Historical Quarterly
LA His S — Louisiana Historical Society. Publications
LA Hist — Louisiana History
LA Hist Quar — Louisiana Historical Quarterly
Lah LJ — Lahore Law Journal
Lah LT — Lahore Law Times
Lahore — All India Reporter, Lahore Series
Lahore L Times — Lahore Law Times
LAIL — Latin American Indian Literatures
LAINA — Laboratory Investigation
LAIS — Labor Arbitration Information System
Lait Belge — Laiterie Belge
Lait Ind Ferme — Laiterie et les Industries de la Ferme
Laits Prod Lait — Laits et Produits Latiers. Vache, Brebis, Chevre
LaK — Literatur als Kunst
LAKAA — Laekartidningen
Laka Ind — Laka Industrija
Lake Mich Water Qual Rep — Lake Michigan Water Quality Report
Lake Reservoir Manage — Lake and Reservoir Management
Lakeside — Lakeside Monthly
Lakes Lett — Lakes Letter
Lake Superior Min Inst Proc — Lake Superior Mining Institute. Proceedings
Lakokras Mater Ikh Primen — Lakokrasochnye Materialy i Ikh Primenenie
L Akt — Linguistik Aktuell
Lal — La Lettura
LAL — Latin America (London)
Lalahan Zootek Arastirma Enst Derg — Lalahan Zootekni Arastirma Enstitusu Dergisi
LA Law — Los Angeles Lawyer
LA Law Rev — Louisiana Law Review
LA Lib Assn Bull — Louisiana Library Association. Bulletin
LA Lib Bul — Louisiana Library Association. Bulletin
Lalit Kala Contemp — Lalit Kala Contemporary
LALJ — Latin American Indian Literature Journal
LA LJ — Louisiana Law Journal
LA Los Alamos Nat Lab — LA. Los Alamos National Laboratory
LALR — Latin American Literary Review
LA LR — Louisiana Law Review
LA L Rev — Louisiana Law Review
Lam — Lampas. Tijdschrift voor Nederlandse Classici
LaM — Langues Modernes
LAM — L'Approdo Musicale
LAM — Latino America. Anuario de Estudios Latinoamericanos (Mexico)
LAM — London's Australian Magazine
LAMAA — Lakokrasochnye Materialy i Ikh Primenenie
Lamb Arch — Lambard's Archeion
LAMEA — Laval Medical
LAMIE7 — Letters in Applied Microbiology
LAMM — Leitfaeden fuer Angewandte Mathematik und Mechanik
La Molina Peru Estac Exp Agric Inf — La Molina Peru Estacion Experimental Agricola. Informe
Lamont A Met — Annalen fuer Meteorologie, Erdmagnetismus, und Verwandte Gegenstaende. Lamont
Lamp — Lampetten
Lampang Rep — Lampang Reports
LAMR — Latin American Music Review
LAMSAS — Linguistic Atlas of the Middle and South Atlantic States
LAN — Language
LAN — Latin America Newsletters
LAN — Latin American Newsletters
LAN — Life Association News
Lanbau Vol — Lanbauforschung Volkenrode
LANC — Land. Newsletter. Lands Directorate. Environment Canada

LANCA — Lancet
Lancaster Co Hist Soc Pap — Lancaster County Historical Society. Papers
Lancette Fr — Lancette Francaise
Lanchow Univ J Nat Sci — Lanchow University Journal. Natural Sciences
Lanc L Rev — Lancaster Law Review
LANCS — Linguistic Atlas of the North Central States
Land — Land and Land News
Land — Land. Bureau of Land Management
Land — Landskap
Land A — Landarzt
Land & Water LR — Land and Water Law Review
Land & Water L Rev — Land and Water Law Review
Land App Ct Cas — Land Appeal Court Cases
Landarb — Landarbeit
Landarb Tech — Landarbeit und Technik
Land Arch — Landscape Architecture
L & B — Literature and Belief
Landbauforsch Voelkenrode — Landbauforschung Voelkenrode
Landbauforsch Voelkenrode Sonderh — Landbauforschung Voelkenrode. Sonderheft
L & B Bull — Daily Law and Bank Bulletin
Landb Courant — Landbouw Courant
Landbouwet S Afr Agroanimalia — Landbouwetenskap in Suid-Afrika. Agroanimalia
Landbouwet S Afr Agrochemophysica — Landbouwetenskap in Suid-Afrika. Agrochemophysica
Landbouwet S Afr Agroplantae — Landbouwetenskap in Suid-Afrika. Agroplantae
Landbouwet S Afr Phytophylactica — Landbouwetenskap in Suid-Afrika. Phytophylactica
Landbouwhogesch Wageningen Meded — Landbouwhogeschool Wageningen. Mededelingen
Landbouwhogesch Wageningen Misc Pap — Landbouwhogeschool Wageningen. Miscellaneous Papers
Landbouwkd Tijdschr — Landbouwkundig Tijdschrift
Landbouwk Tijdschr The Hague — Landbouwkundig Tijdschrift. Nederlandsch Genootschap voor Landbouwwetenschap (The Hague)
Landbouwk Tijdschr Wageningen Groningen — Landbouwkundig Tijdschrift (Wageningen and Groningen)
Landbouwmechan — Landbouwmechanisatie
Landbouwproefstn Suriname Bull — Landbouwproefstation Suriname. Bulletin
Landbouwproefstn Suriname Meded — Landbouwproefstation Suriname. Mededeling
Landbouwvoorl — Landbouwvoorlichting
Landbouwvoorlichting — Rijkslandbouwvoorlichtingsdienst
Landbrugsokonomiske Stud Copenh Vet Landbohojsk Okon Inst — Landbrugsokonomiske. Studier. Copenhagen Veterinaer. Og Landbohojskole. Okonomisk Institut
Landb Wereldnieuws — Landbouw Wereldnieuws. Nederlands Ministerie van Landbouw, Visserij en Voedselvoorziening
L and C — Language and Communication
L & C — Lefroy and Cassel's Practice Cases
L & Comp Tech — Law and Computer Technology [*Later, Law/Technology*]
L & Comp Technol — Law and Computer Technology [*Later, Law/Technology*]
Land Conserv Ser Dep NT — Land Conservation Series. Department of the Northern Territory
L & Contemp Prob — Law and Contemporary Problems
L and Contemp Probl — Law and Contemporary Problems
L & CONTEM PROB — Law and Contemporary Problems
Land Econ — Land Economics
Landerbank — Landerbank Economic Bulletin
Landesanst Immissions Bodennutzungsschutz Landes Nordrhein — Landesanstalt fuer Immissions- und Bodennutzungsschutz des LandesNordrhein-Westfalen. Jahresbericht
Landesanst Immissionsschutz Nordrhein Westfalen Schriftenr — Landesanstalt fuer Immissionsschutz Nordrhein-Westfalen. Schriftenreihe
Landesanst Wasser Boden Lufthyg Berlin Dahlem Mitt — Landesanstalt fuer Wasser-, Boden-, und Lufthygiene zu Berlin-Dahlen.Mitteilungen
Landesanst Wasserhyg Berlin Dahlem Mitt — Landesanstalt fuer Wasserhygiene zu Berlin-Dahlem. Mitteilungen
Land Forstwirtsch Forsch Oesterr — Land- und Forstwirtschaftliche Forschung in Oesterreich
L & G — Latina et Graeca
L & H — Literature and History
L & Human Behav — Law and Human Behavior
L & I — Literature and Ideology
Landis & Gyr Rev — Landis and Gyr Review
Land Issues Probl VA Polytech Inst State Univ Coop Ext Serv — Land Issues and Problems. Virginia Polytechnic Institute and State University. Cooperative Extension Service
L & Just — Law and Justice
L & L — Lehrproben und Lehrgaenge
L & L — Life and Letters
L & L — Lingua e Literatura
L & L — Linguistica et Litteraria
L&Le — Life and Letters
L and Lin M — Language and Linguistics in Melanesia
Land Loon — Het Oude Land van Loon. Jaarboek van de Federatie der Geschied-en Oudheidkundige Kringen van Limburg
Land L Serv — Land Laws Service
L & M — Literature and Medicine
L and M — Literature and Medicine
Landmasch-Markt — Landmaschinen-Markt
Landmasch Rundsch — Landmaschinen-Rundschau
Landmasch-Rundschau — Landmaschinen-Rundschau
Land Miner Surv — Land and Minerals Surveying

Land Newsl — Land Newsletter
Landoekonom Forsoglab Aarbog (Copenhagen) — Landoekonomisk Forsogslaboratorium Aarbog (Copenhagen)
Land of Sun — Land of Sunshine
Landokon Forsogslab Efterars — Landoekonomisk Forsogslaboratoriums Efterarsmode
Landowning in Scot — Landowning in Scotland
L & P — Literature and Psychology
L & Pol Int'l Bus — Law and Policy in International Business
Land Reform — Land Reform, Land Settlement, and Cooperatives
Land Resour Dev Cent Proj Rec (Surbiton UK) — Land Resources Development Centre. Project Record (Surbiton, United Kingdom)
Land Resour Dev Cent Tech Bull — Land Resources Development Centre. Technical Bulletin
Land Resour Div Dir Overseas Surv Land Resour Study — Land Resources Division. Directorate of Overseas Surveys. Land Resource Study
Land Resour Div Dir Overseas Surv Tech Bull — Land Resources Division. Directorate of Overseas Surveys. Technical Bulletin
Land Resour Manage Ser Div Land Resour Manage CSIRO — Land Resources Management Series. Division of Land Resources Management. Commonwealth Scientific and Industrial Research Organisation
Land Resour Mgmt Ser Div Land Resour Mgmt CSIRO — Land Resources Management Series. Division of Land Resources Management. Commonwealth Scientific and Industrial Research Organisation
Land Resour Stud Land Resour Div Dir Overseas Surv — Land Resource Study. Land Resources Division. Directorate of Overseas Surveys
Land Res Ser Commonw Sci Industr Res Organ (Aust) — Land Research Series. Commonwealth Scientific and Industrial Research Organisation (Melbourne, Australia)
Land Res Ser CSIRO — Land Research Series. Commonwealth Scientific and Industrial Research Organisation
Land Res Ser CSIRO (Aust) — Land Research Series. Commonwealth Scientific and Industrial Research Organisation (Australia)
L and S — Language and Speech
L & S — Lingua e Stile
Landscape Arch — Landscape Architecture
Landscape Archit — Landscape Architecture
Landscape Archre — Landscape Architecture
Landscape Des — Landscape Design
Landscape Intl — Landscape International
Landscape J — Landscape Journal
Landscape Plann — Landscape Planning
Landscape Res — Landscape Research
Landsc Arch — Landscape Architecture
Landschaftsentwickl Umweltforsch — Landschaftsentwicklung und Umweltforschung
Landslides J Jpn Landslide Soc — Landslides. Journal. Japan Landslide Society
L & Soc Order — Law and the Social Order
L and Soc Rev — Law and Society Review
Land Subsidence Proc Int Symp — Land Subsidence. Proceedings. International Symposium on Land Subsidence
Landtech — Landtechnik
Landtech Forsch — Landtechnische Forschung
Landtmannen Sven Land — Landtmannen. Svenskt Land
Land-Tuinbouw Jaarb — Land en Tuinbouw Jaarboek
L & U — Lion and the Unicorn
LANDUP — Alberta Land Use Planning Data Bank
Land Use and Env L Rev — Land Use and Environment Law Review
Land Use Built Form Stud Inf Notes — Land Use Built Form Studies. Information Notes
Land Use Built Form Stud Reps — Land Use Built Form Studies. Reports
Land Use Built Form Stud Wking Paps — Land Use Built Form Studies. Working Papers
Land Use Built Form Tech Notes — Land Use Built Form Studies. Technical Notes
Land Use Law and Zoning Dig — Land Use Law and Zoning Digest
Landw Ann Mecklenburg Patriot Vereins — Landwirthschaftliche Annalen des Mecklenburgischen Patriotischen Vereins
Land Water Int — Land and Water International
Landw Ber Mitteldeutschl — Landwirthschaftliche Berichte aus Mitteldeutschland
Landw Blaett Zoegl Bildungs Anst Ungarisch Altenburg — Landwirthschaftliche Blaetter, den Zoeglingen der Bildungs-Anstalt in Ungarisch-Altenburg Gewidmet
LandwBl Oldenburg — Landwirthschafts. Blatt fuer das Herzogtum Oldenburg
Landw Fo — Landwirtschaftliche Forschung
Landw Forsch — Landwirtschaftliche Forschung
Landw G — Landwirtschaftsgesetz
Landwirt — Landwirtschaft
Landwirt-Angew Wiss Bundesmin Ernahr Landwirt Forsten — Landwirtschaft-Angewandte Wissenschaft. Bundesministerium fuer Ernaehrung, Landwirtschaft, und Forsten
Landwirt Forsch Sonderh — Landwirtschaftliche Forschung. Sonderheft
Landwirtsch Angew Wiss — Landwirtschaft-Angewandte Wissenschaft
Landwirtsch Brennerei Ztg — Landwirtschaftliche Brennerei-Zeitung
Landwirtsch Chem Bundesversuchsanst (Linz) Veroeff — Landwirtschaftlich-Chemische Bundesversuchsanstalt (Linz). Veroeffentlichungen
Landwirtsch Forsch — Landwirtschaftliche Forschung
Landwirtsch Forsch Sonderh — Landwirtschaftliche Forschung. Sonderheft
Landwirtsch Jahrb — Landwirtschaftliche Jahrbuecher
Landwirtsch Jahrb Bayern — Landwirtschaftliches Jahrbuch fuer Bayern
Landwirtsch Jahrb Schweiz — Landwirtschaftliches Jahrbuch der Schweiz
Landwirt Schriftenr Boden Pflanze — Landwirtschaftliche Schriftenreihe. Boden und Pflanze
Landwirtsch Schriftenr Boden Pflanze Tier — Landwirtschaftliche Schriftenreihe. Boden, Pflanze, Tier

Landwirtsch Vers Stn — Landwirtschaftlichen Versuchs-Stationen
Landwirt Ver Stn — Landwirtschaftlichen Versuchs-Stationen
Landwirtsch Ztg (Fuehlings) — Landwirtschaftliche Zeitung (Fuehlings)
Landwirt Zentralbl — Landwirtschaftliches Zentralblatt
Landw Jahrb — Landwirtschaftliche Jahrbuecher
Landw Jb Bay — Landwirtschaftliches Jahrbuch fuer Bayern
Landw Jb Schweiz — Landwirtschaftliches Jahrbuch der Schweiz
L and W LR — Land and Water Law Review
Landw Mh — Landwirtschaftliche-Monatshefte
Landw Versuchsstat — Die Landwirtschaftlichen Versuchsstationen
Landw Wbl Kurhessen-Waldeck — Landwirtschaftliches Wochenblatt fuer Kurhessen-Waldeck
Landw Wbl (Muenchen) — Landwirtschaftliches Wochenblatt (Muenchen)
Landw Wbl Westf Lippe — Landwirtschaftliches Wochenblatt fuer Westfalen und Lippe
Landw Zeitung Augsburg — Landwirtschaftliche Zeitung (Augsburg)
Landw Z Oesterr Schlesien — Landwirtschaftliche Zeitschrift fuer das Oesterreichische Schlesien
LANE — Labrador Nor-Eastern
LANE — Linguistic Atlas of New England
Lang — Langages
Lang — Language
LANG — Language. Linguistics Society of America
L Ang — Los Angeles Medical Journal
LangA — Language and Automation
LangAb — Language and Language Behavior Abstracts
Lang and C — Language and Culture
Lang and Commun — Language and Communication
Lang & L — Language and Literature
Lang & S — Language and Style
Lang & Speech — Language and Speech
Lang Arts — Language Arts
Lang Assoc East Afr Jnl — Language Association of Eastern Africa. Journal
Lang Autom — Language and Automation
Langenbeck — Langenbecks Archiv fuer Chirurgie
Langenbecks Arch Chir — Langenbecks Archiv fuer Chirurgie
Langenbecks Arch Chir Suppl — Langenbecks Archiv fuer Chirurgie. Supplement
Langenbecks Arch Chir Suppl Kongressbd — Langenbecks Archiv fuer Chirurgie. Supplement. Kongressband
Langenbecks Arch Klin Chir — Langenbecks Archiv fuer Klinische Chirurgie
Lang Fr — Langue Francaise
LangL — Language Learning
Lang Lang Behav Abstr — Language and Language Behavior Abstracts. LLBA
Lang Learn — Language Learning
Lang Literature Series — Language and Literature Series
Lang Mod — Langues Modernes
LangMono — Language Monographs
Lang Plan News — Language Planning Newsletter
LangQ — Language Quarterly
Lang R — Language Research
Lang S — Language and Style
LangS — Language Sciences
Lang Soc — Language in Society
Lang Speech — Language and Speech
Lang Speech & Hearing Serv Sch — Language, Speech, and Hearing Services in Schools
Lang Speech Hear Serv Sch — Language, Speech, and Hearing Services in Schools
Lang Style — Language and Style
LangTAb — Language Teaching Abstracts [*Later, Language Teaching and Linguistics Abstracts*]
Lang Teach — Language Teaching
Lang Teach & Ling Abstr — Language Teaching and Linguistics Abstracts
Lang Teach Linguist Abstr — Language Teaching and Linguistics Abstracts
Language Soc — Language in Society
Langue et Culture — Notre Langue et Notre Culture
Langue Raison Calc — Langue, Raisonnement, Calcul
Langues et L — Langues et Linguistique
LAN Harris — Local Area Networks. A Harris Perspective
LanM — Langues Modernes
Lans — Lansing's Reports
Lantbrhoegsk Ann — Lantbrukshoegskolans Annaler
Lantbrhogsk Annlr — Lantbrukshogskolans Annaler
Lantbrhogsk Meddn — Lantbrukshogskolans Meddelanden
Lantbruksakad Ekon Avd Medd — Lantbruksakademien. Ekonomiska Avdelning. Meddelande
Lantbruksakad Tek Avd Medd — Lantbruksakademien. Tekniska Avdelning. Meddelande
Lantbruksakad Traedgaardsavd Medd — Lantbruksakademien. Traedgaardsavdelning. Meddelande
Lantbruksakad Vetenskapsavd Medd — Lantbruksakademien. Vetenskapsavdelning. Meddelande
Lantbruks-Hoegsk Ann — Lantbruks-Hoegskolans Annaler
Lantbrukshoegsk Husdjursfoersoeksanst Medd — Lantbrukshoegskolan, Husdjursfoersoeksanstalten. Meddelande
Lantbrukshoegsk Jordbruksfoersoeksanst Medd — Lantbrukshoegskolan Jordbruksfoersoeksanstalten Meddelanden
Lantbrukshogsk Ann — Lantbrukshogskolans Annaler
Lantbrukshogsk Husdjursforsoksanst Medd — Lantbrukshogskolan Husdjursforsoksanstalten Meddelanden
Lantbrukshogsk Inst Vaextodling Rapp Avh — Lantbrukshogskolan. Institutionen foer Vaextodling. Rapporter ochAvhandlingar
Lantbrukshogsk Meddel — Lantbrukshogskolans Meddelanden
Lantbrukshogsk Medd Ser A — Lantbrukshogskolans Meddelanden. Series A
Lantbrukshogsk Medd Ser B — Lantbrukshogskolans Meddelanden. Series B

Lantbrukshogsk Vaxtskyddsrapp Jordbruk — Lantbrukshogskolan Vaxtskyddsrapport Jordbruk

Lantbrukshogsk Vaxtskyddsrapp Jordbruk (Uppsala) — Lantbrukshogskolan. Vaxtskyddsrapporter Jordbruk (Uppsala)

Lantbrukshogsk Vaxtskyddsrapp Tradg — Lantbrukshogskolan Vaxtskyddsrapporter Tradgard

Lantbruksstyr Medd — Lantbruksstyrelsen. Meddelanden

Lantbrukstidskr Dalarne — Lantbrukstidskrift foer Dalarne. Kopparbergs Laens Hushallningssaellskap

Lantbrukstidskr Jaemtland Haerjedalen — Lantbrukstidskrift foer Jaemtland och Haerjedalen

Lantbrukstidskr Stockholms Lan Stad — Lantbrukstidskrift foer Stockholms Lan och Stad

L'Ant Cl — Antiquite Classique

L Ant Clas — Antiquite Classique

Lanterne Med — Lanterne Medicale

Lanthanide Actinide Res — Lanthanide and Actinide Research

L Anthrop — Anthropologie

Lantm Andelsfolk — Lantman och Andelsfolk

LANZA — Landarzt

L A of Alta Bul — Library Association of Alberta. Bulletin

LA Off Public Works Water Resour Basic Rec Rep — Louisiana. Office of Public Works. Water Resources Basic Records Report

La Off Public Works Water Resour Spec Rep — Louisiana. Office of Public Works. Water Resources Special Report

La Off Public Works Water Resour Tech Rep — Louisiana. Office of Public Works. Water Resources Technical Report

Laogr — Laographia

LAP — Latin American Perspectives

LaPar — La Parisienne

LA Phil — Los Angeles Philharmonic. Program Notes

LA Phil Sym Mag — Los Angeles Philharmonic Orchestra. Symphony Magazine

Lapidary J — Lapidary Journal

Lapidary Jour — Lapidary Journal

LA Plant Sugar Manuf — Louisiana. Planter and Sugar Manufacturer

LAPLD — Landscape Planning

Lap Lemb Penelit Kehutanan — Laporan. Lembaga Penelitian Kehutanan

LAPMAU — Lectures in Applied Mathematics

LAPO — Litteratures Anciennes du Proche-Orient

Laporan Lembaga Metall Nas (Indones) — Laporan. Lembaga Metallurgi Nasional (Indonesia)

LAPR — Latin America Political Report

Lap Sept — Lapidarium Septentrionale

LAPUG — Liber Annualis. Pontificia Universitas Gregoriana

LAQ — Library Administration Quarterly

LAQ — Livres et Auteurs Quebecois

LaR — La Rassegna

LAr — Leibniz-Archiv

LAR — Library Association. Record

L Arb — Linguistische Arbeiten

LARC Med — LARC [Lille, Amiens, Rouen, Caen] Medical

LARC Rep — LARC Reports

LaRe — Land Reformer

LA Reg — Louisiana Register

La Republica Supl Dominical — La Republica. Suplemento Dominical

La Rev Stat Ann (West) — West's Louisiana Revised Statutes Annotated

LARFEN — Agricultural Research Organization. Division of Forestry. Ilanot Leaflet

Large Open Pit Min Conf — Large Open Pit Mining Conference

Large Scale Struct Nonlinear Phys Proc Workshop — Large Scale Structures in Nonlinear Physics. Proceedings. Workshop

Large Scale Syst — Large Scale Systems

Large Scale Syst Theory and Appl — Large Scale Systems. Theory and Applications

Lar Li — Pariosse et Liturgie

LarM — Larousse Mensuel

LArm — Literaturnaia Armeniia. Ezhemesiachnyi Literaturno-Khudozhestvennyi i Obshchestvenno-Politicheskii Zhurnal

Lar Mens — Larousse Mensuel

Larousse Mens — Larousse Mensuel

LARR — Latin American Research Review

L Arte Riv Stor A Med & Mod — L'Arte. Rivista di Storia dell'Arte Medievale e Moderna

LA Rural Econ — Louisiana Rural Economist. Louisiana State University. Department of Agriculture and Agribusiness

LARYA — Laryngoscope

Laryngol Rhinol Otol — Laryngologie, Rhinologie, Otologie

Laryngol Rhinol Otol Ihre Grenzgeb — Laryngologie, Rhinologie, Otologie, und Ihre Grenzgebiete

Laryngol Rhinol Otol (Stuttg) — Laryngologie, Rhinologie, Otologie (Stuttgart)

Laryngo-Rhino-Otol — Laryngo- Rhino- Otologie

Laryngoscop — Laryngoscope

La S — Language and Speech

La S — Language and Style

LAS — Leipziger Aegyptologische Studien

LAS — Life Association News

LaS — Louisiana Studies

LASD — Labor Agreement Settlement Data

Laser Ablation Electron Mater — Laser Ablation of Electronic Materials. Basic Mechanisms and Applications

Laser Ablation Mater Synth Symp — Laser Ablation for Materials Syntheseis. Symposium

Laser Adv Appl Proc Nat Quantum Electron Conf — Laser Advances and Applications. Proceedings. National Quantum Electronics Conference

Laser & Unconv Opt J — Laser and Unconventional Optics Journal

Laser Anemom Int Conf — Laser Anemometry. Advances and Applications. International Conference on Laser Anemometry, Advances, and Applications

Laser Appl — Laser Applications

Laser Appl Med Biol — Laser Applications in Medicine and Biology

Laser Chem — Laser Chemistry

Laser Diode Technol Appl — Laser Diode Technology and Applications

Laser Elektro-Opt — Laser und Elektro-Optik

Laser Foc — Laser Focus Buyers Guide

Laser Focus Electro Opt Mag — Laser Focus Including Electro-Optics Magazine

Laser Focus Fiberopt Commun — Laser Focus with Fiberoptic Communications

Laser Focus Fiberoptic Commun — Laser Focus with Fiberoptic Communications

Laser Focus Fiberoptic Technol — Laser Focus with Fiberoptic Technology

Laser Focus Fiberopt Technol — Laser Focus with Fiberoptic Technology

Laser Focus (Littleton Mass) — Laser Focus (Littleton, Massachusetts)

Laser Focus (Newton Mass) — Laser Focus (Newton, Massachusetts)

Laser Foc W — Laser Focus World

Laser F Wld — Laser Focus World

Laser Handb — Laser Handbook

Laser Induced Damage Opt Mater Annu Boulder Damage Symp — Laser-Induced Damage in Optical Materials. Annual Boulder Damage Symposium

Laser Inst Am LIA — Laser Institute of America. LIA

Laser Interact Relat Plasma Phenom — Laser Interaction and Related Plasma Phenomena

Laser J — Laser Journal

Laser Light Scattering Biochem — Laser Light Scattering in Biochemistry

Laser Microtechnol Laser Diagn Surf Int Workshop — Laser Microtechnology and Laser Diagnostics of Surfaces. International Workshop

Laser Optoelektron — Laser und Optoelektronik

Laser Part — Laser and Particle Beams

Laser Part Beam Chem Process Microelectron Symp — Laser and Particle Beam Chemical Processing for Microelectronics.Symposium

Laser Part Beams — Laser and Particle Beams

Laser Phys — Laser Physics

Laser Phys Proc NZ Summer Sch Laser Phys — Laser Physics. Proceedings. New Zealand Summer School in Laser Physics

Laser Phys Proc NZ Symp Laser Phys — Laser Physics. Proceedings. New Zealand Symposium on Laser Physics

Laser Rep — Laser Report

Laser Rev — Laser Review

Lasers & App — Lasers and Applications. A High Tech Publication

Lasers Eng — Lasers in Engineering

Lasers Med Sci — Lasers in Medical Science

Lasers Microelectron Manuf — Lasers in Microelectronic Manufacturing

Lasers Opt Non Conv — Lasers et Optique Non Conventionnelle

Laser Spectrosc Int Conf — Laser Spectroscopy. International Conference

Laser Spectrosc Nonlinear Opt Solids — Laser Spectroscopy and Nonlinear Optics of Solids

Laser Spectros Proc Int Conf — Laser Spectroscopy. Proceedings. International Conference

Lasers Phys Chem Biophys Proc Int Meet Soc Chim Phys — Lasers in Physical Chemistry and Biophysics. Proceedings. InternationalMeeting. Societe de Chimie Physique

Lasers Proc Int Conf — Lasers. Proceedings. International Conference

Lasers Surg Med — Lasers in Surgery and Medicine

Lasers Surg Med Suppl — Lasers in Surgery and Medicine. Supplement

Laser Surg — Lasers in Surgery and Medicine

Laser Tech Bull Spectra Phys — Laser Technical Bulletin. Spectra Physics

Laser und Angew Strahlentech — Laser und Angewandte Strahlentechnik

Laser und Elektro-Opt — Laser und Elektro-Optik

Laser und Optoelektron — Laser und Optoelektronik

LA Sess Law Serv (West) — Louisiana Session Law Service (West)

LASH — List of Australian Subject Headings

LA Ship — Latin American Shipping

LASIE — Information Bulletin. Library Automated Systems Information Exchange

LASLK — Leben und Ausgewaehlte Schriften der Vaeter und Begruender der Lutherischen Kirche

LASORS — Literature Analysis System on Road Safety

LAsR — Library Association Record

LASRB — Laser Review

LASRK — Leben und Ausgewaehlte Schriften der Vaeter und Begruender der Reformierten Kirche

La State Bd Health Q Bul — Louisiana State Board of Health. Quarterly Bulletin

La State Dep Conserv Geol Bull — Louisiana State Department of Conservation. Geological Bulletin

La State Dep Conserv Geol Surv Dep Public Works Water Resour — Louisiana. State Department of Conservation. Geological Survey and Department of Public Works. Water Resources Bulletin

La State Med Soc — Louisiana State Medical Society

La State Med Soc J — Louisiana State Medical Society. Journal

La State Univ Agric Mech Coll Div Eng Res Bull — Louisiana State University and Agricultural and Mechanical College.Division of Engineering Research. Bulletin

La State Univ Agric Mech Coll Eng Exp Stn Bull — Louisiana State University and Agricultural and Mechanical College. EngineeringExperiment Station. Bulletin

La State Univ Agric Mech Coll Eng Exp Stn Repr Ser — Louisiana State University and Agricultural and Mechanical College. EngineeringExperiment Station. Reprint Series

LA State Univ and Agr Mech Coll Tech Rept — Louisiana State University and Agricultural and Mechanical College. Technical Reports

LA State Univ Div Eng Res Bull — Louisiana State University. Division of Engineering Research. Bulletin

LA State Univ Div Eng Res Eng — Louisiana State University. Division of Engineering Research. Engineering Research Bulletin

LA State Univ Div Eng Res Eng Res Bull — Louisiana State University. Division of Engineering Research. Engineering Research Bulletin.

La State Univ Eng Exp Stn Repr Ser — Louisiana State University and Agricultural and Mechanical College. EngineeringExperiment Station. Reprint Series

LA State Univ Eng Expt Sta Bull Studies Phys Sci Ser — Louisiana State University. Engineering Experiment Station. Bulletin. Studies. Physical Science Series

LA State Univ Proc Annu For Symp — Louisiana State University. Proceedings. Annual Forestry Symposium

LA State Univ Stud Biol Sci Ser — Louisiana State University. Studies. Biological Science Series

LA State Univ Stud Coastal Stud Ser — Louisiana State University. Studies. Coastal Studies Series

La St B Assn Proc — Louisiana State Bar Association. Proceedings

La St B Assn Rep — Louisiana State Bar Association. Reports

LA St Exp Sta G Agr LA — Louisiana State Experiment Stations. Geology and Agriculture of Louisiana

LA Stud — Louisiana Studies

LA St Univ An Rp Sup — Louisiana State University. Annual Report of the Superintendent

LA SUQ — Louisiana State University. Quarterly

Las Vegas Rev J — Las Vegas Review. Journal

Lat — Lateranum

LAT — Latin America Regional Reports

Lat — Latinite. Revue des Pays d'Occident

Lat — Latomus

LaT — La Torre

LAT — Los Angeles Times

LatA — Latinskaia Amerika

LatAm — Index to Latin American Periodicals

Lat Am — Latin America

Lat Am Appl Res — Latin American Applied Research

Lat Am Econ Bus — Latin American Economy and Business

Lat Amer — Latin American Perspectives

Lat Amer Mg — Latin American Monographs

Lat Amer Persp — Latin American Perspectives

Lat Amer Times — Latin American Times

Lat Am Ind — Latin American Indian Literatures

Lat Am Ind Lit — Latin American Indian Literatures

Lat Am J Chem Eng Appl Chem — Latin American Journal of Chemical Engineering and Applied Chemistry

Lat Am J Chem Engng Appld Chem — Latin American Journal of Chemical Engineering and Applied Chemistry

Lat Am J Heat Mass Transfer — Latin American Journal of Heat and Mass Transfer

Lat Am Lit — Latin American Literary Review

Lat Am Min Lett — Latin American Mining Letter

Lat Am Mon Econ Indic — Latin American Monthly Economic Indicators

Lat Am Mus — Latin American Music Review

Lat Am Mus R — Latin American Music Review

Lat Am Res — Latin American Research Review

Lat Am Res R — Latin American Research Review

Lat Am Res Rev Austin — Latin American Research Review (Austin, Texas)

Lat Am Sch Phys — Latin American School of Physics

Lat Am Spec Rep — Latin American Special Reports

Lat Am Symp Surf Phys — Latin-American Symposium on Surface Physics

Lat Am Thea — Latin American Theater Review

LATBR — Los Angeles Times Book Review

Lateinam Anders — Lateinamerika Anders

Lateinamer Ber — Lateinamerika-Berichte

Lateinam-Studien — Lateinamerika-Studien

LatH — Lateinamerika Heute

La Them LC — La Themis (Lower Canada)

Lati — Latinitas

LATIA — Landbouwkundig Tijdschrift

LA Times — Los Angeles Times

Latin Am and Empire Rept — NACLA's [*North American Congress on Latin America*] Latin America and Empire Report

Latin Amer — Latinskaja Amerika

Latin Amer Anthrop Rev — Latin American Anthropology Review

Latin Amer Antiq — Latin American Antiquity

Latin Amer Exec Rep — Latin American Executive Report

Latin Amer Indian Lit J — Latin American Indian Literatures Journal

Latin Amer P — Latin American Perspectives

Latin Amer Perspect — Latin American Perspectives

Latin Amer Res R — Latin American Research Review

Latin Amer Res Rev — Latin American Research Review

Latin Amer Stud Tokyo — Latin American Studies. Association for Latin American Studies (Tokyo)

Latin Am Perspectives — Latin American Perspectives

Latin Am Research R — Latin American Research Review

Latin Am Res R — Latin American Research Review

Latin Am Times — Latin American Times

Latinsk Amer — Latinskaja Amerika

Lat M — Latimer Monographs

Latomus — Latomus; Revue d'Etudes Latines

LATR — Latin American Theater Review

La Trobe Library J — La Trobe Library Journal

La Trobe Univ Sch Agric Semin Pap — La Trobe University. School of Agriculture. Seminar Paper

LatT — Latin Teaching

Latte Latticini Conserve Anim — Latte, Latticini, e Conserve Animali

Lattice Defects Cryst Int Summer Sch Defects — Lattice Defects in Crystals. International Summer School on Defects

Lattice Defects Dryst Proc Int Summer Sch — Lattice Defects in Crystals. Proceedings. International Summer School on Lattice Defects in Crystals

Latv Arkhit — Latvijas Arkhitektura

Latv Augstsk Raksti — Latvijas Augstskolas Raksti

Latv Ent — Latvijas Entomologs

Latv Fil Vses Ova Pochvovedov Sb Tr — Latviiskii Filial Vsesoyuznogo Obshchestva Pochvovedov Sbornik Trudov

Latv Fiz Teh Z — Latvijas Fizikas un Tehnisko Zurnals

Latv Fiz Tekh Zh — Latviiskii Fiziko-Tekhnicheskii Zhurnal

Latviisk Gos Univ Ucen Zap — Latviiskii Gosudarstvennyi Universitet Imeni Petra Stucki Ucenyi Zapiski

Latviisk Mat Ezegodnik — Latviiskii Matematiceskii Ezegodnik

Latvijas PSR Zinatn Akad Vestis — Latvijas PSR Zinatnu Akademijas. Vestis

Latvijas PSR Zinatn Akad Vestis Fiz Tehn Zinatn Ser — Latvijas PSR Zinatnu Akademijas. Vestis. Fizikas un Tehnisko Zinatnu Serija

Latvijas Valsts Univ Zinatn Raksti — PSRS Augstakas Izglitibas Ministrija. Petera Stuckas Latvijas Valsts Universitate. Zinatniskie Raksti

Latv Inz & Teh Kongr Biroja Zurnals — Latvijas Inzenieru un Tehniku Kongresa Biroja Zurnals

Latv J Chem — Latvian Journal of Chemistry

Latv J Phys Tech Sci — Latvian Journal of Physics and Technical Sciences

Latv Khim Zh — Latviiskii Khimicheskii Zhurnal

Latv Kim Z — Latvijas Kimijas Zurnals

Latv Lauksaimn Akad LLA Raksti — Latvijas Lauksaimniecibas Akademija. LLA Raksti

Latv Lauksaimn Akad Raktsi — Latvijas Lauksaimniecibas Akademijas Raktsi

Latv Lopkopibas Vet Inst Raksti — Latvijas Lopkopibas un Veterinarijas Zinatniski Petnieciska Instituta Raksti

Latv Lopkopibas Vet Zinat Petnieciska Inst Raksti — Latvijas Lopkopibas un Veterinarijas Zinatniski Petnieciska Instituta Raksti

Latv Mat Ezheg — Latvijskij Matematicheskij Ezhegodnik

Latv Mat Ezhegodnik — Latviiskii Gosudarstvennyi Universitet Imeni Petra Stucki Latviiskii Matematicheskii Ezhegodnik

Latv PSR Zinat Akad Biol Inst Dzivnieku Fiziol Sekt Raksti — Latvijas PSR Zinatnu Akademija. Biologijas Instituts. Dzivnieku Fiziologijas Sektora Raksti

Latv PSR Zinat Akad Biol Inst Raksti — Latvijas PSR Zinatnu Akademija. Biologijas Instituta Raksti

Latv PSR Zinat Akad Fiz Inst Raksti — Latvijas PSR Zinatnu Akademija Fizikas Instituta Raksti

Latv PSR Zinat Akad Geol Geogr Inst Raksti — Latvijas PSR Zinatnu Akademija Geologijas un Geografijas InstitutaRaksti

Latv PSR Zinat Akad Kim Inst Zinat Raksti — Latvijas PSR Zinatnu Akademija. Kimijas Instituta Zinatniskie Raksti

Latv PSR Zinat Akad Mezsaimn Probl Inst Raksti — Latvijas PSR Zinatnu Akademija Mezsaimniecibas Problemu InstitutaRaksti

Latv PSR Zinat Akad Mezsaimn Probl Koksnes Kim Inst Raksti — Latvijas PSR Zinatnu Akademija. Mezsaimniecibas Problemu un Koksnes Kimijas Instituta Raksti

Latv PSR Zinat Akad Vestis — Latvijas PSR Zinatnu Akademijas. Vestis

Latv PSR Zinat Akad Vestis Fiz Teh Ser — Latvijas PSR Zinatnu Akademijas. Vestis. Fizikas un Tehnisko Zinatnu Serija

Latv PSR Zinat Akad Vestis Fiz Teh Zinat Ser — Latvijas PSR Zinatnu Akademijas. Vestis. Fizikas un Tehnisko Zinatnu Serija

Latv PSR Zinat Akad Vestis Kim Ser — Latvijas PSR Zinatnu Akademijas. Vestis. Kimijas Serija

Latv PSR Zinat Akad Zootech Zoohig Inst Raksti — Latvijas PSR Zinatnu Akademija Zootechnikas un Zoohigienas InstitutaRaksti

Latv Univ Bot Darza Raksti — Latvijas Universitates Botaniska Darza Raksti

Latv Univ Raksti — Latvijas Universitates Raksti

Latv Univ Raksti Kim Fak Ser — Latvijas Universitates Raksti. Kimijas Fakultates Serijas

Latv Univ Raksti Lauksaimn Fak Ser — Latvijas Universitates Raksti. Lauksaimniecibas Fakultates Serija

Latv Univ Raksti Mat Dabas Zinat Fak Ser — Latvijas Universitates Raksti. Matematikas un Dabas Zinatnu. Fakultates Serija

Latv Univ Raksti Med Fak Ser — Latvijas Universitates Raksti. Medicinas Fakultates Serija

Latv Univ Zinat Raksti — Latvijas Universitates Zinatniskie Raksti

Latv U Raksti — Latvijas Universitatis Raktsi

Latv Valsts Univ Bot Darza Raksti — Latvijas Valsts Universitates Botaniska Darza Raksti

Latv Valsts Univ Zinat Raksti — Latvijas Valsts Universitate. Zinatniskie Raksti

Latv Zinat Akad Vestis — Latvijas Zinatnu Akademijas Vestis

Latv Zinat Akad Vestis B — Latvijas Zinatnu Akademijas Vestis. B Dala. Dabaszinatnes

LAUM — Linguistic Atlas of the Upper Midwest

Laund News — Laundry News

Laundry Dry Clean J Can — Laundry and Dry Cleaning Journal of Canada

Lau R — Laurel Review

Laur — Laurentianum

Laur Aqu — Laureae Aquincenses

Laus Bll S Vd — Bulletin des Seances de la Societe Vaudoise des Sciences Naturelles (Lausanne)

Laus C R S Suisse — Comptes Rendus de la Societe Suisse (Lausanne)

Lausitz Mschr — Lausitzische und Neue Lausitzische Monatsschrift. Organ der Oberlausitzischen Gesellschaft der Wissenschaften

Lausiz Monatsschr — Lausizische Monatsschrift

Laus S Vd Bll — Bulletin des Seances de la Societe Vaudoise des Sciences Naturelles (Lausanne)

Lavaggio Ind — Lavaggio Industriale

Laval Med — Laval Medical

Laval Theol — Laval Theologique et Philosophique

Laval Theol Phil — Laval Theologique et Philosophique

Laval Univ For Res Found Contrib — Laval University Forest Research Foundation. Contributions

Lav Arroz — Lavoura Arrozeira
Lav Ist Anat Istol Patol (Perugia) — Lavori. Istituto di Anatomia e Istologia Patologica. Universita degli Studi (Perugia)
Lav Ist Anat Istol Patol Univ Studi (Perugia) — Lavori. Istituto di Anatomia e Istologia Patologica. Universita degli Studi (Perugia)
Lav Ist Bot Giardino Colon Palermo — Lavori. Istituto Botanico Giardino Coloniale di Palermo
Lav Ist Bot Reale Univ Cagliari — Lavori. Istituto Botanico. Reale Universita di Cagliari
LAVMA — Lavoro e Medicina
Lav Med — Lavoro e Medicina
Lav Neuropsichiatr — Lavoro Neuropsichiatrico
Lavori Ist Anat Istol Patol Univ Studi (Perugia) — Lavori. Istituto di Anatomia e Istologia Patologica. Universita degli Studi (Perugia)
LavTP — Laval Theologique et Philosophique
Lav Um — Lavoro Umano
Lav Um Suppl — Lavoro Umano. Supplemento
Law — Alabama Lawyer
LAW — Lexikon der Alten Welt
Law — London Law Magazine
Law Am — Lawyer of the Americas
Law Amdt J — Law Amendment Journal
Law Amer — Lawyer of the Americas
Law Americas — Lawyer of the Americas
Law Am Jour — Law Amendment Journal
Law & Bank — Lawyers' and Bankers' Quarterly
Law & Banker — Lawyer and Banker and Central Law Journal
Law & Bk Bull — Weekly Law and Bank Bulletin
Law & Comp Tech — Law and Computer Technology [*Later, Law/Technology*]
Law & Comput Tech — Law and Computer Technology [*Later, Law/Technology*]
Law & Comput Technol — Law and Computer Technology [*Later, Law/Technology*]
Law and Con Pr — Law and Contemporary Problems
Law & Contemp Prob — Law and Contemporary Problems
Law and Housing J — Law and Housing Journal
Law and Hum Behav — Law and Human Behavior
Law & Int Aff — Law and International Affairs
Law and Just — Law and Justice
Law & Lab — Law and Labor
Law & L N — Lawyer and Law Notes
Law & Mag — Lawyer and Magistrate Magazine
Law & Mag Mag — Lawyer and Magistrate Magazine
Law and Policy Internat Bus — Law and Policy in International Business
Law and Pol Int Bus — Law and Policy in International Business
Law & Pol Int'l Bus — Law and Policy in International Business
Law and Poly Intl Bus — Law and Policy in International Business
Law and Poly Q — Law and Policy Quarterly
Law and Psych Rev — Law and Psychology Review
Law and Society R — Law and Society Review
Law & Soc Ord — Law and the Social Order
Law & Soc Order — Law and the Social Order
Law & Soc R — Law and Society Review
Law & Soc Rev — Law and Society Review
Law and Socy Rev — Law and Society Review
Law Anthrop — Law and Anthropology
LAWASIA — LAWASIA. Journal of the Law Association for Asia and the Western Pacific
LAWASIA CLB — LAWASIA [*Law Association for Asia and the Pacific*] Commercial Law Bulletin
LAWASIA LJ — LAWASIA [*Law Association for Asia and the Pacific*] Law Journal
LAWASIA (NS) — LAWASIA [*Law Association for Asia and the Pacific*] (New Series)
LA Water Resour Res Inst Bull — Louisiana Water Resources Research Institute. Bulletin
Law Bul — Law Bulletin
Law Bul & Br — Law Bulletin and Brief
Law Bul IA — Law Bulletin. State University of Iowa
Law Bull — Law Bulletin
Law Bull — Weekly Law Bulletin
Law Chr — Law Chronicle
Law Chr & Jour Jur — Law Chronicle and Journal of Jurisprudence
Law Cl — Law Clerk
Law Contemp Probl — Law and Contemporary Problems
Law Contemp Probl Ser — Law and Contemporary Problems Series
Law Cont Pr — Law and Contemporary Problems
Law Council Newsl — Law Council Newsletter
Law Dig — Law Digest
Law Ex J — Law Examination Journal
LAWFA — Landwirtschaftliche Forschung
Law Gaz — Law Gazette
Law Guild M — Lawyers Guild Monthly
Law Guild Rev — Lawyers Guild Review
Law Hum Behav — Law and Human Behavior
Law Hum Genome Rev — Law and the Human Genome Review
Law in Cont — Law in Context
Law Inst J — Law Institute Journal
Law J — Lawyers Journal
Law Ja — Law in Japan
Law Jour — Law Journal
Law Lib — Law Librarian
Law Lib J — Law Library Journal
Law Lib Jour — Law Library Journal
Law Libn — Law Librarian
Law Lib N — Law Library News
Law Libr J — Law Library Journal

Law Librn — Law Librarian
Law Mag — Law Magazine
Law Mag & Law Rev — Law Magazine and Law Review
Law Mag & R — Law Magazine and Review
Law Mag & Rev — Law Magazine and Review
Law Man on Prof Conduct ABA/BNA — Lawyers' Manual on Professional Conduct. American BarAssociation/Bureau of National Affairs
Law Med & Health Care — Law, Medicine, and Health Care
Law Med Health Care — Law, Medicine, and Health Care
Law Med J — Lawyer's Medical Journal
Law Mo — Western Law Monthly (Reprint)
Law M R — Law Magazine and Review
Law N — Law News
Law N — Law Notes
Lawn Gard Mark — Lawn and Garden Marketing
Lawn Gardn — Lawn and Garden Marketing
Law Off Econ & Management — Law Office Economics and Management
Law Off Econ and Mgt — Law Office Economics and Management
Law Off Information Service — Law Office Information Service
Law Phil — Law and Philosophy
Law Q — Law Quarterly Review
Law Q R — Law Quarterly Review
Law Q Rev — Law Quarterly Review
Law Quar Rev — Law Quarterly Review
Law Quart — Law Quarterly Review
Law Quart R — Law Quarterly Review
Law Quart Rev — Law Quarterly Review
LAWR — Latin America Weekly Report
Law R — Law Review
LAWR — Weekly Report (Latin American)
Law Rec — Irish Law Recorder
Lawrence Berkeley Lab Rep LBL — Lawrence Berkeley Laboratory. Report LBL
Lawrence Livermore Lab Rep — Lawrence Livermore Laboratory. Report
Lawrence Rev Nat Prod — Lawrence Review of Natural Products
Lawrence Rev Nat Prod Monogr Syst — Lawrence Review of Natural Products. Monograph System
Law Rev — Law Review
Law Rev & Qu J — Law Review and Quarterly Journal
Law Rev Dig — Law Review Digest
Law Rev Qu — Law Review Quarterly
Law Rev U Det — Law Review. University of Detroit
Law School Rev — Law School Review. Toronto University
Law Ser MO Bull — University of Missouri. Bulletin. Law Series
Law Soc Bull — Law Society. Bulletin
Law Soc G — Law Society. Gazette
Law Soc Gaz — Law Society's Gazette
Law Soc J — Law Society. Journal
Law Soc Jo — Law Society of Massachusetts. Journal
Law Soc Prob — Law and Social Problems
Law Soc R — Law and Society Review
Law Socy Gaz — Law Society. Gazette
Law Socy J — Law Society. Journal
Law Soc'y Scotl — Law Society of Scotland. Journal
Law State — Law and State
Law Stud — Law Student
Law Stud Mag — Law Students' Magazine
Law Stud Mag NS — Law Students' Magazine. New Series
Law Stu H — Law Students' Helper
Law Tcher — Law Teacher
Law Tech — Law/Technology
Law/Technol — Law/Technology
Law Times (NS) — Law Times. New Series
Law Title Guar Funds News — Lawyers Title Guaranty Funds News
Law T NS — Law Times. New Series
Law W — Law Weekly
Lawy & LN — Lawyer and Law Notes
Lawyer & Banker — Lawyer and Banker and Central Law Journal
Lawyers Med J — Lawyer's Medical Journal
Lawyers' Rev — Lawyers' Review
Lawy Mag — Lawyers' Magazine
Lawy Med J — Lawyer's Medical Journal
Lawy Rev — Lawyers' Review
La-Yaaran For Israel For Assoc — La-Ya'aran/The Forester. Israel Forestry Association
Lay BS — Layman's Bible Series
Lb — Laboratory, a Weekly Record of Scientific Research
LB — Leuvensche Bijdragen. Tijdschrift voor Modern Philologie [*The Hague*]
LB — Leuvense Bijdragen
LB — Levende Billeder
LB — Liberty Bell
LB — Linguistica Biblica
LB — Living Blues
LB — London Gallery Bulletin
LBANA — Laboratory Animals
LBASA — Laboratory Animal Science
LBB — Leuvense Bijdragen (Bijblad)
L B Cases Bot Index — L. B. Case's Botanical Index. An Illustrated Quarterly Botanical Magazine
LBC News — Law Book Company Ltd. Newsletter
LB Cos Indust Arb Serv — Law Book Company's Industrial Arbitration Service
LB Cos Practical Forms — Law Book Company's Practical Forms and Precedents
LB Cos Tax Serv — Law Book Company's Taxation Service
L Bella — Lingua Bella
LBer — Linguistische Berichte
LB Free P — Long Beach Free Press

LBGP — Literarische Berichte aus dem Gebiete der Philosophie
LBGRPh — Literaturblatt fuer Germanische und Romanische Philologie
Lbh A — Kongelige Veterinaer- og Landbohojskole. Arsskrift
Lbh Aa — Veterinaer- og Landbohojskole Aarskrift
LBIB — Linguistica Biblica
LBIYB — Leo Baeck Institute. Year Book
LBj — Leksykohraficny j Bjuleten
LBL — Literaturblatt fuer Germanische und Romanische Philologie
LBI — Living Blues
LBL Comput Cent Newsl — LBL [*Lawrence Berkeley Laboratory*] Computer Center Newsletter
LBLJA — Labor Law Journal
LBL Newsmag — LBL [*Lawrence Berkeley Laboratory*] Newsmagazine
LBML — Leo Baeck Memorial Lecture
LBMRC Res Newl — LBMRC [*Louis Braille Memorial Research Centre*] Research Newsletter
Lb N — Landbonyt
LBQUDZ — Living Bird Quarterly
LbR — Limba Romana
LBR — Lloyds Bank Review
LBR — Luso-Brazilian Review
Lbr Hist (Australia) — Labour History (Australia)
Lbr Hist (US) — Labor History (United States)
Lbr Law J — Labor Law Journal
Lbr M — Landburgsraadets Meddelelser. Faellesrepraesentation for det Danske Landburgs Hovedorganisationer
Lbr Studies J — Labor Studies Journal
Lbr Today — Labor Today
LBS — Labour and Society
LBSEDV — Leiden Botanical Series
LBT — Landbouwkundig Tijdschrift
LBWTAP — Food Science and Technology
LC — Las Ciencias
LC — Letterature Contemporanea
LC — Library Chronicle
LC — Library of Congress
LC — Literatura Chilena. Creacion y Critica
LC — Living Church
LCAN — Lancashire and Cheshire Antiquarian Notes
LC & M Gaz — Lower Courts and Municipal Gazette
LCA Q — LCA [*Lawyers for the Creative Arts*] Quarterly
LCB — Centraal Bureau voor de Statistiek. Bibliotheek en Documentatiedienst. Lijst van Aanwinsten
LCBEP — Libri Confirmationum ad Beneficia Ecclesiastica Pragensem per Archidiocesim
LCC — Labor Case Comments
LCC — Library of Christian Classics
LCC (NSW) — Land Appeal Court Cases (New South Wales)
LCCP — Linguistic Circle of Canberra. Publications
LCD — (La) Ciudad de Dios Revista Agustiniana
LCD — Litterarisches Centralblatt fuer Deutschland
LCE — Literatura Chilena en el Exilio
LCFBA — Lahey Clinic Foundation. Bulletin
LCG — Lower Courts Gazette
LCh — Liberte Chretienne
LCHNB8 — Lichenologist
LCHP — Lancaster County Historical Society. Papers
LChQ — Lutheran Church Quarterly
LChr — Logotechnika Chronika
LChR — [*The*] Lutheran Church Review
L Chr I — Lexikon der Christlichen Ikonographie
LCHS — Lancaster County Historical Society. Papers
LC Inf Bul — United States. Library of Congress. Information Bulletin
LCL — Loeb Classical Library
LC Listy Cukrov — LC. Listy Cukrovarnicke
LCLJ — Lower Canada Law Journal
LCL Jo — Lower Canada Law Journal
LCM — Literary Criterion (Mysore)
LCM — Liverpool Classical Monthly
LCMF — Lettre aux Communautes de la Mission de France
LCN — Law Council Newsletter
LCOM — Local Committee Operations Manual
L Coop Ext Serv Kans State Univ — L. Cooperative Extension Service. Kansas State University
LCP — Latinitas Christianorum Primaeva
LCP — Law and Contemporary Problems
LCP — Library Chronicle. University of Pennsylvania
LCPC Note Inf Tech — Laboratoire Central des Ponts et Chaussees. Note d'Information Technique
LC Pract — LC [*Liquid Chromatography*] in Practice
LCQ — Lutheran Church Quarterly
LCQJCA — Library of Congress. Quarterly Journal of Current Acquisitions
LCR — Land Compensation Reports
LCR — Lutheran Church Review
LCRI — Library of Congress Rule Interpretations
LCrit — Literary Criterion
LCSCF — Libera Cattedra di Storia della Civilta Fiorentina
LCT — Library of Contemporary Theology
LCub — Libros Cubanos
LCUP — Library Chronicle. University of Pennsylvania
LCUT — Library Chronicle. University of Texas
LCW — Lutheran Churches of the World
LD — Landschaftsdenkmale der Musik
LD — Language Dissertations
LD — Legislative Digest. Forecast and Review

LD — Light and Dark
LD — Listin Diario
LD — Literary Digest
LD — Lithuanian Days
LD — Lituanistikos Darbai
LD — Livres Disponibles
LDA — Letras del Azuay
LDAA — Lexikographikon Deltion Akademias Athenon
LDA J — Louisiana Dental Association. Journal
Ld Bi — Im Lande der Bibel
LDBMA — Landbouwmechanisatie
LdD — Letras de Deusto
L de Muz — Lucrari de Muzicologie
LDG — Korte Berichten over Handel, Ambacht, Dienstverlening, Toerisme, Middenbedrijf,en Kleinbedrijf
LDL — Letopis Doma Literatorov
LdM — Lautbibliothek der Deutschen Mundarten
LdM — Lexikon des Mittelalters
LDM — Lingue del Mondo
LDN — London Daily News
LDO — Documentatiecentrum voor Overheidspersoneel. Literatuuroverzicht
LdP — Livros de Portugal
LDPK — Last Days of the Palace at Knossos
LdProv — Lettore de Provincia
LdProv — Lettore di Provincia. Testi, Ricerche, Critica
Ld QR — London Quarterly Review
LdR — Livre des Rois d'Egypte
Ld R — London Review
LDRC Bulletin — LDRC [*Libel Defense Resource Center*] Bulletin
Ld Rec — London Recusant
LDRP — Liber Diurnus Romanorum Pontificum
LDS — Leadership
LDS — London Divinity Series
LDSNT — London Divinity Series. New Testament Series
LDSOT — London Divinity Series. Old Testament Series
Ldwirtsch Jb Bayern — Landwirtschaftliches Jahrbuch fuer Bayern
Ldwirtsch Wbl — Landwirtschaftliches Wochenblatt
Le — Asia-Philippines Leader
LE — Lagina Ephemeris Aegyptiaca et Universa
LE — Land Economics
LE — Lands East
LE — Language
LE — Learning Exchange
LE — Les Echos
LE — Liberal Education
LE — Linguistica Extranea
LE — Literarisches Echo
LE — Literaturnaia Entsiklopediia
Lea — Leadership
LEA — Leathergoods
Lead Abstr — Lead Abstracts
Lead Prod (Washington DC) — Lead Production (Washington, D.C.)
Lead Res Dig — Lead Research Digest
Leafl Agric Exp Stn Ala Polytech Inst — Leaflet. Agricultural Experiment Station. Alabama Polytechnic Institute
Leafl Ala Agric Exp Stn Ala Polytech Inst — Leaflet. Alabama Agricultural Experiment Station. Alabama Polytechnic Institute
Leafl Ala Agric Exp Stn Auburn Univ — Leaflet. Alabama Agricultural Experiment Station. Auburn University
Leafl Amat Ent Soc — Leaflet. Amateur Entomologist's Society
Leafl Anim Prod Div Kenya Minist Agric — Leaflet. Animal Production Division. Kenya Ministry of Agriculture
Leafl Bot Observ Crit — Leaflets of Botanical Observation and Criticism
Leafl Br Isles Bee Breeders Ass — Leaflet. British Isles Bee Breeders' Association
Leafl Calif Agric Exp Stn — Leaflet. California Agricultural Experiment Station
Leafl Calif Agric Exp Stn Ext Serv — Leaflet. California Agricultural Experiment Station. Extension Service
Leafl Commonw For Timb Bur (Canberra) — Leaflet. Commonwealth Forestry and Timber Bureau (Canberra)
Leafl Coop Ext Serv Cook Coll Rutgers State Univ NJ — Leaflet. Cooperative Extension Service. Cook College. Rutgers. The State University of New Jersey
Leafl Coop Ext Serv Mont State Univ — Leaflet. Cooperative Extension Service. Montana State University
Leafl Coop Ext Serv Univ GA — Leaflet. Cooperative Extension Service. University of Georgia
Leafl Coop Ext Univ Calif — Leaflet. Cooperative Extension. University of California
Leafl Dep Agric (Ceylon) — Leaflet. Department of Agriculture (Ceylon)
Leafl Dep Agric Fish (Ire) — Leaflet. Department of Agriculture and Fisheries (Irish Republic)
Leafl Dep Agric Tech Instruct Ire — Leaflet. Department of Agriculture and Technical Instruction for Ireland
Leafl Div Agric Sci Univ Calif — Leaflet. Division of Agricultural Sciences. University of California
Leafl Div Eng Res Dev Univ RI — Leaflet. Division of Engineering Research and Development. University of Rhode Island
Leaflet US Dep Agric — Leaflet. United States Department of Agriculture
Leafl Ext Serv Utah St Univ — Leaflet. Extension Service. Utah State University
Leafl For Comm (UK) — Leaflet. Forestry Commission (United Kingdom)
Leafl Forest Dept Trinidad Tobago — Leaflet. Forest Department. Trinidad and Tobago
Leafl Forests Dep West Aust — Leaflet. Forests Department. Western Australia
Leafl For Timb Bur — Leaflet. Forestry and Timber Bureau
Leafl Israel Agric Res Organ Div For (Ilanot) — Leaflet. Israel Agricultural Research Organization. Division of Forestry (Ilanot)

Leafl L Tex Agric Exp Stn — Leaflet L. Texas Agricultural Experiment Station
Leafl L Tex Agric Ext Serv Tex AM Univ Syst — Leaflet L. Texas Agricultural Extension Service. Texas A & M University System
Leafl Minist Agric (Nth Ire) — Leaflet. Ministry of Agriculture (Northern Ireland)
Leafl Montreal Bot Gdn — Leaflet. Montreal Botanical Garden
Leafl Okla State Univ Agr Appl Sci Agr Ext Serv — Leaflet. Oklahoma State University of Agriculture and Applied Science. Agricultural Extension Service
Leafl Pa State Univ Coop Ext Serv — Leaflet. Pennsylvania State University. Cooperative Extension Service
Leafl PA State Univ Ext Serv — Leaflet. Cooperative Extension Service. Pennsylvania State University
Leafl Purdue Univ Dep Agric Ext — Leaflet. Purdue University. Department of Agricultural Extension
Leafl Rutgers State Univ Coll Agr Environ Sci Ext Serv — Leaflet. Rutgers State University. College of Agriculture and Environmental Science. Extension Service
Leafl Ser Fla Dep Nat Resour Mar Res Lab — Leaflet Series. Florida Department of Natural Resources. MarineResearch Laboratory
Leafl Tex Agric Exp Stn — Leaflet. Texas Agricultural Experiment Station
Leafl Tin Res Inst — Leaflet. Tin Research Institute
Leafl Univ Calif Coop Ext Serv — Leaflet. University of California. Cooperative Extension Service
Leafl Univ Hawaii Coop Ext Serv — Leaflet. University of Hawaii. Cooperative Extension Service
Leafl Univ Ky Agric Ext Serv — Leaflet. University of Kentucky. Agricultural Extension Service
Leafl Univ Ky Coll Agric Coop Ext Serv — Leaflet. University of Kentucky. College of Agriculture. Cooperative Extension Service
Leafl US Dep Agric — Leaflet. United States Department of Agriculture
Leafl VBBA — Leaflet. Village Bee Breeders Association
Leafl W Bot — Leaflets of Western Botany
Leafl West Bot — Leaflets of Western Botany
Leafl YANR Auburn Univ Ala Coop Ext Serv — Leaflet YANR. Auburn University. Alabama Cooperative Extension Service
Leafl YCRD Ala Coop Ext Serv Auburn Univ — Leaflet YCRD. Alabama Cooperative Extension Service. Auburn University
Leafl YEX Auburn Univ Ext Serv — Leaflet YEX. Auburn University Extension Service
Leafl YF Ala Coop Ext Serv Auburn Univ — Leaflet YF. Alabama Cooperative Extension Service. Auburn University
Leafl YHE Ala Coop Ext Serv Auburn Univ — Leaflet YHE. Alabama Cooperative Extension Service. Auburn University
Leafl YM Ala Coop Ext Serv Auburn Univ — Leaflet YM. Alabama Cooperative Extension Service. Auburn University
League Arab States Arab Pet Congr Collect Pap — League of Arab States. Arab Petroleum Congress. Collection of Papers
League Exch — League Exchange
League Int Food Educ Newsl — League for International Food Education. Newsletter
League Nations Bull Health Org — League of Nations. Bulletin of the Health Organization
League of Nations Off J — League of Nations. Official Journal
League of Nations OJ — League of Nations. Official Journal
League of Nations OJ Spec Supp — League of Nations. Official Journal. Special Supplement
LE & W — Literature East and West
LEAP — Libri Erectionum Archidioecesis Pragensis
Lea Rel — Leaders of Religion
Learn — Learning
Learn & Motiv — Learning and Motivation
Learn Exch — Learning Exchange
Learn Mem — Learning & Memory [*Cold Spring Harbor, NY*]
Learn Motiv — Learning and Motivation
Learn Res Bull — Learning Resources Bulletin
Learn Today — Learning Today
LEAT — Lea Transit Compendium
Leather Chem — Leather Chemistry
Leather Chem Dandong Peoples Repub China — Leather Chemicals (Dandong, People's Republic of China)
Leather Ind — Leather Industries
Leather Ind Res Inst S Afr J — Leather Industries Research Institute of South Africa. Journal
Leather Manuf — Leather Manufacturer
Leather Sci Eng — Leather Science and Engineering
Leather Sci (Madras) — Leather Science (Madras)
Leather Sci Technol — Leather Science and Technology
Leather Trades Circ Rev — Leather Trades Circular and Review
Leath Sci — Leather Science
Leath Shoe — Leather and Shoes
Leaves Paint Res Noteb — Leaves from a Paint Research Notebook
LeB — Leo Baeck Institute Yearbook
Leban Med J — Lebanese Medical Journal
Lebanon — Lebanon County Legal Journal
Lebanon Co Hist Soc Pap — Lebanon County Historical Society. Historical Papers and Addresses
Lebanon Co LJ (PA) — Lebanon County Legal Journal
Leban Pharm J — Lebanese Pharmaceutical Journal
Leben Erde — Lebendige Erde
Lebensbild Bayer Schwaben — Lebensbilder aus dem Bayerischen Schwaben
Lebensm Biotechnol — Lebensmittel- und Biotechnologie
Lebensm Ernaehrung — Lebensmittel und Ernaehrung
Lebensm Ind — Lebensmittel-Industrie
Lebensmittelchem Gerichtl Chem — Lebensmittelchemie und Gerichtliche Chemie
Lebensmittelchemie u Gerichtl Chemie — Lebensmittelchemie und Gerichtliche Chemie
Lebensmittelchem Lebensmittelqual — Lebensmittelchemie, Lebensmittelqualitaet

Lebensmittel-Ind — Lebensmittel-Industrie
Lebensmittelind Milchwirtsch — Lebensmittelindustrie und Milchwirtschaft
Lebensm-Wiss Technol — Lebensmittel-Wissenschaft Technologie
Lebensm Wiss Technol Food Sci Technol — Lebensmittel-Wissenschaft und Technologie/Food Science and Technology
Lebensversicher Med — Lebensversicherungs Medizin
Leben Umwelt (Aarau) — Leben und Umwelt (Aarau)
Leben Umwelt (Aarau Switz) — Leben und Umwelt (Aarau, Switzerland)
Leben Umwelt (Wiesb) — Leben und Umwelt (Wiesbaden)
Leber Mag D — Leber Magen Darm
Lebertag Sozialmed — Lebertagung der Sozialmediziner
Leb Pharm J — Lebanese Pharmaceutical Journal
Leb Zeug — Lebendiges Zeugnis
LEC — Land Economics
LEC — Les Etudes Classiques
LeC — Lingua e Cultura
Lecciones Popular Mat — Lecciones Populares de Matematicas
Lech Diagn Primen Radioakt Izot Tr Ukr Konf — Lechebnoe i Diagnosticheskoe Primenenie Radioaktivnykh Izotopov. TrudyUkrainskoi Konferentsii
Lech Kurortakh Zabaik — Lechenie na Kurortakh Zabaikal'ya
Lech Kurortakh Zabaikalya — Lechenie na Kurortakh Zabaikal'ya
Lec Ilus — Lecciones Ilustradas
Lec Ser Div Appl Geomech CSIRO — Lecture Series. Division of Applied Geomechanics. Commonwealth Scientific and Industrial Research Organisation
Lect — Lecturas
Lect — Lectures. Revue Mensuelle de Bibliographie Critique
Lect & A — Lectura y Arte
Lect Anniv Symp Inst Math Sci Madras — Lectures Presented. Anniversary Symposium. Institute of Mathematical Sciences. Madras
Lect Appl Math — Lectures in Applied Mathematics
Lect Biblioth — Lecture et Bibliotheques
Lect Cent Ass Beekrps — Lecture to Central Association of Bee-Keepers
Lect Chania Conf — Lectures Presented at the Chania Conference
Lect Colloq Environ Prot Mech Eng — Lectures. Colloquium on Environmental Protection in MechanicalEngineering
Lect Conf Tribol — Lectures. Conference on Tribology
Lect Congr Mater Test — Lectures. Congress on Material Testing
Lect Contrib Pap Symp Plasma Heat Toroidal Devices — Lectures and Contributed Papers. Symposium on Plasma Heating in Toroidal Devices
Lect Coral Gables Conf Fundam Interact High Energy — Lectures from the Coral Gables Conference on Fundamental Interactions at High Energy
Lect Czech Pol Colloq Chem Thermodyn Phys Org Chem — Lectures. Czech-Polish Colloquium on Chemical Thermodynamics and Physical Organic Chemistry
Lect DECHEMA Annu Meet Biotechnol — Lectures. DECHEMA Annual Meeting of Biotechnologists
Lect FAO/SIDA Train Course Mar Pollut Relat Prot Living Res — Lectures Presented at the FAO/SIDA Training Course on Marine Pollutionin Relation to Protection of Living Resources
Lect Hall Chem Pharmacol — Lecture Hall for Chemistry and Pharmacology
Lect Heterocycl Chem — Lectures in Heterocyclic Chemistry
Lect High Energy Phys Lect Summer Meet Nucl Phys — Lectures on High Energy Physics. Lectures Delivered. Summer Meeting of Nuclear Physicists
Lect Int Symp Migr — Lectures. International Symposium on Migration
Lect Mat — Lecturas Matematicas
Lect Math Life Sci — Lectures on Mathematics in the Life Sciences
Lect Monogr Rep R Inst Chem — Lectures, Monographs, and Reports. Royal Institute of Chemistry
Lect Notes Biomath — Lecture Notes in Biomathematics
Lect Notes Chem — Lecture Notes in Chemistry
Lect Notes Coastal Estuarine Stud — Lecture Notes on Coastal and Estuarine Studies
Lect Notes Comput Sci — Lecture Notes in Computer Science
Lect Notes Div Tech Conf Soc Plast Eng Vinyl Plast Div — Lecture Notes Division. Technical Conference. Society of Plastics Engineers. Vinyl Plastics Divisions
Lect Notes Earth Sci — Lecture Notes in Earth Sciences
Lect Notes Math — Lecture Notes in Mathematics
Lect Notes Phys — Lecture Notes in Physics
Lect Notes Suppl Phys — Lecture Notes and Supplements in Physics
LectPT — Lectures Pour Tous
Lect Sci Basis Med — Lectures on the Scientific Basis of Medicine
Lect Theor Phys — Lectures in Theoretical Physics
Lect Thermodyn Stat Mech Winter Meet Stat Phys — Lectures on Thermodynamics and Statistical Mechanics. Winter Meeting on Statistical Physics
Lect Tous — Lectures pour Tous
Lecturas Econ — Lecturas de Economia
Lecture Notes and Suppl in Phys — Lecture Notes and Supplements in Physics
Lecture Notes Earth Sci — Lecture Notes in Earth Sciences
Lecture Notes in Biomath — Lecture Notes in Biomathematics
Lecture Notes in Chem — Lecture Notes in Chemistry
Lecture Notes in Comput Sci — Lecture Notes in Computer Science
Lecture Notes in Control and Information Sci — Lecture Notes in Control and Information Sciences
Lecture Notes in Econom and Math Systems — Lecture Notes in Economics and Mathematical Systems
Lecture Notes in Engrg — Lecture Notes in Engineering
Lecture Notes in Math — Lecture Notes in Mathematics
Lecture Notes in Med Inform — Lecture Notes in Medical Informatics
Lecture Notes in Phys — Lecture Notes in Physics
Lecture Notes in Phys New Ser M Monogr — Lecture Notes in Physics. New Series M. Monographs
Lecture Notes in Pure and Appl Math — Lecture Notes in Pure and Applied Mathematics

Lecture Notes in Statist — Lecture Notes in Statistics
Lecture Notes Logic — Lecture Notes in Logic
Lecture Notes Numer Appl Anal — Lecture Notes in Numerical and Applied Analysis
Lecture Notes Particles Fields — Lecture Notes on Particles and Fields
Lecture Notes Sci Univ Tokyo — Lecture Notes of the Science University of Tokyo
Lecture Notes Ser Comput — Lecture Notes Series on Computing
Lectures in Appl Math — Lectures in Applied Mathematics
Lectures in Math — Lectures in Mathematics
Lectures LSUC — Special Lectures. Law Society of Upper Canada
Lectures Math ETH Zuerich — Lectures in Mathematics ETH Zuerich
Lectures Math Life Sci — Lectures on Mathematics in the Life Sciences
Lect y V — Lectura y Vida
LED — Literatuuroverzicht Medezeggenschap
Ledeburs Arch — Allgemeines Archiv fuer die Geschichtskunde des Preussischen Staates
Leder Beil — Leder. Beilage
Lederbl — Lederbladet
Lederindustrie Tech Beil — Lederindustrie. Technische Beilage
Lederle Bull — Lederle Bulletin
Leder O Lons — Lederskab og Lonsomhed
Leder Schuhwarind UdSSR — Leder- und Schuhwarenindustrie der UdSSR
Ledertech Rundsch (Berlin) — Ledertechnische Rundschau (Berlin)
Ledertech Rundsch (Zurich) — Ledertechnische Rundschau (Zurich)
Le Div — Lectio Divina
L Ed US — Supreme Court Reports, Lawyer's Edition
LEE — Leefmilieu
LeE — Livre et l'Estampe
LEEC — Lettres Edifiantes et Curieuses Ecrites par des Missionaires de la Compagnie de Jesus
Leeds A Cal — Leeds Art Calendar
Leeds Dent J — Leeds Dental Journal
Leeds G As Tr — Leeds Geological Association. Transactions
Leeds Lyon Symp Tribol Proc — Leeds-Lyon Symposium on Tribology. Proceedings
Leeds Northr Tech J — Leeds and Northrup Technical Journal
Leeds Northrup Tech J — Leeds and Northrup Technical Journal
Leeds Phil Lit Soc Lit Hist Sec Proc — Leeds Philosophical and Literary Society. Literary and History Section. Proceedings
LeedsSE — Leeds Studies in English
Lee Found Nutr Res Rep — Lee Foundation for Nutritional Research. Report
Leeuwenhoek Ned Tijdschr — Leeuwenhoek Nederlandsch Tijdschrift
Left Rev — Left Review
Leg Aid R — Legal Aid Review
Leg Aid Rev — Legal Aid Review
Legal Aid Rev — Legal Aid Review
Legal Aspects Med Prac — Legal Aspects of Medical Practice
Legal Bul — Legal Bulletin
Legal Bull — Legal Bulletin
Legal Econ — Legal Economics
Legal Educ Newsl — Legal Education Newsletter
Legal Gaz (PA) — Legal Gazette (Pennsylvania)
Legal Int — Legal Intelligencer
Legal Intel — Legal Intelligencer
Legal Intell — Legal Intelligencer
Legal Malpract Rep — Legal Malpractice Reporter
Legal Med Ann — Legal Medicine Annual
Legal Med Q — Legal Medical Quarterly
Legal Res J — Legal Research Journal
Legal Serv Bull — Legal Service Bulletin
Legal Service Bul — Legal Service Bulletin
Legal Services Bul — Legal Services Bulletin
Legal Stud — Legal Studies
Legal Sys Let — Legal Systems Letter
Legal Times Wash — Legal Times of Washington
Leg Aspects Med Pract — Legal Aspects of Medical Practice
Leg Contents LC — Legal Contents. LC
Leg Ec — Legal Economics
Leg Econ — Legal Economics
Legensgesch Wiss — Lebensgeschichten aus der Wissenschaft
Leg Exam WR — Legal Examiner Weekly Reporter
Leg Exec — Legal Executive
Leg Gaz — Legal Gazette
Leg Gaz Re — Campbell's Legal Gazette Reports
Legge — Legge's Supreme Court Cases
Leg Inf Bul — Legal Information Bulletin
Leg Inf Manage Index — Legal Information Management Index
Leg Int — Legal Intelligencer
Leg Intel — Legal Intelligencer
Leg Intell — Legal Intelligencer
Leg Intelligencer — Legal Intelligencer Weekly [Philadelphia]
Leg Intl — Legal Intelligencer
Legionella Proc Int Symp — Legionella. Proceedings. International Symposium
Legion Hon — Legion d'Honneur
Legisl Netw Nurses — Legislative Network for Nurses
Legisl Stud Quart — Legislative Studies Quarterly
LEGISNET — National Legislative Network
Legis Roundup — Legislative Roundup
Legis Stud Q — Legislative Studies Quarterly
Leg Issues — Legal Issues of European Integration
Leg J — Pittsburgh Legal Journal
Leg Jour — Pittsburgh Legal Journal
Legka Promst — Legka Promislovist
Legka Tekst Promst — Legka i Tekstilna Promislovist
Legk Met — Legkie Metally

Legk Pishch Promst Podmoskov'ya — Legkaya i Pishchevaya Promyshlennost Podmoskov'ya
Legk Promst (Kaz) — Legkaya Promyshlennost (Kazakhstana)
Legk Promst (Kiev) — Legkaya Promyshlennost (Kiev)
Legk Promst (Moscow) — Legkaya Promyshlennost (Moscow)
Legk Splavy Metalloved Term Obrab Lite Obrab Davleniem Mater — Legkie Splavy Metallovedenie Termicheskaya Obrabotka. Lit'e iObrabotka Davleniem. Materialy Vsesoyuznoi Konferentsii
Legk Tekst Promst — Legkaya i Tekstil'naya Promyshlennost
Leg Med — Legal Medicine
Leg Med Annu — Legal Medicine Annual [Later, Legal Medicine]
Leg Med Annual — Legal Medicine Annual
Leg Med Q — Legal Medicine Quarterly
Leg News — Legal News
Leg Notes and View Q — Legal Notes and Viewpoints Quarterly
Leg Obs — Legal Observer and Solicitor's Journal
Legon J Humanities — Legon Journal of the Humanities
LegPer — Index to Legal Periodicals
Leg Period Dig — Legal Periodical Digest
Leg Pract & Sol J — Legal Practitioner and Solicitor's Journal
Leg Ref Serv Q — Legal Reference Services Quarterly
Leg Rep SL — Legal Reporter Special Leave Supplement
Leg Res J — Legal Research Journal
Leg Resour Index — Legal Resource Index
Leg Rev — Legal Review
Leg Sacr — Leges Graecorum Sacrae e Titulis Collectae
Leg Ser B — Legal Service Bulletin
Leg Serv Bull — Legal Service Bulletin
Leg Stud Q — Legislative Studies Quarterly
Legume Res — Legume Research
Leg YB — Legal Year Book
Leh — Lehigh County Law Journal
Leh Co LJ (PA) — Lehigh County Law Journal
Lehigh Alumni Bull — Lehigh Alumni Bulletin
Lehigh Co LJ — Lehigh County Law Journal
Lehigh LJ — Lehigh County Law Journal
Lehigh Univ Pub — Lehigh University Publications
Leh LJ — Lehigh County Law Journal
Lehrb Allg Geogr — Lehrbuch der Allgemeinen Geographie
Lehrb Anthropol — Lehrbuch der Anthropologie
Lehrb Handb Ingenieurwiss — Lehr- und Handbuecher der Ingenieurwissenschaften
Lehrb Spez Zool — Lehrbuch der Speziellen Zoologie
Lehrbuch Math — Lehrbuch Mathematik
Lehrbuecher Monograph Didakt Math — Lehrbuecher und Monographien zur Didaktik der Mathematik
Lehrbuecher Monograph Geb Exakten Wissensch Math Reihe — Lehrbuecher und Monographien aus dem Gebiete der Exakten Wissenschaften [LMW]. Mathematische Reihe
Lehrbuecher Monogr Didakt Math — Lehrbuecher und Monographien zur Didaktik der Mathematik
Lehrprogrammb Hochschulstud Chem — Lehrprogrammbuecher Hochschulstudium. Chemie
Lei — Leitura
Leibesuebungen & Koerperl Erz — Leibesuebungen und Koerperliche Erziehung
Leica Fot — Leica Fotographie
Leica Fotogr (Engl Ed) — Leica Fotografie (English Edition)
Leicester Chem Rev — Leicester Chemical Review
Leichhardt Hist J — Leichhardt Historical Journal
Leiden Bot Ser — Leiden Botanical Series
Leidsche Geol Meded — Leidsche Geologische Mededeelingen [Later, Leidse Geologische Mededelingen]
Leidse Geol Meded — Leidse Geologische Mededelingen
Leids Ksthist Jb — Leids Kunsthistorisch Jaarboek
Leiegouw — Verslagen en Mededeelingen van de Leiegouw
Leip Nf Gs Sb — Sitzungsberichte der Naturforschenden Gesellschaft zu Leipzig
Leipz Faerber Ztg — Leipziger Faerber-Zeitung
Leipz Hist Abhandl — Leipziger Historische Abhandlungen
Leipzig Bienenzt — Leipziger Bienenzeitung
Leipzig Bienenztg — Leipziger Bienenzeitung
Leipzig Charivari — Leipziger Charivari
Leipziger Gel Zeitungen — Leipziger Gelehrte Zeitungen
Leipziger Mag Naturk Math — Leipziger Magazin zur Naturkunde, Mathematik, und Oekonomie
Leipziger Vjschr Suedosteur — Leipziger Vierteljahrsschrift fuer Suedosteuropa
Leipz Monatsschr Text Ind — Leipziger Monatsschriften fuer Textil-Industrie
Leipz Rechtswiss Stud — Leipziger Rechtswissenschaftliche Studien
Leipz Roman Studien — Leipziger Romanischen Studien
Leipz Semit St — Leipziger Semitische Studien
Leipz Zeitsch F Deut Recht — Leipziger Zeitschrift fuer Deutsches Recht
Leipz Zs Dt R — Leipziger Zeitschrift fuer Deutsches Recht
Leipz Ztg Wiss Beil — Leipziger Zeitung. Wissenschaftliche Beilage
Leis and Move — Leisure and Movement
Leis Hour — Leisure Hour
Leis Recreat Tour Abstr — Leisure, Recreation, and Tourism Abstracts
Leis Rec Tourism Abs — Leisure, Recreation, and Tourism Abstracts
Leis Stud — Leisure Studies
Leis Stud Centre Rev — Leisure Studies Centre. Review
Leistung — Leistung in Zahlen
Leisure Ele — Leisure Time Electronics
Leisure Mgmt — Leisure Management
Leisure Stud — Leisure Studies
Leit — Leiturgia
Leitfaden Elektrotech — Leitfaeden der Elektrotechnik

Leitfaeden Angew Math Mech — Leitfaeden der Angewandten Mathematik und Mechanik

Leitfaeden Inform — Leitfaeden der Informatik

Leitfaeden Monographien Inform — Leitfaeden und Monographien der Informatik

Leitfaeden Monogr Inform — Leitfaeden und Monographien der Informatik

Leit Livr Rio — Leitores e Livros (Rio de Janeiro)

Leitz-Mitt Wiss & Tech — Leitz-Mitteilungen fuer Wissenschaft und Technik

Leitz-Mitt Wissen Technik — Leitz-Mitteilungen fuer Wissenschaft und Technik

Leitz Mitt Wiss Tech — Leitz-Mitteilungen fuer Wissenschaft und Technik

Leitz Sci and Tech Inf — Leitz Scientific and Technical Information

Lejeunia Mem — Lejeunia. Revue de Botanique. Memoire

Leka Promst — Leka Promishlenost

Leka Promst Tekst — Leka Promishlenost. Tekstil

Lekarn Listy — Lekarnicke Listy

Lekarsk — Lekarski

Lek Fak Univ P J Safarika Kosice Zb — Lekarska Fakulta Univerzity P. J. Safarika Kosice. Zbornik

Lek Inf — Lekarstvena Informatsiya

Lek Listy — Lekarske Listy

Lek Obz — Lekarsky Obzor

Lek Pr — Lekarske Prace

Lek Rast — Lekarstvennye Rasteniya

Lek Sirovine — Lekovite Sirovine

Lek Sredstva Dal'nego Vostoka — Lekarstvennye Sredstva Dal'nego Vostoka

Lek Syrevye Resur Irkutsk Obl — Lekarstvennye i Syrevye Resursy Irkutskoi Oblasti

Lektsii Mezhdunar Shk Vopr Ispolz EVM Yad Issled — Lektsii Mezhdunarodnoi Shkoly po Voprosam Ispol'zovaniya EVM vYadernykh Issledovaniyakh

Lek Veda Zahr — Lekarska Veda v Zahranici

Lek Wojsk — Lekarz Wojskowy

Lek Zpr — Lekarsky Zpravy

Lek Zpr Lek Fak Karlovy Univ Hradci Kralove — Lekarske Zpravy Lekarske Fakulty Karlovy University v Hradci Kralove

Leland Stanford Jr Univ Pub — Leland Stanford Junior University. Publications

LEM — Le Matin

Lembaga Ilmu Pengetahuan Indones Lembaga Metall Nas Laporan — Lembaga Ilmu Pengetahuan Indonesia. Lembaga Metallurgi Nasional.Laporan

Lembaga Metall Nas Laporan — Lembaga Metallurgi Nasional. Laporan

Lembaran Publ Lemigas — Lembaran Publikasi Lemigas

LEMIT An — LEMIT [Laboratorio de Ensayo de Materiales e Investigaciones Tecnologicas] Anales

LEMIT An Ser 2 — LEMIT [Laboratorio de Ensayo de Materiales e Investigaciones Tecnologicas] Anales. Serie 2

LeMo — Letterature Moderne

LEN — Land and Environment Notes

LenauA — Lenau Almanach

Lenauf — Lenau Forum

LenC — Lenguaje y Ciencias

Lend a H — Lend a Hand

Lending LF — Lending Law Forum

Lend LF — Lending Law Forum

LengM — Lenguas Modernas

Leninabad Gos Ped Inst Ucen Zap — Leninabadskii Gosudarstvennyi Pedagogiceskii Institut Ucenye Zapiski

Lenin Acad Agric Sci Agro Soil Inst Proc Leningrad Lab — Lenin Academy of Agricultural Science. Agro-Soil Institute. Proceedings. Leningrad Laboratory

Lenin Acad Agric Sci Gedroiz Inst Fert Agro Soil Sci Proc — Lenin Academy of Agricultural Sciences. Gedroiz Institute ofFertilizers and Agro-Soil Science. Proceedings. Leningrad Department

Leningrad Gorn Inst Zap — Leningrad Gornyy Institut Zapiski

Leningrad Gos Ped Inst Ucen Zap — Leningradskii Gosudarstvennyi Pedagogiceskii Institut Imeni A. I. Gercena Ucenye Zapiski

Leningrad Gos Univ Ucen Zap — Leningradskii Gosudarstvennyi Ordena Lenina Universitet Imeni A. A. Zdanova Ucenye Zapiski

Leningrad Gos Univ Ucen Zap Ser Mat Nauk — Leningradskii Gosudarstvennyi Ordena Lenina Universitet Imeni A. A. Zdanova Ucenye Zapiski Serija Matematiceskih Nauk

Leningrad Inz-Ekonom Inst Trudy — Leningradskii Inzenerno-Ekonomiceskii Institut Imeni Pal'miro Tol'jatti Trudy

Leningrad Inz-Stroitel Inst Sb Trudov — Leningradskii Inzhenerno-Stroitel'skii Institut Sbornik Trudov

Leningrad Meh Inst Sb Trudov (LMI) — Leningradskii Mekhaniceskii Institut Sbornik Trudov (LMI)

Leningrad Politehn Inst Trudy — Leningradskii Politehniceskii Institut Imeni M. I. Kalinina Trudy LPI

Leningrad Univ Vestn Geol Geogr — Leningradskii Universitet Vestnik Geologiya i Geografiya

Leningr Elektrotekh Inst Im VI Ulyanova Izv — Leningradskii Elektrotekhnicheskii Institut Imeni V. I. Ul'yanova.Izvestiya

Leningr Gidrometeorol Inst Sb Nauchn Tr — Leningradskii Gidrometeorologicheskii Institut. Sbornik NauchnykhTrudov

Leningr Gidrometeorol Inst Tr — Leningradskii Gidrometeorologicheskii Institut. Trudy

Leningr Gos Inst Usoversh Vrachei Im SM Kirova Nauchn Tr — Leningradskii Gosudarstvennyi Institut Usovershenstvovaniya VracheiImeni S. M. Kirova. Nauchnye Trudy

Leningr Gos Pedagog Inst Im M N Pokrovskogo Uch Zap — Leningradskii Gosudarstvennyi Pedagogicheskii Institut Imeni M. N.Pokrovskogo. Uchenye Zapiski

Leningr Gos Univ Im A A Zhdanova Uch Zap Ser Fiz Geol Nauk — Leningradskii Gosudarstvennyi Universitet Imeni A. A. Zhdanova. UchenyeZapiski. Seriya Fizicheskikh i Geologicheskikh Nauk

Leningr Inst Aviats Priborostr Tr — Leningradskii Institut Aviatsionnogo Priborostroeniya. Trudy

Leningr Inst Gig Tr Tekh Bezop Byull — Leningradskii Institut Gigieny Truda i Tekhniki Bezopasnosti. Byulleten

Leningr Inst Gig Tr Tekh Bezop Tr Mater — Leningradskii Institut Gigieny Trudy i Tekhniki Bezopasnosti. Trudy iMaterialy

Leningr Inst Sov Torg Sb Tr — Leningradskii Institut Sovetskoi Torgovli Sbornik Trudov

Leningr Inst Tochn Mekh Opt Tr — Leningradskii Institut Tochnoi Mekhaniki i Optiki Trudy

Leningr Inst Usoversh Vet Vrachei Sb Nauchn Tr — Leningradskii Institut Usovershenstvovaniya Veterinarnykh Vrachei.Sbornik Nauchnykh Trudov

Leningr Inzh Mezhvuz Temat Sb Tr — Leningradskii Inzhenerno-Stroitel'nyi Institut Mezhvuzovskii Tematicheskii Sbornik Trudov

Leningr Inzh Stroit Inst Mezhvuz Temat Sb — Leningradskii Inzhenerno-Stroitel'nyi Institut Mezhvuzovskii Tematicheskii Sbornik

Leningr Inzh Stroit Inst Sb Tr — Leningradskii Inzhenerno-Stroitel'nyii Institut Sbornik Trudov

Leningr Korablestroit Inst Tr — Leningradskii Korablestroitel'nyi Institut. Trudy

Leningr Lesotekh Akad Im S M Kirova Nauchn Tr — Leningradskaya Lesotekhnicheskaya Akademiya Imeni S. M. Kirova.Nauchnye Trudy

Leningr Mekh Inst Sb Tr — Leningradskii Mekhanicheskii Institut Sbornik Trudov

Leningr Met Zavod Tr — Leningradskii Metallicheskii Zavod Trudy

Leningr Mezhdunar Semin — Leningradskii Mezhdunarodnyi Seminar

Leningr Nauchno Issled Inst Gematol Pereliv Krovi Sb Tr — Leningradskii Nauchno-Issledovatel'skii Institut Gematologii i Perelivaniya Krovi Sbornik Trudov

Leningr Nauchno Issled Inst Lesn Khoz Sb Nauchn Tr — Leningradskii Nauchno-Issledovatel'skii Institut Lesnogo Khozyaistva Sbornik Nauchnykh Trudov

Leningr Nauchno Issled Konstr Inst Khim Mashinostr Tr — Leningradskii Nauchno-Issledovatel'skii i Konstruktorskii Institut Khimicheskogo Mashinostroeniya Trudy

Leningr Ovo Estestvoispyt Tr — Leningradskoe Obshchestvo Estestvoispytatelei. Trudy

Leningr Politekh Inst im M I Kalinina Tr — Leningradskii Politekhnicheskii Institut imeni M. I. Kalinina. Trudy

Leningr Sanit Gig Med Inst Tr LSGMI — Leningradskii Sanitarno-Gigienicheskii Meditsinskii Institut. TrudyLSGMI

Leningr Semin Kosmofiz Mater — Leningradskii Seminar po Kosmofizike. Materialy

Leningr Skh Inst Nauchn Tr — Leningradskii Sel'skokhozyaistvennyi Institut. Nauchnye Trudy

Leningr Tekhnol Inst Tsellyul Bum Promsti Tr — Leningradskii Tekhnologicheskii Institut Tsellyulozno-Bumazhnoi PromyshlennostiTrudy

Leningr Vet Inst Sb Nauchn Rab — Leningradskii Veterinarnyi Institut. Sbornik Nauchnykh Rabot

Len Konop — Len i Konopliya

LeNo — Lettres Nouvelles

Lens Eye Toxic Res — Lens and Eye Toxicity Research

Lens Res — Lens Research

Lenzinger Ber — Lenzinger Berichte

Lenz N — Lenzburger Neujahrsblaetter

Leo — Leonardo

Leo Baeck Inst Jews Germ Yrbk — Leo Baeck Institute of Jews from Germany. Yearbook

Leo Baeck Inst Yearb — Leo Baeck Institute Yearbook

Leod — Leodium

Leon — Leonardo

Leonardo Rass Bibliog — Leonardo. Rassegna Bibliografica

Leonardo Rass Mens Colt It — Leonardo. Rassegna Mensile della Coltura Italiana

Leonardo Saggi & Ric — Leonardo. Saggi e Ricerche

Leonard U Bronn N Jb — Neues Jahrbuch fuer Mineralogie, Geognosie, Geologie, und Petrefaktenkunde. Leonhard und Bronn

Leonhards Zschr — Zeitschrift fuer Mineralogie (By K. C. Von Leonhard)

Leonhar Eul Opera Omnia Ser 2 — Leonharki Euleri Opera Omnia. Series Secunda

LEP — Latin America Weekly Report

LEPDAV — Lepidoptera

LEPMJS — London, Edinburgh, and Dublin Philosophical Magazine and Journal of Science

Lep Rev — Leprosy Review

Lepr India — Leprosy in India

Leprosy Rev — Leprosy Review

Lepr Rev — Leprosy Review

Lepton Photon Interact Int Symosium — Lepton-Photon Interactions. International Symosium

Le Puy A S Ag — Annales de la Soci t d'Agriculture, Sciences, Arts et Commerce du Puy (Le Puy)

Le Puy S Ag A — Annales de la Soci t d'Agriculture, Sciences, Arts et Commerce du Puy (Le Puy)

Ler — Lerindustrien

LEREA — Leprosy Review

LERS (Lab Etud Rech Synthelabo) Monogr Ser — LERS (Laboratoires d'Etudes et de Recherches Synthelabo) Monograph Series

LERS Monogr Ser — LERS [Laboratoires d'Etudes et de Recherches Synthelabo] Monograph Series

Les — Lesonenu. Quarterly of Hebrew

LES — Library of Ecumenical Studies

LeS — Lingua e Stile

LES — London Evening Standard

LES — Los Ensayistas

Lesbian T — Lesbian Tide

Les Khoz — Lesnoe Khozyaistvo

Leslies Illus News — Leslie's Illustrated News

Lesnaya Prom — Lesnaya Promyshlennost

Lesn Bum Derevoobrab Promst (Kiev) — Lesnaya Bumazhnaya i Derevoobrabatyvayushchaya Promyshlennost (Kiev)
Lesn Cas — Lesnicky Casopis
Lesn Hoz — Lesnoe Hozjajstvo
Lesnictvi Cesk Akad Zemed Ustav Vedeckotech Inf Zemed — Lesnictvi. Ceskoslovenska Akademie Zemedelska Ustav Vedeckotechnickych Informaci pro Zemedelstvi
Lesn Ind — Lesnaya Industriya
Lesn Khoz — Lesnoe Khozyaistvo
Lesn Khoz Agrolesomelior Kaz — Lesnoe Khozyaisto i Agrolesomelioratsiya v Kazakhstane
Lesn Khoz Lesn Bum Derevoobrab Promst — Lesnoe Khozyaistvo, Lesnaya, Bumazhnaya i DerevoobrabatyvayushchayaPromyshlennost
Lesnoe Khoz — Lesnoe Khozyaistvo
Lesn Pr — Lesnicka Prace
Lesn Prace — Lesnicka Prace
Lesn Prom — Lesnaja Promyslennost
Lesn Prom-St — Lesnaya Promyshlennost
Lesn Zahr — Lesnictvi v Zahranici
Lesn Zh (Archangel USSR) — Lesnoi Zhurnal (Archangel, USSR)
Lesokhim Podsochka — Lesokhimiya i Podsochka
Lesokhim Promst — Lesokhimicheskaya Promyshlennost
Lesoprom Delo — Lesopromyshlennoe Delo
Lesotho Notes Recs — Lesotho Notes and Records
Lesoved — Lesovedenie
Lesoved Lesn Khoz — Lesovedenie i Lesnoe Khozyaistvo
Lesovod Agrolesomelior — Lesovodstvo i Agrolesomelioratsiia
Lesovod Agrolesomelior Resp Mezhved Temat Sb — Lesovodstvo i Agrolesomelioratsiya Respublikanskii Mezhvedomstvennyi Tematicheskii Sbornik
Lesovod Nauchn Soobshch — Lesovodstvenno-Nauchnye Soobshcheniya
L'Esprit — L'Esprit Createur
Les Prom — Lesnaya Promyshlennost
Lessing Yb — Lessing Yearbook
LEst — Le Lingue Estere
Les Zh — Lesnoi Zhurnal
Let — Le Temps
Let — Letteratura
Let — Livre de l'Etudiant
LetD — Letras de Deusto
LetE — Letras del Ecuador
LetF — Lettres Francaises
LetFB — Lettres Francaises (Buenos Aires)
LetG — Lettres (Geneva)
Let It — Lettere Italiane
LetM — Lettres Modernes
LetM — Lettrisme Mensuel
Let Mat Srp — Letopis Matice Srpske
LetMs — Letopis Matice Srpske
LetN — Lettres Nouvelles
LetNa — Letras Nacionales
Letn Raboty — Letnija Raboty. Travaux des Vacances. Station Biologique du Wolga
Letopisi Khig-Epidemiol Inst — Letopisi na Khigienno-Epidemiologichnite Instituti
Letopisi Khig-Epidemiol Sluzhba — Letopisi na Khigienno-Epidemiologichnata Sluzhba
Letopis Jschr Serb Volksforsch — Letopis Jahresschrift des Instituts fuer Serbische Volksforschung
Letop Nauc Rad Poljopriv Fak Novi Sad — Letopis Naucnih Radova. Poljoprivredni Fakultet. Novi Sad
LetP — Lettres. Poesie, Philosophie, Litterature, Critique
Letr Art Maracaibo — Letras y Artes (Maracaibo)
LetrasC — Letras (Caracas)
Letr Curitiba — Letras (Curitiba, Brazil)
Letr Lima — Letras (Lima)
Letr Mex Mex — Letras de Mexico (Mexico)
Letr Nac Bogota — Letras Nacionales (Bogota)
Let Rom — Lettres Romanes
Lett — Letteratura
Lett Alb — Lettres Albanaises
Lett & A — Lettres et les Arts
Lett & Not Inter J Eng Prov SJ — Letters and Notices. The Internal Journal of the English Provinces of the Society of Jesus
Lett Appl and Eng Sci — Letters in Applied and Engineering Sciences
Lett Appl Eng Sci — Letters in Applied and Engineering Sciences
Lett Appl Microbiol — Letters in Applied Microbiology
Lett Bot — Lettres Botaniques
Lett Brew — Letters on Brewing
Lett Bull Ethnomed — Lettre du Bulletin ?d'Ethnomedecine
Lett Fr — Lettres Francaises
Lett Heat and Mass Transfer — Letters in Heat and Mass Transfer
Lett Heat Mass Transf — Letters in Heat and Mass Transfer
Lett Heat Mass Transfer — Letters in Heat and Mass Transfer
Lett Inf Bur Rech Geol Min — Lettre d'Information. Bureau de Recherches Geologiques et Minieres
Lett It — Lettere Italiane
Lett Ital — Lettere Italiane
Lett It Contemp — Letteratura Italiana Contemporanea
Lett Math Phys — Letters in Mathematical Physics
Lett Med Tours — Lettre Medicale de Tours
Lett Mod — Letterature Moderne
Lett Mod — Universita Bocconi. Letterature Moderne. Rivista di Varia Umanita
Lett Nuov C — Lettere al Nuovo Cimento
Lett Nuovo Cim — Lettere al Nuovo Cimento
Lett Nuovo Cimento — Lettere al Nuovo Cimento

Lett Nuovo Cimento Soc Ital Fis — Lettere al Nuovo Cimento. Societa Italiana di Fisica
Lett Pap Agric Bath Soc — Letters and Papers on Agriculture, Planting, etc. Selected from the Correpondence-Book. Bath and West and Southern Counties Society
Lett Pept Sci — Letters in Peptide Science
Lett Pharm — Lettre Pharmaceutique
Lettre Inf — Lettre d'Information
Lettres Fr — Lettres Francaises
Lettres Fr BA — Lettres Francaises. Buenos-Aires
Lettres Fr Mo — Lettres Francaises. Montevideo
Lettres Rom — Lettres Romanes
Lett Roman — Lettres Romanes
Lettura Oft — Lettura Oftalmologica
Lett Vinc — Lettura Vinciana
Leu Bij — Leuvense Bijdragen
Leucocyte Cult Conf Proc — Leucocyte Culture Conference. Proceedings
Leukemia Abstr — Leukemia Abstracts
Leuk Lymphoma — Leukemia and Lymphoma
Leuk Lymphoma Res — Leukaemia and Lymphoma Research
Leukocytes Host Def Proc Meet Int Leukocyte Cult Conf — Leukocytes and Host Defense. Proceedings. Meeting. International Leukocyte Culture Conference
Leuk Res — Leukemia Research
Leuk Soc Am Res Inc Annu Scholar Fellow Meet — Leukemia Society of America Research, Inc. Annual Scholar Fellow Meeting
Leuv Bijd — Leuvensche Bijdragen
Leuv Bijdr — Leuvense Bijdragen
Levant Recursos Nat Proj Radam (Bras) — Levantamento de Recursos Naturais. Projecto Radam (Brasil)
Leveltari Kozlem — Leveltari Kozlemenyei
Leveltari Sz — Leveltari Szemle
Levende Kst — Levende Kunst
Levende Nat — Levende Natuur
LEVID — Leviathan
Levnedsmbl — Levnedsmiddelbladet
Levnedsmiddelstyr Publ — Levnedsmiddelstyrelsen Publikation
LevT — Levende Talen
LEW — (La) Educacion (Washington, D. C.)
LEW — Lateinisches Etymologisches Woerterbuch
LEW — Literature East and West
LEW Nachr — LEW [*Lokomotivbau-Elektrotechnische Werke*] Nachrichten
Lex — Lexis
Lex AW — Lexikon der Alten Welt
Lex Cap — Lexicon Capuccinum
Lexington Hist Soc Proc — Lexington Historical Society. Proceedings
Lex Jud — Lexikon des Judentums
Lex Myth — Ausfuehrliches Lexikon der Griechischen und Roemischen Mythologie
L Exr — Launceston Examiner
L Exr (Newspr) (Tas) — Launceston Examiner (Newspaper) (Tasmania)
Lex Sci — Lex et Scientia
Lex Th Q — Lexington Theological Quarterly
Lex TQ — Lexington Theological Quarterly
Lex Vindob — Lexicon Vindobonense
Leybold Polarogr Ber — Leybold Polarographische Berichte
Leyte-Samar Stud — Leyte-Samar Studies
LF — Le Figaro
LF — Letras Femeninas
LF — Lettres Francaises
LF — Lia Fail
LF — Limesforschungen
LF — Listy Filologicke
LF — Literarhistorische Forschungen
LF — Literaturen Front
LF — Liturgiegeschichtliche Forschungen
LF — University of Illinois. Law Forum
LFA — Lolland Falsters Historiske Samfund. Arbog
LF Aa — Lolland-Falsters Historiske Samfunds Aarbog
LFAR — Liberal and Fine Arts Review
LFE — Lexikon des Fruegriechischen Epos
L Fem — Letras Femeninas
LFFTD — Laser Focus with Fiberoptic Technology
L Fgr E — Lexikon des Fruegriechischen Epos
LFIl — Listy Filologicke
LFQ — Literature/Film Quarterly
LFr — Langue Francaise
Lfr — Lettres Francaises (Buenos Aires)
LF(RA) — Listy Filologicke. Supplement. Revue Archeologique
L Front — Literaturen Front
LFS — Lettres Francaises
LfSC — Librarians for Social Change. Journal
LF Stiftsm — Lolland-Falsters Stiftsmuseums Arsskrift
LFT — Ley Federal de Trabajo
Lg — Language
Lg — Language. Linguistics Society of America
LG — Lateinische Grammatik
LG — Literary Guide
LG — Literaturnaya Gazeta
LG — London Gazette
LGATR — Local Government Appeals Tribunal Reports
LGATR (NSW) — Local Government Appeals Tribunal Reports (New South Wales)
LGB — Local Government Bulletin
LGBBA3 — Acta Botanica Horti Bucurestiensis
LGBW — Lexikon des Gesamten Buchwesens
LGC Occas Pap — LGC [*Laboratory of the Government Chemist*] Occasional Paper

LGE — Food and Nonfood. Fachzeitschrift fuer Unternehmer und Fuhrungskrafte Moderner Grossformen in Lebensmittelhandel
LGF — Lunder Germanistische Forschungen
LGJ — Lost Generation Journal
LGL & P — Local Government Law and Practice
LGM — Lexica Graeca Minora
LGM — Local Government Management
LGO — Local Government Officer
LGO — Local Government Ordinances
Lgoru Inf Bull — Lgoru Information Bulletin
LGP — Lexikon zur Geschichte und Politik des 20. Jahrhunderts
LGPIT — Leningrad Pedagogical Institute of Foreign Languages. Transactions
LGr — Literaturnaya Gruziya
LGR — New South Wales Local Government Reports
LGRA — Local Government Reports of Australia
LGRED — Local Government Review
LG Rev — Local Government Review
LGR (NSW) — Local Government Law Reports (New South Wales)
LGRP — Literaturblatt fuer Germanische und Romanische Philologie
LGRPh — Literaturblatt fuer Germanische und Romanische Philologie
LGRR — Last Generation of the Roman Republic
LGS — Leges Graecorum Sacrae e Titulis Collectae
LGSHA — Language, Speech, and Hearing Services in Schools
LGTRA — Logistics and Transportation Review
LGU — Leningrad State University. Philology Series. Transactions
LGVI — List of Greek Verse Inscriptions down to 400 BC
LH — Labour History
LH — Liceo de la Habana
LH — Lincoln Herald
LH — Literarischer Handweiser
LH — Livres Hebdomadaires
LH — Lodging Hospitality
LH — Lone Hand
LH — Lykisch und Hittitisch
LHB — Laboratory Hazards Bulletin
LHB — Lock Haven Bulletin
LHBEDM — Law and Human Behavior
LHD — Library of History and Doctrine
L Herle — Land van Herle
LHJ — Ladies' Home Journal
LHMA — Lateinische Hymnen des Mittelalters
LHQ — Louisiana Historical Quarterly
LHR — Lectures on the History of Religions
LHR — Lock Haven Review
LHSb — Literarnohistoricky Sbornik
LHSI — Litteraria Historica Slovaca
LHSSP — Les Houches Summer School Proceedings
LHW — Literarischer Handweiser
LHY — Literary Half-Yearly
LI — Legal Intelligencer
LI — Legislative Instrument
LI — Lessico Ittito
LI — Lettere Italiane
Li — Libri
LI — Libro Italiano
Li — Limia
Li — Lingua
Li — Listener
LI — Literature and Art
LI — Luce Intellettuale
Liai — Liaison
Liaison Rep Commonw Geol Liaison Off — Liaison Report. Commonwealth Geological Liaison Office
Liaisons Soc — Liaisons Sociales
Liais Serv Note For Res Lab (Winnipeg) — Liaison and Services Note. Forest Research Laboratory (Winnipeg)
LIANEI — Liver Annual
LIAR — Report. Labrador Inuit Association
Lib — Liberation [Paris daily]
Lib — Libraries
LIB — Library
Lib — Libya
Lib AE — Libyca [Alger]. Archeologie, Epigraphie
LibAnt — Libya Antiqua
Lib APE — Libyca [Alger]. Anthropologie, Prehistoire, Ethnographie
Lib Arts J Nat Sci Tottori Univ — Liberal Arts Journal. Natural Science. Tottori University
Lib Assn Alta Bull — Library Association of Alberta. Bulletin
Lib Assn R — Library Association. Record
Lib Assn Rec — Library Association. Record
Lib Assn Yrbk — Library Association. Yearbook
Lib Assoc Rec — Library Association. Record
LibB — Libre Belgique
Lib Bicentenaire Revolution Francaise — Librarie du Bicentenaire de la Revolution Francaise
Lib Binder — Library Binder
Lib Brow — Librarians' Browser
LibC — Library Chronicle
Lib Chron — Library Chronicle
Lib Coll J — Library College Journal
Lib Colon — Libri Coloniarum
Lib Cong Inf Bull — Library of Congress. Information Bulletin
Lib Cong Q J — Library of Congress. Quarterly Journal
Lib Cong Q J Cur Acq — Library of Congress. Quarterly Journal of Current Acquisitions

LibE — Liberte de l'Esprit
LIB ED — Libertarian Education: A Magazine for the Liberation of Learning
Lib Educ — Liberal Education
Lib Engrg Math — Library of Engineering Mathematics
Liber — Liberation
Liberal Arts J Tottori Univ — Liberal Arts Journal. Tottori University/Tottori Daigaku Gakugeibu Kenkyu Hokoku
Liberal Ed — Liberal Education
Liberal Educ — Liberal Education
Liberal Geol Soc Cross Sec Type Log — Liberal Geological Society. Cross Sections. Type Log
Liberation Bull — Liberation Bulletin
LIBER Bull — Ligue des Bibliotheques Europeennes de Recherche. Bulletin
Liberia Bull — Liberia Bulletin
Liberian Econ Mgmt Rev — Liberian Economic and Management Review
Liberian LJ — Liberian Law Journal
LiberianSJ — Liberian Studies Journal
Liberian Stud J — Liberian Studies Journal
Liber Stud J — Liberian Studies Journal
Libertas Math — Libertas Mathematica
LiberteP — Liberte (Paris)
Libert Math — Libertas Mathematica. American Romanian Academy of Arts and Sciences
Lib F A — Library of the Fine Arts
Lib Giorn — Libri del Giorno
Lib Herald — Library Herald
Lib Hist — Library History
Libica Archeol — Libyca. Serie Archeologie-Epigraphique
Lib Inf Bull — Library Information Bulletin
Lib Inf News — Library Information Newsletter
Lib Inf Sci — Library and Information Science
LibJ — Library Journal
Lib Jot — Library Jottings
Lib Jour — Library Journal
Lib Jud — Liberal Judaism
Lib Leaves — Library Leaves from the Library of Long Island University
LibLit — Library Literature
Lib (London) — Library (London)
Lib Manage Bul — Library Management Bulletin
LibN — Library Notes
Libn & Bk W — Librarian and Book World
Lib News Bul — Library News Bulletin
Lib Occurrent — Library Occurrent
Lib Op — Library Opinion
Lib Opinion — Liberal Opinion
Lib Opinion — Library Opinion
Lib Period Round Table Newsletter — Library Periodicals Round Table. Newsletter
Lib Prog — Library Progress
Lib Pty Aust NSW Div Res Bull — Liberal Party of Australia. New South Wales Division. Research Bulletin
Lib Q — Library Quarterly
Lib Qtr — Library Quarterly
Libr — Librarium
Libr — Library and Library Chronicle (London)
Lib R — Library Review
Libr Acquis Pract and Theory — Library Acquisitions. Practice and Theory
Libr and Inf Sci — Library and Information Science
Libr AR — Library Association. Record
Library J — Library Journal
Library Mag — Library Magazine
Library Op — Library Opinion
Library Sci (Japan) — Library Science (Japan)
Libr Ass Aust Univ Coll Libr Sect News Sh — Library Association of Australia. University and College Libraries Section. News Sheet
Libr Assoc Rec — Library Association. Record
Libr Ass Rec — Library Association. Record
Libr Binder — Library Binder
Libr Bull Univ Lond — Library Bulletin. University of London
Libr Chron — Library Chronicle
Libr Chron Univ Tex — Library Chronicle. University of Texas
Libr Chron UTA — Library Chronical. University of Texas at Austin
Libr Coll J — Library College Journal
Libr Comput Equip Rev — Library Computer Equipment Review
Libr Congr Acquis Manuscr Div — Library of Congress Acquisitions. Manuscript Division
Libr Congr Inf Bull — Library of Congress. Information Bulletin
Lib Res — Library Research
Lib Resources & Tech Serv — Library Resources and Technical Services
Lib Resources and Tech Services — Library Resources and Technical Services
Lib Res Tec — Library Resources and Technical Services
Lib Rev — Library Review
Libr Her — Library Herald
Libr Hist — Library History
Libri & Doc — Libri e Documenti
Libr Inf Bull — Library and Information Bulletin
Libr Inf Sci Abstr — Library and Information Science Abstracts
Libri Oncol — Libri Oncologici
LIBRIS — Library Information System
Libr J — Library Journal
Libr Jour NY — Library Journal (New York)
Libr Lit — Library Literature
Libr Mater Afr — Library Materials on Africa
Libr Mater Africa — Library Materials on Africa
Libr News Bull — Library News Bulletin

Libr Newsl — Librarians' Newsletter
Libr Notes R Commonw Soc — Library Notes. Royal Commonwealth Society
Libro Actas Congr Nac Med Hig Segur Trab — Libro de Actas. Congreso Nacional de Medicina, Higiene, y Seguridad delTrabajo
Libro Pueblo Mex — El Libro y el Pueblo (Mexico)
Libr Q — Library Quarterly
Libr Quart — Library Quarterly
Libr Resour and Tech Serv — Library Resources and Technical Services
Libr Resources Tech Serv — Library Resources and Technical Services
Libr Resources Tech Servs — Library Resources and Technical Services
Libr Resour Tech Serv — Library Resources and Technical Services
Libr Rev — Library Review
Libr Rev For Comm (Lond) — Library Review. Forestry Commission (London)
Libr Sci Abstr — Library Science Abstracts
Libr Sci Slant Doc — Library Science with a Slant to Documentation
Libr Sci Slant Docum — Library Science with a Slant to Documentation
Libr Technol Rep — Library Technology Reports
Libr Trends — Library Trends
Libr W — Library World
Libr Wld — Library World
Lib Scene — Library Scene
Lib Sci — Library Science
LibSciAb — Library and Information Science Abstracts
Lib Sci Slant Doc — Library Science with a Slant to Documentation
Lib Sci Update — Library Science Update
Libt — Libertaire
LibT — Library Trends
Lib Tech Rep — Library Technology Reports
Lib Trends — Library Trends
Lib W — Library World
Libya Ant — Libya Antiqua
Libya Minist Ind Geol Sec Bull — Libya. Ministry of Industry. Geological Section. Bulletin
Libya Minist Ind Geol Sect Bull — Libya. Ministry of Industry. Geological Section. Bulletin
Libyan J Agric — Libyan Journal of Agriculture
Libyan J Earth Sci — Libyan Journal of Earth Science
Libyan J Sci — Libyan Journal of Science
Libyan Stud — Libyan Studies
Lic — Licorne
LIC — Life Insurance in Canada
Licensing L and Bus Rep — Licensing Law and Business Report
Licens Int — Licensing International
Licentiate All-India Mon J Med Surg — Licentiate All-India Monthly Journal of Medicine and Surgery
LICH — Lichenologist
Lichenol Prog Probl Proc Int Symp — Lichenology. Progress and Problems. Proceedings. InternationalSymposium
Licht-Forsch — Licht-Forschung
Lichttech — Lichttechnik
Lick Obs Bull — Lick Observatory Bulletin
Lick Obs Ct — Contributions from the Lick Observatory
LicP — Liceus de Portugal
LiD — Literatur im Dialog
LIDM — L.I.D. (League for Industrial Democracy) Monthly
Lidoflazin Int Lidoflazin Symp — Lidoflazin. Clinium. Internationales Lidoflazin Symposion
LIE — Lectures in Economics. Theory, Institutions, Policy
LIE — Legal Issues of European Integration
Lieb A — Annalen der Chemie und Pharmacie. Liebig
Liebigs Ann — Liebigs Annalen. Organic and Bioorganic Chemistry
Liebigs Ann Chem — Liebigs Annalen der Chemie
Liebigs Ann Recl — Liebigs Annalen/Recueil. Organic and Bioorganic Chemistry. A European Journal
Liege A Ac — Annales Academiae Leodiensis (Liege)
Liege Mm S Sc — Memoires de la Societe Royale des Sciences, de l'Agriculture, et des Arts a Liege
Liege S Gl Blg A — Annales de la Societe Geologique de Belgique (Liege)
Liege S Sc Mm — Memoires de la Societe Royale des Sciences, de l'Agriculture, et des Arts a Liege
Lie Groups Appl — Lie Groups and their Applications
Lie Groups Hist Frontiers and Appl — Lie Groups. History. Frontiers and Applications
Lie Groups Hist Frontiers and Appl Ser A — Lie Groups. History, Frontiers, and Applications. Series A
Lie Groups Hist Frontiers and Appl Ser B Systems Inform Contr — Lie Groups. History, Frontiers, and Applications. Series B. Systems Informationand Control
Liet — Lietuvos TSR Mokslu Akademijos Darbai
Liet Archeol — Lietuvos Archeologija
Liet Fiz Rink — Lietuvos Fizikos Rinkinys
Liet Fiz Rinkinys — Lietuvos Fizikos Rinkinys
Liet Fiz Z — Lietuvos Fizikos Zurnalas
Liet Geol Mokslines Konf Medziaga — Lietuvos Geologu Mokslines Konferencijos Medziaga
Liet Geol Mokslinio Tyrimo Inst Darb — Lietuvos Geologijos Mokslinio Tyrimo Institutas Darbai
Liet Gyvulinink Mokslinio Tyrimo Inst Darb — Lietuvos Gyvulininkystes Mokslinio Tyrimo Instituto Darbai
Liet Gyvulinink Vet Mokslinio Tyrimo Inst Darb — Lietuvos Gyvulininkystes ir Veterinarijos Mokslinio Tyrimo Instituto Darbai
Liet Hidrotech Melior Mokslinio Tyrimo Inst Darb — Lietuvos Hidrotechnikos ir Melioracijos Mokslinio Tyrimo Instituto Darbai
Liet Hidrotech Melior Mokslinio Tyrimo Inst Mokslines Konf — Lietuvos Hidrotechnikos ir Melioracijos Mokslinio Tyrimo InstitutoMokslines Konferencijos Sutrumpintu Pranesimu Medziaga

Liet Ist Metrastis — Lietuvos Istorijos Metrastis
Liet Mat Rink — Lietuvos Matematikos Rinkinys
Liet Mech Rinkinys — Lietuvos Mechanikos Rinkinys
Liet Misku Ukio Mokslinio Tyrimo Inst Darb — Lietuvos Misku Ukio Mokslinio Tyrimo Instituto Darbai
Liet Mokslu Akad Biol — Lietuvos Mokslu Akademija. Biologija
Liet Mokslu Akad Ekol — Lietuvos Mokslu Akademija. Ekologija
Liet Mokslu Akad Eksp Biol — Lietuvos Mokslu Akademija. Eksperimentine Biologija
Liet TSR Aukst Mokslo Darb Chem Chem Technol — Lietuvos TSR Aukstuju Mokyklu Mokslo Darbai. Chemija ir Chemine Technologija
Liet TSR Aukst Mokyklu Moksl Darb Ultragarsas — Lietuvos TSR Aukstuju Mokyklu Mokslo Darbai. Ultragarsas
Liet TSR Aukst Mokyklu Moksliniai Darb Radioelektron — Lietuvos TSR Aukstuju Mokyklu Moksliniai Darbai. Radioelektronika
Liet TSR Aukst Mokyklu Mokslo Darb Biol — Lietuvos TSR Aukstuju Mokyklu Mokslo Darbai. Biologija
Liet TSR Aukst Mokyklu Mokslo Darb Chem Chem Technol — Lietuvos TSR Aukstuju Mokyklu Mokslo Darbai. Chemija ir Chemine Technologija
Liet TSR Aukst Mokyklu Mokslo Darb Elektrotech Autom — Lietuvos TSR Aukstuju Mokyklu Mokslo Darbai. Elektrotechnika ir Automatika
Liet TSR Aukst Mokyklu Mokslo Darb Elektrotech Mech — Lietuvos TSR Aukstuju Mokyklu Mokslo Darbai. Elektrotechnika ir Mechanika
Liet TSR Aukst Mokyklu Mokslo Darb Geogr — Lietuvos TSR Aukstuju Mokyklu Mokslo Darbai. Geografija
Liet TSR Aukst Mokyklu Mokslo Darb Geogr Geol — Lietuvos TSR Aukstuju Mokyklu Mokslo Darbai. Geografija ir Geologija
Liet TSR Aukst Mokyklu Mokslo Darb Geol — Lietuvos TSR Aukstuju Mokyklu Mokslo Darbai. Geologija
Liet TSR Aukst Mokyklu Mokslo Darb Mech — Lietuvos TSR Aukstuju Mokyklu Mokslo Darbai. Mechanika
Liet TSR Aukst Mokyklu Mokslo Darb Mech Technol — Lietuvos TSR Aukstuju Mokyklu Mokslo Darbai. Mechanine Technologija
Liet TSR Aukst Mokyklu Mokslo Darb Med — Lietuvos TSR Aukstuju Mokyklu Mokslo Darbai. Medicina
Liet TSR Aukst Mokyklu Mokslo Darb Statyba Archit — Lietuvos TSR Aukstuju Mokyklu Mokslo Darbai. Statyba ir Architektura
Liet TSR Aukst Mokyklu Mokslo Darb Tekst Odos Technol — Lietuvos TSR Aukstuju Mokyklu Mokslo Darbai. Tekstiles ir Odos Technologija
Liet TSR Aukst Mokyklu Mokslo Darb Ultragarsas — Lietuvos TSR Aukstuju Mokyklu Mokslo Darbai. Ultragarsas
Liet TSR Aukst Mokyklu Mokslo Darb Vibrotech — Lietuvos TSR Aukstuju Mokyklu Mokslo Darbai. Vibrotechnika
Liet TSR Chem Anal Mokslines Konf Darb — Lietuvos TSR Chemiku Analitiku Mokslines Konferencijos Darbai
Liet TSR Geogr Draugija Geogr Metrastis — Lietuvos TSR Geografine Draugija. Geografinis Metrastis
Liet TSR Mokslu Akad Bot Inst Bot Klausimai — Lietuvos TSR Mokslu Akademiya Botanikos Institutas. Botanikos Klausimai
Liet TSR Mokslu Akad Bot Inst Straipsniu Rinkinys — Lietuvos TSR Mokslu Akademija Botanikos Institutas Straipsniu Rinkinys
Liet TSR Mokslu Akad Darb — Lietuvos TSR Mokslu Akademijos Darbai
Liet TSR Mokslu Akad Darbai B — Lietuvos TSR Mokslu Akademijos Darbai. Serija B
Liet TSR Mokslu Akad Darb Ser A — Lietuvos TSR Mokslu Akademijos Darbai A Serija
Liet TSR Mokslu Akad Darb Ser B — Lietuvos TSR Mokslu Akademijos Darbai. Serija B
Liet TSR Mokslu Akad Darb Ser C — Lietuvos TSR Mokslu Akademijos Darbai. Serija C
Liet TSR Mokslu Akad Darb Ser C Biol Mokslai — Lietuvos TSR Mokslu Akademijos Darbai. Serija C. Biologijos Mokslai
Liet TSR Mokslu Akad Eksp Med Inst Darb — Lietuvos TSR Mokslu Akademijos Eksperimentines Medicinos Instituto Darbai
Liet TSR Mokslu Akad Geogr Skyrius Moksliniai Pranesimai — Lietuvos TSR Mokslu Akademija Geografijos Skyrius Moksliniai Pranesimai
Liet TSR Mokslu Akad Geol Geogr Inst Moksliniai Pranesimai — Lietuvos TSR Mokslu Akademija Geologijos Geografijos Instituta Moksliniai Pranesimai
Liet TSR Mokslu Akad Melior Inst Darb — Lietuvos TSR Mokslu Akademija Melioracijos Institutas Darbai
Liet TSR Mokslu Akad Zinynas — Lietuvos TSR Mokslu Akademijos Zinynas
Lietuvos Mok Akad Darbai — Lietuvos TSR Mokslu Akademijos Darbai
Liet Vet Akad Darb — Lietuvos Veterinarijos Akademijos Darbai
Liet Vet Mokslinio Tyrimo Inst Darb — Lietuvos Veterinarijos Mokslinio Tyrimo Instituto Darbai
Liet Zemdirbystes Mokslinio Tyrimo Inst Darb — Lietuvos Zemdirbystes Mokslinio Tyrimo Instituto Darbai
Liet Zemdir Moks Tyrimo Inst Darb — Lietuvos Zemdirbystes Mokslinio Tyrimo Instituto Darbai
Liet Zemes Ukio Akad Moksliniai Darb — Lietuvos Zemes Ukio Akademijos Moksliniai Darbai
Liet Zemes Ukio Akad Mokslo Darb — Lietuvos Zemes Ukio Akademija Mokslo Darbai
Liet Zemes Ukio Akad Mokslo Darbu Rinkiniai — Lietuvos Zemes Ukio Akademija Mokslo Darbu Rinkiniai
Life & Lab Bul — Life and Labor Bulletin
Life & Lett — Life and Letters
Life Aust — Life Australia
Life Chem Rep — Life Chemistry Reports
Life Chem Rep Suppl Ser — Life Chemistry Reports. Supplement Series
Life D — Life Digest
Life Dig — Life Digest
Life Environ — Life and Environment
Life Health & Accid Ins Cas 2d CCH — Life, Health, and Accident Insurance Cases. Second. Commerce ClearingHouse

Life Ins Courant — Life Insurance Courant
Life Insur Index — Life Insurance Index
Lifelong Learn — Lifelong Learning
Lifelong Learn Adult Years — Lifelong Learning: The Adult Years
Life Sci — Life Sciences
Life Sci Adv — Life Science Advances
Life Sci Adv Biochem — Life Science Advances. Biochemistry
Life Sci Agric Exp Stn Tech Bull (Maine) — Life Sciences and Agriculture Experiment Station. Technical Bulletin (Maine)
Lifesci Biotechnol (Tokyo) — Lifescience and Biotechnology (Tokyo)
Life Sci Collect — Life Sciences Collection
Life Sci Inst Kivo Jochi Daigaku Seimei Kagaku Kenkyusho — Life Science Institute Kivo/Jochi Daigaku Seimei Kagaku Kenkyusho
Life Sci Monogr — Life Sciences Monographs
Life Sci Part I — Life Sciences. Part I. Physiology and Pharmacology
Life Sci Part II — Life Sciences. Part II. Biochemistry. General and Molecular Biology
Life Sci Part II Biochem Gen Mol Biol — Life Sciences. Part II. Biochemistry. General and Molecular Biology
Life Sci Part I Physiol Pharmacol — Life Sciences. Part I. Physiology and Pharmacology
Life Sci Res Rep — Life Sciences Research Reports
Life Sci Res Space Proc Eur Symp — Life Sciences Research in Space. Proceedings. European Symposium
Life Sci Space Res — Life Sciences and Space Research
Life Sci Sp Res — Life Sciences and Space Research
Life Sci Symp — Life Sciences Symposium
Life Sci Symp Environ Solid Wastes — Life Sciences Symposium. Environment and Solid Wastes
Lifeskills Teach Mag — Lifeskills Teaching Magazine
Life Span Dev Behav — Life-Span Development and Behavior
Life Support Biosphere Sci — Life Support and Biosphere Science
Life Support Syst — Life Support Systems
Life-Threat — Life-Threatening Behavior
Lifetime Data Anal — Lifetime Data Analysis
Life with Mus — Life with Music
LIFSA — Life Sciences
Lift Elevator Lift Ropeway Eng — Lift, Elevator Lift, and Ropeway Engineering
LiG — Literatur in der Gesellschaft
Ligand Q — Ligand Quarterly
Ligand Rev — Ligand Review
Light and Light — Light and Lighting
Light and Light and Environ Des — Light and Lighting and Environmental Design
Light Aust — Lighting in Australia
Light Biol Med Proc Congr Eur Soc Photobiol — Light in Biology and Medicine. Proceedings. Congress. European Society for Photobiology
Light Des Appl — Lighting Design and Application
Light Des Appl LD A — Light Design and Application. LD & A
Light Equip News — Lighting Equipment News
Light Flowering Process Proc Int Symp Br Photobiol Soc — Light and the Flowering Process. Proceedings. International Symposium. British Photobiology Society
Light Ind — Light Industry
Lighting Des Applic — Lighting Design and Application
Lighting Design & Appl — Lighting Design and Application
Lighting Equip News — Lighting Equipment News
Lighting Res & Technol — Lighting Research and Technology
Lighting Res Tech — Lighting Research and Technology
Light J — Lighting Journal
Light Light — Light and Lighting
Light Light Environ Des — Light and Lighting and Environmental Design
Light Met Age — Light Metal Age
Light Met Bull — Light Metals Bulletin
Light Met (London) — Light Metals (London)
Light Met Met Ind — Light Metals and Metal Industry
Light Met (Moscow) — Light Metals (Moscow)
Light Met (New York) — Light Metals: Proceedings of Sessions. American Institute of Mining, Metallurgical, and Petroleum Engineers. Annual Meeting (New York)
Light Met (NY) — Light Metals (New York)
Light Met Res — Light Metals Research
Light Met Rev — Light Metals Review
Light Met (Tokyo) — Light Metals (Tokyo)
Light Met (Warrendale Pa) — Light Metals (Warrendale, Pennsylvania) Proceedings. Technical Sessions.
Light Mtl — Light Metal Age
Light Plant Dev Proc Univ Nottingham Easter Sch Agric Sci — Light and Plant Development. Proceedings. University of Nottingham Easter School in Agricultural Science
Light Rail Transit Plann Technol Proc Conf — Light-Rail Transit Planning and Technology. Proceedings. Conference
Light Res and Technol — Lighting Research and Technology
Light Res Technol — Lighting Research and Technology
Light Scattering Liq Surf Complementary Tech — Light Scattering by Liquid Surfaces and Complementary Techniques
Lightwood Res Conf Proc — Lightwood Research Conference. Proceedings
Lightwood Res Coord Counc Proc — Lightwood Research Coordinating Council. Proceedings
Lignite Symp Proc — Lignite Symposium. Proceedings
LI Hist Soc Memoirs — Long Island Historical Society. Memoirs
LiI — Nieuwe Linie
Liiketal Aikakausk — Liiketaloudellinen Aikakauskirja
LIINEO — Livestock International
LIJ — Law Institute Journal
Lijec Vjesn — Lijecnicki Vjesnik
Lijec Vjesn (Engl Transl) — Lijecnicki Vjesnik (English Translation)

Lijec Vjesn Zagrebu — Lijecnicki Vjesnik u Zagrebu
LiK — Liaudies Kuryba
LIK — Literatura ir Kalba
Likvatsionnye Yavleniya Steklakh Tr Vses Simp — Likvatsionnye Yavleniya v Steklakh. Trudy Vsesoyuznogo Simpoziuma
LiL — Limba si Literatura
LiLi — Zeitschrift fuer Literaturwissenschaft und Linguistik
Lilla — Lillabulero
Lille Chir — Lille Chirurgical
Lille Med — Lille Medical
Lille Med Actual — Lille Medical. Actualites
Lille Med Suppl — Lille Medical Supplement
Lille Mm — M moires de la Soci t Royale des Sciences, de l'Agriculture et des Arts,
Lille Mm S — M moires de la Soci t Royale des Sciences, de l'Agriculture et des Arts,
Lille Se Pbl — Seances Publiques de la Societe des Amateurs (Lille)
Lille S Mm — M moires de la Soci t Royale des Sciences, de l'Agriculture et des Arts,
Lille Tr — Recueil des Travaux de la Societe d'Amateurs des Sciences, de l'Agriculture, et des Arts a Lille
Lille Tr Mm — Travaux et Memoires de l'Universite de Lille
Lilly Sci Bull — Lilly Scientific Bulletin
Lil Reg — Lilly's Practical Register
Lily Yearb North Am Lily Soc — Lily Yearbook. North American Lily Society
Lily Year Book — Lily Year-Book. Royal Horticultural Society
LiM — Lingue del Mondo
LiM — Literatura i Marksizm
LiM — Literatura i Mastatsva
Lima Bean Bull — Lima Bean Bulletin. California Lima Bean Growers' Association
LIMC — Lexicon Iconographicum Mythologiae Classicae
Li Men — Literatura ir Menas
Limerick Fld Cl J — Limerick Field Club Journal
Limits Life Proc College Park Colloq Chem Evol — Limits of Life. Proceedings. College Park Colloquium on ChemicalEvolution
Limn Ocean — Limnology and Oceanography
Limnol & Oceanog — Limnology and Oceanography
Limnol & Oceanogr — Limnology and Oceanography
Limnol Donau — Limnologie der Donau
Limnol Donauforschungen Ber Int Konf Limnol Donau — Limnologische Donauforschungen Berichte der Internationalen Konferenzzur Limnologie der Donau
Limnol Flussstn Freudenthal Ber — Limnologische Flussstation Freudenthal. Berichte
Limnol Issled Dunaya Dokl Mezhdunar Konf Limnol Izuch Dunaya — Limnologicheskie Issledovaniya Dunaya. Doklady MezhdunarodnoiKonferentsii po Limnologicheskomu Izucheniyu Dunaya
Limnol Oceanogr — Limnology and Oceanography
Limnol Oceanogr Suppl — Limnology and Oceanography. Supplement
Limnol Soc South Afr J — Limnological Society of Southern Africa. Journal
LimR — Limba Romana
LIN — Lingua
LIn — Linguistic Inquiry
Linacre — Linacre Quarterly
Linacre Q — Linacre Quarterly
Lin Alg App — Linear Algebra and Its Applications
Lin Aragon — Linajes de Aragon
Linc Farm Conf Proc — Lincoln College. Farmers' Conference. Proceedings
Linc LR — Lincoln Law Review
Lincoln L R — Lincoln Law Review
Lincoln L Rev — Lincoln Law Review
Lincoln Rec Soc — Lincoln Record Society
Lincolnshire Hist Arch — Lincolnshire History and Archaeology
Lincolnshire Pop — Lincolnshire Population
Lincs AA Soc Rep — Lincolnshire Architectural and Archaeological Society. Reports and Papers
Lincs Hist & Archaeol — Lincolnshire History and Archaeology
Lindane Suppl — Lindane Supplement
Lindbergia J Bryol — Lindbergia. A Journal of Bryology
Linde-Ber Tech Wiss — Linde-Berichte aus Technik und Wissenschaft
Lindenau Z — Zeitschrift fuer Astronomie und Verwandte Wissenschaften. Lindenau
Linde Reports Sci & Technol — Linde Reports on Science and Technology
Linde Rep Sci and Technol — Linde Reports on Science and Technology
Linde Rep Sci Technol — Linde Reports on Science and Technology
L'Ind Ital del Cemento — L'Industria Italiana del Cemento
Lind Temp Chron — Lindische Tempelchronik
Linear Algebra and Appl — Linear Algebra and Its Applications
Linear Algebra Appl — Linear Algebra and Its Applications
Linear Algebra Its Appl — Linear Algebra and Its Applications
Linear Multilin Algebra — Linear and Multilinear Algebra
Linear Topol Spaces Complex Anal — Linear Topological Spaces and Complex Analysis
Lineinye Uskorit — Lineinye Uskoriteli
Linen News — Linen Supply News
Lines Rev — Lines Review
Ling — Linguistica
Ling — Linguistique
Ling A — Linguistic Analysis
Ling & Lit Stud E Europe — Linguistic and Literary Studies in Eastern Europe
Ling & P — Linguistics and Philosophy
LingB — Linguistische Berichte
LingBib — Linguistica Biblica
Ling Bibl — Linguistica Biblica
LingC — Linguistic Communications
Ling Cal — Linguistic Calculation
Ling Doc — Linguistics in Documentation

Ling e L — Lingua e Literatura
Ling Est — Lingue Estere
LingH — Linguistics (The Hague)
LingI — Linguistic Inquiry
Ling Inq — Linguistic Inquiry
Ling Inquiry — Linguistic Inquiry
Ling Inv — Linguisticae Investigationes
Ling Lit — Linguistics in Literature
Ling Litt — Linguistica et Litteraria
Lingnan Sci J — Lingnan Science Journal
Lingnan Univ Sci Bull — Lingnan University Science Bulletin
LingP — Linguistique (Paris)
Ling Phil — Linguistics and Philosophy
Ling Philos — Linguistics and Philosophy
Ling R — Linguistic Reporter
Ling Stile — Lingua e Stile
Linguist An — Linguistic Analysis
Linguist Ber — Linguistische Berichte
Linguistic Circle Manitoba and N Dak Proc — Linguistic Circle of Manitoba and North Dakota. Proceedings
Linguist In — Linguistic Inquiry
Linguist Lang Behav Abstr — Linguistics and Language Behavior Abstracts. LLBA
Lingv Sb — Lingvisticeskij Sbornik
Lin Invest — Linguisticae Investigationes. Supplementa. Studies in French and General Linguistics
L in Japan — Law in Japan
LINK — Library and Information Network
Linkoeping Stud Sci Tech Diss — Linkoeping Studies in Science and Technology. Dissertations
Linkoping Stud Arts Sci — Linkoping Studies in Arts and Sciences
Lin Lit S — Linguistic and Literary Studies in Eastern Europe
Linnaean Soc Proc — Linnaean Society Proceedings
Linn Belg — Linneana Belgica
Linneana Belg — Linneana Belgica
Linnean Soc Biol J — Linnean Society. Biological Journal
Linnean Soc NSW Proc — Proceedings. Linnean Society of New South Wales
Linn Fern Bull — Linnaean Fern Bulletin
Linn Soc J Zool — Linnean Society. Journal. Zoology
Linn Soc Lond Biol J — Linnean Society of London. Biological Journal
Linn Soc Lond Zool J — Linnean Society of London. Zoological Journal
Linn Soc NSW Proc — Linnean Society of New South Wales. Proceedings
Linn Soc Symp Ser — Linnean Society. Symposium Series
LINQ — Literature in North Queensland
L Inst J — Law Institute Journal
L Inst J Vict — Law Institute Journal of Victoria
L in Trans — Law in Transition
L in Trans Q — Law in Transition Quarterly
Linz AF — Linzer Archaeologische Forschungen
Linzer Biol Beitr — Linzer Biologische Beitraege
Liofilizzazione Criobiol Appl Criog — Liofilizzazione Criobiologia Applicazioni Criogeniche
Lion Unicor — Lion and the Unicorn
Liouv J — Journal de Mathematiques Pures et Appliquees, fonde par Joseph Liouville
Liouv J Mth — Journal de Mathematiques Pures et Appliquees, fonde par Joseph Liouville
LIPES — Les Informations Politiques et Sociales
Lipid Metab Compr Biochem — Lipid Metabolism. Comprehensive Biochemistry
Lipidnyi Obmen Skh Zhivotn Sb Dokl Vses Simp — Lipidyui Obmen u Sel'skokhozyaistvennykh Zhivotnykh Sbornik DokladovVsesoyuznogo Simpoziuma po Lipidnomu Obmenu u Sel'skokhozyaistvennykh Zhivo
Lipid Rev — Lipid Review
Lipids Lipid Metab — Lipids and Lipid Metabolism
Lipid Technol — Lipid Technology
LIPL — Living Places
LIPP — Lippincott's Monthly
Lippay Janos Tud Ulesszak Eloadasai — Lippay Janos Tudomanyos Ulesszak Eloadasai
Lippinc — Lippincott's Magazine
Lippincotts M — Lippincott's Magazine
Lippincott's Med Sci — Lippincott's Medical Science
Lippincotts Mo M — Lippincott's Monthly Magazine
Lippincotts Mthly Mag — Lippincott's Monthly Magazine
Liq Chromatogr Biomed Anal — Liquid Chromatography in Biomedical Analysis
Liq Chromatogr HPLC Mag — Liquid Chromatography and HPLC Magazine
Liq Cryst — Liquid Crystals
Liq Cryst Mater Devices Appl — Liquid Crystal Materials, Devices, and Applications
Liq Cryst Ordered Fluids — Liquid Crystals and Ordered Fluids
Liq Fuels Tech — Liquid Fuels Technology
Liq Matter Conf — Liquid Matter Conference
Liq Matter Proc Liq Matter Conf Eur Phys Soc — Liquid Matter. Proceedings. Liquid Matter Conference. European Physical Society
Liq Met Invited Contrib Pap Int Conf — Liquid Metals. Invited and Contributed Papers. International Conference on Liquid Metals
Liq Scintill Count — Liquid Scintillation Counting
Liq Scintill Counting — Liquid Scintillation Counting
Liquefied Nat Gas — Liquefied Natural Gas
Liquor Cont L Rep CCH — Liquor Control Law Reports. Commerce Clearing House
Liquor Hbk — Liquor Handbook
LIR — Limba Romana
LIR — Linguistics and International Review
Li R — Literaturnaja Rossija
LiRe — Literary Review

LIS — Language in Society
LIS — Lessons in Islam Series
LIS — Life Insurance Selling
LIs — Lingua Islandica
LIS — Linguisticae Investigationes. Supplementa. Studies in French and General Linguistics
Lis — Listener
LISA — Library and Information Science Abstracts
Li Sa — Litteratur og Samfund
Lisb Ac Sc Mm — Historia e Memorias da Academia Real das Sciencias de Lisboa
Lisb A Mar — Annaes Maritimos e Coloniaes (Lisboa)
LIS Ber — LIS-Berichte
Lis Fil — Listy Filologike
LISk — Literary Sketches
LISL — Amsterdam Studies in the Theory and History of Linguistic Science. Series V. Library and Information Sources in Linguistics
LISL — Letopis Instituta za Serbski ludospyt w Budysinje pri Nemskej Akademiji Wedo-Moscow w Berlinje Rjad A Rec A Literatura
LISP Symb Comput — LISP and Symbolic Computation
LISR — Legal Information Service. Reports. Native Law Centre. University of Saskatchewan
List — Listener
List — List Sdruzeni Moravskych Spisovatelu
List Bks Access Pd Art Index Wash — List of Books Accessioned and Periodical Articles Indexed. Columbus Memorial Library. Pan American Union (Washington, DC)
Liste Abbrev Mots Titres — Liste d'Abbreviations de Mots des Titres de Periodiques
Listener BBC Telev Rev — Listener and BBC (British Broadcasting Corporation) Television Review
List of Stat Instr — List of Statutory Instruments
Listprokatnoe Proizvod — Listoprokatnoe Proizvodstvo
Listvennitsa Ee Ispolz Nar Khoz — Listvennitsa i Ee Ispol'zovanie v Narodnom Khozyaistve
Listy Cukrov — Listy Cukrovarnicke
Listy Cukrov Reparske — Listy Cukrovarnicke a Reparske
Listy Fil — Listy Filologicke
Listy Pomol — Listy Pomologicke
Listy Zahradn — Listy Zahradnicke
LIt — Lettere Italiane
LIt — Libro Italiano
Lit — Litaunus
Lit — Literarisches
Lit — Literarium
Lit — Literatur
Lit — Litigation
Lit — Litteraire
Lit — Litterature
Lit — Litteris
Lit — Liturgia
LitA — Literaturnaya Armeniya
Lit A — Liturgical Arts
LITA ITAL — LITA [*Library and Information Technology Association*] Information Technology and Libraries
LItal — Lettere Italiane
Lit & Maksla — Literatura un Maksla
Lit & Psychol — Literature and Psychology
Lit & Theo R — Literary and Theological Review
LitAP — Literarni Archiv Pamatniku Narodniho Pisemnictvi
Lit Arg BA — La Literatura Argentina (Buenos Aires)
Lit Arts — Liturgical Arts
Lit AS — Literatur als Sprache. Literaturtheorie-Interpretation-Sprachkritik
Lit Automat — New Literature on Automation
Lit B — Liturgia (Burgos)
Lit Ber Dent Med — Literaturbericht ueber Neue Veroeffentlichungen auf dem Gebiete der Dentalmedizin
Lit Blaett Boersenhalle — Literarische Blaetter der Boersenhalle
Litbl f Germ u Rom Phil — Literaturblatt fuer Germanische und Romanische Philologie
Litbl Or Philol — Literaturblatt fuer Orientalische Philologie
Lit C — Literarisches Zentralblatt fuer Deutschland
Lit Criterion — Literary Criterion
Lit Crit Regist — Literary Criticism Register. LCR
Litcy Disc — Literacy Discussion
Lit D — Literary Digest
Lit Dig — Literary Digest
Lit Digest — Literary Digest
Lit Digest Intern Book Revw — Literary Digest International Book Review
LitDokAB — Literaturdokumentation zur Arbeitsmarkt- und Berufsforschung
Lit E — Literary Endeavour
LitE — Literatur. Monatsschrift fuer Literaturfreunde
Lit E — Liturgy (Elsberry, MO)
Liteinoe Proizvod — Liteinoe Proizvodstvo
Liteinoe Prozvod — Liteinoe Proizvodstvo
Literaturber Wasser — Literaturberichte ueber Wasser, Abwasser, Luft, und Boden
Literaturbl — Literaturblatt fuer Romanische und Germanische Philologie
Literature — Literature East and West
Liter Discussion — Literacy Discussion
LitEW — Literature East and West
Lit/Film Q — Literature/Film Quarterly
Lit/F Q — Literature/Film Quarterly
Lit/F Quarterly — Literature/Film Quarterly
Lit Gaz — Literary Gazette
Lit Gaz — Literaturnaja Gazeta

Lit Gaz & J B Lett A Sci — Literary Gazette and Journal of Belles Lettres, Arts, Sciences
Lit Half — Literary Half-Yearly
Lit Hdweiser — Literarischer Handweiser
Lit Hist — Literature and History
Lit Hist Soc Quebec Tr — Literary and Historical Society of Quebec. Transactions
Lith Jew — Lithuanian Jew
Lith J Phys — Lithuanian Journal of Physics
Lith Min Resour — Lithology and Mineral Resources
Lithol Issled Kaz — Lithologicheskie Issledovanniya v Kazakhstane
Lithol Miner Resour — Lithology and Mineral Resources
Lithuanian Math J — Lithuanian Mathematical Journal
Lithuanian Math Trans — Lithuanian Mathematical Transactions
Lit Hw — Literarischer Handweiser Zunaechst fuer das Katholische Deutschland
Lit J — Literary Journal
Lit Jb — Liturgisches Jahrbuch
Lit J London — Literary Journal. A Review of Literature, Sciences, Manners, Politics (London)
Lit Krit — Literaturnyy Kritik
Lit Krit — Literatur und Kritik
LitL — Letteratura Italiana Laterza
LitL — Literarni Listy
LitL — Literatura Ludowa
Lit Letter — Literary Letter
Lit Ludow — Literatura Ludowa
LitM — Literarni Mesicnik
LitM — Literaturnaya Mysl
Lit M — Liturgia (Mainz)
Lit Mat Sb — Litovskii Matematiceskii Sbornik
Lit Mod Art — LOMA. Literature on Modern Art
Lit Mus Fin — Literature, Music, Fine Arts
Lit Mus Register A Sci & General Lit — Literary Museum or Register of Arts, Sciences, and General Literature
Lit Mys — Literatura i Mystectvo
LitN — Literarni Noviny
Litodin Litol Geomorfol Shelfa 1976 — Litodinamika, Litologiya i Geomorfologiya Shel'fa. 1976
Litol Geokhim Osad Form Uzb — Litologiya i Geokhimiya Osadochnykh Formatsii Uzbekistana [monograph]
Litol Geokhim Paleogeogr Neftegazonosn Osad Form Uzb — Litologiya, Geokhimiya, i Paleogeografiya Neftegazonosn Osadochnykh Formatsii Uzbekistana
Litol Geokhim Polezn Iskop Osad Obraz Tyan Shanya — Litologiya, Geokhimiya i Poleznye Iskopaemye Osadochnykh Obrazovanii Tyan-Shanya
Litol i Polez Iskop — Litologiya i Poleznye Iskopaemye
Litol Paleozoiskikh Otlozh Est — Litologiya Paleozoiskikh Otlozhenii Estonii
Litov Fiz Sb — Litovskii Fizicheskii Sbornik
Litov Fiz Zh — Litovskii Fizicheskii Zhurnal
Litov Mekh Sb — Litovskii Mekhanicheskii Sbornik
Litov Nauchno Issled Inst Tekst Promsti Nauchno Issled Tr — Litovskii Nauchno-Issledovatel'skii Institut Tekstil'noi Promyshlennosti. Nauchno-Issledovatel'skie Trudy
Litovsk Mat Sb — Litovskii Matematiceskii Sbornik
LitP — Literature and Psychology
LitP — Literature in Perspective
LitP — Litterair Paspoort. Tijdschrift voor Boeken uit de Oude en Nieuvve Wereld
Lit Per — Literary Perspectives
Lit Ph Soc NY Tr — Literary and Philosophical Society of New York. Transactions
Lit Psych — Literature and Psychology
Lit Psychol — Literature and Psychology
Lit R — Literary Review
Lit Rdsch — Literarische Rundschau fuer das Katholische Deutschland
Lit Res New — Literary Research Newsletter
Lit Rev — Literary Review
Lit Rev Oils Fats — Literature Review on Oils and Fats
LitS — Literatura i Sucanist
LitS — Literatura Sovietica
Lit Steam Pwr — Light Steam Power
LitSup — Literary Supplement
Litt — Litteraria
Litt — Litterature [Paris]
Litt — Liturgiques
Litt — Litteris
Lit T — Liturgia (Torino)
Litt Denkwuerdigk — Litterarische Denkwuerdigkeiten oder Nachrichten von Neuen Buechern und KleinenSchriften Besonders der Chursaechsischen Universitaeten, Schulen, und Lande
Litt J Altona — Litteratur-Journal (Altona)
LittK — Litterae (Kuemmerle)
Little M — Little Magazine
Little Mag — Little Magazine
Little Math Lib — Little Mathematics Library
LittleR — Little Review
Little Rev — Little Review
Little Wld Bull — Little World Bulletin
Little Wld Stud — Little World Studies
Litt Orient — Litterae Orientales
Lit U — Literaturna Ukrajina
Liturg A — Liturgical Arts
Liturg Arts — Liturgical Arts
Liturgical Rev — Liturgical Review
LitW — Literatura (Warsaw, Poland)
Lit W (Bost) — Literary World (Boston)
Litwiss Jb — Literaturwissenschaftliches Jahrbuch
Lit Wiss Ling — Literaturwissenschaft und Linguistik

Lit Wochenbl Boersenhalle — Literarisches Wochenblatt der Boersenhalle
Lit Wschr — Literarische Wochenschrift
Lit Zeitung Berlin — Literarische Zeitung (Berlin)
Lit ZentB — Literarisches Zentralblatt
Lit Zentralbl — Literarisches Zentralblatt
LitZs — Liturgische Zeitschrift
Liv — Livres. Bulletin Bibliographique Mensuel
LivA — Living Age
LivAC — Livres et Auteurs Canadiens
LIv Age — Littell's Living Age
Liv Ann — Annals of Archaeology and Anthropology (Liverpool)
Liv Blues — Living Blues
Liv Church — Living Church
Liv Condit Hlth — Living Conditions and Health
Live Adv — Livestock Advisor
Liver Ann — Liver Annual
Liver Cirrhosis Proc Falk Symp — Liver Cirrhosis. Proceedings. Falk Symposium
Liverp Manch Geol J — Liverpool and Manchester Geological Journal
Liverpool AAA — Annals of Archaeology and Anthropology (Liverpool)
Liverpool An Archaeol & Anthropol — Liverpool Annals of Archaeology and Anthropology
Liverpool and Manchester Geol Jour — Liverpool and Manchester Geological Journal
Liverpool Bull — Liverpool Bulletin
Liverpool Class Mthly — Liverpool Classical Monthly
Liverpool G As Tr J — Liverpool Geological Association. Transactions. Journal
Liverpool Geog Soc Tr An Rp — Liverpool Geographical Society. Transactions and Annual Report of the Council
Liverpool G Soc Pr — Liverpool Geological Society. Proceedings
Liverpool L Rev — Liverpool Law Review
Liverpool Manchester Geol J — Liverpool and Manchester Geological Journal
Liverpool Med Inst Trans Rep — Liverpool Medical Institution. Transactions and Reports
Liverpool School Trop Med Mem — Liverpool School of Tropical Medicine. Memoirs
Liver Quant Aspects Struct Func — Liver: Quantitative Aspects of Structure and Function. Proceedings of the International Gstaad Symposium
Liver Transpl — Liver Transplantation
Liver Transpl Surg — Liver Transplantation and Surgery
Livest Advis — Livestock Adviser
Livest Int — Livestock International
Live Stock Bul — Live Stock Bulletin
Live Stock J and Fancier's Gaz — Live Stock Journal and Fancier's Gazette
Livest Prod Day La Agric Exp Stn Anim Sci Dep — Livestock Producers' Day. Louisiana Agricultural Experiment Station. Animal Science Department
Livest Prod Sci — Livestock Production Science
Lives Women Sci — Lives of Women in Science
LivF — Livres de France
Liv for Young Home — Living for Young Homemakers
Living A — Living Arts
Living Bird Q — Living Bird Quarterly
Living Cell Four Dimens Int Conf — Living Cell in Four Dimensions. International Conference
Living Cold Int Symp — Living in the Cold. International Symposium
Living Mus — Living Museum
LIVJA5 — Lijecnicki Vjesnik
LivL — Livres et Lectures. Revue Bibliographique
Liv L Mag — Livingston's Law Magazine
Liv Med Chir J — Liverpool Medico-Chirurgical Journal
Livre A — Livre d'Art
Livre & Est — Livre et l'Estampe
Livre de l Et — Livre de l'Etudiant
Livre de l Etud — Livre de l'Etudiant
Liv Wild — Living Wilderness
Liv Wildn — Living Wilderness
LIWA/YWA — Yearbook of World Affairs. London Institute of World Affairs
LJ — Hall's American Law Journal
LJ — Law Journal. New Series
LJ — Library Journal
LJ — Limburg's Jaarboek
LJ — Limes u Jugoslaviji
LJ — Liturgisches Jahrbuch
LJ — Lower Canada Law Journal
LJ — Luther-Jahrbuch
LJ — New York Law Journal
LJ — Ohio State Law Journal
LJA — Ljetopis Jugoslavenske Akademije
LJb — Literaturwissenschaftliches Jahrbuch der Goerres-Gesellschaft
L-Jb — Luther-Jahrbuch
Ljetopis JAZU — Ljetopis Jugoslavenske Akademije Znanosti i Umjetnosti
LJ Exch in Eq (Eng) — English Law Journal. Exchequer in Equity
LJG — Landesjagdgesetz
LJGG — Literaturwissenschaftliches Jahrbuch der Goerres-Gesellschaft
LJH — Legon Journal of the Humanities
L J Hum — Lamar Journal of the Humanities
LJI — Legal Journals Index
LJKB — Law Journal Reports. King's Bench. New Series
LJKBOS — Law Journal Reports. King's Bench. Old Series
LJLC — Law Journal (Lower Canada)
LJLT — Law Journal (Law Tracts)
LJN — Library Journal (New York)
LJ of the Marut Bunnag Internat L Off — Law Journal. Marut Bunnag International Law Office
LJOSMC — Law Journal, Old Series, Magistrates' Cases
LJR — Low Jet Routes

LJSAA — Literatura na Jazykach Stran Azii i Afriki
LJSCAA — Annuaire Agricole de la Suisse
LJ/SLJ — Library Journal/School Library Journal
LJ Spec Rep — LJ [*Library Journal*] Special Report
LJUC — Law Journal of Upper Canada
LJZ — Leipziger Juedische Zeitung
LK — Leipziger Kommentar das Reichsstrafgesetzbuch
LK — Literatura ir Kalba
LK — Literatur als Kunst
LK — Literaturnyj Kritik
LK — Literaturny Kirgizstan
L K — Literatur og Kritik
L K — Literatur und Kritik
LKAAAN — Annual Report. Laboratory of Algology
LKD — Litteratur des Katholischen Deutschland
LKHOAW — Lesnoe Khozyaistvo
LKI — Is Lietuviu Kulturos Istorijos
LKK — Lietuviu Kalbotyros Klausimai
LKM — Lesnoe Khoziaistvo (Moscow)
LKTRD — Elektro-Tehniek
LL — Labor Letter
LL — Lakeside Leader
LL — La Ley. Revista Juridica Argentina
LL — Language Learning
LL — Letras (Lima)
LL — Liber Lovaniensis
LL — Library Literature
LL — Life and Letters
LL — Lifelong Learning: The Adult Years
LL — Limba si Literatura
LL — Literatur und Leben
LL — Liturgical Library
LL — Livres et Lectures
LL — Lloyd's List
LLA — Leshonenu La'am
LL and C — Language Learning and Communication
LLB — Lawyers Liberation Bulletin
LLBA — Linguistics and Language Behavior Abstracts
LIC — Llen Cymru
LLF — Les Lettres Francaises
LLG — Labor Law Guide
LLG — Luggage and Travelware
L Lib — Law Librarian
L Lib J — Law Library Journal
L Libr J — Law Library Journal
LLJ — Labor Law Journal
LLJ — Lahore Law Journal
LLJ — LaTrobe Library Journal
LLJ — Law Library Journal
LLJ — Liberia Law Journal
LLL — Langages. Litteratures. Linguistique
LLM — Langues et Lettres Modernes
LLM — Limba si Literatura Moldoveneasca Chisinau
LLM — Linden Lane Magazine
LI Mar LN — Lloyd's Maritime Law Newsletter
LLOYA2 — Lloydia
Lloydia — Lloydia. Lloyd Library and Museum
Lloydia J Nat Prod — Lloydia. Journal of Natural Products
Lloyds AE — Lloyd's Aviation Economist
Lloyds Bank R — Lloyds Bank Review
Lloyds Bk — Lloyds Bank Review
Lloyd's Corp Secur Int — Lloyd's Corporate Security International
Lloyds Mar and Com LQ — Lloyd's Maritime and Commercial Law Quarterly
Lloyd's Mar LN — Lloyd's Maritime Law Newsletter
Lloyds Mex — Lloyd's Mexican Economic Report
LLR — High Court of Lagos Law Reports
LLR — Lancaster Law Review
LLR — Liberian Law Reports
LLR — Luzerne Legal Register
LLRGDY — Allergy
LLRTD5 — Allertonia
LLS — Land Laws Service
LLSEE — Linguistic and Literary Studies in Eastern Europe
LLT — Lahore Law Times
LLT — Library of Living Theology
LLud — Literatura Ludowa
LLZg — Leipziger Lehrerzeitung
LL Zt — Leipziger Lehrerzeitung
LM — Labour Monthly
LM — Lady's Magazine
LM — Language Monographs
LM — Langues Modernes
LM — Larousse Mensuelle
LM — Leisure Monthly Magazine
LM — Le Monde
LM — Letterature Moderne
LM — Lexikon der Marienkunde
LM — London Law Magazine
LM — London Magazine
LM — London Mercury
LM — Lucrari de Muzicologie
LM — Ludus Magistralis
LM — Luna Monthly
LM — Lutherische Monatshefte
LM — Universita Bocconi. Letterature Moderne. Rivista di Varia Umanita

LMA — Le Moyen Age
LMA — Lexikon des Mittelalters
LMA — Liverpool Monographs in Archaeology and Oriental Studies
LMAD — Lietuvos TSR Mokslu Akademijos Darbai. Serija A
L Mag — London Law Magazine
L Mag — London Magazine
Lmag — Longman's Magazine
L Mag & LR — Law Magazine and Law Review
L Mag & Rev — Law Magazine and Review
LMags — Index to Little Magazines
LMAI — Leaflets. Museum of the American Indian. Heye Foundation [*New York*]
LM & LR — Law Magazine and Law Review
LMAOS — Liverpool Monographs in Archaeology and Oriental Studies
LM BI — Lueneburger Museumsblaetter
LMC — Las Misiones Catolicas [*Barcelona*]
LMC — Life Magazine (Chicago)
LMC — Literature, Meaning, Culture
LMD — Australian Legal Monthly Digest
LMD — La Maison-Dieu
LMD — Les Missions Dominicaines [*Paris-Kain*]
L Md Ps J — Medical and Physical Journal (London)
L Med and Health — Law, Medicine, and Health Care
L Med Q — Legal Medical Quarterly
L Mer — London Mercury
LMF — Le Monde Francais
LMFA — Literature Music Fine Arts
LMGL — Lippische Mitteilungen aus Geschichte und Landeskunde
LMG Rep Data and Word Process Libr — LMG [*Library Management Group*] Report on Data and Word Processing for Libraries
LMH — Lebensmittelzeitung
LMI — Larousse Mensuel Illustre
LMi — Literaturna Misel
LMJ — Leningrad Mathematical Journal
LMJ — Lutherisches Missions Jahrbuch
LMJ B — Lutherisches Missions-Jahrbuch fuer die Jahre (Berlin)
LMK — Lexikon der Marienkunde
LMKF — Litterarisches Magazin fuer Katholiken und deren Freunde
LMLG — Luther. Mitteilungen der Luthergesellschaft
LMLP — La Monda Lingvo-Problemo
LMLSA — Language Monographs. Linguistic Society of America
LMNTD — Elements
L Mod — Langues Modernes
LMod — Lettres Modernes
LMold — Limba si Literatura Moldoveneasca
LMQ — Legal Medical Quarterly
LMRT — Library of Modern Religious Thought
LMS — Last Mycenaeans and Their Successors
LMS — Letopis Matice Srpske. Novi Sad
LMS — London Mediaeval Studies
LMSCEZ — Lasers in Medical Science
LMSLA — Lantmannen (Sweden)
LMT — Library Management
L Mth S P — Proceedings of the London Mathematical Society
LN — (La) Nacion
LN — La Nature
LN — Law Notes
LN — Legal News
LN — Lettres Nouvelles
LN — Leyes Nacionales
LN — Library Notes
LN — Lingua Nostra
LN — Literaturnoe Nasledstvo
LNA — Limen (Argentina)
LnA — London Aphrodite
L Nations J — League of Nations Journal
LNB — Leipziger Namenkundliche Beitraege
LNB — Loteria. Loteria Nacional de Beneficencia
LNB/L — Loteria. Loteria Nacional de Beneficencia
LNCR — (La) Nacion (Costa Rica)
LNCSEA — Lecture Notes on Coastal and Estuarine Studies
LNDR — Land Reform
LNI — La Nuova Italia
LNL — Langues Neo-Latines
LNL — Les Nouvelles Litteraires
LNLJ — Linguistic Notes from La Jolla
LnM — London Mercury
LNMVA — Learning and Motivation
LNN — Leipziger Neueste Nachrichten
LNo — Lingua Nostra
Lno Penko-Dzhutovaya Promst — Lno Penko-Dzhutovaya Promyshlennost
LNos — Lingua Nostra
L Notes — Law Notes [*London*]
L Notes (NY) — Law Notes (New York)
LNouv — Lettres Nouvelles
LNP — Lecture Notes in Physics
LNQ — Lincolnshire Notes and Queries
LNS — Lundastudier i Nordisk Sprakvetenskap
LNS — Lutheran News Service
LNU — Negentien Nu
LO — Lex Orandi
LO — Limnology and Oceanography
LO — Literaturnoe Obozrenie
Lo — Lochlann
LO — L'Oltremare
LO — Louisiana Musician

LOAF — Look at Finland
Lo B — Light of Buddha
LOC — Catalog of Books represented by Library of Congress Printed Cards
LOC — Liturgiarum Orientalium Collectio
Loc — Locus
Local Curr Their Appl Proc Informal Conf — Local Currents and Their Applications. Proceedings. Informal Conference
Local Fin — Local Finance
Local Fin (The Hague) — Local Finance (The Hague)
Local Gov Adm — Local Government Administration
Local Gov in South Aust — Local Government in South Australia
Local Gov in Sthn Afr — Local Government in Southern Africa
Local Gov J of Western Aust — Local Government Journal of Western Australia
Local Gov Rev — Local Government Review
Local Gov South Aust — Local Government in South Australia
Local Gov Stud — Local Government Studies
Local Govt — Local Government
Local Govt Adm — Local Government Administration
Local Govt Admin — Local Government Administration
Local Govt B — Local Government Bulletin
Local Govt Chron — Local Government Chronicle
Local Govt Eng — Local Government Engineer
Local Govt Forum — Local Government Forum
Local Govt IULA Newsl — Local Government - IULA [*International Union of Local Authorities*] Newsletter
Local Govt Manpower — Local Government Manpower
Local Govt News — Local Government News
Local Govt Policy Making — Local Government Policy Making
Local Govt Q — Local Government Quarterly
Local Govt R Austl — Local Government Reports of Australia
Local Govt Rev — Local Government Review
Local Govt R Japan — Local Government Review in Japan
Local Govt Stud — Local Government Studies
Local Hist — Local Historian
Local Pop Stud — Local Population Studies
Local Popul Stud — Local Population Studies Magazine and Newsletter
Locat Rep Div Miner Chem CSIRO — Location Report. Division of Mineral Chemistry. Commonwealth Scientific and Industrial Research Organisation
Locc Prot — Loccumer Protokolle
Loc Ct Gaz — Local Courts and Municipal Gazette
Loc Finance — Local Finance
Locgov Dig — Locgov Digest
Loc Gov Rev — Local Government Review
Loc Govt Q — Local Government Quarterly
Loc Govt Rev — Local Government Review
Locke News — Locke Newsletter
Lockheed GA Q — Lockheed Georgia Quarterly
Lockheed Horiz — Lockheed Horizons
Lockheed Symp Magnetohydrodyn — Lockheed Symposia on Magnetohydrodynamics
Lockwood Dir — Lockwood's Directory of the Paper and Allied Trades
Loco J — Locomotive Journal
Locomotive Eng J — Locomotive Engineers' Journal
Loc Self Gov — Local Self-Government
Locust Newsl FAO Plant Prod Prot Div — Locust Newsletter. FAO. Plant Production and Protection Division
LOD — Leadership and Organization Development Journal
Lo D — Light of Dharma
Lodg Ind — United States Lodging Industry
L Od S T — Transactions of the Odontological Society (London)
Lodzki Num — Lodzki Numizmatyk
Lodzk Stud Etnogr — Lodzkie Studia Etnograficzne
Lodz Stud Etnogr — Lodzkie Studia Etnograficzne
Lodz Tow Nauk Pr Wydz 3 — Lodzkie Towarzystwo Naukowe Prace Wydzialu 3. Nauk Matematyczno-Przyrodniczych
Lodz Tow Nauk Pr Wydz 3 Nauk Mat-Przyr — Lodzkie Towarzystwo Naukowe Prace Wydzialu 3. Nauk Matematyczno-Przyrodniczych
Lodz Tow Nauk Pr Wydz 4 — Lodzkie Towarzystwo Naukowe Prace Wydzialu 4. Nauk Lekarskich
Loeb Class Libr — Loeb Classical Library
LoF — Library of Fathers of the Holy Catholic Church
LOFC — Ligues Ouvrieres Feminines Chretiennes
L Off Ec and Mgmt — Law Office Economics and Management
L Off Econ & Man — Law Office Economics and Management
LOG — Lawn-O-Gram
Log — Logos. Internationale Zeitschrift fuer Philosophie und Kultur
Log Anal — Log Analyst
Log Anal — Logique et Analyse
Log & Saw — Logging and Sawmilling Journal
Loggers Handb Pac Logging Congr — Loggers Handbook. Pacific Logging Congress
Logic Comput Philos — Logic and Computation in Philosophy
Logic Log Philos — Logic and Logical Philosophy
Logic Teor Ci — Logica y Teoria de la Ciencia
Logik Grundlagen Math — Logik und Grundlagen der Mathematik
Logiko Inf Resheniya Geol Zadach — Logiko-Informatsionnye Resheniya Geologicheskikh Zadach
LOGIN — Local Government Information Network
Logique Anal — Logique et Analyse
Logique et Anal NS — Logique et Analyse. Nouvelle Serie
Logique Math Inform — Logique. Mathematiques. Informatique
Logist & Transp Rev — Logistics and Transportation Review
Logist Spectrum — Logistics Spectrum
Logoped Phoniatr Vocol — Logopedics, Phoniatrics, Vocology
Logos — Logos Journal

Log Spec — Logistics Spectrum
LoH — Louisiana History
Lohnuntern Land-Forstwirt — Lohnunternehmen in Land- und Forstwirtschaft
Loisir et Soc — Loisir et Societe
LOL — Luzac's Oriental List and Book Review
Lollipops — Lollipops, Ladybugs, and Lucky Stars
Lo LR — Loyola Law Review
LOMa — London Magazine
LoN — Logos (Naples)
Lond A — London Archaeologist
Lond Clin Med J — London Clinic Medical Journal
Londe Electr — L'onde Electrique
L'Ondes Electr — L'Ondes Electronique
Lond Gaz — London Gazette
Lond J — London Journal
Lond LM — London Law Magazine
Lond M — London Magazine
Lond Mag — London Magazine
Lond Math Soc Lect Note Ser — London Mathematical Society. Lecture Note Series
Lond Math Soc Monogr — London Mathematical Society. Monographs
Lond Med Gaz — London Medical Gazette
Lond Med St — London Mediaeval Studies
Lond Med Surg J — London Medical and Surgical Journal
Lond Mercury — London Mercury
Lond Mis Soc Chr — London Missionary Society. Chronicle
Lond Nat — London Naturalist
London Archaeol — London Archaeologist
London Archit — London Architect
London Archt — London Architect
London Bull — London Bulletin
London Bus Mag — London Bus Magazine
London Bus School J — London Business School. Journal
London Chron — London Chronicle
London Commun Wk Serv Newsl — London Community Work Service Newsletter
London Docklands Dev Newsl — London Docklands Development Newsletter
London Edinburgh Dublin Philos Mag J Sci — London, Edinburgh, and Dublin Philosophical Magazine and Journal of Science
London Edinburgh Philos Mag J Sci — London and Edinburgh Philosophical Magazine and Journal of Science
London Ednl R — London Educational Review
London Hlth News — London Health News
London Ind Centre News — London Industrial Centre News
London J — London Journal
London Jnl — London Journal
London Labour Brief — London Labour Briefing
London Lesbian Newsl — London Lesbian Newsletter
London L Rev — City of London Law Review
London Mag — London Magazine
London Math Soc Lecture Note Ser — London Mathematical Society. Lecture Note Series
London Math Soc Monographs — London Mathematical Society. Monographs
London Math Soc Stud Texts — London Mathematical Society Student Texts
London Meas Rates Mat Prices — London Measured Rates and Materials Prices
London Med J — London Medical Journal
London Med Repos — London Medical Repository
London Middlesex Archaeol Soc Spec Pap — London and Middlesex Archaeological Society. Special Papers
London Natur — London Naturalist
London Passenger Transp — London Passenger Transport
London Physiol J — London Physiological Journal
London Quar Rev — London Quarterly Review
London Quart Wld Aff — London Quarterly of World Affairs
London Rev Bks — London Review of Books
London Rev Public Admin — London Review of Public Administration
London Shellac Res Bur Bull — London Shellac Research Bureau. Bulletin
London Shellac Res Bur Tech Pap — London Shellac Research Bureau. Technical Paper
London Soc — London Society
London Soc Jnl — London Society. Journal
London Stud — London Studies
London Volunt News — London Voluntary News
Lond Q — London Quarterly Review
LondQHolbR — London Quarterly and Holborn Review
Lond QHR — London Quarterly and Holborn Review
Lond Q R — London Quarterly and Holborn Review
Lond School Trop Med Research Mem Ser — London School of Tropical Medicine. Research Memoir Series
Lond Studio — London Studio
Lond Topog Rec — London Topographical Record
Long Ashton Int Symp — Long Ashton International Symposium
Long Ashton Res Stn Rep — Long Ashton Research Station. Report
Long Ashton Symp Proc — Long Ashton Symposium. Proceedings
Long Dst L — Long-Distance Letter
Longest R — Longest Revolution
Longev — Longevita
Long Island Agron — Long Island Agronomist
Long Island J Philos — Long Island Journal of Philosophy. And Cabinet of Variety
Long Island M J — Long Island Medical Journal
Long Isl B — Long Island Business
Long Isl Forum — Long Island Forum
Long Isl Hortic News — Long Island Horticulture News
Longm — Longman's Magazine
Long Point Bird Obs Annu Rep — Long Point Bird Observatory. Annual Report
Long Range Plan — Long-Range Planning

Long Range Plann — Long-Range Planning
Long-Rang P — Long-Range Planning
Long Rev — Longest Revolution
Long Term Care Health Serv Adm Q — Long Term Care and Health Services Administration. Quarterly
Long Term Care Q — Long-Term Care Quarterly
LonM — London Magazine
Lon Mag — London Magazine
LonMer — London Mercury
Lon R Bks — London Review of Books
Loodusuurijate Selts Tappistead Sekts Toim — Loodusuurijate Selts Tappisteaduste Sektsiooni Toimetised
Loodusuur Seltsi Aastar — Loodusuurijate. Seltsi Aastaraaman
Look Ahead Proj Highlights — Looking Ahead and Projection Highlights
Look Jpn — Look Japan
Look Lab (Hawaii) — Look Laboratory (Hawaii)
Loonb Land-Tuinbouw — Loonbedrijf in Land- en Tuinbouw
Lopatochnye Mash Struinye Appar — Lopatochnye Mashiny i Struinye Apparaty
LOPh — Literaturblatt fuer Orientalische Philologie
LOR — Long-Range Planning
Lore & L — Lore and Language
Lore Lang — Lore and Language
Lorenz Rep — Lorenz's Ceylon Reports
Lor Inst — Lorimer. Institutes of Law
LORS — Luzac's Oriental Religions Series
LoS — Life of Spirit
LOS — Literary Onomastics Studies
LOS — London Oriental Series
LoS — Louisiana Studies
Los Ang Cty Mus Contrib Sci — Los Angeles County Museum. Contributions in Science
Los Angeles BAB — Los Angeles Bar Association. Bulletin
Los Angeles B Assn Bul — Los Angeles Bar Association. Bulletin
Los Angeles B Bull — Los Angeles Bar Bulletin
Los Angeles Bus and Econ — Los Angeles Business and Economics
Los Angeles Chron — Los Angeles Chronicle
Los Angeles Co Emp — Los Angeles County Employee
Los Angeles Counc Eng Sci Proc Ser — Los Angeles Council of Engineers and Scientists. Proceedings Series
Los Angeles County Mus Contr Sci — Los Angeles County Museum. Contributions in Science
Los Angeles County Mus Nat History Quart — Los Angeles County Museum of Natural History. Quarterly
Los Angeles Ed Res B — Los Angeles Educational Research Bulletin
Los Angeles L Rev — Los Angeles Law Review
Los Angeles Munic Leag Bul — Los Angeles Municipal League. Bulletin
Los Angeles Mus Art Bull — Los Angeles County Museum. Bulletin of the Art Division
Los Angeles Mus Bul — Los Angeles County Museum. Bulletin of the Art Division
Los Angeles Mus Q — Los Angeles County Museum of History, Science, and Art. Quarterly
Los Angeles Sch J — Los Angeles School Journal
Loss & Dam Rev — Loss and Damage Review
Loss Pre — Loss Prevention
Loss Prev — Loss Prevention: A CEP Technical Manual
Loss Prev Saf Promot Process Ind Proc Int Symp — Loss Prevention and Safety Promotion in the Process Industries. Proceedings. International Symposium on Loss Prevention and Safety Promotio the Process Industries
LOT — Leadership and Organization Development Journal
LOT — Library of Orthodox Theology
Lotta Antiparass — Lotta Antiparassitaria
Lotta Contro Tuberc — Lotta Contro la Tubercolosi
Lotta Contro Tuberc Mal Polm Soc — Lotta Contro la Tubercolosi e le Malattie Polmonari Sociali
Lotta Tuberc — Lotta Contro la Tubercolosi
Lotta Tuberc Mal Polm Soc — Lotta Contro la Tubercolosi e le Malattie Polmonari Sociali
Lotus Int — Lotus International
Loughborough Univ Technol Chem Eng J — Loughborough University of Technology. Chemical Engineering Journal
Loughborough Univ Technol Chem Eng Soc J — Loughborough University of Technology. Chemical Engineering Society. Journal
Loughborough Univ Technol Dep Transp Technol TT Rep — Loughborough University of Technology. Department of Transport Technology. TT Report
Louisiana Agric Exp Sta Hort Res Circ — Louisiana Agricultural Experiment Station. Horticultural Research Circular
Louisiana Agric Exp Sta N Louisiana Exp Sta Annual Rep — Louisiana Agricultural Experiment Station. North Louisiana Experiment Station. Annual Report
Louisiana Geol Surv Bull — Louisiana. Geological Survey. Bulletin
Louisiana Hist — Louisiana History
Louisiana Jnl — Louisiana Journal
Louisiana L Rev — Louisiana Law Review
Louisiana Rev — Louisiana Revue
Louisiana Univ Agric Coll Forest Dept Annual Ring — Louisiana University and Agricultural and Mechanical College. Forestry Department. The Annual Ring
Louisiana Water Resources Research Inst Bull — Louisiana Water Resources Research Institute. Bulletin
Louisville Law — Louisville Lawyer
Louisville Med — Louisville Medicine
Louisville Med News — Louisville Medical News
Louisvl Mg — Louisville Magazine
Lou Leg N — Louisiana Legal News
Lou L Jour — Louisiana Law Journal
Lou L Rev — Louisiana Law Review

Lou Revy — Louisiana Revy
Louth Arch J — County Louth Archaeological Journal
Louvain A Ac — Annales Academiae Lovaniensis
Louvain Stds — Louvain Studies
Louvain Univ Inst Geol Mem — Louvain Universite. Institut Geologique. Memoires
Louv Med — Louvain Medical
LouvSt — Louvain Studies
Louv Univ Inst Geol Mem — Louvain Universite. Institut Geologique. Memoires
Lovens Lit Inf — Lovens Litteratur Information
Low Can LJ — Lower Canada Law Journal
Low Count H — Low Countries History. Yearbook
Lower Dimens Syst Mol Electron — Lower-Dimensional Systems and Molecular Electronics
Low-Level Radioact Waste Technol Newsl — Low-Level Radioactive Waste Technology Newsletter
Low Pay Bull — Low Pay Bulletin
Low Pay Rev — Low Pay Review
Low Rank Fuels Symp — Low-Rank Fuels Symposium
Low Temp Electr Gener Cool — Low-Temperature Electric Generator Cooling
Low Temp Phys (Kiev) — Low Temperature Physics (Kiev)
Low Temp Phys Proc Summer Sch — Low Temperature Physics. Proceedings. Summer School
Low Temp Res Stn (Camb) Annu Rep — Low Temperature Research Station (Cambridge). Annual Report
Low Temp Sci Ser A — Low Temperature Science. Series A. Physical Sciences
Low Temp Sci Ser B Biol Sci — Low Temperature Science. Series B. Biological Sciences
Loy Chi LJ — Loyola University of Chicago. Law Journal
Loy Con Prot J — Loyola Consumer Protection Journal
Loy LA Int'l and Comp L Ann — Loyola of Los Angeles. International and Comparative Law Annual
Loy LA Int'l & Comp LJ — Loyola of Los Angeles. International and Comparative Law Journal
Loy LA L Rev — Loyola University of Los Angeles [*later, Loyola Marymount University*]. Law Review
Loy LJ — Loyola Law Journal
Loy LR — Loyola Law Review
Loy L Rev — Loyola Law Review
Loy LR LA — Loyola of Los Angeles. Law Review
Loyola L J — Loyola Law Journal
Loyola LJ — Loyola Law Journal
Loyola Los A L Rev — Loyola of Los Angeles. Law Review
Loyola Los Ang Int'l & Comp L Ann — Loyola of Los Angeles. International and Comparative Law Annual
Loyola L Rev — Loyola Law Review
Loyola of Los Angeles L Rev — Loyola of Los Angeles. Law Review
Loyola U Chi LJ — Loyola University of Chicago. Law Journal
Loyola ULA L Rev — Loyola University of Los Angeles [*later, Loyola Marymount University*]. Law Review
Loyola ULJ (Chicago) — Loyola University Law Journal (Chicago)
Loyola ULJ (Chicago) — Loyola University. Law Review (Chicago)
Loyola UL Rev (LA) — Loyola University of Los Angeles [*later, Loyola Marymount University*]. Law Review
Loyola Univ of Chicago LJ — Loyola University of Chicago. Law Journal
Loy R — Loyola Law Review
Loy U Chi LJ — Loyola University of Chicago. Law Journal
Lozar Vinar — Lozarstvo Vinarstvo
LP — (La) Palabra
LP — Lesnaja Promyslennost
LP — Lesnicka Prace
Lp — Letopis
LP — Liber Pontificalis
LP — Lingua Portuguesa
LP — Lingua Posnaniensis
LP — Literature and Psychology
LP — Litho-Printer Magazine
LP — Poetarum Lesbiorum Fragmenta
LPA — (La) Prensa (Argentina)
L Paed (B) — Lexikon fuer Paedagogik (Bern)
L Paed (F) — Lexikon der Paedagogik (Freiburg)
L Paed R — Lexikon der Paedagogik. Herausgegeben von Maximilian Roloff
LPB — Laser and Particle Beams
LPB — Lunar and Planetary Bibliography
LPer — Literature in Performance
LPFMRD — Lingvisticheskie Problemy Funktsional'nogo Modelirovaniia Rechevoi Deiatel'nosti
LPG — Landpachtgesetz
LPG — Lexikon der Paedagogik der Gegenwart
L Ph — Lehrbuch der Philosophie
LPHLA — Laporan. Lembaga Penelitian Hasil Hutan
LPI — Law and Policy in International Business
LPI Contribution — Lunar and Planetary Institute. Contribution
LPI Technical Report — Lunar and Planetary Institute. Technical Report
Lpldina — Leopoldina. Amtliches Organ der Kaiserlichen Leopoldino-Carolinischen Deutschen Akademie der Naturforscher
L PI G — Landesplanungsgesetz
LPLP — Language Problems and Language Planning
LPM — Leipziger Messe Journal
LPM — Liber Pontificalis, Prout Exstat in Codice Manuscripto Dertusensi
L Pol Mg — Polytechnic Magazine and Journal of Science, Literature, and the Fine Arts (London)
Lpool BI S P & T — Proceedings and Transactions of the Liverpool Biological Society
Lpool Lt Ph S P — Proceedings of the Literary and Philosophical Society of Liverpool

Lpool Md Chir J — Liverpool Medico-Chirurgical Journal
LPosn — Lingua Posnaniensis
LPP — La Parola del Passato
LPPTS — Library. Palestine Pilgrims Text Society
LPR — Linea de Pensamiento de la Reduccion
LPR — London Property Register
L Ps — Lexikon der Psychologie
L Ps S P — Proceedings of the Physical Society of London
L Psy R — Law and Psychology Review
LPT — Library of Protestant Thought
LP Th — Library of Philosophy and Theology
LPTN — Litteratures Populaires de Toutes les Nations [Paris]
LPTV — Lapin Tutkimusseura Vuosikirja
LPU — Legal Practices Update
LPW — [The] Age. Large Print Weekly
LPW — Lexikon Paepstlicher Weisungen
Lpz Aeg Stud — Leipziger Aegyptologische Studien
Lpz Bien Zt — Leipziger Bienenzeitung
LQ — International and Comparative Law Quarterly
LQ — Library Quarterly
LQ — Liturgiegeschichtliche Quellen
LQ — London Quarterly
LQ — Loquela Mirabilis
LQ — Lutheran Quarterly
LQC — Library Quarterly (Chicago)
LQF — Liturgiegeschichtliche Quellen und Forschungen
LQHR — London Quarterly and Holborn Review
LQR — Law Quarterly Review
LQR — London Quarterly Review
L Q Rev — Law Quarterly Review
LQUADW — Ligand Quarterly
LR — Alabama Law Review
LR — Law Reports
LR — Law Review
LR — Lector
LR — Left Review
LR — Les Lettres Romanes
LR — Liberaal Reveil
LR — Library Review
LR — Limba Romina
LR — Literarische Rundschau
LR — Literary Review
LR — Literaturnaya Rossiya
LR — Lutherische Rundschau
LRA — Library Record of Australasia
Lrab Hasarakakan Gitutyun — Lraber Hasarakakan Gitutyunneri
LRAC — Labrador. Resources Advisory Council. Newsletter
LRB — La Revue Bibliographique
L Rb — Lutherischer Rundblick
Lr B — Lutherische Rundschau. Beiheft
LRBC — Late Roman Bronze Coinage
LRC — (La) Revista Catolica
LRC — Library of Religion and Culture
LRE — La Recherche
LRe — Linguistische Reihe
LR E & I App — Law Reports. English and Irish Appeals
LRESDD — Legume Research
L Rev — Law Review
L Rev & Quart J — Law Review and Quarterly Journal
L Rev U Detroit — Law Review. University of Detroit
LRH — Logos. Revista de Humanidades
LRI — Libri e Riviste d'Italia
LRIF — Logos. Rivista Internazionale di Filosofia
LRIr — Law Reports, Ireland
LRKB — Quebec Official Reports, King's Bench
LRKD — Literarische Rundschau fuer das Katholische Deutschland
LRMPDA — Australia. Commonwealth Scientific and Industrial Research Organisation. Land Resources Management. Technical Paper
LRN — Land Reborn. The Holy Land and the Contemporary Near East (New York)
LRN — Literary Research Newsletter
LRNPDF — Lawrence Review of Natural Products
LRNSEP — Lawrence Review of Natural Products. Monograph System
LR (NSW) — Law Reports (New South Wales)
LR (NSW) B & P — Law Reports (New South Wales). Bankruptcy and Probate
LR (NSW) D — Law Reports (New South Wales). Divorce
LR (NSW) Eq — Law Reports (New South Wales). Equity
LR (NSW) Vice-Adm — Law Reports (New South Wales). Vice-Admiralty
L Rom — Limba Romana
LROTD — Laryngologie, Rhinologie, Otologie
LRP — Long-Range Planning
LR PC — Privy Council. Law Reports
LRR — Labor Relations Reporter
LRRM BNA — Labor Relations Reference Manual. Bureau of National Affairs
LRS — Leipziger Rechtswissenschaftliche Studien
LRS — Leipziger Romanistischer Studien
LRS — Lincoln Record Society
LRS — Living Religion Series
LRS — Ljudska Republika Slovenije
LR(SA) — Law Reports (South Australia)
LRSA — South Australian Law Reports
LRsch — Lutherische Rundschau
LRTS — Library Resources and Technical Services
LRVSA — Landmaschinen-Rundschau
LRW — Labor Relations Week
LRWS — Leipziger Rechtswissenschaftliche Studien

LS — Language and Speech
LS — Language in Society
LS — Lapidarium Septentrionale
LS — Lebendige Schule
LS — Lebendige Seelsorge
LS — Leksikograficeskij Sbornik
LS — Le Soir
LS — Le Soleil
LS — Libro e la Stampa
LS — Lingua e Stile
LS — Lingue Straniere
LS — Linguistica Slovaca
LS — Literatura v Shkole
LS — Literaturny Sovremennik
LS — Local Scripts of Archaic Greece
LS — Lusitania Sacra
LS — Lute Society of America. Journal
LS — Lysistrata
LS — Spectator (London)
LSA — Lebende Sprachen. Zeitschrift fuer Fremde Sprachen in Wissenschaft und Praxis
LSA — Letras (Argentina)
LSA — Library Science Abstracts
LSA — Libre Service Actualites
LSa — Lusitania Sacra
LSAA — Literatura o Stranach Azii i Afriki
LSAB — Linguistic Society of America. Bulletin
LSADDN — Life Science Advances
LSA Exp Stn Tech Bull (Maine) — LSA [Life Sciences and Agricultural] Experiment Station. Technical Bulletin (Maine)
LSAG — Local Scripts of Archaic Greece
LSA/L — Language. Journal of the Linguistic Society of America
LSAM — Lois Sacrees de l'Asie Mineure
LSAN — Lute Society of America Newsletter
LSAQ — Lute Society of America Quarterly
LSARA — Landscape Architecture
LSB — La Sainte Bible
LSB — Legal Service Bulletin
LSb — Leksikograficeskij Sbornik
LSB — Linguistic Survey Bulletin
LSB — Sitzungsberichte. Saechsische Akademie der Wissenschaften (Leipzig)
LSBC — Libri della Scoperta. Biografie di Capolavori
LSBCA — Lucrari Stiintifice ale Institutului Agronomic "Nicolae Balcescu" (Bucuresti). Seria C
LSB (SA) — Law Society. Bulletin (South Australia)
LSBT — Literary Society of Bombay. Transactions
LSC — Libre Service Actualites
L'scape — Landscape
LSCG — Lois Sacrees des Cites Grecques
LSci — Language Sciences
LSD — Litteraria; Studie a Dokumenty
LSE — Leeds Studies in English and Kindred Languages
LSE — Lexikon Strassenverkehrsrechtlicher Entscheidungen
LSE — Lund Studies in English
LSEBA — LSE [Laurence, Scott, & Electromotors Ltd.] Engineering Bulletin
LSE Eng Bull — LSE [Laurence, Scott, & Electromotors Ltd.] Engineering Bulletin
LSEMSA — London School of Economics. Monographs on Social Anthropology
LSE Quart — LSE [London School of Economics] Quarterly
LSFS — Learned Society of Fars, Shiraz
LSG — Law Society. Gazette
LS Gaz — Law Society's Gazette
LSGI — Local Self-Government Institute. Quarterly Journal
LSh — Literatura v Shkole
LSI — Lexique Stratigraphique International
LSIB — London State Information Bank
LSI Contrib — LSI [Lunar Science Institute] Contribution
L si L — Limba si Literatura
LSJ — Labor Studies Journal
LSJ — Law Society. Journal
LSJ — Litterae Societatis Jesu
LSJ — Lute Society. Journal
LSJB — Linnaean Society. Journal of Botany
LSJS — Law Society Judgement Scheme
LS Judg Sch — Law Society Judgement Scheme
LSJZ — Linnaean Society. Journal of Zoology
LsL — Limba si Literatura
LSI — Linguistica Slovaca
LSlov — Livre Slovene
LSLT — Li-Shih Lun-Ts'ung
LSMEDI — Lasers in Surgery and Medicine
LSM News — Liberation Support Movement News
LSMT — Lancaster Series on the Mercersburg Theology
LsNs — Letras Nuevas
LSNS — Lundastudier i Nordisk Sprakvetenskap
LSoc — Language in Society
L Soc Gaz — Law Society's Gazette
L Soc J — Law Society. Journal
L Soc'y Gaz — Law Society. Gazette
Lsp — Landinspektoren
LSp — Language and Speech
LSp — Lebende Sprachen
LSP — Leitsaetze fuer die Preisermittlung
LSP — Letras (Peru)
LSP — Lingvisticeskij Sbornik. Petrozavodsk
LSPPA — Life Sciences. Part I. Physiology and Pharmacology

L Spr — Lebende Sprachen
LSR — Lettera di Sociologia Religiosa
LSR — Lone Star Review
LSR — Luttrell Society. Reprints
Ls S — Letopis' Zurnal'nych Statej
LSS — Leyte-Samar Studies
LSSk — Laerde Selskabs Skrifter
LSSkT — Laerde Selskabs Skrifter. Teologiske Skrifter
LSSS — Lutheran Studies Series
LS St — Leipziger Semitistische Studien
LSSYD6 — Life Support Systems
LSSZB7 — Institutul Agronomic Timisoara Lucrari Stiintifice. Seria Zootehnie
LSt — Leipziger Studien zur Classischen Philologie
LSt — Lingue Straniere
LST — Listener
L Stu Mag — Law Students' Magazine
L Stu Mag NS — Law Students' Magazine. New Series
L Stu Mag OS — Law Students' Magazine. Old Series
L St VG — Bayerisches Landesstraf- und Verordnungsgesetz
LSty — Language and Style
LSU Forest Notes — LSU Forestry Notes. Louisiana Agricultural Experiment Station
LSU For Note LA Sch For — LSU Forestry Notes. Louisiana State University. School of Forestry and WildlifeManagement
LSU For Notes LA Agric Exp Stn — LSU [*Louisiana State University*] Forestry Notes. Louisiana Agricultural Experiment Station
LSUHS — Louisiana State University. Humanistic Series
L Sup M Inst Pr — Lake Superior Mining Institute. Proceedings
LSUS — Louisiana State University Studies
LSUSH — Louisiana State University Studies. Humanities Series
LSUSHS — Louisiana State University. Studies. Humanities Series
LSUSS — Louisiana State University Studies. Social Science Series
LSU Wood Util Note LA Sch For — LSU Wood Utilization Notes. Louisiana State University. School of Forestry and Wildlife Management
LSU Wood Util Notes Agric Exp Stn Res Release La State Univ — LSU Wood Utilization Notes. Agricultural Experiment Station Research Release. Louisiana State University and A & M College
LSV — Lettres du Scolasticat de Vals
Lsvl Orch — Louisville Orchestra Program Notes
LSW — Ludowa Spoldzielnia Wydawnicza
LSZODB — Lehrbuch der Speziellen Zoologie
LT — La Torre
L T — Law Times
LT — Law Times Journal
LT — Law Times Newspaper
LT — Levende Talen
LT — Literary Review
LT — Logos (Tuebingen)
LTB — Laboratory Techniques in Biochemistry and Molecular Biology
LTBA — Lexikalischen Tafelserien der Babylonier und Assyrer
LTBA — Linguistics of the Tibeto-Burman Area
LTCO — London Transactions. International Congress of Orientalists
LTE — Tunisie Economique
L Teach — Law Teacher
L Teacher — Law Teacher. Journal of the Association of Law Teachers, London
LTECA — Landtechnik
L T (Eng) — Law Times Journal (England)
LTF Res Progr — LTF [*Lithographic Technical Foundation*] Research Progress
Ltg Des Appl — Lighting Design and Application
Ltg Equip News — Lighting Equipment News
Ltg J (Thorn) — Lighting Journal (Thorn)
Ltg Res Tech — Lighting Research and Technology
L Th — La Themis
L Th — Library of Theology
L Th K — Lexikon fuer Theologie und Kirche
LTHPA — Lectures in Theoretical Physics
LThPh — Laval Theologique et Philosophique
LTHS — La Trobe Historical Studies
LTIED — Ekspress-Informatsiya Laboratornye Tekhnologicheskie Issledovaniya i Obogashchenie Mineral'nogo Syr'ya
L Times — Law Times
LTimesLS — Times Literary Supplement (London)
LTJ — Law Times Journal
LT Jo — Law Times
LT Jo (Eng) — Law Times Journal (England)
LT Jour — Law Times
LTK — Lexikon fuer Theologie und Kirche
Lt L — Leksykolohiia ta Leksykohrafiia Mizhvidomchyi Zbirnyk
LTL — London Theological Library
LTLA — Language Teaching and Linguistics Abstracts
LTLJ — La Trobe Library Journal
LTLS — London Times Literary Supplement
Lt Ltg — Light and Lighting
LTM — Leeds Texts and Monographs
LT NS — Law Times. New Series
LT NS (Eng) — Law Times. New Series
LTNT — Lipsius und Tischer's Neusprachliche Texte. Englische Reihe
LTP — Laval Theologique et Philosophique
LTP — Long-Term Projections
Lt Prod Engng — Light Production Engineering
LTQ — Lexington Theological Quarterly
LTR — Law Times Reports
LTR — Leather. International Journal of the Industry
LTR — Levant Trade Review
LTR — Library Technology Reports

LTR — Logistics and Transportation Review
L Trans Q — Law in Transition Quarterly
LTROS — Law Times Reports. Old Series
LTS — London Times Literary Supplement
LTSB — Low Temperature Science. Series B. Biological Sciences
LTSR Med — LTSR Medicina
LTU — Library Trends (Urbana, Illinois)
LTU — Luvische Texte in Umschrift
LTW — List Taschenbuecher der Wissenschaft
Lu — Lusiada
Lu — Lusitania. Revista de Estudos Portugueses
LUA — Acta Universitatis Lundensis
LUA — Lunds Universitet. Arsskrift
LUAC Mon — LUAC [*Life Underwriters Association of Canada*] Monitor
Lubr Eng — Lubrication Engineering
Lubric Eng — Lubrication Engineering
Lubric Engng — Lubrication Engineering
Lubric Engrg — Lubrication Engineering
Lubr Sci — Lubrication Science
Luc — Luceafarul
Lucas Engng Rev — Lucas Engineering Review
Lucas Eng Rev — Lucas Engineering Review
Lucca At Ac — Atti della Reale Accademia Lucchese di Scienze, Lettere, ed Arti (Lucca)
Lucrari Muzicol — Lucrari de Muzicologie
Lucrari Sti Inst Ped Galati — Lucrari Stiintifice. Institutul Pedagogic Galati
Lucr Cercet Inst Cercet Ind Chim Aliment — Lucrari de Cercetare. Institutul de Cercetari pentru Industrie si Chimie Alimentara
Lucr Cercet Inst Cercet Project Aliment — Lucrari de Cercetare. Institutul de Cercetari si Projectari Alimentare
Lucr Cercet Inst Chim Aliment — Lucrari de Cercetare. Institutul de Chimie Alimentara
Lucr Conf Natl Farm — Lucrarile Prezentate la Conferinta Nationala de Farmacie
Lucr Grad Bot (Bucuresti) — Lucrarile Gradinii Botanice (Bucuresti)
Lucr Gradinii Bot (Bucur) — Lucrarile Gradinii Botanice (Bucuresti)
Lucr ICPE — Lucrarile ICPE
Lucr Inst Cercet Alim — Lucrarile Institutului de Cercetari Alimentare
Lucr Inst Cercet Aliment — Lucrarile Institutului de Cercetari Alimentare
Lucr Inst Cercet Vet Bioprep Pasteur — Lucrarile Institutului de Cercetari Veterinare si Biopreparate Pasteur
Lucr Inst Pet Gaze Bucuresti — Lucrarile Institutului de Petrol si Gaze din Bucuresti
Lucr Inst Pet Gaz Geol Bucuresti — Lucrarile Institutului de Petrol, Gaze, si Geologie din Bucuresti
Lucr Semin Mat Fiz Inst Politeh "Traian Vuia" (Timisoara) — Lucrarile Seminarului de Matematica si Fizica. Institutului Politehnic "Traian Vuia" (Timisoara)
Lucr Ses Stiint Inst Agron Nicolae Balcescu — Lucrarile Sesiunii Stiintifice. Institutul Agronomic "Nicolae Balcescu"
Lucr Ses Stiint Inst Agron Nicolae Balcescu Ser C — Lucrarile Sesiunii Stiintifice. Institutul Agronomic "Nicolae Balcescu" (Bucuresti). Seria C. Zootehnie si Medicina Veterinara
Lucr Simp Biodeterior Clim — Lucrarile. Simpozion de Biodeteriorare si Climatizare
Lucr Simp Clim Biodeterior — Lucrarile. Simpozion de Climatizare si Biodeteriorare
Lucr Sti Inst Agron Dr Petru Groza (Cluj) — Lucrari Stiintifice. Institutul Agronomic "Dr. Petru Groza" (Cluj)
Lucr Sti Inst Agron Dr Petru Groza (Cluj) Ser Agr — Lucrari Stiintifice. Institutul Agronomic "Dr. Petru Groza" (Cluj). Seria Agricultura
Lucr Sti Inst Agron Ion Ionescu de la Brad (Iasi) — Lucrari Stiintifice. Institutul Agronomic "Ion Ionescu de la Brad" (Iasi)
Lucr Sti Inst Agron N Balcescu (Bucuresti) Ser A B C — Lucrari Stiintifice. Institutul Agronomic "Nicolae Balcescu" (Bucuresti). SeriaA, B, C
Lucr Sti Inst Agron Professor Ion Ionescu de la Brad — Lucrari Stiintifice. Institutul Agronomic "Professor Ion Ionescu de la Brad"
Lucr Sti Inst Agron Timisoara (Bucuresti) — Lucrari Stiintifice. Institutul Agronomic Timisoara (Bucuresti)
Lucr Sti Inst Agron "T Vladimirescu" (Craiova) — Lucrari Stiintifice. Institutul Agronomic "T. Vladimirescu" (Craiova)
Lucr Sti Inst Cercet Zooteh — Lucrarile Stiintifice. Institutului de Cercetari Zootehnice
Lucr Stiint Cent Exp Ingrasaminte Bact (Bucharest) — Lucrari Stiintifice. Centrul Experimental de Ingrasaminte Bacteriene (Bucharest)
Lucr Stiint Inst Agron (Bucuresti) Ser A — Lucrari Stiintifice. Institutul Agronomic "Nicolae Balcescu" (Bucuresti). Seria A. Agronomie
Lucr Stiint Inst Agron (Bucuresti) Ser B — Lucrari Stiintifice. Institutul Agronomic "Nicolae Balcescu" (Bucuresti). SeriaB. Horticultura
Lucr Stiint Inst Agron (Bucuresti) Ser C — Lucrari Stiintifice. Institutul Agronomic "Nicolae Balcescu" (Bucuresti). SeriaC. Zootehnie si Medicina Veterinara
Lucr Stiint Inst Agron (Bucuresti) Ser D Zooteh — Lucrari Stiintifice. Institutul Agronomic "Nicolae Balcescu" (Bucuresti). SeriaD. Zootehnie
Lucr Stiint Inst Agron (Cluj) — Lucrari Stiintifice. Institutul Agronomic "Dr. Petru Groza" (Cluj)
Lucr Stiint Inst Agron (Cluj) Ser Agric — Lucrari Stiintifice. Institutul Agronomic "Dr. Petru Groza" (Cluj). Seria Agricultura
Lucr Stiint Inst Agron (Cluj) Ser Med Vet — Lucrari Stiintifice. Institutul Agronomic "Dr. Petru Groza" (Cluj). Seria Medicina Veterinari
Lucr Stiint Inst Agron (Cluj) Ser Med Vet Zooteh — Lucrari Stiintifice. Institutul Agronomic "Dr. Petru Groza" (Cluj). Seria Medicina Veterinara si Zootehnie
Lucr Stiint Inst Agron (Cluj) Ser Zooteh — Lucrari Stiintifice. Institutul Agronomic "Dr. Petru Groza" (Cluj). Seria Zootehnie
Lucr Stiint Inst Agron (Iasi) — Lucrarile Stiintifice. Institutul Agronomic "Professor Ion Ionescu de la Brad" (Iasi)

Lucr Stiint Inst Agron Ion Ionescu de la Brad (Iasi) — Lucrarile Stiintifice. Institutul Agronomic "Professor Ion Ionescu de la Brad" (Iasi)

Lucr Stiint Inst Agron N Balcescu — Lucrari Stiintifice ale Institutului Agronomic N. Balcescu. Bucuresti. Seria C

Lucr Stiint Inst Agron N Balcescu (Bucuresti) Ser C — Lucrari Stiintifice ale Institutului Agronomic "Nicolae Balcescu" (Bucuresti). Seria C

Lucr Stiint Inst Agron N Balcescu (Bucur) Ser C — Lucrari Stiintifice ale Institutului Agronomic "Nicolae Balcescu" (Bucuresti). Seria C

Lucr Stiint Inst Agron "Nicolae Balcescu" Agron — Lucrari Stiintifice. Institutul Agronomic "Nicolae Balcescu." Seria A. Agronomie

Lucr Stiint Inst Agron "Nicolae Balcescu" Hortic — Lucrari Stiintifice. Institutul Agronomic "Nicolae Balcescu." Horticultura

Lucr Stiint Inst Agron "Nicolae Balcescu" Imbunatatiri Fun — Lucrari Stiintifice. Institutul Agronomic "Nicolae Balcescu." Imbunatatiri Funciare

Lucr Stiint Inst Agron "Nicolae Balcescu" Med Vet — Lucrari Stiintifice. Institutul Agronomic "Nicolae Balcescu." Medicina Veterinara

Lucr Stiint Inst Agron "Nicolae Balcescu" Zooteh — Lucrari Stiintifice. Institutul Agronomic "Nicolae Balcescu." Seria D. Zootehnie

Lucr Stiint Inst Agron (Timisoara) Seri Medna Vet — Lucrari Stiintifice. Institutul Agronomic (Timisoara). Seria Medicina Veterinara

Lucr Stiint Inst Agron (Timisoara) Ser Med Vet — Lucrari Stiintifice. Institutul Agronomic (Timisoara). Seria Medicina Veterinara

Lucr Stiint Inst Agron (Timisoara) Ser Zooteh — Lucrari Stiintifice. Institutul Agronomic (Timisoara). Seria Zootehnie

Lucr Stiint Inst Cercet Zooteh — Lucrarile Stiintifice. Institutului de Cercetari Zootehnice

Lucr Stiint Inst Cerc Zooteh — Lucrarile Stiintifice. Institutului de Cercetari Zootehnice

Lucr Stiint Inst Mine Petrosani — Lucrarile Stiintifice. Institutului de Mine Petrosani

Lucr Stiint Inst Mine Petrosani Ser 4 — Lucrarile Stiintifice. Institutului de Mine Petrosani. Seria 4. Stiinte de Cultura Tehnica Generala

Lucr Stiint Inst Mine Petrosani Ser 5 — Lucrarile Stiintifice. Institutului de Mine Petrosani. Seria 5. Geologie

Lucr Stiint Inst Mine Petrosani Ser 6 — Lucrarile Stiintifice. Institutului de Mine Petrosani. Seria 6. Stiinte Sociale

Lucr Stiint Inst Patol Ig Anim — Lucrarile Stiintifice. Institutului de Patologie si Igiena Animala

Lucr Stiint Inst Pedagog Oradea Ser Mat Fiz Chim — Lucrari Stiintifice. Institutul Pedagogic din Oradea. Seria Matematica, Fizica,Chimie

Lucr Stiint Inst Politeh (Cluj) — Lucrarile Stiintifice. Institutul Politehnic (Cluj)

Lucr Stiint Inst Politeh (Galati) — Lucrarile Stiintifice. Institutul Politehnic (Galati)

Lucr Stiint Inst Seruri Vacc Pasteur (Bucur) — Lucrarile Stiintifice. Institutului de Seruri si Vaccinuri Pasteur (Bucuresti)

Lucr Stiint Ser B Hortic — Lucrari Stiintifice. Seria B. Horticultura

Lucr Stiint Ser C VII — Lucrari Stiintifice. Seria C VII. Zootehnie si Medicina Veterinara

Lucr Stiint Ser Zooteh Med Vet — Lucrari Stiintifice. Seria Zootehnie si Medicina Veterinara

Lucr Stiint Stn Cent Cercet Sericic Apic — Lucrari Stiintifice. Statiunea Centrala de Cercetari pentru Sericicultura si Apicultura

Lucr Stint Inst Agron (Timisoara) Ser Agron — Lucrari Stiintifice. Institutul Agronomic (Timisoara). Seria Agronomie

LUCS — Land Use in Canada Series

LUD — (La) Universidad

LuD — Linguistik und Didaktik

Ludoviciana Contr Herb — Ludoviciana. Contributions de l'Herbier Louis-Marie. Faculte d'Agriculture. Universite Laval

Ludwigsburg Geschbl — Ludwigsburger Geschichtsblaetter

LUeAMA — Leipziger Uebersetzungen und Abhandlungen zum Mittelalter

Lue B — Lueneburger Blaetter

Luebeck Mushft — Luebecker Museumshefte

Lueneberger Musbl — Lueneburger Museumsblaetter

Lueneb Nt Vr Jh — Jahreshefte des Naturwissenschaftlichen Vereins fuer das Fuerstenthum Lueneberg

Lueneburger B — Lueneburger Blaetter

LueZ — Zeitschrift des Vereins fuer Luebecker Geschichte und Altertumskunde

LUF — Librairie de l'Universite de Fribourg

LUF — Librairie Universelle de France

LUFBBK — Fonds de Recherches Forestieres. Universite Laval. Bulletin

Luftfahrttech Raumfahrttech — Luftfahrttechnik, Raumfahrttechnik

Luft- Kaeltetech — Luft- und Kaeltetechnik

Luft und Kaeltetech — Luft- und Kaltetechnik

LuG — Literatur und Geschichte. Eine Schriftenreihe

LUH — Ledermarkt und Hautemarkt mit Gerbereiwissenschaft und Praxis. Das Wochenjournal fuer die Lederindustrie, den Hautegrosshandel und Ledergrosshandel

LUIA — London University Institute of Archaeology

LuJ — Limes u Jugoslaviji

Lu J — Luther Jahrbuch

LUK — Literatur und Kritik

LuL — Literatur und Leben

LuM — Literatura un Maksla

Lu m — Liturgie und Moenchtum

Lum — Lumen

Lum — Lumiere

Lum Elect — Lumiere Electrique. Journal Universel d'Electricite

Lumen — Lumen Vitae

Lumiere — Lumiere et Vie

Lumin Cryst Mol Solutions Proc Int Conf — Luminescence of Crystals, Molecules, and Solutions. Proceedings. International Conference on Luminescence

Lumin Tech Chem Biochem Anal — Luminescence Techniques in Chemical and Biochemical Analysis

LumVie — Lumiere et Vie

LumViSup — Lumiere et Vie. Supplement Biblique

LumVit — Lumen Vitae

Lunar and Planetary Explor Colloquium Proc — Lunar and Planetary Exploration Colloquium. Proceedings

Lunar Sci Inst Contrib — Lunar Science Institute. Contribution

Lund Acta Un — Acta Universitatis Lundensis. Lunds Universitets Ars-Skrift. Afdelningen for Mathematik och Naturvetenskap

Lund Phys Sallsk Arsb — Physiographiska Sallskapets Arsberattelse (Lund)

Lund Phys Sallsk Ts — Physiografiska Sallskapets Tidskrift (Lund)

Lunds Univ Arsskr — Acta Universitatis Lundensis. Lunds Universitets Arsskrift. Afdelningen for Mathematik och Naturvetenskap

Lunds Univ Arsskr Avd 2 — Lunds Universitet. Arsskrift. Avdelningen 2. Kungliga Fysiografiska Salskapets i Lund. Handlinger

Lunds Univ Arsskr NF Andra Afd Med — Acta Universitatis Lundensis. Lunds Universitets Arsskrift. Afdelningen foer Mathematik och Naturvetenskap. Ny Foeljd. Andra Afdelningen. Medicin Sam Matematiska och Naturvetenskapliga Aemnen

Lund Un Acta — Acta Universitatis Lundensis. Lunds Universitets Ars-Skrift. Afdelningen for Mathematik och Naturvetenskap

Lung Biol Health Dis — Lung Biology in Health and Disease

Lung Cancer Progr Ther Res — Lung Cancer. Progress in Therapeutic Research

Lun Ger For — Lunder Germanistische Forschungen

Lung Perspect — Lung Perspectives

Lunker Gaz — Lunker Gazette

Luonnon Tutk — Luonnon Tutkija

LuQ — Lutheran Quarterly

LuR — Literature und Reflexion

LUR — Petera Stuckas Latvijas Valsts Universitate Zinatniskie Raksti. Filologijas Zinatnes. A Serija (Riga)

LURB — List of Unlocated Research Books

Lu S — Lehre und Symbol

LusB — Luso-Brazilian Review

Luso Braz Rev Madison — Luso-Brazilian Review (Madison, Wisconsin)

Luso J Sci Tech — Luso Journal of Science and Technology

Lus Sac — Lusitania Sacra

Lus S Sc Nt — Societe des Sciences Naturelles du Grand-Duche de Luxembourg

Lustige Bl — Lustige Blaetter

Lute Soc J — Lute Society. Journal

Luth — Lutheran

Luth — Luthertum. Erlangen

LuthChQ — Lutheran Church Quarterly

Luth Ch Quar — Lutheran Church Quarterly

Luth Church R — Lutheran Church Review

Luth Educ — Lutheran Education

Lutheran Q — Lutheran Quarterly

Luther-Jahrb — Luther-Jahrbuch

Lutherjb — Lutherjahrbuch

Luth For — Lutheran Forum

Luth H Conf — Lutheran Historical Conference. Essays and Reports

LuthJB — Luther-Jahrbuch

LuthMonh — Lutherische Monatshefte

LuthQ — Lutheran Quarterly

LuthRu — Lutherische Rundschau

Luth S — Lutheran Standard

Luth St — Luther-Studien

Luth Th J — Lutheran Theological Journal

Luth W — Lutheran Witness

LuthW — Lutheran World

LutJ — Luther-Jahrbuch

Lutte Cancer — Lutte Contre le Cancer

Lutt L — Lutterworth Library

Lu W — Lehre und Wehre

LuW — Literatur und Wirklichkeit

LuW — Luftfahrt und Wissenschaft

Luxemb Bienenztg — Luxemburgische Bienen-Zeitung

Lux I Pb — Publications de l'Institut Royal Grand-Ducal de Luxembourg. Section des Sciences Naturelles et Mathematiques

Lux Pb I — Publications de l'Institut Royal Grand-Ducal de Luxembourg. Section des Sciences Naturelles et Mathematiques

Lux S Sc Mm — Societe des Sciences Naturelles du Grand-Duche de Luxembourg

Luzerne Leg Reg (PA) — Luzerne Legal Register

Luzerne LJ (PA) — Luzerne Law Journal

Luz Law T — Luzerne Law Times

Luz Leg Reg — Luzerne Legal Register

Luz LJ — Luzerne Law Journal

Luz LR — Luzerne Legal Register

Luz LT (NS) — Luzerne Law Times. New Series

Luz LT (OS) — Luzerne Law Times. Old Series

LUZR — Petera Stuckas Latvijas Valsts Universitate Zinatniskie Raksti

LV — La Vanguardia

LV — Leningradskij Universitet Vestnik Serija Istorii, Literatury, i Jazyka

LV — Levensverzekering

LV — Lumen Vitae

LV — Lumiere et Vie

LVB — Lumiere et Vie (Bruges)

LVE — Liverpool Echo

LVE — Lumen Vitae. English Edition

LVF — Lumen Vitae. Edition Francaise

LVI Saatotek Tutkimussemin — LVI-Saatotekniikan Tutkimusseminaari

L'viv Zootekh Vet Inst Nauk Pr — L'vivskii Zootekhnichno-Veterinarnii Institut. Naukovi Pratsi

LVKJ — Latviesu Valodas Kulturas Jautajumi

LVL — Lumiere et Vie (Lyon)

LVLG — Luther. Vierteljahrsschrift der Luthergesellschaft

Lv Lns — Live Lines

L'vov Politehn Inst Naucn Zap Ser Fiz-Mat — L'vovskii Politehniceskii Institut. Naucnye Zapiski. Serija Fiziko-Matematiceskaja
L'vov Torg Ekon Inst Nauchn Zap — L'vovskii Torgovo-Ekonomicheskii Institut. Nauchnye Zapiski
LVR — Land and Valuation Court Reports
LVS — Larousse du XX Siecle
LvS — Literatura v Shkole
LvSK — Literatura v Shkole
LVWN — Livable Winter Newsletter
LW — Law Weekly
LW — Literarische Wochenschrift
LW — Living Wilderness
LW — Lutheran World
LW — Lydisches Woerterbuch
LW — United States Law Week
LWC — Living World Commentary
LWF Doc — LWF [*Lutheran World Federation*] Documentation
LWF Rep — LWF [*Lutheran World Federation*] Report
LWJ — Literaturwissenschaftliches Jahrbuch der Goerres-Gesellschaft
LwJB — Landwirtschaftliches Jahrbuch fuer Bayern
LWK — Leerblad. Vakblad voor de Lederwarenbranche en Reisartikelenbranche in de Beneluxlanden
LWL — Lexikon der Weltliteratur im 20. Jahrhundert
LWLR — Land and Water Law Review
LWLRD — Land and Water Law Review
LWN — Landbouwwereldnieuws
LWorld — Lutheran World
LWQF — Liturgiewissenschaftliche Quellen und Forschungen
LWR — Land and Water Law Review
LWS — Lutheran World. Supplement
LWU — Literatur in Wissenschaft und Unterricht
LWZ — Lederwaren Zeitung
LXAAAC — Annual Report. Laboratory of Experimental Algology and Department of Applied Algology
LY — Lessing Yearbook
LY — Li-shih Yen-chiu
Ly — Lychnos
Ly — Lyra
LyC — Lenguaje y Ciencias
Lych — Lychnos
Lychnos Lardomshist Samf Arsb — Lychnos Lardomshistoriska Samfundets Arsbok
Lyc N H NY An Pr — Lyceum of Natural History of New York. Annals. Proceedings
Lycoming Coll Mag — Lycoming College Magazine
LydgN — Lydgate Newsletter

Lyd Wb — Lydisches Woerterbuch
Lying-In J Reprod Med — Lying-In Journal of Reproductive Medicine
LyL — Lanzas y Letras
Lymph Cyt R — Lymphokine and Cytokine Research
Lymphokine Cytokine Res — Lymphokine and Cytokine Research
Lymphokine Res — Lymphokine Research
Lymphokines Thymic Horm Their Potential Util Cancer Ther — Lymphokines and Thymic Hormones. Their Potential Utilization in Cancer Therapeutics
Lyngb — Lyngby-Bogen
Lynx Suppl (Prague) — Lynx Supplementum (Prague)
LyON — Lyric Opera News
Lyon Ac Mm — Memoires de l'Academie des Sciences, Belles-Lettres, et Arts de Lyon. Classe des Sciences
Lyon Ac Mm Sc — Memoires de l'Academie des Sciences, Belles-Lettres, et Arts de Lyon. Classe des Sciences
Lyon Ac Sc Mm — Memoires de l'Academie des Sciences, Belles-Lettres, et Arts de Lyon. Classe des Sciences
Lyon A S L — Annales de la Societe Linneene de Lyon
Lyon Chir — Lyon Chirurgical
Lyon Med — Lyon Medical
Lyon Mm Ac — Memoires de l'Academie des Sciences, Belles-Lettres, et Arts de Lyon. Classe des Sciences
Lyon Mm Ac Sc — Memoires de l'Academie des Sciences, Belles-Lettres, et Arts de Lyon. Classe des Sciences
Lyon Pharm — Lyon Pharmaceutique
Lyon S Ag A — Annales des Sciences Physiques et Naturelles, d'Agriculture et d'Industrie, publiees par la Societe d'Agriculture (Lyon)
Lyons Fac Sci Lab Geol Doc — Lyons. Faculte des Sciences. Laboratoires de Geologie. Documents
Lyon S Sc Md Mm — Memoires et Comptes-Rendus de la Societe des Sciences Medicales de Lyon
Lyon Un A — Annales de l'Universite de Lyon
LyP — Libro y Pueblo
Lysosomes Biol Pathol — Lysosomes in Biology and Pathology
Lyumin Mater Osobo Chist Veshchestva — Lyuminestsentnye Materialy i Osobo Chistye Veshchestva. Sbornik Nauchnykh Trudov
LZ — Literarisches Zentralblatt
LZ — Literarisches Zentralblatt fuer Deutschland
LZ — Literaturen Zbor
LZ — Literaturnye Zapiski
LZAV — Latvijas PSR Zinatnu Akademijas. Vestis
LZB — Literarisches Zentralblatt fuer Deutschland
LZD — Literarisches Zentralblatt fuer Deutschland
LZNAAN — Acta Zoologica Colombiana
LzT — Listy z Teatru

M

M — All India Reporter, Madras Series
M — Maasbode
M — Magistratuur
M — Mankind
M — Man [*London*]
M — Manuscripts
M — Marketing
M — Masquerade
M — Memorial; Journal Officiel du Grand Duche de Luxembourg
M — Merkur
M — M. Gentle Men for Gender Justice
M — Missiology
M — Mnemosyne
M — Monde
M — M; the Civilized Man
M — Museon. Revue d'Etudes Orientales
M — Museum. Maandblad voor Philologie en Geschiedenis
M — Musica
M — Musicology
M3 Archaeol — M3 Archaeology
MA — Al-Mustami Al-Arabi
MA — Maandblad voor Accountancy en Bedrijfshuishoudkunde
MA — Mackenzie News
MA — Madison Avenue
MA — Magazine of Art
MA — Mairena
MA — Management Abstracts
MA — Maroc Antique
Ma — Maryland Music Educator
MA — Masters Abstracts
MA — Materiale si Cercetari Arheologice
MA — Medical Annual
MA — Medium Aevum
MA — Microfilm Abstracts
M-A — Mid-America: An Historical Review
MA — Military Affairs
MA — Modern Age
MA — Monographs in Anaesthesiology
MA — Monumenta Americana [*Berlin*]
MA — Monumenta Archaeologica
MA — Monumenta Archaeologica (Prague)
MA — Moyen Age
MA — Musical America
MA — Musical Antiquary
MAA — Maatschappijbelangen
MAA — Management Accounting
MAA — Managing
MAA — Mededeelingen. Koninklijke Nederlandsche Akademie van Wetenschappen te Amsterdam
MAA — Memoires. Academie des Sciences, Agriculture, Arts, et Belles-Lettres d'Aix
MAAA — Memoirs. American Anthropological Association
MAAL — Monumenti Antichi. Reale Accademia Nazionale dei Lincei
MAAN — Memorie. Reale Accademia di Archeologia, Lettere, e Belle Arti di Napoli
Maandber Proefstn JavasuikInd — Maandbericht ven het Proefstation voor de Javasuikerindustrie
Maandber Zuiderzeewkn — Maandbericht Betreffende de Zuiderzeewerken
Maandbl Geest Volksgezondh — Maandblad voor de Geestelijke Volksgezondheid
Maandbl Landbouwvoorlichtingsdienst (Neth) — Maandblad voor de Landbouwvoorlichtingsdienst (Netherlands)
Maandbl LandbVoorlDienst — Maandblad voor de Landbouwvoorlichtingsdienst
Maandbl Natuurl Genoot Limburg — Maandblad Uitgegeven door het Natuurhistorisch Genootschap in Limburg
Maandbl Natuurhist Genootsch Limburg — Maandblad. Uitgegeven Door Het Natuurhistorisch Genootschap in Limburg
Maandbl Natuurw — Maandblad voor Natuurwetenschappen. Genootschap ter Bevordering van Natuur-, Genees- en Heelkunde te Amsterdam
Maandbl Ned Natuurh Vereen — Maandblad der Nederlandsche Natuurhistorische Vereeniging
Maandbl Ned Optn — Maandblad voor den Nederlandschen Opticien
Maandbl Ned Pomol Vereen — Maandblad der Nederlandsche Pomologische Vereeniging
Maandbl Ned Vereen Ing — Maandblad van de Nederlandsche Vereeniging van Ingenieurs
Maandbl Oud Utrecht — Maandblad van Oud-Utrecht
Maandbl Pieper — Maandblad de Pieper

Maandbl V Ber En Reclasseer — Maandblad voor Berechting en Reclasseering van Volwassenen en Kinderen
Maandbl Vervalsch — Maandblad tegen de Vervalschingen
Maandbl Vlaam Bieenb — Maandblad van de Vlaamse Bieenbond
Maandbl Vlaam Imkersb — Maandblad van de Vlaamse Imkersbond
Maandbl Ziekenverpl — Maandblad voor Ziekenverpleging
Maandel Meded StToez Volksgezondh — Maandelijkse Mededelingen. Staatstoezicht op de Volksgezondheid
Maandschr Bijent — Maandschrift voor Bijenteelt
Maandschr Econ — Maandschrift Economie
Maandschr Kindergeneesk — Maandschrift voor Kindergeneeskunde
Maandschr Kindergeneeskd — Maandschrift voor Kindergeneeskunde
Maandschr Ned Maatsch Tuinb — Maandschrift van de Nederlandsche Maatschappij voor Tuinbouw en Plantkunde
Maandschr Ned Maatsch Tuinb PlKunde — Maandschrift van de Nederlandsche Maatschappij voor Tuinbouw en Plantkunde
Maandschr Tuinb — Maandschrift voor Tuinbouw
Maandsrapp Smitts Sygd Husdyr Kbh — Maanedsrapport Angaaende Smittsomme Sygdomme hos Hysdyrene. Landbruksministerium (Kjobenhavn)
MAAR — Memoirs. American Academy at Rome
Maasg — Maasgouw
MAA Stud Math — MAA [*Mathematical Association of America*] Studies in Mathematics
Maat — Maatstaf. Maanblad voor Letteren
Maatalouden Karjanhoitol — Maatalouden Karjanhoitolehti
Maatalouden Tutkimuskeskuksen Aikak — Maatalouden Tutkimuskeskuksen Aikakauskirja
Maatalouden Tutkimuskeskus Maantutkimuslaitos Agrogeol Julk — Maatalouden Tutkimuskeskus. Maantutkimuslaitos. Agrogeologisia Julkaisuja
Maatalouden Tutkimuskeskus Maantutkimuslaitos Agrogeol Kart — Maatalouden Tutkimuskeskus. Maantutkimuslaitos. Agrogeologisia Karttoja
Maatalouden Tyotehos Julk — Maatalouden Tyotehoseuran Julkaisuja
Maataloushal Aikakausk — Maataloushallinon Aikakauskirja
Maatalouskoel Maatutkim — Maatalouskoelaitoksen Maatutkimusosasto
Maatalouskoel Tiet Julk — Maatalouskoelaitoksen Tieteellisia Julkaisuja
Maatalous Koetoim — Maatalous ja Koetoiminta
Maatalousminist Julk — Maatalousministerion Julkaisuja
Maatalousminist Tuotanto Osaston Julk — Maatalousministerion Tuotanto-Osaston Julkaisu
Maatalouss Neuv Liiton Puutarhaammatt Julk — Maatalousseuran Neuvojain Liiton Puutarhaammattiosaston Julkaisuja
Maatalouss Valiaik Koneterkastusl Julk — Maatalousseurojen Valiaikaisen Konetarkastuslaitoksen Julkaisuja
Maataloust Aikakausk — Maataloustieteelinen Aikakauskirja
Maataloustiet Aikak — Maataloustieteelinen Aikakauskirja
Maataloustieteelinen Aikak — Maataloustieteelinen Aikakauskirja
Maatsch Lettknd Bijdr Hand — Maatschappij van Letterkunde. Bijdragen tot de Handelingen
Maatsch Vl Biblioph — Maatschappij der Vlaamsche Bibliophielen
MAB — Maandblad voor Accountancy en Bedrijfshuishoudkunde
MAB — Magazine of Bank Administration
MAb — Masters Abstracts
MAB — Memoires. Academie Royale de Belgique
MAB — Memoires. Association Bretonne
MABBA — Memoires. Academie Royale de Belgique. Classe des Beax-Arts
MABC — Monthly Agricultural Bulletin (Cairo)
MABFAI — Muenchener Beitraege zur Abwasser-, Fischerei-, und Flussbiologie
MABL — Memoires. Academie Royale de Belgique. Classe des Lettres et des Sciences Morales et Politiques
MABP — Medii Aevi Bibliotheca Patristica
MABy — Monuments de l'Art Byzantin
MA Byz — Monuments de l'Art Byzantin
MAC — Commercial Courier
MAC — Macabre
Mac — Maclean's
Mac — Macmillan's Magazine
Mac — Macula
MAC — MAC [*Media Agencies Clients*]/Western Advertising
MAC — Management Accounting
MAC — Measurement and Control
Mac — Media, Agencies, Clients [*Later, Adweek*]
MAC — Memoires. Academie Nationale des Sciences, Arts, et Belles-Lettres de Caen
MAC — Memorias. Academia das Ciencias de Lisboa. Classe de Letras
MAC — Mergers and Acquisitions
MAC — Monumenti dell'Antichita Cristiana

MAC — Motor Accidents Cases
M Ac A — Memoires. Academie des Sciences, Belles-Lettres, et Arts d'Angers
Mac Acta A — Macedoniae Acta Archaeologica
Macaroni J — Macaroni Journal
Macaulay Inst Soil Res Annu Rep — Macaulay Institute for Soil Research. Annual Report
Macaulay Inst Soil Res Collect Pap — Macaulay Institute for Soil Research. Collected Papers
MACBAB — Memorias. Real Academia de Ciencias y Artes de Barcelona
Macch Mot Agric — Macchine e Motori Agricole
Macch Motori Agr — Macchine e Motori Agricoli
M Accounting — Management Accounting
MACD — Metabolic Aspects of Cardiovascular Disease
MACDA — Michigan Academician
M Ac Dijon — Memoires. Academie des Sciences, Arts, et Belles Lettres de Dijon
Macdonald Coll J — Macdonald College Journal
Macdonald Coll Repr — Macdonald College Reprints
Macdonald Fm J — Macdonald Farm Journal
MACEJ — Manitoba Association of Confluent Education. Journal
MA Celt — Memoires. Academie Celtique
Macequece Min News — Macequece Mining News
Macewen Meml Lect — Macewen Memorial Lecture. University of Glasgow
MACF — Memoires. Academie des Sciences, Belles Lettres, et Arts de Clermont-Ferrand
MAC Forester — M.A.C. (Michigan Agricultural College) Forester
Mach — Al-Machriq
Mach — Machinery [Later, Machinery and Production Engineering]
Mach Acctg Data Process — Machine Accounting and Data Processing
Mach Age — Machine Age
Mach Agric — Machine Agricole
Mach Agric Equip Rural — Machinisme Agricole et Equipement Rural
Mach Agric Fr — Machine Agricole Francaise
Mach Agric Mod — Machine Agricole Moderne
Mach Agric Trop — Machinisme Agricole Tropical
Mach Agr Trop — Machinisme Agricole Tropical
Mach and Prod Eng — Machinery and Production Engineering
Mach & Prod Engng — Machinery and Production Engineering
Mach and Tool — Machines and Tooling
Mach Build Ind — Machine Building Industry
Mach Bus — Machinery Business
Mach Des — Machine Design
Mach Design — Machine Design
Mach Equip Food Ind — Machinery and Equipment for Food Industry
Machinaal Melk — Machinaal Melken
Machine D — Machine Design
Machinery Chron — Machinery Chronicle
Machinery Elect Export Markt — Machinery-Electrical Export-Markt
Machinery Mkt — Machinery Market and the Machinery and Engineering Materials Gazette
Machinery Mkt Trades Index — Machinery Market Trades Index
Machinery Mkt Yb — Machinery Market Yearbook
Machinery Prod Engng — Machinery and Production Engineering
Machinerys Die Cast Suppl — Machinery's Die-Casting Supplement
Machinery Shipbldg — Machinery and Shipbuilding
Machinisme Agric — Machinisme Agricole et Equipement Rural
Machinists Mon J — Machinists' Monthly Journal
Mach Intell Pattern Recogn — Machine Intelligence and Pattern Recognition
Mach Korea — Machinery Korea
Mach Learn — Machine Learning
Mach Lloyd Int Rev Eng Equip — Machinery Lloyd. International Review of Engineering Equipment
Mach Mag — Mach Magazine
Mach Market — Machinery Market
Mach Mod — Machine Moderne
Mach Outil Angl — Machine-outil Anglaise
Mach Outil Fr — Machine Outil Francaise
Mach Outil Outill — Machine-outil. Outillage
Mach Prod E — Machinery and Production Engineering
Mach Prod Eng — Machinery and Production Engineering
Mach Sci Technol — Machining Science and Technology
Machs Fr — Machines Francaises
Mach Shop — Machine Shop
Mach Shop Eng Manuf — Machine Shop and Engineering Manufacture
Mach Shop Mag — Machine Shop Magazine
Mach Shop Yb — Machine Shop Year Book
Machs Main D Oeuvre Agric — Machines et Main-d'Oeuvre Agricoles
Machs Outill Agric — Machines et Outillages Agricoles
Machs Outils — Machines-Outils et Outillage General
Mach Steel — Machinery and Steel
Machs Tool — Machines and Tooling
Mach Tech Constr — Machines et Techniques de Construction
Mach Tool — Machines and Tooling
Mach Tool Blue Bk — Machine Tool Blue Book
Mach Tool Blue Book — Machine and Tool Blue Book
Mach Tool Eng — Machine Tool Engineering
Mach Tool Engl Transl — Machines and Tooling. English Translation of Stanki i Instrument
Mach Tool Engng Prod News — Machine Tool Engineering and Production News
Mach Tool News — Machine Tool News
Mach Tool R — Machine Tool Review
Mach Tool Rev — Machine Tool Review
Mach Tools — Machine Tools
Mach Tools & Tools — Machine Tools and Tools
Mach Tools Increase Prod — Machine Tools to Increase Production
Mach Transl — Machine Translation

Mach Vision Appl — Machine Vision and Applications
Mach Woodwkr — Machine Woodworker
MACL — Memoires. Academie d'Histoire de la Culture de Leningrad
MACL — Memorias. Academia das Ciencias de Lisboa. Classe de Letras
MACLCL — Memorias. Academia das Ciencias de Lisboa. Classe de Letras
MACLL — Memorias. Academia das Ciencias de Lisboa. Classe de Letras
Macl Mag — Maclean's Magazine
Maclurean Lyc Contr — Maclurean Lyceum. Contributions
M Ac M — Memoires. Academie de Metz
Macmil — Macmillan's Magazine
Macmillan Lect Br Columb Univ — Macmillan Lectures. British Columbia University
Macm M — Macmillan's Magazine
Macon Ac A — Annales de l'Academie de Macon, Societe des Arts, Sciences, Belles-Lettres et d'Agriculture
Macon S Ag C R — Compte Rendu des Travaux de la Societe d'Agriculture, des Sciences, Arts, et Belles-Lettres de Macon
Macon S C R — Compte Rendu des Travaux de la Societe d'Agriculture, des Sciences, Arts, et Belles-Lettres de Macon
Mac R — Macedonian Review
MACR — Molecular Aspects of Cell Regulation
MACr — Monumenti di Antichi Cristiana
MAC Rec — M.A.C. (Michigan Agricultural College) Record
Macromol Behav — Macromolecules and Behavior
Macromol Chem Phys — Macromolecular Chemistry and Physics
Macromol Chem Phys Suppl — Macromolecular Chemistry and Physics. Supplement
Macromolec — Macromolecules
Macromol Phys — Macromolecular Physics
Macromol R — Macromolecular Reviews. Part D. Journal of Polymer Science
Macromol Rapid Commun — Macromolecular Rapid Communications
Macromol Rep — Macromolecular Reports. International Rapid Publication Supplement to the Journal of Macromolecular Science. Pure and Applied Chemistry
Macromol Rev — Macromolecular Reviews
Macromols — Macromolecules
Macromol Specif Biol Mem — Macromolecular Specificity and Biological Memory
Macromol Symp — Macromolecular Symposia
Macromol Synth — Macromolecular Syntheses
Macromol Synth Order Adv Prop — Macromolecules. Synthesis, Order, and Advanced Properties
Macromol Theory Simul — Macromolecular Theory and Simulations
M Ac S — Memoires. Academie de Stanislas
M Ac Savoie — Memoires. Academie des Sciences, Belles-Lettres, et Arts de Savoie
MAC/WA — MAC [Media Agencies Clients]/Western Advertising
Mad — Madamina
MAD — Materials for the Assyrian Dictionary
MAD — Memoires. Academie des Sciences, des Arts, et des Belles-Lettres de Dijon
Madagascar Dir Ind Mines Rapp Act Geol — Madagascar. Direction de l'Industrie et des Mines. Rapports d'Activite. Geologie
Madagascar Med — Madagascar Medical
Madagascar Rev Geogr — Madagascar. Revue de Geographie
Madagascar Revue de Geogr — Madagascar. Revue de Geographie
Madagascar Serv Mines Ann Geol — Madagascar. Service des Mines. Annales Geologiques
Madaus Jber — Madaus Jahresbericht
Made in Mex — Made in Mexico
Madem — Mademoiselle
Maden Tetkik Arama Enst Mecm — Maden Tetkik ve Arama Enstitusu Mecmuasi
Maden Tetkik Arama Enst Yayin — Maden Tetkik ve Arama Enstitusu Yayinlarindan
Maden Tetkik Arama Enst Yayinlarindan — Maden Tetkik ve Arama Enstitusu Yayinlarindan
Maden Tetkik Arama Enst Yayin Seri A — Maden Tetkik ve Arama Enstitusu Yayinlarindan. Seri A. Bildirigler
Maden Tetkik Arama Enst Yayin Seri B — Maden Tetkik ve Arama Enstitusu Yayinlarindan. Seri B. Irdeller
Maden Tetkik Arama Enst Yayin Seri C — Maden Tetkik ve Arama Enstitusu Yayinlarindan. Seri C. Monografiler
Maden Tetkik Arama Enst Yayin Seri D — Maden Tetkik ve Arama Enstitusu Yayinlarindan. Seri D. Jeolojik Harta Materye-Leri
Madhya Bharati J Univ Saugar Part 2 Sect B Nat Sci — Madhya Bharati. Journal of the University of Saugar. Part 2. Section B. NaturalSciences
Madhya Bharati Part 2 Sect A Phys — Madhya Bharati. Part 2. Section A. Physical Sciences
Madhya Bharati Pt 2 Sect A — Madhya Bharati. Part 2. Section A. Physical Sciences
MADIS — Burda-Marketing Info System
Madison Av — Madison Avenue
Madison Ave — Madison Avenue
Madjalah Inst Tek Bandung Proc — Madjalah Institut Teknologi Bandung Proceedings
Madjalleh Behdasht Rav — Madjalleh Behdasht Ravany
Madjelis Ilmu Pengetahuan Indones Penerbitan — Madjelis Ilmu Pengetahuan Indonesia Penerbitan
Madj Ilm — Madjalah Ilmiah
Madj Kedokt Indonesia — Madjalah Kedokteran Indonesia
Madj Keseh Angk Perang — Madjalah Kesehatan Angkatan Perang
Madj Keseh Mulut Gigi — Madjalah Kesehatan Mulut dan Gigi
Madj Persat Dokt Gigi Indones — Madjalah Persatuan Dokter Gigi Indonesia
Madj Persat Dokt Gigi Indonesia — Madjalah Persatuan Dokter Gigi Indonesia
Madj Pert — Madjalah Pertanian
Madj Pharm — Madjalah Pharmasi
Mad LJ — Madras Law Journal

Mad LT — Madras Law Times
Mad LW — Madras Law Weekly
Madness — Madness Network News
MADNV — Mitteilungsblatt. Allgemeiner Deutsche Neuphilologenverband
Madoqua Ser I — Madoqua. Series I
Madoqua Ser II — Modoqua. Series II
Mad Q — Madison Quarterly
Mad R — Madras Review
Madras Agric Cal — Madras Agricultural Calendar
Madras Agric J — Madras Agricultural Journal
Madras Agri J — Madras Agriculture Journal
Madras Agr J — Madras Agricultural Journal
Madras Eng Rp — Reports. Corps of Engineers of the Madras Presidency
Madras Fish Bull — Madras Fisheries Bulletin
Madras Forest Bull — Madras Forest Bulletin
Madras Forest Coll Mag — Madras Forest College Magazine
Madras J — Madras Journal of Literature and Science
Madras J Lit Sci — Madras Journal of Literature and Science
Madras LJ — Madras Law Journal
Madras LJ — Madras Law Journal and Reports
Madras Med Coll Mag — Madras Medical College Magazine
Madras Med J — Madras Medical Journal
Madras M J — Madras Medical Journal
Madras Vet Coll Annu — Madras Veterinary College. Annual
Madras Vet J — Madras Veterinary Journal
Madr Cient — Madrid Cientifico
Madresfield Agric Clubs Q — Madresfield Agricultural Club's Quarterly
Madrid Ac Ci Mm — Memorias de la Real Academia de Ciencias (Madrid)
Madrid A H Nt — Anales de Historia Natural (Madrid)
Madrider Mitt — Madrider Mitteilungen. Deutsches Archaeologisches Institut. Madrider Abteilung
Madrid Forsch — Madrider Forschungen
Madrid Mitt — Madrider Mitteilungen
Madrid Mm — Memorias de la Real Academia de Ciencias (Madrid)
Madrid Rv — Revista de los Progresos de las Ciencias Exactas, Fisicas, y Naturales (Madrid)
Madrid S H Nt A — Anales de la Sociedad Espanola de Historia Natural (Madrid)
Madrid Univ Fac Med Arch — Madrid Universidad. Facultad de Medicina. Archivos
Madr Mitt — Mitteilungen. Deutsches Archaeologische Institut. Abteilung Madrid
Madrono West Am J Bot — Madrono. West American Journal of Botany
Mad WN — Madras Weekly Notes
Mad WNCC — Madras Weekly Notes, Criminal Cases
MADZAK — Koninklijk Museum voor Midden-Afrika [*Tervuren, Belgie*]. Zoologische Documentatie
MAE — Maize
MAE — Medium Aevum
MAE — Ministero degli Affari Esteri. Monografie e Rapporto Coloniale
MAE — Ministry of Agriculture. Egypt
MAEB — Ministry of Agriculture. Egypt. Bulletin
MAECA — Modern Aspects of Electrochemistry
MAECDR — Marine Ecology. Pubblicazioni della Stazione Zoologica di Napoli. I
Maehr Schles Heimat — Maehrisch-Schlesische Heimat
Maehr Tagbl — Maehrisches Tagblatt
MAEL — Memoires. Societe Archeologique d'Eure-et-Loire
MAeM — Medium Aevum Monographs
MAEQA — Meetings on Atomic Energy
Maerisch-Schlesische Heimat — Maerisch-Schlesische Heimat. Vierteljahresschrift fuer Kultur und Wirtschaft
Maerk F — Maerkische Forschungen
Maerk Naturschutz — Maerkische Naturschutz
Maerk Tierwelt — Maerkische Tierwelt
MAES — Memoirs. American Ethnological Society
MAeS — Mitteilungen aus der Aegyptischen Sammlung
MAES — Monographs. American Ethnological Society
Maes Rural Mex — El Maestro Rural (Mexico)
MAe St — Muenchener Aegyptologische Studien
MAETB — Ministry of Agriculture. Egypt. Technical Bulletin
MAEUDD — Meddelanden fran Avdelningen foer Ekologisk Botanik Lunds Universitet
MAev — Medium Aevum
MAF — Memoires. Societe Nationale des Antiquaires de France
MAFA — Monographs on Archaeology and Fine Arts
MAFES Res Highlights Miss Agric For Exp Stn — MAFES Research Highlights. Mississippi Agricultural and Forestry Experiment Station
Mafic Dykes Emplacement Mech Proc Int Dyke Conf — Mafic Dykes and Emplacement Mechanisms. Proceedings. International Dyke Conference
MAFLS — Memoires. American Folklore Society
MAFR — Marine Fisheries Review
MAFR — Marriage and Family Review
MAFSA9 — Mitteilungen. Arbeitsgemeinschaft fuer Floristik in Schleswig-Holstein und Hamburg
MAG — Magazine Article Guide
Mag — [*The*] Magistrate
Mag — Magistratuur
MAG — Manager's Magazine
MAG — Managing
MAG — Mesoamerica
MAG — Mitteilungen. Altorientalische Gesellschaft
Mag A — Magazine of Art
MagA — Magazine of Art
Magadan Zon Nauchno Issled Inst Selsk Khoz Sev Vostoka Tr — Magadanskii Zonal'nyi Nauchno-Issledovatel'skii Institut Sel'skogo Khozyaistva Severo-Vostoka. Trudy
Mag Age — Magazine Age

Mag Ak Ets — Magyar Akademiai Ertesito. A Mathematikai es Termeszettudomanyi Osztalyok Kozlonye
Mag Ak Ets Mth Term — Magyar Akademiai Ertesito. A Mathematikai es Termeszettudomanyi Osztalyok Kozlonye
Magallah Tibb Mastir — Magallah Tibbiah el Masstiriah
Mag Amer Hist — Magazine of American History
Mag Am Hist — Magazine of American History
Mag Antiq — Magazine of Antiques
Mag Arbeitsr — Magazin fuer Arbeitsrecht, Sozialpolitik, und Verwandte Gebiete
Mag Art — Magazine of Art
Magasin Modes Nouv Fr & Angl — Magasin des Modes Nouvelles Francaises et Anglaises
Mag Asvanyolaj Foldgaz Kiserl Intez Kozl — Magyar Asvanyolaj-es Foldgaz Kiserleti Intezet Koezlemenyei
Mag Ausl Lit Gesammten Heilk — Magazin der Auslaendischen Literatur der Gesammten Heilkunde, und Arbeiten des Aerztlichen Vereins zu Hamburg
Magazin Ag — Magazine Age
Magazin Tech IndPolit — Magazin fuer Technik und Industriepolitik
Mag Bank Adm — Magazine of Bank Administration
Mag Belorv Arch Ideggyogy Sz — Magyar Belorvosi Archivum es Ideggyogyaszati Szemle
Mag Bihar Agr Coll — Magazine. Bihar Agricultural College
Mag Biol Kutatointez Munkai — Magyar Biologiai Kutatointezet Munkai
Mag Bl — Magical Blend
Mag Bldg — Magazine of Building
Mag Blundells Sch Sci Soc — Magazine of the Blundell's School Science Society
Mag Build Equip — Magazine of Building Equipment
Mag Bus — Magazine of Business
Mag Coll Agric — Magazine. College of Agriculture
Mag Coll Indig Med Colombo — Magazine. College of Indigenous Medicine (Colombo)
Mag Concrete Res — Magazine of Concrete Research
Mag Concr R — Magazine of Concrete Research
Mag Concr Res — Magazine of Concrete Research
MAGD — Mitteilungen der Afrikanische Gesellschaft in Deutschland
MAGDA — Mechanisms of Ageing and Development
Mag Datenverarb — Magazin fuer Datenverarbeitung
Magdeb Forsch — Magdeburger Forschungen
Magdebg Geschbll — Magdeburger Geschichtsblaetter
Mag Dortmund — Magazin von und fuer Dortmund
Magellanic Clouds Proc Symp Int Astron Union — Magellanic Clouds. Proceedings. Symposium. International Astronomical Union
Mag Enc — Magazine Encyclopedique
Mag F A — Magazine of Fine Arts
Mag Fantasy & Sci Fict — Magazine of Fantasy and Science Fiction
Mag Fil Sz — Magyar Filozofiai Szemle
Mag Freunde Naturl — Magazin fuer Freunde der Naturlehre und Naturgeschichte, Scheidekunst, Land- und Stadtwirthschaft, Volks- und Staatsarznei
Mag Geogr — Magazin fuer die Geographie, Staatenkunde, und Geschichte
Mag Geogr Argent — Magazine Geografico Argentino
Mag Gr — Magna Graecia
Mag Gyogyszeresztud Tarsasag Ert — Magyar Gyogyszeresztudomanyi Tarsasag Ertesitoje
Mag Hist — Magazine of History with Notes and Queries
Mag Hort — Magazine of Horticulture
Mag Hort Bot — Magazine of Horticulture, Botany, and All Useful Discoveries and Improvements in Rural Affairs
Maghreb — Maghreb-Machrek
Maghreb Develop — Maghreb Developpement
Maghreb Math Rev — Maghreb Mathematical Review
Maghreb Rev — Maghreb Review
Mag I — Magazine Index
MAGIC — Marketing and Advertising General Information Centre
Mag Index — Magazine Index
Mag Int Wohnen — Magazin fuer Internationales Wohnen
Mag Istor — Magazin Istoric
Mag Ital — Magazzino Italiano Che Contiene Storia
MAGJB — Magyar Allami Eoetvoes Lorand Geofizikai Intezet. Evi Jelentese
Mag Ke'm Foly — Magyar Kemiai Folyoira
Mag Kem Lapja — Magyar Kemikusok Lapja
Mag Kir Szolo Borgazd Kozp Kiserl Allomas Ampelol Intez Evk — Magyar Kir. Szolo es Borgazdasagi Kozponti Kiserleti Allomas (Ampelologiai Intezet) Evkonyve
Mag Kozlekedes Mely Vizepites — Magyar Kozlekedes. Mely es Vizepites
Mag Kst — Magazin Kunst
MagL — Magazine Litteraire
Mag Landb Kruidk — Magazijn voor Landbouw en Kruidkunde
Mag Litt — Magazine Litteraire
Mag Litter Scientif — Magazin Litteraire et Scientifique
Mag Lond Elect Bd — Magazine. London Electricity Board
Mag London — Magazine of London
Mag Lond (Roy Free Hosp) School Med Women — Magazine. London (Royal Free Hospital) School of Medicine for Women
Mag Lt — Magazine of Light
Mag Macl — Magazine Maclean
Mag Magnes — Magazine of Magnesium
MAGMA NY — MAGMA (New York). Magnetic Resonance Materials in Physics, Biology, and Medicine
Magmat Glubinnoe Str Zemnoi Kory Sredn Azii — Magmatizm i Glubinnoe Stroenie Zemnoi Kory Srednei Azii
Magmat Polezn Iskop Sev Vost Korei Yuga Primorya — Magmatizm i Poleznye Iskopaemye Severo-Vostochnoi Korei i Yuga Primor'ya
Mag Mern Epitesz Egylet Kozl — Magyar Mernok es Epitesz Egylet Koezloenye
Mag Min Health Saf MESA — Magazine of Mining Health and Safety. MESA
MagN — Magyar Nyelvor

Magn Aarb — Magnetisk Aarbog. Dansk Meteorologisk Institut
Magn Aarb Gronl — Magnetisk Aarbog. Gronland
Mag Nagpur Agr Coll — Magazine. Nagpur Agricultural College
Mag Nat Hist — Magazine of Natural History
Mag Nat Hist Naturalist — Magazine of Natural History and Naturalist
Mag Naturk Helv — Magazin fuer die Naturkunde Helvetiens
Magn Ceram — Magnetic Ceramics
Magn Eigenschaften Festkoerpern Vortr Metalltag DDR — Magnetische Eigenschaften von Festkoerpern. Vortraege gehalten auf der Metalltagung der DDR
Magn Electr Sep — Magnetic and Electrical Separation
Mag N Entdeck Ges Naturk — Magazin fuer die Neuesten Entdeckungen in der Gesammten Naturkunde
Magnesium Bull — Magnesium. Bulletin
Magnesium Mon Rev — Magnesium Monthly Review
Magnesium Relevant Ion Eur Congr Magnesium — Magnesium. A Relevant Ion. European Congress on Magnesium
Magnesium Rev Abstr — Magnesium Review and Abstracts
Magnes Lecture Ser — Magnes Lecture Series
Magnes Prod — Magnesium Products
Magnes Res — Magnesium Research
Magnes Rev Abstr — Magnesium Review and Abstracts
Magnes Tabloid — Magnesium Tabloid. Magnesium Company of Canada
Magnetismo Ipnot — Magnetismo ed Ipnotismo
Magnetismo Terr Filip — Magnetismo Terrestre en Filipinas
Magnetogr Hourly Val US Cst Geod Surv — Magnetograms and Hourly Values. U.S. Coast and Geodetic Survey
Magnetogr Wingst — Magnetogramme Wingst
Magnetohydrodyn — Magnetohydrodynamics
Magnetohydrodynamics Hemisphere Publ Corp — Magnetohydrodynamics (Hemisphere Publishing Corporation)
Magnetohydrodyn Process Metall Proc Symp — Magnetohydrodynamics in Process Metallurgy. Proceedings. Symposium
Magnetos Phenom Astrophys — Magnetospheric Phenomena in Astrophysics
Mag Neuen Erfind — Magazin aller Neuen Erfindungen, Entdeckungen, und Verbesserungen
Mag Neueste Gesch Evang Missions Bibelges — Magazin fuer die Neueste Geschichte der Evangelischen Missionsund Bibelgesellschaften
Mag Neuesten Erfahr Entdeckungen Berichtigungen Geb Pharm — Magazin fuer die Neuesten Erfahrungen. Entdeckungen und Berichtigungen im Gebiete der Pharmacie
Mag Neuesten Erfind — Magazin der Neuesten Erfindungen, Entdeckungen, und Verbesserungen
Mag Neuesten Interessantesten Reisebeschreib — Magazin der Neuesten und Interessantesten Reisebeschreibungen
Magn Gidrodin — Magnitnaya Gidrodinamika
Mag N H — Magazine of Natural History
Magn Hydrodyn — Magnetohydrodynamics
Magnit Gidrodinamika — Akademija Nauk Latviiskoi SSR. Magnitnaja Gidrodinamika
Magnitogidrodin Metod Poluch Elektroenergii — Magnitogidrodinamicheskii Metod Polucheniya Elektroenergii
Magnitogidrodin Metod Preobraz Energ — Magnitogidrodinamicheskii Metod Preobrazovaniya Energii
Magn Lett — Magnetism Letters
Magnl Met Atmos Elect Seism Obsns Govt Obs Bombay Alibag — Magnetical, Meteorological, Atmospheric Electric, and Seismological Observations made at the Government Observatories of Bombay and Alibag
Magnl Met Seism Obsns Govt Obs Bombay Alibag — Magnetical, Meteorological, and Seismological Observations made at the Government Observatories. Bombay and Alibag
Magn Lovushki — Magnitnye Lovushki
Magn Magn Mater Dig — Magnetism and Magnetic Materials Digest
Magn Met Beob Klagenf — Magnetische und Meteorologische Beobachtungen zu Klagenfurt
Magn Mol Mater — Magnetic Molecular Materials
Magn Opt Spektrosk Miner Gorn Porod — Magnitnaya i Opticheskaya Spektroskopiya Mineralov i Gornykh Porod
Magn Rasatl Yill — Magnetizmi Rasatlari Yilligi
Magn Rep Helwan Obs — Magnetic Report. Helwan Observatory
Magn Resonance Rev — Magnetic Resonance Review
Magn Reson Annu — Magnetic Resonance Annual
Magn Reson Chem Biol Lect Ampere Int Summer Sch — Magnetic Resonance in Chemistry and Biology. Based on Lectures at the Ampere International Summer School
Magn Reson Food Sci — Magnetic Resonance in Food Science
Magn Reson Imaging — Magnetic Resonance Imaging
Magn Reson Imaging Clin N Am — Magnetic Resonance Imaging Clinics of North America
Magn Reson Med — Magnetic Resonance in Medicine
Magn Reson Q — Magnetic Resonance Quarterly
Magn Reson Rev — Magnetic Resonance Review
Magn Results Amberley Obs — Magnetic Results. Amberley Observatory
Magn Results Apia Obs — Magnetic Results. Apia Observatory
Magn Results Dom Obs Ottawa — Magnetic Results. Dominion Observatory (Ottawa)
Magn Results Nurmijarvi Geophys Obs — Magnetic Results from Nurmijarvi Geophysical Observatory
Magn Results R Obs Hong Kong — Magnetic Results. Royal Observatory. Hong Kong
Magn Soc India Newsl — Magnetics Society of India. Newsletter
Magn Soc India Trans — Magnetics Society of India. Transactions
Mag of Art — Magazine of Art
Mag of Business — Magazine of Business
Mag of Hist — Magazine of History

Mag of Stand — Magazine of Standards
Mag of Wall St — Magazine of Wall Street
Magon Inst Rech Agron Publ Ser Sci — Magon Institut de Recherches Agronomiques. Publication. Serie Scientifique
Magon Inst Rech Agron Publ Ser Tech — Magon Institut de Recherches Agronomiques. Publication. Serie Technique
Mag Pesca Caza — Magazine de Pesca y Caza
Mag Pharm — Magazin fuer Pharmacie und die Dahin Einschlagenden Wissenschaften
Mag Pittoresque — Magazine Pittoresque
Mag Popular Sci J Useful Arts — Magazine of Popular Science and Journal of the Useful Arts
Mag Psz Sz — Magyar Pszichologiai Szemle
Mag R Free Hosp Sch Med — Magazine of the Royal Free Hospital School of Medicine
M Agric Ext Serv Univ Minn — M. Agricultural Extension Service. University of Minnesota
MagS — Magasin du Spectacle. Revue Mensuelle du Theatre et du Cinema
Mag Soc Milit Med Sci — Magazine. Society of Military Medical Science
Mag Soc Milit Med Sci Tokyo — Magazine of the Society of Military Medical Science (Tokyo)
Mag Stand — Magazine of Standards
Mag Std — Magazine of Standards
Mag Traumatol Orthop Helyreallito Sebesz — Magyar Traumatologia, Orthopaedia, es Helyreallito-Sebeszet
Mag Tud Akad 5 Otodik Orv Tud Oszt Kozl — Magyar Tudomanyos Akademia. 5 Otodik Orvosi Tudomanyok Osztalyanak Koezlemenyei
Mag Tud Akad Agrartud Oszt Kozl — Magyar Tudomanyos Akademia. Agrartudomanyok Osztalyanak Koezlemenyei
Mag Tud Akad Biol Tud Oszt Kozl — Magyar Tudomanyos Akademia. Biologiai Tudomanyok Osztalyanak Koezlemenyei
Mag Tud Akad Kem Tud Oszt Kozl — Magyar Tudomanyos Akademia. Kemiai Tudomanyok Osztalyanak Koezlemenyei
Mag Tud Akad Kozp Fiz Kut Intez Kozl — Magyar Tudomanyos Akademia. Kozponti Fizikai Kutato Intezetenek Koezlemenyei
Mag Tud Akad Kozp Kem Intez Kozl — Magyar Tudomanyos Akademia. Kozponti Kemiai Kutato Intezetenek Koezlemenyei
Mag Tud Akad Mat Fiz Tud Oszt Kozl — Magyar Tudomanyos Akademia. Matematikai es Fizikai Tudomanyok Osztalyanak Koezlemenyei
Mag Tud Akad Musz Tud Oszt Kozl — Magyar Tudomanyos Akademia. Mueszaki Tudomanyok Osztalyanak Koezlemenyei
Mag Tud Ak Etk Mth — Ertekezesek a Mathematikai Osztaly Korebol. Kiadja a Magyar Tudomanyos Akademia
Mag Tud Ak Etk Termt — Ertekezesek a Termeszettudomanyok Korebol. Kiadja a Magyar Tudomanyos Akademia
Mag Tud Ak Ets — A Magyar Tudomanyos Akademia
Mag Tud Ak Evk — A' Magyar Tudos Tarsasag' Evkonyvei
Mag v H — Magazijn van Handelsrecht
MAGW — Mitteilungen. Anthropologische Gesellschaft in Wien
Mag Wall St — Magazine of Wall Street
Mag Wall Street — Magazine of Wall Street
Mag Western Hist — Magazine of Western History
Mag Westphalen — Magazin fuer Westphalen
MAG Wien — Mitteilungen. Anthropologische Gesellschaft in Wien
MagWJ — Magazin fuer die Wissenschaft des Judentums
Magy Agyagipar — Magyar Agyagipar
Magy Allami Eoetvoes Lorand Geofiz Intez Evi Jelentese — Magyar Allami Eoetvoes Lorand Geofizikai Intezet. Evi Jelentese
Magy Allami Foldt Intez Evk — Magyar Allami Foldtani Intezet Evkonvye
Magy Allatorv Lap — Magyar Allatorvosok Lapja
Magy Allatorv Lapja — Magyar Allatorvosok Lapja
Magy Allatorv Lap Kueloenszama — Magyar Allatorvosok Lapja Kueloenszama
Magy Allatten — Magyar Allattenyesztes
Magy All Eotvos Lorand Geofiz Intez Evi Jel — Magyar Allami Eoetvoes Lorand Geofizikai Intezet. Evi Jelentese
Magy All Foldt Intez Evi Jel — Magyar Allami Foldtani Intezet. Evi Jelentese
Magy All Foldt Intez Evk — Magyar Allami Foldtani Intezet. Evkoenyve
Magy All Foldt Intez Modszertani Kozl — Magyar Allami Foldtani Intezet. Modszertani Koezlemenyek
Magy Alum — Magyar Aluminium
Magyar Akad Ertes — Magyar Academiai Ertesitoe
Magyar Allami Foeldt Intez Evi Jel — A Magyar Allami Foeldtani Intezet evi Jelentesei/Annual Report. Hungarian Geological Institute
Magyaraz Magyarorsz Geol Talajism Terkep — Magyarazatok Magyarorszag Geologiai es Talajismereti Terkepeihez
Magyar Biol Kutatoint Munkai — Magyar Biologiai Kutatointezet Munkai/Arbeiten des Ungarischen Biologischen Forschungsinstituts
Magyar Bor Gyuem — Magyar Bor es Gyuemoelcs
Magyar Filoz Szle — Magyar Filozofiai Szemle
Magyar Fil Szemle — Magyar Filozofiai Szemle
Magyar Fiz Foly — Magyar Fizikai Folyoirat
Magyar Gyuem — A Magyar Gyuemoelcz
Magyar Kem Lapja — Magyar Kemikusok Lapja
Magyar Kert Budapest — Magyar Kertesz (Budapest)
Magyar Kir Allami Foeldt Intez Evi Jel — A Magyar Kiralyi Allami Foeldtani Intezet Evi Jelentesei
Magyar Kir Kert Akad Koezlem — Magyar Kiralyi Kerteszeti Akademia Koezlemenyei/Mitteilungen der Koeniglichen Ungarischen Gartenbau-Akademie/Bulletin. Academie Royale Hongroise d'Horticulture/Bulletin. Royal Hungarian Horticultural College
Magyar Kir Koezp Szoelesz Kiserl Allomas Ampelol Intez Evk — A Magyar Kiralyi Koezponti Szoeleszeti Kiserleti Allomas es Ampelologiai Intezet Evkoenyve. Annales. Institut Ampelologique Royal Hongrois
Magyar Koenyvsz — Magyar Koenyvszemle
Magyar Nemzeti Gal Evkoenyve — Magyar Nemzeti Galeria Evkoenyve

Magyar Nemzeti Gal Koezlemenyei — Magyar Nemzeti Galeria Koezlemenyei

Magyar Noevenyt Lapok — Magyar Noevenytani Lapok

Magyar Num Tars Ev — Magyar Numizmatikai Tarsulat Evkoenyve

Magyarorszag Foldmiv — Magyarorszag Foldmivelesugye

Magyarorsz Allatvilaga — Magyarorszag Allatvilaga

Magyarorsz Borterm Keszit Targyazo Folyoir — Magyarorzag Bortermeszteset 's Kesziteset Targyazo Folyoiras/Z Weinbau Weinbereitung Ungarn. Z Weinbau Weinbereitung Ungarn Siebenbuergen

Magyarorsz Eghajl — Magyarorszag Eghajlata. Orszagos Meteorologiai Intezet

Magyarorsz Foldrengesek — Magyarorszagi Foldrengesek

Magyarorsz Mezogazd Statiszt — Magyarorszagainak Mezogazdasagi Statisztikaja

Magyarorsz Mueml Topogr — Magyarorszag Muemleki Topografiaja

Magyarorsz Viragtalan Noeven Meghat Kezikoenyve — Magyarorszag Viragtalan Noeveneinek Meghatarozo Kezikoenyve

Magyar Orv Termesz Nagy Gyuel Munk — Magyar Orvosok es Termeszetvizsgalok Nagy Gyuelesemek Munkalatai. Die Versammlung Ungarischer Aerzte und Naturforscher

Magyar Pszichol Szle — Magyar Pszichologiai Szemle

Magyar Textiltech — Magyar Textiltechnika

Magyar Tud Akad Biol Agrartud Oszt Koezlem — A Magyar Tudomanyos Akademia Biologiai es Agrartudomanyi Osztalyanak Koezlemenyei

Magyar Tud Akad Biol Csoport Koezlem — Magyar Tudomanyos Akademia Biologiai Csoportjanak Koezlemenyei

Magyar Tud Akad Evk — A Magyar Tudomanyos Akademia Evkoenyvei

Magyar Tud Akad Filoz-Tort Oszt Kozlem — Magyar Tudomanyos Akademia. Filozofiai-Torteneti Osztalyanak Koezlemenyei

Magyar Tud Akad Mat Fiz Oszt Koezl — Magyar Tudomanyos Akademia. Matematikai es Fizikai Tudomanyok Osztalyanak Koezlemenyei

Magyar Tud Akad Tihanyi Biol Kutatoint Evk — Magyar Tudomanyos Akademia Tihanyi Biologiai Kutatointezetenek Evkoenyve. Annales Instituti Biologici Tihany Hungaricae Academiae Scientiarum

Magyar Tudomanyos Akad Nyelv & Irodalmi Tudomanyok Osztalyana — Magyar Tudomanyos Akademia Nyelv es Irodalmi Tudomanyok Osztalyanak Koezlemenyei

Magy Asvanyolaj-Foeldgazkiserl Intez Koezl — Magyar Asvanyolaj-es Foeldgazkiserleti Intezet Koezlemenyei

Magy Asvanyolaj Foldgaz Kiserl Intez Kiadv — Magyar Asvanyolaj-es Foldgaz Kiserleti Intezet Kiadvanyai

Magy Asvanyolaj Foldgaz Kiserl Intez Kozl — Magyar Asvanyolaj-es Foldgaz Kiserleti Intezet Koezlemenyei

Magy Baln Ert — Magyar Balneologiai Ertesito

Magy Banyaujs — Magyar Banyaujsag

Magy Belorv Arch — Magyar Belorvosi Archivum

Magy Belorv Archvm — Magyar Belorvosi Archivum es Ideggyogyaszati Szemle

Magy Biol Kutato Intezet Munkai — Magyar Biologiai Kutato Intezet Munkai

Magy Biztositastud Szle — Magyar Biztositastudomanyi Szemle

Magy Boripar — Magyar Boripar

Magy Bork — Magyar Borkereskedelem

Magy Bot Lap — Magyar Botanikai Lapok

Magy Chem Folyoirat — Magyar Chemiai Folyoirat

Magy Csillag Egyes Nepsz Foly — Magyar Csillagaszati Egyesulet Nepszeru Folyoirata

Magy Czip Ujs — Magyar Czipesz-Ujsag

Magy Czukoripar — Magyar Czukoripar

Magy Doh Ujs — Magyar Dohany-Ujsag

Magy Drog — Magyar Drogista

Magy Drog Ujs — Magyar Drogista Ujsag

Magy EnergGazd — Magyar Energiagazdasag

Magy Epitoeipar — Magyar Epitoeipar

Magy Epitom Egyes Ert — Magyar Epitomesterek Egyesulete Ertesitoje

Magy Epitomuv — Magyar Epitomuveszet

Magy Erdesz — Magyar Erdesz

Magy Fem es Gepipar — Magyar Fem- es Gegipar

Magy Fenykep — Magyar Fenykepeszes

Magy Fenykep Bpesti Fenykep Ipart Hivat Lap — Magyar Fenykepesz a Budapesti Fenykepeszek es Fenykepnagyitok Ipartestulete Hivatalos Lapja

Magy Fenykep Lap — Magyar Fenykepeszek Lapja

Magy Fiz Foly — Magyar Fizikai Folyoirat

Magy Fogasz Szle — Magyar Fogaszati Szemle

Magy Fogorv Lap — Magyar Fogorvosok Lapja

Magy Fogtech — Magyar Fogtechnikus

Magy Fogtech Kozl — Magyar Fogtechnikusok Kozlonye

Magy Foldm — Magyar Foldmivelo

Magy Foldm Bpest — Magyar Foldmuves (Budapest)

Magy Foldm Gyuro — Magyar Foldmives (Gyuro)

Magy Foldr Jel — Magyar Foldrengesi Jelentes

Magy Foly Repert — Magyar Folyoiratok Repertoriuma

Magy Fotogr — Magyar Fotografia

Magy Geofiz — Magyar Geofizika

Magy Gepipar — Magyar Gepipar

Magy Gepvasar — Magyar Gepvasar

Magy Gomb Lap — Magyar Gombaszati Lapok

Magy Gumi Hirl — Magyar Gumi Hirlap

Magy Gummi es Asbestujs — Magyar Gummi- es Asbestujsag

Magy Gyogyzerestud Tarsas Ert — Magyar Gyogyszerestudomanyi Tarsasag Ertesito

Magy Hivaddstech — Magyar Hivadastechnika

Magy Husipar Lap — Magyar Husiparosok Lapja

Magy Iparmuv — Magyar Iparmuveszet

Magy Iparokt — Magyar Iparoktatas

Magy K Allatorv Foisk — Magyar Kiralyi Allatorvosi Foiskola

Magy K All Rov Allomas — Magyar Kiralyi Allami Rovartani Allomas

Magy K Csillagv Intez Nagy Kiad — Magyar Kiralyi Csillagvizsgalo-Intezet Nagyobb Kiadvanyai

Magy Kem Fo — Magyar Kemiai Folyoirat

Magy Kem Foly — Magyar Kemiai Folyoirat

Magy Kem Folyoirat — Magyar Kemiai Folyoirat

Magy Kem Lap — Magyar Kemikusok Lapja

Magy Kem Lapja — Magyar Kemikusok Lapja

Magy Kerekp Szov Ert — Magyar Kerekparos-Szovetseg Ertesitoje

Magy Kertez Szolesz Foisk Kozl — Magyar Kerteszeti es Szoleszeti Foiskola Kozlemenyei

Magy Kir Szolo Borgazd Kozp Kiserl Allomas Ampelol Intez Evk — Magyar Kir. Szolo es Borgazdasagi Kozponti Kiserleti Allomas. Ampelologiai Intezet Evkonyve

Magy K Kozp Szolesz Kiserl Allom Ampel Intez Kozl — Magyar Kiralyi Kozponti Szoleszeti Kiserleti Allomas es Ampelologiai Intezet Kozlemenyei

Magy Koenyvszle — Magyar Koenyvszemle

Magy Ko Es Marvanyujs — Magyar Ko- es Marvanyujsag

Magy Koezl — Magyar Koezloeny

Magy Konyvker Evk — Magyar Konyvkereskedok Evkonyve

Magy Konyvk Konyvker Orsz Egyes Megbiz — Magyar Konyvkiadok es Konyvkereskedok Orszagos Egyesulete Megbizasabol

Magy Konyvszle — Magyar Konyvszemle

Magy Korhaz — Magyar Korhaz

Magy K Orsz Kozeg Intez Osszeg Kozl — Magyar Kiralyi Orszagos Kozegeszsegugyi Intezet Osszegyujtott Kozlemenyei

Magy K Orsz Met Foldmagn Intez Evk — Magyar Kiralyi Orszagos Meteorologiai es Foldmagnessegi Intezet Evkonyve

Magy K Orsz Met Foldmagn Intez Hivat Kiad — Magyar Kiralyi Orszagos Meteorologiai es Foldmagnessegi Intezet Hivatalos Kiadvanyai

Magy K Orsz Met Foldmagn Intez Idoj Napijel — Magyar Kiralyi Orszagos Meteorologiai es Foldmagnessegi Intezet Idojarasi Napijelentesei

Magy K Orsz Met Foldmagn Intez Jel — Magyar Kiralyi Orszagos Meteorologiai es Foldmagnessegi Intezet Jelentesei

Magy K Orsz Met Foldmagn Intez Konyv Czimjeg — Magyar Kiralyi Orszagos Meteorologiai es Foldmagnessegi Intezet Konyvtaranak Czimjegyzeke

Magy K Orsz Met Foldmagn Intez Nepsz Kiad — Magyar Kiralyi Orszagos Meteorologiai es Foldmagnessegi Intezet Nepszeru Kiadvanyai

Magy K Orsz Met Foldmagn Intez Terk Idoj Surgonyjel — Magyar Kiralyi Orszagos Meteorologiai es Foldmagnessegi Intezet Terkepes Idojarasi Surgonyjelentesei

Magy Kozgazdtud Intez Kiad — Magyar Kozgazdatastudomanyi Intezet Kiadvanyai

Magy Kozlek Mely Es Vizepites — Magyar Kozlekedes, Mely- es Vizepites

Magy K Technol Iparmuz Kozl — Magyar Kiralyi Technologiai Iparmuzeum, Kozlemenyei

Magy K Tisza Istvan Tudom Egyet Met Intez Kozl — Magyar Kiralyi Tisza Istvan Tudomany Egyetem Meteorologiai Intezetenek Kozlemenyei

Magy Kult — Magyarorszag Kulturflora

Magy Kulturfloraja — Magyarorszag Kulturfloraja

Magy Malom Es Gazd Ert — Magyar Malom- es Gazdasagi Ertesito

Magy Malom Kozl — Magyar Malom-Kozlony

Magy Mat Kongr Kozl — Magyar Matematikai Kongresszus Kozlemenyei

Magy Meh — Magyar Meh

Magy Mern Es Epit Egyl Heti Ert — Magyar Mornok- es Epitesz-Egylet Heti Ertesitoje

Magy Mern Es Epit Egyl Kozl — Magyar Mernok- es Epitesz-Egylet Kozlonye

Magy Mezoegazd — Magyar Mezoegazdasag

Magy Mezogazd Szovetkez Uzl Ert — Magyar Mezogazdak Szovetkezetenek Uzleti Ertesitoje

Magy Mukert — Magyar Mukertesz

Magy Mukert Kerteszgazd — Magyar Mukerteszek es Kerteszgazdak Orszagos Szakkozlonye

Magy Nemesfem Ipar — Magyar Nemesfem-Ipar

Magy Nemz Biblfia — Magyar Nemzeti Bibligrafia

Magy Nemz Muz Nepr Gyujtem — Magyar Nemzeti Muzeum Neprajzi Gyujtemenye

Magy Nemz Muz Nepr Osztal Ert — Magyar Nemzeti Muzeum Neprajzi Osztalyanak Ertesitoje

Magy Nemz Muz Nepr Tar Ert — Magyar Nemzeti Muzeum Neprajzi Tar Ertesitoje

Magy Nemz Muz Termeszetr Osztal Foly — Magyar Nemzeti Muzeum Termeszetrajzi Osztalyanak Folyoirata

Magy Nepr Tarsas Keleti Szakosztal Kiad — Magyar Neprajzi Tarsasag Keleti Szakosztalyanak Kiadvanyai

Magy Noeorv Lap — Magyar Noeorvosok Lapja

Magy Noeorv Lapja — Magyar Noeorvosok Lapja

Magy Noorvos Lap — Magyar Noorvosok Lapja

Magy Nyomd — Magyar Nyomdaszat

Magy Onkol — Magyar Onkologia

Magy Orv Archvm — Magyar Orvosi Archivum

Magy Orv Bibliogr — Magyar Orvosi Bibliografia

Magy Orv Lap — Magyar Orvosok Lapja

Magy Orv Nagy — Magyar Orvosi Nagyhet

Magy Orv Revue — Magyar Orvosi Revue

Magy Orv Termeszetv Nagygyul Evk — Magyar Orvosok es Termeszetvizsgalok Nagygyulesenek Evkoenyvei

Magy Orv Termeszetv Nagygyul Tort Vazl Munk — Magyar Orvosok es Termeszetvizsgalok Nagygyulesenek Torteneti Vazlata es Munkalatai

Magy Orv Termeszetv Vandorgyul Tort — Magyar Orvosok es Termeszetvizsgalok Vandorgyulesenek Tortenete

Magy Posta Es Tavirda Szakl — Magyar Posta- es Tavirda Szaklap

Magy Pszichol Szemle — Magyar Pszichologiai Szemle

Magy Pszichol Szle — Magyar Pszichologiai Szemle

Magy Radio — Magyar Radio

Magy Radiol — Magyar Radiologia

Magy Reumatol — Magyar Reumatologia

Magy Rontg Kozl — Magyar Rontgen Kozlony

Magy Seb — Magyar Sebeszet

Magy Sebesz — Magyar Sebeszet

Magy Sebeszet — Magyar Sebeszet

Magy Szeszterm — Magyar Szesztermelo
Magy Tech — Magyar Technika
Magy Tejgazd Lap — Magyar Tejgazdasagi Lapok
Magy Textilipar — Magyar Textilipar
Magy Textiltech — Magyar Textiltechnika
Magy Text Tech — Magyar Textiltechnika
Magy Traumatol Orthop — Magyar Traumatologia, Orthopaedia, es Helyreallito-Sebeszet
Magy Traumatol Orthop Helyreallito Sebesz — Magyar Traumatologia, Orthopaedia, es Helyreallito-Sebeszet
Magy Traumatol Ortop Kezseb Plasztikai Seb — Magyar Traumatologia, Ortopedia, Kezsebeszet, Plasztikai Sebeszet
Magy Traumat Orthop Helyreal Sebeszet — Magyar Traumatologia, Orthopaedia es Helyreallito Sebeszet
Magy Tud — Magyar Tudomany
Magy Tud Akad 3 Oszt Fiz Kozl — Magyar Tudomanyos Akademia. 3. Osztalyanak Fizikai Kozlemenyei
Magy Tud Akad Agrartud Osztal Kozl — Magyar Tudomanyos Akademia. Agrartudomanyok Osztalyanak Koezlemenyei
Magy Tud Akad Atommag Kut Intez Kozl — Magyar Tudomanyos Akademia Atommag Kutato Intezet. Kozlemenyek
Magy Tud Akad Biol Csoportjanak Kozlem (Budapest) — Magyar Tudomanyos Akademia. Biologiai Csoportjanak Koezlemenyei (Budapest)
Magy Tud Akad Biol Orv Tud Oszt Kozl — Magyar Tudomanyos Akademia. Biologiai es Orvosi Tudomanyok Osztalyanak Koezlemenyei
Magy Tud Akad Biol Tud Oszt Koezl — Magyar Tudomanyos Akademia. Biologiai Tudomanyok Osztalyanak Koezlemenyei
Magy Tud Akad Kem Tud Oszt Kozlem — Magyar Tudomanyos Akademia. Kemiai Tudomanyok Osztalyanak Koezlemenyei
Magy Tud Akad Kozp Fiz Kut Intez Kozl — Magyar Tudomanyos Akademia Kozponti Fizikai Kutato Intezetenek Koezlemenyei
Magy Tud Akad Mat Fiz Tud Oszt Kozlem — Magyar Tudomanyos Akademia. Matematikai es Fizikai Tudomanyok Osztalyanak Koezlemenyei
Magy Tud Akad Mat Kut Intez Kozlem — Magyar Tudomanyos Akademia. Matematikai Kutato Intezetenek Koezlemenyei
Magy Tud Akad Muesz Fiz Kut Intez Koezl — Magyar Tudomanyos Akademia. Mueszaki Fizikai Kutato Intezetenek Koezlemenyei
Magy Tud Akad Muszaki Tud Oszt Kozlem — Magyar Tudomanyos Akademia. Mueszaki Tudomanyok Osztalyanak Koezlemenyei
Magy Tud Akad Tihanyi Biol Kutatointez Evk — Magyar Tudomanyos Akademia. Tihanyi Biologiai Kutatointezet Evkoenyve
Magy Tud Akad Veszpremi Akad Bizottsaganak Ert — Magyar Tudomanyos Akademia. Veszpremi Akademiai Bizottsaganak Ertesitoje
Magy Tud Int Koez — Magyar Tudomanyos Akademia Regeszeti Intezetenek Koezlemenyei
Magy Tudom — Magyar Tudomany
Magy Tudom Akad Agrartud Osztal Kozl — Magyar Tudomanyos Akademia Agrartudomanyok Osztalyanak Kozlemenyei
Magy Tudom Akad Alkalm Mat Intez Kozl — Magyar Tudomanyos Akademia Alkalmazott Matematikai Intezetenek Kozlemenyei
Magy Tudom Akad Alm — Magyar Tudomanyos Akademia Almanach
Magy Tudom Akad Biol Agrartud Osztal Kozl — Magyar Tudomanyos Akademia Biologiai es Agrartudomanyi Osztalyanak Kozlemenyei
Magy Tudom Akad Biol Csoporty Kozl — Magyar Tudomanyos Akademia Biologiai Csoportyanak Kozlemenyei
Magy Tudom Akad Biol Orv Tudom Osztal Kozl — Magyar Tudomanyos Akademia Biologiai es Orvosi Tudomanyok Osztalyanak Kozlemenyei
Magy Tudom Akad Biol Osztal Kozl — Magyar Tudomanyos Akademia. Biologiai Osztalyanak Koezlemenyei
Magy Tudom Akad Csillago Intez Kozl — Magyar Tudomanyos Akademia Csillagvizsgalo Intezetenek Kozlemenyei
Magy Tudom Akad III Es VI Osztaly Vgyeszesot Kozl — Magyar Tudomanyos Akademia III es VI Osztaly Vgyeszesotortjanak Kozlemenyei
Magy Tudom Akad Kem Tudom Osztal Kozl — Magyar Tudomanyos Akademia Kemiai Tudomanyok Osztalyanak Kozlemenyei
Magy Tudom Akad Kozp Fiz Kut Intez Kozl — Magyar Tudomanyos Akademia Kozponti Fizikai Kutato Intezetenek Kozlemenyei
Magy Tudom Akad Mat Fiz Osztal Kozl — Magyar Tudomanyos Akademia Matematikai es Fizikai Osztalyanak Kozlemenyei
Magy Tudom Akad Mat Kut Intez Kozl — Magyar Tudomanyos Akademia Matematikai Kutato Intezetenek Kozlemenyei
Magy Tudom Akad Musz Tudom Osztal Kozl — Magyar Tudomanyos Akademia Muszaki Tudomanyok Osztalyanak Kozlemenyei
Magy Tudom Akad Orv — Magyar Tudomanyos Akademia Orvosi
Magy Tud Osz Koez — Magyar Tudomanyos Akademia Filozofiai es Tortenettudomanyi. Osztalyanak Koezlemenyei
Magy Urol — Magyar Urologia
Magy Uveg Es Agyagujs — Magyar Uveg- es Agyagujsag
Magy Uvegipar — Magyar Uvegipar
Magy Vadaszujs — Magyar Vadaszujsag
Magy Vas Es Gepus — Magyar Vas- es Gepujsag
Magy Vasutas — Magyar Vasutas
Magy Villamos Muevek Troeszt Koezl — Magyar Villamos Muevek Troeszt Koezlemenyei
MAGZ — Mitteilungen. Antiquarische Gesellschaft in Zurich
Mah — Maryland Historian
MaH — Maryland Historical Magazine
MAH — Medical Abbreviations Handbook
MAH — Melanges d'Archeologie et d'Histoire
MAH — Metaal en Techniek. Vakblad voor de Metaalnijverheid
MAH — Mid-America. An Historical Review
Maharaja Sayajirao Mem Lect — Maharaja Sayajirao Memorial Lectures
Maharashtra Coop Q — Maharashtra Cooperative Quarterly
Maharashtra LJ — Maharashtra Law Journal
Maharashtra Med J — Maharashtra Medical Journal

Maharastra Coop Quart — Maharashtra Cooperative Quarterly
Mahatma Phule Agric Univ Res J — Mahatma Phule Agricultural University. Research Journal
MAHC — Memoria de Alfonso Hernandez Cata
MAHC — Monographies en Archeologie et Histoire Classique
MAHi — Memorias. Academia de la Historia
Mah LJ — Maharashtra Law Journal
Mah Med J — Maharashtra Medical Journal
MAHR — Mid-America: An Historical Review
MAHS — Mitteilungen der Auslandhochschule an der Universitaet Berlin
MAI — Magyar Tudomanyos Akademia Regeszeti Intezetenek Koezlemenyei
MAI — Memoires. Institut National de France. Academie des Inscriptions et Belles-Lettres
MAI — Mitteilungen des Deutschen Archaeologischen Instituts
MAI — Moskovskij Archeologiceskij Institut
MAIBL — Memoires. Academie des Inscriptions et Belles-Lettres
MAIBL — Memoires Presentes par Divers Savants. Academie des Inscriptions et Belles-Lettres
MAIBLA — Memoires Presentes par Divers Savants. Academie des Inscriptions et Belles-Lettres. Antiquites de la France
MAIBLE — Memoires Presentes par Divers Savants. Academie des Inscriptions et Belles-Lettres. Sujets Divers d'Erudition
MAIBLIF — Memoires. Academie des Inscriptions et Belles Lettres. Institut de France
MAID — Market Analysis and Information Database
MAIK — Mitteilungen des Deutschen Archaeologischen Instituts. Abteilung Kairo
Mailleraye Olii Trasform — Mailleraye e gli Olii per Trasformatori
Main — Mainstream
MAIN — Maritime Industries. Massachusetts Institute of Technology
Main Curr M — Main Currents in Modern Thought
Main Curr Mod Thought — Main Currents in Modern Thought
Maine Ag Dept B — Maine. Department of Agriculture. Quarterly Bulletin
Maine Ag Exp — Maine. Agricultural Experiment Station. Publications
Maine Agric Exp Sta Abstr Recent Publ — Maine Agricultural Experiment Station. Abstracts of Recent Publications
Maine Agric Exp Sta Mimeogr Rep — Maine Agricultural Experiment Station. Mimeographed Report
Maine Agric Exp Stn Bull — Maine. Agricultural Experiment Station. Bulletin
Maine Agric Exp Stn Misc Publ — Maine. Agricultural Experiment Station. Miscellaneous Publication
Maine Agric Exp Stn Misc Rep — Maine. Agricultural Experiment Station. Miscellaneous Report
Maine Agric Exp Stn Official Inspect — Maine. Agricultural Experiment Station. Official Inspections
Maine Agric Exp Stn Off Inspect — Maine. Agricultural Experiment Station. Official Inspections
Maine Agric Exp Stn Tech Bull — Maine. Agricultural Experiment Station. Technical Bulletin
Maine Basic Data Rep Ground Water Ser — Maine. Basic-Data Reports. Ground-Water Series
Maine Dept Mar Res Fish Bull — Maine Department of Marine Resources. Fisheries Bulletin
Maine Dept Mar Res Fish Circ — Maine Department of Marine Resources. Fisheries Circulars
Maine Dept Mar Res Res Bull — Maine Department of Marine Resources. Research Bulletin
Maine Farm Res — Maine Farm Research
Maine Field Nat — Maine Field Naturalist
Maine For Rev — Marine Forest Review
Maine Geol — Maine Geology
Maine Geol Surv Spec Econ Ser — Maine. Geological Survey. Special Economic Series
Maine Geol Surv Spec Econ Stud Ser Bull — Maine. Geological Survey. Special Economic Studies Series. Bulletin
Maine Hist Soc Coll — Maine Historical Society. Collections
Maine Lib Assn Bul — Maine Library Association. Bulletin
Maine Life Agric Exp Stn Tech Bull — Maine. Life Sciences and Agricultural Experiment Station. Technical Bulletin
Maine Life Mag — Maine Life Magazine
Maine Life Sci Agric Exp Stn Bull — Maine. Life Sciences and Agricultural Experiment Station. Bulletin
Maine Life Sci Agric Exp Stn Off Inspect — Maine. Life Sciences and Agricultural Experiment Station. Official Inspections
Maine Life Sci Agric Exp Stn Tech Bull — Maine. Life Sciences and Agricultural Experiment Station. Technical Bulletin
Maine L R — Maine Law Review
Maine L Rev — Maine Law Review
Maine Potato Yearb — Maine Potato Yearbook
Maine State Bar Assn Proc — Maine State Bar Association. Proceedings
Maine Technol Exp Stn Univ Maine Pap — Maine. Technology Experiment Station. University of Maine. Paper
Maine Technology Expt Sta Bull Paper — Maine. Technology Experiment Station. Bulletin. Papers
Mainfraenk Hft — Mainfraenkische Hefte
Mainfraenk Jahrb — Mainfraenkisches Jahrbuch fuer Geschichte und Kunst
Mainfraenk Jb Gesch & Kst — Mainfraenkisches Jahrbuch fuer Geschichte und Kunst
Mainfraenk Jb Gesch Kunst — Mainfraenkisches Jahrbuch fuer Geschichte und Kunst
Mainfr Jb — Mainfraenkisches Jahrbuch fuer Geschichte und Kunst
Main Group Chem — Main Group Chemistry
Mainly Anim — Mainly about Animals
Main Rds — Main Roads
MA Inst Ung Ak — Mitteilungen. Archaeologisches Institut der Ungarischen Akademie der Wissenschaften

Maint — Maintenant
Maint — Maintenant. Cahiers d'Art et de Litteratur
Maint Eng — Maintenance Engineering
Maint Eng (London) — Maintenance Engineering (London)
Maint Engng — Maintenance Engineering
Maint Mgmt Internat — Maintenance Management International
Mainzer Geowiss Mitt — Mainzer Geowissenschaftliche Mitteilungen
Mainzer Naturwiss Arch — Mainzer Naturwissenschaftliches Archiv
Mainzer Zeitschr — Mainzer Zeitschrift
Mainz Z — Mainzer Zeitschrift
Mainz Zs — Mainzer Zeitschrift
Maipu Chile Estac Exp Agron Bol Tec — Maipu, Chile. Estacion Experimental Agronomica. Boletin Tecnico
MAIR — Memorie. Classe di Scienze Morali, Storiche, e Filologiche. Accademia d'Italia (Roma)
MAIS — Missione Archeologica Italiana in Siria
MAISBP — Marine Invertebrates of Scandinavia
Mais D — La Maison-Dieu
Mais Dieu — La Maison-Dieu
Maison Fr — Maison Francaise. Revue Nationale de l'Habitation Moderne
Maison Sante Fr — Maison de Sante de France
Maitotal Lehti — Maitotalouden Lehti
MaitrePhon — Maitre Phonetique
Maitrise Text — Maitrise Textile
Mait Sp — Maitres Spirituels
Maize Biol Res — Maize for Biological Research
Maize Genet Coop News Lett — Maize Genetics Cooperation. News Letter
MAJA — Monographs. American Jewish Archives
Majalah Kedokt Surabaya — Majalah Kedokteran Surabaya
MAJBAC — Muelleria
Maj Batan — Majalah Batan
Maj Daneshgah e Tehran Daneshkade ye Darusazi — Majallah. Daneshgah- e Tehran. Daneshkade- ye Darusazi
Maj Demog Indo — Majalah Demografi Indonesia
Maj Farm Indones — Majalah Farmasi Indonesia
Majocchi A Fis C — Annali di Fisica, Chimica, e Matematiche, col Bullettino dell' Industria Meccanica e Chimica. Majocchi
Major Activ Atom Energy Progms US — Major Activities in the Atomic Energy Programs. U.S. Atomic Energy Commission
Major Amer Univ PhD Qualif Questions Solut — Major American Universities Ph.D. Qualifying Questions and Solutions
Major Biogeochem Cycles Their Interact — Major Biogeochemical Cycles and Their Interactions
Major Genes Reprod Sheep Int Workshop — Major Genes for Reproduction in Sheep. International Workshop
Majority — Majority Report
Majorossy Imre Muz Ertesitoje — Majorossy Imre Muzeumanak Ertesitoje
Major Probl Clin Pediatr — Major Problems in Clinical Pediatrics
Major Probl Clin Surg — Major Problems in Clinical Surgery
Major Probl Intern Med — Major Problems in Internal Medicine
Major Probl Obstet Gynecol — Major Problems in Obstetrics and Gynecology
Major Probl Pathol — Major Problems in Pathology
Mak — Makedonika
MAK — Materialy po Arkheologii Kavkaza
MAKA — Maulana Abul Kalam Azad. A Memorial Volume
Maked — Makedonika
Maked Folkl — Makedonski Folklor
Maked Med Pregl — Makedonski Medicinski Pregled
Makedon Akad Nauk Umet Oddel Mat-Tehn Nauk Prilozi — Makedonska Akademija na Naukite i Umetnostite Oddelenie za Matematichki-Tehnichki Nauki. Prilozi
Makedon Akad Nauk Umet Oddel Prirod-Mat Nauk Prilozi — Makedonska Akademija na Naukite i Umetnostite Oddelenie za Prirodo-Matematicki Nauki Prilozi
Makedon Folki — Makedonski Folklor
Makedon Med Pregl — Makedonski Medicinski Pregled
Makedonska Rev — Makedonska Revija
Makerere Hist J — Makerere Historical Journal
Makerere Hist Jnl — Makerere Historical Journal
Makerere J — Makerere Journal
Makerere LJ — Makerere Law Journal
Makerere Med J — Makerere Medical Journal
Mak F NY — Making Films in New York
MAKIA — Maandschrift voor Kindergeneeskunde
Making Mus — Making Music
Making NZ — Making New Zealand
Mak LJ — Makerere Law Journal
Mak P — Makedonika [*Thessalonike*]. Paratema
M Ak R — Marburger Akademische Reden
Makr Ch — Makromolekulare Chemie
Makrom Chem — Makromolekulare Chemie
Makromol Chem — Makromolekulare Chemie
Makromol Chem Macromol Symp — Makromolekulare Chemie. Macromolecular Symposia
Makromol Chem Rapid Commun — Makromolekulare Chemie. Rapid Communications
Makromol Chem Suppl — Makromolekulare Chemie. Supplement
Makromol Chem Theory Simul — Makromolekulare Chemie. Theory and Simulations
Makromolek Chem — Makromolekulare Chemie
Makromolek Latky — Makromolekularni Latky
Makromol Granitse Razdela Faz — Makromolekuly na Granitse Razdela Faz
Mak Tas — Maktab-i-Tasiju'
MAKW — Mitteilungen. Altertumskommission fuer Westphalen

MAL — Atti. Accademia Nazionale dei Lincei. Memorie. Classe di Scienze Morali, Storiche, e Filologiche
MAL — Markenartikel. Zeitschrift fuer die Markenartikelindustrie
MAL — Mirador Amazonico [*Bogota*]
MAL — Modern Austrian Literature
MAL — Monografie di Archeologia Libica
MAL — Monumenti Antichi. Accademia Nazionale dei Lincei
Malacol Int J Malacol — Malacologia. International Journal of Malacology
Malacolog Soc London Proc — Malacological Society of London. Proceedings
Malacol Rev — Malacological Review
Malacol Soc Aust J — Malacological Society of Australia. Journal
Malacol Soc L Pr — Malacological Society of London. Proceedings
Mala Econ R — Malayan Economic Review
Malagasy Rapp Annu Serv Geol — Malagasy. Rapport Annuel du Service Geologique
Malahat Rev — Malahat Review
Malakol Abh (Dres) — Malakologische Abhandlungen (Dresden)
MalaR — Malahat Review
Malaria Internat Arch (Leipzig) — Malaria. International Archives (Leipzig)
Malaria (Roma) — Malaria e Malattie dei Paesi Caldi (Roma)
Malar Mal Paesi Caldi — Malaria e Malattie dei Paesi Caldi
Malar Mon — Malaria Monthly
Malati Medici Med — Malati-Medici-Medicina
Malatt Cardiovasc — Malattie Cardiovascolari
Malatt Infez — Malattie de Infezione
Malawian Geogr — Malawian Geographer
Malawi Annu Rep Dep Agric — Malawi. Annual Report of the Department of Agriculture
Malawi Dep Agric Fish Annu Rep Fish Part 2 — Malawi. Department of Agriculture and Fisheries. Annual Report. Fisheries Research. Part 2
Malawi For Res Inst Res Rec — Malawi Forest Research Institute. Research Record
Malawi Geol Surv Dep Bull — Malawi. Geological Survey Department. Bulletin
Malawi Geol Surv Dep Mem — Malawi. Geological Survey Department. Memoir
Malawi J Sci Technol — Malawi Journal of Science and Technology
Malawi Nat Bib — Malawi National Bibliography
Malaya Dep Agric Bull — Malaya. Department of Agriculture. Bulletin
Malaya For Res Inst Res Pam — Malaya. Forest Research Institute. Research Pamphlet
Malaya Geol Surv Dep Mem — Malaya. Geological Survey Department. Memoir
Malay Agric J — Malayan Agricultural Journal
Malay Agric Statist — Malayan Agricultural Statistics
Malay Agri Hort Ass Mag — Malayan Agri-Horticulture Association Magazine
Malaya Law R — Malaya Law Review
Malaya LR — Malaya Law Review
Malaya L Rev — Malaya Law Review
Malaya Med J — Malaya Medical Journal
Malayan Ag J — Malayan Agricultural Journal
Malayan Agric J — Malayan Agricultural Journal
Malayan Agr J — Malayan Agricultural Journal
Malayan Econ R — Malayan Economic Review
Malayan Econ Rev — Malayan Economic Review
Malayan Gard Pl — Malayan Garden Plants
Malayan J Tr Geog — Malayan Journal of Tropical Geography
Malayan J Trop Geogr — Malayan Journal of Tropical Geography
Malayan Lib J — Malayan Library Journal
Malayan LJ — Malayan Law Journal
Malayan Sci Bull — Malayan Science Bulletin
Malay Archit — Malayan Architect
Malay Bldr Engr — Malayan Builder and Engineer
Malay Dep Agric Bull — Malaya. Department of Agriculture. Bulletin
Malay Econ Rev — Malayan Economic Review
Malay Fish — Malayan Fisheries
Malay For — Malayan Forester
Malay Forester — Malayan Forester
Malay Forest Rec — Malayan Forest Records
Malay For Rec — Malayan Forest Records
Malay Hist J — Malayan Historical Journal
Malay Ind Equip News — Malayan Industrial Equipment News
Malay J Ed — Malaysian Journal of Education
Malay J Trop Geogr — Malayan Journal of Tropical Geography
Malay Med J — Malayan Medical Journal and Estate Sanitation
Malay Nat — Malayan Naturalist
Malay Nat J — Malayan Nature Journal
Malay Orchid Rev — Malayan Orchid Review
Malay Pharm J — Malayan Pharmaceutical Journal
Malay Plg Man — Malayan Planting Manual
Malay Radio Rev — Malayan Radio Review
Malay Rep For Admin — Malay Report on Forest Administration
Malays Agric J — Malaysian Agricultural Journal
Malays Annu Rep Inst Med Res — Malaysia. Annual Report. Institute for Medical Research
Malays Appl Bio — Malaysian Applied Biology
Malays Appl Biol Biol Gunaan Malays — Malaysian Applied Biology/Biologi Gunaan Malaysia
Malays Biochem Soc Conf Proc — Malaysian Biochemical Society Conference. Proceedings
Malays Borneo Reg Annu Rep Geol Surv — Malaysia. Borneo Region. Annual Report of the Geological Survey
Malay Sci Bull — Malayan Science Bulletin
Malays Div Agric Bull — Malaysia. Division of Agriculture. Bulletin
Malays For — Malaysian Forester
Malays For Res Inst Kepong Res Pam — Malaysia. Forest Research Institute. Kepong Research Pamphlet
Malays Geol Surv Annu Rep — Malaysia. Geological Survey. Annual Report

Malays Geol Surv Borneo Reg Annu Rep — Malaysia. Geological Survey. Borneo Region. Annual Report
Malays Geol Surv Borneo Reg Bull — Malaysia. Geological Survey. Borneo Region. Bulletin
Malays Geol Surv Borneo Reg Mem — Malaysia. Geological Survey. Borneo Region. Memoir
Malays Geol Surv Borneo Reg Rep — Malaysia. Geological Survey. Borneo Region. Report
Malays Geol Surv Dist Mem — Malaysia. Geological Survey. District Memoir
Malays Geol Surv Map Bull — Malaysia. Geological Survey. Map Bulletin
Malays Geol Surv Rep — Malaysia. Geological Survey. Report
Malay Shell — Malayan Shell
Malaysia Hist — Malaysia in History
Malaysian Agric Res — Malaysian Agricultural Research
Malaysian Numi Soc Newslett — Malaysian Numismatic Society Newsletter
Malaysian Rubb Rev — Malaysian Rubber Review
Malays Inst Med Res Annu Rep — Malaysia Institute for Medical Research. Annual Report
Malays Inst Penylidikan Perubatan Lapuran Tahunan — Malaysia Institiut Penylidikan Perubatan Lapuran Tahunan
Malays J Biochem Mol Biol — Malaysian Journal of Biochemistry and Molecular Biology
Malays J Pathol — Malaysian Journal of Pathology
Malays J Reprod Health — Malaysian Journal of Reproductive Health
Malays J Sci — Malaysian Journal of Science
Malays J Sci Ser A — Malaysian Journal of Science. Series A. Life Sciences
Malays J Sci Ser B — Malaysian Journal of Science. Series B. Physical and Earth Sciences
Malays Minist Agric Co-Op Bull — Malaysia. Ministry of Agriculture and Co-Operatives. Bulletin
Malays Minist Agric Fish Bull — Malaysia. Ministry of Agriculture and Fisheries. Bulletin
Malays Minist Agric Lands Bull — Malaysia. Ministry of Agriculture and Lands. Bulletin
Malays Minist Agric Lands Tech Leafl — Malaysia. Ministry of Agriculture and Lands. Technical Leaflet
Malays Minist Agric Rural Dev Bull — Malaysia. Ministry of Agriculture and Rural Development. Bulletin
Malays Minist Agric Rural Dev Fish Bull — Malaysia. Ministry of Agriculture and Rural Development. Fisheries Bulletin
Malays Minist Agric Rural Dev Risalah Penerangan — Malaysia. Ministry of Agriculture and Rural Development. Risalah Penerangan
Malays Minist Agric Tech Leafl — Malaysia. Ministry of Agriculture. Technical Leaflet
Malays Minist Lands Mines Annu Rep Geol Surv Malays — Malaysia. Ministry of Lands and Mines. Annual Report of the Geological Survey of Malaysia
Malays Rep For Admin West Malaysia — Malaysia. Report on Forest Administration in West Malaysia
Malays Soc Biochem Mol Biol Annu Conf Proc — Malaysian Society for Biochemistry and Molecular Biology. Annual Conference. Proceedings
Malays Vet J — Malaysian Veterinary Journal
Malay Tin Rubber J — Malayan Tin and Rubber Journal
Malay Tin Rubb J — Malayan Tin and Rubber Journal
Mal Cardiovasc — Malattie Cardiovascolari
Mal Cuore Vasi — Malattie del Cuore e dei Vasi
Mal Econ R — Malayan Economic Review
Malernes Fagbl — Malernes Fagblad
MALFB — Memoires. Academie Royale de Langue et de Litterature Francaises de Belgique
Malgache Repub Ann Geol Madagascar — Malgache Republique. Annales Geologiques de Madagascar
Malgache Repub Rapp Annu Serv Geol — Malgache Republique. Rapport Annuel. Service Geologique
MALGI — Micul Atlas Lingvistic al Graiurilor Istoromine
MALHC — Mensuario de Arte, Literatura, Historia, y Ciencia
Mal Hist — Malaysia in History
Malig Hyperthermia Curr Concepts — Malignant Hyperthermia. Current Concepts
MALinc — Atti. Accademia Nazionale dei Lincei. Memorie. Classe di Scienze Morali, Storiche, e Filologiche
MA Linc — Memorie. Accademia Nazionale dei Lincei
MALincei — Atti. Accademia Nazionale dei Lincei. Memorie. Classe di Scienze Morali, Storiche, e Filologiche
Mal Infez — Malattie da Infezione
Mal Law R — Malaya Law Review
Mallee Hort Dig — Mallee Horticulture Digest
Mallee Hortic Dig — Mallee Horticulture Digest
Mall Iron Facts — Malleable Iron Facts
Mal LJ — Malayan Law Journal
Malmohus Lans Hushallningssallsk Kvartallsskr — Malmoehus Laens Hushallningssaellskaps Kvartallsskrift
Mal O Mael — Mal og Maele
Mal Pharm J — Malayan Pharmaceutical Journal
Malpract Dig — Malpractice Digest
Mal R — Malahat Review
Mal Rub Dv — Malaysian Rubber Developments
Mal Rub R — Malaysian Rubber Review
Malta Plan — Malta Guidelines for Progress Development Plan, 1980-1985
M Altar — Musik und Altar
Malt Brew — Malting, Brewing, and Allied Processes
MALT Bulletin — Montana. Association of Language Teachers. Bulletin
Maltechnik Rest — Maltechnik, Restauro
Malting Brew Allied Processes — Malting, Brewing, and Allied Processes
Malt Res Inst Publ — Malt Research Institute. Publication
Malvern Phys Ser — Malvern Physics Series
Maly Poradn Konstr — Maly Poradnik Konstruktora

MAM — Machinery Market
MAM — Memoires. Academie de Metz
MAM — Mission Archeologique de Mari
MaM — Music and Musicians
MAMA — Monumenta Asiae Minoris Antiqua
M Am Acad Rome — Memoirs. American Academy in Rome
MAMAD — Manager Magazin
MAME — Mawdsley Memoirs
M Am H — Magazine of American History
M Am Hist — Magazine of American History
MAMIDH — Marine Micropaleontology
MAMLAN — Mammalia
Mamm — Mammalia. Morphologie, Biologie, Systematique des Mammiferes
Mammalia Pleistoc — Mammalia Pleistocaenica
Mammal Inf — Mammalogical Informations
Mammal Rev — Mammal Review
Mamm Cell Cult — Mammalian Cell Culture
Mamm Depicta — Mammalia Depicta
Mamm Depicta Beih Z Saeugetierkd — Mammalia Depicta. Beihefte zur Zeitschrift fuer Saeugetierkunde
Mamm Genome — Mammalian Genome
Mamm Mutagen Study Group Commun — Mammalian Mutagenicity Study Group Communications
Mamm Reprod — Mammalian Reproduction
Mamm Species — Mammalian Species
MAMS — Marine Mammal Science
MAN — Manage
Man — Management
MAN — Management Focus
MAN — Manitoba Business
Man — Mankind
Man — Mannus. Zeitschrift fuer Vorgeschichte
Man — Manuscripta
MAN — Memoires. Academie de Nimes
MAN — Men's Antisexist Newsletter
MAN — Mensario. Arquivo Nacional. Ministerio da Justica. Arquivo Nacional. Divisao dePublicacoes
MAN — Men's Association News
MANAAT — Man: A Monthly Record of Anthropological Science
Man Acts — Acts of Manitoba
MANADW — Manitoba Nature
Manag — Management
Manage Abstr — Management Abstracts
Manage Account — Management Accounting
Manage Advis — Management Adviser
Manage Assess Peat Energy Resour Exec Conf Proc — Management Assessment of Peat as an Energy Resource. Executive Conference Proceedings
Manage Contents — Management Contents
Manage Controls — Management Controls
Manage Datamatics — Management Datamatics
Manage Decis — Management Decision
Manage e Inf — Management e Informatica
Manage Focus — Management Focus
Manage Gov — Management in Government
Manage Index — Management Index
Manage Inf — Management Informatics
Manage Inf Anal Cent Proc Forum — Management of Information Analysis Centers. Proceedings. Forum
Manage Inf Syst — Management Information Systems
Manage Inf Syst Q — Management Information Systems Quarterly
Manage Int Rev — Management International Review
Manage Market Abstr — Management and Marketing Abstracts
Management D — Management Digest
Management Inf Serv — Management Information Services
Management NZ — Management. New Zealand Institute of Management
Management's Bibliog Data — Management's Bibliographic Data
Management Sci — Management Science
Management Servs — Management Services
Manage News — Management News
Manage Objectives — Management by Objectives
Manage Plann — Managerial Planning
Manage Plng — Managerial Planning
Manage Res — Management Research
Manage Rev — Management Review
Manage Rev Dig — Management Review and Digest
Managerial and Decision Econ — Managerial and Decision Economics
Managerial Decis Econ — Managerial and Decision Economics
Managerial Fin — Managerial Finance
Managerial Plan — Managerial Planning
Manage Sci — Management Science
Manage Serv — Management Services
Manage Serv Gov — Management Services in Government
Manage Today — Management Today
Manage Uncontrolled Hazard Waste Sites — Management of Uncontrolled Hazardous Waste Sites
Manage World — Management World
Managing Mod Lab — Managing the Modern Laboratory
Manag Int R — Management International Review
Manag Japan — Management Japan
Manag Objectives — Management by Objectives
Manag Sci — Management Science
Manag Sci A — Management Science. Series A. Theory
Manag Sci B — Management Science. Series B. Application
Manag Today — Management Today

Man & Ry KB — Manning and Ryland's English King's Bench Reports
Man & Soc — Man and Society
Man B — Mannus-Buecherei
Man Bar News — Manitoba Bar News
ManBl Svenska Gasverksfor — Manadsblad. Svenska Gasverksforeningen
Man B New — Manitoba Bar News
Man B News — Manitoba Bar News
Man Calc Chlor Inst — Manual. Calcium Chloride Institute
Manch — Manchester Literary Club. Papers
MancheL — Manche Libre
Man Chem — Manufacturing Chemist and Pharmaceutical and Fine Chemical Trade Journal
Manchester — Manchester School of Economic and Social Studies
Manchester Assoc Eng Trans — Manchester Association of Engineers. Transactions
Manchester G Soc Tr — Manchester Geological Society. Transactions
Manchester Lit Phil Soc Mem Proc — Manchester Literary and Philosophical Society. Memoirs and Proceedings
Manchester Lit Ph Soc Mem — Manchester Literary and Philosophical Society. Memoirs and Proceedings
Manchester Med Gaz — Manchester Medical Gazette
Manchester M Soc Tr — Manchester Mining Society. Transactions
Manchester Rev — Manchester Review
Manchester Sch Econ Soc Stud — Manchester School of Economic and Social Studies
Manchester Sch Ed Gazette — University of Manchester. School of Education. Gazette
Manchester School — Manchester School of Economic and Social Studies
Manchester Univ Pub Hist Ser — University of Manchester. Publications. Historical Series
Manch Gl S T — Transactions of the Manchester Geological Society
Manch Guard — Manchester Guardian Weekly
Manch Lit Phil Soc Mem Proc — Manchester Literary and Philosophical Society. Memoirs and Proceedings
Manch Lt Ph S Mm — Memoirs of the Literary and Philosophical Society of Manchester
Manch Lt Ph S Mm & P — Memoirs and Proceedings of the Manchester Literary and Philosophical Society
Manch Lt Ph S P — Proceedings of the Literary and Philosophical Society of Manchester
Manch Mcr S Rp — Manchester Microscopical Society. Annual Report
Manch Mcr S T — Manchester Microscopical Society. Transactions and Annual Report
Manch Med Gaz — Manchester Medical Gazette
Manch Mm Ph S — Memoirs of the Literary and Philosophical Society of Manchester
Manch Ph S Mm — Memoirs of the Literary and Philosophical Society of Manchester
Manch Ph S P — Proceedings of the Literary and Philosophical Society of Manchester
Manch Q — Manchester Quarterly
Manchr Geol Min Soc Trans — Manchester Geological and Mining Society Transactions
Manchr Med Gaz — Manchester Medical Gazette
Manchr Med Rev — Manchester Medical Review
Manchr Med Stud Gaz — Manchester Medical Students' Gazette
Manchr Rev — Manchester Review
Manchr Univ Chem Soc Mag — Manchester University Chemical Society Magazine
Manchr Univ Engng Soc Mag — Manchester University Engineering Society Magazine
Manchr Univ Med Sch Gaz — Manchester University Medical School Gazette
Manch S Mm — Memoirs of the Literary and Philosophical Society of Manchester
Manch S P — Proceedings of the Literary and Philosophical Society of Manchester
Manch Univ Med Sch Gaz — Manchester University. Medical School. Gazette
Manchuria Geol Min Rev — Manchuria Geological and Mining Review
Man Conch — Manual of Conchology
Man Couns — Manitoba Counsellor
M&B Lab Bull — M&B (May and Baker) Laboratory Bulletin
M&B Pharm Bull — M&B (May and Baker) Pharmaceutical Bulletin
M&B Vet Rev — M. and B. (May and Baker) Veterinary Review
M & C — Maintenance and Cure
M & C — Media and Consumer
M & C — Memory and Cognition
M&C Apprent Mag — M. and C. (Mavor and Coulson) Apprentices' Magazine [Glasgow]
M&C Mach Min — M. and C. (Mavor and Coulson) Machine Mining [Glasgow]
M & Eval Guid — Measurement and Evaluation in Guidance
M & GA — Meteorological and Geoastrophysical Abstracts
M & H — Mediaevalia et Humanistica
MAN Diesel Eng News — M.A.N. (Maschinenfabrik Augsburg-Nuernberg A.G.) Diesel Engine News
M & L — Music and Letters
M&M — Masses and Mainstream
M&R — Martyrdom and Resistance
M & R — Mediaeval and Renaissance Studies
M & R — Milton and the Romantics
M & RS — Mediaeval and Renaissance Studies
Mandschr Kindergeneeskd — Mandschrift voor Kindergeneeskunde
M&W — Man and World
M & W Law Dic — Mozley and Whiteley's Law Dictionary
MANE — Monographs on the Ancient Near East
Man Ed Res C Res B — Manitoba Educational Research Council. Research Bulletins
Maneds Bors — Maneds Borsen
Manedsskr Prakt Laegegern — Manedsskrift foer Praktisk Laegegerning

Man EG — Manuale di Eteo Geroglifico
MANEX — Management Experten-Nachweis
Man Farm — Manual Farmaceutico
Manf Eng Trans — Manufacturing Engineering Transactions
Man For — Management Forum
MAN ForschHft — M.A.N. (Maschinenfabrik Augsburg-Nuernberg A.G.) Forschungsheft
MAN Forsch Planen Bauen — MAN [Maschinenfabrik Augsburg-Nuernberg] Forschen, Planen, Bauen
Manganese Dioxide Symp Proc — Manganese Dioxide Symposium. Proceedings
Manganese Lit Rev — Manganese Literature Review
Manganese Nodules Dimens Perspect — Manganese Nodules. Dimensions and Perspectives
Mangt Today — Management Today
Manhat — Manhattan
Man His Environ — Man and His Environment
Man Hort — Manual of Horticulture
MANIAJ — Man in India
Manica Min J — Manica Mining Journal
Manila Hlth Dep Bull — Manila Health Department Bulletin
Mani LJ — Manitoba Law Journal
Man Ill Div Nat Hist Surv — Manual. Illinois Division of the Natural History Survey
Man Ind — Man in India
Man India — Man in India
Manit CoOp — Manitoba Co-Operator
Manit Dep Mines Nat Resour Mines Branch Publ — Manitoba. Department of Mines and Natural Resources. Mines Branch. Publication
Manit Entomol — Manitoba Entomologist
Manit Med Rev — Manitoba Medical Review
Manit Nat — Manitoba Nature
Manitoba Agric Ext News — Manitoa Agricultural Extension News
Manitoba B — Manitoba Business
Manitoba Dep Mines Natur Resour Mines Br Publ — Manitoba. Department of Mines and Natural Resources. Mines Branch. Publication
Manitoba Eng — Manitoba Engineer
Manitoba Ent — Manitoba Entomologist
Manitoba Hort — Manitoba Horticulturist
Manitoba LJ — Manitoba Law Journal
Manitoba Med Ass Bull — Manitoba Medical Association Bulletin
Manitoba Med Rev — Manitoba Medical Review
Man J R Anthropol Inst — Man. Journal of the Royal Anthropological Institute
Mankind Monogr — Mankind Monographs
Mankind Q — Mankind Quarterly
Mankind Quart — Mankind Quarterly
MANL — Memorie. Accademia Nazionale dei Lincei
Man Life — Man and Life
Man LittTips Svenska PlastFor — Manadens Litteraturtips. Svenska Plastforeningen
Man L J — Manitoba Law Journal
Man LS Chron — Manchester Law Students' Chronicle
Man LSJ — Manchester Law Students' Journal
Man LSJ — Manitoba Law School. Journal
Man-Made T — Man-Made Textiles in India
Man Made Text — Man-Made Textiles
Man Mag — Manager Magazin
Man Math T — Manitoba Math Teacher
Man Med — Man and Medicine
Man ML — Manson Memorial Lecture
Man MLJ — Manitoba Modern Language Journal
Man Mon Rec Anthropol Sci — Man: A Monthly Record of Anthropological Science
Man Mus Ed — Manitoba Music Educator
Man Nat — Man and Nature
M Ann D C — Medical Annals of the District of Columbia
Man NE — Man in the Northeast
Mannesmann Forschungsber — Mannesmann Forschungsberichte
Mannheim Geschbl — Mannheimer Geschichtsblaetter. Monatschrift fuer die Geschichte, Altertums- und Volkskunde Mannheims und der Pfalz
Mannheim Hefte — Mannheimer Hefte
Mannichfaltigk Lit — Mannichfaltigkeiten aus dem Gebiete der Literatur, Kunst, und Natur
Manns Paed Mag — Mann's Paedagogisches Magazin
ManOvers Vaderlek Finl — Manadsoversikt af Vaderleken i Finland
ManOvers Vaderlek Sver — Manadsoversikt af Vaderleken i Sverige
Manp App Psychol — Manpower and Applied Psychology
Manpower J — Manpower Journal
Manpower Unemployment Res Afr Newsl — Manpower and Unemployment Research in Africa. Newsletter
Manpower Unempl Res Afr — Manpower and Unemployment Research in Africa: A Newsletter
Man Pract Fed Sew Wks Ass — Manual of Practice. Federation of Sewage Works Association
MAN Print Mach News — M.A.N. (Maschinenfabrik Augsburg-Nuernberg A.G.) Printing Machinery News
Man Q — Manchester Quarterly
ManR — Manchester Review
MANR — Manitoba Reports
MANRA Newsl — MANRA Newsletter. British Rayon Research Association
MAN Res Eng Manuf — MAN [Maschinenfabrik Augsburg-Nuernberg] Research, Engineering, Manufacturing
MansBl — Mansfelder Blaetter
Man Sci — Management Science
Man Sci Teach — Manitoba Science Teacher
Man Ser Asph Inst — Manual Series. Asphalt Institute
Man Soc Sci T — Manitoba Social Science Teacher
Man/Soc/Tech — Man/Society/Technology

Mansoura Sci Bull — Mansoura Science Bulletin
Mansoura Sci Bull A Chem — Mansoura Science Bulletin. A. Chemistry
Man Spectra — Manitoba Spectra
Man Steril Disinf — Manual of Sterilization, Disinfection, and Related Surgical Techniques
Mant — Manteiea
M Ant — Monumenti Antichi
Man Teach — Manitoba Teacher
ManTech — ManTech Journal. US Army
Mantech Anal — Mantech Analysis
ManTech J — ManTech Journal. US Army
Man Text Ind Can — Manual of the Textile Industry of Canada
Man Textos Univ Cienc — Manuales y Textos Universitarios. Ciencias
M Ant Fr — Memoires. Societe Nationale des Antiquaires de France
Man Ther — Manual Therapy
M Anthr G Wien — Mitteilungen. Anthropologische Gesellschaft in Wien
M Anthrop Ges Wien — Mitteilungen. Anthropologische Gesellschaft in Wien
Mant Med — Mantova Medica
Mantova Med — Mantova Medica
Man Tr — Manual Training Magazine
Man Train Mag — Manual Training Magazine
Manual Arts Bul — Manual Arts Bulletin for Teachers in Secondary Schools
Manual Calif Agr Exp Sta — Manual. California Agricultural Experiment Station
Manuale A Radiom — Manuale Annuario Radiometeorico
Manuale Lact — Manuale Lactis
Manuales Tec — Manuales Tecnicos
Manual Inst For (Chile) — Manual. Instituto Forestal (Santiago De Chile)
Manuals Engng Pract — Manuals of Engineering Practice. American Society of Civil Engineers
Manual Train — Manual Training Magazine
Manualul Ing Chim — Manualul Inginerului Chimist
Manuel Annu Sante — Manuel-Annuaire de la Sante
Manuel Gen Ind Auto — Manuel General de l'Industrie Automobile
Manuels Inform Masson — Manuels Informatiques Masson
Manufact — Manufacturer
Manufact Ind — Manufacturing Industry
Manufacturing Ind — Manufacturing Industries
Manuf & Management — Manufacturing and Management
Manuf Appl Lasers — Manufacturing Applications of Lasers
Manuf Bul — Manufacturers' Bulletin
Manuf Ch Ae — Manufacturing Chemist and Aerosol News
Manuf Chem — Manufacturing Chemist
Manuf Chem — Manufacturing Chemist and Aerosol News
Manuf Chem Assoc Chem Saf Data Sheet — Manufacturing Chemists' Association. Chemical Safety Data Sheet
Manuf Chemist — Manufacturing Chemist
Manuf Confect — Manufacturing Confectioner
Manuf Eng — Manufacturing Engineering
Manuf Eng & Mgt — Manufacturing Engineering and Management [Later, Manufacturing Engineering]
Manuf Engin — Manufacturing Engineer
Manuf Eng Manage — Manufacturing Engineering and Management [Later, Manufacturing Engineering]
Manuf Ind — Manufacturing Industries
Manuf Manage — Manufacturing Management
Manuf Mat Manage — Manufacturing and Materials Management
Manuf Milk Prod J — Manufactured Milk Products Journal
Manuf Mo — Manufacturers' Monthly
Manuf Mon — Manufacturers' Monthly
Manuf Perfum — Manufacturing Perfumer
Manuf Rec — Manufacturers' Record
Manuf Res Plann — Manufacturing Resource Planning
Manuf Rev — Manufacturing Review
Manuf Syst — Manufacturing Systems
Manuf Technol Horiz — Manufacturing Technology Horizons
Manuf Week — Manufacturing Week
Man Univ — Manuali per l'Universita
Man Univ Calif Agric Ext Serv — Manual. University of California. Agricultural Extension Service
Manusc Math — Manuscripta Mathematica
Manuscr — Manuscripta
Manuscr Geod — Manuscripta Geodaetica
Manuscripta Math — Manuscripta Mathematica
Manuscr Rep Abstr Okla Agric Exp Stn — Manuscript Report Abstracts. Oklahoma Agricultural Experiment Station
Manuscr Rep McGill Univ (Montreal) Mar Sci Cent — Manuscript Report. McGill University (Montreal). Marine Sciences Centre
Manutent Mec Automn — Manutention Mecanique et Automation
Manx Herring Fish Rep — Manx Herring Fishery Report
Manx J Agr — Manx Journal of Agriculture
Manx J Agric — Manx Journal of Agriculture
Manx Mus Pamph — Manx Museum Pamphlets
MaNy — Magyar Nyelvor
Many Body Probl Proc Mallorca Int Sch Phys — Many-Body Problem. Proceedings. Mallorca International School of Physics
MAO — Monografie Archivii Orientalniho
MAOB — Marine Observer
MAoG — Mitteilungen. Altorientalische Gesellschaft
Ma O Mo — Mark og Montre
Ma Opf & St — Mathematische Operationsforschung und Statistik
Ma P — Makedonski Pregled
MAP — Marketing Action Planner
MAP — Materialy po Arkheologii Rossii
MAP — Mediaeval Academy Publications
Mapas Mens Litoral Peru — Mapas Mensuales del Litoral Peruano

Mapas Obscoes Obs Joao Capelo — Mapas das Observacoes Efectuadas neste Observatorio Joao Capelo
Map Chart Ser NY St Mus Sci Serv — Map and Chart Series. New York State Museum and Science Service
Ma PF — Mainzer Philosophische Forschungen
Maple Syrup Dig — Maple Syrup Digest
MAPMA — Muenchener Archiv fuer Philologie des Mittelalters und der Renaissance
MAPP — Materialy po Arkheologii Pivnichnoho Prychornomor'ia
Map Read — Map Reader
MAPS — Medium Aevum. Philologische Studien
MAPS — Memoirs. American Philosophical Society
MAQ — Maandnotities Betreffende de Economische Toestand
MaQ — Mankind Quarterly
Maq Metais — Maquinas e Metais
MAQR — Michigan Alumni Quarterly Review
Maquinas — Maquinas & Metais
Maquin Nav — Maquinista Naval
MAR — Managed Accounts Report
Mar — Mar del Sur
Mar — Marges. Revue de Litterature et d'Art
Mar — Marianum
MAR — Marketing
MAR — Markeur. Marketing Magazine voor Universiteit en Bedrijfsleven
MAR — Materialy po Archeologii Rossii
M Ar — Medieval Archaeology
MAR — Memoires. Academie Roumaine
MAR — Mining Annual Review
MAR — Monumenta Artis Romanae
MAR — Municipal Association Record
MAR — Municipal Association Reports
MAR A — Mythology of All Races
Mar A — Maritime Art
Mar Activ N — Marine Activities in the North
Mar Advocate & Busy E — Maritime Advocate and Busy East
Mar Aero Models — Marine and Aero Models
Mar Aerztl Kriegserfahr — Marineaerztliche Kriegserfahrungen. Medizinalabteilung der Admiralitaet
Marathwada U J — Marathwada University Journal
Marathwada Univ J Sci — Marathwada University. Journal of Science
Marathwada Univ J Sci Sect A Phys Sci — Marathwada University. Journal of Science. Section A. Physical Sciences
Marathwada Univ J Sci Sect B Biol Sci — Marathwada University. Journal of Science. Section B. Biological Sciences
MARB — Memoires. Academie Royale de Belgique
MARBAI — Morris Arboretum. Bulletin
Mar Behav and Physiol — Marine Behaviour and Physiology
Mar Behav Physiol — Marine Behaviour and Physiology
Marb Geogr Schr — Marburger Geographische Schriften
Mar Bio Ass Ind J — Marine Biological Association of India Journal
Mar Biol — Marine Biology. International Journal of Life in Oceans and Coastal Waters
Mar Biol Assoc India J — Marine Biological Association of India. Journal
Mar Biol (Berl) — Marine Biology (Berlin)
Mar Biol Lett — Marine Biology Letters
Mar Biol (NY) — Marine Biology (New York)
Mar Biol Rep Cape Tn — Marine Biological Report (Cape Town)
Mar Biol (Vladivostok) — Marine Biology (Vladivostok)
Mar BJ — Maryland Bar Journal
Marb Jb — Marburger Jahrbuch fuer Kunstwissenschaft
Marb Jb Kunstwiss — Marburger Jahrbuch fuer Kunstwissenschaft
Marb Jb Kw — Marburger Jahrbuch fuer Kunstwissenschaft
MARBL — Memoires. Academie Royale de Belgique. Lettres
M Arb R — Magazin fuer Arbeitsrecht, Sozialpolitik, und Verwandte Gebiete
Marb Schr — Schriften der Gesellschaft zur Befoerderung der Gesammten Naturwissenschaften zu Marburg
Marburger Geogr Schr — Marburger Geographische Schriften
Marburg Jb Kstgesch — Marburger Jahrbuch fuer Kunstgeschichte
Marburg Jb Kstwiss — Marburger Jahrbuch fuer Kunstwissenschaft
Marburg Winckelmann Programm — Marburger Winckelmann-Programm
Marb Winck Prog — Marburger Winckelmann-Programm
Marb W Pr — Marburger Winckelmann-Programm
MArch — Medieval Archaeology
March Dimes Birth Defects Found Birth Defects Orig Artic Ser — March of Dimes Birth Defects Foundation. Birth Defects Original Article Series
Mar Chem — Marine Chemistry
Mar Chem (Neth) — Marine Chemistry (Netherlands)
Marche Romane — Marche Romane. Cahiers de l'ARULg. Association des Romanistes de l'Universite de Liege
March India — March of India
March Mach Agri — Marchand de Machines Agricoles
March Repar Tract Mach Agric — Marchand Reparateur de Tracteurs et Machines Agricoles
Mar Coat Conf Proc — Marine Coatings Conference. Proceedings
Marconi Instrum — Marconi Instrumentation
Marconi Instrumn — Marconi Instrumentation
Marconi Rev — Marconi Review
Mar Corros Offshore Struct Pap Symp — Marine Corrosion on Offshore Structures. Papers Presented. Symposium
Mar Crp G — Marine Corps Gazette
Marcus Beck Lab Rep — Marcus Beck Laboratory Reports
Mar D Int — Maritime Defence. The Journal of International Naval Technology
Mar Ecol Prog Ser — Marine Ecology. Progress Series
Mar Ecol (Pubbl Stn Zool Napoli I) — Marine Ecology (Pubblicazioni Stazione Zoologica di Napoli. I)
Maremma Agric — Maremma Agricola

Mar Eng — Marine Engineering
Mar Eng — Marine Engineering/Log
Mar Eng Cat — Marine Engineering/Log. Catalog and Buyer's Guide
Mar Eng/Log — Marine Engineering/Log
Mar Eng Nav Architect — Marine Engineer and Naval Architect
Mar Engng Can — Marine Engineering of Canada
Mar Engng/Log — Marine Engineering/Log
Mar Engng Lond — Marine Engineering (London)
Mar Engng NY — Marine Engineering (New York)
Mar Engng Shipbldg Abstr — Marine Engineering and Shipbuilding Abstracts
Mar Eng Rev — Marine Engineers Review
Mar Engr MotShip Bldr — Marine Engineer and Motorship Builder
Mar Engr Offrs Mag — Marine Engineer Officers' Magazine
Mar Engrs J — Marine Engineers Journal
Mar Engrs Rev — Marine Engineers Review
Mar Eng Yrb — Marine Engineering/Log. Yearbook and Maritime Review
Mar Environ Res — Marine Environmental Research
Mar Equip — Marine Equipment
Mar Equip News — Marine Equipment News and Marine Engineering Digest
MA Rev — Massachusetts Review
Mar Fish Abstr — Marine Fisheries Abstracts
Mar Fish Re — Marine Fisheries Review
Mar Fish Res Univ Miami — Marine Fisheries Research. Marine Laboratory. University of Miami
Mar Fish Ser Div Fish Game Mass — Marine Fisheries Series. Division of Fisheries and Game. Massachusetts Department of Conservation
Mar Food Chains Proc Symp — Marine Food Chains. Proceedings. Symposium
Mar Fr — Marine Francaise
Mar Freshwater Res — Marine and Freshwater Research
Marg — Marginales. Revue Bimestrielle des Idees et des Lettres
Margaretol J Cent Bead Res — Margaretologist. The Journal of the Center for Bead Research
Mar Geol — Marine Geology
Mar Geophys Res — Marine Geophysical Researches
Mar Georesources Geotechnol — Marine Georesources and Geotechnology
Mar Geotech — Marine Geotechnology
Mar Geotechnol — Marine Geotechnology
Marginalia Dermatol — Marginalia Dermatologica
Mar I — March of India
Mari — Marianne. Grand Hebdomadaire Politique et Litteraire Illustre
MARI — Publications. Middle American Research Institute
Mariani Found Paediatr Neurol Ser — Mariani Foundation Paediatric Neurology Series
Marian Libr Stud — Marian Library Studies
Marian Stds — Marian Studies
Maricopa Oil Rev — Maricopa Oil Review
Mari Gos Ped Inst Ucen Zap — Mariiskii Gosudarstvennyi Pedagogiceskii Institut. Ucenye Zapiski
Marijuana Rev — Marijuana Review
MariM — Marianne Magazine
Marina Ital — Marina Italiana
Marine Aff Jnl — Marine Affairs Journal
Marine Bio — Marine Biology
Marine Biol Assn UK J — Marine Biological Association of the United Kingdom. Journal
Marine Biol Assoc J — Marine Biological Association Journal
Marine Eng — Marine Engineering
Marine Eng/Log — Marine Engineering/Log
Marine Fisheries R — Marine Fisheries Review
Marine Geotech — Marine Geotechnology
Marine Geotechnol — Marine Geotechnology
Marineh T — Marinehistorisk Tidsskrift
Marine March — Marine Marchande
Marine Rdsch — Marine-Rundschau
Mariner Engng Rec — Mariner and Engineering Record
Mariner Mir — Mariner's Mirror
Mariners Mir — Mariner's Mirror
Mariners Weath Log — Mariners' Weather Log
Marine Tech Soc J — Marine Technology Society. Journal
Marineverordgsbl — Marine-Verordnungsblatt
Mar Invertebr Scand — Marine Invertebrates of Scandinavia
Mar Invest S Afr — Marine Investigations in South Africa. Department of Agriculture
Mariol St — Mariologische Studien
Marion County Med Soc Bull — Marion County Medical Society. Bulletin
Marisia — Marisia Studii si Materiale Arheologice. Istorie. Etnografie
Marit Aviat Mag — Maritime and Aviation Magazine
Marit Aviat Rev — Maritime and Aviation Review
Marit Fmr — Maritime Farmer
Maritime Sediments Atlantic Geol — Maritime Sediments and Atlantic Geology
Marit Import Export Mag — Maritime and Import-Export Magazine
Marit Med News — Maritime Medical News
Marit Min Rec — Maritime Mining Record
Marit Policy & Manage — Maritime Policy and Management
Marit Sediments — Maritime Sediments [Later, Maritime Sediments and Atlantic Geology]
Marit Sediments & Atl Geol — Maritime Sediments and Atlantic Geology
Marit Sediments Atl Geol — Maritime Sediments and Atlantic Geology
Marit Tidsskr — Maritimt Tidsskrift
Mar J — Marine Journal
Mark — Mark Twain Journal
Mark Adjust Wood — Market Adjusted Wood. New Approaches in Forestry and Sawmills. Elmia Wood 81
Mark Bull US Dep Agric — Marketing Bulletin. US Department of Agriculture
Mark Commun — Marketing Communications
Market Adv Res Newsl — Marketing Advertising Research Newsletter

Market Bull — Market Bulletin. Florida Department of Agriculture
Market Com — Marketing Communications
Market Comm Rep — Marketing Communications Report
Market Eur — Market Research Europe
Marketing — Marketing Magazine
Marketing Res Rep USDA — Marketing Research Report. United States Department of Agriculture
Marketing Ser Agr Marketing Adv (India) — Marketing Series. Agricultural Marketing Adviser (India)
Market Intell Eur — Market Intelligence Europe
Market J — Marketing Journal
Market Research Soc J — Journal. Market Research Society
Market Res Rep — Market Research Report
Market Rev — Market Review
Market Week — Adweek's Marketing Week
Markgr Jb — Markgraefler Jahrbuch
Mark Grow J — Market Grower's Journal
Markham R — Markham Review
Markham Rev — Markham Review
Mark Hung — Marketing in Hungary
Marking Ind — Marking Industry
Mark Media Decis — Marketing and Media Decisions
Mark Mix — Marketing Mix
Mark News — Marketing News
Mark og Montre — Mark og Montre fra Sydvestjydske Museer
Markov Process Related Fields — Markov Processes and Related Fields
MarkR — Markham Review
Mark Res Abstr — Market Research Abstracts
Mark Res Rep US Dep Agric — Marketing Research Report. United States Department of Agriculture
Mark Twain — Mark Twain Journal
Mar L and Com — Journal of Maritime Law and Commerce
Mar Law — Maritime Lawyer
Mar Life — Marine Life
Mar LJ — Maryland Law Journal and Real Estate Record
Mar Log — Marine Log
Mar L Rev — Maryland Law Review
MarLuftfl Rdsch — Marineluftflotten-Rundschau
Mar M — Marbacher Magazin
Mar Mag — Marine Magazine
Mar Mamm Sci — Marine Mammal Science
Marmara Univ Eczacilik Derg — Marmara Universitesi Eczacilik Dergisi
MARMDK — Marine Mining
Mar Med — Maroc Medical
Mar Met Rep Hakodate — Marine Meteorological Report. Hakodate Marine Observatory
Mar Micropaleontol — Marine Micropaleontology
Mar Min — Marine Mining
Mar Mining — Marine Mining
MarMinist Kundgor Sovaern — Marineministeriets Kundgorelser for Sovaernet
Mar Mirror — Mariner's Mirror
Mar Models — Marine Models
Mar Moore N — Marianne Moore Newsletter
Mar Muz Jud Mur — Marisia. Muzeul Judetean Mures
Mar News — Marine News
Mar Obs — Marine Observer
Maroc Med — Maroc Medical
Maroc Serv Geol Notes Mem Serv Geol — Maroc. Service Geologique. Notes et Memoires du Service Geologique
MArOr — Monographs. Archiv Orientalni
Mar Pet Geol — Marine and Petroleum Geology
Mar Policy — Marine Policy
Mar Policy Manage — Marine Policy and Management
Mar Pollut Bull — Marine Pollution Bulletin
Mar Pollut Res Titles — Marine Pollution Research Titles
Mar Prod Month — Marine Products Month/Shui Ch'an Yueeh K'an (Fu Kan)
Mar Psyiat Q — Maryland Psychiatric Quarterly
Marq Int — Marques Internationales
Marq LR — Marquette Law Review
Marq L Rev — Marquette Law Review
Marquette Busin R — Marquette Business Review
Marquette Bus R — Marquette Business Review
Marquette Engr — Marquette Engineer
Marquette Geologists Assoc Bull — Marquette Geologists Association. Bulletin
Marquette Law R — Marquette Law Review
Marquette Law Rev — Marquette Law Review. College of Law. Marquette University
Marquette L R — Marquette Law Review
Marquette L Rev — Marquette Law Review
Marquette Med Rev — Marquette Medical Review
Marquette Slav Stud — Marquette Slavic Studies
Mar Rd — Marine-Rundschau
Mar Rdsch — Marine Rundschau
MARRDZ — Marine Research. Department of Agriculture and Fisheries for Scotland
Mar Rec — Marine Record
Mar Res — Marine Research. Scottish Home Department. Fisheries Division
Mar Res Dep Agric Fish Scotl — Marine Research. Department of Agriculture and Fisheries for Scotland
Mar Res Indones — Marine Research in Indonesia
Mar Res Indonesia — Marine Research in Indonesia
Mar Res Lab Educ Ser (St Petersburg FL) — Marine Research Laboratory. Educational Series (St. Petersburg, Florida)
Mar Res Lab Invest Rep (S-W Afr) — Marine Research Laboratory. Investigational Report (South-West Africa)

Mar Res Lab Prof Pap Ser (St Petersburg Florida) — Marine Research Laboratory. Professional Papers Series (St. Petersburg, Florida)
Mar Res Lab Spec Sci Rep (St Petersburg FL) — Marine Research Laboratory. Special Scientific Report (St. Petersburg, Florida)
Mar Res Lab Tech Ser (St Petersburg FL) — Marine Research Laboratory. Technical Series (St. Petersburg, Florida)
Mar Res Ser Scott Home Dep — Marine Research Series. Scottish Home Department
Mar Rev — Marine Review
Marr Fam Liv — Marriage and Family Living
Marr Hyg — Marriage Hygiene
Marriage — Marriage and Family Living
Marriage Fam Rev — Marriage and Family Review
Marriage Hyg — Marriage Hygiene
MarS — Marian Studies
Mars — Marseillaise
MARS — PTS [*Predicasts*] Marketing and Advertising Reference Service
MARSB2 — Maritime Sediments [*Later, Maritime Sediments and Atlantic Geology*]
Mars Bull — Mars Bulletin. Military Amateur Radio System. US Department of Defence
Mars Chir — Marseille Chirurgical
Mar Sci Cent Manuscr Rep McGill Univ (Montreal) — Marine Sciences Centre. Manuscript Report. McGill University (Montreal)
Mar Sci Commun — Marine Science Communications
Mar Sci Comtex — Marine Sciences. Comtex
Mar Sci Contents Tables — Marine Science Contents Tables
Mar Sci Cont Tab — Marine Science Contents Tables
Mar Sci Instrum — Marine Sciences Instrumentation
Mar Sci Newsl — Marine Sciences Newsletter
Mar Sci (NY) — Marine Science (New York)
Mar Sci Res Cent Spec Rep (Stony Brook) — Marine Sciences Research Center. Special Report (Stony Brook)
Mar Sci Res Cent (Stony Brook) Tech Rep — Marine Sciences Research Center (Stony Brook). Technical Report
MARSD4 — Marine Science
Marseille Chir — Marseille Chirurgical
Marseille Hyg — Marseille Hygiene
Marseille Med — Marseille Medical
Marseille Med Scient — Marseille Medico-Scientifique. Annuaire
Marseille Mm S Em — Memoires de la Societe d'Emulation de la Provence (Marseille)
Mars Fac Sc A — Annales de la Faculte des Sciences de Marseille
Mar S Lima — Mar del Sur (Lima)
Mar St — Marian Studies
Mar Stud San Pedro Bay Calif — Marine Studies of San Pedro Bay, California
Mar Sur Lima — Mar del Sur (Lima)
MArt — Magazine of Art
Mart — Mart Magazine
MART — Meaning and Art
MArt — Mundus Artium
MArte — Musica y Arte
Mar Technol — Marine Technology
Mar Technol Soc Annu Conf Prepr — Marine Technology Society. Annual Conference. Preprints
Mar Technol Soc Annu Conf Proc — Marine Technology Society. Annual Conference. Proceedings
Mar Technol Soc J — Marine Technology Society. Journal
Mar Tech S J — Marine Technology Society. Journal
Martigny J — Martigny-Journal
Martin Centre for Archtl & Urban Studies Trans — Martin Centre for Architectural and Urban Studies. Transactions
Martin Ctr Archit Urban Stud — Martin Centre for Architectural and Urban Studies. Transactions
Martinus Nijhoff Philos Lib — Martinus Nijhoff Philosophy Library
MART J — Manitoba Association of Resource Teachers. Journal
Martonv Novenysl Kut Intez Evk — Martonvasare Novenyslesmelesi Kutato Intezet Evkonyne
MarTropMed — Marches Tropicaux et Mediterraneens
Mar Week — Marine Week
Marx Antropol — Marxistisk Antropologi
Marx Bl — Marxistische Blaetter
Marxist Blaet Probl Ges — Marxistische Blaetter fuer Probleme der Gesellschaft
Marxistische Bl — Marxistische Blaetter fuer Probleme der Gesellschaft, Wirtschaft, und Politik
Marxist Persp — Marxist Perspectives
Marxist Quar — Marxist Quarterly
Marx Td — Marxism Today
Maryland Ac T — Transactions of the Maryland Academy of Sciences and Letters
Maryland Agric Coll Nat Stud Bull — Maryland Agricultural College. Nature Study Bulletin
Maryland Agric Exp Sta Misc Publ — Maryland Agricultural Experiment Station. Miscellaneous Publication
Maryland Agric Exp Sta Popular Bull — Maryland Agricultural Experiment Station. Popular Bulletin
Maryland Geol Survey County Geol Map — Maryland. Geological Survey. County Geologic Map
Maryland Geol Survey Rept Inv — Maryland. Geological Survey. Report of Investigations
Maryland Gl Sv — Maryland Geological Survey
Maryland Hist Mag — Maryland Historical Magazine
Maryland L Rev — Maryland Law Review
Maryland Med J — Maryland Medical Journal
Maryland MJ — Maryland State Medical Journal
Maryland Res — Maryland Researcher
Mary L Rev — Maryland Law Review

Maryl St Med J — Maryland State Medical Journal
Maryl St MJ — Maryland State Medical Journal
Mar Zool — Marine Zoologist
Mas — Al-Masarra. Al-Macarrat
MAS — Magazine Article Summaries
M As — Melanges Asiatiques
MAS — Memoires. Academie de Stanislas
MAS — Mission Archeologique au Soudan
MAS — Modern Asian Studies
MAS — Muenchener Aegyptologische Studien
MAS — Survey of Economic Conditions in Japan
Masalah Bang — Masalah Bangunan
MASB — Memoirs. Asiatic Society of Bengal
MAS Bo — Monograph. Asiatic Society of Bombay
MAS Bull — M.A.S. (Michigan Academy of Science) Bulletin
MASCA J — MASCA [*Museum Applied Science Center for Archaeology*] Journal. Universityof Pennsylvania
MASCA Journ — MASCA Journal. Museum Applied Science Center for Archaeology. University Museum
MASCA Journal — Museum Applied Science Center for Archaeology. Journal
MASCAP — Museum Applied Science Center for Archaeology. Pamphlet
MASCAR — Museum Applied Science Center for Archaeology. Report
MASCA Res Pap Sci Archaeol — MASCA [*Museum Applied Science Center for Archaeology*] Research Papers in Science and Archaeology
MASCF — Memoires. Academie des Sciences, Belles-Lettres, et Arts de Clermont-Ferrand
MaschBau Betr — Maschinenbau-der Betrieb
MaschBau Kleineisenind — Maschinenbau und Kleineisenindustrie
MaschBau Waermew — Maschenbau und Waermewirtschaft
Masch Buchhalt — Maschinen-Buchhaltung
Masch Elektrotech — Maschinenwelt Elektrotechnik
Maschinenbau Betr — Maschinenbau der Betrich
Maschinenbautech — Maschinenbautechnik
Maschintec — Maschinenbautechnik
Masch Konstr BetrTech — Maschinen-Konstrukteur-Betriebstechnik
Masch KraftZeug U Eisenmarkt — Maschinen-, Kraftfahrzeug-, und Eisenmarkt
MaschMarkt Landw — Maschinenmarkt fuer die Landwirtschaft
Maschst Heiz — Maschinist und Heizer
Masch U Geraetepruef Reichsnaehrst — Maschinen- und Geraetepruefungen des Reichsnaehrstandes
Masch U MetallindZtg — Maschinen- und Metallindustriezeitung
Masch U WerkzExport Bp — Maschinen- und Werkzeug-Export (Budapest)
MaschWelt Elektrotech — Maschinenwelt und Elektrotechnik
Masch Werkz — Maschine und Werkzeug
Masch Werkzeung — Maschine und Werkzeug
MaschZtg Landw — Maschinenzeitung fuer fie Landwirtschaft und deren Technische Nebenbetriebe
Mash Appar Khim Tekhnol — Mashiny i Apparaty Khimicheskoi Tekhnologii
Mashina Derev — Mashina v Derevne
Mashinostroit Khim Metalloobrab Promsti — Mashinostroiteli dlya Khimicheskoi i Metalloobrabatyvayushchei Promyshlennosti
Mashinostroit Remesl Vest — Mashinostroitel'nyi i Remeslennyi Vestnik
Mash Tekhnol Pererab Polim — Mashiny i Tekhnologiya Pererabotki Polimerov
Mash Trakt Sta — Mashino-Traktornaya Stantsiya
MASI — Memoirs. Archaeological Survey of India
MASIB — Memoire. Accademia delle Scienze. Istituto di Bologna
MASIBM — Memoire. Accademia delle Scienze. Istituto di Bologna. Classe di Scienze Morali
MASIF — Memoires. Academie des Sciences de l'Institut de France
MASJ — Midcontinent American Studies. Journal
MaskBefalsforb Tidskr — Maskinbefalsforbundets Tidskrift
Mask Ind — Maskin-Industrien
Maskin J — Maskinjournalen
Mask Koth — Maske und Kothurn
MASL — Memoirs. Anthropological Society (London)
Maslob Delo — Masloboinoe Delo
Maslob Zhir Delo — Masloboino Zhirovoe Delo
Maslob Zhirov Delo — Masloboino-Zhirovoe Delo
Maslob Zhirov Prom — Masloboino Zhirovaya Promyshlennost [*Later, Maslozhirovaya Promyshlennost*]
Maslob Zhir Promst — Masloboino Zhirovaya Promyshlennost [*Later, Maslozhirovaya Promyshlennost*]
Maslob Zir Prom — Masloboino Zhirovaya Promyshlennost
Maslo Sapunena Promst — Maslo Sapunena Promyshlennost
Maslo Zhir Promst — Maslozhirovaya Promyshlennost [*Formerly, Masloboino Zhirovaya Promyshlennost*]
Masl Zhir Prom — Masloboino Zhirovaya Promyshlennost [*Later, Maslozhirovaya Promyshlennost*]
MASM — Memoires. Academie des Sciences et Lettres de Montpellier. Section des Lettres
MASMDP — Mississippi-Alabama Sea Grant Consortium. MASGP
MASMP — Memoires. Academie des Sciences Morales et Politiques
MASNC — Minerals Availability System
MASO — Meijerbergs Arkiv foer Svensk Ordforskning
MASP — Materialy po Arkheologii Severnogo Prichernomor'ia
Mass — Massachusetts Reports
Massachusetts Stud Engl — Massachusetts Studies in English
Massage J — Massage Journal
Mass Ag Exp — Massachusetts Agricultural Experiment Station. Publications
Mass Agric — Massachusetts Agriculture
Mass Agric Exp Sta Bienn Rep — Massachusetts Agricultural Experiment Station. Biennial Report
Mass Agric Exp Sta Bull Circ — Massachusetts Agricultural Experiment Station Bulletin. Circular

Mass Agric Exp Stn Bull — Massachusetts Agricultural Experiment Station. Bulletin

Mass Agric Exp Stn Control Ser Bull — Massachusetts Agricultural Experiment Station. Control Series. Bulletin

Mass Agric Exp Stn Ext Serv Publ — Massachusetts Agricultural Experiment Station. Extension Service Publication

Mass Agric Exp Stn Monogr Ser — Massachusetts Agricultural Experiment Station. Monograph Series

Mass Ann Laws (Law Co-Op) — Annotated Laws of Massachusetts (Lawyers' Co-Op)

Mass App Ct — Massachusetts Appeals Court Reports

Mass App Dec — Appellate Decisions (Massachusetts)

Mass App Div — Appellate Division Reports (Massachusetts)

Mass App Div Adv Sh — Appellate Division Advance Sheets (Massachusetts)

Mass Basic Data Rep Ground Water Ser — Massachusetts Basic Data Report. Ground Water Series

Mass Dent Soc J — Massachusetts Dental Society. Journal

Mass Dep Nat Resour Div Mar Fish Monogr Ser — Massachusetts Department of Natural Resources. Division of Marine Fisheries. Monographs Series

Mass Dept Correc Q — Massachusetts Department of Corrections. Quarterly

Mass Dept Ment Dis Bul — Massachusetts Department of Mental Diseases. Bulletin

Mass DIA — Massachusetts. Department of Industrial Accidents. Bulletin

Mass Div Mar Fish Tech Ser — Massachusetts. Division of Marine Fisheries. Technical Series

Mass Educ B — Mass Education Bulletin

Masses Ouvr — Masses Ouvrieres

Massey Agric Coll Dairyfarm Annu — Massey Agricultural College. Dairyfarming Annual

Massey Agric Coll Sheepfarm Annu — Massey Agricultural College. Sheepfarming Annual

Massey-Ferguson R — Massey-Ferguson Review

Mass Fruit Grow Assoc Rep Annu Meet — Massachusetts Fruit Growers' Association. Report of the Annual Meeting

Mass Gen L — General Laws of the Commonwealth of Massachusetts

Mass Gen Laws Ann (West) — Massachusetts General Laws Annotated (West)

Mass Hist Soc Coll — Massachusetts Historical Society. Collections

Mass Hist Soc Proc — Massachusetts Historical Society. Proceedings

Mass Hlth J — Massachusetts Health Journal

Mass H R — Massachusetts House of Representatives

Mass Hydrol Data Rep — Massachusetts Hydrologic Data Report

Mass Inst Tech Dep Civ Eng Hydrodyn Lab Rep — Massachusetts Institute of Technology. School of Engineering. Department of Civil Engineering. Hydrodynamics Laboratory. Report

Mass Inst Tech Dep Civ Eng Res Earth Phys Res Rep — Massachusetts Institute of Technology. School of Engineering. Department of Civil Engineering. Research in Earth Physics. Research Report

Mass Inst Tech Dep Civ Eng Soils Publ — Massachusetts Institute of Technology. School of Engineering. Department of Civil Engineering. Soils Publication

Mass Inst Tech Dep Nav Architect Mar Eng Rep — Massachusetts Institute of Technology. Department of Naval Architecture and Marine Engineering. Report

Mass Inst Tech Fluid Mech Lab Publ — Massachusetts Institute of Technology. Fluid Mechanics Laboratory. Publication

Mass Inst Technology Abs Theses — Massachusetts Institute of Technology. Abstracts of Theses

Mass Inst Technology and Woods Hole Oceanog Inst Paper — Massachusetts Institute of Technology and Woods Hole Oceanographic Institution.Papers

Mass Inst Technol Res Lab Electron Tech Rep — Massachusetts Institute of Technology. Research Laboratory of Electronics. Technical Report

Mass Inst Tech Res Lab Electron Tech Rep — Massachusetts Institute of Technology. Research Laboratory of Electronics. Technical Report

Mass J Osteop — Massachusetts Journal of Osteopathy

Mass Law Quar — Massachusetts Law Quarterly

Mass Lib Assn Bul — Massachusetts Library Association. Bulletin

Mass Loss Stars Proc Trieste Colloq Astrophys — Mass Loss from Stars. Proceedings. Trieste Colloquium on Astrophysics

Mass L Q — Massachusetts Law Quarterly

Mass LR — Massachusetts Law Review

Mass L Rev — Massachusetts Law Review

Mass M — Massachusetts Magazine

Mass Med — Massachusetts Medicine

Mass Med J — Massachusetts Medical Journal

Mass Med Newsl — Mass Media Newsletter

M Assn S Africa J — Medical Association of South Africa. Journal

Mass Nurse — Massachusetts Nurse

Massoobmennye Protsessy Appar Khim Tekhnol — Massoobmennye Protsessy i Apparaty Khimicheskoi Tekhnologii

Massoobmennye Protsessy Khim Tekhnol — Massoobmennye Protsessy Khimicheskoi Tekhnologii

Mass Ouvr — Masses Ouvrieres

Mass Prod — Mass Production

Mass Q — Massachusetts Quarterly Review

Mass R — Massachusetts Review

Mass Reg — Massachusetts Register

Mass Regs Code — Code of Massachusetts Regulations

Mass Res — Massachusetts Researcher

Mass Rev — Massachusetts Review

Mass Spect Bull — Mass Spectrometry Bulletin

Mass Spectrom — Mass Spectrometry

Mass Spectrom Bull — Mass Spectrometry Bulletin

Mass Spectrom New Instrum Tech — Mass Spectrometry New Instruments and Techniques

Mass Spectrom Part A B — Mass Spectrometry. Part A-B

Mass Spectrom Rev — Mass Spectrometry Reviews

Mass Spectrosc — Mass Spectroscopy

Mass St Bd Educ — Massachusetts State Board of Education

Mass Stud E — Massachusetts Studies in English

Mass Supp — Supplement (Massachusetts)

Mass Transp — Mass Transportation

Mass Transpn — Mass Transportation

Mass Tribut — Massimario Tributario

Mass Univ Coll Food Nat Resour Agric Exp Stn Res Bull — Massachusetts University. College of Food and Natural Resources. Agricultural Experiment Station. Research Bulletin

Mass Univ Dep Geol Contrib — Massachusetts University. Department of Geology. Contribution

Mass Univ Dept Geology and Mineralogy Special Dept Pub — Massachusetts University. Department of Geology and Mineralogy. Special Department Publication

Mass Wildl — Massachusetts Wildlife

MAST — Memorie. Reale Accademia delle Scienze di Torino

MASTA — Medical Advisory Services for Travellers Abroad

Mastatstva Belarus — Mastatstva Belarusi

Mast Draw — Master Drawings

Mas Teh Glas — Masinsko-Tehnicki Glasnik

Mas Teh Glasn — Masinsko-Tehnicki Glasnik

Mastera Isk Isk — Mastera Iskusstva ob Iskusstve

Master Bldr — Master Builder

Master Bldr Archit Engr — Master Builder and Architectural Engineer [London]

Master Bldr Mod Archit — Master Builder and Modern Architect [London]

Master Bldrs Ass J — Master Builders' Associations Journal [London]

Master Bldrs J — Master Builders' Journal. Federation of Master Builders and Master Builders' Federation [London]

Master Carriers NSW — Master Carriers of New South Wales

Master Draw — Master Drawings

Master Drgs — Master Drawings

Master Painter Aust — Master Painter of Australia

Master Plumber of SA — Master Plumber of South Australia

Master Print A — Master Printer's Annual [London]

Masters Abstr — Masters Abstracts

Master Sh Metal Wkrs J — Master Sheet Metal Workers' Journal [Philadelphia]

Masters Modern Phys — Masters of Modern Physics

Mast in Art — Masters in Art

Mast in Music — Masters in Music

MAST J — Manitoba Association of School Trustees. Journal

MASTM — Memorie. Royale Academia delle Scienze di Torino. Classe di Scienze Morali, Storiche, e Filologiche

Mas Trakt St — Masino-Traktornaja Stancija

Masya Indo — Masyarakat Indonesia

MASYDR — MRC . Laboratory Animals Centre. Symposia

Ma T — Marxism Today

Mat — Matrix

Mat — Matulu

MAT — Memoires. Academie des Sciences, Inscriptions, et Belles-Lettres de Toulouse

MAT — Memorie. Reale Accademia delle Scienze di Torino

Mat A — Materialy Archeologiczne

Mat AB — Materialien aus der Arbeitsmarkt und Berufsforschung

Mat & Issledovaniya Arkheol SSSR — Materialy i Issledovaniya po Arkheologii SSSR

Mat Apl Comput — Matematica Aplicada e Computacional

Mat Arch — Materialy Archeologiczne

Mat Arh — Materiale si Cercetari Arheologice

Matarj Vyvuc Fleery Fauny Belarusi — Matar'jaly da Vyvucen'nja Fleery i Fauny Belarusi/Beitraege zur Erforschung derFlora und Fauna Weissrusslands

Mat Ark Gruz Kav — Materialy po Arkheologii Gruzii i Kavkaza

Mat Arkheol Ros — Materialy po Arkheologii Rossii

Mat Arkh SO — Materialy po Arkheologii i Drevnei Istorii Severnoi Osetii

Mat A Sev Pric — Materialy po Archeologii Severnogo Pricernomor'ja

Mat Bibl — Matematicka Biblioteka

Mat Bilten — Matematicki Bilten

Mat Cas — Matematicky Casopis

Mat Casopis Sloven Akad Vied — Matematicky Casopis Slovenskej Akademie Vied

Mat-Child Nurs J — Maternal-Child Nursing Journal

Mat Contemp — Matematica Contemporanea

Mat Cult Notes — Material Culture Notes

Mat Des — Materials and Design

Matematika Period Sb Perevodov Inostran Statei — Matematika. Periodiceskii Sbornik Perevodov Inostrannyh Statei

Mat Engng — Materials Engineering

Mat Ensenanza — Matematicas y Ensenanza

Mat Ensenanza Univ — Matematica Ensenanza Universitaria

Mater Archeol Cracow — Materialy Archeologiczne. Muzeum Arkheologiczne (Cracow)

Mater Assoc Direct Energy Convers Proc Symp — Materials Associated with Direct Energy Conversion. Proceedings. Symposium

Mater Aust — Materials Australia

Mater Australas — Materials Australasia

Mater Badaq Inst Gospod Wodnej — Materialy Badaqcze Instytut Gospodarki Wodnej

Mater Badaw Ser Gospod Wodna Ochr Wod — Materialy Badawcze. Seria. Gospodarka Wodna i Ochrona Wod

Mater Biblfii Russk Nauch Trud Belgr — Materialy dyla Bibliografii Russkikh Nauchnykh Trudov za Rubezhom (Belgrade)

Mater Biobiblfii Uchen SSSR — Materialy k Biobibliografii Uchenykh SSSR

Mater Biobibliogr Ucen SSSR Ser Biol Nauk Bot — Materialy k Biobibliografii Ucenyh SSSR. Serija Biologiceskih Nauk. Botanika

Mater Biogeogr SSSR — Materialy po Biogeografii SSSR

Mater Budow — Materialy Budowlane

Mater Carte Geol Alger — Materiaux pour la Carte Geologique de l'Algerie
Mater Charact — Materials Characterization
Mater Charact Syst Perform Reliab — Materials Characterization for Systems Performance and Reliability
Mater Charact Thermomech Anal — Materials Characterization by Thermomechanical Analysis
Mater Chem — Materials Chemistry
Mater Chem and Phys — Materials Chemistry and Physics
Mater Compon Fossil Energy Appl — Materials and Components in Fossil Energy Applications
Mater Compon Newsl — Materials and Components Newsletter
Mater Constr (Bucharest) — Materiale de Constructs (Bucharest)
Mater Constr (Madrid) — Materiales de Construccion (Madrid)
Mater Constr Mater Struct — Materiaux et Constructions/Materials and Structures
Mater Constr (Paris) — Materiaux et Constructions (Paris)
Mater Contam Control Pap Symp — Materials and Contamination Control. Papers Presented. Symposium
Mater Corros — Materials and Corrosion
Mater Des — Materials and Design
Mater Des Eng — Materials in Design Engineering
Mater Des Engng — Materials in Design Engineering
Mater Des (Surrey) — Materials and Design (Surrey)
Mater Dev Elect Commun Lab Tokyo — Materials for the Development of the Electrical Communications Laboratory (Tokyo)
Mater Dev Res Elect Commun Lab Tokyo — Materials for the Development of Researches of the Electrical Communications Laboratory (Tokyo)
Mater Docum Archit — Materiaux et Documents de l'Architecture
Mater Ekol Fiziol Rast Ural Flory — Materialy po Ekologii i Fiziologii Rastenii Ural'skoi Flory
Mater Eng — Materials Engineering
Mater Eng (Cleveland) — Materials Engineering (Cleveland)
Mater Eng Modena Italy — Materials Engineering (Modena, Italy)
Mater Eng (Surrey) — Materials in Engineering (Surrey)
Mater Ermittlung Sanierung Altlasten — Materialien zur Ermittlung und Sanierung von Altlasten
Mater Etnogr Gruz — Materialy po Etnografii Gruzii
Mater Etnogr Inst Narod Severa — Materialy po Ethografii. Institut Narodov Severa im P. G. Smidovicha
Mater Etnogr Ross Gosud Russk Muz — Materialy po Etnografii (Rossii). Gosudarstvenniyi Russkii Muzei
Mater Etude Calam — Materiaux pour l'Etude des Calamites Publies par les soins de la Societe de Geographie de Geneve
Mater Etude Fl Geogr Bot Orient — Materiaux pour Servir a l'Etude de la Flore et de la Geographie Botanique de l'Orient. Missions du Ministere de l'Instruction Publique en 1904 et en 1906
Mater Eval — Materials Evaluation
Mater Evaluation — Materials Evaluation
Mater Evol Fiziol — Materialy po Evolyutsionnoi Fiziologii
Mater Faune Ekol Pochvoobitayushchikh Bespozvon — Materialy po Faune i Ekologii Pochvoobitayushchikh Bespozvonochnykh
Mater Fizjogr Kraju — Materialy do Fizjografii Kraju. Documenta Physiographica Polonica
Mater Floryst Geobot — Materialy Florystyczne i Geobotaniczne
Mater Flow — Material Flow
Mater Forum — Materials Forum
Mater Genet Eksp Miner — Materialy po Geneticheskoi i Eksperimental'noi Mineralogii
Mater Geol Dalnevost Kraya — Materialy po Geologii Dal'nevostochnogo Kraya
Mater Geol Kavk — Materialy dlya Geologii Kavkaza
Mater Geol Mestorozhd Redk Elem Zarub Stranakh — Materialy po Geologii Mestorozhdenii Redkikh Elementov v Zarubezhnykh Stranakh
Mater Geol Metallog Kol'sk Poluostrova — Materialy po Geologii i Metallogenii Kol'skogo Poluostrova
Mater Geol Obsz Slaskokrakow — Materialy do Geologii Obszaru Slaskokrakowskiego
Mater Geol Polez Iskop Daln Vost — Materialy po Geologii i Poleznym Iskopaemym Dal'nyego Vostoka
Mater Geol Polez Iskop Yakutsk — Materialy po Geologii i Poleznym Iskopaemym. Gornotekhnicheskaya Kontora (Yakutsk)
Mater Geol Polezn Iskop Buryat ASSR — Materialy po Geologii i Poleznym Iskopaemym Buryatskoi ASSR
Mater Geol Polezn Iskop Chit Obl — Materialy po Geologii i Poleznym Iskopaemym Chitinskoi Oblasti
Mater Geol Polezn Iskop Dal'nevost Kraya — Materialy po Geologii i Poleznym Iskopaemym Dal'nevostochnogo Kraya
Mater Geol Polezn Iskop Irkutsk Obl — Materialy po Geologii i Poleznym Iskopaemym Irkutskoi Oblasti
Mater Geol Polezn Iskop Krasnoyarsk Kraya — Materialy po Geologii i Poleznym Iskopaemym Krasnoyarskogo Kraya
Mater Geol Polezn Iskop Sev Vostoka Evr Chasti SSSR — Materialy po Geologii i Poleznym Iskopaemym Severo Vostoka Evropeiskoi Chasti SSSR
Mater Geol Polezn Iskop Sev Zapada RSFSR — Materialy po Geologii i Poleznym Iskopaemym Severo-Zapada RSFSR
Mater Geol Polezn Iskop Sev Zapada SSSR — Materialy po Geologii i Poleznym Iskopaemym Severo-Zapada SSSR
Mater Geol Polezn Iskop Tsentr Raionov Evr Chasti SSSR — Materialy po Geologii i Poleznym Iskopaemym Tsentral'nykh Raionov Evropeiskoi Chasti SSSR
Mater Geol Polezn Iskop Urala — Materialy po Geologii i Poleznym Iskopaemym Urala
Mater Geol Polezn Iskop Vost Sib — Materialy po Geologii i Poleznym Iskopaemym Vostochnoi Sibiri
Mater Geol Polezn Iskop Yakutsk ASSR — Materialy po Geologii i Poleznym Iskopaemym Yakutskoi ASSR

Mater Geol Polezn Iskop Yuzhn Kaz — Materialy po Geologii i Poleznym Iskopaemym Yuzhnogo Kazakhstana
Mater Geol Polezn Iskop Yuzhn Urala — Materialy po Geologii i Poleznym Iskopaemym Yuzhnogo Urala
Mater Geol Polezn Iskop Zapadn Kaz — Materialy po Geologii i Poleznym Iskopaemym Zapadnogo Kazakhstana
Mater Geol Polezy Iskop Kaz — Materialy po Geologii i Poleznym Iskopaemym Kazakhstana
Mater Geol Ross — Materialy dlya Geologii Rossii
Mater Geol Sred Azii — Materialy po Geologii Srednei Azii
Mater Geol Suisse — Materiaux pour la Geologie de la Suisse
Mater Geol Suisse Geophys — Materiaux pour la Geologie de la Suisse. Geophysique
Mater Geol Tsentr Kaz — Materialy po Geologii Tsentral'nogo Kazakhstana
Mater Geol Tuvinskoi ASSR — Materialy po Geologii Tuvinskoi ASSR
Mater Geol Tyan Shanya — Materialy po Geologii Tyan-Shanya
Mater Geol Zapadno Sib Nizmennosti — Materialy po Geologii Zapadno Sibirskoi Nizmennosti
Mater Geol Zapadn Sib — Materialy po Geologii Zapadnoi Sibiri
Mater Geol Zapad Sib Kraya — Materialy po Geologii Zapadno-Sibirskogo Kraya
Mater Geomorf Paleogeogr SSSR — Materialy po Geomorfologii i Paleogeografii SSSR
Mater Gidrol Dalnevost Kraya — Materialy po Gidrologii Dal'nevostochnogo Kraya
Mater Handl & Storage — Materials Handling and Storage
Mater Handl Biblphy — Materials Handling Bibliography [*London*]
Mater Handl Data — Materials Handling Data
Mater Handl Distrib — Materials Handling and Distribution [*New York*]
Mater Handl Eng — Material Handling Engineering
Mater Handl Man — Materials Handling Manual [*London*]
Mater Handl Mgmt — Materials Handling and Management
Mater Handl News — Materials Handling News
Mater Handl Pyrometall Proc Int Symp — Materials Handling in Pyrometallurgy. Proceedings. International Symposium
Mater High Temp — Materials at High Temperatures
Materiae Veg — Materiae Vegetabiles. Acta Culturae et Praeparationis Plantarum
Materiale — Materiale si Cercetari Arheologice
Materiale Clim Rom — Materiale Pentou Climatologia Romanici
Material Forvalt — Material-Forvalteren
Material H — Material Handling Engineering Package/Material Handling Interaction. Special Issue
Material Handl Engng — Material Handling Engineering
Materiali Bulg Arkhit Nasl — Materiali ot Bulgarskoto Arkhitekturno Nasledstvo
Materiali Costr — Materiali da Costruzione
Materialien Stereochem — Materialien der Stereochemie
Materialkd-Tech Reihe — Materialkundliche-Technische Reihe
Materialn — Materialnyt
Materialozn Tekhnol — Materialoznanie i Tekhnologiya
Materialpruef — Materialpruefung
Materials Eng — Materials Engineering
Materials Eval — Materials Evaluation
Materialy Arch — Materialy Archeologiczne
Materialy Sem Kibernet — Materialy Seminara po Kibernetike
Materia Med Nordmark — Materia Medica Nordmark
Materiel Agric — Materiel Agricole
Materiel Colon — Materiel Colonial
Materiel Lourd Cent Elect — Materiel Lourd pour Centrales Electriques
Materie Plast — Materie Plastiche
Mater Inst Tech Batim Trav Publ — Materiaux. Institut Technique du Batiment et des Travaux Publics
Mater Interact Relevant Pulp Pap Wood Ind Symp — Materials Interactions Relevant to the Pulp, Paper, and Wood Industries. Symposium
Mater Int Symp Biokybern — Materialien des Internationalen Symposiums Biokybernetik
Mater Issled Petrograd Kraya — Materialy po Issledovaniyu Petrogradskogo Kraya, Izdavaemye Kommissiei po Izucheniyu Estestvennykh Proizvoditel'nyk sil Rossii
Mater Issled Pomoshch Proekt Stroit Karakum Kanala — Materialy Issledovanii v Pomoshch Proektirovaniyu i Stroitelstvu Karakumskogo Kanala
Mater Istor Fauny Flory Kazakhst — Materialy po Istorii Fauny i Flory Kazakhstana
Mater Istor Flory Rastit SSSR — Materialy po Istorii Flory i Rastitel'nosti SSSR
Mater Istor Zemled SSSR — Materialy po Istorii Zemledeliya SSSR
Mater I Vsesoju Sez Izuch Poved Chelov — Materialy Imperial Vsesoju sez Izucheniia Poveda Chelovedke
Materiyaly Etnol — Materiyaly do Etnolohiyi
Materiyaly Etnol Antrop — Materiyaly do Etnolohiyi i Antropolohiyi
Materiyaly Heofiz Kharakt Ukr — Materiyaly do Heofizychnoi Kharakteristyky Ukrainy
Materiyaly Istor Ukr Etnohr — Materiyaly do Istorii Ukrayins'koyi Etnohrafii</PHR>%
Materiyaly Poraion Vyvch Dribn Zvir — Materiyaly do Poraionovoho Vyvchennya Dribynkh Zviriv ta Ptakhiv Shcho Nymy Zhyvlyat'sya
Materiyaly Ukr Raion Heol Rozvid Upr — Materiyaly. Ukrayins'ka Raionova Heoloho-Rozvidkova Uprava
Materiyaly Ukr Rus Etnol — Materiyaly do Ukrayins'ko-Rus'koyi Etnol'ohii
Materiyaly Vyvch Mynul Faun URSR — Materiyaly do Vyvchennya Mynulykh Faun URSR
Materiyaly Zahal Zastot Heol Ukr — Materiyaly do Zahal'noyi ta Zastotovanoyi Heolohii Ukrayiny
Mater Izuc Estestv Priozv Sil Rossii — Materialy dlja Izucenija Estestvennyh Proizvoditel'nyh sil Rossii/Materiaux pour l'Etude des Ressources Naturelles de la Russie
Mater Izuch Arkt — Materialy po Izucheniyu Arktiki
Mater Izuch Estest Proizv Sil Ross — Materialy dlya Izucheniya Estestvennykh Proizvoditel'nykh sil Rossi, Izdavaemyya Komissiei pri Rossiiskoi Akademii Nauk

Mater Izuch Lech Miner Vod Gryazei Balneotekh — Materialy po Izucheniyu Lechebnykh Mineral'nykh Vod i Gryazei i Bal'neotekhnike

Mater Izuch Perm Kraya — Materialy po Izucheniyu Permskago Kraya

Mater Izuch Russk Pochv — Materialy po Izucheniyu Russkikh Pochv

Mater Izuch Stavrop Kraya — Materialy po Izucheniyu Stavropol'skogo Kraya

Mater Izuch Vredn Nasek — Materialy po Izucheniyu Vrednykh Nasekomykh. Nasekomyya, Povrezhdavshiya Polya, Sady i Ogorody Moskovskoi Gubernii

Mater Izuch Zhen'shenya Drugikh Lek Sredstv Dal'nego Vostoka — Materialy k Izucheniyu Zhen'shenya i Drugikh Lekarstvennykh Sredstv Dal'nego Vostoka

Mater J SAMPE Quart — Materials Journal. SAMPE [*Society for the Advancement of Material and Process Engineering*] Quarterly

Mater Khar'k Otd Geogr Ova Ukr — Materialy Khar'kovskogo Otdela Geograficheskogo Obshchestva Ukrainy

Mater Klimatogr Galicyi — Materialy do Klimatografii Galicyi Zebrane przez Sekcye Meteorologiczna Komisyi Fizyograficznej

Mater Klim Pridnepr Seti — Materialy po Klimatologii Pridneprovskoi Seti

Mater Kom Eksped Issled — Materialy Komissii Ekspeditsionnykh Issledovanii

Mater Komiss Eksped Issl — Materialy Komissii Ekspedicionnykh Issledovanij

Mater Komiss Izuc Jakutsk Avton SSR — Materialy Komissii po Izuceniju Jakutskoj Avtonomnoj SSR/Materiaux de la Commission pour l'Etude de la Republique Autonome Sovietique Socialiste Jakoute

Mater Kom Issled Mongol Tuvin Narod Respub — Materialy Komissii po Issledovaniyu Mongol'skoi i Tuvinskoi Narodnuikh Respublik

Mater Kom Izuch Yakut Avton Sov Sots Respub — Materialy Komissii po Izucheniyu Yakutskoi Avtonomnoi Sovetskoi Sotsialisticheskoi Respubliki

Mater Kom Mineral Geochem Karpato Balk Geol Assoz — Materialien der Komission fuer Mineralogie und Geochemie. Karpato-Balkanische Geologische Assoziation

Mater Kom Mineral Geokhim Karpato Balk Geol Assots — Materialy Komissii Mineralogii i Geokhimii Karpato-Balkanskaya GeologicheskayaAssotsiatsiya

Mater Kompleksn Izuch Belogo Morya — Materialy po Kompleksnomu Izucheniyu Belogo Morya

Mater Konf Molodykh Biol Kirg — Materialy Konferentsii Molodykh Biologov Kirgizii

Mater Konf Molodykh Uch Spets Akad Nauk Arm SSR — Materialy Konferentsii Molodykh Uchenykh i Spetsialistov. Akademiya Nauk Armyanskoi SSR

Mater Konf Rab Vuzov Zavod Lab Yugo Vostoka SSSR Vopr Obshch — Materialy Konferentsii Rabotnikov Vuzov i Zavodskikh Laboratorii Yugo-Vostoka SSSR po Voprosam Obshchei Khimii. Khimicheskoi Tekhnologii i Khimiko-Analiticheskogo Kontrolya Proizvodstva

Mater Krajowego Semin Magn Mater Amorficznych — Materialy Krajowego Seminarium na temat Magnetycznych Materialow Amorficznych

Mater Kult Tadzhik — Material'naya Kul'tura Tadzhikistana

Mater Lab Issled Merz Grunt — Materialy po Laboratornym Issledovaniyam Merzlykh Gruntov

Mater Lett — Materials Letters

Mater Leve Geobot Suisse — Materiaux pour le Leve Geobotanique de la Suisse

Mater Life — Materials Life

Mater Manage J Rev — Material Management Journal and Review

Mater Manuf Process — Materials and Manufacturing Processes

Mater Maquinaria Metodos Constr — Materiales Maquinaria y Metodos para la Construccion

Mater Marstov Sess Akad Navuk BSSR — Materialy Marstovskoi Sessii Akademii Nauk BSSR

Mater Mech Eng — Materials for Mechanical Engineering

Mater Med Nordmark — Materia Medica Nordmark

Mater Med Pol — Materia Medica Polona

Mater Med Pol Engl Ed — Materia Medica Polona (English Edition)

Mater Meth — Materials and Methods

Mater Meth Man — Materials and Methods Manual [*New York*]

Mater Met Konstr — Materialy po Metallicheskim Konstruktsiyam

Mater Metod Tekh Geologorazved Rab — Materialy po Metodike i Tekhnike Geologorazved Rabot

Mater Mezhresp Soveshch Koord Nauchno Issled Rab Khlopkovod — Materialy Mezhrespublikanskogo Soveshchaniya po Koordinatsii Nauchno-Issledovatel'skikh Rabot po Khlopkovodstvu

Mater Mikol Fitopatol Rossii — Materialy po Mikologii i Fitopatologii Rossii

Mater Mikol Fitopat Ross — Materialy po Mikologii i Fitopatologii Rossii

Mater Mikol Obsled Ross — Materialy po Mikologicheskomu Obsledovaniyu Rossii

Mater Mineral Geokhim Petrogr Zabaik — Materialy po Mineralogii, Geokhimii, i Petrografii Zabaikal'ya

Mater Mineral Geokhim Petrogr Zabaikal'ya — Materialy po Mineralogii, Geokhimii, i Petrografii Zabaikal'ya

Mater Mineral Kol'sk Poluostrova — Materialy po Mineralogii Kol'skogo Poluostrova

Mater Mineral Petrogr Polezn Iskop Zapadn Sib — Materialy po Mineralogii, Petrografii, i Poleznym Iskopaemym Zapadnoi Sibiri

Mater Mol Res Div Newsl — Materials and Molecular Research Division. Newsletter

Mater Mosk Gor Konf Molodykh Uch — Materialy Moskovskoi Gorodskoi Konferentsii Molodykh Uchenykh

Maternal-Child Nurs J — Maternal-Child Nursing Journal

Maternal Child Welf — Maternal and Child Welfare

Maternal Child Welf Surv — Maternal and Child Welfare Survey

Matern & Child Welf — Maternity and Child Welfare

Mater Nauchn Konf Gruz Zootekh Vet Uchebn Issled Inst — Materialy Nauchnoi Konferentsii Posvyashchennoi 50-Letiyu Velikoi Oktyabr'skoi Sotsialisticheskoi Revolyutsii. Gruzinskii Zootekhnichesko-Veterinarnyi Uchebno-Issledovatel'skii Institut

Mater Nauchn Konf Molodykh Uch Kuban Gos Med Inst — Materialy Nauchnoi Konferentsii Molodykh Uchenykh. Kubanskii Gosudarstvennyi Meditsinskii Institut

Mater Nauchn Konf Selsk Khoz — Materialy Nauchnoi Konferentsii po Sel'skomu Khozyaistvu

Mater Nauchn Konf Voronezh Skh Inst — Materialy Nauchnoi Konferentsii Voronezhskii Sel'skokhozyaistvennyi Institut

Mater Nauchno Prakt Konf Oftalmol Sev Kavk — Materialy Nauchno-Prakticheskoi Konferentsii Oftal'mologov Severnogo Kavkaza

Mater Nauchno Tekh Konf Leningr Elektrotekh Inst Svyazi — Materialy Nauchno-Tekhnicheskoi Konferentsii Leningradskogo Elektrotekhnicheskogo Instituta Svyazi

Mater Nauchn Stud Konf Smolensk Gos Med Inst — Materialy Nauchnoi Studencheskoi Konferentsii, Posvyashchennoi 50-letiyu Smolenskogo Gosudarstvennogo Meditsinskogo Instituta

Mater Nauc Konfer Aspir Azerb Pedag Inst Im Lenina — Materialy Naucnoi Konferencii Aspirantov Posvjascennoj Poluvekovomu Jubileju Azerbajdzanskogo Pedagogiceskogo Instituta Imeni V. I. Lenina

Mater Nauk Krajowego Zjazdu Endokrynol Pol — Materialy Naukowe Krajowego Zjazdu Endokrynologow Polskich

Matern Child Health J — Maternal and Child Health Journal

Matern Child Nurs J — Maternal-Child Nursing Journal

Mater New Process Technol Photovoltaics Proc Symp — Materials and New Processing Technologies for Photovoltaics. Proceedings. Symposium

Matern Inf — Maternita ed Infanzia

Matern Infanc — Maternidade e Infancia

Maternita Infanz — Maternita ed Infanzia

Maternity Child Welf — Maternity and Child Welfare

Maternity Child Welf Surv — Maternity and Child Welfare Survey

Mater Note Aust Aeronaut Res Lab — Australia. Aeronautical Research Laboratories. Materials Note

Mater Nouv Aeronaut CR Trav Congr Int Aeronaut — Materiaux Nouveaux pour l'Aeronautique. Compte Rendu des Travaux. Congres International Aeronautique

Mater Nouv Tech Mond — Materiels Nouveaux et Techniques Mondiales

Mater Obl Konf NTO Selsk Khoz — Materialy Oblastnoi Konferentsii NTO (Nauchno-Tekhnicheskoe Obshchestva) Sel'skogo Khoyvaistva

Mater Obmenu Opytom Nauchn Dostizh Med Promsti — Materialy po Obmenu Opytom i Nauchnymi Dostizheniyami v Meditsinskoi Promyshlennosti

Mater Obmenu Peredovym Opytom Nauchn Dostizh Med Promsti — Materialy po Obmenu Peredovym Opytom i Nauchnymi Dostizheniyamiv Meditsinskoi Promyshlennosti

Mater Obshch Merzlotoved Mezhduved Soveshch Merzlotoved — Materialy po Obshchemu Merzlotovedeniyu, Mezhduvedomstvennoe Soveshchanie po Merzlotovedeniyu

Mater Obshch Prikl Geol — Materialy po Obshchei i Prikladnoi Geologii

Mater Ogniotrwale — Materialy Ogniotrwale

Mater Ogolnopol Semin Magn Rezon Jad Jego Zastosow — Materialy Ogolnopolskiego Seminarium na temat. Magnetycznego Rezonansu Jadrowego i Jego Zastosowan

Mater Opis Russk Rek — Materialy dlya Opisaniya Russkikh Rek

Mater Org — Material und Organismen

Mater Organ — Material und Organismen

Mater Org Beih — Materials und Organismen Beihefte

Mater Org (Berl) — Material und Organismen (Berlin)

Mater Org Suppl — Materiaux et Organismes. Supplement

Mater Osnov Paleont — Materialy k Osnovam Paleontologii

Mater Osnov Uchen Merz Zon Zemn Kory — Materialy k Osnovam Ucheniya o Merzlykh Zonakh Zemnoi Kory

Mater Osob Kom Issled Soyuz Avton Respub — Materialy Osobogo Komiteta po Issledovaniyu Soyuznykh i Avtonomnykh Respublik

Mater Osob Komiteta Issl Sojuzn Avton Respubl — Materialy Osobogo Komiteta po Issledovaniju Sojuznyh i Avtonomnyh Respublik

Mater Otrasl Konf Pererab Vysokosernistykh Neftei — Materialy Otraslevoi Konferentsii po Pererabotke Vysokosernistykh Neftei

Mater Otsenki Zemel Vologod Gub — Materialy dlya Otsenki Zemel Vologodskoi Gubernii

Mater Perf — Materials Performance

Mater Perform — Materials Performance

Mater Performance — Materials Performance

Mater Perform Maint Proc Int Symp — Materials Performance Maintenance. Proceedings. International Symposium

Mater Plast (Bucharest) — Materiale Plastice (Bucharest)

Mater Plast Elastomeri — Materiale Plastice ed Elastomeri

Mater Plast Elastomeri Fibre Sint — Materiale Plastice, Elastomeri, Fibre Sintetice

Mater Plast Milan — Materie Plastiche (Milan)

Mater Plenuma Geomorfol Kom Akad Nauk SSSR — Materialy Plenuma Geomorfologicheskoi Komissii. Akademiya Nauk SSSR

Mater Podzespoly Magn Konf — Materialy i Podzespoly Magnetyczne. Konferencja

Mater Pol Czech Szk Stereochem Pept — Materialy z Polsko-Czechoslowackiej Szkoly Stereochemii Peptydow

Mater Polit Bildung — Materialien zur Politischen Bildung

Mater Posymp Symp Metal Proszkow — Materialy Posympozjalne. Sympozjum Metalurgii Proszkow

Mater Povolzh Konf Fiziol Uchastiem Biokhim Farmakol Morfol — Materialy, Povolzhskaya Konferentsiya Fiziologov s Uchastiem Biokhimikov, Farmakologov, i Morfologov

Mater Poznaniyu Fauny Flory SSSR Otd Bot — Materialy k Poznaniyu Fauny i Flory SSSR Otdel Botanicheskii

Mater Poznaniyu Fauny Flory SSSR Otd Zool — Materialy k Poznaniyu Fauny i Flory SSSR Otdel Zoologicheskii

Mater Pozn Fauny Flory SSSR — Materialy k Poznaniyu Fauny i Flory SSSR

Mater Pozn Fauny Fl Rossijsk Imperii Otd Bot — Materialy k Poznaniyu Fauny i Flory Rossijskoj Imperii. Otdel Botanickeskij

Mater Pozn Fauny Nizh Povolzhya — Materialy k Poznaniyu Fauny Nizhnego Povolzh'ya

Mater Pozn Fauny Yugo-Zapad Ross — Materialy k Poznaniyu Fauny Yugo-Zapadnoi Rossii

Mater Pozn Geol Stroen Ross Imp — Materialy k Poznaniyu Geologicheskago Stroeniya Rossiiskoi Imperii

Mater Pozn Geol Stroen SSSR — Materialy k Poznaniyu Geologicheskogo Stroeniya SSSR

Mater Pozn Prir Orlov Gub — Materialy k Poznaniyu Prirody Orlovskoi Gubernii

Mater Pr Antrop — Materialy i Prace Antropologiczne

Mater Pr Antropol — Materialy i Prace Antropologiczne

Mater Pribalt Nauchn Konf Zashch Rast — Materialy k Pribaltiiskoi Nauchnoi Konferentsii po Zashchite Rastenii

Mater Pribalt Nauchno Koord Konf Vopr Parazitol — Materialy Pribaltiiskoi Nauchno-Koordinatsionnoi Konferentsii po Voprosam Parazitologii

Mater Pr Inst Geofiz Pol Akad Nauk — Materialy i Prace. Instytut Geofizyki. Polska Akademia Nauk

Mater Prirod Uslov Sel Khoz Yugo Zap Yakut ASSR — Materialy o Prirodnykh Usloviyakh i Sel'skom Khozyaistve Yugo-Zapada Yakutskoi ASSR

Mater Process Comput Age Proc Int Symp — Materials Processing in the Computer Age. Proceedings. International Symposium

Mater Process Eng — Materials and Processing Engineering

Mater Processes Microelectron Syst — Materials and Processes for Microelectronic Systems

Mater Process Technol — Materials and Process Technology

Mater Process Theory Pract — Materials Processing. Theory and Practices

Mater Proizvod Silam Uzb — Materialy po Proizvoditel'nym Silam Uzbekistana

Mater Proizv Silam Uzbek — Materialy po Prizvoditel'nym Silam Uzbekistana

Mater Prot — Materials Protection [*Later, Materials Performance*]

Mater Prot Perform — Materials Protection and Performance [*Later, Materials Performance*]

Mater Prot Performance — Materials Protection and Performance [*Later, Materials Performance*]

Mater Prot Wuhan Peoples Repub China — Materials Protection (Wuhan, People's Republic of China)

Mater Pr Pol Akad Nauk Inst Geofiz — Materialy i Prace. Polska Akademia Nauk. Instytut Geofizyki

Materpruefengsamt Bauw Tech Hochsch Muenchen Ber — Materialpruefengsamt fuer das Bauwesen der Technischen Hochschule Muenchen. Bericht

Mater Pruef Mat Test — Materialpruefung/Materials Testing

Mater Pr Zakl Geofiz Pol Akad Nauk — Materialy i Prace. Zaklad Geofizyki Polska Akademia Nauk

Mater Rab Opyt Melior Chasti — Materialy Rabot Opytno-Meliorativnoi Chasti

Mater Rab Soveshch Stat Fiz — Materialy Rabochego Soveshchaniya po Statisticheskoi Fizike

Mater Rab Soveshch Tekh Puzyrkovykh Kamer — Materialy Rabochego Soveshchaniya po Tekhnike Puzyr'kovykh Kamer

Mater Reliab Issues Microelectron Symp — Materials Reliability Issues in Microelectronics. Symposium

Mater Rep Aust Aeronaut Res Lab — Australia. Aeronautical Research Laboratories. Materials Report

Mater Rep Univ Mus Univ Tokyo — Material Reports. University Museum. University of Tokyo

Mater Res AECL — Materials Research in AECL

Mater Res and Stand — Materials Research and Standards

Mater Res At Energy Can Ltd — Materials Research in Atomic Energy of Canada Limited

Mater Res Bull — Materials Research Bulletin

Mater Res Bull Spec Issue — Materials Research Bulletin. Special Issue

Mater Res Innovations — Materials Research Innovations

Mater Res Lab Tech Note MRL TN Aust — Materials Research Laboratory. Technical Note. MRL-TN (Australia)

Mater Res Lab Tech Rep MRL TR — Materials Research Laboratory Technical Report. MRL-TR

Mater Resp Konf Biokhim Genet Fiziol Rast Zhivotn Chel — Materialy Respublikanskoi Konferentsii po Biokhimii, Genetike, i Fiziologii Rastenii. Zhivotnykh i Cheloveka

Mater Resp Konf Elektrokhim Lit SSR — Materialy Respublikanskoi Konferentsii Elektrokhimikov Litovskoi SSR

Mater Resp Konf Molodykh Uch Fiz — Materialy Respublikanskoi Konferentsii Molodykh Uchenykh po Fizike

Mater Resp Konf Okhr Prir — Materialy Respublikanskoi Konferentsii po Okhrane Prirody

Mater Resp Konf Poroshk Metall — Materialy k Respublikanskoi Konferentsii po Poroshkovoi Metallurgii

Mater Resp Konf Probl Mikroelem Med Zhivotnovod — Materialy Respublikanskoi Konferentsii po Probleme Mikroelementy v Meditsine i Zhivotnovodstve

Mater Resp Konf Tekst Khim — Materialy Respublikanskoi Konferentsii po Tekstil'noi Khimii

Mater Resp Nauchn Konf Agrokhim Gruz — Materialy Respublikanskoi Nauchnoi Konferentsii Agrokhimikov Gruzii

Mater Resp Nauchn Konf Fiziol Vyssh Uchebn Zaved Gruz — Materialy Respublikanskoi Nauchnoi Konferentsii Fiziologov Vysshikh Uchebnykh Zavedenii Gruzii

Mater Resp Nauchn Konf Stomatol Gruz — Materialy Respublikanskoi Nauchnoi Konferentsii Stomatologov Gruzii

Mater Resp Nauchno Prakt Konf Probl Term Porazhenii — Materialy Respublikanskoi Nauchno-Prakticheskoi Konferentsii po Probleme Termicheskikh Porazhenii

Mater Resp Nauchno Proizvod Konf Zashch Rast Kaz — Materialy Respublikanskoi Nauchno-Proizvodstvennoi Konferentsii po Zashchite Rastenii v Kazakhstane

Mater Resp Nauchno Tekh Konf Primen Polim Mater Promsti — Materialy Respublikanskoi Nauchno-Tekhnicheskoi Konferentsii po Primeneniyu Polimernykh Materialov v Promyshlennosti

Mater Resp Onkol Konf — Materialy Respublikanskoi Onkologicheskoi Konferentsii

Mater Resp Rasshir Konf Farmakol Gruz — Materialy Respublikanskoi Rasshirennoi Konferentsii Farmakologov Gruzii

Mater Resp Semin Din Tepl Protsessov — Materialy Respublikanskogo Seminara po Dinamike Teplovykh Protsessov

Mater Resp Sezda Gematol Transfuziol Beloruss — Materialy Respublikanskogo S'ezda Gematologov i Transfuziologov Belorussii

Mater Resp Soveshch Neorg Khim — Materialy Respublikanskogo Soveshchaniya po Neorganicheskoi Khimii

Mater Res Soc Symp Proc — Materials Research Society. Symposia. Proceedings

Mater Res Stand — Materials Research and Standards

Mater Rizh Soveshch Magn Gidrodin — Materialy. Predstavlennye dlya Obsuzhdeniya na Rizhskom Soveshchanii po Magnitnoi Gidrodinamike

Mater Rybokhoz Issled Sev Basseina — Materialy Rybokhozyaistvennykh Issledovanii Severnogo Basseina

Mater Sb Statni Vyzk Ustav Mater — Materialovy Sbornik Statni Vyzkumny Ustav Materialu

Mater Sci — Materials Science

Mater Sci and Eng — Material Science and Engineering

Mater Sci Concr — Materials Science of Concrete

Mater Sci E — Materials Science and Engineering

Mater Sci Energy Technol — Materials Science in Energy Technology

Mater Sci Eng — Materials Science and Engineering

Mater Sci Eng A — Materials Science and Engineering. A. Structural Materials. Properties, Microstructure, and Processing

Mater Sci Eng A Struct Mater — Materials Science and Engineering. A. Structural Materials. Properties, Microstructure, and Processing

Mater Sci Eng A Struct Mater Prop Microstruct Process — Materials Science and Engineering. A. Structural Materials. Properties, Microstructure, and Processing

Mater Sci Eng B — Materials Science and Engineering. B. Solid-State Materials for Advanced Technology

Mater Sci Eng B Solid State Adv Technol — Materials Science and Engineering B. Solid-State Materials for Advanced Technology

Mater Sci Eng B Solid State Mater — Materials Science and Engineering. B. Solid State Materials for Advanced Technology

Mater Sci Eng C Biomimetic Mater Sens Syst — Materials Science and Engineering C. Biomimetic Materials, Sensors, and Systems

Mater Sci Eng R Rep — Materials Science and Engineering. R. Reports

Mater Sci Forum — Materials Science Forum

Mater Sci Found — Materials Science Foundations

Mater Sci High Temp Polym Microelectron Symp — Materials Science of High Temperature Polymers for Microelectronics. Symposium

Mater Sci Monogr — Materials Science Monographs

Mater Sci NY — Materials Science (New York)

Mater Sci Phys Non Conv Energy Sources — Materials Science and Physics of Non-Conventional Energy Sources

Mater Sci Prog — Materials Science Progress

Mater Sci Rep — Materials Science Reports

Mater Sci Res — Materials Science Research

Mater Sci Res Int — Materials Science Research International

Mater Sci Semicond Process — Materials Science in Semiconductor Processing

Mater Sci Space Proc Eur Symp — Material Sciences in Space. Proceedings. European Symposium on Material Sciences in Space

Mater Sci T — Materials Science and Technology

Mater Sci Technol — Materials Science and Technology

Mater Sci Technol (Sofia) — Materials Science and Technology (Sofia)

Mater Semin Kibern — Materialy Seminara po Kibernetike

Mater Ses Nauk Inst Ochr Rosl (Poznan) — Materialy Sesji Naukowej Instytutu Ochrony Roslin (Poznan)

Mater Sess Obedin Sess Nauchno Issled Inst Zakavk Resp Stroit — Materialy Sessii. Ob'edinennaya Sessiya Nauchno-Issledovatel'skikh Institutov Zakavkayskikh Republik Stroitel'stvu

Mater Sezda Farm B SSR — Materialy S'ezda Farmatsevtov Belorusskoi SSR

Mater Sezda Farm Kaz — Materialy S'ezda Farmatsevtov Kazakhstana

Mater Sezda Karpato Balk Geol Assots — Materialy S'ezda Karpato-Balkanskoi Geologicheskoi Assotsiatsii

Mater Sezda Karpato Balk Geol Assots Dokl Sov Geol — Materialy S'ezda Karpato-Balkanskoi Geologicheskoi Assotsiatsii. Doklady Sovetskikh Geologov

Mater Sezda Vses Entomol Ova — Materialy S'ezda Vsesoyuznogo Entomologicheskogo Obshchestva

Mater Sib Soveshch Spektrosk — Materialy Sibirskogo Soveshchaniya po Spektroskopii

Mater Simp Biokhim Funkts Sist Kletochnykh Organell — Materialy Simpoziuma Biokhimicheskie Funktsii v Sisteme Kletochnykh Organell

Mater Simp Biokhim Mitokhondrii — Materialy Simpoziuma po Biokhimii Mitokhondrii

Mater Simp Mikol Likhenolgov Pribalt Resp — Materialy Simpoziuma Mikologov i Likhenologov Pribaltiiskikh Respublik

Mater Simp Mitokhondriyam — Materialy Simpoziuma po Mitokhondriyam

Mater Simp Solyanoi Tekton — Materialy Simpoziuma po Solyanoi Tektonike

Mater Simp Spektrosk Krist — Materialy Simpoziuma po Spektroskopii Kristallov

Mater Slovets Obshch Kraev — Materialy. Slovetskoe Obshchestvo Kraevedeniya

Mater Sluzh Ucheta Vredit Bolez Sel Khoz Rast — Materialy po Sluzhbe Ucheta Vreditelei i Boleznei Sel'sko-Khozyaistvennykh Rastenii

Mater Soc — Materials and Society

Mater Sov Antarkt Eksped — Materialy Sovetskoi Antarkticheskoi Ekspeditsii

Mater Soveshch Lyumin Kristallofsfory — Materialy Soveshchaniya po Lyuminestsentsii. Kristallofsfory

Mater Soveshch Mekh Ingib Tsepnykh Gazov Reakts — Materialy Soveshchaniya po Mekhanizmu Ingibirovaniya Tsepnykh Gazovykh Reaktsii

Mater Soveshch Parenter Pitan — Materialy Soveshchaniya po Parenteral'nomu Pitaniyu

Mater Soveshch Prob Gisto Gematicheskikh Barerov — Materialy Soveshchaniya po Probleme Gisto-Gematicheskikh Bar'erov

Mater Soveshch Rab Lab Geol Organ — Materialy k Soveshchaniyu Rabotnikov Laboratorii Geologicheskikh Organizatsii

Mater Soveshch Redkozem Met Splavam Soedin — Materialy Soveshchaniya po Redkozemel'nym Metallam. Splavam i Soedineniyam

Mater Soveshch Spektrosk — Materialy Soveshchaniya po Spektroskopii

Mater Stalnym Konstr — Materialy po Stal'nym Konstruktsiyam

Mater Struct — Materials and Structures

Mater Studia Inst Masz Przepl — Materialy i Studia Instytutu Maszyn Przeplywowych

Mater Studia Kom Elektryf Pol — Materialy i Studia Komisji Elektryfikacji Polski

Mater Stud Nauchn Ova Khar'k Politekh Inst — Materialy Studencheskogo Nauchnogo Obshchestva. Khar'kovskii Politekhnicheskii Institut

Mater Study Foss Fauna Ukr SSR — Materials for the Study of the Fossil Fauna of the Ukraine SSR

Mater Symp Natl SAMPE Symp — Materials Symposium. National SAMPE [*Society for the Advancement of Materialand Process Engineering*] Symposium

Mater Symp Paliw Plynnych Prod Smarowych Gospod Morsk — Materialy na Sympozjum Paliw Plynnych i Produktow Smarowych w Gospodarce Morskiej

Mater Tag Karpato Balk Geol Assoz — Materialien der Tagung der Karpato-Balkanischen Geologischen Assoziation

Mater Tech — Materiaux et Techniques

Mater Tech Duebendorf Switz — Material and Technik (Duebendorf, Switzerland)

Mater Technol Test — Materials and Technology Testing

Mater Tech (Paris) — Materiaux et Techniques (Paris)

Mater Tekh Snabzhenie — Material'no Tekhnicheskoe Snabzhenie

Mater Teknol (Sofia) — Materialoznavie i Tekhnologiya (Sofia)

Mater Teor Klin Med — Materialy Teoreticheskoi i Klinicheskoi Meditsiny

Mater Test — Materials Testing

Mater Tezisy VI Konf Khim Sel' Khoz — Materialy i Tezisy VI Konferentsii po Khimizatsii Sel'skogo Khozyaistva

Mater Ther — Materia Therapeutica

Mater Tid — Material-Tidende

Mater Tikhookean Nauchn Kongr Sekts Morsk Biol — Materialy Tikhookeanskogo Nauchnogo Kongressa. Sektsiya Morskaya Biologiya

Mater Today — Materials Today

Mater Toksikol Radioakt Veshchestv — Materialy po Toksikologii Radioaktivnykh Veshchestv

Mater Trans JIM — Materials Transactions. JIM (Japan Institute of Metals)

Mater Tsent Muz TSSR — Materialy Tsentral'nogo Muzeya TSSR

Mater Tsent Nauchno Issled Geol Razved Inst — Materialy. Tsentral'nogo Nauchno-Isslefovatel'skogo Geologo-Razvedochnogo Instituta

Mater Tsentr Nauchno Issled Inst Bum Promsti — Materialy Tsentral'nogo Nauchno-Issledovatel'skogo Instituta Bumazhnoi Promyshlennosti

Mater Tsentr Nauchno Issled Inst Tekst Promsti — Materialy Tsentral'nogo Nauchno-Issledovatel'skogo Instituta Tekstil'noi Promyshlennosti

Mater Tsentr Nauchno Issled Inst Tsellyul Bum Promsti — Materialy Tsentral'nogo Nauchno-Issledovatel'skogo Instituta Tsellyuloznoi i Bumazhnoi Promyshlennosti

Mater Uch Merzlykh Zonakh Zemnoi Kory — Materialy k Ucheniyu o Merzlykh Zonakh Zemnoi Kory

Mater Ukr Tsent Inst Endokr Organoter — Materialy. Ukrainskii Tsentral'nyi Institut Endokrinologii i Organoterapii

Mater Umweltbundesamt (Ger) — Materialien - Umweltbundesamt (Germany)

Mater u Organ — Material und Organismen

Mater Ural Soveshch Spektrosk — Materialy Ural'skogo Soveshchaniya po Spektroskopii

Mater Veg — Materiae Vegetabiles

Mater Vologod Oblast Sel Khoz Opyt Sta — Materialy. Vologodskaya Oblastnaya Sel'skokhozyaistvennaya Opytnaya Stantsiya

Mater Vopr Prom Toksikol Klin Prof Bolezn — Materialy po Voprosam Promyshlennoi Toksikologii i Kliniki Professional'nykh Boleznei

Mater Vseross Sezda Farm — Materialy Vserossiiskogo S'ezda Farmatsevtov

Mater Vseross Soveshch Okhr Materinstva Mladench — Materialy Vserossiiskago Soveshchaniya po Okhrane Materinstva i Mladenchestva

Mater Vses Konf Din Stereokhim Konform Anal — Materialy Vsesoyuznoi Konferentsii po Dinamicheskoi Stereokhimii i Konformatsionnomu Analizu

Mater Vses Konf Elektron Mikrosk — Materialy Vsesoyuznoi Konferentsii po Elektronnoi Mikroskopii

Mater Vses Konf Elektronnoluchevoi Svarke — Materialy Vsesoyuznoi Konferentsii po Elektronnoluchevoi Svarke

Mater Vses Konf Farm — Materialy Vsesoyuznoi Konferentsii Farmatsevtov

Mater Vses Konf Farmakol Protivoluchevykh Prep — Materialy Vsesoyuznoi Konferentsii Farmakologiya Protivoluchevykh Preparatov

Mater Vses Konf Fiziol Biokhim Osn Povysh Prod Skh Zhivotn — Materialy Vsesoyuznoi Konferentsii po Fiziologicheskim i Biokhimicheskim Osnovam Povysheniya Produktivnosti Sel'skokhozyaistvennykh Zhivotnykh

Mater Vses Konf Geol Metallog Tikhookean Rudn Poyasa — Materialy k Vsesoyuznoi Konferentsii po Geologii i Metallogenii Tikhookeanskogo Rudnogo Poyasa

Mater Vses Konf Issled Str Org Soedin Fiz Metodami — Materialy Vsesoyuznoi Konferentsii po Issledovaniyu Stroeniya Organicheskikh Soedinenii Fizicheskimi Metodami

Mater Vses Konf Khim Biokhim Uglevodov — Materialy Vsesoyuznoi Konferentsii po Khimii i Biokhimii Uglevodov

Mater Vses Konf Neitr Fiz — Materialy Vsesoyuznoi Konferentsii po Neitronnoi Fizike

Mater Vses Konf Okisleniyu Org Soedin Zhidk Faze — Materialy Vsesoyuznoi Konferentsii po Okisleniyu Organicheskikh Soedinenii v Zhidkoi Faze

Mater Vses Konf Plazmennym Uskorit — Materialy Vsesoyuznoi Konferentsii po Plazmennym Uskoritelyam

Mater Vses Konf Poroshk Metall — Materialy Vsesoyuznoi Konferentsii po Poroshkovoi Metallurgii

Mater Vses Konf Primen Tunnelnykh Diodov Vychisl Tekh — Materialy Vsesoyuznoi Konferentsii po Primeneniyu Tunnel'nykh Diodov v Vychislitel'noi Tekhnike

Mater Vses Konf Probl Khim Obmen Uglevodov — Materialy Vsesoyuznoi Konferentsii po Probleme Khimiya i Obmen Uglevodov

Mater Vses Konf Sovrem Probl Biokhim Dykhaniya Klin — Materialy Vsesoyuznoi Konferentsii Sovremennye Problemy Biokhimii Dykhaniya i Klinika

Mater Vses Konf Vopr Metod Tekh Ultrazvuk Spektrosk — Materialy Vsesoyuznoi Konferentsii po Voprosam Metodiki i Tekhniki Ul'trazvukovoi Spektrosopii

Mater Vses Konf Vopr Pozharnoi Zashch Nar Khoz Strany — Materialy Vsesoyuznoi Konferentsii po Voprosam Pozharnoi Zashchity Narodnogo Khozyaistva Strany

Mater Vses Konf Vzaimodeistviyu At Chastits Tverd Telom — Materialy Vsesoyuznoi Konferentsii po Vzaimodeistviyu Atomnykh Chastits s Tverdym Telom

Mater Vses Litol Konf — Materialy Vsesoyuznoi Litologicheskoi Konferentsii

Mater Vses Litol Soveshch — Materialy Vsesoyuznogo Litologicheskogo Soveshchaniya

Mater Vses Mezhvuz Konf Ozonu — Materialy. Vsesoyuznaya Mezhvuzovskaya Konferentsiya po Ozonu

Mater Vses Nauchn Konf Mekh Gorn Porod — Materialy Vsesoyuznoi Nauchnoi Konferentsii po Mekhanike Gornykh Porod

Mater Vses Nauchn Konf Sud Med — Materialy Vsesoyuznoi Nauchnoi Konferentsii Sudebnykh Medikov

Mater Vses Nauchn Konf Vopr Gig Toksikol Svyazi Khim Nar Khoz — Materialy Vsesoyuznoi Nauchnoi Konferentsii po Voprosam Gigieny i Toksikologii v Svyazi s Khimizatsiei Narodnogo Khozyaistva

Mater Vses Nauchno Issled Geol Inst — Materialy Vsesoyuznogo Nauchno-Issledovatel'skogo Geologicheskogo Instituta

Mater Vses Nauchno Issled Inst Bum Tsellyul Prom — Materialy Vsesoyuznogo Nauchno-Issledovatel'skogo Instituta Bumazhnoi i Tsellyuloznoi Promyshlennosti

Mater Vses Nauchno Issled Inst Bum Tsellyul Promsti — Materialy Vsesoyuznogo Nauchno-Issledovatel'skogo Instituta Bumazhnoi i Tsellyuloznoi Promyshlennosti

Mater Vses Nauchno Prakt Konf Gorenie Probl Tusheniya Pozharov — Materialy Vsesoyuznoi Nauchno-Prakticheskoi Konferentsii Gorenie i Problemy Tusheniya Pozharov

Mater Vses Nauchno Tekh Geofiz Konf — Materialy Vsesoyuznoi Nauchno-Tekhnicheskoi Geofizicheskoi Konferentsii

Mater Vses Nauchno Tekh Konf Kompoz Mater — Materialy Vsesoyuznoi Nauchno-Tekhnicheskoi Konferentsii Kompozitsionnye Materialy

Mater Vses Nauchn Stud Konf Stud Nauchno Tekh Prog Khim — Materialy Vsesoyuznoi Nauchnoi Studencheskoi Konferentsii Student i Nauchno-Tekhnicheskii Progress. Khimiya

Mater Vses Reol Simp — Materialy Vsesoyuznogo Reologicheskogo Simpoziuma

Mater Vses Semin Teor Tekhnol Pressovaniya Poroshk — Materialy Vsesoyuznogo Seminara po Teorii i Tekhnologii Pressovaniya Poroshkov

Mater Vses Shk Fiz Elektron At Stolknovenii — Materialy Vsesoyuznoi Shkoly po Fizike Elektronnykh i Atomnykh Stolknovenii

Mater Vses Shk Fiz Elem Chastits Vys Energ — Materialy Vsesoyuznoi Shkoly po Fizike Elementarnykh Chastits i Vysokikh Energii

Mater Vses Shk Gologr — Materialy Vsesoyuznoi Shkoly po Golografii

Mater Vses Simp Biokhim Mitokhondrii — Materialy Vsesoyuznogo Simpoziuma po Biokhimii Mitokhondrii

Mater Vses Simp Goreniyu Vzryvu — Materialy Vsesoyuznogo Simpoziuma po Goreniyu i Vzryvu

Mater Vses Simp Khimioprofil Khimioter Grippa — Materialy Vsesoyuznogo Simpoziuma po Khimioprofilaktike i Khimioterapii Grippa

Mater Vses Simp Mekhanoemiss Mekhanokhim Tverd Tel — Materialy Vsesoyuznogo Simpoziuma po Mekhanoemissii i Mekhanokhimii Tverdykh Tel

Mater Vses Simp Okeanogr Aspekty Okhr Vod Khim Zagryaz — Materialy Vsesoyuznogo Simpoziuma Okeanograficheskie Aspekty Okhrany Vod ot Khimicheskikh Zagryaznenii

Mater Vses Simp Poluprovodn Slozhnogo Sostava — Materialy Vsesoyuznogo Simpoziuma po Poluprovodnikam Slozhnogo Sostava

Mater Vses Simp Probl Gistofiziol Soedin Tkani — Materialy Vsesoyuznogo Simpoziuma po Problemam Gistofiziologii Soedinitel'noi Tkani

Mater Vses Simp Rasprostr Uprugikh Uprugoplast Voln — Materialy Vsesoyuznogo Simpoziuma po Rasprostraneniyu Uprugikh i Uprugoplasticheskikh Voln

Mater Vses Simp Sovrem Probl Samoochishcheniya Regul Kach Vody — Materialy Vsesoyuznogo Simpoziuma po Sovremennym Problemam Samoochishcheniya i Regulirovaniya Kachestva Vody

Mater Vses Simp Strukt Funkts Kletochnogo Yadra — Materialy Vsesoyuznogo Simpoziuma Struktura i Funktsii Kletochnogo Yadra

Mater Vses Simp Strukt Funkts Organ Mozzhechka — Materialy Vsesoyuznogo Simpoziuma. Posvyashchennogo Strukturnoi i Funktsional'noi Organizatsii Mozzhechka

Mater Vses Simp Tsitoplazmaticheskoi Nasledstvennosti — Materialy Vsesoyuznogo Simpoziuma po Tsitoplazmaticheskoi Nasledstvennosti

Mater Vses Soveshch Biokhim Genet Ryb — Materialy Vsesoyuznogo Soveshchaniya po Biokhimicheskoi Genetike Ryb

Mater Vses Soveshch Biol Deistviyu Ultrafiolet Izluch — Materialy Vsesoyuznogo Soveshchaniya po Biologicheskomu Deistviyu Ul'trafioletovogo Izlucheniya

Mater Vses Soveshch Defoliatsii Desikatsii Skh Kult — Materialy Vsesoyuznogo Soveshchaniya po Defoliatsii i Desikatsii Sel'skokhozyaistvennykh Kul'tur

Mater Vses Soveshch Diagrammam Sostoyaniya — Materialy Vsesoyuznogo Soveshchaniya po Diagrammam Sostoyaniya

Mater Vses Soveshch Elektrolyumin — Materialy Vsesoyuznogo Soveshchaniya po Elektrolyuminestsentsii

Mater Vses Soveshch Fiz Zhidk — Materialy Vsesoyuznogo Soveshchaniya po Fizike Zhidkostei

Mater Vses Soveshch Izuch Chetvertichn Perioda — Materialy Vsesoyuznogo Soveshchaniya po Izucheniyu Chetvertichnogo Perioda

Mater Vses Soveshch Khim Karbenov Ikh Analogov — Materialy Vsesoyuznogo Soveshchaniya po Khimii Karbenov i Ikh Analogov

Mater Vses Soveshch Pnevmoavgomatike — Materialy Vsesoyuznogo Soveshchaniya po Pnevmoavgomatike

Mater Vses Soveshch Polyarogr Anal — Materialy Vsesoyuznogo Soveshchaniya po Polyarograficheskomu Analizu

Mater Vses Soveshch Psevdoozhizhennomu Sloyu — Materialy Vsesoyuznogo Soveshchaniya po Psevdoozhizhennomu Sloyu

Mater Vses Soveshch Relaks Yavleniyam Polim — Materialy Vsesoyuznogo Soveshchaniya po Relaksatsionnym Yavleniyam v Polimerakh

Mater Vses Soveshch Rostu Nesoversh Met Krist — Materialy Vsesoyuznogo Soveshchaniya po Rostu i Nesovershenstvam Metallicheskikh Kristallov

Mater Vses Soveshch Soedin Tkani — Materialy Vsesoyuznogo Soveshchaniya po Soedinitel'noi Tkani

Mater Vses Soveshch Spektrosk Anal Tsvetn Metall — Materialy Vsesoyuznogo Soveshchaniya Spektroskopistov-Analitikov Tsvetnoi Metallurgii

Mater Vses Soveshch Svarke Raznorodnykh Kompoz Mnogosloinykh — Materialy Vsesoyuznogo Soveshchaniya po Svarke Raznorodnykh, Kompozitsionnykh, i Mnogosloinykh Materialov

Mater Vses Soveshch Tseolitam — Materialy Vsesoyuznogo Soveshchaniya po Tseolitam

Mater Vses Soveshch Tverd Goryuch Iskop — Materialy Vsesoyuznogo Soveshchaniya po Tverdym Goryuchim Iskopaemym

Mater Vses Soveshch Vopr Landshaftoved — Materialy k Vsesoyuznomu Soveshchaniyu po Voprosam Landshaftovedeniya

Mater Vses Soveshch Vopr Primen Mikroelem Selsk Khoz Med — Materialy Vsesoyuznogo Soveshchaniya po Voprosam Primeneniya Mikroelementov v Sel'skom Khozyaistve i Meditsine

Mater Vses Teplofiz Konf — Materialy Vsesoyuznoi Teplofizicheskoi Konferentsii

Mater Vses Teplofiz Konf Svoistvamveshchestv pri Vys Temp — Materialy Vsesoyuznoi Teplofizicheskoi Konferentsii po Svoistvamveshchestv pri Vysokikh Temperaturakh

Mater Vses Teplofiz Konf Svoistvam Veshchestv Vys Temp — Materialy Vsesoyuznoi Teplofizicheskoi Konferentsii po Svoistvam Veshchestv pri Vysokikh Temperaturakh

Mater Vses Vulkanol Soveshch — Materialy Vsesoyuznogo Vulkanologicheskogo Soveshchaniya

Mater World — Materials World

Mater Yield Improved Technol Summ Proc Conf Forg — Material Yield and Improved Technology. A Summary. Proceedings. Conference on Forging

Mater Yubileinoi Nauchno Prakt Konf Kurortol Fizioter Sev Oset — Materialy Yubileinoi Nauchno-Prakticheskoi Konferentsii Kurortologov i Fizioterapevtov Severnoi Osetii

Mater Zachodniopomorskie Muz Pomorza Zachodniego — Materialy Zachodniopomorskie. Muzeum Pomorza Zachodniego

Mater Zent Wiss Forschungsinst Papierind — Materialien des Zentralen Wissenschaftlichen Forschungsinstituts der Papierindustrie

Mater Zimnei Shk Fiz Poluprovodn — Materialy Zimnei Shkoly po Fizike Poluprovodnikov

Mater Zimnei Shk LIYaF Fiz Yadra Elem Chastits — Materialy Zimnei Shkoly LIYaF (Leningradskii Institut Yadernoi Fiziki) po Fizike Yadra i Elementarnykh Chastits

Mater Zimnei Shk Teor Yadra Fiz Vys Energ — Materialy Zimnei Shkoly po Teorii Yadra i Fizike Vysokikh Energii

Mat Etn Gruz — Materialy po Etnografii Gruzii

Mat Eval — Materials Evaluation

Mat Fak Univ Kiril Metodij (Skopje) Godisen Zb — Matematicki Fakultet Univerzitetot Kiril i Metodij (Skopje). Godisen Zbornik

Mat Fiz — Akademiya Nauk Ukrainskoi SSR. Institut Matematiki. Matematicheskaya Fizika

Mat Fiz Astron — Matematyka, Fizyka, Astronomia

Mat Fiz Chem — Matematyka, Fizyka, Chemia

Mat Fiz i Funkcional Anal — Matematiceskaja Fizika i Funkcional'nyi Analiz

Mat Fiz List Ucenike Srednjih Sk — Matematicko Fizicki List za Ucenike Srednjih Skola

Mat Fiz Nelinein Mekh — Matematicheskaya Fizika i Nelineinaya Mekhanika

Mat Fiz Politech Slaska — Matematyka-Fizyka. Politechnika Slaska

Mat Fiz Sof — Matematika i Fizika (Sofiya)

Mat Fiz Sred Shk — Matematika i Fizika v (Srednei) Shkole

Mat-Fys Med — Matematisk-Fysiske Meddelelser. Kongelige Danske Videnskabernes Selskab

Mat-Fys Medd Danske Vid Selsk — Matematisk-Fysiske Meddelelser. Kongelige Danske VidenskabernesSelskab

Mat-Fys Medd Dan Vidensk Selsk — Matematisk-Fysiske Meddelelser. Kongelige Danske Videnskabernes Selskab

Mat Fys Medd K Dan Vidensk Selsk — Matematisk-Fysiske Meddelelser - Kongelige Danske Videnskabernes Selskab

Mat Fys Meddr — Matematisk-Fysiske Meddelelser

Mat Fys Skr — Matematisk-Fysiske Skrifter Udgivet af det Kongelige Danske Videnskabernes Selskab

Mat Fyz Cas — Matematicko-Fyzikalny Casopis

Mat-Fyz Cas Slov Akad Vied — Matematicko-Fyzikalny Casopis. Slovenskej Akademie Vied

Mat Fyz Sb Bratisl — Matematicko-Fyzikalny Sbornik (Bratislava)

MATH — Mathematics Abstracts

Math — Mathesis

Math Abh — Mathematische Abhandlungen aus dem Verlag Mathematischer Modelle von Martin Schilling

Math Agoge — Mathematike Agoge

Math Algorithms — Mathematical Algorithms

Math and Comp in Simulation — Mathematics and Computers in Simulation

Math and Comput Educ — Mathematics and Computer Education

Math and Comput Simulation — Mathematics and Computers in Simulation

Math Ann — Mathematische Annalen

Math Annal — Mathematische Annalen

Math AnnIn — Mathematische Annalen

Math Anwendungen Phys Tech — Mathematik und Ihre Anwendungen in Physik und Technik

Math Appl — Mathematics and Its Applications

Math Appl East European Ser — Mathematics and its Application (East European Series)

Math Appl Japanese Ser — Mathematics and its Applications (Japanese Series)

Math Appl Polit Sci — Mathematical Applications in Political Science

Math Appl Soviet Ser — Mathematics and its Applications (Soviet Series)

Math Approaches Geophys — Mathematical Approaches to Geophysics

Math-Arbeitspapiere — Mathematik-Arbeitspapiere

Math Arbeitspap Univ Bremen — Mathematik-Arbeitspapiere. Universitaet Bremen

Math Astronom Blaetter NF — Mathematisch-Astronomische Blaetter. Neue Folge

Math Balk — Mathematica Balkanica

Math Balkanica — Mathematica Balkanica

Math Balkanica NS — Mathematica Balkanica. New Series

Math Biblthek — Mathematische Bibliothek

Math Biol — Mathematics in Biology

Math Biosci — Mathematical Biosciences

Math Bohem — Mathematica Bohemica

Math Bul — Mathematics Bulletin

Math CAD — Mathematics and CAD

Math Cent Amsterdam Rekenafd — Mathematisch Centrum Amsterdam Rekenafdeling

Math Centre Tracts — Mathematical Centre. Tracts

Math Chem Ser — Mathematical Chemistry Series

Math Chron — Mathematical Chronicle. University of Auckland

Math Chronicle — Mathematical Chronicle

Math Civilis — Mathematiques et Civilisation

Math Colloq Univ Cape Town — Mathematics Colloquium. University of Cape Town

Math Comp — Mathematics of Computation

Math Comput — Mathematics of Computation

Math Comput Ed — Mathematics and Computer Education

Math Comput Modelling — Mathematical and Computer Modelling

Math Comput Simul — Mathematics and Computers in Simulation

Math Comput Simulation — Mathematics and Computers in Simulation

Math Concepts and Methods in Sci and Engrg — Mathematical Concepts and Methods in Science and Engineering

Math Concepts Methods Sci Eng — Mathematical Concepts and Methods in Science and Engineering

Math Concepts Methods Sci Engrg — Mathematical Concepts and Methods in Science and Engineering

Math Control Signals Systems — Mathematics of Control, Signals, and Systems

Math Dept Rep — Mathematics Department Report

Math Didaktik Unterrichtspraxis — Mathematik. Didaktik und Unterrichtspraxis

Math Dynam Astronom Ser — Mathematical and Dynamical Astronomy Series

Math Ecol — Mathematical Ecology

Math Ed for Teaching — Mathematical Education for Teaching

Math Ed Lib — Mathematics Education Library

Math Education — Mathematics Education

Math Educ Teach — Mathematical Education for Teaching

Mathematica Jap — Mathematica Japonicae

Mathematica Scand — Mathematica Scandinavica

Mathematik Naturw Tech — Mathematik fuer Naturwissenschaft und Technik

Mathematik Tech Wirt — Mathematik, Technik, Wirtschaft

Math Eng Ind — Mathematical Engineering in Industry

Math Engrg Indust — Mathematical Engineering in Industry

Mathesis Gand — Mathesis. Recueil Mathematique (Gand)

Mathesis Pol — Mathesis Polska

Mathesis S Grav — Mathesis. Tijdschrift voor Wiskunde. 's Gravenhage

Math Finance — Mathematical Finance

Math ForschBer — Mathematische Forschungsberichte

Math Forschungsber — Mathematische Forschungsberichte

Math Forum — Mathematical Forum

Math Fys Meddr — Mathematisk-Fysiske Meddelelser

Math Gazette — Mathematical Gazette

Math Geol — Mathematical Geology

Math Grundlagen Math Phys Ingen — Mathematische Grundlagen fuer Mathematiker, Physiker, und Ingenieure

Math Inform Sci Humaines — Mathematiques Informatique et Sciences Humaines

Math Ingen — Mathematik fuer Ingenieure

Math Ingen Naturwiss — Mathematik fuer Ingenieure und Naturwissenschaftler

Math Ingen Naturwiss Oekonom Landwirte — Mathematik fuer Ingenieure, Naturwissenschaftler, Oekonomen, und Landwirte

Math Ingen Naturwiss Okonom Sonstige Anwendungsorient Berufe — Mathematik fuer Ingenieure, Naturwissenschaftler, Oekonomen, und Sonstige Anwendungsorientierte Berufe

Math Ing Naturwiss Okon Landwirte — Mathematik fuer Ingenieure, Naturwissenschaftler, Oekonomen, und Landwirte

Math in School — Mathematics in School

Math Intellig — Mathematical Intelligencer

Math Intelligencer — Mathematical Intelligencer

Mat Hist Bull — Material History Bulletin

Mat Hist Primet Nat Homme — Materiaux pour l'Histoire Primitive et Naturelle de l'Homme

Math Japon — Mathematica Japonicae

Math J Okayama Univ — Mathematical Journal. Okayama University

Math J Toyama Univ — Mathematics Journal of Toyama University

Math Kibernet Zogierth Sakith Gamokw — Mathematikuri Kibernetikis Zogierthi Sakithxis Gamokwewa

Mathl Biophys Monogr Ser — Mathematical Biophysics Monograph Series

Math Lecture Note Ser — Mathematics Lecture Note Series

Math Lecture Ser — Mathematics Lecture Series

Math Lehrb Monogr I — Mathematische Lehrbuecher und Monographien. I. Abteilung. Mathematische Lehrbuecher

Math Lehrbuecher Monogr I Abt Math Lehrbuecher — Mathematische Lehrbuecher und Monographien. I. Abteilung. Mathematische Lehrbuecher

Math Lehrbuecher Monogr II Abt Math Monogr — Mathematische Lehrbuecher und Monographien. II. Abteilung. Mathematische Monographien

Math Lehrer — Mathematik fuer Lehrer

Math Leitfaeden — Mathematische Leitfaeden

Mathl Expos — Mathematical Expositions

Mathl Gaz — Mathematical Gazette

Mathl J Okayama Univ — Mathematical Journal of Okayama University

Mathl Mag — Mathematical Magazine

Mathl Notes — Mathematical Notes

Math Logic Quart — Mathematical Logic Quarterly

Mathl Quest Solut — Mathematical Questions and Solutions from the Educational Times

Mathl Rev — Mathematical Reviews

Mathl Survs — Mathematical Surveys

Mathl Tabl Br Ass Advmt Sci — Mathematical Tables. British Association for the Advancement of Science

Mathl Tabl Natn Phys Lab — Mathematical Tables. National Physical Laboratory [*London*]

Math Mag — Mathematics Magazine

Math Math Phys (Washington DC) — Mathematics and Mathematical Physics (Washington, DC)

Math Math Sci — Mathematics of Mathematical Science

Math Mech Solids — Mathematics and Mechanics of Solids

Math Medley — Mathematical Medley

Math Methoden Tech — Mathematische Methoden in der Technik

Math Methods Appl Sci — Mathematical Methods in the Applied Sciences

Math Methods Oper Res — Mathematical Methods of Operations Research

Math Methods Statist — Mathematical Methods of Statistics

Math Miniaturen — Mathematische Miniaturen

Math Mo — Mathematical Monthly

Math Model — Mathematical Modeling

Math Modeling Comput Experiment — Mathematical Modeling and Computational Experiment

Math Modelling — Mathematical Modelling

Math Modelling Sci Comput — Mathematical Modelling and Scientific Computing

Math Models Methods Appl Sci — Mathematical Models and Methods in Applied Sciences

Math Model Systems — Mathematical Modelling of Systems

Math Monograph — Mathematische Monographien

Math Monographs Univ Cape Town — Mathematical Monographs of the University of Cape Town

Math Monogr Berl — Mathematische Monographien (Berlin)

Math Montisnigri — Mathematica Montisnigri

Math Nachr — Mathematische Nachrichten

Math Naturw Ber Ung — Mathematische und Naturwissenschaftliche Berichte aus Ungarn

Math Naturw Bl — Mathematisch-Naturwissenschaftliche Blaetter

Math Naturwiss Anz Ung Akad Wiss — Mathematischer und Naturwissenschaftlicher Anzeiger der Ungarischen Akademie der Wissenschaften

Math Naturwiss Ber Ung — Mathematische und Naturwissenschaftliche Berichte aus Ungarn

Math Naturwiss Ber Ungarn — Mathematische und Naturwissenschaftliche Berichte aus Ungarn

Math-Naturwiss Bibliothek — Mathematisch-Naturwissenschaftliche Bibliothek

Math-Naturwiss Taschenb — Mathematisch-Naturwissenschaftliche Taschenbuecher

Math Naturwiss Tech — Mathematik fuer Naturwissenschaft und Technik

Math Naturwiss Unterr — Mathematische und Naturwissenschaftliche Unterricht

Math Naturw Mitt — Mathematisch-Naturwissenschaftliche Mitteilungen

Math Naturw Unterr — Mathematische und Naturwissenschaftliche Unterricht

Math Natwiss Bll — Mathematisch-Naturwissenschaftliche Blaetter

Math Notae — Mathematicae Notae

Math Notes — Mathematical Notes

Math Notes Acad Sci (USSR) — Mathematical Notes. Academy of Sciences (USSR)

Math Numer Sin — Mathematica Numerica Sinica

Math Numer Sinica — Mathematica Numerica Sinica

Math of Comput — Mathematics of Computation

Math Operationsforsch Stat — Mathematische Operationsforschung und Statistik

Math Operationsforsch Statist — Mathematische Operationsforschung und Statistik

Math Operationsforsch Statist Ser Optim — Mathematische Operationsforschung und Statistik. Series Optimization

Math Operationsforsch Statist Ser Optimization — Mathematische Operationsforschung und Statistik. Series Optimization

Math Operationsforsch Statist Ser Statist — Mathematische Operationsforschung und Statistik. Series Statistik

Math Operationsforsch und Stat — Mathematische Operationsforschung und Statistik

Math Operationsforsch und Stat Ser Optimiz — Mathematische Operationsforschung und Statistik. Series Optimization

Math Operationsforsch und Stat Ser Stat — Mathematische Operationsforschung und Statistik. Series Statistik

Math Oper Res — Mathematics of Operations Research

Math Pannon — Mathematica Pannonica

Math Phys — Mathematik fuer Physiker

Math Phys — Mathematiques pour la Physique

Math Phys Appl Math — Mathematical Physics and Applied Mathematics

Math Phys Electron J — Mathematical Physics Electronic Journal

Math Physiker — Mathematik fuer Physiker

Math Phys Monograph Ser — Mathematical Physics Monograph Series

Math Phys Monogr Ser — Mathematical Physics Monograph Series

Math Phys Phys Math Proc Int Symp — Mathematical Physics and Physical Mathematics. Proceedings. International Symposium

Math Phys Schr Ing Stud — Mathematisch-Physikalische Schriften fuer Ingenieure und Studierende

Math-Phys Semesterber — Mathematisch-Physikalische Semesterberichte

Math Phys Soc Egypt Proc — Mathematical and Physical Society of Egypt. Proceedings

Math Phys Stud — Mathematical Physics Studies

Math Population Stud — Mathematical Population Studies

Math Practice Theory — Mathematics in Practice and Theory

Math Probl Theor Phys Proc Int Conf — Mathematical Problems in Theoretical Physics. Proceedings. International Conference on Mathematical Physics

Math Proc C — Mathematical Proceedings. Cambridge Philosophical Society

Math Proc Camb Philos Soc — Mathematical Proceedings. Cambridge Philosophical Society

Math Proc Cambridge Philos Soc — Mathematical Proceedings. Cambridge Philosophical Society

Math Proc Cambridge Phil Soc — Mathematical Proceedings. Cambridge Philosophical Society

Math Prog — Mathematical Programming

Math Progr — Mathematical Programming

Math Program — Mathematical Programming

Math Programming — Mathematical Programming

Math Programming Stud — Mathematical Programming Studies

Math Program Stud — Mathematical Programming Studies

Math Publ — Mathematical Publications

MathR — Mathematical Reviews

Math Reihe — Mathematische Reihe

Math Rep — Mathematical Reports

Math Rep College General Ed Kyushu Univ — Mathematical Reports. College of General Education. Kyushu University

Math Rep Kyushu Univ — Mathematical Reports. College of General Education. Kyushu University

Math Rep Toyama Univ — Toyama University. Mathematics Reports

Math Res — Mathematical Research

Math Research — Mathematical Research

Math Res Lett — Mathematical Research Letters

Math Rev — Mathematical Reviews

Math Rev Sect — Mathematical Reviews Sections

Maths Bul — Mathematics Bulletin for Teachers in Secondary Schools

Math Scand — Mathematica Scandinavica

Math Schuelerbuecherei — Mathematische Schuelerbuecherei

Math Sci — Mathematical Sciences

Math Sci — Mathematical Scientist

Math Sci Eng — Mathematics in Science and Engineering

Math Sci Engrg — Mathematics in Science and Engineering

Math Scientist — Mathematical Scientist

Math Sci Hum — Mathematiques et Sciences Humaines

Math Sci Humaines — Centre de Mathematique Sociale. Ecole Pratique des Hautes Etudes. Mathematiqueset Sciences Humaines

Math Sci Ref Ser — Mathematical Sciences Reference Series

Math Sci Res Inst Publ — Mathematical Sciences Research Institute Publications

Math Sci Washington DC — Mathematical Sciences (Washington, DC)

Maths Comput — Mathematics of Computation

Math Sem — Mathematics Seminar

Math Semesterber — Mathematische Semesterberichte

Math Seminar — Mathematics Seminar

Math Sem Notes Kobe Univ — Mathematics Seminar. Notes. Kobe University

Math Sem Notes Kobe Univ Second Ed — Kobe University. Mathematics Seminar Notes. Second Edition

Math Ser — Mathematics Series

Math Slovaca — Mathematica Slovaca

Maths Mag — Mathematics Magazine

Maths News Lett — Mathematics News Letter

Math Soc — Mathematical Society [*Banaras Hindu University*]

Math Social Sci — Mathematical Social Sciences

Math Soc Sci — Mathematical Social Sciences

Math Spectrum — Mathematical Spectrum

Maths Stud — Mathematics Student

Maths Symp — Mathematics Symposium. Office of Technical Services [*Washington*]

Maths Teacher — Mathematics Teacher

Maths Teaching — Mathematics Teaching. Association for Teaching Aids in Mathematics [*Sydenham*]

Math Structures Comput Sci — Mathematical Structures in Computer Science

Math Student — Mathematics Student

Math Studienanfaenger — Mathematik fuer Studienanfaenger

Math Surveys — Mathematical Surveys

Math Surveys Monogr — Mathematical Surveys and Monographs

Math Surveys Monographs — Mathematical Surveys and Monographs

Math Syst Econom — Mathematical Systems in Economics

Math Systems in Econom — Mathematical Systems in Economics

Math Systems Theory — Mathematical Systems Theory

Math Syst T — Mathematical Systems Theory

Math Teach — Mathematics Teacher

Math Teach — Mathematics Teaching

Math Teacher — Mathematics Teacher

Math Teaching — Mathematics Teaching

Math Termezettud Ertes — Mathematikai es Termeszettudomanyi Ertesitoe

Math Texte — Mathematische Texte

Math Theory Appl — Mathematics. Theory and Applications

Math Theory Elem Part Proc Conf — Mathematical Theory of Elementary Particles. Proceedings. Conference

Math Today — Mathematics Today

Math Top — Mathematical Topics

Math Trans (Engl Transl) — Mathematical Transactions (English Translation of Matematicheskii Sbornik)
Math USSR Izv — Mathematics of the USSR. Izvestiya
Math USSR Sb — Mathematics of the USSR. Sbornik
Math Vorles Univ Goettingen — Mathematische Vorlesungen an der Universitaet Goettingen
Mathware Soft Comput — Mathware and Soft Computing
Math Wirtschaftswiss — Mathematik fuer Wirtschaftswissenschaftler
Math World — Mathematical World
Math Z — Mathematische Zeitschrift
Matica Srp Zb Prir Nauke — Matica Srpska. Zbornik za Prirodne Nauke
Matiere Mal Condens Ec Ete Phys Theor — Matiere Mal Condensee. Ecole d'Ete de Physique Theorique
Matieres Color — Matieres Colorantes
Matieres Med — Matieres Medicales
Matieres Plast — Matieres Plastiques
Matieres Plast Caoutch — Matieres Plastiques et Caoutchouc
Matieres Plast Med — Matieres Plastiques en Medecine
Mati Iss — Materialy i Issledovaniia po Arkheologii SSSR
Matimyas Mat — Matimyas Matematika
MatIRJa — Materialy i Issledovanija po Istorii Russkogo Jazyka
Mat Iss — Materialy i Issledovaniia po Arkheologii SSSR
Mat Issled — Matematicheskie Issledovaniya
Mat Ist Muz — Materiale de Istorie si Muzeografie
Mat Ist Muz (Bucuresti) — Materiale de Istorie si Muzeografie (Bucuresti)
Mat Kul't Tadzh — Material'naia Kul'tura Tadzhikistana
Mat Kult Tadzhikistana — Material'naya Kul'tura Tadzhikistana
Mat Lap — Matematikai Lapok
Mat Lapok — Matematikai Lapok
Mat Lehrerausbildung — Mathematik fuer die Lehrerausbildung
Mat List — Matematicheskii Listok
Mat Logika Primenen — Matematicheskaya Logika i ee Premeneniya
Matls Sci — Materials Science
Mat Medd Danske Vid Selsk — Matematisk-fysiske Meddelelser. Det Kongelige Danske Videnskabernes Selskab
Mat Mekh Izd Akad Nauk SSSR — Matematika i Mekhanika v Izdaniyakh Akademii Nauk SSSR
Mat Metody Biol Tr Resp Konf — Matematicheskie Metody v Biologii, Trudy Respublikanskoi Konferentsii
Mat Metody Din Kosm App Akad Nauk SSSR Vychisl Tsentr — Matematicheskie Metody v Dinamike Kosmicheskikh Apparatov Akademiya Nauk SSSR Vychisislitel'nyi Tsentr
Mat Metody Fiz Mekh Polya — Matematicheskie Metody i Fiziko-Mekhanicheskie Polya
Mat Metody Geol — Matematicheskie Metody v Geologii
Mat Metody i Fiz-Meh Polja — Akademija Nauk Ukrainskoi SSR L'vovskii Filial Matematiceskoi Fiziki Instituta Matematiki. Matematiceskie Metody i Fiziko-Mehaniceskie Polja
Mat Metody Issled Polim Mater Vses Soveshch — Matematicheskie Metody dlya Issledovaniya Polimerov, Materialy Vsesoyuznogo Soveshehaniya
Mat Metody Khim Mater Vses Konf — Matematicheskie Metody v Khimii, Materialy Vsesoyuznoi Konferentsii
Mat (Minsk) — Materialy po Arkheologii BSSR [*Byelorussian Soviet Socialist Republic*] (Minsk)
Mat Model — Matematicheskoe Modelirovanie. Rossiiskaya Akademiya Nauk
Mat Model Elektr Tsepi — Matematicheskoe Modelirovanie i Elektricheskie Tsepi
Mat Model Teor Elektr Tsepei — Matematicheskoe Modelirovanie i Teoriya Elektricheskikh Tsepei
Mat News Int — Materials News International
Mat Obraz — Matematicheskoe Obrazovanie
Mat (Petrograd) — Materialy po Arkheologii Rossii (Petrograd)
Mat Phys Lap — Matematikai es Physikai Lapok
Mat-Phys Semesterber — Mathematisch-Physikalische Semesterberichte
Mat Plast — Materiale Plastice
Mat Plast Elast — Materie Plastiche ed Elastomeri
Mat po Arkh — Materialy po Arkheologii i Drevnei Istorii Severnoi Osetii
Mat Politech — Matematyka dla Politechnik
Mat Probl Geofiz — Matematicheskie Problemy Geofiziki
Mat Pure Appl Citta Castello — Matematiche Pure ed Applicate (Citta di Castello)
MatRD — Materialy i Issledovanija po Russkoj Dialektologii
Matrices Fibres Polym Nouv Aspects Chim Phys Colloq — Matrices et Fibres Polymeres. Nouveaux Aspects Chimiques et Physiques. Colloque
Mat (Riga) — Materialy i Issledovaniia po Arkheologii Latviiskoi (Riga)
Matrikel Lantmaterist — Matrikel over Lantmateristaten
Matrix and Tensor Q — Matrix and Tensor Quarterly
Matrix Biol — Matrix Biology
Matrix Suppl — Matrix Supplement
Matrix Tensor Q — Matrix and Tensor Quarterly
Matrix Tensor Quart — Matrix and Tensor Quarterly
Matrix Tensor Quart — Tensor Club of Great Britain. Matrix and Tensor Quarterly
Matrl Eng — Materials Engineering
Matrl Hand — Material Handling Engineering
Matrl Perf — Materials Performance
Matr Tens Q — Matrix and Tensor Quarterly
Mat Rus Isk — Materialy po Russkomu Iskusstvu
Mat Sb — Matematicheskie Sbornik
Mat Sb (NS) — Matematiceskii Sbornik (Novaja Serija)
Mat Sb (Tomsk) — Matematiceskii Sbornik (Tomsk)
Matscience Rep — Matscience Report
Matscience Symp Theor Phys — Matscience Symposia on Theoretical Physics
Mat Sci Res Stud Ser — Materials Science Research Studies Series
MATS Flyer — MATS (Military Aviation Transport Service) Flyer [*Washington*]
Mat Shk — Matematika v Shkole
Mat si Cerce Arh — Materiale si Cercetari Arheologice
MatSl — Matica Slovenska

Mats Perf — Materials Performance
Mats Reclam Wkly — Materials Reclamation Weekly
Mats Struct — Materials and Structures
Mat Star — Materialy Starozytne
Mat Star — Materialy Starozytne. Panstwowe Muzeum Archeologiczne
Mat Stos — Matematyka Stosowana
Mat Stos 3 — Roczniki Polskiego Towarzystwa Matematycznego. Seria III. Matematyka Stosowana
Matsushita Electr Works Tech Rep — Matsushita Electric Works. Technical Report
Matsushita Med J — Matsushita Medical Journal
Matsushita Tech J — Matsushita Technical Journal
Mat T — Matematisk Tidsskrift
Mat Tab Bilim Derg — Matematik ve Tabiat Bilimleri Dergisi
Mat Tab Ilim Mecm — Matematik ve Tabii Ilimler Mecmuasi
Mat Tabl Mosk — Matematicheskie Tablitsy (Moskva)
Mat Teor Biol Protsessov Tezisy Dokl Konf — Matematicheskaya Teoriya Biologicheskikh Protsessov. Tezisy Dokladov Konferentsii
Mat Termeszettud Ert — Matematikai es Termeszettudomanyi Ertesito
Mat Termeszettud Ertes — Matematikai es Termeszettudomanyi Ertesitoe
Mat Termeszettud Kozl — Matematikai es Termeszettudomanyi Kozlemenyek, Vonatkozolag a Hazai Viszonyokra
Mat Testi Cl — Materiali e Discussioni per l'Analisi dei Testi Classici
Mat Turcica — Materialia Turcica
Maturation Nerv Syst Proc Int Summer Sch Brain Res — Maturation of the Nervous System. Proceedings. International Summer School of Brain Research
Mat Vesnik — Matematicki Vesnik
Mat Vesn Nova Ser — Matematichki Vesnik. Nova Seriya
Mat Voprosy Kibernet Vychisl Tekhn — Matematicheskie Voprosy Kibernetiki i Vychislitel'noi Tekhniki
Mat Voprosy Upravlen Proizvodstvom — Moskovskii Gosudarstvennyi Universitet. Mehaniko-Matematiceskii Fakul'tet. Matematiceskii Voprosy Upravlenija Proizvodstvom
Mat v Skole — Ministerstvo Prosvescenija RSSR Matematika v Skole
MATYC J — MATYC [*Mathematics Association of Two-Year Colleges*] Journal
Mat Zachodnio-Pomorskie — Materialy Zachodnio-Pomorskie
Mat Zametki — Matematicheskie Zametki
MAU — Monographs. Andrews University
Maudsley Monogr — Maudsley Monographs. Institute of Psychiatry
MAUOA — Music. American Guild of Organists
Maur — Mauretania
Maurice Ewing Ser — Maurice Ewing Series
Mauritius Dep Agric Annu Rep — Mauritius. Department of Agriculture. Annual Report
Mauritius Dep Agric Bull — Mauritius. Department of Agriculture. Bulletin
Mauritius Dep Agric Sci Ser Bull — Mauritius. Department of Agriculture. Scientific Series. Bulletin
Mauritius Dep Agric Sugar Cane Res Stn Annu Rep — Mauritius. Department of Agriculture. Sugar Cane Research Station. Annual Report
Mauritius Econ Bull — Mauritius Economic Bulletin
Mauritius Inst Bull — Mauritius Institute. Bulletin
Mauritius Ministr Agric Nat Resour Annu Rep — Mauritius. Ministry of Agriculture and Natural Resources. Annual Report
Mauritius Sugar Cane Res Stn Annu Rep — Mauritius. Sugar Cane Research Station. Annual Report
Mauritius Sugar Ind Res Inst Annu Rep — Mauritius Sugar Industry Research Institute. Annual Report
Mauritius Sugar Ind Res Inst Bull — Mauritius Sugar Industry Research Institute. Bulletins
Mauritius Sugar Ind Res Inst Leafl — Mauritius Sugar Industry Research Institute. Leaflet
Mauritius Sugar Ind Res Inst Occas Pap — Mauritius Sugar Industry Research Institute. Occasional Paper
Mauritius Sugar Ind Res Inst Tech Circ — Mauritius Sugar Industry Research Institute. Technical Circular
Maurit Sug News Bull — Mauritius Sugar News Bulletin
MAUSB — Metals Australia [*Later, Metals Australasia*]
MAV — Madison Avenue
MAV — Memoires. Academie des Vaucluse
MAW — Mededeelingen. Akademie van Wetenschappen
MAW — Mythologies in the Ancient World
Mawdsley Mem — Mawdsley Memoirs
MAW HTR BE Versuchseinlagerung Bohrloechern Statusber — MAW- und HTR-BE-Versuchseinlagerung in Bohrloechern, Statusbericht
MAX — Maschinenmarkt
Max-Planck-Ges Ber Mitt — Max-Planck-Gesellschaft. Berichte und Mitteilungen
Max Planck Ges Foerd Wiss Projektgruppe Laserforsch Ber PLF — Max-Planck-Gesellschaft zur Foerderung der Wissenschaften.Projektgruppe fuer Laserforschung. Bericht PLF
Max-Planck-Ges Jahrb — Max-Planck-Gesellschaft. Jahrbuch
Max Planck Inst Aeron Mitt — Max-Planck-Institut fuer Aeronomie. Mitteilungen
Max Planck Inst Kernphys Rep MPI H — Max-Planck-Institut fuer Kernphysik. Report MPI H
Max-Planck-Inst Plasmaphys Garching Muenchen Ber IPP JET — Max-Planck-Institut fuer Plasmaphysik. Garching bei Muenchen. Bericht IPP-JET
Max-Planck-Inst Plasmaphys Presseinf — Max-Planck-Institut fuer Plasmaphysik. Presseinformation
Max Planck Inst Quantenop Ber MPQ — Max-Planck-Institut fuer Quantenoptik. Bericht MPQ
Max Planck Inst Stroemungsforsch Ber — Max-Planck-Institut fuer Stroemungsforschung. Bericht
Max Von Pettenkofer Inst Ber — Max-Von-Pettenkofer-Institut. Berichte
Maxwell R — Maxwell Review
MaY — Music at Yale

Maya Res New Orleans — Maya Research (New Orleans)
May Baker Lab Bull — May and Baker Laboratory Bulletin
May Baker Pharm Bull — May and Baker Pharmaceutical Bulletin
Mayo Clin P — Mayo Clinic. Proceedings
Mayo Clin Proc — Mayo Clinic. Proceedings
May Parl — May's Parliamentary Practice
May Rev — Maynooth Review
MAZ — Manager's Magazine
Maz — Mazungumzo
MAZ — Muenchen Allgemeine Zeitung
MAZ — Personal. Mensch und Arbeit in Betrieb
Mazda Data Serv — Mazda Data Service
Mazda Res Bull — Mazda Research Bulletin
Mazda Tech Rev — Mazda Technical Review
MAZOAT — Marine Zoologist
Mazungumzo — Mazungumzo Student Journal of African Studies
MB — Maandblad voor Belastingrecht
MB — Maandblad voor het Boekhouden
MB — Madrider Beitraege. Deutsches Archaeologisches Institut. Abteilung Madrid
MB — Magazine of Building
MB — Mandens Blad
MB — Mare Balticum
MB — Mediaevalia Bohemica
MB — Melanges Baldensperger
MB — Mesaionike Bibliotheke
MB — Miscellanea Barcinonensia
MB — Mission Bulletin
MB — Mitteilungsblatt. Irgun Olej Merkas Europa
MB — Monthly Bulletin of Decisions of the High Court of Uganda
MB — Monumenta Boica
MB — More Books
MB — Musee Belge
MB — Music in Britain
MBA — Europees Parlement. EP Nieuws
MBA — MBA/Masters in Business Administration
MBal — Mare Balticum
MBANA — Methods of Biochemical Analysis
M Bank Admin — Magazine of Bank Administration
MBAS (Calcutta) — Monthly Bulletin. Asiatic Society (Calcutta)
MBB — Deutsche Bundesbank. Monatsberichte mit Statistischen Beiheften
MbBAW — Monatsbericht. Berliner Akademie der Wissenschaft
MBBG — Missionsblatt der Bruedergemeine
Mb Bo — Mededelingenblad Bedrijfsorganisatie
MBBull — Bulletin Bibliographique. Musee Belge
MBB WF-Inf — MBB [*Messerschmitt-Boelkow-Blohm*] WF-Information
MBChrG — Maedchenbildung auf Christlicher Grundlage
MBD — Marching Band Director
MBDL — Muenstersche Beitraege zur Deutschen Literatur
MBE — Monumenta Biblica et Ecclesiastica
MBEA J — Mississippi Business Education Association. Journal
MBEA Today — Michigan Business Education Association Today
M Bel R — Maandblad voor Belastingrecht
MBENA — Medical and Biological Engineering [*Later, Medical and Biological Engineering and Computing*]
MB en R — Maandblad voor Berechtiging en Reclassering van Volwassenen en Kinderen
Mber Dt Akad Wiss Berl — Monatsbericht der Deutschen Akademie der Wissenschaften zu Berlin
Mber Dt Geol Ges — Monatsbericht der Deutschen Geologischen Gesellschaft
Mber Gesamtleist Geb Krankh Harn U SexApp — Monatsbericht ueber die Gesamtleistungen auf dem Gebiet der Krankheiten des Harn- und Sexualapparats
Mber Hess Landesamt Wett U Gewasserk — Monatsbericht des Hessischen Landesamtes fuer Wetter- und Gewasserkunde
Mber HorizPendelstn Taschkent — Monatsbericht der Horizontalpendelstation (Taschkent)
Mber Int Altersforsch Altersbekaempf — Monatsbericht. Internationale Altersforschung und Altersbekaempfung
Mber Koen Preuss Akad Wiss Berlin — Monatsberichte der Koeniglich Preussischen Akademie der Wissenschaften zu Berlin
Mber Kstwiss & Ksthand — Monatsberichte ueber Kunstwissenschaft und Kunsthandel
M Berl Ges Anthrop — Mitteilungen. Berliner Gesellschaft fuer Anthropologie, Ethnologie, und Urgeschichte
Mber NiederschlVerhalt Ndtl — Monatsbericht ueber die Niederschlagsverhaltnisse in Norddeutschland
Mberr Dt Geol Ges — Monatsberichte der Deutschen Geologischen Gesellschaft
Mber Urol — Monatsbericht fuer Urologie
Mber Wiss Hum Kom — Monatsbericht des Wissenschaftlich-Humanitaren Komitees
Mber Witt Saarland — Monatsbericht ueber die Witterung in Saarland
MBF — Materials Business File
MBFLD — Mitteilungsblatt. Bundesanstalt fuer Fleischforschung
MBG — Marburger Beitraege zur Germanistik
MBGBA — Montana. Bureau of Mines and Geology. Bulletin
MBGF — Muenstersche Beitraege zur Geschichtsforschung
MBGRV — Materialien zur Bibelgeschichte und Religioesen Volkskunde des Mittelalters
MBGSA — Montana. Bureau of Mines and Geology. Special Publication
MBI — MBI. Medico-Biologic Information
M Bildung — Musik und Bildung
MBIOAJ — Marine Biology
MBJ — Michigan State Bar Journal
MbJb — Mecklenburger Jahrbuch Schwerin
MBK — Maandblad voor Beeldende Kunsten

MBK — Mitteilungen. Berner Kunstmuseum
MBK — Schouw Vakblad voor Verwarming, Sanitair, en Keukenapparatuur
MBKG — Muenchener Beitraege zur Kunstgeschichte
Mbl — Maandblad van de Centrale Raad van Beroep
MBL — Modern British Literature
MBI — Mouton Blanc
MB Lab Bull — M and B [*May and Baker*] Laboratory Bulletin
Mbl Altert Ver Wien — Monatsblatt des Altertum-Vereins zu Wien
Mbl Bad Schwarzwaldver — Monatsblatt des Badischen Schwarzwaldvereins
MblBBDI — Monatsblaetter des Berliner Bezirksvereins Deutscher Ingenieure
Mbl Bdorg — Mededelingenblad Bedrijfsorganisatie
Mbl Bel Recht — Maandblad voor Belastingrecht
Mbl Berl BezVer Dt Ing — Monatsblatt des Berliner Bezirksvereins Deutscher Ingenieure
Mb Lbs — Mededelingenblad Landbouwschap
MBLED — Marine Biology Letters
MBLED7 — Marine Biology Letters
Mbl Freiheitliche Wirtschaftspol — Monatsblaetter fuer Freiheitliche Wirtschaftspolitik
Mbl GesundhPflege — Monatsblatt fuer Gesundheitspflege
Mbl Goslar Verb Naturw Med Ver — Monatsblatt des Goslarer Verbands Naturwissenschaftlicher und Medizinischer Vereine an Deutschen Hochschulen
MblKRU — Monatsblaetter fuer den Katholischen Religionsunterricht an den Hoeheren Lehranstalten
MBL Lect Biol — MBL (Marine Biological Laboratory) Lectures in Biology
Mbll Hist Ges Posen — Monatsblaetter der Historischen Gesellschaft fuer die Provinz Posen
MBL (Mar Biol Lab) Lect Biol (Woods Hole) — MBL (Marine Biology Laboratory) Lectures in Biology (Woods Hole)
Mbl Nt — Maandblad voor Natuurwetenschappen, Uitgegeven door de Sectie voor Natuurwetenschappen van het Genootschap ter Bevordering van Natuur-, Genees- en Heelkunde
Mbl Obstb — Monatsblatt fuer Obstbau
Mbl Oeff GesundhPflege — Monatsblatt fuer Oeffentliche Gesundheitspflege
MBLPA3 — Mediko-Biologichni Problemi
Mbl Ver Gesch Stadt Wien — Monatsblatt des Vereins fuer Geschichte der Stadt Wien
Mbl Ver Landesk Niederoest — Monatsblatt des Vereins fuer Landeskunde von Niederoesterreich
Mbl V Frueh Gesch — Mitteilungsblatt. Gesellschaft fuer Vor-und Fruehgeschichte
Mbl Wiss Klubs Wien — Monatsblatt des Wissenschaftlichen Klubs in Wien
MBM — Malaysian Business
MBM — Metal Bulletin Monthly
MBM — Molecular Biology and Medicine
MBM — Muenchener Beitraege zur Mediaevistik und Renaissance-Forschung
MB Metaalbewerking — MB. Metaalbewerking
MBMG Mont Bur Mines Geol Spec Publ — MBMG. Montana Bureau of Mines and Geology Special Publication
MBM Met Bull Mon — MBM. Metal Bulletin Monthly
MBMRF — Muenchener Beitraege zur Mediavistik und Renaissance-Forschung
MBNG — Mitteilungen der Bayerischen Numismatischen Gesellschaft
MBO — Maandblad voor Bedrijfsadministratie en Organisatie
MBOP — Moniteur Bibliographique. Bulletin Officiel des Imprimes Publies en Pologne
MBP — Maxima Bibliotheca Veterum Patrum et Antiquorum Scriptorum Ecclesiasticorum
MBP — Muenchener Beitraege zur Papyrusforschung
MBPF — Muenchener Beitraege zur Papyrusforschung und Antiken Rechtsgeschichte
MB Pharm Bull — M and B Pharmaceutical Bulletin
MBPHAX — Marine Behaviour and Physiology
MBPR — Muenchener Beitraege zur Papyrusforschung und Antiken Rechtsgeschichte
MB Prod — MB Produktietechniek
MBQ — Montana Business Quarterly
MBR — Belastingbeschouwingen. Onafhankelijk Maandblad voor Belastingrecht en Belastingpraktijk
MBR — Maandblad voor Berechtiging en Reclassering van Volwassenen en Kinderen
MBR — Multivariate Behavioral Research
MBRA — Mitteilungen der Biologischen Reichsanstalt
MBRMAO — Multivariate Behavioral Research Monograph
MBRP — Muenchener Beitraege zur Romanischen und Englischen Philologie
MBRWA — Monthly Bulletin. International Railway Congress Association
MBS — Memoires. Bibliotheque de la Sorbonne
MBS — Monthly Bulletin of Statistics
MBSG — Marine Biological Station (Ghardaqa, Red Sea) Publications
MB Th — Muenstersche Beitraege zur Theologie
MBU — FAO [*Food and Agriculture Organization of the United Nations*] Monthly Bulletin of Statistics
MBUBW — Maha-Bodhi and the United Buddhist World
Mbuehne — Musikbuehne
Mbull Schweiz Ver Gas U WassFachm — Monatsbulletin. Schweizerischer Verein von Gas- und Wasserfachmaennern
M Bull (US Army Europe) — Medical Bulletin (United States Army, Europe)
MBV — Maandstatistiek van de Binnenlandse Handel en Dienstverlening
MBVF — Muenstersche Beitraege zur Vor- und Fruehgeschichte
MBW — Metaalbewerking Werkplaatstechnisch Vakblad voor Nederland en Belgie
MC — American Maritime Cases
MC — Management Contents
MC — Marketing Communications
MC — McMurray Courier
MC — Medal Collector
MC — Medical Chronicle
MC — Misisons Catholiques [*Lyon*]

MC — Monatliche Correspondenz zur Befoerderung der Erd- und Himmelskunde

MC — Mondo Classico

MC — Monte Carmelo

MC — Monthly Criterion

MC — Monumenta Christiana

MC — United States. Government Printing Office. Monthly Catalog of United States Government Publications

MCA — Materiale si Cercetari Arheologice

MCAB — Memoires Couronnes et Autres Memoires. Academie Royale des Sciences, des Lettres, et Beaux-Arts de Belgique

MCACO — Memoires. Commission des Antiquites de la Cote-D'Or

MCA Cote d'Or — Memoires. Commission des Antiquites du Departement de la Cote d'Or

M Can — Museo Canario

MCar — Monte Carmelo

MCA Radio News Lett — MCA (Ministry of Civil Aviation) News Letter [*London*]

M C Arh — Materiale si Cercetari Arheologice

M Carm — Monte Carmelo

MCASDZ — Instituto Universitario Pedagogico de Caracas. Monografias Cientificas "AugustoPi Suner"

M Cass — Miscellanea Cassinese

MCAT — Musees et Collections Archeologiques de l'Algerie et de la Tunisie

MCAW — Major Companies of the Arab World

MCB — Maandschrift van het Centraal Bureau voor de Statistiek

MCB — Melanges Chinois et Bouddhiques

MCB — Molecular and Cellular Biology

MCBEB — Microbial Ecology

M Cb L — Meddelelser fra Carlsberg Laboratoriet

McBride's — McBride's Magazine

MCC — Mitteilungen der Centralkommission zur Erforschung der Denkmale

McCann-E NR — McCann-Erickson, Inc. News Release

MCCHDC — Specialist Periodical Reports. Macromolecular Chemistry

McCl — McClure's Magazine

McClure — McClure's Magazine

McClure's — McClure's Magazine

McClures M — McClure's Magazine

McClures Mag — McClure's Magazine

McCollum Pratt Inst Johns Hopkins Univ Contrib — McCollum-Pratt Institute. Johns Hopkins University. Contribution

McCQ — McCormick Quarterly

MCDM — Magazin fuer Christliche Dogmatik und Moral

MCDPC — Memoires. Commission Departementale des Monuments Historiques du Pas-de-Calais

MCDW — Monthly Climatic Data for the World

MCER(A) — Mining and Chemical Engineering Review (Australia)

MCG — Marche. L'Hebdomadaire du Dirigeant

MCG — Memoires du Comite Geologique/Trudy Geologicheskogo Komiteta

MCG — Monatshefte der Comenius-Gesellschaft

MCG — Monumenta Conciliorum Generalium Saecli Decimiquinti

McGill Dent Rev — McGill Dental Review

McGill Engr — McGill Engineer. McGill University

McGill J Educ — McGill Journal of Education

McGill L J — McGill Law Journal

McGill Med J — McGill Medical Journal

McGill Med Jnl — McGill Medical Journal

McGill Med Undergrad J — McGill Medical Undergraduate Journal

McGill Rep — McGill Reporter

McGill Sub Arct Res Pap — McGill Sub-Arctic Research Papers. McGill University

McGill Univ Axel Heiberg Isl Res Rep Glaciol — McGill University. Axel Heiberg Island Research Reports. Glaciology

McGill Univ Mar Sci Cent Manuscr — McGill University. Marine Sciences Centre. Manuscript

McGill Univ (Montreal) Mar Sci Cent Manuscr Rep — McGill University (Montreal). Marine Sciences Centre. Manuscript Report

McGill Univ Peter Redpath Mus — McGill University [*Montreal*]. Peter Redpath Museum

McGl — McGloin's Louisiana Courts of Appeal Reports

McG LJ — McGill Law Journal

McGraw 2000 — McGraw-Hill American Economy Prospects for Growth through 2000

McGraw ESH — Annual McGraw-Hill Survey. Investment in Employee Safety and Health

McGraw Hill Med Health — McGraw-Hill's Medicine and Health

McGraw Hill Ser Electr Engrg Circuits Systems — McGraw-Hill Series in Electrical Engineering. Circuits and Systems

McGraw Hill Ser Electr Engrg Commun Inform Theory — McGraw-Hill Series in Electrical Engineering. Communications and Information Theory

McGraw Hill Ser Quantitative Methods Management — McGraw-Hill Series in Quantitative Methods for Management

McGraw Hill Wash Rep Med Health — McGraw-Hill's Washington Report on Medicine and Health

McGraw Ove — McGraw-Hill Overseas Operations of United States Industrial Companies

McGraw PE — McGraw-Hill Annual Survey of Business Plans for New Plants and Equipment

McGraw Pol — McGraw-Hill Annual Pollution Control Expenditures

McGraw RD — McGraw-Hill Annual Survey of Research and Development Expenditures

McGraw ST — McGraw-Hill Publications. US Business Outlook. Short Term

McGraw US — McGraw-Hill United States Business Outlook. Long Term

MCh — Mikrasiatiki Chronika

MCH — Monographs in Church History

MCHAC — Memoires. Cercle Historique et Archeologique de Courtrai

MCHEB — Mechanical and Chemical Engineering Transactions

M Chius — Etrusco Museo Chiusino

MCHL — Mayo Clinic Health Letter

MCHMDI — Manufacturing Chemist

M Chr Lit — Magazine of Christian Literature

MCIC Rep — MCIC [*Metals and Ceramics Information Center*] Report

MCJ — Menologe de la Compagnie de Jesus

MCJ — Mensajero del Corazon de Jesus

MCJ News — Milton Centre of Japan. News

MCK — Monumenta Christiana. Geschriften van de Kerkvaders

MCKBA — Memoirs. College of Science. University of Kyoto. Series B

McKee Pedersen Instrum Appl Notes — McKee-Pedersen Instruments Applications Notes

McKinsey Q — McKinsey Quarterly

McKinsey Quart — McKinsey Quarterly

MCL — Cebecoskoop

MCL — Martin Classical Lectures

MCL — Missions Catholiques (Lyons)

M Cl — Mondo Classico

MCLB — Modern and Classical Language Bulletin

MCLC S&T Sect B Nonlinear Opt — MCLC (Molecular Crystals and Liquid Crystals) Science and Technology. Section B. Nonlinear Optics

McLean Foram Lab Rept — McLean Foraminiferal Laboratory. Reports

McLean Hosp J — McLean Hospital Journal

McLean Paleont Lab Rept — McLean Paleontological Laboratory. Reports

M Clin N Am — Medical Clinics of North America

M Clin North America — Medical Clinics of North America

MCLJ — Mifflin County Legal Journal

MCM — Magic Carpet Magazine

MCM — Marketing Communications

MCM — Miscellanea Classico-Medievale

MCM — Missions Catholiques (Milan)

MCM — Modern Churchman

MCM — Monumenta Christiana. Geschriften uit de Middeleuwen

MCM — Music Clubs Magazine

McMaster Symp Iron Steelmaking Proc — McMaster University. Symposium on Iron and Steelmaking. Proceedings

MCMJ — Michigan Mathematical Journal

MCMP — University of Michigan Contributions in Modern Philology

MCMSM — Modern Analytical and Computational Methods in Science and Mathematics

MCMT — Main Currents in Modern Thought

MCN — American Journal of Maternal Child Nursing

MCN — Motor Cycle News

MCN Am J Matern Child Nurs — MCN. American Journal of Maternal Child Nursing

McNaughts M — McNaught's Monthly

MCNJA — Maternal-Child Nursing Journal

McN L — McNair Lectures

McN R — McNeese Review

MCNYA — Machinery [*Later, Machinery and Production Engineering*]

MCO — Marches Tropicaux et Mediterraneens

MCOFA — Machine Outil Francaise

MCOM — Medical Communications

MCom — Miscelanea Comillas

MCOPB — Methods in Computational Physics

M Copern V — Mitteilungen des Copernicus-Vereins fuer Wissenschaft und Kunst zu Thorn

MCP — Massachusetts CPA [*Certified Public Accountant*] Review

MCP — Materials Chemistry and Physics

MCP — Mensario das Casas do Povo

MCP — Mineral Commodity Profiles. US Bureau of Mines

MCP — Missions Catholiques (Paris)

MCPAAJ — Escuela Nacional de Agricultura [*Chapingo*]. Monografias

MCP Alum — Mineral Commodity Profiles. Aluminum

MCP Chrom — Mineral Commodity Profiles. Chromium

MCP Clays — Mineral Commodity Profiles. Clays

MCP Cobalt — Mineral Commodity Profiles. Cobalt

MCP Columb — Mineral Commodity Profiles. Columbium

MCP Copper — Mineral Commodity Profiles. Copper

MCP Iron — Mineral Commodity Profiles. Iron and Steel

MCP Iron O — Mineral Commodity Profiles. Iron Ore

MCP Lead — Mineral Commodity Profiles. Lead

MCP Mang — Mineral Commodity Profiles. Manganese

MCP Nickel — Mineral Commodity Profiles. Nickel

MCP Plat — Mineral Commodity Profiles. Platinum Group Metals

MCP Potash — Mineral Commodity Profiles. Potash

MCP Silicn — Mineral Commodity Profiles. Silicon

MCP Silver — Mineral Commodity Profiles. Silver

MCP Soda A — Mineral Commodity Profiles. Soda Ash, Sodium Carbonate, and Sodium Sulfate

MCP Tantlm — Mineral Commodity Profiles. Tantalum

MCP Titanm — Mineral Commodity Profiles. Titanium

MCP Vandm — Mineral Commodity Profiles. Vanadium

MCP Zinc — Mineral Commodity Profiles. Zinc

MCQ — Management Communication Quarterly

MCR — Mass Communications Review

MCR — Melbourne Critical Review

MCr — Museum Criticum

MCR and R — Medical Care Research and Review

MCRAPE — Memoires. Centre de Recherches Anthropologique, Prehistorique, et Ethnologage

MCREDA — Multivariate Experimental Clinical Research

MCRFA — Microscope and Crystal Front

MCRHAC — Memoires. Cercle Royal Historique et Archeologique de Courtrai

Mcr J — Quarterly Journal of Microscopical Science

MCR (NZ) — Magistrates' Court Reports (New Zealand)

Mcr S J — Journal of the Royal Microscopical Society
Mcr S T — Transactions of the Microscopical Society of London
MCS — Maandblad. Centraal Bureau Statistiek
MCS — Manchester Cuneiform Studies
MCS — Monumenta Christiana Selecta
MCSN — Materiali e Contributi per la Storia della Narrativa Greco-Latina
MCSR — Monatsschrift fuer Christliche Sozialreform
Mc St — Manchester Cuneiform Studies
MCV — Melanges. Casa de Velazquez
MCVQ Med Coll VA Q — MCVQ. Medical College of Virginia. Quarterly
MCZAAZ — Museum of Comparative Zoology [*Harvard University*]. Annual Report
MD — Denkschriften der Bayerischen Akademie der Wissenschaften zu Muenchen
MD — Mackenzie Drift
MD — Maison-Dieu
Md — Maryland Reports
MD — MD: Medical Newsmagazine
MD — Media Decisions
MD — Modern Drama
MD — Modern Drummer
MD — Musica Disciplina
MDA — Dagbladpers
MDA — Marketing and Distribution Abstracts
MdA — Melanges d'Archeologie Egyptienne et Assyrienne
MDAC — Memoires et Documents Publies par l'Academie Chablaisienne
MDAC — Mystery and Detection Annual
MD Acad Sci Bull — Maryland Academy of Sciences. Bulletin
MD Ac Sc Tr — Maryland Academy of Sciences. Transactions
MDAF — Memoires et Documents Publies par l'Academie Faucigny
MDAFA — Memoires. Delegation Archeologique Francaise de Afghanistan
MD Ag Exp — Maryland. Agricultural Experiment Station. Publications
Md Agric Coll Fm Advis — Maryland Agricultural College Farm Adviser
Md Agric Coll Q — Maryland Agricultural College Quarterly
Md Agric Exp Stn Annu Rep — Maryland. Agricultural Experiment Station. Annual Report
MD Agric Exp Stn Bull — Maryland. Agricultural Experiment Station. Bulletin
Md Agric Exp Stn Misc Publ MP — Maryland Agricultural Experiment Station. Miscellaneous Publication. MP
MD Agric Exp Stn MP — Maryland. Agricultural Experiment Station. MP
MDAI — Mitteilungen. Deutsches Archaeologische Institut
MDAIA — Mitteilungen. Deutsches Archaeologische Institut. Abteilung Athens
MDAI Bag Abt — Baghdader Mitteilungen. Deutsches Archaeologisches Institut. Abteilung Baghdad
MDAIK — Mitteilungen. Deutsches Archaeologische Institut. Abteilung Kairo
MDAI(M) — Madrider Mitteilungen. Deutsches Archaeologisches Institut. Madrider Abteilung
MDAIM — Mitteilungen. Deutsches Archaeologische Institut. Abteilung Madrid
MDAIR — Mitteilungen des Deutschen Archaeologischen Instituts. Roemische Abteilung
MDAIR — Mitteilungen. Deutsches Archaeologische Institut. Abteilung Rome
MDAI RE — Mitteilungen des Deutschen Archaeologischen Instituts. Roemische Abteilung. Ergaenzungsheft
MDAI Rom Abt — Mitteilungen des Deutschen Archaeologischen Instituts. Roemische Abteilung
MDA J (Jefferson City) — MDA [*Missouri Dental Association*] Journal (Jefferson City, Missouri)
MDAM — Majalle(H)-Ye Daneshkade(H)-Ye Adabiyyat-E Mashhad
MDan — Meddelelser fra Dansklaererforeningen
MDAN — Memoires et Dissertations sur les Antiquites Nationales et Etrangeres
MD Anderson Symp Fundam Cancer Res — M.D. Anderson Symposium on Fundamental Cancer Research
Md Ann Code — Annotated Code of Maryland
M Dansklf — Meddelelser fra Dansklaererforeningen
MDAP — Memoirs. Department of Archaeology in Pakistan
Md App — Maryland Appellate Reports
MDAPV — Materialy i Doslidzhenniia z Arkheologi i Prykarpattia i Volyni
MDARC — Medecine et Armees
MDA (Tehran) — Majalle(H)-Ye Daneshkade(H)-Ye Adabiyyat Va Olun-E Ensanie-Ye (Tehran)
MDA Verb — Mitteilungen des Deutschen Archaeologen-Verbandes
MDAW — Monatsberichte der Deutschen Akademie der Wissenschaften zu Berlin
MD BJ — Maryland Bar Journal
Mdbl Amstelodanum — Maandblad Amstelodanum
Mdbl Beeld Kst — Maandblad voor Beeldende Kunsten
Mdbl Bond Heemschut — Maandblad van den Bond Heemschut
Mdbl Ned Leeuw — Maandblad de Nederlandsch Leeuw
Mdbl Oud Utrecht — Maandblad Oud-Utrecht
Md Board Nat Resour Dep Geol Mines Water Resour Bull — Maryland. Board of Natural Resources. Department of Geology, Mines, and Water Resources. Bulletin
MD Bur Mines Ann Rept — Maryland. Bureau of Mines. Annual Report
MDBVK — Mitteldeutsche Blaetter fuer Volkskunde
MDC — Medisch Contact
Md Chir S P — Proceedings of the Royal Medical and Chirurgical Society of London
Md Chir T — Medico-Chirurgical Transactions, published by the Royal Medical and Chirurgical Society of London
MDCNAY — Medicina. Revista do Centro Academico Rocha Lima [*CARL*]. Hospital das Clinicas da Faculdade de Medicina de Ribeirao Preto. Universidade de Sao Paulo
Md Code Ann — Annotated Code of Maryland
Md Comml Fish Hatch Ops — Maryland Commercial Fish Hatchery Operations
MD Comput — MD Computing
MD Conserv — Maryland Conservationist
Md C Us — Medicinisch-Chemische Untersuchungen. Aus dem Laboratorium fuer Angewandte Chemie zu Tuebingen

MDD — Dun's Million Dollar Directory
MDD — Medical Devices, Diagnostics, and Instrumentation Reports: the Gray Sheet
MDD — Middenstand
MD Dep Geol Mines Water Resour Bull — Maryland. Department of Geology. Mines and Water Resources Bulletin
Md Dep Nat Resour Geol Surv Inf Circ — Maryland. Department of Natural Resources. Geological Survey. Information Circular
MD Dept Geology Mines and Water Res Bull County Rept — Maryland. Department of Geology. Mines and Water Resources Bulletin. County Reports
MDE — Management Decision
MDE Digest — Marketing and Distributive Educators' Digest
MDEG — Mitteilungen der Deutschen Entomologischen Gesellschaft
MD Energy Saver — Maryland Energy Saver
Md Entomol — Maryland Entomologist
MDERD — Monatsschrift fuer Deutsches Recht
MdF — Mercure de France
MDF — Metals Datafile
MDF — Mitteldeutsche Forschungen
MdF — Musees de France
Md Fmr — Maryland Farmer
MdFr — Musees de France
Md Fruit Grow — Maryland Fruit Grower
MDG — Monatsschrift fuer das Deutsche Geistesleben
MD Geol Surv Basic Data Rep — Maryland. Geological Survey. Basic Data Report
MD Geol Surv Bull — Maryland. Geological Survey. Bulletin
Md Geol Surv Gen Ser — Maryland Geological Survey. General Series
MD Geol Surv Guideb — Maryland. Geological Survey. Guidebook
MD Geol Surv Inf Circ — Maryland. Geological Survey. Information Circular
MD Geol Surv Quadrangle Atlas — Maryland. Geological Survey. Quadrangle Atlas
MD Geol Surv Rep Invest — Maryland. Geological Survey. Report of Investigations
Md Geol Surv Stratigr Mem — Maryland Geological Survey. Stratigraphical Memoirs
Md Geol Surv Topogr Mem — Maryland Geological Survey. Topographical Memoirs
Md Geol Surv Water Resour Basic Data Rep — Maryland. Geological Survey. Water Resources Basic Data Report
MDGFA — Bulletin. Geological Society of Denmark
MDGNO — Mitteilungen der Deutschen Gesellschft fuer Natur- und Voelkerkunde Ostasiens
MDGNOS — Mitteilungen der Deutschen Gesellschft fuer Natur- und Voelkerkunde Ostasiens. Supplement
MDGNVO — Mitteilungen. Deutsche Gesellschaft fuer Natur- und Voelkerkunde Ostasiens
Md Grapevine — Maryland Grapevine
MD G S Sp Pub — Maryland. Geological Survey. Special Publication
MDGV — Mitteilungen der Deutschen Gesellschaft fuer Volkskunde
MD His M — Maryland Historical Magazine
MD Hist — Maryland Historian
MD Hist M — Maryland Historical Magazine
MD Hist Mag — Maryland Historical Magazine
MD Hist Soc Fund-Publ — Maryland Historical Society. Fund-Publications
MdHM — Maryland Historical Magazine
MdI — Memorie. Instituto di Corrispondenza Archeologica
MDI — Mineral Deposit Inventory Database
MDI — Mitteilungen. Deutsches Archaeologische Institut
MDIA — Mitteilungen. Deutsches Institut fuer Aegyptische Altertumskunde
MDIAA — Mitteilungen des Deutschen Archaeologischen Instituts. Abteilung Kairo
MDIAeA — Mitteilungen des Deutschen Instituts fuer Aegyptische Altertumskunde in Kairo
MDIAK — Mitteilungen des Deutschen Archaeologischen Instituts. Abteilung Kairo
MDIGB — Deutsch-Israelitischer Gemeindebund
MDIIDI — Medical Device and Diagnostic Industry
MDIK — Mitteilungen. Deutsches Institut fuer Aegyptische Altertumskunde (Kairo)
MD Int Symp — MD. International Symposia [*New York*]
MDIOME — Mltteilungsblatt. Irgun Olej Merkas Europa
M Disciplina — Musica Disciplina
MD J — M.D. Journal [*Manila*]
MDJ — Middle East Journal
Md Jb — Medizinische Jahrbuecher. Herausgegeben von der K.K. Gesellschaft der Aerzte in Wien
MdJb — Mitteldeutsches Jahrbuch
MDKG — Monographien zur Deutschen Kulturgeschichte
MDKHD — Mukogawa Joshi Daigaku Kiyo. Yakugaku Hen
Md Kl — Materialdienst des Konfessionskundlichen Institts
MDL — Landbouwdocumentatie
M DI — Maanedsskrift for Dyrlaeger
MDL — Materialien zur Deutschen Literatur
MD Law R — Maryland Law Review
Md Laws — Laws of Maryland
MD LF — Maryland Law Forum
M Dlf — Medlemsblad for den Danske Dyrlaegeforening
MDLG — Mitteilungen der Deutschen Landwirtschafts-Gesellschaft
MD Libr — Maryland Libraries
MDLK — Von Missionsdienst der Lutherischen Kirchen
MD LR — Maryland Law Review
MD L Rev — Maryland Law Review
MDM — Manusia dan Masharakat
MDM — Mededelingenblad Bedrijfsorganisatie
MD Mag — Maryland Magazine
MD Med J — Maryland Medical Journal
MD Med J — M.D. Medical Journal [*New York*]
MD Med Newsmag — M.D. Medical Newsmagazine
MD Moebel Decor — MD Moebel + Decoration
MD Nat — Maryland Naturalist

MD Naturalist — Maryland Naturalist
MDNKA — Miyazaki Daigaku Nogakubu. Kenkyu Hokoku
MDNPAR — Direccion General del Inventario Nacional Forestal. Publicacion
MD Nurse — Maryland Nurse
MDNY — MD. Medical Newsmagazine (New York)
MDO — Mitteilungen. Deutsche Orient-Gesellschaft zu Berlin
MDOG — Mitteilungen. Deutsche Orient-Gesellschaft zu Berlin
M Dom — Memorie Domenicane
MDOrG — Mitteilungen der Deutschen Orient Gesellschaft zu Berlin
MDP — Memoires. Delegation en Perse
MDP — Misiones Dominicanas del Peru
MD Pharm — Maryland Pharmacist
MD Poultryman — Maryland Poultryman
Md Poultryman Coop Ext Serv Univ Md — Maryland Poultryman. Cooperative Extension Service. University of Maryland
Md Psychiat Q — Maryland Psychiatric Quarterly
MDPTB — Medical Progress through Technology
MDPV — Mitteilungen und Nachrichten. Deutscher Palaestina-Verein
MDr — Modern Drummer
MD Reg — Maryland Register
MD Regs Code — Code of Maryland Regulations
MDRP — Mackenzie Delta Research Project
MDS — Memoires Presentes par Divers Savants a l'Academie des Inscriptions et Belles-Lettres
MDS — Mitteilungen der Deutscher Schutzgebiet
MdS — Muse des Saitenspiels
MDSAI — Memoires Presentes par Divers Savants a l'Academie des Inscriptions et Belles-Lettres
MDSC — Medical Self-Care
MDSCAD — Medicina nei Secoli
MDSJA — Medical Service Journal
Mdss F Prak Laeg — Manedsskrift for Praktisk Laegegerning
MD State Med J — Maryland State Medical Journal
Md St B Assn Rep — Maryland State Bar Association. Report
Md St Med J — Maryland State Medical Journal
MDTHA — Medicina Thoracalis
Md Tidewat News — Maryland Tidewater News
MDtShG — Mitteilungen. Deutsche Shakespeare-Gesellschaft
MDU — Monatshefte fuer Deutschen Unterricht
Md Univ Agric Exp Stn Annu Rep — Maryland. University. Agrucultural Experiment Station. Annual Report
Md Univ Agric Exp Stn Bull — Maryland. University. Agricultural Experiment Station. Bulletin
Md Water Resour Res Cent Tech Rep — Maryland. Water Resources Research Center. Technical Report
Md Weath Serv — Maryland Weather Service
MDWV — Mitteilungen des Deutschen Weinbauverbandes
MDY — Milieudefensie
ME — Maandschrift Economie
ME — Maine Reports
ME — Marketing in Europe
Me — Meander
Me — Meaning
ME — Medical Economics
ME — Mennonite Encyclopedia
ME — Mensaje
ME — Metis Newsletter. Metis Association of the Northwest Territories
ME — Middle East Series
ME — Monitor Ecclesiasticus
ME — Musikerziehung
MEA — Accountantadviseur
Mea — Meander
MEA — Middle Eastern Affairs
MEA — Miscelanea de Etnologia e Arqueologia
MeAB — Meteorological Abstracts and Bibliography
Me Acts — Acts, Resolves, and Consitutional Resolutions of the State of Maine
MEAD — Proceedings. Conference on Middle East Agriculture. Middle East Supply Centre Agricultural Report
Mead Johnson Symp Perinat Dev Med — Mead Johnson Symposium on Perinatal and Developmental Medicine
MEAH — Miscelanea de Estudios Arabes y Hebraicos
MEAM — Mainake Estudios de Arqueologia Malaguena
Mean — Meanjin
Mean Atmos Press Cloud Air Temp Sea Surf Temp N Pacif Ocean — Mean Atmospheric Pressure, Cloudiness, Air Temperature, and Sea Surface Temperature of the North Pacific Ocean
Meaning Life — Meaning of Life
Meanjin — Meanjin Quarterly
Meanjin Q — Meanjin Quarterly
Mean Sea Surf Temp Anom Chart Wash — Mean Sea Surface Temperature Anomaly Chart. U.S. Navy Hydrographic Office (Washington)
Mean Sea Surf Temp Chart Wash — Mean Sea Surface Temperature Chart. U.S. Navy Hydrographic Office (Washington)
Meas — Measure
Meas & Autom News — Measurement and Automation News
Meas and Control — Measurement and Control
Meas and Insp Technol — Measurement and Inspection Technology
Meas Contr — Measurement and Control
Meas Control — Measurement and Control
Meas Control (1962-64) — Measurement and Control (1962-64)
Meas Eval G — Measurement and Evaluation in Guidance
Meas Focus — Measurement Focus
Meas Insp Technol — Measurement and Inspection Technology
Meas Instrum Rev — Measurement and Instrument Review

Meas J Int Meas Confed — Measurement. Journal of the International Measurement Confederation
Meas Methods Corros Prot Event Eur Fed Corros — Measuring Methods in Corrosion Protection. Event of the European Federation of Corrosion
Measmt & Eval in Guid — Measurement and Evaluation in Guidance
Measmt Control — Measurement and Control
Measmt Tech Pittsb — Measurement Techniques. Instrument Society of America (Pittsburgh)
Measmt Tech Wash — Measurement Techniques (Washington)
Meas Prog Sci Technol Proc IMEKO Congr Int Meas Confed — Measurement for Progress in Science and Technology. Proceedings. IMEKO Congress. International Measurement Confederation
Meas Sci Technol — Measurement Science and Technolgy
Meas Tech — Measurement Techniques
Meas Tech Engl Transl — Measurement Techniques (English Translation)
Meas Tech R — Measurement Techniques (USSR)
Meas Toxic Relat Air Pollut Proc Int Spec Conf — Measurement of Toxic and Related Air Pollutants. Proceedings of an International Specialty Conference
Meat Facts — Meat Facts. A Statistical Summary about America's Largest Food Industry
Meat Ind — Meat Industry
Meat Ind Bul — Meat Industry Bulletin
Meat Ind J — Meat Industry Journal
Meat Ind J Q — Meat Industry Journal of Queensland
Meat Ind Pretoria — Meat Industry (Pretoria)
Meat Ind Res Conf (NZ) — Meat Industry Research Conference (New Zealand)
Meat Ind Res Inst NZ Rep MIRINZ — Meat Industry Research Institute of New Zealand. Report MIRINZ
Meat Marketing in Aust — Meat Marketing in Australia
Meat Mktg — Meat Marketing
Meat Outlk — Meat Outlook
Meat Proc — Meat Processing
Meat Process — Meat Processing
Meat Process Conf Proc — Meat Processing Conference. Proceedings
Meat Prod & Exp — Meat Producer and Exporter
Meat Prod Exporter — Meat Producer and Exporter
Meat Res Inst Memo — Meat Research Institute. Memorandum
Meat Res News Lett — Meat Research News Letter
Meat Sci — Meat Science
Meat Sci Inst Proc — Meat Science Institute. Proceedings
Meat Situat Outlook — Meat. Situation and Outlook
Meat Trades J Aust — Meat Trades Journal of Australia
Me Audubon Soc Bull — Maine Audubon Society Bulletin
MEAVDO — Eidgenoessische Anstalt fuer das Forstliche Versuchswesen. Mitteilungen
MEB — Mededeelingen. Encyclopaedisch Bureau
MEB — Middle East Bulletin
MEB — Missouri English Bulletin
ME Bd Agr An Rp — Maine. Board of Agriculture. Annual Report
MEBEA — Medical Electronics and Biological Engineering
MEBIEP — Monographs in Epidemiology and Biostatistics
MEC — Ministerio de Educacao e Cultura
MEC — Monitor de la Educacion Comun
MEC — Monumenta Epigraphica Christiana
Mecan Electrif Agr — Mecanizarea si Electrificarea Agriculturii
Mecc Agr — Meccanizzazione Agricola
Meccanica J Ital Assoc Theoret Appl Mech — Meccanica. Journal of the Italian Association of Theoretical and Applied Mechanics
Meccanizz Agr For — Meccanizzazione Agraria e Forestale. Riassunti Analitici della Stampa Tecnica
Meccanizz Agric — Meccanizzazione Agricola
Mecc Ital — Meccanica Italiana
Mec Docum — Mecanique Documentation
Mec Elec — Mecanique Electricite
Mec Elect — Mecanique, Electricite
Mec Electr — Mecanique Electricite
Mec Et Elect — Mecanique et Electricite
Mech Age — Mechanical Age
Mech Age D — Mechanisms of Ageing and Development
Mech Ageing Dev — Mechanisms of Ageing and Development
Mech Anal — Mechanics: Analysis
Mech Anesth Action Skeletal Card Smooth Muscle — Mechanisms of Anesthetic Action in Skeletal, Cardiac, and Smooth Muscle
Mechanical Mus — Mechanical Music
Mechanics Mag — Mechanics' Magazine
Mechanik — Mechanik Miesiecznik Naukowo-Techniczny
Mechanika Bydgoszcz Pol — Mechanika (Bydgoszcz, Poland)
Mechanika Opole Pol — Mechanika (Opole, Poland)
Mechanis Hort — Mechanisation in Horticulture
Mechanis Ser Dep Agric Malaya — Mechanisation Series. Department of Agriculture. Malaya
Mechanite Ind — Mechanite in Industry
Mechanite Metal Cast — Mechanite Metal Castings [London]
Mechanix Ill — Mechanix Illustrated [London]
Mechaniz Constr — Mechanization of Construction
Mechaniz Inz Stavb — Mechanizace na Inzenyrskych Stavbach
Mechaniz Labor Consum Heavy Wk — Mechanization of Labor-Consuming and Heavy Work [Washington]
Mechaniz Zemed — Mechanizace Zemedelstvi
Mech Autom Adm — Mechanizace Automatizace Administrativy
Mech Behav Electromagn Solid Continua Proc IUTAM IUPAP Symp — Mechanical Behavior of Electromagnetic Solid Continua. Proceedings. IUTAM (International Union of Theoretical and Applied Mechanics) IUPAP Symposium
Mech Behav Mater — Mechanical Behavior of Materials

Mech Behav Mater Proc Int Conf — Mechanical Behavior of Materials. Proceedings. International Conference on Mechanical Behavior of Materials

Mech Behav Mater Proc Int Conf — Mechanical Behaviour of Materials. Proceedings. International Conference

Mech Behav Mater Struct Microelectron Symp — Mechanical Behavior of Materials and Structures in Microelectronics. Symposium

Mech Behav Mat Proc Symp — Mechanical Behavior of Materials. Proceedings. Symposium on Mechanical Behaviorof Materials

Mech Boy — Mechanical Boy

Mech Cat — Mechanical Catalog</PHR> %

Mech Chem Engng Trans Instn Engrs (Aust) — Mechanical and Chemical Engineering Transactions. Institution of Engineers (Australia)

Mech Chem Eng Trans — Mechanical and Chemical Engineering Transactions

Mech Chem Eng Trans Inst Eng (Aust) — Mechanical and Chemical Engineering Transactions. Institution of Engineers (Australia)

Mech Chem Prum — Mechanizace v Chemickem Prumyslu

Mech Chem Solid Propellants Proc Symp Nav Struct Mech — Mechanics and Chemistry of Solid Propellants. Proceedings. Symposium on Naval Structural Mechanics

Mech Chromosome Distrib Aneuploidy Proc Int Meet Aneuploidy — Mechanisms of Chromosome Distribution and Aneuploidy. Proceedings. International Meeting on Aneuploidy

Mech Cohesive Frict Mater — Mechanics of Cohesive-Frictional Materials

Mech Compos Mater — Mechanics of Composite Materials

Mech Compos Mater Proc Symp Nav Struct Mech — Mechanics of Composite Materials. Proceedings. Symposium on Naval Structural Mechanics

Mech Compos Mater Struct — Mechanics of Composite Materials and Structures

Mech Comput Mech — Mechanics: Computational Mechanics

Mech Contract — Mechanical Contractor

Mech Control Emesis Proc Int Meet — Mechanisms and Control of Emesis. Proceedings. International Meeting

Mech Corros Prop A Key Eng Mater — Mechanical and Corrosion Properties A. Key Engineering Materials

Mech Corros Prop B Single Cryst Prop — Mechanical and Corrosion Properties B. Single Crystal Properties

Mech Crack Growth Proc Natl Symp Fract Mech — Mechanics of Crack Growth. Proceedings. National Symposium on Fracture Mechanics

Mech Des — Mechanical Design

Mech Dev — Mechanics of Development

Mech Dev — Mechanisms of Development

Mechd Fmg — Mechanised Farming [London]

Mech Dig — Mechanical Digest

Mech Dynam Systems — Mechanics: Dynamical Systems

Mech Elastic Stability — Mechanics of Elastic Stability

Mech Eng — Mechanical Engineering

Mech Eng Bull — Mechanical Engineering Bulletin

Mech Eng Contrib Clean Air Proc Conf — Mechanical Engineer's Contribution to Clean Air. Proceedings. Conference

Mech Eng Marcel Dekker — Mechanical Engineering (Marcel Dekker)

Mech Eng News — Mechanical Engineering News

Mech Eng News (Washington DC) — Mechanical Engineering News (Washington, DC)

Mech Engng — Mechanical Engineering

Mech Engng Bull — Mechanical Engineering Bulletin

Mech Engng Educ Bull — Mechanical Engineering Education Bulletin. Manchester College of Technology

Mech Engng Elect Engng — Mechanical Engineering and Electrical Engineering

Mech Engng J — Mechanical Engineering Journal

Mech Engng News — Mechanical Engineering News

Mech Engng Note Aeronaut Res Labs Aust — Mechanical Engineering Note. Aeronautical Research Laboratories. Australia

Mech Engng Rep Natn Res Coun Can — Mechanical Engineering Report. National Research Council. Canada

Mech Engng Res — Mechanical Engineering Research [Edinburgh, London]

Mech Engng Ser Engng Exp Stn Ariz — Mechanical Engineering Series. Engineering Experiment Station. Arizona

Mech Engng Tech Memor Aeronaut Res Labs Aust — Mechanical Engineering Technical Memorandum. Aeronautical Research Laboratories. Australia

Mech Eng Note Aust Aeronaut Res Lab — Mechanical Engineering Note. Australia. Aeronautical Research Laboratories

Mech Engr — Mechanical Engineer

Mech Eng Rep Aust Aeronaut Res Lab — Mechanical Engineering Report (Australia). Aeronautical Research Laboratories

Mech Eng Rep MP Natl Res Counc Can Div Mech Eng — Mechanical Engineering Report MP. National Research Council of Canada. Divisionof Mechanical Engineering

Mech Eng Rep MS Natl Res Counc Can Div Mech Eng — Mechanical Engineering Report MS. National Research Council Canada. Division of Mechanical Engineering

Mech Engrg — Mechanical Engineering

Mech Engrg Res Stud — Mechanical Engineering Research Studies

Mech Engrg Ser — Mechanical Engineering Series

Mech Engrs Pock Bk — Mechanical Engineers' Pocket Book

Mech Eng Sci Monogr — Mechanical Engineering Science Monograph. Institution of Mechanical Engineers

Mech Eng Technol — Mechanical Engineering Technology

Mech Eng (Tokyo) — Mechanical Engineering (Tokyo)

Mech Eng Tokyo — Mechanical Engineer (Tokyo)

Mech Eng Trans Inst Eng (Aust) — Mechanical Engineering Transactions. Institution of Engineers (Australia)

Mechenye At Issled Pitan Rast Primen Udobr Tr Soveshch — Mechenye Atomy v Issledovaniyakh Pitaniya Rastenii i Primeneniya Udobrenii Trudy Soveshchaniya

Mechenye Biol Atk Veshchestva — Mechenye Biologicheski Atkivnye Veshchestva

Mech Failures Prev Group Meet — Mechanical Failures Prevention Group. Meeting

Mech Fibre Carcinog — Mechanisms in Fibre Carcinogenesis

Mech Fluids Transp Process — Mechanics of Fluids and Transport Processes

Mech Handl — Mechanical Handling

Mech Illus — Mechanix Illustrated

Mech Inorg Organomet React — Mechanisms of Inorganic and Organometallic Reactions

Mech Intest Adapt Proc Int Conf — Mechanisms of Intestinal Adaptation. Proceedings. International Conference on Intestinal Adaptation

Mech Leafl GB Min Agr Fish Food — Mechanisation Leaflet. Great Britain Ministry of Agriculture, Fisheries, and Food

Mech Lymphocyte Act Immune Regul 3 — Mechanisms of Lymphocyte Activation and Immune Regulation 3. Developmmental Biology of Lymphocytes

Mech Lymphocyte Act Proc Int Leucocyte Conf — Mechanisms of Lymphocyte Activation. Proceedings. International Leucocyte Conference

Mech Mach T — Mechanism and Machine Theory

Mech Mach Theory — Mechanism and Machine Theory

Mech Mater — Mechanics of Materials

Mech Math Methods Ser Handbooks Ser I Comput Methods Mech — Mechanics and Mathematical Methods. Series of Handbooks. Series I. Computational Methods in Mechanics

Mech Math Methods Ser Handbooks Ser III Acoust Electromagnet — Mechanics and Mathematical Methods. Series of Handbooks. Series III. Acoustic, Electromagnetic, and Elastic Wave Scattering

Mech Miesiecznik Nauk-Tech — Mechanik Miesiecznik Naukowo-Techniczny

Mech Mies Nauk Tech — Mechanik Miesiecznik Naukowo-Techniczny

Mech Mol Migr — Mechanisms of Molecular Migrations

Mech of Fracture — Mechanics of Fracture

Mech Photosynth Proc Int Congr Biochem — Mechanism of Photosynthesis. Proceedings. International Congress of Biochemistry

Mech Polim — Mechanika Polimerov

Mech Polym Degrad Stab — Mechanisms of Polymer Degradation and Stabilisation [monograph]

Mech Practice — Mechanics and Practice. Lixue Yu Shijian

Mech Princ Enzyme Act — Mechanistic Principles of Enzyme Activity

Mech Prog — Mechanical Progress

Mech Prop Cast Met Works Conf Theory Cast — Mechanical Properties of Cast Metal. Works. Conference on the Theory of Casting

Mech Prop Eng Ceram Proc Conf — Mechanical Properties of Engineering Ceramics. Proceedings. Conference

Mech Prop High Rates Strain Proc Conf — Mechanical Properties at High Rates of Strain. Proceedings. Conference. Mechanical Properties of Materials at High Rates of Strain

Mech React Sulfur Comp — Mechanisms of Reactions of Sulfur Compounds

Mech React Sulfur Compd — Mechanisms of Reactions of Sulfur Compounds

Mech Recent Adv Ther Hypertens Int Symp Nephrol — Mechanisms and Recent Advances in Therapy of Hypertension. International Symposium on Nephrology

Mech Recomb Proc Biol Div Res Conf — Mechanisms in Recombination. Proceedings. Biology Division Research Conference

Mech Res Comm — Mechanics Research Communications

Mech Res Commun — Mechanics Research Communications

Mech Roln — Mechanizacja Rolnictwa

Mech Sci — Mechanical Sciences

Mech Sci — Mechanical Sciences. Mashinovdeniye

Mech Solids — Mechanics of Solids

Mech Solids Engl Transl — Mechanics of Solids (English Translation)

Mech Struct Mach — Mechanics of Structures and Machines

Mech Structures Mach — Mechanics of Structures and Machines

Mech Surface Structures — Mechanics of Surface Structures

Mech Symptom Form Proc Congr Int Coll Psychosom Med — Mechanisms in Symptom Formation. Proceedings. Congress. International College of Psychosomatic Medicine

Mech Syst Signal Processing — Mechanical Systems and Signal Processing

Mech Technol Budowy Masz (Bydgoszcz Pol) — Mechanika, Technologia Budowy Maszyn (Bydgoszcz, Poland)

Mech Teoret Stos — Polskie Towarzystwo Mechaniki Teoretycznej i Stosowana

Mech Teor i Stoso — Mechanika Teoretyczna i Stosowana

Mech Teor i Stosow — Mechanika Teoretyczna i Stosowana

Mech Tests Bitum Mixes Proc Int Symp — Mechanical Tests for Bituminous Mixes. Characterization, Design, and Quality Control. Proceedings. International Symposium

Mech Top — Mechanical Topics

Mech Tox — Mechanisms of Toxicity

Mech Tox Action Some Target Organs Proc Eur Soc Toxicol Meet — Mechanism of Toxic Action on Some Target Organs. Proceedings. European Society of Toxicology Meeting

Mech Tox Metab — Mechanisms of Toxicity and Metabolism

Mech Transl — Mechanical Translation [Cambridge, Massachusetts]

Mech Tumor Promot — Mechanisms of Tumor Promotion

Mech Weld Engr — Mechanical and Welding Engineer [Melbourne]

Mech Wld Engng Rec — Mechanical World and Engineering Record

Mech Wld Monogr — Mechanical World Monographs [Manchester]

Mech Wld Yb — Mechanical World Yearbook [Manchester]

Mech Work Steel Process — Mechanical Working and Steel Processing

Mech Work Steel Process Conf Proc — Mechanical Working and Steel Processing. Conference Proceedings

Mech World Eng Rec — Mechanical World and Engineering Record

Mech Zesz Nauk Politech Krakow — Mechanika, Zeszyty Naukowe Politechniki Krakowskiej

Mec Ind — Mecanique et Industrie

Meckel Arch — Archiv fuer Anatomie und Physiologie. Meckel

Mecklenb Landw Mitt — Mecklenburgische Landwirtschaftliche Mitteilungen

Mecklenb Landw Wbl — Mecklenburgische Landwirtschaftliche Wochenblatt

Mecklenb Landw Ztg — Mecklenburgische Landwirtschaftliche Zeitung

Mecklenb Zeitsch F Rechtspfl Rechtswiss Verwaltung — Mecklenburgische Zeitschrift fuer Rechtspflege, Rechtswissenschaft, Verwaltung
Meckl Vr Nt Arch — Archiv des Vereins der Freunde der Naturgeschichte in Mecklenburg
Meckl Z — Mecklenburgische Zeitschrift fuer Rechtspflege und Rechtswissenschaft
MECM — Materiales para el Estudio de la Clase Media en la America Latina [*Washington*]
Mec-Mat-Elec — Mecanique- Materiaux- Electricite
Mec Mater Electr — Mecanique- Materiaux- Electricite
Mecmuasi Univ Fen Fak (Istanbul) — Mecmuasi Universite. Fen Fakulte (Istanbul)
Mecn Conduct — Mecanicien Conducteur
Mecn Mod — Mecanicien Moderne
Mec Nouv — Mecanique Nouvelle
Mecon J — Mecon Journal
Mec Phys — Mecanique-Physique
Mec Pneumopathies Prof Conf GERP — Mecanismes des Pneumopathies Professionelles. Conference GERP
Mec Roches — Mecanique des Roches
Mec Rur — Mecanique Rurale
Mec Rur Mach Agric Mod — Mecanique Rurale et la Machine Agricole Moderne
MED — Marketing and Media Decisions
Med — Mediations. Revue des Expressions Contemporaines
Med — Medica
MEd — Medical Education
Med — Medico
Med — Mediterranean
Med — Mediterraneo
MED — Middle English Dictionary
M Ed — Monde de l'Education
Med A — Medical Annual
Med A — Medicinsk Arbog
Med Abstr — Medical Abstract Service
Med Abstr Chengtu — Medical Abstracts. Chinese Medical Journal (Chengtu)
Med Abstr J — Medical Abstracts Journal
Med Abstr Philad — Medical Abstracts (Philadelphia)
Med Abstr Rev Shanghai — Medical Abstracts and Reviews (Shanghai)
Med Accid Trav — Medecine des Accidents du Travail
Med Actual — Medicamentos de Actualidad
Med Actuelle — Medecine Actuelle
Med Adv — Medical Advance
Med Advis — Medical Adviser
Med Advoc — Medical Advocate
MedAe — Medium Aevum
Med Aero — Medecine Aeronautique
Med Aeronaut — Medecine Aeronautique
Med Aeronaut Spat Med Subaquat Hyperbare — Medecine Aeronautique et Spatiale, Medecine Subaquatique et Hyperbare
MedAev — Medium Aevum
Med Aevum — Medium Aevum
Med Aevum Quotidianum — Medium Aevum Quotidianum
Med Aff — Medical Affairs
Med Afr Noire — Medecine d'Afrique Noire
Med Age — Medical Age
Med Agric Reg — Medical and Agricultural Register
Med Aktuell — Medizin Aktuell
Med Ak Wet — Mededeelingen der Koninklijke Nederlandse Akademie van Wetenschappen. AfdeelingLetterkunde
Med All Rev — Medical Alliance Review
Med An — Medicinski Anali
Med and Biol Eng — Medical and Biological Engineering [*Later, Medical and Biological Engineering and Computing*]
Med and Biol Eng and Comput — Medical and Biological Engineering and Computing
Med and Comp — Medicine and Computer
Med & Human — Medievalia et Humanistica
Med & Law — Medicine and Law
Med and Phil Comment — Medical and Philosophical Commentaries
Med & Rin — Medioevo e Rinascimento
Med and Sci Sport — Medicine and Science in Sports and Exercise
Med and Surg Monit — Medical and Surgical Monitor
Med & Uman — Medioevo e Umanesimo
Med Anecdot Hist Litt — Medecine Anecdotique, Historique, Litteraire
Medan Ilmu Penget — Medan Ilmu Pengetahuan
Medan Ilmu Pengetahuan Madj Filsafat — Medan Ilmu Pengetahuan Madjalak Filsafat, Ilmu, Ilmu Sosial, Budaja, Pasti dan Alam
Med Ann — Medical Annals
Med Ann DC — Medical Annals of the District of Columbia
Med Ann Distr Columbia — Medical Annals of the District of Columbia
Med Annu — Medical Annual
Med Anthro — Medical Anthropology
Med Anthro Newsl — Medical Anthropology Newsletter
Med Anthrop — Medical Anthropology
Med Anthropol — Medical Anthropology
Med Anthropol Newsletter — Medical Anthropology Newsletter
Med Anthropol Q — Medical Anthropology Quarterly
Med Anthrop Q — Medical Anthropology Quarterly
Med Arb — Medicinsk Arbog
Med Arch — Medicinskij Archiv
Med Arch — Medieval Archaeology
Med Archaeol — Medieval Archaeology
Med Arch Sarajevo — Medical Archives (Sarajevo)
Med Arch Wien Oesterreich Unter Der Enns — Medicinisches Archiv von Wien und Oesterreich unter der Enns
Med Arena — Medical Arena [*Kansas City*]
Med Arh — Medicinski Arhiv

Med Arhiv — Medicinski Arhiv
Med Arkh — Meditsinski Arkhiv
Med Armees — Medecine et Armees
Med Aromat Plants Ind Profiles — Medicinal and Aromatic Plants. Industrial Profiles
Med Art — Medical Art
Med Arts Sci — Medical Arts and Sciences
Med Aspects Drug Abuse — Medical Aspects of Drug Abuse
Med Aspects Exercise Test Train — Medical Aspects of Exercise Testing and Training
Med Aspects Hum Sex — Medical Aspects of Human Sexuality
Med Ass — Zeitschrift fuer Medizinstudenten und Assistenten
Med Assn State Ala Trans — Medical Association. State of Alabama. Transactions
Med Assoc State Ala J — Medical Association of the State of Alabama. Journal
Med Audiovision — Medecine et Audiovision
Med Avh Univ Bergen — Medisinske Avhandlinger. Universitet i Bergen
Med (B) — Medicina (Bogota)
MedBer Wuertt — Medizinalberichte von Wuerttemberg
Med Biblphies — Medical Bibliographies [*Columbia College. New York*]
Med Biochem — Medical Biochemistry
Med Bio Eng — Medical and Biological Engineering [*Later, Medical and Biological Engineering and Computing*]
Med Bio Ill — Medical and Biological Illustration
Med Biol — Medecine et Biologie
Med Biol — Medical Biology
Med Biol Appl Mass Spectrom Proc Symp — Medical and Biological Application of Mass Spectrometry. Proceedings. Symposium
Med Biol Aspects Energ Space Symp — Medical and Biological Aspects of the Energies of Space. Symposium
Med Biol Eff Light — Medical and Biological Effects of Light
Med Biol Eng — Medical and Biological Engineering [*Later, Medical and Biological Engineering and Computing*]
Med Biol Eng Comput — Medical and Biological Engineering and Computing
Med Biol Engng — Medical and Biological Engineering [*Later, Medical and Biological Engineering and Computing*]
Med Biol Environ — Medecine, Biologie, Environnement
Med Biol (Helsinki) — Medical Biology (Helsinki)
Med Biol Illus — Medical and Biological Illustration
Med Biol Illustr — Medical Biology Illustrations
Med Biol Inf — Mediko Biologicheskaya Informatsiya
Med Biol Probl — Mediko-Biologichni Problemi
Med Biol (Tokyo) — Medicine and Biology (Tokyo)
Med Biol Zh — Mediko-Biologicheskii Zhurnal
Med Biul — Meditsinskii Biulleten
Med Bl — Medizinische Blaetter
Med Bl Wien — Medizinische Blaetter. Wochenschrift fuer die Gesamte Heilkunde (Wien)
Med Bohringer Eur — Medico Bohringer. Europa
Med Bookm Hist — Medical Bookman and Historian
Med Brief — Medical Brief
Med Bull — Medical Bulletin
Med Bull Am Red Cross Soc — Medical Bulletin. American Red Cross Society
Med Bull Bombay — Medical Bulletin (Bombay)
Med Bull Cornell Univ — Medical Bulletin. Cornell University Medical College
Med Bull Cow & Gate — Medical Bulletin of Cow and Gate, Ltd
Med Bull Eur Commd US Army — Medical Bulletin of the European Command. U.S. Army
Med Bull Exxon Corp Affil Co — Medical Bulletin. Exxon Corporation and Affiliated Companies
Med Bull Fukuoka Univ — Medical Bulletin. Fukuoka University
Med Bull Istanbul Fac Med Istanbul Univ — Medical Bulletin. Istanbul Faculty of Medicine. Istanbul University
Med Bull Istanbul Med Fac — Medical Bulletin. Istanbul Medical Faculty
Med Bull Istanbul Med Fac Istanbul Univ — Medical Bulletin. Istanbul Medical Faculty. Istanbul University
Med Bull Istanbul Univ — Medical Bulletin. Istanbul University
Med Bull Kuala Lumpur — Medical Bulletin (Kuala Lumpur)
Med Bull May & Baker — Medical Bulletin. May and Baker [*Dagenham*]
Med Bull Natl Med Cent (Seoul) — Medical Bulletin. National Medical Center (Seoul)
Med Bull No Virginia — Medical Bulletin of Northern Virginia
Med Bull NY Univ Coll Med — Medical Bulletin. New York University College of Medicine
Med Bull Providence Hosp (Southfield Mich) — Medical Bulletin. Providence Hospital (Southfield, Michigan)
Med Bull Standard Oil Co — Medical Bulletin. Standard Oil Company
Med Bull Stand Oil Co (NJ) Affil Co — Medical Bulletin. Standard Oil Company (New Jersey) and Affiliated Companies
Med Bull Univ Cincinnati — Medical Bulletin. University of Cincinnati
Med Bull Univ Toronto — Medical Bulletin. University of Toronto
Med Bull (US Army) — Medical Bulletin (United States Army)
Med Bull US Army (Eur) — Medical Bulletin. US Army (Europe)
Med Bull Vet Adm — Medical Bulletin. Veterans Administration
Med Bull Veterans Adm US — Medical Bulletin. Veterans Administration (United States)
Med Bull Wash Univ — Medical Bulletin of Washington University
Med Bur — Medical Bureau [*Calcutta*]
Med Bydr — Mediese Bydraes
Med Bydraes — Mediese Bydraes
Med Care — Medical Care
Med Care Res Rev — Medical Care Research and Review
Med Care Rev — Medical Care Review
Med Cent J Univ Mich — Medical Center Journal. University of Michigan
Med Century — Medical Century
Med Chem — Medicinal Chemistry

Med Chem (Academic Press) — Medicinal Chemistry (Academic Press). A Series of Monographs

Med Chem Adv Proc Int Symp — Medicinal Chemistry Advances. Proceedings. International Symposium on MedicinalChemistry

Med Chem (Leverkusen Ger) — Medizin und Chemie (Leverkusen, Germany)

Med Chem Proc Int Symp — Medicinal Chemistry. Proceedings. International Symposium on Medicinal Chemistry

Med Chem Proc Int Symp Main Lect — Medicinal Chemistry. Proceedings. International Symposium on Medicinal Chemistry. Main Lectures

Med Chem Res — Medicinal Chemistry Research

Med Chem Ser Monogr — Medicinal Chemistry: A Series of Monographs

Med Chem Ser Rev — Medicinal Chemistry: A Series of Reviews

Med Chem Spec Contrib Int Symp — Medicinal Chemistry. Special Contributions. International Symposium on Medicinal Chemistry

Med Chem (Wiley) — Medicinal Chemistry (Wiley)

Med Chien — Medecine du Chien

Med Chir — Medecine et Chirurgie

Med Chir Dig — Medecine et Chirurgie Digestives

Med Chir J R — Medico-Chirurgical Journal and Review

Med Chir Zeitung — Medicinisch-Chirurgische Zeitung

Med Chron — Medical Chronicle

Med Cir — Medicina y Cirugia

Med Cir Bogota — Medicina y Cirurgia (Bogota)

Med Cir Farm — Medicina, Cirugia, Farmacia

Med Cir Gu — Medicina y Cirugia de Guerra

Med Cir Lisbon — Medicina and Cirurgia (Lisbon)

Med Cirugia Pharm — Medicina, Cirugia, Pharmacia

Med Cir Zootech — Medicina y Cirurgia Zootechnicas

Med Class — Medical Classics [*Baltimore*]

Med Clin — Medicina Clinica

Med Clin Barcelona — Medicina Clinica (Barcelona)

Med Clin Chicago — Medical Clinics of Chicago

Med Clin Exp — Medecine Clinique et Experimentale

Med Clinics No Am — Medical Clinics of North America

Med Clin NA — Medical Clinics of North America

Med Clin N Am — Medical Clinics of North America

Med Clin North Am — Medical Clinics of North America

Med Clin Rep Elsie Inglis Meml Matern Hosp — Medical and Clinical Report. Elsie Inglis Memorial Maternity Hospital

Med Clin Rep Natn Matern Hosp Dubl — Medical and Clinical Report. National Maternity Hospital (Dublin)

Med Clin Rep R Wom Hosp Melb — Medical and Clinical Report of the Royal Women's Hospital. Melbourne

Med Clin Rep Simpson Meml Matern Pav R Infirm Edinb — Medical and Clinical Report. Simpson Memorial Maternity Pavilion. Royal Infirmary (Edinburgh)

Med Clins Chicago — Medical Clinics of Chicago

Med Clin Sper — Medicina Clinica e Sperimentale

Med Colon — Medicina Colonial

Med Colon (Madr) — Medicina Colonial (Madrid)

Med Commun — Medical Communications

Med Commun Mass Med Soc — Medical Communications. Massachusetts Medical Society

Med Comp J — Medical Computer Journal

Med Cond — Medico Condotto

Med Condotto — Medico Condotto

Med Consensus — Medical Consensus

Med Consult New Remedies — Medical Consultation and New Remedies

Med Cont — Medicina Contemporanea

Med Contact — Medisch Contact

Med Contemp — Medecine Contemporaine. Journal de l'Hydrotherapie

Med Contemp — Medicina Contemporanea

Med Contemp (Lisbon) — Medicina Contemporanea (Lisbon)

Med Contemp Naples — Medicina Contemporanea (Naples)

Med Contemp Turin — Medicina Contemporanea (Turin)

Med Convers Bl — Medizinisches Conversationsblatt

Med Cor-Bl Bayer Aerzte — Medizinisches Correspondenz-Blatt Bayerischer Aerzte

Med Cor-Bl Rhein u Westfael Aerzte — Medizinisches Correspondenz-Blatt Rheinischer und Westfaelischer Aerzte

Med Cor-Bl Wuerttemb Aerztl Landesver — Medizinisches Correspondenz-Blatt. Wuerttembergischer Aerztliche Landesverein

Med Cor-Bl Wuerttemb Aerztl Ver — Medizinisches Correspondenz-Blatt. Wuerttembergischer Aerztliche Verein

Med Cosmetol — Medical Cosmetology

Med Counterpoint — Medical Counterpoint

Med Crit — Medical Critic

Med Crit Guide — Medical Critic and Guide

Med Cult — Medicina e Cultura

Med Cult (Milan) — Medicina e Cultura (Milan)

Med Cut — Medicina Cutanea [*Later, Medicina Cutanea Ibero-Latino-Americana*]

Med Cutanea — Medicina Cutanea [*Later, Medicina Cutanea Ibero-Latino-Americana*]

Med Cutan Iber Lat Am — Medicina Cutanea Ibero-Latino-Americana

Med C Virg — Medical College of Virginia. Quarterly

Medd Abo Akad Geol Mineral Inst — Meddelanden fran Abo Akademis Geologisk-Mineralogiska Institut

Medd Alnarpsinst Mejeriavd Statens Mejerifoers — Meddelande fran Alnarpsinstitutets Mejeriavdelning och Statens Mejerifoersoek

Med Dames — Medecine des Dames

Medd Avd Ekol Bot Lunds Univ — Meddelanden fran Avdelningen foer Ekologisk Botanik Lunds Universitet

Medd Biotek Inst ATV Afd Bioteknol — Meddelelser fra Bioteknisk Institut. ATV (Akademiet for de Tekniske Videnskaber) Afdelingen for Bioteknologi

MeddBl Arb Fagl Landsorg Krist — Meddelelsesblad. Utgit av Arbeidernes Faglige Landsorganisation (Kristiania)

Medd Carlsberg Lab — Meddelelser fra Carlsberg Laboratorium

Medd Centralanst Foersoeksvaes Jordbruksomraadet — Meddelande fraan Centralanstalten foer Foersoeksvaesendet paa Jordbruksomraadet

Medd Centralstyr Malmohus Lans Forsoks-Vaxtskyddsringar — Meddelande fran Centralstyrelsen foer Malmoehus Laens Foersoeksoch Vaxtskyddsringar

Medd Dan Fisk Havunders — Meddelelser fra Danmarks Fiskfri-og Havundersogelser

Medd Dan Geol Foren — Meddelelser fra Dansk Geologisk Forening

Medd Dansk Geol Forend — Meddelanden fra Dansk Geologiske Forendlingen

Med Decision Making — Medical Decision Making

Med Decis Making — Medical Decision Making

Meddeland Lantbruksakad Traedgardsavd — Meddelande. Lantbruksakademiens Traedgardsavdelningen

Meddeland Lunds Bot Mus — Meddelanden fran Lunds Botaniska Museum

Meddeland Statens Vaextskyddsanst — Meddelande. Statens Vaextskyddsanstalt

Meddel Carlsberg Lab — Meddelelser fra Carlsberg Latoratoriet

Meddelser NCG — Meddelelser fra Ny Carlsberg Glyptotek

Meddelels Krigsarch — Meddelelser fra Krigs-Archiverne

Meddel Goeteborgs Bot Trad — Acta Horti Gothoburgensis. Meddelanden fran Goeteborgs Botaniska Traedgard

Meddel Goeteborgs Bot Traedg — Acta Horti Gothoburgensis. Meddelanden fran Goeteborgs Botaniska Traedgard

Meddel Komm Byggn — Meddelanden fran Statens Kommitte foer Byggnadsforskning

Meddel Lund — Meddelande fran Lunds Universitet Historiska Museum

Meddel Lund — Meddelanden fran Lunds Universitets Historiska Museum

Meddel Lunds U Hist Mus — Meddelanden fra Lunds Universitets Historiska Museum

Meddel Lund U Hist Mus — Meddelande fran Lunds Universitet Historiska Museum

Meddel Ny Carlsberg — Meddelelser fra Ny Carlsberg

Meddel om Gronland — Meddelelser om Groenland

Meddel Skogsfoers Anst — Meddelanden fran Statens Skogsfoersoeksanstalt

Meddel Thorvaldsens Mus — Meddelelser fra Thorvaldsens Museum

Med Dent J — Medical/Dental Journal

Med Dent Jnl — Medical-Dental Journal

Med Dent Mater — Medical and Dental Materials

Med Device & Diagn Ind — Medical Device and Diagnostic Industry

Medd F Arh St — Meddelelser fra Arhus Stift

Medd Geod Inst (Den) — Meddelelse. Geodaetisk Institut (Denmark)

Medd Goeteborgs Bot Traedg — Acta Horti Gothoburgensis. Meddelanden fran Goeteborgs Botaniska Traedgard

Medd Goeteborgs Bot Traedg — Meddelanden fran Goeteborgs Botaniska Traedgaard

Medd Grafiska Forskningslab — Meddelande. Grafiska Forskningslaboratoriet

Medd Groenl — Meddelelser om Groenland

Medd Groenland — Meddelelser om Groenland

Medd Groenl Geosci — Meddelelser om Groenland. Geoscience

Medd Gronl — Meddelelser om Groenland

Medd Havsfiskelab Lysekil — Meddelande fran Havsfiskelaboratoriet Lysekil

Medd Hermetikkind Lab — Meddelelse fra Hermetikkindustriens Laboratorium

Med Dial — Medical Dial

Med Dig Bombay — Medical Digest (Bombay)

Med Dig Lond — Medical Digest (London)

Med Dig Tokyo — Medical Digest (Tokyo)

Med Dig Winnetka — Medical Digest (Winnetka)

Med Dimensions — Medical Dimensions

Medd Ind Centrallab Helsinki — Meddelanden fran Industrins Centrallaboratorium., Helsinki

Medd Inst Maltdrycksforsk — Meddelande fran Institutet foer Maltdrycksforskning

Medd Inst Tek Kemi Aabo Akad — Meddelanden fraan Institutionen foer Teknisk Kemi. Aabo Akademi

Med Dir Tuinb — Mededelingen. Directeur van de Tuinbouw

Medd Jordbrukste Inst — Meddelande-Jordbruksteknisk Institutet

Medd K Lantbruksakad Ekon Avd — Meddelande fraan Kungliga Lantbruksakademiens Ekonomiska Avdelning

Medd K Lantbruksakad Tek Avd — Meddelande fraan Kungliga Lantbruksakademiens Tekniska Avdelning

Medd K Lantbruksakad Traedgaardsavd — Meddelande fraan Kungliga Lantbruksakademiens Traedgaardsavdelning

Medd K Lantbruksakad Vetenskapsavd — Meddelande fraan Kungliga Lantbruksakademiens Vetenskapsavdelning

Medd K Lantbruksstyr — Meddelande fraan Kungliga Lantbruksstyrelsen

Medd K Lantbruksstyr Ser A — Meddelanden. Kungliga Lantbruksstyrelsen. Serie A. Allmaent

Medd K Lantbruksstyr Ser B — Meddelanden. Kungliga Lantbruksstyrelsen. Serie B. Landbruksavdelningen

Medd Komm Dan Fisk Havunders Ser Fisk — Meddelelser fra Kommissionen for Danmarks Fiskeri- og Havundersoegelser. Serie Fiskeri

Medd Komm Dan Fisk Havunders Ser Hydrogr — Meddelelser fra Kommissionen for Danmarks Fiskeri- og Havundersoegelser. Serie Hydrografi

Medd Komm Dan Fisk Havunders Ser Plankton — Meddelelser fra Kommissionen for Danmarks Fiskeri- og Havundersoegelser. Serie Plankton

Medd Komm Havunders Ser Fisk — Meddelelser fra Kommissionen for Havundersoegelser. Serie Fiskeri

Medd Komm Havunders Ser Hydrogr — Meddelelser fra Kommissionen for Havundersoegelser. Serie Hydrografti

Medd Komm Havunders Ser Plankton — Meddelelser fra Kommissionen for Havundersoegelser. Serie Plankton

Medd K Vetenskapsakad Nobelinst — Meddelanden fraan Kungliga Vetenskapsakademiens Nobelinstitut

Medd Kvismare Fagelstn — Meddelande fran Kvismare Fagelstation

Medd Lantbruksstyr — Meddelanden - Lantbruksstyrelsen

Medd Luftfoersvarsfoeren Malmoe — Meddelanden fran Malmoe Luftfoersvarsfoerening

Medd Lunds Geol Mineral Inst — Meddelanden fran Lunds Geologisk-Mineralogiska Institut

Medd Lunds Mineral Geol Inst — Meddelanden fran Lunds Mineralogisk-Geologiska Institution

Medd Lunds Univ Hist Mus — Meddelande fran Lunds Universitet Historiska Museum

Meddn Agrikekon ForsAnst Finl — Meddelanden fran Agrikulturekonomiska Forsoksanstalten i Finland

Meddn Agron For Helsingf — Meddelanden fran Agronomiska Forening (Helsingfors)

Meddn Alnarps Lantbr Mejeri TradgInst — Meddelanden. Alnarps Lantbruks-, Mejeri-, och Tradgardsinstitut

Meddn Alnarps Tradg ForsVerks — Meddelanden fran Alnarps Tradgardars Forsoksverksamhet

Meddn Astr Obs Upps — Meddelanden fran Astronomiske Observatorium. Uppsala

Meddn Cent Anst ForsVas JordbrOmrdd Stockh — Meddelanden fran Centralanstalten for Forsoksvasendet pa Jordbruksomradet (Stockholm)

Meddn Elekt StandardKomm Stockh — Meddelanden. Elektriska Standardiseringskommitten (Stockholm)

Meddn Finl UtsadFor — Meddelanden fran Finlands Utsadesforening

Meddn Finska KemSamf — Meddelanden fran Finska Kemistsamfundet

Meddn Finska Skogsv For Tapio — Meddelanden Utgifna af Finska Skogsvards Forenigen Tapio

Meddn Flyg O Navmed Namnd — Meddelanden fran Flyg- och Navalmedicinska Namnden

Meddn Flygtek ForsAnst — Meddelanden. Flygtekniska Forsoksanstalten

Meddn For Vaxtforadl Frukttrad — Meddelanden. Foreningen for Vaxtforadling av Frukttrad

Meddn For Vaxtforadl Skogstrad — Meddelanden af Foreningen for Vaxtforadling av Skogstrad

Meddn Geogr For Finl — Meddelanden af Geografiska Foreningen i Finland

Meddn Geogr For Goteborg — Meddelanden fran Geografiska Foreningen i Goteborg

Meddn Geogr Inst Stockh Hogsk — Meddelanden fran Geografiska Institutet vid Stockholms Hogskola

Meddn Hydrogr Byr Helsingf — Meddelanden fran Hydrografiska Byran (Helsingfors)

Meddn Hydrogr Byr Stockh — Meddelanden fran Hydrografiska Byran (Stockholm)

Meddn Ind CentLab Helsinki — Meddelanden fran Industriens Centrallaboratorium (Helsinki)

Meddn IndStyr Finl — Meddelanden fran Industristyrelsen i Finland

Meddn IngVetenskAkad — Meddelanden fran Ingeniorsvetenskapsakademi

Meddn Insp Fisk Finl — Meddelanden fran Inspektoren for Fiskerierna i Finland

Meddn Inst Husdjursforadl — Meddelanden fran Institutet for Husdjursforadling

Meddn Instn Brobyggn — Meddelanden. Institutionen for Brobyggnad

Meddn JordbrDep Stockh — Meddelanden. Jordbruksdepartement (Stockholm)

Meddn Jordbrtek For Upps — Meddelanden fran Jordbrukstekniska Foreningen (Uppsala)

Meddn Jordbrtek Inst Upps — Meddelanden. Jordbrukstekniska Institutet (Uppsala)

Meddn K LantbrAkad Ekon Avd — Meddelanden fran Kunliga Lantbruksakademiens Ekonomiska Avdelning

Meddn K LantbrAkad TradgAvd — Meddelanden fran Kunliga Lantbruksakademiens Tradgardsavdelning

Meddn K LantbrAkad VetenskAvd — Meddelanden fran Kunliga Lantbruksakademiens Vetenskapsavdelning

Meddn K Lantbrhogsk Lantbrfors Jordbrfors — Meddelanden fran Kungliga Lantbrukshogskolan och [Statens] Lantbruksforsok Jordbruksforsok

Meddn K LantbrStyr — Meddelanden fran Kunliga Lantbruksstyrelsen

Meddn K Svenska VetenskAkad Nobelinst — Meddelanden fran Kunliga Svenska Vetenskapsakademiens Nobelinstitut

Meddn K Tek Hogsk MaterProfnAnst — Meddelanden fran Kunliga Tekniska Hogskolans Materialprofningsanstalt

Meddn Landtm — Meddelanden till Landtman

Meddn LantbrHogsk HusdjursforsAnst Norrtalje — Meddelanden fran Lantbrukshogskolans Husdjursforsoksanstalten (Norrtalje)

Meddn LantbrHogsk JordbrForsAnst Norrtalje — Meddelanden fran Lantbrukshogskolans Jordbruksforsoksanstalten (Norrtalje)

Meddn Lunds Astr Obs — Meddelanden fran Lunds Astronomiska Observatorium

Meddn Lunds Bot Mus — Meddelanden fran Lunds Botaniska Museum

Meddn Lunds Geogr Instn — Meddelanden fran Lunds Geografiska Institution

Meddn Lunds Geol Faltklub — Meddelanden fran Lunds Geologiska Faltklub

Meddn Lunds Geol Miner Instn — Meddelanden fran Lunds Geologisk-Mineralogiska Institution

Meddn Lunds Univ Limnol Instn — Meddelanden fran Lunds Universitets Limnologiska Institution

Meddn Lunds Univ Mat Semin — Meddelanden fran Lunds Universitets Matematiska Seminarium

Meddn Maria Sjukhus Med Avd — Meddelanden fran Maria Sjukhus Medicinska Avdelning

Meddn MedStyr — Meddelanden fran Medicinalstyrelsen

Meddn Nord Mus — Meddelanden fran Nordiska Museet

Meddn Oceanogr Inst Goteborg — Meddelanden fran Oceanografiska Institutet i Goteborg

Medd Nor Farm Selsk — Meddelelser fra Norsk Farmaceutisk Selskap

Medd Nor Inst Skogforsk — Meddelelser fra Norsk Institute foer Skogforskning

Medd Nor Myrselsk — Meddelelser fra det Norske Myrselskab

Medd Nor Sk — Meddelelser fra det Norske Skogforsoeksvesen

Medd Nor Skogforsoksves — Meddelelser fra det Norske Skogforsoeksvesen

Medd Norsk Tretekn Inst — Meddelelser Norsk Treteknisk Institutt

Medd Nor Viltforsk — Meddelelser fra Norsk Viltforskning

Meddn Perm Komm FruktodlFors — Meddelanden fran Permanenta Kommitten for Fruktodlingsforsok

Meddn Sallsk Psyk Forsk Helsingf — Meddelanden utgifna af Sallskapet for Psykisk Forskning i Helsingfors

Meddn Skanes NaturskFor — Meddelanden fran Skanes Naturskyddsforening

Meddn Skansens Obs — Meddelanden fran Skansens Observatorium

Meddn Soc Fauna Flora Fenn — Meddelanden af Societas pro Fauna et Flora Fennica

Meddn Stift Rasforadl Skogstr — Meddelanden. Stiftelsen for Rasforadling av Skogstrad

Meddn St Inst Folkhals — Meddelanden fran Statens Institut for Folkhalsan

Meddn St Komm ByggnForsk — Meddelanden. Statens Kommittee for Byggnadsforskning

Meddn St Lantbrkem Kontrollanst — Meddelanden. Statens Lantbrukskemiska Kontrollanstalt

Meddn St MaskProvn — Meddelanden. Statens Maskinprovningar

Meddn St Mejerifors — Meddelanden fran Statens Mejeriforsok

Meddn St Methydrogr Anst — Meddelanden fran Statens Meteorologiskhydrografiska Anstalt

Meddn St Namnd ByggnForsk — Meddelanden. Statens Namnd for Byggnadsforskning

Meddn St ProvnAnst — Meddelanden fran Statens Provningsanstalt

Meddn St Sjohist Mus — Meddelanden fran Statens Sjohistoriska Museum

Meddn St SkeppsprovnAnst — Meddelanden fran Statens Skeppsprovningsanstalt

Meddn St SkogsforsAnst — Meddelanden fran Statens Skogsforsoksanstalt

Meddn St Skogsforskinst (Stockholm) — Meddelanden fran Statens Skogsforskningsinstitut (Stockholm)

Meddn St TradgFors Alnarp — Meddelanden fran Statens Tradgardsforsok (Alnarp)

Meddn St Unders O ForsAnst SotvattFisk — Meddelanden fran Statens Undersoknings- och Forsogsanstalt for Sotvattenfisket

Meddn St Vaginst — Meddelanden. Statens Vaginstitut

Meddn St VaxtskAnst — Meddelanden fran Statens Vaxtskyddsanstalt

Meddn St Vet Med Anst — Meddelanden fran Statens Veterinarmedicinska Anstalt

Meddn Svenska Tek VetenskAkad Finl — Meddelanden. Svenska Tekniska Vetenskapsakademien i Finland

Meddn Svenska TextForskInst — Meddelanden fran Svenska Textilforskningsinstitutet

Meddn Sverig FroeodlFoerb — Meddelanden fran Sveriges Froeodlarefoerbund

Meddn Sver IndForb — Meddelanden fran Sveriges Industriforbund

Meddn Sver Kom IndKont — Meddelanden fran Sveriges Kemiska Industrikontor

Meddn Sver MaskIndFor StandKomm — Meddelanden fran Sveriges Maskinindustriforenings Standardkommittee

Meddn Sver Met Hydrol Inst — Meddelanden fran Sveriges Meteorologiska och Hydrologiska Institute

Meddn Sver Yngre Vet For — Meddelanden fran Sveriges Yngre Veterinarers Forening

Meddn TEFO — Meddelanden fran TEFO

Meddn Telmat Stn Agard — Meddelanden fran Telmatologiska Stationen Agard

Meddn TranspForskKomm — Meddelanden fran Transportforskningskommission

Meddn Ultuna Landtbrlnst — Meddelanden fran Ultuna Landtbruksinstitut

Meddn Upps LantbrHogsk Baljvaxtlab — Meddelanden fran Uppsala Lantbrukshogskolans Baljvaxtlaboratorium

Meddn Upps Univ Fys Instn — Meddelanden fran Uppsala Universitets Fysiska Institution

Meddn Upps Univ Geogr Instn — Meddelanden fran Uppsala Universitets Geografiska Institution

Meddn Upps Univ Met Instn — Meddelanden fran Uppsala Universitets Meteorologiska Institution

Meddn Upps Univ Min Geol Instn — Meddelanden fran Uppsala Universitets Mineralogisk-Geologiska Institution

Meddn Varmlands Naturh For — Meddelanden fran Varmlands Naturhistoriska Forening

Meddn VetHogsk — Meddelanden fran Veterinarhogskolan

Med Doc — Medical Documentation

Med Dok — Medizinische Dokumentation

Medd Om Konserv — Meddelelser om Konservering

Med Dosim — Medical Dosimetry

Med Dosw Mikrobiol — Medycyna Doswiadczalna i Mikrobiologia

Med Dosw Mikrobiol (Transl) — Medycyna Doswiadczalna i Mikrobiologia (Translation)

Med Dosw Spoleczna — Medycyna Doswiadczalna i Spoleczna

Medd Papirind Forskningsinst — Meddelelse fra Papirindustriens Forskningsinstitutt

Meddr Akad ArkitForen — Meddelelser fra Akademisk Arkitektforening

Meddr Autogummibrchn — Meddelelser for Autogummibranchen

Meddr Betongkom Norsk Ing Foren — Meddelelser. Betongkomite. Norsk Ingeniorforening

Meddr Carlsberg Lab — Meddelelser fra Carlsberg Laboratoriet

Meddr Danm Antrop — Meddelelser om Danmarks Antropologi, udgivet af den Antropologiske Komite

Meddr Danm Fisk og Havunders — Meddelelser fra Danmarks Fiskeri- og Havundersogelser

Meddr Danm Geod Inst — Meddelelser fra Danmarks Geodaetiske Institut

Meddr Dansk Astronaut Foren — Meddelelser. Dansk Astronautisk Forening

Meddr Dansk Byplanlab — Meddelelser. Dansk Byplanlaboratorium

Meddr Dansk Geol Foren — Meddelelser fra Dansk Geologisk Forening

Meddr Dansk Interplanet Selsk — Meddelelser. Dansk Interplanetarisk Selskab

Meddr Dansk Met Inst — Meddelelser fra Dansk Meteorologisk Institut

Meddr Dansk Selsk RumfForsk — Meddelelser. Dansk Selskab for Rumfartsforskning

Meddr Dr F G Gades Path Anat Lab — Meddelelser fra Dr. F. G. Gade's Pathologisk-Anatomiske Laboratorium i Bergen

Meddr Finsens Med Lysinst — Meddelelser. Finsen's Medicinske Lysinstitut

Meddr FiskMinist ForsLab — Meddelelser fra Fiskeriministeriets Forsogslaboratorium

Meddr Foren Svampekundsk Fremme — Meddelelser fra Foreningen til Svampekundskabens Fremme

Meddr Gronland — Meddelelser om Gronland, af Kommissionen for Ledelsen af de Geologiske og Geografiske Undersogelser i Gronland

Meddr Hermetikkind Lab — Meddelelser fra Hermetikkindustriens Laboratorium

Meddr IndForen Kbh — Meddelelser. Industriforeningen i Kjobenhavn og Industriraadet

Meddr Inst SterilForsk — Meddelelser. Institut for Sterilitetsforskning

Meddr Kaninkontrolstn Favrholm — Meddelelser fra Kaninkontrolstation pa Favrholm

Meddr Kbh Univ Patol Anat Inst — Meddelelser fra Kobenhavns Universitets Patologisk-Anatomiske Institut

Meddr Kbh Univ Psyk Klin — Meddelelser fra Kobenhavns Universitets Psykiatriske Klinik og Psykiatrisk Laboratorium

Meddr K Danske Haveselsk — Meddelelser fra det Kunliga Danske Haveselskab

Meddr Kommn Danm Fisk Og Havunders — Meddelelser fra Kommissionen for Danmarks Fiskeri og Havundersogelser

Meddr Kommn Havunders — Meddelelser fra Kommissionen for Havundersogelser

Meddr Kristiania FodsStift — Meddelelser fra Kristiania Fodselsstiftelse

Meddr K Vet Og Landbohojsk Serumlab — Meddelelser fra den Kungliga Veterinaer- og Landbohojskoles Serumlaboratorium

Meddr Lab BygnTek Danm Tek Hojsk — Meddelelser. Laboratoriet for Bygningsteknik, Danmarks Tekniske Hojskole

Meddr Landokon Driftsbur — Meddelelser. Landokonomiske Driftsbureau

Meddr Lydtek Lab — Meddelelser fra Lydteknisk Laboratorium

Meddr Mejerier — Meddelelser til de Mejerier

Meddr Metall Kom Norg Tek Naturv ForskRad — Meddelelser. Metallurgisk Komite, Norges Teknisk-Naturvitenskapelige Forskningsrad

Meddr Met Inst Charlottenlund — Meddelelser. Meteorologisk Institut (Charlottenlund)

Meddr Naturh Mus Aarhus — Meddelelser fra Naturhistorisk Museum. Aarhus

Meddr Norg LandbrHoisk MaskProveanst — Meddelelser. Norges Landbrukshoiskolens Maskinproveanstalt

Meddr Norg Svalb Og Ishavsunders — Meddelelser. Norges Svalbard- og Ishavsundersokelser

Meddr Norsk Bot Foren — Meddelelser. Norsk Botanisk Forening

Meddr Norsk Dampkjelforen — Meddelelser fra den Norsk Dampkjelforening

Meddr Norske ElektVkrs Foren — Meddelelser. Norske Elektricitesverkers Forening

Meddr Norske Myrselsk — Meddelelser fra det Norske Myrselskap

Meddr Norske NatnForen Tuberk — Meddelelser fra den Norske Nationalforening mot Tuberkulosen

Meddr Norsk Ent Foren — Meddelelser fra Norsk Entomologisk Forening

Meddr Norske Skogsfors Ves — Meddelelser fra det Norske Skogforsoeksvesen

Meddr Norske Sykehusforen — Meddelelser fra den Norske Sykehusforening

Meddr Norsk Farm Selsk — Meddelelser fra Norsk Farmaceutisk Selskap</PHR>%

Meddr Norsk Polarinst — Meddelelser om Norsk Polarinstitutt

Meddr Norsk Tretek Inst — Meddelelser. Norsk Treteknisk Institutt

Meddr Ole Romer Obs — Meddelelser. Ole Romer-Observatoriet

Meddr Oslo Kommun Sykehuser — Meddelelser fra Oslo Kommunale Sykehuser

Meddr PapInd ForskInst — Meddelelser fra Papirindustriens Forskningsinstitut

Meddr Prod Tek ForskInst — Meddelelser fra Produksjonsteknisk Forskningsinstitut

Meddr Shipsmodelltanken Norg Tek Hogsk — Meddelelser. Skipsmodelltanken, Norges Tekniske Hogskole

Meddr SjofKont — Meddelelser fra Sjofartskontoret

Meddr Skalling Lab — Meddelelser fra Skalling-Laboratoriet

Meddr Smitts Husdyr — Meddelelser om Smittsomme hos Husdyrene

Meddr St ForsVirks PlKult — Meddelelser fra Statens Forsoksvirksomhed i Plantekultur

Meddr StProveanst — Meddelelser. Statsproveanstalt

Meddr St RedskProv — Meddelelser. Statens Redskabsprover

Meddr St Seruminst — Meddelelser fra Statens Seruminstitut

Meddr St Vet Serumlab — Meddelelser fra Statens Veterinaere Serumlaboratorium

Meddr St Viltunders — Meddelelser fra Statens Viltundersokelser

Meddr St Vitam Lab — Meddelelser fra Statens Vitamin-Laboratorium

Meddr SundhStyr — Meddelelser fra Sundhedsstyrelsen

Meddr Udv Unders Midler Mod Traeodelaeg — Meddelelser. Udvalget til Undersogelse af Midler Mod Traeodelaeggende Organismer

Meddr Univ Hyg Inst Kbh — Meddelelser fra Universitets Hygieniske Institut (Kjobenhavn)

Meddr Univ Psyk Lab Kbh — Meddelelser fra Universitetets Psykiatriske Laboratorium og Kommunehospitalets Nervesindssygeafdeling (Kobenhavn)

Meddr Vejdir — Meddelelser fra Vejdirektoren

Meddr Vejlab — Meddelelser fra Vejlaboratoriet

Meddr Vejlefjord Sanat Brystsyge — Meddelelser fra Vejlefjord Sanatorium for Brystsyge

Meddr Vestland Forstl ForsStn — Meddelelser fra Vestlandets Forstlige Forsoksstatjion

Meddr Zool Mus Oslo — Meddelelser fra det Zoologiske Museum (Oslo)

Medd Statens Lantbrukskem Lab — Meddelande. Statens Lantbrukskemiska Laboratorium

Medd Statens Mejerifoers (Swed) — Meddelande fran Statens Mejerifoersoek (Sweden)

Medd Statens Planteavsforsog — Meddelelse Statens Planteavlsforsog

Medd Statens Provningsanst Stockholm — Meddelande fraan Statens Provningsanstalt. Stockholm

Medd Statens Skeppsprovningsanst — Meddelanden fran Statens Skeppsprovningsanstalt

Medd Statens Skogsforskningsinst — Meddelanden fran Statens Skogsforskningsinstitut

Medd Statens Skogsforskningsinst (Swed) — Meddelanden fran Statens Skogsforskningsinstitut (Sweden)

Medd Statens Tek Forskningscent Textillab — Meddelande. Statens Tekniska Forskningscentral. Textillaboratoriet

Medd Statens Traedgaardsfoers — Meddelanden fran Statens Traedgaardsfoersoek

Medd Statens Vaextskyddsanst — Meddelanden. Statens Vaextskyddsanstalt

Medd Statens Viltunders — Meddelelser fra Statens Viltundersokelser

Medd Statens Viltunders (Pap Norw State Game Res Inst) — Meddelelser fra Statens Viltundersokelser (Papers. Norwegian State GameResearch Institute)

Medd Stat Forskningsanst Lantmannabyggnader — Meddelande fran Statens Forskningsanst Lantmannabyggnader

Medd Stiftelsens Aabo Akad Forskningsinst — Meddelanden fraan Stiftelsens foer Aabo Akademi Forskningsinstitut

Medd Stift Rasforadl Skogstrad — Meddelanden fran Stiftelsen foer Rasforadling av Skogstrad

Medd Sven Forskningsinst Cem Betong K Tek Hoegsk Stockholm — Meddelanden. Svenska Forskningsinstitutet foer Cement och Betong vid Kungliga Tekniska Hoegskolan i Stockholm

Medd Sven Mejeriernas Riksfoeren Produkttek Avd — Meddelande. Svenska Mejeriernas Riksfoerening. Produkttekniska Avdelningen

Medd Svenska Tek Vetenskapsakad Finl — Meddelande Svenska Tekniska Vetenskapsakademien i Finland

Medd Svenska TraforsknInst Tratek Avd — Meddelanden. Svenska Traforskningsinstitutets Tratekniska Avdelning

Medd Svenska Traforskn Inst (Trakem PappTekn) — Meddelanden fran Svenska Traforskningsinstitutet (Trakemi och Papperteknik)

Medd Sven Text — Meddelande fran Svenska Textilforskninginstitutet

Medd Sven Textilforskningsinst — Meddelanden fran Svenska Textilforskningsinstitutet

Medd Sven Traskyddsinst — Meddelanden fran Svenska Traskyddsinstitutet

Medd Sver Kem Industrikontor — Meddelanden fran Sveriges Kemiska Industrikontor

Medd Thorvaldsen Mus — Meddelelser fra Thorvaldsens Museum

Medd Traedgaardsfoers — Meddelanden fran Traedgaardsfoersoek

Medd Vaextekol Inst Lund Univ — Meddelanden fran Vaextekologiska Institutionen Lunds Universitet

Medd Vestland Forstl Forsokssta — Meddelelser fra Vestlandets Forstlige Forsoeksstasjon

Medd Vestl Forstl Forsoeksstn — Meddelelser fra Vestlandets Forstlige Forsoeksstasjon

MEDEA — Medecine

Medec Fr — Medecine de France

Med Echo — Medical Echo

Medecin Als Lorr — Medecin d'Alsace et de Lorraine

Medecin Campagne — Medecin de Campagne

Medecin Estomac — Medecin de l'Estomac

Medecin Fr — Medecin de France

Medecin Fr Bourg La Reine — Medecin Francais (Bourg-la-Reine)

Medecin Fr Lyon — Medecin Francais (Lyon)

Medecin Fr Paris — Medecin Francais (Paris)

Medecin Paris — Medecin de Paris

Medecin Pratn — Medecin Praticien

Medecin Synd — Medecin Syndicaliste

Medecin Usine — Medecin d'Usine

Med Eclairee Sci Phys — La Medicine Eclairee par les Sciences Physiques, ou Journal des Decouvertes Relatives aux Differentes Parties de l'Art de Guerir

Med Econ — Medical Economics

Med Econst — Medical Economist

Med Econ Surgeons — Medical Economics for Surgeons

Meded — Mededelingen. Nederlandsch Historisch Institut te Rome

Meded Acad Marine Belgie — Mededelingen van de Marine Academie van Belgie

Meded Afd Docum Dep Landb — Mededelingen van de Afdeling Documentatie. Departement van Landbouw, Visserij en Voedselvoorziening

Meded Afd GezondhZoig Ned Inst Praev Geneesk Leiden — Mededelingen uit de Afdeling Gezondheitszoig van het Nederlands Instituut voor Praeventive Geneeskunde te Leiden

Meded Afd Landb Ned Indie — Mededelingen van de Afdeling Landbouw. Departement van Landbouw, Nederlandsch-Indie

Meded Afd Nijv Ned Indie — Mededelingen van de Afdeling Nijverheid. Departement van Landbouw in Nederlandsch-Indie

Meded Afd PlZiekt Buitenz — Mededelingen van de Afdeling voor Plantenziekten (Buitenzorg)

Meded Afd Rubber Res Proefstn West Java — Mededeelingen van de Afdeeling Rubber Research van het Proefstation West-Java

Meded Afd Vissch Dep Landb — Mededelingen. Afdeling Visscherijen. Departement van Landbouw

Meded Agric Chem Lab Buitenz — Mededelingen van het Agricultuur-Chemisch Laboratorium (Buitenzorg)

Meded Akad Mar Belg — Mededelingen. Akademie der Marine van Belgie

Meded Alg Proefstat Java — Mededeelingen. Algemeen Proefstation op Java

Meded Alg Proefstn Alg Rubberplant Oostkust Sumatra Alg Ser — Mededeelingen van het Algemeen Proefstation der Algemeene Rubberplanters ter Oostkust van Sumatra, Algemeene Serie

Meded Alg Proefstn AVROS — Mededeelingen. Algemeen Proefstation der AVROS

Meded Alg Proefstn AVROS Alg Ser — Mededeelingen van het Algemeen Proefstation der AVROS. Algemeene Serie

Meded Alg Proefstn AVROS Rubber Ser — Mededeelingen van het Algemeen Proefstation der AVROS, Rubber Serie

Meded Alg Proefstn Java Salatiga — Mededeelingen van het Algemeen Proefstation op Java te Salatiga

Meded Alg Proefstn Landb Buitenz — Mededelingen van het Algemeen Proefstation voor den Landbouw (Buitenzorg)

Meded Alg Tech Comm KeurInst WatLeidArt — Mededelingen. Algemeene Technische Commissie, Keuringsinstituut voor Waterleidingsartikelen

Meded Alg Vlaam Geneesheerenverb — Mededelingen van het Algemeen Vlaamsch Geneesheerenverbond

Meded Arbor Landb Hoogesch Wageningen — Mededelingen van het Arboretum, Landbouwhoogeschool te Wageningen

Meded Belg Cent Technol Onderz Leid — Mededelingen. Belgisch Centrum voor Technologisch Onderzoek van Leidingen

Meded Belg Natuurkd Ver — Mededelingen van Belgische Natuurkundige Vereniging

Meded Ber Geldersch Overijs Maatsch Landb — Mededelingen en Berichten der Gelderschoverijselsche Maatschappij van Landbouw

Meded Besoek Proefstn — Mededelingen van het Besoekisch Proefstation

Meded Besoek Proefstn Rubb Ser — Mededelingen van het Besoekisch Proefstation. Rubber Serie

Meded Best AVROS — Mededelingen van het Bestuur der A.V.R.O.S

Meded Biol Stat Wijster — Mededelingen van het Biologisch Station te Wijster

MededBl Ned Maatsch Bevord Tandheelk — Mededelingenblad van de Nederlandsche Maatschappij tot Bevordering der Tandheelkunde

Mededbl Ned Ver Vrienden Cer — Mededelingenblad Nederlandse Vereniging van Vrieden van Ceramiek

MededBl Vereen Zoogdierk — Mededelingenblad van de Vereeniging voor Zoogdierkunde en Zoogdierbescherming

Meded Bot Inst Rijksuniv Gent — Mededelingen. Botanisch Instituut. Rijksuniversiteit te Gent

Meded Bot Lab Herb Rijks Univ Utrecht — Mededelingen van het Botanisch Laboratorium en Herbarium van de Rijks-Universiteit te Utrecht

Meded Bot Lab Rijks Univ Utrecht — Mededelingen van het Botanisch Laboratorium der Rijks-Universiteit te Utrecht

Meded Bot Tuinen Belmonte Arbor Wageningen — Mededelingen van de Botanische Tuinen en het Belmonte Arboretum der L. S. H. te Wageningen

Meded Burgerl Geneeskd Dienst Ned Indie — Mededelingen van den Burgerlijken Geneeskundigen Dienst in Nederlandsch-Indie

Meded Burg Geneesk Dienst Ned Indie — Mededelingen van den Burgerlijken Geneeskundigen Dienst in Nederlandsch-Indie

Meded Cent Inst MaterOnderz — Mededelingen. Centraal Instituut voor Materiaalonderzoek

Meded Centr Inst Landbouwk Onderz — Mededelingen. Centraal Instituut voor Landbouwkundig Onderzoek

Meded Cent Rubberstn — Mededeelingen. Centraal Rubberstation

Meded Com Bestud Bestrijd Iepenziekte — Mededelingen van het Comite inzake Bestudeering en Bestrijding van de Iepenziekte

Meded Com Bestud Bestrijd InsectPlag Bosschen — Mededelingen van het Comite ter Bestudeering en Bestrijding van Insectenplagen in Bosschen

Meded Com Bestud Bestrijd Ziekt Iepen — Mededelingen van het Comite ter Bestudeering en Bestrijding van Ziekten in Iepen en andere Boomsoorten

Meded Com Faun Onderz Zuidersee Polders — Mededelingen van de Commissie voor het Faunistisch Onderzoek der Zuidersee Polders

Meded Comm Filterconstr KeurInst WatLeidArt — Mededelingen. Commissie Filterconstructies, Keuringsinstituut voor Waterleidingsartikelen

Meded Comm KeurEisen WatleidArt — Mededelingen. Commissie voor Keuringseisen van Waterleidingartikelen, Keuringsinstituut voor Waterleidingartikelen

Meded Comm Niet Metal Leid KeurInst WatLeidArt — Mededelingen. Commissie Niet-Metalen Leidingen, Keuringsinstituut voor Waterleidingartikelen

Meded Comm Veldgeg Ijz Leid KeurInst WatLeidArt — Mededelingen. Commissie Veldgegevens Ijzeren Leidingen, Keuringsinstituut voor Waterleidingartikelen

Meded Comm Vorst KeurInst WatLeidArt — Mededelingen. Commissie Vorst, Keuringsinstituut voor Waterleidingartikelen

Meded Comm WatVerlies KeurInst WatLeidArt — Mededelingen. Commissie Waterverlies, Keuringsinstituut voor Waterleidingartikelen

Meded Corros Inst TNO — Mededelingen. Corrosie-Instituut. T.N.O

Meded CultTuin Buitenz — Mededelingen uit den Cultuurtuin (Buitenzorg)

Meded Deli Plrs Vereen — Mededelingen Uitgegeven door de Deli Planters Vereeniging

Meded Deli Proefstn Medan — Mededelingen van het Deli-Proefstation te Medan

Meded Dep Econ Zak Ned Indie — Mededelingen van het Departement van Economische Zaken in Nederlandsch-Indie

Meded Dep Landb Ned Indie — Mededelingen Uitgeven van het Departement van Landbouw in Nederlandsch-Indie

Meded Dep Landb Suriname — Mededelingen. Departement van den Landbouw in Suriname

Meded Dept Landb Ned Indiee — Mededeelingen Uitgeven. Departement van Landbouw in Nederlandsch-Indiee

Meded Dienst Kst & Wet Gemeente s Gravenhage — Mededelingen van de Dienst voor Kunsten en Wetenschappen der Gemeente 's-Gravenhage

Meded Dienst Volksgezondh Ned Indie — Mededelingen van den Dienst der Volksgezondheid in Nederlandsch-Indie

Meded Dienst Volksgezond Ned Indie — Mededelingen van den Dienst der Volksgezondheid in Nederlandsch-Indie

Meded Directeur Tuinb — Mededeelingen. Directeur van de Tuinbouw

Meded Dir Tuinb — Mededeelingen. Directeur van de Tuinbouw

Meded Dir Tuinbouw (Neth) — Mededelingen. Directie Tuinbouw (Netherlands)

Mededeelingen — Mededeelingen der Koninklijke Nederlandse Akademie van Wetenschappen. AfdeelingLetterkunde

Mededeel V D Dienst D Volksgezondh In Nederl Indie — Mededelingen van den Dienst der Volksgezondheid in Nederlandsch-Indie

Meded Electrostoom — Mededelingen van Electrostoom

Mededel Neder Inst Rom — Mededelingen. Nederlandsch Historisch Instituut te Rome

Meded Fac Diergeneeskd Rijksuniv (Gent) — Mededelingen. Faculteit Diergeneeskunde Rijksuniversiteit (Gent)

Meded Fac Landbouwwet Rijksuniv (Gent) — Mededelingen. Faculteit Landbouwwetenschappen. Rijksuniversiteit (Gent)

Meded Fac LandWet (Gent) — Mededelingen. Faculteit Landbouwwetenschappen. Rijksuniversiteit (Gent)

Meded Fonds Pluimveebel — Mededelingen van het Fonds voor Pluimveebelangen

Meded Gemeentemus Den Haag — Mededelingen Gemeentemuseum Den Haag

Meded Geneesk Lab Weltevr — Mededelingen uit het Geneeskundig Laboratorium te Weltevreden

Meded Geol Bur Mijngeb Heerlen — Mededelingen. Geologisch Bureau voor het Mijngebied te Heerlen

Meded Geol Inst Univ Amst — Mededelingen. Geologisch Instituut. Universiteit van Amsterdam

Meded Geol Mijnbouwkd Dienst Suriname — Mededeling. Geologishe Mijnbouwkundige Dienst van Suriname

Meded Geol Mijnbouwk Dienst Suriname — Mededelingen van de Geologisch-Mijnbouwkundige Dienst van Suriname

Meded Geol Ned — Mededelingen Omtrent de Geologie van Nederland

Meded Geol Sticht — Mededelingen. Geologische Stichting

Meded Geol Stichting Ser C — Mededelingen. Geologische Stichting. Serie C. Uitkomsten van het Geologie-Palaeontologie. Onderzoek van de Ondergrond van Nederland

Meded Geol Sticht Nieuwe Ser (Neth) — Mededelingen. Geologische Stichting. Nieuwe Serie (Netherlands)

Meded Gesch & Oudhdknd Kring Leuven & Omgev — Mededelingen van de Geschied- en Oudheidkundige Kring voor Leuven en Omgeving

Meded Indones Inst Rubberonderz — Mededeelingen. Indonesisch Instituut voor Rubberonderzoek

Meded InlichtBur Chilisalp — Mededelingen van het Inlichtingsbureau voor Chilisalpeter

Meded Ins Ratio Suikerprod — Mededelingen. Instituut voor Rationele Suikerproductie

Meded Inst Bewar Verwerk TuinbProd — Mededelingen van het Instituut voor Bewaring en Verwerking van Tuinbouwproducten

Meded Inst Biol Scheik Onderz LandbGewass — Mededelingen. Instituut voor Biologisch en Scheikundig Onderzoek van Landbouwgewassen

Meded Inst Biol Scheik Onderz Landbougewassen (Wageningen) — Mededelingen. Instituut voor Biologisch en Scheikundig Onderzoek van Landbouwgewassen (Wageningen)

Meded Inst CultTech WatHuish — Mededelingen. Institut voor Cultuurtechniek en Waterhuishouding

Meded Inst Graan Meel Brood TNO (Wageningen) — Mededeling. Instituut voor Graan. Meel en Brood TNO [*Toegepast Natuurwetenschappelijk Onderzoek*] (Wageningen)

Meded Inst Mod Veevoeding De Schothorst Hoogland Amersfoorst — Mededeling. Instituut voor Moderne Veevoeding "De Schothorst" te Hoogland bij Amersfoorst

Meded Inst Phytopath — Mededelingen. Instituut voor Phytopathologie te Wageningen

Meded Inst Phytopath Lab BloembollOnderz Lisse — Mededelingen van het Instituut voor Phytopathologie. Laboratorium voor Bloembollenonderzoek te Lisse

Meded Inst Phytopath Lab Mycol Aardappelonderz — Mededelingen van het Instituut voor Phytopathologie. Laboratorium voor Mycologie en Aardappelonderzoek

Meded Inst Plantenziekten Onderz — Mededelingen van het Instituut voor Plantenziektenkundig Onderzoek

Meded Inst PlVered — Mededelingen van het Instituut voor Plantenveredeling

Meded Inst PlZiekt Buitenz — Mededelingen van het Instituut voor Plantenziekten (Buitenzorg)

Meded Inst PlZiektenk Onderz — Mededelingen. Instituut voor Plantenziektenkundig Onderzoek

Meded Inst Ration Suikerprod — Mededelingen. Instituut voor Rationele Suikerproductie

Meded Inst Rat Suik Prod — Mededelingen. Instituut voor Rationele Suikerproductie

Meded Inst SuikBietTeelt — Mededelingen van het Instituut voor Suikerbietenteelt

Meded Inst Suikerprod — Mededelingen van het Instituut voor Suikerproductie

Meded Inst Toegep Biol Onderz Nat — Mededelingen. Instituut voor Toegepast Biologisch Onderzoek in der Natuur

Meded Inst Trop Geneesk — Acta Leidensia. Edita Cura et Sumptibus Medicinae Tropicae. Mededeelingen uit het Instituut voor Tropische Geneeskunde

Meded Inst Vered TuinbGewass — Mededelingen van het Instituut voor de Veredeling van Tuinbouwgewassen

Meded Inst Warmte Econ TNO — Mededelingen van het Instituut voor Warmte-Economie. T.N.O

Meded Javasuikind — Mededelingen uit de Java-Suikerindustrie. Proefstation van den Java-Suikerindustrie

Meded K Acad Geneeskd Belg — Mededelingen. Koninklijke Academie voor Geneeskunde van Belgie

Meded K Acad Wet Lett en Schone Kunsten Belg — Mededelingen. Koninklijke Academie voor Wetenschappen. Letteren en Schone Kunsten van Belgie

Meded K Acad Wet Lett Schone Kunsten Belg Kl Wet — Mededelingen. Koninklijke Academie voor Wetenschappen. Letteren en Schone Kunsten van Belgie. Klasse der Wetenschappen

Meded K Belg Inst Natuurwet — Mededelingen. Koninklijk Belgisch Instituut voor Natuurwetenschappen

Meded Keram Inst TNO — Mededelingen. Keramisch Instituut TNO

Meded KeurInst WatLeidArt — Mededelingen. Keuringsinstituut voor Waterleidingartikelen

Meded Kina Proefstn — Mededelingen van het Kina Proefstation

Meded K Inst Trop Afd Trop Prod — Mededeling. Koninklijk Instituut voor de Tropen. Afdeling Tropische Producten

Meded Koffiebessenboeboek Fonds — Mededelingen van het Koffiebessenboeboek-Fonds

Meded Kolon Inst Amst — Mededelingen van het Koloniaal Instituut te Amsterdam

Meded Kolon Inst Amsterdam Afd Trop Hyg — Mededeeling. Koloniaal Instituut te Amsterdam. Afdeeling Tropische Hygiene

Meded Kon Akad Wet Afd Lettknd — Mededelingen der Koninklijke Academie van Wetenschappen. Afdeeling Letterkunde

Meded Kon Akad Wetensch Afd Lettk — Mededeelingen der Koninklijke Akademie van Wetenschappen Afdeeling Letterkunde

Meded Kon Akad Wetensch Lett Sch Kunst Belgie Kl Wetensch — Mededeelingen van de Koninklijke Academie voor Wetenschappen, Letteren, en Schone Kunsten van Belgie. Klasse der Wetenschappen

Meded Kon Ned Akad Wet — Mededelingen van de Koninklijke Nederlandse Akademie voor Wetenschappen

Meded Kon Nederl Ak Wetensch — Mededeelingen. Koninklijke Nederlandsche Akademie van Wetenschappen

Meded Kon Veren Indisch Inst — Mededeeling Koninklijke Vereeniging Indisch Instituut

Meded Kon Vl Ak Wetensch — Mededeelingen. Koninklijke Vlaamse Akademie van Wetenschappen

Meded K Ver Indisch Inst Afd Handelsmus — Mededeling. Koninklijke Vereniging Indisch Instituut. Afdeling Handelsmuseum

Meded K Ver Indisch Inst Afd Trop Hyg — Mededeling. Koninklijke Vereniging Indisch Instituut. Afdeling Tropische Hygiene

Meded K Ver Kolon Inst Afd Handelsmus — Mededeeling. Koninklijke Vereeniging Koloniaal Instituut. Afdeeling Handelsmuseum

Meded K Ver Kolon Inst Afd Trop Hyg — Mededeeling. Koninklijke Vereeniging Koloniaal Instituut. Afdeeling Tropische Hygiene

Meded K Vlaam Acad Wet Lett Schone Kunsten Belg Kl Wet — Mededelingen. Koninklijke Vlaamse Academie voor Wetenschappen. Letterenen Schone Kunsten van Belgie. Klasse der Wetenschappen

Meded Lab Aero En Hydrodyn Delft — Mededelingen uit het Laboratorium voor Aero- en Hydrodynamics (Delft)

Meded Lab Agrogeol Grondonderz Weltevr — Mededelingen van het Laboratorium voor Agrogeologie en Grondonderzoek (Weltevreden)

Meded Lab Bloembollenonderz — Mededeelingen. Laboratorium voor Bloembollenonderzoek

Meded Lab Ent Wageningen — Mededelingen. Laboratorium voor Entomologie (Wageningen)

Meded Lab Fysiol Chem Univ Amsterdam — Mededelingen. Laboratorium voor Fysiologische Chemie. Universiteit van Amsterdam

Meded Lab Houttechnol Gent — Mededelingen van het Laboratorium voor Houttechnologie (Gent)

Meded Lab Houttechnol Rijkslandbouwhogesch (Gent) — Mededelingen. Laboratorium voor Houttechnologie. Rijkslandbouwhogeschool (Gent)

Meded Lab Path Anat Bact Weltevr — Mededelingen uit het Laboratorium voor Pathologische Anatomie en Bacteriologie te Weltevreden

Meded Lab Physiol Chem Univ Amst — Mededelingen uit het Laboratorium voor Physiologische Chemie der Universiteit van Amsterdam

Meded Lab Physiol Chem Univ Amsterdam — Mededelingen. Laboratorium voor Physiologische Chemie. Universiteit van Amsterdam

Meded Lab Physiol Chem Univ Amsterdam Ned Inst Volksvoed — Mededelingen. Laboratorium voor Physiologische Chemie. Universiteit van Amsterdam et Nederlands Instituut voor Volksvoeding

Meded Lab Phytopath — Mededelingen. Laboratorium voor Phytopathologie

Meded Lab Plphysiol Onderz Wageningen — Mededelingen van het Laboratorium voor Plantenphysiologisch Onderzoek, Landbouwhoogeschool te Wageningen

Meded Lab PlZiekt Buitenz — Mededelingen van het Laboratorium voor Plantenziekten (Buitenzorg)

Meded Lab Scheikd Onderz Buitenzorg — Mededeeling. Laboratorium voor Scheikundig Onderzoek te Buitenzorg

Meded Lab Scheik Onderz Bogor — Mededelingen van het Laboratorium voor Scheikundig Onderzoek (Bogor)

Meded Lab TuinbPlTeelt Wageningen — Mededelingen van het Laboratorium voor Tuinbouwplantenteelt, Landbouwhoogeschool te Wageningen

Meded LandbHogesch OpzoekStns Gent — Mededelingen. Landbouwhogeschool en Opzoekingsstations van de Staat te Gent

Meded Landbhogesch Wageningen — Mededelingen. Landbouwhogeschool te Wageningen

Meded Landbouwhogesch (Ghent) — Mededelingen. Landbouwhogeschool (Ghent)

Meded Landbouwhogeschool — Mededeelingen van de Landbouwhogeschool

Meded Landbouwhogesch Opzoekingssta (Ghent) — Mededelingen. Landbouwhogeschool en Opzoekingsstations (Ghent)

Meded Landbouwhogesch Opzoekingsstn Staat Gent — Mededelingen. Landbouwhogeschool en Opzoekingsstations van de Staat te Gent

Meded Landbouwhogesch Wageningen — Mededelingen. Landbouwhogeschool te Wageningen

Meded Landbouwhoogeschool Onderzoekingstat Staat Gent — Mededeelingen van de Landbouwhoogeschool en de Onderzoekingstations van den Staat te Gent

Meded Landbouwk Bur Ned Stikstofmeststoffen Ind — Mededelingen van het Landbouwkundig Buereau der Nederlandse Stikstofmeststoffen-Industrie

Meded LandbVoorlDienst Buitenz — Mededelingen van den Landbouwvoorlichtingsdienst (Buitenzorg)

Meded LandbVoorlDienst Den Haag — Mededelingen van den Landbouwvoorlichtingsdienst (Den Haag)

Meded LandProefstn Suriname — Mededelingen. Landbouwproefstation in Suriname

Meded Lds PlTuin Batavia — Mededelingen uits Lands Plantentuin (Batavia)

Meded Lederinst TNO — Mededelingen. Lederinstituut TNO

Meded L Vlaam Acad Wet Belg Kl Wet — Mededelingen. Koninklijke Vlaamse Academie voor Wetenschappen. Letteren en Schone Kunsten van Belgie. Klasse der Wetenschappen

Meded Nat Coop Aan- Verkoopver Landbouw Cen Bur — Mededelingen. Nationale Cooperatieve Aan- en Verkoopvereniging voor de LandbouwCentral Bureau

Meded Natn Com Brouwgerst — Mededelingen van het Nationaal Comite voor Brouwgerst

Meded Natuur — Mededeelingen uit het Gebied van Natuur, Wetenschapen, en Kunst

Meded Ned Alg KeurDienst LandbZaken Aardappelpootg — Mededelingen van de Nederlandse Algemeene Keuringsdienst voor Landbouwzaken en Aardappelpootgoed

Meded Ned Alg Keuringsdienst Landbouwz — Mededelingen. Nederlandse Algemene Keuringsdienst voor Landbouwzaden en Aardappelpootgoed

Meded Ned Hist Inst Rome — Mededelingen van het Nederlands Historisch Instituut te Rome

Meded Ned Indisch Inst Rubberonderz — Mededelingen van het Nederlandsch-Indisch Instituut voor Rubberonderzoek

Meded Ned Inst Rome — Mededelingen van het Nederlands Instituut te Rome

Meded Ned Mycol Vereen — Mededelingen. Nederlandsche Mycologische Vereeniging

Meded Ned Vacuumver — Mededelingenblad. Nederlandse Vacuumvereniging

Meded Ned Vereen Diet — Mededelingen der Nederlandsche Vereeniging van Dietisten

Meded Ned Vereen Koeltech — Mededelingen. Nederlandsche Vereeniging voor Koeltechniek

Meded Ned Ver Koeltech — Mededelingen. Nederlande Vereeniging voor Koeltechniek

Meded Ned Vlasinst — Mededelingen. Nederlands Vlasinstituut

Meded Overdr Inst Bewar Verwerk TuinProd — Mededelingen en Overdrukken van het Instituut voor Bewaring en Verwerking van Tuinbouwprodukten

Meded Path Lab Medan — Mededelingen uit het Pathologisch Laboratorium te Medan

Meded Phytopath Lab Willie Commelin Scholten — Mededelingen uit het Phytopathologisch Laboratorium Willie Commelin Scholten

Meded Plantn Res Dep US Rubb Plantns Buitenz — Mededelingen. Plantation Research Department der United States Rubber Plantations, Inc (Buitenzorg)

Meded Plrs Com Medan — Mededelingen. Planters Comite (Medan)

Meded PlZiektenk Dienst Wageningen — Mededelingen van den Plantenziektenkundigen Dienst te Wageningen

Meded Proefstat Boschw — Mededeelingen van het Proefstation voor het Boschwezen

Meded Proefstat Java Suikerindustr — Mededeelingen. Proefstation voor de Java Suikerindustrie

Meded Proefstat Rijst — Mededeelingen van het Proefstation voor Rijst

Meded Proefstat Rubber — Mededelingen. Proefstation voor Rubber

Meded Proefstn Akker- en Weideb — Mededelingen. Proefstation voor de Akker- en Weidebouw

Meded Proefstn Akker Weidebouw — Mededeling. Proefstation foor de Akker- en Weidebouw

Meded Proefstn Boschw Batavia — Mededelingen. Proefstation voor het Boschwezen (Batavia)

Meded Proefstn Groent En Fruitteelt Glas — Mededelingen van het Proefstation voor de Groenten- en Fruitteelt onder Glas

Meded Proefstn Groenteelt Volle Grond — Mededelingen. Proefstation voor de Groenteelt in de Volle Grond

Meded Proefstn Groenteelt Vollegrond Ned — Mededeling. Proefstation voor de Groenteelt in de Vollegrond in Nederland

Meded Proefstn Java Suikerind — Mededelingen. Proefstation voor de Java Suikerindustrie

Meded Proefstn Java Suiklnd — Mededelingen van het Proefstation voor de Java-Suikerindustrie

Meded Proefstn Malang — Mededelingen van het Proefstation Malang

Meded Proefstn Rubber — Mededelingen van het Proefstation voor Rubber

Meded Proefstn Thee Buitenz — Mededelingen van het Proefstation voor Thee (Buitenzorg)

Meded Proefstn Vorstenl Tab — Mededelingen van het Proefstation voor Vorstenlandsche Tabak

Meded Proefstn Vorstenl Tabak Klaten — Mededelingen van het Proefstation voor Vorstenlandsche Tabak. Klaten

Meded Raad Bijst Samenwk WatLeidLab — Mededelingen. Raad van Bijstand van de Samenwerkende Waterleidinglaboratoria, Keuringsinstituut voor Waterleidingartikelen

Meded Rijksbur DrinkwatVoorz — Mededelingen. Rijksbureau voor Drinkwatervoorziening

Meded Rijksfac Landbouwwet Gent — Mededelingen. Rijksfaculteit Landbouwwetenschappen te Gent

Meded Rijks Geol Dienst — Mededelingen. Rijks Geologische Dienst

Meded Rijks Geol Dienst Nieuwe Ser (Neth) — Mededelingen. Rijks Geologische Dienst. Nieuwe Serie (Netherlands)

Meded Rijks Herb — Mededelingen van Rijks-Herbarium

Meded Rijks Hoogere Land Boschbouwsch — Mededelingen. Rijks Hoogere Land-, Tuin-, en Boschbouwschool

Meded Rijks Inst Brandstoff Econ — Mededelingen van het Rijks-Instituut voor Brandstoffen-Economie

Meded Rijks Inst Pharm Ther Onderz — Mededelingen. Rijks Instituut voor Pharmaco-Therapeutisch Onderzoek

Meded Rijksinst Pluimveeteelt — Mededelingen. Rijksinstituut voor Pluimveeteelt

Meded Rijks Inst Volksgezondh — Mededelingen uit het Rijks-Instituut voor Volksgezondheid te Utrecht

Meded Rijks Landbouwhoogeschool — Mededeelingen. Rijks Landbouwhoogeschool en de Daaraan Verbonden Instituten

Meded Rijksmus Gesch Natuurw — Mededelingen uit het Rijksmuseum voor de Geschiedenis der Natuurwetenschappen te Leiden

Meded Rijksmus Volk — Mededeelingen. Rijksmuseum voor Volkenkunde

Meded Rijksopspor Delfstoff — Mededelingen van de Rijksopsporing van Delfstoffen

Meded Rijksproefstat Zaadcontr (Wageningen) — Mededeling. Rijksproefstation voor Zaadcontrole (Wageningen)

Meded Rijksproefstn Zaadcontrole — Mededelingen. Rijksproefstation voor Zaadcontrole

Meded Rijksseruminricht — Mededeelingen van de Rijksseruminrichting

Meded Rijksstn Zeeviss Oostende Belg — Mededelingen van het Rijksstation voor Zeevisserij (Oostende, Belgium)

Meded RijkstuinbConsul — Mededelingen van het Rijkstuinbouwconsulentschap
Meded Rijksuniv Gent Fak Landbouwkd Toegep Biol Wet — Mededelingen. Faculteit Landbouwkundige en Toegepaste Biologische Wetenschappen
Meded RijksvoorlDienst Behoeve RubbHandel Delft — Mededelingen van den Rijksvoorlichtingsdienst ten Behoeve van den Rubberhandel en de Rubbernijverheid te Delft
Meded RijksvoorlDienst Behoeve Vezelhandel Delft — Mededelingen van het Rijksvoorlichtingsdienst ten Behoeve van den Vezelhandel en de Vezelnijverheid te Delft
Meded Rijksvoorlichtingsdienst Rubberhandel Rubbernijverheid — Mededeelingen van de Rijksvoorlichtingsdienst ten behoeve van den Rubberhandel en de Rubbernijverheid te Delft
Meded RojksboschbProefstn — Mededelingen van het Rijksboschbouwproefstation
Meded Rom — Mededelingen van het Nederlands Historisch Instituut te Rome
Meded Rubb Buitenz — Mededelingen over Rubber. Departement van Landbouw (Buitenzorg)
Meded Rubber — Mededeelingen over Rubber
Meded Rubber Sticht Amsterdam — Mededelingen van de Rubber-Stichting, Amsterdam
Meded Rubber-Sticht (Delft) — Mededelingen. Rubber-Stichting (Delft)
Meded RubbSticht — Mededelingen van de Rubberstichting
Meded Scheik Lab StBedr Artill Inricht — Mededelingen. Scheikundig Laboratorium van het Staatsbedrijf der Artillerie-Inrichtingen
Meded Sterrenk Inst Univ Gent — Mededelingen van het Sterrenkundig Instituut der Universiteit te Gent
Meded Stichting Nederl Graan-Cent — Mededeling. Stichting Nederlands Graan-Centrum
Meded Stichting Ned Graancentrum — Mededelingen van de Stichting Nederlands Graancentrum
Meded Stichting Plantenveredeling (Wageningen) — Mededelingen. Stichting voor Plantenveredeling (Wageningen)
Meded Sticht Jacob Campo Weyerman — Mededelingen van de Stichting Jacob Campo Weyerman
Meded Sticht MaterOnderz — Mededelingen. Stichting voor Materiaalonderzoek
Meded Sticht Ned Indisch Inst Rubberonderz — Mededeelingen. Stichting Nederlandsch-Indisch Instituut voor Rubberonderzoek
Meded Sticht Oliehoud Zaden — Mededelingen. Stichting voor Oliehoudende Zaden
Meded Sticht PlVered — Mededelingen. Stichting voor Plantenveredeling
Meded Stud Comm Metal Leid KeurInst WatLeidArt — Mededelingen. Studie-Commissie Metalen Leidingen, Keuringsinstituut voor Waterleidingartikelen
Meded Subcomm Tuinsproeiers KeurInst WatLeidArt — Mededelingen Subcommissie Tuinsproeiers, Keuringsinstituut voor Waterleidingartikelen
Meded TuinbVoorlDienst — Mededelingen van den Tuinbouwvoorlichtingsdienst
Med Educ — Medical Education
Med Educ Bull — Medical Education Bulletin. W.H.O. Regional Office for South East Asia
Med Educ (Oxf) — Medical Education (Oxford)
Meded Uitv Com Ned Wegen Congr — Mededelingen uitg. door het Uitvoerend Comite. Nederlandsch Wegen-Congres
Meded Vakgroep Landbouwplantenteelt Graslandkd — Mededeling Vakgroep Landbouwplantenteelt en Graslandkunde
Meded Veeartsenijk Dienst — Mededelingen. Veeartsenijkundige Dienst
Meded Veeartsenijsch Rijksuniv Gent — Mededelingen. Veeartsenijschool. Rijksuniversiteit te Gent
Meded VeeartsSch Rijksuniv Gent — Mededelingen der Veeartsenijschool van de Rijksuniversiteit te Gent
Meded Vereen Dordt Ing — Mededelingen. Vereeniging van Dordtsche Ingenieurs
Meded Vereen Luchtbehand — Mededelingen. Vereeniging voor Luchtbehandelingen
Meded Versl VisschInsp — Mededelingen en Verslagen der Visscherijinspectie
Meded Vezelinst TNO — Mededeling. Vezelinstituut TNO
Meded Vissch — Mededelingen over Visscherij
Meded VisschStn Batavia — Mededelingen van het Visscherijstation te Batavia
Meded Vlaam Chem Ver — Mededelingen. Vlaamse Chemische Vereniging
Meded Vlaam Chem Vereen — Mededelingen der Vlaamsche Chemische Vereeniging
Meded Vl Topon Ver — Mededeelingen Uitgegeven. Vlaamse Toponymische Vereniging
Meded Werkgrp Meteoren Ned Vereen Weer En Steerenk — Mededelingen. Werkgroep Meteoren van de Nederlandse Vereeniging voor Weer- en Sterrenkunde
Meded Wiskd Genoot — Mededelingen van het Wiskundig Genootschap
Meded Zeevaartk Geb Ned Oost Indie — Mededelingen op Zeevaartkundig Gebied over Nederlandsch Oost-Indie
Meded Zeew — Mededelingen Betreffende het Zeewezen
Meded Zittingen K Acad Overzeese Wet (Brussels) — Mededelingen der Zittingen. Koninklijke Academie voor Overzeese Wetenschappen (Brussels)
Meded Zuiderzee Comm Ned Dierk Vereen — Mededelingen van de Zuiderzee-Commissie, Nederlandsche Dierkundige Vereeniging
Meded Zuid-Nederl Dial Centr — Mededeelingen. Zuid-Nederlandsche Dialect Centrale
Med Eksp Biol Tr Mosk Konf Molodykh Uch — Meditsina i Eksperimental'naya Biologiya. Trudy Moskovskoi Konferentsii Molodykh Uchenykh
Med Elec — Medical Electronics
Med Elec — Medical Electronics and Data
Med Elect — Medecine Electrique
Med Electrol Radiol — Medical Electrology and Radiology
Med Electron — Medical Electronics
Med Electron Biol Eng — Medical Electronics and Biological Engineering
Med Electron Data — Medical Electronics and Data
Med Electron Microsc — Medical Electron Microscopy
Med Electron (Tokyo) — Medical Electronics (Tokyo)
Med Electropath — Medecine Electropathique

Medelhavs Mus B — Medelhavsmuseet Bulletin
Medelhavsmus Bull — Medelhavsmuseet Bulletin
Medelh Bull — Bulletin. Medelhausmuseet
Med Entomol Zool — Medical Entomology and Zoology
Med Era Chicago — Medical Era (Chicago)
Med Era (St Louis) — Medical Era (St. Louis)
Med Ernaehr — Medizin und Ernaehrung
Med Esp — Medicina Espanola
Med Espan — Medicina Espanola
Med Esporte — Medicina do Esporte
Med Essays and Obs (Edinb) — Medical Essays and Observations (Edinburgh)
Med et Hum — Mediaevalia et Humanistica
Med Exam — Medical Examiner
Med Exam Practnr — Medical Examiner and Practitioner
Med Exp — Medicina Experimentalis
Med Exp Int J Exp Med — Medicina Experimentalis. International Journal of Experimental Medicine
Med Exp (Kharkov) — Medecine Experimentale (Kharkov)
MedF — Medecine de France
Med F — Medicinsk Forum
Med Fem Norm — Medecine Feminine Normale
Med Fis Rehabil — Medicina Fisica y Rehabilitacion
Med Folge Ber Osteur Inst Freien Univ Berlin — Medizinische Folge der Berichte des Osteuropa-Institut an der Freien Universitaet Berlin
Medford Hist Reg — Medford Historical Register. Medford Historical Society
Med Forsch — Medizinische Forschung
Med Fortn — Medical Fortnightly
Med Forum — Medical Forum
Med Forum — Medicinsk Forum
Med Foyer — Medecine du Foyer
Med Fr — Medecin de France
Med Fr — Medecine Francaise
Med Free Press — Medical Free Press
Med Gaz Canton — Medical Gazette. Dr. Sun Yat-Sen Medical College (Canton)
Med Gaz Cleveland — Medical Gazette (Cleveland)
Med Gaz St Louis — Medical Gazette (St. Louis, Mo.)
Med Geriatr — Medicina Geriatrica
Med Ges — Medizin und Gesellschaft
Med Glas — Medicinski Glasnik
Med Group Manage — Medical Group Management
Med Group News — Medical Group News
Med Grundlagenforsch — Medizinische Grundlagenforschung
Med Guild Q — Medical Guild Quarterly
Med Gynaecol Androl Sociol — Medical Gynaecology, Andrology, and Sociology
Med Gynaecol Sociol — Medical Gynaecology and Sociology
MedH — Medical History
Med Hammare Fackla — Med Hammare och Fackla
Med Harbinger — Medical Harbinger
Med Health Care Philos — Medicine, Health Care, and Philosophy
Med Her — Medical Heritage
Med Her New Albany — Medical Herald (New Albany)
Med Her St Joseph — Medical Herald (St. Joseph)
Med Heute Osaka — Medizin von Heute (Osaka)
Med Hist — Medical History
Med Hist Arsb — Medicinhistorisk Arsbok
Med Hist Suppl — Medical History. Supplement
Med Hlth Rep Aden — Medical and Health Report. Colony of Aden
Med Hoje — Medicina de Hoje
Med Hum — Mediaevalia et Humanistica
Med Hupe UERJ — Medicina Hupe-UERJ
Med Hyg — Medecine et Hygiene
Med Hyg Anvers — Medecine et Hygiene (Anvers)
Med Hyg Brux — Medecine et Hygiene (Bruxelles)
Med Hyg (Geneve) — Medecine et Hygiene (Geneve)
Med Hypnoanal — Medical Hypnoanalysis
Med Hypotheses — Medical Hypotheses
Media — Mediafile
MediA — Medicinhistorisk Arsbok
Media, C & S — Media, Culture, and Society
Media Culture Soc — Media, Culture, and Society
Media Eco — Media Ecology Review
Media Educ and Dev — Media in Education and Development
Mediaevalia Phil Polonorum — Mediaevalia Philosophica Polonorum
Mediaeval Philos Texts Transl — Mediaeval Philosophical Texts in Translation
Mediaeval Renaiss Stud Warburg Inst — Mediaeval and Renaissance Studies. Warburg Institute
Mediaeval Stud — Mediaeval Studies
Mediaev Philos Pol — Mediaevalia Philosophica Polonorum
Mediaev St — Mediaeval Studies
Mediaev Stud — Mediaeval Studies
Media Ind N — Media Industry Newsletter
Media in Educ Dev — Media in Education and Development
Media Inf Aust — Media Information Australia
Media L Notes — Media Law Notes
Media L Rep BNA — Media Law Reporter. Bureau of National Affairs
Media Manage Jnl — Media Management Journal
Media Per — Media Perspektiven
Media Rep — Media Reporter
Media Rev — Media Review
Media Rev Dig — Media Review Digest
Media Rpt — Media Report to Women
Mediators Inflammation — Mediators of Inflammation
Mediators Pulm Inflammation — Mediators of Pulmonary Inflammation
Medical — Medical Self-Care
Medical J Aust — Medical Journal of Australia

Medicamenta (Ed Farm) — Medicamenta (Edicion para el Farmaceutico)
Medicam Mod — Medicamentos Modernos
Medicat Mart — Medication Martiale
Medicat Nouv — Medication Nouvelle
Medic Educ Brief — Medical Education Briefing
Medic Educ Newsl — Medical Education Newsletter
Medicent Man — Medicenter Management
Medic Hist — Medical History
Medicina (Rijeka Yugosl) — Medicina (Rijeka, Yugoslavia)
Medicine Ill — Medicine Illustrated
Medicine Lab Prog — Medicine and Laboratory Progress
Medicine Monogr — Medicine Monographs
Medicine Sci Law — Medicine, Science, and Law
Medicine Surg — Medicine and Surgery
Medicine Yr — Medicine of the Year
Medico Ital — Medico Italiano
Medicolegal Dig — Medicolegal Digest
Medico Legal J — Medico-Legal Journal
Medico-Legal Soc Proc — Medico-Legal Society. Proceedings
Medico-Legal Soc VIC Proc — Medico-Legal Society of Victoria. Proceedings
Medicoleg Libr — Medicolegal Library
Medicoleg News — Medicolegal News
Medico Prat — Medico Pratico
Medico Prat Contemp — Medico Pratico Contemporaneo
Medico Vet (Torino) — Il Medico Veterinario (Torino)
Medien — Medien und Erziehung
Medien Jnl — Medien Journal
Mediev A — Medieval Archaeology
Medieval Arch — Medieval Archaeology
Medieval Archaeol — Medieval Archaeology
Medieval Ceram — Medieval Ceramics
Medievalia Hum — Medievalia et Humanistica. Studies in Medieval and Renaissance Culture
Medieval Renaiss Stud Univ N Carolina — Medieval and Renaissance Studies. University of North Carolina
Mediev et Hum — Mediaevalia et Humanistica
Mediev Humanist — Medievalia et Humanistica
Med Image Anal — Medical Image Analysis
Med Image Process — Medical Image Processing
Med Imaging — Medical Imaging
Med Imaging Instrum — Medical Imaging and Instrumentation
Med Imaging VI Image Capture Formatting Disp — Medical Imaging VI. Image Capture, Formatting, and Display
Med Imaging VI Image Process — Medical Imaging VI. Image Processing
Med Imaging VI Instrum — Medical Imaging VI. Instrumentation
Med Imaging VI PACS Des Eval — Medical Imaging VI. PACS Design and Evaluation
Med Immunol — Medical Immunology
Med Immunsuppr Arbeitstag — Medikamentoese Immunsuppression, Arbeitstagung
Med Index Hosp Equip — Medical Index of Hospital Equipment
Med Inf — Medecine et Informatique
Med Inf — Medical Informatics
Med Infant — Medecine Infantile
Med Inf (Lond) — Medecine et Informatique (London)
Med Inform Statist — Medizinische Informatik und Statistik
Med Inst Lufthyg Silikoseforsch Jahresber — Medizinisches Institut fuer Lufthygiene und Silikoseforschung. Jahresbericht
Med Instrum — Medical Instrumentation
Med Instrum (Arlington) — Medical Instrumentation (Arlington, VA)
Med Insur Hlth Conserv — Medical Insurance and Health Conservation
Med Int — Medecine Internationale
Med Int — Medicine International
Med Interna — Medicina Interna
Med Interna (Buchar) — Medicina Interna (Bucharest)
Med Interne — Medecine Interne
Med Interne (Paris) — Medecine Interne (Paris)
Med Intern Radiat Dose Comm Pam — Medical Internal Radiation Dose Committee, Pamphlets
Medisch Cont — Medisch Contact
Medische Ber Semarang — Medische Berichten (Semarang)
Medisch Maandbl — Medisch Maandblad
Medisch Pharm Nieuws — Medisch en Pharmaceutish Nieuws
Medisch Weekbl — Medisch Weekblad voor Nord- en Zuid-Nederland
Medi Sci — Medi Science
MEDISTAT — Banque de Donnees Socio-economiques des Pays Mediterraneens
Med Istraz — Medicinska Istrazivanja
Med Istraz Suppl — Medicinska Istrazivanja. Supplementum
Medit — Mediterraneo
Med Ital — Medicina Italiana. Rivista di Pediatria e Malattie Infettive
Medit Archaeol — Mediterranean Archaeology
MEDITEC — Medizinische Technik
Mediterranean Electrotechnical Conf - MELECON — Mediterranean Electrotechnical Conference. MELECON
Mediterr Congr Rheumatol — Mediterranean Congress of Rheumatology
Mediterr Med — Mediterranee Medicale
Medit Naturalist — Mediterranean Naturalist. A Monthly Journal of Natural Science
Meditsin Referat Zh — Meditsinskii Referatinynyi Zhurnal
Medium Aev — Medium Aevum
Medium Energy Antiprotons Quark Gluon Struct Hadrons — Medium-Energy Antiprotons and the Quark-Gluon Structure of Hadrons
Medizinalkalender Berl — Medizinalkalender (Berlin)
Medizinal Statist Nachr — Medizinalstatistische Nachrichten
Medizin Chem — Medizin und Chemie
Medizin Ernaehr — Medizin und Ernaehrung

Medizinhist J — Medizinhistorisches Journal
Medizin SowjUn Volksdemokr Ref — Medizin der Sowjetunion und der Volksdemokratien im Referat
M Ed J — Music Educators Journal
MEDJA — Music Educators Journal
Med J Abstr — Medical Journal Abstracts
Med J Armed Forces (India) — Medical Journal. Armed Forces (India)
Med J Aserb — Medizinishes Journal von Aserbaidshan
Med J Assist Med Practnr Serv Suva — Medical Journal of the Assistant Medical Practitioner Service (Suva)
Med J Aust — Medical Journal of Australia
Med J Austral — Medical Journal of Australia
Med J Aust Supp — Medical Journal of Australia. Supplement
Med J Cairo Univ — Medical Journal. Cairo University
Med J Charlotte — Medical Journal (Charlotte)
Med J Chulalongkorn Hosp Med Sch (Bangkok) — Medical Journal. Chulalongkorn Hospital Medical School (Bangkok)
Med J Columbus — Medical Journal (Columbus)
Med J Commun — Medical Journal for Communication
Med J EAC — Medical Journal. Emilio Aguinaldo College of Medicine
Med J Egypt Armed Forces — Medical Journal of the Egyptian Armed Forces
Med J Emilio Aguinaldo Coll Med — Medical Journal. Emilio Aguinaldo College of Medicine
Med J (Engl Transl Lijec Vjesn) — Medical Journal (English Translation of Lijecnicki Vjesnik)
Med J Fraternity Mem Hosp — Medical Journal. Fraternity Memorial Hospital
Med J Han-Il Hosp — Medical Journal. Han-Il Hospital
Med J Hiroshima Prefect Hosp — Medical Journal. Hiroshima Prefectural Hospital
Med J Hiroshima Univ — Medical Journal. Hiroshima University
Med J Kagoshima Univ — Medical Journal. Kagoshima University
Med J Kinki Univ — Medical Journal. Kinki University
Med J Kobe Univ — Medical Journal. Kobe University
Med Jl S Afr — Medical Journal of South Africa
Med Jl SW — Medical Journal of the South-West [Bristol]
Med J Mag — Medical Journal Magazine
Med J Malaya — Medical Journal of Malaya [Later, Medical Journal of Malaysia]
Med J Malays — Medical Journal of Malaysia
Med J Malaysia — Medical Journal of Malaysia
Med J Med Assoc Siam — Medical Journal. Medical Association of Siam
Med J Med Ass Siam — Medical Journal. Medical Association of Siam
Med J Minami Osaka Hosp — Medical Journal. Minami Osaka Hospital
Med J Mut Aid Ass Tokyo — Medical Journal of the Mutual Aid Association (Tokyo)
Med J Mutual Aid Assoc — Medical Journal. Mutual Aid Association
Med J Natl Hosp Sanat Jpn — Medical Journal. National Hospitals and Sanatoriums of Japan
Med J Neth Indies — Medical Journal for the Netherlands Indies
Med J Osaka Univ — Medical Journal. Osaka University
Med J Osaka Univ (Engl Ed) — Medical Journal. Osaka University (English Edition)
Med J Osaka Univ (Jpn Ed) — Medical Journal. Osaka University (Japanese Edition)
Med Jour And Rec — Medical Journal and Record
Med J Rec — Medical Journal and Record
Med J Shimane Cent Hosp — Medical Journal. Shimane Central Hospital
Med J Shinshu Univ — Medical Journal. Shinshu University
Med J Siamese Red Cross — Medical Journal. Siamese Red Cross
Med J Siam Red Cross — Medical Journal of the Siamese Red Cross
Med J So Africa — Medical Journal of South Africa
Med J South West — Medical Journal. South West
Med J Sumitomo Hosp — Medical Journal. Sumitomo Hospital
Med J (Ukr) — Medical Journal (Ukraine)
Med J Zambia — Medical Journal of Zambia
Med Klin — Medizinische Klinik
Med Klin (Berlin) — Medizinische Klinik (Berlin)
Med Klin (Muenchen) — Medizinische Klinik (Muenchen)
Med Klin Norddtsch Ausg — Medizinische Klinik. Norddeutsche Ausgabe
Med Klin Sueddtsch Ausg — Medizinische Klinik. Sueddeutsche Ausgabe
Med Klin Suppl — Medizinische Klinik. Supplement
Med Kosmet — Medizinische Kosmetik
Med Krit Bl — Medizinisch-Kritische Blaetter
Med (L) — Medicina (Lisbon)
Med Lab — Medecine et Laboratoire
Med Lab — Medizinische Laboratorium
Med Lab Observer — Medical Laboratory Observer
Medical Laboratory Advisory — Medical Laboratory Advisory Service
Med Lab Sci — Medical Laboratory Sciences
Med Lab (Stuttg) — Medizinische Laboratorium (Stuttgart)
Med Lab Tec — Medical Laboratory Technology
Med Lab Technol — Medical Laboratory Technology
Med Lab World — Medical Laboratory World
Med Lasers Syst — Medical Lasers and Systems
Med Lav — Medicina del Lavoro
Med Law — Medicine and Law
Med Leaves — Medical Leaves
Med Leg & Crimin R — Medico-Legal and Criminological Review
Med Leg & Crim Rev — Medico-Legal and Criminological Review
Med Leg Assicur — Medicina Legale e delle Assicurazioni
Med Leg Bull — Medico-Legal Bulletin
Med-Leg Criminol Rev — Medico-Legal and Criminological Review
Med Leg Dommage Corpor — Medecine Legale et Dommage Corporel
Med Leg Hop Congr Acad Int Med Leg Med Soc — Medecine Legale a l'Hopital. Congres. Academie Internationale de Medecine Legale et de Medecine Sociale
Med Leg J — Medico-Legal Journal
Med-Leg J (London) — Medico-Legal Journal (London)

Med-Leg J (NY) — Medico-Legal Journal (New York)
Med Leg N — Medico-Legal News
Med Leg Soc Tr — Medico-Legal Society. Transactions
Med Leg Soc Trans — Transactions. Medico-Legal Society
Med Leg Soc Victoria Proc — Medico-Legal Society of Victoria. Proceedings
Med Leg Toxicol — Medecine Legale. Toxicologie
Med Leg Vic Proc — Medico-Legal Society of Victoria. Proceedings
Medlemsbl Dan Dyrlaegeforen — Medlemsblad foer den Danske Dyrlaegeforening
Medlemsbl Foren Danske LandbrKand — Medlemsblad. Foreningen af Danske Landbrugskandidater
Medlemsbl Nor Veterinaerforen — Medlemsblad den Norske Veterinaerforening
Medlemsbl Sver Veterinaerfoerb — Medlemsblad. Sveriges Veterinaerfoerbund
Medlemsbl Sver VetFoerb — Medlemsblad foer Sveriges Veterinaerfoerbund
Medlemsskr Stiftelsen Glasinst (Vaexjoe Swed) — Medlemsskrift. Stiftelsen Glasinstitutet (Vaexjoe, Sweden)
Medlesmbl Danske Dyrlaegeforen — Medlemsblad for den Danske Dyrlaegeforening
Med Lett — Medical Letter
Med Lett Drugs Ther — Medical Letter on Drugs and Therapeutics
Med Liability Advisory — Medical Liability Advisory Service
Med Liab R — Medical Liability Reporter
Med Lib Assn Bul — Medical Library Association. Bulletin
Med Lib Assn Bull — Medical Library Association. Bulletin
Med Libr — Medical Libraries
Med Libr Hist J — Medical Library and Historical Journal
Med Librs — Medical Libraries
Med Life — Medical Life
Med LJ — Medico-Legal Journal
Med L Rptr — Media Law Reporter
Med Maandbl — Medisch Maandblad
Med Mag Lond — Medical Magazine (London)
Med Mag Tel Aviv — Medical Magazine (Tel-Aviv)
MEDMAL — Medical Malpractice Lawsuit Filings
Med Malpract Cost Containment J — Medical Malpractice Cost Containment Journal
Med Market Media — Medical Marketing and Media
Med Mark Media — Medical Marketing and Media
Med Markt — Medical Marketing and Media
Med Markt Acta Medicotech — Medizinal-Markt/Acta Medicotechnica
Med Medecins — Medecine et Medecins
MED Media Educ and Dev — MED. Media in Education and Development
Med Meetings — Medical Meetings
Med Mentor — Medical Mentor
Med Met Ber — Medizin-Meteorologischer Berichte
Med Met Ergaenz Zehntaeg NW Dt WittBer — Medizin-Meteorologische Ergaenzungen zum Zehntaegigen Nordwestdeutscher Witterungsbericht
Med Met Hft — Medizin-Meteorologische Hefte
Med Microbi — Medical Microbiology and Immunology
Med Microbiol — Medical Microbiology
Med Microbiol Hyg — Medical Microbiology and Hygiene
Med Microbiol Immunol — Medical Microbiology and Immunology
Med Microbiol Lett — Medical Microbiology Letters
Med Midway — Medicine on the Midway
Med Milit Rev — Medico-Military Review
Med Mirror — Medical Mirror
Med Misc — Medical Miscellany
Med Missions Home Abroad — Medical Missions at Home and Abroad
Med Missions India — Medical Missions in India
Med Mkt — Medical Marketing and Media
Med Mod — Medecine Moderne
Med Mod — Medicina Moderna
Med Mod Can — Medecine Moderne du Canada
Med Moderne — Medecine Moderne
Med Mod (Paris) — Medecine Moderne (Paris)
Med Mon — Medical Monthly
Med Monatsschr — Medizinische Monatsschrift
Med Monatsschr Pharm — Medizinische Monatsschrift fuer Pharmazeuten
Med Monatssp — Medizinischer Monatsspiegel
Med Monatsspiegel — Medizinischer Monatsspiegel
Med Monde — Medecine dans le Monde
Med Morale — Medicina e Morale
Med Mundi — Medica Mundi
Med Mycol — Medical Mycology [Oxford]
Med Mysl Uzbekistana — Meditsinskaia Mysl Uzbekistana
Medna Cient — Medicina Cientifica
Medna Cirug Barcelona — Medicina y Cirugia (Barcelona)
Medna Cirug Bogota — Medicina y Cirugia (Bogota)
Medna Cirug Guerra — Medicina y Cirugia de Guerra
Medna Cirug Occid — Medicina y Cirugia de Occidente [Guadalajara]
Medna Cirug Ortop — Medicina, Cirugia, Ortopedica
Medna Cirug Zootec — Medicina y Cirugia Zootecnicas
Medna Cirurg Farm — Medicina, Cirurgia, Farmacia
Medna Cirurg Porto Alegre — Medicina e Cirurgia (Porto Alegre)
Medna Cirurg Recife — Medicina e Cirurgia (Recife)
Medna Clin — Medicina Clinica
Medna Clin Sper — Medicina Clinica e Sperimentale
Medna Colon — Medicina Colonial
Medna Contemp — Medicina Contemporanea
Medna Deporte Trab — Medicina del Deporte y del Trabajo
Mednae Novit — Medicinae Novitates
Medna Esp — Medicina Espanola
Medna Exp — Medicina Experimentalis
Medna Farm — Medicina y Farmacia
Medna Fenn — Medicina Fennica
Medna Fis Rehabil — Medicina Fisica y Rehabilitacion

Medna Homeop Mex — Medicina Homeopatica Mexicana
Medna Hoy — Medicina de Hoy
Medna Infant — Medicina Infantile
Medna Infort Lav — Medicina degli Infortuni del Lavoro e delle Malattie Professionali
Medna Interna — Medicina Interna [Bucuresti]
Medna Int Parigi — Medicina Internazionale (Parigi)
Medna Int Paris — Medicina Internacional (Paris)
Medna Ital Milano — Medicina Italiana (Milano)
Medna Ital Napoli — Medicina Italiana (Napoli)
Medna Jurispr Accid Trab — Medicina y Jurisprudencia de Accidentes del Trabajo
Medna Latina Habana — Medicina Latina (Habana)
Medna Latina Madr — Medicina Latina (Madrid)
Medna Lav — Medicina del Lavoro
Medna Leg — Medicina Legal
Medna Libr — Medicina y Libros
Medna Milit — Medicina Militar
Medna Milit Esp — Medicina Militar Espanola
Medna Milit Medna Civ — Medicina Militar, Medicina Civil
Medna Mod Barcelona — Medicina Moderna (Barcelona)
Medna Mod Genova — Medicina Moderna (Genova)
Medna Mod Porto — Medicina Moderna (Porto)
Medna Mod Valencia — Medicina Moderna (Valencia)
Medna Mod Valparaiso — Medicina Moderna (Valparaiso)
Medna Ninos — Medicina de los Ninos
Medna Nuova — Medicina Nuova
Medna Paises Calid — Medicina de los Paises Calidos
Medna Panam — Medicina Panamericana
Medna Pop — Medicina Popolare
Medna Pract Barcelona — Medicina Practica (Barcelona)
Medna Pract Zaragoza — Medicina Practica (Zaragoza)
Medna Prat Napoli — Medicina Pratica (Napoli)
Medna Prat Paris — Medicina Pratica (Paris)
Medna Prev — Medicina Preventiva
Medna Prog — Medicina y sus Progresos
Medna Psicosom — Medicina Psicosomatica
Medna Revta — Medicina em Revista
Medna Rur — Medicina Rural
Medna Sec XX — Medicina nel Secolo XX
Medna Segur Trab — Medicina y Seguridad del Trabajo
Medna Soc Lima — Medicina Social (Lima)
Medna Soc Napoli — Medicina Sociale (Napoli)
Medna Soc Torino — Medicina Sociale (Torino)
Med Nat — Medecine Naturelle
Med Naturw Arch — Medizinisch-Naturwissenschaftliches Archiv
Med Naturw Gesell Zu Jena Denks — Medizinisch-Naturwissenschaftliche Gesellschaft zu Jena. Denkschriften
Med Naturwiss Arch — Medizinisch-Naturwissenschaftliches Archiv
Medna Vet Porto Alegre — Medicina Veterinaria (Porto Alegre)
Medna Vet Valladolid — Medicina Veterinaria (Valladolid)
Med NC — Meddelelser fra Ny Carlsberg Glyptotek
Med Nederl Hist Inst Rom — Mededelingen van het Nederlandsch Historisch Instituut te Rome
Med Ned Ver Int R — Mededelingen van de Nederlandse Vereniging voor Internationaal Recht
Med News — Medical News
Med News Cincinn — Medical News (Cincinnati)
Med Newsl — Medical Newsletter
Med Newsmag — MD Medical Newsmagazine
Med News NY — Medical News (New York)
Med NI Rome — Mededelingen. Nederlandsch Historisch Instituut te Rome
Mednl Chem — Medicinal Chemistry
Mednlhist Dokum — Medicinalhistoriske Dokumenter
Med Norm — Medecine Normale
Med Notes — Medical Notes
Med Notes Quer — Medical Notes and Queries
Med Nouv — Medecine Nouvelle
Med Nucl — Medecine Nucleaire
Med Nucl Radiobiol Lat — Medicina Nucleare. Radiobiologica Latina
Med Nucl Radiobiol Lat Suppl — Medicina Nucleare. Radiobiologica Latina. Supplement
Med Nucl Suppl — Medecine Nucleaire. Supplementum
Med Nutr — Medecine et Nutrition
Med Nutr Res Commun — Medical and Nutritional Research Communications
Med Obozr — Meditsinskoe Obozrainie
Med Obozr — Meditsinskoe Obozrienio Sprimona
Med Obsr Dig — Medical Observer and Digest
Med Occidente — Medicina de Occidente
Med Off — Medical Officer
Med Officer — Medical Officer
Med Offr — Medical Officer
Med Oncol — Medical Oncology
Med Oncol Tumor Pharmacother — Medical Oncology and Tumor Pharmacotherapy
Med Opin Rev — Medical Opinion and Review
Med Oral — Medecine Orientale
Med Orient — Medecine Orientale et les Archives Orientales de Medecine et de Chirurgie
Med Orthop Tech — Medizinisch-Orthopaedische Technik
Med Other Appl Proc Int Congr Isozymes — Medical and Other Applications. Proceedings. InternationalCongress on Isozymes
Medoty Vysokomolek Org Khim — Metody Vysokomolekulyarnoi Organicheskoi Khimii
Med Outl — Medical Outlook
Med (P) — Medicina (Parma)

Med Paedag Mschr Ges Sprachheilk — Medizinisch-Paedagogische Monatsschrift fuer die Gesamte Sprachheilkunde

Med Paedagog Jugendkd — Medizinische und Paedagogische Jugendkunde

Med Paises Calidos — Medicina de los Paises Calidos

Med Pamph Med Soc Indiv Psychol — Medical Pamphlets. Medical Society of Individual Psychology

Med Panam — Medicina Panamericana

Med Parazitol — Meditsinskaya Parazitologiya i Parazitarnye Bolezni

Med Parazitol Parazit Bolezni — Meditsinskaya Parazitologiya i Parazitarnye Bolezni

Med Pediatr Oncol — Medical and Pediatric Oncology

Med Pediatr Oncol Suppl — Medical and Pediatric Oncology. Supplement

Med Pharm — Medical Pharmacy

Med Pharmacol Exp — Medicina et Pharmacologia Experimentalis

Med Pharmacol Exp Int J Exp Med — Medicina et Pharmacologia Experimentalis. International Journal of ExperimentalMedicine

Med Pharm Crit Guide — Medico-Pharmaceutical Critic and Guide

Med Pharm J Brooklyn — Medico-Pharmaceutical Journal (Brooklyn)

Med Pharm J Philadel — Medico-Pharmaceutical Journal (Philadelphia)

Med Philos — Medicina Philosophica

Med Phys — Medical Physics

Med Phys — Medica Physica

Med Phys Bull — Medical Physics Bulletin

Med Phys Forsch Prax Wiss Tag Dtsch Ges Med Phys — Medizinische Physik in Forschung und Praxis. Wissenschaftliche Tagungder Deutschen Gesellschaft fuer Medizinische Physik

Med Phys Handb — Medical Physics Handbooks

Med Physiol — Medical Physiology

Med Phys J — Medical and Physical Journal

Med Pickwick — Medical Pickwick

Med Podmladak — Medicinski Podmladak

Med Pop — Medecine Populaire

Med Post — Medical Post

Med Pr — Medycyna Pracy

Med Pract Let — Medical Practice Letter

Med Prat — Medecine Praticienne

Med Prat — Medecine Pratique

Med Prat (Napoli) — Medicina Pratica (Napoli)

Med Pratne — Medecine Praticienne

Med Pregl — Medicinski Pregled

Med Press — Medical Press

Med Press and Circ — Medical Press and Circular

Med Press Egypt — Medical Press of Egypt

Med Princ Pract — Medical Principles and Practice

Med Prisma — Medizinische Prisma

Med Probl — Medicinski Problemi

Med Probl Performing Artists — Medical Problems of Performing Artists

Med Proc — Medical Proceedings

Med Prod Sales — Medical Products Sales

Med Prod Salesman — Medical Products Salesman

Med Prof — Medical Profession

Med Prof Womans J — Medical and Professional Woman's Journal

Med Prog A — Medical Progress Annual

Med Prog Lond — Medical Progress (London)

Med Prog Louisville — Medical Progress (Louisville)

Med Prog (NY) — Medical Progress (New York)

Med Prog Technol — Medical Progress through Technology

Med Prom-St SSSR — Meditsinskaya Promyshlennost SSSR

Med Pr Tech — Medical Progress through Technology

Med Psicosom — Medicina Psicosomatica

Med Psychiatry — Medical Psychiatry

Med Publ Found Symp Ser — Medicine Publishing Foundation Symposium Series

Med Publs Leland Stanford Jun Univ — Medical Publications. Leland Stanford Junior University

Med Q Dep Sold Civ Re Establ Ottawa — Medical Quarterly. Department of Soldiers' Civil Re-establishment. Canada (Ottawa)

Med Q Indiana Univ Sch Med — Medical Quarterly. Indiana University. School of Medicine

Med Q Kingston — Medical Quarterly (Kingston)

Med Quart Rev — Medical Quarterly Review

Med R — Medioevo Romanzo

MedR — Mediterranean Review

Med Radiogr Photogr — Medical Radiography and Photography

Med Radiol — Meditsinskaya Radiologiya

Med Radiol (Mosk) — Meditsinskaia Radiologiia (Moskva)

Med Radiol Radiats Bezop — Meditsinskaya Radiologiya i Radiatsionnaya Bezopasnost

Med Radiol (USSR) — Medical Radiology (USSR)

Med Razgledi — Medicinski Razgledi

Med Rec — Medical Record

Med Rec Ann — Medical Record and Annals

Med Rec Health Care Inf J — Medical Record and Health Care Information Journal

Med Rec Mississippi — Medical Record of Mississippi

Med Rec News — Medical Record News

Med Rec (NY) — Medical Record (New York)

Med Recorder — Medical Recorder

Med Rec Pontefract — Medical Record. Association of Medical Record Officers (Pontefract)

Med Ref Serv Q — Medical Reference Services Quarterly

Med Ren — Mediaeval and Renaissance Studies

Med Ren St — Mediaeval and Renaissance Studies

Med Rep Br Hond — Medical Reports. British Honduras

Med Rep Br Hosp Mothers Babies — Medical Reports. British Hospital for Mothers and Babies

Med Rep Cent Lond Throat Ear Hosp — Medical Reports of the Central London Throat and Ear Hospital (London)

Med Rep Charles Univ Med Fac Hradec Kralove — Medical Reports. Charles University Medical Faculty at Hradec Kralove

Med Rep China Imp Marit Customs — Medical Reports. China Imperial Maritime Customs

Med Rep Cornell Univ Dispens — Medical Reports. Cornell University Medical College Dispensary

Med Rep Durand Hosp — Medical Reports of the Durand Hospital for the McCormick Institute [Chicago]

Med Rep FMS — Medical Reports. Federated Malay States

Med Rep Gen Lying In Hosp Lambeth — Medical Reports. General Lying-in Hospital. York Road. Lambeth [London]

Med Rep Grenada — Medical Reports. Grenada

Med Rep Hlth Sanit Cond Nth Rhod — Medical Reports on Health and Sanitary Conditions. Northern Rhodesia

Med Rep Japan — Medical Reports of Japan

Med Rep Madras Govt Matern Hosp — Medical Reports. Madras Government Maternity Hospital

Med Reposit — Medical Repository

Med Rep R Matern Wom Hosp Glasg — Medical Reports. Royal Maternity and Women's Hospital (Glasgow)

Med Rep R Samaritan Hosp Wom — Medical Reports. Royal Samaritan Hospital for Women

Med Rep Sch Aviat US Air Force — Medical Reports. School of Aviation. U.S. Air Force

Med Rep Sheppard Enoch Pratt Hosp — Medical Reports of the Sheppard and Enoch Pratt Hospital [Baltimore]

Med Rep Showa Med Sch — Medical Reports. Showa Medical School

Med Rep St Negri Sembilan — Medical Reports for the State of Negri Sembilan

Med Rep St Pahang — Medical Reports of the State of Pahang

Med Rep St Perak — Medical Reports for the State of Perak

Med Rep Str Settl — Medical Reports. Straits Settlements

Med Rep St Selangor — Medical Reports for the State of Selangor

Med Res — Medicinal Research

Med Res Bull Repat Dept — Repatriation Department. Medical Research Bulletin

Med Res Cent (Nairobi) Annu Rep — Medical Research Centre (Nairobi). Annual Report

Med Res Colon — Medical Research in the Colonies, Protectorates, and Mandated Territories [London]

Med Res Counc Clin Res Cent Symp (UK) — Medical Research Council. Clinical Research Centre Symposium (United Kingdom)

Med Res Counc (GB) Annu Rep — Medical Research Council (Great Britain). Annual Report

Med Res Counc (GB) Ind Health Res Board Rep — Medical Research Council (Great Britain). Industrial Health Research Board Report

Med Res Counc (GB) Lab Anim Cent Man Ser — Medical Research Council (Great Britain). Laboratory Animals Centre. Manual Series

Med Res Counc (GB) Lab Anim Cent Symp — Medical Research Council (Great Britain). Laboratory Animals Centre. Symposia

Med Res Counc (GB) Memo — Medical Research Council (Great Britain). Memorandum

Med Res Counc (GB) Monit Rep — Medical Research Council (Great Britain). Monitoring Report

Med Res Counc (GB) Spec Rep Ser — Medical Research Council (Great Britain). Special Report Series

Med Res Counc Mon Bull — Medical Research Council. Monthly Bulletin

Med Res Coun Memo — Medical Research Council Memorandum [London]

Med Res Coun War Memo — Medical Research Council War Memorandum [London]

Med Res Eng — Medical Research Engineering

Med Res Index — Medical Research Index

Med Res Inst Tokyo Med Dent Univ Annu Rep — Medical Research Institute. Tokyo Medical and Dental University. Annual Report

Med Res Memo Natn Coal Bd Med Serv — Medical Research Memoranda. National Coal Board Medical Service [London]

Med Res Photosens Dyes Kyoto — Medical Researches for Photosensitizing Dyes. Kyoto University Institute of Pathology

Med Res Photosensit Dyes — Medical Researches for Photosensitizing Dyes

Med Res Proj — Medical Research Projects

Med Res Rev — Medicinal Research Reviews

Med Res Ser Monogr — Medicinal Research: A Series of Monographs

Med Res Veterans Adm US — Medical Research in the Veterans Administration. U.S. Veterans Administration

Med Rev (Belgr) — Medicinska Revija (Belgrade)

Med Rev (Bergen) — Medicinsk Revue (Bergen)

Med Rev CARL — Medicina. Revista do CARL

Med Rev Cent Acad Rocha Lima (Sao Paulo) — Medicina. Revista do Centro Academico Rocha Lima [CARL] (Sao Paulo)

Med Rev (Chiba Jpn) — Medicina Revuo (Chiba, Japan)

Med Rev Edinb — Medical Review (Edinburgh)

Med Rev Lond — Medical Review (London)

Med Rev Mens Estud Trab Prof Ed Farm — Medicamenta. Revista Mensual de Estudios y Trabajos Profesionales.Edicion para el Farmaceutico

Med Rev Mex — Medicina Revista Mexicana

Med Rev Revs Calcutta — Medical Review of Reviews (Calcutta)

Med Rev Revs NY — Medical Review of Reviews (New York)

Med Rev St Louis — Medical Review (St. Louis)

Med Rev Tokyo — Medical Review (Tokyo)

Med Riv Encicl Med Ital — Medicina. Rivista della Enciclopedia Medica Italiana

MedRom — Medioevo Romanzo

MedS — Mediaeval Studies

MedS — Medical Socioeconomic Research Sources. American Medical Association

Med (S) — Medizinische (Stuttgart)

Med Sanit Rep Bahama Isl — Medical and Sanitary Report. Bahama Islands

Med Sanit Rep Gilbert Ellice Isl — Medical and Sanitary Report. Gilbert and Ellice Islands
Med Sanit Rep Hong Kong — Medical and Sanitary Report. Hong Kong
Med Sanit Rep Leeward Isl — Medical and Sanitary Report. Leeward Islands
Med Sanit Rep Nth Sth Prov Nigeria — Medical and Sanitary Report of the Northern and Southern Provinces. Nigeria
Med Sanit Rep St Christopher Nevis — Medican and Sanitary Report. St. Christopher and Nevis
Med Sanit Rep Trin — Medical and Sanitary Report. Trinidad and Tobago
Med Sanit Rep Zanzibar — Medical and Sanitary Report. Zanzibar
Med Scandinavia — Medieval Scandinavia
Medsche Klin (Muenchen) — Medizinische Klinik (Muenchen)
Medsche Kosm — Medizinische Kosmetik
Medsche Lit — Medizinische Literatur
Medsche Mitt Schering Kahlbaum — Medizinische Mitteilungen. Schering-Kahlbaum A.G
Medsche Mschr NY — Medizinische Monatsschrift (New York)
Medsche Mschr (Stuttg) — Medizinische Monatsschrift (Stuttgart)
Medsche Mschr Stuttg — Medizinische Monatsschrift (Stuttgart)
Medsche Novit — Medizinische Novitaeten
Medsche Rdsch — Medizinische Rundschau
Medsches KorrBl Wuertt Aerztl Landesver — Medizinisches Korrespondenzblatt des Wuerttembergischen Aerztlichen Landesvereins
Medsches Lit U Schriftst Vadem — Medizinisches Literatur- und Schriftsteller-Vademecum
Medsche Welt (Stuttg) — Medizinische Welt (Stuttgart)
Med Schl — Medical School Rounds
Med Sci — Medical Science
Med Sci Abstr Rev — Medical Science Abstracts and Reviews
Med Sci & L — Medicine, Science, and the Law
Med Scient — Medecine Scientifique
Med Scient Archs Adelaide Hosp — Medical and Scientific Archives of the Adelaide Hospital
Med Sci Law — Medicine, Science, and the Law
Med Sci Madras — Medical Science (Madras)
Med Sci Monit — Medical Science Monitor
Med Sci Res — Medical Science Research
Med Sect Sports — Medicine and Science in Sports
Med Sci Sports Exerc — Medicine and Science in Sports and Exercise
Med Sci Spt — Medicine and Science in Sports
Med Sci Symp Ser — Medical Science Symposia Series
Med Sci Tokyo — Medical Science. Science of the Living Body (Tokyo)
Med Scol — Medecine Scolaire
Med Searchlight — Medical Searchlight
Med Secoli — Medicina nei Secoli
Med Sect Proc — Medical Section Proceedings [Washington, DC]
Med Segur Trab (Madr) — Medicina y Seguridad del Trabajo (Madrid)
Med Sens — Medecine des Sens et de leurs Organes
Med Sent — Medical Sentinel
Med Ser Air Hyg Fdn Am — Medical Series. Air Hygiene Foundation of America
Med Serv — Medical Service
Med Services J (Canada) — Medical Services Journal (Canada)
Med Serv J (Can) — Medical Service Journal (Canada)
Med Servs J Can — Medical Services Journal. Canada
Med Sestra — Meditsinskaya Sestra
Medska Beseda — Meditsinska Beseda
Medska For Tidskr — Medicinska Foreningens Tidskrift
Medska Misul — Meditsinska Misul'
Medsk Arsb — Medicinsk Arsbok
Medskaya Beseda — Meditsinskaya Beseda
Medskaya Biblfiya — Meditsinskaya Bibliografiya
Medskaya Gaz — Meditsinskaya Gazeta
Medskaya Kn — Meditsinskaya Kniga
Medskaya Lit SSSR — Meditsinskaya Literatura SSSR
Medskaya Mysl Rostov — Meditsinskaya Mysl' (Rostov-na-Donu)
Medskaya Mysl Tashk — Meditsinskaya Mysl' (Tashkent)
Medskaya Parazit — Meditsinskaya Parazitologiya i Parazitarnye Bolezni
Medskaya Prom SSSR — Meditsinskaya Promyshlennost' SSSR
Medskaya Radiol — Meditsinskaya Radiologiya
Medskaya Sestra — Meditsinskaya Sestra
Medske Fremskridt — Medicinske Fremskridt
Medsk Forum — Medicinsk Forum
Medsk Hist Smaaskr — Medicinsk-Historiske Smaaskrifter
Medski Arh — Medicinski Arhiv
Medski Feld — Meditsinski Feldsher
Medski Glasn — Medicinski Glasnik
Medskii Byull — Meditsinskii Byulleten'
Medskii Rab — Meditsinskii Rabotnik
Medskii Ref Zh — Meditsinskii Referativnii Zhurnal
Medskii Sovrem — Meditsinskii Sovremennik
Medskii Zh — Meditsinskii Zhurnal
Medskii Zh Dr Oksa — Meditsinskii Zhurnal Doktora Oksa
Medskii Zh Uzbek — Meditsinskii Zhurnal Uzbekistana
Medski Let — Meditsinski Letopisi
Medski Napr — Meditsinski Napreduk
Medski Podml — Meditsinski Podmladak
Medski Pregl Beogr — Medicinski Pregled (Beograd)
Medski Pregl Novi Sad — Medicinski Pregled (Novi Sad)
Medskiya Pribavl Morsk Sb — Meditsinskiya Pribavleniya k Morskomu Sborniku, Izdavaemyya pod Nablyudeniem Flota General-Shtab-Doktora
Medsk ManRevy — Medicinsk Manadsrevy
Medskoe Obozr Nizhn Povolzh — Meditsinskoe Obozrenie Nizhnyago Povolzh'ya
Medskoe Obozr Sprimona — Meditsinskoe Obozrenie Sprimona
Medsko Spis — Meditsinsko Spisanie
Medsk Revue — Medicinsk Revue

Medsk Selsk Fyens Stifts Forh — Medicinsk Selskab for Fyens Stifts Forhandlinger
MEDSOC — Medical Socioeconomic Research Sources. American Medical Association
Med Soc — Medicina Sociale
Med Socioecon Res Source — Medical Socioeconomic Research Sources
Med Soc New Jersey J — Medical Society of New Jersey. Journal
Med Soc PA Tr — Medical Society of the State of Pennsylvania. Transactions
Med Soc Prev — Medecine Sociale et Preventive
Med Soc Prof — Medecine Sociale et Professionelle
Med Soc Tenn Trans — Medical Society of Tennessee. Transactions
Med Soc (Turin) — Medicina Sociale (Turin)
Med Soc Va Trans — Medical Society of Virginia. Transactions
Med Soldier — Medical Soldier
Med Sper — Medicina Sperimentale
Med Sper Arch Ital — Medicina Sperimentale. Archivio Italiano
Med Spin — Mededelingen van Wege het Spinozahuis
Med Sport — Medecine du Sport
Med Sport (Basel) — Medicine and Sport (Basel)
Med Sport (Berl) — Medizin und Sport (Berlin)
Med Sport (Berlin) — Medizin und Sport (Berlin)
Med Sportiva — Medicina Sportiva
Med Sport (Paris) — Medecine du Sport (Paris)
Med Sport Sci — Medicine and Sport Science
Med Sport (Turin) — Medicina dello Sport (Turin)
Med St — Mediaeval Studies
Med Stand — Medical Standard
Med Statist Nachr — Medizinal-Statistische Nachrichten
Med Strucni Cas Zlh Podruznica Rijeka — Medicina Strucni Casopis Zlh Podruznica Rijeka
Med Stud — Medieval Studies
Med Stud Mag — Medical Students' Magazine
Med Stud Opin — Medical Student Opinion
Med Summ — Medical Summary
Med Suppl Rev Foreign Press — Medical Supplement to the Review of the Foreign Press
Med Surg — Medicine and Surgery
Med Surg Bull — Medical and Surgical Bulletin
Med Surg J Trop — Medico-Surgical Journal of the Tropics
Med Surg Monit — Medical and Surgical Monitor
Med Surg Path Rep R Sth Hosp — Medical, Surgical, and Pathological Reports of the Royal Southern Hospital [Liverpool]
Med Surg Pediatr — Medical and Surgical Pediatrics
Med Surg Rep — Medical and Surgical Reporter
Med Surg Rep Bellevue All Hosps — Medical and Surgical Report of Bellevue and Allied Hospitals in the City of New York
Med Surg Rep Boston Cy Hosp — Medical and Surgical Report of the Boston City Hospital
Med Surg Rep Buffalo Gen Hosp — Medical and Surgical Report. Buffalo General Hospital
Med Surg Rep Episc Hosp Philad — Medical and Surgical Report. Episcopal Hospital. Philadelphia
Med Surg Rep Presb Hosp NY — Medical and Surgical Report. Presbyterian Hospital in the City of New York
Med Surg Rep Roosevelt Hosp — Medical and Surgical Report of the Roosevelt Hospital
Med Surg Rep St Lukes Hosp — Medical and Surgical Report of St. Luke's Hospital
Med Surg Sugg — Medico-Surgical Suggestions
Med Surg Yb Physns Hosp Plattsburgh — Medical and Surgical Year Book. Physicians' Hospital of Plattsburgh
Med Teach — Medical Teacher
Med Tech — Medizinische Technik
Med Tech Bull — Medical Technicians Bulletin
Med Tech J — Medico-Technologisches Journal
Med Tech Mitt Geb Instrum Tech — Medizinisch-Technische Mitteilungen aus den Gebieten der Instrumentellen Technik
Med Technol — Medical Technology
Med Technol Aust — Medical Technology in Australasia
Med Technol Aust — Medical Technology in Australia
Med Technol Australas — Medical Technology in Australasia
Med Technol Rev — Medical Technology Review
Med Technol Ser — Medical Technology Series
Med Technol (Tokyo) — Medical Technology (Tokyo)
Med Techns Bull — Medical Technicians Bulletin
Med Tech Publ Co Int Rev Sci Biochem — Medical and Technical Publishing Company. International Review of Science. Biochemistry
Med Tekh — Meditsinskaya Tekhnika
Med Tekh (Moscow) — Meditsinskaya Tekhnika (Moscow)
Med Tekh (Sofia) — Meditsinska Tekhnika (Sofia)
Med Temp Rev — Medical Temperance Review
Med Term Climatol — Medicina Termale e Climatologia
Med Therm Clim — Medecine Thermale et Climatique
Med Thorac — Medicina Thoracalis
Med Times — Medical Times
Med Times and Gaz (London) — Medical Times and Gazette (London)
Med Times Chicago — Medical Times (Chicago)
Med Times Denver — Medical Times (Denver)
Med Times Hosp Gaz — Medical Times and Hospital Gazette
Med Times (London) — Medical Times (London)
Med Times (NY) — Medical Times (New York)
Med Times Regist — Medical Times and Register
Med Top Chicago — Medical Topics (Chicago)
Med Top Melb — Medical Topics (Melbourne)
Med Toxicol — Medical Toxicology

Med Toxicol Adverse Drug Exper — Medical Toxicology and Adverse Drug Experience
Med Toxicol Proc EUROTOX Congr Meet — Medical Toxicology. Proceedings. EUROTOX Congress Meeting
Med Tradic — Medicina Tradicionale
Med Trav — Medecine du Travail
Med Trav Ergon — Medecine du Travail & Ergonomie
Med Treat (Tokyo) — Medical Treatment (Tokyo)
Med Trial Technique Q — Medical Trial Technique Quarterly
Med Trial Tech Q — Medical Trial Technique Quarterly
Med Trib — Medical Tribune
Med Trib Med N — Medical Tribune and Medical News
Med Trop — Medecine Tropicale
Med Trop (Madr) — Medicina Tropical (Madrid)
Med Trop (Madrid) — Medicina Tropical (Madrid)
Med Trop (Mars) — Medecine Tropicale (Marseilles)
Med Trop (Marseille) — Medecine Tropicale (Marseille)
Med Tr Prom Ekol — Meditsina Truda i Promyshlennaya Ekologiya
Med Tr TQ — Medical Trial Technique Quarterly
M Educators J — Music Educators Journal
MEDUD2 — Medical Education
Medullary Thyroid Carcinoma Proc Eur Congr — Medullary Thyroid Carcinoma. Proceedings. European Congress on Medullary Thyroid Carcinoma
Med Ultrasound — Medical Ultrasound
Med Univers — Medicina Universal
Med Universalis — Medicus Universalis
Med Univ Pleven Sci Works — Medical University of Pleven. Scientific Works
Medun Probl — Medunarodni Problemi
Med Unserer Zeit — Medizin in Unserer Zeit
Med Utilization Rev — Medical Utilization Review
Med VBN — Mededelingen van het Verbond der Belgische Nijverheid
Med Veg — Medecine Vegetale
Med Versuche Bemerk Ges Edinburgh — Die Medizinischen Versuche, Nebst Bemerkungen, Welche von Einer Gesellschaft inEdinburgh Durchgesehen und Herausgegeben Werden
Med Versuche u Bemerk (Edinb) — Medizinischen Versuche und Bemerkungen (Edinburgh)
Med Vet Entomol — Medical and Veterinary Entomology
Med Vet Hell — Medecine Veterinaire Hellenique
Med Vet Que — Medecin Veterinaire du Quebec
Med View — Medical View
Med Virol Proc Int Symp — Medical Virology. Proceedings. International Symposium
Med Visitor — Medical Visitor
Med Vital — Medecine Vitaliste
Med Vjesnik — Medicinski Vjesnik
Med W — Medizinische Woche
Med War — Medicine and War
Med Welt — Medizinische Welt
Med Weter — Medycyna Weterynaryjna
Med Wkly — Medical Weekly
Med Wld Lond — Medical World (London)
Med Wld News — Medical World News
Med Wld Newsl — Medical World Newsletter
Med Wld N Psychiat — Medical World News for Psychiatrists
Med Wld Philad — Medical World (Philadelphia)
Med Wochenbl Aerzte — Medicinisches Wochenblatt fuer Aerzte, Wundaerzte, und Apotheker
Med Womans J — Medical Woman's Journal
Med Wom J — Medical Woman's Journal
Med World — Medical World News
Med World News — Medical World News
Medycyna Dosw Mikrobiol — Medycyna Doswiadczalna i Mikrobiologia
Medycyna Dosw Spol — Medycyna Doswiadczalna i Spoleczna
Medycyna Kron Lek — Medycyna i Kronika Lekarska
Medycyna Pr — Medycyna Pracy
Medycyna Prakt — Medycyna Praktyczna
Medycyna Wet — Medycyna Weterynaryjna
Med Zb (Sarajevo) — Medicinski Zbornik (Sarajevo)
Med Zh (Kiev) — Medichnii Zhurnal (Kiev)
Med Zh (Ukr) — Medichnii Zhurnal (Ukraine)
Med Zh Uzb — Meditsinskii Zhurnal Uzbekistana
Medzinar Konf Org Povlakoch Pr — Medzinarodna Konferencia o Organickych Povlakoch. Prace
Medzinar Konf Praskovej Metal Zb Prednasok — Medzinarodna Konferencia o Praskovej Metalurgii. Zbornik Prednasok
Medzinar Konf Preduprave Mater Pr — Medzinarodna Konferencia o Preduprave Materialov. Prace
Medzinar Konf Text Chem — Medzinarodna Konferencia Textilnych Chemikov
Medzinar Symp Klznom Ulozeni Zb Prednasok — Medzinarodne Sympozium o Klznom Ulozeni. Zbornik Prednasok
Medzinar Symp Metrol — Medzinarodne Sympozium Metrologie
Med Ztg — Medizinische Zeitung
Med Ztg Russlands — Medizinische Zeitung. Russlands
Me E — Maria et Ecclesia
MEE — Megale Hellenike Enkyklopaideia
MEE — Middle East Economist
MEE — Middle East Executive Reports
MEECA — Messager Evangelique de l'Eglise de la Confession d'Augsbourg
MEEC Miss State Univ Coop Ext Serv — MEEC. Mississippi State University. Cooperative Extension Service
ME Eco Hbk — Middle East Economic Handbook
MEED — Middle East Economic Digest
Meehans Mon — Meehan's Monthly
MEEP — Middle East Economic Papers

MEEPA — Methods of Experimental Physics
Meeresk Beob Ergebn Dt Feuerschiffen — Meereskundliche Beobachtungen (afterwards und Ergebnisse) auf Deutschen Feuerschiffen der Nord und Ostsee
Meeresk Beob Ergebn Dt Hydrogr Inst — Meereskundliche Beobachtungen und Ergebnisse. Deutsches Hydrographisches Institut
Meerestech Mar Tech — Meerestechnik/Marine Technology
Meerestech Mar Technol — Meerestechnik/Marine Technology
Meerestechnik Mar Technol — Meerestechnik/Marine Technology
MEES — Memoirs. Egypt Exploration Society
Meet Adrenergic Mech Proc — Meeting on Adrenergic Mechanisms. Proceedings
Meet Am Psychopathol Assoc — Meeting. American Psychopathological Association
Meet East Afr Sub Comm Soil Correl Land Eval — Meeting. Eastern African Sub-Committee for Soil Correlation andLand Evaluation
Meet EULAR Standing Comm Int Clin Stud — Meeting. EULAR Standing Committee on International Clinical Studies
Meeting Nw — Meeting News
Meet Isr Opt Eng — Meeting in Israel on Optical Engineering
Meet Jpn Assoc Anim Cell Technol — Meeting. Japanese Association for Animal Cell Technology
Meet Mycol Wkrs India — Meetings of Mycological Workers in India. Department of Agriculture
Meet Pap Annu Conv Gas Process Assoc — Meeting Papers. Annual Convention. Gas Processors Association
Meet Place J R Ont Mus — Meeting Place Journal. Royal Ontario Museum
Meet Plasma Protein Group — Meeting. Plasma Protein Group
Meet Vet Offrs Lahore — Meetings of Veterinary Officers (Lahore, Calcutta)
Me F — Le Monde et la Foi
MEF — Middle East Forum
MEF — Mideast File
Me Fmr — Maine Farmer
ME Fm Res — Maine Farm Research
MEFo — Middle East Focus
MEFO — Miscelanea de Estudios Dedicados a Fernando Ortiz por Sus Discipulos
MEFR — Melanges d'Archeologie et d'Histoire. Ecole Francaise de Rome
MEFRA — Melanges. Ecole Francaise de Rome. Antiquite
MEFRM — Melanges. Ecole Francaise de Rome. Moyen Age. Temps Modernes
MEGA Membr Ekol Geol Anal — MEGA. Membrany, Ekologie, Geologie, Analytika
Meggendorf Bl — Meggendorfer Blaetter
Meggendorf Humorist Bl — Meggendorfers Humoristische Blaetter
Megyei Monogr — Megyei Monografiak
MEH — Materials Handling News
MeH — Medievalia et Humanistica
Mehanika Period Sb Perevodov Inostran Statei — Mehanika. Periodiceskii Sbornik Perevodov Inostrannyh Statei
Mehanika Polimerov — Akademija Nauk Latviiskoi SSR. Institut Mehaniki Polimerov. Mehanika Polimerov
Meh Autom — Mehanizacija i Automatizacija
MEHBA — Meteorology and Hydrology
Mehesz Kozl — Meheszeti Kozlony
ME His S — Maine Historical Society. Collections
Mehran Univ Res J Eng and Technol — Mehran University. Research Journal of Engineering and Technology
Meh Tverd Tela — Mehanika Tverdogo Tela
MEHUA — Memoirs. Faculty of Engineering. Hokkaido University
MEHYA — Mental Hygiene
MEI — Media Info
Meiden Rev (Int Ed) — Meiden Review (International Edition)
Meidensha Rev (Int Ed) — Meidensha Review [later, Meiden Review] (International Edition)
MEIFD — Minerva Ecologica, Idroclimatologica, Fisicosanitaria
Meijeritiet Aikak — Meijeritieteellinen Aikakauskirja
Meijeritiet Aikakausk — Meijeritieteellinen Aikakauskirja
Meijertiet Aikak Finn J Dairy Sci — Meijeritieteellinen Aikakauskirja/Finnish Journal of Dairy Science
MEINA — Metal Industry
ME I P — Institution of Mechanical Engineers. Proceedings
MEISA — Minzoku Eisei
Meisner A — Annalen der Allgemeinen Schweizerischen Gesellschaft fuer die Gesammten Naturwissenschaften. Meisner
Meisner Az — Naturwissenschaftlicher Anzeiger der Allgemeinen Schweizerischen Gesellschaft fuer die Gesammten Naturwissenschaften. Meisner
MEITAL — Medecine Interne
MEJ — Middle East Journal
MEJ — Music Educators Journal
Mejeritek Medd — Mejeritekniska Meddelanden
Mejeritek Meddn — Mejeritekniske Meddelanden
Mejeritidskr Finl Svenskbygd — Mejeri-Tidskrift for Finlands Svenskbygd
MEJOAB — Lijecnicki Vjesnik
MEK — Melk
MEKAW — Mitteilungen der Erdbebenkommission der Akademie der Wissenschaften in Wien
MEKEA — Memoirs. Faculty of Science. Kyushu University. Series E. Biology
MEKGR — Monatshefte fuer Evangelische Kirchengeschichte des Rheinlandes
Mekh & Avtom Proiz — Mekhanizatsiya i Avtomatizatsiya Proizvodstva
Mekhan Elektrif Sots Sel'Khoz — Mekhanizatsiya Elektrifikatsiya Sotsialisticheskogo Sel'skogo Khozyaistva
Mekhanika Tverd Tela Tr Vses Sezda Teor Prikl Mekh — Mekhanika Tverdogo Tela. Trudy Vsesoyuznogo S'ezda po Teoreticheskoi iPrikladnoi Mekhanike
Mekhanoemiss Mekhanokhim Tverd Tel Dokl Vses Simp — Mekhanoemissiya i Mekhanokhimiya Tverdykh Tel. Doklady VsesoyuznogoSimpoziuma po Mekhanoemissii i Mekhanokhimii Tverdykh Tel
Mekh Armir Plast — Mekhanika Armirovannykh Plastikov
Mekh Avtom Proizvod — Mekhanizatsiya i Avtomatizatsiya Proizvodstva
Mekh Avtom Upr — Mekhanizatsiya i Avtomatizatsiya Upravleniya

Mekh Deform Tverd Tel — Mekhanika Deformiruemykh Tverdykh Tel
Mekh Elektrif Sel'sk Khoz — Mekhanizatsiia i Elektrifikatsiia Sel'skogo Khoziaistva
Mekh Grunt — Mekhanika Gruntov
Mekh i Avtom Proizvod — Mekhanizatsiya i Avtomatizatsiya Proizvodstva
Mekh i Avtom Upr — Mekhanizahriya i Avtomahzatsiya Upravleniya
Mekh Katal Reakts Mater Vses Konf — Mekhanizm Kataliticheskikh Reaktsii. Materialy Vsesoyuznoi Konferentsii
Mekh Khlopkovod — Mekhanizatsiya Khlopkovodstva
Mekh Kompozitnykh Mater — Mekhanika Kompozitnykh Materialov
Mekh Kompoz Mater — Mekhanika Kompozitnykh Materialov
Mekh Kompoz Mater Rizh Politekh Inst — Mekhanika Kompozitnykh Materialov. Rizhskii Politekhnicheskii Institut
Mekh Kompoz Mater (Zinatne) — Mekhanika Kompozitnykh Materialov (Zinatne)
Mekh Mashinost — Mekhanika I Mashinostroenie
Mekh Nek Patol Protsessov — Mekhanizmy Nekotorykh Patologicheskikh Protsessov
Mekh Obrab Drev — Mekhanicheskaya Obrabotka. Drevesiny
Mekh Patol Protsessov — Mekhanizmy Patologicheskikh Protsessov
Mekh Polim — Mekhanika Polimerov
Mekh Prir Modif Radiochuvstvitel'nosti — Mekhanizmy Prirodnoi i Modifitsirovannoi Radiochuvstvitel'nosti
Mekh Razrusheniya Metal Nauk Ukr SSR Repub Mezhvedom Sb — Mekhanizm Razrusheniya Metallov Akademiya Nauk Ukrainskoi SSR Republikanskii Mezhvedomstvennyi Sbornik
Mekh Silsk Hospod — Mekhanizatsiia Sil's'koho Hospodarstva
Mekh Tepl Svoistva Str Neorg Stekol Mater Vses Simp — Mekhanicheskie i Teplovye Svoistva i Stroenie NeorganicheskikhStekol. Materialy Vsesoyuznogo Simpoziuma
Mekh Tverd Tela — Akademiya Nauk Ukrainskoi SSR. Institut Prikladnoi Matematikii, Mekhaniki. Mekhanika Tverdogo Tela
Mekh Tverd Tela — Mekhanika Tverdogo Tela
Mekh Ustalost Met Mater Mezhdunar Kollok — Mekhanicheskaya Ustalost Metallov. Materialy MezhdunarodnogoKollokviuma
Mekh Zhidk Gaza — Mekhanika Zhidkosti i Gaza
Mekh Zhidk Gaza Itogi Nauki Tekh — Mekhanika Zhidkosti i Gaza. Itogi Nauki i Tekhniki
MEKLA — Medizinische Klinik
MEKMA — Memoirs. Faculty of Engineering. Kumamoto University
MEKOA — Metallurgiya i Koksokhimiya
Mekong Bull — Mekong Bulletin
MEKSA — Memoirs. Faculty of Engineering. Kyushu University
Mek Tidssk — Mekanisk Tidsskrift
MEKYA — Memoirs. Faculty of Engineering. Kyoto University
Mel — Melanges
MEL — Metal Bulletin
MEL — Meyers Enzyklopaedisches Lexikon
MeL — Musique et Liturgie
ME L — University of Maine. Law Review
MELAA — Medicina del Lavoro
MELADG — Medicine and Law
MelAL — Melanges. Abel Lefranc
Melanesian Law J — Melanesian Law Journal
Melanesian LJ — Melanesian Law Journal
Melang Ecole Fr Rome Moyen Age — Melanges. Ecole Francaise de Rome. Moyen Age, Temps Modernes
Melanges — Melanges d'Archeologie et d'Histoire. Ecole Franciase de Rome
Melanges Archeol Hist — Melanges d'Archeologie et d'Histoire. Ecole Franciase de Rome
Melanges Biol Bull Phys Math Acad Imp Sci Saint Petersbourg — Melanges Biologiques Tires du Bulletin Physico-Mathematique. Academie Imperialedes Sciences de Saint-Petersbourg
Melanges Chamard — Melanges d'Histoire Litteraire de la Renaissance Offerts a Henri Chamard
Melanges Hoepffner — Melanges de Philologie Romane et de Litterature Medievale Offerts a Ernest Hoepffner
Melanges Roques — Melanges de Linguistique et de Litterature Romanes Offerts a Mario Roques
Melanges Univers Saint-Joseph Beyrouth — Melanges. Universite Saint-Joseph Beyrouth
Melanges Univ SJ — Melanges. Universite Saint-Joseph
Melang Fac Orient Univ St Joseph — Melanges de la Faculte Orientale. Universite St. Joseph
Melang Soc Emul Bruges — Melanges. Societe d'Emulation de Bruges
Melanoma Res — Melanoma Research
MELA Notes — Middle East Librarians' Association Notes
Mel Archaeol & Hist Ecole Fr Rome — Melanges d'Archeologie et d'Histoire. L'Ecole Francaise de Rome
Mel Archeol et Hist — Melanges d'Archeologie et d'Histoire. Ecole Franciase de Rome
Mel Arch Hist — Melanges d'Archeologie et d'Histoire. Ecole Francaise de Rome
Mel Asiat — Melanges Asiatiques
ME Laws — Laws of the State of Maine
MelBB — Melanges. Bernard Bouvier
Melb Chamber of Commerce Yrbk — Melbourne Chamber of Commerce. Yearbook
Melb City Mission Rec — Melbourne City Mission Record
Melb Critical R — Melbourne Critical Review
Melb Crit R — Melbourne Critical Review
Mel (Beyrouth) — Melanges. Universite Saint Joseph (Beyrouth)
Melb Grad — Melbourne Graduate
Melb Graduate — Melbourne Graduate
Melb Hist J — Melbourne Historical Journal
Melb Hosp Clin Rep — Melbourne Hospital Clinical Reports
Melb Legacy Week Bul — Melbourne Legacy Week. Bulletin

Melb Metro Board Works Monograph — Monograph. Melbourne and Metropolitan Board of Works
Melb Mon Mag — Melbourne Monthly Magazine
Melbourne Critical Rev — Melbourne Critical Review
Melbourne Hist J — Melbourne Historical Journal
Melbourne Hist Jnl — Melbourne Historical Journal
Melbourne J Politics — Melbourne Journal of Politics
Melbourne Pap Aust Def — Melbourne Papers on Australian Defence
Melbourne Slavon Stud — Melbourne Slavonic Studies
Melbourne Stud Educ — Melbourne Studies in Education
Melbourne Stud in Educ — Melbourne Studies in Education
Melbourne ULR — Melbourne University. Law Review
Melbourne Univ Dep Civ Eng Transp Sect Bull — University of Melbourne. Department of Civil Engineering. Transport Section. Bulletin
Melbourne Univ Dep Civ Eng Transp Sect Spec Rep — University of Melbourne. Department of Civil Engineering. Transport Section. Special Report
Melbourne Univ Dep Mech Eng Hum Factors Group HF Rep — University of Melbourne. Department of Mechanical Engineering. Human Factors Group. HF Report
Melbourne Univ Law Rev — Melbourne University. Law Review
Melbourne Univ L Rev — Melbourne University. Law Review
Melb Rev — Melbourne Review
MelbSS — Melbourne Slavonic Studies
Melb Stud Educ — Melbourne Studies in Education
Melb Studies in Educ — Melbourne Studies in Education
Mel Bull Mnmtl — Melanges du Bulletin Monumental
Melb UL Rev — Melbourne University. Law Review
Melb Univ Circ to Sch — Melbourne University. Circular to Schools
Melb Univ Elect Engng Dep Rep — University of Melbourne. Department of Electrical Engineering. Report
Melb Univ Gaz — Melbourne University. Gazette
Melb Univ Law R — Melbourne University. Law Review
Melb Univ Law Rev — Melbourne University. Law Review
Melb Univ LR — Melbourne University. Law Review
Melb Univ L Rev — Melbourne University. Law Review
Melb Univ Mag — Melbourne University. Magazine
Melb Univ Sch For Bull — University of Melbourne. School of Forestry. Bulletin
Melb Walker — Melbourne Walker
Melb Zool Gard Annu Rep — Melbourne Zoological Gardens. Annual Report
MelCA — Melanges. Charles Andler
Mel Carthage — Melanges de Carthage
Mel Casa Velazquez — Melanges. Casa de Velazquez
MelCD — Melanges Charles Drouhet
MelCW — Melanges. Carl Wahlund
Mel d Arch — Melanges d'Archeologie et d'Histoire. Ecole Francaise de Rome
Meld Biol Stn Sollia — Meldinger. Biologisk Stasjon Sollia
Mel del' Ec Fr de Rom — Melanges d'Archeologie et d'Histoire. Ecole Francaise de Rome
Meld Hermetikkind Lab — Melding fra Hermetikkindustriens Laboratorium
Mel Dimce Koko — Melanges Dimce Koko
Meld Landbruksteknisk Inst — Melding-Landbruksteknisk Institut
MelDM — Melanges. Daniel Mornet
Meld Meierlinst Nor Landbrukshogsk — Melding-Meieriinstituttet. Norges Landbrukshogskole
Meld Norg Landbrukshogsk — Meldinger fra Norges Landbrukshogskole
Meld Nor Landbrukshogsk — Meldinger fra Norges Landbrukshogskole
Meld Nor Landbrukshogsk Inst Blomsterdyrk Veksthusforsok — Melding-Norges Landbrukshogskole. Institutt foer Blomsterdyrking og Veksthusforsok
Meld St ForsGard Kvithamar — Melding Statens Forsoksgard Kvithamar
Meld St ForsStn Gronsakdyrk — Meldinger fra Statens Forsoksstasjon Gronsakdyrking
Meld St Plpatol Inst — Meldinger fra Statens Plantepatologiske Institutt
Meld St PlVern — Meldinger fra Statens Plantevern
Mel Ecole Fr Rome Ant — Melanges de l'Ecole Francaise de Rome. Antiquite
Mel Ecole Fr Rome Moyen Age Temps Mod — Melanges de l'Ecole Francaise de Rome. Moyen Age. Temps Modernes
Me Legis Serv — Maine Legislative Service
MelEH — Melanges. Edmond Huguet
Melekess Gos Ped Inst Ucen Zap — Melekesskii Gosudarstvennyi Pedagogiceskii Institut. Ucenye Zapiski
MelFB — Melanges. Ferdinand Brunot. Societe Nouvelle de Librairie et d'Edition
MelFBa — Melanges. Ferdinand Baldensperger. Champion
MelGB — Melanges. Gaston Boissier. Fontemoing
MelGL — Melanges. Gustave Lanson. Hachette
Mel Gr — Melanges Greco-Romains. Tire du Bulletin Historico-Philologique. Academie Imperiale des Sciences de St. Petersbourg
MelH — Melbourne Historical Journal
MelHC — Melanges. Henri Chamard. Nizet
Mel Hist — Melita Historica
Melhor Prod Sementes Hort — Melhoramento e Produccao de Sementes de Algumas Hortalicas
ME Li — Monumenta Ecclesiae Liturgica
Mel Inst Dominicain Etud Orient Caire — Melanges de l'Institut Dominicain d'Etudes Orientales du Caire
Meliorace Prehl Lit Zemed Lesn Melior — Meliorace. Prehled Literatury Zemedelskych a Lesnickych Melioraci
Meliorat Acker- Pflanzenbau — Melioration Acker- und Pflanzenbau
Melior Delo — Meliorativnoe Delo
Melior Ispol'z Osushennykh Zemel — Melioratsiya i Ispol'zovaniya Osushennykh Zemel
Melior Rolne — Melioracje Rolne
Melior Torf — Melioratsiya i Torf
Melior Vodn Khoz — Melioratsiya Vodnoe Khozyaistva
Meliss Ellas — Melissokomike Ellas

MeliT — Melita Theologica. The Reviews of the Royal University Students' Theological Association

Melita Hist — Melita Historica

MelitaT — Melita Theologica. The Reviews of the Royal University Students' Theological Association

Melittologists' Bull — Melittologists' Bulletin

Melk Sudostr — Melkoe Sudostroenie

MelLA — Melanges. Louis Arnould. Poitiers. Societe Francaise d'Imprimerie et de Librairie

Melliand Int — Melliand International

Mellliands TextBer — Mellliands Textilberichte

Melliand TextBer — Melliand Textilberichte

Melliand TextBer Engl Edn — Melliand Textilberichte (English Edition)

Melliand Textilber — Melliand Textilberichte

Melliand Textilber — Melliand Textilberichte International

Melliand Textilber Int — Melliand Textilberichte International

Melliand Textilber Int Text Rep Ger Ed — Melliand Textilberichte/International Textile Reports. German Edition

Melliand Textilchem — Melliand Textilchemie

Melliand Text Mon — Melliand Textile Monthly

Mell Textil — Melliand Textilberichte

MelM — Melanges Malraux Miscellany

Mel Maker — Melody Maker

MelMR — Melanges. Mario Roques

Melos NeueZM — Melos. Neue Zeitschrift fuer Musik

MelPHLJ — Melanges de Philosophie et de Litterature Juives

ME L Rev — Maine Law Review

Mel Rom — Melanges d'Archeologie et d'Histoire. Ecole Francaise de Rome

MelScR — Melanges de Science Religieuse

Melsheimer Entomol Ser — Melsheimer Entomological Series

Melsheimer Ent Ser — Melsheimer Entomological Series

Mel Stiennon — Melanges Stiennon

Mel St J — Melanges. Universite Saint-Joseph

Mel St Joseph — Melanges. Universite Saint-Joseph

Melsunger Med Mitt — Melsunger Medizinische Mitteilungen

Melsunger Med Pharm Mitt Wiss Prax — Melsunger Medizinisch Pharmazeutische Mitteilungen aus Wissenschaft und Praxis

Melsunger Med Pharm Mitt Wiss Prax Suppl — Melsunger Medizinisch Pharmazeutische Mitteilungen aus Wissenschaft und Praxis.Supplement

Melts Meth — Melts and Methods

Mel Univ St Joseph — Melanges. Universite Saint Joseph

MelUSJ — Melanges. Universite Saint Joseph

Mel U St Joseph — Melanges de l'Universite Saint-Joseph

Melyepitestud Sz — Melyepitestudomanyi Szemle

Melyepitestud Szle — Melyepitestudomanyi Szemle

MeM — Materiales en Marcha

MEM — Mensch en Maatschappij

MEM — Mens en Maatschappij. Tijdschrift voor Sociale Wetenschappen

MeM — Mens en Melodie

MeM — Mens en Muziek

MEM — Middle Eastern Monographs

MeM — Moines et Monasteres

Mem AAR — Memoirs. American Academy in Rome

Mem Acad Chir — Memoires. Academie de Chirurgie

Mem Acad Cienc Artes Barcelona — Memorias. Academia de Ciencias y Artes de Barcelona

Mem Acad Cienc Lisb Cl Cienc — Memorias. Academia das Ciencias de Lisboa. Classe de Ciencias

Mem Acad Cienc Madrid — Memorias. Real Academia de Ciencias Exactas, Fisicas, y Naturales deMadrid

Mem Acad Cienc Zaragoza — Memorias. Academia de Ciencias de Zaragoza

Mem Acad Ci Lisboa Cl Ci — Memorias da Academia das Ciencias de Lisboa. Classe de Ciencias

Mem Acad Delphin — Memoires de l'Academie Delphinale

Mem Acad des Inscript — Institut de France. Academie des Inscriptions et Belles-Lettres. Memoires

Mem Acad Fr — Memoires de l'Academie Francaise

Mem Acad Geogr Hist S Jose — Memoria. Academia de Geografia e Historia de Costa Rica (San Jose)

Mem Acad Imp Sci Saint Petersbourg Ser 6 Sci Math Seconde Pt — Memoires. Academie Imperiale des Sciences de Saint-Petersbourg. Sixieme Serie. Sciences Mathematiques, Physiques, et Naturelles. Seconde Part Sciences Naturelles

Mem Acad Imp Sci St Petersbourg Hist Acad — Memoires. Academie Imperiale des Sciences de St. Petersbourg. Avec l'Histoire de l'Academie

Mem Acad Inscr — Memoires. Academie des Inscriptions et Belles Lettres

Mem Acad Inscr & B Lett — Memoires de l'Academie des Inscriptions et Belles-Lettres

Mem Acad Int Geogr Bot — Memoires de l'Academie Internationale de Geographie Botanique

Mem Acad Malgache — Memoires. Academie Malgache

Mem Acad Marseille — Memoires Publies par l'Academie de Marseille

Mem Acad Med (Paris) — Memoires. Academie de Medecine (Paris)

Mem Acad Metz — Memoires de l'Academie de Metz

Mem Acad Mex Estud Num — Memorias. Academia Mexicana de Estudios Numismaticos

Mem Acad Montpellier — Memoires de l'Academie de Montpellier

Mem Acad Nac Hist — Memorias. Academia Nacional de Historia y Geografia

Mem Acad Nac Hist Geogr Mex — Memoria. Academia Nacional de Historia y Geografia (Mexico)

Mem Acad Nat Metz — Memoires de l'Academie Nationale de Metz

Mem Acad Natn Sci Caen — Memoires de l'Academie Nationale des Sciences, Arts, et Belles-Lettres de Caen

Mem Acad Nimes — Memoires. Academie de Nimes

Mem Acad Pol Sci Lett Cl Sci Math Nat Ser A — Memoires. Academie Polonaise des Sciences et des Lettres. Classedes Sciences Mathematiques et Naturelles. Serie A. Sciences Mathematiques

Mem Acad Pol Sci Lett Cl Sci Math Nat Ser B — Memoires. Academie Polonaise des Sciences et des Lettres. Classedes Sciences Mathematiques et Naturelles. Serie B. Sciences Naturelles

Mem Acad R Belg Cl Sci 4 — Memoires de l'Academie R. de Belgique. Classe des Sciences. Collection in -4

Mem Acad R Belg Cl Sci 4o Ser II — Memoires. Academie Royale de Belgique. Classe des Sciences. Collection in Quarto. Deuxleme Serie

Mem Acad R Belg Cl Sci 8 — Memoires de l'Academie R. de Belgique. Classe des Sciences. Collection in -8

Mem Acad R Belg Cl Sci Collect 4o — Memoires. Academie Royale de Belgique. Classe des Sciences. Collection in Quarto

Mem Acad R Med Belg — Memoires. Academie Royale de Medecine de Belgique

Mem Acad Royale Belgique Cl B A — Memoires de l'Academie Royale de Belgique. Classe des Beaux-Arts

Mem Acad Royale Belgique Cl Sci — Memoires de l'Academie Royale de Belgique. Classe des Sciences

Mem Acad Royale Sci & B Lett [Berlin] — Memoires de l'Academie Royale des Sciences et Belles-Lettres [Berlin]

Mem Acad Royale Sci & Lett Danemark — Memoires de l'Academie Royale des Sciences et Lettres du Danemark

Mem Acad Royale Sci Lett & B A — Memoires de l'Academie Royale des Sciences, des Lettres, et des Beaux-Arts de Belgique. Classe des Beaux-Arts

Mem Acad Roy Metz — Memoires de l'Academie Royale de Metz. Lettres, Sciences, Arts, Agriculture

Mem Acad Roy Prusse Anat Avignon — Memoires. Academie Royale de Prusse. Concernant l'Anatomie, la Physiologie, la Physique, l'Histoire Naturelle, la Botanique, la Mineralogie (Avignon)

Mem Acad Roy Sci Colon Cl Sci Nat — Memoires. Academie Royale des Sciences Coloniales. Classe des Sciences Naturelles et Medicales. Verhandelingen. Koninklike Academie voor Koloniale Wetenschappen. Klasse der Natuur- en Geneeskundige Wetenschappen

Mem Acad Roy Sci Hist Berlin — Memoires de l'Academie Royale des Sciences et Belles Lettres Depuis l'Avenementde Frederic Guillaume II au Throne. Avec l'Histoire (Berlin)

Mem Acad Roy Sci Lett Belg — Memoires. Academie Royale des Sciences, des Lettres, et des Beaux-Arts de Belgique

Mem Acad Roy Sci Outre-Mer (Brussels) — Memoires. Academie Royale des Sciences d'Outre-Mer (Brussels)

Mem Acad Roy Sci Paris — Memoires. Academie Royale des Sciences (Paris)

Mem Acad Roy Sci Turin — Memoires de l'Academie Royale des Sciences (Turin)

Mem Acad R Sci Colon Cl Sci Nat Med 4 — Memoires. Academie R. des Sciences Coloniales. Classe des Sciences Naturelles et Medicales. Collection in -4

Mem Acad R Sci Colon Cl Sci Nat Med 8 — Memoires. Academie R. des Sciences Coloniales. Classe des Sciences Naturelles et Medicales. Collection in -8

Mem Acad R Sci Colon Cl Sci Tech 4 — Memoires. Academie R. des Sciences Coloniales. Classe des Sciences Techniques. Collection in -4

Mem Acad R Sci Colon Cl Sci Tech 8 — Memoires. Academie R. des Sciences Coloniales. Classe des Sciences Techniques. Collection in -8

Mem Acad R Sci D Outre Mer Cl Sci Nat Med 4 — Memoires. Academie R. des Sciences d'Outre-Mer. Classe des Sciences Naturelles et Medicales. Collection in -4

Mem Acad R Sci D Outre Mer Cl Sci Nat Med 8 — Memoires. Academie R. des Sciences d'Outre-Mer. Classe des Sciences Naturelles et Medicales. Collection in -8

Mem Acad R Sci D Outre Mer Cl Sci Tech 4 — Memoires. Academie R. des Sciences d'Outre-Mer. Classe des Sciences Techniques. Collection in -4

Mem Acad R Sci D Outre Mer Cl Sci Tech 8 — Memoires. Academie R. des Sciences d'Outre-Mer. Classe des Sciences Techniques. Collection in -8

Mem Acad R Sci Lett Belg — Memoires de l'Academie R. des Sciences, des Lettres, et des Beaux-Arts de Belgique

Mem Acad R Sci Lett Dan Sect Sci — Memoires. Academie Royale des Sciences et des Lettres de Danemark.Section des Sciences

Mem Acad R Sci Outr Mer Cl Sci Tech Collect (Brussels) — Memoires. Academie Royale des Sciences d'Outre-Mer. Classe des Sciences Techniques. Collection in 8 (Brussels)

Mem Acad Sci — Memoires. Academie des Sciences. Institut de France

Mem Acad Sci A & B Lett Dijon — Memoires de l'Academie des Sciences, Arts, et Belles-Lettres de Dijon

Mem Acad Sci Agric Aix — Memories de l'Academie des Sciences, Agriculture, Arts, et Belles-Lettres d'Aix

Mem Acad Sci Angers — Memoires. Academie des Sciences et Belles-Lettres d'Angers

Mem Acad Sci Arts Belles Lett Dijon — Memoires. Academie des Sciences, Arts, et Belles-Lettres de Dijon

Mem Acad Sci Arts Dijon — Memoires de l'Academie des Sciences, Arts, et Belles-Lettres de Dijon

Mem Acad Sci Belles Lett Amiens — Memories de l'Academie des Sciences, Belles-Lettres, et des Arts d'Amiens

Mem Acad Sci Belles Lett Angers — Memoires de l'Academie des Sciences, Belles-Lettres, et Arts d'Angers

Mem Acad Sci Belles Lett Clermont Ferrand — Memoires de l'Academie des Sciences, Belles-Lettres, et Arts de Clermont-Ferrand

Mem Acad Sci Belles Lett Lyon — Memoires de l'Academie des Sciences, Belles-Lettres, et Arts de Lyon

Mem Acad Sci B Lett & A Angers — Memoires de l'Academie des Sciences, Belles-Lettres, et Arts d'Angers

Mem Acad Sci B Lett & A Clermont Ferrand — Memoires de l'Academie des Sciences, Belles-Lettres, et Arts de Clermont-Ferrand

Mem Acad Sci B Lett & A Marseille — Memoires de l'Academie des Sciences, Belles-Lettres, et Arts de Marseille

Mem Acad Sci B Lett & A Savoie — Memoires de l'Academie des Sciences, Belles-Lettres, et Arts de Savoie

Mem Acad Sci Dijon — Memoires de l'Academie des Sciences, Arts et Belles-Lettres de Dijon

Mem Acad Sci Inscr B-Lett Toulouse — Memoires. Academie des Sciences, Inscriptions, et Belles-Lettres de Toulouse

Mem Acad Sci Inscript Belles Lett Toulouse — Memoires. Academie des Sciences, Inscriptions et Belles-Lettres de Toulouse

Mem Acad Sci Inscriptions B L Toulouse — Memoires. Academie des Sciences, Inscriptions, et Belles-Lettres de Toulouse

Mem Acad Sci Inst Fr — Memoires. Academie des Sciences. Institut de France

Mem Acad Sci Toulouse — Memoires. Academie des Sciences, Inscriptions, et Belles-Lettres de Toulouse

Mem Acad Sci Turin — Memoires. Academie des Sciences de Turin

Mem Acad Sci Ukr SSR — Memoirs. Academy of Sciences. Ukrainian SSR

Mem Acad Stanislas — Memoires de l'Academie de Stanislas

Mem Acad Vaucluse — Memoires de l'Academie de Vaucluse

Mem Accad Agric Sci Lett Verona — Memorie. Accademia de Agricoltura, Scienze, e Lettere di Verona

Mem Accad Archeol Lett & B A Napoli — Memorie dell'Accademia di Archeologia, Lettere, e Belle Arti di Napoli

Mem Accad Imp Sci Genova — Memorie dell' Accademia Imperiale delle Scienze e Belle Arti di Genova

Mem Accad Lincei — Memorie. Reale Accademia Nazionale dei Lincei. Classe di ScienzeFisiche, Matematiche, e Naturali

Mem Accad Patavina Sci Lett & A — Memorie dell'Accademia Patavina di Scienze, Lettere, ed Arti

Mem Accad Patav Sci Lett Arti — Memorie. Accademia Patavina di Scienze, Lettere, ed Arti

Mem Accad Sci Genova — Memorie. Accademia delle Scienze, Lettere, ed Arti di Genova

Mem Accad Sci Ist Bologna Cl Sci Fis — Memorie. Accademia delle Scienze. Istituto di Bologna. Classe di Scienze Fisiche

Mem Accad Sci Med Chir (Naples) — Memorie. Accademia di Scienze Mediche e Chirurgiche (Naples)

Mem Accad Sci (Modena) — Memorie. Reale Accademia di Scienze, Lettere, ed Arti (Modena)

Mem Accad Sci Torino Cl Sci Fis Mat Nat — Memorie. Accademia delle Scienze di Torino. Classe di Scienze Fisiche, Matematiche, e Naturali

Mem Accad Sci Torino Cl Sci Fis Mat Nat Ser 4A — Memorie. Accademia delle Scienze di Torino. Classe di Scienze Fisiche, Matematiche, e Naturali. Serie 4A

Mem Accad Sci Torino Cl Sci Fis Mat Natur — Memorie. Accademia delle Scienze di Torino. Classe di Scienze Fisiche, Matematiche, e Naturali

Mem Accad Sci Torino Cl Sci Fis Mat Natur 4 — Memorie. Accademia delle Scienze di Torino. Classe di Scienze Fisiche, Matematiche, e Naturali. Serie 4

Mem Accad Sci Torino Cl Sci Fis Mat Natur 5 — Accademia delle Scienze di Torino. Memorie. Classe di Scienze Fisiche, Matematiche, e Naturali. Serie 5

Mem Acc Bologna — Memorie. Accademia delle Scienze. Istituto di Bologna

Mem Acc It — Memorie. Accademia Nazionale dei Lincei (Italia)

Mem Acc Linc — Memorie. Accademia Nazionale dei Lincei

Mem Acc Linc — Memorie. Atti della Accademia Nazionale dei Lincei. Classe de Scienze Morali, Storiche, e Filologiche

Mem Acc Linc d'Italia — Memorie. Accademia Nazionale dei Lincei (Italia)

Mem Acc Nap — Memorie. Accademia di Archeologia, Lettere, e Belle Arti di Napoli

Mem Acc Napoli — Memorie. Accademia di Archeologia, Lettere, e Belle Arti di Napoli

Mem Acc Naz Linc — Memorie. Accademia Nazionale dei Lincei

Mem Ac Inscr — Memoires Presentes par Divers Savants a l'Academie des Inscriptions et Belles Lettres

Mem Agric Exp Stn (Ithaca NY) — Memoirs. Agricultural Experiment Station (Ithaca, New York)

Mem Agric Oecon Arts — Memoirs of Agriculture and Other Oeconomical Arts

Mem Agric Soc Centr Agric France — Memoires d'Agriculture, d'Economie Rurale et Domestique. Societe Centrale d'Agriculture de France

Mem Agric Soc Roy Agric Paris — Memoires d'Agriculture, d'Economie Rurale et Domestique. Societe Royale d'Agriculture de Paris

Mem Akita Univ — Memoirs. Akita University

Mem AL — Memorie. Accademia Nazionale dei Lincei

Mem Am Ac — Memoirs. American Academy in Rome

Mem Am Acad Arts Sci — Memoirs. American Academy of Arts and Sciences

Mem Am Acad Rome — Memoirs. American Academy in Rome

Mem Am Ac Rome — Memoirs. American Academy in Rome

Mem Am Assoc Pet Geol — Memoir. American Association of Petroleum Geologists

Mem Am Entomol Inst (Ann Arbor) — Memoirs. American Entomological Institute (Ann Arbor)

Mem Am Entomol Inst (Gainesville) — Memoirs. American Entomological Institute (Gainesville)

Mem Am Entomol Soc — Memoirs. American Entomological Society

Mem Amer Acad Rome — Memoirs. American Academy in Rome

Mem Amer Assoc Advancem Sci — Memoirs. American Association for the Advancement of Science

Mem Amer Math Soc — Memoirs. American Mathematical Society

Mem Amer Mus Nat Hist — Memoirs of the American Museum of Natural History

Mem Amer Philos Soc — Memoirs. American Philosophical Society

Mem Am Math — Memoirs. American Mathematical Society

Mem Am Philos Soc — Memoirs. American Philosophical Society

Mem & C R Soc Ingen Civ France — Memoires et Compte-Rendu de la Societe des Ingenieurs Civils en France

Mem & Diss Ant N & Etrang — Memoires et Dissertations sur les Antiquites Nationales et Etrangeres

Mem & Doc Soc Savois Hist & Archeol — Memoires et Documents Publies par la Societe Savoisienne d'Histoire et d'Archeologie

Mem Angers — Memoires. Academie des Sciences, Belles-Lettres, et Arts d'Angers

Mem Ant — Memoria Antiquitatis. Acta Musei Petrodavensis. Revista Muzeului Arheologic Piatra Neamt

Mem Antiq — Memoria Antiquitatis Acta Musei Petrodavensis. Revista Muzeului Archeologic Piatra Neamt

Mem Anual Mus Nac Hist Nat Bernardino Rivadavia — Memoria Anual. Museo Nacional de Historia Natural Bernardino Rivadavia

Mem Artillerie Fr — Memorial de l'Artillerie Francaise

Mem Artillerie Fr Sci Tech Armement — Memorial de l'Artillerie Francaise. Sciences et Techniques de l'Armement

Mem Asiat Soc Beng — Memoirs of the Asiatic Society of Bengal

Mem Asiat Soc Bengal — Memoirs. Asiatic Society of Bengal

Mem Asoc Latinoam Prod Anim — Memoria. Asociacion Latinoamericana de Produccion Animal

Mem Ass Ing Ec Liege — Memoires de l'Association des Ingenieurs Sortis de l'Ecole de Liege

Mem Ass Int Ponts Charp — Memoires. Association Internationale des Ponts et Charpentes

Mem Assoc Int Hydrogeol — Memoires. Association Internationale des Hydrogeologues

Mem Assoc Int Hydrogeol Reunion Istanbul — Memoires. Association Internationale des Hydrogeologues. Reunion d'Istanbul

Mem Astron Soc India — Memoirs. Astronomical Society of India

Mem Astron Soc London — Memoirs. Royal Astronomical Society of London

Mem Astr Soc Japan — Memoirs of the Astronomical Society of Japan

Mem Athenee Orient — Memoires de Athenee Oriental Fonde en 1864

Mem Atti Cent Studi Ing Agrar — Memorie ed Atti. Centro di Studi per l'Ingegneria Agraria

Mem Aust Mus — Memoirs. Australian Museum

Mem Austral Mus — Memoirs of the Australian Museum

Mem Barcel A — Memoria. Universidad de Barcelona. Instituto de Arqueologia y Prehistoria

MEMBBM — Methods in Membrane Biology

Memb Bull Cott Rayon Merch Ass — Members' Bulletin. Cotton and Rayon Merchants' Association

Memb Bull Soc Nav Archit Mar Engrs — Member's Bulletin. Society of Naval Architects and Marine Engineers

Memb Circ Br Fed Mast Print — Members' Circular. British Federation of Master Printers

Mem Bd Maori Ethnol Res — Memoirs of the Board of Maori Ethnological Research

Mem Bernice Pauahi Bishop Mus — Memoirs. Bernice Pauahi Bishop Museum of Polynesian Ethnology and Natural History

Mem Bernice P Bishop Mus — Memoirs of the Bernice P. Bishop Museum

Mem Biol Lab Johns Hopkins Univ — Memoirs from the Biological Laboratory of the Johns Hopkins University

Mem Biol Mar Oceanogr — Memorie di Biologia Marina e di Oceanografia

Mem Bologna — Atti. Accademia delle Scienze. Istituto di Bologna. Memorie

Mem Boston Soc Nat Hist — Memoirs. Boston Society of Natural History

Mem Botan Surv S Afr — Memoirs. Botanical Survey of South Africa

Mem Bot Opname S-Afr — Memoirs. Botaniese Opname van Suid-Afrika

Mem Bot Surv S Afr — Memoir. Botanical Survey of South Africa

Membrane Biochem — Membrane Biochemistry

Mem Br Astr Ass — Memoirs of the British Astronomical Association

Membr Biochem — Membrane Biochemistry

Membr Cell Biol — Memrane and Cell Biology (Basel)

Membr Def Attack Complement Perforins — Membrane Defenses against Attack by Complement and Perforins

Mem Br E Afr Met Serv — Memoirs. British East Africa Meteorological Service

Mem BRGM — Memoires. Bureau de Recherches Geologiques et Minieres

Membr Interact HIV — Membrane Interactions of HIV. Implications for Pathogensis and Therapy in AIDS

Mem Brooklyn Bot Gdn — Memoirs of the Brooklyn Botanic Garden

Membr Proteins — Membrane Proteins

Membr Sci Technol — Membrane Science and Technology

Membr Sci Technol Ser — Membrane Science and Technology Series

Membr Sep Sci Technol — Membrane Separations. Science and Technology

Membr Struct Funct Fed Eur Biochem Soc Meet — Membranes. Structure and Function. Federation of European BiochemicalSocieties Meeting

Membr Transp Processes — Membrane Transport Processes

Mem Bull Soc Med Chir Bordeaux — Memoires et Bulletins de la Societe de Medecine et de Chirurgie de Bordeaux

Mem Bur Mines Geol Mont — Memoir. Bureau of Mines and Geology. Montana

Mem Bur Rech Geol Minieres — Memoires. Bureau de Recherches Geologiques et Minieres

Mem CACO — Memoires. Commission des Antiquites du Departement de la Cote d'Or

Mem Caledonian Hort Soc — Memoirs. Caledonian Horticultural Society

Mem Calif Acad Sci — Memoirs. California Academy of Sciences

Mem Camb Univ Sch Agric — Memoirs. Cambridge University School of Agriculture

Mem Can Soc Pet Geol — Memoir. Canadian Society of Petroleum Geologists

Mem Carnegie Mus — Memoirs of the Carnegie Museum

Mem Carneg Mus — Memoirs of the Carnegie Museum

Mem Carte Geol Tunis — Memoires de la Carte Geologique de la Tunisie

MEMCB — Miscelanea de Estudos a Memoria de Claudio Basto

Mem Cent Met Obs Tokyo — Memoirs. Central Meteorological Observatory (Tokyo)

Mem Cent Natl Rech Metall Sect Hainaut — Memoires. Centre National de Recherches Metallurgiques. Section du Hainaut

Mem Cent Nat Rech Metall Sect Hainaut — Memoires. Centre National de Recherches Metallurgiques. Section du Hainaut

Mem Challenger Soc — Memoirs of the Challenger Society

Mem Chalon S — Memoires. Societe d'Histoire et d'Archeologie de Chalon-sur-Saone

Mem Chubu Electr Power Co Ltd — Memoirs. Chubu Electric Power Company Limited

Mem Chubu Inst Technol — Memoirs. Chubu Institute of Technology

Mem Chubu Inst Technol A — Memoirs. Chubu Institute of Technology. Series A

Mem Chukyo Women's Coll Chukyo Women's J Coll — Memoirs. Chukyo Women's College. Chukyo Women's Junior College

Mem Cl Sci Acad R Belg Coll 8 — Memoires. Classe des Sciences. Academie Royale de Belgique. Collection in 8

Mem Cl Sci Acad R Belg Collect 4 — Memoires. Classe des Sciences. Academie Royale de Belgique. Collection in 4

Mem Cl Sci Acad R Belg Collect 8o — Memoires. Classe des Sciences. Academie Royale de Belgique. Collection in Octavo

Mem Cl Sci Math Inst Natl France — Memoires. Classe des Sciences Mathematiques et Physiques. Institut National de France

Mem Cl Sci Morali Stor Filol Accad Naz Lincei — Memorie Classe di Scienze, Morali, Storiche, et Filologiche. Accademia Nazionale dei Lincei

Mem Cl Sci Mor Stor & Filol — Memorie della Classe di Scienze Morali, Storiche, e Filologiche

Mem Coal Surv Un S Afr — Memoirs. Coal Survey. Union of South Africa

Mem Cognit — Memory and Cognition

Mem Cognition — Memory and Cognition

Mem Coll Agric Ehime Univ — Memoirs. College of Agriculture. Ehime University

Mem Coll Agric Kyoto Univ — Memoirs. College of Agriculture. Kyoto University

Mem Coll Agric Kyoto Univ Agric Econ Ser — Memoirs. College of Agriculture. Kyoto University. Agricultural Economy Series

Mem Coll Agric Kyoto Univ Anim Sci Ser — Memoirs. College of Agriculture. Kyoto University. Animal Science Series

Mem Coll Agric Kyoto Univ Bot Ser — Memoirs. College of Agriculture. Kyoto University. Botanical Series

Mem Coll Agric Kyoto Univ Chem Ser — Memoirs. College of Agriculture. Kyoto University. Chemical Series

Mem Coll Agric Kyoto Univ Entomol Ser — Memoirs. College of Agriculture. Kyoto University. Entomological Series

Mem Coll Agric Kyoto Univ Fish Ser — Memoirs. College of Agriculture. Kyoto University. Fisheries Series

Mem Coll Agric Kyoto Univ Food Sci Technol Ser — Memoirs. College of Agriculture. Kyoto University. Food Science and Technology Series

Mem Coll Agric Kyoto Univ Genet Ser — Memoirs. College of Agriculture. Kyoto University. Genetical Series

Mem Coll Agric Kyoto Univ Hortic Ser — Memoirs. College of Agriculture. Kyoto University. Horticultural Series

Mem Coll Agric Kyoto Univ Phytopathol Ser — Memoirs. College of Agriculture. Kyoto University. Phytopathological Series

Mem Coll Agric Kyoto Univ Plant Breed Ser — Memoirs. College of Agriculture. Kyoto University. Plant Breeding Series

Mem Coll Agric Kyoto Univ Wood Sci Technol Ser — Memoirs. College of Agriculture. Kyoto University. Wood Science and Technology Series

Mem Coll Agric Natl Taiwan Univ — Memoirs. College of Agriculture. National Taiwan University

Mem Coll Agric Natl Taiwan Univ — Memoirs. College of Agriculture. National Taiwan University/Kuo Li Taiwan Ta Hsueeh Nung Hsueeh Yuean Yen Chiu Pao K'an

Mem Coll Agric Natn Taiwan Univ — Memoirs of the College of Agriculture. National Taiwan University

Mem Coll Agr Kyoto Univ — Memoirs. College of Agriculture. Kyoto University

Mem Collect 8 Inst R Colon Belg Cl Sci Tech — Memoires. Collection in Octavo. Institut Royal Colonial Belge. Classe desSciences Techniques

Mem College Ed Akita Univ Natur Sci — Memoirs of the College of Education. Akita University. Natural Science

Mem Coll Eng Chubu Univ — Memoirs. College of Engineering. Chubu University

Mem Coll Eng Kyoto Imp Univ — Memoirs. College of Engineering. Kyoto Imperial University

Mem Coll Eng Kyushu Imp Univ — Memoirs. College of Engineering. Kyushu Imperial University

Mem Coll Engng Kyoto Univ — Memoirs of the College of Engineering. Kyoto Imperial University

Mem Coll Engng Kyushu Imp Univ — Memoirs of the College of Engineering. Kyushu Imperial University

Mem Coll Med Natl Taiwan Univ — Memoirs. College of Medicine. National Taiwan University

Mem Coll Sci Eng Waseda Univ — Memoirs. College of Science and Engineering. Waseda University

Mem Coll Sci Kyoto Imp Univ — Memoirs. College of Science. Kyoto Imperial University

Mem Coll Sci Kyoto Imp Univ Ser A — Memoirs. College of Science. Kyoto Imperial University. Series A

Mem Coll Sci Kyoto Imp Univ Ser B — Memoirs. College of Science. Kyoto Imperial University. Series B

Mem Coll Sci Univ Kyoto Ser A — Memoirs. College of Science. University of Kyoto. Series A

Mem Coll Sci Univ Kyoto Ser A Math — Memoirs. College of Science. University of Kyoto. Series A. Mathematics

Mem Coll Sci Univ Kyoto Ser B — Memoirs. College of Science. University of Kyoto. Series B

Mem Coll Sci Univ Kyoto Ser B Geol Biol — Memoirs. College of Science. University of Kyoto. Series B. Geology andBiology

Mem Col Nac Mex — Memoria de El Colegio Nacional (Mexico)

Mem Colombo Mus — Memoirs of the Colombo Museum

Mem Com Geol (Rom) — Memoriile Comitetului Geologic (Romania)

Mem Comm Ant Dept Cote d Or — Memoires de la Commission des Antiquites du Departement de la Cote-d'Or

Mem Comm Dept Mnmts Hist Pas de Calais — Memoires de la Commission Departementale des Monuments Historiques du Pas-de-Calais

Mem Comun Inst Geol (Barcelona) — Memorias y Comunicaciones. Instituto Geologico (Barcelona)

Mem Conf Anu Asoc Tec Azucar Cuba — Memoria. Conferencia Anual. Asociacion de Tecnicos Azucarerosde Cuba

Mem Conf Anu ATAC — Memoria. Conferencia Anual de la ATAC

Mem Conf Int Pesqui Cacau — Memorias. Conferencia Internacional de Pesquisas em Cacau

Mem Cong Ibero Lat Am Dermatol — Memorias. Congreso Ibero Latino Americano de Dermatologia

Mem Cong Med Latino-Am (Buenos Aires) — Memoria. Congreso Medico Latino-Americano (Buenos Aires)

Mem Congr Int Gaz Nat Liquefle — Memoires. Congres International sur le Gaz Naturel Liquefie

Mem Congr Int Lepra — Memoria. Congreso Internacional de la Lepra

Mem Congr Int Quim Pura Apl — Memorias. Congreso Internacional de Quimica Pura y Aplicada

Mem Congr Latinoam Sider — Memoria. Congreso Latinoamericano de Siderurgia

Mem Congr Mex Anestesiol — Memorias. Congreso Mexicano de Anestesiologia

Mem Congr Mond Pet — Memoires. Congres Mondial du Petrole

Mem Congr Mund Cardiol — Memorias. Congreso Mundial de Cardiologia

Mem Congr Nac Med Vet Zootec — Memorias. Congreso Nacional de Medicina Veterinaria y Zootecnia

Mem Conn Acad Arts Sci — Memoirs. Connecticut Academy of Arts and Sciences

Mem Connecticut Acad Arts — Memoirs. Connecticut Academy of Arts and Sciences

Mem Cons Oceanogr Ibero Am — Memorias. Consejo Oceanografico Ibero-Americano

Mem Cornell Univ Agric Exper Station — Memoirs. Cornell University. Agricultural Experiment Station

Mem Cornell Univ Agric Exp Stn — Memoirs. Cornell University. Agricultural Experiment Station

Mem Cote D'Or — Memoires. Commission des Antiquites du Departement de la Cote-D'Or

Mem Couronnes — Memoires Couronnes

Mem Couronnes Autres Mem Acad Roy Sci Belgique — Memoires Couronnes et Autres Memoires. Academie Royale des Sciences, Lettres etBeaux-Arts de Belgique

Mem Couronnes Mem Savants Etrangers Acad Roy Sci Bruxelles 8 — Memoires Couronnes et Memoires des Savants Etrangers. Academie Royale des Sciences et Belles-Lettres de Bruxelles. In Octavo

Mem CR Congr Bois Charb Bois Util Carb — Memoires et Comptes Rendus. Congres du Bois et du Charbon de Bois Utilises Comme Carburants

Mem CR Congr Natn Ensil Fourr — Memories et Comptes Rendus. Congres National de l'Ensilage des Fourrages

Mem Creuse — Memoires. Societe des Sciences Naturelles et Archeologiques de la Creuse

Mem CR Seanc Congr Natn Pech Marit — Memoires et Comptes Rendus des Seances. Congres National des Peches Maritimes

Mem C R Soc R Can — Memoires et Comptes Rendus. Societe Royale du Canada

Mem CR Soc Scient Litt Alais — Memoires et Comptes Rendus de la Societe Scientifique et Litteraire d'Alais

Mem CR Soc Sci Med Lyon — Memoires et Comptes Rendus de la Societe des Sciences Medicales de Lyon

Mem CR Trav Soc Ing Civ Fr — Memoires et Compte Rendu des Travaux. Societe des IngenieursCivils de France

Mem Cyprus Geol Surv Dep — Memoir. Cyprus. Geological Survey Department

Mem Def Acad — Memoirs. Defense Academy

Mem Def Acad (Jap) — Memoirs. Defense Academy (Japan)

Mem Def Acad Math Phys Chem Eng — Memoirs. Defense Academy. Mathematics, Physics, Chemistry, and Engineering

Mem Def Acad Math Phys Chem Eng (Yokosuka Jpn) — Memoirs. Defense Academy. Mathematics, Physics, Chemistry, and Engineering (Yokosuka, Japan)

Mem Defense Acad — Memoirs. Defense Academy. Mathematics, Physics, Chemistry, and Engineering

Mem del'Acad d Inscr — Memoires Presentes par Divers Savants. Academie des Inscriptions et Belles-Lettres. Institut de France

Mem Del Archeol Fr Afghanistan — Memoires de la Delegation Archeologique Francaise en Afghanistan

Mem de la Soc d Emul du Doubs — Memoires de la Societe d'Emulation du Department du Doubs

Mem Dep Agric India Bacteriol Ser — Memoirs. Department of Agriculture in India. Bacteriological Series

Mem Dep Agric India Bact Ser — Memoirs of the Department of Agriculture in India. Bacteriological Series

Mem Dep Agric India Bot Ser — Memoirs. Department of Agriculture in India. Botanical Series

Mem Dep Agric India Chem Ser — Memoirs. Department of Agriculture in India. Chemical Series

Mem Dep Agric India Entomol Ser — Memoirs. Department of Agriculture in India. Entomological Series

Mem Dep Agric India Ent Ser — Memoirs of the Department of Agriculture in India. Entomological Series

Mem Dep Agric India Vet — Memoirs of the Department of Agriculture in India. Veterinary Series

Mem Dep Agric Iraq — Memoirs of the Department of Agriculture. Iraq

Mem Dep Agric Queb — Memoires du Departement de l'Agriculture de Quebec

Mem Dep Agric Sth Rhod — Memoirs of the Department of Agriculture. Southern Rhodesia

Mem Dep Agric Trin — Memoirs of the Department of Agriculture. Trinidad and Tobago

Mem Dep Cote d'Or — Memoires. Commission des Antiquites du Departement de la Cote d'Or

Mem Dep Eng Kyoto Imp Univ — Memoirs. Department of Engineering. Kyoto Imperial University

Mem Dep Geol Sci Va Polytech Inst State Univ — Memoir. Department of Geological Sciences. Virginia PolytechnicInstitute and State University

Mem Dep Mineral Univ Geneve — Memoire. Departement de Mineralogie. Universite de Geneve

Mem Dep Miner Ceylon — Memoirs. Department of Mineralogy. Ceylon

Mém Dep Mines Inds Un S Afr — Memoirs of the Department of Mines and Industries. Union of South Africa

Mem Dep Mines SW Afr — Memoirs. Department of Mines of South-West Africa

Mem Dep Zool Univ Punjab — Memoirs of the Department of Zoology. University of the Punjab

Mem Descr Carta Geol Ital — Memorie Descrittive della Carta Geologica d'Italia

Mem Differential Equations Math Phys — Georgian Academy of Sciences. A. Razmadze Mathematical Institute. Memoirs on Differential Equations and Mathematical Physics

Mem Dijon — Memoires. Academie des Sciences, Arts, et Belles Lettres de Dijon

Mem Discuss Congr Natn Period Gynec Obstet Paediat — Memoires et Discussions. Congres National Periodique de Gynecologie, d'Obstetrique, et de Paediatrie

Mem Doc Acad Sci Besancon — Memoires et Documents. Academie des Sciences, Belles-Lettres, et Arts de Besancon

Mem Domenicane — Memoriae Domenicane

Mem Domenicane — Memorie Domenicane

Mem Ecol Soc Aust — Memoirs. Ecological Society of Australia

Mem Econ Acad Real Sci Lisboa — Memorias Economicas. Academia Real das Sciencias de Lisboa

Me Med J — Maine Medical Journal

Mem Ehime Univ — Memoirs. Ehime University

Mem Ehime Univ Nat Sci Ser B (Biol) — Memoirs. Ehime University. Natural Science. Series B (Biology)

Mem Ehime Univ Nat Sci Ser C — Memoirs. Ehime University. Natural Science. Series C

Mem Ehime Univ Nat Sci Ser D — Memoirs. Ehime University. Natural Science. Series D. Earth Science

Mem Ehime Univ Natur Sci Ser A — Memoirs. Ehime University. Natural Science. Series A

Mem Ehime Univ Sect 2 Nat Sci — Memoirs. Ehime University. Section 2. Natural Science

Mem Ehime Univ Sect 2 Ser C — Memoirs. Ehime University. Section 2. Natural Science. Series C. Chemistry

Mem Ehime Univ Sect 3 Eng — Memoirs. Ehime University. Section 3. Engineering

Mem Ehime Univ Sect 3 Engrg — Memoirs. Ehime University. Section 3. Engineering

Mem Ehime Univ Sect 6 Agr — Memoirs. Ehime University. Section 6. Agriculture

Mem Ehime Univ Sect 6 (Agric) — Memoirs. Ehime University. Section 6 (Agriculture)

Memento Def Cult Rabat — Memento. Defense des Cultures. Direction Generale de l'Agriculture (Rabat)

Mem Entomol Soc Can — Memoirs. Entomological Society of Canada

Mem Entomol Soc Que — Memoirs. Entomological Society of Quebec

Mem Entomol Soc South Afr — Memoirs. Entomological Society of Southern Africa

Mem Entomol Soc Sthn Afr — Memoirs. Entomological Society of Southern Africa

Mem Entomol Soc Wash — Memoirs. Entomological Society of Washington

Memento Serv Met AOF — Memento. Service Meteorologique de l'A.O.F

Mementos Ther — Mementos Therapeutiques

Mem Ent S C — Memoirs. Entomological Society of Canada

Mem Ent Soc Can — Memoirs. Entomological Society of Canada

Mem Estud Mus Zool Univ Coimbra — Memorias e Estudos. Museu Zoologico. Universidade de Coimbra

MeMeth — Media and Methods

Mem Etud Sci Rev Metall — Memoires et Etudes Scientifiques de la Revue de Metallurgie

Mem Exc — Memorias. Junta Superior de Excavaciones y Antiquedades

Mem Explic Cartes Geol Min Belg — Memoires pour Servir a l'Explication des Cartes Geologiques et Minieres de la Belgique

MEMFA — Metallurgia and Metal Forming

Mem Fac Agr Hokkaido U — Memoirs. Faculty of Agriculture. Hokkaido University

Mem Fac Agr Hokkaido Univ — Memoirs. Faculty of Agriculture. Hokkaido University

Mem Fac Agric Hokkaido Univ — Memoirs. Faculty of Agriculture. Hokkaido University

Mem Fac Agric Kagawa Univ — Memoirs. Faculty of Agriculture. Kagawa University

Mem Fac Agric Kagoshima Univ — Memoirs. Faculty of Agriculture. Kagoshima University

Mem Fac Agric Kinki Univ — Memoirs. Faculty of Agriculture. Kinki University

Mem Fac Agric Kochi Univ — Memoirs. Faculty of Agriculture. Kochi University

Mem Fac Agric Miyazaki Univ — Memoirs of the Faculty of Agriculture. Miyazaki University

Mem Fac Agric Natl Taiwan Univ — Memoirs. Faculty of Agriculture. National Taiwan University/Kuo Li Tai Wan Ta Hsueeh Nung Hsueeh Yuean Yen Chiu Pao Kao

Mem Fac Agric Natn Taiwan Univ — Memoirs of the Faculty of Agriculture. National Taiwan University

Mem Fac Agric Niigata Univ — Memoirs. Faculty of Agriculture. Niigata University

Mem Fac Agric Taihoku Imp Univ — Memoirs. Faculty of Agriculture. Taihoku Imperial University

Mem Fac Agric Univ Miyazaki — Memoirs. Faculty of Agriculture. University of Miyazaki

Mem Fac Agr Kagawa Univ — Memoirs. Faculty of Agriculture. Kagawa University

Mem Fac Agr Kinki Univ — Memoirs. Faculty of Agriculture. Kinki University

Mem Fac Agr Univ Miyazaki — Memoirs. Faculty of Agriculture. University of Miyazaki

Mem Fac Ed Kumamoto Univ Natur Sci — Kumamoto University. Faculty of Education. Memoirs. Natural Science

Mem Fac Ed Kumamoto Univ Sect 1 — Memoirs. Faculty of Education. Kumamoto University. Section 1 (Natural Science)

Mem Fac Ed Miyazaki Univ — Memoirs. Faculty of Education. Miyazaki University

Mem Fac Ed Shiga Univ Natur Sci — Shiga University. Faculty of Education. Memoirs. Natural Science

Mem Fac Ed Shiga Univ Natur Sci Ped Sci — Memoirs. Faculty of Education. Shiga University. Natural Science and Pedagogic Science

Mem Fac Ed Shimane Univ Natur Sci — Shimane University. Faculty of Education. Memoirs. Natural Science

Mem Fac Educ Akita Univ — Memoirs. Faculty of Education. Akita University

Mem Fac Educ Akita Univ Nat Sci — Memoirs. Faculty of Education. Akita University. Natural Science

Mem Fac Educ Kagawa Univ — Memoirs. Faculty of Education. Kagawa University

Mem Fac Educ Kumamoto Univ — Memoirs. Faculty of Education. Kumamoto University

Mem Fac Educ Kumamoto Univ Nat Sci — Memoirs. Faculty of Education. Kumamoto University. Natural Science

Mem Fac Educ Kumamoto Univ Sect 1 (Nat Sci) — Memoirs. Faculty of Education. Kumamoto University. Section 1 (Natural Science)

Mem Fac Educ Mie Univ — Memoirs. Faculty of Education. Mie University

Mem Fac Educ Niigata Univ — Memoirs. Faculty of Education. Niigata University

Mem Fac Educ Shiga Univ Nat Sci — Memoirs. Faculty of Education. Shiga University. Natural Science

Mem Fac Educ Shiga Univ Nat Sci Pedagog Sci — Memoirs. Faculty of Education. Shiga University. Natural Science and Pedagogic Science

Mem Fac Educ Toyama Univ — Memoirs. Faculty of Education. Toyama University

Mem Fac Educ Yamanashi Univ — Memoirs. Faculty of Education. Yamanashi University

Mem Fac Eng Des Kyoto Inst Technol Ser Sci Technol — Memoirs. Faculty of Engineering and Design. Kyoto Institute of Technology. Series of Science and Technology

Mem Fac Eng Ehime Univ — Memoirs. Faculty of Engineering. Ehime University

Mem Fac Eng Fukui Univ — Memoirs. Faculty of Engineering. Fukui University

Mem Fac Eng Hiroshima Univ — Memoirs. Faculty of Engineering. Hiroshima University

Mem Fac Eng Hokkaido Imp Univ — Memoirs. Faculty of Engineering. Hokkaido Imperial University

Mem Fac Eng Hokkaido Univ — Memoirs. Faculty of Engineering. Hokkaido University

Mem Fac Eng Hokkaido Univ (Sapporo Jpn) — Memoirs. Faculty of Engineering. Hokkaido University (Sapporo, Japan)

Mem Fac Eng Kagoshima Univ — Memoirs. Faculty of Engineering. Kagoshima University

Mem Fac Eng Kobe Univ — Memoirs. Faculty of Engineering. Kobe University

Mem Fac Eng Kumamoto Univ — Memoirs. Faculty of Engineering. Kumamoto University

Mem Fac Eng Kyoto Univ — Memoirs. Faculty of Engineering. Kyoto University

Mem Fac Eng Kyushu Imp Univ — Memoirs. Faculty of Engineering. Kyushu Imperial University

Mem Fac Eng Kyushu Univ — Memoirs. Faculty of Engineering. Kyushu University

Mem Fac Eng Miyazaki Univ — Memoirs. Faculty of Engineering. Miyazaki University

Mem Fac Eng Nagoya Univ — Memoirs. Faculty of Engineering. Nagoya University

Mem Fac Eng Nagoya Univ — Memoirs. Nagoya University. Faculty of Engineering

Mem Fac Engng Hiroshima Univ — Memoirs of the Faculty of Engineering. Hiroshima University

Mem Fac Engng Hokkaido Univ — Memoirs of the Faculty of Engineering. Hokkaido University

Mem Fac Engng Kobe Univ — Memoirs of the Faculty of Engineering. Kobe University

Mem Fac Engng Kumamoto Univ — Memoirs of the Faculty of Engineering. Kumamoto University

Mem Fac Engng Kyoto Univ — Memoirs. Faculty of Engineering. Kyoto University

Mem Fac Engng Kyushu Univ — Memoirs. Faculty of Engineering. Kyushu University

Mem Fac Engng Miyazaki Univ — Memoirs of the Faculty of Engineering. Miyazaki University

Mem Fac Engng Nagoya Univ — Memoirs of the Faculty of Engineering. Nagoya University

Mem Fac Engng Osaka Cy Univ — Memoirs of the Faculty of Engineering. Osaka City University

Mem Fac Eng Okayama Univ — Memoirs. Faculty of Engineering. Okayama University

Mem Fac Eng Osaka City Univ — Memoirs. Faculty of Engineering. Osaka City University

Mem Fac Engrg Design Kyoto Inst Tech Ser Sci Tech — Memoirs of the Faculty of Engineering and Design. Kyoto Institute of Technology. Series of Science and Technology

Mem Fac Engrg Hiroshima Univ — Memoirs of the Faculty of Engineering. Hiroshima University

Mem Fac Engrg Kyoto Univ — Memoirs. Faculty of Engineering. Kyoto University

Mem Fac Engrg Miyazaki Univ — Memoirs. Faculty of Engineering. Miyazaki University

Mem Fac Eng Tamagawa Univ — Memoirs. Faculty of Engineering. Tamagawa University

Mem Fac Eng Tehran Univ — Memoirs. Faculty of Engineering. Tehran University

Mem Fac Eng Tokyo Metrop Univ — Memoirs of Faculty of Engineering. Tokyo Metropolitan University

Mem Fac Eng Yamaguchi Univ — Memoirs. Faculty of Engineering. Yamaguchi University

Mem Fac Fish Hokkaido Univ — Memoirs. Faculty of Fisheries. Hokkaido University

Mem Fac Fish Kagoshima Univ — Memoirs. Faculty of Fisheries. Kagoshima University

Mem Fac Gen Ed Kumamoto Univ Natur Sci — Memoirs. Kumamoto University. Faculty of General Education. Natural Sciences

Mem Fac Gen Educ Hiroshima Univ — Memoirs. Faculty of General Education. Hiroshima University

Mem Fac Gen Educ Kumamoto Univ — Memoirs. Faculty of General Education. Kumamoto University

Mem Fac Ind Arts Kyoto Tech Univ — Memoirs. Faculty of Industrial Arts. Kyoto Technical University. Science and Technology

Mem Fac Ind Arts Kyoto Tech Univ Sci and Technol — Memoirs. Faculty of Industrial Arts. Kyoto Technical University. Science and Technology

Mem Fac Indust Arts Kyoto Tech Univ Sci and Tech — Memoirs. Faculty of Industrial Arts. Kyoto Technical University. Science and Technology

Mem Fac Intgr Arts Sci Hiroshima Univ — Memoirs. Faculty of Integrated Arts and Sciences. Hiroshima University

Mem Fac Lib Arts Educ Akita Univ Nat Sci — Memoirs. Faculty of Liberal Arts and Education. Akita University.Natural Science

Mem Fac Lib Arts Educ Miyazaki Univ — Memoirs. Faculty of Liberal Arts Education. Miyazaki University

Mem Fac Lib Arts Educ Miyazaki Univ Nat Sci — Memoirs. Faculty of Liberal Arts and Education. Miyazaki University. Natural Science

Mem Fac Lib Arts Educ Part 2 Yamanashi Univ — Memoirs. Faculty of Liberal Arts and Education. Part 2. Mathematics andNatural Sciences. Yamanashi University

Mem Fac Lib Arts Fukui Univ — Memoirs. Faculty of Liberal Arts. Fukui University

Mem Fac Liberal Arts Educ Yamanashi Univ — Memoirs. Faculty of Liberal Arts and Education. Yamanashi University

Mem Fac Lit Sci Shimane Univ Nat Sci — Memoirs. Faculty of Literature and Science. Shimane University. Natural Sciences

Mem Fac Lit Sci Shimane Univ Natur Sci — Memoirs. Faculty of Literature and Science. Shimane University. Natural Sciences

Mem Fac Med Natl Taiwan Univ — Memoirs. Faculty of Medicine. National Taiwan University

Mem Fac Med Natn Taiwan Univ — Memoirs of the Faculty of Medicine. National Taiwan University

Mem Fac Sci Agric Taihoku Imp Univ — Memoirs. Faculty of Science and Agriculture. Taihoku Imperial University

Mem Fac Sci Engng Waseda Univ — Memoirs of the Faculty of Science and Engineering. Waseda University

Mem Fac Sci Eng Waseda Univ — Memoirs. Faculty of Science and Engineering. Waseda University

Mem Fac Sci Kochi Univ Ser A Math — Kochi University. Faculty of Science. Memoirs. Series A. Mathematics

Mem Fac Sci Kochi Univ Ser C — Memoirs. Faculty of Science. Kochi University. Series C. Chemistry

Mem Fac Sci Kochi Univ Ser D Biol — Memoirs. Faculty of Science. Kochi University. Series D. Biology

Mem Fac Sci Kyoto Univ Ser — Memoirs. Faculty of Science. Kyoto University. Series of Physics, Astrophysics,Geophysics, and Chemistry

Mem Fac Sci Kyoto Univ Ser Biol — Memoirs. Faculty of Science. Kyoto University. Series of Biology

Mem Fac Sci Kyoto Univ Ser Geol Mineral — Memoirs. Faculty of Science. Kyoto University. Series of Geology and Mineralogy

Mem Fac Sci Kyoto Univ Ser Phys Astrophys Geophys Chem — Memoirs. Faculty of Science. Kyoto University. Series of Physics, Astrophysics,Geophysics, and Chemistry

Mem Fac Sci Kyushu Univ — Memoirs. Faculty of Science. Kyushu University

Mem Fac Sci Kyushu Univ B — Memoirs. Faculty of Science. Kyushu University. Series B

Mem Fac Sci Kyushu Univ C — Memoirs. Faculty of Science. Kyushu University. Series C

Mem Fac Sci Kyushu Univ Ser A — Memoirs. Faculty of Science. Kyushu University. Series A. Mathematics

Mem Fac Sci Kyushu Univ Ser B — Memoirs. Faculty of Science. Kyushu University. Series B. Physics

Mem Fac Sci Kyushu Univ Ser C — Memoirs. Faculty of Science. Kyushu University. Series C. Chemistry

Mem Fac Sci Kyushu Univ Ser D — Memoirs. Faculty of Science. Kyushu University. Series D. Geology

Mem Fac Sci Kyushu Univ Ser D Geol — Memoirs. Faculty of Science. Kyushu University. Series D. Geology

Mem Fac Sci Kyushu Univ Ser E — Memoirs. Faculty of Science. Kyushu University. Series E. Biology

Mem Fac Sci Kyushu Univ Ser E Biol — Memoirs. Faculty of Science. Kyushu University. Series E. Biology

Mem Fac Sci Natn Taiwan Univ — Memoirs of the Faculty of Science. National Taiwan University

Mem Fac Sci Shimane Univ — Shimane University. Faculty of Science. Memoirs

Mem Fac Sci Taihoku Imp Univ — Memoirs. Faculty of Science and Agriculture. Taihoku Imperial University/Rino-Gaku-Bu Kiyo

Mem Fac Technol Kagoshima Univ — Memoirs. Faculty of Technology. Kagoshima University

Mem Fac Technol Kanazawa Univ — Memoirs. Faculty of Technology. Kanazawa University

Mem Fac Technol Tokyo Metrop Univ — Memoirs. Faculty of Technology. Tokyo Metropolitan University

Mem Fac Tech Tokyo Metropolitan Univ — Memoirs. Faculty of Technology. Tokyo Metropolitan University

Mem Facul Fish — Memoir of the Faculty of Fisheries

Mem Fd Invest Bd — Memoirs of the Food Investigation Board. Department of Scientific and Industrial Research [London]

Mem Fed Soc Hist & Archeol Aisne — Memoires de la Federation des Societes d'Histoire et d'Archeologie de l'Aisne

Mem Fed Soc Hist & Archeol Paris & Ile de France — Memoires de la Federation des Societes Historiques et Archeologiques de Paris et de l'Ile-de-France

Mem Fed Soc Paris & Ile de France — Memoires de la Federation des Societes de Paris et de l'Ile-de-France

Mem Fiji Geol Surv Dep — Memoir. Fiji. Geological Survey Department

Mem Fis Istoria Nat — Memorie Sopra la Fisica e Istoria Naturale di Diversi Valentuomini

Mem Fld Div Minist Agric Sudan — Memoirs of the Field Division. Ministry of Agriculture. Sudan

Mem For Div Sudan — Memoirs of Forestry Division. Ministry of Agriculture. Sudan

Mem Gakugei Fac Akita Univ Nat Sci — Memoirs of Gakugei Faculty. Akita University. Natural Science

Mem Gen Inst Geol Min Esp — Memoria General. Instituto Geologico y Minero de Espana

Mem Geogr Brch Can — Memoirs. Geographical Branch. Department of Mines and Technical Surveys. Canada

Mem Geol Dep Mysore — Memoirs of the Geological Department. Mysore State

Mem Geol Div Res Coun Alberta — Memoirs. Geological Division. Research Council of Alberta

Mem Geol Soc Am — Memoir. Geological Society of America

Mem Geol Soc Amer — Memoirs. Geological Society of America

Mem Geol Soc China — Memoir. Geological Society of China

Mem Geol Soc India — Memoir. Geological Society of India

Mem Geol Soc Jpn — Memoirs. Geological Society of Japan

Mem Geol Soc Lond — Memoirs of the Geological Society of London

Mem Geol Surv Brch Can — Memoirs of the Geological Survey Branch. Department of Mines. Canada

Mem Geol Surv Brch Can Anthrop Ser — Memoirs of the Geological Survey Branch. Department of Mines. Canada. Anthropological Series

Mem Geol Surv Br Solomon Isl — Memoirs of the Geological Survey of the British Solomon Islands

Mem Geol Surv Can — Memoirs. Geological Survey of Canada

Mem Geol Surv China Ser A — Memoirs. Geological Survey of China. Series A

Mem Geol Surv China Ser B — Memoirs. Geological Survey of China. Series B

Mem Geol Surv Dep Br Terr Borneo — Memoirs of the Geological Survey Department. British Territories in Borneo

Mem Geol Surv Dep Cyprus — Memoirs. Geological Survey Department. Cyprus

Mem Geol Surv Dep Fed Malaya — Memoirs of the Geological Survey Department. Federation of Malaya

Mem Geol Surv Dep Nyasald — Memoirs. Geological Survey Department. Nyasaland

Mem Geol Surv Dep (Sudan) — Memoirs. Geological Survey Department (Sudan)

Mem Geol Surv Dep Tanganyika — Memoirs. Geological Survey Department. Tanganyika

Mem Geol Surv GB Engl Wales Explan Sheet — Memoirs. Geological Survey of Great Britain. England and Wales Explanation Sheet

Mem Geol Surv GB (Scotl) — Memoirs. Geological Survey of Great Britain (Scotland)

Mem Geol Surv GB Spec Rep Miner Resour GB — Memoirs. Geological Survey of Great Britain. Special Reports on theMineral Resources of Great Britain

Mem Geol Surv Gold Cst — Memoirs of the Geological Survey of the Gold Coast

Mem Geol Surv Gt Br — Memoirs. Geological Survey of Great Britain

Mem Geol Surv India — Memoirs. Geological Survey of India

Mem Geol Surv India Palaeont Indica — Memoirs of the Geological Survey of India. Palaeontologia Indica

Mem Geol Surv Japan — Memoirs of the Geological Survey of Japan

Mem Geol Surv Kenya — Memoir. Geological Survey of Korea

Mem Geol Surv North Irel — Memoir. Geological Survey of Northern Ireland

Mem Geol Surv NSW — Memoirs. Geological Survey of New South Wales

Mem Geol Surv NSW Geol — New South Wales. Geological Survey. Memoirs. Geology

Mem Geol Surv NSW Palaeontol — Memoirs. Geological Survey of New South Wales. Palaeontology

Mem Geol Surv Nth Ire — Memoirs of the Geological Survey. Northern Ireland

Mem Geol Surv NZ — Memoirs. Geological Survey of New Zealand

Mem Geol Surv of NSW — Memoirs. Geological Survey of New South Wales

Mem Geol Surv of NSW Geol — Memoirs. Geological Survey of New South Wales. Department of Mines. Geology

Mem Geol Surv Papua New Guinea — Memoirs. Geological Survey of Papua New Guinea

Mem Geol Surv S Afr — Memoirs. Geological Survey of South Africa

Mem Geol Surv South West Afr — Memoir. Geological Survey of South West Africa

Mem Geol Surv UK — Memoirs of the Geological Survey of the United Kingdom

Mem Geol Surv Un S Afr — Memoirs. Geological Survey. Union of South Africa

Mem Geol Surv Vic — Memoirs. Geological Survey of Victoria

Mem Geol Surv Vict — Memoirs. Geological Survey of Victoria

Mem Geol Surv Victoria — Memoir. Geological Survey of Victoria

Mem Geol Surv West Aust — Memoirs. Geological Survey of Western Australia

Mem Geol Surv Wyo — Memoir. Geological Survey of Wyoming

Mem Geopaleontol Univ Ferrara — Memorie Geopaleontologiche. Universita di Ferrara

Mem Gifu Tech Coll — Memoirs. Gifu Technical College

Mem Gov Ind Res Inst Nagoya — Memoirs. Government Industrial Research Institute. Nagoya

Mem Gov Ind Res Inst Sikoku — Memoirs. Government Industrial Research Institute. Sikoku

Mem Govt Ind Res Inst Nagoya — Memoirs. Government Industrial Research Institute (Nagoya)

Mem Grad Sch Eng Tokyo Metrop Univ — Memoirs of Graduate School of Engineering. Tokyo Metropolitan University

Mem Grassl Res Inst (Hurley Engl) — Memoir. Grassland Research Institute (Hurley, England)

Mem Gray Herb — Memoirs of the Gray Herbarium. Harvard University

Mem Herb Boissier — Memoires de l'Herbier Boissier

Mem Himeji Tech Coll — Memoirs. Himeji Technical College

Mem Hist Ant — Memorias de Historia Antigua. Universidad de Oviedo

Mem Hist Nat Acad Real Ci Lisboa — Memorias de Historia Natural, de Quimica, de Agricultura, Artes, e Medicina. Lidas na Academia Real das Ciencias de Lisboa

Mem Hist Nat Anim Pl — Memoires pour Servir a l'Histoire Naturelle des Animaux et des Plantes

Mem Hist Nat Emp Chin — Memoires Concernant l'Histoire Naturelle de l'Empire Chinois

Mem Hokkaido Automot Jr Coll — Memoirs. Hokkaido Automotive Junior College

Mem Hokkaido Inst Technol — Memoirs. Hokkaido Institute of Technology

Mem Hong Kong Biol Circle — Memoirs of the Hong Kong Biological Circle

Mem Hong Kong Nat Hist Soc — Memoirs of the Hong Kong Natural History Society

Mem Hors Ser Soc Geol Fr — Memoire Hors-Serie. Societe Geologique de France

Mem Hort Soc NY — Memoirs of the Horticultural Society of New York

Mem Hourglass Cruises — Memoirs. Hourglass Cruises

Mem Hyogo Univ Agric — Memoirs. Hyogo University of Agriculture

Mem ICF — Memoires ICF

Memies Serv Met Catal — Memories. Servei Meteorologic de Catalunya

Mem IFAO — Memoires. Institut Francais d'Archeologie Orientale

Mem Imp Acad Tokyo — Memoirs of the Imperial Academy (Tokyo)

Mem Imp Mar Observ — Memoirs. Imperial Marine Observatory

Mem Imp Mineral Soc St Petersburg — Memoirs. Imperial Mineralogical Society of St. Petersburg

Mem Imp Reale Ist Veneto Sci — Memorie. Imperiale Reale Istituto Veneto di Scienze, Lettere, ed Arti

Mem INAH — Memorias del Instituto Nacional de Antropologia e Historia

Mem Indian Bot Soc — Memoirs. Indian Botanical Society

Mem Indian Civ Vet Dep — Memoirs of the Indian Civil Veterinary Department

Mem Indian Inst Sci — Memoirs of the Indian Institute of Science

Mem Indian Met Dep — Memoirs of the Indian Meteorological Department

Mem Indian Mus — Memoirs. Indian Museum

Mem Ind Met Tokyo — Memoirs of Industrial Meteorology (Tokyo)

Mem Inst — Memoires. Institut Francais d'Archeologie Orientale

Mem Inst Agron For Etat Belarussie — Memoires. Institut Agronomique et Forestier d'Etat de la Belarussie

Mem Inst Agron Univ Louvain — Memoires de l'Institut Agronomique de l'Universite Catholique de Louvain

Mem Inst Astr Shanghai — Memoirs. Institute of Astronomy. National Research Institute of China (Shanghai)

Mem Inst Biocien Univ Fed Pernambuco — Memorias. Instituto de Biociencias. Universidade Federal dePernambuco

Mem Inst Butantan — Memorias. Instituto Butantan

Mem Inst Butantan (Sao Paulo) — Memorias. Instituto Butantan (Sao Paulo)

Mem Inst Chem Acad Sci Ukr SSR — Memoirs. Institute for Chemistry. Academy of Sciences. Ukrainian SSR

Mem Inst Chem Technol Acad Sci Ukr SSR — Memoirs. Institute of Chemical Technology. Academy of Sciences of theUkrainian SSR

Mem Inst Chem Ukr Acad Sci — Memoirs. Institute of Chemistry. Ukrainian Academy of Sciences

Mem Inst Cor Arch — Memorie. Instituto di Corrispondenza Archeologica

Mem Inst Egypt — Memoires de l'Institut Egyptien

Mem Inst Egypt — Memoires. Institut d'Egypte

Mem Inst Egypte — Memoires. Institut d'Egypte

Mem Inst Esp Oceanogr — Memorias. Instituto Espanol de Oceanografia

Mem Inst Estud Cat Seccio Hist Arqueol — Memories de l'Institut d'Estudis Catalans. Seccion Historico-Arqueologic

Mem Inst Ethnol — Memoires de l'Institut d'Ethnologie

Mem Inst Etud Centrafr — Memoires de l'Institut d'Etudes Centrafricaines

Mem Inst Etud Marit Belg — Memoires. Institut d'Etudes Maritimes de Belgique

Mem Inst Fr Afrique Noire Cent Cameroun — Memoires de l'Institut Francais d'Afrique Noire. Centre du Cameroun

Mem Inst Fr Afrique Noire Mel Ethnol — Memoires de l'Institut Francais d'Afrique Noire. Melanges Ethnologiques

Mem Inst Fr Afr Noire — Memoires de l'Institut Francais d'Afrique Noire

Mem Inst Franc — Memoires. Institut Francais d'Archeologie Orientale

Mem Inst Franc Afrique Noire — Memoires de l'Institut Francais d'Afrique Noire

Mem Inst Francais Arch Or — Memoires. Institut Francais d'Archeologie Orientale

Mem Inst Franc Archeol Or Caire — Memoires Publies. Membres. Institut Francais d'Archeologie Orientale au Caire

Mem Inst France Acad Inscr & B Lett — Memoires de l'Institut de France. Academie des Inscriptions et Belles-Lettres

Mem Inst Fr Archeol — Memoires de l'Institut Francais d'Archeologie

Mem Inst Gen Psychol — Memoires de l'Institut General Psychologique

Mem Inst Geod Dan — Memoires. Institut Geodesique de Danemark

Mem Inst Geol Bassin Aquitaine — Memoires. Institut de Geologie du Bassin d'Aquitaine

Mem Inst Geol Esp — Memoria. Instituto Geologico de Espana

Mem Inst Geol Min Esp — Memorias. Instituto Geologico y Minero de Espana

Mem Inst Geol Peking — Memoirs of the Institute of Geology. Academia Sinica (Peking)

Mem Inst Geol (Rom) — Memoires. Institut Geologique (Romania)

Mem Inst Geol (Rom) — Memorii. Institutul Geologic (Romania)

Mem Inst Geol Rom — Memoriile Institutului Geologic al Romaniei

Mem Inst Geol Shanghai — Memoirs of the Institute of Geology. National Research Institute of China (Shanghai)

Mem Inst Geol Univ Louv — Memoires. Institut Geologique. Universite de Louvain

Mem Inst Geol Univ Louvain — Memoires de l'Institut Geologique de l'Universite de Louvain

Mem Inst High Speed Mech Tohoku Univ — Memoirs. Institute of High Speed Mechanics. Tohoku University

Mem Inst Invest Cient Mocambique Ser A Cienc Biol — Memorias. Instituto de Investigacao Cientifica de Mocambique. Serie A. CienciasBiologicas

Mem Inst Invest Ci Mocambique — Memorias. Instituto de Investigacao Cientifica de Mocambique

Mem Inst Metrol Stand URSS Presentes Com Int Poids Mes — Memoires. Institut de Metrologie et de Standardisation de l'URSS Presentes au Comite International des Poids et Mesures

Mem Inst Met Shanghai — Memoirs. Institute of Meteorology. National Research Institute of China (Shanghai)

Mem Inst Min Technol New Mex — Memoirs. Institute of Mining Technology. New Mexico State Bureau of Mines and Mineral Resources

Mem Inst Nat Fr — Memoires. Institut National de France

Mem Inst Nat France — Memoires de l'Institut National de France. Academie des Inscriptions et Belles-Lettres

Mem Inst Natl Pol Econ Rurale — Memoires. Institut National Polonais d'Economie Rurale

Mem Inst Natl Sci Sci Math — Memoires de l'Institut National des Sciences et Arts. Sciences Mathematiques etPhysiques

Mem Inst Natn Genev — Memoires de l'Institut National Genevois

Mem Inst Oceanogr Indoch — Memoires de l'Institut Oceanographique de l'Indochine

Mem Inst Oceanogr (Monaco) — Memoires. Institut Oceanographique (Monaco)

Mem Inst Oceanogr Nhatrang — Memoires de l'Institut Oceanographique de Nhatrang

Mem Inst Org Chem Technol Acad Sci Ukr SSR — Memoirs. Institute of Organic Chemistry and Technology. Academy of Sciences. Ukrainian SSR

Mem Inst Oswaldo Cruz — Memorias. Instituto Oswaldo Cruz

Mem Inst Oswaldo Cruz (Rio De J) — Memorias. Instituto Oswaldo Cruz (Rio De Janeiro)

Mem Inst Paleont Suisse — Memoires de l'Institut Paleontologique Suisse

Mem Inst Plant Prot Belgrade — Memoirs. Institute for Plant Protection. Belgrade

Mem Inst Protein Res Osaka Univ — Memoirs. Institute of Protein Research. Osaka University

Mem Inst Quim (Rio De Janeiro) — Memoria. Instituto de Quimica (Rio De Janeiro)

Mem Inst R Colon Belge Sect Sci Nat Med 4 — Memoires de l'Institut Royal Colonial Belge. Section des Sciences Naturelles et Medicales. Collection in -4

Mem Inst R Colon Belge Sect Sci Nat Med 8 — Memoires de l'Institut Royal Colonial Belge. Section des Sciences Naturelles et Medicales. Collection in -8

Mem Inst R Colon Belge Sect Sci Tech 4 — Memoires de l'Institut Royal Colonial Belge. Section des Sciences Techniques. Collection in -4

Mem Inst R Colon Belge Sect Sci Tech 8 — Memoires de l'Institut Royal Colonial Belge. Section des Sciences Techniques. Collection in -8

Mem Inst Rech Sci Madagascar Ser A Biol Anim — Memoires. Institut de Recherche Scientifique de Madagascar. Serie A. Biologie Animale

Mem Inst Rech Sci Madagascar Ser B Biol Veg — Memoires. Institut de Recherche Scientifique de Madagascar. Serie B. Biologie Vegetale

Mem Inst Rech Sci Madagascar Ser F Oceanogr — Memoires. Institut de Recherche Scientifique de Madagascar. Serie F. Oceanographie

Mem Inst Roy Colon Belge Sect Sci Nat 4 — Memoires. Institut Royal Colonial Belge. Section des Sciences Naturelles et Medicales. Verhandelingen. Koninklijk Belgisch Koloniaal Instit Afdeeling der Natuur- en Geneeskundige Wetenschappen. In Quarto

Mem Inst Sci Divers Savans Sci Math — Memoires Presentes a l'Institut des Sciences, Lettres, et Arts par Divers Savans, et lus dans ses Assemblees. Sciences Mathematiques et Physiques

Mem Inst Sci Engrg Ritsumeikan Univ — Memoirs of the Institute of Science and Engineering. Ritsumeikan University

Mem Inst Sci Ind Res Osaka Univ — Memoirs. Institute of Scientific and Industrial Research. Osaka University

Mem Inst Sci Madagascar Ser B — Memoires. Institut de Recherche Scientifique de Madagascar. Serie B. Biologie

Mem Inst Sci Madagascar Ser B Biol Veg — Memoires. Institut Scientifique de Madagascar. Serie B. Biologie Vegetale

Mem Inst Sci Madagascar Ser D — Memoires. Institut de Recherche Scientifique de Madagascar. Serie D. Sciences de la Terre

Mem Inst Sci Technol Meiji Univ — Memoirs. Institute of Sciences and Technology. Meiji University

Mem Inst Suisse Rech For — Memoires. Institut Suisse de Recherches Forestieres

Mem Int Assoc Hydrogeol — Memoirs. International Association of Hydrogeologists

Mem Int Soc Sugar Cane Technol — Memoirs. International Society of Sugar Cane Technologists

Mem Ist Geol Mineral Univ Padova — Memorie. Istituti di Geologia e Mineralogia. Universita di Padova

Mem Ist Geol Paleontol Univ Padov — Memorie. Istituto di Geologia e Paleontologia. Universita diPadova

Mem Ist Geol Univ Padova — Memorie. Istituto Geologico. Universita di Padova

Mem Ist Ital Idrobiol — Memorie. Istituto Italiano di Idrobiologia

Mem Ist Ital Idrobiol Dott Marco De Marchi — Memorie. Istituto Italiano di Idrobiologia Dottore Marco De Marchi

Mem Ist Ital Idrobiol Dott Marco De Marchi (Pallanza Italy) — Memorie. Istituto Italiano di Idrobiologia Dottore Marco De Marchi (Pallanza, Italy)

Mem Ist Ital Idrobiol Dott Marco Marchi — Memorie. Istituto Italiano di Idrobiologia Dottore Marco De Marchi

Mem Ist Lombardo Accad Sci Lett Cl Sci Mat Natur — Memorie. Istituto Lombardo Accademia di Scienze e Lettere. Classe di Scienze Matematiche e Naturali

Mem Ist Lomb Sc — Memorie. Istituto Lombardo di Scienze e Lettere, Scienze, Morali e Storiche

Mem Ist Svizz Ric For — Memorie. Istituto Svizzero di Ricerche Forestali

Mem Ist Ven Sci Lett & A — Memorie dell'Istituto Veneto di Scienze, Lettere, ed Arti

Me M J — Maine Medical Journal

Mem Jornadas Agron — Memoria Jornadas Agronomicas

Mem Jpn Meteorol Agency — Memoirs. Japan Meteorological Agency

Mem Junta Direct Soc Nac Agrar — Memoria. Junta Directiva. Sociedad Nacional Agraria

Mem Junta Exc — Memorias. Junta Superior de Excavaciones y Antiquedades

Mem Junta Invest Cient Ultramar Ser II — Memorias. Junta de Investigacoes Cientificas do Ultramar. Serie II

Mem Junta Invest Ultramar (Port) — Memorias. Junta de Investigacoes do Ultramar (Portugal)

Mem Junta Invest Ultramar Ser II — Memorias. Junta de Investigacoes do Ultramar. Serie II

Mem Junta Missoes Geogr Invest Ultramar (Port) — Memorias. Junta das Missoes Geograficas e de Investigacoes do Ultramar (Portugal)

Mem Kagawa Agric Coll — Memoirs. Kagawa Agricultural College

Mem Kakioka Magn Obs — Memoirs. Kakioka Magnetic Observatory

Mem Kanazawa Inst Technol — Memoirs. Kanazawa Institute of Technology

Mem Kanazawa Tech Coll — Memoirs. Kanazawa Technical College

Mem Kitami Coll Technol — Memoirs. Kitami College of Technology

Mem Kitami Inst Tech — Memoirs. Kitami Institute of Technology

Mem Kobe Mar Observ — Memoirs. Kobe Marine Observatory

Mem Kobe Mar Obs (Kobe Jpn) — Memoirs. Kobe Marine Observatory (Kobe, Japan)

Mem Kodaikanal Obs — Memoirs of the Kodaikanal Observatory

Mem Konan Univ Sci Ser — Memoirs. Konan University. Science Series

Mem Kyancutta Mus — Memoirs. Kyancutta Museum

Mem Kyoto Tech Univ Sci Tech — Memoirs. Faculty of Industrial Arts. Kyoto Technical University. Science and Technology

Mem Kyushu Inst Technol Eng — Memoirs. Kyushu Institute of Technology. Engineering

Mem Lab Anthrop S Fe — Memoirs. Laboratory of Anthropology (Santa Fe)

Mem Lab Biol Agric Inst Pasteur — Memoires du Laboratoire de Biologie Agricole de l'Institut Pasteur

Mem Lab Essais Soc Fr Photogr — Memoires du Laboratoire d'Essais de la Societe Francaise de Photographie

Mem Lab Nac Eng Civ (Port) — Memoria. Laboratorio Nacional de Engenharia Civil (Portugal)

Mem Lancs Sea Fish Comm — Memoirs of the Lancashire Sea Fisheries Committee

Meml Artillerie Fr Sci Tech Armement — Memorial de l'Artillerie Francaise. Sciences et Techniques de l'Armement

Meml Artill Fr — Memorial de l'Artillerie Francaise

Meml Dir Obr Sanit Nac B Aires — Memorial del Directorio. Obras Sanitarias de la Nacion (Buenos Aires)

Memle Inst Geol Rom — Memoriile Institutului Geologic al Romaniei

Memle Inst Met Cent Rom — Memoriile Institutului Meteorologic Central al Romaniei

Memle Sect Stiint Acad Rom — Memoriile Sectiunii Stiintifice. Academia Romana

Meml Genie Marit — Memorial du Genie Maritime

Mem Linc — Memorie. Accademia Nazionale dei Lincei

Meml Ing Ejerc — Memorial de Ingenieros del Ejercito

Meml Inst Cent Met Vars — Memorial de l'Institut Central Meteorologique (Varsovie)

Mem Lit Soc Manchester — Memoirs. Literary and Philosophical Society of Manchester

Mem LJ — Memphis Law Journal

Meml Lect Chem Soc — Memorial Lectures Delivered Before the Chemical Society

Meml Meteorol Natl — Memorial de la Meteorologie Nationale

Meml Mfs Etat Tab Allum — Memorial des Manufactures de l'Etat Tabacallumettes

Meml Off Natn Met Fr — Memorial de l'Office National Meteorologique de France

Mem Lowell Obs — Memoirs of the Lowell Observatory [*Flagstaff, Arizona*]

Mem Low Temp Res Stn Trin — Memoirs. Low Temperature Research Station. Saint Augustine, Trinidad

Meml Poud — Memorial des Poudres

Meml Poudres — Memorial des Poudres

Meml Poudres Salpetres — Memorial des Poudres et Salpetres

Meml Sci Math — Memorial des Sciences Mathematiques

Meml Sci Phys — Memorial des Sciences Physiques

Meml Serv Chim Etat — Memorial des Services Chimiques de l'Etat

Meml Serv Exploit Ind Tab — Memorial du Service d'Exploitation Industrielle des Tabacs et des Allumettes

Meml Serv Exploit Ind Tab Allumettes Ser B — Memorial du Service d'Exploitation Industrielle des Tabacs et des Allumettes. Serie B. Publications. Institut Experimental des Tabacs de Bergerac

Meml Serv Geogr Armee — Memorial du Service Geographique de l'Armee

Meml Serv Poudres — Memorial du Service des Poudres

Meml Servs Chim Etat — Memorial des Services Chimiques de l'Etat

Meml Tec Ejerc Chile — Memorial Tecnico del Ejercito de Chile

Meml Ther Appl — Memorial de Therapeutique Appliquee

Mem MA — Memorias de los Museos Arqueologicos Provinciales

Mem Malaysia Geol Surv Borneo Region — Memoir. Malaysia Geological Survey. Borneo Region

Mem MAP — Memorias. Museos Arqueologicos Provinciales

Mem MA Prov — Memorias de los Museos Arqueologicos Provinciales

Mem Mat Fis Soc Ital Sci Modena Pt Mem Fis — Memorie di Matematica e di Fisica. Societa Italiana delle Scienze Residente in Modena. Parte Contenente le Memorie di Fisica

Mem Math Phys Acad Roy Sci Divers Scavans — Memoires de Mathematique et de Physique. Presentes a l'Academie Royale des Sciences par Divers Scavans

Mem Mat Inst Jorge Juan — Memorias de Matematica. Instituto Jorge Juan

Mem Med Soc London — Memoirs. Medical Society of London

Mem Meteorol Natl — Memorial de la Meteorologie Nationale

Mem Midi — Memoires. Societe Archeologique du Midi de la France

Mem Miner Resour Div (Tanzania) — Memoirs. Mineral Resources Division (Tanzania)

Mem Miner Resour Geol Surv Szechuan — Memoirs of Mineral Resources. Geological Survey of Szechuan

Memming Geschbl — Memminger Geschichtsblaetter. Zwanglos Erscheinende Mitteilungen der Heimatpflege Memmingen

Mem Miss Caire — Memoires Publies par les Membres de la Mission Archeologique Francaise au Caire

Mem Miyakonojo Tech Coll — Memoirs. Miyakonojo Technical College

Mem Mont Bur Mines Geol — Memoir. Montana Bureau of Mines and Geology

Mem Muroran Inst Tech — Memoirs. Muroran Institute of Technology

Mem Muroran Inst Technol — Memoirs. Muroran Institute of Technology

Mem Muroran Inst Technol Sci Eng — Memoirs. Muroran Institute of Technology, Science, and Engineering

Mem Mururan Univ Eng — Memoirs. Mururan University of Engineering

Mem Mus Amer Ind — Memoirs of the Museum of the American Indian

Mem Mus Anthropol U MI — Memoirs of the Museum of Anthropology. University of Michigan

Mem Mus A Provinc — Memorias. Museos Arqueologicos Provinciales

Mem Mus Arq — Memorias de los Museos Arqueologicos Provinciales

Mem Mus Arqu Provinciales — Memorias. Museos Arqueologicos Provinciales

Mem Mus Caucase — Memoires du Musee du Caucase

Mem Mus Civ Stor Nat Verona — Memorie. Museo Civico di Storia Naturale di Verona

Mem Mus Civ Stor Nat Verona IIA Ser Sez Sci Vita — Memorie. Museo Civico di Storia Naturale di Verona. IIA Serie. Sezione Scienze della Vita

Mem Mus Comp Zool Harv Coll — Memoirs. Museum of Comparative Zoology at Harvard College

Mem Mus Dr Alvaro De Castro — Memorias. Museu Dr. Alvaro De Castro

Mem Mus Hist Nat — Memoires du Museum d'Histoire Naturelle

Mem Mus Hist Nat "Javier Prado" — Memorias. Museo de Historia Natural "Javier Prado"

Mem Mus Hist Nat (Paris) Ser C — Memoires. Museum National d'Histoire Naturelle (Paris). Serie C. Sciences de laTerre

Mem Mus Mar Ser Zool — Memorias. Museu do Mar. Serie Zoologica

Mem Mus Natl His Nat Ser C Sci Terre — Memoires. Museum National d'Histoire Naturelle. Serie C. Sciences de la Terre

Mem Mus Natl Hist Nat — Memoires. Museum National d'Histoire Naturelle

Mem Mus Natl Hist Nat Ser A (Paris) — Memoires. Museum National d'Histoire Naturelle. Serie A. Zoologie (Paris)

Mem Mus Natl Hist Nat Ser A Zool — Memoires. Museum National d'Histoire Naturelle. Serie A. Zoologie

Mem Mus Natl Hist Nat Ser B Bot — Memoires. Museum National d'Histoire Naturelle. Serie B. Botanique

Mem Mus Natl Hist Nat Ser C Geol — Memoires. Museum National d'Histoire Naturelle. Serie C. Geologie

Mem Mus Natl Hist Nat Ser C (Paris) — Memoires. Museum National d'Histoire Naturelle. Serie C. Sciences de la Terre (Paris)

Mem Mus Natl Hist Nat Ser C Sci Terre — Memoires. Museum National d'Histoire Naturelle. Serie C. Sciences de la Terre

Mem Mus Natl Hist Nat Ser D (Paris) — Memoires. Museum National d'Histoire Naturelle. Serie D. Sciences Physico-Chimiques (Paris)

Mem Mus Natn Hist Nat (Paris) — Memoires. Museum National d'Histoire Naturelle (Paris)

Mem Mus Parana — Memorias. Museo de Parana

Mem Mus R Hist Nat Belg — Memoires du Musee Royal d'Histoire Naturelle de Belgique

Mem Mus Stor Nat Venezia Tridentina — Memorie. Museo di Storia Naturale della Venezia Tridentina

Mem Mus Tridentino Sci Nat — Memorie. Museo Tridentino di Scienze Naturali

Mem Mus Victoria — Memoirs. Museum of Victoria

Mem Nap — Memorie. Accademia di Archeologia, Lettere, e Belle Arti di Napoli

Mem Napoli — Memorie. Accademia di Archeologia, Lettere, e Belle Arti di Napoli

Mem Nara Univ — Memoirs. Nara University

Mem Nas Mus Bloemfontein — Memoirs. Nasionale Museum Bloemfontein

Mem Nat Cult Res San-In Reg — Memoirs of Natural and Cultural Researches of the San-In Region

Mem Nat Defense Acad — Memoirs. National Defense Academy. Mathematics, Physics, Chemistry, and Engineering

Mem Natl Def Acad — Memoirs. National Defense Academy

Mem Natl Inst Polar Res Ser E Biol Med Sci — Memoirs. National Institute of Polar Research. Series E. Biology and Medical Science

Mem Natl Inst Polar Res Spec Issue (Jpn) — Memoirs. National Institute of Polar Research. Special Issue (Japan)

Mem Natl Inst Zool Acad Sin Bot Ser — Memoirs. National Institute of Zoology and Botany. Academica Sinica. Botanical Series

Mem Natl Mus Vict — Memoirs. National Museum of Victoria

Mem Natl Mus Victoria — Memoirs. National Museum of Victoria

Mem Natl Mus Victoria Melbourne — Memoirs. National Museum of Victoria. Melbourne

Mem Natl Sci Mus (Jpn) — Memoirs. National Science Museum (Japan)

Mem Natl Sci Mus (Tokyo) — Memoirs. National Science Museum (Tokyo)

Mem Nat Mus VIC — Memoirs. National Museum of Victoria

Mem Natn Acad Sci — Memoirs of the National Academy of Sciences [*Washington*]

Mem Natn Astr Obs Athens — Memoirs of the National Astronomical Observatory. Athens

Mem Natn Geogr Soc — Memoirs. National Geographic Society

Mem Natn Mus (Melb) — Memoirs. National Museum (Melbourne)

Mem Natn Mus Sth Rhod — Memoirs. National Museum of Southern Rhodesia

Mem Natn Mus Vict — Memoirs of the National Museum of Victoria

Mem Natn Res Inst Chem Shanghai — Memoirs. National Research Institute of Chemistry (Shanghai)

Mem Natn Res Inst Engng Shanghai — Memoirs. National Research Institute of Engineering (Shanghai)

Mem Natn Res Inst Geol Shanghai — Memoirs of the National Research Institute of Geology (Shanghai)

Mem Natn Tokai Kinki Agric Exp Stn — Memoirs of the National Tokai-Kinki Agricultural Experiment Station

Mem Nat Sci — Memoirs of Natural Sciences. Museum. Brooklyn Institute of Arts and Sciences

Mem Nat Sci Mus Brooklyn Inst — Memoirs of Natural Sciences. The Museum of the Brooklyn Institute of Arts and Sciences

Mem Niihama Natl Coll Technol — Memoirs of Niihama National College of Technology

Mem Niihama Natl Coll Technol Sci Eng — Memoirs. Niihama National College of Technology, Science, and Engineering

Mem Niihama Tech Coll — Memoirs. Niihama Technical College

Mem Niihama Tech Coll Nat Sci — Memoirs. Niihama Technical College. Natural Sciences

Mem Niihama Tech Coll Sci Eng — Memoirs. Niihama Technical College. Science and Engineering

Mem NM Bur Mines Miner Resour — Memoir. New Mexico Bureau of Mines and Mineral Resources

Mem Note Ist Geol Appl Univ Napoli — Memorie e Note. Istituto di Geologia Applicata. Universita di Napoli

Mem Notic Mus Miner Geol Univ Coimbra — Memorias e Noticias. Museu e Laboratorio Mineralogico e Geologico. Universidadede Coimbra

Mem Not Publ Mus Lab Mineral Geol Univ Coimbra — Memorias e Noticias Publicacoes. Museu e Laboratorio Mineralogico e Geologico. Universidade de Coimbra

Mem Not Publ Mus Lab Miner Geol Univ Coimbra — Memorias e Noticias. Museu e Laboratorio Mineralogico e Geologico. Universidadede Coimbra

Mem Not Univ Coimbra Mus Lab Mineral Geol Cent Estud Geol — Memorias e Noticias. Universidade de Coimbra. Museu e LaboratorioMineralogico e Geologico e Centro de Estudos Geologicas

Mem Nova Scotia Dep Mines — Memoirs. Nova Scotia Department of Mines

Mem NS Dep Mines — Memoirs. Nova Scotia Department of Mines

Mem NSW Nat Club — Memoirs of the New South Wales Naturalists' Club

Mem Numazu Coll Technol — Memoirs. Numazu College of Technology

Mem Numer Math — Memoirs of Numerical Mathematics

Mem Nuttall Orn Club — Memoirs of the Nuttall Ornithological Club

Mem NY Acad Sci — Memoirs. New York Academy of Sciences

Mem NY Agr Exp Sta — Memoir. New York Agricultural Experiment Station

Mem NY Agric Exp Stn (Ithaca) — Memoirs. New York. Agricultural Experiment Station (Ithaca)

Mem NY Bot Gard — Memoirs. New York Botanical Gardens

Mem NY Bot Gdn — Memoirs of the New York Botanical Garden

Mem NY State Mus Sci Serv — Memoirs. New York State Museum and Science Service

Mem NY St Mus Nat Hist — Memoirs of the New York State Museum of Natural History

Mem NZ Oceanogr Inst — Memoirs. New Zealand Oceanographic Institute

MEMO — Mirovaya Ekonomika i Mezhdunarodnyye Otnosheniya

MEMOA — Medizinische Monatsschrift

Mem Obs Ebre — Memoires de l'Observatoire de l'Ebre sis a Roquetas

Mem Observ Soc Oecon Berne — Memoires et Observations Recueilles. Societe Oeconomique de Berne

Mem Obsns Czech Astr Soc — Memoirs and Observations of the Czech (Czechoslovak) Astronomical Society

Memo Chf Engr Manchr Steam Us Ass — Memoranda by Chief Engineer. Manchester Steam Users' Association

Memo Dep Geogr Univ Coll Aberystwyth — Memoranda. Department of Geography. University College. Aberystwyth

Memo Div Chem Eng CSIRO — Memorandum. Division of Chemical Engineering. Commonwealth Scientific and Industrial Research Organisation

Memo Div Chem Engng CSIRO — Memorandum. Division of Chemical Engineering. Commonwealth Scientific and Industrial Research Organisation

Memo Emerg Med Servs Lond — Memoranda. Emergency Medical Services London

Memo Fed Dept Agr Res (Nigeria) — Memorandum. Federal Department of Agricultural Research (Nigeria)

Mem Off Natn Anti Acrid Alger — Memoires de l'Office National Anti-Acridien (Alger)

Mem Off Rech Sci Tech Outre-Mer — Memoires. Office de la Recherche Scientifique et Technique d'Outre-Mer

Mem Off Scient Tech Pech Marit — Memoires. Office Scientifique et Technique des Peches Maritimes

Mem Ofic Estud Espec Min Agr Dir Agr Pesca (Chile) — Memoria. Oficina de Estudios Especiales. Ministerio de Agricultura. Direccion de Agricultura y Pesca (Chile)

Memo Indian Tea Assoc Tocklai Exp Stn — Memorandum. Indian Tea Association. Tocklai Experimental Station

Memoir Ser Am Anthrop Ass — Memoir Series. American Anthropological Association

Memoir Ser Lond Sch Hug Trop Med — Memoir Series of the London School of Hygiene and Tropical Medicine

Memo Meat Res Inst — Memorandum. Meat Research Institute

Memo Med Res Counc — Memorandum. Medical Research Council

Memo Nav Met Brch — Memoranda. Naval Meteorological Branch [London]

Memo Nav Weath Serv Dep — Memoranda. Naval Weather Service Department [London]

Memo Nor Landbrukshogsk Inst Landbruksokom — Memorandum. Norges Landbrukshogskole Institutt foer Landbruksokonomi

Memo Notes Br Portl Cem Ass — Memoranda and Notes. British Portland Cement Association

Memo Orig Plan Results Fld Exp Rothamsted Exp Stn — Memoranda of the Origin, Plan, and Results of the Field and other Experiments. Rothamsted Experimental Station

Memo Print Ind Res Ass — Memoranda. Printing Industry Research Association

Memorabilia Zool — Memorabilia Zoologica

Memorab Zool — Memorabilia Zoologica

Memorandum Ser Bur Mines Can — Memorandum Series. Bureau of Mines. Department of Mines and Resources. Canada

Memorandum Ser Mines Brch Can — Memorandum Series. Mines Branch. Department of Mines and Technical Surveys. Canada

Memo R Armament Res Dev Establ (GB) — Memorandum. Royal Armament Research and Development Establishment (Great Britain)

Memo Res Div Dep Natn Hlth Welf Can — Memoranda. Research Division. Department of National Health and Welfare. Canada

Memorial Hist Esp — Memorial Historico Espanol

Memorial Univ Newfoundland Occas Pap Biol — Memorial University of Newfoundland. Occasional Papers in Biology

Memorie Accad Agric Sci Verona — Memorie dell'Accademia d'Agricoltura, Scienze, Lettere, Arti e Commercio di Verona

Memorie Accad Lunig Sci Giovanni Capellini — Memorie dell'Accademia Lunigianese de Scienze Giovanni Capellini

Memorie Accad Pont Nuovi Lincei — Memorie dell'Accademia Pontificia dei Nuovi Lincei

Memorie Accad Sci Torino — Memorie della Accademia delle Scienze di Torino

Memorie Astr Oss Astr Capodimonte — Memorie Astronomiche. Osservatorio Astronomico di Capodimonte

Memorie Astr R Oss Astr Capodimonte — Momorie Astronomiche. R. Osservatorio Astronomico di Capodimonte

Memorie Atti Cent Studi Ingegn Agr — Memorie ed Atti. Centro di Studi per l'Ingegneria Agraria

Memorie Biogeogr Adriat — Memorie di Biogeografica Adriatica

Memorie Biol Mar Oceanogr — Memorie di Biologia Marina e di Oceanografia

Memorie Congr Ass Oftal Ital — Memorie del Congresso dell'Associazione Oftalmologica Italiana

Memorie Descr Carta Geol Ital — Memorie Descrittive della Carta Geologica d'Italia

Memorie Dir Gen Pesca — Memorie. Direzione Generale della Pesca e del Demanio Marittimo

Memorie Geogr Antrop — Memorie di Geografia Antropica

Memorie Geogr Econ — Memorie di Geografia Economica

Memorie Lincei — Memorie. Accademia Nazionale dei Lincei

Memorie Mat Fis Soc Ital Sci — Memorie di Matematica e di Fisica della Societa Italiana delle Scienze

Memorie R Accad Sci Lett Modena — Memorie della Reale Accademia di Scienze, Lettere, ed Arti in Modena

Memorie R Accad Sci Lett Zelanti — Memorie della Reale Accademia di Scienze, Lettere, ed Arti Degli Zelanti

Memorie Rapp Ist Sper Metalli Legg — Memorie e Rapporti dell'Istituto Sperimentale dei Metalli Leggeri

Memorie R Com Talassogr Ital — Memorie. Reale Comitato Talassografico Italiano

Memorie R Ist Veneto Sci — Memorie del Reale Istituto Veneto di Scienze, Lettere, ed Arti

Memorie R Oss Astr Capodimonte — Memorie del Reale Osservatorio Astronomico di Capodimonte in Napoli

Memorie R Staz Patol Veg — Memorie della Reale. Stazione di Patologia Vegetale

Memorie R Uff Cent Met Geofis — Memorie del Regio Ufficio Centrale di Meteorologia e Geofisica

Memories Inst Catal Hist Nat — Memories de la Institucio Catalana d'Historia Natural

Memories Inst Estud Catal — Memories. Institut d'Estudis Catalans

Memories Mus Cienc Nat Barcelona — Memories del Museu de Ciencies Naturals de Barcelona

Memorie Soc Astr Ital — Memorie della Societa Astronomica Italiana

Memorie Soc Ent Ital — Memorie. Societa Entomologica Italiana

Memorie Soc Geogr Ital — Memorie della Societa Geografica Italiana

Memorie Soc Geol Ital — Memorie della Societa Geologica Italiana

Memorie Soc Ital Sci Nat — Memorie della Societa Italiana di Scienze Naturali e del Museo Civico di Storia Naturale di Milano

Memorie Soc Ital Sci XL — Memorie della Societa Italiana delle Scienze detta dei XL

Memorie Soc Lunig G Capellini Stor Nat — Memorie della Societa Lunigianese G. Capellini per la Storia Naturale

Memorie Soc Nat Mat Modena — Memorie della Societa dei Naturalisti e Matematici di Modena

Memorie Soc Spettrosc Ital — Memorie della Societa degli Spettroscopisti Italiani

Memorie Soc Tosc Sci Nat — Memorie della Societa Toscana di Scienze Naturali

Memories Soc Catal Cienc Fis — Memories. Societat Catalana de Ciencies Fisiques

Memorie Studi Ist Idraul Milano — Memorie e Studi dell'Istituto di Idraulica e Costruzioni Idrauliche del Politecnico di Milano

Mem Orig Revue Metall — Memoires Originaux de la Revue de Metallurgie

Mem ORSTOM — Memoires. Office de la Recherche Scientifique et Technique d'Outre-Mer

Mem Osaka Inst Technol Ser A — Memoirs of the Osaka Institute of Technology. Series A. Science and Technology

Mem Osaka Inst Technol Ser A Sci Technol — Memoirs. Osaka Institute of Technology. Series A. Science and Technology

Mem Osaka Inst Tech Ser A — Memoirs. Osaka Institute of Technology. Series A. Science and Technology

Mem Osaka Kyoiku Univ — Memoires. Osaka Kyoiku University

Mem Osaka Kyoiku Univ III Nat Sci Appl Sci — Memoirs. Osaka Kyoiku University. III. Natural Science and Applied Science

Mem Osaka Kyoiku Univ III Natur Sci Appl Sci — Memoirs. Osaka Kyoiku University. III. Natural Science and Applied Science

Mem Osaka Kyoiku Univ Ser 3 — Memoirs of Osaka Kyoiku University. Series 3. Natural Science and Applied Science

Mem Osaka Univ Lib Arts Educ — Memoirs of the Osaka University of the Liberal Arts and Education

Mem Osaka Univ Lib Arts Educ B Natur Sci — Memoirs. Osaka University of Liberal Arts and Education. B. Natural Science

Memo Scripps Instn Oceanogr — Memoranda. Scripps Institution of Oceanography

Memo Soc Fauna Flora Fenn — Memoranda Societatis pro Fauna et Flora Fennica

Memo Soc Promot Nat Reserv — Memoranda. Society for the Promotion of Nature Reserves

Memo Tech Off Natn Etud Rech Aeronaut — Memo Technique. Office National d'Etudes et de Recherches Aeronautiques

Memo Tocklai Exp Stn Indian Tea Ass — Memoranda. Tocklai Experimental Station of the Indian Tea Association

Memo Univ Coll Wales Dept Geogr — Memorandum. University College of Wales. Department of Geography

Memo Util Coal Comm Instn Min Engrs — Memoranda. Utilization of Coal Committee. Institution of Mining Engineers

Memo W Afr Maize Rust Res Unit — Memoranda. West African Maize Rust Research Unit

Mem Pac Coast Entomol Soc — Memoirs. Pacific Coast Entomological Society

Mem Pacif Cst Ent Soc — Memoirs of the Pacific Coast Entomological Society [San Francisco]

Mem Palaeontol Ser Geol Surv (NSW) — Memoirs. Palaeontology Series. Geological Survey (New South Wales)

MEMPB — Moessbauer Effect Methodology. Proceedings of the Symposium

Mem Peabody Mus — Memoirs. Peabody Museum of Yale University

Mem Peabody Mus Archaeol & Ethnol — Memoirs of the Peabody Museum of Archaeology and Ethnology

Mem Peabody Mus Harv — Memoirs of the Peabody Museum of American Archaeology and Ethnology of Harvard University

Mem Peabody Mus Yale — Memoirs of the Peabody Museum of Yale University

Memphis Bs — Memphis Business Journal

Memphis J Med Sc — Memphis Journal of the Medical Sciences

Memphis LJ — Memphis Law Journal

Memphis Med J — Memphis Medical Journal

Memphis Med Mo — Memphis Medical Monthly

Memphis Med Mon — Memphis Medical Monthly

Memphis Med Month — Memphis Medical Monthly

Memphis Med Monthly — Memphis Medical Monthly

Memphis Med Rec — Memphis Medical Recorder

Memphis Mid S Med J — Memphis and Mid-South Medical Journal

Memphis Mid-South Med J — Memphis and Mid-South Medical Journal

Memphis M J — Memphis Medical Journal

Memphis State UL Rev — Memphis State University. Law Review

Memphis State Univ L Rev — Memphis State University. Law Review

Memphis St U L Rev — Memphis State University. Law Review

Mem Phys — Memoires de Physique

Mem Phys Chim Soc Arcueil — Memoires de Physique et de Chimie. Societe d'Arcueil

Mem Phys Ukr — Memoires de Physique Ukrainiens

Memp LJ — Memphis Law Journal

Mem Polynes Soc — Memoirs of the Polynesian Society

Mem Pont Acc — Atti. Pontificia Accademia Romana di Archeologia. Memorie

Mem Pont Accad Romana Archeol — Memorie della Pontificia Accademia Romana di Archeologia

Mem Poudres — Memorial des Poudres

Mem Pres AIM — Memoires Presentes a l'A.I.M [Liege]

Mem Pres Div Sav Acad Sci Inst Fr — Memoires Presentes par Divers Savants a l'Academie des Sciences de l'Institut de France

Mem Proc Manchester Lit Philos Soc — Memoirs and Proceedings. Manchester Literary and Philosophical Society

Mem Proc Manchr Lit Phil Soc — Memoirs and Proceedings of the Manchester Literary and Philosophical Society

Mem Propellants Explos Rocket Mot Establ (Wescott Engl) — Memorandum. Propellants, Explosives, and Rocket Motor Establishment(Westcott, England)

Mem Publies Inst Prot Plant — Memoires Publies. Institut pour la Protection des Plantes

Mem Publ Soc Sci Arts Lett Hainaut — Memoires et Publications. Societe des Sciences, des Arts, et des Lettres du Hainaut

Mem Pub Soc Sci Arts Lett Hainaut — Memoires et Publications. Societe des Sciences, des Arts, et des Lettres du Hainaut

Mem Punjab Irrig Res Inst — Memoirs. Punjab Irrigation Research Institute

Mem Punjab Irrig Res Lab — Memoirs. Punjab Irrigation Research Laboratory

Mem Qd Mus — Memoirs. Queensland Museum

Mem Queensland Mus — Memoirs. Queensland Museum

Mem Queensl Mus — Memoirs. Queensland Museum

Mem R Acad Cienc Artes Barc — Memorias. Real Academia de Ciencias y Artes de Barcelona

Mem R Acad Cienc Exactas Fis Nat Madrid — Memorias. Real Academia de Ciencias Exactas, Fisicas, y Naturales de Madrid

Mem R Acad Cienc Exactas Fis Nat Madrid Ser Cienc Exactas — Memorias. Real Academia de Ciencias Exactas, Fisicas, y Naturales de Madrid. Serie de Ciencias Exactas

Mem R Acad Cienc Exactas Fis Nat Madrid Ser Cienc Fis-Quim — Memorias. Real Academia de Ciencias Exactas, Fisicas, y Naturales de Madrid. Serie de Ciencias Fisico-Quimicas

Mem R Acad Cienc Exactas Fis Nat Madrid Ser Cienc Nat — Memorias. Real Academia de Ciencias Exactas, Fisicas, y Naturales de Madrid. Serie de Ciencias Naturales

Mem R Acad Cienc Exactas Fis Nat Madr Ser Cienc Nat — Memorias. Real Academia de Ciencias Exactas, Fisicas, y Naturales de Madrid. Serie de Ciencias Naturales

Mem R Accad Ital Cl Sci Fis Mat Nat — Memorie. Reale Accademia d'Italia. Classe di Scienze Fisiche, Matematiche, e Naturali

Mem R Accad Ital Cl Sci Fis Mat Nat Biol — Memorie. Reale Accademia d'Italia. Classe di Scienze Fisiche, Matematiche, e Naturali. Biologia

Mem R Accad Ital Cl Sci Fis Mat Nat Chim — Memorie. Reale Accademia d'Italia. Classe di Scienze Fisiche, Matematiche, e Naturali. Chimica

Mem R Accad Ital Cl Sci Fis Mat Nat Fis — Memorie. Reale Accademia d'Italia. Classe di Scienze Fisiche, Matematiche, e Naturali. Fisica

Mem R Accad Ital Cl Sci Fis Mat Nat Ing — Memorie. Reale Accademia d'Italia. Classe di Scienze Fisiche, Matematiche, e Naturali. Ingegneria

Mem R Accad Ital Cl Sci Fis Mat Nat Mat — Memorie. Reale Accademia d'Italia. Classe di Scienze Fisiche, Matematiche, e Naturali. Matematica

Mem R Accad Naz Lincei Cl Sci Fis Mat Nat — Memorie. Reale Accademia Nazionale dei Lincei. Classe di ScienzeFisiche, Matematiche, e Naturali

Mem R Accad Sci Ist Bologna Cl Sci Fis — Memorie. Reale Accademia delle Scienze. Istituto di Bologna. Classe di Scienze Fisiche

Mem R Accad Sci Lett Arti (Modena) — Memorie. Reale Accademia di Scienze, Lettere, ed Arti (Modena)

Mem Raffles Mus — Memoirs of the Raffles Museum

Mem RAH — Memorias. Real Academia de la Historia

Mem Raman Res Inst — Memoirs. Raman Research Institute

Mem Rapp Serv Epiphyt — Memoires et Rapports du Service des Epiphyties

Mem R Asiat Soc Bengal — Memoirs. Royal Asiatic Society of Bengal

Mem R Astron Soc — Memoirs. Royal Astronomical Society

Mem Real Acad B Let Barcelona — Memorias de la Real Academia de Buenas Letras de Barcelona

Mem Real Acad Ci Art Barcelona — Memorias. Real Academia de Ciencias y Artes de Barcelona

Mem Real Acad Ci Barcelona — Memorias. Real Academia de Ciencias y Artes de Barcelona

Mem Real Acad Cienc Artes Barcelona — Memorias. Real Academia de Ciencias y Artes de Barcelona

Mem Real Acad Ci Exact Fis Natur Madrid — Memorias. Real Academia de Ciencias Exactas, Fisicas, y Naturales de Madrid. Serie de Ciencias Exactas

Mem Real Acad Hist — Memorias de la Real Academia de la Historia

Mem Reale Accad Archeol Lett & B A Soc Reale Napoli — Memorie della Reale Accademia di Archeologia, Lettere, e Belle Arti. Societa Reale di Napoli

Mem Reale Accad Sci Ist Bologna Cl Sci Fis — Memorie. Reale Accademia delle Scienze. Istituto di Bologna. Classe di Scienze Fisiche

Mem Reale Accad Sci Ist Bologna Cl Sci Mor — Memorie della Reale Accademia di Scienze dell'Istituto di Bologna. Classe di Scienze Morau

Mem Reale Accad Sci Modena — Memorie della Reale Accademia di Scienze, Lettere, e d' Arti di Modena

Mem Reale Accad Sci Torino — Memorie della Reale Accademia delle Scienze di Torino

Mem Reale Comitato Talassogr Ital — Memorie. Reale Comitato Talassagrafico Italiano

Mem Real Ist Lombardo Sci Lett & A — Memorie del Reale Istituto Lombardo di Scienze, Lettere, ed Arti

Mem Real Soc Econ Mallorquina Amigos Pais — Memorias. Real Sociedad Economica Mallorquina de Amigos del Pais

Mem Real Soc Esp Hist Nat — Memorias de la Real Sociedad Espanola de Historia Natural

Mem Rend Accad Zel Acireale — Memorie e Rendiconti. Accademia di Scienze, Lettere, e Belle Arti degli Zelanti e dei Dafnici di Acireale

Mem Rend Ist Sci Bologna — Memorie e Rendiconti. Istituto delle Scienze di Bologna

Mem Res Depart Toyo Bunko — Memoirs. Research Department. Toyo Bunko

Mem Res Dept Tokio — Memoires. Research Dept. Toyo Bunko (Tokio)

Mem Res Dept Toyo Bunko — Memoirs of the Research Department of the Toyo Bunko

Mem Res Div Dep Agric Uganda — Memoirs of the Research Division. Department of Agriculture. Uganda

Mem Res Div Minist Agric Sudan — Memoirs of Research Division. Ministry of Agriculture. Sudan

Mem Res Inst Acoust Sci Osaka Univ — Memoirs. Research Institute of Acoustical Science. Osaka University

Mem Res Inst Fd Sci Kyoto Univ — Memoirs of the Research Institute for Food Science. Kyoto University

Mem Res Inst Food Sci Kyoto Univ — Memoirs. Research Institute for Food Science. Kyoto University

Mem Res Inst Sci and Eng Ritsumeikan Univ — Memoirs. Research Institute of Science and Engineering. Ritsumeikan University

Mem Res Inst Sci Engrg Ritsumeikan Univ — Memoirs of the Research Institute of Science and Engineering Ritsumeikan University

Mem Res Inst Sci Eng Ritsumeikan Univ — Memoirs. Research Institute of Science and Engineering. Ritsumeikan University

Mem Reun Tec Nac Mania — Memoria. Reunion Tecnica Nacional de Mania

Mem Rev Acad Nac Cienc — Memorias y Revista. Academia Nacional de Ciencias

Mem Rev Acad Nac Cienc "Antonio Alzate" — Memorias y Revista. Academia Nacional de Ciencias "Antonio Alzate"

Mem Rev Acad Nac Cien Mex — Memorias y Revista. Academia Nacional de Ciencias (Mexico)

Mem Rev Soc Cient Antonio Alzate — Memorias y Revista. Sociedad Cientifica "Antonio Alzate"

Mem Roger Williams Park Mus — Memoirs. Roger Williams Park Museum

Mem Romane Ant & B A — Memorie Romane di Antichita e di Belle Arti

Mem Roy Astron Soc Lond — Memoirs. Royal Astronomical Society of London

Mem Roy Soc South Australia — Memoirs. Royal Society of South Australia

Mem Ryojun Coll Eng — Memoirs. Ryojun College of Engineering

Mem Ryojun Coll Engng — Memoirs. Ryojun College of Engineering

Mems A Estac Exp Agric Canete — Memorias Anuales. Estacion Experimental Agricola (Canete)

Mem S Afr Geol Surv — Memoir. South Africa Geological Survey

Mem S Afr Inst Med Res — Memoirs of the South African Institute for Medical Research

Mem Sagami Inst Technol — Memoirs. Sagami Institute of Technology

Mems A Inst Mec Hidraul Agric B Aires — Memorias Anuales. Instituto de Mecanica y Hidraulica Agricola (Buenos Aires)

Mems A Inst Med Exp Estud Trat Cancer — Memorias Anuales. Instituto de Medicina Experimental para el Estudio y el Tratamiento del Cancer

Mems A Jta Cienc Nat Barcelona — Memorias Anuales. Junta de Ciencies Naturals (Barcelona)

Mems A Mus Nac Hist Nat B Aires — Memorias Anuales. Museo Nacional de Historia Natural (Buenos Aires)

Mem Sch Biol Oriented Sci Technol Kinki Univ — Memoirs of the School of Biology-Oriented Science and Technology of Kinki University

Mem Sch Eng Okayama Univ — Memoirs. School of Engineering. Okayama University

Mem School Engrg Okayama Univ — Memoirs. School of Engineering. Okayama University

Mem School Sci Engrg Waseda Univ — Memoirs. School of Science and Engineering. Waseda University

Mem School Sci Eng Waseda Univ — Memoirs. School of Science and Engineering. Waseda University

Mem Sch Sci and Eng Waseda Univ — Memoirs. School of Science and Engineering. Waseda University

Mem Sch Sci Engng Waseda Univ — Memoirs. School of Science and Engineering. Waseda University

Mem Sch Sci Eng Waseda Univ — Memoirs. School of Science and Engineering. Waseda University

Mem Sci Dept Univ Tokyo — Memoirs. Science Department. University of Tokyo

Mem Scient Revue Metall — Memoires Scientifiques de la Revue de Metallurgie

Mem Sci Geol — Memorie di Scienze Geologiche

Mem Sci Geol Inst Geol Univ Louis Pasteur Strasbourg — Memoire. Sciences Geologiques. Institut de Geologie. Universite LouisPasteur de Strasbourg

Mem Sci Phys — Memoires de Sciences Physiques

Mem Sci Rev Met — Memoires Scientifiques de la Revue de Metallurgie

Mem Sci Rev Metall — Memoires Scientifiques de la Revue de Metallurgie

Mem Sci Soc China — Memoirs. Science Society of China/Chung Kuo K'o Hsueeh She Yen Chin Ts'ung K'an

Mems Comn Invest Paleont Prehist (Madr) — Memorias. Comision de Investigaciones Paleontologicas y Prehistoricas. Instituto Nacional de Ciencias Fisico-Naturales (Madrid)

Mems Comn Of Semill Montev — Memorias de la Comision Oficial de Semillas (Montevideo)

Mems Comun Inst Geol Barcelona — Memorias y Comunicaciones. Instituto Geologico (Barcelona)

Mems Congr Interam Cardiol — Memorias del Congreso Interamericano de Cardiologia

Mems Congr Pan Am Ferrocarr — Memorias. Congreso Panamericano de Ferrocarriles

Mems Congr Venez Med — Memorias. Congreso Venezolano de Medicina

Mems Cons Oceanogr Ibero Am — Memorias del Consejo Oceanografico Ibero-Americano

Mems Cons Sup Invest Cient Barcelona — Memorias. Consejo Superior de Investigaciones Cientificas. Delegacion de Barcelona

Mems Cons Sup Invest Cient Madr — Memorias. Consejo Superior de Investigaciones Cientificas (Madrid)

Mems Cons Sup Salubr Mex — Memorias del Consejo Superior de Salubridad (Mexico)

Mems Conv Nac Ass Nac Prod Maderas Pino — Memorias de la Convencion Nacional, Associacion Nacional de Productores de Maderas de Pino

Mems Cpo Ing Civ Lima — Memorias del Cuerpo de Ingenieros Civiles (Lima)

Mems Cpo Med Escol Montev — Memorias del Cuerpo Medico Escolar (Montevideo)

Mems Dep Nac Ing Montev — Memorias del Departamento Nacional de Ingenieros (Montevideo)

Mems Dep Salubr Publ Mex — Memorias. Departamento de Salubridad Publica (Mexico)

Mem S Diego Soc Nat Hist — Memoirs of the San Diego Society of Natural History

Mems Dir Frutas B Aires — Memorias de la Direccion de Frutas, Hortalizas y Flores (Buenos Aires)

Mems Dir Gen Minas Geol Hidrol B Aires — Memorias. Direccion General de Minas, Geologia y Hidrologia (Buenos Aires)

Mems Dir Gen Montes Caza Pesca Fluv — Memorias. Direccion General de Montes, Caza y Pesca Fluvial

Mems Dir Gen Tierr Colon B Aires — Memorias de la Direccion General de Tierras y Colonias (Buenos Aires)

Mem Sears Fdn Mar Res — Memoirs. Sears Foundation for Marine Research. Yale University

Mem Sect Chim Miner Congr Int Chim Pure Appl — Memoires Presentes a la Section de Chimie Minerale. CongresInternational de Chimie Pure et Appliquee

Mem Sect Sti Acad Romane — Memoriile Sectiunii Stiintifice Academia Romana

Mem Sect Stiint Acad Repub Soc Rom — Memoriile Sectiilor Stiintifice. Academia Republicii Socialiste Romania

Mem Sect Stiint Acad Repub Soc Romania Ser IV — Memoriile Sectiilor Stiintifice. Academia Republicii Socialiste Romania. Seria IV

Mem Sect Stiint Acad Romana Ser IV — Memoriile Sectiilor Stiintifice. Academia Romana. Seria IV

Mem Seitoku Jr Coll Nutr — Memoirs. Seitoku Junior College of Nutrition

Mem Semin Lat Am Quim — Memorias. Seminario Latino Americano de Quimica

Mem Semin Latino-Amer Irrig — Memoria. Seminario Latino-Americano de Irrigacion

Mem Ser Calcutta Math Soc — Memoir Series. Calcutta Mathematical Society

Mem Serv Carte Geol Alsace Lorraine — Memoires. Service de la Carte Geologique d'Alsace et de Lorraine

Mem Serv Carte Geol Als Lorr — Memoires du Service de la Carte Geologique d'Alsace et de Lorraine

Mem Serv Carte Geol Det Fr — Memoires du Service de la Carte Geologique Detaillee de la France

Mem Serv Carte Geol Tunis — Memoires du Service de la Carte Geologique de la Tunisie

Mem Serv Chim Etat — Memorial des Services Chimiques de l'Etat

Mem Serv Geol Belg — Memoire. Service Geologique de Belgique

Mem Serv Geol Congo Belge — Memoires. Service Geologique du Congo Belge et Ruanda-Urundi

Mem Serv Geol Geophys (Belgrade) — Memoires. Service Geologique et Geophysique (Belgrade)

Mem Serv Geol Geophys Serb — Memoires du Service Geologique et Geophysique. Serbie

Mem Serv Geol Grece — Memoires du Service Geologique de Grece

Mem Serv Geol Indoch — Memoires du Service Geologique de l'Indo-Chine

Mem Serv Geol Port — Memorias. Servicos Geologicos de Portugal

Mem Serv Geol Yougosl — Memoires du Service Geologique du Royaume de Yougoslavie

Mem Serv Hydromet Yougosl — Memoires. Service Hydrometeorologique de Yougoslavie

Mem Servir Explication Carte Geol Detaill Fr — Memoires pour Servir a l'Explication de la Carte Geologique Detaillee de la France

Mem Servir Explication Cartes Geol Min Belg — Memoires pour Servir a l'Explication des Cartes Geologiques et Minieres de la Belgique

Mems Esc Nac Agric Lima — Memorias. Escuela Nacional de Agricultura (Lima)

Mems Estac Agric Exp Palmira — Memorias. Estacion Agricola Experimental de Palmira (Palmira)

Mems Estac Exp Agric Canete — Memorias. Estacion Experimental Agricola. Canete

Mems Estac Exp Agric La Molina — Memorias. Estacion Experimental Agricola de La Molina

Mems Estac Exp Agric Soc Nac Agr Lima — Memorias. Estacion Experimental Agricola. Sociedad Nacional Agraria (Lima)

Mems Estud Mus Zool Univ Coimbra — Memorias e Estudos. Museu Zoologico. Universidade de Coimbra

Mems Fac Agron Vet Univ Nac La Plata — Memorias de la Facultad de Agronomia y Veterinaria. Universidad Nacional de la Plata

Mems Fac Cienc Fis Mat Astr Univ Nac La Plata — Memorias de la Facultad de Ciencias Fisicas, Matematicas, y Astronomicas. Universidad Nacional de la Plata

Mems Fac Cienc Med B Aires — Memorias de la Facultad de Ciencias Medicas de Buenos Aires

Mems Fund Inst Biol Med Exp B Aires — Memorias de la Fundacion Instituto de Biologia y Medicina Experimental (Buenos Aires)

Mems Gen Inst Geol Min Esp — Memorias Generales. Instituto Geologico y Minero de Espana

Mems Ginec Mex — Memorias de Ginecologia. Academia de Medicina de Mexico (Mexico)

Mem S Industr Sci Inst Kagoshima Univ — Memoirs. South Industrial Science Institute. Kagoshima University/Nanpo-Sango Kagaku Kenkyujo Hokoku. Kagoshima Daigaku

Mems Insp Gen Tierr Colon Chile — Memorias de la Inspeccion General de Tierras y Colonizacion (Santiago de Chile)

Mems Inst Agropec Nac Guatem — Memorias del Instituto Agropecuario Nacional (Guatemala)

Mems Inst Nac Fis Clim Montev — Memorias del Instituto Nacional Fisico-Climatologico (Montevideo)

Mems Inst Oswaldo Cruz — Memorias. Instituto Oswaldo Cruz

Mems Jta Invest Ultramar — Memorias. Junta de Investigacoes do Ultramar

Mems Lab Nac Engenh Civ — Memorias. Laboratorio Nacional de Engenharia Civil

Mems Lab Transp Mec Suelo Madrid — Memorias. Laboratorio del Transporte y Mecanica del Suelo (Madrid)

Mem S Ling — Memoires. Societe de Linguistique de Paris

Mems Med Casa Orates Chile — Memorias de los Medicos de la Casa de Orates de Santiago de Chile

Mems Minist Agric Com Bogota — Memorias del Ministerio de Agricultura y Comercio (Bogota)

Mems Minist Agric Cria Caracas — Memorias. Ministerio de Agricultura y Cria (Caracas)

Mems Minist Agric Ind C Rica — Memorias del Ministerio de Agricultura y Industrias. Costa Rica

Mems Minist Agric Nac B Aires — Memorias del Ministerio de Agricultura de la Nacion (Buenos Aires)

Mems Minist Corr Telegr Bogota — Memorias. Ministerio de Correos y Telegrafos (Bogota)

Mems Minist Gob Fom La Paz — Memorias del Ministerio de Gobierno y Fomento (La Paz)

Mems Minist Hacienda Asuncion — Memorias del Ministerio de Hacienda (Asuncion)

Mems Minist Ind Def Agric Montev — Memorias del Ministerio de Industrias. Defensa Agricola (Montevideo)

Mems Minist Ind Obr Publ Chile — Memorias del Ministerio de Industria y Obras Publicas (Santiago de Chile)

Mems Minist Minas Petrol Bogota — Memorias del Ministerio de Minas y Petroleos (Bogota)

Mems Minist Obr Publ Caracas — Memorias del Ministerio de Obras Publicas (Caracas)

Mems Minist Obr Publ Montev — Memorias del Ministerio de Obras Publicas (Montevideo)

Mems Minist Salubr Agric Cria Caracas — Memorias del Ministerio de Salubridad y de Agricultura y Cria (Caracas)

Mems Minist Salud Publ B Aires — Memorias. Ministerio de Salud Publica (Buenos Aires)

Mems Minist Sanid Asist Soc Caracas — Memorias del Ministerio de Sanidad y Asistencia Social (Caracas)

Mems Minist Trab Comun Caracas — Memorias del Ministerio de Trabajo y Comunicaciones (Caracas)

Mems Mus Bocage — Memorias do Museu Bocage [*Lisboa*]

Mems Mus Dr Alvaro de Castro — Memorias do Museu Dr. Alvaro de Castro [*Lourenco Marques*]

Mems Mus Entre Rios — Memorias del Museo de Entre Rios

Mems Mus Hist Nat Javier Prado — Memorias del Museo de Historia Natural Javier Prado. Universidad Nacional Mayor de San Marcos [*Lima*]

Mems Mus Paraense Hist Nat Ethnogr — Memorias do Museu Paraense de Historia Natural e Ethnographia [*Para*]

Mem Soc Acad Agric Sci A & B Lett Dept Aube — Memoires de la Societe Academique d'Agriculture, des Sciences, Arts, et Belles-Lettres du Departement de l'Aube

Mem Soc Acad Archeol Dep Oise — Memoires. Societe Academique d'Archeologie, Sciences, et Arts du Departement del'Oise

Mem Soc Acad Archeol Sci & A Dep Oise — Memoires de la Societe Academique d'Archeologie, Science, et Arts du Departement de l'Oise

Mem Soc Acad Sci Falaise — Memoires. Societe Academique des Sciences, Arts, et Belles-Lettres de Falaise

Mem Soc AF — Memoires. Societe Nationale des Antiquaires de France

Mem Soc Agric Arrondissement Valenciennes — Memoires. Societe d'Agriculture, des Sciences, et des Arts de l'Arrondissement de Valenciennes

Mem Soc Agric Commer Sci Arts (Marne) — Memoires. Societe d'Agriculture, Commerce, Sciences, et Arts du Departement de la Marne (Chalons Sur Marne)

Mem Soc Agric Ind Sci Falaise — Memoires de la Societe d'Agriculture, d'Industrie, des Sciences, et des Arts de Falaise

Mem Soc Agricrs Fr — Memoires de la Societe des Agriculteurs de France

Mem Soc Agric Sci & A Angers — Memoires de la Societe d'Agriculture, Sciences, et Arts d'Angers

Mem Soc Agric Sci & A Cent N Seant a Douai — Memoires de la Societe d'Agriculture, Sciences, et Arts Centrale du Nord, Seant a Douai

Mem Soc Agric Sci Angers — Memoires de la Societe d'Agriculture, Sciences, et Arts d'Angers

Mem Soc Agric Sci Orleans — Memoires de la Societe d'Agriculture, Sciences, Belles-Lettres et Arts d'Orleans

Mem Soc Amer Archaeol — Memoirs of the Society for American Archaeology

Mem Soc A Midi — Memoires. Societe Archeologique de Midi de la France

Mem Soc Ant — Memoires. Societe Nationale des Antiquaires de France

Mem Soc Anthrop Paris — Memoires de la Societe d'Anthropologie de Paris

Mem Soc Antiq Ouest — Memoires. Societe des Antiquaires de l'Ouest

Mem Soc Antiqua Cent — Memoires de la Societe des Antiquaires du Centre

Mem Soc Antiqua Ouest — Memoires de la Societe des Antiquaires de l'Ouest

Mem Soc Ant Picardie — Memoires. Societe des Antiquaires de Picardie

Mem Soc Archeol & Hist Moselle — Memoires de la Societe d'Archeologie et d'Histoire de la Moselle

Mem Soc Archeol Champenoise — Memoires de la Societe Archeologique Champenoise

Mem Soc Archeol Litt Sci Avranches — Memoires de la Societe d'Archeologie, de Litterature, Sciences et Arts d'Avranches et de Mortain

Mem Soc Archeol Midi France — Memoires de la Societe d'Archeologie du Midi de la France

Mem Soc Archeol Montpellier — Memoires de la Societe d'Archeologie de Montpellier

Mem Soc Archeol Sci & A Dept Oise — Memoires de la Societe d'Archeologie, Sciences, et Arts du Departement de l'Oise

Mem Soc Archeol Touraine — Memoires de la Societe Archeologique de Touraine

Mem Soc Arts Sci Carcassonne — Memoires de la Societe des Arts et des Sciences de Carcassonne

Mem Soc Astr Anvers — Memoires de la Societe d'Astronomie d'Anvers

Mem Soc Astron Ital — Memorie. Societa Astronomica Italiana

Mem Soc Astronom Ital NS — Memorie. Societa Astronomica Italiana. Nuova Serie

Mem Soc Belge Geol — Memoires. Societe Belge de Geologie, de Paleontologie

Mem Soc Belge Geol Paleont Hydrol Bull — Memoires de la Societe Belge de Geologie, de Paleontologie, et d'Hydrologie. Bulletin

Mem Soc Belge Geol Paleontol Hydrol Ser 4 — Memoires de la Societe Belge de Geologie, de Paleontologie, et d'Hydrologie. Serie 4

Mem Soc Belge Geol Paleontol Hydrol Ser 8 — Memoires de la Societe Belge de Geologie, de Paleontologie, et d'Hydrologie. Serie in Octavo

Mem Soc Belge Geol Ser 8 — Memoires de la Societe Belge de Geologie, de Paleontologie, et d'Hydrologie. Serie 8

Mem Soc Biogeogr — Memoires de la Societe de Biogeographie

Mem Soc Bot Fr — Memoires. Societe Botanique de France

Mem Soc Bourguignonne Geog & Hist — Memoires de la Societe Bourguignonne de Geographie et d'Histoire

Mem Soc Broteriana — Memorias. Sociedade Broteriana

Mem Soc Centr Agric France — Memoires. Societe Centrale d'Agriculture de France

Mem Soc Centr Med Vet — Memoires. Societe Centrale de Medecine Veterinaire

Mem Soc Chalon — Memoires. Societe d'Histoire et d'Archeologie de Chalon-Sur-Saone

Mem Soc Cienc Nat (La Salle) — Memoria. Sociedad de Ciencias Naturales (La Salle)

Mem Soc Cien Nat La Salle Caracas — Memoria. Sociedad de Ciencias Naturales La Salle (Caracas)

Mem Soc Cient "Antonio Alzate" — Memorias. Sociedad Cientifica "Antonio Alzate"

Mem Soc Ci Nat La Salle — Memoria. Sociedad de Ciencias Naturales (La Salle)

Mem Soc Cubana Hist Nat "Felipe Poey" — Memorias. Sociedad Cubana de Historia Natural "Felipe Poey"

Mem Soc Cubana Hist Nat F Poey Hab — Memorias. Sociedad Cubana de Historia Natural Felipe Poey (La Habana)

Mem Soc de Ling de Paris — Memoires. Societe de Linguistique de Paris

Mem Soc Eduenne — Memoires. Societe Eduenne

Mem Soc Emul Doubs — Memoires de la Societe d'Emulation du Doubs

Mem Soc Emul Montbeliard — Memoires de la Societe d'Emulation de Montbeliard

Mem Soc Endocrinol — Memoirs. Society for Endocrinology

Mem Soc Entomol Can — Memoires. Societe Entomologique du Canada

Mem Soc Entomol Ital — Memorie. Societa Entomologica Italiana

Mem Soc Entomol Que — Memoires. Societe Entomologique du Quebec

Mem Soc Ethnogr — Memoires de la Societe d'Ethnographie

Mem Soc Etud Hist Geogr Isthme Suez — Memoires. Societe d'Etudes Historiques et Geographiques de l'Isthme de Suez

Mem Soc Etud Paleont Palethnogr Provence — Memoires de la Societe d'Etudes Paleontologiques et Palethnographiques de Provence

Mem Soc Fr Hist Med — Memoires de la Societe Francaise d'Histoire de la Medecine

Mem Soc Frib Sci Nat Bacteriol — Memoires. Societe Fribourgeoise des Sciences Naturelles.Bacteriologie

Mem Soc Frib Sci Nat Bot — Memoires. Societe Fribourgeoise des Sciences Naturelles. Botanique

Mem Soc Frib Sci Nat Chim — Memoires. Societe Fribourgeoise des Sciences Naturelles. Chimie

Mem Soc Frib Sci Nat Geol Geogr — Memoires. Societe Fribourgeoise des Sciences Naturelles. Geologie et Geographie

Mem Soc Frib Sci Nat Math Phys — Memoires. Societe Fribourgeoise des Sciences Naturelles. Mathematique et Physique

Mem Soc Frib Sci Nat Physiol Hyg Bacteriol — Memoires. Societe Fribourgeoise des Sciences Naturelles. Physiologie, Hygiene, Bacteriologie

Mem Soc Frib Sci Nat Zool — Memoires. Societe Fribourgeoise des Sciences Naturelles. Zoologie

Mem Soc Geol Belg — Memoires. Societe Geologique de Belgique

Mem Soc Geol Belgique — Memoires. Societe Geologique de Belgique

Mem Soc Geol Fr — Memoires. Societe Geologique de France

Mem Soc Geol Fr Nouv Ser — Memoires. Societe Geologique de France. Nouvelle Serie

Mem Soc Geol Fr Paleont — Memoires de la Societe Geologique de France. Paleontologie

Mem Soc Geol Ital — Memorie. Societa Geologica Italiana

Mem Soc Geol Mineral Bretagne — Memoires. Societe Geologique et Mineralogique de Bretagne

Mem Soc Geol Miner Bretagne — Memoires. Societe Geologique et Mineralogique de Bretagne

Mem Soc Geol N — Memoires de la Societe Geologique du Nord

Mem Soc Geol Nord — Memoires de la Societe Geologique du Nord

Mem Soc Helv Sci Nat — Memoires. Societe Helvetique des Sciences Naturelles

Mem Soc Hist & Archeol Bretagne — Memoires de la Societe d'Histoire et d'Archeologie de Bretagne

Mem Soc Hist & Archeol Pontoise Val Oise & Vexin — Memoires de la Societe Historique et Archeologique de Pontoise, du Val d'Oise, et du Vexin

Mem Soc Hist & Litt Tournai — Memoires de la Societe Historique et Litteraire de Tournai

Mem Soc Hist Cher — Memoires de la Societe Historique du Cher

Mem Soc Hist Litt & Sci Cher — Memoires de la Societe Historique, Litteraire, et Scientifique du Cher

Mem Soc Hist Litt Scient Cher — Memoires de la Societe Historique, Litteraire, et Scientifique du Cher

Mem Soc Hist Nat Afrique N Hors Ser — Memoires. Societe d'Histoire Naturelle de l'Afrique du Nord. Hors Serie

Mem Soc Hist Nat Afr N — Memoires de la Societe d'Histoire Naturelle de l'Afrique du Nord

Mem Soc Hist Nat Afr Nord — Memoires. Societe d'Histoire Naturelle de l'Afrique du Nord

Mem Soc Hist Nat Auvergne — Memoires de la Societe d'Histoire Naturelle d'Auvergne

Mem Soc Hist Nat Dep Moselle — Memoires de la Societe d'Histoire Naturelle du Departement de la Moselle

Mem Soc Hist Nat Doubs — Memoires de la Societe d'Histoire Naturelle du Doubs

Mem Soc Hist Natur Afr Nord — Memoires. Societe d'Histoire Naturelle de l'Afrique du Nord

Mem Soc Hist Paris & Ile de France — Memoires de la Societe de l'Histoire de Paris et de l'Ile-de-France

Mem Soc Iber Ci Nat — Memorias. Sociedad Iberica de Ciencias Naturales

Mem Soc Imp Antiqua France — Memoires de la Societe Imperiale des Antiquaires de France

Mem Soc Imp Mineral — Memoires. Societe Imperiale de Mineralogie

Mem Soc Ing Civ Fr — Memoires. Societe des Ingenieurs Civils de France

Mem Soc Ital Sci Nat Mus Civ Stor Nat Milano — Memorie. Societa Italiana di Scienze Naturali e Museo Civico di Storia Naturaledi Milano

Mem Soc Lett Metz — Memoires de la Societe des Lettres, Sciences, et Arts et d'Agriculture de Metz

Mem Soc Lett Sci & Art Bar le Duc — Memoires de la Societe des Lettres, Sciences, et Arts de Bar-le-Duc

Mem Soc Lett Sci Aveyron — Memoires de la Societe des Lettres, Sciences, et Arts de l'Aveyron

Mem Soc Lett Sci Bar Le Duc — Memoires de la Societe des Lettres, Sciences, et Arts de Bar-le-Duc

Mem Soc Lett Sci St Dizier — Memoires de la Societe des Lettres, Sciences, Arts, de l'Agriculture, et de l'Industrie de St-Dizier

Mem Soc Ling — Memoires. Societe de Linguistique de Paris

Mem Soc Linn Calvados — Memoires. Societe Linneenne de Calvados

Mem Soc Linn N Fr — Memoires de la Societe Linneenne du Nord de la France

Mem Soc Linn Normandie — Memoires de la Societe Linneenne de Normandie

Mem Soc Linn Provence — Memoires de la Societe Linneenne de Provence

Mem Soc Litt Grenoble — Memoires. Societe Litteraire de Grenoble

Mem Soc Math France NS — Memoire. Societe Mathematique de France. Nouvelle Serie

Mem Soc Med Toulouse — Memoires de la Societe de Medecine de Toulouse

Mem Soc N Antiqua France — Memoires de la Societe Nationale des Antiquaires de France

Mem Soc Nat Antiqu France — Memoires. Societe Nationale des Antiquaires de France

Mem Soc Nationale Antiq Fr — Memoires. Societe Nationale des Antiquaires de France

Mem Soc Nat Kiev — Memoires. Societe des Naturalistes de Kiev

Mem Soc Natl Agric Angers — Memoires. Societe Nationale d'Agriculture, Sciences, et Arts d'Angers

Mem Soc Natl Agric France — Memoires. Societe Nationale d'Agriculture de France

Mem Soc Natl Sci Nat Math Cherbg — Memoires. Societe Nationale des Sciences Naturelles et Mathematiques de Cherbourg

Mem Soc Natn Acad Cherbourg — Memoires de la Societe Nationale Academique de Cherbourg

Mem Soc Natn Agric Fr — Memoires de la Societe Nationale d'Agriculture de France

Mem Soc Natn Agric Sci Angers — Memoires de la Societe Nationale d'Agriculture, Science, et Arts d'Angers

Mem Soc Natn Agric Sci Dep N — Memoires de la Societe Nationale d'Agriculture, Sciences, et Arts, Centrale du Departement du Nord

Mem Soc Natn Sci Nat Math Cherbourg — Memoires de la Societe Nationale des Sciences Naturelles et Mathematiques de Cherbourg

Mem Soc Neuchatel Geogr — Memoires de la Societe Neuchateloise de Geographie

Mem Soc Neuchatel Sci Nat — Memoires. Societe Neuchateloise des Sciences Naturelles

Mem Soc Orn Fr — Memoires de la Societe Ornithologique de France et de l'Union Francaise

Mem Soc Orn Mammal Fr — Memoires de la Societe Ornithologique et Mammalogique de France

Mem Soc Paleont Russ — Memoires de la Societe de Paleontologie de Russie

Mem Soc Philomath Verdun — Memoires de la Societe Philomathique de Verdun

Mem Soc Phys Hist Nat Geneve — Memoires de la Societe de Physique et d'Histoire Naturelle de Geneve

Mem Soc Prehist Fr — Memoires de la Societe Prehistorique Francaise

Mem Soc R Belge Entomol — Memoires. Societe Royale Belge d'Entomologie

Mem Soc R Bot Belg — Memoires. Societe Royale de Botanique de Belgique

Mem Soc R Can — Memoires. Societe Royale du Canada

Mem Soc R Ent Belg — Memoires. Societe Royale Entomologique de Belgique

Mem Soc R Geogr Egypte — Memoires de la Societe R. de Geographie d'Egypte

Mem Soc R Malac Belg — Memoires de la Societe R. Malacologique de Belgique

Mem Soc Roy Acad Savoie — Memoires. Societe Royale Academique de Savoie

Mem Soc Roy Arras — Memoires. Societe Royale d'Arras pour l'Encuragement des Sciences, des Lettres,et des Arts

Mem Soc Roy Liege — Memorandum. Societe Royale de Liege

Mem Soc Roy Sci Liege Coll in-8o — Memoires. Societe Royale des Sciences de Liege. Collection in Octavo

Mem Soc Roy Sci Nancy — Memoires. Societe Royale des Sciences et Belles-Lettres de Nancy

Mem Soc R Sci Boheme — Memoires de la Societe R. des Sciences de Boheme

Mem Soc R Sci Liege — Memoires. Societe Royale des Sciences de Liege

Mem Soc R Sci Liege 4o — Memoires. Societe Royale des Sciences de Liege. Collection in Quarto

Mem Soc R Sci Liege 8o — Memoires. Societe Royale des Sciences de Liege. Collection in Octavo

Mem Soc R Sci Liege Collect 8 — Memoires. Societe Royale des Sciences de Liege. Collection in Octavo

Mem Soc R Sci Liege Vol Hors Ser — Memoires. Societe Royale des Sciences de Liege. Volume Hors Serie

Mem Soc Russe Mineral — Memoires. Societe Russe de Mineralogie

Mem Soc R Zool Malac Belg — Memoires de la Societe R. Zoologique et Malacologique de Belgique

Mem Soc Sci Agric Lille — Memoires de la Societe des Sciences, de l'Agriculture, et des Arts de Lille

Mem Soc Sci & Lett Loir et Cher — Memoires de la Societe des Sciences et des Lettres de Loir-et-Cher

Mem Soc Sci Arts Bayeux — Memoires de la Societe des Sciences, Arts, et Belles-Lettres de Bayeux

Mem Soc Sci Arts Vitry Le Francois — Memoires. Societe des Sciences et Arts de Vitry-le-Francois

Mem Soc Sci Loir Et Cher — Memoires de la Societe des Sciences et Lettres de Loir-et-Cher

Mem Soc Sci Nancy — Memoires. Societe des Sciences de Nancy

Mem Soc Sci Nat Archeol Creuse — Memoires de la Societe des Sciences Naturelles et Archeologiques de la Creuse

Mem Soc Sci Nat Cherbourg — Memoires. Societe des Sciences Naturelles de Cherbourg

Mem Soc Sci Nat Hist Cannes — Memoires de la Societe des Sciences Naturelles et Historiques de Cannes

Mem Soc Sci Nat Maroc — Memoires. Societe des Sciences Naturelles du Maroc

Mem Soc Sci Nat Phys Maroc Bot — Memoires. Societe des Sciences Naturelles et Physiques du Maroc. Botanique

Mem Soc Sci Nat Phys Maroc Zool — Memoires. Societe des Sciences Naturelles et Physiques du Maroc. Zoologie

Mem Soc Sci Nat Seine Et Oise — Memoires de la Societe des Sciences Naturelles de Seine-et-Oise

Mem Soc Sci Nat Strasbourg — Memoires. Societe des Sciences Naturelles de Strasbourg

Mem Soc Sci Phys Nat Bordeaux — Memoires. Societe des Sciences Physiques et Naturelles de Bordeaux

Mem Soc Sci Strasbourg — Memoires. Societe des Sciences, Agriculture, et Arts de Strasbourg

Mem Soc Toscana Sci Nat Pisa — Memorie. Societa Toscana di Scienze Naturali Residente in Pisa

Mem Soc Vaudoise Sci Nat — Memoires. Societe Vaudoise des Sciences Naturelles

Mem Soc Zool Fr — Memoires. Societe Zoologique de France

Mem Soc Zool Tchec Prague — Memoires. Societe Zoologique Tchecoslovaque de Prague

Mem Soil Res Inst (Kumasi Ghana) — Memoir. Soil Research Institute (Kumasi, Ghana)

Mem Sous Commn Alliag Legers Commn Perm Etud Aeronaut — Memoires de la Sous-Commission des Alliages Legers et Ultralegers de la Commission Permanente d'Etudes Aeronautiques

Mem South Calif Acad Sci — Memoirs. Southern California Academy of Sciences

Mems R Acad Cienc Artes Barcelona — Memorias de la Real Academia de Ciencias y Artes de Barcelona

Mems R Acad Cienc Exact Fis Nat Madr — Memorias de la Real Academia de Ciencias Exactas, Fisicas y Naturales de Madrid

Mems R Acad Sci Lisb — Memorias da Real Academia das Sciencias de Lisboa

Mem S R Met — Memoires Scientifiques de la Revue de Metallurgie

Mems R Soc Esp Hist Nat — Memorias de la Real Sociedad Espanola de Historia Natural

Mems Soc Astr Esp Am — Memorias de la Sociedad Astronomica de Espana y America

Mems Soc Broteriana — Memorias da Sociedade Broteriana [*Coimbra*]

Mems Soc Cienc Nat La Salle — Memorias de la Sociedad de Ciencias Naturales La Salle

Mems Soc Cub Hist Nat Felipe Poey — Memorias de la Sociedad Cubana de Historia Natural Felipe Poey

Mems Soc Ent Esp — Memorias de la Sociedad Entomologica de Espana

Mems Soc Estud Vascos — Memorias de la Sociedad de Estudios Vascos

Mems Soc Geogr Nac Secc Cienc Suelo Madr — Memorias. Sociedad Geografica Nacional. Seccion de la Ciencia del Suelo (Madrid)

Mems Soc Iber Cienc Nat — Memorias de la Sociedad Iberica de Ciencias Naturales

Mems Soc Nac Agric Chile — Memorias de la Sociedad Nacional de Agricultura (Santiago de Chile)

Mems Soc Rur Argent — Memorias de la Sociedad Rural Argentina

Mems Tareas Soc Estud Clin Habana — Memorias de las Tareas, que han Ocupado a la Sociedad de Estudios Clinicos de la Habana

Mem St Bur Mines Miner Resour (New Mex) — Memoirs. State Bureau of Mines and Mineral Resources (New Mexico)

Mem Sth Calif Acad Sci — Memoirs. Southern California Academy of Sciences

Mem Stor Dioc Brescia — Memorie Storiche della Diocesi di Brescia

Mem Stor Dioc Milano — Memorie Storiche della Diocesi di Milano

Mem Stor Forogiuliesi — Memorie Storiche Forogiuliesi

Mem St Petersbourg — Memoires. Academie Imperiale des Sciences de St-Petersbourg

Mems Trab Cent Invest Cient Algod — Memorias e Trabalhos. Centro de Investigacao Cientifica Algododeira

Mems Trab Inst Invest Cient Angola — Memorias e Trabalhos. Instituto de Investigacao Cientifica de Angola

Mems Trab Langosta Montev — Memorias de los Trabajos Contra la Langosta. Ministerio de Industrias. Defensa Agricola (Montevideo)

Mems Trab Patron Alfonso el Sabo Mat Fis Quim — Memorias de los Trabajos del Patronato Alfonso el Sabo de Matematicas Fisica y Quimica

Mems Trab Real Inst Nac Invest Agron — Memorias de los Trabajos Realizados. Instituto Nacional de Investigaciones Agronomicas

Mems Trab Vulg Cient Estac Sism Obs Cartuja — Memorias y Trabajos de Vulgarizacion Cientifica. Estacion Sismologica y el Observatorio Astronomico y Meteorologico de Cartuja

Mem St ULR — Memphis State University. Law Review

Mem Sudan Met Serv — Memoirs. Sudan Meteorological Service

Mem Suffolk Nat Soc — Memoirs of the Suffolk Naturalists Society

Mem Suisses Paleontol — Memoires Suisses de Paleontologie

Mem Suzuka Coll Technol — Memoirs. Suzuka College of Technology

Mem Svizz Paleontol — Memorie Svizzere di Paleontologia

Mem Tanaka Citrus Exp Sta — Memoirs. Tanaka Citrus Experiment Station/ Tanaka Kankitsu Shiken-Jo. Mino-Mura,Fukuoka-Ken

Mem Tanaka Citrus Exp Stn — Memoirs of the Tanaka Citrus Experiment Station

Mem Tec Congr Latinoam Sider — Memoria Tecnica. Congreso Latinoamericano de Siderurgia

Mem Tech Cent Tech Ind Mec — Memoires Techniques. Centre Technique des Industries Mecaniques

Mem Tech CETIM — Memoires Techniques. CETIM

Mem Tech Meet Corros Eng Div Soc Mater Sci Jpn — Memoirs. Technical Meeting of Corrosion Engineering Division. Society of Materials Science. Japan

Mem Tec ILAFA Congr Latinoam Sider — Memoria Tecnica. ILAFA. Congreso Latinoamericano de Siderurgia

Mem Tercer Semin Lat Am Quim — Memorias. Tercer Seminario Latino Americano de Quimica

Mem Tohoku Inst Technol Ser 1 — Memoirs. Tohoku Institute of Technology. Series 1. Science andEngineering

Mem Tokai Hort Exp Stn — Memoirs of the Tokai Horticultural Experiment Station

Mem Tokyo Metrop Coll Aeronaut Eng — Memoirs. Tokyo Metropolitan College of Aeronautical Engineering

Mem Tokyo Univ Agr — Memoirs. Tokyo University of Agriculture

Mem Tokyo Univ Agric — Memoirs. Tokyo University of Agriculture

Mem Tomakomai Tech Coll — Memoirs. Tomakomai Technical College

Mem Torrey Bot Club — Memoirs. Torrey Botanical Club

Mem Tottori Agric Coll — Memoirs. Tottori Agricultural College

Mem Toulouse — Memoires. Academie des Sciences, Inscriptions, et Belles-Lettres de Toulouse

Mem Touraine — Memoires. Societe Archeologique de Touraine

Mem Trav Cons Perm Int Explor Mer — Memoires sur les Travaux du Conseil Permanent International pour l'Exploration de la Mer

Mem Trav Fac Cath — Memoires et Travaux. Facultes Catholiques de Lille

Mem Trav Soc Hydrotech Fr — Memoires et Travaux. Societe Hydrotechnique de France

Mem Trav Soc Hydrot France — Memoires et Travaux. Societe Hydrotechnique de France

Mem Trav Soc Ind N Fr — Memoires et Travaux de la Societe Industrielle du Nord de la France

Mem Trevoux — Memoires de Trevoux

Mem Tsetse Res Ser Tanganyika — Memoirs. Tsetse Research Series. Department of Tsetse Research. Tanganyika Territory

Mem Univ Calif — Memoirs. University of California

Mem Univ Etat Extreme Orien — Memoires. Universite d'Etat a l'Extreme-Orient

Mem Univ Lab Phys Chem Med Public Health Har Univ — Memoirs. University Laboratory of Physical Chemistry Related to Medicine and Public Health. Harvard University

Mem Un Soc Sav Bourges — Memoires de l'Union des Societes Savantes de Bourges
Memu Obshch Lyub Estest Antrop Etnogr — Memuary Obshchestva Lyubitelei Estestvoznaniya, Antropologii I Etnografii
Mem U Saint Joseph — Memoires de l'Universite Saint-Joseph
Mem Vald — Memorie Valdarnesi
Mem Va Polytech Inst State Univ Dep Geol Sci — Memoir. Virginia Polytechnic Institute and State University. Departmentof Geological Sciences
Mem Vivre — Memoire Vivre
Mem Wakayama Natl Coll Technol — Memoirs. Wakayama National College of Technology
Mem Wakayama Tech Coll — Memoirs. Wakayama Technical College
Mem Wistar Inst Anat — Memoirs of the Wistar Institute of Anatomy
MEN — Meatworks Extension News
Menabo — Menabo di Letteratura
Menarini Ser Immunopathol — Menarini Series on Immunopathology
Me Nat — Maine Naturalist
Mendel Bull — Mendel Bulletin
Mendel Chem J — Mendeleev Chemistry Journal
Mendeleev Chem J — Mendeleev Chemistry Journal
Mendeleev Chem J (Engl Transl) — Mendeleev Chemistry Journal (English Translation)
Mendeleev Commun — Mendeleev Communications
Mendeleevsk Sezd Obshch Prikl Khim — Mendeleevskii S'ezd po Obshchei i Prikladnoi Khimii
Mendel J — Mendel Journal
Mendel Newsl — Mendel Newsletter
Mendel Newslett — Mendel Newsletter
Mendel Pasteur Rev — Mendel and Pasteur Review
Men Dis LR — Mental Disability Law Reporter
Mendocino Rev — Mendocino Review
Me Ne — Meroitic Newsletter
Menemui Mat — Menemui Matematik
Mengen Spurenelem Arbeitstag — Mengen- und Spurenelemente, Arbeitstagung
M Engy Rev — Monthly Energy Review
MenJ — Menorah Journal
Men Meth Res — Men and Methods in Research
Menn — Mennonite
Menn Enc — Mennonite Encyclopedia
Menn HS — Mennonite Historical Series
Menninger Q — Menninger Quarterly
Menn L — Mennonite Life
Menn Lex — Mennonitisches Lexikon
Menn Life — Mennonite Life
Menn o Mil — Menneske og Miljo
Mennonite Q R — Mennonite Quarterly Review
Mennonite Quar Rev — Mennonite Quarterly Review. Goshen College
Mennonite Quart Rev — Mennonite Quarterly Review
Mennonit Gesch Bl — Mennonitische Geschichtsblaetter
Menn Q R — Mennonite Quarterly Review
Menn R — Mennonitische Rundschau
MENOA — Metano, Petrolio, e Nuove Energie
Menomonie Rev — Menomonie Review
Menorah — Menorah Journal
Menorah J — Menorah Journal
Menorah Journ — Menorah Journal
MenQ — Mennonite Quarterly Review
Men Retard — Mental Retardation
MENS — Man-Environment Systems
Mensaje Bol Inf Fed Iberoam Parques — Mensaje Boletin Informativo. Federacion Iberoamericana de Parques Zoologicos
Mensajero Agric — Mensajero Agricola
Mensajero For — Mensajero Forestal
Mensaj For — Mensajero Forestal
Mens en Mel — Mens en Melodie
Mens en Mij — Mens en Maatschappij
Men's Fit — Men's Fitness
MensM — Mens en Melodie
Mens Maat — Menschen Maatschappij
Mens Maatsch — Mens en Maatschappij
Mens Maatschap — Mens en Maatschappij
Mens Mij Twee Tijdschr — Mens en Maatschappy Tweedmaandelijks Tydschrift
Mens Ond — Mens en Onderneming
Mens Ondern — Mens en Onderneming
Mental Disab L Rep — Mental Disability Law Reporter
Mental Health in Aust — Mental Health in Australia
Mental Hyg — Mental Hygiene
Mental Hyg Lond — Mental Hygiene (London)
Mental Reta — Mental Retardation
Menth — Mentalhygiejne
Ment Health — Mental Health
Ment Health Aust — Mental Health in Australia
Ment Health Book Rev Index — Mental Health Book Review Index
Ment Health Bul — Mental Health Bulletin. Pennsylvania Department of Welfare
Ment Health Bul Ill — Mental Health Bulletin. Illinois Society for Mental Hygiene
Ment Health Obs — Mental Health Observer. Massachusetts Society for Mental Hygiene
Ment Health Program Rep — Mental Health Program Reports
Ment Health Res Inst Univ Mich Annu Rep — Mental Health Research Institute. University of Michigan. Annual Report
Ment Health Serv Res — Mental Health Services Research
Ment Health Soc — Mental Health and Society
Ment Health Stat Note — Mental Health Statistical Note
Ment Hlth Baltimore — Mental Health (Baltimore)
Ment Hlth Bull Chicago — Mental Health Bulletin (Chicago)

Ment Hlth Bull Danville — Mental Health Bulletin. Danville State Hospital
Ment Hlth Lond — Mental Health (London)
Ment Hlth S Afr — Mental Health. South Africa
Ment Hlth Ser US Publ Hlth Serv — Mental Health Series. US Public Health Service
Ment Hlth Servs J — Mental Health Services Journal [London]
Ment Hlth Stat — Mental Health Statistics
Ment Hosp — Mental Hospitals
Ment Hyg — Mental Hygiene
Ment Hyg (Arlington VA) — Mental Hygiene (Arlington, Virginia)
Ment Phys Disabil Law Rep — Mental and Physical Disability Law Reporter
Ment Ret — Mental Retardation
Ment Retard — Mental Retardation
Ment Retard Abstr — Mental Retardation Abstracts
Ment Retard Abstr Dev Disab Abstr — Mental Retardation and Developmental Disabilities Abstracts
Ment Retard Absts — Mental Retardation Abstracts
Ment Retard Dev Disabil — Mental Retardation and Developmental Disabilities
Ment Retard Dev Disabil Res Rev — Mental Retardation and Developmental Disabilities Research Reviews
Ment Ret Bul — Mental Retardation Bulletin
Ment Welf — Mental Welfare. Central Association for Mental Welfare [London]
Me/NZ — Melos/Neue Zeitschrift fuer Musik
MENZA — Methods in Enzymology
MEO — Middle East Opinion
MEOC — Methods of Elemento-Organic Chemistry
MEOC News — Middle East Outreach Coordinators' Newsletter
MEOL — Mededeelingen Ex Oriente Lux
MEOL — Mededelingen en Verhandelingen van het Voor-Aziatisch-Egyptisch Genootschap
MeP — Mekedonski Pregled. Spisanie za Nauka. Literatura i Obteostven Zivot
MEP — MEP: Multicultural Education Papers
MEPR — Messager de l'Exarchat du Patriarche Russe en Europe Occidentale
ME Proc Conf Mater Eng — ME Proceedings. Conference on Materials Engineering
MEQ — Metal Bulletin Monthly
MER — Malayan Economic Review
Mer — Mercer Law Review
Mer — Merian
Mer — Meridiens
MER — MER (Marine Engineers Review)
MER — Middle East Record
MER — Midwest English Review
MER — Monthly Energy Review
MERA — Maeventec Employers Rated Almanac
MERADO N — MERADO [Mechanical Engineering Research and Development Organisation] News
Meran Dok Vortr Int Fortbildungskurs Prakt Wiss Pharm — Meran. Dokumentation der Vortraege. Internationaler Fortbildungskursfuer Praktische und Wissenschaftliche Pharmazie
Mera Publs — Mera Publications [St. Albans]
MerB — Meridian Books
Merc — London Mercury
Merc — Mercuriale
Merc — Mercury
Mercer — Mercer County Law Journal
Mercer Beasley L Rev — Mercer Beasley Law Review
Mercer BL Rev — Mercer Beasley Law Review
Mercer Dent Soc Newsl — Mercer Dental Society. Newsletter
Mercer Law — Mercer Law Review
Mercer Law Rev — Mercer Law Review
Mercer L Rev — Mercer Law Review
Mercersb — Mercersburg Review
Merc France — Mercure de France
Merch — Merchandising
Merchand Vision — Merchandising Vision
Merch Mo — Merchandising Monthly
Merch Navy J — Merchant Navy Journal
Merch W — Merchandising Week [Later, Merchandising]
Mercian Geol — Mercian Geologist
Merck Agr Memo — Merck Agricultural Memo
Merck Rep — Merck Report
Mercks Annln — Mercks Annalen
Mercks Archs — Merck's Archives
Mercks A Rep Rec Adv Pharm Chem Ther — Merck's Annual Report of Recent Advances in Pharmaceutical Chemistry and Therapeutics
Merck Sharp Dohme Semin Rep — Merck, Sharp, and Dohme. Seminar Report
Merck Symp — Merck-Symposium
Merc LJ — Mercantile Law Journal
Merc LR — Mercer Law Review
Merc (Newspr) (Tas) — Mercury Reports (Newspaper) (Tasmania)
Merc S Arch — Mercury Series. Archaeological Survey of Canada. Papers
Merc S Ethn — Mercury Series. Ethnology Division. Papers
Mercure — Mercure de France
Mercure Fr — Mercure de France
Mercurio Peru — Mercurio Peruano
Mercur Peru Lima — Mercurio Peruano (Lima)
Mercy Med — Mercy Medicine
MERDD — Monthly Energy Review
Merentutkimuslaitoksen Julk — Merentutkimuslaitoksen Julkaisu
Meres Autom — Meres es Automatika
Meres es Autom — Meres es Automatika
Meresuegyi Koezl — Meresuegyi Koezlemenyek
Me Rev Stat Ann — Maine Revised Statutes Annotated
MERF — Melanges. Ecole Roumaine en France

MerF — Mercure de France
MerFl — Mercure de Flandre
Merg and Acq — Mergers and Acquisitions
Merger & A I — Mergers and Acquisitions Almanac and Index
Mergers — Mergers and Acquisitions
Mergers Acquis — Mergers and Acquisitions
Mergers & Acquis — Mergers and Acquisitions
Merino Breed J — Merino Breeders' Journal
MERIP — MERIP [*Middle East Research and Information Project*] Reports
MERIP Rep — MERIP Reports
MERIP Reports — Middle East Research and Information Project Reports
MERIT Newsl — MERIT [*Monitored Earth Rotation and Intercompared Techniques*] Newsletter
MERJD — Moessbauer Effect Reference and Data Journal
Merk — Merkur
Merkaz Volkani Bul (Bet Dagan Isr) — Merkaz Volkani. Buletin (Bet Dagan, Israel)
Merkbl Abt Forstschutz Tier Schaedl Inst Forstw Berl — Merkblaetter. Abteilung Forstschutz gegen Tierische Schaedlinge. Institut fuer Forstwissenschaften. Deutsche Akademie der Landwirtschaftswissenschaften (Berlin)
Merkbl Angew Parasitenkd Schaedlingsbekaempf — Merkblaetter ueber Angewandte Parasitenkunde und Schaedlingsbekaempfung
Merkblatt Imker Verb Kleingaertner Siedler Kleintierz — Merkblatt. Imker des Verbandes der Kleingaertner, Siedler, und Kleintierzuechter
Merkbl Bayer Landesanst PflBau PflSchutz — Merkblaetter der Bayerischen Landesanstalt fuer Pflanzenbau und Pflanzenschutz
Merkbl Biol Bundesanst Land Forstwirtsch — Merkblatt. Biologische Bundesanstalt fuer Land und Forstwirtschaft
Merkbl Biol Bundesanst Land Forstwirtsch (Braunschweig) — Merkblatt. Biologische Bundesanstalt fuer Land und Forstwirtschaft (Braunschweig)
Merkbl Biol Bundesanst Ld U Forstw Braunschw — Merkblaetter. Biologische Bundesanstalt fuer Land- und Forstwirtschaft in Braunschweig
Merkbl Biol Reichsanst Ld U Forstw — Merkblaetter. Biologische Reichsanstalt fuer Land- und Forstwirtschaft
Merkbl Bundesanst Forst Holzwirtsch — Merkblaetter der Bundesanstalt fuer Forst- und Holzwirtschaft
Merkbl Bundesanst Forst U Holzw — Merkblaetter der Bundesanstalt fuer Forst- und Holzwirtschaft
Merkbl Deutsch Landwirtsch Ges — Merkblatt. Deutsche Landwirtschafts-Gesellschaft
Merkbl Dt Waldarb — Merkblaetter fuer die Deutsche Waldarbeit
Merkbl Hauptstelle Forstl PflSchutz — Merkblaetter der Hauptstelle fuer Forstlichen Pflanzenschutz
Merkbl Herst Pappdaechern — Merkblaetter fuer die Herstellung von Pappdaechern
Merkbl Inst Forstw Eberswalde Tharandt — Merkblaetter. Institute fuer Forstwissenschaften, Eberswalde, und Tharandt. Deutsche Akademie der Landwirtschaftswissenschaften
Merkbl Inst Schiffs U TropKrankh — Merkblaetter. Institut fuer Schiffs- und Tropenkrankheiten
Merkbl Reichsinst Forst Holzwirtsch — Merkblaetter der Reichsinstitutes fuer Forst- und Holzwirtschaft
Merkbl Ver Zellst Chem — Merkblatt. Verein der Zellstoff- und Papier-Chemiker und -Ingenieure
Merkbl Zentralinst Forst Holzwirtsch — Merkblaetter der Zentralinstitutes fuer Forst- und Holzwirtschaft
Merkur Ungarn — Merkur von Ungarn, oder Litterarzeitung fuer das Koenigreich Ungarn und Dessen Kronlaender
Merkwuerd Abh Holl Aerzte — Merkwuerdige Abhandlungen Hollaendischer Aerzte
Merlewood Res Dev Pap — Merlewood Research and Development Paper
Merlewood Res Stn Merlewood Res Dev Pap — Merlewood Research Station. Merlewood Research and Development Paper
MERL Fluids Rep — MERL (Mechanical Engineering Research Laboratory) Fluids Report. Fluid Mechanics Division [*London*]
Mer LJ — Mercantile Law Journal
MERL Plast Rep — MERL (Mechanical Engineering Research Laboratory) Plasticity Report. Plasticity Division [*London*]
MERL Rep AB Div — MERL (Mechanical Engineering Research Laboratory) Report AB Div. Mechanics and Materials Division [*London*]
MERL Rep Mech Met — MERL (Mechanical Engineering Research Laboratory) Report Mech/Met. Machanisms, Metrology, and Noise Control Division [*London*]
MERL Res Summ — MERL (Mechanical Engineering Research Laboratory) Research Summary [*London*]
MER (Mar Eng Rev) — MER (Marine Engineers Review)
Mernoekgeol Sz — Mernoekgeologiai Szemle
Meroitic Newsl — Meroitic Newsletter
Mer O-Mer — Mer-Outre-Mer
Merova Tech — Merova Technika
MerP — Mercurio Peruano
Merrill ML — Merrill Lynch Market Letter
Merrill-Palmer Q — Merrill-Palmer Quarterly
Merril-Pal — Merrill-Palmer Quarterly
MERRSU — Modern Encyclopedia of Religions in Russia and the Soviet Union
MERSDW — Marine Environmental Research
Mersey Quart — Mersey Quarterly
MERSL — Modern Encyclopedia of Russian and Soviet Literature
MERTB — Mental Retardation
Mer (Tokyo) Bull Soc Fr Jpn Oceanogr — Mer (Tokyo). Bulletin de la Societe Franco-Japonaise d'Oceanographie
MERU — Monatsblaetter fuer den Evangelischen Religionsunterricht
M Erz — Musikerziehung
Merzlotnye Issled — Merzlotnye Issledovaniya
MES — Harvard Middle Eastern Studies
MES — Medical Economics
Mes — Mesopotamia
Mes — Message

Mes — Mesures
MES — Middle Eastern Studies
MESA Bull — Middle East Studies Association Bulletin
MESA Mag Min Health Saf — MESA [*Mining Enforcement and Safety Administration*] Magazine of Mining Health and Safety
MESA NY Bight Atlas Monogr — MESA [*Marine Ecosystems Analysis*] New York. Bight Atlas Monograph
Mesa Redonda Asoc Invest Tec Ind Papelera Esp — Mesa Redonda. Asociacion de Investigacion Tecnica de la IndustriaPapelera Espanola
MESCAK — Memoires. Societe Entomologique du Canada
Mes Controle Ind — Mesures et Controle Industriel
Mes Cope St — Mesopotamia. Copenhagen Studies in Assyriology
MESEDT — Marine Ecology. Progress Series
Mese Sanit — Mese Sanitario
Mes Fid — Messager des Fideles
Mesic Prehl Met Pozor — Mesicni Prehled Meteorologickych Pozorovani
MesO — Messages d'Orient
Mesoam Notes Mex — Mesoamerican Notes (Mexico)
Meson Reson Relat Electromagn Phenom Proc Int Conf — Meson Resonances and Related Electromagnetic Phenomena. Proceedings.International Conference
Mesons Light Nucl Proc Int Symp — Mesons and Light Nuclei. Proceedings. International Symposium
Mesopo — Mesopotamia. Rivista di Archeologia
Mesopot Agric — Mesopotamia Agriculture
Mesopotamia J Agric — Mesopotamia Journal of Agriculture
MESPBQ — Medizin und Sport
Mes Reg Aut — Mesures, Regulation, Automatisme
Mes Regul Autom — Mesures, Regulation, Automatisme
Mes Regul Automat — Mesures, Regulation, Automatisme
Mess — Messenger
Messager Sci & A — Messager des Sciences et des Arts
Messager Sci Arts Gand — Messager des Sciences et des Arts. Recueil Publie. Societe Royale des Beaux-Arts et des Lettres, et par Celle d'Agriculture et de Botanique de Gand
Messager Sci Hist — Messager des Sciences Historiques
Messager Sci Hist Belgique — Messager des Sciences Historiques de Belgique
Messager Tech Econ — Messager Technico-Economique
Messag Med Lyon — Messager Medical (Lyon)
Messag Med Paris — Messager Medical (Paris)
Messag Photogr — Messager de la Photographie
Messag Vinic — Messager Vinicole
Mess Math — Messenger of Mathematics
Mess Mth — Messenger of Mathematics
Mess Pruef — Messen und Pruefen
Mess Pruef Autom — Messen und Pruefen/Automatik
Mess Pruefen Autom — Messen, Pruefen, Automatisieren
Mess Pruef Ver Autom — Messen und Pruefen Vereinigt mit Automatik
Mess-Steuern-Regeln — Messen-Steuern-Regeln
Mess Steuern Regeln mit Automatisierungsprax — Messen, Steuern, Regeln mit Automatisierungspraxis
Messtech BetrUeberw WassWkn — Messtechnik und Betriebsueberwachung in Wasserwerken
Messtech Korrosionschutz Veranst Eur Foed Korros — Messtechnik im Korrosionschutz. Veranstaltung der EuropaeischenFoederation Korrosion
MessTec Spez — MessTec Spezial
Mes-Steuern-Regeln — Messen-Steuern-Regeln
Mess und Pruef — Messen und Pruefen
Mess U Prueftech — Mess- und Prueftechnik
MESTARABH — Miscelanea de Estudios Arabes y Hebraicos
Me St B Assn Proc — Maine State Bar Association. Proceedings
Mes Terap — Mes Terapeutico
Mestn Promysl Chud Prom — Mestnaja Promyslennost' i Chudozestvennye Promysly
Mest Topl — Mestnoe Toplivo
ME St Water Storage Comm An Rp — Maine. State Water Storage Commission. Annual Report
Mesur Controle Ind — Mesures et Controle Industriel
Mesz Hent Lap — Meszarosok es Hentesek Lapja
MET — Econometrica
Met — Metall
Met — Metals Abstracts
Met — Metroeconomica
MET — Monthly Energy Review
Met A — Meteorologiske Annaler
Metaalinst TNO Circ — Metaalinstituut TNO [*Nederlands Centrale Organisatie voor Toegepast-Natuurwetenschappelijk Onderzoek*]. Circulaire
Metaalinst TNO Commun — Metaalinstituut TNO [*Nederlands Centrale Organisatie voor Toegepast-Natuurwetenschappelijk Onderzoek*]. Communications
Metaalinst TNO Publ — Metaalinstituut TNO [*Nederlands Centrale Organisatie voor Toegepast-Natuurwetenschappelijk Onderzoek*]. Publikatie
Metaal Tech — Metaal en Techniek
Met Aarb — Meteorologisk Aarbog. Dansk Meteorologisk Institut
MetAb — Metals Abstracts
METAB — Metalurgija
Metab Aspects Cardiovasc Dis — Metabolic Aspects of Cardiovascular Disease
Metab Azota Skh Zhivotn Dokl Simp — Metabolizm Azota u Sel'skokhozyaistvennykh Zhivotnykh, Doklady izSimpoziuma ob Azotistom Metabolizme Sel'skokhozyaistvennykh Zhivotnykh
Metab Biochem — Metabolic Biochemistry
Metab Bone Dis Relat Res — Metabolic Bone Disease and Related Research
Metab Brain Dis — Metabolic Brain Disease
Metab Clin Exp — Metabolism - Clinical and Experimental
Metab Dis — Metabolism and Disease
Metab Eau Electrol — Metabolisme de l'Eau et des Electrolytes
Metab Eng — Metabolic Engineering

Metab Enzymol Nucleic Acids Proc Int Symp — Metabolism and Enzymology of Nucleic Acids. Proceedings. International Symposium on Metalolism and Enzymology of Nucleic Acids

Metab Eye Dis Proc Int Symp — Metabolic Eye Disease. Proceedings. International Symposium on Metabolic Eye Diseases

Met Abh Hamb Sternw Bergedorf — Meteorologische Abhandlungen auf der Hamburger Sternwarte in Bergedorf

Met Abh Inst Met Geophys Berl — Meteorologische Abhandlungen. Institut fuer Meteorologie und Geophysik. Freie Universitaet Berlin

Metab Interconvers Enzymes Int Symp — Metabolic Interconversion of Enzymes. International Symposium

Metab Interrelat Trans Conf — Metabolic Interrelations. Transactions of the Conference

Metab Interrel Trans Confs Josiah Macy Jr Fdn — Metabolic Interrelations. Transactions of Conferences. Josiah Macy Jr Foundation [New York]

Met ABM — Metalurgia. ABM

Metab Miokarda Mater Sov Am Simp — Metabolizm Miokarda. Materialy Sovetsko-Amerikanskogo Simpoziuma

Metab Nerv Syst Proc Int Neurochem Symp — Metabolism of the Nervous System. Proceedings. International Neurochemical Symposium

Metab Nutr Azotes Symp Int — Metabolisme et Nutrition Azotes. Symposium International

Metabolism — Metabolism - Clinical and Experimental

Metab Ophthalmol — Metabolic Ophthalmology

Metab Ophthalmol Pediatr Syst — Metabolic Ophthalmology, Pediatric, and Systemic

Metab Parietis Vasorum CR Congr Int Angeiol — Metabolismus Parietis Vasorum. Comptes Rendus du Congres International d'Angeiologie

Metab Pathways — Metabolic Pathways

Metab Pediatr Ophthalmol — Metabolic and Pediatric Ophthalmology

Metab Pediatr Syst Ophthalmol — Metabolic, Pediatric, and Systemic Ophthalmology

Met Abstr — Metallurgical Abstracts

Met Abstr Biblphy — Meteorological Abstracts and Bibliography

Met Aciers Spec Met Alliages — Metaux. Aciers Speciaux. Metaux et Alliages

META J — Manitoba Elementary Teachers' Association. Journal

Metal ABM — Metalurgia. ABM

Metal & Electr — Metalurgia y Electricidad

Metal Bul — Metal Bulletin

Metal Bull — Metal Bulletin

Metal Bull Mon — Metal Bulletin Monthly

Metal Cast — Metal Casting

Metal Clean Biblphical Abstr — Metal Cleaning Bibliographical Abstracts

Metal Clean Finish — Metal Cleaning and Finishing

Metal Cons — Metal Construction

Metal Constr Br Weld J — Metal Construction and British Welding Journal [Later, Metal Construction]

Metal Constr Mas — Metalurgia si Constructia de Masini

Metal Electr — Metalurgia y Electricidad

Metal Eng Q — Metals Engineering Quarterly

Metal Fin — Metal Finishing

Metal Fing — Metal Finishing Guidebook and Directory

Metal Finish — Metal Finishing

Metal Finish Abstr — Metal Finishing Abstracts

Metal Form — Metal Forming

Metal Ind — Metal Industry

Metal Ind Handb — Metal Industry Handbook

Metal Ind Lond — Metal Industry (London)

Metal Ind NY — Metal Industry (New York)

Metal Ions Biol Syst — Metal Ions in Biological Systems

Metall — Metallurgist

Metall Abstr — Metallurgical Abstracts

Metall Anal — Metallurgical Analysis

Metall & Metal Form — Metallurgia and Metal Forming

Metall Australas Proc Annu Conf Aust Inst Met — Metallurgy in Australasia. Proceedings. Annual Conference. Australian Instituteof Metals

Metall Chem Eng — Metallurgical and Chemical Engineering

Metall Chem Engng — Metallurgical and Chemical Engineering

Metall Chern Met — Metallurgiya Chernykh Metallov

Metall Club R Coll Sci Technol J — Metallurgical Club. Royal College of Science and Technology Journal

Metall Constr Mec — Metallurgie et la Construction Mecanique

Metall Eng — Metallurgical Engineer

Metall Eng Bombay — Metallurgical Engineer (Bombay)

Metall Eng Consult J — Metallurgical and Engineering Consultants. Journal

Metall Eng IIT (Bombay) — Metallurgical Engineer. Indian Institute of Technology (Bombay)

Metall Engng Dig — Metallurgical Engineering Digest

Metall Ereunes — Metallourgikes Ereunes

Metallges Mitt Arbeitsbereich — Metallgesellschaft. Mitteilungen aus dem Arbeitsbereich

Metallges Period Rev — Metallgesellschaft. Periodic Review

Metallges Rev Act — Metallgesellschaft. Review of the Activities

Metallges Rev Activ — Metallgesellschaft AG [Frankfurt/Main]. Review of the Activities

Metall Giessereitech — Metallurgie und Giessereitechnik

Metall Gornorudn Promst — Metallurgicheskaya i Gornorudnaya Promyshlennost

Metallilab Tied Valt Tek Tutkimuskeskus — Metallilaboratorio. Tiedonanto. Valtion Teknillinen Tutkimuskeskus

Metalli Legg Applic — Metalli Leggeri e loro Applicazioni

Metallind Rdsch — Metallindustrielle Rundschau

Metalli Non Ferr Ferroleghe — Metalli Non Ferrose e Ferroleghe

Metall Iskusst Vseobshch — Metallicheskoe Iskusstvo i Vseobshchaya Torgovlya

Metall Ital — Metallurgia Italiana

Metall J — Metallurgical Journal

Metallk GiessWes — Metallkunde und Giessereiwesen

Metall Khim Prom Kaz — Metallurgicheskaya i Khimicheskaya Promyshlennost Kazakhstana

Metall Khim Titana — Metallurgiya i Khimiya Titana

Metall Koksokhim — Metallurgiya i Koksokhimiya

Metall Masch — Metall und Maschine. Technische Ausgabe B der Deutschen Werkmeisterzeitung

Metall Mater Technol — Metallurgist and Materials Technologist

Metall Mater Trans A — Metallurgical and Materials Transactions A. Physical Metallurgy and Materials Science

Metall Mater Trans B — Metallurgical and Materials Transactions B. Process Metallurgy and Materials Processing Science

Metall Met — Metallurgia and Metal Forming

Metall Metalloved Alma Ata — Metallurgiya i Metallovedenie (Alma-Ata)

Metall Metalloved Chist Met — Metallurgiya i Metallovedenie Chistykh Metallov

Metall Metalloved Chist Met Sb Nauchn Rab — Metallurgiya i Metallovedenie Chistykh Metallov Moskovskij Inzhenerno-Fizicheskij Institut Sbornik Nauchnykh Rabot

Metall Met Form — Metallurgia and Metal Forming

Metall Note Aust Aeronaut Res Lab — Metallurgy Note. Australia. Aeronautical Research Laboratories

Metall Numis — Metallurgy in Numismatics

Metalloberfl — Metalloberflaeche-Angewandte Elektrochemie

Metalloberflaeche-Angew Elektrochem — Metalloberflaeche-Angewandte Elektrochemie

Metallofiz — Metallofizika

Metallofizika Akad Nauk Ukr SSR Inst Metallofiz — Metallofizika. Akademiya Nauk Ukrainskoi SSR. Institut Metallofiziki

Metallofizika Akad Nauk Ukr SSR Otd Fiz Astron — Metallofizika. Akademiya Nauk Ukrainskoi SSR. Otdelenie Fiziki i Astronomii

Metallofiz Noveishie Tekhnol — Metallofizika i Noveishie Tekhnologii

Metallog Dokembr Shchitov Drevnikh Podvizhnykh Zon Dokl Vses — Metallogeniya Dokembriiskikh Shchitov i Drevnikh Podvizhnykh Zon. Doklady Vsesoyuznoi Ob'edinennoi Sessii po Zakonomernostyam Razmeshcheniya Poleznykh Iskopaemykh i Prognoznym Kartam

Metallog Geol Issled — Metallogenicheskie i Geologicheskie Issledovaniya

Metallogr Inst ForskVerks — Metallografiska Institutets Forskningsverksamhet

Metallogr Metalwkg — Metallography and Metalworking

Metallogr Rev — Metallographic Review

Metalloorg Khim — Metalloorganicheskaya Khimiya

Metallotech Revue — Metallotechnische Revue

Metalloved Fiz Khim Metallofiz Sverkhprovodn Tr Soveshch — Metallovedenie. Fiziko-Khimiya i Metallofizika Sverkhprovodnikov. Trudy Soveshchanii po Metallovedeniyu. Fiziko-Khimii i Metallofizike Sverkhprovodnikov

Metalloved i Term Obrab Met — Metallovedenie i Termicheskaya Obrabotka Metallov

Metalloved Korroz Met — Metallovedenie i Korroziya Metallov

Metalloved Obrab Met — Metallovedenie i Obrabotka Metallov

Metalloved Prochn Mater — Metallovedenie i Prochnost Materialov

Metalloved Sb Statei — Metallovedenie. Sbornik Statei

Metalloved Term Obrab — Metallovedenie i Termicheskaya Obrabotka

Metalloved Term Obrab Itogi Nauki Tekh — Metallovedenie i Termicheskaya Obrabotka. Itogi Nauki i Tekhniki

Metalloved Term Obrab (Kalinin USSR) — Metallovedenie i Termicheskaya Obrabotka (Kalinin, USSR)

Metalloved Term Obrab Met — Metallovedenie i Termicheskaya Obrabotka Metallov

Metalloved Term Obrab (Moscow) — Metallovedenie i Termicheskaya Obrabotka (Moscow)

Metallov i Term Obrab Metal — Metallovedenie i Termicheskaya Obrabotka Metallov

Metallov Obrab Metall — Metallovedenie i Obrabotka Metallov

Metallov Term Obrab Metall — Metallovedenie i Termicheskaya Obrabotka Metallov

Metall Plant Technol — Metallurgical Plant and Technology

Metall Plant Technol Int — Metallurgical Plant and Technology International

Metall Proizvod — Metallurgicheskoe Proizvodstvo

Metall Qual Proc Annu Conf — Metallurgy and Quality. Proceedings. Annual Conference

Metall-Reinig Vorbehandl — Metall-Reinigung und Vorbehandlung

Metall Rep Aeronaut Res Lab Aust — Australia. Aeronautical Research Laboratories. Metallurgy Report

Metall Rep CRM — Metallurgical Reports. CRM

Metall Rep Geol Surv S Aust — Metallurgical Reports. Geological Survey. S. Australia

Metall Res Athens — Metallurgical Research (Athens)

Metall Rev — Metallurgical Reviews (Supplement to Metals and Materials)

Metall Rev MMIJ — Metallurgical Review. MMIJ

Metall Sb Statei — Metallurgiya. Sbornik Statei

Metall Sci Technol — Metallurgical Science and Technology

Metall Slags Fluxes Int Symp Proc — Metallurgical Slags and Fluxes. International Symposium. Proceedings

Metall Soc AIME Proc — Metallurgical Society of AIME Proceedings

Metall Soc Conf — Metallurgical Society. Conferences

Metall Soc Conf Proc — Metallurgical Society. Conferences. Proceedings

Metall Soc Confs NY — Metallurgical Society Conferences. Metals Branch. American Institute of Mining Engineers (New York)

Metall Spec (Paris) — Metallurgie Speciale (Paris)

Metall SSSR — Metallurgiya SSSR

Metall T-A — Metallurgical Transactions. A. Physical Metallurgy and Materials Science

Metalltag DDR — Metalltagung der DDR

Metall T-B — Metallurgical Transactions. B. Process Metallurgy

Metall Tech Memo Aust Aeronaut Res Lab — Australia. Aeronautical Research Laboratories. Metallurgy Technical Memorandum

Metall Teplotekh — Metallurgicheskaya Teplotekhnika
Metall Teplotekh Oborud Izmer Kontrol Avtom Metall Proizvod — Metallurgicheskaya Teplotekhnika, Oborudovanie, Izmereniya, Kontrol i Avtomatizatsiya v Metallurgicheskom Proizvodstve
Metall Topl — Mettallurgija i Toplivo
Metall Trans — Metallurgical Transactions
Metall Trans A — Metallurgical Transactions. A
Metall Trans B — Metallurgical Transactions. B
Metall u Erz — Metall und Erz
Metallurg — Metallurgia
Metallurgia Ital — Metallurgia Italiana
Metallurgia Mecc — Metallurgia e Meccanica
Metallurgie Constr Mec — Metallurgie et la Construction Mecanique
Metallurgie GiessTech — Metallurgie und Giessereitechnik
Metallurgiste Bordel — Metallurgiste Bordelais
Metallurgiya Topl — Metallurgiya i Toplivo
Metallurgy Note Aeronaut Res Labs Aust — Metallurgy Note. Aeronautical Research Laboratories. Australia
Metallverarb Handwk — Metallverarbeitendes Handwerk
Metallwaren Ind Galvanotech — Metallwaren-Industrie und Galvanotechnik
Metallwar Ind Galvano Tech — Metallwaren-Industrie und Galvano-Technik
Metallwirt Metallwiss Metalltech — Metallwirtschaft, Metallwissenschaft, Metalltechnik
Metallwirtsch — Metallwirtschaft, Metallwissenschaft, Metalltechnik
Metallwirtsch Metallwiss Metalltech — Metallwirtschaft, Metallwissenschaft, Metalltechnik
Metallwirtsch Wiss Tech — Metallwirtschaft, Metallwissenschaft, Metalltechnik
Metall Wirt Wiss Tech — Metall. Wirtschaft, Wissenschaft, Technik
Metally Splavy Elektrotekh — Metally i Splavy v Elektrotekhnike
Metal Mater — Metalurgia and Materials
Metal Miner Mkts — Metal and Mineral Markets
Metal Mod — Metalurgia Moderna
Metal Odlew — Metalurgia i Odlewnictwo
Metalozn Obrob Cieplna — Metaloznawstwo i Obrobka Cieplna
Metalozn Obrob Cieplna Inz Powierzchni — Metaloznawstwo, Obrobka Cieplna, Inzynieria Powierzchni
Metal Powder Ind Fed Stand — Metal Powder Industries Federation. MPIF Standard
Metal Powd News — Metal Powder News
Metal Powd Rep — Metal Powder Report
Metal Process Bull — Metal Processing Bulletin
Metal Prod Mfg — Metal Products Manufacturing
Metal Prog — Metal Progress
Metal Proszkow — Metalurgia Proszkow
Metal Rec Electropl — Metal Record and Electroplater
Metal Reptr — Metal Reporter
Metal Resour Circ Ont — Metal Resources Circular. Department of Mines. Ontario Province
Metals Abstr Index — Metals Abstracts Index
Metals Aust — Metals Australia [Later, Metals Australasia]
Metal Sci — Metal Science
Metal Sci H — Metal Science and Heat Treatment
Metal Sci Heat Treat — Metal Science and Heat Treatment
Metal Sci Heat Treat Metals — Metal Science and Heat Treatment of Metals
Metal Sci J — Metal Science Journal [Later, Metal Science]
Metals Eng Quart — Metals Engineering Quarterly
Metals Handb — Metals Handbook. American Society for Metals
Metals Jpn Inst Met — Metals. Japan Institute of Metals
Metals Mater — Metals and Materials
Metals Mats — Metals and Materials
Metals Miner Int — Metals and Minerals International
Metal Spray — Metal Spraying
Metals Rev — Metals Review
Metals Soc Wld — Metals Society World
Metal Stamp — Metal Stamping
Metal Stat — Metal Statistics
Metal Statist — Metal Statistics
Metal Statist Dig — Metal Statistical Digest
Metals Tech — Metals Technology
Metals Technol — Metals Technology
Metal Trades J — Metal Trades Journal
Metal Treat — Metal Treating
Metalurgia Constr Mas — Metalurgia si Constructia de Masini
Metalurgia Electr — Metalurgia y Electricidad
Metalurgia Mec — Metalurgia y Mecanica
Metalurgija Sisak Yugosl — Metalurgija (Sisak, Yugoslavia)
Metalwkg Bull — Metalworking Bulletin
Metalwkg Prod — Metalworking Production
Metalwork Econ — Metalworking Economics
Metalwork Interfaces — Metalworking Interfaces
Metalwork Manag — Metalworking Management
Metalwork Prod — Metalworking Production
Metalwrkg Prod — Metalworking Production
Met Anal Outlook — Metals Analysis and Outlook
Met & Eng — Metal and Engineering
Met & GeoAb — Meteorological and Geoastrophysical Abstracts
Met Ann — Meteorologiske Annaler
Met Annr Oslo — Meteorologiske Annaler (Oslo)
Met Annu Conf Australas Inst Met — Metals. Annual Conference. Australasian Institute of Metals
Metano Pet Nuove Energ — Metano, Petrolio, e Nuove Energie
Metano Petrol Nuove Energ — Metano, Petrolio e Nuove Energie
Metaphilos — Metaphilosophy
Met Aust — Metals Australasia
Met Aust — Metals Australia [Later, Metals Australasia]

Met Australas — Metals Australasia
Metaux Alliages Mach — Metaux, Alliages et Machines
Metaux Civil — Metaux et Civilisations
Metaux Corros — Metaux et Corrosion
Metaux (Corros-Ind) — Metaux (Corrosion-Industries)
Metaux Corros Inds — Metaux, Corrosion, Industries
Metaux Corros Usure — Metaux, Corrosion-Usure
Metaux Deform — Metaux Deformation
Metaux Inds — Metaux et Industries
Metaux Mach — Metaux et Machines
Metaxa A Md Chir — Annali Medico-Chirurgici. Metaxa
Met Based Drugs — Metal-Based Drugs
Met Beob Dt Feuerschiffen N U Ostsee — Meteorologische Beobachtungen von Deutschen Feuerschiffen der Nord- und Ostsee
Met Beob Hamb Sternw Bergedorf — Meteorologische Beobachtungen auf der Hamburger Sternwarte in Bergedorf
Met Beob Mosk — Meteorologische Beobachtungen in Moskau
Met Beob Palaest — Meteorologische Beobachtungen in Palaestina
Met Beob WettWarte Saarbr — Meteorologische Beobachtungen. Wetterwarte Saarbruecken
Met Beob Wuertt — Meteorologische Beobachtungen in Wuerttemberg
Met Biblphy — Meteorological Bibliography
Met Bil Riga — Meteoroloogiskais Biletens (Riga)
Met Bull — Metal Bulletin
Met Bull Dubl — Meteorological Bulletin for Dublin City
Met Bull Inst Geophys Technol St Louis — Meteorological Bulletin. Institute of Geophysical Technology (St. Louis)
Met Bull London — Metal Bulletin (London)
Met Bull (Loosdrecht Netherlands) — Metallic Bulletin (Loosdrecht, Netherlands)
Met Bull Manila Cent Obs — Meteorological Bulletin. Manila Central Observatory
Met Bull Mon — Metal Bulletin Monthly
Met Bur Bull — Bureau of Meteorology. Bulletin
Met Bur Met Study — Bureau of Meteorology. Meteorological Study
Met Bur Met Summ — Bureau of Meteorology. Meteorological Summary
Met Bur Proj Rep — Bureau of Meteorology. Project Report
Met Bur Working Paper — Bureau of Meteorology. Working Paper
Met Byull Geof Obs Kazan — Meteorologicheskii Byulleten' Geofizicheskoi Observatorii Kazanskogo Gosudarstvennogo Universiteta
Met Byull Irkutsk Magn Met Obs — Meteorologicheskii Byulleten'. Irkutskaya Magnitnaya i Meteorologicheskaya Observatoriya
Met Ceram Inf Cent Rep — Metals and Ceramics Information Center. Report
Met Chem Metallwoche — Metall und Chemie. Metallwoche
Met Civilis — Metaux et Civilisations
Met Clean Finish — Metal Cleaning and Finishing
Met Const — Metal Construction
Met Constr — Metal Construction
Met Constr Br Weld J — Metal Construction and British Welding Journal [Later, Metal Construction]
Met Constr Mec — Metallurgie et la Construction Mecanique
Met Corros — Metaux and Corrosion
Met (Corros-Ind) — Metaux (Corrosion-Industries)
Met Corros Usure — Metaux. Corrosion. Usure
Met Data Antarct Ocean — Meteorological Data of the Antarctic Ocean
Met Data Indones Aerodr — Meteorological Data of Indonesian Aerodromes
Met Data Palest — Meteorological Data for Palestine
Met Deform — Metaux Deformation
Met Dep Pap Cairo — Meteorological Department Papers. Cairo
Met Dep Tech Notes Transcontinental West Air — Meteorological Department Technical Notes. Transcontinental and Western Air [Kansas City]
METEE — Publications. Metropolitan Museum of Art. Egyptian Expedition
Met Electr (Madrid) — Metalurgia y Electricidad (Madrid)
Met Elements N Pacif Ocean — Meteorological Elements on the North Pacific Ocean. Central Meteorological Observatory [Tokyo]
Met Eng — Metals in Engineering
Met Eng Q — Metals Engineering Quarterly
Met Eng (Tokyo) — Metals in Engineering (Tokyo)
Meteor & Geoastrophys Abstr — Meteorological and Geoastrophysical Abstracts
Meteor Forschungsergeb Reihe A — Meteor Forschungsergebnisse. Reihe A. Allgemeines, Physik, und Chemie des Meeres
Meteor Forschungsergeb Reihe AB — Meteor Forschungsergebnisse. Reihe A/B. Allgemeines, Physik, und Chemie des Meeres. Maritime Meteorologie
Meteor Forschungsergeb Reihe B — Meteor Forschungsergebnisse. Reihe B. Meteorologie und Aeronomie
Meteor Forschungsergeb Reihe C — Meteor Forschungsergebnisse. Reihe C. Geologie und Geophysik
Meteor Forschungsergeb Reihe D Biol — Meteor Forschungsergebnisse. Reihe D. Biologie
Meteor Forschungsergen Reihe B — Meteor Forschungsergebnisse. Reihe B. Meteorologie und Aeronomie
Meteor Gidrol Inf Byull — Meteorologiya i Gidrologiya. Informatsionnyi Byulleten
Meteoric Stone Meteoric Iron — Meteoric Stone and Meteoric Iron
Meteoritica (Engl Transl) — Meteoritica (English Translation)
Meteorit Planet Sci — Meteoritics and Planetary Science
Meteorit Soc Contr — Meteoritical Society. Contributions
Meteor Klimat Gidrol — Meteorologiya, Klimatologija, i Gidrologija
Meteor Mag — Meteorological Magazine
Meteornoe Rasprostr Radiovoln — Meteornoe Rasprostranenie Radiovoln
Meteorol Abh Inst Meteorol Geophys Freie Univ (Berl) — Meteorologische Abhandlungen. Institut fuer Meteorologie und Geophysik. Freie Universitaet (Berlin)
Meteorol Abst and Biblio — Meteorological Abstracts and Bibliography
Meteorol Abst Bibliogr — Meteorological Abstracts and Bibliography
Meteorol Ann — Meteorologiske Annaler
Meteorol Bull — Meteorological Bulletin

Meteorol Dienst DDR Veroeff — Meteorologischer Dienst der Deutschen Demokratischen Republik. Veroeffentlichungen
Meteorol Geoastrophys Abstr — Meteorological and Geoastrophysical Abstracts
Meteorol Gidrol — Meteorologiya i Gidrologiya
Meteorol Gidrol Inf Byull — Meteorologiya i Gidrologiya Informatsionnyi Byulleten
Meteorol Gidrolog — Meteorologiya i Gidrologiya
Meteorol Hydrol — Meteorology and Hydrology
Meteorol i Gidrol — Meteorologiya i Gidrologiya
Meteorol Issled — Meteorologicheskie Issledovaniya
Meteorol Izv — Meteorologicheskie Izvestiya
Meteorol Mag — Meteorological Magazine
Meteorol Monogr — Meteorological Monographs
Meteorologia Clim Colon Cabo Verde — Meteorologia e Climatologia. Colonia de Cabo Verde
Meteorologia Corresp — Meteorologia Por Correspondencia
Meteorologia Hidrol — Meteorologia si Hidrologia
Meteorologia Hidrol Gospod Apel — Meteorologia, Hidrologia si Gospodarinea Apelar
Meteorologia Prat — Meteorologia Pratica
Meteorology Aust — Meteorology of Australia
Meteorology Bombay Presid — Meteorology of the Bombay Presidency
Meteorology Circ Un Air Lines — Meteorology Circular. United Air Lines
Meteorology Hydrol — Meteorology and Hydrology
Meteorology Mysore — Meteorology in Mysore
Meteorology Nott — Meteorology of Nottingham
Meteorology NZ — Meteorology of New Zealand
Meteorology Shrops — Meteorology of Shropshire
Meteoroloji Rasatl — Meteoroloji Rasatlari
Meteoroloji Sism Mikn Rasatl — Meteoroloji, Sismoloji ve Miknati Rasatlari
Meteoroloji Sism Rasatl — Meteoroloji ve Sismoloji Rasatlari
Meteorol Rundsch — Meteorologische Rundschau
Meteorol Soc Jpn J — Meteorological Society of Japan. Journal
Meteorol Stud — Meteorological Study
Meteorol Stud Meteorol Bur — Bureau of Meteorology. Meteorological Study
Meteorol Z — Meteorologische Zeitschrift
Meteorol Zpr — Meteorologicke Zpravy
Meteor Rund — Meteorologische Rundschau
MetErz — Metall und Erz
Met Erz Beil — Metall und Erz. Beilage
Met Ezheg Kostroma — Meteorologicheskii Ezhegodnik. Materialy po Izucheniyu Klimata Kostromskoi Gubernii (Kostroma)
Met Fabr News — Metal Fabricating News
Met Feljegyz — Meteorologiai Feljegyzesck
Met Finish — Metal Finishing
Met Finish Abstr — Metal Finishing Abstracts
Met Finish Assoc India Trans — Metal Finishers' Association of India. Transactions
Met Finishing Abstr — Metal Finishing Abstracts
Met Finish J — Metal Finishing Journal
Met Finish Pract — Metal Finishing Practice
Met Finish Sci — Metal Finishing Science
Met Form — Metal Forming
Met Form Drop Forger — Metal Forming, Incorporating the Drop Forger
Met Forum — Metals Forum
Met Gaz — Metals Gazette
Met Geoastrophys Abstr — Meteorological and Geoastrophysical Abstracts
Met Gidrol Nabl Transp Pakhtusov — Meteorologicheskiya i Gidrologicheskiya Nablyudeniya, Proizvedennyya na Transporte Pakhtusov
Met Godis Beogr — Meteoroloski Godisnjak. Hidrometeoroloska Sluzba
Met God Sof — Meteorologichen Godishnik. Tsentralen Meteorologichen Institut (Sofiya)
MetH — Mediaevalia et Humanistica
MetH — Methodist History
Meth — Methodos
Meth Appar Bur Int Etal Phys Chim — Methodes et Appareils en Usage au Bureau International des Etalons Physico-Chimiques
Meth Biochem Analysis — Methods of Biochemical Analysis
Meth Cancer Res — Methods in Cancer Research
Meth Enzym — Methods in Enzymology
Meth Feder Social Serv Social Serv Bul — Methodist Federation for Social Service. Social Service Bulletin
Meth Geomath — Methods in Geomathematics
MethH — Methodist History
Meth Inf Med — Methods of Information in Medicine
ME Th K — Magazine fuer Evangelische Theologie und Kirche
Meth M — Methodist Magazine
Meth Mag — Methodist Magazine
Meth Med Res — Methods in Medical Research
Meth Membrane Biol — Methods in Membrane Biology
Meth Mol Biol — Methods in Molecular Biology
Method Appraisal Phys Sci — Method and Appraisal in the Physical Sciences
Method Chim — Methodicum Chimicum
Methode Mes CRR — Methode de Mesure CRR (Centre de Recherches Routieres, Brussels)
Methoden Verfahren Math Phys — Methoden und Verfahren der Mathematischen Physik
Methodes Math Inform — Methodes Mathematiques de l'Informatique
Methodes Math Ingr — Methodes Mathematiques pour l'Ingenieur
Methodes Phys Anal — Methodes Physiques d'Analyse
Methodes Prat Ingen — Methodes et Pratiques de l'Ingenieur
Method Fortschr Med Lab — Methodische Fortschritte im Medizinischen Laboratorium
Method Inf Med — Methodik der Information in der Medizin
Methodist Hosp Dallas Med Staff Bull — Methodist Hospital of Dallas. Medical Staff. Bulletin

Methodist Period Index — Methodist Periodical Index
Methodol Dev Biochem — Methodological Developments in Biochemistry
Methodol Sci — Methodology and Science
Methodol Surv — Methodological Surveys
Methodol Surv Bioanal Drugs — Methodological Surveys in Bioanalysis of Drugs
Methodol Surv Biochem — Methodological Surveys in Biochemistry
Methodol Surv Biochem Anal — Methodological Surveys in Biochemistry and Analysis
Methodol Surv Sub Ser A — Methodological Surveys. Sub-series A. Trace-Organic Analysis
Methodol Surv Sub Ser B — Methodological Surveys. Sub-series B. Biochemistry
Method Phys Anal — Methodes Physiques d'Analyse
Methods Achiev Exp Pathol — Methods and Achievements in Experimental Pathology
Methods Anim Exp — Methods of Animal Experimentation
Methods Appl Anal — Methods and Applications of Analysis
Methods Biochem Anal — Methods of Biochemical Analysis
Methods Biotechnol — Methods in Biotechnology
Methods Cancer Res — Methods in Cancer Research
Methods Carbohydr Chem — Methods in Carbohydrate Chemistry
Methods Cell Biol — Methods in Cell Biology
Methods Cell Physiol — Methods in Cell Physiology
Methods Cell Sci — Methods in Cell Science
Methods Cell Sep — Methods of Cell Separation
Methods Chromatogr — Methods in Chromatography
Method Sci — Methodology and Science
Methods Clin Pharmacol — Methods in Clinical Pharmacology
Methods Comput Chem — Methods in Computational Chemistry
Methods Comput Phys — Methods in Computational Physics. Advances in Research and Applications
Methods Diabetes Res — Methods in Diabetes Research
Methods Elem Org Chem — Methods of Elemento-Organic Chemistry
Methods Enzymol — Methods in Enzymology
Methods Exam Waters Assoc Mater — Methods for the Examination of Waters and Associated Materials
Methods Experiment Phys — Methods of Experimental Physics
Methods Exp Phys — Methods of Experimental Physics
Methods Find Exp Clin Pharmacol — Methods and Findings in Experimental and Clinical Pharmacology
Methods Forensic Sci — Methods of Forensic Science
Methods Free Radical Chem — Methods in Free Radical Chemistry
Methods Funct Anal Topology — Methods of Functional Analysis and Topology
Methods Geochem Geophys — Methods in Geochemistry and Geophysics
Methods Hematol — Methods in Hematology
Methods Horm Radioimmunoassay — Methods of Hormone Radioimmunoassay [*monograph*]
Methods Horm Res — Methods in Hormone Research
Methods Immunol Immunochem — Methods in Immunology and Immunochemistry
Methods Inf Med — Methods of Information in Medicine
Methods Inf Med (Suppl) — Methods of Information in Medicine (Supplement)
Methods Invest Diagn Endocrinol — Methods in Investigative and Diagnostic Endocrinology
Methods Lab Med — Methods in Laboratory Medicine
Methods Mech Prod Ions Large Mol — Methods and Mechanisms for Producing Ions from Large Molecules
Methods Med Res — Methods in Medical Research
Methods Membr Biol — Methods in Membrane Biology
Methods Microbiol — Methods in Microbiology
Methods Mod Biom — Methods of Modern Biometrics
Methods Mod Math Phys — Methods of Modern Mathematical Physics
Methods Mol Biol — Methods in Molecular Biology
Methods Mol Biol Totowa NJ — Methods in Molecular Biology (Totowa, New Jersey)
Methods Mol Cell Biol — Methods in Molecular and Cellular Biology
Methods Mol Med — Methods in Molecular Medicine
Methods Mycoplasmol — Methods in Mycoplasmology
Methods Neurochem — Methods of Neurochemistry
Methods Neurosci — Methods in Neurosciences
Methods Oper Res — Methods of Operations Research
Methods Pharmacol — Methods in Pharmacology
Methods Phenom Their Appl Sci Technol — Methods and Phenomena. Their Applications in Science and Technology
Methods Physiol Psychol — Methods in Physiological Psychology
Methods Physiol Ser — Methods in Physiology Series
Methods Princ Med Chem — Methods and Principles in Medicinal Chemistry
Methods Psychobiol — Methods in Psychobiology
Methods Stereochem Anal — Methods in Stereochemical Analysis
Methods Subnucl Phys — Methods in Subnuclear Physics
Methods Surf Charact — Methods of Surface Characterization
Methods Virol — Methods in Virology
Meth Per Ind — Methodist Periodical Index
Meth Probl Med Educ — Methods and Problems of Medical Education
Meth Q — Methodist Quarterly
Meth Q R — Methodist Quarterly Review
Meth Quar Rev — Methodist Quarterly Review
Meth R — Methodist Review
Meth Rec — Methodist Recorder
Meth Rev — Methodist Review
Meth Virol — Methods in Virology
METI — Metis
METIA — Medical Times
Met Iakttag Abisko — Meteorologiska Iakttagelser i Abisko
Met Iakttag Riksgransen — Meteorologiska Iakttagelser i Riksgransen
Met Iakttag Sver — Meteorologiska Iakttagelser i Sverige
Met Ind — Metaux et Industries

Met Ind (China) — Metal Industries (China)
Met Ind (Johannesburg) — Metal Industries (Johannesburg)
Met Ind Kaohsing Taiwan — Metal Industries (Kaohsing, Taiwan)
Met Ind (London) — Metal Industry (London)
Met Ind London Suppl — Metal Industry (London). Supplement
Met Ind Rev — Metal Industries Review
Met Inf Med — Methods of Information in Medicine
Met Intez Tudom Kozl — Meteorologiai Intezetenek Tudomanyos Kozlemenyei
Met Ions Biol — Metal Ions in Biology
Met Ions Biol Med Proc Int Symp — Metal Ions in Biology and Medicine. Proceedings. International Symposium on Metal Ions in Biology and Medicine
Met Ions Biol Syst — Metal Ions in Biological Systems
Met Isvj Zagr — Meteoroloski Isvjestaj. Geofizicki Institut (Zagreb)
Met Ital — Metallurgia Italiana
Met Izv Akad Nauk SSSR — Metally Izvestiya Akademi Nauk SSSR
Met Jaarb — Meteorologisch Jaarboek
Met Jb Eesti — Meteorologisches Jahrbuch fuer Eesti
Met Jb Finnl — Meteorologisches Jahrbuch fuer Finnland
Met J Univ Strathclyde Glasgow — Metallurgical Journal. University of Strathclyde, Glasgow
Met Konstr Ispyt Sooruzh — Metallicheskie Konstruktsii i Ispytaniya Sooruzhenii
Metl Bul M — Metal Bulletin Monthly
Met Leggeri Loro Appl — Metalli Leggeri e Loro Applicazioni
Met Life Stat Bull — Metropolitan Life Insurance Company. Statistical Bulletin
Metl Ind N — Metals Industry News
Met Lyonn — Meteorologie Lyonnaise
MET M — Metropolitan Magazine
Met Mach — Metaux et Machines
Met Mag (Lond) — Meteorological Magazine (London)
Met Mag Nanking — Meteorological Magazine (Nanking)
Met Magn Pozor — Meteorologicka a Magneticka Pozorovani
Met Magn Table Rep Falmouth Obs — Meteorological and Magnetical Table and Reports. Falmouth Observatory
Met Mark Place Met Congr — Metals in the Market Place. Metals Congress
Met Mark Rev — Metal Market Review
Met Mater — Metals and Materials
Met Mater (Bratislava) — Metallic Materials (Bratislava)
Met Mater Inst Met — Metals and Materials. Institute of Metals
Met Mater Manuf Pap Annu Conf Australas Inst Met — Metals Materials Manufacturing. Papers Presented. Annual Conference. Australasian Institute of Metals
Met Mater Met Soc — Metals and Materials (Metals Society)
Met Mater Processes — Metals, Materials, and Processes
Met Mater Seoul — Metals and Materials (Seoul)
Met/Mater Today — Metals/Materials Today
Met Mber Zagreb — Meteorologischer Monatsbericht (Zagreb)
Met Mber Zuerich — Meteorologischer Monatsbericht (Zuerich)
METMD — Metamedicine
Met Memo Nav Intell Brch — Meteorological Memoranda. Naval Intelligence Branch [London]
Met Mem Peking — Meteorological Memoirs (Peking)
Met Miner Mark — Metal and Mineral Markets
Met Miner Process — Metals and Minerals Processing
Met Miner Rev — Metals and Minerals Review
Met Miner Rev (Calcutta) — Metals and Minerals Review (Calcutta)
Met Monogr — Meteorological Monographs. American Meteorological Society
Met Mus Bul — Metropolitan Museum of Art. Bulletin
Met Mus Bull — Metropolitan Museum of Art. Bulletin
Met Mus J — Metropolitan Museum. Journal
Met Mus Stud — Metropolitan Museum Studies
Met Nabl Enis Gub — Meteorologicheskiya Nablyudeniya Eniseiskoi Gubernii
Met Nabl Sta Inst Sel Khoz Lesov Nov Aleks — Meteorologicheskiya Nablyudeniya, Proizvedennyya na Stanstii Instituta Sel'skago Khozyaistva i Lesovodstva v Novoi Aleksandrii
Met News (India) — Metal News (India)
Met No Ferreos — Metales No Ferreos
Met Note Aust Aeronaut Res Lab — Australia. Aeronautical Research Laboratories. Metallurgy Note
Met Notes Israel — Meteorological Notes. Meteorological Service. State of Israel
Met Notes Kyoto Univ — Meteorological Notes. Meteorological Research Institute. Kyoto University
Met Notes Loyola Univ — Meteorological Notes. Loyola University
Met Notes Nigeria — Meteorological Notes. Nigeria
Met Notes Rhod Nyasald — Meteorological Notes. Department of Meteorological Services. Rhodesia and Nyasaland
Met Notes Tabl Falmouth — Meteorological Notes and Tables. Falmouth Observatory
Met Obozr Evr Ross — Meteorologicheskoe Obozrenie Evropeiskoi Rossii
Met Obozr Glav Fiz Obs — Meteorologicheskoe Obozrenie. Izd. Glavnoi Fizicheskoi Observatorii
Met Obozr Odessa — Meteorologicheskoe Obozrenie. Trudy Meteorologicheskoi seti Yugozapada Rossii (Odessa)
Met Obsns Adelaide Obs — Meteorological Observations made at the Adelaide Observatory
Met Obsns Amman — Meteorological Observations at Amman
Met Obsns Antigua — Meteorological Observations. Antigua
Met Obsns Ascension Isl — Meteorological Observations at Ascension Island
Met Obsns Bahama Isl — Meteorological Observations. Bahama Islands
Met Obsns Barbados — Meteorological Observations. Barbados
Met Obsns Basutoland — Meteorological Observations. Basutoland
Met Obsns Bathurst — Meteorological Observations Taken at Bathurst, Gambia
Met Obsns Bechuanald — Meteorological Observations. Bechuanaland
Met Obsns Bermuda — Meteorological Observations. Bermuda
Met Obsns Br Caribb — Meteorological Observations. British Caribbean Meteorological Service

Met Obsns Br E Afr — Meteorological Observations. British East Africa
Met Obsns Br Guiana — Meteorological Observations. British Guiana
Met Obsns Br Hond — Meteorological Observations. British Honduras
Met Obsns Cairo — Meteorological Observations. Cairo
Met Obsns Carriacoa Obs — Meteorological Observations. Carriacoa Observatory. Grenada
Met Obsns Cent Met Stn Kaunas — Meteorological Observations at the Central Meteorological Station. Kaunas
Met Obsns Ceylon — Meteorological Observations in Ceylon
Met Obsns Clim Summ R Alfred Obs Maurit — Meteorological Observations and Climatological Summaries. Royal Alfred Observatory. Mauritius
Met Obsns Cumberland Bay — Meteorological Observations taken at Cumberland Bay, South Georgia
Met Obsns Cyprus — Meteorological Observations. Cyprus
Met Obsns Falkland Isl — Meteorological Observations. Falkland Islands
Met Obsns Fanning Isl — Meteorological Observations at Fanning Island
Met Obsns Fiji — Meteorological Observations. Fiji
Met Obsns FMS — Meteorological Observations. Federated Malay States
Met Obsns Funafuti — Meteorological Observations at Funafuti, Ellice Islands
Met Obsns Gambia — Meteorological Observations. Gambia Colony
Met Obsns Gibraltar — Meteorological Observations. Gibraltar
Met Obsns Gold Cst — Meteorological Observations. Gold Coast
Met Obsns Govt Obs Wellington — Meteorological Observations. Government Observatory (Welllington)
Met Obsns Grenada — Meteorological Observations. Grenada
Met Obsns Guernsey — Meteorological Observations. Guernsey
Met Obsns Hongkong Obs — Meteorological Observations. Hongkong Observatory
Met Obsns Jamaica — Meteorological Observations. Jamaica
Met Obsns Leeward Isl — Meteorological Observations. Leeward Islands
Met Obsns Malta — Meteorological Observations. Malta
Met Obsns Manila — Meteorological Observations. Manila
Met Obsns Maurit — Meteorological Observations. Mauritius
Met Obsns Milit Hosp Freetown — Meteorological Observations. Military Hospital. Freetown
Met Obsns Nigeria — Meteorological Observations. Nigeria
Met Obsns Nth Rhod — Meteorological Observations. Northern Rhodesia
Met Obsns Nyasald — Meteorological Observations. Nyasaland Protectorate
Met Obsns NZ — Meteorological Observations in New Zealand
Met Obsns Ocean Isl — Meteorological Observations at Ocean Island
Met Obsns Off Met Stn Davos — Meteorological Observations. Official Meteorological Station. Davos
Met Obsns Palest — Meteorological Observations. Palestine
Met Obsns Palest Transjordan — Meteorological Observations. Palestine and Transjordan
Met Obsns Perth Obs — Meteorological Observations made at the Perth Observatory. Western Australia
Met Obsns Rep Br Colon — Meteorological Observations, Reports, etc., made in British Colonies and Protectorates
Met Obsns Singapore — Meteorological Observations. Singapore
Met Obsns Somalild — Meteorological Observations. Somaliland
Met Obsns St Clari Exp Stn — Meteorological Observations. Saint Clair Experiment Station [Port of Spain]
Met Obsns St Helena — Meteorological Observations. Saint Helena
Met Obsns Sth Rhod — Meteorological Observations. Southern Rhodesia
Met Obsns St Lucia — Meteorological Observations. Saint Lucia
Met Obsns St Met Bur Riga — Meteorological Observations. State Meteorological Bureau (Riga)
Met Obsns Stns Second Order — Meteorological Observations at Stations of the Second Order [London]
Met Obsns St Vincent — Meteorological Observations. Saint Vincent
Met Obsns St Xaviers Coll — Meteorological Observations. St. Xavier's College. Calcutta
Met Obsns Suva — Meteorological Observations taken at Suva
Met Obsns Swazild — Meteorologial Observations. Swaziland
Met Obsns Tanganyika — Meteorological Observations. Tanganyika Territory
Met Obsns Totland Bay — Meteorological Observations. Totland Bay [Isle of Wight]
Met Obsns Trin — Meteorological Observations. Trinidad
Met Obsns Uganda — Meteorological Observations. Uganda
Met Obsns Wellington — Meteorological Observations. Wellington, N.Z
Met Obsns Welsh Pl Breed Stn Aberystwyth — Meteorological Observations Made at the Welsh Plant Breeding Station. Aberystwyth
Met Obsns Zanzibar — Meteorological Observations. Zanzibar Sultanate
Met Obsns ZikaWei — Meteorological Observations. Zi-ka-Wei
Met Obsns Zomba — Meteorological Observations. Zomba
Met Obsrs Handb — Meteorological Observer's Handbook
Met Oceanogr Waarn Ned Lichtschepp Noordzee — Meteorologische en Oceanografische Waarnemingen verricht aan board van Nederlandse Lichtscheppen in de Noordzee
Metod Fiziol Issled I P Pavlova — Metodiki Fiziologicheskikh Issledovanii Akademika I. P. Pavlova i ego Shkoly
Metodi Anal Acque — Metodi Analitici per le Acque
Metod Mater Inst Mineral Geokhim Kristallokhim Redk Elem Aka — Metodicheskie Materialy. Institut Mineralogii. Geokhimii i Kristallokhimii Redkikh Elementov. Akademiya Nauk SSSR
Metod Mater Nauchn Soobshch — Metodicheskie Materialy i Nauchnye Soobshcheniya
Metod Mater Nauchn Soobshch Vses Nauchno Issled Inst Zhelezno — Metodicheskie Materialy i Nauchnye Soobshcheniya. Vsesoyuznyi Nauchno-Issledovatel'skii Institut Zheleznodorozhnoi Gigieny
Metodol Probl Nauki — Metodologiceskie Problemy Nauki
Metodol Sots Probl Tekh Tekh Nauk — Metodologicheskie i Sotsial'nye Problemy Tekhniki i Tekhnicheskikh Nauk
Metod Prepod Inostr Yazykov Vuze — Metodika Prepodavaniya Inostrannykh Yazykov v Vuze

Metod Prepod Khim — Metodika Prepodavaniya Khimii
Metod Prirucky Exp Bot — Metodicke Prirucky Experimentalni Botaniky
Metod Tekh Razved — Metodika i Tekhnika Razvedki
Metod Ukazaniya Geol S'emke Masshtaba 1:50000 — Metodicheskie Ukazaniya po Geologicheskoi S'emke Masshtaba 1:50,000
Metod Vopr Nauki — Metodologiceskie Voprosy Nauki
Metody Anal Khim Reakt Prep — Metody Analiza Khimicheskikh Reaktivov i Preparatov
Metody Anal Kontrolya Kach Prod Khim Promsti — Metody Analiza i Kontrolya Kachestva Produktsii v Khimicheskoi Promyshlennosti
Metody Anal Kontrolya Proizvod Khim Promsti — Metody Analiza i Kontrolya Proizvodstva v Khimicheskoi Promyshlennosti
Metody Anal Org Soedin Nefti Ikh Smesei Proizvodnykh — Metody Analiza Organicheskikh Soedinenii Nefti Ikh Smesei i Proizvodnykh
Metody Anal Org Soedin Neft Ikh Smesei Proizvodnykh — Metody Analiza Organicheskikh Soedinenii Nefti Ikh Smesei i Proizvodnykh
Metody Anal Redkomet Miner Rud Gorn Porod — Metody Analiza Redkometal'nykh Mineralov Rud i Gornykh Porod
Metody Anal Veshchestv Osoboi Chist Monokrist — Metody Analiza Veshchestv Osoboi Chistoty i Monokristallov
Metody Diskret Anal — Metody Diskretnogo Analiza
Metody Diskret Analiz — Metody Diskretnogo Analiza
Metody Eksp Bot — Metody Eksperimental'noi Botaniki
Metody Ispyt Detalei Mash Prib — Metody Ispytanii Detalei Mashin i Priborov
Metody Issled Katal Katal Reakts — Metody Issledovaniya Katalizatorov i Kataliticheskikh Reaktsii
Metody Issled Vinodel — Metody Issledovaniya v Vinodelii
Metody Izuch Veshchestv Sostava i Ikh Primen — Metody Izucheniya Veshchestvennogo Sostava i Ikh Primenenie
Metody Khim Anal Miner Syr'ya — Metody Khimicheskogo Analiza Mineral'nogo Syr'ya
Metody Kompleksn Izuch Fotosint — Metody Kompleksnogo Izucheniya Fotosinteza
Metody Lyumin Anal Mater Soveshch — Metody Lyuminestsentnogo Analiza. Materialy Soveshchaniya poLyuminestsentsii
Metody Opred Absol Vozrasta Geol Obraz — Metody Opredeleniya Absolyutnogo Vozrasta Geologicheskikh Obrazovanii
Metody Opred Issled Sostoyaniya Gazov Met Dokl Vses Simp — Metody Opredeleniya i Issledovaniya Sostoyaniya Gazov v Metallakh.Doklady na Vsesoyuznom Simpoziume po Metodam Analiza Gazov v Metallakh
Metody Opred Issled Sostoyaniya Gazov Met Vses Konf — Metody Opredeleniya i Issledovaniya Sostoyaniya Gazov v Metallakh.Vsesoyuznaya Konferentsiya
Metody Opred Pestits Vode — Metody Opredeleniya Pestitsidov v Vode
Metody Paleogeogr Issled — Metody Paleogeograficheskikh Issledovanii
Metody Pochody Chem Technol — Metody a Pochody Chemicke Technologie
Metody Poluch Khim Reak Prep — Metody Polucheniya Khimicheskikh Reaktivov i Preparatov
Metody Prib Anal Sostava Veshchestva — Metody i Pribory dlya Analiza Sostava Veshchestva
Metody Prib Avtom Nerazrushayushchego Kontrolya — Metody i Pribory Avtomaticheskogo Nerazrushayushchego Kontrolya
Metody Probl Ekotoksikol Model Prognozirovaniya Mater Vses — Metody i Problemy Ekotoksikologicheskogo Modelirovaniya iPrognozirovaniya. Materialy Vsesoyuznogo Rabochego Soveshchaniya poMezhdunarodnoi Programme YUNESKO Chelovek i Biosfera
Metody Protsessy Khim Tekhnol — Metody i Protsessy Khimicheskoi Tekhnologii
Metody Prots Khim Tekhnol — Metody i Protsessy Khimicheskoi Tekhnologii
Metody Razved Geofiz — Metody Razvedochnoi Geofiziki
Metody Rudn Geofiz — Metody Rudnoi Geofiziki
Metody Sredstva Issled Mater Konstr Rab Vozdeistv Radiats — Metody i Sredstva Issledovaniya Materialov i Konstruktsii.Rabotayushchikh pod Vozdeistviem Radiatsii
Metody Vychisl — Leningradskii Ordena Lenina Gosudarstvennyi Imeni A. A. Zhdanova Metody Vychislenii
Metody Vycisl — Metody Vycislenii
Metod Zavadeni Vysledku Vyzk Praxe — Metodiky pro Zavadeni Vysledku Vyzkumu do Praxe
Metod Zavadeni Vysledku Vyzk Zemed Praxe — Metodiky pro Zavadeni Vysledku Vyzkumu do Zemedelske Praxe
Metod Zavad Vysled Vyzk Praxe — Metodiky pro Zavadeni Vysledku Vyzkumu do Praxe
Met Off Circ — Meteorological Office Circular
Met Off Note NZ — Meteorological Office Note. New Zealand Meteorological Service
Met Papers — Metropolitan Papers
Met Pap Lond — Meteorological Papers. Meteorological Office (London)
Met Pap MIT — Meteorological Papers. Massachusetts Institute of Technology
Met Pap NY Univ — Meteorological Papers. New York University College of Engineering
Met Perform Reliab Issues VLSI ULSI — Metallization. Performance and Reliability Issues for VLSI and ULSI
Met Phys — Metal Physics
Met Phys Lect Inst Metall Refresher Course — Metal Physics. Lectures Delivered at the Institution of Metallurgists RefresherCourse
Met Phys Semin — Metal Physics Seminar
Met Plast — Metallized Plastics. Fundamental and Applied Aspects
Met Powder Rep — Metal Powder Report
Met Prod Manuf — Metal Products Manufacturing
Met Prog — Metal Progress
Met Prog Datab — Metal Progress Databook
Met Prop Counc Publ — Metal Properties Council. Publication
Metr — Metropolis
M Etr — Monumenti Etruschi
Met Radar Stud — Meteorological Radar Studies. Blue Hill Meteorological Observatory. Harvard University

Met Rdsch — Meteorologische Rundschau
Met Read New Guinea — Meteorological Readings. New Guinea
Met Rec Br E Afr — Meteorological Records. British East Africa
Met Rec Electroplat — Metal Records and Electroplater
Met Rec Malta — Meteorological Records. Malta
Met Rec R Met Soc — Meteorological Record of the Royal Meteorological Society [London]
Met Register Govt Lab Antigua — Meteorological Register kept at the Government Laboratory. St. Johns, Antigua
Met Register McCarthy Isl — Meteorological Register. McCarthy Island, Gambia
Met Register Rainf Returns Dominica — Meteorological Register and Rainfall Returns for the Botanic Gardens. Dominica
Met Reinig Vorbehandl — Metall-Reinigung und Vorbehandlung
Met Reinig Vorbehandl Oberflaechentech Form — Metall-Reinigung, Vorbehandlung, Oberflaechentechnik, Formung
Met Rep Barbados — Meteorological Report. Barbados
Met Rep Cairo — Meteorological Report. Cairo
Met Rep Colombo Obs — Meteorological Report. Colombo Observatory
Met Rep Dover — Meteorological Report. Dover
Met Rep Fiji — Meteorological Report. Fiji
Met Rep Lond — Meteorological Report. London
Met Rep Nat Hist Soc Northampton — Meteorological Report. Natural History Society. Northampton
Met Rep Nth Rhod — Meteorological Report. Northern Rhodesia
Met Rep Perth — Meteorological Report. Perth, W.A
Met Rep Richmond Hill Obs Grenada — Meteorological Report. Richmond Hill Observatory. Grenada
Met Rep Sth Rhod — Meteorological Report. Southern Rhodesia
Met Rep Teignmouth — Meteorological Report. Teignmouth
Met Rep Torquay — Meteorological Report. Torquay
Met Rep Wellington — Meteorological Report. Wellington. N.Z
Met Results R Obs Hong Kong — Meteorological Results. Royal Observatory. Hong Kong
Met Returns Basutold — Meteorological Returns. Basutoland
Met Returns Br N Borneo — Meteorological Returns. British North Borneo
Met Returns R Bot Gdns Trin — Meteorological Returns. Royal Botanic Gardens. Trinidad
Met Returns Surv Dep Nigeria — Meteorological Returns. Survey Department. Nigeria
Met Rev — Metals Review
Met Rev Cent Geophys Obs Leningr — Meteorological Review. Central Geophysical Observatory (Leningrad)
Met Rev (Suppl Metals Mater) — Metallurgical Reviews (Supplement to Metals and Materials)
Metric Bul — Metric Bulletin
Metric Info — Metric Information
Metr Mus J — Metropolitan Museum. Journal
Metr Mus Stud — Metropolitan Museum Studies
Metr Mus Studies — Metropolitan Museum Studies
Metro — Metronome
Metroecon — Metroeconomica
Metrohm Bull — Metrohm Bulletin
Metrol — Metrologia
Metrol Apl — Metrologia Aplicata
Metrol Insp — Metrology and Inspection
Metrol Poverochn Delo — Metrologiya i Poverochnoe Delo
Metrol Script — Metrologicorum Scriptorum Reliquiae
Metrol Tekhnol Issled Kach Poverkhn — Metrologicheskie i Tekhnologicheskie Issledovaniya KachestvaPoverkhnosti
Metronidazole Proc Int Symp Metronidazole — Metronidazole. Proceedings. International Symposium on Metronidazole
Metron Int Rev Statist — Metron. International Review of Statistics
Metrop — Metropolitan
Metrop Detroit Sci Rev — Metropolitan Detroit Science Review
Metrop Mus — Metropolitan Museum of Art. Bulletin
Metropolitan Life Insur Co Stat Bul — Metropolitan Life Insurance Company. Statistical Bulletin
Metropolitan Life Stat Bul — Metropolitan Life Insurance Company. Statistical Bulletin
Metropolitan Life Statis Bul — Metropolitan Life Insurance Company. Statistical Bulletin
Metropolitan Toronto Bd Trade J — Metropolitan Toronto Board of Trade. Journal
Metropolitan Toronto Bus J — Metropolitan Toronto Business Journal
Metropol M — Metropolitan Magazine
Metrop Vickers Gaz — Metropolitan-Vickers Gazette
Metrop Vickers Res Ser — Metropolitan-Vickers Research Series
Metrop Wat — Metropolitan Water [London]
Metrosect Accel — Metrosection Accelerator. Society of Automotive Engineers [New York]
METS — Monographs. Evangelical Theological Society
Metsanduse Tead Uurim Lab Metsandusl Uurim — Metsanduse Teadusliku Uurimise Laboratoorium. Metsanduslikud Uurimused
Metsanduslik Uurim — Metsanduslikud Uurimused
Metsand Uurim — Metsandustikud Uurimused. Zoologia ja Botanika Instituut
Metsantutkimuslaitoksen Julk — Metsantutkimuslaitoksen Julkaisuja
Metsatal Aikakausl — Metsataloudellinen Aikakauslehti
Metsataloud Aikak — Metsataloudellinen Aikakauslehti
Metsatehon Tied — Metsatehon Tiedoituksia
Metsatieteellisen Koelaitoken Julk — Metsatieteellisen Koelaitoken Julkaisuja
Metsatieteellisen Tutkimuslaitoksen Julk — Metsatieteellisen Tutkimuslaitoksen Julkaisuja
Metsatiet Tutkimuslait Julk — Metsatieteellisen Tutkimuslaitoksen Julkaisuja
METSC — Metal Science
Met Sci — Metal Science
Met Sci and Heat Treat — Metal Science and Heat Treatment

Met Sci Heat Treat — Metal Science and Heat Treatment
Met Sci Heat Treat Met — Metal Science and Heat Treatment of Metals
Met Sci Heat Treat Met (Engl Transl) — Metal Science and Heat Treatment of Metals (English Translation)
Met Sci Heat Treat Met (USSR) — Metal Science and Heat Treatment of Metals (USSR)
Met Sci Heat Treat (USSR) — Metal Science and Heat Treatment (USSR)
Met Sci J — Metal Science Journal [*Later, Metal Science*]
Met Sel Khoz Byull Pridnepr Met Seti — Meteorologicheskii I Sel'sko-Khozyaistvennyi Byulleten' Pridneprovskoi Meteorologicheskoi Seti
Met Serv Israel — Meteorological Service. Israel
Metsniereba Tekh — Metsniereba da Tekhnika
Met Soc AIME Conf — Metallurgical Society. American Institute of Mining, Metallurgical, and Petroleum Engineers. Conferences
Met Soc AIME Inst Metals Div Spec Rep — Metallurgical Society. American Institute of Mining, Metallurgical, and Petroleum Engineers. Institute of Metals Division. Special Report
Met Soc AIME TMS Pap — Metallurgical Society. American Institute of Mining, Metallurgical, and Petroleum Engineers. TMS Papers
Met Soc Book — Metals Society Book
Met Soc World — Metals Society World
Met Space Age Plansee Proc Pap Plansee Semin De Re Met — Metals for the Space Age. Plansee Proceedings. Papers Presented at thePlansee Seminar. De Re Metallica
Met S QJ — Quarterly Journal of the Royal Meteorological Society
Met Stamp — Metal Stamping
Met Statist St Lucia — Meteorological Statistics. Saint Lucia
Met Study Bur Met — Bureau of Meteorology. Meteorological Study
Met Summ Apia Obs — Meteorological Summary. Apia Observatory. Western Samoa
Met Summary Met Bur — Bureau of Meteorology. Meteorological Summary
Met Summ Cyprus — Meteorological Summary of Cyprus
Met Summ Mon Clim Bull Aust — Meteorological Summary. Monthly Climatological Bulletin. Bureau of Meteorology. Australia
Met Summ Mon Clim Rec Melb — Meteorological Summary. Monthly Climatological Records. Melbourne
Met Summ Monsoon Period — Meteorological Summary of the Monsoon Period
Met Summ Mon Statist Summ Melb — Meteorological Summary. Monthly Statistical Summary [*Melbourne*]
Met Summ Rainf Montserrat — Meteorological Summary and Rainfall. Montserrat
Met Summ Select Clim Stns Melb — Meteorological Summary for Selected Climatological Stations [*Melbourne*]
Met Summs Geneva Airport — Meteorological Summaries of Geneva Airport
Met Summs Palest — Meteorological Summaries. Palestine
Met Summs Rhod Nyasald — Meteorological Summaries. Rhodesia and Nyasaland Meteorological Service
Met Summs Suriname — Meteorological Summaries. Suriname
Met Summs Zurich Airport — Meteorological Summaries of Zurich Airport
Met Summ Tonga — Meteorological Summary. Tonga
Met Synopsis Univ Calif Stud Obs — Meteorological Synopsis of University of California Students' Observatory
Met Tabl Falkland Isl — Meteorological Tables. Falkland Islands and Dependencies Meteorological Service
Met Tech Inf — Metokika a Technika Informaci
Met Technol — Metals Technology
Met Technol (Jpn) — Metals and Technology (Japan)
Met Technol (London) — Metals Technology. Institute of Metals (London)
Met Technol (NY) — Metals Technology (New York)
Met Technol (Tokyo) — Metals and Technology (Tokyo)
Met Trans — Metallurgical Transactions
Met Transl — Meteorological Translations. Division of Meteorological Services. Air Services Branch. Department of Transport. Canada
Met Treat — Metal Treating
Met Treat Drop Forg — Metal Treatment and Drop Forging
Met Treat (London) — Metal Treatment (London)
Met Treat (Rocky Mount NC) — Metal Treating (Rocky Mount, North Carolina)
Met Tr J — Metal Trades Journal
METU Faculty of Archre Occasional Paper Series — METU [*Middle East Technical University*] Faculty of Architecture. Occasional Paper Series
METU J Pure Appl Sci — Middle East Technical University. Journal of Pure and Applied Sciences
METU Studies Develop — Middle East Technical University. Studies in Development
Met Vest — Meteorologicheskii Vestnik. Izd. Russkim Geograficheskim Obshchestvom i Glavnym Gidrograficheskim Upravleniem. Petrograd
Met Vodom Nabl G Galiche — Meteorologicheskiya i Vodomernyya Nablyudeniya v g. Galiche i na Galichskom Ozere
Met Waarn Dep Landb Suriname — Meteorologische Waarnemingen. Department van Landbouw. Suriname
Met Waarnem Met Stns Suriname Curac — Meteorologische Waarnemingen gedaan op de Meteorologische Stations in de Kolonien Suriname en Curacao
Met Week — Metals Week
Met Woche — Metall Woche
Met Work Press — Metal Working Press
Metwork Prod — Metalworking Production
Met Yb Tehran — Meteorological Yearbook. Iranian Meteorological Department (Tehran)
Met Z — Meteorologische Zeitschrift
Metz Ac Mm — Memoires de l'Academie Royale, Imperiale de Metz
Met Zb Ljubl — Meteoroloski Zbornik. Drustvo Meteorologov Slovenije (Ljubljana)
Metz Mm Ac — Memoires de l'Academie Royale, Imperiale de Metz
Met Zpr — Meteorologicke Zprava
MEUBAR — Ehime Daigaku Kiyo Shizenkagaku. B. Shirizu Seibutsugaku
Meunerie Franc — La Meunerie Francaise
Meun Fr — Meunerie Francaise

MEUP — Member's Update. Canadian Arctic Resources Committee
MEWEA — Medizinische Welt
MEWOA — Medical World
MEX — Marketing in Europe
Mex Agr — Mexico Agricola
Mex Am R — Mexican-American Review [*Later, Mex-Am Review*]
Mex Art Life Mex — Mexican Art and Life (Mexico)
Mex BI Gg — Boletin del Instituto Nacional de la Sociedad Mexicana de Geografia y Estadistica de la Republica Mexicana
Mex Bosques — Mexico y Sus Bosques
Mex Com Dir Invest Recur Miner Bol — Mexico. Comite Directivo para la Investigacion de los Recursos Minerales. Boletin
Mex Com Fom Min Bol — Mexico. Comision de Fomento Minero. Boletin
Mex Cons Rec Nat No Ren Sem Int Anu Expl Geol Min Mem — Mexico. Consejo de Recursos Naturales No Renovables. Seminario Interno Anual sobre Exploracion Geologico-Minera. Memoria
Mex Cons Recur Nat No Renov Bol — Mexico. Consejo de Recursos Naturales No Renovables. Boletin
Mex Cons Recur Nat No Renov Publ — Mexico. Consejo de Recursos Naturales No Renovables. Publicacion
Mex En Arte Mex — Mexico en el Arte (Mexico)
Mex Farm — Mexico Farmaceutico. Defensor de la Farmacia Mexicana
Mex Fin Rep — Mexican Financial Report
Mex Flkways — Mexican Folkways
Mex Folkways — Mexican Folkways
Mex For — Mexico Forestal
Mex Gg BI — Boletin del Instituto Nacional de la Sociedad Mexicana de Geografia y Estadistica de la Republica Mexicana
Mexicn Rev — Mexican-American Review [*Later, Mex-Am Review*]
Mexico Anales Inst Biologia — Mexico. Anales del Instituto de Biologia
Mexico & Cost — Mexico y sus Costumbres
Mexico Ant — Mexico Antiguo
Mexico Com Fomento Min Bol — Mexico. Comision de Fomento Minero. Boletin
Mexico Consejo Rec Naturales No Renovables Bol Pub — Mexico. Consejo de Recursos Naturales No Renovables. Boletin. Publicaciones
Mexico Escuela Nac Cienc Biol Anales — Mexico. Escuela Nacional de Ciencias Biologicas. Anales
Mexico Forest — Mexico Forestal. Sociedad Forestal Mexicana
Mexico Inst Nac Inv Rec Minerales Bol — Mexico. Instituto Nacional para la Investigacion de Recursos Minerales. Boletin
Mexico Q Rev — Mexico Quarterly Review
Mexico Univ Nac Autonoma Inst Geografia Bol — Mexico. Universidad Nacional Autonoma. Instituto de Geografia. Boletin
Mexico Univ Nac Autonoma Inst Geologia Bol — Mexico. Universidad Nacional Autonoma. Instituto de Geologia. Boletin
Mex I G — Mexico. Instituto Geologico
Mex Inst Nac Invest Recur Miner Bol — Mexico. Instituto Nacional para la Investigacion de Recursos Minerales. Boletin
Mex Marit — Mexico Maritimo
Mex Min Fomento An — Mexico. Ministerio de Fomento. Anales
Mex Min J — Mexican Mining Journal
Mex M J — Mexican Mining Journal
Mex Obs BI — Ministerio de Fomento de la Republica Mexicana. Boletin Mensual del Observatorio Meteorologico-Magnetico Central de Mexico
Mex S Alzate Mm — Memorias de la Sociedad Cientifica Antonio Alzate
Mex Sec Fomento Bol — Mexico. Secretaria de Fomento. Boletin
Mex Secr Agric Ganad Of Estud Espec Foll Divul — Mexico. Secretaria de Agricultura y Ganaderia. Oficina de Estudios Especiales. Folleto de Divulgacion
Mex Secr Agric Ganad Of Estud Espec Foll Misc — Mexico. Secretaria de Agricultura y Ganaderia. Oficina de Estudios Especiales. Folleto Miscelaneo
Mex Secr Agric Ganad Of Estud Espec Foll Tec — Mexico. Secretaria de Agricultura y Ganaderia. Oficina de Estudios Especiales. Folleto Tecnico
Mex Stud — Mexican Studies
Mex Univ Nac Auton Inst Geol Paleontol Mex — Mexico. Universidad Nacional Autonoma. Instituto de Geologia. Paleontologia Mexicana
Mex Univ Nac Auton Inst Geol Rev — Mexico. Universidad Nacional Autonoma. Instituto de Geologia. Revista
Mex Univ Nac Auton Inst Geol Ser Divulg — Mexico. Universidad Nacional Autonoma. Instituto de Geologia. Serie Divulgacion
Mex Univ Nac R Mens — Mexico Universidad Nacional. Revista Mensual
Meyler Pecks Drug Induced Dis — Meyler and Peck's Drug-Induced Diseases
Meyler's Side Eff Drugs — Meyler's Side Effects of Drugs
Mey Lex — Meyers Lexikon
MEYNA — Meyniana
Mezd Otnosenija — Mezdunarodni Otnosenija
Mezdun Ezeg Polit Ekon — Mezdunarodnyj Ezegodnik. Politika i Ekonomika
Mezdun Zizn — Mezdunarodnaja Zizn
Mezei Gazd Baratja — Mezei Gazdak Baratja
Mezhdunar Agroprom Zh — Mezhdunarodnyi Agropromyshlennyi Zhurnal
Mezhdunar Entomol Kongr Tr — Mezhdunarodnyi Entomologicheskii Kongress. Trudy
Mezhdunar Gazov Kongr — Mezhdunarodnyi Gazovyi Kongress
Mezhdunar Geokhim Kongr Dokl — Mezhdunarodnyi Geokhimicheskii Kongress. Doklady
Mezhdunar Geol Kongr — Mezhdunarodnyi Geologicheskii Kongress
Mezhdunar Kollok Mekh Ustalost Met — Mezhdunarodnyi Kollokvium. Mekhanicheskaya Ustalost Metallov
Mezhdunar Kollok Tonkim Magn Plenkam — Mezhdunarodnyi Kollokvium po Tonkim Magnitnym Plenkam
Mezhdunar Konf Amorfnym Zhidk Poluprovodn — Mezhdunarodnyi Konferentsiya po Amorfnym Zhidkum Poluprovodnikam
Mezhdunar Konf Fiz Tyazh Ionov — Mezhdunarodnaya Konferentsiya po Fizike Tyazhelykh Ionov
Mezhdunar Konf Fiz Vys Energ — Mezhdunarodnaya Konferentsiya po Fizike Vysokikh Energii

Mezhdunar Konf Koord Khim Tezisy Dokl — Mezhdunarodnaya Konferentsiya po Koordinatsionnoi Khimii. TezisyDokladov

Mezhdunar Konf Merzlotoved — Mezhdunarodnaya Konferentsiya po Merzlotovedeniyu

Mezhdunar Konf Merzlotoved Mater — Mezhdunarodnaya Konferentsiya po Merzlotovedeniyu. Materialy

Mezhdunar Konf Meteorol Karpat Tr — Mezhdunarodnaya Konferentsiya po Meteorologii Karpat. Trudy

Mezhdunar Konf MGD Preobraz Energ — Mezhdunarodnaya Konferentsiya po MGD [*Magnetogidrodinamika*]-Preobrazovaniyu Energii

Mezhdunar Konf Op Rentgenovskikh Luchei Mikroanal — Mezhdunarodnaya Konferentsiya po Optike Rentgenovskikh Luchei iMikroanalizu

Mezhdunar Konf Poroshk Metall — Mezhdunarodnaya Konferentsiya po Poroshkovoi Metallurgii

Mezhdunar Konf Primen Sint Almazov Promsti — Mezhdunarodnaya Konferentsiya po Primeneniyu Sinteticheskikh Almazov vPromyshlennosti

Mezhdunar Konf Radiats Fiz Poluprovodn Rodstvennykh Mater — Mezhdunarodnaya Konferentsiya po Radiatsionnoi Fizike Poluprovodnikov iRodstvennykh Materialov

Mezhdunar Konf Teor Plazmy — Mezhdunarodnaya Konferentsiya po Teorii Plazmy

Mezhdunar Konf Titanu — Mezhdunarodnaya Konferentsiya po Titanu

Mezhdunar Konf Tuberk Tr — Mezhdunarodnaya Konferentsiya po Tuberkulezu. Trudy

Mezhdunar Kongr Antropol Etnogr Nauk Tr — Mezhdunarodnyi Kongress Antropologicheskikh i Etnograficheskikh Nauk.Trudy

Mezhdunar Kongr Astronavt Dokl — Mezhdunarodnaya Kongress po Astronavtike Doklady

Mezhdunar Kongr Efirnym Maslam Mat — Mezhdunarodnyi Kongress po Efirnym Maslam. Materialy

Mezhdunar Kongr Gerontol — Mezhdunarodnyi Kongress Gerontologov

Mezhdunar Kongr Katal — Mezhdunarodnyi Kongress po Katalizu

Mezhdunar Kongr Khim Tsem — Mezhdunarodnyi Kongress po Khimii Tsementa

Mezhdunar Kongr Koloristov — Mezhdunarodnyi Kongress Koloristov

Mezhdunar Kongr Liteishchikov Dokl — Mezhdunarodnyi Kongress Liteishchikov. Doklady

Mezhdunar Kongr Lugovod — Mezhdunarodnyi Kongress po Lugovodstvu

Mezhdunar Kongr Miner Udobr Dokl Plenarnykh Zased — Mezhdunarodnyi Kongress po Mineralnym Udobreniyam. Doklady naPlenarnykh Zasedaniyakh

Mezhdunar Kongr Miner Udobr Dokl Sov Uchastnikov Kongr — Mezhdunarodnyi Kongress Mineralnym Udobreniyam. Doklady SovetskikhUchastnikov Kongressa

Mezhdunar Kongr Obogashch Polezn Isko Sb — Mezhdunarodnyi Kongress po Obogashcheniyu Poleznykh Iskopaemykh.Sbornik

Mezhdunar Kongr Obogashch Polezn Isko Tr — Mezhdunarodnyi Kongress po Obogashcheniyu Poleznykh Iskopaemykh. Trudy

Mezhdunar Kongr Obogashch Uglei — Mezhdunarodnyi Kongress po Obogashcheniyu Uglei

Mezhdunar Kongr Org Geokhim — Mezhdunarodnyi Kongress po Organicheskoi Geokhimii

Mezhdunar Kongr Pochvovedov Probl Pochvoved — Mezhdunarodnyi Kongress Pochvovedov. Problemy Pochvovedeniya

Mezhdunar Kongr Poverkhn Akt Veshchestvam — Mezhdunarodnyi Kongress po Poverkhnostno-Aktivnym Veshchestvam

Mezhdunar Kongr Term Obrab Mater — Mezhdunarodnyi Kongress po Termicheskoi Obrabotke Materialov

Mezhdunar Kongr Zashch Rast — Mezhdunarodnyi Kongress po Zashchite Rastenii

Mezhdunar Kongr Zashch Rast Dokl — Mezhdunarodnyi Kongress po Zashchite Rastenii. Doklady

Mezhdunar Mineral Assots Sezd — Mezhdunarodnaya Mineralogicheskaya Assotsiatsiya S'ezd

Mezhdunar Nauch Suvesh Kheterozisa — Mezhdunarodno Nauchno Suveshtanie po Kheterozisa

Mezhdunar Ptits Zh — Mezhdunarodnyi Ptitsevodnyi Zhurnal

Mezhdunar Sel-Khoz Zh — Mezhdunarodnyi Sel'skokhozyaistvennyi Zhurnal

Mezhdunar Sel'skokhoz Zh — Mezhdunarodnyi Sel'skokhozyaistvennyi Zhurnal

Mezhdunar Selskostop Spis — Mezhdunarodno Selskostopansko Spisanie

Mezhdunar Semin Probl Fiz Vys Energ Kvantovoi Teor Polya — Mezhdunarodnyi Seminar po Problemam Fiziki Vysokikh Energii i KvantovoiTeorii Polya

Mezhdunar Semin Probl Fiz Vys Energ Obz Dokl — Mezhdunarodnyi Seminar po Problemam Fiziki Vysokikh Energii. ObzornyeDoklady

Mezhdunar Sezd Infekts Patol Soobshch — Mezhdunarodnyi S'ezd po Infektsionnoi Patologii. Soobshcheniya

Mezhdunar Shk Biol Monit — Mezhdunarodnaya Shkola Biologicheskogo Monitoringa

Mezhdunar Shk Kogerentnoi Opt Gologr Varna — Mezhdunarodnaya Shkola po Kogerentnoi Optike i Golografii-Varna

Mezhdunar Shk Molodykh Uch Fiz Vys Energ Mater — Mezhdunarodnaya Shkola Molodykh Uchenykh po Fizike Vysokikh Energii.Materialy

Mezhdunar Shk Neitr Fiz — Mezhdunarodnaya Shkola po Neitronnoi Fizike

Mezhdunar Shk OIYaI TsERN Fiz Tr — Mezhdunarodnaya Shkola OIYaI-TsERN po Fizike. Trudy

Mezhdunar Shk Protsessam Perenosa Nepodvizhnykh — Mezhdunarodnaya Shkola po Protsessam Perenosa v Nepodvizhnykh iPsevdoozhizhennykh Zernistykh Sloyakh

Mezhdunar Shk Semin Lazernaya Diagn Plazmy — Mezhdunarodnaya Shkola Seminar Lazernaya Diagnostika Plazmy

Mezhdunar Shk Semin Mat Modeli Anal Chislennn Metody Teor — Mezhdunarodnaya Shkola Seminar Matematicheskie Modeli, Analiticheskie iChislennye Metody v Teorii Perenosa

Mezhdunar Shk Semin Metody Lazernoi Diagn Odnofaznykh — Mezhdunarodnaya Shkola Seminar Metody Lazernoi Diagnostiki Odnofaznykhi Mnogofaznykh Techenii

Mezhdunar Shk Semin Teplo Massoobmen Khim Reagiruyushchikh — Mezhdunarodnaya Shkola Seminar Teplo i Massoobmen v KhimicheskiReagiruyushchikh Sistemakh

Mezhdunar Shk Spets Rostu Krist — Mezhdunarodnaya Shkola Spetsialistov po Rostu Kristallov

Mezhdunar Shk Stran Chlenov SEV Svarka Poroshk Provolokoi — Mezhdunarodnaya Shkola Stran-Chlenov SEV Svarka Poroshkovoi Provolokoi

Mezhdunar Shk Vopr Ispol EVM Yad Issled — Mezhdunarodnaya Shkola po Voprosam Ispol'zovaniya EVM v YadernykhIssledovaniyakh

Mezhdunar Simp Borbe Seroi Gnilyu Vinograda — Mezhdunarodnyi Simpozium po Bor'be s Serois Gnil'yu Vinograda

Mezhdunar Simp Boru — Mezhdunarodnyi Simpozium po Boru

Mezhdunar Simp Elektron Strukt Perekhodnykh Met Ikh Splavov — Mezhdunarodnyi Simpozium po Elektronnoi Strukture PerekhodnykhMetallov. Ikh Splavov i Intermetallicheskikh Soedinenii. Materialy

Mezhdunar Simp Fiz Luny Planet — Mezhdunarodnyi Simpozium po Fizike Luny i Planet

Mezhdunar Simp Fiz Vys Energ Elem Chastits — Mezhdunarodnyi Simpozium po Fizike Vysokikh Energii i ElementarnykhChastits

Mezhdunar Simp Fotogr Zhelatine Tezisy Dokl — Mezhdunarodnyi Simpozium po Fotograficheskoi Zhelatine. Tezisy Dokladov

Mezhdunar Simp Geterog Katal Tr — Mezhdunarodnyi Simpozium po Geterogennomu Katalizu Trudy

Mezhdunar Simp IFAK Avtom Upr Prostanstve — Mezhdunarodnyi Simpozium IFAK po Avtomaticheskomu Upravleniyu vProstanstve

Mezhdunar Simp Immunol Reprod — Mezhdunarodnyi Simpozium po Immunologii Reproduktsii

Mezhdunar Simp Izbr Probl Stat Mekh Tr — Mezhdunarodnyi Simpozium po Izbrannym Problemam StatisticheskoiMekhaniki. Trudy

Mezhdunar Simp Khim Voloknam — Mezhdunarodnyi Simpozium po Khimicheskim Voloknam

Mezhdunar Simp Kompoz — Mezhdunarodnoe Simpozium Kompozity

Mezhdunar Simp Kompoz Met Mater — Mezhdunarodnyi Simpozium po Kompozitsionnym Metallicheskim Materialam

Mezhdunar Simp Kosm Meteorol — Mezhdunarodnyi Simpozium po Kosmicheskoi Meteorologii

Mezhdunar Simp Meteorol Aspekty Radioakt Zagryaz Atmos Tr — Mezhdunarodnyi Simpozium Meteorologicheskie Aspekty RadioaktivnogoZagryazneniya Atmosfery. Trudy

Mezhdunar Simp Metody Prikl Geokhim — Mezhdunarodnyi Simpozium Metody Prikladnoi Geokhimii

Mezhdunar Simp Nauchno Tekh Probl Kombikormovoi Promsti — Mezhdunarodnyi Simpozium po Nauchno-Tekhnicheskim ProblemamKombikormovoi Promyshlennosti

Mezhdunar Simp Polikondens — Mezhdunarodnyi Simpozium Polikondensatsii

Mezhdunar Simp Stran Chlenov SEV — Mezhdunarodnyi Simpozium Stran-Chlenov SEV

Mezhdunar Simp Svyazi Gomogennym Geterog Katal — Mezhdunarodnyi Simpozium po Svyazi mezhdu Gomogennym i GeterogennymKatalizom

Mezhdunar Simp Yad Elektron Tr — Mezhdunarodnyi Simpozium po Yadernoi Elektronike. Trudy

Mezhdunar Simp Zharoprochn Met Mater — Mezhdunarodnyi Simpozium po Zharoprochnym Metallicheskim Materialam

Mezhdunar Simp Zimnemu Betonirovaniyu Dokl — Mezhdunarodnyi Simpozium po Zimnemu Betonirovaniyu. Doklady

Mezhdunar Skh Kogerentnoi Opt Gologr Varna — Mezhdunarodnaya Shkola po Kogerentnoi Optike i Golografii-Varna

Mezhdunar S-Kh Zh — Mezhdunarodnyi Sel'skokhozyaistvennyi Zhurnal

Mezhdunar Soveshch Probl Kvantovoi Teor Polya — Mezhdunarodnoi Soveshchanie po Problemam Kvantovoi Teorii Polya

Mezhduved Geofiz Kom — Mezhduvedomstvennyi Geofizicheskikh Komitet

Mezhmol Vzaimodeistvie Konform Mole Tezisy Dokl Vses Simp — Mezhmolekulyarnoe Vzaimodeistvie i Konformatsii Molekul. TezisyDokladov Vsesoyuznogo Simpoziuma

Mezhneironnaya Peredacha Veg Nervn Sist Tr Vses Simp Vopr — Mezhneironnaya Peredacha v Vegetativnoi Nervnoi Sisteme. TrudyVsesoyuznogo Simpoziuma po Voprosam Obshchei Fiziologii Nervnoi Sistemy

Mezhved Geofiz Kom Prezidiume Akad Nauk Ukr SSR Inf Byull — Mezhvedomstvennyi Geofizicheskii Komitet pri Prezidiume Akademii Nauk Ukrainskoi SSR Informatsionnyi Byulleten

Mezhved Sb Lenengr Gidrometeorol Inst — Mezhvedomstvennyi Sbornik. Leningradskii GidrometeorologicheskiiInstitut

Mezhved Soveshch Probl Metamorfog Rudoobraz — Mezhvedomstvennoe Soveshchanie po Probleme MetamorfogennogoRudoobrazovaniya

Mezhved Temat Sb Mosk Energ Inst — Mezhvedomstvennyi Tematicheskii Sbornik. Moskovskii EnergeticheskiiInstitut

Mezhvuz Gistol Konf Probl Reakt Plast Epiteliya Soedin Tkani — Mezhvuzovskaya Gistologicheskaya Konferentsiya po Probleme. Reaktivnosti Plastichnost Epiteliya i Soedinietlnoi Tkani v Normalnykh EksperimentalnyPatologicheskikh Usloviyakh

Mezhvuz Konf Vopr Ispareniya Goreniya Gazov Din Dispersnykh — Mezhvuzovskaya Konferentsiya po Voprosam Ispareniya, Goreniya, iGazovoi Dinamiki Dispersnykh Sistem. Materialy

Mezhvuz Nauchn Konf Kaunas Med Inst — Mezhvuzovskaya Nauchnaya Konferentsiya Kaunasskogo MeditsinskogoInstituta

Mezhvuzovskii Sbornik Nauchn Tr Permsk Politekh Inst — Mezhvuzovskii Sbornik Nauchnykh Trudov. Permskii PolitekhnicheskiiInstitut

Mezhvuzovskii Tematicheskii Sb-Yaroslavskii Gos Univ — Mezhvuzovskii Tematicheskii Sbornik-Yaroslavskii Gosudarstvennyi Universitet

Mezhvuz Sb Nauchn Metod Tr Yarosl Gos Pedagog Inst — Mezhvuzovski Sbornik Nauchnykh i Metodicheskikh Trudov. YaroslavskiiGosudarstvennyi Pedagogicheskii Institut Imeni K. D. Ushinskogo

Mezhvuz Sb Nauchn Tr Erevan Politekh Inst Im K Marksa Ser 17 — Mezhvuzovskii Sbornik Nauchnykh Trudov Erevanskii PolitekhnicheskiiInstitut Imeni K. Marksa. Seriya 17. Radiotekhnika, Elektronika

Mezhvuz Sb Nauchn Tr Erevan Politekh Inst Im K Marksa Ser 18 — Mezhvuzovskii Sbornik Nauchnykh Trudov Erevanskii PolitekhnicheskiiInstitut Imeni K. Marksa. Seriya 18. Gornoe Delo i Metallurgiya

Mezhvuz Sb Nauchn Tr Erevan Politekh Inst Im K Marksa Ser 19 — Mezhvuzovskii Sbornik Nauchnykh Trudov Erevanskii PolitekhnicheskiiInstitut Imeni K. Marksa. Seriya 19. Khimicheskaya Tekhnologiya

Mezhvuz Sb Nauchn Tr Erevan Politekh Inst Ser 19 — Mezhvuzovskii Sbornik Nauchnykh Trudov. Erevanskii Politekhnicheskii Institut. Seriya 19. Khimicheskaya Tekhnologiya

Mezhvuz Sb Nauchn Tr Leningr Tekhnol Inst Im Lensoveta Mash — Mezhvuzovskii Sbornik Nauchnykh Trudov Leningradskii TekhnologicheskiiInstitut Imeni Lensoveta. Mashiny i Tekhnologiya Pererabotki Polimerov

Mezhvuz Sb Nauchn Tr Yarosl Gos Pedagog Inst — Mezhvuzovskii Sbornik Nauchnykh Trudov Yaroslavskii GosudarstvennyiPedagogicheskii Institut Imeni K. D. Ushinskogo

Mezhvuz Sb Tr Biol Kafedry Kirg Univ Ser Bot — Mezhvuzovskii Sbornik Trudov Biologicheskoi Kafedry Kirgizskogo Universiteta Seriya Botanicheskaya

Mezhvuz Sb Ural Politekh Inst Im S M Kirova Magnitogorsk — Mezhvuzovskii Sbornik. Uralskii Politekhnicheskii Institut Imeni S. M.Kirova i Magnitogorskii Gorno-Metallurgicheskii Institut Imeni G. I. Nosova

Mezhvuz Temat Sb Leningr Inzh Stroit Inst — Mezhvuzovskii Tematicheskii Sbornik Leningradskii Inzhenerno Stroitel'nyi Institut

Mezhvuz Temat Sb Nauchn Tr Leningr Inzh Stroit Inst — Mezhvuzovskii Tematicheskii Sbornik Nauchnykh Trudov Leningradskii InzhenernoStroitel'nyi Institut

Mezhvuz Temat Sb Tr Leningr Inzh Stroit Inst — Mezhvuzovskii Tematicheskii Sbornik Trudov Leningradskii Inzhenerno Stroitel'nyi Institut

Mezhvuz Temat Sb Tr Tyumen Gos Univ Tyumen Ind Inst — Mezhvuzovskii Tematicheskii Sbornik. Tyumenskii GosudarstvennyiUniversitet i Tyumenskii Industrial'nyi Institut

Mezhvuz Temat Sb Yarosl Gos Univ — Mezhvuzovskii Tematicheskii Sbornik-Yaroslavskii Gosudarstvennyi Universitet

Mezin Vztahy — Mezinarodni Vztahy

Mezoegazd Kiserl Koezp Evk — Mezoegazdasagi Kiserletuegyi Koezpont Evkoenyve

Mezoegazd Kut — Mezoegazdasagi Kutatasok

Mezoegazd Kutat — Mezoegazdasagi Kutatasok

Mezoegazd Kutatas — Mezoegazdasagi Kutatasok

Mezogazd Alkalm Lap — Mezogazdasagi Alkalmazottak Lapja

Mezogazd Ert — Mezogazdasagi Ertesitoje

Mezogazd Gepesitesi Tanulmanyok Mezogazd Gepkiserl Intez — Mezogazdasagi Gepesitesi Tanulmanyok A. Mezogazdasag Gepkiserleti Intezet

Mezogazd Gepesit Tanulm — Mezogazdasagi Gepesitesi Tanulmanyok

Mezogazd Gepesz Foisk Kiad — Mezogazdasagi Gepeszmernoki Foiskola Kiadvanyai

Mezogazd Gepkis Intez Evk — Mezogazdasagi Gepkiserleti Intezet Evkonyve

Mezogazd Ip — Mezogazdasag es Ipar

Mezogazd Tech — Mezoegazdasagi Technika

Mezogazd Tud Kozl — Mezogazdasagi Tudomanyos Koezlemenyek

Mezogazd Vilagirod — Mezoegazdasagi Vilagirodalom

Mezogazd Vilagirodalom — Mezoegazdasagi Vilagirodalom

Mezsaimn Probl Inst Raksti — Mezsaimniecibas Problemu Instituta Raksti

Mezzogiorn — Mezzogiorno d'Europa

Mezzogiorno d'Europa Q R — Mezzogiorno d'Europa. Quarterly Review

MF — Maandblad van Financien

MF — Makedonski Folklor

MF — Mercure de France

MF — Midwest Folklore

MF — Miscellanea Francescana

MF — Misiones Franciscanos

MF — Musikforschung

MFA — Museum Francisceum Annales

MfA — Musik fuer Alle

MFA AR — Annual Report. Museum of Fine Arts

MFA B — Bulletin. Museum of Fine Arts

MfAb — Microfilm Abstracts

MFA Bull — MFA Bulletin. Museum of Fine Arts

MFB — Europese Investeringsbank. Mededelingen

MFB — Madras Fisheries Bulletin

M F B — Monthly Film Bulletin

MFBMA — Mitteilungen. Forstliche Bundes-Versuchsanstalt (Mariabrunn)

MFC — Manufacturing Chemist, Incorporating Chemical Age

MFC — Motor Freight Controller

MFCBAC — Montana. Forest and Conservation Experiment Station. Bulletin

MFCG — Mitteilungen und Forschungsbeitraege. Cusanus-Gesellschaft

MFCL — Memoire et Travaux Publies par les Facultes Catholiques de Lille

MFCNAE — Montana. Forest and Conservation Experiment Station. Note

MF Coop Ext Serv Kans State Univ Manhattan — MF. Cooperative Extension Service. Kansas State University. Manhattan

MFCSAT — Montana. Forest and Conservation Experiment Station. Special Publication

MFCusanusG — Mitteilungen und Forschungsbeitraege. Cusanus-Gesellschaft

Mfd Fishery Prod — Manufactured Fishery Products

Mfd Gas Ind — Manufactured Gas Industry

MFDGAW — Communications. Faculte de Medecine Veterinaire. Universite de l'Etat Gand

MFDU — Monatshefte fuer Deutschen Unterricht

MFE — Mazingira. The World Forum for Environment and Development

MFEHA — Memoirs. Faculty of Engineering. Hiroshima University

MFEKA — Memoirs. Faculty of Engineering. Kobe University

MFEMA — Manufacturing Engineering and Management [*Later, Manufacturing Engineering*]

MFENAO — Montana. Forest and Conservation Experiment Station. Research Note

Mfg — Manufacturing

MFG — Middle East Observer

Mfg Chem — Manufacturing Chemist

Mfg Chem Aerosol News — Manufacturing Chemist and Aerosol News

Mfg Cloth — Manufacturing Clothier

Mfg Confect — Manufacturing Confectioner

MFGEB — Manufacturing Engineering

Mfg Eng — Manufacturing Engineering

Mfg Eng Manage — Manufacturing Engineering and Management [*Later, Manufacturing Engineering*]

Mfg Inds — Manufacturing Industries

Mfg Optn — Manufacturing Optician

Mfg Perf — Manufacturing Perfumer

Mfg Rec — Manufacturing Record

Mfg Tech H — Manufacturing Technology Horizons

MFH — Mitteilungen. Institut fuer Handelsforschung. Universitaet zu Koeln

MFI — Managerial Finance

MF(I) — Midwest Folklore (Indiana University)

MFITD — Fukui Kogyo Daigaku Kenkyu Kiyo

MFIZA — Metallofizika

MFJ — Municipal Finance Journal

MFKCA — Memoirs. Faculty of Science. Kyushu University. Series C

MFKDA — Memoirs. Faculty of Science. Kyushu University. Series D. Geology

MfKh — Monatsschrift fuer Kinderheilkunde

MFKLDH — Progress in Applied Microcirculation

MFKPA — Memoirs. Faculty of Science. Kyoto University. Series of Physics, Astrophysics,Geophysics, and Chemistry

MFL — Marriage and Family Living

MFLB — Massachusetts Foreign Language Bulletin

MFLRA — Mededelingen. Faculteit Landbouwwetenschappen. Rijksuniversiteit (Gent)

MfM — Monatshefte fuer Musikgeschichte

MFME — Mora Ferenc Muzeum Evkoenyve

MFM Mod Fototech — MFM. Moderne Fototechnik

MF MP Milchforsch Milchprax — MF-MP. Milchforschung-Milchpraxis

MFN — Metal Fabricating News

MFN — Mitteilungen fuer Namenskunde

MFNV — Meddelelser fra Norsk Viltforskning

MFO — Melanges. Universite Saint-Joseph

MFOB — Melanges. Faculte Orientale de Beyrouth

M Forskning — Musik und Forskning

M Forum — Music Forum

MFOUJ — Melanges. Faculte Orientale. Universite de St. Joseph

MfP — Monatsschrift fuer Pastoraltheologie

MFP — Monographs in Fetal Physiology

MFP Alum — Mineral Facts and Problems. Preprint. Aluminum

MFP Antim — Mineral Facts and Problems. Preprint. Antimony

MFP Arsenc — Mineral Facts and Problems. Preprint. Arsenic

MFP Asbsts — Mineral Facts and Problems. Preprint. Asbestos

MFP Barite — Mineral Facts and Problems. Preprint. Barite

MFP Beryl — Mineral Facts and Problems. Preprint. Beryllium

MFP Bis — Mineral Facts and Problems. Preprint. Bismuth

MFP Boron — Mineral Facts and Problems. Preprint. Boron

MFP Bromin — Mineral Facts and Problems. Preprint. Bromine

MFP Cadm — Mineral Facts and Problems. Preprint. Cadmium

MFP Clays — Mineral Facts and Problems. Preprint. Clays

MFP Columb — Mineral Facts and Problems. Preprint. Columbium

MFP Copper — Mineral Facts and Problems. Preprint. Copper

MFP C Stone — Mineral Facts and Problems. Preprint. Crushed Stone

MFP Diamnd — Mineral Facts and Problems. Preprint. Diamond - Industrial

MFP Dime S — Mineral Facts and Problems. Preprint. Dimension Stone

MFP Feldsp — Mineral Facts and Problems. Preprint. Feldspar

MFP Gallm — Mineral Facts and Problems. Preprint. Gallium

MFP Garnet — Mineral Facts and Problems. Preprint. Garnet

MFP Germnu — Mineral Facts and Problems. Preprint. Germanium

MFP Gold — Mineral Facts and Problems. Preprint. Gold

MFP Gypsum — Mineral Facts and Problems. Preprint. Gypsum

MFP Indium — Mineral Facts and Problems. Preprint. Indium

MFP Iodine — Mineral Facts and Problems. Preprint. Iodine

MFP Iron O — Mineral Facts and Problems. Preprint. Iron Ore

MFP Lead — Mineral Facts and Problems. Preprint. Lead

MFP Magn — Mineral Facts and Problems. Preprint. Magnesium

MFP Mang — Mineral Facts and Problems. Preprint. Manganese

MFP Mica — Mineral Facts and Problems. Preprint. Mica

MFP Moly — Mineral Facts and Problems. Preprint. Molybdenum

MFP Peat — Mineral Facts and Problems. Preprint. Peat

MFP Perlit — Mineral Facts and Problems. Preprint. Perlite

MFP Prepnt — Mineral Facts and Problems. Preprints

MFP Quartz — Mineral Facts and Problems. Preprint. Quartz

MFP Rubid — Mineral Facts and Problems. Preprint. Rubidium

MFPSA — Monographies Francaises de Psychologie

MFP Salt — Mineral Facts and Problems. Preprint. Salt

MFP Sand — Mineral Facts and Problems. Preprint. Sand and Gravel

MFP Sel — Mineral Facts and Problems. Preprint. Selenium

MFP Silicn — Mineral Facts and Problems. Preprint. Silicon

MFP Silver — Mineral Facts and Problems. Preprint. Silver

MFP Soda A — Mineral Facts and Problems. Preprint. Soda Ash and Sodium Sulfate

MFP Stront — Mineral Facts and Problems. Preprint. Strontium

MFP Sulfur — Mineral Facts and Problems. Preprint. Sulfur

MFP Tellur — Mineral Facts and Problems. Preprint. Tellurium

MFP Thorm — Mineral Facts and Problems. Preprint. Thorium

MFP Tin — Mineral Facts and Problems. Preprint. Tin
MFP Titanm — Mineral Facts and Problems. Preprint. Titanium
MFP Tungst — Mineral Facts and Problems. Preprint. Tungsten
MFP Vandm — Mineral Facts and Problems. Preprint. Vanadium
MFP Vermic — Mineral Facts and Problems. Preprint. Vermiculite
MFP Zinc — Mineral Facts and Problems. Preprint. Zinc
MFP Zirc — Mineral Facts and Problems. Preprint. Zirconium and Hafnium
MFR — Maltese Folklore Review
Mfr — Manufacture
MFr — Mercure de France
MFr — Miscellanea Francescana
M Fra — Moyen Francais
Mfr Bldr — Manufacturer and Builder
MfrChemAer — Manufacturing Chemist and Aerosol News
M Freiberger Altert V — Mitteilungen des Freiberger Altertumsvereins
MFRVA — Microform Review
MFS — Manufacturing Systems
MFS — Meddelanden fran Strindbergssaellskapet
MFS — Mescellanea Francescana di Storia, di Lettere, di Arti
MFS — Modern Fiction Studies
MFSF — Magazine of Fantasy and Science Fiction
MFSJP — Monografia das Festas do S. Joao em Portugal
MF Soc Manuf Eng — MF. Society of Manufacturing Engineers
MFSV — Meddelelser fra Statens Viltundersokelser
MFVFF — Meddelelser fra Vestlandets Forstlige Forsoeksstasjon
MG — Magna Graecia
MG — Manchester Guardian
MG — Mandaeische Grammatik
MG — Massorah Magna
MG — Memminger Geschichtsblaetter
MG — Methods in Geomathematics
MG — Migne Series. Graeca
MG — Molodaya Gvardiya
MG — Mouvement Geographique
MG — Musikantengilde
MGA — Maandblad Gemeente-Administratie
MGA — Meteorological and Geoastrophysical Abstracts
MGA — Mitteilungen. Gesamtarchiv der Deutschen Juden
MGA Bull — MGA Bulletin. Mushroom Growers' Association
MGADJ — Mitteilungen. Gesamtarchiv der Deutschen Juden
MGAEU — Mitteilungen der Berliner Gesellschaft fuer Anthropologie, Ethnologie, und Urgeschichte
MGAGB — Montana Geological Society. Annual Field Conference. Guidebook
MGAGES — Monografie di Genetica Agraria
MGAJA — Magyar Allami Foldtani Intezet. Evi Jelentese
MGATC — Modern German Authors. Texts and Contexts
MGB — Mennonitische Geschichtsblaetter
MGB — Muenchener Germanistische Beitraege
MGbl — Muehlhauser Geschichtsblaetter
MGCN Main Group Chem News — MGCN. Main Group Chemistry News
Mg C Pop Cr — Monographs. Carolina Population Center
MGD — Guardian
MGD — Musik und Gottesdienst
MGD Teor Energ Tekhnol — MGD Teoriya Energetika Tekhnologiya
MGEB — Mitteilungen der Gesellschaft fuer Erdkunde zu Berlin
MGEK — Mitteilungen. Gesellschaft zur Erforschung Judischer Kunstdenkmaeler
M Geneve — Musees de Geneve
MGeolGW — Mitteilungen der Geologischen Gesellschaft Wien
M Ges — Musik und Gesellschaft
MGESA — Mededelingen. Geologische Stichting. Nieuwe Serie
M Ges Salzb — Mitteilungen. Gesellschaft fuer Salzburger Landeskunde
MGF — Men's Guide to Fashion
MGFIAL — Annales. Instituti Geologici Publici Hungarici
MGFIB — Morskie Gidrofizicheskie Issledovaniya
MGG — Methods in Geochemistry and Geophysics
MGG — MGG. Molecular and General Genetics
MGG — Mitteilungen. Geographische Gesellschaft
MGG — Musik in Geschichte und Gegenwart
MGGH — Mitteilungen der Geographischen Gesellschaft in Hamburg
MGGM — Mitteilungen der Geographischen Gesellschaft in Muenchen
MGG Mol Gen Genet — MGG. Molecular and General Genetics
MGGT — Mitteilungen der Geographischen Gesellschaft zu Jena
MGGW — Mitteilungen. Geographische Gesellschaft in Wien
MGGZ — Mitteilungen der Geographisch-Ethnographischen Gesellschaft (Zuerich)
MGH — International Management
MGH — Monumenta Germaniae Historica
MGHAA — Monumenta Germaniae Historica. Auctores Antiquissimi
MGHB — Monumenta Germaniae Historica. Briefe der Deutschen Kaiserzeit
MGH Const — Monumenta Germaniae Historica. Constitutiones
MGH DRG — Monumenta Germaniae Historica. Diplomata Regnum Germaniae ex Stirpe Karolinorum
MGH LL — Monumenta Germaniae Historica. Libelli de Lite
MGH News — Montreal General Hospital. News
MGH SRG — Monumenta Germaniae Historica. Scriptores Rerum Germanicarum
MGI — Mitteilungen des Grabmann-Instituts
MGI — Musei e Gallerie d'Italia
MGITA2 — Meteorologiya i Gidrologiya Informatsionnyi Byulleten
MGJ — Monatsschrift fuer die Geschichte und Wissenschaft des Judentums
MGJF — Mitteilungen. Gesellschaft fuer Juedische Familienforschung
MGJFF — Mitteilungen. Gesellschaft fuer Juedische Familienforschung
MgJL — Mining Journal (London)
MGJOAP — Market Grower's Journal
MGJV — Mitteilungen. Gesellschaft fuer Juedische Volkskunde
MGKFA3 — Hungarian Journal of Chemistry
MGkK — Monatsschrift fuer Gottesdienst und Kirchliche Kunst

MGL — Mycenaeae Graecitatis Lexicon
MG Lex — Mycenaeae Graecitatis Lexicon
M Gl F — Meddelelser fra Dansk Geologisk Forening
MGM — Manchester Guardian (Manchester)
MGM — Miscellanea Giovanni Mercati
MgML — Mining Magazine (London)
MGMNw — Mitteilungen zur Geschichte der Medizin und Naturwissenschaften
MGMPA — Memorie. Istituti di Geologia e Mineralogia. Universita di Padova
Mgmt Acct — Management Accounting
Mgmt Bus Automn — Management and Business Automation
Mgmt Dec — Management Decision
Mgmt Engng — Management Engineering
Mgmt Focus — Management Focus
Mgmt in Govt — Management in Government
Mgmt Prac — Management Practice
Mgmt Printing — Management in Printing
Mgmt Publs Br Columb Game Commn — Management Publications. British Columbia Game Commission
Mgmt Res News — Management Research News
Mgmt Rev — Management Review
Mgmt Rev Dig — Management Review and Digest
Mgmt Sci — Management Science
Mgmt Serv — Management Services
Mgmt Serv Govt — Management Services in Government
Mgmt Today — Management Today
Mgmt World — Management World
MGMV — Molecular Genetics, Microbiology, and Virology
MGN — Finish
Mgng Engr — Managing Engineer
Mgng Print — Managing Printer
MGNM — Mitteilungen. Germanisches Nationalmuseum
MGNVO — Mitteilungen. Gesellschaft fuer Natur- und Voelkerkunde Ostasiens
MGOKL — Mededeelingen. Geschied- en Oudheidkundige Kring voor Leuven en Omgeving
MGOKLeuven — Mededeelingen. Geschied- en Oudheidkundige Kring voor Leuven en Omgeving
MGottesdienst — Musik und Gottesdienst
MGP — Monumenta Germaniae Paedagogica
MGPGA — Monatsblaetter. Gesellschaft fuer Pommersche Geschichte und Altertumskunde
MGPNA — Metallurgicheskaya i Gornorudnaya Promyshlennost
MGQ — Management Science
MGR — Miscellanea Greca e Romana
M Gr — Monographies Gregoriennes
MGR — Monumenta Musicae Byzantinae
MGRCAT — Medicina Geriatrica
M Grecs — Monuments Grecs. Association des Etudes Grecques
Mgrl Plan — Managerial Planning
MGS — Mededeelingen van de Geologische Stichting
MGS — Michigan Germanic Studies
MGSACU — Geological Survey of Malaysia. Annual Report
MGSchL — Mitteilungen der Gesellschaft Schweizerischer Landwirte
MGSDA — Annual Statistical Summary. Michigan Geological Survey Division
MGSH — Mitteilungen. Geologische Staatsinstitut (Hamburg)
MGSI — Memoires. Geological Survey of India
MGSKG — Magazin zum Gebrauch der Staaten und Kirchengeschichte
MGSL — Minas Gerais. Suplemento Literario
MGSL — Mitteilungen der Gesellschaft fuer Salzburger Landeskunde
MGSLK — Mitteilungen. Gesellschaft fuer Salzburger Landeskunde
MGSM — Marburger Geographische Schriften (Marburg)
MGSMC — Michigan. Geological Survey Division. Miscellany
Mg Soc Anth — Monographs on Social Anthropology
MGSVAN — Geological Survey of Victoria. Memoir
Mg S Wld — Monograph Series in World Affairs. University of Denver
Mgt Accounting — Management Accounting
Mgt Acct — Management Accounting
Mgt Adviser — Management Adviser
MGTC — Mitteilungen der Gesellschaft Teilhard de Chardin fuer den Deutschen Sprachraum
Mgt Controls — Management Controls
Mgt Decision — Management Decision
Mgt Educ & Dev — Management, Education, and Development
Mgt Focus — Management Focus
Mgt Info Service Rept — Management Information Service Report
Mgt in Govt — Management in Government
Mgt Internat R — Management International Review
Mgt Int R — Management International Review
Mgt Methods — Management Methods
MGTOA — Magyar Tudomanyos Akademia. Kemiai Tudomanyok Osztalyanak Koezlemenyei
Mgt Q — Management Quarterly
Mgt R — Management Review
Mgt Rec — Management Record
Mgt Sci — Management Science
Mgt Ser — Management Services
Mgt Services — Management Services
Mgt Services in Govt — Management Services in Government
Mgt Today — Management Today
Mgt World — Management World
MGV — Maandblad voor de Geestelijke Volksgezondheid
MGv — Molodaia Gvardiia. Ezhemesiachnyi Literaturno-Khudozhestvennyi i Obshchestvenn-Politicheskii Zhurnal
MGV — Mycenaean Greek Vocabulary
MGVK — Mitteilungsblatt der Gesellschaft fuer Voelkerkunde
MGVL — Mitteilungsblatt der Gesellschaft fuer Voelkerkunde (Leipzig)

MGW — Manchester Guardian Weekly
MGWJ — Monatsschrift fuer die Geschichte und Wissenschaft des Judentums
MGZ — Edelmetaal, Uurwerken, Edelstenen. Maandblad voor de Edelmetaalbranche, Uurwerkenbranche, Edelstenenbranche, en Diamantbranche
MGZ — Management-Zeitschrift
MH — Mediaevalia et Humanistica
MH — Mental Hygiene
MH — Methodist History
MH — Michigan History Magazine
MH — Minnesota History
MH — Missionalia Hispanica
MH — Missionary Herald
MH — Monde Hebdomadaire
MH — Mundo Hispanico
MH — Museum Helveticum
MH — Museum Helveticum. Revue Suisse pour l'Etude de l'Antiquite Classique
MH — Musichandel
MHA — Missionalia Hispanica
MHAGB — Mittheilungen der Historischen und Atiquarischen Gesellschaft zu Basel
MHAR — Memoires. Section Historique. Academie Roumaine
MHB — Mennonite Historical Bulletin
MHB — Museum Ha'aretz Bulletin
Mh Baukunst Stadteb — Monatshefte fuer Baukunst und Stadtebau
MHBRI — Mental Health Book Review Index
MHC — Modern Healthcare
Mh Chem — Monatshefte fuer Chemie und Verwandte Teile Anderer Wissenschaften
MhChrPK — Monatshefte fuer Christliche Politik und Kultur
MHCT — Monumentorum ad Historiam Concilii Tridentini
MHD — Maandstatistiek van de Buitenlandse Handel per Land
MHD — Museo del Hombre Dominicano
MHD/B — Boletin. Museo del Hombre Dominicano
MHD Int Conf Electr Power Gener — MHD. International Conference on Electrical Power Generation
MHD Int Conf Magnetohydrodyn Electr Power Gener — MHD. International Conference on Magnetohydrodynamic Electrical PowerGeneration
MHE — Manufacturers Hanover Economic Report
MHE — Memorial Historico Espanol
MHE — Middle East Economic Survey
MHETA J — Manitoba Home Economics Teachers' Association. Journal
Mh Evang Kirchengesch Rheinl — Monatschefte fuer Evangelische Kirchengeschichte des Rheinlandes
MHF — Materialy do Historii Filozofii Stredniowiecznej w Polsce
MHF — Monuments Historiques de la France
Mh Fisch — Monatshefte fuer Fischerei
Mhft Baukst & Staedtebau — Monatshefte fuer Baukunst und Staedtebau
Mhft Kstwiss — Monatshefte fuer Kunstwissenschaft
MHG — Mitteilungen. E. T. A. Hoffman-Gesellschaft
Mhh Christl Polit — Monatshefte fuer Christliche Politik und Kultur
MHH I — Monumenta Hungariae Historica. Irok
Mhh Kunstwiss — Monatshefte fuer Kunstwissenschaft
MHH O — Monumenta Hungariae Historica. Okmanytarak
Mhh Prakt Dermatol — Monatshefte fuer Praktische Dermatologie
MHHPT — Museum Haganum Historico-Philologico-Theologicum
MHIDAS — Major Hazard Incident Data Service
M His — Magazine of History
MHis — Mundo Hispanico
MHisp — Mundo Hispanico
M Hist Ver Pfalz — Mitteilungen des Historischen Vereins der Pfalz
MHJ — Malayan Historical Journal
MHJ — Medizin-Historisches Journal
MHJ — Melbourne Historical Journal
MHJ — Monumenta Hungariae Judaica
MHKK — Mededelingen. Historische Kring Kesteren en Omstreken
MHL — Medical History (London)
MHL — Mitteilungen aus der Historischen Literatur
MHL — Mitteilungen. Bundesstelle fuer Aussenhandelsinformation
MHL — Modern Hebrew Literature
Mh Landw — Monatshefte fuer Landwirtschaft
MHLS — Mid-Hudson Language Studies
MHM — Maryland Historical Magazine
MHM — Michigan History Magazine
Mh Math — Monatshefte fuer Mathematik
MhMPh — Monatshefte fuer Mathematik und Physik
MH News Lett — MH (Mental Health) News Letter. National Council for Mental Health [London]
MHO — Maandblad voor het Handelsonderwijs
MHOSA — Mental Hospitals
MHP — Bedrijfskunde Tijdschrift voor Management
MHP — Materials Handling and Packaging
MHP — Miscellanea Historiae Pontificiae
MHPT — Museum Historico-Philologico-Theologicum
MHQ — Military History Quarterly
MHR — Missouri Historical Review
MHRA — Modern Humanities Research Association
MHRA Bull — Modern Humanities Research Association. Bulletin
MHRADS — Modern Humanities Research Association. Dissertation Series
MHRev — Malahat Review
MHRKg — Monatshefte fuer Rheinische Kirchengeschichte
MHRM — Microcomputers in Human Resource Management
MHS — Melanges d'Histoire Sociale
MHS — Monatsschrift fuer Hoehere Schulen
MHS — Monumenta Hispaniae Sacra
MHS — Moravian Historical Society. Transactions

MHSB — Missouri Historical Society. Bulletin
MHSch — Monatsschrift fuer Hoehere Schulen
Mh Seide Kunstseide — Monatshefte fuer Seide und Kunstseide
MHSI — Mosaics of Hagia Sophia at Istanbul
MHSJ — Monumenta Historica Societatis Jesu
MHS L — Monumenta Hispaniae Sacra. Serie Liturgica
MHSM — Monumenta Spectantia Historiam Slavorum Meridionalium
MHSo — Melanges d'Histoire Sociale
MHS S — Monumenta Hispaniae Sacra. Subsidia
MHT — Metalworking Production
MHT Financ — Manufacturers Hanover Trust Co. Financial Digest
M HT Gjen — Meddelelser fra Historisk-Topografisk Selskab for Gjentofte Kommune
Mh Tierheilk — Monatshefte fuer Tierheilkunde
MHTRA — Metal Science and Heat Treatment of Metals
MHU — Marketing in Hungary
MHum — Mediaevalia et Humanistica
MHV — Monumenta Hispaniae Vaticana
MHVDF — Mitteilungen des Historischen Vereins der Dioezese Fulda
Mh VetMed — Monatshefte fuer Veterinaermedizin
MHVP — Mitteilungen des Historischen Vereins der Pfalz
MHVS — Mitteilungen des Historischen Vereins des Kantons Schwyz
MHVS — Mitteilungen des Historischen Vereins fuer Steiermark
MHW — Maandblad voor Handelswetenschappen en Administratieve Praktijk
MHYPDB — Medical Hypnoanalysis
MI — Management Index
MI — Man in India
MI — Marketing Insights
MI — Memorie. Istituto di Corrispondenza Archeologica
Mi — Mind
Mi — Missiology
MI — Missouri School Music Magazine
MI — Mitteilungen des Deutschen Archaeologischen Instituts
MI — Monde Illustre
MI — Musikindustrie
MIA — Materialy i Issledovanija po Arkheologii SSSR
MIA — Media Information Australia
MIA — Middle East Economic Digest
MIA — Mitteilungen des Deutschen Archaeologischen Instituts. Athenische Abteilung
MIA — Mitteilungen. Institut fuer Auslandsbeziehungen
MIAB — Mitteilungen des Instituts fuer Allgemeine Botanik
MIAB — Mitteilungen. Institut fuer Auslandsbeziehungen
MIAH — Hamburg. Institut fuer Asienkunde. Mitteilungen
MIAHDA — Mitteilungen aus dem Institut fuer Allgemeine Botanik
MIAKB — Myakkangaku
Miami Geol Soc Annu Field Trip (Guideb) — Miami Geological Society. Annual Field Trip (Guidebook)
Miami Heral — Miami Herald
Miami Int Conf Altern Energy Sources — Miami International Conference on Alternative Energy Sources
Miami Int Congr Energy Environ — Miami International Congress on Energy and Environment
Miami LQ — Miami Law Quarterly
Miami L Rev — Miami Law Review
Miami Med — Miami Medicine
Miami Revw — Miami Review
Miami Univ Sch Marine Atmos Sci Annu Rep — Miami University. School of Marine and Atmospheric Science. Annual Report
Miami Winter Symp — Miami Winter Symposium
MIASA — Mineralogical Magazine and Journal of the Mineralogical Society
Miasn Ind SSSR — Miasnaia Industriia SSSR
MIB — Memorie. Accademia delle Scienze. Istituto di Bologna
MIB — Moneta Imperii Byzantini
MIB Miner Ind Bull — MIB. Mineral Industries Bulletin
MIBNAU — Instituut voor Toegepast Biologisch Onderoek in de Natuur [Institute for Biological Field Research]. Mededeling
MIBS — Memoirs of the Indian Botanical Society
MIBT — Muzej Istocne Bosne u Tuzli
MIBUB — Mikrobiyoloji Bulteni
MIBUBI — Bulletin of Microbiology
MiC — Man in Community
Mic — Michigan Music Educator
MIC — Modeling Identification and Control
MIC — Monumenta Iuris Canonici
MICA — Memoirs. International Congress of Anthropology
MicA — Michigan Academician
Micafil Nachr — Micafil-Nachrichten
MICCC — Monograph Series. International Council for Computer Communications
Miceti Patog — Miceti Patogeni dell'Uomo e degli Animali
MIC G — Monumenta Iuris Canonici. Corpus Glossatorum
MicH — Michigan History
Mich — Michigan Reports
MichA — Michigan Academician
Mich Acad — Michigan Academician
Mich Acad Sci Arts & Lett Pap — Michigan Academy of Science, Arts, and Letters. Papers [New York]
Mich Acad Sci Pap — Michigan Academy of Science, Arts, and Letters. Papers
Mich Acad Sci Papers — Michigan Academy of Science, Arts, and Letters. Papers
Mich Ac Sc Rp An Rp — Michigan Academy of Science. Report. Annual Report
Mich Admin Code — Michigan Administrative Code
Mich Agric Exp — Michigan. Agricultural Experiment Station. Publications
Mich Agric Coll Exp Stn Q Bull — Michigan Agricultural College. Experiment Station. Quarterly Bulletin
Mich Agric Exp Stn Annu Rep — Michigan. Agricultural Experiment Station. Annual Report
Mich Agric Exp Stn Mem — Michigan. Agricultural Experiment Station. Memoir

Mich Agric Exp Stn Q Bull — Michigan. Agricultural Experiment Station. Quarterly Bulletin

Mich Agric Exp Stn Spec Bull — Michigan. Agricultural Experiment Station. Special Bulletin

Mich Agric Exp Stn Tech Bull — Michigan. Agricultural Experiment Station. Technical Bulletin

Mich Alumni Quar Rev — Michigan Alumni Quarterly Review

Mich App — Michigan Appeals Reports

Mich Archit Engr — Michigan Architect and Engineer

Mich Assn Chiefs Police Proc — Michigan Association of Chiefs of Police. Proceedings

Mich Audubon News — Michigan Audubon News

Mich Audubon Newsl — Michigan Audubon Newsletter

Mich BJ — Michigan Bar Journal

Mich Bot — Michigan Botanist

Mich Bus Pap — Michigan Business Papers

Mich Bus R — Michigan Business Review

Mich Bus Rep — Michigan Business Reports

Mich Bus Stud — Michigan Business Studies

Mich Comp Laws — Michigan Compiled Laws

Mich Comp Laws Ann (West) — Michigan Compiled Laws, Annotated (West)

Mich Conserv — Michigan Conservation

Mich Corp Finance and Bus LJ — Michigan Corporate Finance and Business Law Journal

Mich Crop Rep — Michigan Crop Report

Mich Dent Assoc J — Michigan Dental Association. Journal

Mich Dent J — Michigan Dental Journal

Mich Dep Conserv Game Div Rep — Michigan. Department of Conservation. Game Division Report

Mich Dep Conserv Geol Surv Div Annu Stat Summ — Michigan. Department of Conservation. Geological Survey Division. Annual Statistical Summary

Mich Dep Conserv Geol Surv Div Prog Rep — Michigan Department of Conservation. Geological Survey Division. Progress Report

Mich Dep Conserv Geol Surv Div Publ — Michigan Department of Conservation. Geological Survey Division.Publication

Mich Dep Conserv Geol Surv Div Water Invest — Michigan. Department of Conservation. Geological Survey Division. Water Investigation

Mich Dep Nat Resour Geol Surv Div Misc — Michigan Department of Natural Resources. Geological Survey Division. Miscellany

Mich Dry Bean Dig — Michigan Dry Bean Digest

Mich Econ — Michigan Economy

Mich Ed J — Michigan Education Journal

Mich Energy — Michigan Energy

Mich Engr — Michigan Engineer

Mich Ent — Michigan Entomologist

Mich Entomol — Michigan Entomologist

Mich Farm Econ — Michigan Farm Economics. Michigan State University. Cooperative Extension Service

Mich Fem Stud — Michigan Feminist Studies

Mich Fish — Michigan Fisheries

Mich Fmr — Michigan Farmer and State Journal of Agriculture

Mich For — Michigan Forestry

Mich Geol Surv Bull — Michigan. Geological Survey. Bulletin

Mich Geol Surv Circ — Michigan. Geological Survey. Circular

Mich Geol Surv Div Annu Stat Summ — Michigan Geological Survey Division. Annual Statistical Summary

Mich Geol Surv Div Bull — Michigan. Geological Survey Division. Bulletin

Mich Geol Surv Div Misc — Michigan. Geological Survey Division. Miscellany

Mich Geol Surv Div Prog Rep — Michigan. Geological Survey Division. Progress Report

Mich Geol Surv Div Publ — Michigan. Geological Survey Division. Publication

Mich Geol Surv Div Rep Invest — Michigan Geological Survey Division. Report of Investigation

Mich Geol Surv Div Water Invest — Michigan. Geological Survey Division. Water Investigation

Mich Geol Surv Rep Invest — Michigan. Geological Survey. Report of Investigation

Mich Gov Stud — Michigan Governmental Studies

Mich G S Rp — Michigan. Geological Survey. Michigan State Board of Geological Survey. Report

MichH — Michigan History Magazine

Mich His Col — Michigan Historical Commission. Collections

Mich His M — Michigan History Magazine

Mich Hist — Michigan History

Mich Hist Coll — Michigan Historical Collections. Michigan Historical Commission

Mich Hist M — Michigan History Magazine

Mich Hist Mag — Michigan History Magazine. Michigan Historical Commission

Mich Hist Soc Coll — Michigan Pioneer and Historical Society Collections

Mich Hlth — Michigan Health

Mich Hosp — Michigan Hospitals

Michigan Agric Exp Sta Element Sci Bull — Michigan Agricultural Experiment Station. Elementary Science Bulletin

Michigan Agric Exp Sta Folder — Michigan Agricultural Experiment Station. Folder

Michigan Agric Exp Sta Res Bull — Michigan Agricultural Experiment Station. Research Bulletin

Michigan Agric Exp Sta Special Bull — Michigan Agricultural Experiment Station. Special Bulletin

Michigan Bu — Michigan Business

Michigan Geol Biol Surv Publ Biol Ser — Michigan Geological and Biological Survey Publication. Biological Series

Michigan Geol Survey Ann Statistical Summ — Michigan. Geological Survey. Annual Statistical Summary

Michigan Geol Survey Rept Inv — Michigan. Geological Survey. Report of Investigation

Michigan Geol Survey Water Inv — Michigan. Geological Survey. Water Investigation

Michigan Law Rev — Michigan Law Review

Michigan Med — Michigan Medicine

Michigan Univ Mus Paleontology Contr — Michigan University. Museum of Paleontology. Contributions

Michigan Univ Mus Zoology Occasional Paper — Michigan University. Museum of Zoology. Occasional Papers

Mich Int Bus Stud — Michigan International Business Studies

Mich Inv — Michigan Investor

Mich Law R — Michigan Law Review

Mich Law Rev — Michigan Law Review

Mich Legis Serv — Michigan Legislative Service

Mich Leg News — Michigan Legal News

Mich Libn — Michigan Librarian

Mich Lib News — Michigan Library News

Mich Librn — Michigan Librarian

Mich LJ — Michigan Law Journal

Mich LR — Michigan Law Review

Mich L Rev — Michigan Law Review

Mich Manuf Fin Rec — Michigan Manufacturer and Financial Record

Mich Math J — Michigan Mathematical Journal

Mich Med — Michigan Medicine

Mich Med News — Michigan Medical News

Mich Med Soc J — Michigan Medical Society. Journal

Mich Mfr — Michigan Manufacturer and Financial Record

Mich Miner — Michigan Miner

Mich Mol Inst Press Symp Ser — Michigan Molecular Institute Press. Symposium Series

Mich M Soc J — Michigan State Medical Society. Journal

Mich Munic Leag Proc — Michigan Municipal League. Proceedings

Mich Munic R — Michigan Municipal Review

Mich Mus Educ — Michigan Music Educator

Mich Nat Resour Mag — Michigan Natural Resources Magazine

Mich Nurse — Michigan Nurse

Mich Nurse Newsl — Michigan Nurse Newsletter

Michoacan Mex Com For Bol Ser Tec — Michoacan, Mexico. Comision Forestal. Boletin. Serie Tecnica

Mich Occup Hlth — Michigan's Occupational Health

Mich Out Of Doors — Michigan Out-of-Doors

Mich Pap Geogr — Michigan Papers in Geography

Mich Papy — Michigan Papyri

Mich Police J — Michigan Police Journal. Michigan Association of Chiefs of Police

Mich Prob Assn Proc — Michigan Probation Association. Proceedings

Mich Pub Acts — Public and Local Acts of the Legislature of the State of Michigan

Mich Publ Hlth — Michigan Public Health

MichQR — Michigan Quarterly Review

Mich Q Rev — Michigan Quarterly Review

Mich Quart Rev — Michigan Quarterly Review

Mich Rds Forests — Michigan Roads and Forests

Mich Reg — Michigan Register

Mich Res — Michigan Researcher

Mich SBA Jo — Michigan State Bar Association. Journal

Mich S B J — Michigan State Bar Journal

Mich Sci Action Mich Agric Exp Stn — Michigan Science in Action. Michigan Agricultural Experiment Station

Mich Sheriffs Assn Proc — Michigan Sheriffs Association. Proceedings

Mich Stat Abstr — Michigan Statistical Abstract

Mich Stat Ann (Callaghan) — Michigan Statutes, Annotated (Callaghan)

Mich State Bar Jour — Michigan State Bar Journal

Mich State Coll Agric Appl Sci Agric Exp Stn Q Bull — Michigan State College of Agricultural and Applied Science.Agricultural Experiment Station. Quarterly Bulletin

Mich State Coll Agric Appl Sci Agric Exp Stn Spec Bull — Michigan State College of Agricultural and Applied Science.Agricultural Experiment Station. Special Bulletin

Mich State Coll Agric Appl Sci Agric Exp Stn Tech Bull — Michigan. State College of Agricultural and Applied Science. Agricultural Experiment Station. Technical Bulletin

Mich State Coll Vet — Michigan State College Veterinarian

Mich State Dent Assoc J — Michigan State Dental Association. Journal

Mich State Dent Soc Bull — Michigan State Dental Society. Bulletin

Mich State Dent Soc J — Michigan State Dental Society. Journal

Mich State Econ Rec — Michigan State Economic Record

Mich State Univ Agric Exp Stn Annu Rep — Michigan State University. Agricultural Experiment Station. Annual Report

Mich State Univ Agric Exp Stn Mem — Michigan. State University. Agricultural Experiment Station. Memoir

Mich State Univ Agric Exp Stn Q Bull — Michigan. State University. Agricultural Experiment Station. Quarterly Bulletin

Mich State Univ Agric Exp Stn Spec Bull — Michigan. State University. Agricultural Experiment Station. Special Bulletin

Mich State Univ Agric Exp Stn Tech Bull — Michigan. State University. Agricultural Experiment Station. Technical Bulletin

Mich State Univ Lat Am Stud Cent Occ Pap — Michigan State University. Latin American Studies Center. Occasional Papers

Mich St BJ — Michigan State Bar Journal

Mich St Coll Vet — Michigan State College Veterinarian

Mich St Univ Vet — Michigan State University Veterinarian

Mich Technol Univ Ford For Cent Res Notes — Michigan Technological University. Ford Forestry Center. Research Notes

Mich Univ Eng Res Inst Eng Res Bull — Michigan University. Engineering Research Institute. Engineering Research Bulletin

Mich Univ Inst Sci Technol Rep — Michigan University. Institute of Science and Technology. Report

Mich Univ Mus Zool Oc P — Michigan University. Museum of Zoology. Occasional Papers

Mich Water Res Comm Rept — Michigan Water Resources Commission. Report
Mich Wat Wks News — Michigan Water Works News
Mich Wildl — Michigan Wildlife
Mich Wood Technol — Michigan Wood Technology
Mich YB Int'l Legal Stud — Michigan Yearbook of International Legal Studies
MiCIS — Microbial Culture Information Service
MIC Model Identif Control — MIC. Modeling, Identification, and Control
MICOB — Micron
Micol Ital — Micologia Italiana
Micro — Microprocessing and Microprogramming
Micro-6502/6809 J — Micro - The 6502/6809 Journal
Microb Comp Genomics — Microbial and Comparative Genomics
Microb Drug Resist — Microbial Drug Resistance
Microb Drug Resist Larchmont NY — Microbial Drug Resistance (Larchmont, New York)
Microbeam Anal — Microbeam Analysis. Proceedings. Annual Conference. Microbeam AnalysisSociety
Microbeam Anal Deerfield Beach Fla — Microbeam Analysis (Deerfield Beach, Florida)
Microbeam Anal Soc Annu Conf Proc — Microbeam Analysis Society. Annual Conference. Proceedings
Microb Ecol — Microbial Ecology
Microb Ecol Health Dis — Microbial Ecology in Health and Disease
Microb Ecol Phylloplane Pap Int Symp Microbiol Leaf Surf — Microbial Ecology of the Phylloplane. Papers Read at the InternationalSymposium on the Microbiology of Leaf Surfaces
Microbes Infect — Microbes and Infection
Microb Genet Bull — Microbial Genetics Bulletin
Microb Geochem — Microbial Geochemistry
Microb Growth C1 Compounds Proc Int Symp — Microbial Growth on C1 Compounds. Proceedings. International Symposium
Microbiol Abstr — Microbiological Abstracts
Microbiol Aliments Nutr — Microbiologie, Aliments, Nutrition
Microbiol Bull Dep Agric Jamaica — Microbiological Bulletin. Department of Agriculture. Jamaica
Microbiol Circ Dep Sci Agric Jamaica — Microbiological Circular. Department of Science and Agriculture. Jamaica
Microbiol Civ Eng Proc Fed Eur Microbiol Soc Symp — Microbiology in Civil Engineering. Proceedings. Federation of European Microbiological Societies Symposium
Microbiol Ecology — Microbiological Ecology
Microbiol Esp — Microbiologia Espanola
Microbiol Fish Meat Curing Brines Proc Int Symp — Microbiology of Fish and Meat Curing Brines. Proceedings. InternationalSymposium on Food Microbiology
Microbiol Immun — Microbiology and Immunology
Microbiol Immunol — Microbiology and Immunology
Microbiol Mol Biol Rev — Microbiology and Molecular Biology Reviews
Microbiolog — Microbiology
Microbiologia Esp — Microbiologia Espanola
Microbiologia Parazit Epidem — Microbiologia, Parazitologia, Epidemiologia
Microbiology (Engl Transl Mikrobiologiya) — Microbiology (English Translation of Mikrobiologiya)
Microbiol Parazitol Epidemiol — Microbiologia, Parazitologia, Epidemiologia
Microbiol Parazitol Epidemiol (Buchar) — Microbiologia, Parazitologia, Epidemiologia (Bucharest)
Microbiol Res — Microbiological Research
Microbiol Rev — Microbiological Reviews
Microbiol Sci — Microbiological Sciences
Microbiol Ser — Microbiology Series
Microbiol Series — Microbiology Series
Microbios L — Microbios Letters
Microbios Lett — Microbios Letters
Microb Pathog — Microbial Pathogenesis
Microb Releases — Microbial Releases. Viruses, Bacteria, Fungi
Microcard Bull — Microcard Bulletin
Microchem J — Microchemical Journal
Microchem J Symp Ser — Microchemical Journal. Symposium Series
Microcirc Endothelium Lymphatics — Microcirculation, Endothelium, and Lymphatics
Microcirculation (NY) — Microcirculation (New York)
Microcomp Dig — Microcomputer Digest
Microcompos Nanophase Mater Proc Symp — Microcomposites and Nanophase Materials. Proceedings. Symposium
Microcompu — Microcomputing
Microcomput Civ Eng — Microcomputers in Civil Engineering
Microcomput Index — Microcomputer Index
Microcomput Inf Manage — Microcomputers for Information Management
Microcomput Printout — Microcomputer Printout
Micro Copy Cards Microfich — Micro-copy Cards and Microfiches
Micro Decis — Micro Decision
Microdial Neurosci — Microdialysis in the Neurosciences
Microecol Ther — Microecology and Therapy
Microelectron and Reliab — Microelectronics and Reliability
Microelectron Eng — Microelectronic Engineering
Microelectronics Engl Transl — Microelectronics. English Translation
Microelectron Int — Microelectronics International
Microelectron J — Microelectronics Journal
Microelectron Reliab — Microelectronics and Reliability
Microelectron Signal Process — Microelectronics and Signal Processing
Microel Rel — Microelectronics and Reliability
Microfiche Fdn Newsl — Microfiche Foundation. Newsletter
Microfilm Abstr — Microfilm Abstracts
Microform Publ Geol Soc Am — Microform Publication. Geological Society of America

Microform R — Microform Review
Microform Rev — Microform Review
Microgravity Sci Technol — Microgravity Science and Technology
Microgr Newsl — Micrographics Newsletter
Microgr Prep — Micrographie Preparateur
Micro Jrl — Microwave Journal
Microlepid Palearct — Microlepidoptera Palaearctica
Microlithogr World — Microlithography World
Micro Mktw — Micro Marketworld
Micronesian Rep — Micronesian Reporter
Micronesica J Coll Guam — Micronesica. Journal of the College of Guam
Micronesica J Univ Guam — Micronesica. Journal of the University of Guam
Micrones Reporter — Micronesian Reporter
Micron Microsc Acta — Micron and Microscopica Acta
Microorg Ferment — Microorganisms and Fermentation
Microorg Ind — Microorganisms and Industry
Microorg Infect Dis — Microorganisms and Infectious Diseases
Micropaleon — Micropaleontology
Micropaleont Bull — Micropaleontology Bulletin
Micropaleontolog Spec Publ — Micropaleontology. Special Publication
Microporous Mater — Microporous Materials
Microporous Mesoporous Mater — Microporous and Mesoporous Materials
Microprobe Anal — Microprobe Analysis
Micro Proc Annu Workshop Microprogram — Micro Proceedings. Annual Workshop on Microprogramming
Microprocess and Microprogram — Microprocessing and Microprogramming
Microprocess and Microsyst — Microprocessors and Microsystems
Microprocess Microprogram — Microprocessing and Microprogramming
Microprocessors Microsysts — Microprocessors and Microsystems
Microprocess Software Q — Microprocessor Software Quarterly
Microprocess Work — Microprocessors at Work
Micro Pub — Micro Publisher
Microsc — Microscope
Microsc Act — Microscopica Acta
Microsc Acta — Microscopica Acta
Microsc Acta Suppl — Microscopica Acta. Supplement
Microscale Thermophys Eng — Microscale Thermophysical Engineering
Microsc Aspects Adhes Lubr Proc Int Meet Soc Chim Phys — Microscopic Aspects of Adhesion and Lubrication. Proceedings.International Meeting. Society de Chimie Physique
Microsc Bull — Microscopical Bulletin and Science News
Microsc Cryst Front — Microscope and Crystal Front
Microsc Electron Biol Cel — Microscopia Electronica y Biologia Celular
Microsc Entomol Mon — Microscope and Entomological Monthly
Microsc Handb — Microscopy Handbooks
Microsc J Quekett Microsc Club — Microscopy. Journal of the Quekett Microscopical Club
Microsc Microanal — Microscopy and Microanalysis
Microsc Microanal Microstruct — Microscopy, Microanalysis, Microstructures
Microscope Entomol Monthly — Microscope and Entomological Monthly
Microsc Oxid Proc Int Conf — Microscopy of Oxidation. Proceedings. International Conference
Microsc Res Tech — Microscopy Research and Technique
Microsc Semicond Mater 1991 Proc Inst Phys Conf — Microscopy of Semiconducting Materials 1991. Proceedings. Institute of Physics Conference
Microsc Soc Can Bull — Microscopical Society of Canada. Bulletin
Microsc Today — Microscopy Today
Microsomal Part Protein Synth Pap Symp — Microsomal Particles and Protein Synthesis. Papers Presented at the Symposium
Microsomes Drug Oxid Chem Carcinog Int Symp Microsomes Drug — Microsomes, Drug Oxidations, and Chemical Carcinogenesis. InternationalSymposium on Microsomes and Drug Oxidations
Micros Soc Can Proc — Microscopical Society of Canada. Proceedings
Micros Symp Proc — Microscopy Symposium. Proceedings
Microstruct Sci — Microstructural Science
Microsymp Macromol Polyvinyl Chloride — Microsymposium on Macromolecules Polyvinyl Chloride
Micro Syst — Micro Systems
Microsystm — Microsystems
Microtec — Microtecnic
Microvasc R — Microvascular Research
Microvasc Res — Microvascular Research
Microwave Energy Appl Newsl — Microwave Energy Applications Newsletter
Microwave J — Microwave Journal
Microwave Opt Technol Lett — Microwave and Optical Technology Letters
Microwave Res Inst Symp Ser Polytech Inst Brooklyn — Microwave Research Institute Symposia Series. Polytechnic Institute of Brooklyn
Microwave Res Inst Symp Ser Polytech Inst NY — Microwave Research Instutute Symposia Series. Polytechnic Institute of New York
Microwaves Opt Acoust — Microwaves, Optics, and Acoustics
Microwaves Opt Antennas — Microwaves, Optics, and Antennas
Microwaves Theory Appl Mater Process — Microwaves. Theory and Application in Materials Processing
Microwave Syst News — Microwave Systems News
Microw Opt Technol Lett — Microwave and Optical Technology Letters
Microw Syst News — Microwave Systems News
MIC S — Monumenta Iuris Canonici. Subsidia
MID — March of India (Delhi)
MID — Midland Bank Review
Mid — Midstream
Mid — Midway
MidA — Mid-America: An Historical Review
MIDAD — NIDA Research Monograph
MiDAIK — Mitteilungen. Deutsches Archaeologisches Institut. Abteilung Kairo
Mid-Am — Mid-America: An Historical Review

Mid Amer Rev Sociol — Mid-American Review of Sociology
Mid-Am Hist — Mid-America: An Historical Review
Mid-Am Oil Gas Rep — Mid-America Oil and Gas Reporter
Mid Am Outlk — Mid-American Outlook
Mid Am Res Rec New Orleans — Middle American Research Records (New Orleans)
Mid-Am Spectrosc Symp Proc — Mid-America Spectroscopy Symposium. Proceedings
Mid-Atl Ind Waste Conf — Mid-Atlantic Industrial Waste Conference
Mid-Atl Ind Waste Conf Proc — Mid-Atlantic Industrial Waste Conference. Proceedings
MIDC Bull — MIDC (Metals Industry Development Centre) Bulletin
MIDCD — Modeling Identification and Control
Midcon Conf Rec — Midcon Conference Record
Mid-Cont — Mid-Continent
Mid Cont Bk — Mid-Continent Banker
Midcontinent Am Studies Jour — Midcontinent American Studies. Journal
Midcont J Archaeol — Midcontinental Journal of Archaeology
Mid-Cont Lepid Ser — Mid-Continent Lepidoptera Series
MidCR — Mid-Century Review
Middle Am Res Rec — Middle American Research Records
Middle Atlant Fish — Middle Atlantic Fisheries
Middlebury Hist Soc Papers and Pr — Middlebury [*Vermont*] Historical Society. Papers and Proceedings
Middle E — Middle East
Middle Eas — Middle East
Middle East Abstr Index — Middle East. Abstracts and Index
Middle East Archtl Design — Middle East Architectural Design
Middle East Bus Wkly — Middle East Business Weekly
Middle East Comp — Middle East Computing
Middle East Dent Oral Health — Middle East Dentistry and Oral Health
Middle East Econ Dig — Middle East Economic Digest
Middle East Electron — Middle East Electronics
Middle East Exec Repts — Middle East Executive Reports
Middle East J — Middle East Journal
Middle East J Anaesthesiol — Middle East Journal of Anaesthesiology
Middle East Med Assem Proc — Middle East Medical Assembly. Proceedings
Middle East R — Middle East Review
Middle East Tech Univ J Pure Appl Sci — Middle East Technical University. Journal of Pure and Applied Sciences
Middle E Executive Rep — Middle East Executive Reports
Middle E J — Middle East Journal
Middle E Mg — Middle Eastern Monographs
Middle E St — Middle Eastern Studies
Middle States Assn Col & Sec Sch Proc — Middle States Association of Colleges and Secondary Schools. Proceedings
Middle States Council for Social Studies Proc — Middle States Council for the Social Studies. Proceedings
Middle Thames Nat — Middle-Thames Naturalist
Middletonian Med Mag — Middletonian Medical Magazine
Middx Hosp J — Middlesex Hospital Journal
Middx Hosp Rep Med Surg Path Regist — Middlesex Hospital. Reports of the Medical, Surgical, and Pathological Registrars
MIDE — Methods in Investigative and Diagnostic Endocrinology
MidE — Middle East Journal
MidEast — Middle East
Mid East Ann Rev — Middle East Annual Review
Mid East Annu R — Middle East Annual Review
Mid East E — Middle East and African Economist
Mid East Elect — Middle East Electricity
Mid East Fin Dir — Middle East Financial Directory
Mid East Forum — Middle East Forum
Mid East J — Middle East Journal
Mid East J Anaesthesiol — Middle East Journal of Anaesthesiology
Mid East R — Middle East Review
Mid East Stud — Middle Eastern Studies
Mid E J — Middle East Journal
MIDEO — Melanges. Institut Dominicain d'Etudes Orientales
Mid E Stud — Middle Eastern Studies
Mid E Stud Assoc Bull — Middle Eastern Studies Association Bulletin
Mid E Studies — Middle Eastern Studies
MIDGA — Mitsubishi Denki Giho
Mid Health Visit Com Nurs — Midwife, Health Visitor, and Community Nurse
Midi Agric Vitic — Midi Agricole et Viticole
Midland — Midland Monthly
Midland Bank R — Midland Bank Review
Midland Bank Rev — Midland Bank Review
Midland Hist — Midland History
Midland Sch — Midland Schools
Midl Drug Pharm Rev — Midland Druggist and Pharmaceutical Review
Midl Macromol Monogr — Midland Macromolecular Monographs
Midl Med Rev — Midland Medical Review
Midl Med Surg Reporter Topogr Statist J — Midland Medical and Surgical Reporter. And Topographical and Statistical Journal
Midl Naturalist — Midland Naturalist
Midm — Midstream
MidM — Midwest Monographs
Mid Pacif Mag — Mid-Pacific Magazine
MidQ — Midwest Quarterly
MidR — Midwest Review
MIDr — Modern International Drama
Mid-S F — Mid-South Folklore
Mid South Neurosci Dev Group Publ — Mid-South Neuroscience Development Group Publication
Mid-South Q Bus R — Mid-South Quarterly Business Review

Mid W Banker — Mid-Western Banker [*Milwaukee*]
Midw Constr News — Midwest Construction News
Midw Engr — Midwest Engineer
Mid West Bank — Mid-western Banker
Mid-West Bnk — Mid-Western Banker
Midwest Conf Endocrinol Metab — Midwest Conference on Endocrinology and Metabolism
Midwest Conf Throid Endocrinol — Midwest Conference on the Thyroid and Endocrinology
Midwest Dent — Midwestern Dentist
Midwest Eng — Midwest Engineer
Midwest Folk — Midwest Folklore
Midwest J — Midwest Journal
Midwest J Phil — Midwest Journal of Philosophy
Midwest Mus Conf Am Assoc Mus Q — Midwest Museums Conference. American Association of Museums. Quarterly
Midwest Q — Midwest Quarterly
Midwest R Publ Adm — Midwest Review of Public Administration
Midwest Stud Phil — Midwest Studies in Philosophy
Midwest Symp Circuits Syst — Midwest Symposium on Circuits and Systems
Midw Fmr — Midwest Farmer
Midwife Health Visit — Midwife and Health Visitor [*Later, Midwife, Health Visitor, and Community Nurse*]
Midwife Health Visit Community Nurse — Midwife, Health Visitor, and Community Nurse
Midwives Chron — Midwives Chronicle
Midw Jour Pol Sci — Midwest Journal of Political Science
Midw Q — Midwest Quarterly
Midw Quar — Midwest Quarterly
Midw Stud P — Midwest Studies in Philosophy
MIE — Memoires. Institut d'Egypte
MIE — Middle East and African Economist
Miel Fr — Miel de France
Mie Med J — Mie Medical Journal
Mie Med J Suppl — Mie Medical Journal. Supplement
Mie Med Sci — Mie Medical Science
MIENDE — Minerals and the Environment
MiER — Middle East Review
Mies Galic Tow Ochr Zwierz — Miesiecznik Galicyjskiego Towarzystwa Ochrony Zwierzat
Mies Sad Ogrod — Miesiecznik Sadowniczo-Ogrodniczy
Mies Terap — Miesiecznik Terapeutyczny
Mie Univ Fac Bioresour Bull — Mie University. Faculty of Bioresources. Bulletin
MIF — Memoires. Institut de France
MIF — Munshi Indological Felicitation Volume. Bharatiya Vidya
MIFAN — Memoires. Institut Francais d'Afrique Noire
MIFAO — Memoires Publies par les Membres de l'Institut Francais d'Archeologie Orientaledu Caire
MIFAOC — Memoires Publies par les Membres de l'Institut Francais d'Archeologie Orientaledu Caire
MIFFK — Materialy po Istorii Fauny i Flory Kazakhstana
MIG — Management in Government
MIGFW — Mitteilungen. Institut fuer Geschichtsforschung und Archivwissenschaft in Wien
MIGKA — Mineralogiya i Geokhimiya
Miglior Genet — Miglioramento Genetica. Istituto di Allevamento Vegetale per la Cerealcoltura
MIGMUP — Memorie dell'Istituto Geologico e Mineralogia della Universita di Padova
Migne P G — Patrologia Graeca (Migne)
Migne P L — Patrologia Latina (Migne)
MIGRA — Miscellanea Graeca
Migraine Symp — Migraine Symposium
Migr dans le Monde — Migrations dans le Monde
Migr Int — Migrations Internationales
Migr Today — Migration Today
MIHC — Mensajes. Institucion Hispanocubana de Cultura
MIHP — Memoires et Bulletins. Institut Historique de Provence
MII — Man in India
MIIGA — Mie Igaku
MIIMA — Memorie. Istituto Italiano di Idrobiologia Dottore Marco De Marchi
MIIMD — Microbiology and Immunology
MIJL — Memoirs of the International Journal of American Linguistics, or Indiana University Publications in Anthropology and Linguistics
Mijloc Farm — Mijlocitorul Farmaceutic
MIKKA — Metody Issledovaniya Katalizatorov i Kataliticheskikh Reaktsii
Mikkelin Laan Maanviljelyss Vuosik — Mikkelin Laanin Maanviljelysseuran Vuosikirja Kertomus
Mikol Fitopat — Mikologiya i Fitopatologiya
Mikol Fitopatol — Mikologiya i Fitopatologiya
Mikrobiol — Mikrobiologiya
Mikrobiol Derg — Mikrobiologi Dergisi
Mikrobiol Inst Zinat Rak — Mikrobiologijas Instituta Zinatniskie Raksti
Mikrobiol Nar Gospod Med Mater Zizdu Ukr Mikrobiol Tov — Mikrobiologiya dlya Narodnogo Gospodarstva i Meditsini. Materiali ZizduUkrainskogo Mikrobiologichnogo Tovaristva
Mikrobiol Proizvod Dokl Konf Mikrobiol Lit SSR — Mikrobiologiya i Proizvodstvo. Doklady Dolozhennye na KonferentsiiMikrobiologov Litovskoi SSR
Mikrobiol Prom Ref Sb — Mikrobiologicheskaya Promyshlennost Referativnyi Sbornik
Mikrobiol Protsessy Pochvakh Mold — Mikrobiologicheskie Protsessy v Pochvakh Moldavii
Mikrobiol Sb — Mikrobiologicheskii Sbornik
Mikrobiol Sint — Mikrobiologicheskii Sintez
Mikrobiol Sint Sb Inf Mater — Mikrobiologicheskii Sintez Sbornik Informatsii Materialov

Mikrobiol Z — Mikrobiolohichnyi Zhurnal
Mikrobiol Zh — Mikrobiologichnyi Zhurnal
Mikrobiol Zh (Kiev) — Mikrobiolohichnyi Zhurnal (Kiev)
Mikrobiol Zurn — Mikrobiologicnyj Zurnal/Journal de Microbiologie
Mikrobiyol Bul — Mikrobiyoloji Bulteni
Mikrobiyol Bul Suppl — Mikrobiyoloji Bulteni. Supplement
Mikrob Umwelt Antimikrob Massnahmen — Mikrobielle Umwelt und Antimikrobielle Massnahmen
Mikroch Act — Mikrochimica Acta
Mikrochem Acta — Mikrochemica Acta
Mikrochemie Mikrochem Acta — Mikrochemie Vereinigt mit Mikrochemica Acta
Mikrochem Ver Mikrochim Acta — Mikrochemie Vereinigt mit Mikrochimica Acta
Mikrochim Acta — Mikrochimica Acta
Mikrochim Acta Suppl — Mikrochimica Acta. Supplement
Mikrochim Ichnoanal Acta — Mikrochimica et Ichnoanalytica Acta
Mikro Comp — Mikrocomputer-Zeitschrift
MikroComp Praxis — MikroComputer-Praxis
Mikroehlektron — Mikroehlektronika
Mikroelektronika Akad Nauk SSSR — Mikroelektronika Akademiya Nauk SSSR
Mikroelektronika Izd Sov Radio — Mikroelektronika Izdatelstvo Sovetskoe Radio
Mikroelektron Kongr Int Elektron Arbeitskreises Vortr — Mikroelektronik. Kongress des InternationalenElektronik-Arbeitskreises. Vortraege
Mikroelem Med — Mikroelementy v Meditsine
Mikroelem Miner — Mikroelementy v Mineralakh
Mikroelem Pochvakh Sov Soyuza — Mikroelementy v Pochvakh Sovetskogo Soyuza
Mikroelem Prod Rast — Mikroelementy v Produktivnost' Rastenii
Mikroelem Rastenievod Tr Inst Biol Akad Nauk Latv SSR — Mikroelementy v Rastenievodstve. Trudy Instituta Biologii. AkademiyaNauk Latviiskoi SSR
Mikroelem Sel Khoz Med Resp Mezhved Sb (Kiev) — Mikroelementy v Selskom Khozyaistve i Meditsine Respublikanskii Mezhvedomstvennyi Sbornik (Kiev)
Mikroelem Selsk Khoz Dokl Resp Soveshch — Mikroelementy v Selskom Khozyaistve. Doklady RespublikanskogoSoveshchaniya
Mikroelem Sel'sk Khoz Med — Mikroelementy v Selskom Khozyaistve i Meditsine
Mikroelem Selsk Khoz Med Dokl Vses Soveshch — Mikroelementy v Selskom Khozyaistve i Meditsine. Doklady VsesoyuznogoSoveshchaniya po Mikroelementam
Mikroelem Selsk Khoz Med Mater Vses Soveshch — Mikroelementy v Selskom Khozyaistve i Meditsine. Materialy VsesoyuznogoSoveshchaniya po Voprosam Primeneniya Mikroelementov v Selskom KhozyaistveMeditsine
Mikroelem Selsk Khoz Med Tr Vses Soveshch — Mikroelementy v Selskom Khozyaistve i Meditsine. Trudy VsesoyuznogoSoveshchaniya po Mikroelementam
Mikroelem Sib — Mikroelementy v Sibiri
Mikroelem Sib Inf Byull — Mikroelementy v Sibiri Informatsionnyi Byulleten
Mikroelem SSSR — Mikroelementy v SSSR. Naucnyj Sovet po Probleme Biologiceskaja rol' Mikroelementov v Zizni Rastenij, Zivotnyh i Celoveka
Mikroelem Vost Sib Dal'nem Vostoke — Mikroelementy v Vostochnoi Sibiri i na Dal'nem Vostoke
Mikroelem Zhivotnovod Rastenievod — Mikroelementy v Zhivotnovodstve i Rastenievodstve
Mikroelem Zhizni Rast Zhivotn Tr Konf — Mikroelementy v Zhizni Rastenii i Zhivotnykh. Trudy Konferentsii poMikroelementam
Mikrogeom Ekspl Svoistva Mash — Mikrogeometriya i Ekspluatatsionnye Svoistva Mashin
Mikro-Klein Comput — Mikro-Klein Computer
Mikrooekol Ther — Mikrooekologie und Therapie
Mikroorg i Rast — Mikroorganizmy i Rasteniya
Mikroorg Rast Trudy Inst Mikrobiol Akad Nauk Latvii SSR — Mikroorganizmy i Rasteniya. Trudy Instituta Mikrobiologii Akademii Nauk Latviiskoi SSR
Mikroorg Selsk Khoz Tr Mezhvuz Nauchn Konf — Mikroorganizmy v Selskom Khozyaistve. Trudy Mezhvuzovskoi NauchnoiKonferentsii
Mikroprovod Prib Sopr — Mikroprovod i Pribory Soprotivleniya
Mikrosc Naturfr — Mikroscopie fuer Naturfreunde
Mikroskop Naturfr — Mikroskopie fuer Naturfreunde
Mikrotom Nachr — Mikrotom-Nachrichten
Mikrowelin — Mikroweilen and Military Electronics
Mikrowellen Mag — Mikrowellen Magazin
Mikrozirk Forsch Klin — Mikrozirkulation in Forschung und Klinik
MIL — Memorie. Istituto Lombardo
MIL — Memorie. Istituto Lombardo di Scienze e Lettere, Scienze, Morali e Storiche
Mi L — Michigan Law Review
MIL — Middle East
Mil — Militaergeschichte
Mi L — University of Miami. Law Review
MilA — Military Affairs
Mil Aff — Military Affairs
Mil Affairs — Military Affairs
Milano Riv Mens Com — Milano. Rivista Mensile del Comune
Milano Tec — Milano Tecnica
Milan Semin Mat Fis Rend — Milan. Seminario Matematico e Fisico. Rendiconti
Mil At Aten — Atti dell' Ateneo, gia Accademia Fisico-Medico-Statistica di Milano
Mil At Cagnola — Atti della Fondazione Scientifica Cagnola dalla sua Istituzione in Poi (Milano)
Mil At S It — Atti della Societa Italiana di Scienze Naturali (Milano)
Milbank Mem — Milbank Memorial Fund. Quarterly
Milbank Mem Fund Annu Rep — Milbank Memorial Fund. Annual Report
Milbank Mem Fund Q — Milbank Memorial Fund. Quarterly
Milbank Mem Fund Q Bull — Milbank Memorial Fund. Quarterly Bulletin
Milbank Meml Fund Q Bull — Milbank Memorial Fund Quarterly Bulletin
Milbank Meml Fund Q Health Soc — Milbank Memorial Fund. Quarterly. Health and Society
Milbank Memor Fund Quart — Milbank Memorial Fund. Quarterly
Milbank Q — Milbank Quarterly
Milb Mem Fund Q — Milbank Memorial Fund. Quarterly

Mil Chapl Rev — Military Chaplains' Review
Milch Butter Ind — Milch- und Butter-Industrie
Milchforsch-Milchprax — Milchforschung-Milchpraxis
Milch Prax Rindermast — Milch Praxis und Rindermast
Milchw Anz — Milchwirtschaftlicher Anzeiger
Milchw Forsch — Milchwirtschaftliche Forschungen
Milchwirtsch Ber Bundesanst Wolfpassing Rotholz — Milchwirtschaftliche Berichte aus dem Bundesanstalten Wolfpassing und Rotholz
Milchwirtsch Forsch — Milchwirtschaftliche Forschungen
Milchwirtsch Forschgg — Milchwirtschaftliche Forschungen
Milchwirtsch Zentralbl — Milchwirtschaftliches Zentralblatt
Milchwirtsch Ztg — Milchwirtschaftliche Zeitung
Milchwirtsch Ztg Alpen Sudeten Donauraum — Milchwirtschaftliche Zeitung fuer den Alpen-, Sudeten- und Donauraum
Milchwiss — Milchwissenschaft
Milchwiss Ber — Milchwissenschaftliche Berichte
Milchwissenschaft Milk Sci Int — Milchwissenschaft. Milk Science International
Milchw LitBer — Milchwirtschaftlicher Literaturbericht
Milchw Taschenb — Milchwirtschaftliches Taschenbuch
Milchw Umsch — Milchwirtschaftliche Umschau
Milchw Zentbl — Milchwirtschaftliches Zentralblatt
Milchw Ztg — Milchwirtschaftliche Zeitung
Milch Ztg — Milch-Zeitung
Mildura Cultiv — Mildura Cultivator
Mil Effem — Effemeridi Astronomiche di Milano. Con Appendice di Osservazioni e Memorie Astronomiche
Mil Effem As — Effemeridi Astronomiche di Milano. Con Appendice di Osservazioni e Memorie Astronomiche
Mil Electron — Military Electronics
Mil Electron/Countermeas — Military Electronics/Countermeasures
Mil Eng — Military Engineer
Mil Engin — Military Engineer
Mil Engineer — Military Engineer. Society of Military Engineers
Miles Int Symp Ser — Miles International Symposium Series
Miles Mag — Miles Magazine. Miles Aircraft Ltd [*Reading*]
Milestones Conn Agr Home Econ — Milestones in Connecticut Agricultural and Home Economics
Mil Fib Opt N — Military Fiber Optics News
Mil G I Lomb — Giornale dell' I. R. Istituto Lombardo di Scienze, Lettere, ed Arti e Biblioteca Italiana. Compilata da Varj Dotti Nazionali e Stranieri (Milano)
Mil G S Inc — Giornale della Societa d' Incorragiamento delle Scienze. Stabilita in Milano
Mil Hist J — Military History Journal
Mil I Lomb G — Giornale dell' I. R. Istituto Lombardo di Scienze, Lettere, ed Arti e Biblioteca Italiana. Compilata da Varj Dotti Nazionali e Stranieri (Milano)
Mil I Lomb Mm — Memorie dell' I. R. Istituto Lombardo di Scienze, Lettere ed Arti.(Milano)
Mil I Lomb Rd — Reale Istituto Lombardo di'Scienze e Lettere. Rendiconti (Milano)
Militaergesch — Militaergeschichte
Militaerpol Dok — Militaerpolitik Dokumentation
Militaert T — Militaert Tidsskrift
Milit Aff — Military Affairs
Militararztl Publn — Militaeraerztliche Publikationen
Militarmed Arztl Kriegswiss — Militaermedizin und Aerztliche Kriegswissenschaft
Militarwiss Tech Mitt — Militaerwissenschaftliche und Technische Mitteilungen
Military Law R — Military Law Review
Military LJ — Military Law Journal
Military M — Military Market Annual
Military R — Military Review
Milit Dent J — Military Dental Journal
Milit Engr — Military Engineer
Milit Geneesk Tijdschr — Militair-Geneeskundig Tijdschrift
Milit Hist Tex Southwest — Military History of Texas and the Southwest
Milit Hosps Commn Bull Ottawa — Military Hospitals Commission Bulletin (Ottawa)
Milit LR — Military Law Review
Milit Med — Military Medicine
Milit Med J Iraq — Military Medical Journal of Iraq
Milit Musikerztg — Militaer-Musikerzeitung
Milit Rev — Military Review
Milit Surg — Military Surgeon [*Washington*]
Miliz For — Milizia Forestale
Milk Board J — Milk Board Journal
Milk Dairy Res Rep — Milk and Dairy Research. Report
Milk Dlr — Milk Dealer
Milk Ind — Milk Industry
Milk Ind Found Conv Proc Lab Sect — Milk Industry Foundation. Convention Proceedings. Laboratory Section
Milk Ind Found Conv Proc Milk Supplies Sect — Milk Industry Foundation. Convention Proceedings. Milk Supplies Section
Milk Ind Found Conv Proc Plant Sect — Milk Industry Foundation. Convention Proceedings. Plant Section
Milk Insp — Milk Inspector
Milk Intolerances Rejection Symp Gastroenterol Nutr Milk — Milk Intolerances and Rejection. Symposium of Gastroenterology andNutrition on Milk Intolerances
Milk Mag — Milk Magazine
Milk Messgr — Milk Messenger
Milk Plant Mo — Milk Plant Monthly
Milk Plant Mon — Milk Plant Monthly
Milk Pl Mon — Milk Plant Monthly
Milk Prod — Milk Producer
Milk Prod J — Milk Products Journal
Milk Prodr — Milk Producer
Milk Sanit — Milk Sanitarian

Milk Sci Int — Milk Science International
Milk Shorth J — Milking Shorthorn Journal
Milk Trade Gaz — Milk Trade Gazette
Milk Trade J — Milk Trade Journal
Milkweed Chron — Milkweed Chronicle
Mill Ambrosiano — Millenino Ambrosiano
Millers Gaz — Millers' Gazette
Millers J Australasia — Millers' Journal of Australasia
Millers Rev — Millers' Review
Mill Fact — Mill and Factory
Millgate Mo — Millgate Monthly
Mill Grain News — Milling and Grain News
Milling — Milling and Baking News
Milling F & F — Milling Feed and Fertilizer
Milling Feed Fert — Milling Feed and Fertiliser
Milling S — Changing Face of Breadstuffs (Milling and Baking News. Special Edition)
MillN — Mill Newsletter
Mill News — Mill Newsletter
Mill News Lett — Mill News Letter
Mil LR — Military Law Review
Mil L Rep — Military Law Reporter
Mil L Rev — Military Law Review
Mill Wks Pract Engng News — Mill and Works Practice and Engineering News
Mil Med — Military Medicine
Mil Med Pharm Rev (Belgrade) — Military Medical and Pharmaceutical Review (Belgrade)
Mil Mm I Lomb — Memorie dell' I. R. Istituto Lombardo di Scienze, Lettere ed Arti (Milano)
Mil Mm I Lomb Ven — Memorie dell' I. R. Istituto del Regno Lombardo-Veneto (Milano)
Miloticky Hospod — Miloticky Hospodar. Milotice nad Becvou
Mil Rev — Military Review
Mil R Ts — Militair Rechtelijk Tijdschrift
MILS — Mineral Industry Location System
Mil Sci Tech — Military Science and Technology
Mil S It At — Atti della Societa Italiana di Scienze Naturali (Milano)
Mil Surg — Military Surgeon
Mil Surgeon — Military Surgeon
Mil T — Militaert Tidsskrift
MILT — Minister's Letter. Letter to Indian People on Current Issues. Minister of Indian Affairs and Northern Development
MILTA — Militaertechnik
Miltitzer Ber Ather Ole — Miltitzer Berichte uber Atherische Ole. Riechstoffe
Milt Law R — Military Law Review
Milton Keynes J Archaeol Hist — Milton Keynes Journal of Archaeology and History
Milton N — Milton Newsletter
Milton Q — Milton Quarterly
Milton S — Milton Studies
Milton Stud — Milton Studies
Miltron — Miltronics
Milupa AG Wiss Abt Wiss Inf — Milupa AG. Wissenschaftliche Abteilung. Wissenschaftliche Information
Milupa Med Wiss Abt Wiss Inf — Milupa Med. Wissenschaftliche Abteilung. Wissenschaftliche Information
Milwau Jl — Milwaukee Journal
Milwaukee Med J — Milwaukee Medical Journal
Milwaukee Med Soc Times — Milwaukee Medical Society Times
Milwaukee Med Times — Milwaukee Medical Times
Milw BAG — Milwaukee Bar Association. Gavel
Milw Public Mus Contrib Biol Geol — Milwaukee Public Museum. Contributions in Biology and Geology
Milw Public Mus Occas Pap Nat Hist — Milwaukee Public Museum. Occasional Papers. Natural History
Milw Public Mus Publ Biol Geol — Milwaukee Public Museum. Publications in Biology and Geology
Milw Public Mus Spec Publ Biol Geol — Milwaukee Public Museum. Special Publications in Biology and Geology
Mi M — Mineralogical Magazine and Journal. Mineralogical Society
MIM — Mining and Industrial Magazine
MIM — Mining Magazine
MIM — Monatsblaetter fuer Innere Mission
MIM — Monatsschrift fuer Innere Mission
MIMA News — MIMA (Magnesia-Silica Insulation Manufacturers Association) News
MIMBD — Montanaro d'Italia - Monti e Boschi
MIMEA — Minerva Medica
Mimeo AS Indiana Agr Exp Sta — Mimeo AS. Indiana Agricultural Experiment Station
Mimeo AY Indiana Agr Exp Sta — Mimeo AY. Indiana Agricultural Experiment Station
Mimeo Circ NS Dep Agric — Mimeographed Circular Service. Nova Scotia Department of Agriculture and Marketing
Mimeo Circ Wyo Agric Exp Stn — Mimeograph Circular. Wyoming Agricultural Experiment Station
Mimeo Co-Op Ext Serv Purdue Univ — Mimeo. Co-Operative Extension Service. Purdue University
Mimeo EC Purdue Univ Coop Ext Serv — Mimeo EC. Purdue University. Cooperative Extension Service
Mimeograms Harv Coll Obs — Mimeograms. Harvard College Observatory
Mimeogr Bull A-E Ohio State Univ Dept Agr Econ Rural Sociol — Mimeograph Bulletin A-E. Ohio State University. Department of Agricultural Economics and Rural Sociology
Mimeogr Circ Okla Agric Exp Stn — Mimeograph Circular. Oklahoma Agricultural Experiment Station

Mimeogr Circ Res Counc Alberta — Mimeographed Circular. Research Council of Alberta
Mimeogr Circ Univ RI Ext Serv Agr Home Econ — Mimeograph Circular. University of Rhode Island. Extension Service in Agriculture and Home Economics
Mimeogr Circ Wyo Agr Exp Sta — Mimeograph Circular. Wyoming Agricultural Experiment Station
Mimeogr Circ Wyo Agric Exp Stn — Mimeograph Circular. Wyoming Agricultural Experiment Station. Wyoming University
Mimeogr Circ Res Coun Alberta — Mimeographed Circular. Research Council of Alberta
Mimeogrd Publ Commonw Bur Past Fld Crops — Mimeographed Publications. Commonwealth Bureau of Pastures and Field Crops
Mimeogrd Publs Commonw Bur Past Fld Crops — Mimeographed Publications. Commonwealth Bureau of Pastures and Field Crops
Mimeogrd Publs Commonw Bur Past Forage Crops — Mimeographed Publications. Commonwealth (formerly Imperial) Bureau of Pastures and Forage Crops
Mimeogrd Publs Commonw Mycol Inst — Mimeographed Publications. Commonwealth Mycological Institute
Mimeogrd Rep Fm Mgmt Serv Univ Minn — Mimeographed Reports. Farm Management Service. University of Minnesota
Mimeogr New Hamps Agric Exp Stn — Mimeograph. New Hampshire Agricultural Experiment Station
Mimeogr Publ Commonwealth Bur Pastures Field Crops — Mimeographed Publications. Commonwealth Bureau of Pastures and Field Crops
Mimeogr Publ Hawaii Univ Dept Hort — Mimeographed Publication. Hawaii University. Department of Horticulture
Mimeogr Publs Agric Econ Brch Ottawa — Mimeograph Publications. Agriculture Economics Branch. Ottawa
Mimeogr Rep Cambridge Univ Sch Agr Farm Econ Br — Mimeographed Report. Cambridge University. School of Agriculture. Farm Economics Branch
Mimeogr Ser Ark Agr Exp Sta — Mimeograph Series. Arkansas Agricultural Experiment Station
Mimeogr Ser Ark Agric Exp Stn — Mimeograph Series. Arkansas Agricultural Experiment Station
Mimeogr Ser Arkansas Agric Exp Stn — Mimeograph Series. Arkansas. Agricultural Experiment Station
Mimeogr Ser Bull W Va Geol Surv — Mimeograph Series Bulletin. West Virginia Geological Survey
Mimeogr Ser GA Agr Exp Sta — Mimeograph Series. Georgia Agricultural Experiment Station
Mimeogr Ser GA Agric Exp Stn — Mimeograph Series. Georgia Agricultural Experiment Station
Mimeogr Ser Southwest Mo State Univ State Fruit Exp Stn — Mimeograph Series. Southwest Missouri State University. State Fruit Experiment Station
Mimeogr Ser Univ Arkansas Agric Exp Stn — Mimeograph Series. University of Arkansas. Agricultural Experiment Station
Mimeogr Ser Utah Agr Exp Sta — Mimeograph Series. Utah Agricultural Experiment Station
Mimeogrs Forest Prod Labs Can — Mimeographs. Forest Product Laboratories. Canada
Mimeogrs US Bur Ent — Mimeographs. US Bureau of Entomology
Mimeogr Univ Ga Agric Exp Stns — Mimeograph. University of Georgia Agricultural Experiment Stations
Mimeo ID Purdue Univ Dept Agr Ext — Mimeo ID. Purdue University. Department of Agricultural Extension
Mimeo Rep Dep Soils Agric Exp Stn Univ Fl — Mimeo Report. Department of Soils. Agricultural Experiment Station.University of Florida
Mimeo Rep Fla Dep Agric Econ — Mimeo Report. Department of Agricultural Economics. Florida Agricultural Experiment Stations
Mimeo Rep Fla Everglades Exp Sta — Mimeo Report. Florida Everglades Experiment Station
MIMN — Micmac News
MIMS — Memoires. Institut Scientifuge de Madagascar
MIMS — Monthly Index of Medical Specialities
MIMSA — Minerva Medica. Supplemento
Mim Ulama — Mimbar Ulama
MIN — Korte Berichten voor Milieu
MIN — Media Industry Newsletter
Min — Minerva
Min — Minerve Francaise
Min Act Dig — Mining Activity Digest
Min Age — Mining Age
Min Am — Mining American
Minamata Dis — Minamata Disease
Min & Geol J — Mining and Geological Journal
Min & Met — Mining and Metallurgy
Min & Mtrl — Minerals and Materials: A Monthly Survey
Min Annu Rev — Mining Annual Review
Minas Gerais Braz Inst Agron Circ — Minas Gerais, Brazil. Instituto Agronomicao. Circular
Minas Odont — Minas Odontologica
Min B — Mining Bulletin
Min Boliv — Mineria Boliviana
Min Can — Mining in Canada
Min Chem Engng Rev — Mining and Chemical Engineering Review
Min Chem Eng Rev — Mining and Chemical Engineering Review
Min Coking Coal Proc Conf — Mining and Coking of Coal. Proceedings of the Conference
Min Cong J — Mining Congress Journal
Min Congr J — Mining Congress Journal
Min Contract Rev — Mining and Contracting Review
Min Cuba — Mineria en Cuba
MInd — Metting Index

Minden Heimatbl — Mindener Heimatblaetter
Min Dep Mag Univ Nott — Mining Department Magazine. University of Nottingham
Min Dep Mag Univ Nottingham — Mining Department Magazine. University of Nottingham
Min Deposit — Mineralium Deposita
Mindeskr Japetus Steenstrups Fods — Mindeskrift. Japetus Steenstrups Fodsel
Mind Gyuejt — Mindenee Gyuejtemeny
Mind Med Monogr — Mind and Medicine Monographs
Mind Tissue Proc Conf — Mind as a Tissue. Proceedings of a Conference
Mind Your Own Bus — Mind Your Own Business
Mine & Quarry Eng — Mine and Quarry Engineering
Mine Data Sheets Metallog Map 1:250000 — Mine Data Sheets to Accompany Metallogenic Map 1:250,000
Mine Dev Mon — Mine Development Monthly
Mine Drain Proc Int Mine Drain Symp — Mine Drainage. Proceedings. International Mine Drainage Symposium
Mine Inj Worktime Q — Mine Injuries and Worktime Quarterly
Min Elect Mech Engr — Mining Electrical and Mechanical Engineer
Min Electr Mech Eng — Mining, Electrical, and Mechanical Engineer
Min Electr Rec — Mining and Electrical Record
Min Eng — Mining Engineering
Min Eng (Colorado) — Mining Engineering (Colorado)
Min Eng Electr Rec — Mining Engineering and Electrical Record
Min Eng (Harare) — Mining and Engineering (Harare)
Min Eng (Littleton Colo) — Mining Engineering (Littleton, Colorado)
Min Eng (Lond) — Mining Engineer (London)
Min Engng — Mining Engineering
Min Engng Elect Rec — Mining, Engineering, and Electrical Record
Min Engng NY — Mining Engineering (New York)
Min Engng Rec — Mining and Engineering Record
Min Engng Rev Melb — Mining and Engineering Review (Melbourne)
Min Engng Rev S Francisco — Mining and Engineering Review (San Francisco)
Min Engng Wigan — Mining Engineering (Wigan)
Min Engng Wld — Mining and Engineering World
Min Eng (NY) — Mining Engineering (New York)
Min Engr — Mining Engineer
Min Eng Rec — Mining and Engineering Record
Min Eng Rev — Mining and Engineering Review
Min Eng World — Mining and Engineering World
Mine Pet & Gaze (Bucharest) — Mine, Petrol, si Gaze (Bucharest)
Mine Pet Gaze — Mine, Petrol, si Gaze
Mine Pet Gaze (Bucharest) — Mine, Petrol, si Gaze (Bucharest)
Mine Quarry Engng — Mine and Quarry Engineering
Mine Quarry Mech — Mine and Quarry Mechanisation
Min Equip — Mining Equipment
Min Equip Int — Mining Equipment International
Minerac Metall — Mineracao e Metallurgia
Mineragr Invest CSIRO Aust — Mineragraphic Investigations. C.S.I.R.O. Australia
Mineragr Invest Tech Pap CSIRO Aust — Mineragraphic Investigations Technical Paper C.S.I.R.O. Australia
Mineral Abstr — Mineralogical Abstracts
Mineral Aspekty Petro Rudog — Mineralogicheskie Aspekty Petro- i Rudogeneza
Mineral Assoc Can Short Course Handb — Mineralogical Association of Canada. Short Course Handbook
Mineral Collect — Mineral Collector
Mineral Geokhim — Mineralogiya i Geokhimiya
Mineral Ind — Mineral Industry
Mineral Ind Br Commonw — Mineral Industry of the British Commonwealth and Foreign Countries
Mineral Inds — Mineral Industries
Mineral Inds J — Mineral Industries Journal
Mineral Industries Jour — Mineral Industries Journal
Mineral Inf Serv Calif — Mineral Information Service. Division of Mines and Geology. California
Mineral Issled — Mineralogicheskie Issledovaniya
Mineral J (Tokyo) — Mineralogical Journal (Tokyo)
Mineral Kriter Svyazi Kislogo Magnat Rudn Miner Mater Sezda — Mineralogicheskie Kriterii Svyazi Kislogo Magnatizma s RudnoiMineralizatsiei. Materialy Sezda MMA
Mineral Mag — Mineralogical Magazine
Mineral Mag J Mineral Soc (1876-1968) — Mineralogical Magazine and Journal of the Mineralogical Society (1876-1968)
Mineral Mag Suppl — Mineralogical Magazine and Journal. Mineralogical Society. Supplement
Mineral Mitteilungsbl Landesmus Joanneum — Mineralogisches Mitteilungsblatt. Landesmuseum Joanneum
Mineral News Serv Philipp — Mineral News Service. Bureau of Mines. Republic of the Philippines
Mineralog Abstr — Mineralogical Abstracts
Mineralog et Petrog Acta — Mineralogica et Petrographica Acta
Mineralogical Mag — Mineralogical Magazine
Mineralog J Sapporo — Mineralogical Journal. Mineralogical Society of Japan (Sapporo)
Mineralog Mag — Mineralogical Magazine
Mineralog Petrogr Mitt — Mineralogische und Petrographische Mitteilungen
Mineralog Sb Lvov — Mineralogicheskii Sbornik (L'vov)
Mineralog Soc America Spec Paper — Mineralogical Society of America. Special Paper
Mineralog Soc Utah Bull — Mineralogical Society of Utah. Bulletin
Mineral Oil Wld — Mineral and Oil World
Mineralol Ber — Mineralol-Berichte
Mineral Osad Obraz — Mineralogiya Osadochnykh Obrazovanii
Mineral Petrogr Acta — Mineralogica et Petrographica Acta
Mineral Petrogr Mitt — Mineralogische und Petrographische Mitteilungen

Mineral Petrogr Mitt — Tschermaks Mineralogische und Petrographische Mitteilungen
Mineral Petrogr Mitt Tschermaks — Mineralogische und Petrographische Mitteilungen Tschermaks
Mineral Petrogr Urala — Mineralogiya i Petrografiya Urala
Mineral Petrol — Mineralogy and Petrology
Mineral Plann — Mineral Planning
Mineral Pol — Mineralogia Polonica
Mineral Process Extr Metall Rev — Mineral Processing and Extractive Metallurgy Review
Mineral Process Inf Note — Mineral Processing Information Note
Mineral Rec — Mineralogical Record
Mineral Rep Okla Geol Surv — Mineral Reports. Oklahoma Geological Survey
Mineral Resour Chosen — Mineral Resources of Chosen
Mineral Resour Circ Kans — Mineral Resources Circular. Kansas State Geological Survey
Mineral Resour Circ Univ Tex — Mineral Resources Circulars. Bureau of Economic Geology. University of Texas
Mineral Resour Circ Va — Mineral Resources Circular. Division of Geology. Virginia State Department of Conservation and Economic Development
Mineral Resour Inf Circ Can — Mineral Resources Information Circular. Mineral Resources Division. Department of Mines and Technical Surveys. Canada
Mineral Resour Mich — Mineral Resources of Michigan
Mineral Resour NSW — Mineral Resources of New South Wales
Mineral Resour Ore — Mineral Resources of Oregon
Mineral Resour Pamph Br Guiana — Mineral Resources Pamphlet. Geological Survey Department. British Guiana
Mineral Resour Pamph Somalild — Mineral Resources Pamphlet. Geological Survey. Somaliland Protectorate
Mineral Resour Philipp Isl — Mineral Resources of the Philippine Islands
Mineral Resour Rep Idaho — Mineral Resources Report. Idaho State Bureau of Mines and Geology
Mineral Resour Rep Va — Mineral Resources Report. Virginia Division of Mineral Resources
Mineral Resour Ser Sth Rhod — Mineral Resources Series. Geological Survey. Southern Rhodesia
Mineral Resour Tasm — Mineral Resources. Tasmania Geological Survey
Mineral Resour US — Mineral Resources of the United States. Geological Survey. Bureau of Mines
Mineral Resour West Aust — Mineral Resources of Western Australia
Mineral Sb (Baku) — Mineralogicheskii Sbornik (Baku)
Mineral Sb (Lvov) — Mineralogicheskii Sbornik (Lvov)
Mineral Sb (L'vov Gos Univ) — Mineralogicheskiy Sbornik (L'vovskiy Gosudarstvennyy Universitet)
Mineral Sb (Sverdlovsk) — Mineralogicheskii Sbornik (Sverdlovsk)
Minerals Eng — Minerals Engineering
Mineral Slovaca — Mineralia Slovaca
Minerals News Serv Philipp Isl — Minerals News Service. Bureau of Mines. Phililpine Islands
Mineral Soc Am Short Course Notes — Mineralogical Society of America. Short Course Notes
Mineral Soc Am Spec Pap — Mineralogical Society of America. Special Paper
Mineral Soc Bull — Mineralogical Society. Bulletin
Mineral Soc Jpn Spec Pap — Mineralogical Society of Japan. Special Paper
Mineral Soc Monogr — Mineralogical Society Monograph
Minerals Res CSIRO — Minerals Research in Commonwealth Scientific and Industrial Research Organisation
Mineral Surv Mex — Mineral Survey (Mexico)
Minerals Yb — Minerals Yearbook [*Washington*]
Mineral Tadzh — Mineralogiya Tadzhikistana
Mineral T N — Mineral Trade Notes
Mineralwasser Fabr — Mineralwasser-Fabrikant
Mineralwasser Fabr Brunnen Haendler — Mineralwasser-Fabrikant und Brunnen-Haendler
MineralwasserfabrZtg — Mineralwasserfabrikantenzeitung
Mineral Zh — Mineralogicheskiy Zhurnal
Miner Assess Rep Inst Geol Sci — Mineral Assessment Report. Institute of Geological Sciences
Miner Bioprocess Proc Conf — Mineral Bioprocessing. Proceedings. Conference
Miner Boliviana La Paz — Mineria Boliviana (La Paz)
Miner Brief Br Geol Surv — Mineral Brief. British Geological Survey
Miner Bull — Mineral Bulletin
Miner Bull Energy Mines Resour Can — Mineral Bulletin. Energy, Mines, and Resources Canada
Miner Chem Engr — Miner, Chemist, and Engineer
Miner Commod Profiles — Mineral Commodity Profiles
Miner Deposita — Mineralium Deposita
Miner Deposits — Mineral Deposits
Miner Deposits Alps Alp Epoch Eur Proc Int Symp — Mineral Deposits of the Alps and of the Alpine Epoch in Europe. Proceedings. International Symposium on Mineral Deposits of the Alps
Miner Deposits Circ Ontario Geol Surv — Mineral Deposits Circular. Ontario Geological Survey
Miner Dossier Miner Resour Consult Comm — Mineral Dossier. Mineral Resources Consultative Committee
Miner Dressing Notes — Mineral Dressing Notes
Miner Dress J — Minerals Dressing Journal
Miner Duengem Insektofungic — Mineralische Duengemittel und Insektofungicide
Miner Econ Ser (Indiana Geol Surv) — Mineral Economics Series (Indiana Geological Survey)
Miner Electrolyte Metab — Mineral and Electrolyte Metabolism
Miner Energy Bull — Minerals and Energy Bulletin
Miner Energy Resour — Mineral and Energy Resources
Miner Eng — Minerals Engineering
Miner Eng Soc Tech Mag — Minerals Engineering Society Technical Magazine

Miner Environ — Minerals and the Environment
Miner Fert Insectofungi — Mineral Fertilizers and Insectofungicides
Miner Fossiles — Mineraux et Fossiles
Miner Fossiles Guide Collect — Mineraux et Fossiles. Guide du Collectionneur
Mineria Boliv — Mineria Boliviana
Mineria Metal (Madrid) — Mineria y Metalurgia (Madrid)
Mineria Met (Mexico City) — Mineria y Metalurgia (Mexico City)
Miner Ind — Mineral Industries
Miner Ind Bull — Mineral Industries Bulletin
Miner Ind Bull Colo Sch Mines — Mineral Industries Bulletin. Colorado School of Mines
Miner Ind J — Mineral Industries Journal
Miner Ind NSW — Mineral Industry of New South Wales
Miner Ind (NY) — Mineral Industry (New York)
Miner Ind Q South Aust — Mineral Industry Quarterly. South Australia
Miner Ind Res Lab Rep Univ Alaska — Mineral Industry Research Laboratory Report. University of Alaska
Miner Ind Res Lab Univ Alaska Rep — Mineral Industries Research Laboratory. University of Alaska. Report
Miner Ind Surv Alum — Mineral Industry Surveys. Aluminum
Miner Ind Surv Alum Baux — Mineral Industry Surveys. Aluminum and Bauxite
Miner Ind Surv Antimony — Mineral Industry Surveys. Antimony
Miner Ind Surv Bauxite — Mineral Industry Surveys. Bauxite
Miner Ind Surv Bismuth — Mineral Industry Surveys. Bismuth
Miner Ind Surv Cadmium — Mineral Industry Surveys. Cadmium
Miner Ind Surv Carbon Black — Mineral Industry Surveys. Carbon Black
Miner Ind Surv Cem — Mineral Industry Surveys. Cement
Miner Ind Surv Chromium — Mineral Industry Surveys. Chromium
Miner Ind Surv Cobalt — Mineral Industry Surveys. Cobalt
Miner Ind Surv Coke Coal Chem — Mineral Industry Surveys. Coke and Coal Chemicals
Miner Ind Surv Copper Ind — Mineral Industry Surveys. Copper Industry
Miner Ind Surv Copper Prod — Mineral Industry Surveys. Copper Production
Miner Ind Surv Copper Sulfate — Mineral Industry Surveys. Copper Sulfate
Miner Ind Surv Copper US — Mineral Industry Surveys. Copper in the United States
Miner Ind Surv Explos — Mineral Industry Surveys. Explosives
Miner Ind Surv Ferrosilicon — Mineral Industry Surveys. Ferrosilicon
Miner Ind Surv Fluorspar — Mineral Industry Surveys. Fluorspar
Miner Ind Surv Fuel Oils Sulfur Content — Mineral Industry Surveys. Fuel Oils by Sulfur Content
Miner Ind Surv Gold Silver — Mineral Industry Surveys. Gold and Silver
Miner Ind Surv Gypsum — Mineral Industry Surveys. Gypsum
Miner Ind Surv Iron Ore — Mineral Industry Surveys. Iron Ore
Miner Ind Surv Iron Steel Scrap — Mineral Industry Surveys. Iron and Steel Scrap
Miner Ind Surv Lead Ind — Mineral Industry Surveys. Lead Industry
Miner Ind Surv Lead Prod — Mineral Industry Surveys. Lead Production
Miner Ind Surv Lime — Mineral Industry Surveys. Lime
Miner Ind Surv Magnesium — Mineral Industry Surveys. Magnesium
Miner Ind Surv Manganese — Mineral Industry Surveys. Manganese
Miner Ind Surv Mercury — Mineral Industry Surveys. Mercury
Miner Ind Surv Molybdenum — Mineral Industry Surveys. Molybdenum
Miner Ind Surv Nat Gas — Mineral Industry Surveys. Natural Gas
Miner Ind Surv Nat Gas Liq — Mineral Industry Surveys. Natural Gas Liquids
Miner Ind Surv Nickel — Mineral Industry Surveys. Nickel
Miner Ind Surv PAD Dist Supply/Demand — Mineral Industry Surveys. PAD Districts Supply/Demand
Miner Ind Surv Pet Statement — Mineral Industry Surveys. Petroleum Statement
Miner Ind Surv Phosphate Rock — Mineral Industry Surveys. Phosphate Rock
Miner Ind Surv Platinum — Mineral Industry Surveys. Platinum
Miner Ind Surv Selenium — Mineral Industry Surveys. Selenium
Miner Ind Surv Silicon — Mineral Industry Surveys. Silicon
Miner Ind Surv Sodium Compd — Mineral Industry Surveys. Sodium Compounds
Miner Ind Surv Sulfur — Mineral Industry Surveys. Sulfur
Miner Ind Surv Tin — Mineral Industry Surveys. Tin
Miner Ind Surv Tin Ind — Mineral Industry Surveys. Tin Industry
Miner Ind Surv Titanium — Mineral Industry Surveys. Titanium
Miner Ind Surv Tungsten — Mineral Industry Surveys. Tungsten
Miner Ind Surv Vanadium — Mineral Industry Surveys. Vanadium
Miner Ind Surv Wkly Coal Rep — Mineral Industry Surveys. Weekly Coal Report
Miner Ind Surv Zinc Ind — Mineral Industry Surveys. Zinc Industry
Miner Ind Surv Zinc Oxide — Mineral Industry Surveys. Zinc Oxide
Miner Ind Surv Zinc Prod — Mineral Industry Surveys. Zinc Production
Miner Ind Surv Zirconium Hafnium — Mineral Industry Surveys. Zirconium and Hafnium
Miner Ind (University Park PA) — Mineral Industries (University Park, Pennsylvania)
Miner Mag — Mineral Magazine and Journal. Mineralogical Society
Miner Mater — Minerals and Materials
Miner Metal — Mineracao, Metalurgia
Miner Metall Process — Minerals and Metallurgical Processing
Miner Metalur Rio — Mineracao e Metalurgia (Rio de Janeiro)
Miner Met Environ Pap Int Conf — Minerals, Metals, and the Environment. Papers. International Conference Minerals, Metals, and the Environment
Miner Met Rev — Minerals and Metals Review
Miner News Serv (Philipp) — Minerals News Service. Bureau of Mines (Philippines)
Minero Mex — Minero Mexicano
Miner Perspect US Bur Mines — Mineral Perspectives. United States Bureau of Mines
Miner Plann — Mineral Planning
Miner Policy Background Pap Miner Resour Branch (Ontario) — Mineral Policy Background Paper. Mineral Resources Branch (Ontario)
Miner PriceWatch — Mineral PriceWatch
Miner Process — Minerals Processing

Miner Process Des — Mineral Processing Design
Miner Process Inf Note Warren Spring Lab — Mineral Processing Information Note. Warren Spring Laboratory
Miner Process Int Miner Process Congr Proc — Mineral Processing. International Mineral Processing Congress. Proceedings
Miner Process Proc Int Cong — Mineral Processing. Proceedings. International Congress
Miner Process Technol Rev — Mineral Processing and Technology Review
Miner Prod Abstr — Mineral Products Abstracts
Miner Rec — Mineralogical Record
Miner Reconnaissance Programme Rep Br Geol Surv — Mineral Reconnaissance Programme Report. British Geological Survey
Miner Reconnaissance Programme Rep Inst Geol Sci — Mineral Reconnaissance Programme Report. Institute of Geological Sciences
Miner Rep Can Miner Resour Branch — Mineral Report. Canada. Mineral Resources Branch
Miner Res CSIRO — Minerals Research in Commonwealth Scientific and Industrial Research Organisation
Miner Res CSIRO (Aust) — Minerals Research in Commonwealth Scientific and Industrial Research Organisation (Australia)
Miner Res Explor Inst Turk Bull — Mineral Research and Exploration Institute of Turkey. Bulletin
Miner Res (Nagpur) — Mineral Research (Nagpur)
Miner Resour Bull (Geol Surv West Aust) — Mineral Resources Bulletin (Geological Survey of Western Australia)
Miner Resour Bull LA Geol Surv — Mineral Resources Bulletin. Louisiana Geological Survey
Miner Resour Bull Louisiana Geol Surv — Mineral Resources Bulletin. Louisiana Geological Survey
Miner Resour Bull (Saudi Arabia) — Mineral Resources Bulletin. Directorate General of Mineral Resources (Saudi Arabia)
Miner Resour Bull Saudi Arabia Dir Gen Miner Resour — Mineral Resources Bulletin. Saudi Arabia. Directorate General of Mineral Resources
Miner Resour Circ (Univ Tex Austin Bur Econ Geol) — Mineral Resource Circular (University of Texas at Austin. Bureau of Economic Geology)
Miner Resour Consult Comm Miner Dossier (GB) — Mineral Resources Consultative Committee. Mineral Dossier (Great Britain)
Miner Resour Geol Geophys Bur 1:250000 Geol Ser — Mineral Resources. Geology and Geophysics. Bureau of 1:250,000 Geological Series
Miner Resour Geol Surv NSW — New South Wales. Geological Survey. Mineral Resources
Miner Resour Min Ind Cyprus Bull — Mineral Resources and Mining Industry of Cyprus. Bulletin
Miner Resour Pam Geol Surv Dep Br Guiana — Mineral Resources Pamphlet. Geological Survey Department. British Guiana
Miner Resour Pam Geol Surv Guyana — Mineral Resources Pamphlet. Geological Survey of Guyana
Miner Resour Rep — Mineral Resources Report. Bureau of Mineral Resources. Geology and Geophysics
Miner Resour Rep Botswana Geol Surv Dep — Mineral Resources Report. Botswana Geological Survey Department
Miner Resour Rep Commonw Geol Liaison Off — Mineral Resources Report. Commonwealth Geological Liaison Office
Miner Resour Rep Geol Surv Dep (Botswana) — Mineral Resources Report. Geological Survey Department (Botswana)
Miner Resour Rep Idaho Bur Mines Geol — Mineral Resources Report. Idaho. Bureau of Mines and Geology
Miner Resour Rep Invest Saudi Arabia Dir Gen Miner Resour — Mineral Resources Report of Investigation. Saudi Arabia Directorate General of Mineral Resources
Miner Resour Rep NM Bur Mines Miner — Mineral Resources Report. New Mexico Bureau of Mines and MineralResources
Miner Resour Rep PA Topogr Geol Surv — Mineral Resource Report. Pennsylvania Topographic and Geologic Survey
Miner Resour Rep Va Div Miner Resour — Mineral Resources Report. Virginia Division of Mineral Resources
Miner Resour Res Dir Gen Miner Resour (Saudi Arabia) — Mineral Resources Research. Directorate General of Mineral Resources (Saudi Arabia)
Miner Resour Rev — Mineral Resources Review. Department of Mines. South Australia
Miner Resour Rev Dep Mines S Aust — Mineral Resources Review. Department of Mines. South Australia
Miner Resour Rev South Aust Dep Mines — Mineral Resources Review. Department of Mines. South Australia
Miner Resour Rev South Aust Dep Mines Energy — Mineral Resources Review. South Australia Department of Mines andEnergy
Miner Resour Sect Educ Ser (NC) — Mineral Resources Section. Educational Series (North Carolina)
Miner Resour Ser Div Geol (SC) — Mineral Resources Series. Division of Geology (South Carolina)
Miner Resour Ser Rhod Geol Surv — Mineral Resources Series. Rhodesia Geological Survey
Miner Resour Ser SC Div Geol — Mineral Resources Series. South Carolina. Division of Geology
Miner Resour Ser WV Geol Econ Surv — Mineral Resources Series. West Virginia Geological and Economic Survey
Miner Resour Surv (NH Div Econ Dev) — Mineral Resources Survey (New Hampshire Division of Economic Development)
Miner Resursy Zarub Stran — Mineral'nye Resursy Zarubezhnykh Stran
Miner Rev — Minerales Revista
Miner Rocks — Minerals and Rocks
Miner Rohst — Mineralische Rohstoffe
Miner Rohst Nichteisenmet — Mineralische Rohstoffe und Nichteisenmetalle
Miner Sci Eng — Minerals Science and Engineering

Miner Sci Eng (Johannesburg) — Minerals Science and Engineering (Johannesburg)
Miners Circ — Miners' Circular. Bureau of Mines [*Washington*]
Miner Slovaca — Mineralia Slovaca
Miner Slovaca Monogr — Mineralia Slovaca. Monografia
Miner Syr'e — Mineral'noe Syr'e
Miner Syr'e Ego Pererab — Mineral'noe Syr'e i Ego Pererabotka
Miner Syre Pererab — Mineral'noe syr'e i ego Pererabotka
Miner Syre Tsvet Metally — Mineral'noe syr'e i tsvetnye Metally
Miner Syr'e Tsvetn Met — Mineral'noe syr'e i Tsvetnye Metally
Miner Syr'e Vses Inst Miner Syr'ya — Mineral'noe Syr'e. Vsesoyuznyi Institut Mineral'nogo Syr'ya
Miner Syr'e Vses Nauchno Issled Inst Miner Syr'ya — Mineral'noe Syr'e. Vsesoyuznyi Nauchno-Issledovatel'skii Institut Mineral'nogo Syr'ya
Miner Trade Notes — Mineral Trade Notes
Miner Udobr Insektofung — Mineral'nye Udobreniya i Insektofungitsidy
Miner Udobr Insektofungis — Mineral'nye Udobreniya i Insektofungisidy
Minerva Aerosp — Minerva Aerospaziale
Minerva Agr — Minerva Agraria
Minerva Anest — Minerva Anestesiologica
Minerva Anestesiol — Minerva Anestesiologica
Minerva Bioepistemol — Minerva Bioepistemologica
Minerva Biol — Minerva Biologica
Minerva Cardioangiol — Minerva Cardioangiologica
Minerva Chir — Minerva Chirurgica
Minerva Derm — Minerva Dermatologica
Minerva Dermatol — Minerva Dermatologica
Minerva Diet — Minerva Dietologica
Minerva Dietol — Minerva Dietologica [*Later, Minerva Dietologica e Gastroenterologica*]
Minerva Dietol Gastroenterol — Minerva Dietologica e Gastroenterologica
Minerva Ecol Idroclimatol Fisicosanit — Minerva Ecologica, Idroclimatologica, Fisicosanitaria
Minerva Ecol Idroclimatol Fis Nucl — Minerva Ecologia, Idroclimatologica, Fisiconucleare
Minerva Ecol Idroclimatol Fis Sanit — Minerva Ecologia, Idroclimatologica, Fisicosanitaria
Minerva Endocrinol — Minerva Endocrinologica
Minerva Farm — Minerva Farmaceutica
Minerva Fisiconucl — Minerva Fisiconucleare
Minerva Fisiconucl G Fis Sanit Prot Radiaz — Minerva Fisiconucleare. Giornale di Fisica, Sanitaria, e Protezione Contro le Radiazioni
Minerva Fisioter — Minerva Fisioterapica
Minerva Fisioter Radiobiol — Minerva Fisioterapica e Radiobiologica
Minerva Gastroent — Minerva Gastroenterologica
Minerva Gastroenterol — Minerva Gastroenterologica
Minerva Ginec — Minerva Ginecologica
Minerva Ginecol — Minerva Ginecologica
Minerva Idroclimatol — Minerva Idroclimatologica
Minerva Med — Minerva Medica
Minerva Med Eur Med — Minerva Medica. Europa Medica
Minerva Med Guiliana — Minerva Medica Guiliana
Minerva Medicoleg — Minerva Medicolegale
Minerva Med Rass Ipnosi Med Psicosom — Minerva Medica. Rassegna Ipnosi e Medicina Psicosomatica
Minerva Med (Roma) — Minerva Medica (Roma)
Minerva Med Sicil — Minerva Medica Siciliana
Minerva Med Suppl — Minerva Medica. Supplemento
Minerva Med Suppl Minerva Fisioter — Minerva Medica. Supplement. Minerva Fisioterapica
Minerva Med Suppl Minerva Fisioter Radiobiol — Minerva Medica. Supplement. Minerva Fisioterapica e Radiobiologica
Minerva Med Suppl Minerva Med Sicil — Minerva Medica. Supplemento. Minerva Medica Siciliana
Minerva Nefrol — Minerva Nefrologica
Minerva Neurochir — Minerva Neurochirurgica
Minerva Nipiol — Minerva Nipiologica
Minerva Nucl — Minerva Nucleare
Minerva Nucl J Nucl Biol Med — Minerva Nucleare. Journal of Nuclear Biology and Medicine
Minerva Oftalmol — Minerva Oftalmologica
Minerva ORL — Minerva Otorinolaringologica
Minerva Ortognatod — Minerva Ortognatodontica
Minerva Ortop — Minerva Ortopedica
Minerva Otorinolar — Minerva Otorinolaringologica
Minerva Otorinolaringol — Minerva Otorinolaringologica
Minerva Paediat — Minerva Paediatrica
Minerva Ped — Minerva Pediatrica
Minerva Pediatr — Minerva Pediatrica
Minerva Pneumol — Minerva Pneumologica
Minerva Psichiatr — Minerva Psichiatrica
Minerva Psichiatr Psicol — Minerva Psichiatrica e Psicologica [*Later, Minerva Psichiatrica*]
Minerva Radiol — Minerva Radiologica
Minerva Radiol Fisioter Radio-Biol — Minerva Radiologica. Fisioterapica e Radio-Biologica
Minerva Stomat — Minerva Stomatologica
Minerva Stomatol — Minerva Stomatologica
Minerva Urol — Minerva Urologica
Minerva Urol Nefrol — Minerva Urologica e Nefrologica
Minerva Z — Minerva-Zeitschrift
Miner Vody Vost Sib — Mineral'nye Vody Vostochnoi Sibiri
Miner Waste Util Symp Proc — Mineral Waste Utilization Symposium. Proceedings
Miner Wealth (Athens) — Mineral Wealth (Athens)

Miner Wealth Gujarat Dir Geol Min — Mineral Wealth. Gujarat Directorate of Geology and Mining
Miner Wealth (India) — Mineral Wealth (India)
Miner YB 2 — Minerals Yearbook. Volume 2. Area Reports, Domestic
Miner YB 3 — Minerals Yearbook. Volume 3. Area Reports, International
Miner Yearb — Minerals Yearbook
Miner Yrbk — Minerals Yearbook. Volume 1. Metals and Minerals
Mine Safety & Health Rep BNA — Mine Safety and Health Reporter. Bureau of National Affairs
Mine Saf Health — Mine Safety and Health
Mines Annu Rep Dep Mines West Aust — Mines Annual Report. Department of Mines. Western Australia
Mines Branch Inf Circ — Mines Branch Information Circular
Mines Branch Monogr — Mines Branch Monograph
Mines Branch Res Rep — Mines Branch Research Report
Mines Branch Tech Bull — Mines Branch Technical Bulletin
Mines Brch Invest Can — Mines Branch Investigations. Department of Mines. Canada
Mines Carr Gr Entrepr — Mines, Carrieres, Grandes Entreprises
Mines Carrieres Tech — Mines and Carrieres les Techniques
Mines Colon — Mines Coloniales [*Bruxelles*]
Mines Dep Bull Sth Rhod — Mines Department Bulletin. Department of Mines and Public Works. Southern Rhodesia
Mines Dep Victoria Groundwater Invest Program Rep — Mines Department. Victoria Groundwater Investigation Program Report
Mines Geol — Mines et Geologie
Mines Geol Energ — Mines, Geologie et Energie
Mines Geol Energie (Maroc) — Mines, Geologie, et Energie (Royaume du Maroc)
Mines Geol Rabat — Mines et Geologie. Direction des Mines et de la Geologie (Rabat)
Mines Hanb — Mines Handbook [*New York*]
Mines Mag — Mines Magazine
Mines Met — Mines et Metallurgie
Mines Metall — Mines et Metallurgie
Mines Meth — Mines and Methods
Mines Min — Mines and Mining
Mines Miner (Nagpur India) — Mines and Minerals (Nagpur, India)
Mines Miner (Scranton PA) — Mines and Minerals (Scranton, Pennsylvania)
Mines Prospects Map Ser Idaho Bur Mines Geol — Mines and Prospects Map Series. Idaho Bureau of Mines and Geology
Mines Quarr — Mines and Quarries
Mines Rhod — Mines of Rhodesia
Mines Statem NZ — Mines Statement. Ministry of Mines. New Zealand
Mine Subsidence Control Proc Bur Mines Technol Transfer Semin — Mine Subsidence Control. Proceedings. Bureau of Mines Technology Transfer Seminar
Mines Year-End Rev Bur Mines (Philipp) — Mines Year-End Review. Bureau of Mines and Geo-Sciences (Philippines)
Mine Vent — Mine Ventilation
MI News — MI (Metal Industries) News
Min Ext Instr Pamph Univ W Va — Mining Extension Instruction Pamphlet. University of West Virginia</PHR> %
MINF — Memoires. Institut National de France
Minfacts Minist Nat Resour (Ontario) — Minfacts. Ministry of Natural Resources (Ontario)
MINFDZ — Medecine et Informatique
MINFDZ — Medical Informatics
Mingays Electrical W — Mingay's Electrical Weekly
Min Gaz Houghton Mich — Mining Gazette (Houghton, Michigan)
Min Gaz Kimberley — Mining Gazette (Kimberley)
Min Geol — Mining Geology
Min Geol Base Met Symp — Mining Geology and the Base Metals. A Symposium
Min Geol J — Mining and Geological Journal
Min Geol (Soc Min Geol Jap) — Mining Geology (Society of Mining Geologists of Japan) Journal
Min Geol Spec Issue (Tokyo) — Mining Geology [*Society of Mining Geologists of Japan*] Special Issue (Tokyo)
Min Geol Tokyo — Mining Geology (Tokyo)
Ming Stud — Ming Studies
MinH — Minnesota History
Min Hdb — Minerva Handbuecher
Min Her Colliery Eng — Mining Herald and Colliery Engineer
Mini Applic — Minicomputer Applications Analyzer
Miniat Camera — Miniature Camera
Miniat Camera Mag — Miniature Camera Magazine
Miniat Camera Wld — Miniature Camera World
Miniature Camera Mag — Miniature Camera Magazine
Miniature Camera World — Miniature Camera World
Miniature Opt Lasers — Miniature Optics and Lasers
Minicam Photogr — Minicam Photography
Minicomput Comput Chem Rep Workshop — Minicomputer and Computations in Chemistry. Report on the Workshop
Minicomput Rev — Minicomputer Review
Miniera Ital — Miniera Italiana
Mini-Micro — Mini-Micro Systems
Minimicro Bull — Mini-Micro Bulletin
Mini Micro S — Mini-Micro Systems Special Peripherals Digest. Fall, 1983
Mini-Micro Syst — Mini-Micro Systems
Minim Invasive Neurosurg — Minimally Invasive Neurosurgery
Minimum Effluent Mills Symp — Minimum Effluent Mills Symposium
Min Ind Mag South Afr — Mining and Industrial Magazine of Southern Africa
Min Ind Mag Sth Afr — Mining and Industrial Magazine of Southern Africa
Min Ind Prov Queb — Minind Industry of the Province of Quebec
Min Ind Q — Mineral Industry Quarterly
Min Ind Quebec — Mining Industry in Quebec

Min Ind Rec — Mining and Industrial Record
Min Ind Rev — Mining and Industrial Review
Min Ind Technol — Mining Industry Technology
Mining & Chem Eng R — Mining and Chemical Engineering Review
Mining Congr J — Mining Congress Journal
Mining Elec Mech Eng — Mining, Electrical, and Mechanical Engineer
Mining Eng (London) — Mining Engineer (London)
Mining Eng (NY) — Mining Engineering (New York)
Mining Jrl — Mining Journal
Mining Mag — Mining Magazine
Mining Met Quart — Mining and Metallurgy. Quarterly
Mining Mg — Mining Magazine
Mining Miner Eng — Mining and Minerals Engineering
Mining R — Mining Review
Mining Rev — Mining Annual Review
Mining Technol — Mining Technology
Min Invest Mine Insp Alaska — Mining Investigations and Mine Inspection in Alaska
Miniplant Sider Trab Congr ILAFA Miniplant — Miniplantas Siderurgicas. Trabajos presentados al Congreso ILAFA (Instituto Latinoamericano del Fierro y el Acero) Miniplantas
Mini Soft — Mini-Micro Software
Minist Agric Aliment Ont Bull (Ed Fr) — Ministere de l'Agriculture et de l'Alimentation de l'Ontario. Bulletin (EditionFrancaise)
Minist Agric Fish Food Bull GB — Ministry of Agriculture, Fisheries, and Food. Bulletin (Great Britain)
Minist Agric Fish Food Publ RVG (UK) — Ministry of Agriculture, Fisheries, and Food. Publication RVG (United Kingdom)
Minist Agric Fish Food Ref Book GB — Ministry of Agriculture, Fisheries, and Food. Reference Book (Great Britain)
Minist Agric Fish Food Tech Bull — Ministry of Agriculture, Fisheries, and Food. Technical Bulletin
Minist Agric Inst Colomb Agropecu Programa Nac Entomol — Ministerio de Agricultura. Instituto Colombiano Agropecuario. Programa Nacionalde Entomologia
Minist Agric Inst Nac Invest Agron Spain Cuad — Ministerio de Agricultura. Instituta Nacional de Investigaciones Agronomicas (Spain). Cuaderno
Minist Agric Mktg Guide — Marketing Guide. Ministry of Agriculture
Minist Agric Nat Resour Cent Agric Stn Res Rep (Guyana) — Ministry of Agriculture and Natural Resources. Central Agricultural Station. Research Report (Guyana)
Minist Agric Rural Dev Dep Bot Publ (Tehran) — Ministry of Agriculture and Rural Development. Department of Botany. Publication (Tehran)
MinistBl K Preuss Verw Landw — Ministerialblatt der Koeniglichen Preussischen Verwaltung fuer Landwirtschaft, Domaenen, und Forsten
MinistBl MedAngeleg — Ministerialblatt fuer Medizinalangelegenheiten
Minist Conserv Victoria Environ Stud Ser — Ministry for Conservation. Victoria. Environmental Studies Series
Minist Cult Educ Fund Miguel Lillo Misc — Ministerio de Cultura y Educacion. Fundacion Miguel Lillo. Miscelanea
Minist Energ Ressour Etude Spec ES (Que) — Ministere de l'Energie et des Ressources. Etude Speciale ES (Quebec)
Minist Energy Mines Pet Resour Pap BC — Ministry of Energy, Mines, and Petroleum Resources. Paper (British Columbia)
Minist Fd Bull Dom Sci Teach — Ministry of Food Bulletin for Domestic Science Teachers
Minist Fom Obras Publicas Peru Inst Nac Invest Fom Min Bol — Ministerio de Fomento y Obras Publicas (Peru). Instituto Nacional de Investigacion y Fomento Mineros. Boletin
Minist Fr Outre Mer Dir Agric Elev For Bull Agron — Ministere de la France d'Outre Mer. Direction de l'Agriculture de l'Elevage et des Forets. Bulletin Agronomique
Minist Fr Outre Mer Dir Agric Elev For Bull Sci — Ministere de la France d'Outre Mer. Direction de l'Agriculture de l'Elevage et des Forets. Bulletin Scientifique
Minist Ganad Agric Cent Invest Agric Alberto Boerger Bol Tec — Ministerio de Ganaderia y Agricultura. Centro de Investigaciones Agricolas "Alberto Boerger." Boletim Tecnico
Minist Ind Commer Que Rapp Annu — Ministere de l'Industrie et du Commerce du Quebec. Rapport Annuel
Minist Justicia R (Venezuela) — Revista. Ministerio de Justicia (Venezuela)
Minist Mar Merc Mem — Ministero della Marina Mercantile. Memoria
Minist Munit J — Ministry of Munitions Journal [*London*]
Minist Obras Publicas Lab Nac Eng Civ Port Mem — Ministerio das Obras Publicas. Laboratorio Nacional de Engenharia Civil (Portugal). Memoria
Minist Richesses Nat Que Etude Spec ES — Ministere des Richesses Naturelles du Quebec. Etude Speciale ES
Minist Salud Publica Hosp Psiquiatr Habana Bol Psicol — Ministerio de Salud Publica. Hospital Psiquiatrico de la Habana. Boletin de Psicologia
Minist Sante Publique (Fr) Rapp SCPRI — Ministere de la Sante Publique (France). Rapport SCPRI
Minist Selsk Khoz Uzb SSR Gl Upr Skh Nauki Tr — Ministerstvo Sel'skogo Khozyaistva Uzbekskoi SSR. Glavnoe Upravlenie Sel'skokhozyaistvennoi Nauki. Trudy
Minist Trab Ind Comer Inst Nac Tecnol Publ Rio de Janeiro — Ministerio do Trabalho. Industria e Comercio. Instituto Nacional de Tecnologia.Publicacoes (Rio de Janeiro)
Minist Vyssh Sredn Spets Obraz Az SSR Uch Zap Ser Biol Nauk — Ministerstvo Vysshego i Srednego Spetsial'nogo Obrazovaniya Azerbaidzhanskoi SSR. Uchenye Zapiski. Seriya Biologicheskikh Nauk
Minist Vyssh Sredn Spets Obraz Az SSR Uch Zap Ser Khim Nauk — Ministerstvo Vysshego i Srednego Spetsial'nogo Obrazovaniya Azerbaidzhanskoi SSR. Uchenye Zapiski. Seriya Khimicheskikh Nauk
Mini Sys — Mini-Micro Systems
Miniwatt Dig — Miniwatt Digest
Miniwatt Setmakers Bull — Miniwatt Setmakers' Bulletin

Miniwatt Tech Bull — Miniwatt Technical Bulletin
Min J — Mining Journal
Min J (Lond) — Mining Journal (London)
Min J (London) — Mining Journal (London)
Min J Phoenix — Mining Journal (Phoenix)
Min J Wash — Mining Journal (Washington)
Min Leafl NZ — Mining Leaflet. New Zealand Department of Mines
Min Mag — Mining Magazine
Min Mag Bargoed — Mining Magazine (Bargoed)
Min Mag Lond — Mining Magazine (London)
Min Mag NY — Mining Magazine (New York)
Min Man Min Yb — Mining Manual and Mining Year Book
Min Metal — Mineracao, Metalurgia
Min Metal — Mineria y Metalurgia
Min Metal Geol — Mineracao, Metalurgia, Geologia
Min Metall — Mining and Metallurgy
Min Metall Eng — Mining and Metallurgical Engineering
Min Metall Invest Carnegie Inst Technol — Mining and Metallurgical Investigations. Carnegie Institute of Technology
Min Metall Invest Utah Engng Exp Stn — Mining and Metallurgical Investigations. Technical Paper. Utah Engineering Experiment Station
Min Metall J — Mining and Metallurgical Journal
Min Metall Nanking — Mining and Metallurgy. Chinese Institute of Mining and Metallurgy (Nanking)
Min Metall NY — Mining and Metallurgy (New York)
Min Metall Q — Mining and Metallurgy. Quarterly
Min Metall Q Engl Transl — Mining and Metallurgy Quarterly (English Translation)
Min Metall Soc America Bull — Mining and Metallurgical Society of America. Bulletin
Min Metal (Madrid) — Mineria y Metalurgia (Madrid)
Min Metal (Mexico City) — Mineria y Metalurgia (Mexico City)
Min Metal Plast Electr — Mineria y Metalurgia, Plasticos y Electricidad
Min Metal (Taipei) — Mining and Metallurgy (Taipei)
Min Met Rev — Minerals and Metals Review
Min Mex — Minero Mexicano
Min Min Dev — Minerals and Mineral Development
Min Miner Eng — Mining and Minerals Engineering
Min Miner Engng — Mining and Minerals Engineering
Min Mirror — Mining Mirror
Min Mon — Mining Monthly
Minn — Minnesota Reports
Minn Acad Sci J — Minnesota Academy of Science. Journal
Minn Acad Sci Proc — Minnesota Academy of Science. Proceedings
Minn Ac N Sc B — Minnesota Academy of Natural Sciences. Bulletin
Minn Ac Sc Bll — Bulletin of the Minnesota Academy of Natural Sciences
Minn Ag Exp — Minnesota. Agricultural Experiment Station. Publications
Minn Agric Econ Minn Ext Serv Univ Minn — Minnesota Agricultural Economist. Minnesota Extension Service. University of Minnesota
Minn Agric Economist — Minnesota Agricultural Economist
Minn Agric Exp Stn Bull — Minnesota. Agricultural Experiment Station. Bulletin
Minn Agric Exp Stn Misc Rep — Minnesota. Agricultural Experiment Station. Miscellaneous Report
Minn Agric Exp Stn Stn Bull — Minnesota. Agricultural Experiment Station. Station Bulletin
Minn Agric Exp Stn Tech Bull — Minnesota. Agricultural Experiment Station. Technical Bulletin
Minn Beekpr — Minnesota Beekeeper
Minn Bot Stud — Minnesota Botanical Studies
Minn Bs Jl — Minnesota Business Journal
Minn Cities — Minnesota Cities
Minn Conserv — Minnesota Conservationist
Minn Dep Agric Annu Feed Bull — Minnesota. Department of Agriculture. Annual Feed Bulletin
Minn Dep Conserv Div Game Fish Sect Res Plann Invest Rep — Minnesota. Department of Conservation. Division of Game and Fish. Section on Research and Planning. Investigational Report
Minn Dep Conserv Div Waters Bull — Minnesota. Department of Conservation. Division of Waters. Bulletin
Minn Dep Conserv Tech Bull — Minnesota. Department of Conservation. Technical Bulletin
Minn Dep Nat Resour Div Fish Wildl Sect Wildl Wildl Res Q — Minnesota. Department of Natural Resources. Division of Fish and Wildlife. Section of Wildlife. Wildlife Research Quarterly
Minn Dep Nat Resour Div Game Fish Sect Tech Serv Invest Rep — Minnesota. Department of Natural Resources. Division of Game and Fish. Section of Technical Services. Investigational Report
Minn Dep Nat Resour Game Res Proj Q Prog Rep — Minnesota. Department of Natural Resources. Game Research Project. Quarterly Progress Report
Minn Dep Nat Resour Sect Fish Invest Rep — Minnesota. Department of Natural Resources. Section of Fisheries. Investigational Report
Minn Dept Conserv Div Waters Bull Tech Paper — Minnesota. Department of Conservation. Division of Waters. Bulletin. Technical Paper
Minn Div Waters Bull — Minnesota. Division of Waters. Bulletin
Minn Div Waters Soils Miner Bull — Minnesota. Division of Waters, Soils, and Minerals. Bulletin
Minneap Dist Dent J — Minneapolis District Dental Journal
Minneap Distr Dent J — Minneapolis District Dental Journal
Minneapolis Inst A Bull — Minneapolis Institute of Arts Bulletin
Minneapolis Inst Bul — Minneapolis Institute of Arts. Bulletin
Minneap Steel Mach Co Bull — Minneapolis Steel Machinery Co. Bulletin
Minn Engr — Minnesota Engineer
Minnesota Agric Exp Sta Misc Rep — Minnesota Agricultural Experiment Station. Miscellaneous Report
Minnesota Agric Exp Sta Techn Bull — Minnesota Agricultural Experiment Station. Technical Bulletin

Minnesota Geol Survey Misc Map — Minnesota. Geological Survey. Miscellaneous Map

Minnesota Geol Survey Rept Inv — Minnesota. Geological Survey. Report of Investigations

Minnesota Geol Survey Spec Pub Ser — Minnesota. Geological Survey. Special Publication Series

Minnesota L Rev — Minnesota Law Review

Minnesota Med — Minnesota Medicine

Minnesota Min Dir — Minnesota Mining Directory

Minnesota Pl Stud — Minnesota Plant Studies

Minnesota Stud Biol Sci — Minnesota Studies in the Biological Sciences

Minnesota Stud Philos Sci — Minnesota Studies in the Philosophy of Science

Minnesota Univ Water Resources Research Center Bull — University of Minnesota. Graduate School. Water Resources Research Center. Bulletin

Min Neurochir — Minerva Neurochirurgica

Min News Croydon Qd — Mining News (Croydon, Queensland)

Min Newsletter — Mining Newsletter

Minn Farm & Home Sci — Minnesota Farm and Home Science

Minn Farm Home Sci — Minnesota Farm and Home Science

Minn Fish Game Invest Fish Ser — Minnesota Fish and Game Investigations. Fish Series

Minn Fish Invest — Minnesota Fisheries Investigations

Minn Fm Home Fact Sh Ent — Minnesota Farm and Home Science. Entomology Fact Sheet

Minn Fm Rev — Minnesota Farm Review

Minn Forest Insect Dis Surv — Minnesota Forest Insect and Disease Survey

Minn Forestry Res Note — Minnesota Forestry Research Notes

Minn For Notes — Minnesota Forestry Notes

Minn For Res Notes — Minnesota Forestry Research Notes

Minn Geol Surv Bull — Minnesota. Geological Survey. Bulletin

Minn Geol Surv Inf Circ — Minnesota Geological Survey. Information Circular

Minn Geol Surv Rep Invest — Minnesota. Geological Survey. Report of Investigations

Minn Geol Surv Spec Publ Ser — Minnesota. Geological Survey. Special Publication Series

Minn G S — Minnesota. Geological and Natural History Survey

Minn H — Minnesota History

Minn Highw J — Minnesota Highway Journal

Minn His — Minnesota History

Minn His B — Minnesota History. Bulletin

Minn His S — Minnesota Historical Society. Collections

Minn Hist — Minnesota History

Minn Hist B — Minnesota History. Bulletin

Minn Hist Bul — Minnesota History Bulletin

Minn History — Minnesota History

Minn Hist Soc Educ Bull — Minnesota Historical Society. Educational Bulletin

Minn Holst Fries — Minnesota Holstein Friesian

Minn Home Fm Sci — Minnesota Home and Farm Science

Minn Hort — Minnesota Horticulturist

Minn Hortic — Minnesota Horticulturist

Minn Insect Life — Minnesota Insect Life

Minn Inst Arts Bul — Minneapolis Institute of Arts. Bulletin

Minn Inst Bul — Minneapolis Institute of Arts. Bulletin

Minn J Ed — Minnesota Journal of Education

Minn J of Ed — Minnesota Journal of Education

Minn Jour Sci — Minnesota Journal of Science

Minn J Sci — Minnesota Journal of Science

Minn Law J — Minnesota Law Journal

Minn Law R — Minnesota Law Review

Minn Law Rev — Minnesota Law Review. Law School. University of Minnesota

Minn Laws — Laws of Minnesota

Minn Lib — Minnesota Libraries

Minn Libr — Minnesota Libraries

Minn LJ — Minnesota Law Journal

Minn L R — Minnesota Language Review

Minn LR — Minnesota Law Review

Minn L Rev — Minnesota Law Review

Minn Med — Minnesota Medicine

Minn Munic — Minnesota Municipalities

Minn Nurs Accent — Minnesota Nursing Accent

Minn Nutr Conf Proc — Minnesota Nutrition Conference. Proceedings

Minno Delo Metal — Minno Delo i Metalurgiya

Minn Off Iron Range Resour Rehabil Rep Inventory — Minnesota. Office of Iron Range Resources and Rehabilitation. Report of Inventory

Minn Optom — Minnesota Optometrist

Minn Pharm — Minnesota Pharmacist

Minn Pl Stud — Minnesota Plant Studies

MinnR — Minnesota Review

Minn R — Minnesota Rules

Minn Reg — Minnesota State Register

Minn Rep Univ Minn Agric Exp Stn — Minnesota Report. University of Minnesota. Agricultural Experiment Station

Minn Rev — Minnesota Review

Minn Sch Mines Exp Sta B — Minnesota School of Mines. Experiment Station. Bulletin

Minn Sci — Minnesota Science

Minn Sci Agric Exp Stn Univ Minn — Minnesota Science. Agricultural Experiment Station. University of Minnesota

Minn Sci Minn Agric Exp Stn — Minnesota Science. Minnesota Agricultural Experiment Station

Minn Sess Law Serv (West) — Minnesota Session Law Service (West)

Minn Star — Minnesota Star and Tribune

Minn Stat — Minnesota Statutes

Minn Stat Ann (West) — Minnesota Statutes, Annotated (West)

Minn State Florists Bull — Minnesota State Florists' Bulletin

Minn St Bd Con Q — Minnesota State Board of Control. Quarterly

Minn St Conf Soc Wk Proc — Minnesota State Conference of Social Work. Proceedings

Minn St Fed Lab Yrbk — Minnesota State Federation of Labor. Yearbook

Minn St P B — Minneapolis-St. Paul City Business

Minn Stud Phil Sci — Minnesota Studies in the Philosophy of Science

Minn Stud Pl Sci — Minnesota Studies in Plant Science

Minn Symp Child Psychol — Minnesota Symposia on Child Psychology

Minn Technolog — Minnesota Technolog

Minn Univ Agric Exp Stn Tech Bull — Minnesota. University. Agricultural Experiment Station. Technical Bulletin

Minn Univ Agric Ext Serv Ext Bull — Minnesota University. Agricultural Extension Service. Extension Bulletin

Minn Univ Agric Ext Serv Ext Folder — Minnesota University. Agricultural Extension Service. Extension Folder

Minn Univ Eng Exp Stn Bull — Minnesota University. Engineering Experiment Station. Bulletin

Minn Univ Eng Exp Stn Tech Pap — Minnesota University. Engineering Experiment Station. Technical Paper

Minn Univ Min Symp — Minnesota University. Mining Symposium

Minn Univ Q B — Minnesota University. Quarterly Bulletin

Minn Univ St Anthony Falls Hydraul Lab Proj Rep — Minnesota University. St. Anthony Falls Hydraulic Laboratory. Project Report

Minn Univ St Anthony Falls Hydraul Lab Tech Pap — Minnesota University. St. Anthony Falls Hydraulic Laboratory. Technical Paper

Minn Univ Water Resour Res Cent Bull — Minnesota University. Water Resources Research Center. Bulletin

Minn Wildl Dis Invest — Minnesota Wildlife Disease Investigation

Minoes Megbizh — Minoeseg es Megbizhatosag

Min Oil Bull — Mining and Oil Bulletin

Min Oil Rec — Mining and Oil Record

Minor Planet Circ — Minor Planet Circulars/Minor Planets and Comets

Min Pediat — Minerva Pediatrica

MINPROC — Mineral Processing Technology

Min Proc Inst Civ Engin — Minutes of the Proceedings of the Institution of Civil Engineers

Min Qua Engng — Mine and Quarry Engineering

Min R — Mining Review

Min Rec — Mining Record

Min Record — Mining Record

Min Reptr — Mining Reporter

Min Res Bur 1 Mile Geol Ser — Bureau of Mineral Resources. 1 Mile Geological Series

Min Res Bur 1:250000 Geol Ser — Bureau of Mineral Resources. 1:250,000 Geological Series

Min Res Bur Bull — Bureau of Mineral Resources. Bulletin

Min Res Bur Geol Map — Bureau of Mineral Resources. Geological Map

Min Res Bur Geophys Obs Rep — Bureau of Mineral Resources. Geophysical Observatory Report

Min Res Bur Pamph — Bureau of Mineral Resources. Pamphlet

Min Res Bur Petrol Search Pub — Bureau of Mineral Resources. Petroleum Search Subsidy Acts. Publication

Min Res Bur Petrol Search Publ — Bureau of Mineral Resources. Petroleum Search Subsidy Acts. Publication

Min Res Bur Petrol Search Public — Bureau of Mineral Resources. Petroleum Search Subsidy Acts. Publication

Min Res Bur Rep — Bureau of Mineral Resources. Report

Min Res Bur Sum Rep — Bureau of Mineral Resources. Summary Report

Min Res Explor Inst Turk Bull — Mining Research and Exploration Institute of Turkey. Bulletin

Min Res Proc — Mining Research. Proceedings

Min Rev — Mining Review

Min Rev (Adelaide) — Mining Review (Adelaide). South Australia Department of Mines

Min Rev Metall — Mining Review and Metallurgist

Min Rev Salt Lake City — Mining Review (Salt Lake City)

Min Saf — Mining and Safety

Minsai Geppo — Minji Saiban Geppo

Min Sci — Mining Science

Min Scient Press Lond — Mining and Scientific Press (London)

Min Scient Press S Francisco — Mining and Scientific Press (San Francisco)

Min Sci Press — Mining and Scientific Press

Minshu — Saiko Saibansho Minji Hanreishu

Minsk Gos Med Inst Sb Nauchn Rab — Minskii Gosudarstvennyi Meditsinskii Institut Sbornik Nauchnykh Rabot

Minsk Vrach Izv — Minskiya Vrachebnyya Izvestiya

Min Soc Mag Univ Nott — Mining Society Magazine. University of Nottingham

Min St — Ministery Studies

Min St — Ministry Studies

M Inst Rech Sci Mad — Memoires. Institut de Recherche Scientifique de Madagascar

Min Surv — Mining Survey

Min Surv (Johannesb) — Mining Survey (Johannesburg)

MINTEC — Mining Technology Abstracts

Min Tech Dig — Mining Technical Digest

Min Techn — Mineraloel-Technik

Min Technol — Mining Technology

Min Technol NY — Mining Technology (New York)

Min Technol (Taipei) — Mining Technology (Taipei)

Mintec Min Technol Abstr — Mintec. Mining Technology Abstracts

MINTEK Res Dig — MINTEK [*Council for Mineral Technology*] Research Digest

MINUA — Minerva Nucleare

Minufiya J Agric Res — Minufiya Journal of Agricultural Research

Minut A Mtgs Atlant St Mar Fish Commn — Minutes of Annual Meetings. Atlantic States Marine Fisheries Commission

Minut Bd Agric Trin — Minutes of the Board of Agriculture. Trinidad
Minut Conch Club Sth Calif — Minutes of the Conchological Club of Southern California
Minut Dent Bd UK — Minutes of the Dental Board of the United Kingdom
Minutes — Minutes. Seminar in Ukrainian Studies
Minutes Annu Meet Natl Plant Board — Minutes. Annual Meeting. National Plant Board
Minutes Int Symp Cyclodextrins — Minutes. International Symposium on Cyclodextrins
Minutes Meet PA Electr Assoc Eng Sect — Minutes. Meeting. Pennsylvania Electric Association. Engineering Section
Minutes Proc Inst Civ Eng — Minutes and Proceedings. Institution of Civil Engineers
Minut Gen Med Coun — Minutes of the General Medical Council [London]
Minut Proc Aberd Ass Civ Engrs — Minutes of Proceedings of the Aberdeen Association of Civil Engineers
Minut Proc Bradford Engng Soc — Minutes of Proceedings of the Bradford Engineering Society
Minut Proc Cap Soc Civ Engrs — Minutes of Proceedings. Cape Society of Civil Engineers
Minut Proc Cent Bd Irrig India — Minutes of Proceedings. Central Board of Irrigation. India
Minut Proc Engng Ass NSW — Minutes of Proceedings of the Engineering Association of New South Wales
Minut Proc Froghopper Invest Comm — Minutes and Proceedings of the Froghopper Investigation Committee [Trinidad]
Minut Proc Instn Aeronaut Engrs — Minutes of Proceedings. Institution of Aeronautical Engineers [London]
Minut Proc Instn Civ Engrs — Minutes of Proceedings of the Institution of Civil Engineers [London]
Minut Proc Natn Ass Colliery Mgrs — Minutes of Proceedings. National Association of Colliery Managers [London]
Minut Proc Punjab Engng Congr — Minutes of Proceedings. Punjab Engineering Congress
Minut Proc S Afr Instn Civ Engrs — Minutes of Proceedings. South African Institution of Civil Engineers
Minut Proc S Afr Soc Civ Engrs — Minutes of Proceedings. South African Society of Civil Engineers
Minut Sess Advis Comm Comun Transit Geneva — Minutes of Sessions. Advisory Committee for Communications and Transit (Geneva)
Minut Sess Air Transp Coop Comm Geneva — Minutes of Sessions. Air Transport Co-operation Committee (Geneva)
Min Week — Mining Week
Min World — Mining World
Min Yearb (Denver) — Mining Yearbook (Denver)
Min Year Book — Mining Year Book
Min Zimbabwe — Mining in Zimbabwe
Minzokugaku — Minzokugaku-Kenkyu
MIO — Akademie der Wissenschaften. Berlin. Institut fuer Orientforschung. Mitteilungen
MIO — Mitteilungen des Instituts fuer Orientforschung
MIO — Musee Imperial Ottoman
MIODAWB — Deutsche Akademie der Wissenschaften zu Berlin. Institut fuer Orientforschung. Mitteilungen
MIOe — Mitteilungen des Instituts fuer Oesterreichische Geschichtsforschung
MIOEA — Mineraloel
MI Oe G — Mitteilungen. Institut fuer Oesterreichische Geschichtsforschung
MIOeG — Mitteilungen, Oesterreichisches Institut fuer Geschichtsforschung
MIOeG E — Mitteilungen des Instituts fuer Oesterreichische Geschichtsforschung. Ergaenzungsband
MIOF — Mitteilungen. Institut fuer Orientforschung. Deutsche Akademie der Wissenschaften zu Berlin
MIOFP — Melanges de l'Institut Orthodoxe Francais de Paris
MIOG — Mitteilungen. Institut fuer Oesterreichische Geschichtsforschung
MIOGF — Mitteilungen. Institut fuer Oesterreichische Geschichtsforschung
MI Or — Mitteilungen. Institut fuer Orientforschung
MIOTA — Minerva Otorinolaringologica
MIP — Marketing Intelligence and Planning
MIPEA — Minerva Pediatrica
MIPS — Magazine of Intelligent Personal Systems
MIPS — Martinsreid Institute for Protein Sequence Data
MIQ — Medieval India Quarterly
Miquel BII — Bulletin des Sciences Physiques et Naturelles en Neerlande. Miquel, Mulder, Wenckebach
MIR — Management International Review
MIR — Middle East Executive Reports
Mi R — Minnesota Review
Mir — Miracle Science and Fantasy Stories
MIR — Mitteilungen des Deutschen Archaeologischen Instituts. Roemische Abteilung
Mircen J Appl Microbiol Biotechnol — Mircen Journal of Applied Microbiology and Biotechnology
MIRD — Materialy i Issledovanija po Russkoj Dialektologii
Mir Ek Mezd Otnos — Mirovaja Ekonomika i Mezdunarodnye Otnosenija
Mir Ekon Mezdun Otnos — Mirovaja Ekonomika i Mezdunarodnye Otnosenija
MIRINZ Rep — MIRINZ [Meat Industry Research Institute. New Zealand] Report
Mir Isk — Mir Iskusstva
MIRL Rep Univ Alaska — MIRL (Mineral Industry Research Laboratory) Report. University of Alaska
MIRNA8 — Koninklijk Belgisch Instituut voor Natuurwetenschappen. Verhandelingen
Mirovaya Ekon Mezhdunar Otnosheniya — Mirovaya Ekonomikai i Mezhdunarodnye Otnosheniya
MIRPR — Monograph. Institute for Research in Psychology and Relgion
Mir Rybolovstvo — Mirovoe Rybolovstvo

MIRSDQ — MTP [Medical & Technical Publishing Co.] International Review of Science.Series One. Physiology
MIRV — Mining Review
MIS — Management Information Systems Quarterly
MIS — Misset's Pakblad
MIS — Mississippi Music Educator
MIS — Muenchener Indologische Studien
MIS Abr — Mineral Industry Surveys. Abrasive Materials
Misaki Mar Biol Inst Kyoto Univ Spec Rep — Misaki Marine Biological Institute. Kyoto University. Special Report
Misaki Mar Biol Sta Contr — Misaki Marine Biological Station. Contributions
MIS Alum — Mineral Industry Surveys. Aluminum
MIS Antim — Mineral Industry Surveys. Antimony
MIS Asbsts — Mineral Industry Surveys. Asbestos
MIS Asphlt — Mineral Industry Surveys. Asphalt
MIS Barite — Mineral Industry Surveys. Barite
MIS Baux — Mineral Industry Surveys. Bauxite
MIS Bauxit — Mineral Industry Surveys. Bauxite
MIS Beryl — Mineral Industry Surveys. Beryllium
MIS Bis — Mineral Industry Surveys. Bismuth
MIS B Mica — Mineral Industry Surveys. Block and Film Mica
MIS Boron — Mineral Industry Surveys. Boron. Annual Advance Summary
MIS Bromin — Mineral Industry Surveys. Bromine
Misc — Miscellanea
Misc — New York Miscellaneous Reports
Misc 2d — New York Miscellaneous Reports. Second Series
Misc A — Miscellanea d'Arte. Rivista Mensile di Storia dell'Arte Medievale e Moderna
MIS Cadm — Mineral Industry Surveys. Cadmium
MiscAgost — Miscellanea Agostiniana
MIS Calcm — Mineral Industry Surveys. Calcium and Calcium Compounds
Misc A Mataro — Miscellanies Arqueologiques sobre Mataro i el Maresme
Misc Antrop Ecuator — Miscelanea Antropologica Ecuatoriana
Misc Antropol Ecuator — Miscelanea Antropologica Ecuatoriana
MiscBarc — Miscellanea Barcinonensia
Misc Bavar Monacensia — Miscellanea Bavarica Monacensia
Misc Bav Mon — Miscellanea Bavarica Monacensia
Misc Bib Hertz — Miscellanea Bibliothecae Hertzianae
MiscBibl — Miscellanea Biblica Edita a Pontificio Instituto Biblico ad Celebrandum Annum XXV ex quo Conditum est Institutum
Misc Bryol Lichenol — Miscellanea Bryologica et Lichenologica
Misc Bull Botanic Gdn (Adelaide) — Botanic Gardens (Adelaide). Miscellaneous Bulletin
Misc Bull Coun Agric Res (India) — Miscellaneous Bulletins. Council of Agricultural Research (India)
Misc Bull Div Market Econ Dep Agric NSW — Miscellaneous Bulletin. Division of Marketing and Economics. Department of Agriculture. New South Wales
Misc Bull Ser Econ Serv Branch Dep Primary Ind — Miscellaneous Bulletin Series. Economic Services Branch. Department of Primary Industries
Misc Byz Mon — Miscellanea Byzantina Monacensia
Misc Circ USDA — Miscellaneous Circular. United States Department of Agriculture
Misc Com — Miscelanea Comillas
Misc Comillas — Miscelanea Comillas. Universidad Pontificia de Comillas
Misc Cur Ephem Med Phys German Acad Imp Leop Nat Cur — Miscellanea Curiosa Sive Ephemeridum Medico-Physicarum Germanicarum Academiae Imperialis Leopoldinae Naturae Curiosorum
Miscelanea Mat — Miscelanea Matematica
MIS Cement — Mineral Industry Surveys. Cement
MIS Cesium — Mineral Industry Surveys. Cesium and Rubidium
Misc Estud Arab & Heb — Miscelanea de Estudios Arabes y Hebraicos
Misc Ext Publ NC Univ Ext Serv — Miscellaneous Extension Publication. North Carolina University. Extension Service
Misc Fac Lett Y Torino — Miscellanea della Facolta di Lettere dell'Universita di Torino
Misc Florent Erud & Stor — Miscellanea Fiorentina di Erudizione e Storia
Misc For Adm Nac Bosques (Argent) — Miscelaneas Forestales. Administracion Nacional de Bosques (Buenos Aires, Argentina)
Misc Forest — Miscelaneas Forestales. Administracion Nacional de Bosques
Misc Fr — Miscellanea Francescana
Misc Franc — Miscellanea Francescana
Misc Francesc — Miscellanea Francescana
Misc Fund Miguel Lillo — Miscelanea. Fundacion Miguel Lillo
Misc Geol Surv Div Mich — Miscellany. Geological Survey Division. Michigan
Misc Graec — Miscellanea Graeca
MIS Chrom — Mineral Industry Surveys. Chromium
MIS Cl — Mineral Industry Surveys. Copper Industry
Misc Inform Tokyo Univ Forests — Miscellaneous Information. Tokyo University Forests/Ehshurin. Tokyo Daigaku Nogakubu Enshurin
Misc Inf Tokyo Univ For — Miscellaneous Information. Tokyo University Forests
Misc Invest Appl Sci Res Corp Thailand — Miscellaneous Investigation. Applied Scientific Research Corporation of Thailand
Misc Lau — Miscellanea Laurentiana
MIS Clays — Mineral Industry Surveys. Clays
Misc Lub — Miscellanea Lubecensia
Misc Med — Miscellanea Mediaevalia
Misc Mich Geol Surv — Miscellany. Michigan. Geological Survey
Misc Mon — Miscellanea Bavarica Monacensia
Misc Mus — Miscellanea Musicologica
Misc Musicol — Miscellanea Musicologica
Misc Neuesten Ausl Lit — Miscellen aus der Neuesten Auslaendischen Literatur
MIS Cobalt — Mineral Industry Surveys. Cobalt
MIS Columb — Mineral Industry Surveys. Columbium and Tantalum
MIS Copper — Mineral Industry Surveys. Copper
MIS Corund — Mineral Industry Surveys. Corundum

Misc Paper D US Army Eng Waterw Exp Stn — Miscellaneous Paper D. US Army Engineer Waterways Experiment Station

Misc Pap Exp For Taiwan Univ — Miscellaneous Papers. Experimental Forest. National Taiwan University

Misc Pap Fd Invest Bd — Miscellaneous Papers. Food Investigation Board

Misc Pap Fm Econ Brch Sch Agric Univ Camb — Miscellaneous Papers. Farm Economics Branch School of Agriculture. University of Cambridge (Cambridge)

Misc Pap Geol Soc (London) — Miscellaneous Paper. Geological Society (London)

Misc Pap Gronl Geol Unders — Miscellaneous Papers. Gronlands Geologiske Undersogelse

Misc Pap Hort Inst Taihoku Imp Univ — Miscellaneous Papers. Horticultural Institute. Taihoku Imperial University/Taihoku Teikoku Daigaku Rinogakubu Engeigaku Kiyoshitsu Zappo

Misc Pap Koenigstuhl Sternw — Miscellaneous Papers of the Koenigstuhl-Sternwarte

Misc Pap Landbouwhogesch Wageningen — Miscellaneous Papers. Landbouwhogeschool Wageningen

Misc Pap Met Serv Israel — Miscellaneous Papers. Meteorological Service. Israel

Misc Pap Ont Div Mines — Miscellaneous Paper. Ontario Division of Mines

Misc Pap Ont Geol Surv — Miscellaneous Paper. Ontario Geological Survey

Misc Pap Oreg Dep Geol Miner Ind — Miscellaneous Paper. Oregon Department of Geology and Mineral Industries

Misc Pap Oreg State Coll Agr Exp Sta — Miscellaneous Paper. Oregon State College. Agricultural Experiment Station

Misc Pap Pac Southwest Forest Range Exp Sta US Forest Serv — Miscellaneous Paper. Pacific Southwest Forest and Range Experiment Station. US Forest Service

Misc Pap Pa Topogr Geol Surv — Miscellaneous Papers. Pennsylvania Topographic and Geologic Survey

Misc Pap Univ Obs Oxf — Miscellaneous Papers of the University Observatory. Oxford

Misc Pap US Army Eng Waterw Exp Stn — Miscellaneous Paper. United States Army Engineers. Waterways Experiment Station

Misc Pap Vict Fish Game Dep — Miscellaneous Papers. Victoria Fisheries and Game Department

Misc Publ Agric Exp Stn Okla State Univ — Miscellaneous Publication. Agricultural Experiment Station. Oklahoma State University

Misc Publ Aust Entomol Soc — Miscellaneous Publication. Australian Entomological Society

Misc Publ Aust Ent Soc — Miscellaneous Publication. Australian Entomological Society

Misc Publ Bur Stand — Miscellaneous Publication. Bureau of Standards

Misc Publ Dept Nat Sci Los Angeles County Mus — Miscellaneous Publications. Department of Natural Sciences. Los Angeles County Museum

Misc Publ Entomol Soc Am — Miscellaneous Publications. Entomological Society of America

Misc Publ Exp Res Stn Cheshunt UK — Miscellaneous Publications. Experimental and Research Station (Cheshunt, United Kingdom)

Misc Publ Genet Soc Can — Miscellaneous Publications. Genetics Society of Canada

Misc Publ Geol Surv India — Miscellaneous Publications. Geological Survey of India

Misc Publ Hawaii Univ Coop Ext Serv — Miscellaneous Publication. Hawaii University. Cooperative Extension Service

Misc Publ Hokkaido Natl Agric Exp Stn — Miscellaneous Publication. Hokkaido National Agricultural Experimentation Station

Misc Publ Hort Res Sta — Miscellaneous Publication. Horticultural Research Station/Rinji Hokoku

Misc Publ Int Tin Res Dev Counc — Miscellaneous Publications. International Tin Research and Development Council

Misc Publ Land Resour Div Dir Overseas Surv — Miscellaneous Publication. Land Resources Division. Directorate of Overseas Surveys

Misc Publ MP Tex Agric Exp Stn — Miscellaneous Publication MP. Texas Agricultural Experiment Station

Misc Publ Mus Zool Univ Mich — Miscellaneous Publications. Museum of Zoology. University of Michigan

Misc Publ Natl Bur Stand — Miscellaneous Publication. National Bureau of Standards

Misc Publ Natl Inst Agric Sci Jpn Ser B — Miscellaneous Publication. National Institute of Agricultural Sciences (Japan).Series B. Soils and Fertilizers

Misc Publ Natl Inst Agric Sci Ser D Physiol Genet — Miscellaneous Publication. National Institute of Agricultural Sciences. SeriesD. Physiology and Genetics

Misc Publ Nursery Mark Gard Ind Dev Soc Exp Res Stn — Miscellaneous Publications. Nursery and Market Garden Industries Development Society. Experimental and Research Station

Misc Publ Okla State Univ Agr Exp Sta — Miscellaneous Publication. Oklahoma State University. Agricultural Experiment Station

Misc Publs Agric Exp Stn Univ Vt — Miscellaneous Publications. Agricultural Experiment Station. University of Vermont

Misc Publs Alaska Agric Coll Sch Mines — Miscellaneous Publications. Alaska Agricultural College and School of Mines

Misc Publ S Carol Ext Serv — Miscellaneous Publications. South Carolina Extension Service

Misc Publs Dep Agric NSW — Miscellaneous Publications of the Department of Agriculture. New South Wales

Misc Publs Dep Agric Scotl — Miscellaneous Publications. Department of Agriculture for Scotland

Misc Publs Dep Agric Un S Afr — Miscellaneous Publications. Department of Agriculture. Union of South Africa

Misc Publs Dep Hort Nott Univ Sch Agric — Miscellaneous Publications. Department of Horticulture. Nottingham University School of Agriculture

Misc Publs Edinb E Scotl Coll Agric — Miscellaneous Publications. Edinburgh and East of Scotland College of Agriculture

Misc Publs Ent Soc Am — Miscellaneous Publications. Entomological Society of America

Misc Publs Exp Res Stn Cheshunt — Miscellaneous Publications. Experimental and Research Station. Nursery and Market Garden Industries Development Society. Cheshunt

Misc Publs Flood Control Coord Comm Berkeley — Miscellaneous Publications. Flood Control Co-ordinating Committee (Berkeley)

Misc Publs For Brch Can — Miscellaneous Publications. Forestry Branch. Division of Forest Research. Canada

Misc Publs Forest Dep West Aust — Miscellaneous Publications. Forests Department. Western Australia

Misc Publs Forests Commn Vict — Miscellaneous Publications. Forests Commission. Victoria

Misc Publs Hokkaido Univ Coll Exp Forests — Miscellaneous Publications. Hokkaido University College Experiment Forests

Misc Publs Inst Fish Res Univ Mich — Miscellaneous Publications. Institute for Fisheries Research. University of Michigan

Misc Publs Inst For Teheran — Miscellaneous Publications. Institute of Forestry (Teheran)

Misc Publs Mus Zool Univ Mich — Miscellaneous Publications. Museum of Zoology. University of Michigan

Misc Publs Natn Bur Stand — Miscellaneous Publications of the National Bureau of Standards [*Washington*]

Misc Publs Natn Ready Mix Concr Ass — Miscellaneous Publications. National Ready Mixed Concrete Association [*Washington*]

Misc Publs Neb Agric Exp Stn — Miscellaneous Publications. Nebraska Agricultural Experiment Station

Misc Publs Newcomen Soc Am Brch — Miscellaneous Publications. Newcomen Society. American Branch

Misc Publs Nth Rocky Mount Forest Range Exp Stn — Miscellaneous Publications. Northern Rocky Mountains Forest and Range Experiment Station

Misc Publs Okla Agric Exp Stn — Miscellaneous Publications. Oklahoma Agricultural Experiment Station

Misc Publs Pakist Ass Advmt Sci — Miscellaneous Publications. Pakistan Association for the Advancement of Science

Misc Publs Potato Mktg Bd — Miscellaneous Publications. Potato Marketing Board [*London*]

Misc Publs R Alfred Obs Mauritius — Miscellaneous Publications of the Royal Alfred Observatory. Mauritius

Misc Publs Rhode Isl Agric Exp Stn — Miscellaneous Publications. Rhode Island Agricultural Experiment Station

Misc Publs R Ont Mus Zool — Miscellaneous Publications. Royal Ontario Museum of Zoology

Misc Publs Stand Ass Aust — Miscellaneous Publications. Standards Association of Australia

Misc Publs Storrs Agric Exp Stn — Miscellaneous Publications. Storrs Agricultural Experiment Station

Misc Publs Tex Agric Exp Stn — Miscellaneous Publications. Texas Agricultural Experiment Station

Misc Publs Univ Bristol Res Stn Campden — Miscellaneous Publications. University of Bristol Research Station. Campden

Misc Publs Univ ME — Miscellaneous Publications. University of Maine

Misc Publs US Dep Agric — Miscellaneous Publications. United States Department of Agriculture

Misc Publs US Dep Agric Soil Conserv Serv — Miscellaneous Publications. United States Department of Agriculture. Soil Conservation Service

Misc Publs US Publ Hlth Mar Hosp Serv — Miscellaneous Publications of the United States Public Health and Marine Hospital Service

Misc Publ Tex Agr Exp Sta — Miscellaneous Publications. Texas Agricultural Experiment Station

Misc Publ Univ KY Co-Op Ext Serv Agr Home Econ HE — Miscellaneous Publication. University of Kentucky. Cooperative Extension Service. Agriculture and Home Economics. HE

Misc Publ Univ Maine Agric Exp Stn — Miscellaneous Publication. University of Maine. Agricultural Experiment Station

Misc Publ Univ MD Agr Exp Sta — Miscellaneous Publication. University of Maryland. Agricultural Experiment Station

Misc Publ Univ NC State Coll Agr Eng Dept Agr Econ — Miscellaneous Publication. University of North Carolina. State College of Agriculture and Engineering. Department of Agricultural Economics

Misc Publ USDA — Miscellaneous Publication. United States Department of Agriculture

Misc Publ US Dep Agric — Miscellaneous Publication. United States Department of Agriculture

Misc Publ Wash State Univ Coll Agr Ext Serv — Miscellaneous Publication. Washington State University. College of Agriculture.Extension Service

Misc Publ W Va Univ Agric For Exp Stn — Miscellaneous Publication. West Virginia University. Agricultural and Forestry Experiment Station

Misc Publ W Va Univ Coll Agr Agr Ext Serv — Miscellaneous Publication. West Virginia University. College of Agriculture. Agricultural Extension Service

Misc Pub US Dep Agric — Miscellaneous Publication. United States Department of Agriculture

Misc Puig Cadafalch — Miscellania Puig i Cadafalch

Misc Quad Neoclass — Miscellanea. Quaderni sul Neoclassico

Misc Release Cent St Forest Exp Stn — Miscellaneous Release. Central States Forest Experiment Station

Misc Rep Agric Exp Stn Univ Minn — Miscellaneous Report. Agricultural Experiment Station. University of Minnesota

Misc Rep (Arusha) Trop Pestic Res Inst — Miscellaneous Report (Arusha). Tropical Pesticides Research Institute

Misc Rep Cent Overseas Pest Res UK — Miscellaneous Report. Centre for Overseas Pest Research (United Kingdom)

Misc Rep Lab Gov Chem (GB) — Miscellaneous Report. Laboratory of the Government Chemist (Great Britain)

Misc Rep Life Sci Agric Exp Stn Univ Maine — Miscellaneous Report. Life Sciences and Agriculture Experiment Station. University of Maine

Misc Rep Maine Agr Exp Sta — Miscellaneous Report. Maine Agricultural Experiment Station

Misc Rep Minn Agric Exp Stn — Miscellaneous Report. Minnesota Agricultural Experiment Station

Misc Rep Nebr Agr Exp Sta — Miscellaneous Report. Nebraska Agricultural Experiment Station

Misc Rep Ohio Div Geol Surv — Miscellaneous Report. Ohio Division of Geological Survey

Misc Rep Phytopathol Lab Fac Sci Taihoku Imp Univ — Miscellaneous Reports. Phytopathological Laboratory. Faculty of Science and Agriculture. Taihoku Imperial University

Misc Rep Res Inst Nat Resourc (Tokyo) — Miscellaneous Reports. Research Institute for Natural Resources (Tokyo)

Misc Rep Saskatchewan Energy Mines — Miscellaneous Report. Saskatchewan Energy and Mines

Misc Rep Univ Maine Agric Exp Stn — Miscellaneous Report. University of Maine Agricultural Experiment Station

Misc Rep Univ Minn Agr Exp Sta — Miscellaneous Report. University of Minnesota. Agricultural Experiment Station

Misc Rep Univ Minn Agric Exp Stn — Miscellaneous Report. University of Minnesota. Agricultural Experiment Station

Misc Rep Yamashina Inst Ornithol — Miscellaneous Reports. Yamashina Institute for Ornithology

Misc Rep Yamashina's Inst Ornithol Zool — Miscellaneous Reports. Yamashina's Institute for Ornithology and Zoology

MIS Cs — Mineral Industry Surveys. Copper Sulfate

Misc Scient Pap Allegheny Obs — Miscellaneous Scientific Papers of the Allegheny Observatory

Misc Scient Pap Perkins Obs — Miscellaneous Scientific Papers of the Perkins Observatory

Misc Ser Circ Mich St Univ Coop Ext Serv — Miscellaneous Series Circular. Michigan State University Cooperative Extension Service

Misc Ser Conn St Geol Nat Hist Surv — Miscellaneous Series. Connecticut State Geological and Natural History Survey

Misc Ser Cps Engrs US Army — Miscellaneous Series. Corps of Engineers. US Army

Misc Ser Dom Forest Serv — Miscellaneous Series. Dominion Forest Service

Misc Ser Middle Am Res Inst — Miscellaneous Series. Middle American Research Institute

Misc Ser Miyazaki Univ — Miscellaneous Series. Miyazaki University

Misc Ser ND Geol Surv — Miscellaneous Series. North Dakota Geological Survey

Misc Soc Romana Stor Patria — Miscellanea della Societa Romana di Storia Patria

Misc Spec Publ Fish Mar Serv Can — Miscellaneous Special Publication. Fisheries and Marine Service (Canada)

Misc Spec Publ Fish Res Board Can — Miscellaneous Special Publication. Fisheries Research Board of Canada

Misc St L Crist Ant — Miscellanea di Studi di Letteratura Cristiana Antica

Misc Stor It — Miscellanea di Storia Italiana

Misc Stor Lig — Miscellanea di Storia Ligure

Misc Stor Sen — Miscellanea Storica Senese

Misc Stor Ven — Miscellanea di Storia Veneta

Misc Stor Ven Trident — Miscellanea di Storia Veneto-Tridentina

Misc Stud Dep Agric Econ Univ Reading — Miscellaneous Studies. Department of Agricultural Economics. University of Reading

Misc Univ Nac Tucuman Fac Agron — Miscelanea. Universidad Nacional de Tucuman. Facultad de Agronomia

Misc Univ Nac Tucuman Fac Agron Zootech — Miscelanea. Universidad Nacional de Tucuman. Facultad de Agronomia y Zootecnia

Misc Var Lett — Miscellanea di Varia Letteratura

Misc Volterrana — Miscellanea Volterrana

Misc Wilbouriana — Miscellanea Wilbouriana

Misc Wildl Publs Ore St Game Commn — Miscellaneous Wildlife Publications. Oregon State Game Commission

Misc Zool — Miscelanea Zoologica

Misc Zool Hung — Miscellanea Zoologica Hungarica

MIS Diamnd — Mineral Industry Surveys. Diamond - Industrial

MIS Diato — Mineral Industry Surveys. Diatomite

MIS Dime S — Mineral Industry Surveys. Dimension Stone in 1982

MISDM — Misdemeanor and Cure

Mises A Jour Med Prat — Mises a Jour de Medecine Pratique

Mises Au Point Chim Analyt Pure Appl — Mises au Point de Chimie Analytique, Pure et Appliquee et d'Analyse Bromatologique

Mises Jour Cardiol — Mises a Jour Cardiologiques

Mises Jour Sci — Mises a Jour Scientifiques

Mises Point Biochim Pharmacol — Mises au Point de Biochimie Pharmacologique

Mises Point Chim Anal Org Pharm Bromatol — Mises au Point de Chimie Analytique, Organique, Pharmaceutique, et Bromatologique

Mises Point Chim Anal Pure Appl Anal Bromatol — Mises au Point de Chimie Analytique, Pure, et Appliquee et d'Analyse Bromatologique

Mis Ex — Misiones Extranjeras

MIS Explsv — Mineral Industry Surveys. Explosives

MIS Feldsp — Mineral Industry Surveys. Feldspar and Related Minerals

MIS Ferro — Mineral Industry Surveys. Ferroalloys

MIS Ferros — Mineral Industry Surveys. Ferrosilicon

MIS Fluor — Mineral Industry Surveys. Fluorspar in 1975

MIS F Mtls — Mineral Industry Surveys. Ferrous Metals Supply and Demand Data

Mis Fra — Miscellanea Francescana

MIS Gallm — Mineral Industry Surveys. Gallium

MIS Garnet — Mineral Industry Surveys. Garnet

MIS Gem — Mineral Industry Surveys. Gem Stones. Annual Advance Summary

MIS Gem St — Mineral Industry Surveys. Gem Stones

MisGM — Miscellanea. Guido Mazzoni. Florence

MIS Gold — Mineral Industry Surveys. Gold and Silver

MIS Graph — Mineral Industry Surveys. Natural Graphite

MIS Grapht — Mineral Industry Surveys. Graphite

MIS Gyp Mn — Mineral Industry Surveys. Gypsum Mines and Calcining Plants

MIS Gypsum — Mineral Industry Surveys. Gypsum

MisH — Missouri Historical Review

MISIA — Memoirs. Institute of Scientific and Industrial Research. Osaka University

MIS I & S — Mineral Industry Surveys. Iron and Steel Scrap

MIS Iodine — Mineral Industry Surveys. Iodine. Annual Advance Summary

MIS Iron — Mineral Industry Surveys. Iron and Steel

MIS Iron O — Mineral Industry Surveys. Iron Ore

MIS Ir Ox — Mineral Industry Surveys. Iron Oxide Pigments

Misku Dep Metras — Misku Departamento Metrastis

MIS Kyan — Mineral Industry Surveys. Kyanite and Related Minerals

M Isl — Melanges Islamologiques

MIS Lead — Mineral Industry Surveys. Lead Industry

MIS Lead P — Mineral Industry Surveys. Lead Production

MIS Lime — Mineral Industry Surveys. Lime

MIS Lith — Mineral Industry Surveys. Lithium

MIS Magn — Mineral Industry Surveys. Magnesium and Magnesium Compounds

MIS Mang — Mineral Industry Surveys. Manganese

MIS Mercry — Mineral Industry Surveys. Mercury

MIS Mercury — Mineral Industry Surveys. Mercury

MIS Mica — Mineral Industry Surveys. Mica

MIS Moly — Mineral Industry Surveys. Molybdenum

MIS Nickel — Mineral Industry Surveys. Nickel

MIS Nitro — Mineral Industry Surveys. Nitrogen

MIS Nonfer — Mineral Industry Surveys. Nonferrous Metals

MIS Nonfl M — Mineral Industry Surveys. Raw Nonfuel Mineral Production

MISO — Materialy i Issledovanija Smolenskoj Oblasti

MisP — Miscellanea Phonetica

MIS Peat — Mineral Industry Surveys. Advance Data on Peat

MIS Peat P — Mineral Industry Surveys. Peat Producers in the United States in 1980

MIS Perlit — Mineral Industry Surveys. Perlite

MIS Phos R — Mineral Industry Surveys. Phosphate Rock

MIS Plat — Mineral Industry Surveys. Platinum

MIS P Magn — Mineral Industry Surveys. Primary Magnesium

MIS Potash — Mineral Industry Surveys. Potash. Annual Advance Summary

MIS Pumice — Mineral Industry Surveys. Pumice and Volcanic Cinder

MIS Qtly — Mineral Industry Surveys. Quarterly

MIS Quartz — Mineral Industry Surveys. Quartz Crystals

Mis R — Missionary Review of the World

MIS Rhenm — Mineral Industry Surveys. Rhenium

Miss — Missiology

Miss — Mississippi Reports

Miss Acad Sci J — Mississippi Academy of Sciences. Journal

Miss Acad Sci Jour — Mississippi Academy of Sciences. Journal

Miss Ag Exp — Mississippi. Agricultural Experiment Station. Publications

Miss Agr Exp Sta B — Mississippi. Agricultural Experiment Station. Bulletin

Miss Agric Exp Stn Annu Rep — Mississippi. Agricultural Experiment Station. Annual Report

Miss Agric Exp Stn Bull — Mississippi. Agricultural Experiment Station. Bulletin

Miss Agric Exp Stn Circ — Mississippi. Agricultural Experiment Station. Circular

Miss Agric Exp Stn Tech Bull — Mississippi. Agricultural Experiment Station. Technical Bulletin

Miss Agric For Exp Stn Annu Rep — Mississippi. Agricultural and Forestry Experiment Station. Annual Report

Miss Agric For Exp Stn Bull — Mississippi. Agricultural and Forestry Experiment Station. Bulletin

Miss Agric For Exp Stn Res Rep — Mississippi. Agricultural and Forestry Experiment Station. Research Report

Miss Agric For Exp Stn Tech Bull — Mississippi. Agricultural and Forestry Experiment Station. Technical Bulletin

MIS Salt — Mineral Industry Surveys. Salt

MIS Sand — Mineral Industry Surveys. Sand and Gravel

Miss & Roc — Missiles and Rockets

Miss B — Mission Bulletin

Miss Board Water Comm Bull — Mississippi. Board of Water Commissioners. Bulletin

Miss Board Water Comm Cty Rep — Mississippi Board of Water Commissioners. County Report

Miss BT — Missionary Bulletin. Tokyo

Miss Bus Jnl — Mississippi Business Journal

Miss Bus R — Mississippi Business Review

Miss Catt — Missioni Cattoliche

Miss CL Rev — Mississippi College. Law Review

Miss Code Ann — Mississippi Code Annotated

Miss Col LR — Mississippi College. Law Review

Miss Demonstr — Mississippi Demonstrator

Miss Dent Assoc J — Mississippi Dental Association. Journal

Miss Doct — Mississippi Doctor

MIS Sel — Mineral Industry Surveys. Selenium

Missels Zuivelbereid En Hand — Missels Zuivelbereiding en- Handel

Miss Farm Res — Mississippi Farm Research. Mississippi Agricultural Experiment Station

Miss Fm News — Mississippi Farm News

Miss Fm Res — Mississippi Farm Research

MissFR — Mississippi Folklore Register

Miss Game Fish — Mississippi Game and Fish

Miss Gem — Missionierende Gemeinde

Miss Geol — Mississippi Geology

Miss Geol Econ Topogr Surv Inf Ser MGS — Mississippi. Geological, Economic, and Topographical Survey. Information SeriesMGS

Miss Geol Surv Bull — Mississippi. Geological, Economic, and Topographical Survey. Bulletin

Miss G S B — Mississippi. Geological Survey. Bulletin

MissHisp — Missionalia Hispanica
Miss His S — Mississippi Historical Society. Publications
Miss Hist Soc Publ — Mississippi Historical Society. Publications
Miss H Soc P — Mississippi Historical Society Publications
Missile Des Dev — Missile Design and Development
Missile Engng — Missile Engineering
MIS Silicn — Mineral Industry Surveys. Silicon
Miss Ind Inst Bull — Mississippi Industrial Institute Bulletin
Miss Int — Missie Integraal
Missio — Missiology
Missionalia Hisp — Missionalia Hispanica. CSIC (Consejo Superior de Investigaciones Cientificas)
MissionArchFrMem — Memoire. Mission Archeologique Francaise au Caire
Missionary R — Missionary Review
Mission Hisp — Missionalia Hispanica
Mission Hosp — Mission Hospital [*London*]
Mission Jnl — Mission Journal
Mission Rev — Missionary Review
Mission Rev Of The World — Missionary Review of the World
Mission Scient Omo — Mission Scientifique de l'Omo, 1932-33 [*Paris*]
Missionswiss Religionswiss — Missionswissenschaft und Religionswissenschaft
Mississipi — Mississippi Business Journal
Mississippi Agric Coll Techn Bull — Mississippi Agricultural College. Technical Bulletin
Mississippi Agric Exp Sta Bull — Mississippi Agricultural Experiment Station. Mississippi Agricultural and Mechanical College. Bulletin
Mississippi Farm Res — Mississippi Farm Research. Mississippi Agricultural Experiment Station
Mississippi Geol Econ and Topog Survey Bull — Mississippi. Geological, Economic, and Topographical Survey. Bulletin
Mississippi Med Monthly — Mississippi Medical Monthly. Mississippi State Medical Association and Its Component Societies
Mississippi Med Rec — Mississippi Medical Record
Mississippi's Bus — Mississippi's Business
Mississippi Val J Busin Econ — Mississippi Valley Journal of Business and Economics
Mississippi Valley Hist Rev — Mississippi Valley Historial Review
Missi Valley Hist Rev — Mississippi Valley Historical Review
MIS Slag — Mineral Industry Surveys. Slag, Iron, and Steel
Miss Law J — Mississippi Law Journal
Miss Law Jour — Mississippi Law Journal
Miss Law Rev — Mississippi Law Review
Miss Laws — General Laws of Mississippi
Miss Lib News — Mississippi Library News
Miss L J — Mississippi Law Journal
Miss Med — Missouri Medicine
Miss Med Mon — Mississippi Medical Monthly
Miss Med Rec — Mississippi Medical Record
MIS Sod C — Mineral Industry Surveys. Sodium Compounds Annual
MIS Sodium — Mineral Industry Surveys. Sodium Compounds
Missouri Agric Coll Fmr — Missouri Agricultural College Farmer
Missouri Agric Exp Sta Circ — Missouri Agricultural College. Agricultural Experiment Station. Circular
Missouri Agric Exp Sta Inform — Missouri Agricultural College. Agricultural Experiment Station. Circular of Information
Missouri Agric Exp Sta Special Rep — Missouri Agricultural College. Agricultural Experiment Station. Special Report
Missouri Arch — Missouri Architect
Missouri Bot Garden Annals — Missouri Botanical Garden. Annals
Missouri Bur Geol Mines — Missouri Bureau of Geology and Mines
Missouri Conserv — Missouri Conservationist
Missouri Drugg — Missouri Druggist
Missouri Fmr — Missouri Farmer
Missouri Geol Survey and Water Resources Educ Ser — Missouri. Geological Survey and Water Resources. Educational Series
Missouri Geol Survey and Water Resources Inf Circ — Missouri. Geological Survey and Water Resources. Information Circular
Missouri Geol Survey and Water Resources Report — Missouri. Geological Survey and Water Resources. Report
Missouri Geol Survey and Water Resources Rept Inv — Missouri. Geological Survey and Water Resources. Report of Investigations
Missouri Geol Survey and Water Resources Spec Pub — Missouri. Geological Survey and Water Resources. Special Publication
Missouri Geol Surv Wat Resour — Missouri Geological Survey and Water Resources
Missouri Hist R — Missouri Historical Review
Missouri J Math Sci — Missouri Journal of Mathematical Sciences
Missouri Law R — Missouri Law Review
Missouri Med Assn J — Missouri Medical Association. Journal
Missouri State Agric Coll Bull — Missouri State Agricultural College. Bulletin
Missouri Tax Rev — Missouri Tax Review
MissQ — Mississippi Quarterly
Miss Quart — Mississippi Quarterly
Miss R — Mississippi Review
Miss R — Missouri Review
Miss Rag — Mississippi Rag
Miss Rev Wld — Missionary Review of the World
Miss River Fish — Mississippi River Fisheries. US Fish and Wildlife Service
Miss RN — Mississippi RN
Miss Rom — Missale Romanum
Miss R World — Missionary Review of the World
Miss State Coll Agric Exp Stn Annu Rep — Mississippi State College. Agricultural Experiment Station. Annual Report
Miss State Coll Agric Exp Stn Bull — Mississippi State College. Agricultural Experiment Station. Bulletin

Miss State Coll Agric Exp Stn Circ — Mississippi State College. Agricultural Experiment Station. Circular
Miss State Geol Surv Bull — Mississippi State Geological Survey. Bulletin
Miss State Geol Survey Bull Circ — Mississippi State Geological Survey. Bulletin. Circular
Miss State Univ Agr Expt Sta Tech Bull — Mississippi State University. Agricultural Experiment Station. Technical Bulletin
Miss State Univ Agric Exp Stn Annu Rep — Mississippi State University. Agricultural Experiment Station. Annual Report
Miss State Univ Agric Exp Stn Bull — Mississippi State University. Agricultural Experiment Station. Bulletin
Miss St B Assn Rep — Mississippi State Bar Association. Reports
Miss Tid — Missionstidning
Misstofvereniging S Afr J — Misstofvereniging van Suid-Afrika Joernaal
MIS Stone — Mineral Industry Surveys. Stone
MIS Stront — Mineral Industry Surveys. Strontium
MIS Sulf U — End Uses of Sulfur and Sulfuric Acid in 1982. Mineral Industry Survey
MIS Sulfur — Mineral Industry Surveys. Sulfur
Miss Val Hist Assn Proc — Mississippi Valley Historical Association. Proceedings
Miss Val Hist R — Mississippi Valley Historical Review
Miss Val Hist Rev — Mississippi Valley Historical Review. A Journal of American History
Miss Valley Hist Rev — Mississippi Valley Historical Review. Mississippi Valley Historical Association
Miss Vall Med J — Mississippi Valley Medical Journal
Miss Val Med J — Mississippi Valley Medical Journal
Miss V His As — Mississippi Valley Historical Association. Proceedings
Miss V His R — Mississippi Valley Historical Review
Miss V Med J — Mississippi Valley Medical Journal
Miss W — Missiewerk
Miss Water Resour Conf Proc — Mississippi Water Resources Conference. Proceedings
MIS Talc — Mineral Industry Surveys. Talc, Soapstone, and Pyrophyllite
MISTB — Transactions. Missouri Academy of Science
MIS Tin — Mineral Industry Surveys. Tin
MIS Titanm — Mineral Industry Surveys. Titanium
Mist Mun — Historia Mundi
MIS Tungst — Mineral Industry Surveys. Tungsten
MIS Uranm — Mineral Industry Surveys. Uranium
MIS Van — Mineral Industry Surveys. Vanadium
MIS Vandm — Mineral Industry Surveys. Vanadium
MIS Vermic — Mineral Industry Surveys. Vermiculite
MIS Zinc — Mineral Industry Surveys. Zinc Industry
MIS Zinc O — Mineral Industry Surveys. Zinc Oxide
MIS Zinc P — Mineral Industry Surveys. Zinc Production
MIS Zirc — Mineral Industry Surveys. Zirconium and Hafnium
Mita J Econ — Mita Journal of Economics
Mitau Arb Kurlaend Gs — Arbeiten der Kurlaendischen Gesellschaft fuer Literatur und Kunst (Mitau)
Mitb — Mitbestimmung
Mitb Gespr — Mitbestimmungsgespraech
Mitchell Rep — Mitchell Report. Mitchell Engineering Ltd. [*London*]
Mitchurin Beweg — Mitchurin Bewegung
MIT Fluid Mech Lab Publ — Massachusetts Institute of Technology. Fluid Mechanics Laboratory. Publication
MitG — Mitteilungen der Oberhessischen Geschichtsverein
MIT Hydrodyn Lab Tech Rep — MIT [*Massachusetts Institute of Technology*] Hydrodynamics Laboratory. Technical Report
MitI — Mitteilungen des Instituts fuer Oesterreichische Geschichtsforschung
Mit J — Mittellateinisches Jahrbuch
MIT (Mass Inst Technol) Press Res Monogr — MIT (Massachusetts Institute of Technology) Press. Research Monograph
MIT (Mass Inst Technol) Stud Am Polit Public Policy — MIT (Massachusetts Institute of Technology) Studies in American Politics and Public Policy
Mit MR — Mitchell's Maritime Register
Mitochondria Struct Funct Fed Eur Biochem Soc Meet — Mitochondria. Structure and Function. Federation of European Biochemical Societies Meeting
Mitokhondrii Biokhim Morfol Mater Simp — Mitokhondrii, Biokhimiya i Morfologiya, Materialy Simpoziuma Struktura i Funktsii Mitokhondrii
Mitokhondrii Ferment Protsessy Ikh Regul Mater Simp — Mitokhondrii, Fermentativnye Protsessy, i Ikh Regulyatsiya. Materialy Simpoziuma Struktura i Funktsii Mitokhondrii
M i TOM — Metallovedenie i Termicheskaja Obrabotka Metallov
MIT Press Energy Lab Ser — MIT [*Massachusetts Institute of Technology*] Press Energy Laboratory Series
MIT Press Res Monogr — MIT [*Massachusetts Institute of Technology*] Press. Research Monograph
MIT Press Ser Artificial Intelligence — MIT Press Series in Artificial Intelligence
MIT Press Ser Comput Sci — MIT [*Massachusetts Institute of Technology*] Press. Series in Computer Science
MIT Press Ser Comput Syst — MIT Press Series in Computer Systems
MIT Press Ser Found Comput — MIT Press Series in the Foundations of Computing
MIT Press Ser Logic Program — MIT Press Series in Logic Programming
MIT Press Ser Sci Comput — MIT Press Series in Scientific Computation
MIT Press Ser Signal Process Optim Control — MIT [*Massachusetts Institute of Technology*] Press. Series in Signal Processing. Optimization and Control
MIT Ralph M Parsons Lab Water Resour Hydrodyn Rep — Massachusetts Institute of Technology. School of Engineering. Ralph M. Parsons Laboratory for Water Resources and Hydrodynamics. Report
Mitr Art — Mitropolia Ardealului
Mitr Ban — Mitropolia Banatului
Mitre Corp Tech Rep MTR — Mitre Corporation. Technical Report MTR
MIT Res J — MIT (Mindanao Institute of Technology) Research Journal

Mitre Tech Rep — Mitre Technical Report
MitrOlt — Mitropolia Olteniei
Mitrop Olteniei — Mitropolia Olteniei
MIT Sea Grant Rep MITSG — MIT (Massachusetts Institute of Technology) Sea Grant Report MITSG
Mitsubishi Chem Res Dev Rev — Mitsubishi Chemical Research and Development Review
Mitsubishi Denki Lab Rep — Mitsubishi Denki Laboratory Reports
Mitsubishi Denki Tech Rev — Mitsubishi Denki Technical Review
Mitsubishi Electr Adv — Mitsubishi Electric Advance
Mitsubishi Electr Eng — Mitsubishi Electric Engineer
Mitsubishi Heavy Ind Mitsubishi Tech Bull — Mitsubishi Heavy Industries. Mitsubishi Technical Bulletin
Mitsubishi Heavy Ind Tech Rev — Mitsubishi Heavy Industries Technical Review
Mitsubishi Kasei Corp Res Dev Rev — Mitsubishi Kasei Corporation Research and Development Review
Mitsubishi Kasei R D Rev — Mitsubishi Kasei R & D Review
Mitsubishi Plast Technol — Mitsubishi Plastics Technology
Mitsubishi Steel Manuf Tech Rev — Mitsubishi Steel Manufacturing Technical Review
Mitsubishi Tech Bull — Mitsubishi Technical Bulletin
Mitsubishi Tech Rev — Mitsubishi Heavy Industries Technical Review
Mitsui Tech Rev — Mitsui Technical Review
Mitsui Zosen Tech Rev — Mitsui Zosen Technical Review
Mitt — Mitteilungen des Deutschen Archaeologischen Instituts
Mitt Aargau Natfd Ges — Mitteilungen der Aargauischen Naturforschenden Gesellschaft
Mitt Aargau Naturf Ges — Mitteilungen der Aargauischen Naturforschenden Gesellschaft
Mitt Aarg Nat Ges — Mitteilungen der Aargauischen Naturforschenden Gesellschaft
Mitt Abt Ackerbau Staatl Inst Exp Agron Leningrad — Mitteilungen der Abteilung fuer Ackerbau des Staatlichen Instituts fuer Experimentelle Agronomie. Leningrad
Mitt Abt Bekaempf Kurpfusch — Mitteilungen der Abteilung zur Bekaempfung der Kurpfuscherei und des Geheimmittelwesens
Mitt Abt Berbg Geol Palaeont Landes Mus Joanneum — Mitteilungen der Abteilung fuer Bergbau, Geologie und Palaeontologie des Landes-Museums Joanneum
Mitt Abt Bergbau Geol Palaeontol Landesmus Joanneum — Mitteilungen der Abteilung fuer Bergbau, Geologie und Palaeontologie des Landesmuseums Joanneum
Mitt Abt Gesteins Erz Kohle U Salzunters — Mitteilungen der Abteilung fuer Gesteins-, Erz-, Kohle- und Salz-Untersuchungen
Mitt Abt Mech Schwing StrForschStelle Prof Risch — Mitteilungen der Abteilung fuer Mechanische Schwingungen, Strassenforschungsstelle von Professor C. Risch
Mitt Abt Mineral Landesmus Joanneum — Mitteilungen der Abteilung fuer Mineralogie am Landesmuseum Joanneum
Mitt (Agen) — Mitteilungen (Agen)
Mitt Agrarwiss Fak Mosonmagyarovar (Ung) — Mitteilungen. Agrarwissenschaftliche Fakultaet zu Mosonmagyarovar (Ungarn)
Mitt Agrarwiss Hochsch Mosonmagyarovar (Ung) — Mitteilungen. Agrarwissenschaftliche Hochschule zu Mosonmagyarovar (Ungarn)
Mitt Akad Wiss UdSSR — Mitteilungen. Akademie der Wissenschaften der UdSSR
Mitt Allg Pathol Pathol Anat — Mitteilungen ueber Allgemeine Pathologie und Pathologische Anatomie
Mitt Alpenl Geol Ver — Mitteilungen. Alpenlaendischer Geologische Verein
Mitt Alter Kom Westfalen — Mitteilungen der Altertums Kommission fuer Westfalen
Mitt Altertver Zwickau — Mitteilungen des Altertumvereins fuer Zwickau und Umgebung
Mitt Alt Komm Westfalen — Mitteilungen der Altertums Kommission fuer Westfalen
Mitt Ant Gesell — Mitteilungen der Antiquarischen Gesellschaft in Zurich
Mitt Anthr Ges — Mitteilungen der Anthropologischen Gesellschaft in Wien
Mitt Anthrop Ges W — Mitteilungen. Anthropologische Gesellschaft in Wien
Mitt Anthrop Ges Wien — Mitteilungen der Anthropologischen Gesellschaft in Wien
Mitt Anthropol Ges Wien — Mitteilungen. Anthropologische Gesellschaft in Wien
Mitt Anthrop Ver Schles Holst — Mitteilungen des Anthropologischen Vereins in Schleswig-Holstein
Mitt Antiqua Ges Zuerich — Mitteilungen der Antiquarischen Gesellschaft Zuerich
Mitt Arbeitsbereich Metallges AG — Mitteilungen aus dem Arbeitsbereich Metallgesellschaft AG
Mitt Arbeitsgem Florist Kartierung Bayerns — Mitteilungen. Arbeitsgemeinschaft zur Floristischen Kartierung Bayerns
Mitt Arbeitsgem Florist Schleswig-Holstein Hamb — Mitteilungen. Arbeitsgemeinschaft fuer Floristik in Schleswig-Holstein und Hamburg
Mitt Arbeitsgem Florist Schleswig-Holstein Hamburg — Mitteilungen. Arbeitsgemeinschaft fuer Floristik in Schleswig-Holstein und Hamburg
Mitt Arbeitsgem Geobot Schleswig-Holstein Hamburg — Mitteilungen. Arbeitsgemeinschaft Geobotanik in Schleswig-Holstein und Hamburg
Mitt Arbeitsmarkt U Berufsforsch — Mitteilungen aus der Arbeitsmarkt -und Berufsforschung
Mitt ArbGeb Felten und Guillaume Lahmeyerwke — Mitteilungen aus dem Arbeitsgebiete der Felten und Guillaume-Lahmeyerwerke A.G.
Mitt ArbGemein Foerd Futterb — Mitteilungen der Arbeitsgemeinschaft zur Foerderung des Futterbaues
Mitt ArbGemein Naturw Sibiu Hermannstadt — Mitteilungen der Arbeitsgemeinschaft fuer Naturwissenschaften Sibiu-Hermannstadt
Mitt Arb KK Chem Physiol VersStn Klosterneuburg — Mitteilungen ueber die Arbeiten der K.K. Chemisch-Physiologischen Versuchsstation fuer Wein- und Obstbau zu Klosterneuburg bei Wien
Mitt ArbKreis Wald Wass — Mitteilungen des Arbeitskreises Wald und Wasser
Mitt Archaeol Inst Ung Akad Wiss — Mitteilungen. Archaeologisches Institut der Ungarischen Akademie der Wissenschaften
Mitt Archit U IngVer Hamb — Mitteilungen des Architekten- und Ingenieurvereins zu Hamburg

Mitt Archit U IngVer Kassel — Mitteilungen des Architekten- und Ingenieurvereins zu Kassel
Mitt Arch Schiffb Schiffahrt — Mitteilungen des Archivs fuer Schiffbau und Schiffahrt
Mitt Astr Ges — Mitteilungen. Astronomische Gesellschaft
Mitt Astr Ges Hamb — Mitteilungen der Astronomischen Gesellschaft (Hamburg)
Mitt Astr Inst Univ Tuebingen — Mitteilungen des Astronomischen Instituts der Universitaet Tuebingen
Mitt Astron Ges — Mitteilungen. Astronomische Gesellschaft
Mitt Astrophys Obs Potsdam — Mitteilungen des Astrophysikalischen Observatoriums (Potsdam)
Mitt Astr Recheninst Berl — Mitteilungen des Astronomischen Recheninstituts (Berlin-Dahlem)
Mitt Athener Akad Sitz — Mitteilungen der Athener Akademie Sitzung
Mitt Augenklin Carol Med Chir Inst Stockh — Mitteilungen aus der Augenklinik des Carolinischen Medico-Chirurgischen Instituts zu Stockholm
Mitt Augenklin Jurjew — Mitteilungen aus der Augenklinik in Jurjew
Mitt Aus D Deutschen Schutzgeb — Mitteilungen aus den Deutschen Schutzgebieten
Mitt Ausk U BeratStelle TeerstrBau — Mitteilungen. Auskunft- und Beratungstelle fuer Teerstrassenbau
Mitt Aussch Bekaempf Dasselplage — Mitteilungen des Ausschusses zur Bekaempfung der Dasselplage
Mitt Aussch Tech Forstw — Mitteilungen des Ausschusses fuer Technik in der Forstwirtschaft. Deutscher Forstverein
Mitt Ausschuss Pulvermetall — Mitteilungen aus dem Ausschuss fuer Pulvermetallurgie
Mitt B — Mitteilungen des Bundesdenkmalamtes
Mitt Bad Bot Ver — Mitteilungen des Badischen Botanischen Vereins
Mitt Bad Bot Vereins — Mitteilungen des Badischen Botanischen Vereins
Mitt Bad Ent Ver — Mitteilungen der Badischen Entomologischen Vereinigung
Mitt Bad Forstl VersAnst — Mitteilungen der Badischen Forstlichen Versuchsanstalt
Mitt Bad Geol Landesanst — Mitteilungen. Badische Geologische Landesanstalt
Mitt Bad Geol Ldsanst — Mitteilungen der Badischen Geologischen Landesanstalt
Mitt Bad Landessternw Heidelb — Mitteilungen der Badischen Landessternwarte zu Heidelberg
Mitt Bad Landesvereins Naturk Naturschutz Freiburg — Mitteilungen des Badischen Landesvereins fuer Naturkunde und Naturschutz e. V. in Freiburg im Breisgau
Mitt Bad Landesver Naturk — Mitteilungen des Badischen Landesvereins fuer Naturkunde
Mitt Bad Landesver Naturkd Naturschutz (Freib Br) — Mitteilungen des Badischen Landesvereins fuer Naturkunde und Naturschutz EV (Freiburg Im Breisgau)
Mitt Bad Zool Ver — Mitteilungen des Badischen Zoologischen Vereins
Mitt Balt Gesch — Mitteilungen aus der Baltischen Geschichte
Mitt Baron Brukenthal Mus — Mitteilungen aus dem Baron Brukenthalischen Museum
Mitt Basl Bot Ges — Mitteilungen der Basler Botanischen Gesellschaft
Mitt Bastfaserind — Mitteilungen fuer die Bastfaserindustrie
Mitt Bayer Bot Ges — Mitteilungen der Bayerischen Botanischen Gesellschaft zur Erforschung der Heimischen Flora
Mitt Bayer Landesanst Tier Grub Muenchen — Mitteilungen. Bayerische Landesanstalt fuer Tierzucht in Grub bei Muenchen
Mitt Bayer Landesanst Tierz Grub — Mitteilungen. Bayerische Landesanstalt fuer Tierzucht in Grub bei Muenchen
Mitt Bayer Landesanst Tierzucht — Mitteilungen der Bayerischen Landesanstalt fuer Tierzucht
Mitt Bayer Landesverb Bekaempf Tuberk — Mitteilungen des Bayerischen Landesverbands zur Bekaempfung der Tuberkulose
Mitt Bayer Numi Ges — Mitteilungen der Bayerischen Numismatischen Gesellschaft
Mitt Bayer Staatssamml Palaeontol Hist Geol — Mitteilungen. Bayerische Staatssammlung fuer Palaeontologie und Historische Geologie
Mitt BEFA — Mitteilungen der BEFA (Beratungsstelle fuer Autogentechnik)
Mitt Ber Delliwa Ver — Mitteilungen und Berichte des Deliwa-Vereins
Mitt Berg Kom NatDenkmPflege — Mitteilungen des Bergischen Komitees fuer Naturdenkmalpflege
Mitt Berg U Huettenm Ver Siegen — Mitteilungen des Berg- und Huettenmaennischen Vereins zu Siegen
Mitt Berg U Huettenm Ver Wetzlar — Mitteilungen des Berg- und Huettenmaennischen Vereins fuer die Lahn-, Dill- und Benachbarten Reviere (Wetzlar)
Mitt Ber Landw Akad Bonn Poppelsdorf — Mitteilungen und Berichte der Landwirtschaftlichen Akademie zu Bonn-Poppelsdorf
Mitt Berl Anhalt MaschBau AG — Mitteilungen der Berlin-Anhaltischen Maschinenbau-Aktien-Gesellschaft
Mitt Berl BezVer Dt Ing — Mitteilungen des Berliner Bezirksvereins Deutscher Ingenieure
Mitt Berl ElektWerke — Mitteilungen der Berliner Elektrizitaetswerke
Mitt Berl Ges Anthrop Ethnol Urgesch — Mitteilungen der Berliner Gesellschaft fuer Anthropologie, Ethnologie, und Urgeschichte
Mitt Berl Ges Anthropol — Mitteilungen. Berliner Gesellschaft fuer Anthropologie, Ethnologie, und Urgeschichte
Mitt Berliner Ges Anthropol Ethnol u Urgesch — Mitteilunged der Bberliner Gesellschaft fuer Anthropologie, Ethnologie, und Urgeschichte
Mitt Berl Malak — Mitteilungen der Berliner Malakologen
Mitt B Fors — Mitteilungen. Bundesforschungsanstalt fuer Forst- und Holzwirtschaft
Mitt Biochem — Mitteilungen ueber Biochemie
Mitt Biol Bund Anst Ld- u Forstw — Mitteilungen. Biologische Bundesanstalt fuer Land- und Forstwirtschaft
Mitt Biol Bundesanst Land-Forstwirt (Berlin-Dahlem) — Mitteilungen. Biologische Bundesanstalt fuer Land- und Forstwirtschaft (Berlin-Dahlem)

Mitt Biol Bundesanst Land-Forstwirtsch (Berl-Dahlem) — Mitteilungen. Biologische Bundesanstalt fuer Land- und Forstwirtschaft (Berlin-Dahlem)

Mitt Biol Bundesanst Land- u Forstw — Mitteilungen. Biologische Bundesanstalt fuer Land- und Forstwirtschaft

Mitt Biol Landw Inst Amani — Mitteilungen aus dem Biologisch-Landwirtschaftlichen Institut Amani

Mitt Biol Reichsanst Land Forstwirtsch Berlin Dahlem — Mitteilungen aus der Biologischen Reichsanstalt fuer Land- und Forstwirtschaft.Berlin-Dahlem

Mitt Biol Reichsanst Ld U Forstw — Mitteilungen der Biologischen Reichsanstalt fuer Land- und Forstwirtschaft

Mitt Biol Stn Wijster — Mitteilungen der Biologischen Station Wijster

Mitt Biol VersAnst Bot Abt Wien — Mitteilungen aus der Biologischen Versuchsanstalt der K. Akademie der Wissenschaften. Botanische Abteilung (Wien)

Mitt Biol Zentralanst Land Forstwirtsch Berlin Dahlem — Mitteilungen aus der Biologischen Zentralanstalt fuer Land- und Forstwirtschaft, Berlin-Dahlem

MittBl Bad Geol Landesanst — Mitteilungsblatt der Badischen Geologischen Landesanstalt

Mitt Bl Ber Zahn Ae — Mitteilungsblatt der Berliner Zahnaerzte

MittBl Bundesanst WassBau — Mitteilungsblatt der Bundesanstalt fuer Wasserbau

MittBl Chem Ges DDR — Mitteilungsblatt. Chemische Gesellschaft der Deutschen Demokratischen Republik

MittBl Dt Amts Mass Gewicht — Mitteilungsblatt des Deutschen Amts fuer Mass und Gewicht

Mitt Bl Dt Gem Parad Fschg — Mitteilungsblatt der Deutschen Arbeitsgemeinschaft fuer Paradentose-Forschung

MittBl Dt Keram Ges — Mitteilungsblatt der Deutschen Keramischen Gesellschaft

Mitt Bl DVW — Mitteilungsblatt. Deutscher Verein fuer Vermessungswesen

MittBl ForschGes StrWes Oest Ing U ArchitVer — Mitteilungsblatt der Forschungsgesellschaft fuer das Strassenwesen imischen Ingenieur- und Architektenverein

MittBl Freunde Schweiz Keram — Mitteilungsblatt. Freunde der Schweizer Keramik

MittBl Hydrogr Dienst Ost — Mitteilungsblatt. Hydrographischer Dienst in Oesterreich

MittBl Int StudKommn Motorlos Flug — Mitteilungsblatt. Internationale Studienkommission fuer den Motorlosen Flug

Mittbl Ker Freunde Schweiz — Mitteilungsblatt. Keramik-Freunde der Schweiz

Mitt Bl Math Stat — Mitteilungsblatt fuer Mathematische Statistik

MittBl Math Statist — Mitteilungsblatt fuer Mathematische Statistik und ihre Anwendungsgebiete

MittBl Oest Ver VermessWes Oest Ges Photogramm — Mitteilungsblatt. Oesterreichischer Verein fuer Vermessungswesen und Oesterreichische Gesellschaft fuer Photogrammetrie

Mittbl Ver Bndkrimbeamt Oesterreichs — Mitteilungsblatt. Vereinigung der Bundeskriminalbeamten Oesterreichs

Mitt Bochum BezVer Dt Ing — Mitteilungen des Bochumer Bezirksvereins Deutscher Ingenieure

Mitt Bosnien — Wissenschaftliche Mittheilungen aus Bosnien und der Herzegowina

Mitt Bot Gart Berlin Dahlem — Mitteilungen aus dem Botanischen Garten und Museum Berlin-Dahlem

Mitt Bot Gart Mus Berl-Dahlem — Mitteilungen. Botanischer Garten und Museum Berlin-Dahlem

Mitt Bot Gart St Gallen — Mitteilungen aus dem Botanischen Garten St. Gallen

Mitt Bot Gart Zuerich — Mitteilungen des Botanischen Gartens in Zuerich

Mitt Bot Inst Tech Hochsch Wien — Mitteilungen des Botanischen Instituts der Technischen Hochschule. Wien

Mitt Bot Muenchen — Mitteilungen. Botanische Staatssammlung Muenchen

Mitt Bot Mus Hamb — Mitteilungen aus dem Botanischen Museum (Hamburg)

Mitt Bot Mus Univ Zuerich — Mitteilungen aus dem Botanischen Museum der Universitaet Zuerich

Mitt Bot Staatsinst Hamburg — Mitteilungen aus den Botanischen Staatsinstituten in Hamburg

Mitt Bot Staatssamml Muench — Mitteilungen. Botanische Staatssammlung Muenchen

Mitt Bot Staatssamml Muenchen — Mitteilungen aus der Botanischen Staatssammlung Muenchen

Mitt Bot StSamml Muench — Mitteilungen aus der Botanischen Staatssammlung (Muenchen)

Mitt Bot VersLab Klosterneuburg — Mitteilungen aus dem Botanischen Versuchs-Laboratorium und Laboratorium fuer Pflanzenkrankheiten des Oenologisch-Pomologisch Instituts in Klosterneuburg

Mitt Braunschw BezVer Dt Ing — Mitteilungen des Braunschweiger Bezirksvereins Deutscher Ingenieure

Mitt Brennkrafttech Ges — Mitteilungen aus der Brennkrafttechnischen Gesellschaft

Mitt Brenn Presshefefabr — Mitteilungen fuer Brennerei und Presshefefabrikation

Mitt Brennstoffinst (Freiberg) — Mitteilungen. Brennstoffinstitut (Freiberg)

Mitt Breslau BezVer Dt Ing — Mitteilungen des Breslauer Bezirksvereins Deutscher Ingenieure

Mitt BundAnst PflSchutz Wien — Mitteilungen aus der Bundesanstalt fuer Pflanzenschutz (Wien)

Mitt Bund Dt Archit — Mitteilungen des Bundes Deutscher Architekten

Mitt Bundesanst Forst Holzwirtsch — Mitteilungen der Bundesanstalt fuer Forst- und Holzwirtschaft

Mitt Bundesdenk — Mitteilungen des Bundesdenkmalamtes

Mitt Bundesforschanst Forst- u Holzw — Mitteilungen. Bundesforschungsanstalt fuer Forst- und Holzwirtschaft

Mitt Bundesforsch (Reinbek Hamburg) — Mitteilungen. Bundesforschungsanstalt fuer Forst- und Holzwirtschaft (Reinbek bei Hamburg)

Mitt Bundesforschungsanst Forst Holzwirtsch — Mitteilungen. Bundesforschungsanstalt fuer Forst- und Holzwirtschaft

Mitt BundForschAnst Fisch — Mitteilungen der Bundesforschungsanstalt fuer Fischerei

Mitt BundForschAnst Forst U Holzw — Mitteilungen der Bundesforschungsanstalt fuer Forst- und Holzwirtschaft

Mitt BundVers U PruefAnst Wien — Mitteilungen der Bundesversuchs- und Pruefungsanstalt (Wien)

Mitt Burgenl Landesmus — Mitteilungen des Burgenlaendischen Landesmuseums

Mitt Carl Schenck MaschFabr — Mitteilungen. Carl Schenck Mascheninfabrik

Mitt ChemFachaussch Ges Dt Metallh U Bergl — Mitteilungen des Chemiker-Fachausschusses der Gesellschaft Deutscher Metallhuetten- und Bergleute

Mitt Chem Forsch Inst Ind — Mitteilungen des Chemischen Forschungs-Instituts der Industrie

Mitt Chem ForschInst Wirt Oest — Mitteilungen des Chemischen Forschungs-Instituts der Wirtschaft Oesterreichs

Mitt Chem Forschungsinst Ind Oesterr — Mitteilungen des Chemischen Forschungsinstitutes der Industrie Oesterreichs

Mitt Chem Forschungsinst Wirtsch Oesterr — Mitteilungen. Chemisches Forschungsinstitut der Wirtschaft Oesterreichs

Mitt Chem Tech Inst Tech Hochsch Karlsruhe — Mitteilungen des Chemisch-Technischen Instituts der Technischen Hochschule Karlsruhe

Mitt Chem Tech VersStn H Passow Blankenese — Mitteilungen aus der Chemisch-Technischen Versuchsstation von H. Passow in Blankenese

Mitt Chir Klin Tuebingen — Mitteilungen aus der Chirurgischen Klinik zu Tuebingen

Mitt Christ Kst — Mitteilungen fuer Christliche Kunst

Mitt Copernicus Inst Berl — Mitteilungen des Copernicus-Instituts (Berlin-Dahlem)

Mitt Copernicus Ver Wiss & Kst Thorn — Mitteilungen des Copernicus-Vereins fuer Wissenschaft und Kunst zu Thorn

Mitt Copernikusver Thorn — Mitteilungen des Copernicus-Vereins fuer Wissenschaft und Kunst zu Thorn

Mitt Dachpappen Ind — Mitteilungen aus der Dachpappen-Industrie

Mitt DAI — Mitteilungen des Deutschen Archaeologischen Instituts

Mitt D Arch Inst — Mitteilungen. Deutschen Archaeologischen Instituts. Roemische Abteilung

Mitt DDR — Mitteilungen. Wissenschaftlichen Bibliothekswesen der Deutschen DemokratischenRepublik

Mitt Dendrol Ges Oest Ung — Mitteilungen der Dendrologischen Gesellschaft zur Foerderung der Gehoelzkunde und Gartenkunst in Oesterreich-Ungarn

Mitt der Basler Afrika Bibliographien — Mitteilungen der Basler Afrika Bibliographien

Mitt Deut Arch Instzu Athen — Mitteilungen des Deutschen Archaeologischen Instituts. Athenische Abteilung

Mitt Deut Landwirt Ges — Mitteilungen. Deutsche Landwirtschafts Gesellschaft

Mitt Deutsch Boehmerwaldbundes — Mitteilungen des Deutschen Boehmerwaldbundes

Mitt Deutschen Ges M Orients — Mitteilungen. Deutsche Gesellschaft fuer Musik des Orients

Mitt Deutsch Ges Natur Voelkerk Ostasiens — Mitteilungen der Deutschen Gesellschaft fuer Natur- und Voelkerkunde Ostasiens

Mitt D Industrie U Handelskammer Berlin — Mitteilungen der Industrie- und Handelskammer zu Berlin

Mitt Direktor Osterr Nat Bank — Mitteilungen. Direktorium der Oesterreichischen National Bank

Mitt DLG — Mitteilungen. Deutsche Landwirtschafts Gesellschaft

Mitt d Numismat Ges in Wien — Mitteilungen der Oesterreichischen Numismatischen Gesellschaft

Mitt DOG — Mitteilungen der Deutschen Orient-Gesellschaft

Mitt DokumZent Tech Wirt Wien — Mitteilungen des Dokumentationszentrums der Technik und Wirtschaft (Wien)

Mitt Draegerwk — Mitteilungen aus dem Draegerwerk

Mitt D Sem F Orient Sp — Mitteilungen des Seminars fuer Orientalische Sprachen

Mitt Dt Am Tech Verb — Mitteilungen des Deutsch-Amerikanischen Technikerverbands

Mitt Dt Archaeol Inst — Mitteilungen des Deutschen Archaeologischen Instituts

Mitt Dt Archaeol Inst Abt Kairo — Mitteilungen des Deutschen Archaeologischen Instituts. Abteilung Kairo

Mitt Dt Archaeol Inst Ath Abt — Mitteilungen des Deutschen Archaeologischen Instituts. Athenische Abteilung

Mitt Dt Archaeol Inst Athen Abt — Mitteilungen des Deutschen Archaeologischen Instituts. Athenische Abteilung

Mitt Dt Archaeol Inst Roem Abt — Mitteilungen des Deutschen Archaeologischen Instituts. Roemische Abteilung

Mitt Dt BoehmWaldb — Mitteilungen des Deutschen Boehmerwaldbundes

Mitt Dt Brauerb — Mitteilungen des Deutschen Brauerbundes

Mitt Dt Dendrol Ges — Mitteilungen der Deutschen Dendrologischen Gesellschaft

Mitt Dt Ent Ges — Mitteilungen. Deutsche Entomologische Gesellschaft

Mitt Dt Flottenver — Mitteilungen des Deutschen Flottenvereins

Mitt Dt ForschInst TextInd Dresd — Mitteilungen des Deutschen Forschungs-Instituts fuer Textilindustrie in Dresden

Mitt Dt ForschInst TextInd Reutlingen — Mitteilungen des Deutschen Forschungs-Instituts fuer Textilindustrie (Reutlingen)

Mitt Dt ForschInst TextStoffe Karlsruhe — Mitteilungen aus dem Deutschen Forschungs-Institut fuer Textilstoffe in Karlsruhe

Mitt Dt Forstver — Mitteilungen des Deutschen Forstvereins

Mitt Dt Geophys Ges — Mitteilungen der Deutschen Geophysikalischen Gesellschaft

Mitt Dt Germ Verb — Mitteilungen des Deutschen Germanisten-Verbandes

Mitt Dt Ges Bekaempf GeschlKrankh — Mitteilungen der Deutschen Gesellschaft zur Bekaempfung der Geschlechtskrankheiten

Mitt Dt Ges Bekaempfg Geschlechtkrkht — Mitteilungen der Deutschen Gesellschaft zur Bekaempfung der Geschlechtskrankheiten

Mitt Dt Kstgewver Hamburg — Mitteilungen des Deutschen Kunstgewerbevereins zu Hamburg

Mitt Dt LandsGes (Frankfurt/Main) — Mitteilungen. Deutsche Landwirtschafts Gesellschaft (Frankfurt/Main)

Mitt Dt Landw Ges — Mitteilungen. Deutsche Landwirtschafts Gesellschaft

Mitt Dt MaterPruefAnst — Mitteilungen der Deutschen Material-Pruefungsanstalten

Mitt Dt Milchw Reichsverb — Mitteilungen des Deutschen Milchwirtschaftlichen Reichsverbands

Mitt Dt Norm — Mitteilungen aus der Deutschen Normung. Deutscher Normenausschuss

Mitt Dt NormAussch — Mitteilungen des Deutschen Normenausschusses

Mitt Dt Oest AlpVer — Mitteilungen des Deutschen und Oesterreichischen Alpenvereins

Mitt Dt Orientges — Mitteilungen der Deutschen Orient-Gesellschaft

Mitt Dt Orient Ges — Mitteilungen der Deutschen Orient-Gesellschaft zu Berlin

Mitt Dt Orient Inst — Mitteilungen des Deutschen Orient-Instituts

Mitt Dt PatAnwaelte — Mitteilungen der Deutschen Patentanwaelte

Mitt Dt Pharm Ges — Mitteilungen. Deutsche Pharmazeutische Gesellschaft

Mitt Dt Pharm Ges Pharm Ges DDR — Mitteilungen der Deutschen Pharmazeutischen Gesellschaft und Pharmazeutischen Gesellschaft der DDR

Mitt Dt Reichs ErdbDienst — Mitteilungen des Deutschen Reichs-Erdbebendienstes

Mitt Dtsch Archaeol Inst Abt Kairo — Mitteilungen. Deutsches Archaeologische Institut. Abteilung Kairo

Mitt Dtsch Dendrol Ges — Mitteilungen. Deutsche Dendrologische Gesellschaft

Mitt Dtsche Ges Musik Orients — Mitteilungen. Deutsche Gesellschaft fuer Musik des Orients

Mitt Dtsch Email Verb — Mitteilungen des Deutschen Email Verbandes e.V

Mitt Dtsch Entomol Ges — Mitteilungen. Deutsche Entomologische Gesellschaft

Mitt Dtsch Forschungsanst Luft Raumfahrt — Mitteilung. Deutsche Forschungsanstalt fuer Luft- und Raumfahrt

Mitt Dtsch Forschungsgem Komm Erforsch Luftverunreinig — Mitteilung. Deutsche Forschungsgemeinschaft, Kommission zur Erforschung der Luftverunreinigung

Mitt Dtsch Forschungsgem Komm Pruef Fremder Stoff Lebensm — Mitteilung. Deutsche Forschungsgemeinschaft. Kommission zur Pruefung Fremder Stoffe bei Lebensmitteln

Mitt Dtsch Forschungsgem Komm Pruef Rueckstaenden Lebensm — Mitteilung. Deutsche Forschungsgemeinschaft, Kommission zur Pruefung von Rueckstaenden in Lebensmitteln

Mitt Dtsch Forschungsges Blechverarb Oberflaechenbehandl — Mitteilungen. Deutsche Forschungsgesellschaft fuer Blechverarbeitung und Oberflaechenbehandlung

Mitt Dtsch Forschungsinst Textilind Dresden — Mitteilungen. Deutsches Forschungsinstitut fuer Textilindustrie in Dresden

Mitt Dtsch Forsch Versuchsanst Luft Raumfahrt — Mitteilung. Deutsche Forschungs- und Versuchsanstalt fuer Luft- und Raumfahrt

Mitt Dtsch Ges Holzforsch — Mitteilungen. Deutsche Gesellschaft fuer Holzforschung

Mitt Dtsch Landwirtsch Ges — Mitteilungen. Deutsche Landwirtschafts Gesellschaft

Mitt Dtsch Malakozool Ges — Mitteilungen der Deutschen Malakozoologischen Gesellschaft

Mitt Dtsch Pharm Ges — Mitteilungen. Deutsche Pharmazeutische Gesellschaft

Mitt Dtsch Pharm Ges Pharm Ges DDR — Mitteilungen der Deutschen Pharmazeutischen Gesellschaft und der Pharmazeutischen Gesellschaft der DDR

Mitt Dt Schutzgeb — Mitteilungen aus den Deutschen Schutzgebieten

Mitt Dt SeefischVer — Mitteilungen des Deutschen Seefischereivereins

Mitt Dt Ver WohnWes Staedteb Raumplan — Mitteilungen des Deutschen Verbandes fuer Wohnungswesen, Staedtebau und Raumplanung

Mitt Dt Ver Gas U WassFachm — Mitteilungen des Deutschen Vereins von Gas- und Wasserfachmaennern und des Verbandes der Deutschen Gas- und Wasserwerke

Mitt Dt Ver Ton Zem U Kalkind — Mitteilungen des Deutschen Vereins fuer Ton-, Zement- und Kalkindustrie

Mitt Dt Weinbauverbd — Mitteilungen des Deutschen Weinbauverbandes

Mitt Dt WeinbVer — Mitteilungen des Deutschen Weinbauvereins

Mitt Dt WettDienst — Mitteilungen des Deutschen Wetterdienstes

Mitt Dt WettDienst US Zone — Mitteilungen des Deutschen Wetterdienstes in der US Zone

Mitt Eidg GesundhAmt — Mitteilungen des Eidgenoessischen Gesundheitsamtes

Mitt Eidg Inst Schnee U LawinForsch — Mitteilungen des Eidgenoessischen Instituts fuer Schnee- und Lawinenforschung

Mitt Eidg MaterPruefAnst Zuerich — Mitteilungen der Eidgenoessischen Materialpruefungsanstalt am Schweizerischen Polytechnikum in Zuerich

Mitteil d Inst f Oesterr Geschichtsforschung in Wien — Mitteilungen des Institut fuer Oesterreiches Geschichtsforschung in Wien

Mitteilungsbl Abt Mineral Landesmus Joanneum — Mitteilungsblatt. Abteilung fuer Mineralogie am Landesmuseum Joanneum

Mitteilungsbl Amtl Materialpruef Niedersachsen — Mitteilungsblatt fuer die Amtliche Materialpruefung in Niedersachsen

Mitteilungsbl Bundesanst Fleischforsch — Mitteilungsblatt. Bundesanstalt fuer Fleischforschung

Mitteilungsbl Bundesanst Wasserbau (Fed Repub Ger) — Mitteilungsblatt der Bundesanstalt fuer Wasserbau (Federal Republic of Germany)

Mitteilungsbl Chem Ges DDR — Mitteilungsblatt. Chemische Gesellschaft der Deutschen Demokratischen Republik

Mitteilungsbl Chem Ges Dtsch Demokr Repub Beih — Mitteilungsblatt. Chemische Gesellschaft der Deutschen Demokratischen Republik.Beiheft

Mitteilungsbl Dtsch Ges Sonnenenergie — Mitteilungsblatt. Deutsche Gesellschaft fuer Sonnenenergie

Mitteilungsbl Dtsch Keram Ges — Mitteilungsblatt. Deutsche Keramische Gesellschaft

Mitteilungsbl Fraunhofer-Ges — Mitteilungsblatt. Fraunhofer-Gesellschaft zur Foerderung der Angewandten Forschung EV

Mitteilungsbl Fraunhofer-Ges Foerd Angew Forsch — Mitteilungsblatt. Fraunhofer-Gesellschaft zur Foerderung der Angewandten Forschung EV

Mitteilungsbl GDCh Fachgruppe Lebensmittelchem Gerichtl Chem — Mitteilungsblatt. GDCh [*Gesellschaft Deutscher Chemiker*] Fachgruppe Lebensmittelchemie und Gerichtliche Chemie

Mitteilungsbl Ges Dtsch Chem Fachgruppe Anal Chem — Mitteilungsblatt. Gesellschaft Deutscher Chemiker. Fachgruppe Analytische Chemie

Mitteilungsbl Ges Dtsch Chem Fachgruppe Chem Inf — Mitteilungsblatt. Gesellschaft Deutscher Chemiker. Fachgruppe Chemie-Information

Mitteilungsbl Ges Dtsch Chem Fachgruppe Chem Inf Comput — Mitteilungsblatt. Gesellschaft Deutscher Chemiker, Fachgruppe, Chemie-Information-Computer

Mitteilungsbl Jungen Gerberei Tech — Mitteilungsblaetter fuer den Jungen Gerberei-Techniker

Mitteilungsbl Oesterr Orchideenges — Mitteilungsblatt der Oesterreichischen Orchideengesellschaft

Mitteilungsbl Strahlungsmessgeraete — Mitteilungsblaetter Strahlungsmessgeraete

Mitteilungsbl Ver Dtsch Ing Br Zone — Mitteilungsblatt der Vereins Deutscher Ingenieure in der Britischen Zone

Mitt EisenbVer Berl — Mitteilungen des Eisenbahnvereins zu Berlin

Mitt Eisenhuettenmaenn Inst Tech Hochsch (Aachen) — Mitteilungen. Eisenhuettenmaennisches Institut der Technischen Hochschule (Aachen)

Mitt Eisenhuettenm Inst Aachen — Mitteilungen aus dem Eisenhuettenmaennischen Institut der Koenigl. Technischen Hochschule. Aachen

Mitt Eisenhuettenm Inst Breslau — Mitteilungen aus dem Eisenhuettenmaennischen Institut der Koenigl. Technischen Hochschule. Breslau

Mitt Eisen Stahl Spundwand Hoesch — Mitteilungen ueber die Eisen- Stahl- Spundwand Hoesch

Mitteldt BergbZtg — Mitteldeutsche Bergbauzeitung

Mitteldt ObstbZtg — Mitteldeutsche Obstbauzeitung

Mitt Elektroind — Mitteilungen der Elektroindustrie

Mitt Elektrotech Lab Aschaffenb — Mitteilungen des Elektrotechnischen Laboratoriums. Aschaffenburg

Mitt Elektrotech Verein Lpz — Mitteilungen der Elektrotechnischen Vereiningung zu Leipzig

Mitteleur WittBer — Mitteleuropaischer Witterungsbericht

Mittellat Jb — Mittellateinisches Jahrbuch

Mitt Els Loth BezVer Dt Ing — Mitteilungen des Elsass-Lothringer Bezirksvereins Deutscher Ingenieure

Mitt Ent Ges (Basel) — Mitteilungen. Entomologische Gesellschaft (Basel)

Mitt Ent Ges Halle — Mitteilungen aus der Entomologischen Gesellschaft zu Halle a. S

Mitt Entomol Ges (Basel) — Mitteilungen. Entomologische Gesellschaft (Basel)

Mitt Entomol Ges BRD — Mitteilungen. Entomologische Gesellschaft in der Bundesrepublik Deutschland

Mitt Ent Ver Bremen — Mitteilungen aus dem Entomologischen Verein in Bremen

Mitt Ent Ver Polyxena — Mitteilungen des Entomologischen Vereins Polyxena

Mitt Ent Zuerich — Mitteilungen der Entomologia Zuerich und Umgebung

Mitt ErdbKommn Wien — Mitteilungen der Erdbebenkommission der K. Akademie der Wissenschaften in Wien

Mitternb — Mitternachtsbuecher

Mitt Ernst Heinkel FlugzWke — Mitteilungen. Ernst Heinkel Flugzeugwerke

Mitt Fachaussch Holzfragen — Mitteilungen des Fachausschusses fuer Holzfragen beim Verein Deutscher Ingenieure und Deutschen Forstverein

Mitt Fachverb Metall GiessTech — Mitteilungen. Fachverband Metallurgie und Giessereitechnik

Mitt Farbstoffkomm Dtsch Forschungsgem — Mitteilung der Farbstoffkommission. Deutsche Forschungsgemeinschaft

Mitt Farbstoff Kommn Dt ForschGemein — Mitteilungen. Farbstoff-Kommission der Deutschen Forschungsgemeinschaft

Mitt FischVer Prov Brandenb — Mitteilungen der Fischereivereine fuer die Provinz Brandenburg

Mitt Florist-Soziol Arbeitsgem — Mitteilungen. Floristisch-Soziologische Arbeitsgemeinschaft

Mitt Florist Soziol Arbeitsgem Niedersachsen — Mitteilungen der Floristisch-Soziologischen Arbeitsgemeinschaft in Niedersachsen

Mitt Flor Soz Arb — Mitteilungen. Floristisch-Soziologische Arbeitsgemeinschaft

Mitt Flor Soz ArbGemein — Mitteilungen der Florist-Soziologischen Arbeitsgemeinschaft. Zentralstelle fuer Vegetationskantierung

Mitt ForschAbt Angew Kohlenpetrogr — Mitteilungen der Forschungsabteilung fuer Angewandte Kohlenpetrographie und Kohlenaufbereitung

Mitt ForschAnst Dt Reichspost — Mitteilungen aus der Forschungsanstalt der Deutschen Reichspost

Mitt ForschAnstn GutehoffnHuette — Mitteilungen aus den Forschungsanstalten. Gutehoffnungshuette. Aktienverein fuer Bergbau und Huettenbetrieb

Mitt ForschArb Geb IngWes — Mitteilungen ueber Forschungsarbeiten auf dem Gebiet des Ingenieurwesens

Mitt Forscharb Ing Wesens — Mitteilungen ueber Forschungsarbeiten auf dem Gebiete des Ingenieur-Wesens

Mitt ForschGes Blechverarb — Mitteilungen der Forschungsgesellschaft Blechverarbeitung

Mitt ForschHeim Waermeschutz — Mitteilungen aus dem Forschungsheim fuer Waermeschutz

Mitt ForschInst Elektrowaermetech Hannover — Mitteilungen. Forschungsinstitut fuer Elektrowaermetechnik. Technische Hochschule (Hannover)

Mitt ForschInst MaschWes Baubetr — Mitteilungen des Forschungsinstituts fuer Maschinenwesen beim Baubetrieb. Technische Hochschule

Mitt ForschInst Phys Strahlantr — Mitteilungen aus dem Forschungsinstitut Physik der Strahlantriebe

Mitt ForschInst ProbAmt Edelmetalle. Gmuend — Mitteilungen des Forschungsinstituts und Probieramts fuer Edelmetalle der Staatlichen Hoeheren Fachschule Schwaeb (Gmuend)

Mitt ForschInst Sorau Verb Dt Leinen Ind — Mitteilungen des Forschungsinstituts Sorau des Verbands Deutscher Leinen-Industrieller

Mitt ForschInst Ver Dt Eisenportlandzem Wke — Mitteilungen des Forschungsinstituts des Vereins Deutscher Eisenportlandzement-Werke

Mitt ForschInst Ver Stahlwke AG — Mitteilungen aus dem Forschungsinstitut. Vereinigte Stahlwerke Aktiengesellschaft

Mitt ForschInst WassBau WassKraft — Mitteilungen des Forschungsinstituts fuer Wasserbau und Wasserkraft

Mitt Forsch Konstr Stahlb — Mitteilungen ueber Forschung und Konstruktion im Stahlbau

Mitt Forsch Konstr Stahlbau — Mitteilungen ueber Forschung und Konstruktion in Stahlbau

Mitt ForschLab Agfa — Mitteilungen aus den Forschungslaboratorien der Agfa Aktiengesellschaft fuer Photofabrikation

Mitt ForschReis Gelehrt Dt Schutzgeb — Mitteilungen von Forschungsreisenden und Gelehrten aus den Deutschen Schutzgebieten

Mitt ForschStelle StrBau Braunschw — Mitteilungen der Forschungsstelle fuer Strassenbau an der Technischen Hochschule zu Braunschweig

Mitt Forschungsanst Gutehoffnungshuette Konzerns — Mitteilungen. Forschungsanstalten von Gutehoffnungshuette-Konzerns

Mitt Forschungsbeitr Cusanus Ges — Mitteilungen und Forschungsbeitraege der Cusanus Gesellschaft

Mitt Forschungsges Blechverarb — Mitteilungen der Forschungsgesellschaft Blechverarbeitung

Mitt Forschungsinst Luftfahrtmaterialpruefung Moscow — Mitteilungen des Forschungsinstituts fuer Luftfahrtmaterialpruefung. Moscow

Mitt Forschungsinst Pflanzenzuecht Pflanzenbau Sopronhorpacs — Mitteilungen. Forschungsinstituts fuer Pflanzenzuechtung und Pflanzenbau in Sopronhorpacs

Mitt Forschungsinst Ung Zuckerind — Mitteilungen des Forschungsinstituts der Ungarischen Zuckerindustrie

Mitt Forschungsinst Ver Stahlwerke Ag (Dortmund) — Mitteilungen. Forschungsinstitut der Vereinigten Stahlwerke Aktiengesellschaft(Dortmund)

Mitt Forschungslab AGFA Gevaert AG (Leverkusen Muenchen) — Mitteilungen. Forschungslaboratorien der AGFA-Gevaert AG (Leverkusen-Muenchen)

Mitt Forschungslab AGFA (Leverkusen) — Mitteilungen. Forschungslaboratorium AGFA (Leverkusen)

Mitt Forschungsreis Gelehrt Dt Schtzgebiet — Mitteilungen von Forschungsreisenden und Gelehrten aus den Deutschen Schutzgebieten

Mitt ForsteinrichtAmts Koblenz — Mitteilungen des Forsteinrichtungsamts Koblenz

Mitt Forstl Bundesversuchsanstalt (Mariabrunn) — Mitteilungen. Forstliche Bundes-Versuchsanstalt (Mariabrunn)

Mitt Forstl Bundes-Versuchsanst (Mariabrunn) — Mitteilungen. Forstliche Bundes-Versuchsanstalt (Mariabrunn)

Mitt Forstl Bundes-Versuchsanst (Wien) — Mitteilungen. Forstliche Bundes-Versuchsanstalt (Wien)

Mitt Forstl BundVersAnst Mariabrunn — Mitteilungen aus der Forstlichen Bundesversuchsanstalt. Mariabrunn

Mitt Forstl Forschungsanst Schwed — Mitteilungen der Forstlichen Forschungsanstalt Schwedens

Mitt Forstl VersAnst — Mitteilungen. Forstliche Bundes-Versuchsanstalt

Mitt Forstl VersWes Badens — Mitteilungen aus dem Forstlichen Versuchswesen Badens

Mitt Forstl VersWes Oest — Mitteilungen aus dem Forstlichen Versuchswesen Oesterreichs

Mitt Forstl VerWes Preuss — Mitteilungen aus dem Forstlichen Versuchswesen Preussens

Mitt Forsttech Akad — Mitteilungen der Forsttechnischen Akademie

Mitt Forst U Kameralverw Hessen — Mitteilungen der Forst- und Kameralverwaltung des Volksstaates Hessen

Mitt Forstw Forstwiss — Mitteilungen aus Forstwirtschaft und Forstwissenschaft

Mitt Fraenk Geogr Ges — Mitteilungen der Fraenkischen Geographischen Gesellschaft

Mitt Franzius Inst — Mitteilungen. Franzius-Institut. Hannoversche Versuchsanstalt fuer Grundbau und Wasserbau

Mitt Fraunhofer Inst — Mitteilungen aus dem Fraunhofer Institut

Mitt Fr Geogr Ges — Mitteilungen der Fraenkischen Geographischen Gesellschaft

Mitt Gaehrphysiol Lab Klosterneuburg — Mitteilungen aus dem Gaehrungsphysiologischen Laboratorium der K.K. Chemisch-Physiologischen Versuchsstation fuer Wein- und Obstbau in Klosterneuburg bei Wien

Mitt Geb Feuerloeschw — Mitteilungen auf dem Gebiet des Feuerloeschwesens

Mitt Geb Lebensmittelunters Hyg — Mitteilungen aus dem Gebiete der Lebensmitteluntersuchung und Hygiene

Mitt Geb Lebensmittelunters Hyg Trav Chim Aliment Hyg — Mitteilungen aus dem Gebiete der Lebensmitteluntersuchung und Hygiene. Travaux de Chimie Alimentaire et d'Hygiene

Mitt Geb Lebensmittelunters U Hyg — Mitteilungen aus dem Gebiet der Lebensmitteluntersuchung und -Hygiene

Mitt Geb Naturwiss Tech — Mitteilungen aus den Gebieten der Naturwissenschaft und Technik

Mitt Gebn Holzbearb Saeg — Mitteilungen aus den Gebieten der Holzbearbeitung und Saegerei

Mitt Gebn Naturw Tech — Mitteilungen aus den Gebieten der Naturwissenschaften und der Technik

Mitt Geb Seew — Mitteilungen aus dem Gebiet des Seewesens

Mitt Geburtsh Gynaek Prax — Mitteilungen zur Geburtshilfe und Gynaekologie fuer die Praxis

Mitt Geb WassBau Grundbforsch — Mitteilungen aus dem Gebiete des Wasserbaues und der Grundbauforschung

Mitt Gegenstaende Artill U Geniew — Mitteilungen ueber Gegenstaende des Artillerie- und Geniewesens

Mitt Gegenstde Artillw — Mitteilungen ueber Gegenstaende des Artillerie- und Geniewesens

Mitt Geodaet Inst Tech Univ Graz — Mitteilungen. Geodaetische Institut der Technischen Universitaet Graz

Mitt Geodaet Inst Zuerich — Mitteilungen aus dem Geodaetischen Institut. Eidgenoessische Technische Hochschule (Zuerich)

Mitt Geog Ges Hamburg — Mitteilungen der Geographischen Gesellschaft in Hamburg

Mitt Geogr Ethnogr Ges Zuerich — Mitteilungen der Geographisch-Ethnographischen Gesellschaft in Zuerich

Mitt Geogr Ethnol Ges Basel — Mitteilungen der Geographisch-Ethnologischen Gesellschaft in Basel

Mitt Geogr Ges Hamb — Mitteilungen. Geographische Gesellschaft in Hamburg

Mitt Geogr Ges Muench — Mitteilungen der Geographischen Gesellschaft in Muenchen

Mitt Geogr Ges Muenchen — Mitteilungen. Geographische Gesellschaft in Muenchen

Mitt Geogr Ges Naturhist Mus Luebeck — Mitteilungen der Geographischen Gesellschaft und des Naturhistorischen Museums in Luebeck

Mitt Geogr Ges Naturh Mus Luebeck — Mitteilungen der Geographischen Gesellschaft und des Naturhistorischen Museums in Luebeck

Mitt Geogr Ges Thueringen Jena — Mitteilungen der Geographischen Gesellschaft fuer Thueringen zu Jena

Mitt Geol Ges Wien — Mitteilungen. Geologische Gesellschaft in Wien

Mitt Geol Inst Eidg Tech Hochsch Univ Zurich — Mitteilungen. Geologisches Institut der Eidgenoessischen Technischen Hochschuleund der Universitaet Zuerich

Mitt Geol Palaeontol Inst Univ Hamburg — Mitteilungen. Geologisch-Palaeontologische Institut. Universitaet Hamburg

Mitt Geol Staatsinst Hamb — Mitteilungen. Geologisches Staatsinstitut in Hamburg

Mitt Geo Palaon — Mitteilungen aus dem Geologische-Palaontologischen

Mitt Georgischen Abt Akad Wiss USSR — Mitteilungen der Georgischen Abteilung der Akademie der Wissenschaften der USSR

Mitt Georg Sticker Inst Gesch Med — Mitteilungen des Georg Sticker-Instituts fuer Geschichte der Medizin

Mitt Germ Nationalmus Nuernbg — Mitteilungen des Germanischen Nationalmuseums (Nuernberg)

Mitt Germ Verb — Mitteilungen des Deutschen Germanisten-Verbandes

Mitt Ger Nmus — Mitteilungen aus dem Germanischen Nationalmuseum

Mitt Ges Angew Math Mech — Mitteilungen der Gesellschaft fuer Angewandte Mathematik und Mechanik

Mitt Ges Bayerische Mg — Mitteilungsblatt. Gesellschaft fuer Bayerische Musikgeschichte

Mitt Ges Braunkohl U Mineraloelforsch — Mitteilungen. Gesellschaft fuer Braunkohlen- und Mineraloelforschung. Technische Hochschule

Mitt Gesch & Altertver Liegnitz — Mitteilungen des Geschichts- und Altertumsvereins zu Liegnitz

Mitt Gesch Dt Boehmen — Mitteilungen der Geschichte der Deutschen in Boehmen

Mitt Gesch Med Naturwiss — Mitteilungen zur Geschichte der Medizin und der Naturwissenschaften

Mitt Gesch Med Naturwiss Tech — Mitteilungen zur Geschichte der Medizin der Naturwissenschaften und Technik

Mitt Gesch Med Naturw Tech — Mitteilungen zur Geschichte der Medizin und der Naturwissenschaften und der Technik

Mitt Ges Dt NatForsch Aerzte — Mitteilungen der Gesellschaft Deutscher Naturforscher und Aerzte

Mitt Ges Erdk KolonWes Strassb — Mitteilungen der Gesellschaft fuer Erdkunde und Kolonialwesen zu Strassburg

Mitt Ges Erdk L — Mitteilungen der Gesellschaft fuer Erdkunde zu Leipzig

Mitt Ges Erdk Lpz — Mitteilungen der Gesellschaft fuer Erdkunde zu Leipzig

Mitt Ges Erhaltung Gesch Dkml Elsass — Mitteilungen der Gesellschaft fuer Erhaltung der Geschichtlichen Denkmale in Elsass

Mitt Ges Foerd Dt Wiss Boehm — Mitteilungen der Gesellschaft zur Foerderung Deutscher Wissenschaft, Kunst und Literatur in Boehmen

Mitt Ges Foerd Forsch Zuerich — Mitteilungen der Gesellschaft zur Foerderung der Forschung. Eidgenoessische Technische Hochschule (Zuerich)

Mitt Ges Foerd Wasserw Harze — Mitteilungen der Gesellschaft zur Foerderung der Wasserwirtschaft im Harze

Mitt Ges Geol Bergbaustud Oesterr — Mitteilungen. Gesellschaft der Geologie- und Bergbaustudenten in Oesterreich

Mitt Ges Geol Bergbaustud Wien — Mitteilungen. Gesellschaft der Geologie- und Bergbaustudenten in Wien

Mitt Ges Ges Ther — Mitteilungen der Gesellschaft fuer die Gesamte Therapie

Mitt Ges Hist Kostuem U Waffenkde — Mitteilungen der Gesellschaft fuer Historische Kostuem- und Waffenkunde

Mitt Ges Inn Med Kinderheilk — Mitteilungen der Gesellschaft fuer Innere Medizin und Kinderheilkunde

Mitt Ges Inn Med Wien — Mitteilungen der Gesellschaft fuer Innere Medizin in Wien

Mitt Gesn Siemens & Halske Siemens Schuckertwke — Mitteilungen aus den Gesellschaften Siemens & Halske, Siemens-Schuckertwerke

Mitt Ges Prakt Aerzte Riga — Mitteilungen aus der Gesellschaft Praktischer Aerzte zu Riga

Mitt Ges Salzb Landesk — Mitteilungen der Gesellschaft fuer Salzburger Landeskunde

Mitt Ges Salzburg Landesknd — Mitteilungen der Gesellschaft fuer Salzburger Landeskunde

Mitt Ges Schweiz Landw — Mitteilungen der Gesellschaft Schweizerischer Landwirte

Mitt Ges Schweiz Ldwirte — Mitteilungen der Gesellschaft Schweizerischer Landwirte

Mitt Ges Tierpsychol — Mitteilungen der Gesellschaft fuer Tierpsychologie

Mitt Ges Vergl Kstforsch Wien — Mitteilungen der Gesellschaft fuer Vergleichende Kunstforschung in Wien

Mitt Ges Vervielfalt Kst — Mitteilungen der Gesellschaft fuer Vervielfaltigende Kunst

Mitt Ges Vorratsschutz — Mitteilungen der Gesellschaft fuer Vorratsschutz

Mitt Ges Waermew — Mitteilungen der Gesellschaft fuer Waermewirtschaft

Mitt Gew Hyg Mus Wien — Mitteilungen des Gewerbe-Hygienischen Museums in Wien

Mitt Giess Inst Aachen — Mitteilungen aus dem Giesserei-Institut. Aachen

Mitt Grenzgeb Med Chir — Mitteilungen aus den Grenzgebieten der Medizin und Chirurgie

Mitt Grenzgeb Med u Chir — Mitteilungen aus den Grenzgebieten der Medizin und Chirurgie

Mitt Grossforschungszentrum Chemieanlagen — Mitteilungen. Grossforschungszentrum Chemieanlagen

Mitt Grossherz Mecklenb Geol Landesanst — Mitteilungen aus der Grossherzoglichen Mecklenburgischen Geologischen Landesanstalt

Mitt Grossherz Sternw Heidelb — Mitteilungen der Grossherzoglichen Sternwarte zu Heidelberg

Mitt Gruppe Dtsch Kolonialwirtsch Unternehm — Mitteilungen der Gruppe Deutscher Kolonialwirtschaftlicher Unternehmungen

Mitt Gynaek Klin Prof Otto Engstroem Helsingf — Mitteilungen aus der Gynaekologischen Klinik des Prof. Otto Engstroem in Helsingfors

Mitt Hamb Bot StInst — Mitteilungen aus dem Hamburgischen Botanischen Staatsinstitut

Mitt Hamb Staatskrankenanst — Mitteilungen. Hamburgische Staatskrankenanstalten

Mitt Hamb Sternw Bergedorf — Mitteilungen der Hamburger Sternwarte in Bergedorf

Mitt Hamb St Krankenanst — Mitteilungen aus den Hamburgischen Staats-Krankenanstalten

Mitt Hamb Zool Mus Inst — Mitteilungen. Hamburgisches Zoologische Museum und Institut

Mitt Hannover VersAnst Grundb WassBau — Mitteilungen der Hannoverschen Versuchsanstalt fuer Grundbau und Wasserbau

Mitt Hans Pfitzner Ges — Mitteilungen. Hans-Pfitzner-Gesellschaft

Mitt Hauptstn ErdbForsch Hamb — Mitteilungen der Hauptstation fuer Erdbebenforschung am Physikalischen Staatslaboratorium zu Hamburg

Mitt Hauptver Dt Ing Tschech Repub — Mitteilungen. Hauptverein Deutscher Ingenieure in der Tschechoslowakischen Republik

Mitth d Arch Instzu Athen — Mitteilungen des Deutschen Archaeologischen Instituts. Athenische Abteilung

Mitt Hermann Goering Akad Deutsch Forstwiss — Mitteilungen der Hermann-Goering-Akademie der Deutschen Forstwissenschaft

Mitt Hermsdorf Schomburg Isolat — Mitteilungen. Hermsdorf-Schomburg Isolatoren G.m.b.H

Mitt Hess Landesforstverw — Mitteilungen. Hessische Landesforstverwaltung

Mitth Flora Ges Bot Dresden — Mittheilungen ueber Flora. Gesellschaft fuer Botanik und Gartenbau in Dresden

Mitth Gesammtgeb Bot — Mittheilungen aus dem Gesammtgebiete der Botanik

Mitt Hist Ver Kant Schwyz — Mitteilungen des Historischen Vereins des Kantons Schwyz

Mitt Hist Ver Osnabr — Mitteilungen des Historischen Vereins fuer Osnabrueck

Mitt Hist Ver Pfalz — Mitteilungen des Historischen Vereins der Pfalz

Mitth Justus Perthes Geogr Anst Ergaenzungsband — Mittheilungen aus Justus Perthes' Geographischer Anstalt ueber Wichtige Neue Erforschungen auf dem Gesammtgebiete der Geographie. Ergaenzungsband

Mitth Landw — Mittheilungen aus dem Gebiete der Landwirthschaft

Mitth Med — Mittheilungen aus dem Gebiete der Medizin, Chirurgie, und Pharmacie

Mitth Naturwiss Vereine Neu Vorpommern — Mittheilungen aus dem Naturwissenschaftlichen Vereine von Neu-Vorpommern und Ruegen

Mitth Naturwiss Vereins Freiberg — Mittheilungen des Naturwissenschaftlichen Vereins zu Freiberg in Sachsen

Mitt Hoehlenk — Mitteilungen fuer Hoehlenkunde

Mitt HoehlKomm Wien — Mitteilungen der Hoehlenkommission (Wien)

Mitt Hoehl U Karstforsch — Mitteilungen ueber Hoehlen- und Karstforschung

Mitt Hoh Bundeslehr- u VersAnst Wein- Obst- u Gartenb — Mitteilungen der Hoeheren Bundeslehr- und Versuchsanstalten fuer Wein-, Obst-, und Gartenbau

Mitt HolzforschStelle Darmstadt — Mitteilungen der Holzforschungsstelle an der Technischen Hochschule. Darmstadt

Mitth HopfenbVerb Saaz — Mitteilungen des Hopfenbauverbands in Saaz

Mitth Philom Ges Elsass Lothringen — Mittheilungen der Philomatischen Gesellschaft in Elsass-Lothringen

Mitth Theor Erdk — Mittheilungen aus dem Gebiete der Theoretischen Erdkunde

Mitth Thurgauischen Naturf Vereins Thaetigk — Mittheilungen des Thurgauischen Naturforschenden Vereins ueber Seine Thaetigkeit

Mitth Verh Ges Naturf Freunde Berlin — Mittheilungen aus den Verhandlungen der Gesellschaft Naturforschender Freunde zu Berlin

Mitth Verh Naturwiss Ges Hamburg — Mittheilungen aus den Verhandlungen der Naturwissenschaftlichen Gesellschaft inHamburg

Mitt Hydraul Inst Muench — Mitteilungen des Hydraulischen Instituts der Technischen Hochschule. Muenchen

Mitt Hydrogr Bur Finnl — Mitteilungen vom Hydrographischen Bureau der Oberverwaltung der Wege- und Wasserbauten in Finnland

Mitt Hyg Inst K Univ Jurjew — Mitteilungen aus dem Hygienischen Institut der K. Universitaet zu Jurjew

Mitt Ind Forschungszent Chemieanlagen — Mitteilungen. Industrie-Forschungszentrum Chemieanlagen

Mitt IngKom — Mitteilungen des Ingenieurkomitees

Mitt Inst Aerodyn — Mitteilungen. Institut fuer Aerodynamik an der Eidgenoessischen Technischen Hochschule in Zuerich

Mitt Inst Aerodyn Zuerich — Mitteilungen. Institut fuer Aerodynamik. Eidgenoessische Technische Hochschule (Zuerich)

Mitt Inst Allg Anorg Chem Bulg Akad Wiss — Mitteilungen des Instituts fuer Allgemeine und Anorganische Chemie. BulgarischeAkademie der Wissenschaften

Mitt Inst Allg Anorg Chem Org Chem Bulg Akad Wiss — Mitteilungen. Institute fuer Allgemeine und Anorganische Chemie und Organische Chemie. Bulgarische Akademie der Wissenschaften

Mitt Inst Allg Bot (Hamb) — Mitteilungen aus dem Institut fuer Allgemeine Botanik (Hamburg)

Mitt Inst Allgemeine Bot (Hamb) — Mitteilungen aus dem Institut fuer Allgemeine Botanik (Hamburg)

Mitt Inst Angew Geod — Mitteilungen des Instituts fuer Angewandte Geodasie

Mitt Inst Angew Math — Mitteilungen aus dem Institut fuer Angewandte Mathematik

Mitt Inst Angew Math Zuerich — Mitteilungen aus dem Institut fuer Angewandte Mathematik. Eidgenossische Technische Hochschule (Zuerich)

Mitt Inst Angew Mikrobiol Wien — Mitteilungen des Instituts fuer Angewandte Mikrobiologie (Wien)

Mitt Inst Auslandsbezieh — Institute fuer Auslandsbeziehungen. Mitteilungen

Mitt Inst Ausl Kolon Forstw Tharandt — Mitteilungen des Instituts fuer Auslaendische und Koloniale Forstwirtschaft an der Forstlichen Hochschule, Tharandt

Mitt Inst Baustatik — Mitteilungen. Institut fuer Baustatik. Eidgenoessische Technische Hochschule inZuerich

Mitt Inst Baustat Zuerich — Mitteilungen aus dem Institut fuer Baustatik. Eidgenoessische Technische Hochschule (Zuerich)

Mitt Inst Bautech — Mitteilungen. Institut fuer Bautechnik

Mitt Inst Chemieanlagen — Mitteilungen. Institute fuer Chemieanlagen

Mitt Inst Chem Kaelteausruest VVB Chem Klimaanlagen Ausg A — Mitteilungen des Institutes fuer Chemie- und Kaelteausruestungen der VVB Chemie- und Klimaanlagen. Ausgabe A

Mitt Inst Colombo-Aleman Invest Cient "Punta De Betin" — Mitteilungen. Instituto Colombo-Aleman de Investigaciones Cientificas "Punta DeBetin"

Mitt Inst Dkmlpf Schwerin — Mitteilungen des Institutes fuer Denkmalpflege Schwerin

Mitt Inst Dr Carl Spengler Davos — Mitteilungen aus dem Institut Dr. Carl Spengler in Davos

Mitt Inst Dt ForschGes Bodenmech — Mitteilungen des Instituts der Deutsche Forschungsgesellschaft fuer Bodenmechanik. Technische Universitaet, Berlin-Charlottenburg

Mitt Inst Dt Ges Forsch Graph Gew — Mitteilungen des Instituts. Deutsche Gesellschaft fuer Forschung im Graphischen Gewerbe

Mitt Inst ElektromaschBau Zuerich — Mitteilungen aus dem Institut fuer Elektromaschinenbau. Eidgenoessische Technische Hochschule (Zuerich)

Mitt Inst FlugzStat FlugzBau Zuerich — Mitteilungen aus dem Institut fuer Flugzeugstatik und Glugzeugbau. Eidgenoessische Technische Hochschule (Zuerich)

Mitt Inst FlugzStat Leichtb Zuerich — Mitteilungen aus dem Institut fuer Flugzeugstatik und Leichtbau. Eidgenoessische Technische Hochschule (Zuerich)

Mitt Inst Forstwiss Budapest — Mitteilungen des Institutes fuer Forstwissenschaft. Budapest

Mitt Inst Geophys Zuerich — Mitteilungen aus dem Institut fuer Groophysik. Eidgenossische Technische Hochschule (Zuerich)

Mitt Inst Geschforsch & Archwiss Wien — Mitteilungen des Instituts fuer Geschichtsforschung und Archivwissenschaft in Wien

Mitt Inst Gesch Med Univ Wurzb — Mitteilungen aus dem Institut fuer Geschichte der Medizin an der Universitaet Wuerzburg

Mitt Inst Grundbau Bodenmech Eidg Tech Hochsch (Zurich) — Mitteilungen. Institut fuer Grundbau und Bodenmechanik. Eidgenoessische Technische Hochschule (Zurich)

Mitt Inst Handelsforsch Univ Koeln — Mitteilungen des Instituts fuer Handelsforschung an der Universitaet Koeln

Mitt Inst HochfreqTech Zuerich — Mitteilungen aus dem Institut fuer Hochfrequenztechnik. Eidgenossische Technische Hochschule (Zuerich)

Mitt Inst Hydraul Gewaesserkd — Mitteilungen. Institut fuer Hydraulik und Gewaesserkunde. Technische Hochschule

Mitt Inst Hydraul Hydraul Masch Zuerich — Mitteilungen aus dem Institut fuer Hydraulik und Hydraulischen Maschinen. Eidgenossische Technische Hochschule (Zuerich)

Mitt Inst Hydraul Masch Anl Zuerich — Mitteilungen aus dem Institut fuer Hydraulischen Maschinen und Anlagen. Eidgenossische Technische Hochschule (Zuerich)

Mitt Inst KohlVergas NebenprodGewinn Wien — Mitteilungen des Instituts fuer Kohlenvergasung und Nebenproduktengewinnung (Wien)

Mitt Inst KraftWes Dresden — Mitteilungen aus dem Institut fuer Kraftfahrwesen der Saechsischen Technischen Hochschule (Dresden)

Mitt Inst Massivb Hannover — Mitteilungen aus dem Institut fuer Massivbau. Technische Hochschule, Hannover

Mitt Inst Oesterreich Geschforsch — Mitteilungen des Instituts fuer Oesterreichische Geschichtsforschung

Mitt Inst Oesterr Gesch Forsch — Mitteilungen des Instituts fuer Geschichtsforschung und Archivwissenschaft in Wien

Mitt Inst Oesterr Gesch Forsch — Mitteilungen des Instituts fuer Oesterreichische Geschichtsforschung

Mitt Inst Oesterr Gesch Forsch — Mitteilungen des Oesterreichischen Instituts fuer Geschichtsforschung

Mitt Inst Or F — Mitteilungen des Instituts fuer Orientforschung

Mitt Inst Orient F — Mitteilungen des Instituts fuer Orientforschung

Mitt Inst Orientforsch — Mitteilungen. Institutes fuer Orientforschung

Mitt Inst Orientforsch Dtsch Akad Wiss Berl — Mitteilungen. Institut fuer Orientforschung. Deutsche Akademie der Wissenschaften zu Berlin

Mitt Inst Radiumforsch Wien — Mitteilungen aus dem Institut fuer Radiumforschung (Wien)

Mitt Inst Raumforsch — Mitteilungen aus dem Institut fuer Raumforschung

Mitt Inst Raumforsch Raumordn — Mitteilungen aus dem Institut fuer Raumforschung und Raumordnung

Mitt Inst Seefisch — Mitteilungen. Institut fuer Seefischerei

Mitt Inst StrBau Zuerich — Mitteilungen aus dem Institut fuer Strassenbau. Eidgenossische Technische Hochschule (Zuerich)

Mitt Inst StromMasch Karlsruhe — Mitteilungen. Institut fuer Stromungsmaschinen. Badische Technische Hochschule (Karlsruhe)

Mitt Inst Syst Bot Martin Luther Univ Halle Wittenberg — Mitteilungen aus dem Institut fuer Systematische Botanik und Pflanzengeographieder Martin-Luther-Universitaet Halle-Wittenberg

Mitt Inst Tech Mech Bulg Akad Wiss — Mitteilungen des Instituts fuer Technische Mechanik. Bulgarische Akademie der Wissenschaften

Mitt Inst Tech Phys Zuerich — Mitteilungen aus dem Institut fuer Technische Physik. Eidgenoessische Technische Hochschule (Zuerich)

Mitt Inst Textiltechnol Chemiefasern Rudolstadt — Mitteilungen. Institut fuer Textiltechnologie der Chemiefasern Rudolstadt

Mitt Inst TextMaschBau TextInd Zuerich — Mitteilungen aus dem Institut fuer Textilmaschinenbau und Textilindustrie. Eidgenossische Technische Hochschule (Zuerich)

Mitt Inst Text Tech — Mitteilungen aus dem Institut fuer Textiltechnik

Mitt Inst Thermodyn VerbrennMotBau Zuerich — Mitteilungen. Institut fuer Thermodynamik und Verbrennungsmotorenbau. Eidgenossische Technische Hochschule (Zuerich)

Mitt Inst Therm Turbomasch — Mitteilungen. Institut fuer Thermische Turbomaschinen. Eidgenoessische Technische Hochschule

Mitt Inst WassBau Berl — Mitteilungen aus dem Institut fuer Wasserbau. Technische Hochschule (Berlin)

Mitt Inst WassBau WassWirt Berl — Mitteilungen aus dem Institut fuer Wasserbau und Wasserwirtschaft (Berlin)

Mitt Inst Wasserbau Wasserwirtsch Rheinisch Westfael Tech Hoch — Mitteilungen des Instituts fuer Wasserbau und Wasserwirtschaft der Rheinisch-Wesfaelischen Techninen Hochschule Aachen

Mitt Inst Wasserwirtsch Bauwes Bulg Akad Wiss — Mitteilungen. Instituts fuer Wasserwirtschaft und Bauwesen. Bulgarische Akademie der Wissenschaften

Mitt Int Bodenkd Ges — Mitteilungen der Internationalen Bodenkundlichen Gesellschaft

Mitt Int Entomol Ver EV (Frankf) — Mitteilungen des Internationalen Entomologischen Vereins EV (Frankfurt)

Mitt Intern Kriminal Vereing — Mitteilungen der Internationalen Kriminalistischen Vereinigung

Mitt Int Landw Inst Presse — Mitteilungen des Internationalen Landwirtschaftlichen Instituts an die Presse

Mitt Int Math UnterrKommn — Mitteilungen der Internationalen Mathematischen Unterrichtskommission

Mitt Int Moor-Torf-Ges — Mitteilungen. Internationale Moor- und Torf-Gesellschaft

Mitt Int Stiftung Mozarteum — Mitteilungen. Internationale Stiftung Mozarteum

Mitt Int Verein Theor Angew Limnol — Mitteilungen der Internationalen Vereinigung fuer Theoretische und Angewandte Limnologie

Mitt Int Ver Saatgutpruef — Mitteilungen. Internationale Vereinigung fuer Saatgutpruefung

Mitt Int Ver Saatgutpruefung — Mitteilungen. Internationale Vereinigung fuer Saatgutpruefung

Mitt Int Ver Samenkontrolle — Mitteilungen der Internationalen Vereinigung fuer Samenkontrolle

Mitt Int Ver Theor Angew Limnol — Mitteilungen. Internationale Vereinigung fuer Theoretische und Angewandte Limnologie

Mitt IOeG — Mitteilungen. Oesterreichisches Institut fuer Geschichtsforschung

Mitt Jahrb K Ung Geol Anst — Mitteilungen des Jahrbuches der Koeniglichen Ungarischen Geologischen Anstalt

Mitt JahrVersamml Frei Verein Bayer Vertr Angew Chem — Mitteilungen aus der Jahresversammlung der Freien Vereinigung Bayerischer Vertreter der Angewandten Chemie

Mitt Jap Ges Gynak — Mitteilungen der Japanischen Gesellschaft fuer Gynakologie

Mitt Jap Med Hochsch Mukden — Mitteilungen aus der Japanischen Medizinischen Hochschule zu Mukden

Mitt Josef Haas Ges — Mitteilungsblatt. Josef-Haas-Gesellschaft

Mitt (Kairo) — Mitteilungen. Deutsches Institut fuer Aegyptische Altertumskunde (Kairo)

Mitt Kaiser Wilhelm Inst Eisenforsch Duesseldorf — Mitteilungen. Kaiser-Wilhelm-Institut fuer Eisenforschung zu Duesseldorf

Mitt Kali Forsch Anst — Mitteilungen. Kali-Forschungs-Anstalt

Mitt K Anst Land-u Forstw — Mitteilungen. Kaiserliche Anstalt fuer Land- und Forstwirtschaft

Mitt Kautsch Stift Delft — Mitteilungen der Kautschuk-Stiftung. Delft

Mitt Kinderaerz — Mitteilungen fuer Kinderaerzte

Mitt Kirov Forsttech Akad — Mitteilungen der Kirov Forsttechnischen Akademie

Mitt K Landesanst Wasserhyg Berlin Dahlem — Mitteilungen aus der Koeniglichen Landesanstalt fuer Wasserhygiene zu Berlin-Dahlen

Mitt Kl Math Naturwiss Med Tschech Akad Wiss Kuenste — Mitteilungen. Klasse der Mathematik, der Naturwissenschaften und der Medizin. Tschechische Akademie der Wissenschaften und Kuenste

Mitt (Klosterneuburg) — Mitteilungen (Klosterneuburg)

Mitt Klosterneuburg Rebe Wein Obs Fruecht — Mitteilungen Klosterneuburg. Rebe und Wein, Obstbau und Fruechteverwertung

Mitt Klosterneuburg Ser A — Mitteilungen (Klosterneuburg). Serie A. Rebe und Wein

Mitt K Materialpruef Berlin Lichterfelde West — Mitteilungen aus dem Koeniglichen Materialpruefungsamt zu Berlin-Lichterfelde West

Mitt Koenigl Mineral Geol Mus Dresden — Mitteilungen aus dem Koeniglich Mineralogisch-Geologischen und PraehistorischenMuseum zu Dresden

Mitt Koen Saechs Altertver — Mitteilungen des Koeniglichen-Saechsischen Altertumsvereins

Mitt Kohle Eisenforsch GmbH — Mitteilungen. Kohle- und Eisenforschung GmbH

Mitt Kohlenforschungsinst Prag — Mitteilungen des Kohlenforschungsinstituts in Prag

Mitt Komm Erforsch Luftverunreinig Dtsch Forschungsgem — Mitteilung. Kommission zur Erforschung der Luftverunreinigung. Deutsche Forschungsgemeinschaft

Mitt Komm Pruef Stoffe Lebensm Dtsch Forschungsgem — Mitteilung. Kommission zur Pruefung Fremder Stoffe bei Lebensmitteln, Deutsche Forschungsgemeinschaft

Mitt Komm Pruef Rueckstaenden Lebensm Dtsch Forschungsgem — Mitteilung. Kommission zur Pruefung von Rueckstaenden in Lebensmitteln. Deutsche Forschungsgemeinschaft

Mitt Komm Wasserforsch Dtsch Forschungsgem — Mitteilung der Kommission fuer Wasserforschung. Deutsche Forschungsgemeinschaft

Mitt Kornbrenn Presshefefabr — Mitteilungen fuer Kornbrennerei und Presshefefabrikation

Mitt K Pruefungsanst Wasserversorg Abwaesserbeseit Berlin — Mitteilungen aus der Koeniglichen Pruefungsanstalt fuer Wasserversorgung und Abwaesserbeseitigung zu Berlin

Mitt Kraftwerksanlagenbau (DDR) — Mitteilungen. Kraftwerksanlagenbau (DDR)

Mitt KreisgeflugelzAnst Erding — Mitteilungen der Kreisgeflugelzuchtanstalt Erding

Mitt Krems Stadtarchvs — Mitteilungen des Kremser Stadtarchivs

Mitt Ksr Koen Cent Comm Erforsch & Erhaltung Baudkml — Mitteilungen der K.-K. [Kaiserlich-Koeniglichen] Central-Commission zur Erforschung und Erhaltung des Baudenkmale

Mitt Ksr Koen Maehr Schles Ackerbauges — Mitteilungen der K.-K. [Kaiserlich-Koeniglichen] Maehrisch-Schlesischen Ackerbaugesellschaft

Mitt Ksr Koen Oesterreich Mus Kst & Indust — Mitteilungen der K.-K. [Kaiserlich-Koeniglichen] Oesterreichischen Museums fuer Kunst und Industrie

Mitt Ksr Koen Zent Comm Erforsch & Erhaltung Kst & Hist Dkml — Mitteilungen der K.-K. [Kaiserlich-Koeniglichen] Zentral-Commission zur Erforschung und Erhaltung der Kunst- und Historischen Demkmale

Mitt Ksthist Inst Florenz — Mitteilungen des Kunsthistorischen Instituts in Florenz

Mitt K Tech Versuchsanst Berlin — Mitteilungen aus den Koeniglichen Technischen Versuchsanstalten zu Berlin

Mitt Kuehland Landw Ver — Mitteilungen des Kuehlander Landwirtschaftlichen Vereins, Neutitschein

Mitt Kunst — Mitteilungen des Kunsthistorischen Instituts in Florenz

Mitt Kunst Kunstgew — Mitteilungen fuer Kunst und Kunstgewerbe

Mitt Lab Geol Dienstes Berlin — Mitteilungen aus den Laboratorien des Geologischen Dienstes. Berlin

Mitt Lab Geol Dienstes (DDR) — Mitteilungen. Laboratorien des Geologischen Dienstes (DDR)

Mitt Labn Preuss Geol Landesanst — Mitteilungen aus den Laboratorien der Preussischen Geologischen Landesanstalt

Mitt Lab Preuss Geol Landesanst — Mitteilungen aus den Laboratorien der Preussischen Geologischen Landesanstalt

Mitt Lab Preuss Geol Landesanst — Mitteilungen. Laboratorien der Preussischen Geologischen Landesanstalt

Mitt Landbau — Mitteilungen fuer den Landbau

Mitt Landbau Agric Bull — Mitteilungen fuer den Landbau. Agricultural Bulletin

Mitt Landesanst Tierz Grub — Mitteilungen. Landesanstalt fuer Tierzucht in Grub

Mitt Landesanst Wass Boden U Lufthyg — Mitteilungen aus der Landesanstalt fuer Wasser-, Boden-, und Lufthygiene

Mitt Landesanst Wasser Boden Lufthyg Berlin Dahlem — Mitteilungen aus der Landesanstalt fuer Wasser-, Boden- und Lufthygiene zu Berlin-Dahlem

Mitt Landesanst Wasserhyg Berlin Dahlem — Mitteilungen aus der Landesanstalt fuer Wasserhygiene zu Berlin-Dahlem

Mitt Landesforstverw Bayerns — Mitteilungen aus der Landesforstverwaltung Bayerns

Mitt Landesstelle Spinnpfl Berl — Mitteilungen der Landesstelle fuer Spinnpflanzen (Berlin)

Mitt Landesverb ZiegenzVer Wurtt — Mitteilungen des Landesverbands der Ziegenzuchtvereine Wurttembergs

Mitt Landesver Saechs Heimatschutz — Mitteilungen des Landesvereins Saechsischer Heimatschutz

Mitt Land U Forstw ForschRats Bad Godesberg — Mitteilungen des Land- und Forstwirtschaftlichen Forschungsrats (Bad Godesberg)

Mitt Land U ForstwVerb Prov Ostpreuss — Mitteilungen des Land- und Forstwirtschaftsverbands der Provinz Ostpreussen

Mitt Landw (Berl) — Mitteilungen fuer die Landwirtschaft (Berlin)

Mitt LandwGes Wien — Mitteilungen der Landwirtschaftsgesellschaft in Wien

Mitt Landw Inst Koenigl Univ Breslau — Mitteilungen der Landwirtschaftlichen Institute der Koeniglichen Universitaet Breslau

Mitt Landw Inst Univ Lpz — Mitteilungen des Landwirtschaftlichen Instituts der Universitaet Leipzig

Mitt Landwirtsch — Mitteilungen fuer die Landwirtschaft

Mitt Landwirtsch Versuchsstellen (Ung) A — Mitteilungen. Landwirtschaftliche Versuchsstellen (Ungarn). A. Pflanzenbau

Mitt Landwirtsch Versuchsstellen Ung B — Mitteilungen der Landwirtschaftlichen Versuchsstellen Ungarns. B. Tierzucht

Mitt Landwirtsch Versuchsstellen (Ung) C — Mitteilungen. Landwirtschaftliche Versuchsstellen (Ungarn). C. Gartenbau

Mitt LandwKamm Sachs Gotha — Mitteilungen der Landwirtschaftskammer fuer Sachsen-Gotha

Mitt Landw Kreisver Dresden — Mitteilungen des Landwirtschaftlichen Kreisvereins zu Dresden

Mitt Landw Kreisver Erzgebirge — Mitteilungen des Landwirtschaftlichen Kreisvereins im Erzgebirge

Mitt Landw Mannheim — Mitteilungen fuer die Landwirtschaft (Mannheim)

Mitt Landw Physiol Lab Univ Koenigsb — Mitteilungen aus dem Landwirtschafts-Physiologischen Laboratorium der Universitaet Koenigsberg

Mitt Lausitz BezVer Ver Dt Ing — Mitteilungen des Lausitzer Bezirksvereins des Vereins Deutscher Ingenieure

Mitt Ldsver Saechs Heimatsch — Mitteilungen des Landesvereines fuer Saechsischen Heimatschutz

Mitt Litau Lit Ges — Mitteilungen der Litauischen Literarischen Gesellschaft

Mitt Liv U Estland Bur Landeskult — Mitteilungen des Liv- und Estlandischen Bureaus fuer Landeskultur

Mitt LMU — Mitteilungen aus dem Gebiete der Lebensmitteluntersuchung und Hygiene

Mitt Lokomob — Mitteilungen ueber Lokomobilen

Mitt Lpz BezVer Ver Dt Ing — Mitteilungen des Leipziger Bezirksvereins des Vereins Deutscher Ingenieure

Mitt Luftschiffb Schutte Lanz — Mitteilungen aus dem Luftschiffbau Schutte-Lanz

Mitt Maehr LandesFischVer — Mitteilungen des Maehrischen Landesfischereivereins

Mitt Markscheidew — Mitteilungen aus dem Markscheidewesen

Mitt Markscheidewes — Mitteilungen aus dem Markscheidewesen

Mitt MaschLab Winterthur — Mitteilungen aus dem Maschinenlaboratorium am Kantonalen Technikum in Winterthur

Mitt Materialpruef Berlin Dahlem — Mitteilungen aus dem Materialpruefungsamt zu Berlin-Dahlem

Mitt Materialpruefgsamt — Mitteilungen des Materialpruefungsamtes

Mitt Materialpruefungsanst Tech Hochsch (Darmstadt) — Mitteilungen. Materialpruefungsanstalt. Technische Hochschule (Darmstadt)

Mitt MaterPrufAmt Berl Dahlem — Mitteilungen aus dem Materialpruefungsamt und dem Kaiser Wilhelm-Institut fuer Metallforschung zu Berlin-Dahlem

Mitt MaterPrufAnst Darmstadt — Mitteilungen der Materialprufungsanstalt an der Technischen Hochschule, Darmstadt

Mitt Math Ges (DDR) — Mitteilungen. Mathematische Gesellschaft (Deutsche Demokratische Republik)

Mitt Math Ges Deut Demokr Republ — Mitteilungen der Mathematischen Gesellschaft der Deutschen Demokratischen Republik

Mitt Math Gesellsch (Hamburg) — Mitteilungen. Mathematische Gesellschaft (Hamburg)

Mitt Math Ges Hamb — Mitteilungen der Mathematischen Gesellschaft in Hamburg

Mitt Math Sem (Giessen) — Mitteilungen. Mathematisches Seminar (Giessen)

Mitt Math Semin Univ Giessen — Mitteilungen des Mathematischen Seminars der Universitaet Giessen

Mitt Max Eyth Ges Foerd Landtech — Mitteilungen. Max Eyth-Gesellschaft zur Foerderung der Landtechnik

Mitt Max-Planck-Ges — Mitteilungen. Max-Planck-Gesellschaft

Mitt Max-Planck-Ges Foerd Wiss — Mitteilungen. Max-Planck-Gesellschaft zur Foerderung der Wissenschaften

Mitt Max Planck Inst Aeron — Mitteilungen aus dem Max-Planck-Institut fuer Aeronomie

Mitt Max Planck Inst Aeronomie — Mitteilungen aus dem Max-Planck-Institut fuer Aeronomie

Mitt Max Planck Inst Eisenforsch — Mitteilungen aus dem Max-Planck-Institut fuer Eisenforschung

Mitt Max Planck Inst Phys Stratosph — Mitteilungen aus dem Max-Planck-Institut fuer Physik der Stratosphare

Mitt Max-Planck-Inst Stroemungsforsch Aerodyn Versuchsanst — Mitteilungen. Max-Planck-Institut fuer Stroemungsforschung und der Aerodynamischen Versuchsanstalt

Mitt Max Plank Inst StromForsch — Mitteilungen aus dem Max-Planck-Institut fuer Stromungsforschung und der Aerodynamischen Versuchsanstalt

Mitt Max Reger Inst — Mitteilungen. Max Reger Institut

Mitt Med Akad Keijo — Mitteilungen aus der Medizinischen Akademie zu Keijo

Mitt Med Akad Kioto — Mitteilungen aus der Medizinischen Akademie zu Kioto

Mitt Med Biol Ges Dresden — Mitteilungen der Medizinisch-Biologischen Gesellschaft (Dresden)

Mitt Med Fac Kaiserl Jap Univ — Mitteilungen aus der Medicinischen Facultaet der Kaiserlich-Japanischen Universitaet/Teikoku Daigaku Ika Kiyo

Mitt Med Fak Tok — Mitteilungen aus der Medizinischen Fakultaet der Kaiserlichen Japanischen Universitaet zu Tokio

Mitt Med Ges Chiba — Mitteilungen der Medizinischen Gesellschaft zu Chiba

Mitt Med Gesellsch Tokyo — Mitteilungen. Medizinische Gesellschaft zu Tokyo

Mitt Med Ges Nagoya — Mitteilungen der Medizinischen Gesellschaft zu Nagoya

Mitt Med Ges Okayama — Mitteilungen der Medizinischen Gesellschaft zu Okayama

Mitt Med Ges Osaka — Mitteilungen der Medizinischen Gesellschaft zu Osaka

Mitt Med Ges Tokyo — Mitteilungen. Medizinische Gesellschaft zu Tokyo

Mitt Met Inst Univ Helsingf — Mitteilungen des Meteorologischen Instituts der Universitaet Helsingfors

Mitt Mikrol Ver Linz — Mitteilungen des Mikrologischen Vereins in Linz

Mitt Milchw Ver Algau — Mitteilungen des Milchwirtschaftlichen Vereins im Algau

Mitt Miner Geol Inst Reichsuniv Groningen — Mitteilungen aus dem Mineralogisch-Geologischen Institut der Reichsuniversitaet zu Groningen

Mitt Miner Geol StInst Hamb — Mitteilungen aus dem Mineralogisch-Geologischen Staatsinstitut in Hamburg

Mitt Mitglieder Tech Ueberwach-Ver (Bayern) — Mitteilungen fuer die Mitglieder des Technischen Ueberwachungs-Vereins (Bayern)

Mitt Mitgl ObstbVersRings — Mitteilungen fuer die Mitglieder des Obstbauversuchrings

Mitt Mittelrhein FabrVer — Mitteilungen fuer den Mittelrheinischen Fabrikantenverein

Mitt Montan Ver Oest — Mitteilungen fuer Montanistische Vereine Oesterreichs

Mitt Moor U Torfw — Mitteilungen fuer Moor- und Torfwirtschaft

Mitt MPI Aeron — Mitteilungen. Max-Planck-Institut fuer Aeronomie

Mitt MPI Stroemungsforsch Aerodyn Versuchsanst — Mitteilungen. Max-Planck-Institut fuer Stroemungsforschung und der Aerodynamischen Versuchsanstalt

Mitt Muench Ent Ges — Mitteilungen. Muenchener Entomologische Gesellschaft

Mitt Muench Entomol Ges — Mitteilungen. Muenchener Entomologische Gesellschaft

Mitt Mus Bergbau Geol Tech Landesmus Joanneum Graz — Mitteilungen des Museums fuer Bergbau, Geologie und Technik am Landesmuseum Joanneum. Graz

Mitt Mus Bergb Geol Tech Graz — Mitteilungen des Museums fuer Bergbau, Geologie und Technik am Landesmuseum Joanneum (Graz)

Mitt Mus Bild Kst Leipzig — Mitteilungen aus dem Museum der Bildenden Kuenste Leipzig

Mitt Musealveins Krain — Mitteilungen des Musealvereins fuer Krain

Mitt Mus fuer Voelkerkunde Hamburg — Mitteilungen aus dem Museum fuer Voelkerkunde Hamburg

Mitt Mus fuer Voelkerkunde Leipzig — Mitteilungen aus dem Museum fuer Voelkerkunde Leipzig

Mitt Mus Hallstatt — Mitteilungen aus dem Museum in Hallstatt

Mitt Mus Miner Geol Vorgesch Dresden — Mitteilungen aus dem Museum fuer Mineralogie, Geologie und Vorgeschichte zu Dresden

Mitt Mus Naturk Danzig — Mitteilungen aus dem Museum fuer Naturkunde in Danzig

Mitt Mus Naturk Vorgesch Magdeb — Mitteilungen aus dem Museum fuer Naturkunde und Vorgeschichte und dem Naturwissenschaftlichen Arbeitkreis (Magdeburg)

Mitt MusVer Krain — Mitteilungen des Musealvereins fuer Krain

Mitt Mus Vlkerknd Hamburg — Mitteilungen des Museums fuer Voelkerkunde in Hamburg

Mitt Mus Voelkerk Hamburg — Mitteilungen. Museum fuer Voelkerkunde in Hamburg

Mitt Mus Voelkerk Leipzig — Mitteilungen. Museum fuer Voelkerkunde zu Leipzig

Mitt Mus Volkerk Lpz — Mitteilungen aus dem Museum fuer Volkerkunde (Leipzig)

Mitt Nachr Dt PalastinaVer — Mitteilungen und Nachrichten des Deutschen Palastina-Vereins

Mitt Nachrr Evgl Kirche Russld — Mitteilungen und Nachrichten fuer die Evangelische Kirche Russlands

Mitt Na Kde — Mitteilungen fuer Namenkunde

Mitt Naturdenkmalpflege Prov Grenzmark Posen Westpreussen — Mitteilungen ueber Naturdenkmalpflege in der Provinz Grenzmark Posen-Westpreussen

Mitt Naturf Ges Bern — Mitteilungen der Naturforschenden Gesellschaft in Bern

Mitt Naturf Ges Kanton Glarus — Mitteilungen der Naturforschenden Gesellschaft des Kantons Glarus

Mitt Naturf Ges Luzern — Mitteilungen der Naturforschenden Gesellschaft in Luzern

Mitt Naturf Ges Schaffhausen — Mitteilungen der Naturforschenden Gesellschaft Schaffhausen

Mitt Naturf Ges Solothurn — Mitteilungen der Naturforschenden Gesellschaft in Solothurn

Mitt Naturforsch Ges Bern — Mitteilungen. Naturforschende Gesellschaft in Bern

Mitt Naturh Ges Nuernb — Mitteilungen der Naturhistorischen Gesellschaft in Nuernberg

Mitt Naturh Mus Hamb — Mitteilungen aus dem Naturhistorischen Museum in Hamburg

Mitt Naturk Naturschutz — Mitteilungen fuer Naturkunde und Naturschutz

Mitt Naturk Vorgesch Mus KultGesch Magdeb — Mitteilungen fuer Naturkunde und Vorgeschichte aus dem Museum fuer Kulturgeschichte in Magdeburg

Mitt Naturk Vorgesch Mus Kulturgesch Naturwiss Arbeitskreis — Mitteilungen fuer Naturkunde und Vorgeschichte aus dem Museum fuer Kulturgeschichte und dem Naturwissenschaftlichen Arbeitskreis

Mitt Naturw ArbGemein Haus Nat Salzb — Mitteilungen der Naturwissenschaftlichen Arbeitsgemeinschaft vom Haus der Natur in Salzburg

Mitt Naturw Ges Isis Bautzen — Mitteilungen aus der Naturwissenschaftlichen Gesellschaft Isis in Bautzen

Mitt Naturw Ges Isis Meissen — Mitteilungen der Naturwissenschaftlichen Gesellschaft Isis in Meissen

Mitt Naturw Ges Thun — Mitteilungen der Naturwissenschaftlichen Gesellschaft Thun

Mitt Naturw Ges Winterthur — Mitteilungen der Naturwissenschaftlichen Gesellschaft in Winterthur

Mitt Naturwiss Ges Isis Bautzen — Mitteilungen aus der Naturwissenschaftlichen Gesellschaft Isis in Bautzen

Mitt Naturwiss Ges Winterthur — Mitteilungen. Naturwissenschaftliche Gesellschaft in Winterthur

Mitt Naturwiss Mus Stadt Aschaffenburg — Mitteilungen. Naturwissenschaftliches Museum der Stadt Aschaffenburg

Mitt Naturwiss Vereins Aschaffenburg — Mitteilungen des Naturwissenschaftlichen Vereines in Aschaffenburg

Mitt Naturwiss Vereins Univ Wien — Mitteilungen des Naturwissenschaftlichen Vereins der Universitaet Wien

Mitt Naturwiss Ver Steiermark — Mitteilungen. Naturwissenschaftlicher Verein fuer Steiermark

Mitt Naturw Mus Aschaffenb — Mitteilungen des Naturwissenschaftlichen Museums der Stadt Aschaffenburg

Mitt Naturw Ver Aschaffenb — Mitteilungen des Naturwissenschaftlichen Vereins zu Aschaffenburg

Mitt Naturw Ver Dusseld — Mitteilungen des Naturwissenschaftlichen Vereins zu Dusseldorf

Mitt Naturw Ver Neu Vorpomm — Mitteilungen des Naturwissenschaftlichen Vereins fuer Neu-Vorpommern und Rugen in Greifswald

Mitt Naturw Ver Schneeberg — Mitteilungen des Naturwissenschaftlichen Vereins fuer Schneeberg

Mitt Naturw Ver Steierm — Mitteilungen des Naturwissenschaftlichen Vereins fuer Steiermark

Mitt Naturw Ver Troppau — Mitteilungen des Naturwissenschaftlichen Vereins in Troppau

Mitt Naturw Ver Univ Wien — Mitteilungen des Naturwissenschaftlichen Vereins an der Universitaet Wien

Mitt Natwiss Ver Steierm — Mitteilungen des Naturwissenschaftlichen Vereins fuer die Steiermark

Mitt Niederl Ahnengemeinschaft — Mitteilungen der Niederlaendischen Ahnengemeinschaft. Hamburg

Mitt Niederoest Forstver — Mitteilungen des Niederoesterreichischen Forstvereins

Mitt Niederrhein BezVer Ver Dt Ing — Mitteilungen des Niederrheinischen Bezirksvereins des Vereins Deutscher Ingenieure

Mitt Niedersaechs Landesforstverwalt — Mitteilungen aus der Niedersaechsischen Landesforstverwaltung

Mitt Nikolai Hauptsternwarte Pulkowo — Mitteilungen der Nikolai-Hauptsternwarte Pulkowo

Mitt Nikolai Hauptsternw Pulkowo — Mitteilungen der Nikolai-Hauptsternwarte Pulkowo

Mitt Nordfries Ver Heimatkde — Mitteilungen des Nordfriesischen Vereins fuer Heimatkunde

Mitt NormAussch Dt Ind — Mitteilungen des Normenausschusses der Deutschen Industrie

Mitt Num Ges — Mitteilungen. Numismatische Gesellschaft

Mitt Numismat Ges Wien — Mitteilungen der Numismatischen Gesellschaft in Wien

Mitt Oberhess Geschver — Mitteilungen des Oberhessischen Geschichtsvereins

Mitt Oberoesterr Landesarch — Mitteilungen des Oberoesterreichischen Landesarchivs

Mitt Oberschles BezVer Dt Ing — Mitteilungen des Oberschlesischen Bezirksvereins des Vereins Deutscher Ingenieure und des Oberschlesischen Elektrotechnischen Vereins

Mitt Obstbauversuchsring Alten Landes — Mitteilungen. Obstbauversuchsring des Alten Landes

Mitt ObstbVersAnst — Mitteilungen der Obstbauversuchsanstalt

Mitt ObstbVersuchsr Alten Landes — Mitteilungen. Obstbauversuchsring des Alten Landes

Mitt Obst Gart — Mitteilungen. Obst und Garten

Mitt Obst Garten — Mitteilungen Obst und Garten

Mitt Oest Arbeitsg — Mitteilungen der Oesterreichischen Arbeitsgemeinschaft fuer Urund Fruehgeschichte

Mitt Oest Berbg — Mitteilungen ueber den Oesterreichischen Bergbau

Mitt Oest DokumZent Tech Wirt — Mitteilungen des Oesterreichischen Dokumentationszentrums fuer Technik und Wirtschaft

Mitt Oesterreich Gal — Mitteilungen der Oesterreichischen Galerien

Mitt Oesterreich Ges Mw — Mitteilungen. Oesterreichische Gesellschaft fuer Musikwissenschaft

Mitt Oesterreich Inst Geschforsch — Mitteilungen des Oesterreichischen Instituts fuer Geschichtsforschung

Mitt Oesterr Geogr Ges — Mitteilungen der Oesterreichischen Geographischen Gesellschaft

Mitt Oesterr Geol Ges — Mitteilungen. Oesterreichische Geologische Gesellschaft

Mitt Oesterr Ges Holzforsch — Mitteilungen. Oesterreichische Gesellschaft fuer Holzforschung

Mitt Oesterr Ges (Vienna) — Institut fuer Oesterreichische Geschichtsforschung. Mitteilungen (Vienna)

Mitt Oesterr Mineral Ges — Mitteilungen. Oesterreichische Mineralogische Gesellschaft

Mitt Oesterr Mykol Ges — Mitteilungen der Oesterreichischen Mykologischen Gesellschaft

Mitt Oesterr Numismat Ges — Mitteilungen der Oesterreichischen Numismatischen Gesellschaft

Mitt Oesterr Sanitaetsverwalt (Vienna) — Mitteilungen. Oesterreichische Sanitaetsverwaltung (Vienna)

Mitt Oesterr Staatsarch — Mitteilungen des Oesterreichischen Staatsarchivs

Mitt Oester Ver Bibliothw — Mitteilungen des Oesterreichischen Vereins fuer Bibliothekswesen

Mitt Oest Fachaussch Holzfragen — Mitteilungen des Oesterreichischen Fachausschusses fuer Holzfragen

Mitt Oest Geogr Ges — Mitteilungen der Oesterreichischen Geographischen Gesellschaft

Mitt Oest SanitWes — Mitteilungen des Oesterreichischen Sanitaetswesens

Mitt O Geog — Mitteilungen. Oesterreichische Geographische Gesellschaft

Mitt Or Ges — Mitteilungen der Deutschen Orient Gesellschaft zu Berlin

Mitt Ost Bodenk Ges — Mitteilungen. Oesterreichische Bodenkundliche Gesellschaft

Mitt Osterlande — Mitteilungen aus dem Osterlande. Naturforschende Gesellschaft des Osterlandes zu Altenburg

Mitt Osterreich Geol Ges — Mitteilungen der Oesterreichischen Geologischen Gesellschaft

Mitt Ostschweiz Geogr Komm Ges St Gallen — Mitteilungen der Ostschweizerischen Geographisch-Kommerziellen Gesellschaft in St. Gallen

Mitt Path Inst Med Fak Niigata — Mitteilungen aus dem Pathologischen Institut der Medizinischen Fakultaet. Niigata

Mitt Pfaelz Vereins Naturk Pollichia — Mitteilungen des Pfaelzischen Vereins fuer Naturkunde Pollichia

Mitt Pfaelz Ver Naturk Pollichia — Mitteilungen des Pfaelzischen Vereins fuer Naturkunde Pollichia

Mitt Pharm Forsch Inst — Mitteilungen des Pharmazeutischen Forschungs-Institutes

Mitt Photogr Privatlab Hugo Hinterberger — Mitteilungen aus dem Photographischen Privatlaboratorium des Universitats-Lehrers Hugo Hinterberger

Mitt Phys Ges Zuerich — Mitteilungen der Physikalischen Gesellschaft (Zuerich)

Mitt Physik Techn Reichsanst — Mitteilungen der Physikalisch-Technischen Reichsanstalt

Mitt Phys Mech Inst Prof M Th Edelmann — Mitteilungen. Physikalisch-Mechanisches Institut von Prof. Dr. M. Th. Edelmann und Sohn

Mitt Phys StLab Hamb — Mitteilungen aus dem Physikalischen Staatslaboratorium in Hamburg

Mitt Pollichia — Mitteilungen der Pollichia

Mitt Pollichia Pfaelz Ver Naturkd Naturschutz — Mitteilungen. Pollichia des Pfaelzischen Vereins fuer Naturkunde und Naturschutz

Mitt Pollichia Pfaelz Ver Naturk NatSchutz — Mitteilungen der Pollichia des Pfaelzischen Vereins fuer Naturkunde und Naturschutz

Mitt Porzellanfabr Hermsdorf Freiburg — Mitteilungen der Porzellanfabriken Hermsdorf-Freiburg

Mitt Porzellanfabr Ph Rosenthal — Mitteilungen der Porzellanfabrik Ph. Rosenthal und Co. A.G

Mitt Posen BezVer Ver Dt Ing — Mitteilungen des Posener Bezirksvereins des Vereins Deutscher Ingenieure

Mitt Praehis Komm Wien — Mitteilungen der Praehistorischen Kommission. Akademie der Wissenschaften. Wien

Mitt Praehist Komm Oesterreich Akad Wiss — Mitteilungen der Praehistorischen Kommission der Oesterreichischen Akademie der Wissenschaften

Mitt Praehist Komm Vienna — Mitteilungen der Praehistorien Kommission der Oesterreichischen Akademie der Wissenschaften (Vienna)

Mitt Praeh Kom — Mitteilungen der Praehistorischen Kommission der Kaiserlichen Akademie der Wissenschaften

Mitt Praeh Kom — Mitteilungen. Praehistorische Kommission. Akademie der Wissenschaften

Mitt Prahist Kommn Wien — Mitteilungen der Praehistorischen Kommission der Oesterreichischen Akademie der Wissenschaften (Wien)

Mitt Prax Dampfkessel U DampfmaschBetr — Mitteilungen aus der Praxis des Dampfkessel- und Dampfmaschinenbetriebs (Berlin)

Mitt Pressluftind — Mitteilungen fuer die Pressluftindustrie

Mitt Preuss VersAnst Wasserb Schiffb — Mitteilungen der Preussischen Versuchsanstalt fuer Wasserbau und Schiffbau

Mitt Progas Un — Mitteilungen. Progas-Union

Mitt Provinzialstelle Naturdenkmalpflege Hannover — Mittlungen der Provinzialstelle fuer Naturdenkmalpflege Hannover

Mitt ProvMus Sachs — Mitteilungen aus dem Provinzialmuseum der Prov. Sachsen

Mitt PruefAnst Heiz U LuftAnl Berl — Mitteilungen der Pruefungsanstalt fuer Heizungs- und Luftungsanlagen der Technischen Hochschule zu Berlin

Mitt PruefAnst Schweiz Polytech Zuerich — Mitteilungen der Pruefungsanstalt des Schweizerischen Polytechnikums in Zuerich

Mitt PruefAnst WassVersorg Abwasserbeseit Berl — Mitteilungen der Pruefungsanstalt fuer Wasservorsorgung und Abwasserbeseitigung zu Berlin

Mitt Pruefgsanst Wasserversorg Berl — Mitteilungen aus der Koeniglichen Pruefungsanstalt fuer Wasserversorgung und Abwaesserbeseitigung zu Berlin

Mitt Pruef U VersAnst Baustoffe Wien — Mitteilungen der Pruef- und Versuchs-Anstalt fuer Baustoffe in Wien

Mitt Pueckler Ges — Mitteilungen der Pueckler-Gesellschaft

Mitt Rebe Wein — Mitteilungen. Rebe und Wein

Mitt Rebe Wein Obstbau Fruechteverwert — Mitteilungen. Rebe und Wein, Obstbau und Fruechteverwertung

Mitt Reichsamts Bodenforsch Zweigstelle Wien — Mitteilungen. Reichsamt Bodenforschung. Zweigstelle Wien

Mitt Reichsamts Bodenforsch Zweigst Freiberg — Mitteilungen des Reichsamts fuer Bodenforschung. Zweigstelle Freiberg

Mitt Reichsamts Bodenforsch Zweigst Wien — Mitteilungen des Reichsamts fuer Bodenforschung. Zweigstelle Wien

Mitt Reichsamts Landesaufn — Mitteilungen des Reichsamts fuer Landesaufnahme

Mitt Reichsanst ErdbForsch — Mitteilungen der Reichsanstalt fuer Erdbebenforschung

Mitt Reichsanst Mass Gewicht — Mitteilungen der Reichsanstalt fuer Mass und Gewicht

Mitt Reichsbd Dt Techn — Mitteilungen des Reichsbunds Deutscher Techniker

Mitt Reichsbund Dt Tech — Mitteilungen des Reichsbundes Deutscher Technik

Mitt ReichsforstwRats — Mitteilungen des Reichsforstwirtschaftsrats

Mitt Reichsinst Forst U Holzw — Mitteilungen des Reichsinstituts fuer Forst- und Holzwirtschaft

Mitt ReichspostzentAmts — Mitteilungen des Reichspostzentralamts

Mitt Reichsstelle Bodenforsch — Mitteilungen der Reichsstelle fuer Bodenforschung

Mitt Reichsstelle Bodenforsch Zweigstelle Freiburg — Mitteilungen der Reichsstelle fuer Bodenforschung. Zweigstelle Freiburg

Mitt Reichsstelle Bodenforsch Zweigstelle Wien — Mitteilungen der Reichsstelle fuer Bodenforschung. Zweigstelle Wien

Mitt Reichsstelle Bodenforsch Zweigst Munch — Mitteilungen der Reichsstelle fuer Bodenforschung. Zweigstelle Muenchen

Mitt Reichsverb Brenntorferz — Mitteilungen des Reichsverbandes der Brenntorferzeuger

Mitt Reichsverb LandmaschHand — Mitteilungen des Reichsverbandes des Landmaschinenhandels

Mitt RG — Mitteilungen der Raabe-Gesellschaft

Mitt Rheinische Mg — Mitteilungen. Arbeitsgemeinschaft fuer Rheinische Musikgeschichte

Mitt Roemermus Hildesheim — Mitteilungen aus dem Roemermuseum. Hildesheim

Mitt Roland — Mitteilungen des Roland

Mitt Rosenthal Isolat — Mitteilungen. Rosenthal-Isolatoren

Mitt Saarpfaelz Vereins Naturk Pollichia Bad Duerkheim — Mitteilungen des Saarpfaelzischen Vereins fuer Naturkunde und Naturschutz Pollichia mit dem Sitz in Bad Duerkheim

Mitt Saarpfaelz Ver Naturk NatSchutz — Mitteilungen des Saarpfaelzischen Vereins fuer Naturkunde und Naturschutz Pollichia mit dem Sitz in Bad Durkheim

Mitt Saechs Forstl VersAnst Tharandt — Mitteilungen aus der Saechsischen Forstlichen Versuchsanstalt zu Tharandt

Mitt Saechs Kstsamml — Mitteilungen aus den Saechsischen Kunstsammlungen

Mitt Saechs PruefStn Landw Masch — Mitteilungen der Saechsischen Pruefungsstation fuer Landwirtschaftliche Maschinen und Geraete in Leipzig

Mitt Saechs Thuer Ver Erdk — Mitteilungen des Saechsisch-Thueringischen Vereins fuer Erdkunde zu Halle a. S

Mitt Sammelstelle Schmarotzerbest VDEV — Mitteilungen der Sammelstelle fuer Schmarotzerbestimmung des V.D.E.V

Mitt Schles Ges Volksk — Mitteilungen der Schlesischen Gesellschaft fuer Volkskunde

Mitt Schles KohlForschInst Breslau — Mitteilungen aus dem Schlesischen Kohlenforschungsinstitut der Kaiser-Wilhelm-Gesellschaft in Breslau

Mitt Schmalspurbranche — Mitteilungen aus der Schmalspurbranche

Mitt SchrAustausch Geol Landesamt Schlesw Holst — Mitteilungen. Schriftenaustausch des Geologischen Landesamtes Schleswig-Holstein

Mitt Schweiz Anst Forstl Versuchsw — Mitteilungen. Schweizerische Anstalt fuer das Forstliche Versuchswesen

Mitt Schweiz Anst Forstl Versuchswes — Mitteilungen. Schweizerische Anstalt fuer das Forstliche Versuchswesen

Mitt Schweiz Anst Forstl VersWes — Mitteilungen der Schweizerischen Anstalt fuer das Forstliche Versuchswesen

Mitt Schweiz Apoth Ver — Mitteilungen. Schweizerischer Apotheker-Verein

Mitt Schweiz AzetVer — Mitteilungen des Schweizerischen Azetylenvereins

Mitt Schweiz Braunviehzuchtverb — Mitteilungen des Schweizerischen Braunviehzuchtverbands

Mitt Schweiz Ent Ges — Mitteilungen. Schweizerische Entomologische Gesellschaft

Mitt Schweiz Entomol Ges — Mitteilungen. Schweizerische Entomologische Gesellschaft

Mitt Schweiz Entomol Ges Bull Soc Entomol Suisse — Mitteilungen. Schweizerische Entomologische Gesellschaft. Bulletin de la Societe Entomologique Suisse

Mitt Schweiz Fleckviehzuchtverb — Mitteilungen. Schweizerischer Fleckviehzuchtverband

Mitt Schweiz Heiz U MaschVerb — Mitteilungen des Schweizerischen Heizer- und Maschinistenverbands

Mitt Schweiz Kakteen Ges — Mitteilungen der Schweizerischen Kakteen-Gesellschaft

Mitt Schweiz Landw — Mitteilungen fuer die Schweizerische Landwirtschaft

Mitt Schweiz Landwirt — Mitteilungen fuer die Schweizerische Landwirtschaft

Mitt Schweiz Landwirtsch — Mitteilungen fuer die Schweizerische Landwirtschaft

Mitt Schweiz Mf Ges — Mitteilungsblatt. Schweizerische Musikforschende Gesellschaft

Mitt Schweiz StudKommn Elekt Bahnbetr — Mitteilungen der Schweizerischen Studienkommission fuer Elektrischen Bahnbetrieb

Mitt Schweiz Zentralanst Forstl Versuchswes — Mitteilungen. Schweizerische Zentralanstalt fuer das Forstliche Versuchswesen

Mitt Schw LW — Mitteilungen fuer die Schweizerische Landwirtschaft

Mitt Seismos Ges — Mitteilungen. Seismos-Gesellschaft

Mitt Seism Stn Darmstadt — Mitteilungen der Seismischen Station. Darmstadt

Mitt Sekt Naturk Oest TourKlubs — Mitteilungen der Sektion fuer Naturkunde des Oesterreichischen Touristenklubs

Mitt Semin Or Spr Westas St — Mitteilungen des Seminars fuer Orientalische Sprachen. Westasiatische Studien

Mitt Senatskomm Wasserforsch Dtsch Forschungsgem — Mitteilung der Senatskommission fuer Wasserforschung. Deutsche Forschungsgemeinschaft

Mitt SFV — Mitteilungen. Schweizerische Anstalt fuer das Forstliche Versuchswesen

Mitt Siebenb Aerztever — Mitteilungen des Siebenbuergischen Aerztevereins

Mitt Sonderforschungsbereichs 79 Wasserforsch Kuestenbereich — Mitteilungen des Sonderforschungsbereichs 79 fuer Wasserforschung im Kuestenbereich der Technischen Universitaet Hannover

Mitt SonnObs Kanzelhohe — Mitteilungen des Sonnenobservatoriums. Kanzelhohe

Mitt Staatl Heimat Schlossmus Burgk/Saale — Mitteilungen. Staatliches Heimat und Schlossmuseum Burgk/Saale

Mitt Staatsinst Allg Bot (Hamb) — Mitteilungen. Staatsinstitut fuer Allgemeine Botanik (Hamburg)

Mitt Staatsinst Allg Bot (Hamburg) — Mitteilungen. Staatsinstitut fuer Allgemeine Botanik (Hamburg)

Mitt Stadtarchv Koeln — Mitteilungen aus dem Stadtarchiv von Koeln

Mitt Stand Kom Unters SchlagwettFrag Wien — Mitteilungen des Standigen Komitees zur Untersuchung von Schlagwetterfragen in Wien

Mitt St Blasien Wett U Sonnenw — Mitteilungen. St. Blasien Wetter- und Sonnenware

Mitt Steiermarkisches Landesmus (Graz) Mus Bergbau Geol Tec — Mitteilung-Steiermarkisches Landesmuseum (Graz). Museum fuer Bergbau, Geologie,und Technik

Mitt Sternw Berl Babelsb — Mitteilungen der Sternwarte Berlin-Babelsberg

Mitt Sternw Bpest Szabadsaghegy — Mitteilungen der Sternwarte, Budapest-Szabadsaghegy

Mitt Sternw Koenigstuehl Heidelb — Mitteilungen der Sternwarte Koenigstuehl-Heidelberg

Mitt Sternw Munch — Mitteilungen der Sternwarte Muenchen

Mitt Sternw Sonneberg — Mitteilungen der Sternwarte zu Sonneberg in Thueringen

Mitt Sternw Ung Akad Wiss — Mitteilungen der Sternwarte der Ungarischen Akademie der Wissenschaften

Mitt Sternw Univ Turku — Mitteilungen der Sternwarte der Universitaet Turku

Mitt Stforstverw Bayerns — Mitteilungen. Staatsforstverwaltung Bayern

Mitt St Mus Naturk Stuttg — Mitteilungen aus dem Staatlichen Museum fuer Naturkunde in Stuttgart

Mitt St Petersb Augenheilanst — Mitteilungen aus der St. Petersburger Augenheilanstalt

Mitt St Sternw Heidelb Koenigstuehl — Mitteilungen der Staatlichen Sternwarte Heidelberg-Koenigstuehl

Mitt StudGes Windkr — Mitteilungen der Studiengesellschaft Windkraft e. V

Mitt Tageslit EisenbWes — Mitteilungen aus der Tagesliteratur des Eisenbahnwesens

Mitt Tech Hochsch Budapest — Mitteilungen der Technischen Hochschule. Budapest

Mitt Tech Inst St Tung Chi Univ — Mitteilungen des Technischen Instituts. Staatliche Tung-Chi Universitaet

Mitt Tech Kommn Schweiz Stahlverb — Mitteilungen der Technischen Kommission der Schweizer Stahlverbandes

Mitt Tech Mikrosk Lab Wien — Mitteilungen aus dem Technisch-Mikroskopischen Laboratorium der Technischen Hochschule in Wien

Mitt Techn Mikroskop Lab TH Wien — Mitteilungen aus dem Technisch-Mikroskopischen Laboratorium der Technischen Hochschule in Wien

Mitt Tech Univ Braunschweig — Mitteilungen. Technische Universitaet Carolo-Wilhelmina zu Braunschweig

Mitt Tech Univ Carolo-Wilheimina — Mitteilungen. Technische Universitaet Carolo-Wilheimina

Mitt Tech Univ Carolo Wilhelmina Braunschweig — Mitteilungen. Technische Universitaet Carolo-Wilhelmina zu Braunschweig

Mitt Tech Univ Schwerind Miskolc Hung — Mitteilungen. Technische Universitaet fuer Schwerindustrie (Miskolc, Hungary)

Mitt Tech Univ Schwerind Miskolc Hung Foreign Lang Ed — Mitteilungen der Technischen Universitaet fuer Schwerindustrie (Miskolc, Hungary) (Foreign Language Edition)

Mitt Tech Wiss Ver Lpz — Mitteilungen der Technisch-Wissenschaftlichen Vereine Leipzigs, Bezirksverein d. Vereins Deutscher Ingenieure (Leipzig)

Mitt Tech Wiss Ver Nuernberg — Mitteilungen der Technisch-Wissenschaftlichen Vereine in Nuernberg

Mitt Telegrtech Reichsamt — Mitteilungen aus dem Telegraphentechnischen Reichsamt

Mitt Textilforsch Anst Krefeld — Mitteilungen. Textilforschungs-Anstalt Krefeld

Mitt Text Ind — Mitteilungen ueber Textil-Industrie

Mitt Thurgau Natforsch Ges — Mitteilungen der Thurgauischen Naturforschenden Gesellschaft

Mitt Thurg Natf Ges — Mitteilungen der Thurgauischen Naturforschenden Gesellschaft

Mitt Tieraerztl Fak Reichsuniv Gent — Mitteilungen. Tieraerztliche Fakultaet der Reichsuniversitaet Gent

Mitt Tieraerztl Fak Staatsuniv Gent — Mitteilungen der Tieraerztlichen Fakultaet der Staatsuniversitaet Gent

Mitt Tieraerztl Hochsch Staatsuniv Gent — Mitteilungen der Tieraerztlichen Hochschule der Staatsuniversitaet Gent

Mitt Tieraerztl Praxis Preuss Staate — Mitteilungen. Tieraerztliche Praxis im Preussischen Staate

Mitt Typogr — Mitteilungen des Typograph

Mitt Ung Forschungsinst Bergbau — Mitteilungen des Ungarischen Forschungsinstitutes fuer Bergbau

Mitt Ung Verb Materialpruef — Mitteilungen des Ungarischen Verbands fuer Materialpruefung

Mitt Ung Zentralinst Entwickl Bergbaus — Mitteilungen des Ungarischen Zentralinstituts fuer die Entwicklung des Bergbaus

Mitt Univ Brasov Ser C — Mitteilungen der Universitaet zu Brasov. Serie C

Mitt Univ Bund — Mitteilungen. Universitaetsbund Marburg

Mitt Universitaetsbibl Dortmund — Mitteilungen aus der Universitaetsbibliothek Dortmund

Mitt Univ Sternw Bonn — Mitteilungen der Universitaets-Sternwarte. Bonn

Mitt UnivSternw Breslau — Mitteilungen der Universitaetssternwarte zu Breslau

Mitt UnivSternw Frankf A M — Mitteilungen der Universitaetssternwarte zu Frankfurt a. M.

Mitt Univ Sternw Goettingen — Mitteilungen der Universitaets-Sternwarte. Goettingen

Mitt UnivSternw Innsbruck — Mitteilungen der Universitaetssternwarte in Innsbruck

Mitt UnivSternw Jena — Mitteilungen der Universitaetssternwarte in Jena

Mitt Univ Sternw Muenster — Mitteilungen der Universitaetssternwarte. Muenster

Mitt Univ Sternw Wien — Mitteilungen der Universitaets-Sternwarte. Wien

Mitt Unterabt GesundhWes Wien — Mitteilungen der Unterabteilung Gesundheitswesen (Wien)

Mitt Vaterl Gesch St Gall — Mitteilungen zur Vaterlaendischen Geschichte. Historischer Verein in St. Gallen

Mitt Vbd Dt Ver Volkskde — Mitteilungen des Verbandes Deutscher Vereine fuer Volkskunde

Mitt Ver Aerzte Steierm — Mitteilungen des Vereins der Aerzte in Steiermark

Mitt Ver Bad Tieraerzte — Mitteilungen des Vereins Badischer Tieraerzte

Mitt Ver Bauhutte Stuttg — Mitteilungen des Vereins Bauhutte zu Stuttgart

Mitt Verb Dt Archit U IngVer — Mitteilungen des Verbands Deutscher Architekten- und Ingenieurvereine

Mitt Verb Dt Biol — Mitteilungen des Verbands Deutscher Biologen

Mitt Verb Dt Boehm TextInd Reichinb — Mitteilungen des Verbands der Deutschboehmischen Textilindustriellen in Reichenberg und des Maehrisch-Schlesischen Verbands Deutscher Textilindustriellen in Jaegerndorf

Mitt Verb Dt Diploming — Mitteilungen des Verbands Deutscher Diplomingenieure

Mitt Verb Dt Glasmal — Mitteilungen des Verbands Deutscher Glasmalereien

Mitt Verb Dt PatAnwalte — Mitteilungen des Verbands Deutscher Patentanwalte

Mitt Verb Dt SpiritInteress — Mitteilungen des Verbands Deutscher Spiritus- und Spirituoseninteressenten

Mitt Ver Befoerd Landw Gew Hohenz Landen — Mitteilungen des Vereins zur Befoerderung der Landwirtschaft und der Gewerbe in den Hohenzollernschen Landen

Mitt Verb Ehem Graz Tech — Mitteilungen des Verbands Ehemal Grazer Techniker

Mitt Ver Bekaempf Schwinds Chemnitz — Mitteilungen des Vereins zur Bekaempfung der Schwindsucht in Chemnitz

Mitt Ver Berg U Huettenm Interessen Aachen Bez — Mitteilungen des Vereins fuer die Berg- und Huettenmannischen Interessen im Aachener Bezirk

Mitt Verb Handl Landw Masch Dtl — Mitteilungen des Verbands der Handler Landwirtschaftlicher Maschinen und Geraete Deutschlands

Mitt Verb Landw MaschPrufAnst — Mitteilungen des Verbands Landwirtschaftlicher Maschinenprufungsanstalten

Mitt Verb Oest Liqueur Spirit U Essigfabr — Mitteilungen des Verbandsischer Liqueur-, Spirituosen-, und Essigfabrikanten

Mitt Verb Optikergehilf Dtl — Mitteilungen des Verbands der Optiker-Gehilfen Deutschlands

Mitt Verb Saaz HopfProdGem — Mitteilungen des Verbands der Saazer Hopfen-Produktions-Gemeinden

Mitt Verb Schles TextInd — Mitteilungen des Verbands Schlesischer Textilindustrieller

Mitt Verb Tech Wiss Ver Magdeb — Mitteilungen des Verbands Technisch-Wissenschaftlicher Vereine zu Magdeburg

Mitt Ver Chemnitz Gesch — Mitteilungen des Vereins fuer Chemnitzer Geschichte

Mitt Ver Dt Eisen U Stahlind — Mitteilungen des Vereins Deutscher Eisen- und Stahlindustrieller

Mitt Ver Dt Emailfachl — Mitteilungen des Vereins Deutscher Emailfachleute

Mitt Ver Dtsch Emailfachl — Mitteilungen. Verein Deutscher Emailfachleute

Mitt Ver Dtsch Emailfachl — Mitteilungen. Verein Deutscher Emailfachleute

Mitt Ver Dtsch Emailfachleute Dtsch EMAIL Zent — Mitteilungen des Vereins Deutscher Emailfachleute und des Deutschen EMAIL-Zentrums

Mitt Ver Dt Spiegelglas Fabr — Mitteilungen des Vereins Deutscher Spiegelglas-Fabriken

Mitt Ver Dt StrBahn U Kleinbahnverw — Mitteilungen des Vereins Deutscher Strassenbahn- und Kleinbahnverwaltungen

Mitt Verein Dt GewassSchutz — Mitteilungen. Vereinigung Deutscher Gewasserschutz

Mitt Verein Dt Landw VersStnen — Mitteilungen der Vereinigung Deutscher Landwirtschaftlicher Versuchsstationen

Mitt Verein Dt Schweinez — Mitteilungen der Vereinigung Deutscher Schweinezuechter

Mitt Verein ElektWke — Mitteilungen der Vereinigung der Elektrizitatswerke

Mitt Verein Freund Astr Kosm Phys — Mitteilungen der Vereinigung von Freunden der Astronomie und Kosmischen Physik

Mitt Verein Grosskesselbesitzer — Mitteilungen der Vereinigung der Grosskesselbesitzer

Mitt Verein Schweiz Versicherungsmath — Vereinigung Schweizerischer Versicherungsmathematiker. Mitteilungen

Mitt Verein Schweiz VersichMath — Mitteilungen der Vereinigung Schweizerischer Versicherungs-Mathematiker

Mitt Vereins Forstl Standortsk — Mitteilungen des Vereins fuer Forstliche Standortskunde und Forstpflanzenzuechtung

Mitt Vereins Forstl Standortskart — Mitteilungen des Vereins fuer Forstliche Standortskartierung

Mitt Verein Tech Oberbeamt Dt Stadte — Mitteilungen der Vereinigung der Technischen Oberbeamten Deutscher Stadte

Mitt Ver Erdk Dresden — Mitteilungen des Vereins fuer Erdkunde zu Dresden

Mitt Ver Erdk Halle — Mitteilungen des Vereins fuer Erdkunde zu Halle

Mitt Ver Erdk Lpz — Mitteilungen des Vereins fuer Erdkunde zu Leipzig

Mitt Ver Foerd Lokal U StrBahnw Wien — Mitteilungen des Vereins fuer die Foerderung des Lokai- und Strassenbahnwesens (Wien)

Mitt Ver Foerd Moorkult Dt Reiche — Mitteilungen des Vereins zur Foerderung der Moorkultur im Deutschen Reiche

Mitt Ver Forstl Standortskunde ForstpflZucht — Mitteilungen. Verein fuer Forstliche Standortskunde und Forstpflanzenzuechtung

Mitt Ver Frde Human Gymn — Mitteilungen des Vereins der Freunde des Humanistischen Gymnasiums

Mitt Ver Geogr Univ Lpz — Mitteilungen des Vereins der Geographen an der Universitaet Leipzig

Mitt Ver Geol Saalfeld — Mitteilungen des Vereins fuer Geologie in Saalfeld in Thueringen

Mitt Ver Gesch & Altertknd Westfalens & Landesmus Prov Westfa — Mitteilungen des Vereins fuer Geschichte und Altertumskunde Westfalens und des Landesmuseums der Provinz Westfalen

Mitt Ver Gesch Berlin — Mitteilungen des Vereins fuer die Geschichte Berlins

Mitt Ver Gesch Berlins — Mitteilungen des Vereins fuer die Geschichte Berlins

Mitt Ver Gesch Dresdens — Mitteilungen des Vereins fuer Geschichte Dresdens

Mitt Ver Gesch Dt Boehmen — Mitteilungen des Vereins fuer Geschichte der Deutschen in Boehmen

Mitt Ver Gesch Kahla — Mitteilungen des Vereins fuer Geschichte und Altertumskunde (Von Kahla und Roda)

Mitt Ver Gesch Naturw Sangerhausen — Mitteilungen des Vereins fuer Geschichte und Naturwissenschaft in Sangerhausen

Mitt Ver Gesch Nbg — Mitteilungen des Vereins fuer Geschichte der Stadt Nuernberg

Mitt Ver Gesch Stadt Nuernberg — Mitteilungen des Vereins fuer Geschichte der Stadt Nuernberg

Mitt Ver Gesch Stadt Wien — Mitteilungen des Vereins fuer Geschichte der Stadt Wien

Mitt Ver Gesch Wien — Mitteilungen des Vereins fuer Geschichte der Stadt Wien

Mitt Ver Grosskesselbesitzer — Mitteilungen. Vereinigung der Grosskesselbesitzer

Mitt Ver Grosskesselbetr — Mitteilungen. Vereinigung der Grosskesselbetreiber

Mitt Ver Grosskraftwerksbetr — Mitteilungen der Vereinigung der Grosskraftwerksbetreiber

Mitt Verh LandwRats Wien — Mitteilungen ueber die Verhandlungen des Landwirtschaftsrats (Wien)

Mitt Ver Hoeh Forstbeamten Bayerns — Mitteilungen des Vereins der Hoeheren Forstbeamten Bayerns

Mitt Ver Hohlenk Ost — Mitteilungen des Vereins fuer Hohlenkunde in

Mitt Verh Sekt Ld U Forstw Wien — Mitteilungen ueber die Verhandlungen der Sektion fuer Land- und Forstwirtschaft und Montanwesen des Industrie- und Landwirtschaftsrats (Wien)

Mitt Ver Kupferschm Dtl — Mitteilungen des Vereins der Kupferschmiedereien Deutschlands

Mitt Ver Luebeck Gesch — Mitteilungen des Vereins fuer Luebecker Geschichte

Mitt Ver Luebeck Gesch & Altertknd — Mitteilungen des Vereins fuer Luebeckische Geschichte und Alterthumskunde

Mitt Ver Math Naturw Ulm — Mitteilungen des Vereins fuer Mathematik und Naturwissenschaften in Ulm

Mitt Ver Metallwerke Ranshofen Berndorf — Mitteilungen. Vereinigte Metallwerke Ranshofen-Berndorf

Mitt Ver Naturfr Modling — Mitteilungen des Vereins der Naturfreunde in Modling

Mitt Ver Naturfr Reichenb — Mitteilungen aus dem Verein der Naturfreunde in Reichenberg

Mitt Ver Naturk Krefeld — Mitteilungen des Vereins fuer Naturkunde zu Krefeld

Mitt Ver Naturk NatSchutz Westmark Pollichia — Mitteilungen des Vereins fuer Naturkunde und Naturschutz in der Westmark Pollichia

Mitt Ver Naturk Vegesack — Mitteilungen des Vereins fuer Naturkunde fuer Vegesack

Mitt Ver Naturw Unterh Cassel — Mitteilungen des Vereins fuer Naturwissenschaftliche Unterhaltung zu Cassel

Mitt Ver Reichsland Feldmess — Mitteilungen des Vereins Reichslandischer Feldmesser

Mitt Ver Saechs Orn — Mitteilungen des Vereins Saechsischer Ornithologen

Mitt VersAnst BauingWes Braunschw — Mitteilungen der Versuchsanstalt fuer Bauingenieurwesen an der Technischen Hochschule zu Braunschweig

Mitt VersAnst Dt Luxemb Bergwks U Huetten AG Dortmund — Mitteilungen aus der Versuchsanstalt der Deutsch-Luxemburgischen Bergwerks- und Huetten A.G. Dortmunder Union

Mitt VersAnst GarGew Wien — Mitteilungen der Versuchsanstalt fuer Gaerungsgewerbe und des Instituts fuer Angewandte Mikrobiologie (Wien)

Mitt VersAnst StrBau Stuttg — Mitteilungen der Versuchsanstalt fuer Strassenbau (Stuttgart)

Mitt VersAnst WassBau Erdbau Zuerich — Mitteilungen der Versuchanstalt fuer Wasserbau und Erdbau (Zuerich)

Mitt VersAnst WassBau Munch — Mitteilungen der Versuchsanstalt fuer Wasserbau (Muenchen)

Mitt VersAnst WassBau Schiffb Berl — Mitteilungen der Versuchsanstalt fuer Wasserbau und Schiffbau in Berlin

Mitt Ver Schlesw Holst Arzte — Mitteilungen fuer den Verein Schleswig-Holsteinischer Arzte

Mitt Vers Eisenbeton Aussch Oest Ing U ArchitVer — Mitteilungen ueber Versuche, Ausgefuehrt vom Eisenbeton-Ausschuss des Oesterreichischen Ingenieur- und Architektenvereins

Mitt Ver Stud Geogr Univ Berl — Mitteilungen des Vereins der Studierenden der Geographie an der Universitaet Berlin

Mitt Versuchsanst Gaerungsgewerbe Inst Angew Mikrobiol — Mitteilungen der Versuchsanstalt fuer das Gaerungsgewerbe und des Institutes fuer Angewandte Mikrobiologie

Mitt Versuchsergeb Bundesanst Pflanzenbau Samenpruf Wien — Mitteilungen. Versuchsergebnissen der Bundesanstalt fuer Pflanzenbau und Samenpruefung in Wien

Mitt Versuchsstat Gaerungsgewerbe Inst Angew Mikrobiol — Mitteilungen der Versuchsstation fuer das Gaerungsgewerbe sowie des Institutes fuer Angewandte Mikrobiologie

Mitt Versuchsstn Gaerungsgewerbe Wein — Mitteilungen. Versuchsstation fuer das Gaerungsgewerbe in Wien

Mitt Vers Wasserbau Hydrol Glaziologie — Mitteilungen. Versuchsanstalt fuer Wasserbau, Hydrologie, und Glaziologie

Mitt Ver Verbreiterg Natwiss Kenntn — Mitteilungen des Vereins zur Verbreiterung Naturwissenschaftlicher Kenntnis Noerdlich der Elbe

Mitt Ver Verbreit Landw Kennt — Mitteilungen des Vereins zur Verbreitung Landwirtschaftlicher Kenntnisse

Mitt Ver Vergl Kstforsch — Mitteilungen des Vereins fuer Vergleichende Kunstforschung

Mitt Ver Verhuet Seuch Tierkrankh — Mitteilungen des Vereins fuer Verhuetung von Seuchen und Tierkrankheiten

Mitt VGB — Mitteilungen der VGB

Mitt VGB (Tech Ver Grosskraftwerksbetr) — Mitteilungen. VGB (Technische Vereinigung der Grosskraftwerksbetreiber)

Mitt VGN — Mitteilungen des Vereins fuer Geschichte der Stadt Nuernberg

Mitt Vhdlgg Ges Natfd Frde Berlin — Mittheilungen aus den Verhandlungen der Gesellschaft Naturforschender Freunde zu Berlin

Mitt VOB — Mitteilungen. Vereinigung Oesterreichischer Bibliothek

Mitt Vorderas Ges — Mitteilungen. Vorderasiatisch-Aegyptischen Gesellschaft

Mitt VWF — Verband der Wissenschaftler an Forschungsinstituten. Mitteilungen

Mitt Walde Niedersachs Landesforstverw — Mitteilungen aus dem Walde der Niedersaechsischen Landesforstverwaltung

Mitt Warmestelle Ver Dt Eisenhuettenl — Mitteilungen der Warmestelle. Verein Deutscher Eisenhuettenleute

Mitt Warmetech Inst Darmstadt — Mitteilungen des Warmetechnischen Instituts an der Technischen Hochschule. Darmstadt

Mitt Wasserbau — Mitteilungen aus dem Gebiete des Wasserbaues und der Grundbauforschung

Mitt Weinb Kellerw — Mitteilungen ueber Weinbau und Kellerwirtschaft

Mitt Westf BerggewerkschKasse — Mitteilungen der Westfaelischen Berggewerkschaftskasse

Mitt Westpreuss FischVer — Mitteilungen des Westpreussischen Fischereivereins

Mitt Westpreuss Geschver — Mitteilungen des Westpreussischen Geschichtsvereins

Mitt Wien Altertver — Mitteilungen des Wiener Altertumsvereins

Mitt Wien Heilstatte Lupuskranke — Mitteilungen aus der Wiener Heilstatte fuer Lupuskranke

Mitt Wien Med DoktKoll — Mitteilungen des Wiener Medizinischen Doktorenkollegiums

Mitt Wien Miner Ges — Mitteilungen der Wiener Mineralogischen Gesellschaft

Mitt Wien Sternw — Mitteilungen der Wiener Sternwarte

Mitt Wirks Estland GartenbVer — Mitteilungen ueber die Wirksamkeit des Estlandischen Gartenbauvereins

Mitt WirtErgebn Herz Braunschw Forstverw — Mitteilungen ueber die Wirtschaftsergebnisse der Herzoglich Braunschweigischen Forstverwaltung

Mitt Wiss Ver Schneeb — Mitteilungen des Wissenschaftlichen Vereins fuer Schneeberg und Umgebung (Schneeberg)

Mitt Wohler Inst — Mitteilungen des Wohler-Instituts. Braunschweig

Mitt Wuertt BezVer Ver Dt Ing — Mitteilungen des Wuerttembergischen Bezirksvereins des Vereins Deutscher Ingenieure

Mitt Wuerttemberg Forstl Versuchsanst — Mitteilungen der Wuerttembergischen Forstlichen Versuchsanstalt

Mitt Wuertt Forstl VersAnst — Mitteilungen der Wuerttembergischen Forstlichen Versuchsanstalt

Mitt Wuertt GeomVer — Mitteilungen des Wuerttembergischen Geometervereins

Mitt Wuertt Met ZentStn Stuttg — Mitteilungen der Wuerttembergischen Meteorologischen Zentralstation in Stuttgart

Mitt WWI — Mitteilungen des Wirtschaftswissenschaftlichen Instituts der Gewerkschaften

MittZem Beton U Eisbetonb — Mitteilungen ueber Zement, Beton- und Eisenbetonbau

Mitt ZentBur Int Seism Ass — Mitteilungen des Zentralbureaus der Internationalen Seismologischen Assoziation

Mitt ZentInst Forst und Holzw — Mitteilungen des Zentralinstituts fuer Forst- und Holzwirtschaft

Mitt ZentKommn Schweiz Landesk — Mitteilungen der Zentralkommission fuer Schweizerische Landeskunde

Mitt Zentralanst Forst Holzwirtsch — Mitteilungen der Zentralanstalt fuer Forst- und Holzwirtschaft

Mitt Zentralinst Schweisstech DDR — Mitteilungen. Zentralinstitut fuer Schweisstechnik der Deutschen DemokratischenRepublik

Mitt Zentr Soz Arbeitsgemeinsch — Mitteilungsblatt. Zentrale Sozialistische Arbeitsgemeinschaft

Mitt ZentStelle Foerd Dt PortlZemInd — Mitteilungen der Zentralstelle zur Foerderung der Deutschen Portland-Zement-Industrie

Mitt ZentStelle Landw Gew Hohenz — Mitteilungen der Zentralstelle fuer Landwirtschaft und Gewerbe in Hohenzollern

Mitt ZentStelle Preuss LandwKamm — Mitteilungen der Zentralstelle der Preussischen Landwirtschaftskammern

Mitt ZentStelle Wiss Tech Unters — Mitteilungen der Zentralstelle fuer Wissenschaftlich-Technische Untersuchungen

Mitt ZentVerein Archit Wien — Mitteilungen der Zentralvereinigung der Architekten der im Reichsrat Vertretenden Koenigreiche und Laender (Wien)

Mitt ZentVer Fluss U Kanalschiff Ost — Mitteilungen des Zentralvereins fuer Fluss- und Kanalschiffahrt in, vormals Donauvereins

Mitt Zool Gart Dresden — Mitteilungen aus dem Zoologischen Garten zu Dresden

Mitt Zool Gart Halle — Mitteilungen aus dem Zoologischen Garten zu Halle

Mitt Zool Gart Lpz — Mitteilungen aus dem Zoologischen Garten zu Leipzig

Mitt Zool Inst Muenster — Mitteilungen aus dem Zoologischen Institut der Westfaelischen Wilhelms-Universitaet zu Muenster i. W

Mitt Zool Mus Berl — Mitteilungen. Zoologisches Museum in Berlin

Mitt Zool Mus Hamb — Mitteilungen aus dem Zoologischen Museum in Hamburg

Mitt Zool Mus Hambg — Mitteilungen des Zoologischen Museums. Hamburg

Mitt Zool Mus Univ Kiel — Mitteilungen aus dem Zoologischen Museum der Universitaet Kiel

Mitt Zool Samml Mus Naturk Berl — Mitteilungen aus der Zoologischen Sammlung des Museums fuer Naturkunde in Berlin

Mitt Zool StInst Hamb — Mitteilungen aus dem Zoologischen Staatsinstitut und Zoologischen Museum in Hamburg

Mitt Zool Stn Neapel — Mitteilungen aus der Zoologischen Station zu Neapel

Mitt Ztrstelle Dt Persongesch — Mitteilungen der Zentralstelle fuer Deutsche Personen- und Familiengeschichte

Mitt Zurich — Mitteilungen der Antiquarischen Gesellschaft in Zurich

MIV — Materialy po i Zuceniju Vostoka

MIV — MIV - Museerne i Viborg Amt

MIW — Modern India and the West. A study of the Interaction of their Civilizations

MIWF — Mitteilungen des Instituts fuer den Wissenschaftlichen Film

Miwi Ber — Milchwissenschaftliche Berichte

MIWPD — Mid-Atlantic Industrial Waste Conference. Proceedings

Mixed Convect Heat Transfer 1991 Natl Heat Transfer Conf — Mixed Convection Heat Transfer 1991. National Heat Transfer Conference

Mixed Valency Syst Appl Chem Phys Biol — Mixed Valency Systems. Applications in Chemistry, Physics, and Biology

Mixing Part Solids Eur Symp — Mixing of Particulate Solids. European Symposium

Mixing Polym Process — Mixing in Polymer Processing

Mixing Proc Eur Conf — Mixing. Proceedings. European Conference

Miyagi Prefect Inst Public Health Annu Rep — Miyagi Prefectural Institute of Public Health. Annual Report

MIZ — Journal. Arab Maritime Transport Academy

MIZG — Monatsblaetter fuer Innere Zeitgeschichte

Miz Had — Mizrah He-Hadas

MJ — Le Monde Juif

MJ — Makedonski Jazik

MJ — Makerere Journal

MJ — Menorah Journal

MJ — Midwest Journal

MJ — Mining Journal

MJ — Minister van Justitie

MJ — Mittellateinisches Jahrbuch

MJ — Modern Judaism

MJ — Monde Juif

MJ — Moudjahik

MJ — Municipal Journal

MJ — Museum Journal

MJ — Musica Judaica

MJ — Music Journal

MJA — Medical Journal of Australia

MJAGDE — Mesopotamia Journal of Agriculture

MJASA — Mysore Journal of Agricultural Sciences

Mjasn Ind — Mjasnaja Industrija SSSR

MJAUA — Medical Journal of Australia

MJ Australia — Medical Journal of Australia

M Jb — Mainfraenkisches Jahrbuch fuer Geschichte und Kunst

MJB — Mindener Jahrbuch

MJB — Muenchener Jahrbuch der Bildenden Kunst

MJBK — Muenchener Jahrbuch der Bildenden Kunst

MJC — Manitoba Journal of Counselling

MJDSA — Mukogawa Joshi Daigaku Kiyo. Shizenkagakuhen

M Jeu — Musique en Jeu

MJGK — Mainfraenkisches Jahrbuch fuer Geschichte und Kunst

MJGL — Magazin fuer Juedische Geschichte und Literatur

MJH — Michigan Jewish History

MJHSE — Miscellanies. Jewish Historical Society of England

MJIMB — Major Problems in Internal Medicine

MJJ — Materialy po Jafeticeskomu Jazykoznaniju

MJL — Marketing Journal

MJLF — Midwestern Journal of Language and Folklore

MJLS — Madras Journal of Literature and Science

MJMLAI — Medical Journal of Malaysia

MJN — Muenchener Juedische Nachrichten

MJP — Management Japan

MJP — Museums Journal. Organ of the Museums Association of Pakistan (Peshawar, West Pakistan)

MJPGA — Mitteilungen aus Justus Perthes' Geographischer Anstalt

MJPS — Midwest Journal of Political Science

MJR — Missouri Journal of Research in Music Education

MJSExc — Memorias. Junta Superior de Excavaciones y Antiquedades

MJSFA — Mises a Jour Scientifiques

MJTG — Malayan Journal of Tropical Geography

MJTOA — Mineralogical Journal (Tokyo)

MJudaica — Musica Judaica

MJugend — Musikalische Jugend

MJULAO — Communications. Instituti Forestalis Fenniae

MJV — Mitteilungen. Gesellschaft fuer Juedische Volkskunde

MJV — Mitteilungen zur Juedischen Volkskunde

MJVK — Mitteilungen fuer Juedischen Volkskunde

MK — Mackenzie Times

MK — Magyar Koenyvszemle

MK — Mededelingen van het Kadaster

MK — Medizinische Klinik

MK — Miesiecznik Koscielny

MK — Minzokugaku-Kenkyu

MK — Moskovskij Kraeved

Mk — Musik. Monatsschrift

MK — Mysl Karaimska

Mk Aerztl Fortb — Monatskurse fuer die Aerztliche Fortbildung

MKAI — Majallat Kulliyat al-Adab, al-Iskandariyyah

MKARAH — Mitteilungen der Hoeheren Bundeslehr- und Versuchsanstalten fuer Wein-, Obst-, und Gartenbau [*Klosterneuburg*]. Serie A. Rebe und Wein

Mkarte Nortatlant Ozean — Monatskarte fuer den Nordatlantischen Ozean

MKASA — Mikrochimica Acta. Supplement

MKAW — Mededeelingen. Koninklijke Nederlandsche Akademie van Wetenschappen. Afdeling Letterkunde

MKAWA — Mededeelingen. Koninklijke Academie voor Wetenschappen. Letteren en Schone Kunsten van Belgie. Klasse der Wetenschappen

MKB — Materialien zur Kunde des Buddhismus

MKBOAD — Mitteilungen der Hoeheren Bundeslehr- und Versuchsanstalten fuer Wein- und Obstbau [*Klosterneuburg*]. Serie B. Obst und Garten

MKD — Handelspartner. Nederlands Duitse Handelscourant

MKDKA — Muroran Kogyo Daigaku Kenkyu Hokoku

MKE — Market Research Europe

MKE — Muzeum es Konyvtari Ertesito

MKEMA — Mikroelementy v Meditsine

MK Ert — Muzeum es Konyvtari Ertesito

Mkg — Musikerziehung

MKHA — Meddelanden fran Kyrkohistoriska Arkivet i Lund

MKhIF — Mitteilungen des Kunsthistorischen Instituts Florenz

M Khr — Mikrasiatika Chronika

MKIF — Mitteilungen. Kunsthistorisches Institut. Florence

MKIMP — Mirovoe Khoziaistvo i Mirovaia Politika

M Kirche — Musik und Kirche

MKK — Mal Kwa Kul

MKK — Mobelkultur. Fachzeitschrift fuer die Mobelwirtschaft

MKKG — Mitteilungen der K. K. Geographische Gesellschaft in Wien

MKKM — Monatshefte fuer Katholische Kirchenmusik

MKKZ — Muenchener Katholische Kirchenzeitung fuer das Erzbistum Muenchen und Freising

MKL — Mededelingen. Koninklijke Nederlandse Academie van Wetenschappen. Afdeling Letterkunde

M KI — Medizinische Klinik

MKMP — Morovoe Khoziastvo i Moravaia Politica

MKNA — Mededeelingen. Koninklijke Nederlandsche Akademie van Wetenschappen. Afdeling Letterkunde

MKNAL — Mededeelingen. Koninklijke Nederlandsche Akademie van Wetenschappen. Afdeling Letterkunde

MKNAWL — Mededeelingen. Koninklijke Nederlandsche Akademie van Wetenschappen. Afdeling Letterkunde

MKO — Machinery Korea

MKOH — Mededeelingen. Kunst- en Oudheidkundigen Kring van Herenthals

MKOUA — Memoirs. Konan University. Science Series

MKP — Monatsschrift fuer Kirchliche Praxis

MKQUA4 — Mankind Quarterly

MKR — Militair Keuringsreglement

MKR Schriften — MKR [*Mitteldeutscher Kulturrat*] Schriften

MKrStr — Monatsschrift fuer Kriminalpsychologie und Strafrechtsreform

MKS — Marketing Science

MKS — Mitteilungsblatt der Keramikfreunde der Schwiez

MKS — Mon-Khmer Studies

M Kszle — Magyar Koenyvszemle

Mkt — Marketing

MKT — Marketing Times

MKT — Mathematische Keilschrifttexte

Mkt & Media Decisions — Marketing and Media Decisions

MKTG — Marketing

Mktg and DE Today — Marketing and Distributive Education Today

Mktg Dec — Marketing and Media Decisions

Mktg Dec S — Marketing and Media Decisions. Special Seasonal Edition

Mktg Demonst Leafl Minist Agric — Marketing Demonstration Leaflet. Ministry of Agriculture and Fisheries

Mktg Educator's N — Marketing Educator's News

Mktg Eur — Marketing in Europe

Mktg Hung — Marketing in Hungary

Mktg Leafl Minist Agric — Marketing Leaflet. Ministry of Agriculture and Fisheries

Mktg News — Marketing News

Mktg Revw — Marketing Review
Mkt Grow — Market Grower
Mkt Grow J — Market Growers' Journal
Mktg Times — Marketing Times
Mktg (UK) — Marketing (United Kingdom)
Mktg Ungarn — Marketing in Ungarn
Mktg Week — Marketing Week
Mkt Inform Guide — [*The*] Marketing Information Guide
Mkt Res — Market Research
Mkts Traders S Asia — Markets and Traders in South Asia
MKTW — Marketing Week
MKUBA — Memoirs. College of Agriculture. Kyoto University
M Ku Hist Florenz — Mitteilungen des Kunsthistorischen Instituts in Florenz
M Kultist Florenz — Mitteilungen. Kunsthistorisches Institut. Florence
MKVAB — Mededeelingen. Koninklijke Vlaamse Akademie van Wetenschappen, Letteren en Schone Kunsten v Belgie
MKW — Monatshefte fuer Kunstwissenschaft
MKWL — Monatshefte der Kunstwissenschaftlichen Literatur
MKZU — Menschen der Kirche in Zeugnis und Urkunde
ML — Man (London)
ML — Mennonite Life
MI — Mladost
ML — Modern Language Journal
ML — Modern Languages
ML — Modern Liturgy
ML — Month (London)
ML — Monthly Letter EMG
ML — Museon (Louvain). Revue d'Etudes Orientales. Etudes Philologiques, Historiques, et Religieuses
ML — Museum Lessianum
ML — Music and Letters
MLA — MLA [*Modern Language Association of America*] International Bibliography of Books and Articles on the Modern Languages and Literature
MLA — Modern Language Abstracts
MLAANZ Newsletter — Maritime Law Association of Australia and New Zealand. Newsletter
M Labor R — Monthly Labor Review
M Lab R — Monthly Labor Review
Mlad Misl — Mladezka Misl
MLA Int Bibl — Modern Language Association of America. International Bibliography
MLA Int Bibliogr Books Artic Mod Lang Lit — MLA [*Modern Language Association*] International Bibliography of Books andArticles on the Modern Languages and Literatures
MI Airbase — Military Airbase
MI Airport — Military Airports
MLA-L — MLA (Music Library Association) List [*Online*]
MLAM — Monumenta Linguarum Asiae Maioris
MLAN — Music Library Association. Newsletter
MLAN — Music Library Association. Notes
MLANCCN — MLA (Music Library Association) Northern California Chapter Newsletter
M Lang — Modern Languages
MLA Q — Missouri Library Association. Quarterly
MlatJb — Mittellateinisches Jahrbuch
M Lauriacum — Mitteilungen des Museumsvereins "Lauriacum"
MLB — Maritime Law Book Key Number Data Base
MLB — Suesswarenmarkt. Fachzeitschrift fuer Markt, Marketing, und Merchandising von Suesswaren
MI Balance — Military Balance
MLD — Maandstatistiek van de Landbouw
MLD — Mitteilungen des Medizinischen Literatur-Dienstes
ML Dig & R — Monthly Law Digest and Reporter
MLDMA — Melody Maker
MLEGB — Metallurgical Engineer. Indian Institute of Technology (Bombay)
Mlek Letac — Mlekarsky Letacek
Mlek Listy — Mlekarske Listy
MI Eng — Military Engineer
MLetters — Music and Letters
MLF — Microlog Fiche Service from Micromedia
MLF — Modern Language Forum
MLF — Modersmalslararnas Foreming. Arsskrift
MLF — Skrifter utgivet av Modersmalslaerarnas Foerening
MLFA — Modersmalslararnas Foreming. Arsskrift
MLG — Mitteilungen aus der Livlandischen Geschichte
MLH — Monumenta Linguarum Hispanicarum
ML H — Museum Lessianum. Section Historique
MLI — Metropolitan Life Insurance Company. Statistical Bulletin
MLI — Monumenta Linguae Ibericae
M Life — Medical Life
MLIHB — Mitteilungen des Landwirtschaftlichen Instituts der Hochschule fuer Bodenkultur
MLIHfB — Mitteilungen des Landwirtschaftlichen Instituts der Hochschule fuer Bodenkultur
M Ling — Modeles Linguistiques
MI Intel — Military Intelligence
MLISB — Medical Instrumentation
Mlit — Maitres des Litteratures
MLit — Miesiecznik Literacki
MLJ — Madras Law Journal
MLJ — Makerere Law Journal
MLJ — Malayan Law Journal
MLJ — Manitoba Law Journal
MLJ — Memphis Law Journal
MLJ — Mississippi Law Journal

MLJ — Modern Language Journal
MLJ — Modern Language Review
MLJ Supp — Malayan Law Journal. Supplement
Mlkt — Maelkeritidende
Mlle — Mademoiselle
MLM — Melanges Louis Massignon
MLM (Mound Facil) — MLM (Mound Facility)
MLMN — Mal-i-Mic News. Metis and Non-Statute Indians in New Brunswick
MLN — Modern Language Notes
MLN Bull — MLN [*Minnesota League for Nursing*] Bulletin
M L New — Malcolm Lowry Newsletter
MLNSBP — Mammalian Species
MLO — Medical Laboratory Observer
Mlody Tech — Mlody Technik
MLOSA — Mededelingen. Landbouwhogeschool en Opzoekingsstations van de Staat te Gent
MLP — Monthly List of Publications
ML P — Museum Lessianum. Section Philosophique
ML Ph — Muirhead Library of Philosophy
MLP OT — Monumenta Liturgiae Polychoralis. Ordinarium Missae cum Tribus Choris
MLPSA — Monthly List of Publications of South Australian Interest Received in the StateLibrary of South Australia
MLQ — Malabar Law Quarterly
MLQ — Modern Language Quarterly
MIR — Mladinska Revija
MLR — Modern Language Review
MLR — Modern Law Review
MLR — Monthly Labor Review
MI Rev — Military Review
MLS — Marian Library Studies
MLS — MLS: Marketing Library Services
MLS — Modern Language Studies
MLS — Moskovskij Letopisnyj Svod Konca
MLS — Multinational Business
MLS — Paris. Universite. Memoires lus a la Sorbonne dans les Seances Extraordinaires du Comite. Histoire, Philologie, et Sciences Morales
MLSaeH — Mitteilungen des Landesvereines fuer Saechsischen Heimatschutz
MLST — Mittellateinische Studien und Texte
MLT — Madras Law Times
MLT — Malaysia Industrial Digest
ML Tech — Military Technology
MLUHM — Meddelanden fran Lunds Universitets Historiska Museum de Lund
MLV — Bedrijfsontwikkeling; Maandblad voor Agrarische Produktie, Verwerking, en Afzet
MLVBA — Metallverarbeitung
MLVS — Mededelingen mit de Leidse Verzameling van Spijkerschrift Inscripties
MLV/T — Tribus. Veroeffentlichungen des Linden-Museums. Museum fuer Laender- und Voelkerkunde
MLW — Madras Law Weekly
MLW — Mittellateinisches Woerterbuch
MLW — Mountain Life and Work
Mlyn L — Mlynarske Listy
Mlyn Listy — Mlynarske Listy
Mlyn Nov — Mlynarske Noviny
Mlyn Pek Prum Tech Skladovani Obili — Mlynsko-Pekarensky Prumysl a Technika Skladovani Obili
Mlyn Pol — Mlynarz Polski
Mlynsko-Pekar Prum Tech Sklad Obili — Mlynsko-Pekarensky Prumysl a Technika Skladovani Obili
MM — Acta et Diplomata Graeca Medii Aevi
MM — Maal og Minne
MM — Maclean's Magazine
MM — Macmillan's Magazine
MM — Madrider Mitteilungen
MM — Magyar Muzeum
MM — Maitland Mercury
MM — Maitres de la Musique
MM — Manufacturers' Monthly
MM — Mariner's Mirror
MM — Massachusetts Music News
MM — Masses and Mainstream
MM — Media and Methods
MM — Melody Maker
MM — Mens en Maatschappij
MM — Meteorological Magazine
MM — Mining Magazine
MM — Miscellanea Mediaevalia
MM — Miscellaneous Man
MM — Mitteilungen. Internationale Stiftung Mozarteum
MM — Modern Music
MM — Monuments et Memoires Publies par l'Academie des Inscriptions et Belles-Lettres
MM — Moody Monthly
MM — Muenchener Museum
MM — Muenchner Museum fuer Philologie des Mittelalters und der Renaissance
MM — Music and Musicians
MM — Music Magazine
MMA — Management Accounting
MMA — Management and Marketing Abstracts
MMA — Minoan and Mycenaean Art
MMA — Miscellanea Musicologica
MMA — Monographs on Mediterranean Antiquity
MMAB — Metropolitan Museum of Art Bulletin
MMAD — Macallat al-Macma al-Limi al-Arabi Dimasq

MMADA — Modern Materials. Advances in Development and Applications
MMAE — Memorial. Mision Arqueologica Espanola en Egypto
MMAF — Memoires. Mission Archeologique Francaise au Caire
MMAF — Memoires Publies. Membres. Mission Archeologique Francaise au Caire
MMAFC — Memoires. Mission Archeologique Francaise au Caire
MMAI — Memoires. Mission Archeologique en Iran
MMAI — Monuments et Memoires Publies par l'Academie des Inscriptions et Belles-Lettres
MMAIBL — Monuments et Memoires Publies par l'Academie des Inscriptions et Belles-Lettres
MMAJ — Metropolitan Museum Journal
MMAP — Memoires. Mission Archeologique en Perse
MMAP — Memorias. Museos Arqueologicos Provinciales
MMASA — Modern Machine Shop
MMB — Monumenta Musicae Belgicae
MMB — Monumenta Musicae Byzantinae
MMB — Muenzen- und Medaillensammler Berichte aus allen Gebieten der Geld-, Muenzen-, und Medaillenkunde
MMBB — Molecular Marine Biology and Biotechnology
MMC — Miscellanea Musicologica
MMC — Monuments Illustrating Old and Middle Comedy
MMCI — Monde Musulman Contemporain. Initiations
M Mcr J — Monthly Microscopical Journal
MMCSNV — Memorie del Museo Civico di Storia Naturale di Verona
MMDPB7 — Mammalia Depicta
MME — Minnesota Messenia Expedition
MMEDA — Military Medicine
MMEDDC — Man and Medicine
M Medii Aevi — Musica Medii Aevi
MMERD — MER (Marine Engineers Review)
MMER Rep Dep Mech Eng Monash Univ — MMER Report. Department of Mechanical Engineering. Monash University
M Met Soc Am B — Mining and Metallurgical Society of America. Bulletin
MMFC — Memoires Publies par les Membres. Mission Archeologique Francaise au Caire
Mm Fis Sperim — Memorie di Fisica Sperimentale
MMFN — Manitoba Metis Federation News
MMFQ — Milbank Memorial Fund. Quarterly. Health and Society
MMFSBQ — Museo Civico di Storia Naturale di Verona. Memorie. Fuori Serie
MMG — Manager Magazin
M Mg — Monatshefte fuer Musikgeschichte
Mm Gl Sv — Memoirs of the Geological Survey of Great Britain and of the Museum of Economic Geology in London
MMGS — Melbourne Monographs in Germanic Studies
MMH — Montana: The Magazine of Western History
MMI — Maintenance Management International
MMI — Medical Microbiology and Immunology
MM Industriej — MM [Metall und Maschinenindustrie] Industriejournal
M Minima — Musica Minima
M Misc — Midwestern Miscellany
MMJM — Marisia. Muzeul Judetean Mures
MMJ MD Med J — MMJ. Maryland Medical Journal
MMK — Materialy Mongol'skoj Kommissii
MMK — Mideast Markets
MML — Mineralogical Magazine and Journal of the Mineralogical Society (London)
MMLA — Majallat Majma al-Lughah al-Arabiyah
MMLI — Majallat al-Majma al-Limi al-Iraqi
MMLMP — Materialy po Matematiceskoj Lingvistike i Masinnomu Perevodu
MMLRAI — Mammal Review
MMLS — Memoirs and Proceedings. Manchester Literary and Philosophical Society
MMM — Medical Marketing and Media
MMM — Melanges Malraux Miscellany
MMM — Textes et Monuments Figures Relalifs aus Mysteres de Mithra
MMMA — Monumenta Monodica Medii Aevi
Mm Md Mil — Recueil de Memoires de Medecine, de Chirurgie, et de Pharmacie Militaires, redige sous le Surveillance du Conseil de Sante
MM Minoes Megbizh — MM. Minoeseg es Megbizhatosag
MMMOEI — Monographs of Marine Mollusca
MMMSM — Millenaire Monastique du Mont Saint-Michel
MMN — Marianne Moore Newsletter
MMN — Mitteilungen zur Geschichte der Medizin und der Naturwissenschaft
MMNCAH — Memoires. Museum National d'Histoire Naturelle. Serie C. Sciences de la Terre
MMNPAM — Manitoba. Department of Mines and Natural Resources. Mines Branch. Publication
MMNRW — Manitoba. Department of Mines, Natural Resources, and Environment. Wildlife Research MS Reports
MMOSD — Molybdenum Mosaic
MMP — Memoires. Museum National d'Histoire Naturelles (Paris)
MMP — Microform Market Place
MMPAIBL — Monuments et Memoires Publies. Academie des Inscriptions et Belles-Lettres
MMPD — Money Manager Profile Diskettes
MMPJAE — Manufactured Milk Products Journal
MMQ — Management Quarterly
MMQ — Metalectrovisie
MM Qual Zuverlaessigk Sonderausg — MM. Qualitaet und Zuverlaessigkeit. Sonderausgabe
MMQUB — Mining and Metallurgy. Quarterly
MMr — Mariner's Mirror
MMR — Military Media Review
MMR — Minerva Medica. Rivista delle Riviste di Scienze Mediche (Rome and Turin)
MMR — Minoan-Mycenaean Religion and its Survival in Greek Religion
MMR — Monthly Musical Record
MMRI — Multi-Media Reviews Index

MMR Miner Met Rev — MMR. Minerals and Metals Review
MMRSA — Methods in Medical Research
M Ms — Medizinische Monatsschrift
MMS — Medizinische Monatsschrift (Stuttgart)
MMS — Metropolitan Museum. Studies
MMS — Muenstersche Mittelalter-Schriften
MMSCEC — Marine Mammal Science
M Msch W — Mitteilungen aus dem Markscheidewesen
MMSJ — Monumenta Missionum Societatis Jesu
MM St — Metropolitan Museum Studies
MM St — Mitteilungsblatt fuer Mathematische Statistik und Ihre Anwendungsgebiete
MMT — Majaleye Musighi (Tehran)
MMT — Management Technology
Mmt Int Rev — Management International Review
M Mus Lauriacum — Mitteilungen des Museumsvereins "Lauriacum"
M Muzeum — Magyar Muzeum
MMV — Matzke Memorial Volume. (Palo Alto, Stanford University)
MMVH — Mittheilungen aus dem Museum fuer Voelkerlunde [Hamburg]
MMVIEB — Memoirs. Museum of Victoria
MMVKH — Mitteilungen aus dem Museum fuer Voelkerkunde in Hamburg
MMV Laur — Mitteilungen des Museumsvereins. Lauriacum
MMW — Muenchener Medizinische Wochenschrift
MMWL — Monthly Magazine. Muslim World League
MMW Muench Med Wochenschr — MMW. Muenchener Medizinische Wochenschrift
MMWOA — Muenchener Medizinische Wochenschrift
MMWOAU — Muenchener Medizinische Wochenschrift
MMWR — Morbidity and Mortality Weekly Report
MMWR CDC Surveill Summ — MMWR [Morbidity and Mortality Weekly Report] - CDC Surveillance Summaries
MMWR Morb Mortal Wkly Rep — MMWR. Morbidity and Mortality Weekly Report
MMWR Surveill Summ — MMWR [Morbidity and Mortality Weekly Report] Surveillance Summaries
MM Zt — Militaer-Musikerzeitung
MN — Malawi News
MN — Man
MN — Manchester Evening News
MN — Miscellanea Numismatica
Mn — Mnemosyne
MN — Monumenta Nipponica
MN — Moscow News
MN — Museum News
MN — Museum Notes. American Numismatic Society
MNA — Medizinisch-Naturwissenschaftliches Archiv
MNA — Megafon (Argentina)
MNANS — Museum Notes. American Numismatic Society
MNAW — Mededelingen der Nederlandse Akademie van Wetenschappen
MNAWA — Mededeelingen der Koninklijke Nederlandse Akademie van Wetenschappen. AfdeelingLetterkunde
MNAWL — Mededeelingen. Koninklijke Nederlandsche Akademie van Wetenschappen. Afdeling Letterkunde
MN Bl — Mathematisch-Naturwissenschaftliche Blaetter
MNC — Monde Non-Chretien
MNC — Monuments Illustrating New Comedy
MNC — Nederlands College voor Belastingconsulenten. Nationale Associatie van Accountantsadministratieconsulenten, Nederlandse Vereniging van Boekhoudbureaux en Administratiekantoren. Mededelingenblad
MNCBAY — Comunicaciones Botanicas. Museo de Historia Natural de Montevideo
MNCDN — Mededeelingen. Nijmeegse Centrale voor Dialecten Naamkunde
MNCR/V — Vinculos. Revista de Antropologia. Museo Nacional de Costa Rica
MND — Monde
MNDI — Mitteilungen des Normenausschusses der Deutschen Industrie
MNDMG — Monatsblatt der Norddeutschen Missions-Gesellschaft
MNDPV — Mitteilungen und Nachrichten. Deutscher Palaestina-Verein
Mnem — Mnemosyne. Bibliotheca Classica Batava
MNEMA9 — Manitoba Entomologist
Mnemos — Mnemosyne. Bibliotheca Classica Batava
Mnemosyne — Mnemosyne. Bibliotheca Classica Batava
M Neuchatel — Musee Neuchatelois. Recueil d'Histoire Nationale et d'Archeologie Neuchatel
MNF — Textilia
MNfP — Music News from Prague
M Nfr VH — Mitteilungen. Nordfriesischer Verein fuer Heimatkunde
MNFS — Meddelelser fra Norsk Forening foer Sprog-Videnskap
MNFSA — Meddelelser fra Norsk Farmaceutisk Selskap
Mngb — Menighedsbladet
MNGBA — Mitteilungen. Naturforschende Gesellschaft in Bern
MNGMD — Management
Mngmt Dec — Management Decision
MNGPM — Magazin fuer die Neuste Geschichte der Protestantischen Missionsund Bibelgesellschaft
MNGS — Manitoba Geographical Series
MnH — Minnesota History
MNHIR — Mededeelingen. Nederlandsch-Historisch Institut le Rome
MN Hist — Minnesota History
MNHNP — Museum National d'Histoire Naturelle (Paris)
MNI — Modern Asia
MNI — Muslim News International
MNI Microcomput News Int — MNI. Microcomputer News International
MNip — Monumenta Nipponica
MNIR — Mededeelingen. Nederlandsch-Historisch Institut le Rome
MNIS — Mitteilungen aus dem Koeniglichen Naturwissenschaftlichen Institut (Sofia)
MNJ — Mining Journal
MNKMA5 — Mankind Monographs
MNKP — Materialy po Nacional'no - Kolonial'nym Problemam

MNLAB9 — Arquivos. Museu Bocage
MN LR — Minnesota Law Review
MNM — Monumenta Nipponica Monographs
MNMCA — Memoires. Societe Nationale des Sciences Naturelles et Mathematiques de Cherbourg
Mn Mg — Mineralogical Magazine and Journal of the Mineralogical Society of Great Britain and Ireland
Mnmt & Landschappen — Monumenten en Landschappen
Mnmt Ant Lincei — Monumenti Antichi. Pubblicati per Cura della Reale Accademia dei Lincei
Mnmt Archaeol — Monumenta Archaeologica
Mnmt Bergomensia — Monumenta Bergomensia
Mnmt Chart Pap Hist Illus — Monumenta Chartae Papyraceae Historiam Illustrantia
Mnmt Ger Hist — Monumenta Germaniae Historiam
Mnmt Nipponica — Monumenta Nipponica
Mnmts A & Hist — Nos Monuments d'Art et d'Histoire
Mnmt Serica — Monumenta Serica
Mnmts Hist — Monuments Historiques
Mnmts Hist France — Monuments Historiques de la France
Mnmts Piot — Monuments Piot
MNN — Muenchener Neueste Nachrichten
MNNA — Manitoba Nature
MNNMBL — Museo Nacional de Historia Natural. Noticiario Mensual
MNNTB8 — Man and Nature
MNO — Meubelecho
MNo — Monde Nouveau
MNOIM — Missionsnachrichten der Ostindischen Missionsanstalt zu Halle
M Not R Ast — Monthly Notices. Royal Astronomical Society
MNP — Monde Nouveau-Paru
MNPAAS — Morfologia Normala si Patologica
MNpar — Monde Nouveau-Paru
MNRAA — Monthly Notices. Royal Astronomical Society
MNRLD — Mineraloel
MNRLSM — Manitoba. Department of Natural Resources. Library Service Manuscripts
MNRTA — Mental Retardation
MNSKA — Meddelelser fra det Norske Skogforsoeksvesen
MNSPBL — Medecine du Sport
MNSV — Meddelelser fra Norsk Forening foer Sprog-Videnskap
MNTC — Moffatt New Testament Commentary
Mntl Pt — Mental Patients Liberation/Therapy
Mntn Life — Mountain Life and Work
Mntp A Clin — Annales Cliniques de la Societe Medicale Pratique de Montpellier
Mntp Ac Mm — Academie des Sciences et Lettres de Montpellier. Memoires de la Section des Sciences
Mntp Ac Sc Mm — Academie des Sciences et Lettres de Montpellier. Memoires de la Section des Sciences
Mntp Mm Ac Sect Sc — Academie des Sciences et Lettres de Montpellier. Memoires de la Section des Sciences
Mntp Mm Sc — Academie des Sciences et Lettres de Montpellier. Memoires de la Section des Sciences
Mntp Rec Bll — Recueil des Bulletins Publies par la Societe Libre des Sciences de Montpellier
Mntp S Lang Gg Bll — Societe Languedocienne de Geographie. Bulletin (Montpellier)
MNU — Monatsschrift fuer Naturwissenschaftlichen Unterricht
Mnu — Mundo Nuevo
MNUGD6 — Memorias e Noticias Publicacoes. Museu e Laboratorio Mineralogico e Geologico. Universidade de Coimbra
MNU Math Naturwiss Unterr — MNU. Mathematische und Naturwissenschaftliche Unterricht
MNUSD — Museum Notes. University of South Dakota Museum
MNV — Montalban (Venezuela)
Mnva — Minerva
MNVAD — Mededelingenblad. Nederlandse Vacuumvereniging
MNW — Marketing News
MNy — Magyar Nyelv
MNy — Magyar Nyelvjarasok
MNY — Messager de New York
M Ny C G — Meddelelser fra Ny Carlsberg Glyptotek
MNyj — Magyar Nyelvjarasok
M Nyor — Magyar Nyelvoer
MO — Miscellanea Orientalia
MO — Missionerskoe Obozrienie
MO — Missouri Reports
MO — Modern Occasions
Mo — Monat
MO — Monatshefte
MO — Monde Oriental
Mo — Money
MO — Moniteur Officiel
Mo — Moskva
MO — Movimento Operaio
MO — Musica d'Oggi
MO — Musical Opinion
MoA — Modern Asian Studies
Mo Acad Sci Bull Suppl — Missouri Academy of Science. Bulletin. Supplement
MO Acad Sci Occas Pap — Missouri Academy of Science. Occasional Paper
MO Ag Bd — Missouri State Board of Agriculture. Publications
MO Ag Exp — Missouri. Agricultural Experiment Station. Publications
MO Agric Exp Stn Bull — Missouri. Agricultural Experiment Station. Bulletin
MO Agric Exp Stn Res Bull — Missouri. Agricultural Experiment Station. Research Bulletin

MO Agric Exp Stn Spec Rep — Missouri. Agricultural Experiment Station. Special Report
Mo Ann Stat (Vernon) — Vernon's Annotated Missouri Statutes
MO App — Missouri Appeal Reports
MO Archaeologist — Missouri Archaeologist
MO Archaeol Soc Mem — Missouri Archaeological Society Memoir
Mo Aust Dem R — Monthly Australian Demographic Review
MoB — Monde de la Bible
MOB — Mortgage Banking
MO Bar J — Missouri Bar. Journal
Mo B Assn Proc — Missouri Bar Association. Proceedings
MO B G — Missouri Bureau of Geology and Mines
Mobil Country J — Mobil Country Journal
Mobile Med Surg J — Mobile Medical and Surgical Journal
Mobile Part Syst — Mobile Particulate Systems
Mobil Ind Rev — Mobil Industrial Review. Mobil Oil Co. [London]
Mobilization Reassem Genet Inf — Mobilization and Reassembly of Genetic Information
Mobil Ph N — Mobile Phone News
Mobil Rdsch — Mobil Rundschau. Mobil Oil A.G [Hamburg]
Mobil Rev — Mobil Review
Mobil Tech Ser — Mobil Technical Series. Mobil Oil Co. [London]
MO B J — Missouri Bar. Journal
MO Bot Gard Ann — Missouri Botanical Garden. Annals
MO Bot Gard Bull — Missouri Botanical Garden. Bulletin
Mo Bur Geol Mines Rep — Missouri. Bureau of Geology and Mines. Reports
MOC — Bedrijfshuishouding. Magazine voor Interne en Civiele Diensten
Mocambique Missao Combate Tripanossomiases Annu Rep — Mocambique Missao de Combate as Tripanossomiases. Annual Report
Mocambique Prov Dir Serv Geol Minas Mem Commun Bol — Mocambique. Provincia. Direccao dos Servicos de Geologia e Minas. Memorias e Communicacoes. Boletim
Mocambique Prov Serv Ind Geol Ser Geol Minas Mem Commun Bol — Mocambique. Provincia. Servicos de Industria e Geologia. Serie de Geologia e Minas. Memorias e Communicacoes. Boletim
MOCC — Magnum Oecumenicum Constantiense Concilium
Moccasin Tel — Moccasin Telegraph
MO Code Regs — Missouri Code of State Regulations
MO Conserv — Missouri Conservationist
MOCRA — Molecular Crystals
MOCT — Moccasin Telegraph
Mod — Modilianum
Mod A — Modern Age
Mod Ac Sc Mm — Memorie della Regia Accademia di Scienze, Lettere, ed Arti di Modena
Mod Age — Modern Age
Mod Aging Res — Modern Aging Research
Mod Agric Athens — Modern Agriculture (Athens)
Mod Agric Equip Ser — Modern Agricultural Equipment Series
Mod Airports — Modern Airports
Mod Anal Antibiot — Modern Analysis of Antibiotics
Mod Approaches Chem React Searching Proc Conf — Modern Approaches to Chemical Reaction Searching. Proceedings. Conference
Mod Arts News — Modern Arts News
Mod Arzneim Ther — Moderne Arzneimittel-Therapie
Mod Asian S — Modern Asian Studies
Mod Asian Stud — Modern Asian Studies
Mod Aspects Electrochem — Modern Aspects of Electrochemistry
Mod Aspects Neurosurg — Modern Aspects of Neurosurgery
Mod Aspects Part Phys Collect Lect Spring Sch Theor Exp Phys — Modern Aspects of Particle Physics. Collection of Lectures. Spring School of Theoretical and Experimental Physics
Mod Aspects Ser Chem — Modern Aspects Series of Chemistry
Mod Aspects Vitreous State — Modern Aspects of the Vitreous State
Mod As Stud — Modern Asian Studies
Mod Ath and Coach — Modern Athlete and Coach
Mod Athl Coach — Modern Athlete and Coach
Mod Aust L — Modern Austrian Literature
Mod Austrian Lit — Modern Austrian Literature
Mod B — Modern Boating
Mod Bauformen — Moderne Bauformen
Mod Beekeep — Modern Beekeeping
Mod Biol — Modern Biology
Mod Brew — Modern Brewer
Mod Brew Age — Modern Brewery Age
Mod Brew M — Modern Brewery Age. Magazine Section
Mod Bus Law — Modern Business Law
Mod Camera Mag — Modern Camera Magazine
Mod Cast — Modern Castings
Mod Cast Am Foundryman — Modern Casting and American Foundryman
Mod C Cardi — Modern Concepts of Cardiovascular Disease
Mod Cell Biol — Modern Cell Biology
Mod Ch — Modern Churchman
Mod Chem — Modern Chemistry
Mod Chem Eng — Modern Chemical Engineering
Mod Chem Ind — Modern Chemical Industry
Mod China — Modern China
Mod China Stud — Modern China Studies
Mod Chin Lit Newsl — Modern Chinese Literature Newsletter
Mod Chirop — Modern Chiropody
Mod Chlor Alkali Technol — Modern Chlor-Alkali Technology
Mod Chlor Alkali Technol Pap Int Chlorine Symp — Modern Chlor-Alkali Technology. Papers Presented at the International Chlorine Symposium
ModChm — Modern Churchman
Mod Clin — Modern Clinics

Mod Comput Tech Their Impact Chem Eng Pap Tutzing Symp — Modern Computer Techniques and Their Impact on Chemical Engineering. Papers. Tutzing Symposium

Mod Concepts Cardiovasc Dis — Modern Concepts of Cardiovascular Disease

Mod Concepts Penicillium Aspergillus Classif — Modern Concepts in Penicillium and Aspergillus Classification

Mod Concepts Pract Fiber Refin Proc Annu Pulp Pap Conf — Modern Concepts and Practices of Fiber Refining. Proceedings. Annual Pulp and Paper Conference

Mod Concepts Psychiatr Surg Proc World Congr — Modern Concepts in Psychiatric Surgery. Proceedings. World Congress of Psychiatric Surgery

Mod Concr — Modern Concrete

ModD — Modern Drama

Mod Dairy — Modern Dairy

Mod Data — Modern Data

Mod Dent — Modern Dentistry

Mod Dev Powder Metall — Modern Development in Powder Metallurgy

Mod Dev Shock Tube Res Proc Int Shock Tube Symp — Modern Developments in Shock Tube Research. Proceedings. International Shock Tube Symposium

ModDr — Modern Drama

Mod Drama — Modern Drama

Mod Drug Encycl Ther Index Suppl — Modern Drug Encyclopedia and Therapeutic Index. Supplement

Mod Drugg — Modern Druggist

Mod Drugs — Modern Drugs

Mode — Modern Office and Data Equipment

Mode Action Anti Parasit Drugs — Mode of Action of Anti-Parasitic Drugs

Mod East Asian Stud — Modern East Asian Studies

Mod Ed — Modern Education

Model Aircr — Model Aircraft

Model Anal Simul Commande — Modelisation. Analyse. Simulation. Commande

Model Biol Med Resp Mezhved Sb — Modelirovanie v Biologii i Meditsine Respublikanskii Mezhvedomstvennyi Sbornik

Model Cast Weld Adv Solidif Processes V Proc Int Conf — Modeling of Casting, Welding, and Advanced Solidification Processes V. Proceedings. International Conference on Modeling of Casting and Welding Processes

Model Deform Cryst Solids Proc Symp — Modeling the Deformation of Crystalline Solids. Proceedings. Symposium

Mod Elect Mech — Modern Electrics and Mechanics

Model Eng — Model Engineer

Model Engr — Model Engineer

Model EVM Defektov Krist — Modelirovanie na EVM Defektov v Kristallakh

Model Identif Control — Modeling Identification and Control

Modelirovanie Ekonom Processov — Otdelenie Ekonomiceskoi Kivernetiki Ekonomiceskogo Fakul'teta Moskovogo Gosudarstvennogo Universiteta Imeni M. V. Lomonosova. Modelirovanie Ekonomiceskih Processov

Model Khim Reakt Tr Vses Konf Khim Reakt — Modelirovanie Khimicheskikh Reaktorov. Trudy Vsesoyuznoi Konferentsii po Khimicheskim Reaktoram

Modell Control Biotechnol Processes Proc IFAC Symp — Modelling and Control of Biotechnological Processes. Proceedings. IFAC Symposium

Modell Control Biotech Processes Proc IFAC Workshop — Modelling and Control of Biotechnical Processes. Proceedings. IFAC Workshop

Modell Ecotoxicol — Modelling in Ecotoxicology

Modell Eff Clim Electr Mech Eng Equip Int Symp — Modelling the Effect of Climate on Electrical and Mechanical Engineering Equipment. International Symposium

Modell Environ Chem — Modelling in Environmental Chemistry

Modell Environ Eff Electr Gen Eng Equip Summ Int Symp — Modelling of Environmental Effects on Electrical and General Engineering Equipment. Summary. International Symposium

Modell Meas Control A — Modelling, Measurement, and Control A. General Physics, Electronics. Electrical Engineering

Modell Meas Control B — Modelling, Measurement, and Control B. Solid and Fluid Mechanics and Thermics. Mechanical Systems

Modell Meas Control C — Modelling, Measurement, and Control C. Energetics, Chemistry, Earth. Environmental and Biomedical Problems

Modell Meas Control D — Modelling, Measurement, and Control D. Manufacturing, Management. Human and Socio-Economic Problems

Modell Simul Mater Sci Eng — Modelling and Simulation in Materials Science and Engineering

Model Mech — Model Mechanic

Model Optim Khim Protsessov — Modelirovanie i Optimizatsiya Khimicheskikh Protsessov

Model R — Model Railroader

Models Dermatol — Models in Dermatology

Model Simul Proc Annu Pittsburgh Conf — Modeling and Simulation. Proceedings. Annual Pittsburgh Conference

Models Lab Rep Dep Archit Sci Syd Univ — Models Laboratory Reports. Department of Architectural Science. University of Sydney

Mod Eng — Modern Engineer

Mod Engl Jnl — Modern English Journal

Mod Engr — Modern Engineer

MO Dent J — Missouri Dental Journal

Mo Dep Bus Adm Div Geol Surv Water Resour Inf Circ — Missouri Department of Business and Administration. Division of Geological Survey and Water Resources. Information Circular

MO Dep Conserv Terr Ser — Missouri. Department of Conservation. Terrestrial Series

Modern Approaches Geophys — Modern Approaches in Geophysics

Modern Boating — Modern Boating and Seacraft

Modern Drum — Modern Drummer

Moderne Lehrtexte Wirtschaftswiss — Moderne Lehrtexte. Wirtschaftswissenschaften

Moderne Math Elem Darstellung — Moderne Mathematik in Elementarer Darstellung

Moderne Metallbearb — Moderne Metallbearbeitung

Modern European Philos — Modern European Philosophy

Modern Lit — Modern Liturgy

Modern LR — Modern Law Review

Modern L Rev — Modern Law Review

Modern Med Minneapolis — Modern Medicine. The Newsmagazine of Medicine (Minneapolis)

Modern O — Modern Occasions

Modern Phil — Modern Philology

Modern Phys Lett A — Modern Physics Letters. A. Particles and Fields, Gravitation, Cosmology, Nuclear Physics

Modern Phys Lett B — Modern Physics Letters. B. Condensed Matter Physics, Statistical Physics, Applied Physics

Modern Plastics Int — Modern Plastics International

Modern P S — Modern Poetry Studies

Modern Railw — Modern Railways

Modern Sci Vedic Sci — Modern Science and Vedic Science

Modern Vocational Trends Career Mon — Modern Vocational Trends. Career Monographs

Mode Sel Chem Proc Jerusalem Symp Quantum Chem Biochem — Mode Selective Chemistry. Proceedings. Jerusalem Symposium on Quantum Chemistry and Biochemistry

Mod Explor Tech Proc Symp — Modern Exploration Techniques. Proceedings. Symposium

Mod Farmer — Modern Farmer

Mod Farming — Modern Farming

Mod Farming Cent Afr — Modern Farming in Central Africa

Mod Fict St — Modern Fiction Studies

Mod Fict Stud — Modern Fiction Studies

Mod Fluoresc Spectrosc — Modern Fluorescence Spectroscopy

Mod Fm Equip — Modern Farm Equipment

Mod Fmg Lond — Modern Farming (London)

Mod Fmg New Orl — Modern Farming (New Orleans)

Mod Fmg Nott — Modern Farming (Nottingham)

Mod Fndry — Modern Foundry

Mod Genet — Modern Genetics

Mod Geol — Modern Geology

Mod Gladiolus Grow — Modern Gladiolus Grower

Mod Health — Modern Healthcare

Mod Healthcare — Modern Healthcare

Mod Heb Lit — Modern Hebrew Literature

Mod Highw — Modern Highway

Mod Holzverarb — Moderne Holzverarbeitung

Mod Hosp — Modern Hospital

Mod Hosp News Lett — Modern Hospital News Letter

Modif Inf Content Plant Cells Proc John Innes Symp — Modification of the Information Content of Plant Cells. Proceedings. John Innes Symposium

Modif Polim Mater — Modifikatsiya Polimernykh Materialov

Modif Polym — Modification of Polymers

Mod Illus — Moderniste Illustre

Mod Ind — Modern Industry

Mod Ind Energy — Modern Industrial Energy

Mod Ind Furnaces — Modern Industrial Furnaces

Mod Ind Press — Modern Industrial Press

Mod Instrum Methods Elem Anal Pet Prod Lubr — Modern Instrumental Methods of Elemental Analysis of Petroleum Products and Lubricants

Mod Int Dr — Modern International Drama

MO Div Geol Land Surv Rep Invest — Missouri Division of Geology and Land Survey. Report of Investigations

Mo Div Geol Surv Water Resour Rep — Missouri. Division of Geological Survey and Water Resources. Reports

Mod Jud — Modern Judaism

Mod Judaism — Modern Judaism

Mod Kemi — Modern Kemi

Mod Knit — Modern Knitting Management

Mod Lan — Modern Language Notes

Mod Lang — Modern Languages

Mod Lang Abstr — Modern Language Abstracts

Mod Lang Assn Pub — Modern Language Association of America. Publications

Mod Lang For — Modern Language Forum

Mod Lang Forum — Modern Language Forum

Mod Lang J — Modern Language Journal

Mod Lang N — Modern Language Notes

Mod Lang Notes — Modern Language Notes

Mod Lang Q — Modern Language Quarterly

Mod Lang Quarterly — Modern Language Quarterly

Mod Lang Quartl — Modern Language Quarterly

Mod Lang R — Modern Language Review

Mod Lang Rev — Modern Language Review

Mod Lang Scot — Modern Languages in Scotland

Mod Lang St — Modern Language Studies

Mod Law R — Modern Law Review

Mod Law Rev — Modern Law Review

Mod Law Soc — Modern Law and Society

Mod Libn — Modern Librarian

Mod Lit — Modern Liturgy

Mod Lithography — Modern Lithography

Mod Lithogr NY — Modern Lithography (New York)

Mod Lithogr Offset Print — Modern Lithographer and Offset Printer

Mod LR — Modern Law Review

Mod L Rev — Modern Law Review

Mod M — Modern Motor

Mod Mach — Modern Machinery

Mod Mach Shop — Modern Machine Shop

Mod Mater — Modern Materials

Mod Mater Adv Dev Appl — Modern Materials. Advances in Development and Applications
Mod Mater Handl — Modern Materials Handling
Mod Mat H — Modern Materials Handling
Mod Meat Mktg — Modern Meat Marketing and Imported Food Journal
Mod Mech — Modern Mechanic
Mod Mechs Invent — Modern Mechanics and Inventions
Mod Med — Moderne Medizin
Mod Med — Modern Medicine
Mod Med A — Modern Medicine Annual
Mod Med Asia — Modern Medicine of Asia
Mod Med Aust — Modern Medicine of Australia
Mod Med Battle Creek — Modern Medicine (Battle Creek, Michigan)
Mod Med (Chicago) — Modern Medicine (Chicago)
Mod Med Cleveland Ohio — Modern Medicine (Cleveland, Ohio)
Mod Med Gt Br — Modern Medicine of Great Britain
Mod Med (Jpn) — Modern Medicine (Japan)
Mod Med Lab — Modern Medical Laboratory
Mod Med Lond — Modern Medicine (London)
Mod Med (Minneapolis) — Modern Medicine (Minneapolis)
Mod Med Osaka — Modern Medicine (Osaka)
Mod Med Sci — Modern Medical Science
Mod Met — Modern Metals
Mod Metal Finish — Modern Metal Finishing
Mod Metals — Modern Metals
Mod Met Finish — Modern Metal Finishing
Mod Method Plant Anal New Ser — Modern Methods of Plant Analysis. New Series
Mod Methods Igneous Petrol Understanding Magmat Processes — Modern Methods of Igneous Petrology. Understanding Magmatic Processes
Mod Methods Pharmacol — Modern Methods in Pharmacology
Mod Methods Plant Anal — Modern Methods of Plant Analysis
Mod Methods Polym Charact — Modern Methods of Polymer Characterization
Mod Methods Protein Nucleic Acid Res — Modern Methods in Protein and Nucleic Acid Research. Review Articles
Mod Mfg — Modern Manufacturing
Mod Miller — Modern Miller
Mod Miller Bakers News — Modern Miller and Bakers News
Mod Min — Modern Mining
Mod Mm Ac Sc — Memorie della Regia Accademia di Scienze, Lettere, ed Arti di Modena
Mod Mm S — Memorie di Matematica e di Fisica della Societa Italiana delle Scienze (Modena)
Mod Mm S It — Memorie di Matematica e di Fisica della Societa Italiana delle Scienze (Modena)
Mod Mon — Modern Monthly
Mod Mot — Modern Motor
Mod Motor — Modern Motor
Mod Muhely — Modern Muhely
Mod Mus — Modern Music
Mod Music — Modern Music
Mod Muveszet — Modern Muveszet
Mod NMR Tech Their Appl Chem — Modern NMR Techniques and Their Application in Chemistry
Mod Nurs Home — Modern Nursing Home
Mod Nutr — Modern Nutrition
Mod Off — Modern Office Procedures
Mod Off — Modern Office Technology
Mod Off and Data Manage — Modern Office and Data Management
Mod Off Dat Man — Modern Office and Data Management
Mod Off Proc — Modern Office Procedures
Mod Off Proced — Modern Office Procedures
Mod Off Procedures — Modern Office Procedures
Mod Packag — Modern Packaging
Mod Packag Encycl — Modern Packaging Encyclopedia
Mod Packag Encycl Issue — Modern Packaging Encyclopedia Issue
Mod Paint — Modern Paint and Coatings
Mod Paint Coat — Modern Paint and Coatings
Mod Painters — Modern Painters
Mod Pathol — Modern Pathology
Mod Perspect Psychiatry — Modern Perspectives in Psychiatry
Mod Perspect Thermoelectr Relat Mater Symp — Modern Perspectives on Thermoelectrics and Related Materials. Symposium
Mod Pet Technol — Modern Petroleum Technology
Mod Pharm — Modern Pharmacology
Mod Pharm — Modern Pharmacy
Mod Pharmacol — Modern Pharmacology
Mod Pharmacol Toxicol — Modern Pharmacology-Toxicology
Mod Phil — Modern Philology
Mod Philol — Modern Philology
Mod Phot — Modern Photography
Mod Photogr — Modern Photography
Mod Photogr Cincinnati — Modern Photography (Cincinnati)
Mod Photogr Lond — Modern Photography (London)
Mod Phys Lett A — Modern Physics Letters A. Particles and Fields, Gravitation, Cosmology, NuclearPhysics
Mod Phys Lett B — Modern Physics Letters B. Condensed Matter Physics, Statistical Physics and Applied Physics
Mod Phys Monogr Ser — Modern Physics Monograph Series
Mod Phys Tech Mater Technol — Modern Physical Techniques in Materials Technology
Mod Phytochem Methods — Modern Phytochemical Methods
Mod Pkg — Modern Packaging
Mod Pkg En — Modern Packaging Encyclopedia and Buyer's Guide Issue
Mod Plas — Modern Plastics

Mod Plast — Modern Plastics
Mod Plast Encycl — Modern Plastics Encyclopaedia and Engineer's Handbook
Mod Plastics — Modern Plastics
Mod Plast Int — Modern Plastics International
Mod Pl Oper Maint — Modern Plant Operation and Maintenance
Mod Plst Int — Modern Plastics International
Mod Poetry Stud — Modern Poetry Studies
Mod Poet St — Modern Poetry Studies
Mod Poult Keep — Modern Poultry Keeping
Mod Powder Diffr — Modern Powder Diffraction
Mod Power and Eng — Modern Power and Engineering
Mod Power Eng — Modern Power and Engineering
Mod Power Syst — Modern Power Systems
Mod Pract Derm — Modern Practice in Dermatology
Mod Pract Gas Chromatogr — Modern Practice of Gas Chromatography
Mod Pract Infect Fev — Modern Practice in Infectious Fevers
Mod Pract Ophthal — Modern Practice in Ophthalmology
Mod Pract Psychol Med — Modern Practice in Psychological Medicine
Mod Pract Tuberc — Modern Practice in Tuberculosis
Mod Precis — Modern Precision
Mod Probl Act Struct Cent Nerv Syst — Modern Problems of the Activity and Structure of the Central Nervous System
Mod Probl Nutr — Modern Problems of Nutrition
Mod Probl Ophthalmol — Modern Problems in Ophthalmology
Mod Probl Paediatr — Moderne Probleme der Paediatrie
Mod Probl Paediatr — Modern Problems in Paediatrics
Mod Probl Pharmacopsychiatry — Modern Problems of Pharmacopsychiatry
Mod Probl Pharmakopsychiatr — Moderne Probleme der Pharmakopsychiatrie
Mod Probl Surf Phys Int Sch Condens Matter Phys Lect — Modern Problems of Surface Physics. International School on Condensed Matter Physics. Lectures
Mod Prob Ophth — Modern Problems in Ophthalmology
Mod Psychoanal — Modern Psychoanalysis
Mod Psychol — Modern Psychology
Mod Psychologist — Modern Psychologist
Mod Pwr — Modern Power
Mod Pwr Engng — Modern Power and Engineering
Mod Q — Modern Quarterly
Mod Quart Misc — Modern Quarterly Miscellany
Mod Quart Res SE A — Modern Quarterly Research in Southeast Asia
Mod Quat Res SE Asia — Modern Quaternary Research in Southeast Asia
Mod R — Modern Review
Mod Railw — Modern Railways
Mod R (Calcutta) — Modern Review (Calcutta)
Mod Refrig — Modern Refrigeration
Mod Refrig Air Cond — Modern Refrigeration and Air Conditioning
Mod Refrig Air Control — Modern Refrigeration and Air Control
Mod Refrig Air Control News — Modern Refrigeration and Air Control News
Mod Relazione — Relazione delle Adunanze della R. Accademia di Scienze, Lettere, ed Arti di Modena
ModRev — Modern Review
Mod Roentgen-Fotogr — Moderne Roentgen-Fotografie
Mod Rr — Modern Railroads
ModS — Modern Schoolman
Mod Sanit Bldg Maint — Modern Sanitation and Building Maintenance
Mod Sch — Modern Schoolman
Mod Schoolm — Modern Schoolman
Mod Schoolman — Modern Schoolman
Mod Sci — Modern Science
Mod Shoemkg — Modern Shoemaking
Mod S It Mm — Memorie di Matematica e di Fisica della Societa Italiana delle Scienze (Modena)
Mod S Nt An — Annuario della Societa dei Naturalisti in Modena
Mod S Nt At — Atti della Societa dei Naturalisti di Modena
Mod S Nt At Rd — Atti della Societa dei Naturalisti di Modena. Rendiconti delle Adunanze
Mod Soil Microbiol — Modern Soil Microbiology
Mod Solid State Phys Simon Fraser Univ Lect — Modern Solid State Physics. Simon Fraser University. Lectures
Mod Sp — Moderne Sprachen
Mod Steel Constr — Modern Steel Construction
Mod Steelwk — Modern Steelwork
Mod St Lit — Modernist Studies. Literature and Culture, 1920-1940
Mod Stomat — Modern Stomatology
Mod Stud — Modernist Studies
Mod Stud Assoc Yearb — Modern Studies Association Yearbook
Mod Sugar Plant — Modern Sugar Planter
Mod Sunlight — Modern Sunlight
Mod Synth Methods — Modern Synthetic Methods. Conference Paper. International Seminar on Modern Synthetic Methods
Modszertani Kozl Mag All Foldt Intez — Modszertani Kozlemenyek. Magyar Allami Foldtani Intezet
Mod Teach — Modern Teacher
Mod Teach — Modern Teaching
Mod Tech Comput Chem MOTECC 90 — Modern Techniques in Computational Chemistry. MOTECC-90
Mod Tech Comput Chem MOTECC 91 — Modern Techniques in Computational Chemistry. MOTECC-91
Mod Technol Treib Explosivst — Moderne Technologie von Treib- und Explosivstoffen
Mod Tech Surg Abdom Surg — Modern Technics in Surgery. Abdominal Surgery
Mod Tech Surg Card Thor Surg — Modern Technics in Surgery. Cardiac-Thoracic Surgery
Mod Tech Surg Plastic Surg — Modern Technics in Surgery. Plastic Surgery
Mod Tex B — Modern Textile Business
Mod Text — Modern Textiles

Mod Text — Modern Textiles Magazine
Mod Textil — Modern Textiles
Mod Text Mag — Modern Textiles Magazine
Mod Theor Chem — Modern Theoretical Chemistry
Mod Ther — Modern Therapy
Mod Tire Dealer — Modern Tire Dealer
Mod Tramw — Modern Tramway
Mod Tramway — Modern Tramway
Mod Transp — Modern Transport
Mod Treat — Modern Treatment
Mod Treat Gen Pract — Modern Treatment in General Practice
Mod Treat Gen Pract Yb — Modern Treatment in General Practice Yearbook
Mod Treat Yb — Modern Treatment Year Book
Mod Trends Anaesth — Modern Trends in Anaesthesia
Mod Trends Cardiol — Modern Trends in Cardiology
Mod Trends Cyber Syst Proc Int Congr — Modern Trends in Cybernetics and Systems. Proceedings. International Congress of Cybernetics and Systems
Mod Trends Dermatol — Modern Trends in Dermatology
Mod Trends Drug Depend Alcohol — Modern Trends in Drug Dependence and Alcoholism
Mod Trends Endocrinol — Modern Trends in Endocrinology
Mod Trends Forensic Med — Modern Trends in Forensic Medicine
Mod Trends Gastro Ent — Modern Trends in Gastro-Enterology
Mod Trends Gastroenterol — Modern Trends in Gastroenterology
Mod Trends Hum Leuk 2 — Modern Trends in Human Leukemia 2. Biological, Immunological, Therapeutical, and Virological Aspects
Mod Trends Hum Leuk 3 — Modern Trends in Human Leukemia 3. Newest Results in Clinical and Biological Research
Mod Trends Hum Leuk 4 Wiselde Jt Meet Pediatr Oncol — Modern Trends in Human Leukemia 4. Newest Results in Clinical and Biological Research Including Pediatric Oncology. Wiselde Joint Meeting on Pediatric Oncology
Mod Trends Hum Reprod Physiol — Modern Trends in Human Reproductive Physiology
Mod Trends Immunol — Modern Trends in Immunology
Mod Trends Med Virol — Modern Trends in Medical Virology
Mod Trends Neurol — Modern Trends in Neurology
Mod Trends Obstet — Modern Trends in Obstetrics
Mod Trends Oncol — Modern Trends in Oncology
Mod Trends Orthop — Modern Trends in Orthopaedics
Mod Trends Paediatr — Modern Trends in Paediatrics
Mod Trends Pharmacol Ther — Modern Trends in Pharmacology and Therapeutics
Mod Trends Plast Surg — Modern Trends in Plastic Surgery
Mod Trends Psychosom Med — Modern Trends in Psychosomatic Medicine
Mod Trends Radiother — Modern Trends in Radiotherapy
Mod Trends Rheumatol — Modern Trends in Rheumatology
Mod Trends Ser Psychosom Med — Modern Trends Series. Psychosomatic Medicine
Mod Trends Surg — Modern Trends in Surgery
Mod Trends Toxicol — Modern Trends in Toxicology
Modular I St — Modular Instruction in Statistics
Modular Texts Mol Cell Biol — Modular Texts in Molecular and Cell Biology
Modulated Struct Mater — Modulated Structure Materials
Modulation Cell Interact Vitam A Deriv Retinoids — Modulation of Cellular Interactions by Vitamin A and Derivatives (Retinoids)
Modulation Mediation Cancer Vitam Proc Int Conf — Modulation and Mediation of Cancer by Vitamins. Proceedings. International Conference on the Modulation and Mediation of Cancer by Vitam
Modulators Exp Carcinog Proc Symp — Modulators of Experimental Carcinogenesis. Proceedings. Symposium
Modules Appl Math — Modules in Applied Mathematics
Modul Q — Modular Quarterly
Mod Un — Modern Unionist
Mod Unfallverhuet — Moderne Unfallverhuetung
Mod Util Infrared Technol — Modern Utilization of Infrared Technology
Mod Util Infrared Technol Civ Mil — Modern Utilization of Infrared Technology. Civilian and Military
Mod Vet Pract — Modern Veterinary Practice
Mod Welt — Moderne Welt
Mod Wireless — Modern Wireless
Mod World — Modern World
Mod Ytbehandling — Modern Ytbehandling
MOE — Molecular Endocrinology
Moebel Decor — Moebel Decoration
Moeglinsche Ann Landw — Moeglinsche Annalen der Landwirthschaft
MOeGMMK — Mitteilungen der Oesterreichischen Gesellschaft fuer Muenz- und Medaillenkunde
MOEIG — Mitteilungen. Oesterreichisches Institut fuer Geschichtsforschung
MOeIG E — Mitteilungen des Oesterreichischen Instituts fuer Geschichtsforschung. Ergaengsband
MOEMDJ — Motivation and Emotion
MOENG — Mitteilungen der Oesterreichischen Numismatischen Gesellschaft
M Oe Num Ges — Mitteilungen der Oesterreichischen Numismatischen Gesellschaft
MOeSA E — Mitteilungen des Oesterreichischen Staatsarchivs. Ergaenzungband
Moessbauer Eff Methodol — Moessbauer Effect Methodology
Moessbauer Eff Methodol Proc Symp — Moessbauer Effect Methodology. Proceedings of the Symposium
Moessbauer Eff Proc Int Conf — Moessbauer Effect. Proceedings. International Conference on the Moessbauer Effect
Moessbauer Eff Ref Data J — Moessbauer Effect Reference and Data Journal
Moessbauer Spectrosc — Moessbauer Spectroscopy
Moessbauer Spectrosc Appl Inorg Chem — Moessbauer Spectroscopy Applied to Inorganic Chemistry
M Oe Ur Frueh Gesch — Mitteilungen der Oesterreichischen Arbeitgemeinschaft fuer Ur- und Fruehgeschichte

M of Art — Magazine of Art
M Offic — Medical Officer
M of Hist — Magazine of History
MOFPH — Monumenta Ordinis Fratrum Praedicatorum Historica
MOG — Mitteilungen des Oberhessischen Geschichtsvereins
MOGA — Mitteilungen. Oesterreichische Gesellschaft fuer Anthropologie, Ethnologie, undPraehistorie
MO Geol Surv Rep Invest — Missouri. Geological Survey. Report of Investigations
Mo Geol Surv Water Resour Ground Water Rep — Missouri Geological Survey and Water Resources. Ground Water Report
MO Geol Surv Water Resour Inf Circ — Missouri. Geological Survey and Water Resources. Information Circular
MO Geol Surv Water Resour Inform Circ — Missouri. Geological Survey and Water Resources. Information Circular
MO Geol Surv Water Resour Misc Publ — Missouri. Geological Survey and Water Resources. Miscellaneous Publication
MO Geol Surv Water Resour Rep — Missouri. Geological Survey and Water Resources. Report
MO Geol Surv Water Resour Rep Invest — Missouri. Geological Survey and Water Resources. Report of Investigations
MO Geol Surv Water Resour Spec Publ — Missouri. Geological Survey and Water Resources. Special Publication
MO Geol Surv Water Resour Water Resour Rep — Missouri. Geological Survey and Water Resources. Water Resources Report
MOGMS — Meddelelser om Groenland. Man and Society
MOGR — Meddelelser om Groenland
MO G S MO Bur G Mines — Missouri. Geological Survey. Missouri Bureau of Geology and Mines
MOH — Magazine of Horror
MoH — Monatshefte
MOhGV — Mitteilungen des Oberhessischen Geschichtsvereins
MO His Col — Missouri Historical Society. Collections
MO His R — Missouri Historical Review
MO Hist Rev — Missouri Historical Review
MO Hist Soc Bull — Missouri Historical Society. Bulletin
MO Hlth Rep — Missouri Health Report
MOHOA — Modern Hospital
Mo I — March of India
MOI — Moniteur du Commerce International
MOIED — Modern Industrial Energy
MOIG — Mitteilungen. Oesterreichisches Institut fuer Geschichtsforschung
MOIGF — Mitteilungen. Oesterreichisches Institut fuer Geschichtsforschung
Moigno Cosmos — Cosmos. Revue Encyclopedique Hebdomadaire des Progres des Sciences. Moigno
Mo Illust — Monthly Illustrator
MOIMER — Minia. Orgao do Instituto Minhoto de Estudos Regionais
Moirs Aust Investments — Moir's Australian Investments
MoiS — Mois Suisse. Litteraire, Artistique, Politique, Economique, Scientifique
Mois — Mois. Synthese de l'Activite Mondiale
Mois Aeronaut — Mois Aeronautique
Mois Afr — Le Mois en Afrique
Mois Agric — Mois Agricole
Mois Agric Vitic — Mois Agricole et Viticole
Mois Biol — Mois Biologique
Mois Chim Electrochim — Mois Chimique et Electrochimique
Mois Colon Marit — Mois Colonial et Maritime
Mois Econ et Fin — Mois Economique et Financier
Mois Ethnogr Fr — Mois d'Ethnographie Francaise
Mois Med — Mois Medical
Mois Med Chir — Mois Medico-Chirurgical
Mois Minier Metall — Mois Minier et Metallurgique
Mois Min Metall — Mois Minier et Metallurgique
Mois Oenol — Mois Oenologique
Mois Scient — Mois Scientifique
Mois Scient Ind — Mois Scientifique et Industriel
Mois Sci Ind — Mois Scientifique et Industriel
Moist Fert — Moisture and Fertility. American Potash Institute
Mois Ther — Mois Therapeutique
Moisture Frost Relat Soil Prop — Moisture and Frost-Related Soil Properties
Mo J — Modern Judaism
Mo J Australian-American Assoc — Australian-American Association. Monthly Journal
Mojave Reveg Notes — Mojave Revegetation Notes
Mo J Med Sci — Monthly Journal of Medical Science
MOJOD — Mother Jones
MO J Res Mus Ed — Missouri Journal of Research in Music Education
Mo Jur — Monthly Jurist
MOK — Oesterreichisches Institut fuer Wirtschaft Forschung. Monatsberichte
MOKIA — Monatsschrift fuer Kinderheilkunde
MOKOAI — Moskovskii Kolkhoznik
Mokslas Tech — Mokslas ir Technika
Mokslin Pranes — Moksliniai Pranesimai
Mokslo Darb Vilniaus Valstybinis Pedagog Inst — Mokslo Darbai. Vilniaus Valstybinis Pedagoginis Institutas
Mokuzai Gak — Mokuzai Gakkaishi
Mokuzai Gakkai Shi/J Jap Wood Res Soc — Mokuzai Gakkai Shi/Journal. Japan Wood Research Society
MO L — Missouri Law Review
MOL — Molenaar Weekblad voor de Graanverwerkende Industrie en Veevoederindustrie
Mol — Molieriste
MOLAA — Monatsschrift fuer Ohrenheilkunde und Laryngo-Rhinologie
Mo Labor R — Monthly Labor Review
Mo Labor Rev — Monthly Labor Review
Mo Lab Rev — Monthly Labor Review

Mol Androl — Molecular Andrology
Mol Aspects Cell Regul — Molecular Aspects of Cellular Regulation
Mol Aspects Inflammation — Molecular Aspects of Inflammation
Mol Aspects Med — Molecular Aspects of Medicine
Mol Aspects Monooxygenases Bioact Toxic Compd — Molecular Aspects of Monooxygenases and Bioactivation of Toxic Compounds
Mo Law Rep — Monthly Law Reporter
Mo Laws — Laws of Missouri
Mol Basis Bact Metab — Molecular Basis of Bacterial Metabolism
Mol Basis Hum Cancer — Molecular Basis of Human Cancer
Mol Basis Microb Pathog — Molecular Basis of Microbial Pathogenicity. Report of the Molecular Basis of the Ineffective Process, Berlin, 1979
Mol Beam Epitaxy Proc Int Symp — Molecular Beam Epitaxy. Proceedings. International Symposium
Mol Biochem Parasitol — Molecular and Biochemical Parasitology
Mol Biol — Molecular Biology
Mol Biol — Molekulyarnaya Biologiya
Mol Biol & Med — Molecular Biology and Medicine
Mol Biol Atheroscler Proc Steenbock Symp — Molecular Biology of Atherosclerosis. Proceedings. Steenbock Symposium
Mol Biol B Cell Dev — Molecular Biology of B Cell Developments
Mol Biol Biochem Biophys — Molecular Biology, Biochemistry, and Biophysics
Mol Biol Cell — Molecular Biology of the Cell
Mol Biol Cyanobacteria — Molecular Biology of Cyanobacteria
Mol Biol Diabetes — Molecular Biology of Diabetes
Mol Biol Engl Transl Mol Biol (Mosc) — Molecular Biology. English Translation of Molekulyarnaya Biologiya (Moscow)
Mol Biol Erythropoiesis — Molecular Biology of Erythropoiesis
Mol Biol Evol — Molecular Biology and Evolution
Mol Biol Free Radical Scavenging Syst — Molecular Biology of Free Radical Scavenging Systems
Mol Biol Int Ser Monogr Textb — Molecular Biology; an International Series of Monographs and Textbooks
Mol Biol Itogi Nauki Tekh — Molekulyarnaya Biologiya. Itogi Nauki i Tekhniki
Mol Biol (Kiev) — Molekulyarnaya Biologiya (Kiev)
Mol Biol Mamm Gene Appar — Molecular Biology of the Mammalian Genetic Apparatus
Mol Biol Med — Molecular Biology and Medicine
Mol Biol (Mosc) — Molekulyarnaya Biologiya (Moscow)
Mol Biol Physiol Insulin Insulin Like Growth Factors — Molecular Biology and Physiology of Insulin and Insulin-Like Growth Factors
Mol Biol Plant Dev — Molecular Biology of Plant Development
Mol Biol Proc Int Conf — Molecular Biology. Proceedings. International Conference
Mol Biol Rep — Molecular Biology Reports
Mol Biol Rp — Molecular Biology Reports
Mol Biol Tumour Res Annu Meet Arbeitsgem Gen Diagn — Molecular Biology in Tumour Research. Annual Meeting. Arbeitsgemeinschaft fuer Gen-Diagnostik
Mol Biotechnol — Molecular Biotechnology
Mol Brain Res — Molecular Brain Research
Mol Breed — Molecular Breeding
Mo Lbr R — Monthly Labor Review
Mol Carcino — Molecular Carcinogenesis
Mol Carcinog — Molecular Carcinogenesis
Mol C Bioch — Molecular and Cellular Biochemistry
Mol Cell — Molecular Cell
Mol Cell Biochem — Molecular and Cellular Biochemistry
Mol Cell Biol — Molecular and Cellular Biology
Mol Cell Biol Hum Dis Ser — Molecular and Cell Biology of Human Diseases Series
Mol Cell Biol Res Commun — Molecular Cell Biology Research Communications
Mol Cell Differ — Molecular Cell Differentiation
Mol Cell Endocr — Molecular and Cellular Endocrinology
Mol Cell Endocrinol — Molecular and Cellular Endocrinology
Mol Cell Neurosci — Molecular and Cellular Neurosciences
Mol Cell Pathol — Molecular Cell Pathology
Mol Cell Probes — Molecular and Cellular Probes
Mol Cells — Molecules and Cells
Mol C Endoc — Molecular and Cellular Endocrinology
Mol Chem Ne — Molecular and Chemical Neuropathology
Mol Chem Neuropathol — Molecular and Chemical Neuropathology
Mol Complexes — Molecular Complexes
Mol Comp Physiol — Molecular Comparative Physiology
Mol Cryst — Molecular Crystals
Mol Cryst and Liq Cryst — Molecular Crystals and Liquid Crystals
Mol Cryst and Liq Cryst Lett — Molecular Crystals and Liquid Crystals. Letters
Mol Cryst and Liq Cryst Suppl Ser — Molecular Crystals and Liquid Crystals. Supplement Series
Mol Cryst Liq Cryst — Molecular Crystals and Liquid Crystals
Mol Cryst Liq Cryst Incorporating Nonlinear Opt — Molecular Crystals and Liquid Crystals Incorporating Nonlinear Optics
Mol Cryst Liq Cryst Lett — Molecular Crystals and Liquid Crystals. Letters
Mol Cryst Liq Cryst Lett Sect — Molecular Crystals and Liquid Crystals. Letters Section
Mol Cryst Liq Cryst Sci Technol Sect A — Molecular Crystals and Liquid Crystals Science and Technology. Section A. Molecular Crystals and Liquid Crystals
Mol Cryst Liq Cryst Sci Technol Sect A Mol Crys Liq Cryst — Molecular Crystals and Liquid Crystals Science and Technology. Section A. Molecular Crystals and Liquid Crystals
Mol Cryst Liq Cryst Sci Technol Sect B Nonlinear Opt — Molecular Crystals and Liquid Crystals Science and Technology Section B. Nonlinear Optics
Mol Cryst Liq Cryst Sci Technol Sect C — Molecular Crystals and Liquid Crystals Science and Technology. Section C. Molecular Materials
Mol Cytogenet Proc Annu Biol Div Res Conf — Molecular Cytogenetics. Proceedings. Annual Biology Division Research Conference
Molded Prod — Molded Products

Mol Des Electrode Surf — Molecular Design of Electrode Surfaces
Mol Des Model Concepts Appl Part A — Molecular Design and Modeling. Concepts and Applications. Part A. Proteins, Peptides, and Enzymes
Mol Diabetol — Molecular Diabetology
Mol Diagn — Molecular Diagnosis
Molding Tech Release — Molding Technical Release. Plastics Department. Union Carbide International Company
Mol Divers — Molecular Diversity
Mol Diversity — Molecular Diversity
Molec Biol — Molecular Biology
Molec Cryst — Molecular Crystals and Liquid Crystals
Mol Ecol — Molecular Ecology
Molec Pharm — Molecular Pharmacology
Molec Phys — Molecular Physics
Molecular Phys — Molecular Physics
Mo Leg Exam — Monthly Legal Examiner
MO Legis Serv — Missouri Legislative Service
Molekularbiol Biochem Biophys — Molekularbiologie, Biochemie, und Biophysik
Mol Electron Bioelectron — Molecular Electronics and Bioelectronics
Mol Electron Mol Electron Devices — Molecular Electronics and Molecular Electronic Devices
Mol Endocrinol — Molecular Endocrinology
Mol Eng — Molecular Engineering
Moleschtt Us — Untersuchungen zur Naturlehre des Menschen und der Thiere. Moleschott
Mol Fiz Biofiz Vodn Sist — Molekulyarnaya Fizika i Biofizika Vodnykh Sistem
Mol Fiz Biofiz Vod Sis — Molekulyarnaya Fizika i Biofizika Vodnykh Sistem
Mol Genet Biofiz — Molekulyarnaya Genetika i Biofizika
Mol Genet Dev Neurobiol Taniguchi Symp Brain Sci — Molecular Genetics in Developmental Neurobiology. Taniguchi Symposium on Brain Sciences
Mol Genet Genomics — Molecular Genetics and Genomics
Mol Genet Med — Molecular Genetic Medicine
Mol Genet Metab — Molecular Genetics and Metabolism
Mol Genet Mikrobiol Virusol — Molekulyarnaya Genetika, Mikrobiologiya, i Virusologiya
Mol Gen Genet — Molecular and General Genetics
Mol G Genet — Molecular and General Genetics
Mol Hum Reprod — Molecular Human Reproduction
MO Lib Assn Newsl — Missouri Library Association. Newsletter
MO Lib Assn Q — Missouri Library Association. Quarterly
MO Libr Ass Q — Missouri Library Association. Quarterly
Mol Immunobiol Self React — Molecular Immunobiology of Self-Reactivity
Mol Immunol — Molecular Immunology
Molini Ital — Molini d'Italia
Molin Panad — Molineria y Panaderia
Mol Insect Sci Proc Int Symp — Molecular Insect Science. Proceedings. International Symposium on Molecular Insect Science
Mol Interact — Molecular Interactions
MOLJA — Modern Language Journal
Molk Kaeserei Ztg — Molkerei- und Kaeserei- Zeitung
Molk U Kas Ztg — Molkerei- und Kaserei-Zeitung
Molk Ztg (Berlin) — Molkerei-Zeitung (Berlin)
Molk Ztg (Hildesheim Ger) — Molkerei-Zeitung (Hildesheim, Germany)
Molk Ztg Welt Milch — Molkerei-Zeitung Welt der Milch
Molluscs Archaeol Recent — Molluscs in Archaeology and the Recent. Department of Zoology. University of British Columbia
Mo L Mag — Monthly Law Magazine
Mol Mar Biol Biotechnol — Molecular Marine Biology and Biotechnology
Mol Mater — Molecular Materials
Mol Mech Cell Growth Differ — Molecular Mechanisms in Cellular Growth and Differentiation [*monograph*]
Mol Mech Immune Regul — Molecular Mechanisms of Immune Regulation
Mol Mech Insectic Resist — Molecular Mechanisms of Insecticide Resistance
Mol Mech Their Clin Appl Malig — Molecular Mechanisms and Their Clinical Application in Malignancies
Mol Mech Transp Proc Bari Meet Bioenerg Int Symp — Molecular Mechanisms of Transport. Proceedings. Bari Meeting on Bioenergetics. International Symposium
Mol Med — Molecular Medicine
Mol Med Cambridge Mass — Molecular Medicine (Cambridge, Massachusetts)
Mol Med NY — Molecular Medicine (New York)
Mol Med Sofia — Molekulyarna Meditsina (Sofia)
Mol Med Today — Molecular Medicine Today
Mol Mekh Genet Protsessov Tr — Molekulyarnye Mekhanizmy Geneticheskikh Protsessov. Trudy
Mol Membr Biol — Molecular Membrane Biology
Mol Microbiol — Molecular Microbiology
Mol Neurobiol — Molecular Neurobiology
Mol Neuropharmacol — Molecular Neuropharmacology
Mol Neurosci Proc Galveston Neurosci Symp — Molecular Neuroscience. Expression of Neural Genes. Proceedings. Galveston Neuroscience Symposium
Moln Lap — Molnarok Lapja
Moloch Khoz — Molochnoe Khozyaistvo, Skotovodstvo, Lugovodstvo, Travoseyanie i Svinevodstvo
Moloch Myas Zhiv — Molochnoe i Myasnoe Zhivotnovodstvo
Moloch Myas Zhivotnovod — Molochnoe i Myasnoe Zhivotnovodstvo
Molochn Myasn Skotovod (Moscow) — Molochnoe i Myasnoe Skotovodstvo (Moscow)
Molochn Myasn Zhivotnovod — Molochnoe i Myasnoe Zhivotnovodstvo
Molochno Masloden Promst — Molochno-Maslodel'naya Promyshlennost
Molochno Myasn Skotovod (Kiev) — Molochnoe i Myasnoe Skotovodstvo (Kiev)
Molochn Prom-St — Molochnaya Promyshlennost
Moloch Prom — Molochnaya Promyshlennost'
Moloch Prom SSSR — Molochnaya Promyshlennost' SSSR

Molodoi Nauchn Rab Estestv Nauki — Molodoi Nauchnyi Rabotnik. Estestvennye Nauki

Mol Online — Molecules Online

Mol Pathog Gastrointest Infect — Molecular Pathogenesis of Gastrointestinal Infections

Mol Pathol — Molecular Pathology

Mol Pharmacol — Molecular Pharmacology

Mol Pharmacol Recept — Molecular Pharmacology of Receptors

Mol Photoch — Molecular Photochemistry

Mol Photochem — Molecular Photochemistry

Mol Phylogenet Evol — Molecular Phylogenetics and Evolution

Mol Phys — Molecular Physics

Mol Physiol — Molecular Physiology

Mol Phys Rep — Molecular Physics Reports

Mol Plant Microbe Interact — Molecular Plant-Microbe Interactions

Mol Plant Microb Interact MPMI — Molecular Plant-Microbe Interactions. MPMI

Mol Psychiatry — Molecular Psychiatry

MO LR — Missouri Law Review

Mol Reprod Dev — Molecular Reproduction and Development

MO L Rev — Missouri Law Review

Mol Sieves — Molecular Sieves

Mol Simul — Molecular Simulation

Mol Spectros — Molecular Spectroscopy

Mol Spectrosc Electron Struct Intramol Interact — Molecular Spectroscopy, Electronic Structure, and Intramolecular Interactions

Mol Spectrosc Mod Res — Molecular Spectroscopy. Modern Research

Mol Spectrosc Proc Conf — Molecular Spectroscopy. Proceedings. Conference

Mol Spektrosk — Molekulyarnaya Spektroskopiya

Mol Struct Diffr Methods — Molecular Structure by Diffraction Methods

Mol Struct Dimens — Molecular Structures and Dimensions

Mol Struct Dimensions Ser A — Molecular Structures and Dimensions. Series A

Mol Struct Energ — Molecular Structure and Energetics

Mol Strukt — Molekulyarnaya Struktura [*monograph*]

Mol Supramol Photochem — Molecular and Supramolecular Photochemistry

Mol Tech Taxon — Molecular Techniques in Taxonomy

Molten Met — Molten Metal

Molten Salt Chem Technol — Molten Salt Chemistry and Technology

Mol Ther — Molecular Therapy

Mol Toxicol — Molecular Toxicology

Mol Urol — Molecular Urology

Mol Vis — Molecular Vision

Mol Vision — Molecular Vision [*Electronic Publication*]

Molybdenum Agric Newsl — Molybdenum Agricultural Newsletter. Climax Molybdenum Co

Molysulfide Newslett — Molysulfide Newsletter

MoM — Maal og Minne

MOM — Mobelmarkt. Fachzeitschrift fuer die Mobelwirtschaft

MOM — Modern Office

MOMA Bull — Museum of Modern Art Bulletin

Mo M Assn J — Missouri Medical Association. Journal

MOMEA — Montpellier Medical

MO Med — Missouri Medicine

Momenti Probl Storia Pensiero — Momenti e Problemi della Storia del Pensiero

Mo Micro J — Monthly Microscopical Journal

Mo Munic R — Missouri Municipal Review

Mo Mus Rec — Monthly Musical Record

MON — Ministerstvo Oborony Narodowej

MON — Money

Mon — [*The*] Monist

Mon — Moniteur Belge

Mon — Moniteur Congolais

Mon — Month (London)

Mon — Monumenti Annali e Bullettini Pubblicati. Instituto di Correspondenza Archaeologica

Mon — Monumenti Inediti. Pubblicati dell'Instituto di Correspondenza Archeologica

Mon Abstr Bull Kodak Res Labs — Monthly Abstract Bulletin from the Kodak Research Laboratories

Mon Abstr Bull Res Lab Eastman Kodak Co. — Monthly Abstract Bulletin. Research Laboratory. Eastman Kodak Co.

Mon Abstr Met Obsns Manila — Monthly Abstracts of Meteorological Observations made at Manila

Mon Abstr Natn Smelt Co — Monthly Abstracts. National Smelting Co.

Mon Abstr Obsns Malay Met Serv — Monthly Abstract of Observations. Malayan Meteorological Service

Monaco Med — Monaco Medical

Monaco Mus Anthropol Prehist Bull — Monaco. Musee d'Anthropologie Prehistorique. Bulletin

MonAeg — Monumenta Aegyptiaca

Mon Agric Bull Iraq — Monthly Agricultural Bulletin. Department of Agriculture. Iraq

Mon Agric Bull Palest — Monthly Agricultural Bulletin. Palestine

Mon Agric News Bull Nanking — Monthly Agricultural News Bulletin (Nanking)

Mon Agric Rep Lond — Monthly Agricultural Report (London)

Mon Agric Rep Nth Ire — Monthly Agricultural Report. Government of Northern Ireland Ministry of Agriculture

Mon Agric Rep Scotl — Monthly Agricultural Report. Department of Agriculture for Scotland

MonAL — Monumenti Antichi Pubblicati dell'Accademia dei Lincei

Monaldi Arch Chest Dis — Monaldi Archives for Chest Disease

Mon Analyt Bull Inter-Afr Bur Soils — Monthly Analytical Bulletin. Inter-African Bureau for Soils

Mon Angl — Monasticon Anglicanum

Mon Ann Bull — Monumenti Annali e Bullettini Pubblicati. Instituto di Correspondenza Archaeologica

Mon Ann d Inst — Monumenti Annali e Bullettini Pubblicati. Instituto di Correspondenza Archaeologica

Mon A (Novi Sad) — Monumenta Archaeologica (Novi Sad)

Mon Ant — Monumenti Antichi

Mon Ant Linc — Monumenti Antichi. Accademia Nazionale dei Lincei

Mon Ant Lincei — Monumenti Antichi. Accademia Nazionale dei Lincei

Mon A (Prague) — Monumenta Archaeologica (Prague)

Mon A Rainf Statist Sudan — Monthly and Annual Rainfall Statistics. Sudan

Mon A Rainf Table Un Prov Agra Oudh — Monthly and Annual Rainfall Table in the United Provinces of Agra and Oudh

Mon A Rainf Thailand — Monthly and Annual Rainfall of Thailand

Mon Arch — Monumenta Archaeologica (Prague)

Mon Arte Ant — Monumenti d'Arte Antica

Monash LR — Monash University. Law Review

Monash UL Rev — Monash University. Law Review

Monash Univ Chem Eng Dep Rep — Monash University. Chemical Engineering Department. Report

Monash Univ Gaz — Monash University. Gazette

Monash Univ L Rev — Monash University. Law Review

Mon As Min Ant — Monumenta Asiae Minoris Antiqua

Mon Astr News Lett Harv Coll Obs — Monthly Astronomical News-Letter. Committee for the Distribution of Astronomical Literature. Harvard College Observatory

Monat — Monatshefte; a Journal Devoted to the Study of German Language and Literature

Monat f Deut Unt — Monatshefte fuer Deutschen Unterricht

Monathl Fruechte Gel Ges Ungern — Monathliche Fruechte einer Gelehrten Gesellschaft in Ungern

Monatl ErdbBer Geophys Obs Georgiens — Monatlicher Erdbebenbericht des Geophysikalischen Observatoriums Georgiens

Monatl Mitt Baugew — Monatliche Mitteilungen fuer das Baugewerbe

Monatl Mitt Hauptstn ErdbForsch Hamb — Monatliche Mitteilungen der Hauptstation fuer Erdbebenforschung zu Hamburg

Monatl Mitth Gesammtgeb Naturwiss — Monatliche Mittheilungen aus dem Gesammtgebiete der Naturwissenschaften

Monatl Weltkarte SeewettAmt — Monatliche Weltkarte. Seewetteramt

Monats — Monatshefte

Monatsb Berl — Monatsberichte der Deutschen Akademie der Wissenschaften zu Berlin

Monatsber Deut Akad Wiss Berlin — Monatsberichte. Deutsche Akademie der Wissenschaften zu Berlin

Monatsber Dtsch Akad Wiss Berl — Monatsberichte. Deutsche Akademie der Wissenschaften zu Berlin

Monatsber Dtschen Bundesbank — Monatsberichte. Deutsche Bundesbank

Monatsber Int Altersforsch Altersbekaempf — Monatsberichte fuer Internationale Altersforschung und Altersbekaempfung

Monatsber Oesterr Inst Wirtsch-Forsch — Monatsberichte. Oesterreichisches Institut fuer Wirtschaftsforschung

Monatsber Verh Ges Erdk Berlin — Monatsberichte ueber die Verhandlungen der Gesellschaft fuer Erdkunde zu Berlin

Monatsblaett Freiheitliche Wirtsch Polit — Monatsblaetter fuer Freiheitliche Wirtschafts-Politik

Monats Blatt Landw Vereins Oberdonau Kreis Koenigr Bayern — Monats-Blatt des Landwirthschaftlichen Vereins fuer den Oberdonau-Kreis im Koenigreiche Bayern

Monatsbl D Deut Reichsverb F Gerichtshilfe — Monatsblaetter des Deutschen Reichsverbands fuer Gerichtshilfe, Gefangenen- und Entlassenenfuersorge

Monats Chem — Monatshefte fuer Chemie

Monatschr Brauwiss — Monatsschrift fuer Brauwissenschaft

Monatschr Geburtsh u Gynak — Monatsschrift fuer Geburtshilfe und Gynaekologie

Monatschr Lungenkrankh Tuberkulosebekaempf — Monatsschrift fuer Lungenkrankheiten und Tuberkulosebekaempfung

Monatschr Ornithol Vivarienkd Ausg B — Monatsschrift fuer Ornithologie und Vivarienkunde. Ausgabe B. Aquarien und Terrarien

Monatschr Psychiat u Neurol — Monatsschrift fuer Psychiatrie und Neurologie

Monatsh Ausw Politik — Monatshefte fuer Auswaertige Politik

Monatsh Chem — Monatshefte fuer Chemie

Monatsh Chem Verw Teile Anderer Wiss — Monatshefte fuer Chemie und Verwandte Teile Anderer Wissenschaften

Monatsh Comen Ges — Monatshefte der Comenius. Gesellschaft

Monatshefte — Monatshefte fuer Deutschen Unterricht. Deutsche Sprache und Literatur

Monatsh Math — Monatshefte fuer Mathematik

Monatsh Math Phys — Monatshefte fuer Mathematik und Physik

Monatsh Montan Hochsch Leoben — Monatshefte fuer der Montanistischen Hochschule in Leoben

Monatsh Naturwiss Unterr Aller Schulgattungen Natur Sch — Monatshefte fuer den Naturwissenschaftlichen Unterricht Aller Schulgattungen und Natur und Schule

Monatsh Prakt Dermat — Monatshefte fuer Praktische Dermatologie

Monatsh Prakt Dermatol — Monatschefte fuer Praktische Dermatologie

Monatsh Prakt Tierh — Monatshefte fuer Praktische Tierheilkunde

Monatsh Seide Kunstseide — Monatshefte fuer Seide und Kunstseide

Monatsh Seide Kunstseide Zellwolle — Monatshefte fuer Seide und Kunstseide. Zellwolle

Monatsh Tierheilkd — Monatshefte fuer Tierheilkunde

Monatsh Vet — Monatshefte fuer Veterinaermedizin

Monatsh Veterinaermed — Monatshefte fuer Veterinaermedizin

Monatsh Veterinarmed — Monatshefte fuer Veterinaermedizin

Monats Kind — Monatsschrift fuer Kinderheilkunde

Monatskurse Aerztl Fortbild — Monatskurse fuer die Aerztliche Fortbildung

Monats Math — Monatshefte fuer Mathematik

Monats Schnellber — Monats-Schnellbericht

Monatsschr Brau — Monatsschrift fuer Brauerei

Monatsschr Brauerei — Monatsschrift fuer Brauerei

Monatsschr Deutsch Kakteen Ges — Monatsschrift der Deutschen Kakteen-Gesellschaft

Monatsschr Dtsch Recht — Monatsschrift fuer Deutsches Recht

Monatsschr Dtsch Zahnarzte Freie Zahnarzt — Monatsschrift Deutscher Zahnarzte der Freie Zahnarzt

Monatsschr Geburshilfe Gynaekol — Monatsschrift fuer Geburtshilfe und Gynaekologie

Monatsschr Kinderheilkd — Monatsschrift fuer Kinderheilkunde

Monatsschr Krebsbekaempf — Monatsschrift fuer Krebsbekaempfung

Monatsschr Lungenkr Tuberk-Bekaempf — Monatsschrift fuer Lungenkrankheiten und Tuberkulose-Bekaempfung

Monatsschr Med — Monatsschrift fuer Medicin, Augenheilkunde, und Chirurgie

Monatsschr Obst Weinbau — Monatsschrift fuer Obst- und Weinbau

Monatsschr Ohrenheilkd Kehlkopf Nasen Rachenkrankh — Monatsschrift fuer Ohrenheilkunde sowie fuer Kehlkopf-, Nasen-,Rachenkrankheiten

Monatsschr Ohrenheilkd Laryngo-Rhinol — Monatsschrift fuer Ohrenheilkunde und Laryngo-Rhinologie

Monatsschr Ornithol Vivarienkd Ausg B Aquarien Terrarien — Monatsschrift fuer Ornithologie und Vivarienkunde. Ausgabe B. Aquarien und Terrarien

Monatsschr Pomol Prakt Obstbau — Monatsschrift fuer Pomologie und Praktischen Obstbau

Monatsschr Psychiatr Neurol — Monatsschrift fuer Psychiatrie und Neurologie

Monatsschr Text Ind — Monatsschrift fuer Textil-Industrie

Monatsschr Text Ind Beil — Monatsschrift fuer Textil-Industrie. Beilage

Monatsschr Unfallheilkd Versicher-Versorg Verkehrsmed — Monatsschrift fuer Unfallheilkunde. Versicherungs-, Versorgungs-, und Verkehrsmedizin

Monatsschr Unfallheilkd — Monatsschrift fuer Unfallheilkunde

Monatsschr Unfallheilkd Versicher Versorg Verkehrsmed — Monatsschrift fuer Unfallheilkunde. Versicherungs-, Versorgungs-, und Verkehrsmedizin

Monats Unfa — Monatsschrift fuer Unfallheilkunde

Mon B — Moniteur Belge

MONBA — Monatsschrift fuer Brauerei

Mon Biblphical Bull Inter Afr Bur Soils Rur Econ — Monthly Bibliographical Bulletin. Inter-African Bureau for Soils and Rural Economy

Mon Biblphy Curr Period Lit Saf Mines Res Test Bd — Monthly Bibliography of Current Periodical Literature. Safety in Mines Research and Testing Board [*Sheffield*]

Mon Biblphy Rlys — Monthly Bibliography of Railways. International Railway Congress

Mon Boica — Monumenta Boica

Mon Bull Agric Econ Statist — Monthly Bulletin of Agricultural Economics and Statistics

Mon Bull Agric Intell Plant Dis — Monthly Bulletin of Agricultural Intelligence and Plant Disease

Mon Bull Agric Intell Pl Dis — Monthly Bulletin of Agricultural Intelligence and Plant Diseases. International Institute of Agriculture

Mon Bull Agric Sci Pract — Monthly Bulletin of Agricultural Science and Practice

Mon Bull Agric Statist Ottawa — Monthly Bulletin of Agricultural Statistics (Ottawa)

Mon Bull Agric Statist Res Toyko — Monthly Bulletin of Agricultural Statistics and Research (Tokyo)

Mon Bull Am Bakers Assoc — Monthly Bulletin. American Bakers Association

Mon Bull Am Iron Steel Inst — Monthly Bulletin of the American Iron and Steel Institute

Mon Bull Ariz St Bd Hlth — Monthly Bulletin of the Arizona State Board of Health

Mon Bull Avic Soc Aust — Monthly Bulletin of the Avicultural Society of Australia

Mon Bull Boston Soc Civ Engrs — Monthly Bulletin of the Boston Society of Civil Engineers

Mon Bull Br Boot Shoe Res Ass — Monthly Bulletin. British Boot Shoe and Allied Trades' Research Association

Mon Bull Br Coal Util Res Ass — Monthly Bulletin. British Coal Utilisation Research Association

Mon Bull Br Iron Steel Fed — Monthly Bulletin. British Iron and Steel Federation

Mon Bull Br Rd Fed — Monthly Bulletin of the British Road Federation

Mon Bull Calif Bd Hlth — Monthly Bulletin. California Board of Health

Mon Bull Calif Commn Hort — Monthly Bulletin. California Commission of Horticulture

Mon Bull Calif Dep Agric — Monthly Bulletin. California Department of Agriculture

Mon Bull Can Inst Min Metall — Monthly Bulletin. Canadian Institute of Mining and Metallurgy

Mon Bull Can Min Inst — Monthly Bulletin. Canadian Mining Institute

Mon Bull Ceram Ind — Monthly Bulletin for the Ceramic Industry

Mon Bull Chabot Obs — Monthly Bulletin. Chabot Observatory

Mon Bull Chicago Munic Tuberc Sanat — Monthly Bulletin of the Chicago Municipal Tuberculosis Sanatorium

Mon Bull Coff Bd Kenya — Monthly Bulletin. Coffee Board of Kenya

Mon Bull Coffee Board Kenya — Monthly Bulletin. Coffee Board of Kenya

Mon Bull Combust Appl Mkrs Ass — Monthly Bulletin. Combustion Appliance Makers' Association [*London*]

Mon Bull Denver Hlth Bur — Monthly Bulletin. Denver Health Bureau

Mon Bull Dep Agric (Calif) — Monthly Bulletin. Department of Agriculture (California)

Mon Bull Dep Hlth Cy NY — Monthly Bulletin of the Department of Health of the City of New York

Mon Bull Dep Publ Hlth Philad — Monthly Bulletin of the Department of Public Health and Charities of the City of Philadelphia

Mon Bull Dep Publ Hlth S Diego — Monthly Bulletin of the Department of Public Health. City of San Diego

Mon Bull Di Cyan Brown — Monthly Bulletin. Di Cyan and Brown

Mon Bull Div Zool Pa Dep Agric — Monthly Bulletin. Division of Zoology. Pennsylvania Department of Agriculture

Mon Bull East Bur L O N Hlth Org — Monthly Bulletin of the Eastern Bureau. League of Nations Health Organisation

Mon Bull Econ Soc Intell — Monthly Bulletin of Economic and Social Intelligence. International Institute of Agriculture

Mon Bull Emerg Publ Hlth Lab Serv — Monthly Bulletin of the Emergency Public Health Laboratory Service [*London*]

Mon Bull Emerg Public Health Lab Serv — Monthly Bulletin. Emergency Public Health Laboratory Service

Mon Bull Emp Inds Ass — Monthly Bulletin. Empire Industries Association [*London*]

Mon Bull Fd Agric Statist — Monthly Bulletin of Food and Agricultural Statistics [*Washington, Rome*]

Mon Bull Fd Drugs Ga — Monthly Bulletin. Food and Drugs. Georgia Department of Agriculture

Mon Bull Fed St Med Bds US — Monthly Bulletin. Federation of State Medical Boards of the undS

Mon Bull Fla St Pl Bd — Monthly Bulletin. Florida State Plant Board

Mon Bull Ga Dep Agric — Monthly Bulletin of the Georgia Department of Agriculture

Mon Bull Glass Ind — Monthly Bulletin for the Glass Industry

Mon Bull Hawaii Volc Obs — Monthly Bulletin. Hawaiian Volcano Observatory

Mon Bull Hlth Anim Brch Dep Agric Can A — Monthly Bulletin. Health of Animals Branch. Department of Agriculture. Canada. A. Contagious Diseases Division

Mon Bull Hlth Anim Brch Dep Agric Can B — Monthly Bulletin. Health of Animals Branch. Department of Agriculture. Canada. B. Meat and Canned Foods Division

Mon Bull Hlth Dep Boston — Monthly Bulletin of the Health Department of the City of Boston

Mon Bull Ill Bd Hlth — Monthly Bulletin. Illinois Board of Health

Mon Bull Ill St Dent Soc — Monthly Bulletin of the Illinois State Dental Society

Mon Bull Imp Mar Lab Kobe — Monthly Bulletin. Imperial Marine Laboratory (Kobe)

Mon Bull Indiana Bd Hlth — Monthly Bulletin. Indiana Board of Health

Mon Bull Inf Int Cargo Handl Coord Ass — Monthly Bulletin of Information. International Cargo Handling Coordination Association

Mon Bull Inf Int Coun Scient Un — Monthly Bulletin of Information. International Council of Scientific Unions

Mon Bull Inf Refrig — Monthly Bulletin of Information on Refrigeration

Mon Bull Inst Med Lab Technol — Monthly Bulletin of the Institute of Medical Laboratory Technology

Mon Bull Int Advis Comm Docum Termin Pure Appl Sci — Monthly Bulletin of the International Advisory Committee on Documentation and Terminology in Pure and Applied Sciences

Mon Bull Int Assoc Refrig — Monthly Bulletin. International Association of Refrigeration

Mon Bull Int Ass Print Ho Craftsm — Monthly Bulletin. International Association of Printing House Craftsmen

Mon Bull Int Fed Agric Prod — Monthly Bulletin. International Federation of Agricultural Producers

Mon Bull Int Railw Congr Assoc — Monthly Bulletin. International Railway Congress Association

Mon Bull Int Railw Congr Assoc (Engl Ed) — Monthly Bulletin. International Railway Congress Association (English Edition)

Mon Bull Int Rly Congr Ass — Monthly Bulletin of the International Railway Congress Association

Mon Bull Int Ry Congr Ass Cybern Electron Ry — Monthly Bulletin. International Railway Congress Association. Cybernetics and Electronics of the Railways

Mon Bull Int Scient Radio Un — Monthly Bulletin of the International Scientific Radio Union

Mon Bull Iran Forest Serv — Monthly Bulletin. Iranian Forest Service

Mon Bull Jap Agric Ass Calif — Monthly Bulletin. Japanese Agricultural Association of California

Mon Bull Kans Cy SW Clin Soc — Monthly Bulletin. Kansas City Southwest Clinical Society

Mon Bull La Bd Hlth — Monthly Bulletin. Louisiana Board of Health

Mon Bull Ld Util Surv Br — Monthly Bulletin. Land Utilisation Survey of Britain [*London*]

Mon Bull Leag Red Cross Socs — Monthly Bulletin. League of Red Cross Societies

Mon Bull Leath Inds Res Inst — Monthly Bulletin. Leather Industries Research Institute

Mon Bull Mass Soc Ment Hyg — Monthly Bulletin. Massachusetts Society for Mental Hygiene

Mon Bull Med Dep Cyprus — Monthly Bulletin of the Medical Department. Cyprus

Mon Bull Miner Inds Lab Columbia — Monthly Bulletin. Mineral Industries Laboratory (Columbia)

Mon Bull Minist Health Emerg Public Health Lab Serv — Monthly Bulletin. Ministry of Health and the Emergency Public Health LaboratoryService

Mon Bull Minist Health Public Health Lab — Monthly Bulletin. Ministry of Health and the Public Health Laboratory

Mon Bull Minist Health Public Health Lab Serv — Monthly Bulletin. Ministry of Health and the Public Health Laboratory Service

Mon Bull Minist Hlth — Monthly Bulletin of the Ministry of Health and Public Health Laboratory Service

Mon Bull Minist Hlth — Monthly Bulletin of the Ministry of Health and the Emergency Public Health Laboratory Service

Mon Bull Minneap Dep Hlth — Monthly Bulletin. Minneapolis Department of Health

Mon Bull Minst Mines Hydrocarbons (Caracas) — Monthly Bulletin. Ministry of Mines and Hydrocarbons (Caracas)

Mon Bull Mo St Bd Agric — Monthly Bulletin. Missouri State Board of Agriculture

Mon Bull Natn Inst Poult Husb — Monthly Bulletin. National Institute of Poultry Husbandry [*Newcastle-upon-Tyne*]

Mon Bull Natn Inst Telecommun Res — Monthly Bulletin. National Institute for Telecommunications Research

Mon Bull Natn Lumber Mfrs Ass — Monthly Bulletin. National Lumber Manufacturers' Association [*Washington*]

Mon Bull Natn Varnish Mfrs Ass — Monthly Bulletin. National Varnish Manufacturers' Association [*Philadelphia*]

Mon Bull Natn Warm Air Heat Vent Ass — Monthly Bulletin of the National Warm Air, Heating, and Ventilating Association [*Columbus, Ohio*]

Mon Bull New Haven Dep Hlth — Monthly Bulletin. New Haven Department of Health

Mon Bull NY Cy Bd Hlth — Monthly Bulletin. New York City Board of Health

Mon Bull NY Fmrs New Jersey Agric Soc — Monthly Bulletin. New York Farmer's and New Jersey Agricultural Society

Mon Bull Path Bact Lab Assts Ass — Monthly Bulletin of the Pathological and Bacteriological Laboratory Assistants' Association

Mon Bull Penrith Distr Nat Hist Soc — Monthly Bulletin. Penrith and District Natural History Society

Mon Bull Philipp Hlth Serv — Monthly Bulletin of the Philippine Health Service

Mon Bull Philipp Weath Bur — Monthly Bulletin. Philippine Weather Bureau

Mon Bull R Alfred Obs — Monthly Bulletin. Royal Alfred Observatory [*Mauritius*]

Mon Bull Schweiz Ver Gas Wasserfachmaennern — Monats-Bulletin des Schweizerischen Vereins von Gas- undWasserfachmaennern

Mon Bull St Bd Hlth Mass — Monthly Bulletin of the State Board of Health of Massachusetts

Mon Bull Swed Engrs Soc Chicago — Monthly Bulletin of the Swedish Engineers Society of Chicago

Mon Bull Tenn Dep Agric — Monthly Bulletin. Tennessee Department of Agriculture

Mon Bull Tsingtao Obs — Monthly Bulletin Tsingtao Observatory

Mon Bull Ulster Agric Org Soc — Monthly Bulletin. Ulster Agricultural Organization Society

Mon Bull West Wash Agric Substn — Monthly Bulletin. Western Washington Agricultural Substation

Mon Bull W Suffolk Agric Educ — Monthly Bulletin. West Suffolk Agricultural Education Committee

Moncalieri Oss Bll — Bullettino Meteorologico dell' Osservatorio del R. Collegio Carlo Alberto in Moncalieri

Mon Carb Black Rep — Monthly Carbon Black Report

Mon Cat US Gov Publ — Monthly Catalog of United States Government Publications

Mon Cat US Gov Publications — Monthly Catalog of United States Government Publications

Mon Checkl State Publ — Monthly Checklist of State Publications

Mon Circ Br Goat Soc — Monthly Circular. British Goat Society

Mon Circ Docum Termin Nat Sci — Monthly Circular on Documentation and Terminology in the Natural Sciences

Mon Circ Exp Res Stn Lea Vall Distr Nurserym Grow Ass — Monthly Circular. Experiment and Research Station. Lea Valley and District Nurseryman's and Grower's Association

Mon Circ Huddersf Nat Soc — Monthly Circular. Huddersfield Naturalists' Society

Mon Circ Inf Dep Agric Fiji — Monthly Circular of Information. Department of Agriculture. Fiji

Mon Circ Leath Inds Res Inst — Monthly Circular. Leather Industries Research Institute

Mon Circ Memb UNESCO Comm Docum Nat Sci — Monthly Circular for Members of UNESCO Committees and Collaborating Bodies Concerned with Documentation of the Natural Sciences

Mon Circ Socs R Photogr Soc — Monthly Circular of Societies Affiliated to the Royal Photographic Society [*London*]

Mon Clim Bull Baghdad — Monthly Climatological Bulletin [*Baghdad*]

Mon Clim Bull Met Inst Athens — Monthly Climatological Bulletin of the Meteorological Institute. National Observatory (Athens)

Mon Clim Data Damascus — Monthly Climatological Data (Damascus)

Mon Clim Data Wld — Monthly Climatic Data for the World by Continents

Mon Clim Summ Manila — Monthly Climatological Summary (Manila)

Mon Coal Bull India — Monthly Coal Bulletin. India

Mon Coal Statist Summ — Monthly Coal Statistical Summary [*Geneva*]

Mon Common Insect Mag — Monthly Common Insect Magazine

Mon Corresp Befoerd Erd Himmelskunde — Monatliche Correspondenz zur Befoerderung der Erd und Himmelskunde

Mon Crop Livestk Rep Toronto — Monthly Crop and Livestock Report (Toronto)

Mon Crop Rep Wash — Monthly Crop Report (Washington, D.C.)

Mon Crop Weath Rep — Monthly Crop Weather Report [*London*]

Mon Crude Refin Rep — Monthly Crude Refinery Report [*Washington*]

Mon Cyclop Med Bull — Monthly Cyclopaedia and Medical Bulletin [*Philadelphia*]

Mon Cyclop Pract Med — Monthly Cyclopaedia of Practical Medicine [*Philadelphia*]

Mon Dairy Rep Toronto — Monthly Dairy Report (Toronto)

Mon Dairy Rev Ottawa — Monthly Dairy Review (Ottawa)

Monda Ling-Prob — Monda Lingvo-Problemo

Monde Agric — Monde Agricole

Monde Alpin Rhod — Monde Alpin et Rhodanien

Monde Alp Rhodan — Monde Alpin et Rhodanien

Monde Apic — Monde Apicole

Monde Avic — Monde Avicole

MondeB — Monde. Hebdomadaire d'Information Litteraire, Artistique, Scientifique, Economique, et Sociale

Monde Colon Illus — Monde Colonial Illustre

Monde de l'Educ — Monde de l'Education

Monde Dent — Monde Dentaire

Monde Dent — Monde Dental

Monde Elect Ind — Monde Electrique et Industriel

MondeF — Mondes Francais

Monde For — Monde Forestier

Monde Fr — Monde Francais

MondeH — Monde (ed. Hebdomadaire)

Monde Illus — Monde Illustre

Monde Ind — Monde Industriel

Monde Iran & Islam — Monde Iranien et l'Islam

MondeL — Monde Libertaire

Mon dell'Inst — Monumenti Annali e Bullettini Pubblicati. Instituto di Correspondenza Archaeologica

Mon dell'Inst — Monumenti Inediti. Pubblicati dell'Instituto di Correspondenza Archeologica

Monde Med — Monde et Medicine

Monde Med (Paris) — Monde Medical (Paris)

Monde Med Pharm — Monde Medical et Pharmaceutique

Monde Miner — Monde et les Mineraux

Monde Min Metall — Monde Minier et Metallurgique

Monde Mod — Monde Moderne

Monde Nouv — Monde Nouveau

Monde Ois — Monde des Oiseaux

Monde Orient — Monde Oriental

Monde Pharm Med — Monde Pharmaceutique et Medical

Monde Pl — Monde des Plantes. Revue Mensuelle de Botanique. Organe. Academie Internationale de Geographie Botanique

Monde Plant — Monde des Plantes

Mondes Asiat — Mondes Asiatiques

Mondes Dev — Mondes en Developpement

Mondes en Develop — Mondes en Developpement

Mondes et Cult — Mondes et Cultures

Mondes et Dev — Mondes et Development

Monde Souterr — Monde Souterrain

Monde Text (Ghent) — Monde Textile (Ghent)

Monde Therm — Monde Thermal

Mondl — Monumenti Annali e Bullettini Pubblicati. Instituto di Correspondenza Archaeologica

Mond I — Monumenti Inediti. Pubblicati. Instituto di Correspondenza Archeologica

Mon Dig Br Leath Mfrs Res Ass — Monthly Digest. British Leather Manufacturers' Research Association

Mon Dig Fed Paint Varn Prod Clubs — Monthly Digest. Federation of Paint and Varnish Production Clubs [*Philadelphia*]

Mond Inst — Monumenti Annali e Bullettini Pubblicati. Instituto di Correspondenza Archaeologica

Mond Inst — Monumenti Inediti. Pubblicati dell'Instituto di Correspondenza Archeologica

MondL — Monumenti Antichi. Accademia Nazionale dei Lincei

Mond Mag — Mond Magazine. Mond Nickel Co.

Mond Nickel Bull — Mond Nickel Bulletin

Mondo Agric — Mondo Agricolo

Mondo Class — Mondo Classico

Mondo Econ — Mondo Economico

Mondo Fin — Mondo Finanziario

Mondo Med — Mondo Medico

Mondo Odontostomatol — Mondo Odontostomatologico

Mondo Ortod — Mondo Ortodontico

Mondo Sotterr — Mondo Sotterraneo

Mondo Sotterraneo Pubbl Nuova Ser — Mondo Sotterraneo. Circolo Speleologico e Idrologico Friulano. Pubblicazione. Nuova Serie

Mondo Tess — Mondo Tessile

Mon Econ Lett — Monthly Economic Letter

Moneda y Cred — Moneda y Credito

Mon Energy Rev — Monthly Energy Review

Mon Epidem Rep L O N — Monthly Epidemiological Report of the Health Section of the Secretariat. League of Nations

Mon E Rap Col — Monitore e Rapporti Coloniali

Moneta e Cred — Moneta e Credito

Mon Etr — Monumenti Etruschi

Mon Even Sky Map — Monthly Evening Sky Map

MonF — Monde Francais

Mon Film Bull — Monthly Film Bulletin of the British Film Institute

Mon Freq Tabl E Afr Met Serv — Monthly Frequency Tables. East African Meteorological Service

Mon Freq Tabl Horiz Visib Pakist — Monthly Frequency Tables on Horizontal Visibility. Pakistan

Mon Freq Tabl Hydrogr Serv Bangkok — Monthly Frequency Tables. Hydrographic Service. Bangkok

Mon Freq Tabl India Met Dep — Monthly Frequency Tables. India Meteorological Department

Mon Freq Tabl Met Brch Aust — Monthly Frequency Tables. Meteorological Branch. Australia

Mon Freq Tabl Met Off Lond — Monthly Frequency Tables. Meteorological Office (London)

Mon Freq Tabl Met Off Un S Afr — Monthly Frequency Tables. Meteorological Office. Union of South Africa

Mon Freq Tabl Pakist Met Dep — Monthly Frequency Tables. Pakistan Meteorological Department

Mon Freq Tabl Pilot Balloon Stns India Met Dep — Monthly Frequency Tables. Pilot Balloon Stations. India Meteorological Department

Mon Freq Tabl Willis Isl — Monthly Frequency Tables. Willis Island. Meteorological Branch. Australia

MONG — Mitteilungen. Oesterreichische Numismatische Gesellschaft

Mon Germ Hist Auct Ant — Monumenta Germaniae Historica. Scriptores. Auctores Antiquissimi

Mon Gr — Monuments Grecs. Association des Etudes Grecques

Mongrafias Inst Eduardo Torroja Constr Cem — Monografias. Instituto Eduardo Torroja de la Construccion y del Cemento

Mong Stud — Mongolian Studies

Mon Health Bull — Monthly Health Bulletin

Mon Homoeop Rev — Monthly Homoeopathic Review [*London*]

Mon In — Monumenti Inediti a Illustrazione della Storia degli Antichi Popoli Italiani

Mon In — Monumenti Inediti. Pubblicati. Instituto di Correspondenza Archeologica

Mon Index Curr Fndry Lit — Monthly Index to Current Foundry Literature. Institute of British Foundrymen

Mon Index Pap Radio Telegr Teleph Scient Press — Monthly Index of Papers on Radio Telegraphy and Telephony Appearing in the Scientific Press

Mon Index Russ Acc Libr Congr — Monthly Index of Russian Accessions. Library of Congress

Mon Inf Bull Caribb Commn — Monthly Information Bulletin of the Caribbean Commission

Mon Inf Scient Mus — Monthly Informations. Scientific Museums

Mon Inf Sh Br Stand Instn — Monthly Information Sheet. British Standards Institution

Mon Inst — Monumenti Annali e Bullettini Pubblicati. Instituto di Correspondenza Archaeologica

Mon Ist — Monumenti Inediti Pubblicati dell'Istituto di Corrispondenza Archeologica

Monit — Moniteur Belge

Monit Afr — Moniteur Africain

Monit Agric Ouest — Moniteur Agricole de l'Ouest

Monit Aliment — Moniteur de l'Alimentation

Monit Archit — Moniteur des Architects

Monit Assess Res Cent Rep — Monitoring and Assessment Research Centre. Report

Monit Belge — Moniteur Belge

Monit Ceram Verr — Moniteur de la Ceramique, de la Verrerie et Journal du C ramiste et du Chaufournier (R unis)

Monit Ceram Verrerie J Ceram Chaufournier Reunis — Moniteur de la Ceramique et de la Verrerie et Journal du Ceramiste et de Chaufournier Reunis

Monit Cordonn Cuir — Moniteur de la Cordonnerie et du Cuir

Monit Educ Comun BA — El Monitor de la Educacion Comun (Buenos Aires)

Monit Elect — Moniteur de l'Electicite

Monit Entrepr Ind — Moniteur de l'Entreprise et de l'Industrie

Moniteur Cer Verrerie — Moniteur de la Ceramique et de la Verrerie

Moniteur Commer Internat — Moniteur du Commerce International

Moniteur Univl — Moniteur Universel

Monit Farm Ter — Monitor de la Farmacia y de la Terapeutica

Monit Fils Tissus — Moniteur des Fils et Tissus, des Apprets et de la Teinture

Monit Gen Quinc Outill — Moniteur General de la Quincaillerie et de l'Outillage

Monit Hop — Moniteur des Hopitaux

Monit Hort Arboric Vitic — Moniteur d'Horticulture, Arboriculture, Viticulture, Sciences, Arts, et Industries Horticoles

Monit Hort Belge — Moniteur Horticole Belge

Monit Hyg Salubr Publique — Moniteur d'Hygiene et de Salubrite Publique

Monit Ind — Moniteur Industriel

Monit Maille — Moniteur de la Maille

Monit Mecn — Moniteur du Mecanicien

Monit Mec Rur — Moniteur de la Mecanique Rurale et la Machine Agricole Moderne

Monit Mol Neurosci Proc Int Conf In Vivo Methods — Monitoring Molecules in Neuroscience. Proceedings. International Conference on In Vivo Methods

Monitore Elettromeop — Monitore dell'Elettromeopatia

Monitore Farm Ag Leoni — Monitore Farmaceutico dell'Agenzia Leoni e De Lorenzo

Monitore Ostet Ginec — Monitore Ostetrico-Ginecologico

Monitore Tec — Monitore Tecnico

Monitore Terap — Monitore Terapeutico

Monitore Zool Ital — Monitore Zoologico Italiano

Monitore Zool Ital Monogr — Monitore Zoologico Italiano [*Italian Journal of Zoology*]. Monografia

Monitor Farm Terap — Monitor de la Farmacia y de la Terapeutica

Monitor For — Monitor Forestier

Monitor Morar — Monitor Morarilor

Monitor Petrol Rom — Monitor Petrolului Roman

Monitor Proc Inst Radio Electron Eng (Aust) — Monitor. Proceedings. Institution of Radio and Electronics Engineers (Australia)

Monitor Sanit — Monitor Sanitario

Monitor Socs Anon Pat Invenc B Aires — Monitor de Sociedades Anonimas y Patentes de Invencion (Buenos Aires)

Monit Ostet-Ginecol — Monitore Ostetrico-Ginecologico

Monit Ostet-Ginecol Endocrinol Metab — Monitore Ostetrico-Ginecologico di Endocrinologia e del Metabolismo

Monit Papet Belge — Moniteur de la Papeterie Belge

Monit Papet Fr — Moniteur de la Papeterie Francaise

Monit Pap Fr — Moniteur de la Papeterie Francaise

Monit Peint — Moniteur de la Peinture

Monit Petrol — Moniteur des Petroles, du Gaz Acetylene, des Huiles Minerales et Vegetales

Monit Pet Roman — Monitorul Petrolului Roman

Monit Pet Roum — Moniteur du Petrole Roumain

Monit Photogr — Moniteur de la Photographie

Monit Poisson — Moniteur du Poisson

Monit Pol — Monitor Polski

Monit Prod Chim — Moniteur des Produits Chimiques

Monit Prof Elect — Moniteur Professionel de l'Electricite

Monit Prof Electr Electron — Moniteur Professionnel de l'Electricite et Electronique

Monit Prog Agric Vitic — Moniteur du Progres Agricole et Viticole

Monit Sci Doct Quesneville — Moniteur Scientifique du Docteur Quesneville

Monit Scient — Moniteur Scientifique

Monit Soies — Moniteur des Soies

Monit Tec — Monitore Tecnico

Monit Tein Apprets Impress Tissus — Moniteur de la Teinture des Apprets et de l'Impression des Tissus

Monit Teint — Moniteur de la Teinture et de l'Impression des Tissus

Monit Ther — Moniteur Therapeutique, Recueil des Medications Nouvelles

Monit Tiss Mec — Moniteur du Tissage Mecanique

Monit Trav Publ Batim — Moniteur des Travaux Publics et du Batiment

Monit Trav Publics Batim — Moniteur des Travaux Publics et du Batiment

Monit Zool Ital — Monitore Zoologico Italiano

Monit Zool Ital/Ital J Zool New Ser — Monitore Zoologico Italiano/Italian Journal of Zoology. New Series

Monit Zool Ital/Ital J Zool New Ser Suppl — Monitore Zoologico Italiano/Italian Journal of Zoology. New Series. Supplement

Monit Zool Ital Monogr — Monitore Zoologico Italiano [*Italian Journal of Zoology*]. Monografia

Monit Zool Ital Suppl — Monitore Zoologico Italiano [*Italian Journal of Zoology*]. Supplemento

Mon J Br Goat Soc — Monthly Journal. British Goat Society

Mon J Chamb Mines West Aust — Monthly Journal. Chamber of Mines. Western Australia

Mon J Elect Commun Lab Tokyo — Monthly Journal of the Electrical Communication Laboratory (Tokyo)

Mon J Engrs Club Baltimore — Monthly Journal of the Engineers' Club of Baltimore

Mon J Inst Ind Sci Tokyo — Monthly Journal. Institute of Industrial Science. University of Tokyo

Mon J Inst Ind Sci Univ Tokyo — Monthly Journal. Institute of Industrial Science. University of Tokyo

Mon J Inst Metals — Monthly Journal. Institute of Metals

Mon J Psychiatry Neurol — Monthly Journal of Psychiatry and Neurology

Mon Labor Rev — Monthly Labor Review

Mon Lab Re — Monthly Labor Review

Mon Law Mag — Monthly Law Magazine

Mon Law Rep — Monthly Law Reporter

Mon Lett Bur Agric Res Econ Armour & Co — Monthly Letter. Bureau of Agricultural Research and Economics. Armour and Company

Mon Lett Rothamsted Exp Stn — Monthly Letter. Rothamsted Experimental Station. Imperial Bureau of Soil Science

Mon Linc — Monumenti Antichi. Accademia Nazionale dei Lincei

Mon Lincei — Monumenti Antichi. Accademia Nazionale dei Lincei

Mon List Acc Sci Mus Libr — Monthly List of Accessions. Science Museum Library [*London*]

Mon List Geogr Publs — Monthly List of Geographical Publications [*Buffalo*]

Mon List Publs US Dep Agric — Monthly List of Publications. US Department of Agriculture. Division of Publications

Mon L R — Monash University. Law Review

Mon L Rev — Monash University. Law Review

Mon L Rev — Montana Law Review

Mon Mag Circ N Engl Hort Soc — Monthly Magazine and Circular. North of England Horticultural Society

Mon Mag Pharm Chem Med — Monthly Magazine of Pharmacy, Chemistry, Medicine [*London*]

Mon Means Br W Afr Met Serv — Monthly Means. British West African Meteorological Service

Mon Means Certain Stns E Afr Met Serv — Monthly Means at Certain Stations. East African Meteorological Service

Mon Means Met Sect Kuwait — Monthly Means. Meteorological Section. Government Research Station. Kuwait

Mon Means Pilot Balloon Data Pakist — Monthly Means of Pilot Balloon Data. Pakistan

Mon Memor Paint Res Stn (Taddington) — Monthly Memorandum. Paint Research Station (Taddington)

Mon Memor Tech Serv Libr — Monthly Memorandum. Technical Service Library [*London*]

Mon Met Bull Bangkok — Monthly Meteorological Bulletin (Bangkok)

Mon Met Bull Canton — Monthly Meteorological Bulletin (Canton)

Mon Met Bull Inst Met Pei Chi Ko — Monthly Meteorological Bulletin. Institute of Meteorology (Pei-Chi-Ko)

Mon Met Bull Liberia — Monthly Meteorological Bulletin. Liberia Meteorological Service

Mon Met Bull Nanking — Monthly Meteorological Bulletin (Nanking)

Mon Met Bull R Obs Hongkong — Monthly Meteorological Bulletin. Royal Observatory (Hongkong)

Mon Met Charts Indian Ocean — Monthly Meteorological Charts of the Indian Ocean (East Indian Seas) [*London*]

Mon Met Charts N Atlant Mediterr — Monthly Meteorological Charts of the North Atlantic and Mediterranean [*London*]

Mon Met Data Ten Degr Sq Atlant Indian Oceans — Monthly Meteorological Data for Ten-Degree Squares in the Atlantic and Indian Oceans [*Utrecht*]

Mon Met Data Ten Degr Sq Oceans — Monthly Meteorological Data for Ten-Degree Squares in the Oceans [*Utrecht*]

Mon Met Rep Balboa Hts — Monthly Meteorological Report. Balboa Heights [*Canal Zone*]

Mon Met Return Br N Borneo — Monthly Meteorological Return. British North Borneo

Mon Met Return Dar Es Salaam — Monthly Meteorological Return. Dar-es-Salaam

Mon Met Return Nth Nigeria — Monthly Meteorological Return. Principal Medical Officer. Northern Nigeria

Mon Met Summ Apia Obs — Monthly Meteorological Summary. Apia Observatory [*Samoa*]

Mon Met Summ Aviat Bangkok — Monthly Meteorological Summary for Aviation (Bangkok)

Mon Met Summ Calgary — Monthly Meteorological Summary. Calgary

Mon Met Summ Toronto — Monthly Meteorological Summary. Toronto

Mon Met Summ Weath Bur Off St Louis — Monthly Meteorological Summary. Weather Bureau Office. St. Louis, Missouri

Mon Min Handb — Monthly Mining Handbook [*London*]

Monmouth Ant — Monmouthshire Antiquary

Monmouth County Med Soc Newsletter — Monmouth County Medical Society. Newsletter

Monmouth Hist — Monmouth Historian

Monmouth Rev — Monmouth Review

Monmouthshire Ant — Monmouthshire Antiquary. Proceedings. Monmouthshire and Caerleon Antiquarian Society

Monmouthshire Antiq — Monmouthshire Antiquary

MonN — Monumenta Nipponica

Mon Nat Gasol Rep — Monthly Natural Gasoline Report. US Bureau of Mines [*Washington*]

Mon News Bull Tex Dep Agric — Monthly News Bulletin of the Texas Department of Agriculture

Mon Newsl Civ Aviat India — Monthly Newsletter on Civil Aviation in India

Mon Newsl Div Forest Prod CSIR Aust — Monthly Newsletter. Division of Forest Products. Council for Scientific and Industrial Research. Australia

Mon Newsl NZ Forest Serv — Monthly Newsletter. New Zealand Forest Service

Mon News Serv Int Fed Agric — Monthly News Service. International Federation of Agricultural Producers

Monn Gr — Monnaies Grecques

Mon Nipp — Monumenta Nipponica

Mon Not — Moniteur du Notariat et de l'Enregistrement. Journal de Legislation et de Jurisprudence

Mon Not Astron Soc S Afr — Monthly Notes. Astronomical Society of Southern Africa

Mon Not Astr Soc India — Monthly Notices of the Astronomical Society of India

Mon Notes Astron Soc South Afr — Monthly Notes. Astronomical Society of Southern Africa

Mon Notes Astr Soc Sth Afr — Monthly Notes of the Astronomical Society of Southern Africa

Mon Notes R Bot Gdn Edinb — Monthly Notes. Royal Botanic Garden. Edinburgh

Mon Notes Util Duck Club — Monthly Notes. Utility Duck Club [*Portishead*]

Mon Not Pap R Soc Tasmania — Monthly Notices of Papers. Royal Society of Tasmania

Mon Not R Astron Soc — Monthly Notices. Royal Astronomical Society

Mon Not R Astr Soc — Monthly Notices of the Royal Astronomical Society [*London*]

Mon Not R Astr Soc Geophys Suppl — Monthly Notices of the Royal Astronomical Society. Geophysical Supplement [*London*]

Mon Not Roy Astron Soc — Monthly Notices. Royal Astronomical Society

Monogr Acad Ci Exact Fis Quim Nat Zaragoza — Monografias de la Academia de Ciencias Exactas, Fisicas, Quimicas, y Naturales de Zaragoza

Monogr Acad Nat Sci Phila — Monographs. Academy of Natural Sciences of Philadelphia

Monogr Acad Nat Sci Philad — Monographs. Academy of Natural Sciences of Phiadelphia

Monografias Dep Agric Com P Rico — Monografias del Departamento de Agricultura y Comercio. Puerto Rico

Monografias Div Geol Miner Bras — Monografias do Divisao Geologico e Mineralogico. Ministeria de Agricultura. Brasil

Monografias Fac Cienc Mat Fis Quim Nat Ind Univ Nac Litoral — Monografias Publicadas por la Facultad de Ciencia Matematicas, Fisico-Quimicas y Naturales Aplicadas a la Industria. Universidad Nacional del Litoral

Monografias Geol Univ Oviedo — Monografias Geologicas. Instituto de Geologia. Universidad de Oviedo

Monografias Inst Antonio Aurelio Costa Ferriera — Monografias do Instituto Antonio Aurelio da Costa Ferriera

Monografias Inst Biol Univ Nac Mex — Monografias del Instituto de Biologia. Universidad Nacional (Mexico)

Monografias Inst Butantan — Monografias do Instituto Butantan [*Sao Paulo*]

Monografias Inst Estud Geogr Univ Nac Tucuman — Monografias del Instituto de Estudios Geograficos. Universidad Nacional (Tucuman)

Monografias Inst Geofis Univ Nac Mex — Monografias del Instituto de Geofisica, Universidad Nacional Autonoma de Mexico

Monografias Inst Hyg Secc Parasit Mex — Monografias del Instituto de Hygiene. Seccion de Parasitologia. Departamento de Salubridad Publica de la Republica Mexicana

Monografias Inst Oswaldo Cruz — Monografias do Instituto Oswaldo Cruz

Monografias Inst Salubr Enferm Trop Mex — Monografias do Instituto de Salubridad y Enfermedades Tropicales (Mexico)

Monografias Inst Tec Constr Cem — Monografias Instituto Tecnico de la Construccion del Cemento

Monografias Lab Biol Mar Havana — Monografias. Laboratorio de Biologia Marina. Universidad Catolica de Santo Tomas de Villanereva (Havana)

Monografias Serv Geol Minas Geraes — Monografias do Servico Geologico. Estado de Minas Geraes

Monografie Dziej Nauki Tech — Monografie z Dziejow Nauki I Techniki

Monografie Geofis — Monografie di Geofisica

Monografie Mat — Monografie Matematyczne

Monografie Nauk Panst Rada Ochr Przyr — Monografie Naukowe. Panstwowa Rada Ochrony Przyrody

Monografie R Com Talassogr Ital — Monografie. Reale Comitato Talassografico Italiano

Monografie Scient Aeronaut — Monografie Scientifiche di Aeronautica

Monografie Scient Aeronaut Suppl Tec — Monografie Scientifiche di Aeronautica. Supplementi Tecnici

Monografie Tecnol Staz Sper Ind Conserve Aliment — Monografie di Tecnologia della Stazione Sperimentale per l'Industria delle Conserve Alimentari

Monografii Fiz — Monografii de Fizica

Monografii Inst Cerc Pisc Rom — Monografii. Institutul de Cercetari Piscicole al Romaniei

Monografii Kom Izuch Estestv Proizvod Sil Ross — Monografii, Izdavaemyya Komissiei po Izucheniyu Estestvennykh Proizvoditel'nykh sil Rossii

Monografii Med — Monografii Medicale [*Bucuresti*]

Monografii Paleont — Monografii po Paleontologii SSSR

Monografii Volzh Biol Sta Saratov — Monografii Volzhskoi Biologischeskoi Stantsii Saratovskogo Obshchestva Estestvoispytatelei (Saratov)

Monografije Seizm Zav — Monografije. Seizmoloski Zavod FNR Jugoslavije u Beogradu

Monografine Ser Geol Geogr Inst — Monografine Serija. Geologijos in Geografijos Institutas [*Vilnius*]

Monograf Inst Mat — Monografias. Instituto de Matematicas

Monograf Mat — Monografie Matematyczne

Monograf Math — Monografias de Matematica

Monograf Mat Pura Apl — Monografias de Matematicas Pura e Aplicada

Monograf Psych — Monografie Psychologiczne

Monograf Sec Cien — Monografies de la Seccio de Ciencies

Monograf Soc Paranaense Mat — Monografias da Sociedade Paranaense de Matematica

Monograf Soc Paran Mat — Monografias da Sociedade Paranaense de Matematica

Monogr Allergy — Monographs in Allergy

Monogr Am Assoc Ment Defic — Monographs. American Association on Mental Deficiency

Monogr Am Assoc Ment Retard — Monographs. American Association on Mental Retardation

Monogr Am Coll Nutr — Monographs. American College of Nutrition

Monogr Amer Phytopathol Soc — Monograph. American Phytopathological Society

Monogr Am Ethnol Soc — Monographs. American Ethnological Society

Monogr Am Fish Soc — Monograph. American Fisheries Society

Monogr Am Heart Ass — Monographs. American Heart Association

Monogr Am Mus Nat Hist — Monographs of the American Museum of Natural History

Monogr Am Oil Chem Soc — Monograph. American Oil Chemists' Society

Monogr Am Soc Agron — Monographs. American Society of Agronomy

Monogr Am Soc Mammal — Monographs. American Society of Mammalogists

Monogr Am Soc Pl Physiol — Monographs. American Society of Plant Physiologists

Monogr Anaesthesiol — Monographs in Anaesthesiology

Monogr Anal — Monographs in Analysis

Monogr Angew Entomol — Monographien zur Angewandten Entomologie

Monogr Ann Radiol — Monographies des Annales de Radiologie

Monogr Annu Soc Fr Biol Clin — Monographie Annuelle. Societe Francaise de Biologie Clinique

Monograph Br Crop Prot Counc — Monograph. British Crop Protection Council

Monograph Enseign Math — Monographies de l'Enseignement Mathematique

Monographiae Act Derm — Monographiae Actorum Dermatologicorum

Monographiae Biol — Monographiae Biologicae

Monographiae Bot — Monographiae Botanicae

Monographieen Rijksinst Pharm Ther Onderz — Monographieen van het Rijksinstituut voor Pharmaco-Therapeutisch Onderzoek

Monographies A Belge — Monographies de l'Art Belge

Monograph Linguist Math — Monographies de Linguistique Mathematique

Monograph Math — Monographies de Mathematique

Monograph Modernen Math — Monographien zur Modernen Mathematik

Monograph Rep Ser Inst Metals — Monograph and Report Series. Institute of Metals [*London*]

Monographs Adv Texts Surveys Pure Appl Math — Monographs, Advanced Texts, and Surveys in Pure and Applied Mathematics

Monographs by the Bibliogr Soc — Monographs by the Bibliographic Society

Monograph Sci Maison Franco-Japon — Monographies Scientifiques de la Maison Franco-Japonaise

Monograph Ser Am Ass Cereal Chem — Monograph Series. American Association of Cereal Chemists

Monograph Ser Am Ass Conserv Vision — Monograph Series. American Association for the Conservation of Vision

Monograph Ser Am Chem Soc — Monograph Series. American Chemical Society

Monograph Ser Am J Hyg — Monograph Series. American Journal of Hygiene

Monograph Ser Am Boston Psychoanal Soc — Monograph Series. Boston Psychoanalytic Society

Monograph Ser Egypt Soc Gynaec Obstet — Monograph Series. Egyptian Society of Gynaecology and Obstetrics

Monograph Ser NY Cy Hlth Dep — Monograph Series of the New York City Health Department

Monograph Ser Res Inst Appl Elect Hokkaido Univ — Monograph Series of the Research Institute of Applied Electricity. Hokkaido University

Monograph Ser Soviet Union — Monograph Series on Soviet Union

Monograph Ser St Etnogr Mus Stockh — Monograph Series. Statens Etnografiska Museum (Stockholm)

Monograph Ser Utah St Agric Coll — Monograph Series. Utah State Agricultural College

Monograph Ser Utah St Univ — Monograph Series. Utah State University

Monograph Ser WHO — Monograph Series. World Health Organisation

Monographs Phys Chem Mater — Monographs on the Physics and Chemistry of Materials

Monographs Population Biol — Monographs in Population Biology

Monographs Statist Appl Probab — Monographs on Statistics and Applied Probability

Monographs Stud Math — Monographs and Studies in Mathematics

Monographs Surveys Water Res Engrg — Monographs and Surveys in Water Resource Engineering

Monographs Textbooks Mech Solids Fluids Mech Anal — Monographs and Textbooks on Mechanics of Solids and Fluids. Mechanics Analysis

Monographs Textbooks Mech Solids Fluids Mech Continua — Monographs and Textbooks on Mechanics of Solids and Fluids. Mechanics of Continua

Monographs Textbooks Mech Solids Fluids Mech Dynam Systems — Monographs and Textbooks on Mechanics of Solids and Fluids. Mechanics of Dynamical Systems

Monographs Textbooks Mech Solids Fluids Mech Fluids Transport — Monographs and Textbooks on Mechanics of Solids and Fluids. Mechanics of Fluidsand Transport Processes

Monographs Textbooks Mech Solids Fluids Mech Genesis Method — Monographs and Textbooks on Mechanics of Solids and Fluids. Mechanics of Genesis and Method

Monographs Textbooks Mech Solids Fluids Mech Plastic Solids — Monographs and Textbooks on Mechanics of Solids and Fluids. Mechanics of Plastic Solids

Monographs Textbooks Phys Sci — Monographs and Textbooks in Physical Science

Monographs Textbooks Phys Sci Lecture Notes — Monographs and Textbooks in Physical Science. Lecture Notes

Monographs Textbooks Pure Appl Math — Monographs and Textbooks in Pure and Applied Mathematics

Monograph Wissenschaftstheorie Grundlagenforsch — Monographien zur Wissenschaftstheorie und Grundlagenforschung

Monogr Appl Toxicol — Monographs in Applied Toxicology

Monogr Atheroscler — Monographs on Atherosclerosis

Monogr Baker Inst Med Res — Monographs of the Baker Institute of Medical Research</PHR> %

Monogr Bd Scient Ind Res Palest — Monographs. Board of Scientific and Industrial Research. Palestine

Monogr Bell Telph Syst — Monographs. Bell Telephone System

Monogr Biochem — Monografie Biochemiczne

Monogr Biol — Monographiae Biologicae

Monogr Biol Soc Pakist — Monographs. Biological Society of Pakistan

Monogr BIPM — Monographie. BIPM

Monogr Bldg Res Inst Wash — Monographs. Building Research Institute. National Research Council (Washington)

Monogr Bot — Monographiae Botanicae

Monogr Br Crop Prot Counc — Monograph. British Crop Protection Council

Monogr Br Plant Growth Regul Group — Monograph. British Plant Growth Regulator Group

Monogr Calif Policy Semin — Monograph. California Policy Seminar

Monogr Cent Actual Sci Tech INSA — Monographies. Centre d'Actualisation Scientifique et Technique de l'INSA

Monogr Chem Tech Lab Gwalior — Monographs from the Chemical and Technical Laboratory. Gwalior

Monogr Clin Cytol — Monographs in Clinical Cytology

Monogr Clin Neurol Neurosurg — Monographs on Clinical Neurology and Neurosurgery

Monogr Clin Neurosci — Monographs in Clinical Neuroscience

Monogr Com Invest Cient Prov Buenos Aires — Monografias. Comision de Investigaciones Cientificas de la Provincia deBuenos Aires

Monogr Comput Sci — Monographs in Computer Science

Monogr Conserv Coun Tex Acad Sci — Monographs. Conservation Council. Texas Academy of Science

Monogr Contemp Math — Monographs in Contemporary Mathematics

Monogr Dep Zool Univ Sydney — Monographs. Department of Zoology. University of Sydney

Monogr Dev Biol — Monographs in Developmental Biology

Monogr Dev Pediatr — Monographs in Developmental Pediatrics

Monogr Dir Geol Min Uttar Pradesh — Monograph. Directorate of Geology and Mining. Uttar Pradesh

Monogr Div Geol Mineral (Braz) — Monografia. Divisao de Geologia e Mineralogia (Brazil)

Monogr Drugs — Monographs on Drugs

Monogr Econ Dev — Monographs in the Economics of Development

Monogr Endocrinol — Monographs on Endocrinology

Monogr Epidemiol Biostat — Monographs in Epidemiology and Biostatistics

Monogr Eur Brew Conv — Monograph. European Brewery Convention

Monogr Fauny Pol — Monografie Fauny Polski

Monogr Fd Res Ass — Monographs. Food Research Association

Monogr Fed Coun Br Med Coun Aust — Monographs of the Federal Council of the British Medical Council in Australia

Monogr Fetal Physiol — Monographs in Fetal Physiology

Monogr Forschungszent Juelich — Monographien des Forschungszentrums Juelich

Monogr Franklin Inst Penn — Monographs. Franklin Institute of the State of Pennsylvania for the Promotion of Mechanic Arts

Monogr Genet Agrar — Monografie di Genetica Agraria

Monogr Geol Dep Hunter Mus — Monographs of the Geological Department of the Hunterian Museum

Monogr Geol Surv Ala — Monographs of the Geological Survey of Alabama

Monogr Geol Surv Alabama — Monograph. Geological Survey of Alabama

Monogr Geol Surv Ill — Monographs of the Geological Survey of Illinois

Monogr Geom Topology — Monographs in Geometry and Topology

Monogr Georgetown Coll Obs — Monographs. Georgetown College Observatory

Monogr Gesamtgeb Neurol Psychiatr — Monographien. Gesamtgebiete der Neurologie und Psychiatrie

Monogr Gesamtgeb Psychiatr — Monographien. Gesamtgebiete der Psychiatrie

Monogr Gesamtgeb Psychiatr (Berlin) — Monographien. Gesamtgebiete der Psychiatrie. Psychiatry Series (Berlin)

Monogr Giovanni Lorenzini Found — Monographs. Giovanni Lorenzini Foundation

Monogr Glass Technol — Monographs on Glass Technology

Monogr Groupe Etude Main — Monographies. Groupe d'Etude de la Main

Monogr Harmon Anal — Monographs in Harmonic Analysis

Monogr Hist Cult — Monographs in History and Culture

Monogr Hum Genet — Monographs in Human Genetics

Monogr Hunter Valley Res Fdn — Monograph. Hunter Valley Research Foundation

Monogr Hunter Valley Res Found — Monograph. Hunter Valley Research Foundation

Monogr Illum Engng Soc — Monographs. Illuminating Engineering Society

Monogr Indian Geogr Soc — Monographs. Indian Geographical Society

Monogr INIA — Monografias. INIA

Monogr Inst Butantan (Sao Paulo) — Monografias. Instituto Butantan (Sao Paulo)

Monogr Inst Eduardo Torroja Constr Cem — Monografias. Instituto Eduardo Torroja de la Construccion y delCemento

Monogr Inst Estud Geogr — Monografias del Instituto de Estudios Geograficos

Monogr Inst Oswaldo Cruz (Rio De J) — Monografias. Instituto Oswaldo Cruz (Rio De Janeiro)

Monogr Inst Soc Hist Med — Monographs. Institute on Social and Historical Medicine

Monogr Int Un Geod Geophys — Monographs. International Union of Geodesy and Geophysics

Monogr Kans Agric Exp Stn — Monograph. Kansas Agricultural Experiment Station

Monogr Koebenhavns Univ H C Oersted Inst Fys Lab — Monograph. Koebenhavns Universitet. H. C. Oersted Institutet. FysiskLaboratorium

Monogr Lav Neuropsichiatr — Monografie de il Lavoro Neuropsichiatrico

Monogr Mar Mollusca — Monographs of Marine Mollusca

Monogr Mat — Monografie Matematyczne

Monogr Mater Soc — Monographs in Materials and Society

Monogr Math Phys Tata Inst — Monographs on Mathematics and Physics. Tata Institute of Fundamental Research

Monogr Med Baltimore — Monographs in Medicine (Baltimore)

Monogr Med Publ Hlth Harvard — Monographs in Medicine and Public Health. Harvard University

Monogr Med Sci — Monographies Medicales et Scientifiques

Monogr Med Univ Chicago — Monographs in Medicine. University of Chicago

Monogr Memo Natl Res Inst Mach Des (Bechovice Czech) — Monographs and Memoranda. National Research Institute for Machine Design (Bechovice, Czechoslovakia)

Monogr Metallic Mater — Monographs on Metallic Materials. Royal Aeronautical Society of Great Britain [London]

Monogr Mineral Soc — Monograph. Mineralogical Society

Monogr Miner Resour — Monographs on Mineral Resources. Imperial Institute [London]

Monogr Mod Chem — Monographs in Modern Chemistry

Monogr MS Cem Res Inst India — Monograph MS. Cement Research Institute of India

Monogrn Abh Int Revue Ges Hydrobiol Hydrogr — Monographien und Abhandlungen zur Internationalen Revue der Gesamten Hydrobiologie

Monogrn Afr PflFam U Gatt — Monographien Afrikanischer Pflanzenfamilien und Gattungen

Monogrn Angew Chem — Monographien zu Angewandte Chemie und Chemie-Ingenieur-Technik

Monogrn Angew Elektrochem — Monographien uber Angewandte Elektrochemie

Monogrn Angew Ent — Monographien zur Angewandten Entomologie

Monogr Natl Bur Stand (US) — Monograph. National Bureau of Standards (United States)

Monogr Natl Cancer Inst — Monographs. National Cancer Institute

Monogrn Chem Appar — Monographien zur Chemischen Apparatur

Monogrn Chem Tech Fabr Meth — Monographien uber Chemisch-Technische Fabrikationsmethoden

Monogr Ned Entomol Ver — Monografieen van de Nederlandse Entomologische Vereniging

Monogrn Einheim Tiere — Monographien Einheimischer Tiere

Monogr Neoplast Dis Various Sites — Monographs on Neoplastic Disease at Various Sites

Monogrn Erdk — Monographien zur Erdkunde

Monogr Neural Sci — Monographs in Neural Sciences

Monogrn Exp Theor Phys — Monographien der Experimentellen und Theoretischen Physik

Monogrn Feuer Tech — Monographien zur Feuerungstechnik

Monogrn Frauenk — Monographien zur Frauenkunde und Eugenetik und Konstitutionsforschung, Sexualbiologie und Vererbungslehre

Monogrn Geb Fettchem — Monographien aus dem Gebiete de Fettchemie

Monogrn Geol Palaeont — Monographien zur Geologie und Palaeontologie

Monogrn Gesamtgeb Ent — Monographien aus dem Gesamtgebiet der Entomologie

Monogrn Gesamtgeb Neurol Psychiat — Monographien aus dem Gesamtgebiet der Neurologie u. Psychiatrie

Monogrn Gesamtgeb Physiol Pfl Tiere — Monographien aus dem Gesamtgebiet der Physiologie der Pflanzen und der Tiere

Monogrn Gesamtgeb Wiss Bot — Monographien aus dem Gesamtgebiet der Wissenschaftlichen Botanik

Monogrn Gesch Chem — Monographien aus der Geschichte der Chemie

Monogrn KautschTech — Monographien zur Kautschuktechnik

Monogrn Kunstgew — Monographien des Kunstgewerbes

Monogrn Landw Nutztiere — Monographien Landwirtschaftlicher Nutztiere

Monogrn PflSchutz — Monographien zum Pflanzenschutz

Monogr Nucl Med Biol — Monographs on Nuclear Medicine and Biology

Monogr Nucl Med Biol Ser — Monographs on Nuclear Medicine and Biology Series

Monogr Numer Anal — Monographs on Numerical Analysis

Monogrn Voelkerk — Monographien zur Voelkerkunde

Monogrn Wildsaeugetiere — Monographien der Wildsaeugetiere

Monogr Oceanogr Methodol — Monographs on Oceanographic Methodology

Monogr Ophthalmol — Monographs in Ophthalmology

Monogr Oral Sci — Monographs in Oral Science

Monogr Paediatr — Monographs in Paediatrics

Monogr Parazytol — Monografie Parazytologiczne

Monogr Pathol — Monographs in Pathology

Monogr Percy Fitzpatrick Inst Afr Ornithol — Monographs. Percy Fitzpatrick Institute of African Ornithology

Monogr Pharmacol Physiol — Monographs in Pharmacology and Physiology

Monogr Phys Chem Mater — Monographs on the Physics and Chemistry of Materials

Monogr Physiol Causale — Monographie de Physiologie Causale

Monogr Physiol Soc — Monographs. Physiological Society

Monogr Physiol Soc Phila — Monographs. Physiological Society of Philadelphia

Monogr Physiol Soc Philadelphia — Monographs. Physiological Society of Philadelphia

Monogr Physiol Veg — Monographies de Physiologie Vegetale

Monogr Plast — Monographs on Plastics

Monogr Politech Krakow Im Tadeusza Kosciuszki — Monografia. Politechnika Krakowska Imeni Tadeusza Kosciuszki

Monogr Popul Biol — Monographs in Population Biology

Monogr Primatol — Monographs in Primatology

Monogr Programa Reg Desarrollo Cient Tecnol Ser Biol — Monografia. Programa Regional de Desarrollo Cientifico y Tecnologico.Serie de Biologia

Monogr Programa Reg Desarrollo Cient Tecnol Ser Fis — Monografia. Programa Regional de Desarrollo Cientifico y Tecnologico.Serie de Fisica

Monogr Programa Reg Desarrollo Cient Tecnol Ser Quim — Monografia. Programa Regional de Desarrollo Cientifico y Tecnologico.Serie de Quimica

Monogr Psychiatr Clin Helsinki Univ Cent Hosp — Monographs. Psychiatric Clinic. Helsinki University Central Hospital

Monogr Psychiatr Fenn — Monographs of Psychiatria Fennica

Monogr Quekett Microsc Club — Monographs. Quekett Microscopical Club

Monogr Radiol — Monographies de Radiologie

Monogr Rep Ser Inst Met (London) — Monograph and Report Series. Institute of Metals (London)

Monogr Roger Williams Park Mus — Monographs of the Roger Williams Park Museum

Monogr R Soc NSW — Monograph. Royal Society of New South Wales

Monogr Rutgers Cent Alcohol Stud — Monographs. Rutgers Center of Alcohol Studies

Monogr Saito Ho On Kai — Monographs. Saito Ho-on Kai

Monogr Saito Ho On Kai Repr Ser — Monographs. Saito Ho-on Kai. Reprint Series

Monogrs Cent Natn Rech Agron — Monographies. Centre National de Recherches Agronomiques

Monogr Sch Am Res Santa Fe — Monographs of the School of American Research (Santa Fe, Mexico)

Monogr Semicond Phys — Monographs in Semiconductor Physics

Monogr Ser Am Assoc Cereal Chem — Monograph Series. American Association of Cereal Chemists

Monogr Ser Australas Inst Min Metall — Monograph Series. Australasian Institute of Mining and Metallurgy

Monogr Ser Eur Organ Res Treat Cancer — Monograph Series. European Organization for Research on Treatment ofCancer

Monogr Ser Inst Bot Acad Sin — Monograph Series. Institute of Botany. Academia Sinica

Monogr Ser Int Brain Res Organ — Monograph Series. International Brain Research Organization

Monogr Ser Int Conf Coord Chem — Monograph Series of the International Conferences on Coordination Chemistry held Periodically at Smolenice in Slovakia

Monogr Ser Miner Deposits — Monograph Series on Mineral Deposits

Monogr Ser Nat Sci Bull Coll Sci Sun Yatsen Univ — Monographic Series. Natural Sciences Bulletin. College of Science. Sun Yatsen University/Kuo Li Chung Shan Ta Hsueeh Tzu Jan K'o Hsueeh K'o

Monogr Ser Res Inst Appl Electr Hokkaido Univ — Monograph Series. Research Institute of Applied Electricity. Hokkaido University

Monogr Ser Text Inst (Manchester UK) — Monograph Series. Textile Institute (Manchester, UK)

Monogr Ser Weed Sci Soc Am — Monograph Series. Weed Science Society of America

Monogrs Inst Interuniv Sci Nucl — Monographies. Institut Interuniversitaire des Science Nucleaires

Monogrs Inst Pasteur — Monographies de l'Institut Pasteur

Monogrs Med Scient — Monographies Medicales et Scientifiques

Monogrs Met Natn — Monographies de la Meteorologie Nationale

Monogrs Obs R Belg — Monographies. Observatoire Reale de Belgique

Monogr Soc Anal Chem — Monograph. Society for Analytical Chemistry

Monogr Soc Anthrop — Monographs on Social Anthropology

Monogr Soc Appl Anthrop — Monographs. Society for Applied Anthropology

Monogr Soc Chem Ind (London) — Monograph. Society of Chemical Industry (London)

Monogr Soc Ind Appl Math — Monographs of the Society for Industrial and Applied Mathematics

Monogr Soc Res Child Dev — Monographs. Society for Research in Child Development

Monogrs Reg Inst Rech Sahar — Monographies Regionales. Institut de Recherches Sahariennes

Monogrs Revue Chim Ind — Monographies de la Revue de Chimie Industrielle

Monogr Srpska Akad Nauka — Monografii Srpska Akademija Nauka

Monogrs Sect Seism UGGI — Monographie. Section de Seismologie. Union Geodesique et Geophysique Internationale

Monogr Steel Cast Res Trade Assoc — Monograph. Steel Castings Research and Trade Association

Monogrs Trav Scient Com Natn Roy Serb Sect Seism — Monographies et Travaux Scientifiques du Comite National do Royaume des Serbes, Croates, et Slovenes, Section de Seismologie

Monogr Stud Entomol — Monographs. Studies in Entomology

Monogr Stud Inst Phys — Monographs for Students. Institute of Physics

Monogr Suppl J Speech Hear Disorders — Monograph Supplements. Journal of Speech and Hearing Disorders

Monogr Surg — Monographs on Surgery

Monogr Surg Sc — Monographs in the Surgical Sciences

Monogr Surg Sci — Monographs in the Surgical Sciences

Monogr Teach — Monographs for Teachers

Monogr Tea Prod Ceylon — Monographs on Tea Production in Ceylon

Monogr Tech Util Aciers Spec — Monographies Techniques sur l'Utilisation des Aciers Speciaux

Monogr Textb Mater Sci — Monographs and Textbooks in Material Science

Monogr Textb Mech Solids Fluids Mech Anal — Monographs and Textbooks on Mechanics of Solids and Fluids. Mechanics Analysis

Monogr Textb Mech Solids Fluids Mech Elast Stab — Monographs and Textbooks on Mechanics of Solids and Fluids. Mechanics of Elastic Stability

Monogr Textb Mech Solids Fluids Mech Surf Struct — Monographs and Textbooks on Mechanics of Solids and Fluids. Mechanics of Surface Structures

Monogr Textbooks Phys Sci Lecture Notes — Monographs and Textbooks in Physical Science. Lecture Notes

Monogr Textbooks Pure Appl Math — Monographs and Textbooks in Pure and Applied Mathematics

Monogr Texts Phys Astron — Monographs and Texts in Physics and Astronomy

Monogr Theor Appl Genet — Monographs on Theoretical and Applied Genetics

Monogr Theory Photogr — Monographs on the Theory of Photography from the Research Laboratory of the Eastman Kodak Company

Monogr Ther Squiff Inst — Monographs on Therapy. Squiff Institute of Medical Research

Monogr T Kosciuszko Tech Univ Cracow — Monograph. T. Kosciuszko Technical University of Cracow

Monogr Univ Bristol Res Stn Campden — Monographs. University of Bristol Research Station. Campden, Gloucestershire

Monogr Univ P Rico Phys Biol Sci — Monographs of the University of Puerto Rico. Series B. Physical and Biological Sciences

Monogr US Geol Surv — Monographs of the US Geological Survey

Monogr Ustav Vyzk Vyuziti Paliv (Bechovice Czech) — Monografie. Ustav pro Vyzkum a Vyuziti Paliv (Bechovice,Czechoslovakia)

Monogr UVP — Monografie. Ustav pro Vyzkum a Vyuziti Paliv

Monogr Vinyl Prod — Monographs. Vinyl Products

Monogr Virol — Monographs in Virology

Monogr Vis Commun — Monographs in Visual Communication

Monogr Volzsk Biol Stancii — Monografii Volzskoj Biologiceskoj Stancii/Monographien der Biologischen Wolga-Station

Monogr Wash Acad Sci — Monographs. Washington Academy of Sciences

Monogr West Found Vertebr Zool — Monographs. Western Foundation of Vertebrate Zoology

Monogr Wilmer Ophthal Inst — Monographs. Wilmer Ophthalmological Institute

Monokrist Stsintill Org Lyuminofory — Monokristally. Stsintillyatory i Organicheskie Lyuminofory

Monokrist Tekh — Monokristally i Tekhnika

Mo Notes — Monthly Notes. Australian School of Pacific Administration

Monotype Nachr — Monotype Nachrichten

Monotype News Lett — Monotype News Letter

Monotype Rec — Monotype Recorder

Monotype Tech Bull — Monotype Technical Bulletin

Monoufeia J Agric Res — Monoufeia Journal of Agricultural Research

Mon Paediat — Monographs in Paediatrics

Mon Period Index — Monthly Periodical Index

Mon Petrol Forecasts US — Monthly Petroleum Forecasts. U.S. Bureau of Mines

Mon Petrol Statem US — Monthly Petroleum Statements. U.S. Bureau of Mines

Mon Pet Statement — Monthly Petroleum Statement

Mon Photo J Tokyo — Monthly Photo-Journal (Tokyo)

Mon Pilot Charts N Atlant Mediterr — Monthly Pilot Charts of the North Atlantic and Mediterranean. Meteorological Office [London]

Mon Piot — Monuments et Memoires Publies par l'Academie des Inscriptions et Belles-Lettres. Fondation Piot

Mon Pitt — Monumenti della Pittura Antica Scoperti in Italia

Mon Print Tokyo — Monthly Print. Japanese Society of Printing Technology (Tokyo)

Mon Prog Rep Emerg Publ Hlth Lab Serv — Monthly Progress Report. Emergency Public Health Laboratory Service [London]

Mon Prog Rep Geol Surv Vict — Monthly Progress Report. Geological Survey of Victoria [Melbourne]

Mon Prog Rep Soc Mot Mfrs — Monthly Progress Report. Society of Motor Manufacturers and Traders [London]

Mon Rainf India — Monthly Rainfall of India [Calcutta]

Mon Rainf Statem Palest — Monthly Rainfall Statement. Palestine

Mon Rec Dent Sci Pract Misc — Monthly Record of Dental Science. Practice and Miscellany

Mon Rec Dent Sci Tokyo — Monthly Record of Dental Science (Tokyo)

Mon Rec Met Obsns Can — Monthly Record of Meteorological Observations in Canada

Mon Rec Scient Lit — Monthly Record of Scientific Literature [New York]

Mon Regist Soc Pract Astr — Monthly Register of the Society for Practical Astronomy [Chicago]

Mon Rep Agric Met Scheme — Monthly Report. Agricultural Meteorological Scheme [London]

Mon Rep Am Ass Var Star Obsrs — Monthly Report of the American Association of Variable Star Observers

Mon Rep Can Miner Ind — Monthly Report. Canadian Mineral Industry

Mon Rep Cent Met Obs Japan — Monthly Report of the Central Meteorological Observatory of Japan

Mon Rep Chamb Mines Vict — Monthly Report. Chamber of Mines of Victoria [Melbourne]

Mon Rep Chamb Mines West Aust — Monthly Report. Chamber of Mines of Western Australia

Mon Rep Civ Eng Res Inst Hokkaido Dev Bur — Monthly Report. Civil Engineering Research Institute of Hokkaido. Development Bureau

Mon Rep Dep Hlth Panama Canal — Monthly Report of the Department of Health of the Panama Canal

Mon Rep Dly Weath Values Liberia — Monthly Report of Daily Weather Values. Liberia

Mon Rep Earthq Osaka — Monthly Report of Earthquakes. Osaka District Meteorological Observatory (Osaka)

Mon Rep Fruit Veg Crops — Monthly Report on Fruit and Vegetable Crops [London]

Mon Rep Ikomasan Sol Obs — Monthly Report. Ikomasan Solar Observatory of Kyoto University

Mon Rep Jap Cott Spinn Ind — Monthly Report of Japanese Cotton Spinning Industry

Mon Rep Jpn Perfum Flavour Assoc — Monthly Report. Japan Perfumery and Flavouring Association

Mon Rep Manchr Steam Eng Mkrs Soc — Monthly Report. Manchester Steam Engine Makers' Society

Mon Rep Met Obs Osaka — Monthly Report of the Meteorological Observatory. Osaka

Mon Rep Minist Agric Nth Ire — Monthly Report. Ministry of Agriculture. Northern Ireland

Mon Rep Minist Inds China — Monthly Report. Ministry of Industries. China

Mon Rep Oil Gas Sect W Va Dep Mines — Monthly Report. Oil and Gas Section. West Virginia Department of Mines

Mon Rep Proc Br Acet Weld Ass — Monthly Report of Proceedings. British Acetylene and Welding Association

Mon Rep Seism Osaka — Monthly Report of Seismology (Osaka)

Mon Rep Transpn Tokyo — Monthly Report of Transportation. Technical Research Institute (Tokyo)

Mon Rep Univ Hlth Serv Univ Mich — Monthly Report of the University Health Service. University of Michigan

Mon Rep Un Soc Boilermkrs Iron Shipbldrs — Monthly Report. United Society of Boilermakers and Iron Shipbuilders [Newcastle]

Mon Res Fish Tokyo — Monthly Research of Fisheries. Fisheries Research Institute (Tokyo)

Mon Return Sea Fish — Monthly Return of Sea Fisheries [London]

Mon Returns Natn Epidem Prev Bur Peking — Monthly Returns. National Epidemic Prevention Bureau (Peking)

Mon Rev — Monthly Review

Mon Rev Am Electroplat Soc — Monthly Review. American Electroplaters' Society

Mon Rev Can Fish Statist — Monthly Review of Canadian Fisheries Statistics

Mon Rev Div Ind Hyg Saf Stand NY St — Monthly Review of the Division of Industrial Hygiene and Safety Standards of the New York State Department of Labor

Mon Rev Fed Reserve Bank Kans City — Monthly Review. Federal Reserve Bank of Kansas City

Mon Rev Inc Soc Insp Wghts Meas — Monthly Review. Incorporated Society of Inspectors of Weights and Measures [Louth]

Mon Rev Mod Mach Shop Pract — Monthly Review of Modern Machine Shop Practice [Coventry]

Mon Rev Psychiatry Neurol — Monthly Review of Psychiatry and Neurology

Mon Rev Tech Lit Br Rlys — Monthly Review of Technical Literature. British Railways

Mon Rev Wheat Situ — Monthly Review of the Wheat Situation [Ottawa]

Mon S — Monastic Studies

Mons Antiqua — Monmouthshire Antiquary

Monsanto Int — Monsanto International

Monsanto Mag — Monsanto Magazine

Monsanto R — Monsanto Review

Monsanto Res Corp Mound Facil Rep MLM — Monsanto Research Corporation. Mound Facility. Report MLM

Monsanto Res Corp Mound Lab Rep MLM — Monsanto Research Corporation. Mound Laboratory. Report MLM

Monsanto Res Corp Mound Lab Res Dev Rep — Monsanto Research Corporation. Mound Laboratory. Research andDevelopment Report

Monsanto Tech Rev — Monsanto Technical Review

Mon Sc — Moniteur Scientifique

Mon Seas Precip Calif Sect US Weath Bur — Monthly and Seasonal Precipitation. California Section. U.S. Weather Bureau

Mon Seism Bull R Obs Hongkong — Monthly Seismological Bulletin. Royal Observatory (Hongkong)

Mon Seism Rep Fordham Univ — Monthly Seismological Report. Fordham University

Mon Ser — Monumenta Serica

Mon Serv Bull Fish Dep West Aust — Monthly Service Bulletin. Fisheries Department. Western Australia

Monsoon Rainf Summ Poona — Monsoon Rainfall Summary. Poona

Monspel Hippocrates — Monspeliensis Hippocrates

Mon S Res C — Monographs. Society for Research in Child Development

Mon Statist Bull Br Iron Steel Fed — Monthly Statistical Bulletin. British Iron and Steel Federation

Mon Statist Bull Rubb Prod Coun Malaya — Monthly Statistical Bulletin. Rubber Producers' Council of the Federation of Malaya

Mon Statist Rep Jap Govt Fish Statist — Monthly Statistical Report. Japanese Government Fishery Statistics

Mon Stud — Monastic Studies

Mon Summ Auto Engng Lit — Monthly Summary of Automobile Engineering Literature. Motor Industry Research Association [Lindley]

Mon Summ Chem Engng Inf — Monthly Summary of Chemical Engineering Information. British Chemical Plant Manufacturers' Association [London]

Mon Summ Clim Data Bangkok — Monthly Summary of Climatic Data (Bangkok)

Mon Summ Curr Lit Antibiot — Monthly Summary of Current Literature on Antibiotics. Distillers' Co. [Epsom]

Mon Summ Curr Lit Distill Co — Monthly Summary of Current Literature. Distillers' Co. [Epsom]

Mon Summ Fishery Prod US — Monthly Summary. Fishery Products. US Fish and Wildlife Service

Mon Summ Import Events Fld Transp Commun — Monthly Summary of Important Events in the Field of Transport and Communications [Lake Success]

Mon Summ Met Obsns Cebu Cy — Monthly Summary of Meteorological Observations. Cebu City

Mon Summ Met Obsns Davao Cy — Monthly Summary of Meteorological Observations. Davao City

Mon Summ Met Obsns Forecast Cent Nichols Fld Paranaque — Monthly Summary of Meteorological Observations. Forecasting Centre. Nichols Field. Paranaque

Mon Summ Met Obsns Iloilo Cy — Monthly Summary of Meteorological Observations. Iloilo City

Mon Summ Met Obsns Laoag — Monthly Summary of Meteorological Observations. Laoag. Ilocos Norte

Mon Summ Met Obsns Legaspi Cy — Monthly Summary of Meteorological Observations. Legaspi City

Mon Summ Met Obsns Manila Cent Off — Monthly Summary of Meteorological Observations. Manila Central Office

Mon Summ Met Obsns Puerta Princesa — Monthly Summary of Meteorological Observations. Puerta Princesa, Palawan

Mon Summ Met Obsns Surigao — Monthly Summary of Meteorological Observations. Surigao

Mon Summ Met Obsns Weath Bur Forecast Cent Manila — Monthly Summary of Meteorological Observations. Weather Bureau Forecasting Center. Manila

Mon Summ Met Obsns Zamboang Cy — Monthly Summary of Meteorological Observations. Zamboanga City

Mon Summ Pl Pests Dis Engl Wales — Monthly Summary of Plant Pests and Diseases in England and Wales

Mon Summ Rainf Ghana — Monthly Summary of Rainfall. Ghana

Mon Summ Rainf Gold Cst — Monthly Summary of Rainfall in the Gold Coast

Mon Summ Rainf Nigeria — Monthly Summary of Rainfall in Nigeria

Mon Summ Rec Temp Rainf Fiji WPHC Stns — Monthly Summary of Records of Temperature and Rainfall. Fiji and W.P.H.C. Stations

Mon Summ Rep DSIR — Monthly Summary of Reports. Department of Scientific and Industrial Research [London]

Mon Summ Weath Condit Schipol Aerodr — Monthly Summary of Weather Conditions. Schipol Aerodrome

Mont — Montana Reports

Mont — Montana: The Magazine of Western History

Mont Acad Sci Proc — Montana Academy of Sciences. Proceedings

Mont Admin R — Administrative Rules of Montana

Mont Ag Exp — Montana. Agricultural Experiment Station. Publications

Mont Agresearch Mont Agric Exp Stn Mont Univ — Montana Agresearch. Montana Agricultural Experiment Station. Montana University

Mont Agric Exp Stn Bull — Montana. Agricultural Experiment Station. Bulletin

Mont Agric Exp Stn Circ — Montana. Agricultural Experiment Station. Circular

Montana Acad Sci Proc — Montana Academy of Sciences. Proceedings

Montana Agric Exp Sta Circ — Montana College of Agriculture and Mechanic Arts. Agricultural Experiment Station. Circular

Montana Agric Exp Sta Misc Publ — Montana State College. Agricultural Experiment Station. Miscellaneous Publication

Montana Agric Exp Sta Special Rep — Montana State College. Agricultural Experiment Station. Special Report

Montana Bur Mines and Geology Bull — Montana. Bureau of Mines and Geology. Bulletin

Montana Bur Mines and Geology Spec Pub — Montana. Bureau of Mines and Geology. Special Publication

Montana Fmr — Montana Farmer

Montana Lib — Montana Libraries

Montana Lib Q — Montana Library Quarterly

Montana Live Stk Sanit Bd — Montana Live Stock Sanitary Board

Montana L Rev — Montana Law Review

Montana Oil Min J — Montana Oil and Mining Journal

Montanaro Ital-Monti Boschi — Montanaro d'Italia - Monti e Boschi

Montana St Poultrym — Montana State Poultryman

Montana Wildl Bull — Montana Wildlife Bulletin

Montana Wool Grow — Montana Wool Grower

Montana Wyo Oil Miner J — Montana-Wyoming Oil and Mineral Journal

Montanistica Metal — Montanistica si Metalurgie

Montan Rdsch — Montanistische Rundschau

Montan Rdsch — Montan-Rundschau

Montan-Rundsch — Montan-Rundschau

Montan Rundsch Suppl — Montanistische Rundschau. Supplement

Montan-Ztg — Montan-Zeitung

Montanztg Oest Ung — Montanzeitung fuer Oesterreich-Ungarn, die Balkanlaender und das Deutsche Reich

Montazhn Rab Stroit — Montazhnye Raboty v Stroitel'stve

Montazhn Spet Rab Stroit — Montazhnye i Spetsial'nye Raboty v Stroitel'stve

Montazh Spets Rab Stroit — Montazhnye i Spetsializirovannye Raboty v Stroitel'stve

Mont B Assn Proc — Montana Bar Association. Proceedings

Mont Bur Mines Geol Bull — Montana. Bureau of Mines and Geology. Bulletin

Mont Bur Mines Geol Mem — Montana. Bureau of Mines and Geology. Memoir

Mont Bur Mines Geol Misc Contrib — Montana. Bureau of Mines and Geology. Miscellaneous Contributions

Mont Bur Mines Geol Spec Publ — Montana. Bureau of Mines and Geology. Special Publication

Mont Bus Q — Montana Business Quarterly

Mont Code Ann — Montana Code Annotated

Mont Co LR — Montgomery County Law Reporter

Mont Co L Rep — Montgomery County Law Reporter

Monte Carlo Methods Appl — Monte Carlo Methods and Applications

Montecatini Edison SpA Ist Ric Agrar Contrib — Montecatini Edison. S.p.A. Istituto de Ricerche Agrarie. Contributi

Mon Tech Bull Int Combust — Monthly Technical Bulletin. International Combustion Ltd. [Derby]

Montech Conf — Montech Conferences

Mon Tech Rev — Monthly Technical Review

Mont Ed — Montana Education

Mont Educ — Montana Education

Monterrey Med — Monterrey Medico

Montevideo U Arquit Rev — Montevideo Universidad de Arquitectura Revista

Mont Fish Game Dep Tech Bull — Montana. Fish and Game Department. Technical Bulletin

Mont For Conserv Exp Stn Bull — Montana. Forest and Conservation Experiment Station. Bulletin

Mont For Conserv Exp Stn Lubrecht Ser — Montana. Forest and Conservation Experiment Station. Lubrecht Series

Mont For Conserv Exp Stn Note — Montana. Forest and Conservation Experiment Station. Note

Mont For Conserv Exp Stn Res Note — Montana. Forest and Conservation Experiment Station. Research Note

Mont For Conserv Exp Stn Spec Publ — Montana. Forest and Conservation Experiment Station. Special Publication

Mont For Conserv Exp Stn Study Rep — Montana. Forest and Conservation Experiment Station. Study Report

Mont Forest Ind News — Montana Forest Industry News

Montfort — Montfort. Vierteljahresschrift fuer Geschichte und Gegenwartskunde Vorarlbergs

Mont G — Montana Gothic

Montg — Montgomery County Law Reporter

Montg Co — Montgomery County Law Reporter

Montg Co Law Rep'r — Montgomery County Law Reporter

Montg Co LR — Montgomery County Law Reporter

Mont'g Co L Rep — Montgomery County Law Reporter

Montg Co L Rep'r — Montgomery County Law Reporter

Montg Co LR (PA) — Montgomery County Law Reporter (Pennsylvania)

Mont Geol Soc Annu Field Conf Guideb — Montana Geological Society. Annual Field Conference. Guidebook

Mont'g L Rep — Montgomery County Law Reporter

Montgomeryshire Collect — Montgomeryshire Collections

Montg (PA) — Montgomery County Law Reporter (Pennsylvania)

Montg Rep Ser Med Res Coun — Monitoring Report Series. Medical Research Council

Montguide MT Agric Mont State Univ Coop Ext Serv — Montguide MT. Agriculture. Montana State University. Cooperative Extension Service

Montguide MT Hum Resour Dev Mont State Univ Coop Ext Serv — Montguide MT. Human Resource Development. Montana State University. CooperativeExtension Service

Month Bus Rev — Monthly Business Review

Mont His S — Montana Historical Society. Contributions

Month JL — Monthly Journal of Law

Month Jur — Monthly Jurist

Month Lab Rev — Monthly Labor Review

Month Law Bul — Monthly Law Bulletin

Month L Bull (NY) — Monthly Law Bulletin (New York)

Month Leg Ex — Monthly Legal Examiner

Month Leg Exam — Monthly Legal Examiner

Month Leg Exam (NY) — Monthly Legal Examiner (New York)

Month LJ — Monthly Journal of Law

Month LM — Monthly Law Magazine

Month L Rep — Monthly Law Reporter

Month L Rep — Monthly Law Reports

Month L Rev — Monthly Law Review

Monthly Am J G — Monthly American Journal of Geology and Natural Science

Monthly Arch Med Sci — Monthly Archives. Medical Sciences

Monthly Catalog US Govt Publ — Monthly Catalog of United States Government Publications

Monthly Cat US Govt Pub — Monthly Catalog of United States Government Publications

Monthly Coal Bull — Monthly Coal Bulletin

Monthly Crit Gaz — Monthly Critical Gazette

Monthly Crop Rep — Monthly Crop Report

Monthly F Bull — Monthly Film Bulletin

Monthly Labor R — Monthly Labor Review

Monthly Labor Rev — Monthly Labor Review

Monthly L Bul — New York Monthly Law Bulletin

Monthly Mag — Monthly Magazine

Monthly Mus Rec — Monthly Musical Record

Monthly Notices Roy Astronom Soc — Monthly Notices. Royal Astronomical Society

Monthly R — Monthly Review

Monthly Rev — Monthly Review

Monthly Rev Dental Surg — Monthly Review of Dental Surgery

Monthly Statist Rev — Monthly Statistical Review

Monthly Vital Stat Rep — Monthly Vital Statistics Report

Monthly Weather Rev — Monthly Weather Review

Month West Jur — Monthly Western Jurist

Mon Times — Monetary Times

Mont Ind — Monthly Index to Reporters

Mont Instal — Montajes e Instalaciones

Mont Law Re — Montana Law Review

Mont Laws — Laws of Montana

Mont'LR — Montana Law Review

Mont L Rev — Montana Law Review

Mont Mag Hist — Montana: The Magazine of Western History

Mont ML — Montefiore Memorial Lecture

Montpellier Med — Montpellier Medical

Montpell Med — Montpellier Medical

Montpel Med — Montpellier Medical

Montr — Montemora

Mon Trans Am Inst Electr Eng — Monthly Transactions. American Institute of Electrical Engineers

Montreal Med — Montreal Medicine

Montreal Med J — Montreal Medical Journal

Montreal Mus Bull — Montreal Museum Bulletin

Montreal Pharm J — Montreal Pharmaceutical Journal

Montreal Univ Service Biogeographie Bull — Montreal Universite. Service de Biogeographie. Bulletin

Montroll Memorial Lecture Ser Math Phys — Montroll Memorial Lecture Series in Mathematical Physics

Mont Rural Electr News — Montana Rural Electric News

Montsaml — Montsamlernyt

Mont Sicil — Montagne Siciliano

Mont State Coll Agric Exp Stn Bull — Montana State College. Agricultural Experiment Station. Bulletin

Mont State Coll Eng Exp Stn Bull — Montana State College. Engineering Experiment Station. Bulletin

Mont Univ B — Montana University. Bulletin

Mont Univ Jt Water Resour Res Cent MWRRC Rep — Montana University Joint Water Resources Research Center. MWRRCReport

Mont Water Resour Res Cent MWRRC Rep — Montana Water Resources Research Center. MWRRC Report

Mont Wool Grow — Montana Wool Grower

MONU — Monumentum. International Council of Monuments and Sites

Mon ULR — Monash University. Law Review

Monum Archit J — Monumental and Architectural Journal

Monum Archit Stone J — Monumental-Architectural Stone Journal

Monumenta Med — Monumenta Medica

Monumenta Nip — Monumenta Nipponica

Monuments Piot — Academie des Inscriptions et Belles-Lettres. Fondation Eugene Piot. Monuments et Memoires

MO Num Ges — Mitteilungen der Oesterreichischen Numismatischen Gesellschaft

Monum J — Monumental Journal and Commemorative Art

Monum Nippon — Monumenta Nipponica

Mon Upper Air Charts — Monthly Upper Air Charts [London]

MO Nurse — Missouri Nurse

Mon Values Certain Met Elem Select Stns Cairo — Monthly Values of Certain Meteorological Elements at Selected Stations (Cairo)

Mon Vital Stat Rep — Monthly Vital Statistics Report

Mon Weath Bull Kabul — Monthly Weather Bulletin (Kabul)

Mon Weath Bull Nanking — Monthly Weather Bulletin. National Southeastern University (Nanking)

Mon Weath Data Burma — Monthly Weather Data. Burma

Mon Weather Rev — Monthly Weather Review

Mon Weath Map Can — Monthly Weather Map [Toronto]

Mon Weath Rep Baghdad — Monthly Weather Report (Baghdad)

Mon Weath Rep Cairo — Monthly Weather Report (Cairo)

Mon Weath Rep Dubl — Monthly Weather Report (Dublin)

Mon Weath Rep Ghana — Monthly Weather Report. Ghana

Mon Weath Rep Israel — Monthly Weather Report. Israel

Mon Weath Rep Lond — Monthly Weather Report of the Meteorological Office (London)

Mon Weath Rep Nigeria — Monthly Weather Report. Nigeria

Mon Weath Rep Saudi Arab — Monthly Weather Report. Saudi Arabia

Mon Weath Rep Sierra Leon Gambia — Monthly Weather Report. Sierra Leone and the Gambia

Mon Weath Rep Un S Afr — Monthly Weather Report. Union of South Africa

Mon Weath Rev — Monthly Weather Review

Mon Weath Rev Met Dep India — Monthly Weather Review. Meteorological Department. India

Mon Weath Rev Met Serv Can — Monthly Weather Review. Meteorological Service. Canada

Mon Weath Rev US Dep Agric — Monthly Weather Review. U.S. Department of Agriculture

Mon Weath Summ SE Asia West Pacif — Monthly Weather Summary. Southeast Asia and the Western Pacific

Mon Weath Summ Seoul — Monthly Weather Summary. Central Meteorological Observatory (Seoul)

Mon Weath Summ Synopt Stns Tehran — Monthly Weather Summary for Synoptic Stations (Tehran)

Mon WJ — Monthly Western Jurist

Mon Zoll — Monumenta Zollerana

Moody — Moody's Magazine

Moody M — Moody Monthly

Moody's Inv Serv — Moody's Investors Service

Moons L T — Moons and Lion Tailes

Moorgate Wall St — Moorgate and Wall Street

Moorg Wal S — Moorgate and Wall Street

Moot Ct Bull — University of Illinois. Moot Court Bulletin

MOP — Mary's Own Paper

MOP — Modern Office Procedures

MOP — Modern Office Technology

MOP — Modern Plastics International

M Opinion — Musical Opinion

MOPLD — Moon and the Planets

MOR — Mathematics of Operations Research

MOR — Mining and Oil Review

MoR — Modern Review

M Or — Monde Oriental

Mo R — Monthly Review

Mor — Moradas. Revista de las Artes y de las Letras

Mor — Moreana

Mor — Morris' Reports

Mora Ferenc Muz Ev — Mora Ferenc Muzeum Evkoenyve

Mora Ferenc Muz Evk — A Mora Ferenc Muzeum Evkoenyve/Jahrbuch des Ferenc Mora Museums/Les Les Annales. Musee Ferenc Mora

Moral Ed — Moral Education

Morav Hospod — Moravsky Hospodar

Moravian Mus — Moravian Music Foundation. Bulletin

Moravian Mus — Moravian Music Journal

Morav Miss — Moravian Missions

Morav Num Zpr — Moravske Numismaticke Zpravy

Moravske Num Zpravy — Moravske Numismaticke Zpravy

Morav Slez Cas Zubni Tech — Moravsko-Slezsky Casopis pro Zubni Techniku

Morav Th S Bul — Moravian Theological Seminary. Bulletin

Morbidity Mortality Wkly Rep US Dep Hlth Educ Welf — Morbidity and Mortality Weekly Report. United States Department of Health, Education, and Welfare

Morbid Mortal Weekly Rep — Morbidity and Mortality Weekly Report

Mord Gos Univ Uch Zap — Mordovskii Gosudarstvennyi Universitet. Uchenye Zapiski

MO Reg — Missouri Register

More Import Insect Rec — More Important Insect Records [*Washington*]

Mo Rel M — Monthly Religious Magazine

Mo Rev — Monthly Review

Mo Review — Monthly Review

MO Rev Stat — Missouri Revised Statutes

More Zhizn — More i ego Zhizn'

MORFA — Morskoi Flot

Morf Norm Patol Buc — Morfologia Normala si Patologica (Bucuresti)

Morfog Regener — Morfogenez i Regeneratsiya

Morfol Chel Zhivotn Antropol — Morfologiya Cheloveka i Zhivotnykh. Antropologiya

Morfol Chel Zhivotn Embriol — Morfologiya Cheloveka i Zhivotnykh. Embriologiya

Morfol Norm Patol — Morfologia Normala si Patologica

Morfol Norm Patol (Buchar) — Morfologia Normala si Patologica (Bucharest)

Morfol Norm si Pat — Morfologia Normala si Patologica

Morfol Osn Mikrotsirk (Moscow) — Morfologicheskie Osnovy Mikrotsirkulyatsii (Moscow)

Morfol Reakt Izmen Perifer Nervn Sist Usloviyakh Eksp — Morfologiya Reaktivnykh Izmenenii Pericheskoi Nervnoi Sistemy v Usloviyakh Eksperimenta

Morgan Gty — Morgan Guaranty Survey

Morgan Kaufmann Ser Data Management Systems — Morgan Kaufmann Series in Data Management Systems

Morgantown Energy Res Cent Spec Publ MERC SP US Dep Energy — Morgantown Energy Research Center. Special Publication. MERC/SP. UnitedStates Department of Energy

Morgantown Energy Technol Cent Rep DOE METC US Dep Energy — Morgantown Energy Technology Center. Report DOE/METC. United States Department of Energy

Morgenl — Morgenland

Morioka Tab Shikenjo Hokoku — Morioka Tabako Shikenjo Hokoku

Morks Mag — Morks Magazijn

MorMJ — Moravian Music Journal

Morning Chron — Morning Chronicle

Morn Watch — Morning Watch

Morocco Serv Geol Notes Mem — Morocco. Service Geologique. Notes et Memoires

Morot J Bot — Journal de Botanique (L. Morot, Editor)

Morph Jb — Morphologisches Jahrbuch

Morphol Embryol — Morphologie et Embryologie

Morphol Embryol (Bucur) — Morphologie et Embryologie (Bucurest)

Morphol Igazsagugyi Orv Sz — Morphologiai es Igazsagugyi Orvosi Szemle

Morphol Jahrb — Morphologisches Jahrbuch

Morphol Jb — Morphologisches Jahrbuch

Morphol Med — Morphologia Medica

Morphol Polym Proc Europhys Conf Macromol Phys — Morphology of Polymers. Proceedings. Europhysics Conference onMacromolecular Physics

Morris Arbor Bull — Morris Arboretum. Bulletin

Morris Arbor Monogr — Morris Arboretum Monographs [*Philadelphia*]

Morsk Fl — Morskoi Flot

Morsk Flot — Morskoi Flot

Morsk Gidrofiz Issled — Morskie Gidrofizicheskie Issledovaniya

Morski Inst Rybacki Pr Ser A — Morski Instytut Rybacki. Prace. Seria A. Oceanografia i Biologia Rybacka

Morsko Ribarst — Morsko Ribarstvo

Morsk Rech Flot — Morskoi i Rechnoi Flot

Morsk Sb — Morskoi Sbornik

Morsk Sb Bizerta — Morskoi Sbornik (Bizerta)

Morsk Sb Leningr — Morskoi Sbornik (Leningrad)

Morsk Sb Med Pribav — Morskoi Sbornik. Meditsinskiya Pribavleniya

Morsk Sudostr — Morskoe Sudostroenie

Morsk Vrach — Morskoi Vrach

Morsk Zh — Morskoi Zhurnal

Mort Banker — Mortgage Banker

Mort Banking — Mortgage Banking

Mortg Bank — Mortgage Banking

Mortg Bnkr — Mortgage Banker

MorTid — Morgen-Tidningen

Morton Arbor Q — Morton Arboretum Quarterly

MOS — Methods in Organic Synthesis

Mos — Mosaic

MOSA — Mitteilungen. Oesterreichisches Staatsarchiv

Mosaic J Molybdenum Metall — Mosaic. Journal of Molybdenum Metallurgy

Mos Ant It — Mosaici Antichi in Italia

Mosc Bll S Nt — Bulletin de la Societe Imperiale des Naturalistes (Moscou)

Mosc Cm S Ps Md — Commentationes Societatis Physico-Medicae apud Universitatem Mosquensem Institutae

MOSCEQ — Moscosoa

MO Sch Mines Metall Bull Gen Ser — Missouri School of Mines and Metallurgy. Bulletin. General Series

MO Sch Mines Metall Bull Tech Ser — Missouri School of Mines and Metallurgy. Bulletin. Technical Series

Moschr — Monatsschrift

Mosc N Mm — Nouveaux Memoires de la Societe Imperiale des Naturalistes de Moscou

Mosc Obs A — Annales de l'Observatoire de Moscou

Moscosoa Contrib Cient Jard Bot Nac Dr Rafael M Moscosoa — Moscosoa. Contribuciones Cientificas. Jardin Botanico Nacional Dr. Rafael M. Moscosoa

Moscow Int Compos Conf — Moscow International Composites Conference

Moscow Nar — Press Bulletin. Moscow Narodny Bank Ltd.

Moscow Narodny Bank Q R — Moscow Narodny Bank. Quarterly Review

Moscow Univ Biol Sci Bull (Engl Transl) — Moscow University. Biological Sciences Bulletin (English Translation)

Moscow Univ Bull Ser 3 — Moscow University. Bulletin. Series 3. Physics and Astronomy

Moscow Univ Chem Bull Engl Transl — Moscow University. Chemistry Bulletin. English Translation

Moscow Univ Comput Math and Cybern — Moscow University. Computational Mathematics and Cybernetics

Moscow Univ Comput Math Cybernet — Moscow University Computational Mathematics and Cybernetics

Moscow Univ Geol Bull (Engl Transl) — Moscow University. Geology Bulletin (English Translation)

Moscow Univ Math Bull — Moscow University. Mathematics Bulletin

Moscow Univ Math Bull (Engl Transl) — Moscow University. Mathematics Bulletin (English Translation)

Moscow Univ Mech Bull — Moscow University. Mechanics Bulletin

Moscow Univ Mech Bull (Engl Transl) — Moscow University. Mechanics Bulletin (English Translation of Vestnik Moskovskogo Universiteta. Mekhanika)

Moscow Univ Phys Bull — Moscow University. Physics Bulletin

Moscow Univ Phys Bull Engl Transl — Moscow University. Physics Bulletin. English Translation

Moscow Univ Soil Sci Bull (Engl Transl) — Moscow University. Soil Science Bulletin (English Translation)

Mosc S Nt Bll — Bulletin de la Societe Imperiale des Naturalistes (Moscou)

Mosc S Nt Mm — Memoires de la Societe Imperiale des Naturalistes de Moscou

Mosc S Nt N Mm — Nouveaux Memoires de la Societe Imperiale des Naturalistes de Moscou

Mosc S Sc Bll — Bulletin of the Imperial Society of Lovers of Natural Science, Anthropology, and Ethnography, in connection with the Imperial University of Moscow

Mosc Univ Biol Sci Bull — Moscow University. Biological Sciences Bulletin

Mosc Univ Biol Sci Bull (Engl Transl Vestn Mosk Univ Biol) — Moscow University. Biological Sciences Bulletin (English Translation of Vestnik. Moskovskogo Universiteta. Biologiya)

Mosc Univ Chem Bull — Moscow University. Chemistry Bulletin

Mosc Univ Comput Math Cybern — Moscow University. Computational Mathematics and Cybernetics

Mosc Univ Geol Bull — Moscow University. Geology Bulletin

Mosc Univ Math Bull — Moscow University. Mathematics Bulletin

Mosc Univ Mech Bull — Moscow University. Mechanics Bulletin

Mosc Univ Phys Bull — Moscow University. Physics Bulletin

Mosc Univ Soil Sci Bull — Moscow University. Soil Science Bulletin

Mosc Un Mm — Scientific Memoirs of the Imperial University of Moscow

Mosc Un Mm Ps Mth — Scientific Memoirs of the Imperial University of Moscow. Physico-Mathematical Section

Moser ML — Hans Joachim Moser Musik-Lexikon

Mosher Period Index — Mosher Periodical Index

Mosk Aviats Inst Im Sergo Ordzhonikidze Temat Sb Nauchn Tr — Moskovskii Aviatsionnyi Institut Imeni Sergo Ordzhonikidze.Tematicheskii Sbornik Nauchnykh Trudov

Mosk Aviats Inst Im Sergo Ordzhonikidze Tr — Moskovskii Aviatsionnyi Institut Imeni Sergo Ordzhonikidze. Trudy

Mosk Energ Inst Mezhved Temat Sb — Moskovskii Energeticheskii Institut. Mezhvedomstvennyi TematicheskiiSbornik

Mosk Fiz Tekh Inst Tr MFTI Ser Radiotekh Elektron — Moskovskii Fiziko-Tekhnicheskii Institut. Trudy MFTI. SeriyaRadiotekhnika i Elektronika

Mosk Fiz Tekh Inst Tr Ser Obshch Mol Fiz — Moskovskii Fiziko-Tekhnicheskii Institut. Trudy. Seriya "Obshchaya i Molekulyarnaya Fizika"

Mosk Gidromelior Inst Nauchn Zap — Moskovskii Gidromeliorativnyi Institut. Nauchnye Zapiski

Mosk Gos Pedagog Inst Uch Zap — Moskovskii Gosudarstvennyi Pedagogicheskii Institut. Uchenye Zapiski

Mosk Gos Univ im M V Lomonosova Uch Zap — Moskovskii Gosudarstvennyi Universitet imeni M. V. Lomonosova. UchenyeZapiski

Mosk Inst Elektron Mashinostr Tr — Moskovskii Institut Elektronnogo Mashinostroeniya. Trudy

Mosk Inst Inzh Zheleznodorozhn Transp Tr — Moskovskii Institut Inzhenerov Zheleznodorozhnogo Transporta. Trudy

Mosk Inst Khim Mashinostr Tr — Moskovskii Institut Khimicheskogo Mashinostroeniya. Trudy

Mosk Inst Nar Khoz Sverdl Fil Sb Nauchn Tr — Moskovskii Institut Narodnogo Khozyaistva. Sverdlovskii Filial. Sbornik Nauchnykh Trudov

Mosk Inst Neftekhim Gazov Promsti Im I M Gubkina Tr — Moskovskii Institut Neftekhimicheskoi i Gazovoi Promyshlennosti ImeniI. M. Gubkina. Trudy

Mosk Inst Stali Sb — Moskovskii Institut Stali. Sbornik

Mosk Inst Stali Splavov Nauchn Tr — Moskovskii Institut Stali i Splavov. Nauchnye Trudy

Mosk Inst Stali Splavov Sb — Moskovskii Institut Stali i Splavov. Sbornik

Mosk Inst Tonkoi Khim Tekhnol Im M V Lomonosova Tr Inst — Moskovskii Institut Tonkoi Khimicheskoi Tekhnologii Imeni M. V.Lomonosova. Trudy Instituta

Mosk Inst Tonkoi Khim Tekhnol Tr — Moskovskii Institut Tonkoi Khimicheskoi Tekhnologii. Trudy

Mosk Inzh Stroit Inst Im V V Kuibysheva Sb Tr — Moskovskii Inzhenerno-Stroitel'nyi Institut Imeni V. V. Kuibysheva.Sbornik Trudov

Mosk Khim Tekhnol Inst Im D I Mendeleeva Tr — Moskovskii Khimiko-Tekhnologicheskii Institut Imeni D. I. Mendeleeva.Trudy

Mosk Kolkhozn — Moskovskii Kolkhoznik

Mosk Lesotekh Inst Nauchn Tr — Moskovskii Lesotekhnicheskii Institut. Nauchnye Trudy

Mosk Med Zh — Moskovskii Meditsinskii Zhurnal

Mosk Nauchn Konf Osnovn Probl Gig Tr — Moskovskaya Nauchnaya Konferentsiya po Osnovnym Problemam Gigieny Truda

Mosk Nauchno Issled Inst Gig Im F F Erismana Sb Nauchn Tr — Moskovskii Nauchno-Issledovatel'skii Institut Gigieny Imeni F. F. Erismana. Sbornik Nauchnykh Trudov

Mosk Nauchno Issled Inst Gig Uch Zap — Moskovskii Nauchno-Issledovatel'skii Institut Gigieny. Uchenye Zapiski

Mosk Nauchno Issled Inst Psikhiatr Tr — Moskovskii Nauchno-Issledovatel'skii Institut Psikhiatrii. Trudy

Mosk Neft Inst Tr — Moskovskii Neftyanoi Institut. Trudy

Mosk Obl Pedagog Inst Im N K Krupskoi Uch Zap — Moskovskii Oblastnoi Pedagogicheskii Institut Imeni N. K. Krupskoi.Uchenye Zapiski

Moskov Aviacion Inst Ordzonikidze Trudy — Moskovskii Ordena Lenina Aviacionnyi Institut Imeni Sergo Ordzonikidze. Trudy

Moskov Gos Ped Inst Ucen Zap — Moskovskii Gosudarstvennyi Pedagogiceskii Institut Imeni V. I. Lenina. Ucenye Zapiski

Moskov Gos Univ Soobsc Gos Astronom Inst Sternberg — Moskovskii Gosudarstvennyi Universitet Imeni M. V. Lomonosova. Soobscenija Gosudarstvennogo Astronomiceskogo Instituta Imeni P. K. Sternberga

Moskov Gos Univ Soobshch Gos Astronom Inst Sternberga — Moskovskii Gosudarstvennyi Universitet Imeni M. V. Lomonosova. Soobshcheniya Gosudarstvennogo Astronomicheskogo Instituta Imeni P. K. Sternberga

Moskov Gos Univ Trudy Gos Astronom Inst Sternberg — Moskovskii Gosudarstvennyi Universitet Imeni M. V. Lomonosova. Trudy Gosudarstvennogo Astronomiceskogo Instituta Imeni P. K. Sternberga

Moskov Gos Zaocn Ped Inst Sb Naucn Trudov — Moskovskii Gosudarstvennyi Zaocnyi Pedagogiceskii Institut. Sbornik Naucnyh Trudov

Moskov Inst Elektron Masinostroenija-Trudy MIEM — Moskovskii Institut Elektronnogo Masinostroenija. Trudy MIEM

Moskov Inst Inz Zeleznodoroz Transporta Trudy — Moskovskii Institut Inzenerov Zeleznodoroznogo Transporta. Trudy

Moskov Inz-Stroitel Inst Sb Trudov — Moskovskii Inzenerno-Stroitelskii Institut Imeni V. V. Kuibyseva. Sbornik Trudov

Moskov Lesotehn Inst Naucn Trudy — Moskovskii Lesotehniceskii Institut. Naucnye Trudy

Moskov Oblast Ped Inst Ucen Zap — Moskovskii Oblastnoi Pedagogiceskii Institut. Ucenye Zapiski

Mosk O-Vo Ispyt Prir Byull Otd Geol — Moskovskoye Obshchestvo Ispytateley Prirody. Byulleten. Otdel Geologicheskiy

Mosk Skh Akad Im K A Timiryazeva Dokl TSKhA — Moskovskaya Sel'skokhozyaistvennaya Akademiya Imeni K. A. Timiryazeva.Doklady TSKhA

Mosk Skh Akad Im K A Timiryazeva Sb Nauchn Tr — Moskovskaya Sel'skokhozyaistvennaya Akademiya Imeni K. A. Timiryazeva.Sbornik Nauchnykh Trudov

Mosk Tekhnol Inst Legk Promsti Nauchn Tr — Moskovskii Tekhnologicheskii Institut Legkoi Promyshlennosti. NauchnyeTrudy

Mosk Univ Vestn Ser 6 Biol Pochvoved — Moskovskiy Universitet. Vestnik. Seriya 6. Biologiya. Pochvovedeniye

Mosk Univ Vestn Ser Geogr — Moskovskiy Universitet. Vestnik. Seriya Geografii

Mosk Univ Zool Muz Sb Tr — Moskovskii Universitet. Zoologicheskii Muzei. Sbornik Trudov

Mosk Vet Akad Im K I Skryabina Sb Nauchn Tr — Moskovskaya Veterlnarnaya Akademiya Imeni K. I. Skryabina. SbornikNauchnykh Trudov

Mosk Vet Akad Tr — Moskovskaya Veterinarnaya Akademiya. Trudy

Mosk Vyssh Tekh Uchil Im N E Baumana Sb — Moskovskoe Vysshee Tekhnicheskoe Uchilishche Imeni N. E. Baumana.Sbornik

Mosk Vyssh Tekh Uchil Im N E Baumana Sb Tr — Moskovskoe Vysshee Tekhnicheskoi Uchilishche Imeni N. E. Baumana.Sbornik Trudov

Mosk Vyssh Tekh Uchil Im N E Baumana Tr — Moskovskoe Vysshee Tekhnicheskoi Uchilishche Imeni N. E. Baumana.Trudy

Mosk Zaochn Poligr Inst Nauchn Tr — Moskovskii Zaochnyi Poligraficheskii Institut. Nauchnye Trudy

Moslem W — Moslem World

Mosl R — Moslemische Revue

Mosonmagy Agrartud Foisk Kozl — Mosonmagyarovari Agrartudomanyi Foiskola Kozlemenyei

Mosonmagyarovari Agrartud Foiskola Kozl — Mosonmagyarovari Agrartudomanyi Foiskola Kozlemenyei

Mosonmagyarovari Mezogazdasagtud Kar Kozl — Mosonmagyarovari Mezogazdasagtudomanyi Kar Kozlemenyei

Mosonmagy Mesogazd Akad Kozl — Mosonmagyarovari Mesogazdasagi Akademia Kozlemenye

MO Speleology — Missouri Speleology

MOSQAU — Mosquito News

Mosq Control Res Annu Rep — Mosquito Control Research. Annual Report

Mosq News — Mosquito News

Mosq Syst — Mosquito Systematics

Mosq Syst News Lett — Mosquito Systematics News Letter

Mosquito Ne — Mosquito News

M Ostens — Musik des Ostens

Mo Stethoscope Med Rep — Monthly Stethoscope and Medical Reporter

MOstf — Marburger Ostforschungen

Mostra — Mostra dell'Arte e della Civilta Etrusca

Mostra Etr — Mostra dell'Arte e della Civilta Etrusca

Mostra Int Conserve Imballaggi Congr — Mostra Internazionale delle Conserve ed Imballaggi. Congressi

Mostra Int Conserve Relativi Imballaggi Congr — Mostra Internazionale delle Conserve e Relativi Imballaggi. Congressi

Mostra Int Ind Conserve Aliment Congr — Mostra Internazionale delle Industrie per le Conserve Alimentari. Congressi

Mo Summary Aust Cond — Monthly Summary of Australian Conditions

MOSVA — Mitteilungen. Oesterreichische Sanitaetsverwaltung

Mosvodokanalniiproekt Tr — Mosvodokanalniiproekt. Trudy

Mo Tax Features — Monthly Tax Features

Mot Boat — Motor Boat

Mot Boating — Motor Boating

Mot Boat Yacht — Motor Boat and Yachting

Mot Body — Motor Body

Mot Body Bldg — Motor Body Building and Vehicle Construction

Mot Car Wld — Motor Car World

Mot Commerce Ind — Motor Commerce and Industry

Mot Cycl — Motor Cycling

Mot Cycle — Motor Cycle

Mot Cycl Motg — Motor Cycling and Motoring

Mot Gasturb Luftf — Motor und Gasturbine in der Luftfahrt

Motg Equip News — Motoring Equipment News

Moth Earth — Mother Earth News

Mother J — Mother Jones

Moth Jones — Mother Jones

Moths Am North Mex — Moths of America, North of Mexico

Motil Dig Tract Proc Int Symp Gastrointest Motil — Motility of the Digestive Tract. Proceedings. International Symposiumon Gastrointestinal Motility

Mot Ind — Motor Industry

Mot Ind Gt Br — Motor Industry of Great Britain

Motion Pict Engng Tokyo — Motion Picture Engineering (Tokyo)

Motion Pict Tech Bull — Motion Picture Technical Bulletin

Motiv Emotion — Motivation and Emotion

Motive Pwr Chicago — Motive Power (Chicago)

Motive Pwr NY — Motive Power (New York)

Motn Life — Mountain Life and Work

Mot Oil Medium — Motor Oil Medium

Motor B — Motor Boating

Motor B & S — Motor Boating and Sailing

Motor Bus — Motor Business

Motorcycle Scoot Three Wheel Mech — Motorcycle, Scooter, and Three-Wheeler Mechanics

MotorIntnl — Motor Report International

Motoris Agr — Motorisation Agricole

Motoris Agric — Motorisation Agricole

Motor M — Motor Manual

Motorola Tech Dev — Motorola Technical Developments

Motorola Tech Disclosure Bull — Motorola Technical Disclosure Bulletin

Motor Serv (Chicago) — Motor Service (Chicago)

Motor T — Motor Trend

Motortech Z — Motortechnische Zeitschrift

Motor Trade J — Motor Trade Journal

Motor Transp — Motor Transport

Mo Trade & Shipping R — Monthly Trade and Shipping Review

Mot Rdsch — Motor-Rundschau

MOT Schriftenr Med Orthop Tech — MOT. Schriftenreihe der Medizinisch-Orthopaedischen Technik

Mot Serv Chicago — Motor Service (Chicago)

Mot Serv Lond — Motor Service (London)

Mot Ship — Motor Ship

MotShip Diesel Boat — Motorship and Diesel Boating

Mot Ship Mot Boat — Motor Ship and Motor Boat

Mot Ship Ref Bk — Motor Ship Reference Book

MotShips Wld — Motorships of the World

Mot Sk — Motor Skills. Theory into Practice

Mot Skills Res Exch — Motor Skills Research Exchange. Department of Psychology. University of Louisville

Mot Tractn — Motor Traction

Mot Trader — Motor Trader

Mot Transp — Motor Transport

Mot Veh Insp Bull — Motor Vehicle Inspection Bulletin

Mot Veh Res — Motor Vehicle Research

Mot Wld Ind Veh Rev — Motor World and Industrial Vehicle Review

Mot Wld NY — Motor World (New York)

MOU — Monografie Orientalniho Ustavu

MOU — Motor Business

Mound Facil Rep MLM — Mound Facility. Report MLM

Mound Lab Rep MLM — Mound Laboratory. Report MLM

Mo Univ Agric Exp Stn Res Bull — Missouri University. Agricultural Experiment Station. ResearchBulletin

Mo Univ Coll Agric Agric Exp Stn Bull — Missouri University. College of Agriculture. Agricultural ExperimentStation. Bulletin

MO Univ Coll Agric Agric Exp Stn Spec Rep — Missouri. University. College of Agriculture. Agricultural Experiment Station. Special Report

MO Univ Eng Exp Stn Eng Repr Ser — Missouri University. Engineering Experiment Station. Engineering Reprint Series

MO Univ Eng Exp Stn Eng Ser Bull — Missouri. University. Engineering Experiment Station. Engineering Series Bulletin

MO Univ Sch Mines Metall Bull Gen Ser — Missouri University. School of Mines and Metallurgy. Bulletin. General Series

Mountain Geol — Mountain Geologist

Mount Biol Stn Notes Wellington — Mountain Biological Station Notes (Wellington)

Mount Plains Libr Q — Mountain Plains Library Association. Quarterly

Mount Rev — Mountain Review

Mount St Fm Live Stk J — Mountain States Farm and Live Stock Journal [Salt Lake City]

Mount Wld — Mountain World

Mous — Mouseion. International Museum Office

Mous — Mouseion. Rivista di Scienze Classiche

MouS — Mouvement Social

MO U Sch Mines & Met Bul Tech Ser — University of Missouri. School of Mines and Metallurgy. Bulletin. Technical Series

Mouth — Mouth of the Dragon

Mo Utopia — Modern Utopia

Mouvement Soc — Mouvement Social

Mouvement Synd Mond — Mouvement Syndical Mondial

Mouv Int Engr Prod Chim — Mouvement International des Engrais et des Produits Chimiques. Institut International d'Agriculture [*Rome*]
Mouv Marit — Mouvement Maritime [*Bruxelles*]
Mouv Med Paris — Mouvement Medical (Paris)
Mouv Med Univ Toulouse — Mouvement Medical a l'Universite de Toulouse
Mouv Psych — Mouvement Psychique, Revue Medicale et Scientifique
MouvS — Mouvement Social. Revue Catholique Internationale
Mouv Sanit — Mouvement Sanitaire
Mouv Siderurg Belge — Mouvement Siderurgique Belge
Mouv Soc — Mouvement Social
Mov — Movoznavstvo
MOVB — Mitteilungen. Oesterreichischer Verein fuer Bibliothekwesen
MOVBW — Mitteilungen. Oesterreichischer Verein fuer Bibliothekwesen
Mov Casa Orat Santiago — Movimiento de la Casa de Orates de Santiago
Mov Disord — Movement Disorders
Movietone — Movietone News
Movietone N — Movietone News
Mov Im — Moving Image
Mov Liberaz Ital — Il Movimento di Liberazione in Italia
Mov M — Movie Maker
MOV Nachr — MOV [*Marine-Offizier-Vereinigung*] Nachrichten
Mov Operaio — Movimento Operaio
Mov Operaio Soc — Movimento Operaio e Socialista
Mo Water Sewerage Conf J — Missouri Water and Sewerage Conference. Journal
Mo W Jur — Monthly Western Jurist
Moy Mens Serv Met AOF — Moyennes Mensuelles. Service Meteorologique de l'A.O.F
Moy Mens Stn Met Cent Brazzaville — Moyennes Mensuelles a la Station Meteorologique Centrale de Brazzaville
Moy Tot Extr Serv Met Cameroun — Moyennes Totaux et Extremes. Service Meteorologique. Cameroun
Mozambique Dir Serv Geol Minas Mem Commun Bol — Mozambique. Direccao dos Servicos de Geologia e Minas. Memorias eCommunicacoes. Boletim
Mozambique Serv Geol Minas Ser Geol Minas Mem Commun Bol — Mozambique. Servicos de Geologia e Minas. Serie de Geologia e Minas. Memorias eCommunicacoes. Boletim
Mozambique Serv Ind Minas Geol Ser Geol Minas Mem Commun Bol — Mozambique. Servicos de Industria, Minas, e Geologia. Serie de Geologiae Minas. Memorias e Communicacoes. Boletim
MozartJb — Mozart-Jahrbuch
MozJ — Mozart-Jahrbuch
Moz Jb — Mozart-Jahrbuch
Mozoegazd Kiserletugyi Kozp Evk — Mozoegazdasagi Kiserletugyi Kozpont Evkonyve
MP — Mackenzie Pilot
MP — Maitre Phonetique
MP — Masinnyj Perevod Trudy Instituta Tocnoj Mechaniki i Vycislitel Hoj Techniki Akademiy Nauk SSR
MP — Medical Press and Circular
MP — Mercurio Peruano
MP — Methods and Phenomena
MP — Modern Packaging
MP — Modern Philology
MP — Monuments Piot. Monuments et Memoires Publies par l'Academie des Inscriptions et Belles-Lettres
MP — Museo de Pontevedra
MP — Mycenaean Pottery
MPA — American Review of Public Administration
MPA — Materialy i Prace Antropologiczne
MPA — Michigan CPA
MPA — Monatsberichte der Preussischen Akademie der Wissenschaften zu Berlin
MPAC — Mission Pelliot en Asie Centrale
M Pad — Memorie. Reale Accademia di Scienze, Lettere, ed Arti di Padova
MPANL — Memorie. Pontificia Accademia dei Nuovi Lincei
MPARA — Memorie. Pontificia Accademia Romana di Archeologia
MP Arkansas Univ Coop Ext — MP - University of Arkansas. Cooperative Extension Service
MPASI — Monumenti della Pittura Antica Scoperti in Italia
MPAW — Monatsberichte der Koenigliche Preussischen Akademie der Wissenschaften
MPB — Moderne Predigt-Bibliothek
MP Bl — Muensterisches Pastoralblatt
MP Bl — Musikpaedagogische Blaetter
MPC — Manuali del Pensiero Cattolico
MPC — Medical Press and Circular
MPC — Metal Pi Complexes
MPCPC — Mathematical Proceedings. Cambridge Philosophical Society
MPD — Monographs in Psychobiology and Disease
MPEEA — Moniteur Professionnel de l'Electricite et Electronique
MPer — Mercurio Peruano
MPer — Music Perception
MPESA7 — Mar y Pesca
MPETA J — Manitoba Physical Education Teachers' Association. Journal
MPF — Monographien zur Philosophischen Forschung
MPFEE8 — Psychiatria Fennica Monografiasarja
MPG — Patrologiae Cursus Completus. Series Graeca
MPG (Max-Planck-Ges) Spiegel Aktuel Inf — MPG (Max-Planck-Gesellschaft) Spiegel. Aktuelle Informationen
MPG News — MPG. News. Maine Potato Growers, Inc.
MPG Presseinf — MPG [*Max-Planck-Gesellschaft*] Presseinformation
MPG Spiegel Aktuele Inf — MPG [*Max-Planck-Gesellschaft*] Spiegel. Aktuele Informationen
MPh — Maitre Phonetique
MPh — Modern Philology
MPh — Museum. Maanblad voor Philologie en Geschiedenis

MPHAE6 — Medical Physics Handbooks
MPHEB — Memoires pour Servir de Preuves a l'Histoire Ecclesiastique et Civile de Bretagne
M Phil — Modern Philology
MPHL — Mercurio Peruano de Historia, Literatura, y Noticias Publicas
MPhL — Museum Philologum Londiniense
M Ph LJ — Melanges de Philosophie et de Litterature Juives
MPHML — Melanges de Philosophie, d'Histoire, de Morale, et de Litterature
MPhon — Maitre Phonetique
M Photo — Modern Photography
MPhP — Mediaevalia Philosophica Polonorum
M Ph T — Monastere de Phoebammon dans la Thebaide
MPI — Methodist Periodical Index
MPI — Militaerpsykologiska Institutet
MPI Appl Notes — MPI [*McKee-Pedersen Instruments*] Applications Notes
MPICE — Minutes of Proceedings. Institution of Civil Engineers
MPiKL — Masinnyj Perevod i Prikladnaja Lingvistika
MPI (McKee Pedersen Instrum) Appl Notes — MPI (McKee-Pedersen Instruments) Applications Notes
MPIPEM — Memoires Publies. Institut pour la Protection des Plantes
MP i PL — Masinnyj Perevod i Prikladnaja Lingvistika
Mpisi Ser — Mpisi Series. Livestock and Agricultural Department. Swaziland
M P It — Monumenta Polyphoniae Italicae
MPK — Mitteilungen der Praehistorischen Kommission der Oesterreichischen Akademie derWissenschaften
MPL — Managerial Planning
MPL — Monumenta Polyphoniae Liturgicae Sanctae Ecclesiae Romanae
MPL — Muenchener Papiere zur Linguistik
MPL — Musician, Player, and Listener
MPLJ — Melanges de Philosophie et de Litterature Juives
MPLL — Michigan. University. Publications in Language and Literature
MPLMB — Modifikatsiya Polimernykh Materialov
MPLR — Municipal and Planning Law Reports
MPM — Medical Parasitology and Parasitic Diseases/Meditsinskaia Parazitologiia i Parazitarnye Bolezni (Moscow)
MP MD Agric Exp Stn — MP. Maryland Agricultural Experiment Station
MPMLPS — Memoirs and Proceedings. Manchester Literary and Philosophical Society
MPMTA — Tschermaks Mineralogische und Petrographische Mitteilungen
MPNBAZ — Marine Pollution Bulletin
MPO — Marine Policy. The International Journal of Ocean Affairs
MPOBA — Monographs in Population Biology
MPologne — Musique en Pologne
M Pont — Museo de Pontevedra
MPOTB — Modern Problems in Ophthalmology
MPOUA — Memorial des Poudres
MPP — Mediaevalia Philosophica Polonorum
MPPA — Medical Problems of Performing Artists
MPPAA — Moderne Probleme der Paediatrie
MPPAEC — Medical Problems of Performing Artists
MPR — Mervyn Peake Review
MPR — Miscellanea Paul Rivet Octogenario Dicata [*Mexico*]
MPR — Muenchener Beitraege zur Papyrusforschung und Antiken Rechtsgeschichte
M Press — Medical Press and Circular
M Pr Hist Kom (Wien) — Mitteilungen der Praehistorischen Kommission der Oesterreichischen Akademie derWissenschaften (Wien)
M Pr Lg — Maanedsskrift for Praktisk Laegegerning og Social Medicin
MPR Met Powder Rep — MPR. Metal Powder Report
M Pr T — Monatsschrift fuer Praktische Tierheilkunde
MPrTh — Monatsschrift fuer Praktische Tierheilkunde
MPS — Mathematical Programming Studies
MPS — Modern Poetry Studies
MPSG — Mitteilungen aus der Papyrussammlung der Giessener Universitaetsbibliothek
M Ps N — Monatsschrift fuer Psychiatrie und Neurologie
MPSOA — Preprint Series. Institute of Mathematics. University of Oslo
MPSSA — Meditsinskaya Promyshlennost SSSR
MPSSP — Modern Problems in Solid State Physics
MPSZA — Magyar Pszichologiai Szemle
MPT — Manuels et Precis de Theologie
MPTh — Monatsschrift fuer Pastoraltheologie
MPTHDI — Monographs in Ophthalmology
MPT Metall Plant Technol — MPT. Metallurgical Plant and Technology
MPTP — Materials Processing. Theory and Practices
MP Univ Arkansas Coop Ext Serv — MP. University of Arkansas. Cooperative Extension Service
MP Univ Mo Ext Div — MP. University of Missouri. Extension Division
MP Univ Nebr Agric Exp Stn — MP. University of Nebraska. Agricultural Experiment Station
MPV — Monumenta Poloniae Vaticana
MP Vt Agric Exp Stn — MP. Vermont Agricultural Experiment Station
MPWSEX — West Virginia University. Agriculture and Forestry Experiment Station. Miscellaneous Publication
MQ — Management Quarterly Magazine
MQ — Massachusetts Law Quarterly
MQ — Midwest Quarterly
MQ — Milton Quarterly
MQ — Modern Quarterly
MQ — Musical Quarterly
MQA — Manuel des Questions Actuelles
MQELA — Mecanique Electricite
MQG — Mitteilungen. Rheinisch-Westfaelisches Institut fuer Wirtschaftsforschung
Mq L — Marquette Law Review
Mq LR — Marquette Law Review
MQNY — Musical Quarterly. New York

MQR — Mennonite Quarterly Review
MQR — Methodist Quarterly Review
MQR — Mexico Quarterly Review
MQR — Michigan Quarterly Review
M Q Rev Montreal Mus F A — M. A Quarterly Review of the Montreal Museum of Fine Arts
MQRYA — Mine and Quarry
MQU — Management Quarterly
MQU — Multinational Business
MR — Mainzer Reihe
MR — March
MR — Marche Romane
MR — Marine-Rundschau
MR — Massachusetts Review
MR —.Mathematical Reviews
Mr — Meander
MR — [The] Media Report
MR — Mester
MR — Methodist Review
MR — Microform Review
MR — Minnesota Review
MR — Missale Romanum
MR — Missionswissenschaft und Religionswissenschaft
MR — Modern Review
MR — Montana Law Review
MR — Monthly Review
MR — Music Review
Mr — Musikrevy
MR — Mythes et Religions
MRA — Mainzer Romanistische Arbeiten
MRA — Mental Retardation Abstracts
MRA — Messtechnik, Regelunstechnik, Automatik
MRAL — Memorie. Reale Accademia Nazionale dei Lincei
MR & D — Management Review and Digest
MRATCAB — Murray River and Tributaries - Current Awareness Bulletin
MRATE — Money Market Rates
MRAZBN — Musee Royal de l'Afrique Centrale [Tervuren, Belgique]. Annales. Serie inOctavo. Sciences Zoologiques
MRBDT — Mitteilungen des Reichsbunds Deutscher Technik
MRBIR — Municipal Registered Bond Interest Record
MRBOAS — Marine Biology
MRC — Mediaeval and Renaissance Classics
MRCHB — Marine Chemistry
MRCHBD — Marine Chemistry
MRC Lab Anim Cent Symp — MRC . Laboratory Animals Centre Symposium
MRCLBP — Marcellia
MRC (Med Res Counc) (GB) Lab Anim Cent Symp — MRC (Medical Research Council) (Great Britain). Laboratory Animals Centre. Symposia
MRC Memo — MRC [Medical Research Council. Great Britain] Memorandum
MRCOD — Mechanics Research Communications
MRC Rev — MRC [Media Research Council] Review
MRCSA — Medical Research Council. Special Report Series
MRC War Memo — MRC [Medical Research Council. Great Britain] War Memorandum
MRCYA — Mercury
MRD — Media Review Digest
MRD — Memoirs. Research Department. Toyo Bunko
MRDDD8 — Mental Retardation and Developmental Disabilities
MRDS — Mineral Resources Data System
MRDTB — Memoirs. Research Department. Toyo Bunko
MRE — Management Review
MRE — Monographies Reine Elisabeth
M Rec — Medical Record
MRED — Mountain Research and Development
Mr Eng/Log — Marine Engineering/Log
MREO — Museion. Revue d'Etudes Orientales
M Reporter — Mining Reporter
MRERB — Marine Engineers Review
MRev — Mediterranean Review
MRev — Monthly Review
MRF — Manager Magazin
MRF — Music Research Forum
MRFWA4 — Malaysia. Report on Forest Administration in West Malaysia
MRG — Militaerregierungsgesetz
MRG — Mitteilungen der Raabe-Gesellschaft
MRGB — Mittelrheinische Geschichtsblaetter
MRGGAT — Morgagni
MRGRAS — Musee Royal de l'Afrique Centrale [Tervuren, Belgique]. Rapport Annuel. Departement de Geologie et de Mineralogie
MRGTAY — Marine Geotechnology
MRI — Maandstatistiek van de Brijzen
MRINAQ — Marine Research in Indonesia
MRINCS — Multidisciplinary Research
MRIR — Medellin. Revista. Instituto Pastoral del Celam
MRIS — Maritime Research Information Service
MRI Technical Report Series — Mineral Resources Institute. Technical Report Series
MRIW — Mitteilungen des Rumaenischen Instituts an der Universitaet Wien
MRJ — Mennonite Research Journal
MRK — Marketing. Zeitschrift fuer Forschung und Praxis
MRK — Military Review (Kansas)
MRKG — Monatshefte fuer Rheinische Kirchengeschichte
MRKTD — Marktforschung
MRL — Monthly Retail Trade. Current Business Report
MRL — Mutation Research Letters

MRLAA2 — Marine Research Laboratory. Investigational Report
MRLAB — Mededelingen. Rijksfaculteit Landbouwwetenschappen te Gent (Belgium)
MRL Bull Res Dev — MRL [Materials Research Laboratories] Bulletin of Research and Development
MRLTAP — Murrelet
MR Miss Agr Exp Sta — MR. Mississippi Agricultural Experiment Station
MRo — Marche Romane
M R Of R — Medical Review of Reviews
MRom — Marche Romane
MRP — American Review of Public Administration
MRP — Magazin fuer Religionsphilosophie, Exegese, und Kirchengeschichte
MRP — Musee de Rethelois et du Porcien
MRPS — Matricularum Regni Poloniae Summaria
MRR — Mad River Review
MRR — Magristrates of the Roman Republic
MRR — Market Research Great Britain
MRREDD — Medicinal Research Reviews
MRRTS — Manitoba. Department of Renewable Resources and Transportation Services. Research Branch. Reports
MRRVB — Meteornoe Rasprostranenie Radiovoln
MRS — Materials Research Society. Symposia. Proceedings
MRS — Mediaeval and Renaissance Studies
MRS — Michigan Romance Studies
MRS — Mission de Ras Shamra
MRS Bull — MRS [Materials Research Society] Bulletin
MRSHAO — Marine Research Series. Scottish Home Department
MRS Internet J Nitride Semicond Res — MRS Internet Journal of Nitride Semiconductor Research
MRSLA2 — Memoires. Societe Royale des Sciences de Liege. Collection in Octavo
MRSPD — Materials Research Society. Symposia. Proceedings
MRSQ — Medical Reference Services Quarterly
MRT — Magyarorszag Regeszeti Topografiaja
MRT — Militair Rechtelijk Tijdschrift
MRTMBB — Maritimes
Mr V — Metallreinigung Vorbehandlung, Oberflaechentechnik, Formung
MRV — Mex-Am Review
MRV — Montan-Rundschau. Zeitschrift fuer Bergbau und Huettenwesen (Vienna)
MRVNAN — RIVON [Rijksinstituut voor Veldbiologische Onderzoek ten Behoeve van het Natuurbehoud] Jaarverslag
MRVO — Militaerregierungsverordnung
MRW — Missionary Review of the World
MRW — Monthly Review
MRW — Museum fuer Religionswissenschaft in Ihrem Ganzen Umfange
MRWKA — Marine Week
MRX — National Bank of Ethiopia. Quarterly Bulletin. New Series
MRYAA — Memoirs. Royal Astronomical Society
MRYIBO — Miscellaneous Reports. Yamashina Institute for Ornithology and Zoology
MRZGA — Metody Razvedochnoi Geofiziki
MS — Maandblad N. Samson. Gewijd aan de Belangen der Gemeenteadministratie
MS — Magasin du Spectacle
MS — Mail on Sunday
MS — Manchester School of Economic and Social Studies
MS — Mar del Sur
MS — Mediaeval Studies
M/S — Media/Scope
MS — Melanges Syriens Offerts a Monsieur Rene Dussaud
MS — Memorias Succintas. Kahal Kados
MS — Metrologicorum Scriptorum Reliquiae
MS — Microstructural Science
MS — Midnight Sun. Igloolik
MS — Mitteilungen aus dem Gebiete der Statistik
MS — Moderna Sprak
MS — Modern Scot
Ms — Mois Suisse
MS — Monde Slave
MS — Monografias Sociologicas. Universidad Nacional de Colombia
MS — Monumenta Serica
MS — Mouvement Sociologique
Ms — Ms Magazine
MS — MS. Manuscript
MS — Mundo Social
MS — Musica Sacra
MS — Music Survey
MS — Muttersprache
M S — Muzikal'niy Sovremennik
MS — Mythic Society. Quarterly Journal
MSA — Monographs on Social Anthropology
MSA — Societe Academique d'Agriculture, des Sciences, et Belles Lettres du Departement de l'Aube. Memoires
MSA — Vakblad voor de Handel in Aardappelen, Groenten, en Fruit
MSAA — Memoirs. Society for American Archaeology
MSAAEQ — American Group Psychotherapy Association. Monograph Series
MSAC — Memoires. Societe des Arts et des Sciences de Carcassonne
MSAC — Societe des Antiquaires du Centre. Memoires
MSA Charente — Memoires. Societe Archeologique et Historique de la Charente
M Sacra — Musica Sacra
M Sacrae Ministerium — Musicae Sacrae Ministerium
MSAC Res J — MSAC [Mountain State Agricultural College] Research Journal
MSAeDG — Marburger Studien zur Aelteren Deutschen Geschichte
MSAF — Memoires. Societe Nationale des Antiquaires de France
MSAFV — Mitteilungen der Schweizerischen Anstalt fuer das Forstliche Versuchswesen
MSAg — Societe Archeologique et Historique de l'Agenais. Memoires
MSAGD9 — Maritime Sediments and Atlantic Geology

MSALH — Memoires et Publications. Societe des Sciences, des Arts et des Lettres du Heimat

MSAM — Memoires. Societe des Antiquaires de la Morinie

MSAM — Societe d'Agriculture, Commerce, Science, et Arts du Departement de la Marne. Memoires

MSA Marne — Memoires. Societe d'Agriculture, Commerce, Sciences, et Arts du Departement de la Marne

MSAMF — Memoires. Societe Archeologique du Midi de la France

MSAO — Memoires. Societe des Antiquaires de l'Ouest

MSAP — Memoires de la Societe des Americanistes de Paris

MSAP — Memoires. Societe des Antiquaires de Picardie

MSAPD2 — MIT [*Massachusetts Institute of Technology*] Studies in American Politicsand Public Policy

MSAR — Memoires. Societe Archeologique Imperiale Russe

MSARLRP — McGill Sub-Arctic Research Laboratory. Research Paper

MSASB — Monographs Series. Royal Asiatic Society of Bengal

MSATA — Societa Astronomica Italiana. Memorie

MSAv — Societe d'Archeologie, Litterature, Sciences, et Arts des Arrondissements d'Avranches et de Mortain. Memoires

MSAVAH — Institut Suisse de Recherches Forestieres. Memoires

MSB — Mass Spectrometry Bulletin

MSB — Mededelingen van de Schoolraad voor de Scholen met de Bijbel

MSB — Messager de Saint Benoit

MSB — Mongolian Studies. Journal of the Mongolia Society

MSB — Mongolia Society. Bulletin

MSB — Sitzungsberichte der Bayerischen Akademie der Wissenschaften. Muenchen

MSBCD2 — Marine Studies of San Pedro Bay, California

MSBG-A — Masalah Bangunan

MSBIDK — Methodological Surveys in Biochemistry

MSBMRS — Marine Sciences Branch. Manuscript Report Series. Canada Department of Energy,Mines, and Resources

MS Bres — Monografie di Storia Bresciana

MSBTA — Memoires. Academie des Sciences, Inscriptions, et Belles-Lettres de Toulouse

MSC — Maitres de la Spiritualite Chretienne

MSC — Management Science

MSC — Manizales (Colombia)

M Sc — Musik in der Schule

MScan — Mediaeval Scandinavia

MSCDA — Monographs. Society for Research in Child Development

MSCE — Miscellanea di Storia e Cultura Ecclesiastica

M Scene — Music Scene

MSch — Modern Schoolman

M Schallplatte — Musica Schallplatte

Mschr Brau — Monatsschrift fuer Brauerei

Mschr Christl Polit — Monatsschrift fuer Christliche Politik und Kultur

Mschr Dt KaktGes — Monatsschrift der Deutschen Kakteen-Gesellschaft

Mschr EisenbVer Hannover — Monatsschrift der Eisenbahnvereine des Direktionsbezirks Hannover

Mschr ElektHomoop — Monatsschrift fuer Elektro-Homoopathie

Mschr Feinmech Opt — Monatsschrift fuer Feinmechanik und Optik

Mschr GartenbVer Darmstadt — Monatsschrift des Gartenbauvereins, Darmstadt

Mschr Geburtsh Gynak — Monatsschrift fuer Geburtshilfe und Gynakologie

Mschr Gesch & Wiss Judenthums — Monatsschrift fuer Geschichte und Wissenschaft des Judenthums

Mschr Ges Heimatkde Brandbg — Monatsschrift der Gesellschaft fuer Heimatkunde der Provinz Brandenburg

Mschr GesundhPflege — Monatsschrift fuer Gesundheitspflege

Mschr Handelsr Bankw — Holdheims Monatsschrift fuer Handelsrecht und Bankwesen. Steuerund Stempelfragen

Mschr Harnkrankh Sex Hyg — Monatsschrift fuer Harnkrankheiten und Sexuelle Hygiene

Mschr Hist Ver Oberbayern — Monatsschriften des Historischen Vereins von Oberbayern

Mschr Hyg Aufklaer Reform — Monatsschrift fuer Hygienische Aufklaerung und Reform

Mschr Kakteenk — Monatsschrift fuer Kakteenkunde

Mschr Kinderheilk — Monatsschrift fuer Kinderheilkunde

Mschr Klin Kinderheilk — Monatsschrift fuer Klinische Kinderheilkunde

Mschr Krebsbekaempf — Monatsschrift fuer Krebsbekaempfung

Mschr Kriminalpsych — Aschaffenburgs Monatsschrift fuer Kriminalpsychologie

Mschr KrimPsychol — Monatsschrift fuer Kriminalpsychologie

Mschr Lit Wiss Judent — Monatsschrift fuer Literatur und Wissenschaft des Judentums

Mschr Miner Gesteins U PetrifSamml — Monatsschrift fuer Mineralien-, Gesteins-, und Petrifaktensammler

Mschr Ohrenheilk Lar Rhinol — Monatsschrift fuer Ohrenheilkunde und Laryngo-Rhinologie

Mschr Orthop Chir — Monatsschrift fuer Orthopaedische Chirurgie und Physikalische Heilmethoden

Mschr Pastoraltheol — Monatsschrift fuer Pastoraltheologie

Mschr Phys Diat Heilmeth — Monatsschrift fuer die Physikalisch-Diatetische Heilmethoden

Mschr Prakt WassHeilk — Monatsschrift fuer Praktische Wasserheilkunde und Physikalische Heilmethoden

Mschr Psychiat Neurol — Monatsschrift fuer Psychiatrie und Neurologie

Mschrr Comeniusges — Monatsschriften der Comenius-Gesellschaft

Mschr Soz Med — Monatsschrift fuer Soziale Medizin

Mschr TextInd — Monatsschrift fuer Textilindustrie

Mschr TuberkBekaempf — Monatsschrift fuer Tuberkulosebekaempfung

Mschr Unfallheilk Invalidenw — Monatsschrift fuer Unfallheilkunde und Invalidenwesen

Mschr Unfallheilk VersichMed — Monatsschrift fuer Unfallheilkunde und Versicherungsmedizin

Mschr Ung Med — Monatsschrift Ungarischer Mediziner

Mschr Ver Tieraerzte Ost — Monatsschrift des Vereins der Tieraerzte in Oesterreich

Mschr Wien Tieraerztl — Monatsschrift Wiener Tieraerztliche

Mschr Wuertt Ver Bauk — Monatsschrift des Wuerttembergischen Vereins fuer Baukunde

Mschr Zahnheilk — Monatsschrift fuer Zahnheilkunde

Mschr Zahnheilk Zahntech — Monatsschrift fuer Zahnheilkunde und Zahntechnik

Mschr Zahntech — Monatsschrift fuer Zahntechnik und Verwandte Gebiete

M Science — Mining Science

M Sci Rel — Melanges de Science Religieuse

MSCN — Memorias de la Sociedad de Ciencias Naturales La Salle [*Caracas*]

MSCOA — Metallurgical Society. Conferences

M Sc Press — Mining and Scientific Press

MScRel — Melanges de Science Religieuse

MSCS — Mankato State College [*later Mankato State University*] Studies

MSCT — Marine Science Contents Tables

MSCTS — Monograph Series. Calvin Theological Seminary

MSD — Musica Sacra

MSD — Societe d'Etudes Scientifiques et Archeologiques de Draguignan. Memoires

MSDC News — MSDC (Medical Society of the District of Columbia) News

MS Diss — Manuscript Dissertation

MSDS — Material Safety Data Sheets

MSE — Maandblad voor Sociaal Economiese. Wetenschappen

MSE — Malaja Sovetskaja Enciklopedija

MSE — Massachusetts Studies in English

MSE — Mathematical Studies in Economics and Statistics in the USSR and Eastern Europe

MSE — Memoires. Societe Eduenne

MSE — Muslims of the Soviet East

MSEC — Memoires. Societe d'Emulation de Cambrai

MSEC — Societe Toulousaine d'Etudes Classiques. Melanges

MSED — Memoires. Societe d'Emulation du Doubs

MSEG — Mitteilungen der Schweizerischen Entomologischen Gesellschaft

MSEJ — Memoires. Societe des Etude Japonaises, Chinoises, Tartares, et Indochinoises aParis

MSEJ — Memoires. Societe des Etudes Juives

MSEP — Memoires de la Societe d'Ethnographie de Paris

MSER — Memoires. Societe d'Emulation de Roubaix

MSer — Monumenta Serica

M Ser M — Monumenta Serica. Monograph Series

MSESS — Manchester School of Economic and Social Studies

MSEWA — Memoirs. School of Science and Engineering. Waseda University

M S Ex — Melville Society. Extracts

MSF — Marvel Science Fiction

MSF — Memorie Storiche Forogiuliesi

MSFFF — Memoranda Societatis pro Fauna et Flora Fennica

MSFL — Metodologia delle Scienze e Filosofia del Linguaggio

MSFO — Memoires. Societe Finno-Ougrienne

MSForogiuliesi — Memorie Storiche Forogiuliesi

MSFOu — Memoires. Societe Finno-Ougrienne

MSG — Mitteilungen. Sonzino-Gesellschaft

MSG — Musici Scriptores Graeci

MSGE — Memoires. Societe de Geographie d'Egypte

Ms Gesch Jud — Monatsschrift fuer Geschichte und Wissenschaft des Judentums

MSGF — Memoires de la Societe Geologique de France

MSGFOK — Mitteilungen. Schweizerische Gesellschaft der Freunde Ostasiatischer Kultur

MSGI — Memoria delle Societa Geografica Italiana

MSG News — Maghrib Studies Group. Newsletter

MSGSB — Gijutsu Shiryo. Mitsubishi Sekiyu Kabushiki Kaisha

MSGV — Mitteilungen. Schlesische Gesellschaft fuer Volkskunde

MSGVK — Mitteilungen der Schlesischen Gesellschaft fuer Volkskunde

MSGW — Mitteilungen der Sevcenko-Gesellschaft in Lemberg

MSH — Musica Sacro-Hispana

MSHAB — Memoires. Societe d'Histoire et d'Archeologie de Bretagne

MSHAL — Memoires. Societe Historique et Archeologique de Langres

MSH Chalon — Memoires. Societe d'Histoire et d'Archeologie de Chalon-sur-Saone

MSHD — Memoires. Societe pour l'Histoire de Droit et des Institutions des Anciens PaysBourguignons, Comtois et Romands

MSHDI — Memoires. Societe pour l'Histoire du Droit et des Institutions des Anciens Pays Bourguignons, Comtois, et Romands

MSHG — Societe d'Histoire et d'Archeologie de Geneve. Memoires et Documents

Ms Hoeh Sch — Monatsschrift fuer Hoehere Schulen

MSHP — Memoires. Societe de l'Histoire de Paris et de l'Ile-de-France

MSH Th — Muenchener Studien zur Historischen Theologie

MSI — Miscellanea di Storia Italiana

MSI — Moody Street Irregulars

MSIA — Societe Imperiale des Antiquaires de France. Memoires

MS Insul Reptr — MS Insulation Reporter. Magnesia-Silica Insulation Manufacturers' Association

Ms J — Museum Journal. University Museum. University of Pennsylvania

MS JI — M.S. Journal [*Calcutta*]

MSJMAZ — Mount Sinai Journal of Medicine

MSK — Mitteilungen. Stadtarchiv von Koeln

MSKEDJ — Japanese Journal of Michurin Biology

MSL — Manchester School of Economic and Social Studies

MSL — Materials for the Sumerian Lexicon

MSL — Memoires. Societe Linguistique de Paris

MSL — Miscellanea di Storia Ligure

M Sl — Monde Slave

MSLAVA J — Manitoba School Library Audio-Visual Association. Journal

MSLBA — Muscle Biology

MSLC — Miscellanea di Studi di Letteratura Cristiana Antica

MSLC — Modernist Studies. Literature and Culture, 1920-1940

MSLCA — Miscellanea di Studi Letteratura Cristiana Antica
MS LJ — Mississippi Law Journal
MSLL — Minnesota. University. Studies in Language and Literature
MSLL — Monograph Series on Languages and Linguistics. Georgetown University
MSLOB — Mineralia Slovaca
MSLP — Memoires. Societe Linguistique de Paris
MSLund — Meddelanden fran Seminarierna foer Slaviska Sprak, Jamforande Sprakforskning och Finsk-Ugriska Sprak vis Lunds Universitet
MSM — Materials Science Monographs
MSM — Memoires. Societe d'Agriculture, Commerce, Sciences, et Arts du Departement de la Marne
MSM — Miscellanea di Studi Muratoriani. Convegno di Studi in Onore di L. A. Muratori
MSM — Modern Schoolman
MsM — Ms Magazine
MSMarne — Memoires. Societe d'Agriculture, Commerce, Sciences, et Arts du Departement de la Marne
MSMC — Masterkey. Southwest Museum (Los Angeles, California)
MSMCDN — Medical Research Council (Great Britain). Laboratory Animals Centre. Manual Series
MSMHD — Medecine Aeronautique et Spatiale, Medecine Subaquatique et Hyperbare
MSMND — South African Medical Equipment News
MSMSD — Mechanics of Materials
MSN — Microwave Systems News
MSN — Monthly Science News
MS N — Musica Sacra
MSNAF — Memoires. Societe Nationale des Antiquaires de France
MSNAFr — Memoires. Societe Nationale des Antiquaires de France
MS News — M.S. News. Multiple Sclerosis Society [London]
MSNH — Memoires. Societe Neophilologique de Helsinki
MSNM — Memoires de la Societe des Naturalistes de Moscou
MSN Microwave Syst News — MSN. Microwave Systems News
MSO — Memoires. Section des Orientalistes. Socite Imperiale Russe d'Archeologie
MSO — Societe d'Agriculture, Sciences, Belles-Lettres, et Arts d'Orleans. Memoires
M Soc NJ J — Medical Society of New Jersey. Journal
M Soc NS J — Mining Society of Nova Scotia. Journal
MSOeRK — Mitteilungen aus der Studienabteilung des Oekumenischen Rates der Kirchen
MSOS — Mitteilungen des Seminars fuer Orientalische Sprachen an der Friedrich-Wilhelms-Universitaet zu Berlin
MSOS — Mitteilungen. Seminar fuer Orientalische Sprachen zu Berlin
MSOSAfr — Mitteilungen des Seminars fuer Orientalische Sprachen. Afrikanische Studien
MSOSD — Mathematical Social Sciences
M Sp — Militaire Spectator
MSP — Monumenta Sacra et Profana
MSp — Muttersprache
MSPA — Missinipe Achimowin. Churchill River Information
MSPAIRS — Missinipe Achimowin. Interim Report Supplement
MSPP — Maharastra Sahitya Parisad Patrika
MSpr — Moderna Sprak
MSpra — Moderne Sprachen
MSprak — Moderna Sprak
MSQSAK — Mosquito Systematics
MSR — Industrie- und Handelsrevue
MSR — Malone Society. Reprints
MSR — Melanges de Science Religieuse
MSR — Mobile Satellite Reports
MsR — Muslim Review
MSR C — Melanges de Science Religieuse. Cahier Supplement
MSRC — Memoires. Societe Royale du Canada
MS Rep — M.S. Reports. Department of Atomic Energy. Ministry of Supply [London]
MSR Mess Steuern Regeln — MSR. Messen, Steuern, Regeln
MSRN — Mountain Safety Research Newsletter
MSRS — Medical Socioeconomic Research Sources
MSRS — Monatsschrift fuer die Reformierte Schweiz
MSRT J — MSRT [Michigan Society for Respiratory Therapy] Journal
MSS — Manuscripts
MSS — Marvel Science Stories
MSS — Muenchener Studien zur Sprachwissenschaft
MSS B — Muenchener Studien zur Sprachwissenschaft. Beiheft
MSSCD — Microstructural Science
MSSCEK — Medicine and Sport Science
MSSLA — Missili
MSSLC — Memoires. Societe des Sciences et Lettres de Loir-et-Cher
MSSM — Monumenta Servorum Sanctae Mariae
MSS Mid E — Manuscripts of the Middle East
MSSNC — Memoires. Societe des Sciences Naturelles et Archeologiques de la Creuse
MSSNTS — Monograph Series. Society for New Testament Studies
MSSOTS — Monograph Series. Society for Old Testament Studies
MSSYBF — Specialist Periodical Reports. Mass Spectrometry
M St — Mariologische Studien
MST — Middle East Transport
MSt — Mitteldeutsche Studien
MST — Mittellateinische Studien und Texte
MSt — Monastic Studies
MST — Societe Archeologique de Touraine. Memoires
MStLAB — Mitteilungen des Statistischen Landesamts des Koenigreichs Boehmen
MST News Pol — MST (Microsystem Technology) News Poland
MSTPS/R — Revista Mexicana del Trabajo. Secretaria del Trabajo y Prevision Social
MStud — Milton Studies

MSU — Mitteilungen. Septuaginta Unternehmen
MSU — MSU [Michigan State University] Business Topics
MSUB — Maharaja Sayajirao University of Baroda. Oriental Institute. Journal
MSUBOIJ — Maharaja Sajajirao. University of Baroda. Oriental Institute Journal
MSU Bus To — MSU [Michigan State University] Business Topics
MSU Bus Top — MSU [Michigan State University] Business Topics
MSU Bus Topics — MSU [Michigan State University] Business Topics
MSU (Mich State Univ) Bus Topics — MSU (Michigan State University) Business Topics
MSV — Maandstatistiek Verkeer en Vervoer
MSV — Miscellanea Storica della Valdelsa
Ms Val — Miscellanea Storica della Valdelsa
MSVSN — Memoires de la Societe Vaudoise des Sciences Naturelles
MSV Z Met Schmuckwaren Fabr Verchrom — MSV. Zeitschrift fuer Metall- und Schmuckwaren-Fabrikation sowieVerchromung
MSWFA — Messwerte
MSYNAB — Mosquito Systematics News Letter
MSzA — Mainzer Studien zur Amerikanistik
MSZS — Muenchener Studien zur Sprachwissenschaft
MT — Machine Translation
MT — Management Today
MT — Marvel Tales
MT — Marxism Today
MT — Matematisk Tidsskrift
MT — Mathematics Teacher
MT — Mechanical Translation
MT — Medical Times and Gazette
mt — Meerestechnik
MT — Megiddo Tombs
MT — Melanges Theologiques
MT — Moccasin Telegraph. Fort Chipewyan
MT — Motor Trend Magazine
MT — Museum Tusculanum
MT — Musical Times
MT — Music Theory Spectrum
MT — Mycenae Tablets
MTA — Maden Tetkik ve Arama Enstitusu Dergisi/Journal of the Mining Research and Exploration Institute of Turkey
MTA — Magyar Tudomanyos Akademia Filozofiai es Tortenettudomanyi. Osztalyanak Koezlemenyei
MTA — Magyar Tudomanyos Akademia. Nyelv-es Irodalomtudomanyi Osztalyanak. Koezlemenyei
MTA — Materials Engineering
MTAEB — Maden Tetkik ve Arama Enstitusu. Bulletin (Ankara)
MTAEY — Maden Tetkik ve Arama Enstitusu Yayinlari/Publications of the Mining Research and Exploration Institute of Turkey
MTAFTO — Magyar Tudomanyos Akademia Filozofiai es Tortenettudomanyi. Osztalyanak Koezlemenyei
MTAFTOK — Magyar Tudomanyos Akademia Filozofiai es Tortenettudomanyi. Osztalyanak Koezlemenyei
MTAII Oszt Koezl — Magyar Tudomanyos Akademia Filozofiai es Tortenettudomanyi. Osztalyanak Koezlemenyei
MTAI Oszt Koezl — Magyar Tudomanyos Akademia Nyelv es Irodalomtudomanyi Osztalyanak Koezlemenyei
MTAJ — MTA [Motor Traders Association of New South Wales] Official Journal
MTAK — Magyar Tudomanyos Akademia Filozofiai es Tortenettudomanyi. Osztalyanak Koezlemenyei
MTAK — Magyar Tudomanyos Akademia. Nyelv-es Irodalomtudomanyi Osztalyanak. Koezlemenyei
M T & Long Island M J — Medical Times & Long Island Medical Journal
MTANIOK — Magyar Tudomanyos Akademia Nyelv es Irodalomtudomanyi Osztalyanak Koezlemenyei
MTA Nyelv Irod OK — Magyar Tudomanyos Akademia Nyelv es Irodalomtudomanyi Osztalyanak Koezlemenyei
MTatD — Materialy po Tatarskoj Dialektologii
MTB — Memoirs. Research Department. Toyo Bunko
MTB — Tokyo. Toyo Bunko [Oriental Library]. Research Department. Memoirs
Mt Blanc Obs A — Annales de l'Observatoire Meteorologique Physique et Glaciaire du Mont Blanc
MTCA — Magazine. Texas Commission on Alcoholism
MTCPCI — Marine Technology Society. Annual Conference. Preprints
MTD — Management Decision
MTD — Market Trends Digest
MTDFA — Metal Treatment and Drop Forging
MTD Mag — M.T.D. (Midland Tar Distillers) Magazine
MTDYA — Modern Trends in Dermatology
MTE JI — MTE (Medical Training Establishment) Journal. Royal Air Force [Harrogate]
MTG — Medical Times and Gazette
Mt Geol — Mountain Geologist
MTGRB — Metallographic Review
Mt Grow — Mountaineer Grower
MTGSA — Mitteilungen aus dem Arbeitsbereich. Metallgesellschaft AG
MTGU — Australian Master Tax Guide Updater
M Th — Melita Theologica
MTH — Musiktheorie
Mth A — Mathematische Annalen
Mtherapie — Musiktherapie
Mthly Bull Constr Indices (Bldg Civil Engng) — Monthly Bulletin of Construction Indices (Building and Civil Engineering)
Mthly Dig Transp News — Monthly Digest of Transport News
Mthly Lab R — Monthly Labor Review
Mthly Mag — Monthly Magazine
Mthly Publ Opin Surv — Monthly Public Opinion Surveys
Mthly R — Monthly Review

MThM — Meddelelser fra Thorvaldsens Museum
Mth N B Ung — Mathematische und Naturwissenschaftliche Berichte aus Ungarn
M Thorv Mus — Meddelelser fra Thorvaldsens Museum
MThS — Muenchener Theologische Studien
M Th SH — Muenchener Theologische Studien. Historische Abteilung
M Th SHE — Muenchener Theologische Studien. Historische Abteilung. Ergaenzungsband
M Th SK — Muenchener Theologische Studien. Kanonistische Abteilung
M Th SS — Muenchener Theologische Studien. Systematische Abteilung
M Th St — Marburger Theologische Studien
Mth Term Ets — Mathematikai es Termeszettudomanyi Ertesito
Mth Termt Ets — Mathematikai es Termeszettudomanyi Ertesito
Mth Ts — Mathematisk Tidsskrift
M Th Z — Muenchener Theologische Zeitschrift
MTI — Maeventec Travel Information
MTIAA — Metalurgiya
M Tijdschr Werktuigkunde — M-Tijdschrift. Werktuigkunde
M Times — Musical Times
M Times & Long Island M J — Medical Times and Long Island Medical Journal
M Times NY — Medical Times (New York)
M Tire Dealr — Modern Tire Dealer
MTJ — Mark Twain Journal
MTK — Monatsschrift fuer Theologie und Kirche
MTLGA — Metallurgie
MTM — Journal of Methods-Time Measurement
MTM — Management Team
MTM — Marches Tropicaux et Mediterraneens
MTM — Marketing Times
MTNG — Mitteilungen der Thurgauischen Naturforschenden Gesellschaft
Mtn St Bank — Mountain States Banker
MTO — Management Today
Mtone News — Movietone News
Mt Ostld — Mittheilungen aus dem Osterlande
MTP — Music Therapy Perspectives
MTP Int Rev Sci Biochem — MTP [Medical & Technical Publishing Co.] International Review of Science.Biochemistry
MTP Int Rev Sci Physiol — MTP [Medical and Technical Publishing Company] International Review of Science. Physiology
Mt Plains Lib Assn Q — Mountain Plains Library Association. Quarterly
MTP (Med Tech Publ Co) Int Rev Sci Ser One Physiol — MTP (Medical and Technical Publishing Company) International Review of Science.Series One. Physiology
MTQ — Mark Twain Quarterly
MTR — Mitsubishi Bank Review
MTr — Music Trades
Mt Res Dev — Mountain Research and Development
MTS — Marine Technology Series
MTS — Microcard Theological Studies
MTS — Monuments Illustrating Tragedy and Satyr Plays
MTS — Most Thrilling Science Ever Told
MTSHB5 — Morioka Tabako Shikenjo Hokoku
Mt Sinai J — Mount Sinai Journal of Medicine
Mt Sinai J Med — Mount Sinai Journal of Medicine
MTSJBB — Marine Technology Society. Journal
Mt States Min Age — Mountain States Mining Age
Mt States Miner Age — Mountain States Mineral Age
Mt Stromlo Obs Repr — Mount Stromlo Observatory Reprints [Canberra]
MTTKA — Meteoritika
MTTMA — Memoirs. Faculty of Technology. Tokyo Metropolitan University
MTTQ — Medical Trial Technique Quarterly
MTU — Muenchener Texte und Untersuchungen zur Deutschen Literatur des Mittelalters
M Tud — Magyar Tudomany
MTUDLM — Muenchener Texte und Untersuchungen zur Deutschen Literatur des Mittelalters
MTVA — Mitteilungen des Staatlichen Technischen Versuchsamtes
Mt Wash Obs News Bull — Mount Washington Observatory News Bulletin
MTW Mitt — MTW Mitteilungen. Zeitschrift zur Pflege der Beziehungen Zwischen Mathematik, Technik, Wirtschaft
MTWOA — Metalworking
MTY — MTM. Journal of Methods Time Measurement
MTZ — Motortechnische Zeitschrift
MTZ — Muenchener Theologische Zeitschrift
MTZ Motortech Z — MTZ. Motortechnische Zeitschrift
MU — Moniteur Universel
Mu — Mulino
Mu — Musica
Mu — Muttersprache. Zeitschrift zur Pflege und Erforschung der Deutschen Sprache
MuA — Musica Antiqua
MU(B) — Melanges. Universite Saint Joseph (Beyrouth)
MuB — Musik und Bildung
MUBBDD — Moscow University. Biological Sciences Bulletin
Mubers Witt Oest — Monatsuebersicht der Witterung in Oesterreich
MUBM — Mitteilungen des Universitaetsbundes Marburg
MuC — MusiCanada
Muck Shift Publ Wks Dig — Muck Shifter and Public Works Digest
Muebers Saechs Landeswetterw — Monatsuebersicht der Saechsischen Landeswetterwarte
Muegy Koezl Magy K Josef Nador Musz Gazdasagtud Egy — Muegyetemi Koezlemenyek. Magyar Kir. Josef Nador Mueszaki es Gazdasagtudomanyi Egyetem
Muegy Kozl (Budapest) — Muegyetemi Kozlemenyek (Budapest)
MUEHA — Muehle
Muehandis Mak — Muehandis ve Makina
Muehandis Mekt Mecm — Muehandis Mektebi Mecmuasi

Muehle Mischfuttertech — Muehle und Mischfuttertechnik
Muehlen U Speicherb — Muehlen- und Speicherbau
Muehlen Ztg — Muehlen-Zeitung
Muehlhaeuser Geschbl — Muehlhaeuser Geschichtsblaetter
MueJ — Muenchner Jahrbuch der Bildenden Kunst
MuEJ — Music Educators Journal
Mue Jb — Muenchner Jahrbuch der Bildenden Kunst
MUELC — Mundo Electronico
Muell Abfall Beih — Muell und Abfall. Beihefte
Mueller Arch — Archiv fuer Anatomie, Physiologie, und Wissenschaftliche Medicin. Mueller, Reichert, Du Bois-Reymond
Muen — Muenster
Muench Ab — Abhandlungen der Mathematisch-Physikalischen Classe der Koenigl. Bayerischen Akademie der Wissenschaften (Muenchen)
Muench Aerztl Anz — Muenchener Aerztliche Anzeiger
Muench Ak Ab — Abhandlungen der Mathematisch-Physikalischen Classe der Koenigl. Bayerischen Akademie der Wissenschaften (Muenchen)
Muench Bauztg — Muenchener Bauzeitung
Muench Beit Abwasser-Fisch- Flussbiol — Muenchener Beitraege zur Abwasser-, Fischerei-, und Flussbiologie
Muench Beitr — Muenchener Beitraege zur Romanischen und Englischen Philologie
Muench Beitr — Muenchener Beitraege zur Papyrusforschung und Antiken Rechtsgeschichte
Muench Beitr Abwasser Fisch Flussbiol — Muenchener Beitraege zur Abwasser-, Fischerei-, und Flussbiologie
Muench Beitr Gesch Lit Naturw Med — Muenchener Beitraege zur Geschichte und Literatur der Naturwissenschaften und Medizin
Muench Beitr z Pap — Muenchener Beitraege zur Papyrusforschung und Antiken Rechtsgeschichte
Muench Brautech Zentbl — Muenchener Brautechnisches Zentralblatt
Muench D — Denkschriften der Koenigl. Bayerischen Akademie der Wissenschaften zu Muenchen
Muenchen Augsb Abendztg — Muenchen-Augsburger Abendzeitung
Muenchener Med Wochens — Muenchener Medizinische Wochenschrift
Muenchener Theol Z — Muenchener Theologische Zeitschrift
Muenchen Med Wchnschr — Muenchener Medizinische Wochenschrift
Muenchen Theol Z — Muenchener Theologische Zeitschrift
Muench Gelehrte Az — Gelehrte Anzeigen. Herausgegeben von Mitgliedern der Koenigl. Bayerischen Akademie der Wissenschaften (Muenchen)
Muench Geogr Abh — Muenchener Geographische Abhandlungen
Muench Geogr Stud — Muenchener Geographische Studien
Muench Gs Mph Pl Sb — Sitzungsberichte der Gesellschaft fuer Morphologie und Physiologie in Muenchen
Muench Jahr Bild Kunst — Muenchener Jahrbuch der Bildenden Kunst
Muench Jarhb Bild K — Muenchner Jahrbuch der Bildenden Kunst
Muench Klebst Veredel Semin — Muenchener Klebstoff- und Veredelungs-Seminar
Muench Koleopt Z — Muenchener Koleopterologische Zeitschrift
Muench Med Abh — Muenchener Medizinische Abhandlungen
Muench Med Wochenschr — Muenchener Medizinische Wochenschrift
Muench Med Wschr — Muenchener Medizinische Wochenschrift
Muenchn Beitr Abwass Fisch Flussbiol — Menchner Beitraege zur Abwasser-, Fischerei-, und Flussbiologie
Muenchn Beitr Vor & Fruegesch — Muenchner Beitraege zur Vor- und Fruegeschichte
Muenchener Beitr Abwasser Fisch Flussbiol — Muenchener Beitraege zur Abwasser-, Fischerei-, und Flussbiologie
Muenchner Jahrb — Muenchner Jahrbuch der Bildenden Kunst
Muenchner Jb Bild Kunst — Muenchner Jahrbuch der Bildenden Kunst
Muench Geogr Hft — Muenchener Geographische Hefte
Muenchn Illus Presse — Muenchner Illustrierte Presse
Muenchn Jb Bild Kst — Muenchner Jahrbuch der Bildenden Kunst
Muenchn Jb Kstgesch — Muenchner Jahrbuch der Kunstgeschichte
Muenchn Jugend — Muenchner Jugend
Muenchn Mus Philol Mittelalt & Ren — Muenchner Museum fuer Philologie des Mittelalters und der Renaissance
Muenchn Neuesten Nachr — Muenchner Neuesten Nachrichten
Muench Nt Tech Com Ab — Abhandlungen der Naturwissenschaftlich-Technischen Commission bei der Koenigl. Baierischen Akademie (Muenchen)
Muench St Spr Wiss — Muenchener Studien zur Sprachwissenschaft
Muench Stud Psychol Phil — Muenchener Studien zur Psychologie und Philosophie
Muench Symp Exp Orthop — Muenchner Symposion fuer Experimentelle Orthopaedie
Muench Tieraerztl Wochenschr — Muenchener Tieraerztliche Wochenschrift
Muench Tieraerztl Wschr — Muenchener Tieraerztliche Wochenschrift
Muench Z Archt — Zeitschrift des Bayerischen Architecten- und Ingenieur-Vereins (Muenchen)
Muenster Forsch Geol Palaeontol — Muenstersche Forschungen zur Geologie und Palaeontologie
Muenster Numi Ztg — Muenstersche Numismatische Zeitung
Muenstersche Forsch Geol Palaeontol — Muenstersche Forschungen zur Geologie und Palaeontologie
Muenstersche N Z — Muenstersche Numismatische Zeitung
Muenz Med — Muenzen und Medaillen
Mue PF — Muenchner Philosophische Forschungen
Mueszaki Terv — Mueszaki Tervezes
Mueszeruegyi Merestech Koezl — Mueszeruegyi es Merestechnikai Koezlemenyek
Muesz Koezl Lang Gepgyar Muesz Gazd Tajek — Mueszaki Koezlemenyek. Lang Gepgyar Mueszaki es Gazdasagi Tajekoztatoja
Muesz Tud — Mueszaki Tudomany
Mue TZ — Muenchner Theologische Zeitschrift
Mueved — Muemlekvedelem

Mueves Ertes — Muveszettorteneti Ertesito
Muevtort Ert — Muveszettorteneti Ertesito
MUFOB — Metempirical UFO [*Unidentified Flying Object*] Bulletin
MuG — Musik und Gesellschaft
MU Gazette — Melbourne University. Gazette
Muhendis Mektebi Mecm — Muhendis Mektebi Mecmuasi
MUHLA2 — Muehlenzeitung
Muhle Mischfuttertech — Muehle und Mischfuttertechnik
Mul — Music Index
Mul — Musikinstrument
Muirhead Tech — Muirhead Technique
Muirh Lib P — Muirhead Library of Philosophy
MUIS — Madras University Islamic Series
MUJ — Madras University. Journal
MUJ — Melanges. Faculte Orientale. Universite de St. Joseph
MuJ — Music Journal
MUJA — Madras University. Journal. Section A. Humanities
MUJB — Madras University. Journal. Section B. Science
Mu Jb — Muenchner Jahrbuch der Bildenden Kunst
MUJSAX — Marathwada University. Journal of Science. Section A. Physical Sciences
MUJSBY — Marathwada University. Journal of Science. Section B. Biological Sciences
MUJWRRC Rep — MUJWRRC [*Montana University Joint Water Resources Research Center*] Report
MuK — Maske und Kothurn
MuK — Musik und Kirche
MUK — Wirtschaftlichkeit
Mukom Elevat Prom — Mukomol'no-Elevatornaya Promyshlennost
Mukom Elevat Sklad Khoz — Mukomol'e i Elevatorno-Skladskoe Khozyaistvo
Mukomole Elevat Skladskoe Khoz — Mukomol'e i Elevatorno-Skladskoe Khozyaistvo
Mukomol' -Elevator Prom — Mukomol'no-Elevatornaya Promyshlennost'
Mukomolno Elevat Kombikormovaya Promst — Mukomol'no Elevatornaya i Kombikormovaya Promyshlennost
Mukomolno Elevat Promst — Mukomol'no-Elevatornaya Promyshlennost'
Mul — Mulino
MuL — Music and Letters
MU Law R — Melbourne University. Law Review
Mulder Arch — Natuur- en Scheikundig Archief. Mulder, Wenckebach
Mulford Vet Bull — Mulford Veterinary Bulletin
Mulhouse Bll — Bulletin de la Societe Industrielle de Mulhouse
Mulhouse Bll S In — Bulletin de la Societe Industrielle de Mulhouse
Mulhouse S In Bll — Bulletin de la Societe Industrielle de Mulhouse
Mu LJ — Municipal Law Journal
Mullard Outl — Mullard Outlook
Mullard Rev — Mullard Review
Mullard Tech Bull — Mullard Technical Bulletin
Mullard Tech Commun — Mullard Technical Communications
Mullard Tech Handb — Mullard Technical Handbook
Mullard Tech Handb Bull — Mullard Technical Handbook Bulletin
Mullard Tech Rep — Mullard Technical Report
Mullard Wld Rev — Mullard World Review
MULR — Malayan Union Law Reports
MULR — Melbourne University. Law Review
MULRA6 — Muellerei
MULS — Minnesota Union List of Serials
Multicult — Multiculturalism
Multicult Ed — Multicultural Education
Multicult Ed J — Multicultural Education Journal
Multicult Educ Abstr — Multicultural Education Abstracts
Multidimens Systems Signal Process — Multidimensional Systems and Signal Processing
Multidimens Syst Signal Proc — Multidimensional Systems and Signal Processing
Multidisciplinary Res — Multidisciplinary Research
Multidiscip Res — Multidisciplinary Research
Multilayer Ceram Devices — Multilayer Ceramic Devices
Multi Media Rev Index — Multi Media Reviews Index
Multi Mon — Multinational Monitor
Multinational Bus — Multinational Business
Multinatl — Multinational Monitor
Multinatl Monit — Multinational Monitor
Multipart Dyn Int Symp — Multiparticle Dynamics. International Symposium
Multiphase Sci Technol — Multiphase Science and Technology
Multiple Sclerosis Indicative Abstr — Multiple Sclerosis Indicative Abstracts
Multipurp Util Miner Resour — Multipurpose Utilization of Mineral Resources
Multi Scler Abstr — Multiple Sclerosis Abstracts
Multivar Behav Res — Multivariate Behavioral Research
Multivar Behav Res Monogr — Multivariate Behavioral Research Monograph
Multiv Be R — Multivariate Behavioral Research
Mult Mon — Multinational Monitor
Mult Scler — Multiple Sclerosis
Mult Scler Abstr — Multiple Sclerosis Abstracts
MUM — Melbourne University. Magazine
Mu M — Muenzen und Medaillen
MUM — Music Ministry
MuM — Music and Musicians
MUMEB — Music Clubs Magazine
MUMED9 — Museum Memoir
MUMEEA — Mundo Medico
MUMSCMR — McGill University [*Montreal*]. Marine Sciences Centre. Manuscript Report
MUMUA — Music and Musicians
MUN — Memoires de l'Universite de Neuchatel
MUN — Musical Newsletter

MunArt — Mundus Artium
Mun Att'y — Municipal Attorney
Munca Sanit — Munca Sanitara
Munch Beitr z Pap — Muenchner Beitraege zur Papyrusforschung und Antiken Rechtsgeschichte
Munchner Jahrb — Muenchner Jahrbuch der Bildenden Kunst
MunchThZ — Muenchener Theologische Zeitschrift
Munc M — Muenzen und Medaillen
Mund — Mundus Artium
Mundo A — Mundo de Arte
Mundo Aeronaut — Mundo Aeronautico
Mundo Agric — Mundo Agricola
Mundo Apic — Mundo Apicola
Mundo Avic — Mundo Avicola
Mundo Azuc — Mundo Azucarero
Mundo Cient — Mundo Cientifico
Mundo Electron — Mundo Electronico
Mundo Ilus — Mundo Ilustrado
Mundo Ind — Mundo Industrial
Mundo Mader — Mundo Maderero
Mundo Med — Mundo Medico
Mundo Text Argent — Mundo Textil Argentino
MuNDPV — Mittheilungen und Nachrichten. Deutscher Palaestina-Verein
MundusA — Mundus Artium
Mundus Art — Mundus Artium
MUNFA — Moderne Unfallverhuetung
Munger Africana Lib Notes — Munger Africana Library Notes
Munger Africana Libr Notes — Munger Africana Library Notes
Munibe — Munibe. Sociedad de Ciencias Naturales Aranzadi
Munic Adm Eng — Municipal Administration and Engineering
Munic Aff — Municipal Affairs
Munic & Co Eng — Municipal and County Engineering
Munic and Public Services J — Municipal and Public Services Journal
Munic & Road Board Gaz — Municipal and Road Board Gazette
Munic & Road Board Gazette — Municipal and Road Board Gazette
Munic Bldg Mgmt — Municipal Building Management
Munic Cty Eng — Municipal and County Engineering
Munic Cty Engng — Municipal and County Engineering
Munic Eng — Municipal Engineer
Munic Eng Aust — Municipal Engineering in Australia
Munic Eng in Aust — Municipal Engineering in Australia
Munic Eng (Indianapolis) — Municipal Engineering (Indianapolis)
Munic Eng J — Municipal Engineers Journal
Munic Eng (London) — Municipal Engineering (London)
Munic Eng Mot Public Health — Municipal Engineering. Motor and Public Health
Munic Engng — Municipal Engineering
Munic Engng Indianap — Municipal Engineering (Indianapolis)
Munic Engng Lond — Municipal Engineering. Cleansing and Public Health (London)
Munic Engr — Municipal Engineer
Munic Engrs J — Municipal Engineers' Journal
Munic Engrs Specif — Municipal Engineers' Specification
Munich Symp Biol Connect Tissue — Munich Symposium on Biology of Connective Tissue
Munich Symp Microbiol — Munich Symposia on Microbiology
Munic Improv — Municipal Improvements
Munic Index — Municipal Index
Munic Ind Waste — Municipal and Industrial Waste
Munic Ind Waste Annu Madison Waste Conf — Municipal and Industrial Waste. Annual Madison Waste Conference
Munic Info — Municipal Information
Munic J — Municipal Journal
Munic J Eng — Municipal Journal and Engineer
Munic J Engr — Municipal Journal and Engineer [*New York*]
Munic J NY — Municipal Journal (New York)
Munic J Public Works — Municipal Journal and Public Works
Munic J Publ Wks — Municipal Journal and Public Works [*New York*]
Munic J Publ Wks Engr — Municipal Journal and Public Works Engineer [*London*]
Munic Manage Dir — Municipal Management Directory
Munic Mirror — Municipal Mirror and Queensland Shire Record
Munic News — Municipal News
Munic News Water Works — Municipal News and Water Works
Munic News Wat Wks — Municipal News and Water Works [*Chicago*]
Munic R Can — Municipal Review of Canada
Munic Ref & Res Center Notes — New York City Municipal Reference and Research Center. Notes
Munic Ref Lib Notes — New York City Public Library. Municipal Reference Library. Notes
Munic Rev — Municipal Review
Munic Sanit — Municipal Sanitation
Munic Sewage Treat Plant Sludge Manage — Municipal Sewage Treatment Plant Sludge Management
Munic Util — Municipal Utilities
Munic Util Mag — Municipal Utilities Magazine
Muni Fin J — Municipal Finance Journal
Munkaved Munka Uezemeue — Munkavedelem. Munka-es Uezemegeszseguegy
Mun L Ct Dec — Municipal Law Court Decisions
Mun LJ — Municipal Law Journal
MUNOPB — Memorial University of Newfoundland. Occasional Papers in Biology
Mun Ord Rev — Municipal Ordinance Review
Mun Plan L Rep — Municipal and Planning Law Reports
MUNSDM — Marathwada University. Journal of Science
Munsey — Munsey's Magazine
Munseys M — Munsey's Magazine
MU Oddfellows Mag — Manchester Unity Oddfellows' Magazine

Muon Catal Fusion — Muon Catalyzed Fusion
MUOX — Musk-Ox
MUOXD — Musk-Ox
MUR — Al-Mustansiriya University. Review
MUR — Marburger Universitaetsreden
Mur — Murray's Reports
MUREAV — Mutation Research. Section on Environmental Mutagenesis and Related Subjects
Murex Rev — Murex Review
Murm Olenevodcheskaya Opytn Stn Sb Nauchn Rab — Murmanskaya Olenevodcheskaya Opytnaya Stantsiya. Sbornik Nauchnykh Rabot
Muromsk Gos Ped Inst Ucen Zap — Muromskii Gosudarstvennyi Pedagogiceskii Institut. Ucenye Zapiski
Murp & H — Murphy and Hurlstone's English Exchequer Reports
Murr — Murray's Reports
Murray — Murray's Magazine
Murray VA — Murray Valley Annual
MURT — Murrelet
MUS — Multinational Services
Mus — Museon. Revue d'Etudes Orientales
Mus — Museum. Maanblad voor Philologie en Geschiedenis
Mus — Museum of Foreign Literature
Mus — Musica
Mus — Musician
MUS — Music Now
MusA — Musical America
Mus A Ann Arbor MI U MI Mus A Bull — Museum of Art. Ann Arbor, Michigan. University of Michigan Museum of Art Bulletin
Mus Academy Jl — Music Academy. Journal
Mus Afr — Museum Africum
Mus Al — Musik und Altar
Mus Alt — Museum der Altertumswissenschaft
Mus Am — Musical America
Mus Anal — Musical Analysis
Mus Analysis — Music Analysis
Mus & Artists — Music and Artists
Mus & A Washington — Museum and Arts Washington
Mus & Dance — Music and Dance
Mus & Fit — Muscle & Fitness
Mus and Let — Music and Letters
Mus & Lett — Music and Letters
Mus & Mus — Music and Musicians
Mus Antropol Etnogr — Museo di Antropologia ed Etnografia
Mus Appl Arts Sci Sydney Res Essent Oils Aust Flora — Museum of Applied Arts and Sciences. Sydney. Researches on Essential Oils of the Australian Flora
Mus Appl Sci Cent Archaeol J — Museum Applied Science Center for Archaeology Journal
Mus Appl Sci Cent Archaeol Res Pap Sci Archaeol — Museum Applied Science Center for Archaeology Research Papers in Science and Archaelogy
Mus Archivist — Museum Archivist
Mus Archivists Newslett — Museum Archivists' Newsletter
Mus Assoc Proc — Musical Association Proceedings
Mus at Home — Music at Home
Mus Australia — Museums Australia
MusB — Musee Belge
MUSBDU — Moscow University. Soil Science Bulletin
Mus Belg — Musee Belge. Revue de Philologie Classique
Mus Belge — Musee Belge. Revue de Philologie Classique
Mus Bot Leide — Musee Botanique de Leide
Mus Bull — Museum Bulletin
Mus Bull Can Geol Surv — Museum Bulletin. Canada Geological Survey
Mus Bull Natn Mus Sci Art Dubl — Museum Bulletin. National Museum of Science and Art (Dublin)
Mus Bull NY State Mus — Museum Bulletin. New York State Museum
Mus Bull Staten Island Inst Arts — Museum Bulletin. Staten Island Institute of Arts and Science
Mus Bull Staten Isl Ass Arts Sci — Museum Bulletin of the Staten Island Association of Arts and Sciences
Mus Bull Univ Neb — Museum Bulletin. University of Nebraska
Muscan — Musicanada
Musc Dystr J — Muscular Dystrophy Journal
Mus Chius — Etrusco Museo Chiusino
MU Sci R — Melbourne University. Science Review
Mus Civ Stor Giacomo Doria Ann — Museo Civico di Storia Naturale Giacomo Doria. Annali
Mus Civ Stor Nat Trieste Atti — Museo Civico di Storia Naturale di Trieste. Atti
Mus Civ Stor Nat Verona Mem Fuori Ser — Museo Civico di Storia Naturale di Verona. Memorie. Fuori Serie
Mus Clas Ant — Museum of Classical Antiquites
Muscle Biol — Muscle Biology
Muscle Nerve Suppl — Muscle and Nerve. Supplement
Mus Clubs Mag — Music Clubs Magazine
Mus Colon Marseille Ann — Musee Colonial de Marseille. Annales
Mus Comp Zool (Harv Univ) Annu Rep — Museum of Comparative Zoology (Harvard University). Annual Report
Mus Comp Zool Mem — Museum of Comparative Zoology [Harvard University]. Memoirs
Mus Conde — Musee Conde
Mus Cour — Musical Courier
Mus Crit — Museum Criticum
Muscular Dystrophy Abstr — Muscular Dystrophy Abstracts
Mus Dealer — Music Dealer
Mus Denmark — Musical Denmark
Mus Dev — Muscular Development

Mus Disc — Musica Disciplina
Mus Disc RN — Musica Disciplina. Renaissance News
Mus Div — Musica Divina
Mus d'Oggi — Musica d'Oggi. Rassegna di Vita e di Cultura Musicale
Muse Annu Mus A & Archaeol U MO Columbia — Muse. Annual of the Museum of Art and Archaeology. University of Missouri. Columbia
Mus Ed J — Music Educators Journal
Mus Educ J — Music Educators Journal
Musee Guimet Annales Bibl d'Etud — Musee Guimet. Annales. Bibliotheque d'Etudes
Musee Guimet Annales Bibl de Vulg — Musee Guimet. Annales. Bibliotheque de Vulgarisation
Musee Nat Homme Centre Canad Et Culture Trad — Musee National de l'Homme. Centre Canadien d'Etudes sur la Culture Traditionnelle
Musee Neuchat — Musee Neuchatelois. Recueil d'Histoire Nationale et d'Archeologie
Museo Chius — Etrusco Museo Chiusino
Museo Nac de Hist Nat de Buenos Aires Anales — Museo Nacional de Historia Natural de Buenos Aires. Anales
Mus Esp Ant — Museo Espanol de Antiguedades
Mus et Coll Alg Tun — Musees et Collections Archeologiques de l'Algerie et de la Tunisie
Mus et Coll Al Tun — Musees et Collections Archeologiques de l'Algerie et de la Tunisie
Mus Ethnographers Grp Newslett — Museum Ethnographers Group Newsletter
Mus et Lit — Musique et Liturgie
Museum — Mosaic Museum
Museum Comp Zool Memoirs — Harvard University. Museum of Comparative Zoology. Memoirs
Museum d'Hist Nat de Lyon Archives — Museum d'Histoire Naturelle de Lyon. Archives
Museum J — Museum Journal
Museums Jnl — Museums Journal
Museumskde — Museumskunde
Museum Stud — Museum Studies
Museum UNESCO — Museum. A Quarterly Review Published by UNESCO
Mus Events — Musical Events
Mus F A Bull — Museum of Fine Arts Bulletin
Mus FA Houston Bull — Museum of Fine Arts. Houston. Bulletin
Mus Families — Musee des Families
Mus Far E Ant Bull — Museum of Far Eastern Antiquities Bulletin
Mus Far East Antiq Bull — Museum of Far Eastern Antiquities Bulletin
Mus Felipe Poey Acad Cienc Cuba Trab Divulg — Museo "Felipe Poey." Academia de Ciencias de Cuba. Trabajos de Divulgacion
Mus Ferrar Boll Annu — Musei Ferraresi. Bollettino Annuale
Mus F Holb O Om — Museet for Holbaek og Omegn. Arsberetning
Mus Forum — Music Forum
Mus Fr — Musees de France
Mus France — Musees de France
Mus Gal It — Musei e Gallerie d'Italia
Mus Geneve — Musees de Geneve
Mus Gr — Musici Scriptores Graeci
Mus Guimet Ann Bibl Etudes — Musee Guimet. Annales. Bibliotheque d'Etudes
Mus Guimet Ann Bibl Vulg — Musee Guimet. Annales. Bibliotheque de Vulgarisation
MUSHA — Music Trades
Mus Haaretz — Museum Ha'aretz [Tel-Aviv] Yearbook
Mus Ha'aretz Bull — Museum Ha'aretz Bulletin
Mus Helv — Museum Helveticum
Mus Helvet — Museum Helveticum
Mus Heude Notes Bot Chin — Musee Heude. Notes de Botanique Chinoise
Mus Heute — Museum Heute
Mus High Educ — Music in Higher Education
Mus Hist Nat Grigore Antipa Trav — Museum d'Histoire Naturelle Grigore Antipa. Travaux
Mus Hist Nat Lyon Nouv Arch — Museum d'Histoire Naturelle de Lyon. Nouvelles Archives
Mus Hist Nat Lyon Nouv Arch Suppl — Museum d'Histoire Naturelle de Lyon. Nouvelles Archives. Supplement
Mus Hist Nat Mars Bull — Museum d'Histoire Naturelle de Marseille. Bulletin
Mus Hist Quito — Museo Historico (Quito)
Mushr News — Mushroom News [Worthing]
Mushroom J — Mushroom Journal
Mushroom Sci — Mushroom Science
Mushr Sci — Mushroom Science. International Conference on Scientific Aspects of Mushroom Growing
Mus I — Music Index
Musical Quar — Musical Quarterly
Musical Times — Musical Times and Singing-Class Circular
Music Am — Music America
Music Artic Guide — Music Article Guide
Music Disci — Musica Disciplina
Music Ed Jnl — Music Educators Journal
Music Educ — Music Educators Journal
Musicl — Music Index
Music Ind — Music Index
Music in Ed — Music in Education
Music J — Music Journal
Music Lett — Music and Letters
Music Lib Assn Notes — Music Library Association. Notes
Music Libr Ass Notes — Music Library Association. Notes
Music Man — Music and Man
Musicol — Musicology
Musicol Slovaca — Musicologica Slovaca
Music Quart — Musical Quarterly

Music R — Music Review
Music Rev — Music Review
Music (SMA) — Music (Schools of Music Association)
Music Teach — Music and the Teacher
Music Time — Musical Times
Music Trad — Music Trades
Musikbll Anbruch — Musikblaetter des Anbruch
Musikf — Musikforschung
Musikforsch — Musikforschung
Musikk Mag Ballade — Musikkmagasinet Ballade
Musil S — Musil Studien
Mus Ind Dir — Music Industry Directory
Mus Industry — Music Industry
Mus in Ed — Music in Education
Mus in Schule — Musik in der Schule
Mus Int — Musik International - Instrumentenbau-Zeitschrift
MUSIP — Marquette University. Slavic Institute. Papers
Mus It — Museo Italiano di Antichita Classica
MUSJ — Melanges. Universite Saint Joseph
Mus J — Museum Journal
Mus J — Museums Journal
Mus J — Music Journal
Mus Jazz — Musica Jazz
Mus J Ber Mus — Museums Journal. Berichte aus den Museen
Mus Jeu — Musique en Jeu
Mus Jl — Music Journal
Mus J Organ Mus Assoc — Museums Journal. The Organ of the Museums Association
Mus Judaica — Musica Judaica
Mus J Univ Penn — Museum Journal. University of Pennsylvania
MUSKA — Music in Education
Mus Koeln — Museen in Koeln. Bulletin
Mus Kulturgesch Abh Ber Naturk Vorgesch — Museum fuer Kulturgeschichte. Abhandlungen und Berichte fuer Naturkunde und Vorgeschichte
MusL — Music and Letters
Musl Cour — Muslim Courier
Musl Dig — Muslim Digest
Mus Leader — Musical Leader
Mus Leafl S Barbara Mus Nat Hist — Museum Leaflet. Santa Barbara Museum of Natural History
Mus Lett — Music and Letters
Mus Lib Assn Notes — Music Library Association. Notes
Muslim Assoc Adv Sci Proc — Muslim Association for the Advancement of Science. Proceedings
Muslim Mag — Muslim Magazine
Muslim Sci — Muslim Scientist
Muslim W — Muslim World
Muslim Wld — Muslim World
Muslim Wrld — Muslim World
Mus Lit — Music and Liturgy
Mus Livre — Musee du Livre
Musl R — Muslim Review
MuslW — Muslim World
MusM — Music and Musicians
Mus Mag — Music Magazine
Mus Mak — Music Maker
Mus Mem (Salisbury) — Museum Memoir (Salisbury)
Mus Midden-Afr Ann Reeks in 8O Geol Wet — Museum voor Midden-Afrika. Annalen. Reeks in Octavo. Geologische Wetenschappen
Mus Min — Music Ministry
Mus Mod Art Bul — New York City Museum of Modern Art. Bulletin
Mus N — Museum News
Mus Nac Hist Nat Bol (Santiago) — Museo Nacional de Historia Natural. Boletin (Santiago)
Mus Nac Hist Nat Bol (Santiago De Chile) — Museo Nacional de Historia Natural. Boletin (Santiago De Chile)
Mus Nac Hist Nat Notic Mens (Santiago) — Museo Nacional de Historia Natural. Noticiario Mensual (Santiago)
Mus Nac Hist Nat Not Mens (Santiago) — Museo Nacional de Historia Natural. Noticiario Mensual (Santiago)
Mus Nac Hist Nat (Santiago De Chile) Publ Ocas — Museo Nacional de Historia Natural (Santiago De Chile). Publicacion Ocasional
Mus Nac Hist Natur Buenos Aires An — Museo Nacional de Historia Natural de Buenos Aires. Anales
Mus Nac Mex An — Museo Nacional de Mexico. Anales
Mus Nac Pubs Avulas — Museu Nacional. Publicacoes Avulsas
Mus Nat Homme Publ Ethnol — Musee National de l'Homme. Publications d'Ethnologie
Mus Nat Homme Public Archeol — Musee National de l'Homme. Publications d'Archeologie
Mus Natl Hist Nat Bull — Museum National d'Histoire Naturelle. Bulletin
Mus Natl Hist Nat Bull Lab Marit Dinard — Museum National d'Histoire Naturelle. Bulletin du Laboratoire Maritime de Dinard
Mus Natl Hist Nat Bull Sect B Bot Biol Ecol Veg Phytochim — Museum National d'Histoire Naturelle. Bulletin. Section B. Botanique, Biologie et Ecologie Vegetales, Phytochimie
Mus Natl Hist Nat Bull Sect C — Museum National d'Histoire Naturelle. Bulletin. Section C. Sciences de la Terre, Paleontologie, Geologie, Mineralogie
Mus Natl Hist Nat Mem Ser A (Paris) — Museum National d'Histoire Naturelle. Memoires. Serie A. Zoologie (Paris)
Mus Natl Hist Nat Not Syst — Museum National d'Histoire Naturelle. Notulae Systematicae
Mus Natl Hist Nat Paris Bull — Museum National d'Histoire Naturelle. (Paris). Bulletin.

Mus Natl Hist Nat (Paris) Mem Ser C — Museum National d'Histoire Naturelle. Memoires. Serie C. Sciences de la Terre (Paris)
Mus Natl Histoire Nat Bull — Museum National d'Histoire Naturelle. Bulletin
Mus Natl Hung Ann Hist-Nat — Museum Nationale Hungaricum. Annales Historico-Naturales
Mus Natnl Hist Nat (Paris) Mem Ser C — Museum National d'Histoire Naturelle. Memoires. Serie C (Paris)
Mus Naturgesch Helv — Museum der Naturgeschichte Helvetiens
Mus Natur Heimatk Magdeburg Abh Ber — Museum fuer Naturkunde und Heimatkunde zu Magdeburg. Abhandlungen und Berichte
Mus Neuchatel Rev Hist Reg — Musee Neuchatelois. Revue d'Histoire Regionale
Mus News — Musical Newsletter
Mus News — Music News
Mus News Brooklyn Inst Arts Sci — Museum News. Brooklyn Institute of Arts and Sciences
Mus News Cleveland Hlth Mus — Museum News. Cleveland Health Museum
Mus News Cleveland Mus Nat Hist — Museum News. Cleveland Museum of Natural History
Mus News Prague — Music News from Prague
Mus News Tech Bull — Museum News Technical Bulletin
Mus News Toledo Mus A — Museum News. Toledo Museum of Art
Mus News Wash — Museum News (Washington, D.C.)
Mus New Zealand — Music in New Zealand
Mus North Ariz Bull — Museum of Northern Arizona. Bulletin
Mus North Ariz Res Cent (Flagstaff) Annu Rep — Museum of Northern Arizona and Research Center (Flagstaff). Annual Report
Mus Not — Museum Notes. American Numismatic Society
Mus Not Am Num Soc — Museum Notes. American Numismatic Society
Mus Notes Mus A RI — Museum Notes. Museum of Art. Rhode Island
Mus Notes Mus Nth Ariz — Museum Notes. Museum of Northern Arizona
Mus Notes News Idaho State Coll — Museum Notes and News. Idaho State College
Mus Notes Vancouver — Museum Notes (Vancouver)
Mus Observer — Musical Observer
Mus Oggi — Musica d'Oggi. Rassegna di Vita e di Cultura Musicale
Mus Op — Musical Opinion
Mus Paleontol Pap Paleontol — Museum of Paleontology. Papers on Paleontology
Mus P & L — Musician, Player, and Listener
Mus Pap Ala Mus Nat Hist — Museum Paper. Alabama Museum of Natural History
Mus Pap Geol Surv Ala — Museum Paper. Geological Survey of Alabama
Mus Parade — Music Parade
Mus Para Emilio Goeldi Bol Geol — Museu Paraense Emilio Goeldi. Boletim. Geologia
Mus Para Emilio Goeldi Publ Avulsas — Museu Paraense Emilio Goeldi. Publicacoes Avulsas
Mus Par E Goeldi Pub Avulsas — Museu Paraense Emilio Goeldi. Publicacoes Avulsas
Mus Patavinum — Museum Patavinum
Mus Perc — Music Perception
Mus Philipon — Musee Philipon
Mus Pontevedra — Museo de Pontevedra
Mus Psych — Musikpsychologie
Mus Publs Manchr Mus — Museum Publications. Manchester Museum
Mus Publs Mar Mus Newport News — Museum Publications. Mariners' Museum (Newport News)
Mus Q — Musical Quarterly
Mus Qu — Musical Quarterly
Mus R — Music Review
Mus R Afr Centr (Tervuren Belg) Rapp Annu Dep Geol Mineral — Musee Royal de l'Afrique Centrale (Tervuren, Belgique). Rapport Annuel du Departement de Geologie et de Mineralogie
Mus R Afr Cent Tervuren Belg Ann Ser 8 Sci Geol — Musee Royal de l'Afrique Centrale. Tervuren. Belgique. Annales, Serie in 8. Sciences Geologiques
Mus R Afr Cent (Tervuren Belg) Ann Ser Octavo Sci Geol — Musee Royal de l'Afrique Centrale (Tervuren, Belgique). Annales. Serie in Octavo. Sciences Geologiques
Mus R Afr Cent (Tervuren Belg) Ann Ser Octavo Sci Zool — Musee Royal de l'Afrique Centrale (Tervuren, Belgique). Annales. Serie in Octavo. Sciences Zoologiques
Mus R Afr Cent (Tervuren Belg) Doc Zool — Musee Royal de l'Afrique Centrale (Tervuren, Belgique). Documentation Zoologique
Mus R Afr Cent (Tervuren Belg) Do Zool — Musee Royal de l'Afrique Centrale (Tervuren, Belgique). Documentation Zoologique
Mus R d'Hist Nat Belgique B — Musee Royal d'Histoire Naturelle de Belgique. Bulletin
Mus Ref Serv — Music Reference Services Quarterly
Mus Reg Sci Nat Boll — Museo Regionale di Scienze Naturali. Bollettino
Mus Rev — Music Review
Mus Rev Trimest — Museum. Revue Trimestrielle Publiee par l'UNESCO [United Nations Educational, Scientific, and Cultural Organisation]
Mus Roy Afr Cent Dep Geol Mineral Rap Ann — Musee Royal de l'Afrique Centrale. Departement de Geologie et de Mineralogie. Rapport Annuel
Mus Royaux B A Belgique Bull — Musees Royaux des Beaux-Arts de Belgique. Bulletin
Mus Rusticum Commerciale Leipzig — Museum Rusticum et Commerciale oder Auserlesene Schriften, den Ackerbau, die Handlung, die Kuenste und Manufacturen Betreffend (Leipzig)
Mus Rusticum Commerciale London — Museum Rusticum et Commerciale (London)
MUSS — Madras University Sanskrit Series
MusS — Musees Suisses
Mus Sacra — Musica Sacra
Mus Scene — Music Scene
Mus Schall — Musica Schallplatte. Zeitschrift fuer Schallplattenfreunde
Mus Sci — Museologia Scientifica

Mus Slovaca — Musicologica Slovaca
Mus Soc Arg Bol — Museo Social Argentino. Boletin
Mus Stadt Koeln — Museen der Stadt Koeln
Mus Stor Nat Ven Tridentia Studi Trentini Sci Nat — Museo di Storia Naturale della Venezia Tridentina. Studi Trentini di Scienze Naturali
Mus Stud — Museum Studies. Art Institute of Chicago
Mus Stud J — Museum Studies Journal
Mus Stud Jnl — Museum Studies Journal
Mus Stud Tokyo — Museum Studies. Japanese Association of Museums (Tokyo)
Mus Superv J — Music Supervisors Journal
Mus Survey — Music Survey
Mus T — Musical Times
Mus Talk S Barbara Mus Nat Hist — Museum Talk. Santa Barbara Museum of Natural History
Mus Tcr — Music Teacher and Piano Student
Mus Teach Nat Assn Proc — Music Teachers National Association. Proceedings
Mus Technol Appl Sci Sydney Res Essent Oils Aust Flora — Museum of Technology and Applied Science. Sydney Researches on Essential Oils of the Australian Flora
Mus Teyler Archiv — Musee Teyler. Archives
Mus Theory Spectrum — Music Theory Spectrum
Mus Therapy — Music Therapy
Mus Thera Um — Musiktherapeutische Umschau
Mus Times — Musical Times
Mus Today Nl — Music Today Newsletter
Mus Topogr Vaterlandsk Oesterr Kaiserstaates — Museum fuer Topographische Vaterlandskunde des Oesterreichischen Kaiserstaates
Mus Trade Rev — Music Trade Review
Mus Trades — Music Trades
Mus Tridentino Sci Nat Mem — Museo Tridentino di Scienze Naturali. Memorie
Mus Tusc — Museum Tusculanum
Mus u Bild — Musik und Bildung
Mus u Ges — Musik und Gesellschaft
Mus u Gottesd — Musik und Gottesdienst
Mus u Kir — Musik und Kirche
Mus Univ — Musica Universita
Mus Univl — Museo Universal
Mus USA — Music USA. Review of the Music Industry and Amateur Music Participation
Mus West — Music of the West Magazine
Mus Wk — Museum Work. Including the Proceedings of the American Association of Museums
Mus y Artes — Boletin de Musica y Artes Visuales
Musz Egy Novenyt Intez Kozl — Muszaki Egyetem Novenytani Intezetenek Kozlemenyei
Musz Elet — Muszaki Elet
Muszerugyi Merestech Kozl — Muszerugyi es Merestechnikai Kozlemenyek
Musz Fiz Kut Intez Evk Magy Tud Akad — Muszaki Fizikai Kutato Intezet. Evkonyv. Magyar Tudomanyos Akademia
Musz Kozl — Muszaki Kozlemenyek
Musz Lap — Muszaki Lapja
Mus Zpravy Prazskeho Kraje — Musejni Zpravy Prazskeho Kraje
Musz Szle — Muszaki Szemle
Musz Termeszettud Egy Szov Ert — Muszaki es Termeszettudomanyi Egyesuletek Szovetsege Ertesito
Musz Tud — Muszaki Tudomany
Musz Vil — Muszaki Vilag
Musz Vivm — Muszaki Vivmanyok
Mut — Muttersprache
Mutagens Their Toxic — Mutagens and Their Toxicities
Mutagens Toxicol (Tokyo) — Mutagens and Toxicology (Tokyo)
Mutat Res — Mutation Research
Mutat Res DNAging Genet Instab — Mutation Research. DNAging. Genetic Instability and Aging
Mutat Res DNA Repair — Mutation Research. DNA Repair
Mutat Res DNA Repair Rep — Mutation Research. DNA Repair Reports
Mutat Res Environ Mutagen Relat — Mutation Research. Environmental Mutagenesis and Related Subjects Including Methodology
Mutat Res Fundam Mol Mech Mutagen — Mutation Research. Fundamental and Molecular Mechanisms of Mutagenesis
Mutat Res Genet Toxicol Test — Mutation Research; Genetic Toxicology Testing
Mutat Res Int J Mutagen Chromosome Breakage Relat Subj — Mutation Research. International Journal on Mutagenesis, Chromosome Breakage, and Related Subjects
Mutat Res Lett — Mutation Research Letters
Mutat Res Rev Genet Toxicol — Mutation Research. Reviews in Genetic Toxicology
Mutat Res Sect Environ Mutagen — Mutation Research. Section on Environmental Mutagenesis and Related Subjects
Mutat Res Sect Environ Mutagenesis Relat Subj — Mutation Research. Section on Environmental Mutagenesis and Related Subjects
Mutat Res Sect Environ Mutagen Relat Subj — Mutation Research Section on Environmental Mutagenesis and Related Subjects
Mutech Chem Eng J — Mutech Chemical Engineering Journal
MUTED — Muszaki Tervezes
Mut Funds Guide CCH — Mutual Funds Guide. Commerce Clearing House
Mutisia Acta Bot Colomb — Mutisia. Acta Botanica Colombiana
MUTSA — Music Teacher
MUTSAF — Acta Botanica Colombiana
MUUJA — Musart
Muved — Muemlekvedelem
Muvelt Hagyomany — Muveltseg es Hagyomany
Muves Ertes — Mueveszettoerteneti Ertesitoe
Muvesz Lapja — Muveszetok Lapja
MUY — Management International Review

Mu Z — Malerei und Zeichnung der Griechen
Muz — Muzeon
Muz Akademiya — Muzykal'naya Akademiya
Muz & Wetenschap — Muziek & Wetenschap
Muz Arch Krakow Mat Arch — Muzeum Archeologiczne. Krakow. Materialy Archeologiczne
Muz Delo — Muzeinoe Delo [Leningrad]
Muz F — Muzykal'naya Fol'kloristika
Muz Fuz Erd Nemz Muz Asvanyt Ert — Muzeumi Fuzetek. Az Erdelyi Nemzeti Muzeum Asvanytaranak Ertesitoje [Kolozsvar]
Muz Fuz Kiadja Erd Muz Egy — Muzeumi Fuzetek. Kiadja az Erdelyi Muzeum-Egyesulet. Az Erdelyi Nemzeti Muzeum Termeszettarainak, etc., Ertestitoje [Kolozsvar]
Muz Glasnik — Muzejski Glasnik
Muz Haaretz Bull — Museum Haaretz. Bulletin
Muzikol Zbornik — Muzikoloski Zbornik
Muz Istor Munic Bucur — Muzeul de Istorie al Municipiului Bucuresti
Muz Nat — Muzeul National
Muz Pam Kul — Muzei i Pametnizi na Kulturata
Muz Pam Kult — Muzei i Pametnizi na Kulturata
Muz Pitesti — Muzeul din Pitesti. Studii si Comunicari. Istorie-Stiintele Naturii
Muz Soucas — Muzeum a Soucasnost
Muz Stiint Naturii Bacau Stud Comun — Muzeul de Stiintele Naturii Bacau Studii si Comunicari
Muz Vlastivedna Prace — Muzejni a Vlastivedna Prace
Muz Zbornik — Muzikoloski Zbornik - Musicological Annual
Muzzio Sci — Muzzio Scienze
MV — Minority Voices
MV — Mykenische Vasen
MvA — Memorie van Antwoord
MVAA — Monumenti Vaticani di Archeologia e d'Arte
MVAeG — Mitteilungen. Vorderasiatisch-Aegyptische Gesellschaft
MVAG — Mitteilungen der Vorderasiatischen Gesellschaft
MVAG — Mitteilungen. Vorderasiatisch-Aegyptische Gesellschaft
MvA I — Memorie van Antwoord aan de Eerste Kamer
MvA II — Memorie van Antwoord aan de Tweede Kamer
MVAW — Mededeelingen. Vlaamsche Academie voor Wetenschappen, Letteren, en Schoone Kunsten van Belgie
MVAW L — Mededeelingen van de Vlaamsche Academie voor Wetenschappen, Letteren en SchooneKunsten van Belgie. Klasse der Letteren
MVAW SK — Mededeelingen van de Vlaamsche Academie voor Wetenschappen, Letteren en SchooneKunsten van Belgie. Klasse der Schoone Kunsten
MVB — Jahrbuch der Absatz- und Verbrauchsforschung
MvB — Maandblad voor Belastingrecht
MVB — Musica Viva Billetin
MV/BA — Baessler-Archiv. Museen fuer Voelkerkunde
MvB en R — Maandblad voor Berechtiging en Reclassering
MVBI — Mitteilungen. Verband Ehemaliger Breslauer und Schlesier in Israel
MVBRAV — Multivariate Behavioral Research
MVC Rep — MVC (Miljoevardscentrum) Report
MvDeurw — Maandblad voor de Vereniging van Deurwaarders
MVDM — Mitteilungen des Verbandes Deutscher Musikkritiker
MVDVV — Mitteilungen des Verbandes Deutscher Vereine fuer Volkskunde
M Vej — Meddelelser fra Vejlaboratoriet
MVEJDP — Malaysian Veterinary Journal
MVEL — Mitteilungen des Vereins fuer Erdkunde Leipzig
MVEL — Monatsblatt der Vereinigung der Evangelisch-Lutherischen Innerhalb der Preussischen Landeskirche
M V E Leipzig — Mitteilungen des Vereins fuer Erdkunde Leipzig
MVEOL — Mededeelingen en Verhandelingen Ex Oriente Lux
MVEQDC — Medecin Veterinaire du Quebec
Mverz Dt Univ Tech Hochsch Ersch Schr — Monatsverzeichnis der an den Deutschen Universitaeten und Technischen Hochschulen Erschienenen Schriften
MVFC — Mitteilungen des Vereins der Freunde Carnuntums
MVG — Mitteilungen. Vorderasiatisch-Aegyptischen Gesellschaft
MVG — Mitteilungen zur Vaterlaendische Geschichte
MVGAFr — Mitteilungen. Verein fuer Geschichte und Altertumskunde in Frankfurt-Am-Main
MVGB — Mitteilungen des Vereins fuer die Geschichte Berlins
MVGBH — Mitteilungen des Vereins fuer Geschichte und Landeskunde zu Bad Homburg vor derHoehe
MVGDB — Mitteilungen. Verein fuer Geschichte der Deutschen in Boehmen
MVGGA — Mitteilungen. Versuchsstation fuer das Gaerungsgewerbe in Wien (Austria)
MVGKA — Mitteilungen. Vereinigung der Grosskesselbesitzer
MVGKB — Mitteilungen. VGB
MVGM — Mitteilungen des Vereins fuer Geschichte der Stadt Meissen
MVGN — Mitteilungen des Vereins fuer Geschichte der Stadt Nuernberg
MVGOW — Mitteilungen. Verein fuer Geschichte von Ost- und West Preussen
MVGSN — Mitteilungen. Verein fuer Geschichte der Stadt Nuernberg
MvH — Magazijn van Handelsrecht
MVH — Munzautomat Mainz
MVHB — Mitteilungen des Vereins fuer Heimatkunde in Landkreis Birkenfeld
MVHG — Mitteilungen. Verein der Freunde des Humanistischen Gymnasiums
MVHR — Mississippi Valley Historical Review
MVHRH — Monumenta Vaticana Historiam Regni Hungariae Illustrantia
MVHSchl — Mitteilungen des Vereins fuer Heimatschutz, Innsbruck
MVI — Maandblad der Vereniging van Inspecteurs van Financien
MVKAUO — Mitteilungen. Verein fuer Kunst und Altertum in Ulm und Oberschwaben Ulm
MVL — Maandschrift voor Liturgie
MVL — Monografieen over Vlaamse Letterkunde
MVLA — Monumenta Veteris Liturgiae Ambrosianae
MVLCA — Mededeelingen. Vlaamse Chemische Vereniging

MVLNOe — Monatsblatt des Vereins fuer Landeskunde von Niederoesterreich und Wien

MVN — Materiali per il Vocabolario Neosumerico

MVN — Mededeelingen. Vereniging Naamkunde te Leuven en Commissie Naamkunde te Amsterdam

MVNAG — Mitteilungen. Verein fuer Nassauische Altertumskunde und Geschichts-Forschung

MVNLA — Mededeelingen. Vereniging Naamkunde te Leuven en Commissie Naamkunde te Amsterdam

Mvorhersage Dt WettDienst — Monatsvorhersage. Deutscher Wetterdienst

MVP Ber — MVP [Max-Von-Pettenkofer-Institut] Berichte

MVPhW — Mitteilungen. Verein Klassischer Philologen in Wien

MVR — Motor Vehicle Reports

MVSA J — MVSA (Fertilizer Society of South Africa) Joernaal (Afrikanns)

MVV — Dibevo

MVVV — Mitteilungen des Verbandes der Vereine fuer Volkskunde

MVW — Uitvaartwezen

MVW/AV — Archiv fuer Voelkerkunde Museum fuer Voelkerkunde in Wien und von Verein Freunde der Voelkerkunde

MVZADA — Mitteilungen. Verein zur Abwehr des Antisemitismus

MW — Management World

MW — Meisterwerke der Griechischen Plastik

Mw — Meisterwerke Griechischer Kunst

MW — Middle Way. Buddhist Society

MW — Miscellanea Wilbouriana. Brooklyn Museum

MW — Moslem World

MW — Music Weekly Magazine

MW — Muslim World

MWA — Men's Wear

MWAT — Missionswissenschaftliche Abhandlungen und Texte

MWBI — Musikalisches Wochenblatt

MWBWA — Mededelingen. Koninklijke Vlaamse Academie voor Wetenschappen. Letterenen Schone Kunsten van Belgie. Klasse der Wetenschappen

MWD — Metalworking Digest

MWDI — Master Water Data Index

M Weather R — Monthly Weather Review

M Weath Rev — Monthly Weather Review

MWERA — Mechanical World and Engineering Record

M West Hist — Magazine of Western History

MWFL — Midwest Folklore

MWFL — Missionswissenschaftliche Forschungen (Leipzig)

MWG — Mensch, Welt, Gott

MWG E — Mensch, Welt, Gott. Ergaenzungsband

MWJ — Magazin fuer die Wissenschaft des Judentums

MWK — Muslim World (Karachi)

MWKA — Mitteilungen der Wiener Katholischen Akademie

MWL — Management World

MWM — Milla Wa-Milla

MWM Nachr — MWM (Motoren-Werke Mannheim A.G.) Nachrichten

MWN — Madras Weekly Notes

MWN — Medical World News

MWNCC — Madras Weekly Notes, Criminal Cases

MWOGA2 — Montana Wool Grower

M World — Medical World

M World — Mining World

MWP — Marburger Winckelmann-Programm

MWPL — Montreal Working Papers in Linguistics

MWPr — Marburger Winckelmann-Programm

MWQ — Midwest Quarterly

MWR — Monthly Wholesale Trade

MWRRC Rep — MWRRC [Montana Water Resources Research Center] Report

MWS — Muslim World Series

MWW — Marquis Who's Who

MWW — Metall. Internationale Zeitschrift fuer Technik und Wirtschaft

My — All India Reporter, Mysore Series

MY — May

MY — Missiology

Myas Ind SSSR — Myasnaya Industriya SSSR

Myas Khoz SSSR — Myasnoe Khozyaistvo SSSR

Myas Moloch Prom SSSR — Myasnaya i Molochnaya Promyshlennost' SSSR

Myasn Ind SSSR — Myasnaya Industriya SSSR

Myasn Khoz SSSR — Myasnoe Khozyaistvo SSSR

Myasn Molochn Promst SSSR — Myasnaya i Molochnaya Promyshlennost SSSR

My C — Mystere Chretien

MYCGA — Memory and Cognition

Mycol — Mycologia

Mycol Abstr — Mycological Abstracts

Mycol Bull Columbus — Mycological Bulletin (Columbus)

Mycol Helv — Mycologia Helvetica

Mycol J — Mycological Journal

Mycol J Nagao Inst — Mycological Journal of Nagao Institute

Mycol Leafl Tanganyika — Mycological Leaflet (Tanganyika)

Mycol Mem — Mycologia Memoir

Mycol Notes Lloyd Libr Mus — Mycological Notes of the Lloyd Library and Museum [Cincinnati]

Mycol Pap — Mycological Papers

Mycol Pap Commonw Mycol Inst — Mycological Papers. Commonwealth Mycological Institute

Mycol Plant Pathol Rep Victoria Univ Wellington Bot Dep — Mycology and Plant Pathology Report. Victoria University of Wellington. Botany Department

Mycol Res — Mycological Research

Mycol Ser — Mycology Series

Mycol Soc Amer Year Book — Mycological Society of America. Year Book

Mycol Zcntralbl — Mycologisches Zentralblatt

Mycopath Mycol Appl — Mycopathologia et Mycologia Applicata

Mycopathol Mycol Appl — Mycopathologia et Mycologia Applicata

Mycopathol Mycol Appl Suppl — Mycopathologia et Mycologia Applicata. Supplementum

Mycopathol Mycol Appl Suppl Iconogr Mycol — Mycopathologia et Mycologia Applicata. Supplementum Iconographia Mycologica

Mycopatholo — Mycopathologia

Mycotoxin Res — Mycotoxin Research

MYEAA — Minerals Yearbook

MYG — Food Analysis

MYH — Milieuhygiene

MYHEED — Mycologia Helvetica

MYK — Metrovisie

Mykol Sb — Mykologicky Sbornik

Mykol Unters Ber — Mykologische Untersuchungen u. Berichte

Mykol Untersuch — Mykologische Untersuchungen

Mykol Zentbl — Mykologisches Zentralblatt

Mykol Zprav — Mykologicky Zpravodaj

Mykrobiol Zh — Mykrobiolchichniyi Zhurnal

MYL — Monthly Labor Review

My LJ — Mysore Law Journal

MYOGA — Materialy Ogniotrwale

Myonj-Ji Univ J Nat Sci — Myonj-Ji University. Journal of Natural Science

Myotis Mitteilungsbl Fledermauskundler — Myotis Mitteilungsblatt fuer Fledermauskundler

MYP Alum — Minerals Yearbook. Preprint. Aluminum

MYP A M — Minerals Yearbook. Preprint. Abrasive Materials

MYP Antim — Minerals Yearbook. Preprint. Antimony

MYP Asbsts — Minerals Yearbook. Preprint. Asbestos

MYP Barite — Minerals Yearbook. Preprint. Barite

MYP Bauxit — Minerals Yearbook. Preprint. Bauxite

MYP Beryl — Minerals Yearbook. Preprint. Beryllium

MYP Bis — Minerals Yearbook. Preprint. Bismuth

MYP Boron — Minerals Yearbook. Preprint. Boron

MYP Bromin — Minerals Yearbook. Preprint. Bromine

MYP Cadm — Minerals Yearbook. Preprint. Cadmium

MYP Calcm — Minerals Yearbook. Preprint. Calcium and Calcium Compounds

MYP Cement — Minerals Yearbook. Preprint. Cement

MYP Chrom — Minerals Yearbook. Preprint. Chromium

MYP Clays — Minerals Yearbook. Preprint. Clays

MYP Cobalt — Minerals Yearbook. Preprint. Cobalt

MYP Columb — Minerals Yearbook. Preprint. Columbium and Tantalum

MYP Copper — Minerals Yearbook. Preprint. Copper

MYP C Stone — Minerals Yearbook. Preprint. Crushed Stone

MYP Diato — Minerals Yearbook. Preprint. Diatomite

MYP Dime S — Minerals Yearbook. Preprint. Dimension Stone

MYP Felsp — Minerals Yearbook. Preprint. Feldspar, Nepheline, Syenite, and Aplite

MYP Ferro — Minerals Yearbook. Preprint. Ferroalloys

MYP Fluor — Minerals Yearbook. Preprint. Fluorspar

MYP Gallm — Minerals Yearbook. Preprint. Gallium

MYP Gem St — Minerals Yearbook. Preprint. Gem Stones

MYP Gold — Minerals Yearbook. Preprint. Gold

MYP Grapht — Minerals Yearbook. Preprint. Graphite

MYP Gypsum — Minerals Yearbook. Preprint. Gypsum

MYP Helium — Minerals Yearbook. Preprint. Helium

MYP I & S S — Minerals Yearbook. Preprint. Iron and Steel Scrap

MYP Iodine — Minerals Yearbook. Preprint. Iodine

MYP Iron — Minerals Yearbook. Preprint. Iron and Steel

MYP Iron O — Minerals Yearbook. Preprint. Iron Ore

MYP Iron S S — Minerals Yearbook. Preprint. Iron and Steel Slag

MYP Ir Ox — Minerals Yearbook. Preprint. Iron Oxide Pigments

MYP Kyan — Minerals Yearbook. Preprint. Kyanite and Related Materials

MYP Lead — Minerals Yearbook. Preprint. Lead

MYP Lime — Minerals Yearbook. Preprint. Lime

MYP Lith — Minerals Yearbook. Preprint. Lithium

MYP Magn C — Minerals Yearbook. Preprint. Magnesium Compounds

MYP Mercry — Minerals Yearbook. Preprint. Mercury

MYP Mica — Minerals Yearbook. Preprint. Mica

MYP Mining — Minerals Yearbook. Preprint. Mining and Quarrying Trends in the Metal and Nonmetal Industries

MYP M N Mtl — Minerals Yearbook. Preprint. Minor Nonmetals

MYP Moly — Minerals Yearbook. Preprint. Molybdenum

MYP Nitro — Minerals Yearbook. Preprint. Nitrogen

MYP Nonfl M — Minerals Yearbook. Preprint. Nonfuel Minerals Survey Methods

MYP O Mtl — Minerals Yearbook. Preprint. Other Metals

MYP O Nmtl — Minerals Yearbook. Preprint. Other Nonmetals

MYP Peat — Minerals Yearbook. Preprint. Peat

MYP Phos R — Minerals Yearbook. Preprint. Phosphate Rock

MYP Platnm — Minerals Yearbook. Preprint. Platinum - Group Metals

MYP Potash — Minerals Yearbook. Preprint. Potash

MYP Prod — Minerals Yearbook. Preprint. Products

MYP Pumic — Minerals Yearbook. Preprint. Pumice and Volcanic Cinder

MYP Pumice — Minerals Yearbook. Preprint. Pumice and Pumicite

MYP Rev — Minerals Yearbook. Preprint. Review of the Mineral Industry

MYP Rhenm — Minerals Yearbook. Preprint. Rhenium

MYP Salt — Minerals Yearbook. Preprint. Salt

MYP Sand — Minerals Yearbook. Preprint. Sand and Gravel

MYP Silver — Minerals Yearbook. Preprint. Silver

MYP Slag — Minerals Yearbook. Preprint. Slag - Iron and Steel

MYP Sodium — Minerals Yearbook. Preprint. Sodium and Sodium Compounds

MYP State — Minerals Yearbook. Preprint. Area Reports. Individual States

MYP Stat S — Minerals Yearbook. Preprint. Statistical Summary

MYP Stone — Minerals Yearbook. Preprint. Stone

MYP Sulfur — Minerals Yearbook. Preprint. Sulfur and Pyrites

MYP Talc — Minerals Yearbook. Preprint. Talc, Soapstone, and Pyrophyllite

MYP Terr — Minerals Yearbook. Preprint. Territorial Mineral Industry of Puerto Rico, Virgin Islands, and Pacific Islands
MYP Thorm — Minerals Yearbook. Preprint. Thorium
MYP Tin — Minerals Yearbook. Preprint. Tin
MYP Titanm — Minerals Yearbook. Preprint. Titanium
MYP Tungst — Minerals Yearbook. Preprint. Tungsten
MYP Vandm — Minerals Yearbook. Preprint. Vanadium
MYP Vermic — Minerals Yearbook. Preprint. Vermiculite
MYP Wld Min — Minerals Yearbook. Preprint. Minerals in the World Economy
MYP Zinc — Minerals Yearbook. Preprint. Zinc
MYP Zirc — Minerals Yearbook. Preprint. Zirconium and Hafnium
My Sal — Mysterium Salutis
Mys LJ — Mysore Law Journal
Mysl Lotn — Mysl Lotnicza
Mysore Agric Cal Yb — Mysore Agricultural Calendar and Yearbook
Mysore Agric J — Mysore Agricultural Journal
Mysore Agr J — Mysore Agricultural Journal
Mysore Archaeol Dept Annu Rep — Mysore Archaeological Department Annual Report
Mysore Dep Mines Geol Bull — Mysore. Department of Mines and Geology. Bulletin
Mysore Dep Mines Geol Geol Stud — Mysore. Department of Mines and Geology. Geological Studies
Mysore Econ J — Mysore Economic Journal
Mysore Econ R — Mysore Economic Review
Mysore J Agric Sci — Mysore Journal of Agricultural Sciences
Mysore LJ — Mysore Law Journal

Mysore Met Mem — Mysore Meteorological Memoirs
Mysore Or — Mysore Orientalist
Mystetstvoz Zbirn — Mystetstvoznavstvo Zbirnyk
Mys WN — Mysore Weekly Notes
MYT — Mysterious Traveler Mystery Reader
Myth Bibl — Mythologische Bibliothek
Myth Gr — Mythographi Graeci
Myth Graec — Mythographi Graeci
MythosP — Mythos Papers
MYV — Maandstatistiek van de Industrie
MYZ — Mix. Ijzerwaren, Doe het Zelf
MZ — Magdeburger Zeitung
MZ — Mainzer Zeitschrift
MZ — Malerei und Zeichnung der Griechen
MZ — Malerei und Zeichnung der Klassischen Antike
MZ — Meteorologische Zeitschrift
MZ — Mundaiz
MZ — Muzikoloski Zbornik - Musicological Annual
MZDKP — Materialy Zrodlowe do Dziejow Kosciola w Polsce
MZISA — Monitore Zoologico Italiano [*Italian Journal of Zoology*]. Supplemento
M Zizn — Muzikal'naja Zizn
MZMB — Mitteilungen aus dem Zoologischen Museum (Berlin)
MZOHDT — Miscellanea Zoologica Hungarica
MZoMB — Mitteilungen des Zoologischen Museums. Berlin
MZOODG — Miscellanea Zoologica
MZWMA — Molkerei-Zeitung Welt der Milch
Mz Zts — Mainzer Zeitschrift

N

N — All India Reporter, Nagpur Series
N — Nada
N — Nation
N — Nationalzeitung
N — Nature
N — Neophilologus
N — November
N60ES — North of 60. Environmental Studies
NA — Names
NA — Nassauische Annalen. Verein fuer Nassauische Altertumskunde und Geschictsforschung
Na — Nation
NA — Nationalmuseets Arbejdsmark
NA — Nation and Athenaeum
Na — Naturalia
Na — Nature
NA — Nederlands Archievenblad
NA — Neues Archiv der Gesellschaft fuer Aeltere Deutsche Geschichtskunde
NA — Neutestamentliche Abhandlungen
NA — New Adelphi
NA — New African
NA — New Alliance
NA — News Agencies
NA — North American Archaeologist
NA — North American Review
NA — Note d'Archivio per la Storia Musicale
NA — Notes Africaines
NA — Noticias Agricolas
NA — Nuova Antologia
NA — Nuova Antologia di Scienze, Lettere, ed Arti
NA — Nuovi Argomenti
NAA — Narody Azii i Afriki
NAA — Notices d'Archeologie Armoricaine
NAAB News — N.A.A.B. (National Association of Artificial Breeders) News [Columbia]
NAA Bul — National Association of Accountants. Bulletin
NAACP Newsl — NAACP [National Association for the Advancement of Colored People] Newsletter
NAAeDG — Neues Archiv der Gesellschaft fuer Aeltere Deutsche Geschichtskunde
NAAF — Nouvelles Archives de l'Art Francais
NA Anarch — North American Anarchist
NAAS — Newsletter. Association for Asian Studies
NAAS Advis Pap — National Agricultural Advisory Service. Advisory Papers
NAAS Poult Sect Q J — N.A.A.S. (National Agricultural Advisory Service) Poultry Section Quarterly Journal
NAAS Prog Rep — National Agricultural Advisory Service. Progress Report
NAAS Q Rev — NAAS [National Agricultural Advisory Service] Quarterly Review
NAAS Quart Rev — NAAS [National Agricultural Advisory Service] Quarterly Review
NAAS Tech Rep — N.A.A.S. (National Agricultural Advisory Service) Technical Report [London]
NAB — Nation's Business
NAB — Nederlandsch Archievenblad
NAb — Neues Abendland
NABTE Rev — NABTE [National Association for Business Teacher Education] Review
NAC — Management Accounting
Nac — Nacion
NAC — National Association of College Wind and Percussion Instructors. Journal
NAC — Nationalmuseets Arbejdsmark (Copenhagen)
NAC — Numismatica e Antichita Classiche
NACA Rep — NACA (US National Advisory Committee for Aeronautics) Reports
NACA Res Memor — NACA (National Advisory Committee for Aeronautics) Research Memoranda [Washington]
NACA Tech Memo — NACA [US National Advisory Committee for Aeronautics] Technical Memorandum
NACA Tech Rep — NACA (US National Advisory Committee for Aeronautics) Technical Report
NacC — Nacional (Caracas)
NACCALJ — National Association of Claimants' Compensation Attorneys. Law Journal
NAC (C & O) — Reports of the Decisions of the Native Appeal Courts, Cape Province and the Orange Free State [South Africa]
NACF Mag — National Art Collections Fund Magazine
NACF Rev — National Art Collections Fund Review
Nachb — Nachbarn

Nach Elek — Nachrichtentechnik-Elektronik
Nach Elktr — Nachrichten-Elektronik und Telematik
Nachr Aerztl Miss — Nachrichten aus der Aerztlichen Mission
Nachr Akad Wiss Goettingen — Nachrichten. Akademie der Wissenschaften zu Goettingen
Nachr Akad Wiss Goettingen Math-Phys Kl II — Nachrichten. Akademie der Wissenschaften zu Goettingen. II. Mathematisch-Physikalische Klasse
Nachr Akad Wiss Goettingen Philol Hist Kl — Nachrichten der Akademie der Wissenschaften in Goettingen. Philologisch-Historische Klasse
Nachr Akad Wiss Goettingen Philol Hist Klasse — Nachrichten der Akademie der Wissenschaften in Goettingen. Philologisch-Historische Klasse
Nachr Akad Wiss Goett Philologisch-Hist Kl — Nachrichten. Akademie der Wissenschaften zu Goettingen. Philologisch-Historische Klasse
Nachr Akad Wiss UdSSR — Nachrichten. Akademie der Wissenschaften der UdSSR
Nachr Akad Wiss UkrSSR — Nachrichten der Akademie der Wissenschaften der UkrSSR
Nachr Ak Goett — Nachrichten. Akademie der Wissenschaften in Goettingen
Nachr Arb Gem Ges Wes — Nachrichten der Arbeitsgemeinschaft fuer das Gesundheitswesen
Nachrbl — Nachrichtenblatt
Nachr Bl Bay Ent — Nachrichtenblatt der Bayerischen Entomologen
NachrBl Bayer Ent — Nachrichtenblatt der Bayerischen Entomologen
Nachrbl Dkmlpf Baden Wuerttemberg — Nachrichtenblatt der Denkmalpflege in Baden-Wuerttemberg
NachrBl Dt Pflschutzdienst (Berl) — Nachrichtenblatt. Deutscher Pflanzenschutzdienst (Berlin)
NachrBl Dt PflSchutzdienst (Berlin) — Nachrichtenblatt. Deutschen Pflanzenschutzdienst (Berlin)
Nachrbl Dt Pflschutzdienst (Stuttg) — Nachrichtenblatt. Deutschen Pflanzenschutzdienst (Stuttgart)
NachrBl Dt PflSchutzdienst (Stuttgart) — Nachrichtenblatt. Deutschen Pflanzenschutzdienst (Stuttgart)
Nachrbl Dtsch Pflschdienst (Berlin) — Nachrichtenblatt. Deutschen Pflanzenschutzdienst (Berlin)
Nachrbl Dtsch Pflschdienst (Braunschweig) — Nachrichtenblatt. Deutschen Pflanzenschutzdienst (Braunschweig)
Nachrbl Ges Wiss Goettingen Philos Hist Kl — Nachrichtenblatt der Gesellschaft der Wissenschaften zu Goettingen. Philosophisch-Historische Klasse
NachrBl PflSchutzdienst DDR — Nachrichtenblatt fuer den Pflanzenschutzdienst in der DDR
Nachrbl Soc Annensis E V — Nachrichtenblatt der Societas Annensis e. V
Nachr Chem Tech — Nachrichten aus Chemie und Technik [Later, Nachrichten aus Chemie, Technik, und Laboratorium]
Nachr Chem Tech Lab — Nachrichten aus Chemie, Technik, und Laboratorium [Formerly, Nachrichten aus Chemie und Technik]
Nachr Chem Tech Laborat — Nachrichten aus Chemie, Technik, und Laboratorium
Nachr Dok — Nachrichten fuer Dokumentation
Nachr Dokum — Nachrichten fuer Dokumentation
Nachr Dtsch Geol Ges — Nachrichten. Deutsche Geologische Gesellschaft
Nachr Elektroind — Nachrichten der Elektroindustrie
Nachr Elektron — Nachrichten-Elektronik
Nachr Elektron and Telematik — Nachrichten-Elektronik und Telematik
Nachr Forschungszent Karlsruhe — Nachrichten. Forschungszentrum Karlsruhe
Nachr Fortgange Naturf Ges Jena — Nachricht von dem Fortgange der Naturforschenden Gesellschaft zu Jena
Nachr fuer Dok — Nachrichten fuer Dokumentation
Nachr Gel Sachen — Nachrichten von Gelehrten Sachen. Herausgegeben von der Akademie zu Erfurt
Nachr Ges N Vk Ostas — Nachrichten der Gesellschaft fuer Natur und Voelkerkunde Ostasiens
Nachr Ges Wiss Goett — Nachrichten. Akademie der Wissenschaften zu Goettingen
Nachr Ges Wiss Goettingen Geschaeftliche Mitt — Nachrichten von der Gesellschaft der Wissenschaften zu Goettingen. Geschaeftliche Mitteilungen
Nachr Ges Wiss Goettingen Jahresber — Nachrichten von der Gesellschaft der Wissenschaften zu Goettingen. Jahresbericht
Nachr Ges Wiss Goettingen Math Phys Kl — Nachrichten. Gesellschaft der Wissenschaften zu Goettingen. Mathematisch-Physikalische Klasse
Nachr Ges Wiss Goettingen Math Phys Kl Fachgruppe 1 — Nachrichten von der Gesellschaft der Wissenschaften zu Goettingen. Mathematisch-Physikalische Klasse. Fachgruppe 1. Mathematik
Nachr Ges Wiss Goettingen Math-Phys Kl Fachgruppe 2 — Nachrichten. Gesellschaft der Wissenschaften zu Goettingen. Mathematisch-Physikalische Klasse. Fachgruppe 2. Physik, Astronomie, Geophysik, Technik

Nachr Ges Wiss Goettingen Math Phys Kl Fachgruppe 3 — Nachrichten. Gesellschaft der Wissenschaften zu Goettingen. Mathematisch-Physikalische Klasse. Fachgruppe 3. Chemie, Einschliesslich Physikalische Chemie

Nachr Ges Wiss Goettingen Math Phys Kl Fachgruppe 4 — Nachrichten. Gesellschaft der Wissenschaften zu Goettingen. Mathematisch-Physikalische Klasse. Fachgruppe 4. Geologie und Mineralogie

Nachr Ges Wiss Goettingen Math Phys Kl Fachgruppe 6 — Nachrichten. Gesellschaft der Wissenschaften zu Goettingen. Mathematisch-Physikalische Klasse. Fachgruppe 6. Biologie

Nachr Ges Wiss Goetting Math Phys Kl Fachgruppe 1 — Nachrichten. Gesellschaft der Wissenschaften zu Goettingen. Mathematisch-Physikalische Klasse. Fachgruppe 1. Mathematik

Nachr (Giessen) — Nachrichtenblatt fuer Deutsche Vorzeit (Giessen)

Nachr Giessen — Nachrichten der Giessener Hochschulgesellschaft

Nachr Giessener Hochschulges — Nachrichten der Giessener Hochschulgesellschaft

Nachr Goettingen — Nachrichten. Akademie der Wissenschaften zu Goettingen

Nachrichtenbl Deut Pflanzenschutzdienst (Berlin) — Nachrichtenblatt. Deutscher Pflanzenschutzdienst (Berlin)

Nachrichtenbl Deut Pflanzenschutzdienst (Stuttgart) — Nachrichtenblatt. Deutschen Pflanzenschutzdienst (Stuttgart)

Nachrichtenbl Deutsch Ges Gesch Med — Nachrichtenblatt der Deutschen Gesellschaft fuer Geschichte der Medizin, Naturwissenschaft und Technik

Nachrichtenbl Deutsch Kakteenges — Nachrichtenblatt der Deutschen Kakteengesellschaft

Nachrichtenbl Dtsch Ges Gesch Med Naturwiss Tech — Nachrichtenblatt. Deutsche Gesellschaft fuer Geschichte der Medizin. Naturwissenschaft und Technik

Nachrichtenbl Dtsch Pflanzenschutzdienst (Berlin) — Nachrichtenblatt. Deutschen Pflanzenschutzdienst (Berlin)

Nachrichtenbl Dtsch Pflanzenschutzdienst (Braunschw) — Nachrichtenblatt des Deutschen Pflanzenschutzdienstes (Braunschweig)

Nachrichtenbl Dtsch Pflanzenschutzdienstes (Braunschweig) — Nachrichtenblatt. Deutschen Pflanzenschutzdienst (Braunschweig)

Nachrichtenbl Goldschmiede Juwelier Graveur Handwerk — Nachrichtenblatt fuer das Goldschmiede-, Juwelier-, und Graveur-Handwerk

Nachrichtenbl Opt Handwerk — Nachrichtenblatt fuer das Optiker-Handwerk

Nachrichtenbl Pflanzenschutz DDR — Nachrichtenblatt fuer den Pflanzenschutz in der DDR

Nachrichtenbl Pflanzenschutzdienst DDR — Nachrichtenblatt fuer den Pflanzenschutzdienst in der DDR

Nachrichtenbl Photogr Handwerk — Nachrichtenblatt fuer das Photographen Handwerk

Nachrichtentech-Elektron — Nachrichtentechnik-Elektronik

Nachrichtentech Elektronik — Nachrichtentechnik-Elektronik

Nachrichtentech Fachber — Nachrichtentechnische Fachberichte

Nachrichtentech Fachber Beih NTZ — Nachrichtentechnische Fachberichte. Beihefte der Nachrichtentechnische Zeitschrift

Nachrichtentech Ges Fachber — Nachrichtentechnische Gesellschaft. Fachberichte

Nachrichtentech Z — Nachrichtentechnische Zeitung

Nachr K Ges Wiss Goettingen Math Phys Kl — Nachrichten von der Koeniglichen Gesellschaft der Wissenschaften zu Goettingen.Mathematisch-Physikalische Klasse

Nachr Kgl Ges WG — Nachrichten der Koeniglichen Gesellschaft der Wissenschaften zu Goettingen

Nachr Koenigl Ges Wiss Goettingen Geschaeftl Mitt — Nachrichten von der Koeniglichen Gesellschaft der Wissenschaften zu Goettingen.Geschaeftliche Mitteilungen

Nachr Koenigl Ges Wiss Goettingen Math Phys Kl — Nachrichten von der Koeniglichen Gesellschaft der Wissenschaften zu Goettingen.Mathematisch-Physikalische Klasse

Nachr Mensch Umwelt — Nachrichten Mensch-Umwelt

Nachr Metallind — Nachrichten Metallindustrie

Nachr Naturwiss Mus Stadt (Aschaffenburg) — Nachrichten. Naturwissenschaftliches Museum der Stadt (Aschaffenburg)

Nachr Naturw Mus (Aschaffenb) — Nachrichten. Naturwissenschaftliches Museum der Stadt (Aschaffenburg)

Nachr Niedersachs Urgesch — Nachrichten aus Niedersachsens Urgeschichte

Nachr/Nouv/Notiz — Nachrichten/Nouvelles/Notizie

Nachrrdienst Dt Ver Oefftl Fuers — Nachrichtendienst des Deutschen Vereins fuer Oeffentliche und Private Fuersorge

Nachrr Ges Wiss Goettg — Nachrichten der Koeniglichen Gesellschaft der Wissenschaften zu Goettingen

Nachr RVA — Nachrichten des Reichsversicherungsamts

Nachr Stand — Nachrichten fuer Standardisierung

Nachrtech — Nachrichtentechnisch

Nachrtech Z — Nachrichtentechnische Zeitschrift

Nachr Telefonbau & Normalzeit — Nachrichten der Telefonbau und Normalzeit

Nachr Trop Med (Tiflis) — Nachrichten der Tropischen Medizin (Tiflis)

Nachr Venereol Dermatol Moscow — Nachrichten ueber Venerologie und Dermatologie (Moscow)

Nachr Verein Schweizer Bibl — Nachrichten. Vereinigung Schweizerischer Bibliothekare

Nachr Wiss Bib — Nachrichten fuer Wissenschaftliche Bibliotheken

Nachr Z — Nachrichtentechnische Zeitschrift

Nach Zeit — Nachrichtentechnische Zeitschrift

NACLA — NACLA (North American Congress of Latin America) Report on the Americas

NACLA Rep Amer — NACLA Reports on the Americas

NACN — Native Canadian

NAC (N & T) — Decisions of the Native Appeal and Divorce Court (Transvaal and Natal)

NAC (NE) — Decisions of the Native Appeal Court (North Eastern Division)

NAC News Pestic Rev — NAC [*National Agriculture Chemicals Association*] News and Pesticide Review

NACR (SR) — Native Appeal Court Reports (Southern Rhodesia)

NAC (S) — Selected Decisions of the Native Appeal Court (Southern Division)

NACTA J Natl Assoc Coll Teach Agric — NACTA Journal. National Association of Colleges and Teachers of Agriculture

NACWPI — NACWPI [*National Association of College Wind and Percussion Instructors*]Journal

NAD — Nielson Audience Demographic Report

NADA — Native Affairs Department. Annual

Nadezn i Kontrol'kacestva — Nadeznost i Kontrol'kacestva

NADGA — Nagoya Kogyo Daigaku Gakuho

NADKA — Nagasaki Daigaku Suisan-Gakubu Kenkyu Hokoku

NADL J — NADL [*National Association of Dental Laboratories*] Journal

N Adm T — Nordisk Administrativt Tidsskrift

NADS — Newsletter. American Dialect Society

NAE — Nova Acta Eruditorum

NAEBJ — National Association of Educational Broadcasters. Journal

Naehr — Naehrung. Chemie, Biochemie, Mikrobiologie, Technologie

NAEP — National Assessment of Educational Progress

NAERI — National Agricultural Economic Research Inventory

Naeringsforskning Suppl — Naeringsforskning. Supplement

NAE S — Nova Acta Eruditorum. Supplementum

NAESDI — NATO [*North Atlantic Treaty Organization*] ASI Series. Series E. Applied Sciences

NAF — National Forum. Phi Kappa Phi Journal

NAF — New African

NA f G — Neues Archiv der Gesellschaft fuer Aeltere Deutsche Geschichtskunde

NAfr — Notes Africaines

Naft Gazova Promst — Naftova i Gazova Promislovist

NAG — Nachrichten. Akademie der Wissenschaften zu Goettingen

NAG — Neues Archiv der Gesellschaft fuer Aeltere Deutsche Geschichtskunde

NAGADGK — Neues Archiv der Gesellschaft fuer Aeltere Deutsche Geschichtskunde

Nagasaki Igakkai Zasshi Suppl — Nagasaki Igakkai Zasshi. Supplement

Nagasaki Med J — Nagasaki Medical Journal

NAGBA — National Gas Bulletin

NAGDA — Nara Gakugei Daigaku Kiyo

Nag Ig Zass — Nagasaki Igakkai Zasshi

Nag J Med Sci — Nagoya Journal of Medical Science

Nag LJ — Nagpur Law Journal

NAGMA — College of Agriculture (Nagpur). Magazine

Nag Math J — Nagoya Mathematical Journal

NagoKR — Nagoya Daigaku Bungakubu Kenkyu Ronshu

Nagoya Gakuin Univ Rev Humanit Nat Sci — Nagoya Gakuin University Review. Humanities. Natural Science

Nagoya J Med Sci — Nagoya Journal of Medical Science

Nagoya Math J — Nagoya Mathematical Journal

Nagoya Med J — Nagoya Medical Journal

Nagoya Univ Dep Earth Sci Collect Pap Earth Sci — Nagoya University. Department of Earth Sciences. Collected Papers on Earth Sciences

Nagoya Univ Inst Plasma Phys Annu Rev — Nagoya University. Institute of Plasma Physics. Annual Review

Nagoya Univ Inst Plasma Phys Rep IPPJ AM — Nagoya University. Institute of Plasma Physics. Report IPPJ-AM

Nagoya Univ Inst Plasma Phys Rep IPPJ REV — Nagoya University. Institute of Plasma Physics. Report IPPJ-REV

Nagoya Univ Jour Earth Sci — Nagoya University. Journal of Earth Sciences

Nagpur Agric Coll Mag — Nagpur Agricultural College. Magazine

Nagpur Coll Agric Mag — Nagpur College of Agriculture Magazine

Nagpur Univ J — Nagpur University. Journal

NAGR — National Geographic Research

Nagra Bull — Nagra Bulletin

Nagra Inf — Nagra Informiert

NAGSHKP — Neues Archiv fuer die Geschichte der Stadt Heidelberg und der Kurpfalz

NAGSHRP — Neues Archiv fuer die Geschichte der Stadt Heidelberg und der Rheinischen Pfalz

Nag UCL Mag — Nagpur University. College of Law. Magazine

NAGZA — Nagasaki Igakkai Zasshi

NAH — Noticiario Arqueologico Hispanico

NAHE — Nova Acta Historico-Ecclesiastica

NAHIA News — National Association of Historians of Islamic Art. Newsletter

NAHID3 — Instituto Nacional para la Conservacion de la Naturaleza. Naturalia Hispanica

NA Hisp — Noticiario Arqueologico Hispanico

NAHQAO — Nebraska. University. College of Agriculture and Home Economics. Quarterly

Nahr Ernaehr — Nahrung und Ernaehrung

Nahrungsm Ind — Nahrungsmittel-Industrie

NAIGA — Nagoya Igaku

NAIG AR — NAIG [*Nippon Atomic Industry Group*] Annual Review

NAIKAB — Internal Medicine

Naika Hok — Naika Hokan

Nairobi J Med — Nairobi Journal of Medicine

NAJHS — News. American Jewish Historical Society

NA Jl Expl Agric — New Zealand Journal of Experimental Agriculture

NAJMDP — North American Journal of Fisheries Management

NAJN — North American Journal of Numismatics

NAk — Narodopisne Aktuality

NAK — Nederlandsch Archief voor Kerkgeschiedenis

NAkG — Nachrichten. Akademie der Wissenschaften zu Goettingen

NAKG — Nederlandsch Archief voor Kerkgeschiedenis

N Akkad Proj Rep — Northern Akkad Project Reports

NAL — Newspapers in Australian Libraries

NAI — Nova Alvorada
NALA — Native Library Advocate
NALC — Nova Acta Academiae Caesareae Leopoldino-Carolinae Germanicae Naturae Curiosorum
NALCO Abstr Curr Art Wat Treat — NALCO (National Aluminum Corporation) Abstracts of Current Articles on Water Treatment [*Chicago*]
NALF — Negro American Literature Forum
N Al J C — Neues Allgemeines Journal der Chemie
NALLDJ — National Association of Language Laboratory Directors. Journal
NALSDJ — NATO [*North Atlantic Treaty Organization*] ASI Series. Series A. Life Sciences
NAM — Narodi Ameriki. A.V. Efimov and S.A. Tokarev [*Moskva*]
NAM — Nouvelles Archives des Missions Scientifiques et Litteraires
N Am Bird Bander — North American Bird Bander
NAMC — Notiziario Archeologico del Ministero delle Colonie
N Amer Archaeol — North American Archaeologist
NAmerR — North American Review
N Amer Rev — North American Review
N Am Fauna — North American Fauna
N Am Flora — North American Flora
N Am Flora Ser II — North American Flora. Series II
Namibia N — Namibia News
N Am J Fish Manage — North American Journal of Fisheries Management
NAMOA9 — Natura Mosana
NA Monthly — North Australian Monthly
N Am R — North American Review
N Am Rev — North American Review
NAMRU — US Naval Medical Research Unit [*Cairo*]
NAMS — Nouvelles Archives des Missions Scientifiques et Litteraires
N A Mth — Nouvelles Annales de Mathematiques
N Am Vet — North American Veterinarian
NAMZ — Neue Allgemeine Missionszeitschrift
NAN — Nachrichten fuer Dokumentation. Zeitschrift fuer Information und Dokumentation
NAN — Nassauische Annalen
NAN — Neues Archiv fuer Niedersachsen
Nan Ching Ta Hsueeh Hsueeh Pao — Acta Universitatis Nankinensis Scientiarum Naturalium/Nan Ching Ta Hsueh Hsueh Pao
Nancy Mm Ac Stanislas — Academie de Stanislas. Memoires de la Societe Royale des Sciences, Lettres et Arts (Nancy)
Nancy Mm S Sc — Memoires de la Societe Royale des Sciences, Lettres, et Arts de Nancy
Nancy S Sc Bll — Bulletin de la Societe des Sciences de Nancy
Nancy Tr S Sc — Precis Analytique des Travaux de la Societe Royale des Sciences, Arts, et Agriculture de Nancy
N & A — Nation and Athenaeum
N & C — Nigeria and the Classics
N & PEIR — Newfoundland and Prince Edward Island Reports
N & Q — Notes and Queries
N & S — Nicholls and Stops' Reports
N & S — Nord und Sued
N & V — Nova et Vetera
NANED — Neuropathology and Applied Neurobiology
Nankai Lectures Math Phys — Nankai Lectures on Mathematical Physics
Nankai Ser Pure Appl Math Theoret Phys — Nankai Series in Pure, Applied Mathematics and Theoretical Physics
Nankai Univ Res Lab Appl Chem Rep — Nankai University. Research Laboratory of Applied Chemistry. Reports
Nanking J — Nanking Journal
N Ann Sc Nat (Bologna) — Nuovi Annali delle Scienze Naturali (Bologna)
Nanostruct Mater — Nanostructured Materials
Nansei Reg Fish Res Lab Bull — Nansei Regional Fisheries Research Laboratory. Bulletin
N Ant — Nuova Antologia
NAnt — Nuova Antologia di Scienze, Lettere, ed Arti
Nanta Math — Nanta Mathematica
Nantes A S Ac — Annales de la Societe Academique de Nantes et du Departement de la Loire Inferieure (Nantes)
NANTIS News Bull — Nottingham and Nottinghamshire Technical Information Service. News Bulletin
N Antol Sc — Nuova Antologia di Scienze, Lettere, ed Arti
Nantucket Hist Assoc Proc — Nantucket Historical Association. Proceedings
Nanyang Q — Nanyang Quarterly
Nanyang Univ J Part III — Nanyang University. Journal. Part III. Natural Sciences
Nanzan Stud Cult Anthrop — Nanzan Studies in Cultural Anthropology
NAO JI — N.A.O. (National Association of Opticians) Journal [*Glasgow*]
Na Okika O Hawaii Hawaii Orchid J — Na Okika O Hawaii/Hawaii Orchid Journal
Naoukovi Zapiski Kievskogo Inst Naradnogo Gospod — Naoukovi Zapiski Kievskogo Institutul Naradnogo Gospod
Nap Ac Asp A — Annali dell' Accademia degli Aspiranti Naturalisti (Napoli)
Nap Ac At — Atti della Reale Accademia delle Scienze e Belle Lettere. Sezione della Societa R. Barbonica (Napoli)
Nap Ac Pont At — Atti dell' Accademia Pontaniana di Napoli
Nap Ac Sc Mm — Memorie della R. Accademia delle Scienze (Napoli)
Nap At Ac — Atti della Reale Accademia delle Scienze e Belle Lettere. Sezione della Societa R. Barbonica (Napoli)
Nap At Ac Sc — Atti della Reale Accademia delle Scienze e Belle Lettere. Sezione della Societa R. Barbonica (Napoli)
Nap At I Inc — Atti del Real Istituto d' Incorraggiamento alle Scienze Naturali di Napoli
Nap Bll Ac Asp — Bullettino dell' Accademia degli Aspiranti Naturalisti (Napoli)
NAPEHE Proc — NAPEHE [*National Association for Physical Education in Higher Education*] Proceedings
Nap I Inc At — Atti del Real Istituto d' Incorraggiamento alle Scienze Naturali di Napoli

Naples Sta Zool Pubbl — Naples. Stazione Zoologica. Pubblicazioni
Nap Ms — Museo di Letteratura e Filosofia (Napoli)
NAPN — Native Authority Public Notice
Nap Nobil — Napoli Nobilissima
Napoli Nob — Napoli Nobilissima. Rivista Bimestrale di Arte Figurativa, Archeologia, e Urbanistica
Napoli Riv Mun — Napoli Rivista Municipale
Nap Pres — Napier. Prescription
Napravlennyi Sint Tverd Veshchestv — Napravlennyi Sintez Tverdykh Veshchestv
Nap Rd — Rendiconto dell' Accademia delle Scienze Fisiche e Matematiche (Napoli)
Nap Rd — Rendiconto delle Adunanze e de' Lavori della Reale Accademia delle Scienze Fic. o Mat. di Napoli
Napred Pcel — Napredno Pcelarstvo
Nap S Nt Bll — Bollettino della Societa di Naturalisti in Napoli
NAPT Bull — NAPT (National Association for the Prevention of Tuberculosis) Bulletin [*London*]
NAPT Commonw Hlth Mess — NAPT (National Association for the Prevention of Tuberculosis) Commonwealth Health Messenger [*London*]
NAPT Commonw Mess — NAPT (National Association for the Prevention of Tuberculosis) Commonwealth Messenger [*London*]
NAPT J — NAPT [*National Association of Physical Therapists*] Journal
NAPT Mass Radiogr Newsl — NAPT (National Association for the Prevention of Tuberculosis) Mass Radiography Newsletter [*London*]</PHR> %
NaR — Nasa Rec
NAR — New American Review [*Later, American Review*]
NAR — North American Review
NAR — Norwegian Archaeological Review
NAR — Nuova Antologia di Scienze, Lettere, ed Arti
NAr — Nuovi Argomenti
NAR — Nutrition Abstracts and Reviews
NARAS Inst Jnl — NARAS [*National Academy of Recording Arts and Sciences*] Institute Journal
Nar Azii i Afriki — Narody Azii i Afriki
N Arch Wisk — Nieuw Archief voor Wiskunde
Narcolepsy Proc Int Symp — Narcolepsy. Proceedings. International Symposium on Narcolepsy
NAREB — Nature and Resources
NaRev — Nassau Review
N Arg — Nuovi Argomenti
NARHA — Nucleic Acids Research
Narisi Istor Prirodoznav i Tekhn — Narisi z Istorii Prirodoznavstva i Tekhniki
Narisi Istor Prirodozn Tekh — Narisi z Istorii Prirodoznavstva i Tekhniki
Narisi Istor Tekh Prirodozn — Narisi z Istorii Tekhniki i Prirodoznavstva
Nar Khoz Sov Latv — Narodnoe Khozyaistvo Sovetskoi Latvii
Nar Khoz Uzb — Narodnoe Khozyaistvo Uzbekistana
NARM Relay Symp Pap — NARM (National Association of Relay Manufacturers) Relay Symposium Papers [*Belleroe, New York*]
Nar Muz (Prague) Cas Oddil Prirodoved — Narodni Muzeum. Casopis. Oddil Prirodovedny (Prague)
Narod Aktual — Narodopisne Aktuality
Narod Azii Afriki — Narody Azii i Afriki
Narod Khoz Uzbek — Narodnoe Khozyaistvo Uzbekistana
Narod Vestn Csl — Narodopisny Vestnik Ceskoslovensky
Narody AA — Narody Azii i Afriki
Narody Azii Afr — Narody Azii i Afriki
Naropa Mag — Naropa Magazine
Narragansett Mar Lab Collect Repr — Narragansett Marine Laboratory. Collected Reprints. Graduate School of Oceanography. University of Rhode Island
Narrag Hist Reg — Narragansett Historical Register
Narrag Reg — Narragansett Historical Register
NARS — Narrative Accomplishment Reporting System
NARS — National Automated Accounting Research System
Na Rs Rev — Naval Research Reviews
Nar Sumar — Narodni Sumar
Nar Tvorch Etnohr — Narodna Tvorchist' ta Etnohrafiya
Nar Tvor ta Etnogr — Narodna Tvorcist' ta Etnografija
Nar Umjetn — Narodna Umjetnost
Nar Zdrav — Narodno Zdravlje
Nar Zdravlje — Narodno Zdravlje
NAS — Natuursteen
NAS — Norwegian-American Studies
NAS — Notizie degli Archivi di Stato
NASABW — Noticias Agricolas. Servicio Shell para el Agricultor
NASA Conf Publ — NASA [*National Aeronautics and Space Administration*] Conference Publication
NASA Contract Rep — NASA [*National Aeronautics and Space Administration*] Contractor Report
NASA Memo — NASA [*National Aeronautics and Space Administration*] Memorandum
NASA Memor — NASA (National Aeronautics and Space Administration) Memoranda [*Washington*]
NASA Ref Publ — NASA [*National Aeronautics and Space Administration*] Reference Publication
NASA Rep — NASA (National Aeronautics and Space Administration) Report
NASA Rep Ed — NASA [*National Aeronautics and Space Administration*] Report to Educators
NASA Republ — NASA [*National Aeronautics and Space Administration*] Republication
NASA Republn — NASA (National Aeronautics and Space Administration) Republication [*Washington*]
NASA Spec Publ — NASA [*National Aeronautics and Space Administration*] Special Publications
NASA Spec Publ SP — NASA [*US National Aeronautics and Space Administration*] Special Publication SP

NASA Tech Brief — NASA [*National Aeronautics and Space Administration*] Technical Briefs

NASA Tech Briefs — NASA [*National Aeronautics and Space Administration*] Technical Briefs

NASA Tech Memo — NASA [*National Aeronautics and Space Administration*] Technical Memorandum

NASA Tech Memor — NASA (National Aeronautics and Space Administration) Technical Memorandum [*Washington*]

NASA Tech Note — NASA [*National Aeronautics and Space Administration*] Technical Note

NASA Tech Pap — NASA [*National Aeronautics and Space Administration*] Technical Paper

NASA Tech Publ Announce — NASA (US National Aeronautics and Space Administration) Technical Publications Announcements

NASA Tech Rep — NASA [*National Aeronautics and Space Administration*] Technical Report

NASA Tech Transl — NASA [*National Aeronautics and Space Administration*] Technical Translation

NASCA — NASA [*National Aeronautics and Space Administration*] Technical Note

N A Sc Nt — Nuovi Annali delle Scienze Naturali

NASD J — Journal. National Association for Staff Development in Further and Higher Education

NASD Newsl — NASD [*National Association of Securities Dealers*] Newsletter

NASEDC — NATO [*North Atlantic Treaty Organization*] Advanced Study Institutes Series. Series E. Applied Science

NASG — Neues Archiv fer Saechsische Geschichte und Altertumskunde

NASGA — Neues Archiv fuer Saechsische Geschichte und Altertumskunde

NASGAK — Neues Archiv fuer Saechsische Geschichte und Altertumskunde

NASGEJ — NATO [*North Atlantic Treaty Organization*] ASI Series. Series G. Ecological Sciences

Nashville J Med Surg — Nashville Journal of Medicine and Surgery

Nashville Monthly Rec Med Phys Sci — Nashville Monthly Record of Medical and Physical Science

Nas Inst Metall Repub S Afr Versl — Nasionale Instituut vir Metallurgie. Republiek van Suid-Afrika. Verslag

NASL — Nuova Antologia di Scienze, Lettere, ed Arte [*Roma*]

NASM — National Association of Schools of Music. Proceedings

Nas Mus Bloemfontein Jaarversl — Nasionale Museum Bloemfontein Jaarverslag

NAS-NRC D Chem Chem Technol Annu Rep — National Academy of Sciences - National Research Council. Division of Chemistry and Chemical Technology. Annual Report

NAS-NRC Div Chem Chem Technol Annu Rep — National Academy of Sciences - National Research Council. Division of Chemistry and Chemical Technology. Annual Report

NAS-NRC Nucl Sci Ser Rep — National Academy of Sciences - National Research Council. Nuclear Sciences Series. Report

NAS-NRC Publ — National Academy of Sciences - National Research Council. Publication

NASPA J — NASPA [*National Association of Student Personnel Administrators*] Journal

Nas Prz — Nasza Przeszlose

NASPSPA Newsl — NASPSPA [*North American Society for Psychology of Sport and Physical Activity*] Newsletter

NASR — Norwegian-American Studies and Records

NASRA — National Academy of Sciences - National Research Council. Publication

Nass Ann — Nassauische Annalen

Nassau Ann — Nassauische Annalen

Nassau Cty Med Cent Proc — Nassau County Medical Center Proceedings

Nassauische An — Nassauische Annalen

Nassauischer Ver Naturk Jb — Nassauischer Verein fuer Naturkunde. Jahrbuecher

Nassau L — Nassau Lawyer

Nassau Mag — Nassau Magazine

NASSDK — NATO [*North Atlantic Treaty Organization*] Advanced Study Institutes Series. Series A. Life Sciences

Nass Heim — Nassauische Heimatblaetter

Nass Jb — Jahrbuecher des Vereins fuer Naturkunde im Herzogthum Nassau

NASSP-B — National Association of Secondary-School Principals. Bulletin

NASSP Bull — NASSP [*National Association of Secondary School Principals*] Bulletin

Nass Vr Jb — Jahrbuecher des Vereins fuer Naturkunde im Herzogthum Nassau

NAST — Native Art Studies Association of Canada. Newsletter

NASTOCK — North American Stock Market

Na Stroikakh Ross — Na Stroikakh Rossii

N Astr T — Nordisk Astronomisk Tidsskrift

Nas Versnellersentrum Nuus — Nasionale Versnellersentrum Nuus

NASW N — NASW [*National Association of Social Workers*] News

Nat — Nation

NAT — National Association of Teachers of Singing. Bulletin

Nat — Naturalist

Nat — Nature

Nat A — Nationalmuseets Arbeidsmark

Nat Acad Sci Biog Mem — National Academy of Sciences. Biographical Memoirs

Nat Acad Sci Lett — National Academy of Science Letters

Nat Acad Sci Nat Res Counc Publ — National Academy of Sciences - National Research Council. Publication

Nat Acad Sci Proc — National Academy of Sciences. Proceedings

Nat Agr — Nation's Agriculture

Nat Air Space Mus Res Rep — National Air and Space Museum. Research Report

Natal Inst Eng J — Natal Institute of Engineers. Journal

Natal LJ — Natal Law Journal

Natal LM — Natal Law Magazine

Natal LQ — Natal Law Quarterly

Natal Mus Ann — Natal Museum. Annals

Natal Mus J Human — Natal Museum Journal of Humanities

Natal UL Rev — Natal University. Law Review

Natal Univ Law Rev — Natal University. Law Review

Natal Univ Sci — Natal University Science

Nat Am — Native Americans

Nat & A — Natura ed Arte

Nat Appl Sci Bull — Natural and Applied Science Bulletin

Nat Areas J — Natural Areas Journal

Nat Art Ed Assn Yrbk — National Art Education Association. Yearbook

Nat Art Educ Assn Res Monogr — National Art Education Association. Research Monograph

Nat Arthritis N — National Arthritis News

Nat Assn Attys Gen Proc — National Association of Attorneys General. Proceedings [*Chicago*]

Nat Assn Deans Women J — National Association of Deans of Women. Journal

Nat Assn Prev Study Tuberc Bul — National Association for the Prevention and Study of Tuberculosis. Bulletin

Nat Assn Sec-Sch Prin Bul — National Association of Secondary-School Principals. Bulletin

Nat Assn State Univs Trans & Proc — National Association of State Universities. Transactions and Proceedings

Nat Assn Stud Council Yrbk — National Association of Student Councils. Yearbook

Nat Assoc of Inspectors and Ednl Advisers J — National Association of Inspectors and Educational Advisers. Journal

Nat Astron Bull — National Astronomical Bulletin

Nat Bank Austsia M Summ — National Bank of Australasia. Monthly Summary of Australian Conditions

Nat Bank Egypt Econ Bul — National Bank of Egypt. Economic Bulletin

Nat Bank Ethiopia Q Bul ns — National Bank of Ethiopia. Quarterly Bulletin. New Series

Nat Banking R — National Banking Review

Nat Bank Yugoslavia Q Bul — National Bank of Yugoslavia. Quarterly Bulletin

Nat Bar Bull — National Bar Bulletin

Nat Bar Exam Dig — National Bar Examination Digest

Nat Bar J — National Bar Journal

Nat B Belg — National Bank of Belgium. Report

Nat Bee Krs Dig — National Bee Keepers Digest

Nat Belg — Naturalistes Belges

Nat Biol — Natura. Seria Biologie

Nat Biotechnol — Nature Biotechnology

Nat BJ — National Bar Journal

Nat Bk (Aus) — National Bank. Monthly Summary (Australia)

Nat Bldgs Organisation Jnl — National Buildings Organisation. Journal

Nat Bldr — National Builder

Nat Bot Res Inst Lucknow Bull — National Botanical Research Institute. Lucknow. Bulletin

Nat Bottlers' Gaz — National Bottlers' Gazette

Nat Bsns Ed Q — National Business Education Association. Quarterly

Nat Bsns Ed Yrbk — National Business Education Association. Yearbook

Nat Bsns Woman — National Business Woman

Nat Builder — National Builder

Nat Bur Stand Appl Math Ser — National Bureau of Standards. Applied Mathematics Series

Nat Bur Standards TNB — National Bureau of Standards. Technical News Bulletin

Nat Bur Stand Bldg Sci Ser — National Bureau of Standards. Building Science Series

Nat Bur Stand Handb — National Bureau of Standards. Handbook

Nat Bur Stand Misc Pubs — National Bureau of Standards. Miscellaneous Publications

Nat Bur Stand Monogr — National Bureau of Standards. Monographs

Nat Bur Stand Spec Publ — National Bureau of Standards. Special Publication

Nat Bur Stand Tech News Bull — National Bureau of Standards. Technical News Bulletin

Nat Bur Stand Tech Note — National Bureau of Standards. Technical Note

Nat Bus Educ Yrbk — National Business Education Association. Yearbook

Nat Butter & Cheese J — National Butter and Cheese Journal

Nat Butter J — National Butter Journal

Nat Cambridgeshire — Nature in Cambridgeshire

Nat Cambs — Nature in Cambridgeshire

Nat Can — Nature Canada

Nat Canada — Nature Canada

Nat Cancer Inst J — National Cancer Institute. Journal

Nat Cancer Inst Monogr — National Cancer Institute. Monographs

Nat Can I M — National Cancer Institute. Monographs

Nat Can (Ottawa) — Nature Canada (Ottawa)

Nat Can Que — Naturaliste Canadien (Quebec). Revue d'Ecologie et de Systematique

Nat Can (Quebec) — Naturaliste Canadien (Quebec)

Nat Cath Ed Assn Bul — National Catholic Educational Association. Bulletin

Nat Cath Ed Assn Proc — National Catholic Educational Association. Proceedings

Nat Cath Rep — National Catholic Reporter

Nat Cell Biol — Nature Cell Biology

Nat Cheese J — National Cheese Journal

Nat Child Labor Com Proc — National Child Labor Committee. Proceedings

Nat Christ Coun R — National Christian Council. Review

Nat Cities — Nation's Cities

Nat Civic R — National Civic Review

Nat Civic Rev — National Civic Review

Nat Civ Rev — National Civic Review

Nat Coffee — National Coffee Drinking Survey

Nat Comm Teach Ed & Prof Stand Off Rep — National Commission on Teacher Education and Professional Standards. Official Report

Nat Comp Conf Proc — National Computer Conference Proceedings

Nat Conf City Govt — National Conference for Good City Government. Proceedings

Nat Conf Publ Inst Eng Aust — National Conference Publication. Institution of Engineers of Australia

Nat Conf Publs Instn Engrs Aust — National Conference Publications. Institution of Engineers of Australia

Nat Conf Social Work Proc — National Conference of Social Work. Proceedings

Nat Conf Soc Work — National Conference of Social Work. Proceedings

Nat Conserv Branch Transvaal Bull — Nature Conservation Branch. Transvaal Bulletin

Nat Conserv News — Nature Conservancy News

Nat Convect Enclosures Natl Heat Transfer Conf — Natural Convection in Enclosures. National Heat Transfer Conference

Nat Corp Rep — National Corporation Reporter

Nat Council O — National Council Outlook

Nat Council Social Stud Yrbk — National Council for the Social Studies. Yearbook

Nat Council Teach Math Yrbk — National Council of Teachers of Mathematics. Yearbook

Nat Cult — Nature and Culture

Nat Development — National Development

Nat Dev Q — National Development Quarterly

Nat E Africa — Nature in East Africa. The Bulletin. East Africa Natural History Society

Nat Econ Surv — Nation Economic Survey

Nat Ed Assn Proc — National Education Association. Addresses and Proceedings

Nat Ed Assn Res Bul — National Education Association. Research Bulletin

Nat Educ Assn J — National Education Association. Journal

Nat Educ Assn Proc — National Education Association. Proceedings and Addresses

Nat Elec Mfr Ass Stand Publ — National Electrical Manufacturers Association. Standards Publication

Nat El Prin — National Elementary Principal

NAtenea — Nueva Atenea

Nat Eng — National Engineer

Nat Eng Lab Rep — National Engineering Laboratory. Report

Nat Environ Res Counc Inst Geol Sci Overseas Mem — Natural Environment Research Council. Institute of Geological Sciences. Overseas Memoir

Nat Environ Res Counc Inst Geol Sci Rep (UK) — Natural Environment Research Council. Institute of Geological Sciences. Report (United Kingdom)

Nat Environ Res Counc Inst Terr Ecol Annu Rep — Natural Environment Research Council. Institute of Terrestrial Ecology. Annual Report

Nat Environ Res Counc News J — Natural Environment Research Council. News Journal

Nat Environ Res Counc Publ Ser D UK — Natural Environment Research Council. Publications Series D (U.K.)

Nat F — National Forum

NatF — Nation Francaise

Nat Field Clubs J — Naturalist and Field Clubs Journal

Nat Fmrs Un Annu Conf — National Farmers' Union. Annual Conference

Nat Forum — National Forum

Nat Found March Dimes Birth Defects Orig Artic Ser — National Foundation. March of Dimes. Birth Defects Original Article Series

NATGA — Natuurwetenschappelijk Tijdschrift (Ghent)

Nat Gall SA Bull — National Gallery of South Australia. Bulletin

Nat Gall VIC A Bull — National Gallery of Victoria. Annual Bulletin

Nat Gal Rep — National Gallery of Art. Report

Nat Gas — Natural Gas

Nat Gas A — Natural Gas Annual, 1983

Nat Gas As Am Pr — Natural Gas Association of America. Proceedings

Nat Gas Bul — National Gas Bulletin

Nat Gas Bull — National Gas Bulletin

Nat Gas Chem Ind — Natural Gas Chemical Industry

Nat Gas Cincinnati — Natural Gas (Cincinnati)

Nat Gas Convers Proc Nat Gas Convers Symp — Natural Gas Conversion. Proceedings. Natural Gas Conversion Symposium

Nat Gas (Energy Data Rep) — Natural Gas (Energy Data Report)

Nat Gas/Fuel Forecast Ser A — Natural Gas/Fuel Forecast. Series A. Geographic

Nat Gas/Fuel Forecast Ser B — Natural Gas/Fuel Forecast. Series B. Industrial

Nat Gas Gasoline J — Natural Gas and Gasoline Journal

Nat Gas Ind — Natural Gas Industry

Nat Gas Liq — Natural Gas Liquids

Nat Gas Mag — Natural Gas Magazine

Nat Gas Mon — Natural Gas Monthly

Nat Gas Mon Rep Energy Data Rep — Natural Gas Monthly Report (Energy Data Report)

Nat Gas Process Assoc Proc Annu Conv Tech Pap — Natural Gas Processors Association. Proceedings. Annual Convention. Technical Papers

Nat Gas Res Technol Proc Conf — Natural Gas Research and Technology. Proceedings. Conference

Nat Genet — Nature Genetics

Nat Geo — National Geographic Magazine

Nat Geog — National Geographic Magazine

Nat Geog J Ind — National Geographical Journal of India

Nat Geog M — National Geographic Magazine

Nat Geog R — National Geographic Research

Nat Geogr Mag Wash — National Geographic Magazine (Washington, DC)

Nat Geog Soc Nat Geog Mon — National Geographic Society. National Geographic Monographs

Nat Geog World — National Geographic World

Nat Geo J Ind — National Geographic Journal of India

Nat Grac — Naturaleza y Gracia

Nat Health Serv Inf Bul — National Health Services Information Bulletin

Nat Heimat — Natur und Heimat

Nat Herb NSW Contrib — National Herbarium of New South Wales. Contributions

Nat Hisp — Naturalia Hispanica

Nat Hispan — Naturalia Hispanica

Nat Hist — Natural History

Nat Hist Bull Siam Soc — Natural History Bulletin. Siam Society

Nat Hist Guides Boston Soc Nat Hist — Natural History Guides. Boston Society of Natural History

Nat Hist Mag — Natural History Magazine

Nat Hist Mag — Natural History Magazine. British Museum. Natural History

Nat Hist Misc (Chic) — Natural History Miscellanae (Chicago)

Nat Hist Mus Los Ang Cty Contrib Sci — Natural History Museum of Los Angeles County. Contributions in Science

Nat Hist Mus Los Ang Cty Sci Bull — Natural History Museum of Los Angeles County. Science Bulletin

Nat Hist Mus Los Ang Cty Sci Ser — Natural History Museum of Los Angeles County. Science Series

Nat Hist Mus Los Angeles Cty Sci Bull — Natural History Museum of Los Angeles County. Science Bulletin

Nat Hist Natl Parks Hung — Natural History of the National Parks of Hungary

Nat Hist (NY) — Natural History (New York)

Nat Hist Rennell Isl Br Solomon Isl — Natural History of Rennell Island, British Solomon Islands

Nat Hist Rev — Natural History Review. A Quarterly Journal of Biological Science

Nat Hlth Bul — Natural Health Bulletin

Nat Hort M — National Horticultural Magazine

Nat Hosp — National Hospital

Nat Hospital — National Hospital

Nath T — Naturhistorisk Tidende

Nat I Anim — National Institute of Animal Health. Quarterly

Nat Immun — Natural Immunity

Nat Immun Cell Growth Regul — Natural Immunity and Cell Growth Regulation

Nat Immunol — Nature Immunology

Nat Inc Tax Mag — National Income Tax Magazine

Nat Insects Tokyo — Nature and Insects (Tokyo)

Nat Inst Arch Ed Bul — National Institute for Architectural Education. Bulletin

Nat Inst B Pr Pr N S — National Institution for the Promotion of Science. Bulletin of the Proceedings.Proceedings. New Series

Nat Inst Bull — Bulletin. Proceedings. National Institution for the Promotion of Science

Nat Inst Econ R — National Institute Economic Review

Nat Inst Econ Rev — National Institute Economic Review

Nat Inst Educ Res B — National Institute for Educational Research. Bulletin

Nat Inst Soc Sci — National Institute of Social Sciences. Proceedings

Nat Interest — National Interest

Nation Acad Sci Proc — National Academy of Sciences. Proceedings [*Washington, D.C.*]

National Inst Health Bull US Pub Health Serv — National Institute of Health. Bulletin. United States Public Health Service

Nationalmus Arbejdsmark — Nationalmuseets Arbejdsmark

Nationalztg — Nationalzeitung

Nation and Ath — Nation and Athenaeum

Nation Athen — Nation and Athenaeum

Nation Educ Assoc Jour — National Education Association of the United States. Journal

Nation Geneal Soc Quar — National Genealogical Society. Quarterly [*Arlington, Virginia*]

Nation Geog Mag — National Geographic Magazine [*Washington, D.C.*]

Nation (Lond) — Nation and Athenaeum (London)

Nation Mus Canad Rep — National Museum of Canada. Annual Report

Nation Research Council Bul — National Research Council. Bulletin. National Academy of Sciences [*Washington, D.C.*]

Nation Rev — National Review

Nation Rev — Nation Review

Nation's Ag — Nation's Agriculture

Nation's Agric — Nation's Agriculture

Nation's Bus — Nation's Business

Nations Nouv — Nations Nouvelles

Nation's Sch — Nation's Schools

Nation Univ Law Rev — National University Law Review. National University Law School [*San Diego*]

Nation U Staat — Nation und Staat

Nation Wirtsch — Nationale Wirtschaft

Native Affairs Dep A — NADA. Native Affairs Department Annual. Rhodesia Ministry of Internal Affairs

Native Affairs Dept Annu — Native Affairs Department Annual

Native Sch Bul — Native School Bulletin

Nat J — National Journal

Nat J Crim Def — National Journal of Criminal Defense

Nat J Criminal Defense — National Journal of Criminal Defense

Nat J Leg Ed — National Journal of Legal Education

Nat J Shanghai — Nature Journal (Shanghai)

Nat Jutl — Natura Jutlandica

Nat Jutlandica — Natur Jutlandica

Nat Kuenstliche Alterung Kunstst Donaulaendergespraech — Natuerliche und Kuenstliche Alterung von Kunststoffen. Donaulaendergespraech

NATLA — Nauchnye Trudy Leningradskaya Lesotekhnicheskaya Akademiya Imeni S. M. Kirova

NATLA — Newsletter. American Theological Library Association

Natl Acad Med Sci (India) Ann — National Academy of Medical Sciences (India). Annals

Natl Acad Sci Advis Cent Toxicol Rep NAS ACT US — National Academy of Sciences. Advisory Center on Toxicology. Report NAS/ACT (United States)

Natl Acad Sci Biog Mem Proc — National Academy of Sciences. Biographical Memoirs. Proceedings

Natl Acad Sci Comm Polar Res Rep US Antarc Res Act Rep SCAR — National Academy of Sciences. Committee on Polar Research. Report of United States Antarctic Research Activities. Report to SCAR

Natl Acad Sci (India) Annu Number — National Academy of Sciences (India). Annual Number

Natl Acad Sci Lett — National Academy of Science and Letters

Natl Acad Sci Lett (India) — National Academy of Science. Letters (India)

Natl Acad Sci Natl Res Counc — National Academy of Sciences-National Research Council

Natl Acad Sci Natl Research Council Pub — National Academy of Sciences - National Research Council. Publication

Natl Acad Sci Proc — National Academy of Sciences. Proceedings

Natl Acad Sci Pub — National Academy of Sciences. Publication

Natl Acad Sci Technol Repub Philipp Trans — National Academy of Science and Technology. Republic of the Philippines. Transactions

Natl Acad Sci USA Biogr Mem — National Academy of Sciences of the United States of America. Biographical Memoirs

Natl Accel Cent News — National Accelator Centre. News

Natl Advis Comm Aeronaut Annu Rep — National Advisory Committee for Aeronautics. Annual Report

Natl Advis Comm Aeronaut Rep — National Advisory Committee for Aeronautics. Reports

Natl Advis Comm Aeronaut Tech Memo — National Advisory Committee for Aeronautics. Technical Memorandum

Natl Advis Comm Aeronaut Tech Notes — National Advisory Committee for Aeronautics. Technical Notes

Natl Advis Comm Aeronaut Tech Rep — National Advisory Committee for Aeronautics. Technical Report

Natl Advis Comm Aeronaut US Res Abstr Reclassif Not — National Advisory Committee for Aeronautics (United States). Research Abstracts and Reclassification Notice

Natl Advisory Comm Research Geol Sci — National Advisory Committee on Research in the Geological Sciences

Natl Aeronaut Establ Mech Eng Rep MS (Can) — National Aeronautical Establishment. Mechanical Engineering Report MS (Canada)

Natl Aeronaut Space Adm — National Aeronautics and Space Administration

Natl Aerosp Electron Conf Proc — National Aerospace Electronics Conference. Proceedings

Natl Aerosp Lab Misc Publ NLR MP (Neth) — National Aerospace Laboratory. Miscellaneous Publication NLR MP (Netherlands)

Natl Aerosp Lab Neth Rep NLR TR — National Aerospace Laboratory. Netherlands. Report NLR TR

Natl Agric Soc Ceylon J — National Agricultural Society of Ceylon. Journal

Natl Air Pollut Control Adm Publ APTD Ser US — National Air Pollution Control Administration Publication. APTD (Air Pollution Technical Data) Series (United States)

Natl Air Pollut Control Adm (US) Publ AP Ser — National Air Pollution Control Administration (United States). Publication. AP Series

Natl Air Pollut Control Adm (US) Publ APTD Ser — National Air Pollution Control Administration (United States). Publication. APTD [*Air Pollution Technical Data*] Series

Natl Air Pollut Symp Proc — National Air Pollution Symposium. Proceedings

Natl Am Miller — National and American Miller

Nat Lamp — National Lampoon

Nat Land — Natur und Land

Nat Landschaft — Natur und Landschaft

Nat Landschap — Natuur en Landschap Tijdschrift van de Contact Commissie voor Natuur- en Landschapsbescherming

N Atlantic Reg Bus L Rev — North Atlantic Regional Business Law Review

Natl Asphalt Pavement Assoc Qual Improv Program QIP Rep — National Asphalt Pavement Association. Quality Improvement Program. QIP Report

Natl Assn Sec-Schl Princ — National Association of Secondary-School Principals. Bulletin

Natl Assoc Corros Eng Conf — National Association of Corrosion Engineers. Conference

Natl Assoc Corros Eng Int Corros Conf Ser — National Association of Corrosion Engineers. International Corrosion ConferenceSeries

Natl Assoc Corros Eng Int Symp — National Association of Corrosion Engineers International Symposium

Natl Assoc Margarine Manuf Bull — National Association of Margarine Manufacturers. Bulletin

Nat Law Guild Q — National Lawyers Guild Quarterly

Natl Biomed Sci Instrum Symp Proc — National Biomedical Sciences Instrumentation Symposium. Proceedings

Natl Bitum Concr Assoc Qual Improv Program Publ — National Bituminous Concrete Association. Quality Improvement Program. Publication

Natl Bitum Concr Assoc Qual Improv Program Publ QIP — National Bituminous Concrete Association. Quality Improvement Program. Publication QIP

Natl Board Examiner — National Board Examiner

Natl Board Fire Underwrit Res Rep — National Board of Fire Underwriters. Research Report

Natl Board Fire Underwrit Tech Surv — National Board of Fire Underwriters. Technical Survey

Natl Bot Gard (Lucknow) Annu Rep — National Botanic Gardens (Lucknow). Annual Report

Natl Bottlers Gaz — National Bottlers' Gazette

Natl Build Stud Res Pap — National Building Studies. Research Paper

Natl Bur Stand Annu Rep (US) — National Bureau of Standards. Annual Report (United States)

Natl Bur Stand Tech Rep NBSIR US — National Bureau of Standards. Technical Report NBSIR (United States)

Natl Bur Stand US Build Sci Ser — National Bureau of Standards (United States). Building Science Series

Natl Bur Stand (US) Circ — National Bureau of Standards (United States). Circular

Natl Bur Stand US Dimens — National Bureau of Standards (United States). Dimensions

Natl Bur Stand (US) Handb — National Bureau of Standards (United States). Handbook

Natl Bur Stand (US) J Res — National Bureau of Standards (United States). Journal of Research

Natl Bur Stand (US) Misc Publ — National Bureau of Standards (United States). Miscellaneous Publication

Natl Bur Stand (US) Monogr — National Bureau of Standards (United States). Monograph

Natl Bur Stand (US) Spec Publ — National Bureau of Standards (United States). Special Publication

Natl Bur Stand (US) Tech News Bull — National Bureau of Standards (United States). Technical News Bulletin

Natl Bur Stand (US) Tech Note — National Bureau of Standards (United States). Technical Note

Natl Bus Educ Yrbk — National Business Education Association. Yearbook

Natl Bus Woman — National Business Woman

Natl Butter Cheese J — National Butter and Cheese Journal

Natl Butter J — National Butter Journal

Natl Cact Succ J — National Cactus and Succulent Journal

Natl Cactus Succulent J — National Cactus and Succulent Journal

Natl Cancer Conf Proc — National Cancer Conference. Proceedings

Natl Cancer Inst Carcinog Tech Rep Ser (US) — National Cancer Institute. Carcinogenesis Technical Report Series (United States)

Natl Cancer Inst J — National Cancer Institute. Journal

Natl Cancer Inst Monogr — National Cancer Institute. Monographs

Natl Cancer Inst Res Rep — National Cancer Institute. Research Report

Natl Canners Assoc Circ — National Canners' Association. Circulars

Natl Canners' Assoc Res Lab Bull — National Canners' Association. Research Laboratory. Bulletin

Natl Canners' Assoc Res Lab Circ — National Canners' Association. Research Laboratory. Circular

Natl Catal Symp Proc — National Catalysis Symposium. Proceedings

Natl Cent Air Pollut Control Publ APTD Ser US — National Center for Air Pollution Control Publication. APTD Series (United States)

Natl Cent Sci Res Vietnam Proc — National Centre for Scientific Research of Vietnam. Proceedings

Natl Cent Univ Bull Geophys Taiwan — National Central University. Bulletin of Geophysics (Taiwan)

Natl Cent Univ Sci Rep Ser A — National Central University Science Reports. Series A. Mathematics, Physics, and Chemistry

Natl Cent Univ Sci Rep Ser B — National Central University Science Reports. Series B. Biological Sciences

Natl Cheese J — National Cheese Journal

Natl Chem Eng Conf — National Chemical Engineering Conference

Natl Chem Pet Instrum Symp — National Chemical and Petroleum Instrumentation Symposium

Natl Civic Rev — National Civic Review

Natl Civ Rev — National Civic Review

Natl Clay Prod Quarrying — National Clay Products and Quarrying

Natl Cleaner Dyer — National Cleaner and Dyer

Natl Clgh Poison Control Cent Bull — National Clearinghouse for Poison Control Centers. Bulletin

Natl Comput Conf — National Computer Conference

Natl Comput Phys Conf — National Computational Physics Conference

Natl Conf Acceptable Sludge Disposal Tech Proc — National Conference on Acceptable Sludge Disposal Techniques. Proceedings

Natl Conf Adm Res Proc — National Conference on the Administration of Research. Proceedings

Natl Conf At Spectrosc Invited Pap — National Conference on Atomic Spectroscopy. Invited Papers

Natl Conf Aust Inst Energy — National Conference. Australian Institute of Energy

Natl Conf Complete WateReuse Proc — National Conference on Complete WateReuse. Proceedings

Natl Conf Control Hazard Mater Spills — National Conference on Control of Hazardous Material Spills

Natl Conf Dent Public Relat — National Conference on Dental Public Relations

Natl Conf Earth Sci Pap (Alberta Univ) — National Conference on Earth Science. Papers (Alberta University)

Natl Conf Electron Probe Anal Proc — National Conference on Electron Probe Analysis. Proceedings

Natl Conf Electroplat Met Finish — National Conference on Electroplating and Metal Finishing

Natl Conf Energy Environ — National Conference on Energy and the Environment

Natl Conf Environ Eff Aircr Propul Syst — National Conference on Environmental Effects on Aircraft and Propulsion Systems

Natl Conf Environ Eng — National Conference on Environmental Engineering [*New York*]

Natl Conf Fluid Power — National Conference on Fluid Power

Natl Conf Fract — National Conference on Fracture

Natl Conf Hazard Waste Manage Proc — National Conference about Hazardous Waste Management. Proceedings

Natl Conf Hazard Wastes Hazard Mater — National Conference on Hazardous Wastes and Hazardous Materials [*Silver Spring, Maryland*]

Natl Conf IC Engines Combust — National Conference on I.C. Engines and Combustion

Natl Conf IC Engines Combust Proc — National Conference on IC [*Internal Combustion*] Engines and Combustion. Proceed ings

Natl Conf Individ Onsite Wastewater Syst Proc — National Conference for Individual Onsite Wastewater Systems. Proceedings

Natl Conf Instrum Iron Steel Ind — National Conference. Instrumentation for the Iron and Steel Industry

Natl Conf Metall Sci Technol — National Conference on Metallurgical Science and Technology

Natl Conf Packag Wastes Proc — National Conference on Packaging Wastes. Proceedings

Natl Conf Publ Inst Eng Aust — National Conference Publications. Institution of Engineers of Australia

Natl Conf Sludge Manage Disposal Util — National Conference on Sludge Management Disposal and Utilization

Natl Conf Therm Spray Conf Proc — National Conference on Thermal Spray. Conference Proceedings

Natl Conf Wheat Util Res Rep — National Conference on Wheat Utilization Research. Report

Natl Congr Ital Headache Assoc Pap — National Congress. Italian Headache Association. Papers

Natl Congr Oncol Rep — National Congress of Oncology. Reports

Natl Congr Pressure Vessels Piping Sel Pap Fuel Elem Anal — National Congress on Pressure Vessels and Piping. Selected Papers. Fuel Element Analysis

Natl Congr Theor Appl Mech Proc — National Congress on Theoretical and Applied Mechanics. Proceedings

Natl Conv Combust Environ — National Convention on Combustion and Environment

Natl Coop Highw Res Program Rep — National Cooperative Highway Research Program. Report

Natl Coop Highw Res Program Synth Highw Pract — National Cooperative Highway Research Program. Synthesis of Highway Practice

Natl Corn Handb — National Corn Handbook

Natl Council Social Stud Yrbk — National Council for the Social Studies. Yearbook

Natl Council Teach Math Yrbk — National Council of Teachers of Mathematics. Yearbook

Natl Counc Pap Ind Air Stream Improv Spec Rep — National Council. Paper Industry for Air and Stream Improvement. Special Report

Natl Counc Radiat Prot Meas Annu Meet — National Council on Radiation Protection and Measurements. Annual Meeting

Natl Counc Radiat Prot Meas US Rep — National Council on Radiation Protection and Measurements (U.S.). Report

Natl Counc Res Dev Rep NCRD (Isr) — National Council for Research and Development. Report NCRD (Israel)

Natl Cycling — National Cycling

Natl Dairy Counc Dairy Counc Dig — National Dairy Council. Dairy Council Digest

Natl Dairy Res Inst (Karnal) Annu Rep — National Dairy Research Institute (Karnal). Annual Report

Natl Def — National Defense

Natl Def Med J (Tokyo) — National Defense Medical Journal (Tokyo)

Natl Dent Assoc J — National Dental Association. Journal

Natl Dent Health Conf — National Dental Health Conference

Natl Dev — National Development

Natl Dist Heat Assoc Off Proc — National District Heating Association. Official Proceedings

Natl Drug — National Druggist

Natl Drug Abuse Conf Proc — National Drug Abuse Conference. Proceedings

Nat Leag Compul Educ Offic Proc — National League of Compulsory Education Officials. Proceedings [US]

Natl Eclectic Med Q — National Eclectic Medical Quarterly

Natl Eco — National Institute Economic Review

Natl Educ — National Education

Natl Electr Light Assoc Bull — National Electric Light Association. Bulletin

Natl Electron Conf Proc — National Electronics Conference. Proceedings

Natl Electron Rev — National Electronics Review

Natl El Prin — National Elementary Principal

Natl Eng — National Engineer

Natl Eng Lab Rep (GB) — National Engineering Laboratory. Report (Great Britain)

Nat LF — Natural Law Forum

Natl Fabric Altern Forum Proc — National Fabric Alternatives Forum. Proceedings

Natl Fall Conf Am Soc Nondestr Test — National Fall Conference. American Society for Nondestructive Testing

Natl Farm Chemurg Counc Bull — National Farm Chemurgic Council. Bulletin

Natl Farm Chemurg Counc Chemurg Pap — National Farm Chemurgic Council. Chemurgic Papers

Natl Farm Gard Mag — National Farm and Garden Magazine

Natl Fert Dev Cent Bull Y (US) — National Fertilizer Development Center. Bulletin Y (United States)

Natl Fert Rev — National Fertilizer Review

Natl Fire Codes — National Fire Codes

Natl Fire Prot Assoc Q — National Fire Protection Association. Quarterly

Natl Fisherman — National Fisherman

Natl Food Eng Conf Proc — National Food Engineering Conference Proceedings

Natl Food Rev — National Food Review

Natl Food Rev NFR US Dep Agric Econ Res Serv — National Food Review NFR. US Department of Agriculture. Economic Research Service

Natl Forum Hosp Health Aff — National Forum on Hospital and Health Affairs

Natl Found Cancer Res Cancer Res Assoc Symp — National Foundation for Cancer Research. Cancer Research Association Symposia

Natl Found March Dimes Birth Defects Orig Artic Ser — National Foundation. March of Dimes. Birth Defects Original Article Series

Natl Fuels Lubr Mtg — National Fuels and Lubricants Meeting

Natl Gas Bull — National Gas Bulletin

Natl Gas Bull (Melbourne) — National Gas Bulletin (Melbourne)

Natl Gas Turbine Establ Rep (UK) — National Gas Turbine Establishment. Report (United Kingdom)

Natl Genoss Lagerung Radioakt Abfaelle Inf — Nationale Genossenschaft fuer die Lagerung Radioaktiver Abfaelle Informiert

Natl Genoss Lagerung Radioakt Abfaelle Tech Ber — Nationale Genossenschaft fuer die Lagerung Radioaktiver Abfaelle. Technischer Bericht

Natl Geographic Mag — National Geographic Magazine

Natl Geogr Mag — National Geographic Magazine

Natl Geogr Res — National Geographic Research

Natl Geogr Soc Res Rep — National Geographic Society. Research Reports

Natl Geol Surv China Gen Statement Min Ind — National Geological Survey of China. General Statement Mining Industry

Natl Geol Surv China Mem Ser C — National Geological Survey of China. Memoirs. Series C

Natl Geol Surv China Spec Rep — National Geological Survey of China. Special Report

Natl Geophys Res Inst (Hyderabad India) Bull — National Geophysical Research Institute (Hyderabad, India). Bulletin

Natl Glass — National Glass Budget

Natl Glass Budget — National Glass Budget

Natl Ground Water Qual Symp Proc — National Ground Water Quality Symposium. Proceedings

Nat L Guild Q — National Lawyers Guild Quarterly

Natl Health Insur Jt Comm Med Res Comm (GB) Spec Rep Ser — National Health Insurance Joint Committee. Medical Research Committee (Great Britain). Special Report Series

Natl Health Insur Rep — National Health Insurance Reports

Natl Health Med Res Counc (Canberra) Med Res — National Health and Medical Research Council (Canberra). Medical Research

Natl Health Med Res Counc (Canberra) Med Res Proj — National Health and Medical Research Council (Canberra). Medical Research Projects

Natl Health Med Res Counc (Canberra) Rep — National Health and Medical Research Council (Canberra). Report

Natl Heat Mass Transfer Conf Proc — National Heat and Mass Transfer Conference. Proceedings

Natl Heat Transfer Conf — National Heat Transfer Conference

Natl Heat Transfer Conf Prepr AIChE Pap — National Heat Transfer Conference. Preprints of AIChE [*American Institute ofChemical Engineers*] Papers

Natl Hortic Mag — National Horticultural Magazine

Natl Hosp Health Care — National Hospital Health Care

Nat Libr Wales J — National Library of Wales. Journal

Natl I Eco — National Institute Economic Review

Nat Life Nobel Conf — Nature of Life. Nobel Conference

Nat Life Southeast Asia — Nature and Life in Southeast Asia

Nat Lime Ass Bull — National Lime Association. Bulletin

Natl Incinerator Conf Proc — National Incinerator Conference. Proceedings

Natl Ind Res Inst Annu Rep — National Industrial Research Institute. Annual Report

Natl Ind Res Inst (Seoul) Rev — National Industrial Research Institute (Seoul). Review

Natl Inst Agric Bot (Camb) Rep Acc — National Institute of Agricultural Botany (Cambridge). Report and Accounts

Natl Inst Agric Sci Jpn Misc Publ Ser B — National Institute of Agricultural Sciences (Japan). Miscellaneous Publication. Series B. Soils and Fertilizers

Natl Inst Alcohol Abuse Alcohol Res Monogr — National Institute on Alcohol Abuse and Alcoholism. Research Monograph

Natl Inst Anim Health Q — National Institute of Animal Health. Quarterly

Natl Inst Anim Health Q (Yatabe) — National Institute of Animal Health. Quarterly (Yatabe)

Natl Inst Drug Abuse Res Monogr Ser — National Institute on Drug Abuse. Research Monograph Series

Natl Inst Econ R — National Institute Economic Review

Natl Inst Econ Rev — National Institute Economic Review

Natl Inst Environ Stud Jpn Rep Spec Res — National Institute for Environmental Studies. Japan. Report of Special Research

Natl Inst Fusion Sci Nagoya — National Institute for Fusion Science (Nagoya)

Natl Inst Genet (Mishima) Annu Rep — National Institute of Genetics (Mishima). Annual Report

Natl Inst Geol Min Bandung Indones Bull — National Institute of Geology and Mining. Bandung. Indonesia. Bulletin

Natl Inst Health Consensus Dev Conf Summ — National Institutes of Health. Consensus Development Conference. Summaries

Natl Inst Health Publ US — National Institutes of Health Publication (United States)

Natl Inst Metall Repub S Afr Rep — National Institute for Metallurgy. Republic of South Africa. Report

Natl Inst Nutr Annu Rep — National Institute of Nutrition. Annual Report

Natl Inst Oceanol Oceanogr Cruise Rep Indones — National Institute of Oceanology. Oceanographical Cruise Report (Indonesia)

Natl Inst Polar Res Mem Ser C Earth Sci — National Institute of Polar Research. Memoirs. Series C. Earth Sciences

Natl Inst Polar Res Mem Spec Issue — National Institute of Polar Research. Memoirs. Special Issue

Natl Inst Polar Res Mem Spec Issue (Jpn) — National Institute of Polar Research. Memoirs. Special Issue (Japan)

Natl Inst Polar Res Symp Antarct Meteorites — National Institute of Polar Research Symposium on Antarctic Meteorites

Natl Inst Polar Res (Tokyo) Antarct Geol Map Ser — National Institute of Polar Research (Tokyo). Antarctic Geological Map Series

Natl Inst Public Health Ann (Norw) — National Institute of Public Health Annals (Norway)

Natl Inst Radiol Sci Rep NIRSM Jpn — National Institute of Radiological Sciences. Report NIRS-M (Japan)

Natl Inst Res Dairy Bienn Rev UK — National Institute for Research in Dairying. Biennial Reviews (United Kingdom)

Natl Inst Res Dairy Rep (Engl) — National Institute for Research in Dairying. Report (England)

Natl Inst Res Dairy Tech Bull (UK) — National Institute for Research in Dairying. Technical Bulletin (United Kingdom)

Natl Inst Res Nucl Sci (GB) Rep — National Institute for Research in Nuclear Science (Great Britain). Report

Natl Inst Sci India Trans — National Institute of Sciences of India. Transactions

Natl Inst Stand Technol J Res — National Institute of Standards and Technology. Journal of Research

Natl Inst Stand Technol Spec Publ — National Institute of Standards and Technology Special Publication

Natl Inst Steenkolennijverheid Bull Tech Houille Deriv — Nationaal Instituut voor de Steenkolennijverheid. Bulletin Technique. Houille et Derives

Natl Inst Water Supply (Neth) Q Rep — National Institute for Water Supply (Netherlands). Quarterly Report

Nat Lith — National Lithographer

Nat Lit Soc J — National Literary Society Journal

Nat LJ — Natal Law Journal

Natl J — National Journal

Natl J Crim Def — National Journal of Criminal Defense

Natl Jt Comm Fert Appl Proc Annu Meet — National Joint Committee on Fertilizer Application. Proceedings of the Annual Meeting

Natl Lab High Energy Phys KEK (Jpn) — National Laboratory for High Energy Physics. Report KEK (Japan)

Natl Lab High Energy Phys Proc — National Laboratory for High Energy Physics. Proceedings [*Japan*]

Nat'l Law Guild Prac — National Lawyers Guild. Practitioner

Nat'l Legal Mag — National Legal Magazine

Natl Libr Wales J — National Library of Wales. Journal

Natl Lime Assoc Azbe Award — National Lime Association. Azbe Award

Natl Lithogr — National Lithographer

Nat'l LJ — National Law Journal

Natl Lubr Grease Inst Spokesman — National Lubricating Grease Institute. Spokesman

Natl Lucht Ruimtevaartlab Misc Publ NLR MP Neth — National Lucht- en Ruimtevaartlaboratorium. Miscellaneous Publication NLR MP (Netherlands)

Natl Lucht Ruimtevaartlab Rapp — Nationaal Lucht- en Ruimtevaartlaboratorium. Rapport

Natl Lucht Ruimtevaartlab Rapp NLR TR — National Lucht- en Ruimtevaartlaboratorium. Rapport NLR TR

Natl Lucht Ruimtevaartlab Versl Verh — Nationaal Lucht- en Ruimtevaartlaboratorium. Verslagen en Verhandelingen

Natl Luchtvaartlab Misc Publ NLR MP Neth — National Luchtvaartlaboratorium. Miscellaneous Publication NLR MP (Netherlands)

Nat LM — Natal Law Magazine

Natl M — National Magazine

Natl Mar Fish Serv Spec Sci Rep Fish Ser — National Marine Fisheries Service. Special Scientific Report Fisheries Series

Natl Mar Fish Serv (US) Circ — National Marine Fisheries Service (US). Circular

Natl Mar Fish Serv (US) Spec Sci Rep Fish — National Marine Fisheries Service (US). Special Scientific Report-Fisheries

Natl Market Rep — National Marketing Report

Natl Mastitis Counc Annu Meet — National Mastitis Council. Annual Meeting

Natl Mater Advis Board Publ NMAB — National Materials Advisory Board. Publication NMAB

Nat'l M (Bost) — National Magazine (Boston)

Natl Meas Lab Tech Pap (Aust) — National Measurement Laboratory. Technical Paper (Australia)

Natl Meas Lab Tech Pap CSIRO Aust — Australia. Commonwealth Scientific and Industrial Research Organisation. National Measurement Laboratory. Technical Paper

Natl Med Care Utilization and Expenditure Survey — National Medical Care Utilization and Expenditure Survey

Natl Med Chem Symp Am Chem Soc Proc — National Medicinal Chemistry Symposium. American Chemical Society. Proceedings

Natl Med J China (Beijing) — National Medical Journal of China (Beijing)

Natl Med J India — National Medical Journal of India

Natl Meet Am Chem Soc Div Environ Chem — National Meeting. American Chemical Society. Division of Environmental Chemistry

Natl Meet APhA Acad Pharm Sci — National Meeting. APhA Academy of Pharmaceutical Sciences

Natl Meet Biophys Biotechnol Finl Proc — National Meeting on Biophysics and Biotechnology in Finland. Proceedings

Natl Meet Biophys Med Eng Finl Proc — National Meeting on Biophysics and Medical Engineering in Finland. Proceedings

Natl Meet S Afr Inst Chem Eng Pap Programme — National Meeting. South African Institution of Chemical Engineers. Papers and Programme

Natl Metall Lab Jamshedpur India Tech J — National Metallurgical Laboratory. Jamshedpur, India. Technical Journal

Natl Miller — National Miller

Natl Miller Am Miller — National Miller and American Miller

Nat'l Mun Rev — National Municipal Review

Natl Mus Bloemfontein Annu Rep — National Museum Bloemfontein. Annual Report

Natl Mus Bloemfontein Res Mem — National Museum Bloemfontein. Researches Memoir

Natl Mus Canada Bull — National Museum of Canada Bulletin

Natl Mus Can Bull — National Museum of Canada. Bulletin

Natl Mus Can Nat Hist Pap — National Museum of Canada. Natural History Papers

Natl Mus Korea Art Mag — National Museum of Korea. Art Magazine

Natl Mus Nat Sci (Ottawa) Publ Biol Oceanogr — National Museum of Natural Sciences (Ottawa). Publications in Biological Oceanography

Natl Mus Nat Sci (Ottawa) Publ Bot — National Museum of Natural Sciences (Ottawa). Publications in Botany

Natl Mus Nat Sci (Ottawa) Publ Nat Sci — National Museum of Natural Sciences (Ottawa). Publications in Natural Sciences

Natl Mus Nat Sci (Ottawa) Publ Palaeontol — National Museum of Natural Sciences (Ottawa). Publications in Palaeontology

Natl Mus Nat Sci (Ottawa) Publ Zool — National Museum of Natural Sciences (Ottawa). Publications in Zoology

Natl Mus NZ Misc Ser — National Museum of New Zealand. Miscellaneous Series

Natl Mus NZ Rec — National Museum of New Zealand. Records

Natl Mus South Rhod Occas Pap — Periodical Museums of Southern Rhodesia. Occasional Papers

Natl Mus South Rhod Occas Pap Ser B — National Museum of Southern Rhodesia. Occasional Papers. Series B. Natural Sciences

Natl Mus Victoria Mem — National Museum of Victoria. Memoirs

Natl Newsp Index — National Newspaper Index

Natl Nosocomial Infect Study — National Nosocomial Infections Study

Natl Nucl Data Cent Rep BNL NCS US — National Nuclear Data Center. Report BNL-NCS (United States)

Natl Nucl Energy Ser Manhattan Proj Tech Sect Div 1 — National Nuclear Energy Series. Manhattan Project Technical Section. Division 1. Electromagnetic Separation Project

Natl Nucl Energy Ser Manhattan Proj Tech Sect Div 2 — National Nuclear Energy Series. Manhattan Project Technical Section. Division 2. Gaseous Diffusion Project

Natl Nucl Energy Ser Manhattan Proj Tech Sect Div 3 — National Nuclear Energy Series. Manhattan Project Technical Section. Division 3.

Natl Nucl Energy Ser Manhattan Proj Tech Sect Div 4 — National Nuclear Energy Series. Manhattan Project Technical Section. Division 4. Plutonium Project

Natl Nucl Energy Ser Manhattan Proj Tech Sect Div 5 — National Nuclear Energy Series. Manhattan Project Technical Section. Division 5. Los Alamos Project

Natl Nucl Energy Ser Manhattan Proj Tech Sect Div 6 — National Nuclear Energy Series. Manhattan Project Technical Section. Division 6. University of Rochester Project

Natl Nucl Energy Ser Manhattan Proj Tech Sect Div 7 — National Nuclear Energy Series. Manhattan Project Technical Section. Division 7. Materials Procurement Project

Natl Nucl Energy Ser Manhattan Proj Tech Sect Div 8 — National Nuclear Energy Series. Manhattan Project Technical Section. Division 8. Manhattan Project

Natl Nucl Energy Ser Manhattan Proj Tech Sect Div 9 — National Nuclear Energy Series. Manhattan Project Technical Section. Division 9. Thermal Diffusion Project

Natl Nucl Instrum Conf Proc — National Nuclear Instrumentation Conference. Proceedings

Natl Observer — National Observer

Natl Oceanic Atmos Adm (US) Circ — National Oceanic and Atmospheric Administration (United States). Circular

Natl Oceanic Atmos Adm (US) Fish Bull — National Oceanic and Atmospheric Administration (United States). Fishery Bulletin

Natl Oceanic Atmos Adm (US) Spec Sci Rep Fish — National Oceanic and Atmospheric Administration (United States). Special Scientific Report. Fisheries

Natl Oceanic Atmos Adm (US) Tech Rep Natl Mar Fish Serv Circ — National Oceanic and Atmospheric Administration (US) Technical Report. NationalMarine Fisheries Service Circular

Natl Open Hearth Basic Oxygen Steel Conf Proc — National Open Hearth and Basic Oxygen Steel Conference. Proceedings

Natl Organ Black Chem Chem Eng Annu Natl Conf — National Organization for Black Chemists and Chemical Engineers. Annual National Conference

Natl Paint Bull — National Paint Bulletin

Natl Painters Mag — National Painters Magazine

Natl Paint Varn Lacquer Assoc Abstr Rev — National Paint, Varnish, and Lacquer Association. Abstract Review

Natl Paint Varn Lacquer Assoc Sci Sect Circ — National Paint, Varnish, and Lacquer Association. Scientific Section. Circulars

Natl Paint Varn Lacquer Assoc Tech Div Abst Rev — National Paint, Varnish, and Lacquer Association. Technical Division. Abstract Review

Natl Palace Mus Q — National Palace Museum Quarterly

Natl Parks — National Parks Magazine [*Formerly, National Parks and Conservation Magazine*]

Natl Parks Conserv Mag — National Parks and Conservation Magazine [*Later, National Parks Magazine*]

Natl Parks Mag — National Parks Magazine [*Formerly, National Parks and Conservation Magazine*]

Natl Pecan Assoc Rep Proc Annu Conv — National Pecan Association. Report. Proceedings. Annual Convention

Natl Pecan Grow Assoc Rep Proc Annu Conv — National Pecan Growers Association. Report. Proceedings. Annual Convention

Natl Pet News — National Petroleum News

Natl Pet Refin Assoc Tech Pap — National Petroleum Refiners Association. Technical Papers

Natl Pet Refin Assoc Tech Publ — National Petroleum Refiners Association. Technical Publication

Natl Pet Refiners Assoc Pap — National Petroleum Refiners Association. Papers

Natl Pet Refiners Assoc Tech Publ — National Petroleum Refiners Association. Technical Publication

Natl Petroleum Bibliography — National Petroleum Bibliography

Natl Pharm Dagen Versl Int Symp Controle Pharm Spec — Nationale Pharmaceutische Dagen. Verslagen. Internationaal Symposium over de Controle van de Pharmaceutische Specialiteiten

Natl Phys Lab Div Chem Stand NPL Rep Chem (UK) — National Physical Laboratory. Division of Chemical Standards. NPL Report Chem (United Kingdom)

Natl Phys Lab Div Inorg Met Struct NPL Rep IMS — National Physical Laboratory. Division of Inorganic and Metallic Structure. NPL Report IMS

Natl Phys Lab Div Mater Appl NPL Rep DMA UK — National Physical Laboratory. Division of Materials Applications. NPL Report DMA (United Kingdom)

Natl Phys Lab Div Mater Metrol NPL Rep DMMA UK — National Physical Laboratory. Division of Materials Metrology. NPL Report DMM(A) (United Kingdom)

Natl Phys Lab Div Mech Opt Metrol NPL Rep MOM UK — National Physical Laboratory. Division of Mechanical and Optical Metrology. NPL Report MOM (United Kingdom)

Natl Phys Lab Div Quantum Metrol NPL Rep QU (UK) — National Physical Laboratory. Division of Quantum Metrology. NPL Report QU (United Kingdom)

Natl Phys Lab India Tech Bull — National Physical Laboratory (India). Technical Bulletin

Natl Phys Lab Notes Appl Sci (UK) — National Physical Laboratory. Notes on Applied Science (United Kingdom)

Natl Phys Lab Rep — National Physical Laboratory. Reports

Natl Phys Lab UK Collect Res — National Physical Laboratory (U.K.). Collected Researches

Natl Phys Lab (UK) Div Chem Stand Rep — National Physical Laboratory (United Kingdom). Division of Chemical Standards. Report

Natl Phys Lab (UK) Proc Symp — National Physical Laboratory (United Kingdom). Proceedings of a Symposium

Natl Phys Lab (UK) Rep — National Physical Laboratory (United Kingdom). Report

Natl Phys Lab UK Rep CMMTA — National Physical Laboratory (United Kingdom). Report. CMMT(A)

Natl Phys Lab (UK) Symp — National Physical Laboratory (United Kingdom). Symposium

Natl Prior — Setting National Priorities. The 19- Budget

Natl Prov — National Provisioner

Natl Provis — National Provisioner

Natl Pub Empl Rep Lab Rel Press — National Public Employment Reporter. Labor Relations Press

Nat LQ — Natal Law Quarterly

Natl Quantum Electron Conf — National Quantum Electronics Conference

Nat LR — Natal Law Reports

Natl Racq — National Racquetball

Natl Radiol Prot Board Instrum Eval UK — National Radiological Protection Board. Instrument Evaluation (United Kingdom)

Natl Radiol Prot Board Rep NRPB IE UK — National Radiological Protection Board. Report NRPB-IE (United Kingdom)

Natl Radiol Prot Board Rep NRPB R UK — National Radiological Protection Board. Report NRPB-R (United Kingdom)

Natl Ready Mixed Concr Assoc Publ — National Ready Mixed Concrete Association. Publication

Natl Real Estate Investor — National Real Estate Investor

Natl Res Cent Disaster Prev Rep — National Research Center for Disaster Prevention. Report

Natl Res Counc Advis Cent Toxicol Rep NAS ACT (US) — National Research Council. Advisory Center on Toxicology. Report NAS/ACT (United States)

Natl Res Counc Build Res Advis Board Tech Rep — National Research Council. Building Research Advisory Board. Technical Report

Natl Res Counc Bull Can — National Research Council Bulletin (Canada)

Natl Res Counc Can Aeronaut Rep — National Research Council of Canada. Aeronautical Report

Natl Res Counc Can Annu Rep — National Research Council of Canada. Annual Report

Natl Res Counc Can Assoc Comm Sci Criter Environ Qual Publ — National Research Council of Canada. Associate Committee on Scientific Criteriafor Environmental Quality. Publication

Natl Res Counc Can Bull — National Research Council of Canada. Bulletin

Natl Res Counc Can Div Build Res Can Build Dig — National Research Council of Canada. Division of Building Research. Canadian Building Digest

Natl Res Counc Can Div Build Res DBR Pap — National Research Council of Canada. Division of Building Research. DBR Paper

Natl Res Counc Can Div Build Res Fire Study — National Research Council of Canada. Division of Building Research. Fire Study

Natl Res Counc Can Div Build Res Res Pap — National Research Council of Canada. Division of Building Research. Research Paper

Natl Res Counc Can Div Build Res Tech Pap — National Research Council of Canada. Division of Building Research. Technical Paper

Natl Res Counc Can Div Build Res Tech Rep — National Research Council of Canada. Division of Building Research. Technical Report

Natl Res Counc Can Div Mech Eng Energy — National Research Council of Canada. Division of Mechanical Engineering. Energy

Natl Res Counc Can Div Mech Eng Energy Newsl — National Research Council of Canada. Division of Mechanical Engineering. EnergyNewsletter

Natl Res Counc Can Div Mech Eng Lab Tech Rep — National Research Council of Canada. Division of Mechanical Engineering. Laboratory Technical Report

Natl Res Counc Can Div Mech Eng Mech Eng Rep — National Research Council of Canada. Division of Mechanical Engineering. Mechanical Engineering Report

Natl Res Counc Can Div Mech Eng Mech Eng Rep MP — National Research Council of Canada. Division of Mechanical Engineering. Mechanical Engineering Report. Series MP

Natl Res Counc Can Div Mech Eng Mech Eng Rep MS — National Research Council of Canada. Division of Mechanical Engineering. Mechanical Engineering Report MS

Natl Res Counc Can Div Mech Eng Q Bull — National Research Council of Canada. Division of Mechanical Engineering. Quarterly Bulletin

Natl Res Counc Can Div Mech Gen Newsl — National Research Council of Canada. Division of Mechanical Engineering. General Newsletter

Natl Res Counc Can Environ Secr Publ — National Research Council of Canada. Environmental Secretariat. Publication

Natl Res Counc Can Mar Anal Chem Stand Program Rep — National Research Council Canada. Marine Analytical Chemistry Standards Program. Report

Natl Res Counc Can Mech Eng Rep MP — National Research Council of Canada. Mechanical Engineering Report. Series MP

Natl Res Counc Can Radio Electr Eng Div Bull — National Research Council of Canada. Radio and Electrical Engineering Division. Bulletin

Natl Res Counc Can Rep — National Research Council of Canada. Report

Natl Res Counc Can Rep NRCC — National Research Council Canada. Report NRCC

Natl Res Counc Can Tech Transl — National Research Council of Canada. Technical Translation

Natl Res Counc Can Unsteady Aerodyn Lab Lab Tech Rep — National Research Council of Canada. Unsteady Aerodynamics Laboratory. Laboratory Technical Report

Natl Res Counc Chem Biol Coord Cent Rev (US) — National Research Council. Chemical-Biological Coordination Center. Review (United States)

Natl Res Counc Comm Probl Drug Depend Proc Annu Sci Meet US — National Research Council. Committee on Problems of Drug Dependence. Proceedings. Annual Scientific Meeting (United States)

Natl Res Counc Curr Issues Stud (US) — National Research Council. Current Issues and Studies (United States)

Natl Res Counc Highw Res Board Res Abstr — National Research Council. Highway Research Board. Research Abstracts

Natl Res Council Annual Rep Chairm Div Biol — National Research Council. Annual Report. Chairman. Division of Biology and Agriculture

Natl Res Council Publ — National Research Council Publications. National Academy of Sciences

Natl Res Counc Issues Stud (US) — National Research Council. Issues and Studies (United States)

Natl Res Counc Natl Mater Advis Board Publ NMAB — National Research Council. National Materials Advisory Board. Publication NMAB

Natl Res Counc Philipp Bull — National Research Council of the Philippines. Bulletin

Natl Res Counc Philipp Res Bull — National Research Council. Philippines. Research Bulletin

Natl Res Counc Rev — National Research Council. Review

Natl Res Counc Thailand J — National Research Council of Thailand. Journal

Natl Res Counc Transp Res Board Spec Rep — National Research Council. Transportation Research Board. Special Report

Natl Res Counc Transp Res Board Transp Res Rec — National Research Council. Transportation Research Board. Transportation Research Record

Natl Res Counc US Bull — National Research Council (US). Bulletin

Natl Res Counc US Publ — National Research Council (US). Publication

Natl Res Inst Occup Dis S Afr Med Res Counc Annu Rep — National Research Institute for Occupational Diseases. South African Medical Research Council. Annual Report

Natl Res Inst Pollut Resour Jpn Rep — National Research Institute for Pollution and Resources. Japan. Report

Nat L Rev — National Law Review

Natl Rev — National Review

Natl Rural Letter Carrier — National Rural Letter Carrier

Natl Saf — National Safety

Natl Saf Congr Trans — National Safety Congress. Occupational Health Nursing Section. Transactions

Natl Saf News — National Safety News

Natl SAMPE Symp Exhib Proc — National SAMPE [*Society for the Advancement of Material and Process Engineering*] Symposium and Exhibition. Proceedings

Natl SAMPE Tech Conf — National SAMPE [*Society for the Advancement of Material and Process Engineering*] Technical Conference

Natl Sand Gravel Assoc NSGA Circ — National Sand and Gravel Association. NSGA Circular

Natl Sci Counc Mon — National Science Council. Monthly

Natl Sci Counc Mon (Taipei) — National Science Council Monthly (Taipei)

Natl Sci Counc Proc Part 2 (Taiwan) — National Science Council. Proceedings. Part 2. Biological, Medical, and Agricultural Sciences (Taiwan)

Natl Sci Counc Repub China Proc — National Science Council. Republic of China. Proceedings

Natl Sci Counc Repub China Proc Part A Appl Sci — National Science Council. Republic of China. Proceedings. Part A. Applied Sciences

Natl Sci Counc Repub China Proc Part A Phys Sci Eng — National Science Council. Republic of China. Proceedings. Part A. Physical Science and Engineering

Natl Sci Counc Repub China Proc Part B Basic Sci — National Science Council. Republic of China. Proceedings. Part B. Basic Science

Natl Sci Counc Repub China Proc Part B Life Sci — National Science Council. Republic of China. Proceedings. Part B. Life Sciences

Natl Sci Counc (Taipei) Proc Part 1 Nat Math Sci — National Science Council (Taipei). Proceedings. Part 1. Natural and Mathematical Sciences

Natl Sci Dev Board Philipp Sci Bull — National Science Development Board (Philippines). Science Bulletin

Natl Sci Dev Board Technol J Philipp — National Science Development Board. Technology Journal (Philippines)

Natl Sci Found Annu Rep — National Science Foundation. Annual Report

Natl Sci Found Civ Environ Eng Rep NSF CEE (US) — National Science Foundation. Civil and Environmental Engineering. Report NSF/CEE (United States)

Natl Sci Found NSF — National Science Foundation. NSF

Natl Sci Found NSF US — National Science Foundation. Publication NSF (United States)

Natl Sci Found Res Appl Natl Needs Rep NSF RANN US — National Science Foundation. Research Applied to National Needs. Report NSF/RANN (United States)

Natl Sci Found Res Appl Natl Needs Rep NSF/RA (US) — National Science Foundation. Research Applied to National Needs. Report NSF/RA(US)

Natl Sci Found Sci Manpower Bull — National Science Foundation. Scientific Manpower Bulletin

Natl Sci Mus Bull Ser C Geol Tokyo — National Science Museum. Bulletin. Series C. Geology (Tokyo)

Natl Sci Mus Bull Ser C (Tokyo) — National Science Museum. Bulletin. Series C. Geology (Tokyo)

Natl Sci Mus (Tokyo) Bull Ser C Geol Paleontol — National Science Museum (Tokyo). Bulletin. Series C. Geology and Paleontology

Natl Sci Mus (Tokyo) Mem — National Science Museum (Tokyo). Memoirs

Natl Sci Technol Auth Technol J — National Science and Technology Authority Technology Journal

Natl Seed Symp — National Seed Symposium

Natl Semin Immobilized Enzyme Eng Proc — National Seminar on Immobilized Enzyme Engineering. Proceedings

Natl Semin Nitrogen Crop Prod Proc — National Seminar on Nitrogen in Crop Production. Proceedings

Natl Sfty News — National Safety News

Natl Shade Tree Conf Proc — National Shade Tree Conference. Proceedings

Natl Soc Clean Air Annu Conf Proc — National Society for Clean Air. Annual Conference. Proceedings

Natl Soc Stud Educ Yrbk — National Society for the Study of Education. Yearbook

Natl Sol Energy Conv Proc — National Solar Energy Convention. Proceedings

Natl Speleol Soc Bull — National Speleological Society. Bulletin

Natl Speleol Soc Occasional Paper — National Speleological Society. Occasional Paper

Natl Stand Lab Tech Pap CSIRO Aust — Australia. Commonwealth Scientific and Industrial Research Organisation. National Standards Laboratory. Technical Paper

Natl Stand Ref Data Ser Natl Bur Stand — National Standard Reference Data Series. National Bureau of Standards

Natl Stand Ref Data Ser NBS — National Standard Reference Data Series. US National Bureau of Standards

Natl Stand Ref Data Ser US Natl Bur Stand — National Standard Reference Data Series. United States National Bureau of Standards

Natl Stand Ref Data Syst LBL — National Standard Reference Data System. Lawrence Berkeley Laboratory. University of California

Natl State of the Art Symp Am Chem Soc — National State of the Art Symposium. American Chemical Society

Natl Swed Build Res Doc — National Swedish Building Research. Document

Natl Sym — National Symphony Program Notes

Natl Symp Appl Isot Tech Hydrol Hydraul — National Symposium on Application of Isotope Techniques in Hydrology and Hydraulics

Natl Symp Aquifer Restor Ground Water Monit — National Symposium on Aquifer Restoration and Ground Water Monitoring

Natl Symp At Energy Jpn — National Symposium on Atomic Energy. Japan

Natl Symp Biol Manage Centrarchid Basses — National Symposium on the Biology and Management of the Centrarchid Basses

Natl Symp Dev Irradiat Test Technol Pap — National Symposium on Developments in Irradiation Testing Technology. Papers

Natl Symp Fiber Front — National Symposium on Fiber Frontiers

Natl Symp Food Process Wastes — National Symposium on Food Processing Wastes

Natl Symp Ind Isot Radiogr Proc — National Symposium on Industrial Isotope Radiography. Proceedings

Natl Symp Refrig Air Cond — National Symposium on Refrigeration and Air Conditioning

Natl Symp Reliab Qual Control Trans — National Symposium on Reliability and Quality Control. Transactions

Natl Symp Tech Use Radioisot — National Symposium on Technical Use of Radioisotopes

Natl Tax J — National Tax Journal

Natl Tech Assoc J — National Technical Association. Journal

Natl Tech Conf Book Pap AATCC — National Technical Conference. Book of Papers. AATCC

Natl Tech Inf Serv Search — National Technical Information Service Search

Natl Tech Rep — National Technical Report

Natl Tech Rep Matsushita Electr Ind Co — National Technical Report. Matsushita Electric Industrial Co.

Natl Tech Rep (Matsushita Electr Ind C Osaka) — National Technical Report (Matsushita Electric Industrial Co., Osaka)

Natl Therm Spray Conf — National Thermal Spray Conference [*Materials Park, Ohio*]

Natl Toxicol Program Tech Rep Ser — National Toxicology Program. Technical Report Series

Natl Toxicol Program Tox Rep Ser — National Toxicology Program Toxicity Report Series

Natl Tree News — National Tree News. National Arborist Association

Nat Lucht Ruimtevaartlab — National Lucht- en Ruimtevaartlaboratorium

Nat Lucht-Ruimtevaartlab Verslagen en Verhandel — Nationaal Lucht- en Ruimtevaartlaboratorium. Verslagen en Verhandelingen

Natl Underwrit (Life Health) — National Underwriter (Life and Health Insurance Edition)

Natl Underwrit (Life Health Insur Ed) — National Underwriter (Life and Health Insurance Edition)

Natl Univ Peiping Coll Agric Res Bull — National University of Peiping. College of Agriculture. Research Bulletin

Natl Univ Singapore Dep Chem Semin — National University of Singapore. Department of Chemistry. Seminar

Natl Vac Symp Trans — National Vacuum Symposium. Transactions

Natl Veg Res Stn Annu Rep (Wellsbourne) — National Vegetable Research Station. Annual Report (Wellsbourne)

Natl Vital Stat Rep — National Vital Statistics Report [*Hyattsville, MD*]

Natl Vitam Found Annu Rep — National Vitamin Foundation. Annual Report

Natl Vitam Found Nutr Monogr Ser — National Vitamin Foundation. Nutrition Monograph Series

Natl Vitam Found Nutr Symp Ser — National Vitamin Foundation. Nutrition Symposium Series

Natl Vitamin Found Annu Rep — National Vitamin Foundation. Annual Report

Natl Waste News — National Waste News

Natl Waste Process Conf Proc — National Waste Processing Conference. Proceedings

Natl Water Supply Improv Assoc Annu Conf Tech Proc — National Water Supply Improvement Association. Annual Conference. Technical Proceedings

Natl Water Supply Improv Assoc J — National Water Supply Improvement Association Journal

Natl Weeds Conf S Afr Proc — National Weeds Conference of South Africa. Proceedings

Natl Westminster Bank Q Rev — National Westminster Bank. Quarterly Review

Natl Wildl — National Wildlife

Natl Wool Grow — National Wool Grower

Nat M — National Magazine

NATMA — NASA [*National Aeronautics and Space Administration*] Technical Memorandum

Nat Mag — National Magazine

Nat Mag — Nature Magazine

Nat Malays — Nature Malaysiana

Nat Malgache — Naturaliste Malgache

Nat Map Bull — National Mapping Bulletin

Nat Med — Natural Medicines

Nat Med — Nature Medicine

Nat Med Assn J — National Medical Association. Journal

Nat Med NY — Nature Medicine (New York)

Nat Med Tokyo — Natural Medicines (Tokyo)

Nat Mensch — Natuur en Mensch

Nat Mensch (Nuernb) — Natur und Mensch (Nuernberg)

Nat Monspel — Naturalia Monspeliensia

Nat Monspeliensia Ser Bot — Naturalia Monspeliensia. Serie Botanique

Nat Monspel Rev Bot Gen Mediterr — Naturalia Monspeliensia. Revue de Botanique Generale et Mediterraneenne

Nat Monspel Ser Bot — Naturalia Monspeliensia. Serie Botanique

Nat Mosana — Natura Mosana

Nat Mosana Suppl B Bot — Natura Mosana. Supplement B. Botanique

Nat Mosana Suppl CD Zool — Natura Mosana. Supplement CD. Zoologie

Nat Munic R — National Municipal Review

Nat Munic Rev — National Municipal Review

Nat Mun Rev — National Municipal Review

Nat Mus — Natur und Museum

Nat Mus Council Bul — National Music Council. Bulletin

Nat Mus Senckenb Naturforsch Ges — Natur und Museum. Senckenbergische Naturforschende Gesellschaft

Nat Mus VIC Mem — National Museum of Victoria. Memoirs

Nat Mus Wales Ann Rep — National Museum of Wales. Annual Report

Natn Bldr — National Builder

Natn Coun Outlook — National Council Outlook

Nat Neurosci — Nature Neuroscience

Nat New Biol — Nature: New Biology

NATNews — NATNews. National Association of Theatre Nurses

Natn Geogr — National Geographic Magazine

Natn Geogr Mag — National Geographic Magazine

Natn Guardian — National Guardian

Natn Jewish Mon — National Jewish Monthly

Natn Munic Rev — National Municipal Review

NAT Nor Apotekerforen Tidsskr — NAT. Norges Apotekerforenings Tidsskrift

Nat Notes Grand Canyon — Nature Notes from the Grand Canyon

Natn Petrol News — National Petroleum News

Natn Res Progm Agric Res Serv — National Research Program. Agricultural Research Service

Natn Rev — National Review

Natns Bus — Nation's Business

Natns Restr — Nation's Restaurant News

Natn Symp Hydrol — National Symposium on Hydrology

Natn Times — National Times

NATO 16 — NATO's Sixteen Nations. North Atlantic Treaty Organization

NATO Adv Sci Inst Ser F Comput Systems Sci — NATO Advanced Science Institute Series F. Computer and Systems Sciences

NATO Adv Sci Inst Ser G Ecolog Sci — NATO Advanced Science Institutes Series. Series G. Ecological Sciences

NATO Adv Sci Inst Ser Ser 3 — NATO Advanced Science Institutes Series. Series 3. High Technology

NATO Adv Sci Inst Ser Ser A — NATO Advanced Science Institutes Series. Series A. Life Sciences

NATO Adv Sci Inst Ser Ser G — NATO Advanced Science Institutes Series. Series G. Ecological Sciences

NATO Adv Sci Inst Ser Ser H — NATO Advanced Science Institutes Series. Series H. Cell Biology

NATO Adv Study Inst — NATO Advanced Study Institute

NATO Adv Study Inst Ser B — NATO [*North Atlantic Treaty Organization*] Advanced Study Institutes. Series B. Physics

NATO Adv Study Inst Ser B Physics — NATO [*North Atlantic Treaty Organization*] Advanced Study Institutes. Series B. Physics

NATO Adv Study Inst Ser C — NATO [*North Atlantic Treaty Organization*] Advanced Study Institutes. Series C. Mathematical and Physical Sciences

NATO Adv Study Inst Ser D — NATO [*North Atlantic Treaty Organization*] Advanced Study Institutes. Series D. Behavioural and Social Sciences

NATO Adv Study Inst Ser D Behav Soc Sci — NATO Advanced Study Institute Series D. Behavioural and Social Sciences

NATO Adv Study Inst Ser E — NATO [*North Atlantic Treaty Organization*] Advanced Study Institutes. Series E. Applied Sciences

NATO Adv Study Inst Ser Ser A — NATO Advanced Study Institute Series. Series A. Life Sciences

NATO Adv Study Inst Ser Ser A Life Sci — NATO [*North Atlantic Treaty Organization*] Advanced Study Institutes Series. Series A. Life Sciences

NATO Adv Study Inst Ser Ser E Appl Sci — NATO [*North Atlantic Treaty Organization*] Advanced Study Institutes Series. Series E. Applied Science

NATO Adv Study Inst Sol Eclipses Ionos — NATO Advanced Study Institute on Solar Eclipses and the Ionosphere

NATO ASI (Adv Sci Inst) Ser Ser A Life Sci — NATO [*North Atlantic Treaty Organization*] ASI (Advanced Science Institutes) Series. Series A. Life Sciences

NATO ASI (Adv Sci Inst) Ser Ser E Appl Sci — NATO [*North Atlantic Treaty Organization*] ASI (Advanced Science Institutes) Series. Series E. Applied Sciences

NATO ASI (Adv Sci Inst) Ser Ser G Ecol Sci — NATO [*North Atlantic Treaty Organization*] ASI (Advanced Science Institutes) Series. Series G. Ecological Sciences

NATO ASI Ser 1 — NATO ASI Series 1. Disarmament Technologies

NATO ASI Ser Ser 2 Environ — NATO ASI Series. Series 2. Environment

NATO ASI Ser Ser 3 — NATO ASI Series. Series 3. High Technology

NATO ASI Ser Ser A — NATO [*North Atlantic Treaty Organization*] ASI Series A. Life Sciences

NATO ASI Ser Ser B — NATO ASI Series. Series B. Physics

NATO ASI Ser Ser C — NATO ASI Series. Series C. Mathematical and Physical Sciences
NATO ASI Ser Ser E — NATO ASI Series. Series E. Applied Sciences
NATO ASI Ser Ser G — NATO ASI Series. Series G. Ecological Sciences
NATO ASI Ser Ser H Cell Biol — NATO ASI Series. Series H. Cell Biology
NATO ASI Ser Ser I — NATO ASI Series. Series I. Global Environmental Change
NATO/CCMS Air Pollut — NATO/CCMS [*North Atlantic Treaty Organization/ Committee on the Challenges of Modern Society*] Air Pollution
NATO Challenges Mod Soc — NATO Challenges of Modern Society
NATO Comm Challenges Mod Soc Air Pollut — NATO [*North Atlantic Treaty Organization*]/Committee on the Challenges of Modern Society. Air Pollution
NATO Comm Challenges Mod Soc Tech Rep CCMS — North Atlantic Treaty Organization. Committee on the Challenges of Modern Society. Technical Report CCMS
NATO Comm Challenges Mod Soc Tech Rep NATO CCMS — North Atlantic Treaty Organization. Committee on the Challenges of Modern Society. Technical Report NATO/CCMS
NATO Conf Ser 1 — NATO Conference Series. 1. Ecology
NATO Conf Ser 4 — NATO [*North Atlantic Treaty Organization*] Conference Series 4. Marine Sciences
NATO Conf Ser 6 — NATO Conference Series. 6. Materials Science
NATO Conf Ser II Systems Sci — NATO Conference Series II. Systems Science
NATO Conf Ser IV — NATO Conference Series IV. Marine Sciences
Nat -Okon Tss — Nationalokonomisk Tidsskrift
Natok T — Nationalokonomisk Tidsskrift
Nat O Milj — Natur Og Miljo
NATO Sci Ser 3 — NATO Sciences Series 3. High Technology
NATO's Fift Nations — NATO's [*North Atlantic Treaty Organization*] Fifteen Nations
NATO War P — NATO [*North Atlantic Treaty Organization*] and the Warsaw Pact Force Comparisons
Nat P — Nationalities Papers
Nat Pal Mus B — National Palace Museum. Bulletin
Nat Parent-Teach — National Parent-Teacher
Nat Parks — National Parks Magazine [*Formerly, National Parks and Conservation Magazine*]
Nat Parks & Con Mag — National Parks and Conservation Magazine [*Later, National Parks Magazine*]
Nat Pet N — National Petroleum News
Nat Petrol Refiners Ass Tech Papers — National Petroleum Refiners Association. Technical Papers
Nat Philos — Natural Philosopher
Nat Phys Lab (Gt Brit) Notes Appl Sci — National Physical Laboratory (Great Britain). Department of Scientific and Industrial Research. Notes on Applied Science
Nat Phys Lab UK Collect Res — National Physical Laboratory (United Kingdom). Collected Researches
Nat Phys Universe Nobel Conf — Nature. Physical Universe. Nobel Conference
Nat Plants (Tokyo) — Nature and Plants (Tokyo)
Nat Police Offic — National Police Officer [*St. Louis*]
Nat Poult Impr Plan Rep US Dept Agric Sci Educ Admin — National Poultry Improvement Plan. Report. United States Department of Agriculture. Science and Education Administration
Nat Prob Assn Proc — National Probation Association. Proceedings [*New York*]
Nat Prob Assn Yrbk — National Probation Association. Yearbook [*New York*]
Nat Probation Assn Yrbk — National Probation and Parole Association. Yearbook
Nat Prod Lett — Natural Product Letters
Nat Prod RD — Natural Products R and D
Nat Prod Rep — Natural Product Reports
Nat Prod Rep J Curr Dev Bio Org Chem — Natural Product Reports. A Journal of Current Developments in Bio-Organic Chemistry
Nat Prod Res Dev — Natural Product Research and Development
Nat Prod Sci — Natural Product Sciences
Nat Prot Nat Toxicants Food — Natural Protectants and Natural Toxicants in Food
Nat Public Accountant — National Public Accountant
Nat Pur Rev — National Purchasing Review
Nat Q — National Quarterly Review
Nat Q R — National Quarterly Review
Nat Q Rev — National Quarterly Review
Nat R — National Review
Nat R — Nation Review
NATRA — Nature
Nat Racq — National Racquetball
Nat Radiat Environ Int Symp — Natural Radiation Environment. International Symposium on the Natural RadiationEvironment
Nat Real Estate Invest — National Real Estate Investor
Nat Real Estate Investor — National Real Estate Investor
Nat Rep — National Republic
Nat Repub — National Republic [*Washington, D.C.*]
Nat Res Counc Bldg Res Adv Bd Tech Rep — National Research Council. Building Research Advisory Board. Technical Report
Nat Res Counc Can Aeronaut Rep — National Research Council of Canada. Aeronautical Report
Nat Res Counc Can Annu Rep — National Research Council of Canada. Annual Report
Nat Res Counc Can Ass Comm Geod Geophys Proc Hydrol Symp — National Research Council of Canada. Associate Committee on Geodesy and Geophysics. Proceedings of Hydrology Symposium
Nat Res Counc Can Ass Comm Geotech Res Tech Memo — National Research Council of Canada. Associate Committee on Geotechnical Research. Technical Memorandum
Nat Res Counc Can Div Bldg Res Bibliogr — National Research Council of Canada. Division of Building Research. Bibliography
Nat Res Counc Can Div Mech Eng Mech Eng Rep — National Research Council of Canada. Division of Mechanical Engineering. Mechanical Engineering Report

Nat Res Counc Can Mech Eng Rep ME — National Research Council of Canada. Mechanical Engineering Report. ME
Nat Res Counc Can Unsteady Aerodyn Lab Lab Tech Rep — National Research Council of Canada. Unsteady Aerodynamics Laboratory. Laboratory Technical Report
Nat Res Counc Comm Probl Drug Depend Proc Annu Sci Meet (US) — National Research Council. Committee of Problems of Drug Dependence. Proceedings. Annual Scientific Meeting (United States)
Nat Res Counc Conf Elec Insul Annu Rep — National Research Council. Conference on Electrical Insulation. Annual Report
Nat Res Council Bul — National Research Council. Bulletin [*Washington, D.C.*]
Nat Res Council Can Div Mech Engng Gen — National Research Council of Canada. Division of Mechanical Engineering. General Newsletter
Nat Res Counc Nat Acad Sci Rep — Research Council. National Academy of Sciences. Reports
Nat Res J — Natural Resources Journal
Nat Res Law — Natural Resources Law
Nat Res Lawyer — Natural Resources Lawyer
Nat Resour — Nature and Resources
Nat Resources Forum — Natural Resources Forum
Nat Resources J — Natural Resources Journal
Nat Resources Jour — Natural Resources Journal
Nat Resources Law — Natural Resources Lawyer
Nat Resources L Newsl — Natural Resources Law Newsletter
Nat Resour Earth Sci — Natural Resources and Earth Sciences. Abstract Newsletter
Nat Resour Environ Ser — Natural Resources and the Environment Series
Nat Resour Forum — Natural Resources Forum
Nat Resour Forum Libr — Natural Resources Forum Library
Nat Resour J — Natural Resources Journal
Nat Resour Lawyer — Natural Resources Lawyer
Nat Resour Res — Natural Resources Research
Nat Resour Res (Paris) — Natural Resources Research (Paris)
Nat Retail Dryg Assn Proc — National Retail Drygoods Association. Proceedings [*Philadelphia*]
Nat Rev — National Review
Nat Rev — Nation Review
Nat Rev Genet — Nature Reviews. Genetics
Nat Rev Mol Cell Biol — Nature Reviews. Molecular Cell Biology
Nat Rev Neurosci — Nature Reviews. Neuroscience
Nat Rubber — Natural Rubber News
Nat Rubber Background — Natural Rubber Background
Nat Rubber Tech Bull — Natural Rubber Technical Bulletin
Nat Rubber Technol — Natural Rubber Technology
Nat Rubb News — Natural Rubber News
NATS — National Association of Teachers of Singing. Bulletin
Nat Safety News — National Safety News
Nat Saf News — National Safety News
Nats Akad Nauk Ukrain Inst Mat Preprint — Natsional'na Akademiya Nauk Ukraini. Institut Matematiki. Preprint
Nat Sand Gravel Ass NSGA Circ — National Sand and Gravel Association. NSGA Circular
Nat Savings and Loan League J — National Savings and Loan League. Journal
NATS Bul — NATS [*National Association of Teachers of Singing*] Bulletin
NATS Bull — National Association of Teachers of Singing. Bulletin
Nat Sc As Staten Island Pr — Natural Science Association of Staten Island. Proceedings
Nat Sch — Nation's Schools
Nat Schedule Rates — National Schedule of Rates
Nat Sci — Natural Science
Nat Sci — Natural Sciences
Nat Sci Ann — Nature. Science Annual
Nat Sci Bull Univ Amoy — Natural Science Bulletin. University of Amoy
Nat Sci J Hunan Norm Univ — Natural Sciences Journal of Hunan Normal University
Nat Sci J Xiangtan Univ — Natural Science Journal of Xiangtan University
Nat Sci Mus — Natural Science and Museum/Shizen Kagaku no Hakubutsukan
Nat Sci Prog — Nature. Science Progress
Nat Sci Rep Ochanomizu Univ — Natural Science Report. Ochanomizu University
Nat Sci Res Nat Sci Inst Chosun Univ — Natural Science Research. Natural Science Institute. Chosun University
Nat Sculp R — National Sculpture Review
Nat Sculpt — National Sculpture Review
Nat Sec R — National Security Record
Nat Seedsman — National Seedsman
Nat Sicil — Naturalista Siciliano
NATSJ — National Association of Teachers of Singing. Journal
Nats Konf At Spektrosk Dokl — Natsional'naya Konferentsiya po Atomnoi Spektroskopii. Doklady
Nats Konf Salmonelite Salmonelozite — Natsionalna Konferentsiya po Salmonelite i Salmonelozite
Nats Konf Vodopodgot Voden Rezhim Koroz TETs AETs Sb Dokl — Natsionalna Konferentsiya po Vodopodgotovka, Voden Rezhim i Koroziya v TETs i AETs. Sbornik Dokladi
Nats Kongr Onkol Sb Dokl — Natsionalen Kongres po Onkologiya. Sbornik Dokladi
Nats Kongr Teor Prilozh Mekh Dokl — Natsionalen Kongres po Teoretichna i Prilozhna Mekhanika. Dokladi
Nats Nauchna Ses Khim Med Profil Dokl — Natsionalna Nauchna Sesiya na Khimitsite s Meditsinski Profil. Dokladi
Nat Soc Med Res Bull — National Society for Medical Research. Bulletin
Nat Soc Pen Inf NY Bul — National Society of Penal Information of New York. News Bulletin
Nat Soc Study Ed Yrbk — National Society for the Study of Education. Yearbook
Nat Stock & F — National Stockman and Farmer

Nat Struct Biol — Nature Structural Biology
Nat Study — Nature Study
Nat Synth Gas Energy Data Rep — Natural and Synthetic Gas (Energy Data Report)
Nat Synth Zusatzst Nahr Menschen Int Symp — Natuerliche und Synthetische Zusatzstoffe in der Nahrung des Menschen. Internationales Symposion
Nat T — National Times
Nat Tax J — National Tax Journal
Nat Tax Mag — National Tax Magazine
Nat Tech — Natur und Technik
Nat Tech — Natuur en Techniek
Nat Tech Beek Neth — Natuur en Techniek (Beek, Netherlands)
Nat Tech (Maastricht Neth) — Natuur en Technik (Maastricht, Netherlands)
Nat Tech Rep — National Technical Report
Nat Tech Zurich — Natur und Technik (Zurich)
Nat Times — National Times
Nat T Mag — National Times Magazine
Nat Toxins — Natural Toxins
Nat Toxins Proc Int Symp Anim Plant Microb Toxins — Natural Toxins. Proceedings. International Symposium on Animal, Plant, and Microbial Toxins
Nat Toxins Proc World Congr Anim Plant Microb Toxins — Natural Toxins. Characterization, Pharmacology, and Therapeutics. Proceedings. World Congress on Animal, Plant, and Microbial Toxins
Nat Trust — National Trust
Nat Trust Aust Bull — National Trust of Australia. Bulletin
Nat Trust Bul — National Trust Bulletin
Nat Trust Studies — National Trust Studies
Nat Tuberc Assn Bul — National Tuberculosis Association. Bulletin
Nat Tuberc Assn Trans — National Tuberculosis Association. Transactions
NATUA — Nature
Nat UL Rev — Natal University. Law Review
Nat UL Rev — National University. Law Review
Nat Underw — National Underwriter
Nat Underw (Fire Ed) — National Underwriter (Fire and Casualty Insurance Edition)
Nat Underw (Life) — National Underwriter (Life and Health Insurance Edition)
Nat Underw (Life Ed) — National Underwriter (Life and Health Insurance Edition)
Nat Underw (Prop Ed) — National Underwriter (Property and Casualty Insurance Edition)
Nat Underw (Property Ed) — National Underwriter (Property and Casualty Insurance Edition)
Natura Biol — Natura. Seria Biologie
Natural Food Fmg — Natural Food and Farming
Natural Gard — Natural Gardening
Natural Gas Ind — Natural Gas for Industry
Natural Hi — Natural History
Natural Hist — Natural History. Journal of the American Museum of Natural History
Naturalia Monspel Ser Bot — Naturalia Monspeliensia. Serie Botanique
Naturaliste Can — Naturaliste Canadien
Naturaliste Canad — Le Naturaliste Canadien. Bulletin de Recherches, Observations et Decouvertes seRapportant a l'Histoire Naturelle du Canada
Naturalists J London 1893-99 — Naturalist's Journal (London 1893-99)
Natural L F — Natural Law Forum
Natural Resources J — Natural Resources Journal
Natural Resources Jnl — Natural Resources Journal
Natural Resources Law — Natural Resources Lawyer
Natural Resources Lawy — Natural Resources Lawyer
Natur & Gesell — Natur und Gesellschaft
Natur Belges — Naturalistes Belges
Nature and Life SE Asia — Nature and Life in Southeast Asia
Nature and Sci Ed R — Nature and Science Education Review
Naturegp Ocean Guide Books — Naturegraph Ocean Guide Books
Naturegr Ocean Guide Books — Naturegraph Ocean Guide Books
Nature (London) New Biol — Nature (London). New Biology
Nature (London) Phys Sci — Nature (London). Physical Science
Nature Mag — Nature Magazine
Nature New Biol — Nature: New Biology
Naturens Verd — Naturens Verden
Nature: Phys Sci — Nature: Physical Science
Nature Syst — Nature and System
Naturf Ges Bamberg Ber — Naturforschende Gesellschaft in Bamberg. Bericht
Naturf Gesell Basel Verh — Naturforschende Gesellschaft in Basel. Verhandlungen
Naturf Gesell Bern Mitt Neue Folge — Naturforschende Gesellschaft in Bern. Mitteilungen. Neue Folge
Naturf Gesell Zurich Vierteljahrsschr — Naturforschende Gesellschaft in Zuerich. Vierteljahresschrift
Naturforsch Ges Basel Verh — Naturforschende Gesellschaft in Basel. Verhandlungen
Naturforsch Ges Freib im Breisgau Ber — Naturforschende Gesellschaft zu Freiburg im Breisgau. Berichte
Naturforsch Ges Zuerich Vierteljahrsschr — Naturforschende Gesellschaft in Zuerich. Vierteljahrsschrift
Natur Hist — Natural History
Naturhist Ges Hannover Ber — Naturhistorische Gesellschaft zu Hannover. Bericht
Naturhist Ges Nuernberg Ber — Naturhistorische Gesellschaft Nuernberg e. V. Bericht
Naturhist Ges Nuernberg Jahresber — Naturhistorische Gesellschaft Nuernberg. Jahresbericht
Naturhist Mus (Bern) Jahrb — Naturhistorisches Museum (Bern). Jahrbuch
Naturhist Mus Stadt Bern Jahrb — Naturhistorisches Museum der Stadt Bern. Jahrbuch
Naturhist Mus Wien Ann — Naturhistorisches Museum in Wien. Annalen
Naturhist Mus Wien Veroeff Neue Folge — Naturhistorisches Museum in Wien. Veroeffentlichungen. Neue Folge
Naturh-Med Ver Heidelberg Verh — Naturhistorisch-Medicinischer Verein zu Heidelberg. Verhandlungen

Naturh Ver Preus Rheinl Verh — Naturhistorischer Verein der Preussischen Rheinlande und Westphalens. Verhandlungen
Naturh Ver Preus Rheinl Verh (Niederrhein Ges Bonn) Szb — Naturhistorischer Verein der Preussischen Rheinlande. Verhandlungen (Niederrheinische Gesellschaft fuer Naturund Heilkunde in Bonn). Sitzungsberichte
Natur J — Nature Journal
Naturkamp — Naturkampen
Naturk Jb Stadt Linz — Naturkundliches Jahrbuch der Stadt Linz
Natur Landsch — Natur und Landschaft
Natur Landschaft — Natur und Landschaft
Natur Mensch — Natur und Mensch / La Nature et l'Homme / La Natura e l'Uomo
Natur Mus (Arhus) — Natur og Museum (Arhus)
Natur Mus (Frankf) — Natur und Museum (Frankfurt)
Natur Res J — Natural Resources Journal
Natur Res L — Natural Resources Lawyer
Natur Resou — Natural Resources Lawyer
Natur Resource Modeling — Natural Resource Modeling
Natur Resources Forum — Natural Resources Forum
Natur Resources J — Natural Resources Journal
Natursch Naturp — Naturschutz- und Naturparke
Naturschutzarbeit Berlin Brandenburg Beih — Naturschutzarbeit in Berlin und Brandenburg. Beiheft
Naturschutzarbeit Naturk Heimatf Bez Rostock — Naturschutzarbeit und Naturkundliche Heimatforschung in den Bezirken Rostock-Schwerin-Neubrandenburg
Naturschutz Landschaftspflege Niedersachsen Beih — Naturschutz und Landschaftspflege in Niedersachsen. Beiheft
Natur Sci J Harbin Normal Univ — Natural Sciences Journal of Harbin Normal University
Natur Sci J Xiangtan Univ — Natural Science Journal of Xiangtan University
Natur Sci Rep Ochanomizu Univ — Natural Science Report. Ochanomizu University
Natur Study — Nature Study
Natur Syst — Nature and System
Natur Techn Vienna — Natur und Technik (Vienna)
Natur Techn Zurich — Natur und Technik. Schweizerische Zeitschrift fuer Naturwissenschaften (Zurich)
Natur u Mus — Natur und Museum
Natur u Volk — Natur und Volk
Naturw Abh — Naturwissenschaftliche Abhandlungen
Naturwiss — Naturwissenschaften
Naturwiss Abh Tuebingen — Naturwissenschaftliche Abhandlungen (Tuebingen)
Naturwiss Anz Allg Schweiz Ges Gesammten Naturwiss — Naturwissenschaftlicher Anzeiger der Allgemeinen Schweizerischen Gesellschaft fuer die Gesammten Naturwissenschaften
Naturwissen — Naturwissenschaften
Naturwissenschaft Med — Naturwissenschaft und Medizin
Naturwiss Fak Muenich Univ Inaug-Diss — Naturwissenschaftliche Fakultaet Muenich Universitaet. Inaugural-Dissertation
Naturwiss Ges Isis Meissen Mitt Sitzungen — Naturwissenschaftliche Gesellschaft Isis in Meissen. Mitteilungen aus den Sitzungen
Naturwiss Med — Naturwissenschaft und Medizin
Naturwiss Monatsh Biol Chem Geogr Geol Unterr — Naturwissenschaftliche Monatshefte fuer den Biologischen, Chemischen, Geographischen, und Geologischen Unterricht
Naturwiss Rdsch — Naturwissenschaftliche Rundschau
Naturwiss Rundsch — Naturwissenschaftliche Rundschau
Naturwiss Rundschau Stuttgart — Naturwissenschaftliche Rundschau (Stuttgart)
Naturwiss Umsch Chem Ztg — Naturwissenschaftliche Umschau der Chemiker-Zeitung
Naturwiss Unterr Chem — Naturwissenschaften im Unterricht Chemie
Naturwiss Unterr Phys/Chem — Naturwissenschaften im Unterricht (Teil) Physik/Chemie
Naturwiss Unterr Phys Chem Biol — Naturwissenschaften im Unterricht. Physik/Chemie/Biologie
Naturwiss Ver Bremen Abh — Naturwissenschaftlicher Verein zu Bremen. Abhandlungen
Naturwiss Verein (Darmst) Ber — Naturwissenschaftlicher Verein (Darmstadt). Bericht
Naturwiss Ver Schleswig-Holstein Schr — Naturwissenschaftlicher Verein fuer Schleswig-Holstein. Schriften
Naturwiss Wochenschr — Naturwissenschaftliche Wochenschrift
Naturwiss Z Forst Landwirtsch — Naturwissenschaftliche Zeitschrift fuer Forst- und Landwirtschaft
Naturwiss Z Lotos — Naturwissenschaftliche Zeitschrift Lotos
Naturw Rdsch — Naturwissenschaftliche Rundschau
Naturw Rdsch (Stuttg) — Naturwissenschaftliche Rundschau (Stuttgart)
Naturw Ver (Halle) Jber — Naturwissenschaftlicher Verein (Halle). Jahresberichte
Naturw Ver Neuvorpommern und Ruegen in Greifswald Mitt — Naturwissenschaftlicher Verein fuer Neuvorpommern und Ruegen in Greifswald. Mitteilungen
Naturw Ver Steiermark Mitt — Naturwissenschaftlicher Verein fuer Steiermark. Mitteilungen
Naturw Wchnschr — Naturwissenschaftliche Wochenschrift
Naturw Wochens — Naturwissenschaftliche Wochenschrift
Naturw Wochensch — Naturwissenschaftliche Wochenschrift
Naturw Z Forst u Landw — Naturwissenschaftliche Zeitschrift fuer Forst- und Landwirtschaft
Naturw Z Land-u Forstw — Naturwissenschaftliche Zeitschrift fuer Land- und Forstwirtschaft
Natuur Geneesk Arch Ned Indiee — Natuur- en Geneeskundig Archief voor Nederlandsch-Indie
Natuurh Maandbl — Natuurhistorisch Maandblad
Natuurh Maandbl — Natuurhistorisch Maandblad
Natuurkd Voordr — Natuurkundige Voordrachten

Natuur Konstkab — Natuur- en Konstkabinet

Natuurk Tijdschr Ned-Indie — Natuurkundig Tijdschrift voor Nederlandsch-Indie

Natuurk Verh Kon Maatsch Wetensch Haarlem — Natuurkundige Verhandelingen. Koninglijke Maatschappy der Wetenschappen te Haarlem

Natuurk Verh Maatsch Wetensch Haarlem — Natuurkundige Verhandelingen van de Maatschappy der Wetenschappen te Haarlem

Natuurwet Studiekring Suriname Ned Antillen Uitg — Natuurwetenschappelijke Studiekring voor Suriname en de Nederlandse Antillen. Uitgaven

Natuurwet Tijdschr — Natuurwetenschappelijk Tijdschrift

Natuurwet Tijdschr Ned Indie — Natuurwetenschappelijk Tijdschrift voor Nederlandsch-Indie

Natuurwet Werkgroep Nederlandse Antillen Uitgaven — Natuurwetenoohappolijko Workgroep Nodorlandoo Antillen Uitgaven

Natuurw Tijdschr Ned Indiee — Natuurwetenschappelijk Tijdschrift voor Nederlandsch-Indiee

Nat V — Naturens Verden

Nat Verden — Naturens Verden

Nat Vivante — Nature Vivante

Nat Volk — Natur und Volk

Nat Volk (Frankf) — Natur und Volk (Frankfurt)

Natv Self — Native Self-Sufficiency

Nat Wales — Nature in Wales

Nat W Bank — National Westminster Bank. Quarterly Review

Nat West Bank Q Rev — National Westminster Bank. Quarterly Review

Nat Westminster Bank Q R — National Westminster Bank. Quarterly Review

Nat Westminster Bank Quart R — National Westminster Bank Quarterly Review

Nat Wetlands Newsletter — National Wetlands Newsletter

Nat Wildlife — National Wildlife

Natwiss Wschr — Naturwissenschaftliche Wochenschrift

NatZLF — Naturwissenschaftliche Zeitschrift fuer Land- und Forstwirtschaft

Nauc Bjulletin Leningrad — Naucnyj Bjulletin Leningradskogo Gosud. Universiteta

Nauc Dokl Vyss Skoly Filos Nauki — Naucnye Doklady Vyssej Skoly Filosofskie Nauki

Nauc Dokl Vyss Skoly Nauc Kommunizma — Naucnye Doklady Vyssej Skoly Naucnyj Kommunizma

Nauch Dokl Vysshei Shkoly Biol Nauk — Nauchnye Doklady Vysshei Shkoly Biologicheskie Nauki

Nauche J Du Galvan — Journal du Galvanisme, de Vaccine, etc. Nauche

Nauch Konf Yadern Meteor (Obninsk) — Nauchnaya Konferentsiya po Yadernoi Meteorologii (Obninsk)

Nauchn Appar — Nauchnaya Apparatura

Nauchn Avtomot Inst Izd — Nauchnyi Avtomotornyi Institut. Izdaniya

Nauchn Avtomot Inst Tr — Nauchnyi Avtomotornyi Institut. Trudy

Nauchn Byull Leningr Gos Univ — Nauchnye Byulleten Leningradskogo Gosudarstvennogo Universiteta

Nauchn Byull Vses Nauchno Issled Inst Khlopku — Nauchni Byulleten Vsesoyuznogo Nauchno Issledovatel'skogo Instituta po Khlopku

Nauchn Dokl Ross Akad Nauk Ural Otd Komi Nauchn Tsentr — Nauchnye Doklady. Rossiiskaya Akademiya Nauk. Ural'skoe Otdelenie. Komi Nauchnyi Tsentr

Nauchn Dokl Vyssh Shk Biol Nauki — Nauchnye Doklady Vysshei Shkoly Biologicheskie Nauki

Nauchn Dokl Vyssh Shk Elektromekh Avtom — Nauchnye Doklady Vysshei Shkoly Elektromekhanika i Avtomatika

Nauchn Dokl Vyssh Shk Energ — Nauchnye Doklady Vysshei Shkoly Energetika

Nauchn Dokl Vyssh Shk Fiz Mat Nauki — Nauchnye Doklady Vysshei Shkoly Fiziko-Matematicheskie Nauki

Nauchn Dokl Vyssh Shk Geol Geogr Nauki — Nauchnye Doklady Vysshei Shkoly Geologo-Geograficheskie Nauki

Nauchn Dokl Vyssh Shk Gorn Delo — Nauchnye Doklady Vysshei Shkoly Gornoe Delo

Nauchn Dokl Vyssh Shk Khim Khim Tekhnol — Nauchnye Doklady Vysshei Shkoly Khimiya i Khimicheskaya Tekhnologiya

Nauchn Dokl Vyssh Shk Lesoinzh Delo — Nauchnye Doklady Vysshei Shkoly Lesoinzhenernoe Delo

Nauchn Dokl Vyssh Shk Mashinostr Priborostr — Nauchnye Doklady Vysshei Shkoly Mashinostroenie i Priborostroenie

Nauchn Dokl Vyssh Shk Metall — Nauchnye Doklady Vysshei Shkoly Metallurgiya

Nauchn Dokl Vyssh Shk Radiotekh Elektron — Nauchnye Doklady Vysshei Shkoly Radiotekhnika i Elektronika

Nauchn Dokl Vyssh Shk Stroit — Nauchnye Doklady Vysshei Shkoly Stroitel'stvo

Nauchn Ezheg Chernovits Univ — Nauchnyi Ezhegodnik Chernovitskogo Universiteta

Nauchn Ezheg Chernovits Univ Biol Fak Chernovtsy — Nauchnye Ezhegodnik Chernovitskogo Universiteta Biologicheskii Fakul'tet Chernovtsy

Nauchn Ezheg Odess Gos Univ Biol Fak — Nauchnyi Ezhegodnik Odesskii Gosudarstvennyi Universitet Biologicheskii Fakul'tet

Nauchn Ezheg Odess Gos Univ Khim Fak — Nauchnyi Ezhegodnik Odesskii Gosudarstvennyi Universitet Khimicheskii Fakul'tet

Nauchn Ezheg Odess Univ — Nauchnyi Ezhegodnik Odesskogo Universiteta

Nauchni Dokl Yubileina Nauchna Ses Vissh Med Inst Varna — Nauchni Dokladi. Yubileina Nauchna Sesiya. Vissh Meditsinski Institut-Varna

Nauchn Inf Beloruss Tekhnol Inst — Nauchnaya Informatsiya. Belorusskii Tekhnologicheskii Institut

Nauchn i Prikl Fotogr i Kinematogr — Zhurnal Nauchnoi i Prikladnoi Fotografii i Kinematografii

Nauchn Issled Klin Lab — Nauchnye Issledovaniya v Klinikakh I V Laboratoriyakh

Nauchni Tr Inst Konservna Promst Plovdiv — Nauchni Trudove. Institut po Konservna Promishlenost. Plovdiv

Nauchni Tr Inst Mlechna Promst (Vidin Bulg) — Nauchni Trudove. Institut po Mlechna Promishlenost (Vidin, Bulgaria)

Nauchni Tr Inst Pochv Izsled — Nauchni Trudove. Instituta za Pochveni Izsledvaniya

Nauchni Tr Inst Rastit Masla Protein Mieshti Sredstva Sofiya — Nauchni Trudove. Institut po Rastitelni Masla, Protein, i Mieshti Sredstva-Sofiya

Nauchni Tr Inst Spets Usuvursh Lek — Nauchni Trudove. Institut za Spetsializatsiya i Usuvurshenstvuvane na Lekarite

Nauchni Tr ISUL — Nauchni Trudove na ISUL

Nauchni Tr Nauchnoizsled Inst Durzh Kontrol Lek Sredstva — Nauchni Trudove. Nauchnoizsledovatelski Institut za Durzhaven Kontrol na Lekarstvenite Sredstva

Nauchni Tr Nauchnoizsled Inst Konservna Promst (Plovdiv) — Nauchni Trudove. Nauchnoizsledovatelski Institut po Konservna Promishlenost (Plovdiv)

Nauchni Tr Nauchnoizsled Inst Okhr Tr Prof Zabol — Nauchni Trudove. Nauchnoizsledovatelskiya Instituta po Okhrana na Truda i Profesialnite Zabolyavaniya

Nauchni Tr Nauchnoizsled Inst Pediatr — Nauchni Trudove. Nauchnoizsledovatelskiya Institut po Pediatriya

Nauchni Tr Nauchnoizsled Inst Radiobiol Radiats Khig — Nauchni Trudove. Nauchnoizsledovatelski Institut po Radiobiologiya i Radiatsionna Khigiena

Nauchni Tr Nauchnoizsled Inst Ribar Ribna Promst Varna — Nauchni Trudove. Nauchnoizsledovatelski Institut po Ribarstvo i Ribna Promishlenost. Varna

Nauchni Tr Nauchnoizsled Inst Vinar Pivovar Promst (Sofia) — Nauchni Trudove. Nauchnoizsledovatelski Institut po Vinarska i Pivovarna Promishlenost (Sofia)

Nauchni Tr Plovdivski Univ — Nauchni Trudove. Plovdivski Universitet

Nauchni Tr Plovdivski Univ Mat Fiz Khim Biol — Nauchni Trudove. Plovdivski Universitet. Matematika, Fizika, Khimiya, Biologiya

Nauchni Tr Selskostop Akad Georgi Dimitrov Agron Fak — Nauchni Trudove. Selskostopanska Akademiya Georgi Dimitrov. Agronomicheski Fakultet

Nauchni Tr Selskostop Akad Georgi Dimitrov Zootekh Fak — Nauchni Trudove. Selskostopanska Akademiya Georgi Dimitrov. Zootekhnicheski Fakultet

Nauchni Tr Selskostop Akad (Sofia) Ser Rastenievud — Nauchni Trudove. Selskostopanska Akademiya "Georgi Dimitrov" (Sofia) Seriya. Rastenievudstvo

Nauchni Tr Transp Med — Nauchni Trudove po Transportna Meditsina

Nauchni Tr Tsentr Nauchnoizsled Inst Tekhnol Mashinostr — Nauchni Trudove. Tsentralniya Nauchnoizsledovatelski Institut po Tekhnologiya na Mashinostroineto

Nauchni Trud Minist Zemed Gorite — Nauchni Trudove. Ministerstvo na Zemedelieto i Gorite

Nauchni Trudove Ser Gorsko Stop — Nauchni Trudove. Seriia Gorsko Stopanstvo

Nauchni Trud Vissh Lesotekh Inst — Nauchni Trudove. Vissh Lesotekhnicheski Institut

Nauchni Trud Vissh Selskostop Inst "Vasil Kolarov" — Nauchni Trudove. Vissh Selskostopanski Institut "Vasil Kolarov"

Nauchni Tr Vissh Inst Khranit Vkusova Promst (Plovdiv) — Nauchni Trudove. Vissh Institut po Khranitelna i Vkusova Promishlenost (Plovdiv)

Nauchni Tr Vissh Lesotekh Inst (Sofia) — Nauchni Trudove. Vissh Lesotekhnicheski Institut (Sofia)

Nauchni Tr Vissh Lesotekh Inst (Sofia) Ser Gorsko Stop — Nauchni Trudove. Vissh Lesotekhnicheski Institut (Sofia). Seriya Gorsko Stopanstvo

Nauchni Tr Vissh Lesotekh Inst (Sofia) Ser Mekh Tekhnol Durv — Nauchni Trudove. Vissh Lesotekhnicheski Institut (Sofia). Seriya Mekhanichna Tekhnologiya na Durvesinata

Nauchni Tr Vissh Lesotekh Inst (Sofia) Ser Ozelenyavane — Nauchni Trudove. Vissh Lesotekhnicheski Institut (Sofia). Seriya Ozelenyavane

Nauchni Tr Vissh Med Inst (Sofia) — Nauchni Trudove na Visshiya Meditsinski Institut (Sofia)

Nauchni Tr Vissh Med Inst (Varna) — Nauchni Trudove na Visshiya Meditsinski Institut (Varna)

Nauchni Tr Vissh Pedagog Inst (Plovdiv) Mat Fiz Khim Biol — Nauchni Trudove. Vissh Pedagogicheski Institut (Plovdiv). Matematika, Fizika, Khimiya, Biologiya

Nauchni Tr Vissh Selskostop Inst (Plovdiv) — Nauchni Trudove. Vissh Selskostopanski Institut "Vasil Kolarov" (Plovdiv)

Nauchni Tr Vissh Selskostop Inst (Sofia) Agron Fak — Nauchni Trudove. Vissh Selskostopanski Institut "Georgi Dimitrov" (Sofia). Agronomicheski Fakultet

Nauchni Tr Vissh Selskostop Inst Sofia Agron Fak Rastenievyd — Nauchni Trudove. Vissh Selskostopanski Institut (Sofia). Agronomicheski Fakultet. Seriya Rastenievydstvo

Nauchni Tr Vissh Selskostop Inst (Sofia) Zootekh Fak — Nauchni Trudove. Vissh Selskostopanski Institut "Georgi Dimitrov" (Sofia). Zootekhnicheski Fakultet

Nauchni Tr Vissh Selskostop Inst Vasil Kolarov Plovdiv — Nauchni Trudove. Vissh Selskostopanski Institut Vasil Kolarov. Plovdiv

Nauchni Tr Vissh Veterinarnomed Inst Prof Dr G Pavlov — Nauchni Trudove. Vissh Veterinarnomeditsinski Institut Prof. Dr G. Pavlov

Nauchni Tr Vissh Veterinarnomed Inst (Sofia) — Nauchni Trudove. Vissh Veterinarnomeditsinski Institut "Prof. Dr. G. Pavlov" (Sofia)

Nauchni Tr Yubileina Nauchna Ses Vissh Med Inst Varna — Nauchni Trudove. Yubileina Nauchna Sesiya. Vissh Meditsinski Institut. Varna

Nauchn Konf Geol Litvy Mater — Nauchnaya Konferentsiya Geologov Litvy. Materialy

Nauchn Konf Izuch Vnutr Vodoemov Pribaltiki — Nauchnaya Konferentsiya po Izucheniyu Vnutrennikh Vodoemov Pribaltiki

Nauchn Konf Molodykh Uch Morfol Moskvy — Nauchnaya Konferentsiya Molodykh Uchenykh-Morfologov Moskvy

Nauchn Konf Mosk Otd Vses Mineral Ova — Nauchnaya Konferentsiya Moskovskogo Otdeleniya Vsesoyuznogo Mineralogicheskogo Obshchestva

Nauchn Konf Parazit Ukr SSR — Nauchnaya Konferentsiya Parazitologov Ukrainskoi SSR

Nauchn Konf Selen Biol — Nauchnaya Konferentsiya Selen v Biologii

Nauchno Agron Zh — Nauchno Agronomicheskii Zhurnal

Nauchno Inf Byull Nauchno Issled Otd Kiev Ind Inst — Nauchno-Informatsionnyi Byulleten Nauchno-Issledovatel'skogo Otdeleniya Kievskogo Industrial'nogo Instituta

Nauchno Inf Byull Tsentr Nauchno Issled Aptechn Inst — Nauchno-Informatsionnyi Byulleten Tsentral'nogo Nauchno-Issledovatel'skogo Aptechnogo Instituta

Nauchno Issled Gornorazved Inst NIGRIZoloto Tr — Nauchno-Issledovatel'skii Gornorazvedochnyi Institut NIGRIZoloto. Trudy

Nauchno Issled Inst Biol Biofiz Tomsk Gos Univ Tr — Nauchno-Issledovatel'skii Institut Biologii i Biofiziki pri Tomskom Gosudarstvennom Universitete. Trudy

Nauchno Issled Inst Elektron Ionnoi Tekhnol Tr Tbilisi — Nauchno-Issledovatel'skii Institut Elektronno-Ionnoi Tekhnologii. Trudy (Tbilisi)

Nauchno-Issled Inst Epidemio Mikrobiol Tr (Sofia) — Nauchno-Issledovatel'skii Institut Epidemiologii i Mikrobiologii Trudy (Sofia)

Nauchno Issled Inst Geol Arktiki Tr — Nauchno-Issledovatel'skiy Institut Geologii Arktiki Trudy

Nauchno Issled Inst Gig Tr Profzabol im NI Makhviladze Sb Tr — Nauchno-Issledovatel'skii Institut Gigieny Truda i Profzabolevanii imeni N. I. Makhviladze. Sbornik Trudov

Nauchno Issled Inst Kamnya Silik Sb Nauchn Rab Aspir Soiskate — Nauchno-Issledovatel'skii Institut Kamnya i Silikatov. Sbornik Nauchnykh Rabot Aspirantov i Soiskatelei

Nauchno Issled Inst Kartofel Khoz Tr — Nauchno-Issledovatel'skii Institut Kartofel'nogo Khozyaistva. Trudy

Nauchno Issled Inst Kraev Patol Tr Alma Ata — Nauchno-Issledovatel'skii Institut Kraevoi Patologii. Trudy (Alma-Ata)

Nauchno Issled Inst Kurortol Fizioter im IG Koniashvili Tr — Nauchno-Issledovatel'skii Institut Kurortologii i Fizioterapii imeni I.G. Koniashvili. Trudy

Nauchno Issled Inst Monomerov Sint Kauch Sb Nauchn Tr — Nauchno-Issledovatel'skii Institut Monomerov dlya Sinteticheskogo Kauchuka. Sbornik Nauchnykh Trudov

Nauchno Issled Inst Onkol Tr (Tbilisi) — Nauchno-Issledovatel'skii Institut Onkologii. Trudy (Tbilisi)

Nauchno Issled Inst Osn Podzemn Sooruzh Sb — Nauchno-Issledovatel'skii Institut Osnovanii i Podzemnykh Sooruzhenii. Sbornik

Nauchno Issled Inst Pchelovod Tr — Nauchno-Issledovatel'skii Institut Pchelovodstva. Trudy

Nauchno Issled Inst Pochvoved Agrokhim Melior Tr Tbilisi — Nauchno-Issledovatel'skii Institut Pochvovedeniya. Agrokhimii i Melioratsii. Trudy (Tbilisi)

Nauchno Issled Inst Pochvoved Agrokhim Tr (Yerevan) — Nauchno-Issledovatel'skii Institut Pochvovedeniya i Agrokhimii. Trudy (Yerevan)

Nauchno Issled Inst Prikl Mat Mekh Tomsk Gos Univ Tr — Nauchno-Issledovatel'skii Institut Prikladnoi Matematiki i Mekhaniki pri Tomskom Gosudarstvennom Universitete. Trudy

Nauchno Issled Inst Prom Stroit Sb Tr — Nauchno-Issledovatel'skii Institut Promyshlennogo Stroitel'stva. Sbornik Trudov

Nauchno Issled Inst Prom Stroit Tr Inst — Nauchno-Issledovatel'skii Institut Promyshlennogo Stroitel'stva. Trudy Instituta

Nauchno Issled Inst Rentgenol Radiol Onkol Tr — Nauchno-Issledovatel'skii Institut Rentgenologii, Radiologii i Onkologii. Trudy

Nauchno Issled Inst Sanit Gig im GM Natadze Sb Tr — Nauchno-Issledovatel'skii Institut Sanitarii i Gigieny imeni G.M. Natadze. Sbornik Trudov

Nauchno Issled Inst Sint Spirtov Org Prod Sb Tr — Nauchno-Issledovatel'skii Institut Sinteticheskikh Spirtov i Organicheskikh Produktov. Sbornik Trudov

Nauchno Issled Inst Sint Spirtov Org Prod Tr — Nauchno-Issledovatel'skii Institut Sinteticheskikh Spirtov i Organicheskikh Produktov. Trudy

Nauchno Issled Inst Stroit Arkhit Tr Yerevan — Nauchno-Issledovatel'skii Institut Stroitel'stva i Arkhitektury. Trudy (Yerevan)

Nauchno Issled Inst Stroit Fiz Tr — Nauchno-Issledovatel'skii Institut Stroitel'noi Fiziki. Trudy

Nauchno Issled Inst Stroit Mater Sb Nauchn Rab — Nauchno-Issledovatel'skii Institut Stroitel'nykh Materialov. Sbornik Nauchnykh Rabot

Nauchno Issled Inst Tekh Ekon Issled Sb Tr — Nauchno-Issledovatel'skii Institut Tekhniko-Ekonomicheskikh Issledovanii. Sbornik Trudov

Nauchno Issled Inst Zashch Rast Tr (Tbilisi) — Nauchno-Issledovatel'skii Institut Zashchity Rastenii. Trudy (Tbilisi)

Nauchno Issled Inst Zemled Echmiadzin Arm SSR Sb Nauchn Tr — Nauchno-Issledovatel'skii Institut Zemledeliya, Echmiadzin. Armenian SSR. Sbornik Nauchnykh Trudov

Nauchno Issled Kozhno Venerol Inst Sb Nauchn Tr (Minsk) — Nauchno-Issledovatel'skii Kozhno-Venerologicheskii Institut. Sbornik Nauchnykh Trudov (Minsk)

Nauchno Issled Kozhno Venerol Inst Sb Tr Tbilisi — Nauchno-Issledovatel'skii Kozhno-Venerologicheskii Institut. Sbornik Trudov (Tbilisi)

Nauchno-Issled Lab Geol Zarubezh Stran Tr — Nauchno-Issledovatel'skaya Laboratoriya Geologii Zarubezhnykh Stran Trudy

Nauchno Issled Proektn Inst Tsvetn Metall Armniprotsvetmet Tr — Nauchno-Issledovatel'skii i Proektnyi Institut Tsvetnoi Metallurgii Armniprotsvetmet. Trudy

Nauchno Issled Rab Otrasli Bum Tsellyul — Nauchno-Issledovatel'skie Raboty po Otrasli Bumagi i Tsellyulozy

Nauchno-Issled Rab Vses Nauchno Issled Inst Torf Promsti — Nauchno-Issledovatel'skie Raboty Vsesoyuznogog Nauchno-Issledovatel'skogo Instituta Torfyanoi Promyshlennosti

Nauchno Issled Tekhnokhim Inst Bytovogo Obsluzhivaniya Tr — Nauchno-Issledovatel'skii Tekhnokhimicheskii Institut Bytovogo Obsluzhivaniya. Trudy

Nauchno-Issled Tr Ivanov Tekst Inst — Nauchno-Issledovatel'skie Trudy Ivanovskii Tekstil'nye Institut

Nauchno-Issled Tr Kalinin Nauchno-Issled Inst Tekst Promsti — Nauchno-Issledovatel'skie Trudy Kalininskii Nauchno-Issledovatel'skii InstitutTekstil'noi Promyshlennosti

Nauchno-Issled Tr Latv Nauchno-Issled Inst Legk Promsti — Nauchno-Issledovatel'skie Trudy Latviiskii Nauchno-Issledovatel'skii Institut Legkoi Promyshlennosti

Nauchno-Issled Tr Litov Nauchno-Issled Inst Tekst Promsti — Nauchno-Issledovatel'skie Trudy Litovskii Nauchno-Issledovatel'skii Institut Tekstil'noi Promyshlennosti

Nauchno-Issled Tr Mosk Tekst Inst — Nauchno-Issledovatel'skie Trudy Moskovskii Tekstil'nyi Institut

Nauchno Issled Tr Nauchno Issled Inst Mekhovoi Promsti — Nauchno-Issledovatel'skie Trudy. Nauchno-Issledovatel'skii Institut Mekhovoi Promyshlennosti

Nauchno Issled Tr Nauchno Issled Inst Sherst Promsti — Nauchno-Issledovatel'skie Trudy. Nauchno-Issledovatel'skii Institut SherstyanoiPromyshlennosti

Nauchno-Issled Tr Tsentr Inst Nauchno-Tekh Inf Legk Promsti — Nauchno-Issledovatel'skie Trudy Tsentral'nyi Institut Nauchno-Tekhnicheskoi Informatsii Legkoi Promyshlennosti

Nauchno-Issled Tr Tsentr Nauchno-Issled Inst Sherst Promsti — Nauchno-Issledovatel'skie Trudy Tsentral'nyi Nauchno-Issledovatel'skii Institut Sherstyanoi Promyshlennosti

Nauchno Issled Tr Ukr Nauchno Issled Inst Kozh Obuvn Promsti — Nauchno-Issledovatel'skie Trudy. Ukrainskii Nauchno-Issledovatel'skii Institut Kozhevenno-Obuvnoi Promyshlennosti

Nauchno-Issled Tr Vses Nauchno-Issled Inst Mekhovoi Promsti — Nauchno-Issledovatel'skie Trudy Vsesoyuznyi Nauchno-Issledovatel'skii InstitutMekhovoi Promyshlennosti

Nauchno Issled Tr Vses Nauchno Issled Inst Shveinoi Promsti — Nauchno-Issledovatel'skie Trudy. Vsesoyuznyi Nauchno-Issledovatel'skii InstitutShveinoi Promyshlennosti

Nauchno Issled Vet Inst Tr Dushanbe USSR — Nauchno-Issledovatel'skii Veterinarnyi Institut. Trudy (Dushanbe, USSR)

Nauchnoizsled Inst Epidemiol Mikrobiol Tr — Nauchnoizsledovatelski Institut po Epidemiologiya i Mikrobiologiya. Trudove

Nauchnoizsled Inst Konservna Promst Plovdiv Nauchni Tr — Nauchnoizsledovatelski Institut po Konservna Promishlenost. Plovdiv. Nauchni Trudove

Nauchnoizsled Inst Okeanogr Ribno Stop Varna Izv — Nauchnoizsledovatelski Institut po Okeanografiya i Ribno Stopanstvo. Varna. Izvestiya

Nauchnoizsled Inst Okhr Tr Prof Zabol Tr — Nauchnoizsledovatelski Institut po Okhrana na Truda i Profesionalnite Zabolyavaniya. Trudove

Nauchnoizsled Inst Radiobiol Radiats Khig Nauchni Tr — Nauchnoizsledovatelski Institut po Radiobiologiya i Radiatsionna Khigiena. Nauchni Trudove

Nauchnoizsled Inst Stroit Mater Tr (Sofia) — Nauchnoizsledovatelski Institut po Stroitelni Materiali Trudove (Sofia)

Nauchnoizsled Inst Tsvetna Metal (Plovdiv) God — Nauchnoizsledovatelski Institut po Tsvetna Metalurgiya (Plovdiv). Godishnik

Nauchnoizsled Khim Farm Inst Tr — Nauchnoizsledovatelski Khimiko-Farmatsevtichen Institut. Trudove

Nauchnoizsled Proektno Konstr Inst Tsvetna Metal Plovdiv God — Nauchnoizsledovatelski i Proektno-Konstruktorski Institut po Tsvetna Metalurgiya(Plovdiv). Godishnik

Nauchnoizsled Tr Inst Tekst Promost (Sofia) — Nauchnoizsledovatelski Trudove na Instituta po Tekstilna Promishlenost (Sofia)

Nauchno Metod Konf Probl Prepod VUZ — Nauchno-Metodicheska Konferentsiya po Problemite na Prepodavane vuv VUZ

Nauchno Metod Konf Vupr Obuchenieto VUZ — Nauchno-Metodicheska Konferentsiya po Vuprosite na Obuchenieto vuv VUZ

Nauchno-Prakt Inf Tsentr Aptechn Nauchno-Issled Inst — Nauchno-Prakticheskaya Informatsiya. Tsentral'nyi Aptechnyi Nauchno-Issledovatel'skii Institut

Nauchn Osn Materialoved Dokl Sess — Nauchnye Osnovy Materialovedeniya. Doklady Prochitannye na Sessii Nauchnye Osnovy Materialovedeniya

Nauchn Osn Okhr Prir — Nauchnye Osnovy Okhrany Prirody

Nauchn Osn Prakt Ispolz Tipomorfizma Miner Mater Sezda MMA — Nauchnye Osnovy i Prakticheskoe Ispol'zovanie Tipomorfizma Mineralov. MaterialyS'ezda MMA

Nauchn Osn Razvit Zhivotnovod Beloruss — Nauchnye Osnovy Razvitiya Zhivotnovodstva v Belorussii

Nauchn Osn Tekhnol Obrab Vody — Nauchnye Osnovy Tekhnologii Obrabotki Vody

Nauchno Tekh Biul Vses Nauchno Issled Inst Mekh Sel'sk Khoz — Nauchno-Tekhnicheskii Biulleten. Vsesoiuznyi Nauchno-Issledovatel'skii InstitutMekhanizatsii Sel'skogo Khoziaistva

Nauchno-Tekh Byull Agron Fiz — Nauchno-Tekhnicheskii Byulleten' po Agronomicheskoi Fizike

Nauchno-Tekh Byull Nauchno-Issled Inst Mekh Rybn Promsti — Nauchno-Tekhnicheskii Byulleten Nauchno-Issledovatel'skogo Instituta Mekhanizatsii Rybnoi Promyshlennosti

Nauchno-Tekh Byull Nauchno-Issled Inst Teploenerg Priborostr — Nauchno-Tekhnicheskii Byulleten Nauchno-Issledovatel'skii Institut Teploenergeticheskogo Priborostroeniya

Nauchno Tekh Byull Sib Nauchno Issled Inst Khim Selsk Khoz — Nauchno-Tekhnicheskii Byulleten. Sibirskii Nauchno-Issledovatel'skii Institut Khimizatsii Sel'skogo Khozyaistva

Nauchno-Tekh Byull SoyuzNIKhI — Nauchno-Tekhnicheskii Byulleten SoyuzNIKhI

Nauchno-Tekh Byull Tsentr Genet Lab — Nauchno-Tekhnicheskii Byulleten' Tsentral'noi Geneticheskoi Laboratorii

Nauchno-Tekh Byull Vses Nauchno-Issled Inst Khlopkovod — Nauchno-Tekhnicheskii Byulleten. Vsesoyuznyi Nauchno-Issledovatel'skii InstitutKhlopkovodstva

Nauchno-Tekh Byull Vses Sel-Genet Inst — Nauchno-Tekhnicheskii Byulleten' Vsesoyuznogo Selektsionno-Geneticheskogo Instituta

Nauchno-Tekh Inf — Nauchno-Tekhnicheskaya Informatsiya

Nauchno-Tekh Inf Byull Leningr Politekh Inst — Nauchno-Tekhnicheskii Informatsionnyi Byulleten Leningradskogo Politekhnicheskogo Instituta

Nauchno-Tekh Inf Byull Nauchn Inst Udobr Insektofungits — Nauchno-Tekhnicheskii Informatsionnyi Byulleten Nauchnogo Instituta po Udobreniyam i Insektofungitsidam

Nauchno Tekh Inf Gos Nauchno Tekh Kom Sov Minist Est SSR — Nauchno-Tekhnicheskaya Informatsiya. Gosudarstvennyi Nauchno-Tekhnicheskii Komitet Soveta Ministrov Estonskoi SSR

Nauchno-Tekh Inf Litov Nauchno-Issled Vet Inst — Nauchno-Tekhnicheskaya Informatsiya Litovskii Nauchno-Issledovatel'skii Veterinarnyi Institut

Nauchno-Tekh Inf Ser 1 — Nauchno-Tekhnicheskaya Informatsiya. Seriya 1. Organizatsiya i Metodika Informatsionnoi Raboty

Nauchno-Tekh Inf Ser 2 — Nauchno-Tekhnicheskaya Informatsiya. Seriya 2. Informatsionnye Protsessy i Sistemy

Nauchno-Tekh Inf (Sofia) — Nauchno-Tekhnicheskaya Informatsiya (Sofia)

Nauchno Tekh Inf Tsellyul Bum Gidroliz Lesokhim Promsti — Nauchno-Tekhnicheskaya Informatsiya po Tsellyulozno-Bumazhnoi. Gidroliznoi i Lesokhimicheskoi Promyshlennosti

Nauchno Tekh Inf VINTI — Nauchno-Tekhnicheskaya Informatsiya. Vsesoyuznyi Institut Nauchnoi i Tekhnicheskoi Informatsii

Nouohno Tokh Konf Iopolz Ioniz Izluoh Nar Khoz Dokl — Nauchno-Tekhnicheskaya Konferentsiya po Ispol'zovaniyu Ioniziruyushchikh Izluchenii v Narodnom Khozyaistve. Doklady

Nauchno Tekh Konf Issled Vikhrevogo Eff Ego Primen Tekh — Nauchno-Tekhnicheskaya Konferentsiya po Issledovaniyu Vikhrevogo Effekta i Ego Primeneniyu v Tekhnike

Nauchno Tekh Konf Raschet Konstr Primen Radiats Trub Promsti — Nauchno-Tekhnicheskaya Konferentsiya. Raschet, Konstruirovanie i Primenenie Radiatsionnykh Trub v Promyshlennosti

Nauchno Tekh Konf Steklo Tonkaya Keram — Nauchno-Tekhnicheskaya Konferentsiya Steklo i Tonkaya Keramika

Nauchno Tekh Konf Stuklo Fina Keram — Nauchno-Tekhnicheska Konferentsiya Stuklo i Fina Keramika

Nauchno Tekh Konf Zavaryavane Stroit Montazha Dokl — Nauchno-Tekhnicheska Konferentsiya po Zavaryavane v Stroitelstvoto i Montazha. Dokladi

Nauchno Tekh Obedin GruzNIIstrom Sb Tr — Nauchno-Tekhnicheskoe Ob'edinenie GruzNIIstrom Sbornik Trudov

Nauchno-Tekh Obz Ser Geol Razved Gaz Gazokondens Mestorozhd — Nauchno-Tekhnicheskii Obzor. Seriya. Geologiya, Razvedka Gazovykh, i Bazokondensatnykh Mestorozhdenii

Nauchno Tekh Obz Ser Geol Razved Gazov Gazokondens Mestorozh — Nauchno-Tekhnicheskii Obzor. Seriya. Geologiya i Razvedka Gazovykh i Gazokondensatnykh Mestorozhdenii

Nauchno Tekh Obz Ser Ispolz Gaza Nar Khoz — Nauchno-Tekhnicheskii Obzor. Seriya. Ispol'zovanie Gaza v Narodnom Khozyaistve

Nauchno-Tekh Obz Ser Pererab Gaza Gazov Kondens — Nauchno-Tekhnicheskii Obzor. Seriya. Pererabotka Gaza i Gazovogo Kondensata

Nauchno Tekh Obz Ser Transp Khranenie Gaza — Nauchno-Tekhnicheskii Obzor. Seriya. Transport i Khranenie Gaza

Nauchno-Tekh Ova SSSR — Nauchno-Tekhnicheskie Obshchestva SSSR

Nauchno-Tekh Probl Goreniya Vzryva — Nauchno-Tekhnicheskie Problemy Goreniya i Vzryva

Nauchno Tekh Prog Profil Med Mater Nauchn Konf Klin Kafedr — Nauchno-Tekhnicheskii Progress i Profilakticheskaya Meditsina. Materialy Nauchnoi Konferentsii Klinicheskikh Kafedr

Nauchno Tekh Ref Sb Drozhzhevaya Promst — Nauchno-Tekhnicheskii Referativnyi Sbornik. Drozhzhevaya Promyshlennost

Nauchno Tekh Ref Sb Krakhmalo Patochn Promst — Nauchno-Tekhnicheskii Referativnyi Sbornik. Krakhmalo-Patochnaya Promyshlennost

Nauchno Tekh Ref Sb Maslo Zhir Promst — Nauchno-Tekhnicheskii Referativnyi Sbornik. Maslo-Zhirovaya Promyshlennost

Nauchno Tekh Ref Sb Sakh Promst — Nauchno-Tekhnicheskii Referativnyi Sbornik. Sakharnaya Promyshlennost

Nauchno Tekh Ref Sb Ser Avtom Khim Proizvod — Nauchno-Tekhnicheskii Referativnyi Sbornik. Seriya. Avtomatizatsiya Khimicheskikh Proizvodstv

Nauchno Tekh Ref Sb Ser Azotn Promst — Nauchno-Tekhnicheskii Referativnyi Sbornik. Seriya. Azotnaya Promyshlennost

Nauchno Tekh Ref Sb Ser Fosfornaya Promst — Nauchno-Tekhnicheskii Referativnyi Sbornik. Seriya Fosfornaya Promyshlennost

Nauchno Tekh Ref Sb Ser Kaliinaya Promst — Nauchno-Tekhnicheskii Referativnyi Sbornik. Seriya. Kaliinaya Promyshlennost

Nauchno Tekh Ref Sb Ser Khim Tekhnol Lyuminoforov Neorg Mater — Nauchno-Tekhnicheskii Referativnyi Sbornik. Seriya. Khimiya i Tekhnologiya Lyuminoforov i Chistykh Neoganicheskikh Materialov

Nauchno Tekh Ref Sb Ser Kislorodn Promst — Nauchno-Tekhnicheskii Referativnyi Sbornik. Seriya. Kislorodnaya Promyshlennost

Nauchno Tekh Ref Sb Ser Proizvod Pererab Plastmass Sint Smol — Nauchno-Tekhnicheskii Referativnyi Sbornik. Seriya. Proizvodstvo i Pererabotka Plastmass i Sinteticheskikh Smol

Nauchno Tekh Ref Sb Ser Promst Gornokhim Syrya — Nauchno-Tekhnicheskii Referativnyi Sbornik. Seriya. Promyshlennost Gornokhimicheskogo Syr'ya

Nauchno Tekh Ref Sb Ser Promst Khim Volokon — Nauchno-Tekhnicheskii Referativnyi Sbornik. Seriya. Promyshlennost Khimicheskikh Volokon

Nauchno Tekh Ref Sb Ser Promst Tovarov Bytovoi Khim — Nauchno-Tekhnicheskii Referativnyi Sbornik. Seriya. Promyshlennost Tovarov Bytovoi Khimii

Nauchno Tekh Ref Sb Ser Reakt Osobo Chist Veshchestva — Nauchno-Tekhnicheskii Referativnyi Sbornik. Seriya. Reaktivy i Osobo Chistye Veshchestva

Nauchno Tekh Ref Sb Ser Toksikol Sanit Khim Plastmass — Nauchno-Tekhnicheskii Referativnyi Sbornik. Seriya. Toksikologiya i Sanitarnaya Khimiya Plastmass

Nauchno Tekh Ref Sb Spirt Likero Vodochn Promst — Nauchno-Tekhnicheskii Referativnyi Sbornik. Spirtovaya i Likero-Vodochnaya Promyshlennost

Nauchno Tekh Ref Sb Vinodel Promst — Nauchno-Tekhnicheskii Referativnyi Sbornik. Vinodel'cheskaya Promyshlennost

Nauchno-Tekh Sb Dobyche Nefti — Nauchno-Tekhnicheskii Sbornik po Dobyche Nefti

Nauchno-Tekh Sb Geol Razrab Transp Ispolz Prir Gaza — Nauchno-Tekhnicheskii Sbornik po Geologii, Razrabotke, Transportu, i Ispol'zovaniyu Prirodnogo Gaza

Nauchno Tekh Sb Gos Izd Lit Obl At Nauki Tekh — Nauchno-Technicheskii Sbornik. Gosudarstvennoe Izdatel'stvo Literatury v Oblasti Atomnoi Nauki i Tekhniki

Nauchno-Temat Sb Ufim Neft Inst — Nauchno-Tematicheskii Sbornik. Ufimskii Neftyanoi Institut

Nauchn Prikl Probl Energ — Nauchnye i Prikladnye Problemy Energetiki

Nauchn Rab Inst Okhr Tr Vses Tsentr Sov Prof Soyuz — Nauchnye Raboty Institutov Okhrany Truda Vsesoyuznogo Tsentral'nogo Soveta Professional'nykh Soyuzov

Nauchn Rab Inst Okhr Tr Vses Tsentr Sov Prof Soyuzov — Nauchnye Raboty Institutov Okhrany Truda Vsesoyuznogo Tsentral'nogo Soveta Professional'nykh Soyuzov

Nauchn Rab Inst Okhr Tr VTsSPS — Nauchnye Raboty Institutov Okhrany Truda VTsSPS

Nauchn Rab Stud Gorn Gorno Geol Fak Novocherk Politekh Inst — Nauchnye Raboty Studentov Gornogo i Gorno-Geologicheskogo Fakul'tetov. Novocherkasskii Politekhnicheskii Institut

Nauchn Rab Stud Khim Tekhnol Fak Novocherk Politekh Inst — Nauchnye Raboty Studentov Khimiko-Tekhnologicheskogo Fakul'teta. Novocherkasskii Politekhnicheskii Institut

Nauchn Rab Stud Mosk Farm Inst — Nauchnye Raboty Studentov Moskovskogo Farmatsevticheskogo Instituta

Nauchn Rab Stud Mosk Gorn Inst — Nauchnye Raboty Studentov Moskovskogo Gornogo Instituta

Nauchn Rab Stud Mosk Med Stomatol Inst — Nauchnye Raboty Studentov Moskovskogo Meditsinskogo Stomatologicheskogo Instituta

Nauchn Rab Stud Mosk Vet Akad — Nauchnye Raboty Studentov. Moskovskaya Veterinarnaya Akademiya

Nauchn Rab Stud Novocherk Politekh Inst — Nauchnye Raboty Studentov Novocherkasskii Politekhnicheskii Institut

Nauchn Rab Stud Sverdl Gorn Inst — Nauchnye Raboty Studentov Sverdlovskii Gornyi Institut

Nauchn Rab Stud Sverdl Gorn Inst im V V Vakhrusheva — Nauchnye Raboty Studentov. Sverdlovskii Gornyi Institut imeni V. V. Vakhrusheva

Nauchn Rab Vrach Mord SSSR — Nauchnye Raboty Vrachei Mordovskoi SSSR

Nauchn Rab Vses Nauchno Issled Ugoln Inst — Nauchnye Raboty. Vsesoyuznyi Nauchno-Issledovatel'skii Ugol'nyi Institut

Nauchn Semin Poluch Issled Svoistv Soedin Redkozem Met — Nauchnyi Seminar po Polucheniyu i Issledovaniyu Svoistv Soedinenii Redkozemel'nykh Metallov

Nauchn Sess Khim Tekhnol Org Soedin Sery Sernistykh Neftei P — Nauchnaya Sessiya po Khimii i Tekhnologii Organicheskikh Soedinenii Sery i Sernistykh Neftei. Plenarnye Doklady

Nauchn Soobshch Akad Nauk SSSR Sib Otd Yakutsk Fil — Nauchnye Soobshcheniya. Akademiya Nauk SSSR. Sibirskoe Otdelenie. Yakutskii Filial

Nauchn Soobshch Arm Nauchno Issled Inst Stroit Mater Sooruzh — Nauchnye Soobshcheniya Armyanskii Nauchno-Issledovatel'skii Institut Stroitel'nykh Materialov i Sooruzhenii

Nauchn Soobshch Armniprotsvetmeta — Nauchnye Soobshcheniya Armniprotsvetmeta

Nauchn Soobshch Gos Vses Nauchno Issled Inst Tsem Prom-Sti — Nauchnye Soobshcheniya Gosudarstvennyi Vsesoyuznyi Nauchno-Issledovatel'skii Institut Tsementnoi Promyshlennosti

Nauchn Soobshch Inst Fiziol Akad Nauk SSSR — Nauchnye Soobshcheniya Instituta Fiziologii Akademii Nauk SSSR

Nauchn Soobshch Inst Geol Geogr Akad Nauk Lit SSR — Nauchnye Soobshcheniya Instituta Geologii i Geografii. Akademiya Nauk LitovskoiSSR

Nauchn Soobshch Inst Gorn Dela Im A A Skochinskogo — Nauchnye Soobshcheniya Institut Gornogo Dela Imeni A. A. Skochinskogo

Nauchn Soobshch Inst Gorn Dela (Moscow) — Nauchnye Soobshcheniya Institut Gornogo Dela (Moscow)

Nauchn Soobshch Sarat Avtomob Dorozhn Inst — Nauchnye Soobshcheniya. Saratovskii Avtomobil'no-Dorozhnyi Institut

Nauchn Soobshch Vses Nauchno Issled Inst Tsem Promsti — Nauchnye Soobshcheniya Vsesoyuznyi Nauchno-Issledovatel'skii Institut Tsementnoi Promyshlennosti

Nauchn Soobshch Yakutsk Fil Akad Nauk SSSR — Nauchnye Soobshcheniya. Yakutskii Filial Akademiya Nauk SSSR

Nauchn Sprav Agrar Univ — Nauchnyi Spravochnik Agrarnogo Universiteta

Nauchn Stud Zh Geol Fak Mosk Gos Univ — Nauchnyi Studencheskii Zhurnal. Geologicheskii Fakul'tet. Moskovskii Gosudarstvennyi Universitet

Nauchn Tr Akad Kommunal'n Khoz — Nauchnye Trudy Akademii Kommunal'nogo Khozyaistva

Nauchn Tr Akad Kommunaln Khoz im K D Pamfilova — Nauchnye Trudy. Akademiya Kommunal'nogo Khozyaistva imeni K. D. Pamfilova

Nauchn Tr Arkhang Lesotekh Inst — Nauchnye Trudy. Arkhangel'skii Lesotekhnicheskii Institut

Nauchn Tr Arm Nauchno Issled Inst Zhivotnovod Vet — Nauchnye Trudy. Armyanskii Nauchno-Issledovatel'skii Institut Zhivotnovodstva i Veterinarii

Nauchn Tr Aspir Odess Skh Inst — Nauchnye Trudy Aspirantov Odesskii Sel'skokhozyaistvennyi Institut

Nauchn Tr Aspir Ordinatorov Pervogo Mosk Med Inst — Nauchnye Trudy Aspirantov i Ordinatorov Pervogo Moskovskogo Meditsinskogo Instituta

Nauchn Tr Aspir Tashk Gos Univ — Nauchnye Trudy Aspirantov. Tashkentskii Gosudarstvennyi Universitet

Nauchn Tr Bashk Gos Med Inst — Nauchnye Trudy Bashkirskogo Gosudarstvennogo Meditsinskogo Instituta

Nauchn Tr Bashk Med Inst — Nauchnye Trudy Bashkirskogo Meditsinskogo Instituta

Nauchn Tr Beloruss Inst Inzh Zheleznodorozhn Transp — Nauchnye Trudy. Belorusskii Institut Inzhenerov Zheleznodorozhnogo Transporta

Nauchn Tr Beloruss Inst Mekh Selsk Khoz — Nauchnye Trudy. Belorusskii Institut Mekhanizatsii Sel'skogo Khozyaistva

Nauchn Tr Beloruss Inst Zhivotnovod — Nauchnye Trudy. Belorusskii Institut Zhivotnovodstva

Nauchn Tr Beloruss Nauchno Issled Inst Zhivotnovod — Nauchnye Trudy. Belorusskii Nauchno-Issledovatel'nstut Institut Zhivotnovodstva

Nauchn Tr Bukharestskii Skh Inst Bukharest Ser Agron — Nauchnye Trudy. Bukharestskii Sel'skokhozyaistvennyi Institut imeni N. Belchesku. Bukharest. Seriya. Agronomiya

Nauchn Tr Bukhar Gos Pedagog Inst — Nauchnye Trudy Bukharskii Gosudarstvennyi Pedagogicheskii Institut

Nauchn Tr Bykovskoi Bakhchevoi Opytn Stn — Nauchnye Trudy Bykovskoi Bakhchevoi Opytnai Stantsii

Nauchn Tr Chelyab Obl Klin Bol'n — Nauchnye Trudy Chelyabinskoi Oblastnoi Klinicheskoi Bol'nitsy

Nauchn Tr Dnepropetr Metall Inst — Nauchnye Trudy Dnepropetrovskii Metallorgicheskii Institut

Nauchn Tr Donskoi Zon Nauchno Issled Inst Sel'sk Khoz — Nauchnye Trudy Donskoi Zonal'nyi Nauchno-Issledovatel'skii Institut Sel'skogo Khozyaistva

Nauchn Tr Ekon Fak Cheshskobudeevitskogo Skh Inst Biol Ser — Nauchnye Trudy Ekonomicheskogo Fakul'teta Cheshskobudeevitskogo Sel'skokhozyaistvennogo Instituta. Biologicheskaya Seriya

Nauchn Tr Erevan Gos Univ Ser Geol Nauk — Nauchnye Trudy Erevanskii Gosudarstvennyi Universitet Seriya Geologicheskikh Nauk

Nauchn Tr Erevan Gos Univ Ser Khim Nauk — Nauchnye Trudy Erevanskii Gosudarstvennyi Universitet Seriya Khimicheskikh Nauk

Nauchn Tr Erevan Politekh Inst — Nauchnye Trudy Erevanskogo Politekhnicheskogo Instituta

Nauchn Tr Giredmeta — Nauchnye Trudy Giredmeta

Nauchn Tr Gos Inst Usoversh Vrachei im S M Kirova — Nauchnye Trudy Gosudarstvennogo Instituta Usovershenstvovaniya Vrachei imeni S. M. Kirova

Nauchn Tr Gos Nauchno Issled Inst Tsvetn Met — Nauchnye Trudy. Gosudarstvennyi Nauchno-Issledovatel'skii Institut Tsvetnykh Metallov

Nauchn Tr Gos Nauchno-Issled Proektn Inst Redkomet Prom-Sti — Nauchnye Trudy Gosudarstvennyi Nauchno-Issledovatel'skii i Proektnyi Institut Redkometallicheskoi Promyshlennosti

Nauchn Tr Gos Nikitsk Bot Sad — Nauchnye Trudy. Gosudarstvennyi Nikitskii Botanicheskii Sad

Nauchn Tr Gruz Politekh Inst im V I Lenina — Nauchnye Trudy. Gruzinskii Politekhnicheskii Institut imeni V. I. Lenina

Nauchn Tr Gruz Skh Inst — Nauchnye Trudy Gruzinskii Sel'skokhozyaistvennyi Institut

Nauchn Tr Inst Avtom — Nauchnye Trudy Instituta Avtomatiki

Nauchn Tr Inst Chern Metall (Dnepropetrovsk) — Nauchnye Trudy Institut Chernoi Metallurgii (Dnepropetrovsk)

Nauchn Tr Inst Entomol Fitopatol — Nauchnye Trudy Instituta Entomologii i Fitopatologii

Nauchn Tr Inst Entomol Fitopatol Akad Nauk Ukr SSR — Nauchnye Trudy Instituta Entomologii i Fitopatologii Akademii Nauk Ukrainskoi SSR

Nauchn Tr Inst Fiziol Rast Agrokhim Akad Nauk Ukr SSR — Nauchnye Trudy Institut Fiziologii Rastenii i Agrokhimii. Akademiya Nauk Ukrainskoi SSR

Nauchn Tr Inst Giprotsvetmetobrabotka — Nauchnye Trudy Instituta Giprotsvetmetobrabotka

Nauchn Tr Inst Gorn Dela Akad Nauk SSSR Sib Otd — Nauchnye Trudy Instituta Gornogo Dela. Akademiya Nauk SSSR. Sibirskoe Otdelenie

Nauchn Tr Inst Mekh Mosk Gos Univ — Nauchnye Trudy. Institut Mekhaniki. Moskovskii Gosudarstvennyi Universitet

Nauchn Tr Inst Mineral Resur (Ukrainian SSR) — Nauchnye Trudy Instituta Mineral'nykh Resursov (Ukrainian SSR)

Nauchn Tr Inst Pochv Issled — Nauchnye Trudy Instituta Pochvennykh Issledovaniya

Nauchn Tr Inst Rastit Masel Proteina Moyushch Sredstv Sofiya — Nauchnye Trudy. Institut Rastitel'nykh Masel. Proteina i Moyushchikh Sredstv-Sofiya

Nauchn Tr Inst Sibtsvetmetniiproekt — Nauchnye Trudy. Instituta Sibtsvetmetniiproekt

Nauchn Tr Irkutsk Gos Med Inst — Nauchnye Trudy Irkutskii Gosudarstvennyi Meditsinskii Institut

Nauchn Tr Irkutsk Gos Nauchno Issled Inst Redk Met — Nauchnye Trudy Irkutskii Gosudarstvennyi Nauchno-Issledovatel'skii Institut Redkikh Metallov

Nauchn Tr Irkutsk Gos Nauchno Issled Inst Redk Tsvetn Met — Nauchnye Trudy Irkutskii Gosudarstvennyi Nauchno-Issledovatel'skii Institut Redkikh i Tsvetnykh Metallov

Nauchn Tr Irkutsk Med Inst — Nauchnye Trudy Irkutskii Meditsinskii Institut

Nauchn Tr Irkutsk Nauchno Issled Inst Epidemiol Mikrobiol — Nauchnye Trudy. Irkutskii Nauchno-Issledovatel'skii Institut Epidemiologii i Mikrobiologii

Nauchn Tr Irkutsk Politekh Inst — Nauchnye Trudy Irkutskogo Politekhnicheskogo Instituta

Nauchn Tr Ivanov Gos Med Inst — Nauchnye Trudy Ivanovskogo Gosudarstvennogo Meditsinskogo Instituta

Nauchn Tr Kalmytskii Nauchno Issled Inst Myasn Skotovod — Nauchnye Trudy. Kalmytskii Nauchno-Issledovatel'skii Institut Myasnogo Skotovodstva

Nauchn Tr Kamenets Podol'sk Skh Inst — Nauchnye Trudy Kamenets Podol'skii Sel'skokhozyaistvennyi Institut

Nauchn Tr Karagand Fil Inst Obogashch Tverd Goryuch Iskop — Nauchnye Trudy Karagandinskii Filial Instituta Obogashcheniya Tverdykh Goryuchikh Iskopaemykh

Nauchn Tr Karagand Nauchno Issled Ugol'n Inst — Nauchnye Trudy Karagandinskii Nauchno-Issledovatel'skii Ugol'nyi Institut

Nauchn Tr Karsh Gos Pedagog Inst — Nauchnye Trudy. Karshinskii Gosudarstvennyi Pedagogicheskii Institut

Nauchn Tr Kazan Gos Med Inst — Nauchnye Trudy. Kazanskii Gosudarstvennyi Meditsinskii Institut

Nauchn Tr Kazan Gos Vet Inst im N E Baumana — Nauchnye Trudy. Kazanskogo Gosudarstvennogo Veterinarnogo Instituta imeni N. E.Baumana

Nauchn Tr Kazan Med Inst — Nauchnye Trudy Kazanskogo Meditsinskogo Instituta

Nauchn Tr Kaz Skh Inst — Nauchnye Trudy. Kazakhskii Sel'skokhozyaistvennyi Institut

Nauchn Tr Khark Gorn Inst — Nauchnye Trudy Khar'kovskii Gornyi Institut

Nauchn Tr Khar'k Inst Inzh Kommunal'n Stroit — Nauchnye Trudy Khar'kovskii Institut Inzhenerov Kommunal'nogo Stroitel'stva

Nauchn Tr Khark Inst Inzh Zheleznodorozhn Transp — Nauchnye Trudy. Khar'kovskogo Instituta Inzhenerov Zheleznodorozhnogo Transporta

Nauchn Tr Khar'k S-Kh Inst — Nauchnye Trudy Khar'kovskogo Sel'skokhozyaistvennogo Instituta

Nauchn Tr Kirg Med Inst — Nauchnye Trudy Kirgizskogo Meditsinskogo Instituta

Nauchn Tr Konf Astrakh Tekh Inst Rybn Promsti Khoz — Nauchnye Trudy Konferentsii. Posvyashchennoi 100-letiyu so Dnya Rozhdeniya V. I. Lenina. Astrakhanskii Tekhnicheskii Institut Rybnoi Promyshlennosti i Khozyaistva. Astrakhan

Nauchn Tr Krasnodar God Pedagog Inst — Nauchnye Trudy Krasnodarskogo Gosudarstvennogo Pedagogicheskogo Instituta

Nauchn Tr Krasnodar Gos Pedagog Inst — Nauchnye Trudy. Krasnodarskii Gosudarstvennyi Pedagogicheskii Institut

Nauchn Tr Krasnodar Nauchno Issled Inst Sel'sk Khoz — Nauchnye Trudy Krasnodarskogo Nauchno-Issledovatel'skogo Instituta Sel'skogo Khozyaistva

Nauchn Tr Krasnodar Nauchno Issled Vet Stn — Nauchnye Trudy Krasnodarskoi Nauchno-Issledovat'skoi Veterinarnoi Stantsii

Nauchn Tr Krasnodar Politekh Inst — Nauchnye Trudy. Krasnodarskogo Politekhnicheskogo Instituta

Nauchn Tr Krym Gos Med Inst — Nauchnye Trudy Krymskii Gosudarstvennyi Meditsinskii Institut

Nauchn Tr Kuban Gos Med Inst — Nauchnye Trudy Kubanskogo Gosudarstvennogo Meditsinskogo Instituta

Nauchn Tr Kuban Gos Univ — Nauchnye Trudy Kubanskii Gosudarstvennyi Universitet

Nauchn Tr Kuibyshev Gos Pedagog Inst im V V Kuibysheva — Nauchnye Trudy. Kuibyshevskii Gosudarstvennyi Pedagogicheskii Institut imeni V.V. Kuibysheva

Nauchn Tr Kurgan S-Kh Inst — Nauchnye Trudy Kurganskogo Sel'skokhozyaistvennogo Instituta

Nauchn Tr Kursk Gos Pedagog Inst — Nauchnye Trudy Kurskij Gosudarstvennyj Pedagogicheskij Institut

Nauchn Tr Kursk Gos Skh Optn Stn — Nauchnye Trudy Kurskoi Gosudarstvennoi Sel'skokhozyaistvennoi Opytnoi Stantsii

Nauchn Tr Kursk Gos Skh Opytn Stn — Nauchnye Trudy Kurskoi Gosudarstvennoi Sel'skokhozyaistvennoi Opytnoi Stantsii

Nauchn Tr Kursk Politekh Inst — Nauchnye Trudy Kurskii Politekhnicheskii Institut

Nauchn Tr Kursk Selkh Inst — Nauchnye Trudy Kurskogo Sel'skokhozyaistvennogo Instituta

Nauchn Tr Kursk SKhI — Nauchnye Trudy Kurskogo SKhI

Nauchn Tr KuzNIIUgleobogashcheniya — Nauchnye Trudy. KuzNIIUgleobogashcheniya

Nauchn Tr Leningr Gorn Inst Nov Issled Khim Metall Obogashch — Nauchnye Trudy Leningradskii Gornyi Institut Novye Issledovaniya v Khimii, Metallurgii, i Obogashchenii

Nauchn Tr Leningr Gos Inst Usoversh Vrachei — Nauchnye Trudy Leningradskogo Gosudarstvennogo Instituta Usovershenstvovaniya Vrachei

Nauchn Tr Leningr Gos Inst Usoversh Vrachei im S M Kirova — Nauchnye Trudy Leningradskogo Gosudarstvennogo Instituta Usovershenstvovaniya Vrachei imeni S. M. Kirova

Nauchn Tr Leningr Inst Tochn Mekh Opt — Nauchnye Trudy Leningradskii Institut Tochnoi Mekhaniki i Optiki

Nauchn Tr Leningr Inst Usoversh Vrachei Im S M Kirova — Nauchnye Trudy Leningradskogo Instituta Usovershenstvovaniya Vrachei Imeni S. M. Kirova

Nauchn Tr Leningr Inzh Stroit Inst — Nauchnye Trudy Leningradskii Inzhenerno-Stroitel'nyi Institut

Nauchn Tr Leningr Lesotekh Akad — Nauchnye Trudy Leningradskoi Lesotekhnicheskoi Akademii

Nauchn Tr Leningr Lesotekh Akad im S M Kirova — Nauchnye Trudy. Leningradskaya Lesotekhnicheskaya Akademiya imeni S. M. Kirova

Nauchn Tr Leningr Nauchno Issled Inst Pereliv Krovi — Nauchnye Trudy Leningradskii Nauchno-Issledovatel'skii Institut Perelivaniya Krovi

Nauchn Tr Leningr Skh Inst — Nauchnye Trudy Leningradskogo Sel'skokhozyaistvennogo Instituta

Nauchn Tr Leningr Tekhnol Inst Im Lensoveta — Nauchnye Trudy Leningradskogo Tekhnologicheskogo Instituta Imeni Lensoveta

Nauchn Tr Lesokhoz Fak Ukr Skh Akad — Nauchnye Trudy Lesokhozyaistvennogo Fakul'teta Ukrainskoi Sel'skokhozyaistvennoi Akademii

Nauchn Tr Litov S-Kh Akad — Nauchnye Trudy Litovskoi Sel'skokhozyaistvennoi Akademii

Nauchn Tr L'vov Lesotekh Inst — Nauchnye Trudy L'vovskogo Lesotekhnicheskogo Instituta

Nauchn Tr Lvov Skh Inst — Nauchnye Trudy. L'vovskii Sel'skokhozyaistvennyi Institut

Nauchn Tr L'vov Zoovet Inst — Nauchnye Trudy L'vovskii Zooveterinarnyi Institut

Nauchn Tr Magnitogorsk Gornometall Inst — Nauchnye Trudy. Magnitogorskii Gornometallurgicheskii Institut

Nauchn Tr Melitopol'skoi Opytn Stn Sadovod — Nauchnye Trudy Melitopol'skoi Opytnoi Stantsii Sadovodstva

Nauchn Tr Melitop Opytn Stn Sadovod — Nauchnye Trudy Melitopol'skoi Opytnoi Stantsii Sadovodstva

Nauchn Tr Mosk Energ Inst — Nauchnye Trudy. Moskovskii Energeticheskii Institut

Nauchn Tr Mosk Gor Klin Bol'n N 52 — Nauchnye Trudy Moskovskoi Gorodskoi Kliniceskci Bol'nitsy N 52

Nauchn Tr Mosk Gorn Inst — Nauchnye Trudy Moskovskogo Gornogo Instituta

Nauchn Tr Mosk Inst Nar Khoz — Nauchnye Trudy. Moskovskii Institut Narodnogo Khozyaistva

Nauchn Tr Mosk Inst Radioelektron Gorn Elektromekh — Nauchnye Trudy Moskovskii Institut Radioelektroniki i Gornoi Elektromekhaniki

Nauchn Tr Mosk Inst Stali Splavov — Nauchnye Trudy. Moskovskii Institut Stali i Splavov

Nauchn Tr Mosk Inzh Ekon Inst — Nauchnye Trudy Moskovskogo Inzhenerno-Ekonomicheskogo Instituta

Nauchn Tr Mosk Lesotekh Inst — Nauchnye Trudy Moskovskogo Lesotekhnicheskogo Instituta

Nauchn Tr Mosk Nauchno-Issled Inst Vaktsin Syvorot — Nauchnye Trudy Moskovskogo Nauchno-Issledovatel'skogo Instituta Vaktsin i Syvorotok

Nauchn Tr Mosk Poligr Inst — Nauchnye Trudy Moskovskii Poligraficheskii Institut

Nauchn Tr Mosk Tekhnol Inst Legk Promsti — Nauchnye Trudy Moskovskogo Tekhnologicheskogo Instituta Legkoi Promyshlennosti

Nauchn Tr Mosk Zaochn Poligr Inst — Nauchnye Trudy. Moskovskii Zaochnyi Poligraficheskii Institut

Nauchn Tr Nauchno Issled Gornometall Inst (Yerevan) — Nauchnye Trudy Nauchno-Issledovatelskii Gornometallurgicheskii Institut (Yerevan)

Nauchn Tr Nauchno-Issled Inst Gorn Sadovod Tsvetovod — Nauchnye Trudy Nauchno-Issledovatel'skogo Instituta Gornogo Sadovodstva i Tsvetovodstva

Nauchn Tr Nauchno-Issled Inst Karakulevod — Nauchnye Trudy. Nauchno-Issledovatel'skii Institut Karakulevodstva

Nauchn Tr Nauchno-Issled Inst Kartofel'n Khoz — Nauchnye Trudy Nauchno-Issledovatel'skii Institut Kartofel'nogo Khoziaistva

Nauchn Tr Nauchno Issled Inst Konservn Promsti Plovdiv — Nauchnye Trudy. Nauchno-Issledovatel'skii Institut Konservnoi Promyshlennosti. Plovdiv

Nauchn Tr Nauchno Issled Inst Materi Rebenka — Nauchnye Trudy. Nauchno-Issledovatel'skii Institut Materi i Rebenka

Nauchn Tr Nauchno-Issled Inst Pediatr — Nauchnye Trudy Nauchno-Issledovatel'skogo Instituta po Pediatrii

Nauchn Tr Nauchno-Issled Inst Pushnogo Zverovod Krolikovod — Nauchnye Trudy Nauchno-Issledovatel'skii Institut Pushnogo Zverovodstva i Krolikovodstva

Nauchn Tr Nauchno-Issled Inst Radiol Radiats Gig — Nauchnye Trudy Nauchno-Issledovatel'skii Institut Radiologii i Radiatsionnoi Gigieny

Nauchn Tr Nauchno Issled Inst Rastenievod Pieshtyany — Nauchnye Trudy Nauchno-Issledovatel'skogo Instituta Rastenievodstva v G. Pieshtyany

Nauchn Tr Nauchno-Issled Inst Sel'sk Khoz Yugo Vostoka — Nauchnye Trudy Nauchno-Issledovatel'skii Institut Sel'skogo Khozyaistva Yugo-Vostoka

Nauchn Tr Nauchno-Issled Inst S-Kh Yugo-Vost — Nauchnye Trudy Nauchno-Issledovatel'skogo Instituta Sel'skokhozyaistva Yugo-Vostoka

Nauchn Tr Nauchno Issled Inst Stroit Fiz — Nauchnye Trudy. Nauchno-Issledovatel'skii Institut Stroitel'noi Fiziki

Nauchn Tr Nauchno Issled Vet Inst (Minsk) — Nauchnye Trudy Nauchno-Issledovatel'skogo Veterinarnogo Instituta (Minsk)

Nauchn Tr Nizhnednepr Nauchno Issled Stn Obleseniyu Peskov V — Nauchnye Trudy. Nizhnedneprovskoi Nauchno-Issledovatel'skoi Stantsii po Obleseniyu Peskov i Vinogradarstvu na Peskakh

Nauchn Tr Novocherk Politekh Inst im Sergo Ordzhonikidze — Nauchnye Trudy. Novocherkasskogo Politekhnicheskogo Instituta imeni Sergo Ordzhonikidze

Nauchn Tr Novosib Gos Pedagog Inst — Nauchnye Trudy Novosibirskogo Gosudarstvennogo Pedagogicheskogo Instituta

Nauchn Tr Novosib Med Inst — Nauchnye Trudy Novosibirskogo Meditsinskogo Instituta

Nauchn Tr Novosib Nauchno Issled Vet Stn — Nauchnye Trudy Novosibirskoi Nauchno-Issledovatel'skoi Veterinarnoi Stantsii

Nauchn Tr Obninskii Otd Geogr Ova SSSR — Nauchnye Trudy Obninskii Otdel Geograficheskogo Obshchestva SSSR

Nauchn Tr Obogashch Briket Uglei — Nauchnye Trudy po Obogashcheniyu i Briketirovaniyu Uglei

Nauchn Tr Odess Gos Med Inst — Nauchnye Trudy. Odesskii Gosudarstvennyi Meditsinskii Institut

Nauchn Tr Omsk Gos Med Inst im M I Kalinina — Nauchnye Trudy. Omskii Gosudarstvennyi Meditsinskii Institut imeni M. I. Kalinina

Nauchn Tr Omsk Inst Inzh Zheleznodorozhn Transp — Nauchnye Trudy. Omskii Institut Inzhenerov Zheleznodorozhnogo Transporta

Nauchn Tr Omsk Med Inst — Nauchnye Trudy Omskii Meditsinskii Institut

Nauchn Tr Omsk Med Inst im M I Kalinina — Nauchnye Trudy. Omskii Meditsinskii Institut imeni M. I. Kalinina

Nauchn Tr Omsk S-Kh Inst — Nauchnye Trudy Omskogo Sel'skokhozyaistvennogo Instituta

Nauchn Tr Omsk Vet Inst — Nauchnye Trudy Omskogo Veterinarnogo Instituta

Nauchn Tr Orlov Obl Skh Opytn Stn im P I Lisitsyna — Nauchnye Trudy. Orlovskaya Oblastnaya Sel'skokhozyaistvennaya Opytnaya Stantsiya imeni P. I. Lisitsyna

Nauchn Tr Orlov Ob Skh Opytn Stn — Nauchnye Trudy Orlovskaya Oblastnaya Sel'skokhozyaistvennaya Opytnaya Stantsiya

Nauchn Tr Permsk Farm Inst — Nauchnye Trudy Permskogo Farmatsevticheskogo Instituta

Nauchn Tr Permsk Gorn Inst — Nauchnye Trudy. Permskii Gornyi Institut

Nauchn Tr Permsk Gos Farm Inst — Nauchnye Trudy. Permskii Gosudarstvennyi Farmatsevticheskii Institut

Nauchn Tr Permsk Med Inst — Nauchnye Trudy Permskogo Meditsinskogo Instituta

Nauchn Tr Permsk Nauchno Issled Ugoln Inst — Nauchnye Trudy Permskii Nauchno Issledovatel'skii Ugol'nye Institut

Nauchn Tr Permsk Politekh Inst — Nauchnye Trudy Permskii Politekhnicheskii Institut

Nauchn Tr Poltav Skh Inst — Nauchnye Trudy Poltavskii Sel'skokhozyaistvennyi Institut

Nauchn Tr Primorsk S-Kh Inst — Nauchnye Trudy Primorskogo Sel'skokhozyaistvennogo Instituta

Nauchn Tr Ptitsevod Nauchno-Issled Inst Ptitsevod — Nauchnye Trudy Ptitsevodstvo Nauchno-Issledovatel'skii Institut Ptitsevodstva

Nauchn Tr Rizh Nauchno Issled Inst Travmatol Ortop — Nauchnye Trudy Rizhskii Nauchno-Issledovatel'skii Institut Travmatologii i Ortopedii

Nauchn Tr Rostov Na Donu Inzh Stroit Inst — Nauchnye Trudy Rostovskii-Na-Donu Inzhenerno-Stroitel'nyi Institut

Nauchn Tr Ryazan Med Inst — Nauchnye Trudy Ryazanskii Meditsinskii Institut

Nauchn Tr Ryazan Med Inst im Akad I P Pavlova — Nauchnye Trudy. Ryazanskii Meditsinskii Institut imeni Akademika I. P. Pavlova

Nauchn Tr Samark Gos Univ — Nauchnye Trudy Samarkandskogo Gosudarstvennogo Universiteta

Nauchn Tr Samark Koop Inst Tsentrosoyuza — Nauchnye Trudy Samarkandskogo Kooperativnogo Instituta Tsentrosoyuza

Nauchn Tr Samark Koop Inst Tsentrosoyuza im V V Kuibysheva — Nauchnye Trudy. Samarkandskogo Kooperativnyi Institut Tsentrosoyuza imeni V. Kuibysheva

Nauchn Tr Samark Med Inst — Nauchnye Trudy Samarkandskogo Meditsinskogo Instituta

Nauchn Tr Samark Skh Inst — Nauchnye Trudy Samarkandskii Sel'skokhozyaistvennyi Institut

Nauchn Tr Samark Univ — Nauchnye Trudy Samarkandskogo Universiteta

Nauchn Tr Sarat Inst Mekh Selsk Khoz — Nauchnye Trudy Saratovskogo Instituta Mekhanizatsii Sel'skogo Khozyaistva

Nauchn Tr Sarat Politekh Inst — Nauchnye Trudy Saratovskii Politekhnicheskii Institut

Nauchn Tr Sev-Zapadn Nauchno-Issled Inst Sel'sk Khoz — Nauchnye Trudy Severo-Zapadnogo Nauchno-Issledovatel'skogo Instituta Sel'skogoKhozyaistva

Nauchn Tr Sib Gos Nauchno Issled Proekt Inst Tsvet Metall — Nauchnye Trudy Sibirskii Gosudarstvennyi Nauchno-Issledovatel'skii i ProektnyiInstitut Tsvetnoi Metallurgii

Nauchn Tr Sib Gos Nauchno Issled Proektn Inst Tsvetn Metall — Nauchnye Trudy Sibirskii Gosudarstvennyi Nauchno-Issledovatel'skii i ProektnyiInstitut Tsvetnoi Metallurgii

Nauchn Tr Sib Nauchno Issled Inst Khim Selsk Khoz — Nauchnye Trudy. Sibirskii Nauchno-Issledovatel'skii Institut Khimizatsii Sel'skogo Khozyaistva

Nauchn Tr Sib Nauchno Issled Inst Selsk Khoz — Nauchnye Trudy Sibirskii Nauchno Issledovatel'skii Institut Sel'skogo Khozyaistva

Nauchn Tr Skh Akad Sofia Ser Rastenievod — Nauchnye Trudy. Sel'skokhozyaistvennaya Akademiya. Sofia. Seriya. Rastenievodstvo

Nauchn Tr Skh Inst Arm SSR — Nauchnye Trudy. Sel'skokhozyaistvennogo Instituta Armyanskoi SSR

Nauchn Tr Skh Inst Sofia Agron Fak — Nauchnye Trudy. Sel'skokhozyaistvennyi Institut. Sofia. Agronomicheskii Fakul'tet

Nauchn Tr S'kh Inst (Sofia) Agron Fak Ser Obshch Zemled — Nauchnye Trudy. Sel'skokhozyaistvennyi Institut (Sofia). Agronomicheskii Fakul'tet. Seriya Obshchee Zemledelie

Nauchn Tr Skh Inst Sofia Agron Fak Ser Rastenievod — Nauchnye Trudy. Sel'skokhozyaistvennyi Institut. Sofia. Agronomicheskii Fakultet. Seriya Rastenievodstrvo

Nauchn Tr Stavrop Gos Pedagog Inst — Nauchnye Trudy. Stavropol'skii Gosudarstvennyi Pedagogicheskii Institut

Nauchn Tr Stavrop S-Kh Inst — Nauchnye Trudy Stavropol'skogo Sel'skokhozyaistvennogo Instituta

Nauchn Tr Stud Gruz Skh Inst — Nauchnye Trudy Studentov Gruzinskii Sel'skokhozyaistvennyi Institut

Nauchn Tr Stud Gruz Ssk Inst — Nauchnye Trudy Studentov Gruzinskogo Sel'skokhozyaistvennogo Instituta

Nauchn Tr Sverdl Gos Pedagog Inst — Nauchnye Trudy Sverdlovskii Gosudarstvennyi Pedagogicheskii Institut

Nauchn Tr Tashk Gos Univ — Nauchnye Trudy Tashkentskogo Gosudarstvennogo Universiteta

Nauchn Tr Tashk Gos Univ Im V I Lenina — Nauchnye Trudy Tashkentskii Gosudarstvennyi Universitet Imeni V. I. Lenina

Nauchn Tr Tashk Inst Inzh Zheleznodorozhn Transp — Nauchnye Trudy. Tashkentskii Institut Inzhenerov Zheleznodorozhnogo Transporta

Nauchn Tr Tashk Politekh Inst — Nauchnye Trudy. Tashkentskii Politekhnicheskii Institut

Nauchn Tr Tashk Skh Inst — Nauchnye Trudy. Tashkentskii Sel'skokhozyaistvennyi Institut

Nauchn Tr Tashk Tekst Inst — Nauchnye Trudy Tashkentskogo Tekstil'nogo Instituta

Nauchn Tr Tsentr Inst Usoversh Vrachei — Nauchnye Trudy Tsentral'nogo Instituta Usovershenstovaniya Vrachei

Nauchn Tr Tsentr Nauchno Issled Inst Mekh Obrab Drev — Nauchnye Trudy Tsentral'nyi Nauchno Issledovatel'skii Institut Mekhanicheskoi Obrabotki Drevesiny

Nauchn Tr Tsentr Nauchno Issled Inst Morsk Flota — Nauchnye Trudy. Tsentral'nyi Nauchno-Issledovatel'skii Institut Morskogo Flota

Nauchn Tr Tsentr Nauchno-Issled Inst Olovyannoi Promsti — Nauchnye Trudy Tsentral'nyi Nauchno-Issledovatel'skii Institut Olovyannoi Promyshlennosti

Nauchn Tr Tsentr Nauchno Issled Inst Tsellyul Bum Promsti — Nauchnye Trudy Tsentral'nyi Nauchno-Issledovatel'skii Institut Tsellyuloznoi i Bumazhnoi Promyshlennosti

Nauchn Tr Tul Gorn Inst — Nauchnye Trudy Tul'skogo Gornogo Instituta

Nauchn Tr Tul Gos Pedagog Inst — Nauchnye Trudy Tulskogo Gosudarstvennogo Pedagogicheskogo Instituta

Nauchn Tr Tyumen Gos Univ — Nauchnye Trudy. Tyumenskii Gosudarstvennyi Universitet

Nauchn Tr Tyumen Ind Inst — Nauchnye Trudy. Tyumenskii Industrial'nyi Institut

Nauchn Tr Tyumen Skh Inst — Nauchnye Trudy Tyumenskogo Sel'skokhozyaistvennogo Instituta

Nauchn Tr Uch Prakt Vrachei Uzb — Nauchnye Trudy Uchenykh i Prakticheskikh Vrachei Uzbekistana

Nauchn Tr Ukr Inst Eksp Vet — Nauchnye Trudy Ukrainskii Instituta Eksperimental'noi Veterinarii

Nauchn Tr Ukr Inst Gidrotekh Melior — Nauchnye Trudy Ukrainskogo Instituta Gidrotekhniki i Melioratsii

Nauchn Tr Ukr Nauchno Issled Inst Eksp Vet — Nauchnye Trudy Ukrainskii Nauchno-Issledovatel'skii Institut Eksperimental'noi Veterinarii

Nauchn Tr Ukr Nauchno Issled Inst Fiziol Rast — Nauchnye Trudy Ukrainskii Nauchno-Issledovatel'skii Institut Fiziologii Rastenii

Nauchn Tr Ukr Nauchno Issled Inst Gig Tr Profzabol — Nauchnye Trudy Ukrainskii Nauchno-Issledovatel'skii Institut Gigieny Truda i Profzabolevanii

Nauchn Tr Ukr Nauchno Issled Inst Lesn Khoz Agrolesomelior — Nauchnye Trudy Ukrainskii Nauchno-Issledovatel'skogo. Instituta Lesnogo Khozyaistva i Agrolesomelioratsii

Nauchn Tr Ukr Nauchno Issled Inst Mekh Obrab Drev — Nauchnye Trudy Ukrainskii Nauchno-Issledovatel'skii Institut Mekhanicheskoi Obrabotki Drevesiny

Nauchn Tr Ukr Nauchno Issled Inst Pochvoved — Nauchnye Trudy Ukrainskii Nauchno-Issledovatel'skii Institut Pochvovedeniya

Nauchn Tr Ukr Nauchno Issled Inst Rastenievod Sel Genet — Nauchnye Trudy Ukrainskogo Nauchno-Issledovatel'skogo Instituta RastenievodstvaSelestsii i Genetiki

Nauchn Tr Ukr Nauchno Issled Inst Sadovod — Nauchnye Trudy Ukrainskii Nauchno-Issledovatel'skii Institut Sadovodstva

Nauchn Tr Ukr Nauchno Issled Inst Ugleobogashch — Nauchnye Trudy Ukrainskogo Nauchno-Issledovatel'skogo Instituta Ugleobogashcheniya

Nauchn Tr Ukr Nauchno Issled Inst Vinograd Vinodel — Nauchnye Trudy Ukrainskogo Nauchno-Issledovatel'skogo Instituta Vinogradarstva i Vinodeliya

Nauchn Tr Ukr Nauchno Issled Inst Zashch Rast — Nauchnye Trudy Ukrainskii Nauchno-Issledovatel'skii Institut Zashchity Rastenii

Nauchn Tr Ukr Nauchno Issled Stn Vinograd Osvo Peskov — Nauchnye Trudy Ukrainskoi Nauchno-Issledovatel'skoi Stantsii Vinogradarstva i Osvoeniya Peskov

Nauchn Tr Ukr Nauchno Issled Uglekhim Inst — Nauchnye Trudy. Ukrainskii Nauchno-Issledovatel'skii Uglekhimicheskii Institut

Nauchn Tr Ukr Skh Akad — Nauchnye Trudy Ukrainskaya Sel'skokhozyaistvennaya Akademiya

Nauchn Tr Ural Lesotekh Inst — Nauchnye Trudy Ural'skogo Lesotekhnicheskogo Instituta

Nauchn Tr USKhA — Nauchnye Trudy USKhA (Ukrains'ka Sil's'kohospodars'ka Akademiia)

Nauchn Tr Uzb Skh Inst — Nauchnye Trudy Uzbekskogo Sel'skokhozyaistvennogo Instituta

Nauchn Tr UzNIVI — Nauchnye Trudy UzNIVI

Nauchn Tr Vopr Pererab Kach Uglei — Nauchnye Trudy Voprosam Pererabotki i Kachestva Uglei

Nauchn Tr Voronezh Inzh Stroit Inst — Nauchnye Trudy Voronezhskii Inzhenerno-Stroitel'nyi Institut

Nauchn Tr Voronezh Lesotekh Inst — Nauchnye Trudy Voronezhskogo Lesotekhnicheskogo Instituta

Nauchn Tr Vost Nauchno Issled Uglekhim Inst — Nauchnye Trudy. Vostochnyi Nauchno-Issledovatel'skii Uglekhimicheskii Institut

Nauchn Tr Vrachei Magnitogorsk — Nauchnye Trudy Vrachei Magnitogorsk

Nauchn Tr Vses Nauchn Issled Inst Tsellyul Bum Promsti — Nauchnye Trudy Vsesoyuznogo Nauchno-Issledovatel'skogo Instituta Tsellyulozno-Bumazhnoi Promyshlennosti

Nauchn Tr Vses Nauchno Issled Inst Asbestovoi Promsti — Nauchnye Trudy. Vsesoyuznyi Nauchno-Issledovatel'skii Institut Asbestovoi Promyshlennosti

Nauchn Tr Vses Nauchno Issled Inst Farm — Nauchnye Trudy. Vsesoyuznyi Nauchno-Issledovatel'skii Institut Farmatsii

Nauchn Tr Vses Nauchno Issled Inst Gidrotekh Melior — Nauchnye Trudy. Vsesoyuznogo Nauchno-Issledovatel'skogo Instituta Gidrotekhnikii Melioratsii

Nauchn Tr Vses Nauchno Issled Inst Podzemn Gazif Uglei — Nauchnye Trudy Vsesoyuznyi Nauchno-Issledovatel'skii Institut Podzemnoi Gazifikatsii Uglei

Nauchn Tr Vses Nauchno Issled Inst Sakh Svekly — Nauchnye Trudy Vsesoyuznogo Nauchno-Issledovatel'skogo Instituta Sakharnoi Svekly

Nauchn Tr Vses Nauchno Issled Inst Sazhevoi Promsti — Nauchnye Trudy Vsesoyuznyi Nauchno-Issledovatel'skii Institut Sazhevoi Promyshlennosti

Nauchn Tr Vses Nauchno Issled Inst Skh Mashinostr — Nauchnye Trudy Vsesoyuznogo Nauchno-Issledovatel'skogo Instituta Sel'skokhozyaistvennogo Mashinostroeniya

Nauchn Tr Vses Nauchno Issled Inst Zernobobovykh Kult — Nauchnye Trudy Vsesoyuznyi Nauchno-Issledovatel'skii Institut Zernobobovykh Kul'tur

Nauchn Tr Vses Sel Genet Inst — Nauchnye Trudy Vsesoyuznogo Selektsionno Geneticheskogo Instituta

Nauchn Tr Vses Zaochn Mashinostroit Inst — Nauchnye Trudy Vsesoyuznyi Zaochnyi Mashinostroitel'nyi Institut

Nauchn Tr Vyssh Inst Zootekh Vet Med Zootekh Fak Stara Zagor — Nauchnye Trudy. Vysshii Institut Zootekhniki i Veterinarnoi Meditsiny. Zootekhnicheskii Fakul'tet-Stara Zagora

Nauchn Tr Vyssh Lesotekh Inst Sofiya Ser Lesn Khoz — Nauchnye Trudy. Vysshii Lesotekhnicheskii Institut. Sofiya. Seriya Lesnoe Khozyaistvo

Nauchn Tr Vyssh Lesotekh Inst Sofiya Ser Mekh Tekhnol Drev — Nauchnye Trudy. Vysshii Lesotekhnicheskii Institut. Sofiya. Seriya Mekhanicheskaya Tekhnologiya Drevesiny

Nauchn Tr Vyssh Lesotekh Inst Sofiya Ser Ozelenenie — Nauchnye Trudy. Vysshii Lesotekhnicheskii Institut. Sofiya. Seriya Ozelenenie

Nauchn Tr Vyssh Skh Inst Sofia Zootekh Fak — Nauchnye Trudy. Vysshii Sel'skokhozyaistvennyi Institut. Sofia. Zootekhnicheskii Fakul'tet

Nauchn Tr Vyssh Uchebn Zaved Lit SSR Biol — Nauchnye Trudy Vysshykh Uchebnykh Zavedenii Litovskoi SSR Biologiya

Nauchn Tr Vyssh Uchebn Zaved Lit SSR Elektrotekh Avtom — Nauchnye Trudy Vysshikh Uchebnykh Zavedenii Litovskoi SSR. Elektrotekhnika i Avtomatika

Nauchn Tr Vyssh Uchebn Zaved Lit SSR Elektrotekh Mekh — Nauchnye Trudy Vysshikh Uchebnykh Zavedenii Litovskoi SSR. Elektrotekhnika i Mekhanika

Nauchn Tr Vyssh Uchebn Zaved Lit SSR Geogr — Nauchnye Trudy Vysshikh Uchebnykh Zavedenii Litovskoi SSR. Geografiya

Nauchn Tr Vyssh Uchebn Zaved Lit SSR Geogr Geol — Nauchnye Trudy Vysshikh Uchebnykh Zavedenii Litovskoi SSR. Geografiya i Geologiya

Nauchn Tr Vyssh Uchebn Zaved Lit SSR Geol — Nauchnye Trudy Vysshikh Uchebnykh Zavedenii Litovskoi SSR. Geologiya

Nauchn Tr Vyssh Uchebn Zaved Lit SSR Khim Khim Tekhnol — Nauchnye Trudy. Vysshikh Uchebnykh Zavedenii Litovskoi SSR. Khimiya i Khimicheskaya Tekhnologiya

Nauchn Tr Vyssh Uchebn Zaved Lit SSR Med (Vilnius) — Nauchnye Trudy Vysshykh Uchebnykh Zavedenii Litovskoi SSR Meditsina (Vilnius)

Nauchn Tr Vyssh Uchebn Zaved Lit SSR Mekh — Nauchnye Trudy Vysshikh Uchebnykh Zavedenii Litovskoi SSR. Mekhanika

Nauchn Tr Vyssh Uchebn Zaved Lit SSR Mekh Tekhnol — Nauchnye Trudy. Vysshikh Uchebnykh Zavedenii Litovskoi SSR. Mekhanicheskaya Tekhnologiya

Nauchn Tr Vyssh Uchebn Zaved Lit SSR Stroit Arkhit — Nauchnye Trudy Vysshikh Uchebnykh Zavedenii Litovskoi SSR. Stroitel'stvo i Arkhitektura

Nauchn Tr Vyssh Uchebn Zaved Lit SSR Ultrazvuk — Nauchnye Trudy Vysshikh Uchebnykh Zavedenii Litovskoi SSR Ultrazvuk

Nauchn Tr Vyssh Uchebn Zaved Lit SSR Vibrotekh — Nauchnye Trudy Vysshikh Uchebnykh Zavedenii Litovskoi SSR Vibrotekhnika

Nauchn Tr Vyssh Vet Med Inst im Prof D ra G Pavlova — Nauchnye Trudy. Vysshii Veterinarno-Meditsinskii Institut imeni Prof. D-ra G. Pavlova

Nauchn Tr Zhitomir Skh Inst — Nauchnye Trudy Zhitomirskii Sel'skokhozyaistvennyi Institut

Nauchn Tr Zootekhnol Fak Zoovet Inst — Nauchnye Trudy Zootekhnologicheskogo Fakulteta Zooveterinarnogo Instituta

Nauchn Tr Zootekhnologicheskogo Inst — Nauchnye Trudy Zootekhnologicheskogo Instituta

Nauchn Vestn Univ Agrar Nauk Gedelle Vengriya — Nauchnyi Vestnik Universiteta Agrarnykh Nauk. Gedelle. Vengriya

Nauchnye Zap Dnepropetr Gos Univ — Nauchnye Zapiski Dnepropetrovskogo Gosudarstvennogo Universiteta

Nauchn Zap Belotserk Skh Inst — Nauchnye Zapiski Belotserkovskogo Sel'skokhozyaistvennogo Instituta

Nauchn Zap Cherk Gos Pedagog Inst — Nauchnye Zapiski. Cherkasskii Gosudarstvennyi Pedagogicheskii Institut

Nauchn Zap Chernovits Gos Med Inst — Nauchnye Zapiski Chernovitskii Gosudarstvennyi Meditsinskii Institut

Nauchn Zap Dermatol Venerol Vrachei Kubani — Nauchnye Zapiski po Dermatologii i Venerologii Vrachei Kubani

Nauchn Zap Dnepropetr Gos Univ — Nauchnye Zapiski Dnepropetrovskogo Gosudarstvennogo Universiteta

Nauchn Zap Donetsk Inst Sov Torg — Nauchnye Zapiski Donetskogo Instituta Sovetskoi Torgovli

Nauchn Zap Fiz Mat Fak Odess Gos Pedagog Inst — Nauchnye Zapiski Fiziko-Matematicheskogo Fakul'teta. Odesskii Gosudarstvennyi Pedagogicheskii Institut

Nauchn Zap Gos Eksp Inst Sakh Promsti — Nauchnye Zapiski Gosudarstvennogo Eksperimentnogo Instituta Sakharnoi Promyshlennosti

Nauchn Zap Gos Nauchno-Issled Proektn Inst Ugol'n Prom-Sti — Nauchnye Zapiski Gosudarstvennyi Nauchno-Issledovatel'skii i Proektnyi InstitutUgol'noi Promyshlennosti

Nauchn Zap Kafedr Mat Fiz Estestvozn Odess Gos Pedagog Inst — Nauchnye Zapiski Kafedr Matematiki. Fiziki i Estestvoznaniya. Odesskii Gosudarstvennyi Pedagogicheskii Institut

Nauchn Zap Khar'k Aviats Inst — Nauchnye Zapiski Khar'kovskogo Aviatsionnogo Instituta

Nauchn Zap Khar'k Inst Mekh Elektrif Sel'sk Khoz — Nauchnye Zapiski Khar'kovskii Institut Mekhanizatsii i Elektrifikatsii Sel'skogo Khozyaistva

Nauchn Zap Khar'k Inst Mekh Sel'sk Khoz — Nauchnye Zapiski Khar'kovskii Institut Mekhanizatsii Sel'skogo Khozyaistva

Nauchn Zap Khar'k Inst Mekh Sots Sel'sk Khoz — Nauchnye Zapiski Khar'kovskii Institut Mekhanizatsii Sotsialisticheskogo Sel'skogo Khozyaistva

Nauchn Zap Khar'k Poligr Inst — Nauchnye Zapiski Khar'kovskii Poligraficheskii Institut

Nauchn Zap Kherson Gos Pedagog Inst — Nauchnye Zapiski Khersonskogo Gosudarstvennogo Pedagogicheskogo Instituta

Nauchn Zap Kherson Skh Inst Im A D Tsiurupy — Nauchnye Zapiski Khersonskogo Sel'skokhozyaistvennogo Instituta Imeni A. D. Tsiurupy

Nauchn Zap Kiev Gos Univ — Nauchnye Zapiski. Kievskii Gosudarstvennyi Universitet

Nauchn Zap Lugansk Skh Inst — Nauchnye Zapiski Luganskogo Sel'skokhozyaistvennogo Instituta

Nauchn Zap Lvov Politekh Inst — Nauchnye Zapiski L'vovskogo Politekhnicheskogo Instituta

Nauchn Zap L'vov Skh Inst — Nauchnye Zapiski L'vovskogo Sel'skokhozyaistvennogo Instituta

Nauchn Zap L'vov Torg Ekon Inst — Nauchnye Zapiski L'vovskogo Torgovo Ekonomicheskogo Instituta

Nauchn Zap Mosk Gidromelior Inst — Nauchnye Zapiski Moskovskii Gidromeliorativnyi Institut

Nauchn Zap Nezhin Gos Pedagog Inst — Nauchnye Zapiske. Nezhinskii Gosudarstvennyi Pedagogicheskii Institut

Nauchn Zap Odess Gos Pedagog Inst — Nauchnye Zapiski. Odesskii Gosudarstvennyi Pedagogicheskii Institut

Nauchn Zap Odess Politekh Inst — Nauchnye Zapiski Odesskii Politekhnicheskii Institut

Nauchn Zap Sakh Promsti — Nauchnye Zapiski po Sakhnarnoi Promyshlennosti

Nauchn Zap Sakh Promsti Agron Vyp — Nauchnye Zapiski po Sakharnoi Promyshlennost Agronomicheskii Vypusk

Nauchn Zap Sakh Promsti Tekhnol Vyp — Nauchnye Zapiski po Sakharnoi Promyshlennosti Tekhnologicheskii Vypusk

Nauchn Zap Stalinskogo Inst Sov Torg — Nauchnye Zapiski Stalinskogo Instituta Sovetskoi Torgovli

Nauchn Zap Ukr Poligr Inst — Nauchnye Zapiski Ukrainskii Poligraficheskii Institut

Nauchn Zap Uzhgorod Gos Univ — Nauchnye Zapiski Uzhgorodskogo Gosudarstvennogo Universiteta

Nauchn Zap Voronezh Lesokhim Inst — Nauchnye Zapiski Voronezhskogo Lesokhimicheskogo Instituta

Nauchn Zap Voronezh Lesotekh Inst — Nauchnye Zapiski Voronezhskogo Lesotekhnicheskogo Instituta

Nauchn Zap Voronezh Otd Geogr Ova SSSR — Nauchnye Zapiski Voronezhskogo Otdela Geograficheskogo Obshchestva SSSR

Nauchn Zap Voronezh Otd Vses Bot Ova — Nauchnye Zapiski Voronezhskogo Otdeleniya Vsesoyuznogo Botanicheskogo Obshchestva

Nauchn Zap Voroshilovgr Skh Inst — Nauchnye Zapiski Voroshilovgradskogo Sel'skokhozyaistvennogo Instituta

Nauchn Zh Politekh Inst Tun Tsei — Nauchnye Zhurnal Politekhnicheskogo Instituta Tun-Tsei

Nauchn Zh Sev Zapadn Skh Inst — Nauchnyi Zhurnal. Severo-Zapadnogo Sel'skokhozyaistvennogo Instituta

Nauch Soobshch Inst Fiziol Pavlov — Nauchnye Soobshcheniya Institut Fiziologii Imeni I. P. Pavlova

Nauch-Tekh Inf — Nauchno-Tekhnicheskaya Informatsiya

Nauch Tr Dobrudzhan Selskostop Nauchnoizsled Inst — Nauchni Trudove na Dobrudzhanskiya Selskostopanski Nauchnoizsledovatelski Institut

Nauch Tr Poltav Nauch-Issled Inst Svinovod — Nauchnye Trudy Poltavskii Nauchno-Issledovatel'skii Institut Svinovodstva

Nauch Trudy — Nauchnye Trudy

Nauch Trudy Altaisk Nauchno-Issled Inst Sel Khoz — Nauchnye Trudy Altaiskogo Nauchno-Issledovatel'skogo Instituta Sel'skogo Khozyaistva

Nauch Trudy Kuibyshev Gos Pedagog Inst Zhivot Povolzh'ya — Nauchnye Trudy Kuibyshevskii Gosudarstvennyi Pedagogicheskii Institut ZhivotnyePovolzh'ya

Nauch Trudy Kuibyshevskii Gos Ped Inst — Nauchnye Trudy Kuibyshevskii Gosudarstvennyi Pedagogicheskii Institut Imeni V.V. Kuibysheva

Nauch Trudy Nauchno-Issled Inst Pchel — Nauchnye Trudy Nauchno-Issledovatel'skii Institut Pchelovodstva

Nauch Trudy Stavropol Sek'Khoz Inst — Nauchnye Trudy Stavropol'skogo Sel'Skokhozyaistvennogo Instituta

Nauch Trudy Ukr Nauchno-Issled Inst Les Khoz Agrolesomelior — Nauchnye Trudy Ukrainskogo Nauchno-Issledovatel'skogo Instituta Lesnogo Khozyaistva i Agrolesomelioratsii

Nauch Trudy Ukr Nauchno-Issled Inst Pochv — Nauchnye Trudy Ukrainskogo Nauchno-Issledovatel'skogo Instituta Pochvovedeniya

Nauch Trudy Ukr Sel'Khoz Akad — Nauchnye Trudy Ukrainskoi Sel'Skokhozyaistvennoi Akademii

Nauch Trudy Voronezh Sel'Khoz Inst — Nauchnye Trudy Voronezhskii Sel'skokhozyaistvennyi

Nauch Tr Veselopodol Opyt-Selek Sta — Nauchnye Trudy Veselopodolyanskoi Opytno-Selektsionnoi Stantsii

Nauch Tr Vissh Selskostop Inst "Georgi Dimitrov" Agron Fak — Nauchni Trudove. Vissh Selskostopanski Institut "Georgi Dimitrov." Agronomicheski Fakultet

Nauch Tr Vissh Selskostop Inst "Georgi Dimitrov" Zootekh Fak — Nauchni Trudove. Vissh Selskostopanski Institut "Georgi Dimitrov" (Sofia). Zootekhnicheski Fakultet

Nauch Tr Vissh Selskostop Inst "Vasil Kolarov" — Nauchni Trudove. Vissh Selskostopanski Institut "Vasil Kolarov"

Naucn Obozr Bitner — Naucnoe Obozrenie. Ezenedel'nyi Naucnyj Zurnal (V.V. Bitner, Editor)

Naucno-Teh Pregl — Naucno-Tehnicki Pregled

Naucn Tr Mosk Nauchno-Issled Inst Vaktsin Syvorotok — Nauchnye Trudy Moskovskogo Nauchno-Issledovatel'skogo Instituta Vaktsin i Syvorotok

Nauc Trud Lesoteh Inst (Ser Gorsko Stop) — Naucni Trudove Vissh Lesotehniceski Institut (Serija Gorsko Stopanstvo)

Nauc Trud Lesoteh Inst (Ser Meh Tehn Darv) — Naucnye Trudove Vissh Lesotehniceski Institut (Serija Mehanicna Tehnologija na Darvesinata)

Nauc Trudy Kursk Pedag Inst — Naucnye Trudy Kurskogo Pedagogiceskogo Instituta

Nauc Trudy Leningr Lesoteh Akad — Naucnye Trudy Leningradskaja Ordena Lenina Lesotehniceskja Akademija Imeni S. M. Kirova

Nauc Trudy (Novosib Gos Pedag Inst) — Naucnye Trudy (Novosibirskij Gosudarstvennyj Pedagogiceskij Institut)

Nauc Trudy Novosib Pedag Inst — Naucnye Trudy Novosibirskogo Pedagogiceskogo Instituta

Nauc Trudy Saratov Politehn Inst — Naucnye Trudy Saratovskogo Politehniceskogo Instituta

Nauc Trudy Sverdlovsk Pedag Inst — Naucnye Trudy Sverdlovskogo Pedagogiceskogo Instituta

Nauc Trudy Sverdlovsk Pedag Inst Sociol Probl — Naucnye Trudy Sverdlovskogo Pedagogiceskogo Instituta. Sociologiceskogo Problemi

Nauc Trudy (Taskent Pedag Inst) — Naucnye Trudy (Taskentskij Pedagogiceskij Institut)

Nauc Trudy Taskent Univ — Naucnye Trudy Taskentskogo Universiteta

Nauc Trudy Tjumensk Univ — Naucnye Trudy Tjumenskogo Universiteta

Nauc Trudy Vyss Uceb Zaved Litov SSR — Naucnye Trudy Vyssyh Ucebnyh Zavedennij Litovskoj SSR

Nauc Upravl Obsc — Naucnye Upravlenie Obscestva

Nauheimer Fortbild-Lehrgaenge — Nauheimer Fortbildungs-Lehrgaenge

NAUI News — NAUI (National Association of Underwater Instructors) News

NAUJA — Nagpur University. Journal

Nauk & Inf — Naukovedenie i Informatika

Nauka Pered Opyt Sel'Khoz — Nauka i Peredovoi Opyt v Sel'skom Khozyaistve

Nauka Peredovoi Opyt Sel'sk Khoz — Nauka i Peredovoi Opyt v Sel'skom Khozyaistve

Nauka Pol — Nauka Polska

Nauka Proizvod (Tiflis) — Nauka Proizvodstvu (Tiflis)

Nauka Selsk Khoz — Nauka Sel'skomu Khozyaistvu

Nauka Skh Proizvod — Nauka Sel'skohozyaistvennomu Proizvodstvu

Nauka Teh Bezb — Nauka Tehnika Bezbednost

Nauka Tekh Gor Khoz — Nauka i Tekhnika v Gorodskom Khozyaistve

Nauka Tekh (Leningrad) — Nauka i Tekhnika (Leningrad)

Nauka Tekh Riga — Nauka i Tekhnika (Riga)

Nauka Zemi Ser Geol — Nauka o Zemi. Seria Geologica

Nauka Zhivotnovod — Nauka Zhivotnovodstvu

Nauki Tech Mech Czestochowa Pol — Nauki Techniczne. Mechanika (Czestochowa, Poland)

Naukoved Inf — Naukovedenie i Informatika

Nauk Pr Aspir Ukr Akad Sil's'kogospod Nauk — Naukovi Pratsi Aspirantiv Ukrains'ka Akademiya Sil's'kogospodars'kikh Nauk

Nauk Pratsi Ukr Sil-Hospod Akad — Naukovi Pratsi Ukrayins'ka Sil's'kohospodars'ka Akademiya

Nauk Pr Inst Entomol Fitopatol Akad Nauk Ukr RSR — Naukovi Pratsi Institut Entomologii ta Fitopatologii Akademii Nauk Ukrains'koiRSR

Nauk Pr Inst Livarnogo Virobnitstva Akad Nauk Ukr RSR — Naukovi Pratsi Institutu Livarnogo Virobnitstva Akademiya Nauk Ukrains'koi RSR

Nauk Pr Kamenets Podol'sk Sil's'kogospod Inst — Naukovi Pratsi Kamenets-Podol'skii Sil's'kogospodars'kii Institut

Nauk Pr Khark Inst Inzh Kommunaln Budiv — Naukovi Pratsi. Kharkivs'kii Institut Inzheneriv Kommunal'nogo Budivnitstva

Nauk Pr Khark Sil's'kogospod Inst — Naukovi Pratsi Kharkivs'kii Sil's'kogospodars'kii Institut

Nauk Pr Kiiv Vet Inst — Naukovi Pratsi Kiivs'kogo Veterinarnogo Institutu

Nauk Pr L'viv Sil's'kogospod Inst — Naukovi Pratsi L'vivs'kii Sil's'kogospodars'kii Institut

Nauk Pr L'viv Zootekh Vet Inst — Naukovi Pratsi L'vivs'kii Zootekhnichno-Veterinarnii Institut

Nauk Pr L'viv Zoovet Inst — Naukovi Pratsi L'vivs'kii Zooveterinarnii Institut

Nauk Pr Nauchn Tr Derzh Sil's'kohospod Dosl Stn — Naukovi Pratsi Nauchnye Trudy Derzhavna Sil's'kohospodars'ka Doslidna Stantsiya

Nauk Pr Poltav Sil's'kogospod Inst — Naukovi Pratsi Poltavs'kogo Sil's'kogospodars'skogo Institutu

Nauk Pr Sums'ka Derzh Sil's'kogospod Dosl Stn — Naukovi Pratsi. Sums'ka Derzhavna Sil's'kogospodars'ka Doslidna Stantsiya

Nauk Pr Ukr Inst Eksp Vet — Naukovi Pratsi Ukrains'kii Institut Eksperimental'noi Veterinarii

Nauk Pr Ukr Nauk Dosl Inst Eksp Vet — Naukovi Pratsi Ukrains'kii Naukovo-Doslidnii Institut Eksperimental'noi Veterinarii

Nauk Pr Ukr Nauk Dosl Inst Fiziol Rosl — Naukovi Pratsi Ukrains'kii Naukovo-Doslidnii Institut Fiziologii Roslin

Nauk Pr Ukr Nauk Dosl Inst Sadivn — Naukovi Pratsi Ukrains'kii Naukovo-Doslidnii Institut Sadivnitstva

Nauk Pr Ukr Nauk Dosl Inst Zakhistu Rosl — Naukovi Pratsi Ukrains'kii Naukovo-Doslidnii Institut Zakhistu Roslin

Nauk Pr Ukr Nauk Dosl Inst Zemlerob — Naukovi Pratsi Ukrainskii Naukovo-Doslidnoi Institut Zemlerobstva

Nauk Pr Ukr Sil'kohospod Akad — Naukovi Pratse Ukrayins'ka Sil's'kohospodars'ka Akademiya

Nauk Pr USGA — Naukovi Pratsi USGA

Nauk Pr Vet Fak L'viv Zoovet Inst — Naukovi Pratsi Veterinarnogo Fakul'tetu L'vivs'kii Zooveterinarnii Institut

Nauk Pr Vet Fak Ukr Sil's'kohospod Akad — Naukovi Pratsi Veterynarnoho Fakul'tetu Ukrayins'koyi Sil's'kohospodars'koyi Akademii

Nauk Pr Volyn Derzh Sil's'kohospód Doslid Sta — Naukovi Pratsi Volyns'ka Derzhavna Sil's'kohospodars'ka Doslidna Stantsiya

Nauk Pr Zhitomir Silskogospod Inst — Naukovi Pratsi Zhitomirs'kogo Sil's'kogospodars'kogo Institutu

Nauk Pr Zhytomyr Sil's'kohospod Inst — Naukovi Pratsi Zhytomyrs'koho Sil's'kohospodars'koho Instytutu

Nauk Pr Zootekh Fak Kamenets Podol'sk Sil's'kogospod Inst — Naukovi Pratsi Zootekhnichnogo Fakul'tetu Kamenets-Podol'skii Sil's'kogospodars'kii Institut

Nauk Shchorichnik Kiiv Derzh Univ Im T G Shevchenka — Naukovii Shchorichnik. Kiivs'kii Derzhavnii Universitet Imeni T. G. Shevchenka

Nauk-Tekh Visn — Naukovo-Tekhnichnii Visnik

Nauk Tov im Shevchenka Khem Biol Med Sekts Proc — Naukove Tovaristvo imeni Shevchenka. Khemichno-Biologichna-Medichna Sektsiya. Proceedings

Nauk Za L'viv Derzh Pedagog Inst — Naukovi Zapysky L'vivs'koho Derzhavnoho Pedagogichnoho Instytutu

Nauk Zap Cherk Derzh Pedagog Inst — Naukovi Zapysky Cherkas'koho Derzhavnoho Pedagogichnoho Instytutu

Nauk Zap Chernivets Derzh Univ — Naukovi Zapiski. Chernivets'kii Derzhavnii Universitet

Nauk Zap Dnepropetr Derzh Univ — Naukovi Zapiski Dnepropetrovs'kii Derzhavnii Universitet

Nauk Zap Ivano Frankivs'kii Derzh Med Inst — Naukovi Zapiski Ivano-Frankivs'kii Derzhavnii Medichnii Institut

Nauk Zap Katerinosl Nauk Dosl Katedri Khem — Naukovi Zapiski Katerinoslavs'koi Naukovo-Doslidchoi Katedri Khemii

Nauk Zap Kherson Derzh Pedagog Inst — Naukovi Zapiski Khersons'kogo Derzhavnogo Pedagogichnogo Instituta

Nauk Zap Kiiv Derzh Univ — Naukovi Zapiski Kiivs'kii Derzhavnii Universitet

Nauk Zap Kiiv Derzh Univ Pr Bot Sadu — Naukovi Zapiski Kiivs'kii Derzhavnii Universitet Pratsi Botanichniy Sadu

Nauk Zap Kiiv Vet Inst — Naukovi Zapiski Kiivs'kogo Veterinarnogo Institutu

Nauk Zap Krivoriz Derzh Pedagog Inst — Naukovi Zapiski Krivoriz'kogo Derzhavnogo Pedagogichnogo Instituta

Nauk Zap Kyjivsk Derzhavn Univ Sevcenka — Naukovi Zapysky. Kyjivs'kyj Derzavnyj Universytet imeny T.G. Sevcenka. BulletinScientifique. Universite d'Etat de Kiev

Nauk Zap L'viv Derzh Pedagog Inst — Naukovi Zapysky L'vivs'koho Derzhavnoho Pedagogichnoho Instytutu

Nauk Zap Lviv Derzh Univ Khim Zb — Naukovi Zapiski. L'vivs'kii Derzhavnii Universitet. Khimichnii Zbirnik

Nauk Zap L'viv Derzh Univ Ser Biol — Naukovi Zapiski L'vivs'kii Derzhavnii Universitet Seriya Biologichna

Nauk Zap L'viv Derzh Univ Ser Fiz Mat — Naukovi Zapiski L'vivs'kii Derzhavnii Universitet Seriya Fiziko-Matematichna

Nauk Zap L'viv Derzh Univ Ser Geol — Naukovi Zapiski L'vivs'kii Derzhavnii Universitet Seriya Geologichna

Nauk Zap Lviv Derzh Univ Ser Khim — Naukovi Zapiski. L'vivs'kii Derzhavnii Universitet. Seriya Khimichna

Nauk Zap Lviv Politekh Inst — Naukovi Zapiski. L'vivs'kii Politekhnichnii Institut

Nauk Zap Lviv Silskogospod Inst — Naukovi Zapiski L'vivs'kogo Sil's'kogospodars'kogo Institutu

Nauk Zap L'viv Torg Ekon Inst — Naukovi Zapiski L'vivs'kogo Torgovo-Ekonomichnogo Institutu

Nauk Zap Nizhin Derzh Pedagog Inst — Naukovi Zapiski Nizhins'kii Derzhavnii Pedagogichnii Institut

Nauk Zap Nizhyns'koho Derzh Pedagog Inst — Naukovi Zapysky Nizhyns'koho Derzhavnoho Pedagogichnoho Institutu

Nauk Zap Odes Biol Stn Akad Nauk Ukr RSR — Naukovi Zapiski Odes'koi Biologichnoi Stantsii Akademiya Nauk Ukrains'koi RSR

Nauk Zap Odes Derzh Pedagog Inst — Naukovi Zapiski Odes'kii Derzhavnii Pedagogichnii Institut

Nauk Zap Odes Politekh Inst — Naukovi Zapiski Odes'kii Politekhnichnii Institut

Nauk Zap Stanisl Derzh Med Inst — Naukovi Zapiski Stanislavs'kii Derzhavnii Medichnii Institut

Nauk Zap Sumskogo Derzh Pedagog Inst — Naukovi Zapiski Sumskogo Derzhavnego Pedagogicheskogo Instituta

Nauk Zap Tsukrovoi Promsti — Naukovi Zapiski z Tsukrovoi Promislovosti

Nauk Zap Ukr Biokhem Inst — Naukovi Zapiski Ukrains'kogo Biokhemichnogo Instituta

Nauk Zap Ukr Poligr Inst — Naukovi Zapiski Ukrains'kii Poligrafichnii Institut

Nauk Zap Ukr Tekh Gospod Inst (Munich) — Naukovi Zapiski Ukrains'kii Tekhnichno-Gospodars'kii Institut (Munich)

Nauk Zap Uzhgorod Derzh Univ — Naukovi Zapiski Uzhgorods'kogo Derzhavnogo Universitetu

Nauk Zap Uzhorod Derzh Univ — Naukovi Zapysky Uzhorods'koho Derzhavnoho Universytetu

Nauk Zap Zhitomir Silskogospod Inst — Naukovi Zapiski Zhitomirs'kogo Sil's'kogospodars'kogo Institutu

Naunyn Schmied Arch Pharmacol — Naunyn Schmiedeberg's Archives of Pharmacology

Naunyn-Schmiedebergs Arch Exp Pathol Pharmakol — Naunyn-Schmiedebergs Archiv fuer Experimentelle Pathologie und Pharmakologie

Naunyn-Schmiedebergs Arch Exp Path Pharmak — Naunyn-Schmiedebergs Archiv fuer Experimentelle Pathologie und Pharmakologie

Naunyn-Schmiedebergs Arch Pharmacol — Naunyn-Schmiedeberg's Archives of Pharmacology

Naunyn-Schmiedebergs Arch Pharmakol — Naunyn-Schmiedebergs Archiv fuer Pharmakologie [*Formerly, Naunyn-Schmiedebergs Archiv fuer Pharmakologie und Experimentelle Pathologie*]

Naunyn-Schmiedebergs Arch Pharmakol Exp Pathol — Naunyn-Schmiedebergs Archiv fuer Pharmakologie und Experimentelle Pathologie [*Later, Naunyn-Schmiedebergs Archiv fuer Pharmakologie*]

N Aust M — North Australian Monthly

N Aust Res Bull — North Australia Research Bulletin

Naut — Nautilus

Nau Tekh Inf Ser 1 — Nauchno-Tekhnicheskaya Informatsiya. Seriya 1. Organizatsiya i Metodika Informatsionnoi Raboty

Nau-T Inf 1 — Nauchno-Tekhnicheskaya Informatsiya. Seriya 1. Organizatsiya i Metodika Informatsionnye Raboty

Nau-T Inf 2 — Nauchno-Tekhnicheskaya Informatsiya. Seriya 2. Informatsionnye Protessy i Sistemy

Naut M — Nautical Magazine

Nav — Navorscher

NAV — Neues aus Alt-Villach

NAV — Nouvelles Annales des Voyages

NAV — Nuovo Archivio Veneto

Nav Abstr — Naval Abstracts

NAVAIRNEWS — Naval Aviation News

Navajo Rptr — Navajo Reporter

Navajo Trib Code — Navajo Tribal Code

Naval Eng J — Naval Engineers' Journal

Naval Engr J — Naval Engineers Journal

Naval Engrs J — American Society of Naval Engineers. Journal

Naval F — Naval Forces

Naval Res Logist — Naval Research Logistics

Naval Res Logist Quart — Naval Research Logistics. Quarterly

Naval Res Log Quart — Naval Research Logistics. Quarterly

Naval Stores R — Naval Stores Review

Naval Stores Rev — Naval Stores Review

Naval War College R — Naval War College. Review

Nav Archit — Naval Architect

Nav Av Nws — Naval Aviation News

NA Ven — Archivio Veneto

Nav Eng J — Naval Engineers' Journal

Navig — Navigation

Navig Int — Navigation Interieure

Navitecnia Comer Marit — Navitecnia y Comercio Maritimo

Navitecnia Mot Mar — Navitecnia y Motores Marinos

Navl Eng J — Naval Engineers' Journal

Nav M — Naval Magazine

NAVMAG — Naval Magazine

Nav Ocean Syst Cent Tech Doc US — Naval Ocean Systems Center. Technical Document (United States)

Nav Ordnance Lab Symp Ammonia Batteries — Naval Ordnance Laboratory Symposium on Ammonia Batteries

Navorsinge Nas Mus (Bloemfontein) — Navorsinge van die Nasionale Museum (Bloemfontein)

Navorsingsversl Wet Nywerheidnavorsingsraad (S Afr) — Navorsingsverslag. Wetenskaplike en Nywerheidnavorsingsraad (South Africa)

Navors Nas Mus (Bloemfontein) — Navorsinge van die Nasionale Museum (Bloemfontein)

Nav Reserv — Naval Reservist

Nav Res Lab Memo Rep US — Naval Research Laboratory Memorandum Report (United States)

Nav Res Log — Naval Research Logistics. Quarterly

Nav Res Logist — Naval Research Logistics

Nav Res Logistics Q — Naval Research Logistics. Quarterly

Nav Res Logist Q — Naval Research Logistics. Quarterly

Nav Res Rev — Naval Research Reviews

Nav Stores Rev — Naval Stores Review

Nav Train Bull — Naval Training Bulletin

Nav War Col Rev — Naval War College. Review

Navy Dep RAN Rep — Department of the Navy. RAN [*Royal Australian Navy*] Reports

Navy Intnl — Navy International

Navy League J — Navy League Journal

Navy Med — Navy Medicine

Navy News — Navy News and Undersea Technology

Navy Rec Soc Publ — Navy Records Society. Publications

Navy Tech F S — Navy Technology Transfer Fact Sheet

NAWDAC Journal — National Association for Women Deans, Administrators, and Counselors. Journal

NAWG — Nachrichten. Akademie der Wissenschaften zu Goettingen. Philologisch-Historische Klasse

NAWGott — Nachrichten. Akademie der Wissenschaften zu Goettingen

NAZ — Neueste Auslaendische Zeitschriften

NAZ — Norddeutsche Allgemeine Zeitung

Nazemn Vodn Ekosist — Nazemnye i Vodnye Ekosistemy

NB — Nachrichtenblatt. Deutscher Verein vom Heiligen Lande

NB — Namm och Bygd

NB — Namn og Bygd

NB — Nationalbibliothek

NB — Neues Beginnen. Zeitschrift der Arbeiterwohlfahrt

NB — New Brunswick Reports

NB — Niels Bohr. Collected Works

NB — Nihon Bukkyo

NB — Notebooks for Knossos

NB 2d — New Brunswick Reports, Second Series

NBA — Bach, Johann Sebastian. Neue Ausgabe Saemtlicher Werke

NBA — National Bank. Monthly Summary

NBAC — Nuovo Bulletino di Archeologia Cristiana

NB Acts — Acts of New Brunswick

NBAE — Nouvelle Bibliotheque des Auteurs Ecclesiastiques

N B Arch Christ — Nuova Bulletino di Archeologia Cristiana

NBATS — Neue Beitraege von Alten und Neuen Theologischen Sachen

N Bay Ms — Niederbayerische Monatsschrift

NBB — Central Bank of Libya. Economic Bulletin

NBB — Neue Beitraege zur Bausparmathematik

NBB — Norsk Bibliografisk Bibliotek

NBBMAN — Neurobiology

NBC — Babylonian Inscriptions in the Collection of James B. Nies. Yale University

NBC — Nelson's Bible Commentary

NBD — Nuntiaturbericht aus Deutschland

NB Dep Nat Resour Miner Resour Branch Rep Invest — New Brunswick. Department of Natural Resources. Mineral Resources Branch. Report of Investigation

NB Dep Nat Resour Miner Resour Branch Top Rep — New Brunswick. Department of Natural Resources. Mineral Resources Branch. Topical Report

NB Dep Nat Resour Repr — New Brunswick. Department of Natural Resources. Reprint

NB Dict — New Bible Dictionary

NBE — National Bank of Egypt. Economic Bulletin

NBEA Y — National Business Education Association. Yearbook

NBEF — Nova Bibliotheca Ecclesistica Friburgensis

NBER Gen S — National Bureau of Economic Research. General Studies

N Bergm J — Neues Bergmaennisches Journal

NBER Oc P — National Bureau of Economic Research. Occasional Papers

NBFU Res Rep — NBFU [*National Board of Fire Underwriters*] Research Report

NBG — Nouvelle Biographie Generale

Nbg Forsch — Nuernberger Forschungen

NBGPL — Nederlandsche Bijdragen op het Gebied van Germaansche Philologie en Linguistiek

NBGSA — Nippon Butsuri Gakkaishi

NB His S — New Brunswick Historical Society. Collections

NBHPB — Neuroscience and Behavioral Physiology

NBI — Neue Berliner Illustrierte

N Bibl Classique — Nouvelle Bibliotheque Classique

N Biblioth Classique — Nouvelle Bibliotheque Classique

N Biblioth Litt — Nouvelle Bibliotheque Litteraire

N Bibl Ital — Nuova Biblioteca Italiana

N Bibl Litt — Nouvelle Bibliotheque Litteraire

NBIC — News from Behind the Iron Curtain

NBIE — National Burn Information Exchange

NBIL — National Bibliography of Indian Literature

NBJ — National Bar Journal

NBJ — Noord Brabant

NB Jb — Neues Beethoven Jahrbuch

NBK — Niederdeutsche Beitraege zur Kunstgeschichte

Nb L — Nebraska Law Review

NBL — Neue Badener Landeszeitung

NBL — Neue Beitraege zur Literaturwissenschaft

N Bl — New Blackfriars

NBL — Norsk Biografisk Leksikon

NBLB — Nebraska Law Bulletin

Nb LR — Nebraska Law Review

N Bl Sch H Sch W — Nachrichtenblatt fuer das Schleswig-Holsteinische Schulwesen

NBLU — Naucnyj Bjulletin Leningradskogo Universiteta

NB Lub — Nova Bibliotheca Lubecensis

NblVED — Notizblatt des Vereins fuer Erdkunde, Darmstadt
NB Lwss — Neue Beitraege zur Literaturwissenschaft
NB Miner Resour Branch Inf Circ — New Brunswick. Mineral Resources Branch. Information Circular
NB Miner Resour Branch Rep Invest — New Brunswick. Mineral Resources Branch. Report of Investigations
NB Miner Resour Branch Top Rep — New Brunswick. Mineral Resources Branch. Topical Report
NB Mines Branch Inf Circ — New Brunswick. Mines Branch. Information Circular
NB Mus Monogr Ser — New Brunswick Museum. Monographic Series
NBNA Newsl — National Black Nurses Association. Newsletter
NBNZAK — Notas Biologicas. Facultad de Ciencias Exactas, Fisicas, y Naturales. Universidad Nacional del Nordeste. Corrientes Zoologia
NBO — Boekblad
NBP — Notes Biospeologiques (Paris)
NBP — Wonen. Vakblad voor de Woninginrichting
NBR — National Business Review
NBR — Nederlandsche Bank NV. Kwartaalbericht
NBR — New Boston Review
NBR — New Brunswick Reports
NBR 2d — New Brunswick Reports, Second Series
NB Rep — New Brunswick Reports
NB Res Prod Counc Res Note — New Brunswick. Research and Productivity Council. Research Note
NBRI Spec Rep BOU — NBRI (National Building Research Council. South Africa) Special Report BOU
N Bruns — New Brunswick Reports
N Brunsw NH S Bll — Bulletin of the Natural History Society of New Brunswick
NBS — National Bank Monthly Summary
NBS — NBS [*National Bureau of Standards*] Update
NBS — Nuntiaturberichte aus der Schweiz
NBS Annu Rep — NBS (US National Bureau of Standards) Annual Report
NBS Build Sci Ser — National Bureau of Standards. Building Science Series
NBS Handb US — NBS (National Bureau of Standards) Handbook (United States)
NBSMA — National Bureau of Standards. Monographs
NBS Monogr — National Bureau of Standards. Monographs
NBSPN — Nummus. Boletim da Sociedade Portuguesa de Numismatica
NBS Spec Publ — National Bureau of Standards. Special Publication
NBS Tech News Bull — National Bureau of Standards. Technical News Bulletin
NBS Tech Note (US) — NBS [*National Bureau of Standards*] Technical Note (United States)
NBS TN — United States Department of Commerce. National Bureau of Standards. Technical Notes
NBT — Nederlands Bosbouw Tijdschrift Orgaan voor Bosbouw en Landschapsbouw
NBT — Neues Berner Taschenbuch
N Bull Arch Christ — Nuova Bulletino di Archeologia Cristiana
NBW — NABW [*National Association of Bank Women*] Journal
NBW — Nation's Business (Washington, DC)
NBW — Neue Betriebswirtschaft
NBW — Nieuw Burgerlijk Wetboek
NBZ — New Braunfelser Zeitung
NC — Necrocorinthia
NC — New Cambodge
NC — New Criterion
NC — News Chronicle
NC — Nigeria and the Classics
NC — Nineteenth Century
NC — Nineteenth Century and After
NC — Nineteenth Century Music
NC — North Carolina Reports
NC — Noticias Culturales
NC — Nouvelle Clio
NC — Nouvelle Critique
NC — Numismatic Chronicle and Journal
NC — Nuova Corrente
NCA — Nineteenth Century and After
NCA — Nudos (Argentina)
NCA Am Soc Mech Eng — NCA (Noise Control and Acoustics). American Society of Mechanical Engineers
NCAB — National Cyclopaedia of American Biography
NC Admin Code — North Carolina Administrative Code
NC Adv Legis — Advance Legislative Service to the General Statutes of North Carolina
NC Ag Exp — North Carolina. Agricultural Experiment Station. Publications
NC Agric Exp Stn Bull — North Carolina. Agricultural Experiment Station. Bulletin
NC Agric Exp Stn Tech Bull — North Carolina. Agricultural Experiment Station. Technical Bulletin
NC Agric Ext Serv Ext Circ — North Carolina. Agricultural Extension Service. Extension Circular
NC Agric Ext Serv Ext Folder — North Carolina. Agricultural Extension Service. Extension Folder
NC Agric Ext Serv Leafl — North Carolina. Agricultural Extension Service. Leaflet
NC Agric Res Serv Bull — North Carolina. Agricultural Research Service. Bulletin
NC Agric Res Serv Tech Bull — North Carolina. Agricultural Research Service. Technical Bulletin
NC Agr Statist — North Carolina Agricultural Statistics
N Calif Mon — Northern California Monthly
NCan — Nouveau Candide
NC App — North Carolina Court of Appeals Reports
N Car Central LJ — North Carolina Central Law Journal
NC Arch — North Carolina Architect
NCarF — North Carolina Folklore
N Carol Dent Gaz — North Carolina Dental Gazette
N Carolina Lib — North Carolina Libraries
NCAR Q — National Center for Atmospheric Research. Quarterly

NCASI Atm Poll Tech Bull — National Council of the Paper Industry for Air and Stream Improvement. Atmospheric Pollution Technical Bulletin
NCASI Monthly Bull — National Council of the Paper Industry for Air and Stream Improvement. Monthly Bulletin
NCASI Regul Rev — National Council of the Paper Industry for Air and Stream Improvement. Regulatory Review
NCASI Spec Rep — NCASI [*National Council of the Paper Industry for Air and Stream Improvement*] Special Report
NCASI Tech Bull — National Council of the Paper Industry for Air and Stream Improvement. Technical Bulletin
NCASI Tech Bull Atmos Qual Improv Tech Bull — National Council of the Paper Industry for Air and Stream Improvement. Technical Bulletin. Atmospheric Quality Improvement. Technical Bulletin
NCASI Tech Rev — National Council of the Paper Industry for Air and Stream Improvement. Technical Review
N Cat — Notre Catechese
NCathW — New Catholic World
NCB — New Clarendon Bible
NCB — New Comprehensive Biochemistry
NC Bar Newsl — North Carolina Bar Newsletter
NCB NT — New Clarendon Bible. New Testament
NCB OT — New Clarendon Bible. Old Testament
NcC — Nouvelle Clio. Collection
NCCA — North Carolina Christian Advocate
NC Cave Surv — North Carolina Cave Survey
NC Cent LJ — North Carolina Central Law Journal
NC Central L J — North Carolina Central Law Journal
NCCHS — Newsletter. Congregational Christian Historical Society
NCCP — Nouvelle Collection des Classiques Populaires
NCC Proc — National Computer Conference. Proceedings
NCCR — National Christian Council Review
NCC Res Rep Dig — Nature Conservancy Council. Research Reports Digest
NC Dairy Ext Newsl — North Carolina Dairy Extension Newsletter
N C Dent Gaz — North Carolina Dental Gazette
NC Dent J — North Carolina Dental Journal
NC Dep Conserv Dev Bull — North Carolina. Department of Conservation and Development. Bulletin
NC Dep Conserv Dev Div Miner Resour Bull — North Carolina. Department of Conservation and Development. Division of MineralResources. Bulletin
NC Dep Conserv Dev Div Miner Resour Inf Circ — North Carolina. Department of Conservation and Development. Division of MineralResources. Information Circular
NC Dep Conserv Dev Econ Pap — North Carolina. Department of Conservation and Development. Economic Paper
NC Dep Hum Res Ann Rep — North Carolina. Department of Human Resources. Annual Report
NC Dep Nat Econ Resour Geol Miner Resour Sect Spec Publ — North Carolina. Department of Natural and Economic Resources. Geology and Mineral Resources Section. Special Publication
NC Dep Nat Econ Resour Groundwater Sect Rep Invest — North Carolina. Department of Natural and Economic Resources. Groundwater Section. Report of Investigation
NC Dep Nat Econ Resour Reg Geol Ser — North Carolina. Department of Natural and Economic Resources. Regional Geology Series
NC Dep Water Resour Div Ground Water Ground Water Bull — North Carolina. Department of Water Resources. Division of Ground Water. Ground-Water Bulletin
NC Dep Water Resour Div Stream Sanit Hydrol Bull — North Carolina. Department of Water Resources. Division of Stream Sanitation and Hydrology. Bulletin
NC Div Earth Sci Geol Miner Resour Sect Bull — North Carolina. Division of Earth Sciences. Geology and Mineral Resources Section. Bulletin
NC Div Ground Water Ground Water Bull — North Carolina. Division of Ground Water. Ground Water Bulletin
NC Div Ground Water Ground Water Circ — North Carolina. Division of Ground Water. Ground Water Clrcular
NC Div Ground Water Rep Invest — North Carolina. Division of Ground Water. Report of Investigations
NC Div Miner Resour Bull — North Carolina. Department of Conservation and Development. Division of MineralResources. Bulletin
NC Div Miner Resour Econ Pap — North Carolina. Division of Mineral Resources. Economic Paper
NC Div Miner Resour Inf Circ — North Carolina. Division of Mineral Resources. Information Circular
NC Div Resour Plann Eval Miner Resour Sect Bull — North Carolina. Division of Resource Planning and Evaluation. Mineral ResourcesSection. Bulletin
NC Div Resour Plann Eval Miner Resour Sect Educ Ser — North Carolina. Division of Resource Planning and Evaluation. Mineral ResourcesSection. Educational Series
NC Div Resour Plann Eval Miner Resour Sect Reg Geol Ser — North Carolina. Division of Resource Planning and Evaluation. Mineral ResourcesSection. Regional Geology Series
NC Div Resour Plann Eval Reg Geol Ser — North Carolina. Division of Resource Planning and Evaluation. Regional Geology Series
NC Div Water Resour Div Stream Sanit Hydrol Bull — North Carolina. Department of Water Resources. Division of Stream Sanitation and Hydrology. Bulletin
NC Div Water Resour Eng Bull — North Carolina. Division of Water Resources and Engineering. Bulletin
NC Div Water Resour Inlets Coastal Waterw Bull — North Carolina. Division of Water Resources, Inlets, and Coastal Waterways. Bulletin
NCE — New Catholic Encyclopedia
NCE — North Carolina Music Educator
NCEA — Notas del Centro de Estudios Antropologicos [*Santiago de Chile*]
N Ce B — New Century Bible

NCEGA — Noise Control Engineering
N Cen Assn Q — North Central Association. Quarterly
NCent — New Century
N Cent — Nineteenth Century
Ncent — Nineteenth Century and After
N Cent Corn Breed Res Comm Minutes Meet — North Central Corn Breeding Research Committee. Minutes of Meeting
N Cent J Agric Econ — North Central Journal of Agricultural Economics
N Cent School L Rev — North Central School Law Review
NCF — Nineteenth-Century Fiction
NCF — North Carolina Folklore
NCFLN — Northern California Foreign Language Newsletter
NC Folk — North Carolina Folklore
NCFR — National Council on Family Relations. Newsletter
NCFS — Nineteenth-Century French Studies
NCGE/J — Journal of Geography. National Council of Geographic Education
NC Gen Stat — General Statutes of North Carolina
NC Geol Surv Sect Bull — North Carolina. Geological Survey Section. Bulletin
NCGH — Nippon Chugoku Gakkaiho
NCGS — Fra Ny-Carlsberg Glyptoteks Sammlingen
NCGS B — North Carolina Geological Survey. Bulletin
NCh — Numismatic Chronicle
NCHE — National Center for Health Education. Newsletter
NC His As — State Literary and Historical Association of North Carolina. Proceedings
NC His R — North Carolina Historical Review
NC Hist Com Pub — North Carolina Historical Commission. Publications
NC Hist R — North Carolina Historical Review
NC Hist Rev — North Carolina Historical Review
NChn — Numismatic Chronicle
NChr — New Christian
N Chr — New Christianity
NCHR — North Carolina Historical Review
NChr — Numismatic Chronicle
N Chr — Numismatic Chronicle and Journal. Royal Numismatic Society
N Chret Isr — Nouvelles Chretiennes d'Israel
NChrIsr — Nouvelles Chretiennes d'Israel
NCHRP Prog Rep — National Cooperative Highway Research Program. Report
NCHRP Rep — National Cooperative Highway Research Program. Report
NCHRP Synthesis Highw Prac — National Cooperative Highway Research Program. Synthesis of Highway Practice
NCHS (Natl Cent Health Stat) Adv Data — NCHS (National Center for Health Statistics) Advance Data
N Church R — New Church Review
NCI — National Computer Index
NCI — Notiziario Culturale Italiano
NCI — Nouvelles Chretiennes d'Israel
NCIAA — Nuovo Cimento. Sezione A
NCIBA — Nuovo Cimento. Sezione B
N Cim — Nuovo Cimento, Giornale di Fisica, Chimica e Storia Naturale
NCIMA — National Cancer Institute. Monographs
NCI Monogr — NCI [National Cancer Institute] Monographs
NCirc — Numismatic Circular
NCIS — Nuclear Criticality Information System
NCJ Int'l L and Com Reg — North Carolina Journal of International Law and Commercial Regulation
NCJ of L — North Carolina Journal of Law
NCJRS — National Criminal Justice Reference Service
NCL — North Carolina Law Review
NCL — Nossos Classicos
NCL — Notes on Contemporary Literature
NC Law R — North Carolina Law Review
NC Law Rev — North Carolina Law Review. University of North Carolina
NCLC — Nineteenth Century Literary Criticism
NC League Nurs News — NC [North Carolina] League for Nursing News
NC Lib — North Carolina Libraries
NClio — La Nouvelle Clio
NCLIS — National Commission on Libraries and Information Science
NCLJ — North Carolina Law Journal
NCL Occ Newsl — National Central Library. Occasional Newsletter
NCLR — North Carolina Law Review
NC L Rev — North Carolina Law Review
NCM — National Contract Management Journal
NCM — New Church Magazine
NCMBBJ — Novedades Cientificas. Contribuciones Ocasionales del Museo de Historia NaturalLa Salle [Caracas]. Serie Botanica
NCMC Proc — NCMC [Nassau County Medical Center] Proceedings
NC Med J — North Carolina Medical Journal
NCMH — New Cambridge Modern History
NC Miner Resour Sect Educ Ser — North Carolina. Mineral Resources Section. Educational Series
NC Miner Resour Sect Reg Geol Ser — North Carolina. Mineral Resources Section. Regional Geology Series
NC Mus A Bull — North Carolina Museum of Art Bulletin
NCMZAM — Novedades Cientificas. Serie Zoologia
NCN — Netherlands American Trade
NCNR — Greensboro News and Record
NCO — National Council Outlook
NCoHS — Northumberland County Historical Society. Proceedings
NCoHSP — Northumberland County Historical Society. Proceedings
N Col — New Colophon
NConL — Notes on Contemporary Literature
NC Pestic Manual — North Carolina Pesticide Manual
NCR — Cooperatie
NCR — National Catholic Reporter

NCR — National Civic Review
NCR — New-Church Review
NCR — Nineteenth Century Review
NCr — Nouvelle Critique. Revue du Marxisme Militant
N Cr — Numismatic Chronicle and Journal. Royal Numismatic Society
NCR Bus and Econ — North Carolina Review of Business and Economics
NCRD Rep Isr — NCRD (National Council for Research and Development) Report (Israel)
NCRDS — National Coal Resources Data System
N Cr I — Noticias Cristianas de Israel
NCRMM — Nouvelle Critique. Revue du Marxisme Militant
NCRNS — Numismatic Chronicle and Journal of the Royal Numismatic Society
NCRP Rep — National Council on Radiation Protection and Measurements. Reports
NCRR Bull — NCRR [National Center for Resource Recovery] Bulletin
NCRSAQ — US National Clearinghouse for Drug Abuse Information. Report Series
NCSA — Native Counselling Services of Alberta. Newsletter
NCSA — Newsletter. Copyright Society of Australia
NCSC Manual — National Companies and Securities Commission. Manual
NCSDHA Dent Hyg — NCSDHA [Northern California State Dental Hygienists Association] Dental Hygienist
NC Sess Laws — Session Laws. North Carolina
NCSL — North Carolina. University. Studies in Comparative Literature
NCSP — North Carolina. University. Sesqui-Centennial Publications
NCSRLL — North Carolina Studies in Romance Languages and Literatures
NCSS B — National Council for the Social Studies. Bulletin
NCSSG — Novi Commentarii Societatis Scientiarum Gottingensis
NCSS Read — National Council for the Social Studies. Readings
NCSS Res B — National Council for the Social Studies. Research Bulletin
NCSS Yearb — National Council for the Social Studies. Yearbook
NC State Coll Agric Eng Agric Ext Serv Ext Circ — North Carolina State College of Agriculture and Engineering. Agricultural Extension Service. Extension Circular
NC State Coll Agric Eng Eng Exp Stn Bull — North Carolina State College of Agriculture and Engineering. Engineering Experiment Station. Bulletin
NC State Coll Agric Exp Stn Bull — North Carolina State College. Agricultural Experiment Station. Bulletin
NC State Coll Agric Exp Stn Tech Bull — North Carolina State College. Agricultural Experiment Station. Technical Bulletin
NC State Coll Dep Eng Res Bull — North Carolina State College. Department of Engineering Research. Bulletin
NC State Coll Dept Eng Research Bull — North Carolina State College. Department of Engineering Research. Bulletin
NC State Coll Eng Sch Bull — North Carolina State College. Engineering School Bulletin
NC State Coll Rec — North Carolina State College Record
NC State Coll Sch Agric Annu Rep — North Carolina State College. School of Agriculture. Annual Report
NC State Univ Dep Eng Res Bull — North Carolina State University. Department of Engineering. Research Bulletin
NC State Univ Eng Sch Bull — North Carolina State University. Engineering School Bulletin
NC State Univ Miner Res Lab Lab Notes — North Carolina State University. Minerals Research Laboratory. Laboratory Notes
NC State Univ Miner Res Lab Rep — North Carolina State University. Minerals Research Laboratory. Report
NC State Univ Raleigh Agric Exp Stn Bull — North Carolina State University. Raleigh. Agricultural Experiment Station. Bulletin
NC State Univ Raleigh Agric Exp Stn Tech Bull — North Carolina State University at Raleigh. Agricultural Experiment Station. Technical Bulletin
NC State Univ Sch Agric Life Sci Annu Rep — North Carolina State University. School of Agriculture and Life Sciences. Annual Report
NC St B Newsl — North Carolina State Bar Newsletter
NC St B Proc — North Carolina State Bar. Proceedings
NC St BQ — North Carolina State Bar Quarterly
NCTR — Nineteenth-Century Theatre Research
NCUA Q — National Credit Union Administration. Quarterly
NCult — Nuova Cultura
NC Univ Dep Environ Sci Eng ESE Notes — North Carolina. University. Department of Environmental Sciences and Engineering. ESE Notes
NC Visions — North Carolina Visions
NCW — New Catholic World
NCW News — NCW News (National Council of Women of New South Wales)
NCYBD — Nuclear Canada Yearbook
NCYC CAT — National Collection of Yeast Cultures Catalogue
ND — La Nueva Democracia
ND — Negro Digest
ND — Neues Deutschland
ND — New Directions
ND — Night and Day
ND — North Dakota Music Educator
ND — North Dakota Reports
ND — Novissimo Digesto Italiano
ND — Nowe Drogi
ND — Nueva Democracia
ND — Nuovo Didaskaleion
ND Acad Sci Proc — North Dakota Academy of Science. Proceedings
NDADD8 — New Drugs Annual. Cardiovascular Drugs
ND Admin Code — North Dakota Administrative Code
ND Ag Exp — North Dakota. Agricultural Experiment Station. Publications
ND Agric Exp Stn Bull — North Dakota. Agricultural Experiment Station. Bulletin
N Dak Acad Sci Proc — North Dakota Academy of Science. Proceedings
N Dak Agr Coll Exp Sta Bien Rep — North Dakota Agricultural College. Experiment Station. Biennial Report
N Dak Farm Res Bimon Bull — North Dakota Farm Research. Bimonthly Bulletin. North Dakota Agricultural College. Agricultural Experiment Station

N Dak Fm Res — North Dakota Farm Research
N Dak Geol Surv Bull — North Dakota. Geological Survey. Bulletin
N Dak Geol Surv Circ — North Dakota. Geological Survey. Circular
N Dak Geol Surv Misc Ser — North Dakota. Geological Survey. Miscellaneous Series
N Dak Geol Surv Rep Invest — North Dakota. Geological Survey. Report of Investigations
N Dak G S Bien Rp — North Dakota. Geological Survey. Biennial Report
N Dak His S — North Dakota State Historical Society. Collections
N Dak History — North Dakota History
N Dak Lib Notes — North Dakota Library Notes
N Dak M — North Dakota Magazine
N Dak Outdoors — North Dakota Outdoors
N Dak Research Found Bull Circ — North Dakota Research Foundation Bulletin. Circular
N Dame J Ed — Notre Dame Journal of Education
NDAS — New Dictionary of American Slang
NDAT — Nashriyye(H)-Ye Daneshkade(H)-Ye Adabiyyat va Olum-E Ensani-Ye Tabriz
NDB — Neue Deutsche Biographie
NDBKG — Niederdeutsche Beitraege zur Kunstgeschichte
NDBSB — Nogyo Doboku Shikenjo Hokoku
NDBZ — Neue Deutsche Beamtenzeitung
Nd B Zt — Neudeutsche Bauzeitung
NDCAB — Nippon Dental College. Annual Publications
NDCDDI — New Directions for Child Development
ND Cent Code — North Dakota Century Code
Ndd Jb — Niederdeutsches Jahrbuch
NDEJ — Notre Dame English Journal
NDE Nucl Ind Int Conf — NDE [*Nondestructive Evaluation*] in the Nuclear Industry and Equipment/Services Exposition. International Conference
NDF — Nederlands-Duitse Kamer van Koophandel. Mededelingen
NDF — Neue Deutsche Forschung
ND Farm Res — North Dakota Farm Research
ND Farm Res ND Agric Exp Stn — North Dakota Farm Research. North Dakota Agricultural Experiment Station
NDFKAH — Endemic Diseases Bulletin. Nagasaki University
NDFN — Nauchnye Doklady Vysshei Shkoly Filologicheskie Nauki
NDFW — New Directions for Women
ND Geol Surv Bull — North Dakota. Geological Survey. Bulletin
ND Geol Surv Circ — North Dakota. Geological Survey. Circular
ND Geol Surv Educ Ser — North Dakota. Geological Survey. Educational Series
ND Geol Surv Ground Water Stud — North Dakota Geological Survey. Ground-Water Studies
ND Geol Surv Misc Map — North Dakota. Geological Survey. Miscellaneous Map
ND Geol Surv Misc Ser — North Dakota. Geological Survey. Miscellaneous Series
ND Geol Surv Rep Invest — North Dakota. Geological Survey. Report of Investigations
NDGI — Nachrichten. Deutsche Gesellschaft fuer Islamkunde
NDGKA — Nogyo Doboku Gakkai Ronbunshu
NDGNO — Nachrichten der Deutschen Gesellschaft fuer Natur- und Voelkerkunde Ostasiens
NDGXA — Miscellaneous Series. North Dakota Geological Survey
NDH — Neue Deutsche Hefte
NDH — Nordic Economic Outlook
NDH — North Dakota History
NDHi — North Dakota History
ND His Q — North Dakota Historical Quarterly
ND Hist — North Dakota History
NDHQ — North Dakota Historical Quarterly
NDHR — NDH-Rapport. Norland Distrikshogskole
NDI — No-Dig International
NDI — Nuovo Digesto Italiano
N Did — Nuovo Didaskaleion
NDim — Nuove Dimensioni
NDIS — Australian National Drug Information Service
NDJ — Notre Dame Journal
Nd Jb — Niederdeutsches Jahrbuch
Nd Jb — Niederdeutsches Jahrbuch fuer Volkskunde
Nd Kbl — Korrespondenzblatt des Vereins fuer Niederdeutsche Sprachforschung
Nd Kbl — Korrespondenzblatt. Verein fuer Niederdeutsche Sprachforschung
NDKGA — Nippon Daicho Komonbyo Gakkai Zasshi
NDKGAU — Journal. Japan Society of Colo-Proctology
NDKIA — Nagoya Daigaku Kankyo Igaku Kenkyusho Nenpo
Nd Ko Bl — Korrespondenzblatt. Verein fuer Niederdeutsche Sprachforschung
NDKSBX — Journal. Agricultural Laboratory
NDL — Neudrucke Deutscher Literaturwerke
NDL — Neue Deutsche Literatur
NDL — Notre Dame Lawyer
Ndl Arch Ntk — Nederlandsch Archief voor Genees- en Natuurkunde
ND Laws — Laws of North Dakota
Ndl Gast Oogl Vs — Nederlandsch Gasthuis voor Behoeftige en Minvermogende Ooglijders te Utrecht. Verslag
Ndl Kruidk Arch — Nederlandsch Kruidkundig Archief
Ndl Lancet — Nederlandsch Lancet. Tijdschrift aan de Praktische Chirurgieen Oogheelkunde Gewijd
NDLR — North Dakota Law Review
NDL Rev — North Dakota Law Review
ND L Review — North Dakota Law Review
NdM — Niederdeutsche Mitteilungen
NDM — Nye Danske Magazine
NDMG — Norddeutsche Missionsgesellschaft
Nd Mitt — Niederdeutsche Mitteilungen
NDNRS — National Directory of Newsletters and Reporting Services

Ndoesterr Gewerb Vr Vh — Verhandlungen des Niederoesterreichischen Gewerb-Vereins
NDP — Neue Deutsche Presse
NDPB — Norddeutsches Protestantenblatt
NDQ — North Dakota Quarterly
ND Quar J — North Dakota University. Quarterly Journal
NDR — Neue Deutsche Rundschau
NDR — North Dakota Law Review
NDR — Revue de la Navigation Fluviale Europeenne. Ports et Industries
NDRCAJ — Contributions. Department of Geology and Mineralogy. Niigata University
ND REC Mag — North Dakota REC [*Rural Electric Cooperatives*] Magazine
N Drent Volksalm — Nieuwe Drentsche Volksalmanak
ND Res Found Bull — North Dakota Research Foundation Bulletin
ND Res Rep ND Agric Exp Stn — North Dakota Research Report. North Dakota Agricultural Experiment Station
NDRHE4 — Sado Marine Biological Station. Niigata University. Special Publication
Nd Rhein Jb — Niederrheinisches Jahrbuch
NdS — Niederdeutsche Studien
NdS — Notizie degli Scavi di Antichita
NDSA — National Directory of State Agencies
NDSA — Notizie degli Scavi di Antichita
NDSAA — Nuclear Data. Section A
NDSchNG — Neue Denkschriften der Schweizerischen Naturforschenden Gesellschaft
NDSFB — Nogyo Doboku Shikenjo Giho, F. Sogo
Nds GV Bl — Niedersaechsisches Gesetz- und Verordnungsblatt
ND Sjo — Nordiske Domme i Sjofartsanliggender
NDSK — Nydanske Studier. Almen Kommunikationsteori
Nds Rpfl — Niedersaechsische Rechtspflege
ND State Lab Dep Bull — North Dakota. State Laboratories Department. Bulletin
ND State Water Conserv Comm Ground Water Stud — North Dakota. State Water Conservation Commission. Ground-Water Studies
NDT E Int — NDT and E International
Ndt F — Norddeutsche Familienkunde
NDTI — National Disease and Therapeutic Index
NDT Int — Non-Destructive Testing International
NDT Intl — Nondestructive Testing International
NDTI Rev — NDTI [*National Disease and Therapeutic Index*] Review
NDT News — Non-Destructive Testing News
NDTSB — Nuclear Data Sheets
NdtV — Nachrichtenblatt fuer Deutsche Vorzeit
NDV — Nachrichtendienst. Deutscher Verein fuer Oeffentliche und Private Fuersorge
NDV — Notes et Documents Voltaiques
NDVS — Naucnye Doklady Vyssej Skoly
NDVS-F — Naucnye Doklady Vyssej Skoly Filologiceskie Nauki
NDVTB — Nederlands Tijdschrift voor Vacuumtechniek
NDW — Niederdeutsches Wort
NDZKA — Noodzaak
NDZ Neue Deliwa Z — NDZ (Neue Deliwa-Zeitschrift) Neue Deliwa-Zeitschrift
Nd Z Vk — Niederdeutsche Zeitschrift fuer Volkskunde und Blaetter fuer Niedersaechsische Heimatpflege
NE — Near East
NE — Nebraska Music Educator
Ne — Neva
NE — Nordelbingen
NE — North Eastern Reporter
NE — Notices et Extraits des Manuscrits de la Bibliotheque Nationale
NE — Nouvelle Ecole
NE — Novels of Empire
NE — Nueva Estafeta
NE — Numismatica i Epigrafica
N E 2d — North Eastern Reporter. Second Series
NEA — National Energy Accounts
Nea Agrotike Epitheor — Nea Agrotike Epitheoresis
NeaH — Nea Hestia
NEA J — National Education Association. Journal
NEA Jour NY — Journal. National Education Association (New York)
NEAJT — North East Asia Journal of Theology
Ne AKG — Nederlandsch Archief voor Kerkelijke Geschiedenis
NE Am Soc Mech Eng — NE (Nuclear Engineering Division, ASME). American Society of Mechanical Engineers
Neap — Neapolis
Near East — Near East and India
NEA Res Bul — National Education Association. Research Bulletin
NEA Res Div Rept — National Education Association. Research Division. Reports
NEASB — Near East Archaeological Society. Bulletin
NE Asia J Th — Northeast Asia Journal of Theology
Neb — Nebraska Reports
Neb — Nebula Science Fiction
NEB — New England Journal of Business and Economics
Neb Admin R & Regs — Nebraska Administrative Rules and Regulations
Neb Ag Exp — Nebraska. Agricultural Experiment Station. Publications
Neb Agric Exp Stn Annu Rep — Nebraska. Agricultural Experiment Station. Annual Report
Neb Agric Exp Stn Circ — Nebraska. Agricultural Experiment Station. Circular
NEBBA — Neue Bergbautechnik
Neb Ed J — Nebraska Educational Journal
Neb Educ J — Nebraska Educational Journal
NebH — Nebraska History
Neb His — Nebraska History
Neb His M — Nebraska History. Magazine
Neb His S — Nebraska State Historical Society. Collections
Neb Hist — Nebraska History

Neb Hist Mag — Nebraska History Magazine. Nebraska State Historical Society
Neb J Econ and Bus — Nebraska Journal of Economics and Business
Neb Law Bul — Nebraska Law Bulletin. College of Law. University of Nebraska
Neb Laws — Laws of Nebraska
Neb LB — Nebraska Law Bulletin
Neb L Bul — Nebraska Law Bulletin
Neb Leg N — Nebraska Legal News
Neblettes Handb Photogr Reprogr — Neblette's Handbook of Photography and Reprography. Materials, Processes, and Systems
Neb Lib Assn Q — Nebraska Library Association. Quarterly
Neb LR — Nebraska Law Review
Neb L Rev — Nebraska Law Review
Neb Munic R — Nebraska Municipal Review
NEBR — New Breed. Association of Metis and Non-Status Indians of Saskatchewan
Nebr Acad Sci Affil Soc Trans — Nebraska Academy of Sciences and Affiliated Societies. Transactions
Nebr Acad Sci Trans — Nebraska Academy of Sciences. Transactions
Nebr Ac Sc Pub Pr — Nebraska Academy of Sciences. Publications. Proceedings
Nebr Agric Exp Stn Annu Rep — Nebraska. Agricultural Experiment Station. Annual Report
Nebr Agric Exp Stn Bull — Nebraska. Agricultural Experiment Station. Bulletin
Nebr Agric Exp Stn Circ — Nebraska. Agricultural Experiment Station. Circular
Nebr Agric Exp Stn Res Bull — Nebraska. Agricultural Experiment Station. Research Bulletin
Nebr Agric Exp Stn SB — Nebraska. Agricultural Experiment Station. Station Bulletin SB
Nebraska Acad Sci Proc — Nebraska Academy of Sciences and Affiliated Societies. Proceedings
Nebraska Agric Exp Sta Annual Rep — Nebraska Agricultural Experiment Station. Annual Report
Nebraska Agric Exp Sta Circ — Nebraska Agricultural Experiment Station Circular
Nebraska Agric Exp Sta Res Bull — Nebraska Agricultural Experiment Station Research Bulletin
Nebraska Agric Exp Sta Wheat Abstr — Nebraska Agricultural Experiment Station Wheat Abstracts
Nebraska Geol Survey Paper — Nebraska Geological Survey. Paper
Nebraska L Rev — Nebraska Law Review
Nebraska Univ State Mus Bull — Nebraska. University. State Museum. Bulletin
Nebr BA — Nebraska State Bar Journal
Nebr Bird Rev — Nebraska Bird Review
Nebr Conserv Bull — Nebraska Conservation Bulletin
Nebr Energy News — Nebraska Energy News
NEBRET — Nematologia Brasileira
Neb Rev Stat — Revised Statutes of Nebraska
Nebr Exp Stn Q — Nebraska Experiment Station Quarterly
Nebr Farm Ranch Econ — Nebraska Farm Ranch Economics
Nebr Geol Surv Bull — Nebraska Geological Survey. Bulletin
Nebr LB — Nebraska Law Bulletin
Nebr L Rev — Nebraska Law Review
Nebr Med J — Nebraska Medical Journal
Nebr Nurse — Nebraska Nurse
Nebr State Med J — Nebraska State Medical Journal
Nebr State Mus Bull — Nebraska State Museum. Bulletin
Nebr St Bd Agr An Rp — Nebraska State Board of Agriculture. Annual Report
Nebr St Hist Soc Pr — Nebraska State Historical Society. Proceedings and Collections
Nebr St Med J — Nebraska State Medical Journal
Nebr Symp Motiv — Nebraska Symposium on Motivation
Nebr Tractor Test Nebr Agric Exp Stn — Nebraska Tractor Test. Nebraska Agricultural Experiment Station
Nebr Univ Agric Exp Stn Annu Rep — Nebraska. University. Agricultural Experiment Station. Annual Report
Nebr Univ Agric Exp Stn Bull — Nebraska. University. Agricultural Experiment Station. Bulletin
Nebr Univ Agric Exp Stn Res Bull — Nebraska. University. Agricultural Experiment Station. Research Bulletin
Nebr Univ Agric Ext Serv Ext Circ — Nebraska. University. Agricultural Extension Service. Extension Circular
Nebr Univ Coll Agric Home Econ Ext Serv Ext Circ — Nebraska. University. College of Agriculture and Home Economics. Extension Service. Extension Circular
Nebr Univ Coll Agric Home Econ Q — Nebraska. University. College of Agriculture and Home Economics. Quarterly
Nebr Univ Eng Exp Stn Bull — Nebraska. University. Engineering Experiment Station. Bulletin
Nebr Univ Studies — Nebraska. University. Studies
Nebr Un Stud — University Studies. Published by the University of Nebraska
Nebr Water Surv Pap — Nebraska Water Survey Paper
Nebr Wheat Variety Estimate Nebr Grain Impr Ass — Nebraska Wheat Variety Estimate. Nebraska Grain Improvement Association
Neb SBJ — Nebraska State Bar Journal
Neb St BJ — Nebraska State Bar Journal
Neb St MJ — Nebraska State Medical Journal
Neb Sup Ct J — Nebraska Supreme Court Journal
NEBTA — Nederlands Bosbouw Tijdschrift
Neb WCC — Nebraska Workmen's Compensation Court. Bulletin
Necc — Nouvelles Ecclesiastiques, ou Memoires pour Servir a l'Histoire de la Constitution Unigenitus
NECG — New Ecologist
NECH — National Event Clearinghouse Database
N Ecl — New Eclectic
NE Coop Ext Serv Northeast States — NE. Cooperative Extension Services of the Northeastern States
NEC Res and Dev — NEC [Nippon Electric Company] Research and Development
NEC Res Dev — NEC [Nippon Electric Company] Research and Development

NEC Rev — NEC [Nippon Electric Company] Review
Necro — Necrofile
NED — New English Dictionary on Historical Principles
NedA — Nederlandsch Archievenblad
Ned Akad Wet Afd Natuurkd Verh Eerste Reeks — Nederlandse Akademie van Wetenschappen, Afdeling Natuurkunde. Verhandelingen. Eerste Reeks
Ned Akad Wet Proc Ser B — Nederlandse Akademie van Wetenschappen [Koninklijke]. Proceedings. Series B. Physical Sciences
Ned AKG — Nederlandsch Archief voor Kerkgeschiedenis
Ned Ambachts & Nijvhdskstjb — Nederlandsche Ambachts- en Nijverheidskunstjaarboek
Ned Belg Ver Graanonderz Handel — Nederlands-Belgische Vereniging van Graanonderzoekers. Handelingen
Ned Bosbouwtijdschr — Nederlands Bosbouwtijdschrift
Ned Bosb Tijdschr — Nederlands Bosbouw Tijdschrift
Ned Boschbouw Tijdschr — Nederlandsch Boschbouw-Tijdschrift
Ned Cent Organ TNO Comm Hydrol Onderz Versl Meded — Nederlandse Centrale Organisatie voor Toegepast-Natuurwetenschapelijk Onderzoek. Commissie voor Hydrologisch Onderzoek. Verslagen en Mededelingen
Ned Chem Ind — Nederlandse Chemische Industrie
Ned Dendrol Ver Jaarb — Nederlandse Dendrologische Vereniging. Jaarboek
Ned Entomol Ver Jaarb — Nederlandse Entomologische Vereniging. Jaarboek
Nederl Akad Wetensch Indag Math — Koninklijke Nederlandse Akademie van Wetenschappen. Indagationes Mathematicae ex Actis Quibus Titulus
Nederl Akad Wetensch Proc Ser A — Koninklijke Nederlandse Akademie van Wetenschappen. Proceedings. Series A. Mathematical Sciences
Nederl Akad Wetensch Proc Ser B — Koninklijke Nederlandse Akademie van Wetenschappen. Proceedings. Series B. Physical Sciences [Later, Koninklijke Nederlandse Akademie van Wetenschappen. Proceedings. Series B. Palaeontology, Geology, Physics, and Chemistry]
Nederl Akad Wetensch Verslag Afd Natuurk — Koninklijke Nederlandse Akademie van Wetenschappen. Verslag van de Gewone Vergadering van de Afdeling Natuurkunde
Nederlandsch Hist Inst Rome Med — Nederlandsch Historisch Instituut te Rome. Mededeelingen
Nederlandse Oudheidkundige Bond Bull — Nederlandse Oudheidkundige Bond. Bulletin
Nederlands Hist Ins Rome Med — Mededelingen. Nederlandsch Historisch Institut te Rome
Nederlands Kunsthist Jaar — Nederlands Kunsthistorisch Jaarboek
Nederl Arch Geneal Heraldik — Nederlandsch Archief voor Genealogie en Heraldik
Nederl Arch Kerkgesch — Nederlandsch Archief voor Kerkgeschiedenis
Nederl Arch Kerkgeschiedenis — Nederlandsch Archief voor Kerkgeschiedenis
Nederl-Ind Blad Diergeneesk — Nederlandsch-Indische Bladen voor Diergeneeskunde
Nederl Lancet — Nederlandsch Lancet
Ned Gem — Nederlandse Gemeente
Ned Geol Mijnbouwkd Genoot Verh — Nederlands Geologisch Mijnbouwkundig Genootschap [Koninklijk]. Verhandelingen
NedGerefTTs — Nederduitse Gereformeerde Teologiese Tydskrif
NE Dialog — Northeast Dialog
Ned Ind Eigendom — Nederland Industriele Eigendom
Ned Indie Oud & Nieuw — Nederlandsch-Indie oud en Nieuw
Ned Indisch Rubber Thee Tijdschr — Nederlandsch-Indisch Rubber- en Thee-Tijdschrift
Ned Inst Zuivelonderz Rapp — Nederlands Instituut voor Zuivelonderzoek. Rapporten
Ned Inst Zuivelonderz Versl — Nederlands Instituut voor Zuivelonderzoek. Verslag
Ned Jbl — Nederlands Juristenblad
Ned Jpd — Nederlandse Jurisprudentie
Ned Jurbl — Nederlands Juristenblad
Ned Kruidk Arch — Nederlandsch Kruidkundig Archief. Verslagen en Mededelingen der Nederlandsche Botanische Vereeniging
Ned Kruidkd Arch — Nederlandsch Kruidkundig Archief
Ned Kstbode — Nederlandsche Kunstbode
Ned Ksthist Jb — Nederlands(ch) Kunsthistorisch Jaarboek
Ned Ksthist Woordbk — Nederlands Kunsthistorisch Woordenboek
NedL — Nederlandse Leeuw
Ned Leeuw — Nederlandsche Leeuw
Ned Lett Courant — Nederlandsche Letter-Courant
Ned Maandschr Geneeskd — Nederlandsch Maandschrift voor Geneeskunde
Ned Melk Zuiveltijdschr — Nederlands Melk-en Zuiveltijdschrift
Ned Mil Geneeskd Tijdschr — Nederlands Militair Geneeskundig Tijdschrift
Ned Mus — Nederlandsche Museum
NEDO Frcst — National Economic Development Office. Construction Forecasts
Ned Patr — Nederland's Patriciaat
NEdR — New Edinburgh Review
NEDRES — National Environmental Data Referral Service
Ned Rubberind — Nederlandse Rubberindustrie
NEDS — National Emissions Data System
Ned Scheepsstudiecent TNO Rep — Nederlands Scheepsstudiecentrum TNO. Report
Ned Staatscourant — Nederlandse Staatscourant
Ned Stcrt — Nederlandse Staatscourant
Ned Tandartsenbl — Nederlands Tandartsenblad
NedThT — Nederlands Theologisch Tijdschrift
Ned Tijd — Nederlands Tijdschrift voor Internationaal Recht
Ned Tijdschr — Nederlands Tijdschrift voor Internationaal Recht
Ned Tijdschr Geneeskd — Nederlands Tijdschrift voor Geneeskunde
Ned Tijdschr Gerontol — Nederlands Tijdschrift voor Gerontologie
Ned Tijdschr Hyg Microbiol Serol — Nederlandsch Tijdschrift voor Hygiene, Microbiologie, en Serologie
Ned Tijdschr Klin Chem — Nederlands Tijdschrift voor Klinische Chemie
Ned Tijdschr Natuurk — Nederlands Tijdschrift voor Natuurkunde

Ned Tijdschr Natuurk A — Nederlands Tijdschrift voor Natuurkunde. Series A
Ned Tijdschr Natuurkd — Nederlands Tijdschrift voor Natuurkunde
Ned Tijdschr Natuurkd A — Nederlands Tijdschrift voor Natuurkunde. Series A
Ned Tijdschr Psychol — Nederlands Tijdschrift voor de Psychologie en Haar Grensgebieden
Ned Tijdschr Tandheelkd — Nederlands Tijdschrift voor Tandheelkunde
Ned Tijdschr Vacuumtech — Nederlands Tijdschrift voor Vacuumtechniek
Ned Tijdschr Verloskd Gynaecol — Nederlandsch Tijdschrift voor Verloskunde en Gynaecologie
Ned Ts Geneesk — Nederlandsch Tijdschrift voor Geneeskunde
Ned Ts Verlosk — Nederlandsch Tijdschrift voor Verloskunde en Gynaecologie
NedTT — Nederlands Theologisch Tijdschrift
NedTTs — Nederlands Theologisch Tijdschrift
Ned Tulnbouwbl — Nederlandsche Tuinbouwblad
Ned T v Gen — Nederlands Tijdschrift voor Geneeskunde
Ned Ver Klin Chem Tijdschr — Nederlandse Vereniging voor Klinische Chemie. Tijdschrift
NEE — New England Economic Review. Federal Reserve Bank of Boston
Needlework Bul — Needlework Bulletin for Teachers in Secondary Schools
NEELS — National Emergency Equipment Locator System
Ne Engl J Med — New England Journal of Medicine
NEERI N — NEERI [*National Electrical Engineering Research Institute*] News
Nef — Nef: Cahier Trimestriel
NEF — Northeast Folklore
NEF — Notas y Estudios de Filosofia
NEFNB — Neftepererabotka i Neftekhimiya
Neftegazovaya Geol Geofiz — Neftegazovaya Geologiya i Geofizika
Neftegazov Geol Geofiz — Neftegazovaya Geologiya i Geofizika
Neftekhim — Neftekhimiya
Neftepererab Neftekhim Kazan — Neftepererabotka i Neftekhimiya (Kazan)
Neftepererab Neftekhim (Kiev) — Neftepererabotka i Neftekhimiya (Kiev)
Neftepererab Neftekhim (Moscow) — Neftepererabotka i Neftekhimiya (Moscow)
Neftepererab Neftekhim Slantsepererab — Neftepererabotka, Neftekhimiya, i Slantsepererabotka
Neftepererab Neftekhim Vses Obedin Neftekhim — Neftepererabotka i Neftekhimiya. Vsesoyuznoe Ob'edinenie Neftekhim
Neftepromysl Delo — Neftepromyslovoe Delo
Neftepromysl Delo (Moscow) — Neftepromyslovoe Delo (Moscow)
Neftepromysl Delo Ref Nauchno-Tekh Sb — Neftepromyslovoye Delo Referativnyy Nauchno-Tekhnicheskiy Sbornik
Neft Gazova Promst Sredn Azii — Neftyanaya i Gazovaya Promyshlennost Srednei Azii
Neft Gazov Prom-St' — Neftyanaya i Gazovaya Promyshlennost'
Neft Gazov Promst Sredn Azii — Neftyanaya i Gazovaya Promyshlennost Srednei Azii
Neft Khim — Neft i Khimiya
Neft Khim (Burgas Bulg) — Neft i Khimiya (Burgas, Bulgaria)
Neft Khim Sofia — Neft i Khimiya (Sofia)
Neft Khoz — Neftyanoe Khozyaistvo
Neft Promsl Ser Mash Neft Oborud — Neftyanaya Promyshlennost. Seriya Mashiny i Neftyanoe Oborudovanie
Neft Promsl Ser Neftegazov Geol Geofiz — Neftyanaya Promyshlennost. Seriya Neftegazovaya Geologiya i Geofizika
Neft Promsl Ser Neftepromysl Delo — Neftyanaya Promyshlennost. Seriya Neftepromyslovoe Delo
Neft Promsl Ser Neftepromysl Stroit — Neftyanaya Promyshlennost. Seriya Neftepromyslovoe Stroitel'stvo
Neft Promsl Ser Transp Khranenie Nefti Nefteprod — Neftyanaya Promyshlennost. Seriya Transport i Khranenie Nefti i Nefteproduktov
Neft Promst SSSR — Neftyanaya Promyshlennost SSSR
Neft Slants Khoz — Neftyanoe i Slantsevoe Khozyaistvo
Neft Udobr Stimul Mater Vses Soveshch — Neftyanye Udobreniya i Stimulyatory. Materialy Vsesoyuznogo Soveshchaniya
Neft Vuglishtna Geol — Neftena i Vuglishtna Geologiya
NEFZB — Neirofiziologila
NEG — Nederlandse Gemeente
Neg Ed Rev — Negro Educational Review
NegH — Negro History Bulletin
Neg His Bull — Negro History Bulletin
Negro D — Negro Digest
Negro Ed R — Negro Educational Review
Negro Educ R — Negro Educational Review
Negro H B — Negro History Bulletin
Negro His B — Negro History Bulletin
Negro Hist B — Negro History Bulletin
Negro Hist Bul — Negro History Bulletin
Negro Hist Bull — Negro History Bulletin
NEH — Notulae Entomologicae (Helsingfors)
Nehezip Muesz Egy Koezl — Nehezipari Mueszaki Egyetem Koezlemenyei
Nehezip Musz Egy Idegennyelvu Kozl — Nehezipari Muszaki Egyetem Idegennyelvu Kozlemenyei
Nehezip Musz Egy Kozl 1 Sorozat — Nehezipari Muszaki Egyetem Kozlemenyei. 1. Sorozat. Banyaszat
Nehezip Musz Egy Kozl 2 Sorozat — Nehezipari Muszaki Egyetem Kozlemenyei. 2. Sorozat. Kohaszat
Nehezip Musz Egy Kozl 3 Sorozat — Nehezipari Muszaki Egyetem Kozlemenyei. 3. Sorozat. Gepeszet
Nehezip Musz Egy Miskolc Idegennyelvu Kozl — Nehezipari Mueszaki Egyetem, Miskolc, Idegennyelvu Koezlemenyei
Nehezip Musz Egy Miskolc Kozl — Nehezipari Muszaki Egyetem, Miskolc, Koezlemenyei
Nehezip Musz Egy Sopron Banyamern Foldmeromern Karok Kozl — Nehezipari Muszaki Egyetem Sopron. Banyamernoki es Foldmeromernoki Karok Kozlemenyei
Nehezvegyip Kut Intez Kozl — Nehezvegyipari Kutato Intezet Kozlemenyei

NEHGR — New England Historical and Genealogical Register
NEHGR — New England Historical and Genealogical Register and Antiquarian Journal
Nehorlavost Polym Mater — Nehorlavost Polymernych Materialov
NEI — Near East and India
NEI — Nordik Energi Indeks
NEI — Nuclear Engineering International
NEIC — News from Iceland
NEILA8 — Contributions d'Istanbul a la Science Clinique
NEIN — News Inuit. News Releases from Inuit Tapirisat of Canada
NEINEI — NESDIS [*National Environmental Satellite Data and Information Service*] Environmental Inventory
NE INF US Dep Agric For Serv Northeast For Exp Stn — NE-INF. US Department of Agriculture. Forest Service. Northeastern Forest Experiment Station
NEI Rev — NEI [*Northern Engineering Industries*] Review
Neirokhim Fiziol Sinapticheskikh Protsessov — Neirokhimiya i Fiziologiya Sinapticheskikh Protsessov
NEIS — National Engineering Information Service
Neitr Akt Anal Ego Primen Nar Khoz — Neitronno-Aktivatsionnyi Analiz i Ego Primenenie v Narodnom Khozyaistve
Neitr Fiz Mater Vses Konf — Neitronnaya Fizika. Materialy Vsesoyuznoi Konferentsii po Neitronnoi Fizike
NEJ — Northeast Journal of Business and Economics
NEJ Crim and Civ Con — New England Journal on Criminal and Civil Confinement
NEJM — New England Journal of Medicine
NEJMA — New England Journal of Medicine
NEJMAG — New England Journal of Medicine
NEJPA — Neues Jahrbuch fuer Geologie und Palaeontologie. Abhandlungen
Nek Aktual Vopr Biol Med — Nekotorye Aktual'nye Voprosy Biologii i Meditsiny
Nek Aktual Vopr Biol Med Gorkiy — Nekotorye Aktual'nye Voprosy Biologii i Meditsiny (Gorkiy)
Nek Aktual Vopr Biol Med Moscow — Nekotorye Aktual'nye Voprosy Biologii i Meditsiny (Moscow)
Nek Filos Probl Gos Prava — Nekotorye Filosofskie Problemy Gosudarstva i Prava
Nekot Probl Biokibern Primen Elektron Biol Med — Nekotorye Problemy Biokibernetiki Primenenie Elektroniki v Biologii i Meditsine
Nek Vopr Eksp Fiz — Nekotorye Voposry Eksperimental'noi Fiziki
Nek Vopr Fiz Yadra Elem Chastits Yadernofiz Izmer — Nekotorye Voprosy Fiziki Yadra. Elementarnykh Chastits i Yadernofizicheskikh Izmerenii
Nek Vopr Geol Aziat Chasti SSSR — Nekotorye Voprosy Geologii Aziatskoi Chasti SSSR
Nek Vopr Inzh Fiz — Nekotorye Voprosy Inzhenernoi Fiziki
Nek Vopr Sovrem Elektrokhim Kinet — Nekotorye Voprosy Sovremennoi Elektrokhimicheskoi Kinetiki
Nek Vopr Stroit Skvazhin Oslozhnennykh Usloviyakh Uzb — Nekotorye Voprosy Stroitel'stva Skvazhin v Oslozhnennykh Usloviyakh Uzbekistana
NEKZ — Neue Evangelische Kirchenzeitung
NELA Bul — National Electric Light Association. Bulletin
NELA Ncwsl — NELA [*New England Library Association*] Newsletter
N Elec Telesis — Northern Electric Telesis
NELED — Neuroscience Letters
Nelineinaya Opt Tr Vavilovskoi Konf — Nelineinaya Optika. Trudy Vavilovskoi Konferentsii
Nelineinaya Opt Tr Vses Simp — Nelineinaya Optika. Trudy Vsesoyuznogo Simpoziuma po Nelineinoi Optike
Nelineinaya Teor Plastin Obolochek — Nelineinaya Teoriya Plastin i Obolochek
Nelineinye Volny Samoorgan Sb Mater Vses Shk — Nelineinye Volny. Samoorganizatsiya. Sbornik Sostavlen po Materialam Vsesoyuznoi Shkoly po Nelineinym Volnam
NEL Reports — National Engineering Laboratory. Reports
Nelson Gal & Atkins Mus Bull — Nelson Gallery and Atkins Museum Bulletin
Nelson Loose-Leaf Med — Nelson Loose-Leaf Medicine
Nem — Neman
NEM — New England Magazine
NEM — New Mexico Musiclan
Nematodnye Bolezni Skh Rast Itogi Vses Soveshch Fitonematodam — Nematodnye Bolezni Sel'skokhozyaistvennykh Rastenii. Itogi Vsesoyuznogo Soveshchaniya po Fitonematodam
Nematol — Nematologica
Nematol Bras — Nematologia Brasileira
Nematol Mediterr — Nematologia Mediterranea
NEMBR — Notices et Extraits des Manuscrits de la Bibliotheque du Roi
Nemet Polezn Iskop — Nemetallicheskie Poleznye Iskopaemye
NEMSB — Newsletter. Environmental Mutagen Society
Nemzetkozi Anaesthesiol Kongr — Nemzetkozi Anaesthesiologus Kongresszus
Nemzetkozi Kolorista Kongr — Nemzetkozi Kolorista Kongresszus
Nemzetkozi Meres Muszertech Konf Kozl — Nemzetkozi Meres- es Muszertechnikai Konferencia Kozlemenyei
Nemzetkozi Mezogazd Sz — Nemzetkozi Mezogazdasagi Szemle
NEN — Near East (New York)
NENA — New Nation. Manitoba Native Newspaper
NENAD3 — Neue Entomologische Nachrichten
NENBD — New England Business
N Enc Th — Nouvelle Encyclopedie Theologique
N Eng — New Englander
N Eng Hist Geneal Reg — New England Historical and Genealogical Register
N Eng I Mn E T — Transactions of the North of England Institute of Mining Engineers
N Eng J Med — New England Journal of Medicine
N Engl J Med — New England Journal of Medicine
N Engl Bioeng Conf Proc — New England Bioengineering Conference. Proceedings
N Engl Bus — New England Business
N Engl Dairyman — New England Dairyman

N Engl Econ Rev — New England Economic Review
N Engl Eng — New England Engineer
N Engl Fruit Meet Proc Annu Meet Mass Fruit Grow Assoc — New England Fruit Meetings. Proceedings. Annual Meeting. Massachusetts Fruit Growers' Association
N Engl Galaxy — New England Galaxy
N Engl J Med — New England Journal of Medicine
N Engl J Med Med Prog Ser — New England Journal of Medicine. Medical Progress Series
N Engl L Rev — New England Law Review
N Engl Northeast Bioeng Conf Proc — New England (Northeast) Bioengineering Conference. Proceedings
N Engl LR — New England Law Review
N Engl Reg Allergy Proc — New England and Regional Allergy Proceedings
N Eng L Rev — New England Law Review
N Engl Soc Allergy Proc — New England Society of Allergy Proceedings
N Eng Mag — New England Magazine
N Eng Police J — New England Police Journal
N Eng Q — New England Quarterly. An Historical Review of the New England Life and Letters
N Eng Rev — New England Review
N Eng Soc Stud Bull — New England Social Studies Bulletin
N Eng Water Wks Assn J — New England Water Works Association. Journal
NENJA — NERC [National Electronics Research Council] News Journal
NENKA — Nenryo Kyokai-Shi
NENO — News of Norway
NENOA8 — Japanese Journal of Tropical Agriculture
Neo — Neophilologus
NEOLA4 — Neoplasma
NEONA — Nenryo Oyobi Nensho
Neonatal Netw — Neonatal Network
Neonat Network — Neonatal Network. Journal of Neonatal Nursing
Neonat Screening — Neonatal Screening
Neoph — Neophilologus
Neophil — Neophilologus
Neophilolog — Neophilologus
Neoprene Noteb — Neoprene Notebook
Neorg Ionoobmen Mater — Neorganicheskie Ionoobmennye Materialy
Neorg Khim Itogi Nauki Tekh — Neorganicheskaya Khimiya. Itogi Nauki i Tekhniki
Neorg Lyuminofory Prikl Naznacheniya — Neorganicheskie Lyuminofory Prikladnogo Naznacheniya
Neorg Mater — Neorganicheskie Materialy
Neorg Stekla Pokrytiya Mater — Neorganicheskie Stekla, Pokrytiya, i Materialy
Neosan Avic — Neosan Avicola
NEPAB — Neuropaediatrie
Nepalese J Agric — Nepalese Journal of Agriculture
Nepal Gaz — Nepal Gazette
Nepali Math Sci Rep — Nepali Mathematical Sciences Report
NEPEA — Nepegeszseguegy
NEPEEQ — Neuroendocrine Perspectives
Nepeg — Nepegeszseguegy
N Ephem Sem Epigr — Neue Ephemeris fuer Semitische Epigraphik
Nephrol Dial Transplant — Nephrology, Dialysis, Transplantation
Nephrol Klin Prax — Nephrologie in Klinik und Praxis
Nephrol Nurse — Nephrology Nurse
Nephrol Nurs J — Nephrology Nursing Journal
Nephrol Probl Newborn Pediatr Nephrol Symp — Nephrological Problems of the Newborn. Pediatric Nephrology Symposium
Nephrol Rev — Nephrology Reviews
Nephrol Symp Vortr — Nephrologisches Symposium. Vortraege
Nephro Nurse — Nephrology Nurse
N Eph Sem Ep — Neue Ephemeris fuer Semitische Epigraphik
Nepr Ert — Neprajzi Ertesito
Nepr Ertes — Neprajzi Ertesito
Nepr Koezl — Neprajzi Koezlemenyek
NEPS — National Economic Projections Series
Neptunus Inf Mar — Neptunus Info Marine
NEQ — Nederlands Economisch Persbureau en Adviesbureau [NEPAB]. Nieuwsbrief
NEQ — New England Quarterly
NE Quar — New England Quarterly
NER — National and English Review
NER — National Institute Economic Review
NER — New England Review [Later, New England Review and Bread Loaf Quarterly]
NER — New England Review and Bread Loaf Quarterly
N Era — New Era
NERADN — Neuroscience Research
NERC News J — NERC [National Electronics Research Council] News Journal
N Ercolani — Nuovo Ercolani
N E Reg — New England Historical and Genealogical Register
NEREM Rec — NEREM [Northeast Electronics Research and Engineering Meeting] Record
NERIC Bull — NERIC [Nuclear Engineering Research in Cambridge] Bulletin
Nerudn Stroit Mater — Nerudnye Stroitel'nye Materialy
NERVA — Nervenarzt
Nerv Child — Nervous Child
Nerve Impulse Conf Trans — Nerve Impulse. Conference. Transactions
Nerve Membr Proc Taniguchi Int Symp — Nerve Membrane. Biochemistry and Function of Channel Proteins. Proceedings. Taniguchi International Symposium on Structure and Function of Biological Membrane
Nerv Inhib Proc Friday Harbor Symp — Nervous Inhibition. Proceedings. Friday Harbor Symposium
Nervn Sist — Nervnaya Sistema
Nerv Sist — Nervnaia Sistema

Nerv Sist Leningr Gos Univ Fiziol Inst — Nervnaya Sistema Leningradskij Gosudarstvennyj Universitet Imeni A. A. ZhdanovaFiziologicheskij Institut
Nerv Syst Electr Curr — Nervous System and Electric Currents
NES — Nordelbingische Studien
NESADS — Notas e Estudos. Secretaria de Estado das Pescas. Serie Recursos e Ambiente Aquatico
Ne Sci — New Scientist
NESDIS (Natl Environ Satell Data Inf Serv) Environ Inventory — NESDIS (National Environmental Satellite Data and Information Service) Environmental Inventory
NESI — Nesika
Nesoversh Krist Str Martensitnye Prevrashch — Nesovershenstva Kristallicheskogo Stroeniya i Martensitnye Prevrashcheniya
NESP Newsl — NESP [National Environmental Studies Project] Newsletter
NESP Rep — NESP [National Environmental Studies Project] Report
Nest Chr — Nestor-Chronik
Nestels Rosengart — Nestel's Rosengarten
Nestle Found Publ Ser — Nestle Foundation Publication Series
Nestle Nutr Workshop Ser — Nestle Nutrition Workshop Series
Nestle Nutr Workshop Ser Clin Perform Programme — Nestle Nutrition Workshop Series. Clinical & Performance Programme
Nestle Res News — Nestle Research News
NET — Nederlandsch Economisch Tijdschrift
N et D — Notes et Documents Publiee. Direction des Antiquites et Arts de Tunisie
Neth — Netherlands Patent Document
NETHA — Nederlandsch Tijdschrift voor Hygiene, Microbiologie, en Serologie
Neth Appl — Netherlands Application Patent Document
Neth Bur Ind Eigendom Ind Eigendom — Netherlands. Bureau voor de Industriele Eigendom. Industriele Eigendom
Neth Energy Res Found ECN Rep — Netherlands Energy Research Foundation. ECN [Energieonderzoek Centrum Nederland] Report
Netherlands J Agric Sci — Netherlands Journal of Agricultural Science
Netherl Intl L Rev — Netherlands Yearbook of International Law
Neth Fertil Tech Bull — Netherlands Fertilizer Technical Bulletin
Neth Geol Dienst Toelichting Geol Kaart Ned 1:50,000 — Netherlands. Geologische Dienst. Toelichting bij de Geologische Kaart van Nederland 1:50,000
Neth Geol Sticht Meded Nieuwe Ser — Netherlands. Geologische Stichting. Mededelingen. Nieuwe Serie
Neth Inst Sea Res Publ Ser — Netherlands. Institute for Sea Research. Publication Series
Neth J Agric Sci — Netherlands Journal of Agricultural Science
Neth J Agr Sci — Netherlands Journal of Agricultural Science
Neth J Aquat Ecol — Netherlands Journal of Aquatic Ecology
Neth J Intern Med — Netherlands Journal of Internal Medicine
Neth J Med — Netherlands Journal of Medicine
Neth J Nutr — Netherlands Journal of Nutrition
Neth J Plant Pathol — Netherlands Journal of Plant Pathology
Neth J Sea — Netherlands Journal of Sea Research
Neth J Sea Res — Netherlands Journal of Sea Research
Neth J Surg — Netherlands Journal of Surgery
Neth J Vet Sci — Netherlands Journal of Veterinary Science
Neth J Zool — Netherlands Journal of Zoology
Neth Milk D — Netherlands Milk and Dairy Journal
Neth Milk Dairy J — Netherlands Milk and Dairy Journal
Neth Nitrogen Tech Bull — Netherlands Nitrogen Technical Bulletin
Neth Pat Doc Octrooi — Netherlands. Patent Document. Octrooi
Neth Pat Doc Terinzagelegging — Netherlands. Patent Document. Terinzagelegging
Neth Res Cent TNO Shipbuild Navig Commun — Netherlands Research Centre TNO for Shipbuilding and Navigation. Communication
Neth Rijks Geol Dienst Jaarversl — Netherlands. Rijks Geologische Dienst. Jaarverslag
Neth Rijks Geol Dienst Meded Nieuwe Ser — Netherlands. Rijks Geologische Dienst. Mededelingen. Nieuwe Serie
Neth Stat — Statistical Yearbook of the Netherlands
Neth Sticht Bodemkartering Bodemkund Stud — Netherlands. Stichting voor Bodemkartering. Bodemkundige Studies
NETJA — Nederlands Tijdschrift voor Geneeskunde
Ne T T — Nederlands Theologisch Tijdschrift
Network Comp — Network Computing
Networking Jnl — Networking Journal
Network Newsl — Network Newsletter
Network Sci — Network Science
Neuburg Kollktbl — Neuburger Kollektionenblatt. Jahresschrift des Heimatvereins, Historischen Vereins
Neuch Bll — Bulletin de la Societe des Sciences Naturelles de Neuchatel
Neuch S Sc Bll — Bulletin de la Societe des Sciences Naturelles de Neuchatel
NEUDA — Neue Deliwa-Zeitschrift
Neue Ackerbau Zeitung Ackerbau Ges Niederrheins — Neue Ackerbau-Zeitung der Ackerbau-Gesellschaft und der vier Bezirks-Comitien des Niederrheins
Neue Analekten Erd Himmels Kunde — Neue Analekten fuer Erd- und Himmels-Kunde
Neue Ann Blumisterei Gartenbesitz — Neue Annalen der Blumisterei fuer Gartenbesitzer, Kunstgaertner, Samenhaendler,und Blumenfreunde
Neue Arzneim Spez — Neue Arzneimittel und Spezialitaeten
Neue Arzneim Spez Geheimm — Neue Arzneimittel. Spezialitaeten und Geheimmittel
Neue Aspekte Trasylol-Ther — Neue Aspekte der Trasylol-Therapie
Neue Beitr Gesch Deutsch Altert — Neue Beitraege zur Geschichte des Deutschen Altertums
Neue Beitr Gesch Landesknd Tirols — Neue Beitraege zur Geschichtlichen Landeskunde Tirols
Neue Beitr Kenntn Afrika — Neue Beitraege zur Kenntniss von Afrika
Neue Bergbautech — Neue Bergbautechnik

Neue Berlin Monatsschr — Neue Berlinische Monatsschrift
Neue Berlin Mschr — Neue Berlinische Monatsschrift
Neue Betriebswirtsch — Neue Betriebswirtschaft
Neue Beytr Bot — Neue Beytraege zur Botanik
Neue Bib S Wiss & Frejen Kst — Neue Bibliothek der Schoenen Wissenschaften und der Frejen Kuenste
Neue Bl Gemaeldeknd — Neue Blaetter fuer Gemaeldekunde
Neue Btr Gesch Dt Altert — Neue Beitraege zur Geschichte des Deutschen Altertums
Neue Deliwa-Z — Neue Deliwa-Zeitschrift
Neue Deliwa Z Foerd Gas Wasser Elektrizitaetsfaches — Neue Deliwa-Zeitschrift zur Foerderung des Gas-, Wasser- und Elektrizitaetsfaches
Neue Denkschr Allg Schweiz Ges Gesammten Naturwiss — Neue Denkschriften der Allgemeinen Schweizerischen Gesellschaft fuer die Gesammten Naturwissenschaften. Noveaux Memoires de la Societe Helvetique des Sciences Naturelles
Neue Denkschr Naturhist Mus Wien — Neue Denkschriften des Naturhistorischen Museums in Wien
Neue Denkschr Phys Med Soc Erlangen — Neue Denkschriften. Abhandlungen der Physikalisch-Medicinischen Societaet zu Erlangen
Neue Denkschr Schweiz Naturforsch Ges — Neue Denkschriften der Schweizerischen Naturforschenden Gesellschaft
Neue Dt Lit — Neue Deutsche Literatur
Neue Dt Mschr — Neue Deutsche Monatsschrift
Neue Dtsch Pap Ztg — Neue Deutsche Papier-Zeitung
Neue Entomol Nachr — Neue Entomologische Nachrichten
Neue Entwicklungspol — Neue Entwicklungspolitik
Neue Ergeb Primatol Kongr — Neue Erbegnisse der Primatologie. Kongress
Neue Faserst — Neue Faserstoffe
Neue Ges — Neue Gesellschaft
Neue Gesellsch — Neue Gesellschaft
Neue Giesserei Tech Wiss Beih Metallkd Giessereiwes — Neue Giesserei. Technisch-Wissenschaftliche Beihefte. Metallkunde und Giessereiwesen
Neue Hefte Morphol — Neue Hefte zur Morphologie
Neue Hefte Phil — Neue Hefte fuer Philosophie
Neue Heidelberg Jb — Neue Heidelberger Jahrbuecher
Neue Heidelbg Jbb — Neue Heidelberger Jahrbuecher
Neue Heidelb Jahrb — Neue Heidelberger Jahrbuecher
Neue Hist Abh Baier Akad Wiss — Neue Historische Abhandlungen der Baierischen Akademie der Wissenschaften
Neue Hung Quart — Neue Hungarian Quarterly
Neue Illus Ztg — Neue Illustrierte Zeitung
Neue J — Neue Jahrbuecher fuer Antike und Deutsche Bildung
Neue Jahrb — Neue Jahrbuecher fuer Antike und Deutsche Bildung
Neue Jb — Neue Jahrbuecher
Neue Jbb Wiss Jugendbildg — Neue Jahrbuecher fuer Wissenschaft und Jugendbildung
Neue Jenaische Allg Literaturzeitung — Neue Jenaische Allgemeine Literaturzeitung
Neue Jued Mhft — Neue Juedische Monatshefte
Neue Jurist Wochenschr — Neue Juristische Wochenschrift
Neue Jur Wschr — Neue Juristische Wochenschrift
Neue Lausiz Monatsschr — Neue Lausizische Monatsschrift
Neue Mannigfaltigk — Neue Mannigfaltigkeiten
Neue Med Versuche Bemerk Ges Edinburgh — Neue Medizinische Versuche Nebst Bemerkungen, Welche von Einer Gesellschaft in Edinburgh Durchgesehen und Herausgegeben Werden. Aus dem Englischen Uebersetzt
Neue Med W — Neue Medizinische Welt
Neue Med Welt — Neue Medizinische Welt
Neue Methoden Unters Zellkernes Verh Ges Histochem Symp — Neue Methoden zur Untersuchung des Zellkernes. Verhandlungen der Gesellschaft fuer Histochemie auf dem Symposion
Neue Milit Bll — Neue Militaerische Blaetter
Neue Mitt Landwirtsch — Neue Mitteilungen fuer die Landwirtschaft
Neue Monatl Beitr Naturk Schwerin — Neue Monatliche Beitraege zur Naturkunde (Schwerin)
Neue Muench Beitr Gesch Med Medizinhist — Neue Muenchner Beitraege zur Geschichte der Medizin und Naturwissenschaften. Medizinhistorische Reihe
Neue Muench Beitr Gesch Med Naturwiss Medizinhist Reihe — Neue Muenchner Beitraege zur Geschichte der Medizin und Naturwissenschaften. Medizinhistorische Reihe
Neue Mz — Neue Musikzeitung
Neue Nuernberg Gel Zeitung — Neue Nuernbergische Gelehrte Zeitung
Neue Oberdeutsche Allg Litteraturzeitung — Neue Oberdeutsche Allgemeine Litteraturzeitung
Neue Oesterr Z Kinderheilkd — Neue Oesterreichische Zeitschrift fuer Kinderheilkunde
Neue Oest Z Kinderheilk — Neue Oesterreichische Zeitschrift fuer Kinderheilkunde
Neue Ordnung — Neue Ordnung in Kirche, Staat, Gesellschaft, Kultur
Neue Phys — Neue Physik
Neue Phys Bl — Neue Physikalische Blaetter
Neue Polit Lit — Neue Politische Literatur
Neue Pol Lit — Neue Politische Literatur
Neue Pommersche Provinzialbl — Neue Pommersche Provinzialblaetter
Neue Psychol Stud — Neue Psychologische Studien
Neuer Alman Aller Um Hamburg Liegenden Gaert — Neuer Almanach Aller um Hamburg Liegenden Gaerten
Neue Rdsch — Neue Rundschau
Neuere Entwickl Stossspannungsmesstech 2 Vortr PTB Semin — Neuere Entwicklungen der Stossspannungsmesstechnik 2. Vortraege des PTB-Seminars
Neuere Samml Merkwuerd Reisegesch — Neuere Sammlung der Merkwuerdigsten Reisegeschichten

Neueres Forstmag Abth 2 — Neueres Forstmagazin. Zweyte Abtheilung von neuen Aufsaetzen, die Forstsachen und dahin Einschlagende Huelfreiche Wissenschaften Betreffend auch von Aeltern, Mittlern und Neuern Buechern Welche Eigentlich das Forstwesen Behandeln
Neue Rev — Neue Revue
Neue Rund — Neue Rundschau
Neue Rundsch — Neue Rundschau
Neues Abendl — Neues Abendland
Neues Allg Repert Neuesten In Ausl Lit — Neues Allgemeines Repertorium der Neuesten In- und Auslaendischen Literatur
Neue Samml Interessanter Zwekmaessig Abgefasster Reisebeschre — Neue Sammlung Interessanter und Zwekmaessig Abgefasster Reisebeschreibungen fuer die Jugend
Neue Samml Phys Oekon Schriften Oekon Ges Bern — Neue Sammlung. Physisch-Oekonomischer Schriften. Herausgegeben von der Oekonomischen Gesellschaft in Bern
Neue Samml Schriften Groessten Gel Schweden — Neue Sammlung Verschiedener Schriften der Groessten Gelehrten in Schweden
Neues Arch Ges Aeltere Dt Geschkde — Neues Archiv der Gesellschaft fuer Aeltere Deutsche Geschichtskunde
Neues Arch Niedersachs — Neues Archiv fuer Niedersachsen
Neues Arch Saechs Gesch — Neues Archiv fuer Saechsische Geschichte und Altertumskunde
Neues Archv Gesch Stadt Heidelberg & Kurpfalz — Neues Archiv fuer die Geschichte der Stadt Heidelberg und der Kurpfalz
Neues Archv Saechs Gesch & Altertknd — Neues Archiv fuer Saechsische Geschichte und Altertumskunde
Neues Bergmaenn J — Neues Bergmaennisches Journal
Neues Berlin Wochenbl Belehr Unterhalt — Neues Berlinisches Wochenblatt zur Belehrung und Unterhaltung
Neues Berl Jahrb — Neues Berlinisches Jahrbuch
Neues Chem Arch — Neues Chemisches Archiv
Neue Schleswig Holst Provinzialber — Neue Schleswig-Holsteinische Provinzialberichte
Neue Schriften Naturf Ges Halle — Neue Schriften der Naturforschenden Gesellschaft zu Halle
Neues Deutsch Mag — Neues Deutsches Magazin
Neues Goetting Jb — Neues Goettinger Jahrbuch
Neues Hamburg Mag — Neues Hamburgisches Magazin, oder Fortsetzung Gesammleter Schriften, aus der Naturforschung, der Allgemeinen Stadt- und Land-Oekonomie, und den Angenehmen Wissenschaften Ueberhaupt
Neues Jahrb Geologie u Palaeontologie Monatsh — Neues Jahrbuch fuer Geologie und Palaeontologie. Monatshefte
Neues Jahrb Geol Palaeontol Abh — Neues Jahrbuch fuer Geologie und Palaeontologie. Abhandlungen
Neues Jahrb Geol Palaeontol Abh B — Neues Jahrbuch fuer Geologie und Palaeontologie. Abhandlungen B
Neues Jahrb Geol Palaeontol Monatsh — Neues Jahrbuch fuer Geologie und Palaeontologie. Monatshefte
Neues Jahrb Mineral Abh — Neues Jahrbuch fuer Mineralogie. Abhandlungen
Neues Jahrb Mineral Geognosie — Neues Jahrbuch fuer Mineralogie, Geognosie, Geologie, und Petrefaktenkunde
Neues Jahrb Mineral Geol Abh Abt B Geol Palaeontol — Neues Jahrbuch fuer Mineralogie, Geologie und Palaeontologie. Abhandlungen. Abteilung B. Geologie und Palaeontologie
Neues Jahrb Mineral Geol Monatsh Abt B Geol Palaeontol — Neues Jahrbuch fuer Mineralogie, Geologie, und Palaeontologie. Monatshefte. Abteilung B. Geologie, Palaeontologie
Neues Jahrb Mineral Geol Palaeontol Abh Abt A — Neues Jahrbuch fuer Mineralogie, Geologie, und Palaeontologie. Abhandlungen. Abteilung A. Mineralogie, Petrographie
Neues Jahrb Mineral Geol Palaeontol Abh Abt B — Neues Jahrbuch fuer Mineralogie, Geologie, und Palaeontologie. Abhandlungen. Abteilung B. Geologie, Palaeontologie
Neues Jahrb Mineral Geol Palaeontol Abt A — Neues Jahrbuch fuer Mineralogie, Geologie und Palaeontologie. Abteilung A
Neues Jahrb Mineral Geol Palaeontol Beilageband Abt A — Neues Jahrbuch fuer Mineralogie, Geologie, und Palaeontologie. Beilageband. Abteilung A
Neues Jahrb Mineral Geol Palaeontol Beilageband Abt B — Neues Jahrbuch fuer Mineralogie, Geologie und Palaeontologie. Beilageband. Abteilung B
Neues Jahrb Mineral Geol Palaeontol Monatsh Abt 1 — Neues Jahrbuch fuer Mineralogie, Geologie, und Palaeontologie. Monatshefte. Abteilung 1. Mineralogie, Gesteinskunde
Neues Jahrb Mineral Geol Palaeontol Monatsh Abt 2 — Neues Jahrbuch fuer Mineralogie, Geologie, und Palaeontologie. Monatshefte. Abteilung 2. Geologie, Palaeontologie
Neues Jahrb Mineral Geol Palaeontol Ref — Neues Jahrbuch fuer Mineralogie, Geologie, und Palaeontologie. Referate
Neues Jahrb Mineral Geol Ref Abt B Geol Palaeontol — Neues Jahrbuch fuer Mineralogie, Geologie und Palaeontologie. Referate. Abteilung B. Geologie, Palaeontologie
Neues Jahrb Mineral Monatsh — Neues Jahrbuch fuer Mineralogie. Monatshefte
Neues Jahrb Mineralogie Abh — Neues Jahrbuch fuer Mineralogie. Abhandlungen
Neues Jahrb Mineralogie Monatsh — Neues Jahrbuch fuer Mineralogie. Monatshefte
Neues Jahrbuch Geologie u Palaeontologie Abh Monatsh — Neues Jahrbuch fuer Geologie und Palaeontologie. Abhandlungen. Monatshefte
Neues Jahrbuch Geol Palaeontol Abhandl — Neues Jahrbuch fuer Geologie und Palaeontologie. Abhandlungen
Neues Jahrbuch Geol Palaeontol Monatsh — Neues Jahrbuch fuer Geologie und Palaeontologie. Monatshefte
Neues Jahrbuch Mineralogie Abh Monatsh — Neues Jahrbuch fuer Mineralogie. Abhandlungen. Monatshefte
Neues Jb Mineralog — Neues Jahrbuch fuer Mineralogie

Neues Jb Miner Geol Palaeont Mh — Neues Jahrbuch fuer Mineralogie, Geologie, und Palaeontologie. Monatshefte
Neues J Bot — Neues Journal fuer die Botanik
Neues J Pharm — Neues Journal der Pharmacie
Neues J Pharm Aerzte — Neues Journal der Pharmacie fuer Aerzte, Apotheker und Chemiker
Neues J Phys — Neues Journal der Physik
Neues Lausitz Mag — Neues Lausitzisches Magazin
Neues Mag Aerzte — Neues Magazin fuer Aerzte
Neues Nutzbares Geb Haus Landw — Neues und Nutzbares aus dem Gebiete der Haus- und Landwirthschaft
Neues Optiker Jl — Neues Optiker Journal
Neues Schweiz Mus — Neues Schweizerisches Museum
Neueste Beitr Kunde Insel Madagaskar — Neueste Beitraege zur Kunde der Insel Madagaskar
Neuesten Entdeckungen Chem — Neuesten Entdeckungen in der Chemie
Neueste Nord Beytr Phys Geogr Erd Voelkerbeschreib — Neueste Nordische Beytraege zur Physikalischen und Geographischen Erd-und Voelkerbeschreibung, Naturgeschichte und Oekonomie
Neuestes Chem Arch — Neuestes Chemisches Archiv
Neuestes Gart Jahrb — Neuestes Garten-Jahrbuch, nach Le bon Jardinier
Neuestes J Erfind Gesammten Med — Neuestes Journal der Erfindungen, Theorien und Widersprueche in der Gesammten Medizin
Neues Vaterld Arch — Neues Vaterlaendisches Archiv, oder Beitraege zur Kenntnis des Koenigreichs Hannover
Neues Wien Tagbl — Neues Wiener Tagblatt
Neue Tech — Neue Technik
Neue Tech A — Neue Technik. Abteilung A. Automatik und Industrielle Elektronik
Neue Tech B — Neue Technik. Abteilung B. Kerntechnik
Neue Tech Buero — Neue Technik im Buero
Neue Verpack — Neue Verpackung
Neue Versuche Nuetzl Samml Natur Kunst Gesch Ober Sachsen — Neue Versuche Nuetzlicher Sammlungen zu der Natur- und Kunst-Geschichte Sonderlich von Ober-Sachsen
Neue Wirtsch — Neue Wirtschaft
Neue Wiss Bibl — Neue Wissenschaftliche Bibliothek
Neue Zeitungen Gel Sachen — Neue Zeitungen von Gelehrten Sachen
Neue ZFM — Neue Zeitschrift fuer Musik
Neue Z Fuer Missionswissenschaft — Neue Zeitschrift fuer Missionswissenschaft
Neue Z Mission — Neue Zeitschrift fuer Missionswissenschaft/Nouvelle Revue de Science Missionaire
Neue Z Miss Wiss — Neue Zeitschrift fuer Missionswissenschaft
Neue Z Ruebenzucker Ind — Neue Zeitschrift fuer Ruebenzucker-Industrie
Neue Zs Arbeitsr — Neue Zeitschrift fuer Arbeitsrecht
Neue Z Sys Th — Neue Zeitschrift fuer Systematische Theologie und Religionsphilosophie
Neue Zuerch Ztg — Neue Zuercher Zeitung
Neue Zuer Ztg — Neue Zuericher Zeitung
Neue Z Verwaltungsr — Neue Zeitschrift fuer Verwaltungsrecht
Neuheiten Tech — Neuheiten der Technik
NEUIDS — Neurochemistry International
Neujahrsblatt Naturforsch Ges Zur — Neujahrsblatt. Naturforschende Gesellschaft in Zuerich
Neujahrsbl Naturforsch Ges Zuer — Neujahrsblatt. Naturforschenden Gesellschaft in Zuerich
Neujahrsbl Naturforsch Ges Zuerich — Neujahrsblatt Herausgegeben von der Naturforschenden Gesellschaft in Zuerich
Neujahrsbl Sachs — Neujahrsblaetter Herausgegeben von der Historischen Kommission fuer die ProvinzSachsen
Neujbl Feuerwerker Ges Zuerich — Neujahrsblatt der Feuerwerker-Gesellschaft in Zuerich
Neujbl Hist Antiqua Ver & Kstver Schaffhausen — Neujahrsblatt des Historisch-Andiquarischen Vereins und des Kunstvereins in Schaffhausen
Neujbl Hist Ver Kant St Gallen — Neujahrsblatt des Historischen Vereins des Kantons Sankt Gallen
Neujbl Kstges Zuerich — Neujahrsblatt der Kunstgesellschaft Zuerich
Neujbl Stadtbib Zuerich J — Neujahresblatt [herausgegeben] von der Stadtbibliothek in Zuerich auf das Jahre
Neujbl Waisenhauses — Neujahrsblatt des Waisenhauses
Neujbl Zuerich Kstlergesellschaft — Neujahrsblatt der Zuercher Kunstlergesellschaft
Neumol Cir Torax — Neumologia y Cirugia de Torax
NEUND9 — Neurology and Neurobiology
NE Univ Bul — New England University. Bulletin
NE Univ External Stud Gaz — University of New England. External Studies Gazette
NE Univ Union Rec — University of New England. Union Record
NeuP — Neuphilologische Monatsschrift
Neuphil Mit — Neuphilologische Mitteilungen
Neuphilol M — Neuphilologische Mitteilungen
Neuphilol Mitt — Neuphilologische Mitteilungen
NEURA — Neurology
Neural Comput — Neural Computation
Neural Netw — Neural Networks
Neural Parallel Sci Comput — Neural, Parallel, and Scientific Computations
Neural Regul Mech Aging Proc Philadelphia Symp Aging — Neural Regulatory Mechanisms during Aging. Proceedings. Philadelphia Symposium on Aging
NEUREM — Neurourology and Urodynamics
Neurobehav Toxicol — Neurobehavioral Toxicology
Neurobehav Toxicol Teratol — Neurobehavioral Toxicology and Teratology
Neurobiol Aging — Neurobiology of Aging
Neurobiol Basis Learn Mem Taniguchi Symp Brain Sci — Neurobiological Basis of Learning and Memory. Taniguchi Symposium of Brain Sciences
Neurobiol Biochem Morphol — Neurobiology, Biochemistry, and Morphology

Neurobiol Chem Transm Proc Taniguchi Symp Brain Sci — Neurobiology of Chemical Transmission. Proceedings. Taniguchi Symposium of Brain Sciences
Neurobiol Cholinergic Adrenergic Transm Annu OHOLO Biol Conf — Neurobiology of Cholinergic and Adrenergic Transmitters. Annual OHOLO Biological Conference on Neuroactive Compounds and Their Cell Receptors
Neurobiol Control Breathing Nobel Conf Karolinska Inst — Neurobiology of the Control of Breathing. Nobel Conference. Karolinska Institute
Neurobiol Dis — Neurobiology of Disease
Neurobiol Invertebr Int Symp — Neurobiology of Invertebrates. Gastropoda Brain. International Symposium on Invertebrate Neurobiology
Neurobiol Learn Mem — Neurobiology of Learning and Memory
Neurochem Int — Neurochemistry International
Neurochem Pathol — Neurochemical Pathology
Neurochem Res — Neurochemical Research
Neuro Chir — Neuro-Chirurgie
Neurochira — Neurochirurgia
Neuro-Chire — Neuro-Chirurgie
Neurocomput — Neurocomputing
Neuroc Path — Neurochemical Pathology
Neuroendocr — Neuroendocrinology
Neuroendocrinol Lett — Neuroendocrinology Letters
Neuro Endocrinol Reprod Proc Reinier de Graaf Symp — Neuro-Endocrinology of Reproduction. Proceedings. Reinier de Graaf Symposium
Neuroendocr Perspect — Neuroendocrine Perspectives
Neurogastroenterol Motil — Neurogastroenterology and Motility
Neurohorm Invertebr — Neurohormones in Invertebrates
Neurohypophysis Int Conf — Neurohypophysis. International Conference on the Neurohypophysis
Neuroimaging Clin N Am — Neuroimaging Clinics of North America
Neurol Centralbl — Neurologisches Centralblatt
Neurol Clin — Neurologic Clinics
Neurol Clin Neurophysiol — Neurology & Clinical Neurophysiology
Neurol Dis Ther — Neurological Disease and Therapy
Neurol India — Neurology India
Neurol Med-Chir — Neurologia Medico-Chirurgica
Neurol Neurobiol — Neurology and Neurobiology
Neurol Neurobiol (NY) — Neurology and Neurobiology (New York)
Neurol Neurochir Pol — Neurologia i Neurochirurgia Polska
Neurol Neurochir Psychiatr Pol — Neurologia, Neurochirurgia, i Psychiatria Polska
Neurol Neurocir Psiquiatr — Neurologia, Neurocirurgia, Psiquiatria
Neurol Physiol Infect Dis — Neurology, Physiology, and Infectious Diseases
Neurol Proc World Congr — Neurology. Proceedings. World Congress of Neurology
Neurol Psihiatr Neurochir (Buchar) — Neurologia Psihiatria Neurochirurgia (Bucharest)
Neurol Psychiatr (Bucharest) — Neurologie et Psychiatrie (Bucharest)
Neurol Psychiatr (Bucur) — Neurologie et Psychiatrie (Bucuresti)
Neurol Res — Neurological Research
Neurol Ser One Neural Mech Mov — Neurology. Series One. Neural Mechanisms of Movement
Neurol Surg — Neurological Surgery
Neurol Surg Tokyo — Neurological Surgery (Tokyo)
Neuromodulation Brain Funct Proc Biann Capo Boi Conf — Neuromodulation and Brain Function. Proceedings. Biannual Capo Boi Conference
Neuromuscular Dev Dis — Neuromuscular Development and Disease
Neuromuscular Dis Proc Int Congr — Neuromuscular Diseases. Proceedings. International Congress on Neuromuscular Diseases
Neuromuscul Disord — Neuromuscular Disorders
Neuro Nucl Med — Neuro Nuclear Medicine
Neuro-Oncol — Neuro-Oncology
Neuropadiat — Neuropaediatrie
Neurop Ap N — Neuropathology and Applied Neurobiology
Neuropathol Appl Neurobiol — Neuropathology and Applied Neurobiology
Neuropatol Pol — Neuropatologia Polska
Neuropept Basic Clin Aspects Proc Pfizer Int Symp — Neuropeptides. Basic and Clinical Aspects. Proceedings. Pfizer International Symposium
Neuropept Brain Funct — Neuropeptides and Brain Function
Neuropept Psychiatr Disord — Neuropeptides and Psychiatric Disorders
Neuropharm — Neuropharmacology
Neurophysiol Clin — Neurophysiologie Clinique
Neurophysiology (Engl Transl Neirofiziologiya) — Neurophysiology (English Translation of Neirofiziologiya)
Neuropsichiatr Infant — Neuropsichiatria Infantile
Neuropsychiatr Enfance Adolesc — Neuropsychiatrie de l'Enfance et de l'Adolescence
Neuropsychiatry Neuropsychol Behav Neurol — Neuropsychiatry, Neuropsychology, and Behavioral Neurology
Neuropsycho — Neuropsychologia
Neuropsychol Rev — Neuropsychology Review
Neuropsychopharmacol Proc CINP Congr — Neuropsychopharmacology. Proceedings. C.I.N.P. (Collegium Internationale Neuro-Psychopharmacologicum) Congress
Neuropsychopharmacol Trace Amines Exp Clin Aspects — Neuropsychopharmacology of the Trace Amines. Experimental and Clinical Aspects
Neuroptera Int — Neuroptera International
Neuroradiol — Neuroradiology
Neurorehabil Neural Repair — Neurorehabilitation and Neural Repair
Neurosci Approached Cell Cult — Neuroscience Approached through Cell Culture
Neurosci Behav Physiol — Neuroscience and Behavioral Physiology
Neurosci Biobehav Rev — Neuroscience and Biobehavioral Reviews
Neurosci L — Neuroscience Letters
Neurosci Lett — Neuroscience Letters
Neurosci Lett Suppl — Neuroscience Letters. Supplement
Neurosci Net — Neuroscience-Net

Neurosci News — Neuroscience News

Neurosci Res — Neurosciences Research

Neurosci Res Commun — Neuroscience Research Communications

Neurosci Res NY — Neurosciences Research (New York)

Neurosci Res Program Bull — Neurosciences Research. Program Bulletin

Neurosci Res (Shannon Irel) — Neuroscience Research (Shannon, Ireland)

Neurosci Res Suppl — Neuroscience Research. Supplement

Neurosci Res Symp Summ — Neurosciences Research. Symposium Summaries

Neurosci Ser — Neuroscience Series

Neurosci Study Program — Neurosciences. Study Program

Neurosci Symp — Neuroscience Symposia

Neurosci Transl — Neuroscience Translations

Neurosc R C — Neuroscience Research Communications

Neurosecretion Int Symp — Neurosecretion. International Symposium on Neurosecretion

Neurosecretion Proc Int Symp — Neurosecretion. Molecules, Cells, Systems. Proceedings. International Symposiumon Neurosecretion

Neurospora Newsl — Neurospora Newsletter

Neurosurg Clin N Am — Neurosurgery Clinics of North America

Neurosurg Rev — Neurosurgical Review

Neurotoxicol Teratol — Neurotoxicology and Teratology

Neurotoxic Visual Syst Rochester Int Conf Environ Toxic — Neurotoxicity of the Visual System. Rochester International Conference on Environmental Toxicity

Neurourol Urodyn — Neurourology and Urodynamics

NeuS — Neuere Sprachen

Neu Spr — Neuere Sprachen

Neusser Jb Kst Kultgew & Heimatknd — Neusser Jahrbuch fuer Kunst, Kulturgewerbe, und Heimatkunde

Neutrino 81 Proc Int Conf Neutrino Phys Astrophys — Neutrino 81. Proceedings. International Conference on Neutrino Physics and Astrophysics

Neutron Capture Ther Proc Int Symp — Neutron Capture Therapy. Proceedings. International Symposium on Neutron Capture Therapy

Neutron Cross Sect Technol Proc Conf — Neutron Cross Sections and Technology. Proceedings. Conference

Neutron Data Struct Mater Fast React Proc Spec Meet — Neutron Data of Structural Materials for Fast Reactors. Proceedings. Specialists' Meeting

Neutron Induced React Proc Europhys Top Conf — Neutron Induced Reactions. Proceedings. Europhysics Topical Conference

Neutron Induced React Proc Int Symp — Neutron Induced Reactions. Proceedings. International Symposium

Neutron Phys Nucl Data Sci Technol — Neutron Physics and Nuclear Data in Science and Technology

Neutron Radiogr Proc World Conf — Neutron Radiography. Proceedings. World Conference

Neutron Transmutat Doping Conf — Neutron Transmutation Doping Conference

Neutron Transmutat Doping Semicond Mater Proc — Neutron Transmutation Doping of Semiconductor Materials. Proceedings. Neutron Transmutation Doping Conference

Neutron Transmutat Doping Semicond Proc — Neutron Transmutation Doping in Semiconductors. Proceedings. International Conference on Transmutation Doping in Semiconductors

Nev — Nevada Reports

NeV — Nova et Vetera. Revue d'Enseignement et de Pedagogie

Nevada Agric Exp Sta Bull — Nevada. Agricultural Experiment Station. Bulletin

Nevada Agric Exp Sta Forage Grasses Circ — Nevada Agricultural Experiment Station. Forage Grasses Circular

Nevada Bur Mines Map — Nevada. Bureau of Mines. Map

Nevada Hist Soc Quart — Nevada Historical Society Quarterly

Nevada Univ Center Water Resources Research Proj Rept — Nevada University. Desert Research Institute. Center for Water Resources Research. Project Report

Nevada Univ Desert Research Inst Tech Rept — Nevada. University. Desert Research Institute. Technical Report

Nev Admin Code — Nevada Administrative Code

Nev Ag Exp — Nevada. Agricultural Experiment Station. Publications

Nev Agric Exp Stn B — Nevada. Agricultural Experiment Station. B

Nev Agric Exp Stn Bull — Nevada. Agricultural Experiment Station. Bulletin

Nev Agric Exp Stn Circ — Nevada. Agricultural Experiment Station. Circular

Nev Agric Exp Stn R — Nevada. Agricultural Experiment Station. R

Nev Agric Exp Stn Rep T — Nevada. Agricultural Experiment Station. Report T

Nev Agric Exp Stn Ser B — Nevada. Agricultural Experiment Station. Series B

Nev Agric Exp Stn T — Nevada. Agricultural Experiment Station. T

Nev Agric Exp Stn Tech Bull — Nevada. Agricultural Experiment Station. Technical Bulletin

Nev & M — Nevile and Manning's English King's Bench Reports

Nev Bur Mines Bull — Nevada. Bureau of Mines. Bulletin

Nev Bur Mines Geol Bull — Nevada. Bureau of Mines and Geology. Bulletin

Nev Bur Mines Geol Rep — Nevada. Bureau of Mines and Geology. Report

Nev Bur Mines Rep — Nevada. Bureau of Mines. Report

Nev Dep Conserv Nat Resour Water Resour Bull — Nevada. Department of Conservation and Natural Resources. Water Resources Bulletin

Nev Dep Conserv Nat Resour Water Resour Inf Ser — Nevada. Department of Conservation and Natural Resources. Water Resources Information Series

Nev Dep Conserv Nat Resour Water Resour Reconnaissance Ser — Nevada. Department of Conservation and Natural Resources. Water Resources Reconnaissance Series

Nev Div Water Resour Water Resour Bull — Nevada. Division of Water Resources. Water Resources Bulletin

Nev Div Water Resour Water Resour Reconnaissance Ser — Nevada. Division of Water Resources. Water Resources Reconnaissance Series

Nevelestud Kozlem — Nevelestudomanyi Koezlemenyek

Nev Highways and Parks — Nevada Highways and Parks

Nev Nurses Assoc Q Newslett — Nevada Nurses' Association. Quarterly Newsletter

Nev Off State Eng Water Resour Bull — Nevada. Office of the State Engineer. Water Resources Bulletin

Nev R Bus and Econ — Nevada Review of Business and Economics

Nev Rev Stat — Nevada Revised Statutes

Nev Rev Stat Ann (Michie) — Nevada Revised Statutes, Annotated (Michie)

Nev RNformation — Nevada RNformation

Nevrol Psikhiat Nevrokhir — Nevrologiya, Psikhiatriya, i Nevrokhirurgiya

Nevrol Psikhiatr — Nevrologiya i Psikhiatriya

Nevrol Psikhiatr Nevrokhir — Nevrologiya, Psikhiatriya, i Nevrokhirurgiya

Nevropatol Psikhiat — Nevropatologiya i Psikhiatriya

Nevropatol Psikhiatr Psikhogig — Nevropatologiya. Psikhiatriya i Psikhogigiena

Nev SBJ — Nevada State Bar Journal

Nev Stat — Statutes of Nevada

Nev State Engineer's Office Water Res Bull — Nevada. State Engineer's Office. Water Resources Bulletin

Nev State Eng Water Resour Bull — Nevada. State Engineer. Water Resources Bulletin

Nev State Mus Anthropol Pap — Nevada State Museum. Anthropological Papers

Nev St Bar J — Nevada State Bar Journal

Nev Univ Agric Exp Stn Bull — Nevada. University. Agricultural Experiment Station. Bulletin

Nev Univ Agric Exp Stn Circ — Nevada. University. Agricultural Experiment Station. Circular

Nev Univ Dp G M B — Nevada University. Department of Geology and Mining. Bulletin

Nev Univ Max C Fleischmann Coll Agric Agric Exp Stn Tech Bul — Nevada. University. Max C. Fleischmann College of Agriculture. Agricultural Experiment Station. Technical Bulletin

Nev Univ Max C Fleischmann Coll Agric B — Nevada University. Max C. Fleischmann College of Agriculture. Series B

Nev Univ Max C Fleischmann Coll Agric R — Nevada University. Max C. Fleischmann College of Agriculture. Series R

Nev Univ Max C Fleischmann Coll Agric Rep T — Nevada. University. Max C. Fleischmann College of Agriculture. Report T

Nev Wildl — Nevada Wildlife

NEW — National Energy Software

New — New Age

NEW — New England Business

NEW — New English Weekly

NEW — Onderneming

NewA — New African

New A C P — New American and Canadian Poetry

New A Examiner — New Art Examiner

New Afr — New African

New Afr Dev — New African Development

New Africa — New African

New Agric — New Agriculturist

New Alchemy Q — New Alchemy Quarterly

New Am — New America

Now Am Mcroury — New American Mercury

New Ann Reg — New Annual Register

New Approaches Des Antineoplast Agents Proc Annu Med Chem Symp — New Approaches to the Design of Antineoplastic Agents. Proceedings. Annual Medicinal Chemistry Symposium

New Approaches Diagn Manage Cardiovasc Dis Conf — New Approaches in the Diagnosis and Management of Cardiovascular Disease. Conference on Cardiovascular Disease

New Approaches Manage Allerg Dis Symp Coll Int Allergol — New Approaches to the Management of Allergic Diseases. Symposium. Collegium Internationale Allergologicum

New Argent — Newsletter Argentina

Newark Beth Israel Med Cent J — Newark Beth Israel Medical Center. Journal

Newark Eng Notes — Newark Engineering Notes

Newark L Rev — University of Newark. Law Review

New Asia Acad Bull — New Asia Academic Bulletin. New Asia College. Chinese University of Hong Kong

New A'sian Post — New Australasian Post

New Aspects Storage Release Mech Catecholamines Bayer Symp — New Aspects of Storage and Release Mechanisms of Catecholamines. Bayer-Symposium

New Aspects Subnucl Phys Proc Int Sch Subnucl Phys — New Aspects of Subnuclear Physics. Proceedings. International School of Subnuclear Physics

New Aspects Trasylol Ther — New Aspects of Trasylol Therapy

New Astron — New Astronomy

New Astron Rev — New Astronomy Reviews

N E Water Works Assn J — New England Water Works Association. Journal

New Austral Fruit Grower — New Australian Fruit Grower

Newberry Lib Bul — Newberry Library. Bulletin

New Biol — New Biology

New Bkbinder — New Bookbinder

New Blckfrs — New Blackfriars

New Bldg Projects — New Building Projects

New Bot — New Botanist

New Br — New Brunswick Reports

New Br R — New Brunswick Reports

New Brunswick Dept Lands and Mines Ann Rept — New Brunswick. Department of Lands and Mines. Annual Report

New C — New Collage

New Caledonia Bull Geol — New Caledonia. Bulletin Geologique

New Camb Bibliog Eng Lit — New Cambridge Bibliography of English Literature

New Can F — New Canadian Film

New Cardiovasc Drugs — New Cardiovascular Drugs

Newcastle Chamber of Commerce J — Newcastle Chamber of Commerce Journal

Newcastle Ch Comm J — Newcastle Chamber of Commerce Journal

Newcastle C S T — Newcastle-upon-Tyne Chemical Society. Transactions

Newcastle Inst Ed J — Institutes of Education of the Universities of Newcastle Upon Tyne and Durham. Journal
Newcastle Mag — Newcastle Magazine
Newcastle Teach Coll Bul — Newcastle Teachers College. Bulletin
Newcastle Teach Coll Bull — Newcastle Teachers College. Bulletin
Newcastle Univ Gaz — Gazette. University of Newcastle
Newcastle Univ Phys Dep Res Pub — University of Newcastle. Department of Physics. Research Publication
Newcastle Upon Tyne Illus Chron — Newcastle upon Tyne Illustrated Chronicle
New Celtic Rev — New Celtic Review
New Cent Res Inst Electr Power Ind — News. Central Research Institute of Electrical Power Industry
New Cent Rev — New Century Review
New Chem Eng — New Chemical Engineering
New China — New China Magazine
New Church R — New Church Review
New Church Rev — New-Church Review. Massachusetts New-Church Union
New Civ Eng — New Civil Engineer
New Civ Engnr — New Civil Engineer
New Civ Engr — New Civil Engineer
New Civil Engr — New Civil Engineer
Newcomen Soc Study Hist Eng Technol Trans — Newcomen Society for the Study of the History of Engineering and Technology. Transactions
Newcomen Soc Trans — Newcomen Society. Transactions
New Commonw — New Commonwealth
New Commonw Br Car Suppl — New Commonwealth. British Caribbean Supplement
New Commun — New Community
New Compr Biochem — New Comprehensive Biochemistry
New Concepts Allergy Clin Immunol Proc Int Congr Allergol — New Concepts in Allergy and Clinical Immunology. Proceedings. International Congress of Allergology
New Cov — New Covenant
NEWD — Newsday
New Dent — New Dentist
New Des Youth Dev — New Designs for Youth Development
New Dev Appl Opt Radiom Proc Int Conf — New Developments and Applications of Optical Radiometry. Proceedings. International Conference
New Dev Biosci — New Developments in Biosciences
New Developm Agric — New Development on Agriculture. Hatachi Nogyo. Field Agriculture Society
New Dev Ion Exch Proc Int Conf Ion Exch — New Developments in Ion Exchange. Materials, Fundamentals, and Applications. Proceedings. International Conference on Ion Exchange
New Dev Pediatr Res Int Congr Pediatr — New Developments in Pediatric Research. International Congress of Pediatrics
New Dev Stainless Steel Technol Conf Proc — New Developments in Stainless Steel Technology. Conference Proceedings
New Diamond Sci Technol Proc Int Conf — New Diamond Science and Technology. Proceedings. International Conference
New Dir Child Dev — New Directions for Child Development
New Dir Com — New Directions for Community Colleges
New Direct — New Directions
New Direct Com Coll — New Directions for Community Colleges
New Direct Higher Educ — New Directions for Higher Education
New Direct Inst Res — New Directions for Institutional Research
New Dir Hig — New Directions for Higher Education
New Dir Ment Health Serv — New Directions for Mental Health Services
New Dir Youth Dev — New Directions For Youth Development
New Div — New Divinity
New Dom — New Dominion Monthly
New Dr — New Doctor
New Drugs Annu Cardiovasc Drugs — New Drugs Annual. Cardiovascular Drugs
New Drugs Clin — New Drugs and Clinic
New Drugs Clin Rem — New Drugs and Clinical Remedies
Newe — New-England Galaxy
NewE — New England Quarterly
New Ecol — New Ecologist
New Edinburgh Rev — New Edinburgh Review
New Educ — New Education
Newel — Newelectronics
New Electron — New Electronics
New Electr West — New Electrical West
New Eng — New Engineer
New Eng — New Englander
New Eng Adv W — New England Advertising Week
New Eng Bs — New England Business
New Eng Hist — New England Historical and Genealogical Register
New Eng Hist Geneal Reg — New England Historical and Genealogical Register
New Eng J Crim & Civil Confinement — New England Journal on Criminal and Civil Confinement
New Eng J Numis — New England Journal of Numismatics
New Eng Jour Med — New England Journal of Medicine
New Eng J Parapsych — New England Journal of Parapsychology
New Eng J Prison — New England Journal of Prison Law
New Eng J Prison L — New England Journal of Prison Law
New England Bus — New England Business
New England Econ Indicators — New England Economic Indicators
New England Econ R — New England Economic Review
New England J Bus and Econ — New England Journal of Business and Economics
New England J Human Services — New England Journal of Human Services
New England Jl Photogr Hist — New England Journal of Photographic History
New England J Med — New England Journal of Medicine
New England J Prison L — New England Journal of Prison Law

New England L Rev — New England Law Review
New England Mag — New England Magazine
New England Quart — New England Quarterly
New England Water Works Assoc Jour — New England Water Works Association. Journal
New Engld Med Gaz — New England Medical Gazette
New Engl J Hum Serv — New England Journal of Human Services
New Engl J Med — New England Journal of Medicine
New Engl Quart — New England Quarterly
New Eng L Rev — New England Law Review
New Engl Univ Explor Soc Rep — University of New England. Exploration Society. Report
New Eng M — New England Magazine
New Eng Mag — New England Magazine
New Eng M ns — New England Magazine (New Series)
New Eng Q — New England Quarterly
New Eng Quar — New England Quarterly
New Eng Soc Anniv Celeb — New England Society in the City of New York. Anniversary Celebration
New Entomol — New Entomologist
New Ent (Ueda) — New Entomologist (Ueda)
New Equip News — New Equipment News
NewER — New English Review
New Era — New Era in Home and School
New Era Nurs Image Int — New Era Nursing Image International
Newer Methods Nutr Biochem — Newer Methods of Nutritional Biochemistry
Newer Methods Nutr Biochem Appl Interpret — Newer Methods of Nutritional Biochemistry with Applications and Interpretations
Newer Met Ind — Newer Metal Industry
New Fic — New Fiction
New Fl — New Floral/Shin Kaki
New Flavours Proc Moriond Workshop — New Flavours. Proceedings. Moriond Workshop
New Fl Silva — New Flora and Silva
New Food Ind — New Food Industry
New For — New Forests
Newfoundland and Labrador Mineral Resources Div Bull — Newfoundland and Labrador. Department of Mines, Agriculture, and Resources. Mineral Resources Division. Bulletin
Newfoundland Dep Mines Energy Miner Dev Div Rep Act — Newfoundland. Department of Mines and Energy. Mineral Development Division. Report of Activities
Newfoundland Dep Mines Resour Geol Surv Inf Circ — Newfoundland. Department of Mines and Resources. Geological Survey. InformationCircular
Newfoundland Dep Mines Resour Geol Surv Rep — Newfoundland. Department of Mines and Resources. Geological Survey. Report
Newfoundland Geol Surv Bull — Newfoundland Geological Survey. Bulletin
Newfoundland Geol Survey Inf Circ Rept — Newfoundland. Geological Survey. Information Circular. Report
Newfoundland Geol Surv Inf Circ — Newfoundland. Geological Survey. Information Circular
Newfoundland Geol Surv Rep — Newfoundland. Geological Survey. Report
Newfoundland J Geol Educ — Newfoundland Journal of Geological Education
Newfoundland Labrador Miner Dev Div Rep — Newfoundland and Labrador. Mineral Development Division. Report
Newfoundland Labrador Miner Resour Div Inf Circ — Newfoundland and Labrador. Mineral Resources Division. Information Circular
Newfoundland Labrador Miner Resour Div Miner Resour Rep — Newfoundland and Labrador. Mineral Resources Division. Mineral Resources Report
Newfoundland Labrador Mines Branch Miner Resour Rep — Newfoundland and Labrador. Mines Branch. Mineral Resources Report
Newfoundland Miner Dev Div Rep — Newfoundland. Mineral Development Division. Report
Newfoundland Mines Branch Miner Resour Rep — Newfoundland. Mines Branch. Mineral Resources Report
New Fuels Era Proc Energy Technol Conf — New Fuels Era. Proceedings. Energy Technology Conference
New Gener Comput — New Generation Computing
New Gener Quinolones — New Generation of Quinolones
New Ger Cr — New German Critique
New Ger Crit — New German Critique
New Germ — New German Critique
New Germ Crit — New German Critique
New Ger Stud — New German Studies
New Grove — New Grove Dictionary of Music and Musicians
New Grove Jazz — New Grove Dictionary of Jazz
New Grove Mus Inst — New Grove Dictionary of Musical Instruments
New Guinea Agric Gaz — New Guinea Agricultural Gazette
New Guinea Austral Pacific SE Asia — New Guinea and Australia, the Pacific, and South East Asia
New Guinea Res B — New Guinea Research Bulletin
New Hamp BJ — New Hampshire Bar Journal
New Hampshire Agric Exp Sta Circ — New Hampshire Agricultural Experiment Station. Circular
New Hampshire Agric Exp Sta Res Mimeogr — New Hampshire Agricultural Experiment Station. Research Mimeograph
New Hampshire Progr Rep — New Hampshire Progress Report. University of New Hampshire Agricultural Experiment Station
New Harb — New Harbinger
New Haven Geneal Mag — New Haven Genealogical Magazine
New Haven Sym — New Haven Symphony Orchestra. Program Notes
New Hebrides Anglo Fr Condominium Prog Rep Geol Surv — New Hebrides Anglo-French Condominium. Progress Report. Geological Survey
New Hebrides Annu Rep Geol Surv — New Hebrides. Annual Report. Geological Survey

New Hebrides Condominium Geol Surv Rep — New Hebrides Condominium. Geological Survey. Report

New Hebrides Geol Surv Annu Rep — New Hebrides. Geological Survey. Annual Report

New Hebrides Geol Surv Rep — New Hebrides. Geological Survey. Report

New Hor — New Horizons

New Hor Educ — New Horizons in Education

New Horiz — New Horizons

New Horiz Baltimore — New Horizons (Baltimore)

New Horiz Cardiovasc Dis — New Horizons in Cardiovascular Diseases

New Horiz Catal Proc Int Congr Catal — New Horizons in Catalysis. Proceedings. International Congress on Catalysis

New Horiz Educ — New Horizons in Education

New Horiz Oncol — New Horizons in Oncology

New Horizons in Educ — New Horizons in Education

New Horiz Quantum Chem Proc Int Congr Quantum Chem — New Horizons of Quantum Chemistry. Proceedings. International Congress of Quantum Chemistry

New Hungarian Q — New Hungarian Quarterly

New Hungar Quart — New Hungarian Quarterly

New Hung Q — New Hungarian Quarterly

New Hung Rev — New Hungarian Review

New Ideas Psychol — New Ideas in Psychology

New Image Man Med — New Image of Man in Medicine

New Inf Syst Serv — New Information Systems and Services

New Int — New Internationalist

New Int Clin — New International Clinics

New Inter — New Internationalist

New Intl — New International Review

New Int Realities — New International Realities

New Ir Rev — New Ireland Review

New Istanbul Contrib Clin Sci — New Istanbul Contribution to Clinical Science

NewJ — New Jersey History

New J Agric Forest Coll Agric Chinling Univ — New Journal of Agriculture and Forestry. College of Agriculture. Chinling University/Nung Lin Hsin Pao

New J Chem — New Journal of Chemistry

New Jers Beekprs Ass News — New Jersey Beekeepers Association. News

New Jersey Agric Coll Exp Sta Bot Dep Rep — New Jersey Agricultural College Experiment Station. Botany Department Report

New Jersey Agric Coll Exp Sta Mimeogr Circ — New Jersey Agricultural College Experiment Station. Mimeographed Circular

New Jersey Div Water Policy and Supply Spec Rept — State of New Jersey. Department of Conservation and Economic Development. Division of Water Policy and Supply. Special Report

New Jersey Div Water Policy and Supply Water Resources Circ — State of New Jersey. Department of Conservation and Economic Development. Division of Water Policy and Supply. Water Resources Circular

New Jersey LJ — New Jersey Law Journal

New Jersey L Rev — New Jersey Law Review

New Jersey SBA Qu — New Jersey State Bar Association. Quarterly

New Jers St Hort Soc News — New Jersey State Horticultural Society. News

New Journ — New Journalist

New J Stat & Oper Res — New Journal of Statistics and Operational Research

NewL — New Leader

New L — New Letters

New Law J — New Law Journal

New Left — New Left Review

New Left R — New Left Review

New Left Rev — New Left Review

New Lib — New Liberal Review

New Libr Wld — New Library World

New Lib W — New Library World

New Lib World — New Library World

New Lit Autom — New Literature on Automation

New Lit His — New Literary History

New Lit Hist — New Literary History

New Lit Ideol — New Literature and Ideology

New L J — New Law Journal

New Look Tumour Immunol — New Look at Tumour Immunology

NewLR — New Left Review

New Magic Lantern J — New Magic Lantern Journal

New Mater Jpn — New Materials Japan

New Mater New Processes Electrochem Technol — New Materials and New Processes in Electrochemical Technology

New Mater Technol Appl — New Materials. Technology and Applications

New Math Library — New Mathematical Library

New Med J — New Medical Journal

New Med Phys J — New Medical and Physical Journal. Annals of Medicine, Natural History, and Chemistry

New Methods Drug Res — New Methods in Drug Research

New Met Tech — New Metals and Technics

New Mex Anthrop Albuquerque — New Mexico Anthropologist (Albuquerque, New Mexico)

New Mex Geol — New Mexico Geology

New Mex Hist Rev — New Mexico Historical Review

New Mexico Agric Exp Sta Res Rep — New Mexico Agricultural Experiment Station. Research Report. New Mexico State College

New Mexico Anthropol — New Mexico Anthropologist

New Mexico Bur Mines and Mineral Resources Bull — New Mexico. Bureau of Mines and Mineral Resources. Bulletin. New Mexico Institute of Mining and Technology

New Mexico Bur Mines and Mineral Resources Circ — New Mexico. Bureau of Mines and Mineral Resources. Circular. New Mexico Institute of Mining and Technology

New Mexico Bur Mines and Mineral Resources Geol Map — New Mexico. Bureau of Mines and Mineral Resources. Geologic Map. New Mexico Institute of Mining and Technology

New Mexico Bur Mines and Mineral Resources Mem — New Mexico Bureau of Mines and Mineral Resources. Memoir. New Mexico Institute of Mining and Technology

New Mexico Geol Soc Spec Pub — New Mexico Geological Society. Special Publication

New Mexico Hist Rev — New Mexico Historical Review

New Mexico J Sci — New Mexico Journal of Science

New Mexico Libr Bull — New Mexico Library Bulletin

New Mexico L Rev — New Mexico Law Review

New Mexico State Engineer Tech Rept — New Mexico State Engineer. Technical Report

New Mexico Univ Pubs Meteoritics — New Mexico University. Publications in Meteoritics

New Mex L Rev — New Mexico Law Review

New Microbiol — New Microbiologica

New Monthly Mag — New Monthly Magazine and Universal Register

Newm St — Newman-Studien

New Mthly Mag — New Monthly Magazine

New Mus R — New Music Review and Church Music Review

New Nippon Electr Tech Rev — New Nippon Electric Technical Review

New Nucl Phys Adv Tech — New Nuclear Physics with Advanced Techniques

New Options Energy Technol Pap AIAA EEI IEEE Conf — New Options in Energy Technology. Papers. AIAA/EEI/IEEE Conference (Edison Electric Institute)

New O R — New Orleans Review

New Orleans Acad Ophthalmol Trans — New Orleans Academy of Ophthalmology. Transactions

New Orleans Ac Sc Papers — New Orleans Academy of Sciences. Papers

New Orleans J Med — New Orleans Journal of Medicine

New Orleans M & Surg J — New Orleans Medical and Surgical Journal

New Orleans Med Surg J — New Orleans Medical and Surgical Journal

New Orleans Mus — New Orleans Music

New Orleans Port Rec — New Orleans Port Record

New Orl Med News Hosp Gaz — New Orleans Medical News and Hospital Gazette

New Orl Med Surg J — New Orleans Medical and Surgical Journal

New Orl Rev — New Orleans Review

New Pak Med J — New Pakistan Medical Journal

New Pal Soc — New Palaeographical Society

New Perfum J — New Perfumers' Journal

New Per Ind — New Periodicals Index

New Period Index — New Periodicals Index

New Perspect Clin Microbiol — New Perspectives in Clinical Microbiology

New Perspect Powder Metall — New Perspectives in Powder Metallurgy

New Perspect Theophylline Ther — New Perspectives in Theophylline Therapy

New Perspect Weed Sci — New Perspectives in Weed Science

New Pharmacol Vistas Anesth — New Pharmacologie Vistas in Anesthesia

New Phenom Subnucl Phys Int Sch — New Phenomena in Subnuclear Physics. International School of Subnuclear Physics

New Phys — New Physics

New Phys (Korean Phys Soc) — New Physics (Korean Physical Society)

New Phys Suppl — New Physics. Supplement

New Phytol — New Phytologist

New Polit — New Political Science

New Polit — New Politics

New Pol Sci — New Political Science

New Polym Mater — New Polymeric Materials

New Polym React — New Polymerization Reactions

Newport Hist — Newport History

Newport Hist Soc Bul — Newport Historical Society. Bulletin

Newport N H Soc Pr — Newport Natural History Society. Proceedings

Newport Soc — Newport Society

New Princ — New Princeton Review

New Publ Am Math Soc — New Publications. American Mathematical Society

New Publ Bur Mines — New Publications. Bureau of Mines

New Q — New Quarterly Review

New R — [*The*] New Republic

New R — The Review

New Real — New Realities

New Rem Ther — New Remedies and Therapy

New Rena — New Renaissance

New Rep — [*The*] New Republic

New Repub — [*The*] New Republic

New Republ — New Republic

New Res Plant Anat — New Research in Plant Anatomy

New Res Rep — New Research Reports

New Rev — New Review

New Riv R — New River Review

NEWS — New England Weekly Survey

New S — New Scholar

News — News from Nowhere

NewS — New Statesman

News Am Thorac Soc — News. American Thoracic Society

News Bull Indian Dent Assoc — News Bulletin. Indian Dental Association

News Bull Soc Vertebr Paleontol — News Bulletin. Society of Vertebrate Paleontology

Newscast Reg 4 Amer Iris Soc — Newscast Region 4. American Iris Society

New Sch Ex — New Schools Exchange. Newsletter

New Schl — New Schools Exchange. Newsletter

New Schol — New Scholar

New Schol — New Scholasticism

New Scholas — New Scholasticism

New Scholast — New Scholasticism

New Sci — New Scientist
New Scient — New Scientist
New Sci (London) — New Scientist (London)
News CIMMYT — News. Centro Internacional de Mejoramiento de Maiz y Trigo
New Sci Sci J — New Scientist and Science Journal
News Comment — News and Comments
News Ed Am Chem Soc — News Edition. American Chemical Society
News Eng — News in Engineering
News Farmer Coop — News for Farmer Cooperatives
News Farmer Coops — News for Farmer Cooperatives
Newsfront — Newsfront International
News Geotherm Energy Convers Technol — News of Geothermal Energy Conversion Technology
New Silver Technol — New Silver Technology
News Info GSA — News and Information. Geological Society of America
News Int Rice Com — Newsletter. International Rice Commision
News ISAM — Institute for Studies in American Music. Newsletter
News Jrl — News Journal
Newsl Am Acad Health Adm — Newsletter. American Academy of Health Administration
Newsl Am Acad Implant Dent — Newsletter. American Academy of Implant Dentistry
Newsl Am Assoc Equine Pract — Newsletter. American Association of Equine Practitioners
Newsl Amer Dermatoglyph Ass — Newsletter of the American Dermatoglyphics Association
Newsl Am Soc Ref Res — Newsletter. American Society for Reformation Research
Newsl Appl Nucl Methods Biol Agric — Newsletter on the Application of Nuclear Methods in Biology and Agriculture
Newsl Assoc Br Col Drama Educ — Newsletter. Association of British Columbia Drama Educators
Newsl Aust Conserv Fdn — Australian Conservation Foundation. Newsletter
Newsl Aust Conserv Found — Australian Conservation Foundation. Newsletter
Newsl Aust Inst Aborig St — Newsletter. Australian Institute of Aboriginal Studies
Newsl Aust NZ Soc Nucl Med — Newsletter. Australian and New Zealand Society of Nuclear Medicine
Newsl Biomed Saf Stand — Newsletter of Biomedical Safety and Standards
Newsl Br Univ Film Video Counc — Newsletter. British Universities Film and Video Council
Newsl Can Counc Int Coop — Newsletter. Canadian Council for International Cooperation
Newsl Can Pulp Pap Assoc Tech Sec — Newsletter. Canadian Pulp and Paper Association. Technical Section
Newsl Comm Eur Communit — Newsletter. Commission of the European Communities
Newsl Commonw Sci Counc Earth Sci Pragramme — Newsletter. Commonwealth Science Council. Earth Sciences Programme
Newsl Commw Geol Liaison Off — Newsletter. Commonwealth Geological Liaison Office
Newsl Coop Invest Mediterr — Newsletter of the Cooperative Investigations in the Mediterranean
Newsl Counc Eur Doc Ctre Educ Eur — Newsletter. Council of Europe. Documentation Centre for Education in Europe
News Leather Ind Trade — News of Leather Industry and Trade
Newsl Environ Mutagen Soc — Newsletter. Environmental Mutagen Society
News Lepid Soc — News. Lepidopterists' Society
Newslet — Newsletter. American Symphony Orchestra League, Inc.
Newslett Amer Magnolia Soc — Newsletter. American Magnolia Society
Newslett Amer Res Cent Egypt — Newsletter of the American Research Center in Egypt
News Lett Assoc Off Seed Anal — News Letter. Association of Official Seed Analysts
Newslett Assoc Off Seed Analysts — Newsletter. Association of Official Seed Analysts
Newslett Ass Offic Seed Anal — Newsletter. Association of Official Seed Analysis
Newslett Austrl Assoc Hist Phil Sci — Newsletter. Australian Association for the History and Philosophy of Science
Newslett Baluchistan Stud — Newsletter of Baluchistan Studies
News Lett Bulb Soc — News Letter. Bulb Society
Newslett Charles Rennie Mackintosh Soc — Newsletter. Charles Rennie Mackintosh Society
Newsletter ASOR — Newsletter. American Schools of Oriental Research
Newsletter Comp Stud Communism — Newsletter on Comparative Studies of Communism
Newsletter R Aust Hist Soc — Royal Australian Historical Society. Newsletter
Newsletter Ug — Newsletter for Ugaritic Studies
Newsletter WSEO — Newsletter. Washington State Energy Office
News Lett Florence Nightingale Int Nurs Assoc — News Letter. Florence Nightingale International Nurses Association
Newslett Geol Soc New Zealand — Newsletter. Geological Society of New Zealand
Newslett Hawaiian Bot Gard Found — Newsletter. Hawaiian Botanical Garden Foundation
News Lett India Popul Proj UP — News Letter. India Population Project UP
News Lett Int Coll Dent — News Letter. International College of Dentists
Newslett Interdiv Comm Hist IAGA — Newsletters of the Interdivisional Commission on History of the IAGA
Newslett Int Rice Comm — Newsletter. International Rice Commission
News Lett Int Union Biol Sci — News Letter. International Union of Biological Sciences
Newslett Norfolk Bot Gard Soc — Newsletter. Norfolk Botanical Garden Society
Newslett NY Landmarks Conserv — Newsletter. New York Landmarks Conservancy
Newslett Pl Propag Soc — Newsletter. Plant Propagators Society
News Lett Popul Cent (Bangalore) — News Letter. Population Centre (Bangalore)

News Lett Powder Metall Assoc India — News Letter. Powder Metallurgy Association of India
Newslett Program Publ Conc Sci — Newsletter. Program on Public Conceptions of Science
Newslett Soc Study Egyp Ant — Newsletter of the Society for the Study of Egyptian Antiquities
Newslett Stratigr — Newsletter on Stratigraphy
Newslett Tree Impr Introd — Newsletter of Tree Improvement and Introduction
Newsl Eur Shielding Inf Serv — Newsletter. European Shielding Information Service
Newsl Fusion Energy Found — Newsletter. Fusion Energy Foundation
Newsl Geol Soc (London) — Newsletter. Geological Society (London)
Newsl Geol Soc NZ — Newsletter. Geological Society of New Zealand
Newsl Geol Soc Zambia — Newsletter. Geological Society of Zambia
Newsl Geosci Inf Soc — Newsletter. Geoscience Information Society
Newsl Gov West Aus — Newsletter. Government of Western Australia. Mining
Newsl Gypsy Lore Soc N Amer — Newsletter of the Gypsy Lore Society North American Chapter
Newsl Huntington Soc Can — Newsletter. Huntington Society of Canada
Newsl-IGCP Proj 167 — Newsletter. International Geological Correlation Programme. Project 167
Newsl Indian Soc Nucl Tech Agric Biol — Newsletter. Indian Society for Nuclear Techniques in Agriculture and Biology
Newsl Indones Min Assoc — Newsletter. Indonesian Mining Association
Newsl Inst Foresters Aust — Institute of Foresters of Australia. Newsletter
Newsl Int Acad Periodontol — Newsletter. International Academy of Periodontology
Newsl Int Coll Dent India Sect — Newsletter. International College of Dentists. India Section
Newsl Intellectual Freedom — Newsletter on Intellectual Freedom
Newsl Int Geol Correl Programme Proj 156 Phosphorites — Newsletter. International Geological Correlation Programme. Project 156. Phosphorites
Newsl Int Rice Comm — Newsletter. International Rice Commission
Newsl Int Soc Bass — Newsletter. International Society of Bassists
Newsl Int Soc Radiogr Radiol Tech — Newsletter. International Society of Radiographers and Radiological Technicians
Newsl Int Tromb Assoc — Newsletter. International Trombone Association
Newsl Int Union Biol Sci — Newsletter. International Union of Biological Sciences
Newsl Isot Generator Inf Cent — Newsletter. Isotopic Generator Information Centre
News Lit Fashion — News of Literature and Fashion. Journal of Manners and Society, the Drama, the Fine Arts, Literature, Science.
Newsl Lab Hist Assoc — Newsletter. Labour History Association
Newsl Lang Teach Assoc — Newsletter. Language Teachers Association
Newsl League Int Fd Educ — Newsletter. League for International Food Education
Newsl Leg Act — Newsletter on Legislative Activities
Newsl Mar Technol Soc — Newsletter. Marine Technology Society
Newsl Nathaniel Hawthorne Soc — Newsletter. Nathaniel Hawthorne Society
Newsl NEA Comput Program Libr — Newsletter. NEA [National Education Association] Computer Program Library
Newsl NEA Data Bank — Newsletter. NEA [Nuclear Energy Agency] Data Bank
Newsl New Zealand Archaeol Assoc — Newsletter. New Zealand Archaeological Association
Newsl NZ Archaeol Assoc — Newsletter. New Zealand Archaeological Association
Newsl NZ Geochem Group — Newsletter. New Zealand Geochemical Group
Newsl NZ Map Circle — Newsletter. New Zealand Mapkeepers Circle
Newsl Peak Dist Mines Hist Soc — News-Letter. Peak District Mines Historical Society
Newsl R & D Uranium Explor Tech — Newsletter. R and D in Uranium Exploration Techniques
Newsl Somerset Mines Res Group — Newsletter. Somerset Mines Research Group
Newsl Soz Kognit — Newsletter Soziale Kognition
Newsl Springfield Dent Soc — Newsletter. Springfield Dental Society
Newsl Stat Soc Aust — Statistical Society of Australia. Newsletter
Newsl Stratigr — Newsletters on Stratigraphy
Newsl Taiwan Assoc Surf Sci Eng — Newsletter. Taiwan Association of Surface Scientists and Engineers
Newsl Tokyo Bk Dev Cen — Newsletter. Tokyo Book Development Centre
Newsl Wildl Dis Assoc — Newsletter. Wildlife Disease Association
Newsl Wis League Nurs — Newsletter. Wisconsin League for Nursing
News Media and L — News Media and the Law
News Native Calif — News from Native California
News Notes Am Soc Photogramm — News Notes. American Society of Photogrammetry
News Notes Calif Libr — News Notes of California Libraries
News Notes Calif Libs — News Notes of California Libraries
News NSLA — News. Nova Scotia Library Association
News Obser — News and Observer
New Soc — New Society
New Soc (London) — New Society (London)
New South Lit Mess — New Southern Literary Messenger
New South Wales Mag — New South Wales Magazine
New South Wales Soil Conserv Serv J — New South Wales. Soil Conservation Service. Journal
New South Wales Univ Sch Civ Eng UNICIV Rep — University of New South Wales. School of Civil Engineering. UNICIV Report
New So WL — New South Wales Law Reports
New So W St — New South Wales State Reports
New So WWN — New South Wales Weekly Notes
News Pestic Rev Nat Agr Chem Ass — News and Pesticide Review. National Agricultural Chemicals Association
News Physiol Sci — News in Physiological Sciences
NewSt — New Statesman
New States — New Statesman

New Statesm — New Statesman
New Steelmaking Technol Bur Mines Proc Open Ind Briefing — New Steelmaking Technology from the Bureau of Mines. Proceedings. Open IndustryBriefing
New Stsm — New Statesman
New Stsm Natn — New Statesman and Nation
News Views Ohio League Nurs — News and Views. Ohio League for Nursing
Newsw — Newsweek
News W — News Weekly
Newswk — Newsweek
News Xinhua News Agency — News from Xinhua News Agency
New Syndr Part B Annu Rev Birth Defects — New Syndromes. Part B. Annual Review of Birth Defects
New Synth Methods — New Synthetic Methods
New Teach — New Teacher
New Tech — New Techniques
New Tech A — New Techniques. Section A. Automatic Control and Industrial Electronics
New Tech B — New Techniques. Section B. Nuclear Engineering
New Tech Biophys Cell Biol — New Techniques in Biophysics and Cell Biology
New Tech Books — New Technical Books
New Technol — New Technology
New Technol Clin Lab Sci Proc ECCLS Semin — New Technologies in Clinical Laboratory Science. Proceedings. ECCLS (European Committee for Clinical Laboratory Standards) Seminar
New Technol Educ Ser — New Technology Education Series
New Tech Nutr Res — New Techniques in Nutritional Research
New Test Abstr — New Testament Abstracts
New Testam Abstr — New Testament Abstracts
New Test St — New Testament Studies
New Test Stud — New Testament Studies
New Ther Ischemic Heart Dis Int Adalat Symp — New Therapy of Ischemic Heart Disease. International Adalat Symposium
New Times — New Womens Times
New Towns Bull — New Towns Bulletin
New Trends At Phys — New Trends in Atomic Physics
New Trends Biol Chem — New Trends in Biological Chemistry. In Honor of Professor Kunio Yagi on the Occasion of the 70th Birthday Anniversary
New Trends Chem Teach — New Trends in Chemistry Teaching
New Trends Coal Sci — New Trends in Coal Science
New Trends Theor Exp Nucl Phys Predeal Int Summer Sch — New Trends in Theoretical and Experimental Nuclear Physics. Predeal International Summer School
New University — New University and New Education
New Univ Q — New Universities. Quarterly
New Univ Quart — New Universities. Quarterly
New Wld Antiq — New World Antiquity
New Wld Q — New World Quarterly
New Wld Rev — New World Review
New World A — New World Archaeological Record
New World Antiq London — New World Antiquity (London)
New World R — New World Review
New World Rev — New World Review
New W R — New World Review
NewY — New York Historical Society Quarterly
NewYH — New York History
New York — New York Magazine
New York Acad Sci Ann — New York Academy of Sciences Annals
New York Acad Sci Trans — New York Academy of Sciences. Transactions
New York Agric Exp Sta Circ — New York (State) Agricultural Experiment Station. Circular
New York City BA Bul — Bulletin. Association of the Bar of the City of New York
New York City Board Education Curriculum Bull — New York City Board of Education. Curriculum Bulletins
New York City Dept Health W Bul — New York City Department of Health. Weekly Bulletin
New York Eve Post — New York Evening Post
New York Hist — New York History
New York Hort Rev — New York Horticultural Review
New York J Math — New York Journal of Mathematics
New York J Med — New York State Journal of Medicine
New York Law J Dig Annot — New York Law Journal Digest Annotator
New York Law School Law R — New York Law School. Law Review
New York Med J — New York Medical Journal
New York Med Times — New York Medical Times
New York Pub Lib Bull — Bulletin. New York Public Library
New York State Dep Agric Nat Stud Bull — New York State Department of Agriculture. Nature Study Bulletin
New York State Fruit Growers Assoc Proc — New York State Fruit Growers' Association. Proceedings
New York State J Med — New York State Journal of Medicine
New York State Mus and Sci Service Map and Chart Ser — New York State Museum and Science Service. Map and Chart Series
New York State Mus and Sci Service Mem — New York State Museum and Science Service. Memoir
New York State Mus Mem — New York State Museum Memoirs
New York Times Book Rev — New York Times Book Review
New York Times Mag — New York Times Magazine
New York Univ J Internat Law and Politics — New York University. Journal of International Law and Politics
New York Univ Law R — New York University. Law Review
New York Univ Law Rev — New York University Law Review
New York Univ Stud Near East Civiliz — New York University Studies in Near Eastern Civilization

New York Water Resources Comm Bull — New York Conservation Department. Water Resources Commission. Bulletin
New York Water Resources Comm Rept Inv — New York Conservation Department. Water Resources Commission. Report of Investigation
New Y Q — New York Quarterly
New Y R B — New York Review of Books
New Zealand Agric Sci — New Zealand Agricultural Science
New Zealand Archt — New Zealand Architect
New Zealand Econ Pap — New Zealand Economic Papers
New Zealand Genet Soc Newslett — New Zealand Genetical Society Newsletter
New Zealand J Agric — New Zealand Journal of Agriculture
New Zealand J Bot — New Zealand Journal of Botany
New Zealand J For — New Zealand Journal of Forestry
New Zealand J Math — New Zealand Journal of Mathematics
New Zealand Jour Geology and Geophysics — New Zealand Journal of Geology and Geophysics
New Zealand J Publ Adm — New Zealand Journal of Public Administration
New Zealand J Sci Dunedin — New Zealand Journal of Science (Dunedin)
New Zealand J Sci Tech — New Zealand Journal of Science and Technology
New Zealand Math Mag — New Zealand Mathematics Magazine
New Zealand Math Soc Newslett — New Zealand Mathematical Society Newsletter
New Zealand MJ — New Zealand Medical Journal
New Zealand Oper Res — New Zealand Operational Research
New Zealand Pl Gard — New Zealand Plants and Gardens
New Zealand Sci Rev — New Zealand Science Review
New Zealand Soc Wker — New Zealand Social Worker
New Zealand Tobacco Growers J — New Zealand Tobacco Growers Journal. Tobacco Growers Federation
New Zeal Dep Sci Ind Res Bull — New Zealand. Department of Scientific and Industrial Research. Bulletin
New Zeal Geol Surv Bull — New Zealand. Geological Survey. Bulletin
New Zeal J Geol Geophys — New Zealand Journal of Geology and Geophysics
New Zeal LJ — New Zealand Law Journal
New Zeal Med J — New Zealand Medical Journal
Next Year — Next Year Country
NeZ — New Zealand Journal of History
Nezelezne Kovy Technickoekon Zpravodaj — Nezelezne Kovy. Technickoekonomicky Zpravodaj
NEZSA — Bulletin. New Zealand Department of Scientific and Industrial Research
NEZTA — New Zealand Veterinary Journal
NF — Neerlandia Franciskana
NF — Neue Forschungen
NF — Neues Forum
NF — New York Folklore. Quarterly
NF — Nigerian Field
NF — Northeast Folklore
NF — Northland Free Press
NFA — Nachrichten fuer Aussenhandel
NFAIS Bull — NFAIS (National Federation of Abstracting and Information Services) Bulletin
NFAIS Newsl — NFAIS [National Federation of Abstracting and Indexing Services] Newsletter
NFAN — National Flute Association Newsletter
NFAOD — Numerical Functional Analysis and Optimization
NFCR Cancer Res Assoc Symp — NFCR [National Foundation for Cancer Research] Cancer Research Association Symposia
N f D — Nachrichten fuer Dokumentation
NfDV — Nachrichtenblatt fuer Deutsche Vorzeit
NFEFD — Newsletter. Fusion Energy Foundation
NFF — NATO [North Atlantic Treaty Organization] Review
NFI — NFIB [National Federation of Independent Business] Quarterly Economic Report
N Filat T — Nordisk Filatelistik Tidsskrift
Nf J — Nordfriesisches Jahrbuch
NFJGG — Neue Folge des Jahrbuchs der Goethe Gesellschaft
NFL — New Found Land
NFL — Newfoundland and Prince Edward Island Reports
Nfld & PEIR — Newfoundland and Prince Edward Island Reports
Nfld Q — Newfoundland Quarterly
NFMB — Aarsberetning fra Foreningen til Norske Fortidsminders Bevaring
NF Med Dt — Naturforschung und Medizin in Deutschland
NFNLA — NFAIS [National Federation of Abstracting and Indexing Services] Newsletter
NFNV — Notre Foi et Notre Vie
N For — Nordisk Forum
N Forest — Northern Forestry / Hoppo Ringyo
N Forsch — Neue Forschung
NFP — Neue Freie Presse
NFP Jb — Jahrbuch der Neuen Freien Presse
N Franc — Neerlandia Franciscana
NFS — Nottingham French Studies
NFSGWS — Newsletter. Folklore Society of Greater Washington. Supplement
NFT — New Frontiers in Theology
NFTBEA — Netherlands Fertilizer Technical Bulletin
NFU — Unitas. Economic Quarterly Review
NFULDA — Fondation Universitaire Luxembourgeoise. Serie Notes de Recherche
NFV — New Zealand Foreign Affairs Review
NfWB — Nachrichten fuer Wissenschaftliche Bibliotheken
NG — Nederlandse Gemeente
NG — Neue Germanistik
NG — Neue Gesellschaft
NG — Neusumerischen Gerichtsurkunden
NG — New Guard
NG — Nieuwe Gids
NG — Nota Genitiva

NG — Novum Glossarium
NGA Rep & Stud — National Gallery of Art, Reports, and Studies
N Gas M 1990 — Natural Gas Market through 1990
NGAU — Nachrichten der Georg-August-Universitaet
N Gaz & Lit Register — National Gazette and Literary Register
NGBG — Neujahrsblatt. Gesellschaft zur Befoerderung des Guten und Gemeinnuetzingen
NGC — New Generation Computing
NGC — New German Critique
NGC — Nueva Gaceta Cubana
N G Canada Bull — National Gallery of Canada Bulletin
NGEMA — Neuere Geschichte der Evangelischen Missionsanstalten zur Bekehrung der Heiden in Ostindien
N Geog — National Geographic
N Geog Res — National Geographic Research
N Ges — Neue Gesellschaft
NGET — Norsk Geografisk Tidsskrift
NGF — Nomina Geographica Flandrica
NGG — Nachrichten. Gesellschaft der Wissenschaften zu Goettingen
NGgM — National Geographic Magazine
N Ggr T — Norsk Geografisk Tidsskrift
NGGW — Nachrichten. Gesellschaft der Wissenschaften zu Goettingen
NGH — Nachrichten der Giessener Hochschulgesellschaft
NGJI — National Geographic Journal of India
NGKBA — Nogyo Gijutsu Kenkyusho Hokoku. B. Dojo Hiryo
NGKCA — Nogyo Gijutsu Kenkyusho Hokoku. C. Byori Konchu
NGKDA — Nogyo Gijutsu Kenkyusho Hokoku. D. Seiri, Iden, Sakumotsu Ippan
NGKJB — Nippon Genshiryokusen Kaihatsu Jigyodan Nenpo
NGKNA — Nippon Genshiryoku Kenkyusho Nenpo
NGKYA3 — Folia Ophthalmologica Japonica
NGM — National Geographic Magazine
NGML — Novum Glossarium Mediae Latinitatis
NGMSA — Nauchnye Trudy Nauchno-Issledovatel'skii Gornometallurgicheskii Institut
NGN — Nomina Geographica Neerlandica
NGNVO — Nachrichten. Gesellschaft fuer Natur- und Voelkerkunde Ostasiens
NGPI — New Guinea Periodicals Index
NGPSA — Neftyanaya i Gazovaya Promyshlennost'
NGQ — Numismatic Gazette Quarterly
NGREEG — National Geographic Research
NG Research Bul — New Guinea Research Bulletin
NGRPD — GREMP [*Geothermal Reservoir Engineering Management Program*] News
NGS — Neue Geisteswissenschaftliche Studien
NGS — New German Studies
NGS — Nieuw-Guinea Studien
NGS/NGM — National Geographic Magazine. National Geographic Society
NGSQ — National Genealogical Society. Quarterly
N G Tech Bull — National Gallery Technical Bulletin
NGTE Rep — NGTE (National Gas Turbine Establishment) Report
NGTT — Nederduitse Gereformeerde Teologiese Tydskrif
NGu — Neusumerischen Gerichtsurkunden
NGU Publ — NGU (Norges Geologiske Undersoekelse) Publikasjoner
NGU Skr — NGU [*Norges Geologiske Undersoekelse*] Skrifter
NGV BI — Niedersaechsisches Gesetz- und Verordnungsblatt
NGWG — Nachrichten der Gesellschaft der Wissenschaften in Goettingen
NGWG — Nachrichten. Gesellschaft der Wissenschaften zu Goettingen. Philologisch-Historische Klasse
NGW (Goett) — Nachrichten. Gesellschaft der Wissenschaften (Goettingen)
NGWGott — Nachrichten. Gesellschaft der Wissenschaften zu Goettingen
NGWG PH — Nachrichten der Gesellschaft der Wissenschaften in Goettingen. Philologisch-Historische Klasse
NGWR — Nach Gottes Wort Reformiert
NH — Natural History
NH — Nebraska History
NH — Neos Hellenomnemon
NH — New Hampshire Quarter Notes
NH — New Hampshire Reports
NH — Noms des Hittites
NH — Noord-Holland
NH — Northern History
NH — Nueva Historia. Revista de Historia de Chile
NH — Numario Hispanico
NH Ag Exp — New Hampshire Agricultural Experiment Station. Publications
NHAM — North-Holland Series in Applied Mathematics and Mechanics
NHB — Nederlandsche Historiebladen
NHB — Negro History Bulletin
NHB — Neue Herder Bibliothek
NH Basic Data Rep Ground Water Ser — New Hampshire Basic-Data Report. Ground-Water Series
NHB J — New Hampshire Bar Journal
NHBI — Nassauische Heimatblaetter
NH BI — Nederlandsche Historiebladen
NH Bsns — Seacoast New Hampshire. Business Digest
NH Bsns Rv — New Hampshire Business Review
NHCG — North-Holland Series in Crystal Growth
NH Code Admin R — New Hampshire Code of Administrative Rules
NH Dep Resour Econ Dev Bull — New Hampshire Department of Resources and Economic Development. Bulletin
NHDIDW — Nutrition in Health and Disease
NH Div Econ Dev Bull — New Hampshire. Division of Economic Development. Bulletin
NH Div Econ Dev Miner Resour Surv — New Hampshire Division of Economic Development. Mineral Resources Survey

NHE — Nederlandse Energiehuishouding. Witkomsten van Maandtellingen en Kwartaaltellingen
NHE — Nouvelle Histoire de l'Eglise
NHEIAY — Japanese Journal of Smooth Muscle Research
N Herp Foren — Nordisk Herpetologisk Forening
N Hest — Nea Hestia
NHGZA — Nippon Igaku Hoshasen Gakkai Zasshi
NH His S — New Hampshire Historical Society. Proceedings
NH Hydrol Data Rep — New Hampshire Hydrologic-Data Report
N Hisp — Numario Hispanico
N Hist — Northern History
NHJ — Nathaniel Hawthorne Journal
NHJ — Neue Heidelberger Jahrbuecher
NHJ — New Hampshire Bar Journal
NHJ — Nordharger Jahrbuch. Museen der Stadt Halberstadt
NHJB — Neue Heidelberger Jahrbuecher
NHK Lab Note — NHK [*Nippon Hoso Kyokai*] Laboratories Note
NHKNA — Nippon Hoshasen Kobunshi Kenkyu Kyokai Nempo
NHK Tech J — NHK [*Nippon Hoso Kyokai*] Technical Journal
NHK Tech Monogr — NHK [*Nippon Hoso Kyokai*] Technical Monograph
NHK Tech Rep — NHK (Nippon Hoso Kyokai) Technical Report
NH Laws — Laws of the State of New Hampshire
NHLS — North-Holland Linguistic Series
NHMC — Natural History Miscellanea. Chicago Academy of Sciences
NHMDAP — National Health and Medical Research Council [*Canberra*]. Medical Research
NHML — North-Holland Mathematical Library
NHMS — North-Holland Mathematics Studies
NHMT — North-Holland Medieval Translations
NHNY — Natural History. American Museum of Natural History (New York)
NHochland — Neues Hochland
NHOKA — NHK (Nippon Hoso Kyokai) Technical Monograph
NH Progr Rep — New Hampshire Progress Report
NHQ — New Hungarian Quarterly
NHRB — Northern Health Research Bulletin
NH Rev Stat Ann — New Hampshire Revised Statutes Annotated
NHRI Paper — National Hydrology Research Institute. Paper
NH Rulemaking Reg — New Hampshire Rulemaking Register
N H Rv — Natural History Review
NH Rv — Natural History Review and Quarterly Journal of Science
NHSC — North-Holland Systems and Control Series
N H Soc NB B — Natural History Society of New Brunswick. Bulletin
NHSQ — Nevada Historical Society Quarterly
NHSS — North-Holland Studies in Silver
NHSSD — North-Holland Series in Systems and Software Development
NH State Plan Devel Comm Mineral Res Survey — New Hampshire State Planning and Development Commission. Mineral Resources Survey
NH State Plann Dev Comm Miner Resour Surv — New Hampshire State Planning and Development Commission. Mineral Resources Survey
NHT — International Herald Tribune
NHT — Norsk Historisk Tidsskrift
NHT — Nyt Historisk Tidsskrift
NH Univ Eng Exp Stn Eng Publ — New Hampshire University. Engineering Experiment Station. Engineering Publication
NHV — Nea Helliniki Vivliothiki
NHVKSG — Neujahrsblatt. Historischer Verein des Kantons St. Gallen
NHV St Gall — Neujahrsblatt. Historischer Verein des Kantons St. Gallen
NI — Naucno-Issledovatel'skij
NI — New Internationalist
NI — Nuevo Indice
NI — Nuova Italia
NIA — New India Antiquary
NIA — Notas del Instituto de Antropologia. Universidad Nacional de Tucuman
NIAAA Res Monogr — NIAAA (National Institute on Alcohol Abuse and Alcoholism) Research Monograph
NIAACH — New Interpretations of Aboriginal American Culture History. Betty Meggers [*Washington*]
NIA ES — New India Antiquary. Extra Series
Niagara Hist Soc Pub — Niagara Historical Society. Publications
Niagara Hist Soc Publ — Niagara Historical Society. Publications
NIAHAI — National Institute of Animal Health. Quarterly
Ni AKG — Nieuw Archief voor Kerkelijke Geschiedenis
NIB — Navigantium atque Itinerarium Bibliotheca
NIBM — Note dell'Istituto di Biologia Marina di Rovigno d'Istria
NIBN — National Indian Brotherhood. Newsletter
NIBS Bull Biol Res — Nippon Institute for Biological Science. Bulletin. Biological Research
NIC — New International Commentary on the New Testament
Nica Indig Managua — Nicaragua Indigena. Instituto Indigenista Nacional (Managua)
Nicaragua Servicio Geol Nac Bol — Nicaragua Servicio Geologico Nacional. Boletin
Nicar Inst Invest Sism Bol — Nicaragua Instituto de Investigaciones Sismicas. Boletin
Nicar Med — Nicaragua Medica
Nicar Odontol — Nicaragua Odontologica
Nice Hi — Nice Historique
Nice Hist — Nice Historique
Nice Med — Nice Medical
Nice Obs A — Annales de l'Observatoire de Nice
Nic H & C — Nicholl, Hare, and Carrow's Railway and Canal Cases
NICHAS — Journal. Nihon University Medical Association
Nich Ig Zass — Nichidai Igaku Zasshi
Nichiren Gakkai Kaishi Bull Jap Neth Inst — Nichiren-Gakkai Kaishi/Bulletin of the Japanese-Netherlands Institute

Nicholls State Univ Prof Pap Ser Biol — Nicholls State University. Professional Papers Series. Biology
Nicholson J — Journal of Natural Philosophy, Chemistry, and the Arts. Nicholson
NICKA3 — Japanese Journal of Zootechnical Science
Nickel Ber — Nickel Berichte
Nickel Bull — Nickel Bulletin
Nickel Metall Symp Proc — Nickel Metallurgy. Symposium. Proceedings
Nickel Spurenelem Symp — Nickel. Spurenelement-Symposium
Nickel Steel Top — Nickel Steel Topics
Nickel Sulphide Field Conf — Nickel Sulphide Field Conference
Nickel Top — Nickel Topics
Nickos Fruit J — Nicko's Fruit Journal
Nicotine Tob Res — Nicotine & Tobacco Research
NID — National Intelligence Daily
NIDA Res Monogr — National Institute on Drug Abuse. Research Monograph
NIDZA — Nippon Ika Daigaku Zasshi
NIDZAJ — Journal. Nippon Medical School
NIE — Noticiario Indigenista Espanol [*Madrid*]
Niederbayer Mschr — Niederbayerische Monatsschrift
Niederdeu Mit — Niederdeutsche Mitteilungen
Niederdt Beitr Kstgesch — Niederdeutsche Beitraege zur Kunstgeschichte
Niederdt Jb — Jahrbuch des Vereins fuer Niederdeutsche Sprachforschung
Niederdt Kbl — Korrespondenzblatt des Vereins fuer Niederdeutsche Sprachforschung
Niederlausitzer Florist Mitt — Niederlausitzer Floristische Mitteilungen
Niederoest Imker — Niederoesterreichesche Imker
Niederrhein Ges Bonn Szb — Niederrheinische Gesellschaft fuer Natur und Heilkunde zu Bonn. Sitzungsberichte
Niederrhein Jahrb — Niederrheinisches Jahrbuch
Niederrhein Taschenb Liebhaber Schoenen Guten — Niederrheinisches Taschenbuch fuer Liebhaber des Schoenen und Guten
Niedersachs Zahnarztebl — Niedersaechsisches Zahnarzteblatt
Niedersaechs Beitr Kstgesch — Niedersaechsische Beitraege zur Kunstgeschichte
Niedersaechs Dkmlpf — Niedersaechsische Denkmalpflege
Niedersaechs Jahrb Landesgesch — Niedersaechsisches Jahrbuch fuer Landesgeschichte
Niedersaechs Jb — Niedersaechsisches Jahrbuch
Niedersaechs Ministerialbl — Niedersaechsisches Ministerialblatt
Niedersaechs Neue Zeitungen Gel Sachen — Niedersaechsische Neue Zeitungen von Gelehrten Sachen
Niedersaechs Zahnaerztebl — Niedersaechsisches Zahnaerzteblatt
Nied Jb LG — Niedersaechsisches Jahrbuch fuer Landesgeschichte
Niedzica Semin — Niedzica Seminars
Nielson Rs — Nielson Researcher
Niemeyers Zeits F Int Recht — Niemeyers Zeitschrift fuer Internationales Recht
Niem Z — Niemeyers Zeitschrift fuer Internationales Recht
Nien San Ann Univ Cantho — Nien San. Annals. University of Cantho
NieR — Nieuwe Reeks
Niere Blutgerinnung Haemostase Hamb Symp — Niere, Blutgerinnung und Haemostase. Hamburger Symposium ueber Blutgerinnung
Niere Kreislauf Int Symp Dtsch Ges Fortschr Geb Inn Med — Niere im Kreislauf. Internationales Symposion der Deutschen Gesellschaft fuer Fortschritte auf dem Gebiet der Inneren Medizin
Nieren- Hochdruckkr — Nieren- und Hochdruckkrankheiten
NieS — Nietzsche-Studien. Internationales Jahrbuch fuer die Nietzsche-Forschung
NietzscheS — Nietzsche Studien
Nieuw Arch Wisk — Nieuw Archief voor Wiskunde
Nieuwe Drentse Vlksalm — Nieuwe Drentse Volksalmanak
Nieuwe Gids Biblioth — Nieuwe Gids Bibliotheek. Verzameling Oorspronkelijke Bijdragen Op Het Gebied Van Letteren, Kunst, Wetenschap, en Wijsbegeerte
Nieuwe Natuur Geneesk Biblioth — Nieuwe Natuur- en Geneeskundige Bibliotheek
Nieuwe Vaderl Letteroefen — Nieuwe Vaderlandsche Letteroefeningen
Nieuwe Verh Bataafsch Genoot Proefonderv Wijsbegeerte — Nieuwe Verhandelingen van het Bataafsch Genootschap der Proefondervindelijke Wijsbegeerte
Nieuwe WIG — Nieuwe West-Indische Gids
Nieuw Tijdschr Wisk — Nieuw Tijdschrift voor Wiskunde
NIF — Newsletter on Intellectual Freedom
NiF — Niagara Frontier
NIF — Nippon Facts
NIFAA — Nuovo Cimento. Societa Italiana di Fisica. Sezione A
NIFBA — Nuovo Cimento. Societa Italiana di Fisica. Sezione B
NIFCA — Nuovo Cimento. Societa Italiana di Fisica. Sezione C
NIFS PROC Ser Res Rep — NIFS-PROC Series. Research Report
Nig — Nigeria Magazine
NIGAB — Annual Report. National Institute of Genetics
Nig Ann Int'l L — Nigerian Annual of International Law
Nig Bar J — Nigerian Bar Journal
Nig BJ — Nigerian Bar Journal
Niger Agric J — Nigerian Agricultural Journal
Niger Annu Rep Fed Dep Agric Res — Nigeria. Annual Report. Federal Department of Agricultural Research
Niger Annu Rep Geol Surv Dep — Nigeria. Annual Report. Geological Survey Department
Niger Behav Sci J — Nigerian Behavioural Sciences Journal
Niger Dent J — Nigerian Dental Journal
Niger Dep For Res Programme Work — Nigeria. Department of Forest Research. Programme of Work
Niger Dep For Res Tech Note — Nigeria. Department of Forest Research. Technical Note
Niger Dev — Niger Developpement
Niger Entomol Mag — Nigerian Entomologists' Magazine
Niger Fed Annu Rep Geol Surv — Nigeria Federation. Annual Report. Geological Survey

Niger Fed Dep Agric Res Memor — Nigeria Federal Department of Agricultural Research. Memorandum
Niger Fed Inst Ind Res Res Rep — Nigeria. Federal Institute of Industrial Research. Research Report
Niger Fed Inst Ind Res Tech Memo — Nigeria. Federal Institute of Industrial Research. Technical Memorandum
Niger Field — Nigerian Field
Niger Fld — Nigerian Field
Niger For Inform Bull — Nigerian Forestry Information. Bulletin
Niger Geogr J — Nigerian Geographical Journal
Niger Geol Surv Div Annu Rep — Nigeria Geological Survey Division. Annual Report
Niger Geol Surv Rec — Nigeria. Geological Survey. Records
Nigeria Annu Rep Fed Dep Agric Res — Nigeria. Annual Report. Federal Department of Agricultural Research
Nigeria Bar J — Nigerian Bar Journal. Annual Journal of the Nigeria Bar Association
Nigeria Bull Foreign Affairs — Nigeria. Bulletin on Foreign Affairs
Nigeria Cocoa Res Inst Annu Rep — Nigeria Cocoa Research Institute. Annual Report
Nigeria Dep For Res Programme Work — Nigeria. Department of Forest Research. Programme of Work
Nigeria Dep For Res Tech Note — Nigeria. Department of Forest Research. Technical Note
Nigeria Fed Dep Agric Res Memo — Nigeria Federal Department of Agricultural Research. Memorandum
Nigeria Fed Dep Fish Annu Rep — Nigeria Federal Department of Fisheries. Annual Report
Nigeria Fed Dep Fish Fed Fish Occas Pap — Nigeria Federal Department of Fisheries. Federal Fisheries. Occasional Paper
Nigeria Fed Dep For Res Annu Rep — Nigeria Federal Department of Forest Research. Annual Report
Nigeria Fed Dep For Res Res Pap (For Ser) — Nigeria Federal Department of Forest Research. Research Paper (Forest Series)
Nigeria Fed Dep For Res Res Pap (Savanna Ser) — Nigeria Federal Department of Forest Research. Research Paper (Savanna Series)
Nigeria For Inf Bull — Nigeria Forestry Information Bulletin
Nigeria Geogr J — Nigerian Geographical Journal
Nigeria Mag — Nigeria Magazine
Nigerian Agric J — Nigerian Agricultural Journal
Nigerian Agr J — Nigerian Agricultural Journal
Nigerian Bar J — Nigerian Bar Journal
Nigerian Entomol Mag — Nigerian Entomologists' Magazine
Nigeria Newsl — Nigeria Newsletter
Nigerian Geogr J — Nigerian Geographical Journal
Nigerian Inst Oil Palm Res Annu Rep — Nigerian Institute for Oil Palm Research. Annual Report
Nigerian J Contemporary Law — Nigerian Journal of Contemporary Law
Nigerian J Econ and Social Studies — Nigerian Journal of Economic and Social Studies
Nigerian J Econ Soc Stud — Nigerian Journal of Economic and Social Studies
Nigerian J Entomol — Nigerian Journal of Entomology
Nigerian J For — Nigerian Journal of Forestry
Nigerian J Int Affairs — Nigerian Journal of International Affairs
Nigerian J Internat Studies — Nigerian Journal of International Studies
Nigerian J Islam — Nigerian Journal of Islam
Nigerian J Paediatr — Nigerian Journal of Paediatrics
Nigerian J Public Affairs — Nigerian Journal of Public Affairs
Nigerian J Sci — Nigerian Journal of Science
Nigerian Law J — Nigerian Law Journal
Nigerian Lib — Nigerian Libraries
Nigerian Libr — Nigerian Libraries
Nigerian Librs — Nigerian Libraries
Nigerian Libs — Nigerian Libraries
Nigerian LJ — Nigerian Law Journal
Nigerian Med J — Nigerian Medical Journal
Nigerian Stored Prod Res Inst Annu Rep — Nigerian Stored Products Research Institute. Annual Report
Nigeria Savanna For Res Stn Samaru Zaria Annu Rep — Nigeria Savanna Forestry Research Station. Samaru Zaria Annual Report
Nigeria Savanna For Res Stn Ser Res Pap — Nigeria Savanna Forestry Research Station. Series Research Paper
Nigeria Trade J — Nigeria Trade Journal
Niger Inst Oil Palm Res Annu Rep — Nigerian Institute for Oil Palm Research. Annual Report
Niger J Agric Sci — Nigerian Journal of Agricultural Sciences
Niger J Anim Prod — Nigerian Journal of Animal Production
Niger J Biochem — Nigerian Journal of Biochemistry
Niger J Entomol — Nigerian Journal of Entomology
Niger J For — Nigerian Journal of Forestry
Niger J Med Sci — Nigerian Journal of Medical Sciences
Niger J Nat Sci — Nigerian Journal of Natural Sciences
Niger J Nutr Sci — Nigerian Journal of Nutritional Sciences
Niger J Pharm — Nigerian Journal of Pharmacy
Niger J Plant Prot — Nigerian Journal of Plant Protection
Niger J Sci — Nigerian Journal of Science
Niger Mag — Nigeria Magazine
Niger Med J — Nigerian Medical Journal
Niger Nurse — Nigerian Nurse
Niger Pl Dev — Plan Quinquennal de Developpement Economique et Social, 1979-1983 (Niger)
Niger Postgrad Med J — Nigerian Postgraduate Medical Journal
Nig Geogr J — Nigerian Geographical Journal
NIGHAE — Archiv fuer Japanische Chirurgie
Nig J Contemp L — Nigerian Journal of Contemporary Law

NIGLA — Nauchno-Tekhnicheskaya Informatsiya. Tsentral'nyi Institut Nauchno-Tekhnicheskoi Informatsii Bumazhnoi i Drevoobrabatyvayushchei Promyshlennosti, Tsellyulozno-Baumazhnaya, Gidroliznaya i Lesokhimicheskaya Promyshlennost

Nig Lawy Q — Nigeria Lawyer's Quarterly

Nig LJ — Nigerian Law Journal

Nig LQ — Nigeria Lawyer's Quarterly

Nig LQR — Nigerian Law Quarterly Review

NIGM — Nederlandsch-Indische Geografische Mededeelingen

NigM — Nigeria Magazine

NIH — National Institutes of Health. Publications

NIHAE Bull — NIHAE [*National Institute of Health Administration and Education*] Bulletin

NIH Consens Statement — NIH [*National Institute of Health*] Consensus Statement

NIH Consensus Dev Conf Summ — NIH [*National Institutes of Health*] Consensus Development. Conference Summary

NIH Guide Grants Contracts — NIH [*National Institute of Health*] Guide for Grants and Contracts

NIHOD — Nieren- und Hochdruckkrankheiten

Nihon Chikusan Gakkai Ho Jap J Zootech — Nihon Chikusan Gakkai Ho/ Japanese Journal of Zootechnical Science

Nihon Juishikai Zasshi J Jap Vet Med Assoc — Nihon Juishikai Zasshi/Journal. Japan Veterinary Medical Association

Nihonkai Math J — Nihonkai Mathematical Journal

Nihon Kenchiku Gakkai J Archit & Bldg Sci — Nihon Kenchiku Gakkai/Journal of Architecture and Building Science

Nihon Oyo Dobutsu Konchu Gakkai Shi Jap J Appl Entomol Zool — Nihon Oyo Dobutsu Konchu Gakkai Shi/Japanese Journal of Applied Entomology and Zoology

Nihon Ringakkai Shi J Jap For Soc — Nihon Ringakukai Shi. Journal. Japanese Forestry Society

Nihon Sanshigaku Zasshi J Seric Sci Jap — Nihon Sanshigaku Zasshi. Journal of Sericultural Science of Japan

Nihon Seirigaku Zasshi Jap — Nihon Seirigaku Zasshi/Journal. Physiological Society of Japan

Nihon Senchu Kenkyukai Shi Jap J Nematol — Nihon Senchu Kenkyukai Shi/ Japanese Journal of Nematology

Nihon Shokubutsu Byori Gakkaiho Ann Phytopathol Soc Jap — Nihon Shokubutsu Byori Gakkaiho/Annals. Phytopathological Society of Japan

Nihon Univ Dent J — Nihon University. Dental Journal

Nihon Univ J Med — Nihon University. Journal of Medicine

Nihon Univ J Oral Sci — Nihon University Journal of Oral Science

Nihon Univ J Radiat Med Biol — Nihon University. Journal of Radiation Medicine and Biology

Nihon Univ Med J — Nihon University. Medical Journal

Nihon Univ Mishima Coll Humanit Sci Annu Rep Res — Nihon University. Mishima College of Humanities and Sciences. Annual Report of the Researches

Nihon Univ Mishima Coll Humanit Sci Annu Rep Res Nat Sci — Nihon University. Mishima College of Humanities and Sciences. Annual Report of the Researches. Natural Sciences

NIH Publ — NIH (National Institutes of Health) Publication [*US*]

Niigata Agric For Res — Niigata Agriculture and Forestry Research

Niigata Agric Sci — Niigata Agricultural Science

Niigata Agr Sci — Niigata Agricultural Science

Niigata Dent J — Niigata Dental Journal

Niigata Med J — Niigata Medical Journal

Niigata Univ Sci Rep Ser E — Niigata University. Science Reports. Series E (Geology and Mineralogy)

NiJ — Nigerian Journal of Islam

Nijhoff Internat Philos Ser — Nijhoff International Philosophy Series

NIJKA — Nippon Jozo Kyokai Zasshi

NIK — Nyelv-Es Irodalomtudomanyi Koezlemenyek

NIKGA — Nippon Kinzoku Gakkaishi

NIKHD — Niigata-Ken Kogai Kenkyusho Kenkyu Hokoku

NIKKA — Nippon Kogyo Kaishi

Nikkei Wkly — Nikkei Weekly

Nikko Mater — Nikko Materials

Nikolaev Korablestroit Inst Tr — Nikolaevskii Korablestroitel'nyi Institut. Trudy

NIL — Nederland Israel

Niles Reg — Niles' Register

Niles Reg — Niles' Weekly Register

NI Libr — Northern Ireland Libraries

N Ill LR — Northern Illinois University. Law Review

N Ill UL Rev — Northern Illinois University. Law Review

NILQ — Northern Ireland Legal Quarterly

NILR — Netherlands International Law Review

Nil Reg — Niles' Weekly Register

NIL Rev — Netherlands International Law Review

NIMH — National Institute of Mental Health. Publications

NIMHANS Journal — National Institute of Mental Health and Neuro Sciences. Journal

NIMRD — Nuclear Instruments and Methods in Physics Research

NIM Res Dig — NIM [*National Institute for Metallurgy*] Research Digest

NIM Res Rep — NIM (National Institute for Metallurgy. Republic of South Africa) Research Report

Nim S Sc Bll — Bulletin de la Societe d'Etude des Sciences Naturelles de Nimes

NIN — New Products International

Nine Cen Mus — Nineteenth Century Music

Nine Ct — Nineteenth Century

Nine-Ct Fic — Nineteenth-Century Fiction

Nine-Ct Fr — Nineteenth-Century French Studies

Nine Ct Mus — Nineteenth Century Music

Nine Ct The — Nineteenth-Century Theatre Research

Ninet Cent — Nineteenth Century

Nineteenth Cent — Nineteenth Century

Nineteenth Cent After — Nineteenth Century and After

Nineteenth Cent Theat Res — Nineteenth Century Theatre Research

NINF Informasjon Nor Inst Naeringsmidforsk — NINF Informasjon. Norsk Institutt for Naeringsmiddelforskning

NINND2 — Neuroptera International

NINS — Northern Ireland News Service

N Instr Meth — Nuclear Instruments and Methods [*Later, Nuclear Instruments and Methods in Physics Research*]

NINTD — New Internationalist

Ninth District Q — Ninth District Quarterly

NIOGA — Nippon Onkyo Gakkaishi

NIOSH — National Institute of Occupational Safety and Health. Publications

NIOSH/OSHA Current Intell Bull — NIOSH/OSHA Current Intelligence Bulletin

NIOSH Surv — NIOSH [*National Institute for Occupational Safety and Health*] Survey

NIOSH Tech Inf — NIOSH [*National Institute for Occupational Safety and Health*] TechnicalInformation

NIOSHTIC — NIOSH [*National Institute for Occupational Safety and Health*] Technical Infor mation Center Database

NIP — New Ideas in Psychology

NIP — Nouvelle Initiation Philosophique

NIPA — National Income and Product Accounts

NIPAA — Nippon Shokakibyo Gakkai Zasshi

NIPDA — Nihon Daigaku Nojuigakubu Gakujutsu Kenkyu Hokoku

NIPEA — Nippon Genshiryoku Kenkyusho Kenkyu Hokoku

NIPHA — Nippon Hoshasen Gijutsu Gakkai Zasshi

NIPH Ann — NIPH [*National Institute of Public Health*] Annals

NIPH (Natl Inst Public Health) Ann (Oslo) — NIPH (National Institute of Public Health) Annals (Oslo)

Nip Kag Kai — Nippon Kagaku Kaishi

Nippon Acta Radiol — Nippon Acta Radiologica

Nippon Dent Coll Annu Publ — Nippon Dental College. Annual Publications

Nippon Dojo Hiryogaku Zasshi J Sci Soil Manure — Nippon Dojo Hiryogaku Zasshi/Journal of the Science of Soil and Manure

Nippon Electr Co Res Dev — Nippon Electric Company Research and Development

Nippon Kagaku Kaishi J Chem Soc Jap Chem — Nippon Kagaku Kaishi/Journal. Chemical Society of Japan. Chemistry and Industrial Chemistry

Nippon Kokan Tech Bull — Nippon Kokan Technical Bulletin

Nippon Kokan Tech Rep — Nippon Kokan Technical Reports

Nippon Kokan Tech Rep Overseas — Nippon Kokan Technical Reports Overseas

Nippon Nogei Kagakukai Shi J Agric Chem Soc Jap — Nippon Nogei Kagakukai-Shi/Journal. Agricultural Chemical Society of Japan

Nippon Noyaku Gakkaishi/J Pestic Sci — Nippon Noyaku Gakkaishi/Journal of Pesticide Science

Nippon-Orient — Nippon-Orient-Gakkai-Geppo

Nippon Sanso Eng Rep — Nippon Sanso Engineering Report

Nippon Sochi Gakkai Shi J Jap Soc Grassl Sci — Nippon Sochi Gakkai Shi/ Journal. Japanese Society of Grassland Science

Nippon Stainless Tech Rep — Nippon Stainless Technical Report

Nippon Steel Tech Rep — Nippon Steel Technical Report

Nippon Steel Tech Rep (Jpn Ed) — Nippon Steel Technical Report (Japanese Edition)

Nippon Steel Tech Rep (Overseas) — Nippon Steel Technical Report (Overseas)

Nippon Tungsten Rev — Nippon Tungsten Review

NIPRM — National Institute of Polar Research. Memoirs. Special Issue

NIPRMAA — National Institute of Polar Research. Memoirs. Series A. Aeronomy

NIPRMBMT — National Institute of Polar Research. Memoirs. Series B. Meteorology

NIPRMCES — National Institute of Polar Research. Memoirs. Series C. Earth Sciences

NIPRMEB — National Institute of Polar Research. Memoirs. Series E. Biology and Medical Science

NIPRMFL — National Institute of Polar Research. Memoirs. Series F. Logistics

NIPRMS — National Institute of Polar Research. Memoirs. Special Issue

NIPRORUDA Sb Nauchni Tr Ser Obogat — NIPRORUDA [*Nauchnoizsledovatelski i Proektantski Institut za Rudodobiv i Obogatyavane*] Sbornik Nauchni Trudove. Seriya. Obogatyavanne

NIPRSMS — National Institute of Polar Research. Special Map Series

NIQ — National Institute Economic Review

Ni R — Nauka i Religija

NIR — Netherlands International Law Review

NiR — Nihon Rekishi

NIRED — New International Realities

N Ireland Rec Agr Res — Northern Ireland Record of Agricultural Research

N Ire LQ — Northern Ireland Legal Quarterly

N Ir Legal Q — Northern Ireland Legal Quarterly

N Ir LQ — Northern Ireland Legal Quarterly

N Ir Rev Stat — Northern Ireland Revised Statutes

NIRSA — NIRSA. Journal of the National Intramural-Recreational Sports Association

NISAA — Nippon Sakumotsu Gakkai Kiji

NISEA — Nippon Seirigaku Zasshi

NISER — Nigerian Institute of Social and Economic Research

NISFAY — Acta Obstetrica et Gynaecologica Japonica

NISGA — Nisshin Seiko Giho

NISHB — Nichidai Shigaku

Nishinihon J Dermatol — Nishinihon Journal of Dermatology

Nishinihon J Urol — Nishinihon Journal of Urology

NISK (Nor Inst Skogforsk) Rapp — NISK (Norsk Instituut foer Skogforskning) Rapport

N Isl — Notes on Islam

Nissan Diesel Rev — Nissan Diesel Review

Nissan Tech Rev — Nissan Technical Review

Nisseki Tech Rev — Nisseki Technical Review

Nisshin Steel Tech Rep — Nisshin Steel Technical Report

NIST Spec Publ — NIST [*National Institute of Standards and Technology*] Special Publication

NIt — Nuova Italia

NITA — Journal. National Intravenous Therapy Association

NITAJ — Journal. National Intravenous Therapy Association

NITM — National Income Tax Magazine

Nitrate Wirkung Herz Kreislauf Nitrat Symp — Nitrate. Wirkung auf Herz und Kreislauf. Nitrat-Symposion

Nitric Oxide L Arginine Bioregul Syst Proc Symp — Nitric Oxide from L-Arginine. A Bioregulatory System. Proceedings. Symposium

Nitro Compd — Nitro Compounds. Recent Advances in Synthesis and Chemistry

Nitrogen Fixation Res Prog Proc Int Symp — Nitrogen Fixation Research Progress. Proceedings. International Symposium on Nitrogen Fixation

NITTA — Nauchno-Issledovatel'skie Trudy Tsentral'nogo Nauchno-Issledovatel'skogo Instituta Kozhevenno-Obuvnoi Promyshlennosti

NIV — Nivel

NIW — Nieuw Israelitisch Weekblad

NIYB — New International Year Book

Nizkotemp Vak Materialoved — Nizkotemperaturnoe i Vakuumnoe Materialovedenie

NIZO Nieuws — Nederlands Instituut voor Zuiverlonderzoek Nieuws

NIZO Rapp — NIZO [*Nederlands Instituut voor Zuivelonderzoek*] Rapporten

NIZO Versl — NIZO [*Nederlands Instituut voor Zuivelonderzoek*] Verslagen

NJ — Nas Jezik

NJ — Neue Justiz

NJ — New Jersey Reports

NJ — New Judaea

NJ — Niederdeutsches Jahrbuch

NJ — Northern Journal

NJA — Neue Jahrbuecher fuer das Klassische Altertum

NJAB — Neue Jahrbuecher fuer Antike und Deutsche Bildung

NJADB — Neue Jahrbuecher fuer Antike und Deutsche Bildung

NJ Admin — New Jersey Administrative Reports

NJ Admin Code — New Jersey Administrative Code

NJAF — Northern Journal of Applied Forestry

NJ Ag — New Jersey Agriculture

NJ Ag Dept — New Jersey. Department of Agriculture. Publications

NJ Ag Exp — New Jersey. Agricultural Experiment Station. Publications

NJ Agr — New Jersey Agriculture

NJ Agr Expt Sta Bull — New Jersey. Agricultural Experiment Station. Bulletin

NJ Agric — New Jersey Agriculture

NJ Agric Exp Stn Bull — New Jersey. Agricultural Experiment Station. Bulletin

NJ Agric Exp Stn Circ — New Jersey. Agricultural Experiment Station. Circular

N Jahrb — Neue Jahrbuecher fuer Antike und Deutsche Bildung

NJB — Nederlands Juristenblad

NJb — Neue Jahrbuecher fuer Antike und Deutsche Bildung

N Jb — Neue Jahrbuecher fuer das Klassische Altertum

N Jb — Neue Jahrbuecher fuer Philologie und Paedagogik

NJb — Neue Jahrbuecher fuer Wissenschaft und Jugendbildung

NJb — Niederdeutsches Jahrbuch

N Jb A — Neue Jahrbuecher fuer das Klassische Altertum

NJ Bank — New Jersey Banker

N Jb Beil Bd — Neues Jahrbuch fuer Mineralogie, Geologie, und Palaeontologie. Beilage Band

NJbbPh — Neue Jahrbuecher fuer Philologie und Paedagogik

NJBEA Newsletter — New Jersey Business Education Association. Newsletter

N JbF — Nordisk Jordburgsforskning

N Jb KA — Neue Jahrbuecher fuer das Klassische Altertum

N Jb Mn — Neues Jahrbuch fuer Mineralogie, Geologie, und Palaeontologie

NJBO — Nordic Journal of Botany

N Jbt — Nordisk Jordbrugsforskning

NJ Bur Geol Topogr Bull — New Jersey. Bureau of Geology and Topography. Bulletin

NJ Bus — New Jersey Business

N Jb WJ — Neue Jahrbuecher fuer Wissenschaft und Jugendbildung

NjbWJB — Neue Jahrbuecher fuer Wissenschaft und Jugendbildung

NJ Ceram — New Jersey Ceramist

NJCHD — Nouveau Journal de Chimie

NJ Conf Crime Abst — New Jersey Conference on Crime. Abstracts of Addresses

NJ Conf Soc Wk Proc — New Jersey Conference of Social Work. Proceedings

NJ Dep Conserv Econ Dev Div Water Policy Supply Spec Rep — New Jersey. Department of Conservation and Economic Development. Division of Water Policy and Supply. Special Report

NJ Dep Conserv Econ Develop Geol Rep Ser — New Jersey. Department of Conservation and Economic Development. Geologic Report Series

NJ Dep Environ Prot Div Nat Resour Bur Geol Topogr Bull — New Jersey. Department of Environmental Protection. Division of Natural Resources. Bureau of Geology and Topography. Bulletin

NJ Dept Inst & Agencies Pub — New Jersey Department of Institutions and Agencies. Publications

NJ Div Water Policy Supply Spec Rep — New Jersey. Division of Water Policy and Supply. Special Report

NJ Div Water Policy Supply Water Resour Cir — New Jersey. Division of Water Policy and Supply. Water Resources Circular

NJ Div Water Resour Spec Rep — New Jersey. Division of Water Resources. Special Report

NJ Dp Conservation An Rp — New Jersey. Department of Conservation and Development. Annual Report

NJD Th — Neue Jahrbuecher fuer Deutsche Theologie

NJDW — Neue Jahrbuecher fuer Deutsche Wissenschaft

NJe — Nas Jezik

NJE — Nebraska Journal of Economics and Business

NJE — Nigerian Journal of Economic and Social Studies

NJ Eq — New Jersey Equity Reports

NJESS — Nigerian Journal of Economic and Social Studies

N J f M — Neues Jahrbuch fuer Mineralogie

NJ Geneal Mag — Genealogical Magazine of New Jersey. Genealogical Society of New Jersey

NJ Geol Topogr Bull — New Jersey. Bureau of Geology and Topography. Bulletin

NJGKA — Nippon Jinzo Gakkaishi

NJGP — Neues Jahrbuch fuer Geologie und Palaeontologie. Monatshefte

NJ G S — New Jersey. Geological Survey

NJH — New Jersey History

N Jhb — Neue Jahrbuecher fuer Antike und Deutsche Bildung

NJ His S — New Jersey Historical Society. Proceedings

NJ His S Col — New Jersey Historical Society. Collections

NJ Hist — New Jersey History

NJHistS — New Jersey Historical Society. Proceedings

NJ Hist Soc Proc — New Jersey Historical Society. Proceedings

NJHS — New Jersey Historical Society. Proceedings

NJHSP — New Jersey Historical Society. Proceedings

NJIGA — Nippon Jibi-Inko-Ka Gakkai Kaiho Kaiho

NJ Jnl Optom — New Jersey Journal of Optometry

NJ J Pharm — New Jersey. Journal of Pharmacy

NJK — Nastava Jezika i Knjizevnosti u Srednoj Skoli

NJKA — Neue Jahrbuecher fuer das Klassische Altertum

NJKA — Neue Jahrbuecher fuer das Klassische Altertum, Geschichte, und Deutsche Literatur

NJKAGDL — Neue Jahrbuecher fuer das Klassische Altertum, Geschichte, und Deutsche Literatur

NJKIA — Neue Jahrbuecher fuer das Klassische Altertum

NJL — New Jersey Law Reports

NJL — Nordic Journal of Linguistics

NJL — Norwegian Journal of Linguistics

NJ Lab Hld — New Jersey Labor Herald

NJ Law — New Jersey Lawyer

NJ Law J — New Jersey Law Journal

NJ Law Jour — New Jersey Law Journal

NJ Law N — New Jersey Law News

NJ Laws — Laws of New Jersey

NJ Lawy — New Jersey Lawyer

NJ League Nurs News — New Jersey League for Nursing. News

NJ Lib — New Jersey Libraries

NJ Libr — New Jersey Libraries

NJLJ — New Jersey Law Journal

NJ L R — New Jersey Law Review

NJL Rev — New Jersey Law Review

NJM — National Jewish Monthly

NJM — Neue Juedische Monatshefte

NJM — Nouvelles Juives Mondiales

NJ Med — New Jersey Medicine

NJ Med Soc Jour — New Jersey Medical Society. Journal

NJMIA — Neues Jahrbuch fuer Mineralogie. Abhandlungen

NJ Misc — New Jersey Miscellaneous Reports

NJ Mosq Exterm Assoc Proc Annu Meet — New Jersey Mosquito Extermination Association. Proceedings. Annual Meeting

NJ Munic — New Jersey Municipalities

NJN — Neue Juedische Nachrichten

NJ Nurse — New Jersey Nurse

NJOG — Northern Offshore. Norwegian Journal of Oil and Gas

N Jour Med Chir Pharm (Paris) — Nouveau Journal de Medecine, Chirurgie, et Pharmacie (Paris)

N Jour Pharm (Leipzig) — Neues Journal der Pharmacie fuer Aerzte Apotheker und Chemiker (Leipzig)

NJP — Nederlandse Jurisprudentie. Uitspraken in Burgerlijke en Strafzaken

NJP — Neue Jahrbuecher fuer Paedogogik

NJP — Neue Jahrbuecher fuer Philologie und Paedagogik

NJ Ph P — Neue Jahrbuecher fuer Philologie und Paedagogik

NJPP — Neue Jahrbuecher fuer Philologie und Paedagogik

NJ Reg — New Jersey Register

NJ Re Tit N — New Jersey Realty Title News

NJ Rev Stat — New Jersey Revised Statutes

NJS — Netherlands Journal of Sociology

NJS — Norwegian Bankers Association. Financial Review

NJSBAQ — New Jersey State Bar Association. Quarterly

NJSBJ — New Jersey State Bar Journal

NJ Sch Libn — New Jersey School Librarian

NJ Sess Law Serv (West) — New Jersey Session Law Service (West)

NJ SMTS — News/Journal. Saskatchewan Mathematics Teachers' Society

NJSNA News — NJSNA [*New Jersey State Nurses Association*] Newsletter

NJSNA Newsl — NJSNA [*New Jersey State Nurses Association*] Newsletter

NJSRB — Netherlands Journal of Sea Research

NJ Stat Ann (West) — New Jersey Statutes Annotated (West)

NJ St BJ — New Jersey State Bar Journal

NJ Success — New Jersey Success

NJSUD — Netherlands Journal of Surgery

NJ Super — New Jersey Superior Court Reports

NJ Tax — New Jersey Tax Court Reports

NJUGA — Nippon Junkanki Gakushi

NJUZA9 — Japanese Journal of Veterinary Science

NJW — Neue Jahrbuecher fuer Wissenschaft und Jugendbildung

NJW — Neue Juristische Wochenschrift

NJ Water Resour Spec Rep — New Jersey. Division of Water Resources. Special Report

NJWJ — Neue Jahrbuecher fuer Wissenschaft und Jugendbildung

NJ Zinc Co Res Bull — New Jersey Zinc Company. Research Bulletin

NK — Narodna Kultura

NK — Nasza Ksiegarnia

NK — Neprajzi Koezlemenyek [*Budapest*]

NK — Neue Kirche

NK — New Korea
NK — Nowe Kultura
NK — Numizmatikai Koezloeny
NK — Nyelvtudomanyi Koezlemenyek
NKAKB — Nippon Kagaku Kaishi
NK BI — Neuburger Kollektaneenblatt
NKCHD — Nippon Kikai Gakkai Ronbunshu. C Hen
NKEP — Narodnyj Komissariat Elektrostancji i Elektropromyslennosti
NKEZA — Nippon Koshu Eisei Zasshi
NKEZA4 — Japanese Journal of Public Health
NKGAD — Nippon Kikai Gakkai Ronbunshu. A Hen
NKGBD — Nippon Kikai Gakkai Ronbunshu. B Hen
NKGRB — Nippon Kenchiku Gakkai Ronbun Hokoku-shu
NKGWG — Nachrichten der Koeniglichen Gesellschaften der Wissenschaften zu Goettingen
NKGZAE — Acta Haematologica Japonica
NKHJ — Nederlandsch Kunsthistorisch Jaarboek
NKHOAK — Bulletin. Agricultural Chemicals Inspection Station
NKHS — Ny Kirkehistoriske Samlinger
NKJ — Nederlandsch Kunsthistorisch Jaarboek
NKJTL — Neues Kritisches Journal der Theologischen Literatur
NKKGAB — Japanese Poultry Science
NKKOB — Nara Kogyo Koto Senmon Gakko Kenkyu Kiyo
NKK Tech Rev — NKK Technical Review
NKL — Nordisk Konversations Leksikon
N Knife Mag — National Knife Magazine
NKNOB — Bulletin. Koninklijke Nederlandse Oudheidkundige Bond
N Ko Bl H Sch — Neues Korrespondenzblatt fuer die Hoeheren Schulen in Wuerttemberg
NKoeZ — Numizmatikai Kozlony
NKOGA — Nippon Kokoka Gakkai Zasshi
NKOKD — Nichidai Koko Kagaku
NKRA — Neue Keilschriftliche Rechtsurkunden aus der el-Amarna-Zeit
NKRS — Neueste Kirchenrechts-Sammlungen
NKRWA — Neue Koelner Rechtwissenschaftliche Abhandlungen
NKS — Nederlandsche Katholieke Stemmen
NKs — Nowe Ksiazki
NKSA — Newsletter. Kafka Society of America
NKSHB — Naikai-Ku Suisan Kenkyusho Kenkyu Hokoku
NKSKA — Nippon Kagaku Seni Kenkyusho Koenshu
NKT — Norske Klassiker-Tekster
NKT — Nursery and Kindergarten Teachers
NKT — Ny Kyrklig Tidskrift
NKTAD — Journal. Gyeongsang National University. Natural Sciences
NKTRA — Nippon Kokan Technical Reports Overseas
Nku — Naamkunde
NKYLR — Northern Kentucky Law Review
N KY L Rev — Northern Kentucky Law Review
NKYRA — Nippon Kyobu Rinsho
NKyrKTs — Ny Kyrklig Tidsskrift
NKYZA2 — Japanese Journal of Thoracic Diseases
NKZ — Neue Kirchliche Zeitschrift
NKZAA — Nippon Kyobu Geka Gakkai Zasshi
NKZKA — Nippon Kinzoku Gakkai Kaiho
NL — Canadian Communications Network Letter
NL — Natur und Landschaft
NL — Neuland
NL — New Law Journal
NL — New Leader
NL — Northland News
NL — Norwiny Literackie
NL — Nouvelles Litteraires
NL — Nouvelles Litteraires, Artistiques, et Scientifiques
NL — Numismatic Literature
NLA — Nachrichten der Luther-Akademie
NLA — Norsk Litteraer Aarbok
NLADDR — Nachrichten der Lutherakademie in der DDR
NLAS — Nouvelles Litteraires, Artistiques, et Scientifiques
NLauR — New Laurel Review
NLB — Newberry Library. Bulletin
NLB — Northeast Louisiana Business Review
NLB — Numismatisches Literatur-Blatt
NLC — Nederlandsche Landbouwcooperatie
NLC — New London Commentary
NLC — New London Commentary on the New Testament
NLCHAIBS — Newberry Library. Center for the History of the American Indian. Bibliographical Series
NLCK — New Library of Catholic Knowledge
NLE — Nuclear Engineering International
NLETDU — Neuroendocrinology Letters
NLGI Spokesman — NLGI [National Lubricating Grease Institute] Spokesman
NLGQ — National Lawyers Guild Quarterly
NLH — New Literary History
NLing — Notes on Linguistics
N´Listy — Narodni Listy [National News]
NListy — Numismaticke Listy
NLit — Neue Literatur
N Litt — Nouvelles Litteraires, Artistiques, et Scientifiques
NLiW — Nowiny Literackie i Wydawnicze
NLJ — Nagpur Law Journal
NLJ — New Law Journal
NLJ — Nigerian Law Journal
NLJMA — Netherlands Journal of Medicine
Nlles Lit — Nouvelles Litteraires
NLL Rev — NLL Review

NLL Transl Bull — National Lending Library. Translations Bulletin
NLM — National Liberation Movement in India and Bal Gangadhar
NLM — Neues Lausitzisches Magazin
NLMC — National Library of Medicine. Current Catalog
NLM News — National Library of Medicine. News
NLM Tech Bull — National Library of Medicine. Technical Bulletin
NLN — Neo-Latin News
NLN News — NLN (National League for Nursing) News
NLN Publ — National League for Nursing. Publications
NLOB — Numismatik Literatur Osteuropas und das Balkans
NLP — National Productivity Review
NLPGA Times — National LP-Gas Association Times
NLQ — Nigeria Lawyer's Quarterly
NLQR — Nigeria Law Quarterly Review
NLR — Dine Bizaad Nanil' Iih/Navajo Language Review
NLR — National Review (London)
NLR — New Left Review
NLRB Dec CCH — NLRB [National Labor Relations Board] Decisions. Commerce Clearing House
Nl Res Men Health & Behav Sc — Newsletter for Research in Mental Health and Behavioral Sciences
N L Rev — New Literature Review
NLS — Natuur en Milieu
NLSA — Newsletter. Lute Society of America
NLT — Neuland in der Theologie
NLTSD — National Times
NLu — Sainte-Beuve. Nouveaux Lundis [monograph]
NLV — Nacional (Venezuela)
NLW — Neue Literarische Welt
NLW — Nowiny Literackie i Wydawnicze
NLWJ — National Library of Wales. Journal
NLW Journ — National Library of Wales. Journal
NLZ — Numismatische Literatur-Zeitung
NM — National Music Council. Bulletin
NM — Naturwissenschaft und Medizin
NM — Nautical Magazine
NM — Naval Magazine
NM — Nederlandsche Mercuur
NM — Neuphilologische Mitteilungen
NM — Neusprachliche Mitteilungen aus Wissenschaft und Praxis
NM — New Mexico Reports
NM — Niederdeutsche Mitteilungen
NM — Nordiska Museets och Skansens Arsbok
NM — Northern Miner
NM — Northern Miscellany
NM — Numismatiska Meddelanden
NMA — New Mexico Anthropologist
NMA — New Music Articles
NMAA Newsletter — Nursing Mothers' Association of Australia. Newsletter
NM Acad Sci Bull — New Mexico Academy of Science. Bulletin
NMAG — Naval Magazine
NM Ag Exp — New Mexico. Agricultural Experiment Station. Publications
N Mag Hanau — Neues Magazin fuer Hanauische Geschichte
NM Agric Exp Stn Bull — New Mexico. Agricultural Experiment Station. Bulletin
NM Agric Exp Stn Res Rep — New Mexico. Agricultural Experiment Station. Research Report
NMA Journal — National Microfilm Association. Journal
NMAL — Notes on Modern American Literature
NMANDX — Nuclear Medicine Annual
N Mat T — Nordisk Matematisk Tidsskrift
NMB — Neuendettelsauer Missionsblatt
NMBGF — Neue Muensterische Beitraege zur Geschichtsforschung
NMBJD — New Mexico Business Journal
NMBKG — Neue Muenchener Beitraege zur Kunstgeschichte
NMBQAA — Naturalia Monspeliensia. Serie Botanique
NM Bur Mines Miner Resour Bull — New Mexico. Bureau of Mines and Mineral Resources. Bulletin
NM Bur Mines Miner Resour Cir — New Mexico. Bureau of Mines and Mineral Resources. Circular
NM Bur Mines Miner Resour Circ — New Mexico. Bureau of Mines and Mineral Resources. Circular
NM Bur Mines Miner Resour Ground Water Rep — New Mexico. Bureau of Mines and Mineral Resources. Ground Water Report
NM Bur Mines Miner Resour Hydrol Rep — New Mexico. Bureau of Mines and Mineral Resources. Hydrologic Report
NM Bur Mines Miner Resour Mem — New Mexico. Bureau of Mines and Mineral Resources. Memoir
NM Bur Mines Miner Resour Miner Resour Rep — New Mexico. Bureau of Mines and Mineral Resources. Mineral Resources Report
NM Bur Mines Miner Resour Prog Rep — New Mexico. Bureau of Mines and Mineral Resources. Progress Report
NM Bur Mines Miner Resour Target Explor Rep — New Mexico. Bureau of Mines and Mineral Resources. Target Exploration Report
NM Bur Mines Miner Rsour Ground Water Rep — New Mexico. Bureau of Mines and Mineral Resources. Ground Water Report
NM Bus J — New Mexico Business Journal
NMC — Nuclear Medicine Communications
NMC Bul — National Music Council. Bulletin
NMCCFCS — National Museum of Man. Mercury Series. Canadian Centre for Folk Culture Studies. Papers
NMCD — Nutrition, Metabolism, and Cardiovascular Diseases. NMCD
NMCMASC — National Museums of Canada. Mercury Series. Archaeological Survey of Canada. Papers
NMCMCES — National Museums of Canada. National Museum of Man. Mercury Series. Canadian Ethnology Service. Papers

NMCMED — National Museums of Canada. Mercury Series. Ethnology Division. Papers
NMCMSDP — National Museums of Canada. Mercury Series. Directorate Paper
NMCPA — National Museums of Canada. Publications in Archaeology
NMCPB — National Museums of Canada. Publications in Botany
NMCPBO — National Museums of Canada. Publications in Biological Oceanography
NMCPE — National Museums of Canada. Publications in Ethnology
NMCPFC — National Museums of Canada. Publications in Folk Culture
NMCPNS — National Museums of Canada. Publications in Natural Sciences
NMCPZ — National Museums of Canada. Publications in Zoology
NMD — Nahost und Mittelostverein eV. Rundschreiben
NM Dent J — New Mexico Dental Journal
NM Dep Game Fish Bull — New Mexico. Department of Game and Fish. Bulletin
NMDJA — Netherlands Milk and Dairy Journal
NMDTA — Novosti Meditsinskoi Tekhniki
NME — New Middle East
NME — New Musical Express
N Med — Nordisk Medicin
NMEIA — Nauchnye Trudy Moskovskogo Inzhenerno-Ekonomicheskogo Instituta
NMerk — Neue Merkur
NMES — Near and Middle East Series
NMessenger — Numismatic Messenger
NMEU — Notas del Museo Etnografico de la Facultad de Filosofia y Letras de la Universidad de Buenos Aires
N Mex B Assn Proc — New Mexico Bar Association. Proceedings
N Mex Bs Jl — New Mexico Business Journal
N Mex Bur Mines Mineral Resources Bull — New Mexico State Bureau of Mines and Mineral Resources. Bulletin
N Mex Bur Mines Mineral Resources Mem — New Mexico State Bureau of Mines and Mineral Resources. Memoir
N Mex Bus — New Mexico Business
N Mex Bus R — New Mexico Business Review
N Mex Ext N — New Mexico Extension News
N Mex Ext News N Mex State Univ Agr Ext Serv — New Mexico Extension News. New Mexico State University. Agricultural Extension Service
N Mex Geol — New Mexico Geology
N Mex Lib — New Mexico Libraries
N Mex L Rev — New Mexico Law Review
N Mex Miner — National Musei Miner
N Mex State Engineer Office Tech Rept — New Mexico State Engineer's Office. Technical Report
N Mex St B Assn Proc — New Mexico State Bar Association. Proceedings
NM Ext News — New Mexico Extension News
N Mex Univ B G S — New Mexico University. Bulletin. Geological Series
N Mex Univ Pubs Geology Pubs Meteoritics — New Mexico University. Publications in Geology. Publications in Meteoritics
NMFR — New Mexico Folklore Record
NMG — New Management
NM Geol — New Mexico Geology
NM Geol Soc Annu Field Conf Guideb — New Mexico Geological Society. Annual Field Conference Guidebook
NM Geol Soc Field Conf Guideb — New Mexico Geological Society. Field Conference Guidebook
NM Geol Soc Guideb Annu Field Conf — New Mexico Geological Society. Guidebook of Annual Field Conference
NM Geol Soc Spec Publ — New Mexico Geological Society. Special Publication
NMGGA — Field Conference Guidebook. New Mexico Geological Society
N Mg Ntvd — Nyt Magazin for Naturvidenskaberne
NMGTA — Nederlands Militair Geneeskundig Tijdschrift
NMH — Newcastle Morning Herald
NM His R — New Mexico Historical Review
NMHQ — New Mexico Historical Quarterly
NMHR — New Mexico Historical Review
NMHUJ — New Mexico Highlands University. Journal
NMi — Neuphilologische Mitteilungen
NMIA — Norske Meteorologiske Institutt. Meteorologiske Annaler
NMIMA — Norske Meteorologiske Institutt. Meteorologiske Annaler
NMIMAX — Nuclear Medicine
NMIRA — Nursing Mirror
NMis — Nova Misao
N Miss — Nordisk Missions-Tidsskrift
N Mitt — Neuphilologische Mitteilungen
NM J Sci — New Mexico Journal of Science
NML — New Mexico Law Review
NM Laws — Laws of New Mexico
NM Lib Newsl — New Mexico Libraries. Newsletter
NMLR — New Mexico Law Review
NMLR — Nigerian Monthly Law Reports
NML Rev — New Mexico Law Review
NML Tech J — NML [National Metallurgical Laboratory] Technical Journal
NMM — Noveaux Memoires. Missions de la Compagnie de Jesus
NMM — Nuclear Methods Monographs
NM MIRD Pam — NM/MIRD [Society of Nuclear Medicine. Medical Internal Radiation Dose Committee] Pamphlet
NMMMA — Memoir. New Mexico Bureau of Mines and Mineral Resources
NM Nurse — New Mexico Nurse
NMo — Neuphilologische Monatsschrift
N Mon — Neuphilologische Monatsschrift
NMP — Notas del Museo. Antropologia. La Plata
NMQ — New Mexico Quarterly
NMQR — New Mexico Quarterly. Review
NMR — New Magazine Review
NMR — New Mexico Review
NMR Basic Princ Prog — NMR [Nuclear Magnetic Resonance] Basic Principles and Progress

NMR Biomed — NMR in Biomedicine
NMRLIT — Nuclear Magnetic Resonance Literature System
NMRNB — Nuclear Magnetic Resonance
NMRNBE — Specialist Periodical Reports. Nuclear Magnetic Resonance
NMS — National Master Specification
NMS — Nottingham Medieval Studies
NMSCS — Northwest Missouri State College Studies
NM Sol Energy Assoc Southwest Bull — New Mexico Solar Energy Association. Southwest Bulletin
NM Stat Ann — New Mexico Statutes Annotated
NM State Bur Mines Miner Resour Annu Rep — New Mexico State Bureau of Mines and Mineral Resources. Annual Report
NM State Bur Mines Miner Resour Bull — New Mexico State Bureau of Mines and Mineral Resources. Bulletin
NM State Bur Mines Miner Resour Circ — New Mexico State Bureau of Mines and Mineral Resources. Circular
NM State Bur Mines Miner Resour Geol Map — New Mexico State Bureau of Mines and Mineral Resources. Geologic Map
NM State Bur Mines Miner Resour Mem — New Mexico State Bureau of Mines and Mineral Resources. Memoir
NM State Bur Mines Miner Resour Miner Resour Rep — New Mexico State Bureau of Mines and Mineral Resources. Mineral Resources Report
NM State Bur Mines Miner Resour Target Explor Rep — New Mexico State Bureau of Mines and Mineral Resources. Target Exploration Report
NM State Eng Basic Data Rep — New Mexico State Engineer. Basic Data Report
NM State Eng Off Tech Rep — New Mexico State Engineer's Office. Technical Report
NM State Eng Tech Rep — New Mexico State Engineer. Technical Report
NM State Univ Agric Exp Stn Bull — New Mexico State University. Agricultural Experiment Station. Bulletin
NM State Univ Agric Exp Stn Res Rep — New Mexico State University. Agricultural Experiment Station. ResearchReport
NM Stud F A — New Mexico Studies in the Fine Arts [University of Minnesota]
N MT — Nordisk Mejeri-Tidsskrift
NMT — Nordisk Missions-Tidsskrift
NMTSD7 — Nouvelle Revue de Medecine de Toulouse. Supplement
N Munster Antiq J — North Munster Antiquarian Journal
N Munster Antiqua J — North Munster Antiquarian Journal
N Mus Ab — National Musei Arsbok [National Museums Yearbook]
Nmus Arbejdsmk — Nationalmuseets Arbejdsmark
Nmus Bull — Nationalmuseum Bulletin
N Mus Canada Bull — National Museum of Canada. Bulletin
N Music R — New Music Review
N Mus NZ Rec — National Museum of New Zealand Records
Nmus Skrser — Nationalmuseet Skriftserie [National Museum Writing Series]
N M v H — Nieuw Magazijn van Handelsrecht
NMV Not Med Vet — NMV. Noticias Medico-Veterinarias
NMW — Notes on Mississippi Writers
NM Wildl — New Mexico Wildlife
NMZ — Neue Musik Zeitung
NN — New Nigerian
NN — News of the North
NN — Newspaper News
NN — Notarieel Nieuwsbode
NN — Nucleosides and Nucleotides
NN — Numismatic News Weekly
NN — Numismatisches Nachrichtenblatt
NNA — Nordisk Numismatisk Arsskrift
NNAP — New Native People
NNb — Numismatisches Nachrichtenblatt. Organ des Verbandes der Deutschen Muenzvereine
NNBB — Native News and BIA [Bureau of Indian Affairs] Bulletin
NNBW — Nieuw Nederlandsch Biografisch Woordenboek
NNBYA — Nature: New Biology
NND — Neuer Nekrolog der Deutschen
NNEW — New York Newsday
NNF Nytt — NNF. Nytt Meddelelser fra Norsk Numismatisk Forening
NNGNA — Novosti Neftyanoi i Gazovoi Tekhniki, Neftepererabotka, i Neftekhimiya
NNGZAZ — Folia Endocrinologica Japonica
NNGZB — Neujahrsblatt. Naturforschende Gesellschaft in Zuerich
NNGZB2 — Neujahrsblatt. Naturforschende Gesellschaft in Zuerich
NNH — Neuva Narrativa Hispanoamericana
NNKKAA — Journal. Agricultural Chemical Society of Japan
NNKKB — Nainen Kikan
NNL — Nigeria Newsletter
NNM — Neueste Nachrichten aus dem Morgenlande
NNM — Numismatic Notes and Monographs
NNNE — Nigiqpaq Northwind News
N Notes & Queries — Northern Notes and Queries
NNPPA — Neurologia, Neurochirurgia, i Psychiatria Polska
NNRF — Nouvelle Nouvelle Revue Francaise
NNRG — Neueste Nachrichten aus dem Reiche Gottes
NNSU — Nachrichten aus Niedersachsens Urgeschichte
NNTB — Nachrichten von den Neuesten Theologischen Buechern und Schriften
NN Tech Bull — NN [Netherlands Nitrogen] Technical Bulletin
NNUM — Nordisk Numismatisk Unions Medlemsblad
N Num A — Nordisk Numismatisk Arsskrift
N Num U M — Nordisk Numismatisk Unions Medlemsblad
NNVPA — Nauchni Trudove. Nauchnoizsledovatelski Institut po Vinarska i Pivovarna Promishlenost
NNWSDT — Nestle Nutrition Workshop Series
NNY — Nation (New York)
N Nytt — Nord-Nytt
NO — Narodnoe Obrazovanie
NO — National Observer

NO — Nederlandse Onderneming
NO — Neue Orient
NO — Neurooncology
NO — New Orient
NO — New Outlook
NO — New Oxford Outlook
No — Norseman
NO — Northern Times
No — Notes
N O — Nouvel Observateur
NO — Nova Obzorija
N O — Novy Orient. Casopis Orientalniho Ustava v Praze
NO — Nuestro
Noa — Northamptonshire Past and Present
NOAA Tech Rep NMFS Circ — NOAA [*National Oceanic and Atmospheric Administration*] Technical Report. NMFS Circular
NOAA Tech Rep NMFS SSRF — SSRF
NOAA-TR-NMFS-Circ — National Oceanic and Atmospheric Administration Technical Report-National MarineFisheries Service-Circular
NOAA-TR-NMFS-SSRF — National Oceanic and Atmospheric Administration-Technical Report-National MarineFisheries Service-Special Scientific Report Fisheries
NOAD — Northern Adventures
NOAF — Northern Affairs. Ontario Ministry of Northern Affairs
Noah's Ark Toy Libr Handicapped Child Newsletter — Noah's Ark Toy Library for Handicapped Children. Newsletter
NOALA — Nova Acta Leopoldina
NOAM — Nachrichten aus der Ostafrikanischen Mission
No Am — North American Review
No Am R — North American Review
No Am Rev — North American Review
NOAR — Norwegian Archaeological Review
NOARDP — Novitates Arthropodae
NoB — Namm och Bygd
NoB — Namn och Bygd
NOB — New Orient Bimonthly
NOB — Norges Bank. Economic Bulletin
Nobel Found Symp — Nobel Foundation Symposia
Nobelinst Medd K Vetenskapsakad — Nobelinstitut. Meddelanden Kungliga Vetenskapsakademien
Nobel Symp — Nobel Symposium
NOBKSS — Norges Bank. Skrifter Series
No Brit — North British Review
NoC — North Carolina Historical Review
NoC — Nouveaux Cahiers
No Ca Fo — North Carolina Folklore
No Cages — No More Cages
No Car Hist R — North Carolina Historical Review
No Car Hist Rev — North Carolina Historical Review
No Car Law J — North Carolina Law Journal
No Car Law R — North Carolina Law Review
No Car Law Rev — North Carolina Law Review
No Car Med J — North Carolina Medical Journal
No Car State Bd Health Bul — North Carolina State Board of Health. Bulletin
No Cas LJ — Notes of Cases, Law Journal
NoCo — Nouveau Commerce
NOCOA — Noise Control
No Cordilleran — Northern Cordilleran
NOD — News of the Day
NoD — North Dakota History
Noda Inst Sci Res Rep — Noda Institute for Scientific Research. Report
No Dak Hist — North Dakota History
No Dak Hist Quar — North Dakota Historical Quarterly
No Dak Quar — North Dakota Quarterly
NODE — Northern Development, Incorporating Arctic Digest
NoDEA Nonlinear Differential Equations Appl — NoDEA. Nonlinear Differential Equations and Applications
No D Law — Notre Dame Law Review
NoDQ — North Dakota Quarterly
No East As J Theo — Northeast Asia Journal of Theology
NOeB — Neue Oesterreichische Biographie
NOEB — Neue Orientalische und Exegetische Bibliothek
NoEF — Northeast Folklore
NOEN — Northern Engineer
Noerdlinger Bienenztg — Noerdlinger Bienenzeitung
Noevenyegesz Evk — Noevenyegeszyuegyi Evkoenyv/Yearbook. Official Phytosanitary Service/ Jahrbuch des Amtlichen Pflanzengesundheitsdienstes
Noevenyt Koezlem — Noevenytani Koezlemenyek
Noevenyved Koezl — Noevenyvedelmi Koezloeny
Noevenyved Kutato Intez Evkoen (Budapest) — Noevenyvedelmi Kutato Intezet Evkoenyve (Budapest)
Noevenyved Tud Tanacskozas Koezlem — Noevenyved Tudomanyos Tanacskozas Koezlemenyei
NOG — Northern Offshore. Norwegian Journal of Oil and Gas
Nogaku Iho Agric Bull Saga Univ Nogaku-Bu — Nogaku Iho. Agricultural Bulletin of Saga University. Saga Daigaku. Nogaku-Bu
Nogaku Shusho J Agric Sci (Setagoya) — Nogaku Shuho. Journal of Agricultural Science (Setagoya)
NOGDA — Nogyo Doboku Gakkai-Shi
NOGKAV — Agricultural Research
Nograd Megyei Muz Evkonyve — Nograd Megyei Muzeumok Evkonyve [*Nograd County Museums Annual*]
NOGS Log — New Orleans Geographical Society. Log
NOGT — Norsk Geologisk Tidsskrift
NOGU — Norges Geologiske Undersoekelse

NOGUA — Noguchi Kenkyusho Jiho
Nogyo Doboku Shikenjo Hokoku Bull Natl Res Inst Agric Eng — Nogyo Doboku Shikenjo Hokoku/Bulletin. National Research Institute of Agricultural Engineering
Nogyo Gijutsu J Agric — Nogyo Gijutsu/Journal of Agricultural Science
Nogyo Kikai Gakkai Shi J Soc Agric Mach — Nogyo Kikai Gakkai Shi/Journal. Society of Agricultural Machinery
Nogyo Oyobi Engei/Agric Hortic — Nogyo Oyobi Engei/Agriculture and Horticulture
NoH — Northern History
NoH — North Louisiana Historical Association Journal
N Ohio Bus — Northern Ohio Business Journal
N OH Live — Northern Ohio Live
NOHO — Northern Housing
NOHY — Nordic Hydrology
NOIRB — Non-Ionizing Radiation
No Ire L Q — Northern Ireland Legal Quarterly
Noise & Vib Control Worldwide — Noise and Vibration Control Worldwide
Noise Control — Noise Control Proceedings. National Conference on Noise Control Engineering
Noise Control and Vib Reduct — Noise Control and Vibration Reduction [*Later, Noise and Vibration Control Worldwide*]
Noise Control Eng — Noise Control Engineering
Noise Control Eng J — Noise Control Engineering Journal
Noise Control Engrg — Noise Control Engineering
Noise Control Shock Vib — Noise Control, Shock, and Vibration
Noise Control Vib — Noise Control, Vibration Isolation [*Later, Noise and Vibration Control Worldwide*]
Noise Control Vib Isol — Noise Control, Vibration Isolation [*Later, Noise and Vibration Control Worldwide*]
Noise Control Vibr Reduct — Noise Control and Vibration Reduction [*Later, Noise and Vibration Control Worldwide*]
Noise Pollut Publ Abstr — Noise Pollution Publications Abstract
Noise Reg Rep BNA — Noise Regulation Reporter. Bureau of National Affairs
Noise Vib Bull — Noise and Vibration Bulletin
Noise Vib Control — Noise and Vibration Control
Noise Vibr Contr Worldwide — Noise and Vibration Control Worldwide
Noise Vib Worldwide — Noise and Vibration Worldwide
NOJB — Norwegian Journal of Botany
NOJO — Northern Journal
NOJOA — Nordisk Jordbrugsforskning
NOJZ — Norwegian Journal of Zoology
NOKIAB — Journal of Agricultural Meteorology
NOLA Mitt Niederoesterreich Landesarchv — NOLA [*Niederoesterreichische Landesregierung*]. Mitteilungen aus dem Niederoesterreichischen Landesarchiv
NOLD — Northland
NOLI — Northern Lights. Diocese of Yukon
Nom — Nomisma. Untersuchungen auf dem Gebiete der Antiken Munskunde
NoM — Novyj Mir
Nom Chron — Nomismatika Chronika
Nomencl Chim — Nomenclatura Chimica
Nomencl Guide — Nomenclature Guide
No Miner — Northern Miner
NOMIS — National Online Manpower Information System
Nom Khron — Nomismatika Khronika
Nomograficheskii Sb — Nomograficheskii Sbornik
Nomos — Nomos. Yearbook of the American Society of Political and Legal Philosophy
Nonconvex Optim Appl — Nonconvex Optimization and its Applications
Nonconv Yeasts Biotechnol — Nonconventional Yeasts in Biotechnology. A Handbook
Non-Destr T — Non-Destructive Testing
Non-Destr Test — Non-Destructive Testing
Non-Destr Test (Aust) — Non-Destructive Testing (Australia)
Nondestr Test (Chicago) — Non-Destructive Testing (Chicago)
Non-Destr Test (Guilford Eng) — Non-Destructive Testing (Guilford, England)
Non-Destr Test Int — Non-Destructive Testing International
Nondestr Test (Shanghai) — Nondestructive Testing (Shanghai)
Non-Dest Test — Non-Destructive Testing
Nonequilib Eff Ion Electron Transp Proc Int Swarm Semin — Nonequilibrium Effects in Ion and Electron Transport. Proceedings. International Swarm Seminar
Nonequilib Probl Phys Sci Biol — Nonequilibrium Problems in the Physical Sciences and Biology
Nonferrous Cast Curr Ind Rep — Nonferrous Castings. Current Industrial Reports
Nonferrous Met (Beijing) — Nonferrous Metals (Beijing)
Non-Ferrous Met (China) — Non-Ferrous Metals (China)
Non Ferrous Met (Moscow) — Non-Ferrous Metals (Moscow)
Nonferrous Met Soc China Trans — Nonferrous Metals Society of China. Transactions
NonFMerch — Non-Foods Merchandising
Nonfuel M — Future of Nonfuel Minerals in the United States and World. Input-Output Projections, 1980-2030
Noninvasive Tech Cell Biol — Noninvasive Techniques in Cell Biology
Non-Ioniz Radiat — Non-Ionizing Radiation
Nonlinear Anal — Nonlinear Analysis
Nonlinear Anal Theory Appl Proc Int Summer Sch — Nonlinear Analysis. Theory and Applications. Proceedings. InternationalSummer School
Nonlinear Anal Theory Methods and Appl — Nonlinear Analysis. Theory, Methods, and Applications
Nonlinear Coherent Struct Phys Biol Proc Interdiscip Workshop — Nonlinear Coherent Structures in Physics and Biology. Proceedings. Interdisciplinary Workshop
Nonlinear Dyn — Nonlinear Dynamics

Nonlinear Dyn Quantum Phenom Opt Syst Proc Int Workshop — Nonlinear Dynamics and Quantum Phenomena in Optical Systems. Proceedings. International Workshop

Nonlinear Opt — Nonlinear Optics

Nonlinear Opt Proc Vavilov Conf — Nonlinear Optics. Proceedings. Vavilov Conference

Nonlinear Phenom Complex Syst — Nonlinear Phenomena and Complex Systems

Nonlinear Phenom Complex Systems — Nonlinear Phenomena and Complex Systems

Nonlinear Sci Theory Appl — Nonlinear Science. Theory and Application

Nonlinear Sci Today — Nonlinear Science Today

Nonlinear Stud — Nonlinear Studies

Nonlinear Times Digest — Nonlinear Times and Digest

Nonlinear Time Ser Chaos — Nonlinear Time Series and Chaos

Nonlinear Topics Math Sci — Nonlinear Topics in the Mathematical Sciences

Nonlinear Vibr Probl — Nonlinear Vibration Problems

Nonmet Mater Compos Low Temp Proc ICMC Symp — Nonmetallic Meterials and Composites at Low Temperatures. Proceedings. ICMC[*International Cryogenic Materials Conference*] Symposium

Nonmet Miner Process — Nonmetallic Minerals Processing

Non Met Mines — Non-Metallic Mines

Nonmunjip Inha Tech Jr Coll — Nonmunjip. Inha Technical Junior College

Nonp — Nonplus

Nonpet Veh Fuels Symp — Nonpetroleum Vehicle Fuels Symposium

Nonpr Exec — Nonprofit Executive

Nonrenewable Resour — Nonrenewable Resources

NONT — Northern Ontario Business

N Ontario B — Northern Ontario Business

Nonwn Fabr — International Directory of the Nonwoven Fabrics Industry

Nonwoven Pat Dig — Nonwoven Patents Digest

Nonwovens Ind — Nonwovens Industry

Nonwovn In — Nonwovens Industry

NOODDJ — Notulae Odonatologicae

NOP — New Orleans Poetry Journal

NOPA — Norsk Polarinstitutt. Aarbok

NOPE — Northern Perspectives. Canadian Arctic Resources Committee

NOPH — Norsk Polarinstitutt. Polarhandbok

NOPM — Norsk Polarinstitutt. Meddelelser

NOPS — Norsk Polarinstitutt. Skrifter

NOPSA — Nordisk Psykologi

NOQ — Northwest Ohio Quarterly

NoQ — Notes and Queries

NOR — New Orleans Review

NOR — Normalisatie

Nor — Norseman

NoR — Northern Review

NoR — Nouvelle Revue

NORA — National Online Regulatory Access

NORA — Northern Raven

Nor Apotekerforen Tidsskr — Norges Apotekerforenings Tidsskrift

Nor Arch Rev — Norwegian Archaeological Review

N Ord — Neue Ordnung

Nord — Nordia

Nord Adm T — Nordisk Administrativt Tidsskrift

Nord Adm Tss — Nordisk Administrativt Tidsskrift

Nord Arch Natur Arzneywiss — Nordisches Archiv fuer Natur- und Arzneywissenschaft

Nord Betong — Nordisk Betong

Nord Bitidskr — Nordisk Bitidskrift

Nord Bl Chem — Nordische Blaetter fuer die Chemie

Nord Datanytt Data — Nordisk Datanytt Med Data

Nordd J Mv G — Norddeutsches Jahrbuch fuer Muenzkunde und Verwandte Gebiete

Norddsch Farben Ztg — Norddeutsche Farben Zeitung

Norddtsch Farben Ztg — Norddeutsche Farben Zeitung

Nordenfield Kstindustmus Ab — Nordenfieldske Kunstindustrimuseum Arbok

Norden Industritidn — Norden Industritidning

Nordenskioeld Samf T — Nordenskioeld-Samfundets Tidskrift

Nordeuropaeisk Mejeri-Tidsskr — Nordeuropaeisk Mejeri-Tidsskrift

Nord Fortidsminder — Nordiske Fortidsminder

Nord Fotohist Jl — Nordisk Fotohistorisk Journal

Nord High Temp Symp — Nordic High Temperature Symposium

Nord Hydrol — Nordic Hydrology

Nord Hyg Tids — Nordisk Hygiensk Tidsskrift

Nord Hyg Tidskr — Nordisk Hygienisk Tidskrift

Nord Hyg Tidskr Suppl — Nordisk Hygienisk Tidskrift. Supplementum

Nordic Hydrol — Nordic Hydrology

Nordic J Comput — Nordic Journal of Computing

Nordic J Philos Logic — Nordic Journal of Philosophical Logic

Nord Inst Faergforsk Rep — Nordiska Institutet foer Faergforskning. Report

Nordisk Mat Tidskr — Nordisk Matematisk Tidskrift

Nordisk Tid — Nordisk Tidskrift foer Bok- och Bibliosvaesen

Nordisk Tids Bok & Bibl — Nordisk Tidskrift foer Bok- och Bibliosvaesen

Nord J Bot — Nordic Journal of Botany

Nord J Bot Suppl — Nordic Journal of Botany. Supplement

Nord J Doc — Nordic Journal of Documentation

Nord Jordbrforsk — Nordisk Jordbrugsforskning

Nord Jordbrugsforsk — Nordisk Jordbrugsforskning

Nord Jordbrugsforskn Suppl — Nordisk Jordbrugsforskning. Supplement. Nordiska Jordbruksforskares Foerening

Nord Jordbrugsforsk Suppl — Nordisk Jordbrugsforskning. Supplement

Nord J Psychiatry — Nordic Journal of Psychiatry

Nordjyl Kunstmus — Nordjyllands Kunstmuseum

Nord Kemikermoede — Nordiske Kemikermoede

Nord Kemistmoetet Beraett Foeredr — Nordiska Kemistmoetet. Beraettelse och Foeredrag

Nord Kemistmoetet Foerh Foeredr — Nordiska Kemistmoetet. Foerhandlingar och Foeredrag

Nord Kriminalteknisk Tidsk — Nordisk Kriminalteknisk Tidskrift

Nord Kul — Nordisk Kultur

Nord Kult — Nordisk Kultur

Nord Landvaes Landhuushold Mag — Nordisk Landvaesens Og Landhuusholdnings Magasin et Maanedsskrivt

Nord Mat Tidsskr — Nordisk Matematisk Tidsskrift

Nord Med — Nordisk Medicin

Nord Med Ark — Nordiskt Medicinskt Arkiv

Nord Med Ark Afd 2 — Nordiskt Medicinskt Arkiv. Afdeling 2. Inre Medicin. Arkiv foer InreMedicin

Nord Med Ark Afd 2 Med — Nordiskt Medicinskt Arkiv. Afdeling 2. Inre Medicine. Arkiv foer Inre Medicin

Nord Medicinhist Arsb — Nordisk Medicinhistorisk Aarsbok

Nord Med Tidskr — Nordisk Medicinsk Tidskrift

Nord Meet Med Biol Eng — Nordic Meeting on Medical and Biological Engineering

Nord Mejeri Tidsskr — Nordisk Mejeri Tidsskrift

Nord Moetet Biomed Tek — Nordiska Moetet i Biomedicinsk Teknik

Nord Mus — Nordisk Musikkultur

Nord Psykiatr Tidsskr — Nordisk Psykiatrisk Tidsskrift

Nord Psykol — Nordisk Psykologi

Nord Pulp Pap Res J — Nordic Pulp and Paper Research Journal

Nord Semicond Meet — Nordic Semiconductor Meeting

Nordsl Mus — Nordslesvigske Museer

Nord Soc Cell Biol Proc Congr — Nordic Society for Cell Biology. Proceedings. Congress

Nord Symp Comput Simul Nat Sci — Nordic Symposium on Computer Simulations in Natural Science

Nord Symp Comput Simul Phys Chem Biol Math — Nordic Symposium on Computer Simulation in Physics, Chemistry, Biology, and Mathematics

Nord Symp Harskning Fedtstoffer Foeredrag Diskuss — Nordiske Symposium om Harskning af Fedtstoffer, Foeredrag ogDiskussioner

Nord Symp Livsmedels Sens Egenskaper — Nordiska Symposiet Livsmedels Sensoriska Egenskaper

Nord Symp Sens Prop of Foods — Nordic Symposium on Sensory Properties of Foods

Nord T — Nordisk Tidskrift utg. av Letterstedtska Foereningen

Nord T Bok Och Bibilioteksvaes — Nordisk Tidskrift foer Bok- Och Bibliotekvaesen

Nord Tid — Nordisk Tidskrift foer Bok- och Bibliosvaesen

Nord Tids F Straf — Nordisk Tidsskrift for Strafferet

Nord Tidskr — Nordisk Tidskrift foer Bok- och Bibliosvaesen

Nord Tidskr Beteendeterapi — Nordisk Tidskrift foer Beteendeterapi

Nord Tidskr Dov — Nordisk Tidskrift foer Dovundervisningen

Nord Tidskr Fotogr — Nordisk Tidskrift foer Fotografi

Nord Tidskr f Vetensk — Nordisk Tidskrift foer Vetenskap, Konst, och Industri

Nord Tidskrift — Nordisk Tidskrift foer Filologi

Nord Tidskr Medicotek — Nordisk Tidskrift foer Medicoteknik

Nord Tidskr Vet Kst & Indust — Nordisk Tidsskrift for Vetenskap, Konst, och Indsustri

Nord Tidsskr Filol — Nordisk Tidsskrift for Filologi

Nord Tidsskr Kriminalvidensk — Nordisk Tidsskrift foer Kriminalvidenskab

Nord Tidsskr Lervare Sten Ind — Nordisk Tidsskrift foer Lervare- og Sten-Industri

Nord Tidsskr Logop Foniat — Nordisk Tidsskrift foer Logopedi og Foniatri

Nord Tidsskr Straf — Nordisk Tidsskrift for Strafferet

Nord Tidsskr Strafferet — Nordisk Tidsskrift foer Strafferet

Nord T Internat Ret — Nordisk Tidsskrift for International Ret

Nord T Internat Ret — Nordisk Tidsskrift for International Ret og Jus Gentium

Nord Tss Int Ret — Nordisk Tidsskrift for International Ret

Nord u Sued — Nord und Sued

Nord Utredningsser — Nordisk Utredningsserie

Nord Vet Congr Proc — Nordic Veterinary Congress. Proceedings

Nord Veterinaermed — Nordisk Veterinaermedicin

Nord Veterinaermed Suppl — Nordisk Veterinaermedicin. Supplementum

Nord Veterinaermoede Beret — Nordiske Veterinaermoede. Beretning

Nord Vetmed — Nordisk Veterinaermedicin

Nordwestdt Imkerztg — Nordwestdeutsche Imkerzeitung

Nord World — Nordic World

NORED — Norsk Olje Revy

Norelco Rep — Norelco Reporter

Nor Entomol Tidsskr — Norsk Entomologisk Tidsskrift

Nor Fag Foto — Norsk Fag Foto

Nor Farm Tidsskr — Norsk Farmaceutisk Tidsskrift

Nor Fisk — Norges Fiskerier

Nor Fiskeritid — Norsk Fiskeritidende

Norfolk A — Norfolk Archaeology

Norfolk Arch — Norfolk Archaeology

Norfolk Archaeol — Norfolk Archaeology

Norfolk Crime Conf Proc — Norfolk Safety Director's Citizens Committee on Crime. Proceedings of Crime Conference

Nor Fotogr Tidsskr — Norsk Fotografisk Tidsskrift

Nor Gartnerforenings Tidsskr — Norsk Gartnerforenings Tidsskrift

Nor Geol Tidsskr — Norsk Geologisk Tidsskrift

Nor Geol Unders — Norges Geologiske Undersoekelse

Nor Geol Unders Bull — Norges Geologiske Undersoekelse. Bulletin

Nor Geol Unders Publ — Norges Geologiske Undersoekelse. Publikasjoner

Nor Geol Unders Skr — Norges Geologiske Undersoekelse. Skrifter

Norges Bank Econ Bul — Norges Bank. Economic Bulletin

Norg Geol Unders Publ — Norges Geologiske Undersoekelse. Publikasjoner

Norg Geotek Inst Publ — Norges Geotekniske Institut. Publikasjon

Nor Hvalfangst Tid — Norsk-Hvalfangst-Tidende

Nor Hvalfanst Tid — Norsk-Hvalfangst-Tidende

NORIANE — Normes et Reglements Informations Accessibles en Ligne
Nor Inst Tang- Tareforsk Rep — Norsk Institutt for Tang- og Tareforskning. Report
Nor Inst Vannforsk Aarb — Norsk Institutt foer Vannforskning. Aarbok
Nor Inst Vannforsk Rapp — Norsk Institutt foer Vannforskning. Rapport
NORJ — Northward Journal
NORL — Northian Newsletter
Nor Landbrukshogsk Foringsforsok Beret — Norges Landbrukshogskole Foringsforsokene Beretning
N Orlean Bs — New Orleans Business
N Orleans CB — New Orleans City Business
N Orl M & S J — New Orleans Medical and Surgical Journal
N Orl Med and S J — New Orleans Medical and Surgical Journal
Nor Lovtid — Norsk Lovtidend
Nor Lovtid Avd I — Norsk Lovtidend Avdeling I
Norm — Normannia. Revue Bibliographique et Critique d'Histoire de Normandie
Nor Mag Laegevidensk — Norsk Magasin foer Laegevidenskapen
Normalfrequenzen — Normalfrequenzen und Normalzeit der Frequenz-Technischen Zentralstelle der Berliner Post
Nor Met Arb — Norsk Meteorologisk Arbok
Norm Instr and Prim Plans — Normal Instructor and Primary Plans
Norm Pathol Anat (Stuttg) — Normale und Pathologische Anatomie (Stuttgart)
Norm S L BII — Bulletin de la Societe Linneenne de Normandie (Caen)
Nor Myrselsk Medd — Norske Myrselskap. Meddelelser
Nor Nat — Norsk Natur
NOROD — Noroil
Nor Olje Revy — Norsk Olje Revy
Noro-Psikiyatri Ars — Noro-Psikiyatri Arsivi
NORP — Norpic
Nor Pelsdyrbl — Norsk Pelsdyrblad
Nor Polarinst Aarb — Norsk Polarinstitutt. Aarbok
Nor Polarinst Aarbok — Norsk Polarinstitutt. Aarbok
Nor Polarinst Medd — Norsk Polarinstitutt. Meddelelser
Nor Polarinst Polarhandb — Norsk Polarinstitutt. Polarhandbok
Nor Polarinst Skr — Norsk Polarinstitutt. Skrifter
Nor Prin — Northern Principal
Norrlands Skogsvforb Tidskr (Stockh) — Norrlands Skogsvardsforbunds Tidskrift (Stockholm)
NorS — Nordic Sounds
NORS — Norseman
Norsk Artill Tidskr — Norsk Artillerie Tidskrift
Norsk Data — Norsk Datatidende
Norsk Entomol Tidsskr — Norsk Entomologisk Tidsskrift
Norsk Ent Tidsskr — Norsk Entomologisk Tidsskrift
Norske Vid-Akad Oslo Mat-Natur KI Skr — Norske Videnskaps-Akademi i Oslo. Matematisk-Naturvidenskapelig Klasse. Skrifter
Norske Vidensk Akad Mat Naturvidensk KI Avh — Norske Videnskaps-Akademi. Matematisk-Naturvidenskapelig Klasse. Avhandlinger
Norske Vid Selsk Forh (Trondheim) — Kongelige Norske Videnskabers Selskab. Foerhandlinger (Trondheim)
Norske Vid Selsk Skr (Trondheim) — Kongelige Norske Videnskabers Selskab. Skrifter (Trondheim)
Norsk Farm T — Norsk Farmaceutisk Tidsskrift
Norsk Flkmus Ab — Norsk Folkemuseums Arbok
Norsk Geogr Tidsskr — Norsk Geografisk Tidskrift
Norsk Geogr Ts — Norsk Geografisk Tidskrift
Norsk Geog Tid — Norsk Geografisk Tidskrift
Norsk Geol — Norsk Geologisk Tidskrift
Norsk Geol Tids — Norsk Geologisk Tidskrift
Norsk Geol Tidsskr — Norsk Geologisk Tidskrift
Norsk Hagetid — Norsk Hagetidend
Norsk Havetid — Norsk Havetidende. Udgivet of Selskabet Havedyrkningens Venner
Norskind — Norsk Skogindustri
Norsk Ksthist — Norsk Kunsthistorie
Norsk Kstnerleks — Norsk Kunstnerleksikon
Norsk Mag — Norsk Magazin
Norsk Mag Laegevidensk — Norsk Magazin foer Laegevidenskaben
Norsk Mus — Norsk Musikerblad
Nor Skogbruk — Norsk Skogbruk
Nor Skogforsoeksves Medd — Norske Skogforsoeksvesen. Meddelelser
Nor Skogind — Norsk Skogindustri
Norsk Polarinst Aarbok — Norsk Polarinstitutt. Aarbok
Norsk Skog — Norsk Skogindustri
Norsk Skogbr — Norsk Skogbruk
Norsk Tekstiltid — Norsk Tekstiltidende
Norsk T Sjoves — Norsk Tidsskrift for Sjovesen
Norsk Vet Tid — Norsk Veterinaer-Tidsskrift
Norsk Vet-Tidsskr — Norsk Veterinaer-Tidsskrift
NORT — North
Nor Tannlaegeforen Tid — Norske Tannlaegeforenings Tidende
Norte Agron — Norte Agronomico
Nor Tek Naturvitensk Forskningsrad Metall Kom Medd — Norges Teknisk Naturvitenskapelige Forskningsrad. Metallurgisk Komite. Meddelelse
Nor Tek Vitenskapsakad Medd — Norges Tekniske Vitenskapsakademi. Meddelelse
North Am Conf Powder Coat Proc — North American Conference on Powder Coating. Proceedings
North Amer Fauna — North American Fauna
North Amer Revw — North American Review
North Am Flora — North American Flora
North Am Flora Ser II — North American Flora. Series II
North Am For Biol Workshop — North American Forest Biology Workshop
North Am For Biol Workshop Proc — North American Forest Biology Workshop. Proceedings
North Am For Soils Conf — North American Forest Soils Conference

North Am Gladiolus Counc Bull — North American Gladiolus Council. Bulletin
North Am J Fish Manage — North American Journal of Fisheries Management
North Am Manu Res Conf Proc — North American Manufacturing Research Conference. Proceedings
North Am Mentor Mag — North American Mentor Magazine
North Am Metalwork Res Conf Proc — North American Metalworking Research Conference. Proceedings
North Am Miner News — North American Mineral News
Northamp A — Northampton Archaeology
North Am Pomona — North American Pomona
North Am Pract — North American Practitioner
Northampt Arch — Northamptonshire Archaeology
Northamptonshire Archaeol — Northamptonshire Archaeology
North Am R — North American Review
Northamts Past & Present — Northamptonshire Past and Present
North Am Vet — North American Veterinarian
North Am Wildl Nat Resour Conf Trans — North American Wildlife and Natural Resources Conference. Transactions
North Bengal Univ Rev — North Bengal University Review
North Calif Rev Bus Econ — Northern California Review of Business and Economics
North Car J Int'l L & Comm — North Carolina Journal of International Law and Commercial Regulation
North Car Med J — North Carolina Medical Journal
North Carolina Agric Exp Sta Bull — North Carolina Agricultural Experiment Station Bulletin
North Carolina Agric Exp Sta Dept Agron Res Rep — North Carolina Agricultural Experiment Station. Department of Agronomy. Research Report
North Carolina Agric Exp Sta Special Bull — North Carolina Agricultural Experiment Station Special Bulletin
North Carolina Agric Exp Sta Special Publ — North Carolina Agricultural Experiment Station. Special Publication
North Carolina Cent LJ — North Carolina Central Law Journal
North Carolina College LJ — North Carolina College Law Journal
North Carolina Div Ground Water Ground Water Bull — North Carolina. Department of Water and Air Resources. Division of Ground Water. Ground Water Bulletin
North Carolina Div Mineral Resources Geol Map Ser — North Carolina. Department of Conservation and Development. Division of MineralResources. Geologic Map Series
North Carolina Div Mineral Resources Inf Circ — North Carolina. Department of Conservation and Development. Division of MineralResources. Information Circular
North Carolina Div Mineral Resources Spec Pub — North Carolina. Department of Conservation and Development. Division of MineralResources. Special Publication
North Carolina Lib — North Carolina Libraries
North Cavern Mine Res Soc Occas Publ — Northern Cavern and Mine Research Society. Occasional Publication
North Cen Assn Q — North Central Association. Quarterly [*Ann Arbor*]
North Cent Assn Q — North Central Association. Quarterly
North Cent Reg Ext Publ — North Central Regional Extension Publication
North Cent Reg Ext Publ Mich State Univ Coop Ext Serv — North Central Region Extension Publication. Michigan State University. Cooperative Extension Service
North Cent Weed Control Conf Proc — North Central Weed Control Conference. Proceedings
North Co — North Country Anvil
North Country Lib — North Country Libraries
North Dakota Acad Sci Proc — North Dakota Academy of Science. Proceedings
North Dakota Agric Exp Sta Bimonthly Bull — North Dakota Agricultural Experiment Station. Bimonthly Bulletin
North Dakota Agric Exp Sta Bull — North Dakota Agricultural Experiment Station Bulletin
North Dakota Agric Exp Sta Res Rep — North Dakota Agricultural Experiment Station. Research Report
North Dakota Agric Exp Sta Special Bull — North Dakota Agricultural Experiment Station Special Bulletin
North Dakota Geol Survey Bull — North Dakota. Geological Survey. Bulletin
North Dakota Geol Survey Misc Map — North Dakota. Geological Survey. Miscellaneous Map
North Dakota Geol Survey Misc Ser — North Dakota. Geological Survey. Miscellaneous Series
North Dakota Geol Survey Rept Inv — North Dakota. Geological Survey. Report of Investigations
North Dakota L Rev — North Dakota Law Review
North Div Rep NDR UK At Energy Auth — Northern Division Report ND-R. United Kingdom Atomic Energy Authority
Northeast Bioeng Conf Proc — Northeast Bioengineering Conference. Proceedings
Northeast China Peoples Univ J Nat Sci — Northeastern China People's University Journal. Natural Science
North East Coast Inst Eng Shipbuild Trans — North East Coast Institution of Engineers and Shipbuilders. Transactions
Northeast Electron Res Eng Meet Rec — Northeast Electronics Research and Engineering Meeting Record
Northeast Environ Sci — Northeastern Environmental Science
Northeastern Ind World — Northeastern Industrial World
Northeast For Exp Stn For Serv Res Note NE (US) — Northeastern Forest Experiment Station. Forest Service Research Note NE (US)
Northeast Geol — Northeastern Geology
Northeast Gulf Sci — Northeast Gulf Science
Northeast J Agric Resour Econ — Northeastern Journal of Agricultural and Resource Economics
Northeast Math J — Northeastern Mathematical Journal

Northeast Phila Cham Comm Bul — Northeast Philadelphia Chamber of Commerce. Bulletin
Northeast Reg Antipollut Conf — Northeastern Regional Antipollution Conference
Northeast Tech Comm Util Beech Northeast For Exp Stn Beech — Northeastern Technical Committee on Utilization of Beech. Northeastern Forest Experiment Station. Beech Utilization Series
Northeast Weed Control Conf Proc — Northeastern Weed Control Conference. Proceedings
Northeast Weed Sci Soc Proc Annu Meet — Northeastern Weed Science Society. Proceedings. Annual Meeting
Northeast Wood Util Counc Inc Bull — Northeastern Wood Utilization Council, Incorporated. Bulletin
Northeast Wood Util Counc Inc Woodnotes — Northeastern Wood Utilization Council, Incorporated. Woodnotes
North Eng (Fairbanks) — Northern Engineer (Fairbanks)
Northern Archt — Northern Architect
Northern Cal R Bus and Econ — Northern California Review of Business and Economics
Northern Hist — Northern History. A Review of the History of the North of England
Northern Ireland Lib — Northern Ireland Libraries
Northern KY Law R — Northern Kentucky Law Review
Northern L — Northern Lights
Northern Logger — Northern Logger and Timber Processor
Northern Scot — Northern Scotland
Northern Stud — Northern Studies
North For Res Cent (Can) Inf Rep NORX — Northern Forest Research Centre (Canada). Information Report NOR-X
North Fur Trade — Northern Fur Trade
North Hist — Northern History
North-Holland Math Library — North-Holland Mathematical Library
North-Holland Math Stud — North-Holland Mathematics Studies
North-Holland Math Studies — North-Holland Mathematics Studies
North-Holland Ser Appl Math Mech — North-Holland Series in Applied Mathematics and Mechanics
North Holland Ser Cryst Growth — North-Holland Series in Crystal Growth
North Holland Ser Gen Systems Res — North-Holland Series in General Systems Research
North-Holland Ser in Appl Math and Mech — North-Holland Series in Applied Mathematics and Mechanics
North Holland Ser Probab Appl Math — North-Holland Series in Probability and Applied Mathematics
North Holland Ser Statist Probab — North-Holland Series in Statistics and Probability
North Holland Ser System Sci Engrg — North-Holland Series in Systems Science and Engineering
North Holland Syst Control Ser — North-Holland Systems and Control Series
North Ire Hort Cent Ann Rep — Northern Ireland. Horticultural Centre. Annual Report
North Ireland LQ — Northern Ireland Legal Quarterly
North Irel Gov Minist Commer Mem Geol Surv — Northern Ireland. Government. Ministry of Commerce. Memoirs. GeologicalSurvey
North Irel Mem Geol Surv — Northern Ireland. Memoirs. Geological Survey
North Irel Minist Agric Annu Rep Res Tech Work — North Ireland Ministry of Agriculture. Annual Report on Research and Technical Work
North Irel Minist Agric Rec Agric Res — North Ireland Ministry of Agriculture. Record of Agricultural Research
North Irel Minist Agric Rec Agricultural Res — Northern Ireland. Ministry of Agriculture. Record of Agricultural Research
North Irel Minist Agric Res Exper Rec — Northern Ireland. Ministry of Agriculture. Research and Experimental Record
North J Appl For — Northern Journal of Applied Forestry
North Ken'y SL Rev — Northern Kentucky State Law Review
North KY LR — Northern Kentucky Law Review
North Log Timber Process — Northern Logger and Timber Processer
North Med — North Medicine
North Miner — Northern Miner
North Nigeria Reg Res Stn Tech Rep — Northern Nigeria. Regional Research Station. Technical Report
North Niger Reg Res Stn Tech Rep — Northern Nigeria. Regional Research Station. Technical Report
North Nut Grow Assoc Annu Rep — Northern Nut Growers Association. Annual Report
North Offshore — Northern Offshore
North Pac Fur Seal Comm Proc Annu Meet — North Pacific Fur Seal Commission. Proceedings of the Annual Meeting
North Queensl Conf Australas Inst Min Metall — North Queensland Conference. Australasian Institute of Mining and Metallurgy
North Queensl Nat — North Queensland Naturalist
North R — Northern Review
North Rhod Annu Bull Dep Agric — Northern Rhodesia. Annual Bulletin. Department of Agriculture
North Rhod Dep Geol Surv Bull — Northern Rhodesia. Department of Geological Survey. Bulletin
North Rhod Dep Geol Surv Rep — Northern Rhodesia. Department of Geological Survey. Report
North Rhod Geol Surv Bull — Northern Rhodesia. Geological Survey. Bulletin
North Rhod Geol Surv Rep — Northern Rhodesia. Geological Survey. Report
North Rhod Gov Geol Surv Dep Econ Unit Rep — Northern Rhodesia Government. Geological Survey Department. Economic Unit Report
Northrop ULJ Aero Energy and Envt — Northrop University. Law Journal of Aerospace, Energy, and the Environment
North Scot — Northern Scotland
North Scotl Coll Agric Bull — North of Scotland College of Agriculture. Bulletin
North Sea Oil Inf Sheet — North Sea Oil Information Sheet
North Soc Sci Rev — Northern Social Science Review

North Stafford J Field Stud — North Staffordshire Journal of Field Studies
North Staffordshire J Field Stud — North Staffordshire Journal of Field Studies
North Stud — Northern Studies
North UL Rev — Northwestern University. Law Review
Northum — Northumberland County Legal News
Northumb Co — Northumberland County Legal News
Northumberland Co Leg Jour — Northumberland Legal Journal
Northumberland LJ — Northumberland Legal Journal
Northumb Legal J — Northumberland Legal Journal
Northumb LJ — Northumberland Legal Journal News
Northumb LN — Northumberland Legal News
Northum Co Leg N — Northumberland County Legal News
Northum Leg J — Northumberland Legal Journal
Northum Leg J (PA) — Northumberland Legal Journal
Northum Leg N (PA) — Northumberland County Legal News
Northw Agric Bull — Northwest Agricultural Bulletin. National Northwest Agricultural College. Hsi Pei Nung Pao
Northwest Anthropol Res Notes — Northwest Anthropological Research Notes
Northwest Assn Sheriffs & Police Proc — Northwest Association of Sheriffs and Police. Proceedings
Northwest Atl Fish Organ Annu Rep — Northwest Atlantic Fisheries Organization. Annual Report
Northwest Atl Fish Organ Sci Counc Stud — Northwest Atlantic Fisheries Organization. Scientific Council. Studies
Northwest Atl Fish Organ Stat Bull — Northwest Atlantic Fisheries Organization. Statistical Bulletin
North West Branch Pap Inst Chem Eng — North Western Branch Papers. Institution of Chemical Engineers
Northwest China J Agric Sci — Northwest China Journal of Agricultural Science
Northwest Dent — Northwest Dentistry
Northwest Dent Res — Northwestern Dental Research
Northwest Environ J — Northwest Environmental Journal
Northwestern J Internat Law and Bus — Northwestern Journal of International Law and Business
Northwestern UL Rev — Northwestern University. Law Review
Northwestern Univ Dept Geography Studies Geography — Northwestern University. Department of Geography. Studies in Geography
Northwestern Univ Law R — Northwestern University. Law Review
Northwestern Univ L Rev — Northwestern University. Law Review
Northwest Geol — Northwest Geology
Northwest J Int'l L & Bus — Northwestern Journal of International Law and Business
Northwest Lancet — Northwestern Lancet
Northwest Livestock Dir — Northwest Livestock Directory
Northwest Lumberman — Northwestern Lumberman
Northwest Med — Northwest Medicine
Northwest Miller — Northwestern Miller
Northwest Miller Am Baker — Northwestern Miller and American Baker
North West Newsl — North Western Newsletter
Northwest Ohio Q — Northwest Ohio Quarterly
Northwest Police J — Northwest Police Journal
Northwest Sci — Northwest Science
Northwest Sci Off Publ Northwest Sci Assoc — Northwest Science. Official Publication. Northwest Scientific Association
Northwest Univ Dent Res Grad Study Bull — Northwestern University. Dental Research and Graduate Study Bulletin
Northwest Wood Prod Clin Proc — Northwest Wood Products Clinic. Proceedings
North WLJ — Northwestern Law Journal
Northw L Rev — Northwestern University. Law Review
Northw Med — Northwest Medicine
Northw Ohio His Soc Quar Bul — Historical Society of Northwestern Ohio. Quarterly Bulletin
Northw Ohio Quar — Northwest Ohio Quarterly
Northw Orchid Bull — Northwest Orchid Bulletin
Northw U La — Northwestern University. Law Review
Northw Univ Law Rev — Northwestern University. Law Review
Nor Tid Ind Rettsvern Del 1 — Norsk Tidende foer det Industrielle Rettsvern. Del 1. Patenter
Nor Tidsskr Sprogvidenskap — Norsk Tidsskrift for Sprogvidenskap
Norton — Norton's Literary Letter
Nor Tr Bul — Norwegian Trade Bulletin
Nor TT — Norsk Teologisk Tidsskrift
NorTTs — Norsk Teologisk Tidsskrift
NORV — Norveg. Journal of Norwegian Ethnology
Nor Vel — Norges Vel
Nor Veritas Publ — Norske Veritas. Publication
Nor Veterinaertidsskr — Norsk Veterinaertidsskrift
Nor Vet-Tidsskr — Norsk Veterinaer-Tidsskrift
Nor Vidensk Akad Mat Naturvidensk Kl Skr — Norske Videnskaps-Akademi. Matematisk-Naturvidenskapelig Klasse.Skrifter
Nor Vidensk-Akad Oslo Arbok — Norske Videnskaps-Akademi i Oslo. Aarbok
Nor Vidensk-Akad Oslo Mat Natur Kl N Ser — Norske Videnskaps-Akademi i Oslo. Matematisk-Naturvidenskapelig Klasse. Skrifter. Ny Serie
Nor Vidensk-Akad Skr — Norske Videnskaps-Akademi. Skrifter
Nor Vidensk Selsk Mus Misc — Norske Videnskabers Selskab. Museet. Miscellanea
Nor Vidensk Selsk Skr — Norske Videnskabers Selskab. Skrifter
Norv Pharm Acta — Norvegica Pharmaceutica Acta
Norv Sac — Norvegia Sacra
Nor VVS — Norsk VVS
Norw — Norwegian
Norw AR — Norwegian Archaeological Review
Norw Archaeol Rev — Norwegian Archaeological Review
Norway Bud — National Budget of Norway
Norway Geol Undersoekelse Bull — Norway. Geologiske Undersoekelse. Bulletin

Norw Canners Export J — Norwegian Canners' Export Journal
Norwegian — Norwegian American Commerce
Norwegian Am Hist Assoc Pub — Norwegian-American Historical Association Publications
Norwegian-Am Stud and Rec — Norwegian-American Studies and Records
Norwegian Commer Banks Fin R — Norwegian Commercial Banks. Financial Review
Nor'-West F — Nor'-West Farmer
Norw For — Norwegian Forestry
Norw Geotech Inst Publ — Norwegian Geotechnical Institute. Publication
Norw J Agric Sci — Norwegian Journal of Agricultural Sciences
Norw J Agric Sci Suppl — Norwegian Journal of Agricultural Sciences. Supplement
Norw J Bot — Norwegian Journal of Botany
Norw J Chem Min Metall — Norwegian Journal of Chemistry, Mining, and Metallurgy
Norw J Entomol — Norwegian Journal of Entomology
Norw J For — Norwegian Journal of Forestry
Norw J Zool — Norwegian Journal of Zoology
Norw Marit Res — Norwegian Maritime Research
Norw Oil Rev — Norwegian Oil Review
Norw Pat Doc — Norway. Patent Document
Norw Petrol Dir Pap — Norwegian Petroleum Directorate. Paper
Norw Shipp News — Norwegian Shipping News
(Norw) Stat — Statistisk Manedskefte (Norway)
Norw Whaling Gaz — Norwegian Whaling Gazette
Norwy Econ — Economic Policy and Developments in Norway
Norw Yrbk — Statistical Yearbook of Norway
NOS — News on Sunday
Nos C — Nos Cahiers
NOSK — Norsk Skogindustri
NOSKA — Norsk Skogindustri
Nos Oiseaux Bull Romande Etude Prot Oiseaux — Nos Oiseaux. Bulletin de la Societe Romande pour l'Etude et la Protection des Oiseaux
Nosokom Chron — Nosokomeiaka Chronika
Nosokomeiaka Chron — Nosokomeiaka Chronika
NOSTA — Norges Offisielle Statistikk
NOSYAV — Museum National d'Histoire Naturelle. Notulae Systematicae
NOT — Notes on Translation
Not A — Notizie d'Arte
Not Af — Notes Africaines
Not Agric — Noticias Agricolas/Compania Shell de Venezuela. Servicio Shell Para El Agricultor
Not Agric Fund Serv Agric — Noticias Agricolas. Fundacion Servicio para el Agricultor
Not Agric Serv Agric — Noticias Agricolas. Servicio para el Agricultor
Not Agric Serv Shell Agric — Noticias Agricolas. Servicio Shell para el Agricultor
Not A Hisp — Noticiario Arqueologico Hispanico
Nota Inf Inst Nac Invest Forest (Mex) — Nota Informativa. Instituto Nacional de Investigaciones Forestales (Mexico)
Nota Invest Cent Invest Pesq (Bauta Cuba) — Nota sobre Investigaciones. Centro de Investigaciones Pesqueras (Bauta, Cuba)
Not Allumiere — Notiziario. Museo Civico ed Associazione Archeologica di Allumiere
Not Am Math — Notices. American Mathematical Society
Not Ammin Sanit — Notiziario dell'Amministrazione Sanitaria
NOTAMS — Notice to Airmen
Not Arch — Notiziario Archeologico. Ministero delle Colonie
Not Archeol — Notiziario Archeologico
Not Arq Hisp — Notiziario Archeologico del Ministero delle Colonie
Notas Agron — Notas Agronomicas
Notas Algebra Anal — Notas de Algebra y Analisis
Notas Cent Biol Aquat Trop (Lisb) — Notas. Centro de Biologia Aquatica Tropical (Lisbon)
Notas Cient Ser M Mat — Notas Cientificas. Serie M. Matematica
Notas Ci Ser M Mat — Notas Cientificas. Serie M. Matematica
Notas Comun Inst Geol Espana — Notas y Comunicaciones. Instituto Geologico y Minero de Espana
Notas Comun Inst Geol Min Esp — Notas y Comunicaciones. Instituto Geologico y Minero de Espana
Notas Divulg Inst Munic Bot (Buenos Aires) — Notas de Divulgacion del Instituto Municipal de Botanica (Buenos Aires)
Notas Estud Inst Biol Marit (Lisb) — Notas e Estudos. Instituto de Biologia Maritima (Lisbon)
Notas Estud Secr Estado Pescas Ser Recur Ambiente Aquat — Notas e Estudos. Secretaria de Estado das Pescas. Serie Recursos e Ambiente Aquatico
Notas Estud Univ Rio Grande Sul Esc Geol — Notas e Estudos. Universidade do Rio Grande Do Sul. Escola de Geologia
Notas Fis — Notas de Fisica
Notas Fis Cent Bras Pesqui Fis — Notas de Fisica. Centro Brasileiro de Pesquisas Fisicas
Notas Geom Topol — Notas de Geometria y Topologia
Nota Silvic Adm Nac Bosques (Argent) — Notas Silvicolas. Administracion Nacional de Bosques (Buenos Aires, Argentina)
Notas Inst Mat Estatist Univ Sao Paulo Ser Mat — Notas. Instituto de Matematica e Estatistica da Universidade de Sao Paulo. Serie Matematica
Notas Logica Mat — Notas de Logica Matematica
Notas Mat — Notas de Matematica
Notas Mat Discreta — Notas de Matematica Discreta
Notas Mat Simpos — Notas de Matematica y Simposia
Notas Mesoamer — Notas Mesoamericanas
Notas Mimeogr Cent Biol Aquat Trop (Lisb) — Notas Mimeografadas. Centro de Biologia Aquatica Tropical (Lisbon)
Notas Mus La Plata Antropol — Notas. Museo de La Plata. Antropologia

Notas Mus La Plata Bot — Notas. Museo de La Plata. Botanica
Notas Mus La Plata Geol — Notas del Museo de La Plata. Geologia
Notas Mus La Plata Paleontol — Notas. Museo de La Plata. Paleontologia
Notas Mus La Plata Zool — Notas. Museo de La Plata. Zoologia
Notas Pobl — Notas de Poblacion
Notas Prelim Estud Div Geol Mineral (Braz) — Notas Preliminares e Estudos. Divisao de Geologia e Mineralogia (Brazil)
Notas Prelim Estud Serv Geol Mineral Braz — Notas Preliminares e Estudos. Servico Geologico e Mineralogico do Brazil
Notas Prelim Mus La Plata — Notas Preliminares del Museo de La Plata. Universidad Nactional de La Plata
Notas Quir Sanat Deschamps — Notas Quirurgicas. Sanatorio Deschamps
Notas Soc Mat Chile — Notas de la Sociedad de Matematica de Chile
Notas Tec Inst Pesqui Mar (Rio De J) — Notas Tecnicas. Instituto de Pesquisas da Marinha (Rio De Janeiro)
Notas Tec Inst Pesqui Mar (Rio De Janeiro) — Notas Tecnicas. Instituto de Pesquisas da Marinha (Rio De Janeiro)
Notas Tecn Inst Nac Invest Forest — Notas Tecnicas. Instituto Nacional de Investigaciones Forestales
Notas Tecnol For — Notas Tecnologicas Forestales
Notas Tecnol For Dir Invest For (Argent) — Notas Tecnologicas Forestales. Direccion de Investigaciones Forestales (Argentina)
Notat Biol — Notationes Biologicae
Nota Tec For Esc Ingen For Univ Chile — Notas Tecnico Forestales. Escuela de Ingenieria Forestal. Universidad de Chile
Nota Tec Inst For (Chile) — Nota Tecnica. Instituto Forestal (Santiago De Chile)
Nota Tec Inst Nac Invest For (Mex) — Nota Tecnica. Instituto Nacional de Investigaciones Forestales (Mexico)
Nota Tecnol For Adm Nac Bosques (Argent) — Notas Tecnologicas Forestales. Administracion Nacional de Bosques (Buenos Aires, Argentina)
Notatki Ornitol — Notatki Ornitologiczne
Not Bibliot Interamer — Noticiero Bibliotecario Interamericano
Not Biol — Notationes Biologicae
Not Cent Ital Smalti Porcellanati — Notiziario. Centro Italiano Smalti Porcellanati
Not Chianti Class — Notiziario del Chianti Classico
Not Chim Ind — Notiziario Chimico-Industriale
Not Chiostro Mon Magg — Notizie dal Chiostro del Monastero Maggiore
Not CNEN — Notiziario. Comitato Nazionale per l'Energia Nucleare
Not Com Naz Energ Nucl — Notiziario. Comitato Nazionale per l'Energia Nucleare
Not Com Naz Energ Nucl (Italy) — Notiziario. Comitato Nazionale per 'Energia Nucleare (Italy)
NOTEA — Novosti Tekhniki
Note Apunti Sper Ent Agr — Note ed Apunti Sperimentale di Entomologia Agraria
Noteb Empirical Petrol — Notebook of Empirical Petrology
Note CEA-N (Fr) Commis Energ At — Note CEA-N (France). Commissariat a l'Energie Atomique
Not Ecol — Notiziario dell'Ecologia
Note Econ — Note Economiche
Note E Riv Di Psichiat — Note e Riviste di Psichiatria
Note Fruttic — Note de Frutticultura
Note Inf Tech Lab Cent Ponts Chaussees — Note d'Information Technique. Laboratoire Central des Ponts et Chaussees
Note Lab Biol Mar Pesca-Fano — Note. Laboratorio di Biologia Marina e Pesca-Fano
Note Mat — Note di Matematica
Not ENEA — Notiziario dell'ENEA
Not Enol Aliment — Notiziario Enologico ed Alimentare
Not Entomol — Notulae Entomologicae
Note Recens & Not — Note Recensioni e Notizie
Note Rech Dep Exploit Util Bois Univ Laval — Note de Recherches. Departement d'Exploitation et Utilisation des Bois. Universite Laval
Note Rech Miner Explor Res Inst McGill Univ — Note de Recherche. Mineral Exploration Research Institute. McGill University
Note Rec Roy Soc London — Notes and Records. Royal Society of London
Note Riv Psichiat — Note e Riviste di Psichiatria
Note Riv Psichiatr — Note e Riviste di Psichiatria
No Tes — Novum Testamentum
Notes Afr — Notes Africaines
Notes Agric Res Cent Herb (Egypt) — Notes. Agricultural Research Centre Herbarium (Egypt)
Notes & Doc Mus France — Notes et Documents des Musees de France
Notes & Quer — Notes and Queries
Notes and Records Roy Soc London — Notes and Records. Royal Society of London
Notes & Rec Royal Soc London — Notes and Records of the Royal Society of London
Notes Appl Sci NPL — Notes on Applied Science. National Physical Laboratory
Notes Appl Sci UK Natl Phys Lab — Notes on Applied Science. United Kingdom National Physical Laboratory
Notes Bot School Trinity Coll — Notes. Botanical School of Trinity College
Notes Bot Sch Trinity Coll (Dublin) — Notes. Botanical School of Trinity College (Dublin)
Notes Docum UN Unit Apartheid — Notes and Documents. United Nations Unit on Apartheid
Notes Doc Volt — Notes et Documents Voltaiques
Notes Ent Chin — Notes d'Entomologie Chinoise
Note Serv Oceanogr Peches Indochine — Note du Service Oceanographique des Peches de l'Indochine
Notes et Docum Voltaiques — Notes et Documents Voltaiques
Notes et Etud Docum — Notes et Etudes Documentaires
Notes et Etud Docum Ser Problemes Am Latine — Notes et Etudes Documentaires. Serie Problemes d'Amerique Latine
Notes et Mem Moyen-Orient — Notes et Memoires sur le Moyen-Orient
Notes Etud Doc — Notes et Etudes Documentaires
Notes Hisp — Notes Hispaniques

Notes Inf CEA — Notes d'Information CEA
Notes Inform Statist Banque — Notes d'Information et Statistiques. Banque
Notes Inform Statist Banque Centr Afr Ouest — Notes d'Information et Statistiques. Banque Centrale des Etats de l'Afrique de l'Ouest
Notes Inst Oceanogr Ribar (Split) — Notes. Institut za Oceanografiju i Ribarstvo (Split)
Notes Maroc — Notes Marocaines
Notes Mem Moyen-Orient — Notes et Memoires sur le Moyen-Orient
Notes Mem Serv Geol Maroc — Notes et Memoires. Service Geologique du Maroc
Notes Mem Serv Geol (Morocco) — Notes et Memoires. Service Geologique (Morocco)
Notes Mem Serv Geol (Rabat) — Notes et Memoires. Service Geologique (Rabat)
Notes Mem UAR Hydrobiol Dep — Notes and Memoirs. United Arab Republic. Hydrobiological Department
Notes Neurol — Notes on Neurology
Notes Numer Fluid Mech — Notes on Numerical Fluid Mechanics
Notes Off Seed Introd — Notes. Office of Seed and Plant Introduction
Notes on Education Res in Afr Music — Notes on Education and Research in African Music
Notes on Higher Educ — Notes on Higher Education
Notes on Pure Math — Notes on Pure Mathematics
Notes on Sc Build — Notes on the Science of Building
Notes on the Science of Bldg — Notes on the Science of Building
Notes on Univ Ed — Notes on University Education
Notes Pure Math — Notes on Pure Mathematics
Notes Quer — Notes and Queries
Notes Queries Soc West Highl Isl Hist Res — Notes and Queries. Society of West Highland and Island Historical Research
Notes R Bot Gard (Edinb) — Notes. Royal Botanic Garden (Edinburgh)
Notes R Bot Gdn (Edinb) — Notes. Royal Botanic Garden (Edinburgh)
Notes Read — Notes and Queries for Readers and Writers, Collectors, and Librarians
Notes Rech Fond Univ Luxemb — Notes de Recherche. Fondation Universitaire Luxembourgeoise
Notes Rec R — Notes and Records. Royal Society of London
Notes Rec Roy London — Notes and Records. Royal Society of London
Notes Rec Roy Soc Lond — Notes and Records. Royal Society of London
Notes Rec Roy Soc London — Notes and Records. Royal Society of London
Notes Rec R Soc Lond — Notes and Records. Royal Society of London
Notes Rep Comput Sci Appl Math — Notes and Reports in Computer Science and Applied Mathematics
Notes Rep Math Sci Engrg — Notes and Reports in Mathematics in Science and Engineering
Notes Sci Bldg — Notes on the Science of Building
Notes Sci Build — Notes on the Science of Building
Notes Serv Geol Maroc — Notes du Service Geologique du Maroc
Notes Serv Geol (Tunis) — Notes du Service Geologique (Tunisia)
Notes Soil Tech — Notes on Soil Technique
Notes Strybing Arbor — Notes from Strybing Arboretum
Notes Tech Hydrol — Notes Techniques en Hydrologie
Notes Water Pollut (Stevenage) — Notes on Water Pollution (Stevenage)
Notes Water Res — Notes on Water Research
Notes Wat Res — Notes on Water Research
Note Tech Cent Rech Agron Etat (Gembloux) — Note Technique. Centre de Recherches Agronomiques de l'Etat (Gembloux)
Note Tech Centre Tech For Trop — Note Technique. Centre Technique Forestier Tropicale
Note Tech Cent Sci Tech Ind Text Belge — Note Technique. Centre Scientifique et Technique de l'Industrie Textile Belge
Note Tech Cent Tech For Trop (Nogent Sur Marne Fr) — Note Technique. Centre Technique Forestier Tropical (Nogent-Sur-Marne, France)
Note Tech Dep Exploit Util Bois Univ Laval — Note Technique. Departement d'Exploitation et Utilisation des Bois. Universite Laval
Note Tech Inst Rebois Tunis — Note Technique. Institut de Reboisement de Tunis
Note Tech Off Nat Etud Rech Aerosp (Fr) — Note Technique. Office National d'Etudes et de Recherches Aerospatiales (France)
Not Farm — Noticias Farmaceuticas
Not Farm (Coimbra) — Noticias Farmaceuticas (Coimbra)
Not Galapagos — Noticias de Galapagos
Notic Agr Serv Shell Agr — Noticias Agricolas. Servicio Shell para el Agricultor
Notic Arqueol Hispan Prehist — Noticiario Arqueologico Hispanico Prehistoria
Notices Amer Math Soc — Notices. American Mathematical Society
Notic Geomorfol — Noticia Geomorfologica
NOT i Ch — Naucnaja Organizacija Truda i Chozjajstvo
Noticiario Arq Hisp — Noticiario Arqueologico Hispanico
Noticiario Arqu Hispanico — Noticiario Arqueologico Hispanico
Noticiario Inst Forestal — Noticiario Instituto Forestal
Noticiario Mens Santiago — Noticiario Mensual. Museo Nacional de Historial Natural (Santiago)
Noticias — Brasil. Instituto Brasileiro de Bibliographia e Documentacao. Noticias
Not Inf Cent Ital Smalti Porcellanati — Notiziario Informativo. Centro Italiano Smalti Porcellanati
Not Ist Autom Univ Roma — Notiziario. Istituto di Automatica. Universita di Roma
Not Ist Vaccinogeno Antituberc — Notiziario. Istituto Vaccinogeno Antitubercolare
Notiz Arch — Notiziario Archeologico del Ministero delle Colonie
Notizbl Bot Gart Berlin Dahlem — Notizblatt des Botanischen Gartens und Museums zu Berlin-Dahlem
Notizbl Hess Landesamt Bodenforsch Wiesbaden — Notizblatt. Hessisches Landesamtes fuer Bodenforschung zu Wiesbaden
Notizbl Hess Landesamtes Bodenforsch Wiesb — Notizblatt. Hessisches Landesamt fuer Bodenforschung zu Wiesbaden
Notizbl Koenigl Bot Gart Berlin — Notizblatt des Koeniglichen Botanischen Gartens und Museums zu Berlin
Notiz Cam Cam Commer Ind Agr Cuneo — Notiziario Camerale. Camera di Commercio. Industria e Agricoltura di Cuneo

Notiz Farm — Notiziario Farmaceutico
Notizie Scavi — Notizie degli Scavi di Antichita
Notiz IRI — Notizie IRI
Notiz Malatt Piante — Notiziario sulle Malattie delle Piante
Notiz Mal Piante — Notiziario sulle Malattie delle Piante
Not J — Notaries Journal
NOTL — Northline Association of Canadian Universities for Northern Studies
No TM — Norsk Tidsskrift vor Misjon
Not Mal Piante — Notiziario sulle Malattie delle Piante
Not Man A — Not Man Apart
Not Mar — Notes Marocaines
Not Med Vet — Noticias Medico-Veterinarias
Not Mens Mus Nac Hist Nat — Noticiario Mensual. Museo Nacional de Historia Natural
Not Mineral Sicil Calabrese — Notizie di Mineralogia Siciliana e Calabrese
NOTN — Nortext News
Not Nat Acad Nat Sci Philadelphia — Notulae Naturae. Academy of Natural Sciences of Philadelphia
Not Nat (Phila) — Notulae Naturae (Philadelphia)
NOTOA6 — Brain and Nerve
Not Odonatol — Notulae Odonatologicae
NOTP — New Orleans Times-Picayune
Not Pal Albani — Notizie del Palazzo Albani. Rivista Quadrimestrale di Storia dell'Arte
Not Pont — Notizie Pontificie
Not Quim — Noticias Quimicas
Not Quir Sanat Desch — Notas Quirurgicas del Sanatorio Deschamps
NotR — Notes and Records. Royal Society of London
Notr Dame E — Notre Dame English Journal
Notre Dame Eng J — Notre Dame English Journal
Notre Dame Est Plan Inst — Notre Dame Estate Planning Institute. Proceedings
Notre Dame Est Plan Inst Proc — Notre Dame Estate Planning Institute. Proceedings
Notre Dame Inst on Char Giving Found and Tr — Notre Dame Institute on Charitable Giving. Foundations and Trusts
Notre Dame J Formal Logic — Notre Dame Journal of Formal Logic
Notre Dame J Form Log — Notre Dame Journal of Formal Logic
Notre Dame J Leg — Notre Dame Journal of Legislation
Notre Dame L — Notre Dame Lawyer
Notre Dame Law — Notre Dame Lawyer
Notre Dame Law R — Notre Dame Law Review
Notre Dame L Rev — Notre Dame Law Review
Notre Dame Math Lectures — Notre Dame Mathematical Lectures
Notre Dame Sci Q — Notre Dame Science Quarterly
Not Ric Sci — Notiziario de "La Ricerca Scientifica"
Not Saellsk Fauna Fl Fenn Foerh — Notiser ur Saellskapets Pro Fauna et Flora Fennica Foerhandlinger
Not Scavi — Notizie degli Scavi di Antichita
Not Scavi Ant — Notizie degli Scavi dell'Antichita
Not Soc Ital Biochim Clin — Notiziario. Societa Italiana di Biochimica Clinica
Not Soc Ital Fitosoc — Notiziario. Societa Italiana di Fitosociologia
Notstromversorg Batterien Tech Symp — Notstromversorgung mit Batterien. Technisches Symposium
Not Syst — Notulae Systematicae
No TT — Norsk Teologisk Tidsskrift
Nott Fr St — Nottingham French Studies
Nottingham Fr Stud — Nottingham French Studies
Nottingham Medieval Stud — Nottingham Medieval Studies
Nottingham Univ Min Dep Mag — Nottingham University. Mining Department Magazine
Not Trav Acad Gard — Notice des Travaux de l'Academie du Gard
Notulae Entomol — Notulae Entomologicae
Notul Ent — Notulae Entomologicae
Not W — Notarieel Weekblad
Noutati Med Apl Constr Mas — Noutati in Mecanica Aplicata si in Constructia de Masini
Noutati Stiinte Nat Pedagog — Noutati in Stiinte ale Naturii si in Pedagogie
NOUTD — Nordisk Utredningsserie
N Outl — New Outlook
Nouv Annales D Voyages — Nouvelles Annales des Voyages
Nouv Ann Voyages — Nouvelles Annales des Voyages, de la Geographie, et de l'Histoire
Nouv Arch — Nouvelles Archives des Missions Scientifiques
Nouv Arch Hosp — Nouvelles Archives Hospitalieres
Nouv Arch Ital Biol — Nouvelles Archives Italiennes de Biologie
Nouv Arch Miss — Nouvelles Archives des Missions Scientifiques et Litteraires
Nouv Arch Missions Sci Litt — Nouvelles Archives des Missions Scientifiques et Litteraires
Nouv Arch Mus Hist Nat — Nouvelles Archives du Museum d'Histoire Naturelle
Nouv Archvs A Fr — Nouvelles Archives de l'Art Francais
Nouv Archvs Miss Sci — Nouvelles Archives des Missions Scientifiques
Nouv Archvs Mus — Nouvelles Archives du Museum
Nouv Autom — Nouvel Automatisme
Nouv Avic — Nouvelles de l'Aviculture
Nouv Bib — Nouvelles Bibliques
Nouv Bibl Class — Nouvelle Bibliotheque Classique
Nouv Bigarure — La Nouvelle Bigarure
Nouv Cah — Nouveaux Cahiers
Nouv Caledoniennes — Nouvelles Caledoniennes
Nouv Chine — Nouvelle Chine
Nouv Clio — La Nouvelle Clio
Nouv Crit — Nouvelle Critique
Nouv Critique — Nouvelle Critique
Nouveau Cours de Math — Nouveau Cours de Mathematiques
Nouv Ecodevelop — Nouvelles de l'Ecodeveloppement

Nouvel Autom — Nouvel Automatisme
Nouvelle Bibl Sci — Nouvelle Bibliotheque Scientifique
Nouvelliste Oecon Litt — Le Nouvelliste Oeconomique et Litteraire
Nouvelliste Suisse — Nouvelliste Suisse, Historique, Politique, Litteraire et Amusant
Nouv Est — Nouvelles de l'Estampe
Nouv Etud Hongroises — Nouvelles Etudes Hongroises
Nouv Eure — Nouvelles de l'Eure
Nouv Fem France Illus — Nouveau-Femina-France-Illustration
Nouv Grasse — Nouvelles de Grasse
Nouv Hol — Nouvelles de Hollande
Nouv Hongrie — Nouvelles de Hongrie
Nouv J — Nouveau Journal
Nouv J Asiat — Nouveau Journal Asiatique
Nouv J Chim — Nouveau Journal de Chimie
Nouv J Helv — Nouveau Journal Helvetique, Ou Annales Litteraires et Politiques de l'Europe etPrincipalement de la Suisse
NouvLitt — Nouvelles Litteraires
Nouv Litt — Nouvelles Litteraires, Artistiques, et Scientifiques
Nouv Litter — Nouvelles Litteraires, Artistiques, et Scientifiques
Nouv Med — Nouveautes Medicales
Nouv Mel Orient — Nouveaux Melanges Orientaux
Nouv Mem Acad Royale Sci & B Lett — Nouveaux Memoires de l'Academie Royale des Sciences et Belles-Lettres
Nouv Mem Acad Royale Sci & B Lett Bruxelles — Nouveaux Memoires de l'Academie Royale des Sciences et Belles-Lettres. Bruxelles
Nouv Mem Acad Roy Sci Bruxelles — Nouveaux Memoires de l'Academie Royale des Sciences et Belles-Lettres de Bruxelles
Nouv Mem Acad Roy Sci Hist Berlin — Nouveaux Memoires. Academie Royale des Sciences et Belles-Lettres. Avec l'Histoire (Berlin)
Nouv Minerve — Nouvelle Minerve
NouvO — Nouvel Observateur
Nouv Photocinema — Nouveau Photocinema
Nouv Polit Agric Commune — Nouvelles de la Politique Agricole Commune
Nouv Presse — Nouvelle Presse Medicale
Nouv Presse Med — Nouvelle Presse Medicale
Nouv R Deux Mondes — Nouvelle Revue des Deux Mondes
Nouv Repub Lett — Nouvelles de la Republique des Lettres
Nouv Republ Lett — Nouvelles de la Republique des Lettres
Nouv Rev — Nouvelle Revue
Nouv Rev Bretagne — Nouvelle Revue de Bretagne
Nouv Rev Crit — Nouvelle Revue Critique
Nouv Rev d Italie — Nouvelle Revue d'Italie
Nouv Rev Egypte — Nouvelle Revue d'Egypte
Nouv Rev Entomol — Nouvelle Revue d'Entomologie
Nouv Rev Fr — Nouvelle Revue Francaise
Nouv Rev Fr Hematol — Nouvelle Revue Francaise d'Hematologie. Blood Cells
Nouv Rev Fr Hematol Blood Cells — Nouvelle Revue Francaise d'Hematologie. Blood Cells
Nouv Rev Hist Droit Fr — Nouvelle Revue Historique de Droit Francais et Etranger
Nouv Rev Hongrie — Nouvelle Revue de Hongrie
Nouv Rev Med Toulouse — Nouvelle Revue de Medecine de Toulouse
Nouv Rev Med Toulouse Suppl — Nouvelle Revue de Medecine de Toulouse. Supplement
Nouv Rev Opt — Nouvelle Revue d'Optique
Nouv Rev Opt Appl — Nouvelle Revue d'Optique Appliquee
Nouv Rev Psychanal — Nouvelle Revue de Psychanalyse
Nouv Rev Psychoanalyse — Nouvelle Revue de Psychoanalyse
Nouv Rev Retro — Nouvelle Revue Retrospective
Nouv Rev Son — Nouvelle Revue du Son
Nouv Rev Theo — Nouvelle Revue Theologique
Nouv Rev Theol — Nouvelle Revue Theologique
Nouv Rev Tib — Nouvelle Revue Tibetaine
Nouv Revue Des Deux Mondes — Nouvelle Revue Des Deux Mondes
Nouv R F Hem — Nouvelle Revue Francaise d'Hematologie. Blood Cells
Nouv R Francaise — Nouvelle Revue Francaise
Nouv R Int — Nouvelle Revue Internationale
Nouv R Int Centr Afr Ouest — Nouvelle Revue Internationale Centrale des Etats de l'Afrique de l'Ouest
Nouv R Opt — Nouvelle Revue d'Optique
Nouv R Social — Nouvelle Revue Socialiste
Nouv Rythmes Monde — Nouveaux Rythmes du Monde
Nouv Sci Technol — Nouvelles de la Science et des Technologies
Nouv Tech — Nouvelles Techniques
Nouv Tech A — Nouvelles Techniques. A. Automatique et Electronique Industrielle
Nouv Tech B — Nouvelles Techniques. B. Genie Nucleaire
Nov — Novels
Nov — Noverim
Nova Acta Acad Mogunt Sci Util Erfurti — Abhandlungen der Kurfuerstlich-Mainzischen Akademie Nuetzlicher Wissenschaften zu Erfurt/Nova Acta Academiae Electoralis Moguntinae Scientiarum Utilium quae Erfurti Est
Nova Acta Erud — Nova Acta Eruditorum
Nova Acta Erud Suppl — Ad Nova Acta Eruditorum. Quae Lipsiae Publicantur. Supplementa
Nova Acta Leopold — Nova Acta Leopoldina
Nova Acta Leopold Suppl — Nova Acta Leopoldina. Supplementum
Nova Acta Regiae Soc Sci Ups — Nova Acta Regiae Societatis Scientiarum Upsaliensis
Nova Acta Regiae Soc Sci Upsal — Nova Acta Regiae Societatis Scientiarum Upsaliensis
Nova Acta Regiae Soc Sci Ups C — Nova Acta Regiae Societatis Scientiarum Upsaliensis. Seria C
Nova Acta Regiae Soc Sci Ups Ser C — Nova Acta Regiae Societatis Scientiarum Upsaliensis. Seria C. Botany,General Geology, Physical Geography, Paleontology, and Zoology

Nova Acta R Soc Sc Upsaliensis — Nova Acta Regiae Societatis Scientiarum Upsaliensis
Nova Guinea Geol — Nova Guinea. Geology
Nova Hedwig — Nova Hedwigia
Nova Hedwigia Z Kryptogamenkd — Nova Hedwigia Zeitschrift fuer Kryptogamenkunde
Nova Hist — Nova Historia
Nova J Algebra Geom — Nova Journal of Algebra and Geometry
Nova J Math Game Theory Algebra — Nova Journal of Mathematics, Game Theory, and Algebra
Nova Lit Circuli Francon — Nova Literaria Circuli Franconici Oder Fraenkische Gelehrten-Historie
Nova LJ — Nova Law Journal
Nova Proizv — Nova Proizvodnja
Nova Proizvod — Nova Proizvodnya
Novartis Found Symp — Novartis Foundation Symposium
Novartis Found Symp — Novartis Foundation Symposium [*Chichester*]
Nova Scotia Dept Mines Ann Rept Mem — Nova Scotia. Department of Mines. Annual Report. Memoir
Nova Scotia Hist Rev — Nova Scotia Historical Review
Nova Scotia Hist Soc Coll — Nova Scotia Historical Society. Collections
Nova Scotia Med Bull — Nova Scotia Medical Bulletin
Nova Scotian Inst Sci Proc — Nova Scotian Institute of Science. Proceedings
Nova Tech — Nova Technika
Nov Comm Acad Sci Imp Petrop — Novi Commentarii Academiae Scientiarum Imperalis Petropolitanae
NOVDA — Norsk Veterinaer-Tidsskrift
Nov Dannye Geol Boksitov — Novye Dannye po Geologii Boksitov
Nov Dannye Geol Polezn Iskop Zapadn Sib — Novye Dannye po Geologii i Poleznym Iskopaemym Zapadnoi Sibiri
Nov Dannye Miner — Novye Dannye o Mineralakh
Nov Dannye Miner (SSSR) — Novye Dannye o Mineralakh (SSSR)
Nov D I — Nuovo Digesto Italiano
NOVE — NOMOS Verlagskatalog
No Ve — Nova et Vetera
NOVEA — Novenytermeles
Noved Cient Ser Zool — Novedades Cientificas. Serie Zoologia
Noved Econ — Novedades Economicas
Noveishaya Tektonika Noveishie Otlozh Chel — Noveishaya Tektonika. Noveishie Otlozheniya i Chelovek
Noveishaya Tekton Noveishie Otlozh Chel — Noveishaya Tektonika. Noveishie Otlozheniya i Chelovek
Novel Biodegrad Microb Polym — Novel Biodegradable Microbial Polymers
Novelists Mag — Novelist's Magazine
Novenynemes Novenytermesz Kutato Intez Koezl Sopronhorpacs — Novenynemesitesi es Novenytermesztesi Kutato Intezet. Sopronhorpacs Koezlemenyei
Novenytermeles Crop Prod — Novenytermeles/Crop Production
Novenyved Idoszeru Kerdesei — Novenyvedelem Idoszeru Kerdesei
Novenyved Kut Intez Evk — Novenyvedelmi Kutato Intezet Evkonyve
Nove Virobnitstvi Budiv Mater — Nove u Virobnitstvi Budivel'nikh Materialiv
Nov Fiz Metody Obrab Pishch Prod — Novye Fizicheskie Metody Obrabotki Pishchevykh Produktov
Novgorod Golovn Gos Pedagog Inst Uch Zap — Novgorodskii Golovnoi Gosudarstvennyi Pedagogicheskii Institut. Uchenye Zapiski
Novgorod Golovn Gos Ped Inst Ucen Zap — Novgorodskii Golovnoi Gosudarstvennyi Pedagogicheskii Institut. Ucenye Zapiski
Novices Glean Bee Cult — Novices' Gleanings in Bee Culture
Novices Gleanings Bee Cult — Novices' Gleanings in Bee Culture
Novi Comment Acad Sci Inst Bononiensis — Novi Commentarii Academiae Scientiarum Instituti Bononiensis
Novi Comment Soc Regiae Sci Gott — Novi Commentarii Societatis Regiae Scientiarum Gottingensis
NoVidSF — Det Kongelige Norske Videnskabers Selskabs Forhandlinger
Novinky Poligr Prum — Novinky v Poligrafichem Prumyslu
Novi Probl Pediatr — Novi Problemi v Pediatriyata
Nov Issled Khim Metall Obogashch — Novye Issledovaniya v Khimii, Metallurgii, i Ogobashchenii
Nov Issled Metall Khim Obogashch — Novye Issledovaniya v Metallurgii, Khimii, i Obogashchenii
Nov Issled Pedagog Naukakh — Novye Issledovaniya v Pedagogicheskikh Naukakh
Nov Issled Psikhol Vozrastn Fiziol — Novye Issledovaniya v Psikhologii i Vozrastnoi Fiziologii
Novit Arthropodae — Novitates Arthropodae
Novitates Zool — Novitates Zoologicae
Novi Zb Mat Prob — Novi Zbornik Matematickih Problema
Nov Khir Arkh — Novyi Khirurgicheskii Arkhiv
Nov Lek Rast Sib Ikh Lech Prep Primen — Novye Lekarstvennye Rasteniya Sibiri Ikh Lechebnye Preparaty i Primenenie
Nov Lek Sredstva — Novye Lekarstvennye Sredstva
NovM — Novyj Mir
Nov Maloizvestnye Vidy Fauny Sib — Novye i Maloizvestnye Vidy Fauny Sibiri
Nov Mashinostr — Novoe v Mashinostroenii
Nov Med — Novosti Meditsiny
Nov Med Priborostr — Novosti Meditsinskogo Priborostroeniya
Nov Med Tek — Novosti Meditsinskoi Tekhniki
Nov Med Tekh — Novosti Meditsinskoi Tekhniki
Nov Met Modif Biokhim Fiziol Issled Zhivotnovod — Novye Metody i Modifikatsii Biokhimicheskikh i FiziologicheskikhIssledovanii v Zhivotnovodstve
Nov Metody Ispyt Met — Novye Metody Ispytanii Metallov
Nov Metody Rascheta Zhelezobeton Elem — Novye Metody Rascheta Zhelezobetonnykh Elementov [*monograph*]
Nov Nauke Tekh Vitam — Novoe v Nauke i Tekhnike Vitaminov
Nov Neftepererab — Novosti Neftepererabotki

Nov Neft Gazov Tekh Gazov Delo — Novosti Neftyanoi i Gazovoi Tekhniki Gazovoe Delo

Nov Neft Gazov Tekh Geol — Novosti Neftyanoi i Gazovoi Tekhniki. Geologiya

Nov Neft Gazov Tekh Neftepererab Neftekhim — Novosti Neftyanoi i Gazovoi Tekhniki, Neftepererabotka, i Neftekhimiya

Nov Neft Gazov Tekh Neftepromysl Delo — Novosti Neftyanoi i Gazovoi Tekhniki Neftepromyslovoe Delo

Nov Neft Gazov Tekh Transp Khranenie Nefti Nefteprod — Novosti Neftyanoi i Gazovoi Tekhniki Transport i Khranenie Nefti i Nefteproduktov

Nov Neft Gaz Tekh Neft Oborudovanie Sredstva Avtom — Novosti Neftyanoi i Gazovoi Tekhniki Neftyanoe Oborudovanie i Sredstva Avtomatizatsii

Nov Neft Tekh — Novosti Neftyanoi Tekhniki

Nov Neft Tekh Geol — Novosti Neftyanoi Tekhniki. Geologiya

Nov Neft Tekh Neftepererab — Novosti Neftyanoi Tekhniki Neftepererabotka

Nov Neft Tekh Neftepromysl Delo — Novosti Neftyanoi Tekhniki Neftepromyslovoe Delo

Nov Neft Tekh Stroit Montazh — Novosti Neftyanoi Tekhniki Stroitel'stvo i Montazh

Nov Novejs Ist — Novaja i Novejsaga Istorija

Nov Obl Ispyt Mikrotverdost Mater Soveshch Mikrotverdosti — Novoe v Oblasti Ispytanii na Mikrotverdost. Materialy Soveshchaniya poMikrotverdosti

Novocherk Politekh Inst Im Sergo Ordzhonikidze Tr — Novocherkasskii Politekhnicheskii Institut Imeni Sergo OrdzhonikidzeTrudy

Novopazarski Zborn — Novopazarski Zbornik

Novoross Gos Proektnyi Inst Tsem Promsti Sb Tr — Novorossiiskii Gosudarstvennyi Proektnyi Institut TsementnoiPromyshlennosti. Sbornik Trudov

Novosib Gos Med Inst Nauchn Tr — Novosibirskii Gosudarstvennyi Meditsinskii Institut. Nauchnye Trudy

Novosib Gos Med Inst Tr — Novosibirskii Gosudarstvennyi Meditsinskii Institut. Trudy

Novosib Inst Inzh Geod Aerofotos'emki Kartogr Tr — Novosibirskii Institut Inzhenerov Geodezii, Aerofotos'emki, iKartografii. Trudy

Novosib Inst Inzh Zheleznodorozhn Transp Tr — Novosibirskii Institut Inzhenerov Zheleznodorozhnogo Transporta. Trudy

Novosibirsk Gos Ped Inst Naucn Trudy — Novosibirskii Gosudarstvennyi Pedagogiceskii Institut Naucnye Trudy

Novosib Skh Inst Tr — Novosibirskii Sel'skokhozyaistvennyi Institut. Trudy

Novos Taxa Ent — Novos Taxa Entomologicos

Novos Taxa Entomol — Novos Taxa Entomologicos

Nov P Bibl — Novae Patrum Bibliothecae

Nov Pishch Promsti — Novosti Pishchevoi Promyshlennosti

Nov Proizvod Khim Istochnikov Toka — Novoe v Proizvodstve Khimicheskikh Istochnikov Toka

Nov Proizvod Stroit Mater — Novoe v Proizvodstve Stroitel'nykh Materialov

Nov Razrab Elem Radiotekh Ustroistv — Novye Razrabotki Elementov Radiotekhnicheskikh Ustroistv

Nov Reol Polim Mater Vses Simp Reol — Novoe v Reologii Polimerov. Materialy Vsesoyuznogo Simpoziuma poReologii

Nov Sist Nizshikh Rast — Novosti Sistematiki Nizshikh Rastenii

Nov Sorbenty Khromatogr — Novye Sorbenty dlya Khromatografii

Nov Sorbenty Mol Khromatogr — Novye Sorbenty dlya Molekulyarnoi Khromatografii

Nov T — Novum Testamentum

Nov Tekh — Novosti Tekhniki

Nov Tekh Astron — Novaya Tekhnika v Astronomii

Nov Tekh Buren — Novosti Tekhniki Bureniya

Nov Tekh Energ — Novosti Tekhniki. Energetika

Nov Tekh Gornorudn Promst — Novosti Tekhniki. Gornorudnaya Promyshlennost

Nov Tekh Mashinostr — Novosti Tekhniki. Mashinostroenie

Nov Tekh Metall — Novosti Tekhniki. Metallurgiya

Nov Tekh Neftedobychi — Novosti Tekhniki Neftedobychi

Nov Tekhn Montazh Spets Rabot Stroit — Novaya Tekhnika Montazhnykh i Spetsial'nykh Rabot v Stroitel'stve

Nov Tekh Peredovoi Opyt Stroit — Novaya Tekhnika i Peredovoi Opyt v Stroitel'stve

Nov Tekh Stroiind — Novosti Tekhniki Stroiindustriya

Nov Termoyad Issled SSSR Inf Byull — Novosti Termoyadernykh Issledovanii v SSSR Informatsionnyi Byulleten

NovTest — Novum Testamentum

Nov Tselul Khartienata Prom — Novosti v Tselulozno-Khartienata Promishlenost

Novum Gebrauchs — Novum Gebrauchsgraphik

Novum Test — Novum Testamentum

Nov Vidy Kompleksn Udobr — Novye Vidy Kompleksnykh Udobrenii

NovZ — Novyj Zurnal

Nov Zhizni Nauke Tekh Biol — Novoe v Zhizni, Nauke, Tekhnike. Seriya Biologiia

Nov Zhizni Nauke Tekh Khim — Novoe v Zhizni, Nauke, Tekhnike. Khimiya

Nov Zhizni Nauke Tekh Ser 9 Fiz Astron — Novoe v Zhizni, Nauke, Tekhnike. Seriya 9. Fizika, Astronomiya

Nov Zhizni Nauke Tekh Ser Biol — Novoe v Zhizni, Nauke, Tekhnike. Seriya Biologiia

Nov Zhizni Nauke Tekh Ser Fiz — Novoe v Zhizni, Nauke, Tekhnike. Seriya Fizika

Nov Zhizni Nauke Tekh Ser IX Fiz Mat Astron — Novoe v Zhizni, Nauke, Tekhnike. Seriya IX. Fizika, Matematika, Astronomiya

Nov Zhizni Nauke Tekh Ser Khim — Novoe v Zhizni, Nauke, Tekhnike. Seriya Khimiya

Nov Zhizni Nauke Tekh Ser Kosmonavt Astron — Novoe v Zhizni, Nauke, Tekhnike. Seriya Kosmonavtika Astronomiya

Nov Zhizni Nauke Tekh Ser Tekh — Novoe v Zhizni, Nauke, Tekhnike. Seriya Tekhnika

Nowa Tech Inz Sanit — Nowa Technika w Inzynierii Sanitarnej

Nowe Roln — Nowe Rolnictwo

Nowest R — Northwest Review

NOWIS — National Older Workers Information System

Now Lek — Nowiny Lekarskie

Nowsci Weter — Nowosci Weterynarii

NOWR — Northwater. Institute of Water Resources. University of Alaska

NOWT — Northern Women Talk

Noyes — Catalog of New Publications. Noyes Data Corp.

NoZ — Novy Zivot

NP — Nasza Przeszlosc

NP — National Parks

NP — Native Press

NP — Nauka Polska

NP — Nea Poreia

Np — Neophilologus

NP — Neupunische Inschriften

NP — Neuroendocrine Perspectives

NP — New Palestine

NP — New Philosophy

NP — Nueva Politica

NPA — National Public Accountant

NPAC — Northern Pipeline Agency News Releases and Communiques

N Pal Mus Bull — National Palace Museum Bulletin

NPB — Novae Patrum Bibliothecae

NPC — Nicaraguan Perspectives (California)

NPCM — National Parks and Conservation Magazine [Later, National Parks Magazine]

NPD — New Products and Processes Highlights

NPEKR — Nachrichtendienst der Pressestelle der Evangelischen Kirche der Rheinprovinz

NPENRJ — Notas Sobre Portugal. Exposicao Nacional do Rio de Janeiro

NPfG — Nordpfalzer Geschichtsverein

NPh — Neophilologus

N Phil Unt — Neue Philologische Untersuchungen

NphM — Neuphilologische Mitteilungen

Nph Mitt — Neuphilologische Mitteilungen

NPHR — Notice Papers - House of Representatives

NPhU — Neue Philologische Untersuchungen

NPHYBI — Neurophysiology

NphZ — Neuphilologische Zeitschrift

NPI — New Periodicals Index

NPI — Newsletter. Portuguese Industrial Association

NPIRS — National Pesticide Information Retrieval System

NPJO — Northern Projects Journal. British Columbia Hydro

NPKZA — Nippon Kagaku Zasshi

NPL — Neues Paedagogisches Lexikon

NPL — Novgorodskaja Pervaja Letopis' Starsego i Mladsego Izvodov

NP Li — Notes de Pastorale Liturgique

NPlockie — Notatki Plockie

NPLR — Nyasaland Protectorate Law Reports

NPL Rep Chem (UK) Natl Phys Lab Div Chem Stand — NPL Report Chem (United Kingdom). National Physical Laboratory. Divisionof Chemical Standards

NPL Rep DMA UK Nat Phys Lab Div Mater Appl — NPL Report DMA. United Kingdom. National Physical Laboratory. Division of Materials Applications

NPL Rep DMMA UK Natl Phys Lab Div Mater Metrol — NPL Report DMM(A) (United Kingdom. National Pnysical Laboratory. Division of Materials Metrology)

NPL Rep IMS UK Natl Phys Lab Div Inorg Met Struct — NPL Report IMS. United Kingdom. National Physical Laboratory. Division of Inorganic and Metallic Structure

NPL Rep MOM (UK) Natl Phys Lab Div Mech Opt Metrol — NPL Report MOM (United Kingdom). National Physical Laboratory. Divisionof Mechanical and Optical Metrology

NPL Rep QU UK Natl Phys Lab Div Quantum Metrol — NPL Report QU. United Kingdom. National Physical Laboratory. Division of Quantum Metrology

NPL Tech Bull — NPL [National Physical Laboratory] Technical Bulletin

NPM — Neuphilologische Mitteilungen

NPM — Neuphilologische Monatsschrift

NPML — Notas Preliminares del Museo de La Plata

NPN — National Petroleum News

NP News — National Petroleum News

NPNMA — Nevrologiya, Psikhiatriya, i Nevrokhirurgiya

NPO — New Phytologist (Oxford)

NPPA — National and Provincial Parks Association. Newsletter

NP/PP — Nouveau Planete/Plantete Plus

NPQ — New Perspectives Quarterly

NPR — National Productivity Review

NPR — Neue Philologische Rundschau

N Princ — New Princeton Review

NPRRDF — Natural Product Reports

NPS — Nature: Physical Science

NPS — New Palaeographical Society

NPS — Noms Propres Sud-Semitiques

NPS — Notice Papers - Senate

NPSS — Noms Propres Sud-Semitiques

N Ps St — Neue Psychologische Studien

N Psyk — Nordisk Psykologi

N Psykiat Tss — Nordisk Psykiatrisk Tidsskrift

NPT — New Periodical Titles

NPU — Natural Product Update

NPU — Neue Verpackung. Zeitschrift fuer die Gesamte Verpackungswirtschaft des Inlandes und Auslandes

NQ — Notes and Queries

N QD Nat — North Queensland Naturalist

NQKG — Neue Quartalschrift fuer Katholische Geistliche

N Qld Nat — North Queensland Naturalist

NQM — Nuovi Quaderni del Meridione

NQNS — Notes and Queries. New Series

NQ Register — North Queensland Register

NQRW — Notes and Queries for Readers and Writers, Collectors, and Librarians

N Queensland Naturalist — North Queensland Naturalist

N Queensl Nat — North Queensland Naturalist

NR — Nase Rec
NR — Nassau Review
NR — National Reporter
NR — National Review
NR — Nation Review
NR — Naturwissenschaftliche Rundschau
NR — Naucnyj Rabotnik
NR — Nauka i Religija
NR — Neue Rundschau
NR — Neues Reich in Aegypten
NR — New Records
NR — [*The*] New Republic
NR — News Release
NR — Northern News Report
NR — Northwest Review
NR — Nouvelle Revue
NR — Nova Revija
NR — Numismatic Review
NRA — Nouvelle Revue Apologetique
NRam — New Rambler
NRA Report — NRA [*National Restaurant Association*] Washington Report
NRB — Die Neuesten Religionsbegebenheiten mit Unpartheyischen Anmerkungen
NRB — Neue Rundschau (Berlin)
NRB — Nouvelle Revue de Bretagne
NRBGE — Notes from the Royal Botanic Garden (Edinburgh)
NR Bret — Nouvelle Revue de Bretagne
NRC — Nicarauac Revista Cultural
NRC — Nieuwe Rotterdamsche Courant
NRC — Nouvelle Revue Canadienne
NRC — Nouvelle Revue Critique
NRC — Nueva Revista Cubana
NRCAGTM — National Research Council of Canada. Associate Committee on Geotechnical Research. Technical Memorandum
NRCBRN — National Research Council. Building Research Note
NRCBRRP — National Research Council of Canada. Division of Building Research. Research Paper
NRCBRTP — National Research Council of Canada. Division of Building Research. Technical Paper
NRC Bull — NRC [*National Research Council of Canada*] Bulletin
NRCC — Nabozenska Revue Cirkve Ceskoslovenske
NRCC Bull — NRCC [*National Research Council of Canada*] Bulletin
NRCCTT — National Research Council of Canada. Technical Translation
NRCDBP — National Research Council of Canada. Division of Building Research. DBR Paper
NRCD Bull — National Reprographic Centre for Documentation. Bulletin
NRCE — National Research Council of Canada. Associate Committee on Ecological Reserves. Newsletter
NRCEBF — National Research Council of Canada. Associate Committee on Scientific Criteriafor Environmental Quality. Publication
NRCFFRP — National Research Council. Foreign Field Research Program [*Washington, D.C.*]
NRCG — Numismatic Review and Coin Galleries
NRCLAZ — NRCL. National Research Council Laboratories
NRCL Natl Res Counc Lab (Ottawa) — NRCL. National Research Council Laboratories (Ottawa)
NRCMET — National Research Council of Canada. Division of Mechanical Engineering. Transportation Newsletter
NRCN — NRC [*Northern Regions Centre*] Newsletter
NRC (Natl Res Counc Can) Bull — NRC (National Research Council of Canada) Bulletin
NRC (Natl Res Counc Can) Tech Transl — NRC (National Research Council of Canada) Technical Translation
NRCP Res Bull — NRCP [*National Research Council of the Philippines*] Research Bulletin
NRCr — Nouvelle Revue Critique
NRC Res News — National Research Council. Research News
NRC Rev — NRC [*National Research Council of Canada*] Review
NRC Tech Transl — NRC [*National Research Council, Canada*] Technical Translation
NR(Cyprus) — Numismatic Report (Cyprus)
NRD — National Bank of Pakistan. Monthly Economic Letter
N Rd — Neue Rundschau
NRDB — National Resources Database
NRDF — Nouvelle Revue Historique de Droit Francais et Etranger
NRDIP — Nouvelle Revue de Droit International Prive
NRDM — Nouvelle Revue des Deux Mondes
NRDroit — Nouvelle Revue du Droit
NRE — Eco 3. Energies, Environnement, Matieres Premieres
NRE — National Real Estate Investor
NRE — Northern Reporter. Capital Communications Ltd.
NREL — Nouvelle Releve
N Rel — Nouvelles Religieuses
NRena — New Renaissance
NRep — [*The*] New Republic
N Repub — New Republic
NRev — Nouvelle Revue
N Rev de Champagne et de Brie — Nouvelle Revue de Champagne et de Brie
NRevT — Nouvelle Revue Theologique
N Rev Th — Nouvelle Revue Theologique
NRF — Nouvelle Revue Francaise
NRFH — Nueva Revista de Filologia Hispanica
NRFHE8 — Report. Sado Marine Biological Station. Niigata University
NRFOD — Natural Resources Forum
NRG — Neueste Religionsgeschichte
NRG — Northern Rhodesia Gazette

NRGID — Energia
NRGSD — Energiespectrum
NRGXD — Energoexport
NRH — Nouvelle Revue de Hongrie
NRH — Tweewieler
NRHD — Nouvelle Revue Historique de Droit Francais et Etranger
NRHDF — Nouvelle Revue Historique de Droit Francais et Etranger
NRHDFE — Nouvelle Revue Historique de Droit Francais et Etranger
NRI — Nouvelle Revue d'Italie
N Riding Sch Libr Guild Bull — North Riding School Library. Guild Bulletin
NRIM Spec Rep — NRIM (National Research Institute for Metals) Special Report
NRINA — Nippon Rinsho
N Ri St — Nuova Rivista Storica
NRI Symp Mod Biol — NRI [*Nomura Research Institute*] Symposia on Modern Biology
N Riv Dir Comm — Nuova Rivista di Diritto Commerciale, Diritto dell'Economia, Diritto Sociale
N Riv St — Nuova Rivista Storica
N Riv Stor — Nuova Rivista Storica
NRJ — Natural Resources Journal
NRKZ — Neue Reformierte Kirchenzeitung
NRL — Nouvelle Revue de Lausanne
NRL — Nouvelles de la Republ1en des Lettres
NRL Memo Rep — NRL [*US Naval Research Laboratory*] Memorandum Report
NRLQ — Naval Research Logistics. Quarterly
NRM — Nuova Rivista Musicale Italiana
NRMI — Nuova Rivista Musicale Italiana
NRMS — Nottingham Renaissance and Modern Studies
NRMTDA — Nouvelle Revue de Medecine de Toulouse
NRp — New Republic
NRP — Nouvelle Revue Pedagogique
NRP — Nueva Revista del Pacifico
NRPBA — Neurosciences Research. Program Bulletin
NRPRA Tech Bull — NRPRA [*Natural Rubber Producers' Research Association*] Technical Bulletin
NRRBA — Bulletin. Radio and Electrical Engineering Division. National Research Council of Canada
NRRP — Nueva Revista del Rio de la Plata
NRS — National Reporter System
NRS — Naturwissenschaftliche Rundschau (Stuttgart)
NRS — Naucnye Raboty is Oobscenija Akademii Nauk Uzbekskoj SSR, Otdelenie Obscestvennych Nauk
NRs — Neue Rundschau
NRS — North-Holland Research Series in Early Detection and Prevention of Behaviour Disorders
NRS — Nuova Rivista Storica
NRS B — Nuova Rivista Storica. Biblioteca
NRSDA — Science Dimension
NRSHB2 — Annual Report. Hokkaido Branch. Government Forest Experiment Station
NRSM — Nouvelle Revue de Science Missionaire
N Rs S Nt Mm — Memoires de la Societe des Naturalistes de la Nouvelle-Russie
N Rs S Nt Mm Mth — Memoirs of the Mathematical Section of the New Russian Society of Naturalists
NRSVS — Nordisk Tidsskrift for Sprogvidenskab. Supplement
NRSZD — Nippon Rinsho Saibo Gakkai Zasshi
NRT — Nouvelle Revue de Theologie
NRT — Nouvelle Revue Theologique
NR Tech Bull — NR [*Natural Rubber*] Technical Bulletin
N R Technol — Natural Rubber Technology
NRTh — Nouvelle Revue Theologique
NRTL — Neues Repertorium fuer die Theologische Literatur und Kirchliche Statistik
NRTP — Nouvelle Revue des Traditions Populaires
NRu — Neue Rundschau
N Rund — Neue Rundschau
NRUSDD — US National Park Service. Natural Resources Report
NRv — News Review
NRVN — Northern Raven. New Series
NRVU — Nuova Rivista di Varia Umanita
NRZ — Neue Ruhr Zeitung
NS — Nederlandsche Spectator
NS — Nederlandse Staatscourant
NS — Neuere Sprachen
NS — Neukirchener Studienbuecher
NS — New Scholasticism
NS — New Scientist
NS — New Statesman
NS — New Stories
NS — Nietzsche-Studien
NS — Noble Savage
NS — Nordic Sounds
NS — Norsk Skogindustri
NS — Nova Scotia Reports
NS — Novi Svet
NS — NS. NorthSouth NordSud NorteSur NorteSul. Canadian Association of Latin American Studies. University of Ottawa
NS — Nuclear Safety
NS — Nueva Sociedad
NS — Numen Supplements
NS — Numismatica et Sphragistica
NS — Numismaticky Sbornik
NS — Numismatic Studies
NS — Staatsblad van het Koninkrijk der Nederlanden
NSA — Notizie degli Scavi di Antichita
NSA — Nuclear Science Abstracts [*Later, INIS Atomindex*]

NSa — Nueva Sangre
NSA — Numen Supplements. Altera Series
NSA — Numismatisch-Sphragistischer Anzeiger
NSAA — Neue Studien zur Anglistik und Amerikanistik
NSAAB — Nuclear Science and Applications. Series A. Biological Science
NSAC — Notices et Memoires. Societe Archeologique de Constantine
NSAL — Nsukka Studies in African Literature
NSam — Neue Sammlung. Goettinger Blaetter fuer Kultur und Erziehung
NSammlung — Neue Sammlung
NS & N — New Statesman and Nation
NSAPA — Nuclear Science and Applications
NSAR — Nationalmusei Skriftserie. Analecta Reginensia
N-S Arch Ph — Naunyn-Schmiedeberg's Archives of Pharmacology
NSB — Nachrichten des Schweizerischen Burgenvereins
NSB — National Socialist Bulletin
NSB — Neuerwerbungen Stadtbuecherei Nuernberg
NSB — Neue Schwiezer Biographie
NSB — Notes on the Science of Building
NSb — Numismaticky Sbornik
NSBGA — Nippon Shokubutsu Byori Gakkaiho
NSBGAM — Annals. Phytopathological Society of Japan
NSC — Names in South Carolina
NSC — Nederlandse Staatscourant. Officiele Uitgaven van het Koninkrijk der Nederlanden
NSC — New Scholar (California)
NSc — Notizie degli Scavi di Antichita
NSCAA — National Society for Clean Air. Annual Conference. Proceedings
NSCA J — National Strength and Conditioning Association. Journal
NSCA (Natl Soc Clean Air) Year Book — NSCA (National Society for Clean Air) Year Book
N Scav Ant — Notizie degli Scavi di Antichita
NSCBDF — NSCA [National Society for Clean Air] Year Book
NSch — New Scholasticism
N Schol — New Scholasticism
NSchwRundschau — Neue Schweizer Rundschau
N Scientist — New Scientist
N Sci R — New Science Review
NSCISC — National Spinal Cord Injury Statistical Center Database
NSC (Natl Sci Counc) Symp Ser (Taipei) — NSC (National Science Council) Symposium Series (Taipei)
N Scotia I Sc P & T — Proceedings and Transactions of the Nova Scotian Institute of Natural Science
NSCRA — NASA [National Aeronautics and Space Administration] Contractor Report. CR
NSC Rev 1977-8 — NSC [National Science Council] Review 1977-8
NSC Special Publication — National Science Council. Special Publication
NSC Symp Ser — NSC [National Science Council. Taiwan] Symposium Series
NS(Czech) — Numismaticky Sbornik (Czechoslovakia)
NSD — Nova Subsidia Diplomatica
NSDB Technol J — NSDB [National Science Development Board, Philippines] Technology Journal
NS Dep Lands For Annu Rep — Nova Scotia. Department of Lands and Forests. Annual Report
NS Dep Mines Annu Rep Mines — Nova Scotia. Department of Mines. Annual Report on Mines
NS Dep Mines Energy Pap — Nova Scotia. Department of Mines and Energy. Paper
NS Dep Mines Energy Rep — Nova Scotia Department of Mines and Energy. Report
NS Dep Mines Mem — Nova Scotia. Department of Mines. Memoir
NS Dep Mines Pap — Nova Scotia. Department of Mines. Paper
NS Dep Mines Rep — Nova Scotia Department of Mines. Report
NS Dp Mines Rp — Nova Scotia. Department of Mines. Report
NSDVS — Nye Samling af det Danske Videnskabernes Selskabs Skrifter
NSDYA — Nagoya Shiritsu Daigaku Yakugakubu Kenkyu Nempo
NSDYAI — Annual Report. Faculty of Pharmaceutical Sciences. Nagoya City University
NSE — New Statesman (England)
NSE — Norwegian Studies in English
NSE — Notitiae Siciliensium Ecclesiarum
NSEGA — Nippon Seikosho Giho
NSEGB4 — Science Reports. Niigata University. Series E. Geology and Mineralogy
NSEN — Northern Science Education News Service. Scavengers College, Alaska
NSEQ — Nankai Social and Economic Quarterly
NSf — Numizmatika i Sfragistika
NSFC — North Staffordshire Field Club and Archaeological Society. Transactions and Annual Report.
NSF Inform — NSF [Namnden foer Skoglig Flygbildteknik] Information
NSFNB — NSFI [Norges Skipaforsknings Institutt] Nytt
NSF SRS — National Science Foundation. Science Resources Studies Highlights
NSF Svy SE — Postcensal Survey of Scientists and Engineers. National Science Foundation. Report No. 84-330
NSF Univ — Federal Support to Universities, Colleges, and Nonprofit Institutions. Fiscal Year 1982. National Science Foundation. Report No. 84-315
NSFZD — Nippon Sanka Fujinka Gakkai Chugoku Shikoku Godo Chihobukai Zasshi
NSGKA — Nippon Shashin Gakkai Kaishi
NSGSR — North-Holland Series in General Systems Research
NSG Tech Rep — NSG [Nippon Sheet Glass] Technical Report
NSGTK — Neue Studien zur Geschichte der Theologie und Kirche
NSGZD — Nippon Shokaki Geka Gakkai Zasshi
NSH — Norwegian Shipping News
NSHE — New Schaff-Herzog Encyclopedia of Religious Knowledge
NSHIA — Nankyoku Shiryo
NS His S — Nova Scotia Historical Society. Collections
NS Hist — Nova Scotia History

NSHKA — Nippon Shika Ishikai Zasshi
NSHS — Northwestern University Studies. Humanities Series
NSHT — Norsk Slektshistorisk Tidsskrift
NSi — Nea Sion
NSI — Nielsen Station Index
NSI — Numismatic Society of India. Journal
NSIN — NS/Northsouth. Canadian Journal of Latin American Studies
NS Inst N Sc Pr Tr — Nova Scotia Institute of Natural Science. Proceedings and Transactions
NS Inst Sci Proc — Nova Scotian Institute of Science. Proceedings
NSJ — Niedersaechsisches Jahrbuch fuer Landesgeschichte
NSJB — Niedersaechsisches Jahrbuch
NSJBH — Niedersaechsisches Jahrbuch. Hildesheim
NSJFS — North Staffordshire Journal of Field Studies
NSJL — Niedersaechsisches Jahrbuch fuer Landesgeschichte
NSJLG — Niedersaechsisches Jahrbuch fuer Landesgeschichte
NSK — Notulae Systematicae ex Herbario Instituto Botanici Nomine V.L. Komarovii. Academiae Scientiarum USSR
NSKIA — Nippon Soshikigaku Kiroku
NSKSA — Nippon Setchaku Kyokaishi
NSL — Det Norske Sprak-og Litteraturselskap
NSL — New Scientist (London)
NSLFA — Nervnaia Sistema Leningradskii Gosudarstvennii Universitet Imeni A. A. ZhdanovaFiziologicheskii Institut
NS Lit Sc Soc Tr — Nova Scotia Literary and Scientific Society. Transactions
NSL News — Nova Scotia Law News
NSLVA — Novaja Sovetskaja i Inostrannaja Literatura po Voprosam Ateizma i Religii
NSM — Nationalsozialistische Monatshefte
NSM — Neusprachliche Mitteilungen aus Wissenschaft und Praxis
NSM — New Statesman
NSM — Nexos (Mexico)
NSM — Numismatic Scrapbook Magazine
NS Med — Nuovi Studi Medievali
NS Med Bull — Nova Scotia Medical Bulletin
NSMN — New Statesman and Nation
NSMOD2 — US Department of Health and Human Services. National Institute of Mental Health. Science Monographs
NSMPA — Nauchnye Trudy Samarkandskii Meditsinskii Institut Imeni Akademika I. P. Pavlova
NSN — Akten Betreffende Naamloze Vennootschappen
NSN — New Statesman and Nation
NSNN — Northern Science Network Newsletter. UNESCO-MAB Northern Science Network Secretariat
NSNU — Nuntius Socalicii Neotestamentici Upsaliensis
NSO — National School Orchestra Association. Bulletin
NSO — North South (Ottawa, Canada)
NSO — Nueva Sociedad
NSOA — National School Orchestra Association. Bulletin
NSoc — New Society. The Social Science Weekly
N Sov — Nas Sovremennik
NSp — Neuere Sprachen
NSPR — New Studies in the Philosophy of Religion
NS Prov Dep Mines Annu Rep — Nova Scotia Province. Department of Mines. Annual Report
NSR — National Sculpture Review
NSR — National Shorthand Reporter
NSR — Neue Schweizer Rundschau
NSR — North Sea Observer
NSR — Nova Scotia Reports
NSR — Nuclear Structure References
NSR — Numismatic Studies and Researches
NSR 2d — Nova Scotia Reports. Second Series
NSRDA — National Standard Reference Data Series. United States National Bureau of Standards
NSRDS Ref Data Rep — NSRDS [National Standards Reference Data System] Reference Data Report
NSREA — Neurosciences Research
NS Rep — Nova Scotia Reports
NSRPDU — Netherlands Institute for Sea Research. Publication Series
NSS — New Statesman and Society
NSS — Nysvenska Studier
NSS — Statuten der Vereinigingen
NSS Bull — NSS [National Speleological Society] Bulletin
NSS Bulletin — National Speleological Society. Bulletin
NS Sch Bd Assn N — Nova Scotia School Boards Association. Newsletter
NSSJ — New Scientist and Science Journal
NSSJB — New Scientist and Science Journal
NSSN — National Speed Sport News
NSSNAQ — NSS [National Speleological Society] News
NSS (Natl Speleol Soc) News — NSS (National Speleological Society) News
NSSPA — NASA [National Aeronautics and Space Administration] Special Publications
NSSRP Univ Tsukuba Nucl Solid State Res Proj — NSSRP. University of Tsukuba. Nuclear and Solid State Research Project
NSSVD — Naucni Sastanak Slavista u Vulove Dane
NST — New Scientist
NST — New Serial Titles
N St — New Statesman
NSt — Nordische Studien
NST — Nouvelle Serie Theologique
N Staffordshire J Fld Stud — North Staffordshire Journal of Field Studies
NStat — New Statesman
NSTA Technol J — National Science and Technology Authority Technology Journal

NSTA Technol J — NSTA [*National Science and Technology Authority, Philippines*] Technology Journal

N Statesman — New Statesman and Nation

N St B — Neukirchner Studienbuecher

NSTEA — Nuclear Structural Engineering

NS Tech Coll Dep Civ Eng Essays Timber Struct — Nova Scotia Technical College (Halifax). Department of Civil Engineering. Essays on Timber Structures

NStem — Nieuwe Stem

NSTF Rep — NSTF [*National Scholariship Trust Fund*] Report

NSTGThK — Neue Studien zur Geschichte der Theologie und der Kirche

NS Th — Nouvelle Serie Theologique

NStN — New Statesman and Nation

NSTN — Nova Scotia Tourism News

N Studi Med — Nuovi Studi Medievali

NStv — Narodno Stvaralastvo. Folklor

NSU — Uitspraken van de Raad voor de Luchtvaart en Scheepvaart

Nsukka Stud — Nsukka Studies in African Literature

N/Sun Sent — News/Sun - Sentinel

NS (USSR) — Numizmaticheskii Sbornik Materialy k Katalogu Numizmaticheskogo Sobraniia Gosudarstvennyi Istoricheskii Muzei (USSR)

NSV — Akten Betreffende Cooperatieve Verenigingen

NsvS — Nysvenska Studier

NSW Ad — Law Reports (New South Wales). Vice-Admiralty

NSW Adm — Law Reports (New South Wales). Vice-Admiralty

NSW Art Gallery Q — New South Wales Art Gallery Quarterly

NSWB — New South Wales Bankruptcy Cases

NSW Bkptcy Cas — New South Wales Bankruptcy Cases

NSW Carpenters J — New South Wales Carpenters' Journal

NSWCMHJ — New South Wales Council for the Mentally Handicapped. Journal

NSW Contract Reporter — New South Wales Contract Reporter and Prices Current List

NSW Conv R — New South Wales Conveyancing Reports

NSW Country Trader — New South Wales Country Trader and Storekeeper

NSW CRD — New South Wales Court of Review Decisions

NSW Dep Agric Annu Rep — New South Wales. Department of Agriculture. Annual Report

NSW Dep Agric Biol Chem Res Inst Annu Plant Dis Surv — New South Wales. Department of Agriculture. Biological and Chemical Research Institute. Annual Plant Disease Survey

NSW Dep Agric Bull S — New South Wales. Department of Agriculture. Bulletin S

NSW Dep Agric Chem Branch — New South Wales. Department of Agriculture. Chemistry Branch. Bulletin S

NSW Dep Agric Chem Branch Bull S — New South Wales. Department of Agriculture. Chemistry Branch. Bulletin S

NSW Dep Agric Div Sci Serv Entomol Branch Annu Rep — New South Wales. Department of Agriculture. Division of Science Services. Entomology Branch. Annual Report

NSW Dep Agric Div Sci Serv Entomol Branch Insect Pest Leafl — New South Wales. Department of Agriculture. Division of Science Services. Entomology Branch. Insect Pest Leaflet

NSW Dep Agric Plant Dis Surv — New South Wales. Department of Agriculture. Plant Disease Survey

NSW Dep Agric Rep — New South Wales. Department of Agriculture. Report

NSW Dep Agric Sci Bull — New South Wales. Department of Agriculture. Science Bulletin

NSW Dep Agric Tech Bull — New South Wales. Department of Agriculture. Technical Bulletin

NSW Dep Mines Chem Lab Rep — New South Wales. Department of Mines. Chemical Laboratory Report

NSW Dep Mines Coalfields Branch Tech Rep — New South Wales. Department of Mines. Coalfields Branch. Technical Report

NSW Dep Mines Geol Surv Bull — New South Wales. Department of Mines. Geological Survey. Bulletin

NSW Dep Mines Geol Surv Miner Ind NSW — New South Wales. Department of Mines. Geological Survey. Mineral Industry of New South Wales

NSW Dep Mines Geol Surv Rep — New South Wales. Department of Mines. Geological Survey. Report

NSW Dep Mines Mem Geol Surv NSW Geol — New South Wales. Department of Mines. Memoirs of the Geological Survey of New South Wales. Geology

NSW Dep Mines Mem Geol Surv NSW Palaeontol — New South Wales. Department of Mines. Memoirs of the Geological Survey of New South Wales. Palaeontology

NSW Dep Mines Tech Rep — New South Wales. Department of Mines. Technical Report

NSW Dep Mines Tech Rep CF — New South Wales. Department of Mines. Coalfields Branch. Technical Report CF

NSW Dept Mines Chem Lab Rep — New South Wales. Department of Mines. Chemical Laboratory. Report

NSW Ed Gaz — Education Gazette (New South Wales)

NSW Eq — Law Reports (New South Wales). Equity

NSW Fed INS Clubs Gen Newsletter — New South Wales. Federation of Infants and Nursery School Clubs. General Newsletter

NSW Fed INSC News — New South Wales Federation of Infants and Nursery School Clubs. News

NSW For Comm Dir For Mgmt Res Note — New South Wales. Forestry Commission. Division of Forest Management. Research Note

NSW For Comm Div Wood Technol Bull — New South Wales. Forestry Commission. Division of Wood Technology. Bulletin

NSW For Comm Div Wood Technol Leafl — New South Wales. Forestry Commission. Division of Wood Technology. Leaflet

NSW For Comm Div Wood Technol Pamph — New South Wales. Forestry Commission. Division of Wood Technology. Pamphlet

NSW For Comm Div Wood Technol Proj Rep — New South Wales. Forestry Commission. Division of Wood Technology. Project Reports

NSW For Comm Div Wood Technol Tech — New South Wales. Forestry Commission. Division of Wood Technology. Technical Notes

NSW For Comm Div Wood Technol Tech Notes — New South Wales. Forestry Commission. Division of Wood Technology. Technical Notes

NSW For Comm Res Note — New South Wales. Forestry Commission. Research Notes

NSW For Rec — New South Wales Forestry Recorder

NSW Freemason — New South Wales Freemason

NSW Geol Surv 4-Mile Geol Ser — New South Wales. Geological Survey. 4-Mile Geological Series

NSW Geol Surv 1:250 000 Geol Ser — New South Wales. Geological Survey. 1:250,000 Geological Series

NSW Geol Surv Bull — New South Wales. Geological Survey. Bulletin

NSW Geol Surv Mem Geol — New South Wales. Geological Survey. Memoirs. Geology

NSW Geol Surv Mem Palaeontol — New South Wales. Geological Survey. Memoirs. Palaeontology

NSW Geol Surv Mineral Industry of NSW — New South Wales. Geological Survey. Mineral Industry of New South Wales

NSW Geol Surv Miner Resour — New South Wales. Geological Survey. Mineral Resources

NSW Geol Surv Min Res — New South Wales. Geological Survey. Mineral Resources

NSW Geol Surv Q Notes — New South Wales. Geological Survey. Quarterly Notes

NSW Geol Surv Rec — New South Wales. Geological Survey. Records

NSW Geol Surv Rep — New South Wales. Geological Survey. Report

NSWGG — New South Wales Government Gazette

NSW Herb Contr — New South Wales. National Herbarium. Contributions

NSW Herb Contr Flora Ser — New South Wales. National Herbarium. Contributions. Flora Series

NSW High Educ Bd Ann Rep — New South Wales. Higher Education Board. Annual Report

NSWIER Bul — New South Wales Institute for Educational Research. Bulletin

NSWIG — New South Wales Industrial Gazette

NSW Ind Gaz — New South Wales Industrial Gazette

NSW Inst Ed Res Bul — New South Wales Institute for Educational Research. Bulletin

NSW Land App Cas — Land Appeal Court Cases (New South Wales)

NSW Lib Bul — New South Wales Library Bulletin

NSWLR — New South Wales Law Reports

NSWLR — New South Wales Letters of Registration

NSWLVR — New South Wales Land and Valuation Court Reports

NSWOP — New South Wales Official Publications

NSW Parl Deb — New South Wales Parliamentary Debates

NSW Parl Parl Deb — New South Wales. Parliament. Parliamentary Debates

NSWPD — New South Wales Parliamentary Debates

NSW Philatelic Ann — New South Wales Philatelic Annual

NSW Police News — New South Wales Police News

NSW Potato — New South Wales Potato

NSW Presbyterian — New South Wales Presbyterian

NSWR — Industrial Arbitration Reports (New South Wales). New South Wales Reports

N S W R S J — Journal and Proceedings of the Royal Society of New South Wales

N S W R S T — Transactions of the Royal Society of New South Wales

(NSW) SCR (L) — Supreme Court Reports (Law) (New South Wales)

NSWSR — New South Wales State Reports

NSW State Fish Cruise Rep — New South Wales. State Fisheries Cruise Report

NSW Statist Summ — New South Wales Statistical Summary

NSW Stat Reg — New South Wales Statistical Register

NSW St R — New South Wales State Reports

NSW Timber Worker — New South Wales Timber Worker

NSW Univ Engineering Yrbk — University of New South Wales. Faculty of Engineering. Yearbook

NSW Univ Inst Highw Traff Res Res Note — University of New South Wales. Institute of Highway and Traffic Research. Research Note

NSW Univ Sch Civ Eng UNICIV Rep Ser R — New South Wales University. School of Civil Engineering. UNICIV Report. SeriesR

NSW Univ UNICIV Rep — University of New South Wales. School of Civil Engineering. UNICIV Report

NSW Univ Wat Res Lab Rep — University of New South Wales. Water Research Laboratory. Report

NSW Vet Proc — Proceedings. Australian Veterinary Association. New South Wales Division

NSW Wat Conserv Irrig Comm Surv Thirty NSW River Valleys Rep — New South Wales. Water Conservation and Irrigation Commission. Survey of ThirtyNew South Wales River Valleys. Report

NSW Weath Rep — New South Wales Weather Report

NSWWN — New South Wales Weekly Notes

NSYSD6 — NSC [*National Science Council*] Symposium Series

NSZ — Nederlands-Spaanse Kamer van Koophandel. Spaanse Aanvragen voor Handelskontakten met Nederland

NSZFU — Neueren Sprachen. Zeitschrift fuer Forschung Unterricht und Kontaktstudium

NSZKA — Nauchnye Trudy Severo-Zapadnyi Nauchno-Issledovatel'skii Institut Sel'skogo Khozyaistva

NT — National Times

Nt — Nature. A Weekly Illustrated Journal of Science

N T — New Testament

NT — New Times

NT — New Tombs at Dendra near Midea

NT — Nieuwe Taalgids

NT — Nordisk Tidskrift

NT — Nordisk Tidskrift foer Vetenskap, Konst, och Industri

NT — Northern Times

NT — Novum Testamentum

NT — Nuclear Theory
NT — Nuestro Tiempo
NTA — National Times (Australia)
NtA — Neutestamentliche Abhandlungen
NTA — New Testament Abstracts
NT Aa — Nordisk Tidsskrift for Aandsvageforsorg
NT Ab — New Testament Abstracts
NTAbstr — New Testament Abstracts
NTA Bul — Newfoundland Teachers' Association. Bulletin
NTA E — Neutestamentliche Abhandlungen. Ergaenzungsband
NTAJ — Newfoundland Teachers' Association. Journal
NTA J — NTA [*National Technical Association*] Journal
NTA Jnl — NTA [*National Teachers' Association*] Journal
NTAP — Notices to Airmen Publication
NT Apo — Neutestementliche Apokryphen in Deutscher Uebersetzung
NTATN — Neue Theologische Annalen und Theologische Nachrichten
NTAZA — Nippon Taishitsugaku Zasshi
NTB — New Technical Books
NTB — Nordisk Tidsskrift for Bok- ock Biblioteksvaesen
NTBB — Nordisk Tidsskrift foer Bok- och Biblioteksvaesen
NTBBV — Nordisk Tidsskrift foer Bok- och Biblioteksvaesen
NTBEDQ — Scandinavian Journal of Behaviour Therapy
NTC — Economisch Dagblad. Dagblad voor het Management
NTC — Nuevo Texto Critico
NTCNB — Nature Canada
NTCR — Netherlands Trade Colonial Review
NTCS — Newsletter for Targumic and Cognate Studies
NTCS — Nuevo Texto Critico (Stanford, California)
NTD — Das Neue Testament Deutsch
NTD — Netherlands Trade and News Bulletin
NTD — New Tombs at Dendra near Midea
NTE — Narodna Tvorcist' ta Etnografija
NTELA — Nachrichtentechnik-Elektronik
NTemp — Nostro Tempo
NTEU — Nauchnye Trudy Erivanskogo Universiteta
NTF — National Theater File
NTF — Neutestamentliche Forschungen
NTF — Nordisk Tidsskrift for Filologi
NTF — Nuclear Technology/Fusion
NTFDA — Natturufraedingurinn
NTFLDX — Fonds de Recherches Forestieres. Universite Laval. Note Technique
NTF Logop O Fon — Nordisk Tidsskrift for Logopodi og Foniatri
NT f Ta o St — Nordisk Tidsskrift for Tale og Stemme
NTFUD — Nuclear Technology/Fusion
NTG — Nederlandsch Tijdschrift voor Geneeskunde
NTG — Neue Theologische Grundrisse
NTg — Nieuwe Taalgids. Tijdschrift voor Neerlandici
NTG Fachber — NTG [*Nachrichtentechnische Gesellschaft*] Fachberichte
NTGLA — Nauchnye Trudy Tashkentskii Gosudarstvennyi Universitet Imeni V. I. Lenina
NTGNA — Nauchnye Trudy Gosudarstvennyi Nauchno-Issledovatel'skii i Proektnyi Institut Redkometallicheskoi Promyshlennosti
NTHAA7 — Brain and Development
Nth Am Rev — North American Review
Nth Apiar — Northern Apiarist
N Th B — Neue Theologische Bibliothek
N Th Bi — Neueste Theologische Bibliothek
Nth Caro Hist Rev — North Carolina Historical Review
Nth England Inst Min Mech Eng Trans — North of England Institute of Mining and Mechanical Engineering. Transactions
Nth Forest Ranger Coll A — Northern Forest Ranger College Annual
Nth Gdnr — Northern Gardener
Nth Ir Leg Qtr — Northern Ireland Legal Quarterly
N Th J — Neues Theologisches Journal
Nth Logger — Northern Logger
NThM — New Theatre Magazine
Nth Miner — Northern Miner
Nth Munster Antiq J — North Munster Antiquarian Journal
Nth Persp — Northern Perspectives
Nth Rev — Northern Review
NThS — Nieuwe Theologische Studien
NThSt — Nieuwe Theologische Studien
NThT — Nieuwe Theologische Tijdschrift
NThTs — Nederlands Theologisch Tijdschrift
NTI — Futuribles
NTI — Nielsen Television Index
NTIAA — Nauchnye Trudy Instituta Avtomatiki
NTiem — Nuestro Tiempo
NTiFil — Nordisk Tidsskrift for Filologi
NTIPI — Nauchnye Trudy Industrial'no-Pedagogicheskogo Instituta
NTIR — Nederlands Tijdschrift voor Internationaal Recht
NTiR — Nordisk Tidsskrift for International Ret
NTIS Announc — NTIS [*National Technical Information Service*] Trade Announcements
NTIS Mater Sci — NTIS [*National Technical Information Service*] Materials Science
NTJ — National Tax Journal
NTJ — Neues Trierisches Jahrbuch
NTJ — Northern Territory Judgements
NTK — Nauchnye Trudy Krasnodarskogo Pedagogicheskogo Instituta
NTKAA — Neue Technik. Abteilung A. Automatik und Industrielle Elektronik
NTKBA — Neue Technik. Abteilung B. Kerntechnik
NTKPB — Nauchnye Trudy Kurskii Politekhnicheskii Institut
NT Krimv — Nordisk Tidsskrift for Kriminalvidenskab
NTLA — Nytestamentliga Avhandlingar
NTLe — Nordisk Teologisk Leksikon for Kirke og Skole

Ntleza — Naturaleza. Periodico Cientifico de la Sociedad Mexicana de Historia Natural
NTLLDT — Intelligence
NTLTL — Newsletter. Teaching Language through Literature
NTM — New Theatre Magazine
NTM — Norsk Tidsskrift for Misjon
NTM — NTM. Schriftenreihe fuer Geschichte der Naturwissenschaften, Technik, und Medizin
NTM — Nuestro Tiempo (Madrid)
NTMLB — Nauchni Trudove. Vissh Lesotekhnicheski Institut (Sofia). Seriya Mekhanichna Tekhnologiya na Durvesinata (Bulgaria)
NTMSB — NTM. Schriftenreihe fuer Geschichte der Naturwissenschaften, Technik, und Medizin
NTM Schr Geschichte Natur Tech Medizin — NTM. Schriftenreihe fuer Geschichte der Naturwissenschaften, Technik, und Medizin
NTM Schr Geschichte Naturwiss Tech Medizin — NTM. Schriftenreihe fuer Geschichte der Naturwissenschaften, Technik, und Medizin
NTM Schriftenr Gesch Naturwiss Tech Med — NTM. Schriftenreihe fuer Geschichte der Naturwissenschaften, Technik, und Medizin
NTMTA — Nauchnye Trudy Moskovskogo Tekhnologicheskogo Instituta Legkoi Promyshlennosti
NTMUZ — Neues Testament fuer Menschen Unserer Zeit
NTM Zeit — NTM. Zeitschrift fuer Geschichte der Naturwissenschaft, Technik, und Medizin
NTM Z Gesch Naturwiss Tech Med — NTM. Zeitschrift fuerGeschichte der Naturwissenschaften, Technik, und Medizin
NTN — National Towing News
NTN — Nederland Taiwan Nieuws
NTN — Northern Territory News
NTN — NTIS [*National Technical Information Service*] Energy Tech Notes
NT Neue Tech — NT. Neue Technik
NTNKA — Nederlands Tijdschrift voor Natuurkunde
NT Not Tec AMMA — NT. Notiziario Tecnico AMMA
NTNSDQ — Intensivbehandlung
NTOTD — Neurobehavioral Toxicology and Teratology
NTP — Nederlands Tijdschrift voor Psychologie
NTPGB — Nederlands Tijdschrift voor de Psychologie en Haar Grensgebieden
NTPPA — Nauchnye Trudy Permskii Politekhnicheskii Institut
NTPUB — Nauchni Trudove. Plovdivski Universitet. Matematika, Fizika, Khimiya, Biologiya
NTQ — New Theatre Quarterly
NTR — Nachrichten Transportrationalisierung
NTR — Northern Territory Reports
NTR Nisseki Tech Rev — NTR. Nisseki Technical Review
NTS — Naukovo Tovarystvo Imeni Sevcenka
NTS — New Testament Studies
NTS — Nieuwe Theologische Studien
NTS — Norsk Tidsskrift foer Sprogvidenskap
NTS — Novum Testamentum. Supplements
N Ts Fs K — Nyt Tidsskrift for Fysik og Kemi
NTSIAI — Naturalista Siciliano
N Ts Mth — Nyt Tidsskrift for Mathematik
NT Spe Paed — Nordisk Tidsskrift for Special-Paedagogik
NT Spr — Norsk Tidsskrift foer Sprogvidenskap
NTsPsych — Nederlandsch Tijdschrift voor de Psychologie en Haar Grensgebieden
NTSt — New Testament Studies
NTStud — New Testament Studies
NTSuppl — Novum Testamentum. Supplements
NT Suppls — Novum Testamentum. Supplements
NTSV — Nordisk Tidsskrift foer Sprogvidenskap
NTsV — Nordisk Tidskrift foer Vetenskap, Konst, och Industri
NTT — Nederlands Theologisch Tijdschrift
NTT — Nieuw Theologisch Tijdschrift
NTT — Norsk Teologisk Tidsskrift
NTTid — Norsk Teologisk Tidsskrift
NTTij — Nederlands Theologisch Tijdschrift
NTTO — Nordisk Tidsskrift foer Teknisk Okonomi
NTT Rev — NTT [*Nippon Telegraph and Telephone Corporation*] Review
NT Ts — Nederlands Theologisch Tijdschrift
NTTS — New Testament Texts and Studies
NTTS — New Testament Tools and Studies
NTTS — Nordisk Tidsskrift foer Tale og Stemme
NTTSt — New Testament Texts and Studies
NTTSt — New Testament Tools and Studies
NTU — Nordiska Texter och Undersokningar
NTU — Nordisk Teologisk Uppslagsbok for Kyrka och Skola
NTUC — National Trade Union of Coopers
NTULA3 — Naturalia
NTUn — Nordisk Texter och Undersokningar
NTU Phytopathol Entomol — NTU [*National Taiwan University*] Phytopathologist and Entomology
N Tur A — Norske Turistforenings Arbok
NTURB — Natura (Plovdiv, Bulgaria)
NTUWM — National Trade Union of Woodcutting Machinists
NTUWWM — National Trade Union of Wood Working Machinists
NTV — Nordisk Tidskrift for Vetenskap, Konst och Industri
NTVGA — Nederlandsch Tijdschrift voor Verloskunde en Gynaecologie
NTVK — Nederlandsch Tijdschrift voor Volkskunde
NTVMA — Nauchni Trudove na Visshiya Meditsinski Institut
NTW — Nieuw Tijdschrift voor Wiskunde
NTW — Nymphenburger Texte zur Wissenschaft
NT Yb — National Trust Yearbook
NTZ — Nachrichtentechnische Zeitschrift
NTZ — Neue Theologische Zeitschrift
NTZ Arch — NTZ. Nachrichtentechnische Zeitschrift Archiv

NTZ-Commun J — NTZ-Communications Journal
NTZG — Neutestamentliche Zeitgeschichte
NTZ Nachr Z NTZ-Commun J — NTZ. Nachrichtentechnische Zeitschrift/NTZ-Communications Journal
NTZ Rep — NTZ. Nachrichtentechnische Zeitschrift. Report
Nu — Numismatist
NU — Nunatsiaq News
NuA — Nuova Antologia
NUAH — Nutrition and Health. A Journal of Preventive Medicine
NUAPA — Nuclear Applications
NUATA — Nuclear Applications and Technology
NUB — Nuernberger Urkundenbuch
NUBEDX — Nutrition and Behavior
Nubia Christ — Nubia Christiana
NUC — National Union Catalogue
Nu C — Numismatic Chronicle
NUCAD — Nutrition and Cancer
NUCAV — National Union Catalogue of Audio-Visual Materials
Nuc Compact Compact News Nucl Med — Nuc Compact. Compact News in Nuclear Medicine
Nuc Energy — Nuclear Energy
Nuc En Pros — Nuclear Energy Prospects to 2000
NUC:H — National Union Catalogue of Library Materials for the Handicapped
Nucl — Nucleus
Nucl Acid R — Nucleic Acids Research
Nucl Act — Nuclear Active
Nucl Active — Nuclear Active
Nucl Appl — Nuclear Applications
Nucl Appl and Technol — Nuclear Applications and Technology
Nucl Appl Technol — Nuclear Applications and Technology
Nuc L Bull — Nuclear Law Bulletin
Nucl Can/Can Nucl — Nuclear Canada/Canada Nucleaire
Nucl Can Yearb — Nuclear Canada Yearbook
Nucl Chem Waste Manage — Nuclear and Chemical Waste Management
Nucl-Chicago Tech Bull — Nuclear-Chicago Technical Bulletin
Nucl Data A — Nuclear Data. Section A
Nucl Data Sect A — Nuclear Data. Section A
Nucl Data Sect B — Nuclear Data. Section B
Nucl Data Sheets — Nuclear Data Sheets
Nucl Data Tables — Nuclear Data Tables
Nucl Data Tables US AEC — Nuclear Data Tables. United States Atomic Energy Commission
Nucl Dev Corp S Afr Rep — Nuclear Development Corporation of South Africa. Report
Nuclear Eng — Nuclear Engineering International
Nuclear Engng Design — Nuclear Engineering and Design
Nuclear Law Bul — Nuclear Law Bulletin
Nuclear Phys A — Nuclear Physics. A
Nuclear Phys B — Nuclear Physics. B
Nuclear Phys B Proc Suppl — Nuclear Physics B. Proceedings Supplement
Nuclear Sci Abstr — Nuclear Science Abstracts [*Later, INIS Atomindex*]
Nuclear Science Abstr — Nuclear Science Abstracts [*Later, INIS Atomindex*]
Nuclear Sci Engng — Nuclear Science and Engineering
Nucleic Acids Mol Biol — Nucleic Acids and Molecular Biology
Nucleic Acids Res — Nucleic Acids Research
Nucleic Acids Res Spec Publ — Nucleic Acids Research. Special Publication
Nucleic Acids Res Symp Ser — Nucleic Acids Research. Symposium Series
Nucleic Acids Symp Ser — Nucleic Acids Symposium Series
Nucl Electron Detect Technol — Nuclear Electronics and Detection Technology
Nucl Energy — Nuclear Energy
Nucl Energy Br Nucl Energy Soc — Nuclear Energy. British Nuclear Energy Society
Nucl Energy Dig — Nuclear Energy Digest
Nucl Energy Inf Cent (Warsaw) Rev Rep — Nuclear Energy Information Center (Warsaw). Review Report
Nucl Eng — Nuclear Engineer. Institution of Nuclear Engineers
Nucl Eng Abstr — Nuclear Engineering Abstracts
Nucl Eng and Des — Nuclear Engineering and Design
Nucl Eng Bull — Nuclear Engineering Bulletin
Nucl Eng Des — Nuclear Engineering and Design
Nucl Eng Des Fusion — Nuclear Engineering and Design/Fusion
Nucl Eng (Heywood Temple) — Nuclear Engineering (Heywood-Temple)
Nucl Eng In — Nuclear Engineering International
Nucl Eng Inst Nucl Eng — Nuclear Engineer. Institution of Nuclear Engineers
Nucl Eng Int — Nuclear Engineering International
Nucl Engng & Des — Nuclear Engineering and Design
Nucl Engng Int — Nuclear Engineering International
Nucl Engr — Nuclear Engineer
Nucl Engrg Des — Nuclear Engineering and Design
Nucl Eng (Tokyo) — Nuclear Engineering (Tokyo)
Nucl Equation State Part B — Nuclear Equation of State. Part B. QCD and the Formation of the Quark-Gluon Plasma
Nucl Esp — Nuclear Espana. Revista de la Sociedad Nuclear Espanola
Nucl Eur — Nuclear Europe
Nucl Eur Worldscan — Nuclear Europe Worldscan
Nucl F Supplm — Nuclear Fusion. Supplement
Nucl Fuel Cycle — Nuclear Fuel Cycle
Nucl Fuel Cycle Revis Ed — Nuclear Fuel Cycle. Revised Edition
Nucl Fusion — Nuclear Fusion
Nucl Fusion Res Rep — Nuclear Fusion Research Report
Nucl Fusion Spec Publ — Nuclear Fusion. Special Publication
Nucl Fusion Suppl — Nuclear Fusion. Supplement
Nucl Geneeskd Bull — Nucleair Geneeskundig Bulletin
Nucl Geophys — Nuclear Geophysics
Nucl Hematol — Nuclear Hematology

Nucl Hydrogen Energy Technol — Nuclear-Hydrogen Energy and Technology
Nucl Ind — Nuclear Industry
Nucl India — Nuclear India
Nucl Inf — Nuclear Information
Nucl Instr — Nuclear Instruments and Methods [*Later, Nuclear Instruments and Methods in Physics Research*]
Nucl Instrum — Nuclear Instruments
Nucl Instrum and Methods — Nuclear Instruments and Methods [*Later, Nuclear Instruments and Methods in Physics Research*]
Nucl Instrum Methods — Nuclear Instruments and Methods [*Later, Nuclear Instruments and Methods in Physics Research*]
Nucl Instrum Methods Phys Res — Nuclear Instruments and Methods in Physics Research
Nucl Instrum Methods Phys Res Sect A — Nuclear Instruments and Methods in Physics Research. Section A. Accelerators, Spectrometers, Detectors, and Associated Equipment
Nucl Instrum Methods Phys Res Sect B — Nuclear Instruments and Methods in Physics Research. Section B. Beam Interactions with Materials and Atoms
Nucl Issues — Nuclear Issues
Nucl Law Bull — Nuclear Law Bulletin
Nucl Law Bull Suppl — Nuclear Law Bulletin. Supplement
Nucl Magn Reson — Nuclear Magnetic Resonance
Nucl Mater Manage — Nuclear Materials Management. Journal of the Institute of Nuclear Materials Management
Nucl Med — Nuclear Medicine
Nucl-Med — Nuclear-Medizin
Nucl Med (Amsterdam) — Nuclear Medicine (Amsterdam)
Nucl Med Annu — Nuclear Medicine Annual
Nucl Med Biol — Nuclear Medicine and Biology
Nucl Med Commun — Nuclear Medicine Communications
Nucl Med Endocrinol — Nuclear Medicine. Endocrinology
Nucl Med Eur Nucl Med Congr — Nuclear Medicine. Quantitative Analysis in Imaging and Function. European Nuclear Medicine Congress
Nucl Med Semin — Nuclear Medicine Seminar
Nucl Med (Stuttgart) — Nuclear Medicine (Stuttgart)
Nucl-Med (Stuttgart) — Nuclear-Medizin (Stuttgart)
Nucl Med Suppl — Nuclear-Medizin. Supplementum
Nucl-Med Suppl (Stuttgart) — Nuclear-Medizin. Supplementum (Stuttgart)
Nucl Metall — Nuclear Metallurgy
Nucl Methods Monogr — Nuclear Methods Monographs
Nucl Models Lect Summer Meet Nucl Phys — Nuclear Models. Lectures Given at Summer Meeting of Nuclear Physicists
Nucl N — Nuclear News
Nucl News — Nuclear News
Nucl News (Colombo Sri Lanka) — Nuclear News (Colombo, Sri Lanka)
Nucl News (Hinsdale Ill) — Nuclear News (Hinsdale, Illinois)
Nucl News (La Grange Park Ill) — Nuclear News (La Grange Park, Illinois)
Nucl Newsl Switz — Nuclear Newsletter from Switzerland
Nucl Part Phys Annu — Nuclear and Particle Physics. Annual
Nucl Phys — Nuclear Physics
Nucl Phys A — Nuclear Physics. A
Nucl Phys B — Nuclear Physics. B
Nucl Phys B Field Theory and Stat Syst — Nuclear Physics. B. Field Theory and Statistical Systems
Nucl Phys B Part Phys — Nuclear Physics. B. Particle Physics
Nucl Phys London — Nuclear Physics (London)
Nucl Phys Ser Monogr Texts High Energy Low Energy Nucl Phys — Nuclear Physics, a Series of Monographs and Texts in High-Energy and Low-EnergyNuclear Physics
Nucl Phys Solid State Phys (India) — Nuclear Physics and Solid State Physics (India)
Nucl Phys Solid State Phys Symp Proc — Nuclear Physics and Solid State Physics Symposium. Proceedings
Nucl Plant J — Nuclear Plant Journal
Nucl Pow — Nuclear Power
Nucl Power — Nuclear Power
Nucl Power Eng — Nuclear Power Engineering
Nucl Power Tokyo — Nuclear Power (Tokyo)
Nucl Processes Geol Settings Proc Conf — Nuclear Processes in Geologic Settings. Proceedings. Conference
Nucl Processes Oncog — Nuclear Processes and Oncogenes
Nucl Radiat Chem Symp Proc — Nuclear and Radiation Chemistry Symposium. Proceedings
Nucl Radiochem — Nuclear and Radiochemistry
Nucl React — Nuclear Reactions
Nucl React 1 Gas Cooled Water Cooled React Proc Int Conf — Nuclear Reactors 1. Gas-Cooled and Water-Cooled Reactors. Proceedings. International Conference. Peaceful Uses of Atomic Energy
Nucl React Built Being Built Planned — Nuclear Reactors Built, Being Built, or Planned
Nucl Reactor Saf — Nuclear Reactor Safety
Nucl Reactor Theory Proc Symp Appl Math — Nuclear Reactor Theory. Proceedings. Symposium on Applied Mathematics
Nucl React Saf Heat Transfer — Nuclear Reactor Safety Heat Transfer
Nucl Regul Comm Rep NUREG CP US — Nuclear Regulatory Commission. Report. NUREG/CP (United States)
Nucl Res — Nuclear Research
Nucl Res Cent "Democritus" (Rep) — Nuclear Research Center "Democritus" (Report)
Nucl Res Teheran — Nuclear Research (Teheran)
Nucl Saf — Nuclear Safety
Nucl Safety — Nuclear Safety
Nucl Sci — Nuclear Science
Nucl Sci Abstr — Nuclear Science Abstracts [*Later, INIS Atomindex*]
Nucl Sci Abstr Jpn — Nuclear Science Abstracts of Japan

Nucl Sci and Eng — Nuclear Science and Engineering
Nucl Sci Appl — Nuclear Science and Applications
Nucl Sci Appl Dacca — Nuclear Science and Applications (Dacca)
Nucl Sci Appl NY — Nuclear Science and Applications (New York)
Nucl Sci Appl Sect A — Nuclear Science Applications. Section A
Nucl Sci Appl Sect A Short Rev — Nuclear Science Application. Section A. Short Reviews, Research Papers, and Comments
Nucl Sci Appl Sect B — Nuclear Science Applications. Section B
Nucl Sci Appl Ser A — Nuclear Science and Applications. Series A
Nucl Sci Appl Ser B — Nuclear Science and Applications. Series B
Nucl Sci En — Nuclear Science and Engineering
Nucl Sci Eng — Nuclear Science and Engineering
Nucl Sci Inf Jpn — Nuclear Science Information of Japan
Nucl Sci J — Nuclear Science Journal
Nucl Sci J (Bandar Baru Bangi Malays) — Nuclear Science Journal (Bandar Baru Bangi, Malaysia)
Nucl Sci J Bangi Malays — Nuclear Science Journal (Bangi, Malaysia)
Nucl Sci J Malays — Nuclear Science Journal of Malaysia
Nucl Sci J (Taiwan) — Nuclear Science Journal (Taiwan)
Nucl Sci Res Conf Ser — Nuclear Science Research Conference Series
Nucl Sci Ser — Nuclear Science Series
Nucl Sci (Taiwan) — Nuclear Science (Taiwan)
Nucl Sci Tech — Nuclear Science and Techniques/Hewuli
Nucl Sci Technol — Nuclear Science and Technology
Nucl Sci Technol Dordrecht Neth — Nuclear Science and Technology (Dordrecht, Netherlands)
Nucl Shapes Nucl Struct Low Excitation Energ — Nuclear Shapes and Nuclear Structures at Low Excitation Energies
Nucl Ships — Nuclear Ships
Nucl Soc Isr Trans Jt Annu Meet — Nuclear Societies of Israel. Transactions. Joint Annual Meeting
Nucl Solid State Res Proj Univ Tsukuba Rep NSSRP — Nuclear and Solid State Research Project. University of Tsukuba. Report. NSSRP
Nucl Struct Eng — Nuclear Structural Engineering
Nucl Struct Study Neutrons Proc Int Conf — Nuclear Structure Study with Neutrons. Proceedings. International Conference onNuclear Structure Study with Neutrons
Nucl Study — Nuclear Study
Nucl Tech — Nuclear Technology
Nucl Technol — Nuclear Technology
Nucl Technol/Fusion — Nuclear Technology/Fusion
Nucl Technol Suppl — Nuclear Technology. Supplement
Nucl Track Detect — Nuclear Track Detection
Nucl Tracks — Nuclear Tracks
Nucl Tracks and Radiat Meas — Nuclear Tracks and Radiation Measurements
Nucl Tracks Methods Instrum and Appl — Nuclear Tracks. Methods, Instruments, and Applications
NUCOM — National Union Catalogue of Monographs
NUCOMUSIC — National Union Catalogue of Music
NUCOS — National Union Catalogue of Serials
Nuc Pl Saf — Nuclear Plant Safety
NUCSA — Nucleus
NucSciAb — Nuclear Science Abstracts [*Later, INIS Atomindex*]
NUCUA — Nuovo Cimento. Supplemento
NuD — Nuovo Digesto Italiano
NUDIA — Nutritio et Dieta
NUENA — Nuclear Engineering
Nuernb Ab — Abhandlungen der Naturhistorischen Gesellschaft zu Nuernberg
Nuernberg Abhandl — Abhandlungen der Naturhistorischen Gesellschaft zu Nuernberg
Nuernberger Forsch — Nuernberger Forschungen
Nuestra Arquit — Nuestra Arquitectura
Nuestra Arquit BA — Nuestra Arquitectura (Buenos Aires)
Nuestra Hist — Nuestra Historia
Nuestra Ind Rev Tecnol — Nuestra Industria. Revista Tecnologica
Nuestra Tierra — Nuestra Tierra. Paz y Progreso
Nuetzl Bemerk Garten Blumenfr — Nuetzliche Bemerkungen Fuer Garten- und Blumenfreunde
Nuetzl Samml — Nuetzliche Sammlungen
Nuetzl Unterhalt Berlin Wochenbl Buerger Landmann — Nuetzliches und Unterhaltendes Berlinisches Wochenblatt fuer den Gebildeten Buerger und Denkenden Landmann
Nueva Dem NY — Nueva Democracia (New York)
Nueva Enferm — Nueva Enfermeria
Nueva Era Quito — Nueva Era. Revista Interamericana de Educacion y Cultura (Quito)
Nueva Estaf — Nueva Estafeta
Nueva Pol — Nueva Politica
Nueva Prov — Nueva Provincia
Nueva Rev Filol Hisp Mex — Nueva Revista de Filologia Hispanica (Mexico)
Nueva Revta Filol Hispan — Nueva Revista de Filologia Hispanica
Nueva R Filol Hisp — Nueva Revista de Filologia Hispanica
Nueva Soc — Nueva Sociedad
Nuevas Tend — Nuevas Tendencias
Nuevo Amanecer Cult — Nuevo Amanecer Cultural
Nu G Bot Ital — Nuovo Giornale Botanico Italiano
NUH — National Underwriter (Life and Health Insurance Edition)
NUHEA — Nuclear Hematology
Nuisances Environ — Nuisances et Environnement
Nuisances et Environ — Nuisances et Environnement
NUJ — Nagpur University Journal
NUKKA — Nukleonika
Nukl — Nukleonika
Nuklearmedizin Suppl Stuttgart — Nuklearmedizin. Supplementum (Stuttgart)

Nuklearmed Jahrestag Ges Nuclearmed — Nuklearmedizin. Fortschritte der Nuklearmedizin in Klinischer und Technologischer Sicht. Jahrestagung der Gesellschaft fuer Nuclearmedizin
Nuklearmed Symp — Nuklearmedizinisches Symposion
Nukleinovye Kisloty Tr Konf — Nukleinovye Kisloty. Trudy Konferentsii po Nukleinovym Kislotam
Nukl Energ — Nuklearna Energija
Nukl Entsorgung — Nukleare Entsorgung
Nukleonika Suppl — Nukleonika. Supplement
Nukl Inst Jozef Stefan NIJS Porocilo — Nuklearni Institut Jozef Stefan. NIJS Porocilo
Nukl Inst Jozef Stefan NIJS Rep — Nukleari Institut Jozef Stefan. NIJS Report
NUKOA — Nauchno-Issledovatel'skii Trudy Ukrainskii Nauchno-Issledovatel'skii Institut Kozhevenno-Obuvnoi Promyshlennosti
NUL — Northwestern University. Law Review
NULAB — Nuclear Active
NULH — National Underwriter (Life and Health Insurance Edition)
NULR — Northwestern University. Law Review
NUm — Narodna Umjetnost
Num — Numismatist
Num Ant Cl — Numismatica e Antichita Classiche
Num Ant Cl — Numismatica e Antichita Classiche. Quaderni Ticinesi
Num Ant Clas — Quaderni Ticinesi. Numismatica e Antichita Classiche
Numario Hisp — Numario Hispanico. Revista de Investigacion y Hallazgos Monetarios
Num Beitr — Numismatische Beitraege
Num C — Numismatic Chronicle and Journal. Numismatic Society
Num Change — Numismatique et Change
Num Chr — Numismatic Chronicle and Journal. Royal Numismatic Society
Num Chron — Numismatic Chronicle
Num Chron — Numismatic Chronicle and Journal
NumCirc — Numismatic Circular
NUMDA — Nihon University. Journal of Medicine
Num Digest — Numismatic Digest
Num Epigr — Numizmatika i Epigrafika
Num Epigr IA — Numizmatika i Epigrafika. Institut Arkheologii. Akademiia Nauk SSSR
Numer Algorithms — Numerical Algorithms
Numer Comput Methods — Numerical Computer Methods
Numer Control Soc Proc Annu Meet Tech Conf — Numerical Control Society Proceedings. Annual Meeting and Technical Conference
Numer Eng — Numerical Engineering
Numer Funct Anal Optim — Numerical Functional Analysis and Optimization
Numer Funct Anal Optimiz — Numerical Functional Analysis and Optimization
Numer Heat Transfer — Numerical Heat Transfer
Numer Heat Transfer Int J Comput Methodol Part A Appl — Numerical Heat Transfer. An International Journal of Computation and Methodology. Part A. Applications
Numer Heat Transfer Part A — Numerical Heat Transfer. Part A. Applications
Numer Heat Transfer Part B — Numerical Heat Transfer. Part B. Fundamentals
Numer Heat Transfer Part B Fundam — Numerical Heat Transfer. Part B. Fundamentals
Numer Heat Transf Part A Appl — Numerical Heat Transfer. Part A. Applications
Numer Linear Algebra Appl — Numerical Linear Algebra with Applications
Numer Math — Numerische Mathematik
Numer Math Ingenieure Physiker — Numerische Mathematik fuer Ingenieure und Physiker
Numer Math Ingenieure Physiker (Berl) — Numerische Mathematik fuer Ingenieure und Physiker (Berlin)
Numer Math J Chinese Univ — Numerical Mathematics. A Journal of Chinese Universities
Numer Math Sci Comput — Numerical Mathematics and Scientific Computation
Numer Methods Partial Differential Equations — Numerical Methods for Partial Differential Equations
Numer Methods Simul Multi Phase Complex Flow Proc Workshop — Numerical Methods for the Simulation of Multi-Phase and Complex Flow. Proceedings. Workshop
Numer Methods Therm Probl Proc Int Conf — Numerical Methods in Thermal Problems. Proceedings. International Conference
Numero Unico Futur Campari — Numero Unico Futurista Campari
Numer Verfahren Aktion — Numerische Verfahren in Aktion
Num Hisp — Numario Hispanico
Numi & Ant Class — Numismatica e Antichita Classiche
Numi & Philat J Japan — Numismatic and Philatelic Journal of Japan
Numi Chron — Numismatic Chronicle
Numi Epig — Numizmatika i Epigrafika. Institut Arkheologii. Akademiia Nauk SSSR
Numi Int Bull — Numismatics International Bulletin
Numi Lit — Numismatic Literature
Numi Meddel — Numismatiska Meddelanden
Numis — Numismatist
Numi Sborn — Numizmaticheskii Sbornik
Numis Chron 7 Ser — Numismatic Chronicle. Series 7
Numis Chron 7 Ser (Engl) — Numismatic Chronicle. Series 7 (England)
Numis Circ — Numismatic Circular
Numisma (Austral) — Numisma: An Occasional Numismatic Magazine (Australia)
Numisma Rev Soc IA — Numisma. Revista de la Sociedad Ibero-Americana de Estudios Numismaticos
Numismat Chron — Numismatic Chronicle
Numismatica (Rom) — Numismatica (Rome)
Numismatisk Rapp — Numismatisk Rapport
Numismat Lit Osteur U Balkan — Numismatische Literatur Osteuropas und des Balkans
Numism Zs Wien — Numismatische Zeitschrift (Wien)
Num Israel — Numismatics in Israel
Numi Z — Numismatische Zeitschrift

Num J — Numismatic Journal
NumK — Numizmatikai Kozloeny
Num Koezl — Numizmatikai Koezloeny
NumLB — Numismatisches Literatur-Blatt
Num Listy — Numismaticke Listy
Num Lit — Numismatic Literature
Num Math — Numerische Mathematik
NUMMB — Nuclear Materials Management
Num Moravica — Numismatica Moravica
Num Nachr Bl — Numismatisches Nachrichtenblatt
Num Sbor — Numismaticky Sbornik
Num Sfrag — Numizmatika i Sfragistika
Num St — Numismatic Studies. American Numismatic Society
Num Stockholm — Numismatica Stockholmiensia. Annual Reports and Acquisitions of the Royal Coin Cabinet. National Museum of Monetary History
Num Vij — Numizmaticke Vijesti
Num Z — Berliner Numismatische Zeitschrift
Num Z — Numismatische Zeitschrift
Num Zeit — Numismatische Zeitschrift
Num Zeitr — Numismatische Zeitschrift
Num Zeitr Wien — Numismatische Zeitschrift (Wien)
Num Ztschr — Numismatische Zeitschrift
Nuncius Ann Storia Sci — Nuncius. Annali di Storia della Scienza
NUNE — Nunasi News
NUNGAS — Acta Agriculturae Sinica
Nunt Radiol — Nuntius Radiologicus
NUNW — Nutrition Newsletter
Nu O — Natur und Offenbarung
NuoA — Nuova Antologia
Nuo Ant — Nuova Antologia
Nuo G Bot Ital — Nuovo Giornale Botanico Italiano
Nuo Ital — Nuova Italia
NUOL — Nursing Outlook
NUON — Nunavut Onipkaat. Kitikmeot Inuit Association
Nuo Riv Stor — Nuova Rivista Storica
Nuova Agr Lucana — Nuova Agricoltura Lucana
Nuova Ant — Nuova Antologia
Nuova Antol — Nuova Antologia
Nuova Antol — Nuova Antologia di Lettere, Arti, e Scienze
Nuova Bull di Arch Cristiana — Nuova Bulletino di Archeologia Cristiana
Nuova Chim — Nuova Chimica
Nuova Collez Opusc Sci — Nuova Collezione d'Opuscoli Scientifici
Nuova Crit — Nuova Critica. Studi e Rivista di Filosofia delle Scienze
Nuova Econ — Nuova Economia
Nuov Antol — Nuova Antologia di Lettere, Scienze, ed Arti
Nuova Rass — Nuova Rassegna
Nuova Riv Misena — Nuova Rivista Misena
Nuova Riv Mus Ital — Nuova Rivista Musicale Italiana
Nuova Riv Olii Veg Saponi — Nuova Rivista Olii Vegetali e Saponi
Nuova Riv Stor — Nuova Rivista Storica
Nuova RM Italiana — Nuova Rivista Musicale Italiana
Nuova R Stor — Nuova Rivista Storica
Nuova Vet — Nuova Veterinaria
Nuova Veterin — Nuova Veterinaria
Nuov Bull — Nuovo Bulletino di Archeologia Cristiana
Nuov Cim A — Nuovo Cimento. A
Nuov Cim B — Nuovo Cimento. B
Nuov Dir — Nuovo Diritto
Nuovi Allevam — Nuovi Allevamenti
Nuovi Ann Agric — Nuovi Annali dell'Agricoltura
Nuovi Annali Ig Microbiol — Nuovi Annali d'Igiene e Microbiologia
Nuovi Ann Ig Microbiol — Nuovi Annali d'Igiene e Microbiologia
Nuovi Ann Ist Chim-Agr Sper Gorizia Ser 2 — Nuovi Annali. Istituto Chimico-Agrario Sperimentale di Gorizia. Serie 2
Nuovi Saggi Ces Regia Accad Sci Padova — Nuovi Saggi Della Cesareo-Regia Accademia di Scienze, Lettere, ed Arti di Padova
Nuovi Saggi Reale Accad Sci Lett & A Padova — Nuovi Saggi della Reale Accademia di Scienze, Lettere, ed Arti di Padova
Nuovi Studi Sta Chim-Agr Sper Udine — Nuovi Studi. Stazione Chimico-Agraria Sperimentale di Udine
Nuovo Arch Ital ORL — Nuovo Archivio Italiano di Otologia, Rinologia, e Laringologia
Nuovo Arch Ital Otol Rinol Laringol — Nuovo Archivio Italiano di Otologia, Rinologia, e Laringologia
Nuovo Archv Ven — Nuovo Archivio Veneto
Nuovo Boll Archeol Crist — Nuovo Bollettino di Archeologia Cristiana
Nuovo Cim — Nuovo Cimento
Nuovo Cim A — Nuovo Cimento. A
Nuovo Cim B — Nuovo Cimento. B
Nuovo Cim C — Nuovo Cimento. C
Nuovo Cimento A — Nuovo Cimento. Sezione. A
Nuovo Cimento B — Nuovo Cimento. Sezione. B
Nuovo Cimento C 1 — Nuovo Cimento. C. Serie 1
Nuovo Cimento D 1 — Nuovo Cimento. D. Serie 1
Nuovo Cimento Lett — Nuovo Cimento. Lettere
Nuovo Cimento Soc Ital Fis A — Nuovo Cimento. Societa Italiana di Fisica. Sezione A
Nuovo Cimento Soc Ital Fis B — Nuovo Cimento. Societa Italiana di Fisica. Sezione B
Nuovo Cimento Soc Ital Fis C — Nuovo Cimento. Societa Italiana di Fisica. C. Geophysics and Space Physics
Nuovo Cimento Soc Ital Fis D — Nuovo Cimento. Societa Italiana di Fisica. D. Condensed Matter, Atomic, Molecular and Chemical Physics, Biophysics
Nuovo Cimento Suppl — Nuovo Cimento. Supplemento
Nuovo G — Nuovo Giornale

Nuovo G Bot Ital — Nuovo Giornale Botanico Italiano
Nuovo G Bot Ital Boll Soc Bot Ital — Nuovo Giornale Botanico Italiano e Bollettino. Societa Botanica Italiana
Nuovo G Bot Ital (Nuovo Ser) — Nuovo Giornale Botanico Italiano (Nuovo Serie)
Nuovo Giorn Bot Ital — Nuovo Giornale Botanico Italiano
Nuovo Giorn Ligustico Lett — Nuovo Giornale Ligustico di Lettere, Scienze, ed Arti
Nuovo Mag Tosc — Nuovo Magazzino Toscano
Nuov Riv Di Clin Ed Assis Psichiat — Nuova Rivista di Clinica ed Assistenza Psichiatria
Nuov Riv M — Nuova Rivista Musicale Italiana
Nuov Riv St — Nuova Rivista Storica
Nuov Stud Di Dir Econ E Pol — Nuovi Studi di Diritto, Economica, e Politica
NUP — National Underwriter (Property and Casualty Insurance Edition)
NUPBB — Nuclear Physics. B
NUPC — National Underwriter (Property and Casualty Insurance Edition)
NUPSA — Neuropsychologia
NuQ — Nuovi Quaderni del Meridione
NuR — Numismatic Review
NURE — Nunasi Report
NUREG/CR — NUREG/CR (US Nuclear Regulatory Commission) Report CR
Nurs '78 — Nursing '78
Nurs '82 — Nursing '82
Nurs '80/'81 — Nursing '80/'81
Nurs 83/84 — Nursing '83/'84
Nurs 85/86 — Nursing '85/'86
Nurs Abstr — Nursing Abstracts
Nurs Admin Q — Nursing Administration. Quarterly
Nurs Adm Q — Nursing Administration. Quarterly
Nurs Allied Health Index — Nursing and Allied Health Index
Nurs Care — Nursing Care
Nurs Careers — Nursing Careers
Nurs Clin N Am — Nursing Clinics of North America
Nurs Clin North Am — Nursing Clinics of North America
Nurs Dig — Nursing Digest
Nurs Digest — Nursing Digest
Nurs Dime — Nursing Dimensions
Nurs Dimens — Nursing Dimensions
Nurs Econ — Nursing Economics
Nurs Educ Monogr — Nursing Education Monographs
Nurse Educ — Nurse Educator
Nurse Educ Oppor Innov — Nurse Educators Opportunities and Innovations
Nurse Educ Today — Nurse Education Today
Nurse Inquir — Nurse Inquirer
Nurse Isr — Nurse in Israel
Nurse Patient Law — Nurse, the Patient, and the Law
Nurse Pract — Nurse Practitioner
Nurse Practit — Nurse Practitioner
Nurse Res — Nurse Researcher
Nursery Bus — Nursery Business
Nurserym Gdn Cent — Nurseryman and Garden Center
Nurs Focus — Nursing Focus
Nurs Forum — Nursing Forum
Nurs Forum (Auckl) — Nursing Forum (Auckland)
Nurs Health Care — Nursing and Health Care
Nurs Hist Rev — Nursing History Review
Nurs Hlth Care — Nursing and Health Care
Nurs Homes — Nursing Homes
Nursing (Lond) — Nursing (London)
Nurs J — Nursing Journal
Nurs J India — Nursing Journal of India
Nurs J Singapore — Nursing Journal of Singapore
Nurs J (S Toms) — Nursing Journal (Santo Tomas, Manila)
Nurs Law Ethics — Nursing Law and Ethics
Nurs Law Regan Rep — Nursing Law S Regan Report
Nurs Leader — Nurse Leadership
Nurs Leadersh — Nursing Leadership
Nurs Leadership — Nursing Leadership
Nurs Life — Nursing Life
Nurs M — Nursing Management
Nurs Manage — Nursing Management
Nurs Mir — Nursing Mirror
Nurs Mirror — Nursing Mirror and Midwives Journal [*Later, Nursing Mirror*]
Nurs (Montreal) — Nursing (Montreal)
Nurs News (Concord) — Nursing News (Concord)
Nurs News (Conn) — Nursing News (Connecticut)
Nurs News (Hartford) — Nursing News (Hartford)
Nurs News (Meriden) — Nursing News (Meriden)
Nurs News (New Hamp) — Nursing News (New Hampshire)
Nurs News (So Africa) — Nursing News (South Africa)
Nurs Older People — Nursing Older People
Nurs Outlook — Nursing Outlook
Nurs Pap — Nursing Papers
Nurs Papers — Nursing Papers
Nurs Pract — Nursing Practice
Nurs Pulse New Engl — Nursing Pulse of New England
Nurs (Que) — Nursing (Quebec)
Nurs Res — Nursing Research
Nurs Res Conf — Nursing Research Conference
Nurs Res Rep — Nursing Research Report
Nurs Sci — Nursing Science
Nurs Stand — Nursing Standard
Nurs Stud Index — Nursing Studies Index
Nurs Success Today — Nursing Success Today
Nurs Times — Nursing Times

Nurs Update — Nursing Update
NURVA — Nursing Research
NUS — Nebraska. University. University Studies
NuS — Nord und Sued
NUSBA — Nuclear Science and Applications. Series B. Physical Sciences
NU Sci — NU [*Natal University*] Science
NUSH — Northwestern University. Studies in the Humanities
NuSup — Numen Supplements
NUT — Norges Utenrikshandel
NuTi — Nuestro Tiempo. Revista Espanola de Cultura
NUTIA — Nursing Times
Nutida M — Nutida Musik
Nutida Mus — Nutida Musik
NUTN — Nunatext News
NUTN — Nutrition News
NutrAb — Nutrition Abstracts
Nutr Abstr Rev — Nutrition Abstracts and Reviews
Nutr Abstr Rev Ser A Hum Exp — Nutrition Abstracts and Reviews. Series A. Human and Experimental
Nutr Action — Nutrition Action
Nutr Action Health Lett — Nutrition Action Health Letter
Nutr and MD — Nutrition and the MD
Nutr Behav — Nutrition and Behavior
Nutr Brain — Nutrition and the Brain
Nutr Bromatol Toxicol — Nutricion Bromatologia Toxicologia
Nutr Cancer — Nutrition and Cancer
Nutr Clin — Nutricion Clinica. Dietetica Hospitalaria
Nutr Clin — Nutrition Clinics
Nutr Clin Metab — Nutrition Clinique et Metabolisme
Nutr Clin Nutr — Nutrition and Clinical Nutrition
Nutr Conf Feed Manuf — Nutrition Conference for Feed Manufacturers
Nutr Conf Feed Manuf Proc — Nutrition Conference for Feed Manufacturers. Proceedings
Nutr Cycling Agroecosyst — Nutrient Cycling in Agroecosystems
Nutr Defic Ind Countries Symp Group Eur Nutr — Nutritional Deficiencies in Industrialized Countries. Symposium. Group of European Nutritionists
Nutr Dent Health — Nutrition and Dental Health
Nutr Dieta — Nutritio et Dieta
Nutr Dieta Eur Nutr Diet — Nutrio et Dieta. European Review of Nutrition and Dietetics
Nutr Dieta Suppl — Nutritio et Dieta. Supplement
Nutr Diet Catering — Nutrition, Dietetics, Catering
Nutr Ecosyst — Nutrients in Ecosystems
Nutr Food Sci — Nutrition and Food Science
Nutr Food Sci Pres Knowl Util — Nutrition and Food Science. Present Knowledge and Utilization
Nutr Forum — Nutrition Forum
Nutr Found Inc Rep — Nutrition Foundation, Incorporated. Report
Nutr Health — Nutrition and Health
Nutr Health Dis — Nutrition in Health and Disease
Nutr Hosp — Nutricion Hospitalaria
Nutr Int — Nutrition International
Nutr Metab — Nutrition and Metabolism
Nutr Metab Cardiovasc Dis — Nutrition, Metabolism, and Cardiovascular Diseases
Nutr Metab Cardiovasc Dis — Nutrition, Metabolism, and Cardiovascular Diseases. NMCD
Nutr Monit Nutr Status Assess Proc Conf — Nutrition Monitoring and Nutrition Status Assessment. Proceedings. Conference
Nutr Monogr Ser — Nutrition Monograph Series
Nutr Neurosci — Nutritional Neuroscience
Nutr News — Nutrition News
Nutr Notes — Nutrition Notes
Nutr Plann — Nutrition Planning
Nutr Probl — Nutrition Problems
Nutr Proc Int Congr — Nutrition. Proceedings. International Congress
Nutr Prot Crops Pap Colloq Potassium Inst — Nutrition of Protected Crops. Papers. Colloquium. Potassium Institute
Nutr R — Nutrition Reviews
Nutr Rep In — Nutrition Reports International
Nutr Rep Int — Nutrition Reports International
Nutr Requir Dairy Cattle — Nutrient Requirements of Dairy Cattle
Nutr Requir Dogs — Nutrient Requirements of Dogs
Nutr Requir Domest Anim — Nutrient Requirements of Domestic Animals
Nutr Requir Lab Anim — Nutrient Requirements of Laboratory Animals
Nutr Requir Sheep — Nutrient Requirements of Sheep
Nutr Requir Swine — Nutrient Requirements of Swine
Nutr Res — Nutrition Research
Nutr Res Bull — Nutrition Research Bulletin
Nutr Res Los Angeles — Nutrition Research (Los Angeles)
Nutr Res New York — Nutrition Research (New York)
Nutr Res Rev — Nutrition Research Reviews
Nutr Rev — Nutrition Reviews
Nutr Rev Present Knowl Nutr — Nutrition Reviews' Present Knowledge in Nutrition
Nutr Sci — Nutrition Sciences
Nutr Sci Soy Protein Jpn — Nutritional Science of Soy Protein (Japan)
Nutr Soc Aust Proc — Nutrition Society of Australia. Proceedings
Nutr Soc NZ Proc — Nutrition Society of New Zealand. Proceedings
Nutr Soc Proc — Nutrition Society Proceedings
Nutr Support Serv — Nutritional Support Services
Nutr Symp — Nutricia Symposium
Nutr Today — Nutrition Today
Nutr Transition Proc West Hemisphere Nutr Congr — Nutrition in Transition. Proceedings. Western Hemisphere Nutrition Congress
Nutr Update — Nutrition Update
Nutr Week — Nutrition Week

NUTSDT — Nutrition Sciences
NUVN — Nuvuk News
NV — Naamloze Vennootschap
NV — Nase Veda
NV — Nastavni Vjesnik
NV — Neerlands Volksleven
NV — New Verse
NV — Nova et Vetera
NV — Numizmaticke Vijesti
NV — Nuova Rivista Storica
NVA — Norske Videnskaps-Akademi. Aarbok
NVARA — Naval Architect
Nv Archt T — Transactions of the Institution of Naval Architects
NVB — Noise and Vibration Bulletin
NVC — Narodopisny Vestnik Ceskoslovensky
NVC — Naturens Verden (Copenhagen)
NVE — Naamloze Vennootschap
N Veracruz — Norte de Veracruz
N Vet — Nordisk Veterinaermedicin
NVet — Nova et Vetera
NVF — Natur und Volk. Senckenbergische Naturforschende Gesellschaft (Frankfurt-am-Main)
NVFAAB — National Vitamin Foundation. Annual Report
NVHS — Norske Videnskaps-Akademi i Oslo. Hvalradets Skrifter
NVK — Koeltechniek/Klimaatregeling
NVLSA — Nauchni Trudove. Vissh Lesotekhnicheski Institut (Sofia)
N Vorp Mt — Mittheilungen aus dem Naturwissenschaftlichen Vereine von Neu-Vorpommern und Ruegen
NVROB — Nouvelle Revue d'Optique
Nv Sc — Naval Science
NVS Nuus — Nasionale Versnellersentrum Nuus
NVT — Nieuw Vlaams Tijdschrift
NvT — Novum Testamentum
NVV — Recreatie
NVVI — Nekotorye Voprosy Vseobshchei Istorii
Nw — Naturwissenschaften
NW — Neue Weg
NW — Neue Welt
Nw — Newsweek
NW — New Worlds
NW — New Writing
NW — North Western Reporter
NW — Notarieel Weekblad
NW — Nucleonics Week
NWA — New World Antiquity
NWA — New Worlds Science Fiction
NWA — Nieuw Europa. Tijdschrift van de Europese Beweging in Nederland
NWAC — Native Women's Association of Canada. Newsletter
NWAIAH — New South Wales. Department of Agriculture. Division of Science Services. Entomology Branch. Insect Pest Survey. Annual Report
NWAN — Native Women's Association of the NWT [*Northwest Territories, Canada*]. Newsletter
NW Anthrop Res Notes — Northwest Anthropological Research Notes
N War Coll — Naval War College
NWAY — Norway
NWB — New Books and Periodicals
NWB — New Worlds (British)
NWCR — Naval War College Review
NWD — New Writing & Daylight
NWELA — New Electronics
NW Eur Study Group Assess Nitrogen Fert Requir Meet — NW-European Study Group. Assessment of Nitrogen Fertilizer Requirement. Meeting
NWEX — Northwest Explorer. Northwest Territorial Airways
NW Farm Ranch — North West Farmer, Rancher
NWG — Nieuwe West-Indishe Gids
NWGB — New Writers Group Bulletin
NWGPA — Nachrichten. Gesellschaft der Wissenschaften zu Goettingen. Mathematisch-Physikalische Klasse. Fachgruppe 2. Physik, Astronomie, Geophysik, Technik
NWH — Lebensmittel Praxis. Unabhangiges Fachmagazin fuer Unternehmensfuehrung, Werbung, und Verkauf im Lebensmittelhandel
NWHOM — Newsletter. William H. Over Museum
NWI — Nieuws uit Zweden
NWIG — Nieuwe West-Indische Gids
NWJ — New Scientist
Nw J Intl L and Bus — Northwestern Journal of International Law and Business
NWK — Levensmiddelenmarkt
NWK — Newsweek
NWL — Northwestern University. Law Review
NW Law Rev — Northwestern Law Review
NWL Rev — North Western Law Review
Nw LS — Northwestern University. Law Review. Supplement
NwMSCS — Northwest Missouri State College Studies
NWN — Nuclear Waste News
NW Newsl — North Western Newsletter
NWO — New Work Opportunities
NW Ohio Q — Northwest Ohio Quarterly
NWOQ — Northwest Ohio Quarterly
NW Paper News — Northwest Pulp and Paper News
NW Passage — Northwest Passage
NWPR — Northwest Prospector. Northwest Miners and Developers Bulletin
NWPYA — Sae Mulli
NWQ — New Worlds. Quarterly
NWR — Northwest Review

NWRBBE — Basin Planning Report. New York State Water Resources Commission. Series ENB
NWREDP — Water Research Centre. Notes on Water Research
Nw School — New Schools Exchange. Newsletter
NW Sci — Northwest Science
NWSIA J — NWSIA [*National Water Supply Improvement Association*] Journal
NWSIA Newsl — NWSIA [*National Water Supply Improvement Association*] Newsletter
Nws Lettr — News and Letters
Nws Nat — News National
NWT — Naturwissenschaft und Theologie
NWT — Northwest Territories Reports
NW Terr (Can) — Northwest Territories Reports (Canada)
NWTG3 — NWT [*Northwest Territories, Canada*] Gazette. Part III
NWTGII — NWT [*Northwest Territories, Canada*] Gazette. Part II
NWT Rep — Northwest Territories Reports
NWT Rev Ord — Revised Ordinances of the Northwest Territories
NWTWN — NWT [*Northwest Territories, Canada*] Wildlife Notes
NWTWSCR — NWT [*Northwest Territories, Canada*] Wildlife Service. Completion Reports
NWTWSCT — NWT [*Northwest Territories, Canada*] Wildlife Service. Contact Reports
NWTWSFR — NWT [*Northwest Territories, Canada*] Wildlife Service. File Reports
NWTWSPR — NWT [*Northwest Territories, Canada*] Wildlife Service. Progress Reports
NWU — Viewpoint
NWULR — Northwestern University. Law Review
NW U L Rev — Northwestern University. Law Review
NW Univ Law R — Northwestern University. Law Review
NWVO — Notring der Wissenschaftlichen Verbaende Oesterreichs
NwW — Naturwissenschaftliche Wochenschrift
NWW — New World Writing
NWZam — New Writing from Zambia
NY — New York
NY — New Yorker
NY — New York Magazine
NY — New York Reports
NY — School Music News
NY 2d — New York Reports. Second Series
NyA — Nya Argus
Nya Bot Not — Nya Botaniska Notiser
N Y Ac A — Annals of the New York Academy of Sciences, late Lyceum of Natural History
NY Acad Med Bul — New York Academy of Medicine. Bulletin
NY Acad Sci Ann — New York Academy of Sciences. Annals
NY Acad Sci Trans — New York Academy of Sciences. Transactions
NY Acad Sci Trans Ann — New York Academy of Sciences. Transactions. Annals
N Y Ac T — Transactions of the New York Academy of Sciences, late Lyceum of Natural History
NY Aff — New York Affairs
NY Ag Dept — New York Department of Agriculture. Publications
NY Agric Exp Stn (Geneva) Annu Rep — New York. Agricultural Experiment Station (Geneva). Annual Report
NY Agric Exp Stn (Geneva) Bull — New York. Agricultural Experiment Station (Geneva). Bulletin
NY Agric Exp Stn Geneva NY Annu Rep — New York. Agricultural Experiment Station (Geneva, New York). Annual Report
NY Agric Exp Stn (Geneva) Res Circ — New York. Agricultural Experiment Station (Geneva). Research Circular
NY Agric Exp Stn (Geneva) Tech Bull — New York. Agricultural Experiment Station (Geneva). Technical Bulletin
NY Agric Exp Stn (Ithaca) Bull — New York. Agricultural Experiment Station (Ithaca). Bulletin
NY Agric Exp Stn (Ithaca) Mem — New York. Agricultural Experiment Station (Ithaca). Memoir
N Y A Lyceum — Annals of the Lyceum of Natural History of New York
N Y Am Mth S Bll — Bulletin of the American Mathematical Society (New York)
N Y Am Mth S T — Transactions of the American Mathematical Society (Lancaster, Pennsylvania and New York)
NY Anno Dig — New York Annotated Digest
Nya Perspekt — Nya Perspektiv
NY Appl For Res Inst AFRI Misc Rep — New York Applied Forestry Research Institute. AFRI Miscellaneous Report
NY Appl For Res Inst AFRI Res Note — New York Applied Forestry Research Institute. AFRI Research Note
NY Appl For Res Inst AFRI Res Rep — New York Applied Forestry Research Institute. AFRI Research Report
NY Arts J — New York Arts Journal
Nyasa J — Nyasaland Journal
Nyasaland Farmer Forest — Nyasaland Farmer and Forester
Nyasal Farmer For — Nyasaland Farmer and Forester
Nyasal Geol Surv Dep Mem — Nyasaland Protectorate. Geological Survey Department. Memoir
Nyasal Prot Rec Geol Surv Nyasal — Nyasaland Protectorate. Records. Geological Survey of Nyasaland
NY Bd Agr Mem — New York Board of Agriculture. Memoirs
NY Bot Gard Annu Rep — New York Botanical Garden. Annual Report
NY Bot Garden B — New York Botanical Garden. Bulletin
NY Bot Gard Mem — New York Botanical Garden. Memoirs
NYBR — New York Times Book Review
NYCBA — New York City Bar Association. Bulletin
NYCBA Bull — Bulletin. Association of the Bar of the City of New York
NYC Bd Ed Curric Bul — New York City Board of Education. Curriculum Bulletins
NYC Dept Health W Bul — New York City. Department of Health. Weekly Bulletin
NY Cert Pub Acct — New York Certified Public Accountant

NY Ch Sent — New York Chancery Sentinel
NY City Hall Rec — New York City Hall Recorder
NY Civ Proc — New York Civil Procedure
NY Civ Pro R — New York Civil Procedure Reports
NY Civ Pro R NS — New York Civil Procedure Reports, New Series
NY Civ Pr Rep — New York Civil Procedure Reports
NYCKA — Neng Yuan Chi Kan
NY Co Law Assn Yrbk — New York County Lawyers Association. Yearbook
NY Comm St Res Niagara An Rp — New York Commissioners of the State Reservation at Niagara. Annual Report
NY Comp Codes R & Regs — Official Compilation of Codes, Rules, and Regulations of the State of New York
NY Conf Soc Wk Q Bul — New York (City) Conference of Social Work. Quarterly Bulletin
NY Conserv Dep Fish Res Bull — New York. Conservation Department. Fisheries Research Bulletin
NY County B Bull — New York County Lawyers Association. Bar Bulletin
NY County Law Ass'n B Bull — New York County Lawyers Association. Bar Bulletin
NY Dada — New York Dada
NY Daily L Gaz — New York Daily Law Gazette
NY Daily L Reg — New York Daily Law Register
NY Daily Reg — New York Daily Register
NY Daily Tr — New York Daily Transcript, Old and New Series
NY Dep Agric Mark Annu Rep — New York Department of Agriculture and Markets. Annual Report
NY Dep Agric Mark Circ — New York Department of Agriculture and Markets. Circular
NY Dep Environ Conserv Bull — New York. Department of Environmental Conservation. Bulletin
NY Dep Environ Conserv Div Water Resour Bull — New York. Department of Environmental Conservation. Division of Water Resources. Bulletin
NY Dep Transp Res Rep — New York State Department of Transport. Research Report
NyE — Nyelvtudomanyi Ertekezesek
NY Ecclesiologist — New York Ecclesiologist
Ny Elektron — Ny Elektronik
Nyelvtudomanyi Dolg Eotvos Lorand TudomEgy — Nyelvtudomanyi Dolgozatok. Eotvos Lorand Tudomanyegyetum
Nye Oecon Ann — Nye Oeconomiske Annaler
NYEP — New York Evening Post
NYEPLR — New York Evening Post Literary Review
Nye Saml Kongel Danske Vidensk Selsk Skr — Nye Samling af det Kongelige Danske Videnskabers Selskabs Skrifter
Nyeste Saml Kongel Norske Vidensk Selsk Skr — Nyeste Samling Af Det Kongelige Norske Videnskabers-Selskabs Skrifter
NY Eve Post — New York Evening Post
NYF — New York Law Forum
NY Farms & Markets Dept — New York State Department of Farms and Markets. Publications
NY Fd Life Sci Q — New York's Food and Life Sciences Quarterly
NY Fish Game J — New York Fish and Game Journal
NY Folkl — New York Folklore
NY Folklore — New York Folklore
NY Folk Q — New York Folklore. Quarterly
NY Food Life Sci Bull — New York's Food and Life Sciences Bulletin
NY Food Life Sci Q — New York's Food and Life Sciences Quarterly
NYFQ — New York Folklore. Quarterly
NY Geneal And Biog Rec — New York Genealogical and Biographical Record. New York Genealogical and Biographical Society
NY Gov Conf Crime Proc — New York Governor's Conference on Crime, the Criminal, and Society. Proceedings
NY G S — New York Geological Survey
NYGZA — Nippon Yuketsu Gakkai Zasshi
NYH — New York History
NYH — Nueva York Hispano
NY Herald — New York Herald
NY Herald Trib Forum Cur Prob Rep — New York Herald Tribune. Forum on Current Problems. Report
NY Herald Tribune — New York Herald Tribune
NY Herald Tribune Bk R — New York Herald Tribune. Book Review
NY Herald Tribune W Bk R — New York Herald Tribune. Weekly Book Review
NY Her Trib Lively Arts — New York Herald Tribune. Lively Arts Section
NY His — New York History
NY Hist — New York History
NY History — New York History
NY Hist Soc Bul — New York Historical Society. Quarterly Bulletin
NY Hist Soc Coll — New York Historical Society. Collections
NY Hist Soc Q — New York Historical Society. Quarterly
NY Hist Soc Quar — New York Historical Society. Quarterly
NYHS — New York Historical Society. Quarterly
NYHSQ — New York Historical Society. Quarterly
NYHSQB — New York Historical Society. Quarterly Bulletin
NYHT — New York Herald Tribune
NYHTB — New York Herald Tribune. Weekly Book Review
NyIK — Nyelvtudomanyi Intezet Koezlemenyek
NYIL — Netherlands Yearbook of International Law
Nyiregyhazi ME — Nyiregyhazi Josa Andras Muzeum Evkonyve
NY J Dent — New York Journal of Dentistry
Ny J Hush — Ny Journal Uti Hushallningen
NYJ Int'l & Comp L — New York Law School. Journal of International and Comparative Law
NyJME — Nyiregyhazi Josa Andras Muzeum Evkonyve
NY J Med — New York State Journal of Medicine
NyK — Nyelvtudomanyi Koezlemenyek

NYKZAU — Folia Pharmacologica Japonica
NYL — New York University. Law Review
NYLAB — New York Language Association. Bulletin
NY Law Bul — New York Monthly Law Bulletin
NY Law Consol — New York Consolidated Laws Service
NY Law Forum — New York Law Forum
NY Law Gaz — New York Law Gazette
NY Law J — New York Law Journal
NY Law (McKinney) — McKinney's Consolidated Laws. New York
NY Law R — New York Law Review
NY Law Rev — New York Law Review
NY Laws — Laws of New York
NY Leg N — New York Legal News
NY L F — New York Law Forum
NYL Gaz — New York Law Gazette
NY Lib Assn Bul — New York Library Association. Bulletin
NY Lit For — New York Literary Forum
NYLJ — New York Law Journal
NYLR — New York Law Review
NYL Rev — New York Law Review
NylroK — Nyelv-Es Irodalomtudomanyi Koezlemenyek
NY L Sch Intl L Socy J — New York Law School. International Law Society. Journal
NY L Sch J Intl and Comp L — New York Law School. Journal of International and Comparative Law
NY L Sch L Rev — New York Law School. Law Review
NYL School Rev — New York Law School. Law Review
NYLSLR — New York Law School. Law Review
NY L S L Rev — New York Law School. Law Review
NYLS Stud L Rev — New York Law School. Student Law Review
N Y Lyceum A — Annals of the Lyceum of Natural History of New York
N Y Lyceum P — Proceedings of the Lyceum of Natural History in the City of New York
NY Mag — New York Magazine
N Y Md J — New York Medical Journal
N Y Md Rep — Medical Repository of New York
NY Med — New York Medicine
NY Med Coll Flower Hosp Bull — New York Medical College and Flower Hospital Bulletin
NY Med J — New York Medical Journal
NY Med J Obstet Rev — New York Medical Journal and Obstetrical Review
NY Med Phys J — New York Medical and Physical Journal
NY Med Quart — New York Medical Quarterly
NY Micro Soc J — New York Microscopical Society. Journal
NY Miner Club B — New York Mineralogical Club. Bulletin
NY Mo Law Bul — New York Monthly Law Bulletin
NY Mo L Bul — New York Monthly Law Bulletin
NY Mo LR — New York Monthly Law Reports
NY Mo L Rec — New York Monthly Law Record
NY Month L Bul — New York Monthly Law Bulletin
NY Month LR — New York Monthly Law Reports
NY Monthly Law Bul — New York Monthly Law Bulletin
N Y Ms Bll — University of the State of New York. Bulletin of the New York State Museum
N Y Mth S Bll — Bulletin of the New York Mathematical Society
NY Mun Gaz — New York Municipal Gazette
NYMZ — Nytt Magasin foer Zoologi
NY New Tech Bks — New York Public Library. New Technical Books
NYNY — [The] New Yorker (New York)
NYO — New York Observer
N York Herald and Trib Books — New York Herald and Tribune Books
N York J Med — New York Journal of Medicine
N York Med J — New York Medical Journal
N York Med Journ — New York Medical Journal
N York Times Book Revw — New York Times Book Review
NYP — New York Post
NY Phil — New York Philharmonic Program Notes
NYPL Bull — New York Public Library. Bulletin
NYPO — New York Publicity Outlet
Ny Pol — Ny Politik
NY Prod R — New York Produce Review and American Creamery
NY Prod Rev Am Creamery — New York Produce Review and American Creamery
NY Pub Lib Br Lib Bk News — New York Public Library. Branch Library Book News
NY Pub Lib Bul — New York Public Library Bulletin
NY Pub Lib Bull — New York Public Library Bulletin
NY Public Lib Bull — New York City Public Library. Bulletin
NYQ — New York Quarterly
Nyr — Magyar Nyelvor
NYR — New York Reports
NYR — New York Review of Books
NYRB — New York Review of Books
NYR Bks — New York Review of Books
NY Reg — New York Daily Register
NY Reptr — New York Reporter
NY Rev Bks — New York Review of Books
NY Rev Book — New York Review of Books
NY Rev Books — New York Review of Books
NY Review — New York Review of Books
NY Rev of Books — New York Review of Books
NYR of Bk — New York Review of Books
NYS — New York Sun
NyS — Nydanske Studier. Almen Kommunikationsteori
NYS — West's New York Supplement
NYS 2d — West's New York Supplement. Second Series

NYSBA Bull — New York State Bar Association. Bulletin
NY S B BULL — New York State Bar Bulletin
NYSB J — New York State Bar Journal
NY Sea Grant L and Pol'y J — New York Sea Grant Law and Policy Journal
NYSE Fact — New York Stock Exchange. Fact Book
NYSE Guide CCH — New York Stock Exchange Guide. Commerce Clearing House
NYSERDA Rev — NYSERDA [New York State Energy Research and Development Authority] Review
NYSFI Bull — NYSFI (New York State Flower Industries) Bulletin
NY Soc Exp Study Ed Yrbk — New York Society for the Experimental Study of Education. Yearbook
Nys S — Nysvenska Studier
NYSSNTA J — NYSSNTA [New York State School Nurse-Teachers Association] Journal
NY St Agr Soc Tr — New York State Agricultural Society. Transactions
NY St Assn Chiefs Police Proc — New York State Association of Chiefs of Police. Proceedings
NY St Assn Judges Proc — New York State Association of Judges of County Children's Courts. Proceedings
NY St Assn Magistrates Proc — New York State Association of Magistrates. Proceedings
NY State Ag Exp — New York State Agricultural Experiment Station. Publications
NY State Agric Exp Stn Cornell Univ Geneva NY — New York State Agricultural Experiment Station. Cornell University (Geneva, New York)
NY State Agric Exp Stn (Geneva) Annu Rep — New York State Agricultural Experiment Station (Geneva). Annual Report
NY State Agric Exp Stn Geneva NY Bull — New York State Agricultural Experiment Station (Geneva, New York). Bulletin
NY State Agric Exp Stn Seed Res Circ — New York State Agricultural Experiment Station. Seed Research Circular
NY State Agric Exp Stn Spec Rep — New York State Agricultural Experiment Station. Special Report
NY State Agric Exp Stn Spec Rep Geneva — New York State Agricultural Experiment Station. Special Report (Geneva)
NY State Assoc Milk Food Sanit Annu Rep — New York State Association of Milk and Food Sanitarians. Annual Report
NY State Assoc Milk Sanit Annu Rep — New York State Association of Milk Sanitarians. Annual Report
NY State Bar J — New York State Bar Journal
NY State Coll Ceramics Ceramic Expt Sta Bull — New York State College of Ceramics. Ceramic Experiment Station. Bulletin
NY State Coll For Syracuse Univ Bull — New York State College of Forestry. Syracuse University. Bulletin
NY State Coll For Syracuse Univ Tech Publ — New York State University College of Forestry. Syracuse University. Technical Publication
NY State Conserv — New York State Conservationist
NY State Conserv Dep Biol Surv — New York State Conservation Department. Biological Survey
NY State Dent J — New York State Dental Journal
NY State Dep Agric Mark Bull — New York State Department of Agriculture and Markets. Bulletin
NY State Dep Conserv Water Resour Comm Bull — New York State Department of Conservation. Water Resources Commission. Bulletin
NY State Dep Environ Conserv Basin Plann Rep ARB — New York State Department of Environmental Conservation. Basin Planning Report. Series ARB
NY State Dep Environ Conserv Basin Plann Rep BRB — New York State Department of Environmental Conservation. Basin Planning Report. Series BRB
NY State Dep Environ Conserv Basin Plann Rep ORB — New York State Department of Environmental Conservation. Basin Planning Report. Series ORB
NY State Dep Environ Conserv Bull — New York State Department of Environmental Conservation. Bulletin
NY State Dep Environ Conserv Environ Qual Res Dev Unit Tech P — New York State Department of Environmental Conservation. Environmental Quality Research and Development Unit. Technical Paper
NY State Dep Environ Conserv Tech Pap — New York State Department of Environmental Conservation. Technical Paper
NY State Dep Health Annu Rep Div Lab Res — New York State Department of Health. Annual Report. Division of Laboratories and Research
NY State Dep Health Div Lab Res Annu Rep — New York State Department of Health. Division of Laboratories and Research. Annual Report
NY State Dep Health Lab Res Oper Data — New York State Department of Health. Division of Laboratories and Research. Operations Data
NY State Dep Labor Div Ind Hyg Mon Rev — New York State Department of Labor. Division of Industrial Hygiene. Monthly Review
NY State Dep Labor Ind Bull — New York State Department of Labor. Industrial Bulletin
NY State Dep Labor Mon Rev Div Ind Hyg — New York State Department of Labor. Monthly Review. Division of Industrial Hygiene
NY State Ed — New York State Education
NY State Flower Growers Bull — New York State Flower Growers. Bulletin
NY State Flower Ind Bull — New York State Flower Industries. Bulletin
NY State Hist Assoc Jour — New York State Historical Association. Quarterly Journal
NY State Horti Soc Proc — New York State Horticultural Society. Proceedings
NY State J Med — New York State Journal of Medicine
NY State Mus and Sci Service Bull Circ — New York State Museum and Science Service. Bulletin. Circular
NY State Mus Bull — New York State Museum. Bulletin
NY State Mus Circ Handb — New York State Museum Circular. Handbook
NY State Mus Map Chart Ser — New York State Museum. Map and Chart Series
NY State Mus Mem — New York State Museum. Memoir
NY State Mus Sci Serv Bull — New York State Museum and Science Service. Bulletin
NY State Mus Sci Serv Circ — New York State Museum and Science Service. Circular

NY State Mus Sci Serv Educ Leafl — New York State Museum and Science Service. Educational Leaflet

NY State Mus Sci Serv Map Chart Ser — New York State Museum and Science Service. Map and Chart Series

NY State Mus Sci Serv Mem — New York State Museum and Science Service. Memoir

NY State Nurse — New York State Nurse

NY State Sci Service Rept Inv — New York State Science Service. Report of Investigation

NY State Sci Serv Univ State NY Report Invest — New York State Science Service. University of the State of New York. Report of Investigation

NY State Univ Coll For Syracuse Univ Tech Publ — New York State University College of Forestry. Syracuse University. Technical Publication

NY State Water Resour Comm Basin Plann Rep — New York State Water Resources Commission. Basin Planning Report

NY State Water Resour Comm Basin Plann Rep ENB — New York State Water Resources Commission. Basin Planning Report. Series ENB

NY State Water Resour Comm Basin Plann Rep ORB — New York State Water Resources Commission. Basin Planning Report. Series ORB

NY St Ba A — New York State Bar Association. Bulletin

NY St B Assn Bul — New York State Bar Association. Bulletin

NY St B Assn Proc — New York State Bar Association. Proceedings

NY St BJ — New York State Bar Journal

NY St Cab An Rp — New York State Cabinet of Natural History. Annual Report. Regents University

NY St Conf Prob Offic Proc — New York State Conference of Probation Officers. Proceedings

NY St Conf Soc Wk Papers — New York State Conference of Social Work. Papers

NY St Conf Soc Wk Q Bul — New York State Conference of Social Work. Quarterly

NYSTDL — Agricultural Research. Seoul National University

NY St Educ — New York State Education

NY St G An Rp — New York State Geologist. Annual Report

NY St His As — New York State Historical Association. Proceedings

NY St His As Q J — New York State Historical Association. Quarterly Journal

NY St Hist Assn J — New York State Historical Association. Quarterly Journal

NY St J Med — New York State Journal of Medicine

NY St Mus — New York State Museum

NY St Mus An Rp — New York State Museum of Natural History. Annual Report

NY St Reg — New York State Register

NY Sup Ct — Supreme Court Reports (New York)

NySvT — Ny Svensk Tidskrift

NYSZ — New York Staatszeitung

NYT — New York Times

NYT — New York Times Book Review

NYTB — New York Times Book Review

Nyt Biblioth Phys — Nyt Bibliothek for Physik, Medicin, og Oeconomie

Nyt Bibl Laeg — Nyt Bibliothek for Laeger

NYTBIO — New York Times Biographical File

NYTBR — New York Times Book Review

Ny Tek — Ny Teknik

Nyt F Arb — Nyt fra Arbejdsdirektoratet

Nyt F Isl — Nyt fra Island

NY Theat Cr — New York Theatre Critics. Reviews

NYTIA — New York Times

NY Times — New York Times

NY Times — New York Times Book Review

NY Times Biog Service — New York Times Biographical Service

NY Times Bk R — New York Times Book Review

NY Times Book Rev — New York Times Book Review

NY Times M — New York Times Magazine

NY Times Mag — New York Times Magazine

NY Times N — New York Times. National Edition

NY Times NY Ed — [The] New York Times (New York Edition)

NY Times R — New York Times Book Review

NYTKB — Ny Teknik

NYTLS — New York Times Literary Supplement

NYTM — New York Times Magazine

NYTMag — New York Times Magazine

Nyt Mag For Naturvidensk — Nyt Magazin for Naturvidenskaberne

NYTMS — New York Times Magazine Section

NYTRAH — Marine Sciences Research Center [Stony Brook]. Technical Report

Nyt Sprognaevn — Nyt fra Sprognaevnet

Nytt Mag Bot (Oslo) — Nytt Magasin foer Botanikk (Oslo)

Nytt Mag Naturvid — Nytt Magasin foer Naturvidenskapene

Nytt Mag Naturvidensk — Nytt Magasin foer Naturvidenskapene

Nytt Mag Zool (Oslo) — Nytt Magasin foer Zoology (Oslo)

NYU Conf Charitable — New York University. Conference on Charitable Foundations. Proceedings

NYU Conf Charitable Fdn — New York University. Conference on Charitable Foundations. Proceedings

NYU Conf Lab — New York University. Conference on Labor

NYU Educ Q — New York University. Education Quarterly

NYU Eng Res Rev — NYU Engineering Research Review

NYUEQ — New York University. Education Quarterly

NYU Inst Fed Tax — New York University. Institute on Federal Taxation

NYU Inst Fed Taxation — New York University. Institute on Federal Taxation

NYU Inst on Fed Tax — New York University. Institute on Federal Taxation

NYU Intra L Rev — New York University. Intramural Law Review

NYU Intramur L Rev — New York University. Intramural Law Review

NYU J Int L & Pol — New York University. Journal of International Law and Politics

NYU J Int L & Politics — New York University. Journal of International Law and Politics

NYU J Int'l L & Pol — New York University. Journal of International Law and Politics

NYUJ Int'l Law & Pol — New York University. Journal of International Law and Politics

NYU Law Q Rev — New York University. Law Quarterly Review

NYUL Center Bull — New York University. Law Center. Bulletin

NYULQ Rev — New York University. Law Quarterly Review

NYUL Qu Rev — New York University. Law Quarterly Review

NYULR — New York University. Law Review

NYU L Rev — New York University. Law Review

NYU Med Cent N — New York University Medical Center News

NY Univ J Dent — New York University. Journal of Dentistry

NY Univ J of Internat L and Polit — New York University. Journal of International Law and Politics

NY Univ Law Rev — New York University Law Review. New York University

NY Univ L Q R — New York University. Law Quarterly Review

NY Univ LR — New York University Law Review

NY Univ L Rev — New York University. Law Review

NY Univ Res B — New York University. Research Bulletin in Commercial Education

NYU Rev L & Soc — New York University. Review of Law and Social Change

NYU Rev L and Soc Ch — New York University. Review of Law and Social Change

NYU Rev L & Soc Change — New York University. Review of Law and Social Change

NYU Rev Law & Soc C — New York University. Review of Law and Social Change

NYU Slav P — New York University. Slavic Papers

NYU Univ Stud Comp Lit — New York University. Studies in Comparative Literature

Ny Verd — Ny Verden

NYW — New York World

NY Water Power and Control Comm Bull — New York Water Power and Control Commission. Bulletin

NY Water Power Control Comm Bull — New York State Water Power and Control Commission. Bulletin

NY Water Resour Comm Bull — New York State Water Resources Commission. Bulletin

NY Week Dig — New York Weekly Digest

NY Weekly Dig — New York Weekly Digest

NYWJT — New York World Journal Tribune

NY Wkly Dig — New York Weekly Digest

NY World Mag — New York World Magazine

NYZZA3 — Journal. Japan Pharmaceutical Association

NZ — Nasa Zena

NZ — Neue Zeitschrift fuer Musik

NZ — Neuphilologische Zeitschrift

NZ — Novitates Zoologicae

NZ — Novyj Zurnal

NZ — Numismatische Zeitschrift

NZAEI Newsl — NZAEI [New Zealand Agricultural Engineering Institute] Newsletter

NZ Agi Sci — New Zealand Institution of Agricultural Science. Bulletin

NZ Agric Sci — New Zealand Agricultural Science

NZ Agricst — New Zealand Agriculturist

NZ Agr Sci — New Zealand Agricultural Science

NZ Antarct Rec — New Zealand Antarctic Record

NZ Arch — New Zealand Architect

NZ Archit — New Zealand Architect

NZ Architect — New Zealand Architect

NZ Beekeep — New Zealand Beekeeper

NZ Beekpr — New Zealand Beekeeper

NZ Beekprs J — New Zealand Beekeepers' Journal

NZ Bird Banding Scheme Annu Rep — New Zealand Bird Banding Scheme. Annual Report

NZ Bu Econ — New Zealand Building Economist

NZ Bu Insp — New Zealand Building Inspector

NZ Bus Con — New Zealand Business Conditions

NZC — New Zealand Commerce

NZ Cartogr J — New Zealand Cartographic Journal

NZCernU — Naukovi Zapyski Cernivec'koho Derzavnoho Universyteta

NZCerPI — Naukovi Zapyski Cerkas'koho Derzavnoho Pedahohicnoho Instytutu

NZ Chiro J — New Zealand Chiropractic Journal

NZ Coal — New Zealand Coal

NZ Col LJ — New Zealand Colonial Law Journal

N Z Col Ms Gl Sv Rp — Colonial Museum and Geological Survey of New Zealand. Reports of Geological Explorations

NZ Com — New Zealand Commerce

NZ Com Grow — New Zealand Commercial Grower

NZ Commer Grow — New Zealand Commercial Grower

NZ Conc Constr — New Zealand Concrete Construction

NZ Concr Constr — NZ [New Zealand] Concrete Construction

NZ Conf Australas Inst Min Metall — New Zealand Conference. Australasian Institute of Mining and Metallurgy

NZ Crafts — New Zealand Crafts

NZ Dent J — New Zealand Dental Journal

NZ Dep Agric Annu Rep — New Zealand. Department of Agriculture. Annual Report

NZ Dep Agric Rep — New Zealand. Department of Agriculture. Report

NZ Dep Health Spec Rep Ser — New Zealand. Department of Health. Special Report Series

NZ Dep Intern Aff Wldl Publ — New Zealand. Department of Internal Affairs. Wildlife Publication

NZ Dep Sci Ind Res Appl Biochem Div Tech Rep — New Zealand. Department of Scientific and Industrial Research. Applied Biochemistry Division. Technical Report

NZ Dep Sci Ind Res Bull — New Zealand. Department of Scientific and Industrial Research. Bulletin

NZ Dep Sci Ind Res Chem Div Rep — New Zealand. Department of Scientific and Industrial Research. Chemistry Division. Report

NZ Dep Sci Ind Res Crop Res News — New Zealand. Department of Scientific and Industrial Research. Crop Research News

NZ Dep Sci Ind Res Discuss Pap — New Zealand. Department of Scientific and Industrial Research. Discussion Paper

NZ Dep Sci Ind Res Dom Lab Rep DL — New Zealand. Department of Scientific and Industrial Research. Dominion Laboratory. Report DL

NZ Dep Sci Ind Res Geol Surv Paleontol Bull — New Zealand. Department of Scientific and Industrial Research. Geological Survey. Paleontological Bulletin

NZ Dep Sci Ind Res Geophys Div Rep — New Zealand. Department of Scientific and Industrial Research. Geophysics Division. Report

NZ Dep Sci Ind Res Geophys Div Tech Note — New Zealand. Department of Scientific and Industrial Research. Geophysics Division. Technical Note

NZ Dep Sci Ind Res Ind Process Div Rep — New Zealand. Department of Scientific and Industrial Research. Industrial Processing Division. Report

NZ Dep Sci Ind Res Inf Ser — New Zealand. Department of Scientific and Industrial Research. Information Series

NZ Dep Sci Ind Res Rep — New Zealand. Department of Scientific and Industrial Research. Report

NZ Dep Sci Ind Res Soil Bur Bull — New Zealand. Department of Scientific and Industrial Research. Soil Bureau Bulletin

NZ Dep Stat Transp Stat — New Zealand. Department of Statistics. Transport Statistics

NZ Dept Maori Aff Ann Rep — New Zealand. Department of Maori Affairs. Annual Report

NZ Dir Gen For Rep — New Zealand Director-General of Forests. Report

NZDnepU — Naucnye Zapyski Dnepropetrovskogo Gosudarstvennogo Universiteta

NZ Dominion Mus Bull — New Zealand Dominion Museum Bulletin

NZDonPI — Naukovi Zapyski Donec'koho Derzavnoho Pedahohicnoho Instytutu

NZ Draughtsman — New Zealand Draughtsman

NZDrohPI — Naukovi Zapyski Drohobyc'koho Derzavnoho Pedahohicnoho Instytutu

NZ DSIR Inf Ser — NZ DSIR [*New Zealand Department of Scientific and Industrial Research*] Informat ion Series

N Zealand Lib — New Zealand Libraries

NZ Ecol Soc Proc — New Zealand Ecological Society. Proceedings

NZ Econ Stat — New Zealand Economic Statistics

NZ Elect — New Zealand Electron

NZ Elect Rev — New Zealand Electronics Review

NZ Electr J — New Zealand Electrical Journal

NZ Electronics — New Zealand Electronics. Supplement to Electrical Industry

NZ Electron Rev — New Zealand Electronics Review

NZ Energ J — New Zealand Energy Journal

NZ Energy J — New Zealand Energy Journal

NZ Energy Res Dev Comm Newsl — New Zealand Energy Research and Development Committee. Newsletter

NZ Energy Res Dev Comm Rep — New Zealand. Energy Research and Development Committee. Report

NZ Eng — New Zealand Engineering

NZ Eng — NZ [*New Zealand*] Engineering

NZ Eng News — New Zealand Engineering News

NZ Engng — New Zealand Engineering

NZ Ent — New Zealand Entomologist

NZ Entomol — New Zealand Entomologist

NZ Environ — New Zealand Environment

NZEP — New Zealand Economic Papers

NZ Fam Phys — New Zealand Family Physician

NZ Fam Physician — New Zealand Family Physician

NZ Farmer — New Zealand Farmer

NZ Fed Lab Bull — New Zealand. Federation of Labour. Bulletin

NZ Fert — New Zealand Fertiliser Journal

NZ Fert J — New Zealand Fertiliser Journal

NZ Financ Rev — New Zealand Financial Review

NZ Fin Rev — New Zealand Financial Review

NZ Fish Res Div Fish Res Bull — New Zealand Fisheries. Research Division. Fisheries Research Bulletin

NZFL — Naturwissenschaftliche Zeitschrift fuer Forst- und Landwirtschaft

NZfM — Neue Zeitschrift fuer Musik

NZ For Affairs R — New Zealand Foreign Affairs Review

NZ Foreign Aff Rev — New Zealand Foreign Affairs Review

NZ For Res Inst For Serv Mapp Ser 6 — New Zealand Forest Research Institute. Forest Service Mapping. Series 6

NZ For Res Notes — New Zealand Forestry Research Notes

NZ For Serv For Res Inst FRI Symp — New Zealand. Forest Service. Forest Research Institute. FRI Symposium

NZ For Serv For Res Inst Tech Pap — New Zealand. Forest Service. Forest Research Institute. Technical Paper

NZ For Serv Inf Ser — New Zealand. Forest Service. Information Series

NZ For Serv Rep Dir-Gen For — New Zealand. Forest Service. Report of the Director-General of Forests

NZ For Serv Rep For Res Inst — New Zealand. Forest Service. Report of the Forest Research Institute

NZ For Serv Res Leafl — New Zealand. Forest Service. Research Leaflet

NZ For Serv Tech Pap — New Zealand. Forest Service. Technical Paper

NZ Fruit and Prod — New Zealand Fruit and Product Journal

NZFSA — New Zealand Journal of Forestry Science

NZ Furn — New Zealand Furniture

NZ Gard — New Zealand Gardener

NZ Geneal — New Zealand Genealogist

NZ Geochem Group Newsl — New Zealand Geochemical Group. Newsletter

NZ Geogr — New Zealand Geographer

NZ Geol Surv Bull — New Zealand. Geological Survey. Bulletin

NZ Geol Surv Ind Miner Rocks — New Zealand. Geological Survey. Industrial Minerals and Rocks

NZ Geol Surv Misc Ser Map — New Zealand. Geological Survey. Miscellaneous Series. Map

NZ Geol Surv Rep — New Zealand. Geological Survey. Report

NZGG-A — New Zealand Geographer

NZ Grassl Assoc Proc Conf — New Zealand Grassland Association. Proceedings. Conference

NZ He — New Zealand Herald

NZ Herald — New Zealand Herald

NZ Heritage — New Zealand's Heritage

NZhi — Nauka i Zhizn'

NZ Hist Places — New Zealand Historic Places

NZ Home and Bu — New Zealand Home and Building

NZ Home and Bulld — New Zealand Home and Building

NZ Hosp — New Zealand Hospital

NZIE Proc Tech Groups — NZIE [*New Zealand Institution of Engineers*] Proceedings of Technical Groups

NZIE Trans Electr Mech Chem Eng Sect — NZIE (New Zealand Institution of Engineers) Transactions. Electrical/Mechanical/Chemical Engineering Section

NZ Inst Architects J — New Zealand Institute of Architects Journal

NZ Inst Eng Proc Tech Groups — New Zealand Institution of Engineers. Proceedings of Technical Groups

NZ Inst Eng Trans — New Zealand Institution of Engineers. Transactions

NZ Inst Turf Cult Greenkeep Res Comm Rep Greenkeep Res — New Zealand. Institute for Turf Culture. Greenkeeping Research Committee. Reporton Greenkeeping Research

NZ Inter — New Zealand Interface

NZ Int Rev — New Zealand International Review

NZIR — Niemeyers Zeitschrift fuer Internationales Recht

N Z I T — Transactions and Proceedings of the New Zealand Institute

NZIzmPI — Naukovi Zapyski Izmail's'koho Derzavnoho Pedahohicnoho Instytutu

NZ J Adult Learn — New Zealand Journal of Adult Learning

NZ J Agr — New Zealand Journal of Agriculture

NZ J Agric — New Zealand Journal of Agriculture

NZ J Agric Res — New Zealand Journal of Agricultural Research

NZJ Agri Res — New Zealand Journal of Agricultural Research

NZ J Agr Re — New Zealand Journal of Agricultural Research

NZ J Agr Res — New Zealand Journal of Agricultural Research

NZ J Archaeol — New Zealand Journal of Archaeology

NZJB — New Zealand Jewish Bulletin

NZ J Bot — New Zealand Journal of Botany

NZ J Bus — New Zealand Journal of Business

NZJC — New Zealand Jewish Chronicle

NZ J Crop H — New Zealand Journal of Crop and Horticultural Science

NZ J Crop Hortic Sci — New Zealand Journal of Crop and Horticultural Science

NZ J Dairy — New Zealand Journal of Dairy Science and Technology

NZ J Dairy Sci — New Zealand Journal of Dairy Science and Technology

NZJ Dairy Sci Technol — New Zealand Journal of Dairy Science and Technology

NZJ Dairy Technol — New Zealand Journal of Dairy Technology

NZ J Ecol — New Zealand Journal of Ecology

NZ J Educ — New Zealand Journal of Educational Studies

NZ J Educ Stud — New Zealand Journal of Educational Studies

NZ J Exp Agric — New Zealand Journal of Experimental Agriculture

NZ J Fam Plann — New Zealand Journal of Family Planning

NZ J For — New Zealand Journal of Forestry

NZ J For Sci — New Zealand Journal of Forestry Science

NZ J Fr Stud — New Zealand Journal of French Studies

NZ J Geogr — New Zealand Journal of Geography

NZ J Geol — New Zealand Journal of Geology and Geophysics

NZ J Geol Geophys — New Zealand Journal of Geology and Geophysics

NZ J Hist — New Zealand Journal of History

NZJHPER — New Zealand Journal of Health, Physical Education, and Recreation

NZ J Ind Relat — New Zealand Journal of Industrial Relations

NZ J Ind Relations — New Zealand Journal of Industrial Relations

NZ JI Agric — New Zealand Journal of Agriculture

NZ JI Agric Res — New Zealand Journal of Agricultural Research

NZ JI Bot — New Zealand Journal of Botany

NZ JI Sci — New Zealand Journal of Science

NZ JI Sci Technol — New Zealand Journal of Science and Technology

NZ JI Zool — New Zealand Journal of Zoology

NZ J Mar Freshwater Res — New Zealand Journal of Marine and Freshwater Research

NZ J Mar Freshw Res — New Zealand Journal of Marine and Freshwater Research

NZ J Mar Res — New Zealand Journal of Marine and Freshwater Research

NZ J Med Lab Technol — New Zealand Journal of Medical Laboratory Technology

NZ Jnl Bus — New Zealand Journal of Business

NZ Jnl D Sci — New Zealand Journal of Dairy Science and Technology

NZ J Phys Educ — New Zealand Journal of Health, Physical Education, and Recreation

NZ J Physiother — New Zealand Journal of Physiotherapy

NZ J Physiotherapy — New Zealand Journal of Physiotherapy

NZ J Pub Admin — New Zealand Journal of Public Administration

NZJ Publ Adm — New Zealand Journal of Public Administration

NZ J Public Admin — New Zealand Journal of Public Administration

NZJSAB — New Zealand Journal of Science

NZ J Sci — New Zealand Journal of Science

NZ J Sci Technol — New Zealand Journal of Science and Technology

NZ J Sci Technol Sect A — New Zealand Journal of Science and Technology. Section A

NZ J Sci Technol Sect B — New Zealand Journal of Science and Technology. Section B

NZ J Sports Med — New Zealand Journal of Sports Medicine

NZ J Technol — New Zealand Journal of Technology

NZ J Zool — New Zealand Journal of Zoology

NZKamPI — Naukovi Zapyski Kam'jancja-Polil's'koho Derzavnoho Pedahohicnoho Instytutu

NZKG — Neujahrsblatt. Zuercher Kunstgesellschaft

NZKievPIIn — Naucnye Zapyski Kievskogo Pedagogiceskogo Instytutu Inostrannych Jazykov

NZKyiPI — Naukovi Zapyski Kyjivs'koho Derzavnoho Pedahohicnoho Instytutu
NZ Law J — New Zealand Law Journal
NZ Law Soc N — New Zealand Law Society. Newsletter
NZ Lib — New Zealand Libraries
NZ Libr — New Zealand Libraries
NZ Lincoln Coll Tech Publ — New Zealand Lincoln College. Technical Publication
NZ List — New Zealand Listener
NZ Listener — New Zealand Listener
NZ L J — New Zealand Law Journal
NZLJMC — New Zealand Law Journal, Magistrates' Court Decisions
NZ Local Gov — New Zealand Local Government
NZ Loc Govt — New Zealand Local Government
NZM — Neue Zeitschrift fuer Missionswissenschaft
NZM — Neue Zeitschrift fuer Musik
NZ Mar Dep Fish Res Div Bull New Ser — New Zealand Marine Department. Fisheries Research Division. Bulletin. New Series
NZ Mar Dep Fish Tech Rep — New Zealand Marine Department. Fisheries Technical Report
NZ Mar Dep Rep — New Zealand Marine Department. Report
NZ Mar News — New Zealand Marine News
NZ Meat Prod — New Zealand Meat Producer
NZ Med J — New Zealand Medical Journal
NZ Med J Suppl — New Zealand Medical Journal. Supplement
NZ Min Ener Ann Rep — New Zealand. Ministry of Energy. Annual Report
NZ Minist Agric Fish Fish Tech Rep — New Zealand Ministry of Agriculture and Fisheries. Fisheries Technical Report
NZ Minist Agric Fish Rep Fish — New Zealand Ministry of Agriculture and Fisheries. Report on Fisheries
NZMiss — Neue Zeitschrift fuer Missionswissenschaft
NZMissWiss — Neue Zeitschrift fuer Missionswissenschaft
NZMJA — New Zealand Medical Journal
NZMS — Neue Zeitschrift fuer Missionswissenschaft. Supplement
NZMUKS — Naukovyj Zbirnik Museju Ukranjinskoji Kultury v Sydnyku
N Z Musik — Neue Zeitschrift fuer Musik
NZMW — Neue Zeitschrift fuer Missionswissenschaft
NZN — Niedersachsischer Zeitschriftennachweis
NZ Nat Conserv Counc Newsl — New Zealand. Nature Conservation Council. Newsletter
NZ Natl Radiat Lab Environ Radioact Annu Rep — New Zealand. National Radiation Laboratory. Environmental Radioactivity. AnnualReport
NZ Nat Sci — New Zealand Natural Sciences
NZNB — New Zealand National Bibliography
NZ News — New Zealand News
NZ News Rev — New Zealand News Review
NZNJ — New Zealand Numismatic Journal
NZ Num J — New Zealand Numismatic Journal
NZ Nurs Forum — New Zealand Nursing Forum
NZ Nurs J — New Zealand Nursing Journal
NZ Oceanogr Inst Collect Repr — New Zealand Oceanographic Institute. Collected Reprints
NZ Oceanogr Inst Mem — New Zealand Oceanographic Institute. Memoir
NZOI Misc Publ — NZOI [*New Zealand Oceanographic Institute*] Miscellaneous Publications
NZOI Oceanographic Field Report — New Zealand Oceanographic Institute. Oceanographic Field Report
NZOI Oceanogr Sum — NZOI [*New Zealand Oceanographic Institute*] Oceanographic Summary
NZOI Rec — NZOI [*New Zealand Oceanographic Institute*] Records
NZ Oper Res — New Zealand Operational Research
NZOR — New Zealand Operational Research
NZ Paint — New Zealand Painter and Decorator
NZPG — New Zealand Psychic Gazette
NZ Pharm — New Zealand Pharmacy
NZ Plumb — New Zealand Plumbers Journal
NZ Pop — New Zealand Population Review
NZ Pot — New Zealand Potato Bulletin
NZ Potter — New Zealand Potter
N Z Pp & Rp Mn — New Zealand. Papers and Reports Relating to Minerals and Mining
NZ Psychol — New Zealand Psychologist
NZ Purch — New Zealand Purchasing and Materials Management Journal

NZ Railw Obs — New Zealand Railway Observer
NZ Real — New Zealand Real Estate
NZ Sch Dent Ser Gaz — New Zealand School Dental Service. Gazette
NZ Sci Abstr — New Zealand Science Abstracts
NZ Sci Mater Conf Proc — New Zealand Science of Materials Conference. Proceedings
NZ Sci Rev — New Zealand Science Review
NZ Sci Teach — New Zealand Science Teacher
NZ Semin Trace Elem Health Proc — New Zealand Seminar on Trace Elements and Health. Proceedings
NZ Shadows — New Zealand Shadows
NZ Ship — New Zealand Shipping Gazette
NZSJ — New Zealand Slavonic Journal
NZ Slav J — New Zealand Slavonic Journal
NZ Soc Earthquake Eng Bull — New Zealand Society for Earthquake Engineering. Bulletin
NZ Soc Soil Sci Proc — New Zealand Society of Soil Science. Proceedings
NZ Soc Soil Sci Proc Conf — New Zealand Society of Soil Science. Proceedings. Conference
NZ Soil Bur Bibliogr Rep — New Zealand. Soil Bureau. Bibliographic Report
NZ Soil Bur Bull — New Zealand. Soil Bureau. Bulletin
NZ Soil Bur Sci Rep — New Zealand. Soil Bureau. Scientific Report
NZ Soil News — New Zealand Soil News
NZ Soil Surv Rep — New Zealand. Soil Survey Report
NZ Speech Therapist J — New Zealand Speech Therapists' Journal
NZ Speech Ther J — New Zealand Speech Therapists' Journal
NZ Speleol Bull — New Zealand Speleological Bulletin
NZST — Neue Zeitschrift fuer Systematische Theologie
NZSTh — Neue Zeitschrift fuer Systematische Theologie
NZSThR — Neue Zeitschrift fuer Systematische Theologie und Religionsphilosophie
NZ Summer Sch Laser Phys — New Zealand Summer School in Laser Physics
NZ Surv — New Zealand Surveyor
NZ Sys Th — Neue Zeitschrift fuer Systematische Theologie und Religionsphilosophie
NZ Syst T — Neue Zeitschrift fuer Systematische Theologie und Religionsgeschichte
NZSZ — Nationalzeitung und Soldatenzeitung
NZT — Neue Zurcher Zeitung und Schweizerisches Handelsblatt
NZTBA — New Zealand Journal of Science and Technology. Section B. General Research
NZTCA Jnl — NZTCA [*New Zealand Teachers' Colleges Association*] Journal
N Ztg — Nationale Zeitung
NZ Timb — New Zealand Timber Worker
NZ Timber J Wood Prod Rev — New Zealand Timber Journal and Wood Products Review
NZ Timb J — New Zealand Timber Journal
NZ Tob Grow J — New Zealand's Tobacco Growers' Journal
NZ Tour — New Zealand Tourism
NZ Tour Res — New Zealand Tourism Research Newsletter
NZu — Novyj Zurnal
NZU — Voedingsmiddelen Technologie
NZULR — New Zealand Universities Law Review
NZ U L Rev — New Zealand Universities Law Review
NZ Univ Law Rev — New Zealand Universities Law Review
NZ Univ LR — New Zealand Universities Law Review
NZ Univ L Rev — New Zealand Universities Law Review
NZ Univs Law R — New Zealand Universities Law Review
NZURA — Nauchnye Zapiski Gosudarstvennyi Nauchno-Issledovatel'skii i Proektnyi InstitutUgol'noi Promyshlennosti
NZV — Niederdeutsche Zeitschrift fuer Volkskunde
NZ Val — New Zealand Valuer
NZ Vet J — New Zealand Veterinary Journal
NZW — Neue Zeitschrift fuer Wehrrecht
NZ Weed Pest Control Conf Proc — New Zealand Weed and Pest Control Conference. Proceedings
NZ Wehrr — Neue Zeitschrift fuer Wehrrecht
NZ Wheat Rev — New Zealand Wheat Review
NZ Wings — New Zealand Wings
NZ Womans Wkly — New Zealand Woman's Weekly
NZZ — Neue Zuericher Zeitung
NZZ/SRWA — Swiss Review of World Affairs. Neue Zuericher Zeitung
NZZytPI — Naukovi Zapyski Zytomyrs'koho Derzavnoho Pedahohicnoho Instytutu

O

O — Observer
O — October
O — Oktjabr
O — Olissipo
O — Orbis
O — Organum
O — Osteuropa
OA — Oberbayerisches Archiv fuer Vaterlaendische Geschichte
OA — Oceanic Abstracts
OA — Oesterbotten: Aarsbok
OA — Opuscula Archaeologica
OA — Opuscula Atheniensia
OA — Oriens Academicus
OA — Oriens Antiquus
OA — Oriental Art
OA — Orientalisches Archiv
OA — Oroems Antiquus
OA — Os Acores
OAA — Oesterreichisches Bank-Archiv. Zeitschrift fuer das Gesamte Bankwesen und Sparkassenwesen, Borsenwesen, und Kreditwesen
OAA — Oeuvres Afro-Asiatiques
OA (Bud) — Oriens Antiquus (Budapest)
OAC — Ontario Appeal Cases
OAG — Official Airline Guide
OAG — Oil and Gas Journal
OAHQ — Ohio Archaeological and Historical Quarterly
OAI — Orient Ancien Illustre
OAK — Otcety Archeologiceskoj Komissii
Oakland Trib — Oakland Tribune
Oaklnd Bsn — Oakland Business Monthly
OAKR — Oesterreichisches Archiv fuer Kirchenrecht
Oak Rept — Oak Report. A Quarterly Journal on Music and Musicians
Oak Ridge Assoc Univ Inst Energy Anal Rep Proc ORAU/IEA — Oak Ridge Associated Universities. Institute for Energy Analysis. Report and Proceedings. ORAU/IEA
Oak Ridge Nat Lab Radiat Shielding Inf Cent Rep — Oak Ridge National Laboratory. Radiation Shielding Information Center. Report
Oak Ridge Natl Lab Conf Anal Chem Energy Technol — Oak Ridge National Laboratory Conference on Analytical Chemistry in Energy Technology
Oak Ridge Natl Lab Heavy Sect Steel Technol Program Tech Rep — Oak Ridge National Laboratory. Heavy Section Steel Technology Program. Technical Report
Oak Ridge Natl Lab Radiat Shielding Inf Cent Rep ORNL/RSIC US — Oak Ridge National Laboratory. Radiation Shielding Information Center. Report. ORNL/RSIC (United States)
Oak Ridge Natl Lab Rep — Oak Ridge National Laboratory. Report
Oak Ridge Natl Lab Rep ORNL FMP US — Oak Ridge National Laboratory. Report ORNL/FMP (United States)
Oak Ridge Natl Lab Rep ORNL TM (US) — Oak Ridge National Laboratory. Report. ORNL-TM (United States)
Oak Ridge Natl Lab Rep ORNL US — Oak Ridge National Laboratory. Report. ORNL (United States)
Oak Ridge Natl Lab Rev — Oak Ridge National Laboratory. Review
Oak Ridge Natl Lab Rev US — Oak Ridge National Laboratory Review (United States)
Oak Ridge Natl Lab Tech Rep ORNL FE — Oak Ridge National Laboratory. Technical Report. ORNL/FE
Oak Ridge Natl Lab (US) Phys Div Annu Prog Rep — Oak Ridge National Laboratory (United States). Physics Division. Annual Progress Report
Oak Ridge Oper Off Rep ORO — Oak Ridge Operations Office. Report ORO
OAL — Oriental Art (London)
OALS Bulletin — Office of Arid Lands Studies. Bulletin
OAM — OPEC [Organization of Petroleum Exporting Countries] Bulletin
OANAD — Online-ADL Nachrichten
O & G Jour — Oil and Gas Journal. Forecast/Review
O & N — Old and New
OAP — OAPEC [Organization of Arab Petroleum Exporting Countries] News Bulletin
OAPEC News Bull — OAPEC [Organization of Arab Petroleum Exporting Countries] News Bulletin
OAR — Ontario Appeals Report
OAr — Orientalisches Archiv
O Archaeol and H Qtly — Ohio Archaeological and Historical Quarterly
O Arch Q — Ohio Archaeological and Historical Quarterly
OARID — Oesterreichische Abwasser Rundschau. OAR International
OAR Int — OAR (Oesterreichische Abwasser-Rundschau) International

OAS — Oesterreich in Amerikanischer Sicht. Das Oesterreichbild im Amerikanischen Schulunterricht
Oasaycap Chron — Oasaycap Chronicle. Kansas Boys Industrial School
OasSt — Ostasiatische Studien
OAth — Opuscula Atheniensia
Oat Sci Technol — Oat Science and Technology
OAVG — Oberbayerisches Archiv fuer Vaterlaendische Geschichte
OAW PHKD — Denkschriften der Oesterreichischen Akademie der Wissenschaften. Philosophisch-Historische Klasse
OAW PHKS — Oesterreichische Akademie der Wissenschaften. Philosophisch-Historische Klasse.Sitzungsberichte
OAZ Oesterr Apoth Ztg — OAZ. Oesterreichische Apotheker-Zeitung
Ob — Obra
OB — Observer
OB — Official Bulletin. International Commission for Air Navigation
OB — Ord och Bild
OB — Orientalische Bibliographie
OB — Osvedomitel'nyj Bjulleten' Komissii Ekspedicionnych Issledovanij Akademii Nauk SSSR
OB — Out of Bounds
OBA — Oberbayerisches Archiv fuer Vaterlaendische Geschichte
O Bar — Ohio State Bar Association. Report
O Bay A — Oberbayerisches Archiv fuer Vaterlaendische Geschichte
Obd Vcelar Prekl — Obdorne Vcelarske Preklady
Obecna Chem Technol — Obecna Chemicka Technologie
Obedin Inst Yad Issled (Dubna USSR) Prepr — Ob'edinennyi Institut Yadernykh Issledovanii (Dubna, USSR). Preprint
Obedin Konf Gig Organ Zdravookhr Epidemiol Mikrobiol Infekts — Ob'edinennaya Konferentsiya Gigienostov, Organizatorov Zdravookhraneniya, Epidemiologov, Mikrobiologov, i Infektsionistov
Obedin Nauchn Chteniya Kosmonavt — Ob'edinennye Nauchnye Chteniya po Kosmonavtike
Obedin Sess Nauchno Issled Inst Zakavh Resp Stroit — Ob'edinennaya Sessiya Nauchno-Issledovatel'skikh Institutov Zakavkazskikh Respublik po Stroitel'stvu
Oberbayer Archv — Oberbayerisches Archiv
Oberbayer Archv Vaterlaend Gesch — Oberbayerisches Archiv fuer Vaterlaendische Geschichte
Oberdeutsche Allg Litteraturzeitung — Oberdeutsche Allgemeine Litteraturzeitung
Oberdeutsche Beytr Naturl Oekon — Oberdeutsche Beytraege zur Naturlehre und Oekonomie
Oberflaechentech/Metallprax — Oberflaechentechnik/Metallpraxis
Oberflaechen Werkst — Oberflaechen Werkstoffe
Oberflaeche Surf — Oberflaeche Surface
Oberhess Naturwiss Z — Oberhessische Naturwissenschaftliche Zeitschrift
Oberlin Coll Mus Bull — Oberlin College. Allen Memorial Art Museum. Bulletin
Oberoesterreich Heimatbl — Oberoesterreichische Heimatblaetter
Oberoesterreich Kultz — Oberoesterreich Kulturzeitschrift
Oberoest H Bl — Oberoesterreichische Heimatblaetter
Oberoest Imker — Oberoesterreichische Imker
Oberrhein Geol Abh — Oberrheinische Geologische Abhandlungen
Oberrheinische Geol Abh — Oberrheinische Geologische Abhandlungen
Oberrhein Kst — Oberrheinische Kunst
Obesity & Bariatric Med — Obesity and Bariatric Medicine
Obes Res — Obesity Research
OBGNA — Obstetrics and Gynecology
Ob Gr — Ostbairische Grenzmarken
OBGV — Oxford Book of Greek Verse
Ob Gyn — Obstetrics and Gynecology
OB Hi-Tension News — Ohio Brass Hi-Tension News
OBI — Film
OBIMD — Oncodevelopmental Biology and Medicine
Obit — Obiter
Obit — Obituary
OBJ — Oklahoma Bar Association. Journal
Obj Monde — Objets et Monde
Obl — Obliques
OBL — Orientalia et Biblica Lovaniensia
Ob LGS — Entscheidungen des Obersten Bayerischen Landesgerichts in Strafsachen
Ob LGZ — Entscheidungen des Obersten Bayerischen Landesgerichts in Zivilsachen
OBMR — Occasional Bulletin of Missionary Research
OBMRL — Occasional Bulletin. Missionary Resarch Library
Obogashch Briket Koksovanie Uglya — Obogashchenie, Briketirovanie, i Koksovanie Uglya
Obogashch Briket Uglei — Obogashchenie i Briketirovanie Uglei

Obogashch Briket Uglya — Obogashchenie i Briketirovanie Uglya
Obogashchenie Briket Uglei — Obogashchenie i Briketirovanie Uglei
Obogashch Ispolz Uglya — Obogashchenie i Ispol'zovanie Uglya
Obogashch Nemet Polezn Iskop — Obogashchenie Nemetallicheskikh Poleznykh Iskopaemykh
Obogashch Polezn Iskop — Obogashchenie Poleznykh Iskopaemykh
Obogashch Rud — Obogashchenie Rud
Obogashch Rud Chern Met — Obogashchenie Rud Chernykh Metallov
Obogashch Rud (Irkutsk) — Obogashchenie Rud (Irkutsk)
Obogashch Rud (Leningrad) — Obogashchenie Rud (Leningrad)
OBOS — Our Bodies Ourselves
Oboz Psikhiat Nevrol I Reflek — Obozrenie Psikhiatrii, Nevrologii, i Refleksologii
OBP — Organizational Behavior and Human Performance
OBR — Overseas Business Reports
Obrab Interpret Fiz Eksp — Obrabotka i Interpretatsiya Fizicheskikh Eksperimentov
Obrab Metal Davleniem Mashinostr — Obrabotka Metallov Davleniem v Mashinostroenii
Obrab Met Davleniem Mashinostr — Obrabotka Metallov Davleniem v Mashinostroenii
Obrab Met Davleniem Moscow — Obrabotka Metallov Davleniem (Moscow)
Obrab Met Davleniem (Rostov-On-Don) — Obrabotka Metallov Davleniem (Rostov-On-Don)
Obrab Met Davleniem Sverdlovsk — Obrabotka Metallov Davleniem (Sverdlovsk)
Obreens Archf Ned Kstgech — Obreen's Archief voor Nederlandsche Kunstgeschiedenis
Obrh Past Bl — Oberrheinisches Pastoralblatt
Obrobka Plast — Obrobka Plastyczna
Obrob Plast — Obrobka Plastyczna
Obs — Observatory. A Monthly Review of Astronomy
Obs — Observer
Obs — Obsidian
Obs Astronom Univ Nac La Plata Ser Astronom — Observatorio Astronomico de la Universidad Nacional de La Plata. Serie Astronomica
Obsc Nauki Moskva — Obscestvennye Nauki (Moskva)
Obsc Nauki v Uzbek — Obscestvennye Nauki v Uzbekistane
Obsc N Uzbek — Obscestvennye Nauki v Uzbekistane
Observ Bot Descript Pl Nov Herb Van Heurckiani — Observationes Botanicae et Descriptiones Plantarum Novarum Herbarii Van Heurckiani/Recueil d'Observations Botaniques et de Descriptions de Plantes Nouvelles
Observ Econ Finan Rio — Observador Economico e Financiero (Rio de Janeiro)
Observer Des Brief — Observer Design Brief
Observ Fis — Observationes Sobre la Fisica, Historia Natural, y Artes Utiles
Observ Phys — Observations Sur La Physique, Sur l'Histoire Naturelle et Sur Les Arts
Obs Handb Can — Observer's Handbook. Royal Astronomical Society of Canada
Obshcha Sravn Patol — Obshcha i Sravnitelna Patologiya
Obshch At Yad Spets Yad Prakt — Obshchie Atomnyi, Yadernyi, i Spetsial'nyi Yadernyi Praktikumy
Obshch Ekol Biotsenol Gidrobiol — Obshchaya Ekologiya, Biotsenologiya, Gidrobiologiya
Obshch Energ — Obshchaya Energetika
Obshchest Nauk Uzbek — Obshchestvennye Nauki v Uzbekistane
Obshchestv Pitan — Obshchestvennoe Pitanie
Obshch Geol — Obshchaya Geologiya
Obshch Mashinostr — Obshchee Mashinostroenie
Obshch Prikl Khim — Obshchaya i Prikladnaya Khimiya
Obshch Probl Fiz Khim Biol Itogi Nauki Tekh — Obshchie Problemy Fiziko-Khimicheskoi Biologii. Itogi Nauki i Tekhnik
Obshch Probl Mashinostr Tr Mosk Konf Molodykh Uch — Obshchie Problemy Mashinostroeniya, Trudy Moskovskoi Konferentsii Molodykh Uchenykh
Obshch Vopr Fiziol Mekh Tr Mezhdunar Simp Tekh Biol Probl Up — Obshchie Voprosy Fiziologicheskikh Mekhanizmov, Analiz, i Modelirovanie Biologicheskikh Sistem. Trudy Mezhdunarodnogo Simpoziuma po Tekhnicheskim i Biologicheskim Problemam Upravleniya
Obshch Zakonomern Morfog Regener — Obshchie Zakonomernosti Morfogeneza i Regeneratsii
Obshta Sravnitelna Patol — Obshta i Sravnitelna Patologiia
Obshta Sravn Patol — Obshta i Sravnitelna Patologiya
OBSP — Oxford Bibliographical Society. Proceedings
OBSP — Oxford Bibliographical Society. Publications
Obs sur Phys — Observations sur la Physique, sur l'Histoire Naturelle, et sur les Arts
Obs Tests Cosmol Inflation — Observational Tests of Cosmological Inflation
Obstet Ginecol — Obstetrica si Ginecologia
Obstet Ginecol (Buchar) — Obstetrica si Ginecologia (Bucharest)
Obstet Ginecol Lat-Am — Obstetricia y Ginecologia Latino-Americanas
Obstet Gyn — Obstetrics and Gynecology
Obstet Gynec — Obstetrics and Gynecology
Obstet Gynecol — Obstetrics and Gynecology
Obstet Gynecol Amsterdam — Obstetrics and Gynecology (Amsterdam)
Obstet Gynecol Annu — Obstetrics and Gynecology. Annual
Obstet Gynecol Clin North Am — Obstetrics and Gynecology Clinics of North America
Obstet Gynecol Moscow — Obstetrics and Gynecology (Moscow)
Obstet Gynecol NY — Obstetrics and Gynecology (New York)
Obstet Gynecol Surv — Obstetrical and Gynecological Survey
Obstet Gynecol Ther — Obstetrical and Gynecological Therapy
Obstet Gynecol Ther (Osaka) — Obstetrical and Gynecological Therapy (Osaka)
Obstet Gynecol (Tokyo) — Obstetrics and Gynecology (Tokyo)
Obstet Gynecol Surv — Obstetrical and Gynecological Survey
Obst Gemuese Verwert Ind — Obst- und Gemuese-Verwertungs Industrie
Obst Gynec — Obstetrics and Gynecology
Obst Gynec Surv — Obstetrical and Gynecological Survey
Obst J Gr Brit — Obstetrical Journal of Great Britain and Ireland
OBSUA — Oberflaeche Surface

OBU — Ombudsman. Tijdschrift voor Klachtrecht Tegen Overheidsoptreden
OBW — Journal fuer Betriebswirtschaft
Obz At Energ — Obzory po Atomnoi Energii
Obz Dokl Vses Soveshch Mikroelem — Obzornykh Dokladov Vsesoyuznogo Soveshchaniya po Mikroelementam
Obz Elektron Tekh — Obzory po Elektronnoi Tekhnike
Obz Inf Okhr Zashch Lesa — Obzornaya Informatsiya. Okhrana i Zashchita Lesa
Obz Inf Poligr Promst — Obzornaya Informatsiya, Poligraficheskaya Promyshlennost
Obz Inf Ser Okhr Okruzh Sredy Ratsion Ispolz Prir Resur — Obzornaya Informatsiya. Seriya. Okhrana Okruzhayushchei Sredy i Ratsional'noe Ispol'zovanie Prirodnykh Resursov
Obz Mat Fiz — Obzornik za Matematiko in Fiziko
Obzor Bot Dejateln Rossii — Obzor Botaniceskoj Dejatel'nosti v Rossii
Obzornik Mat Fiz — Obzornik za Matematiko in Fiziko
Obzor Prehist — Obzor Praehistoricky Revue Prehistorique
Obz Otd Proizvod Khim Promsti — Obzory po Otdel'nym Proizvodstvam Khimicheskoi Promyshlennosti
Obz Teplofiz Svoistvam Veshchestv — Obzory po Teplofizicheskim Svoistvam Veshchestv
Obz Veng Lesovod Nauki — Obzor Vengerskoi Lesovodstvennoi Nauki
Obz Vysokotemp Sverkhprovodimosti — Obzory po Vysokotemperaturnoi Sverkhprovodimosti
Oc — Occidente
Oc — Oceania
OC — Old Cornwall
OC — Open Court
OC — Opera Canada
OC — Oracle Series. National Museums of Canada and Department of Indian and NorthernAffairs
OC — Oriens Christianus
OC — Orientalia Christiana Analecta
OCA — O'Casey Annual
OCA — Orientalia Christiana Analecta
OCACD — Oceanologica Acta
O Cath D — Official Catholic Directory
OcBul — Occasional Bulletin of Missionary Research
Occ — Occident
Occ — Occidental
OCC — Open Court (Chicago)
Occas Contr Libr Univ Kentucky Lexington — Occasional Contributions. Library (University of Kentucky, Lexington)
Occasional Publ in Math — Occasional Publications in Mathematics
Occas Newsl Lindsay Club — Occasional Newsletter. Lindsay Club
Occas Notes Hongkong Hort Soc — Occasional Notes. Hongkong Horticultural Society
Occas Pap Aging — Occasional Papers on Aging
Occas Pap Am Soc Reform Res — Occasional Papers. American Society for Reformation Research
Occas Pap Ant Gr Vases Getty Mus — Occasional Papers in Antiquities. Greek Vases in the J. Paul Getty Museum
Occas Pap Anthropol — Occasional Papers in Anthropology
Occas Pap BC Prov Mus — Occasional Papers. British Columbia Provincial Museum
Occas Pap Bell Mus Nat Hist Univ Minn — Occasional Papers. Bell Museum of Natural History. University of Minnesota
Occas Pap Bernice Pauahi Bishop Mus — Occasional Papers. Bernice Pauahi Bishop Museum
Occas Pap Boston Soc Nat Hist — Occasional Papers. Boston Society of Natural History
Occas Pap Br Mus — Occasional Paper. British Museum
Occas Pap Buffalo Soc Nat Sci — Occasional Papers. Buffalo Society of Natural Sciences
Occas Pap Calif Acad Sci — Occasional Papers. California Academy of Sciences
Occas Pap C C Adams Cent Ecol Stud West Mich Univ — Occasional Papers. C. C. Adams Center for Ecological Studies. Western Michigan University
Occas Pap Dep Biochem Makerere Univ — Occasional Paper. Department of Biochemistry. Makerere University
Occas Pap Dep Biol Univ Puget Sound — Occasional Papers. Department of Biology. University of Puget Sound
Occas Pap Div Syst Biol Stanford Univ — Occasional Papers. Division of Systematic Biology. Stanford University
Occas Pap Entomol (Sacramento) — Occasional Papers in Entomology (Sacramento)
Occas Pap Environ Can — Occasional Paper. Environment Canada
Occas Pap Fairchild Trop Gard — Occasional Paper. Fairchild Tropical Garden
Occas Pap Farlow Herb Cryptogam Bot Harv Univ — Occasional Papers. Farlow Herbarium of Cryptogamic Botany. Harvard University
Occas Pap Fla State Collect Arthropods — Occasional Papers. Florida State Collection of Arthropods
Occas Pap Geol Surv (New Hebrides) — Occasional Paper. Geological Survey (New Hebrides)
Occas Pap Ind Rel — Occasional Papers in Industrial Relations
Occas Pap Inst Min Metall — Occasional Papers. Institution of Mining and Metallurgy
Occas Pap Jam Geol Surv Dep — Occasional Paper. Jamaica. Geological Survey Department
Occas Pap Lab Gov Chem GB — Occasional Paper. Laboratory. Government Chemist (Great Britain)
Occas Pap Makerere Univ Dep Geogr — Occasional Paper. Makerere University. Department of Geography
Occas Pap Mauritius Sugar Ind Res Inst — Occasional Paper. Mauritius Sugar Industry Research Institute
Occas Pap Minn Mus Nat Hist — Occasional Papers. Minnesota Museum of Natural History

Occas Pap Mo Acad Sci — Occasional Paper. Missouri Academy of Science

Occas Pap Mollusks Mus Comp Zool Harv Univ — Occasional Papers on Mollusks. Museum of Comparative Zoology. Harvard University

Occas Pap Mus Nat Hist Univ Kans — Occasional Papers. Museum of Natural History. University of Kansas

Occas Pap Mus Nat Hist Univ Minnesota — Occasional Papers. Museum of Natural History. University of Minnesota

Occas Pap Mus Nat Hist Univ Puget Sound — Occasional Papers. Museum of Natural History. University of Puget Sound

Occas Pap Mus Victoria — Occasional Papers. Museum of Victoria

Occas Pap Mus Zool LA State Univ — Occasional Papers. Museum of Zoology. Louisiana State University

Occas Pap Mus Zool Univ Mich — Occasional Papers. Museum of Zoology. University of Michigan

Occas Pap Nanyang Univ Coll Grad Stud Inst Nat Sci — Occasional Paper. Nanyang University. College of Graduate Studies. Institute of Natural Sciences

Occas Pap Nat Hist Soc New Brunswick — Occasional Papers. Natural History Society of New Brunswick

Occas Pap Natl Coll Agric Eng — Occasional Paper. National College of Agricultural Engineering

Occas Pap Natl Mus Monum Rhod Ser B Nat Sci — Occasional Papers. National Museums and Monuments of Rhodesia. Series B. Natural Sciences

Occas Pap Natl Mus Rhod Ser B — Occasional Papers. National Museums of Rhodesia. Series B. Natural Sciences

Occas Pap Natl Mus South Rhod Ser B — Occasional Papers. National Museum of Southern Rhodesia. Series B. Natural Sciences

Occas Pap Natl Speleol Soc — Occasional Papers. National Speleological Society

Occas Pap N Mus S Rhodesia — Occasional Papers. National Museum South Rhodesia

Occas Pap Ont Minist Nat Resour — Occasional Paper. Ontario. Ministry of Natural Resources

Occas Pap Rancho Santa Ana Bot Gard — Occasional Papers. Rancho Santa Ana Botanical Garden

Occas Pap R Coll Gen Pract — Occasional Paper. Royal College of General Practitioners

Occas Pap Rhodes Livingstone Mus — Occasional Papers of the Rhodes-Livingstone Museum

Occas Pap R Ont Mus Zool — Occasional Papers. Royal Ontario Museum of Zoology

Occas Pap San Diego Soc Nat Hist — Occasional Papers. San Diego Society of Natural History

Occas Pap Ser Aust Water Resour Counc — Occasional Papers Series. Australian Water Resources Council

Occas Pap S Forest Exp Sta US Forest Serv — Occasional Papers. Southern Forest Experiment Station. United States Forest Service

Occas Pap Technol Pitt Rivers Mus Univ Oxford — Occasional Papers on Technology. Pitt Rivers Museum. University of Oxford

Occas Pap Trop Sci Cent (San Jose Costa Rica) — Occasional Paper. Tropical Science Center (San Jose, Costa Rica)

Occas Pap Univ Arkansas Mus — Occasional Papers. University of Arkansas Museum

Occas Pap Univ Hawaii — Occasional Papers. University of Hawaii

Occas Pap Veg Surv West Aust — Occasional Papers. Vegetation Survey of Western Australia. Department of Agriculture

Occas Pap World Fertil Surv — Occasional Papers. World Fertility Survey

Occas Publ Br Soc Anim Prod — Occasional Publication. British Society of Animal Production

Occas Publ Cl St — Occasional Publications in Classical Studies

Occas Publ Inst Health Adm GA State Univ — Occasional Publications. Institute of Health Administration. Georgia State University

Occas Publ Rowett Res Inst — Occasional Publication. Rowett Research Institute

Occas Publ Univ Alaska Inst Mar Sci — Occasional Publication. University of Alaska. Institute of Marine Science

Occas Rep VA Div For Dep Conserv Econ Dev — Occasional Report. Virginia Division of Forestry. Department of Conservation and Economic Development

Occas Rev — Occasional Review

Occas Ser Univ Manitoba Dep Agric Econ Farm Manage — Occasional Series. University of Manitoba. Department of Agricultural Economics and Farm Management

Occas Symp Br Grassl Soc — Occasional Symposium. British Grassland Society

Occ Bul Miss R — Occasional Bulletin of Missionary Research

Occ Hazards — Occupational Hazards

Occ Heal ANZ — Occupational Health Australia and New Zealand

Occ Health & Sfty — Occupational Health and Safety

Occ Health Nurs — Occupational Health Nursing

Occid — Occidente

Occident Entomol — Occidental Entomologist

Occ N — Occasional Notes, Canada Law Times

Occ Outlook Q — Occupational Outlook Quarterly

Occ Pap Bur For (Philippines) — Occasional Paper. Bureau of Forestry (Manila, Philippines)

Occ Pap Bur Trans Eco — Occasional Paper. Department of Transport (Bureau of Transport Economics)

Occ Pap Calif Acad Sci — Occasional Papers. California Academy of Sciences

Occ Pap Dep Biol Univ Guyana — Occasional Papers. Department of Biology. University of Guyana

Occ Pap Geol Surv Nig — Occasional Papers. Geological Survey of Nigeria

Occ Pap Geol Surv Ug — Occasional Papers. Geological Survey of Uganda

Occ Pap Maurit Sug Ind Res Inst — Occasional Paper. Mauritius Sugar Industry Research Institute

Occ Pap R Anthrop Inst — Occasional Papers. Royal Anthropological Institute

Occ Pap Vegn Surv West Aust — Occasional Paper. Vegetation Survey of Western Australia

Occ Publs Aust Conserv Fdn — Occasional Publications. Australian Conservation Foundation

Occ Publ Sci Hort — Occasional Publications on Scientific Horticulture

Occult Nodal Metastasis Solid Carcinomata Int Symp Cell Oncol — Occult Nodal Metastasis in Solid Carcinomata. International Symposium on Cellular Oncology

Occupational Outlook Q — Occupational Outlook Quarterly

Occup Dermatoses — Occupational Dermatoses

Occup Environ Dermatoses — Occupational and Environmental Dermatoses

Occup Environ Med — Occupational and Environmental Medicine

Occup Hazards — Occupational Hazards

Occup Health — Occupational Health

Occup Health and Saf — Occupational Health and Safety

Occup Health Bull (Ottawa) — Occupational Health Bulletin (Ottawa)

Occup Health Chem Ind Proc Int Congr — Occupational Health in the Chemical Industry. Proceedings. International Congress on Occupational Health in the Chemical Industry

Occup Health J Tokyo — Occupational Health Journal (Tokyo)

Occup Health (Lond) — Occupational Health (London)

Occup Health Nurs — Occupational Health Nursing

Occup Health Nurs (NY) — Occupational Health Nursing (New York)

Occup Health Rev — Occupational Health Review

Occup Health Saf — Occupational Health and Safety

Occup Hlth — Occupational Health

Occup Hlth Nurs — Occupational Health Nursing

Occup Hlth Rev — Occupational Health Review

Occup Hyg — Occupational Hygiene

Occup Hyg Monogr — Occupational Hygiene Monograph

Occup Hzrd — Occupational Hazards

Occup Med — Occupational Medicine

Occup Med Oxf — Occupational Medicine (Oxford)

Occup Med State of the Art Rev — Occupational Medicine. State of the Art Reviews

Occup Ment Health Notes — Occupational Mental Health Notes

Occup Outl Q — Occupational Outlook Quarterly

Occup Psych — Occupational Psychology

Occup Psychol — Occupational Psychology

Occup Saf Health — Occupational Safety and Health

Occup Saf Health Abstr — Occupational Safety and Health Abstracts

Occup Saf Health Ser Int Labour Off — Occupational Safety and Health Series. International Labour Office

Occup Saf Hlth — Occupational Safety and Health

Occup Saf Hlth Admin Sub Service Vols 1 & 4 — Occupational Safety and Health Administration. Subscription Service. Volumes 1 and 4

Occup Therapy — Occupational Therapy and Rehabilitation

Occup Ther Health Care — Occupational Therapy in Health Care

Occup Ther J Res — Occupational Therapy Journal of Research

Occup Ther Ment Health — Occupational Therapy in Mental Health

OCD — Office of Child Development. Publications

OCD — Oxford Classical Dictionary

Oc Dev and Int L — Ocean Development and International Law

OceanAb — Oceanic Abstracts

Ocean Abstr — Oceanic Abstracts

Ocean Abstr Indexes — Oceanic Abstracts with Indexes

Ocean & Shoreline Manage — Ocean and Shoreline Management

Ocean Coastal Manage — Ocean and Coastal Management

Ocean Dev & Int L — Ocean Development and International Law

Ocean Dev and Intl LJ — Ocean Development and International Law Journal

Ocean Devel & Int L — Ocean Development and International Law

Ocean Develop Int Law — Ocean Development and International Law

Ocean Development and Internat Law — Ocean Development and International Law

Ocean Dev I — Ocean Development and International Law

Ocean Drill Program Proc Initial Rep — Ocean Drilling Program. Proceedings. Initial Report

Ocean Drill Program Proc Sci Results — Ocean Drilling Program. Proceedings. Scientific Results

Ocean Dumping Rep Can Dep Fish Oceans — Ocean Dumping Report (Canada. Department of Fisheries and Oceans)

Ocean Energy Annu Conf Mar Technol Soc — Ocean Energy. Annual Conference. Marine Technology Society

Ocean Eng — Ocean Engineering

Ocean Eng Inf Ser — Ocean Engineering. Information Series

Ocean Engng — Ocean Engineering

Ocean Engrg — Ocean Engineering

Ocean Ind — Ocean Industry

Ocean Ling — Oceanic Linguistics

Ocean Manage — Ocean Management

Ocean Mgt — Ocean Management

Oceanogr Abstr Bibliogr — Oceanographic Abstracts and Bibliography

Oceanogr Cruise Rep Indones Natl Inst Oceanol — Oceanographical Cruise Report (Indonesia. National Institute of Oceanology)

Oceanogr Cruise Rep Inst Mar Res (Djakarta) — Oceanographical Cruise Report. Institute of Marine Research (Djakarta)

Oceanogrl Cruise Rep Div Fish Oceanogr CSIRO — Oceanographical Cruise Report. Division of Fisheries and Oceanography. Commonwealth Scientific and Industrial Research Organisation

Oceanogrl Stn List Div Fish Oceanogr CSIRO — Oceanographical Station List. Division of Fisheries and Oceanography. Commonwealth Scientific and Industrial Research Organisation

Oceanogr Mag — Oceanographical Magazine

Oceanogr Mag (Tokyo) — Oceanographical Magazine (Tokyo)

Oceanogr Mar Biol — Oceanography and Marine Biology

Oceanogr Mar Biol Annu Rev — Oceanography and Marine Biology: An Annual Review

Oceanogr Res Inst (Durban) Invest Rep — Oceanographic Research Institute (Durban). Investigational Report

Oceanogr Soc Jap J — Oceanographical Society of Japan. Journal
Oceanogr Trop — Oceanographie Tropicale
Oceanol — Oceanology
Oceanol Acta — Oceanologica Acta
Oceanol Int — Oceanology International
Oceanol Limnol Sin — Oceanologica et Limnologia Sinica
Oceanol Limn Sin — Oceanologia et Limnologia Sinica
Oceanolog Stud — Oceanological Studies
Oceanol Res — Oceanological Researches
Ocean Res (Seoul) — Ocean Research (Seoul)
Ocean Sci Eng — Ocean Science and Engineering
Oceans Mag — Oceans Magazine
Ocean St B — Ocean State Business
Ocean Therm Energy Convers Conf Proc — Ocean Thermal Energy Conversion Conference. Proceedings
Ocean Yearb — Ocean Yearbook
Ocerki Izuc Jakutsk Kraja — Ocerki po Izuceniju Jakutskogo Kraja
O Ch A — Orientalia Christiana Analecta
Ochanomizu Med J — Ochanomizu Medical Journal
Ocherki Fiz-Khim Petrol — Ocherki Fiziko-Khimicheskoi Petrologii
Ocherki Geol Sov Karpat — Ocherki po Geologii Sovetskikh Karpat
Ocherki Istor Estestvoznan Tekhn — Ocherki Istorii Estestvoznaniya i Tekhniki
Ocherki Istor Estestvozn Tekh — Ocherki po Istorii Estestvoznaniya i Tekhniki
Ochistka Povtorn Ispol'z Stochnykh Vod Urale — Ochistka i Povtornoe Ispol'zovanie Stochnykh Vod na Urale
Ochistka Vodn Vozdushn Basseinov Predpr Chern Metall — Ochistka Vodnogo i Vozdushnogo Basseinov na Predpriyatiyakh Chernoi Metallurgii
O Ch P — Orientalia Christiana Periodica
O Chr — One in Christ
O Chr — Oriens Christianus
Ochr Koroz — Ochrona Przed Korozja
Ochr Ovzdusi — Ochrana Ovzdusi. Supplement to Vodni Hospodarstvi. Rada B
OChrP — Orientalia Christiana Periodica
Ochr Powietrza — Ochrona Powietrza
Ochr Powietrza Probl Odpadow — Ochrona Powietrza i Problemy Odpadow
Ochr Pr — Ochrona Pracy
Ochr Prir — Ochrana Prirody
Ochr Przeciwpozarowa Przem Chem — Ochrona Przeciwpozarowa w Przemysle Chemicznym
Ochr Przed Koroz — Ochrona Przed Korozja
Ochr Przyr — Ochrona Przyrody
Ochr Rosl — Ochrona Roslin
Ochr Rostl — Ochrana Rostlin
OCHZA — Oesterreichische Chemiker-Zeitung
OCI — Ocean Industry. Engineering, Construction, and Operations
OcL — Oceanic Linguistics
OCL — Orthodox Christian Library
Oc M — Oceania Monographs
OCM — Ocean Management
OCM — On Communications
OCMA — Occasional Contributions from the Museum of Anthropology. University of Michigan
OCMAA — Oceanographical Magazine
OCMEA — Occupational Medicine
OcMZ — Oesterreichische Musikzeitschrift
OCNA — Ouvrages sur la Culture Nord-Africaine
OCOC — Oceans of Canada
O Con D — Official Congressional Directory
O C Oppervelaktetech Corrosiebestrijd — O&C. Oppervelaktetechnieken en Corrosiebestrijding
OCP — O Comercio do Porto
OCP — Ohio CPA [*Certified Public Accountant*] Journal
OCP — Orientalia Christiana Periodica
Oc P Anth P — Occasional Papers in Anthropology. Pennsylvania State University
Oc P Dev-A — Occasional Papers. Centre for Developing-Area Studies
Oc P Econ H — Occasional Papers in Economic and Social History
Oc P Geog — Occasional Papers in Geography
Oc P Int Af — Occasional Papers in International Affairs
OCPM — Oxford Classical and Philosophical Monographs
OCPPIB — Orientalia. Commentarii Periodici Pontificii Instituti Biblici
Oc P Rur De — Occasional Papers. Rural Development Committee
OCR — Ordini e Congregazioni Religiose
OC Register — Orange County Register
Ocrotirea Nat — Ocrotirea Naturii
Ocrotirea Nat Med Inconjurator — Ocrotirea Naturii si a Mediului Inconjurator
Ocrot Nat — Ocrotierea Naturii
OCS — Oxford and Cambridge Series
OCSAPB — Outer Continental Shelf. Environmental Assessment Program. Arctic Project Bulletin
OCSAPSB — Outer Continental Shelf. Environmental Assessment Program. Arctic Project Special Bulletin
OCSB — Outer Continental Shelf. Environmental Assessment Program. Bering Sea - Gulf of Alaska Newsletter
OCSSB9 — Specialist Periodical Reports. Organic Compounds of Sulphur, Selenium, and Tellurium
Octagon Pap — Octagon Papers
O C Tijdschr Oppervlaktetech Corrosiebestrijd — O&C. Tijdschrift voor Oppervlaktetechnicken en Corrosiebestrijding
Octagon Math Mag — Octagon Mathematical Magazine
Ocul Immunol Inflamm — Ocular Immunology and Inflammation
Ocul Ther Complications Manage — Ocular Therapy. Complications and Management
OCW — Old Cars Weekly
Od — Odrodzenie
OD — Opus Dei

ODCC — Oxford Dictionary of the Christian Church
ODC Plan Rep — ODC [*Oahu Development Conference*] Planning Reports
Odessky Med J — Odessky Meditsinsky Jurnal
ODGKA — Oita Daigaku Gakugeigakubu Kenkyu Kiyo. Shizenkagaku
ODI (Overseas Development Inst) R — ODI (Overseas Development Institute). Review
ODI R — ODI (Overseas Development Institute) Review [*London*]
ODIZA — Osaka Daigaku Igaku Zasshi
Odjel Teh Nauka — Odjeljenje Tehnickih Nauka
ODM — Ostdeutsche Monatshefte
OdNtw — Ostdeutscher Naturwart
ODOKA — Okayama Daigaku Onsen Kenkyusho Hokoku
ODONA — Odontoiatria
Odont Am — Odontologia de America
Odont Arg — Odontologia Argentina
Odonto Est Port — Odontoestomatologia Portuguesa
Odontoiatr Epith — Odontoiatrike Epitheoresis
Odontoiatr Prat — Odontoiatria Pratica
Odontoiatr Rev Iberoam Med Boca — Odontoiatria. Revista Ibero-Americana de Medicina de la Boca
Odontol — Odontologie
Odontol Atual — Odontologia Atual
Odontol Bull — Odontological Bulletin
Odontol Capixaba — Odontologia Capixaba
Odontol Chil — Odontologia Chilena
Odontol Conserv — Odontologie Conservatrice
Odontol Din — Odontologia Dinamica
Odontol Foren Tidskr — Odontologiska Foreningens Tidskrift
Odontol Mbl — Odontologisches Monatsblatt
Odontol (Mexico) — Odontologia (Mexico)
Odontol Mod — Odontologo Moderno
Odontol Peru — Odontologia Peruana
Odontol Pr — Odontologia Practica
Odontol Revy — Odontologisk Revy
Odontol Samf Finl Arsb — Odontologiska Samfundft i Finland Arsbok
Odontol Stomatol — Odontologiya i Stomatologiya
Odontol Tidskr — Odontologisk Tidskrift
Odontol Ts — Odontologisk Tidskrift
Odontol Urug — Odontologia Uruguaya
Odontopr — Odontoprotesi
Odontostomatol Implantoprotesi — Odontostomatologia e Implantoprotesi
Odontostomatol Prog — Odontostomatological Progress
Odontostomatol Proodos — Odontostomatologike Proodos
Odonto-Stomatol Trop — Odonto-Stomatologie Tropicale
ODOPA — Publications. Dominion Observatory (Ottawa)
Odor Control Assoc J — Odor Control Association. Journal
Odor Res — Odor Research
ODS — Ordbog over det Danske Sprog
Odu U Ife J Afr Stud — Odu. University of Ife Journal of African Studies
ODW — Ostdeutsche Wissenschaft
Od Wiss — Ostdeutsche Wissenschaft
O Dwyer New — O'Dwyer's Newsletter
Ody — Odyssey
Odyssey — Odyssey Review
ODZVK — Oberdeutsche Zeitschrift fuer Volkskunde
OE — Office of Education. Publications
OE — Onze Eeuw
OE — Operation Enterprise Newsletter
OE — Oriens Extremus
OE — Oriental Economist
OE — Osteuropa
OE — Overseas Education
OEA Communique — Office Education Association. Communique
Oe A f KR — Oesterreichisches Archiv fuer Kirchenrecht
Oe Al Kairo — Untersuchungen der Zweigstelle Kairo des Oesterreichischen Archaeologischen Institutes
Oe A Kr — Oesterreichisches Archiv fuer Kirchenrecht
OEA News — United States Department of Commerce. News. Office of Economic Affairs
Oe AW — Oesterreichische Akademie der Wissenschaften
OeB — Oesterreichische Bibliographie
OEB — Orientalische und Exegetische Bibliothek
OeBFZ Ph Th — Oekumenische Beihefte zur Freiburger Zeitschrift fuer Philosophie und Theologie
Oe BL — Oesterreichisches Biographisches Lexikon
OEBMAL — Organizacion de los Estados Americanos. Programa Regional de Desarrollo Cientifico y Tecnologico. Serie de Biologia. Monografia
OeBotZ — Oesterreichische Botanische Zeitschrift
Oe Bot Zs — Oesterreichische Botanische Zeitschrift
Oe BZ — Oesterreichische Botanische Zeitschrift
OEC — OECD [*Organization for Economic Cooperation and Development*] Economic Outlook
Oec — Oecumenica
OeC — Oestliche Christentum
OeC — Oeuvres et Critiques
OEC — Oriental Economist
OECD Ber Dtsch Landwirtsch Ges Prufungsabt Landmasch — OCED Bericht-Deutsche Landwirtschafts-Gesellschaft Prufungsabteilung fuer Landmaschinen
OECD Inform — OECD [*Organization for Economic Cooperation and Development*] InformaticsStudies
OECD Newsl Booksellers — OECD [*Organization for Economic Cooperation and Development*] Newsletter to Booksellers
OECD Observer — OECD [*Organization for Economic Cooperation and Development*] Observer

OECD Outlk — OECD [*Organization for Economic Cooperation and Development*] Economic Outlook

OECD Svys — Organization for Economic Cooperation and Development. Economic Surveys of Member Countries

Oe Ch Zg — Oesterreichische Chemiker-Zeitung

Oecol Plant — Oecologia Plantarum

Oecon Ann — Oeconomiske Annaler

Oecon Phys Abh — Oeconomisch-Physikalische Abhandlungen

Oecon Polon — Oeconomica Polona

Oecon Polona — Oeconomica Polona

Oeco Planta — Oecologia Plantarum

OECT — Oxford Early Christian Texts

OECT — Oxford Editions of Cuneiform Texts

Oecum — Oecumenica

OED — Oxford English Dictionary

OEDS — Oxford English Dictionary Supplement

OEeu — Onze Eeuw. Maandschrift voor Staatkunde, Letteren

OEF — Management Totaal

Oeff Anz — Oeffentlicher Anzeiger fuer das Vereinigte Wirtschaftsgebiet

Oeffentl Verwalt — Oeffentliche Verwaltung

Oeff GD — Oeffentliche Gesundheitsdienst

Oeff Gesundheitsdienst — Oeffentliche Gesundheitsdienst

Oeff Gesundheitswes — Oeffentliche Gesundheitswesen

Oeff Jahrestag Arbeitsgem Verstaerkte Kunstst Vorabdruck — Oeffentliche Jahrestagung der Arbeitsgemeinschaft Verstaerkte Kunststoffe. Vorabdruck

Oefftl Sicherht — Oeffentliche Sicherheit

Oeff Verw — Oeffentliche Verwaltung

Oeff Verwalt — Oeffentliche Verwaltung

Oe FH — Oesterreichs Forst- und Holzwirtschaft

Oefvers Fin Vetensk Soc Foerh — Oefversigt af Finska Vetenskaps-Societetens Foerhandlingar

Oefvers Foerh Finska Vetensk Soc — Oefversigt af Foerhandlingar. Finska Vetenskaps-Societeten

OEFZS (Oesterr Forschungszent Seibersdorf) Ber — OEFZS (Oesterreichisches Forschungszentrum Seibersdorf) Berichte

OEGWA — Oeffentliche Gesundheitswesen

Oehlenschlaeger Stud — Oehlenschlaeger Studier

Oe Jh — Jahreshefte. Oesterreichisches Archaeologische Institut in Wien

Oe Jh Beibl — Jahreshefte. Oesterreichisches Archaeologische Institut. Beiblatt

OeJhh — Jahreshefte des Oesterreichischen Archaeologischen Institutes in Wien

OeKB — Oesterreichisches Klerusblatt

OeKC — Die Oekuminischen Konzile der Christenheit

OEKOA — Oel und Kohle

Oekol Umwelttech — Oekologie/Umwelttechnik

Oekol Wirkungskataster Baden Wuerttemb — Oekologisches Wirkungskataster Baden-Wuerttemberg

Oekon Bot Gart J — Oekonomisch-Botanisches Garten-Journal

Oekon Brennst — Oekonomie des Brennstoffes

Oekon Neuigk Verh — Oekonomische Neuigkeiten und Verhandlungen

Oekonom Unternehmensforsch — Oekonometrie und Unternehmensforschung

Oekosystemanal Umweltforsch — Oekosystemanalyse und Umweltforschung

Oek S — Oekumenische Studien

Oel & Gas Feuerungstech — Oel und Gas und Feuerungstechnik

Oel Fett Ind — Oel-und Fett-Industrie

Oelfeuer Tech — Oelfeuer Technik

Oel Gasfeuer — Oel + Gasfeuerung

Oelhydraul Pneum — Oelhydraulik und Pneumatik

OEM — Oxford English Monographs

OEMA — Obras Escohidas de Machado de Assis

OeMCSR — Oesterreichische Monatsschrift fuer Christliche Socialreform

OeMSch — Oesterreichische Mittelschule

OEMZ — Oesterreichische Musikzeitschrift

OEN — Old English Newsletter

OEN — Oxford English Novels

OEO — OECD [*Organization for Economio Cooperation and Development*] Observer

OeO — OEuvres et Opinions

OEP — OEP. Office Equipment and Products

OEP — Osaka Economic Papers

OEP — Oxford Economic Papers

Oerlikon Schweissmitt — Oerlikon Schweissmitteilungen

OES — Oxford English Studies

Oest Bank-Arch — Oesterreichisches Bank-Archiv

Oest Bot Z — Oesterreichische Botanische Zeitschrift

Oester Anwalts Zeit — Oester Anwalts-Zeitung

Oester Anwaltsztg — Oesterreichische Anwalts-Zeitung

Oesterbottnisk Arsb — Oesterbottnisk Arsbok

Oester Mittelschule — Oesterreichische Mittelschule

Oesterr Abwasser Rundsch — Oesterreichische Abwasser Rundschau

Oesterr Aerzteztg — Oesterreichische Aerztezeitung

Oesterr Akad Wiss Erdwissenschaftliche Komm Schriftenr — Oesterreichische Akademie der Wissenschaften. Erdwissenschaftliche Kommission Schriftenreihe

Oesterr Akad Wiss Math Naturwiss Kl Anz — Oesterreichische Akademie der Wissenschaften. Mathematisch-Naturwissenschaftliche Klasse. Anzeiger

Oesterr Akad Wiss Math Naturwiss Kl Denkschr — Oesterreichische Akademie der Wissenschaften. Mathematisch-Naturwissenschaftliche Klasse. Denkschriften

Oesterr Akad Wiss Math Naturwiss Kl Sitzungsber — Oesterreichische Akademie der Wissenschaften. Mathematisch-Naturwissenschaftliche Klasse. Sitzungsberichte

Oesterr Akad Wiss Math-Naturwiss Kl Sitzungsber Abt 1 — Oesterreichische Akademie der Wissenschaften. Mathematisch-Naturwissenschaftliche Klasse. Sitzungsberichte. Abteilung 1. Biologie, Mineralogie, Erdkunde, und Verwandte Wissenschaften

Oesterr Akad Wiss Math Naturwiss Kl Sitzungsber Abt 1 Biol — Oesterreichische Akademie der Wissenschaften. Mathematisch-Naturwissenschaftliche Klasse. Sitzungsberichte. Abteilung 1. Biologie, Mineralogie, Erdkunde und Verwandte Wissenschaften

Oesterr Akad Wiss Math-Naturwiss Kl Sitzungsber Abt 2 — Oesterreichische Akademie der Wissenschaften. Mathematisch-Naturwissenschaftliche Klasse. Sitzungsberichte. Abteilung 2. Mathematik, Astronomie, Physik, Meteorologie, und Technik

Oesterr Akad Wiss Math Naturwiss Kl Sitzungsber Abt 2A — Oesterreichische Akademie der Wissenschaften. Mathematisch-Naturwissenschaftliche Klasse. Sitzungsberichte. Abteilung 2A. Mathematik, Astronomie, Physik, Meteorologie, und Technik

Oesterr Akad Wiss Math Naturwiss Kl Sitzungsber Abt 2B — Oesterreichische Akademie der Wissenschaften. Mathematisch-Naturwissenschaftliche Klasse. Sitzungsberichte. Abteilung 2B. Chemie

Oesterr Akad Wiss Philos-Hist Kl — Oesterreichische Akademie der Wissenschaften. Philosophisch-Historische Klasse

Oesterr Apoth Ztg — Oesterreichische Apotheker Zeitung

Oesterr Apoth Ztg Beil — Oesterreichische Apotheker-Zeitung. Beilage

Oesterr Archaeol Inst Jahresh — Jahreshefte des Oesterreichischen Archaeologischen Institutes in Wien

Oesterr Arch Gesch — Oesterreichisches Archiv fuer Geschichte, Erdbeschreibung, Staatenkunde, Kunst und Literatur

Oesterr Arch Kirchenrecht — Oesterreichisches Archiv fuer Kirchenrecht

Oesterr Bot Wochenbl — Oesterreichisches Botanisches Wochenblatt. Gemeinnuetziges Organ fuer Botanik

Oesterr Bot Z — Oesterreichische Botanische Zeitschrift

Oesterr Brau Hopfenztg — Oesterreichische Brauer-und Hopfenzeitung

Oesterr Chem-Z — Oesterreichische Chemie-Zeitschrift

Oesterr Chem-Ztg — Oesterreichische Chemiker-Zeitung

Oesterreich Akad Wiss Anz Philos Hist Kl — Oesterreichische Akademie der Wissenschaften. Anzeiger der Philosophisch-Historischen Klasse

Oesterreich Akad Wiss Math-Natur Kl Denkschr — Oesterreichische Akademie der Wissenschaften. Mathematisch-Naturwissenschaftliche Klasse. Denkschriften

Oesterreich Akad Wiss Math-Natur Kl S-B 2 — Oesterreichische Akademie der Wissenschaften. Mathematisch-Naturwissenschaftliche Klasse. Sitzungsberichte. Abteilung 2. Mathematik, Astronomie, Physik, Meteorologie, und Technik

Oesterreich Akad Wiss Math-Natur Kl Sitzungsber 2 — Oesterreichische Akademie der Wissenschaften. Mathematisch-Naturwissenschaftliche Klasse. Sitzungsberichte. Abteilung 2. Mathematik, Astronomie, Physik, Meteorologie, und Technik

Oesterreich Akad Wiss Math Naturwiss Kl Denkschr — Oesterreichische Akademie der Wissenschaften. Mathematisch-Naturwissenschaftliche Klasse. Denkschriften

Oesterreich Akad Wiss Math-Naturwiss Kl SB 2 — Oesterreichische Akademie der Wissenschaften. Mathematisch-Naturwissenschaftliche Klasse. Sitzungsberichte. Abteilung 2. Mathematik, Astronomie, Physik, Meteorologie, und Technik

Oesterreich Aquarel — Oesterreichische Aquarellisten

Oesterreich Archaeol Inst Grab — Oesterreichisches Archaeologisches Institut. Grabungen

Oesterreich Bau & Werkkst — Oesterreichische Bau- und Werkkunst

Oesterreich Blasm — Oesterreichische Blasmusik

Oesterreich Geogr Ges Mitt — Oesterreichische Geographische Gesellschaft. Mitteilungen

Oesterreich Gesch & Lit — Oesterreich in Geschichte und Literatur

Oesterreich Gesch Quellen — Oesterreichische Geschichts-Quellen

Oesterreich Geschwiss Gegenwart Selbstdarstell — Oesterreichische Geschichtswissenschaft der Gegenwart in Selbstdarstellungen

Oesterreichische Zs Berg- u Huettenw — Oesterreichische Zeitschrift fuer Berg- und Huettenwesen

Oesterreich Kstb — Oesterreichische Kunstbuecher

Oesterreich Kstdkml — Oesterreichische Kunstdenkmaler

Oesterreich Kstmonographie — Oesterreichische Kunstmonographie

Oesterreich Ksttop — Oesterreichische Kunsttopographie

Oesterreich Osthft — Oesterreichische Osthefte

Oesterreich Rundschau — Oesterreichische Rundschau. Deutsche Kultur und Politik

Oesterreich Ung Kstchron — Oesterreichisch-Ungarische Kunstchronik

Oesterreich Ung Rev — Oesterreichisch-Ungarische Revue. Monatsschrift fuer die Gesamten Kulturinteressen Oesterreich-Ungarns

Oesterreich Z Dkmlpf — Oesterreichische Zeitschrift fuer Denkmalpflege

Oesterreich Z Kst & Dkmlpf — Oesterreichische Zeitschrift fuer Kunst und Denkmalpflege

Oesterreich Z Vlksknd — Oesterreichische Zeitschrift fuer Volkskunde

Oesterr Forschungszent Seibersdorf Ber OEFZS — Oesterreichisches Forschungszentrum Seibersdorf. Berichte OEFZS

Oesterr Forst-Holzwirtsch — Oesterreichs Forst- und Holzwirtschaft

Oesterr Forstzeitung — Oesterreichische Forstzeitung

Oesterr Gel Anz Vienna — Oesterreichische Gelehrte Anzeigen (Vienna)

Oesterr Geol Ges Mitt — Oesterreichische Geologische Gesellschaft. Mitteilungen

Oesterr Gesch Lit — Oesterreich in Geschichte und Literatur

Oesterr Glaserztg — Oesterreichische Glaserzeitung

Oesterr Ing & Archit Z — Oesterreichische Ingenieur und Architekten. Zeitschrift

Oesterr Ing Arch — Oesterreichisches Ingenieur Archiv

Oesterr Ing-Z — Oesterreichische Ingenieur-Zeitschrift

Oesterr Jb Polit — Oesterreichisches Jahrbuch fuer Politik

Oesterr Jb Soziol — Oesterreichische Jahrbuch fuer Soziologie

OesterrJh — Jahreshefte des Oesterreichischen Archaeologischen Instituts

Oesterr Krankenpflegez — Oesterreichische Krankenpflegezeitschrift

Oesterr Kunstst Rundsch — Oesterreichische Kunststoff-Rundschau

Oesterr Kunstst-Z — Oesterreichische Kunststoff-Zeitschrift

Oesterr Landtech — Oesterreichische Landtechnik

Oesterr Leder Haeutewirtsch — Oesterreichische Leder und Haeuterwirtschaft

Oesterr Leder Ztg — Oesterreichische Leder-Zeitung
Oesterr Mh — Oesterreichische Monatshefte
Oesterr Milchwirtsch — Oesterreichische Milchwirtschaft
Oesterr Milchwirtsch Ztg — Oesterreichische Milchwirtschaftliche Zeitung
Oesterr Milit Z — Oesterreichische Militaerische Zeitschrift
Oesterr Mineral Ges Mitt — Oesterreichische Mineralogische Gesellschaft. Mitteilungen
Oesterr Molk Ztg — Oesterreichische Molkerei Zeitung
Oesterr Monatsschr Forstwesen — Oesterreichische Monatsschrift fuer Forstwesen
Oesterr Moorz — Oesterreichische Moorzeitschrift
Oesterr Osth — Oesterreichische Osthefte
Oesterr Papier — Oesterreichische Papier
Oesterr Papier-Ztg — Oesterreichische Papier-Zeitung
Oesterr Pap Ztg — Oesterreichische Papier-Zeitung
Oesterr Patentbl — Oesterreichisches Patentblatt
Oesterr Schwesternztg — Oesterreichische Schwesternzeitung
Oesterr Seifenfachbl — Oesterreichisches Seifenfachblatt
Oesterr Spirit Ztg — Oesterreichische Spirituosen Zeitung
Oesterr Studienges Atomenerg — Oesterreichische Studiengesellschaft fuer Atomenergie
Oesterr Studienges Atomenerg Ber — Oesterreichische Studiengesellschaft fuer Atomenergie. Berichte
Oesterr Studienges Atomenerg SGAE — Oesterreichische Studiengesellschaft fuer Atomenergie. SGAE
Oesterr Textilz — Oesterreichische Textilzeitschrift
Oesterr Tierarzt — Oesterreichische Tieraerzt
Oesterr Tierarzte Ztg — Oesterreichische Tieraerzte-Zeitung
Oesterr Ung Z Zuckerind Landwirtsch — Oesterreichisch-Ungarische Zeitschrift fuer Zuckerindustrie und Landwirtschaft
Oesterr Verwalt Arch — Oesterreichisches Verwaltungsarchiv
Oesterr Vierteljahresschr Forstwes — Oesterreichische Vierteljahresschrift fuer Forstwesen
Oesterr Vierteljahrschr Forstwesen — Oesterreichische Vierteljahrschrift fuer Forstwesen
Oesterr Vrtljschr Wissensch Veterinaerk — Oesterreichische Vierteljahresschrift fuer Wissenschaftliche Veterinaerkunde
Oesterr Wasser Abfallwirtsch — Oesterreichische Wasser- und Abfallwirtschaft
Oesterr Wasserwirtsch — Oesterreichische Wasserwirtschaft
Oesterr Weidwerk — Oesterreichische Weidwerk
Oesterr Wollen Leinen Ind — Oesterreichs Wollen- und Leinen-Industrie
Oesterr Zahnaerzteztg — Oesterreichische Zahnaerzte-Zeitung
Oesterr Zahnprothet — Oesterreichische Zahnprothetik
Oesterr Zahntech — Oesterreichische Zahntechniker
Oesterr Zahntech Handw — Oesterreichische Zahntechniker Handwerk
Oesterr Zahntechnik — Oesterreichische Zahntechniker
Oesterr Z Aussenpolit — Oesterreichische Zeitschrift fuer Aussenpolitik
Oesterr Z Berg Huettenwes — Oesterreichische Zeitschrift fuer Berg- und Huettenwesen
Oesterr Zeits Volksk — Oesterreichische Zeitschrift fuer Volkskunde
Oesterr Z Elektrizitaetswirtsch — Oesterreichische Zeitschrift fuer Elektrizitaetswirtschaft
Oesterr Z Erforsch Bekaempf Krebskr — Oesterreichische Zeitschrift fuer Erforschung und Bekaempfung der Krebskrankheit
Oesterr Z Erforsch Bekaempf Krebskrankh — Oesterreichische Zeitschrift fuer Erforschung und Bekaempfung der Krebskrankheit
Oesterr Z Erforsch Bekaempf Krebskrankheit — Oesterreichische Zeitschrift fuer Erforschung und Bekaempfung der Krebskrankheit
Oesterr Z Kinderheilkd Kinderfuersorge — Oesterreichische Zeitschrift fuer Kinderheilkunde und Kinderfuersorge
Oesterr Z Oeff Recht — Oesterreichische Zeitschrift fuer Oeffentliches Recht
Oesterr Z Onkol — Oesterreichische Zeitschrift fuer Onkologie
Oesterr Zool Z — Oesterreichische Zoologische Zeitschrift
Oesterr Z Pilzk — Oesterreichische Zeitschrift fuer Pilzkunde
Oesterr Z Polit -Wiss — Oesterreichische Zeitschrift fuer Politikwissenschaft
Oesterr Z Stomatol — Oesterreichische Zeitschrift fuer Stomatologie
Oesterr Ztschr Kinderh — Oesterreichische Zeitschrift fuer Kinderheilkunde
Oesterr Z Volkskd — Oesterreichische Zeitschrift fuer Volkskunde
Oester Tuberkfuersbl — Oesterreichisches Tuberkulose-Fuersorgeblatt
Oester Ung Zs Zuckerind — Oesterreich-Ungarische Zeitschrift fuer Zuckerindustrie und Landwirtschaft
Oester Z Pol — Oesterreichische Zeitschrift fuer Politikwissenschaft
Oester Zs Bergw — Oesterreichische Zeitschrift fuer Berg- und Huettenwesen
Oest Forschinst Wirt und Pol Ber — Oesterreichisches Forschungsinstitut fuer Wirtschaft und Politik. Berichte und Informationen
Oest Forschungsinst Sparkassenwesen VJ-Schriftenreihe — Oesterreichisches Forschungsinstitut fuer Sparkassenwesen Viertel Jahres-Schriftenreihe
Oest Ges Statis und Informatik Mitteilungsbl — Oesterreichische Gesellschaft fuer Statistik und Informatik. Mitteilungsblatt
Oest Imker — Oesterreichische Imker
Oest Imkerkal — Oester Imkerkalender
Oest Jahresh — Jahreshefte des Oesterreichischen Archaeologischen Institutes in Wien
Oest Jahrh — Jahreshefte des Oesterreichischen Archaeologischen Institutes in Wien
Oest Mhefte — Oesterreichische Monatshefte
Oest Osthefte — Oesterreichische Osthefte
Oestr Wschr — Oesterreichische Wochenschrift fuer Wissenschaft, Kunst, und Oeffentliches Leben. Beilage zur K. Wiener Zeitung
Oestr Z Brgw — Oesterreichische Zeitschrift fuer Berg- und Huettenwesen
Oest T Ae Zt — Oesterreichische Tieraerzte-Zeitung
Oest Volkswirt — Oesterreichische Volkswirt
Oest Wasserw — Oesterreichische Wasserwirtschaft
Oest Z Aussenpol — Oesterreichische Zeitschrift fuer Aussenpolitik
Oest Z Oe R — Oesterreichische Zeitschrift fuer Oeffentliches Recht

Oest Zool Z — Oesterreichische Zoologische Zeitschrift
Oest Z Politikwiss — Oesterreichische Zeitschrift fuer Politikwissenschaft
Oest Zs Kinderhk — Oesterreichische Zeitschrift fuer Kinderheilkunde und Kinderfuersorge
Oest Zs Verm W — Oesterreichische Zeitschrift fuer Vermessungswesen
Oest Zs Volkskd — Oesterreichische Zeitschrift fuer Volkskunde
Oest Zs Zahn Hlkd — Oesterreichische Zeitschrift fuer Zahnheilkunde
OET — Oxford English Texts
OeTbcFBI — Oesterreichisches Tuberkulose-Fuersorgeblatt
O et C — Oeuvres et Critiques
OeTV Mag — OeTV [*Oeffentliche Dienste. Transport und Verkehr*] Magazin
OEu — OEuvre
OEUNAH — Econometrics and Operations Research
Oeuvre Crit — Oeuvres et Critiques
Oe V — Oeffentliche Verwaltung
OEV — Oesterreichische Volkswirt
OEV — Onder Eigen Vaandel
Oe VD — Oeffentliche Verwaltung und Datenverarbeitung
Oe VE — Oe VE. Oesterreichische Vorschriften fuer die Elektrotechnik
Oevers Fin Vetensk Soc Foerh — Oeversigt af Finska Vetenskaps-Societetens Foerhandlingar
OeVKT — Oesterreichische Vierteljahresschrift fuer Katholische Theologie
OEW — Osteuropa Wirtschaft
OeZB — Oesterreichische Zeitschrift fuer Bibliothekswesen
OeZDP — Oesterreichische Zeitschrift fuer Denkmalpflege
Oe ZE — Oesterreichische Zeitschrift fuer Elektrizitaetswirtschaft
Oe Z E Oesterr Z Elek — Oe Z E/Oesterreichische Zeitschrift fuer Elektrizitaetswirtschaft
Oe Z f Oe R — Oesterreichische Zeitschrift fuer Oeffentliches Recht
Oe ZKD — Oesterreichische Zeitschrift fuer Kunst und Denkmalpflege
OeZKV — Oesterreichische Zeitschrift fuer Volkskunde
Oe Z Oeff R — Oesterreichische Zeitschrift fuer Oeffentliches Recht
Oe Z Oe R — Oesterreichische Zeitschrift fuer Oeffentliches Recht
Oe ZV — Oesterreichische Zeitschrift fuer Volkskunde
OeZVKB — Oesterreichische Zeitschrift fuer Volkskunde. Buchreihe
OF — Offshore Oil International [*Formerly, Offshore Oil Weekly*]
OF — Oil Forum
OF — Olympische Forschungen
OF — Orate Fratres
OF — Orphicorum Fragmenta
OFA — Old Farmer's Almanac
OFB — Oregon Folklore Bulletin
OFC — Offshore Research Focus
OFCA — Offshore Canada. Supplement of Offshore Oil Weekly
OFCCP Fed Cont Compl Man CCH — OFCCP [*Office of Federal Contract Compliance Programs*] Federal Contract Compliance Manual. Commerce Clearing House
OFE — Oxford Economic Papers
OFEN — Offshore Engineer. Incorporating Northern Offshore
OFEND — Offshore Engineer
OFEW — Organ fuer die Fortschritte des Eisenbahnwesens
Off — Office
Off — Officiantbladet
OFF — Offshore Engineer
Offa Ber Mitt — Offa Berichte und Mitteilungen des Museums Vorgeschichtlicher Altertuemer in Kiel
Off Act Plast Caoutch — Officiel des Activites des Plastiques et du Caoutchouc
Off Adm Autom — Office Administration and Automation
Off Air Programs Publ APTD Ser US — Office of Air Programs Publication. APTD Series (United States)
Off Air Programs (US) Publ AP Ser — Office of Air Programs (United States). Publication. AP Series
Off Amer Horseman — Official American Horseman
Off Archit Plann — Official Architecture and Planning
Off Bull Am Soc Hosp Pharm — Official Bulletin. American Society of Hospital Pharmacists
Off Commun Int Soc Soil Sci — Official Communications. International Society of Soil Sciences
Off Dig Fed Paint Varn Prod Clubs — Official Digest. Federation of Paint and Varnish Production Clubs
Off Dig Fed Soc Paint Technol — Official Digest. Federation of Societies for Paint Technology
Offene Briefe Gartenbau — Offene Briefe fuer Gartenbau, Land- und Forstwirtschaft
Off Eng — Offshore Engineer
Offenlegungsschrift Fed Repub Ger — Offenlegungsschrift (Federal Republic of Germany)
Off Gaz — Official Gazette
Off Gaz Pat Off — Official Gazette. United States Patent Office
Off Gaz US Pat Off — Official Gazette. United States Patent Office
Off Gaz US Pat Off Pat — Official Gazette. United States Patent Office. Patents
Off Gaz US Pat Trademark Off Pat — Official Gazette. United States Patent and Trademark Office. Patents
Off Gaz US Pat Trademks Off Pat — Official Gazette. United States Patent and Trademark Office. Patents
Off Gaz US Pat Trademks Off Trademks — Official Gazette. United States Patent and Trademark Office. Trademarks
Off Gesundheitswes — Oeffentliche Gesundheitswesen
Offic Board Markets — Official Board Markets
Office A & A — Office Administration and Automation
Office Adm & Automation — Office Administration and Automation
Office Admin — Office Administration
Office Archit Plann — Official Architecture and Planning
Office Eqp — Office Equipment and Products
Office Exec — Office Executive

Office Int Epizoot Bull — Office International des Epizooties. Bulletin
Office Mgt — Office Management
Office Nat Etud Rech Aerosp (Fr) Publ — Office National d'Etudes et de Recherches Aerospatiales (France). Publication
Office Natl Etud Rech Aerosp Rep — Office National d'Etudes et de Recherches Aerospatiales. Reports
Office Sys — Office Systems
Office Tech People — Office: Technology and People
Offic Gaz US — Official Gazette. United States Patent and Trademark Office
Official Gazette USPO — United States. Patent Office. Official Gazette
Official J Ind Comm Prop — Official Journal of Industrial and Commercial Property
Offic J (Pat) (Gr Brit) — Official Journal (Patents) (Great Britain)
Off Int Epizoot Bull — Office International des Epizooties. Bulletin
Off Int Vigne Vin Bull — Office International de la Vigne et du Vin. Bulletin
Off J Dent Assoc S Afr — Official Journal. Dental Association of South Africa
Off J Eur Communities — Official Journal of the European Communities
Off J Eur Communities Inf Not — Official Journal of the European Communities. Information and Notices. English Edition
Off J Eur Communities Legis — Official Journal of the European Communities. Legislation
Off J Inst Art Educ — Official Journal. Institute of Art Education
Off J Int Assoc Artif Prolongation Hum Specific Lifespan — Official Journal. International Association on the Artificial Prolongation of the Human Specific Lifespan
Off J Jpn Rheum Assoc — Official Journal. Japan Rheumatism Association
Off J Jpn Soc Pediatr Neurol — Official Journal. Japanese Society of Pediatric Neurology
Off Jl (Pat) — Official Journal (Patents)
Off J (Pat) — Official Journal (Patents)
Off J (Pat)(UK) — Official Journal (Patents) (United Kingdom)
Off J Res Inst Med Sci Korea — Official Journal. Research Institute of Medical Science of Korea
Off Kstsamml Basel Jber — Offentliche Kunstsammlung Basel. Jahresbericht
Off Mach Guide — Office Machine Guide
Off Manage — Office Management
Off Meth Mach — Office Methods and Machines
Off Metieres Plast — Officiel des Matieres Plastiques
Off Mitt Int Bodenkd Ges — Offizielle Mitteilungen der Internationalen Bodenkundlichen Gesellschaft
Off Nat Etud Rech Aeronaut Note Tech — Office National d'Etudes et de Recherches Aeronautiques. Note Technique
Off Nat Etud Rech Aeronaut Publ — Office National d'Etudes et de Recherches Aeronautiques. Publication
Off Nat Etud Rech Aerosp (Fr) Note Tech — Office National d'Etudes et de Recherches Aerospatiales (France). Note Technique
Off Natl Etud Rech Aeronaut Diverse Fr — Office National d'Etudes et de Recherches Aeronautiques. Diverse (France)
Off Natl Etud Rech Aeronaut Rapp Tech (Fr) — Office National d'Etudes et de Recherches Aeronautiques. Rapport Technique (France)
Off Natl Etud Rech Aerosp (Fr) Publ — Office National d'Etudes et de Recherches Aerospatiales (France). Publication
Off Natl Etud Rech Aerosp (Fr) Tire Part — Office National d'Etudes et de Recherches Aerospatiales (France). Tire a Part
Off Nav Res (US) Res Rev — Office of Naval Research (United States). Research Review
Off Organ Soc Clin Bacteriol — Official Organ. Society of Clinical Bacteriology
Off Patrol — Offshore Patrol
Off Plast Caout — Officiel des Plastiques et du Caoutchouc
Off Plast Caoutch — Officiel des Plastiques et du Caoutchouc
Off Print Ink Maker — Official Printing Ink Maker
Off Proc Amer Ass Feed Micros — Official Proceedings. American Association of Feed Microscopists
Off Proc Annu Conf Int Dist Heat Assoc — Official Proceedings. Annual Conference. International District Heating Association
Off Proc Annu Meet Am Assoc Feed Microsc — Official Proceedings. Annual Meeting. American Association of Feed Microscopists
Off Proc Annu Meet Int Dist Heat Assoc — Official Proceedings. Annual Meeting. International District Heating Association
Off Proc Annu Meet Livest Conserv Inst — Official Proceedings. Annual Meeting. Livestock Conservation Institute
Off Proc Annu Meet Master Boiler Makers Assoc — Official Proceedings. Annual Meeting. Master Boiler Makers' Association
Off Proc Int Water Conf — Official Proceedings. International Water Conference
Off Proc Natl Dist Heat Assoc — Official Proceedings. National District Heating Association
Off Proc Natl Ginseng Conf — Official Proceedings. National Ginseng Conference
Off Proc Veg Grow Assoc Am — Official Proceedings. Vegetable Growers Association of America
Off Protok Ital Grosschmiedetag — Offizielle Protokolle der Italienischen Grosschmiedetagung
Off Publ Assoc Am Fert Control Off — Official Publication. Association of American Fertilizer Control Officials
Off Publ Assoc Am Plant Food Control Off — Official Publication. Association of American Plant Food Control Officials
Off Rech Sci Tech Outre-Mer Trav Doc ORSTOM — Office de la Recherche Scientifique et Technique d'Outre-Mer. Travaux et Documents de l'ORSTOM
Off Rec WHO — Official Records. World Health Organization
Offshore Abstr — Offshore Abstracts
Offshore Eng — Offshore Engineer
Offshore Engr — Offshore Engineer
Offshore Rep — Offshore Report
Offshore Res Focus — Offshore Research Focus
Offshore Serv — Offshore Services
Offshore Serv Technol — Offshore Services and Technology
Offshore Technol Conf Proc — Offshore Technology Conference. Proceedings

Off Tech Serv (US) AD — Office of Technical Services (US). AD
Off Tech Serv US PB Rep — Office of Technical Services (US). PB Report
Off Yrbk Cwealth Aust — Official Yearbook of the Commonwealth of Australia
Off Yrbk NSW — Official Yearbook of New South Wales
Off Yrbk Queensland — Official Yearbook of Queensland
Off Yrbk WA — Official Yearbook of Western Australia
OFIV — Our Family. Ilavut. Family Newspaper. Diocese of the Arctic
OFKSA — Osaka Furitsu Kogyo Shoreikan Hokoku
OFKYDA — Proceedings. Osaka Prefecture Institute of Public Health. Edition of Pharmaceutical Affairs
OFS — Office Systems
OFS — Offshore. The Journal of Ocean Business
OFSR — Offshore Resources
OFSVA — Offshore Services
Oftalmol Zh — Oftal'mologicheskii Zhurnal
OFZHA — Oftal'mologicheskii Zhurnal
OG — Official Gazette. United States Patent and Trademark Office
OG — Oriental Geographer
OG — Orientalia Gandensia
OG — Ostbairische Grenzmarken. Institut fuer Ostbairische Heimatforschung
OGA — Oesterreichische Gastgewerbe und Hotel Zeitung
OGD — Oriental Geographer (Dacca)
OGE — Ons Geestelijk Erf
OGF — Organic Gardening and Farming
OGI — Oil and Gas Investor
OGI — Ontario Government Information
OGI — Orientis Graeci Inscriptiones Selectae
OGIS — Orientis Graeci Inscriptiones Selectae
OGJ — Oil and Gas Journal
OGK — Onsei Gakkai Kaiho
OGL — Oesterreich in Geschichte und Literatur
OGL — Ons Geestelijk Leven
OGMCAQ — Specialist Periodical Reports. Organometallic Chemistry
Ogneupory Tekh Keram — Ogneupory i Tekhnicheskaya Keramika
OGNPA — Ogneupory
Ogolnopol Konf Kryszt Mol — Ogolnopolska Konferencja "Krysztaly Molekularne 81"
Ogolnopol Semin Mieszanie Skroty Zgloszonych Pr — Ogolnopolskie Seminarium na temat Mieszanie. Skroty Zgloszonych Prac
Ogolnopol Symp Nauk Chem Plazm Pr — Ogolnopolskie Sympozjum Naukowe. Chemia Plazmy. Prace
Ogolnopol Symp Polim Siarkowych — Ogolnopolskie Sympozjum Polimerow Siarkowych
Ogolnopol Symp Termodyn Warstwy Fluid Mater — Ogolnopolski Sympozjon Termodynamika Warstwy Fluidalnej. Materialy
OG Pat Off — Official Gazette. United States Patent Office
OGR — Official Guide of the Railways
OGS — Oxford German Studies
OGSt — Entscheidungen des Obersten Gerichts in Strafsachen
O Gyalla Asps Obs Beob — Beobachtungen Angestellt am Astrophysicalischen und Meteorologischen Observatorium in O-Gyalla in Ungarn
OGZ — Entscheidungen des Obersten Gerichts in Zivilsachen
OH — Oberpfaelzer Heimat
OH — Ohio History
OH — Ontario History
OH — Oriental Herald
OH — Oriental Herald and Journal of General Literature
OH — Orthodoxie Heute
OH — Osteopathic Hospitals
OH — Oud-Holland
OHA — Occupational Hazards
OHEL — Oxford History of English Literature
OhH — Ohio History
OHI — Oral History Index
Ohio — Ohio Reports
Ohio Admin Code — Ohio Administrative Code
Ohio Ag Dept — Ohio. Department of Agriculture. Bulletins
Ohio Ag Exp — Ohio. Agricultural Experiment Station. Publications
Ohio Agric Exp Sta Bull — Ohio Agricultural Experiment Station Bulletin
Ohio Agric Exp Sta Forest Circ — Ohio Agricultural Experiment Station. Forestry Circular
Ohio Agric Exp Sta Res Circ — Ohio Agricultural Experiment Station Research Circular
Ohio Agric Exp Sta Serv Bull — Ohio Agricultural Experiment Station. Service Bulletin
Ohio Agric Exp Stn Res Bull — Ohio. Agricultural Experiment Station. Research Bulletin
Ohio Agric Exp Stn Res Circ — Ohio. Agricultural Experiment Station. Research Circular
Ohio Agric Exp Stn Spec Circ — Ohio. Agricultural Experiment Station. Special Circular
Ohio Agric Res Dev Cent Res Bull — Ohio. Agricultural Research and Development Center. Research Bulletin
Ohio Agric Res Dev Cent Res Circ — Ohio. Agricultural Research and Development Center. Research Circular
Ohio Agric Res Dev Cent Res Summ — Ohio. Agricultural Research and Development Center. Research Summary
Ohio Agric Res Dev Cent Spec Circ — Ohio. Agricultural Research and Development Center. Special Circular
Ohio Agr Res Develop Cent Res Circ — Ohio. Agricultural Research and Development Center. Research Circular
OhioanaQ — Ohioana Quarterly
Ohio App — Ohio Appellate Reports
Ohio App 3d — Ohio Appellate Reports. Third Series
Ohio Archael — Ohio Archaeologist

Ohio Archaeol Hist Q — Ohio Archaeological and Historical Quarterly
Ohio Assn Sch Libn Bull — Ohio Association of School Librarians. Bulletin
Ohio B — Ohio Bar Reports
Ohio Bar — Ohio State Bar Association. Report
Ohio Biol Surv Biol Notes — Ohio Biological Survey. Biological Notes
Ohio Biol Surv Bull — Ohio Biological Survey. Bulletin
Ohio Biol Surv Inf Circ — Ohio Biological Survey. Informative Circular
Ohio Busn — Ohio Business
Ohio Bus Tchr — Ohio Business Teacher
Ohio CC — Ohio Circuit Court Reports
Ohio CC Dec — Ohio Circuit Court Decisions
Ohio Cir Dec — Ohio Circuit Decisions
Ohio Conf Sewage Treat Annu Rep — Ohio Conference on Sewage Treatment. Annual Report
Ohio Conf Water Purif Annu Rep — Ohio Conference on Water Purification. Annual Report
Ohio Dec — Ohio Decisions
Ohio Dec Reprint — Ohio Decisions Reprint
Ohio Dent J — Ohio Dental Journal
Ohio Dep Nat Resour Div Geol Surv Misc Rep — Ohio. Department of Natural Resources. Division of Geological Survey. Miscellaneous Report
Ohio Dep Nat Resour Div Water Ohio Water Plan Inventory Rep — Ohio. Department of Natural Resources. Division of Water. Ohio Water Plan Inventory Report
Ohio Dept — Ohio Department Reports
Ohio Div Geol Surv Bull — Ohio. Division of Geological Survey. Bulletin
Ohio Div Geol Surv Inf Circ — Ohio. Division of Geological Survey. Information Circular.
Ohio Div Geol Surv Inform Circ — Ohio. Division of Geological Survey. Information Circular
Ohio Div Geol Surv Misc Rep — Ohio. Division of Geological Survey. Miscellaneous Report
Ohio Div Geol Surv Rep Invest — Ohio. Division of Geological Survey. Report of Investigations
Ohio Div Water Bull — Ohio. Division of Water. Bulletin
Ohio Div Water Inform Circ — Ohio. Division of Water. Information Circular
Ohio Div Water Ohio Water Plan Inventory Rep — Ohio. Division of Water. Ohio Water Plan Inventory. Report
Ohio Div Water Ohio Water Plan Invent Rep — Ohio. Division of Water. Ohio Water Plan Inventory. Report
Ohio Div Water Rep Ohio Water Table Surv — Ohio. Division of Water. Report on Ohio Water Table Survey
Ohio Div Water Tech Rep — Ohio. Division of Water. Technical Report
Ohio F — Ohio Farmer
Ohio Farm Home Res — Ohio Farm and Home Research
Ohio Fish Monogr — Ohio Fish Monographs
Ohio Fish Wildl Rep — Ohio Fish and Wildlife Report
Ohio Florists Assoc Bull — Ohio Florist's Association. Bulletin
Ohio Florists Assoc Monthly Bull — Ohio Florists Association. Monthly Bulletin
Ohio Fm Home Res — Ohio Farm and Home Research
Ohio Game Monogr — Ohio Game Monographs
Ohio Govt — Ohio Government Reports
Ohio G S B — Ohio. Geological Survey. Bulletin
OhioH — Ohio History
Ohio Herpetol Soc Spec Publ — Ohio Herpetological Society. Special Publication
Ohio Hist — Ohio History
Ohio HQ — Ohio Historical Quarterly
Ohio Jour Sci — Ohio Journal of Science
Ohio J Rel St — Ohio Journal of Religious Studies
Ohio J Sci — Ohio Journal of Science
Ohio Law Bul — Ohio Law Bulletin
Ohio Law Bull — Weekly Law Bulletin
Ohio Law J — Ohio Law Journal
Ohio Laws — State of Ohio. Legislative Acts Passed and Joint Resolutions Adopted
Ohio LB — Weekly Law Bulletin
Ohio L Bull — Ohio Law Bulletin
Ohio Legal N — Ohio Legal News
Ohio Legis Bull — Ohio Legislative Bulletin (Anderson)
Ohio Legis Bull (Anderson) — Ohio Legislative Bulletin (Anderson)
Ohio Legis Serv (Baldwin) — Baldwin's Ohio Legislative Service
Ohio Leg N — Ohio Legal News
Ohio Leg News — Ohio Legal News
Ohio Lib Assn Bul — Ohio Library Association. Bulletin
Ohio Libr Ass Bull — Ohio Library Association. Bulletin
Ohio LJ — Ohio Law Journal
Ohio LR & Wk Bul — Ohio Law Reporter and Weekly Bulletin
Ohio Med J — Ohio Medical Journal
Ohio Misc — Ohio Miscellaneous
Ohio M J — Ohio Mining Journal
Ohio Monthly Rec — Ohio Monthly Record
Ohio Nat — Ohio Naturalist. Ohio State University
Ohio Northern UL Rev — Ohio Northern University. Law Review
Ohio North L Rev — Ohio Northern University. Law Review
Ohio North Univ L Rev — Ohio Northern University. Law Review
Ohio NP — Ohio Nisi Prius Reports
Ohio NUL Rev — Ohio Northern University. Law Review
Ohio N Univ Law R — Ohio Northern University. Law Review
Ohio Nurses Rev — Ohio Nurses Review
Ohio Op — Ohio Opinions
OhioR — Ohio Review
Ohio Rep — Ohio Report
Ohio Rep Res Dev — Ohio Report on Research and Development
Ohio Rep Res Dev Biol Agri Home Econ — Ohio Report on Research and Development in Biology, Agriculture, and Home Economics

Ohio Rep Res Develop — Ohio Report on Research and Development (Biology, Agriculture, Home Economics).Ohio Agricultural Experiment Station
Ohio Rep Res Developm Biol — Ohio Report on Research and Development in Biology, Agriculture, and Home Economics
Ohio Rev — Ohio Review
Ohio Rev Code Ann (Anderson) — Ohio Revised Code Annotated (Anderson)
Ohio Rev Code Ann (Baldwin) — Ohio Revised Code Annotated (Baldwin)
Ohio SBA Bull — Ohio State Bar Association. Bulletin
Ohio Sch — Ohio Schools
Ohio S L J — Ohio State Law Journal
Ohio Sociol — Ohio Sociologist
Ohio St — Ohio State Reports
Ohio St Ac Sc An Rp — Ohio State Academy of Science. Annual Report
Ohio St Ac Sc Pr — Ohio State Academy of Science. Proceedings
Ohio St Ac Sc Sp P — Ohio State Academy of Science. Special Papers
Ohio State Archaeol and Hist Quar — Ohio State Archaeological and Historical Quarterly
Ohio State Law J — Ohio State Law Journal
Ohio State LJ — Ohio State Law Journal
Ohio State Med J — Ohio State Medical Journal
Ohio State Univ Biosci Colloq — Ohio State University. Biosciences Colloquia
Ohio State Univ Coll Eng Bull — Ohio State University. College of Engineering. Bulletin
Ohio State Univ Eng Exp Sta Bull — Ohio State University. Engineering Experiment Station. Bulletin
Ohio State Univ Eng Exp Stn Circ — Ohio State University. Engineering Experiment Station. Circular
Ohio State Univ Eng Exp Stn News — Ohio State University. Engineering Experiment Station. News
Ohio State Univ Inst Polar Studies Rept — Ohio State University. Institute of Polar Studies. Report
Ohio State Univ Inst Polar Stud Rep — Ohio State University. Institute of Polar Studies. Report
Ohio State Univ Math Res Inst Publ — Ohio State University Mathematical Research Institute. Publications
Ohio State Univ Stud Eng Ser Cir — Ohio State University Studies. Engineering Series. Circular
Ohio State Univ Stud Eng Ser Eng Exp Stn Bull — Ohio State University Studies. Engineering Series. Engineering Experiment Station Bulletin
Ohio State Univ Stud Ohio Biol Surv Bull — Ohio State University Studies. Ohio Biological Survey Bulletin
Ohio St BA Rep — Ohio State Bar Association. Report
Ohio St Law — Ohio State Law Journal
Ohio St LJ — Ohio State Law Journal
Ohio St Univ B — Ohio State University. Bulletin
Ohio St Univ Coll Law Law For Ser — Ohio State University. College of Law. Law Forum Series
Ohio St Univ Contrib Hist & Pol Sci — Ohio State University. Contributions in History and Political Science
Ohio St Univ Coop Ext Serv — Ohio State University. Cooperative Extension Service
Ohio St Univ Educ Res Bul — Ohio State University. Educational Research Bulletin
Ohio St Univ L J — Ohio State University. Law Journal
Ohio St Univ Stud B Assn L J — Ohio State University. Students Bar Association. Law Journal
Ohio Swine Res Ind Rep Anim Sci Ser Ohio Agric Res Dev Cent — Ohio Swine Research and Industry Report. Animal Science Series. Ohio Agricultural Research and Development Center
Ohio Water Plan Inventory Rep — Ohio Water Plan Inventory Report
Ohio Welf Bul — Ohio Welfare Bulletin
Ohio Wesleyan Univ Perkins Obs Contrib — Ohio Wesleyan University. Perkins Observatory. Contributions
O His — Ottawa Hispanica
OHJ — Old-House Journal
Oh J Sci — Ohio Journal of Science
OHK — Die Oberhessischen Kloester
Oh L Bul — Ohio Law Bulletin
Oh Leg N — Ohio Legal News
OHLHA9 — Osteuropastudien der Hochschulen des Landes Hessen. Reihe I. Giessener Abhandlungen zur Agrar und Wirtschaftsforschung des Europaeischen Ostens
Oh LJ — Ohio Law Journal
OHLJ — Osgoode Hall. Law Journal
OHM-TADS — Oil and Hazardous Materials Technical Assistance Data System
Oh NU Intra LR — Ohio Northern University. Intramural Law Review
Oh NULR — Ohio Northern University. Law Review
OHOLO Conf Air Pollut Oung Proc — OHOLO Conference on Air Pollution and the Lung. Proceedings
OHQ — Ohio Historical Quarterly
OHQ — Oregon Historical Quarterly
OhR — Ohio Review
OHRJ — Orissa Historical Research Journal
OHRNA — Ontario Hydro-Research News
OHS — Oxford Historical Series
OHSAD — Occupational Health and Safety
Oh SLJ — Ohio State Law Journal
OH State Archaeol & Hist Q — Ohio State Archaeological and Historical Quarterly
Oh St LJ — Ohio State Law Journal
Oh Univ Rev — Ohio University Review
Ohu Univ Dent J — Ohu University Dental Journal
OI — O Instituto
OI — Old Irish
OIAK — Otchet Imperatorskoi Arkheologicheskoi Kommissii
OIAS — Oriental Institute Publications. University of Chicago. Assyriological Studies

OIAZ (Oesterreichische In Archit Z) — OIAZ (Oesterreichische Ingenier und Architekten Zeitschrift)
OIC — One in Christ
OIC — Oriental Institute. Communications
OIC — Polymers, Paint, and Colour Journal
OIEFA — Oil Engineering and Finance
OIF — Online Review
OIHEL — Opuscula Instituti Historico-Ecclesiastici Lundensis
OIKO — Oikos
Oikos Suppl — Oikos. Supplementum
Oil and Gas Compact Bull — Oil and Gas Compact Bulletin
Oil & Gas J — Oil and Gas Journal
Oil & Gas LR — Oil and Gas Law Review
Oil & Gas Tax Q — Oil and Gas Tax Quarterly
OILBA — Oil Bulletin
Oil Bull — Oil Bulletin
Oil Can — Oil in Canada
Oil Chem Pollut — Oil and Chemical Pollution
Oil Colour Chem Assoc (Aust) Proc News — Oil and Colour Chemists' Association (Australia). Proceedings and News
Oil Colour Chem Assoc J — Oil and Colour Chemists' Association. Journal
Oil Colour Chemist Assoc J — Oil and Colour Chemists' Association. Journal
Oil Colour Trades J — Oil and Colour Trades Journal
Oil Eng Finance — Oil Engineering and Finance
Oil Eng Technol — Oil Engineering and Technology
Oil Fat Ind — Oil and Fat Industry
Oil Fat Ind Moscow — Oil and Fat Industry (Moscow)
Oil Field Eng — Oil Field Engineering
Oilfield Rev — Oilfield Review
Oil Gas — Oil and Gas Bulletin
Oil Gas Compact Bull — Interstate Oil and Gas Compact Commission. Committee Bulletin
Oil Gas Compact Bull — Oil and Gas Compact Bulletin
Oil Gas Direct — Oil and Gas Directory
Oil Gas Eur Mag — Oil Gas European Magazine
Oil Gas Europ Mag — Oil Gas European Magazine
Oil Gas Geol — Oil and Gas Geology
Oil Gas Ind Kiev — Oil and Gas Industry (Kiev)
Oil Gas Int — Oil and Gas International
Oil Gas J — Oil and Gas Journal
Oil Gas Mag (Hamburg) — Oil and Gas Magazine (Hamburg)
Oil Gas Mon — Oil and Gas Monthly
Oil Gas Petrochem Equip — Oil, Gas, and Petrochem Equipment
Oil Gas Rep — Oil and Gas Report
Oil Gas Tax Q — Oil and Gas Tax Quarterly
Oil Geophys Prospect — Oil Geophysical Prospecting
Oil Mill Gazet — Oil Mill Gazetteer
Oil Nat Gas Comm Bull — Oil and Natural Gas Commission. Bulletin
Oil Paint Drug Rep — Oil, Paint, and Drug Reporter
Oil Palm Res — Oil Palm Research
Oil Petrochem Pollut — Oil and Petrochemical Pollution
Oil Prog — Oil Progress
OILS — Oilsander. Suncor Incorporated Resources Group. Oil Sands Division
Oil Shale Relat Fuels — Oil Shale and Related Fuels
Oil Shale Symp Proc — Oil Shale Symposium Proceedings
Oils Oilseeds J — Oils and Oilseeds Journal
Oil Spill Intell Rep — Oil Spill Intelligence Report
Oil Stat (Paris) — Oil Statistics (Paris)
Oil Technol — Oil Technologist
Oil Trade J — Oil Trade Journal
OILWA — Oil Weekly
Oil Wkly — Oil Weekly
Oily Press Lipid Lib — Oily Press Lipid Library
OINOD — Energy
OIP — Oriental Institute. Publications
OIPOB — Otkrytiya, Izobrotoniya, Promyshlennye Obraztsy, Tovarnye Znaki
OIR — Oriental Institute. Reports
OIS — Oriental Institute Publications. University of Chicago. Studies in Ancient Oriental Civilization
OIS — Oxford University. Institute of Economics and Statistics. Bulletin
OIS — Studies in Ancient Oriental Civilization. Oriental Institute
Oiseau Rev Fr Ornithol — Oiseau et la Revue Francaise d'Ornithologie
Oita Prefect For Exp Stn Rep — Oita Prefectural Forest Experiment Station. Report
OIUC SAOC — Oriental Institute. University of Chicago. Studies in Ancient Oriental Civilization
OJ — Jahreshefte des Oesterreichischen Archaeologischen Institutes in Wien
OJ — Official Journal of the European Communities
OJ — Oldenburger Jahrbuch. Verein fuer Landesgeschichte und Altertumskunde
OJ — Opera Journal
OJ — Oudheidkundig Jaarboek. Bulletijn Uitgegeven door den Nederlandsen Oudkundigen Bond
Ojb — Oldenburger Jahrbuch
OJBNOB — Oudheidkundig Jaarboek. Bulletijn Uitgegeven door den Nederlandschen Oudkundigen Bond
OJCH — Overijssel Jaarboek voor Cultuur en Historie
OJES — Osmania Journal of English Studies
OJ Eur Comm — Official Journal of the European Communities
OJS — Ohio Journal of Science
OJS — Osar Jehude Sefarad
O Judd Farmer — Orange Judd Farmer
O Judd Ill F — Orange Judd Illinois Farmer
OK — Oklahoma School Music News
OK — Onze Kongo
OK — Orden der Kirche

Okajimas Folia Anat Jpn — Okajimas Folia Anatomica Japonica
Okayama Igakkai Zasshi Suppl — Okayama Igakkai Zasshi. Supplement
Okayama Math Lectures — Okayama Mathematical Lectures
Okayama Univ Adm Cent Environ Sci Technol Rep — Okayama University. Administration Center for Environmental Science and Technology. Report
Okayama Univ Inst Study Earths Inter Tech Rep Ser B — Okayama University. Institute for Study of the Earth's Interior. Technical Report. Series B
Okayama Univ Inst Therm Spring Res Pap — Okayama University. Institute for Thermal Spring Research. Papers
OKDIA — Osaka Kogyo Daigaku Kiyo. Riko-Hen
Okeanol — Okeanologiya
Okeanol Issled — Okeanologicheskie Issledovaniya
OKEHDW — Proceedings. Osaka Prefecture Institute of Public Health. Edition of Public Health
Oken Isis — Isis, oder Encyclopaedische Zeitung. Oken
OKHED4 — Proceedings. Osaka Prefecture Institute of Public Health. Edition of Mental Health
Okhota Okhot Khoz — Okhota i Okhotnich'e Khozyaistvo
Okhr Okruzh Sredy Ratsion Ispolz Prir Resur Obz Inf — Okhrana Okruzhayushchei Sredy i Ratsional'noe Ispol'zovanie Prirodnykh Resursov. Obzornaya Informatsiya
Okhr Okruzh Sredy Zagryaz Prom Vybrosami — Okhrana Okruzhayushchei Sredy ot Zagryazneniya Promyshlennymi Vybrosami
Okhr Okruzh Sredy Zagryaz Prom Vybrosami TsBP — Okhrana Okruzhayushchei Sredy ot Zagryazneniya Promyshlennymi Vybrosami Tsellyulozno-Bumazhnaya Promyshlennost
Okhr Prir — Okhrana Prirody
Okhr Prir Dal'nem Vostoke — Okhrana Prirody na Dal'nem Vostoke
Okhr Prir Mold — Okhrana Prirody Moldavii
Okhr Prir Tsent-Chernozem Polosy — Okhrana Prirody Tsentral'no-Chernozemnoi Polosy
Okhr Prir Tsentr Chernozemn Polosy — Okhrana Prirody Tsentral'no-Chernozemnoi Polosy
Okhr Prir Urale — Okhrana Prirody na Urale
Okhr Prir Vod Urala — Okhrana Prirodnykh Vod Urala
Okhr Tr Okruzh Sredy — Okhrana Truda i Okruzhayushchei Sredy
Okhr Tr Tekh Bezop Chern Metall — Okhrana Truda i Tekhnika Bezopasnosti v Chernoi Metallurgii
Okhr Zashch Lesa Obz Inf — Okhrana i Zashchita Lesa. Obzornaya Informatsiya
Okhr Zdor Detei Podrostkov (Kiev) — Okhrana Zdorov'ya Detei i Podrostkov (Kiev)
Okhr Zdorovya Detei Podrostkov (Kiev) — Okhrana Zdorov'ya Detei i Podrostkov (Kiev)
Oki Tech Rev — Oki Technical Review
Okla — Oklahoma Reports
Okla Acad Sci Proc — Oklahoma Academy of Science. Proceedings
Okla Ag Exp — Oklahoma. Agricultural Experiment Station. Publications
Okla Agric Exp Stn Annu Rep — Oklahoma. Agricultural Experiment Station. Annual Report
Okla Agric Exp Stn Bull — Oklahoma. Agricultural Experiment Station. Bulletin
Okla Agric Exp Stn Mimeogr Circ — Oklahoma. Agricultural Experiment Station. Mimeographed Circular
Okla Agric Exp Stn Misc Publ — Oklahoma. Agricultural Experiment Station. Miscellaneous Publication
Okla Agric Exp Stn M P — Oklahoma. Agricultural Experiment Station. Miscellaneous Publication
Okla Agric Exp Stn Processed Ser — Oklahoma. Agricultural Experiment Station. Processed Series
Okla Agric Exp Stn Process Ser — Oklahoma. Agricultural Experiment Station. Processed Series
Okla Agric Exp Stn Prog Rep — Oklahoma. Agricultural Experiment Station. Progress Report
Okla Agric Exp Stn Res Rep — Oklahoma. Agricultural Experiment Station. Research Report
Okla Agric Exp Stn Tech Bull — Oklahoma. Agricultural Experiment Station. Technical Bulletin
Okla Agric Mech Coll Div Eng Publ — Oklahoma Agricultural and Mechanical College. Division of Engineering. Publication
Okla BA J — Oklahoma Bar Association. Journal
Okla B Ass'n J — Oklahoma Bar Association. Journal
Okla BJ — Oklahoma Bar Journal
Okla Bsns — Oklahoma Business
Okla Bus — Oklahoma Business
Okla Chronicles — Chronicles of Oklahoma
Okla City UL Rev — Oklahoma City University. Law Review
Okla Crim — Oklahoma Criminal Reports
Okla Curr Farm Econ — Oklahoma Current Farm Economics
Okla Dep Hum Serv Ann Stat Rep — Oklahoma. Department of Human Services. Annual Statistical Report
Okla Div Water Resour Bull — Oklahoma. Division of Water Resources. Bulletin
Okla Dp G N H Bien Rp — Oklahoma. Department of Geology and Natural History. Biennial Report
Okla Eng Exp Stn Publ — Oklahoma Engineering Experiment Station. Publication
Okla Gaz — Oklahoma Gazette
Okla Geol Notes — Oklahoma Geology Notes
Okla Geology Notes — Oklahoma Geology Notes
Okla Geol Surv Bull — Oklahoma. Geological Survey. Bulletin
Okla Geol Surv Circ — Oklahoma. Geological Survey. Circular
Okla Geol Surv Map — Oklahoma. Geological Survey. Map
Okla Geol Surv Miner Rep — Oklahoma. Geological Survey. Mineral Report
Okla G S — Oklahoma. Geological Survey
Oklahoma Acad Sci Proc — Oklahoma Academy of Science. Proceedings
Oklahoma Agric Coll Bot Stud — Oklahoma Agricultural and Mechanical College. Botanical Studies

Oklahoma Agric Exp Sta Annual Rep — Oklahoma Agricultural Experiment Station. Annual Report
Oklahoma Agric Exp Sta Forage Crops Leafl — Oklahoma Agricultural Experiment Station Forage Crops Leaflet
Oklahoma Agric Exp Sta Mimeogr Circ — Oklahoma Agricultural Experiment Station. Mimeographed Circular
Oklahoma Geology Notes — Oklahoma Geology Notes. Oklahoma Geological Survey
Oklahoma Geol Survey Guidebook — Oklahoma. Geological Survey. Guidebook
Oklahoma Geol Survey Map — Oklahoma. Geological Survey. Map
Oklahoma L Rev — Oklahoma Law Review
Oklahoma State Med Assoc J — Oklahoma State Medical Association. Journal
Oklahoma Univ Inf Sci Ser Mon — Oklahoma. University. Information Science Series. Monograph
Okla Law R — Oklahoma Law Review
Okla Libn — Oklahoma Librarian
Okla Librn — Oklahoma Librarian
Okla LJ — Oklahoma Law Journal
Okla LR — Oklahoma Law Review
Okla L Rev — Oklahoma Law Review
Okla Med Ne J — Oklahoma Medical News Journal
Okla Munic R — Oklahoma Municipal Review
Okla Nurse — Oklahoma Nurse
Okla Plann Resour Board Div Water Resour Bull — Oklahoma. Planning and Resources Board. Division of Water Resources. Bulletin
OKL Arb Osterreichisches Kuratorium Landtech — OKL-Arbeit-Oesterreichisches Kuratorium fuer Landtechnik
Okla Reg — Oklahoma Register
Okla SBJ — Oklahoma State Bar Journal
Okla Sess Laws — Oklahoma Session Laws
Okla Sess Law Serv (West) — Oklahoma Session Law Service (West)
Okla Stat — Oklahoma Statutes
Okla Stat Ann (West) — Oklahoma Statutes Annotated (West)
Okla State Med Assoc J — Oklahoma State Medical Association. Journal
Okla State Univ Agric Appl Sci Eng Exp Stn Publ — Oklahoma State University of Agriculture and Applied Science. Engineering Experiment Station. Publication
Okla State Univ Agric Exp Stn Misc Publ MP — Oklahoma State University. Agricultural Experiment Station. Miscellaneous Publication MP
Okla St B Assn Proc — Oklahoma State Bar Association. Proceedings
Okla St B J — Oklahoma State Bar. Journal
Okla Univ Research B — Oklahoma State University. Research Bulletin
Okla Water Res Board Bull — Oklahoma. Water Resources Board. Bulletin
Okl LR — Oklahoma Law Review
OK LR — Oklahoma Law Review
OKMD — Oudheidkundige Mededeelingen
Okon og Polit — Okonomi og Politik
Okon Perspekt — Okonomisk Perspektiv
OKRK — Okuruk
Okr Tr — Okhrana Truda
OKS — Ostkirchliche Studien
Okt — Oktjabr
OKT — On the Knossos Tablets
OL — Observer (London)
OL — Oceanic Linguistics
OL — Orbis Litterarum
OL — Outlook (London)
OLA — Orientalia Lovaniensia Analecta
Olaj Szappan Kozmet — Olaj, Szappan, Kozmetika
Ol Ausgr — Ausgrabungen zu Olympia
OLB — Ohio Law Bulletin
Ol Ber — Bericht ueber die Ausgrabungen in Olympia
Ol Corps Gras Lipides — Oleagineux, Corps Gras, Lipides
OLD — Oxford Latin Dictionary
Old Dominion J Med and S — Old Dominion Journal of Medicine and Surgery
Oldelft Sci Eng Q — Oldelft Scientific Engineering Quarterly
Oldenburger Jahrb Oldenburger Landesvereins Gesch Teil 2 — Oldenburger Jahrbuch des Oldenburger Landesvereins fuer Geschichte, Natur- und Heimatkunde. Teil 2
Oldenburg Jb Altertskde — Oldenburger Jahrbuch fuer Altertumskunde
Oldenburg Landwirtschaftsbl — Oldenburgisches Landwirtschaftsblatt
Old Furn — Old Furniture
Old Herborn Univ Semin Monogr — Old Herborn University Seminar Monograph
Old House Jnl — Old-House Journal
Old Kilkenny Rev — Old Kilkenny Review
Old Kilk Rev — Old Kilkenny Review
Old Master Drgs — Old Master Drawings
Old Northw Geneal Q — Old Northwest Genealogical Quarterly
Old Nurs — Old Nursing
Old NW — Old Northwest Genealogical Quarterly
Old Prt Shop Port — Old Print Shop Portfolio
OLDS — Offshore Lease Data System
Old Test Abstr — Old Testament Abstracts
Old Testam Abstr — Old Testament Abstracts
Old-Time N — Old-Time New England
Old-Time N E — Old-Time New England
Old-Time N Eng — Old-Time New England
Old Vetern — Caring for the Older Veteran
Old Westbury Rev — Old Westbury Review
Old Wexford Soc J — Journal. Old Wexford Society
Old Wtrcol Soc Club — Old Water-Colour Society's Club
Oleagineux Rev Int Corps Gras — Oleagineux. Revue Internationale des Corps Gras
O Legal News — Ohio Legal News
Oleodin Pneum — Oleodinamica Pneumatica

Ol Erg — Olympia. Die Ergebnisse der von dem Deutschen Reich Veranstalten Ausgrabung
OIF — Old Fort News
Olfaction Taste Proc Int Symp — Olfaction and Taste. Proceedings of the International Symposium
Ol Forsch — Olympische Forschungen
OLGE — Rechtsprechung der Oberlandesgerichte auf dem Gebiete des Zivilrechts
OLib — Oeuvres Libres
Oli Grassi Deriv — Olii, Grassi, Derivati
Olii Miner Grassi Saponi Colori Vernici — Olii Minerali. Grassi e Saponi. Colori e Vernici
Olii Miner Olii Grassi Colori Vernici — Olii Minerali. Olii e Grassi. Colori e Vernici
OLIM — Olimpiadas
Olit — Oesterreichisches Literaturblatt (Vienna)
O Lit — Orbis Litterarum
OLit — Ouvroir Liturgique
Olive Pink Soc Bull — Olive Pink Society Bulletin
OLI/ZLW — Zeitschrift fuer Lateinamerika (Wien). Oesterreichisches Lateinamerika Institut(Wien)
OLJ — Ohio Law Journal
OLJ — Oudh Law Journal
OL Jour — Ohio Law Journal
OL Jour — Oudh Law Journal
OLL — Oude Land van Loon
OLN — Ohio Legal News
OLoP — Orientalia Lovaniensia Periodica
OLP — Orientalia Lovaniensia Periodica
OLP — Oriental Library Publications
OLPS — Oriental Library Publications. Sanskrit Series
OLR — Ontario Library Review
OLR — Oregon Law Review
OLR — Oxford Literary Review
OLRB — Ontario Labour Relations Board Monthly Report
OL Sch VO — Verordnung ueber Orderlagerscheine
OLSP — Oceanic Linguistics. Special Publications
Oltenia — Oltenia Studii si Comunicari Istorie
Olt R — Oltenia Romana
OLUC — OCLC [*Online Computer Library Center*] Online Union Catalog
OLV — Oil and Gas Journal
OLWE — Oilweek
Oly Message — Olympic Message
Olym Rev — Olympic Review/Revue Olympique
Oly Rev — Olympic Review
OLZ — Orientalistische Literaturzeitung
OM — Objets et Monde
OM — Obrazotvorce Mistectvo
OM — Omega. The Journal of Death and Dying
OM — Only Music
OM — Opus Musicum
OM — Orientalische Miszellen
OM — Oriente Moderno
OM — Osnabruecker Mitteilungen. Verein fuer Geschichte und Landeskunde von Osnabrueck
OM — Ostdeutsche Monatshefte
OM — Oudheidkundige Mededeelingen uit s'Rijksmuseum van Oudheden te Leiden
OM — Oxford Magazine
Omaha World — Omaha World Herald
OMB — Management in Government
OME — Omega
OMEG — Omega. The Journal of Death and Dying
Omega-Int J — Omega - The International Journal of Management Science
Omega J Death Dying — Omega Journal of Death and Dying
O Mh — Ostdeutsche Monatshefte
O Mich — Greek Ostraca in the University of Michigan Collection
OMIKE — Orszagos Magyar Izraelita Kozmuvelodesi Egyesuelet
OMKDK Modsz Kiad — Orszagos Muszaki Konyvtar es Dokumentacios Kozpont. Modszertani Kiadvanyok
OMKMB — Original Mittheilungen aus der Ethnologischen Abtheilung der Koeniglichen Museen. Berlin
OML — Oudheidkundige Mededelingen uit het Rijksmuseum van Oudheden te Leiden
OM Leiden — Oudheidkundige Mededeelingen uit s'Rijksmuseum van Oudheden te Leiden
OMLLM — Oxford Modern Languages and Literature Monographs
OMM — Nouvel Officiel de l'Ameublement
OMMI Kiad Sorozat 1 — OMMI [*Orszagos Mezogazdasagi Minosegvizsgalo Intezet*] Kiadvanyai. Sorozat1. Genetikus Talajterkepek
OMMI (Orsz Mezogazd Minosegvizsgalo Intez) Kiad Sorozat 1 — OMMI (Orszagos Mezogazdasagi Minosegvizsgalo Intezet) Kiadvanyai. Sorozat 1. Genetikus Talajterkepek
OMML — Oudheidkundige Mededeelingen uit s'Rijksmuseum van Oudheden te Leiden
OMNAN — Ontario. Ministry of Northern Affairs. News Release
Omnia Med — Omnia Medica
Omnia Med Suppl — Omnia Medica. Supplemento
Omnia Med Ther — Omnia Medica et Therapeutica
Omnia Med Ther Arch — Omnia Medica et Therapeutica. Archivio
Omnia Ther — Omnia Therapeutica
Omnibus Mag — Omnibus Magazine
OMO — Oesterreichische Monatsschrift fuer den Orient
OMo — Oriente Moderno
Omodel A Un — Annali Universali di Medicina. Omodei, Calderini
OMorD — Ocerki Mordovskich Dialektov
OMRL — Oudheidkundige Mededeelingen uit s'Rijksmuseum van Oudheden te Leiden

OMRM — Oudheidkundige Medede e Lingen uit het Rijksmuseum van Oudheden te Leiden

OMRO — Oudheidkundige Mededelingen uit het Rijksmuseum van Oudheden te Leiden

OMROL — Oudheidkundige Mededelingen uit het Rijksmuseum van Oudheden te Leiden

Omron Tech — Omron Technics

OMR-Org Mag — Organic Magnetic Resonance

OMRR — Oriental Magazine, Review, and Register

OMRTE — Orszagos Magyar Regezeti Tarsulat Evkonyve

OMS — S & P [*Standard & Poor's Corp.*] Options Monitor Service Plus

OMSGM — Ottendorfer Memorial Series of Germanic Monographs

Omsk Gos Med Inst im M I Kalinina Mauchn Tr — Omskii Gosudarstvennyi Meditsinskii Institut imeni M. I. Kalinina. Nauchnye Trudy

Omsk Inst Inzh Zheleznodorozhn Transp Nauchn Tr — Omskii Institut Inzhenerov Zheleznodorozhnogo Transporta. Nauchnye Trudy

Omsk Inst Inz Zeleznodoroz Transporta Naucn Trudy — Omskii Institut Inzenerov Zeleznodoroznogo Transporta. Naucnye Trudy

Omsk Med Inst im M I Kalinina Nauchn Tr — Omskii Meditsinskii Institut imeni M. I. Kalinina. Nauchnye Trudy

Omsk Med Zhurnal — Omskii Meditsinskii Zhurnal

OMS Nouv — Nouvelles. Organisation Mondiale de la Sante

O M Szep Muz Evk — Orszagos Magyar Szepmuveszeti Muzeum Evkonyve

OMT — Oxford Medieval Texts

O Mz — Oesterreichische Musikzeitschrift

OMZSA — Orszagos Magyar Zsido Segitoe Akcio

ON — Old Northwest

ON — Oltner Neujahrsblaetter

On — Onoma

On — Onomastica

ON — Opera News

ON — Orchestra News

ON — Orientalia Neerlandica

ONA J — Orthopedic Nurses' Association. Journal

ONBRDY — Ontogenesis of the Brain

Onc — Oncologia

ONCOA — Oncologia

Oncodev Biol Med — Oncodevelopmental Biology and Medicine

Oncog Res — Oncogene Research

Oncol Abstr — Oncology Abstracts

Oncol Nurs Forum — Oncology Nursing Forum

Oncol Radiol — Oncologia si Radiologia

Oncol Rep — Oncology Reports

Oncol Res — Oncology Research

ONCR — On Campus Review

Onde Elec — Onde Electrique

Onde Electr — Onde Electrique

Onde Electr Suppl — Onde Electrique. Supplement

Onderstepoort J Vet Res — Onderstepoort Journal of Veterinary Research

Onderstepoort J Vet Sci — Onderstepoort Journal of Veterinary Science and Animal Industry

Onderstepoort J Vet Sci Anim Ind — Onderstepoort Journal of Veterinary Science and Animal Industry

Onderst J V — Onderstepoort Journal of Veterinary Research

Ondontol Bonaer — Odontologia Bonaerense

One Ch — One Church

ONERA Note Tech — Office National d'Etudes et de Recherches Aerospatiales. Note Technique

ONERA Publ — Office National d'Etudes et de Recherches Aerospatiales. Publication

ONESJ — Orient. Report of the Society for Near Eastern Studies in Japan

ONEX — Ontario Native Experience

ONGC Bull — ONGC [*Oil and Natural Gas Commission*] Bulletin

OnH — Ontario History

ONIN — Ontario Indian

On Jug — Onomastica Jugoslavica

ONKAA — Onsen Kagaku

ONKIA — Onken Kiyo

ONKLA — Onkologiya

ONKOB — Onsen Kogakkaishi

ONL — Online

ONL — O Nosso Lar

ONLA — Our Native Land

On-Land Drill News — On-Land Drilling News

Online — Online Review

Online ADL-Nachr — Online ADL-Nachrichten

Online CDROM Rev — Online and CDROM Review

Online Data — Online Database Report

Online Database Rep — Online Database Report

Online J Curr Clin Trials — Online Journal of Current Clinical Trials

Online J Issues Nurs — Online Journal of Issues in Nursing

Online Rev — Online Review

On-Line Rv — On-Line Review

ONN — Enkabe Contact

ONNA — Ontario Naturalist

ONO — Oculus

Ono — Onomastica

Onom — Onomastica

Onomast — Onomastica

Onomast Sacra — Onomastica Sacra

Onomast Slavogerm — Onomastica Slavogermanica

ONO Meded — ONO [*Organisatie voor Natuurwetenschappelijk Onderzoek*] Mededeelingen

OnomJug — Onomastica Jugoslavica

Onondaga Ac Sc Pr — Onondaga Academy of Science. Proceedings

Onondaga Hist As Sc S — Onondaga Historical Association. Science Series

Onore Angelo Celli 25o An Insegnamento — Onore del Professore Angelo Celli nel 25o Anno di Insegnamento

ONR Tech Rep — ONR [*Office of Naval Research*] Technical Report

ONS — Oriental Notes and Studies

OnsE — Ons Erfdeel

On Serv — On Service

On SG — Onomastica Slavogermanica

ONSM — Obrazcy Narodnoj Slovesnosti Mongolov

ONSMP — Obrazcy Narodnoj Slovesnosti Mongol'skich Plernen

ONSN — Oriental Numismatic Society. Newsletter

ONSOP — Oriental Numismatic Society. Occasional Paper

Ontario Ag Dept — Ontario. Department of Agriculture. Publication

Ontario Dept Mines Geol Rept — Ontario. Department of Mines. Geological Report

Ontario Dept Mines Indus Mineral Rept — Ontario. Department of Mines. Industrial Mineral Report

Ontario Dept Mines Map — Ontario. Department of Mines. Map

Ontario Dept Mines Mineral Resources Circ — Ontario. Department of Mines. Mineral Resources Circular

Ontario Dept Mines Misc Paper — Ontario. Department of Mines. Miscellaneous Paper

Ontario Dept Mines Prelim Geochem Map — Ontario. Department of Mines. Preliminary Geochemical Map

Ontario Dept Mines Prelim Geol Map — Ontario. Department of Mines. Preliminary Geological Map

Ontario Dept Mines Prelim Map — Ontario. Department of Mines. Preliminary Map

Ontario Field Biol — Ontario Field Biologist. Toronto Field Biologists' Club

Ontario Fuel Board Ann Rept — Ontario Fuel Board. Annual Report

Ontario Hist Soc Papers — Ontario Historical Society. Papers and Records

Ontario Med Rev — Ontario Medical Review

Ontario Miner Policy Background Pap — Ontario Mineral Policy. Background Paper

Ontario R — Ontario Review

Ontario Research Council Rept — Ontario Research Council. Report

Ont Bird Banding — Ontario Bird Banding

Ont Birds — Ontario Birds

Ont Bur Mines An Rp — Ontario. Bureau of Mines. Annual Report

Ont Bur Mines B — Ontario. Bureau of Mines. Bulletin

Ont Bus — Ontario Business

Ont Coll Pharm Bull — Ontario College of Pharmacy. Bulletin

Ont Dent — Ontario Dentist

Ont Dep Agric Bull — Ontario Department of Agriculture. Bulletin

Ont Dep Agric Food Publ — Ontario. Department of Agriculture and Food. Publication

Ont Dep Agric Publ — Ontario. Department of Agriculture. Publication

Ont Dep Mines Annu Rep — Ontario. Department of Mines. Annual Report

Ont Dep Mines Bull — Ontario. Department of Mines. Mines Inspection Branch. Bulletin

Ont Dep Mines Geol Circ — Ontario. Department of Mines. Geological Circular

Ont Dep Mines Geol Rep — Ontario. Department of Mines. Geological Report

Ont Dep Mines Ind Miner Rep — Ontario. Department of Mines. Industrial Mineral Report

Ont Dep Mines Miner Resour Circ — Ontario. Department of Mines. Mineral Resources Circular

Ont Dep Mines Misc Pap — Ontario. Department of Mines. Miscellaneous Paper

Ont Dep Mines North Aff Bull — Ontario Department of Mines and Northern Affairs. Bulletin

Ont Dep Mines North Aff Geol Rep — Ontario. Department of Mines and Northern Affairs. Geological Report

Ont Dep Mines North Aff Ind Miner Rep — Ontario. Department of Mines and Northern Affairs. Industrial Mineral Report

Ont Dep Mines North Aff Misc Pap — Ontario. Department of Mines and Northern Affairs. Miscellaneous Paper

Ont Dep Mines Rep — Ontario. Department of Mines. Report

Ont Dig — Ontario Digest

Ont Div Mines Bull — Ontario Division of Mines. Bulletin

Ont Div Mines Geol Rep — Ontario. Division of Mines. Geological Report

Ont Div Mines Geosci Rep — Ontario. Division of Mines. Geoscience Report

Ont Div Mines Geosci Study — Ontario Division of Mines. Geoscience Study

Ont Div Mines Ind Miner Rep — Ontario. Division of Mines. Industrial Mineral Report

Ont Div Mines Misc Pap — Ontario. Division of Mines. Miscellaneous Paper

Ont Div Mines Prelim Map Geol Ser — Ontario. Division of Mines. Preliminary Map. Geological Series

Ont Div Mines Prelim Map Geophys Ser — Ontario. Division of Mines. Preliminary Map. Geophysical Series

Ont Ed — Ontario Education

ONTED — Ontario Technologist

ONTERIS — Ontario Education Resources Information System

Ont Field Biol — Ontario Field Biologist

Ont Fish Wildl Rev — Ontario Fish and Wildlife Review

Ont Fld Biol — Ontario Field Biologist

Ont For — Ontario Forests

Ont Geography — Ontario Geography

Ont Geol Surv Misc Pap — Ontario. Geological Survey. Miscellaneous Paper

Ont Geol Surv Rep — Ontario Geological Survey. Report

Ont Geol Surv Spec Vol — Ontario Geological Survey. Special Volume

Ont Geol Surv Study — Ontario Geological Survey. Study

Ont His S — Ontario Historical Society. Papers and Records

Ont Hist — Ontario History

Ont Hist Soc Pap — Ontario Historical Society. Papers and Records

Ont Hist Soc Pap Rec — Ontario Historical Society. Papers and Records

Ont Hortic Exp Stn Prod Lab Rep — Ontario. Horticulture Experiment Stations and Products Laboratory. Report

Ont Hydro-Res News — Ontario Hydro-Research News

Ont Hydro-Res Q — Ontario Hydro-Research Quarterly
Ont Hydro Res Rev — Ontario Hydro-Research News. Review
Ont Ind Arts Bul — Ontario Industrial Arts Association. Bulletin
Ont Ind Waste Conf Proc — Ontario Industrial Waste Conference. Proceedings
Ont J Educ Res — Ontario Journal of Educational Research
Ont Lab — Ontario Labour
Ont Law W — Ontario Lawyers Weekly
Ont Lib R — Ontario Library Review
Ont Libr Rev — Ontario Library Review
Ont LJ — Ontario Law Journal
Ont LJ (NS) — Ontario Law Journal, New Series
Ont Math G — Ontario Mathematics Gazette
Ont Med Rev — Ontario Medical Review
Ont Med Technol — Ontario Medical Technologist
Ont Minist Agric Food Publ — Ontario. Ministry of Agriculture and Food. Publication
Ont Minist Environ API Rep — Ontario Ministry of the Environment. API Report
Ont Minist Environ Res Rep — Ontario Ministry of the Environment. Research Report
Ont Minist Nat Resour Occas Pap — Ontario Ministry of Natural Resources. Occasional Paper
Ont Minist Nat Resour Ont Geol Surv Stud — Ontario Ministry of Natural Resources. Ontario Geological Survey Study
Ont Minist Transp Commun Eng Mater Off Rep EM — Ontario. Ministry of Transportation and Communications. Engineering Materials Office. Report EM
Ontog Brain — Ontogenesis of the Brain
Ontog Phylogenet Mech Neuroimmunomodulation — Ontogenetic and Phylogenetic Mechanisms of Neuroimmunomodulation
Ontog Razvit Zhivotn — Ontogeneticheskoe Razvitie Zhivotnykh
Ont Pet Inst Annu Conf Proc — Ontario Petroleum Institute. Annual Conference. Proceedings
Ont R & WN — Ontario Reports and Ontario Weekly Notes
ONTS — Old and New Testament Student
Ont Stat — Ontario Statistics
Ont Technol — Ontario Technologist
Ont Vet Coll Rep — Ontario Veterinary College. Report
Ont Week N — Ontario Weekly Notes
Ont Week R — Ontario Weekly Reporter
Ont Wkly N — Ontario Weekly Notes
Ont WN — Ontario Weekly Notes
ONU — Obshchestvennye Nauki v Usbekistane
ONU Intra LR — Ohio Northern University. Intramural Law Review
ONU LR — Ohio Northern University. Law Review
Onze Kst — Onze Kunst
OO — Oxford Outlook
OOB — OECD [*Organization for Economic Cooperation and Development*] Observer
O O B — Off Our Backs
OoB — Ord och Bild
OOEH — Oberoesterreichische Heimatblaetter
Ooe N — Oberoesterreichische Nachrichten
OOH — Oesterreichische Osthefte
Oologists' Rec — Oologists' Record
OoP — Okonomi og Politik
OOPK — Ookpik
OOQ — Occupational Outlook Quarterly
O Oslo — Ostraca Osloensia. Greek Ostraca in Norwegian Collections
Oostvlaam Zanten — Oostvlaamse Zanten. Tijdschrift van de Koninklijke Bond der Oostvlaamse Volkskundigen
OostvlZanten — Oostvlaamse Zanten
Oost W — Oost en West
OP — L'Orient Philatelique
OP — Obzor Praehistoricky
OP — Obzor Praehistoricky Revue Prehistorique
OP — Oelhydraulik und Pneumatik
O P — Open Places
OP — Opera
OP — Opera News
Op — Opinion. Journal de la Semaine
OP — O Positivismo. Revista de Philosophia
OP — Opsucula Patrum
Op — Opyty
OP — Ost-Probleme
OPA — Onze Pius-Almanak
OpA — Opuscula Archaeologica. Radovi Arheoloskog Instituta
OPAAER — Archaeological Survey of Alberta. Occasional Papers
OPACA — Optica Acta
OPACCD — Occasional Papers. Archibishops' Commission on Christian Doctrine
OPAFD7 — Allan Hancock Foundation. Occasional Papers
Op Arch — Opuscula Archaeologica. Radovi Arheoloskog Instituta
OPARI — Occasional Publications. African and Afro-American Research Institute. University of Texas, Austin
Op Ath — Opuscula Atheniensia
Op Athen — Opuscula Atheniensia
Opb — Opbouw
OPB — Oxford Paperbacks
OPBIA — Occasional Publications. British Institute of Archaeology at Ankara
Opbouw — Opbouwen
OPBSDH — Occasional Papers. Buffalo Society of Natural Sciences
OpC — Opera Canada
OPCBRF — Occasional Papers. Christian Brethren Research Fellowship
OPCCHS — Occasional Publication. Canadian Church Historical Society
OPCMAZ — Specialist Periodical Reports. Organophosphorus Chemistry
OPCOCM Symposium — Symposium on the Occurrence, Prediction, and Control of Outbursts in Coal Mines

OPD — Chemical Marketing Reporter
Op De Uitkijk — Op de Uitkijk. Bijblad van 'De Aarde en Haar Volken'
OPEC Bull — OPEC [*Organization of Petroleum Exporting Countries*] Bulletin
OPEC (Org Petroleum Exporting Countries) Bul — OPEC (Organization of Petroleum Exporting Countries) Bulletin
OPEC (Org Petroleum Exporting Countries) Pas — OPEC (Organization of Petroleum Exporting Countries) Papers
OPEC (Org Petroleum Exporting Countries) R — OPEC (Organization of Petroleum Exporting Countries) Review
Openbare Biblioth — Openbare Bibliotheek
Openb Kstbez — Openbaar Kunstbezit
Open File Rep Geol Surv North Irel — Open-File Report. Geological Survey of Northern Ireland
Open-File Rep US Geol Surv — Open-File Report. United States Geological Survey
Open Hearth Basic Oxygen Steel Conf Proc — Open Hearth and Basic Oxygen Steel Conference. Proceedings
Open Hearth Proc — Open Hearth Proceedings
Open Hearth Proc AIME — Open Hearth Proceedings. Metallurgical Society of AIME [*American Institute of Mining, Metallurgical, and Petroleum Engineers*]. Iron and Steel Division
Open Learn Sys News — Open Learning Systems News
Open Tech Conf Proc Sprinkler Irrig Assoc — Open Technical Conference Proceedings. Sprinkler Irrigation Association
Open Tech Prog News — Open Tech Program News
Open Univ Set Book — Open University Set Book
Opera — Opera and Concert
Opera — Opera News
Opera Biol — Acta Societatis Scientiarum Fennica. Series B. Opera Biologica
Opera Bot — Opera Botanica
Opera Can — Opera Canada
Opera Collecta Cent Bosbiol Onderz Bokrijk-Genk — Opera Collecta. Centrum voor Bosbiologisch Onderzoek. Bokrijk-Genk
Opera J — Opera Journal
Opera N — Opera News
Opera Q — Opera Quarterly
Operational Res Quart — Operational Research Quarterly
Operation Res — Operations Research
Operator Theory Advances and Appl — Operator Theory. Advances and Applications
Operator Theory Adv Appl — Operator Theory. Advances and Applications
Operat Res — Operations Research
Operat Res Q — Operational Research Quarterly
Operat R Q — Operational Research Quarterly
Oper Dent — Operative Dentistry
Oper Miller — Operative Miller
Opernforschung — Jahrbuch fuer Opernforschung
Oper Program Systems Ser — Operating and Programming Systems Series
Oper Res — Operations Research
Oper Res Indust Engrg — Operations Reseearch and Industrial Engineering
Oper Res Lett — Operations Research Letters
Oper Res Q — Operational Research Quarterly
Oper Res Quart — Operational Research Quarterly
Oper Sect Proc Am Gas Assoc — Operating Section Proceedings. American Gas Association
Oper Syst Rev — Operating Systems Review
Oper Theory Adv Appl — Operator Theory. Advances and Applications
OPF — Public Finance. International Quarterly Journal
OPFAEI — Freshwater Biological Association. Occasional Publication
OPFCDN — Great Britain. Forestry Commission. Occasional Paper
Oph — Ophrys
OPh — Opuscula Philologica
OPh — Opuscula Philosophica
OPH — Oriental Studies published in Commemoration of the Fortieth Anniversary of PaulHaupt as Director of the Oriental Seminary. Johns Hopkins Universit
Oph Bb — Ophthalmologische Bibliothek
Ophthal For — Ophthalmic Forum
Ophthal Lit — Ophthalmic Literature
Ophthalmic Epidemiol — Ophthalmic Epidemiology
Ophthalmic Genet — Ophthalmic Genetics
Ophthalmic Lit — Ophthalmic Literature
Ophthalmic Nurs Forum — Ophthalmic Nursing Forum
Ophthalmic Paediatr Genet — Ophthalmic Paediatrics and Genetics
Ophthalmic Physiol Opt — Ophthalmic and Physiological Optics
Ophthalmic Plast Reconstr Surg — Ophthalmic Plastic and Reconstructive Surgery
Ophthalmic Res — Ophthalmic Research
Ophthalmic Semin — Ophthalmic Seminars
Ophthalmic Surg — Ophthalmic Surgery
Ophthalmic Surg Lasers — Ophthalmic Surgery and Lasers
Ophthalmic Toxicol — Ophthalmic Toxicology
Ophthalmola — Ophthalmologica
Ophthalmol Clin North Am — Ophthalmology Clinics of North America
Ophthalmol Ibero Am — Ophthalmologia Ibero-Americana
Ophthalmologica Suppl — Ophthalmologica. Supplement
Ophthalmol Proc Int Congr — Ophthalmology. Proceedings. International Congress
Ophthalmol Times — Ophthalmology Times
Ophthalmol War Years — Ophthalmology in the War Years
Ophthal Opt — Ophthalmic Optician
Ophthal Plast Reconstr Surg — Ophthalmic Plastic and Reconstructive Surgery
Ophthal Res — Ophthalmic Research
Ophth Rec — Ophthalmic Record
Ophth Soc Aust Trans — Ophthalmological Society of Australia. Transactions
OPI — Bibliotheek en Samenleving

Opl — Opus International
Opin Int Commn Zool Nom — Opinions Rendered by the International Commission on Zoological Nomenclature
Opinion N — Opinion Nationale
Opir Mater Teor Sporud — Opir Materialiv i Teoriya Sporud
Opisanie Izobret Avtorskomu Svidet — Opisanie Izobreteniya k Avtorskomu Svidetel'stvu
Opisanie Izobret Pat — Opisanie Izobreteniya k Patentu
Opisanie Sist Inf Obespecheniya Khim Promsti — Opisanie Sistemy Informatsionnogo Obespecheniya v Khimicheskoi Promyshlennosti
Opis Pat Pat Tymczasowego — Opis Patentowy Patentu Tymczasowego
Opis Pat Pol — Opis Patentowy (Poland)
OPJ — O Primeiro de Janeiro
OPL — Osservatore Politico Letterario
OPL — Our Public Lands
OPLA — Our Public Lands
OPLiLL — Occasional Papers in Linguistics and Language Learning
OPLing — Occasional Papers on Linguistics
OPLLL — Occasional Papers in Language, Literature, and Linguistics
OPM — Oriental Philosophy Half-Monthly Magazine
OPML — Occasional Papers in Modern Languages
OpN — Opera News
Op News — Opera News
Opns Res — Operations Research
OPO — OPEC [*Organization of Petroleum Exporting Countries*] Review
OPO — Ophthalmic and Physiological Optics
Opolskie Tow Przyj Nauk Wydz 5 Nauk Med Pr Med — Opolskie Towarzystwo Przyjaciol Nauk. Wydzial 5 Nauk Medycznych. Prace Medyczne
Opolsk Roczn Ekon — Opolskie Roczniki Ekonomiczne
OPPI — Organic Preparations and Procedures International
Oppor Man Made Fibres Pap Shirley Int Semin — Opportunities for Man-Made Fibres. Papers Presented. Shirley International Seminar
Oppor Mat Proc Buhl Int Conf Mater — Opportunities in Materials. Proceedings. Buhl International Conference on Materials
Oppor North Can — Opportunity in Northern Canada
OPR — Operations Research
Op R — Opuscula Romana
Op Res — Operations Research
Op Res Q — Operational Research Quarterly
Op Res Soc J — Operational Research Society Journal
Op Rom — Opuscula Romana
OPRQSL — O Pantheon. Revista Quinzenal de Sciencias e Letras
Opscula Math — Opuscula Mathematica
OPSED — Ophthalmic Seminars
Op Spectra — Optical Spectra
Ops Research — Operations Research
OPSS — Operating and Programming Systems Series
OPT — Optima
OPT — Optimum
Opt Acta — Optica Acta
Opt Act Switching — Optically Activated Switching
Opt Agric — Optics in Agriculture
Opt Alliance — Optical Alliance
Opt and Lasers Eng — Optics and Lasers in Engineering
Opt and Laser Technol — Optics and Laser Technology
Opt & Photonics News — Optics and Photonics News
Opt and Quantum Electron — Optical and Quantum Electronics
Opt and Spectrosc — Optics and Spectroscopy
Opt & Spektrosk — Optika i Spektroskopiya
Opt Appl — Optica Applicata
Opt Commun — Optics Communications
Opt Comput Archit Technol — Optics for Computers. Architectures and Technologies
Opt Data Storage — Optical Data Storage
Opt Data Storage Technol — Optical Data Storage Technologies
Opt Des Process Technol Appl — Optical Design and Processing Technologies and Applications [*Chicago*]
Opt Dev — Optical Developments
Opt Digital GaAs Technol Signal Process Appl — Optical and Digital GaAs Technologies for Signal-Processing Applications
Opt-Electron — Opto-Electronique
Opt Electr Prop Polym Symp — Optical and Electrical Properties of Polymers. Symposium
Opt Eng — Optical Engineering
Opt Engin — Optical Engineering
Opt Engrg — Optical Engineering
Opt Enhancements Comput Technol — Optical Enhancements to Computing Technology
Opteoelektorn and Poluprovodn Tekh — Opteolektronika i Poluprovodnikovaya Tekhnika
Opt Excitons Confined Syst Proc Int Meet — Optics of Excitons in Confined Systems. Proceedings. International Meeting
Opt Express — Optics Express. The International Electronics Journal of Optics
Opt Fabr Test — Optical Fabrication and Testing
Opt Fiber Commun — Optical Fiber Communications
Opt Fibers Med — Optical Fibers in Medicine
Opt Fiber Transm — Optical Fiber Transmission
Opt Fibre Sens Int Conf — Optical Fibre Sensors. International Conference
Optical Engin — Optical Engineering
Optik — Optik. Zeitschrift fuer Licht- und Elektronenoptik
Optikomekh Prom — Optiko-Mekhanicheskaya Promyshlennost'
Opt Illum Image Sens Mach Vision — Optics, Illumination, and Image Sensing for Machine Vision
Optimal Control Appl Methods — Optimal Control Applications and Methods
Optimal Planirovanie — Optimal'noe Planirovanie

Optim Control Appl Methods — Optimal Control Applications and Methods
Optimizacija — Akademija Nauk SSSR. Sibirskoe Otdelenie. Institut Matematiki. Optimizacija
Optimization — Mathematische Operationsforschung und Statistik. Series Optimization
Optim Metall Protsessov — Optimizatsiya Metallurgicheskikh Protsessov
Optim Method Software — Optimization Methods and Software
Opt Inf Process Syst Archit — Optical Information-Processing Systems and Architectures
Options Mediterr — Options Mediterraneennes
Opt Laser Microlithogr — Optical/Laser Microlithography
Opt Lasers Eng — Optics and Lasers in Engineering
Opt Laser Technol — Optics and Laser Technology
Opt Laser Technol Spec Suppl — Optics and Laser Technology. Special Supplement
Opt Lett — Optics Letters
Opt Mass Data Storage Int Conf — Optical Mass Data Storage. International Conference
Opt Mat — Optical Materials
Opt Mater — Optical Materials
Opt Mater Amsterdam — Optical Materials (Amsterdam)
Opt Mater Technol Energy Effic Sol Energy Convers — Optical Materials Technology for Energy Efficiency and Solar Energy Conversion
Opt Mech Ind Leningrad — Optisch-Mechanische Industrie (Leningrad)
Opt-Mekh Prom — Optiko-Mekhanicheskaya Promyshlennost'
Opt-Mekh Prom-St' — Optiko-Mekhanicheskaya Promyshlennost'
Opt Mem Neural Networks — Optical Memory and Neural Networks
Opt Methods Time State Resolved Chem — Optical Methods for Time- and State-Resolved Chemistry
Opt Microlithog — Optical Microlithography
Opt News — Optics News
Opto-Electron — Opto-Electronics
Optoelectron Devices Appl — Optoelectronic Devices and Applications
Optoelectron Devices Technol — Optoelectronics. Devices and Technologies
Optoelectron Environ Sci — Optoelectronics for Environmental Science
Optoelectron Prop Semicond Superlattices — Optoelectronic Properties of Semiconductors and Superlattices
Opto Electron Rev — Opto-Electronics Review
Optoelektron Poluprovodn Tekh — Optoelektronika i Poluprovodnikovaya Tekhnika
Optoelektron Spektrosk — Optoelektronika i Spektroskopiya
Optogalvanic Spectrosc Proc Int Meet — Optogalvanic Spectroscopy. Proceedings. International Meeting
Optom Clin — Optometry Clinics
Optomech Dimens Stab — Optomechanics and Dimensional Stability
Optomet M — Optometric Monthly
Optom Vision Sci — Optometry and Vision Science
Optom Vis Sci — Optometry and Vision Science
Opt Pura Apl — Optica Pura y Aplicada
Opt Pura y Apl — Optica Pura y Aplicada
Opt Quant E — Optical and Quantum Electronics
Opt Quantum Electron — Optical and Quantum Electronics
Opt Rev — Optical Review
Opt Scanning — Optical Scanning
Opt Soc Am J — Optical Society of America. Journal
Opt Soc London Trans — Optical Society. London. Transactions
Opt Space Commun — Optical Space Communication
Opt Spectra — Optical Spectra
Opt Spectrosc (Engl Transl) — Optics and Spectroscopy (English Translation of Optika i Spektroskopiya)
Opt Spectrosc (USSR) — Optics and Spectroscopy (USSR)
Opt Spectry — Optics and Spectroscopy
Opt Spektro — Optika i Spektroskopiya
Opt Spektrosk — Optika i Spektroskopiya
Opt Spektrosk Akad Nauk SSSR Otd Fiz-Mat Nauk — Optika i Spektroskopiya. Akademiya Nauk SSSR. Otdelenie Fiziko-Matematicheskikh Nauk
Opt Surf Resist Severe Environ — Optical Surfaces Resistant to Severe Environments
Opt Syst Adverse Environ — Optical Systems in Adverse Environments
Opt Technol — Optics Technology
Opt Technol Microwave Appl — Optical Technology for Microwave Applications
Op Uitkijk Christ Cult Mabl — Op de Uitkijk. Christelijk Cultureel Maandblad
OPURD7 — Institute of Arctic and Alpine Research. University of Colorado. Occasional Paper
Opus Arch — Opuscula Archaeologica
Opus Ath — Opuscula Atheniensia
Opusc Arch — Opuscula Archaeologica. Radovi Arheoloskog Instituta
Opusc Archaeol — Opuscula Archaeologica. Radovi Arheoloskog Instituta
Opusc Athen — Opuscula Atheniensia. Skrifter Utgivna av Svenska Institutet i Athen - Acta Instituti Atheniensis Regni Sueciae
Opusc Ent — Opuscula Entomologica
Opusc Entomol — Opuscula Entomologica
Opusc Med — Opuscula Medica
Opusc Med Suppl — Opuscula Medica. Supplementum
Opusc Mt Fis — Opuscoli Matematici e Fisici di Diversi Autori
Opusc Scelti Sci Arti — Opusculi Scelti Sulle Scienze e Sulle Arti
Opuscula Archaeol — Opuscula Archaeologia
Opuscula Athen — Opuscula Atheniensia
Opuscula Inst Romani Finland — Opuscula Instituti Romani Finlandiae
Opusc Zool (Bpest) — Opuscula Zoologica (Budapest)
Opusc Zool (Budap) — Opuscula Zoologica (Budapest)
Opusc Zool (Munich) — Opuscula Zoologica (Munich)
Opus Int — Opus International
Opus M — Opus Musicum
Opus Mus — Opus Musicum

Opus Ph — Opuscula Philologica
Opus Rom — Opuscula Romana
Opus Zool (Muenchen) — Opuscula Zoologica (Muenchen)
OpW — Opern Welt
OPWA — Official Publications of Western Australia
OPWA — Oxford Pamphlet on World Affairs
Opyt Izuch Regul Fiziol Funkts — Opyt Izucheniya Regulyatsii Fiziologicheskikh Funktsii
Opytn Agron — Opytnaya Agronomiya
Opyt Paseka — Opytnaya Paseka
Opyt Primen Radioakt Metodov Poiskakh Razved Neradioakt Rud — Opyt Primeneniya Radioaktivnykh Metodov pri Poiskakh i Razvedke Neradioaktivnykh Rud
Opyt Rab Pchel — Opytnaya Rabota Pchelovodov
Opyt Rab Peredovogo Sovkhoznogo Proizvod — Opyt Raboty Peredovogo Sovkhoznogo Proizvodstva
OQ — Ohioana Quarterly
OQDEAN — Orquidea
OR — Odrodzenie i Reformacja w Polsce
OR — Oil and Resource Development Supplement. Fairbanks Daily News Miner
OR — Oklahoma Law Review
OR — Oltenia Romana
OR — Operational Research Quarterly
OR — Operations Research
OR — Opuscula Romana
OR — Orbis
OR — Oregon Music Educator
OR — Oregon Reports
Or — Orient
Or — Orientalia. Commentarii Periodici Pontificii Instituti Biblici
Or — Orientalist
OR — Orient Review
Or — Orizont
Or — Orpheus. Revista pentru Cultura Clasica
OR — Osservatore Romano
OR — Oxford Review
OR — Schweizerisches Obligationenrecht
ORA — OR. Journal of the Operational Research Society
ORA — Outdoor Recreation Action
ORA — Overseas Reports Announcements
OR Admin R — Oregon Administrative Rules
OR Admin R Bull — Oregon Administrative Rules Bulletin
Or Admin R Bull — Oregon Administrative Rules Bulletin
Oral Biol — Oral Biology
Orale Implantol — Orale Implantologie
Oral H — Oral History
Oral Hist — Oral History
Oral Hyg — Oral Hygiene
Oral Implantol — Oral Implantology
Oral Microbiol Basic Microbiol Immunol — Oral Microbiology with Basic Microbiology and Immunology
Oral Microbiol Immunol — Oral Microbiology and Immunology
Oral Oncol — Oral Oncology
Oral Res Abstr — Oral Research Abstracts
Oral Sci Rev — Oral Sciences Reviews
Oral Surg — Oral Surgery, Oral Medicine, and Oral Pathology
Oral Surgery — Oral Surgery, Oral Medicine, and Oral Pathology
Oral Surg O — Oral Surgery, Oral Medicine, and Oral Pathology
Oral Surg Oral Med Oral Pathol — Oral Surgery, Oral Medicine, and Oral Pathology
Oral Surg Oral Med Oral Pathol Oral Radiol Endod — Oral Surgery, Oral Medicine, Oral Pathology, Oral Radiology and Endodontics
Oral Surg Trans Int Conf — Oral Surgery. Transactions. International Conference on Oral Surgery
Oral Ther Pharmacol — Oral Therapeutics and Pharmacology
Or An — Oriens Antiquus
Orang C BJ — Orange County Business Journal
Orange County BJ — Orange County Bar Association. Journal
Orange County Bus — Orange County Business
Orange Cty — Business Press of Orange County
Orange Cty Dent Soc Bull — Orange County [*California*] Dental Society. Bulletin
OrAnt — Oriens Antiquus
OrAntBud — Oriens Antiquus
OR App — Oregon Reports. Court of Appeals
Or Arch — Orientalisches Archiv
Or Art — Oriental Art
Orb Cath — Orbis Catholicus (Wien)
Orb Cath B — Orbis Catholicus (Barcelona)
Orb Chr — Orbis Christianus
Or Bibl — Orientalische Bibliographie
OrBiblLov — Orientalia et Biblica Lovaniensia
OrBibLov — Orientalia et Biblica Lovaniensia
ORBIS — Oregon Business Information System
Orbis Lit — Orbis Litterarum
Orbis Mus — Orbis Musicae
Orb Lit — Orbis Litterarum
Orb Litt — Orbis Litterarum
Orb Rom — Orbis Romanus
Orc — Orchester
Orch — Orchardist
Orchardist NZ — Orchardist of New Zealand
Orchard NZ — Orchardist of New Zealand
Orchid Biol — Orchid Biology
Orchid Dig — Orchid Digest
Orchid J — Orchid Journal

Orchidol Zeylancia — Orchidologia Zeylancia
OrChr — Oriens Christianus
OrChrA — Orientalia Christiana Analecta
Or Christ — Oriens Christianus
Or Chr P — Orientalia Christiana Periodica
OrChrPer — Orientalia Christiana Periodica
ORCODO — Annual Research Reviews. Oral Contraceptives
Or Cr — Oriente Cristiano. Madrid
ORD — Organizational Dynamics
Ord Dept Doc — Ordinance Department Document
Ordenskunde — Ordenskunde Beitraege zur Geschichte der Auszeichnungen
Ordering Surf Interfaces Proc NEC Symp — Ordering at Surfaces and Interfaces. Proceedings. NEC Symposium
Ordo Can — Ordo Canonicus
Ordre des Architectes du Quebec Bull Technique — Ordre des Architectes du Quebec. Bulletin Technique
ORE — Rekreaksie. Vakblad voor Recreatie Ondernemers
Ore Ag Exp — Oregon. Agricultural Experiment Station. Publications
Ore Agric Progr — Oregon's Agricultural Progress
Or Ec — Oriental Economist
OrEcon — Oriental Economist
Ore Conc Ind — Ore-Concentration Industry
Oreg Agric Exp Stn Bull — Oregon. Agricultural Experiment Station. Bulletin
Oreg Agric Exp Stn Cir — Oregon Agricultural Experiment Station. Circular
Oreg Agric Exp Stn Misc Pap — Oregon. Agricultural Experiment Station. Miscellaneous Paper
Oreg Agric Exp Stn Spec Rep — Oregon. Agricultural Experiment Station. Special Report
Oreg Agric Exp Stn Stn Bull — Oregon. Agricultural Experiment Station. Station Bulletin
Oreg Agric Exp Stn Tech Bull — Oregon. Agricultural Experiment Station. Technical Bulletin
Oreg Agric Prog Oreg Agric Exp Stn — Oregon's Agricultural Progress. Oregon Agricultural Experiment Station
Oreg Agr Progr — Oregon's Agricultural Progress
Oreg Bur Mines Min Res Oreg — Oregon. Bureau of Mines and Geology. Mineral Resources of Oregon
Oreg Dep Geol Miner Ind Bull — Oregon. Department of Geology and Mineral Industries. Bulletin
Oreg Dep Geol Miner Ind GMI Short Pap — Oregon. Department of Geology and Mineral Industries. GMI Short Paper
Oreg Dep Geol Miner Ind Misc Pap — Oregon. Department of Geology and Mineral Industries. Miscellaneous Paper
Oreg Dep Geol Miner Ind Misc Paper — Oregon. Department of Geology and Mineral Industries. Miscellaneous Paper
Oregelkunst Vier T — Orgelkunst. Viermaandelijks Tijdschrift
Ore Geol Rev — Ore Geology Reviews
Oreg Fish Comm Contrib — Oregon. Fish Commission. Contributions
Oreg Fish Comm Res Briefs — Oregon. Fish Commission. Research Briefs
Oreg For Prod Lab Bull — Oregon Forest Products Laboratory. Bulletin
Oreg For Prod Lab (Corvallis) Prog Rep — Oregon. Forest Products Laboratory (Corvallis). Progress Report
Oreg For Prod Lab Inf Circ — Oregon Forest Products Laboratory. Information Circular
Oreg For Prod Lab Res Leafl — Oregon Forest Products Laboratory. Research Leaflet
Oreg For Prod Lab Spec Rep — Oregon Forest Products Laboratory. Special Report
Oreg For Prod Res Cent Bull — Oregon Forest Products Research Center. Bulletin
Oreg For Prod Res Cent Inf Circ — Oregon Forest Products Research Center. Information Circular
Oreg For Prod Res Cent Prog Rep — Oregon. Forest Products Research Center. Progress Report
Oreg For Res Cent Inf Circ — Oregon Forest Research Center. Information Circular
Oreg Ground Water Rep — Oregon. Ground Water Report
Oreg Hist Q — Oregon Historical Quarterly
Oreg Insect Contr Handb — Oregon Insect Control Handbook
Oreg L Rev — Oregon Law Review
Oreg Min — Oregon Mineralogist
Oreg Nurs — Oregon Nurse
Oreg Nurse — Oregon Nurse
Oregon Agric Exp Sta Circ — Oregon Agricultural Experiment Station Circular
Oregon Agric Exp Sta Circ Inform — Oregon Agricultural Experiment Station. Circular Information
Oregon Bsn — Oregon Business
Oregon Dep Geol Mineral Ind Oil Gas Invest — Oregon. Department of Geology and Mineral Industries. Oil and Gas Investigation
Oregon Dept Geology and Mineral Industries Bull — Oregon. Department of Geology and Mineral Industries. Bulletin
Oregon Dept Geology and Mineral Industries Geol Map Ser — Oregon. Department of Geology and Mineral Industries. Geological Map Series
Oregon Geol — Oregon Geology
Oregon Hist Q — Oregon Historical Quarterly
Oregon Orchid Soc Bull — Oregon Orchid Society Bulletin
Oregon Ornam Nursery Digest — Oregon Ornamental and Nursery Digest. Oregon Agricultural College. Agricultural Experiment Station
Oregon State Monogr Stud Bot — Oregon State Monographs. Studies in Botany
Oreg SB Bull — Oregon State Bar Bulletin
Oreg State Agric Coll Agric Exp Stn Bull — Oregon State Agricultural College. Agricultural Experiment Station. Bulletin
Oreg State Agric Coll Agric Exp Stn Circ — Oregon State Agricultural College. Agricultural Experiment Station. Circular

Oreg State Agric Coll Eng Exp Stn — Oregon State Agricultural College. Engineering Experiment Station

Oreg State Chapter Phi Kappa Phi Biol Colloq — Oregon State Chapter of Phi Kappa Phi. Biology Colloquium

Oreg State Coll Agric Exp Stn Bull — Oregon State College. Agricultural Experiment Station. Bulletin

Oreg State Coll Agric Exp Stn Circ — Oregon State College. Agricultural Experiment Station. Circular

Oreg State Coll Eng Exp Stn Bull — Oregon State College. Engineering Experiment Station. Bulletin

Oreg State Coll Eng Exp Stn Circ — Oregon State College. Engineering Experiment Station. Circular

Oreg State Coll Eng Exp Stn Repr — Oregon State College. Engineering Experiment Station. Reprint

Oreg State Dent J — Oregon State Dental Journal

Oreg State Dep Geol Miner Ind Spec Pap — Oregon. State Department of Geology and Mineral Industries. Special Paper

Oreg State Eng Ground Water Rep — Oregon State Engineer. Ground Water Report

Oreg State Hortic Soc Ann Rep — Oregon State Horticultural Society. Annual Report

Oreg State Monogr Stud Bacteriol — Oregon State Monographs. Studies in Bacteriology

Oreg State Monogr Stud Bot — Oregon State Monographs. Studies in Botany

Oreg State Monogr Stud Entomol — Oregon State Monographs. Studies in Entomology

Oreg State Monogr Stud Geol — Oregon State Monographs. Studies in Geology

Oreg State Monogr Stud Pol Sci — Oregon State Monographs. Studies in Political Science

Oreg State Monogr Stud Zool — Oregon State Monographs. Studies in Zoology

Oreg State Univ Biol Colloq — Oregon State University. Biology Colloquium

Oreg State Univ Eng Exp Sta Circ — Oregon State University (Corvallis). Engineering Experiment Station. Circular

Oreg State Univ Eng Exp Stn Circ — Oregon State University. Engineering Experiment Station. Circular

Oreg State Univ For Res Lab Annu Rep — Oregon State University. Forest Research Laboratory. Annual Report

Oreg State Univ For Res Lab Bull — Oregon State University. Forest Research Laboratory. Bulletin

Oreg State Univ For Res Lab Prog Rep — Oregon State University. Forest Research Laboratory. Progress Report

Oreg State Univ For Res Lab Res Bull — Oregon State University. Forest Research Laboratory. Research Bulletin

Oreg State Univ For Res Lab Res Pap — Oregon State University. Forest Research Laboratory. Research Paper

Oreg State Univ Sch Agric Symp Ser — Oregon State University. School of Agriculture. Symposium Series

Oreg State Univ Sch For For Res Lab Res Note — Oregon State University. School of Forestry. Forest Research Laboratory. Research Notes

Oreg State Univ Water Resour Res Inst Semin Proc SEMIN WR — Oregon State University. Water Resources Research Institute. Seminar Proceedings. SEMIN WR

Oreg St Univ Agric Exp Stn Stn Bull — Oregon State University. Agricultural Experiment Station. Station Bulletin

Oreg Water Resour Dep Ground Water Rep — Oregon. Water Resources Department. Ground Water Report.

ORE HIS Q — Oregon Historical Society. Quarterly

Ore Hist Q — Oregon Historical Quarterly

Ore Hist Quar — Oregon Historical Quarterly. Oregon Historical Society

Ore Hist Soc Q — Oregon Historical Society. Quarterly

Ore Hist Soc Quar — Oregon Historical Society. Quarterly

Orehovo-Zuev Ped Inst Ucen Zap Kaf Mat — Orehovo-Zuevskii Pedagogiceskii Institut. Ucenye Zapiski Kafedry Matematiki

OreHQ — Oregon Historical Quarterly

Ore H Soc Quar — Oregon Historical Society. Quarterly

Ore Law Rev — Oregon Law Review. University of Oregon

Ore LR — Oregon Law Review

Ore L Rev — Oregon Law Review

Orenb Gos Pedagog Inst Uch Zap — Orenburgskii Gosudarstvennyi Pedagogicheskii Institut. Uchenye Zapiski

Orenburg Gos Ped Inst Ucen Zap — Orenburgskii Gosudarstvennyi Pedagogiceskii Institut Imeni V. P. Ckalova. Ucenye Zapiski

O R (English) — Osservatore Romano (English)

Ores Met — Ores and Metals

Ores Sediments Int Sedimentol Congr — Ores in Sediments. International Sedimentological Congress

Ore St B Bul — Oregon State Bar. Bulletin

Ore St B Bull — Oregon State Bar Bulletin

Or Eu — Oriente Europeo

O Rev — Occasional Review

Or Ex — Oriens Extremus

ORF — Oratorum Romanorum Fragmenta Liberae rei Publicae

ORFE — Ornis Fennica

ORFr — Oratorum Romanorum Fragmenta

ORG — Human Organization

ORG — Official Recreation Guide

Org — Organist

Org — Orgue

Organ Afr Unity Sci Tech Res Comm Publ — Organization of African Unity. Scientific and Technical Research Commission. Publication

Organ Am States Ann — Organization of American States. Annals

Organ Assem Chem Anal — Organized Assemblies in Chemical Analysis

Organ Behav Hum Decis Process — Organizational Behavior and Human Decision Processes

Organ Behav Hum Perform — Organizational Behavior and Human Performance

Organ Behavior & Human Perf — Organizational Behavior and Human Performance

Organ Beh H — Organizational Behavior and Human Performance

Organ Biol — Organ Biology

Organ Christ Kst — Organ fuer Christliche Kunst

OrGand — Orientalia Gandensia

Organ Directed Toxic Anticancer Drugs Proc Int Symp — Organ Directed Toxicities of Anticancer Drugs. Proceedings. International Symposium on Organ Directed Toxicities of Anticancer Drugs

Organ Dyn — Organizational Dynamics

Organ Dynam — Organizational Dynamics

Organ Estados Am Programa Reg Desarrollo Cient Tecnol Monogr — Organizacion de los Estados Americanos. Programa Regional de Desarrollo Cientifico y Tecnologico. Monografia. Seriede Quimica

Organ Estados Am Programa Reg Desarrollo Cient Tecnol Ser Bio — Organizacion de los Estados Americanos. Programa Regional de Desarrollo Cientifico y Tecnologico. Serie de Biologia

Organ Eur Mediterr Prot Plant Bull — Organisation Europeenne et Mediterraneenne pour la Protection des Plantes. Bulletin

Organ Eur Mediterr Prot Plant Publ Ser A — Organisation Europeenne et Mediterraneenne pour la Protection des Plantes. Publications. Serie A

Organ Eur Mediterr Prot Plant Publ Ser D — Organisation Europeenne et Mediterraneenne pour la Protection des Plantes. Publications. Serie D

Organ Eur Rech Nucl Rapp — Organisation Europeenne pour la Recherche Nucleaire. Rapport

Organ Eur Rech Spat Contract Rep — Organisation Europeenne de Recherches Spatiales. Contractor Report

Organ Expression Globin Genes Proc Conf Hemoglobin Switching — Organization and Expression of Globin Genes. Proceedings. Conference on Hemoglobin Switching

Organ Expression Mitochondrial Genome Proc Int Bari Conf — Organization and Expression of the Mitochondrial Genome. Proceedings. International Bari Conference

Organ Fortschr Eisenbahnwes — Organ fuer die Fortschritte des Eisenbahnwesens

Organ Gestosis Int Meet — Organization Gestosis. International Meeting

Organic Gard — Organic Gardening

Organic Gard & F — Organic Gardening and Farming

Organic Geochem — Organic Geochemistry

Organ Ind Res TNO Cent Tech Inst Heat Technol Dep Pap — Organization for Industrial Research TNO. Central Technical Institute. Heat Technology Department. Paper

Organists R — Organists Review

Organized Lab — Organized Labor

Organ Mass Spectr — Organic Mass Spectrometry

Organohalogen Compd — Organohalogen Compounds

Organomet Chem — Organometallic Chemistry

Organomet Chem Rev — Organometallic Chemistry Reviews

Organomet Chem Rev Ann Surv — Organometallic Chemistry Reviews. Annual Surveys. Transition Metals in Organic Synthesis, Organic Reactions of Selected n-Complexes

Organomet Chem Rev Ann Surv Silicon Germanium Tin Lead — Organometallic Chemistry Reviews. Annual Surveys. Silicon-Germanium-Tin-Lead

Organomet Chem Rev Ann Surv Silicon Lead — Organometallic Chemistry Reviews. Annual Surveys. Silicon-Lead

Organomet Chem Rev Ann Surv Silicon Tin Lead — Organometallic Chemistry Reviews. Annual Surveys. Silicon-Tin-Lead

Organomet Chem Rev Organosilicon Rev — Organometallic Chemistry Reviews. Organosilicon Reviews

Organomet Chem Rev Sect A — Organometallic Chemistry Reviews. Section A. Subject Reviews

Organomet Chem Rev Sect B — Organometallic Chemistry Reviews. Section B. Annual Surveys

Organomet Chem Synth — Organometallics in Chemical Synthesis

Organomet News — Organometallic News

Organomet React — Organometallic Reactions

Organomet React Synth — Organometallic Reactions and Syntheses

Organon — Textile Organon

Organophosphorus Chem — Organophosphorus Chemistry

Organosulfur Chem — Organosulfur Chemistry. Synthetic and Stereochemical Aspects

Organ Rada — Organizacija Rada

Organ React — Organic Reactions

Organ Struct Polym Solutions Gels Microsymp Macromol — Organized Structures in Polymer Solutions and Gels. Prague IUPAC Microsymposiumon Macromolecules

Organ Stud — Organization Studies

Organ Yb — Organ Yearbook

Organzr — Organizer

Org Behav and Hum Perform — Organizational Behavior and Human Performance

Org Chem — Organic Chemistry. A Series of Monographs

Org Chem Bull — Organic Chemical Bulletin

Org Chem Ind — Organic Chemical Industry

Org Chem (New York) — Organic Chemistry (New York)

Org Chem Ser Monogr — Organic Chemistry: A Series of Monographs

Org Chem Shanghai — Organic Chemistry (Shanghai)

Org Coat — Organic Coatings. Science and Technology

Org Coatings Appl Polym Sci Proc — Organic Coatings and Applied Polymer Science Proceedings

Org Coat Int Meet Phys Chem — Organic Coatings. International Meeting of Physical Chemistry

Org Coat Plast Chem — Organic Coatings and Plastics Chemistry

Org Comm — Organizational Communication

Org Compd Aquat Environ Rudolfs Res Conf — Organic Compounds in Aquatic Environments. Rudolfs Research Conference

Org Compd Sulphu Selenium Tellurium — Organic Compounds of Sulphur, Selenium, and Tellurium
Org Cryst Chem Pap Symp — Organic Crystal Chemistry. Papers. Symposium on Organic Crystal Chemistry
Org Dyn — Organizational Dynamics
Org Dynamics — Organizational Dynamics
Org Farmer — Organic Farmer
Org Finish — Organic Finishing
ORGG-A — Oriental Geographer
ORGGAH — Oriental Geographer
Org Gard — Organic Gardening
Org Gard Farming — Organic Gardening and Farming
Org Gdng Fmg — Organic Gardening and Farming
Org Geochem — Organic Geochemistry
Org Inst — Organ Institute. Quarterly
Org Inst Q — Organ Institute. Quarterly
Org Katal — Organicheskii Kataliz
Org Lett — Organic Letters
Org Magn Resonance — Organic Magnetic Resonance
Org Mass Sp — Organic Mass Spectrometry
Org Mass Spectrom — Organic Mass Spectrometry
Org Micropollut Aquat Environ Proc Eur Symp — Organic Micropollutants in the Aquatic Environment. Proceedings. European Symposium
Org Militwiss Vereine — Organ der Militaerwissenschaftlichen Vereine
ORGND — Organometallics
Org Photochem — Organic Photochemistry
Org Photochem Synth — Organic Photochemical Syntheses
Org Poluprod Krasiteli — Organicheskie Poluprodukty i Krasiteli
Org Poluprovodn — Organicheskie Poluprovodniki
Org Prep Proced — Organic Preparations and Procedures
Org Prep Proced Int — Organic Preparations and Procedures International
Org Process Res & Dev — Organic Process Research and Development
OrgR — Organist's Review
Org React — Organic Reactions
Org React — Organic Reactivity
Org React (Eng Transl) — Organic Reactivity (English Translation)
Org React Mech — Organic Reaction Mechanisms
Org React (Tartu) — Organic Reactivity (Tartu)
Org React (USSR) — Organic Reactivity (USSR)
ORGREB-Inst Kraftwerke Inf — ORGREB [*Organisation fuer Abnahme, Betriebsfuehrung, und Rationalisierung von Energieanlagen*]-Institut fuer Kraftwerke. Informationen
Or Gr Inscr Sel — Orientis Graeci Inscriptiones Selectae
Or Gr IS — Orientis Graeci Inscriptiones Selectae
Org Sci — Organizational Science
Org Scientifique — Organisation Scientifique
Org Semicond Proc Inter Ind Conf — Organic Semiconductors. Proceedings. Inter-Industry Conference
Org Sulfur Compd — Organic Sulfur Compounds
Org Synt — Organic Syntheses
Org Synth High Pressures — Organic Synthesis at High Pressures
Org Synth Organomet Proc Symp — Organic Synthesis via Organometallics. Proceedings. Symposium
Org Techint Bol Informativo — Organizacion Techint. Boletin Informativo
Org Usloviyakh Giperbarii — Organizm v Usloviyakh Giperbarii
OrH — Oregon Historical Quarterly
ORHEA — Orvosi Hetilap
Or Hlth — Oral Health
ORHPB — Orthopaede
OrHQ — Oregon Historical Quarterly
Orien — Orientierung
Oriens Ant — Oriens Antiquus
Oriens Extrem — Oriens Extremus
Orient — Orientalia. Commentarii de Rebus Assyro-Babylonicis, Arabicis, Aegyptiacis
Orient A — Oriental Art
Orientacion Econ — Orientacion Economica
Orientalistische Lz — Orientalistische Literaturzeitung
Oriental Soc Aust J — Oriental Society of Australia. Journal
Orientam Soc — Orientamenti Sociali
Orient Art — Oriental Art
Orientat Sc — Orientation Scolaire et Professionnelle
Orientat Scol Profes — Orientation Scolaire et Professionnelle
Orient Carpet & Textile Stud — Oriental Carpet and Textile Studies
Orient Cer Soc Hong Kong Bull — Oriental Ceramic Society of Hong Kong. Bulletin
Orient Cer Soc Transl No — Oriental Ceramics Society Translations Number
Orient Christ Period — Orientalia Christiana Periodica
Orient Chr Per — Orientalia Christiana Periodica
Orient Coll Mag — Oriental College Magazine
Orient Cult — Oriental Culture
Orient Cult — Orientamenti Culturali
Oriente Agropecu — Oriente Agropecuario
Orient Econ Caracas — Orientacion Economica (Caracas)
Orient Economist — Oriental Economist
Oriente Crist — Oriente Cristiano
Oriente Eur — Oriente Europeo
Oriente Mod — Oriente Moderno
Orienter Fremtidsforsk — Orientering om Fremtidsforskning
Orient Geo — Oriental Geographer
Orient Geogr — Oriental Geographer
Orient Geogr (Dacca) — Oriental Geographer (Dacca)
Orient Insects — Oriental Insects
Orient Insects Suppl — Oriental Insects. Supplementum
Orient Lit Ztg — Orientalistische Literaturzeitung

Orient Lovan — Orientalia Lovaniensia Analecta
Orient Lovan Per — Orientalia Lovaniensia Periodica
Orient Lovan Per — Orientalia Lovaniensia Periodica
Orient Lovan Period — Orientalia Lovaniensia Periodica
Orient Prof/Voc Guid — Orientation Professionnelle/Vocational Guidance
Orient Repert — Oriental Repertory
Orient Suecana — Orientalia Suecana
Origin Cosmic Rays Proc NATO Adv Study Inst — Origin of Cosmic Rays. Proceedings. NATO Advanced Study Institute
Origin Evol Interplanet Dust Proc Colloq Int Astron Union — Origin and Evolution of Interplanetary Dust. Proceedings. Colloquium. International Astronomical Union
Origins Hum Cancer Book A C — Origins of Human Cancer. Book A-C
Origins Hum Cancer Conf — Origins of Human Cancer Conference
Origins Hum Cancer Origins Hum Cancer Conf — Origins of Human Cancer. A Comprehensive Review. Origins of Human Cancer Conference
Origin Tech J — Origin Technical Journal
Orig Life — Origins of Life
Orig Life Evol Biosph — Origins of Life and Evolution of the Biosphere
ORIL — Orientations Religieuses, Intellectuelles, et Litteraires
ORIMB — Oral Implantology
ORIP — Oriental Research Institute Publications
ORIPS — Oriental Research Institute Publications. Sanskrit Series
Orissa Ed Mag — Orissa Education Magazine
Orissa Hist Res J — Orissa Historical Research Journal
Orissa J Agric Res — Orissa Journal of Agricultural Research
Orissa Rev — Orissa Review
Orissa Vet J — Orissa Veterinary Journal
Orizz Ortop Odie Riabil — Orizzonti della Ortopedia Odierna e della Riabilitazione
Orizz Profess — Orizzonti Professionali
ORK — Orbis. A Journal of World Affairs
Orkester JL — Orkester Journalen
Ork J — Orkester Journalen
ORL — Obergermanisch-Raetische Limes des Roemerreiches
ORL — Operations Research Letters
OrL — Orbis Litterarum. Revue Internationale d'Etudes Litteraires
ORL — Orient. Deutsche Zeitschrift fuer Politik und Wirtschaft des Orients
ORL — ORL - Journal for Oto-Rhino-Laryngology and Its Borderlands
ORLA — Orthodox Alaska
Orlando Bu J — Orlando Business Journal
Orland Sen — Orlando Sentinel
OR Laws — Oregon Laws and Resolutions
OR Laws Spec Sess — Oregon Laws and Resolutions. Special Session
ORLD — Oriental Review and Literary Digest
Orleans Bll — Bulletin des Sciences Physiques, Medicales et d'Agriculture d'Orleans
ORLIA — Oto-Rino-Laringologia Italiana
Or Lit — Orientalistische Literaturzeitung
ORLJAH — ORL
ORL-J Oto R — ORL - Journal for Oto-Rhino-Laryngology and Its Borderlands
ORL J Otorhinolaryngol Relat Spec — ORL. Journal of Oto-Rhino-Laryngology and Its Related Specialties
ORL Oto-Rhino-Laryngol (Basel) — ORL. Oto-Rhino-Laryngology (Basel)
Or Lov — Orientalia Lovaniensia Analecta
Orlov Gos Ped Inst Ucen Zap — Orlovskii Gosudarstvennyi Pedagogiceskii Institut. Ucenye Zapiski
OrLovPer — Orientalia Lovaniensia Periodica
Orl Parish Med Soc Proc — Orleans Parish Medical Society. Proceedings
Or LR — Oregon Law Review
Or L Rev — Oregon Law Review
Or LSJ — Oregon Law School Journal
OrLz — Orientalistische Literaturzeitung
ORm — Oudheidkundige Mededelingen uit het Rijksmuseum van Oudheden te Leiden
Orm Arast Enst Derg — Ormancilik Arastirma Enstituesue Dergisi
Orm Arast Enst Muht Yay — Ormancilik Arastirma Enstituesue Muhtelif Yayinlar Serisi
Orm Arast Enst Tek Buelt — Ormancilik Arastirma Enstituesue Teknik Buelten
Or Med — Oranie Medicale
OrMod — Oriente Moderno
Orm Vitam — Ormoni e Vitamine
Orn Abh — Ornithologische Abhandlungen
Ornamentals Northwest Coop Ext Serv Oreg State Univ — Ornamentals Northwest. Cooperative Extension Service. Oregon State University
Ornamentals Northwest Newsl Coop Ext Serv Oreg State Univ — Ornamentals Northwest. Newsletter. Cooperative Extension Service. Oregon State University
Orn Ber — Ornithologische Berichte
Ornis Fenn — Ornis Fennica
Ornis Scand — Ornis Scandinavica
Ornithol Abh — Ornithologische Abhandlungen
Ornithol Appl — Ornithologie Applique
Ornithol Beob — Ornithologische Beobachter
Ornithol Ber — Ornithologische Berichte
Ornithol Mberr — Ornithologische Monatsberichte
Ornithol Mitt — Ornithologische Mitteilungen
Ornithol Monatsber — Ornithologische Monatsberichte
ORNL TM — Oak Ridge National Laboratory. TM
Orn Mitt — Ornithologische Mitteilungen
ORNRA — Oak Ridge National Laboratory. Review
OrNS — Orientalia. Nova Series
Or Occ — Orient-Occident
Orog Mafic Ultramafic Assoc — Orogenic Mafic and Ultramafic Association
ORom — Opuscula Romana
ORom — Osservatore Romano
ORP — Odrodzenie i Reformacja w Polsce

OrP — Orientamenti Pedagogici
ORPB — Oberrheinisches Pastoralblatt
Orph — Orpheus
Orph — Orpheus. Revista pentru Cultura Clasica
ORPh — Oxford Readings in Philosophy
Orph F — Orphicorum Fragmenta
Orph Frag — Orphicorum Fragmenta
ORQUA7 — Orquidea
ORRBDQ — Oxford Reviews of Reproductive Biology
Or Rep — Oriental Reprints
OR Rev Stat — Oregon Revised Statutes
ORS — Organization Studies
Ors — Oriens
Or S — Orientalia Suecana
ORS — Oriental Religious Series
ORSA/TIMS Bull — ORSA [*Operations Research Society of America*]/TIMS Bulletin
Or SB Bull — Oregon State Bar. Bulletin
ORSC — Ornis Scandinavica
Orsk Gos Ped Inst Ucen Zap — Orskii Gosudarstvennyi Pedagogiceskii Institut Imeni T. G. Sevcenko. Ucenye Zapiski
Or Soc — Orientamenti Sociali
OR Spektrum — Operations Research Spektrum
Or St B Bull — Oregon State Bar Bulletin
Or St C — Oriental Studies. Cambridge, Massachusetts
Orsted Ts — Tidsskrift for Naturvidenskaberne. Orsted
Or St O — Oriental Studies. Oxford
Or St W — Oriental Studies (Washington, DC)
OrSuec — Orientalia Suecana
Or Surg — Oral Surgery, Oral Medicine, and Oral Pathology
OrSyr — Orient Syrien
Orszagos Magyar Szepmuveszeti Muz Evkonyvei — Orszagos Magyar Szepmuveszeti Muzeum Evkonyvei
Orszagos Mezoegazd Minoesegvizsgalo Intez Evkoen — Orszagos Mezogazdasagi Minosegvizsgalo Intezet Evkonyve
Orsz Erdesz Egyes Evk — Az Orszagos Erdeszeti-Egyesuelet Evkoenyve
Orsz Husipari Kut Intez Kozl — Orszagos Husipari Kutato Intezet Kozlemenyei
Orsz Met Intez Hivat Kiad — Orszagos Meteorologiai Intezet Hivatalos Kiadvanyai
Orsz Mezogazd Minosegv Intez Evk — Orszagos Mezogazdasagi Minosegvizsgalo Intezet Evkonyve
Orsz Mezogazd Minosegvizsgalo Intez Kiad Sorozat 1 — Orszagos Mezogazdasagi Minosegvizsgalo Intezet Kiadvanyai. Sorozat 1. Genetikus Talajterkepek
Orsz Orvost Koenyv Koezl — Orszagos Orvostoerteneti Koenyvtar Koezlemenyei
ORT — Orientalia Rheno-Traiectina
Ort — Ortodoxia
OR Tax — Oregon Tax Reports
ORTE — Orszagos Magyar Regezeti Tarsulat Evkonyve
OR Tech — OR Tech: Official Publication of the Association of Operating Room Technicians
Ort Eco Bul — Ort Economic Bulletin
Ort Eco Rev — Ort Economic Review
Or Th — Oriental Thought
Orth — Ortodoksia. Orthodoxia
Orth Beitr — Orthodoxe Beitraege
Orth L — Orthodox Life
Orthod — Orthodontics
Orthod Fr — Orthodontie Francaise
Ortho J Life — Orthodox Jewish Life
Orthomol Ps — Orthomolecular Psychiatry
Orthomol Psychiatry Treat Schizophr — Orthomolecular Psychiatry. Treatment of Schizophrenia
Orthop Clin North Am — Orthopedic Clinics of North America
Orthoped Cl — Orthopedic Clinics of North America
Orthop Lect — Orthopaedic Lectures
Orthop Nurs — Orthopedic Nursing
Orthop Prax — Orthopaodiccho Praxic
Orthop Rev — Orthopaedic Review
Orthop Surg — Orthopedic Surgery
Orthop Trans — Orthopaedic Transactions
Orthop Traumatol — Orthopedics and Traumatology
Orthop Traumatol — Orthopedie Traumatologie
Orthotics Prosthet — Orthotics and Prosthetics
Orthot Pros — Orthotics and Prosthetics
Orth Par — Orthodoxos Pareteretes
Orth Rd — Orthodoxe Rundschau
Orth St — Orthodoxe Stimme
Ortod — Ortodoncia
Ortod Clin — Ortodoncia Clinica
Ortop Maxilar — Ortopedia Maxilar
Ortop Resp Mezhved Sb — Ortopediya Respublikanskii Mezhvedomstvennyi Sbornik
Ortop Traumatol Appar Mot — Ortopedia e Traumatologia dell'Apparato Motore
Ortop Travmatol Prot — Ortopediya, Travmatologiya, i Protezirovaniye
Ortop Travmatol Protez — Ortopediya, Travmatologiya, i Protezirovaniye
Ortop Travmatol (Sofla) — Ortopediya i Travmatologiya (Sofia)
Ortop Travm Protez — Ortopedija, Travmatologija, i Protezirovanie
Or T Rep — Oregon Tax Reporter
Orts KK — Ortskrankenkasse
ORTTDM — Orthopaedic Transactions
Ortung Navig — Ortung und Navigation
ORUCC — Orpheus. Rivista di Umanita Classica e Cristiana
ORV — Operations Research Verfahren
Orv Hetil — Orvosi Hetilap
Orv Hetilap — Orvosi Hetilap
Orv Lap — Orvosok Lapja

Orv Lapja — Orvosok Lapja
Orvostort Kozl — Orvostorteneti Koezlemeneyek. Communicationes de Historia Artis Medicinae
Orvostud Aktual Probl — Orvostudomany Aktualis Problemai
Orvostud Beszam — Orvostudomanyi Beszamolo
Orv Sz — Orvosi Szemle
Orv Szle — Orvosi Szemle
Orv Tech — Orvos es Technika
Orv Termeszettud Ertes — Orvos-Termeszettudomanyi Ertesitoe
Orv Termt Ets — Orvos-Termeszettudomanyi Ertesito a Kolozsvari Orvos-Termeszettudomanyi Tarsulat es az Erdelyi Muzeum-Egylet Termeszettudomanyi Szakosztalyanak
Oryx — Oryx Journal. Fauna Preservation Society
Oryx J Fauna Preserv Soc — Oryx Journal. Fauna Preservation Society
Oryx Sci Bibliogr — Oryx Science Bibliographies
Oryza J Assoc Rice Res Work — Oryza. Journal of the Association of Rice Research Workers
ORZIM — Otkrytija Russkich Zemleprochodcev i Poljarnych Morechodov XVII Veka na Severovostoke Azii
OS — Oekumenische Studien
OS — Onomastica Sacra
OS — Opciones
OS — Orientalia Suecana
OS — Orient Syrien
Os — Osiris
OS — Ostkirchliche Studien
Os — Osvit
OS — Other Side
OS — Oudtestamentische Studien
OSA Coop Ext Univ Calif — One-Sheet Answers. Cooperative Extension. University of California
OSAHQ — Ohio State Archaeological and Historical Quarterly
Osaka City Inst Public Health Environ Sci Annu Rep — Osaka City Institute of Public Health and Environmental Sciences. Annual Report
Osaka City Med J — Osaka City Medical Journal
Osaka City U Econ R — Osaka City University. Economic Review
Osaka Econ Pap — Osaka Economic Papers
Osaka J Mat — Osaka Journal of Mathematics
Osaka J Math — Osaka Journal of Mathematics
Osaka Mus Nat Hist Bull — Osaka Museum of Natural History. Bulletin
Osaka Prefect Univ Bull Ser A Eng Nat Sci — Osaka Prefecture. University. Bulletin. Series A. Engineering and Natural Sciences
Osaka Univ Dent Sch J — Osaka University Dental School. Journal
Osaka Univ J Geosci — Osaka University. Journal of Geosciences
Osaka Univ L Rev — Osaka University. Law Review
OSAUB — Oriental Series. American University of Beirut
OSAWA8 — Anzeiger. Oesterreichische Akademie der Wissenschaften. Mathematisch-Naturwissenschaftliche Klasse
Osawatom — Osawatomie
OSBA Bull — Ohio State Bar Association. Bulletin
OSBIE9 — Oryx Science Bibliographies
Osborne Assn N Bul — Osborne Association. News Bulletin
OSCD — Ontario Securities Commission Decisions
OSCU — Oriental Studies. Columbia University
Os Cy Med J — Osaka City Medical Journal
OSD — OSD. Overseas Standards Digest
OSE — Oslo Studies in English
OSEBE3 — Oxford Surveys in Evolutionary Biology
OSEI — Oekonomische und Soziale Entwicklung Indiens. Sowietische Beitraege zur Indischen Geschichte
OSEND — Ocean Science and Engineering
OsEP — Osaka Economic Papers
OSEQD — Oldelft Scientific Engineering Quarterly
OSF — Orbit Science Fiction
OSFMA — Optika i Spektroskopiya. Akademiya Nauk SSSR. Otdelenie Fiziko-MatematicheskikhNauk
OSFS — Original Science Fiction Stories
OsG — Oesterreich in Geschichte und Literatur
Osgoode Hall L J — Osgoode Hall. Law Journal
Osgoode Hall LSJ — Osgoode Hall Law School. Journal
OSH — Office on Smoking and Health Database
OSHA Compl Guide CCH — OSHA [*Occupational Safety and Health Administration*] Compliance Guide. Commerce Clearing House
Os Hall LJ — Osgoode Hall. Law Journal
OSH Cas BNA — Occupational Safety and Health Cases. Bureau of National Affairs
OSH Dec CCH — Occupational Safety and Health Decisions. Commerce Clearing House
OSHR — Occupational Safety and Health Reporter
OSH Rep (BNA) — Occupational Safety and Health Reporter (Bureau of National Affairs)
OSIA — On Site in Alberta
Os Ikad Zass — Osaka Ikadaigaku Zasshi
OSIPAR — Ospedali Italiani - Pediatria e Specialita Chirurgiche
OSJ — Ordnance Survey of Jerusalem
Osjecki Zb — Osjecki Zbornik. Muzej Slavonije
Os Josh Ikad Zass — Osaka Joshi Ikadaigaku Zasshi
Osj Zbor — Osjecki Zbornik. Muzej Slavonije
OSKR — One Sky Report
OSLJ — Law Journal. Student Bar Association. Ohio State University
Oslo Komm Kstsaml Ab — Oslo Kommunes Kunstsamlinger Arbok
OSLP — Oregon. University. Monographs. Studies in Literature and Philosophy
OSLP — Oxford Slavonic Papers
Osmania J Social Sciences — Osmania Journal of Social Sciences
Os Math J — Osaka Mathematical Journal
OSMDAB — Osteopathic Medicine

OSN — Ocean Science News
Osnab Jbr — Jahresbericht des Naturwissenschaftlichen Vereins zu Osnabrueck
Osnabr Mitt — Osnabruecker Mitteilungen
Osnabrueck Mitt — Osnabruecker Mitteilungen
Osnabrueck Schrift Math — Osnabruecker Schriften zur Mathematik
Osnabrueck Schrift Math Reihe M Math Manuskr — Osnabruecker Schriften zur Mathematik. Reihe M. Mathematische Manuskripte
Osnabrueck Stud Math — Osnabruecker Studien zur Mathematik
Osnabrueck Schrift Math Reihe V Vorlesungsskr — Osnabruecker Schriften zur Mathematik. Reihe V. Vorlesungsskripten
Osn Fundam — Osnovaniya i Fundamenty
Osn Fundam Mekh Gruntov — Osnovaniya, Fundamenty, i Mekhanika Gruntov
Osn Metall — Osnovy Metallurgii
Osnovn Org Sint Neftekhim — Osnovnoi·Organicheskii Sintez i Neftekhimiya
Osnovn Usloviya Eff Primen Udobr — Osnovnye Usloviya Effektivnogo Primeneniya Udobrenii
OsO — Oesterreichische Osthefte
Osob Razvit Ryb Razlichnykh Estestv Eksp Usloviyakh — Osobennosti Razvitiya Ryb v Razlichnykh Estestvennykh i Eksperimental'nykh Usloviyakh
OSP — Oxford Slavonic Papers
OSPADK — Obshta i Sravnitelna Patologiia
Osped Ital Chir — Ospedali d'Italia - Chirurgia
Osped Maggiore — Ospedale Maggiore
Osped Psichiat — Ospedale Psichiatrico
Osp Ital Chir — Ospedali d'Italia - Chirurgia
Osp Ital Pediatr (Spec Chir) — Ospedali Italiani Pediatria (e Specialita Chirurgiche)
Osp Magg — Ospedale Maggiore
Osp Maggiore — Ospedale Maggiore
Osp Magg Novara — Ospedale Maggiore di Novara
Osp Psichiatr — Ospedale Psichiatrico
OsR — Osservatore Romano
OSR Bull — OSR [*Organisation for Scientific Research in Indonesia*] Bulletin
Osr Nauk Prod Mater Polprzewodn Pr — Osrodek Naukowo-Produkcyjny Materialow Polprzewodnikowych. Prace
Osrodek Badaw Rozwojowy Elektron Prozniowej (Pr) — Osrodek Badawczo-Rozwojowy Elektroniki Prozniowej (Prace)
Osrodek Inf Energ Jad Rev Rep — Osrodek Informacji o Energii Jadrowej. Review Report
OsRom — Osservatore Romano
Oss & Mem Oss Astrofis Arcetri — Osservazioni e Memorie. Osservatorio Astrofisico di Arcetri
Osserv — Osservatore
Osservatorio A — Osservatorio delle Arti
Osserv Trib — Osservatore Tributario
Oss Med — Osservatore Medico
OssRom — Osservatore Romano
OSSTF For — OSSTF [*Ontario Secondary School Teachers' Federation*] Forum
OST — Osteuropa. Zeitschrift fuer Gegenwartsfragen des Ostens
Ostasiat Mus Stockholm Bull — Ostasiatiska Museet (Stockholm). Bulletin
Ostasiat Z — Ostasiatische Zeitschrift
Ostas Lloyd — Ostasiatischer Lloyd
Ostbair Grenzmarken — Ostbairische Grenzmarken
Ostbayer Grenzmarken — Ostbayerische Grenzmarken
Ostb Grenzm — Ostbairische Grenzmarken
Ostdeutsch Naturwart — Ostdeutscher Naturwart
Ostdt Familienkde — Ostdeutsche Familienkunde
Ostdt Mhft — Ostdeutsche Monatshefte
Ostdt Wiss — Ostdeutsche Wissenschaft
Osteopath Ann — Osteopathic Annals
Osteopath Hosp Leadership — Osteopathic Hospital Leadership
Osteopath Med — Osteopathic Medicine
Osteopath Prof — Osteopathic Profession
Osteoporos Int — Osteoporosis International
Osteoporosis Int — Osteoporosis International
Osteoporosis Proc Int Symp — Osteoporosis. Proceedings. International Symposium
Osteop Q — Osteopathic Quarterly
Oster Musik — Oesterreichische Musikzeitschrift
Osterr Bot Z — Oesterreichische Botanische Zeitschrift
Osterr Dent Z — Oesterreichische Dentisten Zeitschrift
Osterreichische Ing Z — Oesterreichische Ingenieur Zeitschrift
Osterr Hebammenztg — Oesterreichische Hebammenzeitung
Osterr Krankenpflegez — Oesterreichische Krankenpflegezeitschrift
Osterr Osth — Oesterreichische Osthefte
Osterr Zahntech — Oesterreichische Zahntechniker
Osterr Z Aussenpolit — Oesterreichische Zeitschrift fuer Aussenpolitik
Osterr Z Off Recht — Oesterreichische Zeitschrift fuer Oeffentliches Recht
Osterr Z Polit-Wiss — Oesterreichische Zeitschrift fuer Politikwissenschaft
Osteur — Osteuropa
Osteur Naturwiss — Osteuropa Naturwissenschaft
Osteuropa Wirtsch — Osteuropa Wirtschaft
Osteur Recht — Osteuropa-Recht
Osteur Wirt — Osteuropa Wirtschaft
Osteur Wirtsch — Osteuropa-Wirtschaft
Ost Fries Mannigfaltigk — Ost-Friesische Mannigfaltigkeiten
OSTGU — Oriental Society. Transactions. Glasgow University
OSTI Newsl — Office for Scientific and Technical Information. Newsletter
Ost Jahrh — Jahreshefte des Oesterreichischen Archaeologischen Institutes in Wien
Ostj Hj — Ostjysk Hjemstavn
Ostjydsk Hjemstavn — Ostjydsk Hjemstavnforenings Aarsskrift
Ostkirchl Stud — Ostkirchliche Studien
Ostkirch St — Ostkirchliche Studien
Ost K St — Ostkirchliche Studien
OstM — Ostdeutsche Monatshefte

Ostmaerk Milchwirtsch Ztg — Ostmaerkische Milchwirtschaftliche Zeitung
Ostmaerk Spirit Ztg — Ostmaerkische Spirituosen-Zeitung
OSTO — Oesterreichische Osthefte
Ost Probl — Ost-Probleme
O Stras — Griechische und Griechisch-Demotische Ostraka der Universitaetsund Landesbibliothek zu Strassbourg im Elsass
Ostrava Vys Ak Banska Sb Rada Hornicko-Geol — Ostrava. Vysoka Skola Banska. Sbornik. Rada Hornicko-Geologicka
Ostr Bodl — Greek Ostraca in the Bodleian Library at Oxford and Various Other Collections
OSTRDN — Tropical Dental Journal
Ostrich Suppl — Ostrich. Supplement
Ostr Mich — Greek Ostraca in the University of Michigan Collection
Ostr Strassb — Griechische und Griechisch-Demotische Ostraka der Universitaetsund Landesbibliothek zu Strassbourg im Elsass
Ostr Wilbour — Ostraca Grecs de la Collection Charles-Edwin Wilbour au Musee de Brooklyn
Ostw — Ostwirtschaft
Ostwalds Klassiker Exakt Wiss — Ostwalds Klassiker der Exakten Wissenschaften
OSu — Orientalia Suecana
OsUA — Ortnamnssaellskapets i Uppsala Aarsskrift
OSUCLL — Ohio State University. Contributions in Language and Literature
OSU Curr Rep Okla State Univ Coop Ext Serv — OSU Current Report. Oklahoma State University. Cooperative Extension Service
OSU Ext Facts Coop Ext Serv Okla State Univ — OSU Extension Facts. Cooperative Extension Service. Oklahoma State University
OSUTCB — Ohio State University. Theatre Collection Bulletin
OSV — Our Sunday Visitor
OSVM — Our Sunday Visitor Magazine
OT — L'Orient
OT — Offene Tore
OT — Onze Taaltuin
OT — Onze Tijd
OT — O Tripeiro
OTA — Onze Taal
Otago Acclim Soc Annu Rep — Otago Acclimatisation Society. Annual Report
Otago Law Rev — Otago Law Review
Otago LR — Otago Law Review
Otago L Rev — Otago Law Review
Otago Mus Zool Bull — Otago Museum of Zoology. Bulletin
Otago Pol Gaz — Otago Police Gazette
Otago U Stud Prehist Anthropol — Otago University Studies in Prehistoric Anthropology
OTAM — Ozbek Tili va Adabiet Masalalari
OTAN Newsl — OTAN [*Organization of Tropical American Nematologists*] Newsletter
OTB — On the Boiler
Otbor i Peredaca Informacii — Otbor i Peredaca Informacii. Akademija Nauk Ukrainskoi SSR. Fiziko-MehaniceskiiInstitut
Otbor i Peredacha Inf — Otbor i Peredacha Informatsii
Otbor Pereda Inf — Otbor i Peredacha Informatsii
OTC — Office: Technology and People
Otcet Dejateln Tiflissk Bot Sada — Otcet O Dejatel'nosti Tiflisskago Botaniceskago Sada
Otcet Dejateln Volzsk Biol Stancii — Otcet O Dejatel'nosti Volzskoj Biologiceskoj Stancii/Bericht ueber die Thaetigkeit der Biologischen Wolga-Station
Otcet Prisuzd Akad Nauk — Otcet O Prisuzdenii Akademieju Nauk
Otcet Volzsk Biol Stancii Saratovsk Obsc Estestvoisp — Otcet Volzskoj Biologiceskoj Stancii Saratovskogo Obscestva Estestvoispytatelejl Ljubitelej Estestvoznanija/Compte-Rendu des Travaux des Vacances. Station Biologique du Volga. Organisee Par la Societe des Naturalistes a Saratow
Otchery Mezhdunar O-Va Khim Serna — Otchery Mezhdunarodnogo Obshchestva po Khimii Serna
Otd Tekh — Otdelochnaya Tekhnika
Otemon Econ Stud — Otemon Economic Studies
OTFP — Oriental Translation Fund Publications
O Theb — Theban Ostraca
OTHEL — Opuscula et Textus Historiam Ecclesiae. Serie Liturgica
OTHES — Opuscula et Textus Historiam Ecclesiae. Serie Scholastica et Mystica
Othr Womn — Other Woman
Oth Sce — Other Scenes
OTI — Trend; das Oesterreichische Wirtschaftsmagazin
OTJR — Occupational Therapy Journal of Research
Otkhody Promsti Miner Syre Proizvod Tekh Stroit Mater — Otkhody Promyshlennosti i Mineral'noe Syr'e v Proizvodstve Tekhnicheskikh i Stroitel'nykh Materialov
Otkrytiya Izobret — Otkrytiya, Izobreteniya
Otkrytiya Izobret Prom Obraztsy Tovarnye Znaki — Otkrytiya, Izobreteniya, Promyshlennye Obraztsy, Tovarnye Znaki
Otkryt Izobret — Otkrytiya, Izobreteniya, Promyshlennye Obraztsy, Tovarnye Znaki
OTKT — On the Knossos Tablets
OTL — Old Testament Library
OT Lect — Old Testament Lectures
OTLR — Otago Law Review
OTLV — Onza, Tigra, y Leon. Revista para la Infancia Venezolana
OTM — Old Time Music
OTM — Oxford Theological Monographs
OTMPA — Oberflaechentechnik/Metallpraxis
Otolar Clin — Otolaryngologic Clinics of North America
Oto Laring — Oto-Laringologia
Otolaryngol Clin N Am — Otolaryngologic Clinics of North America
Otolaryngol Clin North Am — Otolaryngologic Clinics of North America
Otolaryngol Head Neck Surg — Otolaryngology and Head and Neck Surgery
Otolaryngol Pol — Otolaryngologia Polska

Otol Fukuoka — Otologia Fukuoka
Otol Fukuoka Jibi To Rinsho — Otologia Fukuoka Jibi To Rinsho
Otol Jpn — Otology Japan
Otol Neurotol — Otology & Neurotology
Oto Noro Oftalmol — Oto-Noro Oftalmoloji
Otoplenie Vent Stroit Teplofiz — Otoplenie. Ventilyatsiya i Stroitel'naya Teplofizika
Oto-Rhino-Laryngol — Oto-Rhino-Laryngology
Oto-Rhino-Laryngol (Tokyo) — Oto-Rhino-Laryngology (Tokyo)
Oto-Rino-Laringol Ital — Oto-Rino-Laringologia Italiana
Oto-Rino-Laringol Oftalmol — Oto-Rino-Laringologie si Oftalmologie
OTPOA — Otolaryngologia Polska
OTRE — Ottawa Report. Canadian Wildlife Federation
OTRLAX — Oto-Rino-Laringologia
OTS — Oudtestamentische Studien
Otsenka Mestorozhd Poiskakh Razved — Otsenka Mestorozhdenii pri Poiskakh i Razvedkakh
OTSt — Old Testament Studies
OTSt — Oudtestamentische Studien
OTT — Technieuws Ottawa. Korte Berichten op Technisch Wetenschappelijk Gebied
Ottawa Bul — Ottawa Bulletin
Ottawa Evening J — Ottawa Evening Journal
Ottawa Field Nat Club Tr — Ottawa Field Naturalists' Club. Transactions
Ottawa Field Naturalists Club Trans — Ottawa Field-Naturalists' Club Transactions
Ottawa Law R — Ottawa Law Review
Ottawa Lit Sc Soc Tr — Ottawa Literary and Scientific Society. Transactions
Ottawa LR — Ottawa Law Review
Ottawa L Rev — Ottawa Law Review
Ottawa Nat — Ottawa Naturalist
Ottawa W — Ottawa Week
Ott LR — Ottawa Law Review
Otto Graf Inst (Stuttgart) Tech Hochsch Schriftenr — Otto-Graf-Institut (Stuttgart). Technische Hochschule. Schriftenreihe
Otto-Graf-Inst (Stutt) Tech Hochsch Schriftenr — Otto-Graf-Institut (Stuttgart). Technische Hochschule. Schriftenreihe
Otto Graf J — Otto Graf Journal. Annual Journal of Research and Testing of Materials
Ott Voronezh Sel-Khoz Inst — Ottisk iz Aapisok Voronezhskogo Sel'skokhozyaistvennogo Instituta
OTW — Out of This World
OTWA — Out of This World Adventures
OTWerkSuidA — Die Ou Testamentiese Werkgemeenskap in Suid-Afrika
OTWSA — Die Ou Testamentiese Werkgemeenskap in Suid-Afrika
OTWSAP — Papers. Ou Testamentiese Werkgemeenskap in Suid-Afrika
OTZ — Oesterreichische Textil Zeitung. Zentralblatt fuer die Gesamte Textilwirtschaft
Ou — Outlook
OUA — Ortnamnssaellskapets i Uppsala Aarsskrift
OUB — Parfums, Cosmetiques, Aromes. L'Unique Journal Francais de Son Secteur
Oude Kst — Oude Kunst
Oude Land Aarschot — Oude Land van Aarschot
Oudhd & Kst — Oudheide en Kunst
Oudhdknd Jb — Ovocheidkundig Jaarboek
Oudhdknd Meded Rijksmus Ouden Leiden — Oudheidkundige Mededelingen uit het Rijksmuseum van Ouden te Leiden
Oudheidk Mededelingen — Oudheidkundige Mededelingen uit het Rijksmuseum van Oudheden te Leiden
Oudh LJ — Oudh Law Journal
Oudh Med — Oudheidkundige Mededeelingen
Oudh Meded — Oudheidkundige Mededeelingen uit s'Rijksmuseum van Oudheden te Leiden
Oudh Wkly N — Oudh Weekly Notes
Oudh WN — Oudh Weekly Notes
OudSt — Oudtestamentische Studien
Ouest Apic — L'Ouest Apicole
Ouest Med — Ouest Medical
OUFADI — Outdoor Facts
OuK — Oper und Konzert
Oulun Yliopiston Ydintek Laitoksen Julk — Oulun Yliopiston Ydintekniikkan Laitoksen Julkaisuja
OuO — Orient und Occident
OUR — Ohio University Review
Our Gener — Our Generation
Ourivesaria Port — Ourivesaria Portuguesa
Ouro Preto Esc Minas Rev — Ouro Preto. Escola de Minas. Revista
Our Q Mag — Our Quarterly Magazine
OURS — Organ of Unemployed, Relief, and Sustenance Workers
Our World W — Our World Weekly
OUS — Ochanomizu University Studies
OuS — Oudtestamentische Studien
OUSE — Odense University Studies in English
Out — Outlands
Out — Outsider
Outdoor Am — Outdoor America
Outdoor Dig — Outdoor Digest
Outdoor Ind — Outdoor Indiana
Outdoor Okla — Outdoor Oklahoma
Outdoor Rev — Outdoor Review
Outd Rec Act — Outdoor Recreation Action
Outdr Rec — Selected Outdoor Recreation Statistics
Outl — Outlook
Outl Agric — Outlook on Agriculture
Outlook Agr — Outlook on Agriculture
Outlook Agric — Outlook on Agriculture

Outlook Bull South Dent Soc NJ — Outlook and Bulletin. Southern Dental Society of New Jersey
Outlook Proc Agric Outlook Conf US Dep Agric — Outlook. Proceedings. Agricultural Outlook Conference. US Department of Agriculture
Outlook United Fresh Fruit Veg Assoc — Outlook. United Fresh Fruit and Vegetable Association
Outok News — Outokumpu News
Outstanding Soviet Sci — Outstanding Soviet Scientists
Outstate Test Circ Univ Nebr Coll Agr Home Econ Agr Exp Sta — Outstate Testing Circular. University of Nebraska. College of Agriculture and Home Economics. Agricultural Experiment Station
OuTWP — Die Ou Testamentiese Werkgemeenskap in Suid-Afrika (Pretoria)
OUV — Openbare Uitgaven
OuW — Ost und West
OuZa — Outchonye Zapiski
OUZZL — Oesterreich-Ungarische Zeitschrift fuer Zuckerindustrie und Landwirtschaft
OV — Oesterreichische Volkswirt
OV — Ovation
Ov — Overland Monthly
Ova — Ovation
OVC — Verwarming en Ventilatie. Maandblad voor Verwarming, Ventilatie, Airconditioning, en Koeling
Ove Arup Ptnrship Newsletter — Ove Arup Partnership. Newsletter
Overland — Overland Monthly
Overland NS — Overland Monthly. New Series
Overs Bus Rep — Overseas Business Reports
Oversea Ed — Overseas Education
Oversea Educ — Oversea Education
Overseas Bldg Notes — Overseas Building Notes
Overseas Geol Miner Resour — Overseas Geology and Mineral Resources
Overseas Geol Miner Resour Suppl Ser Bull Suppl — Overseas Geology and Mineral Resources. Supplement Series. Bulletin Supplement
Overseas Mem Inst Geol Sci — Overseas Memoir. Institute of Geological Sciences
Overseas Mem Inst Geol Sci (GB) — Overseas Memoir. Institute of Geological Sciences (Great Britain)
Overseas Trade Descrip Export & Import Stat — Overseas Trade Descriptions. Export and Import Statistics
Overseas Trade Stat UK — Overseas Trade Statistics of the United Kingdom
Overs K Danske Vidensk Selsk Forh — Oversigt over det Kongelige Danske Videnskabernes Selskabs. Forhandlinger
Overs K Dan Vidensk Selsk — Oversigt over Selskabets Virksomhed. Kongelige Danske Videnskabernes Selskab
Overs K Dan Vidensk Selsk Forh — Oversigt over det Kongelige Danske Videnskabernes Selskabs. Forhandlinger
Overs Kongel Danske Vidensk Selsk Forh Medlemmers Arbeider — Oversigt Over Det Kongelige Danske Videnskabernes Selskabs Forhandlinger Og Dets Medlemmers Arbeider
Overs Selsk Virksomhed K Dan Vidensk Selsk — Oversigt over Selskabets Virksomhed. Kongelige Danske Videnskabernes Selskab
OVGE — Entscheidungen der Oberverwaltungsgerichte fuer das Land Nordrhein-Westfalen inMuenster
OVIR — Otdel Viz i Registratsii
Ovocn Rozhl — Ovocnicke Rozhledy
Ovo Mag — Ovo Magazine
Ov Rspr — Overzicht Rechtspraak
OVS — Kongelige Danske Videnskabernes Selskab. Oversigt over Selskabets Virksomhed
OVS — Oversigt over det Kongelige Danske Videnskabernes Selskabs Forhandlinger
OVT — Overseas Trading
OW — Offshore Oil Weekly [Later, Offshore Oil International]
OW — Open Wheel
OW — Orient/West
OW — Ostatnie Wiadomosci
OW — Ostdeutsche Wissenschaft
OW — Ost und West
OW — Other Worlds
OWB — Civis Mundi
OWG — Ordnungswidrigkeitengesetz
O Wi — Ostdeutsche Wissenschaft
O Wilb — Ostraca Grecs de la Collection Charles-Edwin Wilbour au Musee de Brooklyn
OWN — Office World News
OWN — Ontario Weekly Notes
OWN — Oudh Weekly Notes
OWN — Oudtestamentisch Werkgezelschap in Nederland
OWR — Ontario Weekly Reporter
OWS — Oxford-Warburg Studies
OWW — Internationale Wochenschrift fuer Wissenschaft, Kunst, und Technik
Ox — Oxoniensa
OxAbs — Oxford Abstracts
Ox B Econ S — Oxford Bulletin of Economics and Statistics
Ox Bul Econ Stat — Oxford Bulletin of Economics and Statistics
Ox Econ Pap — Oxford Economic Papers
OXF — Oxford Bulletin of Economics and Statistics
Oxf Class Dict — Oxford Classical Dictionary
Oxf Com — Oxford Commentaries
Oxf Energy Forum — Oxford Energy Forum
Oxf Ger Stud — Oxford German Studies
Oxf Lat Dic — Oxford Latin Dictionary
Oxf Mag — Oxford Magazine
Oxf Med Sch Gaz — Oxford Medical School Gazette
Oxford Agra Stud — Oxford Agrarian Studies
Oxford A J — Oxford Art Journal

Oxford Appl Math Comput Sci Ser — Oxford Applied Mathematics and Computing Science Series
Oxford B Econ Statis — Oxford Bulletin of Economics and Statistics
Oxford Bibliog Soc Proc — Oxford Bibliographical Society. Proceedings
Oxford Biol Readers — Oxford Biology Readers
Oxford/Carol Biol Readers — Oxford/Carolina Biology Readers
Oxford Econ Pa — Oxford Economic Papers
Oxford Econ Pap — Oxford Economic Papers
Oxford Econ Pas — Oxford Economic Papers
Oxford Engrg Sci Ser — Oxford Engineering Science Series
Oxford Eng Sci Ser — Oxford Engineering Science Series
Oxford Hist Soc — Oxford Historical Society
Oxford J Archaeol — Oxford Journal of Archaeology
Oxford J Legal Stud — Oxford Journal of Legal Studies
Oxford Lecture Ser Math Appl — Oxford Lecture Series in Mathematics and its Applications
Oxford Math Monogr — Oxford Mathematical Monographs
Oxford Math Monographs — Oxford Mathematical Monographs
Oxford Pamphl Wld Aff — Oxford Pamphlets on World Affairs
Oxford Psych Ser — Oxford Psychology Series
Oxford R Educ — Oxford Review of Education
Oxford Rev Educ — Oxford Review of Education
Oxford Rev Reprod Biol — Oxford Reviews of Reproductive Biology
Oxford Sci Publ — Oxford Science Publications
Oxford Ser Opt Sci — Oxford Series on Optical Sciences
Oxfordshire Rec Soc — Oxfordshire Record Society
Oxford Slavonic Pa — Oxford Slavonic Papers
Oxford Slavonic Pap — Oxford Slavonic Papers
Oxford Stud Ancient Phil — Oxford Studies in Ancient Philosophy
Oxford Stud Islam A — Oxford Studies in Islamic Art
Oxford Stud Nucl Phys — Oxford Studies in Nuclear Physics
Oxford Stud Probab — Oxford Studies in Probability
Oxford Surv Eukaryotic Genes — Oxford Surveys on Eukaryotic Genes
Oxf Phys Ser — Oxford Physics Series
Oxf R — Oxford Review
Oxf Rev Reprod Biol — Oxford Reviews of Reproductive Biology
Oxf Slav Pap — Oxford Slavonic Papers
Oxf Surv Eukaryot Genes — Oxford Surveys on Eukaryotic Genes

Oxf Surv Evol Biol — Oxford Surveys in Evolutionary Biology
Oxf Surv Plant Mol Cell Biol — Oxford Surveys of Plant Molecular and Cell Biology
Oxf Univ Pitt Rivers Mus Occas Pap Technol — Oxford University. Pitt Rivers Museum. Occasional Papers on Technology
Oxid Combust Rev — Oxidation and Combustion Reviews
Oxid Damage Repair Int Soc Free Radical Res Bienn Meet — Oxidative Damage and Repair. Chemical, Biological, and Medical Aspects. International Society for Free Radical Research. Biennial Meeting
Oxid Met — Oxidation of Metals
Oxidoreduct Plasma Membr Relat Growth Transp — Oxidoreduction at the Plasma Membrane. Relation to Growth and Transport
Oxid Org Chem Part A — Oxidation in Organic Chemistry. Part A
Oxid Rev Abstr — Oxidation Reviews and Abstracts
Oxid Stress Dis — Oxidative Stress and Disease
Ox Lit Rev — Oxford Literary Review
Oxon — Oxoniensia
Ox Prize Ess — Oxford Prize Essays
Oxygen Transfer Atmos Tissues — Oxygen Transfer from Atmosphere to Tissues
OYBSA — Oyo Butsuri
OYCE — Official Yearbook. Church of England
OYGK — Okayama Daigaku Hobungakubu Gakujutsu Kiyo
OZ — Osjecki Zbornik. Muzej Slavonije
OZ — Ostasiatische Zeitschrift
O Zb — Osjecki Zbornik. Muzej Slavonije
OZDP — Oesterreichische Zeitschrift fuer Kunst und Denkmalpflege
Ozean Tech — Ozean und Technik
OZEBA — Oesterreichische Zeitschrift fuer Erforschung und Bekaempfung der Krebskrankheit
OZE Oesterr Z Elektr — Oe Z E/Oesterreichische Zeitschrift fuer Elektrizitaetswirtschaft
OZE Oesterr Z fuer Elektrizitaetswirtsch — OZE. Oesterreichische Zeitschrift fuer Elektrizitaetswirtschaft
OZET — Obshchestvo Remeslennovo i Zemledel'cheskovo Truda
OZET — Obshchestvo Zemleistroistva Evreiskikh Trudiashchchikhsia v SSSR
OZKDP — Oesterreichische Zeitschrift fuer Kunst und Denkmalpflege
OZOKAN — Austrian Journal of Oncology
Ozone Sci Eng — Ozone. Science and Engineering
OZV — Oesterreichische Zeitschrift fuer Volkskunde

P

P — Pacht
P — Pacific Reporter
P — Palacio
P — Palaestra
P — Palestine
P — Palimpsest
P — Pamphleteer
P — Paralipomena
P — Pazmaveb
P — Penguin Parade
P — Pensamiento
P — Perspectives
P — Pesquisas [*Porto Alegre*]
P — Philologus. Zeitschrift fuer Klassische Altertum
P — Philosophy
P — Poetry
P — Polonystyka
P — Ponte
P — Portugalia
P 2d — Pacific Reporter. Second
PA — Onze Pius-Almanak
PA — Pacific Affairs
Pa — Paideia
PA — Palestine Affairs
PA — Pamatky Archeologicke
Pa — Parkett
PA — Parliamentary Affairs
Pa — Paru
PA — Pastoral Music
Pa — Patria. Revista Portuguesa de Cultura
PA — Pedagogia
Pa — Pennsylvania State Reports
PA — Personnel Administrator
PA — Petroleum Abstracts
PA — Philosophische Abhandlungen
PA — Philosophische Arbeiten
PA — Physics Abstracts
PA — Pollution Abstracts
Pa — Polonystyka
PA — Presence Africaine
PA — Pro Alesia. Revue Trimestrielle des Fouilles d'Alise et des Questions Relative a Alesia
PA — Pro Arte
PA — Professional Administration
PA — Professional Agent
PA — Prosopographia Attica
PA — Przeglad Archeologiczny
PA — Psychological Abstracts
PA — Public Administration
PAA — Pragmateiai tes Akademias Athenon
PAA — Praktika tes Akademias Athenon
PAA — Proceedings. American Academy of Arts and Sciences
PAAA — Asian Affairs. An Americaan Review
PAAAS — Proceedings. American Academy of Arts and Sciences
PAAAS — Publication. American Association for the Advancement of Science
PAABS Rev — PAABS [*Pan-American Association of Biochemical Societies*] Revista
PAABS Symp — PAABS [*Pan-American Association of Biochemical Societies*] Symposium
PAABS Symp Ser — PAABS (Pan-American Association of Biochemical Societies) Symposium Series
PAAC — Journal of Aesthetics and Art Criticism
Pa Acad Sci J — Pennsylvania Academy of Science. Journal
PA Acad Sci Proc — Pennsylvania Academy of Science. Proceedings
PA Admin Bull — Pennsylvania Bulletin
PAAF — African Affairs
PAAG — Annals. Association of American Geographers
PA Ag Exp — Pennsylvania. Agricultural Experiment Station. Publications
PA Agric Exp Stn Bull — Pennsylvania. Agricultural Experiment Station. Bulletin
PA Agric Exp Stn Prog Rep — Pennsylvania. Agricultural Experiment Station. Progress Report
PAAH — Praktika tes en Athenais Archaiologikes Hetaireias
PAAJR — Proceedings. American Academy for Jewish Research
PAANA — Proceedings. Australian Society of Animal Production
PAAOD8 — Proceedings. American Association for Cancer Research and American Society of Clinical Oncology

PAAP — Panjabi Adabi Academy. Publication
PAAPS — Proceedings of the American Academy of Political Science
PAAR — African Arts
PAAR — American Academy in Rome. Papers and Monographs
PA Arch — Pennsylvania Archaeologist
PA Archaeol — Pennsylvania Archaeologist
PAAS — Proceedings. American Antiquarian Society
PAATA — Praktika tes Akademias Athenon
PAAZA — Progressive Agriculture in Arizona
PAB — Product Application Bulletins
PAB — Public Affairs Bulletin
PA BA — Pennsylvania Bar Association. Reports
PABAQ — Pennsylvania Bar Association. Quarterly
PA Bar Asso Q — Pennsylvania Bar Association. Quarterly
PA B Ass'n Q — Pennsylvania Bar Association. Quarterly
Pa B Assn Rep — Pennsylvania Bar Association. Reports
PABCA8 — Annual Biology Colloquium
P Aberd — Catalogue of Greek and Latin Papyri and Ostraca in the Possession of the University of Aberdeen
P Abh — Philosophische Abhandlungen
PABIA — Pathologie et Biologie
PABLI — Pages Bleues Informatisees
PABR — Planning Appeals Board. Reports
PA Bsns Survey — Pennsylvania Business Survey
PABT — American Biology Teacher
Pa Bull — Pennsylvania Bulletin
Pa Bur Topogr Geol Surv Atlas — Pennsylvania. Bureau of Topographic and Geologic Survey. Atlas
PA Bur Topogr Geol Surv Miner Resour Rep — Pennsylvania. Bureau of Topographic and Geologic Survey. Mineral Resource Report
PABVA — Pesquisa Agropecuaria Brasileira. Serie Veterinaria
PAC — Canada. Fisheries and Marine Service. Northern Operations Branch. Pacific Region. Data Report Series
Pac — Packaging
Pa C — Pennsylvania County Reports
PAC — Pensamiento y Accion (Colombia)
Pac A — Pacific Affairs
PACA — Proceedings. African Classical Association
PACAB — Pacific Affairs. Current Awareness Bulletin
Pac Aff — Pacific Affairs
Pac Affairs — Pacific Affairs
Pac Arts Newsl — Pacific Arts Newsletter
Pac Asian J Energy — Pacific and Asian Journal of Energy
Pac Bird Obs — Pacific Bird Observer
Pac Builder Eng — Pacific Builder and Engineer
Pac Chem Eng Cong Proc — Pacific Chemical Engineering Congress. Prceedings
Pac Chem Eng Congr — Pacific Chemical Engineering Congress
Pac Chem Metall Ind — Pacific Chemical and Metallurgical Industries
Pac Coast Gas Assoc Proc — Pacific Coast Gas Association. Proceedings
Pac Coast Int — Pacific Coast International
Pac Coast Int — Pacific Coast International [*Portland*]
Pac Coast Int Assn L Enforcement Offic Proc — Pacific Coast International Association of Law Enforcement Officers. Proceedings
Pac Coast J Nursing — Pacific Coast Journal of Nursing
Pac Coast LJ — Pacific Coast Law Journal
Pac Coast Locker Frozen Food News — Pacific Coast Locker and Frozen Food News
Pac Coast Med — Pacific Coast Medicine
Pac Com — Pacific Community
Pac Comm — Pacific Community
Pac Commun — Pacific Community
Pac Def Report — Pacific Defence Reporter
Pac Discov — Pacific Discovery
Pac Discovery — Pacific Discovery
Pac D Rep — Pacific Defence Reporter
PACE — PACE. Pacing and Clinical Electrophysiology
PACE — PACE. Process and Chemical Engineering
Pace LR — Pace Law Review
Pace L Rev — Pace Law Review
PACE Process Chem Eng — PACE. Process and Chemical Engineering
PACE Process Control Eng — PACE
PACERS — Pacing and Cardiac Electrophysiology Retrieval System
PACFDP — Proceedings. Annual Conference on Restoration of Coastal Vegetation in Florida
Pac Fisherman — Pacific Fisherman

Pac Geol — Pacific Geology
PacH — Pacific Historian
Pachart Hist Astronom Ser — Pachart History of Astronomy Series
Pac Health Dialog — Pacific Health Dialog
Pa Chiefs Police Assn Proc — Pennsylvania Chiefs of Police Association. Proceedings
Pac Hist — Pacific Historian
Pac Hist R — Pacific Historical Review
Pac Hist Rev — Pacific Historical Review
Pac Hist Rev — Pacific History Review
Pac Hortic — Pacific Horticulture
PacHR — Pacific Historical Review
PACHS — Publications. American Church History Seminar
Pacif Aff — Pacific Affairs
Pacif Alask Rev — Pacific and Alaskan Review
Pacif Arts — Pacific Arts
Pacif Bldr Engr — Pacific Builder and Engineer
Pacif Bs N — Pacific Business News
Pacif Chem Metall Inds — Pacific Chemical and Metallurgical Industries
Pacif Coa J Nurs — Pacific Coast Journal of Nursing
Pacif Cst Archit — Pacific Coast Architect
Pacif Cst Archit Bldg Rev — Pacific Coast Architect and Building Review
Pacif Cst Avifauna — Pacific Coast Avifauna
Pacif Cst J Homoeop — Pacific Coast Journal of Homoeopathy
Pacif Cst J Nurs — Pacific Coast Journal of Nursing
Pacif Cst Lumberm — Pacific Coast Lumberman
Pacif Cst Mech — Pacific Coast Mechanic
Pacif Cst Miner — Pacific Coast Miner
Pacif Cst St Fish — Pacific Coast States Fisheries
Pacif Dairy Rev — Pacific Dairy Review
Pacif Dent Gaz — Pacific Dental Gazette
Pacif Drug Rev — Pacific Drug Review
Pacif Fisherm — Pacific Fisherman
Pacif Fruit Wld — Pacific Fruit World
Pacif Hist R — Pacific Historical Review
Pacif Hist Rev — Pacific Historical Review
Pacific A — Pacific Arts
Pacific Aff — Pacific Affairs
Pacific A Newslett — Pacific Arts Newsletter
Pacific Architect & Bldr — Pacific Architect and Builder
Pacific Bus — Pacific Business
Pacific CLJ — Pacific Coast Law Journal
Pacific Coast Med — Pacific Coast Medicine
Pacific Disc — Pacific Discovery
Pacific Discov — Pacific Discovery
Pacific His R — Pacific Historical Review
Pacific Hist Rev — Pacific Historical Review
Pacific Hort — Pacific Horticulture
Pacific Islands Com J — Pacific Islands Communication Journal
Pacific Islands M — Pacific Islands Monthly
Pacific Islands Yrbk — Pacific Islands Year Book
Pacific J Math — Pacific Journal of Mathematics
Pacific Ling — Pacific Linguistics
Pacific L J — Pacific Law Journal
Pacific Med J — Pacific Medical Journal
Pacific Med Surg — Pacific Medicine and Surgery
Pacific Northwest Quart — Pacific Northwest Quarterly
Pacific Northw Q — Pacific Northwest Quarterly
Pacific Perspect — Pacific Perspective
Pacific Phil Quart — Pacific Philosophical Quarterly
Pacific R — Pacific Review of Ethnomusicology
Pacific Sci — Pacific Science
Pacific Sci Inform — Pacific Science Information. Bernice P. Bishop Museum
Pacific Sociol R — Pacific Sociological Review
Pacific Stud — Pacific Studies
Pacif Imp — Pacific Imperialism Notebook
Pacif Insects — Pacific Insects
Pacif J Math — Pacific Journal of Mathematics
Pacif Mar Rev — Pacific Marine Review
Pacif Med J — Pacific Medical Journal</PHR> %
Pacif Miner — Pacific Miner
Pacif Miner — Pacific Mineralogist
Pacif Min J — Pacific Mining Journal
Pacif Min News — Pacific Mining News
Pacif Min Oil Reptr — Pacific Mining and Oil Reporter
Pacif Nat — Pacific Naturalist
Pacif Oil Reptr — Pacific Oil Reporter
Pacif Petrol Rec — Pacific Petroleum Record
Pacif Pharmst — Pacific Pharmacist
Pacif Plast — Pacific Plastics
Pacif Plast Mag — Pacific Plastics Magazine
Pacif Print — Pacific Printer
Pacif Pulp Pap Ind — Pacific Pulp and Paper Industry
Pacif Radio News — Pacific Radio News
Pacif Rd Bldr — Pacific Road Builder and Engineering Review
Pacif Rock — Pacific Rockets</PHR> %
Pacif Sci — Pacific Science
Pacif Sociol Rev — Pacific Sociological Review
Pacif Soc Rev — Pacific Sociological Review
Pacif St Bee J — Pacific States Bee Journal
Pacif Stud — Pacific Studies
Pacing Clin Electrophysiol — Pacing and Clinical Electrophysiology
Pac Insects — Pacific Insects
Pac Insects Mongr — Pacific Insects Monograph
Pac Insects Monogr — Pacific Insects Monograph

Pac J Math — Pacific Journal of Mathematics
Pack — Packaging
Packag Abstr — Packaging Abstracts
Packag A Cat Dir — Packaging Annual Catalogue and Directory [London]
Packag Cat — Packaging Catalog [New York]
Packag Des — Packaging Design
Packag Dig — Packaging Digest
Package Dev — Package Development
Package Dev Syst — Package Development and Systems
Package Eng — Package Engineering
Package Engng — Package Engineering
Package Print Diecutting — Package Printing and Diecutting. Flexography, Gravure, Offset
Packag (India) — Packaging (India)
Packag Inst Spec Rep — Packaging Institute. Special Report
Packag News Lond — Packaging News (London)
Packag News Montreal — Packaging News (Montreal)
Packag Packg Rec — Packaging and the Packing Record
Packag Parade — Packaging Parade
Packag Plast — Packaging with Plastics
Packag Rev — Packaging Review
Packag Rev (S Afr) — Packaging Review (South Africa)
Packag Ser Am Mgmt Ass — Packaging Series. American Management Association
Packag Syst — Packaging Systems
Packag Technol (Hillsdale NJ) — Packaging Technology (Hillsdale, New Jersey)
Packag Technol Sci — Packaging Technology and Science
Packag Wld Dig — Packaging World Digest
Packa Rev — Packaging Review
Pack Encyc — Packaging Encyclopedia
Packer Process — Packer, Processor
Packer Shipp — Packer and Shipper
Packg Packag Convey Gaz — Packing, Packaging, and Conveying Gazette
Packg Rec — Packing Record
Packg Shipp — Packing and Shipping
Pack Print and Dyecutting — Package Printing and Dyecutting
Pack Technol — Packaging Technology
Pack Technol Sci — Packaging Technology and Science
Packung — Packung und Transport in der Chemische Industrie
Pac Law Mag — Pacific Law Magazine
Pac Leg N — Pacific Legal News
Pac LJ — Pacific Law Journal
PACM — Poona Agricultural College Magazine
Pac Mar Fish Comm Annu Rep — Pacific Marine Fisheries Commission. Annual Report
Pac Mar Fish Comm Bull — Pacific Marine Fisheries Commission. Bulletin
Pac Mar Sci Rep — Pacific Marine Science Report
Pac Med Surg — Pacific Medicine and Surgery
Pac Miner Rev — Pacific Minerals Review
Pac Mo — Pacific Monthly
Pac Munic — Pacific Municipalities and Counties
PacN — Pacific Northwest Quarterly
P Ac Nat S — Proceedings. Academy of Natural Sciences of Philadelphia
PACNDF — AAZPA [American Association of Zoological Parks and Aquariums] Annual Proceedings
Pac Neighbours — Pacific Neighbours
Pac Northw — Pacific Northwest Quarterly
Pac Northwest — Pacific Northwesterner
Pac Northwesterner — Pacific Northwesterner
Pac Northwest For Range Exp Stn Res Note PNW — Pacific Northwest Forest and Range Experiment Station. Research Note PNW
Pac Northwest For Range Exp Stn Res Pap PNW — Pacific Northwest Forest and Range Experiment Station. Research Paper PNW
Pac Northwest Lab Annu Rep DOE Assist Secr Environ — Pacific Northwest Laboratory Annual Report to the DOE Assistant Secretary for Environment
Pac Northwest Lab Tech Rep PNL — Pacific Northwest Laboratory. Technical Report PNL
Pac Northwest Q — Pacific Northwest Quarterly
Pac Northwest Sea — Pacific Northwest Sea
PacNQ — Pacific Northwest Quarterly
Pac NWQ — Pacific Northwest Quarterly
Pac Ocean — Pacific Ocean
Pa Code — Pennsylvania Code
Pa Commw — Pennsylvania Commonwealth Court Reports
Pa Cons Stat — Pennsylvania Consolidated Statutes
Pa Cons Stat Ann (Purdon) — Pennsylvania Consolidated Statutes Annotated (Purdon)
PACPA — Proceedings. American Catholic Philosophical Association
Pac Pack Rep — Pacific Packers Report
PACPhA — Proceedings. American Catholic Philosophical Association
Pac Pharm — Pacific Pharmacist
Pac Philos Q — Pacific Philosophical Quarterly
Pac Phil Q — Pacific Philosophical Quarterly
Pac Phil Quart — Pacific Philosophical Quarterly
Pac Plast — Pacific Plastics
Pac Police Mag — Pacific Police Magazine
P Ac Poli S — Proceedings. Academy of Political Science
Pac Polym Conf — Pacific Polymer Conference
Pac Pulp Pap Ind — Pacific Pulp and Paper Industry
Pac Purchasor — Pacific Purchasor
PACQ — Atlantic Community Quarterly
Pac Q — Pacific Quarterly
Pac Res — Pacific Research [Formerly, Pacific Research and World Empire Telegram]
Pac Rockets — Pacific Rockets

Pac Rocket Soc Bull — Pacific Rocket Society. Bulletin
Pac Sci — Pacific Science
Pac Sci Congr Proc — Pacific Science Congress. Proceedings
Pac Sci Congr Rec Proc — Pacific Science Congress. Record of Proceedings
Pac Search — Pacific Search
Pac Sociol R — Pacific Sociological Review
Pac Soc R — Pacific Sociological Review
Pac Soc Rev — Pacific Sociological Review
PacSp — Pacific Spectator
Pac Symp Biocomput — Pacific Symposium on Biocomputing
PACT — Prevention des Accidents, Controles Techniques, Hygiene, et Maladies Professionnelles
Pac Tech Conf Soc Plast Eng — Pacific Technical Conference (Society of Plastics Engineers)
PACTIV — Principos Activos
PACT Rixensart Belg — PACT (Rixensart, Belgium). Journal. European Study Group on Physical, Chemical, and Mathematical Techniques Applied to Archaeology
Pac View — Pacific Viewpoint
Pac Viewp — Pacific Viewpoint
Pac Wine Spirit Rev — Pacific Wine Spirit Review
Pa D — Pennsylvania District Reports
PAD — Personnel Administrator
Pa D & C — Pennsylvania District and County Reports
PA Dent J — Pennsylvania Dental Journal
PA Dep Environ Resour Water Resour Bull — Pennsylvania. Department of Environmental Resources. Water Resources Bulletin
PA Dep For Waters Water Resour Bull — Pennsylvania. Department of Forests and Waters. Water Resources Bulletin
PA Dept Int Affairs Monthly Bull — Pennsylvania. Department of Internal Affairs. Monthly Bulletin
Pa Dept Welf M Bul — Pennsylvania Department of Welfare. Monthly Bulletin
Padiatr Pad — Paediatrie und Paedologie
Padova Ac At E Mm — Atti e Memorie della R. Accademia di Scienze, Lettere, ed Arti in Padova. Nuova Serie
Padova & Prov — Padova e la sua Provincia
Padova Mm Ac — Memorie dell' Accademia di Scienze, Lettere, ed Arti di Padova
Padova N Sag — Nuovi Saggi dell' Accademia di Scienze, Lettere, ed Arti di Padova
Padova Rv Period — Rivista Periodica dei Lavori della I. R. Accademia di Scienze, Lettere, ed Arti di Padova
Padova S Sc At — Atti della Societa Veneto-Trentina di Scienze Naturali Residente in Padova
Padova S Sc Bll — Bullettino della Societa Veneto-Trentina di Scienze Naturali (Padova)
PA Dp Agr An Rp — Pennsylvania. Department of Agriculture. Annual Report
PADS — Publications. American Dialect Society
PADSD — Proceedings. Analytical Division. Chemical Society
Pae — Paedagogik
PAe — Probleme der Aegyptologie
PAE — Problemy Arkheologii i Etnografii
PAEA — Publications. American Economic Association
Paedag Anz Russld — Paedagogischer Anzeiger fuer Russland
Paedag Hist — Paedagogica Historica
Paedag Mag — Paedagogisches Magazin
Paedagog — Paedagogik
Paedagog Hist — Paedagogica Historica
Paedagog Hochsch Karl Liebknecht Potsdam Wiss Z — Paedagogische Hochschule Karl Liebknecht Potsdam. Wissenschaftliche Zeitschrift
Paedagogica Hist — Paedagogica Historica
Paedagog Mag — Paedagogisk Magasin
Paedagog Not — Paedagogisk Notater
Paedagog Orienter — Paedagogisk Orientering
Paedagog Run — Paedagogische Rundschau
Paedag Zbl — Paedagogisches Zentralblatt
Paediat Danub — Paediatria Danubiana
Paediat Jap — Paediatria Japonica
Paediatr Anaesth — Paediatric Anaesthesia
Paediatr Drugs — Paediatric Drugs
Paediatr Endocrinol — Paediatric Endocrinology
Paediatr Fortbildungskurse Prax — Paediatrische Fortbildungskurse fuer die Praxis
Paediatr Grenzgeb — Paediatrie und Grenzgebiete
Paediatr Indones — Paediatrica Indonesiana
Paediatr Osteology New Dev Diagn Ther Proc Int Workshop — Paediatric Osteology. New Developments in Diagnostics and Therapy Proceedings of the International Workshop on Paediatric Osteology
Paediatr Paedol — Paediatrie und Paedologie
Paediatr Paedol (Suppl) — Paediatrie und Paedologie (Supplementum)
Paediatr Perinat Epidemiol — Paediatric and Perinatal Epidemiology
Paediatr Univ Tokyo — Paediatria Universitatis Tokyo
Paed Lex — Paedagogisches Lexikon
Paed LexG — Paedagogisches Lexikon. Herausgegeben von Hans-Hermann Groothoff
Paedog Psychol Arb — Paedagogisch-Psychologische Arbeiten
Paed Psyk T — Paedagogisk-Psykologisk Tidsskrift
PaedR — Paedagogische Rundschau
PA Elec Ass Eng Sect Transm Distrib — Pennsylvania Electric Association. Engineering Section. Transmission and Distribution Committee. Minutes
PA Electr Assoc Annu Rep — Pennsylvania Electric Association. Annual Report
PA Electr Assoc Eng Sect Minutes Meet — Pennsylvania Electric Association. Engineering Section. Minutes of the Meeting
PaeM — Publikationen Aelteerer Musik
PA Energy Ext Serv News — Pennsylvania Energy Extension Service. News
Paepst Rdschr — Paepstliche Rundschreiben

PAES — Publications. American Ethnological Society
PAES — Publications. Princeton University Archaeological Expeditions to Syria
PAET — American Ethnologist
PAF — Pacific Affairs
PA F — Pennsylvania Folklife
PAFA — Publications des Annales. Aix-Marseille. Universite. Faculte des Lettres
PAFAI J — PAFAI (Perfumes and Flavours Association of India) Journal
PA Farm Econ — Pennsylvania Farm Economics
PAFEA — Patologicheskaya Fiziologiya i Eksperimental'naya Terapiya
PA Folklife — Pennsylvania Folklife
PA For — Pennsylvania Forests
PA Fruit News — Pennsylvania Fruit News
PAFS — Asian Folklore Studies
PAFS — Publications. American Folklore Society
PAFTE Rev — PAFTE (Philippine Association for Teacher Education) Review
PAFZDW — Fundacao Zoobotanica do Rio Grande Do Sul. Publicacoes Avulsas
PAG — Packaging
Pag — Page's Three Early Assize Rolls, County of Northumberland
PaGa — Printing and Graphic Arts
PAGAA — Pesquisa Agropecuaria Brasileira. Serie Agronomia
Pagan Newslett — Pagan Newsletter
Page A — Page d'Art
Page J — PAGE (Philippine Association for Graduate Education) Journal
PA Gen As — Pennsylvania General Assembly
Pa Geneal Soc Pub — Genealogical Society of Pennsylvania. Publications
PA Geol — Pennsylvania Geology
PA Geol Surv Atlas — Pennsylvania. Geological Survey. Atlas
PA Geol Surv Gen Geol Rep — Pennsylvania. Geological Survey. General Geology Report
Pa Geol Surv Ground Water Rep — Pennsylvania. Geological Survey. Ground Water Report
PA Geol Surv Inf Circ — Pennsylvania. Geological Survey. Information Circular
PA Geol Surv Miner Resour Rep — Pennsylvania. Geological Survey. Mineral Resource Report
PA Geol Surv Prog Rep — Pennsylvania. Geological Survey. Progress Report
PA Geol Surv Water Resour Rep — Pennsylvania. Geological Survey. Water Resource Report
PA-Ger — Pennsylvania-German
PA Ger Folk Soc Yr Bk — Pennsylvania German Folklore Society. Year Book
Pa German Soc Proc — Pennsylvania German Society. Proceedings and Addresses
Pages Engng Wkly — Page's Engineering Weekly
PagesL — Pages Libres
Pages Mag — Page's Magazine
PAGH — Agricultural History
Pagine A — Pagine d'Arte
Pagine Istria — Pagine Istriane
Pagine Stor Med — Pagine di Storia della Medicina
Pagine Strav — Pagine Stravaganti
PagL — Pagine Libere
PA G S — Pennsylvania. Geological Survey
PAGS — Proceedings. Australian Goethe Society
PAGVA — Progres Agricole et Viticole
PAGYB — Pennsylvania Geology
PAGYDY — Pediatric and Adolescent Gynecology
PAH — Pamatky Archaeologicke. Skupina Historicka
PAH — Pompeianarum Antiquitatum Historia
Pahasapa Q — Pahasapa Quarterly
PAHEA — Pharmaceutica Acta Helvetiae
PA His — Pennsylvania History
PA Hist — Pennsylvania History
Pa Hist Soc Memoirs — Pennsylvania Historical Society. Memoirs
Pahlavi Med J — Pahlavi Medical Journal
PAHO/B — Bulletin. Pan American Health Organization
PAHS — Publications. Abertay Historical Society
Pal — Paldela. Rivista Letteraria di Informazione Bibliografica
PAIA — Pamphlets. Anglo-Israel Association
PAIA — Papers. Archaeological Institute of America. American Series
PAIAA — Proceedings. National Academy of Sciences (India). Section A
Paid — Paideia; Rivista Letteraria di Informazione Bibliografica
Paid — Paideuma
Paid Dues — Paid My Dues
Paideia Studies in Nature of Modern Math — Paideia Studies in the Nature of Modern Mathematics
Paideia Stud Philos Math at Large — Paideia Studies in Philosophia Mathematica at Large
Paidiat Klin — Paidiatrike Klinike
PAIDOL — Paidologist
PAIGH/H — Revista de Historia de America. Instituto Panamericano de Geografia e Historia.Comision de Historia
PAIGS — Performing Arts Information Guide Series
Paines Cutl J — Paine's Cutlery Journal
Paine Webb — Paine, Webber, Jackson & Curtis, Inc. Research Notes
Pain Fr — Pain Francais
Pain Rev — Pain Reviews
Pain Suppl — Pain. Supplement
Paint — Paintbrush
Paint Bull N Dak Agric Exp Stn — Paint Bulletin. North Dakota Agricultural Experiment Station
Paint Colour J Master Painter Aust — Paint Colour; Journal of the Master Painter of Australia
Paint Colour Oil Mf — Paint, Colour, Oil, Varnish, Ink, Lacquer Manufacture
Paint Colour Oil Varn Ink Lacquer Manuf — Paint, Colour, Oil, Varnish, Ink, Lacquer, Manufacture
Paint Colour Rec — Paint and Colour Record

Paint Dec J — Painting and Decorating Journal
Paint Decor — Painting and Decorating
Painters J — Painters and Allied Trades Journal
Painters Mag — Painters Magazine
Paintg Decor — Painting and Decorating
Paint Ind — Paint Industry
Paintindia Annu — Paintindia. Annual
Paint Ind Mag — Paint Industry Magazine
Painting Technol (Tokyo) — Painting Technology (Tokyo)
Paint Ink Int — Paint and Ink International
Paint J — Paint Journal
Paint J — Paint Journal of Australia and New Zealand
Paint J Aust NZ — Paint Journal of Australia and New Zealand
Paint Manuf — Paint Manufacture
Paint Manuf Assoc US Ed Bur Sci Sect Circ — Paint Manufacturers Association. United States. Educational Bureau. Scientific Section. Circulars
Paint Manuf Assoc US Tech Circ Educ Bur Sci Sect — Paint Manufacturers Association. United States. Technical Circulars. Educational Bureau. Scientific Section
Paint Manuf Resin News — Paint Manufacture and Resin News
Paint Mf — Paint Manufacture
Paint Oil Chem Rev — Paint Oil and Chemical Review
Paint Oil Colour J — Paint Oil and Colour Journal
Paint Oil Colour Yb — Paint, Oil, and Colour Year-Book
Paint Prog — Paint Progress
Paint Res — Paint and Resin
Paint Resin Int — Paint and Resin International
Paints Pak — Paints in Pakistan
Paints Pigm Varn Resins — Paints, Pigments, Varnishes, and Resins
Paint Technol — Paint Technology
Paint Varn Lacq Mf — Paint, Varnish, Lacquer, Enamel, and Colour Manufacture
Paint Varn Lacquer Curr Ind Rep — Paint, Varnish, and Lacquer. Current Industrial Reports
Paint Varn Lacquer Enamel Colour Manuf — Paint, Varnish, Lacquer, Enamel, and Colour Manufacture
Paint Varn Prod — Paint and Varnish Production
Paint Varn Prod Manager — Paint and Varnish Production Manager
Paint Varn Trades J — Paint and Varnish Trades Journal
Paint Wallpap — Paint and Wallpaper
PAIOC — Proceedings and Transactions. All India Oriental Conference
PAIS — Public Affairs Information Service
PAIS Bull — PAIS [*Public Affairs Information Service*] Bulletin
PAISER — Proceedings. Annual Conference and International Symposium of the North American Lake Management Society
PAIS Foreign Lang Index — PAIS [*Public Affairs Information Service*] Foreign Language Index
PA J — American Academy of Physicians' Assistants. Journal
PA J — PA Journal [*Formerly, Physician's Associate*]
PAJ — Pan-African Journal
PAJA — American Journal of Archaeology
PAJA — Publications. American Jewish Archives
Pajbjerfond Fors O ForaedlArb — Pajbjerfondens Forsogs- och Foraedlingsarbejde
PAJF — American Journal of Family Therapy
PAJH — American Jewish History
PAJHS — Proceedings. American Jewish Historical Society
PAJHS — Publication. American Jewish Historical Society
PAJM — Journal. American Musicological Society
PAJO — American Journal of Psychoanalysis
PAJP — American Journal of Philology
PajP — Pajarita de Papel
PaK — Piano and Keyboard
Pak Acad Sci Mem — Pakistan Academy of Sciences. Memoirs
Pak Acad Sci Proc — Pakistan Academy of Sciences. Proceedings
Pak Acad Sci Trans — Pakistan Academy of Sciences. Transactions
Pak Agric — Pakistan Agriculture
Pak Assoc Adv Sci Annu Rep — Pakistan Association for the Advancement of Science. Annual Report
Pak Assoc Adv Sci Sci Monogr — Pakistan Association for the Advancement of Science. Scientific Monograph
Pak At Energy Cent Rep — Pakistan. Atomic Energy Centre. Report
Pak At Energy Miner Cent Rep — Pakistan. Atomic Energy Minerals Centre. Report
PAKBA — Promyshlennost Armenii
Pak Bar J — Pakistan Bar Journal
Pak Congr Zool Proc — Pakistan Congress of Zoology. Proceedings
Pak Cottons — Pakistan Cottons
Pak Crim LJ — Pakistan Criminal Law Journal
Pak CSIR Bull Monogr — Pakistan Council of Scientific and Industrial Research. Bulletin. Monograph
Pak Dent Rev — Pakistan Dental Review
Pak Dev R — Pakistan Development Review
Pak Dev Rev — Pakistan Development Review
Pak DR — Pakistan Development Review
Pak Econ — Pakistan Economist
Pak Econ Soc Rev — Pakistan Economic Society Review
Pak Ed Rev — Pakistan Educational Review
Pak Eng — Pakistan Engineer
Pak Geogr R — Pakistan Geographical Review
Pak Geogr Rev — Pakistan Geographical Review
Pak Geol Surv Inf Release — Pakistan Geological Survey. Information Release
Pak Geol Surv Interim Geol Rep — Pakistan. Geological Survey. Interim Geological Report
Pak Geol Surv Rec — Pakistan Geological Survey. Records
Pak Horiz — Pakistan Horizon

Pakistan Archaeol — Pakistan Archaeology
Pakistan Develop R — Pakistan Development Review
Pakistan Econ and Social R — Pakistan Economic and Social Review
Pakistan Eng — Pakistan Engineer
Pakistan J Biol Agr Sci — Pakistan Journal of Biological and Agricultural Sciences
Pakistan J For — Pakistan Journal of Forestry
Pakistan J Med Res — Pakistan Journal of Medical Research
Pakistan J Sci — Pakistan Journal of Science
Pakistan J Sci Ind Res — Pakistan Journal of Scientific and Industrial Research
Pakistan J Sci Res — Pakistan Journal of Scientific Research
Pakistan J Soil Sci — Pakistan Journal of Soil Sciences
Pakistan J Statist — Pakistan Journal of Statistics
Pakistan Lib Bull — Pakistan Library Bulletin
Pakistan Lib R — Pakistan Library Review
Pakistan Phil J — Pakistan Philosophical Journal
Pakist Armed Forces Med J — Pakistan Armed Forces Medical Journal
Pakist Cott — Pakistan Cottons
Pakist Cott Bull — Pakistan Cotton Bulletin
Pakist Dent Rev — Pakistan Dental Review
Pakist Geogr Rev — Pakistan Geographical Review
Pakist J Agric Sci — Pakistan Journal of Agricultural Sciences
Pakist J Biol Agric Sci — Pakistan Journal of Biological and Agricultural Sciences
Pakist J Bot — Pakistan Journal of Botany
Pakist J For — Pakistan Journal of Forestry
Pakist J Hlth — Pakistan Journal of Health
Pakist J Med Res — Pakistan Journal of Medical Research
Pakist J Sci — Pakistan Journal of Science
Pakist J Scient Ind Res — Pakistan Journal of Scientific and Industrial Research
Pakist J Scient Res — Pakistan Journal of Scientific Research
Pakist J Surg Gynaec Obstet — Pakistan Journal of Surgery, Gynaecology, and Obstetrics
Pakist J Zool — Pakistan Journal of Zoology
Pakist Med J — Pakistan Medical Journal
Pakistn Pl — Sixth Five-Year Plan, 1983-88 (Pakistan)
Pakist Rev Agric — Pakistan Review of Agriculture
Pakist Weath Rev — Pakistan Weather Review
Pak J Agric Sci — Pakistan Journal of Agricultural Sciences
Pak J Agri Res — Pakistan Journal of Agricultural Research
Pak J Biochem — Pakistan Journal of Biochemistry
Pak J Biochem Mol Biol — Pakistan Journal of Biochemistry and Molecular Biology
Pak J Biol Agric Sci — Pakistan Journal of Biological and Agricultural Sciences
Pak J Bot — Pakistan Journal of Botany
Pak J Fam Plann — Pakistan Journal of Family Planning
Pak J For — Pakistan Journal of Forestry
Pak J Geriatr — Pakistan Journal of Geriatrics
Pak J Health — Pakistan Journal of Health
Pak J Hydrocarb Res — Pakistan Journal of Hydrocarbon Research
Pak J Med Res — Pakistan Journal of Medical Research
Pak J Nematol — Pakistan Journal of Nematology
Pak J Pharm — Pakistan Journal of Pharmacy
Pak J Pharmacol — Pakistan Journal of Pharmacology
Pak J Pharm Lahore — Pakistan Journal of Pharmacy (Lahore)
Pak J Pharm Sci — Pakistan Journal of Pharmaceutical Sciences
Pak J Sci — Pakistan Journal of Science
Pak J Sci and Ind Res — Pakistan Journal of Scientific and Industrial Research
Pak J Sci Ind Res — Pakistan Journal of Scientific and Industrial Research
Pak J Sci Res — Pakistan Journal of Scientific Research
Pak J Surg Gynaecol Obstet — Pakistan Journal of Surgery, Gynaecology, and Obstetrics
Pak J Surg Gyn Obst — Pakistan Journal of Surgery, Gynaecology, and Obstetrics
Pak J Zool — Pakistan Journal of Zoology
Pak Libr Ass Q J — Pakistan Library Association. Quarterly Journal
Pak Libr Rev — Pakistan Library Review
Pak L Rev — Pakistan Law Review
Pak Manage Rev — Pakistan Management Review
Pak Med For — Pakistan Medical Forum
Pak Med Forum — Pakistan Medical Forum
Pak Med J — Pakistan Medical Journal
Pak Med Rev — Pakistan Medical Review
Pak Nurs Health Rev — Pakistan Nursing and Health Review
Pak Philos Congr Proc — Pakistan Philosophical Congress. Proceedings
PakQ — Pakistan Quarterly
PakR — Pakistan Review
Pak Rev — Pakistan Review
Pak Rev Agric — Pakistan Review of Agriculture
Pak Sci Conf Proc — Pakistan Science Conference. Proceedings
Pak Sup Ct Q — Pakistan Supreme Court Law Quarterly
Pak Text J — Pakistan Textile Journal
Pak Vet J — Pakistan Veterinary Journal
Pal — Palaeontographica
Pal — Palimpsest
PAL — Pro Alesia
PA L — University of Pennsylvania. Law Review
Palabra Hom — Palabra y el Hombre
Palaeo — Palaeohistoria. Acta et Communicationes Instituti Bio-Archaeologici Universitatis Groninganae
Palaeobot India — Palaeobotany in India
Palaeobot Lit — Palaeobotanische Literatur
Palaeobot Z — Palaeobotanische Zeitschrift
Palaeoecol Afr Surround Isl — Palaeoecology of Africa and the Surrounding Islands
Palaeogeogr Palaeoclimatol Palaeoecol — Palaeogeography, Palaeoclimatology, Palaeoecology
Palaeogeo P — Palaeogeography, Palaeoclimatology, Palaeoecology

Palaeont — Palaeontographica
Palaeont Abh (Dames u Kayser) — Palaeontologische Abhandlungen (Dames und Kayser)
Palaeont Afr — Palaeontologia Africana
Palaeont Bull Canberra — Palaeontological Bulletin (Canberra)
Palaeont Bull Wellington — Palaeontological Bulletin. Geological Survey (Wellington)
Palaeont Hung — Palaeontologia Hungarica
Palaeont Jugosl — Palaeontologia Jugoslavica
Palaeont Mem Geol Surv Kwangtung Kwangsi — Palaeontological Memoirs of the Geological Survey of Kwangtung and Kwangsi
Palaeont Novit — Palaeontological Novitates
Palaeontogr Abt A — Palaeontographica. Abteilung A. Palaeozoologie-Stratigraphie
Palaeontogr Abt A Palaeozool-Stratigr — Palaeontographica. Abteilung A. Palaeozoologie-Stratigraphie
Palaeontogr Abt B — Palaeontographica. Abteilung B. Palaeophytologie
Palaeontogr Abt B Palaeophytol — Palaeontographica. Abteilung B. Palaeophytologie
Palaeontogr Am — Palaeontographica Americana
Palaeontogr Can — Palaeontographica Canadiana
Palaeontogr Ital — Palaeontographia Italia
Palaeontogr Soc Monogr — Palaeontographical Society. Monographs
Palaeontogr Soc Monogr (Lond) — Palaeontographical Society. Monographs (London)
Palaeontol Abh — Palaeontologische Abhandlungen
Palaeontol Afr — Palaeontologia Africana
Palaeontol Indica — Palaentologia Indica
Palaeontol Jugosl — Palaeontologia Jugoslavica
Palaeontol Jugoslav — Palaeontologia Jugoslavica
Palaeontol Mex Inst Geol (Mex) — Palaeontologia Mexicana. Instituto de Geologia (Mexico)
Palaeontol Pap Publ Geol Surv Queensl — Palaeontology Papers. Geological Survey of Queensland
Palaeontol Pol — Palaeontologia Polonica
Palaeontol Sinica — Palaeontologia Sinica
Palaeontol Sin Ser B — Palaeontologia Sinica. Series B
Palaeontol Sin Ser C — Palaeontologia Sinica. Series C
Palaeontol Sin Ser D — Palaeontologia Sinica. Series D
Palaeontol Soc Japan Trans Proc NS — Palaeontological Society of Japan. Transactions and Proceedings. New Series
Palaeontol Soc Jpn Spec Pap — Palaeontological Society of Japan. Special Papers
Palaeontol Stratigr Lithol — Palaeontology, Stratigraphy, and Lithology
Palaeontol Z — Palaeontologische Zeitschrift
Palaeont Pakist — Palaeontologia Pakistanica
Palaeont Pol — Palaeontologia Polonica
Palaeont Ser Cairo — Palaeontological Series. Survey Department. Cairo
Palaeont Sin — Palaeontologia Sinica. Geological Survey of China
Palaeont Soc Japan Trans and Proc — Palaeontological Society of Japan. Transactions and Proceedings
Palaeont Soc Mon — Palaeontographical Society. Monographs
Palaeont Univers — Palaeontologia Universalis
Palaeont Zeitschr — Palaeontologische Zeitschrift
Palaeont Zs — Palaeontologische Zeitschrift
Palaeovertebrata Mem Extraordinaire — Palaeovertebrata. Memoire Extraordinaire
Palaeovertebr (Montp) — Palaeovertebrata (Montpellier)
Palaiochrist & Byz Archaiol & Tech Kypro — Palaiochristianiki kai Byzantini Archaiologia kai Techni en Kypro
Pa Lang & Lit — Papers on Language and Literature
Palao Trop Biol Stn Stud — Palao Tropical Biological Station Studies
Palastina Jb — Palastina-Jahrbuch
Palat — Palatina. Rivista di Lettere e Arte
Pa Law Finder — Pennsylvania Law Finder
PA Law J — Pennsylvania Law Journal
PA Law Jour — Pennsylvania Law Journal
Pa Laws — Laws of Pennsylvania
Pa Law Ser — Pennsylvania Law Series
PALB — Animal Learning and Behavior
Pal B — Paleontological Bulletins
PALCDR — Annual Lightwood Research Conference. Proceedings
PalCl — Palestra del Clero
PALCOR — Palestine Correspondence
Pal EFA — Palestine Exploration Fund Annual
PA Leg Gaz — Legal Gazette (Pennsylvania)
Pa Legis Serv (Purdon) — Pennsylvania Legislative Service (Purdon)
Paleobiol Cont — Paleobiologie Continentale
Paleolimnol Lake Biwa Jpn Pleistocene — Paleolimnology of Lake Biwa and the Japanese Pleistocene
Paleonapryazhennost Fiz Osn Metody Issled — Paleonapryazhennost. Fizicheskie Osnovy i Metody Issledovaniya
Paleont Contr Univ Kans — Paleontological Contributions. University of Kansas
Paleont Cub — Paleontologia Cubana
Paleont Mex — Paleontologia Mexicana
Paleont Navors Nas Mus Bloemfontein — Paleontologiese Navorsing van die Nasionale Museum. Bloemfontein
Paleont Obosnov Stratigr Paleoz Rud Altaya — Paleontologicheskoe Obosnovanie Stratigrafii Paleozoya Rudnogo Altaya
Paleont Oboz — Paleontologicheskoe Obozrenie
Paleont Evol-Barc Inst Prov Paleontol — Paleontologia y Evolucion-Barcelona. Instituto Provincial de Paleontologia
Paleontol J — Paleontological Journal
Paleontol J (Engl Transl Paleontol Zh) — Paleontological Journal (English Translation of Paleontologicheskii Zhurnal)
Paleontol Mex — Paleontologia Mexicana

Paleontologiya Stratigr BSSR — Paleontologiya i Stratigrafiya BSSR
Paleontol Sb — Paleontologicheskiy Sbornik
Paleontol Sborn Lvov — Paleontologiceskij Sbornik. Lvov
Paleontol Sborn Moscow Leningrad — Paleontologiceskij Sbornik. Moscow and Leningrad
Paleontol Soc Mem — Paleontological Society. Memoir
Paleontol Stratigr Litol — Paleontologiya Stratigrafiya i Litologiya
Paleontol Zh — Paleontologicheskii Zhurnal
Paleont Pap Publs Geol Suv QD — Paleontology Papers. Publications. Geological Survey of Queensland
Paleont Research Lab Special Inv Rept — Paleontological Research Laboratories. Special Investigation. Report
Paleont Stud La Geol Surv — Paleontological Studies. Department of Conservation. Louisiana Geological Survey</PHR> %
Paleont Zh — Paleontologicheskii Zhurnal
Paleont Ziem Pol — Paleontologia Ziem Polskich
Paleopathol Newsl — Paleopathological Newsletter
PalEQ — Palestine Exploration Quarterly
Palermo Ac At — Atti dell' Accademia di Scienze, Lettere, ed Arti di Palermo
Palermo At — Atti dell' Accademia di Scienze, Lettere, ed Arti di Palermo
Palermo Cir Mt Rd — Rendiconti del Circolo Matematico di Palermo
Palermo Effem — Effemeridi Scientifiche e Letterarie per la Sicilia. Coi Lavori del R. Istituto d' Incorraggiamento per la Sicilia (Palermo)
Palermo G I Inc — Giornale del R. Istituto d' Incorragiamento di Agricoltura, Arti in Sicilia. Parte 3. Scienze Fisico-Matematiche e Naturali (Palermo)
Palermo G Sc Nt — Giornale di Scienze Naturali ed Economiche, Pubblicato per Cura del Consiglio di Perfezionamento Annesso al R. Istituto Tecnico di Palermo
Palermo Mm Spet It — Memorie della Societa degli Spettroscopisti Italiana, Raccolte e Pubblicate per Cura del Prof. P. Tacchini (Palermo)
Palest Board Sci Ind Res Rep — Palestine Board for Scientific and Industrial Research. Reports
Palest Citrogr — Palestine Citrograph
Palest Econ — Palestine Economist
Palest Explor Q — Palestine Exploration Quarterly
Palest Expl Quarterly — Palestine Exploration Quarterly
Palest Gaz Agric Suppl — Palestine Gazette. Agricultural Supplement
Palest Gov Board Sci Ind Res Rep — Palestine. Government. Board for Scientific and Industrial Research. Reports
Palestine & Middle E Econ Rev — Palestine and Middle East Economic Review
Palestine Explor Fund Q — Palestine Exploration Fund Quarterly
Palestine Explor Q — Palestine Exploration Quarterly
Palestine Explor Quart — Palestine Exploration Quarterly
Palest J Bot Hortic Sci — Palestine Journal of Botany and Horticultural Science
Palest J Bot Hort Sci — Palestine Journal of Botany and Horticultural Science
Palest J Bot Jerusalem Ser — Palestine Journal of Botany. Jerusalem Series
Palest J Bot Jerus Ser — Palestine Journal of Botany. Jerusalem Series
Palest J Bot Rehovot Ser — Palestine Journal of Botany. Rehovot Series
Palest Mag Med — Palestine Magazine of Medicine
Palestra Del Dir — Palestra del Diritto
Palestra Oftalmol Panam — Palestra Oftalmologica Panamericana
Palestras Agron — Palestras Agronomicas
Palest Trib — Palestine Tribune
Pal Expl Qu — Palestine Exploration Quarterly
Pal Ex Q — Palestine Exploration Quarterly
PA LG — Legal Gazette (Pennsylvania)
PA Lib Assn Bull — Pennsylvania Library Association. Bulletin
Pali Text Soc — Pali Text Society
PalJ — Palaestina-Jahrbuch
PA LJ — Pennsylvania Law Journal
PalJb — Palaestina-Jahrbuch
PA LJR — Clark's Pennsylvania Law Journal Reports
PA LJ Rep — Pennsylvania Law Journal-Reporter
PalL — Palenque Literario
Palladio — Palladio. Rivista di Storia dell'Architettura
Pal Lat — Palaestra Latina
Palliat Med — Palliative Medicine
Pall Mall Gaz — Pall Mall Gazette
Pall Mall M — Pall Mall Magazine
Pal Mus — Paleographie Musicale
Pal Mus Q — Palace Museum Quarterly
Palo Ciego — Palo de Ciego
Palomba Rac — Raccolta di Lettere. Intorno alla Fisica ed alle Mathematiche. Palomba
PA L Rev — University of Pennsylvania. Law Review
PalSb — Palestinskii Sbornik
Pal Sbor — Palestinskii Sbornik
Pal Sborn — Palestinskii Sbornik
PALSD — Program: Automated Library and Information Systems
PALSGR — Palsgrave Dictionary
Pal Soc — Palaeographical Society. Facsimiles of Manuscripts and Inscriptions
PALTREU — Palaestina Treuhandstelle zur Beratung Deutscher Juden
Palyaval Tanacs — Palyavalasztasi Tanacsadas
Palynol Bull — Palynological Bulletin
PAm — Pan American
PA M — Pennsylvania Magazine of History and Biography
PAMA — American Antiquity
Pam A — Pamatky Archeologicke
P Am Ac Ins — Proceedings. American Academy and Institute of Arts and Letters
PA Mag Hist — Pennsylvania Magazine of History and Biography
PA Mag Hist & Biog — Pennsylvania Magazine of History and Biography
PA Mag Hist Biogr — Pennsylvania Magazine of History and Biography
P Am Antiq — Proceedings. American Antiquarian Society
Pam Arch — Pamatky Archeologicke
Pam Archeol — Pamatky Archeologicke

P Am Ass Ca — Proceedings. American Association for Cancer Research
Pamatky Arch — Pamatky Archeologicke
Pamatky Archeol — Pamatky Archeologicke
Pamatky Prir — Pamatky a Priroda
Pamatky Prir Zivot — Pamatky - Priroda - Zivot
PAMB — American Behavioral Scientist
P Am Cath P — Proceedings. American Catholic Philosophical Association
PAMDA — Progress in Atomic Medicine
Pam Div Wood Technol For Comm NSW — Pamphlet. Division of Wood Technology. Forestry Commission. New South Wales
PA Med — Pennsylvania Medicine
PA Med J — Pennsylvania Medical Journal
P Amer Ac — Proceedings. American Academy of Arts and Sciences
PAMF — American Forests
Pam Fizyogr — Pamietnik Fizyograficzny
Pa Mfr J — Pennsylvania Manufacturers Journal
P Amh — Amherst Papyri
Pa M Hist — Pennsylvania Magazine of History and Biography
Pam Idaho Bur Mines Geol — Pamphlet. Idaho. Bureau of Mines and Geology
Pamiet Farm — Pamietnik Farmaceutyczny
Pamiet Konf Nauk Otolaryngol Dzieciecej Zakopane — Pamietnik Konferencji Naukowej Otolaryngologii Dzieciecej Zakopane
Pamietn Akad Umiejetn W Krakowie Wydz Mat Przyr — Pamietnik Akademji Umiejetnosci W Krakowie. Wydzial Matematiczne-Przyrodniczy
Pamietnik L — Pamietnik Literacki
Pamietnik Teat — Pamietnik Teatralny
Pamiet Pulawski — Pamietnik Pulawski
Pamiet Wiad Farm — Pamietnik i Wiadomosci Farmaceutyczne
Pamiet Zjazdu Otolaryngol Pol Katowicach — Pamietnik Zjazdu Otolaryngologow Polskich w Katowicach
Pam Iowa State Univ Sci Tech Coop Ext Serv — Pamphlet. Iowa State University of Science and Technology. Cooperative Extension Service
Pamiroved — Pamirovedeniye
Pa M J — Pennsylvania Medical Journal
Pam Klin Szpit Sw Lazarza — Pamietnik Kliniczny Szpitala Sw. Lazarza
PamL — Pamietnik Literacki
Pam Lewis Carroll — Pamphlets of Lewis Carroll
PAMM — Periodical Accounts Relating to the Moravian Missions
P Am Math S — Proceedings. American Mathematical Society
PAMN — American Midland Naturalist
PAMN — Publicacoes Avulsas do Museu Nacional [Rio de Janeiro]
Pam Panst Inst Nauk Gospod Wiejsk — Pamietnik Panstwowego Instytutu Naukowego Gospodarstwa Wiejskiego
Pamph — Pamphleteer
Pamph Advis Coun Sci Ind Aust — Pamphlet. Advisory Council of Science and Industry. Australia
Pamph Agric Educ Comm [London] — Pamphlet. Agricultural Education Committee [London]
Pamph Alaska Dep Mines — Pamphlet. Alaska Department of Mines
Pamph Ala St Commn For — Pamphlet. Alabama State Commission of Forestry
Pamph Am Agric Chem Co — Pamphlet. Americal Agricultural Chemical Company
Pamph Amat Ent Soc — Pamphlet. Amateur Entomologists' Society
Pamph Am Mar Stand Comm — Pamphlet. American Marine Standards Committee
Pamph Aust Tob Invest — Pamphlet. Australian Tobacco Investigation
Pamph Bath W Sth Cties Soc — Pamphlet. Bath and West and Southern Counties Society [Bath]
Pamph Br Thomson Houston Co — Pamphlet. British Thomson-Houston Company, Ltd.
Pamph Bur Miner Resour Geol Geophys Canberra — Pamphlet. Bureau of Mineral Resources, Geology, and Geophysics (Canberra)
Pamph Commonw Bur Agric Parasit — Pamphlet. Commonwealth Bureau of Agricultural Parasitology
Pamph Concr Util Bur — Pamphlet. Concrete Utilities Bureau
Pamph Dep Agric Fiji — Pamphlet. Department of Agriculture. Fiji
Pamph Dep Agric (Qd) — Pamphlet. Department of Agriculture (Queensland)
Pamph Dep Agric (Tanganyika) — Pamphlet. Department of Agriculture (Tanganyika Territory)
Pamph Dep Agric Tasm — Pamphlet. Department of Agriculture. Tasmania
Pamph Dep Agric Univ Coll N Wales — Pamphlet. Department of Agriculture. University College of North Wales
Pamph Dep Agric Un S Afr — Pamphlet. Department of Agriculture. Union of South Africa
Pamph Dep Sci Agric Barbados — Pamphlet. Department of Science and Agriculture. Barbados
Pamph Div Ent Pl Path Dep Agric Qd — Pamphlet. Division of Entomology and Plant Pathology. Department of Agriculture and Stock. Queensland
Pamph Div Pl Ind Dep Agric Qd — Pamphlet. Division of Plant Industry. Department of Agriculture and Stock. Queensland
Pamph Div Sci Publs Volcani Cent Agric Res Orgn — Pamphlet. Division of Scientific Publications. Volcani Center. Agricultural Research Organisation
Pamph Div Wood Technol For Comm NSW — Pamphlet. Division of Wood Technology. Forestry Commission. New South Wales
Pamph Div Wood Technol NSW For Commn — Pamphlet. Division of Wood Technology. New South Wales Forestry Commission
Pamph Dom Obs Ottawa — Pamphlet. Dominion Observatory (Ottawa)
Pamph Durban Tech Coll — Pamphlet. Durban Technical College
Pamph E Afr Fish Res Org — Pamphlet. East African Fisheries Research Organisation
Pamph For Dep Kenya — Pamphlet. Forestry Department. Kenya Colony
Pamph Forest Dep Trin — Pamphlet. Forest Department. Trinidad and Tobago
Pamph Forest Dep Uganda — Pamphlet. Forest Department. Uganda
Pamph Forest Res Inst Dehra Dun — Pamphlet. Forest Research Institute (Dehra Dun)
Pamph Geol Dep Uganda — Pamphlet. Geological Department. Uganda

Pamph Idaho Bur Mines Geol — Pamphlet. Idaho Bureau of Mines and Geology
P Am Phil S — Proceedings. American Philosophical Society
Pamph Inst Mkrs Explos [Chicago] — Pamphlet of the Institute of Makers of Explosives [Chicago]
Pamph Inst Sci Ind Aust — Pamphlet. Institute of Science and Industry. Australia
Pamph Inter Mount Ass Sug Beet Grow — Pamphlet. Inter-Mountain Association of Sugar Beet Growers [Salt Lake City]
Pamph Junker Co — Pamphlet. Junker and Co. [Dessau]
Pamph Ky Geol Surv — Pamphlet. Kentucky Geological Survey
Pamph Lds Forests Dep Sierra Leone — Pamphlet. Lands and Forests Department. Sierra Leone
Pamph Leeds Univ Dep Agric — Pamphlet. Leeds University Department of Agriculture and the Yorkshire Council for Agricultural Education
Pamphlet Archre — Pamphlet Architecture
Pamphl For Res Educ Proj For Dep (Sudan) — Pamphlet. Forestry Research and Education Project. Forests Department (Khartoum, Sudan)
Pamph Manchr Agric Advis Comm — Pamphlet. Manchester Agricultural Advisory Committee
Pamph Mines Dep Lond — Pamphlet. Mines Department. Board of Trade (London)
Pamph Minist Hlth [London] — Pamphlet. Ministry of Health [London]
Pamph Natn Lime Ass Wash — Pamphlet. National Lime Association (Washington)
Pamph Natn Mus Wales — Pamphlet. National Museum of Wales
Pamph Nova Scot Dep Publ Wks Mines — Pamphlet. Nova Scotia Department of Public Works and Mines
Pamph NY Engng Fdn — Pamphlet. New York Engineering Foundation
Pamph NY St Dep Hlth — Pamphlet. New York State Department of Health
Pamph Qd Forest Serv — Pamphlet. Queensland Forest Service
Pamph Rur Electrif Adm — Pamphlet. Rural Electrification Administration [Washington, D.C.]
Pamph Saf Comm Min Inst Scotl — Pamphlet. Safety Committee. Mining Institute of Scotland
Pamph Saf Longwall Min N Staffs — Pamphlet. Safety in Longwall Mining. Safety in Mines Research Committee. North Staffordshire Institute of Mining Engineers
Pamph Saf Longwall Wkg Nott — Pamphlet. Safety in Longwall Working. Midland Counties Institution of Engineers (Nottingham)
Pamph S Afr Biol Soc — Pamphlet. South African Biological Society
Pamph Seale Hayne Agric Coll — Pamphlet. Seale-Hayne Agricultural College [Newton Abbot]
Pamph Sect Vertebr Paleont Carnegie Mus — Pamphlet. Section of Vertebrate Paleontology. Carnegie Museum [Pittsburgh]
Pamph Ser Dep Agric W Indies — Pamphlet Series. Department of Agriculture. West Indies [Bridgetown]
Pamph Ser E Afr Met Serv — Pamphlet Series. East African Meteorological Service
Pamph Soil Improv Comm Natn Fertil Ass — Pamphlet. Soil Improvement Committee. National Fertiliser Association [Chicago]
Pamph Sth Fertil Ass Soil Improv Comm — Pamphlet. Southern Fertiliser Association Soil Improvement Committee
Pamph Sudan Met Serv — Pamphlet. Sudan Meteorological Service
Pamph Support Wkgs Mines Comm N Engl Inst Min Mech Engrs — Pamphlet. Support of Workings in Mines Committee. North of England Institute of Mining and Mechanical Engineers
Pamph S Wales Monmouth Saf Mines Res Comm — Pamphlet. South Wales and Monmouthshire Safety in Mines Research Committee
Pamph Tea Res Inst Ceyl — Pamphlet. Tea Research Institute of Ceylon
Pamph Tea Res Inst E Afr — Pamphlet. Tea Research Institute of East Africa
Pamph Volcani Inst Agric Res — Pamphlet. Volcani Institute of Agricultural Research
Pamph Vt Agric Exp Stn — Pamphlet. Vermont Agricultural Experiment Station
PAMPM — Publications in Anthropology. Public Museum of the City of Milwaukee
Pam Pulaw — Pamietnik Pulawski
Pam Pulawski — Pamietnik Pulawski
PAMREA — Proceedings. American Association for Cancer Research. Annual Meeting
PAMS — North-Holland Series in Probability and Applied Mathematics
PAMS — Papers. American Musicological Society
PAMS — Proceedings. American Mathematical Society
PAMSB — Pharos of Alpha Omega Alpha Honor Medical Society
P Am S Info — Proceedings. American Society for Information Science
PamSL — Pamietnik Slowianski Czasopismo Naukowe Posiecone Slowianoznawstwu
Pam Slow — Pamietnik Slowianski
Pam Tea Res Inst Ceylon — Pamphlet. Tea Research Institute of Ceylon
Pam Tow Lek Warsz — Pamietnik Towarzystwa Lekarskiego Warszawskiego
Pam Tow Tatrz — Pamietnik Towarzystwa Tatrzanskiego
Pam Turkm — Pam'iatniki Turkmenistana
PA Mus Bull — Pennsylvania Museum Bulletin
Pam Volcani Cent Bet Dagan Isr — Pamphlet. Volcani Center (Bet Dagan, Israel)
Pam Vt Agric Exp Stn — Pamphlet. Vermont Agricultural Experiment Station
Pam Wilen Tow Lek — Pamietnik Wilenskiego Towarzystwa Lekarskiego
PAMWS — Proceedings. Annual Meeting. Western Society for French History
PAMYA — Proceedings. American Mathematical Society
Pamyat Knizh Imp Akad Nauk — Pamyatnaya Knizhka Imperatorskoi Akademii Nauk
Pamyat Knizh Konstant Mezh Inst — Pamyatnaya Knizhka Konstantinovskogo Mezhevogo Instituta
Pamyat Knizh Prakt Gig — Pamyatnaya Knizhka po Prakticheskoi Gigiene
Pamyat Knizh Varsh Vet Obshch — Pamyatnaya Knizhka Varshavskago Veterinarnago Obshchestva
Pam Zakl Badan Drzew Lasu Korniku — Pamietnik Zakladu Badania Drzew i Lasu w Korniku
Pam Zakl Genet Warsz — Pamietnik Zakladu Genetycznego Szkoly Glownej Gospodarstwa Wiejskiego (Warszawa)
PAN — Packaging News

Pan — Panache
Pan — Panorama
PAN — Pastoral Music Notebook
PanA — Pan-Africanist
PanA — Pan-African Journal
Pan Afr J — Pan-African Journal
Pan Afr Jnl — Pan-African Journal
Panama Admin Recursos Minerales Mapa — Republica de Panama. Administracion de Recursos Minerales. Mapa
Panama Canal Rec — Panama Canal Record
Panama Month Panama — Panama This Month (Panama)
Panama Univ Dept Geografia Pub — Panama Universidad. Departamento de Geografia. Publicacion
Panam Comer Wash — Panamericana Comercial (Washington, DC)
Pan American Mag — Pan-American Magazine
Panamer Math J — Panamerican Mathematical Journal
Pan Amer Union Lib Bibliog Ser — Pan-American Union. Library and Bibliography Series
Pan Am Fisherman — Pan American Fisherman
Pan Am Geol — Pan-American Geologist
Pan Am Health Organ Off Doc — Pan American Health Organization. Official Document
Pan Am Health Organ Res Prog — Pan American Health Organization. Research in Progress
Pan Am Health Organ Sci Publ — Pan American Health Organization. Scientific Publication
Pan-Am Inst Geography and History Pub — Pan-American Institute of Geography and History. Publication
Pan Am Inst Min Eng Geol US Sect Tech Pap — Pan American Institute of Mining Engineering and Geology. United States Section. Technical Paper
Pan Am M — Pan American Magazine
Pan Am Mag — Pan American Magazine
Pan Am Mag Wash — Pan American Magazine (Washington, DC)
Pan Am Med Cong Trans — Pan-American Medical Congress. Transactions
Pan Am Med Wom J — Pan-American Medical Woman's Journal
Pan Am Rec — Pan-American Record
Pan Am Surg Med J — Pan-American Surgical and Medical Journal
Pan Am Tegucigalpa — Pan-America (Tegucigalpa)
Pan Am Union Bol Ciencia y Tecnologia — Pan American Union. Boletin de Ciencia y Tecnologia
Pan Am Union Bul — Pan American Union. Bulletin
Pan Am Womans J — Pan American Woman's Journal
PanAR — Pan American Review
Pand B — Pandectes Belges
P and B — Pragmatics and Beyond
P and BR — Patristic and Byzantine Review
P & C — Poet and Critic
P&D — Poetry and Drama
Pander Btr Ntk — Beitraege zur Naturkunde aus den Ostseeprovinzen Russlands. Pander
P & F — Photography and Focus
P & G Jour — Pipeline and Gas Journal
P & G Jour BG — Pipeline and Gas Journal Buyer's Guide Issue Handbook
P & I — Parole e le Idee
P & IF — Paris et Ile-De-France. Memoires
P & L — Philosophy and Literature
P & L — Politics and Letters
P & NGLR — Papua and New Guinea Law Reports
P & P — Past and Present
P and P — Perception and Psychophysics
Pand Per — Pandectes Periodiques
P & P Intnl — Pulp and Paper International Annual Review
P & P Jrl — Pulp and Paper Journal
P & P Qtly — Pulp and Paper Quarterly Statistics
P & PR — Psychoanalysis and the Psychoanalytic Review
P & R — Parks and Recreation
P & R — Philosophy and Rhetoric
P & V Prod — Paint and Varnish Production
PANE — Park News
Panep Math Biblth — Panepistemiake Mathematike Bibliotheke
PAN/ES — Estudios Latinoamericanos. Polska Akademia Nauk
Pan Genoss Pan — Pan. Herausgegeben von der Genossenschaft Pan
Panhandle Bull — Panhandle Bulletin [Goodwell, Oklahoma]
Panhandle Geol Soc Strat Cross Sec — Panhandle Geological Society. Stratigraphic Cross Section
Panhandle Plains Hist Rev — Panhandle-Plains Historical Review
Pan Indian Ocean Sci Congr Proc Sect D Agr Sci — Pan Indian Ocean Science Congress. Proceedings. Section D. Agricultural Sciences
Pan i Prawo — Panstwo i Prawo
Panjab Geogr Rev — Panjab Geographical Review
Panjab Past Pres — Panjab Past and Present
Panjab Univ (Chandigarh) Cent Adv Stu Geol Publ — Panjab University (Chandigarh). Centre of Advanced Study in Geology. Publication
Panjab Univ Dep Zool Bull — Panjab University. Department of Zoology. Bulletin
Panminerva Med — Panminerva Medica
Pann Szle — Pannonhalmi Szemle
Panorama Democr Chr — Panorama Democrate Chretien
Panorama Econ (Chile) 2a Epoca — Panorama Economico (Chile). Segunda Epoca
Panorama Econ (Mexico) — Panorama Economico (Mexico)
Panorama Isk — Panorama Iskusstv
Panorama M Instruments — Panorama de la Musique et des Instruments
Panor Synth — Panoramas et Syntheses
Panor Syntheses — Panoramas et Syntheses
Panp — Panpipes of Sigma Alpha Iota

Pan-Pac Ent — Pan-Pacific Entomologist
Pan-Pac Entomol — Pan-Pacific Entomologist
Pan Pacif — Pan-Pacific [Honolulu]
Pan-Pacif Ent — Pan-Pacific Entomologist
Pan Pipes — Pan Pipes of Sigma Alpha Iota
PANPJ — Polska Akademia Nauk. Komitet Jezykoznawstwa. Prace Jezykoznawcze
PANPKHL — Polska Akademia Nauk. Oddzial w Krakowie. Prace Komisji Historycznoliterackiej
PANPKS — Polska Akademia Nauk. Oddzial w Krakowie. Prace Komisji Slowianoznawstwa
PANR — Antioch Review
Pan Rass Lett A & Musica — Pan. Rassegna di Lettere, Arti, e Musica
P An Rel M — Proceedings. Annual Reliability and Maintainability Symposium
PANS — Ageing and Society
PANS — Pest Articles News Summaries
PANS — Proceedings. Academy of Natural Sciences of Philadelphia
PANS Pest Artic News Summ — PANS. Pest Articles and News Summaries
PANS Sect C Weed Control — PANS. Pest Articles and News Summaries. Section C. Weed Control
Panst Kom Ochr Przyr Pol — Panstwowy Komitet Ochrony Przyrody w Polsce
Panstw Sluzba Geol Panstw Inst Geol Biul — Panstwowa Sluzba Geologiczna. Pantswowy Instytut. Geologiczny Biuletyn
PANT — Antaeus
Pant — Pantainos
Panta J Med — Panta Journal of Medicine
PANTDK — Progress in Anatomy
Panth — Pantheon
Pantheon Litt — Pantheon Litteraire
P Antin — Antinopolis Papyri
Pantnagar J Res — Pantnagar Journal of Research
PA Nurse — Pennsylvania Nurse
Pan Wochschr — Pan. Wochenschrift
Panz Ann — Panzer Annales
PAORB — Problemes Actuels d'Oto-Rhino-Laryngologie
PAOS — Proceedings. American Oriental Society
PAOTA — Problemes Actuels d'Ophtalmologie
PAP — Pamatky Archaeologicke. Skupina Praveka
PAP — Papyrologica
Pap — Papyrus
PaP — Past and Present
PaP — Patterns of Prejudice
PAP — Psychobiology and Psychopathology
PAPA — Proceedings. American Philological Association
PAPA — Publications. Arkansas Philological Association
PAPAA4 — American Psychopathological Association. Proceedings
Pap Addr Am Min Congr — Papers and Addresses. American Mining Congress
Pap Addr Tech Ass Pulp Pap Ind — Papers and Addresses. Technical Association of the Pulp and Paper Industry
Pap A Forum Packag Inst — Papers Presented at Annual Forum. Packaging Institute [New York]
Pap Agric Educ Sub Comm Middx — Papers. Agricultural Education Sub-Committee. Middlesex
Pap Agric Hist Soc — Papers. Agricultural Historical Society
Pap Albany Soc Civ Engrs — Papers. Albany Society of Civil Engineers
Pap Alum Ind Energy Conserv Workshop — Papers. Aluminum Industry Energy Conservation Workshop
Pap Am Ass Text Technol — Papers of the American Association for Textile Technology
Pap Am Chem Soc Div Paint Plast Print Ink — Papers. American Chemical Society. Division of Paint, Plastics, and Printing Ink
Pap Amer Assoc Archit Bibliographers — Papers of the American Association of Architectural Bibliographers
Pap Amer Soc Agr Eng — Paper. American Society of Agricultural Engineers
Pap Am Inst Steel Constr — Papers. American Institute of Steel Construction
Pap Am Sch Ath — Papers. American School of Classical Studies at Athens
Pap Am Soc Ch Hist — Papers. American Society of Church History
Pap Am Soc Mech Engrs — Papers. American Society of Mechanical Engineers
Pap Am Soc Trop Med — Papers. American Society of Tropical Medicine
Pap Anat Lab St Louis Univ — Papers from the Anatomical Laboratory. St. Louis University [St. Louis, Missouri]
Pap & Proc Royal Soc Tasmania — Papers and Proceedings of the Royal Society of Tasmania
Pap Annu Conf Text Inst (Manchester UK) — Papers. Annual Conference. Textile Institute (Manchester, United Kingdom)
Pap Annu Conv West Can Water Sewage Conf — Papers Presented at the Annual Convention. Western Canada Water and Sewage Conference
Pap Annu Meet Air Waste Manage Assoc — Papers from the Annual Meeting. Air and Waste Management Association
Pap Annu Meet Can Pest Manage Soc — Papers. Annual Meeting. Canadian Pest Management Society
Pap Annu Meet Gypsy Lore Soc N Amer — Papers from the Annual Meetings. Gypsy Lore Society North American Chapter
Pap Anthro — Papers in Anthropology
Pap Anthrop — Papers in Anthropology
Pap Anthrop Inst Imp Univ Tokyo — Papers of the Anthropological Institute. College of Science. Imperial University of Tokyo
Pap Appl Fish Lab Univ Wash — Papers. Applied Fisheries Laboratory. University of Washington
Pap Archaeol Inst America — Papers of the Archaeological Institute of America
Pap Archit Sci Unit Univ Queensl — Paper. Architectural Science Unit. University of Queensland
Pap ASAE — Paper. American Society of Agricultural Engineers
Pap Avulsos Dep Zool (Sao Paulo) — Papeis Avulsos. Departamento de Zoologia (Sao Paulo)

Pap Avulsos Dep Zool Secr Agric Ind Comer (Sao Paulo) — Papeis Avulsos. Departamento de Zoologia. Secretaria de Agricultura Industria e Comercio (Sao Paulo)

Pap Avulsos Zool (Sao Paulo) — Papeis Avulsos de Zoologia (Sao Paulo)

Pap Avul Zool — Papeis Avulsos de Zoologia

Pap Belf Ass Engrs — Papers of the Belfast Association of Engineers

Pap Bibliog — Papers. Bibliographical Society of America

Pap Bibliogr Soc Am — Papers. Bibliographical Society of America

Pap Bibliogr Soc Amer — Papers. Bibliographical Society of America

Pap Bibliog Soc Am — Papers. Bibliographical Society of America

Pap Bibl Soc Am — Papers. Bibliographical Society of America

Pap Board Abstr — Paper and Board Abstracts

Pap Borneo Ling — Papers in Borneo Linguistics

Papbrd Pkg — Paperboard Packaging

Pap Brit School Rome — Papers. British School at Rome

Pap Brit Sch Rome — Papers. British School at Rome

Pap Brux — Papyrologica Bruxellensia

Pap BTH Res Lab — Papers. B.T.H. (British Thomson Houston Co.) Research Laboratory

Pap Bur Inf Nickel — Papers. Bureau of Information on Nickel, Ltd. [*London*]

PAPC — Philological Association of the Pacific Coast

Pap Carton Cellul — Papier. Carton et Cellulose

Pap Celul — Papir a Celuloza

Pap Chem — Paper Chemistry

Pap Chicago — Papers on Chicago. Chicago Geographical Society

Pap Coal Util Symp Focus SO$_2$ Emiss Control — Papers. Coal Utilization Symposium. Focus on SO$_2$ Emission Control

Pap Coat Add — Paper Coating Additives

Pap Comm Ceram Sci Ceram — Papers of the Commission on Ceramical Sciences. Ceramics

Pap Commonw Bur Anim Genet — Papers. Commonwealth Bureau of Animal Genetics [*Edinburgh*]

Pap Commonw Bur Fruit Prod — Papers. Commonwealth Bureau of Fruit Production [*East Malling*]

Pap Commonw For Conf — Paper. Commonwealth Forestry Conference

Pap Comm Res Exp Geol Geophys Harv — Papers. Committee on Research in Experimental Geology and Geophysics. Harvard University

Pap Confs Indian Cent Cott Comm — Papers. Conferences. Indian Central Cotton Committee

Pap Congr Aust NZ Assoc Adv Sci — Australian and New Zealand Association for the Advancement of Science. Congress. Papers

Pap Congr Fed Int Precontrainte — Papers. Congress of the Federation Internationale de la Precontrainte

Pap Conservator — Paper Conservator

Pap Conserv Cat — Paper Conservation Catalogue

Pap Conserv News — Paper Conservation News

Pap Conv Am Nurs Assoc — Papers from the Convention. American Nurses' Association

Pap Convert Envel Ind — Paper Converter and Envelope Industry

Pap Converting — Paper Converting

Pap Czech Soil Sci Conf — Papers. Czechoslovak Soil Science Conference

Pap Dep Agric QD Univ — Papers. Department of Agriculture. University of Queensland

Pap Dep Anat Univ Qd — Papers from the Department of Anatomy. University of Queensland

Pap Dep Biol Univ Qd — Papers from the Department of Biology. University of Queensland

Pap Dep Bot McGill Univ — Papers. Department of Botany. McGill University

Pap Dep Bot Univ Qd — Papers from the Department of Botany. University of Queensland

Pap Dep Chem McGill Univ — Papers from the Department of Chemistry. McGill University

Pap Dep Chem Univ Qd — Papers from the Department of Chemistry. University of Queensland

Pap Dep Dent Univ Qd — Papers. Department of Dentistry. University of Queensland

Pap Dep Engng McGill Univ — Papers from the Department of Engineering. McGill University

Pap Dep Entomol Univ Queensl — Papers. Department of Entomology. University of Queensland

Pap Dep Ent Univ Qd — Papers. Department of Entomology. University of Queensland

Pap Dep Genet Carnegie Instn — Papers. Department of Genetics. Carnegie Institution

Pap Dep Geogr Univ Edinb — Papers from the Department of Geography in the University of Edinburgh

Pap Dep Geol Glasg Univ — Papers. Department of Geology. Glasgow University

Pap Dep Geol Miner McGill Univ — Papers from the Department of Geology and Mineralogy. McGill University

Pap Dep Geol QD Univ — Papers. Department of Geology. University of Queensland

Pap Dep Geol Queensl Univ — Papers. Department of Geology. University of Queensland

Pap Dep Geol Univ QD — Papers. Department of Geology. University of Queensland

Pap Dep Mar Biol Carnegie Instn Wash — Papers from the Department of Marine Biology of the Carnegie Institution of Washington

Pap Dep Math McGill Univ — Papers from the Department of Mathematics. McGill University

Pap Dep Math Univ Qd — Papers from the Department of Mathematics. University of Queensland

Pap Dep Metall McGill Univ — Papers from the Department of Metallurgy. McGill University

Pap Dep Met McGill Univ — Papers from the Department of Meteorology. McGill University

Pap Dep Miner McGill Univ — Papers from the Department of Minerology. McGill University

Pap Dep Min McGill Univ — Papers from the Department of Mining. McGill University

Pap Dep Ophthal McGill Univ — Papers from the Department of Ophthalmology. McGill University

Pap Dep Path McGill Univ — Papers from the Department of Pathology. McGill University

Pap Dep Physiol McGill Univ — Papers from the Department of Physiology. McGill University

Pap Dep Physiol Univ Qd — Papers from the Department of Physiology. University of Queensland

Pap Dep Phys McGill Univ — Papers from the Department of Physics. McGill University

Pap Dep Phys Univ Qd — Papers from the Department of Physics. University of Queensland

Pap Dep Scient Ind Res — Papers of the Department of Scientific and Industrial Research [*London*]

Pap Dep Zool McGill Univ — Papers from the Department of Zoology. McGill University

Pap Dep Zool QD Univ — Papers. Department of Zoology. University of Queensland

Pap Dep Zool Univ Qd — Papers. Department of Zoology. University of Queensland

Pap Diesel Engrs Us Ass — Papers. Diesel Engineers and Users' Association

Pap Discuss Ass Mine Mgrs S Afr — Papers and Discussions Association of Mine Managers of South Africa

Pap Discuss Ass Mine Mgrs Transv — Papers and Discussions. Association of Mine Managers of the Transvaal

Pap Discuss Ass Study Snow Ice — Papers and Discussions. Association for the Study of Snow and Ice

Pap Discuss Congr Med Educ — Papers and Discussions. Congress on Medical Education. American Medical Association

Pap Discuss Jt AIEE IRE ACM Computer Conf — Papers and Discussions Presented at the Joint AIEE-IRE-ACM Computer Conference

Pap Discuss Jt AIEE IRE Computer Conf — Papers and Discussions Presented at the Joint AIEE-IRE Computer Conference

Pap Discuss Recup Conf — Papers and Discussions. Recuperator Conference

Pap Discuss Tn Plann Inst — Papers and Discussions. Town Planning Institute

Pap Discuss Vict Engrs Ass — Papers and Discussions of the Victorian Engineers' Association

Pap Div Org Coat Plast Chem Am Chem Soc — Papers. Division of Organic Coatings and Plastics Chemistry. American Chemical Society

Pap Div Polym Chem Am Chem Soc — Papers. Division of Polymer Chemistry. American Chemical Society

Pap Doncaster Engng Soc — Papers of the Doncaster Engineering Society

Pap Druck — Papier und Druck

PAPE — Aperature

Pap Eastbourne Nat Hist Soc — Papers. Eastbourne Natural History Society

Pap Ecol S Afr Cst — Papers on the Ecology of the South African Coast

PAPEDJ — Pesquisa Agropecuaria Pernambucana

Pap Egypt Geol Surv — Paper. Egyptian Geological Survey

Pap Engng Div Instn Civ Engrs — Papers. Engineering Division. Institution of Civil Engineers

Pap Engng Soc Sch Pract Sci Toronto — Papers Read before the Engineering Society of the School of Practical Science (Toronto)

Paper & Board Abs — Paper and Board Abstracts

Paperbd Packag — Paperboard Packaging

Paperboard Packag — Paperboard Packaging

Paperboard Pkg — Paperboard Packaging

Paper Bul — Paper and Packaging Bulletin

Paper Film Foil Conv — Paper, Film, and Foil Converter

Paper Ind Paper Wld — Paper Industry and Paper World

Paper Jour — Paper Trade Journal

Papermakers Conf Proc — Papermakers Conference. Proceedings

Paper Makers Merch Dir — Paper Makers and Merchants. Directory of All Nations

Paper Making — Paper Making and Paper Selling

Paper Making Print — Paper Making and the Printer

Papermkg Abstr Kenley — Papermaking Abstracts. British Paper and Board Industry Research Association (Kenley, Surrey)

Papermkg Abstr NY — Papermaking Abstracts (New York)

Paper Mkr — Paper Maker

Paper Mkr Kalamazoo — Paper Maker (Kalamazoo)

Paper Mkr Lond — Paper Maker and British Paper Trade Journal (London)

Paper Mkrs Circ — Paper Makers' Circular

Paper Mkrs J — Paper Makers' Journal

Paper Mkrs Mon J — Paper Makers' Monthly Journal

Paper Mkr Wilmington — Paper Maker (Wilmington)

Paper Mkt — Paper Market

Paper Print — Paper and Print

Paper Prog Cleveland — Paper Progress (Cleveland, Ohio)

Paper Prog Lond — Paper and Progress (London)

Paper Pulp Mill Catalogue — Paper and Pulp Mill Catalogue/Engineering Handbook

Papers & Proc Roy Soc Tas — Papers and Proceedings. Royal Society of Tasmania

Papers and Proc Roy Soc Tasmania — Papers and Proceedings. Royal Society of Tasmania

Papers & Proc Tas Hist Res Assn — Papers and Proceedings. Tasmanian Historical Research Association

Papers ASA — Papers. American School of Classical Studies at Athens

Papers AS Athens — Papers. American School at Athens

Papers Biblio Soc Am — Papers. Bibliographical Society of America

Papers Brit School Rome — Papers. British School at Rome

Papers Br Sch Rome — Papers. British School at Rome

Papers B S Rome — Papers. British School at Rome
Papers Far East Hist — Papers on Far Eastern History
Papers in Ed (Anstey Coll) — Papers in Education (Anstey College of Physical Education)
Papers Proc Roy Soc Tasmania — Papers and Proceedings. Royal Society of Tasmania
Paper Tech Indus — Paper Technology and Industry
Paper Technol — Paper Technology
Paper Technol Ind — Paper Technology and Industry
Paper Tonbridge UK — Paper (Tonbridge, United Kingdom)
Paper Trade J — Paper Trade Journal
Paper Tr J — Paper Trade Journal
Paper Twine J — Paper and Twine Journal
Paper Yrb — Paper Year Book
Papeterie Numero Spec — Papeterie. Numero Special
Pap Excav Club Camb Mass — Papers. Excavators' Club (Cambridge, Massachusetts)
PapF — Papierfabrikant
Pap Fac Agric Univ Qd — Papers. Faculty of Agriculture. University of Queensland
Pap Fac Engng Univ Qd — Papers. Faculty of Engineering. University of Queensland
Pap Fac Geogr Univ Qd — Papers. Faculty of Geography. University of Queensland
Pap Fac Med Clin Deps Univ Qd — Papers. Faculty of Medicine Clinical Departments. University of Queensland
Pap FAO/IUFRO World Consult For Tree Breed — Paper. FAO [*Food and Agriculture Organization of the United Nations*]/IUFRO World Consultation on Forest Tree Breeding
Pap Far Eas — Papers on Far Eastern History
Pap Far East Hist — Papers on Far Eastern History
Pap Film Foil Converter — Paper, Film, and Foil Converter
Pap Forest Prod Lab Can — Papers. Forest Products Laboratory. Canada
Pap Gen Topol Appl Summer Conf Long Isl Univ — Papers on General Topology and Applications. Summer Conference at Long Island University
Pap Gen Topol Appl Summer Conf Slippery Rock Univ — Papers on General Topology and Applications. Summer Conference at Slippery RockUniversity
Pap Geol Dep Glasg Univ — Papers from the Geological Department of Glasgow University
Pap Geol Dep Univ Lpool — Papers from the Geological Department of the University of Liverpool
Pap Geol Mus Cairo — Papers. Geological Museum (Cairo)
Pap Geol Surv Can — Papers. Geological Survey of Canada
Pap Geol Surv Egypt — Papers. Geological Survey of Egypt
Pap Geol Surv Neb — Papers of the Geological Survey of Nebraska
Pap Geol Surv UAR — Papers. Geological Survey and Mineral Research Department. United Arab Republic
Pap Geophys Lab Carnegie Instn Wash — Papers from the Geophysical Laboratory. Carnegie Institution of Washington
Pap Geophys Lab Carnegie Inst Washington — Papers from the Geophysical Laboratory. Carnegie Institution of Washington
Pap Giannini Fdn Agric Econ — Papers. Giannini Foundation of Agricultural Economics
Pap Gifu Univ Sch Med — Papers. Gifu University. School of Medicine
Pap GM — Papyri Graecae Magicae
Pap Grad Sch Trop Med Univ Calif — Papers from the Graduate School of Tropical Medicine. University of California
Pap Greenock Phil Soc — Papers of the Greenock Philosophical Society
Pap Grt Barrier Reef Comm — Papers. Great Barrier Reef Committee
PAPhilosS — Proceedings. American Philosophical Society
Pap Hist Scient Soc Manitoba — Papers. Historical and Scientific Society of Manitoba
PAPhS — Proceedings. American Philosophical Society
Pap IAALD World Congr — Papers. International Association of Agricultural Librarians and Documentalists. World Congress
Papier (Darmstadt) Beil — Papier (Darmstadt). Beilage
Papierfabr Wochenbl Papierfabr — Papierfabrikant - Wochonblatt fuer Papierfabrikation
Papiergesch — Papier Geschichte
Papiertech Stift Vortragsband — Papiertechnische Stiftung Vortragsband
Papierverarb — Papier- und Kunststoffverarbeiter
Pap Ind — Paper Industry
Pap Ind Moscow — Paper Industry (Moscow)
Pap Ind Pap World — Paper Industry and Paper World
Pap Inf Conf Nucl Energy Mgmt — Papers. Information Conference on Nuclear Energy for Management
Pap Inst Archaeol Lond — Papers from the Institute of Archaeology (London)
Pap Inst Def Anal — Paper. Institute for Defense Analyses
Pap Inst Met Univ Helsinki — Papers. Institute of Meteorology. University of Helsinki
Pap Instn Engng Insp — Papers. Institution of Engineering Inspection
Pap Instn Heat Vent Engrs — Papers. Instituion of Heating and Ventilating Engineers
Pap Instn PO Elect Engrs — Papers. Institution of Post Office Electrical Engineers
Pap Inst Post Off Electr Eng — Printed Papers. Institution of Post Office Electrical Engineers
Pap Inst Therm Spring Res Okayama Univ — Papers. Institute for Thermal Spring Research. Okayama University
Pap Int Conf Fluid Sealing — Paper. International Conference on Fluid Sealing
Pap Int Conf Liquefied Nat Gas — Papers. International Conference on Liquefied Natural Gas
Pap Int Inst Prev Treat Alcohol — Papers. International Institute on the Prevention and Treatment of Alcoholism
Pap Int Inst Prev Treat Drug Depend — Papers. International Institute on the Prevention and Treatment of Drug Dependence
Papirip Magy Grafika — Papiripar es Magyar Grafika

Pap Is Afr — Papers in International Studies. Africa Series. Ohio University
Pap Is Se A — Papers in International Studies. Southeast Asia Series. Ohio University
Pap J — Papir-Journalen
Pap ja Puu — Paperi ja Puu
Pap Karanis — Papyri from Karanis
Pap Kroeber Anthropol Soc — Papers. Kroeber Anthropological Society
Pap Kroeber Anthrop Soc — Papers of the Kroeber Anthropological Society
Pap Lab Arqueol Valencia — Papeles del Laboratorio de Arqueologia di Valencia
Pap Lab Tree-Ring Res Univ Ariz — Papers. Laboratory of Tree-Ring Research. University of Arizona
Pap Lanc Co Hist Soc — Historical Papers. Lancaster County Historical Society
Pap Lang L — Papers on Language and Literature
Pap Lang Lit — Papers on Language and Literature
Pap Ling — Papers in Linguistics
Pap Lugd Bat — Papyrologica Lugduno-Batava
Pap Maker Br Pap Trade J — Paper Maker and British Paper Trade Journal
Pap Maker (London) — Paper Maker and British Paper Trade Journal (London)
Pap Makers Assoc (GB Irel) Proc Tech Sect — Paper Makers' Association (Great Britain and Ireland). Proceedings of the Technical Section
Pap Makers Mon J — Paper Makers' Monthly Journal
Pap Maker (Wilmington Del) — Paper Maker (Wilmington, Delaware)
Pap Making Pap Selling — Paper Making and Paper Selling
Pap Making Printer — Paper Making and the Printer
Pap Making Selling — Paper Making and Selling
Pap Mayo Fdn Med Educ — Papers from the Mayo Foundation for Medical Education and the Medical School. University of Minnesota
Pap Med Dep Sierra Leone — Papers from the Medical Department. Sierra Leone
Pap Meet Am Chem Soc Div Org Coat Plast Chem — Papers. Meeting. American Chemical Society. Division of Organic Coatings and Plastics Chemistry
Pap Meteorol Geophys — Papers in Meteorology and Geophysics
Pap Meteorol Geophys (Tokyo) — Papers in Meteorology and Geophysics (Tokyo)
Pap Met Geo — Papers in Meteorology and Geophysics
Pap Met Geophys Tokyo — Papers in Meteorology and Geophysics (Tokyo)
Pap Met Univ Calif — Papers in Meteorology. University of California
Pap Me Univ Technol Exp Stn — Papers of the Maine University Technology Experiment Station
Pap Mich Acad — Papers. Michigan Academy of Science, Arts, and Letters
Pap Mich Acad Sci — Papers. Michigan Academy of Science, Arts, and Letters
Pap Mich Acad Sci Arts Lett — Papers. Michigan Academy of Science, Arts, and Letters
Pap Mill News — Paper Mill News
Pap Mill Wood Pulp News — Paper Mill and Wood Pulp News
Pap Miner Explor Res Inst McGill Univ — Paper. Mineral Exploration Research Institute. McGill University
Pap Minist Energy Mines Pet Resour (Br Columbia) — Paper. Ministry of Energy, Mines, and Petroleum Resources (Province of British Columbia)
Pap Natl Conf Prof Nurses Physicians — Papers. National Conference for Professional Nurses and Physicians
Pap Natn Brick Advis Coun — Papers. National Brick Advisory Council. Ministry of Works [*London*]
Pap Natn Fm Chemurg Coun — Papers. National Farm Chemurgic Council [*Columbus, Ohio*]
Pap Natn Inst Res Dairy — Papers. National Institute for Research in Dairying [*Reading*]
Pap Natn Vet Med Ass — Papers. National Veterinary Medical Association [*London*]
Pap New World Archaeol Found — Papers and Proceedings of the New World Archaeological Foundation
Pap N Haven Col Hist Soc — Papers. New Haven Colony Historical Society
Pap Nile Control Dep — Papers. Nile Control Department [*Cairo*]
Pap Norw State Game Res Inst — Papers. Norwegian State Game Research Institute
Pap Nova Scotia Dep Mines — Paper. Nova Scotia Department of Mines
Pap NS Dep Mines — Paper. Nova Scotia Department of Mines
Pap NS Dep Mines Energy — Paper. Nova Scotia Department of Mines and Energy
Pap Nth Engng Inst NSW — Papers. Northern Engineering Institute of New South Wales
Pap Nyomdatech — Papir es Nyomdatechnika
Pap Oceanogr Inst Fla St Univ — Papers. Oceanographic Institute. Florida State University
Pap Ont Ind Waste Conf — Papers. Ontario Industrial Waste Conference
Pap Oreg State Univ For Res Lab — Paper. Oregon State University. Forest Research Laboratory
Pap Ox — Oxyrhynchus Papyri
PapOxy — Oxyrhynchus Papyri
Pap Peabody Mus — Papers of the Peabody Museum of American Archaeology and Ethnography
Pap Peabody Mus Archaeol Ethnol Harv Univ — Papers. Peabody Museum of Archaeology and Ethnology. Harvard University
Pap Pedagog Fac Ostrava — Papers. Pedagogical Faculty in Ostrava
Pap Period Ilus — Papal Periodico Ilustrado
Pap Phil Ling — Papers in Philippine Linguistics. Pacific Linguistics. Series A
Pap Phys Oceanogr Met — Papers in Physical Oceanography and Meteorology [*Cambridge, Massachusetts*]
Pap Plast — Paper and Plastics
Pap Pl Genet — Papers on Plant Genetics
Pap Portland Cem Assoc Fellowship Natl Bur Stand — Papers. Portland Cement Association Fellowship at the National Bureau of Standards
Pap Portld Cem Ass Fellowip — Papers. Portland Cement Association Fellowship [*Washington, D.C.*]
Pap Presentations Proc Digital Equip Comput Users Soc — Papers and Presentations-Proceedings. Digital Equipment Computer Users Society

Pap Presented Annu Conf Rural Electr Power Conf — Papers Presented at the Annual Conference. Rural Electric Power Conference
Pap Primer — Papyrological Primer
Pap Print Dig — Paper and Printing Digest
Pap Print Tech — Paper and Printing Technics
Pap Proc Hampsh Fld Club — Papers and Proceedings of the Hampshire Field Club and Archaeological Society
Pap Proc NY St Ass Dairy Insp — Papers and Proceedings. New York State Association of Dairy and Milk Inspectors
Pap Proc Roy Soc Van Diemens Land — Papers and Proceedings. Royal Society of Van Diemen's Land
Pap Proc R Soc Tas — Papers and Proceedings. Royal Society of Tasmania
Pap Proc R Soc Tasm — Papers and Proceedings. Royal Society of Tasmania
Pap Proc R Soc Tasmania — Papers and Proceedings. Royal Society of Tasmania
Pap Proc Tas Hist Res Assoc — Tasmanian Historical Research Association. Papers and Proceedings
Pap Proc US Nav Inst — Papers and Proceedings. United States Naval Institute
Pap Prov NS Dep Mines — Paper. Province of Nova Scotia. Department of Mines
Papp Traevarutidskr Finl — Pappers och Traevarutidskrift foer Finland
Pap Publ Wks Dep Punjab — Papers. Public Works Department. Punjab
Pap Punjab Irrig Brch — Papers. Punjab Irrigation Branch
Pap Puu — Paperi ja Puu - Papper och Tra
Pap Puu A Painos — Paperi ja Puu. A Painos
Pap Puu B Painos — Paperi ja Puu. B Painos
Pap Puu Painos — Paperi ja Puu. A Painos
PAPQ — American Philosophical Quarterly
PAPR — American Poetry Review
Pap Rep Discuss A Conv Elect Veh Ass Am — Papers, Reports, and Discussions. Annual Convention. Electric Vehicle Association of America
Pap Rep Miner Min NZ — Papers and Reports Relating to Minerals and Mining (Wellington, N.Z.)
Pap Res Appl Technol Symp Mined Land Reclam — Papers. Research and Applied Technology Symposium on Mined-Land Reclamation
Pap Res Conf Meat Ind NZ — Papers. Research Conference. Meat Industry of New Zealand
Pap Robert S Peabody Fdn Archaeol — Papers of the Robert S. Peabody Foundation for Archaeology
Pap Royal Inst Brit Archit — Papers of the Royal Institute of British Architects
Pap Roy Soc Tasm — Royal Society of Tasmania. Papers and Proceedings
Pap R Sociol — Papers. Revista de Sociologia
Pap Rural Electr Power Conf — Papers. Rural Electric Power Conference
PAPS — Proceedings. American Philosophical Society
Pap Saf Mines Res Bd — Papers. Safety in Mines Research Board [London]
Pap Sci Ser — Papers in Science Series
Pap SE As Ling — Papers in South East Asian Linguistics. Pacific Linguistics. Series A
Pap SESA — Paper. SESA
Pap Ship Res Inst (Tokyo) — Papers. Ship Research Institute (Tokyo)
Pap Slav Ling — Papers in Slavonic Linguistics
Pap Soc Agric Bact — Papers. Society of Agricultural Bacteriologists [Reading]
Pap Soc Nav Archit Mar Engrs — Papers. Society of Naval Architects and Marine Engineers [New York]
Pap Soil Surv Conf — Papers. Soil Survey Conference [London]
Pap Somerset Archaeol Nat Hist Soc — Papers. Somersetshire Archaeological and Natural History Society
PAPSP — Proceedings. American Philosophical Society (Philadelphia)
Pap S Shields Archaeol Hist Soc — Papers. South Shields Archaeological and Historical Society
P Ap St Dalho — Applied Statistics. Proceedings of Conference at Dalhousie University
Pap Sthn Afr — Paper Southern Africa
PA Psychiatr Q — Pennsylvania Psychiatric Quarterly
Pap Symp Coal Manage Tech — Papers Presented before the Symposium on Coal Management Techniques
Pap Symp Coal Mine Drainage Res — Papers Presented before the Symposium on Coal Mine Drainage Research
Pap Symp Coal Prep Util — Papers Presented before the Symposium on Coal Preparation and Utilization
Pap Symp Coal Prep (Washington DC) — Papers Presented before the Symposium on Coal Preparation (Washington, DC)
Pap Symp Coal Util — Papers Presented before the Symposium on Coal Utilization
Pap Symp Manage — Papers Presented before the Symposium on Management
Pap Symp Manage Coal Conf Expo — Papers. Symposium on Management. Coal Conference and Expo
Pap Symp Mine Prep Plant Refuse Disposal — Papers. Symposium on Mine and Preparation Plant Refuse Disposal
Pap Symp Surf Coal Min Reclam — Papers. Symposium on Surface Coal Mining and Reclamation
Pap Symp Surf Min Reclam — Papers Presented before the Symposium on Surface Mining and Reclamation
Pap Symp Underground Min — Papers Presented before the Symposium on Underground Mining
Pap Synth Conf Proc — Paper Synthetics Conference. Proceedings
PAPTC — Practical Approach to Patents, Trademarks, and Copyrights
Pap Tech Mtg Int Union Conserv Nature — Paper. Technical Meeting. International Union for the Conservation of Nature and Natural Resources
Pap Technol — Paper Technology
Pap Technol — Paper Technology and Industry
Pap Technol Bury UK — Paper Technology (Bury, United Kingdom)
Pap Technol Ind — Paper Technology and Industry
Pap Technol Leatherhead UK — Paper Technology (Leatherhead, UK)
Pap Technol London — Paper Technology (London)
Pap Trade J — Paper Trade Journal
Pap Trade Rev — Paper Trade Review
Papua & NG — Papua and New Guinea Law Reports

Papua Annual Rep — Papua Annual Report
Papua New Guin Agric J — Papua and New Guinea Agricultural Journal
Papua New Guinea Agric Gaz — Papua and New Guinea Agricultural Gazette
Papua New Guinea Agric J — Papua and New Guinea Agricultural Journal
Papua New Guinea Agr J — Papua and New Guinea Agricultural Journal
Papua New Guinea Dep Agric Stock Fish Annu Rep — Papua New Guinea. Department of Agriculture, Stock, and Fisheries. Annual Report
Papua New Guinea Dep Agric Stock Fish Res Bull — Papua New Guinea. Department of Agriculture, Stock, and Fisheries. Research Bulletin
Papua New Guinea Geol Surv Mem — Papua New Guinea. Geological Survey. Memoir
Papua New Guinea Geol Surv Rep — Papua New Guinea. Geological Survey. Report
Papua New Guinea Inst Med Res Monogr Ser — Papua New Guinea. Institute of Medical Research. Monograph Series
Papua New Guinea J Agric For Fish — Papua New Guinea Journal of Agriculture, Forestry, and Fisheries
Papua New Guinea J Ed — Papua and New Guinea Journal of Education
Papua New Guinea Med J — Papua New Guinea Medical Journal
Papua New Guinea Sci Soc Trans — Papua and New Guinea Scientific Society. Transactions
Pap Univ Maine Technol Exp Stn — Paper. University of Maine. Technology Experiment Station
Pap Univ MO-Columbia Dep Agric Econ — Paper. University of Missouri-Columbia. Department of Agricultural Economics
Pap Univ Queensland Dep Geol — Papers. University of Queensland. Department of Geology
Pap US Geol Surv Wat Supply — Paper. United States Geological Survey. Water Supply
Pap West Reg Home Manage Fam Econ Educ Annu Conf — Papers. Western Region Home Management Family Economics Educators. Annual Conference
Pap World — Paper World
Pap Zenon — Selected Papyri from the Archives of Zenon
Pap Ztg — Papier-Zeitung
PAQ — Public Administration Quarterly
PAQT — American Quarterly
PAR — Kosmetiek
Par — Paradosis
Par — Paragone
Par — Paralipomena
Par — Parents' Magazine and Better Family Living [Later, Parents' Magazine]
Par — Parlament
Par — Paru
PAR — Performing Arts Resources
PAR — Performing Arts Review
PAR — Pro Austria Romana
PAR — Public Administration Review
Para — Paralipomena
Par A Cons — Annales du Conservatoire des Arts et Metiers (Paris)
Par Ac Sc Mm — Memoires de l'Academie des Sciences de l'Institut de France (Paris)
Par A Das Sc — Annaes das Sciencias, das Artes, e das Letras por Huma Sociedade de Portuguezes Residentes em Paris
Par A Ec Norm — Annales Scientifiques de l'Ecole Normale Superieure (Paris)
Paraguay Indus Comer Asuncion — Paraguay Industrial y Comercial (Asuncion)
Parallel Comput — Parallel Computing
Parallel Process Lett — Parallel Processing Letters
Paramagn Rezon — Paramagnitnyj Rezonans
Paramaribo-Suriname Agric Exp Stn Bull — Paramaribo-Suriname. Agricultural Experiment Station. Bulletin
Para-Med — Para-Medico
Paramed Int — Paramedics International
Par A Obs — Annales de l'Observatoire de Paris. Memoires
Par A Pon Chauss — Annales des Ponts et Chaussees. Memoires et Documents Relatifs a l'Art des Constructions et au Service de l'Ingenieur (Paris)
Par Arter — Paroi Arterielle-Arterial Wall
Parasit — Parasitica
Parasit Dis — Parasitic Diseases
Parasite Immunol — Parasite Immunology
Parasite Immunol (Oxf) — Parasite Immunology (Oxford)
Parasit Hung — Parasitologia Hungarica
Parasitol — Parasitology
Parasitol Hung — Parasitologia Hungarica
Parasitol Int — Parasitology International
Parasitol Res — Parasitology Research
Parasitol Schriftenr — Parasitologische Schriftenreihe
Parasitol Today — Parasitology Today
Parasit Res — Parasitology Research
Paravia — Corpus Scriptorum Graecorum Paravianum
Parazitol Sb — Parazitologicheskii Sbornik
Parazit Sb — Parazitologiceskii Sbornik
Parazity Zhivotn Rast — Parazity Zhivotnykh i Rastenii
Parbhani Agric Coll Mag — Parbhani Agricultural College. Magazine
Par Bll S Bt — Bulletin de la Societe Botanique de France (Paris)
Par Bll S C — Bulletin de la Societe Chimique de Paris
Par Bll S Encour — Bulletin de la Societe d'Encouragement pour l'Industrie Nationale (Paris)
Par Bll S Gg — Bulletin de la Societe de Geographie (Paris)
Par Bll S Phlm — Bulletin des Sciences de la Societe Philomathique de Paris
Par Bur Long An — Annuaire Publie par le Bureau des Longitudes (Paris)
PARC — Plains Aquatic Research Conference. Proceedings
Par Ch — Parents' Choice
P Arch — Przeglad Archeologiczny
Par Cl Alp Fr An — Annuaire du Club Alpin Francais (Paris)
Par d Pass — Parola del Passato. Rivista di Studi Antichi

PAREA — Pharmacological Reviews
Par Ec Norm A — Annales Scientifiques de l'Ecole Normale Superieure (Paris)
Par Ec Pol Cor — Correspondance sur l'Ecole Polytechnique, a l'usage des Eleves de cette Ecole (Paris)
Par Ec Pol J — Journal de l'Ecole Polytechnique (Paris)
Parent & Cit — Parent and Citizen
Parent Aust — Parent Australia
Parenter Drug Assoc Bull — Parenteral Drug Association. Bulletin
Parenter Drug Assoc J — Parenteral Drug Association. Journal
Parents — Parents' Magazine
Parents Bull — Parents' Buletin
Parents' Mag — Parents' Magazine and Better Family Living [*Later, Parents' Magazine*]
Parfuem Kosmet — Parfuemerie und Kosmetik
Parfuem Ztg — Parfuemerie-Zeitung
Parfum Cosmet Savons — Parfums, Cosmetiques, Savons
Parfum Mod — Parfumerie Moderne
Parfums Cos — Parfums, Cosmetiques, Aromes
Parfums Cosmet Actual — Parfums, Cosmetiques, Actualites
Parfums Cosmet Aromes — Parfums, Cosmetiques, Aromes
Parfums Cosmet Savons — Parfums, Cosmetiques, Savons
Parfums Cosmet Savons Fr — Parfums, Cosmetiques, Savons de France
Parfums Fr — Parfums de France
P Arg — Pays d'Argentan
Par Gg S Bll — Bulletin de la Societe de Geographie (Paris)
PARH — Art History
PARI — Ariel, A Review of International English Literature
Pari I Prawo — Paristwo i Prawo
Par Ing Civ Mm — Memoires et Comptes Rendus des Travaux de la Societe des Ingenieurs Civils (Paris)
Paris — Parisienne. Revue Litteraire Mensuelle
PARIS — Pictorial and Artifact Retrieval and Information System
Paris & Ile-de-France Mem — Paris et Ile-de-France. Memoires Publies par la Federation des Societes Historiques et Archeologiques de Paris et de l'Ile-de-France
Paris J — Paris-Journal
Paris Med — Paris Medical
ParisR — Paris Review
Paris Rev — Paris Review
Paris Univ Lab Micropaleontol Trav — Paris. Universite. Laboratoire de Micropaleontologie. Travaux
Paris Univ Lab Paleontol Trav — Paris. Universite. Laboratoire de Paleontologie. Travaux
PArJ — Performing Arts Journal
Par J Ec Pol — Journal de l'Ecole Polytechnique (Paris)
PARK — Parks. International Journal for Managers of National Parks, Historic Sites, and Other Protected Areas
Park Adm — Park Administration
Parker Cr Cas — Parker's New York Criminal Reports
Parker Cr Cas (NY) — Parker's New York Criminal Reports
Parker Cr R — Parker's New York Criminal Reports
Parker Cr R (NY) — Parker's New York Criminal Reports
Park Pract Grist — Park Practice Grist
Park Pract Prog — Park Practice Program. Design, Grist, Trends. Index
Parks and R — Parks and Recreation
Parks & Rec — Parks and Recreation
Parks & Wild — Parks and Wildlife
Parks Wildl — Parks and Wildlife
ParL — Parisien Libere [*Paris daily*]
Parl — Parlament
Parl — Parliamentarian
Parl Aff — Parliamentary Affairs
Parl Aff J Hans Soc — Parliamentary Affairs. Journal. Hansard Society
Parlam Beil Polit Zeitgesch — Parlament Beilage aus Politik und Zeitgeschichte
Par Lb Hl Tr — Ecole Pratique des Hautes Etudes. Laboratoire d'Histologie du College de France. Travaux (Paris)
Parl Deb — Parliamentary Debates
Parl Deb HC — Parliamentary Debates. House of Commons
Parl Deb HL — Parliamentary Debates. House of Lords
PAR Legis Bul — PAR [*Public Affairs Research*] Legislative Bulletin
Parliam Aff — Parliamentary Affairs
Parliamentary Aff — Parliamentary Affairs
Parliament Pap (Commonw Aust) — Parliamentary Paper (Commonwealth of Australia)
Parliam Liaison Group Altern Energy Strategies Bull — Parliamentary Liaison Group for Alternative Energy Strategies. Bulletin
Parlim Aff — Parliamentary Affairs
PARM — Arts Magazine
Par M — Parents' Magazine
ParM — Paris-Match
Parma A — Parma per l'Arte. Rivista Quadrimestrale d'Arte e Cultura
Parma Econ — Parma Economica
Parma G S Md Chir — Giornale della Societa Medico-Chirurgica di Parma
Par Med — Paris Medical
ParMi — Paris-Midi [*daily*]
Par Miss — Parole et Mission
Par Mm Ac Sc — Memoires de l'Academie des Sciences de l'Institut de France (Paris)
Par Mm De L I — Memoires de la Classe des Sciences Mathematiques et Physiques de l'Institut (Paris)
Par Mm Ing Civ — Memoires et Comptes Rendus des Travaux de la Societe des Ingenieurs Civils (Paris)
Par Mm S L — Memoires de la Societe Linneenne de Paris

Par Mm S Sav — Memoires des Societes Savantes et Litteraires de la Republique Francaise. Recueillis et Rediges par les Citoyens Prany, Parmentier, Duhamel, Garnier, Lausel, Marchais, Doussin-Dubreuil, Tourlet (Paris)
Par Ms H Nt Bll — Bulletin du Museum d'Histoire Naturelle (Paris)
Par Ms H Nt Cent — Centenaire de la Fondation du Museum d'Histoire Naturelle (Paris)
Par Ms H Nt Mm — Memoires du Museum d'Histoire Naturelle (Paris)
Par Ms H Nt N Arch — Nouvelles Archives du Museum d'Histoire Naturelle (Paris)
ParN — Paris-Normandie
Parn — Parnassus
Par Nucl — Particles and Nuclei
Par Obs A — Annales de l'Observatoire de Paris. Memoires
Par Obs A Mm — Annales de l'Observatoire de Paris. Memoires
Parodontol — Parodontologie
Parodontol Acad Rev — Parodontologie and Academy Review
Parodontol Stomatol Nuova — Parodontologia e Stomatologia Nuova
Parola Passato — Parola del Passato. Rivista di Studi Antichi
Parole et Soc — Parole et Societe
Par Or — Parole de l'Orient
ParP — Paris-Presse [*daily*]
Par Pass — Parola del Passato
ParPl — Paris-Presse l'Intransigeant [*daily*]
Par Poids Et Mes PV — Comite International des Poids et Mesures. Proces-Verbaux des Seances (Paris)
Par Poids Et Mes Tr Mm — Travaux et Memoires du Bureau International des Poids et Mesures (Paris)
PAR Pseudo-Allerg React — PAR. Pseudo-Allergic Reactions
PAR Pseudo-Allerg React Involvement Drugs Chem — PAR. Pseudo-Allergic Reactions. Involvement of Drugs and Chemicals
Parques Jard — Parques y Jardines
ParR — Paris Review
ParR — Partisan Review
ParS — Paris-Soir [*daily*]
Par S Bl Mm — Comptes Rendus des Seances et Memoires de la Societe de Biologie (Paris)
Par S Bl Vol Jubil — Cinquantenaire de la Societe de Biologie. Volume Jubilaire (Paris)
Par S C Bll — Bulletin de la Societe Chimique de Paris
Par S Chir Bll Et Mm — Bulletins et Memoires de la Societe de Chirurgie de Paris
Par Se Ec Norm — Seances des Ecoles Normales
Par Se S Ps — Seances de la Societe Francaise de Physique (Paris)
Par S Gg Bll — Bulletin de la Societe de Geographie (Paris)
Par S Gg C R — Compte Rendu des Seances de la Societe de Geographie et de la Commission Centrale (Paris)
Par S Gl Bll — Bulletin de la Societe Geologique de France (Paris)
PARS Info Q — PARS [*Performing Arts Referral Service*] Information Quarterly
Par S Md Em Mm — Memoires de la Societe Medicale d'Emulation (Paris)
Par S Mth Bll — Bulletin de la Societe Mathematique de France (Paris)
Parsons J — Parsons Journal
Par S Phlm Bll — Bulletin des Sciences de la Societe Philomathique de Paris
Par S Phlm Mm Cent — Memoires Publies par la Societe Philomathique a l'Occasion du Centenaire de sa Fondation (Paris)
Par S Phlm N Bll — Nouveau Bulletin des Sciences de la Societe Philomathique de Paris
Par S Phlm PV — Extraits des Proces-Verbaux des Seances de la Societe Philomathique (Paris)
Par S Ps Se — Seances de la Societe Francaise de Physique (Paris)
ParT — Paris-Theatre
Part Accel — Particle Accelerators
Part and Nucl — Particles and Nuclei
Part Charact — Particle Characterization
Part Debris Med Implants — Particulate Debris from Medical Implants. Mechanisms of Formation and Biological Consequences
Part Des Cryst — Particle Design via Crystallization
Particle B — Particleboard and Medium Density Fibreboard. Annual Publication and Shipments
Particleboard/Compos Mater Ser — Particleboard/Composite Materials Series
Partijn Zhizn — Partinaia Zhizn
PartiP — Parti Pris
Partisan R — Partisan Review
Partisan Rev — Partisan Review
Par T Nauk Sc Pam — Pamietnik Towarzystwa Nauk Scislych w Paryzu (Paris)
Part Nucl — Particles and Nuclei
Part Part Syst Charact — Particle and Particle Systems Characterization
Part R — Partisan Review
Par Tr S Amat — Notices des Travaux de la Societe des Amateurs des Sciences Physiques et Naturelles de Paris
Part Sci Technol — Particulate Science and Technology
Part Size Anal — Particle Size Analysis
Part Surf — Particles on Surfaces. Detection, Adhesion, and Removal
Party — Party Newspapers
Part Z — Partiinaya Zhizn
PARWAC — Archivum Veterinarium Polonicum
PARZEP — Pochvoznanie Agrokhimiya i Rastitelna Zashtita
PaS — Pamietnik Slowianski
PAS — Papers. American School of Classical Studies
PAS — Peredneaziatskij Sbornik
PAS — Politics and Society
PAS — Proceedings. Aristotelian Society
PASA — Papers. American School of Classical Studies at Athens
PASA — Publications. American Society for Archeoogical Research in Asia Minor
PAS Ath — Papers. American School of Classical Studies at Athens
PASB — Archives of Sexual Behavior
PASB — Proceedings. Asiatic Society of Bengal
PASBe — Proceedings. Asiatic Society of Bengal

PASC — Parkscan. Parks Canada
Pascal Newsl — Pascal Newsletter
PASCH — Papers. American Society of Church History
PA Sch J — Pennsylvania School Journal
Pa School J — Pennsylvania School Journal
PAS Cl St — Papers. American School of Classical Studies at Athens
Pasc Lxb — Pasicrisie Luxembourgeoise
PASED — Proceedings. Annual Symposium. Society of Flight Test Engineers
PASF — Asian Affairs
PASI — American Studies International
PASJD — Passive Solar Journal
PasKen J — PasKen (Pasuturu Kenkyusho) Journal
Pas L — Pasicrisie Luxembourgeoise
Pa Slow — Pamietnik Slowianski
Pas Lux — Pasicrisie Luxembourgeoise
PASMB — Proceedings. Australian Society for Medical Research
Pas Mus — Pastoral Music
PASO — Acta Sociologica
PASP — American Speech
PasP — Past and Present
PASR — African Studies Review
Passenger Transp — Passenger Transport
Passeng Transp J — Passenger Transport Journal
Passive Sol J — Passive Solar Journal
PassM — Passauer Monatsschrift
PASSV — Pontificiae Academiae Scientiarum Scripta Varia
Past & Pres — Past and Present
Pa Stat Ann — Purdon's Pennsylvania Statutes Annotated
Pa State Coll Agric Exp Stn Bull — Pennsylvania. State College. Agricultural Experiment Station. Bulletin
PA State Coll Miner Ind Exp Stn Bull — Pennsylvania State College. Mineral Industries Experiment Station. Bulletin
PA State Coll Miner Ind Exp Stn Circ — Pennsylvania State College. Mineral Industries Experiment Station. Circular
PA State Coll Stud — Pennsylvania State College. Studies
Pa State Univ Coll Agric Agric Exp Stn Bull — Pennsylvania State University. College of Agriculture. Agricultural ExperimentStation. Bulletin
PA State Univ Coll Agric Agric Exp Stn Prog Rep — Pennsylvania State University. College of Agriculture. Agricultural Experiment Station. Progress Report
PA State Univ Coll Agric Ext Serv Spec Circ — Pennsylvania State University. College of Agriculture. Agricultural Extension Service. Special Circular
PA State Univ Coll Earth Miner Sci Exp Stn Circ — Pennsylvania State University. College of Earth and Mineral Sciences. Experiment Station. Circular
PA State Univ Coll Earth Miner Sci Spec Publ — Pennsylvania State University. College of Earth and Mineral Sciences. Special Publication
PA State Univ Coll Eng Eng Proc — Pennsylvania State University. College of Engineering. Engineering Proceedings
PA State Univ Coll Eng Eng Res Bull — Pennsylvania State University. College of Engineering. Engineering Research Bulletin
PA State Univ Earth Miner Sci Exp Stn Circ — Pennsylvania State University. Earth and Mineral Sciences Experiment Station. Circular
PA State Univ Ind Exp Stn Bull — Pennsylvania State University. Mineral Industries Experiment Station. Bulletin
PA State Univ Miner Ind Exp Stn Circ — Pennsylvania State University. Mineral Industries Experiment Station. Circular
Pa State Univ Miner Sci Exp Stn Spec Publ — Pennsylvania State University. Mineral Sciences Experiment Station. Special Publication
PA State Univ Sch For Resour Res Briefs — Pennsylvania State University. School of Forest Resources. Research Briefs
PA State Univ Stud — Pennsylvania State University. Studies
Past B — Pastor Bonus
PastBl — Pastoralblaetter
Pastbl — Pastoralblatt
Past Care & Couns Abstr — Pastoral Care and Counseling Abstracts
PA St Coll An Rp — Pennsylvania State College. Annual Report
Pasteur Inst South India (Coonoor) Annu Rep Dir Sci Rep — Pasteur Institute of Southern India (Coonoor). Annual Report of the Director and Scientific Report
Past Forum — Pastorales Forum fuer die Seelsorger im Erzbistum Muenchen-Freising
Past Mus — Pastoral Music
Pastoralist — Pastoralist and Grazier
Pastoral Rev — Pastoral Review
Pastoral Rev Graz Rec — Pastoral Review and Graziers' Record
Pastor And — Pastoral Andina
Pastor Bon — Pastor Bonus
Pastor Care Couns Abstr — Pastoral Care and Counseling Abstracts
Pastor Care Educ — Pastoral Care in Education
Past Pres — Past and Present. Studies in the History of Civilization
Past Presen — Past and Present
Past Psych — Pastoral Psychology
Past R — Pastoral Review and Graziers' Record
Past Rev — Pastoral Review and Graziers' Record
PASU — American Studies
Pa Super — Pennsylvania Superior Court Reports
PASYD — Policy Analysis and Information Systems
Pat — All India Reporter, Patna Series
PAT — Paper Trade Journal
PAT — Practical Anthropology (Tarrytown, New York)
PAT — Public Administration and Development
PAT — Public Administration Times
Pat Abr Suppl Aust Off J Pat Trade Marks Des — Patent Abridgments Supplement. Australian Official Journal of Patents. Trade Marks and Designs
Pat and TM Rev — Patent and Trade Mark Review
Pat & Tr Mk Rev — Patent and Trade Mark Review

Pat Bl — Patentblatt
PATC — Patclass
Pat Coop Treaty Int Appl — Patent Cooperation Treaty International Application
Pat Des J Isr Pat Off — Patents and Designs Journal (Israel, Patent Office)
PATDPA — Deutsche Patent Datenbank
Patentbl — Patentblatt
Patentbl Ausg A — Patentblatt. Ausgabe A
Patentbl Ausg B — Patentblatt. Ausgabe B
Patentj Insluitende Handels Merke Modelle — Patentjoornaal Insluitende Handels-Merke en Modelle
Patentj Insluitende Handelsmerke Modelle Outeursreg Rolprent — Patentjoernaal Insluitende Handelsmerke. Modelle en Outeursreg in Rolprente
Patentjoernaal (S Afr) — Patentjoernaal (South Africa)
Patent Off Soc Jour — Patent Office Society. Journal
Patentschr Ausschliessungspat Ger Democr Repub — Patentschrift. Ausschliessungspatent (German Democratic Republic)
Patentschr Fed Repub Ger — Patentschrift (Federal Republic of Germany)
Paters App — Paterson's Appeal Cases
Pat Fiz Eksp Ter — Patologiceskaya Fiziologiya i Eksperimental'naya Terapija
Pat Graec — Patrologiae Cursus Completus. Series Graeca
Path Biol — Pathologie et Biologie
P Athen — Papyri Societatis Archaeologicae Atheniensis
Path Europ — Pathologia Europaea
Path Microb — Pathologia et Microbiologia
Pathobiol Annu — Pathobiology Annual
Pathol — Pathology
Pathol Annu — Pathology Annual
Pathol Biol — Pathologie et Biologie
Pathol Biol (Paris) — Pathologie et Biologie (Paris)
Pathol Biol Sem Hop — Pathologie et Biologie. La Semaine des Hopitaux
Pathol Clin Med (Tokyo) — Pathology and Clinical Medicine (Tokyo)
Pathol Eur — Pathologia Europaea
Pathol Eur Suppl — Pathologia Europaea. Supplement
Pathol Gen — Pathologie Generale
Pathol Immunopathol Res — Pathology and Immunopathology Research
Pathol Int — Patholgy International
Pathol Lab Med — Pathology and Laboratory Medicine
Pathol Microbiol — Pathologia et Microbiologia
Pathol Microbiol Addit — Pathologia et Microbiologia. Additamentum
Pathol Microbiol Suppl — Pathologia et Microbiologia. Supplementum
Pathol Oncol Res — Pathology Oncology Research
Pathol Res Pract — Pathology. Research and Practice
Pathol Soc Phila Proc — Pathological Society of Philadelphia. Proceedings
Pathol Vet — Pathologia Veterinaria
Path Res Pract — Pathology. Research and Practice
Patient Acc — Patient Accounts
Patient Care Manag — Patient Care Management
Patient Couns Health Educ — Patient Counselling and Health Education
Patient Educ Couns — Patient Education and Counseling
Patient Educ Newsl — Patient Education Newsletter
Pat Introd Spain — Patente de Introduccion (Spain)
Pat Invenc (Spain) — Patente de Invencion (Spain)
Pat J — Patent Journal, Including Trademarks and Models
Pat J Incl Trade Marks Des — Patent Journal, Including Trade Marks and Designs
Pat J Incl Trade Marks Des Copyright Cinematogr Films — Patent Journal, Including Trade Marks, Designs, and Copyright in Cinematograph Films
Pat L Ann — Patent Law Annual
Pat Law Rev — Patent Law Review
Pat LJ — Patna Law Journal
Pat LR — Patent Law Review
Pat L Rev — Patent Law Review
Pat LT — Patna Law Times
Pat LW — Patna Law Weekly
Patma-Banasirakan Handes Ist-Filol Zh — Patma-Banasirakan Handes. Istoriko-Filologicheskii Zhurnal
Patna J Med — Patna Journal of Medicine
Pat Off Gaz — Official Gazette. United States Patent Office
Pat Off J — Patent Office Journal
Pat Off Rec Can — Patent Office Record (Canada)
Pat Off Rep — Patent Office Reports
Pat Off Soc J — Patent Office Society. Journal
Patog Ter Dermatozov — Patogenez i Terapiya Dermatozov
Patog Ter Kozhnykh Vener Zabol — Patogenez i Terapiya Kozhnykh i Venericheskikh Zabolevanii
Patol Clin Ostet Ginecol — Patologia e Clinica Ostetrica e Ginecologica
Patol Comp Tuberc — Patologia Comparata della Tubercolosi
Patol Fiziol Eksp Ter — Patologicheskaya Fiziologiya i Eksperimental'naya Terapiya
Patol-Mex — Patologia-Mexico City
Patol Pol — Patologia Polska
Patol Sper — Patologia Sperimentale
Patol Sper Chir — Patologia Sperimentale e Chirurgia
PA Top G S Com — Pennsylvania Topographic and Geologic Survey Commission
Pa Topogr Geol Surv Bull — Pennsylvania. Topographic and Geologic Survey. Bulletin
PA Topogr Geol Surv Bull A — Pennsylvania Topographic and Geologic Survey. Bulletin A. Atlas Series
PA Topogr Geol Surv Bull C — Pennsylvania. Bureau of Topographic and Geologic Survey. Bulletin C
PA Topogr Geol Surv Bull G — Pennsylvania. Bureau of Topographic and Geologic Survey. Bulletin G
PA Topogr Geol Surv Bull M — Pennsylvania Topographic and Geologic Survey. Bulletin M
PA Topogr Geol Surv Bull W — Pennsylvania Topographic and Geologic Survey. Bulletin W

Pa Topogr Geol Surv Cty Rep — Pennsylvania. Topographic and Geologic Survey. County Report
PA Topogr Geol Surv Geol Atlas PA — Pennsylvania. Bureau of Topographic and Geologic Survey. Geologic Atlas of Pennsylvania
Pa Topogr Geol Surv Ground Water Rep — Pennsylvania. Topographic and Geologic Survey. Ground Water Report
PA Topogr Geol Surv Inform Circ — Pennsylvania. Bureau of Topographic and Geologic Survey. Information Circular
PA Topogr Geol Surv Miner Resour Rep — Pennsylvania Topographic and Geologic Survey. Mineral Resources Report
PA Topogr Geol Surv Progr Rep — Pennsylvania. Bureau of Topographic and Geologic Survey. Progress Report
PA Topogr Geol Surv Spec Bull — Pennsylvania. Bureau of Topographic and Geologic Survey. Special Bulletin
Pa Topogr Geol Surv Water Resour Rep — Pennsylvania. Topographic and Geologic Survey. Water Resource Report
Pat Pol — Patologia Polska
PATQ — ATQ. The American Transcendental Quarterly
Pa Trade J — Paper Trade Journal
PATRA Jl — PATRA Journal. Printing, Packaging, and Allied Research Association [London]
PATREU — Palaestina Treuhandstelle zur Beratung Deutscher Juden
Patria Ilus — Patria Ilustrada
Patrim Hist — Patrimonio Historico
Patriot Med — Patriotische Medicus
Patrist Sorb — Patristica Sorbonensia
Pa Tr J — Paper Trade Journal
Patr Lat — Patrologiae Cursus Completus. Series Latina
Patrol Gr — Patrologiae Cursus Completus. Series Graeca
Patronato Biol Anim Rev — Patronato de Biologia Animal. Revista
Patronato Invest Cient Tec "Juan De La Cierva" Mem — Patronato de Investigacion Cientifica y Tecnica "Juan De La Cierva." Memoria
Patronato Invest Cient Tec "Juan De La Cierva" Publ Tec — Patronato de Investigacion Cientifica y Tecnica "Juan De La Cierva." Publicaciones Tecnicas
Patr Or — Patrologia Orientalis
Patr Sec — Patria Secula
Pat Specif Amended Specif UK — Patent Specification. Amended Specification (United Kingdom)
Pat Specif (Aust) — Patent Specification (Australia)
Pat Specif (Petty)(Aust) — Patent Specification (Petty) (Australia)
Pat Spis Czech — Patentovy Spis (Czechoslovakia)
Pat St — Patristic Studies
Pattern Recogn — Pattern Recognition
Pattern Recognit — Pattern Recognition
Pattern Recognition — Journal. Pattern Recognition Society
Pattern Recognition Lett — Pattern Recognition Letters
Pattern Recognit Lett — Pattern Recognition Letters
Pat TM & Copy J — Patent, Trademark, and Copyright Journal
Pat TM & Copyr J of R & Educ — Patent, Trademark, and Copyright Journal of Research and Education
Patt Prejud — Patterns of Prejudice
Pat Trademark & Copyright J BNA — Patents, Trademark, and Copyright Journal. Bureau of National Affairs
Patt Recog — Pattern Recognition
PATUA — Proceedings. Research Institute of Atmospherics. Nagoya University
PAU — Pamietnik Akademii Umiejetnosci Krakowie
PAU — Polska Akademia Umiejetnosci
PAU-AN — Polska Akademia Umiejetnosci. Archivum Neophilologicum
PAUCA — Proceedings. Royal Australian Chemical Institute
Paul Arendts Monatsschr Kakteenk — Paul Arendt's Monatsschrift fuer Kakteenkunde
Pauls Grdr — Grundriss der Germanischen Philologie (Hermann Paul, Editor)
PA Univ Lab Contr — Pennsylvania University. Laboratory Contributions
PA Univ Mus Bul — Pennsylvania University. University Museum. Bulletin
PA Univ Schoolmen's Week Proc — Pennsylvania University. Schoolmen's Week. Proceedings
PAus — Poetry Australia
PAusL — Papers in Australian Linguistics
P Aust Bioc — Proceedings. Australian Biochemical Society
PAUTDL — Proceedings. Australian Society of Sugar Cane Technologists
P Automtn — Process Automation
PAV — Packaging Review
PAV — Philosophica (Valparaiso, Chile)
Pavia Univ Ist Geol Atti — Pavia Universita. Istituto Geologico. Atti
Paving Conf Proc — Paving Conference. Proceedings
Pav J Biol — Pavlovian Journal of Biological Science
Pavlovian J Biol Sci — Pavlovian Journal of Biological Science
Pavlov J Biol Sci — Pavlovian Journal of Biological Science
Pavlov J Higher Nerv Act — Pavlov Journal of Higher Nervous Activity
PAW — Przeglad Antropologiczny (Wroclaw)
PAWI — Parks and Wilderness
Pawl Zs Hoeh Nerv Taet — Pawlow-Zeitschrift fuer Hoehere Nerventaetigkeit
Pax Rom — Pax Romana
Paxtons Fl Gard — Paxton's Flower Garden
PayA — Pays d'Auge
Pays — Paysans
Pays Ange — Pays d'Ange
Pays Elsace — Pays d'Elsace
Pays Gaumais — Pays Gaumais. La Terre et les Hommes. Revue Regionale
Pays Lor — Pays Lorrain
Payt L — Payton Lectures
PAZ — Paper and Packaging Bulletin
Pazm — Pazmaveb
PAZO — American Zoologist
PaZS — Palaeontologische Zeitschrift (Stuttgart)

PAZT — Aztlan
PB — Document PB. National Technical Information Service
PB — Paedagogische Blaetter
PB — Pantheon Babylonicum: Nomina Deorum
PB — Pastor Bonus
PB — Pays de Bourgogne
PB — Physics Briefs
PB — Planen und Bauen
Pb — Playboy
PB — Poetry Bag
PB — Prabuddha Bharata
PB — Praktische Betriebswirt
PB — Pravoslav'nija Bukovyna
PB — Przeglad Biblioteczny
PB — Psychological Bulletin
PB — Publicatieblad
Pb — Publicatieblad van de Europese Gemeenschappen
PB — Publicatieblad van de Nederlandse Antillen
PB — Push from the Bush
PBA — Polska Bibliografia Analityczna
PBA — Proceedings. British Academy
PBA — Schoenvisie. Maandblad voor de Schoenhandel en Schoenindustrie
PBAc — British Academy. Proceedings
P Baden — Veroeffentlichungen aus der Badischen Papyrus-Sammlungen
PBAE — Publications. Bureau of American Ethnology
PBAL — Black American Literature Forum
PBANB — Pathobiology Annual
PBASA — Proceedings. Bihar Academy of Agricultural Sciences
P Basel — Papyrusurkunden der Oeffentlichen Bibliothek der Universitaet zu Basel
P Bat Conf — Proceedings. Battle Conference on Anglo-Norman Studies
PBBCD — Promoclim B. Bulletin du Genie Climatique
PBBHA — Pharmacology, Biochemistry, and Behavior
PBCE — Boston College Environmental Affairs Law Review
PBDA — Publicaciones de la Biblioteca Departamental del Atlantico [Barranquilla]
Pbd Abstr — Paper and Board Abstracts
Pbd Pkg — Paperboard Packaging
PBE — Pravoslavnaia Boggoslovskaia Entsiklopediia
PBE — Problemes Economiques. Selection de Textes Francais et Etrangers
PBEA Newsletter — Pennsylvania Business Education Association. Newsletter
P Bef G — Personenbefoerderungsgesetz
Pb EG — Publicatieblad van de Europese Gemeenschappen
PBELB — Promyshlennost Belorussii
P Berl Leihg — Berliner Leihgabe Griechischer Papyri
PBF — Praehistorische Bronzefunde
PBF — Public Budgeting and Finance
PBFPA — Protides of the Biological Fluids. Proceedings of the Colloquium
PBGC Manual of Opinion Letters — Pension Benefit Guaranty Corporation. Manual of Opinion Letters
PBGS — Proceedings. Bombay Geographical Society
PBH — Patma-Banasirakan Handes. Istoriko-Filologicheskii Zhurnal
PBh — Prabuddha Bharata
PBHS — Publications. Baptist Historical Society
PBI — Public Interest
PBIA — Biblical Archaeologist
PBIB — Biological Bulletin
PBIBA — Pochvy Bashkirii i Puti Ratsional'nogo Ikh Ispol'zovaniya
PBICAG — Publicaciones Biologicas. Instituto de Investigaciones Cientificas UANL
PBIOEM — Plant Biology
PBIP — Paperbound Books in Print
PBIR — Biological Reviews. Cambridge Philosophical Society
PBIS — Pamphlet Bible Series
PBIS — Prospezioni. Bollettino di Informazioni Scientifiche
PBJA — British Journal of Aesthetics
PBJC — British Journal of Criminology
PBJH — British Journal for the History of Science
PDJO — British Journal of Sociology
PBJOD — Plant Biochemical Journal
PBJP — British Journal for the Philosophy of Science
PBJS — British Journal of Political Science
PBK — Pamietnik Biblioteki Kornickiej
PBKL — Booklist
PBL — Papers in Borneo Linguistics
PBL — Pastoralblaetter
PBI — Pastoralblaetter fuer Homiletik, Katechetik, und Seelsorge
PbI — Pastoralblaetter fuer Predigt, Katechetik, und Kirchliche Unterweisung
P BI — Patentblatt
PBL — Praktisches Bibellexikon
Pbl — Publicatieblad van de Europese Gemeenschappen
PBLSA — Publius
PBM — Poetry Book Magazine
PBM — Public Management
PBMAA — Publications. Research Institute for Mathematical Sciences. Series A
PBMEA — Perspectives in Biology and Medicine
PBML — Prague Bulletin of Mathematical Linguistics
PBMOE8 — Progress in Behavior Modification
PBMR — International Bulletin of Missionary Research
PBN — Papyrus Bouriant
PBNS — Prospects Business News Survey
PBO — Polski Biuletyn Orientalistyczny
PBO — Print Business Opportunities
PBOG — Botanical Gazette
PBOR — Botanical Review
P (Boswinkel) — Einige Wiener Papyri (Boswinkel)
P Bour — Papyrus Bouriant
P Bouriant — Papyrus Bouriant

PBP — Paperbound Books in Print
PBP — Paris. Universite. Institut d'Etudes Slaves. Bibliotheque Polonaise
PBP — Pinkas Bractwa Pogrzebowego
PBPM — Black Perspective in Music
PBR — Progress in Brain Research
PBRA — Polska Bibliografja Biblijna Adnotowana
PBRCA — Proceedings. British Ceramic Society
PBREE3 — Plant Breeding Reviews
PB Rep Off Tech Servs — PB Reports. Office of Technical Services [*Wasington, D. C.*]
PBRT — Behaviour Research and Therapy
PBS — Pressedienst fuer das Bauspar
PBS — Publications. Babylonian Section. University Museum. University of Pennsylvania
PBSA — Papers. Bibliographical Society of America
PBSA — Publications. Bibliographical Society of America
PBSAE — Publications. British School of Archeology in Egypt
PBSA SPap — Proceedings. British Academy. Supplement Paper
PBSB — Beitraege zur Geschichte der Deutschen Sprache und Literatur (Hermann Paul und Wilhelm Braune, Editors)
PBSC — Behavioral Science
PBSC — Papers. Bibliographical Society of Canada
PBSED — Proceedings. Bioenergy R and D Seminar
PBSFS — Publications. British Society of Franciscan Studies
PBSFSE — Publications. British Society of Franciscan Studies. Extra Series
PBSR — Papers. British School at Rome
PBSUV — Papers. Bibliographical Society. University of Virginia
PBSW — Proceedings of the Biological Society of Washington, D.C
PBSWA — Proceedings. Biological Society of Washington
PBSY — British Journal of Psychology
PBTO — Boundary 2
PBUZ — Buzzworm. The Environmental Journal
PBUZDC — Publicaciones de Biologia. Universidad de Navarra. Serie Zoologica
PC — Paraula Cristiana
PC — Peake's Commentary on the Bible
PC — Pensiero Critico
PC — People's China
PC — Peuples et Civilisations. Histoire Generale [*monograph*]
PC — Poesia e Critica
PC — Presence Chretienne
PC — Problems of Communism
PCA — Proceedings. Classical Association
PCAABC — Centre for Agricultural Publications and Documentation [*Wageningen*]. Annual Report
PCAAS — Proceedings. Connecticut Academy of Arts and Sciences
PCAC — Publications. Catholic Anthropological Conference
PC AI Intell Solutions Desktop Comput — PC AI Intelligent Solutions for Desktop Computers
P Cair — Cairo Papyri
P Cair Isidor — Archive of Aurelius Isidorus in the Egyptian Museum, Cairo, and the University of Michigan
P (Cair) Zen — Zenon Papyri (Cairo)
P Camb Ph S — Proceedings. Cambridge Philological Society
PCA Res Dev Bull — PCA (Portland Cement Association) Research and Development Bulletin
PCAS — Proceedings. Cambridge Antiquarian Society
PCAS — Proceedings. Central Asian Society
PCAS — Proceedings. Classical Association of Scotland
PCAS — Proceedings of the California Academy of Sciences
PCB — Peake's Commentary on the Bible
PCB — Poetry Chapbook
PCB — Pollution. Environmental News Bulletin
PCBMEM — Progress in Clinical Biochemistry and Medicine
PCBPB — Pesticide Biochemistry and Physiology
PCBQ — Catholic Biblical Quarterly
PCBR — Progress in Clinical and Biological Research
PCBRD — Progress in Clinical and Biological Research
PCBSA2 — Canadian Federation of Biological Societies. Proceedings
PCC — Proceedings. Chicago Congress. Meteorological Section
PCCCD — Proceedings. Annual Allerton Conference on Communication, Control, and Computing
PCCL — Patrologiae Cursus Completus. Series Latina
PCCLAS/P — Proceedings. Pacific Coast Council on Latin American Studies
PCCOA — Professional Contributions. Colorado School of Mines
PCCRD7 — Proceedings. Serono Clinical Colloquia on Reproduction
PCCSD — Proceedings. International Conference on Cybernetics and Society
PCDP — Contemporary Drug Problems
PCDR — Comparative Drama
PCDRR — PC Digest Ratings Report
PCEA Bol Trimest Exp Agropecu — PCEA [*Programa Cooperativo de Experimentacion Agropecuaria*] Boletin Trimestral de Experimentacion Agropecuaria
PCFL — Paul Carus Foundation Lectures
PCFS — Journal of Comparative Family Studies
PCG — Package Engineering
PCGE — Canadian Geographer
PCGLA — Physics and Chemistry of Glasses
PCGO — Canadian Geographic
PCH — Paternoster Church History
P Ch — Planovoe Chozjajstvo
PCHA — Chaucer Review
PCHAA — Philippine Chinese Historical Association. Annals
PCHEA — Petro/Chem Engineer
Pchela Sof — Pchela Sofiya
Pchel Mir — Pchelovodnyi Mir

Pchel Zhizn — Pchelovodnaya Zhizn'
PCHH — Church History
PCHI — Chicago Review
PCHO — Choice
PCH PhysicoChem Hydrodyn — PCH: PhysicoChemical Hydrodynamics
PCHR — Canadian Historical Review
P Ch S — Proceedings. Chemical Society
PCHS — Publications. Church Historical Society
PCHSS — Publications. Church Historical Society. Sources
PCI — Pacific Viewpoint
PCI — Proceedings. Canadian Institute
PCI — Revista de Derecho Puertorriqueno
PCIA — Papoli e Civilta dell'Italia Antica
PCIV — Civil War History
PCIYA — Progress in Clinical Immunology
PCJ — Bangladesh Development Studies
PCJC — Canadian Journal of Criminology
PCJH — Canadian Journal of History
PCJOAU — Pharmaceutical Chemistry Journal
PCJP — Canadian Journal of Philosophy
Pckg Eng En — Package Engineering Encyclopedia, Including Modern Packaging Encyclopedia
Pckgng Eng — Packaging Engineering
Pckgng Rev — Packaging Review
Pckgng Wek — Packaging Week
PCl — Paul Claudel
PCL — Perspectives on Contemporary Literature
P Cl A — Proceedings. Classical Association
PCLAC — Proceedings. California Linguistics Association Conference
PCLA Newsl — PCLA [*Polish Canadian Librarians Association*] Newsletter
PCLC — Journal of Criminal Law and Criminology
PCLI — Canadian Literature
PCLI — Problemi ed Orientamenti Critici di Lingua e di Letteratura Italiana
P Clin North America — Pediatric Clinics of North America
PCLJ — Pacific Coast Law Journal
PCLO — Clio
PCLP — Classical Philology
PCLQ — Classical Quarterly
PCLQA — Physics and Chemistry of Liquids
PCLS — Classical Antiquity
PCLS — Proceedings. Comparative Literature Symposium
PCLT — Children's Literature. An International Journal
PCMH — Community Mental Health Journal
PCMJ — College Mathematics Journal
P Cmp Sc St — Proceedings. Computer Science and Statistics
PCMQ — Communication Quarterly
PCMR — Communication Research
PCMS — Current Musicology
PCN — Players Chess News
PCN — Print Collector's Newsletter
PCNC — Capital and Class
PCNCDH — Publications. Centre National pour l'Exploitation des Oceans. Actes de Colloques
PCNDP — Publication. Centre National de Documentation Pedagogique
PCNFDQ — Publications. Centre National pour l'Exploitation des Oceans. Rapports Scientifiques et Techniques
PCNH — Computers and the Humanities
PCNMDD — Publications. Centre National pour l'Exploitation des Oceans. Resultats des Campagnes a la Mer
PCNT — Conde Nast Traveler
PCO — Proceedings. Congress of Orientalists
PCOAD — Powder Coatings
P Coast LJ — Pacific Coast Law Journal
PCOG — Press Clippings of Greenland
PCOL — College Literature
PCom — Pays Comtois
PCOMB — Physics of Condensed Matter
P Comp Lit — Proceedings. Comparative Literature Symposium
PCONA — Pest Control
PCOR — Corrections Today
P Cornell — Greek Papyri in the Library of Cornell University
PCOS — Comparative Literature Studies
PCOSD2 — Psychoanalysis and Contemporary Science
PCOU — Counseling Psychologist
PCP — Pacific Coast Philology
PCP — Publications in Classical Philology
PCPHA — Plant and Cell Physiology
PCPhS — Proceedings. Cambridge Philological Society
PCPMDN — Annual Research Reviews. Proteins of Animal Cell Plasma Membranes
PCPO — Comparative Politics
PCPP — Plasma Chemistry and Plasma Processing
PCPPD — Plasma Chemistry and Plasma Processing
PCPS — Canadian Journal of Political Science
PCPS — Proceedings. Cambridge Philological Society
PCPSA — Proceedings. Cambridge Philosophical Society
PCPSD — Progress in Colloid and Polymer Science
PCPT — Perception. Canadian Magazine of Social Comment
PCPU — Comparative Political Studies
PCr — Pensamiento Critico
PCR — Professional Casting Report
PCRB — Parks Canada. Research Bulletin
PCRE — Catholic Historical Review
PCRHP — Publications. Centre de Recherches d'Histoire et de Philologie
PCRHP Gr — Publications. Centre de Recherches d'Histoire et de Philologie. Hautes Etudes du Monde Grecoromain

PCRHP H — Publications. Centre de Recherches d'Histoire et de Philologie. Histoire et Civilisation du Livre
PCRHPM — Publications. Centre de Recherches d'Histoire et de Philologie. Hautes Etudes Medievales et Modernes
PCRHPN — Publications. Centre de Recherches d'Histoire et de Philologie. Hautes Etudes Numismatiques
PCRJ — Criminal Justice Ethics
PCR Methods Appl — PCR (Polymerase Chain Reaction) Methods and Applications
PCR Neurosci — PCR (Polymerase Chain Reaction) in Neuroscience
PCRPD8 — Plant Cell Reports
PCRQ — Critical Quarterly
PCRS — Canadian Review of Sociology and Anthropology
PCRSAE — Colston Research Society. Proceedings of the Symposium
PCRS AR — Publications. Catholic Record Society. Annual Report
PCRSB — Proceedings. Canadian Rock Mechanics Symposium
PCRY — Criminology
PCS — Publications. Camden Society
PCS — Revista de Ciencias Sociales
PCSCF — Publications. Center for the Study of Comparative Folklore and Mythology
PCSCL — Pubblicazione. Centro Studi Capuccini Lombardi
PCS Commun — P.C.S. Communication. Research Laboratory for the Physics and Chemistry of Solids. Cavendish Laboratory [*Cambridge*]
PCSIB — Protection Civile et Securite Industrielle
PCSIR Bull Monogr — PCSIR [*Pakistan Council of Scientific and Industrial Research*] Bulletin/Monograph
PCSIR Res Bull — PCSIR (Pakistan Council of Scientific and Industrial Research) Research Bulletin
PCSM — Criticism
PCSNA — Processing
PCSO — Current Sociology
PCSS — Comparative Studies in Society and History
PCSW — Clinical Social Work Journal
PCSY — Canadian Journal of Psychology
PCTCA — Protection
PCTEB — Pennsylvania Council of Teachers of English. Bulletin
PCTE Bull — Pennsylvania Council of Teachers of English. Bulletin
PCTE Bulletin — Pennsylvania Council of Teachers of English. Bulletin
PCT Gaz — PCT (Patent Cooperation Treaty) Gazette. Gazette of International Patent Applications
PCTHDS — Psychoanalysis and Contemporary Thought
PCT Int Appl — PCT (Patent Cooperation Treaty) International Application
PCTNB — Perception
PCTQ — Critique. Studies in Contemporary Fiction
PCTSA — Proceedings. Annual Meeting. Catholic Theological Society of America
PCUR — Cross Currents
PCVDA — Progress in Cardiovascular Diseases
PCYL — Contemporary Literature
PCZ — Zenon Papyri (Cairo)
PD — Paepstliche Dokumente
PD — Paix et Droit
PD — Papier und Druck
PD — Parliamentary Debates
PD — Pennsylvania Dutchman
PD — Poetic Drama
PD — Politische Dokumente aus Kleinasien
PD — Presidential Documents
PD — Probleme der Dichtung
PD — Przemysl Drzewny
PDA — Planning and Development in the Netherlands (Assen)
PDAA — Pictoral Dictionary of Ancient Athens
PDAGA — Pediatriia, Akusherstvo, i Ginekologiia
PDA J Pharm Sci Technol — PDA [*Parental Drug Association*] Journal of Pharmaceutical Science andTechnology
PDAL — Dalhousie Review
PDANB — Pediatric Annals
PD & GLM Rev — P.D. & G.L.M. Review [*Cardiff*]
PDANHS — Proceedings. Dorset Natural History and Archaeological Society
PDAS — Proceedings. Davenport Academy of Sciences
PDB — Pakistan Development Review
PDBA — Publicaciones del Departamento de Bibliotecas y Archivos Nacionales [*Bogota*]
PDBIA — Periodicum Biologorum
PDCH — Dance Chronicle
PDD — Problemas del Desarrollo
PdD — Probleme der Dichtung
PDE — Preliminary Determination of Epicenters
PDEM — Demography
PDENA — Production Engineer
PDF — Packaging Technology
PDHMUA — Publication. Department of History. Muslim University (Aligarh)
PDI — Papeles de la India
PDI — Planned Innovation
PDial — Poetry Dial
PDIO — Diogenes
PDIP — Diplomatic History
PDIS — Proceedings. National Symposia
PDK — Phi Delta Kappan
PdK — Predigt der Kirche
PdL — Provincia di Lucca
PDM — Physicians Drug Manual
PDM — Poetry and Drama Magazine
PDMLA — PDM. Physicians' Drug Manual
PDNPD — Physica D. Nonlinear Phenomena

PdO — Parole d'Orient
PDO — Problemi d'Oggi
PdP — Parola del Popolo
PdP — Punto de Partida
PDPRA — Plastics Design and Processing
PDR — Pakistan Development Review
PDR — Peter De Ridder Press Publications
PDR — Physician's Desk Reference
PDR — Plant Disease Reporter
PD Rev — PD Review. Powell Duffryn, Ltd. [*Cardiff*]
PDRI — Publications. Diaspora Research Institute
PDRJ — Dance Research Journal
PDSD — US Department of State Dispatch
PDSOF IBM — Public Domain Software on File. IBM
PDST — Death Studies
Pd T — Pedagogisk Tidskrift
PDT — Proceedings. European Society of Drug Toxicity
PDTNBH — Paediatrician
PDTRDV — Pediatria
PDV — Punto de Vista
PDVHL — Palaestinahefte des Deutschen Vereins vom Heiligen Lande
PdZ — Perspektiven der Zukunft
PDZBDD — Publicaciones. Departamento de Zoologia
PDZI — Przeglad Zachodni
PDZRA — Prace Dzialu Zywenia Roslin i Nawozenia
PE — Packaging Engineering
PE — Pennsylvania English
PE — Percussionist
PE — Personnel Executive
PE — Petroleum Engineer
PE — Philippine Educator
PE — Plural
PE — Poesia Espanola
PE — Politique Etrangere
PE — Problems of Economics
Pe — Prose
PE — Punta Europa
PEA — Patres Ecclesiae Anglicanae
PeA — Pretre et Apotre
PEABA — Petroleum Abstracts
Peab L Rev — Peabody Law Review
Peab Mus Pap — Peabody Museum Papers
Peabody J E — Peabody Journal of Education
Peabody J Ed — Peabody Journal of Education
Peabody J Educ — Peabody Journal of Education
Peabody Jour Educ — Peabody Journal of Education. George Peabody College for Teachers
Peabody Mus Nat Hist Yale Univ Bull — Peabody Museum of Natural History. Yale University. Bulletin
PEACA — Progress in Nuclear Energy. Series 9
Peace — Peace Newsletter
Peace — Peace/Non-Violence
Peace and Sci — Peace and the Sciences
Peaceful Nucl Explos — Peaceful Nuclear Explosions. Proceedings of a Technical Committee
Peacemak — Peacemaker
Peace Nws — Peace News
Peace Offic — Peace Officer
Peace Offic Assn Calif Proc — Peace Officers Association of California. Proceedings
PeaceResAb — Peace Research Abstracts
Peace Res Abstr J — Peace Research Abstracts Journal
Peace Res Ja — Peace Research in Japan
Peace Res Rev — Peace Research Reviews
Peace Science Soc Internat Pas — Peace Science Society. International Papers
PEAL — Early American Literature
PEAL — Publishing, Entertainment, Advertising, and Allied Fields Law Quarterly
PEALQ — Publishing, Entertainment, Advertising, and Allied Fields Law Quarterly
PEANA — Proceedings. Easter School in Agricultural Science. University of Nottingham
PE & W — Philosophy East and West
Peanut J Nut World — Peanut Journal and Nut World
Peanut Sci — Peanut Science
PEAP — Publications in East Asiatic Philology
PEAr — Publications in Egyptian Archaeology
Pearce-Sellards Ser Tex Mem Mus — Pearce-Sellards Series. Texas Memorial Museum
Pearsons M NY — Pearson's Magazine (New York)
PEAS — Photographische Einzelaufnahmen Antiker Skulpturen
Peasant Stud — Peasant Studies
Peasant Stud Newsl — Peasant Studies Newsletter
Peat Abstr — Peat Abstracts
Peat Ind — Peat Industry
Peat Ind Proc Symp Comm Int Peat Soc — Peat Industry. Proceedings. Symposium of Commission. International Peat Society
Peat Plant Yearb — Peat and Plant Yearbook
Peb — Pebble
PEB — Philippine Economy Bulletin
PEBIDN — Perspectives in Biometrics
PeC — Peuples et Civilisations
PeC — Poesia e Critica
PEC — Polish Economic News
PECAD4 — Pediatric Cardiology
Pecan J — Pecan Journal. Southeastern Pecan Growers Association
Pecan Q — Pecan Quarterly

Pecan South Incl Pecan Q — Pecan South Including Pecan Quarterly
PECC — Journal of Ecclesiastical History
PECG — Economic Geography
PECH — Economic History Review
PECHA — Petroleum Chemistry USSR
Peche Mar — Peche Maritime
Peche Marit — Peche Maritime
PECM — Journal of Ecumenical Studies
PECO — Peace Country
PECO Prod Q — PECO Products Quarterly. Projectile and Engineering Co.
   [London]
PECS — Princeton Encyclopedia of Classical Sites
Pecsi Muesz Sz — Pecsi Mueszaki Szemle
Pecsi Pedagog Foeisk Evk — A Pecsi Pedagogiai Foeiskola Evkoenyve
PECU — Ecumenical Review
Ped — Pedagogia
Ped — Pedagogie, Education, et Culture
PED — Publications. Egyptian Department. University Museum. University of
   Pennsylvania
Pedag i Psihol — Pedagogika i Psihologija
Pedag Meddel — Pedagogiska Meddelanden fran Skoloeverstyrelsen
Pedagog Fak Plzni Sb Chem — Pedagogicka Fakulta v Plzni. Sbornik. Chemie
Pedagog Fak Plzni Sb Ser Chem — Pedagogicka Fakulta v Plzni. Sbornik. Serie
   Chemie
Pedagog Fak Presove Zb — Pedagogicka Fakulta v Presove. Zbornik
Pedagog Fak Usti nad Labem Sb Rada Chem — Pedagogicka Fakulta v Usti nad
   Labem. Sbornik. Rada Chemicka
Pedagog Sem — Pedagogical Seminary
Pedag Szle — Pedagogiai Szemle
Pedag Tidskr — Pedagogisk Tidskrift
Ped Akus Ginek — Pediatriia, Akusherstvo, i Ginekologiia
PEDBA9 — Pediatria
Ped Cal — Pediatria in Calabria
Ped Clin NA — Pediatric Clinics of North America
Ped Ecuat — Pediatria Ecuatoriana
Pedia — Pediatrics
Pediat Akush Ginek — Pediatriia, Akusherstvo, i Ginekologiia
Pediat Clins N Am — Pediatric Clinics of North America
Pediat Inf — Pediatric Infectious Disease
Pediat Nurs — Pediatric Nursing
Pediatr Adolesc Endocrinol — Pediatric and Adolescent Endocrinology
Pediatr Adolesc Gynecol — Pediatric and Adolescent Gynecology
Pediatr Akush Ginekol — Pediatriia, Akusherstvo, i Ginekologiia
Pediatr Allergy Immunol — Pediatric Allergy and Immunology
Pediatr Ann — Pediatric Annals
Pediatr Cardiol — Pediatric Cardiology
Pediatr Clin N Am — Pediatric Clinics of North America
Pediatr Clin North Am — Pediatric Clinics of North America
Pediatr Contin Educ Courses Pract — Pediatric Continuing Education Courses for
   the Practitioner
Pediatr Dent — Pediatric Dentistry
Pediatr Dermatol — Pediatric Dermatology
Pediatr Dev Pathol — Pediatric and Developmental Pathology
Pediatr Electron Pages — Pediatrics Electronic Pages
Pediatr Emerg Care — Pediatric Emergency Care
Pediat Res — Pediatric Research
Pediatr Esp — Pediatria Espanola
Pediatr Hematol Oncol — Pediatric Hematology and Oncology
Pediatria Arch — Pediatria. Archivio di Patologia e Clinica Pediatrica
Pediatria Espan — Pediatria Espanola
Pediatrics Suppl — Pediatrics Supplement
Pediatr Infect Dis — Pediatric Infectious Disease
Pediatr Infect Dis J — Pediatric Infectious Disease Journal
Pediatr Int — Pediatria Internazionale
Pediatr Listy — Pediatricke Listy
Pediatr Med Chir — Pediatria Medica e Chirurgica
Pediatr Mod — Pediatria Moderna
Pediatr Nephrol — Pediatric Nephrology
Pediatr Nephrol Berlin — Pediatric Nephrology (Berlin)
Pediatr Nephrol NY — Pediatric Nephrology (New York)
Pediatr Neurol — Pediatric Neurology
Pediatr Neurosci — Pediatric Neuroscience
Pediatr Neurosurg — Pediatric Neurosurgery
Pediatr News — Pediatric News
Pediatr Nurs — Pediatric Nursing
Pediatr Nurse Pract — Pediatric Nurse Practitioner
Pediatr Panamericana — Pediatria Panamericana
Pediatr Pathol — Pediatric Pathology
Pediatr Pathol Lab Med — Pediatric Pathology and Laboratory Medicine
Pediatr Pathol Mol Med — Pediatric Pathology & Molecular Medicine
Pediatr Pharmacol — Pediatric Pharmacology
Pediatr Pol — Pediatria Polska
Pediatr Prat — Pediatria Pratica
Pediatr Pulmonol — Pediatric Pulmonology
Pediatr Pulmonol Suppl — Pediatric Pulmonology. Supplement
Pediatr Radiol — Pediatric Radiology
Pediatr Res — Pediatric Research
Pediatr Rev — Pediatric Review
Pediatr Surg Int — Pediatric Surgery International
Pediatr Transplant — Pediatric Transplantation
Pediatr Update — Pediatrics Update
PEDIEY — Pedoatrocoam
P Edin Math — Proceedings. Edinburgh Mathematical Society
Ped Int — Pediatria Internazionale
Pedjatr Pol — Pedjatrja Polska

Pedobiolog — Pedobiologia
Pedod Fr — Pedodontie Francaise
Pedology (Leningr) — Pedology (Leningrad)
Ped Panam — Pediatria Panamericana
Ped Psich — Pedagogika ir Psichologija
Ped Sem — Pedagogical Seminary
PEDTAT — Pediatriya
P Educator — Physical Educator
PEEAD — Promoclim E. Etudes Thermiques et Aerauliques
PEECD — Petroleum Economist
PEEH — Journal of European Economic History
PEEH — Publicaciones de la Escuela de Estudios Hispano-Americanos de Sevilla
PEEID — Petroleum Engineer International
Peel Valley Hist Soc J — Peel Valley Historical Society. Journal
PEEQ — East European Quarterly
PEET — Environmental Ethics
PEFA — Palestine Exploration Fund. Annual
PEFEO — Publications de l'Ecole Francaise d'Extreme-Orient
PEFM — Palestine Exploration Fund. Memoirs
PEFQ — Palestine Exploration Fund. Quarterly Statement
PEFQSt — Palestine Exploration Fund. Quarterly Statement
PEFY — Institut d'Etudes Francaises de Yale University. Publications
Peg — Pegaso
PEG — Production Engineering
PEG — Publicatieblad van de Europese Gemeenschappen
PEGEA — Petroleum Geology
Pegmatitovye Redkomet Mestorozhd — Pegmatitovye Redkometal'nye
   Mestorozhdeniya
PEGR — Ethnic Groups
PEGR — Press Extracts on Greenland
PEGS — Ecologist
PEGS — Publications. English Goethe Society
PEGTA — Problemy Endokrinologii i Gormonoterapii
PEGY — Ethnology
PEHI — Journal of Economic History
PEHPA — Progress in Nuclear Energy. Series 12
PEHQ — European History Quarterly
PEHR — English Historical Review
PEHYA — Petroleum and Hydrocarbons
PEI — Haszard and Warburton's Reports. Prince Edward Island
Pel — Parole e le Idee
PEI — Physical Education Index
PEIA — Universidad Nacional de Tucuman. Instituto de Antropologia. Publicaciones
   Especiales
PEI Acts — Acts of Prince Edward Island
PEIC — Essays in Criticism
PEIDD9 — Personality and Individual Differences
PEIG — Eighteenth-Century Studies
PEIL — Essays in Literature
Peine Salzgitter Ber — Peine und Salzgitter Berichte
Peint Cah Theor — Peinture/Cahiers Theoriques
Peint Pigm Vernis — Peintures, Pigments, Vernis
PEI Rev Regs — Revised Regulations of Prince Edward Island
PEJ — Pakistan Economic Journal
PEJ — Personnel Journal
PEJOA — Personnel Journal
PEKI — Ekistics
Peking Min Coll J — Peking Mining College Journal
Peking Nat Hist Bull — Peking Natural History Bulletin
Peking R — Peking Review
Pek Rev — Peking Review
PEL — Penguin English Library
PELAA — Progress in Nuclear Energy. Series 10
P Eleph — Elephantine Papyri
PELN — English Language Notes
PELO — Paris. Ecole Nationale des Langues Orientales Vivantes. Publications
Pelop — Peloponnesiaka
PELOV — Publications de l'Ecole des Languages Orientales Vivantes
Pelt — Peltier's Decisions. Court of Appeal. Parish of Orleans
PeM — Parole e Metodi
PEM — Perfiles Educativos (Mexico)
PEM — Perspectivas de la Economia Mundial
PEM — Perspectives de l'Economie Mondiale
Pemb Eq — Pemberton's Practice in Equity by Way of Revivor and Supplement
Pembroke Mag — Pembroke Magazine
Pemietnik Lit — Pamietnik Literacki
PEMJ — Pemmican Journal
PEMJA — Pesticides Monitoring Journal
PEM Masch Anlagenbau — PEM Maschinen + Anlagenbau
PEMN/R — Revista. Museo Nacional de la Cultura Peruana
PEMO — Ecological Monographs
PEM Process Eng Mag — PEM Process Engineering Magazine
PEMU — Early Music
Pen — Pensamiento
Pen — Pensee. Revue du Rationalisme Moderne
PEN — Petroleum News. Asia's Energy Journal
Pen Affairs — Penal Affairs
PENB — Environment and Behavior
PenC — Pensee Catholique
Pen Cath — Pensee Catholique
Pen Cri — Penseiro Critico
PEND — Endeavour
PENDA — Polish Endocrinology
PENEE4 — Pediatric Neuroscience
Penelitian Indones — Penelitian Laut di Indonesia

Penelitian Laut Indones (Mar Res Indones) — Penelitian Laut di Indonesia (Marine Research in Indonesia)
Penerbitan Tek Pusat Pengembangan Teknol Miner — Penerbitan Teknik. Pusat Pengembangan Teknologi Mineral
PenF — Pensee Francaise
PEng — Pennsylvania English
Penge Investe — Penge og Investering
Pengum Lemb Penelit Kehutanan — Pengumuman. Lembaga Penelitian Kehutanan
PenH — Pennsylvania History
Peninsula Hist Rev — Peninsula Historical Review. Door County Historical Society
Penjelidikan Indones — Penjelidikan Laut di Indonesia
PenM — Pennsylvania Magazine of History and Biography
PenM — Pensamiento (Madrid)
Penna Law Journal — Pennsylvania Law Journal
Penna LJ — Pennsylvania Law Journal
Penn Ba Q — Pennsylvania Bar Association. Quarterly
Penn BAR — Pennsylvania Bar Association. Report
Penn Bar Assc Q — Pennsylvania Bar Association. Quarterly
Penn Beekpr — Pennsylvania Beekeeper
Penn Dent J — Penn Dental Journal
Penn Geol Surv Atlas — Pennsylvania. Geological Survey. Atlas
Penn Geol Surv Bull — Pennsylvania. Geological Survey. Bulletin
Penn Geol Surv Gen Geol Rep — Pennsylvania. Geological Survey. General Geology Report
Penn Geol Surv Ground Water Rep — Pennsylvania. Geological Survey. Ground Water Report
Penn Geol Surv Inform Circ — Pennsylvania. Geological Survey. Information Circular
Penn Geol Surv Progr Rep — Pennsylvania. Geological Survey. Progress Report
Penn German Soc Proc — Pennsylvania German Society. Proceedings
Penn Hist — Pennsylvania History
Penn Hosp Rep — Pennsylvania Hospital Reports
Pennington Cent Nutr Ser — Pennington Center Nutrition Series
Penn Law — Pennsylvania Lawyer
Penn Law Jour — Pennsylvania Law Journal
Penn LG — Pennsylvania Legal Gazette
Penn Lib Assn Bull — Pennsylvania Library Association. Bulletin
Penn LJ — Pennsylvania Law Journal
Penn L Rev — Pennsylvania Law Review
Penn Mag H — Pennsylvania Magazine of History and Biography
Penn Mag Hist Biog — Pennsylvania Magazine of History and Biography
Penn Mo — Penn Monthly
Penn Nurse — Pennsylvania Nurse
Penn Res — Pennsylvania Researcher
PennsF — Pennsylvania Folklife
PennState Agric — PennState Agriculture
Penn State F — Penn State Farmer
Penn State Stud — Penn State Studies
Penn State Univ Exp Sta Bull — Pennsylvania State University. Experiment Station. Bulletin
Penn State Univ Exp Sta Circ — Pennsylvania State University. Experiment Station. Circular
Penn St M Q — Penn State Mining Quarterly
Penn Stock & F — Pennsylvania Stockman and Farmer
Penn St R — Pennsylvania State Reports
Pennsyl M — Pennsylvania Magazine of History and Biography
Pennsylvania Acad Sci Newsletter — Pennsylvania Academy of Science. Newsletter
Pennsylvania Acad Sci Proc — Pennsylvania Academy of Science. Proceedings
Pennsylvania Bus Survey — Pennsylvania Business Survey
Pennsylvania Geol — Pennsylvania Geology
Pennsylvania Geol Survey Bull — Pennsylvania. Geological Survey. Bulletin
Pennsylvania Geol Survey Inf Circ — Pennsylvania. Geological Survey. Information Circular
Pennsylvania Geol Survey Prog Rept — Pennsylvania. Geological Survey. Progress Report
Pennsylvania State Coll Agric Exp Sta Bull — Pennsylvania State College. Agricultural Experiment Station. Bulletin
Pennsylvania State Coll Agric Exp Sta Bull Inform — Pennsylvania State College Agricultural Experiment Station. Bulletin of Information
Pennsylvania State Coll Stud — Pennsylvania State College Studies
Pennsylvania U Mus J — Pennsylvania University Museum Journal
Penn Univ Mus Bul — Pennsylvania University. University Museum. Bulletin
Penny M — Penny Magazine
Penny Mag Soc Diff Useful Knowl — Penny Magazine of the Society for the Diffusion of Useful Knowledge
Penny Mech Chem — Penny Mechanic and the Chemist
PenP — Pensamiento Politico
Pen Pow — Penny Power
PENR — Ethnic and Racial Studies
PENRB — Professional Engineer
Pen Ref League M Rec — Penal Reform League Monthly Record
Pen Ref League Q Rec — Penal Reform League Quarterly Record
Pen Reformer — Penal Reformer
Penrose Ann — Penrose Annual
Penrose Annu — Penrose Annual
Pens — Pensamiento
Pensador Mex — Pensador Mexicano
Pensamiento Econ — Pensamiento Economico
Pensamiento Polit — Pensamiento Politico
Pensam y Accion — Pensamiento y Accion
Pensee Nat — Pensee Nationale
Pensez Plast — Pensez Plastiques
Pensf T — Pensionsforsikringsanstaltens Tidsskrift

Pensiero Giurid Pen — Pensiero Giuridico-Penale
Pensiero Med — Pensiero Medico
Pensiero Polit — Pensiero Politico
Pension Br — Pension Briefings
Pension FA — Pension Fund Sponsors Ranked by Assets
Pension Fc — Pension Facts
Pensions — Pensions and Investments [*Later, Pension & Investment Age*]
Pensions Investm Age — Pensions and Investment Age
Pension Wld — Pension World
Pens Plan Guide CCH — Pension Plan Guide. Commerce Clearing House
Pens Polit — Pensiero Politico
Pentax Photogr — Pentax Photography
P Ent S Ont — Proceedings. Entomological Society of Ontario
P Ent S Was — Proceedings. Entomological Society of Washington
PENV — Journal of Environmental Health
PENVDK — Population and Environment
Pen Wld — Pension World
Penz Inzh Stroit Inst Sb Nauchn Rab — Penzenskii Inzhenerno-Stroitel'nyi Institut. Sbornik Nauchnykh Rabot
Penz Ped Inst Ucen Zap — Penzenskii Pedagogiceskii Institut Imeni V. G. Belinskogo. Ucenye Zapiski
Penz Politehn Inst Ucen Zap Mat Meh — Penzenskii Politehniceskii Institut. Matematika i Mehanika. Ucenye Zapiski
Penzuegyi Szemle — Penzuegyi Szemle
Penzugyi Szle — Penzuegyi Szemle
PEOC — Essays on Canadian Writing
PEOED — Proceedings. European Offshore Petroleum Conference and Exhibition
PEOPD7 — Perspectives in Ophthalmology
Peop J — People's Journal
People — People Weekly
People and Plann — People and Planning
Peoples Cult — People's Culture
Peoples Repub China Pat Doc — People's Republic of China. Patent Document
People Wkly — People Weekly
Peopl Tax — People and Taxes
Peoria Med Month — Peoria Medical Monthly
PEOUD — Petroleum Outlook
Peo World — People's World
PEP — All India Reporter, Patiala and East Punjab States Union Series
PEP Broadsh — P.E.P. Broadsheets [*London*]
PEP Engng Rep — P.E.P. Engineering Reports [*London*]
PEPIA — Physics of the Earth and Planetary Interiors
Pepinier Hortic Maraichers — Pepinieristes, Horticulteurs, Maraichers
Pepperdine LR — Pepperdine Law Review
Pepperdine L Rev — Pepperdine Law Review
Pepp LR — Pepperdine Law Review
PEPSB — Perception and Psychophysics
Pept Anal Protoc — Peptide Analysis Protocols
Pept Chem — Peptide Chemistry. Proceedings. Symposium on Peptide Chemistry
Pept Chem Biol Proc Am Pept Symp — Peptides. Chemistry and Biology. Proceedings. American Peptide Symposium
PEPTDO — Peptides
Pept Horm Action — Peptide Hormone Action [*monograph*]
Peptidergic Neuron Proc Int Symp Neurosecretion — Peptidergic Neuron. Proceedings. International Symposium on Neurosecretion
Pept Pharm — Peptide Pharmaceuticals
Pept Proc Eur Symp — Peptides. Proceedings. European Symposium
Pept Protein Drug Delivery — Peptide and Protein Drug Delivery
Pept Protein Rev — Peptide and Protein Reviews
Pept Res — Peptide Research
Pept Struct Biol Funct Proc Am Pept Symp — Peptides. Structure and Biological Function. Proceedings. American Peptide Symposium
Pept Synth Struct Funct Proc Am Pept Symp — Peptides. Synthesis, Structure, Function. Proceedings. American Peptide Symposium
Pept Target New Drug Dev — Peptides. A Target for New Drug Development [*monograph*]
PEQ — Palestine Exploration Quarterly
PEQL — Palestine Exploration Quarterly (London)
Per — Personalist
PER — Personnel
Per — Perspective
Per — Perspectives
PER — Polish Ecumenical Review
PERA Bull — PERA (Production Engineering Research Association of Great Britain) Bulletin
Per AJ — Performing Arts Journal
Per A R — Performing Arts Review
PERA Rep — PERA (Production Engineering Research Association of Great Britain) Report
Per Arts & Ent Can — Performing Arts & Entertainment in Canada
Per Biol — Periodicum Biologorum
Percep & Motor Skills — Perceptual and Motor Skills
Percep & Psychophys — Perception and Psychophysics
Percept & Motor Skills — Perceptual and Motor Skills
Percept and Mot Sk — Perceptual and Motor Skills
Percept Cogn Dev — Perceptual Cognitive Development
Percept Cognit Devel — Perceptual Cognitive Development
Perceptismo Teor & Polemico — Perceptismo. Teorico y Polemico
Percept Mot Skills — Perceptual and Motor Skills
Percept Psychophys — Perception and Psychophysics
Perc Mot Sk — Perceptual and Motor Skills
Perc Notes — Percussive Notes
Perc Notes Res Ed — Percussive Notes. Research Edition
Percolation Localization Supercond — Percolation, Localization, and Superconductivity

Per Comp T — Personal Computers Today
Perc Psych — Perception and Psychophysics
Peredovoi Opyt Stroit Ekspl Shakht — Peredovoi Opyt v Stroitel'stve i Ekspluatatsii Shakht
Peredovoi Opyt Stroit Eksp Shakht — Peredovoi Opyt v Stroitel'stve i Ekspluatatsii Shakht
Pererab Gaza Gazov Kondens Nauchno-Tekh Obz — Pererabotka Gaza i Gazovogo Kondensata. Nauchno-Tekhnicheskii Obzor
Pererab Margantsevykh Polimet Rud Gruz — Pererabotka Margantsevykh i Polimetallicheskikh Rud Gruzii
Pererab Neft Gazov — Pererabotka Neftyanykh Gazov
Pererab Tverd Topl — Pererabotka Tverdogo Topliva
PE Rev — Physical Education Review
Perf Art C — Performing Arts in Canada
Perf Art J — Performing Arts Journal
Perf Art R — Performing Arts Review
Perf Arts — Performing Arts in Canada
Perf Arts Can — Performing Arts in Canada
Perf Arts R — Performing Arts Review
Perf Eval — Performance Evaluation
Perf Eval Rev — Performance Evaluation Review
Performance Eval — Performance Evaluation
Performance Eval Rev — Performance Evaluation Review
Performance Instr — Performance and Instruction
Perform Eval — Performance Evaluation
Perform Eval Rev — Performance Evaluation Review
Perform High Temp Syst Proc Conf — Performance of High Temperature Systems. Proceedings. Conference
Performing Arts Rev — Performing Arts Review
Perform Instr J — Performance and Instruction Journal
Perform Monit Geotech Constr Symp — Performance Monitoring for Geotechnical Construction. Symposium
Perform Prot Clothing Symp — Performance of Protective Clothing. Symposium
Perf Right — Performing Right
Perftorirovannye Uglerody Biol Med — Perftorirovannye Uglerody v Biologii i Meditsine [*monograph*]
Perfumer — Perfumer and Flavorist
Perfumers J — Perfumers' Journal and Essential Oil Recorder
Perfumes Flavours Assoc India PAFAI J — Perfumes and Flavours Association of India. PAFAI Journal
Perfum Essent Oil Rec — Perfumery and Essential Oil Record
Perfum Flavor — Perfumer and Flavorist
Perfum Flavor Int — Perfumer and Flavorist International
Perfum Flavorist — Perfumer and Flavorist
Perfum Flavorist Int — Perfumer and Flavorist International
Perfum Flavour — Perfumery and Flavouring
Perfum J — Perfumers' Journal
Perfum Kosmet — Perfumerie und Kosmetik
PerG — Persoon en Gemeenschap
Pergamon Gen Psychol Ser — Pergamon General Psychology Series
Pergamon Internat Library Sci Tech Engrg Social Stud — Pergamon International Library of Science, Technology, Engineering, and Social Studies
Pergamon Ser Environ Sci — Pergamon Series on Environmental Science
Pergamon Ser Monogr Lab Tech — Pergamon Series of Monographs in Laboratory Techniques
Pergamon Texts Inorg Chem — Pergamon Texts in Inorganic Chemistry
Perg I S Da — Pergamon International Series on Dance and Related Disciplines
PerH — Perspectives in American History
Pericard Dis — Pericardial Diseases
Pericyclic React — Pericyclic Reactions
Perinat Med — Perinatal Medicine
Perinat Med Clin Biochem Aspects — Perinatal Medicine. Clinical and Biochemical Aspects
Perinat Med Eur Congr — Perinatal Medicine. European Congress
Perinat Med Tokyo — Perinatal Medicine (Tokyo)
Perinat Neonat — Perinatology/Neonatology
Perinatol Neonatol Dir — Perinatology-Neonatology Directory
Perinat Pharmacol Ther — Perinatal Pharmacology and Therapeutics
Perinat Physiol — Perinatal Physiology [*monograph*]
Perinat Thyroid Physiol Dis — Perinatal Thyroid Physiology and Disease
Period Anim Prod — Periodical on Animal Production
Period Biol — Periodicum Biologorum
Period Bull Int Sugar Confect Manuf Assoc Int Off Cocoa Choc — Periodic Bulletin. International Sugar Confectionery Manufacturers' Associationand International Office of Cocoa and Chocolate
Period Guide Comput — Periodical Guide for Computerists
Period Hydrol — Periodical of Hydrology
Period Mat — Periodico di Matematiche
Period Mat 5 — Periodico di Matematiche. Serie V
Period Math Hung — Periodica Mathematica Hungarica
Period Math Hungar — Periodica Mathematica Hungarica
Period Math Phys Astron — Periodicum Mathematico-Physicum et Astronomicum
Period Mineral — Periodico di Mineralogia
Periodont Abstr — Periodontal Abstracts. Journal of the Western Society of Periodontology
Periodont Case Rep — Periodontal Case Reports
Period Polytech — Periodica Polytechnica
Period Polytech Chem Eng — Periodica Polytechnica. Chemical Engineering
Period Polytech Chem Ingenieurwes — Periodica Polytechnica. Chemisches Ingenieurwesen
Period Polytech Civ Eng — Periodica Polytechnica. Civil Engineering
Period Polytech Civ Engng — Periodica Polytechnica. Civil Engineering
Period Polytech Electr Eng — Periodica Polytechnica. Electrical Engineering
Period Polytech Eng — Periodica Polytechnica. Engineering
Period Polytech Khim — Periodica Polytechnica. Khimiya

Period Polytech Masch Bauwes — Periodica Polytechnica. Maschinen- und Bauwesen
Period Polytech Mech Eng — Periodica Polytechnica. Mechanical Engineering
Period Polytech Mech Engng — Periodica Polytechnica. Mechanical Engineering
Period Polytech Phys Nucl Sci — Periodica Polytechnica. Physics and Nuclear Sciences
Period Polytech Stroit — Periodica Polytechnica. Stroitel'stvo
Period Polytech Trans Engng — Periodica Polytechnica. Transportation Engineering
Period Quin TCI — Periodico Quindicinale del Touring Club Italiano
Period Soc Med Quir Cadiz — Periodico. Sociedad Medico-Quirurgica de Cadiz
Period Soc Stor Prov & Ant Dioc Como — Periodico della Societa Storica per la Provincia e Antica Diocesi di Como
Period Speaking — Periodically Speaking
Period Stor Comense — Periodico Storico Comense. Organo della Reale Deputazione di Storia Patria per la Lombardia
Periopr Nurs Q — Perioperative Nursing Quarterly
Periph Dopaminergic Recept Proc Satell Symp — Peripheral Dopaminergic Receptors. Proceedings. Satellite Symposium
Peripher Arterial Chemorecept Proc Int Symp — Peripheral Arterial Chemoreceptors. Proceedings. International Symposium
Peripher Arterial Chemorecept Proc Int Workshop — Peripheral Arterial Chemoreceptors. Proceedings. International Workshop
Peripher Circ Man Ciba Found Symp — Peripheral Circulation in Man. Ciba Foundation Symposium
Peripher Circ Proc Int Symp — Peripheral Circulation. Proceedings. International Symposium on the Peripheral Circulation
Perit Dial Int — Peritoneal Dialysis International
Periton Dia — Peritoneal Dialysis Bulletin
Perk — Perkins Journal
Perkin Elmer Instrum News Sci Ind — Perkin-Elmer Instrument News for Science and Industry
Perkin-Elmer Tech News — Perkin-Elmer Technical News
Perkin Elmer Therm Anal Appl Study — Perkin-Elmer Thermal Analysis Application Study
Perkins J — Perkins School of Theology. Journal
Perkins Obs Contrib — Perkins Observatory Contributions
Perkins Obs Contrib Ser 2 — Perkins Observatory. Contributions. Series 2
Perkin Trans — Perkin Transactions
P Erl — Papyri der Universitaetsbibliothek Erlangen
PerManAb — Personal Management Abstracts
Permanence Org Coat Symp — Permanence of Organic Coatings. Symposium
Permanency Rep — Permanency Report
Permbledhje Stud — Permbledhje Studimesh
Permbledhje Stud Inst Kerkimeve Gjeol Miner — Permbledhje Studimesh. Instituti i Kerkimeve Gjeologjike dhe Minerale
Permbledhje Stud Inst Stud Kerkimeve Ind Miner — Permbledhje Studimesh. Instituti i Studimeve dhe Kerkimeve Industirale e Minerale
Permbledhje Stud Inst Stud Proj Gjeol Min — Permbledhje Studimesh. Instituti i Studimeve dhe i Projektimeve te Gjeologjise dhe te Minierave
Perm Found Med Bull — Permanente Foundation Medical Bulletin
Perm Found Oakland Calif Med Bull — Permanente Foundation (Oakland, California) Medical Bulletin
Perm Gos Ped Inst Ucen Zap — Permskii Gosudarstvennyi Pedagogiceskii Institut. Ucenye Zapiski
Perm Gos Univ Ucen Zap — Permskii Gosudarstvennyi Universitet Imeni A. M. Gor'kogo. Ucenye Zapiski
Perm Politehn Inst Sb Naucn Trudov — Permskii Politehniceskii Institut. Sbornik Naucnyh Trudov
Permsk Gos Farm Inst Nauchn Tr — Permskii Gosudarstvennyi Farmatsevticheskii Institut. Nauchnye Trudy
Permsk Gos Skh Inst Tr — Permskii Gosudarstvennyi Sel'skokhozyaistvennyi Institut. Trudy
Permsk Gos Skh Opytn Stn Sb Nauchn Tr — Permskaya Gosudarstvennaya Sel'skokhozyaistvennaya Opytnaya Stantsiya. Sbornik Nauchnykh Trudov
Permsk Gos Univ im AM Gorkogo Uch Zap — Permskii Gosudarstvennyi Universitet imeni A.M. Gor'kogo. Uchenye Zapiski
Permsk Nauchno Issled Ugoln Inst Nauchn Tr — Permskii Nauchno-Issledovatel'skii Ugol'nyi Institut. Nauchnye Trudy
Permsk Obl Nauchno Tekh Konf Spektrosk — Permskaya Oblastnaya Nauchno-Tekhnicheskaya Konferentsiya po Spektroskopii
Permsk Politekh Inst Nauchn Tr — Permskii Politekhnicheskii Institut. Nauchnye Trudy
Permsk Skh Inst im Akad DN Pryanishnikova Tr — Permskii Sel'skokhozyaistvennyi Institut imeni Akademika D.N. Pryanishnikova. Trudy
Perm Way — Permanent Way
Pernamb Odont — Pernambuco Odontologica
Peroxidases Chem Biol — Peroxidases in Chemistry and Biology
Perpignan Mm S Ag Pyr Orient — Societe Agricole, Scientifique, et Litteraire des Pyrenees-Orientales. Memoires (Perpignan)
Per Poly CE — Periodica Polytechnica. Chemical Engineering
Per Poly EE — Periodica Polytechnica. Electrical Engineering
Per Poly ME — Periodica Polytechnica. Mechanical Engineering
Per Pract B — Personnel Practice Bulletin
Per Psy — Personnel Psychology
Per Rel St — Perspectives in Religious Studies
Pers — Personalist
Pers — Personnel
Pers — Perspective. A Quarterly of Modern Literature
Pers — Perspektiv
Pers Adm — Personnel Administration
Pers Adm — Personnel Administrator
Pers Admin — Personnel Administrator
Pers Am Hist — Perspectives in American History

Persat Biokim Malays Proc Malays Biochem Soc Conf — Persatuan Biokimia Malaysia. Proceedings. Malaysian Biochemical Society Conference
Pers Commun — Personal Communications
Pers Comput World — Personal Computer World
Pers Eng Instrum News — Personal Engineering and Instrumentation News
Perseo — Perseo. Quindicinale di vita Italiana
Pers Finance LQ — Personal Finance Law Quarterly Report
Pers Finance LQ Rep — Personal Finance Law Quarterly Report
Pers Guid J — Personnel and Guidance Journal
Pers Indiv — Personality and Individual Differences
Pers Indiv Dif — Personality and Individual Differences
Pers Individ Differ — Personality and Individual Differences
Pers Inj Ann — Personal Injury Annual
Pers Inj Deskbook — Personal Injury Deskbook
Pers Inj LJ — Personal Injury Law Journal
Pers J — Personnel Journal
Pers Jrl — Personnel Journal
Pers Lit — Personnel Literature
Pers Man — Personnel Management
Pers Manage — Personnel Management
Pers Manage Abstr — Personnel Management Abstracts
Pers Mgmt Abstr — Personnel Management Abstracts
Pers Mgt — Personnel Management
Pers New Mus — Perspectives of New Music
Person — Personalist
Personal & Soc Psychol Bull — Personality and Social Psychology Bulletin
Personhist T — Personhistorisk Tidskrift
Person Manage Abstr — Personnel Management Abstracts
Personnel & Guid J — Personnel and Guidance Journal
Personnel Exec — Personnel Executive
Personnel Guidance J — Personnel and Guidance Journal
Personnel J — Personnel Journal
Personnel Manag (London) — Personnel Management (London)
Personnel Mgmt — Personnel Management
Personnel Mgmt P-H — Personnel Management. Prentice-Hall
Personnel Mgt Abstracts — Personnel Management Abstracts
Personnel Practice B — Personnel Practice Bulletin
Personnel Practice Bul — Personnel Practice Bulletin
Personnel Psych — Personnel Psychology
Personnel Psychol — Personnel Psychology
Personn Pract Bull — Personnel Practice Bulletin
Person Stud Group Behav — Personality Study and Group Behavior
Persp — Perspectives
Persp Biol — Perspectives in Biology and Medicine
Persp Cath — Perspectives de Catholicite
Perspec — Perspective
Perspec Biol & Med — Perspectives in Biology and Medicine
Perspec Ed — Perspectives on Education
Perspect Accredit — Perspectives on Accreditation
Perspect Amer Hist — Perspectives in American History
Perspect Am Hist — Perspectives in American History
Perspect Asthma — Perspectives in Asthma
Perspect Bioavailability Drugs Annu Symp — Perspectives in Bioavailability of Drugs. Therapeutic and Toxicological Significance. Annual Symposium. Canadian Association for Research in Toxicology
Perspect Biol Dyn Theor Med — Perspectives in Biological Dynamics and Theoretical Medicine
Perspect Biol Med — Perspectives in Biology and Medicine
Perspect Biol Med 21st Century — Perspective on Biology and Medicine in the 21st Century
Perspect Biom — Perspectives in Biometrics
Perspect Biophys Ecol — Perspectives of Biophysical Ecology
Perspect Biotechnol — Perspectives in Biotechnology
Perspect Brain Res Proc Int Summer Sch — Perspectives in Brain Research. Proceedings. International Summer School of Brain Research
Perspect Brain Sci — Perspectives in the Brain Sciences
Perspect Cancer Res Treat — Perspectives in Cancer Research and Treatment
Perspect Cardiovasc Res — Perspectives in Cardiovascular Research
Perspect Clin Endocrinol — Perspectives in Clinical Endocrinology
Perspect Clin Pharm — Perspectives in Clinical Pharmacy
Perspect Clin Pharmacol — Perspectives in Clinical Pharmacology
Perspect Coeliac Dis Proc Symp — Perspectives in Coeliac Disease. Proceedings. Symposium on Coeliac Disease
Perspect Comput — Perspectives in Computing
Perspect Cystic Fibrosis Proc Int Cystic Fibrosis Congr — Perspectives in Cystic Fibrosis. Proceedings. International Cystic Fibrosis Congress
Perspect Dev Neurobiol — Perspectives on Developmental Neurobiology
Perspect Drug Discovery Des — Perspectives in Drug Discovery and Design
Perspect Ethol — Perspectives in Ethology
Perspect Exp Biol Proc Anniv Meet Soc Exp Biol — Perspectives in Experimental Biology. Proceedings. Anniversary Meeting. Society for Experimental Biology
Perspect Grassl Ecol — Perspectives in Grassland Ecology
Perspect Hemostasis Sel Proc Symp — Perspectives in Hemostasis. Selected Proceedings. Symposia
Perspect Hum Reprod — Perspectives in Human Reproduction
Perspect Ind Microbiol Proc Symp — Perspectives in Industrial Microbiology. Proceedings. Symposium
Perspect Ind Psychol — Perspectives in Industrial Psychology
Perspect in Educ — Perspectives in Education
Perspect Inherited Metab Dis — Perspectives in Inherited Metabolic Diseases
Perspect Int — Perspectives Internationales
Perspective K — Perspective (Karachi)
Perspectives Biol Med — Perspectives in Biology and Medicine
Perspectives Civ Rights Q — Perspectives. The Civil Rights Quarterly

Perspectives Euro-Afr — Perspectives Euro-Africaines
Perspectives Latino-Am — Perspectives Latino-Americaines
Perspectives New M — Perspectives of New Music
Perspect Math — Perspectives in Mathematics
Perspect Math Logic — Perspectives in Mathematical Logic
Perspect Med — Perspectives in Medicine
Perspect Medicaid Manage — Perspectives on Medicaid Management
Perspect Medicaid Medicare Manage — Perspectives on Medicaid and Medicare Management
Perspect Membr Biol Mex Soc Biochem Symp — Perspectives in Membrane Biology. Mexican Society of Biochemistry Symposium
Perspect Membr Biophys — Perspectives in Membrane Biophysics
Perspect Mol Sieve Sci Symp Chem Congr North Am — Perspective in Molecular Sieve Science. Published in Advance of a Symposium at the Chemical Congress of North America
Perspect Nephrol Hypertens — Perspectives in Nephrology and Hypertension
Perspect Neuroendocr Res — Perspectives in Neuroendocrine Research
Perspect Ophthalmol — Perspectives in Ophthalmology
Perspect Pediatr Pathol — Perspectives in Pediatric Pathology
Perspect Polon — Perspectives Polonaises
Perspect Powder Metall — Perspectives in Powder Metallurgy
Perspect Psychiatr — Perspectives Psychiatriques
Perspect Psychiatr Care — Perspectives in Psychiatric Care
Perspect Quantum Chem Biochem — Perspectives in Quantum Chemistry and Biochemistry
Perspect Rep Ser — Perspective Report Series
Perspect Sci — Perspectives on Science. Historical, Philosophical, Social
Perspect Shock Res Proc Annu Conf Shock — Perspectives in Shock Research. Proceedings. Annual Conference on Shock
Perspect Stand Model Proc Theor Adv Study Inst Elem Part Phys — Perspectives in the Standard Model. Proceedings. Theoretical Advanced Study Institute in Elementary Particle Physics
Perspect Struct Chem — Perspectives in Structural Chemistry
Perspect Supramol Chem — Perspectives in Supramolecular Chemistry
Perspect Toxicol — Perspectives in Toxicology [*monograph*]
Perspect Vertebr Sci — Perspectives in Vertebrate Science
Perspect Virol — Perspectives in Virology
Perspekt Phil — Perspektiven der Philosophie
Perspekt Zakl Vysk Dreva Pr — Perspektivy Zakladneho Vyskuma Dreva. Prace
Persp Medit — Perspectives Mediterraneennes
Persp N Mus — Perspectives of New Music
Persp Pol — Perspectives Polonaises
Pers Prac B — Personnel Practice Bulletin
Pers Prac Bul — Personnel Practice Bulletin
Pers Pract Bull — Personnel Practice Bulletin
Pers Pract Newsl — Personnel Practices Newsletter
Persp Soc — Perspectives Socialistes
Pers Psych — Personnel Psychology
Pers Psych C — Perspectives in Psychiatric Care
Pers Psychol — Personnel Psychology
Pers Psychopathol — Personality and Psychopathology
Persp Teol — Perspectiva Teologica
Persp USA — Perspectives USA
Pers Rep Exec — Personal Report for the Executive
Pers V — Personalvertretung
Pertanika J Trop Agric Sci — Pertanika Journal of Tropical Agricultural Science
Peru Dir Gen Mineria Bol — Peru. Ministerio de Fomento y Obras Publicas. Direccion General de Mineria. Boletin
Perugia Quadrenn Int Conf Cancer Proc — Perugia Quadrennial International Conference on Cancer. Proceedings
Peru Indig — Peru Indigena
Peru Inst Nac Invest Fom Min Bol — Peru. Instituto Nacional de Investigacion y Fomento Mineros. Boletin
Peru Inst Nac Invest Fom Min Ser Memo — Peru. Instituto Nacional de Investigacion y Fomento Mineros. Serie Memorandum
Peru Minist Agric Dir Gen Agric Bol — Peru. Ministerio de Agricultura. Direccion General de Agricultura. Boletin
Peru Minist Agric Dir Gen Invest Agropecu Bol Tec — Peru. Ministerio de Agricultura. Direccion General de Investigaciones Agropecuarias. Boletin Tecnico
Peru Minist Agric Serv Invest Promoc Agrar Bol Tec — Peru. Ministerio de Agricultura. Servicio de Investigacion y Promocion Agraria.Boletin Tecnico
Peru Minist Energ Minas Serv Geol Min Estud Espec — Peru. Ministerio de Energia y Minas. Servicio de Geologia y Mineria. Estudios Especiales
Peru Minist Fom Obras Publicas Inst Nac Invest Fom Min Bol — Peru. Ministerio de Fomento y Obras Publicas. Instituto Nacional de Investigacion y Fomento Mineros. Boletin
Peru Repub Minist Fom OP Dir Min Com Carta Geol Nac Bol — Peru. Republica. Ministerio de Fomento O.P. Direccion de Mineria. Comision Carta Geologica Nacional. Boletin
PerUSA — Perspectives USA
Peru Serv Geol Min Bol — Peru. Servicio de Geologia y Mineria. Boletin
Peru Serv Geol Min Estud Espec — Peru. Servicio de Geologia y Mineria. Estudios Especiales
Peru Serv Geol Min Geodinamica Ing Geol — Peru. Servicio de Geologia y Mineria. Geodinamica e Ingenieria Geologica
Pervyi Globalnyi Eksp PIGAP — Pervyi Global'nyi Eksperiment PIGAP (Programma Issledovaniya Global'nykh Atmosfernykh Protsessov)
PERY — Ethnohistory
PES — Polish Economic Survey
Pesca Mar — Pesca y Marina
Pesca Pesqui — Pesca y Pesquisa
PESC Rec IEEE Annu Power Electron Spec Conf — PESC Record. IEEE Annual Power Electronics Specialists Conference

PESC Rec IEEE Power Electron Spec Conf — PESC Record. IEEE [*Institute of Electrical and Electronics Engineers*] Power Electronics Specialists Conference
Peshawar Univ Dep Geol Geol Bull — Peshawar. University. Department of Geology. Geological Bulletin
Peshchery Gruz — Peshchery Gruzii
PESI — Physical Education/Sports Index
PESOD — Proceedings. Electrochemical Society
PEsp — Poesia Espanola
PESPD — Periodically Speaking
Pesqu — Pesquisas
Pesqui Agropecuar Brasil Ser Agron — Pesquisa Agropecuaria Brasileira. Serie Agronomia
Pesqui Agropecuar Brasil Ser Vet — Pesquisa Agropecuaria Brasileira. Serie Veterinaria
Pesqui Agropecu Bras — Pesquisa Agropecuaria Brasileira
Pesqui Agropecu Bras Ser Agron — Pesquisa Agropecuaria Brasileira. Serie Agronomia
Pesqui Agropecu Bras Ser Vet — Pesquisa Agropecuaria Brasileira. Serie Veterinaria
Pesqui Agropecu Bras Ser Zootec — Pesquisa Agropecuaria Brasileira. Serie Zootecnia
Pesqui Agropecu Nordeste Recife — Pesquisas Agropecuarias do Nordeste Recife
Pesqui Agropecu Pernambucana — Pesquisa Agropecuaria Pernambucana
Pesqui Apl Lat Am — Pesquisa Aplicada Latino Americana
Pesqui Bot (Porto Alegre) — Pesquisas Botanica (Porto Alegre)
Pesqui Commun (Porto Alegre) — Pesquisas Communications (Porto Alegre)
Pesqui Med — Pesquisa Medica
Pesquisa e Planejamento Econ — Pesquisa e Planejamento Economico
Pesquisas Antropol — Pesquisas Antropologia
Pesquisas Univ Fed Rio Grande Sul Inst Geocienc — Pesquisas. Universidade Federal do Rio Grande do Sul. Instituto de Geociencias
Pesqui Secc B Cienc Nat (Porto Alegre) — Pesquisas. Seccao B. Ciencias Naturais (Porto Alegre)
Pesqui Vet Bras — Pesquisa Veterinaria Brasileira
Pesqui Zool (Porto Alegre) — Pesquisas Zoologia (Porto Alegre)
PESR — Earth-Science Reviews
Pest Artic News Summ — Pest Articles and News Summaries
Pest Art News Sum — Pest Articles and News Summaries
Pest Bioch — Pesticide Biochemistry and Physiology
Pest Contr — Pest Control
Pest Contro — Pest Control
Pest Control Circ — Pest Control Circular
PESTD — Proceedings. European Society of Toxicology
PESTDOC — Pest Control Literature Documentation
Pester Med Chir Presse — Pester Medicinisch-Chirurgische Presse
Pestic Abstr — Pesticides Abstracts and News Summary
Pestic Abstr News Sum Sect C Herbic — Pesticides Abstracts and News Summary. Section C. Herbicides
Pestic Anal — Pesticide Analysis
Pestic Aquat Environ — Pesticides in Aquatic Environments
Pestic Biochem Physiol — Pesticide Biochemistry and Physiology
Pestic Chem Proc Int IUPAC Congr Pestic Chem — Pesticide Chemistry. Proceedings. International IUPAC Congress of Pesticide Chemistry
Pestic CIPAC Methods Proc Ser — Pesticides. CIPAC [*Collaborative International Pesticides Analytical Council*] Methods and Proceedings Series
Pestic Doc Bull — Pesticides Documentation Bulletin
Pestic Environ — Pesticides in the Environment
Pestic Formulations Appl Syst — Pesticide Formulations and Application Systems
Pestic Formulations Appl Syst Conf — Pesticide Formulations and Application Systems. Conference
Pestic Formulations Appl Syst Symp — Pesticide Formulations and Application Systems. Symposium
Pesticide A — Pesticides Annual
Pestic Monit J — Pesticides Monitoring Journal
Pestic Progr — Pesticide Progress
Pestic Res Bull — Pesticide Research Bulletin
Pestic Res Rep — Pesticide Research Report
Pestic Res Rep Agric Can — Pesticide Research Report. Agriculture Canada
Pestic Sci — Pesticide Science
Pestic Sci Biotechnol Proc Int Congr Pestic Chem — Pesticide Science and Biotechnology. Proceedings. International Congress of Pesticide Chemistry
Pestic Sel — Pesticide Selectivity
Pestic Tank Mix Appl Conf — Pesticide Tank Mix Applications. Conference
Pestic Tech — Pesticide and Technique
Pestic Toxic Chem News — Pesticide and Toxic Chemical News
Pestic Toxic Subst Mon Rep — Pesticides and Toxic Substances Monitoring Report
Pestic Venom Neurotoxic Sel Pap Int Congr Entomol — Pesticide and Venom Neurotoxicity. Selected Papers from the International Congress of Entomology
Pest Infest Control Lab Rep (Lond) — Pest Infestation Control. Laboratory Report (London)
Pest Infest Control (Lond) — Pest Infestation Control. Laboratory Report (London)
Pest Infest Res Rep Pest Infest Lab Agric Res Counc — Pest Infestation Research Report. Pest Infestation Laboratory. Agricultural Research Council
Pest Leafl Pac For Res Cent — Pest Leaflet. Pacific Forest Research Centre
Pest Manag Sci — Pest Management Science
Pest Mon J — Pesticides Monitoring Journal
Pest Sci — Pesticide Science
Pestyc Swietle Toksykol Srodowiska — Pestycydy w Swietle Toksykologii Srodowiska
PESW — Proceedings of the Entomological Society of Washington, D.C
PESY — People Say. Bimonthly Newsletter
Pet — Peters Notes
Pet Abstr — Petroleum Abstracts

Pet Abstracts — Petroleum Abstracts
Pet Age — Petroleum Age
Pet & Gaze — Petrol si Gaze
PETC — Et Cetera
Pet Chem — Petroleum Chemistry
Pet Chem Ind Conf Rec Conf Pap — Petroleum and Chemical Industry Conference. Record of Conference Papers
Pet Chem Ind Dev — Petroleum and Chemical Industry Developments
Pet Chem Ind Dev Annu — Petroleum and Chemical Industry Developments. Annual
Pet Chem USSR — Petroleum Chemistry USSR
Pet Chem USSR Engl Transl — Petroleum Chemistry USSR (English Translation)
Pet Coal — Petroleum and Coal
Pet Econ — Petroleum Economist
Pet Econ — Petroleum Economy
Pet Energy Bus News Index — Petroleum/Energy Business News Index
Pet Eng — Petroleum Engineer
Pet Eng Dallas — Petroleum Engineer (Dallas)
Pet Eng Int — Petroleum Engineer International
Pet Eng Los Angeles — Petroleum Engineering (Los Angeles)
Pet Eng Manage — Petroleum Engineer for Management
Pet Equip — Petroleum Equipment
Pet Equip Serv — Petroleum Equipment and Services
Petera Stuckas Latv Valsts Univ Bot Darza Raksti — Petera Stuckas Latvijas Valsts Universitates Botaniska Darza Raksti
Peterborough Mus Soc Occas Pap — Peterborough Museum Society. Occasional Papers
Petergof Biol Inst Tr Leningr Gos Univ im AA Zhdanova — Petergofskii Biologicheskii Institut. Trudy (Leningradskii Gosudarstvennyi Universitet imeni A.A. Zhdanova)
Petermanns Geog Mitt — Petermanns Geographische Mitteilungen
Petermanns Geogr Mitt — Petermanns Geographische Mitteilungen
Petermanns Mitt — Petermanns. A. Mitteilungen aus J. Perthes Geographischer Anstalt
Petermanns Mitteil — Petermanns Mitteilungen, aus Justus Perthes Geographischer Anstalt
Petermanns Mitt Erg — Petermanns Mitteilungen. Ergaenzungsheft
Peterm Geog — Petermanns Geographische Mitteilungen
Peterm Mt — Mittheilungen aus Justus Perthes' Geographischer Anstalt ueber Wichtige neue Erforschungen auf dem Gesammtgebiete der Geographie. Petermann
Peter Phot Mag — Petersen's Photographic Magazine
Peters Zschr — Zeitschrift fuer Populaere Mitteilungen aus dem Gebiete der Astronomie und Verwandter Wissenschaften (Von C. A. F. Peters)
Pet Explor Dev — Petroleum Exploration and Development
Pet Front — Petroleum Frontiers
Pet Gas Process — Petroleum and Gas Processing
Pet Gaz — Petroleum Gazette
Pet Gaz (Budapest) — Petrole et Gaz (Budapest)
Pet Gaze — Petrol si Gaze
Pet Gaze Supl — Petrol si Gaze. Supliment
Pet Geogr Mitt — Petermanns Geographische Mitteilungen
Pet Geol — Petroleum Geology
Pet Geol Engl Transl — Petroleum Geology (English Translation)
Pet Geol Taiwan — Petroleum Geology of Taiwan
Pet Global Tecton Pap Meet Princeton Univ Conf — Petroleum and Global Tectonics. Papers Presented at the Meeting. Princeton University Conference
PETH — Ethics
Pet Hydrocarbons — Petroleum and Hydrocarbons
Pet Hydrocarbons Mar Environ Proc ICES Workshop — Petroleum Hydrocarbons in the Marine Environment. Proceedings from ICES Workshop
Pet Ind — Petroleum-Industrie
Pet Ind Aserb — Petroleum-Industrie von Aserbaidshan
Pet Indep — Petroleum Independent
Pet Ind USSR — Petroleum Industry of the USSR
Pet Inf — Petrole Informations
Pet Int — Petroleo Internacional
Pet Interam — Petroleo Interamericano
Pet Interamericano — Petroleo Interamericano
Pet Int Great Neck NY — Petroleo Internacional (Great Neck, New York)
Pet Int Hong Kong — Petroleo Internacional (Hong Kong)
Pet Int (London) — Petroleum International (London)
Pet Int Milan — Petrolieri International (Milan)
Pet Int Tulsa Okla — Petroleo Internacional (Tulsa, Oklahoma)
Pet Ital — Petrolieri d'Italia
Petit Colosse Simi — Petit Colosse de Simi
Petit Fr Illus — Petit Francais Illustre
Petit J Brass — Petit Journal du Brasseur
Petit Paris — Petit Parisien
Petkim Derg — Petkim Dergisi
Petkim Petrokimya AS Arastirma Mudurlugu Tek Bul — Petkim Petrokimya A.S. Arastirma Mudurlugu. Teknik Bulten
Pet Land J — Petroleum Land Journal
Pet Mag — Petroleum Magazine
Pet Manage — Petroleum Management
Pet Mech Eng ASME — Petroleum Mechanical Engineering (ASME)
Pet Microorg (Tokyo) — Petroleum and Microorganisms (Tokyo)
Pet Mitt — Petermanns Mitteilungen
Pet News — Petroleum News
Pet Newsl — Petroleum Newsletter
PETOA — Petrotecnica
Pet Oelschieferind — Petroleum und Oelschieferindustrie
Pet Oil Shale Ind — Petroleum and Oil-Shale Industry
Pet Outlook — Petroleum Outlook
Pet Petrochem — Petroleum and Petrochemicals

Pet Petrochem Int — Petroleum and Petrochemical International
Pet Petrochem (Tokyo) — Petroleum and Petrochemicals (Tokyo)
Pet P M — Petersen's Photographic Magazine
Pet Press Serv — Petroleum Press Service
Pet Press Service — Petroleum Press Service
Pet Process — Petroleum Processing
Pet Process Beijing — Petroleum Processing (Beijing)
Pet Process Eng — Petroleum Process Engineering
PETRASAFE — Petroleum Transport Scheme for Assistance in Freight Emergencies
PETRB — Petroleum Review
PETRD — Petrologie
Pet Refin — Petroleum Refiner
Pet Refin — Petroleum Refining
Pet Refiner — Petroleum Refiner
Pet Refin Petrochem Lit Abstr — Petroleum Refining and Petrochemicals Literature Abstracts
Pet Refin Petrochem Process — Petroleum Refining and Petrochemical Processing
Pet Refin US US Terr — Petroleum Refineries in the United States and U.S. Territories
Pet Rev — Petrocorp Review
Pet Rev — Petroleum Review
Pet Rev Deux Mond Geogr Hist — Petite Revue des Deux Mondes de Geographie et d'Histoire
Petr Inde — Petroleum Independent
PETROCH — Rock Chemical Database
Petro/Chem Eng — Petro/Chem Engineer
Petrochem Equip — Petrochemical Equipment
Petrochem Ind — Petrochemical Industry
Petrochem Technol Beijing — Petrochemical Technology (Beijing)
Petrogr Appl Concr Concr Aggregates — Petrography Applied to Concrete and Concrete Aggregates
Petrogr Tsentr Kaz — Petrografiya Tsentral'nogo Kazakhstana
Petrogr Vost Sib — Petrografiya Vostochnoi Sibiri
Petrokhim Kriter Rudonosn Magmat Kompleksov — Petrokhimiya. Kriterii Rudonosnosti Magmaticheskikh Kompleksov
Petrol Abstr — Petroleum Abstracts
Petrol Eng — Petroleum Engineer
Petrol Eng Int — Petroleum Engineer International
Petroleo — Petroleo Internacional
Petroleos Mexicanos Servicio Inf — Petroleos Mexicanos Servicio de Informacion
Petroleum — Petroleum Economist
Petroleum Gaz — Petroleum Gazette
Petrol Gaz — Petroleum Gazette
Petrol Geol — Petroleum Geology
Petrolieri Int — Petrolieri International
Petrol Independ — Petroleum Independent
Petrol Inform — Petrole Informations
Petrol Int — Petroleo Internacional
Petrol News — Petroleum News
Petrol Ref — Petroleum Refiner
Petrol Rev — Petroleum Review
Petrol Tech — Petrole et Techniques
Petrol Technol — Petroleum Technology
Petrol Tecnol — Petroleo y Tecnologia
Petro Sit — Petroleum Situation
Petro Times — Petroleum Times
Petrozavodsk Gos Univ Ucen Zap — Petrozavodskii Gosudarstvennyi Universitet. Ucenye Zapiski
Petr Prog — Petrole-Progres
Petr Sit — Petroleum Situation
Petr Techn — Petroleum Technology
Petr Times — Petroleum Times
Petr Tm R — Petroleum Times Price Report
Pet Sci Technol — Petroleum Science and Technology
PETSE — Papers. Estonian Theological Society in Exile
Pet Ses Deriv — Petrole et Ses Derives
Pet Soc CIM Annu Tech Meet — Petroleum Society of CIM. Annual Technical Meeting
Pet Statement Energy Data Rep — Petroleum Statement. Energy Data Reports
Pet Substitutes — Petroleum Substitutes
Pet Supply Mon — Petroleum Supply Monthly
PETTA — Petroleum Times
Pet Tech — Petrole et Techniques
Pet Technol — Petroleum Technology
Pet Technol London — Petroleum Technology (London)
Pet Tech Rev — Petroleum Technical Review
Pet Times — Petroleum Times
Pet Today — Petroleum Today
Petty SR — Petty Sessions Review
PETU — Ethnomusicology
Pet W — Petroleum Week
Pet Week — Petroleum Week
Pet Wirtsch — Petroleum-Wirtschaft
Pet World — Petroleum World
Pet World (London) — Petroleum World (London)
Pet World (Los Angeles) — Petroleum World (Los Angeles)
Pet World Oil — Petroleum World and Oil
Pet World Oil Age — Petroleum World and Oil Age
PEUBA — Publikacije Elektrotehnickog Fakulteta Univerziteta u Beogradu. Serija Matematika i Fizika
Peuples Medit Medit Peoples — Peuples Mediterraneens/Mediterranean Peoples
PEUS — Journal of European Studies
PEV — Presencia Ecumenica (Venezuela)

P Evang — Pentecostal Evangel
PEVO — Evolution
PEW — Philosophy East and West
PEW — Politiek Economisch Weekblad
PEY — Papers from the Eranos Yearbooks
Pez & Serpiente — Pez y la Serpiente
PF — Paedagogische Forschungen
PF — Pennsylvania Folklife
PF — Pensee Francaise
PF — Pergamenische Forschungen
PF — Philosophische Forschungen
PF — Philosophy Forum
PF — Poesie Francaise
PF — Polish Folklore
PF — Popular Foodservice
PF — Prace Filologiczne
PF — Psychologische Forschung
PF — Public Finance
PFA — Korte Berichten over Buitenlandse Projecten
PfA — Pfluegers Archiv fuer die Gesamte Physiologie
Pf A — Pfluegers Archiv fuer die Gesamte Physiologie des Menschen und der Tiere
PFA — Public Finance and Accountancy
Pfaelzer H — Pfaelzer Heimat
Pfaelz Gartenzeitung — Pfaelzische Gartenzeitung
Pfaelz Heimat — Pfaelzer Heimat
Pfaelz Rdsch — Pfaelzische Rundschau
Pfaff Mt — Mittheilungen Practische und Kritische Mittheilungen aus dem Gebiete der Medicin, Chirurgie, und Pharmacie. Pfaff
Pfalzbaier Mus — Pfalzbaierisches Museum
Pfalz Heimat — Pfalzer Heimat. Zeitschrift fuer Pfalzische Landeskunde
PFA Q Mag — P.F.A. Quarterly Magazine [Sydney]
PFATA — Problemy Fiziki Atmosfery
P Fay — Fayum Towns and their Papyri
PFBFA — Power Farming and Better Farming Digest (Australia)
PFBI — FBI Law Enforcement Bulletin
P F Bol Inform Patrimonio Forest Estado — PF. Boletin Informativo de Patrimonio Forestal del Estado
PFC — Progressive Fish-Culturist
PFCUA — Progressive Fish-Culturist
PFE — Paper, Film, and Foil Converter
Pfefferkorn Conf — Pfefferkorn Conference
PFEH — Papers on Far Eastern History
PFEM — Feminist Review
PFF Convrt — Paper, Film, and Foil Converter
PFF Convt — Paper, Film, and Foil Converter
PfGg — Professional Geographer
PFGGA — Professional Geographer
PfH — Pfaelzer Heimat
PfH — Pfaelzische Heimatblaetter
PFHEDE — Pfaelzer Heimat
PfHK — Pfaelzische Heimatkunde
PFHS — French Historical Studies
PFI — Profile Index. Micromedia Ltd.
PFII — Prace Filologiczne
PFil — Przeglad Filozoficzny
Pfitzner — Hans Pfitzner-Gesellschaft. Mitteilungen
Pfizer Med Monogr — Pfizer Medical Monographs
PFL — Pennsylvania Folklife
PFL — Publications de la Faculte de l'Universite de Lille
PFLA — Publications. Faculte des Lettres et Sciences Humaines d'Alger
PFLAB — Pfluegers Archiv. European Journal of Physiology
Pflanzenphysiol Untersuch — Pflanzenphysiologische Untersuchungen
Pflanzenschutzber — Pflanzenschutzberichte
Pflanzenschutz-Nachr — Pflanzenschutz-Nachrichten
Pflanzenschutz-Nachr (Am Ed) — Pflanzenschutz-Nachrichten (American Edition)
Pflanzenschutz-Nachr Bayer — Pflanzenschutz-Nachrichten Bayer
Pflanzenschutz Nachr Bayer (Ger Ed) — Pflanzenschutz-Nachrichten Bayer (German Edition)
Pflanzenschutz Schaedlingsbekaempf — Pflanzenschutz und Schaedlingsbekaempfung
Pflanzenschutz Wiss Wirtsch — Pflanzenschutz, Wissenschaft, und Wirtschaft
Pflanz-Nach Bayer — Pflanzenschutz-Nachrichten Bayer
PflBau PflSchutz PflZucht — Pflanzenbau, Pflanzenschutz, Pflanzenzucht
PFLDA — Physics of Fluids
PFLFT — Pubblicazioni. Facolta di Lettere e Filosofia. Universita di Torino
PFLSA — Physics of Fluids. Supplement
PFLSH — Publications. Faculte des Lettres et Sciences Humaines de Paris
Pflueg Arch — Pfluegers Archiv. European Journal of Physiology
Pflueg Arch Pl — Archiv fuer die Gesammte Physiologie des Menschen und der Thiere. Pflueger
Pfluegers Arch — Pfluegers Archiv. European Journal of Physiology
Pfluegers Arch Eur J Physiol — Pfluegers Archiv. European Journal of Physiology
Pfluegers Arch Ges Physiol — Pfluegers Archiv fuer die Gesamte Physiologie
Pfluegers Archiv Gesamte Physiol Menschen Tiere — Pfluegers Archiv fuer die Gesamte Physiologie des Menschen und der Tiere
PFLUS — Publications. Faculte des Lettres. Universite de Strasbourg
PFLUT — Pubblicazioni. Facolta di Lettres e Filosofia. Universita di Torino
PfM — Pfaelzer Museum und Pfaelzische Heimatkunde
PFNA N — PFNA [Pentecostal Fellowship of North America] News
P Fouad — Papyrus Fouad I
PFPR — Federal Probation
PFPXA6 — Pediatric Continuing Education Courses for the Practitioner
PFQ — Public Finance Quarterly
PFR — Polish Fortnightly Review
PFr — Presence Francophone

P Freib — Mitteilungen aus der Freiburger Papyrussammlung
PFRS — French Studies
PFS — Progress in Filtration and Separation
PFS — Strasbourg. Universite. Faculte des Lettres. Publications
P Fsch — Philosophische Forschungen
PFSCL — Papers on French Seventeenth Century Literature
PFSM — Physical Fitness/Sports Medicine
PFSN — Food Sciences and Nutrition
PFSR — Journal of Feminist Studies in Religion
PFT — Pedagogiska Foereningen Tidskrift
PFTUL — Publications. Faculte de Theologie. Universite Lovanium
PFW — Publications. Frederick Webb Hodge Anniversary Publications Fund [*Los Angeles*]
PG — Palestine Gazette
PG — Patrologia Graeca
PG — Pero Galego
PG — Politie-Gids
PG — Przeglad Geograficzny
PGA — Printing and Graphic Arts
PGA — Public General Acts and Church Assembly Measure
PGAEA — Proceedings. Geologists' Association (England)
PGAR — Georgia Review
PGAR — Persian Gulf Administration Report
PGAZA — Petrol si Gaze
PGC — Pelican Gospel Commentaries
PGC — Publicaciones del Grupo de Caracas de la Sociedad Interamericana de Antropologia y Geografia
PGD — Personnel and Guidance Journal
PGDRE — Papyrus Grecs et Demotiques Recueillis en Egypte
PGEB — Papyrus Grecs d'Epoque Byzantine
PGen — Papyrus de Geneve
PGEO — Geography
PGER — Geographical Review
PGFC — Periodical Guide for Computerists
PGfM — Publikationen Aelterer Praktischer und Theoretischer Musik-Werke
PGFS — Pennsylvania German Folklore Society. Bulletin
PGGJ-A — Philippine Geographical Journal
PGgM — Petermanns Geographische Mitteilungen
PGGUDU — Annual Research Reviews. Prostaglandins and the Gut
Pgh Leg Journal — Pittsburgh Legal Journal
PGHTA — Progress in Hemostasis and Thrombosis
PGiess — Griechische Papyri im Museum des Oberhessischen Geschichtsvereins zu Giessen
PGJ — Personnel and Guidance Journal
PGK — Preussischer Gesamtkatalog
PGL — Patristic Greek Lexicon
PGM — Papyri Graecae Magicae
PGM — Petermanns Geographische Mitteilungen
PGM — Postgraduate Medicine
PGM — Program Manager
PGMAPLB — Papyri Graeci Musei Antiquarii Publici Lugduni-Batavi
PGM E — Petermanns Geographische Mitteilungen. Ergaenzungshefte
PGMT — Pelican Guide to Modern Theology
PGN — Piano Guild Notes
PGNGD — Prace Instytutu Gornictwa Naftowego i Gazownictwa
PGNMA — Progress in Nuclear Medicine
PGNO — Government and Opposition
PGNR — Greece and Rome
PGNS — Polar Gas News
PGNY — Journals of Gerontology
PGO — Progressive Grocer
P Goodsp Cair — Greek Papyri from the Cairo Museum. Together with Papyri of Roman Egypt from American Collections. Goodspeed
P Goth — Papyrus Grecs de la Bibliotheque Municipale de Gothenbourg
PGP — Photogeometric Pottery
PGPKA — Problemy Gematologii i Perelivaniya Krovi
PGPRAR — Persian Gulf Political Residency Administration Reports
PGPSDZ — Pergamon General Psychology Series
PGR — Pakistan Geographical Review
PGR — Paradoxographorum Graecorum Reliquiae
P Gr — Patrologia Graeca
PGR — Plant Growth Regulation
Pgr — Progressive Grocer
PGRAA — Progressive Architecture
PGRB — Greek, Roman, and Byzantine Studies
PGRGK — Publikationen der Gesellschaft fuer Rheinische Geschichtskunde
PGRSA Q — PGRSA (Plant Growth Regulator Society of America) Quarterly
PGS — Pennsylvania German Society. Proceedings and Addresses
PGS — Proceedings. Royal Geographical Society
PGSP — Pennsylvania German Society. Proceedings and Addresses
PGST — Grand Street
PGSW — Journal of Gerontological Social Work
PGT — Planned Giving Today
PGTAA — Prager Tieraerztliches Archiv
PGTWA — Petroleum Geology of Taiwan
PGW — Philosophie und Grenzwissenschaften
PH — Paedigogica Historica
PH — Pakistan Horizon
PH — Palabra y el Hombre. Revista de la Universidad Veracruzana
PH — Pennsylvania History
Ph — Philologus. Zeitschrift fuer Klassische Altertum
Ph — Philosophisches Jahrbuch
Ph — Philosophy
Ph — Phoenix
Ph — Phylon

PH — Practical Homeowner
PH — Primitive Heritage. Margaret Mead and Nicolas Calas [*New York*]
PH — Provence Historique
PH — Przeglad Historyczny
PHA — Pharmaceutisch Weekblad
Pha — Philologica
PhA — Philologischer Anzeiger
PhA — Philologischer Anzeiger als Ergaenzung des Philologus
PHA — Philosophia Antiqua
Ph A — Philosophische Abhandlungen
Phab — Philosophic Abstracts
Ph AB — Philosophische Abhandlungen (Berlin)
PhAb — Photographic Abstracts
PHACCK — PHAC. Pathologie Humaine et Animale Comparee
PHAC Pathol Hum Anim Comp — PHAC. Pathologie Humaine et Animale Comparee
PHAGA — Philippine Agriculturist
PHAH — Hispanic American Historical Review
PHal — Dikaiomata. Auszuege aus Alexandrinischen Gesetzen und Verordnungen in einem Papyrus des Philologischen Seminars der Universitaet Halle
Phal — Phalange
P Halle — Dikaiomata. Auszuege aus Alexandrinischen Gesetzen und Verordnungen in einem Papyrus des Philologischen Seminars der Universitaet Halle
P Hamb — Griechische Papyrusurkunden der Hamburger Staats- und Universitaetsbibliothek
Ph & Phen R — Philosophy and Phenomenological Research
Ph & Rh — Philosophy and Rhetoric
Phanerogamarum Monogr — Phanerogamarum Monographiae
Ph Ant — Philosophia Antiqua
Phar — Pharaons
PHARA — Pharmazie
Pharm Abstr — Pharmaceutical Abstracts
Pharmaceutical J — Pharmaceutical Journal and Transactions
Pharmacochem Libr — Pharmacochemistry Library
Pharmacoepidemiol Drug Saf — Pharmacoepidemiology and Drug Safety
Pharmacogn Phytochem Int Congr — Pharmacognosy and Phytochemistry. International Congress
Pharmacog Tit — Pharmacognosy Titles
Pharmacol — Pharmacology
Pharmacol Basis Migraine Ther Pap Int Symp — Pharmacological Basis on Migraine Therapy. Papers. International Symposium
Pharmacol Basis Small Anim Med — Pharmacological Basis of Small Animal Medicine [*monograph*]
Pharmacol Basis Ther — Pharmacological Basis of Therapeutics [*monograph*]
Pharmacol Biochem Behav — Pharmacology, Biochemistry, and Behavior
Pharmacol Biochem Prop Drug Subst — Pharmacological and Biochemical Properties of Drug Substances
Pharmacol Clin — Pharmacologia Clinica
Pharmacol Commun — Pharmacology Communications
Pharmacol Cond Learn Retention Proc Int Pharmacol Meet — Pharmacology of Conditioning, Learning, and Retention. Proceedings. International Pharmacological Meeting
Pharmacol Eating Disord — Pharmacology of Eating Disorders (Monograph). Theoretical and ClinicalDevelopments
Pharmacol Eff Lipids — Pharmacological Effect of Lipids
Pharmacol Med — Pharmacology in Medicine
Pharmacolog — Pharmacologist
Pharmacol Physicians — Pharmacology for Physicians
Pharmacol R — Pharmacological Research Communications
Pharmacol Res — Pharmacological Research
Pharmacol Res Commun — Pharmacological Research Communications
Pharmacol Rev — Pharmacological Reviews
Pharmacol Rev Commun — Pharmacology Reviews and Communications
Pharmacol Skin — Pharmacology and the Skin
Pharmacol Sleep — Pharmacology of Sleep
Pharmacol Ther — Pharmacology and Therapeutics
Pharmacol Ther (B) — Pharmacology and Therapeutics. Part B. General and Systematic Pharmacology
Pharmacol Ther Dent — Pharmacology and Therapeutics in Dentistry
Pharmacol Ther Part A Chemother Toxicol Metab Inhibitors — Pharmacology and Therapeutics. Part A. Chemotherapy, Toxicology, and Metabolic Inhibitors
Pharmacol Ther Part B Gen Syst Pharmacol — Pharmacology and Therapeutics. Part B. General and Systematic Pharmacology
Pharmacol Ther Part C — Pharmacology and Therapeutics. Part C. Clinical Pharmacology and Therapeutics
Pharmacol Toxicol (Amsterdam) — Pharmacology and Toxicology (Amsterdam)
Pharmacol Toxicol (Copenhagen) — Pharmacology and Toxicology (Copenhagen)
Pharmacol Toxicol (Engl Transl) — Pharmacology and Toxicology (English Translation of Farmakologiya Toksikologiya)
Pharmacol Toxicol Mannheim — Pharmacology and Toxicology (Mannheim)
Pharmacol Toxicol (USSR) — Pharmacology and Toxicology (USSR)
Pharmac Res — Pharmacological Research
Pharm Acta Helv — Pharmaceutica Acta Helvetiae
Pharm Act H — Pharmaceutica Acta Helvetiae
Pharma Int — Pharma International
Pharma Int Engl Ed — Pharma International (English Edition)
Pharma Jpn — Pharma Japan
Pharmakeutikon Delt Epistem Ekodosis — Pharmakeutikon Deltion. Epistemonike Ekodosis
Pharmakopsy — Pharmakopsychiatrie Neuro-Psychopharmakologie
Pharmakopsychiatr Neuro-Psychopharmakol — Pharmakopsychiatrie Neuro-Psychopharmakologie
Pharma Med — Pharma Medica
Pharm Aquitaine — Pharmacien d'Aquitaine

Pharm Arch — Pharmaceutical Archives
Pharma Technol J — Pharma Technologie Journal
Pharmazie Beih — Pharmazie. Beihefte
Pharm Ber — Pharmazeutische Berichte
Pharm Betr — Pharmazeutische Betrieb
Pharm Bio B — Pharmacology, Biochemistry, and Behavior
Pharm Bioequivalence — Pharmaceutical Bioequivalence
Pharm Biol — Pharmacien Biologiste
Pharm Biol Lisse Neth — Pharmaceutical Biology (Lisse, Netherlands)
Pharm Biotechnol — Pharmaceutical Biotechnology
Pharm Biotechnol Int — Pharmaceutical Biotechnology International
Pharm Bull — Pharmaceutical Bulletin
Pharm Bull Fukuoka Univ — Pharmaceutical Bulletin. Fukuoka University
Pharm Bull Nihon Univ — Pharmaceutical Bulletin. Nihon University
Pharm Bus News — Pharmaceutical Business News
Pharm Centralbl — Pharmaceutisches Centralblatt
Pharm Chem J — Pharmaceutical Chemistry Journal
Pharm Chem J (Engl Transl Khim Farm Zh) — Pharmaceutical Chemistry Journal (English Translation of Khimiko-Farmatsevticheskii Zhurnal)
Pharm Chem J (USSR) — Pharmaceutical Chemistry Journal (USSR)
PharmChem Newsl (Menlo Park Calif) — PharmChem Newsletter (Menlo Park, California)
Pharm Correspondenzbl Sueddeutschl — Pharmaceutisches Correspondenzblatt fuer Sueddeutschland Nebst Anzeigeblatt
Pharm Cosmet — Pharmaceuticals and Cosmetics
Pharm Cosmet Rev — Pharmaceutical and Cosmetics Review
Pharm Delt Epistem Ekdosis — Pharmkeutikon Deltion Epistemonike Ekdosis
Pharm Dev Technol — Pharmaceutical Development and Technology
Pharm Era — Pharmaceutical Era
Pharm Fr — Pharmacien de France
Pharm Heute — Pharmazie Heute
Pharm Hist — Pharmacy in History
Pharm Hist Gt Br — Pharmaceutical Historian (Great Britain)
Pharm Hosp Fr — Pharmacie Hospitaliere Francaise
Pharm Ind — Pharmazeutische Industrie
Pharm Ind (Shanghai) — Pharmaceutical Industry (Shanghai)
Pharm Ind Yugosl — Pharmaceutical Industry of Yugoslavia
Pharm Int — Pharmacy International
Pharm J — Pharmaceutical Journal
Pharm J (Dunedin NZ) — Pharmaceutical Journal (Dunedin, New Zealand)
Pharm J (Kiev) — Pharmazeutisches Journal (Kiev)
Pharm J NZ — Pharmaceutical Journal of New Zealand
Pharm J Pharm — Pharmaceutical Journal and Pharmacist
Pharm JTPA — Pharmacia-JTPA
Pharm J Trans — Pharmaceutical Journal and Transactions. Pharmaceutical Society of Great Britain
Pharm Libr Bull — Pharmaceutical Library Bulletin
Pharm Manage — Pharmacy Management
Pharm Manage Comb Am J Pharm — Pharmacy Management Combined with the American Journal of Pharmacy
Pharm Manuf Assoc Yearb — Pharmaceutical Manufacturers Association. Yearbook
Pharm Manuf Int — Pharmaceutical Manufacturing International
Pharm Med — Pharmaceutical Medicine
Pharm Med Future Int Meet Pharm Physicians — Pharmaceutical Medicine - the Future. InternationalMeeting of Pharmaceutical Physicians
Pharm Med (Hamps) — Pharmaceutical Medicine (Hampshire)
Pharm Mon — Pharmaceuticals Monthly
Pharm Monatsbl — Pharmazeutische Monatsblaetter
Pharm Monatsh — Pharmazeutische Monatshefte
Pharm Monogr — Pharmaceutical Monographs
Pharm News — Pharmaceutical News
Pharm News Index — Pharmaceutical News Index
Pharm News Langhorne Pa — Pharmaceutical News (Langhorne, Pennsylvania)
Pharm Pak — Pharmacy Pakistan
Pharm Pharmacol Commun — Pharmacy and Pharmacology Communications
Pharm Pharmacol Lett — Pharmaceutical and Pharmacological Letters
Pharm Pharmakol (Moscow) — Pharmazie und Pharmakologie (Moscow)
Pharm Post — Pharmazeutische Post
Pharm Post Beil — Pharmazeutische Post. Beilage
Pharm Prax — Pharmazeutische Praxis
Pharm Presse — Pharmazeutische Presse
Pharm Presse Beil — Pharmazeutische Presse. Beilage
Pharm Presse Wiss Prakt Hefte — Pharmazeutische Presse. Wissenschaftlich-Praktische Hefte
Pharm Prod Pharm — Pharmacie-Produits Pharmaceutiques
Pharm Rep (Beijing) — Pharmacy Reports (Beijing)
Pharm Res — Pharmaceutical Research
Pharm Rev — Pharmaceutical Review
Pharm Rev — Pharmacological Reviews
Pharm Rev (Tokyo) — Pharmaceutical Review (Tokyo)
Pharm Rundsch — Pharmazeutische Rundschau
Pharm Rundsch (Berlin) — Pharmaceutische Rundschau (Berlin)
Pharm Rural — Pharmacien Rural
Pharm Sci — Pharmaceutical Sciences
Pharm Sci Commun — Pharmaceutical Science Communications
Pharm Sci Technol Today — Pharmaceutical Science and Technology Today
Pharm Soc Jpn J — Pharmaceutical Society of Japan. Journal
Pharm Soc (Pilani) J — Pharmaceutical Society (Pilani). Journal
Pharm Tech Assist Heute — Pharmazeutisch-Technische Assistenten Heute
Pharm Tech Jpn — Pharm Tech Japan
Pharm Technol — Pharmaceutical Technology
Pharm Technol Eur — Pharmaceutical Technology Europe
Pharm Technol Int — Pharmaceutical Technology International
Pharm Tijdschr Belg — Pharmaceutische Tijdschrift voor Belgie

Pharm Tijdschr Ned Indie — Pharmaceutisch Tijdschrift voor Nederlandsch-Indie
Pharm Tijdschr Vlaanderen — Pharmaceutisch Tijdschrift van Vlaanderen
Pharm Times — Pharmacy Times
Pharm Tox — Pharmacology and Toxicology
Pharm Unserer Zeit — Pharmazie in Unserer Zeit
Pharm Verfahrenstech Heute — Pharmazeutische Verfahrenstechnik Heute
Pharm Weekbl — Pharmaceutisch Weekblad
Pharm Weekbl Ned — Pharmeceutisch Weekblad voor Nederland
Pharm Weekbl Sci — Pharmaceutisch Weekblad. Scientific Edition
Pharm World & Sci — Pharmacy World and Science
Pharm Zeitung — Pharmazeutische Zeitung
Pharm Zentralhalle — Pharmazeutische Zentralhalle
Pharm Zentralhalle Dtl — Pharmazeutische Zentralhalle fuer Deutschland
Pharm Zentralhalle Dtschl — Pharmazeutische Zentralhalle fuer Deutschland
Pharm Z Russl — Pharmaceutische Zeitschrift fuer Russland
Pharm Ztg — Pharmazeutische Zeitung
Pharm Ztg (Berl) — Pharmazeutische Zeitung (Berlin)
Pharm Ztg Nachr — Pharmazeutische Zeitung Nachrichten
Pharm Ztg Sci Ed — Pharmazeutische Zeitung. Scientific Edition
Pharm Ztg Ver Apotheker-Ztg — Pharmazeutische Zeitung. Vereinigt mit Apotheker-Zeitung
Pharos — Pharos of Alpha Omega Alpha Honor Medical Society
P Harr — Rendel Harris Papyri of Woodbrooke College. Birmingham
PHAS — Harvard Journal of Asiatic Studies
Phase Transitions Crit Phenom — Phase Transitions and Critical Phenomena
Phase Transitions Proc Conf Chem — Phase Transitions. Proceedings. Conference on Chemistry
P Haun — Papyri Graecae Haunienses
P Hawaii En — Proceedings. Hawaiian Entomological Society
PhB — Philobiblon
PhB — Philosophia (Belgrade)
PhB — Philosophical Books
PhB — Philosophische Bibliothek
PHBCD — Physica B + C
PHBHA — Physiology and Behavior
PHBI — Human Biology
PHBIA — Pharmacien Biologiste
PHBLA — Physikalische Blaetter
PhBIKG — Philosophische Blaetter der Kant-Gesellschaft
PHBOA — Physiologia Bohemoslovenica [Later, Physiologia Bohemoslovaca]
PHBS — Publications. Henry Bradshaw Society
PHC — Pelican History of the Church
PHCAA — Physics in Canada
PHCBA — Photochemistry and Photobiology
PHCCA — Progress in Histochemistry and Cytochemistry
PhCL — Pharmacochemistry Library
PHCTB — Photophysiology
PHCYAQ — Specialist Periodical Reports. Photochemistry
PHDK — Phi Delta Kappan
PHDLAQ — Farmakevtikon Dheltion. Edition Sciontifiquo
Ph E — Philosophie in Einzeldarstellungen
PHEC — Human Ecology
PHEDA — Physics Education
Ph E E — Philosophie in Einzeldarstellungen. Ergaenzungsband
PHEF — Human Ecology Forum
PhEJ — Philippine Economic Journal
P Helm Soc — Proceedings. Helminthological Society of Washington
PHEM — Hemingway Review
Phen & Ped — Phenomenology and Pedagogy
Phenom Ioniz Gases Contrib Pap Int Conf — Phenomena in Ionized Gases. Contributed Papers. InternationalConference
PHER — Journal of Heredity
PHESA — Proceedings. Hawaiian Entomological Society
Ph Esp — Philosophie de l'Esprit
P-H Est Plan — Estate Planning (Prentice-Hall, Inc.)
Ph E W — Philosophy East and West
PhF — Philosophical Forum
Ph F — Philosophische Forschungen
PHFEA — Physica Fennica
Ph G — Philosophie und Geschichte
PHG — Progress in Human Geography
Phi — Philosophy
P Hibeh — Hibeh Papyri
Phi Del Kap — Phi Delta Kappan
Phi D K — Phi Delta Kappan
PHIJ — Historical Journal
Phil — Philologus. Zeitschrift fuer Klassische Altertum
Phil — Philosophies
Phil — Philosophy
Phila Bs J — Philadelphia Business Journal
Philad Ac Nt Sc J — Journal of the Academy of Natural Sciences of Philadelphia
Philad Ac Nt Sc P — Proceedings of the Acacemy of Natural Sciences of Philadelphia
Philad Coll Phm J — Journal of the Philadelphia College of Pharmacy
Philadelphia Bot Sentinel Thomsonian Med Revolutionist — Philadelphia Botanic Sentinel and Thomsonian Medical Revolutionist
Philadelphia J Med Phys Sci — Philadelphia Journal of the Medical and Physical Sciences
Philadelphia Med — Philadelphia Medicine
Philadelphia Mus A Bull — Philadelphia Museum of Art. Bulletin
Philad J Ac Nt Sc — Journal of the Academy of Natural Sciences of Philadelphia
Philad J Coll Phm — Journal of the Philadelphia College of Pharmacy
Philad Md Ps J — Philadelphia Medical and Physical Journal
Philad T — Transactions of the American Philosophical Society
Phil Ag — Philippine Agriculturist

Phila Geog Soc Bul — Geographical Society of Philadelpha. Bulletin
Phila Geog Soc Bull — Philadelphia Geographical Society. Bulletin
Phil Ag R — Philippine Agricultural Review
Phila Inqr — Philadelphia Inquirer
Phila J Med Phys Sci — Philadelphia Journal. Medical and Physical Sciences
Phila LJ — Philadelphia Law Journal
Phila Med — Philadelphia Medicine
Phila Med J — Philadelphia Medical Journal
Phila Med Phys J — Philadelphia Medical and Physical Journal
Phila Mus Bull — Philadelphia Museum of Art. Bulletin
Phil Ant — Philosophia Antiqua
Philanthrop — Philanthropist
Phila Orch — Philadelphia Orchestra. Program Notes
Phila Phot — Philadelphia Photographer
Phila Pris R — Philadelphia Prison Review
Phil Arb — Philosophische Arbeiten
Philat Aust — Philately from Australia
Philat Bul — Philatelic Bulletin
Philately from Aust — Philately from Australia
Philat Pregl — Philatelen Pregled
Phil Books — Philosophical Books
Phil Bull — Philatelic Bulletin
(Phil) Busn — Business Journal (Philadelphia)
Phil Bus R — Philippine Business Review
Phil Class — Philologia Classica
Phil Context — Philosophy in Context
Phil Dev — Philippine Development
Phil East West — Philosophy East and West
Phil Ed Forum — Philippine Educational Forum
Phil Educ Proc — Proceedings. Far Western Philosophy of Education Society
Phil Exch — Philosophic Exchange
Phil Forum — Philosophical Forum
Phil Forum (Boston) — Philosophical Forum (Boston)
Phil Forum (De Kalb) — Philosophy Forum (De Kalb)
Phil Geog J — Philippine Geographical Journal
Philhar — Philharmonic
Phil ILJ — Philippine International Law Journal
Phil Ind — Philosopher's Index
Phil Inq — Philosophical Inquiry
Phil Int LJ — Philippine International Law Journal
Phil Invest — Philosophical Investigators
Philip Abstr — Philippine Abstracts
Philip Morris Sci Symp Proc — Philip Morris Science Symposium. Proceedings
Philipp AEC — Philippine Atomic Energy Commission. Publications
Philipp AEC Annu Rep — Philippine Atomic Energy Commission. Annual Report
Philipp AEC Rep — Philippine Atomic Energy Commission. Reports
Philipp Agric — Philippine Agriculturist
Philipp Agric Eng J — Philippine Agricultural Engineering Journal
Philipp Agric Rev — Philippine Agricultural Review
Philipp At Bull — Philippine Atomic Bulletin
Philipp Biochem Soc Bull — Philippine Biochemical Society. Bulletin
Philipp Bur Agric Econ Rep — Philippines. Bureau of Agricultural Economics. Report
Philipp Bur Mines Geo Sci Rep Invest — Philippines. Bureau of Mines and Geo-Sciences. Report of Investigation
Philipp Bur Mines Inf Circ — Philippines. Bureau of Mines. Information Circular
Philipp Bur Mines Rep Invest — Philippines. Bureau of Mines. Report of Investigations
Philipp Bur Mines Spec Proj Ser Publ — Philippines. Bureau of Mines. Special Projects Series. Publication
Philipp Bus Rev — Philippine Business Review
Philipp Dep Agric Nat Resour Bur Mines Inf Circ — Philippines. Department of Agriculture and Natural Resources. Bureau of Mines. Information Circular
Philipp Dep Agric Nat Resour Bur Mines Rep Invest — Philippines. Department of Agriculture and Natural Resources. Bureau ofMines. Report of Investigation
Philipp Dep Agric Nat Resour Bur Mines Spec Proj Ser Publ — Philippines. Department of Agriculture and Natural Resources. Bureau ofMines. Special Projects Series Publication
Philipp Dep Nat Resour Bur Mines Rep Invest — Philippines. Department of Natural Resources. Bureau of Mines. Reportof Investigation
Philipp Ent — Philippine Entomologist
Philipp Entomol — Philippine Entomologist
Philipp Farms Gard — Philippine Farms and Gardens
Philipp For — Philippine Forests
Philipp For Prod Res Ind Dev Comm FORPRIDE Dig — Philippines. Forest Products Research and Industries Development Commission. FORPRIDE Digest
Philipp Geogr J — Philippine Geographical Journal
Philipp Geol — Philippine Geologist
Philippine Ag R — Philippine Agricultural Review
Philippine Agr — Philippine Agriculturist
Philippine Agr Situation — Philippine Agricultural Situation
Philippine Econ J — Philippine Economic Journal
Philippine Economy and Ind J — Philippine Economy and Industrial Journal
Philippine Farm Gard — Philippine Farms and Gardens
Philippine Internat LJ — Philippine International Law Journal
Philippine Int'l LJ — Philippine International Law Journal
Philippine J Nutr — Philippine Journal of Nutrition
Philippine J Plant Ind — Philippine Journal of Plant Industry
Philippine J Pub Adm — Philippine Journal of Public Administration
Philippine J Pub Admin — Philippine Journal of Public Administration
Philippine J Public Admin — Philippine Journal of Public Administration
Philippine J Sci — Philippine Journal of Science
Philippine LJ — Philippine Law Journal
Philippine L Rev — Philippine Law Review

Philippine Planning J — Philippine Planning Journal
Philippine Rice Corn Progr — Philippines Rice and Corn Progress
Philippines Bur Mines Geo-Sci Rep Invest — Philippines. Bureau of Mines and Geo-Sciences. Report of Investigation
Philippines Mag — Philippines Magazine
Philippine Sociol R — Philippine Sociological Review
Philippines Q — Philippines Quarterly
Philippine Stud — Philippine Studies
Philipp J Agric — Philippine Journal of Agriculture
Philipp J Anesthesiol — Philippine Journal of Anesthesiology
Philipp J Anim Ind — Philippine Journal of Animal Industry
Philipp J Cancer — Philippine Journal of Cancer
Philipp J Cardiol — Philippine Journal of Cardiology
Philipp J Coconut Stud — Philippine Journal of Coconut Studies
Philipp J Crop Sci — Philippine Journal of Crop Science
Philipp J Fish — Philippine Journal of Fisheries
Philipp J Food Sci Technol — Philippine Journal of Food Science and Technology
Philipp J For — Philippine Journal of Forestry
Philipp J Intern Med — Philippine Journal of Internal Medicine
Philipp J Nurs — Philippine Journal of Nursing
Philipp J Nutr — Philippine Journal of Nutrition
Philipp J Ophthal — Philippine Journal of Ophthalmology
Philipp J Ophthalmol — Philippine Journal of Ophthalmology
Philipp J Pediat — Philippine Journal of Pediatrics
Philipp J Pediatr — Philippine Journal of Pediatrics
Philipp J Plant Ind — Philippine Journal of Plant Industry
Philipp J Pub Admin — Philippine Journal of Public Administration
Philipp J Sci — Philippine Journal of Science
Philipp J Sci Sect A — Philippine Journal of Science. Section A. Chemical Sciences
Philipp J Sci Sect B — Philippine Journal of Science. Section B. Medical Sciences
Philipp J Sci Sect C — Philippine Journal of Science. Section C. Botany
Philipp J Surg — Philippine Journal of Surgery
Philipp J Surg Obstet Gynecol — Philippine Journal of Surgery, Obstetrics, and Gynecology
Philipp J Surg Surg Spec — Philippine Journal of Surgery and Surgical Specialties
Philipp J Trop Med — Philippine Journal of Tropical Medicine
Philipp J Vet Anim Sci — Philippine Journal of Veterinary and Animal Sciences
Philipp J Vet Med — Philippine Journal of Veterinary Medicine
Philipp Lumberm — Philippine Lumberman
Philipp Med Dent J — Philippine Medical-Dental Journal
Philipp Med World — Philippine Medical World
Philipp Med World (1946-1951) — Philippine Medical World (1946-1951)
Philipp Med World (1952-1962) — Philippine Medical World (1952-1962)
Philipp Met — Philippine Metals
Philipp Min J — Philippine Mining Journal
Philipp Norm Coll Lang Stud Cent Occ Pap — Philippine Normal College Language Study Center. Occasional Paper
Philipp Nucl J — Philippines Nuclear Journal
Philip Popul J — Philippine Population Journal
Philipp Orchid Rev — Philippine Orchid Review
Philipp Phytopathol — Philippine Phytopathology
Philipp Popul J — Philippine Population Journal
Philipp Q Cult Soc — Philippine Quarterly of Culture and Society
Philipp Quart Cult Soc — Philippine Quarterly of Culture and Society
Philipp Rep — Philippine Report
Philipp Sci — Philippine Scientist
Philipp Sci Index — Philippine Science Index
Philipp Sugar Inst Q — Philippine Sugar Institute. Quarterly
Philipp Sugar Inst Quart — Philippine Sugar Institute Quarterly
Philipp Text Dig — Philippine Textile Digest
Philipp Text Inf Dig — Philippine Textile Information Digest
Philipp Weed Sci Bull — Philippine Weed Science Bulletin
Philips — Philips Music Herald
PhilipSa — Philippiana Sacra
Philip Sac — Philippiniana Sacra
Philips Ind Eng Bul — Philips Industrial Engineering Bulletin
Philips J Res — Philips Journal of Research
Philips Res Rep — Philips Research Reports
Philips Res Rep Suppl — Philips Research Reports. Supplements
Philips Serv Sci Ind — Philips Serving Science and Industry
PhilipSt — Philippine Studies
Philips Tech Rev — Philips Technical Review
Philips Tech Rundsch — Philips Technische Rundschau
Philips Tech Rundschau — Philips Technische Rundschau
Philips Tech Tijdschr — Philips Technisch Tijdschrift
Philips Telecommun Rev — Philips Telecommunication Review
Philips Weld Rep — Philips Welding Reporter
Phill S Rev — Philippine Sociological Review
Phil J — Philosophical Journal. Transactions. Royal Philosophical Society of Glasgow
Phil J Ag — Philippine Journal of Agriculture
Phil Jahr — Philosophisches Jahrbuch
Phil Jahrb — Philosophisches Jahrbuch
Phil J Bio — Philippine Journal of Biology
Phil J Comm — Philippine Journal of Commerce
Phil J Ed — Philippine Journal of Education
Phil J Fish — Philippine Journal of Fisheries
Phil J Ling — Philippine Journal of Linguistics
Phil J Pub Admin — Philippine Journal of Public Administration
Phil Jrl — Business Journal (Philippines)
Phil J Sci — Philippine Journal of Science
Phil J Sci Teach — Philippine Journal of Science Teachers
Phil J Voc Ed — Philippine Journal of Vocational Education
Phil Lab R — Philippine Labor Review

Phil Lab Rel J — Philippine Labour Relations Journal
Phil Ling — Philosophical Linguistics
Phillip J — Phillip Journal
Phillip J Sci — Philippine Journal of Science
Phillips Dir — Phillips' Paper Trade Directory of the World
Phil Lit — Philosophy and Literature
Phil Lit R — Philatelic Literature Review
Phil L J — Philippine Law Journal
Phil LJ — Philippine Law Journal
Phil Log — Philosophie et Logique
Phil L Rev — Philippine Law Review
Phil M — Philosophia. Mendoza
Phil Mag — Philosophical Magazine
Phil Math — Philosophia Mathematica
PhilMh — Philosophische Monatshefte
Phil Mus — Philological Museum
Phil Natur — Philosophia Naturalis
Philol — Philologus. Zeitschrift fuer das Klassiche Altertum
Philologus ZKA — Philologus. Zeitschrift fuer Klassische Altertum
Philol Q — Philological Quarterly
Philol Quar — Philological Quarterly. University of Iowa
Philol Quart — Philological Quarterly
Philol Soc Trans — Philological Society Transactions
Philol Trans — Philological Transactions
Philos — Philosophy
Philos Abhandlungen — Philosophische Abhandlungen
Philos & Phenom Res — Philosophy and Phenomenological Research
Philos & Pub Affairs — Philosophy and Public Affairs
Philos Antiq — Philosophia Antiqua
Philos Anz — Philosophischer Anzeiger
Philos Bibliothek — Philosophische Bibliothek
Philos Book — Philosophical Books
Philos Collect R Soc London — Philosophical Collections. Royal Society of London
Philos Curr — Philosophical Currents
Philos East & West — Philosophy East and West
Philos EW — Philosophy East and West
Philos Explor — Philosophical Explorations
Philos Foru — Philosophy Forum
Philos Forum — Philosophical Forum
Philos Forum — Philosophy Forum
Philos Forum Quart — Philosophical Forum. A Quarterly
Philos Frege — Philosophy of Frege
Philos His — Philosophy and History
Philos Hist — Philosophy and History. German Studies Section I
Philosl — Philosopher's Index
Philos Index — Philosopher's Index
Philos J — Philosophical Journal
Philos Jahr — Philosophisches Jahrbuch
Philos Jb — Philosophisches Jahrbuch
Philos Jb Goerresges — Philosophisches Jahrbuch. Goerres-Gesellschaft
Philos Lit — Philosophy and Literature
Philos M — Philosophical Magazine
Philos Mag — Philosophical Magazine
Philos Mag A — Philosophical Magazine A. Physics of Condensed Matter, Defects, and Mechanical Properties
Philos Mag B — Philosophical Magazine B. Physics of Condensed Matter, Electronic, Optical, andMagnetic Properties
Philos Mag Lett — Philosophical Magazine Letters
Philos Mag Suppl — Philosophical Magazine. Supplement
Philos Math — Philosophia Mathematica
Philos Med — Philosophy and Medicine
Philos Mus Ed — Philosophy of Music Education Review
Philos Nat — Philosophia Naturalis
Philos Natur — Philosophia Naturalis
Philosophy of Ed Soc Proc — Philosophy of Education Society of Great Britain. Proceedings
Philos Pap — Philosophical Papers
Philos Phen — Philosophy and Phenomenological Research
Philos Phenomenol Res — Philosophy and Phenomenological Research
Philos Pub — Philosophy and Public Affairs
Philos Publ Aff — Philosophy and Public Affairs
Philos Q — Philosophical Quarterly
Philos Quart — Philosophical Quarterly
Philos R — Philosophical Review
Philos Rd — Philosophische Rundschau
PhilosRdschau — Philosophische Rundschau
Philos Rev — Philosophical Review
Philos Rhet — Philosophy and Rhetoric
Philos Rund — Philosophische Rundschau
Philos Sci — Philosophy of Science
Philos Soc Sci — Philosophy of the Social Sciences
Philos S Sc — Philosophy of the Social Sciences
Philos Stud — Philosophical Studies
Philos Studies — Philosophical Studies
Philos Stud Ser Philos — Philosophical Studies Series in Philosophy
Philos Stds — Philosophical Studies
Philos Tod — Philosophy Today
Philos Top — Philosophical Topics
Philos Trans — Philosophical Transactions. Giving Some Account of the Present Undertakings, Studies, and Labours of the Ingenious in Many Parts of the World
Philos Trans Abr Hutton — Philosophical Transactions Abridged (Hutton, Editor)
Philos Transact Royal Soc — Philsophical Transactions. Royal Society of London
Philos Trans Phys Eng Sci — Philosophical Transactions. Mathematical, Physical, and Engineering Sciences

Philos Trans Roy Soc London Ser A — Philosophical Transactions. Royal Society of London. Series A. Mathematical andPhysical Sciences
Philos Trans R Soc A — Philosophical Transactions. Royal Society of London. Series A. Mathematical and Physical Sciences
Philos Trans R Soc Lond A Math Phys Sci — Philosophical Transactions. Royal Society of London. Series A. Mathematical and Physical Sciences
Philos Trans R Soc Lond B Biol Sci — Philosophical Transactions. Royal Society of London. B. Biological Sciences
Philos Trans R Soc Lond Biol — Philosophical Transactions. Royal Society of London. Series B. Biological Sciences
Philos Trans R Soc London — Philosophical Transactions. Royal Society of London
Philos Trans R Soc London A — Philosophical Transactions. Royal Society of London. Series A. Mathematical andPhysical Sciences
Philos Trans R Soc London Ser A — Philosophical Transactions. Royal Society of London. Series A. Mathematical and Physical Sciences
Philos Trans R Soc London Ser B — Philosophical Transactions. Royal Society of London. Series B. Biological Sciences
Philos Trans R Soc Lond Ser A — Philosophical Transactions. Royal Society of London. Series A. Mathematical andPhysical Sciences
Philos Trans R Soc Lond Ser A — Philosophical Transactions. Royal Society of London. Series B. Biological Sciences
PhilP — Philological Papers
Phil Papers — Philosophical Papers
Phil Patr — Philosophia Patrum
Phil Perspekt — Philosophische Perspektiven
Phil Phenomenol Res — Philosophy and Phenomenological Research
Phil Plan J — Philippine Planning Journal
Phil Pln 87 — Five-Year Philippine Development Plan, 1983-1987
Phil Pol Sci J — Philippine Political Science Journal
Phil Post — Philharmonic Post
Phil Pub Affairs — Philosophy and Public Affairs
Phil Q — Philippines Quarterly
Phil Q — Philosophical Quarterly
Phil Q Cult Soc — Philippine Quarterly of Culture and Society
Phil Quart — Philosophical Quarterly
Phil Qy — Philological Quarterly
Phil R — Philosophical Review
PhilR — Philosophy and Rhetoric
Phil R Bus Econ — Philippine Review of Business and Economics
Phil Reform — Philosophia Reformata
Phil Res Arch — Philosophy Research Archives
Phil Res R — Philips Research Reports
Phil Rev — Philosophical Review
Phil Rev (Taiwan) — Philosophical Review (Taiwan)
Phil Rhet — Philosophy and Rhetoric
Phil Rundsch — Philosophische Rundschau
PhilS — Philosophical Studies
Phil Sacra — Philippine Sacra
Phil Sci — Philosophy of Science
Phil Soc — Philological Society. Transactions
Phil Soc Act — Philosophy and Social Action
Phil Soc Cr — Philosophy and Social Criticism
Phil Soc Crit — Philosophy and Social Criticism
Phil Sociol R — Philippine Sociological Review
Phil Soc Sci — Philosophy of the Social Sciences
Phil Soc Sci Hum R — Philippine Social Sciences and Humanities Review
Phil St — Philologische Studien
Phil Stud — Philippine Studies
Phil Stud — Philologische Studien
Phil Stud — Philosophical Studies
Phil Stud Educ — Philosophical Studies in Education
Phil Stud (Ireland) — Philosophical Studies (Ireland)
PhilT — Philosophy Today
Phil Techn Rd — Philips Technische Rundschau
Phil Techn Rev — Philips Technical Review
Phil Tech R — Philips Technical Review
Phil Today — Philosophy Today
Phil Topics — Philosophical Topics
Phil Trans — Philosophical Transactions
Phil Trans Royal Soc London Ser A — Philosophical Transactions. Royal Society of London. Series A. Mathematical and Physical Sciences
Phil Trans Roy Soc Lond — Philosophical Transactions. Royal Society of London
Phil Trans Roy Soc Lond B — Philosophical Transactions. Royal Society of London. Series B. Biological Sciences
Phil Trans Roy Soc London Ser A Math Phys Sci — Philosophical Transactions. Royal Society of London. Series A. Mathematical andPhysical Sciences
Phil Trans Roy Soc Lond Ser A — Philosophical Transactions. Royal Society. London. Series A
Phil Trans R Soc — Philosophical Transactions. Royal Society of London
Phil Unters — Philologische Untersuchungen
Phil Woch — Philologische Wochenschrift
Phil Wochenschr — Philologische Wochenschrift
Phil Yb Int'l L — Philippine Yearbook of International Law
PHINA — Pharmazeutische Industrie
PHIND — Pharmaceutical and Healthcare Industries News Database
PHIND — Pharmacy International
PHINet — Prentice Hall Information Network
PHIS — History. The Journal of the Historical Association
PhiS — Philippine Studies
PHIS — Princeton History of Ideas Series
PHisp — Poesia Hispanica
Phist — Precis Historiques. Melanges Religieux, Litteraires, et Scientifiques
Phi T Roy A — Philosophical Transactions. Royal Society of London. Series A. Mathematical and Physical Sciences

Phi T Roy B — Philosophical Transactions. Royal Society of London. Series B. Biological Sciences
Ph J — Philosophical Journal
PhJ — Philosophisches Jahrbuch
Ph J — Philosophisches Jahrbuch der Goerres-Gesellschaft
Ph Jb — Philosophisches Jahrbuch
Ph JE — Philosophical Journal (Edinburgh)
PHJH — Historian. A Journal of History
PHJRD — Philips Journal of Research
PHK — Pakistan Horizons. Pakistan Institute of International Affairs (Karachi)
PHK — Pootaardappelwereld
PHKOA — Photographische Korrespondenz (Austria)
Ph L — Philosophia Lovaniensis
Ph La — Philosophischer Literaturanzeiger
PHLBA — Phlebologie
Phl Freep — Philadelphia Free Press
Ph Lit — Philosophischer Literaturanzeiger
PHLTA — Physics Letters
Ph M — Philosophische Monatshefte
PHM — Poesia Hispanica Moderna
PHMAA — Philosophical Magazine
Ph Mag — Philosophical Magazine
PHMBA — Physics in Medicine and Biology
Phm CB — Pharmaceutisches Central-Blatt
PHMDEH — Pharmaceutical Medicine
Ph Med — Philosophes Medievaux
Ph Mg — Philosophical Magazine, or Annals of Chemistry, Mathematics, Astronomy, Natural History, and General Science
PHMGB — Pharmacology
Phm J — Pharmaceutical Journal and Transactions
PHMMA — Physics of Metals and Metallography
PHMODF — Phanerogamarum Monographiae
PHMTD — Previews of Heat and Mass Transfer
Phm Z Russl — Pharmaceutische Zeitschrift fuer Russland
Ph N — Philosophia Naturalis
Ph Nat — Philosophia Naturalis
Ph N B — Philosophia Naturalis. Beiheft
PHNOA — Physica Norvegica
PHNT — History and Theory
PHNTA — Phonetica
PhO — Philologia Orientalis
Phoe — Phoenix
Phoenix BJ — Phoenix Business Journal
Phoenix Bus J — Phoenix Business Journal
PhoenixC — Phoenix: The Classical Association of Canada
Phoenix Ex Or Lux — Phoenix. Bulletin Uitgegeven door het Vooraziatisch-Egyptisch Genootschap Ex Oriente Lux
PhoenixK — Phoenix (Korea)
Phoenix Q — Phoenix Quarterly
Ph Oe Schr — Schriften der Physikalisch-Oekonomischen Gesellschaft zu Koenigsberg
Phoe Sh — Phoenix Shocker
P Holm — Papyrus Graecus Holmensis
Phon — Phonetica
Phonon Scattering Condens Matter Proc Int Conf — Phonon Scattering in Condensed Matter. Proceedings. InternationalConference
Phonons Proc Int Conf — Phonons. Proceedings. International Conference
PhonPr — Phonetica Pragensia
PHOPD — Photobiochemistry and Photobiophysics
Phospho Potas — Phosphorus and Potassium
Phosphore Agric — Phosphore et Agriculture
Phosphor Sulfur Relat Elem — Phosphorus and Sulfur and the Related Elements
Phosphorus — Phosphorus and Potassium
Phosphorus Agric — Phosphorus in Agriculture
Phosphorus Relat Group V Elem — Phosphorus and the Related Group V Elements
Phosphorus Res Bull — Phosphorus Research Bulletin
Phosphorus Sulfur Silicon Relat Elem — Phosphorus, Sulfur, and Silicon and the Related Elements
Phot — Photon
Phot Abstr — Photographic Abstracts
Phot Alle — Photographie fuer Alle
Phot Annu — Photography Annual
Phot Appln Sci — Photographic Applications in Science, Technology, and Medicine
Phot Appl Sci Tech Med — Photographic Applications in Science, Technology, and Medicine
Phot Arch — Photographisches Archiv
Phot Bull — Photographic Bulletin
Phot Centbl — Photographisches Centralblatt
Phot Colr — Photographic Collector
Phot F A J — Photographic and Fine Art Journal
Phot Hippique — Photographie Hippique
Phot Industrie — Photographische Industrie
Phot J — Photographic Journal
Phot J — Photographic Journal, Including the Transactions of the Photographic Society of Great Britain
Phot J Amer — Photographic Journal of America
Phot Ko — Photographische Korrespondenz
Phot Korr — Photographische Korrespondenz
Phot Mosaics — Photographic Mosaics
Phot News — Photographic News
Photo Abstr — Photographic Abstracts
Photo Art Mon — Photo Art Monthly
Photobiochem and Photobiophys — Photobiochemistry and Photobiophysics
Photobiochem Photobiophys — Photobiochemistry and Photobiophysics

Photobiol Bull — Photobiology Bulletin
Photobiol Tech — Photobiological Techniques
Photobl — Photoblaetter
Photo Can — Photo Canada
Photochem Convers Storage Sol Energy Int Conf — Photochemical Conversion and Storage of Solar Energy. International Conference on Photochemical Conversion and Storage of Solar Energy
Photo Chem Mach Photo Chem Etching — Photo Chemical Machining - Photo Chemical Etching
Photochem P — Photochemistry and Photobiology
Photochem Photobiol — Photochemistry and Photobiology
Photochem Photobiol Rev — Photochemical and Photobiological Reviews
Photochem Photophys — Photochemistry and Photophysics
Photo Cine Rev — Photo-Cine-Review
Photo Comm — Photo Communique
Photodermatol — Photo-Dermatology
Photodermatol Photoimmunol Photomed — Photodermatology, Photoimmunology and Photomedicine
Photoelastic J — Photoelastic Journal
Photoelastic Soil Mech J — Photoelastic and Soil Mechanics Journal
Photoelectrochem Photovoltaics Layered Semicond — Photoelectrochemistry and Photovoltaics of Layered Semiconductors
Photoelectr Spectrom Group Bull — Photoelectric Spectrometry Group Bulletin
Photo Engravers Bull — Photo-Engravers' Bulletin
Photo Era Mag — Photo-Era Magazine
Photog Abstr — Photographic Abstracts
Photogr Abstr — Photographic Abstracts
Photogr Alle — Photographie fuer Alle
Photogram Eng Remote Sensing — Photogrammetric Engineering and Remote Sensing
Photogramma — Photogrammetria
Photogramm Eng — Photogrammetric Engineering [Later, Photogrammetric Engineering and Remote Sensing]
Photogramm Eng and Remote Sensing — Photogrammetric Engineering and Remote Sensing
Photogramm Eng Remote Sens — Photogrammetric Engineering and Remote Sensing
Photogramm Eng Remote Sensing — Photogrammetric Engineering and Remote Sensing
Photogrammetric Eng — Photogrammetric Engineering [Later, Photogrammetric Engineering and Remote Sensing]
Photogramm Rec — Photogrammetric Record
Photographie Forsch — Photographie und Forschung
Photogr Appl Sci Technol and Med — Photographic Applications in Science, Technology, and Medicine
Photogr Appl Sci Technol Med — Photographic Applications in Science, Technology, and Medicine
Photogr Canadiana — Photographic Canadiana
Photogr Chron — Photographische Chronik
Photogr Chron Allg Photogr Ztg — Photographische Chronik und Allgemeine Photographische Zeitung
Photogr Collector — Photographic Collector
Photogr Corpusc CR Colloq Int — Photographie Corpusculaire. Comptes-Rendus du Colloque International
Photogr Eng — Photographic Engineering
Photogr E R — Photogrammetric Engineering and Remote Sensing
Photogr Focus — Photography and Focus
Photogr Forsch — Photographie und Forschung
Photogr Ind — Photographische Industrie
Photogr Index — Photography Index
Photogr Ind Tokyo — Photographic Industries (Tokyo)
Photogr Industrie — Photographische Industrie
Photogr J — Photographic Journal
Photogr J Sect A — Photographic Journal. Section A. Pictorial and General Photography
Photogr J Sect B — Photographic Journal. Section B. Scientific and Technical Photography
Photogr Korresp — Photographische Korrespondenz
Photogr Mag — Photography Magazine
Photogr Rundsch Mitt — Photographische Rundschau und Mitteilungen
Photogr Sci and Eng — Photographic Science and Engineering
Photogr Sci Eng — Photographic Science and Engineering
Photogr Sci Photochem — Photographic Science and Photochemistry
Photogr Sci Symp — Photographic Science. Symposium
Photogr Sci Tech — Photographic Science and Technique
Photogr Sensitivity — Photographic Sensitivity
Photogr Soc Am J — Photographic Society of America. Journal
Photogr Soc Am J Sect B — Photographic Society of America. Journal. Section B. Photographic Science and Technique
Photogr Soc Am J Suppl — Photographic Society of America. Journal. Supplement
Photogr Tech Sci Res — Photographic Techniques in Scientific Research
Photogr Welt — Photographische Welt
Photogr Wiss — Photographie und Wissenschaft
Photo Ind — Photographische Industrie
Photo Ind — Photo-Industrie und -Handel
Photo Ind — Wolfman Report on the Photographic Industry in the United States
Photo Kino Chem Ind — Photo-Kino-Chemical Industry
Photo Lab Manag — Photo Lab Management
Photo Lit — Photographic Literature
Photo-M — Photo-Miniature
Photo-Mag — Photo-Magazin
Photomethd — Photomethods
Photo Methods Ind — Photo Methods for Industry
Photo Min — Photo-Miniature

Photo Mkt — Photo Marketing

Photon Correl Tech Fluid Mech Proc Int Conf — Photon Correlation Techniques in Fluid Mechanics. Proceedings.International Conference

Photon Detect Proc Int Symp Tech Comm — Photon-Detectors. Proceedings. International Symposium.Technical Committee

Photonic Meas Photon Detect Proc Int Symp Tech Comm — Photonic Measurements Photon-Detectors. Proceedings. InternationalSymposium. Technical Committee

Photonics Appl Nucl Phys — Photonics Applied to Nuclear Physics

Photonics Sci News — Photonics Science News

Photon Photon Collisions Proc Int Workshop — Photon Photon Collisions. Proceedings. International Workshop onPhoton Photon Collisions

Photophysiol Curr Top — Photophysiology. Current Topics

Photoplay — Photoplay, Movies, and Video

Photo-Rev — Photo-Revue

Photosel Chem — Photoselective Chemistry

Photosensit Mater — Photosensitive Materials

Photo Spec — Photonics Spectra

Photosynthe — Photosynthetica

Photosynth Proc Int Congr — Photosynthesis. Proceedings. International Congress onPhotosynthesis

Photosynth Res — Photosynthesis Research

Photosynth Sol Energy Convers — Photosynthetic Solar Energy Conversion

Photo Tech — Photo Technique

Photovoltaic Gener Space Proc Eur Symp — Photovoltaic Generators in Space. Proceedings. European Symposium

Photovoltaic Sol Energy Conf Proc Int Conf — Photovoltaic Solar Energy Conference. Proceedings. InternationalConference

Phot Sci En — Photographic Science and Engineering

Phot Sci Eng — Photographic Science and Engineering

Phot Sci Tech — Photographic Society of America. Journal. Section B. Photographic Science and Technique

Phot Tech — Photo Technique

Phot Tech Wirt — Photo-Technik und -Wirtschaft

Phot Times [*London*] — Photographic Times [*London*]

Phot Times [*New York*] — Photographic Times [*New York*]

PHP — Peace, Happiness, Prosperity for All

PhP — Philologica Pragensia

PhP — Philologike Protochronia

Ph P — Philosophia Patrum

PHPE — History of Political Economy

PHPh — Bulletin Historique et Philologique du Comite des Travaux Scientifiques

PHPLA — Physiologia Plantarum

Ph Prag — Philologica Pragensia

PHPXA — Pharmazeutische Praxis

Ph Q — Philological Quarterly

PhQ — Philosophical Quarterly

PHR — Pacific Historical Review

PHR — Pharma Japan

PHR — Pharmazeutische Industrie

PHR — Philippine Historical Review

PhR — Philosophical Review

Ph R — Philosophische Rundschau

PHR — United States Public Health Service. Public Health Reports

PHRA — Poverty and Human Resources Abstracts

Ph RB — Philosophische Rundschau. Beiheft

Ph Rdschau — Philosophische Rundschau

PHRE — Public Health Reports

PHREA — Physiological Reviews

Phreat Lang & Creation — Phreatique, Langage, et Creation

Ph Ref — Philosophia Reformata

Ph Rel — Philosophia Religionis

Ph Res — Philosophy and Phenomenological Research

Ph Rev — Philosophical Phenomenological Review

Ph Rev — Philosophical Review

PHRI — Human Rights

Phron — Phronesis

PHRQ — Human Rights Quarterly

Ph Ru — Philosophische Rundschau

PHRV — Public Health Reviews

PHRVA — Physical Review

PHS — Pakistan Historical Society. Journal

PhS — Philologische Studien

Ph S — Philologus. Supplement

PHS — Philosophical and Historical Studies

PhS — Philosophical Studies

PhS — Philosophy of Science

PHS — Public Health Service. Publications

PHS — Schippersweekblad

PHSB — Journal of Health and Social Behavior

PHSBB — Physics Bulletin

PHSCA — Philippine Journal of Science

PHSCW — Publications. Historical Society of the Church in Wales

PHSIA — Physiotherapy

PHSL — Proceedings. Huguenot Society of London

PHSL — Publications. Huguenot Society of London

PHSM — Pakistan Historical Society. Memoir

PHSNA — Philosophia Naturalis

PHSNB — Physics of Sintering

Ph Soc — Philosophy/Social Theory/Sociology

Ph Soc Glasgow Pr — Philosophical Society of Glasgow. Proceedings

Ph Soc Wash B — Philosophical Society of Washington. Bulletin

PhSR — Philippine Sociological Review

PHSS — Publications. History of Science Society

PHSSA — Physica Status Solidi

PhSt — Philosophical Studies

PHSTB — Physica Scripta

Ph Stud — Philosophische Studien Herausgegeben von Wilhelm Wundt

Ph Studien — Philologische Studien

PHSW — Health and Social Work

PHSWA — Proceedings. Helminthological Society of Washington

PHSYB — Photosynthetica

Ph T — Personalhistorisk Tidsskrift

PHT — Personhistorisk Tidskrift

PhT — Philosophy Today

Pht Arch — Photographisches Archiv

PHTEA — Physics Teacher

PHTED — Physiology Teacher

Ph TF — Philologiae Turcicae Fundamenta

Pht Mh — Photographische Monatshefte

PHTOA — Physics Today

PHTR — Harvard Theological Review

Pht S J — Journal of the Photographic Society of London

PHTTA — Philips Technische Tijdschrift

PhU — Philologische Untersuchungen

PHUD — Hudson Review

PHum — Przeglad Humanistyczny

PHUN — Huntington Library Quarterly

PHUZA — Physik in Unserer Zeit

PhW — Philologische Wochenschrift

PHWEA — Pharmaceutisch Weekblad

Ph Wschr — Philologische Wochenschrift

PHXQA — Phoenix Quarterly

Phy — Phylon

PHYBA — Phyton (Buenos Aires)

PHYCA — Physics

Phycol Newslett — Phycological Newsletter. Phycological Society of America

Phycol Res — Phycological Research

PHYCOM — Physician Communications Service

Phyl — Phylon

PHYMA — Phytomorphology

Phys — Physis

Phys 200 TeV — Physics up to 200 TeV

Phys A — Physica A. Europhysics Journal

PHYSA — Physica (Amsterdam)

Phys Abh — Physikalische Abhandlungen

Phys Abh Koenigl Akad Wiss Berlin — Abhandlungen der Koeniglichen Akademie der Wissenschaften in Berlin

Phys Abstr — Physics Abstracts

Phys Acoust — Physical Acoustics. Principles and Methods

Phys Act Coron Heart Dis Paavo Nurmi Symp — Physical Activity and Coronary Heart Disease. Paavo Nurmi Symposium

Phys Act Rep — Physical Activities Report

Phys & Chem — Physics and Chemistry

Phys and Chem Earth — Physics and Chemistry of the Earth

Phys and Chem Glasses — Physics and Chemistry of Glasses. Section B. Journal. Society of Glass Technology

Phys and Chem Liq — Physics and Chemistry of Liquids

Phys and Chem Miner — Physics and Chemistry of Minerals

Phys Antiprotons LEAR ACOL Era Proc LEAR Workshop — Physics with Antiprotons at LEAR [*Low Energy Antiproton Ring*] in the ACOL Era. Proceedings. LEAR Workshop

Phys Appl — Physics and Applications

Phys Appl — Physique Appliquee

Phys Aspects Microsc Charact Mater Proc Pfefferkorn Conf — Physical Aspects of Microscopic Characterization of Materials. Proceedings. Pfefferkorn Conference

Phys At Mol Matiere Interstellaire Ec Ete Phys Theor — Physique Atomique et Moleculaire et Matiere Interstellaire. Ecole d'Ete de Physique Theorique

Phys At Nucl Transl of Yad Fiz — Physics of Atomic Nuclei. Translation of Yadornaya Fizika

Phys Atomic Nuclei — Physics of Atomic Nuclei

Phys Atoms and Molecules — Physics of Atoms and Molecules

Phys B — Physica B. Europhysics Journal. Low Temperature and Solid State Physics

Phys B Condens Matter — Physica B. Condensed Matter

Phys Belust — Physikalische Belustigungen

Phys Belustigungen — Physikalische Belustigungen

Phys Ber — Physikalische Berichte

Phys Biblioth Rostock Wismar — Physikalische Bibliothek. Rostock und Wismar

Phys Bioinorg Chem Ser — Physical Bioinorganic Chemistry Series

Phys Bl — Physikalische Blaetter

Phys Bl Beil — Physikalische Blaetter. Beilage

Phys Bohemoslov — Physiologia Bohemoslovenica [*Later, Physiologia Bohemoslovaca*]

Phys Briefs — Physics Briefs

Phys Bull — Physics Bulletin

Phys Bull Baoding Peoples Repub China — Physics Bulletin (Baoding, People's Republic of China)

Phys Bull (Peking) — Physics Bulletin (Peking)

Phys C — Physica C. Europhysics Journal. Atomic, Molecular, and Plasma Physics Optics

Phys Can — Physics in Canada

Phys C Glas — Physics and Chemistry of Glasses

Phys Chaos Relat Probl Proc Nobel Symp — Physics of Chaos and Related Problems. Proceedings. NobelSymposium

Phys Chem — Physical Chemistry

Phys Chem — Physik und Chemie

Phys Chem Aspects Soil Relat Mater — Physico-Chemical Aspects of Soil and Related Materials

Phys Chem Behav Atmos Pollut Proc Eur Symp — Physico-Chemical Behaviour of Atmospheric Pollutants. Proceedings. European Symposium
Phys Chem Biol — Physico-Chemical Biology
Phys-Chem Biol (Chiba) — Physico-Chemical Biology (Chiba)
Phys Chem Biol Med — Physical Chemical Biology and Medicine
Phys Chem Centralbl — Physikalisch-Chemisches Centralblatt
Phys Chem Earth — Physics and Chemistry of the Earth
Phys Chem Earth Sci Res Rep — Physical, Chemical, and Earth Sciences Research Report
Phys Chem Fast React — Physical Chemistry of Fast Reactions
Phys Chem Fission Proc IAEA Symp — Physics and Chemistry of Fission. Proceedings. IAEA [*International Atomic Energy Agency*] Symposium. Physics and Chemistry of Fission
Phys Chem Foods — Physical Chemistry of Foods
Phys Chem Glasses — Physics and Chemistry of Glasses
Phys Chem Liq — Physics and Chemistry of Liquids
Phys Chem Magmas — Physical Chemistry of Magmas
Phys Chem Mater Layered Struct — Physics and Chemistry of Materials with Layered Structures
Phys Chem Mech Surf — Physics, Chemistry, and Mechanics of Surfaces
Phys Chem Miner — Physics and Chemistry of Minerals
Phys Chem (NY) — Physical Chemistry (New York)
Phys Chem Org Solvent Syst — Physical Chemistry of Organic Solvent Systems
Phys Chem (Peshawar Pak) — Physical Chemistry (Peshawar, Pakistan)
Phys Chem Phys — Physiological Chemistry and Physics
Phys Chem Sci Res Rep — Physical and Chemical Sciences Research Report
Phys Chem Ser Monogr — Physical Chemistry. Series of Monographs
Phys Chem Solids — Physics and Chemistry of Solids
Phys Chem Space — Physics and Chemistry in Space
Phys Chem (Vienna) — Physik und Chemie (Vienna)
Phys Chem (Washington DC) — Physics and Chemistry (Washington, D. C.)
Phys Collision — Physics in Collision. High-Energy ee/ep/pp Interactions
Phys Comp — Physiologia Comparata et Oecologia
Phys Condens Matter — Physics of Condensed Matter
Phys Con Matt — Physics of Condensed Matter
Phys Contemp Needs — Physics and Contemporary Needs. Proceedings. International Summer College
Phys C Supercond — Physica C. Superconductivity
Phys D — Physica D. Nonlinear Phenomena
Phys Data Zentralstelle Atomkernenerg Dok — Physics Data. Zentralstelle fuer Atomkernenergie-Dokumentation
Phys Daten — Physik Daten
Phys Daten Phys Data — Physik Daten/Physics Data
Phys-Diaet Ther — Physikalisch-Diaetetische Therapie
Phys Didak — Physik und Didaktik
Phys Didakt — Physik und Didaktik
Phys Dokl — Physics. Doklady
Phys Dokl Transl of Dokl Akad Nauk — Physics-Doklady. Translation of the Physics Section of Doklady Akademii Nauk
Phys Earth and Planet Inter — Physics of the Earth and Planetary Interiors
Phys Earth Planetary Interiors — Physics of the Earth and Planetary Interiors
Phys Earth Planet Inter — Physics of the Earth and Planetary Interiors
Phys Ed — Physical Educator
Phys Ed Bul — Physical Education Bulletin for Teachers in Secondary Schools
Phys Ed J — Physical Education Journal
Phys Ed News — Physical Education News
Phys Educ — Physical Education
Phys Educ — Physical Educator
Phys Educ — Physics Education
Phys Educ Index — Physical Education Index
Phys Educ Newsl — Physical Education Newsletter
Phys Electron At Collisions Int Conf — Physics of Electronic and Atomic Collisions. International Conference
Phys Electron At Collisions Invited Pap Int Conf — Physics of Electronic and Atomic Collisions. Invited Papers.International Conference
Phys Elem Part At Nucl — Physics of Elementary Particles and Atomic Nuclei
Phys Energ Fortis Phys Nucl — Physica Energiae Fortis et Physica Nuclearis
Phys Energi Fort Phys Nuclear — Physica Energiae Fortis et Physica Nuclearis
Phys Eng Appl Magn — Physics and Engineering Applications of Magnetism
Phys Environ Rep Dep Archit Sci Syd Univ — Physical Environment Report. Department of Architectural Science. University ofSydney
Phys E Plan — Physics of the Earth and Planetary Interiors
Phys Essays — Physics Essays
Phys Failure Electron — Physics of Failure in Electronics
Phys Fenn — Physica Fennica
Phys Fit Newsl — Physical Fitness Newsletter
Phys Fit Res Dig — Physical Fitness Research Digest
Phys Flu A — Physics of Fluids A. Fluid Dynamics
Phys Flu B — Physics of Fluids B. Plasma Physics
Phys Fluids — Physics of Fluids
Phys Fluids A — Physics of Fluids. A. Fluid Dynamics
Phys Fluids B — Physics of Fluids B. Plasma Physics
Phys Fluids Suppl — Physics of Fluids. Supplement
Phys Geom Topol — Physics, Geometry, and Topology
Phys Grundlagen Med Abh Biophys — Physikalische Grundlagen der Medizin. Abhandlungen aus der Biophysik
Phys Grundlage Tech Plenarvortr Physikertag — Physik. Grundlage der Technik. Plenarvortraege der Physikertagung
Phys Halbleiteroberflaeche — Physik der Halbleiteroberflaeche. Tagungsbericht der Arbeitstagung
Phys Hazards Dust Vap Occup Hyg — Physical Hazards, Dust, and Vapours. Occupational Hygiene
Physica A — Physica A. Theoretical and Statistical Physics
Physica B — Physica B. Europhysics Journal. Low Temperature and Solid State Physics

Physica C — Physica C. Europhysics Journal. Atomic, Molecular, and Plasma Physics Optics
Physical Educ J — Physical Education Journal
Physica Schrift Betriebswirtsch — Physica-Schriften zur Betriebswirtschaft
Physica Status Solidi A — Physica Status Solidi. Sectio A. Applied Research
Physica Status Solidi B — Physica Status Solidi. Sectio B. Basic Research
Physician and Surg — Physician and Surgeon
Physician Assist — Physician Assistant [*Later, Physician Assistant/Health Practitioner*]
Physician Assist Health — Physician Assistant/Health Practitioner
Physician Assist Health Pract — Physician Assistant/Health Practitioner
Physician Comput Monthly — Physician Computer Monthly
Physician Exec — Physician Executive
Physicians Drug Man — Physicians' Drug Manual
Physicians Guide Pract Gastroenterol — Physician's Guide to Practical Gastroenterology
Physicians Manage — Physicians Management
Physician Sportsmed — Physician and Sports Medicine
Physicochem Hydrodyn — Physicochemical Hydrodynamics
Physics & Chem — Physics and Chemistry
Physics Ed — Physics Education
Physics Med Biol — Physics in Medicine and Biology
Physics Teach — Physics Teacher
Physikal Zs — Physikalische Zeitschrift
Physikertag Hauptvortr Jahrestag Verb Dtsch Phys Ges — Physikertagung. Hauptvortraege der Jahrestagung des Verbandes Deutscher Physikalischer Gesellschaften
Physikertag Plenarvortr — Physikertagung, Plenarvortraege
Physikertag Vorabdrucke Kurzfassungen Fachber — Physikertagung. Vorabdrucke der Kurzfassungen der Fachberichte
Physikunterr — Physikunterricht
Phys Ind — Physics in Industry
Physiogr Saelsk Mag — Physiographiska Saelskapets Magazin
Physiol Abstr — Physiological Abstracts
Physiol Behav — Physiology and Behavior
Physiol Behav Mar Org Proc Eur Symp Mar Biol — Physiology and Behaviour of Marine Organisms. Proceedings.European Symposium on Marine Biology
Physiol Biochem Cultiv Plants — Physiology and Biochemistry of Cultivated Plants
Physiol Biochem Cult Plants (USSR) — Physiology and Biochemistry of Cultivated Plants (USSR)
Physiol Bohemoslov — Physiologia Bohemoslovaca
Physiol Can — Physiology Canada
Physiol Chem Phys — Physiological Chemistry and Physics [*Later, Physiological Chemistry and Physics and Medical NMR*]
Physiol Chem Phys Med NMR — Physiological Chemistry and Physics and Medical NMR
Physiol Dig Ruminant Pap Int Symp — Physiology of Digestion in the Ruminant. Papers Presented. International Symposium on the Physiology of Digestion in the Ruminant
Physiol Domest Fowl Br Egg Mark Board Symp — Physiology of the Domestic Fowl. British Egg Marketing Board Symposium
Physiol Ecol — Physiology and Ecology
Physiol Ecol (Jpn) — Physiology and Ecology (Japan)
Physiol Ent — Physiological Entomology
Physiol Entomol — Physiological Entomology
Physiol Genet — Physiological Genetics
Physiol Genomics — Physiological Genomics
Physiol Immun — Physiology of Immunity [*monograph*]
Physiol Intest Circ — Physiology of the Intestinal Circulation
Physiol Meas — Physiological Measurement
Physiol Mech Motiv — Physiological Mechanisms of Motivation [*monograph*]
Physiol Menschen — Physiologie des Menschen
Physiol Mol Plant Pathol — Physiological and Molecular Plant Pathology
Physiol Newborn Infant — Physiology of the Newborn Infant [*monograph*]
Physiol Oecol — Physiology and Oecology
Physiologia Comp Oecol — Physiologia Comparata et Oecologia
Physiologia Pl — Physiologia Plantarum
Physiol Pathol Eff Cytokines Proc Int Workshop Cytokines — Physiological and Pathological Effects of Cytokines. Proceedings. InternationalWorkshop on Cytokines
Physiol Pathol Perinat Anim Ferme Exp Journ Grenier Theix — Physiologie et Pathologie Perinatales chez les Animaux de Ferme. Exposes presentes aux Journees du Grenier de Theix
Physiol Pathophysiol Plasma Protein Metab Proc Int Symp — Physiology and Pathophysiology of Plasma Protein Metabolism. Proceedings. International Symposium
Physiol Pathophysiol Plasma Protein Metab Proc Symp — Physiology and Pathophysiology of Plasma Protein Metabolism. Proceedings. Symposium
Physiol Pathophysiol Skin — Physiology and Pathophysiology of the Skin
Physiol Pharmacol Adenosine Deriv Proc Meet — Physiology and Pharmacology of Adenosine Derivatives. Proceedings. Meeting
Physiol Pharmacol Epileptogenic Phenom — Physiology and Pharmacology of Epileptogenic Phenomena
Physiol Pharmacol Microcirc — Physiology and Pharmacology of the Microcirculation
Physiol Pharmacol Physicians — Physiology and Pharmacology for Physicians
Physiol Physicians — Physiology for Physicians
Physiol Pl — Physiologia Plantarum
Physiol Plant Pathol — Physiological Plant Pathology
Physiol Plant Suppl — Physiologia Plantarum. Supplementum
Physiol Prematurity Trans Conf — Physiology of Prematurity. Transactions. Conference
Physiol Prop Plant Protoplasts — Physiological Properties of Plant Protoplasts
Physiol Psychol — Physiological Psychology

Physiol Res — Physiological Research
Physiol Res Prague — Physiological Research (Prague)
Physiol Rev — Physiological Reviews
Physiol Russe — Physiologiste Russe
Physiol Sex Reprod Flowering Plants Int Symp — Physiology of Sexual Reproduction in Flowering Plants. International Symposium
Physiol Soc Philadelphia Monogr — Physiological Society of Philadelphia. Monographs
Physiol Strategies Gas Exch Metab — Physiological Strategies for Gas Exchange and Metabolism
Physiol Teach — Physiology Teacher
Physiol Veg — Physiologie Vegetale
Physiol Zool — Physiological Zoology
Phys Ioniz Gases — Physics of Ionized Gases
Physiother Can — Physiotherapy Canada
Physiother Pract — Physiotherapy Practice
Physiother Res Int — Physiotherapy Research International
Physiother Res Newsl — Physiotherapy Research Newsletter
Physis Riv Internaz Storia Sci — Physis. Rivista Internazionale di Storia della Scienza
Physis Riv Internaz Storia Sci NS — Physis. Rivista Internazionale di Storia della Scienza. Nuova Serie
Physis Secc A Oceanos Org — Physis. Seccion A: Oceanos y Sus Organismos
Physis Secc A Oceanos Sus Org — Physis. Seccion A: Oceanos y Sus Organismos
Physis Secc B Aguas Cont Org — Physis. Seccion B: Aguas Continentales y Sus Organismos
Physis Secc B Aguas Cont Sus Org — Physis. Seccion B: Aguas Continentales y Sus Organismos
Physis Secc C Cont los Org Terr — Physis. Seccion C: los Continentes y los Organismos Terrestres
Physis Secc C Cont Org Terr — Physis. Seccion C: Continentes y Organismos Terrestres
Phys Kondens Mater — Physik der Kondensierten Materie
Phys Latent Image Form Silver Halides Proc Int Symp — Physics of Latent Image Formation in Silver Halides. Proceedings. International Symposium
Physl Behav — Physiology and Behavior
Physl Bohem — Physiologia Bohemoslovaca
Physl Chem — Physiological Chemistry and Physics [Later, Physiological Chemistry and Physics and Medical NMR]
Phys LEP — Physics at LEP (Large Electron-Positron)
Phys Lett — Physics Letters
Phys Lett A — Physics Letters. Section A
Phys Lett B — Physics Letters. Section B
Phys Lett C — Physics Letters. Section C
Phys Letters — Physics Letters
Phys Low Dimens Syst Proc Nobel Symp — Physics of Low-Dimensional Systems. Proceedings of Nobel Symposium
Physl Plant — Physiologia Plantarum
Physl Pl P — Physiological Plant Pathology
Physl Psych — Physiological Psychology
Physl Veget — Physiologie Vegetale
Physl Zool — Physiological Zoology
Phys Mag — Physicalia Magazine
Phys Magmat Processes Proc — Physics of Magmatic Processes. Proceedings
Phys Magn Mater Proc Int Conf — Physics of Magnetic Materials. Proceedings. International Conference on Physicsof Magnetic Materials
Phys Mater Sci High Temp Supercond II — Physics and Materials Science of High Temperature Superconductors. II
Phys Matiere Condens — Physique de la Matiere Condensee
Phys Mech Prop Rocks — Physical and Mechanical Properties of Rocks
Phys Mech Radiat Biol Proc Conf — Physical Mechanisms in Radiation Biology. Proceedings. Conference
Phys Med Abh Koenigl Acad Wiss Berlin — Physikalische und Medicinische Abhandlungen der Koeniglichen Akademie der Wissenschaften zu Berlin
Phys Med and Biol — Physics in Medicine and Biology
Phys Med Atmos Space Proc Int Symp — Physics and Medicine of the Atmosphere and Space. Proceedings. International Symposium
Phys Med Bi — Physics in Medicine and Biology
Phys Med Biol — Physics in Medicine and Biology
Phys Med Rehabil Clin N Am — Physical Medicine and Rehabilitation Clinics of North America
Phys Met — Physics of Metals
Phys Metall — Physical Metallurgy
Phys Metall Beryllium Conf — Physical Metallurgy of Beryllium. Conference
Phys Methods Chem — Physical Methods of Chemistry [monograph]
Phys Methods Chem Anal — Physical Methods in Chemical Analysis
Phys Methods Determ Mineral — Physical Methods in Determinative Mineralogy [monograph]
Phys Methods Heterocycl Chem — Physical Methods in Heterocyclic Chemistry
Phys Methods Macromol Chem — Physical Methods in Macromolecular Chemistry
Phys Methods Mod Chem Anal — Physical Methods in Modern Chemical Analysis
Phys Met Metallogr — Physics of Metals and Metallography
Phys Met Metallogr Engl Transl — Physics of Metals and Metallography (English Translation)
Phys Met (USSR) — Physics of Metals (USSR)
Phys Narrow Gap Semicond Proc Int Conf — Physics of Narrow Gap Semiconductors. Proceedings. International Conference
Phys News — Physics News Bulletin. Indian Physics Association
Phys News Bombay — Physics News (Bombay)
Phys News Mumbai India — Physics News (Mumbai, India)
Phys Non Cryst Solids Int Conf — Physics of Non-Crystalline Solids. International Conference
Phys Nondestr Test Proc Symp — Physics and Nondestructive Testing. Proceedings. Symposium

Phys Non Therm Radio Sources — Physics of Non-Thermal Radio Sources
Phys Norv — Physica Norvegica
Phys Norveg — Physica Norvegica
Phys Notes — Physics Notes
Phys Occup Ther Geriatr — Physical and Occupational Therapy in Geriatrics
Phys Occup Ther Pediatr — Physical and Occupational Therapy in Pediatrics
Phys Oekon Monaths Quartalschr — Physikalisch-Oekonomische Monaths- und Quartalschrifft
Phys Oekon Patriot — Der Physikalische und Oekonomische Patriot oder Bemerkungen und Nachrichten ausder Naturhistorie, der Algemeinen Haushaltungskunst, und der Handlungskunst
Phys Oper — Physical Operations [monograph]
Phys Pap — Physics Papers
Phys Pap Silesian Univ Katowice — Physics Papers. Silesian University in Katowice
Phys Particles Nuclei — Physics of Particles and Nuclei
Phys Plasmas — Physics of Plasmas
Phys Plenarvortr Physikertag — Physik Plenarvortraege der Physikertagung
Phys Princ Tech Protein Chem — Physical Principles and Techniques of Protein Chemistry
Phys Prop Amorphous Mater — Physical Properties of Amorphous Materials [monograph]
Phys Prop Polym — Physical Properties of Polymers
Phys Quantum Electron — Physics of Quantum Electronics
Phys R — Physical Review
Phys Regelm Ber — Physik in Regelmaessigen Berichten
Phys Rep — Physics Reports. Review Section of Physics Letters. Section C
Phys Rep Kumamoto Univ — Physics Reports. Kumamoto University
Phys Rep Phys Lett Sect C — Physics Reports. Physics Letters. Section C
Phys Res — Physical Research
Phys Res Methods Sediment Rocks Miner — Physical Research Methods of Sedimentary Rocks and Minerals
Phys Rev — Physical Review
Phys Rev — Physiological Reviews
Phys Rev A — Physical Review. Section A. General Physics
Phys Rev A 3 — Physical Review. Section A. General Physics. Third Series
Phys Rev A Gen Phys — Physical Review. Section A. General Physics
Phys Rev B 3 — Physical Review. Section B. Condensed Matter. Third Series
Phys Rev B Conden Matt — Physical Review. Section B. Condensed Matter
Phys Rev B Condens Matter — Physical Review. Section B. Condensed Matter
Phys Rev B Solid State — Physical Review B. Solid State
Phys Rev C — Physical Review. Section C. Nuclear Physics
Phys Rev C 3 — Physical Review. Section C. Nuclear Physics. Third Series
Phys Rev C Nucl Phys — Physical Review C. Nuclear Physics
Phys Rev D — Physical Review. Section D. Particles and Fields
Phys Rev D 3 — Physical Review. Section D. Particles and Fields. Third Series
Phys Rev D Part Fields — Physical Review D. Particles and Fields
Phys Rev E — Physical Review E. Statistical Physics, Plasmas, Fluids, and Related Interdisciplinary Topics
Phys Rev E 3 — Physical Review E. Statistical Physics, Plasmas, Fluids, and Related Interdiscplinary Topics. Third Series
Phys Rev E Stat Phys Plasmas Fluids Relat Interdiscip Topics — Physical Review. E. Statistical Physics, Plasmas, Fluids, and Related Interdisciplinary Topics
Phys Rev L — Physical Review. Letters
Phys Rev Lett — Physical Review. Letters
Phys Rev Sect A — Physical Review. Section A. General Physics
Phys Rev Sect B — Physical Review. Section B. Condensed Matter
Phys Rev Suppl — Physical Review. Supplement
Phys Sante Install Nucl Symp — Physique de Sante dans les Installations Nucleaires. Symposium
Phys Schule — Physik in der Schule
Phys Sci Data — Physical Sciences Data
Phys Sci Res Pap US Air Force Cambridge Res Lab — Physical Sciences Research Papers. United States. Air Force Cambridge Research Laboratories
Phys Sci Some Recent Adv Fr US Proc Symp Basic Sci Fr US — Physical Sciences. Some Recent Advances in France and the United States. Proceedings. Symposium on Basic Science in France and the United States
Phys Scr — Physica Scripta
Phys Scripta — Physica Scripta
Phys Scr T — Physica Scripta. T
Phys Selenium Tellurium Proc Int Symp — Physics of Selenium and Tellurium. Proceedings. International Symposium
Phys Semicond Compd Proc Conf — Physics of Semiconducting Compounds. Proceedings. Conference on Physics of Semiconducting Compounds
Phys Semicond CR Congr Int — Physique des Semiconducteurs. Comptes Rendus. Congres International
Phys Semicond Devices Proc Int Workshop — Physics of Semiconductor Devices. Proceedings. International Workshop
Phys Semicond Int Conf — Physics of Semiconductors. International Conference
Phys Semicond Invited Contrib Pap Int Conf — Physics of Semiconductors. Invited and Contributed Papers. International Conference on the Physics of Semiconductors
Phys Semicond Proc Int Conf — Physics of Semiconductors. Proceedings. International Conference
Phys Simul Optoelectron Devices — Physics and Simulation of Optoelectronic Devices
Phys Sintering — Physics of Sintering
Phys Soc Lond Proc — Physical Society of London. Proceedings
Phys Soc Year Book — Physical Society. Year Book
Phys Solariterr — Physica Solariterrestris
Phys Solid Earth (Engl Ed) — Physics of the Solid Earth (English Edition)
Phys Solids High Pressures Proc Int Conf — Physics of Solids at High Pressures. Proceedings. International Conference on the Physics of Solids at High Pressures

Phys Solids Liq — Physics of Solids and Liquids
Phys Solid Surf Proc Symp — Physics of Solid Surfaces. Proceedings. Symposium
Phys Solid Surf Proc Symp Surf Phys — Physics of Solid Surfaces. Proceedings. Symposium on Surface Physics
Phys Sol Prominences Proc Int Astron Union Colloq — Physics of Solar Prominences. Proceedings. International Astronomical Union Colloquium
Phys Star Form Early Stellar Evol — Physics of Star Formation and Early Stellar Evolution
Phys Stat Sol A — Physica Status Solidi. Sectio A. Applied Research
Phys Stat Sol B — Physica Status Solidi. Sectio B. Basic Research
Phys Status Solidi — Physica Status Solidi
Phys Status Solidi A — Physica Status Solidi. Sectio A. Applied Research
Phys Status Solidi B — Physica Status Solidi. Sectio B. Basic Research
Phys Steel Ind Lehigh Univ — Physics in the Steel Industry. Lehigh University
Phys Strength Plast — Physics of Strength and Plasticity
Phys St S-A — Physica Status Solidi. Sectio A. Applied Research
Phys St S-B — Physica Status Solidi. Sectio B. Basic Research
Phys SuperLEAR Proc SuperLEAR Workshop — Physics of SuperLEAR. Proceedings. SuperLEAR Workshop
Phys Taschenb Freunde Naturl Kuenstler — Physikalisches Taschenbuch Fuer Freunde der Naturlehre und Kuenstler
Phys Teach — Physics Teacher
Phys Teacher — Physics Teacher
Phys Tech Biol Res — Physical Techniques in Biological Research
Phys Tech Bundesanst Ber APh — Physikalisch-Technische Bundesanstalt. Bericht APh
Phys Tech Bundesanst Ber ATWD — Physikalisch-Technische Bundesanstalt. Bericht ATWD
Phys Tech Bundesanst Ber Dos — Physikalisch-Technische Bundesanstalt. Bericht Dos
Phys Tech Bundesanst Ber E — Physikalisch-Technische Bundesanstalt. Bericht E
Phys Tech Bundesanst Ber Me — Physikalisch-Technische Bundesanstalt. Bericht Me
Phys Tech Bundesanst Ber ND — Physikalisch-Technische Bundesanstalt. Bericht ND
Phys Tech Bundesanst Ber Opt — Physikalisch-Technische Bundesanstalt. Bericht Opt
Phys Tech Bundesanst Ber PG — Physikalisch-Technische Bundesanstalt. Bericht PG
Phys Tech Bundesanst Ber Ra — Physikalisch-Technische Bundesanstalt. Bericht Ra
Phys Tech Bundesanst Ber SE — Physikalisch-Technische Bundesanstalt. Bericht SE
Phys Tech Bundesanst Ber W — Physikalisch-Technische Bundesanstalt. Bericht W
Phys Technol — Physics in Technology
Phys Tech Semicond — Physics and Technics of Semiconductors
Phys Ther — Physical Therapy
Phys Therapy — Physical Therapy
Phys Therapy Rev — Physical Therapy Review
Phys Thin Films — Physics of Thin Films. Advances in Research and Development
Phys Today — Physics Today
Phys Unserer Zeit — Physik in Unserer Zeit
Phys Upper Atmos — Physics of the Upper Atmosphere
Phys Verh — Physikalische Verhandlungen
Phys World — Physics World
Phys Z — Physikalische Zeitschrift
Phys Z Beih — Physikalische Zeitschrift. Beihefte
Phys Zeit — Physikalische Zeitschrift
Phys Zeitung — Physicalische Zeitung
Phys Zool — Physiological Zoology
Phys Zschr — Physikalische Zeitschrift
Phys Z Sowjetunion — Physikalische Zeitschrift der Sowjetunion
Phyt — Phytopathology
PHYTA — Phytopathology
PHYTB — Physics in Technology
Phytiat Phytopharm — Phytiatrie-Phytopharmacie
Phytiatr-Phytopharm Rev Fr Med Pharm Veg — Phytiatrie-Phytopharmacie. Revue Francaise de Medicine et de Pharmacie des Vegetaux
Phytochem — Phytochemistry
Phytochem Anal — Phytochemical Analysis
Phytochem Eff Environ Compd — Phytochemical Effects of Environmental Compounds
Phytochemistr (Oxf) — Phytochemistry (Oxford)
Phytochem Soc Annu Proc — Phytochemical Society. Annual Proceedings
Phytochem Soc Eur Proc — Phytochemical Society of Europe. Proceedings
Phytochem Soc Eur Symp Ser — Phytochemical Society of Europe. Symposia Series
Phytodepur Use Prod Biomasses Proc Int Congr — Phytodepuration and Use of the Produced Biomasses. Proceedings. International Congress
Phytoma Def Cult — Phytoma. Defense des Cultures
Phytomorph — Phytomorphology
Phytomorphol — Phytomorphology
Phyton Ann Rei Bot — Phyton. Annales Rei Botanicae
Phyton (Aust) — Phyton. Annales Rei Botanicae (Austria)
Phyton Int J Exp Bot — Phyton. International Journal of Experimental Botany
Phyton Rev Int Bot Exp — Phyton. Revista Internacional de Botanica Experimental
Phytoparasit Isr J Plant Prot Sci — Phytoparasitica. Israel Journal of Plant Protection Sciences
Phytopathol — Phytopathology
Phytopathol Knowl — Phytopathological Knowledge
Phytopathol Medit — Phytopathologia Mediterranea
Phytopathol Mediterr — Phytopathologie Mediterranea

Phytopathol News — Phytopathology News
Phytopathol Z — Phytopathologische Zeitschrift
Phytopathol Z Beih — Phytopathologische Zeitschrift. Beiheft
Phytopathol ZJ Phytopathol — Phytopathologische Zeitschrift/Journal of Phytopathology
Phytopath Z — Phytopathologische Zeitschrift
Phytoprot — Phytoprotection
Phytother R — Phytotherapy Research
Phytotronic Newsl — Phytotronic Newsletter
Phyto Zeits — Phytopathologische Zeitschrift
PHYVA — Physiologie Vegetale
PHYZA — Phytopathologische Zeitschrift
PHZAA — Pharmazeutische Zeitung. Vereinigt mit Apotheker-Zeitung
PHZIA — Pharmazeutische Zeitung
PHZOA — Physiological Zoology
PI — Pagine Istriane
PI — Peru Indigena
PI — Philadelphia Inquirer
PI — Philosopher's Index
PI — Pilot. Fort Smith and Simpson
PI — Politica Internacional
PI — Political India
PI — Portugal Ilustrado
PI — Printers' Ink
PI — Psychological Issues
PIA — Pensions and Investment Age
PIA — Proceedings. Irish Academy
PIA — Proceedings. Royal Irish Academy
PIA — Propiedad Industrial y Artistica
PIA Abstr — P.I.A. Abstracts. Chemical Section. Pine Institute of America
PIAAD — Proceedings. Indian Academy of Sciences. Series Chemical Sciences
PIACA — Proceedings. Indiana Academy of Science
PIAE — Publicacoes. Instituto de Antropologia e Etnologia do Para [Belem]
Piaget Theor Help Prof — Piagetian Theory and the Helping Professions
PIAH — International Journal of African Historical Studies
PIAL — International Journal of American Linguistics
PIAMD — Proceedings. Indian Academy of Sciences. Series Mathematical Sciences
PIAND — Proceedings. Indian Academy of Sciences. Series Animal Sciences
Piano Q — Piano Quarterly
Piano Quart — Piano Quarterly
Piano Tech — Piano Technician
PIASB — Proceedings of the Indian Academy of Sciences. Section B. Biology
P I A Sci A — Proceedings. Indian Academy of Sciences. Section A
P I A Sci B — Proceedings. Indian Academy of Sciences. Section B
PIASH — Proceedings. Israel Academy of Sciences and Humanities
PIAUP — Publications de l'Institut d'Art et d'Archeologie de l'Universite de Paris
PIB — Public Information Bulletin
PIB — Publishing Information Bulletin
PIBSB — Proceedings. Indian National Science Academy. Part B. Biological Sciences
PIBTAD — Proceedings. Congress of the International Society of Blood Transfusion
PIC — Perspectives in Computing
PIC — Physical Inorganic Chemistry
PICA — Property Services Agency Information on Construction and Architecture
PICAM — Proceedings. International Congress of Americanists
PICAO JI — PICAO Journal [Montreal]
Picardie — Bulletins. Societe des Antiquaires de Picardie
Picardie Inform — Picardie Information
PICC — Istituto Cristoforo Colombo. Pubblicazioni
PICED — Proceedings. International Conference on Noise Control Engineering
PICI — Publications. Institut de Civilisation Indienne
P I Civ E 1 — Proceedings. Institution of Civil Engineers. Part 1. Design and Construction
P I Civ E 2 — Proceedings. Institution of Civil Engineers. Part 2. Research and Theory
PICJ — Pacific Islands Communication Journal
Picker Clin Scintil — Picker Clinical Scintillator
Pickle Pak Sci — Pickle Pak Science
PICL — Proceedings. International Congress of Linguists
PICM — Publications. Irish Church Missions
PICO — Proceedings. International Congress of Orientalists
Picosecond Phenom Proc Int Conf — Picosecond Phenomena. Proceedings. International Conference on Picosecond Phenomena
PICP — Proceedings. International Congress of Philosophy
Pic Patr — Ricerche Patristiche
PICPS — Proceedings. International Congress of Phonetic Sciences
PICS — International Journal of Comparative Sociology
Pict Atlas Australia — Picturesque Atlas of Australia
Pict Post — Picture Post
PictR — Pictorial Review
Pict Rev — Pictorial Review
PId — Parole e le Idee
PID — Personality and Individual Differences
PID — Prae-Italic Dialects of Italy
PIDA Bull — P.I.D.A. Bulletin [London]
PIDE — Publications de L'Institut du Desert d'Egypte
PIE — Pacific Islands Ecosystems
PIEEA — Proceedings. Institution of Electrical Engineers
P IEEE — Proceedings. Institute of Electrical and Electronics Engineers
P IEE (Lond) — Proceedings. Institution of Electrical Engineers (London)
PIEL — Publicaciones del Instituto de Arqueologia, Linguistica, y Folklore. Dr. Pablo Cabrera (Cordoba, Argentina)
Pieleg Polozna — Pielegniarka i Polozna
PIEM — Publications. Institut d'Etudes Medievales
PIEMO — Publications. Institut d'Etudes Medievales d'Ottawa

Pienpuu Toimikun Julk — Pienpuualan Toimikunnan Julkaisu
PIEO — Publications. Institut d'Etudes Orientales de la Bibliotheque Patriarcale d'Alexandrie
PIEOA — Publications. Institut d'Etudes Orientales d'Alger
PIERS — Port Import/Export Reporting Service
PIESD — Proceedings. Indian Academy of Sciences. Series Earth and Planetary Sciences
Piet Neuzeit — Pietismus und Neuzeit. Ein Jahrbuch zur Geschichte des Neueren Protestantismus
PIEWD — Prace Naukowe Instytutu Energoelektryki Politechniki Wroclawskiej
PIF — Paris et Ile-De-France. Memoires
PIFA — Institut Francais d'Amsterdam. Maison Descartes. Publications
PIFAO — Publications. Institut Francais d'Archeologie Orientale du Caire
PIFAO BEC — Publications. Institut Francais d'Archeologie Orientale. Bibliotheque d'Etudes Coptes
PIFAS — Publicaciones. Instituto de Filologia. Anejo de Sphinx
PIFI — Publications. Institut Francaise d'Indologie
PIFLD — Problemy Yadernoi Fiziki i Kosmicheskikh Luchei
PIFMLL — Proceedings. International Federation for Modern Languages and Literatures
PIFWD — Prace Naukowe Instytutu Fizyki Politechniki Wroclawskiej
Pig — Pig Iron
PIG — Pork Industry Gazette
PIGBA — Proceedings. Royal Institution of Great Britain
Pigm Cell — Pigment Cell
Pigm Cell Biol Proc Conf Biol Norm Atyp Pig Cell Growth — Pigment Cell Biology. Proceedings. Conference on the Biology of Normal and Atypical Pigment Cell Growth
Pigment Cell Res — Pigment Cell Research
Pigment Resin Tech — Pigment and Resin Technology
Pigment Resin Technol — Pigment and Resin Technology
Pigm Handb — Pigment Handbook [*monograph*]
Pigm Pathol — Pigments in Pathology
Pig News Inf — Pig News and Information
Pig Rsn Tech — Pigment and Resin Technology
PIGWA — Prace Instytutu Gospodarki Wodnej
PIHANS — Publications. Institut Historique et Archeologique Neerlandais de Stamboul
PIHI — Journal of Interdisciplinary History
PIHRC — Proceedings. Indian Historical Record Commission
PIHRFSI — Publications of the Institute of Hydrobiologic Research of the Faculty of Science. University of Istanbul
PIHUA — Prace Instytutow Hutniczych
PIIAA — Proceedings. National Institute of Sciences (India). Part A. Physical Sciences
PIICAV — Convenio IICA-ZN-ROCAP [*Instituto Interamericano de Ciencias Agricolas-Zona Norte-Regional Organization for Central America and Panama*] Publicacion Miscelanea
PIID — Publishers' International ISBN [*International Standard Book Number*] Directory
PIJS — Papers. Institute of Jewish Studies
PIKH — Publikasjoner. Institutt for Kirkehistorie
PIKM — PIK. Northern Magazine for Children
PIL — Papers in Linguistics
PIL — Penn Club Internacional (London)
Pillnitzer Merkbl Pflanzenschutz — Pillnitzer Merkblaetter fuer Pflanzenschutz
PILOA — Prace Instytutu Lotnictwa
PILSA — Progress in Immunobiological Standardization
PI Lux — Publications. Section Historique. Institut Royal Grandducal de Luxembourg
PIM — Pacific Islands Monthly
PIM — Politica Internacional (Madrid)
PIM — Progress in Industrial Microbiology
PIMA Mag — PIMA [*Paper Industry Management Association*] Magazine
P I M Assn J — Philippine Islands Medical Association. Journal
PIMA Yrb — PIMA [*Paper Industry Management Association*] Yearbook
PIMBel — Pracy Instytuta Movaznaustva Akademii Nauk Belaruskaj SSR
PIME — Petrofi Irodalmi Muzeum Evkonyve
PIMGA — Production and Inventory Management
PIMR — International Migration Review. IMR
PIMRA — Progress in Industrial Microbiology
PIMSST — Pontifical Institute of Mediaeval Studies. Studies and Texts
PIMST — Pontifical Institute of Mediaeval Studies. Studies and Texts
PIMTB — Proceedings. Annual Technical Meeting. International Metallographic Society, Inc.
Pi Mu Epsilon J — Pi Mu Epsilon Journal
P I N — Palestine Illustrated Newsletter
PIN — Policy Review
PIN — Public Interest
PINA — International Affairs
PINCCA — Price Index Numbers for Current Cost Accounting
Pineal Funct Proc Satell Symp Int Congr Endocrinol — Pineal Function. Proceedings. Satellite Symposium. International Congress of Endocrinology
Pineal Res Rev — Pineal Research Reviews
Pineapple Q — Pineapple Quarterly
PINEDV — Annual Research Reviews. Pineal
Pine Inst Am Abstr Chem Sect — Pine Institute of America. Abstracts. Chemical Section
Pine Inst Am Tech Bull — Pine Institute of America. Technical Bulletin
PINH — Health
PINH — In Health
PINHA3 — Iraq Natural History Museum. Publication
PINQ — Inquiry
PINSA A Proc Indian Natl Sci Acad Part A — PINSA-A. Proceedings of the Indian National Science Academy. Part A. Physical Sciences

PINSA B Proc Indian Natl Sci Acad Part B — PINSA-B. Proceedings of the Indian National Science Academy. Part B. Biological Sciences
Pint Acabados Ind — Pinturas y Acabados Industriales
Pint Acabados Ind — Pinturas y Acabados Industriales. Recubrimientos Organicos y Metalicos
Pint Acabados Ind Secc Recubrimientos Met — Pinturas y Acabados Industriales. Seccion. Recubrimientos Metalicos
Pint Acabados Ind Secc Recubrimientos Org — Pinturas y Acabados Industriales. Seccion. Recubrimientos Organicos
Pint Acabados Ind Secc Trat Quim Electroqulm — Pinturas y Acabados Industriales. Seccion. Tratamientos Quimicos y Electroquimicos
PIOCA — Progress in Inorganic Chemistry
Pio Ist S Spirito Osp Riuniti Roma Cent Reumatol Boll — Pio Istituto di S. Spirito ed Ospedali Riuniti di Roma. Centro di Reumatologia.Bollettino
PIOL — Publications. Institut Orientaliste de Louvain
Pioneering Concepts Mod Sci — Pioneering Concepts in Modern Science
Pioneers' Assoc of SA Pubs — Pioneers' Association of South Australia. Publications
PIOR — International Organization
PIP — Penny Illustrated Paper
PIP — Product Improvement Program
PIPE — Pipeline. Report of the Northern Pipeline Agency
Pipe Gas J — Pipeline and Gas Journal
Pipeline & Gas J — Pipeline and Gas Journal
Pipeline Contractors Assoc Can — Pipeline Contractors Association of Canada
Pipe Line D — Pipeline Annual Directory and Equipment Guide
Pipeline Eng — Pipeline Engineer
Pipeline Eng Int — Pipeline Engineer International
Pipeline Gas J — Pipeline and Gas Journal
Pipe Line Ind — Pipe Line Industry
Pipeline Manage Oper Eng Gas Distrib News — Pipeline Management, Operations, Engineering, and Gas Distribution News
Pipeline Underground Util Constr — Pipeline and Underground Utilities Construction
Pipeln Ind — International Pipe Line Industry
Pipes & Pipelines Int — Pipes and Pipelines International
Pipes Pipelines Int — Pipes and Pipelines International
PIPGH — Publicaciones del Instituto Panamericano de Geografica e Historia [*Mexico*]
Piping Eng — Piping Engineering
Piping Process Mach (Tokyo) — Piping and Process Machinery (Tokyo)
PIPLD — Proceedings. Indian Academy of Sciences. Series Plant Sciences
Pipleine Eng — Pipeline Engineering
PIPQ — International Philosophical Quarterly
PIPR — International Journal for Philosophy of Religion
PIPSD — Preprint. Institut Prikladnoi Matematiki Akademii Nauk SSSR
PIPWA — Paper Industry and Paper World
PIPYDX — Proceedings. International Colloquium on Invertebrate Pathology
PIQUA — Pit and Quarry
PIR — Pecat' i Revoljucija
PIR — Professional Investor Report
PIR — Prosopographia Imperii Romani
PIRA Packag Abstr — PIRA [*Printing Industry Research Association*] Packaging Abstracts
Pirckheimer Jb — Pirckheimer-Jahrbuch
PIRED — Power Industry Research
PIRHT — Publications. Institut de Recherche et d'Histoire des Textes
PIRM — International Review of Mission
Pirprofen Treat Pain Inflammation Proc Int Symp — Pirprofen in the Treatment of Pain and Inflammation. Proceedings. InternationalSymposium
PIRS — Perspectives in Religious Studies
PIS — Prepodavanie Istorii v Shkole
PiS — Proceedings. Iran Society
PiS — Puskin i Ego Sovremenniki
PISA — Publication. Institute of Social Anthropology
PISAA7 — Indian Academy of Sciences. Proceedings. Section A. Earth and Planetary Sciences
Pisa A Un Tosc — Annali delle Universita Toscane. Parte 2da. Scienze Cosmologiche (Pisa)
Pisa A Un Tosc Sc Cosm — Annali delle Universita Toscane. Parte 2da. Scienze Cosmologiche (Pisa)
PISAD — Proceedings. International Symposium on Automotive Technology and Automation
Pisa Misc Md Chir — Miscellanea Medico-Chirurgico-Farmaceutiche Raccolte in Pisa
Pisa N G — Nuovo Giornale de' Letterati (Pisa)
Pisa S Tosc At Mm — Atti della Societa Toscana di Scienze Naturali Residente in Pisa. Memorie
Pisa S Tosc At PV — Atti della Societa Toscana di Scienze Naturali Residente in Pisa. Processi Verbali
PISBAA — Indian Academy of Sciences. Proceedings. Section B
PISC — Impact of Science on Society
PISC XLI — Proceedings of the Forty-first Indian Science Congress
PISC XLII — Proceedings of the Forty-second Indian Science Congress
PISC XLIII — Proceedings of the Forty-third Indian Science Congress
PISC XLVI — Proceedings of the Forty-sixth Indian Science Congress
PISC XXIX — Proceedings of the Twenty-ninth Indian Science Congress
PISEAJ — Proceedings. Research Institute of Pomology [*Skierniewice, Poland*]. Series E. Conferences and Symposia
PISF — Pubblicazioni. Istituto di Storia della Filosofia
Pishch Pererabatyvayushchaya Promst — Pishchevaya i Pererabatyvayushchaya Promyshlenost'
Pishch Prom Kaz — Pishchevaya Promyshlennost Kazakhstana
Pishch Prom Kiev — Pishchevaya Promyshlennost (Kiev)
Pishch Promst — Pishchevaya Promyshlennost

Pishch Promst Kaz Mezhved Resp Nauchno Tekh Sb — Pishchevaya Promyshlennost Kazakhstana Mezhvedomstvennyi Respublikanskii Nauchno Tekhnicheskii Sbornik

Pishch Prom-St (Kiev 1965) — Pishchevaya Promyshlennost (Kiev, 1965)

Pishch Promst (Moscow) — Pishchevaya Promyshlennost (Moscow)

Pishch Prom-St' Nauchno-Proizvod Sb — Pishchevaya Promyshlennost Nauchno-Proizvodstvennyi Sbornik

Pishch Promst Ser 6 Obz Inf — Pishchevaya Promyshlennost. Seriya 6. Maslo-Zhirovaya Promyshlennost. ObzornayaInformatsiya

Pishch Promst Ser 20 Obz Inf — Pishchevaya Promyshlennost. Seriya 20. Maslo-Zhirovaya Promyshlennost. Obzornaya Informatsiya

Pishch Promst Ser Nauchno Tekh Ref Sb — Pishchevaya Promyshlennost. Seriya. Vinodel'cheskaya Promyshlennost. Nauchno-Tekhnicheskii Referativnyi Sbornik

Pishch Promst SSSR — Pishchevaya Promyshlennost SSSR

Pishch Tekhnol — Pishchevaya Tekhnologiya

Pis'ma Astron Zh — Pis'ma v Astronomicheskii Zhurnal

Pis'ma v Astron Zh — Pis'ma v Astronomicheskii Zhurnal

Pis'ma v Zh Eksp i Teor Fiz — Pis'ma v Zhurnal Eksperimental'noi i Teoreticheskoi Fiziki

Pis'ma v Zh Tekh Fiz — Pis'ma v Zhurnal Tekhnicheskoi Fiziki

Pisma Zh Eksper Teoret Fiz — Pis'ma v Zhurnal Eksperimental'noi i Teoreticheskoi Fiziki

Pis'ma Zh Eksp Teor Fiz — Pis'ma v Zhurnal Eksperimental'noi i Teoreticheskoi Fiziki

Pis'ma Zh Tekh Fiz — Pis'ma v Zhurnal Tekhnicheskoi Fiziki

Pisma Zh Tekhn Fiz — Pis'ma v Zhurnal Tekhnicheskoii Fiziki

Pism Pam Vostoka — Pis'mennye Pamiatniki Vostoka

PISQ — International Studies Quarterly

PIStF — Pubbliccazioni. Istituto di Studi Filosofici

Pistoja At Ac — Atti della R. Accademia Pistojese di Scienze, Lettere, ed Arti. Memorie di Matematica e Fisica, per l' anno 1816

PISU — Publications. Institut Slave d'Upsal

PISW — Journal of Interamerican Studies and World Affairs

Pit & Quar — Pit and Quarry

Pitan Drev Rast — Pitanie Drevesnykh Rastenii

Pitanie Udobr Rast — Pitanie i Udobrenie Rastenii

Pitan Korml Ryb Mezhdunar Semin — Pitanie i Kormlenie Ryb. Mezhdunarodnyi Seminar

Pitannya Eksp Bot — Pitannya Eksperimental'noi Botaniki

Pitannya Fiz Tverd Tila — Pitannya Fiziki Tverdogo Tila

Pitannya Geol — Pitannya Geologii

Pitannya Tekhnol Obrob Vodi Promisl Pitnogo Vodopostachannya — Pitannya Tekhnologii Obrobki Vodi Promislovogo ta Pitnogo Vodopostachannya

Pitan Obmen Veshchestv Rast — Pitanie i Obmen Veshchestv u Rastenii

Pitan Prod Rast — Pitanie i Produktivnost Rastenii

Pitan Rast Primen Udobr — Pitanie Rastenii i Primenenie Udobrenii

Pitan Udobr Skh Rast Mold — Pitanie i Udobrenie Sel'skokhozyaistvennykh Rastenii v Moldavii

PITBB — Piano Teachers Journal

Pitblado Lect — Isaac Pitblado Lectures on Continuing Legal Education

Pitch Pine Nat — Pitch Pine Naturalist

PITKA — Proceedings. Institut Teknologi Bandung. Supplement

Pit L — University of Pittsburgh. Law Review

Pitman Monographs Surveys Pure Appl Math — Pitman Monographs and Surveys in Pure and Applied Mathematics

Pitman Res Notes Math Ser — Pitman Research Notes in Mathematics Series

Pit Quarry — Pit and Quarry

Pitt LJ — Pittsburgh Legal Journal

Pitt Rivers Mus Univ Oxford Occas Pap Technol — Pitt Rivers Museum. University of Oxford. Occasional Papers on Technology

Pittsb Bs T — Pittsburgh Business Times-Journal

Pittsbg Bs — Pittsburgh Business Review

Pittsbg P — Pittsburgh Press

Pittsb Leg J — Pittsburgh Legal Journal

Pittsb Leg J NS — Pittsburgh Legal Journal, New Series

Pittsb Leg J (OS) — Pittsburgh Legal Journal, Old Series

Pittsb Leg J (PA) — Pittsburgh Legal Journal

Pittsb LJ — Pittsburgh Legal Journal

Pittsb L Rev — Pittsburgh Law Review

Pittsburgh Bus R — Pittsburgh Business Review

Pittsburgher Mag — Pittsburgher Magazine

Pittsburgh Leg J — Pittsburgh Legal Journal

Pittsburgh Leg Journal — Pittsburgh Legal Journal

Pittsburgh Rec — Pittsburgh Record

Pittsburgh Sch — Pittsburgh Schools

Pittsburgh Univ Bull — Pittsburgh University. Bulletin

Pittsburgh Univ Sch Ed J — Pittsburgh University. School of Education Journal

Pitts Leg J — Pittsburgh Legal Journal

Pitts Leg J (NS) — Pittsburgh Legal Journal, New Series

Pitts Leg Jour — Pittsburgh Legal Journal

Pitts LJ — Pittsburgh Legal Journal

Pitts LJ (NS) — Pittsburgh Legal Journal, New Series

Pitts L Rev — University of Pittsburgh. Law Review

Pitt Sym — Pittsburgh Symphony Orchestra. Program Notes

Pitture Vern — Pitture e Vernici

Pitture Vernici Eur — Pitture e Vernici Europe

Pivovar Cas Kvas — Pivovarsky Casopis Kvas

PivS — Pivnicne Sjajvo

PIW — Petroleum Intelligence Weekly

PIW — Polski Instytut Wydawniczy

PIWCA — Proceedings. International Waste Conference

PIWSD — Proceedings. International Wire and Cable Symposium

PIZK — Pantheon. Internationale Zeitschrift fuer Kunst

PJ — ICC [*Interstate Commerce Commission*] Practitioners' Journal

PJ — Palastinajahrbuch. Deutsches Evangelische Institut fuer Altertumswissenschaft des Heiligen Landes zu Jerusalem

PJ — Personnel Journal

PJ — Pharmaceutical Journal

PJ — Philosophisches Jahrbuch

PJ — Poradnik Jezykowy

PJ — Preussische Jahrbuecher

PJ — Privacy Journal

PJ — Prudhoe Bay Journal

PJa — Papers on Japan

PJAA — Journal. American Academy of Religion

PJAC — Journal of American Culture

PJACA — Proceedings. Japan Academy

PJAH — Journal of African History

PJAIA — Philippine Journal of Animal Industry

P Jap Acad — Proceedings. Japan Academy

PJAR — Journal of Anthropological Research

PJAS — Journal of Asian and African Studies

PJAY — Journal of Asian History

PJB — Palastinajahrbuch. Deutsches Evangelische Institut fuer Altertumswissenschaft des Heiligen Landes zu Jerusalem

PJb — Preussische Jahrbuecher

PJBL — Journal of Biblical Literature

PJBRS — Palestine Journal of Botany. Rehovot Series

PJBS — Journal of British Studies

PJBSA — Pavlovian Journal of Biological Science

PJC — Publications. Jews' College

PJCA — Journal of Contemporary Asia

PJCE — Journal of Comparative Economics

PJCH — Journal of Church and State

PJCJ — Journal of Criminal Justice

PJCL — Journal of Commonwealth Literature

PJCP — Journal of Comparative Psychology

PJCR — Journal of Confict Resolution

PJCS — Journal of Canadian Studies

PJE — Peabody Journal of Education

PJEC — Journal of Ecology

PJEG — JEGP. Journal of English and Germanic Philology

PJEH — Journal of American Ethnic History

PJER — Journal of the Early Republic

PJET — Journal of Contemporary Ethnography

PJez — Prace Jezykoznawcze Polskiej Akademii Nauk

PJFH — Journal of Family History

PJFI — Journal of Family Issues

PJFS — Journal of Food Science

PJGG — Philosophisches Jahrbuch der Goerres-Gesellschaft

PJGNI — Persica. Jaarboek van het Genootschap Nederland-Iran

PJGP — Journal of General Psychology

PJGS — Journal of Genetic Psychology

PJHB — Journal of Rehabilitation Research and Development

PJHG — Journal of Historical Geography

PJHNAW — Pavlov Journal of Higher Nervous Activity

PJHP — Journal of the History of Philosophy

PJHS — Journal of Hellenic Studies

PJHX — Journal of Homosexuality

PJI — Personnel Journal Index

PJIA — Journal of International Affairs

PJJ — Provincial Judges Journal

PJJQ — James Joyce Quarterly

PJJS — Journal of Japanese Studies

PJK — Prace Jezykoznawcze

PJL — Philippine Journal of Linguistics

PJLN — Journal of Linguistics

PJLT — Philippine Journal of Language Teaching

PJMA — Journal of Mammalogy

PJME — Journal of Medical Ethics

PJMF — Journal of Marital and Family Therapy

PJMH — Journal of Military History

PJMP — Journal of Medicine and Philosophy

PJMR — Journal of Medieval and Renaissance Studies

PJMU — Journal of Musicology

PJN — Philippine Journal of Nursing

PJNB — Journal of Nonverbal Behavior

PJNE — Journal of Near Eastern Studies

PJNEE5 — Pakistan Journal of Nematology

PJNU — Journal of Nutrition Education

PJNu — Philippine Journal of Nutrition

PJOPA — Pakistan Journal of Psychology

PJOS — Journal. American Oriental Society

PJOU — Journalism History

P j P — Paperi ja Puu

PJP — Philippine Journal of Pediatrics

PJPA — Journal of Parapsychology

PJPA — Philippine Journal of Public Administration

PJPH — Journal of Pacific History

PJPI — Philippine Journal of Plant Industry

PJPL — Journal of Politics

PJPM — Journal of Policy Analysis and Management

PJPR — Journal of Peace Research

PJPS — Journal of Police Science and Admnistration

PJPY — Journal of Personality

PJRC — Journal of Research in Crime and Delinquency

PJRCM — Philippine Junior Red Cross Magazine

PJRE — Journal of Rehabilitation

PJRL — Journal of Religion

PJRM — Journal of Recreational Mathematics
PJRO — Journal of Roman Studies
PJRS — Journal of Religious Ethics
PJS — Pakistan Journal of Science
PJS — Philippine Journal of Science
PJSchE — Politisches Jahrbuch der Schweizerischen Eidgenossenschaft
PJ Schw E — Politisches Jahrbuch der Schweizerischen Eidgenoessenschaft
PJSE — Journal of Southeast Asian Studies
PJSG — Journal of State Government
PJSH — Journal of Social History
PJSN — Journal of Southern History
PJSP — Journal of Social Policy
PJSR — Journal for the Scientific Study of Religion
PJSR — Pakistan Journal of Scientific Research
PJSRA — Pakistan Journal of Scientific Research
PJSS — Journal of Social, Political, and Economic Studies
PJSS — Philippine Journal of Surgical Specialties
PJST — Journal of Modern African Studies
PJSX — Journal of Sex Research
PJT — Pacific Journal of Theology
PJTP — Planner Journal. Royal Town Planning Institute
PJTS — Journal of Theological Studies
PJUH — Journal of Urban History
P Jur Vj — Prager Juristische Vierteljahrsschrift
PJWM — Journal of Wildlife Management
PJWT — Journal of the West
PJYA — Journal of Youth and Adolescence
PJZSAZ — Agriculturae Conspectus Scientificus
PK — Pam'iatniki Kul'tury. Novye Otkrytiia
PK — Philologike Kypros
PK — Pinkas ha-Kehilot
PK — Plaste und Kautschuk
PK — Politicka Knihovna Ceskoslovenske Strany Lidove
PK — Prawo Kanoniczne
PK — Praxis-Kurier
PK — Problemy Kibernetiki
PK — Promyslovaia Kooperaciia
PK — Przeglad Klasyczny
PK — Przeglad Koscielny
PK — Przeglad Kulturalny
PKAS — Publications. Kroeber Anthropological Society
PKC — Beijing Review
PKCVA — Promyshlennost Khimicheskikh Reaktivov i Osobo Chistykh Veshchestv
PKDR-B — Pakistan Development Review
PKE — Pakistan and Gulf Economist
PKEN — Kenyon Review
PKF — Pytannia Klasychnoi Filologii
PKFil — Pytannia Klasychnoi Filologii
PKG — Propylaeen Kunstgeschichte
Pkg Abstr — Packaging Abstracts
Pkg Eng — Package Engineering
Pkg (India) — Packaging (India)
Pkg (London) — Packaging (London)
Pkg News — Packaging News
Pkg Technol — Packaging Technology and Management
PKH — Publikatieblad van de Europese Gemeenschappen. Handelingen van het Europese Parlement
PKIKA — Praxis der Kinderpsychologie und Kinderpsychiatrie
PKJ — Pitanja Knjizevnosti a Jezika
PKL — Pfaelzisches Kirchenlexikon
P Klein Form — Griechischen Papyrusurkunden Kleineren Formats
PKMKA — Prikladnaya Mekhanika
PKNAW — Proceedings. Koninkllijke Nederlandische Akademie von Wetenschappen
PKO — Parfuemerie und Kosmetik. Internationale Zeitschrift fuer Wissenschaftliche undTechnIsche Grundlagen der Parfuem- und Kosmetika Industrie
PKOM — Publicationen. Kaiserlich Osmanische Museen
PKOMA — Physik der Kondensierten Materie
P Kon Ned A — Proceedings. Koninklijke Nederlandse Akademie van Wetenschappen. SeriesA. Mathematical Sciences
P Kon Ned B — Proceedings. Koninklijke Nederlandse Akademie van Wetenschappen. SeriesB. Physical Sciences
P Kon Ned C — Proceedings. Koninklijke Nederlandse Akademie van Wetenschappen. SeriesC. Biological and Medical Sciences
PKOP — Piscovye Knigi Obonezskoj Pjatiny
PKroll — Ptolemaeische Koenigsurkunden
PKS — Publikatieblad van de Europese Gemeenschappen. Supplement
Pks & Rec — Parks and Recreation
PKSCAT — Parkes Catalogue of Radio Sources
PKSVAG — Pneumokoniosenavorsingseenheid Jaarverslag Pochvoznanie Agrokhimiya i Rastitelna Zashtita
PKTDA — Prace Komisji Technologii Drewna. Poznanskie Towarzystwo Przyjaciol Nauk
PKU — Unpublished Objects from Palaikastro Excavations, 1902-09
PKV — Protokorinthische Vasenmalerei
PKVJA — PKV [Punjabrao Krishi Vidyapeeth] Research Journal
PKVOA — Produktivnost
PKV Res J — PKV [Punjabrao Krishi Vidyapeeth] Research Journal
PKy — Pneumatike Kypros
PKYK — Kyklos. Internationale Zeitschrift fuer Sozialwissenschaften
PKZ — Protestantische Kirchenzeitung
PKZ — Protestantische Kirchenzeitung fuer das Evangelische Deutschland
PKZZD — Problemy Kontryla i Zashchita Atmosfery ot Zagryazneniya
PL — Palaeographia Latina
PL — Pamietnik Literacki

PL — Papers in Linguistics
PL — Patrologiae Cursus Completus. Series Latina
PL — Patrologia Latina
PL — Pays Lorrain
PL — People (London)
PL — Philosophischer Literaturanzeiger
Pl — Planta
Pl — Plateau
PL — Poet Lore
PL — Poetry (London)
PL — Private Label
PL — Private Library
PL — Programming Languages Series
PLA — Philosophischer Literaturanzeiger
PLA — Plana
PLAA — Pueblos
PLAB — Philadelphia Library Association. Bulletin
PLAB — Philippine Library Association. Bulletin
PLABED — Plant Breeding
PLA Bull — PLA [Pennsylvania Library Association] Bulletin
Placenta Suppl — Placenta. Supplement
PLAH — Labor History
Plain/Medieval — Plainsong & Medieval Music
Plain Ra — Plain Rapper
Plains Anthrop — Plains Anthropologist
Plains Anthropol — Plains Anthropologist
Plaisirs France — Plaisirs de France
PLAKA — Planovoe Khozyaistvo
PLAL — Latin American Literary Review
PLAM — Port of London Authority Monthly
PLAMED — Plantas Medicinales
PLA Mon — P.L.A. (Port of London Authority) Monthly
PLAN — Planner Newsletter. NWT [Northwest Territories, Canada] Land Use Planning Commission
PLAN — Polska Ludowa Akcja Niepodleglosci
PLANA — Planta
Plan Can — Plan Canada
Plan Choz — Planovoe Chozjajstvo
Planeacion Reg — Planeacion Regional
Plan E Afr — Plan East Africa
Plan Eksp Dokl Vses Soveshch — Planirovanie Eksperimenta. Doklady. Prochitannye na Vsesoyuznom Soveshchanii
Planen Pruef Investieren PPI — Planen-Pruefen-Investieren. PPI
Planet and Space Sci — Planetary and Space Science
Planet Assoc Clean Energy Newsl — Planetary Association for Clean Energy. Newsletter
Planet Spac — Planetary and Space Science
Planet Space Sci — Planetary and Space Science
Planets Stars Nebulae Stud Photopolarimetry Pap Colloq — Planets, Stars, and Nebulae. Studied with Photopolarimetry. Papers from Colloquium
PLANEX — Planning Exchange
Plan Higher Educ — Planning for Higher Education
Plan Hist Bull — Planning History Bulletin
Plan Hospod — Planovane Hospodarstvi
Plan Hoz — Planovoe Hozjajstvo
Planif Habitat Inform — Planification, Habitat, Information
Plan Inovtn — Planned Innovation
Plan J S Afr Architects — Plan. Journal for South African Architects
Plan Khoz — Planovoe Khozyaistvo
Plann Admin — Planning and Administration
Plann Build Dev — Planning and Building Developments
Planned Innov — Planned Innovation
Planners J — Planners Journal
Planning and Adm — Planning and Administration
Planning Bul — Planning Bulletin
Planning Develop Netherl — Planning and Development in the Netherlands
Planning History Bull — Planning History Bulletin
Plann News — Planning News
Plann Outlook — Planning Outlook
Plann Pam Nat Plann Ass — Planning Pamphlets. National Planning Association
Plann Parenthood Rev — Planned Parenthood Review
Plann Pub Pol — Planning and Public Policy
Plann Transp Abs — Planning and Transportation Abstracts
Plann Uses Manage Land — Planning the Uses and Management of Land
Plan Persp — Planning Perspectives
Plan Q — Planning Quarterly
Plan Rev — Planning Review
Planseeberichte — Planseeberichte fuer Pulvermetallurgie
Planseeber Pulvermet — Planseeberichte fuer Pulvermetallurgie
Plansee Proc Pap Plansee Semin De Re Met — Plansee Proceedings. Papers. Plansee Seminar. De Re Metallica
Plant — Plant Maintenance and Engineering
Planta Med — Planta Medica
Plant & Eng Applications — Plant and Engineering Applications
Plant & Power Services Eng — Plant and Power Services Engineer
Plant Bibliogr — Plant Bibliography
Plant Biochem — Plant Biochemistry [monograph]
Plant Biochem J — Plant Biochemical Journal
Plant Biochem Physiol Symp — Plant Biochemistry and Physiology Symposium
Plant Biochem Tbilisi — Plant Biochemistry (Tbilisi)
Plant Biol — Plant Biology
Plant Biol (NY) — Plant Biology (New York)
Plant Biotechnol Dev — Plant Biotechnology and Development
Plant Biotechnol Tokyo — Plant Biotechnology (Tokyo)
Plant Breed — Plant Breeding

Plant Breed Abstr — Plant Breeding Abstracts
Plant Breed Acclim Seed Prod — Plant Breeding, Acclimatization, and Seed Production
Plant Breed Proc Plant Breed Symp — Plant Breeding. Proceedings. Plant Breeding Symposium
Plant Breed Rev — Plant Breeding Reviews
Plant Breed Symp — Plant Breeding Symposium
Plant Breed Z Pflanzenzucht — Plant Breeding. Zeitschrift fuer Pflanzenzuchtung
Plant Bull Rubber Res Inst Malays — Planters' Bulletin. Rubber Research Institute of Malaysia
Plant C — Plant Cell
Plant Cell Environ — Plant Cell and Environment
Plant Cell Physiol — Plant and Cell Physiology
Plant Cell Physiol (Kyoto) — Plant and Cell Physiology (Kyoto)
Plant Cell Physiol (Tokyo) — Plant and Cell Physiology (Tokyo)
Plant Cell Rep — Plant Cell Reports
Plant Cell Tissue Organ Cult — Plant Cell Tissue and Organ Culture
Plant Cel P — Plant and Cell Physiology
Plant Chron — Planters' Chronicle
Plant Cultiv Repub Argent Inst Bot Agric (B Aires) — Plantas Cultivadas en la Republica Argentina. Instituto de Botanica Agricola (Buenos Aires)
Plant Dis — Plant Disease
Plant Dis Adv Treatise — Plant Disease. An Advanced Treatise
Plant Dis Leafl Dept Agr Biol Br (NSW) — Plant Disease Leaflet. Department of Agriculture. Biological Branch (New South Wales)
Plant Dis Probl Proc Int Symp — Plant Disease Problems. Proceedings. International Symposium on Plant Pathology
Plant Dis R — Plant Disease Reporter
Plant Dis Rep — Plant Disease Reporter
Plant Dis Rep Suppl — Plant Disease Reporter. Supplement
Plant Energy Manage — Plant Energy Management
Plant Eng — Plant Engineer
Plant Eng — Plant Engineering
Plant Eng Barrington III — Plant Engineering (Barrington, Illinois)
Plant Eng (Lond) — Plant Engineer (London)
Plant Engng — Plant Engineering
Plant Engng & Maint — Plant Engineering and Maintenance
Plant Engrg — Plant Engineering
Plant Eng (Tokyo) — Plant Engineer (Tokyo)
Planter — Planter and Sugar Manufacturer
Planters' Bull — Planters' Bulletin. Rubber Research Institute of Malaysia
Plant Field Lab Mimeo Rep Fla Univ — Plantation Field Laboratory Mimeo Report. Florida University
Plant Food Rev — Plant Food Review
Plant Foods Hum Nutr — Plant Foods for Human Nutrition
Plant Foods Hum Nutr Dordrecht Neth — Plant Foods for Human Nutrition (Dordrecht, Netherlands)
Plant Gard — Plants and Gardens
Plant Genet Eng — Plant Genetic Engineering
Plant Genet Resour Lett — Plant Genetic Resources Newsletter
Plant Grow — Plant Growing
Plant Growth Regul — Plant Growth Regulation
Plant Growth Regul Agric — Plant Growth Regulators in Agriculture
Plant Growth Regul Chem — Plant Growth Regulating Chemicals [monograph]
Plant Growth Regul Soc Am Proc — Plant Growth Regulator Society of America. Proceedings
Plant Growth Regul Soc Am Q — Plant Growth Regulator Society of America Quarterly
Plant Growth Subst 1988 Int Conf Plant Growth Subst — Plant Growth Substances 1988. International Conference on Plant Growth Substances
Plant Growth Subst Proc Int Conf — Plant Growth Substances. Proceedings. International Conference on Plant Growth Substances
Pl Anth — Plains Anthropologist
Plant Horm Recept — Plant Hormone Receptors
Plant Horm Their Role Plant Growth Dev — Plant Hormones and Their Role in Plant Growth and Development [monograph]
Plant Husb — Plant Husbandry
Plant Ind Dig (Manila) — Plant Industry Digest (Manila)
Plant Ind Ser Chin-Amer Joint Comm Rural Reconstr — Plant Industry Series. Chinese-American Joint Commission on Rural Reconstruction
Plant Ind Ser J Comm Rural Reconstr China (US Repub China) — Plant Industry Series. Joint Commission on Rural Reconstruction in China (United States and Republic of China)
Plant Info Bul — Plant Information Bulletin
Plant J — Plant Journal
Plant J Cell Mol Biol — Plant Journal for Cell and Molecular Biology
Plant Lipid Biochem Struct Util Proc Int Symp Plant Lipids — Plant Lipid Biochemistry, Structure, and Utilization. Proceedings. International Symposium on Plant Lipids
Plant Maint — Plant Maintenance
Plant Maint Import Substitution — Plant Maintenance and Import Substitution
Plant Manage Eng — Plant Management and Engineering
Plant Med — Planta Medica
Plant Med J Med Plant Res — Planta Medica. Journal of Medicinal Plant Research
Plant Med Phytother — Plantes Medicinales et Phytotherapie
Plant Microb Biotechnol Res Ser — Plant and Microbial Biotechnology Research Series
Plant Microbe Interact — Plant-Microbe Interactions
Plant Mol Biol — Plant Molecular Biology
Plant Mol Biol Rep — Plant Molecular Biology Reporter
Plant Nat — Plant and Nature
Plant Nutr Physiol Appl Proc Int Plant Nutr Colloq — Plant Nutrition. Physiology and Applications. Proceedings. International Plant Nutrition Colloquium
Plant Nutr Proc Int Colloq Plant Anal Fert Probl — Plant Nutrition. Proceedings. International Colloquium on Plant Analysis and Fertilizer Problems

Plant Nutr Proc Int Plant Nutr Colloq — Plant Nutrition. Proceedings. International Plant Nutrition Colloquium
Plant Operations Prog — Plant/Operations Progress
Plant Oper Manage — Plant Operating Management
Plant Path — Plant Pathology
Plant Pathog Bact Proc Int Conf — Plant Pathogenic Bacteria. Proceedings. International Conference on Plant Pathogenic Bacteria
Plant Pathol — Plant Pathology
Plant Pathol — Plant Pathology. An Advanced Treatise [monograph]
Plant Pathol — Plant Pathology Problems and Progress
Plant Pathol Bull — Plant Pathology Bulletin
Plant Pathol (Lond) — Plant Pathology (London)
Plant Pat US Pat Trademark Off — Plant Patent. United States Patent and Trademark Office
Plant Physiol — Plant Physiology
Plant Physiol & Biochem — Plant Physiology and Biochemistry
Plant Physiol (Bethesda) — Plant Physiology (Bethesda)
Plant Physiol Biochem New Delhi — Plant Physiology and Biochemistry (New Delhi)
Plant Physiol Biochem Paris — Plant Physiology and Biochemistry (Paris)
Plant Physiol Commun (Shanghai) — Plant Physiology Communications (Shanghai)
Plant Physiol Engl Transl — Plant Physiology (English Translation)
Plant Physiol (Moscow) — Plant Physiology (Moscow)
Plant Physiol Sofia — Plant Physiology (Sofia)
Plant Physiol Suppl — Plant Physiology. Supplement
Plant Physl — Plant Physiology
Plant Propagat — Plant Propagator
Plant Prot — Plant Protection
Plant Prot Abstr — Plant Protection Abstracts
Plant Prot Belgrade — Plant Protection (Belgrade)
Plant Prot (Budapest) — Plant Protection (Budapest)
Plant Prot Bull — Plant Protection Bulletin
Plant Prot Bull (Ankara) — Plant Protection Bulletin (Ankara)
Plant Prot Bull FAO — Plant Protection Bulletin. FAO [Food and Agriculture Organization] UnitedNations
Plant Prot Bull Faridabad India — Plant Protection Bulletin (Faridabad, India)
Plant Prot Bull (New Delhi) — Plant Protection Bulletin (New Delhi)
Plant Prot Bull (Rome) — Plant Protection Bulletin (Rome)
Plant Prot Bull Taipei — Plant Protection Bulletin (Taipei)
Plant Prot Hum Welfare Int Congr Plant Prot Proc Congr — Plant Protection for Human Welfare. International Congress of Plant Protection.Proceedings of Congress
Plant Prot Leningrad — Plant Protection (Leningrad)
Plant Prot Overseas Rev — Plant Protection Overseas Review
Plant Prot Q — Plant Protection Quarterly
Plant Prot Sofia — Plant Protection (Sofia)
Plant Prot Tokyo — Plant Protection (Tokyo)
Plant Rech Dev — Plantations, Recherche, Developpement
Plant Res Dev — Plant Research and Development
Plant Sci Bull — Plant Science Bulletin
Plant Sci L — Plant Science Letters
Plant Sci Lett — Plant Science Letters
Plant Sci (Limerick Irel) — Plant Science (Limerick, Ireland)
Plant Sci (Lucknow) — Plant Science (Lucknow, India)
Plant Sci (Lucknow India) — Plant Science (Lucknow, India)
Plant Sci Pam Plant Sci Dep Agric Exp Stn SD State Univ — Plant Science Pamphlet. Plant Science Department. Agricultural Experiment Station. South Dakota State University
Plant Sci Pretoria — Plant Sciences (Pretoria)
Plant Sci (Shannon) — Plant Science (Shannon)
Plant Sci (Sofia) — Plant Science (Sofia)
Plants Daylight Spectrum Proc Int Symp Br Photobiol Soc — Plants and the Daylight Spectrum. Proceedings. International Symposium. British Photobiology Society
Plants Gard — Plants and Gardens
Plant Soil — Plant and Soil
Plant Soil Inter Low pH Proc Int Symp — Plant-Soil Interactions at Low pH. Proceedings. International Symposium
Plants Toxic Assess Second Vol — Plants for Toxicity Assessment. Second Volume
Plant Sugar Manuf — Planter and Sugar Manufacturer
Plant Sys E — Plant Systematics and Evolution
Plant Syst Evol — Plant Systematics and Evolution
Plant Syst Evol Suppl — Plant Systematics and Evolution. Supplementum
Plant Tissue Cult Lett — Plant Tissue Culture Letters
Plant Tissue Cult Proc Int Congr Plant Tissue Cell Cult — Plant Tissue Culture. Proceedings. International Congress of Plant Tissue and Cell Culture
Plant Var Seeds — Plant Varieties and Seeds
PLAP — Latin American Perspectives
PLAQ — Modern Language Quarterly
PLAQ — PLA [Private Libraries Association] Quarterly
PLAR — Latin American Research Review
PLARA — Plastverarbeiter
PLASCAMS — Plastics. Computer Aided Materials Selector
Plas Compd — Plastics Compounding
Plas Com R — Plastics Compounding Redbook
Plas Desgn — Plastics Design Forum
Plas Eng — Plastics Engineering
Plas Ind ES — Plastics Industry Europe. Special Report
Plas Ind Eur — Plastics Industry Europe
Plas Ind N — Plastics Industry News
Plasir Fr — Plasir de France
Plasma Astrophys Int Sch Workshop — Plasma Astrophysics. International School and Workshop

Plasma Based Novel Accel Proc Workshop — Plasma-Based and Novel Accelerators. Proceedings. Workshop on Plasma-Based and Novel Accelerators. Nagoya

Plasmabericht Univ Heidelberg Inst Angew Phys — Plasmabericht. Universitaet Heidelberg. Institut fuer Angewandte Physik

Plasma Chem — Plasma Chemistry and Plasma Processing

Plasma Chem Plasma Process — Plasma Chemistry and Plasma Processing

Plasma Devices Oper — Plasma Devices and Operations

Plasma Laser Process Mater Pap Conf — Plasma and Laser Processing of Materials. Papers. Conference

Plasmapheresis Immunobiol Myasthenia Gravis Proc Symp — Plasmapheresis and the Immunobiology of Myasthenia Gravis. Proceedings. Symposium

Plasma Phys — Plasma Physics

Plasma Phys Accel Thermonucl Res — Plasma Physics, Accelerators, Thermonoculear Research

Plasma Phys Contr Nucl Fusion Res Conf Proc — Plasma Physics and Controlled Nuclear Fusion Research. Conference Proceedings

Plasma Phys Control Fusion — Plasma Physics and Controlled Fusion

Plasma Phys Controlled Fusion — Plasma Physics and Controlled Fusion

Plasma Phys Controlled Nucl Fusion Res — Plasma Physics and Controlled Nuclear Fusion Research. Proceedings. International Conference

Plasma Phys Index — Plasma Physics Index

Plasma Phys Rep Transl of Fiz Plazmy Moscow — Plasma Physics Reports. Translation of Fizika Plazmy (Moscow)

Plasma Process Proc Symp — Plasma Processing. Proceedings. Symposium

Plasma Proteins Gastrointest Tract Health Dis Proc Int Symp — Plasma Proteins and Gastrointestinal Tract in Health and Disease. Proceedings. International Symposium

Plasma Protein Turnover Proc Meet Plasma Protein Group — Plasma Protein Turnover. Proceedings. Meeting. Plasma Protein Group

Plasma Sources Sci Technol — Plasma Sources Science and Technology

Plasmas Polym — Plasmas and Polymers

Plas Massy — Plasticheskie Massy

Plasma Surf Eng Pap Int Conf — Plasma Surface Engineering. Papers. International Conference on Plasma Surface Engineering

Plasma Ther — Plasma Therapy

Plasma Ther Transfus Technol — Plasma Therapy and Transfusion Technology

Plas R Surg — Plastic and Reconstructive Surgery

Plas Rubbers Text — Plastics, Rubbers, Textiles

Plas Rub Int — Plastics and Rubber International

Plas Rubr — Plastics and Rubber Weekly

Plast — Plastic

Plast Abstr — Plastic Abstracts

Plast Age — Plastics Age

Plast Age Encycl Shinpo Hen — Plastics Age Encyclopedia. Shinpo Hen

Plast and Polym — Plastics and Polymers

Plast and Rubber — Plastics and Rubber [*Later, Plastics and Rubber International*]

Plast and Rubber Int — Plastics and Rubber International

Plast & Rubber Process & Appl — Plastics and Rubber Processing and Applications

Plast Aust — Plastics in Australia

Plast Aust Suppl — Plastics in Australia. Supplement

Plast Bear Conf Pap — Plastics in Bearings. Conference. Papers

Plast Bldg Constr — Plastics in Building Construction

Plast Build Constr — Plastics in Building Construction

Plast Bull (London) — Plastics Bulletin (London)

Plast Busin — Plastics Business

Plast Compd — Plastics Compounding

Plast Compounding — Plastics Compounding

Plast Corresp — Plastics Correspondence

Plast Des Process — Plastics Design and Processing

Plast Dig — Plastics Digest

PLASTEC Note — PLASTEC [*Plastics Technical Evaluation Center*] Note

PLASTEC Rep — PLASTEC [*Plastics Technical Evaluation Center*] Report

Plaste Kaut — Plaste und Kautschuk

Plast em Rev — Plasticos em Revista

Plast Eng — Plastics Engineering

Plast Eng Brookfield Conn — Plastics Engineering (Brookfield, Connecticut)

Plast Engng — Plastics Engineering

Plast Eng NY — Plastics Engineering (New York)

Plaste u Kaut — Plaste und Kautschuk

Plaste und Kautsch — Plaste und Kautschuk

Plast Flash — Plastiques Flash

Plast Furnit Natl Tech Conf Soc Plast Eng — Plastics in Furniture. National Technical Conference. Society of Plastics Engineers

Plast Hmoty Kauc — Plasticke Hmoty a Kaucuk

Plastiche — Materie Plastiche ed Elastomeri

Plastic IN — Plastics Industry News

Plastico — Noticiero del Plastico

Plastic Prod — Plastic Products

Plastics Engng — Plastics Engineering

Plastics in Aust — Plastics in Australia

Plast Ind — Plastic Industry

Plast Ind (Hong Kong) — Plastics Industry (Hong Kong)

Plast Ind News — Plastics Industry News

Plast Ind News (Jap) — Plastics Industry News (Japan)

Plast Ind (NY) — Plastics Industry (New York)

Plast Ind (Paris) — Plastiques et Industrie (Paris)

Plast Inst Trans — Plastics Institute. Transactions

Plast Inst Trans J — Plastics Institute. Transactions and Journal

Plast Inst Trans J Conf Suppl — Plastics Institute. Transactions and Journal. Conference Supplement

Plast Kauc — Plasty a Kaucuk

Plast M & E — Plastics Machinery and Equipment

Plast Massen — Plastische Massen

Plast Massen Wiss Tech — Plastische Massen in Wissenschaft und Technik

Plast Massy — Plasticheskie Massy

Plast Massy Rezina — Plasticheskie Massy i Rezina

Plast Mater Leningrad — Plastic Materials (Leningrad)

Plast Mater Med — Plastics Materials in Medicine

Plast Mater (Tokyo) — Plastics Materials (Tokyo)

Plast Mat Pat Newsl — Plastics Materials Patents Newsletter

Plast Matr — Plast. Rivista delle Materie Plastiche

Plast Med Surg — Plastics in Medicine and Surgery

Plast Mod — Plasticos Modernos

Plast Mod Elast — Plastiques Modernes et Elastomeres

Plast Mod Elastomeres — Plastiques Modernes et Elastomeres

Plast Mod Latinoam — Plasticos Modernos Latinoamericanos

Plast Molded Prod — Plastics and Molded Products

Plast Neuromuscular Syst — Plasticity of the Neuromuscular System

Plast News — Plastics News

Plast News (Aust) — Plastics News (Australia)

Plast News Briefs — Plastics News. Briefs

Plast Obrab Met Davleniem — Plastichnost i Obrabotka Metallov Davleniem

Plast Opt Fibers — Plastic Optical Fibers

Plast Pack — Plastics Packaging

Plast Paint Rubber — Plastics, Paint, and Rubber

Plast Panorama — Plast Panorama Scandinavia

Plast Panorama Scand — Plast Panorama Scandinavia

Plast Polym — Plastics and Polymers

Plast Polym Conf Suppl — Plastics and Polymers. Conference Supplement

Plast Proc Pat Newsl — Plastics Processing Patents Newsletter

Plast Prod — Plastic Products

Plast Prog India — Plastics Progress in India

Plast Reconstr Surg — Plastic and Reconstructive Surgery

Plast Reconstr Surg Transplant Bull — Plastic and Reconstructive Surgery and the Transplantation Bulletin

Plast Recovery Funct Cent Nerv Syst Proc Conf — Plasticity and Recovery of Function in the Central Nervous System. Proceedings. Conference

Plast Regener Nerv Syst — Plasticity and Regeneration of the Nervous System

Plast Renf Fibres Verre Text — Plastiques Renforces Fibres de Verre Textile

Plast Resinas — Plasticos y Resinas

Plast Resins — Plastics and Resins

Plast Retail Packag Bull — Plastics in Retail Packaging Bulletin

Plast Rubber — Plastics and Rubber [*Later, Plastics and Rubber International*]

Plast Rubber (Budapest) — Plastics and Rubber (Budapest)

Plast Rubber Compos Process Appl — Plastics, Rubber, and Composites Processing and Applications

Plast Rubber Inst Annu Conf — Plastics and Rubber Institute Annual CoOnference

Plast Rubber Inst Annu Natl Conf — Plastics and Rubber Institute. Annual National Conference

Plast Rubber Int — Plastics and Rubber International

Plast Rubber Mater Appl — Plastics and Rubber. Material and Applications

Plast Rubber News — Plastics and Rubber News

Plast Rubber Proc Appl — Plastics and Rubber Processing and Applications

Plast Rubber Process — Plastics and Rubber. Processing

Plast Rubber Process — Plastics and Rubber Processing and Applications

Plast Rubber Process Appl — Plastics and Rubber Processing and Applications

Plast Rubbers Text — Plastics, Rubbers, Textiles

Plast Rubber Wkly — Plastics and Rubber Weekly

Plast Rubb Int — Plastics and Rubber International

Plast Rubb News — Plastics and Rubber News

Plast Rubb Process Appln — Plastics and Rubber Processing and Applications

Plast Rub Wkly — Plastics and Rubber Weekly

Plast (S Afr) — Plastics (Southern Africa)

Plast (S Africa) — Plastics (Southern Africa)

Plast Sci Costr Mem Symp — Plasticita nella Scienza delle Costruzioni. Memorie Presentate al Symposium

Plast Solothurn Switz — Plastics (Solothurn, Switzerland)

Plast South Afr — Plastics Southern Africa

Plast (Sthn Afr) — Plastics (Southern Africa)

Plast Surf Transp Natl Tech Conf Soc Plast Eng — Plastics in Surface Transportation. National Technical Conference. Society of Plastics Engineers

Plast Surg Nurs — Plastic Surgical Nursing

Plast Tech — Plastics Technology

Plast Tech Eval Cent Note — Plastics Technical Evaluation Center. Note

Plast Tech Eval Cent Rep — Plastics Technical Evaluation Center. Report

Plast Technol — Plastics Technology

Plast Telecommun Int Conf — Plastics in Telecommuncations. International Conference

Plast Telecommun Int Conf Prepr — Plastics in Telecommuncations. International Conference. Preprints

Plast Today — Plastics Today

Plast Trends — Plastics Trends

Plast Univers — Plasticos Universales

Plast World — Plastics World

PLATA — Plating

Plat and Surf Finish — Plating and Surface Finishing

Plat Coat — Plating and Coating

Plateau Q Mus North Ariz — Plateau. Quarterly of the Museum of Northern Arizona

Plat Electron Ind — Plating in the Electronics Industry. Symposium

Platelet Immunol Proc Eur Symp — Platelet Immunology. Fundamental and Clinical Aspects. Proceedings. European Symposium on Platelet Immunology

Plating & Surface Finish — Plating and Surface Finishing

Platinum Metals Rev — Platinum Metals Review

Platinum Met Rev — Platinum Metals Review

Platoon Sch — Platoon School

Plat Surf Finish — Plating and Surface Finishing

PLAV — Papeles de Arquelogia
PLAWA — Plastics World
Play — Playboy
PLAY — [*The*] Playgoer
Playb — Playboy
Players Mag — Players Magazine
Playground — Playground and Recreation
Playmate — Children's Playmate Magazine
PLB — Papyrologica Lugduno-Batava
Pl Biochem J — Plant Biochemical Journal
PLBNDJ — Faculte des Sciences Agronomiques. Laboratoire de Biochimie de la Nutrition. Publication
PLBPDP — Contribution on the Paleolimnology of Lake Biwa and the Japanese Pleistocene
Pl Breed Abstr — Plant Breeding Abstracts
Pl Bull — Planters' Bulletin. Rubber Research Institute of Malaya
PLBYD — Plan og Bygg
PIC — Plaines et Collines
PLC — Princeton University. Library. Chronicle
PLCEDV — Plant Cell and Environment
Pl Cell — Plant Cell
Pl Cell Physiol — Plant and Cell Physiology. Nihon Shokubutsu Seiri Gakkai. Japanese Society of Plant Physiologists
PLCHB — Physiological Chemistry and Physics [*Later, Physiological Chemistry and Physics and Medical NMR*]
PLCM & ND — Proceedings. Linguistic Circle of Manitoba and North Dakota
PLCN-A — Plan Canada
PLCNY — Publications. Linguistic Circle of New York
PLCP — Law and Contemporary Problems
PLCPB — Plant and Cell Physiology
PLCS — Proceedings. London Classical Society
PLD — All Pakistan Legal Decisions
PLD — Public Libraries Division. Reporter
Pl Dis Knowl — Plant Disease Knowledge/Zhibing Zhishi (Chih P'ing Chih Shih)
Pl Dis Reporter — Plant Disease Reporter. Bureau of Plant Industry. US Department of Agriculture
PLDRA — Plant Disease Reporter
PLE — Paginas de Literatura y Ensayo
PLEGA — Plant Engineering
PLEGB — Plastics Engineering
P Leg J — Pittsburgh Legal Journal
P Leg Jour — Pittsburgh Legal Journal
PLEI — Journal of Leisure Research
P Leips — Griechische Urkunden der Papyrussammlung zu Leipzig
PLENA — Plant Engineering
Plenarnye Dokl Vses Soveshch Polyarogr — Plenarnye Doklady na Vsesoyuznom Soveshchanii po Polyarografii
Plenar Posterbeitr Tag Forschungsgem Org Festkoerper — Plenar- und Posterbeitraege. Tagung der Forschungsemeinschaft Organische Festkoerper
Plenarvortr Int Kongr Reprogr Inf — Plenarvortraege. Internationaler Kongress fuer Reprographie und Information
Plenarvortr Kurzref Tag Dtsch Arbeitsgem Akust — Plenarvortraege und Kurzreferate der Tagung der Deutschen Arbeitsgemeinschaft fuer Akustik
Plenarvortr Physikertag — Plenarvortraege der Physikertagungen
Plenary Invited Contrib Aust Electrochem Conf — Plenary and Invited Contributions. Australian Electrochemistry Conference
Plenary Lect Indo Sov Symp Chem Nat Prod — Plenary Lectures. Indo-Soviet Symposium on the Chemistry of Natural Products
Plenary Lect Int Congr Pestic Chem — Plenary Lectures. International Congress of Pesticide Chemistry
Plenary Lect Int Symp Org Sulphur Chem — Plenary Lectures. International Symposium on Organic Sulphur Chemistry
Plenary Lect World Conf Non Destr Test — Plenary Lectures. World Conference on Non-Destructive Testing
Plenary Main Lect Int Symp Macromol — Plenary and Main Lectures. International Symposium on Macromolecules
Plenary Main Sect Lect Int Congr Pure Appl Chem — Plenary and Main Section Lectures. International Congress of Pure and Applied Chemistry
Plenary Sess Int Fair Tech Meet Nucl Ind — Plenary Session. International Fair and Technical Meetings of Nuclear Industries
Plenary Sess Lect Congr Int Soc Blood Transfus — Plenary Session Lectures. Congress. International Society of Blood Transfusion
Plenary Sess Lect Congr World Fed Hemophilia — Plenary Session Lectures. Congress. World Federation of Hemophilia
Plenary Sess Pap Int Congr Soil Sci — Plenary Session Papers. International Congress of Soil Science
Plenary Sess Pap Meet Eur Div Int Soc Haematol — Plenary Session Papers. Meeting. European Division of the International Society of Haematology
PLEND — Plumbing Engineer
Plenochn Polim Mater Ikh Primen Mater Kratkosrochnogo Semin — Plenochnye Polimernye Materialy i Ikh Primenenie. Marerialy Kratkosrochnogo Seminara
PLF — Poetarum Lesbiorum Fragmenta
PLF — Public Administration
Plf Adv — Plaintiff's Advocate
PLF Ber — PLF [*Projektgruppe fuer Laserforschung*] Bericht
PLFQ — Literature/Film Quarterly
PLFS — Polarforschung
PLG — Pakistan Labour Gazette
PLG — Plant Management and Engineering
PLG — Poetae Lyrici Graeci
PLG — Probleme de Lingvistica Genarala
PLGAA — Plants and Gardens
Pl Gard — Plants and Gardens. Brooklyn Botanical Garden
PLGFA — Poligrafiya
PLGJA — Pipeline and Gas Journal

PLHID — Plant Hire
PLHJA — Plumbing and Heating Journal
P Lille — Papyrus Grecs. Institut Papyrologique. Universite de Lille
PLINA — Pipe Line Industry
PLing — Papers in Linguistics
PLINK — American People/Link
PLIR — Literary Review
Pliste Rs — Physiologiste Russe
PLit — Prensa Literaria
PLJ — Pacific Law Journal
PLJ — Patna Law Journal
PLJ — Pennsylvania Law Journal
PLJ — Philippine Law Journal
PLJ — Philippine Library Journal
PLJ — Pittsburgh Legal Journal
PLJ NS — Pittsburgh Legal Journal, New Series
PLKAA — Plaste und Kautschuk
PLL — Papers on Language and Literature
PLLAA — Royal Society. Proceedings. Series A. Mathematical and Physical Sciences
Pl Life — Plant Life. American Plant Life Society
PLLP — Polish Literature/Litterature Polonaise
PLLSA — Plzensky Lekarsky Sbornik
PLM — Pacific Law Magazine
PLM — Papers in Linguistics of Melanesia
PLM — Poetae Latini Minores
PLM — Poor Law Magazine
PL Mag — Poor Law Magazine
PLMEA — Planta Medica
PLMSA — Plasticheskie Massy
PLN — Planning
Pln Dealr — Plain Dealer
PLNG — Language
PLNN-A — Plan
PLNP — Literature and Psychology
PLNSW Staff News — Public Library of New South Wales. Staff News
PLO — Pensiero e Linguaggio in Operazioni/Thought and Language in Operations
PLO — Porta Linguarum Orientalium
Plodoovoscn Hoz — Plodoovoscnoe Hozjajstvo
Plodoovoshchn Inst IV Michurina Tr — Plodoovoshchnoi Institut imeni I.V. Michurina. Trudy
Plodorodie Pochv Karelii Akad Nauk SSSR Karel'sk Filial — Plodorodie Pochv Karelii. Akademiya Nauk SSSR. Karel'skii Filial
P Lond Math — Proceedings. London Mathematical Society
PLOP — Policy Options/Options Politiques
Plor — Pays Lorrain
Ploughs — Ploughshares
Plovdiv Univ Naucn Trud — Plovdivski Universitet. Naucni Trudove
Plovdiv Univ Paisii Khilendarski Nauchn Trud Mat — Plovdivski Universitet Paisii Khilendarski. Nauchni Trudove. Matematika
PLP — Parks Library Pamphlets
Pl Path — Plant Pathology
PLPHA — Plant Physiology
PLPHB — Plasma Physics
Pl Physics — Plasma Physics
Pl Physiol (Lancaster) — Plant Physiology (Lancaster)
Pl Physiol (Wash) — Plant Physiology (Washington)
PLPI — Powell Lectures on Philosophy at Indiana University
PIPI — Planete Plus
PLPLS — Proceedings. Leeds Philosophical and Literary Society
PLPLS-LHS — Proceedings. Leeds Philosophical and Literary Society. Literary and Historical Section
PLPLS-SS — Proceedings. Leeds Philosophical and Literary Society. Scientific Section
Pl Propag — Plant Propagator. International Plant Propagators Society
Pl Protect Peking — Plant Protection. Chih Wupao Hu Zhiwu Baohu (Peking)
Pl Prot (Tokyo) — Plant Protection (Tokyo)
PLPS — Proceedings. Leeds Philosophical and Literary Society
PLPSA — Physiological Psychology
PLPSL — Proceedings. Literary and Philosophical Society of Liverpool
PLPUA — Planseeberichte fuer Pulvermetallurgie (Austria)
PLR — Pakistan Law Review
PLR — Palestine Law Reports
PLR — Patent Law Review
PLR — Planning Review
PLR — Plan. Zeitschrift fuer Planen, Bauen, und Umwelt
PLR — University of Pittsburgh. Law Review
PLRCA — Pharmacological Research Communications
PLRE — Prosopography of the Later Roman Empire
PLRS — Publications. London Record Society
PLRSA — Plasticos y Resinas
Plrs' Bull Rubb Res Inst Malaya — Planters' Bulletin. Rubber Research Institute of Malaya
PLS — Patrologiae Latinae Supplementum
PLS — Proceedings of the Linnaean Society
PLSCB — Policy Sciences
PLSCE4 — Plant Science
Pls Gds — Plants and Gardens
PLSL — Proceedings. Linnaean Society (London)
PLSOA — Plant and Soil
Pl Soil — Plant and Soil
PLSR — Law and Society Review
PLSSA — Planetary and Space Science
PLT — Patna Law Times
PLT — Progress in Low Temperature Physics

PLT — Punjab Law Times
PLTEA — Plastics Technology
PLTPA — Progress in Low Temperature Physics
PLTVA — Plastvaerlden
Plucne Bolesti Tuberk — Plucne Bolesti i Tuberkuloza
Plucne Boles Tuberk — Plucne Bolesti i Tuberkuloza
PLUDA — Plutonium-Dokumentation
Plumb Heat J — Plumbing and Heating Journal
Plumbing Eng — Plumbing Engineer
Plumbing Engr — Plumbing Engineer
Plumbing Heat Equip News — Plumbing and Heating Equipment News
Plural Soc — Plural Societies
PluS — Plural Societies
PLUTA — Pollution
Plutonium Abstr — Plutonium Abstracts
Plutonium-Dok — Plutonium-Dokumentation
Pl Var Seeds Gaz — Plant Varieties and Seeds Gazette
PLVDA — Progress in Liver Diseases
PLW — Patna Law Weekly
Pl World — Plant World. A Monthly Journal of Popular Botany
PLYGA — Psychologia: An International Journal of Psychology in the Orient
PLYHD — Polyhedron
Plym I T — Annual Reports and Transactions of the Plymouth Institution and Devon and Cornwall Natural History Society
Plymouth Miner Min Club J — Plymouth Mineral and Mining Club. Journal
Plyn Voda Zdra Tech — Plyn Voda a Zdravotni Technika
Plyw and Plyw Prod — Plywood and Plywood Products
Plyw Plyw Prod — Plywood and Plywood Products
PLZ — Plastics World
Plzen Lek Sb — Plzensky Lekarsky Sbornik
Plzen Lek Sb Suppl — Plzensky Lekarsky Sbornik. Supplementum
Plzen Pedagog Fak Sb Chem — Plzen. Pedagogicka Fakulta. Sbornik. Chemie
PM — International Journal of Psychiatry in Medicine
PM — Palace of Minos
PM — Paleographie Musicale
PM — Paper Maker
PM — Paper Money
P M — Paris Match
PM — Parole et Mission
PM — Petermanns Geographische Mitteilungen
PM — Petermanns Mitteilungen
PM — Peuples Mediterraneens
PM — Philippine Manager
PM — Philosophische Monatshefte
PM — Photo Marketing Magazine
PM — Placer Mining Times
PM — PM. Pharmacy Management
PM — Polish Music
PM — Politica de Mexico
PM — Popular Mechanics
PM — Post Magazine and Insurance Monitor
PM — Prehistoric Macedonia
PM — Presse Medicale
PM — Primitive Man
PM — Process Metallurgy
PM — Province du Maine
PM — Public Management
PMA — Papers. Michigan Academy of Science, Arts, and Letters
PMA — Personnel Management Abstracts
PMA — Proceedings. Royal Musical Association
PMA — Publications. Mediaeval Academy
PMAA — Princeton Monographs in Art and Archaeology
PMAAR — Papers and Monographs. American Academy in Rome
P Mac — Prehistoric Macedonia
PMAE — Medium Aevum
PM Aerosp Def Technol Symp — P/M in Aerospace and Defence Technologies Symposium
PMag — Papyri Graecae Magicae
PMAHD3 — Annual Research Reviews. Peripheral Metabolism and Action of Thyroid Hormones
PMaine — Province du Maine
PMAI News Lett — PMAI [*Powder Metallurgy Association of India*] News Letter
PMAMA — Prikladnaya Matematika i Mekhanika
PMAN — Man
PMA News — PMA [*Pharmaceutical Manufacturers Association*] Newsletter
PMAODO — Proceedings. American Society of Clinical Oncology. Annual Meeting
PMAR — Massachusetts Review
PMASAL — Publications. Michigan Academy of Science, Arts, and Letters
PMB — Bulletin. Palestine Museum
PMB — Polish Maritime News
PMBAA — Publications. Institut Royal Meteorologique de Belgique. Serie A
PMBIDB — Plant Molecular Biology
PMBRAZ — Contributions. General Agricultural Research Station
PMC — Pollution Engineering
PMC — Popular Mechanics (Chicago)
PMC — Progress in Medicinal Chemistry
PMC — Publication. Maitland Club
PMCe — Philosophy in the Mid-Century
PMCL — Periodica de Re Morali Canonica Liturgica
PMCO — Memory and Cognition
PMCR — Mass Comm Review
PMCS — Media, Culture, and Society
PMDA — Peace Messenger. Diocese of Athabasca. Peace River
PMDCA — Progress in Medicinal Chemistry
PME — Petermanns Mitteilungen. Ergaenzungshefte

PME — Prace i Materialy Etnograficzne
PME — Prosopographia Militiarum Equestrium quae Fuerunt ab Augusto ad Gallienum
PMEA — Middle Eastern Studies
PMEA — Publicaciones del Museo de Etnologia y Antropologia [*Santiago de Chile*]
PMEB — Publicaciones del Museo Etnografico de la Facultad de Filosofia y Letras de la Universidad Nacional de Buenos Aires. Serie A
PMEL — MELUS
PMELA — Plastiques Modernes et Elastomeres
P Mel Gr — Poetae Melici Graeci
PMER — Mercury
P Merton — Descriptive Catalogue of the Greek Papyri in the Collection of Wilfred Merton
PMES — International Journal of Middle East Studies
PMF — Paint and Resin News
PMFAA — Pokroky Matematiky, Fyziky, a Astronomie
PMFR — Marriage and Family Review
PMG — Poetae Melici Graeci
PMGM — Physici et Medici Graeci Minores
PMGoE — Periodiske Meddelelser fra Demonstrationslokalet for Gas og Elektricitet
PMH — Modern Humanities Research Association. Publications. Research Series
PMH — Portugaliae Monumenta Historica
PMHB — Pennsylvania Magazine of History and Biography
PMHBA — Polish Medical Science and History Bulletin
PMHS — Proceedings. Massachusetts Historical Society
PMI — Photo Methods for Industry
PMICA — Proceedings. Institute of Medicine of Chicago
P Mich — Michigan Papyri
P Michaelides — Papyri Michaelidae
P Mich Zen — Zenon Papyri in the University of Michigan Collection
P Mil — Papiri Milanesi
PMIN — Mathematical Intelligencer
PM Iowa State Univ Coop Ext Serv — PM. Iowa State University. Cooperative Extension Service
PM Iowa State Univ Sci Technol Coop Ext Serv — PM. Iowa State University of Science and Technology. Cooperative Extension Service
PMIQ — Midwest Quarterly
PMIZG — Protestantische Monatsblaetter fuer Innere Zeitgeschichte
PMJ — Pakistan Medical Journal
PMJ — Project Management Journal
PMJP — Petermanns Mitteilungen aus Justus Perthes Geographischer Anstalt
PML — Peake [*A.S.*] Memorial Lectures
PMLA — Proceedings of the Modern Language Association
PMLA — Publications. Modern Language Association of America
PMLAAm — Publications. Modern Language Association of America
PMLAss — Publications. Modern Language Association of America
PMM — Pall Mall Magazine
PMM — Personnel Management Manual
PMM — Petroleum Marketing Management
PMM — Petroleum Marketing Monthly
PMMA — Publications. Metropolitan Museum of Art. Egyptian Expedition
PMMEA — Prensa Medica Mexicana
PMMF — Presbyterian Medical Mission Fund
PMMLA — Papers. Midwest Modern Language Association
PMN — Publicacoes do Museu Nacional. Serie Linguistica Especial [*Rio de Janeiro*]
PMND — Mind
PMNE — Mnemosyne. Bibliotheca Classica Batava
PMNH — Men's Health
PMNK — Mankind
PMNWA — Pressemitteilung Nordrhein-Westfalen
PMOA — Modern Age
PMOC — Modern China
PMOD — Modern Drama
PMOGA — Progress in Medical Genetics
PMOJ — Pesticides Monitoring Journal
P Monac — Byzantinische Papyri in der Koenigliche Hof- und Staatsbibliothek zu Muenchen
PMONDN — Society of Economic Paleontologists and Mineralogists. Paleontological Monograph
PMOP — Modern Philology
PMOS — Modern Asian Studies
PMOSA — Perceptual and Motor Skills
PMOT — Modern Theology
PMP — Peabody Museum Papers
PMPA — Publications. Missouri Philological Association
PMPGA — Petermanns Mitteilungen aus Perthes' Geographischer Anstalt
PM Pharm Manage — PM (Pharmacy Management)
PMPPEZ — Physiological and Molecular Plant Pathology
PM Przegl Mech — PM. Przeglad Mechaniczny
PMPSE — Proceedings of the Mathematical and Physical Society of Egypt
PMQR — Michigan Quarterly Review
PMR — Philippine Mining Record
PMR — Proceedings. Patristic, Mediaeval, and Renaissance Conference
PMR — Progress in Mutation Research
PMR — Property Monthly Review
PMRGA — Prace Morski Instytut Rybacki w Gdyni
PMRO — Popular Magazine Review Online
PMRS — Progress of Medieval and Renaissance Studies in the United States and Canada
PMS — Perceptual and Motor Skills
PMS — Popular Music and Society
PMS — Proceedings. Malacological Society of London
PMS — Publications in Mediaeval Studies
PMSA — Mosaic
PMSA — Publicaciones del Museo y de la Sociedad Arqueologica de la Serena

PMSC — Mosaic. A Journal for the Interdisciplinary Study of Literature
PMSCD — Proceedings. Microscopical Society of Canada
PMSE — Manchester School of Economic and Social Studies
PMS Public Manage Source — PMS. Public Management Sources
PMSQ — Mississippi Quarterly
PMSS — Progress in Mathematical Social Sciences
PMSTA — Promyshlennoe Stroitel'stvo
PMT — Products, Marketing, and Technology
PMTF Zh Prikl Mekh Tekh Fiz — PMTF. Zhurnal Prikladnoi Mekhaniki Tekhnickeskio Fiziki
PMU — Progress in Medical Ultrasound
PMUCAH — Memorias e Noticias Publicacoes. Museu e Laboratorio Mineralogico e Geologico. Universidade de Coimbra e Centro de Estudos Geologicos
PMUN — Notes
PMUQ — Musical Quarterly
PMUR — Music Review
PMUS — Music and Letters
PMUW — Muslim World
PMVIA — Progress in Medical Virology
PN — Palace of Nestor at Pylos in Western Messenia
PN — Percussive Notes
PN — Petrus Nonius
PN — Phylon
PN — Poe Newsletter
PN — Poesia Nuova
PN — Poetry Northwest
PN — Portsmouth News
PN — Pottery Notebooks for Knossos
Pn — Poznan
PN — Pro Nervia
PN — Psychic News
PN — Publishing News
PNAR — North American Review
PNAS — Proceedings. National Academy of Sciences
PNASc — Proceedings. National Academy of Sciences
P NAS (Ind) A — Proceedings. National Academy of Sciences (India). Section A. Physical Sciences
P NAS (Ind) B — Proceedings. National Academy of Sciences (India). Section B. Biological Sciences
P NAS (US) — Proceedings. National Academy of Sciences (United States of America)
PNB — Pottery Notebooks for Knossos
PNC — Personal Names from Cuneiform Inscriptions of Cappadocia
PNCCA — Proceedings. National Cancer Conference
PNCH — Proceedings. National Conference on Health Education Goals
PNCL — Nineteenth-Century Literature
PNCTD — Proceedings. National Conference on Power Transmission
PNE — Proyeccion (Espana)
PNEC — Proceedings. National Electronics Conference
PNECA — Proceedings. National Electronics Conference
PNEND — Progress in Nuclear Energy
PNEQ — New England Quarterly
PNER — New England Review and Bread Loaf Quarterly
PNEUDZ — Pneumoftiziologie
Pneum Dig & Druckluft Prax — Pneumatic Digest and Druckluft Praxis
Pneumokoniosenavorsingseenheid Jaarversl — Pneumokoniosenavorsingseenheid Jaarverslag
Pneumol Ftiziatr — Pneumologia i Ftiziatria
Pneumolog Hung — Pneumologia Hungarica
Pneumol/Pneumol — Pneumologie/Pneumonology
Pneumonol Alergol Pol — Pneumonologia i Alergologia Polska
Pneumonol Hung — Pneumonologia Hungarica
Pneumonol-P — Pneumonologie/Pneumonology
Pneumonol Pneumonol — Pneumologie/Pneumonology
Pneumonol Pol — Pneumonologia Polska
Pnevmoavtomatika Mater Vses Soveshch Pnevmoavtomatike — Pnevmoavtomatika. Materialy Vsesoyuznogo Soveshchaniya po Pnevmoavtomatike
PNGL — Papers in New Guinea Linguistics
PNG Med J — Papua New Guinea Medical Journal
PNG Natn Mus Rec — PNG (Papua New Guinea) National Museum Record
PNGUA8 — Forest Research Institute [Bogor]. Communication
PNHYD — Perspectives in Nephrology and Hypertension
PNI — Pensions and Investment Age
PNI — Pharmaceutical News Index [UMI/Data Courier]
PNI — Publications. Netherlands Institute of Archaeology and Arabic Studies
PNIIA — Prace Naukowe Instytutu Inzynierii Ochrony Srodowiska Politechniki Wroclawskiej
PNIS — Proceedings of the National Institute of Sciences of India
PNISB — Proceedings of the National Institute of Sciences of India. Part B. Biological Sciences
PNJHS — Proceedings. New Jersey Historical Society
PNL — Przewodnik Naukowy i Literacki
PNLA Q — Pacific Northwest Library Association. Quarterly
PNLH — New Literary History
PNM — Perspectives of New Music
Pnm — Phantom
PNMBA — Progress in Nucleic Acid Research and Molecular Biology
PNMPA — Psychiatrie, Neurologie, und Medizinische Psychologie
PNMRA — Progress in Nuclear Magnetic Resonance Spectroscopy
PNMUB — Perspectives of New Music
PNMUD — PNM Update
PNNQ — Notes and Queries
PNotes — Pynchon Notes
PNOU-A — Planning Outlook

PNOV — Novel. A Forum on Fiction
PNPRA — Progress in Nuclear Energy. Series 3. Process Chemistry
PNPSA — Progress in Neurology and Psychiatry
PNPSD — Prace Naukowe Politechniki Szczecinskiej
PNQ — Pacific Northwest Quarterly
PNR — PN [Poetry Nation] Review
P N Review — Poetry Nation Review
PNSCEI — National Museum of Natural Sciences [Ottawa]. Publications in Natural Sciences
PNSFA — Proceedings. National Shellfisheries Association
PNTEA — Progress in Nuclear Energy. Series 4
PNTQ — New Theatre Quarterly
PNTS — New Testament Studies
PNU — Praxis des Neusprachlichen Unterrichts
PNUED — Preprint. Akademiya Nauk Ukrainskoi SSR Institut Elektrodinamiki
PNUPA — Progress in Nuclear Physics
PNUS — Prace Naukowe Uniwersytetu Slaskiego
PNUT — Nutrition Today
P Nutr Soc — Proceedings. Nutrition Society
PNW Bull — PNW (Pacific Northwest Cooperative) Bulletin
PNW Pac Northwest Ext Publ Oreg State Univ Coop Ext Serv — PNW. Pacific Northwest Extension Publication. Oregon State University. Cooperative Extension Service
PNW RN Res Note US Dep Agric For Serv Pac Northwest Res Stn — PNW-RN Research Note. US Department of Agriculture. Forest Service. Pacific Northwest Research Station
PNY — Poetry New York
PNYMD — Polytechnic Institute of New York. Department of Mechanical and Aerospace Engineering. Report POLY M/AE
Po — Il Politico
PO — Patrologia Orientalis
Po — Poesie
Po — Polet
PO — Poona Orientalist
Po — Population [Paris]
Po — Portucale
PO — Prairie Overcomer
PO — Pravoslavnoe Obozrenie
PO — Przeglad Orientalistyczny
PoA — Polish American Studies
PoAA — Port of Aden Annual
POAA — Problems of the Arctic and the Antarctic
POA Chronicle — Professional Officers' Association Chronicle
POAS — Poems on Affairs of State
POB — Polarboken
POBI — Polar Biology
POBS — Proceedings. Oxford Bibliographical Society
POBUD — Polymer Bulletin
PoC — Problems of Communism
POC — Proche-Orient Chretien
PoC — Sainte-Beuve. Portraits Contemporains
POCE — Oceania
P-O Chr — Proche-Orient Chretien
Poch Urozhai Latv Nauch-Issled Inst Zemled — Pochva i Urozhai. Latviiskii Nauchno-Issledovatel'skii Institut Zemledeliya
Pochv Biogeotsenol Issled Priazove — Pochvenno-Biogeotsenologicheskie Issledovaniya v Priazov'e
Pochv Geogr Landshaftno Geokhim Issled Zone BAM — Pochvenno-Geograficheskie i Landshaftno-Geokhimicheskie Issledovaniya v Zone BAM
Pochv Issled Primen Udobr — Pochvennye Issledovaniya i Primenenie Udobrenii
Pochvoved — Pochvovedenie
Pochvoved Agrokhim — Pochvovedenie i Agrokhimiya
Pochvoved Agrokhim (Moscow) — Pochvovedenie i Agrokhimiya (Moscow)
Pochvozn Agrokhim — Pochvoznanie i Agrokhimiya
Pochvozn Agrokhim Ekol — Pochvoznanie, Agrokhimiya i Ekologiya
Pochvozn Agrokhim Rastit Zasht — Pochvoznanie Agrokhimiya i Rastitelna Zashtita
Pochv Usloviya Eff Udobr — Pochvennye Usloviya i Effektivnost Udobrenii
Pochvy Baskh Puti Ratsion Ikh Ispol'z — Pochvy Bashkirii i Puti Ratsional'nogo Ikh Ispol'zovaniya
Pochvy Biol Prod — Pochvy i Biologicheskaya Produktivnost
Pochvy Kaliningr Obl — Pochvy Kaliningradskoi Oblasti
Pochvy Yuzhn Urala Povolzhya — Pochvy Yuzhnogo Urala i Povolzh'ya
Pochvy Zapadn Sib Povysh Ikh Biol Akt — Pochvy Zapadnoi Sibiri i Povyshenie Ikh Biologicheskoi Aktivnosti
Pocket Pict Guides Clin Med — Pocket Picture Guides to Clinical Medicine
PoCp — Points et Contrepoints
POCS — Oceanus
Pocumtuck Valley Mem Assoc Proc — Pocumtuck Valley Memorial Association. History and Proceedings
Podgot Koksovanie Uglei — Podgotovka i Koksovanie Uglei
Podgot Pererab Gaza Gazov Kondens — Podgotovka i Pererabotka Gaza i Gazovogo Kondensata. Referativnyi Sbornik
Podgot Pererab Gaza Gazov Kondens Nauchno Tekh Obz — Podgotovka i Pererabotka Gaza i Gazovogo Kondensata. Nauchno-Tekhnicheskii Obzor
Podgot Vosstanov Rud — Podgotovka i Vosstanovlenie Rud
Podiplomski Sem Mat — Podiplomski Seminar iz Matematike
Podreczn Akad Elektron Inform Telekom — Podreczniki Akademickie. Elektronika. Informatyka. Telekomunikacja
Podstaw Nauki Tech Monogr — Podstawowe Nauki Techniczne. Monografia
Podstawowe Probl Wspolczesnej Tech — Podstawowe Problemy Wspolczesnej Techniki
Podstawy Teor Wyladowan Elektr Gazach Symp — Podstawy Teorii Wyladowan Elektrycznych w Gazach. Sympozjum

Podst Sterow — Podstawy Sterowania
PODU — Praci Odes'koho Derzavnoho Universytetu
Podvodnye Med Fiziol Issled — Podvodnye Mediko-Fiziologicheskie Issledovaniya
Podzemn Gazif Uglei — Podzemnaya Gazifikatsiya Uglei
Podzemn Gazif Uglei (1934-35) — Podzemnaya Gazifikatsiya Uglei (1934-35)
Podzemn Gazif Uglei (1957-59) — Podzemnaya Gazifikatsiya Uglei (1957-59)
Podzemn Razrab Moshchn Rudn Mestorozhd — Podzemnaya Razrabotka Moshchnykh Rudnykh Mestorozhdenii
Podzemn Vody SSSR — Podzemnye Vody SSSR
Poe — Poesie
Poe — Poetik
PoE — Point de l'Epee
Poe Chpbk — Poetry Chapbook
PoeE — Poesia Espanola
POeHIR — Publikationen des Oesterreichischen Historischen Instituts in Rom
Poel — Poesie I (i.e. Une)
P O Elect Engrs J — Post Office Electrical Engineers. Journal
P O Electr Eng J — Post Office Electrical Engineers. Journal
PoeN — Poesie Nouvelle
PoeP — Poesie Presente
Poe Pal — Poetry Palisade
POERD — Power Engineer
PoeS — Poe Studies
Poe Stud — Poe Studies
Poet — Poetica
Poet — Poetique. Revue de Theorie et d'Analyse Litteraire
Poet — Poetry
Poetalk Quart — Poetalk Quarterly
PoetC — Poet and Critic
Poet Crit — Poet and Critic
Poetics Tod — Poetics Today
Poetik & Herm — Poetik und Hermeneutik
Poet L — Poet Lore
Poet Lyr Gr — Poetae Lyrici Graeci
Poet Mel Gr — Poetae Melici Graeci
Poet Rom Vet — Poetarum Romanorum Veterum Reliquiae
Poetry Aust — Poetry Australia
Poetry Mag — Poetry Magazine
Poetry NW — Poetry Northwest
PoetryQ — Poetry Quarterly
Poetry R — Poetry Review
Poetry Wale — Poetry Wales
Poets — Poets in the South
PoetW — Poetry Wales
PoeV — Poesie Vivante
Poeyana Inst Biol La Habana Ser A — Poeyana Instituto de Biologia. La Habana. Serie A
Poeyana Inst Biol La Habana Ser B — Poeyana Instituto de Biologia. La Habana. Serie B
Poeyana Inst Zool Acad Cienc Cuba — Poeyana Instituto de Zoologia. Academia de Ciencias de Cuba
POF — Prilozi za Orijentalnu Filologiju
POG — Official Gazette. United States Patent Office
Pog — Pogledi
POG — Tableware International
POGCA — Progress in Organic Coatings
POGE — Polar Geography and Geology
Pogg A — Annalen der Physik und Chemie. Poggendorff, Wiedemann
Poggendorffs Ann — Poggendorffs Annalen
Pogran Sloi Slozhnykh Usloviyakh Mater Sib Teplofiz Semin — Pogranichnye Sloi v Slozhnykh Usloviyakh. Materialy Sibirskogo Teplofizicheskogo Seminara
Pohjavesimallinnuksen Semin — Pohjavesimallinnuksen Seminaari
POHR — Ohio Review
POHY — Oral History Review
POI — Politique Etrangere
Poikila Byz — Poikila Byzantina
Poimennye Pochvy Russ Ravniny — Poimennye Pochvy Russkoi Ravniny
Point Defects Defect Interact Met Proc Yamada Conf — Point Defects and Defect Interactions in Metals. Proceedings. Yamada Conference
Point Defects Relat Prop Ceram — Point Defects and Related Properties of Ceramics
Point Magnesium Agric — Point sur...le Magnesium en Agriculture
PointP — Point (Paris)
Point Point Commun — Point-to-Point Communication [*Later, Communication and Broadcasting*]
Point Point Telecommun — Point-to-Point Telecommunications
Points Appui Econ Rhone-Alpes — Points d'Appui pour l'Economie Rhone-Alpes
Point Vet — Point Veterinaire
POJ — Patent Office Journal
Pojednani Kral Ceske Spolecn Nauk — Abhandlungen der Koeniglichen Boehmischen Gesellschaft der Wissenschaften
Pokroky Chem — Pokroky Chemie
Pokroky Mat Fyz Astron — Pokroky Matematiky, Fyziky, a Astronomie
Pokroky Praskove Metal — Pokroky Praskove Metalurgie
Pokroky Praskove Metal VUPM — Pokroky Praskove Metalurgie VUPM
Pokroky Vinohrad Vina- Vysk — Pokroky vo Vinohradnickom a Vinarskom Vyskume
Pol — FS. Political Risk Letter
Pol — Polemon
Pol — Polish [*Patent Document*]
POL — Politica de Venezuela
Pol — Politics
Pol — Polizei
Pol — Polonystyka
PoL — Portraits Litteraires

PolA — Politique Aujourd'hui
PolAb — Pollution Abstracts
Pol Acad Sci Bull Biol — Polish Academy of Sciences. Bulletin. Biology
Pol Acad Sci Bull Biol Sci — Polish Academy of Sciences. Bulletin. Biological Sciences
Pol Acad Sci Bull Chem — Polish Academy of Sciences. Bulletin. Chemistry
Pol Acad Sci Bull Earth Sci — Polish Academy of Sciences. Bulletin. Earth Sciences
Pol Acad Sci Bull Tech Sci — Polish Academy of Sciences. Bulletin. Technical Sciences
Pol Acad Sci Inst Ecol Rep Sci Act — Polish Academy of Sciences. Institute of Ecology. Report on Scientific Activities
Pol Acad Sci Inst Fundam Tech Res Nonlinear Vib Probl — Polish Academy of Sciences. Institute of Fundamental Technical Research. Nonlinear Vibration Problems
Pol Acad Sci Inst Fundam Tech Res Proc Vib Probl — Polish Academy of Sciences. Institute of Fundamental Technical Research. Proceedings of Vibration Problems
Pol Acad Sci Inst Geophys Publ D — Polish Academy of Sciences. Institute of Geophysics. Publications. D. Physics of the Atmosphere
Pol Acad Sci Inst Geophys Publ Ser D — Polish Academy of Sciences. Institute of Geophysics. Publications. Series D. Atmosphere Physics
Pol Acad Sci Inst Nucl Res Rep — Polish Academy of Sciences. Institute of Nuclear Research. Report
Pol Acad Sci Inst Phys Rep — Polish Academy of Sciences. Institute of Physics. Reports
Pol Acad Sci Med Sect Ann — Polish Academy of Sciences. Medical Section. Annals
Pol Acad Sci Publ Inst Geophys D — Polish Academy of Sciences. Publications. Institute of Geophysics. D. Physics of the Atmosphere
Pol Acad Sci Rev — Polish Academy of Sciences. Review
Pol Aff — Political Affairs
Pol Affairs — Political Affairs
Pol Afr — Politique Africaine
Pol Agric Annu — Polish Agricultural Annual
Pol Agric Annu Ser E — Polish Agricultural Annual. Series E. Plant Protection
Pol Agric For Annu — Polish Agricultural and Forest Annual
Pol Akad Nauk Inst Badan Jad Rep — Polska Akademia Nauk. Instytut Badan Jadrowych. Report
Pol Akad Nauk Inst Fiz Pr — Polska Akademia Nauk. Instytut Fizyki. Prace
Pol Akad Nauk Inst Geofiz Mater Pr — Polska Akademia Nauk. Instytut Geofizyki. Materialy i Prace
Pol Akad Nauk Inst Podstawowych Probl Tech Pr — Polska Akademia Nauk. Instytut Podstawowych Problemow Techniki. Prace
Pol Akad Nauk Inst Podstawowych Probl Tech Proc Vib Probl — Polska Akademia Nauk. Instytut Podstawowych Problemow Techniki. Proceedings of Vibration Problems
Pol Akad Nauk Kom Badan Morze Stud Mater Oceanol — Polska Akademia Nauk. Komitet Badan Morza. Studia i Materialy Oceanologiczne
Pol Akad Nauk Kom Biol Nowotworow Konf — Polska Akademia Nauk. Komisja Biologii Nowotworow. Konferencja
Pol Akad Nauk Kom Ceram Pr Ceram — Polska Akademia Nauk. Komisja Ceramiczna. Prace. Ceramika
Pol Akad Nauk Kom Ceram Pr Ser Ceram — Polska Akademia Nauk. Komisja Ceramiczna. Prace. Serja Ceramika
Pol Akad Nauk Kom Geol Acta Geol Pol — Polska Akademia Nauk. Komitet Geologiczny. Acta Geologica Polonica
Pol Akad Nauk Kom Geol Arch Mineral — Polska Akademia Nauk. Komitet Geologiczny. Archiwum Mineralogiczne
Pol Akad Nauk Kom Krystalogr Biul Inf — Polska Akademia Nauk. Komisja Krystalografii. Biuletyn Informacyjny
Pol Akad Nauk Muz Ziemi Pr — Polska Akademia Nauk. Muzeum Ziemi. Prace
Pol Akad Nauk Oddzial Krakowie Folia Quat — Polska Akademia Nauk. Oddzial w Krakowie. Folia Quaternaria
Pol Akad Nauk Oddzial Krakowie Kom Nauk Geol Pr Geol — Polska Akademia Nauk. Oddzial w Krakowie. Komisja Nauk Geologicznych. Prace Geologicane
Pol Akad Nauk Oddzial Krakowie Kom Nauk Mineral Pr Mineral — Polska Akademia Nauk. Oddzial w Krakowie. Komisja Nauk Mineralogicznych. Prace Mineralogiczne
Pol Akad Nauk Oddzial Krakowie Nauka Wszystkich — Polska Akademia Nauk. Oddzial w Krakowie. Nauka dla Wszystkich
Pol Akad Nauk Oddzial Krakowie Nauk Mineral Pr Mineral — Polska Akademia Nauk. Oddzial w Krakowie. Komisja Nauk Mineralogicznych. Prace Mineralogiczne
Pol Akad Nauk Oddzial Krakowie Pr Kom Ceram Ceram — Polska Akademia Nauk. Oddzial w Krakowie. Prace Komisji Ceramicznej. Ceramika
Pol Akad Nauk Oddzial Krakowie Pr Kom Ceram Ser Ceram — Polska Akademia Nauk. Oddzial w Krakowie. Prace Komisji Ceramicznej. Serja Ceramika
Pol Akad Nauk Oddzial Krakowie Pr Kom Metal Odlew Metal — Polska Akademia Nauk. Oddzial w Krakowie. Prace Komisji Metalurgiczno-Odlewniczej. Metalurgia
Pol Akad Nauk Oddzial Krakowie Pr Kom Metal-Odlew Metalurg — Polska Akademia Nauk. Oddzial w Krakowie. Prace Komisji Metalurgiczno-Odlewniczej. Metalurgia
Pol Akad Nauk Oddzial Krakowie Pr Kom Nauk Tech Ser Ceram — Polska Akademia Nauk. Oddzial w Krakowie. Prace Komisji Nauk Technicznych. Serja Ceramica
Pol Akad Nauk Pr Inst Masz Przeplyw — Polska Akademia Nauk. Prace Instytutu Maszyn Przeplywowych
Pol Akad Nauk Pr Kom Nauk Tech Metal Fiz Met Stopow — Polska Akademia Nauk. Prace Komisji Nauk Technicznych Metalurgia Fizyka Metali i Stopow
Pol Akad Nauk Pr Kom Nauk Tech Ser Ceram — Polska Akademia Nauk. Prace Komisji Nauk Technicznych. Serja Ceramika
Pol Akad Nauk Rozpr Wydz Nauk Med — Polska Akademia Nauk. Rozprawy Wydzialu Nauk Medycznych

Pol Akad Nauk Zakl Nauk Geol Stud Geol Pol — Polska Akademia Nauk. Zaklad Nauk Geologicznych. Studia Geologica Polonica

Pol Akad Nauk Zakl Ochr Przyr Stud Nat Ser A — Polska Akademia Nauk. Zaklad Ochrony Przyrody. Studia Naturae. Seria A. Wydawnictwa Naukowe

Pol Akad Nauk Zesz Probl Gorn — Polska Akademia Nauk. Komitet Gornictwa. Zeszyty Problemowe Gornictwa

Pol Akad Nauk Zesz Probl Nauki Pol — Polska Akademia Nauk. Zeszyty Problemowe Nauki Polskiej

Pol Akad Umiejet Kom Wydawn Slask Wydawn Slask Pr Biol — Polska Akademia Umiejetnosci. Komitet Wydawnictw Slaskich. Wydawnictwa Slaskie. Prace Biologiczne

Pol Akad Umiejet Mater Fizjogr Kraju — Polska Akademia Umiejetnosci. Materialy do Fizjografii Kraju

Pol Akad Umiejet Pr Kom Nauk Farm — Polska Akademia Umiejetnosci. Prace Komisji Nauk Farmaceutycznych

Pol Akad Umiejet Pr Muz Przyr — Polska Akademia Umiejetnosci. Prace Muzeum Przyrodniczego

Pol Akad Umiejet Pr Roln Lesne — Polska Akademia Umiejetnosci. Prace Rolniczo-Lesne

Pol Akad Umiejet Rozpr Wydz Lek — Polska Akademia Umiejetnosci. Rozprawy Wydzialu Lekarskiego

Pol Akad Umiejet Rozpr Wydz Mat Przyr Dzial A — Polska Akademia Umiejetnosci. Rozprawy Wydzialu Matematyczno-Przyrodniczego. Dzial A. Nauki Matematyczno-Fizyczne

Pol Akad Umiejet Rozpr Wydz Mat Przyr Dzial B — Polska Akademia Umiejetnosci. Rozprawy Wydzialu Matematyczno-Przyrodniczego. Dzial B. Nauki Biologiezne

Pol Akad Umiejet Wydawn Slask Pr Biol — Polska Akademia Umiejetnosci. Wydawnictwa Slaskie. Prace Biologiczne

Polam LJ — Polamerican Law Journal

Pol Am Stds — Polish American Studies

Pol Anal — Policy Analysis

Poland China — Poland China World

Poland Inst Geol Biul — Poland. Instytut Geologiczny. Biuletyn

Pol and Polit — Policy and Politics

Pol & Soc — Politics and Society

Polar Biol — Polar Biology

Pol Arch Hydrobiol — Polskie Archiwum Hydrobiologii/Polish Archives of Hydrobiology

Pol Arch Med Wewn — Polskie Archiwum Medycyny Wewnetrznej

Pol Arch Wet — Polskie Archiwum Weterynaryjne

Pol Arch Weter — Polskie Archiwum Weterynaryjne

Polarogr Ber — Polarographische Berichte

Polar Rec — Polar Record

Polar Res — Polar Research

Pol A Stud — Polish Art Studies

Pol Bildung — Politische Bildung

Pol Communication and Persuasion — Political Communication and Persuasion

Pol Diritto — Politica del Diritto

Pol Dokum — Politische Dokumentation

POLEA — Polski Tygodnik Lekarski

Pol Ecol Bibliogr — Polish Ecological Bibliography

Pol Ecol Stud — Polish Ecological Studies

Pol Econ — Political Economy

Pol Econ Rev — Political and Economic Review

Pol Endocrinol — Polish Endocrinology

Pol Endocrinol (Engl Transl Endokrynol Pol) — Polish Endocrinology (English Translation of Endokrynologia Polska)

Pol Eng — Polish Engineering

Pol Eng Rev — Polish Engineering Review

Pol Etr — Politique Etrangere

Pol Etrang — Politique Etrangere

Pol Etrangere — Politique Etrangere

Polev Arkheol Issled Tbilisi — Polevyye Arkheologicheskiye Issledovaniya. Akademiya Nauk Gruzinskoy SSR (Tbilisi)

Polev Issled — Polevyye Issledovaniya

Pol Ext — Politica Externa

POLFA — Polarforschung

Pol Fedn Newsl — Police Federation Newsletter

Pol Geol Mag — Polish Geological Magazine

Poll — Politica Internazionale

POLI — Postal Life

POLIA — Polimery

Police & Peace Offic — Police and Peace Officers

Police & Peace Offic J — Police and Peace Officers Journal [San Francisco]

Police Chiefs N Lett — Police Chiefs News Letter

Police Fedn Newsl — Police Federation Newsletter

Police J — Police Journal

Police J Ct — Police Justice's Court

Police J London — Police Journal (London)

Police J NY — Police Journal (New York)

Police Lab Rev — Police Labor Review

Police LQ — Police Law Quarterly

Police Mag — Police Magazine

Police Mag (Syria) — Police Magazine (Syria)

Police Rep — Police Reporter

Police Res Bull — Police Research Bulletin

Police Rev — Police Review

Police Sc Abs — Police Science Abstracts

Police Sci Abstr — Police Science Abstracts

Policewomans Int Bul — Policewoman's International Bulletin

Policewomans R — Policewoman's Review

Policlinico Sez Chir — Policlinico. Sezione Chirurgica

Policlinico Sez Med — Policlinico. Sezione Medica

Policlinico Sez Prat — Policlinico. Sezione Practica

Policlin Infant — Policlinico Infantile

Policy Anal — Policy Analysis [Later, Journal of Policy Analysis and Management]

Policy Pol — Policy and Politics

Policy Polit — Policy and Politics

Policy Publ Rev — Policy Publication Review

Policy R — Policy Review

Policy Rev — Policy Review

Policy Sci — Policy Sciences

Policy Statement R Coll Gen Pract — Policy Statement. Royal College of General Practitioners

Policy Stud — Policy Studies

Policy Studies J — Policy Studies Journal

Policy Studies R — Policy Studies Review

Policy Stud J — Policy Studies Journal

Policy Stud Rev — Policy Studies Review

POLID — Power Line

Polifon BA — Polifonia (Buenos Aires)

Poligr Proizvod — Poligraficheskoe Proizvodstvo

Poligr Promst Obz Inf — Poligraficheskaya Promyshlennost. Obzornaya Informatsiya

Poligr Promst Ref Inf — Poligraficheskaya Promyshlennost. Referativnaya Informatsiya

Polim Cienc Tecnol — Polimeros. Ciencia e Tecnologia

Polim Mashinostr — Polimery v Mashinostroenii

Polim Mater Ikh Issled — Polimernye Materialy i Ikh Issledovanie

Polim Mater Ikh Primen — Polimernye Materialy i Ikh Primenenie

Polim Med — Polimery w Medycynie

Polim Medziagos Ju Tyrimas — Polimerines Medziagos ir Ju Tyrimas

Polim Medziagu Panaudojimas Liaudies Ukyje — Polimeriniu Medziagu Panaudojimas Liaudies Ukyje

Polim Melior Vodn Khoz — Polimery v Melioratsii i Vodnom Khozyaistve

Polim Sb Tr Nauchnoizsled Inst Kauch Plastmasova Promst — Polimeri Sbornik ot Trudove na Nauchnoizsledovatelskiya Institut po Kauchukova i Plastmasova Promishlenost

Polim Sb Tr Nauchnoizsled Inst Prerabotka Plastmasi — Polimeri Sbornik ot Trudove na Nauchnoizsledovatelskiya Institut po Prerabotkkana Plastmasi

Polim Stroit Mater — Polimernye Stroitel'nye Materialy

Polim Tworzwa — Polimery Tworzywa

Polim Tworz Wielk — Polimery-Tworzywa Wielkoczasteczkowe

Polim Tworz Wielkoczast — Polimery-Tworzywa Wielkoczasteczkowe

Polim Tworzywa Wielkoczasteczkowe — Polimery Tworzywa Wielkoczasteczkowe

Polim Vehomarim Plast — Polimerim Vehomarim Plastiim

Pol Inst Geol Bibliogr Geol Pol — Poland. Instytut Geologiczny. Bibliografia Geologiczna Polski

Pol Inst Meteorol Gospod Wodnej Pr — Poland. Instytut Meteorologii i Gospodarki Wodnej. Prace

Pol Int — Politica Internacional. Instituto de Estudios Politicos

Pol Internat — Politique Internationale

Polio Pap Discuss Int Polio Conf — Poliomyelitis. Papers and Discussions Presented at the Interational Poliomyelitis Confernce

Poliplasti Mater Rinf — Poliplasti e Materiali Rinforzati

Poliplasti Plast Rinf — Poliplasti e Plastici Rinforzati

Poli Q — Political Quarterly

POLIS — Parliamentary On-Line Information System

Poli Sci — Political Science

Poli Sci Q — Political Science Quarterly

Polish Acad Sci Fluid Flow — Polish Academy of Sciences. Transactions. Institute of Fluid Flow Machinery

Polish Acad Sci Inst Philos Sociol Bull Sect Logic — Polish Academy of Sciences. Institute of Philosophy and Sociology. Bulletin of the Section of Logic

Polish Am Stud — Polish American Studies

Polish F — Polish Film

Polish J Chem — Polish Journal of Chemistry

Polish J Pharmacol Pharmacy — Polish Journal of Pharmacology and Pharmacy

Polish Mus — Polish Music

Polish Perspect — Polish Perspectives

Polish R — Polish Review

Polish Rev — Polish Review

Polish Sociol B — Polish Sociological Bulletin

Polish Tech & Econ Abstr — Polish Technical and Economic Abstracts

Poli Societ — Politics and Society

Polit Aff — Political Affairs

Polit and Soc — Politics and Society

Polit Arbejdstekst — Politiske Arbejdstekster

Polit Aujourd — Politique d'Aujourd'hui

Polit Belge — Politique Belge

Polit Caracas — Politica (Caracas)

Polit Dir — Politica del Diritto

Politech Bialostoca Zesz Nauk Mat Fiz Chim — Politechnika Bialostocka. Zeszyty Naukowe. Matematyka, Fizyka, Chemia

Politech Czestochow Zesz Nauk Hutn — Politechnika Czestochowska. Zeszyty Naukowe. Hutnictwo

Politech Czestochow Zesz Nauk Nauki Podstawowe — Politechnika Czestochowska. Zeszyty Naukowe. Nauki Podstawowe

Politech Czestochow Zesz Nauk Nauki Tech Ser Mech — Politechnika Czestochowska. Zeszyty Naukowe. Nauki Techniczne. Seria Mechanika

Politech Krakow im Tadeusza Kosciuszki Monogr — Politechnika Krakowska imeni Tadeusza Kosciuszki. Monografia

Politech Krakow Zesz Nauk Chem — Politechnika Krakowska. Zeszyty Naukowe. Chemia

Politech Krakow Zesz Nauk Inz Technol Chem — Politechnika Krakowska, Zeszyt Naukowe, Inzynieria i Technologia Chemiczna

Politech Lodz Zesz Nauk Chem — Politechnika Lodzka. Zeszyty Naukowe. Chemia

Politech Lodz Zesz Nauk Chem Spozyw — Politechnika Lodzka. Zeszyty Naukowe. Chemia Spozywcza
Politech Lodz Zesz Nauk Fiz — Politechnika Lodzka. Zeszyty Naukowe. Fizyka
Politech Lodz Zesz Nauk Inz Chem — Politechnika Lodzka. Zeszyty Naukowe. Inzynieria Chemiczna
Politech Lodz Zesz Nauk Mech — Politechnika Lodzka. Zeszyty Naukowe. Mechanika
Politech Lodz Zesz Nauk Technol Chem Spozyw — Politechnika Lodzka. Zeszyty Naukowe. Technologia i Chemia Spozywcza
Politech Lodz Zesz Nauk Wlok — Politechnika Lodzka. Zeszyty Naukowe. Wlokiennictwo
Politech Rzeszowska Im Ignacego Lukasiewicza Rozpr — Politechnika Rzeszowska Imienia Ignacego Lukasiewicza. Rozprawy
Politech Rzeszowska Zesz Nauk — Politechnika Rzeszowska. Zeszyty Naukowe
Politech Slaska im W Pstrowskiego Skr Uczelniane — Politechnika Slaska imienia W. Pstrowskiego. Skrypty Uczelniane
Politech Slaska Zesz Nauk Hutn — Politechnika Slaska. Zeszyty Naukowe. Hutnictwo
Politech Slaska Zesz Nauk Mat Fiz — Politechnika Slaska. Zeszyty Naukowe. Matematyka-Fizyka
Politech Slaska Zesz Nauk Mech — Politechnika Slaska. Zeszyty Naukowe. Mechanika
Politech Szczecin Pr Nauk — Politechnika Szczecinska. Prace Naukowe
Politech Warsz Inst Fiz Pr — Politechnika Warszawska. Instytut Fizyki. Prace
Politech Warsz Pr Inst Inz Chem — Politechnika Warszawska. Prace Instytutu Inzynierii Chemicznej
Politech Warsz Pr Inst Inz Chem Procesowej — Politechnika Warszawska. Prace Instytutu Inzynierii Chemicznej i Procesowej
Politech Warsz Pr Inst Podstaw Konstr Masz — Politechnika Warszawska. Prace Instytutu Podstaw Konstrukcji Maszyn
Politech Warsz Pr Nauk Chem — Politechnika Warszawska. Prace Naukowe. Chemia
Politech Warsz Pr Nauk Mech — Politechnika Warszawska. Prace Naukowe. Mechanika
Politech Wroclaw Inst Budow Pr Nauk — Politechnika Wroclawska. Instytut Budownictwa. Prace Naukowe
Politech Wroclaw Inst Fiz Pr Nauk — Politechnika Wroclawska. Instytut Fizyki. Prace Naukowe
Politech Wroclaw Inst Inz Ochr Srodowiska Pr Nauk — Politechnika Wroclawska. Instytut Inzynierii Ochrony Srodwoiska. Prace Naukowe
Politech Wroclaw Inst Inz Sanit Wodnej Pr Nauk — Politechnika Wroclawska. Instytut Inzynierii Sanitarnej i Wodnej. Prace Naukowe
Politech Wroclaw Inst Metrol Elektr Pr Nauk — Politechnika Wroclawskiej. Instytut Metrologii Elektrycznej. Prace Naukowe
Politech Wroclaw Inst Tech Cieplnej Mech Plynow Pr Nauk — Politechnika Wroclawska. Instytut Techniki Cieplnej i Mechaniki Plynow. Prace Naukowe
Politech Wroclaw Inst Ukladow Elektromasz Pr Nauk — Politechnika Wroclawska. Instytut Ukladow ELektromaszynowych. Prace Naukowe
Polit Eco — Review of Radical Political Economics
Polit Econ — Politica ed Economia
Polit ed Econ — Politica ed Economia
Politehn Univ Bucharest Sci Bull Ser A Appl Math Phys — Politehnica University of Bucharest. Scientific Bulletin. Series A. Applied Mathematics and Physics
Politehn Univ Bucharest Sci Bull Ser D Mech Engrg — Politehnica University of Bucharest. Scientific Bulletin. Series D. Mechanical Engineers
Polit Ekon — Politicka Ekonomie
Polit Etr — Politique Etrangere
Polit Etrangere — Politique Etrangere
Polit Foisk Kozlem — Politikai Foiskola Kozlemenyei
Polit Gazdasag Tanulmany — Politikai Gazdasagtan Tanulmanyok
PoliticaH — Politica (Havanna)
Politic St — Political Studies - London
Politik u Zeitgesch — Aus Politik und Zeitgeschichte. Beilage zur Wochenzeitung das Parlament
Polit Int — Politique Internationale
Polit Int Milano — Politica Internazionale (Milano)
Polit Int (Roma) — Politica Internazionale (Roma)
Polit Meinung — Politische Meinung
Polit Methodol — Political Methodology
Polit Perspect — Politiek Perspectief
Polit Phys Mag — Politiske Og Physiske Magazin
Polit Q — Political Quarterly
Polit Quart — Political Quarterly
Polit Rdsch — Politische Rundschau
Polit Samoobr — Politiceskoe Samoobrazovanie
Polit Sci — Political Science
Polit Sci Ann — Political Science Annual
Polit Sci Disc Pap — Political Science Discussion Papers
Polit Scientist — Political Scientist
Polit Sci Q — Political Science Quarterly
Polit Sci Quart — Political Science Quarterly
Polit Sci R — Political Science Review
Polit Sci R'er — Political Science Reviewer
Polit Sci (Wellington) — Political Science (Wellington)
Polit Sc Quartl — Political Science Quarterly
Polit Soc — Politics and Society
Polit Soc Econ Rev — Political, Social, Economic Review
Polit Spolecz — Polityka Spoleczna
Polit Stud — Political Studies
Polit Stud — Politische Studien
Polit Theor — Political Theory
Polit Theory — Political Theory
Polit Today — Politics Today
Polit u Zeitgesch — Politik und Zeitgeschichte
Polit Vjschr — Politische Vierteljahresschrift

Polit Vjschr Sonderh — Politische Vierteljahresschrift. Sonderheft
Polizei Arch — Deutsches Polizei-Archiv
Polizeibeamten Bl — Polizeibeamten-Blatt
Pol J — Police Journal
Pol J Anim Sci Technol — Polish Journal of Animal Science and Technology
Pol J Appl Chem — Polish Journal of Applied Chemistry
Pol J Chem — Polish Journal of Chemistry
Pol J Ecol — Polish Journal of Ecology
Pol J Immunol — Polish Journal of Immunology
Pol J Med Pharm — Polish Journal of Medicine and Pharmacy
Poljodjelska Znan Smotra — Poljodjelska Znanstvena Smotra
Poljopriv Pregl — Poljoprivredni Pregled
Poljopriv Sumar — Poljoprivredni i Sumarstvo
Poljopriv Znan Smotra — Poljoprivredna Znanstvena Smotra
Poljopr Naucna Smotra — Poljoprivredna Naucna Smotra
Poljopr Sumar — Poljoprivredna i Sumarstvo
Poljopr Znan Smotra — Poljoprivredna Znanstvena Smotra
Poljopr Znanst Smotra — Poljoprivredna Znanstvena Smotra
Pol J Pathol — Polish Journal of Pathology
Pol J Phar — Polish Journal of Pharmacology and Pharmacy
Pol J Pharmacol — Polish Journal of Pharmacology
Pol J Pharmacol Pharm — Polish Journal of Pharmacology and Pharmacy
Pol J Soil Sci — Polish Journal of Soil Science
Poll — Pollack's Ohio Unreported Judicial Decisions Prior to 1823
Poll — Pollexfen's English King's Bench Reports
PolL — Polonista (Lublin)
POLL — Public Opinion Location Library
Pol Lab Rev — Police Labor Review
Poll Abstr — Pollution Abstracts
Pollack Mihaly Muesz Foeisk Tud Koezl — Pollack Mihaly Mueszaki Foeiskola Tudomanyos Koezlemenyei
Poll CC Pr — Pollock's Practice of the County Courts
POLLD — Pollimo
Pollen Grain US For Serv Southeast Area — Pollen Grain. United States Forest Service. Southeastern Area
Pollen Physiol Fert Symp — Pollen Physiology and Fertilization. Symposium
Pollex — Pollexfen's English King's Bench Reports
Pollexf — Pollexfen's English King's Bench Reports
Pollexfen — Pollexfen's English King's Bench Reports
Polli — Annali di Chimica. Polli
Pollich — Jahresbericht der Pollichia, eines Naturwissenschaftlichen Vereins der Rheinpfalz
Pol LQ — Police Law Quarterly
Pollut Abatement Semin Proc — Pollution Abatement Seminar. Proceedings
Pollut Abstr — Pollution Abstracts
Pollut Abstr Indexes — Pollution Abstracts with Indexes
Pollut Atmos — Pollution Atmospherique
Pollut Control — Pollution Control
Pollut Control Mar Ind Proc Annu Int Conf — Pollution Control in the Marine Industries. Proceedings. Annual International Conference
Pollut Control Technol Oil Gas Drill Prod Oper — Pollution Control Technology for Oil and Gas Drilling and Production Operations
Pollut Eng — Pollution Engineering
Pollut Eng Technol — Pollution Engineering and Technology
Pollution — Pollution Equipment News
Pollut Monitor — Pollution Monitor
Pollut Prev Process Prod Modif — Pollution Prevention via Process and Product Modification
Pollut Rep UK Cent Dir Environ Pollut — Pollution Report. United Kingdom. Central Directorate on Environmental Pollution
Pollut Res — Pollution Research
Pollut Tech — Pollution Technology
Pol Mach Ind — Polish Machine Industry
Pol Mach Ind Offers — Polish Machine Industry Offers
Pol Med Hist Sci Bull — Polish Medical History and Science Bulletin
Pol Med J — Polish Medical Journal
Pol Med J (Engl Transl Pol Arch Med Wewn) — Polish Medical Journal (English Translation of Polskie Archiwum Medycyny Wewnetrznej)
Pol Med Sci Hist Bull — Polish Medical Science and History Bulletin
Pol Meinung — Politische Meinung
Pol Methodol — Political Methodology
Pol Mt — Polytechnische Mittheilungen, unter Mitwirkung von Professoren Hoeherer Technischer Lehranstalten
Pol Mus Geol Mag — Polish Museum Geological Magazine
POLNA — Polnohospodarstvo
Polnohospod — Polnohospodarstvo
Pologne Aff Occid — Pologne et les Affaires Occidentales
Pologne Contemp — Pologne Contemporaine
Poloriz Phenom Nucl React Proc Int Symp — Polorization Phenomena in Nuclear Reactions. Proceedings. International Symposium
Pol'ovnicky Zb — Pol'ovnicky Zbornik
PolP — Polish Perspectives
Pol Pap Ser — Policy Papers Series
Pol Pat Doc — Poland. Patent Document
Pol Perspect — Polish Perspectives
Pol Pismo Entomol — Polskie Pismo Entomologiczne
Pol Pismo Entomol Ser B — Polskie Pismo Entomologiczne. Seria B. Entomologia Stosowana
Pol Pismo Entomol Ser B Entomol Stosow — Polskie Pismo Entomologiczne. Seria B. Entomologia Stosowana
Pol Przegl Chir — Polski Przeglad Chirurgiczny
Pol Przegl Radiol — Polski Przeglad Radiologii i Medycyny Nuklearnej
Pol Przegl Radiol Med Nukl — Polski Przeglad Radiologii i Medycyny Nuklearnej
Pol Psych B — Polish Psychological Bulletin
Pol Q — Political Quarterly

Pol Qtr — Political Quarterly
Pol Quar — Political Quarterly
Pol R — Policy Review
PolR — Polish Review
Pol R — Politisk Revy
POLRA — Polar Record
Pol Res Bull — Police Research Bulletin
Pol Rev — Polish Review
Pol Rev Radiol Nucl Med — Polish Review of Radiology and Nuclear Medicine
Pol Rev Radiol Nucl Med (Engl Transl) — Polish Review of Radiology and Nuclear Medicine (English Translation)
Pol Sac — Polonia Sacra
Pol Sci — Policy Sciences
Pol Sci — Political Science
Pol Sci — Politica Sociale
Pol Science Q — Political Science Quarterly
Pol Sci Learning — Polish Science and Learning
Pol Sci Q — Political Science Quarterly
Pol Sci Quar — Political Science Quarterly
Pol Sci R — Political Science Review
Pol Sci Rev — Political Science Review
Polska Akad Nauk Met — Polska Akademia Nauk. Metalurgia
Polska Akad Nauk Oddzial Krakowie Pr Kom Nauk Tech Ceram — Polska Akademia Nauk. Oddzial w Krakowie. Prace Komisji Nauk Technicznych. Serja Ceramika
Polska Biblio Analit Mech — Polska Bibliografia Analityczna. Mechanika
Polska Gaz Lek — Polska Gazeta Lekarska
Polska Gaz Lekar — Polska Gazeta Lekarska
Polskie Arch Med Wewnetrznej — Polskie Archiwum Medycyny Wewnetrznej
Polskie Archwm Wet — Polskie Archiwum Weterynaryjne
Polskie Pismo Entomol — Polskie Pismo Entomologiczne
Polskie Pismo Entomol Ser B Entomol Stosow — Polskie Pismo Entomologiczne. Seria B. Entomologia Stosowana
Polskie Tow Ent Klucze Oznaczania Owadow Pol — Polskie Towarzystwo Entomologiczne. Klucze do Oznaczania Owadow Polski
Polski Tygod Lek — Polski Tygodnik Lekarski
Pol Soc — Politics and Society
Pol Soc B — Polish Sociological Bulletin
PolSQ — Political Science Quarterly
Pol St — Political Studies
PolST — Politische Studien
Pol Stud — Political Studies
Pol Studien — Politische Studien
Pol Studies — Political Studies
Pol Stud J — Policy Studies Journal
Pol Stud Rev Ann — Policy Studies Review Annual
Pol Szt Lud — Polska Sztuka Ludowa
Pol Tech Abstr — Polish Technical Abstracts
Pol Tech Econ Abstr — Polish Technical and Economic Abstracts
Pol Technol News — Polish Technological News
Pol Tech Rev — Polish Technical Review
Pol Theory — Political Theory
Pol Tijd — Polytechnisch Tijdschrift
Pol Today — Politics Today
Pol Tow Entomol Klucze Oznaczania Owadow Pol — Polskie Towarzystwo Entomologiczne. Klucze do Oznaczania Owadow Polski
Pol Tow Geol Rocz — Polskie Towarzystwo Geologiczne. Rocznik
Pol Tow Glebozn Kom Biol Gleby Pr Kom Nauk — Polskie Towarzystwo Gleboznawcze. Komisja Biologii Gleby. Prace Komisji Naukowych
Pol Tow Glebozn Kom Chem Gleby Pr Kom Nauk — Polskie Towarzystwo Gleboznawcze. Komisja Chemii Gleby. Prace Komisji Naukowych
Pol Tow Glebozn Kom Genezy Klasyf Kartogr Gleb Pr Kom Nauk — Polskie Towarzystwo Gleboznawcze. Komisja Genezy, Klasyfikacji, i Kartografii Gleb. Prace Komisji Naukowych
Pol Tow Glebozn Kom Zyznosci Odzywiania Rosl Pr Kom Nauk — Polskie Towarzystwo Gleboznawcze. Komisja Zyznosci i Odzywiania Roslin. Prace Komisji Naukowych
Pol Trasporti — Politica dei Trasporti
Poltto Voiteluainelab Tied Valt Tek Tutkimuskeskus — Poltto- ja Voiteluainelaboratorio. Tiedonanto. Valtion Teknillinen Tutkimuskeskus
Pol Tyg Lek — Polski Tygodnik Lekarski
Pol Tyg Lek Wiad Lek — Polski Tygodnik Lekarski i Wiadomosci Lekarskie
Poluch Anal Chist Veshchestv — Poluchenie i Analiz Chistykh Veshchestv
Poluch Anal Veshchestv Osoboi Chist Dokl Vses Konf — Poluchenie i Analiz Veshchestv Osoboi Chistoty. Doklady Vsesoyuznoi Konferentsii po Polucheniyu i Analiyu veshchestv Osoboi Chistoty
Poluch Anal Veshchestv Osoboi Chist Mater Vses Konf — Poluchenie i Analiz Veshchestv Osoboi Chistoty. Materialy Vsesoyuznoi Konferentsii po Metodam Polucheniya i Analiza Veshchestv Osoboi Chistoty
Poluch Issled Svoistv Soedin RZM Mater Nauchn Semin — Poluchenie i Issledovanie Svoistv Soedinenii RZM. Materialy Nauchnogo Seminara po Polucheniyu i Issledovaniyu Svoistv Soedinenii Redkozemel'nykh Metallov
Poluch Izdelii Zhidk Met Uskor Krist Dokl Nauchno Tekh Konf — Poluchenie Izdelii iz Zhidkikh Metallov s Uskorennoi Kristallizatsiei. Doklady na Nauchno-Tekhnicheskoi Konferentsii po Voprosam Proizvodstva Chugunnogo Lista i Otlivok iz Magnievogo Chuguna v Mekhanizirovannykh Kokilyakh
Poluch Lateksov Modif Ikh Svoistv Tr Vses Lateksnoi Konf — Poluchenie Lateksov i Modifikatsiya Ikh Svoistv. Trudy Vsesoyuznoi Lateksnoi Konferentsii
Poluch Primen Fermentov Vitam Aminokislt Obz Inf — Poluchenie i Preimenenie Fermentov. Vitaminov i Aminokislot. Obzornaya Informatsiya
Poluch Strukt Svoistva Sorbentov — Poluchenie, Struktura, i Svoistva Sorbentov
Poluch Svoistva Tonkikh Plenok — Poluchenie i Svoistva Tonkikh Plenok
Poluprovdn Prib Tekh Elektrosvyazi — Poluprovodnikovye Pribory v Tekhnike Elektrosvyazi
Poluprovodn Elektron — Poluprovodnikovaya Elektronika

Poluprovodn Ikh Primen Elektrotekh — Poluprovodniki i Ikh Primenenie v Elektrotekhnike
Poluprovodn Prib Ikh Primen — Poluprovodnikovye Pribory i Ikh Primenenie
Poluprovodn Prib Primen — Poluprovodnikovye Pribory i Ikh Primenenie
Poluprovodn Prib Tekh Elektrosvyazi — Poluprovodnikovye Pribory v Tekhnike Elektrosvyazi
Poluprovodn Segnetoelektr — Poluprovodniki-Segnetoelektriki
Poluprovodn Tekh i Mikroelektron — Poluprovodnikovaya Tekhnika i Mikroelektronika
Poluprov Prib Ikh Primen Sb Statei — Poluprovodnikovye Pribory i Ikh Primenenie Sbornik Statei
Poluprov Tekh Mikroelektron — Poluprovodnikovaya Tekhnika i Mikroelektronika
Pol Urzad Pat Wiad Urzedu Pat — Poland. Urzad Patentowy. Wiadomosci Urzedu Patentowego
Pol Vjschr — Politische Vierteljahresschrift
Pol VO — Polizeiverordnung
Poly — Polybiblion. Revue Bibliographique Universelle
POLY-AE/AM Rep (Polytech Inst NY Dep Aerosp Eng Appl Mech) — POLY-AE/AM Report (Polytechnic Institute of New York. Department of Aerospace Engineering and Applied Mechanics)
Polyamines Gastrointest Tract Proc Falk Symp — Polyamines in the Gastrointestinal Tract. Proceedings. Falk Symposium
Polyarn Siyaniya Svechenie Nochnogo Neba — Polyarnye Siyaniya i Svechenie Nochnogo Neba
Polyar Siyaniya — Polyarnye Siyaniya
Pol Yb of Internat L — Polish Yearbook of International Law
PolyEthylene Glycol Chem — Poly(Ethylene Glycol) Chemistry. Biotechnical and Biomedical Applications
Polygr Betr — Polygraphischer Betrieb
Polygr Ind — Polygraphische Industrie
Polyimides Other High Temp Polym Proc Eur Tech Symp — Polyimides and Other High-Temperature Polymers. Proceedings. European TechnicalSymposium on Polyimides and High-Temperature Polymers
Poly L Rev — Poly Law Review
Polym Adv Technol — Polymers for Advanced Technologies
Polym Age — Polymer Age
Polym Anal Charact IV Proc Int Symp — Polymer Analysis and Characterization IV. Proceedings. International Symposium on Polymer Analysis and Characterization
Polym Anal Charact Proc Int Symp — Polymer Analysis and Characterization. Proceedings. International Symposium on Polymer Analysis and Characterization
Polym Appl — Polymer Application
POLYMAT — Polymer Materials
Polym Biol Med — Polymers in Biology and Medicine
Polym Bull — Polymer Bulletin
Polym Bull (Beijing) — Polymer Bulletin (Beijing)
Polym Bull (Berlin) — Polymer Bulletin (Berlin)
Polym Colloid Syst — Polymers as Colloid Systems
Polym Commun — Polymer Communications
Polym Commun Beijing — Polymer Communications (Beijing)
Polym Compat Incompat Pap Midl Macromol Meet — Polymer Compatibility and Incompatibility. Papers. Midland Macromolecular Meeting
Polym Compos — Polymer Composites
Polym Composites — Polymer Composites
Polym Compos Proc Microsymp Macromol — Polymer Composites. Proceedings. Microsymposium on Macromolecules
Polym Compos Stab — Polymer Compositions Stabilizers
Polym Concr Int Congr Proc — Polymers in Concrete. International Congress on Polymers in Concrete. Proceedings
Polym Concr Proc Int Congr — Polymers in Concrete. Proceedings. International Congress on Polymer Concretes
Polym Conserv — Polymers in Conservation
Polym Degradation Stab — Polymer Degradation and Stability
Polym Degradat Stabil — Polymer Degradation and Stability
Polym Dig Tokyo — Polymer Digest (Tokyo)
Polym Eng and Sci — Polymer Engineering and Science
Polym Eng Curric Proc Buhl Int Conf Mater — Polymers in the Engineering Curriculum. Proceedings. Buhl International Conference on Materials
Polym Engng News — Polymer Engineering News
Polym Engng Rev — Polymer Engineering Reviews
Polym Engng Sci — Polymer Engineering and Science
Polym Eng Rev — Polymer Engineering Reviews
Polym Eng S — Polymer Engineering and Science
Polym Eng Sci — Polymer Engineering and Science
Polymerase Chain React Methods Appl — Polymerase Chain Reaction Methods and Applications
Polymer Engng Science — Polymer Engineering and Science
Polymer J — Polymer Journal
Polym Gels Networks — Polymer Gels and Networks
Polym Heterocycl Pap IUPAC Congr — Polymerization of Heterocyclics. Papers Presented at the IUPAC Congress
Polym Int — Polymer International
Polym J — Polymer Journal
Polym J (Jap) — Polymer Journal (Japan)
Polym J Singapore — Polymer Journal (Singapore)
Polym J (Tokyo) — Polymer Journal (Tokyo)
Polym Lett — Polymer Letters
Polym Mater Sci Eng — Polymeric Materials Science and Engineering. Proceedings. ACS Division of Polymeric Materials Sciences and Engineering
Polym Mater Sci Eng Chengdu People's Repub China — Polymeric Materials Science and Engineering (Chengdu, People's Republic of China)
Polym Mater Sci Eng Proc ACS Div Polym Mater Sci Eng — Polymeric Materials Science and Engineering. Proceedings of the ACS Division of Polymeric Materials Science and Engineering

Polym Mech — Polymer Mechanics
Polym Mech (Engl Transl) — Polymer Mechanics (English Translation)
Polym Med — Polymere in Medizin
Polym Med — Polymers in Medicine
Polym Microelectron Proc Int Symp — Polymers for Microelectronics. Science and Technology. Proceedings. International Symposium
Polym Monogr — Polymer Monographs
Polym Networks Blends — Polymer Networks and Blends
Polym News — Polymer News
Polym Paint Col J — Polymers, Paint, and Colour Journal
Polym Paint Colour J — Polymers, Paint, and Colour Journal
Polym Paint Colour J Suppl Adhes Sealants — Polymers, Paint, Colour Journal. Supplement. Adhesives and Sealants
Polym Photochem — Polymer Photochemistry
Polym-Plast — Polymer-Plastics Technology and Engineering
Polym Plast Mater — Polymers and Plastic Materials
Polym-Plast Technol Eng — Polymer-Plastics Technology and Engineering
Polym Prepr Am Chem Soc Div Polym Chem — Polymer Preprints. American Chemical Society. Division of Polymer Chemistry
Polym Preprints — Polymer Preprints
Polym Process Eng — Polymer Process Engineering
Polym Process (Kyoto) — Polymer Processing (Kyoto)
Polym React Eng — Polymer Reaction Engineering
Polym Recycl — Polymer Recycling
Polym Rep — Polymer Report
Polym Rev — Polymer Reviews
Polym Sci Lib — Polymer Science Library
Polym Sci Ser A Ser B Transl of Vysokomol Soedin Ser A Ser B — Polymer Science. Series A and Series B. Translation of Vysokomolekulyarnye Soedineniya. Seriya A i Seriya B
Polym Sci Technol — Polymer Science and Technology
Polym Sci Technol Comtex — Polymer Science and Technology (Comtex)
Polym Sci Technol Tehran — Polymer Science and Technology (Tehran)
Polym Sci USSR — Polymer Science. USSR
Polym Sci USSR Engl Transl — Polymer Science USSR (English Translation)
Polym Solution — Polymers in Solution
Polym Specific Prop Lect Macromol Symp Jpn FRG — Polymers with Specific Properties. New Aspects and Developments. Lectures. Macromolecular Symposium Japan-FRG
Polym Symp — Polymer Symposia
Polym Synth Oxid Processes — Polymer Synthesis Oxidation Processes
Polym Test — Polymer Testing
Polym Theor Abst — Polymer Theory Abstracts
Polym Unusual Prop Proc Northeast Reg Meet Am Chem Soc — Polymers with Unusual Properties. Proceedings. Northeast Regional Meeting. American Chemical Society
Polym Work Annu Natl Conf — Polymers at Work. Annual National Conference
Polym Yearb — Polymer Yearbook
Polyn Soc J — Polynesian Society Journal
Polynucl Aromat Hydrocarbons Chem Charact Carcinog Int Symp — Polynuclear Aromatic Hydrocarbons. Chemistry, Characterization, and Carcinogenesis. International Symposium
Polynucl Aromat Hydrocarbons Nomencl Guide — Polynuclear Aromatic Hydrocarbons Nomenclature Guide
Polynucl Aromat Hydrocarbons Pap Int Symp Pap — Polynuclear Aromatic Hydrocarbons. Mechanisms, Methods, and Metabolism. Papers. International Symposium on Polynuclear Aromatic Hydrocarbons
Polyolefin Plast — Polyolefin and Plastics
Polyphenols Actual — Polyphenols Actualites
Polysaccharides Biol Trans Conf — Polysaccharides in Biology. Transactions of the Conference
Polysar Prog — Polysar Progress
Polyscope Autom und Elektron — Polyscope. Automatik und Elektronik
Polyscope Comput und Elektron — Polyscope. Computer und Elektronik
Polysilicon Thin Films Interfaces Symp — Polysilicon Thin Films and Interfaces. Symposium
Polytech Exch — Polytechnique Exchange
Polytech Inst Brooklyn Microwave Res Inst Symp Ser — Polytechnic Institute of Brooklyn. Microwave Research Institute. Symposia Series
Polytech Inst Bucharest Sci Bull Chem Materials Sci — Polytechnic Institute of Bucharest. Scientific Bulletin. Chemistry and Materials Science
Polytech Inst Bucharest Sci Bull Chem Mater Sci — Polytechnic Institute of Bucharest. Scientific Bulletin. Chemistry and Materials Science
Polytech Inst Bucharest Sci Bull Electr Engrg — Polytechnic Institute of Bucharest. Scientific Bulletin. Electrical Engineering
Polytech Inst N Y Microwave Res Inst Symp Ser — Polytechnic Institute of New York. Microwave Research Institute. Symposia Series
Polytech J — Polytechnisches Journal
Polytechn Journ — Dinglers Polytechnisches Journal
Polytech Notes Artif Intell — Polytechnic Notes on Artificial Intelligence
Polytech Tijdschr Bouwk Wegen- & Waterbouw — Polytechnisch Tijdschrift Bouwkune Wegen- en Waterbouw
Polytech Tijdschr Ed A — Polytechnisch Tijdschrift. Editie A. Werktuigbouwkunde en Elektrotechniek
Polytech Tijdschr Ed B — Polytechnisch Tijdschrift. Editie B
Polytech Tijdschr Ed Procestech — Polytechnisch Tijdschrift. Editie. Procestechniek
Polytech Tijdschr Ed Werktuigbouw — Polytechnisch Tijdschrift. Editie. Werktuigbouw
Polytech Tijdschr Elektrotech — Polytechnisch Tijdschrift. Elektrotechniek.
Polytech Tijdschr Elektrotech Elektron — Polytechnisch Tijdschrift. Elektrotechniek. Elektronica
Polytech Tijdschr Procestech — Polytechnisch Tijdschrift. Procestechniek
Polytech Tijdschr Werktuigbouw — Polytechnisch Tijdschrift. Werktuigbouw

Polytech Weekbl — Polytechnisch Weekblad
Polytek Revy — Polyteknisk Revy
Polyt Rv — Polytechnic Review
Pol Zh Zootekh Tekhnol — Pol'skii Zhurnal Zootekhniki i Tekhnologii
PoM — Palace of Minos
PoM — Patterns of Myth
POM — Proceso (Mexico)
POMDA — Postgraduate Medicine
POMDD — Poznanskie Roczniki Medyczne
POMFE4 — Ontario. Ministry of Agriculture and Food. Publication
POMG — Omega
Pomiary Autom Kontrola — Pomiary Automatyka Kontrola
POMJA — Polish Medical Journal
PoMM — Patterns of Myth. Myth and Experience
Pommersche Biblioth — Pommersche Bibliothek
Pommersches Arch Wiss Geschmaks — Pommersches Archiv der Wissenschaften und des Geschmaks
Pommersfeldener Beitr — Pommersfeldener Beitraege
Pommers Zschr — Schweizerische Zeitschrift fuer Natur- und Heilkunde (C. F. von Pommer, Editor)
Pomme Terre Fr — Pomme de Terre Francaise
POMNDR — Museo Nacional de Historia Natural. Publicacion Ocasional
Pomol Fr — Pomologie Francaise
Pomol Fruit Grow Soc Annu Rep — Pomological and Fruit Growing Society. Annual Report
Pomol Monatsh — Pomologische Monatshefte
Pomona Coll J Econ Bot — Pomona College Journal of Economic Botany, as Applied to Subtropical Horticulture
Pomona J Entomol — Pomona Journal of Entomology
Pomor Ant — Pomorania Antiqua
POMPA — Publications. Mississippi Philological Association
Pompebl — Pompebledon
Pon — Ponte
PON — Public Opinion
PONE — Polar News. Japan Polar Research Association
Po Now — Poetry Now
PONS — Polar Notes
PONSA — Platt's Oilgram News Service
Ponte Riv M — Ponte. Rivista Mensile di Politica e Letteratura
Pontif Acad Sci Acta — Pontificia Academia Scientiarum. Acta
Pontif Acad Sci Comment — Pontificia Academia Scientiarum. Commentarii
Pontif Acad Sci Scr Varia — Pontificia Academia Scientiarum. Scripta Varia
Pontif Accad Sci Acta — Pontificia Accademia Scientiarum. Acta
Pontif Accad Sci Annu — Pontificia Accademia delle Scienze. Annuario
Pontif Accad Sci Commentat — Pontificia Accademia Scientiarum. Commentationes
Pontif Accad Sci Novi Lyncaei Sci Nuncius Radiophonicus — Pontificia Accademia Scientiarum. Novi Lyncaei. Scientiarum Nuncius Radiophonicus
Pontif Univ Catol Ecuador Rev — Pontificia Universidad Catolica del Ecuador. Revista
Pont Rom — Pontificale Romanum
Pooles Index Period Lit — Poole's Index to Periodical Literature
Poona Agr Col Mag — Poona Agricultural College Magazine
Poona Agric Coll Mag — Poona Agricultural College Magazine
Poona Univ J Sci Technol — Poona University Journal. Science and Technology
Po Or — Poona Orientalist
PoP — Patterns of Prejudice
PoP — Political Psychology
POP — Poona Orientalist (Poona)
Pop — Population
Pop As — Popular Astronomy
Pop Astron — Popular Astronomy
Pop Astronomy — Popular Astronomy
Pop B — Population Bulletin
Pop Bul — Population Bulletin
Pop Bull Colo State Univ Agr Exp Sta — Popular Bulletin. Colorado State University. Agricultural Experiment Station
Pop Comput — Popular Computing
POPDA — Polish Psychological Bulletin
Pop Dev — Population and Development Review
Pop Dev R — Population and Development Review
Pop Diff — Popular Difference
Pop Educ — Popular Educator
Pop Electr — Popular Electronics
Pop Elekt — Populaer Elektronik + High Fidelity
Pop Gard — Popular Gardening
Pop Govt — Popular Government
Popl — Population Index
Pop Ind — Population Index
Pop Index — Population Index
Pop Lect Math — Popular Lectures in Mathematics
Pop Mag Rev — Popular Magazine Review
Pop Mech — Popular Mechanics Magazine
Pop Mech M — Popular Mechanics Magazine
Pop Med (Tokyo) — Popular Medicine (Tokyo)
Pop Mo L Tr — Popular Monthly Law Tracts
Pop Mus — Popular Music
Pop Mus & Soc — Popular Music and Society
Pop Music Period Index — Popular Music Periodicals Index
Pop Music S — Popular Music and Society
Pop Mus Per Ind — Popular Music Periodicals Index
POPO — Polar Post. Polar Postal History Society of Great Britain
POPOA — Phosphorus and Potassium
POPPD — Plant/Operations Progress
Pop Per Ind — Popular Periodical Index

Pop Phot — Popular Photography
Pop Photog — Popular Photography
Pop Photogr — Popular Photography
Pop Plast — Popular Plastics
Pop Plast Annu — Popular Plastics Annual
Pop Plast Packag — Popular Plastics and Packaging
Pop Plast Rubber — Popular Plastics and Rubber
POPQ — Opera Quarterly
Pop Rad — Populaer Radio
Pop Rad — Populaer Radio og TV Teknik
Pop Sci — Popular Science Monthly
Pop Sci M — Popular Science Monthly
Pop Sci Mo — Popular Science Monthly
Pop Sci Mon — Popular Science Monthly
Pop Sci Mthly — Popular Science Monthly
Pop Sci (Peking) — Popular Science (Peking)
Pop Sci R — Popular Science Review
Pop Sc Rv — Popular Science Review. A Quarterly Miscellany of Entertaining and Instructive Articles on Scientific Subjects
Pop St — Populations Studies
Pop Stud — Population Studies
Pop Stud (Lo) — Population Studies (London)
Pop Stud (NY) — Population Studies (New York)
Pop Tech Tous — Popular Technique pour Tous
Popul — Population
Popular Govt — Popular Government
Popular M Soc — Popular Music and Society
Popular Sci Rev — Popular Science Review
Population Bul — Population Bulletin
Population Bul UN — Population Bulletin. United Nations
Population R — Population Review
Population Research and Policy R — Population Research and Policy Review
Population Stud — Population Studies
Popul Bull — Population Bulletin
Popul Bull UN Econ Comm West Asia — Population Bulletin. United Nations Economic Commission for Western Asia
Popul B UN Econ Com West Asia — Population Bulletin. United Nations Economic Commission for Western Asia
Popul Counc Annu Rep — Population Council. Annual Report
Popul Data Inf Serv — Population Data Information Service
Popul Develop R — Population and Development Review
Popul Dev Rev — Population and Development Review
Popul Educ News — Population Education News
Popul Environ — Population and Environment
Popul et Avenir — Population et Avenir
Popul et Famille — Population et Famille
Popul et Famille/Bevolk en Gezin — Population et Famille/Bevolking en Gezin
Popul et Societes — Population et Societes
Popul Exposures Proc Midyear Top Symp Health Phys Soc — Population Exposures. Proceedings. Midyear Topical Symposium. Health Physics Society
Popul Forum — Population Forum
Popul Geogr — Population Geography
Popul I — Population Index
Popul Ind — Population Index
Popul Index — Population Index
Popul Newsl — Population Newsletter
Popul Policy Compend — Population Policy Compendium
Popul Pollut Proc Annu Symp Eugen Soc — Population and Pollution. Proceedings. Annual Symposium. Eugenics Society
Popul Rep A — Population Reports. Series A. Oral Contraceptives
Popul Rep B — Population Reports. Series B. Intrauterine Devices
Popul Rep C — Population Reports. Series C. Sterilization. Female
Popul Rep D — Population Reports. Series D. Sterilization (Male)
Popul Rep E — Population Reports. Series E. Law and Policy
Popul Rep F — Population Reports. Series F. Pregnancy Termination
Popul Rep G — Population Reports. Series G. Prostaglandins
Popul Rep H — Population Reports. Series H. Barrier Methods
Popul Rep I — Population Reports. Series I. Periodic Abstinence
Popul Rep J — Population Reports. Series J. Family Planning Programs
Popul Rep K — Population Reports. Series K. Injectables and Implants
Popul Rep L — Population Reports. Series L. Issues in World Health
Popul Rep M — Population Reports. Series M. Special Topics
Popul Rep Ser G — Population Reports. Series G. Prostaglandins
Popul Rep Spec Top Monogr — Population Reports. Special Topics. Monographs
Popul Rev — Population Review
Popul Stud — Population Studies
Popul Today — Population Today
Popul Trends — Population Trends
POPYA — Portugaliae Physica
PoQ — Political Quarterly
POQ — Public Opinion Quarterly
POR — Pack Report. Fachzeitschrift fuer Verpackungs Marketing und Verpackungs (Technik)
POR — Patent Office Reports
PoR — Poetry Review
PoR — Polish Review
POr — Poona Orientalist
PoR — Population Review
POr — Porta Orientale
Por — Portique
Por — Portugale
POr — Przeglad Orientalistyczny
PORADD — Postgraduate Radiology
Poradnik M — Poradnik Muzyczny
PORB — Orbis

PORCD — Population Reports. Series C
PORDB — Ports and Dredging
PORE — Polar Record
POREEQ — Polar Research
Por Jez — Poradnik Jezykowy
Pork Ind Gaz — Pork Industry Gazette
PORLA — Practica Oto-Rhino-Laryngologica
Porodoobrazuyushchie Miner Mater Sezda MMA — Porodoobrazuyushchie Mineraly. Materialy S'ezda MMA
Poroshk Metall — Poroshkovaya Metallurgiya
Poroshk Metall (Kiev) — Poroshkovaya Metallurgiya (Kiev)
Poroshk Metall (Kuibyshev) — Poroshkovaya Metallurgiya (Kuibyshev)
Poroshk Metall Mater Vses Konf — Poroshkovaya Metallurgiya. Materialy Vsesoyuznoi Konferentsii po Poroshkovoi Metallurgii
Poroshk Metall Metalloobrab Mater Resp Nauchno Tekh Semin — Poroshkovaya Metallurgiya i Metalloobrabotka. Materialy Respublikanskogo Nauchno-Tekhnicheskogo Seminara
Poroshk Metall Minsk — Poroshkovaya Metallurgiya (Minsk)
Porosh Met — Poroshkovaya Metallurgiya
Porosim Its Appl — Porosimetry and Its Application
Porozim Jeji Pouziti — Porozimetrie a Jeji Pouziti
Porphyrins Porphyrias Proc Int Congr — Porphyrins and Porphyrias. Proceedings. International Congress on Porphyrins and Porphyrias
PORS — Polar Research
PORS — Publications in Operations Research Series
Port — Portique
Port — Portugale
Port Acta Biol A — Portugaliae Acta Biologica. A. Morfologia, Fisiologia, Genetica, e Biologia Geral
Port Acta Biol Ser A — Portugaliae Acta Biologica. Serie A
Port Acta Biol Ser B — Portugaliae Acta Biologica. Serie B
Port Afr — Portugal em Africa
Port & Artnews Annu — Portfolio and Artnews Annual
Porta Orient — Porta Orientale
Port Electrochim Acta — Portugaliae Electrochimica Acta
Port em Afr — Portugal em Africa
Portfo — Portfolio
Portfo (Den) — Portfolio (Dennie's)
Port Gazette — Melbourne Harbour Trust Port Gazette
Portia L J — Portia Law Journal
Port Junta Invest Cient Ultramar Estud Ensaios Doc — Portugal. Junta de Investigacoes Cientificas do Ultramar. Estudos, Ensaios, e Documentos
Port Lab Nac Eng Civ Mem — Portugal. Laboratorio Nacional de Engenharia Civil. Memoria
Portland Cem Ass Advanced Eng Bull — Portland Cement Association. Advanced Engineering Bulletin
Portland Cem Ass J PCA Res Develop Lab — Portland Cement Association. Journal of the PCA Research and Development Laboratories
Portland Cem Assoc Fellowship Natl Bur Stand Pap — Portland Cement Association Fellowship at the National Bureau of Standards. Papers
Portland Cem Assoc Res Dev Lab Dev Dep Bull D — Portland Cement Association. Research and Development Laboratories. DevelopmentDepartment. Bulletin D
Portland Cem Assoc Res Dev Lab J — Portland Cement Association. Research and Development Laboratories. Journal
Portland Mag — Portland Magazine
Portland Press Proc — Portland Press Proceedings
Portland Roses Fl — Portland Roses and Flowers
Portland Soc N H Pr — Portland Society of Natural History. Proceedings
Portland UL Rev — Portland University. Law Review
Port Melb — Port Of Melbourne
Port Melbourne Quart — Port Of Melbourne Quarterly
Port Melb Q — Port Of Melbourne Quarterly
Port Minist Ultramar Junta Invest Ultramar An — Portugal. Ministerio do Ultramar. Junta de Investigacoes do Ultramar. Anais
Port Minist Ultramar Junta Invest Ultramar Estud Ensaios Doc — Portugal. Ministerio do Ultramar. Junta de Investigacoes do Ultramar. Estudos, Ensaios, e Documentos
Port Minist Ultramar Junta Invest Ultramar Mem Ser Antropol — Portugal. Ministerio do Ultramar. Junta de Investigacoes do Ultramar. Memorias.Serie Antropologica e Etnologica
Port Minist Ultramar Junta Invest Ultramar Mem Ser Bot — Portugal. Ministerio do Ultramar. Junta de Investigacoes do Ultramar. Memorias.Serie Botanica
Port Minist Ultramar Junta Invest Ultramar Mem Ser Botanica — Portugal. Ministerio do Ultramar. Junta de Investigacoes do Ultramar. Memorias.Serie Botanica
Port Minist Ultramar Junta Invest Ultramar Mem Ser Geol — Portugal. Ministerio do Ultramar. Junta de Investigacoes do Ultramar. Memorias.Serie Geologica
Port Minist Ultramar Junta Invest Ultramar Mem Ser Pedol Trop — Portugal. Ministerio do Ultramar. Junta de Investigacoes do Ultramar. Memorias. Serie de Pedologia Tropical
Port Minist Ultramar Mem Junta Invest Ultramar — Portugal. Ministerio do Ultramar. Memorias da Junta de Investigacoes do Ultramar
Port Of Melbourne Q — Port Of Melbourne Quarterly
Port Of Melbourne Quart — Port Of Melbourne Quarterly
Port Of Melb Q — Port Of Melbourne Quarterly
Port Of Melb Quart — Port Of Melbourne Quarterly
Port Of Syd — Port Of Sydney
Port Of Sydney J — Port Of Sydney Journal
Port Phillip Gaz — Port Phillip Gazette
Port Phy — Portugaliae Physica
Port Phys — Portugaliae Physica
Port R — Portland Review
Ports Dredging — Ports and Dredging
Ports Dredging Oil Rep — Ports and Dredging and Oil Report

Port Serv Fom Min Estud Notas Trab — Portugal. Servico de Fomento Mineiro. Estudos, Notas, e Trabalhos
Port Serv Geol Mem — Portugal. Servicos Geologicos. Memoria
Port Syd — Port Of Sydney
Portug Acta Biol — Portugaliae Acta Biologica
Portugal em Afr — Portugal em Africa
Portugaliae Acta Biol Ser A — Portugaliae Acta Biologica. Serie A
Portugal Inf Rev — Portugal. Informative Review
Portugal Math — Portugaliae Mathematica
Portugal Phys — Portugaliae Physica
Portugal Trab Gl Com — Communicacoes da Commissao dos Trabalhos Geologicos de Portugal
Port UL Rev — Portland University. Law Review
POS — Policy Statements
PoS — Political Studies
POS — Population Studies
Pos — Positif. Revue Periodique de Cinema
POS — Pretoria Oriental Series
POS — Professions and Occupations Sourcebook
POS — Pskovskij Oblastnoj Slovar's Istoriceskimi Dannymi
POSB — Polish Sociological Bulletin
POSEA — Peredovoi Opyt v Stroitel'stve i Ekspluatatsii Shakht
Posebna Izdan — Posebna Izdanja
Posebna Izd Biol Inst N R Srb Beograd — Posebna Izdanja Bioloski Institut N R Srbije Beograd
Posebna Izd Filoz Fak Univ Skopje Hidrobiol Zavod Ohrid — Posebna Izdanja. Filoz. Fak. Na Univ. Skopje. Hidrobioloski Zavod Ohrid Editions Speciales. Station Hydrobiologique
Posebna Izd Geol Glas (Sarajevo) — Posebna Izdanja Geoloskog Glasnika (Sarajevo)
Posebna Izd Zavod Geol Hidrogeol Geofiz Geoteh Istraz — Posebno Izdanje. Zavod za Geoloska, Hidrogeoloska, Geofizicka, i Geotehnicka Istrazivanja
POSID — Polyarnye Siyaniya
Position Theses Ecole Chartes — Position des Theses de l'Ecole des Chartes
Positron Annihilation Proc Int Conf — Positron Annihilation. Proceedings. International Conference on Positron Annihilation
Positron Positronium Chem Int Workshop — Positron and Positronium Chemistry. International Workshop
P Oslo — Papyri Osloenses
PosLuth — Positions Lutheriennes
PoSM — Politische Studien. Monatsschrift der Hochschule fuer Politische Wissenschaften (Munich)
PosMSchr — Juristische Monatsschrift fuer Posen, West- und Ostpreussen und Pommern
POSPB — Problemy Osvoeniya Pustyn
Posselt's Text J — Posselt's Textile Journal
Possible Episomes Eukaryotes Proc Lepetit Colloq — Possible Episomes in Eukaryotes. Proceedings. Lepetit Colloquium
POST — Polymer Science and Technology
POSt — Princeton Oriental Studies
POST-A — Population Studies
Post Accid Heat Removal Inf Exch Meet — Post Accident Heat Removal Information Exchange Meeting
Postal Bull — Postal Bulletin. Weekly
Postal Bull US Postal Serv — Postal Bulletin. United States Postal Service
Postal Spvr — Postal Supervisor
PostB — Postilla Bohemica
Post Bioch — Postepy Biochemii
Postdiplom Sem Fiz — Postdiplomski Seminar iz Fizike
Postdiplom Sem Mat — Postdiplomski Seminar iz Matematike
Post Dir — Post's Paper Mill Directory
Postepy Astron — Postepy Astronomii
Postepy Astronaut — Postepy Astronautyki
Postepy Biochem — Postepy Biochemii
Postepy Biol Komorki — Postepy Biologii Komorki
Postepy Cybernet — Postepy Cybernetyki
Postepy Endokrynol Okresu Rozwoj Konf Nauk Mater Nauk — Postepy Endokrynologii Okresu Rozwojowego. Konferencja Naukowa. Materialy Naukowe
Postepy Fiz — Postepy Fizyki
Postepy Fizjol — Postepy Fizjologii
Postepy Fiz Med — Postepy Fizyki Medycznej
Postepy Ftyz Pneumon — Postepy Ftyzjatrii i Pneumonologii
Postepy Hig Med Dosw — Postepy Higieny i Medycyny Doswiadczalnej
Postepy Med — Postepy Medycyny
Postepy Mikrobiol — Postepy Mikrobiologii
Postepy Nauki Roln — Postepy Nauki Rolniczej
Postepy Nauk Roln — Postepy Nauk Rolniczych
Postepy Tech Jad — Postepy Techniki Jadroweki
Postepy Techn Jadr — Postepy Techniki Jadrowej
Postepy Technol Masz Urzadz — Postepy Technologii Maszyn i Urzadzen
Postepy Technol Masz Urzadzen — Postepy Technologii Maszyn i Urzadzen
Postepy Wied Med — Postepy Wiedzy Medycznej
Postepy Wiedzy Med — Postepy Wiedzy Medycznej
Postepy Wiedzy Roln — Postepy Wiedzy Rolniczej
Posters & Designers — Posters and their Designers
Posters & Publ — Posters and Publicity
Poster Sess Prepr Sess — Poster Sessions Preprints. Sessions
Poste's Gai — Poste's Translation of Gaius
Poste Telecommun — Poste e Telecommunicazioni
Poste Telecomun Sviluppo Soc — Poste e Telecomunicazioni nello Sviluppo dello Societa
Postg Med J — Postgraduate Medical Journal
Post Grad Course Int Meet Anaesthesiol Resusc — Post Graduate Course. International Meeting of Anaesthesiology and Resuscitation

Postgrad Courses Pediatr — Postgraduate Courses in Pediatrics
Postgrad Dent Handb Ser — Postgraduate Dental Handbook Series
Postgrad Med — Postgraduate Medicine
Postgrad Med J — Postgraduate Medical Journal
Postgrad Med J Suppl — Postgraduate Medical Journal. Supplement
Postgrad Med Ser — Postgraduate Medicine Series
Postgrad MJ — Postgraduate Medical Journal
Postgrad Paediatr Ser — Postgraduate Paediatrics Series
Postgrad Radiol — Postgraduate Radiology
Postgraduate Bull — Postgraduate Bulletin
Postgr Med — Postgraduate Medicine
Post Harvest Technol Cassava — Post Harvest Technology of Cassava
Post Hist Soc Bull — Postal History Society Bulletin
Posth Tss — Posthistorisk Tidsskrift
Postimplant Dev Mouse — Postimplantation Development in the Mouse
POST-J — Polymer Science and Technology - Journals
Post Mag & Insur Monitor — Post Magazine and Insurance Monitor
Postmasters Adv — Postmasters Advocate
Post Med Archaeol — Post-Medieval Archaeology
Post-Medieval Arch — Post-Medieval Archaeology
Post-Medieval Archaeol — Post-Medieval Archaeology
Post O E E J — Post Office Electrical Engineers. Journal
Post Off Electr Eng J — Post Office Electrical Engineers. Journal
Post Off (GB) Res Dep Rep — Post Office (Great Britain). Research Department Report
Post Office Hist Soc Trans — Post Office Historical Society. Transactions
Post Off Telecommun J — Post Office Telecommunications Journal
POST-P — Polymer Science and Technology - Patents
Post S — Post Script
POStS — Princeton Oriental Studies. Social Science
Post Scr — Post Script
POT — British Telecom Journal
POT — Papper och Trae
Po T — Poetics Today
POT — Princeton Oriental Texts
Potash 90 — Potash 1990. Feast or Famine
Potash J — Potash Journal
Potash Rev — Potash Review
Potash Trop Agric — Potash and Tropical Agriculture
Potassium Inst Ltd Colloq Proc — Potassium Institute Limited. Colloquium Proceedings
Potassium Potasio Kalium Symp — Potassium Potasio Kalium Symposium
Potassium Qual Agric Prod Proc Congr Int Potash Inst — Potassium and the Quality of Agricultural Products. Proceedings. Congress. International Potash Institute
Potassium Qual Prod Agric CR Colloq Reg Inst Int Potasse — Potassium et la Qualite des Produits Agricoles. Comptes Rendus du Colloque Regional. Institute International de la Potasse
Potassium Relat Grassl Prod Proc Reg Conf Int Potash Inst — Potassium in Relation to Grassland Production. Proceedings. Regional Conference. International Potash Institute
Potassium Symp — Potassium. Symposium
Potassium Symp Pap — Potassium Symposium. Papers
Potato Abstr — Potato Abstracts
Potato Grow — Potato Grower
Potato Handb — Potato Handbook
Potato J — Potato Journal
Potato M — Potato Magazine
Potato Res — Potato Research
Pot Aust — Pottery in Australia
P O Telecommun J — Post Office Telecommunications Journal
Potential Anal — Potential Analysis
Potential New Methods Detect Irradiat Food — Potential New Methods of Detection of Irradiated Food
POTF — Publications. Oriental Translation Fund
Potfuzetek Termeszettud Kozl — Potfuzetek a Termeszettudomanyi Kozlonyhoz
POTN — Problems of the North
Potomac Appalachian Trail Club Bull — Potomac Appalachian Trail Club. Bulletin
Potomac L Rev — Potomac Law Review
Potomac R — Potomac Review
Potomac Rev — Potomac Review
Potosi Univ Autonoma Inst Geologia y Metalurgia Fol Tec — Universidad Autonoma Potosina. Instituto de Geologia y Metalurgia. Folleto Tecnico
Potravin Chladici Tech — Potravinarska a Chladici Technika
Potravin Vedy — Potravinarske Vedy
Potsdamer Forsch Reihe B — Potsdamer Forschungen. Reihe B. Naturwissenschaftliche Reihe
Potsdam Tagztg — Potsdamer Tageszeitung
Potter Am Mo — Potter's American Monthly
Pottery — Pottery in Australia
Pottery Aust — Pottery in Australia
Pottery Gaz Glass Trade Rev — Pottery Gazette and Glass Trade Review
Pottery Glass Rec — Pottery and Glass Record
Pottery Glass Trades J — Pottery and Glass Trades Journal
Pottery in Aust — Pottery in Australia
Potvrda Valjanosti Broj Inst Meh Poljopr — Potvrda o Valjanosti Broj-Institut za Mehanizaciju Poljoprivrede
POTWA — Polimery Tworzywa
POUDAY — Poultry Digest
Poughkeepsie Soc N Sc Pr — Poughkeepsie Society of Natural Science. Proceedings
Poult — Poultry Forum
Poult Abstr — Poultry Abstracts
Poult Advis — Poultry Adviser
Poult Bull — Poultry Bulletin

Poult Dig — Poultry Digest
Poult Egg Situat PES US Dep Agric Econ Res Serv — Poultry and Egg Situation. PES. United States Department of Agriculture. Economic Research Service
Poult Health Symp — Poultry Health Symposium
Poult Ind — Poultry Industry
Poultry Dig — Poultry Digest
Poultry Livestock Comment — Poultry and Livestock Comment
Poultry Process — Poultry Processing and Marketing
Poultry Sci — Poultry Science
Poult Sci — Poultry Science
Poult Sci Symp — Poultry Science Symposium
Poult Trials Bull — Poultry Trials Bulletin
Poult Trib — Poultry Tribune
Poult World — Poultry World
Pour Nos Jard — Pour Nos Jardins. Bulletin. Societe d'Horticulture et des Jardins Populaires deFrance
Pour Sci (Paris) — Pour la Science (Paris) (Edition Francaise de Scientific American)
POV — Politica (Venezuela)
Pov & Human Resour Abstr — Poverty and Human Resources Abstracts
Povedenie Mater Usloviyakh Vak Nizk Temp — Povedenie Materialov v Usloviyakh Vakuuma i Nizkikh Temperatur
Poverkhn Yavleniya Polim — Poverkhnostnye Yavleniya v Polimerakh
Poverkhn Yavleniya Zhidk Zhidk Rastvorakh — Poverkhnostnye Yavleniya v Zhidkostyakh i Zhidkikh Rastvorakh
Pov Hum Resour — Poverty and Human Resources
Pov Hum Resour Abstr — Poverty and Human Resources Abstracts
Povolzh Lesotekh Inst Sb Tr — Povolzhskii Lesotekhnicheskii Institut Sbornik Trudov
Povos & Cult — Povos e Culturas
Povysh Eff Primen Tsem Asfaltovykh Betonov Sib — Povyshenie Effektivnosti Primeneniya Tsementnykh i Asfal'tovykh Betonov v Sibiri
Povysh Plodorodiya Pochv Nechernozemn Polosy — Povyshenie Plodorodiya Pochv Nechernozemnoi Polosy
PoW — Polish Western Affairs
Pow Conv — Powell. Conveyancing
Powder Bulk Eng — Powder and Bulk Engineering
Powder Coat — Powder Coatings
Powder Diffr — Powder Diffraction
Powder Eng — Powder Engineering
Powder Handl Process — Powder Handling and Processing
Powder Ind Res — Powder Industry Research
Powder Met — Powder Metallurgy
Powder Metall — Powder Metallurgy
Powder Metall Assoc India News Lett — Powder Metallurgy Association of India. News Letter
Powder Metall Bull — Powder Metallurgy Bulletin
Powder Metall Def Technol — Powder Metallurgy in Defense Technology
Powder Metall Ind — Powder Metallurgy Industry
Powder Metall Int — Powder Metallurgy International
Powder Metall Met Ceram — Powder Metallurgy and Metal Ceramics
Powder Metall Sci & Technol Hyderabad India — Powder Metallurgy Science and Technology (Hyderabad, India)
Powder Metall Technol — Powder Metallurgy Technology
Powder Sci Eng — Powder Science and Engineering
Powder Sci Technol Jpn — Powder Science and Technology in Japan
Powder Technol — Powder Technology
Powder Technol (Lausanne) — Powder Technology (Lausanne)
Powder Technol Publ Ser — Powder Technology Publication Series
Powder Technol (Tokyo) — Powder Technology (Tokyo)
Powd Metall — Powder Metallurgy
Powd Tech — Powder Technology
Power & Works Engng — Power and Works Engineering
Power Appar Syst — Power Apparatus and Systems
PowerConvers Int — PowerConversion International
Powerconvers Intell Motion — Powerconversion and Intelligent Motion
Power Electron Var Speed Drives Int Conf — Power Electronics and Variable-Speed Drives. International Conference
Power Eng — Power Engineering
Power Eng Barrington Ill — Power Engineering (Barrington, Illinois)
Power Eng Finance — Power Engineering and Finance
Power Eng (India) — Power Engineer (India)
Power Eng J — Power Engineering Journal
Power Eng J Acad Sci (USSR) — Power Engineering Journal. Academy of Sciences
Power Eng N Y — Power and the Engineer (New York)
Power Eng (NY Eng Transl) — Power Engineering (New York, English Translation)
Power Eqp — Survey of Power Equipment Requirements of the United States Electric Utility Industry
Power F — Power Farming
Power Farming Aust — Power Farming in Australia
Power Farming Better Farming Dig Aust NZ — Power Farming and Better Farming Digest in Australia and New Zealand [Later, Power Farming]
Power Farming Mag — Power Farming Magazine
Power Fuel Bull — Power and Fuel Bulletin
Power Gener — Power Generation
Power Ind — Power Industry, Including Industrial Power and Industry Power
Power Ind Res — Power Industry Research
Power N — Power News
Power Plant Eng — Power Plant Engineering
Power Plant Eng S Afr — Power and Plant Engineering in South Africa
Power Plant S Afr — Power and Plant in Southern Africa
Power Plant South Afr — Power and Plant in Southern Africa
Power Plant Sthn Afr — Power and Plant in Southern Africa
Power Pl Eng — Power Plant Engineering

Power Radioisot Proc Int Symp — Power from Radioisotopes. Proceedings. International Symposium
Power React Nucl Fuel Dev Corp Tokai Works Annu Prog Rep — Power Reactor and Nuclear Fuel Development Corporation. Tokai Works Annual Progress Report
Power React Nucl Fuel Dev Corp Tokai Works Semi Annu Prog Re — Power Reactor and Nuclear Fuel Development Corporation. Tokai Works Semi-AnnualProgress Report
Power Reactor Technol — Power Reactor Technology
Power Reactor Technol Reactor Fuel Process — Power Reactor Technology and Reactor Fuel Processing
Power Reactor Technol (Tokyo) — Power Reactor Technology (Tokyo)
Power React Technol — Power Reactor Technology
Power React Technol React Fuel Process — Power Reactor Technology and Reactor Fuel Processing
Power Sources Symp Proc — Power Sources Symposium. Proceedings
Power Stn Pumps Fans Int Conf — Power Station Pumps and Fans. International Conference
Power Trans Des — Power Transmission Design
Power Transm Des — Power Transmission Design
Power Works Eng — Power and Works Engineering
Powloki Ochr — Powloki Ochronne
POWTECH Int Powder Technol Bulk Solids Exhib Congr — POWTECH. International Powder Technology and Bulk Solids Exhibition and Congress
Powys N — Powys Newsletter
Powys Rev — Powys Review
P Oxf — Some Oxford Papyri
P Oxford — Some Oxford Papyri
POxy — Oxyrhynchus Papyri
POZBDM — Folia Venatoria
Pozharnaya Okhr — Pozharnaya Okhrana
Pozharnaya Tekh — Pozharnaya Tekhnika
Poznan Agric Univ Ann — Poznan Agricultural University. Annals
Poznan Rocz Med — Poznanskie Roczniki Medyczne
Poznan Stud — Poznan Studies
Poznan Stud Philos Sci Humanities — Poznan Studies in the Philosophy of the Sciences and the Humanities
Poznan Tow Przyj Nauk Kom Biol Pr — Poznanskie Towarzystwo Przyjaciol Nauk. Komisja Biologiczna. Prace
Poznan Tow Przyj Nauk Pr Kom Biol — Poznanskie Towarzystwo Przyjaciol Nauk. Prace Komisji Biologicznej
Poznan Tow Przyj Nauk Pr Kom Farm — Poznanskie Towarzystwo Przyjaciol Nauk. Prace Komisji Farmaceutycznej
Poznan Tow Przyj Nauk Pr Kom Lek — Poznanskie Towarzystwo Przyjaciol Nauk. Prace Komisji Lekarskiej
Poznan Tow Przyj Nauk Pr Kom Mat Przyr — Poznanskie Towarzystwo Przyjaciol Nauk. Prace Komisji Matematyczno-Przyrodniczej
Poznan Tow Przyj Nauk Pr Kom Mat Przyr Pr Chem — Poznanskie Towarzystwo Przyjaciol Nauk. Prace Komisji Matematyczno-Przyrodniczej. Prace Chemiczne
Poznan Tow Przyj Nauk Pr Kom Mat Przyr Ser A — Poznanskie Towarzystwo Przyjaciol Nauk. Prace Komisji Matematyczno-Przyrodniczej. Seria A
Poznan Tow Przyj Nauk Pr Kom Mat Przyr Ser B — Poznanskie Towarzystwo Przyjaciol Nauk. Prace Komisji Matematyczno-Przyrodniczej. Seria B
Poznan Tow Przyj Nauk Pr Kom Med Dosw — Poznanskie Towarzystwo Przyjaciol Nauk. Prace Komisji Medycyny Doswiadczalnej
Poznan Tow Przyj Nauk Pr Kom Nauk Podstawowych Stosow — Poznanskie Towarzystwo Przyjaciol Nauk. Prace Komisji Nauk Podstawowych Stosowanych
Poznan Tow Przyj Nauk Pr Kom Nauk Roln Kom Nauk Lesn — Poznanskie Towarzystwo Przyjaciol Nauk. Prace Komisji Nauk Rolniczych i KomisjiNauk Lesnych
Poznan Tow Przyj Nauk Pr Kom Technol Drewna — Poznanskie Towarzystwo Przyjaciol Nauk. Prace Komisji Technologii Drewna
Poznan Tow Przyj Nauk Spraw — Poznanskie Towarzystwo Przyjaciol Nauk. Sprawozdania
Poznan Tow Przyj Nauk Wydz Lek Pr Kom Farm — Poznanskie Towarzystwo Przyjaciol Nauk. Wydzial Lekarski. Prace Komisji Farmaceutycznej
Poznan Tow Przyj Nauk Wydz Lek Pr Kom Med Doswi — Poznanskie Towarzystwo Przyjaciol Nauk. Wydzial Lekarski. Prace Komisji Medycyny Doswiadczalnej
Poznan Tow Przyj Nauk Wydz Mat-Przyr Kom Biol Pr — Poznanskie Towarzystwo Przyjaciol Nauk. Wydzial Matematyczno-Przyrodniczy. Komisja Biologiczna Prace
Poznan Tow Przyj Nauk Wydz Mat Przyr Pr Kom Biol — Poznanskie Towarzystwo Przyjaciol Nauk. Wydzial Matematyczno-Przyrodniczy PraceKomisji Biologicznej
Poznan Tow Przyj Nauk Wydz Mat Przyr Pr Kom Mat Przyr — Poznanskie Towarzystwo Przyjaciol Nauk, Wydzial Matematyczno-Przyrodniczy PraceKomisji Matematyczno-Przyrodniczej
Pozn St Teol — Poznanskie Studie Teologiczne
PP — Die Palmyrenischen Personennamen
PP — Palestine Post
PP — Pandectes Periodiques
PP — Pan Pipes
PP — Panstwo i Prawo
PP — Papyrusfunde und Papyrusforschung
PP — Parliamentary Paper
PP — Parola del Passato
PP — Patriarchs and Prophets
PP — Philologica Pragensia
PP — Philosophia Patrum
PP — Pinepointer
PP — Pitt Press Series
PP — Poetry and the People
PP — Population (Paris)
PP — Postavy a Problemy

PP — Prace Polonistyczne
PP — Prasa Polska
PP — Presocratic Philosophers
PP — Przeglad Powszechny
PPa — Parola del Passato
PPA — Preussisches Pfarrarchiv
PPA — Proceedings. Pan-American Scientific Congress
PPAAI — Papers on the Physical Anthropology of the American Indian [New York]
PPAD — Public Administration
PPAF — Pacific Affairs
PPAJ — Performing Arts Journal
PP & S — Papers on Poetics and Semiotics
PPAR — Parabola
PParis — Notices et Texts des Papyrus Grecs du Musée du Louvre et de la Bibliotheque Imperiale
PPAS — Proceedings of the Pakistan Academy of Sciences
PPAS — Pubblicazioni. Pontificio Ateneo Salesiano
PPAS — Publications. Philadelphia Anthropological Society
PPATDQ — Pediatric Pathology
PPA Univ KY Coop Ext Serv — PPA. University of Kentucky. Cooperative Extension Service
PPB — Polybiblion. Partie Litteraire
PPBES — Polnyi Pravoslavnyi Bogoslovskii Entsiklopedicheskii Slovar
PPBUA — Personnel Practice Bulletin
PPC — Journal of Pension Planning and Compliance
PPC — Problemes de la Pensee Chretienne
PPC — Profile of Primitive Culture
PPCJ Polym Paint Colour J — PPCJ Polymers Paint Colour Journal
PPC Jrl — Polymers, Paint, and Colour Journal
PPD — Polish Perspectives
PPDR — Population and Development Review
PPDS — Physical Property Data Service
PPeda — Problemi della Pedagogia
PPEI — Parliamentary Papers. East India
PPENA — Plant and Power Services Engineer
PPERB — Progress in Pediatric Radiology
PPESD9 — Proceedings. APRES
PPetr — Flinders Petrie Papyri
PPEW — Philosophy East and West
PPF — Phaenomenologisch-Psychologische Forschungen
PPF — Poetarum Philosophorum Fragmenta
PPFCDY — Proceedings. Southern Pasture and Forage Crop Improvement Conference
PPG — Phoenizisch-Punische Grammatik
PPGE — Professional Geographer
PPGS — Publications. Pennsylvania German Society
PP Guide — Prescription Proprietaries Guide
PPHBD7 — Plant Physiology and Biochemistry
PPHC — Pakistan History Conference. Proceedings
P/P Herald — Palestine Post Herald
PPhF — Pullacher Philosophische Forschungen
PPHID — Plasma Physics Index
P Philad — Papyrus de Philadelphie
P Ph L — Papers in Philippine Linguistics
PPHL — Public Health Reports
PPHPB — Problemy Projektowe Hutnictwa i Przemyslu Maszynowego
PPHQ — Pacific Philosophical Quarterly
PPHR — Pacific Historical Review
PPHR — Planned Parenthood Review
PPHRA — Philosophy and Phenomenological Research
PPHRD — Photochemical and Photobiological Reviews
PPHS — Publications. Presbyterian Historical Society
PPHY — Philosophy
PPHYA — Plant Physiology
PPI — Park Practice Index
PPI — Planen-Pruefen-Investieren
PPI — Popular Periodical Index
PPI — Producer Price Indexes
PPI — Pulp and Paper International
PPIL — Problems in Private International Law
PPI Planen Pruef Investieren — PPI. Planen, Pruefen, Investieren
PPI Pulp Pap Int — PPI. Pulp and Paper International
PPJ — Pakistan Philosophical Journal
PPJ — Philippine Planning Journal
PPJ — Prilozi Proucavanju Jezika
PPKCB — Prace Komisji Ceramicznej. Polskiej Akademii Nauk. Ceramica
PPKGA — Ponpu Kogaku
PPL — Journal of Pension Planning and Compliance
PPL — Polybiblion. Partie Litteraire
PPL — Population Paper Listing
PPL — Prace Polonistyczne (Lodz)
PPLF — Parliamentary Affairs
PPLG — Ploughshares
PPLL — Papers on Language and Literature
PPL Ser Mankind Eng — PPL Series on Mankind and the Engineer
PPM — Pensamiento Politico Mexicano
PPM — Public Personnel Management
PPM — Pulp and Paper Magazine of Canada [Later, Pulp and Paper (Canada)]
PPML — Princeton Publications in Modern Languages
PPMMA — Problemy Prochnosti v Mashinostroenii
PPMMB — Periodica Polytechnica. Mechanical Engineering
PPMNA — Polski Przeglad Radiologii i Medycyny Nuklearnej
PPMRC — Proceedings. PMR Conference. Annual Publication of the International Patristic,Mediaeval, and Renaissance Conference
PPMVA — Pishchevaya Promyshlennost

PPNADY — Pitch Pine Naturalist
PPNCFL — Proceedings. Pacific Northwest Conference on Foreign Languages
PPNM — Perspectives of New Music
PPNP — Past and Present. A Journal of Historical Studies
PPNPD — Progress in Particle and Nuclear Physics
PPNS — Politics and Society
PPNWCFL — Proceedings. Pacific Northwest Conference on Foreign Languages
PPol — Pensiero Politico
PPol — Przeglad Polski
PPOM — Planeacion y Programa. Organizacion y Metodo
PPOR — Parnassus. Poetry in Review
PPOS — Philosophy of Science
PPOTA — Prumysl Potravin
PPOW — Policy Review
PPow — Przeglad Powszechny
PPP — Pipelines, Politics, and People. Capital Communications Ltd.
PPP — Pulp and Paper International
PPPA — Philosophy and Public Affairs
PPPBDD — Iran. Plant Pests and Diseases Research Institute. Department of Botany. Publication
PPPC — Publication. Pakistan Philosophic Congress
PPPE — People, Plans, and the Peace. Peace River Planning Commission
PPPFMC — Pubblicazioni. Provincia Patavina dei Fratri Minori Conventuali
PPPMD — Pishchevaya Promyshlennost. Seriya 12. Spirtavya i Likero-Vodochnaya Promyshlennost
PPPYBC — Physiological Plant Pathology
PPQU — Philological Quarterly
PPQUE8 — Plant Protection Quarterly
PPr — Paedagogische Provinz
PPR — Performance Practice Review
PPR — Philosophy and Phenomenological Research
P Pr — Pionerskaja Pravda
PPR — Plastica (Puerto Rico)
PPR — Public Productivity Review
PPRAA — Polski Przeglad Radiologiczny
PPRE — Paris Review
P Prehist S — Proceedings. Prehistoric Society
PPRFA — Poliplasti e Plastici Rinforzati
P Princet — Papyri in the Princeton University Collections
PPRL — University of Pennsylvania. Publications. Series in Romanic Languages and Literatures
P Proc Hampshire Field Club — Papers and Proceedings. Hampshire Field Club and Archaeological Society
PProv — Padova e la Sua Provincia
PPRPA — Produits et Problemes Pharmaceutiques
PPRRD3 — Peptide and Protein Reviews
PPrStBrt — Perspectives in Probability and Statistics: in Honor of M. S. Bartlett
PPRV — Physiological Reviews
PPS — Pension and Profit-Sharing Tax Journal
PPS — Personnel Psychology
PPS — Pravoslavnyi Palestinskii Sbornik
PPS — Proceedings. Prehistoric Society
PPS — Publications. Philological Society
PPSA — Publikationen aus den Preussischen Staatsarchiven
PPSB — Personality and Social Psychology Bulletin
PPSb — Pravoslavnyj Palestinskij Sbornik
PPSC — Prairie Schooner
PPSC — Proceedings. Pacific Science Congress
PPSE — Petroleum Economist
PPSED3 — Annual Research Reviews. Physiological and Pathological Aspects of Prolactin Secretion
PPSEE4 — Postgraduate Paediatrics Series
PPSJ — Policy Studies Journal
PPSL — Proceedings. Philological Society (London)
PPSP — Publications. Palestine Section. Museum. University of Pennsylvania
PPSQ — Presidential Studies Quarterly
PPSR — Philosophical Review
PPsS — Pastoral Psychology Series
PPSSA — Proceedings. Nuclear Physics and Solid State Physics Symposium
PPST — Physics Teacher
PPSU — Political Studies
PPSY — Psychiatry
PPSYA — Personnel Psychology
PPTA J — PPTA [Post-Primary Teachers Association] Journal
PPTEC — Polymer-Plastics Technology and Engineering
PPTH — Political Theory
P Ptol — Revenue Laws of Ptolemy Philadelphus
PPTR — Partisan Review
PPTS — Palestine Pilgrims Text Society
PPUAES — Publications. Princeton University Archaeological Expeditions to Syria in 1904-5 and 1909
PPUCA4 — Acta Scientiarum Naturalium. Academiae Scientiarum Bohemoslovacae
PPUM — Prilozi Povijesti Umjetnosti u Malmaciju
PPUMD3 — Museum of Paleontology. Papers on Paleontology
PPUR-A — Population Review
PPW — Prace Polonistyczne (Wroclaw)
PPWMA — Progress in Powder Metallurgy
PPWQ — Psychology of Women Quarterly
PPYEE — Publications. Pennsylvania-Yale Expedition to Egypt
PPYSA — Plant Physiology. Supplement
PPZI — Przeglad Pismiennictwa Zagadnien Informacji
PQ — Pakistan Quarterly
PQ — Philological Quarterly
PQ — Philosophical Quarterly
PQ — Piano Quarterly

PQ — Poetry Quarterly
PQ — Political Quotations
PQ — Psychiatric Quarterly
PQ — United States Patent Quarterly
PQBOAK — Pesquisas Botanica
PQCS — Philippine Quarterly of Culture and Society
PQCSD6 — Commissione Internazionale per la Protezione delle Acque Italo-Svizzere. Rapporti
PQK — Pakistan Quarterly (Karachi)
PQL — Pequenos Grandes Libros de Historia Americana [*Lima*]
PQM — Pacific Quarterly (Moana): An International Review of Arts and Ideas
PQR — Peruvian Quarterly Report
PQRB — Quarterly Review of Biology
PQRF — Quarterly Review of Film and Video
PQS — Palestine Exploration Fund. Quarterly Statement
PQTR — Political Quarterly
P Qu — Philippines Quarterly
PQUEA — Progress in Quantum Electronics
PR — Pakistan Review
PR — Paris Review
PR — Partisan Review
PR — Peking Review
PR — Petroleum Review
PR — Pharmaceutical Record
PR — Philosophical Review
PR — Pioneer
PR — Podravska Revija
PR — Poetry Review
Pr — Practitioner
Pr — Press
PR — Press Independent
PR — Press Releases
Pr — Prevention
Pr — Probe
PR — Proceedings. American Society of University Composers
PR — Programme
Pr — Prohemio
Pr — Prometheus
Pr — Prostor
PR — Psychoanalytic Review
PR — Psychological Review
PR — Public Roads
Pr 2 Sekc Slov Akad Vied Ser Biol — Prace 2 Sekcieje Slovenskej Akademie Vied. Seria Biologicka
Pra — Die Praxis des Bundesgerichts
PRA — Parool (Amsterdam)
PrA — Primer Acto
Pra Bhar — Prabuddha Bharata
Pra Bharata — Prabuddha Bharta
PRACA — Practitioner
Prac Acc — Practical Accountant
Prac Accnt — Practical Accountant
Prac Anth — Practical Anthropology
Prac Appr Pat TM and Copyright — Practical Approach to Patents, Trademarks, and Copyrights
Prac Arch — Prace Archeologiczne
Praca Zabezp Spolecz — Praca i Zabezpieczenie Spoleczne
Prace 2 Sekc Slov Akad Vied — Prace 2. Sekcie Slovenskej Akademie Vied
Prace A — Prace Archaeologiczne
Prace & Mat Muz Archeol & Etnog Lodzi — Prace i Materialy Muzeum Archeologicznego i Etnograficznego w Lodzi
Prace Brnenske Zakl Ceskoslov Akad Ved — Prace Brnenske Zakladny Ceskoslovenske Akademie Ved
Prace Hist Sztuki — Prace z Historii Sztuki
Prace Inst Bad Lesn — Prace Instytut Badawezy Lesnictwa
Prace Inst Fiz — Prace Instytutu Fizyki
Prace Inst Maszyn Przeplywowych — Prace Instytutu Maszyn Przeplywowych
Prace Inst Tech Drewna — Prace Instytut Technologii Drewna
Prace Inst Technol Drewna — Prace Instytut Technologii Drewna
Prace Kom Hist Sztuki — Prace Komisji Historii Sztuki
Prace Komis Biol — Prace Komisji Biologiznej. Poznanskie Towarzystwo Przyjaciol Nauk. Wydzial Matematiczno-Przyrodniczy
Prace Komis Hist Med Nauk Przyr Mat — Prace Komisji Historii Medycyny i Nauk Przyrodniczych-Matematicznych
Prace Krajsk Mus V Hradci Kralove — Prace. Krajskeho Musea v Hradci Kralove/Acta Musei Reginaehradicensis
Prace Mat Lodz — Prace i Materialy Muzeum Archeologicznego i Etnograficznego w Lodzi
Prace Morav Prir Spolecn — Prace Moravske Prirodovedecke Spolecnosti. Acta Societatis Scientiarum Naturalium Moraviae
Prace Mt Fiz — Prace Matematyczno-Fizyczne
Prace Muz Przyr — Prace Muzeum Przyrodniczego/Acta Musei Historiae Naturalis
Prace Nauk Akad Ekon Poznan — Prace Naukowe Akademii Ekonomicznej w Poznaniu
Prace Nauk Akad Ekon Wroclaw — Prace Naukowe Akademii Ekonomicznej we Wroclawiv
Prace Nauk Bad Inst Masz Mat — Prace Naukowo-Badawcze Instytutu Maszyn Matematycznych
Prace Nauk Inst Cybernet Techn Politech Wroclaw Ser Konfer — Wroclaw. Politechnika. Instytut Cybernetyki Technicznej. Prace Naukowe. Seria Konferencje
Prace Nauk Inst Cybernet Techn Politech Wroclaw Ser Monograf — Wroclaw. Politechnika. Instytut Cybernetyki Technicznej. Prace Naukowe. Seria Monografie

Prace Nauk Inst Cybernet Techn Wroclaw Ser Stud i Materialy — Wroclaw. Politechnika. Instytut Cybernetyki Technicznej. Prace Naukowe. Seria Studia i Materialy
Prace Nauk Inst Mat Politech Wroclaw Ser Konfer — Wroclaw. Politechnika Wroclawska. Instytutu Matematyki. Prace Naukowe. Seria Konferencje
Prace Nauk Inst Mat Politech Wroclaw Ser Monograf — Prace Naukowe Instytutu Matematyki Politechniki Wroclawskiej. Seria Monografie
Prace Nauk Inst Mat Politech Wroclaw Ser Stud i Materialy — Politechniki Wroclawskiej. Instytutu Matematyki. Prace Naukowe. Seria Studia i Materialy
Prace Nauk Inst Mat Politech Wroclaw Ser Stud Materialy — Politechniki Wroclawskiej. Instytutu Matematyki. Prace Naukowe. Seria Studia i Materialy
Prace Nauk Inst Ochr Rosl — Prace Naukowe Instytutu Ochrony Roslin
Prace Nauk Uniw Slask Katowic — Prace Naukowe Uniwersytetu Slaskiego w Katowicach
Prace Stud Vysokej Skoly Doprav Spojov Ziline Ser Mat-Fyz — Prace a Studie Vysokej Skoly Dopravy a Spojov v Ziline. Seria Matematicko-Fyzikalna
Prace Stud Vysokej Skoly Doprav Ziline Ser Mat-Fyz — Prace a Studie Vysokej Skoly Dopravnej v Ziline. Seria Matematicko-Fyzikalna
Prace Vyzkum Ust Lesn Hosp Mysl — Prace Vyzkumneho Ustavu Lesneho Hospodarstvi a Myslivosti
Prace Wroclaw Towarz Nauk Ser A — Prace Wroclawskiego Towarzystwa Naukowego. Seria A
Prace Zakladu Dendrol W Korniku — Prace. Zakladu Dendrologii i Pomologii w Korniku/Publications. Institute of Dendrology and Pomology
Prace Zakr Nauk Roln Lesn (Poznan) — Prace z Zakresu Nauk Rolniczych i Lesnych (Poznan)
Prac F — Practical Farmer
Prac Forecast — Practical Forecast for Home Economics
Prac Home Econ — Practical Home Economics
Praci Biol Gruntov Fak — Praci Biologo-Gruntovogo Fakul'tetu
Praci Odesk Derzavn Univ Mecnikova — Praci Odes'kogo Derzavnogo Universytetu imeny I. I. Mecnikova/Trudy Odesskogo Gosudarstvennogo Universiteta imeni I. I. Mecnikova
Prac Konf Cesk Fyz Pr — Pracovni Konference Ceskoslovenskych Fyziku. Prace
Prac Law — Practical Lawyer
Prac Lawyer — Practical Lawyer
Prac Lek — Pracovni Lekarstvi
Pract — Practitioner
Pract Account — Practical Accountant
Pract Adm — Practising Administrator
Pract Anaesth — Practice of Anaesthesia
Pract Anthrop — Practical Anthropology
Pract Anthrop — Practicing Anthropology
Pract Appl Biochem Econ Dev Countries Proc FAOB Symp — Practical Applications of Biochemistry to the Economies of Developing Countries. Proceedings. FAOB (Federation of Asian and Oceanian Biochemists) Symposium
Pract Aspects Ind Compaction — Practical Aspects of Industrial Compaction
Pract Biotechnol — Practical Biotechnology
Pract Brew — Practical Brewer (Monograph)
Pract Colloid Chem — Practical Colloid Chemistry
Pract Comput — Practical Computing
Pract Dig — Practice Digest
Pract Electron — Practical Electronics
Pract Electronics — Practical Electronics
Pract Energy — Practical Energy
Pract Eng (Chicago) — Practical Engineer (Chicago)
Pract Eng (London) — Practical Engineering (London)
Pract Farm — Practical Farmaceutica
Pract Gastroenterol — Practical Gastroenterology
Pract Genet — Practical Genetics
Pract Hologr — Practical Holography
Pract Homeowner — Practical Homeowner
Pract Hort — Practical Horticulture/Jissai Engei
Pract House — Practical Householder
Practical Comput — Practical Computing
Practical Lubric Maint — Practical Lubrication and Maintenance
Pract Invest — Practical Investor
Practit — Practitioner
Practition — Practitioner
Pract M — Practical Magazine
Pract Med (Phila) — Practice of Medicine (Philadelphia)
Pract Metallogr — Practical Metallography
Pract Metallogr Spec Issues — Practical Metallography. Special Issues
Pract Methods Electron Microsc — Practical Methods in Electron Microscopy
Pract Mot — Practical Motorist
Pract Neurochem — Practical Neurochemistry
Pract Odontol — Practica Odontologica
Pract Otol (Kyoto) — Practica Otologica (Kyoto)
Pract Otorhinolaryng — Practica Oto-Rhinolaryngologica
Pract Oto-Rhino-Laryngol — Practica Oto-Rhino-Laryngologica
Pract Paps for the Bible Translator — Practical Papers for the Bible Translator
Pract Parent — Practical Parenting
Pract Period Hazard Toxic Radioact Waste Manage — Practice Periodical of Hazardous, Toxic, and Radioactive Waste Management
Pract Pharm (Tokyo) — Practical Pharmacy (Tokyo)
Pract Photographer — Practical Photographer
Pract Plast — Practical Plastics
Pract Plast Aust NZ — Practical Plastics in Australia and New Zealand
Pract Power Farming — Practical Power Farming
Pract Protein Chromatogr — Practical Protein Chromatography
Pract Solar — Practical Solar
Pract Spectrosc — Practical Spectroscopy
Pract Spectrosc Ser — Practical Spectroscopy Series
Pract Surf Technol — Practical Surface Technology

Pract Treat Low Intermed Level Radioact Wastes Proc Symp — Practices in the Treatment of Low- and Intermediate-Level Radioactive Wastes. Proceedings. Symposium
Pract Welder — Practical Welder
Pract Wireless — Practical Wireless
Pract Woodworking — Practical Woodworking
Prac Wel — Practical Welder
PRAED — Practical Energy
PrAeg — Probleme der Aegyptologie
Praehist Asiae Orient — Praehistoria Asiae Orientalis
Praehist Bl — Praehistorische Blaetter
Praehist Z — Praehistorische Zeitschrift
Praehist Zft — Praehistorische Zeitschrift
Praeh Z — Praehistorische Zeitschrift
Praep Pharmazie — Praeparative Pharmazie
Pr Afr — Presence Africaine
PRAG — Research on Aging
PRAGA — Probleme Agricole
Prag Ab — Abhandlungen der Koeniglichen Boehmischen Gesellschaft der Wissenschaften (Prag)
Prag Beibl Ost West — Prag. Beiblaetter zu Ost und West
Prag Ceske Ak Fr Jos Rz — Rozprawy Ceske Akademie Cisare Frantiska Josefa pro Vedy, Slovesnost a Umeni (Prag)
Prag Dt St — Prager Deutsche Studien
PragerAbh — Abhandlungen der Koeniglich Boehmischen Gesellschaft der Wissenschaften (Prag)
Prager Juris Zeitsch — Prager Juristische Zeitschrift
Prager Med Wochenschr — Prager Medizinische Wochenschrift
Prag Fr Jos Ac Sc Bll Mth Nt — Academie des Sciences de l'Empereur Francois Joseph I. Bulletin International. Resume des Travaux Presentes. Sciences Mathematiques et Naturelles (Prag)
Pragmatics & Beyond Companion Ser — Pragmatics and Beyond Companion Series
Prag Micro — Pragmatics Microficke
Prag Narodop Sborn Ceskoslov — Narodopisny Sbornik Ceskoslovansky (Prag)
PR Agric Exp Stn Bull — Puerto Rico. Agricultural Experiment Station. Bulletin
PR Agric Exp Stn Rio Piedras Bull — Puerto Rico. Agricultural Experiment Station. Rio Piedras. Bulletin
PR Agric Exp Stn Tech Pap — Puerto Rico. Agricultural Experiment Station. Technical Paper
Prag Rundschau — Prager Rundschau
Prague Bull Math Linguist — Prague Bulletin of Mathematical Linguistics
Prague Int Symp Child Neurol — Prague International Symposium of Child Neurology
Prague IUPAC Microsymp Macromol — Prague IUPAC (International Union of Pure and Applied Chemistry) Microsympsiumon Macromolecules
Prague St — Studies in English by Members of the English Seminar of the Charles University, Prague
Prague Stud Math Linguist — Prague Studies in Mathematical Linguistics
Prag Vjschr — Vierteljahrschrift fuer die Praktische Heilkunde. Herausg. von der Medicinischen Facultaet in Prag
PraH — Prace Historyczno-Kulturanie
Prahist Bl — Praehistorische Blaetter
PraHS — Pravne-Historicke Studie
P Rain — Mitteilungen aus der Papyrus-Sammlung der Oesterreichischen Nationalbibliothek. Papyrus Erzherzog Rainer
Prairie Gard — Prairie Garden
Prairie Inst Environ Health PIEH — Prairie Institute of Environmental Health. Report PIEH
Prairie Nat — Prairie Naturalist
Prairie Sch — Prairie Schooner
Prairie Schoon — Prairie Schooner
Prairie Sch R — Prairie School Review
Prairie Sch Rev — Prairie School Review
PRAJ — Peace Research Abstracts Journal
Prak Ak Ath — Praktika tes Akademias Athenon
Pra Kan — Prawo Kanoniczne
Prak Athen Arch het — Praktika tes en Athenais Archaiologikes Etaireias
Prakla-Seismos Rep — Prakla-Seismos Report
Prakruti Utkal Univ J Sci — Prakruti Utkal University Journal of Science
Prakt — Praktika tes Akademias Athenon
Prakt Akad — Praktika tes Akademias Athenon
Prakt Akad Athenon — Praktika tes Akademias Athenon
Prakt Ak Ath — Praktika tes Akademias Athenon
Prakt Allergiediagn 2 Neubearb Erweiterte Aufl — Praktische Allergiediagnostik. 2. Neubearbeitete und Erweiterte Auflage
Prakt Anaesth — Praktische Anaesthesie, Wiederbelebung, und Intensivtherapie
Prakt Anwend Enzymimmunoassays Klin Chem Serol — Praktische Anwendung des Enzymimmunoassays in Klinischer Chemie und Serologie
Prakt Arzt — Praktische Arzt
Prakt Blaett Pflanzenbau Pflanzenschutz — Praktische Blaetter fuer Pflanzenbau und Pflanzenschutz
Prakt Bl Bayer Landesanst Pflanzenbau Pflanzenschutz — Praktische Blaetter der Bayerischer Landesanstalt fuer Pflanzenbau und Pflanzenschutz
Prakt Bl Pflanzenbau Pflanzenschutz — Praktische Blaetter fuer Pflanzenbau und Pflanzenschutz
Prakt Chem — Praktische Chemie
Prakt Desinfekt — Praktische Desinfektor
Prakt Energiek — Praktische Energiekunde
Prakt Enzymol Konf Ges Biol Chem — Praktische Enzymologie. Grundlagen, Gesichertes und Grenzen. Konferenz der Gesellschaft fuer Biologische Chemie
Prakt Fiz Kosm Luchei — Praktikum po Fizike Kosmicheskikh Luchei
Prakt Gazov Khromatogr Mater Semin — Prakticheskaya Gazovaya Khromatografiya. Materialy Seminara. Minsk Oc
Prakt Hell Hydrobiol Inst — Praktika. Hellenic Hydrobiological Institute

Praktijkg — Maandblad de Praktijkgids
Praktika — Praktika tes en Athenais Arkhaiologikes Hetairias
Praktika Akad Athen — Praktika tis Akademias Athenon
Praktika Athen Archaiol Etaireias — Praktika tes Archaiologikes Etaireias en Athenais
Praktische Forschft — Praktische Forschungshefte
Prakt Khim Mutagen Sb Tr Vses Soveshch — Praktika Khimicheskogo Mutageneza. Sbornik Trudov Vsesoyuznogo Soveshchaniya poKhimicheskomu Mutagenezu. Institut Khimicheskoi Fiziki. Mo
Prakt Kieferorthop — Praktische Kieferorthopaedie
Prakt Landtech — Praktische Landtechnik
Prakt Lek — Prakticky Lekar
Prakt Metallogr — Praktische Metallographie
Prakt Metallogr Sonderb — Praktische Metallographie. Sonderbaende
Prakt Panelleniou Chem Synedriou — Praktika Panelleniou Chemikou Synedriou
Prakt Rheol Kunstst — Praktische Rheologie der Kunststoffe
Prakt Schadlingsbekampf — Praktische Schadlingsbekampfer
Prakt Sudebnopsikhiatr Ekspert — Praktika Sudebnopsikhiatricheskoi Ekspertizy
Prakt Tepl Mikrosk — Praktika Teplovoi Mikroskopii
Prakt Tier — Praktische Tieraerzt
Prakt Tierarzt — Praktische Tieraerzt
Prakt Tuberk Bl — Praktische Tuberkulose Blaetter
Prakt Vet — Prakticheskaya Veterinariya
Prakt Vet Konevod — Prakticheskaya Veterinariya i Konevodstvo
Prakt Vet (Moskva) — Prakticheskaia Veterinariia (Moskva)
Prakt Wegw Blenenz — Praktischer Wegweiser fuer Bienenzuechter
Prakt Yad Fiz — Praktikum po Yadernoi Fizike
Prakt Zadachi Genet Selsk Khoz — Prakticheskie Zadachi Genetiki v Sel'skom Khozyaistve
Prakt Zubn Lek — Prakticke Zubni Lekarstvi
PRAL — Research in African Literatures
PRAMC — Pramana
PRAN — Proust Research Association. Newsletter
PRANDM — Progress in Anesthesiology
PRAODP — Agricultural Research Organization. Preliminary Report (Bet-Dagan)
PrAPhA — Proceedings. American Philological Association
PraPol — Prace Polonistyczne
PRAR — Raritan
Pr Archeol — Prace Archeologiczne
PRASD3 — Alabama. Agricultural Experiment Station. Progress Report Series (Auburn University)
Pratica Med — Pratica del Medico
Pratika Athen — Praktika tes Akademias Athenon
Prat Ind Mec — Pratique des Industries Mecanique
Prat Lab Moscow — Pratique de Laboratoire (Moscow)
Prat Med — Pratique Medicale
Prat Med Infant — Pratique de la Medicine Infantile
Pratsi Inst Zool Akad Nauk Ukr RSR — Pratsi Institutu Zoologii Akademiya Nauk Ukrains'koi RSR
Pratsi Odes Derzh Univ Ser Biol Nauk — Pratsi Odeskogo Derzhavnogo Universitetu. Seriya Biologichnikh Nauk
Prat Soudage — Pratique du Soudage
Prat Vet Equine — Pratique Veterinaire Equine
PRAUD9 — Agricultural Research Institute Ukiriguru. Progress Report
PRAVA — Pravda
Prav Mis — Pravoslavna Misao
Prav Mysl — Pravoslavnaja Mysl'
Prav Mysl P — Pravoslavnaja Mysl' (Praha)
Pravoslavnyy Palest Sborn — Pravoslavnyy Palestinskiy Sbornik
Prav Rus — Pravoslavnaja Rus
PRAXA — Praxis
Prax Forsch — Praxis und Forschung
Prax Forsch Z — Praxis und Forschung. Zeitschrift fuer den Fortschrittlichen Landwirt
Praxis — Praxis des Neusprachlichen Unterrichts
Praxis D Berufssch — Praxis der Berufsschule
Praxis Int — Praxis International
Praxis Math — Praxis der Mathematik
Prax Kinder — Praxis der Kinderpsychologie und Kinderpsychiatrie
Prax Kinderpsychol Kinderpsychiatr — Praxis der Kinderpsychologie und Kinderpsychiatrie
Prax Kinderpsychol Kinderpsychiatr Beih — Praxis der Kinderpsychologie und Kinderpsychiatrie. Beiheft
Prax Klin Pharm — Praxis der Klinischen Pharmazie
Prax Klin Pneumol — Praxis und Klinik der Pneumologie
Prax Naturw — Praxis der Naturwissenschaften
Prax Naturwiss Chem — Praxis der Naturwissenschaften. Chemie
Prax Naturwiss Phy — Praxis der Naturwissenschaften. Physik
Prax Naturwiss Phys Unterr Sch — Praxis der Naturwissenschaften. Physik im Unterricht der Schulen
Prax Naturwiss Teil 3 — Praxis der Naturwissenschaften. Teil 3. Chemie
Prax Pneumol — Praxis der Pneumologie
Prax Psychother — Praxis der Psychotherapie
Prax Psychother Psychosom — Praxis der Psychotherapie und Psychosomatik
Prax Schriftenreihe Abt Phys — Praxis-Schriftenreihe. Abteilung Physik
Prax Schriftenr Phys — Praxis Schriftenreihe Physik
Prax Sicherheitstech — Praxis der Sicherheitstechnik
Prax Vet — Praxis Veterinaria
Prazosin Eval New Anti Hypertens Agent Proc Symp — Prazosin. Evaluation of a New Anti-Hypertensive Agent. Proceedings. Symposium
Prazske Hospod Noviny — Prazske Hospodarske Noviny
Prazsky Sbor Hist — Prazsky Sbornik Historicky
PRB — Pre-Raphaelite Brotherhood
PRBa — Physiological Review (Baltimore)

Pr Badaw Gl Inst Metal Odlew Gliwice Pol — Prace Badawcze Glownego Instytutu Metalurgii i Odlewnictwa. Gliwice, Poland
Pr Badaw Inst Badaw Lesn — Prace Badawcze Instytutu Badawczego Lesnictwa
PRBCA — Process Biochemistry
PRBCB — Preparative Biochemistry
Pr Belarus Dzyarzh Univ — Pratsi Belaruskaga Dzyarzhaunaga Universiteta
Pr Biol Mol Uniw Jagiellon — Prace z Biologii Molekularnej (Uniwersytet Jagiellonski)
Pr Biol Pol Akad Umiejet Wydawn Slask — Prace Biologiczne. Polska Akademia Umiejetnosci. Wydawnictwa Slaskie
Pr Bl — Praesteforeningens Blad
Pr Bl — Protestantenblatt
PRBMD — Physical Review. Section B. Condensed Matter
Pr Bot Sadu Kiiv Derzh Univ — Pratsi Botanichnogo Sadu Kiivs'kii Derzhavnii Universitet
Pr Bot Uniw Jagiellon — Prace Botaniczne. Uniwersytet Jagiellonski
PRBP — Review of Black Political Economy
Pr Brnenske Zakl Cesk Akad Ved — Prace Brnenske Zakladny Ceskoslovenske Akademie Ved
PRC — Patterns of Religious Commitment
PrC — Proster in Cas
PRCA — Publications. Indiana University Research Center in Anthropology, Folklore, and Linguistics
PRCAD — Primary Care
PRCAFL — Publications. Research Center in Anthropology, Folklore, and Linguistics
Pr Cent Inst Ochr Pr — Prace Centralnege Instytutu Ochrony Pracy
Pr Cent Lab Gazownictwa Ser B — Prace Centralnego Laboratorium Gazownictwa. Seria B
Pr Cesk Vyzk Slevarenskeho — Prace Ceskoslovenskeho Vyzkumu Slevarenskeho
PRCF — Review of Contemporary Fiction
Pr Chem — Prace Chemiczne
Pr Chem Pr Nauk Uniw Slask Katowic — Prace Chemiczne. Prace Naukowe Uniwersytetu Slaskiego w Katowicach
Pr Chem Uniw Slaski Katowicach — Prace Chemiczne Uniwersytet Slaski w Katowicach
PRCI — Proceedings. Royal Colonial Institute
PrCLS — Proceedings. Comparative Literature Symposium
PRCMC — Percussionist
PRCMC — Protective Coatings on Metals
PrCo — Problems of Communism
PR Commonw Water Resour Bull — Puerto Rico Commonwealth. Water Resources Bulletin
Pr CVUT Praze — Prace CVUT v Praze
Pr CVUT Praze 1 — Prace CVUT v Praze. 1. Stavebni
PRD — Production
PRDE — Preliminary Determination of Epicenters
PR Dec — Decisiones de Puerto Rico
PR Dep Health Bull — Puerto Rico. Department of Health. Bulletin
Pr de V — Principe de Viana
Pr Dydakt Katowice — Prace Dydaktyczne (Katowice)
Pr Dzialu Zywenia Rosl Nawoz — Prace Dzialu Zywenia Roslin i Nawozenia
PRE — Paulys Real-Encyclopaedie der Classischen Alterthumswissenschaft
PRE — Personal Radio Exchange
PRE — Protestantische Realencyklopaedie
PRE — Realencyclopaedie fuer Protestantische Theologie und Kirche
PreA — Presence Africaine
PREA — Reason
Prea Com — Preacher's Commentaries
PREBA3 — Proceedings. Royal Society of Edinburgh. Section B. Biological Sciences
PREBD — Population Reports. Series B
PRECA — Pauly-Wissowas Realencyclopaedie der Classischen Altertumswissenschaft
Precamb Res — Precambrian Research
Pre Cambrian Lower Palaeozoic Rocks Wales Rep Symp — Pre-Cambrian and Lower Palaeozoic Rocks of Wales. Report. Symposium
Precambrian Res — Precambrian Research
Precambrian South Hemisphere — Precambrian of the Southern Hemisphere
Precambrian Trough Struct Baikal Amur Reg Their Metallog — Precambrian Trough Structures of the Baikal-Amur Region and Their Metallogeny
Precancerous Lesions Gastrointest Tract Proc Int Symp — Precancerous Lesions of the Gastrointestinal Tract. Proceedings. International Symposium on Precancerous Lesions of the Gastrointestinal Tract
Precast Concr — Precast Concrete
Precious Met — Precious Metals
Precious Met Perform Dig — Precious Metals Performance Digest
Precious Met Proc Int Precious Met Inst Conf — Precious Metals. Proceedings. International Precious Metals Institute Conference
Precious Met Recover Low Grade Resour Proc — Precious Metals Recovery from Low Grade Resources. Proceedings
PRECIS — Preserved Context Index System
Precis Acad Rouen — Precis de l'Academie de Rouen
Precis Analytique Trav Acad Sci Rouen — Precis Analytique des Travaux. Academie des Sciences, Belles-Lettres, et Arts de Rouen
Precis Eng — Precision Engineering
Precis Engng — Precision Engineering
Precis Instrum Des — Precision Instrument Design
Precis Met — Precision Metal
Precis Met Molding — Precision Metal Molding
Precis Surf Metrol — Precision Surface Metrology
Pre Columbian Metall South Am Conf — Pre-Columbian Metallurgy of South America. Conference

Preconc Drying Food Mater Thijssen Meml Symp Proc Int Symp — Preconcentration and Drying of Food Materials. Thijssen Memorial Symposium. Proceedings. International Symposium
Precursor Processing Biosynth Proteins — Precursor Processing in the Biosynthesis of Proteins
Predeal Int Sch — Predeal International School
Predeal Int Summer Sch — Predeal International Summer School
Predel no Dopustimye Konts Atmos Zagryaz — Predel no Dopustimye Kontsentratsii Atmosfernykh Zagryaznenii
Predelno Dopustimye Konts Atmos Zagryaz — Predel'no Dopustimye Kontsentratsii Atmosfernykh Zagryaznenii
Predi — Predicasts Special Study
Predi 161 — Predicasts. Recreational Vehicles Industry Study 161
Predi 162 — Predicasts. World Rubber and Tire Markets Industry Study 162
Predi 163 — Predicasts. Glass and Advanced Fibers Industry Study 163
Predi 165 — Predicasts. Water Treatment Chemicals Industry Study 165
Predi 168 — Predicasts. World Housing Industry Study 168
PredicadorEv — El Predicador Evangelico
Predict Chronic Toxic Short Term Stud Proc Meet — Prediction of Chronic Toxicity from Short Term Studies. Proceedings. Meeting
Predict Depend Liability Stimul Depressant Drugs Proc Conf — Predicting Dependence Liability of Stimulant and Depressant Drugs. Proceedings.Conference
Predict Photosynth Ecosyst Models — Predicting Photosynthesis for Ecosystem Models
Predict Plast Perform Div Tech Conf Soc Plast Eng — Predicting Plastics Performance. Division Technical Conference. Society of Plastics Engineers
Predict Stab Chaos N Body Dyn Syst — Predictability, Stability, and Chaos in N-Body Dynamical Systems
Predi P55 — Predicasts. Industrial Packaging Paper Trends P-55
PREEB — Presence
PREGA — Promyshlennaya Energetika
Pregled Naucnoteh Rad Inform Zavod Tehn Drveta — Pregled Naucnotehnickih Radova i Informacija. Zavod za Tehnologiiu Drveta
Pregl Probl Ment Retard Osoba — Pregled Problema Mentalno Retardiranih Osoba
Pregnancy Proteins Anim Proc Int Meet — Pregnancy Proteins in Animals. Proceedings. International Meeting
Preh — Prehistoire
Prehist Amer — Prehistoric American
Prehist Arieg — Prehistoire Ariegeoise
Prehist Art Arch — Prehistoric Art Archaeology
Prehist Soc Proc — Proceedings. Prehistoric Society
Prehist Speleol Ariegeoises — Prehistoire et Speleologie Ariegeoises
Prehlad Lesnickej Lit — Prehl'ad Lesnickej. Drevarskej. Celulozovej a Papierenskej Literatury
Prehl Lesn Mysliv Lit — Prehled Lesnicke a Myslivecke Literatury
Prehl Zahr Zemed Lit — Prehled Zahranicni Zemedelske Literatury
Prehl Zemed Lit — Prehled Zemedelske Literatury
Prehl Zemed Lit Zahr Domaci — Prehled Zemedelske Literatury Zahranicni i Domaci
Prehrambena Ind — Prehrambena Industrija
Prehrambeno Tehnol Biotehnol Rev — Prehrambeno-Tehnoloska i Biotehnoloska Revija
Prehrambeno Tehnol Rev — Prehrambeno Tehnoloska Revija
PRei — Philosophische Reihe
Preisschr Fuerstl Jablonowskischen Ges Leipzig — Preisschriften, Gekroent und Herausgegeben von der Fuerstlich Jablonowski'schenGesellschaft zu Leipzig
Preist Alp — Preistoria Alpina
PREL — Religion
PRELA — Przeglad Elektroniki
Prelim Rep Dep Mines Prov Que — Preliminary Report. Department of Mines. Province of Quebec
Prelim Rep Dep Nat Resour Prov Que — Preliminary Report. Department of Natural Resources. Province of Quebec
Prelim Rep Dir Gen Mines (Queb) — Preliminary Report. Direction Generale des Mines (Quebec)
Prelim Rep Geol Surv Wyo — Preliminary Report. Geological Survey. Wyoming
Prelim Rep Int Symp Test In Situ Concr Struct — Preliminary Reports. International Symposium on Testing In Situ of Concrete Structures
Prelim Rep Memo Tech Notes Mater Res Counc Summer Conf — Preliminary Reports. Memoranda and Technical Notes. Materials Research Council Summer Conference
Prelim Rep Minist Richesses Nat Que — Preliminary Report. Ministere des Richesses Naturelles (Quebec)
Prelim Rep Rehovot Nat Univ Inst Agr — Preliminary Report. Rehovot. National and University Institute of Agriculture
Prelim Rep Volcani Cent (Bet Dagan Isr) — Preliminary Report. Volcani Center (Bet Dagan, Israel)
Prelim Rep Volcani Inst Agric Res — Preliminary Report. Volcani Institute of Agricultural Research
Premium/Incentive Bus — Premium/Incentive Business
Prem Trav Soc Libre Agric Dep Bas Rhin Strasbourg — Premiers Travaux de la Societe Libre d'Agriculture et d'Economie Interieure du Departement du Bas-Rhin, Seante a Strasbourg
PRENA — Product Engineering
Prenatal Diagn — Prenatal Diagnosis
Prenatal Neonat Med — Prenatal and Neonatal Medicine. The International Journal of Basic and Clinical Research and Practice
Prenat Diagn — Prenatal Diagnosis
PR Enferm — Puerto Rico y Su Enferma
Prensa Med Argent — Prensa Medica Argentina
Prensa Med Mex — Prensa Medica Mexicana
Prentice Hall Inform System Sci Ser — Prentice Hall Information and System Sciences Series

Prentice Hall Internat Ser Acoust Speech Signal Process — Prentice Hall International Series in Acoustics, Speech, and Signal Processing

Prentice Hall Internat Ser Comput Sci — Prentice Hall International Series in Computer Science

Prentice Hall Internat Ser Indust Systems Engrg — Prentice Hall International Series in Industrial and Systems Engineering

Prentice Hall Internat Ser Syst Control Engin — Prentice-Hall International Series in Systems and Control Engineering

Prentice Hall Ser Comput Math — Prentice-Hall Series in Computational Mathematics

Prentice Hall Signal Process Ser — Prentice-Hall Signal Processing Series

P/Rep — Pedagogic Reporter

PREPA — Przeglad Epidemiologiczny

Prep Bioch — Preparative Biochemistry

Prep Biochem — Preparative Biochemistry

Prep Biochem Biotechnol — Preparative Biochemistry and Biotechnology

Prep Bio Med Appl Labeled Mol Proc Symp — Preparation and Bio-Medical Application of Labeled Molecules. Proceedings. Symposium

Prep Catal Proc Int Symp — Preparation of Catalysis. Proceedings. International Symposium

Prep Charact Mater Proc Indo US Workshop — Preparation and Characterization of Materials. Proceedings. Indo-U.S. Workshop

Prep Chromatogr — Preparative Chromatography

Prep Food D — Prepared Foods New Food Products Directory

Prep Foods — Prepared Foods

Prep Inorg React — Preparative Inorganic Reactions

Prep Prop Solid State Mat — Preparation and Properties of Solid State Materials

Prep Prop Solid State Mater — Preparation and Properties of Solid State Materials

Prepr AIChE Pap Natl Heat Transfer Conf — Preprints of AIChE [*American Institute of Chemical Engineers*] Papers. National Heat Transfer Conference

Prepr Am Chem Soc Div Fuel Chem — Preprints. American Chemical Society. Division of Fuel Chemistry

Prepr Am Chem Soc Div Pet Chem — Preprints. American Chemical Society. Division of Petroleum Chemistry

Prepr Amer Wood Pres Ass — Preprint. American Wood Preservers' Association

Prepr Am Soc Lubr Eng — Preprints. American Society of Lubrication Engineers

Prepr Annu Sci Meet Aerosp Med Assoc — Preprints. Annual Scientific Meeting. Aerospace Medical Association

Prep Rapid Diagn — Preparations for Rapid Diagnosis

Prepr Aust Miner Ind Annu Rev — Preprints. Australian Mineral Industry. Annual Review

Prepr Can Symp Catal — Preprints. Canadian Symposium on Catalysis

Prepr Conf Atmos Environ Aerosp Syst Appl Meteorol — Preprints. Conference on Atmospheric Environment of Aerospace Systems and Applied Meteorology

Prepr Conf Australas Corros Assoc — Preprints from Conference. Australasian Corrosion Association

Prepr Daresbury Lab — Preprint. Daresbury Laboratory

Prepr Daresbury Lab DL P — Preprint. Daresbury Laboratory. DL/P

Prepr Div Pet Chem Am Chem Soc — Preprints. American Chemical Society. Division of Petroleum Chemistry

Prepr East Gas Shales Symp — Preprints. Eastern Gas Shales Symposium

Prepr Eur Congr Biotechnol — Preprints. European Congress on Biotechnology

Prepr Eur Symp Powder Metall — Preprints. European Symposium for Powder Metallurgy

Pre Printed Pap Annu Ind Water Waste Conf — Pre-Printed Papers. Annual Industrial Water and Waste Conference

Preprint Inst Eng Aust Conf — Preprint. Institution of Engineers of Australia. Conference

Prepr Int Symp Papermach Headboxes — Preprints. International Symposium on Papermachine Headboxes

Prepr Invited Talks Contrib Pap Symp Solvent Extr Met — Preprints. Invited Talks and Contributed Papers. Symposium on Solvent Extraction of Metals

Prepr Jt Conf Appl Air Pollut Meteorol — Preprints. Joint Conference on Applications of Air Pollution Meteorology

Prepr Jt Inst Nucl Res Dubna USSR — Preprint. Joint Institute for Nuclear Research. Dubna, USSR

Prepr Mezhdunar Simp Khim Voloknam — Preprinty. Mezhdunarodnyi Simpozium po Khimicheskim Voloknam

Prepr Obedin Inst Yad Issled OIYaI — Preprint Ob'edinennogo Instituta Yadernykh Issledovanii. OIYaI

Prepr Pap ACS Natl Meet Am Chem Soc Div Environ Chem — Preprints of Papers presented at the ACS National Meeting. American Chemical Society. Division of Environmental Chemistry

Prepr Pap Am Chem Soc Div Fuel — Preprints of Papers. American Chemical Society. Division of Fuel Chemistry

Prepr Pap Am Chem Soc Div Fuel Chem — Preprints of Papers. American Chemical Society. Division of Fuel Chemistry

Prepr Pap Annu Conf Australas Corros Assoc — Australasian Corrosion Association. Preprinted Papers of the Annual Conference

Prepr Pap Annu Meet Can Pulp Pap Assoc Techn Sect — Preprints of Papers. Annual Meeting. Canadian Pulp and Paper Association. Technical Section

Prepr Pap Annu Meet Tech Sect CPPA — Preprints of Papers. Annual Meeting. Technical Section. CPPA (Canadian Pulp and Paper Association)

Prepr Pap Environ Eng Conf — Preprints of Papers. Environmental Engineering Conference

Prepr Pap Int Miner Process Congr — Preprints of Papers. International Mineral Processing Congress

Prepr Pap Int Symp Free Radicals — Preprints of Papers Read. International Symposium on Free Radicals

Prepr Pap Natl Meet Div Environ Chem Am Chem Soc — Preprints of Papers Presented at National Meeting. Division of Environmental Chemistry. American Chemical Society

Prepr Pap Natl Meet Div Water Air Waste Chem Am Chem Soc — Preprints of Papers Presented at National Meeting. Division of Water, Air, and Waste Chemistry. American Chemical Society

Prepr Pap Oilseed Process Clin — Preprints of Papers. Oilseed Processing Clinic

Prepr Pap Symp Coal Mine Drain Res — Preprints of Papers Presented before Symposium on Coal Mine Drainage Research

Prepr Plansee Semin — Preprints. Plansee Seminar

Prepr Powder Metall Group Meet — Preprint. Powder Metallurgy Group Meeting

Prepr Rubber Technol Conf — Preprint. Rubber Technology Conference

Prepr Sci Pap Int Fed Soc Cosmet Chem Congr — Preprints. Scientific Papers. International Federation of Societies of Cosmetic Chemists Congress

Prepr Sci Program Aerosp Med Assoc — Preprints. Scientific Program. Aerospace Medical Association

Prepr Semin Electrochem — Preprints of Seminar on Electrochemistry

Prepr Ser — Preprint Series. University of Oslo. Institute of Mathematics

Prepr Ser Inst Math Univ Oslo — Preprint Series. Institute of Mathematics. University of Oslo

Prepr Short Contrib Bratislava IUPAC Int Conf Modif Polym — Preprints of Short Contributions. Bratislava IUPAC (International Union of Pureand Applied Chemistry) sponsored International Conference on Modified Polymers

Prepr Symp Atmos Turbul Diffus Air Qual — Preprints. Symposium on Atmospheric Turbulence, Diffusion, and Air Quality

Prepr Univ Timisoara Fac Stiinte Nat — Preprint. Universitatea din Timisoara. Facultatea de Stiinte ale Naturii

Prepr Univ Timisoara Fac Stiinte Nat Ser Chim — Preprint. Universitatea din Timisoara. Facultatea de Stiinte ale Naturii. Serie Chimie

Prepubl Inst Rech Math Av — Prepublication de l'Institut de Recherche Mathematique Avancee

Prepubl Lab Grom Anal — Prepublications du Laboratoire de Geometrie et Analyse

PRER — Prevention Resources

Pre Raphaelite Rev — Pre-Raphaelite Review

Pres — Presbyterian

Pres — Presence

PRES — Review of English Studies

PresA — Presence Africaine

PresAfr — Presence Africaine

Presb & Ref R — Presbyterian and Reformed Review

Presb Hist Soc J — Presbyterian Historical Society. Journal

Presb Q — Presbyterian Quarterly Review

Presb R — Presbyterian Review

Presbyt-St Luke's Hosp Med Bull — Presbyterian-St. Luke's Hospital. Medical Bulletin

Presbyt-St Luke's Hosp Res Rep — Presbyterian-St. Luke's Hospital. Research Report

Pres Carm — Presenza del Carmelo

Pre-Sch Years — Pre-School Years

Pres Coll Physiol Inst J — Presidency College. Physiological Institute Journal

Presence Afr — Presence Africaine

Presen Poesia Cuencana Cuenca — Presencia de la Poesia Cuencana (Cuenca, Ecuador)

Presentation News Raw Mater Mach Symp Proc — Presentation of News. Raw Materials, Machinery. Symposium Proceedings

Present Concepts Intern Med — Present Concepts in Internal Medicine

Present Status Aims Quantum Electrodyn Proc Symp — Present Status and Aims of Quantum Electrodynamics. Proceedings. Symposium

Preserv Doc Pap — Preservation of Documents and Papers

Preserv Food Ioniz Radiat — Preservation of Food by Ionizing Radiation [*monograph*]

Preserv Madeiras — Preservacao de Madeiras

Preserv Madeiras Bol Tec — Preservacao de Madeiras. Boletim Tecnico

Preserv Pap Text Hist Artistic Value Symp — Preservation of Paper and Textiles of Historic and Artistic Value. Symposium

Preserv Transplant Norm Tissues Ciba Found Symp — Preservation and Transplantation of Normal Tissues. Ciba Foundation Symposium

Preserv Wet Harvested Grains Int Symp — Preservation of Wet Harvested Grains. International Symposium

Pres His S — Presbyterian Historical Society. Journal

Pres His SJ — Presbyterian Historical Society. Journal

Presid Stud Quart — Presidential Studies Quarterly

Pres J — Presbyterian Journal

PresL — Presence des Livres

PresLet — Presence des Lettres

Pres Life — Presbyterian Life

Pres Reg — Presbyterian Register

Presse Actual — Presse Actualite

Pressedienst Bundesminist Bild Wiss — Pressedienst. Bundesministerium fuer Bildung und Wissenschaft

PresseM — Presse Medicale

Presse Med — Presse Medicale

Presse Med Belge — Presse Medicale Belge

Pressemitt Nordrh-Westfalen — Pressemitteilung Nordrhein-Westfalen

Presse Sc — Presse Scientifique des Deux Mondes

Presse Therm Clim — Presse Thermale et Climatique

Presse-Umsch — Presse-Umschau

Pressluft Ind — Pressluft Industrie

Pres Studies Q — Presidential Studies Quarterly

Pres Stud Q — Presidential Studies Quarterly

Pressure Eng — Pressure Engineering

Pressure Vessels Piping Comput Program Eval Qualif — Pressure Vessels and Piping Computer Program Evaluation and Qualification

Pressure Vessel Technol — Pressure Vessel Technology

Pressure Vessel Technol Pap Int Conf — Pressure Vessel Technology. Papers Presented at the International Conference onPressure Vessel Technology

Prestel D — Prestel Directory and Magazine

Prestige de la Photogr — Prestige de la Photographie

Pres W — Presbyterian World

Presynaptic Recept Proc Satell Symp — Presynaptic Receptors. Proceedings. Satellite Symposium
Pret — Pretexte
Pre Term Labour Proc Study Group R Coll Obstet Gynaecol — Pre-Term Labour. Proceedings. Study Group. Royal College of Obstetricians and Gynaecologists
Pr Etnogr — Prace Etnograficzne
Pretreat Chem Water Wastewater Treat Proc Gothenburg Symp — Pretreatment in Chemical Water and Wastewater Treatment. Proceedings. Gothenburg Symposium
Pretsiz Splavy — Pretsizionnye Splavy
Preu — Preuves
Preuss Geol Landesanst Abt Gesteins Erz Kohle Salz Unters Mitt — Preussische Geologische Landesanstalt. Abteilung fuer Gesteins-, Erz-, Kohle- und Salz-Untersuchungen. Mitteilungen
Preuss Jahrb — Preussische Jahrbuecher
Preuss Jb — Preussiche Jahrbuecher
Preuss Jbb — Preussische Jahrbuecher
Preuss Justizministbl — Preussisches Justizministerialblatt
Preuss Provinzialbl — Preussische Provinzialblaetter
Preuss Sammler Kaenntn Naturgesch — Der Preussische Sammler. Zur Kaenntnis der Naturgeschichte
Preuss Sitzb — Preussische Akademie der Wissenschaften. Sitzungsbericht
Preuss Verwaltgsbl — Preussisches Verwaltungsblatt
PREV — Medical and Psychological Previews
P Rev — Powys Review
Pr Ev — Predicador Evangelico
P Rev — Revenue Laws of Ptolemy Philadelphus
Prev Accid Controles Tech Hyg Mal Prof — Prevention des Accidents. Controles Techniques. Hygiene et Maladies Professionelles
Prev Assist Dent — Prevenzione e Assistenza Dentale
Prev Detect Cancer Proc Int Symp — Prevention and Detection of Cancer. Proceedings. International Symposium on Detection and Prevention of Cancer
Prev Fract Conf Aust Fract Group — Prevention of Fracture. Conference of the Australian Fracture Group
Prev Hered Large Bowel Cancer Proc Conf — Prevention of Hereditary Large Bowel Cancer. Proceedings. Conference
Prev Hum Serv — Prevention in Human Services
Previdenza Soc — Previdenza Sociale
Previd Soc — Previdenza Sociale
Preview York A G Bull — Preview. York Art Gallery Bulletin
P Rev Laws — Revenue Laws of Ptolemy Philadelphus
Prev L Rep — Preventive Law Reporter
Prev Med — Preventive Medicine
Prev Ment Handicap — Prevention of Mental Handicap. A World View
Prev Occup Cancer — Prevention of Occupational Cancer
Prev Perinat Inj Proc Symp — Preventability of Perinatal Injury. Proceedings. Symposium
Prev Point View — Preventive Point of View [*monograph*]
Prev Psychiatry Int Meet — Prevention in Psychiatry. International Meeting
Prevrashch Splavakh Vzaimodeistvie Faz — Prevrashcheniya v Splavakh i Vzaimodeistvie Faz
Prev Sci — Prevention Science
Prev Soc Santiago — Prevision Social (Santiago)
Prev Stomatol — Prevenzione Stomatologica
Prev Vet M — Preventive Veterinary Medicine
Prev Vet Med — Preventive Veterinary Medicine
PREXA — Personal Report for the Executive
PREXD — Propellants and Explosives
PRF — GPO [*Government Printing Office*] Sales Publications Reference File
PRF — Publications Romanes et Francaises
Pr Farm — Prace Farmaceutyczne
PRFCA — Prisma. Revista de Filosofia, Ciencia e Arte
PRFCA — Products Finishing (Cincinnati)
PRFIA — Product Finishing
Pr Fil — Prace Filologiczne
Pr Fiz Katowice — Prace Fizyczne (Katowice)
Pr Fiz Pr Nauk Uniw Slaskiego Katowic — Prace Fizyczne. Prace Naukowe Uniwersytetu Slaskiego w Katowicach
Pr Fiz Pr Nauk Uniw Slask Katowic — Prace Fizyczne. Prace Naukowe Uniwersytetu Slaskiego w Katowicach
PRFO — Prairie Forum. Journal. Canadian Plains Research Centre
Prft Bldg St — Profit-Building Strategies
PRG — Progresso. Driemaandelijks Tijdschrift van de Nederlands Italiaanse Kamer van Koophandel
PRG — Psychological Readers' Guide
PRGEA — Przeglad Geofizyczny
Pr Geol-Mineral Acta Univ Wratislav — Prace Geologiczno-Mineralogiczne. Acta Universitatis Wratislaviensis
Pr Geol Pol Akad Nauk Kom Nauk Geol — Prace Geologiczne. Polska Akademia Nauk. Komisja Nauk Geologicznych
PRG/I — Pick Resources Guide/International
PRGLB — Prostaglandins
Pr Gl Inst Gorn — Prace Glownego Instytutu Gornictwa
Pr Gl Inst Gorn Komun — Prace Glownego Instytutu Gornictwa. Komunikat
Pr Gl Inst Lotnictwa — Prace Glownego Instytutu Lotnictwa
Pr Gl Inst Metal Gliwice Pol — Prace Glownego Instytutu Metalurgii. Gliwice, Poland
Pr Gl Inst Naft Cracow — Prace Glownego Instytutu Naftowego. Cracow
Pr Gl Inst Przem Rolnego Spozyw — Prace Glownego Instytutu Przemyslu Rolnego i Spozywczego
Pr Gl Inst Wlok Lodz — Prace Glownego Instytutu Wlokiennictwa. Lodz
Pr Gory Goretskaga Navuk Tav — Pratsy Gory Goretskaga Navukov aga Tavarystva
PRGS — Proceedings. Royal Geographical Society

PRGVB — Progressive
PrH — Provence Historique
Pr Hdb — Preacher's Handbook
PR Health Bull — Puerto Rico Health Bulletin
PR Health Rev — Porto Rico Health Review
PR Health Sci J — Puerto Rico Health Sciences Journal
PrHlit — Prace Historycznoliterackie
PRIA — Proceedings. Royal Irish Academy
PRIAA — Proceedings. Royal Irish Academy. Section A. Mathematical and Physical Sciences
PRIBA — Proceedings. Royal Irish Academy. Section B. Biological, Geological, and Chemical Science
PRIBAN — Proceedings. Royal Irish Academy. Section B. Biological, Geological, and Chemical Science
Prib Avtom Sist Upr Kach Tsellyul Bum Prod — Pribory i Avtomatizirovannye Sistemy v Upravlenii Kachestvom Tsellyulozno-Bumazhnoi Produktsii
Prib i Sist Upr — Pribory i Sistemy Upravleniya
Prib i Tekh Eksp — Pribory i Tekhnika Eksperimenta
Pribliz Metod Resen Differencial Uravnen — Priblizennye Metody Resenija Differencial nyh Uravnenii
Prib Metody Anal Izluch — Pribory i Metody Analiza Izluchenii
Prib Metody Izmer Magn Polei Mater Nauchno Tekh Konf — Pribory i Metody Izmereniya Magnitnykh Polei. Materialy Nauchno-Tekhnicheskoi Konferentsii
Priborostr Avtom Kontrol — Priborostroenie i Avtomaticheskii Kontrol
Pribory i Sistemy Avtomat — Pribory i Sistemy Avtomatiki
Prib Sist Avtom — Pribory i Sistemy Avtomatiki
Prib Sist Upr — Pribory i Sistemy Upravleniya
Prib Tekh Eksp — Pribory i Tekhnika Eksperimenta
Prib Tekhn — Pribory i Tekhnika Eksperimenta
Prib Ustroistva Sredstv Avtom Telemekh — Pribory i Ustroistva Sredstv Avtomatiki i Telemekhaniki
Price Waterhouse R — Price Waterhouse Review
Price Waterhouse Rev — Price Waterhouse Review
Pride Inst J Long Term Home Health Care — Pride Institute. Journal of Long Term Home Health Care
Priestley Lect — Priestley Lectures
PRIGA — Prace Instytutu Geologii
Prikladnaya Geofiz — Prikladnaya Geofizika
Prikl Biokhim Mikrobiol — Prikladnaya Biokhimiya i Mikrobiologiya
Prikl Elektrokhim — Prikladnaya Elektrokhimiya
Prikl Fiz Tverd Tela — Prikladnaya Fizika Tverdogo Tela
Prikl Geofiz — Prikladnaya Geofizika
Prikl Geokhim Mineral — Prikladnaya Geokhimiya i Mineralogiya
Prikl Geom i Inzener Grafika — Prikladnaja Geometrija i Inzenernaja Grafika
Prikl Issled Din Vysokotemp Gaza — Prikladnye Issledovaniya po Dinamike Vysokotemperaturnogo Gaza
Prikl Khim Mashinostr — Prikladnaya Khimiya v Mashinostroenii
Prikl Khromatogr — Prikladnaya Khromatografiya
Prikl Mat — Prikladnaya Matematika i Mekhanika
Prikl Mat i Mekh — Prikladnaya Matematika i Mekhanika
Prikl Mat i Programmirovanie — Prikladnaja Matematika i Programmirovanie
Prikl Mat Mekh — Prikladnaya Matematika i Mekhanika
Prikl Meh — Akademija Nauk Ukrainskoi SSR. Otdelenie Matematiki. Mehaniki i Kibernetiki. Prikladnaja Mehanika
Prikl Mekh — Akademiya Nauk Ukrainskoi SSR. Otdelenie Matematiki. Mekhaniki i Kibernetiki. Prikladnaya Mekhanika
Prikl Mekh — Prikladna Mekhanika
Prikl Mekh Priborostr — Prikladnaya Mekhanika v Priborostroenii
Prikl Mekh Tekh Fiz — Prikladnaya Mekhanika i Tekhnicheskaya Fizika
Prikl Problemy Proc i Plast — Gor'kovskii Gosudarstvennyi Universitet Imeni N. I. Lobacevskogo. Prikladnye Problemy Procnosti i Plasticnosti
Prikl Probl Pryamogo Preobraz Energ — Prikladnye Problemy Pryamogo Preobrazovaniya Energii
Prikl Reol — Prikladnaya Reologiya
Prikl Reol Techenie Dispersnykh Sist — Prikladnaya Reologiya i Techenie Dispersnykh Sistem
Prikl Spektrosk — Prikladnaya Spektroskopiya
Prikl Spektrosk Mater Soveshch — Prikladnaya Spektroskopiya. Materialy Soveshchaniya po Spektroskopii
Prikl Teor Khim — Prikladnaya i Teoreticheskaya Khimiya
Prikl Vopr Fiz — Prikladnye Voprosy Fiziki
Prikl Vopr Fiz Goreniya — Prikladnye Voprosy Fiziki Goreniya
Prikl Vopr Teplomassoobmena — Prikladnye Voprosy Teplomassoobmena
Prikl Yad Fiz — Prikladnaya Yadernaya Fizika
Prikl Yad Spektrosk — Prikladnaya Yadernaya Spektroskopiya
Prikl Zadachi Mat Fiz — Prikladnye Zadachi Matematicheskoi Fiziki
Prikl Zadachi Mekh Polim Sist — Prikladnye Zadachi Mekhaniki Polimerov i Sistem
Prikl Zadachi Teor Perenosa — Prikladnye Zadachi Teorii Perenosa
PrilKJIF — Prilozi za Knjizevnost, Jezik, Istoriju, i Folklor
Prilozh Mikrobiol — Prilozhna Mikrobiologiya
Prilozh Sb Nauchn Rab Med Fak Karlova Univ Gradtse Kralove — Prilozhenie k Sborniku Nauchnykh Rabot Meditsinskogo Fakul'teta Karlova Universiteta v Gradtse Kralove
Prilozi — Prilozi za Knjizevnost, Jezik, Istoriju, i Folklor
Prilozi Maked Akad Nauk Umet Odd Biol Med Nauki — Prilozi. Makedonska Akademija na Naukite i Umetnostite. Oddelenie za Bioloski i Medicinski Nauki
Prilozi Maked Akad Nauk Umet Odd Prir Mat Nauki — Prilozi. Makedonska Akademija na Naukite i Umetnostite. Oddelenie za Prirodo-Matematicki Nauki
Prilozi Povijesti Umjetnosti Dalmac — Prilozi Povijesti Umjetnosti Dalmaciji
PrilPJ — Prilozi Proucavanju Jezika
Primaer Packm — Primaer-Packmittel
Primary Cardiol — Primary Cardiology
Primary Care Physicians Guide Pract Gastroenterol — Primary Care Physician's Guide to Practical Gastroenterology

Primary Educ — Primary Education
Primary J — Primary Journal
Primary Maths — Primary Mathematics
Primary Processes Photobiol Proc Taniguchi Symp — Primary Processes in Photobiology. Proceedings. Taniguchi Symposium
Primary Prod Biosphere — Primary Productivity of the Biosphere
Primary Radioact Miner — Primary Radioactive Minerals
Primary Sci Bull — Primary Science Bulletin
Primary Sens Neuron — Primary Sensory Neuron
Primary Tertiary Struct Nucleic Acids Cancer Res — Primary and Tertiary Structure of Nucleic Acids and Cancer Research
Primate Behav — Primate Behavior
Primates Med — Primates in Medicine
Primates Nutr Res Proc Workshop — Primates in Nutritional Research. Proceedings from a Workshop on Primate Nutrition
Primato A It — Primato Artistico Italiano
Primatolog — Primatologia
Prim Ed-Pop Ed — Primary Education - Popular Educator
Prim Educ — Primary Education
Primen Akt Anal Biol Med — Primenenie Aktivatsionnogo Analiza v Biologii i Meditsine
Primen Antibiot Rastenievod Tr Vses Konf — Primenenie Antibiotikov v Rastenievodstve. Trudy Vsesoyuznoi Konferentsii po Izucheniyu i Primeneniyu Antibiotikov v Rastenievodstve
Primen Antibiot Zhivotnovod Mater Soveshch — Primenenie Antibiotikov v Zhivotnovodstve. Materlaly Soveshchanlya
Primen Dobavok Proizvod Keram Stroit Mater — Primenenie Dobavok v Proizvodstve Keramicheskikh Stroitel'nykh Materialov
Primenen Mat Ekonom — Leningradskii Ordena Lenina Gosudarstvennyi Universitet Imeni A. A. Zdanova. Kafedra i Laboratorija Ekonomiko-Matematiceskih Metodov. Primenenie Matematikii v Ekonomike
Primenen Mat Ekonom — Primenenie Matematiki v Ekonomike
Primenen Teor Verojatnost i Mat Statist — Primenenie Teorii Verojatnostei i Matematiceskoi Statistiki
Primen Invariantnykh Sist Avtom Upr Tr Vses Soveshch — Primenenie Invariantnykh Sistem Avtomaticheskogo Upravleniya. Trudy Vsesoyuznogo Soveshchaniya po Teorii Invariantnosti i Ee Primeneniyu v Sistemakh Avtomaticheskogo Upravleniya
Primen Lazerov At Mol Yad Fiz Tr Vses Shk — Primenenie Lazerov v Atomnoi. Molekulyarnoi i Yadernoi Fizike. Trudy Vsesoyuznoi Shkoly
Primen Mat Metodov Biol — Primenenie Matematicheskikh Metodov v Biologii
Primen Mikroelem Sel-Khoz Akad Nauk UkrSSR — Primenenie Mikroelementov Sel'skom Khozyaistve Akademiya Nauk Ukrainskoi SSR
Primen Mikroelem Selsk Khoz Med Tr Vses Soveshch — Primenenie Mikroelementov v Sel'skom Khozyaistve i Meditsine. Trudy Vsesoyuznogo Soveshchaniya po Mikroelementam
Primen Polim Mater Nar Khoz — Primenenie Polimernykh Materialov v Narodnom Khozyaistve
Primen Prizmennykh Beta Spektrom Sb Dokl Vses Semin — Primenenie Prizmennykh Beta-Spektrometrov. Sbornik Dokladov Vsesoyuznogo Seminara po Prizmennym Beta-Spektrometram i Voprosam Ikh Primeneniya
Primen Radioakt Izot Metall — Primenenie Radioaktivnykh Izotopov v Metallurgii
Primen Tsifrovykh Analogovykh Vychisl Mash Yad Fiz Tekh — Primenenie Tsifrovykh i Analogovykh Vychislitel'nykh Mashin v Yadernoi Fizike iTekhnike
Primen Ul'traakust Issled Veshchestva — Primenenie Ul'traakustiki k Issledovaniyu Veshchestva
Primen Ultrazvuka Promsti Dokl Konf — Primenenie Ul'trazvuka v Promyshlennosti. Doklady. Prochitannye na Konferentsii
Primen Vak Metall Tr Soveshch — Primenenie Vakuuma v Metallurgii. Trudy Soveshchaniya po Primeneniyu Vakuuma v Metallurgi
Primitive A Newslett — Primitive Art Newsletter
Primjena Savrem Metoda Ispit Celika Kolok — Primjena Savremenih Metoda u Ispitivanju Celika. Kokokvij
Primordial Nucleosynth Evol Early Universe Proc Int Conf — Primordial Nucleosynthesis and Evolution of Early Universe. Proceedings. International Conference
Primorsk Skh Inst Tr — Primorskii Sel'skokhozyaistvennyi Institut. Trudy
Princ — Princeton Review
Princ Appl Water Chem Proc Rudolfs Res Conf — Principles and Applications of Water Chemistry. Proceedings. Rudolfs Research Conference
Princ Card Toxicol — Principles of Cardiac Toxicology
Princ Cattle Prod Proc Easter Sch — Principles of Cattle Production. Proceedings. Easter School
Princ Desalin — Principles of Desalination
Prince Of Wales Mus Bull — Prince of Wales Museum Bulletin
Prince S B — Princeton Seminary Bulletin
Princess Takamatsu Cancer Res Fund Proc Int Symp — Princess Takamatsu Cancer Research Fund. Proceedings. International Symposium
Princess Takamatsu Symp — Princess Takamatsu Symposia
Princeton Coll B — Princeton College. Bulletin
Princeton Conf Cerebrovasc Dis — Princeton Conference on Cerebrovascular Diseases
Princeton Conf Cereb Vasc Dis — Princeton Conference on Cerebral Vascular Diseases [Later, Princeton Conference on Cerebrovascular Diseases]
Princeton Landmarks Math — Princeton Landmarks in Mathematics
Princeton Landmarks Phys — Princeton Landmarks in Physics
Princeton Math Ser — Princeton Mathematical Series
Princeton Mus Rec — Princeton University. Museum of Historic Art. Record
Princeton R — Princeton Review
Princeton Sci Lib — Princeton Science Library
Princeton Ser Comput Sci — Princeton Series in Computer Science
Princeton Ser Phys — Princeton Series in Physics
Princeton Stud Math Econom — Princeton Studies in Mathematical Economics
Princeton Theol Rev — Princeton Theological Review
Princeton U Lib Chron — Princeton University Library Chronicle

Princeton Univ Lib Chron — Princeton University. Library. Chronicle
Princ Food Rice — Principal Food. Rice
Princ Food Sci Part 1 Food Chem — Principles of Food Science. Part 1. Food Chemistry
Princ Immunol — Principles of Immunology [monograph]
Princ in Counc — Principals in Council
Principia Cardiol — Principia Cardiologica
Principles Comput Sci Ser — Principles of Computer Science Series
Princ Mech Biol Consequences Induct — Principles, Mechanisms, and Biological Consequences of Induction
Princ NS — Princeton Review (New Series)
Pr Incntv — Premium/Incentive Business
Princ Pathobiol — Principles of Pathobiology [monograph]
Princ Pract Diesel Contam Soils — Principles and Practices for Diesel Contaminated Soils
Princ Pract Med — Principles and Practice of Medicine [monograph]
Princ Pract Pediatr Surg Spec — Principles and Practice of the Pediatric Surgical Specialities
PrincSB — Princeton Seminary Bulletin
PrincSemB — Princeton Seminary Bulletin
Princ Tech Hum Res Ther — Principles and Techniques of Human Research and Therapeutics
Princ Tetanus Proc Int Conf — Principles on Tetanus. Proceedings. International Conference on Tetanus
Princ Theol R — Princeton Theological Review
Princ Tribol — Principles of Tribology
Princ Univ Bull — Princeton University. Bulletin
Princ Viana — Principe de Viana
Prindle Weber Schmidt Ser Adv Math — Prindle, Weber, and Schmidt Series in Advanced Mathematics
Prindle Weber Schmidt Ser Math — Prindle, Weber, and Schmidt Series in Mathematics
Prins & Conderlag — Prins and Conderlag's Reports
Pr Inst Badaw Lesn — Prace Instytutu Badawczego Lesnictwa
Pr Inst Celul Papier — Prace Instytutu Celulozowo-Papierniczego
Pr Inst Celul Papier Komun — Prace Instytutu Celulozowo-Papierniczego. Komunikat
Pr Inst Cybern PAN — Prace Instytutu Cybernetyki Stosowanej PAN
Pr Inst Ef Wykorzystania Mater — Prace Instytutu Efektywnosci Wykorzystania Materialow
Pr Inst Elektrotech — Prace Instytutu Elektrotechniki
Pr Inst Elektrotech (Warsaw) — Prace Instytutu Elektrotechniki (Warsaw)
Pr Inst Fiz Pol Akad Nauk — Prace Instytutu Fizyki. Polska Akademia Nauk
Pr Inst Fiz Politech Warsz — Prace Instytutu Fizyki Politechnica Warszawska
Pr Inst Geol Korisnikh Kopalin Akad Nauk Ukr — Pratsi Institut Geologii Korisnikh Kopalin Akademiya Nauk Ukrains'koi
Pr Inst Gidrobiol Akad Nauk Ukr RSR — Pratsi Institutu Gidrobiologii Akademiya Nauk Ukrains'koi RSR
Pr Inst Gorn Naft Gazownictwa Krakow — Prace Instytutu Gornictwa Naftowego i Gazownictwa (Krakow)
Pr Inst Gospod Wodnej — Prace Instytutu Gospodarki Wodnej
Pr Inst Hutn — Prace Instytutow Hutniczych
Pr Inst Inst Przem Wiazacych Mater Budow Opolu — Prace Instytutu. Instytut Przemyslu Wiazacych Materialow Budowlanych w Opolu
Pr Inst Inst Tech Budow Biul Inf — Prace Instytutu. Instytut Techniki Budowlanej. Biuletyn Informacyjny
Pr Inst Inz Chem Politech Warsz — Prace Instytutu Inzynierii Chemicznej Politechniki Warszawskiej
Pr Inst Inz Chem Procesowej Politech Warsz — Prace Instytutu Inzynierii Chemicznej i Procesowej Politechniki Warszawskiej
Pr Inst Jedwabiu Nat — Prace Instytutu Jedwabiu Naturalnego
Pr Inst Krajowych Wlok Nat — Prace Instytutu Krajowych Wlokien Naturalnych
Pr Inst Lab Badaw Przem Spozyw — Prace Instytutow i Laboratoriow Badawczych Przemyslu Spozywczego
Pr Inst Lacznosci — Prace Instytutu Lacznosci
Pr Inst Lotnictwa — Prace Instytutu Lotnictwa
Pr Inst Masz Mat — Prace Instytutu Maszyn Matematycznych
Pr Inst Masz Przeplyw — Prace Instytutu Maszyn Przeplywowych
Pr Inst Masz Przeplyw Pol Akad Nauk — Prace Instytutu Maszyn Przeplywowych. Polska Akademia Nauk
Pr Inst Mech — Prace Instytutow Mechaniki
Pr Inst Mech Precyz — Prace Instytutu Mechaniki Precyzyjnej
Pr Inst Met — Prace Instytutu Metalurgie
Pr Inst Metal Gliwice (Pol) — Prace Instytutu Metalurgii. Gliwice (Poland)
Pr Inst Metal Zelaza — Prace Instytutu Metalurgii Zelaza
Pr Inst Metal Zelaza im Stanislawa Staszica — Prace Instytutu Metalurgii Zelaza imienia Stanislawa Staszica
Pr Inst Meteorol Gospod Wodnej — Prace Instytutu Meteorologii i Gospodarki Wodnej
Pr Inst Met Niezelaz — Prace Instytutu Metali Niezelaznych
Pr Inst Minist Hutn (Pol) — Prace Instytutu Ministerstwa Hutnictwa (Poland)
Pr Inst Naft (Krakow) — Prace Instytutu Naftowego (Krakow)
Pr Inst Obrobki Skrawaniem — Prace Instytutu Obrobki Skrawaniem
Pr Inst Odlew — Prace Instytutu Odlewnictwa
Pr Inst Odlew Zesz Spec — Prace Instytutu Odlewnictwa. Zeszyty Specjalne
Pr Inst Odlew Zesz Specjalne — Prace Instytutu Odlewnictwa. Zeszyty Specjalne
Pr Inst Przem Cukrow — Prace Instytutu Przemyslu Cukrowniczego
Pr Inst Przem Miecz — Prace Instytutu Przemyslu Mieczarskiego
Pr Inst Przem Org — Prace Instytutu Przemyslu Organicznego
Pr Inst Przem Skorzanego — Prace Instytutu Przemyslu Skorzanego
Pr Inst Przem Szkla Ceram — Prace Instytutu Przemyslu Szkla i Ceramiki
Pr Inst Przem Wlok Lykowych — Prace Instytutu Przemyslu Wlokien Lykowych
Pr Inst Sadow Kwiaciarstwa Skierniewicach Ser A Pr — Prace Instytutu Sadownictwa Kwiaciarstwa w Skierniewicach. Seria A. Prace Doswiadczalne z Zakresu Sadownictwa

Pr Inst Sadow Ser E Mater Zjazdow Konf — Prace Instytutu Sadownictwa. Seria E. Materialy Zjazdow i Konferencji
Pr Inst Sadow Skierniew — Prace Instytutu Sadownictwa w Skierniewicach
Pr Inst Sadow Skierniewicach — Prace Instytutu Sadownictwa w Skierniewicach
Pr Inst Sadow Skierniewicach Ser A — Prace Instytutu Sadownictwa w Skierniewicach. Seria A. Prace Doswiadczalne z Zakresu Sadownictwa
Pr Inst Sadow Skierniewicach Ser A Pr Dosw Z Zakresu Sadow — Prace Instytutu Sadownictwa w Skierniewicach. Seria A. Prace Doswiadczalne Z Zakresu Sadownictwa
Pr Inst Sadow Skierniewice Ser E — Prace Instytutu Sadownictwa. Skierniewice. Seria E. Materialy Zjazdow i Konferencji
Pr Inst Tech Budow — Prace Instytutu Techniki Budowlanej
Pr Inst Tech Budow Ser 1 — Prace Instytutu Techniki Budowlanej. Seria 1. Materialy Budowlane i Ich Zastosowanie
Pr Inst Tech Budow Ser 2 — Prace Instytutu Techniki Budowlanej. Seria 2. Konstrukeje Budowlane i Inzynierskie
Pr Inst Tech Ciepl — Prace Instytutu Techniki Cieplnej
Pr Inst Technol Drewna — Prace Instytut Technologii Drewna
Pr Inst Technol Elektron — Prace Instytutu Technologii Elektronowej
Pr Inst Tele- & Radiotech — Prace Instytutu Tele- i Radiotechnicznego
Pr Inst Wlok — Prace Instytutu Wlokiennictwa
Pr Inst Wlok (Lodz) — Prace Instytutu Wlokiennictwa (Lodz)
Print Abstr — Printing Abstracts
Print & Pub — Printing and Publishing
Print Art — Printing Art
Print Art Q — Printing Art Quarterly
Print Bookbind Trade Rev — Printing and Bookbinding Trade Review
Print Circuit Fabr — Printed Circuit Fabrication
Print Coll Q — Print Collector's Quarterly
Printed Circuit Des — Printed Circuit Design
Print Equip Eng — Printing Equipment Engineer
Print Graph Arts — Printing and Graphic Arts
Printing — Printing Impressions
Printing Abs — Printing Abstracts
Printing Abstr — Printing Abstracts
Printing and Pub — Printing and Publishing
Printing Impr — Printing Impressions
Printing Trades J — Printing Trades Journal
Print Mag — Printing Magazine
Print Mag Natl Lithogr — Printing Magazine National Lithographer
Print Manag — Printing Management
Print Manage Print Mag — Printing Management with Printing Magazine
Printout Ann — Printout Annual
Print Prod — Printing Production
Print R — Print Review
Print Reprogr Conf Proc — Printing and Reprography Conference. Proceedings
Print Reprogr Test Conf Proc — Printing Reprography Testing Conference Proceedings
Print Rev — Print Review
Print Sales — Printed Salesmanship
Print Salesmanship — Printed Salesmanship
Prints Metody Mineragenicheskogo Anal — Printsipy i Metody Mineragenicheskogo Analiza
Print Technol — Printing Technology
Print Trades J — Printing Trades Journal
Pr IPO — Prace IPO
Pr IPPT — Prace IPPT (Instytut Podstawowych Problemow Techniki)
PRIRA — Priroda
P R Ir Ac A — Proceedings. Royal Irish Academy. Section A. Mathematical, Astronomical, and Physical Science
P R Ir Ac B — Proceedings. Royal Irish Academy. Section B. Biological, Geological, and Chemical Science
P R Ir Ac C — Proceedings. Royal Irish Academy. Section C. Archaeology, Celtic Studies, History, Linguistics, Literature
PRIRB — Priroda (Sofia, Bulgaria)
Prir Edice — Prirodovedecka Edice
Prir Gaz Sib — Prirodnyi Gaz Sibiri
Prir Istraz Kral Jugoslavije — Prirodoslovna Istrazivanja Kraljevine Jugoslavije
Prir Ivanov Obl — Priroda Ivanovskoi Oblasti
Prir-Mat Fak Univ Kiril Metodij (Skopje) God Zb Biol — Prirodno-Matematicka Fakultet na Univerzitetot Kiril i Metodij (Skopje). Godisen Zbornik. Biologija
Prir Mat Fak Univ Kiril Metodij (Skopje) God Zb Sek A — Prirodno-Matematicka Fakultet na Univerzitetot Kiril i Metodij (Skopje). Godisen Zbornik. Sekcja A. Matematika, Fizika, i Hemija
Prir Miner Sorbenty Tr Soveshch — Prirodnye Mineral'nye Sorbenty. Trudy Soveshchaniya
Prir (Moscow) — Priroda (Moscow)
Prirod-Mat Fak Univ Kiril i Metodij (Skopje) Godisen Zb — Prirodno-Matematicka Fakultet na Univerzitetot Kiril i Metodij (Skopje). Godisen Zbornik
Prirod-Mat Fak Univ Kiril Metodij (Skopje) Godisen Zb — Prirodno-Matematicka Fakultet na Univerzitetot Kiril i Metodij (Skopje). Godisen Zbornik
Prirodonauc Muz Skopje Posebno Izd — Prirodonaucen Muzej Skopje Posebno Izdanie
Prirodsl Istraz Acta Biol — Prirodoslovna Istrazivanja Acta Biologica
Prirodsl Istraz Acta Geol — Prirodoslovna Istrazivanja Acta Geologica
Prirodoved Cas Slezsky — Prirodovedny Casopis Slezsky
Prirodoved Fak Univ J E Purkyne Brne Folia Biol — Prirodovedecka Fakulta Univerzita J. E. Purkyne v Brne. Folia. Biologia
Prirodoved Fak Univ J E Purkyne Brne Folia Phys — Prirodovedecka Fakulta Univerzita J. E. Purkyne v Brne. Folia. Physica
Prirodoved Pr Ustavu Cesk Akad Ved Brne — Prirodovedne Prace Ustavu Ceskoslovenske Akademie Ved v Brne
Prir Org Veshchestva Sovrem Iskop Osadkov Dokl Vses Semin — Priroda Organicheskogo Veshchestva Sovremennykh i Iskopaemykh Osadkov. Doklady Vsesoyuznogo Seminara

Prir Prace Slov Muz — Prirodovedne Prace Slovenskych Muzei. Acta Rerum Naturalium Museorum Slovenicorum
Prir Razpr — Prirodoslovne Razprave
Prir Socialist Hoz — Priroda i Socialisticeskoe Hozjajstvo
Prir (Sofia) — Priroda (Sofia)
Prir Sorbenty Povolzhya — Prirodnye Sorbenty Povolzh'ya
Prir Tatransk Nar Parku — Priroda Tatranskeho Narodneho Parku
Prir Tr Resur Levoberezhnoi Ukr Ikh Ispolz — Prirodnye i Trudot ye Resursy Levoberezhnoi Ukrainy i Ikh Ispolzovanie
Prir Usloviya Zapadn Sib — Prirodnye Usloviya Zapadnoi Sibiri
Prir Znanie — Priroda i Znanie
PRIS — Pest Management Research Information System
PRIS — Physis. Rivista Internazionale di Storia della Scienze
Prisadki Maslam Tr Vses Nauchno Tekh Soveshch — Prisadki k Maslam. Trudy Vsesoyuznogo Nauchno-Tekhnicheskogo Soveshchaniya
Prisadki Smaz Maslam — Prisadki i Smazochnym Maslam
Pris Assn NY Ann Rep — Prison Association of New York. Annual Report
Pris Assn NY Rep — Prison Association of New York. Report
Prisc Lat Mon Epigr — Priscae Latiniatis Monumenta Epigraphica
PRISD — Proceedings. Indian Academy of Sciences. Series Engineering Sciences
Pris J — Prison Journal. Pennsylvania Prison Society
Pris Jrnl — Prisoners Journal
Prism Int — Prism International
Prison L Reptr — Prison Law Reporter
Prison Serv J — Prison Service Journal
Prispevky Probl Rudn Horn — Prispevky k Problematice Rudneho Hornictvi
PrisrAcSci&Hum — Proceedings. Israel Academy of Sciences and Humanities
PRITA — Problems of Information Transmission
Pr ITME — Prace ITME
PriU — Princeton University Library Chronicle
Privacy Rept — Privacy Report
Private Pract — Private Practice
Priv Lib — Private Library
Priv Libr — Private Library
Priv Rev — Privatization Review
Prize Essays Trans Highl Agric Soc Scotland — Prize Essays and Transactions. Highland and Agricultural Society of Scotland
Prize Essays Trans Highl Soc Scotland — Prize Essays and Transactions. Highland Society of Scotland
PrJ — Preussische Jahrbuecher
PRJ — Public Relations Journal
Pr Jb — Preussiche Jahrbuecher
PrJbb — Preussische Jahrbuecher
PR J Public Health Trop Med — Puerto Rico Journal of Public Health and Tropical Medicine
PRK — Pakistan Review (Karachi and Lahore)
PRK — Praktijkgids
Pr Kat — Prediger und Katechet
PRKNA — Progress in Reaction Kinetics
Pr Kom Biol (Poznan) — Prace Komisji Biologicznej (Poznan)
Pr Kom Biol Poznan Tow Przyj Nauk — Prace Komisji Biologicznej. Poznanskie Towarzystwo Przyjaciol Nauk
Pr Kom Ceram Pol Akad Nauk Ceram — Prace Komisji Ceramicznej. Polskiej Akademii Nauk. Ceramica
Pr Kom Farm Poznan Tow Przyj Nauk — Prace Komisji Farmaceutycznej. Poznanskie Towarzystwo Przyjaciol Nauk
Pr Kom Krystalogr Pol Akad Nauk Inst Nisk Temp Badan Strukt — Prace Komitetu Krystalografii. Polska Akademia Nauk. Instytut Niskich Temperatur i Badan Strukturalnych
Pr Kom Lek Poznan Tow Przyj Nauk — Prace Komisji Lekarskiej. Poznanskie Towarzystwo Przyjaciol Nauk
Pr Kom Mat-Przyr Poznan Tow Przyj Nauk — Prace Komisji Matematyczno-Przyrodniczej. Poznanskie Towarzystwo Przyjaciol Nauk
Pr Kom Mat Przyr Poznan Tow Przyj Nauk Pr Chem — Prace Komisji Matematyczno-Przyrodniczej. Poznanskie Towarzystwo Przyjaciol Nauk. Prace Chemiczne
Pr Kom Metal Odlew Metal Pol Akad Nauk — Prace Komisji Metalurgiczno-Odlewniczej. Metalurgia. Polska Akademia Nauk
Pr Kom Nauk Ceram Pol Akad Nauk — Prace Komisji Nauk Ceramicznych. Ceramika. Polska Akademia Nauk
Pr Kom Nauk Lek Bydgoszcz Pol — Prace Komisji Nauk Lekarskich (Bydgoszcz, Poland)
Pr Kom Nauk Podstawowych Stosow Poznan Tow Przyj Nauk — Prace Komisji Nauk Podstawowych Stosowanych. Poznanskie Towarzystwo Przyjaciol Nauk
Pr Kom Nauk Pol Tow Glebozn Kom Biol Gleby — Prace Komisji Naukowych. Polskie Towarzystwo Gleboznawcze. Komisja Biologii Gleby
Pr Kom Nauk Pol Tow Glebozn Kom Chem Gleby — Prace Komisji Naukowych. Polskie Towarzystwo Gleboznawcze. Komisja Chemii Gleby
Pr Kom Nauk Pol Tow Glebozn Kom Glenezy Klasyf Kartogr Gleb — Prace Komisji Naukowych. Polskie Towarzystwo Gleboznawcze. Komisja Genezy, Klasyfikaeji, i Kartografii Gleb
Pr Kom Nauk Pol Tow Glebozn Kom Zyznosci Odzywiania Rosl — Prace Komisji Naukowych. Polskie Towarzystwo Gleboznawcze. Komisja Zyznosci i Odzywiania Roslin
Pr Kom Nauk Roln Biol Bydgoszcz Pol — Prace Komisji Nauk Rolniczych i Biologicznych (Bydgoszcz, Poland)
Pr Kom Nauk Roln Kom Nauk Lesn Poznan Tow Przyj Nauk — Prace Komisji Nauk Rolniczych i Komisji Nauk Lesnych. Poznanskiej Towarzystwo Przyjaciol
Pr Kom Nauk Roln Lesn (Poznan) — Prace Komisji Nauk Rolniczych i Lesnych. Poznanskie Towarzystwo Przyjaciol Nauk(Poznan)
Pr Kom Nauk Tech Pol Akad Nauk Ser Ceram — Prace Komisji Nauk Technicznych. Polska Akademia Nauk. Serja Ceramika
Pr Kom Technol Drewna Poznan Tow Przyj Nauk — Prace Komisji Technologii Drewna. Poznanskie Towarzystwo Przyjaciol Nauk
Pr Konf Elektrochem — Prace Konferencji Elektrochemicznej

PRKPA — Probleme der Kosmichen Physik

PRKRA — Parks and Recreation

Pr KZ — Preussische Kirchenzeitung

PRL — Political Risk Letter

PrIA — Parliamentary Affairs

PRLASR — Population Research Laboratory. University of Alberta. Department of Sociology.Alberta Series Report

PR Laws — Laws of Puerto Rico

PR Laws Ann — Puerto Rico Laws Annotated

PRLEA — Pracovni Lekarstvi

PrLib — Private Library

PrLit — Prace Literackie

PRLKA — Przeglad Lekarski

Pr Lodz Tow Nauk IV — Prace. Lodzkie Towarzystwo Naukowe. Wydzial IV. Nauk Lekarskich

PRLTA — Physical Review. Letters

PRLWCSR — Population Research Laboratory. University of Alberta. Department of Sociology.Western Canada Series Report

PRM — Polski Rocznik Muzykologiczny

PRM — PR Magazin. Public Relations und Informationspolitik in Medien und Gesellschaft

PrM — Protestantische Monatshefte

PRMA — Proceedings. Royal Musical Association

Pr Mac — Prehistoric Macedonia

Pr Man — Primitive Man

Pr Mater Etnogr Wroclaw — Prace i Materialy Etnograficzne. Polskie Towarzystwo Ludoznawcze (Wroclaw)

Pr Mater Nauk Inst Matki Dziecka — Prace i Materialy Naukowe. Instytut Matki i Dziecka

Pr Mater Pershogo Khark Derzh Med Inst — Pratsi i Materiali Pershogo Kharkivs'kogo Derzhavnogo Medichnogo Institutu

Pr Mater Ser Etnogr Lodz — Prace i Materialy Seria. Etnograficzna. Muzeum Archeologiczne i Etnograficzne (Lodz)

Pr Mater Zootech — Prace i Materialy Zootechniczne

Pr Mat Przyr Ser 2 — Prace Matematyczno-Przyrodnicze. Seria 2

PRMCL — Periodica de Re Morali Canonica Liturgica

PRMCLS — Papers. Regional Meeting. Chicago Linguistics Society

PrMe — Progres Medical

PRMEA — Presse Medicale

Pr Med — Presse Medicale

Pr Med Opolskie Tow Przyj Nauk Wyd Nauk Med — Prace Medyczne. Opolskie Towarzystwo Przyjaciol Nauk. Wydzial 5. Nauk Medycznych

Pr Mineral Pol Akad Nauk — Prace Mineralogiczne Polska Akademia Nauk

Pr Mineral Pol Akad Nauk Oddzial Krakowie Kom Nauk Mineral — Prace Mineralogiczne. Polska Akademia Nauk. Oddzial w Krakowie. Komisja Nauk Mineralogicznych

Pr Molodikh Uch Ukr Akad Sil's'kogospod Nauk — Pratsi Molodikh Uchenikh Ukrains'ka Akademiya Sil's'kogospodars'kikh Nauk

Pr Monogr Politech Szczcoin — Prace Monograficzne. Politechnika Szczecinska

Pr Moravskoslezske Akad Ved Prir — Prace Moravskoslezske Akademie Ved Prirodnich

Pr Morsk Inst Rybackiego Ser A — Prace Morskiego Instytutu Rybackiego. Seria A. Oceanografia i Biologia Rybacka

Pr Morsk Inst Rybackiego Ser B — Prace Morskiego Instytutu Rybackiego. Seria B. Technika Rybacka i Technologia Ryb

Pr Morsk Inst Rybacki Gdyni — Prace Morski Instytut Rybacki w Gdyni

PRMP — Review of Metaphysics

PRMSA — Progress in Materials Science

PRMSB — Proceedings. Royal Microscopical Society

PRMSC — Proceedings. Annual Reliability and Maintainability Symposium

PRMSD — Problemy Mashinostroeniya

Pr Muz Przyr Pol Akad Umiejet — Prace Muzeum Przyrodniczego. Polska Akademia Umiejetnosci

Pr Muz Ziemi — Prace Muzeum Ziemi

PRN — Playfulness, Revelry, Nonsense

PRN — PR Newswire

Pr Naturwiss Teil 3 — Praxis der Naturwissenschaften. Teil 3. Chemie

Pr Nauk Akad Ekon im Oskara Langego Wroclawiu — Prace Naukowe Akademii Ekonomicznej imienia Oskara Langego we Wroclawiu

Pr Nauk Akad Ekon Oskara Langego Wroclaw Chem — Prace Naukowe Akademii Ekonomicznej Imienia Oskara Langego we Wroclawiu. Chemia

Pr Nauk Akad Med Wroclawiu — Prace Naukowe Akademii Medycznej we Wroclawiu

Pr Nauk Inst Budow Politech Wroclaw — Prace Naukowe Instytutu Budownictwa Politechniki Wroclawskiej

Pr Nauk Inst Chem Org Biochem Biotechnol Politech Wroclaw — Prace Naukowe Instytutu Chemii Organicznej, Biochemii i Biotechnologii Politechniki Wroclawskiej

Pr Nauk Inst Chem Org Fiz Politech Wroclaw — Prace Naukowe Instytutu Chemii Organicznej i Fizycznej Politechniki Wroclawskiej

Pr Nauk Inst Chem Org Fiz Politech Wroclaw Ser K — Prace Naukowe Instytutu Chemii Organicznej i Fizycznej Politechniki Wroclawskiej. Seria. Konferencje

Pr Nauk Inst Chem Org Fiz Politech Wroclaw Ser Konf — Prace Naukowe Instytutu Chemii Organicznej i Fizycznej Politechniki Wroclawskiej. Seria Konferencje

Pr Nauk Inst Chem Org Fiz Politech Wroclaw Ser S — Prace Naukowe Instytutu Chemii Organicznej i Fizycznej Politechniki Wroclawskiej. Seria Studia i Materialy

Pr Nauk Inst Chem Technol Nafty Wegla Politech Wroclaw — Prace Naukowe Instytutu Chemii i Technologii Nafty i Wegla Politechniki Wroclawskiej

Pr Nauk Inst Cybern Tech Politech Wroclaw Ser K — Prace Naukowe Instytutu Cybernetyki Technicznej Politechniki Wroclawskiej. Seria Konferencje

Pr Nauk Inst Cybern Tech Politech Wroclaw Ser M — Prace Naukowe Instytutu Cybernetyki Technicznej Politechniki Wroclawskiej. Seria Monografie

Pr Nauk Inst Cybern Tech Politech Wroclaw Ser S — Prace Naukowe Instytutu Cybernetyki Technicznej Politechniki Wroclawskiej. Seria Studia i Materialy

Pr Nauk Inst Energoelektr Politech Wroclaw — Prace Naukowe Instytutu Energoelektryki Politechniki Wroclawskiej

Pr Nauk Inst Fiz Politech Wroclaw — Prace Naukowe Instytutu Fizyki Politechniki Wroclawskiej

Pr Nauk Inst Fiz Politech Wroclaw Ser M — Prace Naukowe Instytutu Fizyki Politechniki Wroclawskiej. Seria Monografie

Pr Nauk Inst Fiz Politech Wroclaw Ser Monogr — Prace Naukowe Instytutu Fizyki Politechniki Wroclawskiej. Seria Monografie

Pr Nauk Inst Fiz Politech Wroclaw Ser S — Prace Naukowe Instytutu Fizyki Politechniki Wroclawskiej. Seria Studia i Materialy

Pr Nauk Inst Fiz Tech Politech Wroclaw — Prace Naukowe Instytutu Fizyki Technicznej Politechniki Wroclawskiej

Pr Nauk Inst Geotech Hydrotech Politech Wroclaw — Prace Naukowe Instytutu Geotechniki I Hydrotechniki Politechniki Wroclawskiej

Pr Nauk Inst Geotech Politech Wroclaw — Prace Naukowe Instytutu Geotechniki Politechniki Wroclawskiej

Pr Nauk Inst Gorn Politech Wroclaw — Prace Naukowe Instytutu Gornictwa Politechniki Wroclawskiej

Pr Nauk Inst Gorn Wroclaw — Prace Naukowe Instytutu Gornictwa Politechniki Wroclawskiej

Pr Nauk Inst Inz Chem Urzadz Ciepl Politech Wroclaw Ser M — Prace Naukowe Instytutu Inzynierii Chemicznej i Urzadzen Cieplnych PolitechnikiWroclawskiej. Seria. Monografie

Pr Nauk Inst Inz Chem Urzadzen Cieplnych Politech Wroclaw — Prace Naukowe Instytutu Inzynierii Chemicznej i Urzadzen Cieplnych PolitechnikiWroclawskiej

Pr Nauk Inst Inz Ladowej Politech Wroclaw — Prace Naukowe Instytutu Inzynierii Ladowej Politechniki Wroclawskiej

Pr Nauk Inst Inz Ochr Srodowiska Politech Wroclaw — Prace Naukowe Instytutu Inzynierii Ochrony Srodowiska Politechniki Wroclawskiej

Pr Nauk Inst Inz Ochr Sr Politech Wroclaw — Prace Naukowe Instytutu Inzynierii Ochrony Srodowiska Politechniki Wroclawskiej

Pr Nauk Inst Inz Sanit Wodnej Politech Wroclaw — Prace Naukowe Instytutu Inzynierii Sanitarnej i Wodnej Politechniki Wroclawskiej

Pr Nauk Inst Konstr Ekspl Masz Politech Wroclaw — Prace Naukowe Instytutu Konstrukcji i Eksploatacji Maszyn Politechniki Wroclawskiej

Pr Nauk Inst Materialozn Mech Tech Politech Wroclaw — Prace Naukowe Instytutu Materialoznawstwa i Technicznej Politechniki Wroclawskiej

Pr Nauk Inst Materialozn Mech Tech Politech Wroclaw Ser M — Prace Naukowe Instytutu Materialoznawstwa i Mechaniki Technicznej Politechniki Wroclawskiej. Seria. Monografie

Pr Nauk Inst Materialozn Mech Tech Politech Wroclaw Ser S — Prace Naukowe Instytutu Materialoznawstwa i Mechaniki Technicznej Politechniki Wroclawskiej. Seria. Studia i Materialy

Pr Nauk Inst Mat Politech Wroclaw Ser M — Prace Naukowe Instytutu Matematyki Politechniki Wroclawskiej. Seria Monografie

Pr Nauk Inst Mat Politech Wroclaw Ser S — Prace Naukowe Instytutu Matematyki Politechniki Wroclawskiej. Seria Studia i Materialy

Pr Nauk Inst Metrol Elektr Politech Wroclaw — Prace Naukowe Instytutu Metrologii Elektrycznej Politechniki Wroclawskiej

Pr Nauk Inst Metrol Elektr Politech Wroclaw Ser K — Prace Naukowe Instytutu Metrologii Elektrycznej Politechniki Wroclawskiej. Seria. Konferencje

Pr Nauk Inst Metrol Elektr Politech Wroclaw Ser Konf — Prace Naukowe Instytutu Metrologii Elektrycznej Politechniki Wroclawskiej. Seria Konferencje

Pr Nauk Inst Metrol Elektr Politech Wroclaw Ser M — Prace Naukowe Instytutu Metrologii Elektrycznej Politechniki Wroclawskiej. Seria. Monografie

Pr Nauk Inst Metrol Elektr Politech Wroclaw Ser S — Prace Naukowe Instytutu Metrologii Elektrycznej Politechniki Wroclawskiej. Seria. Studia i Materialy

Pr Nauk Inst Ochr Rosl — Prace Naukowe Instytutu Ochrony Roslin

Pr Nauk Inst Ochr Rosl (Warsz) — Prace Naukowe Instytutu Ochrony Roslin (Warszawa)

Pr Nauk Inst Przem Org (Warsaw) — Prace Naukowe Instytutu Przemyslu Organicznego (Warsaw)

Pr Nauk Inst Tech Ciepl Mech Plynow Politech Wroclaw — Prace Naukowe Instytutu Techniki Cieplnej i Mechaniki Plynow Politechniki Wroclawskiej

Pr Nauk Inst Tech Ciepl Mech Plynow Politech Wroclaw Ser M — Prace Naukowe Instytutu Techniki Cieplnej i Mechaniki Plynow Politechniki Wroclawskiej. Seria. Monografie

Pr Nauk Inst Tech Ciepl Mech Plynow Politech Wroclaw Ser S — Prace Naukowe Instytutu Techniki Cieplnej i Mechaniki Plynow Politechniki Wroclawskiej. Seria. Studia i Materialy

Pr Nauk Inst Technol Budowy Masz Politech Wroclaw — Prace Naukowe Instytutu Technologii Budowy Maszyn Politechniki Wroclawskiej

Pr Nauk Inst Technol Elektron Politech Wroclaw — Prace Naukowe Instytutu Technologii Elektronowej Politechniki Wroclawskiej

Pr Nauk Inst Technol Elektron Politech Wroclaw Ser Monogr — Prace Naukowe Instytutu Technologii Elektronowej Politechniki Wroclawskiej. Seria Monografie

Pr Nauk Inst Technol Elektron Politech Wroclaw Ser S — Prace Naukowe Instytutu Technologii Elektronowej Politechniki Wroclawskiej. Seria. Studia i Materialy

Pr Nauk Inst Technol Nieorg Nawozow Miner Politech Wroclaw — Prace Naukowe Instytutu Technologii Nieorganicznej i Nawozow Mineralnych Politechniki Wroclawskiej

Pr Nauk Inst Technol Org Tworz Sztucz Politech Wroclaw Ser S — Prace Naukowe Instytutu Technologii Organicznej i Tworzyw Sztucznych Politechniki Wroclawskiej. Seria. Studia i Materialy

Pr Nauk Inst Technol Org Tworzyw Sztucznych Politech Wroclaw — Prace Naukowe Instytutu Technologii Organicznej i Tworzyw Sztucznych Politechniki Wroclawskiej

Pr Nauk Inst Telekomun Akust Politech Wroclaw Ser K — Prace Naukowe Instytutu Telekomunikacji i Akustyki Politechniki Wroclawskiej. Seria. Konferencje

Pr Nauk Inst Telekomun Akust Politech Wroclaw Ser M — Prace Naukowe Instytutu Telekomunikacji i Akustyki Politechniki Wroclawskiej. Seria. Monografie

Pr Nauk Inst Telekomun Akust Politech Wroclaw Ser S — Prace Naukowe Instytutu Telekomunikacji i Akustyki Politechniki Wroclawskiej. Seria. Studia i Materialy

Pr Nauk Inst Ukladow Elektromasz Politech Wroclaw — Prace Naukowe Instytutu Ukladow Elektromaszynowych Politechniki Wroclawskiej

Pr Nauk Inst Ukladow Elektromasz Politech Wroclaw Ser S — Prace Naukowe Instytutu Ukladow Elektromaszynowych Politechniki Wroclawskiej. Seria. Studia i Materialy

Pr Nauk Politech Szczecin — Prace Naukowe Politechniki Szczecinskiej

Pr Nauk Politech Warsz Chem — Prace Naukowe. Politechnika Warszawska. Chemia

Pr Nauk Politech Warsz Elektron — Prace Naukowe Politechnika Warszawska Elektronika

Pr Nauk Politech Wroclaw Pr Nauk Inst Budow — Prace Naukowe Politechniki Wroclawskiej. Prace Naukowe Instytutu Budownictwa

Pr Nauk Politech Wroclaw Ser Konf — Prace Naukowe Politechniki Wroclawskiej. Seria Konferencje

Pr Nauk Politech Wroclaw Ser Monogr — Prace Naukowe Politechniki Wroclawskiej. Seria Monografie

Pr Nauk Politech Wroclaw Ser Stud Mater — Prace Naukowe Politechniki Wroclawskiej. Seria Studia i Materialy

Pr Nauk Politech Wroclaw Ser Wspolpraca — Prace Naukowe Politechniki Wroclawskiej. Seria Wspolpraca

Pr Nauk Spolecznych Katowice — Prace z Nauk Spolecznych (Katowice)

Pr Nauk Uniw Slask Katowicach — Prace Naukowe Uniwersytetu Slaskiego w Katowicach

Pr Nauk Uniw Slask Katowic Pr Fiz — Prace Naukowe Uniwersytetu Slaskiego w Katowicach. Prace Fizyczne

Pr Nauk Wyzsza Szk Pedagog Czestochowa Chem — Prace Naukowe. Wyzsza Szkola Pedagogiczna Czestochowa. Chemia

Pr Nauk Wyzsza Szk Pedagog Czestochowie Ser Mat Przyr — Prace Naukowe. Wyzsza Szkola Pedagogiczna w Czestochowie. Seria Matematyczno-Przyrodnicza

Pr Nauk Wyzsz Szk Ekon Wroclawiu — Prace Naukowe Wyzszej Szkoly Ekonomicznej we Wroclawiu

Pr Navuk Tav Vyvuch Belarusi — Pratsa Navukovaga Tavarystva pa Vyvuchen'nyu Belarusi

PRNBA — Proceedings. Research Institute for Nuclear Medicine and Biology

PRNC — Renascence

PRNHA — Professional Nursing Home

PRNJ — Project North Journal

PRNN — Project North Newsletter

PRNQ — Renaissance Quarterly

PRO — Produktnieuws voor Kantoor en Bedrijf. Investeringsinformatie voor Managers

PRO — Professional Report

PRO — Pro Musica

ProA — Proceedings. American Philosophical Society

Pro A & Libris — Pro Arte et Libris

Pro Acad Pol Sci (USA) — Proceedings. Academy of Political Science (USA)

Pro Am Gas Inst — Proceedings. American Gas Institute

ProAOS — Proceedings. American Oriental Society

Probab Anal Nucl React Saf Proc Top Meet — Probabilistic Analysis of Nuclear Reactor Safety. Proceedings. Topical Meeting

Probab Appl — Probability and its Applications

Probab Eng Mech — Probabilistic Engineering Mechanics

Probab Engrg Inform Sci — Probability in the Engineering and Informational Sciences

Probab Math Stat — Probability and Mathematical Statistics

Probab Math Statist — Probability and Mathematical Statistics

Probab Mech Struct Geotech Reliab Proc Spec Conf — Probabilistic Mechanics and Structural and Geotechnical Reliability. Proceedings of the Specialty Conference

Probab Pure Appl — Probability: Pure and Applied

Probab Stochastics Ser — Probability and Stochastics Series

Probab Theory Related Fields — Probability Theory and Related Fields

Prob Actuels ORL — Problemes Actuels d'Oto-Rhino-Laryngologie

Prob Agric Ind Mex — Problemas Agricolas e Industriales de Mexico

Prob and Prop — Probate and Property

Prob Archit — Problemy Architektury

Probation N — Probation News. California Department of Social Welfare

Probat J — Probation Journal

Prob Com — Problems of Communism

Prob Comm — Problems of Communism

Prob Commun — Problems of Communism

Prob Econ — Problems of Economics

Probe Microsc — Probe Microscopy

Prob Izkustwoto — Problemi na Izkustwoto

Prob J — Probation Journal

Prob Khig — Problemi na Khigienata

Probl Actuels Biochim Appl — Problemes Actuels de Biochimie Appliquee

Probl Actuels Biochim Gen — Problemes Actuels de Biochimie Generale

Probl Actuels Dermatol — Problems Actuels de Dermatologie

Probl Actuels Endocrinol Nutr — Problemes Actuels d'Endocrinologie et de Nutrition

Probl Actuels Ophthal — Problemes Actuels d'Ophthalmologie

Probl Actuels Otorhinolaryngol — Problemes Actuels d'Otorhinolaryngologie

Probl Actuels Paediatr — Problemes Actuels de Paediatrie

Probl Actuels Pharmacopsychiatr — Problemes Actuels de Pharmacopsychiatrie

Probl Actuels Phoniatr Logop — Problemes Actuels de Phoniatrie et Logopedie

Probl Actuels Psychotherap — Problemes Actuels de Psychotherapie

Probl Adapt Gig Tr — Problema Adaptsii v Gigiene Truda

Probl Afr Centr — Problemes d'Afrique Centrale

Probl Aging Trans Conf — Problems of Aging. Transactions. Conference

Probl Agr (Bucharest) — Probleme Agricole (Bucharest)

Probl Agric — Probleme Agricole

Probl Agric Ind Mex — Problemas Agricolas e Industriales de Mexico

Probl Agr Indus Mex — Problemas Agricolas e Industriales de Mexico

Probl Agrofitoteh Teor Apl — Probleme de Agrofitotehnie Teoretica si Aplicata

Probl Agrofiz — Problemy Agrofizyki

Probl Akush Ginekol — Problemi na Akusherstvoto i Ginekologiyata

Probl Anal Khim — Problemy Analiticheskoi Khimii

Probl Ark Antark — Problemy Arktiki i Antarktiki

Probl Arkt Antarkt — Problemy Arktiki i Antarktiki

Probl Arktiki Antarkt — Problemy Arktiki i Antarktiki

Probl Arktiki Antarktiki — Problemy Arktiki i Antarktiki

Probl Attuali Sci Cult — Problemi Attuali di Scienza e di Cultura

Prob Law — Probate Lawyer

Probl Azoto Agric — Problemi dell'Azoto in Agricoltura

Probl Biocybern Biomed Eng — Problems of Biocybernetics and Biomedical Engineering

Probl Biol — Problems in Biology

Probl Biol Krajiny — Problemy Biologie Krajiny

Probl Biol Med — Problemes de Biologie et de Medecine

Probl Biol (Oxford) — Problems in Biology (Oxford)

Probl Biol Sofia — Problemi na Biologiyata (Sofia)

Probl Bioniki — Problemy Bioniki

Probl Bioniki Resp Mezhved Nauchno-Tekh Sb — Problemy Bioniki Respublikanskii Mezhvedomstvennyi Nauchno-Tekhnicheskii Sbornik

Probl Bor'by Protiv Burz Ideol — Problemy Bor'by Protiv Burzuaznoj Ideologii

Probl Bot — Problemy Botaniki

Probl Commu — Problems of Communism

Probl Communism — Problems of Communism

Probl Conscious Trans Conf — Problems of Consciousness. Transactions. Conference

Probl Contemp World — Problems of the Contemporary World

Probl Control and Inf Theory — Problems of Control and Information Theory

Probl Control and Inf Theory (Engl Transl Pap Rus) — Problems of Control and Information Theory (English Translation of the Papers in Russian)

Probl Control Inf Theor — Problems of Control and Information Theory

Probl Controv — Problemes et Controverses

Probl Cryolithol — Problems of Cryolithology

Probl Cybern — Problems of Cybernetics

Probl Cybern (Engl Transl) — Problems of Cybernetics (English Translation)

Probl Cybern (USSR) — Problems of Cybernetics (USSR)

Probl Cytol Protistol — Problems of Cytology and Protistology

Probl Dal'nego Vost — Problemy Dal'nego Vostok

Probl Desarr — Problemas del Desarrollo

Probl Desert Dev — Problems of Desert Development

Probl Desert Dev (Engl Transl Probl Osvoeniya Pustyn) — Problems of Desert Development (English Translation of Problemy Osvoeniya Pustyn)

Probl Dialektiki — Problemy Dialektiki

Probl Doc Inf — Probleme de Documentare si Informare

Probl Drug Depend — Problems of Drug Dependence

Probl Drug Depend Proc Annu Sci Meet Comm Probl Drug Depend — Problems of Drug Dependence. Proceedings. Annual Scientific Meeting. The Committee on Problems of Drug Dependence

Probl Early Infancy Trans Conf — Problems of Early Infancy. Transactions. Conference

Probl Ec — Problemes Economiques

Probl Ecol Biocenol — Problems of Ecology and Biocenology

Probl Ecol Monit Ecosyst Modell — Problems of Ecological Monitoring and Ecosystem Modelling

Probl Econ — Problems of Economics

Probl Econ Agric Mex — Problemas Economico Agricolas de Mexico

Probl Econ (Bucharest) — Probleme Economice (Bucharest)

Probl Ekol — Problemy Ekologii

Probl Ekol Monit Model Ekosist — Problemy Ekologicheskogo Monitoringa i Modelirovaniya Ekosistem

Probl Ekon Krakow — Problemy Ekonomiczne (Krakow)

Probl Ekon Morja — Problemy Ekonomiki Morja

Probl Ekon (Warszawa) — Problemy Ekonomiczne (Warszawa)

Probl Elektrokhim Korroz Met — Problemy Elektrokhimii i Korrozii Metallov

Probl Elem Part At Nucl Phys — Problems of Elementary Particle and Atomic Nucleus Physics

Problemas Bras — Problemas Brasileiros

Problem Books in Math — Problem Books in Mathematics

Probleme de Automat — Probleme de Automatizare

Probleme Prot Plantelor — Probleme de Protectia Plantelor

Problemes Eur — Problemes de l'Europe

Problemi Sicurezza Soc — Problemi della Sicurezza Sociale

Problemi Tehn Kibernet — Problemi na Tehniceskata Kibernetika

Problemi Tekhn Kibernet Robot — Problemi na Tekhnicheskata Kibernetika i Robotika

Problems Control Inform Theory/Problemy Upravlen Teor Inform — Problems of Control and Information Theory. Problemy Upravlenija i Teorii Informacii

Problems Econ — Problems of Economics

Problems Inform Transmission — Problems of Information Transmission

Problems in Geometry — Problems in Geometry in the Key Word Index

Problemy Jadern Fiz i Kosm Lucei — Problemy Jadernoi Fiziki i Kosmiceskih Lucei

Problemy Kibernet — Problemy Kibernetiki

Problemy Kosmich Biol Akad Nauk SSSR — Problemy Kosmicheskoi Biologii Akademiya Nauk SSSR

Problemy Mat — Bydgoszcz. Whzsza Szkola Pedagogiczna. Zeszyty Naukowe. Problemy Matematyczne

Problemy Mat Anal Sloz Sistem — Problemy Matematiceskogo Analiza Sloznyh Sistem

Problemy Matematiceskogo Analiza — Problemy Matematiceskogo Analiza

Problemy Mira Sots — Problemy Mira i Sotsializma

Problemy Pered Inf — Problemy Peredachi Informatsii

Problemy Slucain Poiska — Akademija Nauk Latviiskoi SSR. Institut Elektroniki i Vyceslitel'noi Tehniki. Problemy Slucainogo Poiska

Problemy Teor Gravitacii i Element Castic — Problemy Teorii Gravitacii i Elementarnyh Castic

Problemy Yadern Fiz i Kosm Luchei — Problemy Yadernoi Fiziki i Kosmicheskikh Luchei

Probl Endokr Gormonot — Problemy Endokrinologii i Gormonoterapii

Probl Endokrinol — Problemy Endokrinologii

Probl Endokrinol Gormonoter — Problemy Endokrinologii i Gormonoterapii [*Later, Problemy Endokrinologii*]

Probl Endokrinol (Mosk) — Problemy Endokrinologii (Moskva)

Probl Entrep Agric — Problemes de l'Enterprise Agricole

Probl Entwicklungslaender — Probleme der Entwicklungslaender

Probl Ernaehr Lebensmittelwiss — Probleme der Ernaehrungs- und Lebensmittelwissenschaft

Probl Evol — Problems of Evolution

Probl Evol — Problemy Evolyutsii

Probl Evol Funct Enzymochem Excitation Processes — Problems of the Evolution of Functions and Enzymochemistry of Excitation Processes

Probl Farine — Problemes de Farine

Probl Farm — Problemy na Farmatsiyata

Probl Farmakol — Problemi na Farmakologiyata

Probl Farmakol Farm — Probleml na Farmakologiyata i Farmatsiyata

Probl Festkoerperelektron — Probleme der Festkoerperelektronik

Probl Fetalen Endokrinol — Probleme der Fetalen Endokrinologie

Probl Filos Nauc Kommunizma — Problemy Filosofii i Naucnogo Kommunizma

Probl Fiz Atmos — Problemy Fiziki Atmosfery

Probl Fiz Elem Chastits At Yadra — Problemy Fiziki Elementarnykh Chastits i Atomnogo Yadra

Probl Fiziol Biokhim Drev Rast Tezisy Dokl Vses Konf — Problemy Fiziologii i Biokhimii Drevesnykh Rastenii. Tezisy Dokladov Vsesoyuznoi Konferentsii po Fiziologii i Biokhimii Drevesnykh Rastenii

Probl Fiziol Gipotal — Problemy Fiziologii Gipotalamusa

Probl Fiziol Opt — Problemy Fiziologicheskoj Optiki

Probl Fiziol Patol Vyssh Nervn Deyat — Problemy Fiziologii i Patologii Vysshei Nervnoi Deyatel'nosti

Probl Fiz Khim — Problemy Fizicheskoi Khimii

Probl Fiz Khim Petrol — Problemy Fiziko-Khimicheskoi Petrologii

Probl Fiz Org Khim — Problemy Fiziko-Organischeskoi Khimii

Probl Fiz Soedin AIIBVI Mater Vses Soveshch — Problemy Fiziki Soedinenii AIIBVI. Materialy Vsesoyuznogo Soveshchaniya

Probl Fonovogo Monit Sostoyaniya Prir Sredy — Problemy Fonovogo Monitoringa Sostoyaniya Prirodnoi Sredy

Probl Fotosint Dokl Vses Konf Fotosint — Problemy Fotosinteza. Doklady na Vsesoyuznoi Konferentsii po Fotosintezu

Probl Funkts Bolshikh Ekon Sist — Problemy Funktsionirovaniya Bol'shikh Ekonomicheskikh Sistem

Probl Funkts Morfol — Problemy Funktsional'noi Morfologii

Probl Gastroenterol — Problemy Gastroenterologii

Probl Gemat — Problemy Gematologii i Perelivanija Krovi

Probl Gematol Pereliv Krovi — Problemy Gematologii i Perelivaniya Krovi

Probl Geochem Cosmol — Problems of Geochemistry and Cosmology

Probl Geodin Kavk Dokl Semin — Problemy Geodinamiki Kavkaza. Doklady Prochitannye na Seminare po Geodinamike Kavkaza

Probl Geokhim — Problemy Geokhimii

Probl Geokhim Landshaftov — Problemy Geokhimii Landshaftov

Probl Geokhronol Geokhim Izot — Problemy Geokhronologii i Geokhimii Izotopov

Probl Geokhronol Izot Geol — Problemy Geokhronologii i Izotopnoi Geologii

Probl Geol Geogr Sev Vostoka Evr Chasti SSSR — Problemy Geologii i Geografii Severo-Vostoka Evropeiskoi Chasti SSSR

Probl Geol Karelii Kolsk Poluostrova — Problemy Geologii Karelii i Kol'skogo Poluostrova

Probl Geol Kaz — Problemy Geologii Kazakhstana

Probl Geol Metallog Kavk — Problemy Geologii i Metallogenii Kavkaza

Probl Geol Miner Mestorozhd Petrol Mineral — Problemy Geologii Mineral'nykh Mestorozhdenii, Petrologii i Mineralogii

Probl Geol Nefti — Problemy Geologii Nefti

Probl Geol Polezn Isk Sess Mezhdunar Geol Kongr — Problemy Geologii i Poleznykh Iskopaemykh na Sessii Mezhdunarodnogo Geologicheskogo Kongressa

Probl Geol Rossypei Soveshch Dokl — Problemy Geologii Rossypei. Soveshchanie po Geologii Rossypei. Doklady

Probl Geol Sess Int Geol Congr — Problems of Geology. Session. International Geological Congress

Probl Geol Sess Mezhdunar Geol Kongr — Problemy Geologii na Sessii Mezhdunarodnogo Geologicheskogo Kongressa

Probl Geol Tsentr Kaz — Problemy Geologii Tsentral'nogo Kazakhstana

Probl Gestione — Problemi di Gestione

Probl Gidroenerg Vod Khoz — Problemy Gidroenergetiki i Vodnogo Khozyaistva

Probl Gig Organ Zdravookhr Uzb — Problemy Gigieny i Organizatsii Zdravookhraneniya v Uzbekistane

Probl Glubokikh Mikozov — Problemy Glubokikh Mikozov

Probl Gos Prava — Problemy Gosudarstva i Prava

Probl Grippa Ostrykh Respir Zabol — Problemy Grippa i Ostrykh Respiratornykh Zabolevanii

Probl Hematol Blood Transfus — Problems of Hematology and Blood Transfusion

Probl Hematol Blood Transfus (USSR) — Problems of Hematology and Blood Transfusion (USSR)

Probl Hum Reprod — Problems of Human Reproduction

Probl Infancy Child Trans Conf — Problems of Infancy and Childhood. Transactions. Conference

Probl Inf & Doc — Probleme de Informare si Documentare

Probl Inf Doc Engl Issue — Probleme de Informare si Documentare (English Issue)

Probl Inf Docum — Probleme de Informare si Documentare

Probl Infect Parasit Dis — Problems of Infectious and Parasitic Diseases

Probl Influenza Acute Respir Dis — Problems of Influenza and Acute Respiratory Diseases

Probl Inf Med Biol Wiss Kolloq Organ Informationsverarb — Probleme der Informatik in Medizin und Biologie. Wissenschaftliches Kolloquium zur Organisation der Informationsverarbeitung

Probl Inf Transm — Problems of Information Transmission

Probl Inf Transm Engl Transl — Problems of Information Transmission (English Translation)

Probl Inf Transm (USSR) — Problems of Information Transmission (USSR)

Probl Intravenoesen Anaesth Ber Bremer Neuroleptanalg Symp 1 — Probleme der Intravenoesen Anaesthesie. Bericht ueber das Bremer Neuroleptanalgesie-Symposion. Teil 1

Probl Inzh Geol Sev Kavk — Problemy Inzhenernoi Geologii Severnogo Kavkaza

Probl Kamen Litya — Problemy Kamennogo Lit'ya

Probl Khig — Problemi na Khigienata

Probl Khim Kinet — Problemy Khimicheskoi Kinetiki

Probl Khir — Problemi na Khirurgiyata

Probl Khraneneto — Problemi na Khraneneto

Probl Kibern — Problemy Kibernetiki

Probl Kinet Katal — Problemy Kinetiki i Kataliza

Probl Kontrolya Zashch Atmos Zagryaz — Problemy Kontrolya i Zashchita Atmosfery ot Zagryazneniya

Probl Korroz Zashch Met Tr Vses Soveshch — Problemy Korrozii i Zashchity Metallov. Trudy Vsesoyuznogo Soveshchaniya po Korrozii i Zashchite Metallov

Probl Kosm Biol — Problemy Kosmicheskoi Biologii

Probl Kosm Fiz — Problemy Kosmicheskoj Fiziki

Probl Kosm Phys — Probleme der Kosmichen Physik

Probl Kriobiol — Problemy Kriobiologii

Probl Kriolitol — Problemy Kriolitologii

Probl Kriolitologii — Problemy Kriolitologii

Probl Liver Dis — Problems in Liver Diseases

Probl Loesungen Geb Tech Umweltschutzes Dtsch Tuerk Semin — Probleme und Loesungen auf dem Gebiet des Technischen Umweltschutzes. Deutsch-Tuerkisches Seminar

Probl Low Temp Phys Thermodyn — Problems of Low Temperature Physics and Thermodynamics

Probl Mashinostr — Problemy Mashinostroeniya

Probl Mashinostr Nadezhnosti Mash — Problemy Mashinostroeniya i Nadezhnosti Mashin

Probl Mat Fiz — Problemy Matematicheskoj Fiziki

Probl Med Enzimol Mater Vses Simp — Problemy Meditsinskoi Enzimologii. Materialy. Dolozhennye na Vsesoyuznom Simpoziume po Meditsinskoi Enzimologii

Probl Med Genet — Problemy Meditsinskoi Genetiki

Probl Med Khim — Problemy Meditsinskoi Khimii

Probl Med Radiol — Problemy Meditsinskoi Radiologii

Probl Med Wieku Rozwoj — Problemy Medycyny Wieku Rozwojowego

Probl Metallog Rudog — Problemy Metallogenii i Rudogeneza

Probl Metalloved Fiz Met — Problemy Metallovedeniya i Fiziki Metallov

Probl Metalloved Fiz Met Inst Metalloved Fiz Met — Problemy Metallovedeniya i Fiziki Metallov. Institut Metallovedeniya i Fiziki Metallov

Probl Metalloved Term Obrab — Problemy Metallovedeniya i Termicheskoi Obrabotki

Probl Metall Titana — Problemy Metallurgii Titana

Probl Methods Ultrason Interferom Proc All Union Conf — Problems of Methods of Ultrasonic Interferometry. Proceedings. All-Union Conference

Probl Metodol Ist-Filos Issled — Problemy Metodologii Istoriko-Filosofskogo Issledovanija

Probl Mod Chem Technol — Probleme der Modernen Chemischen Technologie

Probl Mod Nucl Phys Proc Probl Symp Nucl Phys　Problems of Modern Nuclear Physics. Proceedings. Problem Symposium on Nuclear Physics

Probl Morfopatol — Probleme de Morfopatologie

Probl Muz — Probleme de Muzeografie

Probl Narodonas Trud Resursov — Problemy Narodonaselenija i Trudovyh Resursov

Probl Nauc Kommunizma (Leningrad) — Problemy Naucnogo Kommunizma (Leningrad)

Probl Nauc Kommunizma (Moskva) — Problemy Naucnogo Kommunizma (Moskva)

Probl Nauc Uprav Soc Processami — Problemy Naucnogo Upravlenija Social'nymi Processami

Probl Neftegazonosn Tadzh — Problemy Neftegazonosnosti Tadzhikistana

Probl Nefti Gaza Tyumeni — Problemy Nefti i Gaza Tyumeni

Probl Neirokhim — Problemy Neirokhimii

Probl Neirokhir — Problemy Neirokhirurgii

Probl Neirokhir (1955-1963) — Problemy Neirokhirurgii (1955-1963)

Probl Neirokhir Resp Mezhved Sb — Problemy Neirokhirurgii Respublikanskii Mezhvedomstvenhyi Sbornik

Probl Neirokibern — Problemy Neirokibernetiki

Probl Neurosurg — Problems of Neurosurgery

Probl Nevrol Psikhiatr Nevrokhir — Problemi na Nevrologiyata, Psikhiatriyata, i Nevrokhirurgiyata

Probl Nevrol Resp Mezhved Sb — Problemy Nevrologii Respublikanskii Mezhvedomstvennyi Sbornik

Probl North — Problems of the North

Probl Nukl Med Radiobiol Radiat — Problemi na Nuklearnata Meditsina, Radiobiologiyata i Radiatsionnata Khigiena

Probl Obogashch Tverd Goryuch Iskop — Problemy Obogashcheniya Tverdykh Goryuchikh Iskopaemykh

Probl Obshch Energ Edinoi Energ Sist — Problemy Obshchei Energetiki i Edinoi Energeticheskoi Sistemy
Probl Obshch Mol Biol — Problemy Obshchei i Molekulyarnoi Biologii
Probl Okhr Ispolz Vod — Problemy Okhrany i Ispol'zovaniya Vod
Probl Okh Vod — Problemy Okhrany Vod
Probl Oncol (Engl Transl) — Problems of Oncology (English Translation)
Probl Oncol (Engl Transl Vopr Onkol) — Problems of Oncology (English Translation of Voprosy Onkologii)
Probl Oncol Kharkov — Problemes d'Oncologie (Kharkov)
Probl Oncol Leningrad — Problems of Oncology (Leningrad)
Probl Onkol (Sofia) — Problemi na Onkologiyata (Sofia)
Probl Ore Deposition Symp Int Assoc Genesis Ore Deposits — Problems of Ore Deposition. Symposium. International Association on the Genesis of Ore Deposits
Probl Organ — Problemy Organizacji
Probl Ornitol Tr Vses Ornitol Konf — Problemy Ornitologii. Trudy Vsesoyuznoi Ornitologicheskoi Konferentsii
Probl Ortop Stomatol — Problemy Ortopedicheskoi Stomatologii
Probl Osad Geol Dokembr — Problemy Osadochnoy Geologii Dokembriya
Probl Osad Rudoobraz — Problemy Osadochnogo Rudoobrazovaniya
Probl Osobo Opasnykh Infekts — Problemy Osobo Opasnykh Infektsii
Probl Osvoeniya Pustyn — Problemy Osvoeniya Pustyn
Probl Osvo Pustyn — Problemy Osvoeniya Pustyn
Probl Paleogidrol — Problemy Paleogidrologii
Probl Parazitol — Problemy Parazitologii
Probl Parazitol Mater Nauchn Konf Parazitol Ukr SSR — Problemy Parazitologii. Materialy Nauchnoi Konferentsii Parazitologov Ukrainskoi SSR
Probl Parazitol Pribaltike Mater Nauchno Koord Konf — Problemy Parazitologii v Pribaltike. Materialy Nauchno-Koordinatsionnoi Konferentsii po Problemam Parazitologii v Pribaltiiskikh Respublikakh
Probl Parazitol Tr Nauchn Konf Parazitol Ukr SSR — Problemy Parazitologii. Trudy Nauchnoi Konferentsii Parazitologov Ukrainskoi SSR
Probl Parenter Pitan Mater Soveshch — Problemy Parenteral'nogo Pitaniya. Materialy Soveshchaniya po Parenteral'nomu Pitaniyu
Probl Patol Comp — Probleme de Patologie Comparata
Probl Ped — Problemi della Pedagogia
Probl Pediatr — Problemy Pediatrii
Probl Pediatr Mother Child Hyg — Problems of Pediatrics and of Mother and Child Hygiene
Probl Peredachi Inf — Problemy Peredachi Informatsii
Probl Pereda Inf — Problemy Peredachi Informatsii
Probl Pererab Vysokosernistykh Neftei Mater Otrasl Konf — Problemy Pererabotki Vysokosernistykh Neftei. Materialy Otraslevoi Konferentsiipo Pererabotke Vysokosernistykh Neftei
Probl Perinat Med — Probleme der Perinatalen Medizin
Probl Perinatol Proc Asia Oceania Congr Perinatol — Problems in Perinatology. Proceedings of Asia Oceania Congress of Perinatology
Probl Petrol Genet Mineral — Problemy Petrologii i Geneticheskoi Mineralogii
Probl Phlebol Ther Int Kongr Phlebol — Probleme Phlebologischer Therapie. Internationaler Kongress fuer Phlebologie
Probl Photosynth Rep All Union Conf Photosynth — Problems of Photosynthesis. Reports of All-Union Conference on Photosynthesis
Probl Physiol Opt — Problems of Physiological Optics
Probl Pnevmol Ftiziatr — Problemi na Pnevmologiyata i Ftiziatriyata
Probl Pochvoved — Problemy Pochvovedeniya
Probl Polesya — Problemy Poles'ya
Probl Polit Soc — Problemes Politiques et Sociaux
Probl Prat Endocrinol — Problemes Pratiques d'Endocrinologie
Probl Prawa Karnego (Katowice) — Problemy Prawa Karnego (Katowice)
Probl Prikl Geokhim Mater Mezhdunar Simp Metody Prikl Geokhim — Problemy Prikladnoi Geokhimii. Materialy Mezhdunarodnogo Simpoziuma Metody Prikladnoi Geokhimii
Probl Proch Mashinostr — Problemy Prochnosti v Mashinostroenii
Probl Prochn — Problemy Prochnosti
Probl Prochn Mashinostr — Problemy Prochnosti v Mashinostroenii
Probl Proj — Problemy Projectowa
Probl Prot Plant — Probleme de Protectia Plantelor
Probl Psychiatry Neuropathol — Problems of Psychiatry and Neuropathology
Probl Psychol (Engl Transl Vopr Psikhol) — Problems of Psychology (English Translation of Voprosy Psikhologii)
Probl Quat Geol — Problems of Quaternary Geology
Probl Quat Geol Sib — Problems of the Quaternary Geology of Siberia
Probl Razrab Polezn Iskop — Problemy Razrabotki Poleznykh Iskopaemykh
Probl Razvit Metall Promsti — Problemy Razvitiya Metallurgicheskoi Promyshlennosti
Probl Rentgenol Radiobiol — Problemi na Rentgenologiyata i Radiobiologiyata
Probl Rudn Aerol — Problemy Rudnichnoi Aerologii
Probl Selsk Khoz Priamurya — Problemy Sel'skogo Khozyaistva Priamur'ya
Probl Ser — Problemy Severa
Probl Sess Pol Acad Sci — Problem Sessions. Polish Academy of Sciences
Probl Sev — Problemy Severa
Probl Sev Khoz — Problemy Severnogo Khozyaistva
Probl Sev Rastenievod — Problemy Severnogo Rastenievodstva
Probl Sib Oil — Problems of Siberian Oil
Probl Sicur Soc — Problemi della Sicurezza Sociale
Probl Soc Aktivnosti — Problemy Social'noj Aktivnosti
Probl Social (Milano) — Problemi del Socialismo (Milano)
Probl Soc Prognoz — Problemy Social'nogo Prognozirovanija
Probl Soc Zair — Problemes Sociaux Zairois
Probl Soc Zairois — Problemes Sociaux Zairois
Probl Soc Zairoises — Problemes Sociaux Zairoises
Probl Sotsialnoi Gig Istor Med — Problemy Sotsialnoi Gigieny i Istoriia Meditsiny
Probl Sov Geol — Problems of Soviet Geology
Probl Sov Geol — Problemy Sovetskoi Geologii
Probl Sov Gos Prava — Problemy Sovetskogo Gosudarstva i Prava

Probl Soviet — Problemes Sovietiques
Probl Sovrem Anal Khim — Problemy Sovremennoi Analiticheskoi Khimii
Probl Sovrem Khim Koord Soedin — Problemy Sovremennoi Khimii Koordinatsionnykh Soedinenii
Probl Sovrem Khim Koord Soedin Leningr Gos Univ — Problemy Sovremennoj Khimii Koordinatsionnykh Soedinenij Leningradskij Gosudarstvennyj Universitet
Probl Sovrem Khim Tekhnol — Problemy Sovremennoi Khimicheskoi Tekhnologii
Probl Sovrem Teor Elem Chastits — Problemy Sovremennmoi Teorii Elementarnykh Chastits
Probl Sovrem Yad Fiz Sb Dokl Probl Simp Fiz Yadra — Problemy Sovremennoi Yadernoi Fiziki. Sbornik Dokladov na Problemnom Simpoziumepo Fizike Yadra
Probl Spets Elektrometall — Problemy Spetsial'noi Elektrometallurgii
Probl Stellar Convect Proc Colloq — Problems of Stellar Convection. Proceedings. Colloquium
Probl Stomatol — Problemi na Stomatologiyata
Probl Stratigr Rannego Dokembr Sredn Sib — Problemy Stratigrafii Rannego Dokembriya Srednei Sibiri
Probl Surdechno Sudovite Zabol — Problemi na Surdechno-Sudovite Zabolyavaniya
Probl Tech Med — Problemy Techniki w Medycynie
Probl Tekh Elektrodin — Problemy Tekhnicheskoi Elektrodinamiki
Probl Tekh Kibern — Problemy na Tekhnicheskata Kibernetika
Probl Tekh Kibern na Robotikata — Problemy na Tekhnicheskata Kibernetika i Robotikata
Probl Teor Gravitatsii Elem Chastits — Problemy Teorii Gravitatsii i Elementarnykh Chastits
Probl Teor Plazmy Tr Mezhdunar Konf — Problemy Teorii Plazmy. Trudy Mezhdunarodnoi Konferentsii po Teorii Plazmy
Probl Teor Prakt Issled Obl Katal — Problemy Teorii i Praktiki Issledovanii v Oblasti Kataliza
Probl Teploenerg Prikl Teplofiz — Problemy Teploenergetiki i Prikladnoi Teplofiziki
Probl Ter — Probleme de Terapeutica
Probl Ter Stomatol — Problemy Terapeuticheskoi Stomatologii
Probl Theor Phys — Problems of Theoretical Physics
Probl Tierz — Probleme der Tierzucht
Probl Tovaroved Pishch Prod Obshchestv Pitan — Problemy Tovarovedeniya Pishchevykh Produktov i Obshchestvennogo Pitaniya
Probl Treniya Iznashivaniya — Problemy Treniya i Iznashivaniya
Probl Tub — Problemy Tuberkuleza
Probl Tuberk — Problemy Tuberkuleza
Probl Vazhneishikh Infekts Zabol — Problemy Vazhneishikh Infektsionnykh Zabolevanii
Probl Venerol Dermatol (Minsk) — Problemy Venerologii i Dermatologii (Minsk)
Probl Vert Metasomaticheskoi Zon — Problemy Vertikal'noi Metasomaticheskoi Zonal'nosti
Probl Vet Immunol — Problemy Veterinarnoi Immunologii
Probl Virol (Engl Transl Vopr Virusol) — Problems of Virology (English Translation of Voprosy Virusologii)
Probl Virol USSR — Problems of Virology (USSR)
Probl V-Tr Med — Problemi na V-Treshtnata Meditsina
Probl Vutr Med — Problemi na Vutreshnata Meditsina
Probl Wonders Chiral Mol — Problems and Wonders of Chiral Molecules
Probl World Nutr Proc Int Congr Nutr — Problems of World Nutrition. Proceedings. International Congress of Nutrition
Probl Yad Fiz Kosm Luchej — Problemy Yadernoj Fiziki i Kosmicheskikh Luchej
Probl Yad Geofiz — Problemy Yadernoi Geofiziki
Probl Zaraznite Parazit Bolesti — Problemi na Zaraznite i Parazitnite Bolesti
Probl Zhivotnovod — Problemy Zhivotnovodstva
Probl Zooteh Vet — Probleme Zootehnice si Veterinare
Prob Sovremennogo Grado Stroitelstva — Problemy Sovremennogo Grado-Stroitel'stva
PRO Bull Men — PROSI [*Public Relations Office of the Sugar Industry*] Bulletin Mensuel
Prob Vostok — Problemy Vostokovedeniia
PROC — Problems of Communism
PROC — Pro Canada
ProC — Proceedings. Consortium for Revolutionary Europe
Proc — Procellaria
Proc 1st Vic Weed Conf — Proceedings. First Victorian Weed Conference
Proc 3rd Int Conf Peaceful Uses Atom Energy — Proceedings. Third International Conference on the Peaceful Uses of Atomic Energy
Proc 31 A Blueberry Open House — Proceedings. 31st Annual Blueberry Open House
Proc 1989 David Colloq — Proceedings of the 1989 David Colloquium
ProcAAAS — Proceedings. American Association for the Advancement of Science
Proc AAHPSSS — Proceedings. Australasian Association for the History, Philosophy, and Social Studies of Science
Proc A Biol Colloq — Proceedings. Annual Biology Colloquium
Proc Abstr Int Conf Polyimides — Proceedings/Abstracts. International Conference on Polyimides
Proc Abstr Soc Biol Chem (Bangalore) — Proceedings and Abstracts. Society of Biological Chemists (Bangalore)
Proc Acad Environ Biol — Proceedings of the Academy of Environmental Biology
Proc Acad Man — Proceedings. Academy of Management
Proc Acad Nat Sci Phil — Proceedings. Academy of Natural Sciences of Philadelphia
Proc Acad Nat Sci Phila — Proceedings. Academy of Natural Sciences of Philadelphia
Proc Acad Nat Sci Philadelphia — Proceedings. Academy of Natural Sciences of Philadelphia
Proc Acad Natur Sci Phil — Proceedings. Academy of Natural Sciences of Philadelphia
Proc Acad Polit Sci — Proceedings. Academy of Political Science
Proc Acad Pol Sci — Proceedings. Academy of Political Science
Proc Acad Sci Amsterdam — Proceedings. Academy of Sciences of Amsterdam

Proc Acad Sci Armenian SSR — Proceedings. Academy of Sciences of the Armenian SSR

Proc Acad Sci Arm SSR — Proceedings. Academy of Sciences. Armenian SSR

Proc Acad Sci Azerb SSR — Proceedings. Academy of Sciences. Azerbaijan SSR

Proc Acad Sci Belarus Power Eng Phys Ser — Proceedings. Academy of Sciences of Belarus. Power Engineering Physical Series

Proc Acad Sci Est SSR Geol — Proceedings. Academy of Sciences. Estonian SSR. Geology

Proc Acad Sci Georgia Biol Ser — Proceedings. Academy of Sciences of Georgia. Biological Series

Proc Acad Sci Georgia Chem Ser — Proceedings. Academy of Sciences of Georgia. Chemical Series

Proc Acad Sci Georgian SSR Biol Ser — Proceedings. Academy of Sciences. Georgian SSR. Biological Series

Proc Acad Sci Georgian SSR Chem Ser — Proceedings. Academy of Sciences. Georgian SSR. Chemical Series

Proc Acad Sci ND — Proceedings. Academy of Science. North Dakota

Proc Acad Sci Turkm — Proceedings of the Academy of Sciences of Turkmenistan

Proc Acad Sci Turkmen SSR Ser Biol Sci — Proceedings. Academy of Sciences. Turkmen SSR. Series of Biological Sciences

Proc Acad Sci Turkm Ser Biol Sci — Proceedings. Academy of Sciences. Turkmenistan. Series of Biological Sciences

Proc Acad Sci Turk SSR Ser Phys Tech Chem Geol Sci — Proceedings. Academy of Sciences. Turkmen SSR. Series of Physico-Technical, Chemical, and Geological Sciences

Proc Acad Sci Turk SSR Ser Soc Sci — Proceedings. Academy of Sciences. Turkmen SSR. Series of Social Sciences

Proc Acad Sci United Prov Agra Oudh India — Proceedings. Academy of Sciences. United Provinces of Agra and Oudh India

Proc Acad Sci USSR Bot Sci Sect — Proceedings. Academy of Sciences. USSR. Botanical Sciences Section

Proc Acad Sci USSR Chem Sect — Proceedings. Academy of Sciences. USSR. Chemistry Section

Proc Acad Sci USSR Chem Technol Sect — Proceedings. Academy of Sciences. USSR. Chemical Technology Section

Proc Acad Sci USSR Geochem Sect — Proceedings. Academy of Sciences of the USSR. Geochemistry Section

Proc Acad Sci USSR Geol Sci Sect — Proceedings. Academy of Sciences. USSR. Geological Sciences Sections

Proc Acad Sci USSR Phys Chem Sect — Proceedings. Academy of Sciences. USSR. Physical Chemistry Section

Proc Acad Sci USSR Sect Agrochem — Proceedings. Academy of Sciences of the USSR. Section Agrochemistry

Proc Acad Sci USSR Sect Appl Phys — Proceedings. Academy of Sciences of the USSR. Section Applied Physics

Proc Acad Sci USSR Sect Biochem — Proceedings. Academy of Science. USSR. Section. Biochemistry

Proc ACM Comput Sci Conf — Proceedings. ACM Computer Science Conference

Proc ACM Conf Hypertext — Proceedings of the ACM Conference in Hypertext

Proc ACM SIGCPR Conf — Proceedings of the ACM SIGCPR Conference

Proc ACM SIGMOD Int Conf Manage Data — Proceedings of the ACM SIGMOD International Conference on Management of Data

Proc A Conv Am Cranberry Growers' Ass — Proceedings. Annual Convention. American Cranberry Growers' Association

Proc Adv Summer Study Inst — Proceedings. Advanced Summer Study Institute

Proc Adv Technol Conf — Proceedings. Advanced Technology Conference

Proc AEC Air Clean Conf — Proceedings. AEC Air Cleaning Conference

Proc Afr Cl Ass — Proceedings. African Classical Associations

Proc Afr Classical Assoc — Proceedings. African Classical Association

Proc Afr Weed Control Conf — Proceedings. African Weed Control Conference

Proc Agassiz Inst Sacramento — Proceedings. Agassiz Institute (Sacramento, CA)

Proc Agric Exp Stn (Palest) — Proceedings. Agricultural Experiment Station (Palestine)

Proc Agric Pestic Soc — Proceedings. Agricultural Pesticide Society

Proc Agric Pestic Tech Soc — Proceedings. Agricultural Pesticide Technical Society

Proc Agric Soc (Trinidad Tobago) — Proceedings. Agricultural Society (Trinidad and Tobago)

Proc Agric Soc Trin Tob — Proceedings. Agricultural Society of Trinidad and Tobago

Proc Agron Soc NZ — Proceedings. Agronomy Society of New Zealand

Proc Agr Outlook Conf — Proceedings. Agricultural Outlook Conference

Proc Agr Pestic Tech Soc — Proceedings. Agricultural Pesticide Technical Society

Proc Aharon Katzir-Katchalsky Conf — Proceedings. Aharon Katzir-Katchalsky Conference

Proc Air Pollut Contr Ass — Proceedings. Air Pollution Control Association

Proc Air Pollut Control Assoc — Proceedings. Air Pollution Control Association

Proc Air Waste Manage Assoc Annu Meet — Proceedings. Air and Waste Management Association. Annual Meeting

Proc Alaskan Sci Conf — Proceedings. Alaskan Science Conference

Proc Alaska Sci Conf — Proceedings. Alaska Science Conference

Proc Alberta Sulphur Gas Res Workshop — Proceedings. Alberta Sulphur Gas Research Workshop

Proc Alfred Benzon Symp — Proceedings. Alfred Benzon Symposium

Proc All Pak Sci Conf — Proceedings. All Pakistan Science Conference

Proc All Union Conf Photoelasticity — Proceedings. All-Union Conference on Photoelasticity

Proc All Union Conf Radiat Chem — Proceedings. All-Union Conference on Radiation Chemistry

Proc All Union Neurochem Conf — Proceedings. All-Union Neurochemical Conference

Proc Alumni Assoc (Malaya) — Proceedings. Alumni Association (Malaya)

Proc Am Acad — Proceedings. American Academy of Arts and Sciences

Proc Am Acad Arts Sci — Proceedings. American Academy of Arts and Sciences

ProcAmAcAS — Proceedings. American Academy of Arts and Sciences

Proc Am Antiq Soc — Proceedings. American Antiquarian Society

Proc Am Ant Soc — Proceedings. American Antiquarian Society

Proc Am Ass Can Res — Proceedings. American Association for Cancer Research

Proc Am Assoc Cancer Res — Proceedings. American Association for Cancer Research

Proc Am Assoc Cancer Res Am Soc Clin Oncol — Proceedings. American Association for Cancer Research and American Society of Clinical Oncology

Proc Am Assoc Cancer Res Annu Meet — Proceedings. American Association for Cancer Research. Annual Meeting

Proc Am Assoc Econ Entomol North Cent States Branch — Proceedings. American Association of Economic Entomologists. North Central States Branch

Proc Am Assoc State Highw Off — Proceedings. American Association of State Highway Officials

Proc Am Chem Soc Symp Anal Calorim — Proceedings. American Chemical Society Symposium on Analytical Calorimetry

Proc Am Concr Inst — Proceedings. American Concrete Institute

Proc Am Congr Surv Mapp — Proceedings. American Congress on Surveying and Mapping

Proc Am Control Conf — Proceedings of the American Control Conference

Proc Am Cotton Congr — Proceedings. American Cotton Congress

Proc Am Cranberry Grow Assoc — Proceedings. American Cranberry Growers' Association

Proc Am Cranberry Growers' Ass — Proceedings. American Cranberry Growers' Association

Proc Am Diabetes Assoc — Proceedings. American Diabetes Association

Proc Am Doc Inst — Proceedings. American Documentation Institute

Proc Am Drug Manuf Assoc Annu Meet — Proceedings. American Drug Manufacturers Association. Annual Meeting

Proc A Meet Coun Fertil Applic — Proceedings. Annual Meeting. Council on Fertilizer Application

Proc A Meeting Sugar Ind Technicians — Proceedings. Annual Meeting of Sugar Industry Technicians

Proc A Meet Pl Physiol Univ MD — Proceedings. Annual Meeting. American Society of Plant Physiologists at the University of Maryland

Proc Am Electroplat Soc — Proceedings. Technical Sessions. Annual Convention. American Electroplaters' Society

Proc Amer Acad A & Sci — Proceedings of the American Academy of Arts and Sciences

Proc Amer Acad Arts Sci — Proceedings. American Academy of Arts and Sciences

Proc Amer Acad Jew Res — Proceedings. American Academy for Jewish Research

Proc Amer Ac Arts — Proceedings. American Academy of Arts and Sciences

Proc Amer Antiqua Soc — Proceedings of the American Antiquarian Society

Proc Amer Ass State Highw Offic — Proceedings. American Association of State Highway Officials

Proc Amer Cath Phil Assoc — Proceedings. American Catholic Philosophical Association

Proc Amer Ethnol Soc — Proceedings. American Ethnological Society

Proc Amer Inst Architects — Proceedings of the American Institute of Architects

Proc Amer Math Soc — Proceedings. American Mathematical Society

Proc Amer Microscop Soc — Proceedings. American Microscopical Society

Proc Amer Peony Soc — Proceedings. American Peony Society

Proc Amer Phil Ass — Proceedings and Addresses. American Philosophical Association

Proc Amer Philosophical Soc — Proceedings. American Philosophical Society

Proc Amer Philos Soc — Proceedings. American Philosophical Society

Proc Amer Phil Soc — Proceedings. American Philosophical Society

Proc Amer Power Conf — Proceedings. American Power Conference

Proc Amer Seed Trade Assoc — Proceedings. American Seed Trade Association

Proc Amer Soc Anim Pro W Sect — Proceedings. American Society of Animal Production. Western Section

Proc Amer Soc Anim Sci W Sect — Proceedings. American Society of Animal Science. Western Section

Proc Amer Soc Bakery Eng — Proceedings. American Society of Bakery Engineers

Proc Amer Soc Biol Chem — Journal of Biological Chemistry

Proc Amer Soc Brew Chem — Proceedings. American Society of Brewing Chemists

Proc Amer Soc Compos Tech Conf — Proceedings. American Society for Composites. Technical Conference

Proc Amer Soc Hort Sci — Proceedings. American Society for Horticultural Science

Proc Amer Soc of Internat L — Proceedings. American Society of International Law

Proc Amer Soc Testing Materials — Proceedings. American Society for Testing and Materials

Proc Amer Soc U Composers — Proceedings. American Society of University Composers

Proc Amer Soybean Assoc — Proceedings. American Soybean Association

Proc Amer Wood-Preserv Ass — Proceedings. American Wood-Preservers' Association

Proc Am Feed Manuf Assoc Nutr Counc — Proceedings. American Feed Manufacturers Association. Nutrition Council

Proc Am Gas Assoc Oper Sect — Proceedings. American Gas Association. Operating Section

Proc Am Gas Inst — Proceedings. American Gas Institute

Proc Am Hortic Congr — Proceedings. American Horticultural Congress

Proc Am Inst Electr Eng — Proceedings. American Institute of Electrical Engineers

Proc Am Math Soc — Proceedings. American Mathematical Society

Proc Am Nucl Soc Conf Environ Aspects Non Conv Energy Resour — Proceedings. American Nuclear Society Conference on Environmental Aspects of Non-Conventional Energy Resources

Proc Am Peanut Res Educ Assoc — Proceedings. American Peanut Research and Education Association

Proc Am Peanut Res Educ Soc — Proceedings. American Peanut Research and Education Society

Proc Am Pept Symp — Proceedings. American Peptide Symposium

Proc Am Pet Inst Div Refining — Proceedings. American Petroleum Institute. Division of Refining

Proc Am Pet Inst Refin Dep — Proceedings. American Petroleum Institute. Refining Department

Proc Am Pet Inst Sect 1 — Proceedings. American Petroleum Institute. Section 1

Proc Am Pet Inst Sect 2 — Proceedings. American Petroleum Institute. Section 2. Marketing

Proc Am Pet Inst Sect 3 — Proceedings. American Petroleum Institute. Section 3. Refining

Proc Am Pet Inst Sect 3 Refining — Proceedings. American Petroleum Institute. Section 3. Refining

Proc Am Pet Inst Sect 4 — Proceedings. American Petroleum Institute. Section 4. Production

Proc Am Pet Inst Sect 5 — Proceedings. American Petroleum Institute. Section 5. Transportation

Proc Am Pet Inst Sect 6 — Proceedings. American Petroleum Institute. Section 6. Interdivisional

Proc Am Pet Inst Sect 8 — Proceedings. American Petroleum Institute. Section 8. Science and Technology

Proc Am Pharm Manuf Assoc Annu Meet — Proceedings. American Pharmaceutical Manufacturers' Association. Annual Meeting

Proc Am Pharm Manuf Assoc Midyear East Sect Meet — Proceedings. American Pharmaceutical Manufacturers' Association. Midyear Eastern Section Meeting

Proc Am Philos Soc — Proceedings. American Philosophical Society

Proc Am Phil Soc — Proceedings. American Philosophical Society

Proc Am Phytopathol Soc — Proceedings. American Phytopathological Society

Proc Am Power Conf — Proceedings. American Power Conference

Proc Am Railw Eng Assoc — Proceedings. American Railway Engineering Association

Proc Am Sci Congr — Proceedings. American Scientific Congress

Proc Am Soc Anim Prod — Proceedings. Annual Meeting. American Society of Animal Production

Proc Am Soc Anim Sci West Sect — Proceedings. American Society of Animal Science. Western Section

Proc Am Soc Brew Chem — Proceedings. American Society of Brewing Chemists

Proc Am Soc Civ Eng — Proceedings. American Society of Civil Engineers

Proc Am Soc Civ Eng Transp Eng J — Proceedings. American Society of Civil Engineers. Transportation Engineering Journal

Proc Am Soc Clin Oncol Annu Meet — Proceedings. American Society of Clinical Oncology. Annual Meeting

Proc Am Soc Compos — Proceedings of the American Society for Composites

Proc Am Soc Enol — Proceedings. American Society of Enologists

Proc Am Soc Hortic Sci — Proceedings. American Society for Horticultural Science

Proc Am Soc Hortic Sci Trop Reg — Proceedings. American Society for Horticultural Science. Tropical Region

Proc Am Soc Hort Sci — Proceedings. American Society for Horticultural Science

Proc Am Soc Inf Sci — Proceedings. American Society for Information Science

Proc Am Soc Munic Improv — Proceedings. American Society for Municipal Improvements

Proc Am Soc Sugar Beet — Proceedings. American Society of Sugar Beet

Proc Am Soc Test & Mater — Proceedings. American Society for Testing and Materials

Proc Am Soc Ther Radiol Annu Meet — Proceedings. American Society of Therapeutic Radiologists' Annual Meeting

Proc Am Vet Med Ass — Proceedings. American Veterinary Medical Association

Proc Am Vet Med Assoc — Proceedings. American Veterinary Medical Association

Proc Am Water Works Assoc — Proceedings. American Water Works Association

Proc Am Water Works Assoc Annu Conf — Proceedings. American Water Works Association Annual Conference

Proc Am Weld Soc — Proceedings. American Welding Society

Proc Am Wood-Preserv Assoc — Proceedings. American Wood-Preservers' Association

Proc Anal Chem Conf — Proceedings. Analytical Chemical Conference

Proc Anal Div Chem Soc — Proceedings. Analytical Division. Chemical Society

Proc and Trans Rhod Sci Assoc — Proceedings and Transactions. Rhodesia Scientific Association

Proc and Tr Liverpool Biol Soc — Proceedings and Transactions. Liverpool Biological Society

Proc Anim Care Panel — Proceedings. Animal Care Panel

Proc Anim Sci Indian Acad Sci — Proceedings. Animal Sciences. Indian Academy of Sciences

Proc Ann AI Syst Gov — Proceeding. Annual AI Systems in Government Conference

Proc Ann Conf High En Nucl Phys — Proceedings. Annual Conference on High Energy Nuclear Physics

Proc Ann Conf Rehab Eng — Proceedings. Annual Conference on Rehabilitation Engineering

Proc Anniv Conf SPI Reinf Plast Compos Div — Proceedings. Anniversary Conference. SPI Reinforced Plastics/Composites Division

Proc Anniv Tech Conf SPI Reinf Plast Div — Proceedings. Anniversary Technical Conference. SPI Reinforced Plastics Division

Proc Annu ACM Symp Princ Distrib Comput — Proceedings of the Annual ACM Symposium on Principles of Distributed Computing

Proc Annu AIChE Southwest Ohio Conf Energy Environ — Proceedings. Annual AIChE [*American Institute of Chemical Engineers*] Southwestern Ohio Conference on Energy and the Environment

Proc Annu AIIE Conf — Proceedings. Annual AIIE Conference. West Virginia University

Proc Annu Air Pollut Control Conf — Proceedings. Annual Air Pollution Control Conference

Proc Annu Alberta Soil Sci Workshop — Proceedings. Annual Alberta Soil Science Workshop

Proc Annu Allerton Conf Circuit Syst Theory — Proceedings. Annual Allerton Conference on Circuit and System Theory [*Later, Proceedings. Annual Allerton Conference on Communication, Control, and Computing*]

Proc Annu Allerton Conf Commun Control Comput — Proceedings. Annual Allerton Conference on Communication, Control, and Computing

Proc Annual Meeting Amer Carnation Soc — Proceedings. Annual Meeting. American Carnation Society

Proc Annual Meeting Caribbean Food Crops Soc — Proceedings. Annual Meeting. Caribbean Food Crops Society

Proc Annual Meetings Soc Promot Agric Sci — Proceedings. Annual Meetings. Society for the Promotion of Agricultural Science

Proc Annu Am Water Resour Conf — Proceedings. Annual American Water Resources Conference

Proc Annu A N Richards Symp — Proceedings. Annual A. N. Richards Symposium

Proc Annu Appalachian Underground Corros Short Course — Proceedings. Annual Appalachian Underground Corrosion Short Course

Proc Annu Aquat Toxic Workshop — Proceedings. Annual Aquatic Toxicity Workshop

Proc Annu Arkansas Water Works Pollut Control Conf Short Sch — Proceedings. Annual Arkansas Water Works and Pollution Control Conference and Short School

Proc Annu ASME Symp NM Sect — Proceedings. Annual ASME Symposium. New Mexico Section

Proc Annu Battery Conf Appl Adv — Proceedings. Annual Battery Conference on Applications and Advances

Proc Annu Battery Res Dev Conf — Proceedings. Annual Battery Research and Development Conference

Proc Annu Biochem Eng Symp — Proceedings. Annual Biochemical Engineering Symposium

Proc Annu Biol Colloq (Oreg State Univ) — Proceedings. Annual Biology Colloquium (Oregon State University)

Proc Annu Biomed Sci Instrum Symp — Proceedings. Annual Biomedical Sciences Instrumentation Symposium

Proc Annu Blueberry Open House — Proceedings. Annual Blueberry Open House

Proc Annu Calif Weed Conf — Proceedings. Annual California Weed Conference

Proc Annu Clin Conf Cancer — Proceedings. Annual Clinical Conference on Cancer

Proc Annu Cli Spinal Cord Inj Conf — Proceedings. Annual Clinical Spinal Cord Injury Conference

Proc Annu Conf Act Sludge Process Control — Proceedings. Annual Conference on Activated Sludge Process Control

Proc Annu Conf Adm Res — Proceedings. Annual Conference on the Administration of Research

Proc Annu Conf Agron Soc NZ — Proceedings. Annual Conference. Agronomy Society of New Zealand

Proc Annu Conf Alcohol — Proceedings. Annual Conference of Alcoholism

Proc Annu Conf Am Water Works Assoc — Proceedings. Annual Conference. American Water Works Association

Proc Annu Conf Assoc Comput Mach — Proceedings. Annual Conference. Association for Computing Machinery

Proc Annu Conf Aust Inst Met — Proceedings. Annual Conference. Australian Institute of Metals

Proc Annu Conf Australas Inst Met — Proceedings. Annual Conference. Australasian Institute of Metals

Proc Annu Conf Autom Control Pet Chem Ind — Proceedings. Annual Conference on Automatic Control in the Petroleum and Chemical Industries

Proc Annu Conf BC Water Waste Assoc — Proceedings. Annual Conference. British Columbia Water and Waste Association

Proc Annu Conf Biol Sonar Diving Mamm — Proceedings. Annual Conference on Biological Sonar and Diving Mammals

Proc Annu Conf Biol Sonar Diving Mammals — Proceedings. Annual Conference on Biological Sonar and Diving Mammals

Proc Annu Conf Br Steel Cast Res Assoc — Proceedings. Annual Conference. British Steel Castings Research Association

Proc Annu Conf Can Nucl Assoc — Proceedings. Annual Conference. Canadian Nuclear Association

Proc Annu Conf Can Soc Stud Educ Coop Assoc — Proceedings. Annual Conference. Canadian Society for the Study of Education andCooperating Associations

Proc Annu Conf Can Tech Asphalt Assoc — Proceedings. Annual Conference of Canadian Technical Asphalt Association

Proc Annu Conf CMES HTI — Proceedings. Annual Conference of CMES HTI

Proc Annu Conf Compos Adv Ceram Mater — Proceedings. Annual Conference on Composites and Advanced Ceramic Materials

Proc Annu Conf Eff Lithium Doping Silicon Sol Cells — Proceedings. Annual Conference on Effects of Lithium Doping on Silicon Solar Cells

Proc Annu Conf Energy Convers Storage — Proceedings. Annual Conference on Energy Conversion and Storage

Proc Annu Conf Eng Med Biol — Proceedings. Annual Conference on Engineering in Medicine and Biology

Proc Annu Conf Environ Chem Hum Anim Health — Proceedings. Annual Conference on Environmental Chemicals. Human and Animal Health

Proc Annu Conf Environ Toxicol — Proceedings. Annual Conference on Environmental Toxicology

Proc Annu Conf Explos Blasting Tech — Proceedings of the Annual Conference on Explosives and Blasting Technique

Proc Annu Conf Fossil Energy Mater — Proceedings. Annual Conference on Fossil Energy Materials

Proc Annu Conf Ind Appl X Ray Anal — Proceedings. Annual Conference on Industrial Applications of X-Ray Analysis

Proc Annu Conf Int Symp N Am Lake Manage Soc — Proceedings. Annual Conference and International Symposium. North American LakeManagement Society

Proc Annu Conf Kidney — Proceedings. Annual Conference on the Kidney

Proc Annu Conf Malays Soc Biochem Mol Biol — Proceedings of the Annual Conference of the Malaysian Society for Biochemistry and Molecular Biology

Proc Annu Conf Manitoba Agron — Proceedings. Annual Conference of Manitoba Agronomists

Proc Annu Conf MD Del Water Sewage Assoc — Proceedings. Annual Conference. Maryland-Delaware Water and Sewage Association

Proc Annu Conf Microbeam Anal Soc — Proceedings. Annual Conference. Microbeam Analysis Society

Proc Annu Conf Natl Soc Clean Air — Proceedings. Annual Conference. National Society for Clean Air

Proc Annu Conf Niger Soc Anim Prod — Proceedings. Annual Conference. Nigerian Society for Animal Production Symposium on Drought

Proc Annu Conf Nutr Soc NZ — Proceedings. Annual Conference. Nutrition Society of New Zealand

Proc Annu Conf Reinf Plast Compos Inst Soc Plast Ind — Proceedings. Annual Conference. Reinforced Plastics/Composites Institute. Society of the Plastics Industry

Proc Annu Conf Res Med Educ — Proceedings. Annual Conference on Research in Medical Education

Proc Annu Conf Restor Coastal Veg Fla — Proceedings. Annual Conference on Restoration of Coastal Vegetation in Florida

Proc Annu Conf Soc Vac Coaters — Proceedings. Annual Conference. Society of Vacuum Coaters

Proc Annu Conf Southeast Assoc Fish Wildl Agencies — Proceedings. Annual Conference. Southeastern Association of Fish and Wildlife Agencies

Proc Annu Conf Southeast Assoc Game Fish Comm — Proceedings. Annual Conference. Southeastern Association of Game and Fish Commissioners

Proc Annu Conf Steel Cast Res Trade Assoc — Proceedings. Annual Conference. Steel Castings Research and Trade Association

Proc Annu Conf Steel Cast Res Trade Assoc St Found Prac — Proceedings. Annual Conference. Steel Castings Research and Trade Association. Steel Foundry Practice

Proc Annu Conf Tex Pecan Grow Assoc — Proceedings. Annual Conference. Texas Pecan Growers Association

Proc Annu Conf US Public Health Serv State Territ Health Off — Proceedings. Annual Conference. United States Public Health Service with the State and Territorial Health Officers

Proc Annu Congr S Afr Sugar Technol Assoc — Proceedings. Annual Congress. South African Sugar Technologists Association

Proc Annu Connector Symp — Proceedings. Annual Connector Symposium

Proc Annu Contract Meet Contam Control Coal Deriv Gas Streams — Proceedings. Annual Contractors Meeting on Contaminant Control in Coal-Derived Gas Streams

Proc Annu Conv Am Assoc Equine Pract — Proceedings. Annual Convention. American Association of Equine Practitioners

Proc Annu Conv Am Railw Eng Assoc — Proceedings. Annual Convention. American Railway Engineering Association

Proc Annu Conv Assoc Am Pestic Control Off — Proceedings. Annual Convention Association. American Pesticide Control Officials

Proc Annu Conv Flavoring Ext Manuf Assoc US — Proceedings. Annual Convention. Flavoring Extract Manufacturers' Association ofthe United States

Proc Annu Conv Ga Fla Pecan Grow Assoc — Proceedings. Annual Convention. Georgia-Florida Pecan Growers Association

Proc Annu Conv Gas Process Assoc Meet Pap — Proceedings. Annual Convention. Gas Processors Association. Meeting Papers

Proc Annu Conv Gas Process Assoc Tech Pap — Proceedings. Annual Convention. Gas Processors Association. Technical Papers

Proc Annu Conv Indones Pet Assoc — Proceedings. Annual Convention. Indonesian Petroleum Association

Proc Annu Conv J Oil Technol Assoc — Proceedings. Annual Convention and Journal. Oil Technologists' Association

Proc Annu Conv Magnesium Assoc — Proceedings. Annual Convention. Magnesium Association

Proc Annu Conv Milk Ind Found — Proceedings. Annual Convention. Milk Industry Foundation

Proc Annu Conv Milk Ind Found Lab Sect — Proceedings. Annual Convention. Milk Industry Foundation. Laboratory Section

Proc Annu Conv Milk Ind Found Milk Supplies Sect — Proceedings. Annual Convention. Milk Industry Foundation. Milk Supplies Section

Proc Annu Conv Milk Ind Found Plant Sect — Proceedings. Annual Convention. Milk Industry Foundation. Plant Section

Proc Annu Conv Nat Gasoline Assoc Am Tech Pap — Proceedings. Annual Convention. Natural Gasoline Association of America. Technical Papers

Proc Annu Conv Nat Gas Process Assoc Tech Pap — Proceedings. Annual Convention. Natural Gas Processors Association. Technical Papers

Proc Annu Conv Natl Fert Assoc — Proceedings. Annual Convention. National Fertilizer Association

Proc Annu Conv Natur Gas Process Ass Tech Pap — Proceedings. Annual Convention. Natural Gas Processors Association. Technical Papers

Proc Annu Conv Oil Technol Assoc — Proceedings. Annual Convention. Oil Technologists Association

Proc Annu Conv Philipp Sugar Assoc — Proceedings. Annual Convention. Philippine Sugar Association

Proc Annu Conv Sci Program Soc Biol Psychiatry — Proceedings. Annual Convention and Scientific Program. Society of Biological Psychiatry

Proc Annu Conv Soc Leather Technol Chem S Afr Sect — Proceedings. Annual Convention. Society of Leather Technologists and Chemists. South African Section

Proc Annu Conv Soc Leather Trades Chem — Proceedings. Annual Convention. Society of Leather Trades Chemists

Proc Annu Conv Southeast Pecan Grow Assoc — Proceedings. Annual Convention. Southeastern Pecan Growers Association

Proc Annu Conv Sugar Technol Assoc India — Proceedings. Annual Convention. Sugar Technologists' Association of India

Proc Annu Conv West Can Water Sewage Conf — Proceedings. Annual Convention. Western Canada Water and Sewage Conference (1960-1975)

Proc Annu Conv West Can Water Wastewater Assoc — Proceedings. Annual Convention. Western Canada Water and Wastewater Association

Proc Annu East Theor Phys Conf — Proceedings. Annual Eastern Theoretical Physics Conference

Proc Annu Educ Symp Instrum Soc Am — Proceedings. Annual Education Symposium. Instrument Society of America

Proc Annu Electron Microsc Colloq — Proceedings. Annual Electron Microscopy Colloquium

Proc Annu Eng Geol Soils Eng Symp — Proceedings. Annual Engineering Geology and Soils Engineering Symposium

Proc Annu Eng Geol Symp — Proceedings. Annual Engineering Geology Symposium

Proc Annu Environ Water Resour Eng Conf — Proceedings. Annual Environmental and Water Resources Engineering Conference

Proc Annu EPRI Contract Conf Coal Liquefaction — Proceedings. Annual EPRI Contractors' Conference on Coal Liquefaction

Proc Annu Fall Meet Am Physiol Soc — Proceedings. Annual Fall Meeting Sponsored by the American Physiological Society

Proc Annu Fall Meet Calif Nat Gasoline Assoc — Proceedings. Annual Fall Meeting. California Natural Gasoline Association

Proc Annu Fall Meet West Gas Process Oil Refin Assoc — Proceedings. Annual Fall Meeting. Western Gas Processors and Oil Refiners Association

Proc Annu Fall Meet West Gas Process Oil Refiners Assoc — Proceedings. Annual Fall Meeting. Western Gas Processors and Oil Refiners Association

Proc Annu For Veg Manage Conf — Proceedings. Annual Forest Vegetation Management Conference

Proc Annu Freq Control Symp — Proceedings. Annual Frequency Control Symposium

Proc Annu Fuel Cells Contract Rev Meet — Proceedings. Annual Fuel Cells Contractors Review Meeting

Proc Annu Fuels Biomass Symp — Proceedings. Annual Fuels from Biomass Symposium

Proc Annu Gas Chromatogr Inst — Proceedings. Annual Gas Chromatography Institute

Proc Annu Gasif Proj Contract Meet — Proceedings. Annual Gasification Projects Contractors Meeting

Proc Annu Gen Meet Int Inst Synth Rubber Prod — Proceedings. Annual General Meeting. International Institute of Synthetic Rubber Producers

Proc Annu Glass Symp — Proceedings. Annual Glass Symposium

Proc Annu Gulf Caribb Fish Inst — Proceedings. Annual Gulf and Caribbean Fisheries Institute

Proc Annu Hardwood Symp Hardwood Res Counc — Proceedings. Annual Hardwood Symposium. Hardwood Research Council

Proc Annu Health Phys Soc Top Symp — Proceedings. Annual Health Physics Society Topical Symposium

Proc Annu Highw Geol Symp — Proceedings. Annual Highway Geology Symposium

Proc Annu Holm Conf Electr Contacts — Proceedings. Annual Holm Conference on Electrical Contacts

Proc Annu Holm Semin Electr Contacts — Proceedings. Annual Holm Seminar on Electrical Contacts

Proc Annu Ind Air Pollut Control Conf — Proceedings. Annual Industrial Air Pollution Control Conference

Proc Annu Ind Fabr Assoc Int Conv — Proceedings. Annual Industrial Fabrics Association International Convention

Proc Annu Ind Pollut Conf — Proceedings. Annual Industrial Pollution Conference

Proc Annu Instrum Conf — Proceedings. Annual Instrumentation Conference

Proc Annu Instrum Soc Am Chem Pet Ind Div Symp — Proceedings. Annual Instrument Society of America Chemical and Petroleum Industries Division Symposium

Proc Annu Int ACM SIGIR Conf Res Dev Inf Retr — Proceedings of the Annual International ACM SIGIR Conference on Research and Development in Information Retrieval

Proc Annu Int Conf Can Nucl Assoc — Proceedings. Annual International Conference. Canadian Nuclear Association

Proc Annu Int Conf Coal Gasif Liquefaction Convers Electr — Proceedings. Annual International Conference on Coal Gasification, Liquefaction, and Conversion to Electricity

Proc Annu Int Conf Fault Tolerant Comput — Proceedings. Annual International Conference on Fault-Tolerant Computing

Proc Annu Int Conf High Energy Phys — Proceedings. Annual International Conference on High Energy Physics

Proc Annu Int Conf Plasma Chem Technol — Proceedings. Annual International Conference of Plasma Chemistry and Technology

Proc Annu Int Conf Pollut Control Mar Ind — Proceedings. Annual International Conference on Pollution Control in the MarineIndustries

Proc Annu Int Game Fish Res Conf — Proceedings. Annual International Game Fish Research Conference

Proc Annu ISA Anal Div Symp — Proceedings. Annual ISA Analysis Division Symposium

Proc Annu ISA Anal Instrum Symp — Proceedings. Annual ISA Analysis Instrumentation Symposium

Proc Annu Leucocyte Cult Conf — Proceedings. Annual Leucocyte Culture Conference

Proc Annu Lightwood Res Conf — Proceedings. Annual Lightwood Research Conference

Proc Annu Loss Prev Symp — Proceedings of the Annual Loss Prevention Symposium

Proc Annu Madison Waste Conf — Proceedings of the Annual Madison Waste Conference

Proc Annu Maine Biomed Symp — Proceedings. Annual Maine Biomedical Symposium

Proc Annu Manage Conf Am Dent Assoc — Proceedings. Annual Management Conference. American Dental Association

Proc Annu Mar Coat Conf — Proceedings. Annual Marine Coatings Conference

Proc Annu Meat Sci Inst — Proceedings. Annual Meat Science Institute

Proc Annu Meet Adhes Soc — Proceedings of the Annual Meeting of the Adhesion Society

Proc Annu Meet AFMA Nutr Counc — Proceedings. Annual Meeting. AFMA Nutrition Council

Proc Annu Meet Agric Pestic Soc — Proceedings. Annual Meeting. Agricultural Pesticide Society

Proc Annu Meet Agric Res Inst — Proceedings. Annual Meeting. Agricultural Research Institute

Proc Annu Meet Air Pollut Control Assoc — Proceedings. Annual Meeting. Air Pollution Control Association

Proc Annu Meet Air Waste Manage Assoc — Proceedings. Annual Meeting. Air and Waste Management Association

Proc Annu Meet Am Assoc Feed Microsc — Proceedings. Annual Meeting. American Association of Feed Microscopists

Proc Annu Meet Am Assoc Study Goiter — Proceedings. Annual Meeting. American Association for the Study of Goiter

Proc Annu Meet Am Assoc Swine Pract — Proceedings. Annual Meeting. American Association of Swine Practitioners

Proc Annu Meet Am Assoc Vet Lab Diagn — Proceedings. Annual Meeting. American Association of Veterinary Laboratory Diagnosticians

Proc Annu Meet Am Coll Nutr — Proceedings. Annual Meeting. American College of Nutrition

Proc Annu Meet Am Coll Psychiatr — Proceedings. Annual Meeting. American College of Psychiatrists

Proc Annu Meet Amer Soc Hort Sci Caribbean Reg — Proceedings. Annual Meeting. American Society for Horticultural Science. Caribbean Region

Proc Annu Meet Am Pet Inst — Proceedings. Annual Meeting. American Petroleum Institute

Proc Annu Meet Am Psychopathol Assoc — Proceedings. Annual Meeting. American Psychopathological Association

Proc Annu Meet Am Sect Int Sol Energy Soc — Proceedings. Annual Meeting. American Section. International Solar Energy Society

Proc Annu Meet Am Soc Anim Sci West Sect — Proceedings. Annual Meeting. American Society of Animal Science. Western Section

Proc Annu Meet Am Soc Bak Eng — Proceedings. Annual Meeting. American Society of Bakery Engineers

Proc Annu Meet Am Soc Bakery Eng — Proceedings. Annual Meeting. American Society of Bakery Engineers

Proc Annu Meet Am Soc Brew Chem — Proceedings. Annual Meeting. American Society of Brewing Chemists

Proc Annu Meet Am Soc Hortic Sci Trop Reg — Proceedings. Annual Meeting. American Society for Horticulture Science. Tropical Region

Proc Annu Meet Am Soc Inf Sci — Proceedings. Annual Meeting. American Society for Information Science

Proc Annu Meet Am Soc Zool — Proceedings. Annual Meetings. American Society of Zoologists

Proc Annu Meet Am Sol Energy Soc Inc — Proceedings. Annual Meeting. American Solar Energy Society, Inc.

Proc Annu Meet Am Soybean Assoc — Proceedings. Annual Meeting. American Soybean Association

Proc Annu Meet Am Vet Med Assoc — Proceedings. Annual Meeting. American Veterinary Medical Association

Proc Annu Meet Am Wood Preserv Assoc — Proceedings. Annual Meeting. American Wood-Preservers' Association

Proc Annu Meet Arkansas State Hortic Soc — Proceedings. Annual Meeting. Arkansas State Horticultural Society

Proc Annu Meet Biochem (Hung) — Proceedings. Annual Meeting of Biochemistry (Hungary)

Proc Annu Meet Can Grains Counc — Proceedings. Annual Meeting. Canada Grains Council

Proc Annu Meet Can Miner Process — Proceedings. Annual Meeting. Canadian Mineral Processors

Proc Annu Meet Can Nucl Assoc — Proceedings. Annual Meeting. Canadian Nuclear Association

Proc Annu Meet Can Soc Agron — Proceedings. Annual Meeting. Canadian Society of Agronomy

Proc Annu Meet Can Soc Biomech — Proceedings. Annual Meeting. Canadian Society for Biomechanics

Proc Annu Meet Chem Spec Manuf Assoc — Proceedings. Annual Meeting. Chemical Specialties Manufacturers Association

Proc Annu Meet Compressed Gas Assoc — Proceedings. Annual Meeting. Compressed Gas Association

Proc Annu Meet Conn Pomol Soc — Proceedings. Annual Meeting. Connecticut Pomological Society

Proc Annu Meet Contin Educ Lect — Proceedings. Annual Meeting and Continuing Education Lectures

Proc Annu Meet Conv Natl Microfilm Assoc — Proceedings. Annual Meeting and Convention. National Microfilm Association

Proc Annu Meet East Psychiatr Res Assoc — Proceedings. Annual Meeting. Eastern Psychiatric Research Association

Proc Annu Meet Electron Beam Symp — Proceedings. Annual Meeting. Electron Beam Symposium

Proc Annu Meet Electron Microsc Soc Am — Proceedings. Annual Meeting. Electron Microscopy Society of America

Proc Annu Meet Eur Acad Allergol Clin Immunol — Proceedings. Annual Meeting. European Academy of Allergology and Clinical Immunology

Proc Annu Meet Fert Ind Round Table — Proceedings. Annual Meeting. Fertilizer Industry Round Table

Proc Annu Meet Fla State Hortic Soc — Proceedings. Annual Meeting. Florida State Horticultural Society

Proc Annu Meet Hawaii Sugar Plant Assoc — Proceedings. Annual Meeting. Hawaiian Sugar Planters Association

Proc Annu Meet Hawaii Sugar Technol — Proceedings. Annual Meeting. Hawaiian Sugar Technologists

Proc Annu Meet Ind Hyg Found Am — Proceedings. Annual Meeting. Industrial Hygiene Foundation of America

Proc Annu Meet Inf Counc Fabr Flammability — Proceedings. Annual Meeting. Information Council on Fabric Flammability

Proc Annu Meeting Amer Soc Int Law — Proceedings. Annual Meeting. American Society of International Law

Proc Annu Meet Inst Environ Sci — Proceedings. Annual Meeting. Institute of Environmental Sciences

Proc Annu Meet Inst Navig — Proceedings of the Annual Meeting. Institute of Navigation

Proc Annu Meet Inst Nucl Mater Manage — Proceedings. Annual Meeting. Institute of Nuclear Materials Management

Proc Annu Meet Int Comm Glass — Proceedings. Annual Meeting. International Commission on Glass

Proc Annu Meet Int Inst Synth Rubber Prod — Proceedings. Annual Meeting. International Institute of Synthetic Rubber Producers

Proc Annu Meet Int Magnesium Assoc — Proceedings. Annual Meeting. International Magnesium Association

Proc Annu Meet Int Soc Pet Ind Biol — Proceedings. Annual Meeting. International Society of Petroleum Industry Biologists

Proc Annu Meet Int Water Conf — Proceedings. Annual Meeting. International Water Conference

Proc Annu Meet Jpn Assoc Anaerobic Infect Res — Proceedings. Annual Meeting. Japanese Association for Anaerobic Infection Research

Proc Annu Meet Jpn Endocrinol Soc — Proceedings. Annual Meeting. Japan Endocrinological Society

Proc Annu Meet Jpn Neurochem Soc — Proceedings. Annual Meeting. Japanese Neurochemical Society

Proc Annu Meet Jpn Soc Med Mycol — Proceedings. Annual Meeting. Japanese Society for Medical Mycology

Proc Annu Meet Lightwood Res Conf — Proceedings. Annual Meeting. Lightwood Research Conference

Proc Annu Meet Lightwood Res Coord Counc — Proceedings. Annual Meeting. Lightwood Research Coordinating Council

Proc Annu Meet Mass Fruit Grow Assoc — Proceedings. Annual Meeting. Massachusetts Fruit Growers' Association

Proc Annu Meet Med Sect Am Counc Life Insur — Proceedings. Annual Meeting. Medical Section. American Council of Life Insurance

Proc Annu Meet Med Sect Am Life Conv — Proceedings. Annual Meeting. Medical Section. American Life Convention

Proc Annu Meet Med Sect Am Life Insur Assoc — Proceedings. Annual Meeting. Medical Section. American Life Insurance Association

Proc Annu Meet Met Powder Assoc — Proceedings. Annual Meeting. Metal Powder Association

Proc Annu Meet Microsc Soc Can — Proceedings. Annual Meeting. Microscopical Society of Canada

Proc Annu Meet Minn Sect AIME — Proceedings. Annual Meeting. Minnesota Section. AIME

Proc Annu Meet Miss River Res Consortium — Proceedings. Annual Meeting. Mississippi River Research Consortium

Proc Annu Meet Nat Assoc Corros Eng — Proceedings. Annual Meeting. National Association of Corrosion Engineers

Proc Annu Meet Nat Ass Wheat Growers — Proceedings. Annual Meeting. National Association of Wheat Growers

Proc Annu Meet Natl Acad Clin Biochem — Proceedings. Annual Meeting. National Academy of Clinical Biochemistry

Proc Annu Meet Natl Counc Radiat Prot Meas — Proceedings. Annual Meeting. National Council on Radiation Protection and Measurements

Proc Annu Meet Natl Jt Comm Fert Appl — Proceedings. Annual Meeting. National Joint Committee on Fertilizer Application

Proc Annu Meet Nat Res Counc Agr Res Inst — Proceedings. Annual Meeting. National Research Council. Agricultural Research Institute

Proc Annu Meet N Cent Weed Contr Conf — Proceedings. Annual Meeting. North Central Weed Control Conference

Proc Annu Meet NJ — Proceedings. Annual Meeting. New Jersey Mosquito Extermination Association

Proc Annu Meet NJ Mosq Control Assoc — Proceedings. Annual Meeting. New Jersey Mosquito Control Association

Proc Annu Meet NJ Mosq Exterm Assoc — Proceedings. Annual Meeting. New Jersey Mosquito Extermination Association

Proc Annu Meet North Cent States Weed Conf — Proceedings. Annual Meeting. North Central States Weed Conference

Proc Annu Meet North Cent Weed Control Conf — Proceedings. Annual Meeting. North Central Weed Control Conference

Proc Annu Meet Northeast Weed Sci Soc — Proceedings. Annual Meeting. Northeastern Weed Science Society

Proc Annu Meet NY State Hort Soc — Proceedings. Annual Meeting. New York State Horticultural Society

Proc Annu Meet Ohio State Hortic Soc — Proceedings. Annual Meeting. Ohio State Horticultural Society

Proc Annu Meet Pac Coast Fertil Soc — Proceedings. Annual Meeting. Pacific Coast Fertility Society

Proc Annu Meet Plant Growth Regul Soc Am — Proceedings. Annual Meeting. Plant Growth Regulator Society of America

Proc Annu Meet Soc Chim Phys — Proceedings. Annual Meeting. Societe de Chimie Physique

Proc Annu Meet Soc Eng Sci — Proceedings. Annual Meeting. Society of Engineering Science

Proc Annu Meet Soc Promot Agric Sci — Proceedings. Annual Meeting. Society for the Promotion of Agricultural Science

Proc Annu Meet Soil Conserv Soc Am — Proceedings. Annual Meeting. Soil Conservation Society of America

Proc Annu Meet South Weed Conf — Proceedings. Annual Meeting. Southern Weed Conference

Proc Annu Meet South Weed Sci Soc — Proceedings. Annual Meeting. Southern Weed Science Society

Proc Annu Meet Southwest Pet Short Course — Proceedings. Annual Meeting. Southwestern Petroleum Short Course

Proc Annu Meet Upper Atmos Stud Opt Methods — Proceedings. Annual Meeting on Upper Atmosphere Studies by Optical Methods

Proc Annu Meet US Anim Health Assoc — Proceedings. Annual Meeting. United States Animal Health Association

Proc Annu Meet Utah Mosq Abatement Assoc — Proceedings. Annual Meeting. Utah Mosquito Abatement Association

Proc Annu Meet West Div Am Dairy Sci Assoc — Proceedings. Annual Meeting. Western Division. American Dairy Science Association

Proc Annu Meet West Sect Am Soc Anim Sci — Proceedings. Annual Meeting. Western Section. American Society of Animal Science

Proc Annu Meet West Soc Fr Hist — Proceedings. Annual Meeting. Western Society for French History

Proc Annu Meet W Farm Econ Ass — Proceedings. Annual Meeting. Western Farm Economics Association

Proc Annu Meet World Maric Soc — Proceedings. Annual Meeting. World Mariculture Society

Proc Annu Mid-Am Spectrosc Symp — Proceedings. Annual Mid-America Spectroscopy Symposium

Proc Annu Midwest Fert Conf — Proceedings. Annual Midwest Fertilizer Conference

Proc Annu Min Metall Group Symp Exhib — Proceedings. Annual Mining and Metallurgy Group Symposium and Exhibit

Proc Annu Miss Water Resour Conf — Proceedings. Annual Mississippi Water Resources Conference

Proc Annu Nat Dairy Eng Conf — Proceedings. Annual National Dairy Engineering Conference

Proc Annu Nat Dairy Food Eng Conf — Proceedings. Annual National Dairy and Food Engineering Conference

Proc Annu Natl Dairy Eng Conf — Proceedings. Annual National Dairy Engineering Conference

Proc Annu North Am Power Symp — Proceedings of the Annual North American Power Symposium

Proc Annu Northeast Reg Antipollut Conf — Proceedings. Annual Northeastern Regional Antipollution Conference

Proc Annu Northwest Wood Prod Clin — Proceedings. Annual Northwest Wood Products Clinic

Proc Annu NSF RANN Trace Contam Conf — Proceedings. Annual NSF-RANN Trace Contaminants Conference

Proc Annu NSF Trace Contam Conf — Proceedings. Annual NSF [*National Science Foundation*] Trace Contaminants Conference

Proc Annu NY State Health Dep Birth Defects Symp — Proceedings. Annual New York State Health Department Birth Defects Symposium

Proc Annu Offshore Technol Conf — Proceedings. Annual Offshore Technology Conference

Proc Annu OHOLO Biol Conf — Proceedings. Annual OHOLO Biological Conference

Proc Annu Pac Northwest Ind Waste Conf — Proceedings. Annual Pacific Northwest Industrial Waste Conference

Proc Annu Pfizer Res Conf — Proceedings. Annual Pfizer Research Conference

Proc Annu Pittsburgh Conf Model Simul — Proceedings. Annual Pittsburgh Conference on Modeling and Simulation

Proc Annu Plant Biochem Physiol Symp — Proceedings. Annual Plant Biochemistry and Physiology Symposium

Proc Annu Power Sources Conf — Proceedings. Annual Power Sources Conference

Proc Annu Program Rev Workshop Va Tech Cent Adhes Sci — Proceedings. Annual Program Review/Workshop. Virginia Tech Center for Adhesion Science

Proc Annu Public Works Congr — Proceedings. Annual Public Works Congress

Proc Annu Pulp Paper Conf — Proceedings. Annual Pulp and Paper Conference

Proc Annu Purdue Air Qual Conf — Proceedings. Annual Purdue Air Quality Conference

Proc Annu Recipro Meat Conf Am Meat Sci Assoc — Proceedings. Annual Reciprocal Meat Conference. American Meat Science Association

Proc Annu Reliab Maintainability Symp — Proceedings. Annual Reliability and Maintainability Symposium

Proc Annu Reliab Maintain Symp — Proceedings. Annual Reliability and Maintainability Symposium

Proc Annu Res Conf Pfizer Agric Res Dev Dep — Proceedings. Annual Research Conference. Pfizer Agricultural Research and Development Department

Proc Annu Rochester Conf High Energy Nucl Phys — Proceedings. Annual Rochester Conference on High Energy Nuclear Physics

Proc Annu Rocky Mount Bioeng Symp — Proceedings. Annual Rocky Mountain Bioengineering Symposium

Proc Annu Rocky Mt Bioeng Symp — Proceedings. Annual Rocky Mountain Bioengineering Symposium

Proc Annu San Franc Cancer Symp — Proceedings. Annual San Francisco Cancer Symposium

Proc Annu Sanit Water Resour Eng Conf — Proceedings. Annual Sanitary and Water Resources Engineering Conference

Proc Annu Sausage Processed Meats Short Course — Proceedings. Annual Sausage and Processed Meats Short Course

Proc Annu Scanning Electron Microsc Symp — Proceedings. Annual Scanning Electron Microscope Symposium

Proc Annu Sci Conf East Afr Med Res Counc — Proceedings. Annual Scientific Conference. East African Medical Research Council

Proc Annu Sci Meet Comm Probl Drug Depend US Nat Res Counc — Proceedings. Annual Scientific Meeting. Committee on Problems of Drug Dependence. United States National Research Council

Proc Annu Senior Staff Conf USARS — Proceedings. Annual Senior Staff Conference. United States Agricultural Research Service

Proc Annu Sess Ceylon Assoc Adv Sci — Proceedings. Annual Session. Ceylon Association for the Advancement of Science

Proc Annu Sess Sri Lanka Assoc Adv Sci — Proceedings. Annual Session. Sri Lanka Association for the Advancement of Science

Proc Annu Southeast Symp Syst Theory — Proceedings of the Annual Southeastern Symposium on System Theory

Proc Annu Southwest Pet Short Course — Proceedings. Annual Southwestern Petroleum Short Course

Proc Annu State Coll Wash Inst Dairy — Proceedings. Annual State College of Washington Institute of Dairying

Proc Annu Stud Conf — Proceedings. Annual Student Conference

Proc Annu Symp Am Coll Cardiol — Proceedings. Annual Symposium. American College of Cardiology

Proc Annu Symp Bot — Proceedings. Annual Symposium in Botany

Proc Annu Symp Comput Appl Med Care — Proceedings. Annual Symposium on Computer Applications in Medical Care

Proc Annu Symp East Afr Acad — Proceedings. Annual Symposium. East African Academy

Proc Annu Symp East Pa Branch Am Soc Microbiol — Proceedings. Annual Symposium. Eastern Pennsylvania Branch. American Society for Microbiology

Proc Annu Symp Energy Res Dev — Proceedings. Annual Symposium Energy Research and Development

Proc Annu Symp Eng Geol Soils Eng — Proceedings. Annual Symposium on Engineering Geology and Soils Engineering

Proc Annu Symp Environ Pollut — Proceedings. Annual Symposium on Environmental Pollution

Proc Annu Symp Eugen Soc — Proceedings. Annual Symposium of the Eugenics Society

Proc Annu Symp Explos Blasting Res — Proceedings of the Annual Symposium on Explosives and Blasting Research

Proc Annu Symp Freq Control — Proceedings. Annual Symposium on Frequency Control

Proc Annu Symp Gynecol Endocrinol — Proceedings. Annual Symposium on Gynecologic Endocrinology

Proc Annu Symp Incremental Motion Control Syst Devices — Proceedings. Annual Symposium. Incremental Motion Control Systems and Devices

Proc Annu Symp Ind Waste Control — Proceedings. Annual Symposium on Industrial Waste Control

Proc Annu Symp Instrum Process Ind — Proceedings. Annual Symposium on Instrumentation for the Process Industries

Proc Annu Symp Physiol Pathol Hum Reprod — Proceedings. Annual Symposium on the Physiology and Pathology of Human Reproduction

Proc Annu Symp Reduct Costs Hand Oper Glass Plants — Proceedings. Annual Symposium on Reduction of Costs in Hand-Operated Glass Plants

Proc Annu Symp Reprod Med — Proceedings. Annual Symposium on Reproductive Medicine

Proc Annu Symp Sci Basis Med — Proceedings. Annual Symposium on the Scientific Basis of Medicine

Proc Annu Symp Spectrosc — Proceedings. Annual Symposium on Spectroscopy

Proc Annu Symp Trace Anal Detect Environ — Proceedings. Annual Symposium Trace Analysis and Detection in the Environment

Proc Annu Tall Timbers Fire Ecol Conf — Proceedings. Annual Tall Timbers Fire Ecology Conference

Proc Annu Tech Conf Soc Vac Coaters — Proceedings. Annual Technical Conference. Society of Vacuum Coaters

Proc Annu Tech Conf SPI Reinf Plast Div — Proceedings. Annual Technical Conference. SPI Reinforced Plastics Division

Proc Annu Tech Manage Conf Soc Plast Ind Reinf Plast Div — Proceedings. Annual Technical and Management Conference. Society of the Plastics Industry. Reinforced Plastics Division

Proc Annu Tech Meet Exhib Am Assoc Contam Control — Proceedings. Annual Technical Meeting and Exhibit. American Association for Contamination Control

Proc Annu Tech Meet Inst Environ Sci — Proceedings. Annual Technical Meeting. Institute of Environmental Sciences

Proc Annu Tech Meet Int Metallogr Soc Inc — Proceedings. Annual Technical Meeting. International Metallographic Society, Inc.

Proc Annu Tech Meet Tech Assoc Graphic Arts — Proceedings. Annual Technical Meeting. Technical Association. Graphic Arts

Proc Annu Tech Semin Chem Spills — Proceedings. Annual Technical Seminar on Chemical Spills

Proc Annu Tex Conf Util At Energy — Proceedings. Annual Texas Conference on the Utilization of Atomic Energy

Proc Annu Tex Nutr Conf — Proceedings. Annual Texas Nutrition Conference

Proc Annu Tokyo Inst Psychiatry Int Symp — Proceedings of the Annual Tokyo Institute of Psychiatry International Symposium

Proc Annu Tri Serv Microwave Conf Biol Eff Microwave Radiat — Proceedings. Annual Tri-Service Microwave Conference on the Biological Effects of Microwave Radiation

Proc Annu Trop Subtrop Fish Technol Conf — Proceedings. Annual Tropical and Subtropical Fisheries Technological Conference

Proc Annu Trop Subtrop Fish Technol Conf Am — Proceedings. Annual Tropical and Subtropical Fisheries Technological Conferenceof the Americas

Proc Annu Tung Ind Conv — Proceedings. Annual Tung Industry Convention

Proc Annu UMR DNR Conf Energy — Proceedings. Annual UMR-DNR Conference on Energy

Proc Annu UMR-MEC Conf Energy — Proceedings. Annual UMR-MEC [*University of Missouri at Rolla Missouri Energy Council*] Conference on Energy

Proc Annu Underground Coal Convers Symp — Proceedings. Annual Underground Coal Conversion Symposium

Proc Annu Underground Coal Gasif Symp — Proceedings. Annual Underground Coal Gasification Symposium

Proc Annu Wash State Univ Inst Dairy — Proceedings. Annual Washington State University Institute of Dairying

Proc Annu Water Conf Eng Soc West Pa — Proceedings. Annual Water Conference. Engineers' Society of Western Pennsylvania

Proc Annu Water Works Sch Univ Kans — Proceedings. Annual Water Works School at the University of Kansas

Proc Annu West Tex Oil Lifting Short Course — Proceedings. Annual West Texas Oil Lifting Short Course

Proc Annu West Weed Control Conf — Proceedings. Annual Western Weed Control Conference

Proc Annu Workshop Pestic Residue Anal West Can — Proceedings. Annual Workshop on Pesticide Residue Analysis. Western Canada

Proc Annu Workshop World Maricult Soc — Proceedings. Annual Workshop. World Mariculture Society

Proc Annu World Conf Magnesium — Proceedings. Annual World Conference on Magnesium

Proc Annu WWEMA Ind Pollut Conf — Proceedings. Annual WWEMA [*Water and Wastewater Equipment Manufacturers Association*] Industrial Pollution Conference

Proc Anthropol Soc Bombay — Proceedings. Anthropological Society of Bombay

Proc APCA Annu Meet — Proceedings. APCA [*Air Pollution Control Association*] Annual Meeting

Proc Appl Bacteriol — Proceedings of Applied Bacteriology

Proc Appl Supercond Conf — Proceedings. Applied Superconductivity Conference

Proc APREA — Proceedings. APREA

Proc APRES (Am Peanut Res Educ Soc) — Proceedings. APRES (American Peanut Research and Education Society)

Proc Arab Annu Vet Congr — Proceedings. Arab Annual Veterinary Congress

Proc Arab Reg Conf Sulphur Its Usages Arab World — Proceedings. Arab Regional Conference on Sulphur and Its Usages in the Arab World

Proc A Razmadze Math Inst — Proceedings of A. Razmadze Mathematical Institute. Georgian Academy of Sciences

Proc Argenteuil Symp — Proceedings. Argenteuil Symposium

Proc Aris Soc — Proceedings. Aristotelian Society

Proc Aristotelian Soc — Proceedings of the Aristotelian Society

Proc Ark Acad Sci — Proceedings. Arkansas Academy of Science

Proc Arkansas Acad Sci — Proceedings. Arkansas Academy of Science

Proc Arkansas Nutr Conf — Proceedings. Arkansas Nutrition Conference

Proc Arkansas Water Works Pollut Control Conf Short Sch — Proceedings. Arkansas Water Works and Pollution Control Conference and Short School

Proc Army Mater Technol Conf — Proceedings. Army Materials Technology Conference

Proc Arnold O Beckman Conf Clin Chem — Proceedings. Arnold O. Beckman Conference in Clinical Chemistry

Proc Artif Reef Conf — Proceedings. Artificial Reef Conference

Proc ASA — Proceedings ASA

Proc ASA Symp Soybean Process — Proceedings. A.S.A. Symposium on Soybean Processing

Proc Asean Soil Conf — Proceedings. Asean Soil Conference

Proc ASHRAE Semiannu Meet — Proceedings. ASHRAE [*American Society of Heating, Refrigerating, and Air-Conditioning Engineers*] Semiannual Meeting

Proc Asian Congr Fluid Mech — Proceedings. Asian Congress of Fluid Mechanics

Proc Asian Congr Obstet Gynaecol — Proceedings. Asian Congress of Obstetrics and Gynaecology

Proc Asian Pac Congr Antisepsis — Proceedings. Asian/Pacific Congress on Antisepsis

Proc Asian-Pac Congr Cardiol — Proceedings. Asian-Pacific Congress of Cardiology

Proc Asian Pac Weed Sci Soc Conf — Proceedings. Asian-Pacific Weed Science Society Conference

Proc Asian Symp Med Plants Spices — Proceedings. Asian Symposium on Medicinal Plants and Spices

Proc Asian Symp Res React — Proceedings. Asian Symposium on Research Reactor

Proc Asia Pac Phys Conf — Proceedings. Asia-Pacific Physics Conference

Proc Asia Pac Symp Environ Occup Toxicol — Proceedings. Asia-Pacific Symposium on Environmental and Occupational Toxicology

Proc Asiat Soc (Bengal) — Proceedings. Asiatic Society (Bengal)

Proc ASIS Annu Meet — Proceedings. ASIS [*American Society for Information Science*] Annual Meeting

Proc ASME JSME Therm Eng Jt Conf — Proceedings. ASME-JSME Thermal Engineering Joint Conference

Proc ASM Heat Treat Surf Eng Conf Eur — Proceedings. ASM Heat Treatment and Surface Engineering Conference in Europe

Proc Aso Symp — Proceedings. Aso Symposium

Proc Ass Asphalt Paving Technol — Proceedings. Association of Asphalt Paving Technologists

Proc Ass Econ Biol — Proceedings. Association of Economic Biologists

Proc Assoc Adv Automot Med — Proceedings. Association for the Advancement of Automotive Medicine

Proc Assoc Am Physicians — Proceedings. Association of American Physicians

Proc Assoc Asphalt Paving Technol — Proceedings. Association of Asphalt Paving Technologists

Proc Assoc Asphalt Paving Technol Tech Sess — Proceedings. Association of Asphalt Paving Technologists. Technical Sessions

Proc Assoc Clin Biochem — Proceedings. Association of Clinical Biochemists

Proc Assoc Comm Agric South States — Proceedings. Association of the Commissioners of Agriculture of the Southern States

Proc Assoc Econ Biol Coimbatore — Proceedings. Association of Economic Biologists. Coimbatore

Proc Assoc Military Surgeons US — Proceedings. Association of Military Surgeons of the US

Proc Assoc Off Seed Anal — Proceedings. Association of Official Seed Analysts

Proc Assoc Off Seed Anal (North Am) — Proceedings. Association of Official Seed Analysts (North America)

Proc Assoc Plant Prot Kyushu — Proceedings. Association for Plant Protection of Kyushu

Proc Assoc Plant Prot Shikoku — Proceedings. Association for Plant Protection of Shikoku

Proc Assoc South Agric Work — Proceedings. Association of Southern Agricultural Workers

Proc Assoc Sugar Technol — Proceedings. Association of Sugar Technologists

Proc Ass Offic Seed Anal — Proceedings. Association of Official Seed Analysts

Proc Ass Plant Prot Hokuriku — Proceedings. Association of Plant Protection of Hokuriku

Proc Ass Plant Prot Kyushu — Proceedings. Association for Plant Protection of Kyushu

Proc Ass Res Nerv Ment Dis — Proceedings. Association for Research in Nervous and Mental Diseases

Proc Ass S Agr Workers — Proceedings. Association of Southern Agricultural Workers

Proc Ass Sth Agric Wkrs — Proceedings. Association of Southern Agricultural Workers

Proc ASTM — Proceedings. American Society for Testing and Materials

Proc Astron Soc Aust — Proceedings. Astronomical Society of Australia

Proc Astr Soc Aust — Proceedings. Astronomical Society of Australia

Proc Atl Workshop — Proceedings. Atlantic Workshop

Proc Aust Ass Clin Biochem — Proceedings. Australian Association of Clinical Biochemists

Proc Aust Assoc Neurol — Proceedings. Australian Association of Neurologists

Proc Aust Biochem Soc — Proceedings. Australian Biochemical Society

Proc Aust Bldg Res Congr — Australian Building Research Congress. Proceedings

Proc Aust Build Res Congr — Australian Building Research Congress. Proceedings

Proc AUSTCERAM — Proceedings. AUSTCERAM

Proc Aust Ceram Conf — Australian Ceramic Conference. Proceedings

Proc Aust Ceramic Conf — Australian Ceramic Conference. Proceedings

Proc Aust Clay Miner Conf — Australian Clay Minerals Conference. Proceedings

Proc Aust Coal Prep Conf — Proceedings. Australian Coal Preparation Conference

Proc Aust Comput Conf — Proceedings. Australian Computer Conference

Proc Aust Conf Electrochem — Proceedings. Australian Conference on Electrochemistry

Proc Aust Conf Nucl Tech Anal — Australian Conference on Nuclear Techniques of Analysis. Proceedings

Proc Aust Grasslds Conf — Proceedings. Australian Grasslands Conference

Proc Aust Inst Min and Metall — Australasian Institute of Mining and Metallurgy. Proceedings

Proc Aust Inst Min Eng — Proceedings. Australian Institute of Mining Engineers

Proc Aust Inst Min Metall — Proceedings. Australasian Institute of Mining and Metallurgy

Proc Aust Physiol Pharmacol Soc — Proceedings. Australian Physiological and Pharmacological Society

Proc Aust Polym Symp — Proceedings. Australian Polymer Symposium

Proc Aust Pulp Pap Ind Tech Assoc — Proceedings. Australian Pulp and Paper Industry Technical Association

Proc Australas Conf Grassland Invertebr Ecol — Proceedings. Australasian Conference on Grassland Invertebrate Ecology

Proc Australas Conf Radiat Biol — Proceedings. Australasian Conference on Radiation Biology

Proc Australas Conf Radiobiol — Proceedings. Australasian Conference on Radiobiology

Proc Australas Corros Assoc Conf — Proceedings. Australasian Corrosion Association Conference

Proc Australasian Poultry Sci Conv — Proceedings. Australasian Poultry Science Convention

Proc Australas Inst Min and Metall — Australasian Institute of Mining and Metallurgy. Proceedings

Proc Australas Inst Min Eng — Proceedings. Australasian Institute of Mining Engineers

Proc Australas Inst Min Metall — Proceedings. Australasian Institute of Mining and Metallurgy

Proc Australas Poult Stock Feed Conv — Proceedings. Australasian Poultry and Stock Feed Convention

Proc Austrian Ital Yugosl Chem Eng Conf — Proceedings. Austrian-Italian-Yugoslav Chemical Engineering Conference

Proc Aust Road Res Bd — Australian Road Research Board. Proceedings

Proc Aust Road Research Board — Australian Road Research Board. Proceedings

Proc Aust Soc Anim Prod — Proceedings. Australian Society of Animal Production

Proc Aust Soc Med Res — Proceedings. Australian Society for Medical Research

Proc Aust Soc Sugar Cane Technol — Proceedings. Australian Society of Sugar Cane Technologists

Proc Aust Thermodyn Conf — Proceedings. Australian Thermodynamics Conference

Proc Aust Weed Conf — Proceedings. Australian Weed Conference

Proc Auto Div Instn Mech Engrs — Proceedings. Institution of Mechanical Engineers. Auto Division

Proc Automob Div Inst Mech Eng — Proceedings. Automobile Division. Institution of Mechanical Engineers

Proc Automot Corros Prev Conf — Proceedings. Automotive Corrosion Prevention Conference

Proc Aviat Mater Res Inst Moscow — Proceedings. Aviation Materials Research Institute. Moscow

Proc AWMA Annu Meet — Proceedings. A and WMA Annual Meeting
Proc AWWA Annu Conf — Proceedings. AWWA [*American Water Works Association*] Annual Conference
Proc AWWA Water Qual Technol Conf — Proceedings. AWWA [*American Water Works Association*] Water Quality Technology Conference
Proc Bakish Mater Corp Publ — Proceedings. Bakish Materials Corporation Publication
Proc Balaton Symp Part Phys — Proceedings. Balaton Symposium on Particle Physics
Proc Balt Symp Mar Biol — Proceedings. Baltic Symposium on Marine Biology
Proc Banff Summer Inst Part Fields — Proceedings. Banff Summer Institute on Particles and Fields
Proc Bangkok Symp Acid Sulphate Soils Int Symp — Proceedings. Bangkok Symposium on Acid Sulphate Soils. International Symposium on Acid Sulphate Soils
Proc Bath Nat Hist Field Club — Proceedings. Bath Natural History and Antiquarian Field Club
Proc Bauxite Symp — Proceedings of Bauxite Symposium
Proc BC Water Waste Sch — Proceedings. British Columbia Water and Waste School
Proc Beijing Int Symp Pyrotech Explos — Proceedings of the Beijing International Symposium on Pyrotechnics and Explosives
Proc Belfast Nat Hist Philos Soc — Proceedings. Belfast Natural History and Philosophical Society
Proc Belg Congr Anesthesiol — Proceedings. Belgian Congress of Anesthesiology
Proc Beltwide Cotton Prod Conf — Proceedings. Beltwide Cotton Production Conference
Proc Beltwide Cotton Prod Res Conf — Proceedings. Beltwide Cotton Production Research Conferences
Proc Berkeley Int Mater Conf — Proceedings. Berkeley International Materials Conference
Proc Berkeley Symp Math Stat Probab — Proceedings. Berkeley Symposium on Mathematical Statistics and Probability
Proc Bewickwhire Nat Club — Proceedings. Berwickshire Naturalists Club
Proc Biannu Int Estuarine Res Conf — Proceedings. Biannual International Estuarine Research Conference
Proc Biannu Natl Nucl Instrum Symp — Proceedings. Biannual National Nuclear Instrumentation Symposium
Proc Bienn Conf Ground Water — Proceedings. Biennial Conference on Ground Water
Proc Bienn Conf Inst Briquet Agglom — Proceedings. Biennial Conference. Institute for Briquetting and Agglomeration
Proc Bienn Conf Int Briquet Assoc — Proceedings. Biennial Conference. International Briqueting Association
Proc Bienn Cornell Electr Eng Conf — Proceedings. Biennial Cornell Electrical Engineering Conference
Proc Bienn Gas Dyn Symp — Proceedings. Biennial Gas Dynamics Symposium
Proc Bienn Gas Dyn Symp Aerothermochem — Proceedings. Biennial Gas Dynamics Symposium on Aerothermochemistry
Proc Bienn Int Estuarine Res Conf — Proceedings. Biennial International Estuarine Research Conference
Proc Bienn Low Rank Fuels Symp — Proceedings. Biennial Low-Rank Fuels Symposium
Proc Bienn Plains Aquat Res Conf — Proceedings. Biennial Plains Aquatic Research Conference
Proc Bienn Symp Cryog Instrum — Proceedings. Biennial Symposium on Cryogenic Instrumentation
Proc Bienn Symp Turbul Liq — Proceedings. Biennial Symposium on Turbulence in Liquids
Proc Bienn Univ Gov Ind Microelectron Symp — Proceedings. Biennial University/Government/Industry Microelectronics Symposium
Proc Bienn Waste Process Conf — Proceedings of the Biennial Waste Processing Conference
Proc Bienn West Conf Anesthesiol — Proceedings. Biennial Western Conference on Anesthesiology
Proc Bihar Acad Agric Sci — Proceedings. Bihar Academy of Agricultural Sciences
Proc Bihar Acad Agr Sci — Proceedings. Bihar Academy of Agricultural Sciences
Proc Bioenergy R & D Semin — Proceedings. Bioenergy R & D Seminar
Proc Bioeng Conf — Proceedings of the Bioengineering Conference
Proc Biol Soc Wash — Proceedings. Biological Society of Washington
Proc Biomass Thermochem Convers Contract Meet — Proceedings. Biomass Thermochemical Conversion Contractor's Meeting
Proc Bipolar BiCMOS Circuits Technol Meet — Proceedings of the Bipolar/BiCMOS Circuits and Technology Meeting
Proc Bipolar Circuits Technol Meet — Proceedings. Bipolar Circuits and Technology Meeting
Proc Bird Control Semin — Proceedings. Bird Control Seminar
Proc Birmingham Nat Hist Soc — Proceedings. Birmingham Natural History and Microscopical Society
Proc Bolton Landing Conf — Proceedings. Bolton Landing Conference
Proc Bos Soc — Proceedings. Bostonian Society
Proc Bot Soc Br Isles — Proceedings. Botanical Society of the British Isles
Proc Bot Soc London — Proceedings. Botanical Society of London
Proc Br Acad — Proceedings. British Academy
Proc Br Acoust Soc — Proceedings. British Acoustical Society
Proc Brasov Int Sch — Proceedings. Brasov International School
Proc Br Assoc Refrig — Proceedings. British Association for Refrigeration
Proc Braz Symp Chem Lignins Other Wood Compon — Proceedings. Brazilian Symposium on the Chemistry of Lignins and Other Wood Components
Proc Br Ceram Soc — Proceedings. British Ceramic Society
Proc Br Crop Prot Conf — Proceedings. 1980 British Crop Protection Conference. Weeds
Proc Br Crop Prot Conf Pests Dis — Proceedings. British Crop Protection Conference. Pests and Diseases

Proc Br Crop Prot Conf Weeds — Proceedings. British Crop Protection Conference. Weeds
Proc Brighton Crop Prot Conf Pests Dis — Proceedings. Brighton Crop Protection Conference. Pests and Diseases
Proc Br Insectic Fungic Conf — Proceedings. British Insecticide and Fungicide Conference
Proc Bristol Nat Soc — Proceedings. Bristol Naturalists Society
Proc Brit Ac — Proceedings. British Academy
Proc Brit Acad — Proceedings. British Academy
Proc Brit Ceram Soc — Proceedings. British Ceramic Society
Proc Brit Insectic Fungic Conf — Proceedings. British Insecticide and Fungicide Conference
Proc British Asso Ja Stud — Proceedings. British Association for Japanese Studies
Proc Brit Weed Contr Conf — Proceedings. British Weed Control Conference
Proc Br Lithium Congr — Proceedings. British Lithium Congress
Proc Br Nucl Energy Soc Eur Conf — Proceedings. British Nuclear Energy Society European Conference
Proc Brown Boveri Symp Nonemissive Electroopt Disp — Proceedings. Brown Boveri Symposium on Nonemissive Electrooptic Displays
Proc Brown Univ Symp Biol Skin — Proceedings. Brown University Symposium on the Biology of Skin
Proc Br Paedod Soc — Proceedings. British Paedodontic Society
Proc Br Pest Control Conf — Proceedings. British Pest Control Conference
Proc Br Soc Anim Prod — Proceedings. British Society of Animal Production
Proc Br Sulphur Corp Int Conf Fert — Proceedings. British Sulphur Corporation's International Conference on Fertilizers
Proc Br Sulphur Corp Int Conf Fert Technol — Proceedings. British Sulphur Corporation's International Conference on Fertilizer Technology
Proc Br Weed Control Conf — Proceedings. British Weed Control Conference
Proc Br West Indies Sugar Technol Conf — Proceedings. British West Indies Sugar Technologists Conference
Proc Buffalo Milan Symp Mol Pharmacol — Proceedings. Buffalo-Milan Symposium on Molecular Pharmacology
Proc Buhl Int Conf Mater — Proceedings. Buhl International Conference on Materials
Proc Cairo Solid State Conf — Proceedings. Cairo Solid State Conference
Proc Calif Acad Nat Sci — Proceedings. California Academy of Natural Sciences
Proc Calif Acad Sci — Proceedings. California Academy of Sciences
Proc Calif Ann Weed Conf — Proceedings. California Annual Weed Conference
Proc Calif Conf Fire Toxic — Proceedings. California Conference on Fire Toxicity
Proc Calif Conf Prod Flammability — Proceedings. California Conference on Product Flammability
Proc Calif Conf Rubber Toughened Plast — Proceedings. California Conference on Rubber-Toughened Plastics
Proc Calif Weed Conf — Proceedings. California Weed Conference
Proc Calif Zool Club — Proceedings. California Zoological Club
Proc Camb Philos Soc — Proceedings. Cambridge Philosophical Society
Proc Camb Phil Soc Math Phys Sci — Proceedings. Cambridge Philosophical Society. Mathematical and Physical Sciences
Proc Cambr — Proceedings. Cambridge Antiquarian Society
Proc Cambridge Antiq Soc — Proceedings. Cambridge Antiquarian Society
Proc Cambridge Antiqua Soc — Proceedings of the Cambridge Antiquarian Society
Proc Cambridge Ant Soc — Proceedings. Cambridge Antiquarian Society
Proc Cambridge Philos Soc — Proceedings. Cambridge Philosophical Society
Proc Cambridge Phil Soc — Proceedings. Cambridge Philological Society
Proc Cambr Phil Soc — Proceedings. Cambridge Philological Society
Proc Canad Oto Soc — Proceedings. Canadian Otolaryngological Society
Proc Canad Phytopathol Soc — Proceedings. Canadian Phytopathological Society
Proc Can Assoc Lab Anim Sci — Proceedings. Canadian Association for Laboratory Animal Science
Proc Can Cancer Res Conf — Proceedings. Canadian Cancer Research Conference
Proc Can Centen Wheat Symp — Proceedings. Canadian Centennial Wheat Symposium
Proc Can Conf Nondestr Test — Proceedings. Canadian Conference on Nondestructive Testing
Proc Can Conf Res Rheum Dis — Proceedings. Canadian Conference on Research in the Rheumatic Diseases
Proc Can Fed Biol Soc — Proceedings. Canadian Federation of Biological Societies
Proc Can Inst — Proceedings. Canadian Institute
Proc Can Natl Power Alcohol Conf — Proceedings. Canadian National Power Alcohol Conference
Proc Can Nat Weed Comm E Sect — Proceedings. Canadian National Weed Committee. Eastern Section
Proc Can Nat Weed Comm W Sect — Proceedings. Canadian National Weed Committee. Western Section
Proc Can Nucl Assoc Annu Int Conf — Proceedings. Canadian Nuclear Association Annual International Conference
Proc Can Phytopathol Soc — Proceedings. Canadian Phytopathological Society
Proc Can Rock Mech Symp — Proceedings. Canadian Rock Mechanics Symposium
Proc Can Soc Forensic Sci — Proceedings. Canadian Society of Forensic Science
Proc Can Soc Pl Physiol — Proceedings. Canadian Society of Plant Physiologists
Proc Can Symp Nonwovens Disposables — Proceedings. Canadian Symposium on Nonwovens and Disposables
Proc Can Symp Water Pollut Res — Proceedings. Canadian Symposium on Water Pollution Research
Proc Can Wood Chem Symp — Proceedings. Canadian Wood Chemistry Symposium
Proc Cardiff Med Soc — Proceedings. Cardiff Medical Society
Proc Caribb Reg Am Soc Hort Sci — Proceedings. Caribbean Region. American Society for Horticultural Science

Proc CAS CERN Accel Sch Adv Accel Phys Course — Proceedings. CAS-CERN Accelerator School. Advanced Accelerator Physics Course

Proc Cath — Proceedings. Catholic Theological Society of America

Proc Cath Phil Ass — Proceedings. American Catholic Philosophical Association

Proc C C Furnas Meml Conf — Proceedings. C. C. Furnas Memorial Conference

Proc Cellul Conf — Proceedings. Cellulose Conference

Proc Cell Wall Meet — Proceedings. Cell Wall Meeting

Proc Centre Math Anal Austral Nat Univ — Proceedings of the Centre for Mathematical Analysis. Australian National University

Proc Cent Stefano Franscini — Proceedings. Centro Stefano Franscini

Proc CERN Accel Sch Adv Accel Phys Course — Proceedings. CERN Accelerator School Advanced Accelerator Physics Course

Proc CERN Accel Sch Gen Accel Phys Course — Proceedings. CERN Accelerator School General Accelerator Physics Course

Proc CERN Sch Comput — Proceedings. CERN School of Computing

Proc Ceylon Branch Asiat Soc — Proceedings. Ceylon Branch. Royal Asiatic Society

Proc Chem Conf — Proceedings. Chemists' Conference

Proc Chem Eng Group Soc Chem Ind London — Proceedings. Chemical Engineering Group. Society of Chemical Industry. London

Proc Chem Soc — Proceedings. Chemical Society

Proc Chem Soc (London) — Proceedings. Chemical Society (London)

Proc Chem Symp India — Proceedings. Chemistry Symposium (India)

Proc Chester Soc Nat Sci — Proceedings. Chester Society of Natural Science, Literature, and Art

Proc Chin Acad Med Sci Peking Union Med Coll — Proceedings. Chinese Academy of Medical Sciences and the Peking Union Medical College

Proc Chin Physiol Soc Chengtu Branch — Proceedings. Chinese Physiological Society. Chengtu Branch

Proc Chromates Symp — Proceedings. Chromates Symposium

Proc C Indian Acad Sci — Proceedings C. Indian Academy of Sciences

Proc Clean Air Conf — Proceedings. Clean Air Conference

Proc Cleveland Inst Eng — Proceedings. Cleveland Institution of Engineers

Proc Cleveland Symp Macromol — Proceedings. Cleveland Symposium on Macromolecules

Proc Clin Dial Transplant Forum — Proceedings. Clinical Dialysis and Transplant Forum

Proc Clin Res Cent Symp — Proceedings. Clinical Research Centre Symposium

Proc Coal Briquet Conf — Proceedings. Coal Briquetting Conference

Proc Coal Mining Inst Amer — Proceedings. Coal Mining Institute of America

Proc Coal Test Conf — Proceedings. Coal Testing Conference

Proc Coastal Eng Conf — Proceedings of the Coastal Engineering Conference

Proc College Park Colloq Chem Evol — Proceedings. College Park Colloquium on Chemical Evolution

Proc Coll Med Univ Philipp — Proceedings. College of Medicine. University of the Philippines

Proc Coll Nat Sci Sect 2 Seoul Nat Univ — Proceedings. College of Natural Sciences. Section 2. Physics, Astronomy. Seoul National University

Proc Coll Nat Sci Sect 3 Seoul Nat Univ — Proceedings. College of Natural Sciences. Section 3. Chemistry. Seoul National University

Proc Coll Nat Sci Sect 4 Biol Sci Seoul Natl Univ — Proceedings. College of Natural Sciences. Section 4. Biological Sciences. SeoulNational University

Proc Coll Nat Sci Sect 4 Life Sci Seoul Natl Univ — Proceedings. College of Natural Sciences. Section 4. Life Sciences. Seoul National University

Proc Coll Nat Sci Sect 4 Seoul Nat Univ — Proceedings. College of Natural Sciences. Section 4. Life Sciences. Seoul National University

Proc Coll Nat Sci Sect 5 Seoul Nat Univ — Proceedings. College of Natural Sciences. Section 5. Geology, Meteorology, and Oceanography. Seoul National University

Proc Coll Nat Sci (Seoul) — Proceedings. College of Natural Sciences (Seoul)

Proc Coll Nat Sci Seoul Natl Univ — Proceedings. College of Natural Sciences. Seoul National University

Proc Colloq AMPERE — Proceedings. Colloque AMPERE (Atomes et Molecules par des Etudes Radio Electriques)

Proc Colloq Int Potash Inst — Proceedings. Colloquium of the International Potash Institute

Proc Colloq Johnson Res Found Univ Pa — Proceedings. Colloquium. Johnson Research Foundation. University of Pennsylvania

Proc Colloq Spectrosc Int — Proceedings. Colloquium Spectroscopicum Internationale

Proc Colloq Thin Films — Proceedings. Colloquium on Thin Films

Proc Coll Radiol Aust — Proceedings. College of Radiologists of Australia

Proc Colorado Sci Soc — Proceedings. Colorado Scientific Society

Proc Colo Sci Sco — Proceedings. Colorado Scientific Society

Proc Columbia River Basalt Symp — Proceedings. Columbia River Basalt Symposium

Proc Comm Int Tech Sucr — Proceedings. Commission International Technique de Sucrerie

Proc Commonw Min Metall Congr — Proceedings. Commonwealth Mining and Metallurgical Congress

Proc Conf Accel Targets Des Prod Neutrons — Proceedings. Conference on Accelerator Targets Designed for the Production of Neutrons

Proc Conf Appl Crystallogr — Proceedings. Conference on Applied Crystallography

Proc Conf Appl Phys Chem — Proceedings. Conference on Applied Physical Chemistry

Proc Conf Appl Phys Sci Food Res Process Preserv — Proceedings. Conference on the Application of Physical Sciences to Food Research, Processing, and Preservation

Proc Conf Appl Small Accel — Proceedings. Conference on Application of Small Accelerators

Proc Conf Artif Intell Appl — Proceedings of the Conference on Artificial Intelligence Applications

Proc Conf Aust Road Res Board — Proceedings. Conference of the Australian Road Research Board

Proc Conf Aust Soc Sugar Cane Technol — Australian Society of Sugar Cane Technologists. Proceedings of the Conference

Proc Conf Carbon — Proceedings. Conferences on Carbon

Proc Conf Catal Org Synth — Proceedings. Conference on Catalysis in Organic Syntheses

Proc Conf Charles Univ Med Fac — Proceedings. Conference of Charles University Medical Faculty

Proc Conf Chem Vap Deposition Int Conf — Proceedings. Conference on Chemical Vapor Deposition. International Conference

Proc Conf Clim Impact Assess Program — Proceedings. Conference on the Climatic Impact Assessment Program

Proc Conf Colloid Chem Mem Ervin Wolfram — Proceedings. Conference on Colloid Chemistry in Memoriam Ervin Wolfram

Proc Conf Coord Chem — Proceedings. Conference on Coordination Chemistry

Proc Conf Cutaneous Toxic — Proceedings. Conference on Cutaneous Toxicity

Proc Conf Des Exp Army Res Dev Test — Proceedings. Conference on the Design of Experiments in Army Research Development and Testing

Proc Conf Dimens Strength Calc — Proceedings. Conference on Dimensioning and Strength Calculations

Proc Conf Distill Feed Res Counc — Proceedings. Conference. Distillers Feed Research Council

Proc Conf Electron Beam Melting Refin State Of The Art — Proceedings. Conference on Electron Beam Melting and Refining. State of the Art

Proc Conf Eng Med Biol — Proceedings. Conference of Engineering in Medicine and Biology

Proc Conf Environ Toxicol — Proceedings. Conference on Environmental Toxicology

Proc Conf Eur Dial Transplant Assoc — Proceedings. Conference. European Dialysis and Transplant Association

Proc Conf Exploding Wire Phenom — Proceedings. Conference on the Exploding Wire Phenomenon

Proc Conf Explos Blast Tech — Proceedings of the Conference on Explosives and Blasting Technique

Proc Conf Exp Med Surg Primates — Proceedings. Conference of Experimental Medicine and Surgery in Primates

Proc Conf Feeds Beverage Distill — Proceedings. Conference on Feeds of the Beverage Distilleries

Proc Conf Fluid Mach — Proceedings. Conference on Fluid Machinery

Proc Conf Front Chem — Proceedings. Conference on Frontiers of Chemistry

Proc Conf Fruit Growers Domin Canada — Proceedings. Conference of Fruit Growers. Dominion of Canada

Proc Conf Ger Biochem Soc — Proceedings. Conference. German Biochemical Society

Proc Conf Ger Soc Biol Chem — Proceedings. Conference. German Society of Biological Chemistry

Proc Conf Glass Probl — Proceedings. Conference on Glass Problems

Proc Conf Great Lakes Res — Proceedings. Conference on Great Lakes Research

Proc Conf Hot Lab Equip — Proceedings. Conference on Hot Laboratories and Equipment

Proc Conf Ind Energy Conserv Technol — Proceedings. Conference on Industrial Energy Conservation Technology

Proc Conf Ind Waste Pac Northwest — Proceedings. Conference on Industrial Waste. Pacific Northwest

Proc Conf Inst Inf Sci — Proceedings. Conference. Institute of Information Scientists

Proc Conf Int Coal Test Conf — Proceedings. Conference. International Coal Testing Conference

Proc Conf Int Organ Citrus Virol — Proceedings. Conference. International Organization of Citrus Virologists

Proc Conf (Int) Solid State Devices — Proceedings. Conference (International) on Solid State Devices

Proc Conf Ion Plat Allied Tech — Proceedings. Conference. Ion Plating and Allied Techniques

Proc Conf Mater Eng — Proceedings. Conference on Materials Engineering

Proc Conf Microcirc Physiol Pathol — Proceedings. Conference on Microcirculatory Physiology and Pathology

Proc Conf Min Coking Coal — Proceedings. Conference on the Mining and Coking of Coal

Proc Conf Nat Gas Res Technol — Proceedings. Conference on Natural Gas Research and Technology

Proc Conf Natl Assoc Corros Eng — Proceedings. Conference. National Association of Corrosion Engineers

Proc Conf Neutron Cross Sect Technol — Proceedings. Conference on Neutron Cross Sections and Technology

Proc Conf Nucl Processes Geol Settings — Proceedings. Conference on Nuclear Processes in Geologic Settings

Proc Conf NZ Grassl Assoc — Proceedings. Conference. New Zealand Grassland Association

Proc Conf Opt Fiber Sens Based Smart Mater Struct — Proceedings. Conference on Optical Fiber Sensor-Based Smart Materials and Structures

Proc Conf Phys — Proceedings. Conference in Physics

Proc Conf Radiocarbon Dating Accel — Proceedings. Conference on Radiocarbon Dating with Accelerators

Proc Conf Radioisot — Proceedings. Conference on Radioisotopes

Proc Conf Rare Earth Res — Proceedings. Conference on Rare Earth Research

Proc Conf React Complex Nucl — Proceedings. Conference on Reactions between Complex Nuclei

Proc Conf Recent Adv Adapt Sens Mater Their Appl — Proceedings. Conference on Recent Advances in Adaptive and Sensory Materials and Their Applications

Proc Conf Reinf Plast Compos Div Soc Plast Ind — Proceedings. Conference. Reinforced Plastics/Composites Division. Society of the Plastics Industry

Proc Conf Remote Syst Technol — Proceedings. Conference on Remote Systems Technology

Proc Conf Rob Remote Syst — Proceedings of the Conference on Robotics and Remote Systems

Proc Conf Silic Ind — Proceedings. Conference on the Silicate Industry

Proc Conf Soc Plast Ind Can — Proceedings. Conference. Society of the Plastics Industry of Canada

Proc Conf Solid State Devices — Proceedings. Conference on Solid State Devices

Proc Conf Toxicol — Proceedings. Conference on Toxicology

Proc Conf Vac Microbalance Tech — Proceedings. Conference on Vacuum Microbalance Techniques

Proc Conf Workshop Embryonic Fetal Antigens Cancer — Proceedings. Conference and Workshop on Embryonic and Fetal Antigens in Cancer

Proc Congenital Anomalies Res Assoc Annu Rep — Proceedings. Congenital Anomalies. Research Association. Annual Report

Proc Cong Mediterr Phytopathol Union — Proceedings. Congress of the Mediterranean Phytopathological Union

Proc Congr Ampere — Proceedings. Congress Ampere

Proc Congr Ann Corp Ingen For (Quebec) — Proceedings. Congres Annuel. Corporation des Ingenieurs Forestiers (Quebec)

Proc Congr Asian Pac Soc Hematol — Proceedings. Congress. Asian and Pacific Society of Hematology

Proc Congr Counc Min Metall Inst — Proceedings. Congress. Council of Mining and Metallurgical Institutions

Proc Congr Eur Brew Conv — Proceedings. Congress. European Brewery Convention

Proc Congr Eur Dial Transplant Assoc — Proceedings. Congress. European Dialysis and Transplant Association

Proc Congr Eur Organ Res Fluorine Dent Caries Prev — Proceedings. Congress. European Organization for Research on Fluorine and Dental Caries Prevention

Proc Congr Eur Soc Comp Physiol Biochem — Proceedings. Congress. European Society for Comparative Physiology and Biochemistry

Proc Congr Eur Soc Haematol — Proceedings. Congress of the European Society of Haematology

Proc Congr Eur Soc Parenter Enteral Nutr — Proceedings. Congress. European Society of Parenteral and Enteral Nutrition

Proc Congr Fed Asian Oceanian Biochem — Proceedings. Congress. Federation of Asian and Oceanian Biochemists

Proc Congr Fed Int Precontrainte — Proceedings. Congress of the Federation Internationale de la Precontrainte

Proc Congr Grassl Soc South Afr — Proceedings. Congress. Grassland Society of Southern Africa

Proc Congr Hung Assoc Microbiol — Proceedings. Congress of the Hungarian Association of Microbiologists

Proc Congr Hung Pharmacol Soc — Proceedings. Congress. Hungarian Pharmacological Society

Proc Congr Hung Soc Endocrinol Metab — Proceedings. Congress. Hungarian Society of Endocrinology and Metabolism

Proc Congr Int Assoc Sci Study Ment Defic — Proceedings. Congress of the International Association for the Scientific Study of Mental Deficiency

Proc Congr Int Comm Opt — Proceedings. Congress of the International Commission for Optics

Proc Congr Int Fed Soc Cosmet Chem — Proceedings. Congress. International Federation of Societies of Cosmetic Chemists

Proc Congr Int Potash Inst — Proceedings. Congress of the International Potash Institute

Proc Congr Int Radiat Prot Soc — Proceedings. Congress. International Radiation Protection Society

Proc Congr Int Soc Blood Transf — Proceedings. Congress of the International Society of Blood Transfusion

Proc Congr Int Soc Blood Transfus — Proceedings. Congress of the International Society of Blood Transfusion

Proc Congr Int Soc Hematol — Proceedings. Congress. International Society of Hematology

Proc Congr Int Soc Rock Mech — Proceedings. Congress. International Society for Rock Mechanics

Proc Congr Int Soc Study Hypertens Pregnancy — Proceedings. Congress. International Society for the Study of Hypertension in Pregnancy

Proc Congr Int Soc Sugar Cane Technol — Proceedings. Congress of the International Society of Sugar Cane Technologists

Proc Congr Int Union For Res Organ — Proceedings. Congress of the International Union of Forest Research Organizations

Proc Congr Jpn Epilepsy Soc — Proceedings of the Congress of the Japan Epilepsy Society

Proc Congr Jpn Soc Cancer Ther — Proceedings. Congress of the Japan Society for Cancer Therapy

Proc Congr Leather Ind — Proceedings. Congress on the Leather Industry

Proc Congr Mediterr Phytopathol Union — Proceedings. Congress. Mediterranean Phytopathological Union

Proc Congr Nac Quim — Proceedings. Congreso Nacional de Quimica

Proc Congr Nord Soc Cell Biol — Proceedings. Congress. Nordic Society for Cell Biology

Proc Congr Obes — Proceedings. Congress of Obesity

Proc Congr Obstet Gynaecol — Proceedings. Congress of Obstetrics and Gynaecology

Proc Congr Pharm Sci — Proceedings. Congress of Pharmaceutical Sciences

Proc Congr S Afr Genet Soc — Proceedings. Congress of the South African Genetic Society

Proc Congr S Afr Sug Technol Ass — Proceedings. Congress of the South African Sugar Technologists' Association

Proc Congr Scand Neurol — Proceedings. Congress of Scandinavian Neurologists

Proc Conn Pomol Soc — Proceedings. Connecticut Pomological Society

Proc Conv Inst Brew Aust NZ Sect — Proceedings. Convention. Institute of Brewing. Australia and New Zealand Section

Proc Conv Int Assoc Fish Wildl Agencies — Proceedings. Convention. International Association of Fish and Wildlife Agencies

Proc Copper Cobre Int Symp — Proceedings. Copper-Cobre International Symposium

Proc Cornell Agric Waste Manage Conf — Proceedings. Cornell Agricultural Waste Management Conference

Proc Cornell Nutr Conf Feed Manuf — Proceedings. Cornell Nutrition Conference for Feed Manufacturers

Proc Cornell Nutr Conf Feed Mfr — Proceedings. Cornell Nutrition Conference for Feed Manufacturers

Proc Corros Prev — Proceedings. Corrosion and Prevention

Proc Cosmic-Ray Res Lab Nagoya Univ — Proceedings. Cosmic-Ray Research Laboratory. Nagoya University

Proc Cotteswold Natur Fld Club — Proceedings. Cotteswold Naturalists' Field Club

Proc Cotton Dust Res Conf Beltwide Cotton Prod Res Conf — Proceedings. Cotton Dust Research Conference. Beltwide Cotton Production Research Conferences

Proc Cotton Res Congr — Proceedings. Cotton Research Congress

Proc Cotton States Assoc Comm Agric — Proceedings. Cotton States Association of Commissioners of Agriculture

Proc Counc Econ AIME — Proceedings. Council of Economics. American Institute of Mining, Metallurgical, and Petroleum Engineers

Proc Course Dev Neurobiol — Proceedings. Course on Developmental Neurobiology

Proc Course Int Sch Intermed Energy Nucl Phys — Proceedings. Course. International School of Intermediate Energy Nuclear Physics

Proc Coventry Dist Natur Hist Sci Soc — Proceedings. Coventry District Natural History and Scientific Society

Proc Crayford Manor Houoo Hict Archaeol Soc — Proceedings. Crayford Manor House Historical and Archaeological Society

Proc Crop Sci Chugoku Br Crop Sci Soc — Proceedings. Crop Science. Chugoku Branch of the Crop Science Society

Proc Crop Sci Soc Jap — Proceedings. Crop Science Society of Japan

Proc Crop Sci Soc Japan — Proceedings. Crop Science Society of Japan / Nihon Sakumotsu Gakkai Kiji

Proc Crop Sci Soc Jpn — Proceedings. Crop Science Society of Japan

Proc Croydon Nat Hist Sci Soc — Proceedings. Croydon Natural History Science Society

Proc Cryog Eng Conf — Proceedings. Cryogenic Engineering Conference

ProcCTS — Proceedings. College Theology Society

ProcCTSA — Proceedings. Catholic Theological Society of America

Proc Cumberland Geol Soc — Proceedings. Cumberland Geological Society

Proc Custom Integr Circuits Conf — Proceedings of the Custom Integrated Circuits Conference

Proc Cybern Sci Symp — Proceedings. Cybernetic Sciences Symposium

PROCD — Processing

Proc Davenport Acad Nat Sci — Proceedings. Davenport Academy of Natural Sciences

Proc Dep Hortic Plant Health Massey Univ — Proceedings. Department of Horticulture and Plant Health. Massey University

Proc Des Autom Conf — Proceedings. Design Automation Conference

Proc Dev Immunol Workshop — Proceedings. Developmental Immunology Workshop

Proc Devon Archaeol Explor Soc — Proceedings of the Devon Archaeological Exploration Society

Proc Devon Archaeol Soc — Proceedings. Devon Archaeological Society

Proc Devon Arch Expl Soc — Proceedings. Devon Archaeological Exploration Society

Proc Devon Arch Soc — Proceedings. Devon Archaeological Society

Proc Diagn Ther Cardiovasc Interventions — Proceedings of Diagnostic and Therapeutic Cardiovascular Interventions

Proc Discuss Int Plast Congr — Proceedings and Discussions. International Plastics Congress

Proc Distill Feed Conf — Proceedings. Distillers Feed Conference

Proc Distill Feed Res Counc Conf — Proceedings. Distillers Feed Research Council Conference

Proc Div Conf Eur Phys Soc Nucl Phys Div — Proceedings. Divisional Conference. European Physical Society. Nuclear Physics Division

Proc Divers' Gas Purity Symp — Proceedings. Divers' Gas Purity Symposium

Proc Div Refin Am Pet Inst — Proceedings. Division of Refining. American Petroleum Institute

Proc DOE NRC Nucl Air Clean Conf — Proceedings. DOE/NRC Nuclear Air Cleaning Conference

Proc DOE Nucl Airborne Wast Manage Air Clean Conf — Proceedings. DOE (Department of Energy) Nuclear Airborne Waste Management and Air cleaning Conference (US)

Proc DOE Nucl Air Clean Conf — Proceedings. DOE (Department of Energy) Nuclear Air Cleaning Conference (US)

Proc Dorset Nat Hist Archaeol Soc — Proceedings. Dorset Natural History and Archaeological Society

Proc Dorset Natur Hist Archaeol Soc — Proceedings. Dorset Natural History and Archaeological Society

Proc Dorset Natur Hist Arch Soc — Proceedings. Dorset Natural History and Archaeological Society

Proc Dorset Soc — Dorset Natural History and Archaeological Society. Proceedings

Proc Dtsch Dtsch Symp Umweltforsch DDR — Proceedings. Deutsch-Deutsches Symposium Umweltforschung in der DDR

Proc Dudley Midl Geol Soc — Proceedings. Dudley and Midland Geological and Scientific Society and Field Club

Proc East Afr Acad — Proceedings. East African Academy

Proc East Afr Weed Control Conf — Proceedings. East African Weed Control Conference

Proc East Afr Weed Sci Conf — Proceedings. East African Weed Science Conference

Proc Easter Sch Agric Sci Univ Nottingham — Proceedings. Easter School in Agricultural Science. University of Nottingham

Proc East Theor Phys Conf — Proceedings. Eastern Theoretical Physics Conference

Proc Ecol Soc Aust — Proceedings. Ecological Society of Australia

Procedes Conf Int Rech Cacaoyeres — Procedes. Conference Internationale sur les Recherches Cacaoyeres

Procedimiento Conf Int Pesqui Cacao — Procedimiento. Conferencia Internacional de Pesquisas en Cacao

Proc Edinburgh Math Soc — Proceedings. Edinburgh Mathematical Society

Proc Edinburgh Math Soc 2 — Proceedings. Edinburgh Mathematical Society. Series 2

Proc Edinburgh Math Soc Edinburgh Math Notes — Proceedings. Edinburgh Mathematical Society. Edinburgh Mathematical Notes

Proceedings NAPEHE — Proceedings. National Association for Physical Education in Higher Education

Proceedings NIRSA — Proceedings. National Intramural Recreational Sports Association

Proceedings of the IEEE — Proceedings. Institute of Electrical and Electronics Engineers

Proceedings SBA — Proceedings. Society of Biblical Archaeology

Proceedngs — Proceedings. United States Naval Institute

Proceed of the Brit Acad — Proceedings. British Academy

Proceed R Philos Soc of Glasgow — Proceedings. Royal Philosophical Society of Glasgow

Proceeds Scotl — Proceedings. Society of Antiquaries of Scotland

Proc EGAS Conf Eur Group At Spectrosc — Proceedings. EGAS Conference. European Group for Atomic Spectroscopy

Proc Egypt Acad Sci — Proceedings. Egyptian Academy of Sciences

Proc Eighth Br Weed Control Conf — Proceedings. Eighth British Weed Control Conference

Proc Einstein Found Internat — Proceedings of Einstein Foundation International

Proc Elctr Electron Insul Conf — Proceedings. Electrical/Electronics Insulation Conference

Proc Electr Furn Conf — Proceedings. Electric Furnace Conference

Proc Electr Ironmelting Conf — Proceedings. Electric Ironmelting Conference

Proc Electrochem Soc — Proceedings. The Electrochemical Society

Proc Electron Beam Symp — Proceedings. Electron Beam Symposium

Proc Electron Compon Conf — Proceedings. Electronic Components Conference

Proc Electron Components Conf — Proceedings. Electronic Components Conference

Proc Electron Compon Symp — Proceedings. Electronic Components Symposium

Proc Electron Compon Technol Conf — Proceedings. Electronic Components and Technology Conference

Proc Electron Microsc Soc Am — Proceedings. Electron Microscopy Society of America

Proc Electron Microsc Soc South Afr — Proceedings. Electron Microscopy Society of Southern Africa

Proc Emp Min Metall Congr — Proceedings. Empire Mining and Metallurgical Congress

Proc Endocr Soc Aust — Proceedings. Endocrine Society of Australia

Proc Endoc Soc Aust — Proceedings. Endocrine Society of Australia

Proc Energy Resour Conf — Proceedings. Energy Resource Conference

Proc Energy Symp — Proceedings. Energy Symposium

Proc Energy Technol Conf — Proceedings. Energy Technology Conference

Proc Eng Found Conf — Proceedings. Engineering Foundation Conference

Proc Eng Found Conf Fundam Adsorpt — Proceedings. Engineering Foundation Conference on Fundamentals of Adsorption

Proc Engl Int Conf Clean Steel — Proceedings in English. International Conference on Clean Steel

Proc Eng Mech — Proceedings of Engineering Mechanics

Proc Eng Soc Hong Kong — Proceedings. Engineering Society of Hong Kong

Proc Eng Soc West PA — Proceedings. Engineers' Society of Western Pennsylvania

Proc Entomol Soc Amer N Cent Br — Proceedings. Entomological Society of America. North Central Branch

Proc Entomol Soc BC — Proceedings. Entomological Society of British Columbia

Proc Entomol Soc Brit Columbia — Proceedings. Entomological Society of British Columbia

Proc Entomol Soc Manit — Proceedings. Entomological Society of Manitoba

Proc Entomol Soc Manitoba — Proceedings. Entomological Society of Manitoba

Proc Entomol Soc Ont — Proceedings. Entomological Society of Ontario

Proc Entomol Soc Ontario — Proceedings. Entomological Society of Ontario

Proc Entomol Soc Wash — Proceedings. Entomological Society of Washington

Proc Entomol Soc Wash DC — Proceedings. Entomological Society of Washington, DC

Proc Ent Soc Br Columb — Proceedings. Entomological Society of British Columbia

Proc Ent Soc Manitoba — Proceedings. Entomological Society of Manitoba

Proc Ent Soc Ont — Proceedings. Entomological Society of Ontario

Proc Ent Soc Wash — Proceedings. Entomological Society of Washington

Proc Environ Eng Sci Conf — Proceedings. Environmental Engineering and Science Conference

Proc Environ Prot Conf — Proceedings. Environmental Protection Conference

Proc Environ Symp — Proceedings. Environmental Symposium

Proc ERDA Air Clean Conf — Proceedings. ERDA [*Office of Exploratory Research and Problem Assessment*]Air Cleaning Conference

Pro CERN Sch Comput — Proceedings. CERN [*Conseil Europeen pour la Recherche Nucleaire*] School of Computing

Process Adv Mater — Processing of Advanced Materials

Process Archit — Process. Architecture

Process Archre — Process Architecture

Process Autom — Process Automation

Process Bio — Process Biochemistry

Process Biochem — Process Biochemistry

Process Biochem Barking UK — Process Biochemistry (Barking, UK)

Process Biochem Int — Process Biochemistry International

Process Chem Eng — Process and Chemical Engineering

Process Control Autom — Process Control and Automation

Process Control Eng PACE — Process and Control Engineering PACE

Process Control Qual — Process Control and Quality

Process Des Dev — Process Design and Development

Process Econ Int — Process Economics International

Processed Ser Okla Agric Exp Stn — Processed Series. Oklahoma. Agricultural Experiment Station

Process Eng — Process Engineering

Process Eng (Coburg Fed Repub Ger) — Process Engineering (Coburg, Federal Republic of Germany)

Process Eng Mag — Process Engineering Magazine

Process Engng — Process Engineering

Process Eng Plant and Control — Process Engineering. Plant and Control

Process Engravers Mon — Process Engravers Monthly

Proc Essex Inst — Proceedings. Essex Institute

Process Fabr Adv Mater High Temp Appl Proc Symp — Processing and Fabrication of Advanced Materials for High Temperature Applications. Proceedings. Symposium

Process Fruits Sci Technol — Processing Fruits. Science and Technology

Process Ind Can — Process Industries Canada

Process Ind Can Mag — Process Industries Canada Magazine

Process Instrum — Process Instrumentation

Process Metall — Process Metallurgy

Process Saf Environ Prot — Process Safety and Environmental Protection

Process Saf Environ Prot Trans Inst Chem Eng Part B — Process Safety and Environmental Protection. Transactions of the Institution of Chemical Engineers. Part B

Process Saf Prog — Process Safety Progress

Process Ser Okla State Univ Agr Exp Sta — Processed Series. Oklahoma State University. Agricultural Experimental Station

Process St — Process Studies

Process Stud — Process Studies

Process Technol Conf — Process Technology Conference

Process Technol Conf Proc — Process Technology Conference Proceedings

Process Technol Int — Process Technology International

Process Technol Proc — Process Technology Proceedings

Process Util High Sulfur Coals Proc Int Conf — Processing and Utilization of High-Sulfur Coals. Proceedings. International Conference

Proc Est Acad Sci Biol — Proceedings. Estonian Academy of Sciences. Biology

Proc Est Acad Sci Biol — Proceedings of the Estonian Academy of Sciences. Biology

Proc Est Acad Sci Biol Ecol — Proceedings of the Estonian Academy of Sciences, Biology, Ecology

Proc Est Acad Sci Chem — Proceedings of the Estonian Academy of Sciences. Chemistry

Proc Est Acad Sci Eng — Proceedings of the Estonian Academy of Sciences. Engineering

Proc Est Acad Sci Phys Math — Proceedings. Estonian Academy of Sciences. Physics, Mathematics

Proces Technol — Proces Technologie

Proc Estonian Acad Sci Phys Math — Proceedings. Estonian Academy of Sciences. Physics. Mathematics

Proces Verbaux & Mem Acad Sci B Lett & A Besancon & Franche C — Proces-Verbaux et Memoires. Academie des Sciences, Belles-Lettres, et Arts de Besancon et de Franche-Comte

Proces Verbaux Mem Acad Sci Besancon — Proces Verbaux et Memoires de l'Academie des Sciences, Belles-Lettres, et Arts.Besancon

Proces-Verb Seances Soc Sci Phys Nat Bordeaux — Proces-Verbaux des Seances. Societe des Sciences Physiques et Naturelles de Bordeaux

Proc Ethylene Prod Conf — Proceedings. Ethylene Producers Conference

Proc Eur Biophys Cong — Proceedings. European Biophysics Congress

Proc Eur Brew Conv — Proceedings. European Brewing Convention

Proc Eur Conf Chem Vap Deposition — Proceedings. European Conference on Chemical Vapor Deposition

Proc Eur Conf Comput Phys — Proceedings. European Conference on Computational Physics

Proc Eur Conf Controlled Fusion Plasma Phys — Proceedings. European Conference on Controlled Fusion and Plasma Physics

Proc Eur Conf Food Chem — Proceedings. European Conference on Food Chemistry

Proc Eur Conf Mixing — Proceedings. European Conference on Mixing

Proc Eur Conf Part Phys — Proceedings. European Conference on Particle Physics

Proc Eur Conf Prenatal Diagn Genet Disord — Proceedings. European Conference on Prenatal Diagnosis of Genetic Disorders

Proc Eur Conf Surf Sci — Proceedings. European Conference on Surface Science

Proc Eur Congr Allergol Clin Immunol — Proceedings. European Congress of Allergology and Clinical Immunology

Proc Eur Congr Biopharm Pharmacokinet — Proceedings. European Congress of Biopharmaceutics and Pharmacokinetics

Proc Eur Congr Biotechnol — Proceedings. European Congress on Biotechnology

Proc Eur Congr Perinat Med — Proceedings. European Congress of Perinatal Medicine

Proc Eur Dial Transplant Assoc — Proceedings. European Dialysis and Transplant Association

Proc Eur Dial Transplant Assoc Eur Renal Assoc — Proceedings. European Dialysis and Transplant Association European Renal Association

Proc Eur Electro Opt Mark Technol Conf — Proceedings. European Electro-Optics Markets and Technology Conference

Proc Eur Electr Propul Conf — Proceedings. European Electric Propulsion Conference

Proc Eur Great Proj Int Semin — Proceedings. European Great Projects International Seminar

Proc Eur Immunol Meet — Proceedings. European Immunology Meeting

Proc Eur Mar Biol Symp — Proceedings. European Marine Biology Symposium

Proc Eur Mediterr Cereal Rusts Conf — Proceedings. European and Mediterranean Cereal Rusts Conference

Proc Eur Meet Bact Transform Transfection — Proceedings. European Meeting on Bacterial Transformation and Transfection

Proc Eur Meet Meat Res Work — Proceedings. European Meeting of Meat Research Workers

Proc Eur Meet Radioisot Prod — Proceedings. European Meeting of Radioisotope Producers

Proc Eur Pept Symp — Proceedings. European Peptide Symposium

Proc Eur Prosthodontic Assoc — Proceedings. European Prosthodontic Association

Proc Eur Reg Conf Electron Microsc — Proceedings. European Regional Conference on Electron Microscopy

Proc Eur Reg Meet Astron — Proceedings. European Regional Meeting in Astronomy

Proc Eur Reg Tech Conf Plast Process — Proceedings. European Regional Technical Conference. Plastics and Processing

Proc Eur Soc Artif Organs Annu Meet — Proceedings. European Society for Artificial Organs. Annual Meeting

Proc Eur Soc Neurochem Meet ESN — Proceedings. European Society for Neurochemistry. Meeting of the ESN

Proc Eur Soc Toxicol — Proceedings. European Society of Toxicology

Proc Eur Space Mech Tribol Symp — Proceedings. European Space Mechanisms and Tribology Symposium

Proc Eur Steril Cong — Proceedings. European Sterility Congress

Proc Eur Symp Bone Tooth — Proceedings. European Symposium on Bone and Tooth

Proc Eur Symp Calcif Tissues — Proceedings. European Symposium on Calcified Tissues

Proc Eur Symp Chem React Eng — Proceedings. European Symposium on Chemical Reaction Engineering

Proc Eur Symp Eng Ceram — Proceedings. European Symposium on Engineering Ceramics

Proc Eur Symp Life Sci Res Space — Proceedings. European Symposium on Live Sciences Research in Space

Proc Eur Symp Mar Biol — Proceedings. European Symposium on Marine Biology

Proc Eur Symp Nucleon Anti Nucleon Interact — Proceedings. European Symposium on Nucleon Anti-Nucleon Interactions

Proc Eur Symp Polym Spectrosc — Proceedings. European Symposium on Polymer Spectroscopy

Proc Eur Symp Poultr Meat Qual — Proceedings. European Symposium on Poultry Meat Quality

Proc Eur Symp Radiopharmacol — Proceedings. European Symposium on Radiopharmacology

Proc Eur Symp Therm Anal — Proceedings. European Symposium on Thermal Analysis

Proc Exxon Eng Symp — Proceedings. Exxon Engineering Symposium

Proc Fac Agric Kyushu Tokai Univ — Proceedings. Faculty of Agriculture. Kyushu Tokai University

Proc Fac Eng Keiogijuku Univ — Proceedings. Faculty of Engineering. Keiogijuku University

Proc Fac Eng Kyushu Univ — Proceedings. Faculty of Engineering. Kyushu University

Proc Fac Eng Tokai Univ — Proceedings. Faculty of Engineering. Tokai University

Proc Fac Eng Tokai Univ (Jpn Ed) — Proceedings. Faculty of Engineering of Tokai University (Japan Edition)

Proc Fac Sci Tokai Univ — Proceedings. Faculty of Science. Tokai University

Proc Fac Technol Novi Sad — Proceedings. Faculty of Technology. Novi Sad

Proc Falk Symp — Proceedings. Falk Symposium

Proc Fall Meet Mater Equip Whitewares Div Am Ceram Soc — Proceedings. Fall Meeting. Materials and Equipment and Whitewares Divisions. American Ceramic Society

Proc Farm Seed Conf — Proceedings. Farm Seed Conference

Proc FEBS Congr — Proceedings. FEBS

Proc FEBS Meet — Proceedings. FEBS [*Federation of European Biochemical Societies*] Meeting

Proc Fed Conf Great Lakes — Proceedings. Federal Conference on the Great Lakes (US)

Proc Fed Inter Agency Sediment Conf — Proceedings. Federal Inter-Agency Sedimentation Conference

Proc Fed Sci Congr — Proceedings. Federal Science Congress

Proc Fert Assoc India Tech Ser — Proceedings. Fertiliser Association of India. Tech Series

Proc Fertil Soc — Proceedings. Fertilizer Society

Proc Fert Ind Round Table — Proceedings. Fertilizer Industry Round Table

Proc Fert Inst Delhi — Proceedings. Fertiliser Institute (Delhi)

Proc Fert Soc Lond — Proceedings. [*The*] Fertiliser Society of London

Proc Fiber Opt Commun — Proceedings. Fiber Optics and Communications

Proc Finn Acad Sci Lett — Proceedings. Finnish Academy of Science and Letters

Proc Finn Dent Soc — Proceedings. Finnish Dental Society of Washington

Proc Finn Summer Sch Theor Phys — Proceedings. Finnish Summer School in Theoretical Physics

Proc Finn Swed Semin Gulf Bothnia — Proceedings. Finnish-Swedish Seminar on the Gulf of Bothnia

Proc Finn US Jt Symp Occup Saf Health Swed Participation — Proceedings. Finnish-US Joint Symposium on Occupational Safety and Healty with Swedish Participation

Proc First Livest Ocean Conf — Proceedings. First Livestock by Ocean Conference

Proc Fla Acad Sci — Proceedings. Florida Academy of Sciences

Proc Fla Anti-Mosq — Proceedings. Florida Anti-Mosquito Association

Proc Fla Lychee Grow Ass — Proceedings. Florida Lychee Growers Association

Proc Flash Radiogr Symp Natl Fall Conf Am Soc Nondestr Test — Proceedings. Flash Radiography Symposium Presented at the National Fall Conference, American Society for Nondestructive Testing

Proc Fla State Hortic Soc — Proceedings. Florida State Horticultural Society

Proc Fla State Hort Soc — Proceedings. Florida State Horticultural Society

Proc Fla St Hort Soc — Proceedings. Florida State Horticultural Society

Proc Florida State Hortic Soc — Florida. State Horticultural Society. Proceedings

Proc Florida Turf Assoc — Proceedings. Florida Turf Association

Proc FOC Fiber Opt Commun — Proceedings. FOC. Fiber Optics and Communications

Proc Food — Processed Prepared Food

Proc Food Conf Inst Food Technol — Proceedings. Food Conference. Institute of Food Technologists

Proc Forage Grassl Conf — Proceedings. Forage and Grassland Conference

Proc Forest Prod Res Soc Natl Meeting — Proceedings. Forest Products Research Society National Meeting

Proc For Microclim Symp Can Dep Fish For — Proceedings. Forest Microclimate Symposium. Canada Department of Fisheries and Forestry

Proc For Prod Res Soc — Proceedings. Forest Products Research Society

Proc For Prod Symp — Proceedings. Forest Products Symposium

Proc For Res Inst Budapest — Proceedings. Forest Research Institute. Budapest

Proc For Symp LA Sch For — Proceedings. Annual Forestry Symposium. Louisiana State University. School of Forestry and Wildlife Management

Proc Forum Fundam Surg Probl Clin Congr Am Coll Surg — Proceedings. Forum on Fundamental Surgical Problems. Clinical Congress of the American College of Surgeons

Proc Forum Geol Ind Miner — Proceedings. Forum on Geology of Industrial Minerals

Proc Found Orthod Res — Proceedings. Foundation for Orthodontic Research

Proc (Fourth) NZ Geogr Conf — Proceedings. (Fourth) New Zealand Geographical Conference

Proc FPLC Symp — Proceedings. FPLC [*Fast Protein, Polypeptide, and Polynucleotide Liquid Chromatography*] Symposium

Proc FRI Symp For Res Inst NZ For Serv — Proceedings. FRI Symposium. Forest Research Institute. New Zealand Forest Service

Proc Front Chem Conf — Proceedings. Frontiers of Chemistry Conference

Proc Front Educ Conf — Proceedings. Frontiers in Education Conference

Proc Front Power Conf — Proceedings. Frontiers of Power Conference

Proc Front Power Technol Conf — Proceedings. Frontiers of Power Technology Conference

Proc Fujihara Mem Fac Eng Keio Univ — Proceedings. Fujihara Memorial Faculty of Engineering. Keio University

Proc Fujihara Mem Fac Eng Keio Univ (Tokyo) — Proceedings. Fujihara Memorial Faculty of Engineering. Keio University (Tokyo)

Proc Fujihara Meml Fac Eng Keio Univ Suppl — Proceedings. Fujihara Memorial Faculty of Engineering. Deio University. Supplement

Proc Fusion Fission Energy Syst Rev Meet — Proceedings. Fusion/Fission Energy Systems Review Meeting

Proc Ga Nutr Conf Feed Ind — Proceedings. Georgia Nutrition Conference for the Feed Industry

Proc Gas Cond Conf — Proceedings. Gas Conditioning Conference

Proc Gastech — Proceedings. Gastech

Proc Gemmol Assoc GB — Proceedings. Gemmological Association of Great Britain

Proc Gen Conf Condens Matter Div Eur Phys Soc — Proceedings. General Conference. Condensed Matter Division. European Physical Society

Proc Genet Soc Can — Proceedings. Genetics Society of Canada

Proc Gen Meet Eur Grassl Fed — Proceedings. General Meeting. European Grassland Federation

Proc Gen Meet Eur Soc Anim Cell Technol — Proceedings. General Meeting. European Society of Animal Cell Technology

Proc Gen Meet Soc Ind Microbiol — Proceedings. General Meeting of the Society for Industrial Microbiology

Proc Geoinst — Proceedings. Geoinstitut

Proc Geol Ass — Proceedings. Geological Association

Proc Geol Ass Can — Proceedings. Geological Association of Canada

Proc Geol Assoc — Proceedings. Geologists' Association

Proc Geol Assoc Am — Proceedings. Geological Association of America

Proc Geol Assoc Can — Proceedings. Geological Association of Canada

Proc Geol Assoc London — Proceedings. Geologists' Association of London

Proc Geol Soc China — Proceedings. Geological Society of China

Proc Geol Soc Lond — Proceedings. Geological Society of London

Proc Geol Soc S Afr — Proceedings. Geological Society of South Africa

Proc Geophys Soc Tulsa — Proceedings. Geophysical Society of Tulsa

Proc Geopressured Geotherm Energy Conf — Proceedings. Geopressured Geothermal Eenrgy Conference

Proc Geosci Inform Soc — Proceedings. Geoscience Information Society

Proc Geosci Inf Soc — Proceedings. Geoscience Information Society

Proc Ger Soc Neurosurg — Proceedings. German Society of Neurosurgery

Proc Ger Sol Energy Forum — Proceedings. German Solar Energy Forum

Proc Ghana Acad Arts Sci — Proceedings. Ghana Academy of Arts and Sciences

Proc Grass Breeders Work Plann Conf — Proceedings. Grass Breeders Work Planning Conference

Proc Grassl Soc South Afr — Proceedings. Grassland Society of Southern Africa

Proc Great Plains Agr Conf — Proceedings. Great Plains Agriculture Conference

Proc Great Plains Agric Counc — Proceedings. Great Plains Agricultural Council

Proc Great Plains Agric Council — Proceedings. Great Plains Agricultural Council

Proc GRI Sulfur Recovery Conf — Proceedings of the GRI (Gas Research Institute) Sulfur Recovery Conference

Proc Gulf Caribb Fish Inst — Proceedings. Gulf and Caribbean Fisheries Institute

Proc Hamps Field Club & Archaeol Soc — Proceedings of the Hampshire Field Club and Archaeological Society

Proc Hampshire Field Club — Proceedings. Hampshire Field Club and Archaeological Society

Proc Hampshire Fld Club Archaeol Soc — Proceedings. Hampshire Field Club and Archaeological Society

Proc Hamp Soc — Proceedings. Hampshire Field Club and Archaeological Society

Proc Hawaii Acad Sci — Proceedings. Hawaiian Academy of Science

Proc Hawaiian Acad Sci — Proceedings. Hawaiian Academy of Science

Proc Hawaii Entomol Soc — Proceedings. Hawaiian Entomological Society

Proc Hawaii Ent Soc — Proceedings. Hawaiian Entomological Society

Proc Hawaii Int Conf Syst Sci — Proceedings. Hawaii International Conference on System Science

Proc Hawaii Top Conf Part Phys — Proceedings. Hawaii Topical Conference in Particle Physics

Proc Health Phys Soc Annu Meet — Proceedings. Health Physics Society. Annual Meeting

Proc Health Policy Forum — Proceedings. Health Policy Forum

Proc Heat Transfer Fluid Mech Inst — Proceedings. Heat Transfer and Fluid Mechanics Institute

Proc Hell Sch Elem Part Phys — Proceedings. Hellenic School on Elementary Partical Physics

Proc Helminthol Soc Wash — Proceedings. Helminthological Society of Washington

Proc Helminthol Soc (Wash DC) — Proceedings. Helminthological Society (Washington, DC)

Proc Helminth Soc Wash — Proceedings. Helminthological Society of Washington

Proche Orient Chret — Proche Orient Chretien

Proc High Energy Phys Symp — Proceedings. High Energy Physics Symposium

Proc High Lysine Corn Conf — Proceedings. High Lysine Corn Conference

Proc High Temp Liq Met Heat Transfer Technol Meet — Proceedings. High-Temperature Liquid-Metal Heat Transfer Technology Meeting

Proc Highw Veh Syst Contract Coord Meet — Proceedings. Highway Vehicle Systems. Contractors' Coordination Meeting

Prochn Deform Mater Neravnomernykh Fiz Polyakh — Prochnost i Deformatsiya Materialov v Neravnomernykh Fizicheskikh Polyakh

Prochn Met Tsikl Nagruzkakh Mater Soveshch Ustalosti Met — Prochnost Metallov pri Tsiklicheskikh Nagruzkakh. Materialy Soveshchaniya po Ustalosti Metallov

Prochnost Din Aviats Dvigatelei — Prochnost i Dinamika Aviatsionnykh Dvigatelei

Prochn Razrushenie Tverd Tel — Prochnost Razrushenie Tverdykh Tel

Proc Hokkaido Symp Plant Breed Crop Sci Soc — Proceedings. Hokkaido Symposium of Plant Breeding and Crop Science Society

Proc Hokuriku Br Crop Sci Soc (Jap) — Proceedings. Hokuriku Branch of Crop Science Society (Japan)

Proc Hortic Soc London — Proceedings. Horticultural Society of London

Proc Hort Soc N Illinois — Proceedings. Horticultural Society of Northern Illinois

Proc Hoshi Coll Pharm — Proceedings. Hoshi College of Pharmacy

Proc Hot Lab Equip Conf — Proceedings. Hot Laboratories and Equipment Conference

Proc Huguenot Soc Lond — Proceedings. Huguenot Society of London

Proc Huguenot Soc London — Proceedings. Huguenot Society of London

Proc Hum Factors Ergon Soc — Proceedings of the Human Factors and Ergonomics Society

Proc Hung Annu Meet Biochem — Proceedings. Hungarian Annual Meeting for Biochemistry

Proc Hung Bioflavonoid Symp — Proceedings. Hungarian Bioflavonoid Symposium

Proc Hung Text Conf — Proceedings. Hungarian Textile Conference

Proc Hydrol Symp — Proceedings. Hydrology Symposium

Proc Hydrotransp — Proceedings of Hydrotransport

Proc IAEA Symp Phys Chem Fission — Proceedings. IAEA [*Internationa Atomic Energy Agency*] Symposium on the Physics and Chemistry of Fission

Proc Iberoam Symp Catal — Proceedings. Iberoamerican Symposium on Catalysis

Proc ICASSP IEEE Int Conf Acoust Speech Signal Process — Proceedings. ICASSP, IEEE International Conference on Acoustics, Speech, and Signal Processing

Proc I Cda — Process Industries Canada

Proc ICE — Proceedings. Institution of Civil Engineers. Parts 1 and 2

Proc ICMR Semin — Proceedings. ICMR [*International Center for Medical Research, Kobe University*] Seminar

Proc IEE-A — Institution of Electrical Engineers. Proceedings. A

Proc IEE-B — Institution of Electrical Engineers. Proceedings. B

Proc IEE-C — Institution of Electrical Engineers. Proceedings. C

Proc IEE D — Institution of Electrical Engineers. Proceedings. D

Proc IEEE — Proceedings. Institute of Electrical and Electronics Engineers

Proc IEEE ASME Jt Railroad Conf — Proceedings of the IEEE/ASME Joint Railroad Conference

Proc IEEE Comput Soc Int Comput Software Appl Conf — Proceedings. IEEE Computer Society's International Computer Software and Applications Conference

Proc IEEE Comput Soc Symp Res Secur Privacy — Proceedings of the IEEE Computer Society Symposium on Research in Security and Privacy

Proc IEEE Conf Decis Control — Proceedings. IEEE Conference on Decision and Control

Proc IEEE Conf Decis Control Incl Symp Adapt Processes — Proceedings. IEEE Conference on Decision and Control Including the Symposium onAdaptive Processes

Proc IEEE Conv Electr Electron Eng Isr — Proceedings. IEEE Convention of Electrical and Electronics Engineers in Israel

Proc IEEE Cornell Conf Adv Concepts High Speed Semicond Devic — Proceedings. IEEE/Cornell Conference on Advanced Concepts in High Speed Semiconductor Devices and Circuits

Proc IEEE Freq Control Symp — Proceedings. IEEE Frequency Control Symposium

Proc IEEE INFOCOM — Proceedings. IEEE INFOCOM

Proc IEEE Int Conf Comput Des VLSI Comput Process — Proceedings. IEEE International Conference on Computer Design. VLSI in Computers and Processors

Proc IEEE Int Conf Rob Autom — Proceedings. IEEE International Conference on Robotics and Automation

Proc IEEE Int Conf Syst Man Cybern — Proceedings of the IEEE International Conference on Systems, Man, and Cybernetics

Proc IEEE Int Freq Control Symp — Proceedings of the IEEE International Frequency Control Symposium

Proc IEEE Int Symp Circuits Syst — Proceedings. IEEE International Symposium on Circuits and Systems

Proc IEEE Micro Electro Mech Syst — Proceedings. IEEE Micro Electro Mechanical Systems

Proc IEEE Mil Commun Conf — Proceedings. IEEE Military Communications Conference

Proc IEEE Minicourse Fusion — Proceedings. IEEE Minicourse on Fusion

Proc IEEE Minicourse Inertial Confinement Fusion — Proceedings. IEEE [*Institute of Electrical and Electronics Engineers*] Minicourse on Inertial Confinement Fusion

Proc IEEE Semicond Therm Meas Manage Symp — Proceedings. IEEE Semiconductor Thermal Measurement and Management Symposium

Proc IEEE Symp Fusion Eng — Proceedings. IEEE Symposium on Fusion Engineering

Proc IEEE Ultrason Symp — Proceedings. IEEE Ultrasonics Symposium

Proc IEE F — Institution of Electrical Engineers. Proceedings. F

Proc IEE G — Institution of Electrical Engineers. Proceedings. G

Proc IEE H — Proceedings. Institution of Electrical Engineers. H

Proc IEE I — Proceedings. Institution of Electrical Engineers. I

Proc IFAC World Congr — Proceedings. IFAC [*International Federation of Automatic Control*] World Congress

Proc III Natn Peanut Res Conf — Proceedings. Third National Peanut Research Conference

Proc III Mining Inst — Proceedings. Illinois Mining Institute

Proc III Min Inst — Proceedings. Illinois Mining Institute

Proc Imp Acad Japan — Proceedings. Imperial Academy of Japan

Proc Imp Acad (Tokyo) — Proceedings. Imperial Academy (Tokyo)

Proc Imp Cancer Res Fund Symp — Proceedings. Imperial Cancer Research Fund Symposium

Proc Ind Acad Sci — Proceedings. Indiana Academy of Sciences

Proc Ind Hyg Found Am — Proceedings. Industrial Foundation of America

Proc Indiana Acad Sci — Proceedings. Indiana Academy of Science

Proc Indian Acad Sci — Proceedings. Indian Academy of Sciences

Proc Indian Acad Sci A — Proceedings. Indian Academy of Sciences. Section A

Proc Indian Acad Sci Anim Sci — Proceedings. Indian Academy of Sciences. Animal Sciences

Proc Indian Acad Sci B — Proceedings. Indian Academy of Sciences. Section B

Proc Indian Acad Sci Chem Sci — Proceedings. Indian Academy of Sciences. Chemical Sciences

Proc Indian Acad Sci Earth and Planet Sci — Proceedings. Indian Academy of Sciences. Earth and Planetary Sciences

Proc Indian Acad Sci Earth Planet — Proceedings. Indian Academy of Sciences. Earth and Planetary Sciences

Proc Indian Acad Sci Earth Planetary Sci — Proceedings. Indian Academy of Sciences. Earth and Planetary Sciences

Proc Indian Acad Sci Earth Planet Sci — Proceedings. Indian Academy of Sciences. Earth and Planetary Sciences

Proc Indian Acad Sci Eng Sci — Proceedings. Indian Academy of Sciences. Engineering Sciences

Proc Indian Acad Sci Math Sci — Proceedings. Indian Academy of Sciences. Mathematical Sciences

Proc Indian Acad Sci Plant Sci — Proceedings. Indian Academy of Sciences. Plant Sciences

Proc Indian Acad Sci Sect A — Proceedings. Indian Academy of Sciences. Section A

Proc Indian Acad Sci Sect A Chem Sci — Proceedings. Indian Academy of Sciences. Section A. Chemical Sciences

Proc Indian Acad Sci Sect A Earth Planetary Sci — Indian Academy of Sciences. Proceedings. Section A. Earth and Planetary Sciences

Proc Indian Acad Sci Sect A Math Sci — Proceedings. Indian Academy of Sciences. Section A. Mathematical Sciences

Proc Indian Acad Sci Sect B — Proceedings. Indian Academy of Sciences. Section B

Proc Indian Acad Sci Sect C — Proceedings. Indian Academy of Sciences. Section C. Engineering Sciences

Proc Indian Assoc Cultiv Sci — Proceedings. Indian Association for Cultivation of Sciences

Proc Indian Natl Sci Acad A — Proceedings. Indian National Science Academy. Part A. Physical Sciences

Proc Indian Natl Sci Acad Part A — Proceedings. Indian National Science Academy. Part A

Proc Indian Natl Sci Acad Part A Phys Sci — Proceedings. Indian National Science Academy. Part A. Physical Sciences

Proc Indian Natl Sci Acad Part B — Proceedings. Indian National Science Academy. Part B. Biological Sciences

Proc Indian Natl Sci Acad Part B Biol Sci — Proceedings. Indian National Science Academy. Part B. Biological Sciences

Proc Indian Nat Sci Acad Part A — Proceedings. Indian National Science Academy. Part A. Physical Sciences

Proc Indian Roads Congr — Proceedings. Indian Roads Congress

Proc Indian Sci Congr — Proceedings. Indian Science Congress

Proc Ind Miner Int Congr — Proceedings. Industrial Minerals International Congress

Proc Indo Ger Semin — Proceedings. Indo-German Seminar

Proc Indo Pac Fish Counc — Proceedings. Indo-Pacific Fisheries Council

Proc Ind Waste Adv Water Solid Waste Conf — Proceedings. Industrial Waste, Advanced Water, and Solid Waste Conference

Proc Ind Waste Conf — Proceedings. Industrial Waste Conference

Proc Ind Waste Conf Purdue Univ — Proceedings. Industrial Waste Conference. Purdue University

Proc Ind Waste Util Conf — Proceedings. Industrial Waste Utilization Conference

Proc Ind Water Waste Conf — Proceedings. Industrial Water and Waste Conference

Proc Inf Comm Hydrol Res CHO TNO — Proceedings and Information. Committee for Hydrological Research, CHO-TNO

Proc Infrared Detect Technol Workshop — Proceedings. Infrared Detector Technology Workshop

Proc Infrared Soc Jpn — Proceeding. Infrared Society of Japan

Proc Infrared Soc Jpn — Proceedings. Infrared Society of Japan

Proc Inst Ash Util Symp Expo — Proceedings. International Ash Utilization Symposium and Exposition

Proc Inst Automob Eng (London) — Proceedings. Institution of Automobile Engineers (London)

Proc Inst Br Foundrymen — Proceedings. Institute of British Foundrymen

Proc Inst Chem (Calcutta) — Proceedings. Institution of Chemists (Calcutta)

Proc Inst Chem GB Irel — Proceedings. Institute of Chemistry of Great Britain and Ireland

Proc Inst Chem India — Proceedings. Institution of Chemists (India)

Proc Inst Civ Eng — Proceedings. Institution of Civil Engineers

Proc Inst Civ Eng Civ Eng — Proceedings of the Institution of Civil Engineers. Civil Engineering

Proc Inst Civ Engin — Proceedings of the Institution of Civil Engineers

Proc Inst Civ Eng (London) Suppl — Proceedings. Institution of Civil Engineers (London). Supplement

Proc Inst Civ Eng Munic Eng — Proceedings of the Institution of Civil Engineers. Municipal Engineering

Proc Inst Civ Eng Part 1 — Proceedings. Institution of Civil Engineers. Part 1. Design and Construction

Proc Inst Civ Eng Part 1 Des — Proceedings. Institution of Civil Engineers. Part 1. Design and Construction

Proc Inst Civ Eng Part 2 — Proceedings. Institution of Civil Engineers. Part 2. Research and Theory

Proc Inst Civ Eng Part 2 Res — Proceedings. Institution of Civil Engineers. Part 2. Research and Theory

Proc Inst Civ Eng Struct Build — Proceedings of the Institution of Civil Engineers. Structures and Buildings

Proc Inst Civ Eng Transp — Proceedings of the Institution of Civil Engineers. Transport

Proc Inst Civ Eng Water Marit Energ — Proceedings of the Institution of Civil Engineers. Water Maritime and Energy

Proc Inst Elec Eng (London) — Proceedings. Institution of Electrical Engineers (London)

Proc Inst Elec Eng Pt B Elec Power Appl — Proceedings. Institution of Electrical Engineers. Part B. Electric Power Applications

Proc Inst Elec Eng Pt C Generation Transmission Distribution — Proceedings. Institution of Electrical Engineers. Part C. Generation-Transmission-Distribution

Proc Inst Elec Eng Pt E Computers Digital Tech — Proceedings. Institution of Electrical Engineers. Part E. Computers and DigitalTechniques

Proc Inst Elec Eng Pt F Commun Radar Signal Process — Proceedings. Institution of Electrical Engineers. Part F. Communications, Radar, and Signal Processing

Proc Inst Elec Eng Pt G Electron Circuits Syst — Proceedings. Institution of Electrical Engineers. Part G. Electronics Circuits and Systems

Proc Inst Elec Eng Pt H Microwaves Opt Antennas — Proceedings. Institution of Electrical Engineers. Part H. Microwaves, Optics, and Antennas

Proc Inst Elec Engrs — Proceedings. Institution of Electrical Engineers

Proc Inst Elect — Proceedings. Institution of Electrical Engineers

Proc Inst Electr Eng — Proceedings. Institution of Electrical Engineers

Proc Inst Electr Eng (London) — Proceedings. Institution of Electrical Engineers (London)

Proc Inst Electr Eng Part 1 — Proceedings. Institution of Electrical Engineers. Part 1. General

Proc Inst Electr Eng Part 2 — Proceedings. Institution of Electrical Engineers. Part 2. Power Engineering

Proc Inst Electr Eng Part 3 — Proceedings. Institution of Electrical Engineers. Part 3. Radio and Communication Engineering

Proc Inst Electr Eng Part 4 — Proceedings. Institution of Electrical Engineers. Part 4. Monographs

Proc Inst Electr Eng Part A — Proceedings. Institution of Electrical Engineers. Part A. Power Engineering

Proc Inst Electr Eng Part A Suppl — Proceedings. Institution of Electrical Engineers. Part A. Supplement

Proc Inst Electr Eng Part B — Proceedings. Institution of Electrical Engineers. Part B. Electronic and Communication Engineering Including Radio Engineering

Proc Inst Electr Eng Part B Suppl — Proceedings. Institution of Electrical Engineers. Part B. Supplement

Proc Inst Electr Eng Part C — Proceedings. Institution of Electrical Engineers. Part C. Monographs

Proc Inst Electr Eng Spec Issue — Proceedings. Institution of Electrical Engineers. Special Issue

Proc Inst Environ Sci — Proceedings. Institute of Environmental Sciences

Proc Inst Environ Sci Technol — Proceedings. Institute of Environmental Sciences and Technology

Proc Inst Fd Sci Technol — Proceedings. Institute of Food Science and Technology

Proc Inst Fish Varna — Proceedings. Institute of Fisheries (Varna)

Proc Inst Food Sci Technol UK — Proceedings. Institute of Food Science and Technology of the United Kingdom

Proc Inst Food Technol — Proceedings. Institute of Food Technologists

Proc Institute Med Chicago — Proceedings. Institute of Medicine of Chicago

Proc Inst Mech Eng — Proceedings. Institution of Mechanical Engineers

Proc Inst Mech Eng Automob Div — Proceedings. Institute of Mechanical Engineers. Automobile Division

Proc Inst Mech Eng H — Proceedings. Institution of Mechanical Engineers. Part H. Journal of Engineering in Medicine

Proc Inst Mech Eng IMechE Conf — Proceedings. Institute of Mechanical Engineers. IMechE Conference

Proc Inst Mech Eng (London) — Proceedings. Institution of Mechanical Engineers (London)

Proc Inst Mech Eng Part 3 — Proceedings. Institute of Mechanical Engineers. Part 3

Proc Inst Mech Eng Part A — Proceedings. Institution of Mechanical Engineers. Part A. Power and Process Engineering

Proc Inst Mech Eng Part A Power — Proceedings. Institution of Mechanical Engineers. Part A. Power and Process Engineering

Proc Inst Mech Eng Part B — Proceedings. Institution of Mechanical Engineers. Part B. Management and Engineering Manufacture

Proc Inst Mech Eng Part B J Eng Manuf — Proceedings of the Institution of Mechanical Engineers. Part B. Journal of Engineering Manufacture

Proc Inst Mech Eng Part B Manage — Proceedings. Institution of Mechanical Engineers. Part B. Management and Engineering Manufacture

Proc Inst Mech Eng Part C — Proceedings. Institution of Mechanical Engineers. Part C. Mechanical Engineering Science

Proc Inst Mech Eng Part D J Automob Eng — Proceedings of the Institution of Mechanical Engineers. Part D. Journal of Automobile Engineering

Proc Inst Mech Eng Part E J Process Mech Eng — Proceedings of the Institution of Mechanical Engineers. Part E. Journal of Process Mechanical Engineering

Proc Inst Mech Eng Part F J Rail Rapid Transit — Proceedings of the Institution of Mechanical Engineers. Part F. Journal of Rail and Rapid Transit

Proc Inst Mech Eng Part H J Eng Med — Proceedings of the Institution of Mechanical Engineers. Part H. Journal of Engineering in Medicine

Proc Inst Mech Engrs — Proceedings. Institution of Mechanical Engineers

Proc Inst Med Chic — Proceedings. Institute of Medicine of Chicago

Proc Inst Med Chicago — Proceedings. Institute of Medicine of Chicago

Proc Inst Nat Sci Nihon Univ — Proceedings. Institute of Natural Sciences. Nihon University

Proc Instn CE — Proceedings. Institution of Civil Engineers

Proc Instn Civ Engrs — Proceedings. Institution of Civil Engineers

Proc Instn Civ Engrs 1 2 — Proceedings. Institution of Civil Engineers. Parts 1 and 2

Proc Instn Elect Engrs — Proceedings. Institution of Electrical Engineers

Proc Inst Neurol Sci Symp Neurobiol — Proceedings. Institute of Neurological Sciences Symposium in Neurobiology

Proc Instn Mech Engrs — Proceedings. Institution of Mechanical Engineers

Proc Instn Mech Engrs Pt B Mgmt Engng Mf — Proceedings. Institution of Mechanical Engineers. Part B. Management and Engineering Manufacture

Proc Instn Mech Engrs Pt C Mech Engng Sci — Proceedings. Institution of Mechanical Engineers. Part C. Mechanical Engineering Science

Proc Instn Mech Engrs Pt D Transp Engng — Proceedings. Institution of Mechanical Engineers. Part D. Transport Engineering

Proc Instn Radio Electron Engrs Aust — Proceedings. Institution of Radio and Electronics Engineers of Australia

Proc Instn Radio Engrs Aust — Proceedings. Institution of Radio Engineers of Australia

Proc Inst Nucl Theory — Proceedings from the Institute for Nuclear Theory

Proc Inst Oceanogr Fish Bulg Acad Sci — Proceedings. Institute of Oceanography and Fisheries. Bulgarian Academy of Sciences

Proc Inst Pet London — Proceedings. Institute of Petroleum (London)

Proc Inst Pomol (Skierniewice Pol) Ser E Conf Symp — Proceedings. Research Institute of Pomology (Skierniewice, Poland). Series E. Conferences and Symposia

Proc Inst Radio Electron Eng Aust — Proceedings. Institution of Radio and Electronics Engineers of Australia

Proc Inst Railw Signal Eng — Proceedings. Institution of Railway Signal Engineers

Proc Inst Refrig — Proceedings. Institute of Refrigeration

Proc Inst Rubber Ind — Proceedings. Institution of the Rubber Industry

Proc Instrum Soc Am — Proceedings. Instrument Society of America

Proc Instrum Soc Am Annu Instrum Autom Conf Exhib — Proceedings. Instrument Society of America. Annual Instrument-Automation Conference and Exhibit

Proc Inst Sci Res Food Ind USSR — Proceedings. Institute for Scientific Research in the Food Industry. USSR

Proc Inst Sewage Purif — Proceedings. Institute of Sewage Purification

Proc Inst Statist Math — Proceedings. Institute of Statistical Mathematics

Proc Inst Teknol Bandung — Proceedings. Institut Teknologi Bandung

Proc Inst Teknol Bandung Suppl — Proceedings. Institut Teknologi Bandung. Supplement

Proc Inst Vitreous Enamellers — Proceedings. Institute of Vitreous Enamellers

Proc Int Acad Oral Pathol — Proceedings. International Academy of Oral Pathology

Proc Int Alum Lithium Conf — Proceedings. International Aluminum-Lithium Conference

Proc Int Asparagus Symp — Proceedings. International Asparagus-Symposium

Proc Int Assoc Milk Dealers — Proceedings. International Association of Milk Dealers

Proc Int Assoc Test Mater — Proceedings. International Association for Testing Materials

Proc Int Assoc Theor Appl Limnol — Proceedings. International Association of Theoretical and Applied Limnology

Proc Int Assoc Vet Food Hyg — Proceedings. International Association of Veterinary Food Hygienists

Proc Int Astronaut Congr — Proceedings. International Astronautical Congress

Proc Int Astron Union Colloq — Proceedings. International Astronomical Union Colloquium

Proc Int Bari Conf Genet Funct Mitochondrial DNA — Proceedings. International Bari Conference on the Genetic Function of Mitochondrial DNA

Proc Int Barley Genet Symp — Proceedings. International Barley Genetics Symposium

Proc Int Battery Symp — Proceedings. International Battery Symposium

Proc Int Bedding Plant Conf — Proceedings. International Bedding Plant Conference

Proc Int Betatron Symp — Proceedings. International Betatron Symposium

Proc Int Bioclimatol Congr — Proceedings. International Bioclimatological Congress

Proc Int Biodegrad Symp — Proceedings. International Biodegradation Symposium

Proc Int Biodeterior Symp — Proceedings. International Biodeterioration Symposium

Proc Int Biotechnol Symp — Proceedings. International Biotechnology Symposium

Proc Int Bot Congr — Proceedings. International Botanical Congress

Proc Int Brick Masonry Conf — Proceedings. International Brick-Masonry Conference

Proc Int Briquet Assoc Bienn Conf — Proceedings. International Briquetting Association. Biennial Conference

Proc Int Catecholamine Symp — Proceedings. International Catecholamine Symposium

Proc Int Cem Semin — Proceedings. International Cement Seminar

Proc Int Cent Heat Mass Transfer — Proceedings of the International Centre for Heat and Mass Transfer

Proc Int Chromosome Conf — Proceedings. International Chromosome Conference

Proc Int Clean Air Conf — Proceedings. International Clean Air Conference

Proc Int Clean Air Congr — Proceedings. International Clean Air Congress

Proc Int Coal Explor Symp — Proceedings. International Coal Exploration Symposium

Proc Int Coal Test Conf — Proceedings. International Coal Testing Conference

Proc Int Cocoa Res Conf — Proceedings. International Cocoa Research Conference

Proc Int CODATA Conf — Proceedings. International CODATA (Committee on Data for Science and Technology) Conference

Proc Int Coelenterate Conf — Proceedings. International Coelenterate Conference

Proc Int Coeliac Symp — Proceedings. International Coeliac Symposium

Proc Int Colloq CNRS — Proceedings. International Colloquium. CNRS (Centre National de la Recherche Scientifique)

Proc Int Colloq Dev Pharmacol — Proceedings. International Colloquium of Developmental Pharmacology

Proc Int Colloq Group Theor Methods Phys — Proceedings. International Colloquium on Group Theoretical Methods in Physics

Proc Int Colloq Invertebr Pathol — Proceedings. International Colloquium on Invertebrate Pathology

Proc Int Colloq Oxygen Isot — Proceedings. International Colloquium on Oxygen Isotopes

Proc Int Colloq Phys Chem Inf Transfer Regul Reprod Aging — Proceedings. International Colloquium on Physical and Chemical Information Transfer in Regulation and Aging

Proc Int Colloq Plant Anal Fert Probl — Proceedings. International Colloquium on Plant Analysis and Fertilizer Problems

Proc Int Colloq Prospect Biol — Proceedings. International Colloquium on Prospective Biology

Proc Int Colloq Renal Lithiasis — Proceedings. International Colloquium on Renal Lithiasis

Proc Int Colloq Soil Zool — Proceedings. International Colloquium on Soil Zoology

Proc Int Colloq Spectrosc — Proceedings. International Colloquium of Spectroscopy

Proc Int Comm Glass — Proceedings. International Commission on Glass

Proc Int Conf Adjuvant Ther Cancer — Proceedings. International Conference on the Adjuvant Therapy of Cancer

Proc Int Conf Alum Health — Proceedings. International Conference on Aluminum and Health

Proc Int Conf Alum Weldments — Proceedings. International Conference on Aluminum Weldments

Proc Int Conf Amorphous Liq Semicond — Proceedings. International Conference on Amorphous and Liquid Semiconductors

Proc Int Conf Appl Charge Coupled Devices — Proceedings. International Conference on the Application of Charge-Coupled Devices

Proc Int Conf Aquacult Nutr — Proceedings. International Conference on Aquaculture Nutrition

Proc Int Conf Aquacult Nutr Biochem Physiol Approaches Shell — Proceedings. International Conference on Aquaculture Nutrition. Biochemical andPhysiological Approaches to Shellfish Nutrition

Proc Int Conf Artif Intell Law — Proceedings of the International Conference on Artificial Intelligence and Law

Proc Int Conf Asthma — Proceedings. International Conference on Asthma

Proc Int Conf At Collisions Solids — Proceedings. International Conference on Atomic Collisions in Solids

Proc Int Conf At Masses — Proceedings. International Conference on Atomic Masses

Proc Int Conf At Masses Fundam Constants — Proceedings. International Conference on Atomic Masses and Fundamental Constants

Proc Int Conf Atmos Electr — Proceedings. International Conference on Atmospheric Electricity

Proc Int Conf At Phys — Proceedings. International Conference on Atomic Physics

Proc Int Conf Autom Cancer Cytol Cell Image Anal — Proceedings. International Conference on the Automation of Cancer Cytology and Cell Image Analysis

Proc Int Conf Beam Foil Spectrosc — Proceedings. International Conference on Beam-Foil Spectroscopy

Proc Int Conf Biochem Lipids — Proceedings. International Conference on the Biochemistry of Lipids

Proc Int Conf Biochem Probl Lipids — Proceedings. International Conference on Biochemical Problems of Lipids

Proc Int Conf Biochem Sep — Proceedings. International Conference on Biochemical Separations

Proc Int Conf Bitum Coal — Proceedings. International Conference on Bituminous Coal

Proc Int Conf Calorim High Energy Phys — Proceedings. International Conference on Calorimetry in High Energy Physics

Proc Int Conf Cem Microsc — Proceedings. International Conference on Cement Microscopy

Proc Int Conf Cent High Energy Form — Proceedings. International Conference. Center for High Energy Forming

Proc Int Conf Chem Uses Molybdenum — Proceedings. International Conference on the Chemistry and Uses of Molybdenum

Proc Int Conf Chem Vap Deposition — Proceedings. International Conference on Chemical Vapor Deposition

Proc Int Conf Chitin Chitosan — Proceedings. International Conference on Chitin/Chitosan

Proc Int Conf Cloud Phys — Proceedings. International Conference on Cloud Physics

Proc Int Conf Clustering Phenom Nucl — Proceedings. International Conference on Clustering Phenomena in Nuclei

Proc Int Conf Coal Res — Proceedings. International Conference on Coal Research

Proc Int Conf Compaction Consol Part Matter — Proceedings. International Conference on the Compaction and Consolidation of Particulate Matter

Proc Int Conf Comp Virol — Proceedings. International Conference on Comparative Virology

Proc Int Conf Conduct Breakdown Dielectr Liq — Proceedings. International Conference on Conduction and Breakdown in DielectricLiquids

Proc Int Conf Conduct Low Mobility Mater — Proceedings. International Conference on Conduction in Low-Mobility Materials

Proc Int Conf Continuum Models Discrete Syst — Proceedings. International Conference on Continuum Models of Discrete Systems

Proc Int Conf Cosmic Rays — Proceedings. International Conference on Cosmic Rays

Proc Int Conf Cryst Electr Field Struct Eff F-Electron Syst — Proceedings. International Conference on Crystalline Electric Field and Structural Effects in F-Electron Systems

Proc Int Conf Cybern Soc — Proceedings. International Conference on Cybernetics and Society

Proc Int Conf Data Eng — Proceedings. International Conference on Data Engineering

Proc Int Conf Defects Semicond — Proceedings. International Conference on Defects in Semiconductors

Proc Int Conf Differ — Proceedings. International Conference on Differentiation

Proc Int Conf Distrib Comput Syst — Proceedings. International Conference on Distributed Computing Systems

Proc Int Conf Eff Corynebacterium Parvum Exp Clin Oncol — Proceedings. International Conference on the Effects of Corynebacterium Parvum in Experimental and Clinical Oncology

Proc Int Conf Eff Hydrogen Behav Mater — Proceedings. International Conference on Effect of Hydrogen on Behavior of Materials

Proc Int Conf Electr Contact Phenom — Proceedings. International Conference on Electrical Contact Phenomena

Proc Int Conf Electr Electron Mater — Proceedings. International Conference on Electrical and Electronic Materials

Proc Int Conf Electrodeposition — Proceedings. International Conference on Electrodeposition

Proc Int Conf Electrodeposition Met Finish — Proceedings. International Conference on Electrodeposition and Metal Finishing

Proc Int Conf Electron Mater — Proceedings. International Conference on Electronic Materials

Proc Int Conf Electron Microsc — Proceedings. International Conference on Electron Microscopy

Proc Int Conf Electron Struct Actinides — Proceedings. International Conference on the Electronic Structure of the Actinides

Proc Int Conf Electrophor — Proceedings. International Conference on Electrophoresis

Proc Int Conf Electrost Precip — Proceedings. International Conference on Electrostatic Precipitation

Proc Int Conf Energy Storage Compression Switching — Proceedings. International Conference on Energy Storage, Compression, and Switching

Proc Int Conf Environ Degrad Eng Mater — Proceedings. International Conference on Environmental Degradation of Engineering Materials

Proc Int Conf Environ Mutagens — Proceedings. International Conference on Environmental Mutagens

Proc Int Conf Erosion Liq Solid Impact — Proceedings. International Conference on Erosion by Liquid and Solid Impact

Proc Int Confer Sinology — Proceedings of the International Conference on Sinology

Proc Int Conf Erythropoiesis — Proceedings. International Conference on Erythropoiesis

Proc Int Conf ESNA Work Group Waste Irradiat — Proceedings. International Conference of ESNA (European Society of Nuclear Methods in Agriculture) Working Group on Waste Irradiation

Proc Int Conf Eur Chem Mark Res Assoc — Proceedings. International Conference. European Chemical Marketing Research Association

Proc Int Conf Fast Neutron Phys — Proceedings. International Conference on Fast Neutron Physics

Proc Int Conf Fatigue Met — Proceedings. International Conference on Fatigue of Metals

Proc Int Conf Finite Elem Flow Probl — Proceedings. International Conference on Finite Elements in Flow Problems

Proc Int Conf Fire Saf — Proceedings. International Conference on Fire Safety

Proc Int Conf Fixed Film Biol Processes — Proceedings. International Conference on Fixed-Film Biological Processes

Proc Int Conf Fluid — Proceedings. International Conference on Fluidization

Proc Int Conf Fluid Bed Combust — Proceedings. International Conference on Fluidized Bed Combustion

Proc Int Conf Fluid Sealing — Proceedings. International Conference on Fluid Sealing

Proc Int Conf Fract — Proceedings. International Conference on Fracture

Proc Int Conf From Theor Phys Biol — Proceedings. International Conference From Theoretical Physics to Biology

Proc Int Conf Fundam Tribol — Proceedings. International Conference on the Fundamentals of Tribology

Proc Int Conf Genet Eng — Proceedings. International Conference on Genetic Engineering

Proc Int Conf Hadron Spectrosc — Proceedings. International Conference on Hadron Spectroscopy

Proc Int Conf Heat Treat Mater — Proceedings. International Conference on Heat Treatment of Materials

Proc Int Conf Heavy Ion Phys — Proceedings. International Conference on Heavy Ion Physics

Proc Int Conf High Energy Accel — Proceedings. International Conference on High-Energy Accelerators

Proc Int Conf High Energy Accel Instrum — Proceedings. International Conference on High-Energy Accelerators and Instrumentation

Proc Int Conf High Energy Collisions — Proceedings. International Conference on High Energy Collisions

Proc Int Conf High Energy Phys — Proceedings. International Conference on High Energy Physics

Proc Int Conf High Energy Rate Fabr — Proceedings. International Conference on High Energy Rate Fabrication

Proc Int Conf Hot Dip Galvanizing — Proceedings. International Conference on Hot Dip Galvanizing

Proc Int Conf Hydraul Transp Solids Pipes — Proceedings. International Conference on the Hydraulic Transport of Solids in Pipes

Proc Int Conf Immunopharmacol — Proceedings. International Conference on Immunopharmacology

Proc Int Conf Indoor Air Qual Clim — Proceedings. International Conference on Indoor Air Quality and Climate

Proc Int Conf Infrared Phys — Proceedings. International Conference on Infrared Physics

Proc Int Conf Inn Shell Ioniz Phenom — Proceedings. International Conference on Inner Shell Ionization Phenomena

Proc Int Conf Insulin Treat Psychiatry — Proceedings. International Conference on the Insulin Treatment in Psychiatry

Proc Int Conf Int Assoc Water Pollut Res — Proceedings. International Conference of the International Association on Water Pollution Research

Proc Int Conf Intern External Prot Pipes — Proceedings. International Conference on the Internal and External Protection of Pipes

Proc Int Conf Ion Beam Modif Mater — Proceedings. International Conference on Ion Beam Modification of Materials

Proc Int Conf Ion Implant Semicond Other Mater — Proceedings. International Conference on Ion Implantation in Semiconductors and Other Materials

Proc Int Conf Ioniz Phenom Gases — Proceedings. International Conference on Ionization Phenomena in Gases

Proc Int Conf Ionos — Proceedings. International Conference on the Ionosphere

Proc Int Conf Ion Plat Allied Tech — Proceedings. International Conference on Ion Plating and Allied Techniques

Proc Int Conf Ion Sources — Proceedings. International Conference on Ion Sources

Proc Int Conf Land Waste Manage — Proceedings. International Conference on Land for Waste Management

Proc Int Conf Lasers — Proceedings. International Conference on Lasers

Proc Int Conf Lattice Dyn — Proceedings. International Conference on Lattice Dynamics

Proc Int Conf Leuk Lymphoma — Proceedings. International Conference on Leukemia-Lymphoma

Proc Int Conf Light Scattering Solids — Proceedings. International Conference on Light Scattering in Solids

Proc Int Conf Liq Atomization Spray Syst — Proceedings. International Conference on Liquid Atomization and Spray Systems

Proc Int Conf Liq Met Technol Energy Prod — Proceedings. International Conference on Liquid Metal Technology in Energy Production

Proc Int Conf Localized Excitations Solids — Proceedings. International Conference on Localized Excitations in Solids

Proc Int Conf Low Temp Phys — Proceedings. International Conference on Low Temperature Physics

Proc Int Conf Low Temp Phys Chem — Proceedings. International Conference on Low Temperature Physics and Chemistry

Proc Int Conf Magn — Proceedings. International Conference on Magnetism

Proc Int Conf Matrix Vesicles — Proceedings. International Conference on Matrix Vesicles

Proc Int Conf Mech Behav Mater — Proceedings. International Conference on Mechanical Behavior of Materials

Proc Int Conf Mech Bioenerg — Proceedings. International Conference on Mechanisms in Bioenergetics

Proc Int Conf Med Electron — Proceedings. International Conference on Medical Electronics

Proc Int Conf Megagauss Magn Field Gener Relat Top — Proceedings. International Conference on Megagauss Magnetic Field Generation and Related Topics

Proc Int Conf Metall Weld Qualif Microalloyed HSLA Steel Weld — Proceedings. International Conference on the Metallurgy, Welding, and Qualification of Microalloyed (HSLA) Steel Weldments

Proc Int Conf Methods Prep Storing Labelled Comp — Proceedings. International Conference on Methods of Preparing and Storing Labelled Compounds

Proc Int Conf MHD Electr Power Gener — Proceedings. International Conference on MHD Electrical Power Generation

Proc Int Conf Modif Surf Prop Met Ion Implant — Proceedings. International Conference on Modification of Surface Properties of Metals by Ion Implantation

Proc Int Conf Moessbauer Eff — Proceedings. International Conference on the Moessbauer Effect

Proc Int Conf Moessbauer Spectrosc — Proceedings. International Conference on Moessbauer Spectroscopy

Proc Int Conf Molten Salt Chem — Proceedings. International Conference on Molten Salt Chemistry

Proc Int Conf Mycoses — Proceedings. International Conference on the Mycoses

Proc Int Conf Mycoses Superficial Cutaneous Subcutaneous Inf — Proceedings. International Conference on the Mycoses. Superficial, Cutaneous, and Subcutaneous Infections

Proc Int Conf Neuropsychol Learn Disord — Proceedings. International Conference on Neuropsychology of Learning Disorders

Proc Int Conf New Front Hazard Waste Manage — Proceedings. International Conference on New Frontiers for Hazardous Waste Management

Proc Int Conf New Nucl Phys Adv Tech — Proceedings. International Conference on New Nuclear Physics with Advanced Techniques

Proc Int Conf Noise Control Eng — Proceedings. International Conference on Noise Control Engineering

Proc Int Conf Nondestr Test — Proceedings. International Conference on Nondestructive Testing

Proc Int Conf Nucl Data React — Proceedings. International Conference on Nuclear Data for Reactors

Proc Int Conf Nucl Far Stab — Proceedings. International Conference on Nuclei Far from Stability

Proc Int Conf Nucl Methods Environ Energy Res — Proceedings. International Conference on Nuclear Methods in Environmental and Energy Research

Proc Int Conf Nucl Methods Environ Res — Proceedings. International Conference on Nuclear Methods in Environmental Research

Proc Int Conf Nucl Photogr Solid State Track Detect — Proceedings. International Conference on Nuclear Photography and Solid State Track Detectors

Proc Int Conf Nucl Phys — Proceedings. International Conference on Nuclear Physics

Proc Int Conf Nucl Power Its Fuel Cycle — Proceedings. International Conference on Nuclear Power and Its Fuel Cycle

Proc Int Conf Nucl Struct — Proceedings. International Conference on Nuclear Structure

Proc Int Conf Numer Methods Fluid Mech — Proceedings. International Conference on Numerical Methods in Fluid Mechanics

Proc Int Conf Nutr Diet Sport — Proceedings. International Conference on Nutrition, Dietetics, and Sport

Proc Int Conf Offshore Mech Arct Eng OMAE — Proceedings of the International Conference on Offshore Mechanics and Arctic Engineering. OMAE

Proc Int Conf Org Chem Selenium Tellurium — Proceedings. International Conference on the Organic Chemistry of Selenium and Tellurium

Proc Int Conf Org Coat Sci Technol Technomic Publ — Proceedings. International Conference in Organic Coatings Science and Technology. Technomic Publication

Proc Int Conf Org Synth — Proceedings. International Conference on Organic Synthesis

Proc Int Conf Parallel Process — Proceedings of the International Conference on Parallel Processing

Proc Int Conf Part Technol — Proceedings. International Conference in Particle Technology

Proc Int Conf Pattern Recognit — Proceedings. International Conference on Pattern Recognition

Proc Int Conf Peaceful Uses At Energy — Proceedings. International Conference on the Peaceful Uses of Atomic Energy

Proc Int Conf Peaceful Uses Atomic Energy — Proceedings. International Conference on the Peaceful Uses of Atomic Energy

Proc Int Conf Permafrost — Proceedings. International Conference on Permafrost

Proc Int Conf Pervaporation Processes Chem Ind — Proceedings. International Conference on Pervaporation Processes in the Chemical Industry

Proc Int Conf Pet Refin Petrochem Process — Proceedings. International Conference on Petroleum Refining and Petrochemical Processing

Proc Int Conf Phase Transform Ferrous Alloys — Proceedings. International Conference on Phase Transformations in Ferrous Alloys

Proc Int Conf Phenom Ioniz Gases — Proceedings. International Conference on Phenomena in Ionized Gases

Proc Int Conf Phonon Scattering Condens Matter — Proceedings. International Conference on Phonon Scattering in Condensed Matter

Proc Int Conf Phonon Scattering Solids — Proceedings. International Conference on Phonon Scattering in Solids

Proc Int Conf Photochem Convers Storage Sol Energy — Proceedings. International Conference on the Photochemical Conversion and Storage of Solar Energy

Proc Int Conf Photocond — Proceedings. International Conference on Photoconductivity

Proc Int Conf Photonucl React Appl — Proceedings. International Conference on Photonuclear Reactions and Applications

Proc Int Conf Phys Electron At Collisions — Proceedings. International Conference on the Physics of Electronic and Atomic Collisions

Proc Int Conf Phys Semicond — Proceedings. International Conference on the Physics of Semiconductors

Proc Int Conf Phys Solids High Pressures — Proceedings. International Conference on the Physics of Solids at High Pressures

Proc Int Conf Plant Growth Regulat — Proceedings. International Conference on Plant Growth Regulation

Proc Int Conf Plant Pathog Bact — Proceedings. International Conference on Plant Pathogenic Bacteria

Proc Int Conf Plutonium — Proceedings. International Conference on Plutonium

Proc Int Conf Plutonium Metall — Proceedings. International Conference on Plutonium Metallurgy

Proc Int Conf PM Aerosp Mater — Proceedings. International Conference on PM Aerospace Materials

Proc Int Conf Port Ocean Eng Under Arct Cond POAC — Proceedings. International Conference on Port and Ocean Engineering Under Arctic Conditions. POAC

Proc Int Conf Positron Annihilation — Proceedings. International Conference on Positron Annihilation

Proc Int Conf Probl Quantum Field Theory — Proceedings. International Conference on the Problems of Quantum Field Theory

Proc Int Conf Prop Water Steam — Proceedings. International Conference on the Properties of Water and Steam

Proc Int Conf Radiat Biol Cancer — Proceedings. International Conference on Radiation Biology and Cancer

Proc Int Conf Radioact Waste Manage — Proceedings. International Conference on Radioactive Waste Management

Proc Int Conf Radiocarbon Dating — Proceedings. International Conference on Radiocarbon Dating

Proc Int Conf Raman Spectrosc — Proceedings. International Conference on Raman Spectroscopy

Proc Int Conf Rapidly Quenched Met — Proceedings. International Conference on Rapidly Quenched Metals

Proc Int Conf React Process Polym — Proceedings. International Conference on Reactive Processing of Polymers

Proc Int Conf React Shielding — Proceedings. International Conference on Reactor Shielding

Proc Int Conf Rob Vision Sens Controls — Proceedings. International Conference on Robot Vision and Sensory Controls

Proc Int Conf Role Formaldehyde Biol Syst — Proceedings. International Conference on the Role of Formaldehyde in BiologicalSystems

Proc Int Conf Sarcoidosis — Proceedings. International Conference on Sarcoidosis

Proc Int Conf Sci Aspects Mushroom Grow — Proceedings. International Conference on Scientific Aspects of Mushroom Growing

Proc Int Conf Silicon Carbide — Proceedings. International Conference on Silicon Carbide

Proc Int Conf Simul Methods Nucl Eng — Proceedings. International Conference on Simulation Methods in Nuclear Engineering

Proc Int Conf Software Eng — Proceedings. International Conference on Software Engineering

Proc Int Conf Soil Mech Found Eng — Proceedings. International Conference on Soil Mechanics and Foundation Engineering

Proc Int Conf Solid Phase Methods Protein Sequence Anal — Proceedings. International Conference on Solid Phase Methods in Protein Sequence Analysis

Proc Int Conf Solid State Nucl Track Detect — Proceedings. International Conference on Solid State Nuclear Track Detectors

Proc Int Conf Solid Surf — Proceedings. International Conference on Solid Surfaces

Proc Int Conf Solid Waste Technol Manage — Proceedings of the International Conference on Solid Waste Technology and Management

Proc Int Conf Spectrosc — Proceedings. International Conference on Spectroscopy

Proc Int Conf Spectrosc Radiofreq — Proceedings. International Conference on Spectroscopy at Radiofrequencies

Proc Int Conf Stable Isot — Proceedings. International Conference on Stable Isotopes

Proc Int Conf Stable Isot Chem Biol Med — Proceedings. International Conference on Stable Isotopes in Chemistry, Biology,and Medicine

Proc Int Conf Stat Prop Nucl — Proceedings. International Conference on Statistical Properties of Nuclei

Proc Int Conf Strength Met Alloys — Proceedings. International Conference on the Strength of Metals and Alloys

Proc Int Conf Study Nucl Struct Neutrons — Proceedings. International Conference on the Study of Nuclear Structure with Neutrons

Proc Int Conf Supercond Quantum Devices — Proceedings. International Conference on Superconducting Quantum Devices

Proc Int Conf Synth Fibrinolytic Thrombolytic Agents — Proceedings. International Conference on Synthetic Fibrinolytic-Thrombolytic Agents

Proc Int Conf Ternary Multinary Compd — Proceedings. International Conference on Ternary and Multinary Compounds

Proc Int Conf Texture — Proceedings. International Conference on Texture

Proc Int Conf Textures Mater — Proceedings. International Conference on Textures of Materials

Proc Int Conf Theor Phys Biol — Proceedings. International Conference on Theoretical Physics and Biology

Proc Int Conf Therm Anal — Proceedings. International Conference on Thermal Analysis

Proc Int Conf Therm Conduct — Proceedings. International Conference on Thermal Conductivity

Proc Int Conf Thermoelectr — Proceedings of the International Conference on Thermoelectrics

Proc Int Conf Thermoelectr Energy Convers — Proceedings. International Conference on Thermoelectric Energy Conversion

Proc Int Conf Titanium — Proceedings. International Conference on Titanium

Proc Int Conf Titanium Prod Appl — Proceedings. International Conference on Titanium Products and Applications

Proc Int Conf Tools Artif Intell — Proceedings of the International Conference on Tools with Artificial Intelligence

Proc Int Conf Toxic Dinoflagellate Blooms — Proceedings. International Conference on Toxic Dinoflagellate Blooms

Proc Int Conf Transmutat Doping Semicond — Proceedings. International Conference on Transmutation Doping in Semiconductors

Proc Int Conf Trichinellosis — Proceedings. International Conference on Trichinellosis

Proc Int Conf Vac Metall — Proceedings. International Conference on Vacuum Metallurgy

Proc Int Conf Vac Metall Electroslag Remelting Processes — Proceedings. International Conference on Vacuum Metallurgy and Electroslag Remelting Processes

Proc Int Conf Vac Ultraviolet Radiat Phys — Proceedings. International Conference on Vacuum Ultraviolet Radiation Physics

Proc Int Conf Vac Web Coat — Proceedings. International Conference on Vacuum Web Coating

Proc Int Conf Valence Instab — Proceedings. International Conference on Valence Instabilities

Proc Int Conf Waste Disposal Mar Environ — Proceedings. International Conference on Waste Disposal in the Marine Environment

Proc Int Conf Wildl Dis — Proceedings. International Conference on Wildlife Disease

Proc Int Cong Phot — Proceedings. International Congress of Photography

Proc Int Congr Acarol — Proceedings. International Congress of Acarology

Proc Int Congr Aeronaut Sci — Proceedings. International Congress in the Aeronautical Sciences

Proc Int Congr Air Pollut — Proceedings. International Congress on Air Pollution

Proc Int Congr Allergol — Proceedings. International Congress of Allergology

Proc Int Congr Anal Sci — Proceedings. International Congress on Analytical Sciences

Proc Int Congr Anim Reprod — Proceedings. International Congress on Animal Reproduction

Proc Int Congr Anim Reprod Artif Insemin — Proceedings. International Congress on Animal Reproduction and Artificial Insemination

Proc Int Congr Appl Mech — Proceedings. International Congress of Applied Mechanics

Proc Int Congr Aviat Space Med — Proceedings. International Congress on Aviation and Space Medicine

Proc Int Congr Biochem — Proceedings. International Congress of Biochemistry

Proc Int Congr Bioelectrochem Bioenerg — Proceedings. International Congress on Bioelectrochemistry and Bioenergetics

Proc Int Congr Catal — Proceedings. International Congress on Catalysis

Proc Int Congr Chem Cem — Proceedings. International Congress on the Chemistry of Cement

Proc Int Congr Chemother — Proceedings. International Congress of Chemotherapy

Proc Int Congr Clin Chem — Proceedings. International Congress on Clinical Chemistry

Proc Int Congr Comp Physiol — Proceedings. International Congress on Comparative Physiology

Proc Int Congr Crop Prot — Proceedings. International Congress on Crop Protection

Proc Int Congr Cybern Syst — Proceedings. International Congress of Cybernetics and Systems

Proc Int Congr Dermatol — Proceedings. International Congress of Dermatology

Proc Int Congr Deterior Conserv Stone — Proceedings. International Congress on Deterioration and Conservation of Stone

Proc Int Congr Diamonds Ind — Proceedings. International Congress on Diamonds in Industry

Proc Int Congr Eng Food — Proceedings. International Congress on Engineering and Food

Proc Int Congr Ent — Proceedings. International Congress of Entomology

Proc Int Congr Entomol — Proceedings. International Congress of Entomology

Proc Int Congr Essent Oils Fragrances Flavours — Proceedings. International Congress of Essential Oils, Fragrances, and Flavours

Proc Int Congr Exfoliative Cytol — Proceedings. International Congress of Exfoliative Cytology

Proc Int Congr Food Sci Technol — Proceedings. International Congress of Food Science and Technology

Proc Int Congr Gastroenterol — Proceedings. International Congress of Gastroenterology

Proc Int Congr Genet — Proceedings. International Congress of Genetics

Proc Int Congr Geront — Proceedings. International Congress on Gerontology

Proc Int Congr Gerontol — Proceedings. International Congress on Gerontology

Proc Int Congr Hair Res — Proceedings. International Congress on Hair Research

Proc Int Congr Heat Treat Mater — Proceedings. International Congress on Heat Treatment of Materials

Proc Int Congr Hematol — Proceedings. International Congress of Hematology

Proc Int Congr High Speed Photogr — Proceedings. International Congress on High Speed Photography

Proc Int Congr High Speed Photogr Photonics — Proceedings. International Congress on High Speed Photography and Photonics

Proc Int Congr Hist Med — Proceedings. International Congress of the History of Medicine

Proc Int Congr Hist Sci — Proceedings. International Congress of the History of Science

Proc Int Congr Horm Steroids — Proceedings. International Congress on Hormonal Steroids

Proc Int Congr Hum Genet — Proceedings. International Congress of Human Genetics

Proc Int Congr Hyg Prev Med — Proceedings. International Congress for Hygiene and Preventive Medicine

Proc Int Congr Hyperbaric Med — Proceedings. International Congress on Hyperbaric Medicine

Proc Int Congr Immunol — Proceedings. International Congress of Immunology

Proc Int Congr Immunol Satell Workshop — Proceedings. International Congress of Immunology. Satellite Workshop

Proc Int Congr Instrum Aerosp Simul Facil — Proceedings. International Congress on Instrumentation in Aerospace Simulation Facilities

Proc Int Congr Int Assoc Hydrogeol — Proceedings. International Congress. International Association of Hydrogeologists

Proc Int Congr Int Comm Opt — Proceedings. International Congress. International Commission for Optics

Proc Int Congr Intern Med — Proceedings. International Congress of Internal Medicine

Proc Int Congr Int Fed Autom Control — Proceedings. International Congress. International Federation of Automatic Control

Proc Int Congr Int Radiat Prot Assoc — Proceedings. International Congress. International Radiation Protection Association

Proc Int Congr Int Soc Hematol — Proceedings. International Congress. International Society of Hematology

Proc Int Congr Int Union Study Soc Insects — Proceedings. International Congress. International Union for the Study of Social Insects

Proc Int Congr Lightweight Concr — Proceedings. International Congress on Lightweight Concrete

Proc Int Congr Lymphol — Proceedings. International Congress of Lymphology

Proc Int Congr Mar Corros Fouling — Proceedings. International Congress on Marine Corrosion and Fouling

Proc Int Congr Meat Sci Technol — Proceedings. International Congress of Meat Science and Technology

Proc Int Congr Med Plant Res — Proceedings. International Congress on Medicinal Plant Research

Proc Int Congr Menopause — Proceedings. International Congress on the Menopause

Proc Int Congr Ment Retard — Proceedings. International Congress on Mental Retardation

Proc Int Congr Microbiol Stand — Proceedings. International Congress for Microbiological Standardization

Proc Int Congr Mil Med Pharm — Proceedings. International Congress of Military Medicine and Pharmacy

Proc Int Congr Muscle Dis — Proceedings. International Congress on Muscle Diseases

Proc Int Congr Mushroom Sci — Proceedings. International Congress on Mushroom Science

Proc Int Congr Nephrol — Proceedings. International Congress of Nephrology

Proc Int Congr Neuro Genet Neuro Ophthalmol — Proceedings. International Congress of Neuro-Genetics and Neuro-Ophthalmology

Proc Int Congr Neuropathol — Proceedings. International Congress of Neuropathology

Proc Int Congr Neuro Pharmacol — Proceedings. International Congress of Neuro-Pharmacology

Proc Int Congr Neuro Psychopharmacol — Proceedings. International Congress of Neuro-Psychopharmacology

Proc Int Congr Neurotoxicol — Proceedings. International Congress on Neurotoxicology

Proc Int Congr Nutr — Proceedings. International Congress of Nutrition

Proc Int Congr Nutr (Hamburg) — Proceedings. International Congress of Nutrition (Hamburg)

Proc Int Congr Obes — Proceedings. International Congress on Obesity

Proc Int Congr Occup Health — Proceedings. International Congress on Occupational Health

Proc Int Congr Org Geochem — Proceedings. International Congress on Organic Geochemistry

Proc Int Congr Parasitol — Proceedings. International Congress of Parasitology

Proc Int Congr Pathol Physiol — Proceedings. International Congress on Pathological Physiology

Proc Int Congr Pharmacol — Proceedings. International Congress on Pharmacology

Proc Int Congr Pharm Sci — Proceedings. International Congress of Pharmaceutical Sciences

Proc Int Congr Pharm Sci FIP — Proceedings. International Congress of Pharmaceutical Sciences of FIP

Proc Int Congr Phosphorus Compd — Proceedings. International Congress on Phosphorus Compounds

Proc Int Congr Photobiol — Proceedings. International Congress on Photobiology

Proc Int Congr Photosynth — Proceedings. International Congress on Photosynthesis

Proc Int Congr Photosynth Res — Proceedings. International Congress on Photosynthesis Research

Proc Int Congr Phys Med — Proceedings. International Congress of Physical Medicine

Proc Int Congr Plant Sci — Proceedings. International Congress of Plant Sciences

Proc Int Congr Plant Tissue Cell Cult — Proceedings. International Congress of Plant Tissue and Cell Culture

Proc Int Congr Polym Concr — Proceedings. International Congress on Polymers in Concrete

Proc Int Congr Primatol — Proceedings. International Congress of Primatology

Proc Int Congr PRO AQUA — Proceedings. International Congress PRO AQUA

Proc Int Congr Protozool — Proceedings. International Congress on Protozoology

Proc Int Congr Psychother — Proceedings. International Congress of Psychotherapy

Proc Int Congr Pure Appl Chem — Proceedings. International Congress of Pure and Applied Chemistry

Proc Int Congr Quantum Electron — Proceedings. International Congress on Quantum Electronics

Proc Int Congr Radiat Prot — Proceedings. International Congress of Radiation Protection

Proc Int Congr Radiat Res — Proceedings. International Congress of Radiation Research

Proc Int Congr Refrig — Proceedings. International Congress of Refrigeration

Proc Int Congr Reprod Immunol — Proceedings. International Congress of Reproductive Immunology

Proc Int Congr Res Burns — Proceedings. International Congress on Research in Burns

Proc Int Congr Rheol — Proceedings. International Congress on Rheology

Proc Int Congr Rock Mech — Proceedings. International Congress on Rock Mechanics

Proc Int Congr Rural Med — Proceedings. International Congress of Rural Medicine

Proc Int Congr Sci Hum Environ — Proceedings. International Congress of Scientists on the Human Environment

Proc Int Congr Soilless Cult — Proceedings. International Congress on Soilless Culture

Proc Int Congr Stereol — Proceedings. International Congress for Stereology

Proc Int Congr Surf Act — Proceedings. International Congress of Surface Activity

Proc Int Congr Surf Act Subst — Proceedings. International Congress on Surface Active Substances

Proc Int Congr Surf Technol — Proceedings. International Congress on Surface Technology

Proc Int Congr Transplant Soc — Proceedings. International Congress. Transplantation Society

Proc Int Congr Virol — Proceedings. International Congress for Virology

Proc Int Congr Zool — Proceedings. International Congress of Zoology

Proc Int Conv Autom Instrum — Proceedings. International Convention on Automation and Instrumentation

Proc Int Convoc Immunol — Proceedings. International Convocation on Immunology

Proc Int Coral Reef Symp — Proceedings. International Coral Reef Symposium

Proc Int Corbicula Symp — Proceedings. International Corbicula Symposium

Proc Int Course Peritoneal Dial — Proceedings. International Course on Peritoneal Dialysis

Proc Int Cryog Eng Conf — Proceedings of the International Cryogenic Engineering Conference

Proc Int Cystic Fibrosis Congr — Proceedings. International Cystic Fibrosis Congress

Proc Int Dist Heat Assoc — Proceedings. International District Heating Association

Proc Int Drying Symp — Proceedings. International Drying Symposium

Proc Int Electrodeposition Conf — Proceedings. International Electrodeposition Conference

Proc Int Electron Beam Process Semin — Proceedings. International Electron Beam Processing Seminar

Proc Int Electron Packag Conf — Proceedings of the International Electronics Packaging Conference

Proc Int EMIS Conf Low Energy Ion Accel Mass Sep — Proceedings. International EMIS [*Electromagnetic Isotope Separation*] Conference on Low Energy Ion Accelerators and Mass Separators

Proc Inter Afr Soils Conf — Proceedings. Inter-African Soils Conference

Proc Inter Am Symp Hemoglobins — Proceedings. Inter-American Symposium on Hemoglobins

Proc Inter Am Symp Space Res — Proceedings. Inter-America Symposium on Space Research

Proc Interdiscip Conf Electromagn Scattering — Proceedings. Interdisciplinary Conference on Electromagnetic Scattering

Proc Inter Guiana Geol Conf — Proceedings. Inter-Guiana Geological Conference

Proc Internat School of Phys Enrico Fermi — Proceedings. International School of Physics "Enrico Fermi"

Proc Inter Nav Corros Conf — Proceedings. Inter-Naval Corrosion Conference

Proc Intersci Conf Antimicrob Agents Chemother — Proceedings. Interscience Conference on Antimicrobial Agents and Chemotherapy

Proc Intersoc Energy Conver Eng Conf — Proceedings. Intersociety Energy Conversion Engineering Conference

Proc Intersoc Energy Convers Eng Conf — Proceedings. Intersociety Energy Conversion Engineering Conference

Proc Interuniv Fac Work Conf — Proceedings. Interuniversity Faculty Work Conference

Proc Int Estuarine Res Conf — Proceedings. International Estuarine Research Conference

Proc Int Europhys Conf High Energy Phys — Proceedings. International Europhysics Conference on High Energy Physics

Proc Int Fab Altern Forum — Proceedings. International Fabric Alternatives Forum

Proc Int Ferment Symp — Proceedings. International Fermentation Symposium

Proc Int Field Emiss Symp — Proceedings. International Field Emission Symposium

Proc Int Fungal Spore Symp — Proceedings. International Fungal Spore Symposium

Proc Int Gas Res Conf — Proceedings. International Gas Research Conference

Proc Int Geochem Explor Symp — Proceedings. International Geochemical Exploration Symposium

Proc Int Grassland Congr — Proceedings. International Grassland Congress

Proc Int Green Crop Drying Congr — Proceedings. International Green Crop Drying Congress

Proc Int Gstaad Symp — Proceedings. International Gstaad Symposium

Proc Int Haarmann Reimer Symp Fragrance Flavor Subst — Proceedings. International Haarmann and Reimer Symposium on Fragrance and Flavor Substances

Proc Int Heat Pipe Conf — Proceedings. International Heat Pipe Conference

Proc Int Heat Trans Conf — Proceedings. International Heat Transfer Conference

Proc Int Heavy Oil Symp — Proceedings. International Heavy Oil Symposium

Proc Int Hort Congr — Proceedings. International Horticultural Congress

Proc Int Hortic Congr — Proceedings. International Horticultural Congress

Proc Int IEEE VLSI Multilevel Interconnect Conf — Proceedings. International IEEE VLSI Multilevel Interconnection Conference

Proc Int Immunobiol Symp — Proceedings. International Immunobiological Symposium

Proc Int Instrum Meas Conf — Proceedings. International Instruments and Measurements Conference

Proc Int Instrum Symp — Proceedings. International Instrumentation Symposium

Proc Int Iron Steel Congr — Proceedings. International Iron and Steel Congress

Proc Int ISA Biomed Sci Instrum Symp — Proceedings. International ISA [*Instrument Society of America*] Biomedical Sciences Instrumentation Symposium

Proc Int ISA Iron Steel Instrum Symp — Proceedings. International ISA [*Instrument Society of America*] Iron and Steel Instrumentation Symposium

Proc Int ISA Power Instrum Symp — Proceedings. International ISA (Instrument Society of America) Power Instrumentation Symposium

Proc Int IUPAC Congr Pestic Chem — Proceedings. International IUPAC [*International Union of Pure and Applied Chemistry*] Congress of Pesticide Chemistry

Proc Int Kilmer Meml Conf Steril Med Prod — Proceedings. International Kilmer Memorial Conference on the Sterilization of Medical Products

Proc Int Kimberlite Conf — Proceedings. International Kimberlite Conference

Proc Int Kongr Tierhyg — Proceedings des Internationalen Kongresses fuer Tierhygiene

Proc Int Kupffer Cell Symp — Proceedings. International Kupffer Cell Symposium

Proc Int Leucocyte Conf — Proceedings. International Leucocyte Conference

Proc Int Leucocyte Cult Conf — Proceedings. International Leucocyte Culture Conference

Proc Int Liver Conf Spec Ref Afr — Proceedings. International Liver Conference with Special Reference to Africa

Proc Int Lymphokine Workshop — Proceedings. International Lymphokine Workshop

Proc Int Mater Symp — Proceedings. International Materials Symposium

Proc Int Meet Biol Stand — Proceedings. International Meeting of Biological Standardization

Proc Int Meet Fast React Saf Relat Phys — Proceedings. International Meeting on Fast Reactor Safety and Related Physics

Proc Int Meet Ferroelectr — Proceedings. International Meeting on Ferroelectricity

Proc Int Meet Future Trends Inflammation — Proceedings. International Meeting on Future Trends in Inflammation

Proc Int Meet Inflammation — Proceedings. International Meeting on Inflammation

Proc Int Meet Int Exhib Sealing Technol — Proceedings. International Meeting and International Exhibition on Sealing Technology

Proc Int Meet Mod Ceram Technol — Proceedings. International Meeting on Modern Ceramics Technologies

Proc Int Meet Neurobiol — Proceedings. International Meeting of Neurobiologists

Proc Int Meet Org Geochem — Proceedings. International Meeting on Organic Geochemistry

Proc Int Meet Soc Chim Phys — Proceedings. International Meeting. Societe de Chimie Physique

Proc Int Microchem Symp — Proceedings. International Microchemical Symposium

Proc Int Microelectron Symp — Proceedings. International Microelectronics Symposium

Proc Int Microsc Symp — Proceedings. International Microscopy Symposium

Proc Int Mine Drain Symp — Proceedings. International Mine Drainage Symposium

Proc Int Mine Water Congr Int Mine Water Assoc — Proceedings. International Mine Water Congress. International Mine Water Association

Proc Int Minisymp Neonat Diarrhea — Proceedings. International Minisymposium on Neonatal Diarrhea

Proc Int Narc Res Conf — Proceedings. International Narcotic Research Conference

Proc Int Neem Conf — Proceedings. International Neem Conference

Proc Int Neurochem Symp — Proceedings. International Neurochemcial Symposium

Proc Int Neuropathol Symp — Proceedings. International Neuropathological Symposium

Proc Int Offshore Polar Eng Conf — Proceedings of the International Offshore and Polar Engineering Conference

Proc Int Ornithol Congr — Proceedings. International Ornithological Congress

Proc Int Particleboard Compos Mater Symp — Proceedings. International Particleboard/Composite Materials Symposium

Proc Int Peat Congr — Proceedings. International Peat Congress

Proc Int Pharmacol Meet — Proceedings. International Pharmacological Meeting

Proc Int Photobiol Congr — Proceedings. International Photobiological Congress

Proc Int Pigm Cell Conf — Proceedings. International Pigment Cell Conference

Proc Int Pl Propag Soc — Proceedings. International Plant Propagators' Society

Proc Int Polarogr Congr — Proceedings. International Polarographic Congress

Proc Int Powder Metall Conf — Proceedings. International Powder Metallurgy Conference

Proc Int Power Sources Symp — Proceedings. International Power Sources Symposium

Proc Int Power Sources Symp (London) — Proceedings. International Power Sources Symposium (London)

Proc Int Precious Met Inst Conf — Proceedings. International Precious Metals Institute Conference

Proc Int Propul Symp — Proceedings. International Propulsion Symposium

Proc Int Pyrotech Semin — Proceedings. International Pyrotechnics Seminar

Proc Int Rapeseed Conf — Proceedings. International Rapeseed Conference

Proc Intra Sci Res Found Symp — Proceedings. Intra-Science Research Foundation Symposium

Proc Int Reindeer Caribou Symp — Proceedings. International Reindeer/Caribou Symposium

Proc Int Res Conf Proteinase Inhib — Proceedings. International Research Conference on Proteinase Inhibitors

Proc Int Rheol Congr — Proceedings. International Rheological Congress

Proc Int Round Table Nucleosides Nucleotides Their Biol Appl — Proceedings. International Round Table on Nucleosides, Nucleotides, and Their Biological Applications

Proc Int Rubber Conf — Proceedings. International Rubber Conference

Proc Int Sch Condens Matter Phys — Proceedings. International School on Condensed Matter Physics

Proc Int Sch Elem Part Phys — Proceedings. International School of Elementary Particle Physics

Proc Int Sch Excited States Transition Elem — Proceedings. International School on Excited States of Transition Elements

Proc Int Sch Mass Spectrom — Proceedings. International School on Mass Spectrometry

Proc Int Sch Phys Enrico Fermi — Proceedings. International School of Physics "Enrico Fermi"

Proc Int Sch Symmetry Struct Prop Condens Matter — Proceedings. International School on Symmetry and Structural Properties of Condensed Matter

Proc Int Sci Congr Cultiv Edible Fungi — Proceedings. International Scientific Congress on the Cultivation of Edible Fungi

Proc Int Sci Tob Congr — Proceedings. International Scientific Tobacco Congress

Proc Int Seaweed Symp — Proceedings. International Seaweed Symposium

Proc Int Seed Test Ass — Proceedings. International Seed Testing Association

Proc Int Seed Test Assoc — Proceedings. International Seed Testing Association

Proc Int Seed Testing Assoc — Proceedings. International Seed Testing Association

Proc Int Semin Cryst Chem Coord Organomet Compd — Proceedings. International Seminar on Crystal Chemistry of Coordination and Organometallic Compounds

Proc Int Semin High Energy Phys Quantum Field Theory — Proceedings. International Seminar on High Energy Physics and Quantum Field Theory

Proc Int Semin Magn — Proceedings. International Seminar on Magnetism

Proc Int Semin Non Destr Exam Relat Struct Integr — Proceedings. International Seminar on Non-Destructive Examination in Relation to Structural Integrity

Proc Int Semin Sampling Assaying Precious Met — Proceedings. International Seminar on Sampling and Assaying of Precious Metals

Proc Int Shade Tree Conf — Proceedings. Annual Meetings. International Shade Tree Conference

Proc Int Shock Tube Symp — Proceedings. International Shock Tube Symposium

Proc Int Soc Citric — Proceedings. International Society of Citriculture

Proc Int Soc Soil Sci — Proceedings. International Society of Soil Science

Proc Int Soc Soil Sci Suppl — Proceedings. International Society of Soil Science. Supplement

Proc Int Soc Sugar Cane Technol — Proceedings. International Society of Sugar Cane Technologists

Proc Int Solid Wastes Conf — Proceedings. International Solid Wastes Conference

Proc Int Spec Symp Yeasts — Proceedings. International Specialized Symposium on Yeasts

Proc Int Spent Fuel Storage Technol Symp Workshop — Proceedings. International Spent Fuel Storage Technology Symposium/Workshop

Proc Int Spore Conf — Proceedings. International Spore Conference

Proc Int Steel Foundry Congr — Proceedings. International Steel Foundry Congress

Proc Int Summer Meet Nucl Phys Nucl Struct — Proceedings. International Summer Meeting of Nuclear Physicists on Nuclear Structure

Proc Int Summer Sch Accurate Determ Neutron Intensities Struc — Proceedings. International Summer School on the Accurate Determination of Neutron Intensities and Structure Factors

Proc Int Summer Sch Crystallogr Computing — Proceedings. International Summer School on Crystallographic Computing

Proc Int Symp Acetabularia — Proceedings. International Symposium on Acetabularia

Proc Int Symp Adv Chromatog — Proceedings. International Symposium on Advances in Chromatography

Proc Int Symp Adv Gas Chromatogr — Proceedings. International Symposium on Advances in Gas Chromatography

Proc Int Symp Adv Mater ULSI — Proceedings. International Symposium on Advanced Materials for ULSI

Proc Int Symp Adv Refract Metall Ind — Proceedings. International Symposium on Advances in Refractories for the Metallurgical Industries

Proc Int Symp Adv Water Eng — Proceedings. International Symposium. Advances in Water Engineering

Proc Int Symp Agglom — Proceedings. International Symposium on Agglomeration

Proc Int Symp Alcohol Fuels Technol — Proceedings. International Symposium on Alcohol Fuels Technology

Proc Int Symp Alcohol Fuel Technol Methanol Ethanol — Proceedings. International Symposium on Alcohol Fuel Technology. Methanol and Ethanol

Proc Int Symp Anaerobic Dig — Proceedings. International Symposium on Anaerobic Digestion

Proc Int Symp Anal Pyrolysis — Proceedings. International Symposium on Analytical Pyrolysis

Proc Int Symp Anim Plant Microb Toxins — Proceedings. International Symposium on Animal, Plant, and Microbial Toxins

Proc Int Symp Antarct Geol — Proceedings. International Symposium on Antarctic Geology

Proc Int Symp Antarct Glaciol — Proceedings. International Symposium on Antarctic Glaciology

Proc Int Symp Antidepressant Drugs — Proceedings. International Symposium on Antidepressant Drugs

Proc Int Symp Aquat Weeds — Proceedings. International Symposium on Aquatic Weeds

Proc Int Symp Aroma Res — Proceedings. International Symposium on Aroma Research

Proc Int Symp Atheroscler — Proceedings. International Symposium on Atherosclerosis

Proc Int Symp At Mol Solid State Theory Quantum Biol — Proceedings. International Symposium on Atomic, Molecular, and Solid-State Theory and Quantum Biology

Proc Int Symp Automot Technol Autom — Proceedings. International Symposium on Automotive Technology and Automation

Proc Int Symp Baboon Its Use Exp Anim — Proceedings. International Symposium on the Baboon and Its Use as an Experimental Animal

Proc Int Symp Ballist — Proceedings. International Symposium on Ballistics

Proc Int Symp Basic Environ Probl Man Space — Proceedings. International Symposium on Basic Environmental Problems of Man in Space

Proc Int Symp Batteries — Proceedings. International Symposium on Batteries

Proc Int Symp Benefic Agglom — Proceedings. International Symposium on Beneficiation and Agglomeration

Proc Int Symp Benzodiazepines — Proceedings. International Symposium on Benzodiazepines

Proc Int Symp Bile Acids Hepatobiliary Gastrointest Dis — Proceedings. International Symposium on Bile Acids in Hepatobiliary and Gastrointestinal Diseases

Proc Int Symp Biochem Parasites Host Parasite Relat — Proceedings. International Symposium on the Biochemistry of Parasites and Host-Parasite Relationships

Proc Int Symp Biocybern — Proceedings. International Symposium on Biocybernetics

Proc Int Symp Biol Chem Basement Membr — Proceedings. International Symposium on the Biology and Chemistry of Basement Membranes

Proc Int Symp Biomater Otol — Proceedings. International Symposium. Biomaterials in Otology

Proc Int Symp Brain Endocr Interact — Proceedings. International Symposium on Brain-Endocrine Interaction

Proc Int Symp Bronchitis — Proceedings. International Symposium on Bronchitis

Proc Int Symp Br Photobiol Soc — Proceedings. International Symposium. British Photobiology Society

Proc Int Symp Calcitonin — Proceedings. International Symposium on Calcitonin

Proc Int Symp Calcium Binding Proteins Calcium Funct Health D — Proceedings. International Symposium on Calcium-Binding Proteins and Calcium Function in Health and Disease

Proc Int Symp Cancer Ther Hyperthermia Radiat — Proceedings. International Symposium on Cancer Therapy by Hyperthermia and Radiation

Proc Int Symp Can Soc Immunol — Proceedings. International Symposium. Canadian Society for Immunology

Proc Int Symp Capillary Chromatogr — Proceedings. International Symposium on Capillary Chromatography

Proc Int Symp Carotenoids — Proceedings. International Symposium on Carotenoids

Proc Int Symp Catecholamines Stress — Proceedings. International Symposium on Catecholamines and Stress

Proc Int Symp Cell Aspects Transplant — Proceedings. International Symposium on Cellular Aspects of Transplantation

Proc Int Symp Cell Chem — Proceedings. International Symposium for Cellular Chemistry

Proc Int Symp Cereb Blood Flow Metab — Proceedings. International Symposium on Cerebral Blood Flow and Metabolism

Proc Int Symp Cereb Sphingolipidoses — Proceedings. International Symposium on the Cerebral Sphingolipidoses

Proc Int Symp Chem Biol Aspects Pyridoxal Catal — Proceedings. International Symposium on Chemical and Biological Aspects of Pyridoxal Catalysis

Proc Int Symp Chem Cem — Proceedings. International Symposium on the Chemistry of Cement

Proc Int Symp Clean Technol Semicond Device Manuf — Proceedings. International Symposium on Cleaning Technology in Semiconductor Device Manufacturing

Proc Int Symp Clin Enzymol — Proceedings. International Symposium on Clinical Enzymology

Proc Int Symp Clin Immunosuppr — Proceedings. International Symposium on Clinical Immunosuppression

Proc Int Symp Coal Oil Mixture Combust — Proceedings. International Symposium on Coal-Oil Mixture Combustion

Proc Int Symp Coal Slurry Fuels Prep Util — Proceedings. International Symposium on Coal Slurry Fuels Preparation and Utilization

Proc Int Symp Comp Biol Reprod — Proceedings. International Symposium on Comparative Biology of Reproduction

Proc Int Symp Comp Endocrinol — Proceedings. International Symposium on Comparative Endocrinology

Proc Int Symp Comp Res Leuk Relat Dis — Proceedings. International Symposium on Comparative Research on Leukemia and Related Diseases

Proc Int Symp Condens Evaporation Solids — Proceedings. International Symposium on Condensation and Evaporation of Solids

Proc Int Symp Cond Meat Qual Pigs — Proceedings. International Symposium on Condition and Meat Quality of Pigs

Proc Int Symp Contam Control — Proceedings. International Symposium on Contamination Control

Proc Int Symp Control Eff Inclusions Residuals Steels — Proceedings. International Symposium on the Control and Effects of Inclusions and Residuals in Steels

Proc Int Symp Controlled Release Bioact Mater — Proceedings. International Symposium on Controlled Release of Bioactive Materials

Proc Int Symp Controlled Release Bioact Mater — Proceedings of the International Symposium on Controlled Release of Bioactive Materials

Proc Int Symp Coral Reefs — Proceedings. International Symposium on Coral Reefs

Proc Int Symp Corros Electron Mater Devices — Proceedings. International Symposium on Corrosion of Electronic Materials and Devices

Proc Int Symp Curare Curare Like Agents — Proceedings. International Symposium on Curare and Curare-Like Agents

Proc Int Symp Detect Prev Cancer — Proceedings. International Symposium on Detection and Prevention of Cancer

Proc Int Symp Diamond Diamond Like Films — Proceedings. International Symposium on Diamond and Diamond-Like Films

Proc Int Symp Discharges Electr Insul Vac — Proceedings. International Symposium on Discharges and Electrical Insulation inVacuum

Proc Int Symp Drying — Proceedings. International Symposium on Drying

Proc Int Symp Dyn Ioniz Gases — Proceedings. International Symposium on Dynamics of Ionized Gases

Proc Int Symp Electr Contact Phenom — Proceedings. International Symposium on Electric Contact Phenomena

Proc Int Symp Electrets — Proceedings. International Symposium on Electrets

Proc Int Symp Electrochem Miner Met Process III — Proceedings. International Symposium on Electrochemistry in Mineral and Metal Processing III

Proc Int Symp Electron Photon Interact High Energ — Proceedings. International Symposium on Electron and Photon Interactions at High Energies

Proc Int Symp Electroslag Other Spec Melting Technol — Proceedings. International Symposium on Electroslag and Other Special Melting Technology

Proc Int Symp Electroslag Remelting Processes — Proceedings. International Symposium on Electroslag Remelting Processes

Proc Int Symp Endem Nephropathy — Proceedings. International Symposium on Endemic Nephropathy

Proc Int Symp Environ Aspects Pestic Microbiol — Proceedings. International Symposium on Environmental Aspects of Pesticide Microbiology

Proc Int Symp Enzyme Chem — Proceedings. International Symposium on Enzyme Chemistry

Proc Int Symp Equine Med Control — Proceedings. International Symposium on Equine Medication Control

Proc Int Symp Essent Oils — Proceedings. International Symposium on Essential Oils

Proc Int Symp Ethanol Biomass — Proceedings. International Symposium on Ethanol from Biomass

Proc Int Symp Exoelectron Emiss Appl — Proceedings. International Symposium on Exoelectron Emission and Applications

Proc Int Symp Exoelectron Emiss Dosim — Proceedings. International Symposium on Exoelectron Emission and Dosimetry

Proc Int Symp Exp Models Pathophysiol Acute Renal Failure — Proceedings. International Symposium on Experimental Models and Pathophysiologyof Acute Renal Failure

Proc Int Symp Extr Metall Alum — Proceedings. International Symposium on the Extractive Metallurgy of Aluminum

Proc Int Symp Fert Higher Plants — Proceedings. International Symposium on Fertilization in Higher Plants

Proc Int Symp Flammability Fire Retard — Proceedings. International Symposium on Flammability and Fire Retardants

Proc Int Symp Flavins Flavoproteins — Proceedings. International Symposium on Flavins and Flavoproteins

Proc Int Symp Flow Visualization — Proceedings. International Symposium on Flow Visualization

Proc Int Symp Fluid — Proceedings. International Symposium on Fluidization

Proc Int Symp Food Irradiation — Proceedings. International Symposium on Food Irradiation

Proc Int Symp Food Microbiol — Proceedings. International Symposium on Food Microbiology

Proc Int Symp Food Preserv Irradiat — Proceedings. International Symposium on Food Preservation by Irradiation

Proc Int Symp Food Prot — Proceedings. International Symposium on Food Protection

Proc Int Symp Fresh Water Sea — Proceedings. International Symposium on Fresh Water from the Sea

Proc Int Symp Gaseous Dielectr — Proceedings. International Symposium on Gaseous Dielectrics

Proc Int Symp Gastrointest Motil — Proceedings. International Symposium on Gastrointestinal Motility

Proc Int Symp Genet Ind Microorg — Proceedings. International Symposium on the Genetics of Industrial Microorganisms

Proc Int Symp Geochem Earths Surf — Proceedings of the International Symposium on the Geochemistry of the Earth's Surface

Proc Int Symp Geod Phys Earth — Proceedings. International Symposium Geodesy and Physics of the Earth

Proc Int Symp Geogr Nephrol — Proceedings. International Symposium on Geographical Nephrology

Proc Int Symp Geol Geochem Manganese — Proceedings. International Symposium on Geology and Geochemistry of Manganese

Proc Int Symp Germfree Res — Proceedings. International Symposium on Germfree Research

Proc Int Symp Glass Capillary Chromatogr — Proceedings. International Symposium on Glass Capillary Chromatography

Proc Int Symp Gnotobiol — Proceedings. International Symposium on Gnotobiology

Proc Int Symp Hist Arabic Sci — Proceedings. International Symposium for the History of Arabic Science

Proc Int Symp Horm Recept Dig Tract Physiol — Proceedings. International Symposium on Hormonal Receptors in Digestive Tract Physiology

Proc Int Symp Hydrotherm React — Proceedings. International Symposium on Hydrothermal Reactions

Proc Int Symp Ind Toxicol — Proceedings. International Symposium on Industrial Toxicology

Proc Int Symp Ind Uses Selenium Tellurium — Proceedings. International Symposium on Industrial Uses of Selenium and Tellurium

Proc Int Symp Inst Biomed Res Am Med Assoc Educ Res Found — Proceedings. International Symposium of the Institute for Biomedical Research. American Medical Association Education and Research Foundation

Proc Int Symp Instrum High Perform Thin Layer Chromatogr — Proceedings. International Symposium on Instrumental High Performance Thin-Layer Chromatography

Proc Int Symp Int Comm Stud Bauxites Oxides Hydroxides — Proceedings. International Symposium. International Committee for Studies of Bauxites, Oxides, and Hydroxides

Proc Int Symp Interact Fast Neutrons Nucl Neutron Gener Appl — Proceedings. International Symposium on the Interaction of Fast Neutrons with Nuclei. Neutron Generators and Application

Proc Int Symp Ionic Mixed Conduct Ceram — Proceedings. International Symposium on Ionic and Mixed Conducting Ceramics

Proc Int Symp Isoelectr Focusing Isotachophoresis — Proceedings. International Symposium on Isoelectric Focusing and Isotachophoresis

Proc Int Symp Isot Sep — Proceedings. International Symposium on Isotope Separation

Proc Int Symp Jpn Weld Soc — Proceedings. International Symposium. Japan Welding Society

Proc Int Symp Large Chem Plants — Proceedings. International Symposium. Large Chemical Plants

Proc Int Symp Lepton Photon Interact High Energ — Proceedings. International Symposium on Lepton and Photon Interactions at High Energies

Proc Int Symp Livest Wastes — Proceedings. International Symposium on Livestock Wastes

Proc Int Symp Magn Mater Processes Devices — Proceedings. International Symposium on Magnetic Materials, Processes, and Devices

Proc Int Symp Mammary Cancer — Proceedings. International Symposium on Mammary Cancer

Proc Int Symp Mass Spectrom Biochem Med — Proceedings. International Symposium of Mass Spectrometry in Biochemistry and Medicine

Proc Int Symp Med Chem Main Lect — Proceedings. International Symposium on Medicinal Chemistry. Main Lectures

Proc Int Symp Med Mycol — Proceedings. International Symposium on Medical Mycology

Proc Int Symp Metab Eye Dis — Proceedings. International Symposium on Metabolic Eye Diseases

Proc Int Symp Microencapsulation — Proceedings. International Symposium of Microencapsulation

Proc Int Symp Microsomes Drug Oxid — Proceedings. International Symposium on Microsomes and Drug Oxidations

Proc Int Symp Miner Deposits Alps — Proceedings. International Symposium on the Mineral Deposits of the Alps

Proc Int Symp Molten Salts — Proceedings. International Symposium on Molten Salts

Proc Int Symp Multipart Dyn — Proceedings. International Symposium on Multiparticle Dynamics

Proc Int Symp Multiparticle Hadrodyn — Proceedings. International Symposium on Multiparticle Hadrodynamics

Proc Int Symp Mult Valued Logic — Proceedings. International Symposium on Multiple-Valued Logic

Proc Int Symp Nat Antioxid Mol Mech Health Eff — Proceedings of the International Symposium on Natural Antioxidants. Molecular Mechanisms and Health Effects

Proc Int Symp Neonat Diarrhea — Proceedings. International Symposium on Neonatal Diarrhea

Proc Int Symp Neuroontog — Proceedings. International Symposium Neuroontogeneticum

Proc Int Symp Neurosecretion — Proceedings. International Symposium on Neurosecretion

Proc Int Symp Neutron Capture Gamma Ray Spectrosc Relat Top — Proceedings. International Symposium on Neutron Capture Gamma Ray Spectroscopy and Related Topics

Proc Int Symp Neutron Capture Ther — Proceedings. International Symposium on Neutron Capture Therapy

Proc Int Symp Nitrite Meat Prod — Proceedings. International Symposium on Nitrite in Meat Products

Proc Int Symp Nucleon Antinucleon Interact — Proceedings. International Symposium on Nucleon-Antinucleon Interactions

Proc Int Symp Nucl Med — Proceedings. International Symposium on Nuclear Medicine

Proc Int Symp Nucl Phys Dyn Heavy Ion Collisions — Proceedings. International Symposium on Nuclear Physics Dynamics of Heavy-Ion Collisions

Proc Int Symp Nucl Quadrupole Reson Spectrosc — Proceedings. International Symposium on Nuclear Quadrupole Resonance Spectroscopy

Proc Int Symp Oilfield Chem — Proceedings. International Symposium on Oilfield Chemistry

Proc Int Symp Olfaction Taste — Proceedings. International Symposium on Olfaction and Taste

Proc Int Symp Org Selenium Tellurium Compd — Proceedings. International Symposium on Organic Selenium and Tellurium Compounds

Proc Int Symp Osteoporosis — Proceedings. International Symposium on Osteoporosis

Proc Int Symp Oxidases Relat Redox Syst — Proceedings. International Symposium on Oxidases and Related Redox Systems

Proc Int Symp Packag Transp Radioact Mater — Proceedings. International Symposium on Packaging and Transportation of Radioactive Materials

Proc Int Symp Parasit Weeds — Proceedings. International Symposium on Parasitic Weeds

Proc Int Symp Passivity — Proceedings. International Symposium on Passivity

Proc Int Symp Phosphogypsum — Proceedings. International Symposium on Phosphogypsum

Proc Int Symp Phys Ice — Proceedings. International Symposium on Physics of Ice

Proc Int Symp Phys Med Atmos Space — Proceedings. International Symposium on the Physics and Medicine of the Atmosphere and Space

Proc Int Symp Plant Pathol — Proceedings. International Symposium on Plant Pathology

Proc Int Symp Poll — Proceedings. International Symposium on Pollination

Proc Int Symp Power Semicond Devices ICs — Proceedings of the International Symposium on Power Semiconductor Devices and ICs

Proc Int Symp Pre Harvest Sprouting Cereals — Proceedings. International Symposium on Pre-Harvest Sprouting in Cereals

Proc Int Symp Princess Takamatsu Cancer Res Fund — Proceedings. International Symposium of the Princess Takamatsu Cancer Research Fund

Proc Int Symp Process Phys Model Semicond Technol — Proceedings. International Symposium on Process Physics and Modeling in Semiconductor Technology

Proc Int Symp Prot Chem War Agents — Proceedings. International Symposium on Protection against Chemical Warfare Agents

Proc Int Symp Psoriasis — Proceedings. International Symposium on Psoriasis

Proc Int Symp Quantum Biol Quantum Pharmacol — Proceedings. International Symposium on Quantum Biology and Quantum Pharmacology

Proc Int Symp Radioimmunol — Proceedings. International Symposium on Radioimmunology

Proc Int Symp Radiol Prot Adv Theory Pract — Proceedings. International Symposium. Radiological Protection. Advances in Theory and Practice

Proc Int Symp Radionuclides Nephrol — Proceedings. International Symposium on Radionuclides in Nephrology

Proc Int Symp Radiopharm — Proceedings. International Symposium on Radiopharmaceuticals

Proc Int Symp Radiosensitizing Radioprot Drugs — Proceedings. International Symposium on Radiosensitizing and Radioprotective Drugs

Proc Int Symp React Solids — Proceedings. International Symposium on the Reactivity of Solids

Proc Int Symp Recent Adv Tumor Immunol — Proceedings. International Symposium on Recent Advances in Tumor Immunology

Proc Int Symp Remote Sens Environ — Proceedings. International Symposium on Remote Sensing of Environment

Proc Int Symp Remote Sensing Environ — Proceedings. International Symposium on Remote Sensing of Environment

Proc Int Symp Reprod Physiol Fish — Proceedings. International Symposium on Reproductive Physiology of Fish

Proc Int Symp Rickettsiae Rickettsial Dis — Proceedings. International Symposium on Rickettsiae and Rickettsial Diseases

Proc Int Symp Ruminant Physiol — Proceedings. International Symposium on Ruminant Physiology

Proc Int Symp Safe Use Solvents — Proceedings. International Symposium on the Safe Use of Solvents

Proc Int Symp Shock Tubes Waves — Proceedings. International Symposium on Shock Tubes and Waves

Proc Int Symp Silicon Mol Beam Epitaxy — Proceedings. International Symposium on Silicon Molecular Beam Epitaxy

Proc Int Symp Silicon On Insul Technol Devices — Proceedings. International Symposium on Silicon-on-Insulator Technology and Devices

Proc Int Symp Skin Senses — Proceedings. International Symposium on the Skin Senses

Proc Int Symp Solid Oxide Fuel Cells — Proceedings. International Symposium on Solid Oxide Fuel Cells

Proc Int Symp Space Technol Sci — Proceedings. International Symposium on Space Technology and Science

Proc Int Symp Spec Anim Fibers — Proceedings. International Symposium on Specialty Animal Fibers

Proc Int Symp Specific Interact Mol Ions — Proceedings. International Symposium on Specific Interactions between Molecules or Ions

Proc Int Symp Steel Prod Process Integr — Proceedings. International Symposium on Steel Product-Process Integration

Proc Int Symp Streptococci Streptococcal Dis — Proceedings. International Symposium on Streptococci and Streptococcal Diseases

Proc Int Symp Stress Alcohol Use — Proceedings. International Symposium on Stress and Alcohol Use

Proc Int Symp Sub Trop Trop Hortic — Proceedings. International Symposium on Sub-Tropical and Tropical Horticulture

Proc Int Symp Synth Fibrinolytic Agents — Proceedings. International Symposium on Synthetic Fibrinolytic Agents

Proc Int Symp Tech Comm Photon Detect Int Meas Confed — Proceedings. International Symposium. Technical Committee on Photon-Detectors. International Measurement Confederation

Proc Int Symp Tech Comm Photonic Meas Photon Detect Int Meas — Proceedings. International Symposium. Technical Committee on Photonic Measurements (Photon-Detectors). International Measurement Confederation

Proc Int Symp Tests Bitumens Bitum Mater — Proceedings. International Symposium devoted to Tests on Bitumens and Bituminous Materials

Proc Int Symp Trace Elem Metab Man Anim — Proceedings. International Symposium on Trace Element Metabolism in Man and Animals

Proc Int Symp Water Desalin — Proceedings. International Symposium on Water Desalination

Proc Int Symp Water Rock Interact — Proceedings. International Symposium on Water-Rock Interaction

Proc Int Symp Weak Electromagn Interact Nucl — Proceedings of the International Symposium on Weak and Electromagnetic Interactions in Nuclei

Proc Int Symp Wine Health — Proceedings. International Symposium on Wine and Health

Proc Int Symp Yeasts — Proceedings. International Symposium on Yeasts

Proc Int Tailing Symp — Proceedings. International Tailing Symposium

Proc Int Tech Commun Conf — Proceedings. International Technical Communication Conference

Proc Int Tech Conf APICS — Proceedings. International Technical Conference. American Production and Inventory Control Society

Proc Int Tech Conf Slurry Transp — Proceedings. International Technical Conference on Slurry Transportation

Proc Int Tech Meet Air Pollut Model Its Appl — Proceedings. International Technical Meeting on Air Pollution Modeling and Its Application

Proc Int Test Conf — Proceedings of the International Test Conference

Proc Int Thyroid Conf — Proceedings. International Thyroid Conference

Proc Int Titanium Cast Semin — Proceedings. International Titanium Casting Seminar

Proc Int Top Conf High Power Electron Ion Beam Res Technol — Proceedings. International Topical Conference on High Power Electron and Ion Beam Research and Technology

Proc Int Top Meet React Therm Hydraul — Proceedings. International Topical Meeting on Reactor Thermal Hydraulics

Proc Int Top Meet Saf Therm React — Proceedings. International Topical Meeting on Safety of Thermal Reactors

Proc Int Transplutonium Elem Symp — Proceedings. International Transplutonium Element Symposium

Proc Int Tungsten Symp — Proceedings. International Tungsten Symposium

Proc Int Turfgrass Res Conf — Proceedings. International Turfgrass Research Conference

Proc Int Union Biochem Int Union Biol Sci Int Symp — Proceedings. International Union of Biochemistry/International Union of Biological Sciences International Symposium

Proc Int Union Biol Sci Ser B — Proceedings. International Union of Biological Sciences. Series B

Proc Int Union Forest Res Organ — Proceedings. International Union of Forest Research Organizations

Proc Int Union Physiol Sci Int Congr — Proceedings. International Union of Physiological Sciences. International Congress

Proc Int Univ Adv Mater Conf — Proceedings. Industry-University Advanced Materials Conference

Proc Int Vac Congr — Proceedings. International Vacuum Congress

Proc Int Vac Metall Conf — Proceedings. International Vacuum Metallurgy Conference

Proc Int Velsicol Symp — Proceedings. International Velsicol Symposium

Proc Int Vet Congr — Proceedings. International Veterinary Congress

Proc Int Water Conf — Proceedings. International Water Conference

Proc Int Water Conf Eng Soc West Pa — Proceedings. International Water Conference. Engineers' Society of Western Pennsylvania

Proc Int Water Qual Symp — Proceedings. International Water Quality Symposium

Proc Int Wheat Genet Symp — Proceedings. International Wheat Genetics Symposium

Proc Int Wheat Surplus Util Conf — Proceedings. International Wheat Surplus Utilization Conference

Proc Int Winter Meet Fundam Phys — Proceedings. International Winter Meeting on Fundamental Physics

Proc Int Wire Cable Symp — Proceedings. International Wire and Cable Symposium

Proc Int Wool Text Res Conf — Proceedings. International Wool Textile Research Conference

Proc Int Work Meet Soil Micromorphol — Proceedings. International Working-Meeting on Soil Micromorphology

Proc Int Workshop Auger Spectrosc Electron Struct — Proceedings. International Workshop on Auger Spectroscopy and Electronic Structure

Proc Int Workshop Basic Prop Clin Appl Transfer Factor — Proceedings. International Workshop on Basic Properties and Clinical Applications of Transfer Factor

Proc Int Workshop Dyn Aspects Cereb Edema — Proceedings. International Workshop on Dynamic Aspects of Cerebral Edema

Proc Int Workshop Genet Host Parasite Interact For — Proceedings. International Workshop on the Genetics of Host-Parasite Interactions in Forestry

Proc Int Workshop Laser Velocimetry — Proceedings. International Workshop on Laser Velocimetry

Proc Int Workshop Nude Mice — Proceedings. International Workshop on Nude Mice

Proc Int Workshop Pers Comput Databases Occup Health — Proceedings. International Workshop on Personal Computers and Databases in Occupational Health

Proc Int Workshop Phys Recoil Sep Detect Arrays — Proceedings of the International Workshop on Physics with Recoil Separators andDetector Arrays

Proc Int Workshop Rare Earth-Cobalt Perm Magnets Their Appl — Proceedings. International Workshop on Rare Earth-Cobalt Permanent Magnets and Their Applications

Proc Int Workshop Rare Earth Magnets Their Appl — Proceedings. International Workshop on Rare-Earth Magnets and Their Applications and the Sixth International Symposium on Magnetic Anisotropy and Coercivity in Rare Earth-Transition Metal Alloys

Proc Int Workshop Software Specif Des — Proceedings. International Workshop on Software Specification and Design

Proc Int Workshop Solenoidal Detect SSC — Proceedings. International Workshop on Solenoidal Detectors for the SSC

Proc Int Zeolite Conf — Proceedings. International Zeolite Conference

Proc Inuyama Symp — Proceedings. Inuyama Symposium

Proc ION GPS — Proceedings of ION GPS

Proc Iowa Acad Sci — Proceedings. Iowa Academy of Science

Proc IPCR Intest Flora — Proceedings. IPCR (Institute of Physical and Chemical Research) Symposium on Intestinal Flora

Proc IPI Congr — Proceedings. IPI [*International Potash Institute*] Congress

Proc IPUAC Symp Photochem — Proceedings. IUPAC [*International Union of Pure and Applied Chemistry*] Symposium on Photochemistry

Proc Iran Congr Chem Eng — Proceedings. Iranian Congress of Chemical Engineering

Proc Iraqi Sci Soc — Proceedings. Iraqi Scientific Societies

Proc IRE — Proceedings. IRE

Proc IREE Aust — Proceedings. IREE (Institution of Radio and Electronics Engineers) Australia

Proc Ir Gene Workshop — Proceedings. Ir Gene Workshop

Proc Irish Ac Section C — Proceedings. Royal Irish Academy. Section C. Archaeology, Celtic Studies, History, Linguistics, Literature

Proc Ironmaking Conf — Proceedings. Ironmaking Conference

Proc Irwin Strasburger Meml Semin Immunol — Proceedings. Irwin Strasburger Memorial Seminar on Immunology

Proc ISA — Proceedings. Instrument Society of America

Proc ISA Int Conf Exhib — Proceedings. ISA International Conference and Exhibit

Proc Isle Man Natur Hist Antiq Soc — Proceedings. Isle of Man Natural History and Antiquarian Society

Proc Isle Wight Natur Hist Archaeol Soc — Proceedings. Isle of Wight Natural History and Archaeological Society

Proc Isr Acad Sci Humanit Sect Sci — Proceedings. Israel Academy of Sciences and Humanities. Section of Sciences

Proc Israel Acad Sci & Human — Proceedings of the Israel Academy of Science and Humanities

Proc Israel Acad Sci Hum — Proceedings. Israel Academy of Sciences and Humanities

Proc Isr Conf Theor Appl Mech — Proceedings. Israel Conference on Theoretical and Applied Mechanics

Proc Isr Symp Desalin — Proceedings. Israel Symposium on Desalination

Proc ISSOL Meet — Proceedings. ISSOL [*International Society for the Study of Origins of Life*] Meeting

Proc IST Symp Electron Ionic Prop Silver Halides — Proceedings. IS and T Symposium on Electronic and Ionic Properties of Silver Halides

Proc Ital Meet Heavy Forg — Proceedings. Italian Meeting on Heavy Forgings

Proc IUB IUBS Int Symp — Proceedings. IUB/IUBS [*International Union of Biochemistry/International Union of Biological Sciences*] International Symposium

Proc IUFRO Conf Wood Qual Util Trop Spec — Proceedings. IUFRO (International Union of Forestry Research Organizations) Conference on Wood Quality and Utilization of Tropical Species

Proc IUPAC Macromol Symp — Proceedings. IUPAC (International Union of Pure and Applied Chemistry) Macromolecular Symposium

Proc JAERI Symp HTGR Technol — Proceedings. JAERI Symposium on HTGR Technologies. Design, Licensing Requirements, and Supporting Technologies

Proc Jap Acad — Proceedings. Japan Academy

Proc Japan Acad — Proceedings. Japan Academy

Proc Japan Acad Ser A Math Sci — Proceedings. Japan Academy. Series A. Mathematical Sciences

Proc Japan Acad Ser B Phys Biol Sci — Proceedings. Japan Academy. Series B. Physical and Biological Sciences

Proc Jap Assoc Advancem Sci — Proceedings. Japanese Association for the Advancement of Science/Nihon Gakujutsu Kyokai Hokoku

Proc Jap Soc Civ Eng — Proceedings. Japan Society of Civil Engineers

Proc John Innes Symp — Proceedings. John Innes Symposium

Proc John Jacob Abel Symp Drug Dev — Proceedings. John Jacob Abel Symposium on Drug Development

Proc Johns Hopkins Workshop Curr Probl Part Theory — Proceedings. Johns Hopkins Workshop on Current Problems in Particle Theory

ProcJPES — Proceedings. Jewish Palestine Exploration Society

Proc Jpn Acad — Proceedings. Japan Academy

Proc Jpn Acad Ser A — Proceedings. Japan Academy. Series A. Mathematical Sciences

Proc Jpn Acad Ser B — Proceedings. Japan Academy. Series B. Physical and Biological Sciences

Proc Jpn Acad Ser B Phys Biol Sci — Proceedings. Japan Academy. Series B. Physical and Biological Sciences

Proc Jpn Am Semin Prospects Organotransition Met Chem — Proceedings. Japanese-American Seminar on Prospects in Organotransition-Metal Chemistry

Proc Jpn At Ind Forum Inc — Proceedings. Japan Atomic Industrial Forum, Incorporated

Proc Jpn Cem Eng Assoc — Proceedings. Japan Cement Engineering Association

Proc Jpn Conf Radioisot — Proceedings. Japan Conference on Radioisotopes

Proc Jpn Congr Mater Res — Proceedings. Japan Congress on Materials Research

Proc Jpn Congr Test Mater — Proceedings. Japanese Congress for Testing Materials

Proc Jpn Natl Congr Appl Mech — Proceedings. Japan National Congress for Applied Mechanics

Proc Jpn Natl Symp Strength Fract Fatigue — Proceedings. Japan National Symposium on Strength, Fracture, and Fatigue

Proc Jpn Pharmacol Soc — Proceedings. Japanese Pharmacology Society

Proc Jpn Physiol Soc — Proceedings. Japanese Physiological Society

Proc Jpn Soc Antimicrob Anim — Proceedings. Japanese Society of Antimicrobials for Animals

Proc Jpn Soc Civ Eng — Proceedings. Japan Society of Civil Engineers

Proc Jpn Soc Clin Biochem Metab — Proceedings. Japan Society of Clinical Biochemistry and Metabolism

Proc Jpn Soc Forensic Med — Proceedings. Japanese Society of Forensic Medicine

Proc Jpn Soc Intern Med — Proceedings. Japanese Society of Internal Medicine

Proc Jpn Soc Med Mass Spectrom — Proceedings. Japanese Society for Medical Mass Spectrometry

Proc Jpn Soc RES — Proceedings. Japan Society of RES

Proc Jpn Soc Reticuloendothel Syst — Proceedings. Japan Society of the Reticuloendothelial System

Proc Jpn Sov Symp Mechanochem — Proceedings. Japan-Soviet Symposium on Mechanochemistry

Proc Jpn Symp Plasma Chem — Proceedings. Japanese Symposium on Plasma Chemistry

Proc Jpn Symp Thermophys Prop — Proceedings. Japan Symposium on Thermophysical Properties

Proc Jpn US Conf Compos Mater — Proceedings. Japan-US Conference on Composite Materials

Proc Jpn US Semin HTGR Saf Technol — Proceedings. Japan-US Seminar on HTGR Safety Technology

Proc Jt Conf Cholera US Jpn Coop Med Sci Program — Proceedings. Joint Conference on Cholera (United States-Japan Cooperative Medical Science Program)

Proc Jt Conf US Jpn Coop Med Sci Program Cholera Panel — Proceedings. Joint Conference. US-Japan Cooperative Medical Science Program. Cholera Panel

Proc Jt Conv All India Sugar Technol — Proceedings. Joint Convention of All India Sugar Technologists

Proc Jt Int Lepton Photon Symp Europhys Conf High Energy Phys — Proceedings. Joint International Lepton-Photon Symposium and Europhysics Conference on High Energy Physics

Proc Jt USA USSR Symp Theory Light Scattering Condens Matter — Proceedings. Joint USA-USSR Symposium on the Theory of Light Scattering in Condensed Matter

Proc Jubilee Sci Meet High Med Inst Varna — Proceedings. Jubilee Scientific Meeting. Higher Medical Institute-Varna

Proc J US Conf Compos Mater — Proceedings. Japan-US Conference on Composite Materials

Proc K Akad Wet Amsterdam — Proceedings. Koninklijke Akademie van Wetenschappen te Amsterdam

Proc Kansai Plant Prot Soc — Proceedings. Kansai Plant Protection Society

Proc Kans Water Sewage Works Assoc — Proceedings. Kansas Water and Sewage Works Association

Proc Kanto-Tosan Plant Prot Soc — Proceedings. Kanto-Tosan Plant Protection Society

Proc KEK Summer Inst High Energy Phenomenol — Proceedings. KEK Summer Institute on High Energy Phenomenology

Proc Kimbrough Urol Semin — Proceedings. Kimbrough Urological Seminar

Proc Kinki Symp Crop Sci Plant Breed Soc — Proceedings. Kinki Symposium of Crop Science and Plant Breeding Society

Proc K Ned Akad Wet — Proceedings. Koninklijke Nederlandse Akademie van Wetenschappen

Proc K Ned Akad Wet B — Proceedings. Koninklijke Nederlandse Akademie van Wetenschappen. Series B. Physical Sciences

Proc K Ned Akad Wet Biol Chem Geol Phys Med Sci — Proceedings of the Koninklijke Nederlandse Akademie van Wetenschappen. Biological Chemical, Geological, Physical, and Medical Sciences

Proc K Ned Akad Wet Nat Sci — Proceedings of the Koninklijke Nederlandse Akademie van Wetenschappen. Natural Sciences

Proc K Ned Akad Wet Ser A — Proceedings. Koninklijke Nederlandse Akademie van Wetenschappen. Series A. Mathematical Sciences

Proc K Ned Akad Wet Ser A Math Sci — Proceedings of the Koninklijke Nederlandse Akademie van Wetenschappen. Series A. Mathematical Sciences

Proc K Ned Akad Wet Ser B — Proceedings. Koninklijke Nederlandse Akademie van Wetenschappen. Series B. Physical Sciences

Proc K Ned Akad Wet Ser B Palaeontol Geol Phys Chem Anthropo — Proceedings. Koninklijke Nederlandse Akademie van Wetenschappen. Series B. Palaeontology, Geology, Physics, Chemistry, Anthropology

Proc K Ned Akad Wet Ser B Phys Sci — Proceedings. Koninklijke Nederlandse Akademie van Wetenschappen. Series B. Physical Sciences

Proc K Ned Akad Wet Ser C — Proceedings. Koninklijke Nederlandse Akademie van Wetenschappen. Series C. Biological and Medical Sciences

Proc K Ned Akad Wet Ser C Biol Med Sci — Proceedings. Koninklijke Nederlandse Akademie van Wetenschappen. Series C. Biological and Medical Sciences

Proc K Ned Wet Ser B Phys — Proceedings. Koninklijke Nederlandse Akademie van Wetenschappen. Series B. Physical Sciences

Proc Ky Coal Refuse Disposal Util Semin — Proceedings. Kentucky Coal Refuse Disposal and Utilization Seminar

Proc LA Acad Sci — Proceedings. Louisiana Academy of Sciences

Proc LA Ass Agron — Proceedings. Louisiana Association of Agronomists

Proc Lake Superior Min Inst — Proceedings. Lake Superior Mining Institute

Proc LAMPF Users Group Meet — Proceedings. LAMPF Users Group Meeting

Proc Lasers Dermatol Tissue Weld — Proceedings of Lasers in Dermatology and Tissue Welding

Proc Lasers Orthop Dent Vet Med — Proceedings of Lasers in Orthopedic, Dental, and Veterinary Medicine

Proc Laser Surg Adv Charact Ther Syst III — Proceedings. Laser Surgery. Advanced Characterization, Therapeutics, and Systems III

Proc Laser-Tissue Interact — Proceedings of Laser-Tissue Interaction

Proc Laser Tissue Interact III — Proceedings. Laser-Tissue Interaction III

Proc Latin Int Biochem Meet — Proceedings. Latin International Biochemical Meeting

Proc Latv Acad Sci — Proceedings. Latvian Academy of Sciences

Proc Latv Acad Sci Part B — Proceedings. Latvian Academy of Sciences. Part B

Proc Latv Acad Sci Sect B — Proceedings of the Latvian Academy of Sciences. Section B. Natural, Exact, and Applied Sciences

Proc Laurance Reid Gas Cond Conf — Proceedings. Laurance Reid Gas Conditioning Conference

Proc Laurentian Horm Conf — Proceedings. Laurentian Hormone Conference

Proc Leatherhead Dist Local Hist Soc — Proceedings. Leatherhead and District Local History Society

Proc Lebedev Phys Inst — Proceedings (Trudy). P. N. Lebedev Physics Institute

Proc Lebedev Phys Inst Acad Sci Russia — Proceedings of the Lebedev Physics Institute. Academy of Sciences of Russia

Proc Lect Annu Oil Gas Power Conf — Proceedings and Lecture. Annual Oil and Gas Power Conference

Proc Lectin Meet — Proceedings. Lectin Meeting

Proc Leeds Lyon Symp Tribol — Proceedings. Leeds-Lyon Symposium on Tribology

Proc Leeds Phil Lit Soc Lit Hist Sect — Proceedings. Leeds Philosophical and Literary Society. Literary and Historical Section

Proc Leeds Phil Lit Soc Sci Sect — Proceedings. Leeds Philosophical and Literary Society. Scientific Section

Proc Leeds Philos & Lit Soc — Proceedings. Leeds Philosophical and Literary Society

Proc Leeds Philos Lit Soc Lit Hist Sect — Proceedings. Leeds Philosophical and Literary Society. Literary and Historical Section

Proc Leeds Philos Lit Soc Sci Sect — Proceedings. Leeds Philosophical and Literary Society. Scientific Section

Proc Lenin Acad Agric Sci USSR — Proceedings. Lenin Academy of Agricultural Sciences. USSR

Proc Leningrad Dep Gedroiz Inst Fert Agro Soil Sci Lenin Acad — Proceedings. Leningrad Department. Gedroiz Institute of Fertilizers and Agro-Soil Science. Lenin Academy of Agricultural Sciences

Proc Leningrad Soc Anat Histol Embryol — Proceedings. Leningrad Society of Anatomists, Histologists, and Embryologists

Proc Lepetit Colloq — Proceedings. Lepetit Colloquium

Proc Leucocyte Cult Conf — Proceedings. Leucocyte Culture Conference

Proc Leuk Marker Conf — Proceedings. Leukemia Marker Conference

Proc L Farkas Mem Symp — Proceedings. L. Farkas Memorial Symposium

Proc L H Gray Conf — Proceedings. L.H. Gray Conference

Proc Lightwood Res Coord Counc — Proceedings. Lightwood Research Coordinating Council

Proc Lincoln Coll Farmers Conf — Proceedings. Lincoln College. Farmer's Conference

Proc Linnean Soc NSW — Proceedings. Linnean Society of New South Wales

Proc Linnean Soc NS Wales — Proceedings. Linnean Society of New South Wales

Proc Linn Soc Lond — Proceedings. Linnean Society of London

Proc Linn Soc London — Proceedings. Linnean Society of London

Proc Linn Soc NSW — Proceedings. Linnean Society of New South Wales

Proc Linn Soc NY — Proceedings. Linnean Society of New York

Proc Liq Cryst Conf Soc Countries — Proceedings. Liquid Crystal Conference. Socialist Countries

Proc Liverpool Bot Soc — Proceedings. Liverpool Botanical Society

Proc Liverpool Geol Soc — Proceedings. Liverpool Geological Society

Proc London Int Carbon Graphite Conf — Proceedings. London International Carbon and Graphite Conference

Proc London Math Soc — Proceedings. London Mathematical Society

Proc London Math Soc 3 — Proceedings. London Mathematical Society. Third Series

Proc Long Ashton Symp — Proceedings. Long Ashton Symposium

Proc Louisiana State Hort Soc — Proceedings. Louisiana State Horticultural Society

Proc Lunar Int Lab Symp — Proceedings. Lunar International Laboratory Symposium

Proc Lunar Planet Sci Conf — Proceedings. Lunar and Planetary Science Conference

Proc Lunar Sci Conf — Proceedings. Lunar Science Conference

Proc Lund Int Conf Elem Part — Proceedings. Lund International Conference on Elementary Particles

Proc Luxemb Conf Psychobiol Aging — Proceedings. Luxembourg Conference on the Psychobiology of Aging

Proc Mach Dyn Semin — Proceedings. Machinery Dynamics Seminar

Proc Magnesium Assoc — Proceedings. Magnesium Association

Proc MA Hist Soc — Proceedings of the Massachusetts Historical Society

Proc Malacol Soc Lond — Proceedings. Malacological Society of London

Proc Malays Biochem Soc Conf — Proceedings. Malaysian Biochemical Society Conference

Proc Manchester Lit Soc — Proceedings. Manchester Literary and Philosophical Society

Proc Mark Milk Conf — Proceedings. Market Milk Conference

Proc Mar Safety Council USCG — Proceedings. Marine Safety Council. United States Coast Guard

Proc Massachusetts Hist Soc — Proceedings. Massachusetts Historical Society

Proc Mass Hist Soc — Proceedings. Massachusetts Historical Society

Proc Master Brew Assoc Am — Proceedings. Master Brewers Association of America

Proc Math Phys Soc (Egypt) — Proceedings. Mathematical and Physical Society (Egypt)

Proc Math Soc — Proceedings of the Mathematical Society

Proc Mayo Clin — Proceedings. Staff Meetings of the Mayo Clinic

Proc Mayo Clin Staff Meet — Proceedings. Mayo Clinic Staff Meeting

Proc MD Del Water Pollut Control Assoc — Proceedings. Maryland-Delaware Water and Pollution Control Association

Proc MD Nutr Conf Feed Manuf — Proceedings. Maryland Nutrition Conference for Feed Manufacturers

Proc Meas Monit Non Criter Toxic Contam Air — Proceedings. Measurement and Monitoring of Non-Criteria (Toxic) Contaminants in Air

Proc Meat Ind Res Conf — Proceedings. Meat Industry Research Conference

Proc Meat Process Conf — Proceedings. Meat Processing Conference

Proc Mech Work Steel Process Conf — Proceedings. Mechanical Working and Steel Processing Conference

Proc Medico-Legal Soc Vict — Proceedings. Medico-Legal Society of Victoria

Proc Meet Adrenergic Mech — Proceedings. Meeting on Adrenergic Mechanisms

Proc Meet Anim Husb Wing Board Agric Anim Husb India — Proceedings. Meeting of the Animal Husbandry Wing. Board of Agriculture and Animal Husbandry in India

Proc Meet Br West Ind Sugar Technol — Proceedings. Meeting of British West Indies Sugar Technologies

Proc Meet Eur Assoc Cancer Res — Proceedings. Meeting. European Association for Cancer Research

Proc Meet Fed Eur Biochem Soc — Proceedings. Meeting. Federation of European Biochemical Societies

Proc Meet Int Collab Adv Neutron Sources — Proceedings. Meeting. International Collaboration on Advanced Neutron Sources

Proc Meet Int Comm Electrochem Thermodyn Kinet — Preoceedings. Meeting. International Committee of Electrochemical Thermodynamics and Kinetics

Proc Meet Int Conf Biol Membr — Proceedings. Meeting. International Conference on Biological Membranes

Proc Meet Int Found Biochem Endocrinol — Proceedings. Meeting. International Foundation for Biochemical Endocrinology

Proc Meet Int Probl Mod Cereal Process Chem — Proceedings. Meeting. International Problems of Modern Cereal Processing and Chemistry

Proc Meet Int Soc Artif Organs — Proceedings. Meeting. International Society for Artificial Organs

Proc Meet Int Soc Hypertens — Proceedings. Meeting. International Society of Hypertension

Proc Meet Int Study Group Steroid Horm — Proceedings. Meeting. International Study Group for Steroid Hormones

Proc Meet Jpn Soc Med Mass Spectrom — Proceedings. Meeting of the Japanese Society for Medical Mass Spectrometry

Proc Meet Maize Sorghum Sect EUCARPIA — Proceedings. Meeting. Maize and Sorghum Section of EUCARPIA (European Association for Research on Plant Breeding)

Proc Meet Mycotoxins Anim Dis — Proceedings. Meeting on Mycotoxins in Animal Disease

Proc Meet Nucl Anal Methods — Proceedings. Meeting on Nuclear Analytical Methods

Proc Meet Plasma Protein Group — Proceedings. Meeting. Plasma Protein Group

Proc Meet P S Biomed Sci Symp — Proceedings. Meeting. P and S Biomedical Sciences Symposia

Proc Meet Text Inf Users Counc — Proceedings. Meeting. Textile Information Users Council

Proc Meet Ultra High Vac Tech Accel Storage Rings — Proceedings. Meeting on Ultra High Vacuum Techniques for Accelerators and Storage Rings

Proc Meet West Indies Sugar Technol — Proceedings. Meeting of West Indies Sugar Technologists

Proc Membr Technol Conf — Proceedings. Membrane Technology Conference

Proc Mem Lect Meet Anniv Found Natl Res Inst Met — Proceedings. Memorial Lecture Meeting on the Anniversary of the Foundation of National Research Institute for Metals

Proc Metall Soc Can Inst Min Metall — Proceedings. Metallurgical Society. Canadian Institute of Mining and Metallurgy

Proc Metall Soc Can Inst Min Metall Pet — Proceedings. The Metallurgical Society. Canadian Institute of Mining, Metallurgy, and Petroleum

Proc Mex Sch Part Fields — Proceedings of the Mexican School of Particles and Fields

Proc Mex Urethane Symp — Proceedings. Mexican Urethane Symposium

Proc Microbiol Res Group Hung Acad Sci — Proceedings. Microbiological Research Group. Hungarian Academy of Science

Proc Microsc Soc Can — Proceedings. Microscopical Society of Canada

Proc Microsc Soc South Afr — Proceedings. Microscopy Society of Southern Africa

Proc Microsc Symp — Proceedings. Microscopy Symposium

Proc Mid Am Spectrosc Symp — Proceedings. Mid-America Spectroscopy Symposium

Proc Mid-Atl Ind Waste Conf — Proceedings. Mid-Atlantic Industrial Waste Conference

Proc Middle East Congr Osteoporosis — Proceedings. Middle East Congress on Osteoporosis

Proc Middle East Oil Show — Proceedings of the Middle East Oil Show

Proc Midwest Conf Endocrinol Metab — Proceedings. Midwest Conference on Endocrinology and Metabolism

Proc Midwest Conf Fluid Mech — Proceedings. Midwest Conference on Fluid Mechanics

Proc Midwest Conf Solid Mech — Proceedings. Midwestern Conference on Solid Mechanics

Proc Midwest Conf Thyroid — Proceedings. Midwest Conference on the Thyroid

Proc Midwest Fert Conf — Proceedings. Midwestern Fertilizer Conference

Proc Midwest Power Conf — Proceedings. Midwest Power Conference

Proc Mid Year Meet Am Pet Inst — Proceedings. Mid-Year Meeting. American Petroleum Institute

Proc Mid Year Meet Chem Spec Manuf Assoc — Proceedings. Mid-Year Meeting. Chemical Specialties Manufacturers Association

Proc Midyear Top Symp Health Phys Soc — Proceedings. Midyear Topical Symposium. Health Physics Society

Proc Mine Med Off Assoc — Proceedings. Mine Medical Officers Association

Proc Mine Med Off Assoc SA — Proceedings. Mine Medical Officers Association of South Africa

Proc Miner Conf — Proceedings. Mineral Conference

Proc Miner Waste Util Symp — Proceedings. Mineral Waste Utilization Symposium

Proc Miniconf Coincidence React Electromagn Probes — Proceedings. Miniconference on Coincidence Reactions with Electromagnetic Probes

Proc Minn Acad Sci — Proceedings. Minnesota Academy of Sciences

Proc Minn Nutr Conf — Proceedings. Minnesota Nutrition Conference

Proc Minutes Ann Meet Agric Res Inst — Proceedings and Minutes. Annual Meeting of the Agricultural Research Institute

Proc Miss Water Resour Conf — Proceedings. Mississippi Water Resources Conference

Proc MoBBEL — Proceedings of MoBBEL (Molekularbiologische und Biotechnologische Entwicklungsliga)

Proc Mont Acad Sci — Proceedings. Montana Academy of Sciences

Proc Mont Livest Nutr Conf — Proceedings. Montana Livestock Nutrition Conference

Proc Mont Natl Bitum Conf — Proceedings. Montana National Bituminous Conference

Proc Mont Nutr Conf — Proceedings. Montana Nutrition Conference

Proc Montpellier Symp — Proceedings. Montpellier Symposium

Proc Mtg Comm For Tree Breeding Can — Proceedings. Meeting of the Committee on Forest Tree Breeding in Canada

Proc Mtg Sect Int Union For Res Organ — Proceedings. Meeting of Section. International Union of Forest Research Organizations

Proc Munich Symp Biol Connect Tissue — Proceedings. Munich Symposium on Biology of Connective Tissue

Proc Munich Symp Microbiol — Proceedings. Munich Symposium on Microbiology

Proc Muslim Assoc Adv Sci — Proceedings. Muslim Association for the Advancement of Science

Proc Mycol Symp Pol Dermatol Soc — Proceedings. Mycological Symposium. Polish Dermatological Society

Proc N Acad Sci — Proceedings of the National Academy of Sciences

Proc Nagano Pref Agr Exp Sta — Proceedings. Nagano Prefectural Agricultural Experiment Station

Proc Nagano Prefect Agric Exp Sta — Proceedings. Nagano Prefectural Agricultural Experiment Station/ Nagano-Ken Nogyo Shikenjo Shuho

Proc Nairobi Sci Soc — Proceedings. Nairobi Scientific and Philosophical Society

Proc NA Sci — Proceedings. National Academy of Sciences

Proc Nassau Cty Med Cent — Proceedings. Nassau County Medical Center

Proc NASSH — Proceedings. North American Society for Sport History

Proc Nat Acad Sc — Proceedings. National Academy of Science

Proc Nat Acad Sci — Proceedings. National Academy of Sciences

Proc Nat Acad Sci (India) Sect A — Proceedings. National Academy of Sciences (India). Section A

Proc Nat Acad Sci (India) Sect B — Proceedings. National Academy of Sciences (India). Section B. Biological Sciences

Proc Nat Acad Sci (USA) — Proceedings. National Academy of Sciences (United States of America)

Proc Nat Acad Sci (USA) Biol Sci — Proceedings. National Academy of Sciences (United States of America). Biological Sciences

Proc Nat Acad Sci (USA) Phys Sci — Proceedings. National Academy of Sciences (United States of America). Physical Sciences

Proc Nat Ass Wheat Growers — Proceedings. National Association of Wheat Growers

Proc Nat Conf AIAS — Proceedings. National Conference. Australian Institute of Agricultural Science

Proc Nat Conf Fluid Power Annu Meet — Proceedings. National Conference on Fluid Power. Annual Meeting

Proc Nat Electron Conf — Proceedings. National Electronics Conference

Proc Nat Food Eng Conf — Proceedings. National Food Engineering Conference

Proc Nat Gas Process Assoc Tech Pap — Proceedings. Natural Gas Processors Association. Technical Papers

Proc Nat Gas Processors Assoc Annu Conv — Proceedings. Natural Gas Processors Association. Annual Convention

Proc Nat Hist Soc Wisconsin — Proceedings. Natural History Society of Wisconsin

Proc Natl Acad Sci — Proceedings. National Academy of Sciences

Proc Natl Acad Sci Belarus Chem Ser — Proceedings of the National Academy of Sciences of Belarus. Chemical Series

Proc Natl Acad Sci (India) — Proceedings. National Academy of Sciences (India)

Proc Natl Acad Sci (India) Sect A — Proceedings. National Academy of Sciences (India). Section A. Physical Sciences

Proc Natl Acad Sci (India) Sect A Phys Sci — Proceedings. National Academy of Sciences (India). Section A. Physical Sciences

Proc Natl Acad Sci (India) Sect B — Proceedings. National Academy of Sciences (India). Section B. Biological Sciences

Proc Natl Acad Sci (India) Sect B Biol Sci — Proceedings. National Academy of Sciences (India). Section B. Biological Sciences

Proc Natl Acad Sci (USA) — Proceedings. National Academy of Sciences (United States of America)

Proc Natl Acad USA — Proceedings. National Academy. United States of America

Proc Natl Agric Plast Congr — Proceedings. National Agricultural Plastics Congress

Proc Natl Air Pollut Symp — Proceedings. National Air Pollution Symposium

Proc Natl Anal Instrum Symp — Proceedings. Mational Analysis Instrumentation Symposium

Proc Natl Asphalt Conf — Proceedings. National Asphalt Conference

Proc Natl Biomed Sci Instrum Symp — Proceedings. National Biomedical Sciences Instrumentation Symposium

Proc Natl Biophys Conf — Proceedings. National Biophysics Conference

Proc Natl Cancer Conf — Proceedings. National Cancer Conference

Proc Natl Cent Sci Res Vietnam — Proceedings. National Centre for Scientific Research of Vietnam

Proc Natl Cent Sci Technol Vietnam — Proceedings of the National Centre for Sciences and Technology of Vietnam

Proc Natl Chem Eng Conf — Proceedings. National Chemical Engineering Conference

Proc Natl Comput Phys Conf — Proceedings. National Computational Physics Conference

Proc Natl Conf Adm Res — Proceedings. National Conference on the Administration of Research

Proc Natl Conf Aerosols — Proceedings. National Conference on Aerosols

Proc Natl Conf Artif Intell — Proceedings of the National Conference on Artificial Intelligence

Proc Natl Conf Control Hazard Mater Spills — Proceedings. National Conference on Control of Hazardous Material Spills

Proc Natl Conf Electron Probe Anal — Proceedings. National Conference on Electron Probe Analysis

Proc Natl Conf Environ Eff Aircr Propul Syst — Proceedings. National Conference on Environmental Effects on Aircraft and Propulsion Systems

Proc Natl Conf Fluid Power — Proceedings. National Conference on Fluid Power

Proc Natl Conf Fluid Power Annu Meet — Proceedings. National Conference on Fluid Power. Annual Meeting

Proc Natl Conf Fract — Proceedings. National Conference on Fracture

Proc Natl Conf Hazard Wastes Hazard Mater — Proceedings National Conference on Hazardous Wastes and Hazardous Materials

Proc Natl Conf Hydraul Eng — Proceedings. National Conference on Hydraulic Engineering

Proc Natl Conf IC Engines Combust — Proceedings. National Conference on IC Engines and Combustion

Proc Natl Conf Individ Onsite Wastewater Syst — Proceedings. National Conference for Individual Onsite Wastewater Systems

Proc Natl Conf Methadone Treat — Proceedings. National Conference on Methadone Treatment

Proc Natl Conf Munic Sludge Manage — Proceedings. National Conference on Municipal Sludge Management

Proc Natl Conf Noise Control Eng — Proceedings. National Conference on Noise Control Engineering

Proc Natl Conf Packag Wastes — Proceedings. National Conference on Packaging Wastes

Proc Natl Conf Sludge Manage Disposal Util — Proceedings. National Conference on Sludge Management Disposal and Utilization

Proc Natl Congr Czech Physiol Soc — Proceedings. National Congress. Czechoslovak Physiological Society

Proc Natl Conv Study Inf Doc — Proceedings. National Convention for the Study of Information and Documentation

Proc Natl Counc Radiat Prot Meas — Proceedings. National Council on Radiation Protection and Measurements

Proc Natl Counc Sci Dev (Repub China) — Proceedings. National Council on Science Development (Republic of China)

Proc Natl Dist Heat Assoc — Proceedings. National District Heating Association

Proc Natl Drain Symp — Proceedings. National Drainage Symposium

Proc Natl Drug Abuse Conf — Proceedings. National Drug Abuse Conference

Proc Natl Electron Conf — Proceedings. National Electronics Conference

Proc Natl Fert Assoc — Proceedings. National Fertilizer Association

Proc Natl Food Eng Conf — Proceedings. National Food Engineering Conference

Proc Natl Forum Mercury Fish — Proceedings. National Forum on Mercury in Fish

Proc Natl Ginseng Conf — Proceedings. National Ginseng Conference

Proc Natl Heat Mass Transfer Conf — Proceedings. National Heat and Mass Transfer Conference

Proc Natl Home Sewage Treat Symp — Proceedings. National Home Sewage Treatment Symposium

Proc Natl Incinerator Conf — Proceedings. National Incinerator Conference

Proc Natl Instrum Soc Am Chem Pet Instrum Symp — Proceedings. National Instrument Society of America. Chemical and Petroleum Instrumentation Symposium

Proc Natl Inst Sci (India) — Proceedings. National Institute of Sciences (India)

Proc Natl Inst Sci (India) A — Proceedings. National Institute of Sciences (India). Part A. Physical Sciences

Proc Natl Inst Sci (India) Part A — Proceedings. National Institute of Sciences (India). Part A. Physical Sciences

Proc Natl Inst Sci (India) Part A Phys Sci — Proceedings. National Institute of Sciences (India). Part A. Physical Sciences

Proc Natl Inst Sci (India) Part A Suppl — Proceedings. National Institute of Sciences (India). Part A. Supplement

Proc Natl Inst Sci (India) Part B — Proceedings. National Institute of Sciences (India). Part B. Biological Sciences

Proc Natl Inst Sci (India) Part B Biol Sci — Proceedings. National Institute of Sciences (India). Part B. Biological Sciences

Proc Natl Meet Biophys Biotechnol Finl — Proceedings. National Meeting on Biophysics and Biotechnology in Finland

Proc Natl Meet Biophys Med Eng Finl — Proceedings. National Meeting on Biophysics and Medical Engineering in Finland

Proc Natl Meet For Prod Res Soc — Proceedings. National Meeting. Forest Products Research Society

Proc Natl Meet Inst Environ Sci — Proceedings. National Meeting. Institute of Environmental Sciences

Proc Natl Meet S Afr Inst Chem Eng — Proceedings. National Meeting. South African Institution of Chemical Engineers

Proc Natl Online Meet — Proceedings. National Online Meeting

Proc Natl Open Hearth Basic Oxygen Steel Conf — Proceedings. National Open Hearth and Basic Oxygen Steel Conference

Proc Natl Peanut Res Conf US — Proceedings. National Peanut Research Conference (US)

Proc Natl Pecan Assoc US — Proceedings. National Pecan Association (US)

Proc Natl Pollut Control Conf (US) — Proceedings. National Pollution Control Conference (US)

Proc Natl Quantum Electron Conf US — Proceedings. National Quantum Electronics Conference (US)

Proc Natl SAMPE Symp — Proceedings. National SAMPE (Society for the Advancement of Material and Process Engineering) Symposium

Proc Natl Sci Counc — Proceedings. National Science Council

Proc Natl Sci Counc (Repub China) — Proceedings. National Science Council (Republic of China)

Proc Natl Sci Counc Repub China B — Proceedings. National Science Council. Republic of China. Part B. Life Sciences

Proc Natl Sci Counc (Repub China) Part A Appl Sci — Proceedings. National Science Council (Republic of China). Part A. Applied Sciences

Proc Natl Sci Counc (Repub China) Part A Phys Sci Eng — Proceedings. National Science Council (Republic of China). Part A. Physical Science and Engineering

Proc Natl Sci Counc (Repub China) Part B Basic Sci — Proceedings. National Science Council (Republic of China). Part B. Basic Science

Proc Natl Sci Counc (Repub China) Part B Life Sci — Proceedings. National Science Council (Republic of China). Part B. Life Sciences

Proc Natl Semin Immobilized Enzyme Eng — Proceedings. National Seminar on Immobilized Enzyme Engineering

Proc Natl Shade Tree Conf — Proceedings. National Shade Tree Conference

Proc Natl Shellfish Assoc — Proceedings. National Shellfisheries Association

Proc Natl Smoke Abatement Soc — Proceedings. National Smoke Abatement Society

Proc Natl Soc Clean Air — Proceedings. National Society for Clean Air

Proc Natl Sol Energy Conv — Proceedings. National Solar Energy Convention

Proc Natl Symp Aquifer Restor Ground Water Monit — Proceedings. National Symposium on Aquifer Restoration and Ground Water Monitoring

Proc Natl Symp ASME Air Pollut Control Div — Proceedings. National Symposium. ASME (American Society of Mechanical Engineers) Air Pollution Control Division

Proc Natl Symp Assess Environ Pollut — Proceedings. National Symposium on Assessment of Environmental Pollution

Proc Natl Symp Catal — Proceedings. National Symposium on Catalysis

Proc Natl Symp Desalin — Proceedings. National Symposium on Desalination

Proc Natl Symp Radioecol — Proceedings. National Symposium on Radioecology

Proc Natl Symp Therm Pollut — Proceedings. National Symposium on Thermal Pollution

Proc Natl Telecommun Conf — Proceedings. National Telecommunications Conference

Proc Natl Top Meet Nucl Process Heat Appl — Proceedings. National Topical Meeting on Nuclear Process Heat Applications

Proc Natl Waste Process Conf — Proceedings. National Waste Processing Conference

Proc Natl Weeds Conf S Afr — Proceedings. National Weeds Conference of South Africa

Proc Natn Acad Sci — Proceedings. National Academy of Sciences

Proc Natn Acad Sci (India) — Proceedings. National Academy of Sciences (India)

Proc Natn Acad Sci (USA) — Proceedings. National Academy of Sciences (United States of America)

Proc Natn Ent Soc (USA) — Proceedings. National Entomological Society (United States of America)

Proc Natn Inst Sci (India) — Proceedings. National Institute of Sciences (India)

Proc NATO Adv Study Inst Feldspars — Proceedings. NATO Advanced Study Institute on Feldspars

Proc NATO Adv Study Inst Mass Spectrom Theory Des Appl — Proceedings. NATO [North Atlantic Treaty Organization] Advanced Study Institute of Mass Spectrometry on Theory, Design, and Application

Proc Nat Silo Ass — Proceedings. National Silo Association

Proc Nat Telemetering Conf — Proceedings. National Telemetering Conference

Proc Natur Gas Processors Ass — Proceedings. Natural Gas Processors Association

Proc Nat Waste Process Conf — Proceedings of National Waste Processing Conference

Proc Nauk Tov im Shevchenka Khem Biol Med Sekts — Proceedings. Naukove Tovaristvo imeni Shevchenka. Khemichno-Biologichna-Medichna Sektsiya

Proc N Cent Brch Am Ass Econ Ent — Proceedings. North Central Branch. American Association of Economic Entomologists

Proc N Cent Brch Ent Soc Am — Proceedings. North Central Branch. Entomological Society of America

Proc ND Acad Sci — Proceedings. North Dakota Academy of Science

Proc N Dak Acad Sci — Proceedings. North Dakota Academy of Science

Proc Near E S Afr Irrig Pract Semin — Proceedings. Near East - South Africa Irrigation Practices Seminar

Proc Nebr Acad Sci — Proceedings. Nebraska Academy of Sciences

Proc Nebr Acad Sci Affil Soc — Proceedings. Nebraska Academy of Sciences and Affiliated Societies

Proc Ned Akad Wet — Proceedings. Koninklijke Nederlandse Akademie van Wetenschappen

Proc N Engl Bioeng Conf — Proceedings. New England Bioengineering Conference

Proc N Engl Northeast Bioeng Conf — Proceedings. New England (Northeast) Bioengineering Conference

Proc N Engl Soils Discuss Grp — Proceedings. North of England Soils Discussion Group

Proc NewC — Proceedings. Society of Antiquaries of New Castle-upon-Tyne

Proc News Aust Oil Colour Chem Assoc — Proceedings and News. Australian Oil and Colour Chemists Association

Proc News Aust Oil Colour Chemists Assoc — Proceedings and News. Australian Oil and Colour Chemists Association

Proc New Zealand Grasslands Assoc — Proceedings. New Zealand Grasslands Association

Proc NH Acad Sci — Proceedings. New Hampshire Academy of Science

Proc Ninth Int Grassld Congr — Proceedings. Ninth International Grassland Congress

Proc NIPR Symp Antarct Meteorites — Proceedings of the NIPR (National Institute of Polar Research) Symposium on Antarctic Meteorites

Proc NJ Hist Soc — Proceedings. New Jersey Historical Society

Proc NJ Mosq Control Assoc — Proceedings. New Jersey Mosquito Control Association

Proc NJ Mosq Control Assoc Suppl — Proceedings. New Jersey Mosquito Control Association. Supplement

Proc NJ Mosq Exterm Assoc — Proceedings. New Jersey Mosquito Extermination Association

Proc N Mex W Tex Phil Soc — Proceedings. New Mexico-West Texas Philosophical Society

Proc NMFA — Procedure. National Microfilm Association

Proc NOBCChE — Proceedings. NOBCChE (National Black Chemists and Chemical Engineers) Annual Meeting

Proc Nobel Symp — Proceedings. Nobel Symposium

Proc Nonlinear Sci — Proceedings in Nonlinear Science

Proc Nord Aroma Symp — Proceedings. Nordic Aroma Symposium

Proc No RD Fert Assoc India — Proceedings. No. R and D. Fertilizer Association of India

Proc Nord Meet Med Biol Eng — Proceedings. Nordic Meeting on Medical and Biological Engineering

Proc North Am Conf Powder Coat — Proceedings. North American Conference on Powder Coating

Proc North Am For Biol Workshop — Proceedings. North American Forest Biology Workshop

Proc North Am For Soils Conf — Proceedings. North American Forest Soils Conference

Proc North Am Metalwork Res Conf — Proceedings. North American Metalworking Research Conference

Proc North Cent Branch Entomol Soc Am — Proceedings. North Central Branch. Entomological Society of America

Proc North Cent Tree Improv Conf — Proceedings. North Central Tree Improvement Conference

Proc North Cent Weed Control Conf — Proceedings. North Central Weed Control Conference

Proc North Dakota Acad Sci — Proceedings. North Dakota Academy of Science

Proc Northeast Weed Contr Conf — Proceedings. Northeastern Weed Control Conference

Proc Northeast Weed Control Conf — Proceedings. Northeastern Weed Control Conference

Proc Northeast Weed Sci Soc — Proceedings. Northeastern Weed Science Society

Proc Northwest Conf Struct Eng — Proceedings. Northwest Conference of Structural Engineers

Proc Northwest Wood Prod Clin — Proceedings. Northwest Wood Products Clinic

Proc NS Inst Sci — Proceedings. Nova Scotian Institute of Science

Proc Ntheast For Tree Impr Conf — Proceedings. Northeastern Forest Tree Improvement Conference

Proc Nucl Conf Feed Manuf — Proceedings. Nutrition Conference for Feed Manufacturers

Proc Nucl Eng Sci Conf — Proceedings. Nuclear Engineering and Science Conference

Proc Nucl Phys Solid State Phys Symp — Proceedings. Nuclear Physics and Solid State Physics Symposium

Proc Nucl Radiat Chem Symp — Proceedings. Nuclear and Radiation Chemistry Symposium

Proc Nucl Therm Hydraul — Proceedings of Nuclear Thermal Hydraulics

Proc Nurs Theory Conf — Proceedings. Nursing Theory Conference

Proc Nut Grow Soc Oreg Wash BC — Proceedings. Nut Growers Society of Oregon, Washington, and British Columbia

Proc Nutr Counc Am Feed Manuf Assoc — Proceedings. Nutrition Council. American Feed Manufacturers Association

Proc Nutr Soc — Proceedings. Nutrition Society

Proc Nutr Soc Aust — Proceedings. Nutrition Society of Australia

Proc Nutr Soc Aust Annu Conf — Proceedings. Nutrition Society of Australia. Annual Conference

Proc Nutr Soc NZ — Proceedings. Nutrition Society of New Zealand

Proc Nutr Soc South Afr — Proceedings. Nutrition Society of Southern Africa

Proc NWWA EPA Natl Ground Water Qual Symp — Proceedings. NWWA-EPA [National Water Well Association Environmental Protection Agency] National Ground Water Quality Symposium

Proc NY St Hist Assn — Proceedings. New York State Historical Association

Proc NY St Hort Soc — Proceedings. New York State Horticultural Society

Proc NZ Ecol Soc — Proceedings. New Zealand Ecological Society

Proc NZ Grassl Assoc — Proceedings. New Zealand Grassland Association

Proc NZ Grassl Assoc Conf — Proceedings. New Zealand Grassland Association. Conference

Proc NZ Grassld Ass — Proceedings. New Zealand Grassland Association

Proc NZ Inst Agr Sci — Proceedings. New Zealand Institute of Agricultural Science

Proc NZ Sci Mater Conf — Proceedings. New Zealand Science of Materials Conference

Proc NZ Semin Trace Elem Health — Proceedings. New Zealand Seminar on Trace Elements and Health

Proc NZ Soc Anim Proc — Proceedings. New Zealand Society of Animal Production

Proc NZ Weed & Pest Control Conf — Proceedings. New Zealand Weed and Pest Control Conference

Proc NZ Weed Conf — Proceedings. New Zealand Weed and Pest Control Conference

Proc NZ Weed Control Conf — Proceedings. New Zealand Weed Control Conference

Proc NZ Weed Pest Contr Conf — Proceedings. New Zealand Weed and Pest Control Conference

Proc Ocean Drill Program Init Rep — Proceedings. Ocean Drilling Program. Initial Reports

Proc Ocean Drill Program Sci Results — Proceedings. Ocean Drilling Program. Scientific Results

Proc Ocean Energy Conf — Proceedings. Ocean Energy Conference

Proc Ocean Therm Energy Convers Conf — Proceedings. Ocean Thermal Energy Conversion Conference

Proc of Preh Soc — Proceedings. Prehistoric Society of East Anglia

Proc of US Mine Vent Symp — Proceedings of the US Mine Ventilation Symposium

Proc Ohio Acad Sci — Proceedings. Ohio Academy of Science

Proc Ohio State Hortic Soc — Proceedings. Ohio State Horticultural Society

Proc Ohio State Hort Soc — Proceedings. Ohio State Horticultural Society

Proc Oil Gas Power Conf — Proceedings. Oil and Gas Power Conference

Proc Oil Recovery Conf Tex Petrol Res Comm — Proceedings. Oil Recovery Conference. Texas Petroleum Research Committee

Proc Oil Shale Symp — Proceedings. Oil Shale Symposium

Proc Okla Acad Sci — Proceedings. Oklahoma Academy of Science

Proc Ont Ind Waste Conf — Proceedings. Ontario Industrial Waste Conference

Proc Opening Sess Plenary Sess Symp Int Congr Plant Prot — Proceedings. Opening Session and Plenary Session Symposium. International Congress of Plant Protection

Proc Oper Sect Am Gas Assoc — Proceedings. Operating Section. American Gas Association

Proc Ophthalmic Technol — Proceedings of Ophthalmic Technologies

Proc Opt Fibers Med — Proceedings of Optical Fibers in Medicine

Proc Opt Methods Tumor Treat Detect Mech Tech Photodyn Ther — Proceedings of Optical Methods for Tumor Treatment and Detection. Mechanisms and Techniques in Photodynamic Therapy

Proc Oreg Acad Sci — Proceedings. Oregon Academy of Science

Proc Oregon Acad Sci — Proceedings. Oregon Academy of Science

Proc Oreg Weed Conf — Proceedings. Oregon Weed Conference

Proc Organ Inst NSW — Proceedings. Organ Institute of New South Wales

Proc Org Coat Symp — Proceedings. Organic Coatings Symposium

Proc Osaka Prefect Inst Public Health Ed Environ Health — Proceedings. Osaka Prefectural Institute of Public Health. Edition of Environmental Health

Proc Osaka Prefect Inst Public Health Ed Environ Hyg — Proceedings. Osaka Prefectural Institute of Public Health. Edition of Environmental Hygiene

Proc Osaka Prefect Inst Public Health Ed Food Sanit — Proceedings. Osaka Prefecture Institute of Public Health. Edition of Food Sanitation

Proc Osaka Prefect Inst Public Health Ed Ind Health — Proceedings. Osaka Prefecture Institute of Public Health. Edition of Industrial Health

Proc Osaka Prefect Inst Public Health Ed Ment Health — Proceedings. Osaka Prefecture Institute of Public Health. Edition of Mental Health

Proc Osaka Prefect Inst Public Health Ed Pharm Aff — Proceedings. Osaka Prefecture Institute of Public Health. Edition of Pharmaceutical Affairs

Proc Osaka Prefect Inst Public Health Ed Public Health — Proceedings. Osaka Prefecture Institute of Public Health. Edition of Public Health

Proc Osaka Public Health Inst — Proceedings. Osaka Public Health Institute

Proc Oxford Chromosome Conf — Proceedings. Oxford Chromosome Conference

Proc PA Acad Sci — Proceedings. Pennsylvania Academy of Science

Proc Pac Basin Conf — Proceedings. Pacific Basin Conference

Proc Pac Basin Conf Nucl Power Dev Fuel Cycle — Proceedings. Pacific Basin Conference on Nuclear Power Development and the FuelCycle

Proc Pac Basin Conf Nucl Power Plant Constr Oper Dev — Proceedings. Pacific Basin Conference on Nuclear Power Plant Construction, Operation, and Development

Proc Pac Chem Eng Congr — Proceedings. Pacific Chemical Engineering Congress

Proc Pac Coast Gas Ass — Proceedings. Pacific Coast Gas Association, Inc.

Proc Pac Int Summer Sch Phys — Proceedings. Pacific International Summer School in Physics

Proc Pac Northwest Fert Conf — Proceedings. Pacific Northwest Fertilizer Conference

Proc Pac Northwest Ind Waste Conf — Proceedings. Pacific Northwest Industrial Waste Conference

Proc Pac Sci Congr — Proceedings. Pacific Science Congress

Proc PA Ger Soc — Proceedings and Addresses. Pennsylvania-German Society

Proc Pak Acad Sci — Proceedings. Pakistan Academy of Sciences

Proc Pak Congr Zool — Proceedings of Pakistan Congress of Zoology

Proc Pakistan Acad Sci — Proceedings of the Pakistan Academy of Sciences

Proc Pakistan Statist Assoc — Proceedings. Pakistan Statistical Association

Proc Pakist Sci Conf — Proceedings. Pakistan Science Conference

Proc Pak Sci Conf — Proceedings. Pakistan Science Conference

Proc Pan Am Congr Endocrinol — Proceedings. Pan-American Congress of Endocrinology

Proc Panam Congr Rheumatol — Proceedings. Panamerican Congress of Rheumatology

Proc Panel Anal Chem Nucl Fuels — Proceedings. Panel on the Analytical Chemistry of Nuclear Fuels

Proc Panel Moessbauer Spectrosc Its Appl — Proceedings. Panel on Moessbauer Spectroscopy and Its Applications

Proc Panel Neutron Stand Ref Data — Proceedings. Panel on Neutron Standard Reference Data

Proc Panel Peaceful Uses Nucl Explos — Proceedings. Panel on the Peaceful Uses of Nuclear Explosions

Proc Panel Pract Appl Peaceful Uses Nucl Explos — Proceedings. Panel on the Practical Applications of the Peaceful Uses of Nuclear Explosions

Proc Panel Radon Uranium Min — Proceedings. Panel on Radon in Uranium Mining

Proc Panel React Burn up Phys — Proceedings. Panel on Reactor Burn-up Physics

Proc Panel Uranium Explor Geol — Proceedings. Panel on Uranium Exploration Geology

Proc Panel Uranium Explor Methods — Proceedings. Panel on Uranium Exploration Methods

Proc Panel Use Nucl Tech Stud Miner Metab Dis Domestic Anim — Proceedings. Panel on the Use of Nuclear Techniques in Studies of Mineral Metabolism and Disease in Domestic Animals

Proc Panel Use Tracer Tech Plant Breed — Proceedings. Panel on the Use of Tracer Techniques for Plant Breeding

Proc Pan Indian Ocean Sci Congr — Proceedings. Pan Indian Ocean Science Congress

Proc Pan Pac Sci Congr — Proceedings. Pan-Pacific Science Congress

Proc Pap Annu Conf Calif Mosq Control Assoc — Proceedings and Papers. Annual Conference. California Mosquito Control Association

Proc Pap Annu Conf Calif Mosq Vector Control Assoc — Proceedings and Papers. Annual Conference. California Mosquito and Vector Control Association

Proc Pap Graphic Arts Conf — Proceedings and Papers. Graphic Arts Conference

Proc Pap Int Union Conserv Nature Nat Resour — Proceedings and Papers. International Union for the Conservation of Nature and Natural Resources

Proc Pap Synth Conf — Proceedings. Paper Synthetics Conference

Proc Pap Tech Meet Int Union Prot Nat — Proceedings and Papers. Technical Meeting. International Union for the Protection of Nature

Proc Path Soc Phila — Proceedings. Pathological Society of Philadelphia

Proc Paving Conf — Proceedings. Paving Conference

Proc Pen Ital — Procedura Penale Italiana

Proc Penn Acad Sci — Proceedings. Pennsylvania Academy of Science

Proc Peoria Acad Sci — Proceedings. Peoria Academy of Science

Proc Perthshire Soc Nat Sci — Proceedings. Perthshire Society of Natural Science

Proc Perugia Quadrenn Int Conf Cancer — Proceedings. Perugia Quadrennial International Conference on Cancer

Proc Pet Comput Conf — Proceedings. Petroleum Computer Conference

Proc Pet Hydrocarbons Org Chem Ground Water Prev Detect Rem Conf — Proceedings of the Petroleum Hydrocarbons and Organic Chemicals in Ground Water. Prevention, Detection, and Remediation Conference

Proc Pfefferkorn Conf — Proceedings. Pfefferkorn Conference

Proc Pfizer Annu Res Conf — Proceedings. Pfizer Annual Research Conference

Proc Pharm Soc Egypt — Proceedings. Pharmaceutical Society of Egypt

Proc Pharm Soc Egypt Sci Ed — Proceedings. Pharmaceutical Society of Egypt. Scientific Edition

Proc Philadelphia Symp Ocul Visual Dev — Proceedings. Philadelphia Symposia on Ocular and Visual Development

Proc Phil As — Proceedings. American Philological Association

Proc Phil Educ Soc Austl — Proceedings. Philosophy of Education Society of Australasia

Proc Phil Educ Soc GB — Proceedings. Philosophy of Education Society of Great Britain

Proc Philip Morris Sci Symp — Proceedings. Philip Morris Science Symposium

Proc Philipp Sugar Assoc — Proceedings. Philippine Sugar Association

Proc Philos Soc Glasgow — Proceedings of the Philosophical Society of Glasgow

Proc Phil Soc — Proceedings. American Philosophical Society

Proc Physiol Soc London — Proceedings. Physiological Society (London)

Proc Phys Math Soc Jpn — Proceedings. Physico-Mathematical Society of Japan

Proc Phys Semin Trondheim — Proceedings. Physics Seminar in Trondheim

Proc Phys Small Syst — Proceedings. Physics of Small Systems

Proc Phys Soc — Proceedings. Physics Society

Proc Phys Soc Edinb — Proceedings. Physical Society of Edinburgh

Proc Phys Soc Jpn — Proceedings. Physical Society of Japan

Proc Phys Soc Lond — Proceedings. Physical Society of London

Proc Phys Soc London — Proceedings. Physical Society of London

Proc Phys Soc London At Mol Phys — Proceedings. Physical Society. London. Atomic and Molecular Physics

Proc Phys Soc London Gen Phys — Proceedings. Physical Society. London. General Physics

Proc Phys Soc London Sect A — Proceedings. Physical Society of London. Section A

Proc Phys Soc London Sect B — Proceedings. Physical Society of London. Section B

Proc Phys Soc London Solid State Phys — Proceedings. Physical Society. London. Solid State Physics

Proc Phytochem Soc — Proceedings. Phytochemical Society

Proc Phytochem Soc Eur — Proceedings. Phytochemical Society of Europe

Proc Phytochem Soc Symp — Proceedings. Phytochemical Society Symposium

Proc Pineapple Technol Soc — Proceedings. Pineapple Technologists' Society

Proc Pittsburgh Sanit Eng Conf — Proceedings. Pittsburgh Sanitary Engineering Conference

Proc Plant Conf Rubber Res Inst Malaya — Proceedings. Planters' Conference. Rubber Research Institute of Malaya

Proc Plant Growth Regul Soc Am — Proceedings. Plant Growth Regulator Society of America

Proc Plant Growth Regul Work Group — Proceedings. Plant Growth Regulator Working Group

Proc Plant Propagators' Soc — Proceedings. Plant Propagators' Society

Proc Plast Pipe Symp — Proceedings. Plastic Pipe Symposium

Proc Plenary Sess Int Congr Biochem — Proceedings. Plenary Sessions. International Congress of Biochemistry

Proc Plenary Sess World Congr Chem Eng — Proceedings. Plenary Sessions. World Congress on Chemical Engineering

Proc PN Lebedev Phys Inst — Proceedings. P. N. Lebedev Physics Institute

Proc PN Lebedev Phys Inst Acad Sci USSR — Proceedings. P. N. Lebedev Physics Institute. Academy of Sciences of the USSR

Proc Pol Conf Ultrason — Proceedings. Polish Conference on Ultrasonics

Proc Porcelain Enamel Inst Tech Forum — Proceedings. Porcelain Enamel Institute. Technical Forum

Proc Post Accid Heat Removal Inf Exch Meet — Proceedings. Post Accident Heat Removal Information Exchange Meeting

Proc Potato Assoc Amer — Proceedings. Potato Association of America

Proc Poult Sci Symp — Proceedings. Poultry Science Symposium

Proc Power Plant Dyn Control Test Symp — Proceedings. Power Plant Dynamics. Control and Testing Symposium

Proc Power Sources Conf — Proceedings of the Power Sources Conference

Proc Power Sources Symp — Proceedings. Power Sources Symposium

Proc PP Shirshov Inst Oceanol Acad Sci USSR — Proceedings. P. P. Shirshov Institute of Oceanology. Academy of Sciences. USSR

Proc Prehist Soc — Proceedings of the Prehistoric Society

Proc Prehist Soc — Proceedings. Prehistoric Society

Proc Pr Hist Soc — Proceedings. Prehistoric Society

Proc Process Inst Meet — Proceedings. Processing Instructors' Meeting

Proc Process Technol Conf — Proceedings. Process Technology Conference

Proc Prod Liability Prev Conf — Proceedings. Product Liability Prevention Conference

Proc Program Int Symp Controlled Release Bioact Mater — Proceedings and Program. International Symposium on Controlled Release of Bioactive Materials

Proc Proton Radiother Workshop — Proceedings. Proton Radiotherapy Workshop

Proc Pr Soc — Proceedings. Prehistoric Society of East Anglia

Proc PS — Proceedings. Prehistoric Society

Proc PS — Proceedings. Prehistoric Society of East Anglia

Proc Psychopharmacol Symp — Proceedings. Psychopharmacology Symposium

Proc Public Health Eng Conf — Proceedings. Public Health Engineering Conference

Proc Public Works Congr — Proceedings. Public Works Congress

Proc Publ Rochester Int Conf Environ Tox — Proceedings. Publication. Rochester International Conference on Environmental Toxicity

Proc Pulp Pap Symp — Proceedings. Pulp and Paper Symposium

Proc Pyroteknikdagen — Proceedings. Pyroteknikdagen

Proc QD Soc Sug Cane Tech — Queensland Society of Sugar Cane Technologists. Proceedings

Proc QD Soc Sug Cane Technol — Proceedings. Queensland Society of Sugar Cane Technologists

Proc Quadrenn Conf Cancer — Proceedings. Quadrennial Conference on Cancer

Proc Quadrenn IAGOD Symp — Proceedings. Quadrennial IAGOD [*International Association on the Genesis of Ore Deposits*] Symposium

Proc Quadrenn Int Ozone Symp — Proceedings. Quadrennial International Ozone Symposium

Proc Quadrenn Meet Int Assoc Study Liver — Proceedings. Quadrennial Meeting. International Association for the Study of the Liver

Proc Queensl Soc Sugar Cane Technol — Proceedings. Queensland Society of Sugar Cane Technologists

Proc Queensl Soc Sug Cane Technol — Queensland Society of Sugar Cane Technologists. Proceedings

Proc Queens Soc Sugar Cane Technol — Queensland Society of Sugar Cane Technologists. Proceedings

Proc R Acad Sci Amsterdam — Proceedings. Royal Academy of Sciences of Amsterdam

Proc Radio Club Am — Proceedings. Radio Club of America

Proc Radioisot Conf — Proceedings. Radioisotope Conference

Proc Radioisot Soc Philipp — Proceedings. Radioisotope Society of the Philippines

Proc R Agric Hort Soc S Aust — Royal Agricultural and Horticultural Society of South Australia. Proceedings

Proc Rajasthan Acad Sci — Proceedings. Rajasthan Academy of Sciences

Proc Rapid Excavation Tunneling Conf — Proceedings. Rapid Excavation and Tunneling Conference

Proc Rare Earth Res Conf — Proceedings. Rare Earth Research Conference

Proc R Aust Chem Inst — Proceedings. Royal Australian Chemical Institute

Proc R Can Inst — Proceedings. Royal Canadian Institute

Proc Real Time Syst Symp — Proceedings. Real-Time Systems Symposium

Proc Refin Dep Am Pet Inst — Proceedings. Refining Department. American Petroleum Institute

Proc Reg Conf Afr — Proceedings. Regional Conference for Africa

Proc Reg Conf Electron Micros Asia Oceania — Proceedings. Regional Conference on Electron-Microscopy in Asia and Oceania

Proc Reg Conf Int Potash Inst — Proceedings. Regional Conference. International Potash Institute

Proc Reg Educ Annu Chem Teach Symp — Proceedings. Regional Educators Annual Chemistry Teaching Symposium

Proc Regge Cut Conf — Proceedings. Regge Cut Conference

Proc Reg Meet Mod Trends Chemother Tuber Symp Rifampicin — Proceedings. Regional Meeting on Modern Trends in Chemotherapy of Tuberculosis and Symposium on Rifampicin

Proc Relay Conf — Proceedings. Relay Conference

Proc Reliab Maint Conf — Proceedings. Reliability and Maintainability Conference

Proc Remote Syst Technol Div ANS — Proceedings. Remote Systems Technology Division of the American Nuclear Society

Proc Rencontre Moriond — Proceedings. Rencontre de Moriond

Proc R Entomol Soc Lond Ser A Gen Entomol — Proceedings. Royal Entomological Society of London. Series A. General Entomology

Proc R Entomol Soc Lond Ser B Taxon — Proceedings. Royal Entomological Society of London. Series B. Taxonomy

Proc R Ent Soc — Proceedings. Royal Entomological Society

Proc R Ent Soc Lond A — Proceedings. Royal Entomological Society of London. A

Proc Rep Ashmolean Nat Hist Soc Oxfordshire — Proceedings and Report. Ashmolean Natural History Society of Oxfordshire

Proc Rep Belfast Nat Hist Philos Soc — Proceedings and Reports. Belfast Natural History and Philosophical Society

Proc Rep S Seedmen's Ass — Proceedings and Reports. Southern Seedmen's Association

Proc Res Conf Counc Res Am Meat Inst Univ Chicago — Proceedings. Research Conference Sponsored by the Council on Research. AmericanMeat Institute. University of Chicago

Proc Res Conf Res Counc Am Meat Inst Found Univ Chicago — Proceedings. Research Conference Sponsored by the Research Council of the American Meat Institute Foundation. University of Chicago

Proc Res Coord Meet Panel Tracer Tech Stud Use Non Protein Ni — Proceedings. Research Coordination Meeting and Panel on Tracer Techniques in Studies on the Use of Non-Protein Nitrogen (NPN) in Ruminants

Proc Res Coord Meet Seed Protein Improv Programme — Proceedings. Research Coordination Meeting. Seed Protein Improvement Programme

Proc Res Inst Atmos Nagoya Univ — Proceedings. Research Institute of Atmospherics. Nagoya University

Proc Res Inst Fish Oceanogr — Proceedings. Research Institute of Fisheries and Oceanography

Proc Res Inst Nucl Med Biol — Proceedings. Research Institute for Nuclear Medicine and Biology

Proc Res Inst Nucl Med Biol Hiroshima — Proceedings. Research Institute for Nuclear Medicine and Biology. Hiroshima

Proc Res Inst Nucl Med Biol Hiroshima Univ — Proceedings. Research Institute for Nuclear Medicine and Biology. Hiroshima University

Proc Res Inst Oceanogr Fish (Varna) — Proceedings. Research Institute of Oceanography and Fisheries (Varna)

Proc Res Inst Pomol (Skierniewice Pol) Ser E Conf Symp — Proceedings. Research Institute of Pomology (Skierniewice, Poland). Series E. Conferences and Symposia

Proc Res Soc Jap Sugar Refin Technol — Proceedings. Research Society of Japan Sugar Refineries' Technologists

Proc Res Soc Jpn Sugar Refineries' Technol — Proceedings. Research Society of Japan Sugar Refineries' Technologists

Proc Res Soc Jpn Sugar Refin Technol — Proceedings. Research Society of Japan Sugar Refineries' Technologists

Proc R Geogr Soc Australas S Aust Br — Proceedings. Royal Geographical Society of Australasia. South Australian Branch

Proc R Geogr Soc Australas South Aust Branch — Proceedings. Royal Geographical Society of Australasia. South Australian Branch

Proc R Geog Soc Aust S Aust Br — Proceedings. Royal Geographical Society of Australasia. South Australian Branch

Proc RGS — Proceedings. Royal Geographical Society

Proc Rhone Poulence Round Table Conf — Proceedings. Rhone-Poulence Round Table Conference

Proc R Hortic Soc — Proceedings. Royal Horticulture Society

Proc R Inst GB — Proceedings. Royal Institution of Great Britain

Proc R Instn Gt Br — Proceedings. Royal Institution of Great Britain

Proc Rio Grande Val Hortic Inst — Proceedings. Rio Grande Valley Horticultural Institute

Proc Rio Grande Valley Hort Soc — Proceedings. Rio Grande Valley Horticultural Society

Proc R Ir Acad — Proceedings. Royal Irish Academy

Proc R Ir Acad A — Proceedings. Royal Irish Academy. Section A. Mathematical, Astronomical, and Physical Science

Proc R Ir Acad Sect A — Proceedings. Royal Irish Academy. Section A. Mathematical and Physical Sciences

Proc R Ir Acad Sect B — Proceedings. Royal Irish Academy. Section B. Biological, Geological, and Chemical Science

Proc R Ir Acad Sect B Biol Geol Chem Sci — Proceedings. Royal Irish Academy. Section B. Biological, Geological, and Chemical Science

Proc R Irish Acad Sect A — Proceedings. Royal Irish Academy. Section A. Mathematical, Astronomical, and Physical Science

Proc R Irish Acad Sect B — Proceedings. Royal Irish Academy. Section B. Biological, Geological, and Chemical Science

Proc Risoe Int Symp Metall Mater Sci — Proceedings. Risoe International Symposium on Metallurgy and Materials Science

Proc R Microsc Soc — Proceedings. Royal Microscopical Society

Proc RNS — Proceedings. Royal Numismatic Society

Proc Robert A Welch Found Conf Chem Res — Proceedings. Robert A. Welch Foundation. Conferences on Chemical Research

Proc Rochester Acad Sci — Proceedings. Rochester Academy of Science

Proc Rochester Conf Coherence Quantum Opt — Proceedings. Rochester Conference on Coherence and Quantum Optics

Proc Rochester Conf Meson Phys — Proceedings. Rochester Conference on Meson Physics

Proc Rocky Mt Coal Min Inst — Proceedings. Rocky Mountain Coal Mining Institute

Proc Royal Anthropol Inst GB & Ireland — Proceedings of the Royal Anthropological Institute of Great Britain and Ireland

Proc Royal Asiat Soc Ceylon Branch — Proceedings of the Royal Asiatic Society. Ceylon Branch

Proc Royal Aust Chem Inst — Proceedings. Royal Australian Chemical Institute

Proc Royal Geog Soc — Proceedings of the Royal Geographical Society

Proc Royal Inst — Proceedings of the Royal Institution

Proc Royal Irish Acad — Proceedings. Royal Irish Academy

Proc Royal M Assoc — Proceedings. Royal Musical Association

Proc Royal Philos Soc Glasgow — Proceedings of the Royal Philosophical Society of Glasgow

Proc Royal Soc Canad — Proceedings. Royal Society of Canada

Proc Royal Soc Edinb — Proceedings. Royal Society of Edinburgh

Proc Royal Soc London Ser A — Proceedings. Royal Society of London. Series A. Mathematical and Physical Sciences

Proc Royal Soc London Series A — Proceedings. Royal Society of London. Series A

Proc Royal Soc Ser A — Proceedings. Royal Society. Series A. Mathematical and Physical Sciences

Proc Royal Soc Ser B — Proceedings. Royal Society. Series B. Biological Sciences

Proc Roy Anthropol Inst — Proceedings. Royal Anthropological Institute

Proc Roy Anthropol Inst Gr Brit Ir — Proceedings. Royal Anthropological Institute of Great Britain and Ireland

Proc Roy Aust Chem Inst — Proceedings. Royal Australian Chemical Institute

Proc Roy Canad Inst — Proceedings. Royal Canadian Institute

Proc Roy Entomol Soc Lond — Proceedings. Royal Entomological Society of London

Proc Roy Entomol Soc Lond C — Proceedings. Royal Entomological Society of London. Series C. Journal of Meetings

Proc Roy Entomol Soc London Ser A — Proceedings. Royal Entomological Society of London. Series A

Proc Roy Geog Soc Austral — Proceedings. Royal Geographical Society of Australia. South Australian Branch

Proc Roy Inst — Proceedings. Royal Institution of Great Britain

Proc Roy Inst Gr Brit — Proceedings. Royal Institution of Great Britain

Proc Roy Ir Acad B C — Proceedings. Royal Irish Academy. Series B and C

Proc Roy Irish Acad — Proceedings. Royal Irish Academy

Proc Roy Irish Acad Sect A — Proceedings. Royal Irish Academy. Section A. Mathematical, Astronomical, and Physical Science

Proc Roy Microsc Soc — Proceedings. Royal Microscopical Society

Proc Roy Philos Soc Glasgow — Proceedings. Royal Philosophical Society of Glasgow

Proc Roy Phys Soc Edinb — Proceedings. Royal Physical Society of Edinburgh

Proc Roy Soc — Proceedings. Royal Society

Proc Roy Soc B — Proceedings. Royal Society of London. Series B. Biological Sciences

Proc Roy Soc Can — Proceedings. Royal Society of Canada

Proc Roy Soc Canada — Proceedings. Royal Society of Canada

Proc Roy Soc Canada 4 — Proceedings. Royal Society of Canada. Fourth Series

Proc Roy Soc Edinb — Proceedings. Royal Society of Edinburgh

Proc Roy Soc Edinb B — Proceedings. Royal Society of Edinburgh. Section B. Biological Sciences

Proc Roy Soc Edinburgh — Proceedings. Royal Society of Edinburgh

Proc Roy Soc Edinburgh Sect A — Proceedings. Royal Society of Edinburgh. Section A. Mathematical and Physical Sciences

Proc Roy Soc Lond A — Proceedings. Royal Society. London. Series A. Physical Sciences

Proc Roy Soc Lond B — Proceedings. Royal Society. London. Series B

Proc Roy Soc London — Proceedings. Royal Society of London

Proc Roy Soc London S B — Proceedings. Royal Society of London. Series B. Biological Sciences

Proc Roy Soc London Ser A — Proceedings. Royal Society of London. Series A. Mathematical and Physical Sciences

Proc Roy Soc Med — Proceedings. Royal Society of Medicine

Proc Roy Soc QD — Royal Society of Queensland. Proceedings

Proc Roy Soc Ser A — Proceedings. Royal Society. Series A

Proc Roy Soc Vict — Royal Society of Victoria. Proceedings

Proc Roy Zool Soc NSW — Royal Zoological Society of New South Wales. Proceedings

Proc R Philos Soc Glasgow — Proceedings. Royal Philosophical Society of Glasgow

Proc R Physiogr Soc Lund — Proceedings. Royal Physiograph Society at Lund

Proc R Phys Soc Edinb — Proceedings. Royal Physical Society of Edinburgh

Proc R RRIM Plant Conf — Proceedings. RRIM [*Rubber Research Institute of Malaysia*] Planters' Conference

Proc R Soc — Proceedings. Royal Society

Proc R Soc A — Proceedings. Royal Society of London. Series A. Mathematical and Physical Sciences

Proc R Soc B — Proceedings. Royal Society of London. Series B. Biological Sciences

Proc R Soc Can — Proceedings. Royal Society of Canada

Proc R Soc Edinb Biol — Proceedings. Royal Society of Edinburgh. Section B. Biology

Proc R Soc Edinb Nat Environ — Proceedings. Royal Society of Edinburgh. Section B. Natural Environment

Proc R Soc Edinb Sect A — Proceedings. Royal Society of Edinburgh. Section A. Mathematical and Physical Sciences [*Later, Proceedings. Royal Society of Edinburgh. Mathematics*]

Proc R Soc Edinb Sect A Math Phys Sci — Proceedings. Royal Society of Edinburgh. Section A. Mathematical and Physical Sciences [*Later, Proceedings. Royal Society of Edinburgh. Mathematics*]

Proc R Soc Edinb Sect B — Proceedings. Royal Society of Edinburgh. Section B. Biological Sciences

Proc R Soc Edinb Sect B — Proceedings. Royal Society of Edinburgh. Section B. Biology

Proc R Soc Edinb Sect B Biol — Proceedings. Royal Society of Edinburgh. Section B. Biology

Proc R Soc Edinb Sect B Nat Environ — Proceedings. Royal Society of Edinburgh. Section B. Natural Environment

Proc R Soc Edinburgh — Proceedings. Royal Society of Edinburgh

Proc R Soc Edinburgh B — Proceedings. Royal Society of Edinburgh. Section B. Biological Sciences

Proc R Soc Edinburgh Biol Sci — Proceedings. Royal Society of Edinburgh. Section B. Biological Sciences

Proc R Soc Edinburgh Sect A — Proceedings. Royal Society of Edinburgh. Section A. Mathematical and Physical Sciences

Proc R Soc Edinburgh Sect A Math — Proceedings. Royal Society of Edinburgh. Section A. Mathematics

Proc R Soc Edinburgh Sect A Math Phys Sci — Proceedings. Royal Society of Edinburgh. Section A. Mathematical and Physical Sciences

Proc R Soc Edinburgh Sect B Biol — Proceedings. Royal Society of Edinburgh. Section B. Biology

Proc R Soc Edinburgh Sect B Biol Sci — Proceedings of the Royal Society of Edinburgh. Section B. Biological Sciences

Proc R Soc Edinburgh Sect B Nat Environ — Proceedings. Royal Society of Edinburgh. Section B. Natural Environment

Proc R Soc Lond — Proceedings. Royal Society of London. Series B. Biological Sciences

Proc R Soc Lond B Biol Sci — Proceedings. Royal Society of London. Series B. Biological Sciences

Proc R Soc Lond Biol — Proceedings. Royal Society of London. Series B. Biological Sciences

Proc R Soc London — Proceedings. Royal Society of London

Proc R Soc London A — Proceedings. Royal Society of London. Series A. Mathematical and Physical Sciences

Proc R Soc London B — Proceedings. Royal Society of London. B. Biological Sciences

Proc R Soc London Ser A — Proceedings. Royal Society of London. Series A. Mathematical and Physical Sciences

Proc R Soc Lond Ser B Biol Sci — Proceedings. Royal Society. London. Series B. Biological Sciences

Proc R Soc Med — Proceedings. Royal Society of Medicine

Proc R Soc Med Suppl — Proceedings. Royal Society of Medicine. Supplement

Proc R Soc NZ — Proceedings. Royal Society of New Zealand

Proc R Soc QD — Proceedings. Royal Society of Queensland

Proc R Soc Queensl — Proceedings. Royal Society of Queensland

Proc R Soc VIC — Royal Society of Victoria. Proceedings

Proc R Soc Vict — Proceedings. Royal Society of Victoria

Proc R Soc Victoria — Proceedings. Royal Society of Victoria

Proc Ruakura Farmers Conf — Proceedings. Ruakura Farmers' Conference

Proc Ruakura Farmers Conf Week — Proceedings. Ruakura Farmers' Conference Week

Proc Rubber Res Inst Malays Plant Conf — Proceedings. Rubber Research Institute of Malaysia Planters' Conference

Proc Rubber Technol Conf — Proceedings. Rubber Technology Conference

Proc Rudolf Virchow Med Soc City NY — Proceedings. Rudolf Virchow Medical Society in the City of New York

Proc Rudolph Virchow Med Soc NY — Proceedings. Rudolph Virchow Medical Society of New York

Proc Russ Acad Sci Ser Biol — Proceedings. Russian Academy of Sciences. Series Biological

Proc R Zool Soc NSW — Proceedings. Royal Zoological Society of New South Wales

Proc S Afr Soc Anim Prod — Proceedings. South African Society of Animal Production

Proc S Afr Sugar Technol Assoc — Proceedings. South African Sugar Technologists' Association

Proc S Afr Sugar Technol Assoc Annu Congr — Proceedings. South African Sugar Technologists Association. Annual Congress

Proc Sagamore Army Mater Res Conf — Proceedings. Sagamore Army Materials Research Conference

Proc San Diego Biomed Eng Symp — Proceedings. San Diego Biomedical Engineering Symposium
Proc San Diego Biomed Symp — Proceedings. San Diego Biomedical Symposium
Proc Sanit Eng Conf — Proceedings. Sanitary Engineering Conference
Proc SA Scot — Proceedings. Society of Antiquaries of Scotland
Proc Satell Symp Int Congr Pharmacol — Proceedings. Satellite Symposium. International Congress of Pharmacology
Proc S Aust Brch R Geogr Soc Australas — Royal Geographical Society of Australasia. South Australian Branch. Proceedings
Proc Scand Congr Cardiol — Proceedings. Scandinavian Congress of Cardiology
Proc Scand Congr Neurol — Proceedings. Scandinavian Congress of Neurology
Proc Scand Corros Congr — Proceedings. Scandinavian Corrosion Congress
Proc Scand Symp Lipids — Proceedings. Scandinavian Symposium on Lipids
Proc Scand Symp Surf Act — Proceedings. Scandinavian Symposium on Surface Activity
Proc Scand Transplant Meet — Proceedings. Scandinavian Transplantation Meeting
Proc SC Hist Assn — Proceedings. South Carolina Historical Association
Proc School Sci Tokai Univ — Proceedings of the School of Science of Tokai University
Proc Sci Assoc Nigeria — Proceedings. Science Association of Nigeria
Proc Sci Assoc Trinidad — Proceedings. Scientific Association of Trinidad
Proc Sci Inst Kinki Univ — Proceedings. Science Institution. Kinki University
Proc Sci Inst Vitam Res Moscow — Proceedings. Scientific Institute for Vitamin Research. Moscow
Proc Sci Meet Med Fac Hyg Charles Univ — Proceedings. Scientific Meeting. Medical Faculty of Hygiene. Charles University
Proc Sci Sect Toilet Goods Assoc — Proceedings. Scientific Section of the Toilet Goods Association
Proc Sci Soc London — Proceedings. Scientific Society of London
Proc Scotts Turfgrass Res Conf — Proceedings. Scotts Turfgrass Research Conference
Proc Scott Univ Summer Sch Phys — Proceedings. Scottish Universities Summer School in Physics
Proc SD Acad Sci — Proceedings. South Dakota Academy of Science
Proc S Dak Acad Sci — Proceedings. South Dakota Academy of Science
Proc Sea Grant Conf — Proceedings. Sea Grant Conference
Proc Sec Int Symp Vet Epidemiol Econ — Proceedings. Second International Symposium on Veterinary Epidemiology and Economics
Proc Second Malays Soil Conf (Kuala Lumpur) — Proceedings. Second Malaysian Soil Conference (Kuala Lumpur)
Proc Sect Sci Is Acad Sci Humanit — Proceedings. Section of Sciences. Israel Academy of Sciences and Humanities
Proc Sect Sci K Ned Akad Wet — Proceedings. Section of Sciences. Koninklijke Nederlandse Akademie van Wetenschappen
Proc Seed Protein Conf — Proceedings. Seed Protein Conference
Proc SEM Conf Exp Mech — Proceedings of the SEM (Society for Experimental Mechanics) Conference on Experimental Mechanics
Proc Semiann Meet AFMA Nutr Counc — Proceedings. Semiannual Meeting. AFMA [*American Feed Manufacturers Association*] Nutrition Council
Proc Semin Arab Stud — Proceedings of the Seminar for Arabian Studies
Proc Semin Biomass Energy City Farm Ind — Proceedings. Seminar on Biomass Energy for City, Farm, and Industry
Proc Semin Comput Methods Quantum Chem — Proceedings. Seminar on Computational Methods in Quantum Chemistry
Proc Semin Dry Val Drill Proj — Proceedings. Seminar on Dry Valley Drilling Project
Proc Semin Electrochem — Proceedings. Seminar on Electrochemistry
Proc Semin Electromagn Interact Nucl Low Medium Energ — Proceedings. Seminar Electromagnetic Interactions of Nuclei at Low and Medium Energies
Proc Semin Nucl Data — Proceedings. Seminar on Nuclear Data
Proc Semin Nucl Fuel Qual Assur — Proceedings. Seminar on Nuclear Fuel Quality Assurance
Proc Semin Nucl Power — Proceedings. Seminar on Nuclear Power
Proc Semin Pestic Environ — Proceedings. Seminar on Pesticides and Environment
Proc Semin Surf Phys — Proceedings. Seminar on Surface Physics
Proc SEM Spring Conf Exp Mech — Proceedings of the SEM (Society for Experimental Mechanics) Spring Conference on Experimental Mechanics
Proc Ser Am Water Resour Assoc — Proceedings Series. American Water Resources Association
Proc Serono Clin Colloq Reprod — Proceedings. Serono Clinical Colloquia on Reproduction
Proc Serono Symp — Proceedings. Serono Symposia
Proc SESA — Proceedings. Society for Experimental Stress Analysis
Proc Shevchenko Sci Soc Sect Chem Biol Med — Proceedings. Shevchenko Scientific Society. Section of Chemistry, Biology, and Medicine
Proc Shikoku Br Crop Sci Soc (Jap) — Proceedings. Shikoku Branch of Crop Science Society (Japan)
Proc Short Course Coal Util — Proceedings. Short Course in Coal Utilization
Proc SID — Proceedings. SID
Proc Sigatoka Workshop — Proceedings. Sigatoka Workshop
Proc Sigrid Juselius Found Symp — Proceedings. Sigrid Juselius Foundation Symposium
Proc Sigrid Juselius Symp — Proceedings. Sigrid Juselius Symposium
Proc Silvic Conf — Proceedings. Silviculture Conference
Proc SLAC KEK Linear Collider Workshop Damping Ring — Proceedings. SLAC/KEK Linear Collider Workshop on Damping Ring
Proc Soc Agric Bacteriol — Proceedings. Society of Agricultural Bacteriologists
Proc Soc Am For — Proceedings. Society of American Foresters
Proc Soc Am For Natl Conv — Proceedings. Society of American Foresters National Convention
Proc Soc Anal Chem — Proceedings. Society for Analytical Chemistry
Proc Soc Anal Chem Conf — Proceedings. Society for Analytical Chemistry Conference

Proc Soc Antiq Scot — Proceedings. Society of Antiquaries of Scotland
Proc Soc Antiq Scotland — Proceedings. Society of Antiquaries of Scotland
Proc Soc Antiqua — Proceedings of the Society of Antiquaries
Proc Soc Antiqua Scotland — Proceedings of the Society of Antiquaries for Scotland
Proc Soc Antiqu London — Proceedings. Society of Antiquaries of London
Proc Soc Appl Bact — Proceedings. Society for Applied Bacteriology
Proc Soc Appl Bacteriol — Proceedings. Society for Applied Bacteriology
Proc Soc Automot Eng — Proceedings. Society of Automotive Engineers
Proc Soc Bibl Archaeol — Proceedings of the Society of Biblical Archaeology
Proc Soc Biol Chem — Proceedings. Society of Biological Chemists
Proc Soc Biol Chem India — Proceedings. Society of Biological Chemists of India
Proc Soc Brit Architects — Proceedings of the Society for British Architects
Proc Soc Can — Proceedings. Royal Society of Canada
Proc Soc Chem Ind Chem Eng Group — Proceedings. Society of Chemical Industry. Chemical Engineering Group
Proc Soc Chem Ind (Victoria) — Proceedings. Society of Chemical Industry (Victoria)
Proc Soc Exp Biol Med — Proceedings. Society for Experimental Biology and Medicine
Proc Soc Exp Biol (NY) — Proceedings. Society for Experimental Biology and Medicine (New York)
Proc Soc Exper Biol Med — Proceedings. Society for Experimental Biology and Medicine
Proc Soc Exp Stress Anal — Proceedings. Society for Experimental Stress Analysis
Proc Soc Exp Stress Analysis — Proceedings. Society for Experimental Stress Analysis
Proc Soc Hortic Sci — Proceedings. Society for Horticultural Science
Proc Soc Ind Microbiol — Proceedings. Society for Industrial Microbiology
Proc Soc Inf Disp — Proceedings. Society for Information Display
Proc Soc Lond — Proceedings. Royal Society of London
Proc Soc Med — Proceedings. Royal Society of Medicine
Proc Soc Photo Opt Instrum Eng — Proceedings. Society of Photo-Optical Instrumentation Engineers
Proc Soc Plast Ind Can — Proceedings. Society of the Plastics Industry in Canada
Proc Soc Promot Agric Sci — Proceedings. Society for the Promotion of Agricultural Science
Proc Soc Protozool — Proceedings. Society of Protozoologists
Proc Soc Psych Res — Proceedings. Society for Psychical Research
Proc Soc Radiol Prot Int Symp Radiol Prot Adv Theory Pract — Proceedings. Society for Radiological Protection. International Symposium. Radiological Protection - Advances in Theory and Practice
Proc Soc Relay Eng — Proceedings. Society of Relay Engineers
Proc Soc Silver Colrs — Proceedings of the Society of Silver Collectors
Proc Soc Soil Diagn — Proceeding. Society of Soil and Plant Diagnosticians
Proc Soc Study Fertil — Proceedings. Society for the Study of Fertility
Proc Soc Study Ind Med — Proceedings. Society for the Study of Industrial Medicine
Proc Soc Vict — Proceedings. Royal Society of Victoria
Proc Soc Water Treat Exam — Proceedings. Society for Water Treatment and Examination
Proc Soil Crop Sci Soc Fla — Proceedings. Soil and Crop Science Society of Florida
Proc Soil Sci Soc Am — Proceedings. Soil Science Society of America
Proc Soil Sci Soc Amer — Proceedings. Soil Science Society of America
Proc Soil Sci Soc Fla — Proceedings. Soil Science Society of Florida
Proc Solvay Conf Phys — Proceedings. Solvay Conference on Physics
Proc Somerset Archaeol & Nat Hist Soc — Proceedings of the Somersetshire Archaeological and Natural History Society
Proc Somerset Arch Natur Hist Soc — Proceedings. Somerset Archaeology and Natural History Society
Proc Sony Res Forum — Proceedings of the Sony Research Forum
Proc SOS Int Congr Food Sci Technol — Proceedings. SOS [*Science of Survival*]. International Congress of Food Science and Technology
Proc South Afr Electron Microsc Soc Verrigtings — Proceedings. Southern African Electron Microscopy Society-Verrigtings
Proc South Conf For Tree Improv — Proceedings. Southern Conference on Forest Tree Improvement
Proc South Dakota Acad Sci — Proceedings. South Dakota Academy of Sciences
Proc Southeast Asian Reg Semin Trop Med Public Health — Proceedings. Southeast Asian Regional Seminar on Tropical Medicine and Public Health
Proc Southeast Conf Appl Sol Energy — Proceedings. Southeastern Conference on Application of Solar Energy
Proc Southeast Conf Theor Appl Mech — Proceedings. Southeastern Conference on Theoretical and Applied Mechanics
Proc Southeastcon Reg 3 (Three) Conf — Proceedings. Southeastcon Region 3 (Three) Conference
Proc Southeast Pecan Grow Assoc — Proceedings. Southeastern Pecan Growers Association
Proc Southeast Semin Therm Sci — Proceedings. Southeastern Seminar on Thermal Sciences
Proc South For Tree Improv Conf — Proceedings. Southern Forest Tree Improvement Conference
Proc South Lond Entom and Nat Hist Soc — Proceedings. South London Entomological and Natural History Society
Proc South Munic Ind Waste Conf — Proceedings. Southern Municipal and Industrial Waste Conference
Proc South Pasture Forage Crop Imp Conf — Proceedings. Southern Pasture and Forage Crop Improvement Conference
Proc South Pasture Forage Crop Improv Conf — Proceedings. Southern Pasture and Forage Crop Improvement Conference
Proc South Staffs Inst Iron Steel Works Managers — Proceedings. South Staffordshire Institute of Iron and Steel Works Managers

Proc South States Assoc Comm Agric Other Agric Work — Proceedings. Southern States Association of Commissioners of Agriculture and Other Agricultural Workers

Proc South Wales Inst Eng — Proceedings. South Wales Institute of Engineers

Proc South Water Resour Pollut Control Conf — Proceedings. Southern Water Resources and Pollution Control Conference

Proc South Weed Conf — Proceedings. Southern Weed Conference

Proc South Weed Sci Soc — Proceedings. Southern Weed Science Society

Proc Southwest Agr Trade Farm Policy Conf — Proceedings. Southwestern Agricultural Trade Farm Policy Conference

Proc Sov Indian Semin Catal Catal Prog Chem Eng — Proceedings. Soviet-Indian Seminar on Catalysis, Catalysis, and Progress in Chemical Engineering

Proc Space Congr — Proceedings. Space Congress. Technology for the New Horizon

Proc SPE Annu Tech Conf Exhib — Proceedings. SPE Annual Technical Conference and Exhibition

Proc Spec Conf Cold Formed Steel Struct — Proceedings. Specialty Conference on Cold-Formed Steel Structures

Proc Spec Conf Control Technol Agric Air Pollut — Proceedings. Specialty Conference. Control Technology for Agricultural Air Pollutants

Proc Spec Conf State of the Art Odor Control Tech — Proceedings. Specialty Conference. State-of-the-Art of Odor Control Technology

Proc Spec Meet High Energy Nucl Data — Proceedings. Specialists' Meeting on High Energy Nuclear Data

Proc Spec Sess Cotton Dust Res Beltwide Cotton Prod Res Conf — Proceedings. Special Session on Cotton Dust Research. Beltwide Cotton Production Research Conference

Proc SPE East Reg Conf Exhib — Proceedings. SPE Eastern Regional Conference and Exhibition

Proc SPE Int Symp Form Damage Control — Proceedings. SPE International Symposium on Formation Damage Control

Proc SPE Symp Form Damage Control — Proceedings. Society of Petroleum Engineers. American Institute of Mining, Metallurgical, and Petroleum Engineers. Symposium on Formation Damage Control

Proc SPE Symp Improv Oil Recovery — Proceedings. Society of Petroleum Engineers. American Institute of Mining, Metallurgical, and Petroleum Engineers. Symposium on Improved Oil Recovery

Proc SPE Symp Reservoir Simul — Proceedings of the SPE Symposium on Reservoir Simulation

Proc SPI Annu Struct Foam Conf — Proceedings. SPI [*Society of the Plastics Industry*] Annual Structural Foam Conference

Proc SPI Annu Tech Conf — Proceedings. SPI [*Society of the Plastic Industry*] Annual Technical Conference

Proc SPI Annu Tech Conf Urethane Div — Proceedings. SPI [*Society of the Plastic Industry*] Annual Technical Conference. Urethane Division

Proc SPI Annu Tech Mark Conf — Proceedings of the SPI (Society of the Plastics Industry) Annual Technical/Marketing Conference

Proc SPI Annu Tech Mark Conf — Proceedings. SPI (Society of the Plastic Industry) Annual Technical/Marketing Conference

Proc SPI Annu Urethane Div Tech Conf — Proceedings. SPI [*Society of the Plastic Industry*] Annual Urethane Division Technical Conference

Proc SPIE Annu Tech Symp — Proceedings. SPIE [*International Society for Optical Engineering*] Annual Technical Symposium

Proc SPIE Int Soc Opt Eng — Proceedings of SPIE. The International Society for Optical Engineering

Proc SPI Int Tech Mark Conf — Proceedings. SPI [*Society of the Plastic Industry*] International Technical/Marketing Conference

Proc SPI Struct Foam Conf — Proceedings. SPI [*Society of the Plastics Industry*] Structural Foam Conference

Proc Spring Supercond Symp — Proceedings. Spring Superconducting Symposium

Proc Spring Syst Symp — Proceedings. Spring Systematics Symposium

Proc Sprinkler Irrig Assoc Tech Conf — Proceedings. Sprinkler Irrigation Association. Technical Conference

Proc SSSA — Proceedings. Soil Science Society of America

Proc St — Process Studies

Proc Staff Meetings Mayo Clin — Proceedings. Staff Meetings of the Mayo Clinic

Proc Staff Meet Mayo Clin — Proceedings. Staff Meeting. Mayo Clinic

Proc Staffs Iron Steel Inst — Proceedings. Staffordshire Iron and Steel Institute

Proc Stapp Car Crash Conf — Proceedings of Stapp Car Crash Conference

Proc State Coll Wash Inst Dairy — Proceedings. State College of Washington. Institute of Dairying

Proc State Horti Assoc PA — Proceedings. State Horticultural Association of Pennsylvania

Proc Staten Island Inst Arts — Proceedings. Staten Island Institute of Arts and Sciences

Proc State of the Art Odor Control Technol Spec Conf — Proceedings. State-of-the-Art Odor Control Technology Specialty Conference

Proc State Of The Art Program Compd Semicond — Proceedings. State-of-the-Art Program on Compound Semiconductors

Proc State Secr Manage Conf Am Dent Assoc — Proceedings. State Secretaries Management Conference. American Dental Association

Proc Statussemin PBWU Forschungsschwerpunkt Waldschaeden — Proceedings. Statusseminar der PBWU zum Forschungsschwerpunkt Waldschaeden

Proc Steelmaking Conf — Proceedings. Steelmaking Conference

Proc Steel Treat Res Soc — Proceedings. Steel Treating Research Society

Proc Steenbock Symp — Proceedings. Steenbock Symposium

Proc Steklov Inst Math — Proceedings. Steklov Institute of Mathematics

Proc St Fe Meet Annu Meet Div Part Fields Am Phys Soc — Proceedings. Santa Fe Meeting. Annual Meeting. Division of Particles and Fields. American Physical Society

Proc Sth Conf For Tree Impr — Proceedings. Southern Conference on Forest Tree Improvement

Proc Sth Weed Control Conf — Proceedings. Southern Weed Control Conference

Proc Sth Weed Sci Soc — Proceedings. Southern Weed Science Society

Proc Stream Workshop — Proceedings. Streams Workshop

Proc Study Fauna Flora USSR Sect Bot — Proceedings on the Study of the Fauna and Flora of the USSR. Section of Botany

Proc Study Group R Coll Obstet Gynaecol — Proceedings. Study Group. Royal College of Obstetricians and Gynaecologists

Proc Suff Inst A — Proceedings. Suffolk Institute of Archaeology

Proc Suffolk Inst Arch — Proceedings. Suffolk Institute of Archaeology

Proc Suffolk Inst Archaeol Hist — Proceedings. Suffolk Institute of Archaeology and History

Proc Sugar Beet Res Assoc — Proceedings. Sugar Beet Research Association

Proc Sugar Process Res Conf — Proceedings. Sugar Processing Research Conference

Proc Sugar Technol Assoc India — Proceedings. Sugar Technologists Association of India

Proc SULPHUR Int Conf — Proceedings of SULPHUR. International Conference

Proc Summer Colloq Electron Transition Lasers — Proceedings. Summer Colloquium on Electronic Transition Lasers

Proc Summer Comput Simul Conf — Proceedings. Summer Computer Simulation Conference

Proc Summer Conf Spectrosc Its Appl — Proceedings. Summer Conference on Spectroscopy and Its Application

Proc Summer Inst Part Phys — Proceedings. Summer Institute on Particle Physics

Proc Summer Sch Elem Part Phys — Proceedings. Summer School on Elementary Particle Physics

Proc Supercomputing Conf — Proceedings of the Supercomputing Conference

Proc S Wales Inst Eng — Proceedings. South Wales Institute of Engineers

Proc SWANAs Annu Landfill Symp — Proceedings from SWANA's (Solid Waste Association of North America) Annual Landfill Symposium

Proc Symp Adv Oxid Processes Treat Contam Water Air — Proceedings. Symposium on Advanced Oxidation Processes for the Treatment of Contaminated Water and Air

Proc Symp Algol — Proceedings. Symposium on Algology

Proc Symp Andean Antarct Volcanol Probl — Proceedings. Symposium on Andean and Antarctic Volcanology Problems

Proc Symp Antarct Meteorites — Proceedings. Symposium on Antarctic Meteorites

Proc Symp Appl Math — Proceedings. Symposia in Applied Mathematics

Proc Symp Arct Biol Med — Proceedings. Symposia on Arctic Biology and Medicine

Proc Symp Autom Integr Circuits Manuf — Proceedings. Symposium on Automated Integrated Circuits Manufacturing

Proc Symp Balt Mar Biol — Proceedings. Symposium. Baltic Marine Biologists

Proc Symp Biol Dep Brookhaven Natl Lab — Proceedings. Symposium by the Biology Department. Brookhaven National Laboratory

Proc Symp Biol Skin — Proceedings. Symposium on the Biology of Skin

Proc Symp Chem Biochem Prostanoids — Proceedings. Symposium on the Chemistry and Biochemistry of Prostanoids

Proc Symp Chem Compos Tob Tob Smoke — Proceedings. Symposium on the Chemical Composition of Tobacco and Tobacco Smoke

Proc Symp Chem Data Append R Aust Chem Inst — Proceedings. Symposium on Chemical Data. Royal Australian Chemical Institute

Proc Symp Chem Physiol Pathol — Proceedings. Symposium on Chemical Physiology and Pathology

Proc Symp Coeliac Dis — Proceedings. Symposium on Coeliac Disease

Proc Symp Comp Biol Reprod — Proceedings. Symposium on Comparative Biology of Reproduction

Proc Symp Coord Chem — Proceedings. Symposium on Coordination Chemistry

Proc Symp Coord Obs Ionos Magnetos Polar Reg — Proceedings. Symposium on Coordinated Observations of the Ionosphere and the Magnetosphere in the Polar Regions

Proc Symp Cosmic Rays Astrophys Geophys Elem Part Phys — Proceedings. Symposium on Cosmic Rays, Astrophysics, Geophysics, and Elementary Particle Physics

Proc Symp Cosmic Rays Elem Part Phys Astrophys — Proceedings. Symposium on Cosmic Rays, Elementary Particle Physics, and Astrophysics

Proc Symp Detonation — Proceedings. Symposium on Detonation

Proc Symp Dev Iron Chelators Clin Use — Proceedings. Symposium on the Development of Iron Chelators for Clinical Use

Proc Symp East Afr Acad — Proceedings. Symposium. East African Academy

Proc Symp Educ Found Am Soc Plast Reconstr Surg — Proceedings. Symposium. Educational Foundation. American Society of Plastic and Reconstructive Surgeons

Proc Symp Effects Ionizing Radiat Seed Signific Crop Impr — Proceedings. Symposium on the Effects of Ionizing Radiation on Seeds and Their Significance for Crop Improvement

Proc Symp Electr Insul Mater — Proceedings of the Symposium on Electrical Insulating Materials

Proc Symp Electrochem Eng Small Scale Electrolytic Process — Proceedings. Symposium on Electrochemical Engineering and Small Scale Electrolytic Processing

Proc Symp Electroexplos Devices — Proceedings. Symposium on Electroexplosive Devices

Proc Symp Electron Beam Technol — Proceedings. Symposium on Electron Beam Technology

Proc Symp Electron Ion Beam Sci Technol Int Conf — Proceedings. Symposium on Electron and Ion Beam Science and Technology. International Conference

Proc Symp Energy Eng Sci — Proceedings of the Symposium on Energy Engineering Sciences

Proc Symp Eng Aspects Magnetohydrodyn — Proceedings. Symposium. Engineering Aspects of Magnetohydrodynamics

Proc Symp Eng Probl Fusion Res — Proceedings. Symposium on Engineering Problems of Fusion Research

Proc Symp Explos Pyrotech — Proceedings. Symposium on Explosives and Pyrotechnics

Proc Symp Fast React Chem Meas — Proceedings. Symposium on Fast Reactions. Chemistry and Measurements

Proc Symp Ferroelectr — Proceedings. Symposium on Ferroelectricity

Proc Symp Fertil Indian Soils — Proceedings. Symposium on Fertility of Indian Soils

Proc Symp Flue Gas Desulfurization — Proceedings. Symposium on Flue Gas Desulfurization

Proc Symp Fract Mech Ceram — Proceedings. Symposia on the Fracture Mechanics of Ceramics

Proc Symp Fusion Eng — Proceedings. Symposium on Fusion Engineering

Proc Symp Fusion Technol — Proceedings. Symposium on Fusion Technology

Proc Symp Geol Rocky Mt Coal — Proceedings. Symposium on the Geology of Rocky Mountain Coal

Proc Symp Ges Nephrol — Proceedings. Symposium. Gesellschaft fuer Nephrologie

Proc Symp Hadron Spectrosc — Proceedings. Symposium on Hadron Spectroscopy

Proc Symp Hazard Chem Handl Disposal — Proceedings. Symposium on Hazardous Chemicals Handling and Disposal

Proc Symp Health Phys — Proceedings. Symposium on Health Physics

Proc Symp High Power Ambient Temp Lithium Batteries — Proceedings. Symposium on High Power, Ambient Temperature Lithium Batteries

Proc Symp High Temp Electrode Mater Charact — Proceedings. Symposium on High Temperature Electrode Materials and Characterization

Proc Symp High Temp Lamp Chem — Proceedings. Symposium on High Temperature Lamp Chemistry

Proc Symp High Temp Met Halide Chem — Proceedings. Symposium on High Temperature Metal Halide Chemistry

Proc Symp Hist Battery Technol — Proceedings. Symposium on History of Battery Technology

Proc Symp Hydrogen Storage Mater Batteries Electrochem — Proceedings. Symposium on Hydrogen Storage Materials, Batteries, and Electrochemistry

Proc Symp Ice Ocean Dyn Mech — Proceedings. Symposium on Ice-Ocean Dynamics and Mechanics

Proc Symp Improved Qual Electron Compon — Proceedings. Symposium. Improved Quality Electronic Components

Proc Symp Ind Cryst — Proceedings. Symposium on Industrial Crystallization

Proc Symp Ind Waste Control — Proceedings. Symposium on Industrial Waste Control

Proc Symp Instrum Process Ind — Proceedings of the Symposium on Instrumentation for the Process Industries

Proc Symp Int Astron Union — Proceedings. Symposium. International Astronomical Union

Proc Symp Int Soc Corneal Res — Proceedings. Symposium. International Society for Corneal Research

Proc Symp Ion Sources Form Ion Beams — Proceedings. Symposium on Ion Sources and Formation of Ion Beams

Proc Symp Ion Sources Ion Appl Technol — Proceedings. Symposium on Ion Sources and Ion Application Technology

Proc Symp Ion Sources Ion Assisted Technol — Proceedings. Symposium on Ion Sources and Ion-Assisted Technology

Proc Symp Irradiat Facil Res React — Proceedings. Symposium on Irradiation Facilities for Research Reactors

Proc Symp Isotop Plant Nutr Physiol (Vienna Austria) — Proceedings. Symposium on Isotopes in Plant Nutrition and Physiology (Vienna, Austria)

Proc Symp Liq Amorphous Mater — Proceedings. Symposium on Liquids and Amorphous Materials

Proc Symp Liq Solid Helium Three — Proceedings. Symposium on Liquid and Solid Helium Three

Proc Symp Logic Comput Sci — Proceedings. Symposium on Logic in Computer Science

Proc Symp Low Temp Electron Device Oper — Proceedings. Symposium on Low Temperature Electronic Device Operation

Proc Symp Mater Sci Res — Proceedings. Symposium on Materials Science Research

Proc Symp Mech Behav Mater — Proceedings. Symposium on Mechanical Behavior of Materials

Proc Symp Med Feeds — Proceedings. Symposium on Medicated Feeds

Proc Symp Med Radioisot Scintigr — Proceedings. Symposium on Medical Radioisotope Scintigraphy

Proc Symp Microdosim — Proceedings. Symposium on Microdosimetry

Proc Symp Mol Biol — Proceedings. Symposium on Molecular Biology

Proc Symp Mol Biol Viruses — Proceedings. Symposium. Molecular Biology of Viruses

Proc Symp Nav Struct Mech — Proceedings. Symposium on Naval Structural Mechanics

Proc Symp Neutron Dosim — Proceedings. Symposium on Neutron Dosimetry

Proc Symp Neutron Dosim Biol Med — Proceedings. Symposium on Neutron Dosimetry in Biology and Medicine

Proc Symp Neutron Inelastic Scattering — Proceedings. Symposium on Neutron Inelastic Scattering

Proc Symp Neutron Monit Radiol Prot — Proceedings. Symposium on Neutron Monitoring for Radiological Protection

Proc Symp Non Destr Test Nucl Technol — Proceedings. Symposium on Non-Destructive Testing in Nuclear Technology

Proc Symp Non Silver Photogr Processes — Proceedings. Symposium on Non-Silver Photographic Processes

Proc Symp Northeast Accel Pers — Proceedings. Symposium of Northeastern Accelerator Personnel

Proc Symp Northwest Sci Assoc Annu Meet — Proceedings. Symposium. Northwest Scientific Association Annual Meeting

Proc Symp Nucl Data — Proceedings. Symposium on Nuclear Data

Proc Sympos Appl Math — Proceedings. Symposia in Applied Mathematics

Proc Sympos Pure Math — Proceedings. Symposia in Pure Mathematics

Proc Symp Packag Electron Devices — Proceedings. Symposium on Packaging of Electronic Devices

Proc Symp Parkinsons Dis Inf Res Cent — Proceedings. Symposium. Parkinson's Disease Information and Research Center

Proc Symp Particleboard — Proceedings. Symposium on Particleboard

Proc Symp Perspect Ind Microbiol — Proceedings. Symposium on Perspectives in Industrial Microbiology

Proc Symp Pests Pestic — Proceedings. Symposium of Pests and Pesticides

Proc Symp Photogr Process — Proceedings. Symposium on Photographic Processing

Proc Symp Photogr Sensitivity — Proceedings. Symposium on Photographic Sensitivity

Proc Symp Phys Nondestr Test — Proceedings. Symposium on Physics and Nondestructive Testing

Proc Symp Plasma Process — Proceedings. Symposium on Plasma Processing

Proc Symp Polar Meteorol Glaciol — Proceedings. Symposium on Polar Meteorology and Glaciology

Proc Symp Pract Treat Low Intermed Level Radioact Wastes — Proceedings. Symposium on Practice in the Treatment of Low- and Intermediate-Level Radioactive Wastes

Proc Symp Prod Res — Proceedings. Symposium on Productivity in Research

Proc Symp Quantum Stat Many Body Probl — Proceedings. Symposium on Quantum Statistics and Many-Body Problems

Proc Symp Radiat Induced Cancer — Proceedings. Symposium on Radiation-Induced Cancer

Proc Symp Reliab Distrib Software Database Syst — Proceedings. Symposium on Reliability in Distributed Software and Database Systems

Proc Symp Reliab Electron — Proceedings. Symposium on Reliability in Electronics

Proc Symp Rock Mech — Proceedings. Symposium on Rock Mechanics

Proc Symp Saf Nucl Ships — Proceedings. Symposium on the Safety of Nuclear Ships

Proc Symp Silicon Nitride Silicon Dioxide Thin Insul Films — Proceedings. Symposium on Silicon Nitride and Silicon Dioxide Thin Insulating Films

Proc Symp Soc Study Inborn Errors Metab — Proceedings. Symposium. Society for the Study of Inborn Errors of Metabolism

Proc Symp Space Nucl Power Syst — Proceedings. Symposium on Space Nuclear Power Systems

Proc Symp Spec Ceram — Proceedings. Symposium on Special Ceramics

Proc Symp Spec Ceram Br Ceram Res Assoc — Proceedings. Symposium on Special Ceramics held by the British Ceramic ResearchAssociation

Proc Symp Struct Solubility Relat Polym — Proceedings. Symposium on Structure-Solubility Relationships in Polymers

Proc Symp Text Flammability — Proceedings. Symposium on Textile Flammability

Proc Symp Thermophys Prop — Proceedings. Symposium on Thermophysical Properties

Proc Symp Toxic Met — Proceedings. Symposium on Toxicity of Metals

Proc Symp Transfer Print — Proceedings. Symposium on Transfer Printing

Proc Symp Transp Phenom — Proceedings. Symposium on Transport Phenomena

Proc Symp Turbul Liq — Proceedings. Symposium on Turbulence in Liquids

Proc Symp Underwater Physiol — Proceedings. Symposium on Underwater Physiology

Proc Symp Upper Mantle Proj — Proceedings. Symposium on Upper Mantle Project

Proc Symp Use Isotop Weed Res — Proceedings. Symposium on the Use of Isotopes in Weed Research

Proc Symp Use Isot Radiat Soil Org Matter Stud — Proceedings. Symposium on the Use of Isotopes and Radiation in Soil Organic-Matter Studies

Proc Symp Use Radioisotop Soil Plant Nutr Stud — Proceedings. Symposium on the Use of Radioisotopes in Soil-Plant Nutrition Studies

Proc Symp Vet Pharmacol Ther — Proceedings. Symposium on Veterinary Pharmacology and Therapeutics

Proc Symp Wakan Yaku — Proceedings. Symposium on Wakan-Yaku

Proc Symp Waste Manage — Proceedings. Symposium on Waste Management

Proc Symp Wastewater Treat — Proceedings. Symposium on Wastewater Treatment

Proc Symp Wound Ballist — Proceedings. Symposium on Wound Ballistics

Proc Symp X Ray Methods Corros Interfacial Electrochem — Proceedings. Symposium on X-Ray Methods in Corrosion and Interfacial Electrochemistry

Proc Symp Yamato Meteorites — Proceedings. Symposium on Yamato Meteorites

Proc Synth Hydrocarbons Conf Am Inst Min Metall Pet Eng Annu — Proceedings. Synthetic Hydrocarbons Conference. American Institute of Mining, Metallurgical, and Petroleum Engineers. Annual Meeting

Proc Synth Pipeline Gas Symp — Proceedings. Synthetic Pipeline Gas Symposium

Proc Syst Symp — Proceedings. Systems Symposium

Proc TAGA — Proceedings. TAGA

Proc Tall Timbers Conf Ecol Anim Control Habitat Manage — Proceedings. Tall Timbers Conference on Ecological Animal Control by Habitat Management

Proc Tall Timbers Fire Ecol Conf — Proceedings. Tall Timbers Fire Ecology Conference

Proc Tbilisi Symp Cereb Circ — Proceedings. Tbilisi Symposium on Cerebral Circulation

Proc Tbilisi Univ — Proceedings. Tbilisi University

Proc Tech Assoc Pulp Pap Ind — Proceedings. Technical Association. Pulp and Paper Industry

Proc Tech Comm Peaceful Uses Nucl Explos — Proceedings. Technical Committee on the Peaceful Uses of Nuclear Explosions

Proc Tech Conf Am Railway Eng Assoc — Proceedings. Technical Conference. American Railway Engineering Association

Proc Tech Conf Irrig Assoc — Proceedings. Technical Conference. Irrigation Association

Proc Tech Conf Soc Vac Coaters — Proceedings. Technical Conference. Society of Vacuum Coaters

Proc Tech Groups NZ Inst Eng — Proceedings of Technical Groups. New Zealand Institution of Engineers

Proc Tech Meet Tech Soc Eng Sci — Proceedings. Technical Meeting. Society of Engineering Science

Proc Tech Meet Tech Assoc Graphic Arts — Proceedings. Technical Meeting. Technical Association. Graphic Arts

Proc Tech Meet West Coast Sect Air Pollut Control Assoc — Proceedings. Technical Meeting. West Coast Section. Air Pollution Control Association

Proc Tech Mtg Int Union Conserv Nature — Proceedings. Technical Meeting. International Union for Conservation of Nature and Natural Resources

Proc Technol Conf — Proceedings. Technological Conference. South India Textile Research Association

Proc Tech Pap Gen Fish Counc Mediterr — Proceedings and Technical Papers. General Fisheries Council for the Mediterranean

Proc Tech Program Annu Int Electron Packag Conf — Proceedings. Technical Program. Annual International Electronics Packaging Conference

Proc Tech Program Electro-Opt Laser Conf Exp — Proceedings. Technical Program. Electro-Optics/Laser Conference and Exposition

Proc Tech Program Electro Opt Laser Conf Expo — Proceedings. Technical Program. Electro-Optics/Laser Conference and Exposition

Proc Tech Program Electro Opt Syst Des Conf — Proceedings. Technical Program. Electro-Optical Systems Design Conference

Proc Tech Program Int Microelectron Conf — Proceedings. Technical Program. International Microelectronics Conference

Proc Tech Program Int Powder Bulk Solids Handl Process — Proceedings. Technical Program. International Powder and Bulk Solids Handling and Processing

Proc Tech Program Natl Electron Packag Prod Conf — Proceedings. Technical Program. National Electronic Packaging and Production Conference

Proc Tech Sect Br Pap Board Makers Assoc — Proceedings. Technical Section. British Paper and Board Makers' Association

Proc Tech Sect Pap Makers Assoc GB Irel — Proceedings. Technical Section. Paper Makers' Association of Great Britain and Ireland

Proc Tech Semin Chem Spills — Proceedings. Technical Seminar on Chemical Spills

Proc Tech Sess Annu Conv Amer Electroplat Soc — Proceedings. Technical Sessions. Annual Convention. American Electroplaters' Society

Proc Tech Sess Bone Char — Proceedings. Technical Sessions on Bone Char

Proc Tech Sess Bone Char Res — Proceedings. Technical Sessions on Bone Char Research

Proc Tech Sess Cane Sugar Refin Res — Proceedings. Technical Session on Cane Sugar Refining Research

Proc Tech Workshop Near Field Perform Assess High Level Waste — Proceedings. Technical Workshop on Near-Field Performance Assessment for High-Level Waste

Proc Tenovus Workshop — Proceedings. Tenovus Workshop

Proc Teratol Symp — Proceedings on the Teratology Symposium

Proc Tex AM Annu Symp Instrum Process Ind — Proceedings. Texas A & M Annual Symposium on Instrumentation for the Process Indtries

Proc Tex Conf Comput Syst — Proceedings. Texas Conference on Computing Systems

Proc Tex Nutr Conf — Proceedings. Texas Nutrition Conference

Proc Tex Pecan Grow Assoc — Proceedings. Texas Pecan Growers Association

Proc TEXTOR Exec Comm — Proceedings. TEXTOR Executive Committee

Proc Tex Water Sewage Works Short Sch — Proceedings. Texas Water and Sewage Works Short School

Proc Tex Water Util Short Sch — Proceedings. Texas Water Utilities Short School

Proc Tex Water Works Sewerage Short Sch — Proceedings. Texas Water Works and Sewerage Short School

Proc Therm Power Conf — Proceedings. Thermal Power Conference

Proc Tihany Symp Radiat Chem — Proceedings. Tihany Symposium on Radiation Chemistry

Proc Tob Health Conf — Proceedings. Tobacco and Health Conference

Proc Tokyo Int Symp Free Electron Lasers — Proceedings. Tokyo International Symposium on Free Electron Lasers

Proc Tokyo Math Phys Soc — Proceedings. Tokyo Mathematico-Physical Society

Proc Top Conf RF Heating Plasma — Proceedings. Topical Conference on RF Heating in Plasma and Workshop on Antennas and Couples

Proc Top Conf RF Plasma heat — Proceedings. Topical Conference on RF Plasma Heating

Proc Top Meet New Horiz Radiat Prot Shielding — Proceedings. Topical Meeting on New Horizons in Radiation Protection and Shielding

Proc Top Meet Technol Controlled Nucl Fusion — Proceedings. Topical Meeting on the Technology of Controlled Nuclear Fusion

Proc Toronto Symp Therm Anal — Proceedings. Toronto Symposium on Thermal Analysis

Proc Trans Br Entomol Nat Hist Soc — Proceedings and Transactions. British Entomological and Natural History Society

Proc Trans Croydon Natur Hist Sci Soc — Proceedings and Transactions. Croydon Natural History and Scientific Society

Proc Trans Liverp Biol Soc — Proceedings and Transactions. Liverpool Biological Society

Proc Trans Nova Scotian Inst Sci — Proceedings and Transactions. Nova Scotian Institute of Science

Proc Trans NS Inst Sci — Proceedings and Transactions. Nova Scotian Institute of Science

Proc Trans Rhod Sci Assoc — Proceedings and Transactions. Rhodesia Scientific Association

Proc Trans Roy Soc Canada — Proceedings and Transactions. Royal Society of Canada

Proc Trans R Soc Can — Proceedings and Transactions. Royal Society of Canada

Proc Trans Tex Acad Sci — Proceedings and Transactions of Texas Academy of Science

Proc Tree Wardens Arborists Util Conf — Proceedings. Tree Wardens, Arborists, and Utilities Conference

Proc Triangle Semin — Proceedings. Triangle Seminar

Proc Trienn Conf Eur Assoc Potato Res — Proceedings. Triennial Conference. European Association for Potato Research

Proc Tri State Dairy Nutr Conf — Proceedings. Tri-State Dairy Nutrition Conference

Proc TRON Proj Symp Int — Proceedings. TRON Project Symposium International

Proc Trop Reg ASHS — Proceedings. Tropical Region ASHS

Proc Tr PN Lebedev Phys Inst — Proceedings (Trudy). P. N. Lebedev Physics Institute

Proc Tr PN Lebedev Phys Inst Acad Sci USSR Engl Transl — Proceedings. Trudy. P.N. Lebedev Physics Institute. Academy of Sciences of the USSR. (English Translation)

Proc (Trudy) P N Lebedev Phys Inst — Proceedings (Trudy). P. N. Lebedev Physics Institute

ProCTS — Proceedings. College Theology Society

Proc Tub Res Coun — Proceedings. Tuberculosis Research Council

Proc Tucson Comet Conf — Proceedings. Tucson Comet Conference

Proc Turbomachinery Symp — Proceedings. Turbomachinery Symposium

Proc Turfgrass Sprinkler Irrig Conf — Proceedings. Turfgrass Sprinkler Irrigation Conference

Proc Turk Ger Environ Eng Symp — Proceedings. Turkish-German Environmental Engineering Symposium

Proc Ultrason Symp — Proceedings. Ultrasonics Symposium

Proc Underground Coal Convers Symp — Proceedings. Underground Coal Conversion Symposium

Proc UNESCO Conf Radioisot Sci Res — Proceedings. UNESCO Conference on Radioisotopes in Scientific Research

Proc UNESCO Int Conf Radioisot Sci Res — Proceedings. UNESCO International Conference on Radioisotopes in Scientific Research

Proc UN Int Conf Peaceful Uses At Energy — Proceedings. United Nations International Conference on the Peaceful Uses of Atomic Energy

Proc Univ Bristol Spelaeol Soc — Proceedings. University of Bristol Spelaeological Society

Proc Univ Durham Philos Soc Ser A — Proceedings. University of Durham Philosophical Society. Series A. Science

Proc Univ Durham Philos Soc Ser B — Proceedings. University of Durham Philosophical Society. Series B. Arts

Proc Univ Durham Phil Soc — Proceedings. University of Durham. Philosophical Society

Proc Univ Ky Tob Health Res Inst Conf Rep — Proceedings. University of Kentucky. Tobacco and Health Research Institute. Conference Report

Proc Univ MD Nutr Conf Feed Mfr — Proceedings. University of Maryland. Nutrition Conference for Feed Manufacturers

Proc Univ MO Annu Conf Trace Subst Environ Health — Proceedings. University of Missouri. Annual Conference on Trace Substances in Environmental Health

Proc Univ Mo Annu Conf Trace Subst Environ Health — Proceedings. University of Missouri's Annual Conference on Trace Substances in Environmental Health

Proc Univ Newcastle Upon Tyne Philos Soc — Proceedings. University of Newcastle-Upon-Tyne Philosophical Society

Proc Univ Nottingham Easter Sch Agric Sci — Proceedings. University of Nottingham Easter School in Agricultural Science

Proc Univ Nottingham Nutr Conf Feed Manuf — Proceedings. University of Nottingham Nutrition Conference for Feed Manufacturers

Proc Univ Otago Med Sch — Proceedings. University of Otago Medical School

Proc UN Symp Dev Use Geotherm Resour — Proceedings. United Nations Symposium on the Development and Use of Geothermal Resources

Proc USAID Ghana Agr Conf — Proceedings. USAID [United States Agency for International Development]. Ghana Agriculture Conference

Proc USA USSR Symp Fract Compos Mater — Proceedings. USA-USSR Symposium on Fracture of Composite Materials

Proc US Dep Energy Environ Control Symp — Proceedings. US Department of Energy Environmental Control Symposium

Proc US Dep Energy Tech Contract Conf Peat — Proceedings. US Department of Energy Technical Contractors' Conference on Peat

Proc US DOE Photovoltaics Technol Dev Appl Program Rev — Proceedings. US DOE [Department of Energy] Photovoltaics Technology Development and Applications Program Review

Proc User Fabr Filtr Equip — Proceedings. User and Fabric Filtration Equipment

Proc US Gulf Coast Geopressured Geotherm Energy Conf — Proceedings. United States Gulf Coast Geopressured-Geothermal Energy Conference

Proc US Jpn Conf Mar Microbiol — Proceedings. United States-Japan Conference on Marine Microbiology

Proc US Jpn Conf Sewage Treat Technol — Proceedings. US-Japan Conference on Sewage Treatment Technology

Proc US Jpn Conf Toxic Micro Org — Proceedings. United States-Japan Conference on Toxic Micro-Organisms. Micotoxins, Botulism

Proc US Jpn Coop Sci Program — Proceedings. United States-Japan Cooperative Science Program

Proc US Jpn Semin Basic Sci Ceram — Proceedings. United States-Japan Seminar on Basic Science of Ceramics

Proc US Jpn Symp Adv Weld Metall — Proceedings. United States-Japan Symposium on Advances in Welding Metallurgy

Proc US Jpn Workshop Adv Plasma Model — Proceedings. US-Japan Workshop on Advanced Plasma Modeling

Proc US Mex Symp At Mol Phys — Proceedings of the US/Mexico Symposium on Atomic and Molecular Physics

Proc US Natl Mus — Proceedings. United States National Museum

Proc US Nat Mus — Proceedings. United States National Museum

Proc US Nav Inst — United States Naval Institute. Proceedings

Proc US N Mus — Proceedings of the United States National Museum

Proc US Nucl Regul Comm Water Reactor Saf Inf Meet — Proceedings. US Nuclear Regulatory Commission Water Reactor Safety Information Meeting

Proc Ussher Soc — Proceedings. Ussher Society

Proc USSR Acad Sci Biol Ser — Proceedings. USSR Academy of Sciences. Biological Series

Proc USSR Acad Sci Geol Ser — Proceedings. USSR Academy of Sciences. Geological Series

Proc US USSR Symp Supercond Power Trans — Proceedings. US-USSR Symposium on Superconducting Power Transmission

Proc US Vet Med Assoc — Proceedings. United States Veterinary Medical Association

Proc Utah Acad Sci — Proceedings. Utah Academy of Sciences, Arts, and Letters

Proc Utah Acad Sci Arts Lett — Proceedings. Utah Academy of Sciences, Arts, and Letters

Proc Va Turfgrass Conf Trade Show — Proceedings. Virginia Turfgrass Conference and Trade Show

Proc Vertebr Pest Conf — Proceedings. Vertebrate Pest Conference

Proc Veterans Adm Spinal Cord Inj Conf — Proceedings. Veterans Administration Spinal Cord Injury Conference

Proc Vib Probl — Proceedings of Vibration Problems

Proc Victoria Inst — Proceedings of the Victoria Institute

Proc VIC Weeds Conf — Proceedings. Victorian Weeds Science Society

Proc Virchow-Pirquet Med Soc — Proceedings. Virchow-Pirquet Medical Society

Proc Virgil Soc — Proceedings. Virgil Society

Proc Visualization — Proceedings Visualization

Proc Vitic Sci Symp — Proceedings. Viticultural Science Symposium

Proc Vol Bakish Mater Corp Publ — Proceedings Volume. Bakish Materials Corporation. Publication

Proc Vol Electrochem Soc — Proceedings Volume. Electrochemical Society

Proc Vol Geol Soc Am — Proceedings Volume. Geological Society of America

Proc Vol Int Conf Miss Val Type Lead Zinc Deposits — Proceedings Volume. International Conference on Mississippi Valley Type Lead-Zinc Deposits

Proc Vt Maple Sugar Makers Assoc — Proceedings. Vermont Maple Sugar Makers' Association

Proc VV Kuibyshev State Univ Tomsk — Proceedings. V. V. Kuibyshev State University of Tomsk

Proc Warsaw Symp Elem Part Phys — Proceedings. Warsaw Symposium on Elementary Particle Physics

Proc Wash Anim Nutr Conf — Proceedings. Washington Animal Nutrition Conference

Proc Wash State Entomol Soc — Proceedings. Washington State Entomological Society

Proc Wash State Hort Assoc — Proceedings. Washington State Horticultural Association

Proc Wash State Hortic Assoc — Proceedings. Washington State Horticultural Association

Proc Wash State Univ Int Particleboard/Compos Mater Ser — Proceedings. Washington State University International Particleboard/Composite Materials Series

Proc Wash State Univ Int Particleboard Compos Mater Symp — Proceedings. Washington State University International Particleboard/Composite Materials Symposium

Proc Wash State Univ Int Symp Part — Proceedings. Washington State University. International Symposium on Particleboard

Proc Wash State Univ Int Symp Particleboard — Proceedings. Washington State University International Symposium on Particleboard

Proc Wash State Univ Symp Particleboard — Proceedings. Washington State University Symposium on Particleboard

Proc Wash St Ent Soc — Proceedings. Washington State Entomological Society

Proc Wash St Hort Ass — Proceedings. Washington State Horticultural Association

Proc Water Borne Higher Solids Coat Symp — Proceedings. Water-Borne and Higher-Solids Coatings Symposium

Proc Water Borne Higher Solids Powder Coat Symp — Proceedings. Water-Borne, Higher-Solids, and Powder Coatings Symposium

Proc Water Econ Res Inst (Warsaw) — Proceedings. Water Economics Research Institute (Warsaw)

Proc Water Environ Fed Annu Conf — Proceedings of the Water Environment Federation Annual Conference and Exposition

Proc Water Qual Conf — Proceedings. Water Quality Conference

Proc Water Qual Technol Conf — Proceedings. Water Quality Technology Conference

Proc Water React Saf Res Inf Meet — Proceedings. Water Reactor Safety Research Information Meeting

Proc Water Reuse Symp — Proceedings. Water Reuse Symposium

Proc Weed Soc NSW — Proceedings. Weed Society of New South Wales

Proc West Afr Int Cacao Res Conf — Proceedings. West African International Cacao Research Conference

Proc West Can Weed Control Conf — Proceedings. Western Canadian Weed Control Conference

Proc West Chapter Int Shade Tree Conf — Proceedings. Western Chapter. International Shade Tree Conference

Proc West Eur Conf Photosyn — Proceedings. Western Europe Conference on Photosynthesis

Proc West For Conserv Ass — Proceedings. Western Forestry Conference. Western Forestry and Conservation Association

Proc West Found Vertebr Zool — Proceedings. Western Foundation of Vertebrate Zoology

Proc West Hemisphere Nutr Congr — Proceedings. Western Hemisphere Nutrition Congress

Proc West Indies Sugar Technol — Proceedings. Meeting of West Indies Sugar Technologists

Proc West Pharmacol Soc — Proceedings. Western Pharmacology Society

Proc West Poult Dis Conf — Proceedings. Western Poultry Disease Conference

Proc West Poult Dis Conf Poult Health Symp — Proceedings. Western Poultry Disease Conference and Poultry Health Symposia

Proc West Poult Dis Conf Poult Heath Symp — Proceedings. Western Poultry Disease Conference and Poultry Health Symposia

Proc West Sect Am Soc Anim Sci — Proceedings. Western Section. American Society of Animal Science

Proc West Snow Conf — Proceedings. Western Snow Conference

Proc West Soc French Hist — Proceedings. Western Society for French History

Proc West Soc Weed Sci — Proceedings. Western Society of Weed Science

Proc West States Corros Semin — Proceedings. Western States Corrosion Seminar

Proc West Virginia Acad Sci — Proceedings. West Virginia Academy of Science

Proc Wind Energy RD Contract Meet — Proceedings. Wind Energy R and D Contractor Meeting

Proc Winter Workshop Pteridines — Proceedings. Winter Workshop on Pteridines

Proc Wis Hist Soc — Proceedings. Wisconsin State Historical Society

Proc Wkly Semin Neurol — Proceedings. Weekly Seminar in Neurology

Proc Wld For Congr — Proceedings. World Forestry Congress

Proc Wld Orchid Conf — Proceedings. World Orchid Conference

Proc Wood Pole Inst Colo State Univ — Proceedings. Wood Pole Institute. Colorado State University

Proc Wood Prod Clin — Proceedings. Wood Products Clinic

Proc Work Meet Radiat Interact — Proceedings. Working Meeting on Radiation Interaction

Proc Workshop Adv Beam Instrum — Proceedings. Workshop on Advanced Beam Instrumentation

Proc Workshop Balloon Borne Exp Supercond Magnet Spectrom — Proceedings. Workshop on Balloon-Borne Experiments with Superconducting Magnet Spectrometers

Proc Workshop Coal Pillar Mech Des — Proceedings. Workshop on Coal Pillar Mechanics and Design

Proc Workshop Direct Methanol Air Fuel Cells — Proceedings. Workshop on Direct Methanol-Air Fuel Cells

Proc Workshop Elem Part Pict Universe — Proceedings. Workshop on Elementary-Particle Picture of the Universe

Proc Workshop Folyl Antifolyl Polyglutamates — Proceedings. Workshop on Folyl and Antifolyl Polyglutamates

Proc Workshop Intensity Front Phys — Proceedings. Workshop on Intensity Frontier Physics

Proc Workshop Jpn Linear Collider — Proceedings. Workshop on Japan Linear Collider

Proc Workshop Mater Sci Phys Non Conv Energy Sources — Proceedings. Workshop on Materials Science and Physics of Non-Conventional Energy Sources. International Centre for Theoretical Physics

Proc Workshop Neutrons Biol KENS — Proceedings. Workshop on Neutrons in Biology at KENS

Proc Workshop Photon Radiat Quarks — Proceedings. Workshop on Photon Radiation from Quarks

Proc Workshop Phys Detect KEK Asymmetric B Fact — Proceedings. Workshop on Physics and Detectors for KEK Asymmetric B-Factory

Proc Workshop Pulsed Neutron Scattering Magn Mater — Proceedings. Workshop on Pulsed Neutron Scattering from Magnetic Materials

Proc Workshop Scattering Exp Extreme Cond — Proceedings. Workshop on Scattering Experiments under Extreme Conditions

Proc Workshop Short Pulse High Curr Cathodes — Proceedings. Workshop on Short Pulse High Current Cathodes

Proc Workshop Struct Eff Electrocatal Oxygen Electrochem — Proceedings. Workshop on Structural Effects in Electrocatalysis and Oxygen Electrochemistry

Proc Workshop Vitam D — Proceedings. Workshop on Vitamin D

Proc Workshop Wendelstein 7 X 4th — Proceedings. Workshop on Wendelstein 7-X. 4th

Proc Workshop Wendelstein 7 X Helias React — Proceedings of the Workshop on Wendelstein 7-X and Helias Reactors

Proc World Conf Clin Pharmacol Ther — Proceedings. World Conference on Clinical Pharmacology and Therapeutics

Proc World Conf Ind Tribol — Proceedings. World Conference in Industrial Tribology

Proc World Congr Agr Res — Proceedings. World Congress of Agricultural Research

Proc World Congr Anaesthesiol — Proceedings. World Congress of Anaesthesiology

Proc World Congr Biol Psychiatry — Proceedings. World Congress of Biological Psychiatry

Proc World Congr Fertil Steril — Proceedings. World Congress on Fertility and Sterility

Proc World Congr Gastroenterol — Proceedings. World Congress of Gastroenterology

Proc World Congr Int Soc Fat Res — Proceedings. World Congress. International Society for Fat Research

Proc World Congr Met Finish — Proceedings. World Congress on Metal Finishing

Proc World Congr Milk Util — Proceedings. World Congress for Milk Utilization

Proc World Congr New Compd Biol Chem Warf Toxicol Eval — Proceedings. World Congress. New Compounds in Biological and Chemical Warfare. Toxicological Evaluation

Proc World Congr Pain — Proceedings. World Congress on Pain

Proc World Congr Psychiatry — Proceedings. World Congress on Psychiatry

Proc World For Congr — Proceedings. World Forestry Congress

Proc World Hydrogen Energy Conf — Proceedings. World Hydrogen Energy Conference

Proc World Maric Soc — Proceedings. World Mariculture Society

Proc World Pet Congr — Proceedings. World Petroleum Congress

Proc World Poultry Congr — Proceedings. World Poultry Congress

Proc World Soybean Res Conf — Proceedings. World Soybean Research Conference

Proc World Tob Sci Congr — Proceedings. World Tobacco Scientific Congress

Proc W Va Acad Sci — Proceedings. West Virginia Academy of Science

Proc WVU Conf Coal Mine Electrotechnol — Proceedings. WVU [*West Virginia University*] Conference on Coal Mine Electrotechnology

Proc Yale Mineral Soc — Proceedings. Yale Mineralogical Society

Proc Yamada Conf Free Radicals — Proceedings. Yamada Conference on Free Radicals

Proc Yorks Geol Soc — Proceedings. Yorkshire Geological Society

Proc Yorkshire Geol Soc — Proceedings. Yorkshire Geological Society
Proc Zool Soc — Proceedings. Zoological Society
Proc Zool Soc (Calcutta) — Proceedings. Zoological Society (Calcutta)
Proc Zool Soc Lond — Proceedings. Zoological Society of London
PROD — Prisoner Rehabilitation on Discharge
Prod — Produktion
Prod Aggregates GB — Production of Aggregates in Great Britain
Prod Agric Fr — Producteur Agricole Francais
Prod Aliment — Prodotti Alimentari. Chimica e Tecnologia
Prod Anal Polariz X Rays — Production and Analysis of Polarized X Rays
Prod and Inventory Manage — Production and Inventory Management
Prod Anim — Produzione Animale
Prod Appl Microb Enzym Prep — Production and Application of Microbial Enzymatic Preparations
Prod Chim Aerosol Sel — Prodotto Chimico and Aerosol Selezione
Prod Ecol Ants Termites — Production Ecology of Ants and Termites [*monograph*]
Prod Eng — Product Engineering
Prod Eng (Cleveland) — Production Engineering (Cleveland)
Prod Eng (Lond) — Production Engineer (London)
Prod Engng — Production Engineering
Prod Eng NY — Product Engineering (New York)
Prod Engr — Production Engineer
Pr Odes Derzh Univ Prir Nauki — Pratsi Odes'kogo Derzhavnogo Universitetu. Prirodnichi Nauki
Pr Odes Derzh Univ Ser Fiz Nauk — Pratsi Odes'kogo Derzhavnogo Universitetu. Seriya Fizichnikh Nauk
Pr Odes Derzh Univ Ser Geol Geogr Nauk — Pratsi Odes'kogo Derzhavnogo Universitetu. Seriya Geologichnikh ta Geografichnikh Nauk
Pr Odes Derzh Univ Ser Khim Nauk — Pratsi Odes'kogo Derzhavnogo Universitetu. Seriya Khimichnikh Nauk
Pr Odes Derzh Univ Zb Biol Fak — Pratsi Odes'kogo Derzhavnogo Universitetu. Zbirnik Biologichnogo Fakul'tetu
Pr Odes Derzh Univ Zb Khim Fak — Pratsi Odes'Kogo Derzhavnogo Universitetu. Zbirnik Khimichnogo Fakul'tetu
Pr Odes Derzh Univ Zb Nauk Rob Aspir — Pratsi Odes'kogo Derzhavnogo Universitetu. Zbirnik Naukovikh Robit Aspirantiv
Pr Odes Derzh Univ Zb Rob Disertantiv — Pratsi Odes'kogo Derzhavnogo Universitetu. Zbirnik Robit Disertantiv Aspirantiv
Pr Odes Derzh Univ Zb Stud Rob — Pratsi Odes'kogo Derzhavnogo Universitetu. Zbirnik Students'kokh Robit
Pr Odes Gidrometeorol Inst — Pratsi Odes'kogo Gidrometeorologichnogo Institutu
Pr Odes Silskogospod Inst — Pratsi Odes'kogo Sil's'kogospodars'kogo Institutu
Prod Finish — Product Finishing
Prod Finish (Cinci) — Product Finishing (Cincinnati)
Prod Finish (Cincinnati) — Products Finishing (Cincinnati)
Prod Finish (Lond) — Product Finishing (London)
Prod G Am J — Producers Guild of America. Journal
Prod Improve Bull — Productivity Improvement Bulletin
Prod Insights — Productivity Insights
Prod Invent Manage — Production and Inventory Management
Prod Invent Manage J — Production and Inventory Management Journal
Prod Lait Mod — Production Laitiere Moderne
Prod Liability Int — Product Liability International
Prod Liab Int — Product Liability International
Prod Liab Rep CCH — Product Liability Reporter. Commerce Clearing House
Prod Manage — Production Management
Prod Market — Product Marketing
Prod Marketing — Produce Marketing
Prod Miner Serv Fom Prod Miner Avulso — Producao Mineral Servico de Fomento da Producao Mineral. Avulso
Prod Miner Serv Fom Prod Miner Bol — Producao Mineral Servico de Fomento da Producao Mineral. Boletim
Prod Mkt — Product Marketing
Prod Mktg — Product Marketing
Prod Mon — Producers Monthly
Prodn Engnr — Production Engineer
Prod Neutralization Negat Ions Beams Int Symp — Production and Neutralization of Negative Ions and Beams. International Symposium
Prodn J — Production Journal
Prod Perf — Productivity and Performance
Prod Pharm — Produits Pharmaceutiques
Prod Plann Control — Production Planning and Control
Prod Probl Pharm — Produits et Problemes Pharmaceutiques
Prod Prod Bull Natl Coal Board Min Dep — Production and Productivity Bulletin. National Coal Board. Mining Department
Prod Proj Trends Bldg — Products, Projects, and Trends in Building
Prod Publ Assoc Off Seed Certifying Agencies — Production Publication. Association of Official Seed Certifying Agencies
Prod Publ Int Crop Impr Ass — Production Publication. International Crop Improvement Association
Prod R & D — Product R & D
Prod Refin Fabr Recycl Light Met Proc Int Symp — Production, Refining, Fabrication, and Recycling of Light Metals. Proceedings. International Symposium
Prod Res Dev R & D — Product Research and Development R & D
Prod Res Rep — Production Research Report
Prod Res Rep US Dep Agric — Production Research Report. United States Department of Agriculture
Prod Res Rep US Dep Agric Agric Res Serv — Production Research Report. US Department of Agriculture. Agricultural ResearchService
Prod Res Rep US Dep Agric Sci Educ Adm — Production Research Report. United States Department of Agriculture. Science and Education Administration
Prod Rev — Producers' Review
Prod Rur Argent — Produccion Rural Argentina

Prod Safety & Liab Rep BNA — Product Safety and Liability Reporter. Bureau of National Affairs
Prod Technol — Productivity and Technology
Prod Tech (Osaka) — Production and Technique (Osaka)
Prod Tech (Suita) — Production and Technique (Suita)
Produccion Anim — Produccion Animal
Producers R — Producers' Review
Producers' Rev — Producers' Review
Product Eng — Product Engineering
Product et Gestion — Production et Gestion
Production — Production Engineering
Product Res Dev — Product Research and Development
Produits Pharm — Produits et Problemes Pharmaceutiques
Prod Util Lignocellul Proc Workshop — Production and Utilization of Lignocellulosics. Plant Refinery and Breeding, Analysis, Feeding to Herbivores, and Economic Aspects. Proceedings. Workshop
Prod Veg Cereale Plante Teh — Productia Vegetala. Cereale si Plante Tehnice
Prod Veg Mec Agric — Productia Vegetala. Mecanizarea Agriculturii
Prod with Safety — Production with Safety
Prod Yb FAO — Production Yearbook FAO
Proefstn Akkerbouw Groenteteelt Volle Grond Versl Interprov P — Proefstation voor de Akkerbouw en de Groenteteelt in de Volle Grond. Verslagen van Interprovinciale Proeven
Proefstn Akkerbouw Lelystad Versl Interprov Proeven — Proefstation voor de Akkerbouw Lelystad. Verslagen van Interprovinciale Proeven
Proefstn Akkerbouw Wageningen Gestencilde Versl Interprov Pro — Proefstation voor de Akkerbouw Wageningen. Gestencilde Verslagen van Interprovinciale Proeven
Proefstn Akkerbouw (Wageningen) Versl Interprov Proeven — Proefstation voor de Akkerbouw (Wageningen). Verslagen van Interprovinciale Proeven
Proefstn Akker Weidebouw Wageningen Gestencilde Versl Interp — Proefstation voor de Akker- en Weidebouw, Wageningen, Gestencilde Verslagen vanInterprovinciale Proeven
Proefstn Akker Weidebouw Wageningen Meded — Proefstation voor de Akker- en Weidebouw, Wageningen. Mededeling
Proefstn Groenteteelt Vollegrond Ned Meded — Proefstation voor de Groenteteelt in de Vollegrond in Nederland. Mededeling
Proefstn Java Suikerind Meded — Proefstation voor de Java-Suikerindustrie. Mededeelingen
Proefstn Rubber Meded — Proefstation voor Rubber. Mededeeling
Proefstn Vorstenl Tab Meded — Proefstation voor Vorstenlandsche Tabak. Mededeelingen
Proektn Nauchno Issled Inst Gipronikel Tr — Proektnyi Nauchno-Issledovatel'skii Institut Gipronikel. Trudy
Proektn Nauchno-Issled Inst Ural Promstroiniiproekt Tr — Proektnyi i Nauchno-Issledovatel'skii Institut "Ural'skii Promstroiniiproekt." Trudy
Pro Engr — Professional Engineer
Prof Admin — Professional Administration
Pro Fam Inf — Pro Familia Informationen
Prof Bolezni Pylevol Etiol — Professional'nye Bolezvi Pylevoi Etiologii
Prof Build — Professional Builder
Prof Build Apartm Bus — Professional Builder and Apartment Business
Prof Builder & Apt Bus — Professional Builder and Apartment Business
Prof Builder/Apt Bus — Professional Builder and Apartment Business
Prof Camera — Professional Camera
Prof Comput — Professional Computing
Prof Contrib Colo Sch Mines — Professional Contributions. Colorado School of Mines
Prof Dev W — Professional Development Week
Prof Eng — Professional Engineering
Prof Eng (Pretoria) — Professional Engineer (Pretoria)
Prof Eng (Wash DC) — Professional Engineer (Washington, DC)
Profess Gard — Professional Garden
Professional Eng — Professional Engineer
Profession Med — Profession Medicale
Professions et Entr — Professions et Entreprises
Profess Pap Ser Florida State Board Conservation Mar Lab — Professional Papers Series. Florida State Board of Conservation. Marine Laboratory
Prof Flashes — Professional Flashes
Prof Geog — Professional Geographer
Prof Geogr — Professional Geographer
Prof Geologist — Professional Geologist
Prof Hortic — Professional Horticulture
Profilak Med — Profilaktichna Meditsina
Profil Carie Dent Simp Int — Profilassi della Carie Dental. Simposio Internazionale
Profile — Profiles
Profile Med Pract — Profile of Medical Practice
Profiles Genius Ser — Profiles of Genius Series
Profiles Hosp Mark — Profiles in Hospital Marketing
Profil Lech Tuberk — Profilaktika i Lechenie Tuberkuleza
Profil Osobo Opasnykh Infekts — Profilaktika Osobo Opasnykh Infektsii
Profils Econ Nord-Pas-De-Calais — Profils de l'Economie Nord-Pas-De-Calais
Prof Inferm — Professioni Infermieristiche
PROFIS — Programminformationssystem Sozialwissenschaften
Prof Lit Fr — Profil Litteraire de la France
Prof Mark Rep — Professional Marketing Report
Prof Med Assist — Professional Medical Assistant
Prof Mon — Professional Monitor
Prof Nurse — Professional Nurse
Prof Nurs Home — Professional Nursing Home
Prof Nutr — Professional Nutritionist
Prof Pap Deputy Minist Miner Resour (Saudi Arabia) — Professional Papers. Deputy Ministry for Mineral Resources (Saudi Arabia)
Prof Pap Geol Surv — Professional Papers. United States Geological Survey

Prof Pap Ser Fla Dep Nat Resour Mar Res Lab — Professional Papers Series. Florida Department of Natural Resources. Marine Research Laboratory
Prof Pap US Geol Surv — Professional Papers. United States Geological Survey
Prof Photogr — Professional Photographer
Prof Prac Man — Professional Practice Management
Prof Pract Man — Professional Practice Management
Prof Print — Professional Printer
Prof Psycho — Professional Psychology
Prof Regulation N — Professional Regulation News
Prof Rpt — Professional Report
Prof Saf — Professional Safety
Prof Safety — Professional Safety
Prof Sanit Manage — Professional Sanitation Management
Prog — Progressive
Prog Aeronaut Sci — Progress in Aeronautical Science
Prog Aerosp Sci — Progress in Aerospace Sciences
Prog Age — Progressive Age
Prog Agric — Progresso Agricolo
Prog Agric Ariz — Progressive Agriculture in Arizona
Prog Agric Vitic — Progres Agricole et Viticole
Prog Agri Fr — Progres Agricole de France
Prog AIDS Pathol — Progress in AIDS Pathology
Prog Allerg — Progress in Allergy
Prog Allergol Jpn — Progress of Allergology in Japan
Prog Allergy — Progress in Allergy
Prog Anaesthesiol Proc World Congr Anaesthesiol — Progress in Anaesthesiology. Proceedings. World Congress of Anaesthesiologists
Prog Anal At Spectrosc — Progress in Analytical Atomic Spectroscopy
Prog Anal Chem — Progress in Analytical Chemistry
Prog Anal Chem Iron Steel Ind — Progress of Analytical Chemistry in the Iron and Steel Industry
Prog Anal Spectros — Progress in Analytical Spectroscopy
Prog Anal Ultracentrifugation — Progress in Analytical Ultracentrifugation
Prog Anat — Progress in Anatomy
Prog Androl — Progres en Andrologie
Prog Anesthesiol — Progress in Anesthesiology
Prog Anesth Mech — Progress in Anesthetic Mechanism
Prog Anim Biometeorol — Progress in Animal Biometeorology
Prog Antimicrob Anticancer Chemother Proc Int Congr Chemother — Progress in Antimicrobial and Anticancer Chemotherapy. Proceedings. International Congress of Chemotherapy
Prog Appl Mater Res — Progress in Applied Materials Research
Prog Appl Microcirc — Progress in Applied Microcirculation
Prog Arch — Progressive Architecture
Prog Archit — Progressive Architecture
Prog Astronaut Aeronaut — Progress in Astronautics and Aeronautics
Prog Astronaut Rocketry — Progress in Astronautics and Rocketry
Prog Astronaut Sci — Progress in the Astronautical Sciences
Prog At Med — Progress in Atomic Medicine
Prog At Spectrosc — Progress in Atomic Spectroscopy
Prog Basic Clin Pharmacol — Progress in Basic and Clinical Pharmacology
Prog Batteries Battery Mater — Progress in Batteries and Battery Materials
Prog Batteries Sol Cell — Progress in Batteries and Solar Cells
Prog Behav Modif — Progress in Behavior Modification
Prog Biochem Biophys — Progress in Biochemistry and Biophysics
Prog Biochem Pharmacol — Progress in Biochemical Pharmacology
Prog Biochim — Progressi in Biochimica
Prog Biocybern — Progress in Biocybernetics
Prog Biol Sci Relat Dermatol — Progress in the Biological Sciences in Relation to Dermatology
Prog Biomass Convers — Progress in Biomass Conversion
Prog Biomed Eng — Progress in Biomedical Engineering
Prog Biomed Polym Proc Am Chem Soc Symp — Progress in Biomedical Polymers. Proceedings. American Chemical Society Symposium
Prog Biometeorol — Progress in Biometeorology
Prog Biometeorol Div A — Progress in Biometeorology. Division A. Progress in Human Biometeorology
Prog Biometeorol Div B — Progress in Biometeorology. Division B. Progress in Animal Biometeorology
Prog Bioorg Chem — Progress in Bioorganic Chemistry
Prog Biophys and Mol Biol — Progress in Biophysics and Molecular Biology
Prog Biophys Biophys Chem — Progress in Biophysics and Biophysical Chemistry
Prog Biophys Mol Biol — Progress in Biophysics and Molecular Biology
Prog Biotechnol — Progress in Biotechnology
Prog Boron Chem — Progress in Boron Chemistry
Prog Bot — Progress in Botany
Prog Bot Fortschr Bot — Progress in Botany-Fortschritt der Botanik
Prog Brain Res — Progress in Brain Research
Prog Build — Progressive Builder
Prog Calorim Therm Anal — Progress in Calorimetry and Thermal Analysis
Prog Cancer Res Ther — Progress in Cancer Research and Therapy
Prog Cardiol — Progress in Cardiology
Prog Cardiol Basel — Progres en Cardiologie (Basel)
Prog Cardiovasc Dis — Progress in Cardiovascular Diseases
Prog Cardiovasc Nurs — Progress in Cardiovascular Nursing
Prog Catal — Progress in Catalysis
Prog Catal Proc Can Symp Catal — Progress in Catalysis. Proceedings. Canadian Symposium on Catalysis
Prog Catecholamine Res Part A Proc Int Catecholamine Symp — Progress in Catecholamine Research. Part A. Basic Aspects and Peripheral Mechanisms. Proceedings. International Catecholamine Symposium
Prog Catecholamine Res Part B Proc Int Catecholamine Symp — Progress in Catecholamine Research. Part B. Central Aspects. Proceedings. International Catecholamine Symposium

Prog Catecholamine Res Part C Proc Int Catecholamine Symp — Progress in Catecholamine Research. Part C. Clinical Aspects. Proceedings. International Catecholamine Symposium
Prog Cell Cycle Res — Progress in Cell Cycle Research
Prog Ceram Sci — Progress in Ceramic Science
Prog Chem Fats — Progress in the Chemistry of Fats and Other Lipids
Prog Chem Fats Other Lipids — Progress in the Chemistry of Fats and Other Lipids
Prog Chem Fibrinolysis Thrombolysis — Progress in Chemical Fibrinolysis and Thrombolysis
Prog Chem Moscow — Progress in Chemistry (Moscow)
Prog Chem Org Nat Prod — Progress in the Chemistry of Organic Natural Products
Prog Chem Toxicol — Progress in Chemical Toxicology
Prog Chim Subst Org Nat — Progres dans la Chimie des Substances Organiques Naturelles
Prog Clay Sci — Progress in Clay Science
Prog Clin Biochem Med — Progress in Clinical Biochemistry and Medicine
Prog Clin Biol Res — Progress in Clinical and Biological Research
Prog Clin Cancer — Progress in Clinical Cancer
Prog Clin Enzymol Proc Int Congr — Progress in Clinical Enzymology. Proceedings. International Congress of Clinical Enzymology
Prog Clin Immunol — Progress in Clinical Immunology
Prog Clin Med — Progress in Clinical Medicine
Prog Clin Neurophysiol — Progress in Clinical Neurophysiology
Prog Clin Parasitol — Progress in Clinical Parasitology
Prog Clin Pathol — Progress in Clinical Pathology
Prog Clin Pharm — Progress in Clinical Pharmacy
Prog Clin Pharmacol — Progress in Clinical Pharmacology
Prog Coll & Polym Sci — Progress in Colloid and Polymer Science
Prog Colloid Polym Sci — Progress in Colloid and Polymer Science
Prog Combus Sci Technol — Progress in Combustion Science and Technology
Prog Comput Sci Appl Logic — Progress in Computer Science and Applied Logic
Prog Concept Control — Progress in Conception Control
Prog Contracep Delivery Syst — Progress in Contraceptive Delivery Systems
Prog Cosmic Ray Phys — Progress in Cosmic Ray Physics
Prog Crit Care Med — Progress in Critical Care Medicine
Prog Cryog — Progress in Cryogenics
Prog Cryst Growth Charact — Progress in Crystal Growth and Characterization
Prog Cryst Growth Charact Mater — Progress in Crystal Growth and Characterization of Materials
Prog Cryst Phys — Progress in Crystal Physics
Prog Dielectr — Progress in Dielectrics
Prog Drug Metab — Progress in Drug Metabolism
Prog Drug Res — Progress in Drug Research
Prog Ecol — Progress in Ecology
Prog Educ — Progress in Education
Prog Educ — Progressive Education
Prog Educ (Poona) — Progress of Education (Poona)
Prog Educ USA — Progress of Education in the United States of America
Prog Electromagn Res — Progress in Electromagnetics Research
Prog Elektrokhim Org Soedin — Progress Elektrokhimii Organicheskikh Soedinenii
Prog Elem Part Cosmic Ray Phys — Progress in Elementary Particle and Cosmic Ray Physics
Prog Endocr Res Ther — Progress in Endocrine Research and Therapy
Prog Energy Combust Sci — Progress in Energy and Combustion Science
Prog Explor Tuberc — Progres de l'Exploration de la Tuberculose
Prog Exp Pers Psychopathol Res — Progress in Experimental Personality and Psychopathology Research
Prog Exp Pers Res — Progress in Experimental Personality Research
Prog Exp Tumor Res — Progress in Experimental Tumor Research
Prog Extr Metall — Progress in Extractive Metallurgy
Prog Ex Tum — Progress in Experimental Tumor Research
Prog F — Progressive Farmer and Farm Woman
Prog Farmer — Progressive Farmer
Prog Farmer West — Progressive Farmer for the West
Prog Farming — Progressive Farming
Prog Farming/Farmer — Progressive Farming/Farmer
Prog Fibrinolysis — Progress in Fibrinolysis
Prog Filtr Sep — Progress in Filtration and Separation
Prog Fire Retard Ser — Progress in Fire Retardancy Series
Prog Fish-C — Progressive Fish-Culturist
Prog Fish-Cult — Progressive Fish-Culturist
Prog Flavour Res Proc Weurman Flavour Res Symp — Progress in Flavour Research. Proceedings. Weurman Flavour Research Symposium
Prog Food Nutr Sci — Progress in Food and Nutrition Science
Prog Fot — Progresso Fotografico
Prog Fotogr (Barcelona) — Progresso Fotografico (Barcelona)
Prog Fotogr (Milan) — Progresso Fotografico (Milan)
Prog Gastroenterol — Progress in Gastroenterology
Prog Geogr — Progress in Geography
Prog Groc — Progressive Grocer
Prog Grocer — Progressive Grocer
Prog Growth Factor Res — Progress in Growth Factor Research
Prog Gynecol — Progress in Gynecology
Prog Hazard Chem Handl Disposal Proc Symp — Progress in Hazardous Chemicals Handling and Disposal. Proceedings. Symposium on Hazardous Chemicals Handling and Disposal
Prog Heat Mass Transf — Progress in Heat and Mass Transfer
Prog Heat Mass Transfer — Progress in Heat and Mass Transfer
Prog Hematol — Progress in Hematology
Prog Hemostasis Thromb — Progress in Hemostasis and Thrombosis
Prog Hemost Thromb — Progress in Hemostasis and Thrombosis
Prog Hepato Pharmacol — Progress in Hepato-Pharmacology
Prog Heterocycl Chem — Progress in Heterocyclic Chemistry

Prog High Polym — Progress in High Polymers
Prog High Temp Phys Chem — Progress in High Temperature Physics and Chemistry
Prog High Temp Supercond Transistors Other Devices — Progress in High-Temperature Superconducting Transistors and Other Devices
Prog Histochem Cytochem — Progress in Histochemistry and Cytochemistry
Prog Hodgkins Dis — Progress in Hodgkin's Disease
Prog Horm Biochem Pharmacol — Progress in Hormone Biochemistry and Pharmacology
Prog Hort — Progressive Horticulture
Prog Hortic — Progressive Horticulture
Prog HPLC — Progress in HPLC
Prog HPLC HPCE — Progress in HPLC [*High-Performance Liquid Chromatography*] - HPCE [*High-Performance Capillary Electrophoresis*]
Prog Human Geogr — Progress in Human Geography
Prog Hum Biometeorol — Progress in Human Biometeorology
Prog Hum Nutr — Progress in Human Nutrition
Prog Immunobiol Stand — Progress in Immunobiological Standardization
Prog Immunol Int Congr Immunol — Progress in Immunology. International Congress of Immunology
Prog Immunol Proc Int Congr Immunol — Progress in Immunology. Proceedings. International Congress of Immunology
Prog Ind Gas Chromatogr Proc Annu Gas Chromatogr Inst — Progress in Industrial Gas Chromatography. Proceedings. Annual Gas Chromatography Institute
Prog Ind Microbiol — Progress in Industrial Microbiology
Prog Ind Tintorie Tess — Progressi nelle Industrie Tintorie e Tessili
Prog Inflammation Res Ther Int Conf Inflammation Res Assoc — Progress in Inflammation Research and Therapy. International Conference. Inflammation Research Association
Prog Infrared Spectrosc — Progress in Infrared Spectroscopy
Prog Inorg Chem — Progress in Inorganic Chemistry
Prog Instr & Ed Tech — Programmed Instruction and Educational Technology
Prog Instr Bul — Programmed Instruction Bulletin
Prog Lantbruk — Progressivt Lantbruk
Prog Learn — Programmed Learning and Educational Technology
Prog Learn Disabil — Progress in Learning Disabilities
Prog Leukocyte Biol — Progress in Leukocyte Biology
Prog Lipid Res — Progress in Lipid Research
Prog Liver Dis — Progress in Liver Diseases
Prog Low Temp Phys — Progress in Low Temperature Physics
Prog Mater Sci — Progress in Materials Science
Prog Mat Sc — Progress in Materials Science
Prog Med — Il Progresso Medico
Prog Med — Progres Medical
Prog Med Chem — Progress in Medicinal Chemistry
Prog Med Ge — Progress in Medical Genetics
Prog Med Genet — Progress in Medical Genetics
Prog Med (Istanbul) — Progressus Medicinae (Istanbul)
Prog Med Microbiol — Progress in Medical Microbiology
Prog Med Parasitol Jpn — Progress in Medical Parasitology in Japan
Prog Med Psychosom — Progres en Medecine Psychosomatique
Prog Med Radiat Phys — Progress in Medical Radiation Physics
Prog Med (Rome) — Progresso Medico (Rome)
Prog Med (Tokyo) — Progress in Medicine (Tokyo)
Prog Med Vi — Progress in Medical Virology
Prog Med Virol — Progress in Medical Virology
Prog Met Phys — Progress in Metal Physics
Prog Migraine Res — Progress in Migraine Research
Prog Mol Subcell Biol — Progress in Molecular and Subcellular Biology
Prog Mutat Res — Progress in Mutation Research
Prog Nat Sci — Progress in Natural Science
Prog Neonatol — Progres en Neonatologie
Prog Neurobiol — Progress in Neurobiology
Prog Neurobiol (NY) — Progress in Neurobiology (New York)
Prog Neurobiol (Oxf) — Progress in Neurobiology (Oxford)
Prog Neurol Psychiatry — Progress in Neurology and Psychiatry
Prog Neurol Surg — Progress in Neurological Surgery
Prog Neuropathol — Progress in Neuropathology
Prog Neuro-Psychopharmacol — Progress in Neuro-Psychopharmacology
Prog Neuro-Psychopharmacol & Biol Psychiatry — Progress in Neuro-Psychopharmacology and Biological Psychiatry
Prog Neuropsychopharmacol Biol Psychiatry — Progress in Neuropsychopharmacology and Biological Psychiatry
Prog Neutron Capture Ther Cancer Proc Int Symp — Progress in Neutron Capture Therapy for Cancer. Proceedings. International Symposium on Neutron Capture Therapy for Cancer
PROGNO — Prognosen-Trends-Entwicklungen
Prog Non Destr Test — Progress in Non-Destructive Testing
Prog Notes Walter Reed Army Med Cent — Progress Notes. Walter Reed Army Medical Center
Prog Nucleic Acid Res — Progress in Nucleic Acid Research
Prog Nucleic Acid Res Mol Biol — Progress in Nucleic Acid Research and Molecular Biology
Prog Nucl Energy — Progress in Nuclear Energy
Prog Nucl Energy Anal Chem — Progress in Nuclear Energy. Analytical Chemistry
Prog Nucl Energy New Ser — Progress in Nuclear Energy. New Series
Prog Nucl Energy Ser 1 — Progress in Nuclear Energy. Series 1. Physics and Mathematics
Prog Nucl Energy Ser 2 — Progress in Nuclear Energy. Series 2. Reactors
Prog Nucl Energy Ser 3 — Progress in Nuclear Energy. Series 3. Process Chemistry
Prog Nucl Energy Ser 4 — Progress in Nuclear Energy. Series 4. Technology, Engineering, and Safety

Prog Nucl Energy Ser 5 — Progress in Nuclear Energy. Series 5. Metallurgy and Fuels
Prog Nucl Energy Ser 6 — Progress in Nuclear Energy. Series 6
Prog Nucl Energy Ser 7 — Progress in Nuclear Energy. Series 7. Medical Sciences
Prog Nucl Energy Ser 7 Med Sci — Progress in Nuclear Energy. Series 7. Medical Sciences
Prog Nucl Energy Ser 8 — Progress in Nuclear Energy. Series 8. The Economics of Nuclear Power Including Administration and Law
Prog Nucl Energy Ser 9 — Progress in Nuclear Energy. Series 9
Prog Nucl Energy Ser 10 — Progress in Nuclear Energy. Series 10. Law and Administration
Prog Nucl Energy Ser 11 — Progress in Nuclear Energy. Series 11. Plasma Physics and Thermonuclear Research
Prog Nucl Energy Ser 12 — Progress in Nuclear Energy. Series 12. Health Physics
Prog Nucl Magn Reson Spectrosc — Progress in Nuclear Magnetic Resonance Spectroscopy
Prog Nucl Med — Progress in Nuclear Medicine
Prog Nucl Phys — Progress in Nuclear Physics
Prog Nucl Tech Instrum — Progress in Nuclear Techniques and Instrumentation
Prog Nurse — Progressive Nurse
Prog Obes Res — Progress in Obesity Research
Prog Obstet Gynecol — Progres in Obstetrique et Gynecologie
Prog Oceanogr — Progress in Oceanography
Prog Odontostomatol — Progres Odonto-Stomatologique
Prog Ophtalmol — Progres en Ophtalmologie
Prog Ophthalmol Otolaryngol — Progress in Ophthalmology and Otolaryngology
Prog Opioid Res Proc Int Narc Res Conf — Progress in Opioid Research. Proceedings. International Narcotics Research Conference
Prog Opt — Progress in Optics
Prog Org Chem — Progress in Organic Chemistry
Prog Org Coat — Progress in Organic Coatings
Prog Org Coatings — Progress in Organic Coatings
Prog Oto-Rhino-Laryngol — Progres en Oto-Rhino-Laryngologie
Prog Pac Polym Sci Proc Pac Polym Conf — Progress in Pacific Polymer Science. Proceedings. Pacific Polymer Conference
Prog Pain Res Manage — Progress in Pain Research and Management
Prog Pancreatol Proc Symp Eur Pancreatic Club — Progress in Pancreatology. Proceedings. Symposium. European Pancreatic Club
Prog Part Nucl Phys — Progress in Particle and Nuclear Physics
Prog Pass Sol Energy Syst — Progress in Passive Solar Energy Systems
Prog Pathol — Progress in Pathology
Prog Pathophysiol Proc Int Congr — Progress in Pathophysiology. Proceedings. International Congress on Pathological Physiology
Prog Pediatr Hematol/Oncol — Progress in Pediatric Hematology/Oncology
Prog Pediatr Pueric — Progresos de Pediatria y Puericultura
Prog Pediatr Radiol — Progress in Pediatric Radiology
Prog Pediatr Surg — Progress in Pediatric Surgery
Prog Pept Res Proc Am Pept Symp — Progress in Peptide Research. Proceedings. American Peptide Symposium
Prog Perfum Cosmet — Progressive Perfumery and Cosmetics
Prog Pestic Biochem — Progress in Pesticide Biochemistry
Prog Pestic Biochem Toxicol — Progress in Pesticide Biochemistry and Toxicology
Prog Pharmacol — Progress in Pharmacology
Prog Pharmacol Clin Pharmacol — Progress in Pharmacology and Clinical Pharmacology
Prog Pharm Biomed Anal — Progress in Pharmaceutical and Biomedical Analysis
Prog Photogr — Progress in Photography
Prog Photosynth Res Proc Int Congr — Progress in Photosynthesis Research. Proceedings. International Congress of Photosynthesis Research
Prog Photosynth Res Proc Int Congr Photosynth — Progress in Photosynthesis Research. Proceedings. International Congress on Photosynthesis
Prog Photovoltaics Res Appl — Progress in Photovoltaics. Research and Applications
Prog Phycol Res — Progress in Phycological Research
Prog Phys — Progress of Physics
Prog Phys Astrophys Repr Ser — Progress in Physics. Astrophysics. A Reprint Series
Prog Phys Berlin — Progress of Physics (Berlin)
Prog Phys Biophys Repr Ser — Progress in Physics. Biophysics. A Reprint Series
Prog Phys Geogr — Progress in Physical Geography
Prog Physiol — Progress in Physiology
Prog Physiol Psychol — Progress in Physiological Psychology
Prog Physiol Sci Beijing — Progress in Physiological Sciences (Beijing)
Prog Physiol Sci (Engl Transl Usp Fiziol Nauk) — Progress in Physiological Sciences (English Translation of Uspekhi Fiziologicheskikh Nauk)
Prog Physiol Sci (USSR) — Progress in Physiological Sciences (USSR)
Prog Phys Org Chem — Progress in Physical Organic Chemistry
Prog Phys Sci (Moscow) — Progress in Physical Sciences (Moscow)
Prog Phys Ther — Progress in Physical Therapy
Prog Phytochem — Progress in Phytochemistry
Prog Plann — Progress in Planning
Prog Plant Prot — Progress in Plant Protection
Prog Plast — Progressive Plastics
Prog Polym Process — Progress in Polymer Processing
Prog Polym Sci — Progress in Polymer Science
Prog Polym Sci Jpn — Progress in Polymer Science. Japan
Prog Powder Metall — Progress in Powder Metallurgy
Prog Protein Lipid Interact — Progress in Protein-Lipid Interactions
Prog Protozool Proc Int Congr Protozool — Progress in Protozoology. Proceedings. International Congress on Protozoology
Prog Psicofarmacol — Progresos en Psicofarmacologia
Prog Psychiatr Drug Treat — Progress in Psychiatric Drug Treatment

Prog Psychiatry — Progress in Psychiatry
Prog Psychobiol Physiol Psychol — Progress in Psychobiology and Physiological Psychology
Prog Quantum Electron — Progress in Quantum Electronics
Prog Radiat Prot — Progress in Radiation Protection
Prog Radiat Ther — Progress in Radiation Therapy
Prog Radiol Symp Invited Pap Int Congr Radiol — Progress in Radiology. Symposia and Invited Papers. International Congress of Radiology
Prog Radiopharm — Progress in Radiopharmacy
Prog Radiopharmacol — Progress in Radiopharmacology
Progr Agr — Progresso Agricolo
Progr Agr Ariz — Progressive Agriculture in Arizona
Progr Agr Vitic — Progres Agricole et Viticole
Progr Allergy — Progress in Allergy
Program — Programmirovanie
Program Abstr Am Soc Parasitol Annu Meet — Program and Abstracts. American Society of Parasitologists. Annual Meeting
Programa Coop Exp Agropecu US Peru Bol Trimest Exp Agropecu — Programa Cooperativo de Experimentacion Agropecuaria. United States and Peru. Boletim Trimestral de Experimentacion Agropecuaria
Program Aid US Dep Agric — Program Aid. United States Department of Agriculture
Program Am Dairy Sci Assoc Annu Meet Branch Abstr — Program. American Dairy Science Association. Annual Meeting and Branch Abstracts
Program and Comput Software — Programming and Computer Software
Programa Reg Desarrollo Cient Tecnol Monogr Ser Quim — Programa Regional de Desarrollo Cientifico y Tecnologico. Monografia. Serie de Quimica
Programa Reg Desarrollo Cient Tecnol Ser Biol — Programa Regional de Desarrollo Cientifico y Tecnologico. Serie de Biologia
Programa Reg Desarrollo Cient Tecnol Ser Fis — Programa Regional de Desarrollo Cientifico y Tecnologico. Serie de Fisica
Program Autom Libr Inf Syst — Program. Automated Library and Information Systems
Program Learn and Educ Technol — Programmed Learning and Educational Technology
Programma Tezis Dokl Soveshch Yad Spektrosk Strukt At Yadra — Programma i Tezisy Dokladov Soveshchaniya po Yadernoi Spektroskopii i StruktureAtomnogo Yadra
Program Mat Fis Elettron — Programma di Matematica, Fisica, Elettronica
Programmed Learning — Programmed Learning and Educational Technology
Programme Pap Rubber Conf — Programme and Papers. Rubber Conference
Programming and Comput Software — Programming and Computer Software
Programming Lang Ser — Programming Languages Series
Programmirovan — Programmirovanie. Akademija Nauk SSSR
Program News Comput Libr — Program. News of Computers in Libraries
Program Notes Assoc Univ Programs Health Adm — Program Notes. Association of University Programs in Health Administration
Program/Proc Natl Horsemen's Semin — Program/Proceedings. National Horsemen's Seminar
Programs Pap Minn Acad Sci — Programs and Papers. Minnesota Academy of Science
Progr Biophys Biophys Chem — Progress in Biophysics and Biophysical Chemistry
Progr Bull Alberta Univ Ext Dept — Progress Bulletin. Alberta University Extension Department
Progr Card — Progress in Cardiovascular Diseases
Progr Cardiovas Dis — Progress in Cardiovascular Diseases
Progr Clin Cancer — Progress in Clinical Cancer
Progr Contr Eng — Progress in Control Engineering
Progr Coop Centroamer Mejor Maiz — Programa Cooperativo Centroamericano para el Mejoramiento del Maiz
Prog React Kinet — Progress in Reaction Kinetics
Prog Rech Cancer — Progres dans les Recherches sur le Cancer
Prog Rech Exp Tumeurs — Progres de la Recherche Experimentale des Tumeurs
Prog Rech Pharm — Progres des Recherches Pharmaceutiques
Prog Refrig Sci Technol Proc Int Congr Refrig — Progress in Refrigeration Science and Technology. Proceedings. International Congress of Refrigeration
Prog Rep Agric Exp Stn Univ Idaho — Progress Report. Agricultural Experiment Station. University of Idaho
Prog Rep Ala Agric Exp Stn — Progress Report. Alabama Agricultural Experiment Station
Prog Rep Ariz Exp Stn — Progress Report. Arizona Experiment Station
Prog Rep Clovers Spec Purpose Legumes Res — Progress Report. Clovers and Special Legumes Research
Prog Rep Clovers Spec Purpose Legumes Res Univ Wis Dep Agron — Progress Report. Clovers and Special Purpose Legumes Research. University of Wisconsin. Department of Agronomy
Prog Rep Colo Exp Stn — Progress Report. Colorado Experiment Station
Prog Rep Dom Apiarist Canad Dep Agric — Progress Report. Dominion Apiarist. Canadian Department of Agriculture
Prog Rep Exp Stn Colorado State Univ — Colorado State University. Experiment Station. Progress Report
Prog Rep Exp Stns (Tanzania) — Progress Reports. Experiment Stations (Tanzania)
Prog Rep Gen Rev World Coal Ind — Progress Report. General Review of the World Coal Industry
Prog Rep Geol Surv Dep Swaziland — Progress Report. Geological Survey Department. Swaziland
Prog Rep Geol Surv New Hebrides Anglo Fr Condominium — Progress Report. Geological Survey. New Hebrides Anglo-French Condominium
Prog Rep Ins Hydrodyn Hydraul Eng — Progress Report. Institute of Hydrodynamics and Hydraulic Engineering
Prog Rep KY Agric Exp Stn — Progress Report. Kentucky Agricultural Experiment Station

Prog Rep Minist Agric Fish Fd Exp Husb Fms Exp Hort Stns — Progress Report. Ministry of Agriculture, Fisheries, and Food. Experimental Husbandry Farms and Experimental Horticulture Stations
Prog Rep NM Bur Mines Miner Resour — Progress Report. New Mexico Bureau of Mines and Mineral Resources
Prog Rep Nucl Energy Res Jpn — Progress Report. Nuclear Energy Research in Japan
Prog Rep PA Agric Exp Stn — Progress Report. Pennsylvania Agricultural Experiment Station
Prog Rep Pa State Univ Agric Exp Stn — Progress Report. Pennsylvania State University. Agricultural Experiment Station
Prog Rep Pa Topogr Geol Surv — Progress Report. Pennsylvania. Topographic and Geologic Survey
Prog Reprod Biol — Progress in Reproductive Biology
Prog Reprod Biol Med — Progress in Reproductive Biology and Medicine
Prog Reprod Med — Progress in Reproductive Medicine
Prog Rep Ser Agric Exp Stn Ala Polytech Inst — Progress Report Series. Agricultural Experiment Station. Alabama Polytechnic Institute
Prog Rep Ser Agric Exp Stn Auburn Univ (Ala) — Progress Report Series. Agricultural Experiment Station. Auburn University (Alabama)
Prog Rep Ser Ala Agric Exp Stn Auburn Ala — Progress Report Series. Alabama. Agricultural Experiment Station (Auburn, Alabama)
Prog Rep Texas Agric Exp Stn — Progress Report. Texas Agricultural Experiment Station
Prog Rep Univ Calif Water Resour Cent — Progress Report. University of California. Water Resources Center
Prog Rep Wash Dep Fish — Progress Report. Washington. Department of Fisheries
Prog Res — Progress thru Research
Progres Arch — Progressive Architecture
Prog Res Clin Appl Corticosteroids Proc Annu Clin Symp — Progress in Research and Clinical Applications of Corticosteroids. Proceedings.Annual Clinical Symposium
Progres Ed — Progressive Education
Prog Res Emphysema Chronic Bronchitis — Progress in Research in Emphysema and Chronic Bronchitis
Progres Med (Paris) — Progres Medical (Paris)
Progreso Med (Habana) — Progreso Medico (Habana)
Prog Respir Res — Progress in Respiration Research
Progres Scientif — Progres Scientifique
Progress in Math — Progress in Mathematics
Progress in Particle and Nuclear Phys — Progress in Particle and Nuclear Physics
Progress in Phys — Progress in Physics
Progressive Archit — Progressive Architecture
Progressive Archre — Progressive Architecture
Progres Soc 3e Ser — Progres Social. Troisieme Serie
Progresso Fotogr — Progresso Fotografico
Progress Organic Coatings — Progress in Organic Coatings
Progress Phytochem — Progress in Phytochemistry
Progressv — Progressive
Progres Techn — Progres Technique
Progres Vet — Progres Veterinaire
Prog Retinal Eye Res — Progress in Retinal and Eye Research
Prog Retinal Res — Progress in Retinal Research
Progr For — Progressive Forensics
Progr Hemat — Progress in Hematology
Prog Rheumatol Int Semin Treat Rheum Dis — Progress in Rheumatology. International Seminar on Treatment of Rheumatic Diseases
Progr Hum Geogr — Progress in Human Geography. International Review of Current Research
Progr Indust Microbiol — Progress in Industrial Microbiology
Progr Learn Educ Technol — Programmed Learning and Educational Technology
Progr Mater Sci — Progress in Materials Science
Progr Math (Allahabad) — Progress of Mathematics (Allahabad)
Progr Math Varanasi — Progress of Mathematics (Varanasi)
Progr Med Microbiol — Progress in Medical Microbiology
Progr Med (Paris) — Progres Medical (Paris)
Progr Med Virol — Progress in Medical Virology
Progr Neurol Psychiat — Progress in Neurology and Psychiatry
Progr Nonlinear Differential Equations Appl — Progress in Nonlinear Differential Equations and their Applications
Progr Nucl Acid Res — Progress in Nucleic Acid Research
Progr Nucl Energy Ser 1 Phys Math — Progress in Nuclear Energy. Series 1. Physics and Mathematics
Progr Nucl Energy Ser 2 Reactors — Progress in Nuclear Energy. Series 2. Reactors
Progr Nucl Energy Ser 3 Process Chem — Progress in Nuclear Energy. Series 3. Process Chemistry
Progr Nucl Energy Ser 4 Technol Eng — Progress in Nuclear Energy. Series 4. Technology and Engineering
Progr Nucl Energy Ser 5 Met Fuels — Progress in Nuclear Energy. Series 5. Metallurgy and Fuels
Progr Nucl Energy Ser 6 — Progress in Nuclear Energy. Series 6. Biological Sciences
Progr Nucl Energy Ser 8 Econ — Progress in Nuclear Energy. Series 8. Economics
Progr Nucl Energy Ser 10 Law Admin — Progress in Nuclear Energy. Series 10. Law and Administration
Progr Nucl Energy Ser 11 Plasma Phys Thermonucl Res — Progress in Nuclear Energy. Series 11. Plasma Physics and Thermonuclear Research
Progr Offic Journee Interreg Recolte Mec Mais-Grain — Programme Officiel. Journee Interregionale de Recolte Mechanique du Mais-Grain
Progr Pap Recycl — Progress in Paper Recycling
Progr Particle and Nuclear Phys — Progress in Particle and Nuclear Physics

Progr Phys — Progress in Physics
Progr Physiol Psych — Progress in Physiological Psychology
Progr Phys Sci — Progress of Physical Sciences
Progr Plast — Progressive Plastics
Progr Polymer Sci — Progress in Polymer Science
Progr Powder Met — Progress in Powder Metallurgy
Progr Probab — Progress in Probability
Progr Prob Statist — Progress in Probability and Statistics
Progr Pure Appl Discrete Math — Progress in Pure and Applied Discrete Mathematics
Progr Rei Bot — Progressus Rei Botanicae/Fortschritte der Botanik/Progres de la Botanique/Progress of Botany
Progr Rep Cereal Breed Lab — Progress Report. Cereal Breeding Laboratory
Progr Rep Colo State Univ Agr Exp Sta — Progress Report. Colorado State University. Agricultural Experiment Station
Progr Rep Conn Agr Exp Sta — Progress Report. Connecticut Agricultural Experiment Station
Progr Rep Idaho Agr Res — Progress Report. Idaho Agricultural Research
Progr Rep KY Agr Exp Sta — Progress Report. Kentucky Agricultural Experiment Station
Progr Rep PA Agric Exp Sta — Progress Report. Pennsylvania State University. Agricultural Experiment Station
Progr Rep PA State Univ Agr Exp Sta — Progress Report. Pennsylvania State University. Agricultural Experiment Station
Progr Rep Ser Ala Agr Exp Sta — Progress Report Series. Alabama Agricultural Experiment Station
Progr Rep Tex Agr Exp Sta — Progress Report. Texas Agricultural Experiment Station
Progr Rep Tohoku Agr Exp Sta — Progress Report. Tohoku Agricultural Experiment Station
Progr Rep Univ Nebr Coll Agr Dept Agr Econ — Progress Report. University of Nebraska. College of Agriculture. Department of Agricultural Economics
Progr Rev For Prod Lab (Ottawa) — Program Review. Forest Products Laboratory (Ottawa)
Progr Rev For Prod Lab (Vancouver) — Program Review. Forest Products Laboratory (Vancouver)
Progr Rubber Plast Technol — Progress in Rubber and Plastics Technology
Progr Rubber Technol — Progress of Rubber Technology
Progr Sci Comput — Progress in Scientific Computing
Progr Soc — Progres Social
Progr Stiintei — Progresele Stiintei
Progr Surg — Progress in Surgery
Progr Systems Control Theory — Progress in Systems and Control Theory
Progr Ter Clin — Progresos de Terapeutica Clinica
Progr Theoret Comput Sci — Progress in Theoretical Computer Science
Progr Theoret Phys — Progress of Theoretical Physics
Progr Theoret Phys Suppl — Progress of Theoretical Physics. Supplement
Prog Rubber Technol — Progress of Rubber Technology
Prog Rural Ext Commun Dev — Progress in Rural Extension and Community Development
Prog Sci — Progres Scientifique
Prog Sci (Amoy) — Progress in Science (Amoy)
Prog Sci Eng Compos Proc Int Conf Compos Mater — Progress in Science and Engineering of Composites. Proceedings. International Conference on Composite Materials
Prog Sci Ind — Progress of Science in India
Prog Sci Tech Froid CR Congr Int Froid — Progres dans la Science et la Technique du Froid. Comptes Rendus. Congres International du Froid
Prog Sci Technol Rare Earths — Progress in the Science and Technology of the Rare Earths
Prog Semicond — Progress in Semiconductors
Prog Sens Physiol — Progress in Sensory Physiology
Prog Sep Purif — Progress in Separation and Purification
Prog Sex Sel Pap Proc Int Congr — Progress in Sexology. Selected Papers. Proceedings. International Congress of Sexology
Prog Soc — Progres Social
Prog Soil Sci (Nanjing Peoples Repub China) — Progress in Soil Science (Nanjing, People's Republic of China)
Prog Soil Zool Proc Int Colloq — Progress in Soil Zoology. Proceedings. International Colloquium on Soil Zoology
Prog Sol Energy — Progress in Solar Energy
Prog Solid State Chem — Progress in Solid State Chemistry
Prog Space Transp Proc Eur Aerosp Conf — Progress in Space Transportation. Proceedings. European Aerospace Conference
Prog Stand — Progress in Standardization
Prog Steel Constr Work Steel Congr — Progress in Steel Construction Work. Steel Congress
Prog Steel Process Steel Congr — Progress in Steel Processing. Steel Congress
Prog Stereochem — Progress in Stereochemistry
Prog Surf Membr Sci — Progress in Surface and Membrane Science
Prog Surf Sci — Progress in Surface Science
Prog Surg — Progress in Surgery
Prog Tech — Progres Technique
Prog Technol — Progress in Technology
Prog Tekhnol Mashinostr — Progressivnaya Tekhnologiya Mashinostroeniya
Prog Ter — Progresso Terapeutico
Prog Theor Biol — Progress in Theoretical Biology
Prog Theor Org Chem — Progress in Theoretical Organic Chemistry
Prog Theor Phys — Progress of Theoretical Physics
Prog Theor Phys Suppl — Progress of Theoretical Physics. Supplement
Prog Thin-Layer Chromatogr Relat Methods — Progress in Thin-Layer Chromatography and Related Methods
Prog Thyroid Res Proc Int Thyroid Conf — Progress in Thyroid Research. Proceedings. International Thyroid Conference
Prog Top Cytogenet — Progress and Topics in Cytogenetics

Prog T Phys — Progress of Theoretical Physics
Prog Transfus Med — Progress in Transfusion Medicine
Prog Underwater Sci — Progress in Underwater Science
Prog Vac Microbalance Tech — Progress in Vacuum Microbalance Techniques
Progve Agric Ariz — Progressive Agriculture in Arizona
Progve Fmg — Progressive Farming
Prog Vet — Progresso Veterinario
Prog Vet Microbiol Immunol — Progress in Veterinary Microbiology and Immunology
Prog Virol Med — Progres en Virologie Medicale
Prog Water Tech — Progress in Water Technology
Prog Water Technol — Progress in Water Technology
Prog Zool — Progress in Zoology
PROH — Promoting Health
Proiskhozhd Shchelochnykh Porod Tr Vses Petrogr Soveshch — Proiskhozhdenie Shchelochnykh Porod. Trudy Vsesoyuznogo Petrograficheskogo Soveshchaniya
Proizv Obuc — Proizvodstvennoe Obucenie
Proizvod Chuguna — Proizvodstvo Chuguna
Proizvod Chuguna Stali — Proizvodstvo Chuguna i Stali
Proizvod Elektrostali — Proizvodstvo Elektrostali
Proizvod Ferrosplavov — Proizvodstvo Ferrosplavov
Proizvod Ispolz Elastomerov — Proizvodstvo i Ispol'zovanie Elastomerov. Nauchno-Tekhnicheskie Dostizheniya i Peredovoi Opyt
Proizvod Issled Stalei Splavov — Proizvodstvo i Issledovanie Stalei i Splavov
Proizvod Issled Stekla Silik Mater — Proizvodstvo i Issledovanie Stekla i Silikatnykh Materialov
Proizvod Koksa — Proizvodstvo Koksa
Proizvod Krupnykh Mash — Proizvodstvo Krupnykh Mashin
Proizvod Lista — Proizvodstvo Lista
Proizvod Nauchno-Issled Inst Inzh Izyskaniyam Stroit Tr — Proizvodstvennyi i Nauchno-Issledovatel'skii Institut po Inzhenernym Izyskaniyam v Stroitel'stve Trudy
Proizvod Obrab Mater — Proizvoditel'naya Obrabotka Materialov
Proizvod Obrab Stali Splavov — Proizvodstvo i Obrabotka Stali i Splavov
Proizvod Ogneuporov — Proizvodstvo Ogneuporov
Proizvod Pererab Plastmass Sint Smol — Proizvodstvo i Pererabotka Plastmass i Sinteticheskikh Smol
Proizvod Primen Mikrobn Fermentn Prep — Proizvodstvo i Primenenie Mikrobnykh Fermentnykh Preparatov
Proizvod Smaz Mater — Proizvodstvo Smazochnykh Materialov
Proizvod Spets Ogneuporov — Proizvodstvo Spetsial'nykh Ogneuporov
Proizvod Stochnye Vody — Proizvodstvennye Stochnye Vody
Proizvod Svarnykh Besshovnykh Trub — Proizvodstvo Svarnykh i Besshovnykh Trub
Proizvod Svarnykh Trub — Proizvodstvo Svarnykh Trub
Proizvod Tekh Stroit Stekla — Proizvodstvo Tekhnicheskogo i Stroitel'nogo Stekla
Proizvod Tolstolistovoi Stali — Proizvodstvo Tolstolistovoi Stali
Proizvod Trub — Proizvodstvo Trub
Proizvod Vysokokach Prokata — Proizvodstvo Vysokokachestvennogo Prokata
Proizv Shin RTI i ATI — Proizvodstvo Shin Rezinotekhnicheskikh i Asbestotekhnicheskikh Izdelii
Proj & Constr — Projeto e Construcao
Proj Angew Oekol — Projekt Angewandte Oekologie
Proj Civ Trav Econ — Projet. Civilisation, Travail, Economie
Project Hist Biobibliog — Project for Historical Biobibliography
Project IUCN/Wld Wldl Fund — Project. International Union for Conservation of Nature. World Wildlife Fund. Joint Project Operations
Projektgruppe Laserforsch Ber PLF — Projektgruppe fuer Laserforschung. Bericht. PLF
Projektrapp Grafiska Forskningslab — Projektrapport. Grafiska Forskningslaboratoriet
Proj RADAMBRAS Levantamento Recursos Nat — Projeto RADAMBRASIL [*Radar da Amazonia, Brasil*]. Levantamento de RecursosNaturais
Proj Rec Land Resour Dev Cent Surbiton UK — Project Record. Land Resources Development Centre (Surbiton, United Kingdom)
Proj Rep Victoria Minist Conserv Environ Stud Program — Victoria. Ministry for Conservation. Environmental Studies Program. Project Report
Prolactin Proc Int Congr — Prolactin. Basic and Clinical Correlates. Proceedings. International Congress on Prolactin
PROLDI — Annual Research Reviews. Prolactin
Prolet Kult — Proletarskaya Kul'tura
Pro LR — Professional Liability Reporter
P Rom — Papers in Romance
Prom — Prometeu. Revista Illustrada de Cultura
Prom — Promotion
PROM — Romanic Review
PROMADATA — Promotions Marketing and Advertising Data
Prom Aerod — Promyshlennaya Aerodinamika
Pro Managr — Program Manager
Pro Med — Pro Medico
Prom Ekon Byull Sov Nar Khoz Ivanov Ekon Adm Raiona — Promyshlenno-Ekonomicheskii Byulleten Sovet Narodnogo Khozyaistva Ivanovskogo Ekonomicheskogo Administrativnogo Raiona
Prom Energ — Promyshlennaya Energetika
Pro Met — Pro Metal
Prometheus — Prometheus. Revista Quadrimestrale di Studi Classici
Promet-Meteorol Fortbild — Promet-Meteorologische Fortbildung
Promoclim A Actual Equip Tech — Promoclim A. Actualites, Equipement, Technique
Promoclim E — Promoclim E. Etudes Thermiques et Aerauliques
Promoclim Ind Therm Aerauliques — Promoclim. Industries Thermiques et Aerauliques
Prom Org Sint — Promyslennyj Organiceskij Sintez
Promot Dent — Promotion Dentaire

Promot Educ — Promotion et Education
Promot Health — Promoting Health
Promozione Soc — Promozione Sociale
Prom Riv Quad Studi Class — Prometheus. Rivista Quadrimestrale di Studi Classici
Prom Sanit Ochistka Gazov — Promyshlennaya i Sanitarnaya Ochistka Gazov
Prom Sint Kauch — Promyshlennost Sinteticheskogo Kauchuka
Promst Arm — Promyshlennost Armenii
Prom-St Arm Sov Nar Khoz Arm SSR Tekh-Ekon Byull — Promyshlennost Armenii Sovet Narodnogo Khozyajstva Armyanskoj SSR Tekhniko-Ekonomicheskij Byulleten
Promst Beloruss — Promyshlennost Belorussii
Prom-St Khim Reaktivov Osobo Chist Veshchestv — Promyshlennost Khimicheskikh Reaktivov i Osobo Chistykh Veshchestv
Promst Khim Reakt Osobo Chist Veshchestv — Promyshlennost Khimicheskikh Reaktivov i Osobo Chistykh Veshchestv
Promst Lub Volokon — Promyshlennost Lubyanykh Volokon
Prom-St Org Khim — Promyshlennost Organicheskoi Khimii
Prom Stroit — Promyshlennoe Stroitel'stvo
Prom Stroit Inzh Sooruzh — Promyshlennoe Stroitel'stvo i Inzhenernye Sooruzheniya
Promst Sint Kauch — Promyshlennost Sinteticheskogo Kauchuka
Promst Stroit Arkhit Arm — Promyshlennost, Stroitel'stvo i Arkhitektura Armenii
Promst Stroit Mater — Promyshlennost Stroitel'nykh Materialov
Promst Stroit Mater Ser 5 — Promyshlennost Stroitel'nykh Materialov. Seriya 5. Keramicheskaya Promyshlennost
Promst Tovarov Bytovoi Khim — Promyshlennost Tovarov Bytovoi Khimii
Prom Teplotekh — Promyshlennaya Teplotekhnika
Pro Mundi A — Pro Mundi Vita Dossiers. Africa
Pro Mundi Vita — Pro Mundi Vita Bulletin
Pro Mundi Vita Africa Dossier — Pro Mundi Vita Dossiers. Africa
Pro Mundi Vita Asia-Australasia Dossier — Pro Mundi Vita Dossiers. Asia and Australasia
Pro Mundi Vita Europe N Am Dossier — Pro Mundi Vita Dossiers. Europe/North America
PromV — Promotion Violette
Prom Zagryaz Vodoemov — Promyshlennye Zagryazneniya Vodoemov
Pro Nat — Pro Natura
Pr ONPMP — Prace ONPMP
Prop — Property
Propag Intensive Laser Radiat Clouds — Propagation of Intensive Laser Radiation in Clouds
Prop & Ex — Propellents, Explosives, and Pyrotechnics
Prop & Ric — Proposte e Ricerche
Propane Can — Propane Canada
Propellants Explos — Propellants and Explosives
Propellants Explos Pyrotech — Propellants, Explosives, Pyrotechnics
Propellants Explos Rocket Mot Establ Memo — Propellants, Explosives, and Rocket Motor Establishment. Memorandum
Property Mthly Rev — Property Monthly Review
Property Tax J — Property Tax Journal
Proph — Prophezei
Proph Sanit Mor — Prophylaxie Sanitaire et Morale
Prophylax Antiven — Prophylaxie Antivenerienne
Prophyl Ment — Prophylaxie Mentale
Prophyl Sanit Morale — Prophylaxie Sanitaire et Morale
Prop Kg — Propylaen Kunstgeschichte
Prop Law — Property Lawyer
Prop Law Bull — Property Law Bulletin
Prop Law NS — Property Lawyer, New Series
Proposte Soc — Proposte Sociali
Propr Agric — Propriete Agricole
Pr Or — Przeglad Orientalistyczny
PrOrChr — Proche-Orient Chretien
Pr O S — Princeton Oriental Series
ProS — Proceedings. South Carolina Historical Society
Pros — Prospero (Lyons)
Pros — Prospetti
Pros J Natl Dist Att'y A — Prosecutor. Journal of the National District Attorneys Association
Pros Mil Eq — Prosopographia Militiarum Equestrium quae Fuerunt ab Augusto ad Gallienum
Pro Soc Water Treat Exam — Proceedings. Society for Water Treatment and Examination
Prosop Att — Prosopographia Attica
Prosop Imp Rom — Prosopographia Imperii Romani
Prosp — Prospettive
Prosp Arch — Prospezioni Archeologiche
Prospects Antisense Nucleic Acid Ther Cancer AIDS — Prospects for Antisense Nucleic Acid Therapy of Cancer and AIDS
Prospect West Aust — Prospect Western Australia
Prospettiva — Prospettiva. Rivista d'Arte Antica e Moderna
Prospett Merid — Prospettive Meridionali
Prospezioni Arch — Prospezioni Archeologiche
Prosp Ind Ital — Prospettive dell'Industria Italiana
Prosp R — Prospective Review
Pros Ptol — Prosopographia Ptolemaica
Pr Osr Badaw-Rozwoj Elektron Prozniowej — Prace Osrodka Badawczo-Rozwojowego Elektroniki Prozniowej
Pr Osr Badaw Rozwoj Przetwornikow Obrazu — Prace Osrodka Badawczo-Rozwojowego Przetwornikow Obrazu
Pr Osr Badaw Rozwoj Tech Telew — Prace Osrodka Badawczo-Rozwojowego Techniki Telewizyjnej
Pr Osr Nauk Prod Mater Polprzewodn — Prace Osrodek Naukowo-Produkcyjny Materialow Polprzewodnikowych

Pr Osrodka Badawczo-Rozwojowego Przetwornikow Obrazu — Prace Osrodka Badawczo-Rozwojowego Przetwornikow Obrazu
Pr Osrodka Badaw Rozwojowego Elektron Prozniowej — Prace Osrodka Badawczo-Rozwojowego Elektroniki Prozniowej
Prostagland — Prostaglandins
Prostaglandins Cardiovasc Syst — Prostaglandins in the Cardiovascular System
Prostaglandins Leukot Essent Fatty Acids — Prostaglandins Leukotrienes and Essential Fatty Acids
Prostaglandins Leukotrienes Med — Prostaglandins, Leukotrienes, and Medicine
Prostaglandins Med — Prostaglandins and Medicine
Prostaglandins Other Lipid Mediat — Prostaglandins and Other Lipid Mediators [New York]
Prostaglandins Relat Compd Int Conf — Prostaglandins and Related Compounds. International Conference
Prostaglandins Relat Lipids — Prostaglandins and Related Lipids
Prostaglandins Res Stud Ser — Prostaglandins Research Studies Series
Prostaglandins Ser — Prostaglandins Series
Prostaglandins Ther — Prostaglandins and Therapeutics
Prostate Cancer Prostatic Dis — Prostate Cancer and Prostatic Diseases
Prostate Suppl — Prostate Supplement
Prosthet and Orthotics Int — Prosthetics and Orthotics International
Prosthet Orthot Int — Prosthetics and Orthotics International
Prot — Protestant
Prot — Protestantesimo
PROTA — Protoplasma
Prot Aer — Protection Aerienne
Prot Civ Secur Ind — Protection Civile et Securite Industrielle
Prot Coat Met — Protective Coatings on Metals
Prot Coat Met Engl Transl — Protective Coatings on Metals (English Translation)
Protease Inhib Proc Int Conf Fibrinolysis — Protease Inhibitors. Proceedings. International Conference on Fibrinolysis
Prot Ecol — Protection Ecology
Protein Abnorm — Protein Abnormalities
Protein Eng — Protein Engineering
Protein Expression Purif — Protein Expression and Purification
Protein Expr Purif — Protein Expression and Purification
Protein Nucl Acid Enzyme — Protein Nucleic Acid Enzyme
Protein Pept Lett — Protein and Peptide Letters
Protein Sci — Protein Science
Protein Sequences Data Anal — Protein Sequences and Data Analysis
Proteins Iron Metab Proc Int Meet — Proteins of Iron Metabolism. Proceedings. International Meeting
Proteins Struct Funct Genet — Proteins. Structure, Function, and Genetics
Protein Struct — Protein Structure
Protein Struct Funct Proc Int Symp — Protein Structure-Function. Proceedings. International Symposium
Protein Struct Predict Des — Protein Structure, Prediction, and Design
Protein Synth — Protein Synthesis
Protein Synth Ser Adv — Protein Syntheses: A Series of Advances
Protein Targeting Proc John Innes Symp — Protein Targeting. Proceedings. John Innes Symposium
Protein Traffic Eukaryotic Cells — Protein Traffic in Eukaryotic Cells. Selected Reviews
Proteinuria Symp Nephrol — Proteinuria. Symposium of Nephrology
Prot Epis His M — Protestant Episcopal Church. Historical Magazine
Protes Dent — Protesista Dental
Protest — Protestantesimo
Protest Mhh — Protestantische Monatshefte
Protet Stomatol — Protetyka Stomatologiczna
Protext V Proc Int Protext Conf — Protext V. Multimedia in Action. Proceedings. International Protext Conference
Proth Werkst Kd — Prothetik und Werkstoffkunde
Protides Biol Fluids Proc Colloq — Protides of the Biological Fluids. Proceedings of the Colloquium
Protides Biol Fluids Proc Colloq (Bruges) — Protides of the Biological Fluids. Proceedings of the Colloquium (Bruges)
Prot Met — Protection of Metals
Prot Metals — Protection of Metals
Prot Met Transl of Zashch Met — Protection of Metals (Translation of Zashchita Metallov)
Prot Met (USSR) — Protection of Metals (Union of Soviet Socialist Republics)
Protoc Hum Mol Genet — Protocols in Human Molecular Genetics
Protok Fischereitech — Protokolle zur Fischereitechnik
Protok Obsc Estestvoisp Imp Tomsk Univ — Protokoly Obscestva Estestvoispytatelej i Vracej pri Imperatorskom Tomskom Universitete
Protok Obsc Isp Prir Imp Harkovsk Univ — Protokoly Obscestva Ispytatelej Prirody pri Imperatorskom Har'kovskom Universitete
Protok OS — Protokoly Obscego Sobranija Akademii Nauk
Protok Ova Estestvoispyt Imp Yurev Univ — Protokoly Obshchestva Estestvoispytatelei pri Imperatorskom Yur'evskomUniversitete
Protok Zased Obsc Estestvoisp Imp Kazansk Univ — Protokoly Zasedanij Obscestva Estestvoispytatelej Pri Imperatorskom Kazanskom Universitete
Protok Zased Soveta Imp Moscovsk Univ — Protokoly Zasedanij Soveta Imperatorskago Moskovskago Universiteta
Proto Oncog Cell Dev — Proto-Oncogenes in Cell Development
Protoplasma Monogr — Protoplasma-Monographien
Protoplasma Suppl — Protoplasma Supplementum
Prot Plant (Havana) — Proteccion de Plantas (Havana)
Prot Rep R8 PR — Protection Report R8-PR
Protsessy Appar Khim Tekhnol — Protsessy i Apparaty Khimicheskoi Tekhnologii
Protsessy Appar Razdeleniya Zhidk Gazov Smesei — Protsessy i Apparaty dlya Razdeleniya Zhidkikh i Gazovykh Smesei
Protsessy Khromatogr Kolonkakh — Protsessy v Khromatograficheskikh Kolonakh
Prot St — Protestantische Studien

Prot Steel Zinc Dust Paints Pap Semin — Protecting Steel with Zinc Dust Paints. Papers. Seminar
Prot Sz — Protestans Szemle
Prot T — Protestanisk Tidende
Prot Vitae — Protectio Vitae
Prouchvaniya Mikroelem Mikrotorovete Bulg — Prouchvaniya vurkhu Mikroelementite i Mikrotorovete v Bulgariya
Prov — Provencal
PROV — Providence Journal-Bulletin
Prov — Provincia
Prov — Provincial
Prov Anjou — Province d'Anjou
Prov Bl — Provinciaal Blad
ProvBlVk — Provinzial-Blaetter fuer Volkskunde
Prov Buenos Aires Com Invest Cient Inf — Provincia de Buenos Aires. Comision de Investigaciones Cientificas. Informes
Prov Buenos Aires Com Invest Cient Mem — Provincia de Buenos Aires. Comision de Investigaciones Cientificas. Memoria
Prov Buenos Aires Com Invest Cient Monogr — Provincia de Buenos Airos. Comision de Investigaciones Cientificas.Monografias
Provebruksmeld Nor Landbruksokonomiske Inst — Provebruksmelding-Norges Landbruksokonomiske Institutt
Prov Econ — Provincial Economies
Provence Hist — Provence Historique
Provence Univ Ann Geol Mediterr — Provence Universite. Annales. Geologie Mediterraneenne
Provence Univ Lab Paleontol Hum Prehist Etud Quat Mem — Provence Universite. Laboratoire de Paleontologie Humaine et de Prehistoire. Etudes Quaternaires. Memoire
Prov Hist — Provence Historique
Providence Hosp Detroit Med Bull — Providence Hospital of Detroit. Medical Bulletin
Providence Hosp (Southfield Mich) Med Bull — Providence Hospital (Southfield, Michigan). Medical Bulletin
Providen JB — Providence Journal-Bulletin
Providen SJ — Providence Sunday Journal
Providnc J — Providence Journal
Provincial Bank Can Econ R — Provincial Bank of Canada. Economic Review
Prov Inher & Gift Tax Rep CCH — Provincial Inheritance and Gift Tax Reporter. Commerce Clearing House
Provins — Bulletin. Societe d'Histoire et d'Archeologie de l'Arrondissement de Provins
Provinsbank Temabl — Provinsbankens Temablad
Prov Judges J — Provincial Judges Journal
Prov Kaohsiung Teach Coll Chem Dep J — Provincial Kaohsiung Teachers College Chemistry Department. Journal
Prov Liege Tour — Province de Liege-Tourisme
Prov Lucca — Provincia di Lucca
Prov Newfoundland Miner Dev Div Rep — Province of Newfoundland. Mineral Development Division. Report
Prov S Pedro P Alegre — Provincia de Sao Pedro (Porto Alegre)
Prov Treviso — Provincia di Treviso
Proyecto Desarrollo Pesq Publ — Proyecto de Desarrollo Pesquero. Publicacion
P Roy Music — Proceedings. Royal Musical Association
Proy Prin Educ UNESCO Hav Santiago — Proyecto Principal de Educacion UNESCO-America Latina (La Habana; Santiago, Chile)
P Roy S Med — Proceedings. Royal Society of Medicine
P Roy Soc A — Proceedings. Royal Society of London. Series A. Mathematical and Physical Sciences
P Roy Soc B — Proceedings. Royal Society of London. Series B. Biological Sciences
PRP — Pamjatniki Russkogo Prava
PrP — Premier Plan
PRP — Progress in Radiopharmacology
Pr Panstw Inst Geol — Prace Panstwowego Instytutu Geologicznego
PRPH — Research in Phenomenology
Pr Phys Soc L — Proceedings. Physical Society of London
Pr PIT — Prace PIT
PRPO — Review of Politics
PrPol — Prace Polonistyczne
Pr Poznan Tow Przyj Nauk Wydz Nauk Roln Lesn — Prace-Poznanskie Towarzystwo Przyjaciol Nauk. Wydzial Nauk Rolniczych i Lesnych
Pr Preh Soc — Proceedings. Prehistoric Society
Pr Primer — Prairie Primer
Pr Przem Inst Elektron — Prace Przemyslowego Instytutu Elektroniki
Pr Przem Inst Elektron (Warsaw) — Prace Przemyslowego Instytutu Elektroniki (Warsaw)
Pr Przem Inst Telekomun — Prace Przemyslowego Instytutu Telekomunikacji
PrPs — Praktische Psychologie
PRPSA — Petroleum Press Service
PRPSB — Progress in Polymer Science
PRPT — Probe Post
PRPTA — Proceedings. Association of Asphalt Paving Technologists
PR Publ Rep Aust Coal Ind Res Lab — PR. Published Report. Australian Coal Industry Research Laboratories
PRPY — Romance Philology
PRPYA — Praxis der Psychotherapie
PRQ — Problems of Communism
PRR — Political Risk Review
PRR — Pre-Raphaelite Review
PRR — Presbyterian and Reformed Review
PRR — Public Relations Review
PRR — Puerto Rico Reports
Pr Rady Nauk-Tech Huty Lenina — Prace Rady Naukowo-Technicznej Huty Imienia Lenina

Pr R & Regs — Commonwealth of Puerto Rico Rules and Regulations
PRRB — Physics Reports. Reprints Book Series
PRREA — Philips Research Reports
PR Rev Public Health Trop Med — Porto Rico Review of Public Health and Tropical Medicine
PRRM — Pensee. Revue du Rationalisme Moderne
Pr Roln Lesne Pol Akad Umiejet — Prace Rolniczo-Lesne. Polska Akademia Umiejetnosci
Pr Roy Soc — Proceedings. Royal Society
Pr RS Med — Proceedings. Royal Society of Medicine
PRS — Perspectives in Religious Studies
PRS — Philosophy of Religion Series
PrS — Prairie Schooner
PRS — Press Summary
PRS — Proceedings of the Royal Society [*London*]
PRSA — Problemi e Ricerche di Storia Antica
Prsb Q — Presbyterian Quarterly Review
PRSC — Proceedings and Transactions. Royal Society of Canada
PRSCF — Publications. Research Scientists' Christian Fellowship
Pr Schae B — Praktische Schaedlingsbekaempfer
PRSE — Proceedings. Royal Society of Edinburgh
P RS Edin A — Proceedings. Royal Society of Edinburgh. Section A. Mathematical and Physical Sciences
P RS Edin B — Proceedings. Royal Society of Edinburgh. Section B. Natural Environment
PR Sent — Sentencias del Tribunal Supremo de Puerto Rico
PRSM — Proceedings. Royal Society of Medicine
PRSMA — Proceedings. Royal Society of Medicine
Prsnrs — Prisoners
Pr Soc Exp Biol Med — Proceedings. Society for Experimental Biology and Medicine
PRSR — Russian Review
PRSSA — Philips Research Reports. Supplements
PRSTA — Progress in Stereochemistry
Pr Statneho Geol Ustavu (Bratisl) — Prace Statneho Geologickeho Ustavu (Bratislava)
Pr Statneho Geol Ustavu (Bratislava) — Prace Statneho Geologickeho Ustavu (Bratislava)
PRSTB — Progresele Stiintei
Pr Stud Vysk Ustav Vodn Hospod (Bratislava) — Prace a Studie. Vyskumny Ustav Vodneho Hospodarstva (Bratislava)
Pr Stud Vys Sk Dopravnej Ziline Ser Strojnicka — Prace a Studie Vysokej Skoly Dopravnej v Ziline. Seria Strojnicka
Pr Stud Vyzk Ustav Vodohospod — Prace a Studie. Vyzkumny Ustav Vodohospodarsky
Pr Stud Zakl Badan Nauk Gorn Okregu Przem Pol Akad Nauk — Prace i Studia Zakladu Badan Naukowych Gornoslaskiego Okregu Przemyslowego Polskiej Akademii Nauk
PRSU — Religious Studies
PRSUA — Plastic and Reconstructive Surgery
PRSUB — Pribory i Sistemy Upravleniya
PR Sugar Man — Puerto Rico Sugar Manual
PRTCD — Progres Technique
Prt Colr — Print Collector
Prt Colr Club — Print Collector's Club
Prt Colr Conoscitore Stampe — Print Collector/Il Conoscitore di Stampe
Prt Colr Newslett — Print Collector's Newsletter
Prt Colr Q — Print Collector's Quarterly
Prt Connoisseur — Print Connoisseur
PRTEA — Pribory i Tekhnika Eksperimenta
PR Tex Agric Exp Stn — PR. Texas Agricultural Experiment Station
PR Texas Agric Exp Stn — PR. Texas Agricultural Experiment Station
Prtg A — Printing Art
PRTHA — Progress in Radiation Therapy
PrThR — Princeton Theological Review
Prt News — Print News
PRT Plast Rubbers Text — PRT. Plastics, Rubbers, Textiles
PRT Polym Age — PRT Polymer Age
Prt Q — Print Quarterly
Prt Rev — Print Review
PRTS — Politisch-Religioese Texte aus der Sargonidenzeit
Prtseller & Colr — Printseller and Collector
PRTUA — Problemy Tuberkuleza
PRu — Paedagogische Rundschau
PRU — Palais Royal d'Ugarit
Pr U — Pravda Ukrainy
Pruefenden Ges Halle Schriften — Pruefenden Gesellschaft zu Halle Herausgegebene Schriften
Pr Ukr Inst Eksp Farm — Pratsi Ukrains'kogo Instituta Eksperimental'noi Farmatsii
Pr Ukr Nauk Dosl Inst Torf Promsti — Pratsi Ukrains'kogo Naukovo-Doslidnogo Instituta TorfovoiPromislovosti
Pr Ukr Nauk Dosl Inst Zernovogo Gospod — Pratsi Ukrains'kogo Naukovo-Doslidnogo Instituta Zernovogo Gospodarstva
PRUM — Papiri. Universita degli Studi di Milano
Prum Potravin — Prumysl Potravin
Prum Potravin Priloha — Prumysl Potravin. Priloha
PRUND — Plastics and Rubber News
PRUS — Rural Sociology
P Russ Georg — Papyri Russischer und Georgischer Sammlungen
Pr Ustavu Geol Inz — Prace Ustavu Geologickeho Inzenyrstvu
Pr Ustavu Naft Vyzk — Prace Ustavu pro Naftovy Vyzkum
Pr Ustavu Vyzk Paliv — Prace Ustavu pro Vyzkum Paliv
Pr Ustavu Vyzk Vyuziti Paliv — Prace Ustavu pro Vyzkum a Vyuziti Paliv
PRV — Personnel Review
PRv — Philosophical Review

Pr V — Praedica Verbum
PrVBl — Preussisches Verwaltungsblatt
Pr Vinnits'k Derzh Med Inst — Pratsi Vinnits'kogo Derzhavnogo Medichnogo Institutu
PRVOA — Pravda Vostoka
PRVR — Poetarum Romanorum Veterum Reliquiae
Prvt Label — Private Label
PRVYD — Polyteknisk Revy
Pr Vyzk Ustavu CS Naft Dolu — Prace Vyzkumneho Ustavu CS Naftovych Dolu
Pr Vyzk Ustavu Geol Inz — Prace Vyzkumneho Ustavu Geologickeho Inzenyrstvi
Pr Vyzk Ustavu Lesn Hospod Myslivosti (Strnady) — Prace Vyzkumneho Ustavu Lesneho Hospodarstvi a Myslivosti (Strnady)
Pr W — Prawda Wostoka
PRW — Purchasing World
PR Water Resour Bull — Puerto Rico. Water Resources Bulletin
PrWCJewSt — Proceedings. World Congress of Jewish Studies
Pr Winter — Probability Winter School. Proceedings of the Fourth Winter School on Probability
Pr Wroclaw Tow Nauk Ser B — Prace Wroclawskiego Towarzystwa Naukowego. Seria B
Pr Wydz 4 Nauk Lek Lod Tow Nauk — Prace Wydzialu 4. Nauk Lekarskich. Lodzkie Towarzystwo Naukowe
Pr Wydz Nauk Przyr Bydgoskie Tow Nauk Ser A — Prace Wydzialu Nauk Przyrodniczych. Bydgoskie Towarzystwo Naukowe.Seria A
Pr Wydz Nauk Tech Bydgoskie Tow Nauk Ser A — Prace Wydzialu Nauk Technicznych. Bydgoskie Towarzystwo Naukowe. Seria A. Technologia Chemiczna
Pr Wydz Nauk Tech Bydgoskie Tow Nauk Ser B — Prace Wydzialu Nauk Technicznych. Bydogoskie Towarzystwo Naukowe. Seria B
Pr Wydz Nauk Tech Bydgoskie Tow Nauk Ser C — Prace Wydzialu Nauk Technicznych. Bydgoskie Towarzystwo Naukowe. Seria C. Elektronika, Elektrotechnika
Pr Wydz Tech (Katowice) — Prace Wydzialu Techniki (Katowice)
Pryamoe Poluch Zheleza Poroshk Metall — Pryamoe Poluchenie Zheleza i Poroshkovaya Metallurgiya
PrZ — Praehistorische Zeitschrift
Prz — Przeglad Filozoficzny
Pr Zakresu Lesn — Prace z Zakresu Lesnictwa
Pr Zakresu Nauk Roln — Prace z Zakresu Nauk Rolniczych
Pr Zakresu Towarozn Chem — Prace z Zakresu Towaroznawstwa i Chemii
Prz Arch — Przeglad Archeologiczny
Przeg Arch — Przeglad Archeologiczny
Przegd St — Przeglad Statystyczny
Przegl A — Przeglad Archeologiczny
Przeglad A — Przeglad Artystyczny
Przeglad Arch — Przeglad Archeologiczny
Przeglad Bibliot — Przeglad Biblioteczny
Przeglad Geog — Przeglad Geograficzny
Przeglad Geogr — Przeglad Geograficzny
Przeglad Hist — Przeglad Historyczny
Przeglad Hist Sztuki — Przeglad Historii Sztuki
Przeglad Kult — Przeglad Kulturalny
Przeglad Mech — Przeglad Mechaniczny
Przeglad Papier — Przeglad Papierniczy
Przeglad Polski — Przeglad Polski Ustawodawstwa Cywilnego i Kriminalnego
Przeglad Statyst — Przeglad Statystyczny
Przeglad Tech — Przeglad Techniczny
Przeglad Wlok — Przeglad Wlokienniczy
Przegl Antrop — Przeglad Antropologiczny
Przegl Antropol — Przeglad Antropologiczny
Przegl Archeol — Przeglad Archeologiczny
Przegl Bibl — Przeglad Biblioteczny
Przegl Bibliogr Chem — Przeglad Bibliograficzny Chemii
Przegl Biul Inst Masz Przeplyw Pol Akad Nauk Gdansku — Przeglad Biuletynow Instytutu Maszyn Przeplywowych Polskiej AkademiiNauk w Gdansku
Przegl Budow — Przeglad Budowlany
Przegl Dermatol — Przeglad Dermatologiczny
Przegl Dermatol Wenerol — Przeglad Dermatologii i Wenerologii
Przegl Derm Wener — Przeglad Dermatologii i Wenerologii
Przegl Dok Ceram Szlachetnej Szkla — Przeglad Dokumentacyjny Ceramiki Szlachetnej i Szkla
Przegl Dok Nafty — Przeglad Dokumentacyjny Nafty
Przegl Dok Ochr Pr — Przeglad Dokumentacyjny Ochrony Prace
Przegl Dok Papier — Przeglad Dokumentacyjny Papiernictwa
Przegl Dokum Chem — Przeglad Dokumentacyjny Chemii
Przegl Dosw Roln — Przeglad Doswiadczalnictwa Rolniczego
Przegl Elektr — Przeglad Elektroniki
Przegl Elektron — Przeglad Elektroniki
Przegl Elektrotech — Przeglad Elektrotechniczny
Przegl Epidemiol — Przeglad Epidemiologiczny
Przegl Geofiz — Przeglad Geofizyczny
Przegl Geogr — Przeglad Geograficzny
Przegl Geogr Pol Geogr Rev — Przeglad Geograficzny/Polish Geographical Review
Przegl Geol — Przeglad Geologiczny
Przegl Gorn — Przeglad Gorniczy
Przegl Gorn Hutn — Przeglad Gorniczo Hutniczy
Przegl Hist — Przeglad Historyczny
Przegl Hodowlany — Przeglad Hodowlany
Przegl Kom — Przeglad Komunikacyjny
Przegl Komunik — Przeglad Komunikacyjny
Przegl Lek — Przeglad Lekarski
Przegl Mech — Przeglad Mechaniczny
Przegl Met Hydrol — Przeglad Meteorologiczny i Hydrologiczny
Przegl Mlecz — Przeglad Mleczarski

Przegl Morski — Przeglad Morski
Przegl Nauk Lit Zootech — Przeglad Naukowej Literatury Zootechnicznej
Przegl Nauk Tech Akad Gorn Hutn Krakowie Ser G — Przeglad Naukowo Techniczny. Akademia Gorniczo Hutnicza w Krakowie. Seria G. Gornictwo
Przegl Nauk Tech Akad Gorn Hutn Krakowie Ser H — Przeglad Naukowo Techniczny. Akademia Gorniczo Hutnicza w Krakowie. Seria H. Hutnictwo
Przegl Odlew — Przeglad Odlewnictwa
Przegl Organ — Przeglad Organizacji
Przegl Papier Dodatek — Przeglad Papierniczy. Dodatek. Przeglad Dokumentacyjny Papiernictwa
Przegl Papiern — Przeglad Papierniczy
Przegl Pol Pism Tech — Przeglad Polskiego Pismiennictwa Technicznego
Przegl Przem Olejowego — Przeglad Przemyslu Olejowego
Przegl Skorzany — Przeglad Skorzany
Przegl Socjol — Przeglad Socjologiczny
Przegl Spawalnictwa — Przeglad Spawalnictwa
Przegl Stat — Przeglad Statystyczny
Przegl Telekomun — Przeglad Telekomunikacyjny
Przegl Wlok — Przeglad Wlokienniczy
Przegl Wlok Tech Wlok — Przeglad Wlokienniczy Technik Wlokienniczy
Przegl Wojsk Ladowych — Przeglad Wojsk Ladowych
Przegl Zachod — Przeglad Zachodni
Przegl Zboz Mlyn — Przeglad Zbozowo Mlynarski
Przegl Zbozowo Mlyn — Przeglad Zbozowo Mlynarski
Przegl Zool — Przeglad Zologiczny
Przejscia Fazowe Zjawiska Kryt — Przejscia Fazowe i Zjawiska Krytyczne. Wyklady z Wiosennego Sympozjum
Przekazy — Przekazy/Opinie
Prz Elektr — Przeglad Elektroniki
Przem Chem — Przemysl Chemiczny
Przem Drzew — Przemysl Drzewny
Przem Drzewny — Przemysl Drzewny
Przem Ferment — Przemysl Fermentacyjny
Przem Ferment Owocowo Warzywny — Przemysl Fermentacyjny i Owocowo-Warzywny
Przem Ferment Rolny — Przemysl Fermentacyjny i Rolny
Przem Naft — Przemysl Naftowy
Przem Roln Spozyw — Przemysl Rolny i Spozywczy
Przem Spozyw — Przemysl Spozywczy
Przem Spozywczy — Przemysl Spozywczy
Przem Wlok — Przemysl Wlokienniczy
Przemy Chem — Przemysl Chemiczny
Przemysl Chem — Przemysl Chemiczny
Prz Fil — Przeglad Filozoficzny
PRZGA — Przeglad Geologiczny
PrzH — Przeglad Humanistyczny
Prz Hi — Przeglad Historyczny
Prz Hist — Przeglad Historyczny
PrzK — Przeglad Kulturalny
PrzKl — Przeglad Klasyczny
Pr Zool Uniw Jagiellon — Prace Zoologiczne. Uniwersytet Jagiellonski
PrzOr — Przeglad Orientalistyczny
PRZPB — Przeglad Psychologiczny
PrzS — Przeglad Socjologiczny
Prz Stat — Przeglad Statystyczny
Przyr Polski Zachodn — Przyroda Polski Zachodniej
PrzZ — Przeglad Zachodni
PS — Pacific Spectator
PS — Palestinskii Sbornik
PS — Pamietnik Slowianski
PS — Partijnaja Shisn
PS — Patrologia Syriaca
PS — Pedagogical Seminary and Journal of Genetic Psychology
PS — Pensiero e Scuola
PS — Philippine Studies
PS — Philosophical Studies
PS — Planet Stories
PS — Ploughshare
PS — Political Studies
PS — Pop Shop Magazine
PS — Popular Science
PS — Population Studies
PS — Post Script
PS — Prairie Schooner
PS — Pravoslavnyi Sobesiednik
PS — Prevision Social [Quito]
PS — Process Studies
PS — Prose Studies 1800-1900
Ps — Psyche
PSA — Papeles de Son Armadans
PSa — Philippiniana Sacra
PSA — Police Science Abstracts
P Sa — Polotitscheskoje Samoorbrasowanije
PSA — Proceedings. Society of Antiquaries of London
PSA — Psychopharmacology Abstracts
PSA Athen — Papyri Societatis Archaeologicae Atheniensis
PSAC — Publications. Societe d'Archeologie Copte
PSACPA — Philosophical Studies. American Catholic Philosophical Association
PSACT — Publications. Societe d'Archeologie Copte. Textes et Documents
PSAC TD — Publications. Societe d'Archeologie Copte. Textes et Documents
Ps Af — Psychopathologie Africaine
PSAF — Publicaciones de la Seccion de Antropologia. Facultad de Filosofia y Letras
PSAF — Studies in American Fiction
PSA J — PSA [Photographic Society of America] Journal

PSA JI — Photographic Society of America. Journal
PSA Journal — Photographic Society of America. Journal
PSA J Sect B — PSA [*Photographic Society of America*] Journal. Section B. Photographic Science and Technique
PSA J Suppl — PSA [*Photographic Society of America*] Journal. Supplement
PSAL — Proceedings. Society of Antiquaries of London
PSAM — Publications. Service des Antiquites du Maroc
PSAN — Proceedings. Society of Antiquaries of New Castle-upon-Tyne
PS and E — Photographic Science and Engineering
PSA/PS — Political Studies. Political Studies Association
PsaQ — Psychoanalytic Quarterly
PSAQ — South Atlantic Quarterly
PsaR — Psychoanalytic Review
PSAS — Papers in International Studies. Africa Series. Ohio University
PSAS — Proceedings. Society of Antiquaries of Scotland
PSAVA — Pribory i Sistemy Avtomatiki
PSb — Palestinskll Sbornik
PSB — Personeelbeleid
PSB — Polski Slownik Biograficzny
PSB — Princeton Seminary Bulletin
PsB — Psychological Bulletin
Ps B — Psychologische Beitraege fuer alle Gebiete der Psychologie
PSB — Sitzungsberichte der Gesellschaft der Wissenschaften in Prag
PSBA — Proceedings. Society of Biblical Archaeology
PSBF — Pubblicazioni. Studium Biblicum Franciscanum
PSBF Ma — Pubblicazioni. Studium Biblicum Franciscanum. Collectio Major
PSBF Mi — Pubblicazioni. Studium Biblicum Franciscanum. Collectio Minor
PSBH — Proceedings. Society of Biblical Archaeology
PSBNDY — Sociedade Brasileira de Nematologia. Publicacao
PSBRA9 — International Committee for Bird Preservation. Pan American Section. Research Report
PSBS — Policy Sciences Book Series
PSBU — Psychopharmacology Bulletin
PSBUA — Psychological Bulletin
Ps Bull — Psychological Bulletin
PSC — Periodico. Societa Storia Comense
PSC — Personal Computing
PSC — Population Studies (Cambridge)
PSc — Publications de Scriptorium
PSCC — Studies in Comparative Communism
PSCE — Publicaciones de la Sociedad Colombiana de Etnologia
PSCF — Publication. Societe Calviniste de France
P Sch — Prairie Schooner
PSCHO — Psychopharmacology
PSCI — Sciences
PSCIA — Peuce. Studii si Communicari de Istorie si Arheologie
PSC III — Third Pakistan Science Conference
PSC IV — Fourth Pakistan Science Conference
PSC IX — Ninth Pakistan Science Conference
PSCKAR — Bulletin of National Fisheries. University of Pusan. Natural Sciences
PSCL — Papers and Studies in Contrastive Linguistics
PSCOB — Psychiatric Communications
P S Conf Co — Proceedings. Southern Conference on Corrections
PScQ — Political Science Quarterly
P Scribe — Portland Scribe
PSCT — Scandinavian Studies
PSCU — Speculum. Journal of Medieval Studies
PSC V — Fifth Pakistan Science Conference
PSC VI — Sixth Pakistan Science Conference
PSC VIII — Eighth Pakistan Science Conference
PSC X — Tenth Pakistan Science Conference
PSD — Physical Sciences Data
PSE — Prague Studies in English
PSE — Princeton Studies in English
PSEAL — Papers in South East Asian Linguistics
PSEBA — Proceedings. Society for Experimental Biology and Medicine
PSEC — International Security
PSEE — Slavic and East European Journal
PSEKUT — Paar Sammukest Eesti Kirjanduse Uurimise Teed
PSEL — Pages de la Societe des Ecrivains Luxembourgeois de Langue Francaise
PSEL — Publications. Societe Egyptologique a l'Universite d'Etat de Leningrad
PSENA — Photographic Science and Engineering
PSEPB — Progress in Separation and Purification
PSER — Slavonic and East European Review
PSEW — Sewanee Review
PsF — Psychologische Forschung
PSFADF — Proceedings. Annual Conference. Southeastern Association of Fish and Wildlife Agencies
PSFF — Science-Fiction Studies
PSFM — Publications. Societe Francaise de Musicologie
PSFS — Studies in Formative Spirituality
PSGA — Sociological Analysis
PSGH — Sociology and Social Research
PSGI — Sociological Inquiry
PSGQ — Sociological Quarterly
PSGR — Sociological Review
PSGY — Sociology. Journal. British Sociological Association
PSH — De Probatis Sanctorum Historiis
PSHADL — Publications. Societe Historique et Archeologique dans le Duche de Limbourg
PSHAL — Publications. Societe Historique et Archeologique dans le Duche de Limbourg
PSHEA — Publications. Societe d'Histoire de l'Eglise d'Alsace
PSHEAS — Publications. Societe d'Histoire de l'Eglise d'Alsace. Sources
PSHED — Psychologie Heute

PSHF — Publications. Societe de l'Histoire de France
PSHIGDL — Publications. Section Historique. Institut Grand-Ducal de Luxembourg
PSHIL — Publications. Section Historique. Institut Grand-Ducal de Luxembourg
PSHL — Publications. Societe Historique et Archeologique dans le Duche de Limbourg
PSHM — Publications. Societe Historique et Archeologique a Maestrich
PSHP — Pennsylvania Journal for Health, Physical Education, and Recreation
PSHP — Studies in History and Philosophy of Science
PSHQ — Southwestern Historical Quarterly
PSHR — Princeton Studies in the History of Religions
PSHR — Southern Humanities Review
PSHS — Shakespeare Studies
PSHU — Shakespeare Survey
PSI — Piccole Storie Illustrate
PSI — Politics and Society in India
PSI — Pubblicazioni. Societa Italiana per la Ricerca dei Papiri Greci e Latini in Egitto
PSIA — Plantation Society in the Americas
PSI Ber — PSI [*Paul Scherrer Institut*] Bericht
PSICD — Proceedings. IEEE Computer Society's International Computer Software and Applications Conference
Psicon Riv Int Archit — Psicon. Rivista Internazionale di Architettura
PSIFL — Pan. Studi dell'Istituto di Filologia Latina
Psihijatr Danas — Psihijatrija Danas
P (Sijp) — Einige Wiener Papyri (Sijpesteijn)
PSI Proc — PSI (Paul Scherrer Institut). Proceedings
PSIR Bull Monogr — PSIR [*Pakistan Council of Scientific and Industrial Research*] Bulletin Monograph
PSIS — Isis
PSJ — Philosophical Studies of Japan
PSJT — Scottish Journal of Theology
PSKAD — Promyshlennost Sinteticheskogo Kauchuka
PSKI — Skeptical Inquirer
PSKJ — Pitanja Savremenog Knjizevnog Jezika
Pskov Gos Pedagog Inst Uch Zap — Pskovskii Gosudarstvennyi Pedagogicheskii Institut. Uchenye Zapiski
Pskov Ped Inst Fiz-Mat Fak Ucen Zap — Pskovskii Pedagogiceskii Institut. Fiziko-Matematiceskii Fakul'tet. Ucenye Zapiski
PSKS — Publications. Soeren Kierkegaard Selskabet
PSL — Personnel Management
PSL — Political Studies (London)
PSL — Polymer Science Library
PSL — Population Studies (London)
PSL — Proceedings. Society of Antiquaries of London
Psl Admr — Personnel Administrator
Psl & Guid J — Personnel and Guidance Journal
PSLC — Pawathy Stare Literatury Ceske
Psl Exec — Personnel Executive
PSLG — Public Service and Local Government
PSLI — Studies in the Literary Imagination
Psl J — Personnel Journal
PSLJ — Southern Literary Journal
Psl Psy — Personnel Psychology
Psl R — Personnel Review
PSM — Pagine di Storia della Medicina
PSM — Philippine Studies (Manila)
PSM — Physician and Sports Medicine
PSM — Popular Science Monthly
PSM — Publicaciones. Seminario Metropolitano
PSM — Public School Magazine
PSM — Pytannja Slov'jans'koho Movoznavstva
PSMDC — Psychological Medicine
Ps Mdd — Physikalske Meddelelser
PSMDEQ — Psychiatric Medicine
PSMEA — Psychosomatic Medicine
PSMG — Salmagundi
PSMHL — Publications. Societe pour la Recherche et la Conservation des Monuments Historiques dans le Grand Duche de Luxembourg
PSMIAM — Pontica. Studii si Materiale de Istorie, Arheologie, si Muzeografie
PSML — Prague Studies in Mathematical Linguistics
PSMMAF — Proceedings. Staff Meeting of the Mayo Clinic
PSMR — Pagine di Storia della Medicina (Rome)
PSMS — Publications. Ethnographical Museum of Sweden. Stockholm Monograph Series
PSMSC — Psychotherapie und Medizinische Psychologie
PSMUD — Psychology of Music
PSN — Proceedings. Society of Antiquaries of New Castle-upon-Tyne
PSNEB — Psychiatric Annals
PSNG — Simulation and Gaming
PSNO — Studies in the Novel
PSNS — Science and Society
PSNT — Pismo Swiete Nowego Testamentu
PSNTA — Progres Scientifique
PsNW — Psychiatrisch-Neurologische Wochenschrift
PSOB — Social Biology
PSoc — Przeglad Socjologiczny
P Soc Exp M — Proceedings. Society for Experimental Biology and Medicine
PSOH — Social History
PSOP — Social Psychology Quarterly
PSOR — Social Research
P Sorb — Papyrus de la Sorbonne
Psoriasis Proc Int Symp — Psoriasis. Proceedings. International Symposium
PSOS — Social Science Journal
PSp — Pacific Spectator
PSP — Princeton Seminary Pamphlets

PSP — Provincia de Sao Pedro
PSPAEW — Psychotherapy Patient
PSPCD — Proceedings. Annual Southwestern Petroleum Short Course
PSPCE4 — Proceedings. Sugar Processing Research Conference
PSPD — Penny Stock Performance Digest
PSPH — Studies in Philology
PSPHA — Psychophysiology
PSPHDI — Psychopharmacology Series
PSPK — Paderborner Schriften zur Paedagogik und Katechetik
PSPOB — Psychiatria Polska
PSPOS — Philological Society. Publications. Occasional Studies
PSPR — Polnoe Sobranie Postanovlenii i Rasporiazhenii po Vedomstvu Pravoslavnogo Ispovedaniia
PS Przegl Spawal — PS. Przeglad Spawalnictwa
PSPSB — Psychotherapy and Psychosomatics
PSPUC — Publications in Semitic Philology. University of California
PSQ — Philologische Studien und Quellen
PSQ — Political Science Quarterly
PSQAA — Psychoanalytic Quarterly
PSQSA — Psychiatric Quarterly. Supplement
PSQUA — Psychiatric Quarterly
PSR — Pacific Sociological Review
PSR — Petty Sessions Review
PSR — Philippine Sociological Review
PSR — Political Science Review
PsR — Psychoanalytic Review
PsR — Psychological Review
PsR — Psychologische Rundschau
PSRAA — Progress in the Science and Technology of the Rare Earths
PSREA — Psychoanalytic Review
PSRED — Psychological Research
Ps Rep — Psychological Report
Ps Rep M — Psychological Report. Monograph Supplement
Ps Rev — Psychological Review
PSRIA — Papers. Ship Research Institute
PSRL — Polnoe Sobranie Russkikh Letopisei
PSRO — Studies in Romanticism
PSRPD — Prakla-Seismos Report
PSRS — Publications. Sussex Record Society
Ps Rv — Physical Review
PSRV — Southern Review
PSRVA — Psychological Review
PSRWD — Policy Studies Review
PSS — Poona Sarvajanik Sabha. Quarterly Journal
PSS — Psychoanalysis and the Social Sciences
PsS — Psychological Studies
PSS — Pubblicazioni. Seminario de Semitistica. Istituto Orientale di Napoli
PSS — Publications. Surtees Society
PSSA — Puteoli. Studi di Storia Antica
PSSAB — Physica Status Solidi. Sectio A. Applied Research
PSSEAS — Papers in International Studies. Southeast Asia Series. Ohio University
PSSFB — Progress in Surface Science
PSSGL — Penn State Series in German Literature
PSSHR — Philippine Social Sciences and Humanities Review
PSSJ — International Social Science Journal
PSSMDE — Proceedings. Symposium of the Society for the Study of Inborn Errors of Metabolism
PSSR — Philippine Social Science Review
PSSR — Social Science Research
PSSS — Proceedings. Shevchenko Scientific Society. Philological Section
PSSS — Publications. School of Sacred Sciences
PSSSP — Proceedings. Shevchenko Scientific Society. Philological Section
PSSSR — Pubblicazioni. Scuola di Studi Storico-Religiosi
PSST — Pismo Swiete Starego Testamentu
PSSTA — Progress in Solid State Chemistry
PSSUE5 — Psychopharmacology. Supplementum
PSSV — Social Service Review
PSSZAG — Psychologie. Schweizerische Zeitschrift fuer Psychologie und Ihre Anwendungen
PST — Philological Society. Transactions
PST — Policy Studies Journal. Policy Studies Institute
PST — Pontifical Institute of Mediaeval Studies. Studies and Texts
PSt — Prose Studies
PSTA — Packaging Science and Technology Abstracts
PSta — Philippine Statistican
PStAC — Publications. St. Antony's College
PSTOA — Psychology Today
PSTP — Social Theory and Practice
P Strasb — Griechische Papyrus der Kaiserlichen Universitaets- und Landesbibliothek zu Strassburg
PStu — Philippine Studies
PSTY — Style
PSU-ADA — Pennsylvania State University-Abstracts of Doctoral Dissertations
P Suffolk I Arch — Proceedings. Suffolk Institute of Archaeology
PSUI — Suicide and Life-Threatening Behavior
PSUPB — Pribory i Sistemy Upravleniya
PSuQ — Philologische Studien und Quellen
PSURA — Progress in Surgery
PSVS — Soviet Studies
PsVTGr — Pseudepigrapha Veteris Testamenti Graecae
PSWEA — Proceedings. South Wales Institute of Engineers
PSWV — Southwest Review
PSWYA — Psychologia Wychowawcza
PSXJ — Sixteenth Century Journal
Psy — Psyche. Revue Internationale de Psychanalyse et des Sciences de l'Homme

Psy — Psychomusicology
PsyAb — Psychological Abstracts
Psy B — Psychological Bulletin
PSYBB — Psychopharmacology Bulletin
PSYCA — Psychiatry
PSYCD — Psychendocrinology
Psych & MLJ — Psychological and Medico-Legal Journal
Psych Bull — Psychological Bulletin
Psych Depend Bayer Symp — Psychic Dependence. Definition, Assessment in Animals and Man. Theoretical and Clinical Implications. Bayer-Symposium
Psychedelic Rev — Psychedelic Review
Psychiat — Psychiatry
Psychiat Cl — Psychiatria Clinica
Psychiat Digest — Psychiatry Digest
Psychiat En Neurol Bl — Psychiatrische en Neurologische Bladen
Psychiat Fo — Psychiatric Forum
Psychiat Me — Psychiatry in Medicine
Psychiat Neurol Wchnschr — Psychiatrisch-Neurologische Wochenschrift
Psychiat Opin — Psychiatric Opinion
Psychiat Q — Psychiatric Quarterly
Psychiatr Ann — Psychiatric Annals
Psychiatr Annals — Psychiatric Annals
Psychiatr Clin — Psychiatria Clinica
Psychiatr Clin (Basel) — Psychiatria Clinica (Basel)
Psychiatr Clin North Am — Psychiatric Clinics of North America
Psychiatr Commun — Psychiatric Communications
Psychiatr Dev — Psychiatric Developments
Psychiatr Enfant — Psychiatrie de l'Enfant
Psychiatr Fenn — Psychiatria Fennica
Psychiatr Fenn Monogr — Psychiatria Fennica. Monografiasarja
Psychiatr Forum — Psychiatric Forum
Psychiatr Genet — Psychiatric Genetics
Psychiatr Hosp — Psychiatric Hospital
Psychiatr J Univ Ottawa — Psychiatric Journal. University of Ottawa
Psychiatr Med — Psychiatric Medicine
Psychiatr Neurol — Psychiatria et Neurologia
Psychiatr Neurol Jpn — Psychiatria et Neurologia Japonica
Psychiatr Neurol Med Psychol — Psychiatrie, Neurologie, und Medizinische Psychologie
Psychiatr Neurol Med Psychol (Leipz) — Psychiatrie, Neurologie, und Medizinische Psychologie (Leipzig)
Psychiatr Neurol Neurochir — Psychiatria, Neurologia, Neurochirurgia
Psychiatr Neurol Wochenschr — Psychiatrisch Neurologische Wochenschrift
Psychiatr Neurol Wschr — Psychiatrisch-Neurologische Wochenschrift
Psychiatr News — Psychiatric News
Psychiatr Nurs Forum — Psychiatric Nursing Forum
Psychiatr Opinion — Psychiatric Opinion
Psychiatr Pol — Psychiatria Polska
Psychiatr Prax — Psychiatrische Praxis
Psychiatr Q — Psychiatric Quarterly
Psychiatr Q (NY) — Psychiatric Quarterly (New York)
Psychiatr Q Suppl — Psychiatric Quarterly. Supplement
Psychiatr Rehabil J — Psychiatric Rehabilitation Journal
Psychiatr Res Rep — Psychiatric Research Reports
Psychiatr Res Rep Am Psychiatr Assoc — Psychiatric Research Reports. American Psychiatric Association
Psychiatr Serv — Psychiatric Services
Psychiatr Soc — Psychiatrie Sociale
Psychiatr Wochenschr — Psychiatrische Wochenschrift
Psychiatry Clin Neurosci — Psychiatry and Clinical Neurosciences
Psychiatry Dig — Psychiatry Digest
Psychiatry Med — Psychiatry in Medicine
Psychiatry Res — Psychiatry Research
Psychiatry Ser (Berlin) — Psychiatry Series (Berlin)
Psychic R — Psychical Review
Psychoanal Beweg — Psychoanalytische Bewegung
Psychoanal Contemp Sci — Psychoanalysis and Contemporary Science
Psychoanal Contemp Thought — Psychoanalysis and Contemporary Thought
Psychoanal Q — Psychoanalytic Quarterly
Psychoanal Quart — Psychoanalytic Quarterly
Psychoanal R — Psychoanalytic Review
Psychoanal Rev — Psychoanalytic Review
Psychoanal Stud Child — Psychoanalytic Study of the Child
Psychoanal Study Child — Psychoanalytic Study of the Child
Psychoanal Study Child Monogr Ser — Psychoanalytic Study of the Child. Monograph Series
Psychoan Q — Psychoanalytic Quarterly
Psychoan Re — Psychoanalytic Review
Psychobiol Psychopathol — Psychobiology and Psychopathology
Psychocultural R — Psychocultural Review
Psych of Music — Psychology of Music
Psychohist Rev — Psychohistory Review
Psychol Abstr — Psychological Abstracts
Psychol Absts — Psychological Abstracts
Psychol Addict Behav — Psychology of Addictive Behaviors
Psychol Afr — Psychologia Africana
Psychol Africana — Psychologia Africana
Psychol Afr Monogr Suppl — Psychologie Africana. Monograph and Supplement
Psychol Aging — Psychology and Aging
Psychol Assess — Psychological Assessment
Psychol B — Psychological Bulletin
Psychol Be — Psychologische Beitraege
Psychol Beitr — Psychologische Beitraege
Psychol Bel — Psychologica Belgica
Psychol Belg — Psychologica Belgica

Psychol Bul — Psychological Bulletin
Psychol Bull — Psychological Bulletin
Psychol Can — Psychologie Canadienne
Psychol Clin — Psychological Clinic [Philadelphia]
Psychol Clinic — Psychological Clinic
Psychol Erz — Psychologie in Erziehung und Unterricht
Psychol Et Vie — Psychologie et la Vie
Psychol Forsch — Psychologische Forschung
Psychol Fr — Psychologie Francaise
Psychol in the Schs — Psychology in the Schools
Psychol Iss — Psychological Issues
Psychol Issues — Psychological Issues
Psychol Issues Monogr — Psychological Issues. Monographs
Psychol Learn & Motiv — Psychology of Learning and Motivation
Psychol Med — Psychological Medicine
Psychol Med — Psychologie Medicale
Psychol Med Monogr Suppl — Psychological Medicine. Monograph Supplement
Psychol Methods — Psychological Methods
Psychol Monogr — Psychological Monographs
Psychol Monogr Gen Appl — Psychological Monographs. General and Applied
Psychology M — Psychology of Music
Psychol Prax — Psychologische Praxis
Psychol R — Psychological Review
Psychol Read Guide — Psychological Reader's Guide
Psychol Rec — Psychological Record
Psychol Rep — Psychological Reports
Psychol Res — Psychological Research
Psychol Rev — Psychological Review
Psychol Rundsch — Psychologische Rundschau
Psychol Sch — Psychology in the Schools
Psychol Schweiz Z Psychol Anwendungen — Psychologie; Schweizerische Zeitschrift fuer Psychologie und Ihre Anwendungen
Psychol Sci — Psychological Science
Psychol St — Psychologische Studien
Psychol Stu — Psychological Studies
Psychol Tod — Psychology Today
Psychol Today — Psychology Today
Psychol U Med — Psychologie und Medizin
Psychol Women Q — Psychology of Women Quarterly
Psychol Women Quart — Psychology of Women Quarterly
Psychometri — Psychometrika
Psychometrika Monogr Suppl — Psychometrika. Monograph Supplement
Psycho Mycol Stud — Psycho-Mycological Studies
Psychon Bull Rev — Psychonomic Bulletin & Review
Psychon Sci — Psychonomic Science
Psychon Sci Sect Anim Physiol Psychol — Psychonomic Science. Section on Animal and Physiological Psychology
Psychon Sci Sect Hum Exp Psychol — Psychonomic Science. Section on Human Experimental Psychology
Psychop Afr — Psychopathologie Africaine
Psychopathol Afr — Psychopathologie Africaine
Psychopathol Expression Suppl Encephale — Psychopathologie de l'Expression. Supplement de l'Encephale
Psychopathol Pict Expression — Psychopathology and Pictorial Expression
Psychopharm — Psychopharmacologia
Psychopharmacol Abstr — Psychopharmacology Abstracts
Psychopharmacol Bull — Psychopharmacology Bulletin
Psychopharmacol Commun — Psychopharmacology Communications
Psychopharmacol Front Proc Psychopharmacol Symp — Psychopharmacology Frontiers. Proceedings. Psychopharmacology Symposium
Psychopharmacology Suppl — Psychopharmacology. Supplementum
Psychopharmacol Ser — Psychopharmacology Series
Psychopharmacol Ser (Dekker) — Psychopharmacology Series (Dekker)
Psychopharmacol Serv Cent Bull — Psychopharmacology Service Center. Bulletin
Psychopharmacol Suppl — Psychopharmacology. Supplementum
Psychopharmacol Suppl Encephale — Psychopharmacologie. Supplement de l'Encephale
Psychoph C — Psychopharmacology Communications
Psychophysl — Psychophysiology
Psychos Med — Psychosomatic Medicine
Psychosoc Aspects Genet Couns Proc Conf — Psychosocial Aspects of Genetic Counseling. Proceedings. Conference
Psychosocial Rehabil J — Psychosocial Rehabilitation Journal
Psychosoc Proc Iss Child Ment Health — Psychosocial Process. Issues in Child Mental Health
Psychosoc Rehabil J — Psychosocial Rehabilitation Journal
Psychosomat — Psychosomatics
Psychosom Med — Psychosomatic Medicine
Psychotherapy (NY) — Psychotherapy (New York)
Psychother Med Psychol — Psychotherapie und Medizinische Psychologie
Psychother Newsl — Psychotherapy Newsletter
Psychother Patient — Psychotherapy Patient
Psychother Psychosom — Psychotherapy and Psychosomatics
Psychother Psychosom Med Psychol — Psychotherapie, Psychosomatik, Medizinische Psychologie
Psychother Theory Res Pract — Psychotherapy: Theory, Research, and Practice
Psychoth MP — Psychotherapie und Medizinische Psychologie
Psychoth Ps — Psychotherapy and Psychosomatics
Psychoth/TR — Psychotherapy: Theory, Research, and Practice
Psych Pract — Psychiatry in Practice
Psych Prax — Psychologische Praxis
Psych Q — Psychiatric Quarterly
Psych Soc — Psychology and Social Theory
Psych Stud — Psychological Studies
Psych Teaching — Psychology Teaching

Psych Today — Psychology Today
Psycul R — Psychocultural Review
Psyk o Erhv — Psykologien og Erhvervslivet
PSYM — Symposium
PSyr — Patrologia Syriaca
Psy R — Proceedings. Society for Psychical Research
PsyR — Psychoanalytic Review
PSYR — Psychological Record
PsyR — Psychological Review
Psy Rund — Psychologische Rundschau
PsyS — Psychonomic Science
PSYSA — Psyche
P Sy St Carletn — Proceedings. Symposium on Statistics and Related Topics. Carleton University
Psy T — Psychology Today
P Sz — Pannonhalmi Szemle
Ps Z — Physikalische Zeitschrift
PSZ — Polnoe Sobranie Zakonov Rossisskoi Imperii
PSZBA — Prace i Studia Zakladu Badan Naukowych Gornoslaskiego Okregu Przemyslowego Polskiej Akademii Nauk
Pszczelnicze Zesz Nauk — Pszczelnicze Zeszyty Naukowe
Pszczel Zesz Nauk — Pszczelnicze Zeszyty Naukowe
PSzL — Polska Sztuka Ludowa
PSZN — Pubblicazioni della Stazione Zoologica di Napoli [Milan]
PT — Pamietnik Teatralny
PT — Petroleum Times
PT — Philosophical Transactions of The Royal Society of London for Improving Natural Knowledge
PT — Poetics Today
PT — Polar Times
PT — Prehistoric Thessaly
PT — Present Tense
PT — Protestantische Texte
PT — Przeglad Teologiczny
PT — Psychology Today
PT — Pytannja Tekstolohiji
PTA — Kunststof en Rubber
PTA — Papyrologische Texte und Abhandlungen
PTA — Personnel and Training Abstracts
PTA — Practical Accountant
PTA Apoth — PTA [Pharmazeutisch-Technische Assistenten] in der Apotheke
PTAIOC — Proceedings and Transactions. All-India Oriental Conferences
PTA Mag — PTA [Parent-Teacher Association] Magazine
PTA Prakt Pharm — PTA [Pharmazeutisch-Technische Assistenten] in der Praktischen Pharmazie. Fachzeitschrift fuer Pharmazeutisch-Technische Assistenten
PTA Prakt Pharm Beil — PTA [Pharmazeutisch-Technische Assistenten] in der Praktischen Pharmazie. Beilage
PTAR — Academie des Sciences, Belles-Lettres, et Arts de Rouen. Precis Analytique des Travaux
PTASB — Photographic Applications in Science, Technology, and Medicine
PTB Ber Abt Allg Tech Wiss Dienste — PTB [Physikalisch-Technische Bundesanstalt]-Bericht. Abteilung Allgemeine Technisch-Wissenschaftliche Dienste
PTB Ber Abt Atomphys — PTB [Physikalisch-Technische Bundesanstalt]-Bericht. Abteilung Atomphysik
PTB Ber Abt Elektr — PTB [Physikalisch-Technische Bundesanstalt]-Bericht. Abteilung Elektrizitaet
PTB Ber Abt Mech — PTB [Physikalisch-Technische Bundesanstalt]-Bericht. Abteilung Mechanik
PTB Ber Abt Opt — PTB [Physikalisch-Technische Bundesanstalt]-Bericht. Abteilung Optik
PTB Ber Abt Sicherstellung Endlagerung Radioakt Abfaelle — PTB [Physikalisch-Technische Bundesanstalt]-Bericht. Abteilung Sicherstellung und Endlagerung Radioaktiver Abfaelle
PTB Ber Abt Waerme — PTB [Physikalisch-Technische Bundesanstalt]-Bericht. Abteilung Waerme
PTB Ber Dosim — PTB [Physikalisch-Technische Bundesanstalt]-Bericht. Dosimetrie
PTB Ber Forsch Messreaktor Braunschweig — PTB [Physikalisch-Technische Bundesanstalt]-Bericht. Forschungs- und Messreaktor Braunschweig
PTB Ber Neutronendosimetrie — PTB [Physikalisch-Technische Bundesanstalt]-Bericht. Neutronendosimetrie
PTB Ber N Phys Tech Bundesanst — PTB-Bericht N. Physikalisch-Technische Bundesanstalt
PTB Ber Phys Grundlagen — PTB [Physikalisch-Technische Bundesanstalt]-Bericht. Physikalische Grundlagen
PTB Ber Radioakt — PTB [Physikalisch-Technische Bundesanstalt]-Bericht. Radioaktivitaet
PTB Ber ThEx Phys Tech Bundesanst — PTB-Bericht ThEx - Physikalisch - Technische Bundesanstalt
PTB Ber W Phys Tech Bundesanst — PTB-Bericht W. Physikalisch-Technische Bundesanstalt
PTB Mitt — PTB [Physikalisch-Technische Bundesanstalt] Mitteilungen. Amts- und Mitteilungsblatt der Physikalisch- Technische Bundesanstalt
PTB Mitt Forsch Pruefen — PTB [Physikalisch-Technische Bundesanstalt] Mitteilungen. Forschen und Pruefen
PTC — Packung und Transport in der Chemischen Industrie
PTC Bull — P.T.C. (Power Transmission Council) Bulletin [New York]
PTCEDJ — Plant Cell Tissue and Organ Culture
PTC J — Patent, Trademark, and Copyright Journal
PTCJB — Postepy Techniki Jadrowej
PTCLA — Presse Thermale et Climatique
Ptd Salesmanship — Printed Salesmanship
PTeb — Tebtunis Papyri

PTEKAA — Klucze do Oznaczania Owadow Polski
Pteridine Chem Proc Int Symp — Pteridine Chemistry. Proceedings. International Symposium
Ptero — Pterodactyl
PText — Papiere zur Textlinguistik
PTFS — Publications. Texas Folklore Society
PTG — Portugal, Belgique, Luxembourg. Informations Economiques
Ptg Art — Printing Art
PTGMA — Photogrammetria
P Th — Pastoraltheologie
PTH — Popes Through History
PTHEA — Physical Therapy
P Thead — Papyrus de Theadelphie
P Th H — Praktisch Theologisches Handbuch
P Th HB S — Praktisch-Theologische Handbibliothek. Sonderband
PTHO — Thought
PThR — Princeton Theological Review
PTHS — Theological Studies
P Th St — Pretoria Theological Studies
PTI — Petroleum Times
PTIND — Paper Technology and Industry
PTJ — Piano Technician's Journal
PTJ — Property Tax Journal
PTJO — Theatre Journal
PTK — Plato's Theory of Knowledge
PTK — Prehistoric Tombs at Knossos
PTM — Practising Manager
PTMRA — Platinum Metals Review
PTMUD — Postepy Technologii Maszyn i Urzadzen
PTNC — Technology and Culture
PTNMA — Protection of Metals
PTNRA8 — Pattern Recognition
PTOC — Progress in Theoretical Organic Chemistry
PTP — Phase Transition Phenomena
PTPFA — Poznanskie Towarzystwo Przyjaciol Nauk. Wydzial Lekarski. Prace Komisji Farmaceutycznej
Pt Phil Gaz — Port Phillip Gazette
PTPKA — Progress of Theoretical Physics (Kyoto)
PTPMA — Poznanskie Towarzystwo Przyjaciol Nauk. Wydzial Lekarski. Prace Komisji Medycyny Doswiadczalnej
PTPN — Poznanskie Towarzystwo Przyjaciol Nauk
PTPRAI — Poznanskie Towarzystwo Przyjaciol Nauk, Wydzial Matematyczno-Przyrodniczy PraceKomisji Biologicznej
PT Procestech — PT [*Polytechnisch Tijdschrift*]-Procestechniek
PTQR — Triquarterly
PTR — Personality Tests and Reviews
PTR — Princeton Theological Review
PTR — Publishing Trade
PTRC — PTRC. Planning and Transport Research and Computation
PTREA — Philips Technical Review
PTREDQ — Proceedings. Technical Session on Cane Sugar Refining Research
PTRI — Theatre Research International
Ptr Ink — Printers' Ink
Ptr Ink Mo — Printers' Ink Monthly
PTRSC — Proceedings and Transactions. Royal Society of Canada
PTS — Pali Text Society
PTSb — Pravoslavny Theologicky Sbornik
Ptsd Asps Obs Pb — Publicationen des Astrophysikalischen Observatoriums zu Potsdam
PTS Forschungsber — PTS [*Papiertechnische Stiftung*] Forschungsbericht
PTSLA — Plant Science Letters
PTSSD5 — US National Park Service. Transactions and Proceedings
PTSTS — Pali Text Society Translation Series
PTSU — Theatre Survey
PTT Bedr — PTT-Bedrijf. Staatsbedrijf der Posterijen, Telegrafie, en Telefonie
PTTDA — Petroleum Today
PTTI Stud — PTTI [*Postal, Telegraph, and Telephone International*] Studies
PTTPD — Bandaoti Xuebao
PTT Tech Mitt — PTT [*Schweizerische Post Telephon und Telegraphenbetrieben*] Technische Mitteilungen
PTT Vesn — PTT Vesnik. Ministarstva Posta i Sindikata Sluzbenike PTT Jugoslavije
Ptuj Zbor — Ptujski Zbornik
PTWL — Tulsa Studies in Women's Literature
PTXS — Texas Studies in Literature and Language
PU — Patna University. Journal
PU — Pequeno Universo
PU — Problemi di Ulisse
PU — Psychologia Universalis
PUA — Public Administration
PUAES — Publications. Service des Antiquites du Maroc
PUAHC — Proceedings. Union of American Hebrew Congregations
PUAQ — Urban Affairs Quarterly
PUASAL — Proceedings. Utah Academy of Sciences, Arts, and Letters
PUASB — Publicaciones de la Universidad Autonoma Simon Bolivar. Cuadernos sobre Derecho y Ciencias Sociales
PUB — Pacific University Bulletin
Pub — Publisher
PubA — Public Administration
PUBA — Universidad de Buenos Aires. Facultad de Filosofia y Letras. Seccion Antropologica. Publicaciones
Pub Adm — Public Administration
Pub Admin — Public Administration
Pub Admin Abstr — Public Administration Abstracts and Index of Articles
Pub Admin Dev — Public Administration and Development
Pub Admin Rev — Public Administration Review

Pub Admin Survey — Public Administration Survey
Pub Adm R — Public Administration Review
Pub Adm Rev — Public Administration Review
Pub Ad Rev — Public Administration Review
Pub Affairs — Public Affairs
Pub Am Stat Assn — Publications. American Statistical Association
Pub Archives Can Report — Public Archives of Canada. Report
Pub Ast S J — Publications. Astronomical Society of Japan
Pub Ast S P — Publications. Astronomical Society of the Pacific
Pubbl (Bergamo) Sta Sper Maiscoltura — Pubblicazioni (Bergamo) Stazione Sperimentale di Maiscoltura
Pubbl Centro Sper Agr Forest ENCC — Pubblicazioni. Centro di Sperimentazione Agricola e Forestale. Ente Nazionale per la Cellulosa e per la Carta
Pubbl Centro Sperim Agric — Pubblicazioni. Centro di Sperimentazione Agricola e Forestale
Pubbl Centro Sup Logica Sci Comparate — Pubblicazioni a Cura del Centro Superiore di Logica e Scienze Comparate
Pubbl Centro Talassogr Tirreno — Pubblicazioni del Centro Talassografico Tirreno
Pubbl Cent Sper Agric For — Pubblicazioni. Centro di Sperimentazione Agricola e Forestale
Pubbl Cent Sper Agric For (Rome) — Pubblicazioni. Centro di Sperimentazione Agricola e Forestale (Rome)
Pubbl Cent Stud Citogenet Veg CNR — Pubblicazioni. Centro di Studio per la Citogenetica Vegetale. Consiglio Nazionale della Ricerche
Pubbl Chim Biol Med Ist "Carlo Erba" Ric Ter — Pubblicazioni Chimiche, Biologiche, e Mediche. Istituto "Carlo Erba" per Ricerche Terapeutiche
Pubbl Comm Ital Geofis — Pubblicazioni. Commissione Italiana per la Geofisica
Pubbl Dip Metod Model Mat Sci Appl Univ Stud Roma Quad — Universita degli Studi di Roma La Sapienza. Dipartimento di Metodi e Modelli Matematica per le Scienze Applicati. Pubblicaziani
Pubbl Ente Naz Cellulosa Carta — Pubblicazioni. Ente Nazionale per la Cellulosa e per la Carta
Pubbl Fac Lett Filos Univ Milano — Pubblicazioni della Facolta di Lettere e Filosofia dell'Universita di Milano
Pubbl Fac Sci Ing Univ Trieste Ser A — Pubblicazioni. Facolta di Scienze e d'Ingegneria. Universita di Trieste. Serie A
Pubbl Fac Sci Ing Univ Trieste Ser B — Pubblicazioni. Facolta di Scienze e d'Ingegneria. Universita di Trieste. Serie B
Pubbl IAC — Pubblicazioni. Istituto per le Applicazioni del Calcolo. Consiglio Nazionale delle Ricerche
Pubbl Ist Chim Agrar Sper Gorizia Nuovi Ann — Pubblicazione. Istituto Chimico Agrario Sperimentale di Gorizia. Nuovi Annali
Pubbl Ist Geofis (Trieste) — Pubblicazione. Istituto Geofisico (Trieste)
Pubbl Ist Geol Mineral Univ Ferrara — Pubblicazioni. Istituto di Geologia e Mineralogia. Universita di Ferrara
Pubbl Ist Geol Paleontol Geogr Fis Univ Milano Ser G — Pubblicazione. Istituto di Geologia, Paleontologia, e GeograficaFisica. Universita di Milano. Serie G
Pubbl Ist Geol Univ Milano Ser G — Pubblicazione. Istituto di Geologia. Universita di Milano. Serie G
Pubbl Ist Italo Lat Am — Pubblicazione. Istituto Italo-Latino Americano
Pubbl Ist Mat Appl Fac Ingegneria Univ Stud Roma — Pubblicazioni. Istituto di Matematica Applicata. Facolta di Ingegneria. Universita degli Studi di Roma
Pubbl Ist Sper Selv (Arezzo) — Pubblicazioni. Istituto Sperimentale per la Selvicoltura (Arezzo, Italy)
Pubbl Ist Sper Talassogr (Trieste) — Pubblicazione. Istituto Sperimentale Talassografico (Trieste)
Pubbl Oss Geofis Trieste — Pubblicazioni. Osservatorio Geofisico di Trieste
Pubbl R Univ Studi Firenze Fac Sci Mat Fis Nat — Pubblicazioni. Reale Universita degli Studi di Firenze. Facolta diScienze Matematiche, Fisiche, e Naturali
Pubbl Ser III — Pubblicazione. Serie III
Pubbl Staz Zool Napoli — Pubblicazioni. Stazione Zoologica di Napoli
Pubbl Stn Sper Granic Sicil Catania — Pubblicazione. Stazione Sperimentale di Granicoltura per laSicilia-Catania
Pubbl Stn Zool Napoli — Pubblicazioni. Stazione Zoologica di Napoli
Pubbl Stn Zool Napoli II — Pubblicazioni della Stazione Zoologica di Napoli. Section II. History and Philosophy of the Life Sciences
Pubbl Univ Ferrara — Pubblicazioni dell'Universita di Ferrara
Pubbl Univ Studi Firenze Fac Sci Mat Fis Nat — Pubblicazioni. Universita degli Studi di Firenze. Facolta di Scienze Matematiche, Fisiche, e Naturali
Pubbl Univ Studi Trieste Fac Econ Commer Ist Merceol — Pubblicazione. Universita degli Studi di Trieste. Facolta di Economiae Commercio. Istituto di Merceologia
Pubbl Univ Stud Perugia Fac Med Vet — Pubblicazioni. Universita degli Studi di Perugia. Facolta di Medicina Veterinaria
Pub Bus — Public Business
Pub Business Detroit — Public Business (Detroit)
Pub Circ — Publishers' Circular and Booksellers' Record
Pub Col Soc Mass — Publications. Colonial Society of Massachusetts
Pub Cont LJ — Public Contract Law Journal
Pub Cont Newsl — Public Contract Newsletter
Pub Contract L J — Public Contract Law Journal
Pub Dep Math Nouvelle Ser — Publications du Departement de Mathematiques. Nouvelle Serie
Pub Dom Ast — Publications. Dominion Astrophysical Observatory
Pub Emp — Public Employee
Pub Employee Bargaining CCH — Public Employee Bargaining. Commerce Clearing House
Pub Ent Adv LQ — Publishing, Entertainment, Advertising, and Allied Fields Law
Pub Health — Public Health
Pub Health Bul — Public Health Bulletin
Pub Health Cong Proc Add Disc — Public Health Congress. Proceedings, Addresses, and Discussions
Pub Health Monogr — Public Health Monographs

Pub Health Nurs — Public Health Nursing
Pub Health Nurse — Public Health Nurse
Pub Health Rep — Public Health Reports
Pub Health Rept — Public Health Reports
Pub Health Rep US Pub Health and Mar Hosp Serv — Public Health Reports. United States Surgeon-General. Public Health and Marine Hospital Service
Pub Health Rep US Pub Health Serv — Public Health Reports. United States Public Health Service
Pub Health Rpts — Public Health Reports
Pub Health Soc B — Public Health Society. Bulletin
Pub Hist — [*The*] Public Historian
Pub Hist Inst Luxembourg — Publications. Section Historique. Institut Grand-Ducal de Luxembourg
Pub Hlth Eng — Public Health Engineer
Pub Int — Public Interest
Pub Interest — Public Interest
Pub Intl L — Public International Law
Pub L — Public Law
Publ Acad Cienc Estado Sao Paulo — Publicacao. Academia de Ciencias. Estado de Sao Paulo
Publ Acad Horti Vitic — Publicationes Academiae Horti- et Viticulturae
Publ ACIESP — Publicacao. Academia de Ciencias. Estado de Sao Paulo
Publ Adm — Public Administration
Publ Adm London — Public Administration (London)
Publ Adm R — Public Administration Review
Publ Adm Re — Public Administration Review
Publ AEEE Sch Agric Econ Ext Educ Univ Guelph — Publication AEEE. School of Agricultural Economics and Extension Education. University of Guelph
Publ Aff — Public Affairs
Publ Aff B — Public Affairs Bulletin
Publ Agraroekon Fak Landwirtsch Univ — Publikation der Agraroekonomischen Fakultaet der LandwirtschaftlichenUniversitaet
Publ Agric (Can) — Publication. Agriculture (Canada)
Publ Agric Ext Serv N Carol St Univ — Publication. Agricultural Extension Service. North Carolina State University
Publ Agric Res Serv US Dep Agric — Publication. Agricultural Research Service. United States Department of Agriculture
Publ Akkeshi Mar Biol Sta — Publications. Akkeshi Marine Biological Station
Publ Alberta Dept Agr — Publication. Alberta Department of Agriculture
Publ Allan Hancock Pacific Exped — Publications. Allan Hancock Pacific Expeditions
Publ Allegheny Obs Univ Pittsburgh — Publications. Allegheny Observatory. University of Pittsburgh
Publ Amakusa Mar Biol Lab Kyushu Univ — Publications. Amakusa Marine Biological Laboratory. Kyushu University
Publ Am Assoc Adv Sci — Publication. American Association for the Advancement of Science
Publ Am Concr Inst — Publication. American Concrete Institute
Publ Amer Ass Advan Sci — Publication. American Association for the Advancement of Science
Publ Amer Assoc Advancem Sci — Publications. American Association for the Advancement of Science
Publ Amer Jew Hist Soc — Publications. American Jewish Historical Society
Publ Amer Univ Beirut Fac Agr Sci — Publication. American University of Beirut. Faculty of Agricultural Sciences
Publ Am Inst Biol Sci — Publication. American Institute of Biological Sciences
Publ Am Inst Hist Pharm — Publication. American Institute of the History of Pharmacy
Publ Am Pet Inst — Publication. American Petroleum Institute
Publ Am Univ Beirut Fac Agric Sci — Publication. American University of Beirut. Faculty of Agricultural Sciences
Publ ANARE Data Rep Ser — Publications. ANARE [*Australian National Antarctic Research Expeditions*] Data Reports Series
Pub Land & Res L Dig — Public Land and Resources Law Digest
Publ Asoc Excurs Romani Sect Sti — Publicatiunile Asociatiei Excursionistilor Romani. Sectiunea Stiintific
Publ Ass For-Cell — Publication. Association Foret-Cellulose
Publ Assoc Etude Paleontol Stratigr Houilleres — Publication. Association pour l'Etude de la Paleontologie et de la Stratigraphie Houilleres
Publ Assoc Ing Fac Polytech Mons — Publications. Association des Ingenieurs. Faculte Polytechnique de Mons
Publ Astron Soc Aust — Publications. Astronomical Society of Australia
Publ Astron Soc Jpn — Publications. Astronomical Society of Japan
Publ Astron Soc Pac — Publications. Astronomical Society of the Pacific
Publ Astron Soc Pacific — Publications. Astronomical Society of the Pacific
Publ Atkins Inst — Publications. Atkins Institution
Publ Aust Natl Univ Res Sch Phys Sci Dep Eng Phys — Australian National University. Research School of Physical Sciences. Department of Engineering Physics. Publication
Publ Australas Inst Min Metall — Publications. Australasian Institute of Mining and Metallurgy
Publ Avulsa FZB Fund Zoobot Rio Grande Sul — Publicacao Avulsa FZB. Fundacao Zoobotanica do Rio Grande Do Sul
Publ Avulsas Cent Pesqui Aggeu Magalhaes (Recife Braz) — Publicacoes Avulsas. Centro de Pesquisas Aggeu Megalhaes (Recife, Brazil)
Publ Avulsas Inst Aggeu Magalhaes (Recife Braz) — Publicacoes Avulsas. Instituto Aggeu Magalhaes (Recife, Brazil)
Publ Avulsas Mus Nac (Rio De J) — Publicacoes Avulsas. Museu Nacional (Rio De Janeiro)
Publ Avulsa Univ Fed Pernambuco Esc Quim Dep Tecnol — Publicacao Avulsa. Universidade Federal de Pernambuco. Escola deQuimica. Departamento de Tecnologia
Publ Avuls Rev Bras Malariol — Publicacoes Avulsas. Revista Brasileira de Malariologia
Pub Law For — Public Law Forum

Publ B Chalmers Tek Hoegsk — Publikation B. Chalmers Tekniska Hoegskola
Publ BC Minist Agric — Publications. British Columbia Ministry of Agriculture
Publ BC Minist Agric Food — Publications. British Columbia Ministry of Agriculture and Food
Publ Beaverlodge Res Stn — Publication. Beaverlodge Research Station
Publ Belg Inst Verbetering Biet — Publikatie. Belgisch Instituut tot Verbetering van de Biet
Publ Biol Dir Gen Invest Cient UANL (Univ Auton Nuevo Leon) — Publicaciones Biologicas. Direccion General de la Investigacion Cientifica UANL(Universidad Autonoma de Nuevo Leon)
Publ Biol Inst Invest Cient UANL (Univ Auton Nuevo Leon) — Publicaciones Biologicas. Instituto de Investigaciones Cientificas UANL (Universidad Autonoma de Nuevo Leon)
Publ Biol Univ Navarra Ser Zool — Publicaciones de Biologia. Universidad de Navarra. Serie Zoologica
Publ Bot — Publications in Botany
Publ Bot Univ Calif Berkeley — Publications in Botany. University of California, Berkeley
Publ Brit Columbia Dept Agr — Publication. British Columbia Department of Agriculture
Publ Bur Etud Geol Minieres Colon (Paris) — Publications. Bureau d'Etudes Geologiques et Minieres Coloniales (Paris)
Publ Bur Rech Geol Geophys Minieres (Fr) — Publications. Bureau de Recherches Geologiques, Geophysiques, et Minieres (France)
Publ Cairo Univ Herb — Publications. Cairo University Herbarium
Publ Calif Dep Agric — Publication. California Department of Agriculture
Publ Calif State Water Resour Control Board — Publication. California State Water Resources Control Board
Publ Canada Dep Agric — Publication. Canada Department of Agriculture
Publ Canada Dep For — Publication. Canada Department of Forestry
Publ Can Dep Agric — Publication. Canada Department of Agriculture
Publ Can Dept Agr — Publication. Canada Department of Agriculture
Publ Can For Serv — Publication. Canadian Forestry Service
Publ Carnegie Inst Wash — Publications. Carnegie Institution of Washington
Publ Carnegie Inst Washington — Publication. Carnegie Institution of Washington
Publ Catedra Hist Med — Publicaciones de la Catedra de Historia de la Medicina. Univeriasd de Buenos Aires
Publ Catedra Lastanosa Inst Est Oscenses — Publicacion de la Catedra Lastanosa. Instituto de Estudios Oscenses
Publ Cent Adv Study Geol (Chandigarh India) — Publication. Centre of Advanced Study in Geology (Chandigarh, India)
Publ Center Medieval Ren Stud UCLA — Publications. Center for Medieval and Renaissance Studies. UCLA
Publ Cent Estud Entomol Univ Chile — Publicaciones. Centro de Estudios Entomologicos. Universidad de Chile
Publ Cent Estud Leprol — Publicacoes. Centro de Estudos Leprologicos
Publ Cent Etude Util Sciures de Bois — Publication. Centre d'Etude pour l'Utilisation des Sciures de Bois
Publ Cent Invest Tecnol (Pando Urug) — Publicacion. Centro de Investigaciones Tecnologicas (Pando, Uruguay)
Publ Cent Invest Tisiol — Publicaciones. Centro de Investigaciones Tisiologicas
Publ Cent Natl Exploit Oceans Actes Colloq — Publications. Centre National pour l'Exploitation des Oceans. Actes de Colloques
Publ Cent Natl Exploit Oceans Rapp Sci Tech — Publications. Centre National pour l'Exploitation des Oceans. Rapports Scientifiques et Techniques
Publ Cent Natl Exploit Oceans Result Campagnes Mer — Publications. Centre National pour l'Exploitation des Oceans. Resultats des Campagnes a la Mer
Publ Cent Natl Exploit Oceans Ser Rapp Sci Tech (Fr) — Publications. Centre National pour l'Exploitation des Oceans. Serie. Rapport Scientifique et Technique (France)
Publ Cent Natl Geol Houillere — Publication. Centre National de Geologie Houillere
Publ Cent Quim Ind (Buenos Aires) — Publicacion. Centro de Quimicos Industriales (Buenos Aires)
Publ Cent Rech Zootech Univ Louvain — Publication. Centre de Recherches Zootechniques. Universite do Louvain
Publ Centre Rech Math Pures — Publications. Centre de Recherches en Mathematiques Pures
Publ Centre Rech Math Pures 1 — Publications. Centre de Recherches en Mathematiques Pures. Serie 1
Publ Centre Rech Math Pures Ser 3 — Publications. Centre de Recherches en Mathematiques Pures. Serie 3
Publ Centre Rech Math Pures Ser IV — Publications du Centre de Recherches en Mathematiques Pures. Serie IV
Publ Centre Tech For Trop — Publication. Centre Technique Forestier Tropical
Publ Cent Stud Citogenet Veg CNR — Pubblicazioni. Centro di Studi per la Citogenetica Vegetale. ConsiglioNazionale delle Ricerche
Publ Cent Tech For Trop (Nogent-Sur-Marne Fr) — Publication. Centre Technique Forestier Tropical (Nogent-Sur-Marne, France)
Publ Chalmers Tek Hoegsk Goeteborg Inst Vattenfoersoerjnings — Publikation. Chalmers Tekniska Hoegskola. Goeteborg. Institutionen foer Vattenfoersoerjnings- och Avloppsteknik
Publ Chile Univ Cent Estud Entomol — Publicaciones. Chile Universidad. Centro de Estudios Entomologicos
Publ Choice — Public Choice
Publ Chusus (Indones) Dir Geol — Publikasi Chusus (Indonesia). Direktorat Geologi
Publ Cient (Alter) — Publicaciones Cientificas (Alter)
Publ Cient Univ Austral Chile (Fac Ingen For) — Publicaciones Cientificas. Universidad Austral de Chile (Facultad de IngenieriaForestal)
Publ Clark — Publications. Clark Library Professorship. University of California at Los Angeles
Publ Cleans — Public Cleansing
Publ CMMI Congr — Publications. CMMI [*Council of Mining and Metallurgical Institutions*] Congress

Publcoes Avuls Mus Parana — Publicacoes Avulsas. Museu Paranaense
Publcoes Cult Co Diam Angola — Publicacoes Culturais. Companhia de Diamantes de Angola
Publcoes Dir Ger Servs Flor Aquic — Publicacoes. Direccao Geral dos Servicos Florestais e Aqueicolas
Publ Coffee Brew Inst — Publication. Coffee Brewing Institute
Publ Colonial Soc Massach — Publications. Colonial Society of Massachusetts
Publ Com Nac Energ At (Argent) Misc — Publicaciones. Comision Nacional de Energia Atomica (Argentina). Miscelanea
Publ Com Nac Energ At (Argent) Ser Fis — Publicaciones. Comision Nacional de Energia Atomica (Argentina). Serie Fisica
Publ Com Nac Energ At (Argent) Ser Geol — Publicaciones. Comision Nacional de Energia Atomica (Argentina). Serie Geologia
Publ Com Nac Energ At (Argent) Ser Inf — Publicaciones. Comision Nacional de Energia Atomica (Argentina).Serie Informe
Publ Com Nac Energ At (Argent) Ser Mat — Publicaciones. Comision Nacional de Energia Atomica (Argentina). Serie Matematica
Publ Com Nac Energ At (Argent) Ser Quim — Publicaciones. Comision Nacional de Energia Atomica (Argentina). Serie Quimica
Publ Conf Geol Caraibes — Publication. Conference Geologique des Caraibes
Publ Cons Recur Nat No Renov (Mex) — Publicacion. Consejo de Recursos Naturales No Renovables (Mexico)
Publ Cons Recursos Miner — Publicacion. Consejo de Recursos Minerales
Publ Contr LJ — Public Contract Law Journal
Publ Coop Ext Serv La State Univ Agric Mech Coll — Publication. Cooperative Extension Service. Louisiana State University and Agricultural and Mechanical College
Publ Coop Ext Serv Miss State Univ — Publication. Cooperative Extension Service. Mississippi State University
Publ Coop Ext Serv Univ Ariz Coll Agric — Publication. Cooperative Extension Service. University of Arizona. College of Agriculture
Publ Coop Ext Serv Wash St Univ — Publication. Cooperative Extension Service. Washington State University
Publ Co-Op Ext Univ Calif — Publication. Cooperative Extension. University of California
Publ Cult — Public Culture
Publ Cult Cia Diamantes Angola — Publicacoes Culturais. Companhia de Diamantes de Angola
Publ de la Soc Hist de l Orient Latin — Publications de la Societe de l'Histoire de l'Orient Latin
Publ De L Ecole D Lang Orient Viv — Publications de l'Ecole des Langues Orientales Vivantes
Publ Dep Agric (Can) — Publication. Department of Agriculture (Ottawa, Canada)
Publ Dep Algebra Fund Univ Murcia — Publicaciones del Departamento de Algebra y Fundamentos. Universidad de Murcia
Publ Dep Cristalogr Mineral (Madrid) — Publicaciones. Departamento de Cristalografia y Mineralogia (Madrid)
Publ Dep Cristalogr Mineral Univ Barcelona — Publicaciones. Departamento de Cristalografia y Mineralogia.Universidad de Barcelona
Publ Dep Cristalogr Miner CSIC (Spain) — Publicaciones. Departamento de Cristalografia y Mineralogia. Consejo Superior de Investigaciones Cientificas (Spain)
Publ Dep Eng Phys Res Sch Phys Sci Aust Natl Univ — Publication. Department of Engineering Physics. Research School of Physical Sciences. Australian National University
Publ Dep Geom Topol — Publicaciones del Departamento de Geometria y Topologia
Publ Dep Mat — Publicacoes do Departamento de Matematica
Publ Dep Math Lyon — Publications. Departement de Mathematiques. Faculte des Sciences de Lyon
Publ Dep Math Nouvelle Ser D — Publications du Departement de Mathematiques. Nouvelle Serie. D
Publ Dep Mat Univ Extremadura — Publicaciones del Departamento de Matematicas. Universidad de Extremadura
Publ Dept Agr (Can) — Publications. Department of Agriculture (Canada)
Publ Dept Agr Conserv (Manitoba) — Publications. Department of Agriculture and Conservation (Manitoba)
Publ Dep Zool (Barc) — Publicaciones. Departamento de Zoologia (Barcelona)
Publ Dir Gen Geol Minas Repub Ecuador — Publicacion. Direccion General de Geologia y Minas. Republica del Ecuador
Publ Dir Gen Invent Nac For (Mex) — Publicacion. Direccion General del Inventario Nacional Forestal (Coyoacan, Mexico)
Publ Diverses Mus Natl Hist Nat — Publications Diverses. Museum National d'Histoire Naturelle
Publ Diverse Spec Serv Peches Sci Mer (Can) — Publication Diverse Speciale. Service des Peches et des Sciences de laMer (Canada)
Publ Dom Astrophys Obs — Publications. Dominion Astrophysical Observatory
Publ Dom Astrophys Obs (Victoria BC) — Publications. Dominion Astrophysical Observatory (Victoria, British Columbia)
Publ Dom Obs (Ottawa) — Publications. Dominion Observatory (Ottawa)
Publ Dushanb Inst Epidemiol Gig — Publikatsiya Dushanbinskogo Instituta Epidemiologii i Gigieny
Publ Earth Phys Branch (Can) — Publications. Earth Physics Branch (Canada)
Publ Earth Phys Branch Dep Energy Mines & Resour — Publications. Earth Physics Branch. Department of Energy, Mines, and Resources
Publ Econometriques — Publications Econometriques
Publ EE Univ Toronto Inst Environ Stud — Publication EE. University of Toronto. Institute for EnvironmentalStudies
Publ Elektrote Fak Univ Beogradu Ser Mat Fiz — Publikacije Elektrotehnickog Fakulteta Univerziteta u Beogradu. Serija Matematika i Fizika
Publ Elektroteh Fak Ser Elektroenerg — Publikacije Elektrotehnickog Fakulteta. Serija Elektroenergetika
Publ Elektroteh Fak Ser Elektron Telekommun Autom — Publikacije Elektrotehnickog Fakulteta. Serija Elektronika Telekommunikacije. Automatika

Publ Elektroteh Fak Ser Mat & Fiz — Publikacije Elektrotehnickog Fakulteta. Serija Matematika i Fizika
Publ Elektroteh Fak Univ Beogr Ser Mat Fiz — Publikacije Elektrotehnickog Fakulteta Univerziteta u Beogradu. Serija Matematika i Fizika
Publ Elisabethville Univ Etat — Publications. Elisabethville. Universite de l'Etat
Publ Energ — Publicacion sobre Energia
Publ Eng Exp St State Univ Agric Appl Sci (Okla) — Publication. Engineering Experiment Station. State University ofAgriculture and Applied Science (Oklahoma)
Publ Ent Adv A — Publishing, Entertainment, Advertising, and Allied Fields Law Quarterly
Publ E Purdue Univ Coop Ext Serv — Publication E. Purdue University. Cooperative Extension Service
Publ Espec Inst Esp Oceanogr — Publicaciones Especiales. Instituto Espanol de Oceanografia
Publ Espec Inst Nac Invest Forest (Mex) — Publicacion Especial. Instituto Nacional de Investigaciones Forestal (Mexico)
Publ Espec Inst Oceanogr (San Paulo) — Publicacao Especial. Instituto Oceanografico (San Paulo)
Publ Espec Serv Nac Trigo Min Agr (Madrid) — Publicaciones Especiales. Servicio Nacional del Trigo. Ministerio de Agricultura (Madrid)
Publ Espec Univ Rio Grande Sul Esc Geol — Publicacao Especial. Universidade do Rio Grande Do Sul. Escola deGeologia
Publ Estac Exp Agric Tucuman — Publicacion. Estacion Experimental Agricola de Tucuman
Publ Ethnol — Publications in Ethnology
Publ Eur Assoc Ani Prod — Publication. European Association for Animal Production
Publ Eur Gem — Publicatieblad van de Europese Gemeenschappen
Publ Ext Serv Israel Min Agric — Israel. Ministry of Agriculture. Extension Service Publication
Publ Fac Agric Univ Ankara — Publications. Faculte de l'Agriculture. Universite d'Ankara
Publ Fac Agron Univ Teheran — Publications. Faculte d'Agronomie. Universite de Teheran
Publ Fac Agr Sci Amer Univ (Beirut) — Publications. Faculty of Agricultural Sciences. American University (Beirut)
Publ Fac Cienc Fisicomat Univ Nac La Plata — Publicaciones. Facultad de Ciencias Fisicomatematicas. UniversidadNacional de La Plata
Publ Fac Cienc Fisicomat Univ Nac La Plata Ser 2 — Publicaciones. Facultad de Ciencias Fisicomatematicas. Universidad Nacional de La Plata. Serie 2. Revista
Publ Fac Dr Econ Amiens — Publications. Faculte de Droit et d'Economie d'Amiens
Publ Fac Dr Sci Polit Soc Amiens — Publications. Faculte de Droit et des Sciences Politiques et Sociales d'Amiens
Publ Fac Electr Engrg Ser Automat Control — Publications of the Faculty of Electrical Engineering. Series. Automatic Control
Publ Fac Electrotech Univ Belgrade Ser Math Phys — Publications. Faculte d'Electrotechnique. Universite a Belgrade. Serie Mathematiques et Physique
Publ Fac Sci Univ Brno — Publications. Faculte des Sciences. Universite a Brno
Publ Fac Sci Univ Clermont Geol Mineral — Publications. Faculte des Sciences. Universite de Clermont. Geologie et Mineralogie
Publ Fac Sci Univ J E Purkyne (Brno) — Publications. Faculte des Sciences. Universite J. E. Purkyne (Brno)
Publ Fac Sci Univ Masaryk — Publications. Faculte des Sciences. Universite Masaryk
Publ FAO/ECE Jt Comm Working Tech — Publication. FAO [*Food and Agriculture Organization of the United Nations*]/ECE Joint Committee on Forest Working Techniques and Training Forest Workers
Publ Far East Reg Inst Sci Res Vladivostok — Publications. Far Eastern Regional Institute for Scientific Research. Vladivostok
Publ Far East State Univ (Vladivostok) — Publications. Far Eastern State University (Vladivostok)
Publ Farm (Sao Paulo) — Publicacoes Farmaceuticas (Sao Paulo)
Publ Fert Soc S Afr — Publication. Fertilizer Society of South Africa
Publ Field Columbian Mus Bot Ser — Publications. Field Columbian Museum. Botanical Series
Publ Finan — Public Finance
Publ Finance — Public Finance
Publ Finance Quart — Public Finance Quarterly
Publ Finn State Agric Res Board — Publications. Finnish State Agricultural Research Board
Publ Fin Q — Public Finance Quarterly
Publ Fis Mat — Publicacoes de Fisica Matematica
Publ Fond Agathon de Potter — Publications. Foundation Agathon de Potter
Publ For Commn NSW — Publication. Forestry Commission of New South Wales
Publ Foreign Agric Serv US Dep Agric — Publication. Foreign Agricultural Service. United States Department of Agriculture
Publ Forest Res Brch Canada Dep For — Publication. Forest Research Branch. Canada Department of Forestry
Publ For Res Inst Finl — Publications. Forest Research Institute in Finland
Publ For Sci — Publications of Forestry Science
Publ For Serv (Can) — Publication. Forestry Service. Department of Fisheries and Forestry (Ottawa, Canada)
Publ Found Sci Res Surinam Neth Antilles — Publications. Foundation for Scientific Research in Surinam and the NetherlandsAntilles
Publ Geol Dep Ext Serv Univ West Aust — Publication. Geology Department and the Extension Service. University of Western Australia
Publ Geol Dep Victoria Univ Wellington — Publication. Geology Department. Victoria University of Wellington
Publ Geol Espec Ingeominas — Publicaciones Geologicas Especiales del Ingeominas
Publ Geol ICAITI — Publicaciones Geologicas. ICAITI
Publ Geol Inst Centroam Invest Tecnol Ind — Publicaciones Geologicas. Instituto Centroamericano de Investigaciony Tecnologia Industrial

Publ Geol Sci Univ Calif — Publications in Geological Sciences. University of California

Publ Geol Surv Queensl — Publication. Geological Survey of Queensland

Publ GRA Rapp Tech — Publications. GRA [*Groupement Francais pour le Developpement des Recherches Aeronautiques*] Rapport Technique

Publ Great Lakes Res Div Univ Mich — Publication. Great Lakes Research Division. University of Michigan

Publ Great Lakes Res Div Univ Michigan Inst Sci — Publications. Great Lakes Research Division. University of Michigan. Institute of Science and Technology

Publ Great Plains Agric Coun — Great Plains Agricultural Council. Publication

Publ Group Adv Psychiatry — Publication. Groups for the Advancement of Psychiatry

Publ Group Av Methodes Spectrogr — Publication. Groupement pour l'Avancement des Methodes Spectrographiques

Publ Gulf Coast Res Lab Mus — Publications. Gulf Coast Research Laboratory. Museum

Publ Haewundae Mar Lab Pusan Fish Coll — Publications. Haewundae Marine Laboratory. Pusan Fisheries College

Publ Hannah Inst Hist Med — Publication. Hannah Institute for the History of Medicine

Publ Hartley Bot Lab — Publications. Hartley Botanical Laboratories

Publ Heal — Public Health: The Journal of the Society of Community Medicine

Publ Heal R — Public Health Reviews

Publ Health Lab — Public Health Laboratory

Publ Hea Re — Public Health Reports

Publ Heb Univ (Jerusalem) — Publications. Hebrew University (Jerusalem)

Publ Henri Poincare Arch — Publikationen des Henri-Poincare-Archivs

Publ Hist — Publishing History

Publ Hlth — Public Health

Publ Hlth Ne — Public Health News

Publ Hlth Rep (Wash) — Public Health Reports (Washington, DC)

Publ HoChiMinh City Math Soc — Publications of the HoChiMinh City Mathematical Society

Publ Hung Cent Inst Dev Min — Publications. Hungarian Central Institute for the Development of Mining

Publ Hung Min Res Inst — Publications. Hungarian Mining Research Institute

Publ Hung Res Inst Mining — Publications. Hungarian Research Institute for Mining

Pub Lib — Public Libraries

Pub Lib Abst — Public Library Abstracts

Pub Lib Op — Public Library Opinion

Pub Lib Rep — Public Library Reporters

Pub Lib Trustee — Public Library Trustee

Publicaciones Dept Agric Costa Rica — Publicaciones. Departamento de Agricultura de Costa Rica

Public Adm — Public Administration

Public Adm Abstr Index Artic (India) — Public Administration Abstracts and Index of Articles (India)

Public Adm Bull — Public Administration Bulletin

Public Admin — Public Administration

Public Admin and Development — Public Administration and Development

Public Admin Bull — Public Administration Bulletin

Public Admin J (Kathmandu) — Public Administration Journal (Kathmandu)

Public Admin R — Public Administration Review

Public Admin Survey — Public Administration Survey

Public Adm R — Public Administration Review

Public Adm Rev — Public Administration Review

Public Affairs Rept — Public Affairs Report

Public Aff Inf Serv Bull — Public Affairs Information Service Bulletin

Public Aff Rep — Public Affairs Report

Public Anal Assoc J — Public Analysts Association. Journal

Publicatie Prov Gallo Romeins Mus Tongeren — Publicatie Provinciaal Gallo-Romeins Museum te Tongeren

Public Budgeting and Fin — Public Budgeting and Finance

Public Clean Tech Rep — Public Cleansing Technical Report

Public Fin — Public Finance

Public Fin Account — Public Finance and Accountancy

Public Fin (Berlin) — Public Finance (Berlin)

Public Fin Q — Public Finance Quarterly

Public Gard J Am Assoc Bot Gard Arbor — Public Garden. Journal. American Association of Botanical Gardens and Arboreta

Public Health Eng — Public Health Engineer

Public Health Eng Abstr — Public Health Engineering Abstracts

Public Health Eng Conf Proc — Public Health Engineering Conference. Proceedings

Public Health Eur — Public Health in Europe

Public Health J — Public Health Journal

Public Health J (Peking) — Public Health Journal (Peking)

Public Health Lab — Public Health Laboratory

Public Health Monogr — Public Health Monograph

Public Health Nurs — Public Health Nursing

Public Health Nutr — Public Health Nutr

Public Health Pap — Public Health Papers

Public Health Rep — Public Health Reports

Public Health Rev — Public Health Reviews

Public Health Revs — Public Health Reviews

Public Health Soc Med Hyg — Public Health. Social Medicine and Hygiene

Public Hlth Engr — Public Health Engineer

Public Inf Circ Geol Surv Wy — Public Information Circular. Geological Survey of Wyoming

Public Inf Circ Iowa Geol Surv — Public Information Circular. Iowa Geological Survey

Public Land Resour Law Dig — Public Land and Resources Law Digest

Public Lib — Public Libraries

Public Light — Public Lighting

Public Manage Source — Public Management Sources

Public Mgt — Public Management

Public Opin — Public Opinion

Public Opinion Q — Public Opinion Quarterly

Public Opin Q — Public Opinion Quarterly

Public Pers Manage — Public Personnel Management

Public Prod Rev — Public Productivity Review

Public Rel — Public Relations Journal

Public Relations R — Public Relations Review

Public Relat J — Public Relations Journal

Public Relat Q — Public Relations Quarterly

Public Relat Rev — Public Relations Review

Public Sect — Public Sector. New Zealand Institute of Public Administration

Public Sector Health Care Risk Manage — Public Sector. Health Care Risk Management

Public Serv Action — Public Service Action

Public TC Review — Public Telecommunications Review

Public Util Fortn — Public Utilities Fortnightly

Public Water Supply Eng Conf Proc — Public Water Supply Engineers Conference. Proceedings

Public Welf — Public Welfare

Public Works Congr Proc — Public Works Congress. Proceedings

Public Works Eng Yearb — Public Works Engineers' Yearbook

Public Works Local Gov Eng — Public Works and Local Government Engineering

Public Works Rev — Public Works Review

Public Works Roads Transp — Public Works, Roads, and Transport

Public Works Ser — Public Works and Services

Public Work (Syd) — Public Works and Services (Sydney)

Publ ID Coop Ext Serv Purdue Univ — Publication. ID Cooperative Extension Service. Purdue University

Publ IEA — Publicacao. Instituto de Energia Atomica

Publikationsr Fortschr Strahlenschutz — Publikationsreihe Fortschritte im Strahlenschutz

Publikationsser B Chalmers Tek Hoegsk — Publikationsserie B. Chalmers Tekniska Hoegskola

Publ Ill Inst Technol — Publications. Illinois Institute of Technology

Publ INCAP — Publicacion. Instituto de Nutricion de Centro America y Panama

Publ INCAR — Publicacion INCAR

Publ Indian Tea Assoc Sci Dept — Publications. Indian Tea Association. Scientific Department

Publ INED — Publications INED

Publ Inst Antart Argent (B Aires) — Publicacion. Instituto Antartico Argentino (Buenos Aires)

Publ Inst Appl Math — Publications of the Institute for Applied Mathematics

Publ Inst Belge Amelior Betterave — Publications. Institut Belge pour l'Amelioration de la Betterave

Publ Inst Biol Apl (Barc) — Publicaciones. Instituto de Biologia Aplicada (Barcelona)

Publ Inst Biol Apl (Barcelona) — Publicaciones. Instituto de Biologia Aplicada (Barcelona)

Publ Inst Bot Bucuresti — Publicatiunile Institutului Botanic Din Bucuresti

Publ Inst Bot Dr Goncalo Sampaio — Publicacoes do Instituto de Botanica Dr. Goncalo Sampaio

Publ Inst Bot "Dr Goncalo Sampaio" Fac Cienc Univ Porto — Publicacoes. Instituto de Botanica "Dr. Goncalo Sampaio." Faculdade de Ciencias. Universidade do Porto

Publ Inst Bot Univ Geneve — Publications. Institut de Botanique de l'Universite de Geneve

Publ Inst Cent Dev Min Hong — Publications. Institut Central de Developpement Minier de Hongrie

Publ Inst Edafol Hidrol Univ Nac Sur (Bahia Blanca) — Publicaciones. Instituto de Edafologia e Hidrologia. Universidad Nacional del Sur (Bahia Blanca)

Publ Inst Elektroind (Sofia) — Publikationen des Institutes der Elektroindustrie (Sofia)

Publ Inst Energ At (Sao Paulo) — Publicacao. Instituto de Energia Atomica (Sao Paulo)

Publ Inst Etud Rech Min Turq — Publications. Institut d'Etudes et de Recherches Minieres de Turquie

Publ Inst Fis "Alonso De St Cruz" — Publicaciones. Instituto de Fisica "Alonso De Santa Cruz"

Publ Inst Fis Univ Nac Tucuman — Publicacion. Instituto de Fisica. Universidad Nacional de Tucuman

Publ Inst Florestal — Publicacao. Instituto Florestal

Publ Inst Found Engng Soil Mech Rock Mech Waterways Constr — Publications. Institute of Foundation Engineering, Soil Mechanics, Rock Mechanics, and Waterways Construction

Publ Inst French Studies — Publications. Institut of French Studies

Publ Inst Fr Pet Collect Colloq Semin — Publications, Institut Francais du Petrole. Collection Colloques et Seminaires

Publ Inst Geogr (Bogota) — Publicacion. Instituto Geografico Agustin Codazzi (Bogota)

Publ Inst Geol (Barcelona) — Publicaciones. Instituto Geologico (Barcelona)

Publ Inst Geol Topogr — Publicaciones. Instituto Geologico Topografico

Publ Inst Geol Univ Chile — Publicaciones. Instituto de Geologia del Universidade de Chile

Publ Inst Geophys Pol Acad Sci — Publication. Institute of Geophysics. Polish Academy of Sciences

Publ Inst Geophys Pol Acad Sci D — Publications. Institute of Geophysics. Polish Academy of Sciences D. Physics ofthe Atmosphere

Publ Inst Geophys Pol Acad Sci Ser A — Publications. Institute of Geophysics. Polish Academy of Sciences. Series A. Physics of the Earth Interior

Publ Inst Geophys Pol Acad Sci Ser B — Publications. Institute of Geophysics. Polish Academy of Sciences. Series B. Seismology

Publ Inst Geophys Pol Acad Sci Ser C — Publications. Institute of Geophysics. Polish Academy of Sciences. Series C. Earth Magnetism

Publ Inst Geophys Pol Acad Sci Ser E — Publications. Institute of Geophysics. Polish Academy of Sciences. Series E. Ionosphere Physics

Publ Inst Geophys Pol Acad Sci Ser F — Publications. Institute of Geophysics. Polish Academy of Sciences. Series F. Planetary Geodesy

Publ Inst Geophys Ser D Pol Acad Sci — Publications. Institute of Geophysics. Polish Academy of Sciences. Series D. Atmosphere Physics

Publ Inst Invest Geol Diputacion Barcelona — Publicaciones. Instituto de Investigaciones Geologicas. Diputacion de Barcelona

Publ Inst Invest Geol Diputacion Prov Barcelona — Publicaciones. Instituto de Investigaciones Geologicas. Diputacion Provincial de Barcelona

Publ Inst Invest Microquim Univ Nac Litoral (Rosario Argent) — Publicaciones. Instituto de Investigaciones Microquimicas. Universidad Nacionaldel Litoral (Rosario, Argentina)

Publ Inst Italo Latinoam — Publicacion. Instituto Italo-Latinoamericano

Publ Inst Mar Sci Nat Fish Univ Busan — Publications. Institute of Marine Sciences. National Fisheries. University of Busan

Publ Inst Mar Sci Natl Fish Univ Busan — Publications. Institute of Marine Sciences. National Fisheries University of Busan

Publ Inst Mar Sci Univ Tex — Publications. Institute of Marine Science. University of Texas

Publ Inst Mar Sci Univ Texas — Publications. Institute of Marine Science. University of Texas

Publ Inst Math (Belgrade) — Publications. Institut Mathematique. Nouvelle Serie (Belgrade)

Publ Inst Math (Belgrad) NS — Institut Mathematique. Publications. Nouvelle Serie (Belgrade)

Publ Inst Math Univ Nancago — Publications. Institut Mathematique. Universite de Nancago

Publ Inst Math Univ Strasbourg — Publications. Institut de Mathematiques. Universite de Strasbourg

Publ Inst Mex Recursos Nat Renov — Publicacion. Instituto Mexicano de Recursos Naturales Renovables

Publ Inst Mineral Paleontol Quat Geol Univ Lund — Publications. Institutes of Mineralogy, Paleontology, and Quaternary Geology. University of Lund

Publ Inst Musee Voltaire — Publications. Institut et Musee Voltaire

Publ Inst Nac Carbon Sus Deriv "Francisco Pintado Fe" — Publicacion. Instituto Nacional del Carbon y Sus Derivados "Francisco Pintado Fe"

Publ Inst Nac Nutr (Argent) Publ Cient — Publicaciones. Instituto Nacional de la Nutricion (Argentina). Publicaciones Cientificas

Publ Inst Nac Pesqui Amazonia Ser Quim — Publicacoes. Instituto Nacional de Pesquisas da Amazonia. SerieQuimica

Publ Inst Nat Etude Agron Congo — Publications. Institut National pour l'Etude Agronomique du Congo

Publ Inst Nat Etude Agron Congo (INEAC) Serie Scientifique — Publications. Institut National pour l'Etude Agronomique du Congo (INEAC). Serie Scientifique

Publ Inst Natl Etude Agron Congo Belge Ser Sci — Publications. Institut National pour l'Etude Agronomique du Congo Belge. Serie Scientifique

Publ Inst Natl Etude Agron Congo Ser Sci — Publications. Institut National pour l'Etude Agronomique du Congo. Serie Scientifique

Publ Inst Natl Etude Agron Congo Ser Tech — Publications. Institut National pour l'Etude Agronomique du Congo. Serie Technique

Publ Inst Nutr Cent Am Panama — Publicacion. Instituto de Nutricion de Centro America y Panama

Publ Inst Opt Madrid — Publicaciones. Instituto de Optica Daza de Valdes de Madrid

Publ Inst Pesqui Energ Nucl — Publicacao. Instituto de Pesquisas Energeticas e Nucleares

Publ Inst Pesqui Mar — Publicacao. Instituto de Pesquisas da Marinha

Publ Inst Pesqui Mar Rio De Janeiro — Publicacao. Instituto de Pesquisas da Marinha (Rio De Janeiro)

Publ Inst Pesqui Tecnol (Estado Sao Paulo) — Publicacao. Instituto de Pesquisas Tecnologicas (Estado de Sao Paulo)

Publ Inst Quim Fis Antonio Gregorio Rocasolano — Publicaciones. Instituto de Quimica Fisica "Antonio GregorioRocasolano"

Publ Inst Quim Fis Rocasolano — Publicaciones. Instituto de Quimica Fisica "Rocasolano"

Publ Inst Rech Agron Liban Ser Sci — Publication. Institut de Recherches Agronomiques du Liban. SerieScientifique

Publ Inst Rech Agron Liban Ser Tech — Publication. Institut de Recherches Agronomiques du Liban. SerieTechnique

Publ Inst Rech Entomol Phytopathol (Teheran) — Publication. Institut de Recherches Entomologiques etPhytopathologiques (Teheran)

Publ Inst Rech Math Av — Publication de l'Institut de Recherche Mathematique Avancee

Publ Inst Rech Math Rennes — Publications de l'Institut de Recherche de Mathematiques de Rennes

Publ Inst Rech Min Hong — Publications. Institut de Recherches Minieres de Hongrie

Publ Inst Rech Sider Ser A — Publications. Institut de Recherches de la Siderurgie. Serie A

Publ Inst Rech Sider Ser B — Publications. Institut de Recherches de la Siderurgie. Serie B

Publ Inst Rech Siderurg Ser A — Publications. Institut de Recherches de la Siderurgie [*Saint-Germain-En-Laye*]. Serie A

Publ Inst R Meteorol Belg A — Publications. Institut Royal Meteorologique de Belgique. Serie A. Format in-4

Publ Inst R Meteorol Belg B — Publications. Institut Royal Meteorologique de Belgique. Serie A. Format in-8

Publ Inst R Meteorol Belg Ser A — Publications. Institut Royal Meteorologique de Belgique. Serie A. Format in-4

Publ Inst R Meteorol Belg Ser B — Publications. Institut Royal Meteorologique de Belgique. Serie B

Publ Inst Soil Rock Mech Univ Fridericiana (Karlsruhe) — Publications. Institute for Soil and Rock Mechanics. University of Fridericiana(Karlsruhe)

Publ Inst Statist Univ Paris — Publications. Institut de Statistique. Universite de Paris

Publ Inst Suflos Agrotec (B Aires) — Publicacion. Instituto de Suflos y Agrotecnia (Buenos Aires)

Publ Inst Tec Constr Cem — Publicaciones. Instituto Tecnico de la Construccion y del Cemento

Publ Inst Tecnol Estud Super Monterrey Ser Cienc Biol — Publicaciones. Instituto Tecnologico y de Estudios Superiores de Monterrey. Serie Ciencias Biologicas

Publ Inst TT Meneses — Publicaciones. Institucion Tello Tellez de Meneses

Publ Inst Zool "Dr Augusto Nobre" Fac Cienc Porto — Publicacoes. Instituto de Zoologia "Dr. Augusto Nobreda." Faculdade de Ciencias. Universidade do Porto

Publ Inst Zootec (Rio De J) — Publicacao. Instituto de Zootecnia (Rio De Janeiro)

Publ Int — Public Interest

Publ Int Ass Scient Hydrol Symp (Budapest) — Publication. International Association of Scientific Hydrology. Symposium (Budapest)

Publ Inter — Public Interest

Publ Interest — Public Interest

Publ Intern Postgrado — Publicaciones Internas del Postgrado

Publ Int Geol Correl Program Proj — Publication. International Geological Correlation Program Project

Publ Int Inst Land Reclam Improv — Publication. International Institute for Land Reclamation andImprovement

Publ Int Tin Res Inst — Publication. International Tin Research Institute

Publ IOM Natl Acad Sci Inst Med — Publication IOM [*Institute of Medicine*]. National Academy of Sciences. Institute of Medicine

Publ IPEN — Publicacao IPEN

Publ IPRNR (Inst Pesqui Recur Nat Renovaveis) — Publicacao. IPRNR (Instituto de Pesquisas de Recursos Naturais Renovaveis)

Publ IPT — Publicacao IPT

Publishers — Publishers' Weekly

Publ Istanbul Univ Obs — Publications. Istanbul University Observatory

Publius J F — Publius. Journal of Federalism

Publ Iwata Inst Pl Biochem — Publications. Iwata Institute of Plant Biochemistry

Publ Jefferson Med Coll Hosp — Publications. Jefferson Medical College Hospital

Publ Jpn Med Res Found — Publication. Japan Medical Research Foundation

Publ Junta Nac Prod Pecu Ser A Ser Cient Invest — Publicacoes. Junta Nacional dos Produtos Pecuarios. Serie A. Serie Cientifica ede Investigacao

Publ K Meteorol Inst Belg Ser A — Publicaties. Koninklijk Meteorologisch Instituut van Belgie. Serie A

Publ K Meteorol Inst Belg Ser B — Publicaties. Koninklijk Meteorologisch Instituut van Belgie. Serie B

Publ Korean Natl Astron Obs — Publications. Korean National Astronomical Observatory

Publ L — Public Law

Publ Lab Biochim Nutr Univ Cathol Louvain Fac Sci Agron — Publication. Laboratoire de Biochimie de la Nutrition. Universite Catholique deLouvain. Faculte des Sciences Agronomiques

Publ Lab Cent Ensayo Mater Constr (Madrid) — Publication. Laboratorio Central de Ensayo de Materiales de Construccion (Madrid)

Publ Lab Ecole Norm Super — Publication des Laboratoires d'Ecole Normale Superieure

Publ Lab Jefferson Med Coll Hosp — Publications. Laboratories of the Jefferson Medical College Hospital

Publ Lab Med Exp Clin Med E Prado Tagle Univ Chile — Publicaciones. Laboratorio de Medicina Experimental. ClinicaMedica del Prof. E. Prado-Tagle. Hospital Clinica San Vicente. Universidad deChile

Publ Lab Photoelasticite Ecole Polytech Fed (Zurich) — Publications. Laboratoire de Photoelasticite. Ecole Polytechnique Federale (Zurich)

Publ Lab Physiol Chem Univ Amsterdam — Publications. Laboratory of Physiological Chemistry. University of Amsterdam

Publ Law (London) — Public Law (London)

Publ Ld Capability Surv Trinidad & Tobago — Publication. Land Capability Survey of Trinidad and Tobago

Publ Ltg — Public Lighting

Publ Manit Dep Mines Nat Resour Mines Branch — Publication. Manitoba Department of Mines and Natural Resources. MinesBranch

Publ Manit Dep Mines Resour Environ Manage Mines Branch — Publication. Manitoba. Department of Mines, Resources, and Environmental Management. Mines Branch

Publ Manitoba Beekprs Ass — Publication. Manitoba Beekeepers' Association

Publ Mar Biol Sta Ghardaga — Publications. Marine Biological Station. Ghardaga, Red Sea. Faculty of Science.Fouad I University

Publ Mar Biol Stn (Al Ghardaqa) — Publications. Marine Biological Station (Al Ghardaqa, Red Sea)

Publ Mar Biol Stn (Ghardaqa Red Sea) — Publications. Marine Biological Station (Al Ghardaqa, Red Sea)

Publ Mar Biol Stn Stalin — Publications. Marine Biological Station of Stalin

Publ Maria Moors Cabot Found Bot Res — Publication. Marie Moors Cabot Foundation for Botanical Research

Publ Mar Lab Pusan Fish Coll — Publications. Marine Laboratory. Pusan Fisheries College

Publ Marsh Bot Gard — Publications. Marsh Botanical Garden. Yale University

Publ Mat — Publicacions Matematiques

Publ Math Debrecen — Publicationes Mathematicae. Universitatis Debreceniensis

Publ Math Fac Sci Besancon — Publications Mathematiques de la Faculte des Sciences de Besancon

Publ Math Orsay 80 — Publications Mathematiques d'Orsay 80

Publ Math Orsay 81 — Publications Mathematiques d'Orsay 81

Publ Math Orsay 82 — Publications Mathematiques d'Orsay 82

Publ Math Res Center Univ Wisconsin — Publications. Mathematics Research Center. University of Wisconsin

Publ Math Res Cent Univ Wis — Publication. Mathematics Research Center. University of Wisconsin

Publ Math Res Cent Univ Wis Madison — Publication. Mathematics Research Center. University ofWisconsin-Madison

Publ Math Res Cent US Army Univ Wis — Publication. Mathematics Research Center. United States Army. University of Wisconsin

Publ Math Res Inst (Istanbul) — Publications. Mathematical Research Institute (Istanbul)

Publ Math Soc Japan — Publications. Mathematical Society of Japan

Publ Math Univ Bordeaux — Publications Mathematiques. Universite de Bordeaux

Publ Math Univ Paris 7 Denis Diderot — Publications Mathematiques de l'Universite Paris 7 (Denis Diderot)

Publ Math Univ Paris VII — Publications Mathematiques. Universite de Paris. VII

Publ Math Univ Pierre et Marie Curie — Publications Mathematiques. Universite Pierre et Marie Curie

Publ Mat Urug — Publicaciones Matematicas del Uruguay

Publ Maya Soc — Publications. Maya Society

Publ McGill Univ Ser 2 Bot — Publications. McGill University. Series 2. Botany

Publ Med — Publicacoes Medicas

Publ Med Exp Univ Chile — Publicaciones de Medicina Experimental. Universidad de Chile

Publ Metaalinst TNO — Publikatie. Metaalinstituut TNO

Publ Mich State Univ Mus Biol Ser — Publications. Michigan State University Museum. Biological Series

Publ Mid South Neurosci Dev Group — Publication. Mid-South Neuroscience Development Group

Publ Min Agr Ser Premios Nac Invest Agr — Publicaciones. Ministerio de Agricultura. Serie. Premios Nacionales de Investigacion Agraria

Publ Miner Res Explor Inst Turk — Publications. Mineral Research and Exploration Institute of Turkey

Publ Miner Resour Div (Winnipeg) — Publication. Mineral Resources Division (Winnipeg)

Publ Minist Agric (Can) — Publication. Ministry of Agriculture (Canada)

Publ Misc Agric Univ Chile Fac Agron — Publicaciones Miscelaneas Agricolas. Universidad de Chile. Facultad de Agronomia

Publ Misc Estac Exp Agr Tucuman — Publicaciones Miscelaneas. Estacion Experimental Agricola de Tucuman

Publ Miss State Univ Agr Ext Serv — Publication. Mississippi State University. Agricultural Extension Service

Publ Mod Lang Ass — Publications. Modern Language Association of America

Publ Mod Lang Assoc — Publications. Modern Languages Association of America

Publ Mus Hist Nat "Javier Prado" Ser A Zool — Publicaciones. Museo de Historia Natural "Javier Prado." Series A. Zoologia

Publ Mus Hist Nat "Javier Prado" Ser B Bot — Publicaciones. Museo de Historia Natural "Javier Prado." Series B. Botanica

Publ Mus Hist Nat Javier Prado Ser C Geol — Publicaciones. Museo de Historia Natural "Javier Prado." Series C. Geologia

Publ Mus Hist Nat J Prado Lima — Publicaciones. Museo de Historia Natural Javier Prado (Lima)

Publ Mus Lab Mineral Geol Fac Cienc Porto — Publicacoes. Museu e Laboratorio Mineralogico e Geologico. Faculdade de Ciencias do Porto

Publ Mus Lab Mineral Geol Univ Coimbra — Publicacoes. Museu e Laboratorio Mineralogico e Geologico.Universidade de Coimbra

Publ Mus Lab Mineral Geol Univ Coimbra Cent Estud Geol — Publicacoes. Museu e Laboratorio Mineralogico e Geologico.Universidade de Coimbra e Centro de Estudos Geologicos

Publ Mus Mich State Univ Biol Ser — Publications. Museum. Michigan State University. Biological Series

Publ Mus Nat Hist Univ Kansas — Publications. Museum of Natural History. University of Kansas

Publ Muz Judatului Hunedoara — Publicatiile Muzeului Judatului Hunedoara

Publ Nantucket Maria Mitchell Assoc — Publications. Nantucket Maria Mitchell Association

Publ Nat Acad Sci Nat Res Counc — Publication. National Academy of Sciences. National Research Council

Publ Natn Acad Sci Natn Res Coun (Wash) — Publication. National Academy of Sciences. National Research Council (Washington)

Publ Natuurhist Genoot Limburg — Publicaties. Natuurhistorisch Genootschap in Limburg

Publnes Misc Minist Agric Ganad Repub Argent — Publicaciones Miscelaneas. Ministerio de Agricultura y Ganaderia. Republica de Argentina

Publ Newton Inst — Publications of the Newton Institute

Publn Inst Nac Tec Agropec (B Aires) — Publicacion. Instituto Nacional de Tecnologia Agropecuaria (Buenos Aires)

Publn Inst Suelos Agrotec — Publicacion. Instituto de Suelos y Agrotecnia

Publ NMAB Natl Mater Advis Board (US) — Publication. NMAB. National Materials Advisory Board (US)

Publ Nordforsk Miljoevardssekr — Publikation. Nordforsk, Miljoevardssekretariatet

Publ Nor Inst Kosm Fys — Publikasjoner. Norske Institutt foer Kosmisk Fysikk

Publ Obs Astr Univ Belgr — Publications. Observatoire Astronomique. Universite de Belgrade

Publ Obs Univ Mich — Publications. Observatory. University of Michigan

Publ Ocas Mus Cienc Nat (Caracas) Zool — Publicaciones Ocasionales. Museo de Ciencias Naturales (Caracas). Zoologia

Publ OECD (Paris) — Publication. OECD [*Organization for Economic Cooperation and Development*] (Paris)

Publ Off Natl Etud Rech Aerosp (Fr) — Publication. Office National d'Etudes et de Recherches Aerospatiales (France)

Publ Okla State Univ Agr Inform Serv — Publication. Oklahoma State University. Agricultural Information Service

Publ Ont Dep Agric — Publication. Ontario Department of Agriculture and Food

Publ Ont Fish Res Lab — Publications. Ontario Fisheries Research Laboratory

Publ Oper Res Ser — Publications in Operations Research Series

Publ Opin Q — Public Opinion Quarterly

Publ Pacif Nth-West Co-Op Ext Serv — Publication. Pacific Northwest Cooperative Extension Service

Publ Palaeontol Inst Univ Upps Spec Vol — Publications. Palaeontological Institution. University of Uppsala. Special Volume

Publ Pedido Privilegio (Braz) — Publicacao de Pedido de Privilegio (Brazil)

Publ Pers M — Public Personnel Management

Publ Personnel Manag — Public Personnel Management

Publ Pharm — Publicacoes Pharmaceuticas

Publ Phil Soc — Publications. Philological Society

Publ Pol — Public Policy

Publ Policy — Public Policy

Publ Prehist Soc — Publications. Prehistoric Society

Publ Puget Sound Biol St Univ Wash — Publications. Puget Sound Biological Station. University of Washington

Publ Puget Sound Mar Stn Univ Wash — Publications. Puget Sound Marine Station. University ofWashington

Publ Purdue Univ Sch Civ Eng — Publication. Purdue University. School of Civil Engineering

Publ R Acad Farm Barcelona Ser A — Publicaciones. Real Academia de Farmacia de Barcelona. Serie A.Anuarios, Memorias, y Discursos Inaugurales de Curso

Publ R Acad Farm Barcelona Ser B — Publicaciones. Real Academia de Farmacia de Barcelona. Serie B.Revista

Publ R Acad Farm Barcelona Ser C — Publicaciones. Real Academia de Farmacia de Barcelona. Serie C.Discurso de Ingreso

Publ Ramanujan Inst — Publications. Ramanujan Institute

Publ Rapeseed Assoc Can — Publication. Rapeseed Association of Canada

Publ R Coll Physicians Edinburgh — Publication. Royal College of Physicians of Edinburgh

Publ Relat Congo Belg Reg Voisines — Publications Relatives au Congo Belge et aux Regions Voisines

Publ Rel J — Public Relations Journal

Publ Rep Aust Coal Ind Res Lab — Published Reports. Australian Coal Industry Research Laboratories

Publ Res Inst Aabo Akad Found — Publication. Research Institute. Aabo Akademi Foundation

Publ Res Inst Math Sci — Publications. Kyoto University. Research Institute for Mathematical Sciences

Publ Res Inst Math Sci Ser A — Publications. Research Institute for Mathematical Sciences. Series A

Publ Res Inst Math Sci Ser B — Publications. Research Institute for Mathematical Sciences. Series B

Publ Rev — Publications Review

Publ Rev Manage Technol Policy — Publications Review. Management and Technology and Policy

Publ Roads — Public Roads

Publ R Obs (Edinburgh) — Publications. Royal Observatory (Edinburgh)

Publ Rom Fr — Publications Romanes et Francaises

Publ R Trop Inst Amsterdam — Publication. Royal Tropical Institute. Amsterdam

Publ S Afr Inst Med Res — Publications. South African Institute for Medical Research

Publs Am Econ Ass — Publications. American Economic Association

Publs Am Folk Soc — Publications. American Folklore Society

Publs ANARE Data Rep Ser — Publications. ANARE [*Australian National Antarctic Research Expeditions*] Data Reports Series

Publs ANARE Interim Rep Ser — Publications. ANARE [*Australian National Antarctic Research Expeditions*] Interim Reports Series

Publs ANARE Sci Rep Ser — Publications. ANARE [*Australian National Antarctic Research Expeditions*] Scientific Reports Series

Publs Aust Soc Soil Sci — Publications. Australian Society of Soil Science

Publs Aust Soc Soil Science — Publications. Australian Society of Soil Science

Publ Sci Assoc Int Bot — Publications Scientifiques. Association Internationale des Botanistes

Publ Scient Univ Alger Ser B — Publications Scientifiques. Universite d'Alger. Serie B. Sciences Physiques

Publ Sci For — Publications des Sciences Forestieres

Publ Sci For Bois — Publications Scientifiques Forestieres et du Bois

Publ Sci Tech Dir Ind Aeronaut (Fr) — Publications Scientifiques et Techniques. Direction des IndustriesAeronautiques (France)

Publ Sci Tech Dir Ind Aeronaut (Fr) Bull Serv Tech — Publications Scientifiques et Techniques. Direction des IndustriesAeronautiques (France). Bulletin. Services Techniques

Publ Sci Tech Dir Ind Aeronaut (Fr) Notes Tech — Publications Scientifiques et Techniques. Direction des IndustriesAeronautiques (France). Notes Techniques

Publ Sci Tech Min Air — Publications Scientifiques et Techniques. Ministere de l'Air

Publ Sci Tech Min Air Bull Serv Tech — Publications Scientifiques et Techniques. Ministere de l'Air. Bulletins des Services Techniques

Publ Sci Tech Min Air Notes Tech — Publications Scientifiques et Techniques. Ministere de l'Air [*France*].Notes Techniques

Publ Sci Tech Minist Air (Fr) — Publications Scientifiques et Techniques. Ministere de l'Air (France)

Publ Sci Tech Minist Air (Fr) Bull Serv Tech — Publications Scientifiques et Techniques. Ministere de l'Air (France). Bulletindes Services Techniques

Publ Sci Tech Res Comm Organ Afr Unity — Publication. Scientific, Technical, and Research Commission.Organization of African Unity

Publ Sci Tech Secr Etat Aviat (Fr) — Publications Scientifiques et Techniques. Secretariat d'Etat a l'Aviation (France)

Publ Sci Tech Secr Etat Aviat (Fr) Bull Serv Tech — Publications Scientifiques et Techniques. Secretariat d'Etat a l'Aviation (France). Bulletin des Services Techniques

Publ Sci Tech Secr Etat Aviat (Fr) Notes Tech — Publications Scientifiques et Techniques. Secretariat d'Etat a l'Aviation (France). Notes Techniques

Publ Sci Univ Alger Ser B — Publications Scientifiques. Universite d'Alger. Serie B. Sciences Physiques

Publ Sci Univ For Bois — Publications Scientifiques. Universite Forestiere et du Bois

Publs Co-Op Ext Univ Mass Coll Agric — Publications. Co-Operative Extension Service. University of Massachusetts. College of Agriculture

Publs Dep Agric (Alberta) — Publications. Department of Agriculture (Alberta)

Publs Dep Agric (Can) — Publicationsii. Department of Agriculture (Canada)

Publ Sec Mat — Publicacions de la Seccio de Mathematiques

Publ Sem Geom Univ Neuchatel Ser 2 — Publications. Seminaire de Geometrie. Universite de Neuchatel. Serie 2

Publ Sem Geom Univ Neuchatel Ser 3 — Publications. Seminaire de Geometrie. Universite de Neuchatel. Serie 3

Publ Semin Arqueol Numism Aragonesa — Publicaciones. Seminario de Arqueologia y Numismatica Aragonesa

Publ Sem Mat Garcia De Galdeano — Publicaciones. Seminario Matematico Garcia De Galdeano

Publ Sem Mat Garcia de Galdeano Ser II — Publicaciones del Seminario Matematico Garcia de Galdeano. Serie II

Publ Sem Math — Publication des Seminaires de Mathematiques

Publ Ser A Inst R Meteorol Belg — Publications. Serie A. Institut Royal Meteorologique de Belgique

Publ Ser B Inst R Meteorol Belg — Publications. Serie B. Institut Royal Meteorologique de Belgique

Publ Ser Eur Fed Chem Eng — Publication Series. European Federation of Chemical Engineering

Publ Serv Agric (Mozambique) — Publicacoes. Servicos de Agricultura. Servicos de Veterinaria (Lourenco Marques, Mozambique)

Publ Serv Carte Geol (Alger) Bull — Publications. Service de la Carte Geologique (Algerie). Bulletin

Publ Serv Carte Geol (Luxemb) — Publications. Service de la Carte Geologique (Luxembourg)

Publ Serv Flor Aqueic (Portugal) — Publicacoes. Direccao Geral dos Servicos Florestais e Aqueicolas (Lisbon, Portugal)

Publ Serv Geol Alger Bull — Publications. Service Geologique de l'Algerie. Bulletin

Publ Serv Geol Luxemb — Publications. Service Geologique de Luxembourg

Publ Serv Geol Luxemb Bull — Publications. Service Geologique de Luxembourg. Bulletin

Publ Serv Met Madag — Publications. Service Meteorologique de Madagascar

Publ Serv Piscic Ser I-C — Publicacao. Servico de Piscicultura. Serie I-C

Publ Serv Plagas For (Madrid) — Publicacion. Servicio de Plagas Forestales (Madrid)

Publ Seto Mar Biol Lab — Publications. Seto Marine Biological Laboratory

Publ Seto Mar Biol Lab Spec Publ Ser — Publications. Seto Marine Biological Laboratory. Special Publication Series

Publs Geol Surv QD — Publications. Geological Survey of Queensland

Publs Geol Surv QD Palaeont Pap — Publications. Geological Survey of Queensland. Palaeontological Papers

Publ Shirley Inst — Publication. Shirley Institute

Publ S III Univ Sch Agr — Publication. Southern Illinois University. School of Agriculture

Publs Indiana Dep Conserv — Publications. Indiana Department of Conservation

Publs Inst Antrop Cordoba — Publicaciones del Instituto de Antropologia. Universidad Nacional de Cordoba

Publs Inst Invest Arqueol San Juan — Publications. Instituto de Investigaciones Arqueologicas y Museo (San Juan)

Publs Inst Natn Etude Agron Congo Ser Sci — Publications. Institut National pour l'Etude Agronomique du Congo. Serie Scientifique

Publs Manitoba Dep Agric — Publications. Manitoba Department of Agriculture

Publs Maria Moors Cabot Fdn Bot Res — Publications. Maria Moors Cabot Foundation for Botanical Research

Publs Met Dep Melb Univ — Publications. Meteorology Department. University of Melbourne

Publ Smithson Inst — Publication. Smithsonian Institution

Publs Mktg Bd — Publications. Empire Marketing Board

Publs Mod Language Ass Amer — Publications. Modern Language Association of America

Publs Mus Natn Hist Nat — Publications. Museum National d'Histoire Naturelle

Publ Soc Bras Nematol — Publicacao. Sociedade Brasileira de Nematologia

Publ Soc Geol Nord — Publication. Societe Geologique du Nord

Publ Soc Nat Romania — Publicatiunile Societatii Naturalistilor din Romania

Publ Soc Savante Alsace Reg Est — Publications. Societe Savante d'Alsace et des Regions de l'Est

Publ Soil Bur (NZ) — Publication. Soil Bureau. Department of Scientific and Industrial Research (NewZealand)

Publs Osaka Mus Nat Hist — Publications. Osaka Museum of Natural History

Publ SP Am Concr Inst — Publication SP. American Concrete Institute

Publs Petrol Search Subsidy Acts — Publications. Petroleum Search Subsidy Acts. Bureau of Mineral Resources, Geology, and Geophysics

Publ Sta Fed Essais Agr (Lausanne) — Publications. Stations Federales d'Essais Agricoles (Lausanne)

Publ State Inst Agric Chem (Finl) — Publications. State Institute of Agricultural Chemistry (Finland)

Publ State Inst Tech Res — Publications. State Institute for Technical Research

Publ Statens Levnedsmiddelinst (Den) — Publikation. Statens Levnedsmiddelinstitut (Denmark)

Publ Stift Vulkaninst Immanuel Friedlaender — Publikationen Herausgegeben von der Stiftung Vulkaninstitut ImmanuelFriedlaender

Publ Stn Fed Essais Agric (Lausanne) — Publications. Stations Federales d'Essais Agricoles (Lausanne)

Publ SUG — Publikace. Statni Ustav Geofysikalni

Publ Sven Inst Konserveringsforsk — Publikation. Svenska Institutet foer Konserveringsforskning

Publ Syst Assoc — Publications. Systematics Association

Publ Systematics Ass — Publication. Systematics Association

Publ Tallinn Inst Technol Ser A — Publications. Tallinn Institute of Technology. Series A

Publ Tartu Astrofiz Obs — Publikatsii Tartuskoi Astrofizicheskoi Observatorii

Publ Tec Estac Exp Agropecuar INTA (Pergamino) — Publicaciones Tecnicas. Estacion Experimental Agropecuaria. INTA [*Instituto Nacional de Tecnologia Agropecuaria*] (Pergamino)

Publ Tec Estac Exp Agropecuar Manfredi (Argentina) — Publicaciones Tecnicas. Estacion Experimental Agropecuaria de Manfredi (Argentina)

Publ Tech Charbon Fr Bull Inf Tech — Publications Techniques des Charbonnages de France. Bulletind'Informations Techniques

Publ Tech Charbon Fr Doc Tech — Publications Techniques des Charbonnages de France. DocumentsTechniques

Publ Tech Charbon Fr Inf Tech — Publications Techniques des Charbonnages de France. Informations Techniques

Publ Tech Inst Belge Amelior Betterave — Publications Techniques. Institut Belge pour l'Amelioration de la Betterave

Publ Tech Inst Belge Amelior Betterave Tirlemont — Publications Techniques. Institut Belge pour l'Amelioration de la Betterave Tirlemont

Publ Technion Israel Inst Technol Agric Eng Fac — Publication-Technion. Israel Institute of Technology. Agricultural Engineering Faculty

Publ Tech Pap Proc Annu Meet Sugar Ind Technol Inc — Publication of Technical Papers and Proceedings. Annual Meeting of Sugar Industry Technologists, Incorporated

Publ Tech Res Cen Finl Mater Process Technol — Publication. Technical Research Centre of Finland. Materials and Processing Technology

Publ Tech Res Cent Finl — Publications. Technical Research Centre of Finland

Publ Tech Res Cent Finl Electr Nucl Technol — Publications. Technical Research Centre of Finland. Electrical and Nuclear Technology

Publ Tech Sci Pap Tech Univ (Brno) A — Publications of Technical and Scientific Papers. Technical University(Brno). A

Publ Tech Sci Pap Tech Univ Brno B — Publications of Technical and Scientific Papers. Technical University. Brno. B

Publ Tech Univ Est Tallinn Ser A — Publications. Technical University of Estonia at Tallinn. Series A

Publ Tech Univ Heavy Ind (Miskolc Hung) — Publications. Technical University for Heavy Industry (Miskolc,Hungary)

Publ Tech Univ Heavy Ind (Miskolc Hung) Foreign Lang Ed — Publications. Technical University for Heavy Industry (Miskolc,Hungary). Foreign Language Edition

Publ Tech Univ Heavy Ind (Miskolc) Ser B Metall — Publications. Technical University for Heavy Industry (Miskolc). Series B. Metallurgy

Publ Tech Univ Heavy Ind Ser A (Miskolc Hung) — Publications. Technical University for Heavy Industry. Series A. Mining(Miskolc, Hungary)

Publ Tech Univ Heavy Ind Ser B (Miskolc Hung) — Publications. Technical University for Heavy Industry. Series B.Metallurgy (Miskolc, Hungary)

Publ Tec Inst Patol Veg (B Aires) — Publicacion Tecnica. Instituto de Patologia Vegetal (Buenos Aires)

Publ Tecn Inst Bot — Publicacion Tecnica. Instituto de Botanica

Publ Tecn Inst Fitotecn Buenos Aires — Publicacion Tecnica. Instituto de Fitotecnia. Buenos Aires

Publ Tec Patronato Invest Cient Tec "Juan De La Cierva" — Publicaciones Tecnicas. Patronato de Investigacion Cientifica y Tecnica "Juan De La Cierva"

Publ Tehn Fak u Sarajevu — Publikacije Tehnickog Fakulteta u Sarajevu

Publ Tek Dir Geol Seri Geol Ekon (Indones) — Publikasi Teknik. Direktorat Geologi. Seri Geologi Ekonomi (Indonesia)

Publ Tex For Serv Part Tex A&M Univ Syst — Publication. Texas Forest Service. [A] Part of the Texas A & M UniversitySystem

Publ Thoresby Soc — Publications. Thoresby Society

Publ Trans Conf Geol Caraibes — Publication. Transactions. Conference Geologique des Caraibes

Publ Transp Int — Public Transport International

Publ Trimest Inst Belge Amelior Betterave — Publication Trimestrielle. Institut Belge pour l'Amelioration de la Betterave

Publ Trimest Univ Pontif Bolivar — Publicacion Trimestral. Universidad Pontificia Bolivariana

Publ UER Math Pures Appl IRMA — Publications. Unites d'Enseignement et de Recherche de Mathematiques Pures et Appliquees. Institut de Recherche de Mathematiques Avancees

Publ Univ Alaska Coop Ext Serv — Publication. University of Alaska. Cooperative Extension Service

Publ Univ Auton St Domingo — Publicaciones. Universidad Autonoma de Santo Domingo

Publ Univ Calif Agric Ext Serv — Publication. University of California. Agricultural Extension Service

Publ Univ Costa Rica Ser Cienc Nat — Publicaciones. Universidad de Costa Rica. Serie Ciencias Naturales

Publ Univers Pennsylv — Publications. University of Pennsylvania

Publ Univ Etat Extreme Orient — Publications. Universite d'Etat a l'Extreme-Orient

Publ Univ Europ — Publications Universitaires Europeennes

Publ Univ Europeennes Ser V Sci Econom — Publications Universitaires Europeennes. Serie V. Sciences Economiques

Publ Univ Eur Ser 8 Chim Div A — Publications Universitaires Europeennes. Serie 8. Chimie. Division A.Pharmacie

Publ Univ Eur Ser 8 Chim Div B — Publications Universitaires Europeennes. Serie 8. Chimie. Division B.Biochimie

Publ Univ Fl Inst Food Agric Sci — Publication. University of Florida. Institute of Food and Agricultural Sciences

Publ Univ Hortic — Publicationes Universitatis Horticulturae

Publ Univ Innsbruck — Publications. University of Innsbruck

Publ Univ Joensuu Ser B — Publications. University of Joensuu. Series B

Publ Univ Joensuu Ser B-I — Publications. University of Joensuu. Series B-I

Publ Univ Joensuu Ser B-II — Publications. University of Joensuu. Series B-II

Publ Univ Kuopio Community Health Ser Orig Rep — Publications. University of Kuopio. Community Health Series. Original Reports

Publ Univ Laval — Publications. Universite Laval

Publ Univ Mass Water Resour Res Cent — Publication. University of Massachusetts. Water Resources ResearchCenter

Publ Univ Nac Litoral Inst Fisiogr Geol — Publicaciones. Universidad Nacional del Litoral. Instituto de Fisiografia y Geologia
Publ Univ Nac Tucuman Fac Agron Zootec — Publicacion. Universidad Nacional de Tucuman. Facultad de Agronomia y Zootecnia
Publ Univ Nac Tucuman Inst Fis — Publicacion. Universidad Nacional de Tucuman. Instituto de Fisica
Publ Univ Nac Tucuman Inst Ing Quim — Publicacion. Universidad Nacional de Tucuman. Instituto de IngenieriaQuimica
Publ Univ Off Congo Elisabethville — Publications. Universite Officielle du Congo a Elisabethville
Publ Univ Off Congo Lubumbashi — Publications. Universite Officielle du Congo a Lubumbashi
Publ Univ Pretoria — Publikasies. Universiteit van Pretoria
Publ Univ Rouen — Publications de l'Universite de Rouen
Publ Univ Sevilla Ser Cienc — Publicaciones. Universidad de Sevilla. Serie Ciencias
Publ Univ Sevilla Ser Med — Publicaciones. Universidad de Sevilla. Serie Medicina
Publ Univ Tech Sci Budapest — Publications. University of Technical Sciences. Budapest
Publ Univ Tex Bur Econ Geol — Publication. University of Texas. Bureau of Economic Geology
Publ Univ Toronto Dep Civ Eng — Publication. University of Toronto. Department of Civil Engineering
Publ Univ Toronto Inst Environ Stud — Publication. University of Toronto. Institute for Environmental Studies
Publ Univ Toulouse-Le Mirail Ser A — Publications. Universite de Toulouse-Le Mirail. Serie A.
Publ Univ Wis Coop Ext Serv — Publication. University of Wisconsin. Cooperative Extension Service
Publ Univ Wis Ext — Publication. University of Wisconsin Extension
Publ Univ Wyo — Publications. University of Wyoming
Publ Univ Zoeloeland Reeks 3 — Publikasies. Universiteit van Zoeloeland. Reeks 3. Vakpublikasies
Publ Univ Zululand Ser 3 — Publications. University of Zululand. Series 3. Specialized Publications
Publ US Agric Res Serv — Publication. United States Agricultural Research Service
Publ US Agric Res Serv East Reg Res Cent — Publication. United States Agricultural Research Service. EasternRegional Research Center
Publ US Int Trade Commn — Publication. United States International Trade Commission
Publ US Natl Tech Inf Serv — United States. National Technical Information Service. Publication
Publ Utah Geol Assoc — Publication. Utah Geological Association
Publ Va Coop Ext Serv — Publication. Virginia Cooperative Extension Service
Publ Va Div Miner Resour — Publication. Virginia Division of Mineral Resources
Publ Virginia Div Miner Resour — Publication. Virginia Division of Mineral Resources
Publ Vulkaninst Immanuel Friedlaender — Publikationen Herausgegeben von der Stiftung Vulkaninstitut Immanuel Friedlaender
Publ W — Publishers' Weekly
Publ Wagner Free Inst Sci Philadelphia — Publications. Wagner Free Institute of Science of Philadelphia
Publ Water Environ Res Inst — Publications. Water and Environment Research Institute
Publ Water Res Inst — Publications. Water Research Institute
Publ Welfar — Public Welfare
Publ Welfare — Public Welfare
Publ West Tex Geol Soc — Publication. West Texas Geological Society
Publ Wiss Filmen Sekt Tech Wiss Naturwiss — Publikationen zu Wissenschaftlichen Filmen. Sektion Technische Wissenschaften. Naturwissenschaften
Publ W J Barrow Res Lab — Publication. W. J. Barrow Research Laboratory
Publ Wkly — Publishers' Weekly
Publ Wks — Public Works
Publ Wks Local Govt Engng — Public Works and Local Government Engineering
Publ W Va Univ Eng Exp Stn — Publication. West Virginia University. Engineering Experiment Station
Publ Zoo — Publications in Zoology
Pub Manag — Public Management
Pub Mgt — Public Management
Pubn Cent Eur Etud Burgundomedianes — Publication du Centre Europeen d'Etudes Burgundomedianes
Pubns Can Archvs — Publications of the Canadian Archives
Pubns Ecole Fr Extreme Orient — Publications de l'Ecole Francaise d'Extreme-Orient
Pubns Jesup N Pacific Expedition — Publications of the Jesup North Pacific Expedition
Pubns Mod Lang Assoc — Publications of the Modern Languages Association
Pubns Soc Hist & Archeol Limbourg Maestricht — Publications de la Societe Historique et Archeologique dans le Limbourg a Maestricht
Pub Opin — Public Opinion
Pub Opinion — Public Opinion
Pub Opinion Q — Public Opinion Quarterly
Pub Opn Q — Public Opinion Quarterly
Pub Op Q — Public Opinion Quarterly
Pub Pers Mgt — Public Personnel Management
Pub Personnel Stud — Public Personnel Studies
Pub Pol — Public Policy
Pub Rel Bull — Public Relations Bulletin
Pub Rel J — Public Relations Journal
Pub Rel Q — Public Relations Quarterly
Pub Rel Rv — Public Relations Review
Pub Roads — Public Roads

Pub Roch Hist Soc — Publication Fund Series. Rochester Historical Society
Pubs Avulsas — Publicacoes Avulsas
Pubs Ceramicas — Publicaciones Ceramicas
Pub Sector — Public Sector
Pub Service J Vic — Public Service Journal of Victoria
Pub Serv Management — Public Service Management
Pubs Mod Lang Ass Am — Publications. Modern Language Association of America
Pub Soc Bras Nematol — Publicacao. Sociedade Brasileira de Nematologia
Pubs Petrol Search Subsidy Acts — Publications. Petroleum Search Subsidy Acts. Bureau of Mineral Resources, Geology, and Geophysics
Pub Technol N — Public Technology News
Pub Util — Public Utilities Fortnightly
Pub Util Fort — Public Utilities Fortnightly
Pub Util Fortnightly — Public Utilities Fortnightly
Pub Verifiche — Pubblicazioni di Verifiche
Pub W — Publishers' Weekly
Pub Wel — Public Welfare
Pub Welf Ga — Public Welfare (Atlanta, Georgia)
Pub Welf N — Public Welfare News. American Public Welfare Association
PUC — Pubblicazioni. Universita Cattolica del Sacro Cuore
PUCaILL — Publications. University of California. Languages and Literature
PUCF — Publications. Clermont-Ferrand. Universite. Faculte des Lettres
PUCODM — Conseil Scientifique International de Recherches sur les Trypanosomiases et leur Controle
PUCP/DA — Debates en Antropologia. Pontificia Universidad Catolica del Peru. Departamentode Ciencias Sociales
PUCS — Pubblicazioni. Milan. Universita Cattolica del Sacro Cuore
PUCSC — Pubblicazioni. Universita Cattolica del Sacro Cuore
PUCVA6 — Pubblicazioni. Centro di Studi per la Citogenetica Vegetale. Consiglio Nazionale delle Ricerche
PUDCPAHM — Poona University and Deccan College Publications in Archaeology and History of Maharashtra
PUDOC Annu Rep — PUDOC [*Centre for Agricultural Publishing and Documentation*] Annual Report
PUDOC (Cent Landbouwpubl Landbouwdoc) Literatuuroverz — PUDOC (Centrum voor Landbouwpublikaties en Landbouwdocumentatie) Literatuuroverzicht
Puebl Indig Educ — Pueblos Indigenas y Educacion
PUEE — Publications. Universite de l'Etat a Elisabethville
Puer Rico — Puerto Rico Libre
Puerto Rico Agric Exp Sta Annual Rep — Puerto Rico Agricultural Experiment Station. Annual Report
Puerto Rico Agric Exp Sta Rep — Puerto Rico Agricultural Experiment Station. Report
Puerto Rico Bus R — Puerto Rico Business Review
Puerto Rico Dept Indus Research Bull — Puerto Rico. Department of Industrial Research. Bulletin
Puerto Rico J Publ Hlth — Puerto Rico Journal of Public Health and Tropical Medicine
Puerto Rico Univ Agr Expt Sta Tech Paper — Puerto Rico University. Agricultural Experiment Station. Technical Paper
Puerto Rico Water Resources Authority Water Resources Bull — Puerto Rico. Water Resources Authority. Water Resources Bulletin
PUF — Pluimveehouderij
PUF — Presses Universitaires de France
PUF — Public Utilities Fortnightly
PU Fort — Public Utilities Fortnightly
PUG — Porzellan und Glas
PUG — Przeglad Ustawodawstwa Gospodarczego
PUG — Publications. Universite de Grenoble
Puget Snd — Puget Sound Business Journal
Puget Sound Mar Sta Publ — Puget Sound Marine Station Publications
Puglia Chir — Puglia Chirurgica
Puglia Paleocrist — Puglia Paleocristiana
PUH — Purchasing
PUHS — Proceedings. Unitarian Historical Society
PUI — Public Interest
PUIAA7 — Atas. Instituto de Micologia da Universidade Federal de Pernambuco
PUJ/U — Universitas. Pontificia Universitates Javeriana. Facultad de Derecho y CienciasSocioeconomicas
PUKOD — Puresutoresuto Konkurito
PUL — Public Ledger
PULC — Princeton University. Library. Chronicle
PULC — Princeton University Literary Chronicle
Pulk Obs Pb — Publications de l'Observatoire Central Nicolas
Pull Groupe Etud Rythmes Biol — Bulletin. Groupe d'Etude des Rythmes Biologiques
Pulm Hypertens Proc Int Symp — Pulmonary Hypertension. Proceedings. International Symposium on Pulmonary Circulation
Pulm Macrophage Epithelial Cells Proc Annu Hanford Biol Symp — Pulmonary Macrophage and Epithelial Cells. Proceedings. Annual Hanford Biology Symposium
Pulm Pharm — Pulmonary Pharmacology
Pulm Pharmacol — Pulmonary Pharmacology
Pulm Pharmacol & Ther — Pulmonary Pharmacology and Therapeutics
Pulm Pharmacol Ther — Pulmonary Pharmacology and Therapeutics
Pulm Surfactant Biochem Funct Regul Clin Concepts — Pulmonary Surfactant. Biochemical, Functional, Regulatory, and Clinical Concepts
Pulp & Pa — Pulp and Paper
Pulp & Pa Can — Pulp and Paper Magazine of Canada [*Later, Pulp and Paper (Canada)*]
Pulp and Pap (Can) — Pulp and Paper (Canada)
Pulp & Pap Eng — Pulp and Paper Engineering
Pulping Conf Proc — Pulping Conference. Proceedings

Pulp Pap — Pulp and Paper

Pulp Pap & Board — Pulp, Paper, and Board

Pulp Pap Board — Pulp, Paper, Board

Pulp Pap (Can) — Pulp and Paper (Canada)

Pulp Paper Mag Can — Pulp and Paper Magazine of Canada [*Later, Pulp and Paper (Canada)*]

Pulp Paper Manual Can — Pulp and Paper Manual of Canada

Pulp Pap Eur — Pulp and Paper Europe

Pulp Pap Ind — Pulp and Paper Industry

Pulp Pap Ind Corros Probl Int Semin — Pulp and Paper Industry Corrosion Problems. International Seminar on Pulp and Paper Industry Corrosion Problems

Pulp Pap Ind Corros Probl Proc Int Symp Corros Pulp Pap Ind — Pulp and Paper Industry Corrosion Problems. Proceedings.International Symposium on Corrosion in the Pulp and Paper Industry

Pulp Pap Int — Pulp and Paper International

Pulp Pap Mag Can — Pulp and Paper Magazine of Canada

Pulp Pap (Sofia) — Pulp and Paper (Sofia)

Pulpudeva — Pulpudeva. Semaines Philippopolitaines de l'Histoire et de la Culture Thrace

Pulpwood Annu — Pulpwood Annual

Pulpwood Prodn — Pulpwood Production and Sawmill Logging

Pulse — Pulse. Montana State Nurses Association

PUM — Publications. University of Manchester

PUM — PW. Maandblad voor Personeelswerk en Arbeidsverhoudingen

PUM — Pytannja Ukrajins'koho Movoznavstva

PUME — Publications. University of Manchester. English Series

PUMEH — Publications. University of Manchester. Economic History Series

PUMF — Publications. University of Manchester. French Series

PUMG — Publications. University of Manchester. Germanic Series

PUMH — Publications. University of Manchester. Historical Series

Pumpen & Verdichter Inf — Pumpen und Verdichter Information

Pump Eng (Tokyo) — Pump Engineering (Tokyo)

Pumps — Pumps-Pompes-Pumpen

Pumps Their Appl — Pumps and Their Applications

PUMRL — Purdue University. Monographs in Romance Languages

PUMSE — Publications. University of Manchester. School of Education

PUMT — Publications. University of Manchester. Theological Series

PUMTA — Trace Substances in Environmental Health

Punime Mat — Punime Matematike

Punjab Fruit J — Punjab Fruit Journal

Punjab Govt Gaz — Punjab Government Gazette

Punjab Hortic J — Punjab Horticultural Journal

Punjab Irrig Res Inst Annu Rep — Punjab Irrigation Research Institute. Annual Report

Punjab Irrig Res Inst Mem — Punjab Irrigation Research Institute. Memoirs

Punjab Irrig Res Inst Res Publ — Punjab Irrigation Research Institute. Research Publication

Punjab Irrig Res Lab Mem — Punjab Irrigation Research Laboratory. Memoirs

Punjab Med J — Punjab Medical Journal

Punjabrao Krishi Vidyapeeth Coll Agric (Nagpur) Mag — Punjabrao Krishi Vidyapeeth. College of Agriculture (Nagpur). Magazine

Punjabrao Krishi Vidyapeeth Res J — Punjabrao Krishi Vidyapeeth. Research Journal

Punjab Univ Bot Publ — Punjab University Botanical Publication

Punjab Univ J Math (Lahore) — Punjab University. Journal of Mathematics (Lahore)

Punjab Univ J Zool — Punjab University Journal of Zoology

Punjab U Res Bull A — Punjab University Research Bulletin (Arts)

Punj Med J — Punjab Medical Journal

PUnP — Poitiers. Universite. Publications

PuO — Public Opinion

P U Otago M — Proceedings. University of Otago Medical School

PUP — Papsturkunden in Portugal

PUP — Pulp and Paper

PuP — Purchas His Pilgrimes, containing a history of the world in sea voyages and lande travels by Englishmen and others. Samuel Purchas

PUQ — Public Relations Quarterly

PUR — Public Utilities Reports

PUR — Purchasing

Pur A Chem — Pure and Applied Chemistry

Pur A Geoph — Pure and Applied Geophysics

PURBA — Panjab University. Research Bulletin (Arts)

Purch Adm — Purchasing Administration

Purchasing — Purchasing World

Purch Prof — Purchasing Professional

Purch (S Afr) — Purchasing (South Africa)

Purdue Ag — Purdue Agriculturist

Purdue Agric Econ Rep Purdue Univ Coop Ext Serv — Purdue Agricultural Economics Report. Purdue University. Cooperative Extension Service

Purdue Air Qual Conf Proc — Purdue Air Quality Conference. Proceedings

Purdue Ind Waste Conf Proc — Purdue Industrial Waste Conference. Proceedings

Purdue Univ Agric Exp Stn Circ — Purdue University. Agricultural Experiment Station. Circular

Purdue Univ Agric Exp Stn Ext Bull — Purdue University. Agricultural Experiment Station. Extension Bulletin

Purdue Univ Agric Exp Stn Ext Leafl — Purdue University. Agricultural Experiment Station. Extension Leaflet

Purdue Univ Agric Exp Stn Insp Rep — Purdue University. Agricultural Experiment Station. Inspection Report

Purdue Univ Agric Exp Stn Res Bull — Purdue University. Agricultural Experiment Station. Research Bulletin

Purdue Univ Agric Exp Stn Res Prog Rep — Purdue University. Agricultural Experiment Station. Research ProgressReport

Purdue Univ Agric Exp Stn Res Stn Circ — Purdue University. Agricultural Experiment Station. Station Circular

Purdue Univ Agric Exp Stn Stn Bull — Purdue University. Agricultural Experiment Station. Station Bulletin

Purdue Univ Agric Ext Serv Ext Bull — Purdue University. Agricultural Extension Service. Extension Bulletin

Purdue Univ Agric Ext Serv Ext Leaflet — Purdue University. Agricultural Extension Service. Extension Leaflet

Purdue Univ Dept Agr Ext Mimeo AY — Purdue University. Department of Agricultural Extension. Mimeo AY

Purdue Univ Eng Bull Eng Ext Ser — Purdue University. Engineering Bulletin. Engineering Extension Series

Purdue Univ Eng Bull Ext Ser — Purdue University. Engineering Bulletin. Extension Series

Purdue Univ Eng Exp Sta Res Bull — Purdue University. Engineering Experiment Station. Research Bulletin

Purdue Univ Eng Ext Ser — Purdue University. Engineering Extension Series

Purdue Univ Ext Publ — Purdue University. Extension Publications

Purdue Univ Sch Aeronaut Astronaut Eng Sci Res Proj — Purdue University. School of Aeronautics, Astronautics, and Engineering Sciences. Research Project

Purdue Univ Sch Civ Eng Publ CE-MAT — Purdue University. School of Civil Engineering. Publication CE-MAT

Purdue Univ Water Resources Research Center Tech Rept — Purdue University. Water Resources Research Center. Technical Report

Purdue Univ Water Resour Res Cent Tech Rep — Purdue University. Water Resources Research Center. Technical Report

Pure and Appl Chem — Pure and Applied Chemistry

Pure and Appl Geophys — Pure and Applied Geophysics

Pure and Appl Math — Pure and Applied Mathematics

Pure Appl Chem — Pure and Applied Chemistry

Pure Appl Cryog — Pure and Applied Cryogenics

Pure Appl Geophys — Pure and Applied Geophysics

Pure Appl Math — Pure and Applied Mathematics

Pure Appl Opt — Pure and Applied Optics

Pure Appl Phys — Pure and Applied Physics

Pure Chem Daiichi — Pure Chemicals Daiichi

Pure Math Manuscript — Pure Mathematics Manuscript

Pure Prod — Pure Products

PURMA — Purasuchikku Materiaru

PUS — Papsturkunden in Spanien

PUS — Przeglad Ubezpieczen Spolecznych

PUSA — Perspectives USA

Pusat Penelitian Pengembangan Geol Bull — Pusat Penelitian dan Pengembangan Geologi. Bulletin

Pusat Pengembangan Teknol Miner Bul — Pusat Pengembangan Teknologi Mineral. Buletin

Pusat Pengembangan Teknol Miner Penerbitan Tek — Pusat Pengembangan Teknologi Mineral. Penerbitan Teknik

Pusat Penyelidikan Getah Malays J Sains — Pusat Penyelidikan Getah Malaysia. Jurnal Sains

PUSC — Pubblicazioni. Universita Cattolica del Sacro Cuore

PUSM — Papiri. Universita degli Studi di Milano

PUSNM — Proceeding. United States National Museum

Pustyni SSSR Ih Osvoenie — Pustyni SSSR i ih Osvoenie

PUSU — Urban Studies

Puti Povysh Intensivn Prod Fotosint — Puti Povysheniya Intensivnosti i Produktivnosti Fotosinteza

Puti Povysh Intensivn Prod Fotosint Resp Mezhved Sb — Puti Povysheniya Intensivnosti i Produktivnosti Fotosinteza Respublikanskii Mezhvedomstvennyi Sbornik

Puti Povysh Urozhainosti Polevykh Kult — Puti Povysheniya Urozhainosti Polevykh Kul'tur

Puti Sint Izyskaniya Protivoopukholevykh Prep — Puti Sinteza i Izyskaniya Protivoopukholevykh Preparatov

Putnam — Putnam's Monthly Magazine

Putnams M — Putnam's Magazine

PUTQ — University of Toronto Quarterly

PUV — Pulp and Paper

PuW — Poesie und Wissenschaft

PUZBAR — Bulletin. Department of Zoology. University of the Panjab. New Series

Puzzles Electroweak Scale Proc Int Warsaw Meet Elem Part Phys — Puzzles on the Electroweak Scale. Proceedings. International Warsaw Meeting on Elementary Particle Physics

PV — Pacific Viewpoint

PV — Periodieke Verzameling van Administratieve en Rechterlijke BeslissingenBetreffende het Openbaar Bestuur in Nederland

PV — Poesia de Venezuela

PV — Poesia e Verita

PV — Povoa de Varzim

PV — Principe de Viana

PV — Problemy Vostokovedenija

PV — Protokorinthische Vasenmalerei

PV Acad Sci (Ukr) — Proces-Verbaux. Academie des Sciences (Ukraine)

PVAGA — Pochvoznanie i Agrokhimiya

PVAM — Virginia Magazine of History and Biography

PVAQ — Virginia Quarterly Review

P Vars — Papyri Varsovienses

PV Aveyron — Proces-Verbaux des Seances. Societe des Lettres, Sciences, et Arts de l'Aveyron

PVB — Jahresbericht. Philologischer Verein zu Berlin

PVBC — Povoa de Varzim. Boletim Cultural

PVBPA — Proceedings of Vibration Problems

PVBRDX — Pesquisa Veterinaria Brasileira

PVC — Points de Vente. Le Magazine des Magasins

PVCP — Victorian Poetry
PVCS — Victorian Studies
PVG — Personalvertretungsgesetz
PVIM — Pedro Vitorino. In Memoriam
PvJ — Paleis van Justitie. Nieuwsblad Gewijd aan Binnen- en BuitenlandseRechtspleging
PVL — Povest' Vremennych Let
PVM — Problemy Vostokovedeniia. Akademiia Nauk SSSR (Moscow)
PVP — Modern Paint and Coatings
PVR — Platte Valley Review
PV Rapp Reun Tech Union Int Prot Nat — Proces-Verbaux et Rapports de la Reunion Technique. UnionInternationale pour la Protection de la Nature
PVS — Politische Vierteljahresschrift
PVS — Proceedings. Virgil Society
PVSCA — Proceedings. Veterans Administration Spinal Cord Injury Conference
PVSCD5 — Perspectives in Vertebrate Science
P-V Seances Com Int Poids Mes — Proces-Verbaux des Seances. Comite International des Poids et Mesures
P-V Seances Soc Sci Phys Nat Bord — Proces-Verbaux des Seances. Societe des Sciences Physiques et Naturellesde Bordeaux
P-V Seances Soc Sci Phys Nat Bordeaux — Proces-Verbaux des Seances. Societe des Sciences Physiques et Naturelles de Bordeaux
PVSLSAA — Proces-Verbaux de la Societe des Lettres, Sciences, et Arts de l'Aveyron
P V Soc Linn Bordeaux — Proces-Verbaux. Societe Linneenne de Bordeaux
PVTG — Pseudepigrapha Veteris Testamenti Graece
PVTM — Victimology
PVTMA — Preventive Medicine
PVU — PR Revue. Schweizerische Zeitschrift fuer Public Relations
PV Ue — Pariser Verbandsuebereinkunft zum Schutze des Gewerblichen Eigentums
PVUM — Publications. Victoria University of Manchester
PVUMH — Publications. Victoria University of Manchester. Historical Series
PVZTA — Plyn
PW — Paedagogische Welt
PW — Pension World
PW — Philologische Wochenschrift
PW — Poetry Wales
PW — Protestant World
PW — Publishers' Weekly
PWA — Polish Western Affairs
PWAF — World Affairs
PWAR — World Archaeology
PWA Rep — PWA. Report fuer Mitarbeiter und Freunde der Papierwerke "Waldhof-Aschaffenburg"
P Warren — Warren Papyri
PWAS — Washingtonian
PWBQ — Wilson Quarterly
PWBU — Wilson Bulletin
PWCJS — Proceedings. Fifth World Congress of Jewish Studies
PWCLA — Proceedings. World Congress for the Lay Apostolate
P'well — Planwell
P West Ph S — Proceedings. Western Pharmacology Society
PWFK — Western Folklore
PWFND — Publikationen zu Wissenschaftlichen Filmen. Sektion Technische Wissenschaften. Naturwissenschaften
PWFU — World Futures
PWG — Propylaeen-Weltgeschichte
PWHQ — Western Historical Quarterly
PWHS — Proceedings. Wesley Historical Society
PWJR — WJR. Washington Journalism Review
PWLT — World Literature Today
PWMBJ — Populaer-Wissenschaftliche Monatsblaetter zur Belehrung ueber das Judentum
PWMC — Proceedings. World Muslim Conference
PWMIB — Powder Metallurgy International
PWMO — World Monitor
PWMQ — William and Mary Quarterly
PWN — Panstwowe Wydawnictwo Naukowe
PWN — Patna Weekly Notes
PWN — Polskie Wydawnictwe Naukowe
PWNE — Women and Environments
PWNH — Women and Health

PWOM — Working Mother
PWOQD — Psychology of Women Quarterly
PWP — Parliamentary White Paper
PWPMA — Politechnika Warszawska, Prace Naukowe. Mechanika
PWPQ — Western Political Quarterly
PWR — Punjab Weekly Reporter
P W Rev — Price Waterhouse Review
Pwr Fmg — Power Farming
Pwr Fmg Aust NZ — Power Farming in Australia and New Zealand and Better Farming Digest
Pwr Fmg Mag — Power Farming Magazine
Pwr Frmg — Power Farming in Australia and New Zealand
Pwr Frmg Aust NZ — Power Farming in Australia and New Zealand
Pwr Wks Engng — Power and Works Engineering
PWsp — Przeglad Wspotczesny
PWSU — Women's Studies
PWT — Panstwowe Wydawnictwo Techniczne
PWTCA — Powder Technology
PWTN — Prace Wroclawskie Towarzystwo Naukowe Wroclaw
PWTN-A — Prace Wroclawskiego Towarzystwa Naukowego. A
P Wuerzb — Mitteilungen aus der Wuerzburger Papyrussammlung
PXPA — Journal of Experimental Psychology. Animal Behavior Processes
PXPG — Journal of Experimental Psychology. General
PXPH — Journal of Experimental Psychology. Human Perception and Performance
PXPL — Journal of Experimental Psychology. Learning, Memory, and Cognition
PYA — Pensamiento y Accion
PYACA — Psychoanalytic Study of the Child
PYAFB — Psychologia Africana
PYAIA — Postepy Astronomii
PYB — Palestine Year Book
PYB — Problems of Economics. A Journal of Translations
PyC — Pueblo y Cultura
PYCHB — Psychology
PYCOA — Phycologia
PYE — Politica y Espiritu
Pyelonephritis Hahnenklee Symp — Pyelonephritis. Hahnenklee-Symposion
PYFS — Yale French Studies
Pyke — Pyke's Lower Canada King's Bench Reports
Pyke LC — Pyke's Lower Canada King's Bench Reports
Pyke's R — Pyke's Lower Canada King's Bench Reports
PYMOA — Psychological Monographs. General and Applied
PYNNA — Psychiatria, Neurologia, Neurochirurgia
PYNS — Youth and Society
PYPYB — Psychophysiology (Baltimore)
Py R — Pyke's Lower Canada King's Bench Reports
Pyr — Pyrenees. Cahiers des Lettres et des Arts
PYRCA — Psychological Record
Pyridine Its Deriv — Pyridine and Its Derivatives
PYRTA — Psychological Reports
PYSCB — Psychology in the Schools
PYSOA — Physiologist
PYSSB — Psychoanalytic Study of Society
PYTCA — Phytochemistry
PZ — Partiinaya Zhizn
PZ — Phytopathologische Zeitschrift
PZ — Praehistorische Zeitschrift
PZ — Przeglad Zachodni
PZBUA — Przeglad Budowlany
PZE — Pamietniki Zjazdow Polskiego Zwiazku Entomologicznego
PZELA — Przeglad Elektrotechniczny
PZKA — Philologus. Zeitschrift fuer Klassische Altertum
PZKP — Philologus. Zeitschrift fuer Klassische Philologie
PZL — Praehistorische Zeitschrift (Leipzig and Berlin)
PZLSA — Prace z Zakresu Lesnictwa
PZM — Pod Znamenem Marksizma
PZMEA — Przeglad Mechaniczny
PZS — Proceedings. Zoological Society
PZS — Przeglad Zagadnien Socjalnych
PZSC — Proceedings of the Zoological Society (Calcutta)
PZTFD — Pis'ma v Zhurnal Tekhnicheskoi Fiziki
PZ Wiss — PZ (Pharmazeutische Zeitung) Wissenschaft
PZWS — Panstwowe Zaklady Wydawnictwo Szkolnych
PZYG — Zygon

Q

Q — Quadragesms [*Year Books of Edward III*]
Q — Quadrivium
Q — Queen's Quarterly
Q — Quest
Q — Quinzaine
QA — Quimera
Q Abh Mittelrh Kg — Quellen und Abhandlungen zur Mittelrheinischen Kirchengeschichte
Q Abstr Ont Vet Coll — Quarterly Abstracts. Ontario Veterinary College
QAC — Quebec Appeal Cases
QACC Mot Trader — QACC [*Queensland Automobile Chamber of Commerce*] Motor Trader
Qad — Qadmonijot/Qadmoniot. Quarterly for the Antiquities of Eretz-Israel and Biblical Land
Qadmoniot Q Ant Eretz Israel & Bibl Lands — Qadmoniot. Quarterly for the Antiquities of Eretz Israel and Biblical Lands
QAGAF — Quellen und Abhandlungen zur Geschichte der Abtei und der Dioezese Fulda
Q Ag J — Queensland Agricultural Journal
QAGSP — Quellen und Abhandlungen zur Geschichte des Schweizerischen Protestantismus
QAIC — Quarterly. Art Institute of Chicago
QAL — Quaderni di Archeologia della Libia
QAMAA — Quarterly of Applied Mathematics
Q Am Petrol Inst — Quarterly. American Petroleum Institute [*New York*]
Q Am Primrose Soc — Quarterly of the American Primrose Society [*Portland*]
QA Mrh K — Quellen und Abhandlungen zur Mittelrheinischen Kirchengeschichte
Q and Q — Quill and Quire
Qantara — Al-Qantara. Revista de Estudios Arabes
Qantas — Quantas Empire Airways
Qantas E Air — Qantas Empire Airways
QAP — Department of Antiquities in Palestine. Quarterly
Q Ap Math — Quarterly of Applied Mathematics
Q Appl Math — Quarterly of Applied Mathematics
Q App Math — Quarterly of Applied Mathematics
QAR — Quaderni di Archeologia Reggiana
QASRG — Quellen und Abhandlungen zur Schweizerischen Reformationsgeschichte
Q Assoc Lig Arch Stor Nav — Quaderni. Associazione Ligure di Archeologia e Storia Navale
Qatar Univ Sci Bull — Qatar University. Science Bulletin
Qatar Univ Sci J — Qatar University Science Journal
Q Bar News — Queensland Bar News
QBCB — Quarterly Bulletin of Chinese Bibliography
QBCDP — Quarterly Bibliography of Computers and Data Processing
QBib — Quarterly Bibliography of Computers and Data Processing
Q Bibliogr Comput Data Process — Quarterly Bibliography of Computers and Data Processing
Q Biblphy Insectic Mater Veg Orig — Quarterly Bibliography on Insecticide Materials of Vegetable Origin [*London*]
Q Bil — Quaderni di Bilychnis
QBIR — Quarterly Printing Industry Business Indicator Report
Qbl Hist Ver Grossherzogtum Hessen — Quartalsblaetter des Historischen Vereins fuer das Grossherzogtum Hessen
QBO — Mail Advertising Service Association International. Quarterly Business Outlook
Q Bottling Suppl — Quarterly Bottling Supplement
QBSAL — Quarterly Bulletin of the South African Library
Q Building Yrbk — Queensland Building Yearbook
Q Bull Aeronaut Labs Ottawa — Quarterly Bulletin. Aeronautical Laboratories. National Research Council (Ottawa)
Q Bull Agric Statist Ottawa — Quarterly Bulletin of Agricultural Statistics (Ottawa)
Q Bull Alp Gdn Soc — Quarterly Bulletin. Alpine Garden Society
Q Bull Amer Inst Architects — Quarterly Bulletin of the American Institute of Architects
Q Bull Am Inst Archit — Quarterly Bulletin of the American Institute of Architects [*Washington*]
Q Bull Am Rhodod Soc — Quarterly Bulletin. American Rhododendron Society
Q Bull Ass Fd Drug Off (US) — Quarterly Bulletin. Association of Food and Drug Officials (United States)
Q Bull Assoc Food Drug Off — Quarterly Bulletin. Association of Food and Drug Officials
Q Bull Assoc Food Drug Off US — Quarterly Bulletin. Association of Food and Drug Officials of the United States[*Later, Quarterly Bulletin. Association of Food and Drug Officials*]

Q Bull Br Natn Carnation Soc — Quarterly Bulletin. British National Carnation Society
Q Bull Br Psychol Soc — Quarterly Bulletin of the British Psychological Society
Q Bull Br Refract Res Ass — Quarterly Bulletin. British Refractories Research Association [*Stoke-on-Trent*]
Q Bull Bur Publ Wks Philipp Isl — Quarterly Bulletin. Bureau of Public Works. Philippine Islands [*Manila*]
Q Bull Calif St Bd Hlth — Quarterly Bulletin. California State Board of Health [*Sacramento*]
Q Bull Can Engng Stand Ass — Quarterly Bulletin. Canadian Engineering Standards Association [*Ottawa*]
Q Bull Can Min Inst — Quarterly Bulletin. Canadian Mining Institute [*Ottawa*]
Q Bull Cent Bd Irrig India — Quarterly Bulletin. Central Board of Irrigation. India
Q Bull Chicago Vet Coll — Quarterly Bulletin. Chicago Veterinary College
Q Bull Coal Statist Eur — Quarterly Bulletin of Coal Statistics for Europe [*Geneva*]
Q Bull Coke Oven Mgrs Ass — Quarterly Bulletin. Coke Oven Managers' Association
Q Bull Comm Aer Surv Forests — Quarterly Bulletin. Committee on Aerial Survey of Forests [*London*]
Q Bull Coun Coord Int Congr Med Sci — Quarterly Bulletin. Council for the Co-ordination of International Congresses of Medical Sciences [*Paris*]
Q Bull Del St Bd Agric — Quarterly Bulletin. Delaware State Board of Agriculture [*Dover*]
Q Bull Dep Agric Calif — Quarterly Bulletin. Department of Agriculture. California
Q Bull Dep Agric Zanzibar — Quarterly Bulletin. Department of Agriculture. Zanzibar
Q Bull Dep Publ Hlth Nova Scotia — Quarterly Bulletin of the Department of Public Health. Nova Scotia [*Halifax*]
Q Bull Diesel Eng Us Ass — Quarterly Bulletin. Diesel Engine Users' Association [*London*]
Q Bull Dir Gen Med Servs RAF — Quarterly Bulletin. Director General of Medical Services. R.A.F
Q Bull Fac Sci Tehran Univ — Quarterly Bulletin. Faculty of Science. Tehran University
Q Bull Fac Sci Univ Tehran — Quarterly Bulletin. Faculty of Science. University of Tehran
Q Bull Geo-Heat Util Cent — Quarterly Bulletin. Geo-Heat Utilization Center
Q Bull Health Organ League Nations — Quarterly Bulletin. Health Organisation. League of Nations
Q Bull IAALD — Quarterly Bulletin. International Association of Agricultural Librarians and Documentalists
Q Bull Indiana Univ Med Cent — Quarterly Bulletin. Indiana University. Medical Center
Q Bull Instn Engrs Aust — Quarterly Bulletin of the Institution of Engineers. Australia [*Sydney*]
Q Bull Int Ass Agric Libr — Quarterly Bulletin. International Association of Agricultural Librarians and Documentalists
Q Bull Int Assoc Agric Libr & Doc — Quarterly Bulletin. International Association of Agricultural Librarians and Documentalists
Q Bull Int Assoc Agric Libr Doc Bull Trimest Assoc Int Bibl — Quarterly Bulletin. International Association of Agricultural Librarians and Documentalists/ Bulletin Trimestriel (Association Internationale des Bibliothecaires et Documentalistes Agricoles)
Q Bull Irish Georg Soc — Quarterly Bulletin of the Irish Georgian Society
Q Bull Kans Cy SW Clin Soc — Quarterly Bulletin. Kansas City Southwest Clinical Society
Q Bull KGF Min Metall Soc — Quarterly Bulletin of the K. G. F. Mining and Metallurgical Society [*Ooregum*]
Q Bull La Bd Hlth — Quarterly Bulletin. Louisiana Board of Health [*New Orleans*]
Q Bull Me Dep Agric — Quarterly Bulletin. Maine Department of Agriculture [*Orono*]
Q Bull Med Supts Soc — Quarterly Bulletin. Medical Superintendents Society [*London*]
Q Bull Mich St Univ Agric Exp Stn — Quarterly Bulletin. Michigan State University. Agricultural Experiment Station
Q Bull Miss St Pl Bd — Quarterly Bulletin of the Mississippi State Plant Board [*Jackson*]
Q Bull Mon Auth Sing — Quarterly Bulletin. Monetary Authority of Singapore
Q Bull Natl Res Counc Can Div Mech Eng — Quarterly Bulletin. National Research Council of Canada. Division of MechanicalEngineering
Q Bull Natn Chrysanth Soc — Quarterly Bulletin of the National Chrysanthemum Society [*London*]
Q Bull New Hamps Bd Hlth — Quarterly Bulletin. New Hampshire Board of Health [*Concord*]
Q Bull Northwest Univ Med Sch — Quarterly Bulletin. Northwestern University. Medical School

Q Bull NWest Univ Med Sch — Quarterly Bulletin. Northwestern University. Medical School
Q Bull NY Cy Dep Hlth — Quarterly Bulletin of the New York City Department of Health
Q Bull Ohio St Bd Hlth — Quarterly Bulletin. Ohio State Board of Health [Columbus]
Q Bull Publ Hlth Sect R Coll Nurs — Quarterly Bulletin. Public Health Section and Occupational Health Section. Royal College of Nursing [London]
Q Bull Rhode Isl Bd Hlth — Quarterly Bulletin of the Rhode Island Board of Health [Providence]
Q Bull R Vict Inst Archit — Quarterly Bulletin. Royal Victorian Institute of Architects [Melbourne]
Q Bull S Afr Libr — Quarterly Bulletin. South African Library
Q Bull S Afr Natl Gall — Quarterly Bulletin. South African National Gallery
Q Bull S Aust Inst Archit — Quarterly Bulletin. South Australian Institute of Architects [Adelaide]
Q Bull Sea Fish Statist Ottawa — Quarterly Bulletin of Sea Fisheries Statistics (Ottawa)
Q Bull Sea View Hosp — Quarterly Bulletin. Sea View Hospital
Q Bull Solar Activ — Quarterly Bulletin on Solar Activity. International Astronomical Union [Zurich]
Q Bull S Pacif Commn — Quarterly Bulletin. South Pacific Commission [Noumea]
Q Bull Steel Statist Eur — Quarterly Bulletin of Steel Statistics for Europe [Geneva]
Q Bull St Louis Coll Pharm — Quarterly Bulletin of St. Louis College of Pharmacy [St. Louis]
Q Bull Sulphur Explor Synd — Quarterly Bulletin. Sulphur Exploration Syndicate [London]
Q Bull Timb Statist — Quarterly Bulletin of Timber Statistics [Geneva]
Q Bull Univ Hawaii — Quarterly Bulletin. University of Hawaii [Honolulu]
Q Bull Va Game Fish Prot Ass — Quarterly Bulletin. Virginia Game and Game Fish Protective Association [Richmond]
Q Bull Va St Crop Pest Commn — Quarterly Bulletin of the Virginia State Crop Pest Commission [Blacksburg]
Q Bull Vt St Med Soc — Quarterly Bulletin. Vermont State Medical Society [St. Johnsbury]
Q Bull Wash Univ Med Dep — Quarterly Bulletin. Washington University Medical Department
Q Bull Wat Resour Mich — Quarterly Bulletin of the Water Resources. Michigan
Q Bull W Va St Dep Hlth — Quarterly Bulletin. West Virginia State Department of Health
QC — Quaderni Catanesi di Studi Classici e Medievali
QC — Quaderni della Critica
QC — Quinzaine Critique
Q Can Studies — Quarterly of Canadian Studies
QCAR — Queensland Criminal Reports
Q Case Note — Queensland Law Reporter Case Note
QCBS — Quarterly Check-List of Biblical Studies
QCC — Quaderni di Cultura Contemporanea
Q Census & Statistics Bul — Australia. Commonwealth Bureau of Census and Statistics. Queensland Office. Bulletin
Q Chicago Med Sch — Quarterly. Chicago Medical School
Q Circ — Quarterly Circular [London]
Q Circ Br WatWks Ass — Quarterly Circular. British Waterworks Association [London]
Q Circ Ceylon Rubb Res Scheme — Quarterly Circular. Ceylon Rubber Research Scheme [Peradeniya]
Q Circ Munic WatWks Ass — Quarterly Circular of the Municipal Waterworks Association
Q Circ Rubber Res Inst Ceylon — Quarterly Circular. Rubber Research Institute of Ceylon
Q Circ Rubb Res Inst Ceylon — Quarterly Circular. Rubber Research Institute of Ceylon [Colombo]
Q Circ Tea Res Inst E Afr — Quarterly Circular. Tea Research Institute of East Africa [Kericho]
QCJ — Quality Circles Journal
Qckslv — Quicksilver Times
QCL — Queensland Conveyancing Library
QCLBS — Quarterly Check-List of Biblical Studies
QCLCS — Quarterly Checklist of Classical Studies
Q Climat Rev Philipp Isl — Quarterly Climatological Review. Climatological Division. Weather Bureau. Philippine Islands [Manila]
QCLLR — Queensland Crown Lands Law Reports
QCLM — Quarterly Checklist of Medievalia
QCLRS — Quarterly Check-List of Renaissance Studies
QCOA — QCOA: Journal of the Queensland Council on the Ageing
Q Coal Rpt — Quarterly Coal Report
Q Colorado Sch Mines — Quarterly. Colorado School of Mines
Q Colo Sch Mines — Quarterly. Colorado School of Mines
Q Contain Packag Ind Rep — Quarterly Containers and Packaging Industry Reports [Washington]
Q Coop — Queensland Co-Operator
Q Countrywoman — Queensland Countrywoman
QCR — Quality Control Reports: the Gold Sheet
QCR — Queensland Criminal Reports
Q Crit — Quaderni della Critica
QCS — Quaderni. Centro di Studi sulla Deportazione e l'Internamento
QCSMA — Quarterly. Colorado School of Mines
QCSS — Quaderni di Cultura e Storia Sociale
Q Cult Triangle UNESCO Sri Lanka Proj — Quarterly of the Cultural Triangle. UNESCO-Sri Lanka Project
Q Cum Index Curr Med Lit — Quarterly Cumulative Index to Current Medical Literature [Chicago]
Q Cum Index Med — Quarterly Cumulative Index Medicus
QCVL — Quellen zum Christlichen Verstaendnis der Liebe

QD — Quaderni Dannunziani
QDA — Quarterly. Department of Antiquities in Palestine
Qd Ag J — Queensland Agricultural Journal
Qd Agric J — Queensland Agricultural Journal
QDAJ — Quarterly. Department of Antiquities of Jordan
QDAP — Quarterly. Department of Antiquities in Palestine
QDAP — Quarterly Journal. Department of Antiquities in Palestine
QDA Pal — Quarterly. Department of Antiquities in Palestine
Qd Bur Invest Tech Bull — Queensland. Department of Public Lands. Bureau of Investigation. Technical Bulletin
Qd Bur Sug Exp Stat Tech Commun — Queensland. Bureau of Sugar Experiment Stations. Technical Communication
Qd Bur Sug Exp Stn Tech Commun — Queensland. Bureau of Sugar Experiment Stations. Technical Communication
QdC — Quaderni della Critica
QDC — Questions Diplomatiques et Coloniales
Qd Chamber Manufacturers Yb — Queensland Chamber of Manufacturers. Yearbook
Qd Dent J — Queensland Dental Journal
Qd Dent Mag — Queensland Dental Magazine
QDEA — Questions Douanieres, Economiques, et Agricoles [Alexandria, Egypt]
QDEKR — Quellen des Deutschen Evangelischen Kirchenrechts
Q Dent Rev — Quarterly Dental Review
Q Dept Ant Palestine — Quarterly of the Department of Antiquities in Palestine
Qd For Dep Adv Leafl — Queensland. Department of Forestry. Advisory Leaflet
Qd For Dep Pamph — Queensland. Department of Forestry. Pamphlet
Qd Forest Bull — Queensland Forest Bulletin
Qd Geogr J — Queensland Geographical Journal
Qd Geol Surv 1:250 000 Geol Ser — Queensland. Geological Survey. 1:250,000 Geological Series
Qd Geol Surv Rep — Queensland. Geological Survey. Report
Qd Govt Min J — Queensland Government Mining Journal
Qd Heritage — Queensland Heritage
QDI — Questioni Disputate
Q Dig Curr Asph Lit — Quarterly Digest of Current Asphalt Literature [New York]
Q Digger — Queensland Digger
Q Dig Rec Res Forest Mgmt Forest Prod — Quarterly Digest of Recent Research in Forest Management and Forest Products [College Station, Texas]
Qd J Agric Anim Sci — Queensland Journal of Agricultural and Animal Sciences
Qd J Agric Sci — Queensland Journal of Agricultural Science [Later, Queensland Journal of Agricultural and Animal Sciences]
Qd L — Queensland Lawyer
Qd Nat — Queensland Naturalist
Qd Prod — Queensland Producer
Qd R — Queensland Reports
QdS — Quaderni di Storia
Qd Surv — Queensland Surveyor
Qd Univ Agric Dep Pap — University of Queensland. Agriculture Department. Papers
Qd Univ Bot Dep Pap — University of Queensland. Botany Department. Papers
Qd Univ Civ Engng Dep Bull — University of Queensland. Department of Civil Engineering. Bulletin
Qd Univ Comput Centre Pap — University of Queensland. Computer Centre. Papers
Qd Univ Ent Dep Pap — University of Queensland. Entomology Department. Papers
Qd Univ Fac Vet Sci Pap — University of Queensland. Faculty of Veterinary Science. Papers
Qd Univ Geol Dep Pap — University of Queensland. Geology Department. Papers
Qd Univ Pap Zool Dep — University of Queensland. Zoology Department. Papers
Qd Univ Zool Dep Pap — University of Queensland. Zoology Department. Papers
Qd Vet Proc — Queensland Veterinary Proceedings
QE — Quaderni Esegetici
QE — Quantum Electronics
QeA — Questo e Alto
QEBG — Quellen und Eroerterungen zur Bayerischen Geschichte
Q Econ Comment — Quarterly Economic Commentary
Q Economic Rev of UK — Quarterly Economic Review of the United Kingdom
Q Econ R — Quarterly Economic Review
Q Econ Rev Algeria — Quarterly Economic Review of Algeria
Q Econ Rev Chile — Quarterly Economic Review of Chile
Q Econ Rev Egypt — Quarterly Economic Review of Egypt
Q Econ Rev Iran — Quarterly Economic Review of Iran
Q Econ Rev Oil West Eur — Quarterly Economic Review. Oil in Western Europe
Q Econ Rev Yugoslavia — Quarterly Economic Review of Yugoslavia
Q Ed Off Gaz — Education Office Gazette. Queensland Department of Education
Q Elec Contractor — Queensland Electrical Contractor
Q Engl J Tech Assoc Refract Jpn — Quarterly English Journal. Technical Association of Refractories. Japan
Q Engng Seism Bull — Quarterly Engineering Seismology Bulletin. US Coast Guard and Geodetic Survey
QER — Quarterly Economic Review
QF — Quellen und Forschungen aus Italienischen Archiven und Bibliotheken
QF — Quellen und Forschungen zur Sprach- und Kulturgeschichte der Germanischen Voelker
QFAB — Quellen und Forschungen aus Italienischen Archiven und Bibliotheken
QFBKG — Quellen und Forschungen zur Bayerischen Kirchengeschichte
QFC — Quaderni di Filologia Classica
Q Fed St Med Bds US — Quarterly of the Federation of State Medical Boards of the United States [Easton, Pennsylvania]
QFG — Quaderni di Filologia Germanica. Facolta di Lettere e Filosofia. Universita di Bologna
QFG — Quellen und Forschungen aus dem Gebiet der Geschichte
QFGBW — Quellen und Forschungen zur Geschichte des Bistums und Hochstiftes Wuerzburg

QFGG — Quellen und Forschungen aus dem Gebiet der Geschichte

QFGLOe — Quellen und Forschungen zur Geschichte, Literatur, und Sprache Oesterreichs

QFGSHG — Quellen und Forschungen der Gesellschaft fuer Schleswig-Holsteinische Geschichte

QFGSM — Quellen und Forschungen zur Geschichte der Stadt Muenster

QFI — Quellen und Forschungen aus Italienischen Archiven und Bibliotheken

QFIAB — Quellen und Forschungen aus Italienischen Archiven und Bibliotheken

Q Film Radio TV — Quarterly of Film, Radio, and Television

QFINBL — Queensland. Department of Harbours and Marine. Fisheries Notes

QFNKW — Quellen und Forschungen zur Natur und Geschichte des Kreises Wiedenbrueck

QFR — Quarterly Financial Report

QFR — Quarterly Financial Report for Manufacturing, Mining, and Trade Companies

QFRG — Quellen und Forschungen zur Reformationsgeschichte

QFRNAV — Queensland. Department of Forestry. Research Note

QFRT — Quarterly of Film, Radio, and Television

Q Fruit & Veg News — Queensland Fruit and Vegetable News

QFSK — Quellen und Forschungen zur Sprach- und Kulturgeschichte der Germanischen Voelker

Q Fuel Effic Rep — Quarterly Fuel Efficiency Report. Ministry of Fuel and Power [London]

Q Fuel Energy Summ — Quarterly Fuel and Energy Summary

QFWG — Quellen und Forschungen zur Westfaelischen Geschichte

QGDOD — Quellen und Forschungen zur Geschichte des Dominikanerordens in Deutschland

Q Geog J — Queensland Geographical Journal

Q Geol Notes — Quarterly Geological Notes

Q Geol Notes Geol Surv South Aust — South Australia. Geological Survey. Quarterly Geological Notes

QGG — Queensland Government Gazette

QGHR — Quellen zur Geschichte des Humanismus und der Reformation in Facsimile-Ausgaben

QGIG — Queensland Government Industrial Gazette

QGJD — Quellen zur Geschichte der Juden in Deutschland

QGJDOe — Quellen und Forschungen zur Geschichte der Juden in Deutsch-Oesterreich

QGKR — Quellensammlung fuer das Geltende Kirchenrecht

QGM — Quellen und Studien zur Geschichte der Mathematik

QGMath — Quellen und Studien zur Geschichte der Mathematik

QGMJA — Queensland Government Mining Journal

QGN — Quellen und Studien zur Geschichte der Naturwissenschaften und der Medizin

Q Gov Indus Gaz — Queensland Government Industrial Gazette

Q Govt Min J — Queensland Government Mining Journal

Q Govt PRB News Bul — Queensland Government. Public Relations Bureau. News Bulletin

QGP — Queensland Government Publications

QGP — Quellenschriften zur Geschichte des Protestantismus

Q Graingrower — Queensland Graingrower

QGRKP — Quellen zur Geschichte des Roemischkanonischen Prozesses im Mittelalter

QGT — Quellen zur Geschichte der Taeufer

QGWT — Quellen zur Geschichte der Wiedertaeufer

Q Gypsum Rep — Quarterly Gypsum Report. US Bureau of Mines [Washington]

QH — Quaker History

QH — Queensland Heritage

Q Health — Queensland's Health

Q Her — Queensland Heritage

Q Hist Soc J — Queensland Historical Society. Journal

QHKG — Quellenhefte zur Kirchengeschichte

QHR — Queensland Historical Review

QHST — Quellen-Handbuch der Systematischen Theologie

QHTA Bull — QHTA [Queensland History Teachers Association] Bulletin

QI — Quaderni d'Italianistica

QI — Quaderni Ibero-Americani

QI — Quarterly Index

QI — Questions d'Israel

QIA — Quaderni Ibero-Americani

QIBA — Quaderni Italiani di Buenos Aires

QIER J — QIER [Queensland Institute for Educational Research] Journal

QIFL — Quaderni. Istituto di Filologia Latina. Universita di Padova

QIG — Quaderni. Istituto di Glottologia

QIG — Queensland Industrial Gazette

QIGB — Quaderni. Istituto di Glottologia (Bologna)

QILCL — Quaderni. Istituto di Lingue e Litteratura Classica

Q III R Inc Archit Scotl — Quarterly Illustrated of the Royal Incorporation of Architects in Scotland

Q Illust — Quarterly Illustrator

QIMA — QIMA. Institute of Municipal Administration, Queensland Division

Q Ind — Queensland Industry

Q Industry — Queensland Industry

QIP Rep Natl Asphalt Pavement Assoc — QIP Report. National Asphalt Pavement Association

QISA — Quaderni. Istituto di Storia dell'Architettura

Q Isr Inst Metals — Quarterly. Israel Institute of Metals

QITLJ — Queensland Institute of Technology. Law Journal

QJ — Quarterly Journal. Library of Congress

QJ — Quarterly Journal. University of North Dakota

QJAAA — Queensland Journal of Agricultural and Animal Sciences

QJ Adm — Quarterly Journal of Administration

QJ Agric Econ — Quarterly Journal of Agricultural Economy

Q Japan Com'l Arb Ass'n — Quarterly. Japan Commercial Arbitration Association

QJBE — Quarterly Journal of Business and Economics

QJCA — Quarterly Journal of Current Acquisitions

Q J Chem Soc London — Quarterly Journal. Chemical Society. London

Q J Comp Legis — Quarterly Journal of Comparative Legislation

Q J Crude Drug Res — Quarterly Journal of Crude Drug Research

QJE — Quarterly Journal of Economics

Q J Econ — Quarterly Journal of Economics

QJ Eng Geol — Quarterly Journal of Engineering Geology

QJEPs — Quarterly Journal of Experimental Psychology

QJewR — Quarterly Jewish Review

QJewSt — Quarterly of Jewish Studies. Jewish Chronicle

Q J Expermntl Psychol — Quarterly Journal of Experimental Psychology

Q J Exp Physiol — Quarterly Journal of Experimental Physiology and Cognate Medical Sciences

Q J Exp Physiol Cogn Med Sci — Quarterly Journal of Experimental Physiology and Cognate Medical Sciences

Q J Exp Psy — Quarterly Journal of Experimental Psychology

Q J Exp Psychol — Quarterly Journal of Experimental Psychology

QJ Exp Psychol A — Quarterly Journal of Experimental Psychology. A. Human Experimental Psychology

QJ Exp Psychol A Hum Exp Psychol — Quarterly Journal of Experimental Psychology. A. Human Experimental Psychology

Q J Exp Psychol B — Quarterly Journal of Experimental Psychology. B. Comparative and Physiological Psychology

QJ Exp Psychol B Comp Physiol Psychol — Quarterly Journal of Experimental Psychology. B. Comparative and Physiological Psychology

Q J Fla Acad Sci — Quarterly Journal. Florida Academy of Sciences

Q J For — Quarterly Journal of Forestry

Q J Forestry — Quarterly Journal of Forestry

Q J Geol Min Metall Soc (India) — Quarterly Journal. Geological, Mining, and Metallurgical Society (India)

Q J Geol Soc — Quarterly Journal. Geological Society

Q J Geol Soc Lond — Quarterly Journal. Geological Society of London

Q J Geol Soc London — Quarterly Journal. Geological Society of London

QJGM — Quarterly Journal of the Geological Mining and Metallurgical Society of India

QJGS — Quarterly Journal. Geological Society

Q J Hist Sci Technol — Quarterly Journal of the History of Science and Technology

Q J Indian Chem Soc — Quarterly Journal. Indian Chemical Society

Q J Indian Inst Sci — Quarterly Journal. Indian Institute of Science

Q J Indones At Energy Agency — Quarterly Journal. Indonesian Atomic Energy Agency

QJ Int Agric — Quarterly Journal of International Agriculture

Q J Jpn Weld Soc — Quarterly Journal. Japan Welding Society

Q Jl Agric Econ Tokyo — Quarterly Journal of Agricultural Economy (Tokyo)

Q Jl Anthrop Kyushu — Quarterly Journal of Anthropology. Kyushu University

Q Jl Belfast Nat Fld Club — Quarterly Journal. Belfast Naturalists Field Club

Q Jl Bgham Univ Min Soc — Quarterly Journal of Birmingham University Mining Society

QJLC — Quarterly Journal. Library of Congress

Q Jl Crude Drug Res — Quarterly Journal of Crude Drug Research

Q Jl Dep Agric Beng — Quarterly Journal of the Department of Agriculture. Bengal [Calcutta]

Q Jl Engng Ass Malaya — Quarterly Journal. Engineering Association of Malaya [Kuala Lumpur]

Q Jl Exp Path — Quarterly Journal of Experimental Pathology

Q Jl Exp Physiol — Quarterly Journal of Experimental Physiology and Cognate Medical Sciences [London]

Q Jl Exp Psychol — Quarterly Journal of Experimental Psychology

Q Jl Fla Acad Sci — Quarterly Journal. Florida Academy of Sciences

Q Jl For — Quarterly Journal of Forestry [London]

Q Jl Geol Min Metall Soc India — Quarterly Journal of the Geological, Mining, and Metallurgical Society of India [Calcutta]

Q Jl Geol Soc Lond — Quarterly Journal of the Geological Society of London

Q J Lib Con — Quarterly Journal. Library of Congress

Q J Lib Congr — Quarterly Journal of the Library of Congress

Q J Lit Sci & A — Quarterly Journal of Literature, Science, and the Arts

Q J Lit Sci Arts — Quarterly Journal of Literature, Science, and the Arts

Q J Liverpool Univer Inst Commer Res Trop — Quarterly Journal. Liverpool University Institute of Commercial Research in theTropics

Q Jl Microsc Sci — Quarterly Journal of Microscopical Science

Q Jl Mysore Forest Ass — Quarterly Journal of the Mysore Forest Association

Q J Local Self Govt Inst — Quarterly Journal. Local Self-Government Institute

Q Jl Pharm Pharmac — Quarterly Journal of Pharmacy and Pharmacology [London]

Q Jl Pure Appl Math — Quarterly Journal of Pure and Applied Mathematics [London]

Q Jl R Agric Soc Kenya — Quarterly Journal. Royal Agricultural Society of Kenya [Nakuru]

Q Jl R Astr Soc — Quarterly Journal of the Royal Astronomical Society [London]

Q Jl R Inc Archit Scotl — Quarterly Journal of the Royal Incorporation of Architects in Scotland [Edinburgh]

Q Jl R Met Soc — Quarterly Journal. Royal Meteorological Society

Q Jl Rubb Res Inst Ceylon — Quarterly Journal. Rubber Research Institute of Ceylon

Q Jl Rubb Res Inst Malaya — Quarterly Journal. Rubber Research Institute of Malaya [Kuala Lumpur]

Q Jl Sci Wu Han Univ — Quarterly Journal of Science. Wu-Han University

Q Jl Seism Tokyo — Quarterly Journal of Seismology (Tokyo)

QJLSGI — Quarterly Journal. Local Self-Government Institute

QJLSI — Quarterly Journal. Local Self-Government Institute

Q Jl Soc Am Indians — Quarterly Journal. Society of American Indians [Washington]

Q Jl Stud Alcohol — Quarterly Journal of Studies on Alcohol

Q Jl Taiwan Mus — Quarterly Journal of the Taiwan Museum

Q Jl Tex St Bd Hlth — Quarterly Journal of the Texas State Board of Health [*Austin*]

Q Jl Univ N Dak — Quarterly Journal of the University of North Dakota [*Grand Forks*]

Q J Math — Quarterly Journal of Mathematics

QJ Mcr Sc — Quarterly Journal of Microscopical Science

QJ Mech and Appl Math — Quarterly Journal of Mechanics and Applied Mathematics

Q J Mech Ap — Quarterly Journal of Mechanics and Applied Mathematics

QJ Mech Appl Math — Quarterly Journal of Mechanics and Applied Mathematics

Q J Med — Quarterly Journal of Medicine

Q J Micro Sc — Quarterly Journal of Microscopical Science

Q J Microsc Sci — Quarterly Journal of Microscopical Science

QJMS — Quarterly Journal. Meteorological Society

QJMS — Quarterly Journal. Mythic Society

QJ Mth — Quarterly Journal of Pure and Applied Mathematics

Q J Myth Soc — Quarterly Journal of the Mythic Society

Q J N Cent Perf A — Quarterly Journal of the National Centre for the Performing Arts

Q Jnl Speech — Quarterly Journal of Speech

Q J Nucl Med — Quarterly Journal of Nuclear Medicine

Q J Pakistan Lib Assn — Quarterly Journal. Pakistan Library Association

QJ Pharm Allied Sci — Quarterly Journal of Pharmacy and Allied Sciences

Q J Pharm Pharmacol — Quarterly Journal of Pharmacy and Pharmacology

QJP (Mag Cas) — Queensland Justice of the Peace (Magisterial Cases)

QJPR — Queensland Justice of the Peace. Reports

QJPSS — Quarterly Journal of Political and Social Science

Q J Psychol Med — Quarterly Journal of Psychological Medicine

Q J Pub Speak — Quarterly Journal of Public Speaking

QJRAA — Quarterly Journal. Royal Astronomical Society

Q J R Astro — Quarterly Journal. Royal Astronomical Society

QJR Astron Soc — Quarterly Journal. Royal Astronomical Society

QJRMA — Quarterly Journal. Royal Meteorological Society

Q J R Meteo — Quarterly Journal. Royal Meteorological Society

Q J R Meteorol Soc — Quarterly Journal. Royal Meteorological Society

QJR Met Soc — Quarterly Journal. Royal Meteorological Society

QJRMS — Quarterly Journal of the Royal Meteorological Society

Q J R Neth Soc Agric Sci — Quarterly Journal. Royal Netherlands Society for AgriculturalScience

Q J Rubber Res Inst Ceylon — Quarterly Journal. Rubber Research Institute of Ceylon

Q J Rubber Res Inst Sri Lanka — Quarterly Journal. Rubber Research Institute of Sri Lanka

QJS — Quarterly Journal of Speech

QJSA — Quarterly Journal of Studies on Alcohol

QJ Sc — Journal of Science and the Arts

Q J Sc — Quarterly Journal of Science

QJ Sc — Quarterly Journal of Science and Annals of Mining

Q J Sc — Quarterly Journal of Science, Literature, and the Arts

Q J Sci Arts — Quarterly Journal of Science and the Arts

QJ Sci Lit Arts — Quarterly Journal of Science, Literature, and the Arts

QJ Seismol — Quarterly Journal of Seismology

QJSp — Quarterly Journal of Speech

QJSPA — Quarterly Journal of Speech

Q J Speech — Quarterly Journal of Speech

Q J Stud Al — Quarterly Journal of Studies on Alcohol

Q J Stud Alcohol — Quarterly Journal of Studies on Alcohol

Q J Stud Alcohol Part A — Quarterly Journal of Studies on Alcohol. Part A

QJ Stud Alcohol Suppl — Quarterly Journal of Studies on Alcohol. Supplement

QJ Surg Sci — Quarterly Journal of Surgical Sciences

Q J Taiwan Mus (Taipei) — Quarterly Journal. Taiwan Museum (Taipei)

QJXPA — Quarterly Journal of Experimental Psychology

Qk Froz Fd — Quick Frozen Foods

QKG — Quartalschrift fuer Katholische Geistliche

QKRG — Quellensammlung zur Kirchlichen Rechtsgeschichte

QKRGK — Quellensammlung zur Kirchlichen Rechtsgeschichte und zum Kirchenrecht

QL — Quaderni Linguistici

QL — Queensland Lawyer

QL — Quinzaine Litteraire

QLat — Quartier Latin

Q Law Soc J — Queensland Law Society. Journal

QL Beor — Beor's Queensland Law Reports

QLCR — Queensland Land Court Reports

Qld Geog J — Queensland Geographical Journal

Qld Govt Indust Gaz — Queensland Government Industrial Gazette

Qld Health — Queensland's Health

Qld Heritage — Queensland Heritage

Qld Ind — Queensland Industry

Qld Law — Queensland Lawyer

Qld Mus Mem — Queensland Museum. Memoirs

Qld Nat — Queensland Naturalist

Qld Nurs — Queensland Nurse

Qld Parl Deb — Queensland Parliamentary Debates

Qld Sci Teach — Queensland Science Teacher

Qld Teach J — Queensland Teachers' Journal

Qld Univ Law J — University of Queensland. Law Journal

QLFCAE — Fonds de Recherches Forestieres. Universite Laval. Contribution

Q Liberal — Queensland Liberal

QLing — Quantitative Linguistics

Q List Pap Natn Phys Lab — Quarterly List of Papers Published. National Physical Laboratory [*Teddington*]

QLit — Quebec. Litteraire

QLJ — Queensland Law Journal

Q LJ — Queen's Law Journal

QLJ (NC) — Queensland Law Journal (Notes of Cases)

QLL — Quaderni di Lingue e Letterature

Q Los Ang Cty Mus — Quarterly. Los Angeles County Museum

QLP — Questions Liturgiques et Paroissiales

QLR — Queensland Law Reporter

QLR — Queensland Law Reports

QLR (Beor) — Queensland Law Reports (Beor)

QLSJ — Queensland Law Society. Journal

QL Soc J — Queensland Law Society. Journal

QMAB — Quaderni. Museo Archeologico F. Ribezzo di Brindisi

Q Magn Reson Biol Med — Quarterly of Magnetic Resonance in Biology and Medicine

Q Master Plumber — Queensland Master Plumber

QMB — Quarterly Management Bulletin

QME — Quarber Merkur

Q Med Clin — Quarterly Medical Clinics

Q Med J Yorks — Quarterly Medical Journal for Yorkshire [*Sheffield*]

Q Med Rev — Quarterly Medical Review

Q Med Rev Bombay — Quarterly Medical Review (Bombay)

Q Met Bull Inst Met Pei Chi Ko — Quarterly Meteorological Bulletin. Institute of Meteorology (Pei-Chi-Ko)

Q Met Bull Tsing Hua Univ — Quarterly Meteorological Bulletin. Tsing Hua University Meteorological Observatory [*Peiping*]

QMGPA — Quarry Management and Products [*Later, Quarry Management*]

QMP — Quarry, Mine, and Pit

QMRKG — Quellen und Abhandlungen zur Mittelrheinischen Kirchengeschichte

QMS — Quarterly Journal. Mythic Society

Q Museum Memoirs — Memoirs. Queensland Museum

QMW Maths Notes — QMW (Queen Mary and Westfield College) Maths Notes

QN — Quarterly Newsletter. American Bar Association

QN — Quarterly Notes

QN — Quarternote

Q Nat Acc Bull — Quarterly National Accounts Bulletin

Q Natl Dent Assoc — Quarterly. National Dental Association

Q Natl Fire Prot Assoc — Quarterly. National Fire Protection Association

Q Natn Dent Ass Tuskegee — Quarterly of the National Dental Association, Inc. Tuskegee Institute

QNCCR — Quarterly Notes on Christianity and Chinese Religion

Q News Bull Geol Soc S Afr — Quarterly News Bulletin. Geological Society of South Africa

Q Newsl Agric Div Ghana — Quarterly Newsletter. Agriculture Division. Ghana

Q Newsl Nyasald Tea Ass — Quarterly Newsletter. Nyasaland Tea Association [*Blantyre*]

Q Newsl Rhod Nurses Assoc — Quarterly Newsletter. Rhodesia Nurses Association

Q Newsl Surv Dep Ceylon — Quarterly Newsletter. Survey Department. Ceylon [*Colombo*]

QNG — Quellen zur Neueren Geschichte

QNL — Quarterly News Letter

QNM — Quilter's Newsletter Magazine

Q Notes Belf Munic Art Gall Mus — Quarterly Notes. Belfast Municipal Art Gallery and Museum

Q Notes Coff Res Exp Stn Lyamungu — Quarterly Notes of the Coffee Research and Experiment Station. Lyamungu, Moshi

Q Notes Dep Agric NW Front — Quarterly Notes. Department of Agriculture. North-West Frontier [*Tarnab*]

Q Notes Gen Forec Br Weath Bur — Quarterly Notes and General Forecasts of the British Weather Bureau [*London*]

Q Notes Geol Surv India — Quarterly Notes of the Geological Survey of India [*Calcutta*]

Q Notes Mildmay Meml Hosp — Quarterly Notes. Mildmay Memorial Hospital [*London*]

Q Notes Sisal Exp Stn — Quarterly Notes of the Sisal Experiment Station [*Tanga*]

QOA — Quai d'Orsay Archives

QODKG — Quellenhefte zur Ostdeutschen und Osteuropaeischen Kirchengeschichte

Q Oil Stat — Quarterly Oil Statistics

QP — Quaderni Portoghesi

Q Pap Archit — Quarterly Papers on Architecture

Q Pap Edinb Med Miss Soc — Quarterly Papers. Edinburgh Medical Missionary Society [*Edinburgh*]

QPB — Quaderni dei Padri Benedettini di San Giorgio Maggiore

QPD — Queensland Parliamentary Debates

Q Pediatr Bull — Quarterly Pediatric Bulletin

Q Philipp Sugar Inst — Quarterly. Philippine Sugar Institute

QPIR — EBRI [*Employee Benefit Research Institute*] Quarterly Pension Investment Report

QPLR — Queensland Planning Law Reports

QPMV — Qualitas Plantarum et Materiae Vegetabilis

Q Police J — Queensland Police Journal

Q Population Bul NZ — Quarterly Population Bulletin (New Zealand)

Q Poul Bull — Quarterly Poultry Bulletin

Q Poult Bull — Quarterly Poultry Bulletin

QPP — Queensland Parliamentary Papers

QPR — Quality Progress

QPR — Queensland Practice Reports

Q Predict — Quarterly Predictions of National Income and Expenditure

Q Prog Rep Br Coal Util Res Ass — Quarterly Progress Report. British Coal Utilisation Research Association [*London*]

Q Prog Rep Brookhaven Natn Lab — Quarterly Progress Report. Brookhaven National Laboratory [*Upton, New York*]

Q Prog Rep Colo St Dep Game Fish — Quarterly Progress Report. Colorado State Department of Game and Fish

Q Prog Rep N Carol Wldl Resour Commn — Quarterly Progress Report. North Carolina Wildlife Resources Commission

Q Prog Rep Pittman Robertson Res Dev Proj — Quarterly Progress Report. Pittman-Robertson Research and Development Projects. Pennsylvania Game Commission [Harrisburg]

Q Prog Rep Radiat Lab US Air Force — Quarterly Progress Report. Radiation Laboratory. United States Air Force

Q Prog Rep Res Lab Electron MIT — Quarterly Progress Report. Research Laboratory of Electronics. Massachusetts Institute of Technology [Boston]

Q Prog Rep Scripps Tuna Oceanogr Res Progm — Quarterly Progress Report. Scripps Tuna Oceanographical Research Programme

Q Prog Rep Solid St Molec Theory Grp MIT — Quarterly Progress Report. Solid State and Molecular Theory Group. Massachusetts Institute of Technology [Cambridge]

Q Prog Rep Trop Test Establ Nigeria — Quarterly Progress Report. Tropical Testing Establishment. Nigeria

Q Prog Rep W Afr Cocoa Res Inst — Quarterly Progress Report. West African Cocoa Research Institute [Tafo]

Q Prog Rep W Afr Inst Oil Palm Res — Quarterly Progress Report. West African Institute for Oil Palm Research [Benin City]

Q Prog Rep Wildl Res Div Pa — Quarterly Progress Report. Wildlife Research Division. Pennsylvania Game Commission [Harrisburg]

Q Prog Rep Wildl Res Lab US Dep Agric — Quarterly Progress Report. Wildlife Research Laboratory. United States Department of Agriculture [Denver]

Q Prog Rep Wis St Bur Engng — Quarterly Progress Report. Wisconsin State Bureau of Engineering [Madison]

Q Prog Rep Wis Wildl Res — Quarterly Progress Report. Wisconsin Wildlife Research [Madison]

Q Publ Am Stat Assoc — Quarterly Publications. American Statistical Association

Q Publs Am Statist Ass — Quarterly Publications of the American Statistical Association [Boston]

QQ — Queen's Quarterly

QR — Quarterly Review

QR — Quaternary Research

QRADA — Quaderni di Radiologia

Q Radiat Bull — Quarterly Radiation Bulletin. World Meteorological Organization [Pretoria]

QR Ag Econ — Quarterly Review of Agricultural Economics

Q R Agric Econ — Quarterly Review of Agricultural Economics

Q Rass Mus — Quaderni della Rassegna Musicale

QR Aust Educ — Quarterly Review of Australian Education

QRB — Quality Review Bulletin

QRB — Quarterly Review of Biology

QRBIA — Quarterly Review of Biology

Q R Biol — Quarterly Review of Biology

Q R Biophys — Quarterly Review of Biophysics

QRD — Quarterly Review of Doublespeak

QRE — Quarterly Review of Economics and Business

QREB — Quarterly Review of Economics and Business

QREBA — Quarterly Review of Economics and Business

Q Rec Lit Phil Soc Newcastle — Quarterly Record of the Literary and Philosophical Society of Newcastle-upon-Tyne

Q R Econ & Bus — Quarterly Review of Economics and Business

Q R Econ Bu — Quarterly Review of Economics and Business

Q Rec R Bot Soc — Quarterly Record of the Royal Botanic Society of London

Q Rep Acoust Lab MIT — Quarterly Report. Acoustics Laboratory. Massachusetts Institute of Technology [Cambridge]

Q Rep Iowa Coop Wildl Fish Res Units — Quarterly Report. Iowa Cooperative Wildlife and Fisheries Research Units [Ames]

Q Rep Ld Util Div Pa — Quarterly Progress Report. Land Utilization Division. Pennsylvania Game Commission [Harrisburg]

Q Rep Miner Dress Metall Div Ottawa — Quarterly Report. Mineral Dressing and Metallurgical Divisions [Ottawa]

Q Rep Oceanogr Invest Tokyo — Quarterly Report of Oceanographical Investigation. Imperial Fisheries Institute (Tokyo)

Q Rep Ohio Coop Wildl Res Unit — Quarterly Report. Ohio Cooperative Wildlife Research Unit

Q Rep Oil Gas Sect W Va Dep Mines — Quarterly Report. Oil and Gas Section. West Virginia Department of Mines [Charleston]

Q Rep Okla Coop Wildl Res Unit — Quarterly Report. Oklahoma Cooperative Wildlife Research Unit [Stillwater]

Q Rep Ore Coop Wildl Res Unit — Quarterly Report. Oregon Co-operative Wildlife Research Unit

Q Rep Pa Coop Wildl Res Unit — Quarterly Report of the Pennsylvania Cooperative Wildlife Research Unit [University Park]

Q Rep Philipp Hlth Serv — Quarterly Report of the Philippine Health Service [Manila]

Q Rep Prog Interst Commn Del River Basin — Quarterly Report of Progress. Interstate Commission on the Delaware River Basin

Q Rep Prog Segreg Camps Med Treat Sleep Sickn Uganda — Quarterly Report on the Progress of Segregation Camps and Medical Treatment of Sleeping Sickness in Uganda [Royal Society, London]

Q Rep Prog Soil Wat Conserv Res US — Quarterly Report. Progress in Soil and Water Conservation Research. Soil and Water Conservation Branch. United States Department of Agriculture [Washington]

Q Rep Pulp Pap Res Inst Can — Quarterly Report of the Pulp and Paper Research Institute of Canada [Montreal]

Q Rep Railw Tech Res Inst (Tokyo) — Quarterly Report. Railway Technical Research Institute (Tokyo)

Q Rep Res Def Soc — Quarterly Report. Research Defence Society [London]

Q Rep Rly Tech Res Inst Tokyo — Quarterly Report. Railway Technical Research Institute (Tokyo)

Q Rep RTRI Jpn — Quarterly Report of RTRI (Railway Technical Research Institute) (Japan)

Q Rep Scient Dep Indian Tea Ass — Quarterly Report. Scientific Department. Indian Tea Association

Q Rep Scient Wk Lancs West Sea Fish Distr — Quarterly Report on the Scientific Work of the Lancashire and Western Sea Fisheries District [Liverpool]

Q Rep Sulfur Chem — Quarterly Reports on Sulfur Chemistry

Q Rep Taihoku Met Obs — Quarterly Report. Taihoku Meteorological Observatory

Q Rep Univ W Indies Sch Agric — Quarterly Report. University of the West Indies. School of Agriculture

Q Rep W Afr Cocoa Res Inst — Quarterly Report. West African Cocoa Research Institute [Tafo]

QRESA — Quaternary Research

Q Res Rep Southeast Asian Fish Dev Cent Aquacult Dep — Quarterly Research Report. Southeast Asian Fisheries DevelopmentCenter. Aquaculture Department

Q Res Surv Pacif Res Bur — Quarterly Research Survey. Pacific Research Bureau [Ithaca]

Q Rev — Quarterly Review

Q Rev Ag Economics — Quarterly Review of Agricultural Economics

Q Rev Agric Econ — Quarterly Review of Agricultural Economics

Q Rev Allergy Appl Immun — Quarterly Review of Allergy and Applied Immunology [Washington]

Q Rev Allergy Appl Immunol — Quarterly Review of Allergy and Applied Immunology

Q Rev Am Electroplat Soc — Quarterly Review. American Electroplaters' Society

Q Rev Aust Ed — Quarterly Review of Australian Education

Q Rev Biol — Quarterly Review of Biology

Q Rev Bioph — Quarterly Reviews of Biophysics

Q Rev Biophys — Quarterly Reviews of Biophysics

Q Rev Chem Soc — Quarterly Reviews. Chemical Society

Q Rev Chem Soc (Lond) — Quarterly Reviews. Chemical Society (London)

Q Rev DC Nurses Assoc — Quarterly Review. District of Columbia Nurses Association

Q Rev Dep Agric Cyprus — Quarterly Review. Department of Agriculture. Cyprus [Nicosia]

Q Rev Derm Syph — Quarterly Review of Dermatology and Syphilology

Q Rev Drill Stat US — Quarterly Review. Drilling Statistics for the United States

Q Rev Drug Metab Drug Interact — Quarterly Reviews on Drug Metabolism and Drug Interactions

Q Rev Econ Bus — Quarterly Review of Economics and Business

Q Rev Environ — Quarterly Review on Environment

Q Rev Essex Pig Soc — Quarterly Review. Essex Pig Society

Q Rev Evan Luth Ch — Quarterly Review. Evangelical Lutheran Church

Q Rev Film — Quarterly Review of Film Studies

Q Rev Forest Prod Labs Can — Quarterly Review. Forest Product Laboratories. Canada

Q Rev F Studies — Quarterly Review of Film Studies

Q Rev Harefuah — Quarterly Review of the Harefuah

Q Rev Hist S — Quarterly Review of Historical Studies

Q Review of F Studies — Quarterly Review of Film Studies

Q Rev Internal Med Derm — Quarterly Review of Internal Medicine and Dermatology

Q Rev Intern Med Dermatol — Quarterly Review of Internal Medicine and Dermatology

Q Rev Juris — Quarterly Review of Jurisprudence

Q Rev Lit — Quarterly Review of Literature

Q Rev Med — Quarterly Review of Medicine

Q Rev NAAS — Quarterly Review NAAS

Q Rev Obstet Gynecol — Quarterly Review of Obstetrics and Gynecology

Q Rev Pediatr — Quarterly Review of Pediatrics

Q Rev Soil Assoc — Quarterly Review. The Soil Association

Q Rev Surg — Quarterly Review of Surgery

Q Rev Surg Obstet Gynecol — Quarterly Review of Surgery. Obstetrics and Gynecology

Q Rev Surg Surg Spec — Quarterly Review of Surgery and Surgical Specialities

Q Rev Urol — Quarterly Review of Urology

Q R Film S — Quarterly Review of Film Studies

QRG — Quellen der Religionsgeschichte

Q R Higher Ed Among Negroes — Quarterly Review of Higher Education among Negroes

QR Higher Ed Negroes — Quarterly Review of Higher Education among Negroes

Q R Hist Stud — Quarterly Review of Historical Studies

QRHS — Quarterly Review of Historical Studies

QR J — QR Journal. Indian Association for Quality and Reliability

QRJOD — QR [Quality and Reliability] Journal

QRL — Quarterly Review of Literature

QRM — Quarterly Review of Marketing

QR of Lit — Quarterly Review of Literature

Q R Rural Economy — Quarterly Review of the Rural Economy

QRTIA — Quarterly Report. Railway Technical Research Institute

QRU — Quarterly Review of Urology

QRUR — Quellenhefte zum Religionsunterricht. Quellen zur Geschichte der Ausserchristlichen Religionen

QS — Qirjat Sefer

QS — Quaderni di Semitistica

QS — Quaderni di Storia

QSAR — Quantitative Structure-Activity Relationships

QSAR Drug Des Toxicol Proc Eur Symp Quan Struct Act Relat — QSAR [Quantitative Structure-Activity Relationships] in Drug Design and Toxicology. Proceedings. European Symposium on Quantitative Structure-Activity Relationships

Qschr — Quartalschrift

QSCR — Queensland. Supreme Court. Reports

QSem — Quaderni di Semantica

QSEt — Quaderni di Studi Etruschi

QSEtP — Quaderni di Studi Etruschi. Richerche Peistoriche in Etruria

QSG — Quellen zur Schweizer Geschichte

QSGA — Quellen zur Schweizer Geschichte. Akten

QSGB — Quellen zur Schweizer Geschichte. Briefe und Denkwuerdigkeiten

QSGC — Quellen zur Schweizer Geschichte. Chroniken
QSGH — Quellen zur Schweizer Geschichte. Handbuecher
QSGHK — Quellen und Studien zur Geschichte der Helvetischen Kirche
QSGLL — Queensland Studies in German Language and Literature
QSGM — Quellen und Studien zur Geschichte der Mathematik, Astronomie, und Physik. Abteilung B. Studien
QSG Math — Quellen und Studien zur Geschichte der Mathematik, Astronomie, und Physik
QSGNM — Quellen und Studien zur Geschichte der Naturwissenschaften und der Medizin
QSGP — Quellen und Studien zur Geschichte der Philosophie
QSJ — Que Sais Je
QSKG — Quellensammlung zur Kulturgeschichte
QSP — Quellen und Studien zur Philosophie
QSR — State Reports (Queensland)
QSRG — Quellen zur Schweizerischen Reformationsgeschichte
QST — Quarterly Statement
QST — Quarterly Statements. Palestine Exploration Fund
QSt — Quellen und Studien zur Geschichte und Kultur des Altertums und des Mittelalters
Q St Ro — Quaderni di Studi Romani
QS Wkly — Quantity Surveyor Weekly
Qt — Quartet
QTDM — Qazaq Tili Tarychy Men Dyalektology Jasinin Moseleleri
Q Teachers J — Queensland Teachers' Journal
Q Tic Num Ant Clas — Quaderni Ticinesi. Numismatica e Antichita Classiche
QTLCG — Quaderni Triestini per il Lessico della Lirica Corale Greca
Q Trans Am Inst Electr Eng — Quarterly Transactions. American Institute of Electrical Engineers
Qtr J Forestry — Quarterly Journal of Forestry
QTTA — Quaderni Triestini sul Teatro Antico
QU — Quaderni dell'Umanesimo
QUA — Quality
QuaB — Quarterly Bulletin. South African Library
Quad — Quadrant
Quad — Quadrivium
Quad — Quadrum. Revue Internationale d'Art Moderne
Quad Accad Chigiana — Quaderni dell'Accademia Chigiana
Quad Acta Neurol — Quaderni di Acta Neurologica
Quad A Libia — Quaderni di Archeologia della Libia
Quad Anat Prat — Quaderni di Anatomia Pratica
Quad Antiqua — Quaderni dell'Antiquariato
Quad Archit & Des — Quaderni di Architettura e Disegno
Quad Arch Libia — Quaderni di Archeologia della Libia
Quad A Reggio — Quaderni d'Archeologia Reggiana
Quad Arqueol & Hist Ciutat — Quaderns d'Arqueologia i Historia de la Ciutat
Quad Arquit & Urb — Quaderns d'Arquitectura i Urbanisme
Quad Azione Soc — Quaderni di Azione Sociale
Quad Bitontini — Quaderni Bitontini
Quad Brera — Quaderni di Brera
Quad Cat — Quaderni Catanesi di Studi Classici e Medievali
Quad Chim CNR (Italy) — Quaderni di Chimica. Consiglio Nazionale delle Ricerche (Italy)
Quad Clin Ostet — Quaderni di Clinica Ostetrica e Ginecologica
Quad Clin Ostet Ginecol — Quaderni de Clinica Ostetrica e Ginecologica
Quad Coagulazione — Quaderni della Coagulazione
Quad Coagulazione Argomenti Connessi — Quaderni della Coagulazione e Argomenti Connessi
Quad Conoscitore Stampe — Quaderni del Conoscitore di Stampe
Quad Cons Naz Ricerche Gruppo Naz Fis Mat — Quaderni del Consiglio Nazionale delle Richerche. Gruppo Nazionale di Fisica Matematica
Quad Criminol Clin — Quaderni di Criminologia Clinica
Quad Econ (Sarda) — Quaderni dell'Economia (Sarda)
Quad Emiliani — Quaderni Emiliani
Quad Ente Naz Semen Elette — Quaderno. Ente Nazionale Sementi Elette
Quaderni della Ra M — Quaderni della Rassegna Musicale
Quad Estud Med — Quaderns d'Estudis Medievals
Quad Exili — Quaderns de l'Exili
Quad Filol Clas — Quaderni di Filologia Classica
Quad Fitoter — Quaderni di Fitoterapia
Quad Fond Camillo Caetani — Quaderni della Fondazione Camillo Caetani
Quad Fond Politec Mezzogiorno Ital — Quaderno. Fondazione Politecnica per il Mezzogiorno d'Italia
Quad Formaz — Quaderni di Formazione
Quad Fruttic — Quaderni del Frutticoltore
Quad Gal N Marche — Quaderni della Galleria Nazionale delle Marche
Quad Geofis Appl — Quaderni di Geofisica Applicata
Quad G Fis — Quaderni del Giornale di Fisica
Quad Ibero Am — Quaderni Ibero-Americani
Quad Ing Chim Ital — Quaderni dell'Ingegnere Chimico Italiano
Quad Ist Bot Univ Lab Crittogam (Pavia) — Quaderni. Istituto Botanico. Universita Laboratorio Crittogamico (Pavia)
Quad Ist Fil Gr — Quaderni dell'Istituto di Filologia Greca
Quad Ist It Cult RAE — Quaderni dell'Istituto Italiano di Cultura per la Repubblica Araba d'Egitto
Quad Ist N Stud Rinascimento Merid — Quaderni dell'Istituto Nazionale di Studi sul Rinascimento Meridionale
Quad Ist Ric Acque — Quaderni. Istituto di Ricerca sulle Acque
Quad Ist Ric Acque Append Metodi Anal Acque — Quaderni. Istituto di Ricerca sulle Acque. Appendice. Metodi Analiticiper le Acque
Quad Ist Stor A Med & Mod — Quaderni dell'Istituto di Storia dell'Arte Medievale e Moderna
Quad Ist Stor Archit — Quaderni dell'Istituto di Storia dell'Architettura
Quad Ist Stor A U Genova — Quaderni dell'Istituto di Storia dell'Arte dell'Universita di Genova

Quad Ist Stud Islam — Quaderni dell'Istituto di Studi Islamici
Quad Ist Top — Quaderni dell'Istituto di Topografia
Quad Ist Top — Quaderni. Istituto di Topografia Antica
Quad Ist Top Ant — Quaderni dell'Istituto di Topografia Antica
Quad Italo Sviz — Quaderni Italo-Svizzeri
Quad Ital Psichiatr — Quaderni Italiani di Psichiatria
Quad Lab Spettrom Massa — Quaderni di Laboratorio di Spettrometria di Massa
Quad Lotus — Quaderni di Lotus
Quad Mathesis Cosenza — Mathesis di Cosenza. Quaderni
Quad Merceol — Quaderni di Merceologia
Quad Merceol Ist Merceol Univ Bari — Quaderni di Merceologia. Istituto di Merceologia. Universita Bari
Quad Mod — Quaderni Modenesi
Quad Neoclass — Quaderni sul Neoclassicismo
Quad Nutr — Quaderni della Nutrizione
Quad Nutr (Bologna) — Quaderni della Nutrizione (Bologna)
Quad Padano — Quadrante Padano
Quad Pal Te — Quaderni del Palazzo del Te
Quad Pal Venezia — Quaderni del Palazzo Venezia
Quad Pignone — Quaderni Pignone
Quad Poro — Quaderni Poro
Quad Radiol — Quaderni di Radiologia
Quadrangle Rep Conn State Geol Nat Hist Surv — Quadrangle Report. Connecticut. State Geological and Natural History Survey
Quadrangle Ser 1:50000 Geol Surv Jap — Quadrangle Series 1:50,000. Geological Survey of Japan
Quadrenn Meet Int Assoc Study Liver — Quadrennial Meeting. International Association for the Study of the Liver
Quad Rest — Quaderni del Restauro
Quad Ricerca Sci — Quaderni de la Ricerca Scientifica
Quad Ric Progettazione — Quaderni di Ricerca e Progettazione
Quad Ric Sci — Quaderni de la Ricerca Scientifica
Quad Roma — Quaderni di Roma
Quad Sardi Econ — Quaderni Sardi di Economia
Quad Sci Loescher — Quaderni Scientifici Loescher
Quad Sclavo Diagn — Quaderni Sclavo di Diagnostica Clinica e di Laboratorio
Quad Sclavo Diagn Clin Lab — Quaderni Sclavo di Diagnostica Clinica e di Laboratorio
Quad Semin Iran U Venezia — Quaderni del Seminario di Iranistica dell'Universita di Venezia
Quad Ser III — Quaderni. Serie III
Quad Sez Perugina Soc Ital Biol Sper — Quaderni. Sezione Perugina. Societa Italiana di Biologia Sperimentale
Quad Sociol — Quaderni di Sociologia
Quad Sopr Archeol Prov Cagliari & Oristano — Quaderni della Soprintendenza Archeologica per le Province di Cagliari e Oristano
Quad Sopr Beni A & Stor Venezia — Quaderni della Soprintendenza di Beni Artistici e Storici di Venezia
Quad Sopr Gal Liguria — Quaderni della Soprintendenza alle Gallerie della Liguria
Quad Stampe — Quaderni con Stampe
Quad St Lun — Quaderni. Centro di Studi Lunesi
Quad Stor — Quaderni di Storia
Quad Stor — Quaderni Storici
Quad Stor Econ Polit — Quaderni di Storia dell'Economia Politica
Quad Storia Crit Sci — Quaderni di Storia e Critica della Scienza
Quad Storia Sci Med Univ Studi Ferrara — Quaderni di Storia della Scienza e della Medicina. Universita degli Studi di Ferrara
Quad Stor Univ Padova — Quaderni per la Storia. Universita di Padova
Quad Stor U Padova — Quaderni per la Storia dell'Universita di Padova
Quad Stud & Ric Rest Archit & Territ — Quaderni di Studi e Ricerche di Restauro Architettonico e Territoriale
Quad Stud Arab — Quaderni di Studi Arabi
Quad Studi Not Soc Gen Ital Edison Elettr — Quaderni di Studi e Notizie. Societa Generale Italiana Edison deElettricita
Quad Tec Sint Spec Org — Quaderni di Tecniche e Sintesi Speciali Organiche
Quad Top Ant — Quaderni. Istituto di Topografia Antica. Universita di Roma
Quad Unione Mat Italiana — Quaderni dell'Unione Matematica Italiana
Quad Urb C — Quaderni Urbinati di Cultura Classica
Quad Urbin — Quaderni Urbinati di Cultura Classica
Quad Urol — Quaderni di Urologia
Quad Vittoriale — Quaderni del Vittoriale
Quaest Ent — Quaestiones Entomologicae
Quaest Entomol — Quaestiones Entomologicae
Quaest Geobiol — Quaestiones Geobiologicae
Quaest Inf — Quaestiones Informaticae
Quaestiones Math — Quaestiones Mathematicae
QuaJ — Quarterly Journal of Speech
QuakerH — Quaker History
Qual Assur — Quality Assurance
Qual Contr Appl Stat — Quality Control and Applied Statistics
Qual Control Appl Stat — Quality Control and Applied Statistics
Qual Control Clin Chem Trans Int Symp — Quality Control in Clinical Chemistry. Transactions. International Symposium
Qual Control Med Proc Int Congr Pharm Sci — Quality Control of Medicines. Proceedings. International Congressof Pharmaceutical Sciences
Qual Control Rem Site Invest Hazard Ind Solid Waste Test — Quality Control in Remedial Site Investigation. Hazardous and Industrial Solid Waste Testing
Qual Eng — Quality Engineer
Qual Eval — Quality Evaluation
Qual Foods Beverages Chem Technol Proc Symp Int Flavor Conf — Quality of Foods and Beverages. Chemistry and Technology. Proceedings.Symposium. International Flavor Conference
Qual Groundwater Proc Int Symp — Quality of Groundwater. Proceedings. International Symposium

Qualitas Pl Pl Fds Human Nutr — Qualitas Plantarum/Plant Foods for Human Nutrition
Qualite Rev Prat Controle Ind — Qualite. Revue Pratique de Controle Industriel
Quality — Quality of Sheffield and South Yorkshire
Quality Prog — Quality Progress
Qual Kernkraftwerken Am Dtsch Sicht Int Tag — Qualitaet von Kernkraftwerken aus Amerikanischer und Deutscher Sicht.Internationale Tagung
Qual Life Res — Quality of Life Research
Qual Plant — Qualitas Plantarum/Plant Foods for Human Nutrition
Qual Plant Mater Veg — Qualitas Plantarum et Materiae Vegetabiles [*Later, Qualitas Plantarum/Plant Foods for Human Nutrition*]
Qual Plant Plant Foods Hum Nutr — Qualitas Plantarum/Plant Foods for Human Nutrition
Qual Pl Mater Veg — Qualitas Plantarum et Materiae Vegetabiles
Qual Poult Meat Proc Eur Symp — Quality of Poultry Meat. Proceedings. European Symposium on Poultry Meat Quality
Qual Prog — Quality Progress
Qual Publ Malting Barley Improv Assoc — Quality Publication. Malting Barley Improvement Association
Qual Quant — Quality and Quantity
Qual Reliab Eng Int — Quality and Reliability Engineering International
Qual Reliab J — Quality and Reliability Journal
Qual Rev Prat Controle Ind — Qualite. Revue Pratique de Controle Industriel
Qual Today — Quality Today
Qual und Zuverlassigkeit — Qualitaet und Zuverlaessigkeit
Qual Zuverlaessigk — Qualitaet und Zuverlaessigkeit
Quan Sociol — Quantitative Sociology
Quant Approaches Drug Des — Quantitative Approaches to Drug Design
Quant Aspects Risk Assess Chem Carcinog Symp — Quantitative Aspects of Risk Assessment in Chemical Carcinogenesis. Symposium
Quant Chem Symp — Quantum Chemistry Symposia
Quant Descr Met Extr Processes — Quantitative Description of Metal Extraction Processes
Quantitative Appl in the Social Sciences — Quantitative Applications in the Social Sciences
Quantitative Meth Unternehmungsplanung — Quantitative Methoden der Unternehmungsplanung
Quantity Surv — Quantity Surveyor
Quant Mass Spectrom Life Sci — Quantitative Mass Spectrometry in Life Sciences. Proceedings. International Symposium
Qu Ant Pal — Quarterly. Department of Antiquities in Palestine
Quant Struct Act Relat — Quantitative Structure-Activity Relationships
Quantum Biol Symp Int J Quantum Chem — Quantum Biology Symposium. International Journal of Quantum Chemistry
Quantum Chaos Stat Nucl Phys Proc — Quantum Chaos and Statistical Nuclear Physics. Proceedings
Quantum Chem Symp — Quantum Chemistry Symposia
Quantum Electron Electro Opt Proc Nat Quantum Electron Conf — Quantum Electronics and Electro-Optics. Proceedings. National Quantum Electronics Conference
Quantum Electron (New York) — Quantum Electronics (New York)
Quantum Electron Plasma Phys Ital Conf — Quantum Electronics and Plasma Physics. Italian Conference
Quantum Electron Proc Int Congr — Quantum Electronics. Proceedings. International Congress
Quantum Meas Opt — Quantum Measurements in Optics
Quantum Mech Fundam Syst — Quantum Mechanics of Fundamental Systems
Quantum Opt — Quantum Optics. Journal of the European Optical Society. Part B
Quantum Opt Proc Int Symp — Quantum Optics. Proceedings. International Symposium
Quantum Semiclassical Opt B — Quantum and Semiclassical Optics. Journal of the European Optical Society. PartB
Quantum Semiclass Optics — Quantum and Semiclassical Optics
Quantum Stat Many Body Probl Proc Symp — Quantum Statistics and the Many-Body Problem. Proceedings. Symposium on QuantumStatistics and Many-Body Problems
Quantum Stat Mech Nat Sci — Quantum Statistical Mechanics in the Natural Sciences
QuaR — Quarterly Review
Quar — Quarterly Review
QuaRe — Quarterly Review
QuaRH — Quarterly Review of Historical Studies
Quar Jour Econ — Quarterly Journal of Economics
Quark Gluon Struct Hadrons Nucl Proc Int Workshop — Quark-Gluon Structure of Hadrons and Nuclei. Proceedings. International Workshop
Quarks Mesons Isobars Nucl Proc Top Sch — Quarks, Mesons, and Isobars in Nuclei. Proceedings. TopicalSchool
Quarks Nucl Struct Proc Klaus Erkelenz Symp — Quarks and Nuclear Structure. Proceedings. Klaus Erkelenz Symposium
Quar R Biol — Quarterly Review of Biology
Quar Rev — Quarterly Review
Quarries Mines Coal Health Saf — Quarries and Mines Other than Coal. Health and Safety
Quarry Aurv Contract J — Quarry and Surveyors' Contractors' Journal
Quarry Manage — Quarry Management
Quarry Manage Prod — Quarry Management and Products [*Later, Quarry Management*]
Quarry Mgmt — Quarry Management
Quarry Mgmt Products — Quarry Management and Products [*Later, Quarry Management*]
Quarry Min News — Quarry and Mining News
Quarry Surv Contract J — Quarry and Surveyors' and Contractors' Journal [*London*]
Quart — Quarterly Review
Quartaer Biblthk — Quartaer-Bibliothek [*Bonn*]

Quart Amer Primrose Soc — Quarterly. American Primrose Society
Quart Appl Math — Quarterly of Applied Mathematics
Quart Bul Ass Food Drug Offic US — Quarterly Bulletin. Association of Food and Drug Officials of the United States[*Later, Quarterly Bulletin. Association of Food and Drug Officials*]
Quart Bull Amer Rhododendron Soc — Quarterly Bulletin. American Rhododendron Society
Quart Bull Int Ass Agric Libr Docum — Quarterly Bulletin. International Association of Agricultural Librarians and Documentalists
Quart Bull Mich Agric Exp Sta — Quarterly Bulletin. Michigan State University. Agricultural Experiment Station
Quart Bull Mich State Univ Agr Exp Sta — Quarterly Bulletin. Michigan State University. Agricultural Experiment Station
Quart Bull Natl Chrysanthemum Soc — Quarterly Bulletin. National Chrysanthemum Society
Quart Bull Northwestern Univ M School — Quarterly Bulletin. Northwestern University Medical School
Quart Bull Sci Educ — Quarterly Bulletin of Science Education. K'o Hsueeh Chiao Hsueeh Chi K'an. Szechuan Provincial Science Education Institute
Quart Bull Stat Asia Pac — Quarterly Bulletin of Statistics for Asia and the Pacific
Quart Charleston Mus — Quarterly. Charleston Museum
Quart Colo Sch Mines — Quarterly. Colorado School of Mines
Quart En Rev Afr — Quarterly Energy Review. Africa
Quart En Rev Aust — Quarterly Energy Review. Far East and Australia
Quart En Rev Mid East — Quarterly Energy Review. Middle East
Quart En Rev NA — Quarterly Energy Review. North America
Quart En Rev West Eur — Quarterly Energy Review. Western Europe
Quarter Horse Dig — Quarter Horse Digest
Quarterly Appl Math — Quarterly of Applied Mathematics
Quarterly J of Mus Teaching — Quarterly Journal of Music Teaching
Quarterly of F R TV — Quarterly of Film, Radio, and Television
Quartermaster Food Container Inst Armed Forces Act Rep — Quartermaster Food and Container Institute for the Armed Forces. Activities Report
Quartermaster Rev — Quartermaster Review. Quartermaster Association [*Washington, D.C.*]
Quart J Adm — Quarterly Journal of Administration
Quart J Agr Econ — Quarterly Journal of Agricultural Economy
Quart J Chin For (Taipei) — Quarterly Journal of Chinese Forestry (Taipei)
Quart J Crude Drug Res — Quarterly Journal of Crude Drug Research
Quart J Curr Acquisitions — Quarterly Journal of Current Acquisitions. Library of Congress
Quart J Econ — Quarterly Journal of Economics
Quart J Econom — Quarterly Journal of Economics
Quart J Exp Physiol — Quarterly Journal of Experimental Physiology
Quart J Exp Psychol — Quarterly Journal of Experimental Psychology
Quart J For — Quarterly Journal of Forestry
Quart J Forest — Quarterly Journal of Forestry
Quart J Illinois State Agric Soc — Quarterly Journal. Illinois State Agricultural Society
Quart J Indian Inst Sci — Quarterly Journal. Indian Institute of Science
Quart J Indian Tea Assoc Sci Dept — Quarterly Journal. Indian Teas Association. Scientific Department
Quart J Libr Congress — Quarterly Journal. Library of Congress
Quart J Math Oxford Ser 2 — Quarterly Journal of Mathematics. Oxford. Second Series
Quart J Mech Appld Math — Quarterly Journal of Mechanics and Applied Mathematics
Quart J Mech Appl Math — Quarterly Journal of Mechanics and Applied Mathematics
Quart J Med — Quarterly Journal of Medicine
Quart J Microscop Soc Victoria — Quarterly Journal. Microscopical Society of Victoria
Quart J Microsc Sci — Quarterly Journal of Microscopical Science
Quart J Micr Sc — Quarterly Journal of Microscopical Science
Quart Jour Cur Acq Wash — Quarterly Journal of Current Acquisitions. Library of Congress (Washington, DC)
Quart J Roy Astron Soc — Quarterly Journal. Royal Astronomical Society
Quart J Roy Meteorol Soc — Quarterly Journal. Royal Meteorological Society
Quart J Sci Lit Arts — Quarterly Journal of Science, Literature, and the Arts
Quart J Soc Aff — Quarterly Journal of Social Affairs
Quart J Taiwan Mus — Quarterly Journal. Taiwan Museum
Quart J Vet Sc India — Quarterly Journal of Veterinary Science in India and Army Animal Management
Quartl Journ Econ — Quarterly Journal of Economics
Quart LJ (VA) — Quarterly Law Journal
Quart L Rev (VA) — Quarterly Law Review
Quartl Statement Palest Expl Fund — Quarterly Statement. Palestine Exploration Fund
Quart Nat Dent Ass — Quarterly. National Dental Association
Quart Nebr Agr Exp Sta — Quarterly. Nebraska Agricultural Experiment Station
Quart Newsl (Dehra Dun) — Quarterly News Letter. Forest Research Institute and Colleges (Dehra Dun)
Quart Philippine Sugar Inst — Quarterly. Philippine Sugar Institute
Quart R — Quarterly Review
Quart R — Quarterly Reviews. Chemical Society
Quart R Agric — Quarterly Review of Agricultural Economics
Quart R Agric Econ — Quarterly Review of Agricultural Economics
Quart R Centr Bank Ireland — Quarterly Review. Central Bank of Ireland
Quart R Econ Busin — Quarterly Review of Economics and Business
Quart Rec Roy Bot Soc London — Quarterly Record. Royal Botanical Society of London
Quart Rep — Quarterly Report
Quart Rep Ry Tech Res Inst — Quarterly Report. Railway Technical Research Institute
Quart Rev — Quarterly Review

Quart Rev — Quarterly Reviews. Chemical Society
Quart Rev Agr Econ — Quarterly Review of Agricultural Economics
Quart Rev Agric Econ — Quarterly Review of Agricultural Economics
Quart Rev Allergy — Quarterly Review of Allergy and Applied Immunology
Quart Rev Biol — Quarterly Review of Biology
Quart Rev Chem Soc — Quarterly Reviews. Chemical Society
Quart Rev Guernsey Soc — Quarterly Review. Guernsey Society
Quart Revs — Quarterly Reviews. Chemical Society
Quart Summary Meteorol Readings Roy Bot Soc London — Quarterly Summary and Meteorological Readings. Royal Botanic Society of London
Quart Suppl Board Trade J — Quarterly Supplement. Board of Trade Journal
Quart Trans Soc Autom Eng — Quarterly Transactions. Society of Automotive Engineers
Quart Univ Nebr Coll Agr Home Econ Agr Exp Sta — Quarterly. University of Nebraska. College of Agriculture and Home Economics. Agricultural Experiment Station
Quasars Gravitational Lenses Proc Liege Int Astrophys Colloq — Quasars and Gravitational Lenses. Proceedings of the Liege International Astrophysical Colloquium
QUASD — Quality Assurance
Quat — Quatember
Quat Archeol Libia — Quaderni di Archeologia di Libia
Quat Deltas India — Quaternary Deltas of India
Quaternary Res — Quaternary Research
Quatern Res — Quaternary Research
Quat Geol Environ China — Quaternary Geology and Environment of China
Quat Res (Jap Assoc Quat Res) — Quaternary Research (Japan Association of Quaternary Research)
Quat Res (NY) — Quaternary Research (New York)
Quat Res (Tokyo) — Quaternary Research (Tokyo)
Quat Sci R — Quaternary Science Reviews
Quat Sci Rev — Quaternary Science Reviews
Qu Bull — Quarterly Bulletin
QUCC — Quaderni Urbinati di Cultura Classica
Qu Chr — Questions for Christians
QuD — Quaderni Dannunziani
Qu Darst Gesch Burschensch — Quellen und Darstellungen zur Geschichte der Burschenschaft und der Deutschen Einheitsbewegung
Quebec Dept Nat Resources Prelim Rept — Quebec. Department of Natural Resources. Preliminary Report
Quebec Dept Nat Resources Spec Paper — Quebec. Department of Natural Resources. Special Paper
Quebec Dept Trade and Commerce Geog Service Pub — Quebec. Department of Trade and Commerce. Geographical Service. Publication
Quebec Hist Soc Trans — Quebec Historical Society. Transactions
Que Cons Rech Dev For Rapp — Quebec. Conseil de la Recherche et du Developpement Forestiers. Rapport
Que Cons Rech Dev For Rapp Annu — Quebec. Conseil de la Recherche et du Developpement Forestiers. Rapport Annuel
Que Dep Ind Commer Annu Rep — Quebec. Department of Industry and Commerce. Annual Report
Que Dep Lands For Res Serv Res Pap — Quebec. Department of Lands and Forest Research Service. Research Paper
Que Dep Natur Resour Geol Rep — Quebec. Department of Natural Resources. Geological Report
Que Dep Natur Resour Prelim Rep — Quebec. Department of Natural Resources. Preliminary Report
Que Dir Geol Trav Terrain — Quebec. Direction de la Geologie. Travaux sur le Terrain
Que Dp Col Mines Br Rp — Quebec. Department of Colonization, Mines, and Fisheries. Mines Branch. Report on Mining Operations
Queen Q — Queen's Quarterly
Queens B Bull — Queens Bar Bulletin
Queens CBA Bull — Queens County Bar Association. Bulletin
Queens Intra LJ — Queen's Intramural Law Journal
Queen's Intramural LJ — Queen's Intramural Law Journal
Queens JP & Loc Auth Jo — Queensland Justice of the Peace and Local Authorities' Journal
Queensl — Queensland Reports
Queensl Agric J — Queensland Agricultural Journal
Queensland Ag J — Queensland Agricultural Journal
Queensland Agr J — Queensland Agricultural Journal
Queensland Bot Bull — Queensland Botanical Bulletin
Queensland Dent Mag — Queensland Dental Magazine
Queensland Dept Agric Div Pl Industr Bull — Queensland Department of Agriculture and Stock. Division of Plant Industry. Bulletin
Queensland Gov Min J — Queensland Government Mining Journal
Queensland Govt Min Jour — Queensland Government Mining Journal
Queensland Hist R — Queensland Historical Review
Queensland J Agr Anim Sci — Queensland Journal of Agricultural and Animal Sciences
Queensland J Ag Sci — Queensland Journal of Agricultural Science [Later, Queensland Journal of Agricultural and Animal Sciences]
Queensland Land Court Rep — Queensland Land Court Reports
Queensland L Soc'y J — Queensland Law Society. Journal
Queensland Pap in Econ Policy — Queensland Papers in Economic Policy
Queensl Archaeol Res — Queensland Archaeological Research
Queensl Dent J — Queensland Dental Journal
Queensl Dep Agric Stock — Queensland. Department of Agriculture and Stock. Annual Report
Queensl Dep Mines Geol Surv Queensl Publ — Queensland. Department of Mines. Geological Survey of Queensland. Publication
Queensl Dep Mines Geol Surv Queensl Rep — Queensland. Department of Mines. Geological Survey of Queensland. Report

Queensl Dep Primary Ind Agric Chem Branch Tech Rep — Queensland. Department of Primary Industries. Agricultural Chemistry Branch. Technical Report
Queensl Dep Primary Ind Div Anim Ind Bull — Queensland. Department of Primary Industries. Division of Animal Industry. Bulletin
Queensl Dep Primary Ind Div Dairy Bull — Queensland. Department of Primary Industries. Division of Dairying. Bulletin
Queensl Dep Primary Ind Div Plant Ind Bull — Queensland. Department of Primary Industries. Division of Plant Industry. Bulletin
Queensl Dep Primary Ind Inf Ser — Queensland. Department of Primary Industries. Information Series
Queensl Fish Serv Res Bull — Queensland. Fisheries Service. Research Bulletin
Queensl Fish Serv Tech Rep — Queensland. Fisheries Service. Technical Report
Queensl Geogr J — Queensland Geographical Journal
Queensl Geol — Queensland Geology
Queensl Geol Surv 1:250000 Geol Ser — Queensland. Geological Survey. 1:250,000 Geological Series
Queensl Geol Surv Publ — Queensland. Geological Survey. Publication
Queensl Geol Surv Rep — Queensland. Geological Survey. Report
Queensl Gov Min J — Queensland Government Mining Journal
Queensl Herit — Queensland Heritage
Queens LJ — Queensland Law Journal and Reports
Queen's L J — Queen's Law Journal
Queensl J Agric & Anim Sci — Queensland Journal of Agricultural and Animal Sciences
Queensl J Agric Anim Sci — Queensland Journal of Agricultural and Animal Sciences
Queensl J Agric Sci — Queensland Journal of Agricultural Science [Later, Queensland Journal of Agricultural and Animal Sciences]
Queensl LJ & R — Queensland Law Journal and Reports
Queensl LJ (Austr) — Queensland Law Journal (Australia)
Queensl LR — Queensland Law Reports
Queensl LSJ — Queensland Law Society. Journal
Queensl L Soc'y J — Queensland Law Society. Journal
Queensl Nat — Queensland Naturalist
Queensl Nurses J — Queensland Nurses Journal
Queens LR — Queensland Law Reports (Beor)
Queensl R S P — Proceedings of the Royal Society of Queensland
Queensl SC (Austr) — Queensland. Supreme Court. Reports (Australia)
Queensl S Ct R — Queensland. Supreme Court. Reports
Queensl Soc Sugar Cane Technol Proc — Queensland Society of Sugar Cane Technologists. Proceedings
Queensl Univ Dep Civ Eng Bull — Queensland University. Department of Civil Engineering. Bulletin
Queensl Univ Dep Geol Pap — Queensland University. Department of Geology. Papers
Queensl Vet Proc — Queensland Veterinary Proceedings (Australian Veterinary Association, Queensland Division)
Queen's Nurs J — Queen's Nursing Journal
Queen's Papers in Pure and Appl Math — Queen's Papers in Pure and Applied Mathematics
Queen's Q — Queen's Quarterly
Queen's Quart — Queen's Quarterly
Queens Univ Therm Fluid Sci Group Rep — Queen's University. Thermal and Fluid Science Group. Report
Quek Mcr Cl J — Journal of the Quekett Microscopical Club
Que Lait — Quebec Laitier
Quellen & Forsch Gesch Kreises Beckum — Quellen und Forschungen zur Geschichte des Kreises Beckum
Quellen Gesch Stadt Wien — Quellen zur Geschichte der Stadt Wien
Quellen Schriften P M Hahn — Quellen und Schriften zu Philipp Matthaus Hahn
Quellenschr Kstgesch — Quellenschriften fuer Kunstgeschichte
Quellen Stud Gesch Arabischen Math — Quellen und Studien ueber die Geschichte der Arabischen Mathematik
Quellenstud Holl Kstgesch — Quellenstudien zur Hollandischen Kunstgeschichte
Quellen Stud Musikgesch Antike Gegenwart — Quellen und Studien zur Musikgeschichte von der Antike bis in die Gegenwart
Quellen Stud Philos — Quellen und Studien zur Philosophie
Quell Stud Gesch Nat — Quellen und Studien zur Geschichte der Mathematik, Astronomie, und Physik
Que Minist Agric Pech Aliment Dir Gen Pech Marit Cah Inf — Quebec. Ministere de l'Agriculture, des Pecheries, et de l'Alimentation. Direction General des Peches Maritimes. Cahier d'Information
Que Minist Agric Pech Aliment Dir Rech Sci Tech Cah Inf — Quebec. Ministere de l'Agriculture, des Pecheries, et de l'Alimentation. Direction de la Recherche Scientifique et Technique. Cahier d'Information
Que Minist Chasse Pech Contrib — Quebec. Ministere de la Chasse et des Pecheries. Contributions
Que Minist Energ Ressour Etude Spec ES — Quebec. Ministere de l'Energie et des Ressources. Etude Speciale ES
Que Minist Energ Ressour Rapp Geol — Quebec. Ministere de l'Energie et des Ressources. Rapport Geologique
Que Minist Energ Ressour Serv Rech For Mem — Quebec. Ministere de l'Energie et des Ressources. Service de la Recherche Forestiere. Memoire
Que Minist Energ Ressour Serv Rech For Note — Quebec. Ministere de l'Energie et des Ressources. Service de la Recherche Forestiere. Note
Que Minist Energ Ressour Serv Rech Mem — Quebec. Ministere de l'Energie et des Ressources. Service de la Recherche. Memoire
Que Minist Ind Commer Dir Rech Cah Inf — Quebec. Ministere de l'Industrie et du Commerce. Direction de la Recherches Cahiers d'Information
Que Minist Ind Commer Rapp Pech — Quebec. Ministere de l'Industrie et du Commerce. Rapport sur les Pecheries
Que Minist Ind Commer Serv Biol Rapp Annu — Quebec. Ministere de l'Industrie et du Commerce. Service de Biologie. Rapport Annuel

Que Minist Richesses Nat Etude Spec — Quebec. Ministere des Richesses Naturelles. Etude Speciale

Que Minist Richesses Nat Etude Spec ES — Quebec. Ministere des Richesses Naturelles. Etude Speciale ES

Que Minist Terres For Serv Rech Mem — Quebec. Ministere des Terres et Forets. Service de la Recherche. Memoire

Que Minist Terres For Serv Rech Note — Quebec. Ministere des Terres et Forets. Service de la Recherche. Note

Que (Prov) Bur Mines Prelim Rep — Quebec (Province). Bureau of Mines. Preliminary Report

Que (Prov) Dep Mines Gen Rep Minist Mines — Quebec (Province). Department of Mines. General Report of the Minister of Mines

Que Prov Dep Mines Geol Rep — Quebec (Province). Department of Mines. Geological Report

Que Prov Dep Mines Prelim Rep — Quebec (Province). Department of Mines. Preliminary Report

Que Prov Dep Nat Resour Geol Rep — Quebec (Province). Department of Natural Resources. Geological Report

Que (Prov) Dep Nat Resour Prelim Rep — Quebec (Province). Department of Natural Resources. Preliminary Report

Que Prov Dep Nat Resour Spec Pap — Quebec (Province). Department of Natural Resources. Special Paper

Que Prov Minist Richesses Nat Rapp Geol — Quebec (Province). Ministere des Richesses Naturelles. Rapport Geologique

Que (Prov) Minist Richesses Nat Rapp Prelim — Quebec (Province). Ministere des Richesses Naturelles. Rapport Preliminaire

QueQ — Queen's Quarterly

Que Rev Regs — Revised Regulations of Quebec

Que Rev Stat — Revised Statutes of Quebec

Query File Commonw Bur Hortic Plant Crops — Query File. Commonwealth Bureau of Horticulture and Plantation Crops

QueS — Quebec 66-68

Que Sais Je — Que Sais-je. Le Point des Connaissances Humaines

Que Sci — Quebec Science

Que Serv Faune Bull — Quebec. Service de la Faune. Bulletin

Que Serv Faune Rapp — Quebec. Service de la Faune. Rapport

Que Soc Prot Plants Rep — Quebec Society for the Protection of Plants. Report

Quest Act Soc — Questions Actuelles du Socialisme

Quest Act Socialisme — Questions Actuelles du Socialisme

Quest Dip — Questions Diplomatiques et Coloniales

Quest Diplom Colon — Questions Diplomatiques et Coloniales

Quest For — Questions of Forestry

QUESTIIO — Quaderns d'Estadistica. Sistemes. Informatica i Investigacio Operativa

Questions Liturg & Paroiss — Questions Liturgiques et Paroissiales

Quest Quat Geol — Questions of Quaternary Geology

Quest Stor Contemp — Questioni di Storia Contemporanea

Quetelet Cor Mth — Correspondance Mathematique et Physique. Publiee par MM. Garnier et Quetelet

Quetico-Super Wilderness Res Cent Annu Rep — Quetico-Superior Wilderness Research Center. Annual Report

Quetico-Super Wilderness Res Cent Tech Note — Quetico-Superior Wilderness Research Center. Technical Note

Queueing Systems Theory Appl — Queueing Systems. Theory and Applications

QUF — National Bank of Yugoslavia. Quarterly Bulletin

Qu Forschgg Sprach Gesch Germ Voelker — Quellen und Forschungen zur Sprach- und Kulturgeschichte der Germanischen Voelker

QU Gazette — Queensland University. Gazette

Qu H Ostdt Osteur Kirchengesch — Quellenhefte zur Ostdeutschen und Osteuropaeischen Kirchengeschichte

QUIBA — Quimica e Industria

Quick Bibliogr Ser US Dep Agric Natl Agric Libr US — Quick Bibliography Series. US Department of Agriculture. National Agricultural Library (US)

QUIJA — Quintessence International

QUILL — QUILL: Queensland Inter-Library Liaison

Quill & Q — Quill and Quire

Quim Anal — Quimica Analitica

Quim Anal Barcelona — Quimica Analitica (Barcelona)

Quim Anal Madrid — Quimica Analitica (Madrid)

Quim Clin — Quimica Clinica

Quim Farm — Quimica y Farmica

Quim Ind — Quimica e Industria

Quim Ind (Barcelona) — Quimica e Industria (Barcelona)

Quim Ind (Bogota) — Quimica e Industria (Bogota)

Quim Ind (Madrid) — Quimica e Industria (Madrid)

Quim Ind (Montevideo) — Quimica Industrial (Montevideo)

Quim Ind (Sao Paulo) — Quimica e Industria (Sao Paulo)

Quim Nova — Quimica Nova

Quinquenn Congr Int Rech Text Lainiere — Quinquennial Congres International de la Recherche Textile Lainiere

Quinquenn Int Wool Text Res Conf Pap — Quinquennial International Wool Textile Research Conference. Papers

Quintessence Dent Technol — Quintessence of Dental Technology

Quintessence Int — Quintessence International

Quintessence Int Dent Dig — Quintessence International Dental Digest

Quintessencia Protese Lab — Quintessencia de Protese de Laboratorio

Quintessenz J — Quintessenz Journal

Quintessenz Zahntech — Quintessenz der Zahntechnik

Quinz Lit — Quinzaine Litteraire

Quivera Soc Pub — Quivera Society. Publications

Quix — Quixote

Qu Jour Int-Amer Rel — Quarterly Journal of Inter-American Relations

QUKO — Quellen und Untersuchungen zur Konfessionskunde der Orthodoxie

Qu Lait — Quebec Laitier

QU Law J — University of Queensland. Law Journal

Qu LJ — Quarterly Law Journal

QULJ — Queensland University. Law Journal

Qu L Rev — Quarterly Law Review

Qu Minist Ind Commer Serv Rech Cah Inf — Quebec. Ministere de l'Industrie et du Commerce. Service de la Recherche. Cahiers d'Information

Qu Minist Terres For Serv Rech Mem — Quebec. Ministere des Terres et Forets. Service de la Recherche. Memoire

Qu Minist Terres For Serv Rech Note — Quebec. Ministere des Terres et Forets. Service de la Recherche. Note

Q Univ Gaz — University of Queensland. Gazette

QUNJA — Queensland Nurses Journal

QUODD — Quodlibet

Qu (Prov) Dep Mines Gen Rep Minist Mines — Quebec (Province). Department of Mines. General Report. Minister of Mines

Qu (Prov) Dep Mines Prelim Rep — Quebec (Province). Department of Mines. Preliminary Report

Qu (Prov) Dep Nat Resour Spec Pap — Quebec (Province). Department of Natural Resources. Special Paper

QuQu — Queen's Quarterly

QURBA — Quarterly Reviews of Biophysics

QUREA — Quarterly Reviews. Chemical Society

Qu Serv Faune Bull — Quebec. Service de la Faune. Bulletin

Qu Serv Faune Rapp — Quebec. Service de la Faune. Rapport

QUSZA — Quintessenz Journal

QV — Quatro Ventos

QV — Quo Vadis

QVGDR — Quellen und Studien zur Verfassungsgeschichte des Deutschen Reichs im Mittelalter und Neuzeit

Q Vit — Quaderni del Vittoriale

QVJVVNW — Quellenverzeichnis der Justizverwaltungsvorschriften des Landes Nordrhein-Westfalen

QVQ — 84 Nouvelle Revue Litteraire

Q W — Quarterly West

QWLD — Quality of Worklife Database

QWN — Weekly Notes. Queensland

R

R — Race
R — Radio (BBC Monitoring)
R — Railway
R — Realites
R — Rechtsstrijd
R — Rep
R — Republika
R — Revue
R — Rig
R — Rio Do Janeiro
R — Romania
R — Runa [*Buenos Aires*]
R — Rydge's
Ra — Raduga
Ra — Rassegna
RA — Rating Appeals
RA — Real Encyclopaedie der Classischen Altertumswissenschaft
RA — Rechtsgeleerde Adviezen
RA — Rechtskundige Adviseur
Ra — Repertorio Americano
RA — Research Abstracts
RA — Reviews in Anthropology
RA — Revista de Antropologia
RA — Revue Administrative
RA — Revue Anglo-Americaine
RA — Revue Archeologique
RA — Revue d'Alger
RA — Revue d'Anthropologie
RA — Revue d'Assyriologie
RA — Revue d'Assyriologie et d'Archeologie Orientale
RA — Revue de l'Administration et du Droit Administratif de la Belgique
RA — Revue des Arts
RA — Rheinisches Archiv
RA — Romanistische Arbeitshefte
RA — Russkij Archiv
RAA — Recueil des Arrets et Avis du Conseil d'Etat
RAA — Rendiconti. Accademia di Archeologia, Lettere, e Belle Arti
RAA — Repertoire d'Art et d'Archeologie
RAA — Revue. Academie Arabe
RAA — Revue Africaine (Algiers)
RAA — Revue Anglo-Americaine
RAA — Revue d'Assyriologie et d'Archeologie Orientale
RAA — Revue de l'Art Ancien et Moderne
RAA — Revue des Arts Asiatiques
RAACA — Radiochimica Acta
RAACE — Recueil des Arrets et Avis du Conseil d'Etat
RAAD — Revue. Academie Arabe de Damas
RAAEAV — South Africa. Department of Agriculture. Entomology Memoir
RAAEC Nletter — Royal Australian Army. Educational Corps. Newsletter
RAAF Reserve — Royal Australian Air Force Reserve. Magazine
RAAGA — Railway Age
RAAG Res Notes — Research Notes and Memoranda of Applied Geometry for Prevenient Natural Philosophy
RAAm — Revue Anglo-Americaine
RAAM — Revue de l'Art Ancien et Moderne
RAAN — Rendiconti. Accademia di Archeologia, Lettere, e Belle Arti (Napoli)
RAANES — Recent Advances in Animal Nutrition
RAAO — Revue d'Assyriologie et d'Archeologie Orientale
RAAP — Revue des Arts Asiatiques (Paris)
RAAQ — Recherches Amerindiennes au Quebec. Bulletin d'Information
RA Art Louvain — Revue des Archeologues et Historiens d'Art de Louvain
RAAs — Revue des Arts Asiatiques
RABA — Revista Americana de Buenos Aires
Rab Azovsko-Chernomorsk Nauchn Rybokhoz Stn — Raboty Azovsko-Chernomorskoi Nauchnoi Rybokhozyaistvennoi Stantsii
RABBAR — Revista. Museo Argentino de Ciencias Naturales Bernardino Rivadavia e Instituto Nacional de Investigacion de las Ciencias Naturales. Ciencias Botanicas
Rab Donetsk Nauchno Issled Ugoln Inst — Raboty Donetskii Nauchno-Issledovatel'skii Ugol'nyi Institut
Rab Fiz Tverd Tela — Raboty po Fizike Tverdogo Tela
Rab Issled Inst Meteorol Gidrol Chast 2 — Raboty i Issledovaniya. Institut Meteorologii i Gidrologii. Chast 2. Gidrologiya
Rab Khim Rastvorov Kompleksn Soedin — Raboty po Khimii Rastvorov i Kompleksnykh Soedinenii
RABM — Revista de Archivos, Bibliotecas, y Museos

RABMA — Radiobiologia si Biologia Moleculara
Rab Metall (Moscow) — Rabochii Metallurg (Moscow)
Rab Molodykh Uch Vses Akad Skh Nauk — Raboty Molodykh Uchenykh Vsesoyuznaya Akademiya Sel'skokhozyaistvennykh Nauk
RABN — Revista de Archivos y Bibliotecas Nacionales [*Lima*]
Rab Neft — Rabochii Neftyanik
RABo — Rendiconto. Accademia della Scienze. Istituto di Bologna
RABOA — Radiation Botany
Rabocij Klass Sovrem Mir — Rabocij Klass i Sovremennyj Mir
RABol — Rendiconto. Accademia delle Scienze. Istituto di Bologna
R Abolit — Revue Abolitionniste
Raboty Oksk Biol Stancii Gorode Murome — Raboty Okskoj Biologiceskoj Stancii v Gorode Murome. Arbeiten der Biologischen Oka-Station
Raboty Volzsk Biol Stancii — Raboty Volzskoj Biologiceskoj Stancii. Arbeiten (aus) der Biologischen Wolga-Station. Travaux. Station Biologique a Volga
RAbr — Rivista Abruzzese
Rab Stavropol Sta Zashch Rast — Raboty Stavropol'skoi Stantsii Zashchity Rastenii
Rab Tyan-Shan Fiz-Geogr Sta — Raboty Tyan-Shan'skoi Fiziko-Geograficheskoi Stantsii. Akademiya Nauk Kirgizskoi SSR
Rab Tyan Shan'skoi Fiz Geogr Stn Akad Nauk Kirg SSR — Raboty Tyan-Shan'skoi Fiziko-Geograficheskoi Stantsii. Akademiya Nauk Kirgizskoi SSR
Rab Volzh Biol Sta — Raboty Volzhskoi Biologicheskoi Stantsii
Rab Zootom Lab Varsh Univ — Raboty iz Zootomicheskoi Laboratorii Varshavskago Universiteta
RAC — Race
Rac — Raceduen
RAC — Reallexikon fuer Antike und Christentum
RAc — Revista Acoriana
RAC — Revue Academique du Centre
RAC — Revue de l'Art Chretien
RAC — Rivista Archeologia. Provincia e Diocesi di Como
RAC — Rivista di Archeologia Cristiana
RACA — Annual Report. American Congregational Association
RACAA — Radiocarbon
R Acad Cienc Exactas Fis Nat Madrid Mem — Real Academia de Ciencias Exactas, Fisicas, y Naturales de Madrid. Memorias
R Acad Cienc Exactas Fis Nat Madrid Mem Ser Cienc Exactas — Real Academia de Ciencias Exactas, Fisicas, y Naturales de Madrid. Memorias. Serie de Ciencias Exactas
R Acad Cienc Exactas Fis Nat Madrid Mem Ser Cienc Nat — Real Academia de Ciencias Exactas, Fisicas, y Naturales de Madrid. Memorias. Serie de Ciencias Naturales
R Acad Cienc y Artes Barcelona Mem — Real Academia de Ciencias y Artes de Barcelona. Memorias
R Acad De Cienc Med Fis Y Nat De La Habana Anales — Real Academia de Ciencias Medicas, Fisicas y Naturales de la Habana. Anales
R Acad Farm Barcelona Discurso Ingreso — Real Academia de Farmacia de Barcelona. Discurso de Ingreso
R Acad Farm Barcelona Discursos Recepcion — Real Academia de Farmacia de Barcelona. Discursos de Recepcion
R Acad Farm Barcelona Publ Ser A — Real Academia de Farmacia de Barcelona. Publicaciones. Serie A. Anuarios, Memorias, y Discursos Inaugurales de Curso
R Acad Farm Barcelona Ses Inaug — Real Academia de Farmacia de Barcelona. Sesion Inaugural
R Acad Galega Cienc Rev — Real Academia Galega de Ciencis. Revista
R Acad Jurispr Legisl — Revista. Real Academia de Jurisprudencia y Legislacion
R Acad Nac Med An Spain — Real Academia Nacional de Medicina. Anales (Spain)
RA C Ant Nat — Revue Archeologique. Centre Consacree aux Antiquites Nationales
RACathHS — Records. American Catholic Historical Society of Philadelphia
RACC — Revista de la Academia Colombiana de Ciencias Exactas, Fisicas, y Naturales Correspondiente de la Espanola [*Bogota*]
R Acc — Revue des Accidents du Travail
R Accad Di Med Di Torino Giorn — Reale Accademia di Medicina di Torino. Giornale
R Accad Sci Lett Arti Modena Mem — Reale Accademia di Scienze, Lettere, ed Arti in Modena. Memorie
Racc Fis-Chim Ital — Raccolta Fisico-Chimica Italiana
R Ac Cienc Habana An — Real Academia de Ciencias Medicas, Fisicas, y Naturales de la Habana. Anales
Racc Memorie Biol — Raccolta di Memorie Biologiche
Racc Memorie Ital Lar Rinol Otoiat — Raccolta di Memorie Italiane sulla Laringologia, Rinologia, ed Otoiatria
Raccoglitore Med Forli — Raccoglitore Medico Fano Forli

Raccogl Med — Raccoglitore Medico
Raccolta Mem Turin Univ Fac Sci Agr — Raccolta di Memorie. Turin. Universita. Facolta di Scienze Agrarie
Racc Opuscoli Sci Filol — Raccolta d'Opuscoli Scientifici e Filologici
Racc Pubbl Scient Ist Med Leg Aeronaut — Raccolta di Pubblicazioni Scientifiche degli Istituti Medico-Legali per l'Aeronautica
Race — Race and Class
Race Clas — Race and Class
Race Hyg — Race Hygiene
Race Rela L R — Race Relations Law Reporter
Race Rela L Sur — Race Relations Law Survey
RACF — Revue Archeologique du Centre de la France
RACh — Reallexikon fuer Antike und Christentum
RACHA — Rassegna Chimica
RACHE — Revista. Academia Colombiana de Historia Ecclesiastica
RACHS — Records. American Catholic Historical Society of Philadelphia
RACHSP — Records. American Catholic Historical Society of Philadelphia
Racing Car Rev — Racing Car Review
RACJ — Revista de la Asociacion Catolica de la Juventud Ecuatoriana [Quito]
Racjon Budow — Racjonalizator Budowlany
RACND3 — Annual Research Reviews. Rheumatoid Arthritis and Related Conditions
RAComo — Rivista Archeologia. Provincia e Diocesi di Como
R A Como — Rivista Archeologica dell'Antica Provincia e Diocesi di Como
RA Cr — Rivista di Archeologia Cristiana
RACrist — Rivista di Archeologia Cristiana
R Action Soc — Revue d'Action Sociale
Rac Uff — Raccolta Ufficiale delle Leggi e dei Decreti della Repubblica Italiana
Rac Uff Corte Cost — Raccolta Ufficiale delle Sentenze e Ordinanze delle CorteCostituzionale
Rac Vinc — Raccolta Vinciana
RACYA — Reviews in Analytical Chemistry
RACZA — Revista. Academia de Ciencias Exactas, Fisico-Quimicas, y Naturales de Zaragoza
Rad — Radical Teacher
Rad — Rad Jugoslavenski Akademija Znanosti i Umjetnosti
RAD — Revue d'Art Dramatique
RadA — Radical America
RADA — Revue de l'Administration et du Droit Administratif de la Belgique
Rad Akad Nauka Umjet Bosne Hercegovine Od Prir Met Nauka — Radovi. Akademija Nauka i Umjetnosti Bosne i Hercegovine. Odjeljenje Prirodnih i Matematickih Nauka
Rad Am — Radical America
Rad Amer — Radical America
RADAR — Repertoire Analytique d'Articles de Revues de Quebec
Radar Bull — Radar Bulletin
Radar Electron — Radar and Electronics
RADBA — Radiobiology
Rad Clinica — Radiologia Clinica
Rad Clin NA — Radiologic Clinics of North America
Rad Diagn — Radiologia Diagnostica
Rad Eng (London) — Radio Engineering (London)
Radex Rdsch — Radex Rundschau
Radex Rundsch — Radex Rundschau
Radex Runsch — Radex Rundschau
Rad Geofiz Inst Zagr — Radovi. Geofizicki Institut, Sveuciliste u Zagrebu
Rad Geofiz Zav Zagr — Rad Geofizickog Zavoda u Zagrebu
Rad Geoinst — Radovi - Geoinstitut
Rad Hist — Radical History Review
Rad Hrvatske Akad Znan Umjet — Rad Hrvatske Akademije Znanosti i Umjetnosti
Rad Human — Radical Humanist
Rad Humanist — Radical Humanist
RADIA — Radiography
Radiac Sol — Radiacion Solar
Radiat and Environ Biophys — Radiation and Environmental Biophysics
Radiata Pine Tech Bull — Radiata Pine Technical Bulletin (Radiata Pine Association of Australia)
Radiat Biol — Radiation Biology
Radiat Bot — Radiation Botany
Radiat Bot Suppl — Radiation Botany. Supplement
Radiat Cell Response Rep John Lawrence Interdiscip Symp Phys — Radiation and Cellular Response. Report. John Lawrence Interdisciplinary Symposium on the Physical and Biomedical Sciences
Radiat Cent Osaka Prefect Tech Rep — Radiation Center of Osaka Prefecture. Technical Report
Radiat Chem Aqueous Syst Proc L Farkas Mem Symp — Radiation Chemistry of Aqueous Systems. Proceedings of the L. Farkas Memorial Symposium
Radiat Chem Proc Tihany Symp — Radiation Chemistry. Proceedings of the Tihany Symposium
Radiat Chem Sapporo — Radiation Chemistry (Sapporo)
Radiat Curing — Radiation Curing
Radiat Data Rep — Radiation Data and Reports
Radiat Detect Their Uses Proc Workshop — Radiation Detectors and Their Uses. Proceedings. Workshop on Radiation Detectors and Their Uses
Radiat Eff — Radiation Effects
Radiat Eff Defects Solids — Radiation Effects and Defects in Solids
Radiat Effects — Radiation Effects
Radiat Eff Express — Radiation Effects Express
Radiat Eff Inf Cent Rep — Radiation Effects Information Center Report
Radiat Eff Lett — Radiation Effects. Letters Section
Radiat Eff Lett Sect — Radiation Effects. Letters Section
Radiat Env — Radiation and Environmental Biophysics
Radiat Environ Biophys — Radiation and Environmental Biophysics
Radiat Meas — Radiation Measurements
Radiat Med — Radiation Medicine

Radiat Oncol Investig — Radiation Oncology Investigations
Radiat Phys and Chem — Radiation Physics and Chemistry
Radiat Phys Chem — Radiation Physics and Chemistry
Radiat Prot — Radiation Protection
Radiat Prot Aust — Radiation Protection in Australia
Radiat Prot Dosim — Radiation Protection Dosimetry
Radiat Prot Dosimetry — Radiation Protection Dosimetry
Radiat Prot ICRP Publ — Radiation Protection. ICRP [International Commission on Radiological Protection] Publication
Radiat Prot Manage — Radiation Protection Management
Radiat Prot (Seoul) — Radiation Protection (Seoul)
Radiat Prot (Taiyuan People's Repub China) — Radiation Protection (Taiyuan, People's Republic of China)
Radiat Recomb Semicond Int Conf Phys Semicond — Radiative Recombination in Semiconductors. International Conference on the Physics of Semiconductors
Radiat Rep — Radiation Report
Radiat Res — Radiation Research
Radiat Res Polym — Radiation Research on Polymers
Radiat Res Polym Tokyo — Radiation Research on Polymers (Tokyo)
Radiat Res Proc Int Congr — Radiation Research. Proceedings. International Congress of Radiation Research
Radiat Res Rev — Radiation Research Reviews
Radiat Res Suppl — Radiation Research. Supplement
Radiats Bezop Zashch AEhS — Radiatsionnaya Bezopasnost' i Zashchita AEhS. Sbornik Statej
Radiats Bezop Zashch AES — Radiatsionnaya Bezopasnost i Zashchita AES [Atomnaya Elektrostantsiya]
Radiats Biol — Radiatsionnaya Biologiya
Radiats Biol Radioecol — Radiatsionnaia Biologiia, Radioecologiia
Radiats Defekty Met Mater Vses Soveshch — Radiatsionnye Defekty v Metallakh. Materialy Vsesoyuznogo Soveshchaniya
Radiats Eff Met Splavakh Mater Vses Soveshch — Radiatsionnye Effekty v Metallakh i Splavakh. Materialy Vsesoyuznogo Soveshchaniya
Radiats Fiz — Radiatsionnaya Fizika
Radiats Fiz Akad Nauk Latv SSR Inst Fiz — Radiatsionnaya Fizika. Akademiya Nauk Latviiskoi SSR. Institut Fiziki
Radiats Fiz Nemet Krist — Radiatsionnaya Fizika Nemetallicheskikh Kristallov
Radiats Fiz Tverd Tela Radiats Materialoved — Radiatsionnaya Fizika Tverdogo Tela i Radiatsionnoe Materialovedenie
Radiats Gig — Radiatsionnaya Gigiena
Radiat Shielding Inf Cent Rep — Radiation Shielding Information Center. Report
Radiats Issled — Radiatsionnye Issledovaniya
Radiats Khim Tekhnol — Radiatsionno-Khimicheskaya Tekhnologiya
Radiats Stimul Yavleniya Tverd Telakh — Radiatsionno-Stimulirovannye Yavleniya v Tverdykh Telakh
Radiats Tekh — Radiatsionnaya Tekhnika
Radiaz Alta Energ — Radiazioni di Alta Energia
Radiaz Radioisot — Radiazioni e Radioisotopi
Radical Am — Radical America
Radical Commun Med — Radical Community Medicine
Radical Educ Dossier — Radical Education Dossier
Radical His — Radical History Review
Radical Hist — Radical History
Radical Scot — Radical Scotland
Radic Phil — Radical Philosophy
Radic Sci — Radical Science
Radic Sci J — Radical Science Journal
Radiesth Scient — Radiesthesie Scientifique
Rad Imunol Zavoda (Zagreb) — Radovi Imunoloskog Zavoda (Zagreb)
Rad Inst Geol-Rud Istraz Ispit Nukl Drugih Miner Sirovina — Radovi Instituta za Geolosko-Rudarska Istrazivanja i Ispitivanja Nuklearnih i Drugih Mineralnih Sirovina
Rad Inst Nauc Istraz Sum Srb — Radovi. Institut za Naucna Istrazivanja u Sumarstvu Srbije
Rad Inst Proucavanje Suzbijanje Alkohol Drugih Narkomanija — Radovi Instituta za Proucavanje i Suzbijanje Alkoholizma i Drugih Narkomanija uZagrebu
Rad Inst Prouc Suzbijanje Alkohol Drugih Narkomanija Zagrebu — Radovi Instituta za Proucavanje i Suzbijanje Alkoholizma i Drugih Narkomanija uZagrebu
Rad Inst Sum Istraz — Radovi Institut za Sumarska Istrazivanja. Sumarskog Fakulteta. Sveuciliste u Zagrebu
Radioact Nucl Beams Proc Int Conf — Radioactive Nuclear Beams. Proceedings. International Conference
Radioact Sea — Radioactivity in the Sea
Radioact Surv Data Jap — Radioactivity Survey Data in Japan
Radioact Waste Disposal Res Ser Inst Geol Sci — Radioactive Waste Disposal. Research Series. Institute of Geological Sciences
Radioact Waste Manage — Radioactive Waste Management
Radioact Waste Manage and Nucl Fuel Cycle — Radioactive Waste Management and the Nuclear Fuel Cycle
Radioact Waste Manage Disposal Proc Eur Community Conf — Radioactive Waste Management and Disposal. Proceedings. European Community Conference on Radioactive Waste Management and Disposal
Radioact Waste Manage Environ Restor — Radioactive Waste Management and Environmental Restoration
Radioact Waste Manage Nucl Fuel Cycle — Radioactive Waste Management and the Nuclear Fuel Cycle
Radioact Waste Manage (Oak Ridge Tenn) — Radioactive Waste Management (Oak Ridge, Tennessee)
Radioact Waste Technol — Radioactive Waste Technology
Radio Aids Mar Navig — Radio Aids to Marine Navigation
Radioakt Isot Klin Forsch — Radioactive Isotope in Klinik und Forschung
Radioaktiv Zivotn Prostr — Radioaktivita a Zivotne Prostredie
Radio Amat Handb — Radio Amateurs Handbook
Radio Amat News — Radio Amateur News

Radio & Electron Constructor — Radio and Electronics Constructor
Radio and Electron Eng — Radio and Electronic Engineer
Radio & Electronic Eng — Radio and Electronic Engineer
Radio and Electron World — Radio and Electronics World
Radio & TV N — Radio and Television News
Radiobiol — Radiobiologiya
Radiobiol Biol Mol — Radiobiologia si Biologia Moleculara
Radiobiol Inf Byull — Radiobiologiya Informatsionnyi Byulleten'
Radiobiol Lat — Radiobiologica Latina
Radiobiol Proc All Union Sci Tech Conf Appl Radioact Isot — Radiobiology. A Portion of the Proceedings. All-Union Scientific and Technical Conference on the Application of Radioactive Isotopes
Radiobiol Proc Australas Conf — Radiobiology. Proceedings. Australasian Conference on Radiobiology
Radiobiol Radioter Fis Med — Radiobiologia, Radioterapia, e Fisica Medica
Radiobiol-Radiother — Radiobiologia-Radiotherapia
Radiobiol-Radiother (Berl) — Radiobiologia-Radiotherapia (Berlin)
Radiobiol-Radiother (Berlin) — Radiobiologia-Radiotherapia (Berlin)
Radiobr — Radiobranchen
Radioch Act — Radiochimica Acta
Radiochem and Radioanal Lett — Radiochemical and Radioanalytical Letters
Radiochem Cent Rev Amersham Eng — Radiochemical Centre. Review (Amersham, England)
Radiochem Radioanal Lett — Radiochemical and Radioanalytical Letters
Radiochim Acta — Radiochimica Acta
Radioch Rad — Radiochemical and Radioanalytical Letters
Radiochuvstvitelnost Mutabilnost Rast — Radiochuvstvitel'nost i Mutabil'nost Rastenii
Radio Circ US Weath Bur — Radio Circular. United States Weather Bureau
Radio Commun — Radio Communication
Radio Commun Pamph — Radio Communication Pamphlets
Radio Constr — Radio Constructor
Radio Constr Depann — Radio Constructeur et Depanneur
Radioekol Vodn Org — Radioekologiya Vodnykh Organizmov
Radio Elec — Radio-Electronics
Radio-Electr — Radio-Electronics
Radio Elect Rev — Radio and Electrical Review
Radio Electron — Radio Electronica
Radio-Electron — Radio-Electronics
Radioelectron and Commun Syst — Radioelectronics and Communication Systems
Radio Electron Commun Syst — Radio Electronics and Communications Systems
Radioelectron Commun Syst Engl Transl — Radioelectronics and Communications Systems. English Translation
Radio Electron Compon — Radio and Electronic Components
Radio Electron Eng — Radio and Electronic Engineer
Radio Electron Eng (London) — Radio and Electronic Engineer (London)
Radio Electron Engng — Radio Electronic Engineering
Radio Electron Ref A — Radio-Electronic Reference Annual
Radio Electron Wld — Radio and Electronics World
Radio Elect Wkly — Radio Electrical Weekly
Radio Elec W — Radio Electrical Weekly
Radio Elektron — Radio Elektronica
Radio Elektroniikkalab Tek Korkeakoulu Kertomus — Radio- ja Elektroniikkalaboratoriot. Teknillinen Korkeakoulu. Kertomus
Radio Elektron Schau — Radio Elektronik Schau
Radio El En — Radio and Electronic Engineer
Radio Eng — Radio Engineering
Radio Eng and Electron Phys — Radio Engineering and Electronic Physics
Radio Eng Electron Engl Transl — Radio Engineering and Electronics. English Translation
Radio Eng Electron Phys — Radio Engineering and Electronic Physics
Radio Eng Electron Phys Engl Transl — Radio Engineering and Electronic Physics. English Translation
Radio Eng Electron (USSR) — Radio Engineering and Electronic Physics (USSR)
Radio Eng Engl Transl — Radio Engineering. English Translation
Radio Engng Lond — Radio Engineering (London, New York)
Radio Engrg Electron Phys — Radio Engineering and Electronic Physics
Radio Eng (USSR) — Radio Engineering (USSR)
Radio es TV Szle — Radio es TV Szemle
Radio Fernsehen Elektron — Radio Fernsehen Elektronik
Radio Freq Power Plasmas — Radio Frequency Power in Plasmas
Radiogr — Radiographer
Radiographer East Melbourne Aust — Radiographer (East Melbourne, Australia)
Radiogr Clin Photogr Lond — Radiography and Clinical Photography (London)
Radiogr Clin Photogr Rochester NY — Radiography and Clinical Photography (Rochester, New York)
Radiogr Today — Radiography Today
Radio Ind — Radio Industria
Radio Ind Brux — Radio-Industrie (Bruxelles)
Radioind Elettron-Telev — Radioindustria Elettronica-Televisione
Radioisot (Praha) — Radioisotopy (Praha)
Radioisot Soc Philipp Proc — Radioisotope Society of the Philippines. Proceedings
Radioisot (Tokyo) — Radioisotopes (Tokyo)
Radio Lab Tech Univ Helsinki Intern Rep — Radio Laboratory. Technical University of Helsinki. Internal Report
Radiol Austriaca — Radiologia Austriaca
Radiol Bras — Radiologia Brasileira
Radiol Cancer Sel Pap Int Congr Radiol — Radiology of Cancer. Selected Papers. International Congress of Radiology
Radiol Clin — Radiologia Clinica
Radiol Clin — Radiologica Clinica et Biologica
Radiol Clin (Basel) — Radiologia Clinica (Basel)
Radiol Clin Biol — Radiologia Clinica et Biologica

Radiol Clin N Am — Radiologic Clinics of North America
Radiol Clin North Am — Radiologic Clinics of North America
Radiol Clin North America — Radiologic Clinics of North America
Radiol Diagn — Radiologia Diagnostica
Radiol Diagn (Berlin) — Radiologia Diagnostica (Berlin)
Radiol Health Data — Radiological Health Data
Radiol Health Data Rep — Radiological Health Data and Reports
Radiol Hlth Data — Radiological Health Data
Radiol Hung — Radiologia Hungarica
Radiol Iugosl (Ljubljana) — Radiologia Iugoslavica (Ljubljana)
Radiol Kozl — Radiologiai Kozlemenyek
Radiol Manage — Radiology Management
Radiol Med — Radiologia Medica
Radiol Med (Torino) — Radiologia Medica (Torino)
Radiol Mitt — Radiologische Mitteilungen
Radiologia Clin — Radiologia Clinica
Radiologia Fis Med — Radiologia e Fisica Medica
Radiologia Med — Radiologia Medica
Radiologia Prat — Radiologia Pratica
Radiologica Cancer — Radiologica-Cancerologica
Radiological Protect Bull — Radiological Protection Bulletin
Radiologica Prat — Radiologica Pratica</PHR> %
Radiologic Rev — Radiologic Review
Radiol Oncol — Radiology and Oncology
Radiol Prakt — Radiologische Praktika
Radiol Prat — Radiologia Pratica
Radiol Proc Congr Eur Assoc Radiol — Radiology. Proceedings of the Congress of the European Association of Radiology
Radiol Prot Bull — Radiological Protection Bulletin
Radiol Rdsch — Radiologische Rundschau
Radiol Rev Chicago Med Rec — Radiological Review and the Chicago Medical Recorder
Radiol Rev Miss Vall Med J — Radiological Review and Mississippi Valley Medical Journal
Radiol Rev Miss Val Med J — Radiological Review and Mississippi Valley Medical Journal
Radiol Sci — Radiological Sciences
Radiol Technol — Radiologic Technology
Radio Mentor Electron — Radio Mentor Electronic
Radiom News — Radiometer News
Radio Mntr — Radio Mentor Electronic
Radio Mosk — Radio (Moskva)
Radiom Polariogr — Radiometer Polariographics
Radiom Polarogr — Radiometer Polarographics
Radio N — Radio News
Radionic Q — Radionic Quarterly
Radionic Ther — Radionic Therapy
Radio Percept — Radio-Perception. The Journal of the British Society of Dowsers
Radioph Rur — Radiophonie Rurale
Radiophys & Quantum Flectron — Radiophysics and Quantum Electronics
Radiophysiol Radiother — Radiophysiologie et Radiotherapie
Radiophys Quantum Electron — Radiophysics and Quantum Electronics
Radiophys Quantum Electron Engl Transl — Radiophysics and Quantum Electronics. English Translation
Radio Sci — Radio Science
Radio Serv Bul — Radio Service Bulletin
Radio S Francisco — Radio (San Francisco)
Radio Sof — Radio (Sofiya)
Radio T — Radio Times
Radio Tech U Export — Radio-Technik und -Export
Radiotehn i Elektron — Akademia Nauk SSSR. Radiotehnika i Elektronika
Radiotehn (Kharkov) — Radiotehnika (Kharkov)
Radiotek El — Radiotekhnika i Elektronika
Radiotekh — Radiotekhnika
Radiotekh Elektron — Radiotekhnika i Elektronika
Radiotekh Elektron Minsk — Radiotekhnika i Elektronika (Minsk)
Radiotekh Elektron (Moscow) — Radiotekhnika i Elektronika (Moscow)
Radiotekh i Elektron — Radiotekhnika i Elektronika
Radiotekhn — Khar'kovskii Ordena Trudovogo Krasnogo Znameni Gosudarstvennyi Universitet Imeni A.M. Gor'kogo Radiotekhnika
Radiotekhn i Elektron — Radiotekhnika i Elektronika. Akademiya Nauk SSSR
Radiotekh Proizvod — Radiotekhnicheskoe Proizvodstvo
Radio Tel & Hobbies — Radio, Television, and Hobbies
Radio Telev — Radio Television
Radio Telev Int Rev — Radio - Television International Review
Radioter Fis Med — Radioterapia e Fisica Medica
Radioter Radiobiol Fis Med — Radioterapia, Radiobiologia, e Fisica Medica
Radiother Oncol — Radiotherapy and Oncology
Radioth Onc — Radiotherapy Oncology
Radio-TV-Electron — Radio-TV-Electronic [Later, RTE. Radio-TV-Electronic]
Radio-TV-Electron Serv — Radio-TV-Electronic Service
Radio TVH — Radio, Television, and Hobbies
Radio TV Serv — Radio-TV-Service [Basle]
Radiovisor Prog — Radiovisor Progress [London]
Radio Wash — Radio (Washington)
Rad Istraz Topola — Radovi na Istrazivanju Topola
Radium Biol Heilk — Radium in Biologie und Heilkunde
Radium Lt — Radium Light
Radium Rep Meml Hosp NY — Radium Report of the Memorial Hospital (New York)
RadJA — Radovi Jugoslavenske Akademije Znanosti i Umjetnosti
Rad Jugosl Akad Znan Umjet — Radovi Jugoslavenske Akademije Znanosti i Umjetnosti
Rad Jugosl Akad Znan Umjetn — Rad Jugoslavenske Akademije Znanosti I Umjetnosti

Rad Jugoslav Akad — Rad Jugoslavenske Akademije
Rad Jugoslav Akad Znan Umjet — Radovi Jugoslavenske Akademije Znanosti i Umjetnosti
Rad Jugoslav Akad Znan Umjet Odjel Prir Nauke — Radovi Jugoslavenske Akademije Znanosti i Umjetnosti. Odjel za Prirodne Nauke
RADKA — Radiokhimiya
Rad Kongr Srp Zemlorad Zadr — Rad Kongresa Srpskih Zemloradnickih Zadruga
RadL — Radyans'ke Literaturoznavstvo
RADLA — Radiology
Radley Nat — Radley Naturalist
R Adm — Revue Administrative
R Adm — Revue de l'Administration et du Droit Administratif de la Belgique
Rad Mat — Radovi Matematicki
Rad Med Fak Rijeka — Radovi Medicinskogo Fakulteta. Rijeka
Rad Med Fak Zagrebu — Radovi Medicinskogo Fakulteta 'u Zagrebu
R Adm Empresas — Revista de Administracao de Empresas
R Admin Empresas — Revista de Administracao de Empresas
R Admin (Paris) — Revue Administrative (Paris)
R Admin Publica — Revista de Administracion Publica
R Adm Municip (Rio De Janeiro) — Revista de Administracao Municipal (Rio De Janeiro)
R Adm Publ (Madrid) — Revista de Administracion Publica (Madrid)
R Adm Publ (Rio De Janeiro) — Revista de Administracao Publica (Rio De Janeiro)
RADOA — Radiobiologiya
Rad OPFFZ — Radovi. Odsjek za Povijest Filozofski Fakultet. Universita Zagreb
Rad O Result — Rad og Resultater
Radovi Inst Povijest Umjetnosti — Radovi Instituta za Povijest Umjetnosti
Radovi JAZU — Radovi Jugoslavenska Akademija Znanosti Umjenosti
Rad Phil — Radical Philosophy
Rad Phil News — Radical Philosopher's Newsjournal
Rad Poljopriv Fak Univ Saraj — Radovi Poljoprivrednog Fakulteta Univerziteta u Sarajevu
Rad Poljopriv Fak Univ Sarajevu — Radovi Poljoprivrednog Fakulteta Univerziteta u Sarajevu
Rad Poljopriv Nauc Istraz Ust — Radovi Poljoprivrednih Naucno-Istrazivackih Ustanova
Rad Poljopriv Sum Fak Univ Saraj — Radovi Poljoprivredno-Sumarskog Fakulteta Univerziteta u Sarajevu
Rad Psihol Inst Zagr — Radovi. Psihologijski Institut, Sveuciliste u Zagrebu
Rad Reg P & F — Radio Regulation. Pike and Fischer
Rad Rel — Radical Religion
Rad Relig — Radical Religion
Rad Sarajevo Univ Poljopr Fak — Radovi Sarajevo Univerzitet. Poljoprivredni Fakultet
Rad Scien — Radical Science Journal
Rad Seizm Zav — Radovi. Seizmoloski Zavod FNR Jugoslavije
Rad Sumar Fak Inst Sumar Sarajevo — Radovi Sumarskog Fakulteta i Instituta za Sumarstvo u Sarajevo
Rad Sum Fak i Inst Sum — Radovi Sumarski Fakultet i Institut za Sumarstvo
Rad Sum Fak Univ Saraj — Radovi Sumarskog Fakulteta Univerziteta Sarajevu
Rad Teach — Radical Teacher
RadTech Rep — RadTech Report
Rad Ther — Issues in Radical Therapy
Rad Thera — Issues in Radical Therapy
Rad Voj Muz — Rad Vojvodanskich Muzeja
Rad Vojvod Muz — Rad Vojvodanskih Muzeja
Radyan Med — Radyans'ka Medytsyna
Radyne Rev — Radyne Review [Wokingham]
Rad Zavoda Fiz — Radovi Zavoda za Fiziku
RadZSF — Radovi Zavoda za Slavensku Filologiju
RAE — Real Academia Espanola. Boletin
RAE — Revista Antioquena de Economia
RAE — Revista Augustiniana de Espiritualidad
RAE — Revue Archeologique de l'Est et du Centre-Est
RAE — Revue d'Art et d'Esthetique
RAECE — Revue Archeologique de l'Est et du Centre-Est
RAEFB — Radiation Effects
RAELA — Radiotekhnika i Elektronika
RAEMD — Revue de l'Association pour l'Etude du Mouvement Dada
RAeRG — Reallexikon der Aegyptischen Religionsgeschichte
R Aeronaut Soc Centen Congr — Royal Aeronautical Society Centenary Congress
RAEsp — Reformistas Antiquos Espanoles
RA Est — Revue Archeologique de l'Est et du Centre-Est
RAEU — Revista. Asociacion de Escribanos del Uruguay
RAf — Revue Africaine
RAF — Royal Air Force
Rafena Tech Comm — Rafena Technical Communications
RAFIA — Radiatsionnaya Fizika. Akademiya Nauk Latviiskoi SSR. Institut Fiziki
RAfr — Revue Africaine
RAFr — Revue de l'Art Francais
R African Pol Economy — Review of African Political Economy
R Afr Manag — Revue Africaine de Management
R Afr Polit Econ — Review of African Political Economy
RAG — Raina un Aspazijas Gadagramata
R Ag (Cuba) — Revista de Agricultura (Cuba)
RAGEA — Razvedochnaya Geofizika
RAgen — Revue de l'Agenais
R Ag France — Revue des Agriculteurs de France
Raggi Ultraviol — Raggi Ultravioletti
Ragg Lav Lab Chim Agr Bologna — Ragguagli sui Lavori Eseguiti nel Laboratorio Chimico-Agario (Bologna)
RagL — Ragguaglio Librario
RAGOA — Rivista di Agronomia
R Agr Econ Mal — Review of Agricultural Economics of Malaysia

R Agric — Revue de l'Agriculture
R Agric Soc (Cairo) Bull Tech Sect — Royal Agricultural Society (Cairo). Bulletin. Technical Section
R Agric Soc Kenya QJ — Royal Agricultural Society of Kenya. Quarterly Journal
RAH — Reviews in American History
RAHA — Annual Report. American Historical Association
RAHBol — Real Academia de la Historia. Boletin
RAHE — Review of Allied Health Education
RAHS — Royal Australian Historical Society. Journal
RAHSJ — Royal Australian Historical Society. Journal and Proceedings
RAI — Rencontre Assyriologique Internationale
RAI — Rendiconti. Classe di Scienze Morali e Storiche. Accademia d'Italia
RAIAA — Asociacion de Ingenieros Agronomos. Revista
RAIB — Rendiconti. Accademia delle Scienze. Istituto di Bologna
Raiffeisen-Rundsch — Raiffeisen-Rundschau
Rail Clerk — Railway Clerk Interchange
Rail Eng — Railway Engineer [Later, Railway Engineer International]
Rail Eng Int — Rail Engineering International
Rail Int — Rail International
RA Illus — Royal Academy Illustrated
Rail M — Railway Magazine
Railroad & Eng J — Railroad and Engineering Journal
Railroad Gaz — Railroad Gazette
Railroad Res Bul — Railroad Research Bulletin
Rail Syst Contr — Railway Systems Control
Rail Tract Bull — Rail Traction Bulletin [London]
Rail Transport Proc — Rail Transportation Proceedings
Railw Age — Railway Age
Railw Age Gaz — Railway Age Gazette
Railway & Corp Law J — Railway and Corporation Law Journal
Railway R — Railway Review
Railways in Aust — Railways in Australia
Railways Union Gaz — Railways Union Gazette
Railway Trans — Railway Transportation
Railw Dev News — Railway Development News
Railw Eng — Railway Engineer [Later, Railway Engineer International]
Railw Eng Int — Railway Engineer International
Railw Eng J — Railway Engineering Journal
Railw Eng Maint — Railway Engineering and Maintenance
Railw Engr — Railway Engineer [Later, Railway Engineer International]
Railw Eng Rev — Railway and Engineering Review
Railw Gaz — Railway Gazette
Railw Gaz Int — Railway Gazette International
Railw Locomot Cars — Railway Locomotives and Cars
Railw Maint Eng — Railway Maintenance Engineer
Railw Manage Rev — Railway Management Review
Railw Mech Eng — Railway Mechanical Engineer
Railw Q — Railway Quarterly
Railw Res Eng N — Railway Research and Engineering News
Railw Rev — Railway Review
Railw Signal Commun — Railway Signalling and Communications
Railw South Afr — Railways Southern Africa
Railw Syst Control — Railway Systems Control
Railw Track Struct — Railway Track and Structures
RAIN — Royal Anthropological Institute News [Later, Anthropology Today]
RAIN — Royal Anthropological Institute. Newsletter
RAINB — Radio Industria
Rainfall Malta — Rainfall. Meteorological Observatory. University of Malta
Rainf Aust — Rainfall in Australia
Rainf Br Hond — Rainfall. British Honduras
Rainf Clim Obsns Sierra Leone — Rainfall and Climatological Observations. Sierra Leone
Rainf Data Java Madura — Rainfall Data. Java and Madura
Rainf Data Outside Java Madura — Rainfall Data Outside Java and Madura
Rainf Distr Headq Burma — Rainfall Recorded at District Headquarters. Burma Meteorological Department
Rainf India — Rainfall of India
Rainf Jamaica — Rainfall of Jamaica
Rainf Japan — Rainfall of Japan
Rainf NZ — Rainfall. New Zealand
Rainf Obsns Sierra Leone — Rainfall Observations. Sierra Leone
Rainf Palest — Rainfall in Palestine
Rainf Rep Nth Rhod — Rainfall Report. Northern Rhodesia
Rainf R Obs Hong Kong — Rainfall at the Royal Observatory [Hong Kong]
Rainf Season Sth Rhod — Rainfall Season. Southern Rhodesia
Rainf Sel Stns E Afr — Rainfall at Selected Stations in East Africa [Nairobi]
Rainf Statist A Summ Agric Dep St Lucia — Rainfall Statistics and Annual Summary. Agricultural Department. St. Lucia
Rainf Summ Monsoon Period — Rainfall Summary of the Monsoon Period [Calcutta]
Rainf West Aust — Rainfall in Western Australia
Rain Map Aust — Rain Map of Australia
Rain Map NSW — Rain Map. New South Wales
Rain Map Qd — Rain Map. Queensland
Rain Map S Aust — Rain Map. South Australia
Rain Map Tasm — Rain Map. Tasmania
Rain Map Vict — Rain Map. Victoria
Rain Map West Aust — Rain Map. Western Australia
Rain Obsns Indones — Rain Observations in Indonesia
Rains Nile Basin — Rains of the Nile Basin and the Nile Flood [Cairo]
Raion Fibre Sint — Raion e Fibre Sintetiche [Milano]
RaiP — Raison Presente
RAIP — Rapport d'Activites. Institut de Phonetique
R Aircr Establ List Reports — Royal Aircraft Establishment. List of Reports

R Aircr Establ Tech Rep GB — Royal Aircraft Establishment. Technical Report (Great Britain)

RAIRO Anal Num — RAIRO [*Revue Francaise d'Automatique, d'Informatique, et de Recherche Operationnelle*] Analyse Numerique

RAIRO Anal Numer — RAIRO [*Revue Francaise d'Automatique, d'Informatique, et de Recherche Operationnelle*] Analyse Numerique

RAIRO Anal Numer Numer Anal — RAIRO [*Revue Francaise d'Automatique, d'Informatique, et de Recherche Operationnelle*] Analyse Numerique/Numerical Analysis

RAIRO Automat — RAIRO [*Revue Francaise d'Automatique, d'Informatique, et de Recherche Operationnelle*] Automatique

RAIRO Autom Syst Anal Control — RAIRO [*Revue Francaise d'Automatique, d'Informatique, et de Recherche Operationnelle*] Automatique/Systems Analysis and Control

RAIRO Autom/Syst Anal et Control — RAIRO [*Revue Francaise d'Automatique, d'Informatique, et de Recherche Operationnelle*] Automatique/Systems Analysis and Control

RAIRO Inf/Comput Sci — RAIRO [*Revue Francaise d'Automatique, d'Informatique, et de Recherche Operationnelle*] Informatique/Computer Science

RAIRO Inform — RAIRO [*Revue Francaise d'Automatique, d'Informatique, et de Recherche Operationnelle*] Informatique

RAIRO Informat — RAIRO [*Revue Francaise d'Automatique, d'Informatique, et de Recherche Operationnelle*] Informatique

RAIRO Informat Theor — RAIRO [*Revue Francaise d'Automatique, d'Informatique, et de Recherche Operationnelle*] Informatique Theorique

RAIRO Inform Theor — RAIRO [*Revue Francaise d'Automatique, d'Informatique, et de Recherche Operationnelle*] Informatique Theorique/Theoretical Informatics

RAIRO Inf Theor Theor Inf — RAIRO [*Revue Francaise d'Automatique, d'Informatique, et de Recherche Operationnelle*] Informatique Theorique/Theoretical Informatics

RAIRO Operations Research — RAIRO [*Revue Francaise d'Automatique, d'Informatique, et de Recherche Operationnelle*] Recherche Operationnelle/Operations Research

RAIRO Rech Oper Oper Res — RAIRO [*Revue Francaise d'Automatique, d'Informatique, et de Recherche Operationnelle*] Recherche Operationnelle/Operations Research

RAIRO Rev Fr Autom Inf Rech Oper — RAIRO. Revue Franciase d'Automatique d'Informatique et de Recherche Operationalle. Analyse Numerique

RAISA — Radioisotopes

RAIT — Rendiconti. Reale Accademia d'Italia

Raitt Yst Kirj — Raittiuden Ystavien Kirjasia

Ra JAH — Rackham Journal of the Arts and Humanities

Rajasthan Agric — Rajasthan Agriculturist

Rajasthan J Agric Sci — Rajasthan Journal of Agricultural Sciences

Rajasthan Med J — Rajasthan Medical Journal

Rajasthan Univ Studies Statist — Rajasthan University. Studies in Statistics. Science Series

Rajasthan Univ Stud Statist — Rajasthan University. Studies in Statistics. Science Series

RAJB — Recueil Annuel de Jurisprudence Belge

RAJC — Annual Report. American Jewish Committee

RAJ Tech Bull — RAJ [*Rhodesia Agricultural Journal*] Technical Bulletin

Raj Univ Stud — Rajshahi University Studies

RaKet — Rahnema-Ye Ketab

Raketentech Raumfahrtforsch — Raketentechnik und Raumfahrtforschung

Raketentech RaumfForsch — Raketentechnik und Raumfahrtforschung

RAK Reichst Aromen Kosmet — RAK. Reichstoffe, Aromen, Kosmetica

Rakstu Krajums Daugavpils Pedagog Inst — Rakstu Krajums. Daugavpils Pedagogiskais Instituts

Ral — Rassegna d'Italia

RAL — Rendiconti. Accademia Nazionale dei Lincei

RAL — Rendiconti. Classe di Scienze Morali e Storiche. Accademia dei Lincei

RAL — Research in African Literatures

RAL — Revista. Academias de Letras

RAL — Revista de Arqueologia (Lima)

RALAB — Revue de l'Aluminum et de Ses Applications

RAlb — Rivista d'Albania

RALF — Repertoire Analytique de Litterature Francaise

R Alg — Revue d'Algerie

R Algerienne Sciences Juridiques Econs et Pols — Revue Algerienne des Sciences Juridiques, Economiques, et Politiques

R Alger Trav — Revue Algerienne du Travail

R Alicante — Revista. Instituto de Estudios Alicantinos

RALinc — Rendiconti. Classe di Scienze Morali e Storiche. Accademia dei Lincei

RALincei — Rendiconti. Classe di Scienze Morali e Storiche. Accademia dei Lincei

R Allem — Revue d'Allemagne

R Allemagne — Revue d'Allemagne

R All Fr — Revue de l'Alliance Francaise

RALP — Revue Algologique (Paris)

RALR — Reale Accademia Nazionale del Lincei. Rome. Classe di Scienze Morali. Rendiconti

RALRend — Rendiconti. Classe di Scienze Morali e Storiche. Accademia dei Lincei

RALS — Resources for American Literary Study

RAls — Revue d'Alsace

RAL Scav — Reale Accademia dei Lincei. Atti. Notizie degli Scavi

RALSH — Revue Algerienne des Lettres et des Sciences Humaines

Ralw & Corp LJ — Railway and Corporation Law Journal

RAM — Radio-Active Magazine

Ra M — Rassegna Musicale

RAm — Repertorio Americano

RAM — Revue d'Ascetique et de Mystique

RAM — Revue de l'Ameublement

RAM — Rock Australia Magazine

Raman Eff — Raman Effect

Raman Res Inst Mem — Raman Research Institute. Memoirs

Raman Spectrosc — Raman Spectroscopy

RAMC — Rassegna di Asetica e Mistica S. Caterina da Siena

RAMEA — Radiologia Medica

RAMED — Reine und Angewandte Metallkunde in Einzeldarstellungen

RAmer — Repertorio Americano

R Am Hist — Reviews in American History

RAMi — Rivista de Ascetica e Mistica

RaMIsr — Rassegna Mensile di Israel

Ramp — Ramparts Magazine

Ramp Mag — Ramparts Magazine

Ram Rep — Ramanathan's Supreme Court Reports

RAM Res Appl Math — RAM. Research in Applied Mathematics

RAMS — Revista do Arquivo Municipal (Sao Paulo)

RAMSEZ — Records. Australian Museum. Supplement

RAMSP — Revista do Arquivo Municipal (Sao Paulo)

RAMTB — Revue ATB [*Assistance Technique Belge*] Metallurgie

RAN — Rangifer. Nordisk Organ foer Reinforskning

RAN — Rendiconti. Accademia di Archeologia, Lettere, e Belle Arti (Napoli)

RAN — Revue Archeologique de Narbonnaise

RANAM — Recherches Anglaises et Americaines

RA Narb — Revue Archeologique de Narbonnaise

RANBDM — Institut des Sciences Agronomiques du Burundi [*ISABU*]. Rapport Annuel et Notes Annexes

RANC — Revista del Archivo Nacional [*Bogota*]

Ranchi Univ J Agric Res — Ranchi University. Journal of Agricultural Research

Ranchi Univ Math J — Ranchi University. Mathematical Journal

Ranch Mag — Ranch Magazine

Rancho Mex — Rancho Mexicano

Rancho Santa Ana Bot Gard Monogr Bot Ser — Rancho Santa Ana Botanic Garden. Monographs. Botanical Series

RANCR — Revista. Archivos Nacionales de Costa Rica

Rand — Selected Rand Abstracts

R & A — Rates and Allotments

R & C — Religioni e Civitia

R & C — Religion y Cultura

Rand Corp Pap — Rand Corporation. Papers

Rand Corp Rep — Rand Corporation. Report

Rand Corp Rep R — Rand Corporation. Report R

R & D Con Mn — Research and Development Contracts Monthly

R and D Manage — R and D [*Research and Development*] Management

R & D Mangt — R and D [*Research and Development*] Management

R & E Res Exp Math — R & E Research and Exposition in Mathematics

R & I — Restaurants and Institutions

R ANDI — Revista ANDI

Rand J Econom — Rand Journal of Economics

R and L — Religion and Literature

R & McG — Income Tax Decisions of Australasia (Ratcliffe and McGrath)

R & McG Ct of Rev — Court of Review Decisions (Ratcliffe and McGrath)

R & O — Roma e l'Oriente

Randolph Co Hist Soc Mag Of Hist — Randolph County Historical Society. Magazine of History and Biography

Random Comput Dynam — Random and Computational Dynamics

Random House Birkhaeuser Math Ser — Random House/Birkhaeuser Mathematics Series

Random Mater Process — Random Materials and Processes

Random Oper Stochastic Equations — Random Operators and Stochastic Equations

R & P News — Rubber and Plastics News

R & P News 2 — Rubber and Plastics News. 2

R&R — Rock & Rap Confidential

Rand Rep R — Rand. Report R

Rand Revw — Rand Research Review

R & T — Recherches et Travaux

R & T — Road and Track

R & T WUIS — DTIC [*Defense Technical Information Center*] Research and Technology Work Unit Information System

RANF Rev — RANF [*Royal Australian Nursing Federation*] Review

Rang Cr LJ — Rangoon Criminal Law Journal

Range Improv Notes US For Serv Intermt Reg — Range Improvement Notes. United States Forest Service. Intermountain Region

Range Improv Stud Div For Calif — Range Improvement Studies. California Division of Forestry. Department of Natural Resources

Range Improv Studies Calif Dep Conserv Div For — Range Improvement Studies. California Department of Conservation. Division of Forestry

Range Impr Stud Calif Div For — Range Improvement Studies. California Division of Forestry

Range Res Rep Pacif NW Forest Exp Stn — Range Research Report. Pacific Northwest Forest Experiment Station [*Portland*]

Range Sci Dep Ser Colo State Univ — Range Science Department Series. Colorado State University

Range Sci Ser Colo State Univ Range Sci Dep — Range Science Series. Colorado State University. Range Science Department

R An Jpd B — Recueil Annuel de Jurisprudence Belge

RANL — Rendiconti. Reale Accademia Nazionale dei Lincei

Rannsoknastofnun Fiskidnadarins Arsskyrs — Rannsoknastofnun Fiskidnadarins Arsskyrsla

RANP — Revista del Archivo Nacional del Peru

RANS — Report. Australian Numismatic Society

R Ant Christ — Reallexikon fuer Antike und Christentum

R Anth — Revue Anthropologique

R Anthr — Revue d'Anthropologie

R Anthr — Revue d'Anthropologie

R Anthrop — Reviews in Anthropology

R Anthrop — Revue Anthropologique

R Antropol (Sao Paulo) — Revista de Antropologia (Sao Paulo)

Ranuzzi An Gg — Annuario Geografico Italiano. Ranuzzi
RAO — Recueil d'Archeologie Orientale
RA Oise — Revue Archeologique de l'Oise
RAONDT — Radiotherapy and Oncology
RAOU Newsl — RAOU [*Royal Australasian Ornithologists Union*] Newsletter
RAP — Revista de Administracion Publica
RAP — Revolutionary Action Power
RAP — Revue Anthropologique
RAp — Revue Apologetique
RAP — Revue Archeologique (Paris)
RAP — Revue d'Archeologie Polonaise
RAP — Revue de l'Action Populaire [*Later, Projet*]
RAP — Revue de l'Assistance Publique et de la Prevoyance Sociale
RAPA — Report. Administration of the Persian Gulf Residency and Muscat Political Agency
Rap Activ Inst Geol Rom — Raport Asupra Activitatei Institutului Geologic al Romaniei
Rapa Nui J — Rapa Nui Journal. The Journal of the Easter Island Foundation
Rap Bur Nutr Anim Elev — Rapport. Bureau de la Nutrition Animale et de l'Elevage
RAPCD — Revista da Associacao Paulista de Cirugioes Dentistas
Rapeseed Assoc Can Publ — Rapeseed Association of Canada. Publication
RapFB — Rapports (Het Franse Boek)
Rap Gen Ig — Raport General Asupra Igienei
RAPGR — Report. Administration of the Persian Gulf Residency
RAPH — Recherches d'Archeologie, de Philologie,et d'Histoire
Rapid Commun Mass Spectrom — Rapid Communications in Mass Spectrometry
Rapidly Quenched Met Proc Int Conf — Rapidly Quenched Metals. Proceedings. International Conference
Rapid Therm Integr Process — Rapid Thermal and Integrated Processing
Rap Inst Fiz Jad Krakow — Raport. Instytut Fizyki Jadrowej (Krakow)
Rap Inst Fiz Tech Jad AGH — Raport. Instytut Fizyki i Techniki Jadrowej AGH
Rap Inst Nat Etude Agron Congo (INEAC) — Rapport. Institut National pour l'Etude Agronomique du Congo (INEAC)
Rap Inst Tech Jad AGH — Raport. Instytut Techniki Jadrowej AGH
Rapp — Rapport
Rapp A Commn Pech Marit Brux — Rapport Annuel de la Commission de Peches Maritimes (Bruxelles)
Rapp A Cons Sup Hyg Prov Queb — Rapport Annuel du Conseil Superieur d'Hygiene de la Province de Quebec
Rapp Act Bur Voltaique Geol Mines — Rapport. Activite du Bureau Voltaique de le Geologie et des Mines
Rapp Activ Ass Dev Cult Fourrag — Rapport d'Activite de l'Association pour le Developpement de la Culture Fourragere
Rapp Activ Ass Suisse Essai Approvis Semenc Pommes Terre — Rapport d'Activite. Association Suisse pour l'Essai et l'Approvisionnement en Semenceaux de Pommes de Terre
Rapp Activ Cent Etud Rech Charb Fr — Rapport sur l'Activite du Centre d'Etudes et Recherches des Charbonnages de France
Rapp Activ Cent Natn Rech Scient — Rapport d'Activite. Centre National de la Recherche Scientifique [*Paris*]
Rapp Activ Inst Geogr Natn — Rapport sur l'Activite de l'Institut Geographique National [*Paris*]
Rapp Activ Inst Interuniv Phys Nucl — Rapport d'Activite. Institut Interuniversitaire de Physique Nucleaire [*Bruxelles*]
Rapp Activ Labs Bellevue — Rapport d'Activite. Laboratoires de Bellevue [*Paris*]
Rapp Activ Stn Cent Genet Amelior Pl — Rapport d'Activite. Station Centrale de Genetique et d'Amelioration des Plantes [*Versailles*]
Rapp Activ Stns Fed Essais Agric — Rapport d'Activite. Stations Federales d'Essais Agricoles [*Lausanne*]
Rapp Act Serv Geol (Madagascar) — Rapport d'Activite. Service Geologique (Madagascar)
Rapp Act Serv Geol (Malagasy) — Rapport d'Activite. Service Geologique (Malagasy)
Rapp Act Stn Amelior Plant Maraicheres — Rapport d'Activite. Station d'Amelioration des Plants Maraicheres
Rapp Afd Toegep Wisk Math Cent — Rapport. Afdeeling Toegepaste Wiskunde. Mathematisch Centrum [*Amsterdam*]
Rapp A Insp Gen Mines Geol Fr — Rapport Annuel. Inspection Generale des Mines et de la Geologie de la France et d'Outre Mer
Rapp A Inst Encour Rech Scient Ind Agric — Rapport Annuel. Institute pour l'Encouragement de la Recherche Scientifique dans l'Industrie et l'Agriculture (I.R.S.I.A.)
Rapp A Inst Interuniv Phys Nucl — Rapport Annuel. Institut Interuniversitaire de Physique Nucleaire
Rapp A Inst Interuniv Sci Nucl — Rapport Annuel. Institut Interuniversitaire des Sciences Nucleaires
Rapp A Inst Natn Rech Agron — Rapport Annuel. Institut National de la Recherche Agronomique
Rapp A Inst Rech Caoutch Cambodge — Rapport Annuel. Institut de Recherches sur le Caoutchouc au Cambodge
Rapp A Inst Rech Caoutch Indochine — Rapport Annuel. Institut des Recherches sur le Caoutchouc en Indochine
Rapp A Inst Rech Huiles Oleag — Rapport Annuel. Institut de Recherches pour les Huiles et Oleagineux
Rapp A Inst Rech Scient Afr Cent — Rapport Annuel. Institut pour la Recherche Scientifique en Afrique Centrale
Rapp A Lab Ent Constantinople — Rapport Annuel. Laboratoire d'Entomologie. Ecole Superieure d'Agriculture (Constantinople)
Rapp A Minist Sante Can — Rapport Annuel du Ministere de la Sante. Canada
Rapp Anal Phys Chim Eau Rhin — Rapport sur les Analyses Physico-Chimiques de l'Eau du Rhin
Rapp Annu AFOCEL (Assoc For Cellul) — Rapport Annuel. AFOCEL (Association Foret-Cellulose)

Rapp Annu Dep Geol Mineral Mus R Afr Cent — Rapport Annuel du Departement de Geologie et de Mineralogie du Musee Royal de l'Afrique Centrale
Rapp Annu Fed Chambres Synd Miner Met Non Ferreux — Rapport Annuel. Federation des Chambres Syndicales des Minerais et des Metaux Non Ferreux
Rapp Annu Inst Geol Hong — Rapport Annuel de l'Institut Geologique de Hongrie
Rapp Annu Inst Interuniv Sci Nucl — Rapport Annuel. Institut Interuniversitaire des Sciences Nucleaires
Rapp Annu Inst Rech Agron Etat Sofia — Rapport Annuel. Institut des Recherches Agronomiques de l'Etat a Sofia
Rapp Annu Serv Geol (Malagasy) — Rapport Annuel. Service Geologique (Malagasy)
Rapp Annu Stn Agron Etat Sofia — Rapport Annuel. Station Agronomique de l'Etat a Sofia
Rapp A Obs Astr Prov — Rapport Annuel sur les Observatoires Astronomiques de Province
Rapp A Obs Paris — Rapport Annuel de l'Observatoire de Paris
Rapp A Obs Univ Toulouse — Rapport Annuel. Observatoire de l'Universite de Toulouse
Rapp A Sect Geol Miner Paleont Mus R Congo Belge — Rapport Annuel de la Section de Geologie, de Mineralogie, et de Paleontologie. Musee Royale du Congo Belge et de la Commission de Geologie du Ministere des Colonies
Rapp A Serv Eaux Forets Chasses Dahomey — Rapport Annuel. Service des Eaux, Forets, et Chasses (Dahomey)
Rapp A Serv Geol Afr Equat Fr — Rapport Annuel du Service Geologique de l'Afrique Equatoriale Francaise
Rapp A Serv Geol Madagascar — Rapport Annuel du Service Geologique. Madagascar
Rapp A Serv Geol Territ Cameroun — Repport Annuel du Service Geologique. Territoire du Cameroun
Rapp A Serv Natn Prod Agric Haiti — Rapport Annuel. Service National de la Production Agricole. Haiti
Rapp A Serv Prov Hyg Queb — Rapport Annuel. Service Provincial d'Hygiene. Province de Quebec
Rapp Assem Gen Cent Int Engrais Chim — Rapports de l'Assemblee Generale. Centre International des Engrais Chimiques
Rapp Assoc Int Chim Cerealiere — Rapports. Association Internationale de Chimie Cerealiere
Rapp A Stn Agron Libano Fr — Rapport Annuel. Station Agronomique Libano-Francaise
Rapp A Stn Fed Essais Vitic Arboric Lausanne — Rapport Annuel. Station Federale d'Essais Viticoles et Arboricoles a Lausanne
Rapp A Stn Rech Piscc Elisabethville — Rapport Annuel. Station de Recherches Piscicoles a Elisabethville
Rapp A Tech Adm Serv Geogr Afr Occid Fr — Rapport Annuel. Technique et Administratif. Service Geographique de l'Afrique Occidentale Francaise
Rapp A Trav Bur Int Heure — Rapport Annuel sur les Travaux Effectues au Bureau International de l'Heure
Rapp Bilans Exerc Com Spec Katanga — Rapport et Bilans d'Exercise. Comite Special du Katanga
Rapp BIPM — Rapport. BIPM
Rapp BosbProefstn Bogor — Rapport. Bosbouwproefstation (Bogor)
Rapp Byggetek Utv — Rapport. Byggeteknisk Utvalg. Norges Teknisknaturvitenskapelige Forskningsrad
Rapp CEA — Rapport CEA. Commissariat a l'Energie Atomique
Rapp CEA R Fr Commis Energ At — Rapport CEA-R. France Commissariat a l'Energie Atomique
Rapp Cent Etude Energ Nucl — Rapport. Centre d'Etude de l'Energie Nucleaire
Rapp Cent Int Engrais Chim — Rapport. Centre International des Engrais Chimiques
Rapp Chalmers Tek Hoegsk Inst Vattenfoersoerjnings Avloppstek — Rapport. Chalmers Tekniska Hoegskola. Institutionen foer Vattenfoersoerjnings- och Avloppsteknik
Rapp Champs Essais Chaire Dep Agric Meurthe Et Moselle — Rapport sur les Champs d'Essais. Chaire Departementale d'Agriculture de Meurthe-et-Moselle
Rapp Champs Exp Commn Met Eure Et Loire — Rapport sur les Champs d'Experience. Commission Meteorologique de l'Eure-et-Loir
Rapp Com Consult Definition Metre Com Int Poids Mes — Rapport du Comite Consultatif pour la Definition du Metre au Comite International des Poids et Mesures
Rapp Com Dir Synd Suisse Etude Voie Navig Rhone Rhin — Rapport du Comite de Direction. Syndicat Suisse pour l'Etude de la Voie Navigable du Rhone au Rhin
Rapp Com Fr Eclair Chauff — Rapport du Comite Francais de l'Eclairage et du Chauffage
Rapp Com Bevord SuikBietent Noord Prov — Rapport van de Commissie ter Bevordering der Suikerebietenteelt in de Noordelijke Provincien
Rapp Comm Infilt Keurinst WatLeidArt — Rapport. Commissie Infiltratie Keuringsinstituut voor Waterleidingartikelen
Rapp Comm Int Mer Mediter — Rapport. Commission Internationale pour la Mer Mediterranee
Rapp Commissar Energie Atom — Rapport. Commissariat a l'Energie Atomique
Rapp Comm KlimReg Gebouwen TNO — Rapport van de Commissie voor de Klimaatregeling in Gebouwen. Nederlandsch Centrale Organisatie voor Toegepast-Natuurwetenschappelijk Onderzoek
Rapp Commn Atom Un Int Chim — Rapport. Commission des Atomes. Union Internationale de la Chimie
Rapp Commn Congr Hyg Scol Pedag Physiol — Rapport et Communications. Congres d'Hygiene Scolaire et de Pedagogie Physiologique
Rapp Commn Etude Relat Phenom Sol Terr — Rapport de la Commission pour l'Etude des Relations entre les Phenomenes Solaires et Terrestres
Rapp Commn Etude Terrasses Surf Aplaniss — Rapport. Commission pour l'Etude des Terrasses et Surfaces d'Aplanissement. Union Geographique Internationale
Rapp Commn Int Elem Chim — Rapport de la Commission Internationale des Elements Chimiques

Rapp Commn Perm Thermochim — Rapport de la Commission Permanente de Thermochimie

Rapp Commn Poids Atom Un Int Chim — Rapport. Commission des Poids Atomiques. Union Internationale de la Chimie

Rapp Commn Scient Tech Fed Int Prod Jus Fruits — Rapport. Commission Scientifique et Technique. Federation Internationale des Producteurs de Jus de Fruits

Rapp Commns Med Prov Brux — Rapport des Commissions Medicales Provinciales (Bruxelles)

Rapp Commn Tech Fonct Off Natn Propr Ind — Rapport de la Commission Technique sur le Fonctionnement de l'Office National de la Propriete Industrielle

Rapp Comm Sci Tech Fed Int Prod Jus Fruits — Rapports. Commission Scientifique et Technique. Federation Internationale des Producteurs de Jus de Fruits

Rapp Commun Journ Eur Diet — Rapports et Communications. Journees Europeennes de Dietetique

Rapp Com Natn Bois Colon — Rapport du Comite National des Bois Coloniaux

Rapp Concours Merite Agric Queb — Rapport. Concours du Merite Agricole (Quebec)

Rapp Concours Regl Chronom — Rapport sur le Concours de Reglage de Chronometres

Rapp Congr Alien Neurol Fr — Rapport. Congres des Alienistes et Neurologistes de France et des Pays de Langue Francaise

Rapp Congr Fr Med — Rapport. Congres Francais de Medecine

Rapp Congr Int Fed Int Soc Ing Tech Automob — Rapport. Congres International. Federation Internationale des Societes d'Ingenieurs des Techniques de l'Automobile

Rapp Congr Int Hyg Med Prev — Rapports. Congres International d'Hygiene et de Medecine Preventive

Rapp Congr Int Pet — Rapporti al Congresso Internazionale del Petrolio

Rapp Congr Regul Bilan Energ Homme — Rapports du Congres sur la Regulation du Bilan d'Energie chez l'Homme

Rapp Cons Exp Rech Agron — Rapport. Conseil de l'Experimentation et des Recherches Agronomiques. Algerie

Rapp Cons Exp Rech Agron Insp Gen Agric (Algeria) — Rapport. Conseil de l'Experimentation et des Recherches Agronomiques. Inspection Generale de l'Agriculture (Algeria)

Rapp Cons Fed Insp Forets Chasse Peche — Rapport du Conseil Federal. Inspection des Forets, Chasse et Peche

Rapp CR Congr Belge Neurol Psychiat — Rapport et Compte Rendu. Congres Belge de Neurologie et de Psychiatrie

Rapp CR Maison Enf Mal Geneve — Rapport et Compte Rendu. Maison des Enfants Malades. Geneve

Rapp Crois Inst Fr Oceanie Sect Oceanogr — Rapport de Croisiere. Institut Francais d'Oceanie. Section Oceanographie

Rapp Dansk Vejlab — Rapport. Dansk Vejlaboratorium

Rapp Discuss Cons Chim Inst Int Chim Solvay — Rapports et Discussions. Conseil de Chimie. Institut International de Chimie Solvay

Rapp Discuss Cons Phys Inst Int Phys — Rapport et Discussions. Conseil de Physique. Institut International de Physique. Solvay

Rapp Discuss Isot Inst Int Chim Solvay Cons Chim — Rapports et Discussions sur les Isotopes. Institut International de Chimie Solvay. Conseil de Chimie

Rapp Etat Agric Prov Hainaut — Rapport sur l'Etat de l'Agriculture dans la Province de Hainaut

Rapp Final Conf Tech OCEAC — Rapport Final. Conference Technique. OCEAC

Rapp Fonct Lab Agric Alger — Rapport sur le Fonctionnement du Laboratoire d'Agriculture et de la Station d'Essais de Semences et d'Amelioration des Plantes (Alger)

Rapp Fonct Servs Inst Pasteur Alger — Rapport sur le Fonctionnement des Services de l'Institut Pasteur d'Algerie

Rapp Fonct Tech Inst Pasteur AOF — Rapport sur le Fonctionnement Technique de l'Institut Pasteur de l'A.O.F

Rapp Fonct Tech Inst Pasteur Brazzaville — Rapport sur le Fonctionnement Technique de l'Institut Pasteur de Brazzaville

Rapp Fonct Tech Inst Pasteur Dakar — Rapport sur le Fonctionnement Technique. Institut Pasteur de Dakar

Rapp Fonct Tech Inst Pasteur Guayane Fr — Rapport sur le Fonctionnement Technique de l'Institut Pasteur de la Guayane Francaise et du Territoire de l'Inini

Rapp Fonct Tech Inst Pasteur Maroc — Rapport sur le Fonctionnement Technique de l'Institut Pasteur du Maroc

Rapp Fonct Tech Inst Pasteur Martinique — Rapport sur le Fonctionnement Technique de l'Institut Pasteur de la Martinique

Rapp Foreami — Rapport Foreami. Fonds Reine Elisabeth pour l'Assistance Medicale aux Indigenes du Congo Belge

Rapp Geluidscomm TNO — Rapport van de Geluidscommissie. Nederlandsch Centrale Organisatie voor Toegepast-Natuurwetenschappelijk Onderzoek

Rapp Gen Acad Med Vacc Revacc — Rapport General de l'Academie de Medecine sur les Vaccinations et Revaccinations Pratiquees en France et Aux Colonies

Rapp Gen Adm Eaux Forets Belg — Rapport General. Administration des Eaux et Forets. Belgique

Rapp Gen Cent Natn Rech Herb Fourr Brux — Rapport General. Centre National de Recherches Herbageres et Fourrageres (Bruxelles)

Rapp Gen Cent Rech Ligue Pomol — Rapport General. Centre de Recherches de la Ligue Pomologique pour la Defense du Fruit Belge sous les Auspices de l'I.R.S.I.A

Rapp Gen Commn Coton — Rapport General de la Commission du Coton [Paris]

Rapp Gen Com Natn Etude Cult Fruit — Rapport General. Comite National pour l'Etude de la Culture Fruitiere Organise sous les Auspices de l'I.R.S.I.A

Rapp Gen Stn Rech Etat Amelior Pl Fruit Maraich — Rapport General. Station de Recherches de l'Etat pour l'Amelioration des Plantes Fruitieres et Maraicheres

Rapp Gen Trav Soc Philom Paris — Rapports Generaux des Travaux. Societe Philomatique de Paris

Rapp Geol Minist Energie Ressour (Quebec) — Rapport Geologique. Ministere de l'Energie et des Ressources (Quebec)

Rapp Geol Que Minist Energ Ressour — Rapport Geologique. Quebec, Ministere de l'Energie et des Ressources

Rapp Geol Que Minist Richesses Nat — Rapport Geologique. Quebec. Ministere des Richesses Naturelles

Rapp Gronl Geol Unders — Rapport. Gronlands Geologiske Undersogelse

Rapp Hydrates Carbone Glucides Conf Union Int Chim CR — Rapports sur les Hydrates de Carbone (Glucides). Conference. Union Internationale de Chimie. Comptes Rendus

Rapp Hyg Publ Congo Belge — Rapport sur l'Hygiene Publique du Congo Belge

Rapp Ind Can Sci Halieutiques Aquat — Rapport a l'Industrie Canadien sur les Sciences Halieutiques et Aquatiques

Rapp Inf LAU X Cent Rech For Laurentides — Rapport d'Information LAU-X. Centre de Recherches Forestieres des Laurentides

Rapp Inf LAU X Laurentian For Res Cent — Rapport d'Information LAU-X. Laurentian Forest Research Centre

Rapp Infs Ass Fr Urol — Rapport et Informations. Association Francaise d'Urologie

Rapp Ing Mines Com Cent Houill Fr — Rapport des Ingenieurs des Mines. Comite Central des Houilleres de France

Rapp Insp Gen Agric Alger — Rapport. Inspection Generale de l'Agriculture. Algerie

Rapp Inst Biol Afr Occid Fr — Rapport de l'Institut de Biologie du Gouvernement General de l'Afrique Occidentale Francaise

Rapp Inst Bodemvruchtbaar — Rapport. Instituut voor Bodemvruchtbaarheid

Rapp Inst Bodemvruchtbaarheid — Rapport. Instituut voor Bodemvruchtbaarheid

Rapp Inst Etud Mar Ostende — Rapport. Institut des Etudes Marines (Ostende)

Rapp Inst Geogr Natn — Rapport. Institut Geographique National [France]

Rapp Inst Gezondheidstech TNO — Rapport. Instituut voor Gezondheidstechniek TNO

Rapp Instn Virkeslara Skogshogsk — Rapporter. Institutionen for Virkeslara. Skogshogskolan

Rapp Inst Oceanogr — Rapport. Institut Oceanographique

Rapp Inst Parcs Natn Congo Belge — Rapport. Institut des Parcs Nationaux du Congo Belge

Rapp Inst Vaextodling Sver Lantbruksuniv — Rapport. Institutionen foer Vaextodling. Sveriges Lantbruksuniversitet

Rapp Inst Warmte Econ — Rapport. Instituut voor Warmte-Economie

Rapp Inter Etude Lab J Dedek Raffinerie Tirlemontoise — Rapport Interieur d'une Etude Effectuee au Laboratoire J. Dedek Raffinerie Tirlemontoise

Rapp Interno Ist Ric Acque — Rapporto Interno. Instituto di Ricerca sulle Acque

Rapp ISTISAN — Rapporti ISTISAN

Rapp IXe Congr Internat Sci Hist — IXe Congres International des Sciences Historiques. Rapports

Rapp Kont Mat Statist St Skogsforsklnst — Rapport. Kontoret for Matematisk Statistik, Statens Skogsforskningsinstitut

Rapp Korrosionsinst — Rapport. Korrosionsinstitutet

Rapp Lab Chim Agric Maine Et Loire — Rapport du Laboratoire de Chimie Agricole de Maine-et-Loire

Rapp Lab Chim Appl Ind Resines Bordeaux — Rapport du Laboratoire de Chimie Appliquee a l'Industrie des Resines (Bordeaux)

Rapp Lab Essais Conserv Natn Arts Metiers — Rapport. Laboratoire d'Essais. Conservatoire National des Arts et Metiers

Rapp Lab Etud Soie Lyon — Rapport du Laboratoire d'Etudes de la Soie (Lyon)

Rapp Lab Klin Stressforsk Karolinska Inst — Rapporter fraan Laboratoriet foer Klinisk Stressforskning. Karolinska Institutet

Rapp Lab Med Leopoldville — Rapport du Laboratoire Medical de Leopoldville

Rapp Lab Prod For Est (Can) — Rapport. Laboratoire des Produits Forestiers de l'Est (Canada)

Rapp Lab Rech Serv Elev Maroc — Rapport du Laboratoire de Recherches du Service de l'Elevage au Maroc

Rapp Medd Sver Geol Unders — Rapporter och Meddelanden. Sveriges Geologiska Undersoekning

Rapp Minist Agric Prov Queb — Rapport. Ministere de l'Agriculture de la Province de Quebec

Rapp Musees Hist Nat Lausanne — Rapport. Musees d'Histoire Naturelle de Lausanne

Rapp Natn LuchtvLab — Rapport. National Luchtvaartlaboratorium

Rapp Naturvaardsverket Swed — Rapport. Naturvaardsverket (Sweden)

Rapp Natuurw Onderz Comm Zwemb — Rapport. Natuurwetenschappelijk Onderzoek-Commissie Zwembaden

Rapp Ned Inst Zuivelonderz — Rapporten van het Nederlands Instituut voor Zuivelonderzoek

Rapp Ned Wegencongr — Rapport. Nederlandsch Wegencongres

Rapp Nord Fettharskningssymp — Rapport fra Nordiske Fettharskningssymposium

Rapp Nord Korrosjonsmoete — Rapport fra Nordiske Korrosjonsmoete

Rapp Norg Branntek Lab — Rapport. Norges Branntekniske Laboratorium

Rapp Norg ByggforskInst — Rapport. Norges Byggforskningsinstitutt

Rapp Obs Cant Neuchatel — Rapport de l'Observatoire Cantonal de Neuchatel

Rapp Obs Univ Bordeaux — Rapport de l'Observatoire de l'Universite de Bordeaux

Rapp Off Biol Queb — Rapport de l'Office de Biologie. Ministere de la Chasse et des Pecheries. Province de Quebec

Rapp Off Int Epizoot — Rapport. Office International des Epizooties

Rapp Off Natn Rech Scient Ind Invent — Rapport de l'Office National des Recherches Scientifiques et Industrielles et des Inventions

Rapp Off Rech Scient Colon — Rapport de l'Office de la Recherche Scientifique Coloniale

Rapport Conjonct — Rapport de Conjoncture

Rapporteur Med — Rapporteur Medical

Rapp Prelim Dir Gen Mines Que — Rapport Preliminaire. Direction Generale des Mines (Quebec)

Rapp Prelim Minist Richesses Nat (Que) — Rapport Preliminaire. Ministere des Richesses Naturelles (Quebec)

Rapp Proc Verb — Rapports et Proces-Verbaux des Reunions

Rapp Proefstn Groenteteelt Vollegrond Ned — Rapport. Proefstation voor de Groenteteelt in de Vollegrond in Nederland

Rapp P V Ass Oceanogr Phys Helsingf — Rapport et Proces-Verbaux. Association d'Oceanographie Physique (Helsingfors)

Rapp PV Reun Comm Int Explor Sci Mer Mediterr (Monaco) — Rapports et Proces-Verbaux des Reunions. Commission Internationale pour l'Exploration Scientifique de la Mer Mediterranee (Monaco)

Rapp P V Reun Commn Int Explor Scient Mer Mediterr — Rapport et Proces-Verbaux des Reunions. Commission Internationale pour l'Exploration Scientifique de la Mer Mediterranee

Rapp P-V Reun Cons Int Explor Mer — Rapports et Proces-Verbaux des Reunions. Conseil International pour l'Exploration de la Mer

Rapp P V Reun Cons Perm Int Explor Mer — Rapport et Proces-Verbaux des Reunions. Conseil Permanent International pour l'Exploration de la Mer

Rapp Quinq Explor Parc Natn Albert — Rapport Quinquennal de l'Exploration du Parc National Albert

Rapp Rech Cent Reg Etud Nucl Kinshasa — Rapport de Recherche. Centre Regional d'Etudes Nucleaires de Kinshasa

Rapp Rech Lab Cent Ponts Chaussees — Rapport de Recherche. Laboratoire Central des Ponts et Chaussees

Rapp Rech Lab Ponts Chaussees — Rapport de Recherche. Laboratoires des Ponts et Chaussees

Rapp Rech LPC — Rapport de Recherche LPC

Rapp Rech Pestic — Rapport de Recherche sur les Pesticides

Rapp Scient Inst Fr Oceanie — Rapport Scientifique. Institut Francais d'Oceanie

Rapp Scient Trav Caisse Rech Scient Melun — Rapport Scientifique sur les Travaux Entrepris au Moyen des Subventions de la Caisse des Recherches Scientifiques (Melun)

Rapp Sci Tech CNEXO (Fr) — Rapports Scientifiques et Techniques. CNEXO [*Centre National pour l'Exploitation des Oceans*] (France)

Rapp Sentralinst Ind Forsk — Rapport. Sentralinstituut foer Industriell Forskning

Rapp Serv Med Eaux Miner Fr — Rapport sur le Service Medical des Eaux Minerales de France

Rapp Serv Vet Sanit Paris — Rapport du Service Veterinaire Sanitaire de Paris et du Departement de la Seine (Paris)

Rapp Soc Agric Le Caire — Rapport de la Societe d'Agriculture (Le Caire)

Rapp Soc Astr Anvers — Rapport de la Societe d'Astronomie d'Anvers

Rapp Soc Belge Otol Lar Rhinol — Rapport. Societe Belge d'Otologie, de Laryngologie, et de Rhinologie

Rapp Soc Encour Cult Orges Brass Houbl Fr — Rapport. Societe d'Encouragement de la Culture des Orges de Brasserie et des Houblons en France, Secobrah

Rapp Soc Int For Min Congo — Rapport. Societe Internationale Forestiere et Miniere du Congo

Rapp Soc Natn Chemins Fer Belg — Rapport. Societe Nationale des Chemins de Fer Belges

Rapp Soc Oceanogr Golfe Gascogne — Rapport. Societe d'Oceanografie, Golfe de Gascogne

Rapp Sous Commn Fr Commn Int Enseign Math — Rapport. Sous-Commission Francaise. Commission Internationale de l'Enseignement Mathematique

Rapp Sous Commn Suisse Commn Int Enseign Math — Rapport. Sous-Commission Suisse. Commission Internationale de l'Enseignement Mathematique

Rapp Stat Biol St Laurent Trois Pistoles — Rapport. Station Biologique du St. Laurent a Trois Pistoles

Rapp Stat Can Hydrogr Sci Oceaniques — Rapport Statistique Canadien sur l'Hydrographie et les Sciences Oceaniques

Rapp Stn Agron Guadeloupe — Rapport. Station Agronomique de Guadeloupe

Rapp Stn Biol Mar Grande Riviere — Rapport. Station de Biologie Marine de Grande-Riviere

Rapp Stn Biol St Laurent — Rapport. Station Biologique du St. Laurent a Trois Pistoles

Rapp Stn Cent Cult Fruit Kindia — Rapport. Station Centrale des Cultures Fruitieres. Institut des Fruits et Agrumes Coloniaux, Guinee Francaise (Kindia)

Rapp Stn Ent Cho Ganh — Rapport. Station Entomologique. Cho-Ganh [*Tonkin*]

Rapp Stn Genet Cult Mais — Rapport. Station de Genetique et de Culture du Mais

Rapp Stn Piscic Djoumouna — Rapport. Station de Pisciculture de la Djoumouna

Rapp Stn Rech For Rabat — Rapport de la Station de Recherches Forestieres de Rabat

Rapp St Skogsforsklnst — Rapport. Statens Skogsforskningsinstitut

Rapp Studi Comm Stud Provvedimenti Conserv Dif — Rapporti e Studi. Commissione di Studio dei Provvedimenti per la Conservazione e Difesa della Laguna e della Citta di Venezia

Rapp St Vaginst — Rapport. Statens Vaginstitut

Rapp Sven Forskningsinst Cem Betong Tek Hoegsk Stockholm — Rapporter. Svenska Forskningsinstitutet foer Cement och Betong vid Tekniska Hoegskolan i Stockholm

Rapp Sven Inst Konserveringsforsk — Rapport. Svenska Institutet foer Konserveringsforskning

Rapp Sven Livsmedel-Sinstitutet — Rapport. Svenska Livsmedelsinstitutet

Rapp Sver Lantbruksuniv Inst Radioekol — Rapport. Sveriges Lantbruksuniversitet. Institutionen foer Radioekologi

Rapp Sver Lantbruksuniv Inst Vaextodling — Rapport. Sveriges Lantbruksuniversitet. Institutionen foer Vaextodling

Rapp Tech Can Sci Halieutiques et Aquat — Rapport Technique Canadien des Sciences Halieutiques et Aquatiques

Rapp Tech Cent Belge Etude Corros — Rapports Techniques. Centre Belge d'Etude de la Corrosion

Rapp Tech Cent Natn Exp Agric Grignon — Rapport Technique. Centre National d'Experimentation Agricole de Grignon

Rapp Tech For Serv Can For — Rapport Technique de Foresterie. Service Canadien des Forets

Rapp Tech Group Fr Dev Rech Aeronaut — Rapport Technique. Groupement Francais pour le Developpement des Recherches Aeronautiques

Rapp Tech Grpmt Fr Dev Rech Aeronaut — Rapport Technique du Groupement Francais pour le Developpement des Recherches Aeronautiques

Rapp Tech Lab Rech Controle Caoutch — Rapport Technique. Laboratoire de Recherches et de Controle Du Caoutchouc

Rapp Tech Nagra — Rapport Technique. Nagra

Rapp Tech Off Natl Etud Rech Aeronaut (Fr) — Rapport Technique. Office National d'Etudes et de Recherches Aeronautiques (France)

Rapp Tech Serv Peches Sci Mer Can — Rapport Technique. Service des Peches et des Sciences de la Mer (Canada)

Rapp Tec Ist Ric Acque — Rapporti Tecnici. Istituto di Ricerca sulle Acque

Rappto Aerol Obs Tateno — Rapporto de la Aerologia Observatorio de Tateno

Rappto Attiv Com Naz Ric Nucl — Rapporto di Attivita. Comitato Nazionale per le Ricerche Nucleari

Rappto CNEN — Rapporto C.N.E.N. Comitato Nazionale per l'Energia Nucleare

Rappto Monogr Colon Cirenaica — Rapporto e Monografie Coloniali della Cirenaica

Rappto Oss Capodimonte — Rapporto dell'Osservatorio di Capodimonte

Rappto Soc Lotta Mal Infett Milano — Rapporto della Societa per la Lotta Contra le Malattie Infettive (Milano)

Rappto Staz Sper Agr Bari — Rapporto della Stazione Sperimentale Agraria de Bari

Rappto Staz Sper Beetic Rovigo — Rapporto della Stazione Sperimentale di Beeticoltura di Rovigo

Rappto Staz Sper Granic Catania — Rapporto della Stazione Sperimentale di Granicoltura di Catania

Rapp Trav Acad Hong Sci — Rapport sur les Travaux de l'Academie Hongroise des Sciences

Rapp Trav Bur Cent Ass Geod Int — Rapport sur les Travaux du Bureau Central de l'Association Geodesique Internationale

Rapp Trav Geod Astr AOF — Rapport sur les Travaux Geodesiques et Astronomiques Executes en A.O.F

Rapp Trav Geod Fr Serv Geogr Armee — Rapport sur les Travaux Geodesiques Executes en France par le Service Geographique de l'Armee

Rapp Trav Inst Natn Mines Frameries Patur — Rapport sur les Travaux. Institut National des Mines, Frameries-Paturages

Rapp Trav Rech Effect Serv Bot Agron Tunis — Rapport sur les Travaux de Recherches Effectues. Service Botanique et Agronomique de Tunisie

Rapp Trav Stn Rech Trevarez — Rapport des Travaux. Station de Recherches de Trevarez

Rapp Univ i Oslo Fys Inst — Rapport. Universitetet i Oslo. Fysisk Institutt

Rapp Uppsats Avd Skogsekol Skogshogsk — Rapporter och Uppsatser. Avdelningen foer Skogsekologi. Skogshogskolan

Rapp Uppsats Instn Skoglig Mat Statist Skogshogsk — Rapporter och Uppsatser. Institutionen foer Skoglig Matematisk Statistik. Skogshogskolan

Rapp Uppsats Instn Skogsforyngr Skogshogsk — Rapporter och Uppsatser. Institutionen foer Skogsforyngring. Skogshogskolan

Rapp Uppsats Instn Skogsgenet Skogshogsk — Rapporter och Uppsatser. Institutionen foer Skogsgenetik. Skogshogskolan

Rapp Uppsats Instn Skogsprod Skogshogsk — Rapporter och Uppsatser. Institutionen foer Skogsproduktion. Skogshogskolan

Rapp Uppsats Instn Skogstax Skogshogsk — Rapporter och Uppsatser. Institutionen foer Skogstaxering. Skogshogskolan

Rapp Uppsats Instn Skogstek Skogshogsk — Rapporter och Uppsatser. Institutionen foer Skogsteknik. Skogshogskolan

Rapp Verhand Rijksinst Vissch Onderz — Rapport en Verhandelingen Uitgegeven door het Rijksinstituut voor Visscherij-Onderzoek

Rapp Vissch Ind Zeeprod Curacao — Rapport. Visscherij en de Industrie van Zeeprodukten in de Kolonie Curacao

RAPRA Abst — RAPRA [*Rubber and Plastics Research Association*] Abstract

RAPRA Abstr — RAPRA [*Rubber and Plastics Research Association*] Abstracts

RAPRA Members J — RAPRA [*Rubber and Plastics Research Association*] Members Journal

RAPRB — Radioprotection

Raptor Res — Raptor Research

RAPV — Russko-Amerikanskij Pravoslavnyj Vestnik

RAq — Revue d'Aquitaine et du Languedoc

RAQ — Wirtschaft und Produktivitaet

R Aquat Sci — Reviews in Aquatic Sciences

RaR — Religion and Reason

RAR — Renaissance and Reformation

R Ar — Revue Archeologique

RAR — Revue Generale des Assurances et des Responsabilites

RAR — Rivista di Antropologia (Roma)

R Ar Av C Et — Recueil des Arrets et Avis du Conseil d'Etat

RARC — Quarterly Register. Organ. Alliance of Reformed Churches

R Arch — Revue Archeologique

R Arch Bibl Mus — Revista de Archivos, Bibliotecas, y Museos

R Arch Bibl Mus Ayunt — Revista del Archivo, Biblioteca, y Museo del Ayuntamiento de Madrid

RArchCr — Rivista di Archeologia Cristiana

R Archeol — Revue Archeologique

R Archeom — Revue d'Archeometrie

R Arch Hist Art Louvain — Revue des Archeologues et Historiens d'Art de Louvain

R Arch Inst — Royal Archaeological Institute

RAREA — Radiation Research

Rare Earth Res Conf — Rare Earth Research Conference

Rare Earths Mod Sci Technol — Rare Earths in Modern Science and Technology

Rarefied Gas Dyn — Rarefied Gas Dynamics

Rarefied Gas Dyn Proc Int Symp — Rarefied Gas Dynamics. Proceedings of the International Symposium

Rare Met Moscow — Rare Metals (Moscow)

Rare Met Tokyo — Rare Metals (Tokyo)

Rare Nucl Processes Proc Europhys Conf Nucl Phys — Rare Nuclear Processes. Proceedings. Europhysics Conference on Nuclear Physics

R Arg De Cienc Pol — Revista Argentina de Ciencias Politicas

R Arg De Neurol Psiquiat Y Med Leg — Revista Argentina de Neurologia, Psiquiatria, y Medicina Legal
R Argent Relac Int — Revista Argentina de Relaciones Internacionales
RARMB — Razrabotka Rudnykh Mestorozhdenii
RARNEB — Recent Achievements in Restorative Neurology
RA Royal Acad Mag — RA. Royal Academy Magazine
RARPC — Roczniki Akademii Rolniczej w Poznaniu
RArq — Revista de Arqueologia
RArqueol — Revista de Arqueologia
RARSA — Radiation Research. Supplement
RArt — Revue de l'Art
R Art C — Revue de l'Art Chretien
R Art Chr — Revue de l'Art Chretien
R Art C S — Revue de l'Art Chretien. Supplement
RArte — Rivista d'Arte
R Arts — Revue des Arts
R Arts As — Revue des Arts Asiatiques
RAS — Radio Science
RAS — Rassegna. Archivi di Stato
RAS — Rassegna della Letteratura Italiana
RaS — Rassegna Storica del Risorgimento
RAS — Readers Advisory Service
RAS — Revue Archeologique Syrienne
RAS — Royal Asiatic Society of Great Britain and Ireland. Journal
RASA — Rassegna Abruzzese di Storia ed Arte
RASB — Royal Asiatic Society. Bombay Branch. Journal
RASCA — Radio Science
R Ascetique & Mystique — Revue d'Ascetique et de Mystique
Raschet Konstr Issled Oborud Proizvod Istochnikov Toka — Raschet. Konstruirovanie i Issledovanie Oborudovaniya Proizvodstva Istochnikov Toka
Raschet Konstr Neftezavod Oborud — Raschet i Konstruirovanie Neftezavodskogo Oborudovaniya
Raschet Konstr Neftezvod Oborudovaniya — Raschet i Konstruirovanie Neftezavodskogo Oborudovaniya
Raschet Konstr Prim Radiats Trub Prom Mater Nauch Tekh Konf — Raschet, Konstruirovanie, i Primenenie Radiatsionnykh Trub v Promyshlennosti. Materialy Nauchno-Tekhnicheskoi Konferentsii
Raschety Prochn — Raschety na Prochnost
RasF — Rassegna di Filosofia
RASHA — RAS. Rohr-Armatur-Sanitaer-Heizung
RasI — Rassegna d'Italia
RasI — Rassegna Italiana
RASIB — Rendiconto. Accademia delle Scienze. Istituto di Bologna
Ras Isr — Rassegna Mensile di Israel
RasL — Rassegna Lucchese
RASL — Revue d'Aquitaine. Scientifique et Litteraire (Poitiers)
RasM — Rassegna Musicale
RASMA — Revue Agricole et Sucriere de l'Ile Maurice
RAsMyst — Revue d'Ascetique et de Mystique
RasN — Rassegna Nazionale
Raspr Gradja Povij Nauka — Rasprave i Gradja za Povijest Nauka
Rass — Rassegna Critica della Letteratura Italiana
RAss — Revue d'Assyriologie et d'Archeologie Orientale
RASS — Rock Analysis Storage System
Rass A — Rassegna d'Arte
Rass A Ant & Mod — Rassegna d'Arte Antica e Moderna
Rass Agr Ital — Rassegna dell'Agricoltura Italiana
Rass Arch Chir — Rassegna ed Archivio di Chirurgia
Rass Archit & Urb — Rassegna di Architettura e Urbanistica
Rass Archv Stato — Rassegna degli Archivi di Stato
Rass A Sen — Rassegna d'Arte Senese
Rass A Sen & Cost — Rassegna d'Arte Senese e del Costume
Rass A Umbra — Rassegna di Arte Umbra
Rass Bact Opo E Sieroter — Rassegna di Bacterio-, Opo-, e Sieroterapia
Rass Biblfica Stampa Ostet Ginec — Rassegna Bibliografica della Stampa Ostetrico-Ginecologica
Rass Biblfica Zool Lav Pubbl Ital — Rassegna Bibliografica Zoologica di Lavori Pubblicati in Italia
Rass Bibliog A It — Rassegna Bibliografica dell'Arte Italiana
Rass Biol Umana — Rassegna di Biologia Umana
Rass Chim — Rassegna Chimica
Rass Cinofila — Rassegna Cinofila
Rass Clin Sci — Rassegna Clinico-Scientifica
Rass Clin Scient Ist Biochim Ital — Rassegna Clinico-Scientifica dell'Istituto Biochimico Italiano
Rass Clin Sci Ist Biochim Ital — Rassegna Clinico-Scientifica. Istituto Biochimico Italiano
Rass Clin Terap — Rassegna di Clinica, Terapia e Scienze Affini
Rass Clin Ter Sci Affini — Rassegna di Clinica Terapia e Scienze Affini
Rass Contemp — Rassegna Contemporanea
Rass Crit Archit — Rassegna Critica di Architettura
Rass Crit d Lett Ital — Rassegna Critica della Letteratura Italiana
RassCult — Rassegna di Cultura
Rass Cult & Vita Scolast — Rassegna di Cultura e di Vita Scolastica
Rass Cult Mil — Rassegna di Cultura Militare
Rassd'A — Rassegna d'Arte Antica e Moderna
Rass dell Arte Ant e Mod — Rassegna dell'Arte Antica e Moderna
Rass del Lav — Rassegna del Lavoro
Rass Dermatol Sifilogr — Rassegna di Dermatologia e di Sifilografia
Rass Derm Sif — Rassegna di Dermatologia e di Sifilografia
Rass di Studi Francesi — Rassegna di Studi Francesi
Rass d'It — Rassegna d'Italia
Rass d Italia — Rassegna d'Italia
Rass Ec — Rassegna Economica
Rass Econ — Rassegna Economica

Rass Econ Afr Ital — Rassegna Economica dell'Africa Italiana
Rass Econ Cam Commer Ind Agr Alessandria — Rassegna Economica. Camera di Commercio, Industria, e Agricoltura di Alessandria
Rass Econ Colon — Rassegna Economica delle Colonie
Rass Econ (Napoli) — Rassegna Economica (Napoli)
Rassegna Bibliog Delle Sci Giurid — Rassegna Bibliografica delle Scienze Giuridiche
Rassegna Di Studi Psichiat — Rassegna di Studi Psichiatrici
Rassegna Di Stud Sess — Rassegna di Studi Sessuali
Rassegna Giurid — Rassegna Giuridico
Rassegna Int Di Clin E Terap — Rassegna Internazionale di Clinica e Terapia
Rassegna Ital — Rassegna Italiana di Lingue e Letterature Classiche
Rassegna Ital Sociol — Rassegna Italiana di Sociologia
Rassegna M Curci — Rassegna Musicale Curci
Rassegna Pen — Rassegna Penale. Dizionario di Dottrina, Giurisprudenza e Legislazione
Rassegna St Salern — Rassegna Storica Salernitana
Rasseyan Energ Kolebaniyakh Mekh Sist Mater Nauchn Soveshch — Rasseyanie Energii pri Kolebaniyakh Mekhanicheskikh Sistem. Materialy NauchnogoSoveshchaniya
RassF — Rassegna di Filosofia
Rass Faun — Rassegna Faunistica
RassFilos — Rassegna di Filosofia
Rass Fisiopat Clin Ter — Rassegna di Fisiopatologia Clinica e Terapeutica
Rass Fisiopat Clin Terap — Rassegna di Fisiopatologia Clinica e Terapeutica
Rass Fisiopatol Clin Ter — Rassegna di Fisiopatologia Clinica e Terapeutica
Rass Fotogr Cinem — Rassegna Fotografica e Cinematografica
Rass Gallara Stor A — Rassegna Gallaratese di Storia dell'Arte
Rass Geol Sci Affini — Rassegna di Geologia e delle Scienze Affini
Rass Giuliana Med — Rassegna Giuliana di Medicina
Rass Giul Med — Rassegna Giuliana di Medicina
Rass Giur Sard — Rassegna Giuridica Sarda
Rass Graf — Rassegna Grafica
Rasshir Tezisy Dokl Vses Konf Teor Vopr Adsorbts — Rasshirennye Tezisy Dokladov na Vsesoyuznoi Konferentsii po Teoreticheskim Voprosam Adsorbtsii
Rasshir Tezisy Dokl Vses Simp Termodin Ionnogo Obmena — Rasshirennye Tezisy Dokladov. Vsesoyuznyi Simpozium po Termodinamike Ionnogo Obmena
Rass IGI — Rassegna Indo-Greco-Italica
Rass Ind Mar — Rassegna dell'Industrie Marinare ed Ausiliarie
Rass Indo Greco Ital — Rasegna Indo-Greco-Italica
Rass Int Clin — Rassegna Internazionale di Clinica e Terapia
Rass Int Clin Ter — Rassegna Internazionale di Clinica e Terapia
Rass Int Elettron Nucl Atti Congr Sci Sez Nucl — Rassegna Internazionale Elettronica e Nucleare. Atti del Congresso Scientifico.Sezione Nucleare
Rass Int Stomatol Prat — Rassegna Internazionale di Stomatologia Pratica
Rass Istr A — Rassegna dell'Istruzione Artistica
Rass It — Rassegna Italiana
Rass It A — Rassegna Italiana dell'Arte
Rass Ital Chir Med — Rassegna Italiana di Chirurgia e Medicina
Rass Ital Gastro-Enterol — Rassegna Italiana di Gastro-Enterologia
Rass Ital Gastro-Enterol Suppl — Rassegna Italiana di Gastro-Enterologia. Supplemento
Rass Ital Ind Gas — Rassegna Italiana dell'Industria del Gas e delle Industrie Affini
Rass Ital Ling Lett Cl — Rassegna Italiana di Lingue e Letterature Classiche
Rass Ital Oncol — Rassegna Italiana di Oncologia
Rass Ital Oto Rino Lar — Rassegna Italiana di Oto-Rino-Laringologia
Rass Ital Ottal — Rassegna Italiana d'Ottalmologia
Rass Ital Ottalmol — Rassegna Italiana d'Ottalmologia
Rass Ital Soc — Rassegna Italiana di Sociologia
Rass Ital Sociol — Rassegna Italiana di Sociologia
Rass Lav Pubbl — Rassegna dei Lavori Pubblici
Rass Lazio — Rassegna del Lazio. Rivista Mensile. Provincia di Roma
Rass Let It — Rassegna della Letteratura Italiana
Rass March — Rassegna Marchigiana
Rass Mat Fis — Rassegna di Matematica e Fisica
Rass Med — Rassegna Medica
Rass Med Abruzzo Molise — Rassegna Medica d'Abruzzo e Molise
Rass Med Appl Lav Ind — Rassegna di Medicina Applicata al Lavoro Industriale
Rass Med Bologna — Rassegna Medica con Bollettino delle Specialita (Bologna)
Rass Med Convivium Sanit — Rassegna Medica - Convivium Sanitatis
Rass Med Cult — Rassegna Medica e Culturale
Rass Med Ind — Rassegna di Medicina Industriale
Rass Med Ind Ig Lav — Rassegna di Medicina Industriale e di Igiene del Lavoro
Rass Med Infort Patol Lav — Rassegna Medica di Infortunistica e Patologia del Lavoro
Rass Med Sarda — Rassegna Medica Sarda
Rass Med Sarda Suppl — Rassegna Medica Sarda. Supplemento
Rass Med Sper — Rassegna di Medicina Sperimentale
Rass Med Sper Suppl — Rassegna di Medicina Sperimentale. Supplemento
Rass Med Traf — Rassegna di Medicina del Traffico
Rass Mens Bot — Rassegna Mensile di Botanica
Rass Mens Clin Patol Ter Vita Prof Med Condotto Med Prat — Rassegna Mensile di Clinica, di Patologia, di Terapia, e di Vita Professionale del Medico Condotto e del Medico Pratico
Rass Mens Israel — Rassegna Mensile di Israel
Rass Mens Lett Odont — Rassegna Mensile della Letteratura Odontoiatrica
Rass Miner Metall Chim — Rassegna Mineraria, Metallurgica, e Chimica
Rass Min Metall Chim — Rassegna Mineraria, Metallurgia, e Chimica
Rass Min Metall Ital — Rassegna Mineraria e Metallurgica Italiana
Rass Mod Lett & A — Rassegna Moderna di Letteratura ed Arte
Rass Mon — Rassegna Monetaria
Rass Mus — Rassegna Musicale
Rass Mus Curci — Rassegna Musicale Curci
Rass N — Rassegna Nazionale
Rass Nazion — Rassegna Nazionale

Rass Neurol Veg — Rassegna di Neurologia Vegetativa
Rass Neuropsich — Rassegna di Neuropsichiatria e Scienze Affini
Rass Neuropsichiatr Sci Affini — Rassegna di Neuropsichiatria e Scienze Affini
R Assoc Canad Educ Langue Franc — Revue. Association Canadienne d'Education de Langue Francaise
Rass Odont — Rassegna di Odontoiatria
Rass Odontotec — Rassegna Odontotecnica
Rass Olii Miner — Rassegna degli Olii Minerali
Rass Ostet Ginec — Rassegna d'Ostetricia e Ginecologia
Rass Patol Appar Resp — Rassegna di Patologia dell'Apparato Respiratio
Rass Patol Appar Respir — Rassegna di Patologia dell'Apparato Respiratorio
Rass Pediat — Rassegna di Pediatria
Rass Penitenziaria Crim — Rassegna Penitenziaria e Criminologica
Rass Petrol — Rassegna Petrolifera
Rass Poste Telegr — Rassegna delle Poste, dei Telegrafi e dei Telefoni e della Telecommunicazione
Rass Prob Archit Amb — Rassegna. Problemi di Architettura dell'Ambiente
Rass Propr Ind Lett Art — Rassegna della Proprieta Industriale, Letteraria, e Artistica
Rass Psicol Gen Clin — Rassegna di Psicologia Generale e Clinica
Rass Pubbl — Rassegna di Diritto Pubblico
R Ass Resp — Revue Generale des Assurances et des Responsabilites
Rass Sanit AOI — Rassegna Sanitaria dell'A.O.I. (Africa Orientale Italiana)
Rass Sanit Imp Addis Ababa — Rassegna Sanitaria dell'Impero (Addis Ababa)
Rass Sanit Roma — Rassegna Sanitaria di Roma
Rass Sc Gl It — Rassegna delle Scienze Geologiche in Italia
Rass Sci Biol — Rassegna delle Scienze Biologiche
Rass Serv Soc — Rassegna di Servizio Sociale
Rass Sind Quad — Rassegna Sindacale. Quaderni
Rass Sov — Rassegna Sovietica
Rass Statis Lav — Rassegna di Statistiche del Lavoro
Rass Stor R — Rassegna Storica del Risorgimento
Rass Stor Risorg — Rassegna Storica del Risorgimento
Rass Stor Salern — Rassegna Storica Salernitana
Rass Stor Tosc — Rassegna Storica Toscana
Rass Stor Toscana — Rassegna Storica Toscana
Rass Stud & Not — Rassegna di Studi e di Notizie
Rass Stud Etiop — Rassegna di Studi Etiopici
Rass Studi Etiop — Rassegna di Studi Etiopici
Rass Studi Psichiat — Rassegna di Studi Psichiatrici
Rass Studi Psichiatr — Rassegna di Studi Psichiatrici
Rass Studi Sess — Rassegna di Studi Sessuali
Rass Tec Ass Naz Ingegn Archit Ital — Rassegna Tecnica. Associazione Nazionale Ingegneri Architetti Italiani
Rass Tec Pugliese — Rassegna Tecnica Pugliese
Rass Terap — Rassegna di Terapia
Rass Terap Patol Clin — Rassegna di Terapia e Patologia Clinica
Rass Ter Patol Clin — Rassegna di Terapia e Patologia Clinica
Rass Trimest Odont — Rassegna Trimestrale di Odontoiatria
Rass Trimest Odontoiatr — Rassegna Trimestrale di Odontoiatria
Rass Urol Nefrol — Rassegna di Urologia e Nefrologia
RAssyr — Revue d'Assyriologie
R Assyr — Revue d'Assyriologie et d'Archeologie Orientale
RAST — Rivista di Agricoltura Subtropicale e Tropicale
Rasteniev'd Nauki — Rasteniev'dni Nauki
Rasteniev Nauki — Rastenievadni Nauki
Rastenievud Nauk — Rastenievudni Nauki
Rastenievud Nauki — Rastenievudni Nauki
Rastermikrosk Materialpruef Vortr Tag — Rastermikroskopie in der Materialpruefung. Vortraege der Tagung
RaStEt — Rassegna di Studi Etiopici
Rastit Belki — Rastitel'nye Belki
Rastiteln SSSR — Rastitel'nost' SSSR. Vegetatio URSS
Rastit Krainego Sev Ee Osvoenie — Rastitel'nost Krainego Severa i Ee Osvoenie
Rastit Krainego Sev SSSR Ee Osvoenie — Rastitel'nost Krainego Severa SSSR i Ee Osvoenie
Rastit Latv SSR — Rastitel'nost Latviiskoi SSR
Rastit Resur — Rastitel'nye Resursy
Rastit Zasht — Rastitelna Zashtita
Rastit Zasht Plant Prot — Rastitelna Zashtita/Plant Protection
Rast Nauki — Rastenievudni Nauki
Rast Prom Sreda — Rasteniya i Promyshlennaya Sreda
Rast Resursy — Rastitel'nye Resursy
R Astron Soc Can J — Royal Astronomical Society of Canada. Journal
R Astron Soc Can Pr — Royal Astronomical Society of Canada. Selected Papers and Proceedings
R Astron Soc Geophys J — Royal Astronomical Society. Geophysical Journal
R Astron Soc Mem — Royal Astronomical Society. Memoirs
R Astron Soc Mon Not — Royal Astronomical Society. Monthly Notices
Rast Zashch — Rastitelna Zashchita
Rasy Nar — Rasy i Narody
RASyr — Revue Archeologique Syrienne
RAT — Revue. Academie Internationale du Tourisme
RAT — Revue des Accidents du Travail et de Droit Industriel et Social
RATEA — Radiotekhnika
RATES — Rapid Access Tariff Expediting Service
RATG — Recueil. Academie des Sciences, Belles-Lettres, et Arts de Tarn-et-Garonne
Ratg Prakt Landw Angora — Ratgeber fuer den Praktischen Landwirt (Angora)
RATIB — Radiologic Technology
Rationalisierung — Monatsschrift des Rationalisierungs
Ration Drug Dev Proc Int Meet Med Advis Pharm Ind — Rationality of Drug Development. Proceedings. International Meeting of Medical Advisers in the Pharmaceutical Industry
Ration Drug Ther — Rational Drug Therapy

Rat Muis — Rat en Muis
Rat News Lett — Rat News Letter
Ratsion Izobr Predlozh Stroit — Ratsionalizatorskie i Izobretatel'skie Predlozheniya v Stroitel'stve
Ratsion Udobr — Ratsional'noe Udobrenie
R Au — Revue d'Auvergne
Rauch Pnt — Rauch Guide to the United States Paint Industry Data
Rauch Staub — Rauch und Staub
RAug — Revue Augustinienne
Raum & Handwk — Raum und Handwerk
Raumforsch Raumordn — Raumforschung und Raumordnung
Raumforsch und Raumordnung — Raumforschung und Raumordnung
Raumforsch u-Ordnung — Raumforschung und Raumordnung
R Aust Chem Inst — Royal Australian Chemical Institute
R Aust Chem Inst J Proc — Royal Australian Chemical Institute. Journal and Proceedings
R Aust Chem Inst J Proc Suppl — Royal Australian Chemical Institute. Journal and Proceedings. Supplement
R Aust Chem Inst Proc — Royal Australian Chemical Institute. Proceedings
R Aust Plann Inst J — RAPIJ: Royal Australian Planning Institute. Journal
RAut & L — Revue des Auteurs et des Livres
RAuv — Revue d'Auvergne
RAv — Revue de l'Avranchin
Rav Bl — Ravensberger Blaetter fuer Geschichts-, Volks-, und Heimatkunde
Raven Press Ser Mol Cell Biol — Raven Press Series on Molecular and Cellular Biology
R Avr — Revue de l'Avranchin
RAW — Raad van Advies voor het Wetenschapsbeleid. Informatiebank. Tweekbericht
RAW — Record of the Arab World
Raw Mater — Raw Material
Raw Mater Elect Cable Making — Raw Materials for Electric Cable-Making. British Insulated Callender's Cables
Raw Materials Survey Res Rept — Raw Materials Survey. Resource Report
Raw Mater Rep — Raw Materials Report
Raw Silk Rev — Raw Silk Review
Raw Vulc Rubb — Raw and Vulcanized Rubber
RAXRA — Radex Rundschau (Austria)
Raymond W Brink Selected Math Papers — Raymond W. Brink Selected Mathematical Papers
Rayon — Rayon and Synthetic Textiles
Rayon J — Rayon Journal
Rayon J Cellul Fibers — Rayon Journal and Cellulose Fibers
Rayon Melliand Text Mon — Rayon and Melliand Textile Monthly
Rayonne Fibranne Fibr Synth — Rayonne, Fibranne, et Fibres Synthetiques (Paris)
Rayonne Fibres Synth — Rayonne et Fibres Synthetiques
Rayonne Fibr Synth Brux — Rayonne et Fibres Synthetiques (Bruxelles)
Rayonne Fibr Synth Paris — Rayonne et Fibres Synthetiques (Paris)
Rayonnem Ionis — Rayonnements Ionisants
Rayonnem Ionis Tech Mes Prot — Rayonnements Ionisants. Techniques de Mesures et de Protection
Rayon Rayon J — Rayon and the Rayon Journal
Rayon Rec — Rayon Record
Rayon Rev — Rayon Revue
Rayon Silk Dir — Rayon and Silk Directory
Rayon Synth Text — Rayon and Synthetic Textiles
Rayon Synth Yarn J — Rayon and Synthetic Yarn Journal
Rayon Text Mon — Rayon Textile Monthly
Rayon Warp Siz Spec — Rayon Warp Sizing Specialist
Rayon Wld Osaka — Rayon World (Osaka)
Rayon Yb — Rayon Year Book
Ray Soc Pub — Ray Society Publications
Ray Soc Publs — Ray Society Publications
RazFe — Razon y Fe
Raziskave Stud Kmetijski Inst Slov — Raziskave in Studije-Kmetijski Institut Slovenije
Razon y Fe — Razon y Fe. Revista Hispano-Americana de Cultura
Razprave SAZU — Razprave. Slovenska Akademija Znanosti i Umetnosti
Razpr Mat Prir Razr Akad Znan Umet Ljubl — Razprave Matematicno-Prirodoslovnego Razreda, Akademija Znanosti in Umetnosti v Ljubljani
Razpr Mat Prir Razr Akad Znan v Ljubljani — Razprave Matematicno-Pri-Rodoslovnega Razreda Akademije Znanosti in Umetnosti vLjubljani
Razpr Slov Akad Znan Umet IV — Razprave. Slovenska Akademija Znanosti in Umetnosti. IV
Razpr Slov Akad Znan Umet Razred Mat Fiz Teh Vede Ser A — Razprave. Slovenska Akademija Znanosti in Umetnosti. Razred za Matematicne, Fizikalne, in Tehnicne Vede. Serija A. Matematicne, Fizikalne, in Kemicne Vede
Razrab Ehkspl Gazov Gazokondens Mestorozhd — Razrabotka i Ehksplutatsiya Gazovykh i Gazokondensatnykh Mestorozhdenij
Razrab Mestorozhd Polezn Iskop (Kiev) — Razrabotka Mestorozhdenii Poleznykh Iskopaemykh (Kiev)
Razrab Mestorozhd Polezn Iskop (Tiflis) — Razrabotka Mestorozhdenii Poleznykh Iskopaemykh (Tiflis)
Razrab Neft Gazov Mestorozhd — Razrabotka Neftyanykh i Gazovykh Mestorozhdenii
Razrab Rudn Mestorozhd — Razrabotka Rudnykh Mestorozhdenii
Razred Mat Fiz Teh Vede Dela — Razred za Matematicne, Fizikalne in Tehnicne Vede Dela
Raz SAZU — Razprave Razreda za Filoloske in Literarne vede Slovenske Akademije Znanoste inUmetnosti
Razved Geofiz — Razvedochnaya Geofizika
Razved Geofiz (Leningrad) — Razvedochnaya Geofizika (Leningrad)
Razved i Okhr Nedr — Razvedka i Okhrana Nedr
Razved Nedr — Razvedka Nedr

Razved Okhr Nedr — Razvedka i Okhrana Nedr
Razved Promysl Geofiz — Razvedochnaya i Promyslovaya Geofizika
Razved Razrab Neft Gazov Mestorozhd — Razvedka i Razrabotka Neftyanykh i Gazovykh Mestorozhdenii
Razvit Pochvoved Kaz Tr Konf — Razvitie Pochvovedeniya v Kazakhstane. Trudy Konferentsii Pochvovedov Kazakhstana
Razvit Proizvod Kovkogo Chuguna Tr Vses Konf — Razvitie Proizvodstva Kovkogo Chuguna. Trudy Vsesoyuznoi Konferentsii po Teoriii Praktike Proizvodstva Otlivok iz Kovkogo Chuguna
Razv Nedr — Razvedka Nedr [*Moskva*]
Razv Okhr Nedr — Razvedka i Okhrana Nedr
R/B — ASE [*National Institute for Automotive Service Excellence*] Test Registration Booklet
RB — Reallexikon der Byzantinistik
RB — Recherches Bibliques
RB — Rechtsgeleerd Bijblad
RB — Religious Broadcasting
RB — Repertorio Boyacense [*Tunja*]
RB — Retail Business
RB — Revista Bibliotecilor
RB — Revue Benedictine
RB — Revue Biblique
RB — Revue Bossuet
RB — Revue Byzantine
RB — Revue de la Banque
Rb — Risicobank
RB — Rivista Biblica
RB — Romanische Buecherei
RB — Round Bobbin
RBA — Revista de Bellas Artes
RBA — Revue Belge d'Archeologie et d'Histoire de l'Art
RBA — Revue de la Banque
RBA — Rivista. Biblioteche e Degli Archivi
RBAA — Revue Belge d'Art et d'Archeologie
RBAADT — Ain Shams University. Faculty of Agriculture. Research Bulletin
RBAAS — Report. British Association for the Advancement of Science
RBAASc — Report. Meeting. British Association for the Advancement of Science
RBAB — Revue des Bibliotheques et des Archives de la Belgique
RBAC — Resumen Bimestral de Arte y Cultura
RBACB — Revista Brasileira de Analises Clinicas
RBAHA — Revue Belge d'Archeologie et d'Histoire de l'Art
RBAM — Revista. Biblioteca, Archivo, y Museo del Ayuntamiento de Madrid
RBAMM — Revista. Biblioteca, Archivo, y Museo del Ayuntamiento de Madrid
R Bancaria — Revista Bancaria
R Bancaria Bras — Revista Bancaria Brasileira
R Banco Republ — Revista. Banco de la Republica
R Banque — Revue de la Banque
RBAPA — Revue du Bois et de Ses Applications
RBArch — Revue Belge d'Archeologie et d'Histoire de l'Art
RBArg — Revista Biblica con Seccion Liturgica
R Bas Poitou — Revue du Bas-Poitou
R Bb — Rechtsgeleerd Bijblad
RBB — Reference Books Bulletin
RBB — Revue Bancaire Belge
RBB — Revue Bibliographique Belge
RBBRD — Revista de Biblioteconomia de Brasilia
RBBu — Revue de Biologie. Academia Republicii Popolare Romine (Bucharest)
RBC — Regulations of British Columbia
RBC — Revista Bimestre Cubana
RBC — Revue du Berry et du Centre
RBC — Rivista di Biologia Coloniale
RBCalb — Revista Biblica. Villa Calbada
RBCM — Reference Book of Corporate Management
RBCPDG — Canadian Forestry Service. Pacific Forest Research Centre. Report BC-X
RBD — Reserve Bank of India. Bulletin
RBD — Revista Bibliografica y Documental
RBdeF — Revista Brasileira de Filosofia
RBDI — Revue Belge de Droit International
RBDM — Revue Belge de Droit Maritime
RBE — Review of Business and Economic Research
R Belg Arch — Revue Belge d'Archeologie et d'Histoire de l'Art
R Belge — Revue Belge
R Belge Archeol — Revue Belge d'Archeologie et d'Histoire de l'Art
R Belge De Police Adm & Jud — Revue Belge de la Police Administrative et Judiciare
R Belge Dr Int — Revue Belge de Droit International
R Belge Droit Internat — Revue Belge de Droit International
R Belge Mus — Revue Belge de Musicologie
R Belge Musicol — Belgisch Tijdschrift voor Muziek-Wetenschap/Revue Belge de Musicologie
R Belge Philol & Hist — Revue Belge de Philologie et d'Histoire
R Belge Securite Soc — Revue Belge de Securite Sociale
R Belge Secur Soc — Revue Belge de Securite Sociale
R Belg Num — Revue Belge de Numismatique et de Sigillographie
R Belg Sec Soc — Revue Belge de Securite Sociale
R Belgue Philol Hist — Revue Belge de Philologie et d'Histoire
RBelPhH — Revue Belge de Philogogie et d'Histoire
RBen — Revue Benedictine
RB en B — Rechtsgeleerde Bijdragen en Bijblad
RBEP — Revista Brazileira de Estudios Politicos
RBER — Review of Business and Economic Research
RBE Rev Bras Eng — RBE. Revista Brasileira de Engenharia
RBF — Revista Brasileira de Filosofia
RBF — Revista Brasileira de Folclore

RBFBS — Report. British and Foreign Bible Society
RBFi — Revista Brasileira de Filologia
RBFilol — Revista Brasileira de Filologia
RBFSA — Revista Brasileira de Fisica
RBG — Revista Brasileira de Geografia [*Rio de Janeiro*]
RBGCA — Revista Brasileira de Geociencias
RBGd — Rocznik Biblioteki Gdanskiej Pan
RBGED3 — Brazilian Journal of Genetics
RBHGPV — Rheinische Beitraege und Hilfsbuecher zur Germanischen Philologie und Volkskunde
RBI — Recherches Bibliques
Rbi — Revue Biblio-Iconographique
RBi — Revue Biblique
RBI — Revue Biblique Internationale
RBI — Rivista Biblica Italiana
RBIB — Reserve Bank of India. Bulletin
RBib — Revue Biblique
Rbib — Revue des Bibliotheques
RBibC — Revista Bibliografica Cubana
RBibIT — Rivista Biblica Italiana
R Bibl — Revue Biblique
RBibl — Revue des Bibliotheques
R Bible — Revue Biblique
R Biblio Brasilia — Revista de Biblioteconomia de Brasilia
R Bibliogr Doc — Revista Bibliografica y Documental
R Bibl Nac (Cuba) — Revista. Biblioteca Nacional de Cuba
RBIC — Repertoire Bibliographique des Institutions Chretiennes
RBilt — Rivista Biblica Italiana
RBILA — Rivista di Biologia
RBIMBZ — Bio-Mathematics
R Bimestre Cubana — Revista Bimestre Cubana
R Bimestr Inform Banque Maroc Com Ext — Revue Bimestrielle d'Informations. Banque Marocaine du Commerce Exterieur
RBJM — Revista Bibliografica Jose Marti
RBK — Reallexikon der Byzantinischen Kunst
RBKr — Rocznik Biblioteki Pan w Krakowie
R Bk Rel — Review of Books and Religion
RBL — Revista Brasileira de Linguistica
RBI — Revue Blanche
RBL — Revue Bleue
RBL — Ruch Biblijny i Liturgiczny
R Black Pol Econ — Review of Black Political Economy
R Black Pol Economy — Review of Black Political Economy
RBLI — Rassegna Bibliografica della Letteratura Italiana
RBLL — Revista Brasileira de Lingua e Literatura
RBM — Revue Belge de Musicologie
RBMA — Repertorium Biblicum Medii Aevi
RBMAS — Rerum Britannicarum Medii Aevi Scriptores
RBML — Rare Books and Manuscripts Librarianship
RBML — Repertorium fuer Biblische und Morgenlaendische Litteratur
RBM Rev Eur Biotechnol Med — RBM. Revue Europeenne de Biotechnologie Medicale
RBMUDD — Research Bulletin. Marathwada Agricultural University
RBMus — Revue Belge de Musicologie
RBN — PTS [*Predicasts*] Regional Business News
RBN — Revista de Bibliografia Nacional
RBN — Revue Belge de Numismatique
RBNC — Revista. Bibilioteca Nacional Jose Marti (Cuba)
RBNC — Revista. Biblioteca Nacional de Cuba
RBNF — Revue Biologique du Nord de la France
RBNH — Revista. Biblioteca Nacional de Cuba
RBNJM — Revista. Biblioteca Nacional Jose Marti
RBNS — Revue Belge de Numismatique et de Sigillographie
R B Num — Revue Belge de Numismatique et de Sigillographie
RBo — Revue Bossuet
RBo — Revue de Boulogne
RBOBDY — Bardsey Observatory Report
R Bolsa Comer Rosario — Revista. Bolsa de Comercio de Rosario
R Bot Garden Edinb Notes — Royal Botanical Garden of Edinburgh. Notes
R Bot Gard (Kew) Notes Jodrell Lab — Royal Botanic Gardens (Kew). Notes from the Jodrell Laboratory
RBour — Revue Bourdaloue
RBP — Repertoire Bibliographique de la Philosophie
RBP — Revue Belge de Philologie et d'Histoire
RBPh — Revue Belge de Philologie et d'Histoire
RBPhil — Revue Belge de Philologie et d'Histoire
RBPL — Repertoire Bibliographique de la Philosophie (Louvain)
RBPL — Revue Bleue, Politique, et Litteraire
RBPMA — Revue Belge de Pathologie et de Medecine Experimentale
RBPoi — Revue du Bas Poitou et des Provinces de l'Ouest
RBPU — Research Bulletin of the Punjab University. East Punjab University. Government College
RBPUZ — Research Bulletin of the Punjab University. Zoology Series
RBQ — Revue de la Banque
RBQSA — Revista Brasileira de Quimica (Sao Paulo)
RBques — Revue des Bibliotheques
RBr — Revista Brasiliense
Rbr — Revue Britannique
RBR — Ricerche Bibliche e Religiose
R Bras Ec — Revista Brasileira de Economia
R Bras Econ — Revista Brasileira de Economia
R Bras Estatistica — Revista Brasileira de Estatistica
R Bras Estud Pol — Revista Brasileira de Estudos Politicos
R Brasil Econ — Revista Brasileira de Economia
R Brasileira — Revista Brasileira de Musica

R Brasil Estatist — Revista Brasileira de Estatistica
R Brasil Estud Polit — Revista Brasileira de Estudos Politicos
R Brasil Geogr — Revista Brasileira de Geografia
R Brasil Polit Int — Revista Brasileira de Politica Internacional
R Bras Mercado Capitals — Revista Brasileira de Mercado de Capitais
R Bras Pol Internac — Revista Brasileira de Politica Internacional
RBRI — Reference Book Review Index
RBRJ — Revista Brasileira (Rio De Janeiro)
RBRLA — Revue Bryologique et Lichenologique
R Bryol & Lichenol — Revue Bryologique et Lichenologique
RBS — Regulae Benedicti Studia
RBS — Revue Bibliographique de Sinologie
RBSEBR — Radiologia
RBSI — Records. Botanical Survey of India
RBSL — Regensburger Beitrage zur Deutschen Sprach- und Literaturwissenschaft
RBSI — Russkij Biograficeskij Slovar
RBSP — Religious Books and Serials in Print
RBSS — Revue Belge de Securite Sociale
RBSt — Regesten der Bischoefe von Strassburg
Rb St Aa — Ribe Stifts Aarbog
RBSTARO — Revue Belge de Statistique, d'Informatique, et de Recherche Operationnelle
RBT — Reviews in Biochemical Toxicology
RBTNA — Revista Brasileira de Tecnologia
RBU — Buro und EDV. Zeitschrift fuer Buroorganisation und Datentechnik
RB Ue — Revidierte Berner Uebereinkunft
R Bus & Econ Res — Review of Business and Economic Research
R Bus and Econ Research — Review of Business and Economic Research
R Bus St John's Univ — Review of Business. St. John's University
R B v N — Rechtskundig Blad voor het Notaris-Ambt
RBWCD9 — Washington State University. Agricultural Research Center. Research Bulletin
RBY — Rotterdam Europoort Delta
RBYOA — Rinsho Byori
R By S — Rutgers Byzantine Series
R Byz — Reallexikon der Byzantinistik
RBZ — Rotterdam
RC — La Revue du Caire
RC — Race and Class
RC — Rekishi Chiri
RC — Respiratory Care
RC — Review of the Churches
RC — Revista Contemporanea
RC — Revista Cubana
RC — Revue Celtique
RC — Revue Charlemagne
RC — Revue Commerciale - Handelsoverzicht. Chambre de Commerce Neerlandaisepour la Belgique et le Luxembourg
RC — Revue Communale de Belgique
RC — Revue Critique
RC — Revue Critique de Legislation et de Jurisprudence de Canada
RC — Revue Critique d'Histoire et de Litterature
RC — Revue du Caire
RC — Rivista Coloniale. Istituto Coloniale Italiano
RC — Rivista delle Colonie
RC — Royal Correspondence in the Hellenistic Period
RC — Ruperto-Carola
RCA — Alimentation Moderne. Revue de la Conserve
RCA — Revista. Colegio de Abogados de Puerto Rico
RCA — Revista Colombiana de Antropologia
RCA — Revue Catholique d'Alsace
RCABA — Revista. Colegio de Abogados de Buenos Aires
Rc Accad Lincei Cl di Sci Mor Stor Fil — Rendiconti. Accademia Nazionale dei Lincei. Classe di Scienze Morali. Storiche e Filologiche
RCADI — Recueil des Cours. Academie de Droit International de La Haye
RCAEB — RCA [*Radio Corporation of America*] Engineer
RCA Eng — RCA [*Radio Corporation of America*] Engineer
RCAFA — Revista Cafetalera
R Caire — Revue du Caire
RCAJ — Royal Central Asian Society. Journal
RCal — Revista Calasancia
RCAls — Revue Catholique d'Alsace
RCAm — Reformed Church of America
RCam — Revista Camoniana
RCan — Revue Canonique
R Canad — Revue Canadienne
R Canad-Amer Et Slaves — Revue Canadienne-Americaine d'Etudes Slaves
R Canad Biol — Revue Canadienne de Biologie
R Canad Et Afr — Revue Canadienne des Etudes Africaines
R Canad Geogr — Revue Canadienne de Geographie
R Can Dent Corps Q — Royal Canadian Dental Corps. Quarterly
R Can Etud Nationalisme — Revue Canadienne des Etudes sur le Nationalisme
R Can Sciences Info — Revue Canadienne des Sciences de l'Information
RCAPA — Revista de Ciencia Aplicada
RCAPDD — Revista de Ciencias Agrarias
RCA R — RCA [*Radio Corporation of America*] Review
RCARC — RCA [*Radio Corporation of America*] Review
RCA Rev — RCA [*Radio Corporation of America*] Review
RCAS — Journal. Royal Central Asian Society
RCat — Revista de Catalunya
RCA Tech Not — RCA [*Radio Corporation of America*] Technical Notes
RCA Tech Notes — RCA [*Radio Corporation of America*] Technical Notes
R Cath — Revue Catholique
Rc Atti Accad Naz Lincei — Rendiconti e Atti. Accademia Nazionale dei Lincei
RCAV — Rozpravy Ceskoslovenske Akademie Ved

RCAVA — Rozpravy Ceskoslovenske Akademie Ved. Rada Matematickych a Prirodnich Ved
RCAVF — Rezpravy. Ceska Academie Ved. Filologicka
RCAVFPH — Rezpravy. Ceska Academie Ved. Pro Vedy Filosoficke, Pravni, a Historicke
RCAVRSV — Rezpravy. Ceska Academie Ved. Rada Spolecenskych Ved
RCB — Revista de Cultura Biblica
RCB — Revista de Cultura Brasilena
RCB — Revue de Champagne et de Brie
RCB — Revue Juridique du Congo Belge
RCBBDA — Revue de Cytologie et de Biologie Vegetales - La Botaniste
RCBIA — Revue Canadienne de Biologie
RCBOA — Radiologia Clinica et Biologica
RCBPEJ — Reviews in Clinical and Basic Pharmacology
RCC — Revista Catolica (Chile)
RCC — Revista de Cultura (Cochabamba)
RCC — Revue des Cours et Conferences
RCCFB — Revista CENIC [*Centro Nacional de Investigaciones Cientificas*]. Ciencias Fisicas
RCCHA — Report. Canadian Catholic Historical Association
RCCM — Rivista di Cultura Classica e Medioevale
RCCMA — Rivista Critica di Clinica Medica
RCCMEF — Revista Costarricense de Ciencias Medicas
RCCS — Revista Catolica de las Cuestiones Sociales
RCCSI — Rede CONSISDATA [*Consultoria, Sistemas, e Processamento de Dados Ltda.*] de Servicos Integrados
RCD — Revista Chilena de Derecho
RCDA — Religion in Communist Dominated Areas
RCDA — Revista Colombiana de Antropologia
RCDIM — Revista Critica de Derecho Inmobiliario Moderno
RCDIP — Revue Critique de Droit International Prive
RCE — Repertoire Canadien sur l'Education [*See also CEI*]
RCE — Reviews in Cancer Epidemiology
RCE — Revista de Ciencia de la Educacion
RCE — Revue Catholique des Eglises
RCEA — Repertoire Chronologique d'Epigraphie Arabe
RCEB — Revista do Circulo de Estudos Bandeirantes
RCED — Revista do Centro de Estudos Demograficos
RCEE — Revista. Centro de Estudios Extemoenos
RCEH — Revista Canadiense de Estudios Hispanicos
RCEI — Revista Canaria de Estudios Ingleses
RCel — Revue Celtique
R Celt — Revue Celtique
R Celtique — Revue Celtique
RCENDR — Revista Colombiana de Entomologia
R Centroam Econ — Revista Centroamericana de Economia
R Centro Est Hist Milit — Revista. Centro de Estudios Historico-Militares del Peru
RCERB — Ricerche di Termotecnica
RCF — Review of Contemporary Fiction
RCF — Revista Colombiana de Folclor
RCF — Revista Cubana de Filosofia
RCF — Revue du Clerge Francais
RCFNA — Revista. Real Academia de Ciencias Exactas, Fisicas, y Naturales de Madrid
RCG — Revue du Chant Gregorien
RCGJA — Royal College of General Practitioners. Journal
RCh — Revue Charlemagne
Rch — Revue Chretienne
Rch Chron — Recherches Chronometriques
R Ch Com Franc Canada — Revue. Chambre de Commerce Francaise au Canada
R Ch Comm Marseille — Revue. Chambre de Commerce de Marseille
RCHE — Recherche
RCHG — Revista Chilena de Historia y Geografia
R Chile Hist Geogr — Revista Chilena de Historia y Geografia
R Chilena — Revista Chilena
R Chilena De Hist Y Geog — Revista Chilena de Historia y Geografia
R Chil Hist Geogr — Revista Chilena de Historia y Geografia
R Ch J — Rencontre. Chretiens et Juifs
RChL — Revista Chilena de Literatura
RCHL — Revue Critique d'Histoire et de Litterature
RCHN — Revista Chilena de Historia Natural
RCHN — Revue Catholique d'Histoire, d'Archeologie et Litterature de Normandie
RCHNT — Reponses Chretiennes aux Hommes de Notre Temps
RChr — Revue Chretienne
RChr — Russie et Chretiente
RCHRA — Revue de Chimie. Academie de la Republique Populaire Roumaine
RchScR — Recherches de Science Religieuse
RCI — Regesta Chartarum Italiae
RCI — Revista delle Colonie Italiane
RCI — Revue Coloniale Internationale
RCI — Rivista del Clero Italiano
RCIBDB — Revista de Ciencias Biologicas
RCICDE — International Whaling Commission. Report of the Commission
RCID — Revue Catholique des Institutions et de Droit
R Cienc Ec — Revista de Ciencias Economicas
R Ciencia Pol — Revista de Ciencia Politica
R Ciencias Econs — Revista de Ciencias Economicas
R Ciencias Juridicas — Revista de Ciencias Juridicas
R Ciencias Socs (Costa Rica) — Revista de Ciencias Sociales (Costa Rica)
R Ciencias Socs (Puerto Rico) — Revista de Ciencias Sociales (Puerto Rico)
R Cienc Polit — Revista de Ciencia Politica
R Cienc Soc (Ceara) — Revista de Ciencias Sociales (Ceara)
R Cienc Soc Fortaleza — Revista de Ciencias Sociales (Fortaleza)
R Cienc Soc (Puerto Rico) — Revista de Ciencias Sociales (Puerto Rico)

RCIESMM — Rapport et Proces-Verbaux des Reunions. Commission Internationale pour l'Exploration Scientifique de la Mer Mediterranee
RCIF — Revue Catholique des Idees et des Faits
RCIFDN — Revista de Ciencias Farmaceuticas
RCIL — Revue Critique des Idees et des Livres
R Cin — Revue du Cinema
R Cin — Revue du Cinema/Image et Son
RCINA — Revista Chilena de Ingenieria
R Cinematografo — Rivista del Cinematografo
RCIPDJ — Revista Cubana de Investigaciones Pesqueras
R Circ Min Just — Recueil des Circulaires, Instructions, et Autres Actes. Ministere de laJustice
RCI Riscaldamento Cond Idrosanit — RCI. Riscaldamento, Condizionamento, Idrosanitaria
RCI Riscaldamento Refrig Cond Idrosanit — RCI (Riscaldamento, Refrigerazione, Condizionamento, Idrosanitaria)
Rc Ist Lomb Scl Lett — Rendiconti. Istituto Lombardo di Scienze e Lettere
Rc Ist Sup Sanita — Rendiconti. Istituto Superiore di Sanita
RCivB — Revista Civilizacao Brasileira
RCJ — Revista de Ciencias Juridicas
RCJ — Revue Critique de Jurisprudence Belge
RCJB — Revue Critique de Jurisprudence Belge
RCJS — Revista de Ciencias Juridicas y Sociales
RCL — Reading-Canada-Lecture
RCL — Religion in Communist Lands
RCL — Review of Contemporary Law
RCL — Revista Chilena de Literatura
RCI — Rivista Clasica
RCLAD — Ricerca in Clinica e in Laboratorio
RCLADN — Investigacion en la Clinica y en el Laboratorio
R CI Afr — Revue du Clerge Africain
RClFr — Revue du Clerge Francais
RCLI — Rassegna Critica della Letteratura Italiana
RCLJ — Revue Critique de Legislation et de Jurisprudence
RCLL — Revista de Critica Literaria Latinoamericana
RCL Mag — RCL [*Ricegrowers' Cooperative Ltd.*] Magazine
RCM — Revista Chilena de Musica
RCM — Royal College of Music. Magazine
RCMLAO — Revista. Facultad de Ciencias Medicas. Universidad Nacional del Litoral Rosario
RCMLDR — Australia. Commonwealth Scientific and Industrial Research Organisation. MarineLaboratories. Report
RCMN — Revista del Colegio Mayor de Nuestra Senora del Rosario [*Bogota*]
RCMP — RCMP [*Royal Canadian Mounted Police*] Quarterly
RCMPQ — Royal Canadian Mounted Police Quarterly
RCMTA — Ricerche di Matematica
RCMUH — Ruperto-Carola. Mitteilungen der Vereinigung der Freunde der Studentenschaft der Universitaet Heidelberg
RCN — Energiespectrum
RCN — Revue Catholique de Normandie
RCNAA — Radiologic Clinics of North America
RCN Bull — RCN [*Reactor Centrum Nederland*] Bulletin
RCN Meded — Reactor Centrum Nederland. Mededeling
RCNMR — Royal Canadian Navy. Monthly Review
RCN Rep — Reactor Centrum Nederland. Report
RCOBA — Revista Chilena de Obstetricia y Ginecologia
RCOCB — Research Communications in Chemical Pathology and Pharmacology
RCOGB — Revista Cubana de Obstetricia y Ginecologia
RCol — Rassegna di Coltura
R Col — Revue de Doctrine et de Jurisprudence Coloniales et Financieres
R Collect Loc — Revue des Collectivites Locales
R Coll For Dep Refor Res Notes — Royal College of Forestry. Department of Reforestation. Research Notes
R Coll Obstet Gynaecol Proc Study Group — Royal College of Obstetricians and Gynaecologists. Proceedings. Study Group
R Coll Pathol Aust Broadsheet — Royal College of Pathologists of Australia. Broadsheet
R Coll Pathol Symp — Royal College of Pathologists Symposia
R Coll Sci Technol (Glasg) Res Rep — Royal College of Science and Technology (Glasgow). Research Report
R Coll Surg Ir J — Royal College of Surgeons in Ireland. Journal
RColt — Rassegna di Coltura
R Com — Revue Communale de Belgique
R Com B — Revue Communale de Belgique
RCOMD6 — Recent Advances in Community Medicine
R Com Ec — Revue Pratique des Questions Commerciales et Economiques
R Comitato G Italia B — Reale Comitato Geologico d'Italia. Bolletino
R Commer — Revue Commerce
Rcon — Revue Contemporaine
RCOND — Resources and Conservation
RCong — Revue Congolaise
R Cong — Revue Juridique du Congo Belge
R Contemp — Revue Contemporaine
R Contemp Sociol — Review of Contemporary Sociology
R Coop Int — Revue de la Cooperation Internationale
R Coree — Revue de Coree
RCOSDO — Revista de Chirurgie, Oncologie, ORL, Radiologie, Oftalmologie, Stomatologie. Seria Stomatologie
RCP — Recrea Plus
RCP — Revista de Ciencia Politica
RCPBO — Research Communications in Psychology, Psychiatry, and Behavior
RCPEA — Revista Chilena de Pediatria
RCPJA — Royal College of Physicians of London. Journal
RCPQ — Regestum Clementis Papae V
RCPRA — Record of Chemical Progress

RCQFAQ — Revista Colombiana de Ciencias Quimico-Farmaceuticas
RCQUD — Revista de Ciencias Quimicas
RCR — Rabbinical Council Record
RC-R — Revista Chicano-Riquena
RCr — Revue Critique
RCr — Revue Critique d'Histoire et de Litterature
RCR — Revue des Communautes Religieusses
RCRADJ — Revista Cubana de Reproduccion Animal
RCRB — Revista da Conferencia dos Religiosos do Brasil
RCRF — Rei Cretariae Romanae Fautorum Acta
RCrit — Ragioni Critiche. Rivista di Studi Linguistici e Letterari
R Crit De Leg Et De Juris — Revue Critique de Legislation et de Jurisprudence
R Crit Dr Int Prive — Revue Critique de Droit International Prive
R Crit Jpd B — Revue Critique de Jurisprudence Belge
RCRS — Annual Report. Catholic Record Society
RcRt — Romantic Reassessment
RCRUA — Revista. Consejo de Rectores. Universidades Chilenas
RCRVA — Russian Chemical Reviews
RCS — Conditionnement Embouteillage. Revue Mensuelle de l'Embouteillage et des Industries du Conditionnement, Traitement, Distribution, Transport
RCS — Revista de Ciencias Sociales
RCS — Revue Catholique Sociale et Juridique
RCSADO — Research Communications in Substances of Abuse
RCSAV — Rozpravy Ceskoslovenske Akademie Ved
RCSCSPL — Russian, Croatian and Serbian, Czech and Slovak, Polish Literature
RCSF — Rivista Critica di Storia della Filosofia
RCSFP — Rivista Critica di Storia della Filosofia. Pubblicazioni
RCSGS — Rivista Critica delle Scienze Giuridiche e Sociali
RCSH — Revue Congolaise des Sciences Humaines
RCSMC — Recent Advances in Studies on Cardiac Structure and Metabolism
RC Soc — Revue du Christianisme Social
RCT — Revista Catalana de Teologia
RCT — Revista de Cultura Teologica
RCTCA — Recherche Technique
RCTEA — Rubber Chemistry and Technology
RCTPA — Russian Castings Production
RCTPS — Revue Canadienne de Theorie Politique et Sociale
RCub — Revista Cubana
RCuBib — Revista de Cultura Biblica
R Cul Cl Medioev — Rivista di Cultura Classica e Medioevale
R Cul Medioev — Rivista di Cultura Classica e Medioevale
R Current Activities Tech Ed — Review of Current Activities in Technical Education
RCuTeol — Revista de Cultura Teologica
RCV — Recreatievoorzieningen. Maandblad voor Recreatie, Milieu, en Landschap
RCVRB — Royal Military College of Canada. Civil Engineering Research Report
RCVS — Rassegna di Cultura e Vita Scolastica
RCVTA — Rozpravy Ceskoslovenske Akademie Ved. Rada Technickych Ved
RCVTB — Recherches Veterinaires
RD — Reader's Digest
RD — Reichdenkmale Deutscher Musik
RD — Renaissance Drama
RD — Revista de Dialectologia y Tradiciones Populares
RD — Revue Historique de Droit Francais et Etranger
RD — Rivista Dalmatica
R d 2 Mds — Revue des Deux Mondes
RDA — Revista de Antropologia [*Sao Paulo*]
RDA — Revue de l'Administration et du Droit Administratif de la Belgique
Rd A — Rivista di Archeologia
Rd Abstr — Road Abstracts
RDAC — Annual Report. Director. Department of Antiquities. Cyprus
RDAC — Report. Department of Antiquities of Cyprus
RDAF — Revue de Droit Administratif et de Droit Fiscal
RdAm — Revista de America
RD & A — Research, Development, and Acquisition
R D Anthropol — Revue d'Anthropologie
RDB — NORD [*National Organization for Rare Disorders*] Services/Rare Disease Database
RDB — Revue de Droit Belge
RdB — Revue des Bibliotheques
RDB — Revue du Bois et de Ses Applications
RDBel — Revue de Droit Belge
RDBGA — Radiobiologia-Radioterapia
RdBL — Revue de Belles Lettres
RDBMD — Review on the Deformation Behavior of Materials
Rdbr Kraftanl — Rundbrief Kraftanlagen
RdC — Recueil des Cours. Academie de Droit International de La Haye
RdC — Resto del Carlino
RdC — Revista de Cuba
RDC — Revista de la Cepal
RDC — Revista Dominicana de Cultura
RDC — Revue de Droit Canonique
RDC — Revue de Droit Compare. Association Quebecoise pour l'Etude Comparative du Droit
RDC — Rochester Diocesan Chronicle
RDCCIF — Recherches et Debats du Centre Catholique des Intellectuels Francais
RdCE — Revue de la Culture Europeenne
R D Civ — Rivista di Diritto Civile
Rd Constr Leafl — Road Construction Leaflet. Cement and Concrete Association
RDCP — Revista de Derecho y Ciencias Politicas
RDCR — Revista de Derecho de Costa Rica
RDCS — Revista de Ciencias Sociales
RDCTD8 — Australia. Commonwealth Scientific and Industrial Research Organisation. Division of Chemical Technology. Research Review
RdDM — Revue des Deux Mondes

RdDxM — Revue des Deux Mondes
RDE — Rassegna di Diritto Ecclesiastico
RDE — Revista de Espiritualidad
RdE — Revista de las Espanas
Rd'E — Revue d'Egyptologie
RdE — Revue des Etudes Islamiques
RDE — Revue d'Esthetique
RdE — Rivista di Estetica
RDEA — Revista de Derecho Espanol y Americano
R de Ag (Cuba) — Revista de Agricultura (Cuba)
RDEC — Revue d'Egyptologie. Cahiers Complementaires
RDEc — Rivista di Diritto Ecclesiastico
R De Cienc Soc — Revista de Ciencias Sociales
R De Crimin E Med Leg — Revista de Criminologia e Medicina Legal
R de D — Revue de Droit. Universite de Sherbrooke
R de D McGill — Revue de Droit de McGill
R De Droit Int Et De Legis Comp — Revue de Droit International et de Legislation Comparee
RDEEA — Radio and Electronic Engineer
R de G — Revista de Guimaraes
R de Geog de Mtl — Revue de Geographie de Montreal
R de Guimaraes — Revista de Guimaraes
RDEH — Revista de Estudios Internacionales
RdeIE — Revista de Ideas Esteticas
RdeInd — Revista de las Indias
R de J — Revue de Jurisprudence
R de Jur — Revue de Jurisprudence
R de L — Revue de Legislation et de Jurisprudence
R De L Ecole D Anthropol De Paris — Revue de l'Ecole d'Anthropologie de Paris
R de L et de J — Revue de Legislation et de Jurisprudence
R De L Hist D Relig — Revue de l'Histoire des Religions
RDELTRI — Regeszeti Dologozatok as Eotvos Lorand Tudomanyegyetem Regeszeti Interetebol
R de l'Univ de Sherbrooke — Revue. Universite de Sherbrooke
R de l'Univ d'Ott — Revue. Universite d'Ottawa
R de l'Univ Laval — Revue. Universite Laval
R De Med Et D Hyg Trop — Revue de Medecine et d'Hygiene Tropicales
R De Med Leg De Cuba — Revista de Medicina Legal de Cuba
R De Med Leg De Psychiat Leg Et De Crimin — Revue de Medicine Legale, de Psychiatrie Legale et de Criminologie
R De Med Rosario — Revista de Medicina (Rosario de Santa Fe, Argentina)
R de MU — Revue de Musicologie
R de Mus — Revue de Musicologie
RDEN — Rivista di Etnografia (Napoli)
R de Paris — Revue de Paris
R De Philol Fr — Revue de Philologie Francaise de Litterature et d'Histoire Anciennes
R Der Cienc Polit — Revista de Derecho y Ciencias Politicas. Universidad de San Marcos
R Der (Concepcion) — Revista de Derecho (Concepcion)
R Derecho Financiero Hacienda Pbl — Revista de Derecho Financiero y de Hacienda Publica
R Derecho Mercantil — Revista de Derecho Mercantil
R Derecho Privado — Revista de Derecho Privado
R Derechos Humanos — Revista de Derechos Humanos
R Der Int Cienc Diplom — Revista de Derecho Internacional y Ciencias Diplomaticas
RDES — Revista de la Educacion Superior
R des Arts — Revue des Arts
R d'Esthetique — Revue d'Esthetique
RdEt — Revista de Etnografia
RDET — Rivista di Etnologia (Torino)
R D Ethnog — Revue d'Ethnographie
R D Ethnog Et De Sociol — Revue d'Ethnographie et de Sociologie
R D Ethnog Et D Trad Pop — Revue d'Ethnographie et des Traditions Populaires
R D Etudes Ethnog — Revue des Etudes Ethnographiques et Sociologiques
R Deux Mondes — Revue des Deux Mondes
R Developpement Internat — Revue du Developpement International
RdF — Renaissance de Fleury
RDF — Revista Dominicana de Filosofia
RDF — Revue de Droit Familial
RDF — Revue de France
RDF — Revue Historique du Droit Francais et Etranger
RdF — Rivista di Filosofia
RDG — Revista de Geografia
RdG — Revue de Geneve
RDGNA — Radiologia Diagnostica
RDGRA — Radiographer
RDGTA — Rational Drug Therapy
RdH — Revista de Historia
RdH — Revue de Hollande
R d'Hist — Revue d'Histoire de l'Amerique Francaise
R D Hist D Mis — Revue d'Histoire des Missions
RDHL — Revista de Derecho, Historia, y Letras [*Buenos Aires*]
R D Hyg — Revue d'Hygiene
RDI — Revista de Indias
RDI — Revue de Droit International et de Legislation Comparee
RDI — Rivista di Diritto Internazionale
RdI — Rivista d'Italia. Lettere, Scienze, ed Arte
R Dialect & Tradic Popul — Revista de Dialectologia y Tradiciones Populares
R Dialectol Trad Popul — Revista de Dialectologia y Tradiciones Populares CSIC (Consejo Superior de Investigaciones Cientificas)
RDIBF — Recent Developments in International Banking and Finance
RDIC — Revue de Droit International et de Droit Compare
RDICP — Revista de Derecho Internacional y Ciencias Diplomaticas

RDIDC — Revue de Droit International et de Droit Compare
RdIE — Rivista di Estetica
RDI et Comp — Revue de Droit International et de Droit Compare
RdIF — Rivista di Filosofia
RDIGA — Reader's Digest
RDIM — Revista de Derecho Inmobiliario (Madrid)
RDIn — Rivista di Diritto Internazionale
RDInt — Revue de Droit International et de Legislation Comparee
RDIntel — Revue de Droit Intellectuel
R Diplomatica — Revista Diplomatica
RDIPP — Rivista di Diritto Internazionale Privato e Processuale
R Dir Adm — Revista de Direito Administrativo
RdJ — Revue des Jeunes
RDJC — Revue de Doctrine et de Jurisprudence Coloniales et Financieres
RDL — Reallexikon der Deutschen Literaturgeschichte
R d L — Recht der Landwirtschaft
RdL — Revista de Letras
RdL — Revista do Livro
RdL — Revue des Lettres
RDLC — Revista de Literatura Cubana
RdLet — Revista de Letras. Serie Literatura
RDLGB — Radiologe
RDLI — Revista de Integracion
Rd Linc — Rendiconti. Accademia Nazionale dei Lincei
R d LR — Revue des Langues Romanes
RDM — Nouvelle Revue des Deux Mondes
RDM — Research and Development in Mexico
RDM — Retail and Distribution Management
RDM — Revue de Droit Minier
RdM — Revue de la Mediterranee
RdM — Revue de Musicologie
RDM — Revue des Deux Mondes
RdMa — Revue de la Manche
RDMAA — R and D [*Research and Development*] Management
R D Mag — R and D Magazine
RDMin — Revue de Droit Minier
RDMO — Recueil de Documents et Memoires Originaux. H. Ternaux-Compans [*Paris*]
RdMu — Revue de Musicologie
RDN — Revue de la Defense Nationale
RDN — Revue du Nord
RDNamur — Revue Diocesaine de Namur
Rd Nap — Rendiconti. Accademia di Archeologia, Lettere, e Belle Arti di Napoli
RDNGB — Ryukyu Daigaku Nogakubu Gakujutsu Hokoku
Rd Notes — Road Notes. Road Research Board
RDO — Rechnungswesen, Datentechnik, Organisation
R Do Brasil — Revista do Brasil
R Dom Cult — Revista Dominicana di Cultura
RDP — Revista de Derecho Puertorriqueno
RDP — Revue de Droit Penal et de Criminologie
RdP — Revue de Paris
R d P — Revue de Philologie, de Litterature, et d'Histoire Anciennes
RDP — Revue du Droit Publique et de la Science Politique en France et a l'Etranger
RdPac — Revista del Pacifico
RDPen — Revue de Droit Penal et de Criminologie
RdPF — Revue de la Pensee Francaise
RDPT — Revista de Dialectologia y Tradiciones Populares
RD Q — Revue de Qumran
RdQ — Revue de Qumran
RdQH — Revue des Questions Historiques
RDR — Ryukoku Daigaku Ronshu
R Dr Cont — Revue de Droit Contemporain
Rd Res — Road Research
Rd Res Bull New Delhi — Road Research Bulletin (New Delhi)
R D Res Dev Cahners — R and D. Research and Development (Cahners)
R/D Res/Develop — R/D. Research/Development
RD Res Dev (Kobe Steel Ltd) — R & D. Research and Development (Kobe Steel Limited)
Rd Res Overseas Bull — Road Research Overseas Bulletin. Road Research Laboratory
RD Rev Toyota RD Cent — R & D Review of Toyota RD Center
R Dr Fam — Revue de Droit Familial
R Dr Homme — Revue des Droits de l'Homme
RDRIA — Radiazioni e Radioisotopi
R Dr Int Dr Comp — Revue de Droit International et de Droit Compare
R Dr Int Sci Dipl — Revue de Droit International de Sciences Diplomatiques et Politiques
RDRKB — Ritsumeikan Daigaku Rikogaku Kenkyusho Kiyo
R Droit Can — Revue de Droit Canonique
R Droit Int — Revue de Droit International
R Droit Int Sci Dipl Pol — Revue de Droit International de Sciences Diplomatiques et Politiques
R Droit Public — Revue du Droit Public et de la Science Politique en France et a l'Etranger
R Droits Homme — Revue des Droits de l'Homme
R Droit Soc — Revue de Droit Social
R Dr Pen Crim — Revue de Droit Penal et de Criminologie
R Dr Prospect — Revue de Droit Prospectif
R Dr Publ Sci Polit — Revue du Droit Public et de la Science Politique en France et a l'Etranger
R Dr Rur — Revue de Droit Rural
R Dr Soc — Revue de Droit Social
RdS — Responsabilita del Sapere
RdS — Revue de Synthese

RDS — Revue du Dix-Huitieme Siecle
RDS — Revue du Droit Social et des Tribunaux du Travail
RDS — Russkaja Demokraticeskaja Satira XVII Veka
Rds Bridges — Roads and Bridges
R D Sci Polit — Revue des Sciences Politiques
Rds Constr — Roads and Construction
Rds Eng Constr — Roads and Engineering Construction
RDSG — Roczniki Dziejow Spoleczno-Gospodarczych
RdSO — Rivista degli Studi Orientali
Rds Rd Constn — Roads and Road Construction
RdSu — Revue de Suisse
RDT — Recreatie-Documentatie. Literatuuroverzicht Inzake Dagrecreatie, Verblijfsrecreatie, en Toerisme
RdT — Revista de Teatro
RDT — Revue de Droit du Travail
RDT — Revue Diococaine de Tournai
Rd Tar — Road Tar
Rd Tar Bull — Road Tar Bulletin. British Road Tar Association
RDTournai — Revue Diocesaine de Tournai
RDTP — Revista de Dialectologia y Tradiciones Populares
R D Trad Pop — Revue des Traditions Populaires
R D Troupes Col — Revue des Troupes Coloniales
RDU — Revista de la UNESCO
R du B — Revue du Barreau
R du B Can — Revue. Barreau Canadien
R Dublin Soc Econ Proc — Royal Dublin Society. Economic Proceedings
R Dublin Soc J Earth Sci — Royal Dublin Society. Journal of Earth Sciences
R Dublin Soc J Life Sci — Royal Dublin Society. Journal of Life Sciences
R Dublin Soc J Sc Pr — Royal Dublin Society. Journal. Scientific Proceedings
R Dublin Soc Rep — Royal Dublin Society. Report
R Dublin Soc Sci Proc — Royal Dublin Society. Scientific Proceedings
RduC — Revue du Caire
R du D — Revue du Droit
R du Louvre — Revue du Louvre et des Musees de France
R Du Monde Musulm — Revue du Monde Musulman
R du N — Revue du Notariat
R du Not — Revue du Notariat
RduR — Revue du Rouergue
R D U S — Revue de Droit. Universite de Sherbrooke
R du XVIe S — Revue du Seizieme Siecle
RDV — Rechentechnik-Datenverarbeitung
RDV — Reglement Dienstvoorwaarden
R d W — Rechtsarchiv der Wirtschaft
RDyTP — Revista de Dialectologia y Tradiciones Populares
RE — Real-Encyclopaedie der Klassischen Altertumswissenschaft
Re — Realidad
Re — Reforme
Re — Reinsurance
RE — Religious Education
He — Renaissance
Re — Republic
Re — Response
RE — Review and Expositor
RE — Review of Ethnology
RE — Revista Eclesiastica
RE — Revue d'Egypte
RE — Revue d'Esthetique
RE — Revue d'Ethnographie
RE — Revue Egyptologique
RE — Revue Encyclopedique
RE — Rijkseenheid
Rea — Realist
Rea — Realites
REA — Revue de l'Egypte Ancienne
REA — Revue des Etudes Anciennes
REA — Revue des Etudes Armeniennes
REA — Revue des Etudes Augustiniennes
REAA — Revista Espanola de Antropologia Americana
REA Bull — REA [*Rural Electrification Administration*] Bulletin
React Cent Ned Bull — Reactor Centrum Nederland-Bulletin
React Cent Ned Meded — Reactor Centrum Nederland-Mededeling
React Cent Ned Rep — Reactor Centrum Nederland. Report
React Core Mater — Reactor Core Materials
React Dosim Proc Int Symp — Reactor Dosimetry. Proceedings of the International Symposium
React Fuel Process — Reactor Fuel Processing
React Fuel-Process Technol — Reactor and Fuel-Processing Technology
React Funct Polym — Reactive and Functional Polymers
React Gaz Liq Gaz Liq Solide — Reacteurs Gaz-Liquide et Gaz-Liquide-Solide
React Intermed — Reactive Intermediates
React Intermed (Plenum) — Reactive Intermediates (Plenum)
React Intermed Wiley — Reactive Intermediates (Wiley)
React Kin C — Reaction Kinetics and Catalysis Letters
React Kinet — Reaction Kinetics [*Later, Gas Kinetics and Energy Transfer*]
React Kinet Catal Lett — Reaction Kinetics and Catalysis Letters
React Kinet Heterog Chem Syst Proc Int Meet Soc Chim Phys — Reaction Kinetics in Heterogeneous Chemical Systems. Proceedings. InternationalMeeting. Societe de Chimie Physique
Reactor Core Mater — Reactor Core Materials
Reactor Fuel Process — Reactor Fuel Processing
Reactor Mater — Reactor Materials
React Polym — Reactive Polymers
React Polym Ion Exch Sorbents — Reactive Polymers, Ion Exchangers. Sorbents
React Res Cent Kalpakkam Rep RRC — Reactor Research Centre, Kalpakkam. Report RRC

React Res Soc News — Reaction Research Society. News
React Res Soc Rep — Reaction Research Society. Report
React Sci — Reactor Science
React Sci Technol — Reactor Science and Technology
React Solids — Reactivity of Solids
React Solids Int Symp — Reactivity of Solids. International Symposium on Reactivity of Solids
React Solids Proc Int Symp — Reactivity of Solids. Proceedings. International Symposium on the Reactivity ofSolids
REACTS Proc Reg Educ Annu Chem Teach Symp — REACTS. Proceedings. Regional Educators Annual Chemistry Teaching Symposium
React Struct Concepts Org Chem — Reactivity and Structure Concepts in Organic Chemistry
React Technol — Reactor Technology
Read Abstr — Reading Abstracts
Read Dig — Reader's Digest
Read Digest — Reader's Digest
Read Disabil Dig — Reading Disability Digest
Read Educ — Reading Education
Reader — Reader Magazine
Readers D — Reader's Digest
Reader's Dig — Reader's Digest
Read Geog — Reading Geographer
Read Glass Hist — Readings in Glass History
Read Guide Period Lit — Readers' Guide to Periodical Literature
Read Improv — Reading Improvement
Reading Educ — Reading Education
Reading List Dyestuffs Div ICI — Reading List. Dyestuffs Division. Imperial Chemical Industries [*Manchester*]
Reading Med Stud — Reading Medieval Studies
Reading Nat — Reading Naturalist
Reading Orn Club Rep — Reading Ornithological Club Reports
Readings Glass Hist — Readings in Glass History
Reading Univ Geol Rep — Reading University. Geological Reports
Read Long Isl Archaeol Ethnohist — Readings in Long Island Archaeology and Ethnohistory
Read Man — Reading Manitoba
Read Math — Readings in Mathematics
Read Psychol — Reading Psychology
Read Res Q — Reading Research Quarterly
Read Teach — Reading Teacher
Read Time — Reading Time
Read Today Int — Reading Today International
Read World — Reading World
ReaE — Realites-English Edition
R E Ag — Revue des Etudes Augustiniennes
REAIU — Revue des Ecoles de l'Alliance Israelite Universelle
Reakt Bull — Reaktor Bulletin
Reaktor Bull — Reaktor Bulletin
Reaktortag (Fachvortr) — Reaktortagung (Fachvortraege)
Reakt Osobo Chist Veshchestva — Reaktivy i Osobo Chistye Veshchestva
Reakts Metody Issled Org Soedin — Reaktsii i Metody Issledovaniya Organicheskikh Soedinenii
Reakts Sposobn Koord Soedin — Reaktsionnaya Sposobnost' Koordinatsionnykh Soedinenii
Reakts Sposobn Mekh Reakts Org Soedin — Reaktsionnaya Sposobnost' i Mekhanizmy Reaktsii Organicheskikh Soedinenii
Reakts Sposobn Org Soedin — Reaktsionnaya Sposobnost' Organicheskikh Soedinenij
Reakts Sposobnost' Org Soedin Tartu Gos Univ — Reaktsionnaya Sposobnost' Organicheskikh Soedinenij. Tartuskij Gosudarstvennyj Universitet
Real — Realta
ReAL — Re Artes Liberales
REAL — Re: Arts and Letters
Real Acad Hist Bol — Real Academia de la Historia. Boletin
Real Anal Exchange — Real Analysis Exchange
Real Assoc Arquitectos Civ & Arqueologos Port Bol Arquit & Ar — Real Associacao dos Arquitectos Civis e Arqueologos Portugueses. Boletim Arquitectonico e de Arqueologia
REALB — REAL. The Yearbook of Research in English and American Literature
Real Clin — Realites Cliniques
Real Econ — Realta Economica
Real Enc — Real Encyclopaedie der Classischen Altertumswissenschaft
Real-Encycl Ges Heilk — Real-Encyclopaedie der Gesammten Heilkunde Medicinisch-Chirurgisches Handwoerterbuch fuer Praktische Aerzte
Realenz Klass Altertswiss — Pauly-Wissowa. Realenzyklopaedie der Klassischen Altertumswissenschaft
Reale Soc Geog Ital Bol — Reale Societa Geografica Italiana. Bollettino
Reales Sitios Rev Patrm N — Reales Sitios. Revista del Patrimonio Nacional
Real Estate & Stock J — Real Estate and Stock Journal
Real Estate Appraiser & Anal — Real Estate Appraiser and Analyst
Real Estate Bull — Real Estate Bulletin
Real Estate Invest Dig — Real Estate Investment Digest
Real Estate J — Real Estate Journal
Real Estate L J — Real Estate Law Journal
Real Estate Quart — Real Estate Quarterly
Real Estate R — Real Estate Review
Real Estate Rec — Real Estate Record
Real Estate Rev — Real Estate Review
Real Est L — Real Estate Law Journal
Real Est LJ — Real Estate Law Journal
Real Est Re — Real Estate Review
Real Est Rev — Real Estate Review
Real Gard — Real Gardening
Realidad Econ — Realidad Economica

Real Ist Veneto Mem — Reale Istituto Veneto di Scienze, Lettere, ed Arti. Memorie
Realites Nouv — Realites Nouvelles
Reallex fur Ant und Christ — Reallexikon fuer Antike und Christentum
Reallexikon — Reallexikon der Aegyptischen Religionsgeschichte
Real M — Realta del Mezzogiorno. Mensile di Politica, Economia, Cultura
RealN — Realta Nuova
Real Prop P — Real Property, Probate, and Trust Journal
Real Prop Prob and Tr J — Real Property, Probate, and Trust Journal
Real Prop Probate & Trust J — Real Property, Probate, and Trust Journal
Real Prop Rep — Real Property Reports
Real Scient Tech Fr — Realites Scientifiques et Techniques Francaises
Real Soc Geog Bol — Real Sociedad Geografica. Boletin
Realta Econ — Realta Economica
Realta Mezzogiorno — Realta del Mezzogiorno
Real Time Signal Process — Real Time Signal Processing
Real Time Syst — Real-Time Systems
Real Vorg — Reallexikon der Vorgeschichte
Real Wr — Realist Writer
REAM — Revista Espanola de Ambos Mundos
REAn — Revue des Etudes Anciennes
REAnc — Revue des Etudes Anciennes
Reanim Med Urgence — Reanimation et Medecine d'Urgence
Reanim Organes Artif — Reanimation et Organes Artificiels
REAP — Revue Mensuelle de l'Ecole d'Anthropologie de Paris
R E Ar — Revue des Etudes Armeniennes
REARA — Recherche Aerospatiale
REArg — Revista Eclesiastica Argentina
REArm — Revue des Etudes Armeniennes
REArmen — Revue des Etudes Armeniennes
REArmNS — Revue des Etudes Armeniennes. Nouvelle Serie
REA (Rural Electr Adm) Bull (US) — REA (Rural Electrification Administration) Bulletin (United States)
REAS — Revista de Estudios Agro Sociales
Reaseheath Rev — Reaseheath Review. Cheshire School of Agriculture
REAug — Revue des Etudes Augustiniennes
REB — Real Estate Business
REB — Resultaten van de Conjunctuurenquete bij het Bedrijfsleven in de Gemeenschap
REB — Review of Regional Economics and Business
ReB — Revista Biblica
REB — Revista Eclesiastica Brasileira
ReB — Revue Biblique
REB — Revue des Etudes Byzantines
REB — Revue Internationale des Etudes Balkaniques
REBK — Repertoire des Banques de Donnees en Conversationnel
REBM — Regesten der Erzbischoefe von Mainz
REBras — Revista Eclesiastica Brasileira
REBUD — Renewable Energy Bulletin
Rebuilt Tire J — Rebuilt Tire Journal
REByz — Revue des Etudes Byzantines
Rec — Record
Rec — Recorder
Rec — Record. Regional College of Education
REC — Recreational and Educational Computing
Rec — Recueil General des Monnaies Grecques d'Asie Mineure
Rec — Recurrence
REC — Retail Control
REC — Revista de Estudios Clasicos
ReC — Russie et Chretiente
RECA — Real Encyclopaedie der Classischen Altertumswissenschaft
RecA — American Catholic Historical Society of Philadelphia
Rec A Conv Br Wood Preserv Ass — Record of the Annual Convention of the British Wood Preservation Association
Rec Agric Res — Record of Agricultural Research
Rec Agric Res (Belfast) — Record of Agricultural Research (Belfast)
Rec Agric Res Minist Agric (Nth Ire) — Record of Agricultural Research. Ministry of Agriculture (Northern Ireland)
Rec Agric Res Stn Rehovot — Records. Agricultural Research Station. Rehovot
Rec Agr Res (N Ireland) — Record of Agricultural Research (Northern Ireland)
Rec Ak Inst Mus — Records. Auckland Institute and Museum
Rec Albany Mus — Record of the Albany Museum
Recalled Life — Recalled to Life [London]
Rec Am Aust Scient Exped Arnhem Ld — Record. American-Australian Scientific Expedition to Arnhem Land
Rec Am Cath Hist Soc — Records. American Catholic Historical Society of Philadelphia
Rec Am Soc Nat — Record of the American Society of Naturalists
Rec A Mus Princeton U — Record of the Art Museum. Princeton University
Rec Anc Cout Belg — Recueil des Anciennes Coutumes de Belgique
Rec Annu Conv Br Wood Preserv Assoc — Record of the Annual Convention. British Wood Preserving Association
Recaoutch Fr — Recaoutchouteur Francais
Rec Arch Orient — Recueil d'Archeologie Orientale
Rec Art Mus — Record. Art Museum. Princeton University
Rec Asilomar Conf Circuits Syst Comput — Record. Asilomar Conference on Circuits, Systems, and Computers
Rec Ass'n Bar City of NY — Record. Association of the Bar of the City of New York
Rec Auckland Inst — Records. Auckland Institute and Museum
Rec Auckland Inst Mus — Records. Auckland Institute and Museum
Rec Auckl Inst Mus — Records. Auckland Institute and Museum
RecAug — Recherches Augustiniennes
Rec Aust Acad Sci — Records. Australian Academy of Science
Rec Aust Mus — Records. Australian Museum
Rec Aust Museum — Records. Australian Museum

Rec Aust Mus Suppl — Records. Australian Museum. Supplement
Rec Austral Acad Sci — Records. Australian Academy of Science
Rec Austral Mus — Records of the Australian Museum
Rec Bare Facts Caradoc Severn Vall Fld Club — Record of Bare Facts. Caradoc and Severn Valley Field Club
Rec Bat — Recueil de la Jurisprudence de la Propriete et du Batiment
Rec Bot Surv India — Records. Botanical Survey of India
Rec Br Coal Dust Exp — Record of the First Series of British Coal Dust Experiments. Mining Association of Great Britain
Rec Buckinghamshire — Records of Buckinghamshire
Rec Bucks — Records of Buckinghamshire
RecC — Records. Columbia Historical Society of Washington, D.C.
ReCC — Russie et Chretiente. Collection
Rec Canterbury Mus — Records. Canterbury Museum
Rec CEDH — Recueil des Decisions de la Commission Europeenne de Droits de l'Homme
Rec Changer — Record Changer
Rec Chem Prog — Record of Chemical Progress
Rec Coll — Record Collector
Rec Commonw Emp Conf Radio Civ Aviat — Record of the Commonwealth and Empire Conference on Radio for Civil Aviation
Rec Conf Pap Annu Pet Chem Ind Conf — Record of Conference Papers. Annual Petroleum and Chemical Industry Conference
Rec Conf Pap Ind Appl Soc Annu Pet Chem Ind Conf — Record of Conference Papers. Industry Applications Society Annual Petroleum and Chemical Industry Conference
Rec Constantine — Recueil des Notices et Memoires. Societe Archeologiques, Historique, et Geographique du Departement de Constantine
Rec Conv Brit Wood Pres Ass — Record of the Annual Convention. British Wood Preserving Association
Rec Dep For NZ — Record. Department of Forestry. New Zealand
Rec Dep Geol Travancore — Record of the Department of Geology of Travancore
Rec Dep Miner Ceylon — Record of the Department of Mineralogy. Ceylon
Rec Dom Mus (Wellington) — Records. Dominion Museum (Wellington, New Zealand)
Recd Res Fac Agr Univ Tokyo — Records of Researches. Faculty of Agriculture. University of Tokyo
Rec Earthq Stn Regis Coll — Record of the Earthquake Station. Regis College [Denver]
Rec Earthq Stn Univ St Louis — Record of the Earthquake Station. University of Saint Louis
Rec Egypt Govt Sch Med — Record of the Egyptian Government School of Medicine
Rec Electr Commun Eng Conversat Tohoku Univ — Record of Electrical and Communication Engineering Conversation. Tohoku University
Rec Eng N — Recovery Engineering News
Recens & Mitt Bild Kst — Recensionen und Mitteilungen ueber Bildende Kunst
Recent Acc Refs Woods Hole Oceanogr Instn — Recent Accessions and References. Woods Hole Oceanographic Institution
Recent Achiev Restorative Neurol — Recent Achievements in Restorative Neurology
Recent Achiev Restor Neurol — Recent Achievements in Restorative Neurology
Recent Addit Libr R Met Soc — Recent Additions to the Library. Royal Meteorological Society [London]
Recent Adv Acarol Proc Int Congr — Recent Advances in Acarology. Proceedings. International Congress of Acarology
Recent Adv Adapt Sens Mater Their Appl — Recent Advances in Adaptive and Sensory Materials and Their Applications
Recent Adv Aerosp Med — Recent Advances in Aerospace Medicine
Recent Adv Anaesth Analg — Recent Advances in Anaesthesia and Analgesia
Recent Advanc Bot — Recent Advances in Botany
Recent Advanc Invert Physiol — Recent Advances in Invertebrate Physiology
Recent Adv Anim Nutr — Recent Advances in Animal Nutrition
Recent Adv Anionic Polym — Recent Advances in Anionic Polymerization
Recent Adv Aquat Mycol — Recent Advances in Aquatic Mycology
Recent Adv Avian Endocrinol — Recent Advances of Avian Endocrinology
Recent Adv Basic Microcirc Res Eur Conf — Recent Advances in Basic Microcirculatory Research. European Conference on Microcirculation
Recent Adv Behcets Dis — Recent Advances in Behcet's Disease
Recent Adv Bile Acid Res — Recent Advances in Bile Acid Research
Recent Adv Biochem Cereals — Recent Advances in the Biochemistry of Cereals
Recent Adv Biochem Fruits Veg — Recent Advances in the Biochemistry of Fruits and Vegetables
Recent Adv Biochem Pathol Toxic Liver Inj — Recent Advances in Biochemical Pathology. Toxic Liver Injury
Recent Adv Biol Membr Stud — Recent Advances in Biological Membrane Studies
Recent Adv Biol Nitrogen Fixation — Recent Advances in Biological Nitrogen Fixation
Recent Adv Biol Psychiatry — Recent Advances in Biological Psychiatry
Recent Adv Biotechnol — Recent Advances in Biotechnology
Recent Adv Blood Coagulation — Recent Advances in Blood Coagulation
Recent Adv Blood Group Biochem — Recent Advances in Blood Group Biochemistry
Recent Adv Bone Marrow Transplant — Recent Advances in Bone Marrow Transplantation
Recent Adv Buffalo Res Dev — Recent Advances in Buffalo Research and Development
Recent Adv Cancer Res Cell Biol Mol Biol Tumor Virol — Recent Advances in Cancer Research. Cell Biology, Molecular Biology, and Tumor Virology
Recent Adv Cancer Treat — Recent Advances in Cancer Treatment
Recent Adv Can Neuropsychopharmacol — Recent Advances in Canadian Neuropsychopharmacology
Recent Adv Capillary Gas Chromatogr — Recent Advances in Capillary Gas Chromatography
Recent Adv Card Arrhythmias — Recent Advances in Cardiac Arrhythmias

Recent Adv Chem Beta Lactam Antibiot Proc Int Symp — Recent Advances in the Chemistry of Beta-Lactam Antibiotics. Proceedings. International Symposium

Recent Adv Chem Biochem Plant Lipids — Recent Advances in the Chemistry and Biochemistry of Plant Lipids

Recent Adv Chem Compos Tob Tob Smoke Symp — Recent Advances in the Chemical Composition of Tobacco and Tobacco Smoke Symposium

Recent Adv Chem Inf — Recent Advances in Chemical Information

Recent Adv Chem Insect Control — Recent Advances in the Chemistry of Insect Control

Recent Adv Chronobiol Allergy Immunol Proc — Recent Advances in the Chronobiology of Allergy and Immunology. Proceedings

Recent Adv Clin Biochem — Recent Advances in Clinical Biochemistry

Recent Adv Clin Microcirc Res Eur Conf — Recent Advances in Clinical Microcirculatory Research. European Conference on Microcirculation

Recent Adv Clin Nucl Med — Recent Advances in Clinical Nuclear Medicine

Recent Adv Clin Nutr — Recent Advances in Clinical Nutrition

Recent Adv Clin Pathol — Recent Advances in Clinical Pathology

Recent Adv Clin Pharmacol — Recent Advances in Clinical Pharmacology

Recent Adv Clin Ther — Recent Advances in Clinical Therapeutics

Recent Adv Coal Process — Recent Advances in Coal Processing

Recent Adv Community Med — Recent Advances in Community Medicine

Recent Adv Core Curric Course — Recent Advances as a Core Curriculum Course

Recent Adv Diabetes — Recent Advances in Diabetes

Recent Adv Diagn Treat Pituitary Tumors — Recent Advances in the Diagnosis and Treatment of Pituitary Tumors

Recent Adv Drug Delivery Syst — Recent Advances in Drug Delivery Systems

Recent Adv Drug Res — Recent Advances in Drug Research

Recent Adv Endocrinol Metab — Recent Advances in Endocrinology and Metabolism

Recent Adv Eng Sci — Recent Advances in Engineering Science

Recent Adv Entomol India — Recent Advances in Entomology in India

Recent Adv Food Irradiat — Recent Advances in Food Irradiation

Recent Adv Food Sci — Recent Advances in Food Science

Recent Adv Gastroenterol — Recent Advances in Gastroenterology

Recent Adv Geriatr Med — Recent Advances in Geriatric Medicine

Recent Adv Germfree Res Proc Int Symp Gnotobiol — Recent Advances in Germfree Research. Proceedings. International Symposium on Gnotobiology

Recent Adv Glaucoma Proc Int Symp Glaucoma — Recent Advances in Glaucoma. Proceedings. International Symposium on Glaucoma

Recent Adv Gut Horm Res — Recent Advances in Gut Hormone Research

Recent Adv Haematol — Recent Advances in Haematology

Recent Adv Heat Transfer Proc Balt Heat Transfer Conf — Recent Advances in Heat Transfer. Proceedings. Baltic Heat Transfer Conference

Recent Adv Hum Biol — Recent Advances in Human Biology

Recent Adv Infect — Recent Advances in Infection

Recent Adv Liq Cryst Polym — Recent Advances in Liquid Crystalline Polymers

Recent Adv Mamm Dev — Recent Advances in Mammalian Development

Recent Adv Mech Synth Aspects Polym — Recent Advances in Mechanistic and Synthetic Aspects of Polymerization

Recent Adv Med — Recent Advances in Medicine

Recent Adv Microcirc Res — Recent Advances in Microcirculatory Research

Recent Adv Mucosal Immun — Recent Advances in Mucosal Immunity

Recent Adv Mucosal Immunol Part A — Recent Advances in Mucosal Immunology. Part A. Cellular Interactions

Recent Adv Mucosal Immunol Part B — Recent Advances in Mucosal Immunology. Part B. Effector Functions

Recent Adv Myology Proc Int Congr Muscle Dis — Recent Advances in Myology. Proceedings. International Congress on Muscle Diseases

Recent Adv Nerv Syst Toxicol — Recent Advances in Nervous System Toxicology

Recent Adv Neuropathol — Recent Advances in Neuropathology

Recent Adv Neuropharmacol — Recent Advances in Neuropharmacology

Recent Adv New Syndr — Recent Advances and New Syndromes

Recent Adv Non Linear Comput Mech — Recent Advances in Non-Linear Computational Mechanics

Recent Adv Nucl Med — Recent Advances in Nuclear Medicine

Recent Adv Nucl Struct Lect Predeal Int Sch — Recent Advances in Nuclear Structure. Lectures. Predeal International School

Recent Adv Numer Methods Fluids — Recent Advances in Numerical Methods in Fluids

Recent Adv Nurs — Recent Advances in Nursing

Recent Adv Obes Diabetes Res — Recent Advances in Obesity and Diabetes Research

Recent Adv Obesity Res — Recent Advances in Obesity Research

Recent Adv Obes Res — Recent Advances in Obesity Research

Recent Adv Occ Hlth — Recent Advances in Occupational Health

Recent Adv Opt Phys — Recent Advances in Optical Physics

Recent Adv Pain Pathophysiol Clin Aspects — Recent Advances on Pain. Pathophysiology and Clinical Aspects

Recent Adv Pediatr Nephrol — Recent Advances in Pediatric Nephrology

Recent Adv Pharmacol Ther — Recent Advances in Pharmacology and Therapeutics

Recent Adv Pharmacol Toxins — Recent Advances in the Pharmacology of Toxins

Recent Adv Physiol — Recent Advances in Physiology

Recent Adv Phytochem — Recent Advances in Phytochemistry

Recent Adv Plant Nutr Proc Colloq Plant Anal Fert Probl — Recent Advances in Plant Nutrition. Proceedings. Colloquium on Plant Analysis and Fertilizer Problems

Recent Adv Polym Blends Grafts Blocks — Recent Advances in Polymer Blends, Grafts, and Blocks

Recent Adv Renal Dis — Recent Advances in Renal Disease

Recent Adv Res Nerv Syst — Recent Advances in Research of Nervous System

Recent Adv RES Res — Recent Advances in RES [Reticuloendothelial System] Research

Recent Adv Rheumatol — Recent Advances in Rheumatology

Recent Adv Sci Technol Mater — Recent Advances in Science and Technology of Materials

Recent Adv Semicond Theory Technol — Recent Advances in Semiconductors. Theory and Technology

Recent Adv Stud Card Struct Metab — Recent Advances in Studies on Cardiac Structure and Metabolism

Recent Adv Tob Sci — Recent Advances in Tobacco Science

Recent Adv Treat Depression — Recent Advances in the Treatment of Depression

Recent Adv Tuber Res — Recent Advances in Tuberculosis Research

Recent Adv Urol — Recent Advances in Urology

Recent Adv Uses Light Phys Chem Eng Med — Recent Advances in the Uses of Light in Physics, Chemistry, Engineering, and Medicine

Recent Adv Weed Res — Recent Advances in Weed Research

Recent Art Petrol — Recent Articles on Petroleum and Allied Substances. United States Bureau of Mines

Recent Dev Aerosol Sci — Recent Developments in Aerosol Science

Recent Dev Alcohol — Recent Developments in Alcoholism

Recent Dev Anal Surfactants — Recent Developments in the Analysis of Surfactants

Recent Dev Cardiovasc Drugs — Recent Developments in Cardiovascular Drugs

Recent Dev Card Muscle Pharmacol — Recent Developments in Cardiac Muscle Pharmacology

Recent Dev Chem Nat Carbon Compd — Recent Developments in the Chemistry of Natural Carbon Compounds

Recent Dev Chromatogr Electrophor — Recent Developments in Chromatography and Electrophoresis

Recent Dev High Energy Phys — Recent Developments in High-Energy Physics

Recent Dev Hist Chem — Recent Developments in the History of Chemistry

Recent Dev Ion Exch 2 Proc Int Conf Ion Exch Processes — Recent Developments in Ion Exchange 2. Proceedings. International Conference onIon Exchange Processes

Recent Dev Lab Identif Tech — Recent Developments in Laboratory Identification Techniques

Recent Dev Mass Spectrom Biochem Med Environ Res — Recent Developments in Mass Spectrometry in Biochemistry, Medicine, and Environmental Research

Recent Dev Neurobiol Hung — Recent Developments of Neurobiology in Hungary

Recent Dev Pharmacol Inflammatory Mediators — Recent Developments in the Pharmacology of Inflammatory Mediators

Recent Dev Pipeline Weld — Recent Developments in Pipeline Welding

Recent Dev Sep Sci — Recent Developments in Separation Science

Recent Dev Soil Analysis — Recent Developments in Soil Analysis

Recent Dev Technol Surfactants — Recent Developments in the Technology of Surfactants

Recent Dev Ther Drug Monit Clin Toxicol — Recent Developments in Therapeutic Drug Monitoring and Clinical Toxicology

Recent Geogr Lit Maps Pap R Geogr Soc — Recent Geographical Literature, Maps, and Papers added to the Society's Collections. Royal Geographical Society [London]

Recentia Med — Recentia Medica

Recenti Prog Med — Recenti Progressi in Medicina

Recent Lit Hazard Environ Ind — Recent Literature on Hazardous Environments in Industry

Recent Med — Recentia Medica

Recent Med Osaka — Recent Medicine (Osaka)

Recent Prog Androl — Recent Progress in Andrology

Recent Prog Antifungal Chemother Proc Int Conf — Recent Progress in Antifungal Chemotherapy. Proceedings. International Conference on Antifungal Chemotherapy

Recent Prog Chem Synth Antibiot — Recent Progress in the Chemical Synthesis of Antibiotics

Recent Prog Endocr Reprod — Recent Progress in the Endocrinology of Reproduction

Recent Prog Horm Res — Recent Progress in Hormone Research

Recent Prog Kinins — Recent Progress on Kinins

Recent Prog Many Body Theor — Recent Progress in Many-Body Theories

Recent Prog Med (Roma) — Recenti Progressi in Medicina (Roma)

Recent Prog Microbiol — Recent Progress in Microbiology

Recent Prog Nat Sci Jap — Recent Progress of Natural Sciences in Japan

Recent Prog Neurol Surg — Recent Progress in Neurological Surgery

Recent Prog Obstet Gynaecol — Recent Progress in Obstetrics and Gynaecology

Recent Prog Pediatr Endocrinol — Recent Progress in Pediatric Endocrinology

Recent Prog Photobiol — Recent Progress in Photobiology

Recent Prog Polyamine Res — Recent Progress in Polyamine Research

Recent Prog Psychiat — Recent Progress in Psychiatry

Recent Prog Psychiatry — Recent Progress in Psychiatry

Recent Progr Hormone Res — Recent Progress in Hormone Research

Recent Progr Microbiol — Recent Progress in Microbiology

Recent Progr Natur Sci Japan — Recent Progress of Natural Sciences in Japan

Recent Prog Study Ther Brain Edema — Recent Progress in the Study and Therapy of Brain Edema

Recent Prog Surf Sci — Recent Progress in Surface Science

Recent Publ Artic — Recently Published Articles. American Historical Association

Recent Publ Gov Probl — Recent Publications on Governmental Problems

Recent Pubns Governmental Problems — Recent Publications on Governmental Problems

Recent Res Carnitine — Recent Research on Carnitine

Recent Res Cast Iron — Recent Research on Cast Iron

Recent Res Climatol — Recent Research in Climatology

Recent Res Geol — Recent Researches in Geology

Recent Res Mech Behav Solids — Recent Research on Mechanical Behavior of Solids

Recent Res Mol Beams — Recent Research in Molecular Beams

Recent Res Neurotransm Recept — Recent Research on Neurotransmitter Receptors

Recent Res Scleroderris Canker Conifers — Recent Research on Scleroderris Canker of Conifers
Recent Results Cancer Res — Recent Results in Cancer Research
Recent Results Cancer Treat Jpn — Recent Results of Cancer Treatment in Japan
Recent Results Pept Horm Androg Steroid Res Proc Congr Hung — Recent Results in Peptide, Hormone, and Androgenic Steroid Research. Proceedings. Congress. Hungarian Society of Endocrinology and Metabolism
Recents Prog Cryotech — Recents Progres en Cryotechnique
Recents Prog Genie Procedes — Recents Progres en Genie des Procedes
Recents Prog Syst Metr — Recents Progres du Systeme Metrique
Recents Prog Vitaminol — Recents Progres en Vitaminologie
Recent Stud Hypothal Funct — Recent Studies of Hypothalamic Function
Recent Surv Genet Toxicol Relat Fields — Recent Survey on Genetic Toxicology and Related Fields
Recent Trends Automot Emiss Control — Recent Trends in Automotive Emissions Control
Recent Trends Clin Pharmacol Natl Clin Pharmacol Conf — Recent Trends in Clinical Pharmacology. National Clinical Pharmacology Conference
Recent Trends Clin Pharmacol Natl Meet Clin Pharmacol — Recent Trends in Clinical Pharmacology. National Meeting on Clinical Pharmacology
Recent Trends Diabetes Res — Recent Trends in Diabetes Research
Recent Trends Toxicol — Recent Trends in Toxicology
Recept & Signal Transduction — Receptors and Signal Transduction
Recept Antibodies Dis — Receptors, Antibodies, and Disease
Recept Biochem — Receptor Biochemistry
Recept Biochem Methodol — Receptor Biochemistry and Methodology
Recept Compr Treatise — Receptors. A Comprehensive Treatise
Recept Eff Coupling — Receptor-Effector Coupling
Recept Horm Action — Receptors and Hormone Action
Recept Ligands Intercell Commun — Receptors and Ligands in Intercellular Communication
Recept Pharmacol — Receptors in Pharmacology
Recept Purif — Receptor Purification
Recept Recognit Ser A — Receptors and Recognition. Series A
Recept Recognit Ser B — Receptors and Recognition. Series B
RECFD — Revista Cubana de Fisica
Rec Gen — Recueil General de l'Enregistrement et du Notariat
Rec Gen Enr et Not — Recueil General de l'Enregistrement et du Notariat
Rec Genet Soc Am — Record. Genetics Society of America
Rec Gen Sci — Records of General Science
Rec Geol Dep St Mysore — Record of the Geological Department of the State of Mysore
Rec Geol Surv Bechuanald — Record. Geological Survey of Bechuanaland
Rec Geol Surv Br Guiana — Records. Geological Survey of British Guiana
Rec Geol Surv Dep North Rhod — Records. Geological Survey Department. Northern Rhodesia
Rec Geol Surv Guyana — Records. Geological Survey of Guyana
Rec Geol Surv India — Records. Geological Survey of India
Rec Geol Surv Malawi — Records. Geological Survey of Malawi
Rec Geol Surv New South Wales — Records. Geological Survey of New South Wales
Rec Geol Surv Niger — Records. Geological Survey of Nigeria
Rec Geol Surv Nigeria — Record of the Geological Survey of Nigeria
Rec Geol Surv NSW — Records. Geological Survey of New South Wales
Rec Geol Surv Nth Rhod — Record of the Geological Survey of Northern Rhodesia
Rec Geol Surv Nyasald — Record of the Geological Survey of Nyasaland
Rec Geol Surv Pak — Records. Geological Survey of Pakistan
Rec Geol Surv Pakist — Record of the Geological Survey of Pakistan
Rec Geol Surv Tanganyika — Records. Geological Survey of Tanganyika
Rec Geol Surv Tasm — Tasmania. Geological Survey. Record
Rec Geol Surv (Zambia) — Records. Geological Survey (Zambia)
Rech — Recherche
RecH — Recusant History
ReCH — Revista de Ciencias Historicas
RechA — Recherches Augustiniennes
Rech A Crac — Recherches Archeologiques. Institut d'Archeologie. Universite de Cracovie
Rech Aeronaut — Recherche Aeronautique
Rech Aerosp — Recherche Aerospatiale
Rech Aerospat — Recherche Aerospatiale
Rech Aerospat English — La Recherche Aerospatiale. English Edition
Rech Afr — Recherches Africaines
Rech Agron — Recherches Agronomiques
Rech Agron (Quebec) — Recherches Agronomiques (Quebec)
Rech Agron Suisse — Recherche Agronomique en Suisse
Rech Amerind — Recherches Amerindiennes
Rech Amerindien Quebec — Recherches Amerindiennes au Quebec
Rech Astr Obs Utrecht — Recherches Astronomiques de l'Observatoire d'Utrecht
Rech Aug — Recherches Augustiniennes
RechBib — Recherches Bibliques. Journees du Colloque Biblique de Louvain
RechBibl — Recherches Bibliques. Journees du Colloque Biblique de Louvain
Rech Chir Eur — Recherches Chirurgicales Europeennes
Rech Clin Lab — Recherche dans la Clinique et le Laboratoire
Rech Clin Ther Epilepsie Hyst Idiot — Recherches Cliniques et Therapeutiques sur l'Epilepsie, l'Hysterie, et l'Idiotie
RechD — Recherches et Debats du Centre Catholique des Intellectuels Francais
Rech de Pap — Recherches de Papyrologie
Rech Diderot & Enc — Recherches sur Diderot et sur l'Encyclopedie
Rech Dix Sept Siecle — Recherches sur le XVIIeme Siecle
Rech Econ Louvain — Recherches Economiques de Louvain
Rech Econ Soc — Recherches Economiques et Sociales
Rechentech Datenverarb — Rechentechnik-Datenverarbeitung
Recherche Aeronaut — Recherche Aeronautique
Recherche Aerospat — La Recherche Aerospatiale

Recherche Agron Madascar — Recherche Agronomique de Madagascar
Recherche Ind Fr — Recherche Industrielle en France
Recherches — Recherches sur la Musique Francaise Classique
Recherche Soc (Paris) — Recherche Sociale (Paris)
Recher Sc Rel — Recherches de Science Religieuse
Rech et Cam — Recherches et Etudes Camerounaises
Rech Eur Toxicol — Recherche Europeenne en Toxicologie
Rech Fertil Stns Agron — Recherches sur la Fertilisation Effectuee par les Stations Agronomiques. Ministere de l'Agriculture [Paris]
Rech Geol Afr — Recherches Geologiques en Afrique
Rech Graphique — Recherche Graphique
Rech Graphique Commun — Recherche Graphique. Communications
Rech Hydraul — Recherches Hydrauliques
Rech Hydrobiol Cont — Recherches d'Hydrobiologie Continentale
Rech Int — Recherches Internationales a la Lumiere du Marxism
Rech Interdisciplinaires — Recherches Interdisciplinaires
Rech Internat Marxisme — Recherches Internationales a la Lumiere du Marxisme
Rech Int Flammes — Recherches Internationales sur les Flammes
Rech Invent — Recherches et Inventions
Rech Math Appl — Recherches en Mathematiques Appliquees
Rechnergestuetzte Anal Labordatensyst Aachener Semin — Rechnergestuetzte Analytik und Labordatensysteme. Aachener Seminar
Rechn Transp — Rechnoi Transport
Rech Oe — Recherches Oecumeniques
Rech Phil — Recherches de Philosophie
Rech Philos Lang — Recherches sur la Philosophie et le Langage
Rech Prod Foret — Recherches sur les Produits de la Foret
RE Chr A — Real-Encyklopaedie der Christlichen Altertuemer
Rech Rentab Agric — Recherches Relatives a la Rentabilite de l'Agriculture
RechS — Recherches Sociographiques
Rech Sci Rel — Recherches de Science Religieuse
Rech Sci Relig — Recherches de Science Religieuse
RechScR — Recherches de Science Religieuse
Rech Sc Relig — Recherches de Science Religieuse
Rech Soc Anonyme Etabl Roure Bertrand Fils Justin Dupont — Recherches. Societe Anonyme des Etablissments Roure Bertrand Fils et Justin Dupont
Rech Sociogr — Recherches Sociographiques
Rech Sociographiques — Recherches Sociographiques
Rech Sociol — Recherches Sociologiques
Rech Soc (Paris) — Recherche Sociale (Paris)
Rech Sol — Recherches sur le Sol
Rech Soviet — Recherches Sovietiques
Rech Spat — Recherche Spatiale
Rech Spatiale — Recherche Spatiale
RechSR — Recherches de Science Religieuse
Rech Tech — Recherche Technique
Recht Elektrizitaetswirtsch — Recht der Elektrizitaetswirtschaft
RechTh — Recherches de Theologie Ancienne et Medievale
Rech Th — Recherches Theologiques
Recht Int Wirtsch — Recht der Internationaler Wirtschaft
Recht Landwirtsch — Recht der Landwirtschaft
Rechtsgeleerd Mag — Rechtsgeleerd Marazin
Rechtsk T Belg — Rechtskundig Tijdschrift voor Belgie
Rechtsk Tijdschr v Belg — Rechtskundig Tijdschrift voor Belgie
Rechtsk Weekbl — Rechtskundig Weekblad
Rechtsmed Forschungsergeb — Rechtsmedizinische Forschungsergebnisse
Rechtsprechg Oberldsger Zivilr — Rechtsprechung der Oberlandesgerichte auf dem Gebiete des Zivilrechts
Recht Steuern Gas-Wasserfach — Recht und Steuern im Gas- und Wasserfach
Rec Hung Agric Exp Stn A — Records. Hungarian Agricultural Experiment Stations. A. Plant Production
Rec Hung Agric Exp Stn B — Records. Hungarian Agricultural Experiment Stations. B. Animal Breeding
Rec Hung Agric Exp Stn C — Records. Hungarian Agricultural Experiment Stations. C. Horticulture
Rec Huntingdonshire — Records of Huntingdonshire
Rec Hunts — Records of Huntingdonshire
Rech Vet — Recherches Veterinaires
Rech Vet (Paris) — Recherches Veterinaires (Paris)
Rec IEEE Int Electromagn Compat Symp — Record. IEEE International Electromagnetic Compatibility Symposium
Rec IEEE PLANS Position Locat Navig Symp — Record. IEEE PLANS. Position Location and Navigation Symposium
RECIFS — Recherches et Etudes Comparatistes Ibero-Francaises de la Sorbonne Nouvelle
Rec Indian Mus — Records. Indian Museum
Rec Indian Mus (Calcutta) — Records. Indian Museum (Calcutta)
R Ec Int — Revue Economique Internationale
Rec Int Congr Instrum Aerosp Simul Facil — Record. International Congress on Instrumentation in Aerospace Simulation Facilities
Rec Intersoc Energy Convers Eng Conf — Records. Intersociety Energy Conversion Engineering Conference
Recipe Period Index — Recipe Periodical Index
Rec Jur CJCE — Recueil de la Jurisprudence de la Cour de Justice des CommunautesEuropeennes
Rec Jur Dr Adm — Recueil de Jurisprudence du Droit Administratif et du Conseil d'Etat
Rec Jur T A Ni — Recueil de Jurisprudence des Tribunaux de l'Arrondissement de Nivelles
Rec L — Recovering Literature
REcL — Revue Ecclesiastique de Liege
Reclam & Reveg Res — Reclamation and Revegetation Research
Reclam Era — Reclamation Era
Reclam Rev — Reclamation Review
Reclam Reveg Res — Reclamation and Revegetation Research

Recl Anc Inventaires — Recueil e'Anciens Inventaires
Recl Brev Invent — Recueil des Brevets d'Invention
Recl Conf Colloq Pharm Ind — Recueil des Conferences du Colloque de Pharmacie Industrielle
Rec Legisl Gen — Recueil de la Legislation Generale en Vigueur en Belgique
Recl J R Neth Chem Soc — Recueil. Journal. Royal Netherlands Chemical Society
Recl Med Vet — Recueil de Medecine Veterinaire
Recl Med Vet Ec Alfort — Recueil de Medecine Veterinaire. Ecole d'Alfort
Recl Mus N [Belgrade] — Recueil du Musee National [Belgrade]
Recl Trav Bot Neerl — Recueil des Travaux Botaniques Neerlandais
Recl Trav Cent Oceanol Bretagne — Recueil des Travaux. Centre Oceanologique de Bretagne
Recl Trav Chim Pays Bas — Recueil des Travaux Chimiques des Pays-Bas
Recl Trav Chim Pays-Bas Belg — Recueil des Travaux Chimiques des Pays-Bas et de la Belgique
Recl Trav Fac Archit U Belgrade — Recueil des Travaux de la Faculte d'Architecture. Universite de Belgrade
Recl Trav Fac Mines Geol Univ Beograd — Recueil des Travaux des Facultes de Mines et de Geologie. Universite de Beograd
Recl Trav Inst Biol (Beogr) — Recueil des Travaux. Institut Biologique (Beograd)
Recl Trav Inst Ecol Biogeogr Acad Serbe Sci — Recueil des Travaux. Institut d'Ecologie et de Biogeographie. Academie Serbe des Sciences
Recl Trav Inst Geol Jovan Zujovic — Recueil Travaux. Institut Geologique Jovan Zujovic
Recl Trav Inst Rech Struct Matiere (Belgrade) — Recueil de Travaux. Institut de Recherches sur la Structure de la Matiere (Belgrade)
Recl Trav Inst Super Med IP Pavlov — Recueil de Travaux de l'Institut Superieur de Medecine I. P. Pavlov
Recl Trav Muz Primenjene Umetnosti — Recueil des Travaux. Muzej za Primenjene Umetnosti
Recl Trav Rech Fac Agron Univ Belgrade — Recueil des Travaux de Recherches. Faculte Agronomique. Universite de Belgrade
Recl Trav Relatifs Philol & Archeol Egyp & Assyr — Recueil des Travaux Relatifs a la Philologie et a l'Archeologie Egyptiennes et Assyriennes
Recl Trav Stn Mar Endoume Fac Sci Mars — Recueil des Travaux. Station Marine d'Endoume. Faculte des Sciences de Marseille
Recl Trav Stn Mar Endoume Marseille Fasc Hors Ser Suppl — Recueil des Travaux. Station Marine d'Endoume-Marseille. Fascicule Hors Serie. Supplement
Recl Trav Stn Mar Endoume-Mars Fasc Hors Ser Suppl — Recueil des Travaux. Station Marine d'Endoume-Marseille. Fascicule Hors Serie.Supplement
Recl Trav Univ Uppsala — Recueil de Travaux Publie par l'Universite d'Uppsala
Rec Malar Surv India — Records of the Malaria Survey of India
Rec Man Handb — Recreation Management Handbook
Rec Math — Recreational Mathematics
Rec Math — Recreations in Mathematics
Rec Med Res Lab Nairobi — Records. Medical Research Laboratories (Nairobi)
Rec Med Vet — Recueil de Medecine Veterinaire
Rec Med Vet Ecole Alfort — Recueil de Medecine Veterinaire. Ecole d'Alfort
Rec Med Vet Exot — Recueil de Medecine Veterinaire Exotique
Rec Mem et Obs Hyg et Med Vet Mil — Recueil des Memoires et Observations sur l'Hygiene et la Medecine Veterinaires Militaires
Rec Mem Med Mil — Recueil des Memoires de Medecine, de Chirurgie, et de Pharmacie Militaires
Rec Mth Moscou — Recueil Mathematique. Publie par la Societe Mathematique de Moscou
Rec N Mus & A G Boroko — Records of the National Museum and Art Gallery. Boroko
Rec Obs Med Hop Mil — Recueil des Observations de Medecine des Hopitaux Militaires
Rec Obs Scripps Inst Oceanogr — Records of Observations. Scripps Institution of Oceanography
Rec Oceanogr Work Japan — Records of Oceanographic Work in Japan
Rec Oceanogr Works Jpn — Records of Oceanographic Works in Japan
Rec Oceanogr Works Jpn Sp Number — Records of Oceanographic Works in Japan. Special Number
Recognit Technol Today — Recognition Technologies Today
Recomb DNA Tech Bull — Recombinant DNA Technical Bulletin
Recomb DNA Tech Bull Suppl — Recombinant DNA Technical Bulletin. Supplement
Recomm Nutr Allowances Domest Anim — Recommended Nutrient Allowances for Domestic Animals
Recomm Rlrd Specif Int Nickel Co — Recommended Railroad Specifications. International Nickel Company
Recon — Reconstructionist
R Econ Agr — Rivista di Economia Agraria
R Econ Banque Nat Paris — Revue Economique. Banque Nationale de Paris
R Econ Centre-Est — Revue de l'Economie du Centre-Est
Reconciliation Quart — Reconciliation Quarterly
R Econ Conditions Italy — Review of the Economic Conditions in Italy
R Econ Condit Italy — Review of the Economic Conditions in Italy
R Econ (Cordoba) — Revista de Economia (Cordoba)
R Econ Dr Immob — Revue d'Economie et de Droit Immobilier
R Econ e Pol Ind — Rivista di Economia e Politica Industriale
R Econ Estadist — Revista de Economia y Estadistica
R Econ et Fin — Revue Economique et Financiere Ivoirienne
R Econ et Soc — Revue Economique et Sociale
R Econ Fr — Revue Economique Francaise
R Econ Franc — Revue Economique Francaise
R Econ Franco-Comtoise — Revue de l'Economie Franc-Comtoise
R Econ Franco-Suisse — Revue Economique Franco-Suisse
R Econ Fr-Suisse — Revue Economique Franco-Suisse
R Econ Gestion — Revue d'Economie et de Gestion
R Econ Industr — Revue d'Economie Industrielle
R Econ Latinoam — Revista de Economia Latinoamericana

R Econ Latinoamer — Revista de Economia Latinoamericana
R Econ Merid — Revue de l'Economie Meridionale
R Econ Nordeste — Revista Economica do Nordeste
R Econ (Paris) — Revue Economique (Paris)
R Econ Polit (Madrid) — Revista de Economia Politica (Madrid)
R Econ Polit (Paris) — Revue d'Economie Politique (Paris)
R Econ Pol (Madrid) — Revista de Economia Politica (Madrid)
R Econ Pol (Paris) — Revue d'Economie Politique (Paris)
R Econ Pol (Sao Paulo) — Revista de Economia Politica (Sao Paulo)
R Econ Region Urb — Revue d'Economie Regionale et Urbaine
R Econ Soc — Revue Economique et Sociale
Recons Surg — Reconstruction Surgery and Traumatology
REConst — Regesta Episcoporum Constantiensium
R Econ Stat — Review of Economics and Statistics
R Econ Statist — Review of Economics and Statistics
R Econ Statistics — Review of Economics and Statistics
Reconstr Surg Traumatol — Reconstruction Surgery and Traumatology
R Econ Stud — Review of Economic Studies
R Econ Sud-Ouest — Revue Economique du Sud-Ouest
Recontr Surg Traumatol — Reconstruction Surgery and Traumatology
R Econ y Estadistica — Revista de Economia y Estadistica
Recopil Dispos Exploit For — Recopilacion de Disposiciones Vigentes sobre Explotaciones Forestales, Assenio, y Mercado de la Madera
Record — Record. Association of the Bar of the City of New York
Record Broward County Med Assoc — Record. Broward County Medical Association
Recorder and Mus — Recorder and Music
Recorder & Mus Mag — Recorder and Music Magazine
Recorder Columbia Med Soc — Recorder. Columbia Medical Society of Richland County
Recorder Mag — Recorder Magazine
Recorder M Magazine — Recorder and Music Magazine
Record of NYCBA — Record. Association of the Bar of the City of New York
Records Buck — Records of Buckinghamshire
Records Queen Museum — Records. Queen Victoria Museum
Records SA Museum — Records. South Australian Museum
RECorses — Revue des Etudes Corses
Recovery Eng News — Recovery Engineering News
Recovery Pulping Chem — Recovery of Pulping Chemicals
RecP — Recherches Philosophiques
RecPap — Recherches de Papyrologie
Rec Papua New Guinea Mus — Records. Papua New Guinea Museum
Rec Past — Records of the Past
RecPh — Recherches Philosophiques
RecPhL — Recherches de Philologie et de Linguistique
Rec PNG Mus — Records of the Papua New Guinea Museum
Rec Proc Am Soc Anim Prod — Record of Proceedings. Annual Meeting. American Society of Animal Production
Rec Queen Vic Mus — Records. Queen Victoria Museum
Rec Queen Vict Mus — Records. Queen Victoria Museum
Rec Queen Victoria Mus — Records. Queen Victoria Museum
Rec Queen Victoria Mus Launceston — Records. Queen Victoria Museum of Launceston
Rec Q Vict Mus — Records. Queen Victoria Museum
RECR — Reclamation Review
Rec R — Record Review
Recreations Agric — Recreations in Agriculture, Natural History, Arts, and Miscellaneous Literature
Rec Res — Record Research
Rec Res Annu Rep East Afr Agric For Res Organ — Record of Research. Annual Report. East African Agriculture and Forestry Research Organisation
Rec Res Fac Agric Univ Tokyo — Records of Researches. Faculty of Agriculture. University of Tokyo
Rec Rev — Records in Review
Recr Sci — Recreative Science
Recryst Grain Growth Multi Phase Part Containing Mater Proc — Recrystallization and Grain Growth of Multi-Phase and Particle Containing Materials. Proceedings. Risoe International Symposium on Metallurgy and Materials Science
RecS — Recorded Sound
Rec S Aust Mus — Records. South Australian Museum
Rec S Aust Mus (Adelaide) — Records. South Australian Museum (Adelaide)
Rec S Austral Mus — Records of the South Australian Museum
Rec Sci Rel — Recherches de Science Religieuse
Rec Scott Church Hist Soc — Records. Scottish Church History Society
Rec Soc J Bodin — Recueil. Societe Jean Bodin
Rec Soc J Bodin — Recueil. Societe Jean Bodin pour l'Histoire Comparative des Institutions
Rec Sound — Recorded Sound
Rec South Aust Mus — Records. South Australian Museum
Rec South Aust Mus (Adelaide) — Records. South Australian Museum (Adelaide)
RecSR — Recherches de Science Religieuse
Rec Symp Electron Ion Laser Beam Technol — Record. Symposium on Electron, Ion, and Laser Beam Technology
RecTh — Recherches de Theologie Ancienne et Medievale
Rec Tomsk State Kuibyshev Univ — Records. Tomsk State Kuibyshev University
RECTR — Restoration and Eighteenth Century Theatre Research
Rec Trav — Recueil des Travaux Relatifs a la Philologie et a l'Archeologie Egyptiennes et Assyriennes
Rec Trav Bot Neerl — Recueil des Travaux Botaniques Neerlandais
Rec Trav Cent Int Trav Liege — Recueil des Travaux. Centre Interfacultaire du Travail. Universitede Liege
Rec Trav Chim — Recueil des Travaux Chimiques des Pays-Bas
Rec Trav Chim Pays-Bas — Recueil des Travaux Chimiques des Pays-Bas
Rec Trav Inst Nat Hyg — Recueil des Travaux. Institut National d'Hygiene

Rec Trav Lab Physiol Veg Fac Sci Bordeaux — Recueil des Travaux. Laboratoire de Physiologie Vegetale. Faculte desSciences de Bordeaux
Rec Trav Sci Med — Recueil de Travaux de Sciences Medicales au Congo Belge
Rec Tr Chim — Recueil des Travaux Chimiques des Pays-Bas
Rec Tr C P Bas — Recueil des Travaux Chimiques des Pays-Bas et de la Belgique
Rec Trib Charl — Recueil de Jurisprudence des Tribunaux de Charleroi
Recu Com Internat Sci Hist — Comite International des Sciences Historiques. Recueil
Recueil — Recueil des Cours. Academie de Droit International
Recueil Actes Seance Publique Acad Imp Sci St Petersbourg — Recueil des Actes de la Seance Publique de l'Academie Imperiale des Sciences deSt. Petersbourg
Recueil Actes Seance Solennelle Acad Imp Sci St Petersbourg — Recueil des Actes de la Seance Solennelle. Academie Imperiale des Sciences de St. Petersbourg
Recueil de Travaux — Recueil de Travaux Relatifs a la Philologie et a l'Archeologie Egyptiennes et Assyriennes
Recueil Inst Bot — Recueil. Institut Botanique. Universite Libre de Bruxelles
Recueil Mem Actes Soc Sci Dep Mont Tonnerre — Recueil des Memoires et Actes. Societe des Sciences et Arts du Departement du Mont-Tonnerre. Seant a Mayence
Recueil Mem Med — Recueil de Memoires de Medecine, de Chirurgie, et de Pharmacie Militaires
Recueil Ophtalmol — Recueil d'Ophtalmologie
Recueil Pieces Seances Acad Roy Nismes — Recueil des Pieces Lues Dans Les Seances Publiques et Particulieres, de l'Academie Royale de Nismes
Recueil Prix Remportes Quest Prop Acad Bruxelles — Recueil des Prix Remportes sur les Questions Proposees Par l'Academie de Bruxelles
Recueil Trav Archeol — Recueil de Travaux Relatifs a l'Archeologie et a la Philologie
Recueil Trav Lab Bot Fac Sci Univ Montpellier Ser Bot — Recueil des Travaux des Laboratoires de Botanique, Geologie, et Zoologie. Faculte des Sciences. Universite de Montpellier. Serie Botanique
Recueil Trav Soc Sci Lille — Recueil des Travaux. Societe des Sciences, d l'Agriculture, et des Arts de Lille
Recur Hidraul — Recursos Hidraulicos
Recur Miner — Recursos Minerales
Recursos Hidraul — Recursos Hidraulicos
Recursos Min — Recursos Minerales
Rec US Dep State — Record. United States Department of State
Recu Soc Jean Bodin Hist Comp Institutions — Recueils.Societe Jean Bodin pour l'Histoire Comparative des Institutions
Rec Vict Archaeol Surv — Records of the Victorian Archaeological Survey
Rec West Aust Mus — Records. Western Australian Museum
Rec West Aust Mus Suppl — Records. Western Australian Museum. Supplement
RECYA — Revue Roumaine d'Embryologie et de Cytologie. Serie d'Embryologie
Recycling Waste Disposal — Recycling and Waste Disposal
Recycl Met Eng Mater Int Symp — Recycling of Metals and Engineered Materials. International Symposium
Recycl Waste Disposal — Recycling and Waste Disposal
Recycl Weltkongr Konf Niederschr — Recycling Weltkongress. Konferenz-Niederschriften
Recycl World Congr Congr Proc — Recycling World Congress. Congress Proceedings
Rec Zool Surv India — Records. Zoological Survey of India
Rec Zool Surv Pak — Records. Zoological Survey of Pakistan
RED — A'Beckett's Reserved Judgements
RED — Radical Education Dossier
RED — R and D (Research and Development) Management
R Ed — Religious Education
RED — Rerum Ecclesiasticarum Documenta
RED — Revue de l'Enregistrement et des Domaines
REDBA — Redbook
REDC — Revista Espanola de Derecho Canonico
Red Cell Proc Int Conf — Red Cell. Proceedings. International Conference on Red Cell Metabolism and Function
Red Cross M — Red Cross Magazine
REDCS — Revista Espanola de Derecho Canonico (Salamanca)
REDEA — Research/Development
Re de J — Revue de Jurisprudence
Re de L — Revue de Jurisprudence et Legislation
RE Der Can — Revista Espanola de Derecho Canonico
REDI — Revue Egyptienne de Droit International
Redia G Zool — Redia Giornale di Zoologia
Redk Elem — Redkie Elementy
Redk Met — Redkie Metally
Redk Met Splavy Tr Vses Soveshch — Redkie Metally i Splavy. Trudy Vsesoyuznogo Soveshchaniya po Splavam Redkikh Metallov
Red Menac — Red Menace
REDO — Red Documental
Redog ForsknStift Skogsarb — Redogorelse. Forskningsstiftelsen Skogsarbeten
Redox Rep — Redox Report
RedR — Red River Valley Historical Review
R Ed Res — Review of Educational Research
ReD Rev Devetsilu — ReD. Revue Devetsilu
R Educ — Review of Education
R Educacion — Revista de Educacion. Ministerio de Educacion Nacional. Desde Marzo-Abril de 1952 Sustituye a la Revista Nacional de Educacion
R Educ (Madrid) — Revista de Educacion (Madrid)
R Educ Res — Review of Educational Research
REDV — Resource Development. Incorporating Northern Development and Oceanic Industries
REE — Resources and Energy
REE — Revista de Economia y Estadistica
REE — Revista de Estudios Extremenos

REE — Rivista di Epigrafia Etrusca
REEDN — Records of Early English Drama. Newsletter
Reed's Mar Equip News Mar Dig — Reed's Marine and Equipment News and Marine Digest
Reeduc Orthophon — Reeducation Orthophonique
Reef Point Gard Bull — Reef Point Gardens Bulletin
REELB — Revista Electricidade
REENA — Refrigerating Engineering
REEP — Revista. Escuela de Estudios Penitenciarios
REES — Revue des Etudes Ethnographiques et Sociologiques
Reeves J — Reeves Journal
Ref — Reformatio
Ref — Reforme
REF — Repertoire Fiscal
REF — Revista de Estudios Franciscanos
REF — Revista de Etnografie si Folclor
REFAA4 — Research and Farming
REFA Nachr — REFA [*Reichsausschuss fuer Arbeitsstudien*] Nachrichten
Ref Book Rev Index — Reference Book Review Index
Ref Chem Ind — Referate aus dem Gebiet der Chemischen Industrie
Ref Ch R — Reformed Church Review
Ref Dokl Mosk Skh Akad — Referaty Dokladov. Moskovskaya Sel'skokhozyaistvennaya Akademiya imeni K.A. Timiryazeva
Ref Dokl Nauchno-Issled Rab Aspir Ukr Skh Akad — Referaty Dokladov o Nauchno-Issledovatel'skoi Rabote Aspirantov. Ukrainskaya Sel'skokhozyaistvennaya Akademiya
Ref Dokl Soobshch Mendeleevsk Sezd Obshch Prikl Khim — Referaty Dokladov i Soobshchenii. Mendeleevskii S'ezd po Obshchei i Prikladnoi Khimii
Ref Dok Mosk Skh Akad — Referaty Dokladov Moskovskaya Sel'skokhozyaistvennaya Akademiya Imeni K. A. Timiryazeva
Ref Dopov Nauk Dosl Rob Aspir Ukr Akad Sil's'kogospod Nauk — Referati Dopovidei pro Naukovo-Doslidnu Robotu Aspirantiv. Ukrains'ka AkademiyaSil's'kogospodars'kikh Nauk
Ref Egy — Reformatus Egyhaz
RefEgyhaz — Reformatus Egyhaz
Referatebl zur Raumentwicklung — Referateblatt zur Raumentwicklung
Referatebl zur Raumordnung — Referateblatt zur Raumordnung
Referatkartei Silikatlit — Referatkartei der Silikatliteratur
Referat Z — Referativnyi Zhurnal
Referat Zh Biol — Referativnyi Zhurnal. Biologiya
Referat Zh Fotokinotekh — Referat Zhurnal Fotokinotekhnika
Referat Zh Zhivot Vet — Referativnyi Zhurnal. Zhivotnovodstvo i Veterinariya
Ref ES — Reformation Essays and Studies
Refin Eng — Refining Engineer
Refiner Nat Gasoline Manuf — Refiner and Natural Gasoline Manufacturer
Ref Inf Avtom Khim Proizvod — Referativnaya Informatsiya. Avtomatizatsiya Khimicheskikh Proizvodstv
Ref Inf Lesokhim Podsochka — Referativnaya Informatsiya. Lesokhimiya i Podsochka
Ref Inf Poligr Promst — Referativnaya Informatsiya. Poligraficheskaya Promyshlennost
Ref Inf Ser Keram Promst — Referativnaya Informatsiya. Seriya. Keramicheskaya Promyshlennost
Refin Nat Gasoline Manuf — Refiner and Natural Gasoline Manufacturer
Ref J — National Association of Referees in Bankruptcy. Journal
Ref J — Reformed Journal
Ref Jugosl Simp Hmeljarstvo — Referati. Jugoslovanski Simpozij za Hmeljarstvo
Ref Komun Zjazd Nauk Nieorg Zwiazki Fosforowe — Referaty i Komunikaty zgloszone na Zjazd Naukowy na temat. Nieorganiczne Zwiazki Fosforowe
REFL — Reference Librarian
Reflect Nurs Leadersh — Reflections On Nursing
Reflets Econ Franc-Comtoise — Reflets de l'Economie Franc-Comtoise
Reflets et Perspectives — Reflets et Perspectives de la Vie Economique
Reflets Perspect Vie Econ — Reflets et Perspectives de la Vie Economique
Ref Libr — Reference Librarian
Ref Lit Music — Reformed Liturgy and Music
Refl Persp Vie Ec — Reflets et Perspectives de la Vie Economique
REFM — Revista de Estudios Franceses (Madrid)
Ref Mag — Referee Magazine
Ref Mater Vopr Gig Tr Prom Toksikol Klin Prof Bolezn — Referativnye Materialy po Voprosam Gigieny Truda. Promyshlennoi Toksikologii i Kliniki Professional'nykh Boleznei
Ref Med — Reforma Medica
REFNA — REFA [*Reichsausschuss fuer Arbeitsstudien*] Nachrichten
Ref Nauchno Issled Rab Inst Biol Akad Nauk B SSR — Referaty Nauchno-Issledovatel'skikh Rabot Instituta Biologii. Akademiya Nauk Belorusskoi SSR
Ref Nauchn Rab Inst Biol Morya Dalnevost Fil Akad Nauk SSSR — Referaty Nauchnykh Rabot Instituta Biologii Morya. Dal'nevostochnyi Filial. Akademiya Nauk SSSR
Ref Nauchn Soobshch Vses Biokhim Sezd — Referaty Nauchnykh Soobshchenii - Vsesoyuznyi Biokhimicheskii S'ezd
Reformatgesch St — Reformationsgeschichtliche Studien
Refor Mon — Reforestation Monthly
Ref Pol — Reformacja w Polsce
Ref Pres W — Reformed and Presbyterian World
Ref Program Nas Byeenkoms S Afr Inst Chem Ing — Referate en Program. Nasionale Byeenkoms van die Suid-Afrikaanse Instituut van Chemiese Ingenieurs
Ref Q — Reformed Quarterly Review
Ref R — Reformed Review
RE Fr — Revue d'Histoire de l'Eglise de France
REFRA — Refractories
Refract Ind Ceram — Refractories and Industrial Ceramics
Refract Inst Tech Bull — Refractories Institute. Technical Bulletin
Refract J — Refractories Journal

Refract Mater — Refractory Materials
Refract Met Proc Symp Annu Meet Miner Met Mater Soc — Refractory Metals. Extraction, Processing, and Applications. Proceedings. Symposium at the Annual Meeting. Minerals, Metals, and Materials Society
Refractories Curr Ind Rep — Refractories. Current Industrial Reports
Refractor J — Refractories Journal
Ref RH — Reformed Review (Holland, MI)
Refrig — Refrigeration
Refrig A — Refrigeration Annual
Refrig Air — Refrigeration and Air Conditioning
Refrig Air Cond & Heat — Refrigeration Journal, Incorporating Air Conditioning and Heating
Refrig Air Cond Gardenvale Que — Refrigeration and Air Conditioning (Gardenvale, Quebec)
Refrig Air Condit — Refrigeration and Air Conditioning
Refrig Air Condit Heat Recovery — Refrigeration, Air Conditioning, and Heat Recovery
Refrig Ann — Refrigeration Annual
Refrig Annual — Refrigeration Annual
Refrig Cold Stor — Refrigeration, Cold Storage, and Air-Conditioning
Refrig Cold Storage — Refrigeration and Cold Storage
Refrig Cold Storage Air Cond — Refrigeration, Cold Storage, and Air-Conditioning
Refrig Eng — Refrigerating Engineering
Refrigeration J — Refrigeration Journal
Refrig Ind — Refrigeration Industry
Refrig J — Refrigeration Journal
Refrig Sci Technol — Refrigeration Science and Technology
Refrig W — Refrigerating World
Ref R Ph — Reformed Review (Philadelphia)
Ref Savetovanja Savez Geol Drus SFR Jugosl — Referati Savetovanja. Savez Geoloskih Drustava SFR Jugoslavije
Ref Sb — Reformacni Sbornik
Ref Sb Azotn Promst — Referativnyi Sbornik. Azotnaya Promyshlennost
Ref Sb Fosfornaya Promst — Referativnyi Sbornik. Fosfornaya Promyshlennost
Ref Sb Khim Tekhnol Izot Mechenykh Soedin — Referativnyi Sbornik. Khimiya i Tekhnologiya Izotopov i Mechenykh Soedinenii
Ref Sb Kislorodn Promst — Referativnyi Sbornik. Kislorodnaya Promyshlennost
Ref Sb Metody Anal Kontrolya Kach Prod Khim Promsti — Referativnyi Sbornik. Metody Analiza i Kontrolya Kachestva Produktsii v Khimicheskoi Promyshlennosti
Ref Sb Proizvod Pererab Plastmass Sint Smol — Referativnyi Sbornik. Proizvodstvo i Pererabotka Plastmass i Sinteticheskikh Smol
Ref Schw — Reformierte Schweiz
Ref Sc Lit Fire — References to Scientific Literature on Fire
Ref Serv R — Reference Services Review
Ref Serv Rev — Reference Services Review
Ref Shelf — Reference Shelf
Ref Source — Reference Sources
Ref Theol R — Reformed Theological Review
Ref Th R — Reformed Theological Review
RefTR — Reformed Theological Review
Ref Tr Ivanov Khim Tekhnol Inst — Referaty Trudov Ivanovskogo Khimiko-Tekhnologicheskogo Instituta
Refu Vet — Refuah Veterinarith
Ref Values Hum Chem Proc Int Colloq Autom Prospect Biol — Reference Values in Human Chemistry. Proceedings. International Colloquium Automatisation and Prospective Biology
Ref W — Reformed World
Ref Z — Referativnyi Zhurnal
Ref Z Fizika — Referativnyi Zhurnal. Fizika
Ref Zh — Referativnyi Zhurnal
Ref Zh Astron — Referativnyi Zhurnal. Astronomiya
Ref Zh Astron Geod — Referativnyi Zhurnal. Astronomiya. Geodeziya
Ref Zh Biol — Referativnyi Zhurnal. Biologiya
Ref Zh Biol Khim — Referativnyi Zhurnal. Biologicheskaya Khimiya
Ref Zh Elek — Referativnyi Zhurnal. Elektrosvyaz
Ref Zh Faramakol Khimioter Sredstva Toksikol — Referativnyi Zhurnal. Farmakologiya. Khimioterapeuticheskie Sredstva. Toksikologiya
Ref Zh Fiz — Referativnyi Zhurnal. Fizika
Ref Zh Fiz-Khim Biol Biotekhnol — Referativnyi Zhurnal. Fiziko-Khimicheskaya Biologiya i Biotekhnologiya
Ref Zh Fotokinotekh — Referativnyi Zhurnal. Fotokinotekhnika
Ref Zh Geod — Referativnyi Zhurnal. Geodeziya
Ref Zh Geod Aerosemka — Referativnyi Zhurnal. Geodeziya i Aeros'emka
Ref Zh Geof — Referativnyi Zhurnal. Geofizika
Ref Zh Geofiz — Referativnyi Zhurnal. Geofizika
Ref Zh Geol — Referativnyi Zhurnal. Geologiya
Ref Zh Geol Geogr — Referativnyi Zhurnal. Geologiya i Geografiya
Ref Zh Inf — Referativnyi Zhurnal. Informatika
Ref Zh Izmer Tekh — Referativnyi Zhurnal. Izmeritel'naya Tekhnika
Ref Zh Khim — Referativnyi Zhurnal. Khimiya
Ref Zh Khim Biol Khim — Referativnyi Zhurnal. Khimiya. Biologicheskaya Khimiya
Ref Zh Khim Kholod Mashinostr — Referativnyi Zhurnal. Khimicheskoe i Kholodil'noe Mashinostroenie
Ref Zh Khim Mashinostr — Referativnyi Zhurnal. Khimicheskoe Mashinostroenie
Ref Zh Korroz — Referativnyi Zhurnal. Korroziya
Ref Zh Korroz Zaschh Korroz — Referativnyi Zhurnal. Korroziya i Zashchita ot Korrozii
Ref Zh Legk Promst — Referativnyi Zhurnal. Legkaya Promyshlennost
Ref Zh Lesoved Lesovod — Referativnyi Zhurnal. Lesovedenie i Lesovodstvo
Ref Zh Mekh — Referativnyi Zhurnal. Mekhanika
Ref Zh Metall — Referativnyi Zhurnal. Metallurgiya
Ref Zh Metrol Izmer Tekh — Referativnyi Zhurnal. Metrologiya i Izmeritel'naya Tekhnika

Ref Zh Nasosostr Kompressorostr — Referativnyi Zhurnal. Nasosostroenie i Kompressorostroenie
Ref Zh Nasosostr Kompressorostr Kholod Mashinostr — Referativnyi Zhurnal. Nasosostroenie i Kompressorostroenie. Kholodil'noe Mashinostroenie
Ref Zh Nauchn Tekh Inf — Referativnyi Zhurnal. Nauchnaya i Teckhnicheskaya Informatsiya
Ref Zh Oborud Tekhnol — Referativnyi Zhurnal. Oborudovanie i Tekhnologiya
Ref Zh Obshch Vop Patol Onkol — Referativnyi Zhurnal. Obshchie Voprosy Patologii. Onkologiya
Ref Zh Okhr Prir Vosproizvod Prir Resur — Referativnyi Zhurnal. Okhrana Prirody i Vosproizvodstvo Prirodnykh Resursov
Ref Zh Pochvoved Agrokhim — Referativnyi Zhurnal. Pochvovedenie i Agrokhimiya
Ref Zh Radiats Biol — Referativnyi Zhurnal. Radiatsionnaya Biologiya
Ref Zh Rastenievod — Referativnyi Zhurnal. Rastenievodstvo
Ref Zh Tekhnol Mashinostr — Referativnyi Zhurnal. Tekhnologiya Mashinostroeniya
Ref Zh Tekhnol Oborud Bum Delatelnogo Poligr Proizvod — Referativnyi Zhurnal. Tekhnologiya i Oborudovanie Bumago-Delatel'nogo iPoligraficheskogo Proizvodstva
Ref Zh Tekhnol Oborud Tsellyul Bum Poligr Proizvod — Referativnyi Zhurnal. Tekhnologiya i OborudovanieTsellyulozno-Bumazhnogo i Poligraficheskogo Proizvodstva
Ref Zh Teploenerg — Referativnyi Zhurnal. Teploenergetika
Ref Zh Toksikol — Referativnyi Zhurnal. Toksikologiya
Ref Zh Vet — Referativnyi Zhurnal. Veterinariya
Ref Zh Yad Reakt — Referativnyi Zhurnal. Yadernye Reaktory
Ref Zh Zhivotnovod Vet — Referativnyi Zhurnal. Zhivotnovodstvo i Veterinariya
Ref Z Math — Referativnyi Zhurnal. Matematika
Ref Z Plutonium Dok — Referate-Zeitschrift Plutonium-Dokumentation
RefZtg — Reform Zeitung
Ref Zurn Biol — Referativnyj Zurnal. Biologija
Ref Zusammenfassung Int Kongr Kinderkrankh — Referate und Zusammenfassung. Internationale Kongress ueberKinderkrankheiten
Reg — Daily Register
Reg — Regains
REG — Regardie's Magazine
REG — Regional Science and Urban Economics
REG — Revista de Etnologia e de Glotologia
REg — Revue d'Egyptologie
REG — Revue des Etudes Grecques
REg — Revue Egyptologique
REgA — Revue de l'Egypte Ancienne
Reg Anaesth — Regional Anaesthesia
Reg Anaesth (Berlin) — Regional-Anaesthesie (Berlin)
Reg Anesth — Regional Anesthesia [Richmond, VA]
Reg Anesth Pain Med — Regional Anesthesia and Pain Medicine
Reg Anesth Pain Med — Regional Anesthesia and Pain Medicine [Secaucus, NJ]
Regan Rep Nurs Law — Regan Report on Nursing Law
Reg Antipollut Conf — Regional Antipollution Conference
Reg Cat Earthquakes — Regional Catalogue of Earthquakes
Reg Conf Ser Appl Math — Regional Conference Series in Applied Mathematics
Reg Dei — Regnum Dei
Reg Dev — Regional Development News
Reg Dev Dial — Regional Development Dialogue
Reg Dol Eot Lor Tudo Reg Int — Regeszeti Dologozatok as Eotvos Lorand Tudomanyegyetem Regeszeti Interetebol
Reg Dolg — Regeszeti Dolgozatok az Eoetvoes Lorand Tudomanyegyetem Regeszeti Lutezeteboel
Reg Dolg Eoetvoes — Regeszeti Dologozatok as Eotvos Lorand Tudomanyegyetem Regeszeti Interetebol
R Eg Dr Int — Revue Egyptienne de Droit International
Regelungstech — Regelungstechnik
Regelungstech Prax — Regelungstechnische Praxis
Regelungstech Prax Prozess-Rechentech — Regelungstechnische Praxis und Prozess-Rechentechnik
Regelungstech Prax und Prozess-Rechentech — Regelungstechnische Praxis und Prozess-Rechentechnik
Regelungstech Prozess-Datenverarb — Regelungstechnik und Prozess-Datenverarbeitung
Regelungstech Prozess-Datenverarbeitung — Regelungstechnik und Prozess-Datenverarbeitung
Regelungstech RT — Regelungstechnik. RT
Regelungstech und Prozess-Datenverarb — Regelungstechnik und Prozess-Datenverarbeitung
Regensb Naturwiss — Regensburger Naturwissenschaften
Regensb Univ-Ztg — Regensburger Universitaets-Zeitung
Regensburger Math Schriften — Regensburger Mathematische Schriften
Reger — Mitteilungen. Max Reger Institut
Reg Erzb Koeln — Regesten der Erzbischoefe von Koeln im Mittelalter
Regeszeti Tan — Regeszeti Tanulmanyok
Reg Fuez — Regeszeti Fuezetek
Reg Furn Soc J — Regional Furniture Society Journal
Reg Fuz — Regeszeti Fuzetek. Magyar Nemzeti Muzeum
Reggae Rept — Reggae Report
Reg Genet Mineral — Regional'naya i Geneticheskaya Mineralogiya
Reg Geol Nek Raionov SSSR — Regional'naya Geologiya Nekotorykh Raionov SSSR
Reg Geol Ser NC Div Resour Plann Eval Miner Resour Sect — Regional Geology Series. North Carolina Division of Resource Planning and Evaluation. Mineral Resources Section
Reg Geol Ser NC Miner Resour Sect — Regional Geology Series. North Carolina Mineral Resources Section
Reg Geol Sredn Azii — Regional'naya Geologiya Srednei Azii
Reg Geol Zapadn Karpat — Regionalna Geologia Zapadnych Karpat

Regia Soc Sci Upsal Nova Acta — Regia Societas Scientiarum Upsaliensis. Nova Acta

Regia Stn Chim Agrar Sper Roma Pubbl — Regia Stazione Chimico-Agraria Sperimentale di Roma. Pubblicazione

Regia Stn Sper Seta Boll Uffic (Italy) — Regia Stazione Sperimentale per la Seta. Bollettino Ufficiale (Italy)

Reg Immunol — Regional Immunology

Regio Ist Super Nav (Napoli) Ann — Regio Istituto Superiore Navale (Napoli). Annali

Regio Ist Univ Nav (Napoli) Ann — Regio Istituto Universitario Navale (Napoli). Annali

Regional Development J — Regional Development Journal

Regional Science and Urban Econ — Regional Science and Urban Economics

Regional Stud — Regional Studies

Region Develop J — Regional Development Journal

Region Sci Urb Econ — Regional Science and Urban Economics

Region Stud — Regional Studies

Region Urb Econ — Regional and Urban Economics Operational Methods

Register of Kentucky Hist Soc — Register. Kentucky Historical Society

Regist KY Hist Soc — Register. Kentucky Historical Society

Reg Jb Aerztl Fortbild — Regensburger Jahrbuch fuer Aerztliche Fortbildung

Reg J Energy Heat Mass Transfer — Regional Journal of Energy, Heat, and Mass Transfer

RegK — Register. Kentucky Historical Society

Reg Meet Amer Filtr Soc — Regional Meeting. American Filtration Society

Regnum Veg — Regnum Vegetabile

REGR — Resources Group Review. Suncor, Inc.

REGr — Revue des Etudes Grecques

Reg Rep New Hebrides Geol Surv — Regional Report. New Hebrides Geological Survey

REGS-A — Regional Studies

Reg Soc Sci Upsal Nova Acta — Regia Societas Scientiarum Upsaliensis. Nova Acta

Reg Stud — Regional Studies

Reg Stud Assoc Newsl — Regional Studies Association. Newsletter

Reg Tan — Regeszeti Tanulmanyok

Reg Tech Conf Soc Plast Eng — Regional Technical Conference. Society of Plastics Engineers

Reg Tech Meet Am Iron Steel Inst — Regional Technical Meetings. American Iron and Steel Institute

Reg Trimestre — Registro Trimestre o Coleccion de Memorias de Historia, Literatura, Ciencias y Artes

Regulatory Action Net — Regulatory Action Network

Regul Bull KY Agr Exp Sta — Regulatory Bulletin. Kentucky Agricultural Experiment Station

Regul Bull Ky Agric Exp Stn — Regulatory Bulletin. Kentucky Agricultural Experiment Station

Regul Bull Univ KY Coll Agric Agric Exp Stn — Regulatory Bulletin. University of Kentucky. College of Agriculture. Agricultural Experiment Station

Regul Chloroplast Biog — Regulation of Chloroplast Biogenesis

Regul Gut Pept Paediatr Gastroenterol Nutr Annu Meet GPGE — Regulatory Gut Peptides in Paediatric Gastroenterology and Nutrition. Annual Meeting. GPGE

Regul Hemoglobin Switching Proc Conf Hemoglobin Switching — Regulation of Hemoglobin Switching. Proceedings. Conference on Hemoglobin Switching

Regul Hepatic Funct Proc Alfred Benzon Symp — Regulation of Hepatic Function. Metabolic and Structural Interactions. Proceedings. Alfred Benzon Symposium

Regul Pept — Regulatory Peptides

Regul Pept Suppl — Regulatory Peptides. Supplement

Regul Toxicol Pharmacol — Regulatory Toxicology and Pharmacology

Regul Toxicol Pharmacol RTP — Regulatory Toxicology and Pharmacology. RTP

Regul Tox P — Regulatory Toxicology and Pharmacology

Regul y Mando Autom — Regulacion y Mando Automatico

Reg Urban Econ — Regional and Urban Economics

Reg Urb Econ — Regional Science and Urban Economics

R Egypt — Revue d'Egyptologie

R Egypt Dr Int — Revue Egyptienne de Droit International

RE H — Recusant History

REH — Revista de Estudios Hispanicos

REH — Revista de Estudos Historicos. Boletim. Instituto de Estudos Historicos da Faculdade de Letras do Porto

REH — Revue des Etudes Historiques

REH — Revue des Etudes Hongroises

REH — Revue. Societe des Etudes Historiques

Rehab — Rehabilitation

Rehab Couns — Rehabilitation Counseling Bulletin

Rehabil Aust — Rehabilitation in Australia

Rehabil Lit — Rehabilitation Literature

Rehabil Nurs — Rehabilitation Nursing

Rehabil Psychol — Rehabilitation Psychology

Rehabil Rec — Rehabilitation Record

Rehabil SA — Rehabilitation in South Africa

Rehabil S Afr — Rehabilitation in South Africa

Rehabil Suppl (Bratisl) — Rehabilitacia Supplementum (Bratislava)

Rehab Lit — Rehabilitation Literature

REHID — Recursos Hidraulicos

Re Hist De — Revue d'Histoire de la Deuxieme Guerre Mondiale

REHJ — Revista de Estudios Historico-Juridicos

REHom — Revue des Etudes Homeriques

REHong — Revue des Etudes Hongroises

REH-PR — Revista de Estudios Hispanicos (Rio Piedras, Puerto Rico)

REHT — Richard Edens' History of Travayle

REI — Real Estate Issues

REI — Recycling

REI — Renewable Energy Index

REI — Revista Economica Interamericana

REI — Revue des Etudes Indo-Europeennes

REI — Revue des Etudes Islamiques

REI — Revue des Etudes Italiennes

REI — Revue Economique Internationale

REI — Rivista di Epigrafia Italica

Reichhold-Albert-Nachr — Reichhold-Albert-Nachrichten

Reichsarbeitsbl — Reichsarbeitsblatt

Reichsber Phys — Reichsberichte fuer Physik

Reichstoff Ind Kosmet — Reichstoff Industrie und Kosmetik

Reichsverwalt Bl — Reichsverwaltungsblatt

REIC (Radiat Eff Inf Cent) Rep — REIC (Radiation Effects Information Center) Report

Rei Cretariae — Rei Cretariae Romanae Fautorum Acta

Rei Cret Rom Faut Acta — Rei Cretariae Romanae Fautorum Acta

Reidel Texts Math Sci — Reidel Texts in the Mathematical Sciences

REIE — Revue des Etudes Indo-Europeennes

Reihe Automatisierungstech — Reihe Automatisierungstechnik

Reihe Informat — Reihe Informatik

Reihe Math — Reihe Mathematik

REIL — Real Estate Investing Letter

REIM — Revue des Etudes Islamiques. Memoires

REIMD — Revista da Imagem

Reims Se Ac — Seances et Travaux de l'Academie de Reims

Reine Angew Geophys — Reine und Angewandte Geophysik

Reine Angew Metallkd Einzeldarst — Reine und Angewandte Metallkunde in Einzeldarstellungen

Rein Foie Mal Nutr — Rein et Foie. Maladies de la Nutrition

Reinf Plast — Reinforced Plastics

Reinf Plast (Boston) — Reinforced Plastics (Boston)

Reinf Plast Compos BPF Bus Conf — Reinforced Plastics Composites. BPF (British Plastics Federation) Business Conference

Reinf Plast Compos World — Reinforced Plastics and Composites World

Reinf Plast (London) — Reinforced Plastics (London)

REIS — Regional Economic Information System

REIsl — Revue des Etudes Islamiques

REIslam — Revue des Etudes Islamiques

Reiss-Davis Clin Bull — Reiss-Davis Clinic. Bulletin

REIt — Revue des Etudes Italiennes

REJ — Revue des Etudes Juives

REJ — Royal Engineers Journal

REJOD — Reeves Journal

REJuiv — Revue des Etudes Juives

REJuivHJud — Revue des Etudes Juives et Historia Judaica

REK — Regesten der Erzbischoefe von Koeln im Mittelalter

Rekom Vopr Pozharnoi Profil — Rekomendatsii po Voprosam Pozharnoi Profilaktiki

REL — Real Estate Law Journal

Rel — Relations

Rel — Religion

Rel — Religionsgeschichtliche Versuche und Vorarbeiten

REL — Review of English Literature

REL — Revista de Estudios Livres

REL — Revue des Etudes Latines

REL — Revue Ecclesiastique de Liege

RELAA — Recht der Landwirtschaft

RelAb — Religious and Theological Abstracts

Relac Int — Relaciones Internacionales

Relaciones Soc Argentina Antropol — Relaciones. Sociedad Argentina de Antropologia

Relais — Relais Statistiques de l'Economie Picarde

Relais Econ Picarde — Relais Statistiques de l'Economie Picarde

Rel & Theol Abstr — Religious and Theological Abstracts

Relat — Relativity

RELat — Revue des Etudes Latines

Relat Annu Inst Geol Publ Hung — Relationes Annuae. Instituti Geologici Publicii Hungarici

Relat Annu Inst Geol Publicii Hung — Relationes Annuae. Instituti Geologici Publicii Hungarici

Relat Annu Inst Geol Regii Hung — Relationes Annuae. Instituti Geologica Regii Hungarici

Relat Aquar Vasco De Gama — Relatorio. Aquario Vasco de Gama

Relata Tech — Relata Technica

Relata Tech Chim Biol Appl — Relata Technica di Chimica e Biologia Applicata

Relat Cient Esc Super Agric Luiz Queiroz Dep Inst Genet — Relatorio Cientifico. Escola Superior de Agricultura Luiz de Queiroz. Departamento e Instituto de Genetica

Relat DNOCS — Relatoria. DNOCS

Relat Ind — Relations Industrielles

Relat Industr — Relations Industrielles

Relat Int — Relations Internationales

Relat Int (Geneve) — Relations Internationales (Geneve)

Relations Inds (Quebec) — Relations Industrielles (Quebec)

Relativ Aspects Nucl Phys — Relativistic Aspects of Nuclear Physics

Relativ Hadrons Cosmic Compact Objects Proc Workshop — Relativistic Hadrons in Cosmic Compact Objects. Proceedings. Workshop

Relax Polym — Relaxation in Polymers

Relay Eng — Relay Engineer

Relaz Accad Accad Zelanti Aci Reale Sci — Relazione Accademica. Accademia Degli Zelanti di Aci-Reale di Scienze, Lettere,ed Arti

Relaz Attivita Stn Sper Pratic Lodi — Relazione sull'Attivita della Stazione Sperimentale di Praticoltura di Lodi

Relaz Attiv Stn Sper Pratic Lodi — Relazione sull'Attivita della Stazione Sperimentale di Praticoltura di Lodi

Relaz Clin Sci — Relazione Clinico Scientifiche

Relazione Comm Dirett Ist Zootec Laziale (Roma) — Relazione. Commissione Direttiva. Istituto Zootecnico Laziale (Roma)
Relaz Soc — Relazioni Sociali
RelB — Religion och Bibel
RelBib — Religion och Bibel
RELC — Quarterly Review. Evangelical Lutheran Church
RELC — RELC [*Regional English Language Centre*] Journal
Rel Cab — Religious Cabinet
RELC J — RELC (Regional English Language Centre) Journal
Rel Comm Lands — Religion in Communist Lands
Rel Cult — Religion y Cultura
Rel Ed — Religious Education
Rel Ed L — Religion in Education (London)
Rel Educ — Religious Education
Rel Enc — Religious Encyclopedia
Relevance Logic Newslett — Relevance Logic Newsletter
Relev Log News — Relevance Logic Newsletter
RELHA — Revista Espanola de Literatura, Historia, y Arte
RELIA — Rehabilitation Literature
Reliab Eng — Reliability Engineering
Reliab Eng Syst Saf — Reliability Engineering and System Safety
Reliability Eng — Reliability Engineering
Reliable P J — Reliable Poultry Journal
Reliab Offshore Oper Proc Int Workshop — Reliability of Offshore Operations. Proceedings. International Workshop
Reliab Risk Anal — Reliability and Risk Analysis
RELiege — Revue Ecclesiastique de Liege
RE Lig — Rivista di Studi Liguri
Relig & Cult — Religion y Cultura
Relig Ed — Religious Education
Relig Educ — Religious Education
Relig Hum — Religious Humanism
Relig Index One Period — Religion Index One. Periodicals
Relig in Life — Religion in Life
Relig Soc — Religion and Society
Relig Sthn Afr — Religion in Southern Africa
Relig Stud — Religious Studies
Relig Theol Abstr — Religious and Theological Abstracts
Relig T J — Religion Teacher's Journal
Rel Ind — Relations Industrielles
Rel Ind One — Religion Index One
RELing — Revista Espanola de Linguistica
Reliquary Il Archaeol — Reliquary and Illustrated Archaeologist
Rel L — Religions (London)
Rel Life — Religion in Life
RELO — Revue. International Organization for Ancient Languages Analysis by Computer
RELO — Revue. Organisation Internationale pour l'Etude des Langues Anciennes parOrdinateur
RELP — Revista de Educacion (La Plata)
RelPerI — Religious Periodicals Index
RELS — Real Estate Listing Service
RelS — Religious Studies
RELSA — Radio Elektronik Schau
Rel Schr — Religioese Schriftenreihe
Rel So Africa — Religion in Southern Africa
Rel Soc — Religion and Society
Rel St — Religious Studies
Rel St R — Religious Studies Review
Rel St Rev — Religious Studies Review
Rel Stud — Religious Studies
RelTAbstr — Religious and Theological Abstracts
Rel Trad — Religious Traditions
RELV — Revue de l'Enseignement des Langues Vivantes
Rel Veru Vorarb — Religionsgeschichtliche Versuche und Vorarbeiten
Rel X Congr Internaz Sci Stor — X Congresso Internazionale di Scienze Storiche. Relazioni
REM — Repertoire d'Epigraphie Meroitique
REM — Research Management
REM — Revista de Educacion (Madrid)
REM — Revue Ecclesiastique de Metz
Rem Actual — Remedes-Actualites
REMARC — Retrospective Machine Readable Cataloging
Remarques Afr — Remarques Africaines
REMC — Revista de Estudios Musicales. Departamento de Musicologia. Universidad Nacional de Cuyo
Rem Corps Ames — Remedes des Corps et des Ames
Remedial Ed — Remedial Education
Remedial Educ — Remedial Education
Rem Educ — Remedial Education
REMOA — Revista. Escola de Minas
Remote Sens Earth Resour Environ — Remote Sensing of Earth Resources and Environment
Remote Sens Environ — Remote Sensing of Environment
Remote Sensing Earth Resour — Remote Sensing of Earth Resources
Remote Sensing Environ — Remote Sensing of Environment
Remote Sensing Yearb — Remote Sensing Yearbook
Rem R — Remington Review
ReMS — Renaissance and Modern Studies
REMUDY — Records. Western Australian Museum
REN — Real Estate Newsletter
Ren — Renaissance
Ren — Renaissances
Ren — Renascence
REN — Revue des Etudes Napoleoniennes

REN — Rural Equipment News
Ren A — Renaissance des Arts
Rena — Renascence
Ren Accad Napoli — Rendiconti. Accademia di Archeologia, Lettere, e Belle Arti di Napoli
RenAF — Renaissance de l'Art Francais et des Industries de Luxe
Ren A Fr & Indust Luxe — Renaissance de l'Art Francais et des Industries de Luxe
Renais News — Renaissance News
Renaissance Q — Renaissance Quarterly
Renaiss Dr — Renaissance Drama
Renaiss Mod Stud — Renaissance and Modern Studies
Renaiss Q — Renaissance Quarterly
Renaiss Quart — Renaissance Quarterly
Renaiss Ref — Renaissance and Reformation
Renaiss Reform — Renaissance and Reformation
Renal Funct Trans Conf — Renal Function. Transactions. Conference
Renal Physiol — Renal Physiology
Renal Physiol Biochem — Renal Physiology and Biochemistry
Ren & Mod Stud — Renaissance and Modern Studies
Ren & R — Renaissance and Reformation
Ren & Ref — Renaissance and Reformation
Ren & Reformation — Renaissance and Reformation
Ren B — Renaissance Bulletin
RenBib — Rencontres Biblique
Renc — Rencontres
RencAL — Rencontres Artistiques et Litteraires
RencAssyrInt — Recontre Assyriologique Internationale. Compte Rendu
RENCB — Revue d'Electroencephalographie et de Neurophysiologie Clinique
Rencontre Biol — Rencontre Biologique
Rencontre Moriond CR — Rencontre de Moriond. Compte Rendu
Rencontre Moriond Proc — Rencontre de Moriond. Proceedings
Rencontres Caraibes Lutte Biol — Rencontres Caraibes in Lutte Biologique
Rencontres Int Chim Ther — Rencontres Internationales de Chimie Therapeutique
Rencontres Phys Vallee Aoste — Rencontres de Physique de la Vallee d'Aoste
RenD — Renaissance Drama
Rend — Rendezvous
Rend — Rendiconti
Rend Accad Lincei — Rendiconti. Accademia Nazionale dei Lincei
Rend Accad Nat Sci XL Mem Sci Fis Natur 5 — Rendiconti della Accademia Nazionale delle Scienze della dei XL. Memorie di Scienze Fisiche e Naturali. Serie V
Rend Accad Naz 40 (Quaranta) — Rendiconti. Accademia Nazionale dei 40 (Quaranta)
Rend Accad Naz Ital Entomol — Rendiconti. Accademia Nazionale Italiana di Entomologia
Rend Accad Naz Lincei — Rendiconti. Accademia Nazionale dei Lincei
Rend Accad Naz Sci XL Mem Mat 5 — Rendiconti. Accademia Nazionale delle Scienze detta dei XL. Serie V. Memorie diMatematica. Parte I
Rend Accad Naz Sci XL Mem Mat Appl 5 — Rendiconti. Accademia Nazionale delle Scienze detta dei XL. Serie V. Memorie diMatematica e Applicazioni. Parte I
Rend Accad Naz XL — Rendiconti. Accademia Nazionale dei XL
Rend Accad Naz XL 4 — Accademia Nazionale dei XL. Rendiconti. Serie 4
Rend Accad Naz XL 5 — Accademia Nazionale dei XL. Rendiconti. Serie 5
Rend Accad Sci Fis Mat (Napoli) — Rendiconto. Accademia delle Scienze Fisiche e Matematiche (Napoli)
Rend Accad Sci Fis Mat Napoli 4 — Societa Nazionale di Scienze, Lettere, ed Arti in Napoli. Rendiconto dell'Accademia delle Scienze Fisiche e Matematiche. Serie 4
Rend Accad Sci Fis Mat Nat Soc R Napoli — Rendiconti. Accademia di Scienze Fisiche, Matematiche, e Naturali.Societa Reale di Napoli
Rend Acc Arch Nap — Rendiconti. Accademia di Archeologia, Lettere, e Belle Arti di Napoli
Rend Acc It — Atti. Reale Accademia d'Italia. Rendiconti. Classe di Scienze Morali
Rend Acc Linc — Rendiconti. Accademia Nazionale dei Lincei
Rend Acc (Napoli) — Rendiconti. Accademia di Archeologia, Lettere, e Belle Arti (Napoli)
Renda Congr Soc Eur Hematol — Renda sobre o Congresso da Sociedade Europeia de Hematologia
Rend Assoc Min Sarda — Rendiconti. Associazione Mineraria Sarda
Rend Atti Accad Sci Med Chir — Rendiconti e Atti. Accademia di Scienze Mediche e Chirurgiche
Rend Bologna — Atti. Accademia delle Scienze. Istituto di Bologna. Rendiconti
Rend Circ Mat Palermo — Rendiconti. Circolo Matematico di Palermo
Rend Circ Mat Palermo 2 — Rendiconti. Circolo Matematico di Palermo. Serie II
Rend Circ Mat Palermo 2 Suppl — Rendiconti del Circolo Matematico di Palermo. Serie II. Supplemento
Rend Gastro — Rendiconti di Gastro-Enterologia
Rendi Accad Archeol Lett & B A — Rendiconti dell'Accademia di Archeologia, Lettere, e Belle Arti
Rendi Accad N Lincei Cl Sci Mor Stor & Filol — Rendiconti dell'Accademia Nazionale dei Lincei. Classe di Scienze Morali, Storiche, e Filologiche
Rendi Adunanze Solenni Accad N Lincei — Rendiconti delle Adunanze Solenni. Accademia Nazionale dei Lincei
Rendic Accad Linc — Rendiconti della Reale Accademia dei Lincei
Rendic Accad Sc Fis e Mat (Napoli) — Rendiconto. Accademia delle Scienze Fisiche e Matematiche (Napoli)
Rendic Acc d'Italia — Rendiconti. Accademia Nazionale dei Lincei
Rendic Acc Lincei — Rendiconti. Accademia Nazionale dei Lincei
Rendic Acc Pont — Atti. Pontificia Accademia Romana di Archeologia
Rendiconti Accad Lincei — Rendiconti. Accademia Nazionale dei Lincei
Rendiconti Pont Acc Arch — Atti. Pontificia Accademia Romana di Archeologia
Rendic R Accad Sc Ist Bologna — Rendiconto. Reale Accademia delle Scienze. Istituto di Bologna

Rendic R Acc Linc — Rendiconti della Reale Accademia dei Lincei

Rendi Pont Accad Romana Archeol — Rendiconti della Pontificia Accademia Romana di Archeologia

Rendi R Accad N Lincei Cl Sci Mor Stor & Filol — Rendiconti della Reale Accademia Nazionale dei Lincei. Classe di Scienze Morali, Storiche, e Filologiche

Rendi Reale Ist Lombardo Sci & Lett — Rendiconti del Reale Istituto Lombardo di Scienze e Lettere

Rend Istit Mat Univ Trieste — Rendiconti. Istituto di Matematica. Universita di Trieste

Rend Ist Lomb — Rendiconti. Istituto Lombardo. Accademia di Scienze e Lettere

Rend Ist Lomb Accad Sci Lett A — Rendiconti. Istituto Lombardo. Accademia di Scienze e Lettere. Sezione A. Scienze Matematiche, Fisiche, e Geologiche

Rend Ist Lomb Accad Sci Lett A Sci Mat Fis Chim Geol — Rendiconti. Istituto Lombardo. Accademia di Scienze e Lettere. Sezione A. Scienze Matematiche, Fisiche, Chimiche, e Geologiche

Rend Ist Lomb Accad Sci Lett B — Rendiconti. Istituto Lombardo. Accademia di Scienze e Lettere. Sezione B. Scienze Biologiche e Mediche

Rend Ist Lomb Accad Sci Lett B Sci Chim Fis Geol Biol Med — Rendiconti. Istituto Lombardo Accademia di Scienze e Lettere. B. Scienze Chimiche e Fisiche, Geologiche, Biologiche, e Mediche

Rend Ist Lomb Accad Sci Lett Parte Gen Atti Uffic — Rendiconti. Istituto Lombardo. Accademia di Scienze e Lettere. Parte Generale eAtti Ufficiali

Rend Ist Lomb Sci — Rendiconti. Istituto Lombardo di Scienze e Lettere

Rend Ist Lomb Sci Lett — Rendiconti. Istituto Lombardo di Scienze e Lettere

Rend Ist Lomb Sci Lett A — Rendiconti. Istituto Lombardo di Scienze e Lettere. Sezione A. Scienze Matematiche, Fisiche, Chimiche, e Geologiche

Rend Ist Lomb Sci Lett A Sci Mat Fis Chim Geol — Rendiconti. Istituto Lombardo di Scienze e Lettere. Sezione A. Scienze Matematiche, Fisiche, Chimiche, e Geologiche

Rend Ist Lomb Sci Lett Cl Sci Mat Nat — Rendiconti. Istituto Lombardo di Scienze e Lettere. Classe di ScienzeMatematiche e Naturali

Rend Ist Lomb Sci Lett Parte Gen Atti Uff — Rendiconti. Istituto Lombardo di Scienze e Lettere. Parte Generale eAtti Ufficiali

Rend Ist Lomb Sci Lett Parte Gen Atti Uffic — Rendiconti. Istituto Lombardo. Accademia di Scienze e Lettere. Parte Generale eAtti Ufficiali

Rend Ist Mat Univ Trieste — Rendiconti. Istituto di Matematica. Universita di Trieste

Rend Ist Sanita Pubblica — Rendiconti. Istituto di Sanita Pubblica

Rend Ist Sci Univ Camerino — Rendiconti. Istituti Scientifici. Universita di Camerino

Rend Ist Super Sanita — Rendiconti. Istituto Superiore di Sanita

Rend Ist Super Sanita Engl Ed — Rendiconti. Istituto Superiore di Sanita. English Edition

Rend Ist Super Sanita Ital Ed — Rendiconti. Istituto Superiore di Sanita. Italian Edition

Rendi Tornate & Lavori Accad Archeol Lett & BA — Rendiconto delle Tornate e dei Lavori dell'Accademia di Archeologia, Lettere, e Belle Arti

Rend Linc — Rendiconti. Reale Accademia dei Lincei

Rend Mat — Rendiconti di Matematica

Rend Mat 6 — Rendiconti di Matematica. Serie VI

Rend Mat 7 — Rendiconti di Matematica. Serie VII

Rend (Nap) — Rendiconti. Reale Accademia di Archeologia, Lettere, ed Arti (Naples)

Rend Pont — Rendiconti. Pontificia Accademia Romana di Archeologia

Rend Pont Acc — Rendiconti. Pontificia Accademia Romana di Archeologia

Rend Pontif Accad — Atti. Pontificia Accademia Romana di Archeologia

Rend R Accad Naz Lincei — Rendiconti. Reale Accademia Nazionale dei Lincei

Ren Drama — Renaissance Drama

Rend R Ist Lomb Sci Lett — Rendiconti. Istituto Lombardo di Scienze e Lettere. Classe di Lettere e ScienzeMorali e Politiche

Rend R Ist Lomb Sci Lett — Rendiconti. Reale Istituto Lombardo di Scienze e Lettere

Rend R Ist Lomb Sci Lett Cl Sci Mat Nat — Rendiconti. Reale Istituto Lombardo di Scienze e Lettere. Classe diScienze Matematiche e Naturali

Rend R Ist Lomb Sci Lett Parte Gen Atti Uffic — Rendiconti. Reale Istituto Lombardo di Scienze e Lettere. ParteGenerale e Atti Ufficiali

Rend Riun Annu Assoc Elettrotec Elettron Ital — Rendiconti. Riunione Annuale. Associazione Elettrotecnica edElettronica Italiana

Rend Riun Annu Assoc Elettrotec Ital — Rendiconti. Riunione Annuale. Associazione Elettrotecnica Italiana

Rend Riunione Assoc Elettrotec Ital — Rendiconti. Riunione Annuale. Associazione Elettrotecnica Italiana

Rend Rom Gastroenterol — Rendiconti Romani di Gastroenterologia

Rend Sc Int Fis Enrico Fermi — Rendiconti. Scuola Internazionale di Fisica "Enrico Fermi"

Rend Sc Int Fis Fermi — Rendiconti. Scuola Internazionale di Fisica "Enrico Fermi"

Rend Scu Int Fis Enrico Fermi — Rendiconti. Scuola Internazionale di Fisica "Enrico Fermi"

Rend Sedute Accad Naz Lincei Cl Sci Fis Mat Nat — Rendiconti delle Sedute della Accademia Nazionale dei Lincei. Classe diScienze Fisiche, Matematiche, e Naturali

Rend Sem Fac Sci Univ Cagliari — Rendiconti. Seminario della Facolta di Scienze. Universita di Cagliari

Rend Semin Fac Sci Univ Cagliari — Rendiconti. Seminario della Facolta di Scienze. Universita di Cagliari

Rend Semin Mat Fis Milano — Rendiconti. Seminario Matematico e Fisico di Milano

Rend Sem Mat Brescia — Rendiconti. Seminario Matematico di Brescia

Rend Sem Mat Fis Milano — Rendiconti. Seminario Matematico e Fisico di Milano

Rend Sem Mat Messina Ser II — Rendiconti del Seminario Matematico di Messina. Serie II

Rend Sem Mat Univ e Politec Torino — Rendiconti. Seminario Matematico. Universita e Politecnico di Torino

Rend Sem Mat Univ Padova — Rendiconti. Seminario Matematico. Universita di Padova

Rend Sem Mat Univ Politec Torino — Rendiconti. Seminario Matematico gia Conferenze di Fisica e di Matematica. Universita e Politecnico di Torino

Rend Soc Chim Ital — Rendiconti. Societa Chimica Italiana

Rend Soc Ital Mineral Petrol — Rendiconti. Societa Italiana di Mineralogia e Petrologia

Rend Soc Ital Sci Accad XL — Rendiconti. Societa Italiana delle Scienze detta Accademia dei XL

Rend Soc Mineral Ital — Rendiconti. Societa Mineralogica Italiana

RenE — Reinare en Espana

RENEA — Revue Neurologique

R Energie — Revue de l'Energie

Renew — Renewal

Renewable Energ — Renewable Energy

Renewable Sustainable Energy Rev — Renewable and Sustainable Energy Reviews

Renew Energy Bull — Renewable Energy Bulletin

REnf — Revue Mensuelle de l'Oeuvre Nationale de l'Enfance

Ren Funct — Renal Function

R Eng J — Royal Engineers Journal

R Engl Lit — Review of English Literature

R Engl Stud — Review of English Studies

REngS — Review of English Studies

R Eng Stud — Review of English Studies

R Eng Stud NS — Review of English Studies. New Series

RENH — Revue des Etudes Neo-Helleniques

RENID3 — Annual Research Reviews. Renin

RENJA — Russian Engineering Journal

RenL — Renaissance Latine

RENLO — Revue. Ecole Nationale des Langues Orientales

Ren M — Renaissance Monographs

Ren Mitt — Renaissance Mitteilungen

Ren Mod St — Renaissance and Modern Studies

Ren Mod Stud — Renaissance and Modern Studies

Ren MS — Renaissance and Modern Studies

RenN — Renaissance News

Ren News — Renaissance News

RENO — Research on Norway

Ren Oe — Recontre Oecumenique

Renovation Esthet — Renovation Esthetique

RenP — Renaissance Papers

RENPA — Radio Engineering and Electronic Physics

Ren Physiol Biochem — Renal Physiology and Biochemistry

RenPL — Renaissance Politique, Litteraire, et Artistique

RenQ — Renaissance Quarterly

RENRA — Rentgenologiya i Radiologiya

Rens — Renaissances. Revue de la Pensee Politique Francaise

Renseign Agric Bull Period (Bulg) — Renseignements Agricoles. Bulletin Periodique du Ministere de'Agriculture et des Domaines (Bulgaria)

Rensselaer Polytech Inst Eng Sci Ser — Rensselaer Polytechnic Institute. Engineering and Science Series

R Ens Sup — Revue de l'Enseignement Superieur

Ren Stud — Renaissance Studies

Rental — Rental Product News

Rent Equip — Rental Equipment Register

Rentgenogr Miner Syr'ya — Rentgenografiya Mineral'nogo Syr'ya

Rentgenol Radiol — Rentgenologiya i Radiologiya

R Entomol Soc London Symp — Royal Entomological Society of London. Symposia

REO — Recueil d'Etudes Orthodoxes

REO — Revue de l'Extreme-Orient

Re O — Rome e l'Oriente

Reo — Te Reo. Linguistic Society of New Zealand

Rep — Republika

ReP — Review of Politics

REP — Revista de Estudios Politicos

REP — Revista de la Economia Politica

REP — Revue d'Economie Politique

REP — Revue d'Ethnographie (Paris)

REp — Revue Epigraphique

Rep AAS (Austral) — Report. Meeting. Association for the Advancement of Science (Australia)

Rep Acad Sci (Lemberg Pol) — Reports. Academy of Science (Lemberg, Poland)

Rep Acad Sci Ukr SSR — Reports. Academy of Sciences of the Ukrainian SSR

Rep Acad Sci Ukr SSR (Engl Transl Dopov Akad Nauk Ukr RSR) — Reports. Academy of Sciences. Ukrainian SSR (English Translation of Dopovidi Akademii Nauk Ukrains'koi RSR)

Rep Acc Natl Coal Board — Report and Accounts. National Coal Board

Rep Accounts Natl Inst Agric Bot — Reports and Accounts. National Institute of Agricultural Botany

Rep Activ Dan Atom Energy Commn — Report. Activities of the Danish Atomic Energy Commission

Rep Act Res Inst Water Resour Budapest — Report. Activities. Research Institute for Water Resources. Budapest

Rep Advis CSIR Alberta — Report. Advisory Council of Scientific and Industrial Research ofAlberta

Rep Aeromed Lab — Reports. Aeromedical Laboratory

Rep Aeronaut Res Inst — Report. Aeronautical Research Institute

Rep Aeronaut Res Inst Univ Tokyo — Report. Aeronautical Research Institute. University of Tokyo

Rep AFL Univ Cincinnati Dep Aerosp Eng — Report AFL. University of Cincinnati. Department of Aerospace Engineering

Rep Agric Coll Swed Ser A — Reports. Agricultural College of Sweden. Series A

Rep Agric Coll Swed Ser B — Reports. Agricultural College of Sweden. Series B

Rep Agric Dept Hong Kong — Report. Agricultural Department (Hong Kong)

Rep Agric Hort Res Stn Univ Bristol — Report. Agricultural and Horticultural Research Station. University of Bristol

Rep Agric Res Coun Radiobiol Lab — Report. Agricultural Research Council. Radiobiological Laboratory

Rep Agron Branch Dep Agric South Aust — Report. Agronomy Branch. Department of Agriculture and Fisheries. South Australia

Rep Aichi Inst Public Health — Report. Aichi Institute of Public Health

Rep Aichi Prefect Inst Public Health — Report. Aichi Prefectural Institute of Public Health

Rep Akita Prefect Inst Public Health — Report. Akita Prefecture. Institute of Public Health

Rep Alaska Div Mines Geol — Report. Alaska Division of Mines and Geology

Rep Alaska Div Mines Miner — Report. Alaska Division of Mines and Minerals

Rep Alberta Res Counc — Report. Alberta Research Council

Rep Alfalfa Improv Conf — Report. Alfalfa Improvement Conference

Rep Alfred Sloan Found — Report. Alfred P. Sloan Foundation

RepAm — Repertorio Americano

Rep Am Mus Nat Hist — Report. American Museum of Natural History

Rep Am Univ Field Staff — Reports. American Universities Field Staff

Rep Anal Artic Rev Que — RADAR. Repertoire Analytique d'Articles de Revues du Quebec

Rep Anal Chem Unit Inst Geol Sci — Report. Analytical Chemistry Unit. Institute of Geological Sciences

Rep Anim Breed Res Organ — Report. Animal Breeding Research Organisation

Rep Anim Hlth Serv G Br — Report on Animal Health Services in Great Britain

Rep Anim Res Div (NZ) — Report. Animal Research Division. Department of Agriculture (New Zealand)

Rep Annu Conf Hawaii Sugar Technol — Reports. Annual Conference. Hawaiian Sugar Technologists

Rep Annu Conf Ontario Dept Agr Ext Br — Report. Annual Conference. Ontario Department of Agriculture. Extension Branch

Rep Annu Date Grow Inst — Report. Annual Date Growers Institute

Rep Annu Gen Meet Scott Soc Res Plant Breed — Report. Annual General Meeting. Scottish Society for Research in Plant Breeding

Rep Annu Meet Wash State Hortic Assoc — Report. Annual Meeting. Washington State Horticultural Association

Rep Appl Geophys Unit Inst Geol Sci — Report. Applied Geophysics Unit. Institute of Geological Sciences

Rep Archit Sci Unit Univ Queensl — Report. Architectural Science Unit. University of Queensland

Rep Ariz Agr Exp Sta — Report. Arizona Agricultural Experiment Station

Rep Ariz Agric Exp Stn — Report. Arizona Agricultural Experiment Station

Rep Ark Agric Exp Stn — Report. Arkansas Agricultural Experiment Station

Rep Army Res Test Lab — Report. Army Research and Testing Laboratory

Rep Asahi Glass Found — Reports. Asahi Glass Foundation

Rep Asahi Glass Found Ind Technol — Reports. Asahi Glass Foundation for Industrial Technology

Rep Assoc Amer Geol — Reports. Association of American Geologists and Naturalists

Rep Ass Occup Ther — Report. Association of Occupational Therapists

Rep Assoc Hawaii Sugar Technol — Reports. Association of Hawaiian Sugar Technologists

Rep Assoc Trimeresurus Res Kagoshima Univ — Reports. Association of Trimeresurus Research. Kagoshima University

Rep Aust Acad Sci — Reports. Australian Academy of Science

Rep Aust At Energy Comm — Report. Australian Atomic Energy Commission

Rep Aust CSIRO Div Text Ind — Australia. Commonwealth Scientific and Industrial Research Organisation. Division of Textile Industry. Report

Rep Aust CSIRO Div Text Ind — Report. Australia Commonwealth Scientific and Industrial ResearchOrganisation. Division of Textile Industry

Rep Aust Def Stand Lab — Report. Australia Defence Standards Laboratories

Rep Aust Gov Anal Lab — Report. Australian Government Analytical Laboratories

Rep Aust Mater Res Lab — Report. Australia. Materials Research Laboratory

Rep Aust NZ Assoc Adv Sci — Report. Australian and New Zealand Association for the Advancement ofScience

Rep Aust Road Res Board — Report. Australian Road Research Board

Rep Basic Sci Chungnam Nat Univ — Reports of Basic Sciences. Chungnam National University

Rep BC-X Can For Serv Pac For Res Cent — Report BC-X. Canadian Forestry Service. Pacific Forest Research Centre

Rep Bd Health Calif — Reports. State Board of Health of California

Rep Bd Health Mass — Annual Reports. State Board of Health of Massachusetts to the Legislature

Rep Bd Health Ohio — Reports. State Board of Health of Ohio

Rep Bibliogr Inst Chret — Repertoire Bibliographique des Institutions Chretiennes

Rep Bibliogr Philos — Repertoire Bibliographique de la Philosophie

Rep Bibl Phil — Repertoire Bibliographique de la Philosophie

RepBibPhil — Repertoire Bibliographique de la Philosophie

Rep Biochem Res Found Franklin Inst — Reports. Biochemical Research Foundation. Franklin Institute

Rep Biomed — Repertoire Biomed

Rep BISRA — Report. BISRA

Rep Bot Dept Hong Kong — Report. Botanical and Forestry Department Hong Kong

Rep Bot Inst Univ Aarhus — Reports. Botanical Institute. University of Aarhus

Rep Bot Soc Brit Isles — Report. Botanical Society. British Isles

Rep Bot Surv Ind — Report. Botanical Survey of India

Rep Bot Surv India — Report. Botanical Survey of India

Rep Br Beekprs Ass — Report. British Beekeepers Association

Rep Brit Ass Adv Sc — Report. British Association for the Advancement of Science

Rep Brit Assoc Advancem Sci — Reports. British Association for the Advancement of Science

Rep Brit Assoc Adv Sci — Report. British Association for the Advancement of Science

Rep Brit Assoc Adv Sci S Africa — Report of the British Association for the Advancement of Science. South Africa

Rep Brit Bryol Soc — Report. British Bryological Society

Rep Brit Canc Camp — Report. British Empire Cancer Campaign

Rep Brit El All Ind Res Ass — Report. British Electrical and Allied Industries Research Association

Rep Brit Mus Natur Hist — Report. British Museum. Natural History

Rep Br Palaeobot & Palynol — Report on British Palaeobotany and Palynology

Rep Bull Agr Exp Sta S Manchuria Ry Co — Research Bulletin. Agricultural Experiment Station. South Manchuria Railway Company

Rep Bur Miner Resour Geol Geophys — Report. [*Australia*] Bureau of Mineral Resources. Geology and Geophysics

Rep Bur Miner Resour Geol Geophys (Aust) — Report. Bureau of Mineral Resources, Geology, and Geophysics (Australia)

Rep Bur Mines Miner Resour Geol Geophys Microform — Report. Bureau of Mines and Mineral Resources. Geology and Geophysics Microform

Rep BWRA — Report BWRA

Rep Cacao Res Imp Coll Trop Agric (St Augustine Trinidad) — Report on Cacao Research. Imperial College of Tropical Agriculture (St.Augustine, Trinidad)

Rep Cacao Res Reg Cent Br Caribb — Report on Cacao Research. Regional Research Centre of the British Caribbean

Rep Calif Water Resour Cent — Report. California Water Resources Center

Rep Calif Water Resour Cent Univ Calif — Report. California Water Resources Center. University of California

Rep Can — Reporter Canadien

Rep Canad Seed Growers Assoc — Report. Canadian Seed Growers' Association

Rep Cant Agric Coll — Report. Canterbury Agricultural College

Rep Cape Cod Cranberry Growers Assoc — Report. Cape Cod Cranberry Growers' Association

Rep C Appl — Repertoire de Chimie Applique

Rep Cast Res Lab — Report. Castings Research Laboratory

Rep Cast Res Lab Waseda Univ — Report. Castings Research Laboratory. Waseda University

Rep CC-X Chem Control Res Inst — Report CC-X. Chemical Control Research Institute

Rep Cent Adv Instrum Anal Kyushu Univ — Report. Center of Advanced Instrumental Analysis. Kyushu University

Rep Cent Customs Lab (Jpn) — Reports. Central Customs Laboratory (Japan)

Rep Cent Insp Inst Weights Meas Tokyo — Report. Central Inspection Institute of Weights and Measures. Tokyo

Rep Cent Inst Met (Leningrad) — Reports. Central Institute of Metals (Leningrad)

Rep CENTO Sci Programme — Report. CENTO [*Central Treaty Organization*] Scientific Programme

Rep Cent Res Inst Chem Hung Acad Sci — Reports. Central Research Institute for Chemistry. Hungarian Academy ofSciences

Rep Cent Res Inst Electr Power Ind Agric Lab — Report. Central Research Institute. Electric Power Industry Agricultural Laboratory

Rep Cent Res Inst Electr Power Ind Tech Lab — Report. Central Research Institute. Electric Power Industry Technical Laboratory

Rep Cent Res Inst Phys (Budapest) — Reports. Central Research Institute for Physics (Budapest)

Rep Cent Res Lab Nippon Suisan Co — Reports. Central Research Laboratory. Nippon Suisan Company

Rep Cesk Akad Ved Ustav Jad Fyz — Report. Ceskoslovenska Akademia Ved. Ustav Jaderne Fyziky

Rep CE Technion-Isr Inst Technol Dep Chem Eng — Report CE. Technion-Israel Institute of Technology. Department of Chemical Engineering

Rep CG D US Coast Guard Off Res Dev — Report CG-D. United States Coast Guard. Office of Research and Development

Rep Chem Branch Mines Dep (West Aust) — Report. Chemical Branch. Mines Department (Western Australia)

Rep Chem Eng Dep Monash Univ — Report. Chemical Engineering Department. Monash University

Rep Chem Fiber Res Inst Kyoto Univ — Report. Chemical Fiber Research Institute. Kyoto University

Rep Chem Lab Am Med Assoc — Reports. Chemical Laboratory. American Medical Association

Rep Chem Lab (West Aust) — Report. Chemical Laboratory (Western Australia)

Rep Chiba Inst Technol — Report. Chiba Institute of Technology

Rep Chiba Inst Technol Sci Ser — Report. Chiba Institute of Technology. Scientific Series

Rep Chiba Prefect Ind Res Inst — Reports. Chiba Prefectural Industrial Research Institute

Rep Chief US Forest Serv — Report of the Chief. United States Forest Service

Rep Chim Ital — Repertorio Chmico Italiano

Rep Class Research — Reporting Classroom Research

Rep Clemson Univ Water Resour Res Inst — Report. Clemson University. Water Resources Research Institute

Rep CLM R UKAEA Culham Lab — Report CLM-R. United Kingdom Atomic Energy Authority.Culham Laboratory

Rep CLM R UKAEA Res Group Culham Lab — Report CLM-R - UKAEA [*United Kingdom Atomic Energy Authority*] Research Group. Culham Laboratory

Rep CLM R UK At Energy Auth Res Group Culham Lab — Report CLM-R. United Kingdom Atomic Energy Authority. Research Group.Culham Laboratory

Rep Cocoa Res Inst (Tafo Ghana) — Report. Cocoa Research Institute (Tafo, Ghana)

Rep Coll Eng Hosei Univ — Report. College of Engineering. Hosei University

Rep Comm Accredit Rehabil Facil — Report. Commission on Accreditation of Rehabilitation Facilities

Rep Commiss Agric — Report. Commissioner of Agriculture

Rep Commonw Conf Plant Pathol — Report. Commonwealth Conference on Plant Pathology

Rep Commonwealth Entomol Conf — Report. Commonwealth Entomological Conference

Rep Commonwealth Mycol Conf — Report. Commonwealth Mycological Conference

Rep Commonw Mycol Conf — Report. Commonwealth Mycological Conference

Rep Comput Centre Univ Tokyo — Report. Computer Centre. University of Tokyo

Rep Comput Cent Univ Tokyo — Report. Computer Centre. University of Tokyo

Rep CONCAWE — Report. CONCAWE

Rep Concr Silic Lab Tech Res Cent Finl — Report. Concrete and Silicate Laboratory. Technical Research Centre of Finland

Rep Conf Role Wheat World Food Supply — Report. Conference on the Role of Wheat in the World's Food Supply

Rep Congr Eur Ass Res Plant Breed — Report. Congress of the European Association for Research on Plant Breeding

Rep Congr Eur Orthod Soc — Report. Congress. European Orthodontic Society

Rep Constr Eng Res Inst Found (Kobe) — Reports. Construction Engineering Research Institute Foundation (Kobe)

Rep Coop Res Chugoku Reg — Report of the Cooperative Research in Chugoku Region

Rep Coop Res Kinki Chugoku Reg — Report. Cooperative Research in Kinki-Chugoku Region

Rep Coord Res Counc Inc — Report. Coordinating Research Council, Incorporated

Rep Counc Miner Technol (Randburg S Afr) — Report. Council for Mineral Technology (Randburg, South Africa)

Rep Crop Res Lesotho — Report on Crop Research in Lesotho

Rep CSIRO Div Fish Oceanogr — Australia. Commonwealth Scientific and Industrial Research Organisation. Division of Fisheries and Oceanography. Report

Rep CSIRO Div Fish Oceanogr (Aust) — Report. Commonwealth Scientific and Industrial Research Organisation. Division of Fisheries and Oceanography (Australia)

Rep CSIRO Div Miner Eng (Aust) — Report. Commonwealth Scientific and Industrial Research Organisation. Division of Mineral Engineering (Australia)

Rep CSIRO Div Text Ind Aust — Australia. Commonwealth Scientific and Industrial Research Organisation. Division of Textile Industry. Report

Rep CSIRO Div Text Ind (Aust) — Report. Commonwealth Scientific and Industrial Research Organization. Division of Textile Industry (Australia)

Rep CSIRO Mar Lab — Report. CSIRO [*Commonwealth Scientific and Industrial Research Organisation*] Marine Laboratories

Rep CSIRO Sol Energy Stud — Report. Commonwealth Scientific and Industrial Research Organisation. Solar Energy Studies

Rep Culham Lab UK At Energy Auth — Report. Culham Laboratory. United Kingdom Atomic Energy Authority

Rep Curators Bot Exch Club Brit Isles — Report. Curators. Botanical Exchange Club. British Isles

Rep Czech Foundry Res — Reports of Czechoslovak Foundry Research

Rep Danish Biol Sta Minist Agric — Report. Danish Biological Station to the Ministry of Agriculture and Fisheries

Rep Def Stand Lab Aust — Australia. Defence Standards Laboratories. Report

Rep Deir-Alla Res Sta — Report. Deir-Alla Research Station

Rep Del Nurses Assoc — Reporter. Delaware Nurses Association

Rep Dep Agric Econ Univ Nebr Agric Exp Stn — Report. Department of Agricultural Economics. University of Nebraska. Agricultural Experiment Station

Rep Dep Agric NSW — Report. Department of Agriculture of New South Wales

Rep Dep Chem Eng Monash Univ — Report. Department of Chemical Engineering. Monash University

Rep Dep Comm Ltg Fact — Report. Departmental Committee on Lighting in Factories

Rep Dep Comm Noise Opn Mech Propelled Veh — Report. Departmental Committee on Noise in the Operation of Mechanically Propelled Vehicles

Rep Dep Fish Fauna West Aust — Report. Department of Fisheries and Fauna. Western Australia

Rep Dep Fish Wildl West Aust — Report. Department of Fisheries and Wildlife. Western Australia

Rep Dep Hist Med Yale Univ — Report. Department of the History of Medicine. Yale University

Rep Dep Hlth Can — Report. Department of Health. Canada

Rep Dep Hlth Eire — Report. Department of Health. Eire

Rep Dep Hlth Newfoundld — Report. Department of Health. Newfoundland

Rep Dep Hlth Ont — Report. Department of Health. Ontario

Rep Dep Hlth Palest — Report. Department of Health. Palestine

Rep Dep Hlth Prov Queb — Report. Department of Health. Province of Quebec

Rep Dep Hlth Publ Welf Manitoba — Report of the Department of Health and Public Welfare. Manitoba

Rep Dep Hlth Scotl — Report. Department of Health for Scotland and the Scottish Health Services Council

Rep Dep Hlth Servs Tasm — Report. Department of Health Services. Tasmania

Rep Dep Hlth Transjordan — Report of the Department of Health. Transjordan

Rep Dep Hlth Un S Afr — Report of the Department of Health. Union of South Africa

Rep Dep Hlth West Samoa — Report. Department of Health. Western Samoa

Rep Dep Hop Res Wye Coll — Report. Department of Hop Research. Wye College

Rep Dep Hort Mysore — Report. Department of Horticulture. Mysore

Rep Dep Hydrol Surv Uganda — Report. Department of Hydrological Survey. Uganda

Rep Dep Inds Bombay — Report. Department of Industries. Bombay

Rep Dep Inds Lab Alberta — Report. Department of Industries and Labour. Alberta

Rep Dep Ld Rec Agric Assam — Report of the Department of Land Records and Agriculture. Assam

Rep Dep Ld Rec Agric Beng — Report of the Department of Land Records and Agriculture. Bengal

Rep Dep Ld Rec Agric Bombay — Report of the Department of Land Records and Agriculture. Bombay

Rep Dep Lds Forests Alberta — Report. Department of Lands and Forests. Alberta

Rep Dep Lds Forests Mines Ont — Report of the Department of Lands, Forests, and Mines. Ontario

Rep Dep Lds Forests Nova Scotia — Report of the Department of Lands and Forests. Nova Scotia

Rep Dep Lds Forests Prov Queb — Report of the Department of Lands and Forests. Province of Quebec

Rep Dep Lds Forests Sierra Leone — Report. Department of Lands and Forests. Sierra Leone

Rep Dep Lds Mines New Brunsw — Report. Department of Lands and Mines. New Brunswick

Rep Dep Ids Mines Prov Alberta — Report of the Department of Lands and Mines of the Province of Alberta

Rep Dep Lds Mines Survs Kenya — Report. Department of Lands, Mines, and Surveys. Kenya

Rep Dep Lds NSW — Report. Department of Lands. New South Wales

Rep Dep Lds S Aust — Report. Department of Lands. South Australia

Rep Dep Lds Surv NZ — Report of the Department of Lands and Survey. New Zealand

Rep Dep Lds Surv S Aust — Report. Department of Lands and Survey. South Australia

Rep Dep Lds Survs Palest — Report. Department of Lands and Surveys. Palestine

Rep Dep Lds Survs St Lucia — Report. Department of Lands and Surveys. St. Lucia

Rep Dep Lds Survs Tanganyika — Report. Department of Lands and Surveys. Tanganyika

Rep Dep Lds Survs Tasm — Report. Department of Lands and Surveys. Tasmania

Rep Dep Lds Tonga — Report. Department of Lands. Tonga

Rep Dep Lds Un S Afr — Report. Department of Lands. Union of South Africa

Rep Dep Ld Surv Mines Tanganyika — Report. Department of Land, Survey, and Mines. Tanganyika Territory

Rep Dep Leath Ind Univ Leeds — Report. Department of Leather Industries. University of Leeds

Rep Dep Livestk Agric Servs Bechuanald — Report. Department of Livestock and Agricultural Services. Bechuanaland

Rep Dep Mar Biol Carnegie Instn — Report. Department of Marine Biology. Carnegie Institution

Rep Dep Mar Fish Can — Report of the Department of Marine and Fisheries. Canada

Rep Dep Med Servs Nth Reg Nigeria — Report on the Department of Medical Services of the Northern Region of Nigeria

Rep Dep Med Servs West Reg Nigeria — Report of the Department of Medical Services of the Western Region of Nigeria

Rep Dep Merid Astr Dudley Obs — Report of the Department of Meridian Astronomy. Dudley Obsesrvatory

Rep Dep Met Servs Fed Rhod Nyasald — Report. Department of Meteorological Services. Federation of Rhodesia and Nyasaland

Rep Dep Met Univ Chicago — Report. Department of Meteorology. University of Chicago

Rep Dep Mines Can — Report of the Department of Mines. Canada

Rep Dep Mines Cyprus — Report. Department of Mines. Cyprus

Rep Dep Mines Energy Gov Newfoundland Labrador — Report. Department of Mines and Energy. Government of Newfoundland and Labrador

Rep Dep Mines Fiji — Report. Department of Mines. Fiji

Rep Dep Mines FMS — Report. Department of Mines. Federated Malay States

Rep Dep Mines Goldflds NZ — Report of the Department of Mines of the Goldfields of New Zealand

Rep Dep Mines Inds Un S Afr — Report. Department of Mines and Industries. Union of South Africa

Rep Dep Mines Jamaica — Report. Department of Mines. Jamaica

Rep Dep Mines Miner Prov Alberta — Report of the Department of Mines and Minerals. Province of Alberta

Rep Dep Mines Nat Resour Manitoba — Report of the Department of Mines and Natural Resources. Manitoba

Rep Dep Mines Nigeria — Report. Department of Mines. Nigeria

Rep Dep Mines (NSc) — Report. Department of Mines (Nova Scotia)

Rep Dep Mines NSW — Report of the Department of Mines. New South Wales

Rep Dep Mines Prov Nova Scotia — Report of the Department of Mines of the Province of Nova Scotia

Rep Dep Mines Publ Wks Sth Rhod — Report. Department of Mines and Public Works. Southern Rhodesia

Rep Dep Mines Qd — Report of the Department of Mines. Queensland

Rep Dep Mines Resour Can — Report of the Department of Mines and Resources. Canada

Rep Dep Mines Resour Newfoundld — Report. Department of Mines and Resources. Newfoundland

Rep Dep Mines West Aust — Report. Department of Mines. Western Australia

Rep Dep Nat Conserv Un S Afr — Report. Department of Nature Conservation. Union of South Africa

Rep Dep Native Ld Settl Swazild — Report. Department of Native Land Settlement. Swaziland

Rep Dep Natn Hlth Welf Can — Report. Department of National Health and Welfare. Canada

Rep Dep Nat Resour Sask — Report of the Department of Natural Resources. Saskatchewan

Rep Dep Nth Affairs Natn Resour Can — Report. Department of Northern Affairs and National Resources. Canada

Rep Dep Nucl Tech Univ Oulu (Finl) — Reports. Department of Nuclear Technics. University of Oulu (Finland)

Rep Dep Path Bact Univ Leeds — Report. Department of Pathology and Bacteriology. University of Leeds

Rep Dep Path Dep Clin Psychiat Cent Indiana Hosp Insane — Report. Department of Pathology and Department of Clinical Psychiatry. Central Indiana Hospital for the Insane

Rep Dep Phys Univ Oulu — Report. Department of Physics. University of Oulu

Rep Dep Pl Path Seale Hayne Agric Coll — Report. Department of Plant Pathology. Seale-Hayne Agricultural College. Newton Abbott. Devon

Rep Dep Pl Path Sect Biochem Rothamsted — Report. Department of Plant Pathology and Section of Biochemistry. Rothamsted Experimental Station

Rep Dep Publ Hlth Alberta — Report. Department of Public Health. Alberta

Rep Dep Publ Hlth Egypt — Report of the Department of Public Health. Egypt

Rep Dep Publ Hlth Egypt Endem Dis Sect — Report. Department of Public Health. Egypt. Endemic Diseases Section

Rep Dep Publ Hlth Nova Scotia — Report. Department of Public Health. Nova Scotia

Rep Dep Publ Hlth NZ — Report. Department of Public Health. New Zealand

Rep Dep Publ Hlth Prince Edward Isl — Report. Department of Public Health. Prince Edward Island

Rep Dep Publ Hlth Sask — Report. Department of Public Health. Saskatchewan

Rep Dep Publ Hlth S Aust — Report. Department of Public Health and Central Board of Health. South Australia

Rep Dep Publ Hlth Tasm — Report of the Department of Public Health. Tasmania

Rep Dep Publ Hlth Un S Afr — Report. Department of Public Health. Union of South Africa

Rep Dep Publ Hlth Vict — Report. Department of Public Health. Victoria

Rep Dep Publ Wks NSW — Report. Department of Public Works. New South Wales

Rep Dep Resour Dev Can — Report of the Department of Resources and Development. Canada

Rep Dep Rur Wat Dev Ghana — Report. Department of Rural Water Development. Ghana

Rep Dep Sci Agric Bahamas — Report. Department of Science and Agriculture. Bahamas

Rep Dep Sci Agric Barbados — Report of the Department of Science and Agriculture. Barbados

Rep Dep Sci Agric Jamaica — Report of the Department of Science and Agriculture. Jamaica

Rep Dep Scient Ind Res Lond — Report of the Department of Scientific and Industrial Research (London)

Rep Dep Scient Ind Res NZ — Report. Department of Scientific and Industrial Research. New Zealand

Rep Dep Sci Siam Thaild — Report. Department of Science. Ministry of Economic Affairs and Industry. Siam (Thailand)

Rep Dep Soil Chem Bact New Jers Agric Coll — Report. Department of Soil Chemistry and Bacteriology. New Jersey Agricultural College Experiment Station

Rep Dep Soil Ld Use Surv Gold Cst — Report. Department of Soil and Land-Use Survey. Gold Coast

Rep Dep St Forests Vict — Report of the Department of State Forests. Victoria

Rep Dep Survs Ld Nth Rhod — Report. Department of Surveys and Land. Northern Rhodesia

Rep Dep Survs Nyasald — Report. Department of Surveys. Nyasaland

Rep Dept Agric (Brit East Africa) — Report. Department of Agriculture (British East Africa)

Rep Dept Ant Cyprus — Report of the Department of Antiquities. Cyprus

Rep Dept Antiquities Cyprus — Report. Department of Antiquities of Cyprus

Rep Dep Technol Cy Guilds Lond Inst — Report. Department of Technology. City and Guilds of London Institute

Rep Dep Terr Magn Carnegie Instn — Report. Department of Terrestrial Magnetism of the Carnegie Institution

Rep Dep Text Ind Bradford Tech Coll — Report. Department of Textile Industries. Bradford Technical College

Rep Dep Thorac Surg Dunedin Hosp — Report. Department of Thoracic Surgery. Dunedin Hospital and University of Otago

Rep Dep Tsetse Control Gold Coast — Report. Department of Tsetse Control. Gold Coast

Rep Dep Tsetse Res Tanganyika — Report. Department of Tsetse Research. Tanganyika

Rep Dep Vet Res Fed Nigeria — Report. Department of Veterinary Research. Federation of Nigeria

Rep Dep Vet Sci Anim Husb Tanganyika — Report of the Department of Veterinary Science and Animal Husbandry. Tanganyika

Rep Dep Vet Servs Anim Ind Nyasald — Report. Department of Veterinary Services and Animal Industry. Nyasaland

Rep Dep Vet Servs Anim Ind Uganda — Report of the Department of Veterinary Services and Animal Industry. Uganda

Rep Dep Vet Servs Fed Rhod Nyasald — Report. Department of Veterinary Services. Federation of Rhodesia and Nyasaland

Rep Dep Vet Servs Kenya — Report of the Department of Veterinary Services. Kenya

Rep Dep Vet Servs Nth Rhod — Report. Department of Veterinary Services. Northern Rhodesia

Rep Dep Vet Servs Swazild — Report. Department of Veterinary Services. Swaziland

Rep Dep Vet Tsetse Control Servs Nth Rhod — Report. Department of Veterinary and Tsetse Control Services. Northern Rhodesia

Rep Dep Wild Life Conserv Sth Rhod — Report. Department of Wild Life Conservation. Southern Rhodesia

Rep Derwent Bd Conserv — Report. Derwent Board of Conservators

Rep Desert Locust Surv Control E Afr — Report. Desert Locust Survey and Control. East Africa

Rep Detroit Tuberc Sanat — Report. Detroit Tuberculosis Sanatorium

Rep Dev Bd Iraq — Report. Development Board. Iraq

Rep Dev Commnrs — Report of the Development Commissioners

Rep Dev Elect Commun Lab Tokyo — Report of the Development of the Electrical Communication Laboratory (Tokyo)

Rep Devon Bird Watch Preserv Soc — Report. Devon Bird Watching and Preservation Society

Rep Devon River Bd — Report. Devon River Board

Rep Diesel Engrs Us Ass — Report. Diesel Engineers and Users' Association

Rep Dir Agric Br Guiana — Report of the Director of Agriculture. British Guiana

Rep Dir Agric Cyprus — Report of the Director of Agriculture. Cyprus

Rep Dir Agric Tonga — Report of the Director of Agriculture. Tonga

Rep Dir Anti Locust Res Cent — Report of the Director. Anti-Locust Research Centre on Locust Research and Control

Rep Dir Arnold Arbor — Report of the Director. Arnold Arboretum

Rep Dir Blue Hill Met Obs — Report of the Director. Blue Hill Meteorological Observatory

Rep Dir Cent Am Coop Corn Improv Proj — Report. Director of Central American Cooperative Corn Improvement Project

Rep Dir Cent Fuel Res Inst — Report. Director. Central Fuel Research Institute

Rep Dir Dep Embryol Carnegie Instn — Report of the Director of the Department of Embryology. Carnegie Institution

Rep Dir Dep Pl Biol Carnegie Instn — Report of the Director of the Department of Plant Biology. Carnegie Institution

Rep Dir Dom Exp Fms Can — Report of the Director. Dominion Experimental Farms. Canada

Rep Direct Gen Hlth Servs India — Report. Directorate General of Health Services. India

Rep Director Vet Serv Dept Agric (Union South Africa) — Report. Director of Veterinary Services and Animal Industry. Department of Agriculture (Union of South Africa)

Rep Dir Exp Fms Serv Can — Report of the Director. Experimental Farms Service. Canada

Rep Dir Ext Serv US Dep Agric — Report of the Director of the Extension Service. United States Department of Agriculture

Rep Dir Fish Hong Kong — Report of the Director of Fisheries. Hong Kong

Rep Dir Fish Philipp Repub — Report of the Director of Fisheries. Bureau of Fisheries. Philippine Republic

Rep Dir Fish Wildl Serv — Report of the Director of the Fish and Wildlife Service

Rep Dir Forests Qd — Report of the Director of Forests. Queensland

Rep Dir Gen Publ Hlth NSW — Report of the Director-General of Public Health. New South Wales

Rep Dir Geophys Lab Carnegie Instn — Report of the Director. Geophysical Laboratory. Carnegie Institution

Rep Dir Gov Chem Lab (West Aust) — Report. Director of Government Chemical Laboratories (Western Australia)

Rep Dir Jeremiah Horrocks Obs — Report of the Director of the Jeremiah Horrocks Observatory

Rep Dir Med Servs Br Guiana — Report. Director of Medical Services. Medical Department. British Guiana

Rep Dir Met Off Lond — Report of the Director of the Meteorological Office (London)

Rep Dir Met Serv Baghdad — Report of the Director. Meteorological Service. Baghdad

Rep Dir Met Servs Sth Rhod — Report of the Director. Meteorological Services. Southern Rhodesia

Rep Dir Mines Govt Geol S Aust — Report of the Director of Mines and Government Geologist. South Australia

Rep Dir Mines (Tasmania) — Report. Director of Mines (Tasmania)

Rep Dir Mint Wash — Report of the Director of the Mint (Washington)

Rep Dir Mt Wilson Palomar Obs — Report of the Director. Mount Wilson and Palomar Observatories

Rep Dir Mt Wilson Sol Obs — Report of the Director. Mount Wilson Solar Observatory

Rep Dir Ohio Dep Nat Resour — Report of the Director of the Ohio Department of Natural Resources

Rep Dir Ont Metal Min Ass — Report of the Director. Ontario Metal Mining Association

Rep Dir Publ Hlth Madras — Report of the Director of Public Health. Madras

Rep Dir Res Allan Hancock Fdn — Report of the Director of Research. Allan Hancock Foundation. University of Southern California

Rep Dir Vet Serv Anim Ind (Onderstepoort) — Report. Director of Veterinary Services and Animal Industry (Onderstepoort)

Rep Diss Agric Coll Swed Dep Plant Husb — Reports and Dissertations. Agricultural College of Sweden. Departmentof Plant Husbandry

Rep Div Aeronaut CSIR Aust — Report. Division of Aeronautics. C.S.I.R. Australia

Rep Div Agric Iowa St Coll Agric — Report. Division of Agriculture. Iowa State College of Agriculture and Mechanic Arts

Rep Div Apic St Coll Wash — Report of the Division of Apiculture. State College of Washington

Rep Div Bact Exp Fms Serv Can — Report. Division of Bacteriology. Experimental Farms Service. Department of Agriculture. Canada

Rep Div Biol Calif Inst Technol — Report. Division of Biology. California Institute of Technology

Rep Div Bldg Res CSIRO — Report. Division of Building Research. Commonwealth Scientific and Industrial Research Organisation

Rep Div Build Res CSIRO — Report. Division of Building Research. Commonwealth Scientific and Industrial Research Organisation

Rep Div Chem Eng CSIRO — Report. Division of Chemical Engineering. Commonwealth Scientific and Industrial Research Organisation

Rep Div Chem Engng CSIRO — Report. Division of Chemical Engineering. Commonwealth Scientific and Industrial Research Organisation

Rep Div Chem Exp Fms Serv Can — Report. Division of Chemistry. Experimental Farms Service. Department of Agriculture. Canada

Rep Div Coal Res CSIRO Aust — Report. Division of Coal Research. C.S.I.R.O. Australia

Rep Div Electrotechnol CSIRO Aust — Report. Division of Electrotechnology. C.S.I.R.O. Australia

Rep Div Engng CSIRO Aust — Report. Division of Engineering. C.S.I.R.O. Australia</PHR> %

Rep Div Ent CSIRO Aust — Report. Division of Entomology. C.S.I.R.O. Australia

Rep Div Ent Dep Agric Un S Afr — Report of the Division of Entomology of the Department of Agriculture. Union of South Africa

Rep Div Ent Dom Exp Fms Can — Report of the Division of Entomology. Dominion Experimental Farms. Canada

Rep Div Ent Pl Path Brisbane — Report. Division of Entomology and Plant Pathology (Brisbane)

Rep Div Fd Preserv CSIRO Aust — Report. Division of Food Preservation. C.S.I.R.O. Australia

Rep Div Fish Oceanogr CSIRO — Report. Division of Fisheries and Oceanography. Commonwealth Scientific and Industrial Research Organisation

Rep Div Fish Res Newfoundld — Report. Division of Fishery Research. Newfoundland

Rep Div Fish Un S Afr — Report. Division of Fisheries. Union of South Africa

Rep Div Fld Husb Exp Fms Serv Can — Report. Division of Field Husbandry. Experimental Farms Service. Department of Agriculture. Canada

Rep Div Forest Prod CSIRO Aust — Report. Division of Forest Products. C.S.I.R.O. Australia

Rep Div For Relat TVA — Report. Division of Forestry Relations. Tennessee Valley Authority

Rep Div For Sth Rhod — Report. Division of Forestry. Southern Rhodesia

Rep Div Hort Res CSIRO — Report. Division of Horticultural Research. Commonwealth Scientific and Industrial Research Organisation

Rep Div Ind Saf Mass Dep Labor Ind — Report of the Division of Industrial Safety. Massachusetts Department of Labor and Industries

Rep Div Labs Res NY St Dep Hlth — Report. Division of Laboratories and Research. New York State Department of Health

Rep Divl Agric Offrs Ceylon — Report of the Divisional Agricultural Officers. Department of Agriculture. Ceylon

Rep Divl Dep Agric Br Guiana — Report. Divisional. Department of Agriculture. British Guiana

Rep Div Ld Res Reg Surv CSIRO Aust — Report. Division of Land Research and Regional Survey. C.S.I.R.O. Australia

Rep Divl Spec Offrs Dep Agric Fiji — Report. Divisional and Specialist Officers. Department of Agriculture. Fiji

Rep Div Mar Fish Mass Dep Conserv — Report. Division of Marine Fisheries. Massachusetts Department of Conservation

Rep Div Mech Engng CSIRO — Report. Division of Mechanical Engineering. Commonwealth Scientific and Industrial Research Organisation

Rep Div Mech Engng Natn Res Coun Can — Report. Division of Mechanical Engineering. National Research Council of Canada

Rep Div Met Phys CSIRO Aust — Report. Division of Meteorological Physics. CSIRO. Australia

Rep Div Miner CSIRO — Report. Division of Mineralogy. Commonwealth Scientific and Industrial ResearchOrganisation

Rep Div Nutr Food Res TNO — Report. Division for Nutrition and Food Research TNO

Rep Div Phys CSIRO Aust — Report. Division of Physics. C.S.I.R.O. Australia

Rep Div Pl Ind CSIRO — Report. Division of Plant Industry. C.S.I.R.O. Australia

Rep Div Soils CSIRO Aust — Report. Division of Soils. C.S.I.R.O. Australia

Rep Div Text Ind CSIRO — Report. Division of Textile Industry. Commonwealth Scientific and Industrial Research Organisation

Rep Div Tribophys CSIRO Aust — Report. Division of Tribophysics. C.S.I.R.O. Australia

Rep Div Trop Past CSIRO Aust — Report. Division of Tropical Pastures. C.S.I.R.O. Australia

Rep Div Tuberc Control Br Columb — Report. Division of Tuberculosis Control. Department of Health and Welfare. British Columbia

Rep Div Vet Sci Mich St Coll — Report of the Division of Veterinary Science. Michigan State College

Rep Div Water Land Dev Hawaii — Report. Division of Water and Land Development. Hawaii

Rep Div Wat Resour Kans St Bd Agric — Report of the Division of Water Resources. Kansas State Board of Agriculture

Rep Div Wat Ways Ill — Report. Division of Waterways. Illinois

Rep DK Pub Rec Ir — Reports. Deputy Keeper. Public Records in Ireland

Rep DL NZ Dep Sci Ind Res Dom Lab — Report DL. New Zealand Department of Scientific and IndustrialResearch. Dominion Laboratory

Rep Dom Agrost Can — Report of the Dominion Agrostologist. Canada

Rep Dom Astr Obs Ottawa — Report of the Dominion Astronomical Observatory (Ottawa)

Rep Dom Astrophys Obs Vict BC — Report. Dominion Astrophysical Observatory (Victoria, B.C.)

Rep Dom Fuel Bd Can — Report. Dominion Fuel Board. Canada

Rep Dom Grain Res Lab Can — Report of the Dominion Grain Research Laboratory. Canada

Rep Dom Lab NZ — Report of the Dominion Laboratory. N.Z.

Rep Dom Phys Lab NZ — Report. Dominion Physical Laboratory. New Zealand

Rep Dove Mar Lab — Report. Dove Marine Laboratory of Kings College. Durham University

Rep Drain Irrig Dep Br Guiana — Report. Drainage and Irrigation Department. British Guiana

Rep Draydon Exp Husb Fm — Report. Draydon Experimental Husbandry Farm

Rep Dry Ice Ind Sigmaringen — Report on the Dry-Ice Industry (Sigmaringen)

Rep Dudley Obs — Reports. Dudley Observatory

Rep Duke Univ Sch For — Report. Duke University School of Forestry

Rep Dumraon Agric Exp Stn — Report of the Dumraon Agricultural Experiment Station. Department of Agriculture

Rep Durban Mus — Report of the Durban Museum

Rep Durham Univ Obs — Report. Durham University Observatory

Rep E Afr Agric Fish Res Coun — Report of the East African Agricultural and Fisheries Research Council

Rep E Afr Agric For Res Org — Report. East African Agricultural and Forestry Research Organisation

Rep E Afr Agric Res Inst — Report. East African Agricultural Research Institute. Amani

Rep E Afr Coun Med Res — Report of the East African Council for Medical Research

Rep E Afr Freshwat Fish Res Org — Report. East African Freshwater Fisheries Research Organization

Rep E Afr Ind Res Org — Report. East African Industrial Research Organization

Rep E Afr Inst Malar — Report. East African Institute of Malaria and Vector-borne Diseases

Rep E Afr Inst Med Res — Report. East African Institute for Medical Research

Rep E Afr Lepr Res Cent — Report. East African Leprosy Research Centre

Rep E Afr Mar Fish Res Org — Report. East African Marine Fisheries Research Organization

Rep E Afr Med Surv — Report. East African Medical Survey

Rep E Afr Med Surv Res Inst — Report. East African Medical Survey and Research Institute

Rep E Afr Met Dep — Report. East African Meteorological Department

Rep E Afr Sisal Ind — Report. East African Sisal Industry

Rep E Afr Trypan Res Org — Report. East African Trypanosomiasis Research Organization

Rep E Afr Tsetse Trypan Res Reclam Org — Report of the East African Tsetse and Trypanosomiasis Research and Reclamation Organization

Rep E Afr Vet Res Org — Report. East African Veterinary Research Organization

Rep E Afr Virus Res Inst — Report. East African Virus Research Institute

Rep Ealing Scient Microsc Soc — Report of the Ealing Scientific and Microscopical Society

Rep Earthq Res Inst Tokyo — Report. Earthquake Research Institute. Tokyo Imperial University

Rep Earth Sci Coll Gen Educ Kyushu Univ — Reports on Earth Science. College of General Education. Kyushu University

Rep Earth Sci Dep Gen Educ Kyushu Univ — Reports on Earth Science. Department of General Education. Kyushu University

Rep East Caribb Fm Inst — Report. Eastern Caribbean Farm Institute

Rep East For Prod Lab (Can) — Report. Eastern Forest Products Laboratory (Canada)

Rep East Malling Res Stn (Maidstone Engl) — Report. East Malling Research Station (Maidstone, England)

Rep East Reg Prod Dev Bd Nigeria — Report. Eastern Regional Production Development Board. Nigeria

Rep East Rockies Forest Conserv Bd — Report. Eastern Rockies Forest Conservation Board

Rep East Winter Hard Wheat Nurs — Repot. Eastern Winter Hardiness Wheat Nurseries

Rep Ecol Conf NZ — Report of Ecological Conference. New Zealand Ecological Society

Rep Econ Biol — Report on Economic Biology

Rep Econ Bot Burma — Report of the Economic Botanist. Burma

Rep Econ Dep W Scotl Agric Coll — Report. Economics Department. West of Scotland Agricultural College

Rep Econ Fibre Prod Div Dom Exp Fms Can — Report. Economic Fibre Production Division. Dominion Experimental Farms. Canada

Rep Econ Fruit Fmg Wye Coll — Report. Economics of Fruit Farming. Wye College

Rep Econ Mycol S East Agric Coll — Report on Economic Mycology. South Eastern Agricultural College

Rep Econ Zool Br Mus — Report on Economic Zoology. Department of Zoology. British Museum

Rep Econ Zool S East Agric Coll — Report on Economic Zoology. South Eastern Agricultural College

REPed — Revista Espanola de Pedagogia

Rep Eden Fishery Bd — Report. Eden Fishery Board

Rep ED Eng Sect CSIRO — Report ED. Engineering Section. Commonwealth Scientific and Industrial ResearchOrganisation

Rep Edgar Allen Inst Med Mech Treat — Report. Edgar Allen Institute for Medico-Mechanical Treatment

Rep Edinb E Scotl Coll Agric — Report. Edinburgh and East of Scotland College of Agriculture

Rep Eg Expl Soc — Report for the Year. Egypt Exploration Society

Rep Egypt Fish — Report of the Egyptian Fisheries

Rep Ehime Prefect Res Inst Environ Sci — Report. Ehime Prefectural Research Institute for Environmental Science

Rep Elast Chem Div E I Du Pont — Report. Elastomer Chemical Division. E. I. Du Pont de Nemours

Rep Elect Accid — Report on Electrical Accidents and their Causes

Rep Elect Commnrs — Report of the Electricity Commissioners

Rep Elect Dep Natn Phys Lab — Report on the Electricity Department. National Physical Laboratory

Rep Elect Engng Res Lab Univ Tex — Report. Electrical Engineering Research Laboratory. University of Texas

Rep Elect Res Ass — Report. Electrical Research Association

Rep Electro Cult Comm Minist Agric — Report of the Electro-Culture Committee. Ministry of Agriculture [London]

Rep Electro Metall Res Lab Wash St Coll — Report. Electrometallurgical Research Laboratory. Washington State College

Rep Elect Supply Commn Un S Afr — Report. Electricity Supply Commission of the Union of South Africa

Rep Elect Supply Comn Sth Rhod — Report. Electricity Supply Commission. Southern Rhodesia

Rep E Malling Res Stn — Annual Report. East Malling Research Station

Rep Emerg Scient Res Bur Dubl — Report. Emergency Scientific Research Bureau (Dublin)

Rep EM Ont Minist Transp Commun Eng Mater Off — Report EM. Ontario Ministry of Transportation and Communications.Engineering Materials Office

Rep Emp For Ass — Report. Empire Forestry Association

Rep Emp Mktg Bd — Report. Empire Marketing Board

Rep Emp Rheum Coun — Report. Empire Rheumatism Council

Rep Eng Inst Fac Eng Tokyo Univ — Report. Engineering Institute. Faculty of Engineering. Tokyo University

Rep Engng Analysis Comput Grp Can — Report. Engineering Analysis and Computation Group. National Research Council of Canada

Rep Engng Dep Natn Phys — Report on the Engineering Department. National Physical Laboratory

Rep Engng Exp Stn Univ Wis — Report. Engineering Experiment Station. University of Wisconsin

Rep Engng Fdn NY — Report. Engineering Foundation (New York)

Rep Engng Res Inst Kyoto Univ — Report. Engineering Research Institute. Kyoto University

Rep Engng Res Inst Tokyo Univ — Report of the Engineering Research Institute. Tokyo University

Rep Engng Scient Ass Ire — Report. Engineering and Scientific Association of Ireland

Rep Engng Sect CSIRO Aust — Report. Engineering Section. C.S.I.R.O. Australia

Rep Engng Soc Wis — Report of the Engineering Society of Wisconsin

Rep Eng Res Lab Obayashi-Gumi Ltd — Report. Engineering Research Laboratory. Obayashi-Gumi Limited

Rep Ent Div Dep Agric Ceylon — Report. Entomological Division. Department of Agriculture. Ceylon

Rep Ent Mandalay Dep Agric — Report of the Entomologist. Mandalay Department of Agriculture. Burma

Rep Ent Minn Univ Exp Stn — Report of the Entomologist. Minnesota University Experiment Station

Rep Ent Soc Ont — Report. Entomological Society of Ontario

Rep Ent US Dep Agric — Report of the Entomologist. United States Department of Agriculture

Rep Environ Prot Serv Ser EPS 3 (Can) — Report. Environmental Protection Service. Series EPS-3 (Canada)

Rep Environ Prot Serv Ser EPS 4 (Can) — Report. Environmental Protection Service. Series EPS-4 (Canada)

Rep Environ Radiat Surveill Wash Dep Soc Health Serv — Report. Environmental Radiation Surveillance. Washington Department ofSocial and Health Services

Rep Environ Res Organ Chiba Univ — Report. Environmental Research Organization. Chiba University

Rep Environ Sci Inst Hyogo Prefect — Report. Environmental Science Institute of Hyogo Prefecture

Rep Environ Sci Inst Kinki Univ — Report. Environmental Science Institute. Kinki University

Rep Environ Sci Inst Mie Prefect — Report. Environment Science Institute. Mie Prefecture

Rep Environ Sci Mie Univ — Report of Environmental Science. Mie University

Rep Environ Sci Res Cent Shiga Prefect — Report. Environmental Science Research Center of Shiga Prefecture

Rep Environ Sci Res Inst Kinki Univ — Report. Environmental Science Research Institute. Kinki University

Rep Environ Sci Tech Lab Nippon Bunri Univ — Reports. Environmental Science and Technology Laboratory. Nippon BunriUniversity

Rep Environ Sci Technol Lab Nippon Bunri Univ — Reports. Environmental Science and Technology Laboratory. Nippon Bunri University

Rep Environ Sci Technol Lab Oita Inst Technol — Reports. Environmental Science and Technology Laboratory. OitaInstitute of Technology

Rep Epiz Abort Exps Oxf — Report on the Epizootic Abortion Experiments. Oxfordshire County Council

Rep EPS Can Environ Prot Serv Solid Waste Manage Branch — Report EPS. Canada. Environmental Protection Service. Solid Waste Management Branch

Rep Epsom Coll Nat Hist Soc — Report of the Epsom College Natural History Society

Reper Am S Jose — Repertorio Americano (San Jose, Costa Rica)

Reperes-Econ Languedoc-Roussillon — Reperes-Economie du Languedoc-Roussillon

Rep ERP/PMRL Phys Metall Res Lab (Can) — Report ERP/PMRL. Physical Metallurgy Research Laboratories (Canada)

Repert Agric Prat Econ Domest — Repertorio di Agricoltura Pratica e di Economica Domestica

Repert Amer — Repertorio Americano

Repert Kstwiss — Repertorium fuer Kunstwissenschaft

Repert Med Farm Ci Auxiliares — Repertorio Medico-Farmaceutico y de Ciencias Auxiliares

Repert Med Prat Ser Biol — Repertoire Medical Pratique. Serie Biologie

Repert Neuesten Wissenswuerd Gesammten Naturk — Repertorium des Neuesten und Wissenswuerdigsten aus der Gesammten Naturkunde

Repertoire Anal Litt Francaise — Repertoire Analytique de Litterature Francaise

Repertorium der Phot — Repertorium der Photographie

Repert Pharm — Repertoire de Pharmacie

Repert Plant Succulentarum — Repertorium Plantarum Succulentarum

Repert Spec Nov Regni Veg — Repertorium Specierum Novarum Regni Vegatabilis. Centralblatt fuer Sammlung undVeroeffentlichung von Einzeldiagnosen Neuer Pflanzen

Repert Spec Nov Regni Veg Sonderbeih A — Repertorium Specierum Novarum Regni Vegetabilis. Sonderbeiheft A

Repert Spec Nov Regni Veg Sonderbeih B — Repertorium Specierum Novarum Regni Vegetabilis. Sonderbeiheft B

Repert Spec Nov Regni Veg Sonderbeih D — Repertorium Specierum Novarum Regni Vegetabilis. Sonderbeiheft D

Rep Essex Bird Watch Preserv Soc — Report of the Essex Bird-Watching and Preservation Society

Rep Essex Inst Agric — Report. Essex Institute of Agriculture

Rep Essex River Bd — Report. Essex River Board

Rep Estac Cent Agron Cuba — Report. Estacion Central Agronomica de Cuba

Rep E Suff Norf River Bd — Report. East Suffolk and Norfolk River Board

Rep E Suss River Bd — Report. East Susses River Board

Rep Ethno Technol Res — Report of Ethno-Technological Research

Rep Eton Coll Nat Hist Soc — Report. Eton College Natural History Society

Rep Eugen Educ Soc — Report of the Eugenics Education Society

Rep Eugen Rec Off Cold Spring Harb — Report of the Eugenics Record Office [Cold Spring Harbor]

Rep Eugen Soc — Report of the Eugenics Society

Rep Eur Civ Aviat Conf — Report. European Civil Aviation Conference [Montreal]

Rep Eur Mediterr Pl Prot Org — Report. European and Mediterranean Plant Protection Organisation

Rep Europe — Report from Europe

Rep Eur Org Nucl Res — Report of the European Organization for Nuclear Research

Rep Eur Orthod Soc — Report. European Orthodontic Society

Rep Eur Paleobot — Report on European Paleobotany

Rep Evol Comm Roy Soc Lond — Report to the Evolution Committee. Royal Society of London

Rep Evol Comm R Soc — Report to the Evolution Committee of the Royal Society [London]

Rep Expert Comm Envir Sanit WHO — Report. Expert Committee on Environmental Sanitation. World Health Organization

Rep Expert Comm Radiat WHO — Report. Expert Committee on Radiation. World Health Organization

Rep Exp Fm Agric Coll Nagpur — Report on the Experimental Farm attached to the Agricultural College. Nagpur

Rep Exp Fms Bihar Orissa — Report. Experimental Farms of Bihar and Orissa

Rep Exp Fms Can — Report on the Experimental Farms. Department of Agriculture. Canada

Rep Exp Fms Cent Prov — Report on the Experimental Farms in the Central Provinces

Rep Exp Fms Cent Prov Nth Plat Circles — Report of Experimental Farms in the Central Provinces. Northern and Plateau Circles

Rep Exp Fms Cent Prov Sth & East Circles — Report of Experimental Farms in the Central Provinces. Southern and Eastern Circles

Rep Exp Fox Ranch Can — Report. Experimental Fox Ranch. Dominion Experimental Farms. Canada

Rep Explos Brch Home Off — Report. Explosives Branch. Home Office

Rep Explos Div Dep Mines Can — Report. Explosives Division. Department of Mines and Technical Surveys. Canada

Rep Exp Res Stn (Cheshunt) — Report. Experimental and Research Station. Nursery and Market Garden IndustriesDevelopment Society, Ltd. (Cheshunt)

Rep Exps Advis Leafl Univ Coll N Wales — Report on the Experiments and Advisory Leaflets. University College of North Wales

Rep Exps Crops Stk Camb Univ Dep Agric — Report on Experiments with Crops and Stock. Cambridge University Department of Agriculture

Rep Exps Crops Stk Midl Agric Dairy Inst — Report on Experiments with Crops and Stock. Midland Agricultural and Dairy Institute

Rep Exp Stn Farnham Queb — Report. Experimental Station. Farnham, Quebec

Rep Exp Stn Kapuskasing — Report. Experimental Station. Kapuskasing

Rep Exp Stn La Ferme — Report. Experimental Station. La Ferme, Quebec

Rep Exp Stn Lennoxville — Report. Experimental Station. Lennoxville

Rep Exp Stn Morden Manitoba — Report. Experimental Station. Morden, Manitoba

Rep Exp Stn Rosthern — Report. Experimental Station. Rosthern, Saskatchewan

Rep Exp Stn S Afr Sug Ass — Report. Experiment Station of the South African Sugar Association

Rep Exp Stns Emp Cott Grow Corp — Reports Received from Experiment Stations. Empire Cotton Growing Corporation [London]

Rep Exp Stns Scient Sect Dep Agric Bihar Orissa — Report on Experiment Stations and Scientific Sections. Department of Agriculture. Bihar and Orissa

Rep Exp Stn Summerland — Report. Experimental Station. Summerland, B.C

Rep Exps Univ Fm Gravel Hill — Report on Experiments at the University Farm. Gravel Hill [Cambridge]

Rep Exp Tow Tank Stevens Inst Technol — Report. Experimental Towing Tank. Stevens Institute of Technology

Rep Exp Wk Agric Stns Bombay — Report of Experimental Work of the Agricultural Stations in the Bombay Presidency

Rep Exp Wk Cott Qd — Report on Experimental Work on Cotton. Department of Agriculture. Queensland

Rep Exp Wk Econ Bot Bombay — Report on Experimental Work by the Economic Botanist and his Staff. Bombay

Rep Exp Wk Ganeshkhind Bot Gdn — Report of the Experimental Work of the Ganeshkhind Botanical Garden

Rep Exp Wk Highw Tech Comm — Report. Experimental Work on Highways (Technical) Committee. Ministry of Transport [London]

Rep Exp Wk Sug Cane Exp Stn Jamaica — Report on the Experimental Work of the Sugar Cane Experiment Station. Jamaica

Rep F — Repertoire Fiscal

RepF — Republique Francaise

Rep Fabrics Coord Res Comm — Report. Fabrics Co-ordinating Research Committee. Department of Scientific and Industrial Research [London]

Rep Fac Agric Shizuoka Univ — Report. Faculty of Agriculture. Shizuoka University/Shizuoka Daigaku Nogakubu Kenkyu Hokoku

Rep Fac Agr Shizuoka Univ — Reports. Faculty of Agriculture. Shizuoka University

Rep Fac Anaesth R Coll Surg — Report. Faculty of Anaesthetists. Royal College of Surgeons of England

Rep Fac Anim Husb Hung Univ Agric Sci (Godollo) — Reports. Faculty for Animal Husbandry. Hungarian University ofAgricultural Science (Godollo)

Rep Fac Eng Himeji Inst Technol — Reports. Faculty of Engineering. Himeji Institute of Technology

Rep Fac Eng Kanagawa Univ — Reports. Faculty of Engineering. Kanagawa University

Rep Fac Eng Kinki Univ Kyushu Sci Technol Sect — Reports. Faculty of Engineering. Kinki University in Kyushu. Scienceand Technology Section

Rep Fac Eng Nagasaki Univ — Reports. Faculty of Engineering. Nagasaki University

Rep Fac Engng Shizuoka Univ — Report. Faculty of Engineering. Shizuoka University

Rep Fac Engrg Kanagawa Univ — Kanagawa University. Faculty of Engineering. Reports

Rep Fac Engrg Oita Univ — Oita University. Faculty of Engineering. Reports

Rep Fac Eng Shizuoka Univ — Reports. Faculty of Engineering. Shizuoka University

Rep Fac Eng Tottori Univ — Reports. Faculty of Engineering. Tottori University

Rep Fac Eng Yamanashi Univ — Reports. Faculty of Engineering. Yamanashi University

Rep Fac Fish Prefect Univ Mie — Report. Faculty of Fisheries. Prefectural University of Mie

Rep Fac Gen Agric Univ Coll Dubl — Report. Faculty of General Agriculture. University College. Dublin

Rep Fac Pharm Kanazawa Univ — Report of the Faculty of Pharmacy. Kanazawa University

Rep Fac Pharm Tokushima Univ — Report of the Faculty of Pharmacy. Tokushima University

Rep Fac Sci Egypt Univ — Report. Faculty of Science. Egyptian University

Rep Fac Sci Engrg Saga Univ Math — Reports. Faculty of Science and Engineering. Saga University. Mathematics

Rep Fac Sci Kagoshima Univ — Reports. Faculty of Science. Kagoshima University

Rep Fac Sci Kagoshima Univ (Earth Sci Biol) — Reports. Faculty of Science. Kagoshima University. Earth Sciences and Biology

Rep Fac Sci Kagoshima Univ Math Phys Chem — Reports. Faculty of Science. Kagoshima University. Mathematics, Physics, and Chemistry

Rep Fac Sci Shizuoka Univ — Reports. Faculty of Science. Shizuoka University

Rep Fac Sci Technol Meijyo Univ — Reports. Faculty of Science and Technology. Meijyo University

Rep Fac Tech Kanagawa Univ — Kanagawa University. Faculty of Technology. Reports

Rep Fac Technol Kanagawa Univ — Reports. Faculty of Technology. Kanagawa University

Rep Fam L — Reports of Family Law

Rep FAO/IAEA Tech Meet (Brunswick-Volkenrode) — Report. FAO [*Food and Agriculture Organization of the United Nations*]/IAEA Technical Meeting (Brunswick-Volkenrode)

Rep Far East State Univ (Vladivostok) — Reports. Far Eastern State University (Vladivostok)

Rep Fd Prod Consumpt CSIRO Aust — Report on Food Production and Consumption. C.S.I.R.O. Australia

Rep Fd Res Inst (Tokyo) — Report. Food Research Institute (Tokyo)

Rep Fed Agric Coops Gt Br — Report. Federation of Agricultural Co-operatives in Great Britain and Ireland

Rep Fed Dep Chem Nigeria — Report. Federal Department of Chemistry. Federation of Nigeria

Rep Fed Exp Stn P Rico — Report of the Federal Experiment Station in Puerto Rico

Rep Fed Fish Serv Nigeria — Report of the Federal Fisheries Service. Federation of Nigeria

Rep Fed Forest Adm Malaya — Report on Federal Forest Administration. Federation of Malaya

Rep Fed Hort Bd Wash — Report of the Federal Horticultural Board [*Washington*]

Rep Fed Railroad Adm — Report. Federal Railroad Administration

Rep Felsted Sch Scient Soc — Report of the Felsted School Scientific Society

Rep Fermented Foods Exp Stn Kagawa Prefect — Report. Fermented Foods Experimental Station. Kagawa Prefecture

Rep Ferment Ind — Report on the Fermentation Industries

Rep Ferment Inds — Report on the Fermentation Industries. Society of Chemical Industry [*London*]

Rep Ferment Res Inst — Report. Fermentation Research Institute

Rep Ferment Res Inst (Chiba) — Report. Fermentation Research Institute (Chiba)

Rep Ferment Res Inst (Tsukuba-Gun Jpn) — Report. Fermentation Research Institute (Tsukuba-Gun, Japan)

Rep Ferment Res Inst (Yatabe) — Report. Fermentation Research Institute (Yatabe)

Rep Fibre Div Exp Fms Serv Can — Report. Fibre Division. Experimental Farms Service. Department of Agriculture. Canada

Rep Field Act Miner Resour Div (Manitoba) — Report of Field Activities. Mineral Resources Division (Manitoba)

Rep Filariasis Res Unit E Afr — Report. Filariasis Research Unit. East Africa

Rep Finn Acad Sci Lett Sodankyla Geophys Obs — Report. Finnish Academy of Science and Letters. Sodankyla Geophysical Observatory

Rep Fire Res Bd — Report of the Fire Research Board [*London*]

Rep Fire Res Inst Jpn — Report. Fire Research Institute of Japan

Rep Fire Technol Lab Tech Res Cent Finl — Reports. Fire Technology Laboratory. Technical Research Centre of Finland

Rep Fisc — Repertoire Fiscal

Rep Fish Board Swed Inst Mar Res — Report. Fishery Board of Sweden. Institute of Marine Research

Rep Fish Board Swed Ser Hydrogr — Reports. Fishery Board of Sweden. Series Hydrography

Rep Fish Brch Can — Report of the Fisheries Branch. Department of Marine and Fisheries. Canada

Rep Fish Brch Maurit — Report of the Fisheries Branch. Colony of Mauritius

Rep Fish Cult Ottawa — Report on Fish Culture. Department of Fisheries. Canada (Ottawa)

Rep Fish Dep East Reg Nigeria — Report. Fisheries Department. Eastern Region Nigeria

Rep Fish Dep Fed Malaya — Report of the Fisheries Department. Federation of Malaya

Rep Fish Dep Ghana — Report. Fisheries Department. Ghana

Rep Fish Dep Singapore — Report of the Fisheries Department. Colony of Singapore

Rep Fish Game Brch TVA — Report. Fish and Game Branch. Division of Forestry Relations. Tennessee Valley Authority

Rep Fish Res Lab Kyushu Univ — Report. Fishery Research Laboratory. Kyushu University

Rep Fla Agric Exp Stn — Report. Florida Agricultural Experiment Station

Rep Fla St Geol Surv — Report of the Florida State Geological Survey

Rep Fld Exps Agric Dep Univ Coll Wales Aberyst — Report on Field Experiments. Agricultural Department. University College of Wales (Aberystwyth)

Rep Fld Exps Cumberld Durh Northumb — Report on Field and other Experiments. Cumberland, Durham, and Northumberland County Councils

Rep Fld Exps Devon — Report on Field Experiments. Devon County Council

Rep Fld Exps E Suffolk — Report on Field Experiments. East Suffolk County Council

Rep Fld Exps Fm Inst Cannington — Report on Field Experiments. Farm Institute. Cannington

Rep Fld Exps Obsn Stud E Midl Reg Minist Agric — Report on Field Experiments and Observation Studies. East Midland Region. Ministry of Agriculture, Fisheries, and Food

Rep Fld Exps Obsn Stud Hort SEast Reg — Report on Field Experiments and Observation Studies in Horticulture. South-Eastern Region [*Reading, Wye.*]

Rep Fld Exps Sug Cane Trin — Report. Field Experiments on Sugar Cane in Trinidad

Rep Fld Exps Univ Coll N Wales — Report on Field Experiments. University College of North Wales

Rep Fld Feedg Exps Camb Univ Dep Agric — Report of Field and Feeding Experiments. Cambridge University Department of Agriculture

Rep Fld Feedg Pot Cult Exps Woburn Exp Stn — Report on Field, Feeding, and Pot Culture Experiments of the Woburn Experimental Station

Rep Fld Husb Res Stn Potchafstroom — Report. Field Husbandry Research Station. College of Agriculture. Potchafstroom

Rep Fld Ops US Bur Soils — Report on Field Operations. United States Bureau of Soils

Rep Fld Res Stn Witwat Univ — Report. Field Research Station. Witwatersrand University [*Johannesburg*]

Rep Fld Stud Coun — Report. Field Studies Council [*London*]

Rep Fld Trials Exps Univ Coll Reading — Report of Field Trials and Experiments. University College. Reading

Rep Fld Trials Gloucs Agric Educ Sub Comm — Report on Field Trials. Gloucestershire Agricultural Education Sub-Committee

Rep Fm Econ Brch Camb Univ — Report. Farm Economics Branch. Department of Agriculture. Cambridge University

Rep Fm Econ Surv Unit Nakura — Report. Farm Economics Survey Unit. Nakura

Rep Fm Mgmt Res Scheme Oxf — Report. Farm Management Research Scheme (Oxford)

Rep FM Univ Calif Berkeley — Report FM. University of California, Berkeley

Rep Fodder Conserv Sect CSIRO Aust — Report. Fodder Conservation Section. C.S.I.R.O. Australia

Rep Food Ind Exp Stn Hiroshima Prefect — Report. Food Industrial Experiment Station. Hiroshima Prefecture

Rep Food Res Inst Niigata Prefect — Report. Food Research Institute. Niigata Prefecture

Rep Food Res Inst (Tokyo) — Report. Food Research Institute (Tokyo)

Rep Food Res Inst Yamanashi Prefect — Report. Food Research Institute. Yamanashi Prefecture

Rep Foot Mouth Dis Res Comm — Report. Foot and Mouth Disease Research Committee. Ministry of Agriculture and Fisheries

Rep Foot Mouth Dis Res Inst — Report. Foot and Mouth Disease Research Institute

Rep For Advis Gambia — Report of the Forestry Adviser. Gambia

Rep Forage Pl Div Dom Exp Fms Can — Report. Forage Plants Division. Dominion Experimental Farms. Canada

Rep For Brch Can — Report of the Forestry Branch. Department of the Interior. Canada

Rep For Brch Sask — Report. Forestry Branch. Department of Natural Resources. Saskatchewan

Rep For Commn — Report of the Forestry Commission

Rep For Commn NSW — Report of the Forestry Commission. New South Wales

Rep For Commn Sth Rhod — Report. Forestry Commission. Southern Rhodesia

Rep For Dep Br Guiana — Report. Forestry Department. British Guiana

Rep For Dep Br Solomon Isl — Report. Forestry Department. British Solomon Islands

Rep For Dep E Afr — Report. Forestry Department. East Africa Protectorate

Rep For Dep Ghana — Report. Forestry Department. Ghana

Rep For Dep Gold Cst — Report. Forestry Department. Gold Coast

Rep For Dep Hong Kong — Report of the Forestry Department. Hong Kong

Rep For Dep Nigeria — Report. Forestry Department. Nigeria

Rep For Dep NSW — Report of the Forestry Department. New South Wales

Rep For Dep Tasm — Report. Forestry Department. Tasmania

Rep For Div Ir Free St — Report. Forestry Division. Department of Lands. Irish Free State

Rep Forest Adm Ajmere Merwara — Report on the Forest Administration. Ajmere-Merwara

Rep Forest Adm Burma — Report on Forest Administration in Burma

Rep Forest Adm Cyprus — Report of the Forest Administration in Cyprus

Rep Forest Adm East Reg Nigeria — Report on the Forest Administration of the Eastern Region. Forestry Department. Nigeria

Rep Forest Adm Nth Reg Nigeria — Report on Forest Administration of the Northern Region. Forestry Department. Nigeria

Rep Forest Adm Orissa — Report on Forest Administration in Orissa

Rep Forest Adm Sierra Leone — Report on the Forest Administration. Colony of Sierra Leone

Rep Forest Adm Util Circle Burma — Report on Forest Administration in the Utilization Circle. Burma

Rep Forest Adm West Reg Nigeria — Report on the Forest Administration of the Western Region. Forestry Department. Nigeria

Rep Forest Brch Br Columb — Report of the Forest Branch Service of the Department of Lands. British Columbia

Rep Forest Dep Br Hond — Report. Forest Department. British Honduras

Rep Forest Dep Cape Good Hope — Report of the Forest Department. Cape of Good Hope

Rep Forest Dep Colony N Borneo — Report. Forest Department. Colony of North Borneo

Rep Forest Dep Colony Singapore — Report of the Forest Department. Colony of Singapore

Rep Forest Dep Fed Malaya — Report of the Forest Department. Federation of Malaya

Rep Forest Dep Fiji — Report. Forest Department. Fiji

Rep Forest Dep FMS — Report of the Forest Department. Federated Malay States

Rep Forest Dep Jamaica — Report. Forest Department. Jamaica

Rep Forest Dep Johore — Report. Forest Department. Johore

Rep Forest Dep Kenya — Report. Forest Department. Kenya

Rep Forest Dep Malay Un — Report of the Forest Department. Malayan Union

Rep Forest Dep Nth Rhod — Report. Forest Department. Northern Rhodesia

Rep Forest Dep Nyasald — Report of the Forest Department. Nyasaland

Rep Forest Dep Sarawak — Report of the Forest Department. Sarawak

Rep Forest Dep Straits Settl — Report of the Forest Department. Straits Settlements [*Kuala Lumpur*]

Rep Forest Dep (Tanganyika) — Report. Forest Department (Tanganyika Territory)

Rep Forest Dep Trin — Report. Forest Department. Trinidad and Tobago

Rep Forest Dep Uganda — Report of the Forest Department. Uganda

Rep Forest Dep Unit Prov Agra Oudh — Report of the Forest Department. United Provinces of Agra and Oudh

Rep Forest Dep Un S Afr — Report of the Forest Department. Union of South Africa

Rep Foresters US Dep Agric — Report of the Foresters. United States Department of Agriculture

Rep Forest Exp Sta Bur Pl Industr Gov Formosa — Report. Forest Experiment Station. Bureau of Plant Industry. Government of Formosa/Ringyo Shiken-Jo Hokoku. Shokusan-Kyoku

Rep Forest Exp Stn Hokkaido — Annual Report. Hokkaido Branch. Government Forest Experiment Station

Rep Forest Fish Game Commnr NY St — Report of the Forest, Fish, and Game Commissioner. New York State

Rep Forest Insect Dis Surv Can — Report of the Forest Insect and Disease Survey. Department of Agriculture. Canada

Rep Forest Insects Queb — Report on Forest Insects (Quebec)

Rep Forest Insect Surv Can — Report of the Forest Insect Survey. Canada

Rep Forest Prod Lab Madison — Report. Forest Products Laboratory (Madison, Wisconsin)

Rep Forest Prod Labs Can — Report. Forest Products Laboratories. Canada

Rep Forest Prod Res Bd — Report. Forest Products Research Board. Department of Scientific and Industrial Research [*London*]

Rep Forest Prod Res Inst — Report. Forest Products Research Institute/Ringyo Shidojo Kenkyu Hokoku

Rep Forest Prod Res Ore — Report. Forest Products Research. Oregon Forest Research Center

Rep Forest Res Cent Weyerhauser Timb Co — Report. Forest Research Center. Weyerhauser Timber Company

Rep Forest Res Coun Ga — Report. Forest Research Council. Georgia

Rep Forest Res Forest Sch Nigeria — Report on Forest Research and the Forest School. Department of Forest Research. Nigeria

Rep Forest Res Glendon Hall — Report. Forest Research Glendon Hall. Faculty of Forestry. Toronto University

Rep Forest Res Inst Bogor — Report of the Forest Research Institute (Bogor)

Rep Forest Res Inst FMS — Report of the Forest Research Institute. F.M.S

Rep Forest Res Inst NZ — Report. Forest Research Institute. New Zealand Forest Service

Rep Forest Res Lond — Report on Forest Research. Forestry Commission [*London*]

Rep Forest Res Ottawa — Report on Forest Research. Forest Research Division (Ottawa)

Rep Forest Resour Inventory Manitoba — Report. Forest Resources Inventory. Forest Service. Manitoba

Rep Forest Resour Inventory Ont — Report. Forest Resources Inventory. Department of Lands and Forests. Ontario

Rep Forest Res Stn Ilanoth — Report. Forest Research Station. Ilanoth

Rep Forests Commn Vict — Report. Forests Commission. Victoria

Rep Forests Dep Sudan — Report. Forests Department. Sudan

Rep Forests Dep West Aust — Report of the Forests Department. Western Australia

Rep Forest Serv Manitoba — Report of the Forest Service. Manitoba

Rep Forest Serv Palest — Report of the Forest Service. Palestine

Rep Forest Serv Qd — Report of the Forest Service. Queensland

Rep Forest Serv US — Report of the Forest Service. United States Department of Agriculture

Rep Forests Ethiopia — Report on the Forests of Ethiopia

Rep Forests Gdns Dep Maurit — Report of the Forests and Gardens Department. Mauritius

Rep Forest Wat Res Proj Pa — Report. Forest and Water Research Project. Department of Forests and Waters. Pennsylvania

Rep For Game Manage Res Inst — Reports. Forestry and Game Management Research Institute

Rep For Prod Res Inst (Bogor Indones) — Report. Forest Products Research Institute (Bogor, Indonesia)

Rep For Prod Res Inst (Hokkaido) — Report. Hokkaido Forest Products Research Institute (Asahikawa, Hokkaido)

Rep For Res — Report on Forest Research

Rep For Resour Reconn Surv Malaya — Report. Forest Resources Reconnaissance Survey of Malaya

Rep Forsknstift Skogsarb — Report. Redogorelse. Forskningsstiftelsen Skogsarbeten

Rep Forsvar Forsklnst — Report. Forsvarets Forskningsinstitutt

Rep Foyle Fish Commn — Report. Foyle Fisheries Commission [*Belfast*]

Rep FPM-X For Pest Manage Inst — Report FPM-X. Forest Pest Management Institute

Rep Frankenweld Fld Res Stn — Report of the Frankenweld Field Research Station. University of Witwatersrand

Rep Franz Theodore Stone Inst Hydrobiol — Report. Franz Theodore Stone Institute of Hydrobiology

Rep Franz Theodore Stone Lab Ohio St Univ — Report of the Franz Theodore Stone Laboratory. Ohio State University

Rep Freedom Hunger Campaign — Report. Freedom from Hunger Campaign. FAO

Rep Freshwat Biol Ass — Report. Freshwater Biological Assocation

Rep Friends Polar Inst — Report. Friends of the Polar Institute [*Cambridge*]

Rep Fruit Grow Ass Nova Scotia — Report of the Fruit Growers' Association of Nova Scotia

Rep Fruit Grow Ass Ont — Report of the Fruit Growers' Association of Ontario

Rep Fruit Res Stn Kodur — Report of the Fruit Research Station. Kodur

Rep Fruit Res Stn Saharanpur — Report. Fruit Research Station. Saharanpur

Rep Fruit Tree Exp Stn Akita — Report. Fruit Tree Experiment Station. Akita

Rep Fruit Veg Cann Quick Freez Res Ass — Report. Fruit and Vegetable Canning and Quick Freezing Research Association [*Chipping Campden*]

Rep Fruit Veg Preserv Res Stn — Report. Fruit and Vegetable Preservation Research Station [*Chipping Campden*]

Rep Fruit Veg Prod Res Comm Can — Report. Fruit and Vegetable Products Research Committee. Department of Agriculture. Canada

Rep Fuel Res Bd Lond — Report of the Fuel Research Board [*London*]

Rep Fuel Res Bd S Afr — Report. Fuel Research Board. South Africa

Rep Fuel Res Comm CSIR India — Report of the Fuel Research Committee. Council of Scientific and Industrial Research. India

Rep Fuel Res Inst — Report. Fuel Research Institute

Rep Fuel Res Inst Japan — Report. Fuel Research Institute. Department of Commerce and Industry. Japan

Rep Fuel Res Inst S Afr — Report. Fuel Research Institute of South Africa

Rep Fuels Lubr Lab Can — Report. Fuels and Lubricants Laboratory. Division of Mechanical Engineering. National Research Council. Canada

Rep Fukushima Prefect Inst Public Health — Report. Fukushima Prefectural Institute of Public Health

Rep Fukushima Prefect Public Health Inst — Report. Fukushima Prefectural Public Health Institute

Rep Fukushima Seric Exp Stn — Report. Fukushima Sericultural Experimental Station

Rep Fulmer Res Inst — Report. Fulmer Research Institute [*Stoke Poges*]

Rep Fungic Insectic Res Coord Serv — Report. Fungicide and Insecticide Research Co-ordination Service

Rep Fur Fms Can — Report on Fur Farms. Canada

Rep Furuncul Comm Scotl — Report. Furunculosis Committee. Scotland

Rep Fys Lab I Tek Hoejsk (Lyngby) — Report. Fysisk Laboratorium I. Danmarks Tekniske Hoejskole (Lyngby)

REPGA — Reprographics

Rep Ga Agric Exp Stn — Report of the Georgia Agricultural Experiment Station

Rep Ga Dep Agric — Report of the Georgia Department of Agriculture

Rep Ga Dep Game Fish — Report. Georgia Department of Game and Fish

Rep GA For Res Coun — Report. Georgia Forest Research Council

Rep Game Commnr Sask — Report on the Game Commissioner. Saskatchewan

Rep Game Conserv Bd Br Columb — Report of the Game Conservation Board of the Province of British Columbia

Rep Game Dep Fed Malaya — Report of the Game Department. Federation of Malaya

Rep Game Dep FMS — Report on the Game Department. Federated Malay States

Rep Game Dep Kenya — Report. Game Department. Colony and Protectorate of Kenya

Rep Game Dep Malay Un — Report on the Game Department. Malayan Union

Rep Game Dep Tanganyika — Report of the Game Department. Tanganyika

Rep Game Preserv Dep Tanganyika — Report. Game Preservation Department. Tanganyika Territory

Rep Game Preserv W Beng — Report on Game Preservation in West Bengal

Rep Game Tsetse Control Dep Nth Rhod — Report. Game and Tsetse Control Department. Northern Rhodesia

Rep Game Ward E Afr — Report of the Game Warden. East African Protectorate

Rep Gas Cylind Res Comm — Report of the Gas Cylinders Research Committee. Department of Scientific and Industrial Research [*London*]

Rep Gas Dyn Sect Div Mech Engng Can — Report. Gas Dynamics Section. Division of Mechanical Engineering. National Research Council. Canada

Rep Gas Explos Comm Br Ass — Report. Gaseous Explosions Committee. British Association [*London*]

Rep Gas Res Bd — Report. Gas Research Board [*London*]

Rep Ga St Coll Agric — Report. Georgia State College of Agriculture [*Atlanta*]

Rep Ga St Engng Exp Stn — Report. Georgia State Engineering Experiment Station [*Atlanta*]

Rep Gen Exp Fms Dep Agric Tanganyika — Report from the General Experimental Farms. Department of Agriculture. Tanganyika

Rep Gen Fish Counc Mediterr — Report. General Fisheries Council for the Mediterranean

Rep Gen Hlth Servs Bd Nth Ire — Report. General Health Services Board. Northern Ireland

Rep Gen Mgr St Coal Mines Vict — Report. General Manager of State Coal Mines. Victoria [*Melbourne*]

Rep Gen Res Comm Monmouth S Wales Coal Own Ass — Report. General Research Committee. Monmouthshire and South Wales Coal Owners' Association

Rep Gen Surv Somalild — Report on the General Survey. Somaliland

Rep Geod Inst (Den) — Report. Geodetic Institute (Denmark)

Rep Geod Surv Can — Report of the Geodetic Survey of Canada

Rep Geol Dep Sierra Leone — Report. Geological Department. Sierra Leone

Rep Geol Dep Uganda — Report. Geological Department. Uganda Protectorate

Rep Geol Div Sask — Report. Geology Division. Department of Mineral Resources. Saskatchewan

Rep Geol Div Tanganyika — Report of the Geological Division. Tanganyika Territory

Rep Geol FMS — Report of the Geologist. Federated Malay States

Rep Geol Miner Explor (Seoul) — Report of Geological and Mineral Exploration (Seoul)

Rep Geol Min Explor — Report of Geological and Mineral Exploration

Rep Geol Min Surv Iran — Report. Geological and Mining Survey of Iran

Rep Geol Surv Ala — Report. Geological Survey of Alabama and State Oil Gas Board

Rep Geol Surv Anglo Egypt Sudan — Report. Geological Survey of the Anglo-Egyptian Sudan

Rep Geol Surv Bd — Report of the Geological Survey Board. Department of Scientific and Industrial Research [London]

Rep Geol Surv Bd Rep Dir — Report of the Geological Survey Board with the Report of the Director [London]

Rep Geol Surv Bechuanald — Report. Geological Survey. Bechuanaland

Rep Geol Surv Borneo Reg Malays — Report. Geological Survey of the Borneo Region, Malaysia

Rep Geol Surv Brch Dep Mines Can — Report. Geological Survey Branch. Department of Mines. Canada

Rep Geol Surv Can — Report. Geological Survey of Canada

Rep Geol Surv Colo — Report of the Geological Survey of Colorado

Rep Geol Surv Dep Br Borneo — Report of the Geological Survey Department. British Territories in Borneo

Rep Geol Surv Dep Br Guiana — Report. Geological Survey Department. British Guiana

Rep Geol Surv Dep Cyprus — Report. Geological Survey Department. Cyprus

Rep Geol Surv Dep Fed Malaya — Report. Geological Survey Department. Federation of Malaya

Rep Geol Surv Dep FMS — Report. Geological Survey Department. Federated Malay States

Rep Geol Surv Dep (Guyana) — Report. Geological Survey Department (Guyana)

Rep Geol Surv Dep Jamaica — Report of the Geological Survey Department. Jamaica

Rep Geol Surv Dep Malay Un — Report. Geological Survey Department. Malayan Union

Rep Geol Surv Dep Nth Rhod — Report of the Geological Survey Department. Northern Rhodesia

Rep Geol Surv Dep Nyasald — Report. Geological Survey Department. Nyasaland

Rep Geol Surv Dep Sudan — Report. Geological Survey Department. Ministry of Mineral Resources. Republic of the Sudan

Rep Geol Surv Dep Tanganyika — Report. Geological Survey Department. Tanganyika

Rep Geol Surv Dep Uganda — Report. Geological Survey Department. Uganda Protectorate

Rep Geol Surv Dep (Zambia) — Report. Geological Survey Department (Zambia)

Rep Geol Surv East Malays — Report. Geological Survey of East Malaysia

Rep Geol Surv Fiji — Report. Geological Survey of Fiji

Rep Geol Surv Ghana — Report of the Geological Survey of Ghana

Rep Geol Surv Gold Cst — Report of the Geological Survey of the Gold Coast

Rep Geol Surv Greenl — Report. Geological Survey of Greenland

Rep Geol Surv Hokkaido — Report. Geological Survey of Hokkaido

Rep Geol Surv Iran — Report. Geological Survey of Iran

Rep Geol Surv Japan — Report of the Geological Survey of Japan

Rep Geol Surv Jpn — Report. Geological Survey of Japan

Rep Geol Surv Kenya — Report. Geological Survey of Kenya

Rep Geol Surv Kwantung Kwangsi — Report. Geological Survey of Kwangtung and Kwangsi [Canton]

Rep Geol Surv Ky — Report of the Geological Survey of Kentucky

Rep Geol Surv Malays — Report. Geological Survey of Malaysia

Rep Geol Surv Mines Dep (Uganda) — Report. Geological Survey and Mines Department (Uganda)

Rep Geol Surv Mo — Report of the Geological Survey of Missouri

Rep Geol Surv Mus Lond — Report on the Geological Survey and Museum, the Science Museum, and the work of the Solar Physics Committee [London]

Rep Geol Surv Newfoundld — Report of the Geological Survey of Newfoundland

Rep Geol Surv Nigeria — Report. Geological Survey. Nigeria

Rep Geol Surv NSW — Report. Geological Survey of New South Wales

Rep Geol Surv NZ — Report. Geological Survey of New Zealand

Rep Geol Surv Papua New Guinea — Report. Geological Survey of Papua, New Guinea

Rep Geol Surv Prov Newfoundld — Report. Geological Survey. Province of Newfoundland

Rep Geol Surv Qd — Report. Geological Survey of Queensland

Rep Geol Surv Queensl — Report. Geological Survey of Queensland

Rep Geol Surv S Aust — Report. Geological Survey of South Australia

Rep Geol Surv S Aust A Rep — Report. Geological Survey. South Australia. Annual Report

Rep Geol Surv Sierra Leone — Report of the Geological Survey of Sierra Leone

Rep Geol Surv Somalild — Report of the Geological Survey. Somaliland Protectorate

Rep Geol Surv Sth Rhod — Report of the Geological Survey of Southern Rhodesia

Rep Geol Surv Tanganyika — Report. Geological Survey of Tanganyika Territory

Rep Geol Surv Tasm — Report. Geological Survey of Tasmania

Rep Geol Surv Transv — Report of the Geological Survey of the Transvaal

Rep Geol Surv Uganda — Report. Geological Survey of Uganda

Rep Geol Surv Un S Afr — Report of the Geological Survey of the Union of South Africa

Rep Geol Surv Vic — Report. Geological Survey of Victoria

Rep Geol Surv Vict — Report. Geological Survey of Victoria

Rep Geol Surv West Aust — Report. Geological Survey of Western Australia

Rep Geol Surv West Aust — Western Australia. Geological Survey. Report

Rep Geol Surv W Va — Report of the Geological Survey of West Virginia

Rep Geol Surv Zambia — Report. Geological Survey of Zambia

Rep Geophys Geochem Explor Geol Surv Korea — Report of Geophysical and Geochemical Exploration. Geological Survey of Korea

Rep Geophys Obs Christchurch — Report. Geophysical Observatory. Christchurch

Rep Geophys Res Stn Kyoto Univ — Reports. Geophysical Research Station. Kyoto University

Rep Geosci Miner Resour — Report on Geoscience and Mineral Resources

Rep Geosci Miner Resour Korea Inst Energy Resour — Report on Geoscience and Mineral Resources. Korea Institute of Energyand Resources

Rep Geosci Miner Resour Korea Res Inst Geosci Miner Resour — Report on Geoscience and Mineral Resources. Korea Research Institute ofGeoscience and Mineral Resources

Rep Germ — Reptertorium Germanicum

Rep Gezira Agric Res Serv Anglo Egypt Sudan — Report of the Gezira Agricultural Research Service. Anglo-Egyptian Sudan

Rep Gezira Bd Sudan — Report. Gezira Board. Sudan

Rep Ghana Geol Surv — Report. Ghana Geological Survey

Rep Ghana Met Serv — Report. Ghana Meteorological Service

Rep Gifu Prefect Inst Public Health — Report. Gifu Pefectural Institute of Public Health

Rep Giza Meml Ophthal Lab — Report of the Giza Memorial Ophthalmic Laboratory [Cairo]

Rep Glam River Bd — Report. Glamorgan River Board [Bridgend]

Rep Glasg W Scotl Tech Coll — Report. Glasgow and West of Scotland Technical College

Rep Glasshouse Crops Res Inst — Report. Glasshouse Crops Research Institute

Rep Glass Res Inst Tohoku Univ — Report. Glass Research Institute. Tohoku University

Rep Gleadthorpe Exp Husb Fm — Report. Gleadthorpe Experimental Husbandry Farm

Rep Godlee Obs — Report of the Godlee Observatory [Manchester]

Rep Gorgas Meml Lab — Report. Gorgas Memorial Laboratory

Rep Gov Chem Ind Res Inst (Tokyo) — Reports. Government Chemical Industrial Research Institute (Tokyo)

Rep Gov Chem Lab (West Aust) — Report. Government Chemical Laboratories (Western Australia)

Rep Gov Forest Exp Sta — Report. Government Forest Experiment Station/Ringyo Shiken Syuho

Rep Gov For Exp Stn — Report. Government Forest Experiment Station

Rep Gov Ind Dev Lab (Hokkaido) — Reports. Government Industrial Development Laboratory (Hokkaido)

Rep Gov Ind Res Inst (Kyushu) — Reports. Government Industrial Research Institute (Kyushu)

Rep Gov Ind Res Inst (Nagoya) — Reports. Government Industrial Research Institute (Nagoya)

Rep Gov Ind Res Inst (Osaka) — Reports. Government Industrial Research Institute (Osaka)

Rep Gov Ind Res Inst (Shikoku) — Reports. Government Industrial Research Institute (Shikoku)

Rep Gov Ind Res Inst (Tohoku) — Reports. Government Industrial Research Institute (Tohoku)

Rep Gov Mech Lab Tokyo — Report. Government Mechanical Laboratory. Tokyo

Rep Gov Mineral Anal Chem (West Aust) — Report. Government Mineralogist, Analyst, and Chemist (Western Australia)

Rep Gov Sugar Exp Sta — Report. Government Sugar Experiment Station/Taiwan Sotokufu Togyo Shikenjo Hokoku

Rep Gov Sugar Exp Stn (Tainan Formosa) — Report. Government Sugar Experiment Station (Tainan, Formosa)

Rep Govt Astr Durban — Report of the Government Astronomer. Durban Observatory

Rep Govt Biol Cape Good Hope — Report of the Government Biologist. Cape of Good Hope

Rep Govt Bot Gdns Pks Madras — Report of the Government Botanic Gardens and Parks. Madras

Rep Govt Botl Gdns Saharanpur — Report of the Government Botanical Gardens. Saharanpur [Allahabad]

Rep Govt Bur Microbiol NSW — Report of the Government Bureau of Microbiology. New South Wales

Rep Govt Ceylon Pearl Oyster Fish Gulf Manaar — Report to the Government of Ceylon on the Pearl Oyster Fisheries of the Gulf of Manaar

Rep Govt Chem Ind Res Inst Tokyo — Report of the Government Chemical and Industrial Research Institute (Tokyo)

Rep Govt Chem Jamaica — Report. Government Chemist. Jamaica

Rep Govt Chem Lond — Report of the Government Chemist (London)

Rep Govt Chem Sudan — Report of the Government Chemist. Sudan

Rep Govt Chem Tanganyika — Report of the Government Chemist. Tanganyika

Rep Govt Cinchona Plantn Fact Beng — Report of the Government Cinchona Plantation and Factory in Bengal

Rep Govt Engr Swazild — Report of the Government Engineer. Swaziland

Rep Govt Ent Cape Good Hope — Report of the Government Entomologist. Cape of Good Hope

Rep Govt Ent Cyprus — Report of the Government Entomologist. Cyprus

Rep Govt Ent Jamaica — Report of the Government Entomologist. Jamaica

Rep Govt Ent Natal — Report of the Government Entomologist. Natal

Rep Govt Geol S Aust — Report of the Government Geologist. South Australia

Rep Govt Geol Swazild — Report of the Government Geologist. Swaziland

Rep Govt Geol Trin — Report of the Government Geologist. Trinidad

Rep Govt Hort Gdns Lucknow — Report on the Government Horticultural Gardens. Lucknow

Rep Govt Ind Res Inst Nagoya — Report of Government Industrial Research Institute (Nagoya)

Rep Govt Ind Res Inst Tokyo — Report of the Government Industrial Research Institute (Tokyo)

Rep Govt Insp Explos Nth Ire — Report. Government Inspectors of Explosives. Northern Ireland

Rep Govt Inst Vet Research (Fusan Chosen) — Report. Government Institute for Veterinary Research (Fusan, Chosen)

Rep Govt Lab Supt Agric Leeward Isl — Report of the Government Laboratory and Superintendent of Agriculture of the Leeward Islands

Rep Govt Mech Lab (Tokyo) — Report. Government Mechanical Laboratory (Tokyo)

Rep Govt Med Sch Rangoon — Report. Government Medical School. Rangoon

Rep Govt Min Engr Un S Afr — Report of the Government Mining Engineer. Union of South Africa

Rep Govt Miner Analyst Chem West Aust — Report of the Government Mineralogist, Analyst, and Chemist. Chemical Branch. Department of Mines. Western Australia

Rep Govt Publ Hlth Dep Br Guiana — Report of the Government Public Health Department. British Guiana

Rep Govt Res Inst Dep Agric Formosa — Report. Government Research Institute. Department of Agriculture. Formosa

Rep Govt Sug Exp Stn Taiwan — Report of the Government Sugar Experiment Station. Taiwan

Rep Govt Surv Mines Dep Swazild — Report of the Government Survey and Mines Department. Swaziland

Rep Govt Vet Bact Un S Afr — Report of the Government Veterinary Bacteriologist. Union of South Africa

Rep Govt Vet Offr Hong Kong — Report of the Government Veterinary Officer. Hong Kong

Rep Govt Vet Surg Ceylon — Report of the Government Veterinary Surgeon. Ceylon

Rep Grain Pests Comm R Soc — Report of the Grain Pests Committee of the Royal Society

Rep Grain Res Lab Winnipeg — Report. Grain Research Laboratory (Winnipeg)

Rep Grain Stor Dep Tanganyika — Report of the Grain Storage Department. Tanganyika

Rep Grassld Improv Stn — Report of the Grassland Improvement Station [*Hurley*]

Rep Grassld Res Inst — Report of the Grassland Research Institute [*Hurley*]

Rep Grassld Res Stn Kitale — Report of the Grassland Research Station. Kitale

Rep Grasslds Agric Res Stn Marandellas — Report. Grasslands Agricultural Research Station. Marandellas. Southern Rhodesia

Rep Gr Brit Agr Res Counc — Report. Great Britain Agricultural Research Council

Rep Gr Brit Colon Pestic Res Unit CPRU/Porton — Report. Great Britain Colonial Pesticides Research Unit. CPRU/Porton

Rep Greeld Exped Univ Mich — Report of the Greenland Expeditions of the University of Michigan, 1926-31

Rep Greenkeep Res NZ Inst Turf Cult Greenkeep Res Comm — Report on Greenkeeping Research. New Zealand Institute for TurfCulture. Greenkeeping Research Committee

Rep Grenfell Ass — Report. Grenfell Association [*London*]

Rep Greshams Sch Nat Hist Soc — Report of the Gresham's School Natural History Society

Rep Group Adv Psychiatry — Report. Group for the Advancement of Psychiatry

Rep Gt Barrier Reef Comm — Report of the Great Barrier Reef Committee

Rep Gt Brit Trop Pestic Res Unit TPRU/Porton — Report. Great Britain Tropical Pesticides Research Unit. TPRU/Porton

Rep Gt Lakes Fishery Commn — Report. Great Lakes Fishery Commission

Rep Gt Ouse River Bd — Report. Great Ouse River Board [*Cambridge*]

Rep Guam Agric Exp Stn — Report of the Guam Agricultural Experiment Station

Rep Gudiyattam SugCane Res Stn — Report. Gudiyattam Sugarcane Research Station [*Madras*]

Rep Guide Dep Agric Univ Camb — Report and Guide. Department of Agriculture. University of Cambridge

Rep Gulf St Mar Fish Commn — Report. Gulf States Marine Fisheries Commission [*New Orleans*]

Rep Gulval Exp Stn — Report. Gulval Experimental Station. Penzance

REPh — Revue de l'Enseignement Philosophique

Rep Haffkine Inst — Report of the Haffkine Institute [*Bombay*]

Rep Hagari Agric Res Stn — Report. Hagari Agricultural Research Station

Rep Haileybury Imp Serv Coll Nat Hist Soc — Report. Haileybury and Imperial Service College Natural History Society [*Hertford*]

Rep Hamps River Bd — Report. Hampshire River Board [*Winchester*]

Rep Hampstead Scient Soc — Report of the Hampstead Scientific Society [*London*]

Rep Hannah Dairy Res Inst — Report. Hannah Dairy Research Institute [*Glasgow*]

Rep Harcourt Butler Inst Publ Hlth — Report of the Harcourt Butler Institute of Public Health [*Rangoon*]

Rep Harper Adams Agric Coll — Report. Harper Adams Agricultural College [*Newport*]

Rep Harper Adams Coll Pig Feed Exp Stn — Report. Harper Adams College Pig Feeding Experiment Station

Rep Hartford Dep Engng — Report of the Hartford Department of Engineering

Rep Harv Seism Stn — Report of the Harvard Seismographic Station

Rep Haslemere Microsc Nat Hist Soc — Report of the Haslemere Microscope and Natural History Society

Rep Hastings St Leonards Nat Hist Soc — Report of the Hastings and St. Leonards Natural History Society

Rep Hatch Agric Exp Stn — Report of the Hatch Agricultural Experiment Station [*Amherst, Massachusetts*]

Rep Hawaii Agric Exp Stn — Report of the Hawaii Agricultural Experiment Station

Rep Hawaiian Sug Plrs Ass Exp Stn — Report. Hawaiian Sugar Planters' Association Experiment Station

Rep Hawaiian Sug Technol — Report. Hawaiian Sugar Technologists

Rep Hawaiian Volc Obs — Report of the Hawaiian Volcano Observatory

Rep Hawaii Div Water Land Dev — Report. Hawaii. Division of Water and Land Development

Rep Hawaii Sugar Technol — Reports. Hawaiian Sugar Technologists

Rep Hawaii Univ Mar Lab — Report. Hawaii University Marine Laboratory

Rep Hayling Mosq Control — Report. Hayling Mosquito Control

Rep Health Soc Subj (Lond) — Reports. Health and Social Subjects (London)

Rep Heat Div Natn Engng Lab — Report. Heat Division. National Engineering Laboratory

Rep Heat Vent Res Ass — Report. Heating and Ventilating Research Association

Rep Heat Vent Res Coun — Report. Heating and Ventilating Research Council

Rep Hell Agric Res Stn — Report of the Hellenic Agricultural Research Station

Rep Helsinki Univ Technol Radio Lab — Report. Helsinki University of Technology. Radio Laboratory

Rep Henderson Res Stn — Report. Henderson Research Station. Mazoe

Rep Henry Lester Inst Med Res — Report. Henry Lester Institute of Medical Research

Rep Henry Phipps Inst Study Treat Prev Tuberc — Report of the Henry Phipps Institute for the Study, Treatment, and Prevention of Tuberculosis

Rep Herbic Comm East Sect Natn Weed Comm Ottawa — Report. Herbicide Committee. Eastern Section. National Weed Committee (Ottawa)

Rep Herring Ind Bd Scotl — Report. Herring Industry Board. Scotland

Rep High Alt Obsn Univ Colo — Report of the High Altitude Observation of the University of Colorado

Rep Highl Isl Med Serv Bd — Report. Highlands and Islands Medical Service Board

Rep Hill Fmg Res Org — Report. Hill Farming Research Organization

Rep Hillsborough Agric Res Inst — Report. Hillsborough Agricultural Research Institute

Rep Himeji Inst Technol — Reports. Himeji Institute of Technology

Rep Himeji Tech Coll — Reports. Himeji Technical College

Rep Hiroshima Prefect Forest Exp Stn — Report. Hiroshima Prefectural Forest Experiment Station

Rep Hlth Army — Report on the Health of the Army [*London*]

Rep Hlth Army India — Report on the Health of the Army in India

Rep Hlth Brch Br Columb — Report. Health Branch. Department of Health and Welfare. British Columbia

Rep Hlth Dep Balt — Report. Health Department. Baltimore

Rep Hlth Dep Mesopot — Report. Health Department. Mesopotamia

Rep Hlth Dep Zanzibar — Report of the Health Department. Zanzibar

Rep Hlth Gibraltar — Report on the Health of Gibraltar

Rep Hlth Maltese Isl — Report on the Health of the Maltese Islands

Rep Hlth Med Servs — Report. Health and Medical Services. Queensland

Rep Hlth Navy — Report on the Health of the Navy

Rep Hlth RAF — Report on the Health of the Royal Air Force [*London*]

Rep Hlth Serv Philipp Isl — Report of the Health Service of the Philippine Islands

Rep Hlth Serv St Lucia — Report on the Health Service. St. Lucia

Rep HM Astr Cape Good Hope — Report of H.M. Astronomer at the Cape of Good Hope. Royal Observatory

Rep HM Chf Insp Mines — Report of H.M. Chief Inspector of Mines [*London*]

Rep HM Elect Insp Mines — Report of H.M. Electrical Inspector of Mines

Rep HM Insps Mines Quarr N East Div — Report. H.M. Inspectors of Mines and Quarries. North Eastern Division

Rep HM Insps Mines Quarr Northumb Cumberl Div — Report. H.M. Inspectors of Mines and Quarries. Northumberland and Cumberland Division

Rep HM Insps Mines Quarr N West Div — Report. H.M. Inspectors of Mines and Quarries. North Western Division

Rep HM Insps Mines Quarr Scot Div — Report. H.M. Inspectors of Mines and Quarries. Scottish Division

Rep HM Insps Mines Quarr S West Div — Report. H.M. Inspectors of Mines and Quarries. South Western Division

Rep HM Insps Mines Quarr W Midl Sth Div — Report. H.M. Inspectors of Mines and Quarries. West Midland and Southern Division

Rep HM Princ Elect Insp Mines — Report of H.M. Principal Electrical Inspector of Mines [*London*]

Rep Hokkaido Branch Gov Forest Exp Sta — Report. Hokkaido Branch. Government Forest Experiment Station/Ringyo Shikenjo Hokkaido Shijo Gyomu Hokoku

Rep Hokkaido Fish Hatchery — Reports. Hokkaido Fish Hatchery

Rep Hokkaido For Prod Res Inst — Report. Hokkaido Forest Products Research Institute

Rep Hokkaido Ind Res Inst — Reports. Hokkaido Industrial Research Institute

Rep Hokkaido Ind Technol Cent — Report. Hokkaido Industrial Technology Center

Rep Hokkaido Inst Environ Sci — Report of Hokkaido Institute of Environmental Sciences

Rep Hokkaido Inst Public Health — Report. Hokkaido Institute of Public Health

Rep Hokkaido Nat Agr Exp Sta — Report. Hokkaido National Agricultural Experiment Station

Rep Hokkaido Natn Agric Exp Stn — Report. Hokkaido National Agricultural Experiment Station

Rep Hokkaido Pref Agr Exp Sta — Report. Hokkaido Prefectural Agricultural Experiment Station

Rep Hokkaido Prefect Agric Exp Stn — Report. Hokkaido Prefectural Agricultural Experiment Stations

Rep Hokkaido Res Inst Environ Pollut — Report. Hokkaido Research Institute for Environmental Pollution

Rep Hokkaido Stn Govt Forest Exp Stn — Report. Hokkaido Station. Government Forest Experiment Station

Rep Hon Companys Bot Gard Calcutta — Report. Honourable Company's Botanic Gardens. Calcutta Royal Botanic Garden

Rep Hong Kong Obs — Report. Hong Kong Observatory

Rep Hood River Brch Exp Stn — Report of the Hood River Branch Experiment Station

Rep Horace Lamb Inst Oceanogr — Report. Horace Lamb Institute of Oceanography

Rep Hormel Inst Univ Minn — Report. Hormel Institute. University of Minnesota

Rep Hort Exp Sta (Ontario) — Report. Horticultural Experiment Station (Ontario)

Rep Hort Exp Stn Prod Lab (Vineland) — Report. Horticultural Experiment Station and Products Laboratory (Vineland Station)

Rep Hort Soc NY — Report of the Horticultural Society of New York

Rep Hort Socs Ont — Report of the Horticultural Societies. Ontario Department of Agriculture

Rep Houldsworth Sch Appl Sci — Report. Houldsworth School of Applied Science. University of Leeds

Rep H Phipps Inst Tuberc — Report. Henry Phipps Institute for the Study, Treatment, and Prevention of Tuberculosis

Rep Hull E Yorks River Bd — Report. Hull and East Yorkshire River Board

Rep Humane Traps Advis Comm — Report of the Humane Traps Advisory Committee. Ministry of Agriculture, Fisheries, and Food

Rep Hung Acad Sci Cent Res Inst Phys — Report. Hungarian Academy of Sciences. Central Research Institute for Physics. Koezponti Fizikai Kutato Intezet

Rep Hung Agric Exp Stn — Reports. Hungarian Agricultural Experiment Station

Rep Hung Biol Stn Tihany — Reports. Hungarian Biological Station at Tihany

Rep Huntingdon Fauna Flora Soc — Report. Huntingdonshire Fauna and Flora Society

Rep Hybrid Corn Ind Res Conf — Report. Hybrid Corn Industry. Research Conference

Rep Hydrobiol Res Unit Univ Khartoum — Report of the Hydrobiological Research Unit. University of Khartoum

Rep Hydrodyn Lab Univ Chicago — Report. Hydrodynamics Laboratory. Department of Meteorology. University of Chicago

Rep Hydro Elect Commn Tasm — Report. Hydro-Electric Commission. Tasmania

Rep Hydro Elect Pwr Commn Prov Ont — Report. Hydro-Electric Power Commission of the Province of Ontario

Rep Hydro Elect Surv India — Report. Hydro-Electric Survey of India

Rep Hydrogr Obsns Fusan — Report of Hydrographical Observations. Fishery Experimental Station. Fusan, Chosen

Rep Hyg Lab Shiga Prefect — Report. Hygiene Laboratory of Shiga Prefecture

Rep Hyogo Prefect For Exp Stn — Report. Hyogo Prefectural Forest Experiment Station

Rep Hyogo Prefect Inst Environ Sci — Report. Hyogo Prefectural Institute of Environmental Science

R Epi — Revue Epigraphique

Rep IA St Apiar — Report of Iowa State Apiarist

Rep Ice Obsg Forecast Progm Wash — Report of the Ice Observing and Forecasting Program. Hydrographic Office (Washington)

Rep IChTJ Ser A — Reporty IChTJ [*Instytut Chemii i Techniki Jadrowej*]. Seria A

Rep IChTJ Ser B — Reporty IChTJ [*Instytut Chemii i Techniki Jadrowej*]. Seria B

Rep ICJ — International Court of Justice. Reports of Judgements, Advisory Opinions, and Orders

Rep ICTIS/ER IEA Coal Res — Report ICTIS/ER [*IEA Coal Research Technical Information Service/Executive Review*] IEA Coal Research

Rep ICTIS/TR IEA Coal Res — Report ICTIS/TR [*IEA Coal Research Technical Information Service/Technical Report*]. IEA Coal Research

Rep Idaho Agric Exp Stn — Report. Idaho Agricultural Experiment Station

Rep Idaho Bur Mines Geol — Report of the Idaho Bureau of Mines and Geology

Rep Idaho Dep Agric — Report of the Idaho Department of Agriculture

Rep Idaho Fish Game Dep — Report. Idaho Fish and Game Department

REpigr — Revue Epigraphique

Rep IGY Met Data Cent — Report. I.G.Y. (International Geophysical Year) Meteorological Data Centre

Rep Ill Agric Exp Stn — Report of the Illinois Agricultural Experiment Station

Rep Ill Beekeep Ass — Report. Illinois Beekeeping Association

Rep Ill Conserv Dep — Report. Illinois Conservation Department

Rep Ill Dep Agric — Report of the Illinois Department of Agriculture

Rep Ill Rivers Lakes Commn — Report of the Illinois Rivers and Lakes Commission

Rep Ill Soc Engrs Surv — Report. Illinois Society of Engineers and Surveyors

Rep Ill St Ent — Report of the Illinois State Entomologist

Rep Imp Agric Bur — Report. Imperial Agricultural Bureau

Rep Imp Bact Muktesar — Report of the Imperial Bacteriologist (Muktesar)

Rep Imp Bur Fish Scient Invest Tokyo — Report. Imperial Bureau of Fisheries Scientific Investigations (Tokyo)

Rep Imp Bur Fish Sci Invest — Report. Imperial Bureau of Fisheries. Scientific Investigation

Rep Imp Bur Soil Sci Rothamsted — Report. Imperial Bureau of Soil Science (Rothamsted)

Rep Imp Cancer Res Fund — Report. Imperial Cancer Research Fund

Rep Imp Coll Sci Technol Lond — Report. Imperial College of Science and Technology (London)

Rep Imp Coll Trop Agric Trin — Report. Imperial College of Tropical Agriculture (St. Augustine, Trinidad)

Rep Imp Coun Agric Res — Report. Imperial Council of Agricultural Research

Rep Imp Dairy Dep India — Report. Imperial Dairy Department. India

Rep Imp Dep Agric India — Report of the Imperial Department of Agriculture. India

Rep Imp Ent Conf — Report on the Imperial Entomological Conference

Rep Imp For Inst Univ Oxf — Report. Imperial Forestry Institute. University of Oxford

Rep Imp Fuel Res Inst (Jpn) — Reports. Imperial Fuel Research Institute (Japan)

Rep Imp Ind Lab Osaka — Report. Imperial Industrial Laboratory (Osaka)

Rep Imp Inst Lond — Report of the Imperial Institute (London)

Rep Imp Inst Vet Res Muktesar — Report of the Imperial Institute of Veterinary Research. Muktesar

Rep Imp Jap Geod Commn — Report. Imperial Japanese Geodetic Commission

Rep Imp Miner Resour Bur — Report. Imperial Mineral Resources Bureau

Rep Imp Mycol Conf — Report. Imperial Mycological Conference

Rep Imp Res Bur Delhi — Report of the Imperial Research Bureau (Delhi)

Rep Imp Vet Conf — Report of the Imperial Veterinary Conference

Rep Imp Vet Res Inst Muktesar — Report. Imperial Veterinary Research Institute. Muktesar and Izatnagar

Rep Imp Zootech Exp Stn Chiba Shi — Report. Imperial Zootechnical Experiment Station (Chiba-Shi)

Rep Ind Coun Agric Res — Report. Indian Council of Agricultural Research

Rep Ind Educ Res Cent Chungnam Natl Univ — Report. Industrial Education Research Center. Chungnam National University

Rep Ind Fatigue Res Bd — Report. Industrial Fatigue Research Board. Scientific and Industrial Research Department

Rep Ind Fatigue Res Bd A Rep — Report. Industrial Fatigue Research Board. Annual Report. Scientific and Industrial Research Department

Rep Ind Hlth Res Bd — Report. Industrial Health Research Board. Scientific and Industrial Research Department

Rep Ind Hlth Res Bd A Rep — Report. Industrial Health Research Board. Annual Report. Scientific and Industrial Research Department

Rep Ind Hlth Res Bo — Report. Industrial Health Research Board

Rep India Min Rur Dev — Report. India Ministry of Rural Development

Rep Indiana Agric Exp Stn — Report of the Indiana Agricultural Experiment Station

Rep Indiana Bd For — Report of the Indiana Board of Forestry

Rep Indiana Dep Conserv — Report of the Indiana Department of Conservation

Rep Indiana Dep Geol Nat Resour — Report of the Indiana Department of Geology and Natural Resources

Rep Indiana Dep Mines Min — Report. Indiana Department of Mines and Mining

Rep Indian Agric Progm — Report. Indian Agricultural Program

Rep Indian Ass Cult Sci — Report of the Indian Association for the Cultivation of Science

Rep Indian Cent Cott Comm — Report. Indian Central Cotton Committee

Rep Indian Cent Cott Comm — Reprints. Indian Central Cotton Committee [*Bombay*]

Rep Indian Cent Jute Comm — Report. Indian Central Jute Committee

Rep Indian Cent SugCane Comm — Report. Indian Central Sugarcane Committee

Rep Indian Chem Soc — Report. Indian Chemical Society

Rep Indian Coff Bd — Report. Indian Coffee Board

Rep Indian Coun Agric Res — Report. Indian Council of Agricultural Research

Rep Indian Dairy Dep — Report of the Indian Dairy Department

Rep Indian Ecol Soc — Report. Indian Ecological Society

Rep Indian Forest Coll — Report of the Indian Forest College. Dehra Dun

Rep Indian Inst Sug Technol — Report. Indian Institute of Sugar Technology

Rep Indian Lac Ass Res — Report of the Indian Lac Association for Research

Rep Indian Lac Cess Comm — Report. Indian Lac Cess Committee

Rep Indian Lac Res Inst — Report of the Indian Lac Research Institute

Rep Indian Min Fed — Report. Indian Mining Federation

Rep Indian Mus Nat Hist Sect — Report of the Indian Museum. Natural History Section

Rep Indian Tea Ass Wk Ross Inst Trop Med — Report to the Indian Tea Association on the Work of the Ross Institute of Tropical Medicine in India

Rep Indian Vet Res Inst Muktesar Izatnager — Report. Indian Veterinary Research Institute Muktesar and Izatnager

Rep Ind Miner Surv Tokyo — Report of the Industrial Mineral Survey (Tokyo)

Rep Ind Orthop Soc — Report. Industrial Orthopaedic Society

Rep Ind Res Advis Coun Hawaii — Report of the Industrial Research Advisory Council. Hawaii

Rep Ind Res Bur India — Report. Industrial Research Bureau. India

Rep Ind Res Cent Shiga Prefect — Reports. Industrial Research Center. Shiga Prefecture

Rep Ind Res Coun Eire — Report. Industrial Research Council. Eire

Rep Ind Res Inst Aichi Prefect Gov — Reports. Industrial Research Institute. Aichi Prefectural Government

Rep Ind Res Inst Hyogo Prefect — Reports. Industrial Research Institute. Hyogo Prefecture

Rep Ind Res Inst Ishikawa — Report. Industrial Research Institute of Ishikawa

Rep Ind Res Inst Kanagawa Prefect — Report. Industrial Research Institute of Kanagawa Prefecture

Rep Ind Res Inst Kumamoto Prefect — Report. Industrial Research Institute. Kumamoto Prefecture

Rep Ind Res Inst Nagano Technol Dev Cent Nagano — Reports. Industrial Research Institute of Nagano and TechnologyDevelopment Center of Nagano

Rep Ind Res Inst Osaka Prefect — Reports. Industrial Research Institute. Osaka Prefecture

Rep Ind Technol Cent Wakayama Prefect — Report. Industrial Technology Center of Wakayama Prefecture

Rep Ind Tech Res Inst — Report. Osaka Industrial Technical Research Institute

Rep Inf Cent Jt Inst Lab Astrophys — Report. Information Center. Joint Institute for Laboratory Astrophysics

Rep Inf Serv CSIRO Aust — Report. Information Service. Commonwealth Scientific and Industrial Research Organization. Australia

Rep Injur Insects Midl Cties — Report on Injurious Insects and other Animals Observed in the Midland Counties [*Birmingham*]

Rep Inld Fish Dep Un S Afr — Report. Inland Fisheries Department. Union of South Africa

Rep Inld Wat Surv Comm — Report. Inland Water Survey Committee

Rep Insectic Fungic Bd US — Report. Insecticide and Fungicide Board. United States Department of Agriculture

Rep Insp Mines Cyprus — Report. Inspector of Mines. Cyprus

Rep Inst Agric Res Tohoku Univ — Reports. Institute for Agricultural Research. Tohoku University

Rep Inst Agr Res (Korea) — Report. Institute of Agricultural Research (Korea)

Rep Inst Anim Physiol — Report. Institute of Animal Physiology

Rep Inst Appl Microbiol Univ Tokyo — Reports. Institute of Applied Microbiology. University of Tokyo

Rep Inst Bas Med Sci — Report. Institute of Basic Medical Sciences

Rep Inst Bewar Verwerk TuinbProd — Report. Instituut voor Bewaring en Verwerking van Tuinbouwproducten

Rep Inst Chem Res Kyoto Univ — Reports. Institute for Chemical Research. Kyoto University

Rep Inst Clin Res Exp Med — Report. Institute of Clinical Research and Experimental Medicine. Middlesex Hospital Medical School

Rep Inst Fish Biol Minist Econ Aff Natl Taiwan Univ — Report. Institute of Fishery Biology. Ministry of Economic Affairs. National Taiwan University

Rep Inst Freshwater Res (Drottningholm) — Report. Institute of Freshwater Research (Drottningholm)

Rep Inst Geol Sci — Report. Institute of Geological Sciences

Rep Inst Geol Sci (UK) — Report. Institute of Geological Sciences (United Kingdom)

Rep Inst High Speed Mech Tohoku Univ — Reports. Institute of High Speed Mechanics. Tohoku University

Rep Inst Ind Sci Univ Tokyo — Report. Institute of Industrial Science. University of Tokyo

Rep Inst Ind Technol Yeung Nam — Report. Institute of Industrial Technology. Yeung Nam University

Rep Inst Ind Technol Yeung Nam Univ — Report. Institute of Industrial Technology. Yeung Nam University

Rep Inst Jpn Chem Fibers Kyoto Univ — Reports. Institute of Japanese Chemical Fibers. Kyoto University

Rep Inst Ld Wat Mgmt Res — Report. Institute for Land and Water Management Research

Rep Inst Mar Res Fish Board Swed — Report. Institute of Marine Research. Fishery Board of Sweden

Rep Inst Med Dent Eng Tokyo Med Dent Univ — Reports. Institute for Medical and Dental Engineering. Tokyo Medicaland Dental University

Rep Inst Med Vet Sci (SA) — Report. Institute of Medical and Veterinary Science (South Australia)

Rep Inst Met (Leningrad) — Reports. Institute of Metals (Leningrad)

Rep Inst Min Res Univ Rhod — Report. Institute of Mining Research. University of Rhodesia

Rep Inst Min Res Univ Zimbabwe — Report. Institute of Mining Research. University of Zimbabwe

Rep Inst Nat Prod Yeungnam Univ — Report. Institute of Natural Products. Yeungnam University

Rep Instn Engrs Shipbldrs Scotl — Report. Institution of Engineers and Ship-Builders in Scotland

Rep Inst Neurol — Report. Institute of Neurology

Rep Instn Heat Vent Engrs — Report. Institution of Heating and Ventilating Engineers

Rep Instn Min Engrs — Report. Institution of Mining Engineers

Rep Instn Struct Engrs — Report of the Institution of Structural Engineers

Rep Inst Nucl Phys (Krakow) — Report. Institute of Nuclear Physics (Krakow)

Rep Inst Ophthal Univ Lond — Report. Institute of Ophthalmology. University of London

Rep Inst Opt Res (Tokyo) — Reports. Institute for Optical Research (Tokyo)

Rep Inst Petrol — Report. Institute of Petroleum

Rep Inst Phys — Report. Institute of Physics

Rep Inst Phys Chem Acad Sci Ukr SSR — Reports. Institute of Physical Chemistry. Academy of Sciences.Ukrainian SSR

Rep Inst Phys Chem Res — Reports. Institute of Physical and Chemical Research

Rep Inst Phys Chem Res (Jpn) — Reports. Institute of Physical and Chemical Research (Japan)

Rep Inst Phys Warsaw Tech Univ — Reports. Institute of Physics. Warsaw Technical University

Rep Inst Pl Ind Indore — Report. Institute of Plant Industry (Indore)

Rep Inst Psychiat — Report. Institute of Psychiatry

Rep Inst Psycho Analysis — Report. Institute of Psycho-Analysis

Rep Inst Publ Hlth Univ Ont — Report. Institute of Public Health. University of Ontario (London, Ontario)

Rep Inst Pulp Pap Ind Shizuoka Prefect — Reports. Institute of the Pulp and Paper Industry. Shizuoka Prefecture

Rep Inst Putref Res Chiba Univ — Report. Institute of Putrefaction Research. Chiba University

Rep Inst Ray Ther Electro Ther — Report. Institute of Ray Therapy and Electro-Therapy

Rep Inst Res Agric Econ Univ Oxf — Report. Institute for Research in Agricultural Economics. University of Oxford

Rep Inst Res Agric Engng Univ Oxf — Report. Institute for Research in Agricultural Engineering. University of Oxford

Rep Inst Res Stor Process Hort Prod Wageningen — Report. Institute for Research on Storage and Processing of Horticultural Produce (Wageningen)

Rep Instrumn Lab MIT — Report. Instrumentation Laboratory. Massachusetts Institute of Technology

Rep Inst Scient Res Manchoukuo — Report of the Institute of Scientific Research. Manchoukuo

Rep Inst Scient Treat Delinq — Report. Institute for the Scientific Treatment of Delinquency

Rep Inst Sci Formosa — Report of the Institute of Science. Formosa

Rep Inst Sci Ind Aust — Report. Institute of Science and Industry. Commonwealth of Australia

Rep Inst Sci Lab Kurashiki — Report of the Institute for Science of Labour (Kurashiki)

Rep Inst Sci Labour (Tokyo) — Reports. Institute for Science of Labour (Tokyo)

Rep Inst Sci Res Manchoukuo — Report. Institute of Scientific Research (Manchoukuo)/Tairiku Kagakuin Kenkyu Hokoku

Rep Inst Sci Technol — Report. Institute of Science and Technology

Rep Inst Sci Technol Sung Kyun Kwan Univ — Report. Institute of Science and Technology. Sung Kyun Kwan University

Rep Inst Sci Technol Tokyo — Report of the Institute of Science and Technology (Tokyo)

Rep Inst Sci Technol Tokyo Univ — Report. Institute of Science and Technology. Tokyo University

Rep Inst Seaweed Res — Report. Institute of Seaweed Research

Rep Inst Sex Res Univ Indiana — Report. Institute for Sex Research. University of Indiana

Rep Inst Soc Med — Report. Institute of Social Medicine

Rep Inst Space Astronaut Sci (Tokyo) — Report. Institute of Space and Astronautical Science (Tokyo)

Rep Inst Statist Univ Oxf — Report. Institute of Statistics. University of Oxford

Rep Inst Syst Des Optim Kans State Univ — Report. Institute for Systems Design and Optimization. Kansas State University

Rep Inst Technol Nihon Univ — Report. Institute of Technology. Nihon University

Rep Inst Theor Astrophys — Report. Institute of Theoretical Astrophysics

Rep Inst Theor Astrophys Univ Oslo — Report. Institute of Theoretical Astrophysics. University of Oslo

Rep Inst Trop Agric Univ P Rico — Report. Institute of Tropical Agriculture. University of Porto Rico

Rep Inst Tuberc Kyushu Univ — Report of the Institute for Tuberculosis. Kyushu University

Rep Inst Upper Atmos Phys Univ Sask — Report. Institute of Upper Atmospheric Physics. University of Saskatchewan

Rep Inst Virus Res Kyoto — Report of the Institute for Virus Research. Kyoto University

Rep Inst Weath Clim Res Oslo — Report. Institute of Weather and Climatic Research (Oslo)

Rep Inst Weld — Report. Institute of Welding

Rep Inst Wine Food Technol Yamanashi Prefect — Report. Institute for Wine and Food Technology. Yamanashi Prefecture

Rep Int Ass Dairy Milk Insp — Report. International Association of Dairy and Milk Inspectors

Rep Int Ass Milk Sanit — Report. International Association of Milk Sanitarians

Rep Int Ass Munic Electns — Report. International Association of Municipal Electricians

Rep Int Assoc Cereal Chem — Reports. International Association of Cereal Chemistry

Rep Int Ass Promot Study Quatern — Report of the International Association for Promoting the Study of Quaternions

Rep Int Ass Rubb Cult Neth Indies — Report. International Association for Rubber and other Cultivations in the Netherlands-Indies

Rep Int Atom Energy Ag — Report. International Atomic Energy Agency

Rep Int Chestnut Commn — Report. International Chestnut Commission

Rep Int Comm Bird Preserv Br Sect — Report of the International Committee for Bird Preservation. British Section

Rep Int Commn Appl Ecol — Report. International Commission on Applied Ecology

Rep Int Comm New Analyt React — Report of the International Committee on New Analytical Reactions and Reagents. Union Internationale de la Chimie

Rep Int Commn NW Atlant Fish — Report. International Commission for Northwest Atlantic Fisheries

Rep Int Commn Whal — Report. International Commission on Whaling

Rep Int Conf Ironmaking — Reports. International Conference on Ironmaking

Rep Int Coun Bird Preserv Br Sect — Report. International Council for Bird Preservation British Section

Rep Int Counc Scient Un — Report. International Council of Scientific Unions

Rep Int Coun Scient Un — Report. International Council of Scientific Unions

Rep Int Crop Improv Ass — Report. International Crop Improvement Association

Rep Inter Afr Bur Epizoot Dis — Report. Inter-African Bureau for Epizootic Diseases

Rep Inter Am Inst Agric Sci — Report. Inter-American Institute of Agricultural Sciences

Rep Inter Am Trop Tuna Commn — Report. Inter-American Tropical Tuna Commission

Rep Intermount Forest Range Exp Stn Ogden — Report. Intermountain Forest and Range Experiment Station. Ogden, Utah

Rep Intern Combust Eng Sub Comm Advis Comm Aeronaut — Report. Internal Combustion Engine Subcommittee. Advisory Committee for Aeronautics

Rep Interst Conf For Aust — Report. Inter-State Conference on Forestry. Australia

Rep Int Fish Commn — Report. International Fisheries Commission

Rep Int Hlth Div Rockefeller Fdn — Report. International Health Division Rockefeller Foundation

Rep Int Hortic Congr — Report. International Horticultural Congress

Rep Int Inst Ld Reclam Improv — Report. International Institute for Land Reclamation and Improvement

Rep Int Litt Art — Repertoire International de la Litterature de l'Art

Rep Int Med Grp Invest Contracept — Report. International Medical Group for the Investigation of Contraception

Rep Int N Pacif Fish Commn — Report. International North Pacific Fisheries Commission

Rep Int Pac Halibut Comm — Report. International Pacific Halibut Commission

Rep Int Pacif Salm Fish Commn — Report. International Pacific Salmon Fisheries Commission

Rep Int Poplar Commn — Report. International Poplar Commission

Rep Introd Improv Agric — Report on Introduction of Improvements in Agriculture

Rep Int Tin Res Coun — Report. International Tin Research Council

Rep Int Whaling Comm — Report. International Whaling Commission

Rep Int Whaling Comm Spec Issue — Report. International Whaling Commission. Special Issue

Rep Int Workshop Int Histocompat Conf — Report. International Workshop. International Histocompatibility Conference

Rep Inventory Minn Off Iron Range Resour Rehabil — Report of Inventory. Minnesota Office of Iron Range Resources andRehabilitation

Rep Invest Ariake Sea — Report of Investigations. Ariake Sea

Rep Invest Aust Gov Anal Lab — Australian Government Analytical Laboratories. Report of Investigations

Rep Invest Bur Econ Geol (Texas) — Report of Investigations. Bureau of Economic Geology (Texas)

Rep Invest Bur Econ Geol Univ Tex — Report of Investigations. Bureau of Economic Geology. University of Texas

Rep Invest Bur Mines Philipp — Report of Investigations. Bureau of Mines of the Philippines

Rep Invest Conn State Geol Nat Hist Surv — Report of Investigations. Connecticut State Geological and NaturalHistory Survey

Rep Invest Delaware Geol Surv — Report of Investigations. Delaware Geological Survey

Rep Invest Del Geol Surv — Report of Investigations. Delaware. Geological Survey

Rep Invest Dep Mines S Aust — Report of Investigations. Department of Mines (Geological Survey). South Australia

Rep Invest Div Geol Surv Ohio — Report of Investigations. Division of Geologocial Survey. Ohio

Rep Invest Div Geol Tenn — Report of Investigations. Division of Geology. Department of Conservation. State of Tennessee

Rep Invest Div Geol Wash St Dep Conserv — Report of Investigations. Division of Geology. Washington State Department of Conservation and Development

Rep Invest Div Miner Resour (VA) — Report of Investigations. Division of Mineral Resources (Virginia)

Rep Invest Fla Bur Geol — Report of Investigations. Florida Bureau of Geology

Rep Invest Fla Geol Surv — Report of Investigations. Florida Geological Survey

Rep Invest Geol Miner Resour Br Solomon Isl — Report on Investigations into the Geology and Mineral Resources of the Protectorate. British Solomon Islands

Rep Invest Geol Surv Div Mich — Report of Investigations. Geological Survey Division of Michigan

Rep Invest Geol Surv Finl — Report of Investigation. Geological Survey of Finland

Rep Invest Geol Surv MO — Report of Investigations. Geological Survey of Missouri

Rep Invest Geol Surv S Aust — Report of Investigations. Geological Survey of South Australia

Rep Invest Geol Surv South Aust — Report of Investigations. Geological Survey of South Australia

Rep Invest Geol Surv Wyo — Report of Investigations. Geological Survey of Wyoming

Rep Invest Geol Surv Wyoming — Report of Investigations. Geological Survey of Wyoming

Rep Invest Gov Chem Labs West Aust — Report of Investigations. Government Chemical Laboratories. Western Australia

Rep Investigacion Inst Mat Cibernet Comput — Reporte de Investigacion del Instituto de Matematica. Cibernetica y Computacion

Rep Invest Ill State Geol Surv — Report of Investigations. Illinois State Geological Survey

Rep Invest Ill State Water Surv — Report of Investigation. Illinois State Water Survey

Rep Invest Ill St Geol Surv — Report of Investigations. Illinois State Geological Survey

Rep Invest Ill St Mus Nat Hist — Report of Investigations. Illinois State Museum of Natural History

Rep Invest Iowa Geol Surv — Report of Investigations. Iowa Geological Survey

Rep Invest Ky Geol Surv — Report of Investigations. Kentucky. Geological Survey

Rep Invest Md Geol Surv — Report of Investigations. Maryland Geological Survey

Rep Invest Mich Geol Surv Div — Report of Investigation. Michigan Geological Survey Division

Rep Invest Minnesota Geol Surv — Report of Investigations. Minnesota Geological Survey

Rep Invest Mo Div Geol Land Surv — Report of Investigations. Missouri Division of Geology and Land Survey

Rep Invest Mo Geol Surv — Report of Investigations. Missouri Geological Survey

Rep Invest Mo Geol Surv Water Resources — Report of Investigations. Missouri Geological Survey and WaterResources

Rep Invest N B Miner Resour Branch — Report of Investigation. New Brunswick. Mineral Resources Branch

Rep Invest NC Div Ground Water — Report of Investigation. North Carolina Division of Ground Water

Rep Invest N Dak Geol Surv — Report of Investigations. North Dakota Geological Survey

Rep Invest ND Geol Surv — Report of Investigations. North Dakota Geological Survey

Rep Invest Ohio Div Geol Surv — Report of Investigations. Ohio Division of Geological Survey

Rep Invest Philipp Bur Mines — Report of Investigation. Philippines. Bureau of Mines

Rep Invest Philipp Bur Mines Geo Sci — Report of Investigation. Philippines Bureau of Mines and Geo-Sciences

Rep Invest R Dep Mines Thailand — Report of Investigations. Royal Department of Mines. Thailand

Rep Invest S Dak Geol Nat Hist Surv — Report of Investigations. South Dakota Geological and Natural History Survey

Rep Invest SD Geol Surv — Report of Investigations. South Dakota Geological Survey

Rep Invest S Hamps Strawberry Probl — Report on Investigations on South Hampshire Strawberry Problems

Rep Invest Shellfish Mass — Report of Investigations of Shellfisheries of Massachusetts

Rep Invest South Aust Geol Surv — Report of Investigations. South Australia Geological Survey

Rep Invest South Australia Geol Surv — Report of Investigations. South Australia Geological Survey

Rep Invest State Water Surv Ill — Report of Investigation. State Water Survey of Illinois

Rep Invest Tenn Div Geol — Report of Investigations. Tennessee Division of Geology

Rep Invest Univ Tex Austin Bur Econ Geol — Report of Investigations. University of Texas at Austin. Bureau of Economic Geology

Rep Invest US Bur Mines — Report of Investigations. United States Bureau of Mines

Rep Invest Va Div Miner Resour — Report of Investigations. Virginia Division of Mineral Resources

Rep Invest WA Govt Chem Labs — Report of Investigations. Government Chemical Laboratories. Western Australia

Rep Invest West Aust Gov Chem Lab — Report of Investigations. Western Australia. Government Chemical Laboratories

Rep Invest W Va Geol Econ Surv — Report of Investigations. West Virginia Geological and Economic Survey

Rep Invest Wyo Geol Surv — Report of Investigations. Wyoming Geological Survey

Rep Ionos & Space Res Jap — Report of Ionosphere and Space Research in Japan

Rep Ionos and Space Res Jpn — Report of Ionosphere and Space Research in Japan

Rep Ionos Res Jpn — Report of Ionosphere Research in Japan [Later, Report of Ionosphere and Space Research in Japan]

Rep Ion Spa — Report of Ionosphere and Space Research in Japan

Rep Iowa Agric Exp Stn — Report of the Iowa Agricultural Experiment Station

Rep Iowa State Univ Eng Res Inst — Report. Iowa State University. Engineering Research Institute

Rep Iowa St Hort Soc — Report. Iowa State Horticultural Society

Rep Iron Steel Consum Coun — Report. Iron and Steel Consumers' Council

Rep Iron Steel Corp Gt Br — Report. Iron and Steel Corporation of Great Britain

Rep Irrig Dep Egypt — Report of the Irrigation Department. Egypt

Rep Irrig Dep Sth Rhod — Report of the Irrigation Department. Southern Rhodesia

Rep Irrig Dep Un S Afr — Report. Irrigation Department. Union of South Africa

Rep Irrig Res Inst Pakist — Report of the Irrigation Research Institute. Pakistan

Rep Irrig Wat Supply Commn Qd — Report. Irrigation and Water Supply Commission. Queensland

Rep Ir Soc Prot Birds — Report of the Irish Society for the Protection of Birds

Rep Isle Man Bd Agric Fish Manx Herring Fish — Report made to the Isle of Man Board of Agriculture and Fisheries on Manx Herring Fisheries

Rep Isle Thanet Fld Club — Report. Isle of Thanet Field-Club

Rep Isle Wight River Bd — Report. Isle of Wight River Board

Rep Isthm Canal Commn — Report. Isthmian Canal Commission

Rep Japan Sea Reg Fish Res Lab — Report. Japan Sea Regional Fisheries Research Laboratory

Rep Jap Bot Gard Assoc — Report. Japanese Botanical Garden Association/ Nippon Shokubutsuen Kyokwai Kaiho

Rep Jap Inst Infect Dis — Report. Japanese Institute for Infectious Diseases

Rep Jap Soc Tuberc — Report. Japanese Society for Tuberculosis

Rep JEDS — Report of JEDS (Japanese Expeditions of Deep Sea)

Rep John & Mary R Markle Fdn — Report. John and Mary R. Markle Foundation

Rep John Innes Hort Instn — Report. John Innes (Horticultural) Institution

Rep Josef Stefan Inst — Report of Josef Stefan Institute

Rep Jpn Inst Baking — Report. Japan Institute of Baking

Rep Jpn Mar Prod Co Res Lab — Reports. Japan Marine Products Company. Research Laboratory

Rep Jpn Spinners Insp Found — Report. Japan Spinners' Inspecting Foundation

Rep Jr Bird Rec Club — Report. Junior Bird Recorders' Club

Rep Jt Advis Comm River Pollut — Report. Joint Advisory Committee on River Pollution [London]

Rep Jt Benz Res Comm — Report of the Joint Benzole Research Committee of the National Benzole Association and the University of Leeds

Rep Jt Coal Bd Aust — Report. Joint Coal Board. Australia

Rep Jt Coal Bd NSW — Report of the Joint Coal Board. Department of Mines New South Wales

Rep Jt FAO WHO Expert Comm Fd Addit — Report. Joint FAO/WHO Expert Committee on Food Additives

Rep Jt FAO WHO Expert Comm Meat Hyg — Report. Joint FAO/WHO Expert Committee on Meat Hygiene

Rep Jt FAO WHO Expert Comm Milk Hyg — Report. Joint FAO/WHO Expert Committee on Milk Hygiene

Rep Jt Fish Res Org Nth Rhod — Report. Joint Fisheries Research Organization. Northern Rhodesia

Rep Jt Inst Lab Astrophys — Report. Joint Institute for Laboratory Astrophysics

Rep Jt Invest Comm Coal Util Jt Coun Solid Smokeless Fuels Fed — Report of the Joint Investigations Committee of the Coal Utilisation Joint Council and the Solid Smokeless Fuels Federation

Rep Jt Stand Comm Res Univ Bgham — Report of the Joint Standing Committee for Research. University of Birmingham

Rep Jute Agric Res Inst — Report of the Jute Agricultural Research Institute. Indian Central Jute Committee

Rep Kagawa Ken Shoyu Exp Stn — Report. Kagawa-Ken Shoyu Experiment Station

Rep Kagawa Prefect Inst Public Health — Report. Kagawa Prefectural Institute of Public Health

Rep Kagawa Prefect Res Cent Environ Pollut Control — Report. Kagawa Prefectural Research Center for Environmental Pollution Control

Rep Kagoshima Prefect Inst Environ Pollut Public Health — Report. Kagoshima Prefectural Institute of Environmental Pollution andPublic Health

Rep Kagoshima Prefect Inst Public Health — Report. Kagoshima Prefectural Institute of Public Health

Rep Kakioka Magn Obs — Report of the Kakioka Magnetic Observatory

Rep Kanagawa Ken Agric Exp Sta — Report. Kanagawa-Ken Agricultural Experiment Station. Kanawaga-Kenritsu Noji Shiken-Jo Moji Shiken Seiseki

Rep Kans Agric Exp Stn — Report of the Kansas Agricultural Experiment Station. Manhattan

Rep Kansas Agric Exper Station — Report. Kansas Agricultural Experiment Station

Rep Kans State Board Agr — Report. Kansas State Board of Agriculture

Rep Kans State Univ Cent Energy Stud — Report. Kansas State University. Center for Energy Studies

Rep Kans State Univ Inst Syst Des Optim — Report. Kansas State University. Institute for Systems Design andOptimization

Rep Kans St Bd Agric — Report of the Kansas State Board of Agriculture

Rep Kans Univ Geol Surv — Report. Kansas University Geological Survey

Rep Kans Water Sewage Works Assoc — Report. Kansas Water and Sewage Works Association

Rep Kasaragod Agric Exp Stn — Report. Kasaragod Agricultural Experiment Station

Rep Kennan Ind Res Inst Tochigi Prefect — Reports. Kennan Industrial Research Institute of Tochigi Prefecture

Rep Kent Essex Sea Fish Comm — Report. Kent and Essex Sea Fisheries Committee

Rep Kent River Bd — Report. Kent River Board

Rep Kenya Fish — Report. Kenya Fisheries

Rep Kenya Mines Geol Dep — Report. Kenya. Mines and Geological Department

Rep Kenya Sisal Grow Ass — Report. Kenya Sisal Growers Association

Rep Kenya Wild Life Soc — Report of the Kenya Wild Life Society

Rep Kevo Subarct Res Stn — Reports. Kevo Subarctic Research Station

Rep Kihara Inst Biol Res — Reports. Kihara Institute for Biological Research

Rep King Edw VII Coll Med Singapore — Report. King Edward VII College of Medicine (Singapore)

Rep King Edw VII Meml Hosp Bermuda — Report. King Edward VII Memorial Hospital (Bermuda)

Rep King Edw VII Meml Pasteur Inst Shillong — Report of the King Edward VII Memorial Pasteur Institute and Medical Research Institute (Shillong)

Rep King Edw VII Sanat Midhurst — Report. King Edward VII Sanatorium. Midhurst

Rep King Edw VII Welsh Natn Meml Ass — Report. King Edward VII Welsh National Memorial Association

Rep King George V Anti Tuberc Leag Bombay — Report. King George V Anti-Tuberculosis League (Bombay)

Rep King Inst Prev Med — Report. King Institute of Preventive Medicine [*Madras*]

Rep Kings Sch Canterb Nat Hist Soc — Report. King's School Canterbury Natural History Society and Field Club

Rep Kitchener Sch Med — Report. Kitchener School of Medicine [*Khartoum*]

Rep Kochi Univ Nat Sci — Reports. Kochi University. Natural Science

Rep Kodaikanal Madras Obs — Report. Kodaikanal and Madras Observatories

Rep Kolar Gold Fld Obs — Report on the Kolar Gold Field Observatory

Rep Krugersdorp Med Offr — Report. Krugersdorp Medical Officer

Rep Kumamoto Prefect Seric Exp Stn — Report. Kumamoto Prefecture Sericulture Experiment Station

Rep Kumaun Govt Gdns — Report of the Kumaun Government Gardens [*Allahabad*]

Rep Kunst W — Repertorium fuer Kunstwissenschaft

RepKw — Repertorium fuer Kunstwissenschaft

Rep Kwangsi Agric Exp Stn — Report. Kwangsi Agricultural Experiment Station

Rep KY Agric Exp Stat — Report. Kentucky Agricultural Experiment Station. University of Kentucky

Rep Ky Agric Exp Stn — Report of the Kentucky Agricultural Experiment Station of the University of Kentucky

Rep Ky Dep Mines Miner — Report. Kentucky Department of Mines and Minerals

Rep Kyotitsu Coll Pharm — Report. Kyotitsu College of Pharmacy

Rep Kyoto Coll Pharm — Report. Kyoto College of Pharmacy

Rep Kyoto Univ For — Reports. Kyoto University Forests

Rep Kyoto Univ Forest — Report. Kyoto University Forest/Kyoto Daigaku Nogakubu Enshurin Iho

Rep Ky Res Fdn — Report. Kentucky Research Foundation

Rep Kyushu Br Crop Sci Soc Jap — Report. Kyushu Branch. Crop Science Society of Japan

Rep Kyushu Univ For — Reports. Kyushu University Forests

Rep La Agric Exp Stn — Report of the Louisiana Agricultural Experiment Station

Rep Lab Biol Taiwan Fish Res Inst — Report. Laboratory of Biology. Taiwan Fisheries Research Institute

Rep Lab Clin Stress Res Karolinska Inst — Reports. Laboratory for Clinical Stress Research. Karolinska Institute

Rep Lab Cy Univ Jt Bd Res Ment Dis Bgham — Report of the Laboratory. City and University Joint Board of Research for Mental Disease (Birmingham)

Rep Lab Exp Limnol Maple — Report of the Laboratory for Experimental Limnology. Southern Research Station (Maple, Ontario)

Rep Lab Govt Chem — Report. Laboratory of the Government Chemist [*London*]

Rep Lab Hydrobiol Univ Taiwan — Report. Laboratory of Hydrobiology. University of Taiwan

Rep Lab Mus Comp Path Zool Soc Philad — Report. Laboratory and Museum of Comparative Pathology of the Zoological Society of Philadelphia

Rep Lab R Coll Physns Edinb — Report from the Laboratory of the Royal College of Physicians. Edinburgh

Rep Lab Servs Div Med Dep Uganda — Report of the Laboratory Services Division of the Medical Department. Uganda

Rep Labs Med Dep Buffalo Univ — Report of the Laboratories. Medical Department. Buffalo University

Rep Lab Soils Fert Fac Agric Okayama Univ — Reports. Laboratory of Soils and Fertilizers. Faculty of Agriculture. Okayama University

Rep Labs Pl Path Exp Fm Ottawa — Report of the Laboratories of Plant Pathology and Economic Botany at the Experiment Farm [*Ottawa*]

Rep Lab Stress Elast Tohoku Univ — Report of the Laboratory for Stress and Elasticity. Tohoku University

Rep Lab Vertebr Biol Univ Mich — Report. Laboratory of Vertebrate Biology. University of Michigan

Rep Lab Vertebr Genet Univ Mich — Report. Laboratory of Vertebrate Genetics. University of Michigan

Rep La Dep Conserv — Report. Louisiana Department of Conservation

Rep La Fruit Truck Exp Stn — Report of the Louisiana Fruit and Truck Experiment Station

Rep Lake St Forest Exp Stn — Report. Lake States Forest Experiment Station [*St. Paul, Minnesota*]

Rep Lake Vict Fish Serv — Report. Lake Victoria Fisheries Service

Rep Lancaster Astr Scient Ass — Report. Lancaster Astronomical and Scientific Association

Rep Lancs Chesh Ent Soc — Report of the Lancashire and Cheshire Entomological Society

Rep Lancs Chesh Fauna Comm — Report of the Lancashire and Cheshire Fauna Committee

Rep Lancs River Bd — Report. Lancashire River Board

Rep Lancs Sea Fish Labs — Report of the Lancashire Sea-Fisheries Laboratories

Rep Lancs West Sea Fish Distr — Report. Lancashire and Western Sea Fisheries District

Rep La St Mus — Report of the Louisiana State Museum

Rep Lat Am For Commn — Report. Latin-American Forestry Commission

Rep Laurent Forest Prot Ass — Report. Laurentian Forest Protective Association [*Quebec*]

Rep Lawrence Livermore Lab — Report. Lawrence Livermore Laboratory. University of California

Rep Ld Adm Bd Qd — Report. Land Administration Board. Queensland

Rep Ld Dep East Nigeria — Report. Land Department. Eastern Nigeria

Rep Ld Fert Comm — Report of the Land Fertility Committee [*London*]

Rep Lds Dev Servs Brch Can — Report of Lands and Development Services Branch. Department of Mines and Resources. Canada

Rep Lds Mines Dep Br Guiana — Report of the Lands and Mines Department. British Guiana

Rep Lds Pks Forests Brch Can — Report of the Lands, Parks, and Forests Branch. Department of Mines. Canada

Rep Lds Surv Brch Br Columb — Report of the Lands and Survey and Water Rights Branches of the Department of Lands. British Columbia</PHR> %

Rep Lds Surv Dep Br N Borneo — Report. Lands and Survey Department. British North Borneo

Rep Lds Survs Dep Trin — Report. Lands and Surveys Department. Trinidad and Tobago

Rep Lds Survs Dep Uganda — Report. Lands and Surveys Department. Uganda Protectorate

Rep Leafl Edinb E Scotl Coll Agric — Report Leaflet. Edinburgh and East of Scotland College of Agriculture

Rep Leag O Natns Hlth Org Soc — Report of the League of Nations Health Organization Society

Rep Leath Inds Res Inst Rhodes Univ — Report. Leather Industries Research Institute. Rhodes University College [*Grahamstown*]

Rep Leeds Phil Lit Soc — Report of the Leeds Philosophical and Literary Society

Rep Lee Fdn Nutr Res — Report. Lee Foundation for Nutritional Research [*Milwaukee*]

Rep Lee Vall Hort Stn — Report. Lee Valley Horticulture Station

Rep Leicester Mus Art Gall — Report of the Leicester Museum and Art Gallery

Rep Leland Stanf Jr Univ — Report of the Leland Stanford Junior University

Rep Lepr Serv Res Unit East Nigeria — Report. Leprosy Service Research Unit. Ministry of Health. Eastern Nigeria

Rep Liais Comm Aeronaut Radio Res US — Report of Liaison Committee on Aeronautic Radio Research. United States Department of Commerce

Rep Lib Arts Fac Shizuoka Univ Nat Sci — Reports. Liberal Arts Faculty. Shizuoka University. Natural Science

Rep Lib Arts Sci Fac Shizuoka Univ — Report. Liberal Arts and Science Faculty. Shizuoka University

Rep Lib Arts Sci Fac Shizuoka Univ Nat Sci — Reports. Liberal Arts and Science Faculty. Shizuoka University. Natural Science

Rep Liberal Arts Fac Shizuoka Univ Ser B Nat Sci — Reports. Liberal Arts Faculty. Shizuoka University. Series B. Natural Science/Shizuoka Daigaku Bunruigakubu Kenkyu Hokuku. B. Shizen Kagaku

Rep Liberal Arts Sci Fac Shizuoka Univ Nat Sci — Reports. Liberal Arts and Science Faculty. Shizuoka University. Natural Science

Rep Lincs Nat Trust — Report of the Lincolnshire Naturalists' Trust

Rep Lincs River Bd — Report. Lincolnshire River Board

Rep Lincs Seed Grow Ass — Report. Lincolnshire Seed Growers' Association

Rep Linen Ind Res Ass — Report. Linen Industry Research Association

Rep Liscombe Exp Husb Fm — Report. Liscombe Experimental Husbandry Farm

Rep Lister Inst Prev Med — Report of the Lister Institute of Preventive Medicine

Rep Live Sav Appar Csts UK — Report on the Life-Saving Apparatus on the Coasts of the United Kingdom

Rep Livestk Agric Dep Swazild — Report of the Livestock and Agricultural Department. Swaziland

Rep Livestk Commn — Report of the Livestock Commission

Rep Livestk Offr Cyprus — Report. Livestock Officer. Cyprus

Rep Livestk Res Stn Hosur — Report of the Livestock Research Station. Hosur

Rep Liv Med Inst — Report. Liverpool Medical Institution

Rep Llandudno Distr Fld Club — Report of the Llandudno and District Field Club

Rep Local Govt Bd (London) — Reports. Local Government Board (London)

Rep Loc Govt Bd Publ Hlth — Report to the Local Government Board on Public Health and Medical Matters [*London*]

Rep Lond Advis Comm Rubb Res Ceylon Malaya — Report of the London Advisory Committee for Rubber Research. Ceylon and Malaya

Rep Lond Nat Hist Soc — Report of the London Natural History Society

Rep Lond Sch Hyg — Report of the London School of Hygiene and Tropical Medicine

Rep Lond Shellac Res Bur — Report. London Shellac Research Bureau

Rep Long Ashton Res Stn — Report. Long Ashton Research Station. University of Bristol

Rep Los Ang St Cty Arbor — Report. Los Angeles State and County Arboretum

Rep Lothians River Purif Bd — Report. Lothians River Purification Board [*Edinburgh*]

Rep Louth Antiq Nat Soc — Report of the Louth Antiquarian and Naturalists' Society

Rep Lower Ottawa Forest Prot Ass — Report. Lower Ottawa Forest Protection Association

Rep Lowestoft N Suff Fld Nat Club — Report. Lowestoft and North Suffolk Field Naturalists' Club

Rep Low Speed Aerodyn Res Ass — Report. Low-Speed Aerodynamics Research Association

Rep Low Temp Lab Natn Res Coun Can — Report. Low Temperature Laboratory. National Research Council. Canada

Rep Low Temp Res Lab Cape Tn — Report. Low Temperature Research Laboratory (Cape Town)

Rep Low Temp Res Stn — Report. Low Temperature Research Station [*Cambridge*]

Rep Lpool Cancer Control Org — Report of the Liverpool Cancer Control Organisation

Rep Lpool Geol Ass — Report of the Liverpool Geological Association

Rep Lpool Mar Biol Comm — Report. Liverpool Marine Biology Committee

Rep Lpool Med Instn — Report of the Liverpool Medical Institution

Rep Lpool Microsc Soc — Report of the Liverpool Microscopical Society

Rep Lpool Obs — Report of the Liverpool Observatory and Tidal Institute

Rep Lpool Sch Trop Med — Report. Liverpool School of Tropical Medicine

Rep Luddington Exp Hort Stn — Report. Luddington Experimental Horticulture Station

Rep Lundy Fld Soc — Report. Lundy Field Society

Rep Lune Bd Conserv — Report. Lune Board of Conservators [*Lancaster*]

Rep Lyallpur Agric Stn — Report on the Lyallpur Agricultural Station [*Lahore*]

REPM — Revista Espanola de Pedagogia (Madrid)

Rep Macaulay Inst Soil Res — Report. Macaulay Institute for Soil Research

Rep Macdonald Agric Coll — Report. Macdonald Agricultural College

Rep Magn Met Obs Toronto — Report of the Magnetic and Meteorological Observatory (Toronto)

Rep Maize Control Bd Sth Rhod — Report. Maize Control Board. Southern Rhodesia

Rep Malar Advis Bd Fed Malaya — Report of the Malaria Advisory Board. Federation of Malaya

Rep Malar Advis Bd FMS — Report of the Malaria Advisory Board. Federated Malay States

Rep Malar Advis Bd Malay Un — Report of the Malaria Advisory Board. Malayan Union

Rep Malar Bur FMS — Report of the Malaria Bureau. Federated Malay States

Rep Malar Comm R Soc — Report of the Malaria Committee of the Royal Society

Rep Malar Erad Scheme Maurit — Report. Malaria Eradication Scheme. Mauritius

Rep Malar Inst India — Report of the Malaria Institute of India

Rep Malar Ops Bombay — Report on Malaria Operations in Bombay

Rep Malar Punjab — Report on Malaria in the Punjab

Rep Malay Met Serv — Report. Malayan Meteorological Service

Rep Malta — Report on the Working of the Museum Department for the Year. Malta Department of Information

Rep Malt Barley Improv Ass — Report. Malting Barley Improvement Association [*Milwaukee*]

Rep Malvern Coll Nat Hist Soc — Report. Malvern College Natural History Society

Rep Malvern Fld Club — Report. Malvern Field Club

Rep Manchr Comm Cancer — Report. Manchester Committee on Cancer

Rep Manchr Distr Radium Inst — Report. Manchester and District Radium Institute

Rep Manchr Geogr Soc — Report. Manchester Geographical Society

Rep Manchr Geol Min Soc — Report. Manchester Geological and Mining Society

Rep Manchr Med Ethic Ass — Report of the Manchester Medico-Ethical Association

Rep Manchr Med Soc — Report of the Manchester Medical Society

Rep Manchr Microsc Soc — Report of the Manchester Microscopical Society

Rep Manchr Steam Users Ass — Report. Manchester Steam Users' Association

Rep Manchuria Res Inst — Report. Manchuria Research Institute

Rep Manchur Plague Prev Serv — Report. Manchurian Plague Prevention Service

Rep Mandalay Agric Coll Fm — Report. Mandalay Agricultural College Farm

Rep Mango Res Scheme Uttar Prad — Report. Mango Research Scheme. Uttar Pradesh

Rep Manitoba Dep Agric — Report of the Manitoba Department of Agriculture

Rep Manur Exp Staffs — Report on Manurial Experiments. Staffordshire County Council

Rep Mar Anal Chem Stand Program Natl Res Counc (Can) — Report. Marine Analytical Chemistry Standards Program. NationalResearch Council (Canada)

Rep Mar Biol Ass China — Report of the Marine Biological Association of China

Rep Mar Biol Ass UK — Report. Marine Biological Association of the United Kingdom

Rep Mar Biol Ass W Scotl — Report. Marine Biological Association of the West of Scotland

Rep Mar Biol Lab — Reports. Marine Biological Laboratory

Rep Mar Biol Stn Bangor — Report. Marine Biology Station. University College of North Wales (Bangor)

Rep Mar Biol Stn Kochi Univ — Report. Marine Biological Station. Kochi University

Rep Mar Biol Stn Port Erin — Report. Marine Biological Station. Port Erin

Rep Marble Lab — Report. Marble Laboratory [*Canton*]

Rep Mar Dep Hong Kong — Report. Marine Department. Hong Kong

Rep Mar Dep Nigeria — Report. Marine Department. Nigeria

Rep Mar Dep NZ — Report. Marine Department. New Zealand

Rep Mar Freshwat Invest Aberyst — Report on Marine and Freshwater Investigations. University College of Wales (Aberystwyth)

Rep Marit Sect Can Inst For — Report. Maritime Section. Canadian Institute of Forestry

Rep Mar Lab Rockport — Report of the Marine Laboratory. Rockport. Texas Game and Fish Commission

Rep Mar Lab Univ Miami — Report. Marine Laboratory. University of Miami

Rep Marlboro Coll Nat Hist Soc — Report of the Marlborough College Natural History Society

Rep Mar Pollut Lab — Report. Marine Pollution Laboratory

Rep Maruter Agric Res Stn — Report. Maruter Agricultural Research Station

Rep Maryland State Hort Soc — Report. Maryland State Horticultural Society

Rep Mass Agric Exp Stn — Report of the Massachusetts Agricultural Experiment Station

Rep Mass Bd Publ Hlth — Report of the Massachusetts Board of Public Health

Rep Mass Dep Agric — Report. Massachusetts Department of Agriculture

Rep Mass Dep Conserv — Report. Massachusetts Department of Conservation

Rep Mass Dep Ment Dis — Report. Massachusetts Department of Mental Diseases

Rep Mass Dep Publ Hlth — Report of the Massachusetts Department of Public Health

Rep Mass Div Sanit Engng — Report of the Massachusetts Division of Sanitary Engineering

Rep Mass Inst Technol — Report. Massachusetts Institute of Technology

Rep Mass Spectromet Conf — Report. Mass Spectrometry Conference

Rep Mass St Forester — Report of the Massachusetts State Forester

Rep Matern Unit East Distr Hosp Glasg — Report. Maternity Unit. Eastern District Hospital (Glasgow)

Rep Mater Res Lab Aust — Australia. Materials Research Laboratories. Report

Rep Mater Sci Technol — Report of Materials Science and Technology

Rep Math Colloq Notre Dame — Report of a Mathematical Colloquium. Notre Dame, Indiana

Rep Mathematical Phys — Reports on Mathematical Physics

Rep Math Log — Reports on Mathematical Logic

Rep Math Logic — Reports on Mathematical Logic

Rep Math Phys — Reports on Mathematical Physics

Rep Maurit Inst — Report of the Mauritius Institute

Rep Maurit Sug Ind Res Inst — Report. Mauritius Sugar Industry Research Institute

Rep Mazoe Citrus Exp Stn — Report. Mazoe Citrus Experimental Station

Rep Md Agric Exp Stn — Report of the Maryland Agricultural Experiment Station

Rep Md Agric Soc — Report of the Maryland Agricultural Society

Rep MD Agr Soc — Report. Maryland Agricultural Society

Rep Md Bd For — Report of the Maryland Board of Forestry

Rep Md Bd Nat Resour — Report. Maryland Board of Natural Resources

Rep MD Beekprs Ass — Report. Maryland Beekeepers' Association

Rep Md Dep Tidewat Fish — Report. Maryland Department of Tidewater Fisheries

Rep Md St Bd Hlth — Report. Maryland State Board of Health

Rep Md St Hort Soc — Report of the Maryland State Horticultural Society

Rep Me Agric Exp Stn — Report of the Maine Agricultural Experiment Station

Rep Mechanis Comm S Afr Sug Ass — Report. Mechanisation Committee. South African Sugar Association

Rep Mechaniz Sug Beet Crop Gt Br — Report on Mechanization of the Sugar Beet Crop in Great Britain

Rep Mech Developm Comm For Comm (Lond) — Report. Mechanical Development Committee. Forestry Commission (London)

Rep Mech Eng Lab (Tokyo) — Report. Mechanical Engineering Laboratory (Tokyo)

Rep Mech Engng Res Bd — Report of the Mechanical Engineering Research Board. D.S.I.R. (Department of Scientific and Industrial Research)

Rep Mech Lab Tokyo — Report. Mechanical Laboratory. Tokyo

Rep Med and Health Dept (Mauritius) — Report. Medical and Health Department (Mauritius)

Rep Med and Health Work Sudan — Report on Medical and Health Work in the Sudan

Rep Med Dep Anglo Iran Oil Co — Report. Medical Department. Anglo-Iranian Oil Co

Rep Med Dep Br N Borneo — Report. Medical Department. British North Borneo

Rep Med Dep Fiji — Report. Medical Department. Fiji

Rep Med Dep FMS — Report. Medical Department. Federated Malay States

Rep Med Dep Hong Kong — Report. Medical Department. Hong Kong

Rep Med Dep Jamaica — Report of the Medical Department. Jamaica

Rep Med Dep Kenya — Report. Medical Department. Kenya

Rep Med Dep Nigeria — Report. Medical Department Nigeria

Rep Med Dep Sierra Leone — Report on the Medical Department. Sierra Leone

Rep Med Dep Singapore — Report. Medical Department. Colony of Singapore

Rep Med Dep Straits Settl FMS — Report of the Medical Department. Straits Settlements and Federated Malay States

Rep Med Dep Tanganyika — Report. Medical Department. Tanganyika Territory

Rep Med Dep Uganda — Report. Medical Department. Uganda Protectorate</ PHR> %

Rep Me Dep Agric — Report of the Maine Department of Agriculture

Rep Med Hlth Dep Bermuda — Report of the Medical and Health Department. Bermuda

Rep Med Hlth Dep Malta — Report. Medical and Health Department. Malta

Rep Med Hlth Dep Maurit — Report of the Medical and Health Department. Mauritius

Rep Med Hlth Dep Seychelles — Report of the Medical and Health Department. Seychelles

Rep Med Insp Hlth Trin — Report of the Medical Inspector of Health. Trinidad and Tobago

Rep Med Insp Sch Bri Columb — Report of the Medical Inspection of Schools. British Columbia

Rep Med Insp Sch Child Scotl — Report on the Medical Inspection of School Children in Scotland

Rep Med Lab Dar Es Salaam — Report of the Medical Laboratory. Dar-es-Salaam

Rep Med Offr Gibraltar — Report of the Medical Officer. Gibraltar

Rep Med Offr Hlth Glasg — Report of the Medical Officer of Health. Glasgow

Rep Med Offr Hlth Munic Colombo — Report of the Medical Officer of Health. Municipality of Colombo

Rep Med Offr Loc Govt Bd — Report of the Medical Officer of the Local Government Board [*London*]

Rep Med Res Coun Ire — Report of the Medical Research Council of Ireland

Rep Med Res Coun Lond — Report of the Medical Research Council [*London*]

Rep Med Res Coun NZ — Report. Medical Research Council. New Zealand

Rep Med Res Inst Gold Cst — Report. Medical Research Institute. Gold Coast

Rep Med Res Inst Nigeria — Report of the Medical Research Institute for Nigeria

Rep Med Res Lab Kenya — Report of the Medical Research Laboratory. Kenya

Rep Med Res Probl Japan Anti Tuberc Ass — Report on Medical Research Problems of the Japan Anti-Tuberculosis Association

Rep Med Res Probl Jpn Anti-Tuberc Assoc — Reports on Medical Research Problems of the Japan Anti-Tuberculosis Association

Rep Med Res Soc Min Smelting Ind — Report. Medical Research Society for Mining and Smelting Industries

Rep Med Sanit Dep Aden — Report. Medical and Sanitary Department. Aden

Rep Med Sanit Dep Barbados — Report. Medical and Sanitary Department Barbados

Rep Med Sanit Dep Grenada — Report on the Medical and Sanitary Department. Grenada

Rep Med Sanit Dep St Lucia — Report of the Medical and Sanitary Department. St. Lucia

Rep Med Sanit Dep Swazild — Report. Medical and Sanitary Department. Swaziland

Rep Med Sanit Dep Trin — Report. Medical and Sanitary Department. Trinidad and Tobago

Rep Med Sanit Divs Zanzibar — Report. Medical and Sanitary Divisions. Zanzibar

Rep Med Serv Nth Terr Aust — Report of the Medical Service. Northern Territory, Australia

Rep Med Servs Br Guiana — Report of the Medical Services in British Guiana

Rep Med Servs Lagos — Report on the Medical Services of the Federal Territory of Lagos

Rep Med Statist NZ — Report on the Medical Statistics. New Zealand

Rep Med Surg Regist Univ Coll Hosp Lond — Report of the Medical and Surgical Registrars. University College Hospital (London)

Rep Meet Am Ass Study Prev Infant Mort — Report of Meetings of the American Association for Study and Prevention of Infant Mortality [*Baltimore*]

Rep Meet Aust NZ Assoc Adv Sci — Report. Meeting. Australian and New Zealand Association for the Advancement of Science

Rep Meet Bombay Med Phys Soc — Report of Meetings. Bombay Medical and Physical Society

Rep Meet Caribb Geol Conf — Report of the Meetings. Caribbean Geological Conference

Rep Meetg Brit Assoc Advanc Sc — Report. Meeting. British Association for the Advancement of Science

Rep Meet Tech Inf Offrs Eur Prod Ag — Report on the Meeting of Technical Information Officers. European Productivity Agency

Rep Me Forest Commn — Report of the Maine Forest Commission

Rep Melb Metrop Board Works — Report. Melbourne and Metropolitan Board of Works

Rep Melb Obs — Report of the Melbourne Observatory

Rep Mellon Inst Ind Res — Report. Mellon Institute of Industrial Research. University of Pittsburgh

Rep Memo Advis Comm Aeronaut — Report and Memoranda. Advisory Committee for Aeronautics

Rep Memo Aeronaut Res Comm Coun — Report and Memoranda. Aeronautical Research Committee (Council) [*London*]

Rep Memo Bldg Inds Natn Coun — Report and Memoranda. Building Industries National Council [*London*]

Rep Ment Hlth Div Can — Report. Mental Health Division. Department of National Health and Welfare. Canada

Rep Ment Hlth Res Inst Univ Mich — Report. Mental Health Research Institute. University of Michigan

Rep Mersey River Bd — Report. Mersey River Board

Rep Me Sea Shore Fish Dep — Report of the Maine Sea and Shore Fisheries Department

Rep Me St Pomol Soc — Report of the Maine State Pomological Society

Rep Metall Aeronaut Res Labs Aust — Report on Metallurgy. Aeronautical Research Laboratories. Australia

Rep Metall Dep Natn Phys Lab — Report on the Metallurgy Department. National Physical Laboratory [*London*]

Rep Met Brch Malay Met Serv — Report. Meteorological Branch. Malayan Meteorological Service

Rep Met Br Guiana — Report on the Meteorology of British Guiana

Rep Met Ceylon — Report on the Meteorology of Ceylon

Rep Met Comm Lond — Report of the Meteorological Committee (London)

Rep Met Commn Cap Tn — Report of the Meteorological Commission (Cape Town)

Rep Met Coun R Soc — Report of the Meteorological Council to the Royal Society [*London*]

Rep Met Dep Burma — Report. Meteorological Department. Burma

Rep Met Dep Govt India — Report. Meteorological Department of the Government of India

Rep Met Obs Govt Gen Chosen — Report. Meteorological Observatory of the Government-General of Chosen

Rep Met Obs Osaka — Report of the Meteorological Observatory. Osaka

Rep Met Off Lond — Report on the Meteorological Office [*London*]

Rep Met Off NZ — Report. Meteorological Office. New Zealand

Rep Met Off Un S Afr — Report. Meteorological Office. Union of South Africa

Rep Met Phys Servs Cairo — Report on the Meteorological and Physical Services. Survey Department (Cairo)

Rep Metrol Dep Natn Phys Lab — Report of the Metrology Department. National Physical Laboratory [*London*]

Rep Metrop Asylums Bd — Report. Metropolitan Asylums Board [*London*]

Rep Metrop Wat Bd — Report of the Metropolitan Water Board [*London*]

Rep Metrop Wat Sewer Drain Bd NSW — Report. Metropolitan Water Sewerage and Drainage Board. New South Wales

Rep Met Seism Obsns Int Latit Obs Mizusawa — Report of the Meteorological and Seismological Observations. International Latitude Observatory of Mizusawa

Rep Met Serv Br E Afr — Report. Meteorological Service. British East Africa

Rep Met Serv Can — Report of the Meteorological Service of Canada

Rep Met Servs Sierra Leone — Report of the Meteorological Services. Sierra Leone

Rep Mich Acad Sci — Report of the Michigan Academy of Science

Rep Mich Agric Exp Stn — Report of the Michigan Agricultural Experiment Station

Rep Mich Anti Tuberc Ass — Report. Michigan Anti-Tuberculosis Association

Rep Mich Ass Prev Tuberc — Report of the Michigan Association for the Prevention and Relief of Tuberculosis

Rep Mich Bd Agric — Report of the Michigan Board of Agriculture

Rep Mich Dep Hlth — Report of the Michigan Department of Health

Rep Mich Dept Conserv Game Div — Report. Michigan Department of Conservation. Game Division

Rep Mich St Hort Soc — Report of the Michigan State Horticultural Society

Rep Mich Tuberc Ass — Report. Michigan Tuberculosis Association

Rep Mich Univ Mus Zool — Report. Michigan University Museum of Zoology

Rep Microbiol Lab Dep Publ Hlth NSW — Report of the Microbiological Laboratory. Department of Public Health. New South Wales

Rep Microwave Commun Jap — Report. Microwave Communication Research Committee in Japan

Rep Middlesb Tuberc Care Comm — Report. Middlesborough Tuberculosis Care Committee

Rep Middx Hosp — Report. Middlesex Hospital [*London*]

Rep Midl Agric Dairy Coll — Report of the Midland Agricultural and Dairy College [*Kingston-on-Soar, Derby*]

Rep Midl Coke Res Comm — Report. Midland Coke Research Committee [*London*]

Rep Midl Reaffor Ass — Report of the Midland Reafforesting Association [*Birmingham*]

Rep Milbank Meml Fund — Report. Milbank Memorial Fund

Rep Milk & Milk Prod Tech Advis Comm — Report. Milk and Milk Products Technical Advisory Committee [*Reading*]

Rep Milk Dairy Res Alnarp — Report. Milk and Dairy Research. Alnarp

Rep Millport Mar Biol Ass — Report. Millport Marine Biological Association

Rep Min Bur Philipp Isl — Report of the Mining Bureau. Philippine Islands

Rep Mine Insp Alaska — Report of the Mine Inspector for the Territory of Alaska

Rep Miner Bur (S Afr) — Report. Minerals Bureau. Department of Mines (South Africa)

Rep Miner Dev Div (Newfoundland) — Report. Mineral Development Division. Department of Mines (Newfoundland)

Rep Miner Ind Educ Div Comm Geophys Educ — Report of the Mineral Industry Education Division's Committee on Geophysics Education. American Institute of Mining and Metallurgical Engineers

Rep Miner Ind Fed Malaya — Report on the Mineral Industry. Federation of Malaya

Rep Miner Ind Res Lab Univ Alaska — Report. Mineral Industry Research Laboratory. University of Alaska

Rep Miner Inds Can — Report on the Mineral Industries of Canada

Rep Minerogr Invest CSIRO Aust — Report. Minerographic Investigations. C.S.I.R.O. Australia

Rep Miner Prod Can — Report on the Mineral Production of Canada

Rep Miner Res Lab CSIRO — Report. Division of Mineralogy. Minerals Research Laboratory. Commonwealth Scientific and Industrial Research Organisation

Rep Miner Resour Alberta — Report on the Mineral Resources of Alberta

Rep Miners Phthisis Bd Un S Afr — Report. Miners Phthisis Board. Union of South Africa

Rep Miners Phthisis Med Bur Un S Afr — Report. Miners Phthisis Medical Bureau. Union of South Africa

Rep Mines Brch Can — Report. Mines Branch. Canada

Rep Mines Dep Ghana — Report of the Mines Department. Ghana

Rep Mines Dep Gold Cst — Report of the Mines Department. Gold Coast

Rep Mines Dep Nth Rhod — Report of the Mines Department. Northern Rhodesia

Rep Mines Dep Sierra Leone — Report of the Mines Department. Sierra Leone

Rep Mines Dep Transv — Report. Mines Department. Transvaal

Rep Mines Dep Uganda — Report of the Mines Department. Uganda

Rep Mines Quarr Dep Egypt — Report. Mines and Quarries Department. Egypt

Rep Min Fiji — Report on Mining. Department of Lands, Mines, and Surveys. Fiji

Rep Min Geol Dep Kenya — Report. Mining and Geological Department. Kenya Colony and Protectorate

Rep Min Ind Idaho — Report. Mining Industry of Idaho

Rep Min Ind Malay Un — Report on Mining Industry in the Malayan Union

Rep Min Ind Natal — Report on the Mining Industry of Natal

Rep Minist Agric Lds Jamaica — Report. Ministry of Agriculture and Lands. Jamaica

Rep Minist Agric Lds Sth Rhod — Report of the Ministry of Agriculture and Lands. Southern Rhodesia

Rep Minist Agric Sudan — Report of the Ministry of Agriculture. Sudan

Rep Minist Comm Agric Fd OEEC — Report. Ministerial Committee for Agriculture and Food. O.E.E.C

Rep Minister Agric Can — Report of the Minister of Agriculture for Canada

Rep Minister Agric Eire — Report of the Minister for Agriculture. Eire

Rep Minister Agric Mines Newfoundld — Report of the Minister of Agriculture and Mines. Newfoundland

Rep Minister Agric Ont — Report of the Minister of Agriculture. Ontario

Rep Minister Fuel Pwr — Report of the Minister of Fuel and Power [*London*]

Rep Minister Lds For Eire — Report of the Minister for Lands and Forestry. Eire

Rep Minister Lds Forests Prov Ont — Report of the Minister of Lands and Forests of the Province of Ontario

Rep Minist Fd Agric India — Report. Ministry of Food and Agriculture. India

Rep Minist Fish Ir Free St — Report. Ministry of Fisheries. Irish Free State (Republic of Ireland)

Rep Minist Hlth Ghana — Report. Ministry of Health. Ghana

Rep Minist Hlth Jordan — Report. Ministry of Health. Jordan

Rep Minist Hlth Lond — Report of the Ministry of Health (London)

Rep Minist Hlth Nth Reg Nigeria — Report of the Ministry of Health. Northern Region. Nigeria

Rep Minist Hlth Uganda — Report. Ministry of Health. Uganda

Rep Minist Publ Wks Egypt — Report of the Ministry of Public Works. Egypt

Rep Minist Pwr Fed Rhod Nyasald — Report. Ministry of Power. Federation of Rhodesia and Nyasaland

Rep Minn Agric Exp Stn — Report of the Minnesota Agricultural Experiment Station

Rep Minn Agric Exp Stn Brch Stns — Report. Minnesota Agricultural Experiment Station Branch Stations

Rep Minn Geol Nat Hist Surv — Report of the Minnesota Geological and Natural History Survey

Rep Minn St Agric Soc — Report of the Minnesota State Agricultural Society

Rep Minn St Ent — Report of the Minnesota State Entomologist

Rep Minn St Forester — Report of the Minnesota State Forester

Rep Min Ops Br Columb — Report of Mining Operations. British Columbia

Rep Min Ops Prov Queb — Report on Mining Operations in the Province of Quebec

Rep Min Quarr Inds Nth Ire — Report on the Mining and Quarrying Industries in Northern Ireland

Rep Min Res Lab Br Colliery Own Res Ass — Report. Mining Research Laboratory. British Colliery Owners Research Association

Rep MINTEK — Report. MINTEK

Rep Miss Agr Exp Sta — Report. Mississippi Agricultural Experiment Station

Rep Miss St Game Fish Commn — Report. Mississippi State Game and Fish Commission

Rep Mo Agric Exp Stn — Report. Missouri Agricultural Experiment Station

Rep Mobile Radio Comm — Report of the Mobile Radio Committee

Rep Mo Bot Gdn — Report. Missouri Botanical Garden

Rep Mo Bur Mines — Report. Missouri Bureau of Mines and Mine Inspection

Rep Mo Conf Wat Purif — Report of the Missouri Conference on Water Purification

Rep Mo Conserv Commn — Report. Missouri Conservation Commission

Rep Mont Agric Exp Stn — Report. Montana Agricultural Experiment Station

Rep Mont Dep Mines — Report. Montana Department of Mines

Rep Mont Fish Game Commn — Report. Montana Fish and Game Commission

Rep Mont Livestk Sanit — Report. Montana Livestock Sanitary Board

Rep Montrose Nat Hist Soc — Report. Montrose Natural History and Antiquarian Society

Rep Mont St Forest Dep — Report. Montana State Forest Department

Rep Mont Univ Jt Water Resour Res Cent — Report. Montana University Joint Water Resources Research Center

Rep Mosq Control Comm Ottawa Distr — Report of the Mosquito Control Committee of the Ottawa District

Rep Mosq Control Serv Br Guiana — Report. Mosquito Control Service. British Guiana

Rep Moss Exch Club — Report of the Moss Exchange Club

Rep Mo St Bd Agric — Report. Missouri State Board of Agriculture

Rep Mot Ind Res Ass — Report. Motor Industry Research Association

Rep Mo Wat Sewer Conf — Report of the Missouri Water and Sewerage Conference

Rep MRL NC State Univ Miner Res Lab — Report MRL. North Carolina State University. Minerals Research Laboratory

Rep MRP MSL Can Cent Miner Energy Technol Miner Res Program — Report MRP/MSL. Canada Centre for Mineral Energy Technology. MineralsResearch Program/Mineral Sciences Laboratories

Rep MRP PMRL (Phys Metall Res Lab) Can — Report MRP/PMRL (Physical Metallurgy Research Laboratories). Canada

Rep Mr Tebbutts Obs — Report of Mr. Tebbutt's Observatory

Rep Mt Desert Isl Biol Lab — Report. Mount Desert Island Biological Laboratory. Salisbury Cove, Maine

Rep Mt Sinai Hosp — Report of the Mount Sinai Hospital

Rep Mt Vernon Hosp — Report of the Mount Vernon Hospital for Consumption and the Radium Institute

Rep Mukden Med Coll — Report. Mukden Medical College

Rep Mult Sclerosis Soc — Report. Multiple Sclerosis Society

Rep Munit Supply Labs Maribyrnong — Report. Munitions Supply Laboratories. Marybyrnong, Victoria

Rep Munit Supply Labs Maribyrnong A Rep — Report. Munitions Supply Laboratories. Marybyrnong, Victoria. Annual Report

Rep Musc Dyst Assoc Can — Reporter. Muscular Dystrophy Association of Canada

Rep Mus Comm Univ Manchr — Report of the Museum Committee. University of Manchester

Rep Mus Comp Zool Harv — Report of the Museum of Comparative Zoology at Harvard University

Rep Museums Brooklyn Inst — Report. Museums of the Brooklyn Institute of Arts and Sciences

Rep Museums Met Obs Bolton — Report of the Museums and Meteorological Observatory (Bolton)

Rep Mushroom Res Stn — Report. Mushroom Research Station

Rep Mus Sci Ind Chicago — Report. Museum of Science and Industry founded by Julius Rosenwald (Chicago)

Rep Mycol Burma — Report of the Mycologist. Burma

Rep Mysore Dep Mines Geol — Report. Mysore Department of Mines and Geology

Rep Mysore Serum Inst — Report of the Mysore Serum Institute

Rep Nagano Prefect Ind Res Inst — Reports. Nagano Prefectural Industrial Research Institute

Rep Nagasaki Mar Obs — Report of the Nagasaki Marine Observatory

Rep Nagpur Agric Coll — Report on the Nagpur Agricultural College

Rep Nagpur Exp Fm — Report on the Nagpur Experimental Farm

Rep Naivasha Livestk Res Stn — Report. Naivasha Livestock Research Station

Rep Nandyal Agric Res Stn — Report. Nandyal Agricultural Research Station

Rep Nankai Reg Fish Res Lab — Report. Nankai Regional Fisheries Research Laboratory

Rep Nantucket Maria Mitchell Ass — Report. Nantucket Maria Mitchell Association

Rep Natal Bot Gard Colon Herb — Report on the Natal Botanic Gardens and Colonial Herbarium

Rep Natal Fish Dep — Report. Natal Fisheries Department

Rep Natal Pks Game Fish Preserv Bd — Report of the Natal Parks, Game, and Fish Preservation Board

Rep Nat Conserv — Report of the Nature Conservancy [*London*]

Rep Nat Dis Inst — Report. Nature of Disease Institute [*London*]

Rep Nat Gas Corp Barbados — Report. Natural Gas Corporation. Barbados

Rep Nat Hist Mus Stanford Univ — Report of the Natural History Museum of Stanford University

Rep Nat Hist Mus Univ Khartoum — Report. Natural History Museum. University of Khartoum

Rep Nat Hist Soc Md — Report of the Natural History Society of Maryland

Rep Nat Hist Soc Northumberland — Reports. Natural History Society of Northumberland, Durham, and Newcastle-upon-Tyne

Rep Nat Inst Nutr — Report. National Institute of Nutrition

Rep Native Lds Fish Commn Fiji — Report. Native Lands and Fisheries Commission. Fiji

Rep Natl Food Res Inst — Report. National Food Research Institute

Rep Natl Food Res Inst (Tokyo) — Report. National Food Research Institute (Tokyo)

Rep Natl Gas Turbine Establ UK — Report. National Gas Turbine Establishment. United Kingdom

Rep Natl Ind Res Inst (Korea) — Report. National Industrial Research Institute (Korea)

Rep Natl Ind Stand Res Inst (Korea) — Report. National Industrial Standards Research Institute (Korea)

Rep Natl Inst Health (Repub Korea) — Report. National Institute of Health (Republic of Korea)

Rep Natl Inst Metall — Report. National Institute for Metallurgy

Rep Natl Inst Metall (S Afr) — Report. National Institute for Metallurgy (South Africa)

Rep Natl Inst Vet Res (Pusan South Korea) — Report. National Institute for Veterinary Research (Pusan, South Korea)

Rep Natl Mus Victoria — Reports. National Museum of Victoria

Rep Natl Radiol Prot Board — Report. National Radiological Protection Board

Rep Natl Res Counc Can Mar Anal Chem Stand Program — Report. National Research Council Canada. Marine Analytical Chemistry StandardsProgram

Rep Natl Res Inst Met — Report. National Research Institute for Metals

Rep Natl Res Inst Police Sci (Jpn) Res Forensic Sci — Reports. National Research Institute of Police Science (Japan). Research on Forensic Science

Rep Natl Res Inst Pollut Resour (Kawaguchi Jpn) — Report. National Research Institute for Pollution and Resources (Kawaguchi, Japan)

Rep Natl Res Lab Metrol — Report. National Research Laboratory of Metrology

Rep Natl Swed Environ Prot Board — Report. National Swedish Environment Protection Board

Rep Natl Water Resour Counc Repub Philipp — Report. National Water Resources Council. Republic of the Philippines

Rep Natn Acad Sci Wash — Report on the National Academy of Sciences (Washington)

Rep Natn Advis Comm Res Geol Sci Can — Report of the National Advisory Committee on Research in the Geological Sciences. Canada

Rep Natn Aeronaut Establ Can — Report. National Aeronautical Establishment. Canada

Rep Natn Agric Res Bur China — Report of the National Agricultural Research Bureau of the Ministry of Industry. China

Rep Natn Ass Ment Hlth — Report. National Association for Mental Health [*London*]

Rep Natn Ass Prev Tuberc — Report of the National Association for the Prevention of Tuberculosis (London)

Rep Natn Auricula Primula Soc Sth Sect — Report. National Auricula and Primula Society. Southern Section

Rep Natn Bot Gdns S Afr — Report of the National Botanic Gardens. South Africa

Rep Natn Bur Stand — Report. National Bureau of Standards [*Washington, D.C.*]

Rep Natn Cancer Inst Can — Report. National Cancer Institute of Canada

Rep Natn Chem Lab — Report of the National Chemical Laboratory [*London*]

Rep Natn Comm Geod Geophys Pakist — Report. National Committee for Geodesy and Geophysics in Pakistan

Rep Natn Comm Vital Hlth Statist US — Report. National Committee on Vital and Health Statistics. US

Rep Natn Comm Wood Util Wash — Report. National Committee on Wood Utilization (Washington)

Rep Natn Conf Fishery Bds — Report. National Conference of Fishery Boards [*Manchester*]

Rep Natn Conf Wghts Meas Wash — Report of National Conference on Weights and Measures (Washington)

Rep Natn Coun Combat Vener Dis — Report. National Council for Combating Venereal Diseases [*London*]

Rep Natn Coun Ment Hyg — Report. National Council for Mental Hygiene [*London*]

Rep Natn Dairy Res Inst Karnal — Report. National Dairy Research Institute. Karnal, Punjab

Rep Natn Fd Res Inst (Jap) — Report. National Food Research Institute (Japan)

Rep Natn Fd Surv Comm — Report of the National Food Survey Committee. Ministry of Agriculture, Fisheries, and Food [*London*]

Rep Natn Fmrs Un — Report of the National Farmers' Union [*London*]

Rep Natn Fmrs Un Scotl — Report. National Farmers' Union of Scotland

Rep Natn Forest Pk Comm — Report. National Forest Park Committee [*London*]

Rep Natn Forest Reserv Commn Wash — Report. National Forest Reservation Commission (Washington)

Rep Natn Fuel Pwr Comm — Report of the National Fuel and Power Committee. Board of Trade [*London*]

Rep Natn Hlth Med Res Coun Aust — Report. National Health and Medical Research Council. Australia

Rep Natn Inst Agric Bot — Report of the National Institute of Agricultural Botany [*Cambridge*]

Rep Natn Inst Agric Engng — Report. National Institute for Agricultural Engineering [*Askham Bryan*]

Rep Natn Inst Agric Engng Scott Mach Test Stn — Report. National Institute of Agricultural Engineering and Scottish Machinery Testing Station

Rep Natn Inst Genet (Misima) — Report. National Institute of Genetics (Misima)

Rep Natn Inst Ind Psychol — Report of the National Institute of Industrial Psychology [*London*]

Rep Natn Inst Ind Psychol A Rep — Report of the National Institute of Industrial Psychology. Annual Report [*London*]

Rep Natn Inst Metall (S Afr) — Report. National Institute for Metallurgy (South Africa)

Rep Natn Inst Nutr Tokyo — Report of the National Institute of Nutrition (Tokyo)

Rep Natn Inst Oceanogr — Report of the National Institute of Oceanography [*Cambridge*]

Rep Natn Inst Res Dairy — Report of the National Institute for Research in Dairying. Reading University [*Shinfield, Reading*]

Rep Natn Mus Sci Arts Dubl — Report of the National Museum of Science and Arts (Dublin)

Rep Natn Mus Sth Rhod — Report. National Museum of Southern Rhodesia

Rep Natn Mus Wales — Report. National Museum of Wales

Rep Natn Oceanogr Coun — Report of the National Oceanographic Council [Cambridge]

Rep Natn Paint Varn Lacq Ass Wash — Report. National Paint, Varnish, and Lacquer Association (Washington)

Rep Natn Phys Lab — Report of the National Physical Laboratory [London]

Rep Natn Pig Progeny Test Bd — Report. National Pig Progeny Testing Board [Arlesey]

Rep Natn Quarant Serv China — Report. National Quarantine Service. China

Rep Natn Radium Trust Commn — Report. National Radium Trust and Radium Commission [London]

Rep Natn Res Coun Can — Report of the National Research Council. Canada

Rep Natn Res Coun Can A Rep — Report of the National Research Council. Canada. Annual Report

Rep Natn Res Coun Japan — Report. National Research Council of Japan

Rep Natn Res Coun Labs Can Radio Elect Engng Div — Report of the National Research Council Laboratories of Canada. Radio and Electrical Engineering Division

Rep Natn Res Coun Philipp Isl — Report. National Research Council of the Philippine Islands

Rep Natn Res Coun Wash — Report of the National Research Council (Washington)

Rep Natn Resour Plann Bd Wash — Report. National Resources Planning Board (Washington)

Rep Natn Sci Fdn — Report. National Science Foundation [Washington]

Rep Nat Ophthal Treat Bd — Report. National Ophthalmic Treatment Board [London]

Rep Nat Res Inst Police Sci — Reports. National Research Institute of Police Science

Rep Nat Res Inst Police Sci Res Traffic Saf Regul — Reports. National Research Institute of Police Science. Research on Traffic Safety and Regulation

Rep Nat Res Inst Pollut Resour (Jpn) — Report. National Research Institute for Pollution and Resources (Japan)

Rep Nat Resour Bd Nth Rhod — Report. Natural Resources Board. Northern Rhodesia

Rep Nat Resour Bd Sth Rhod — Report. Natural Resources Board. Southern Rhodesia

Rep Nat Rubb Dev Bd — Report. Natural Rubber Development Board [London]

Rep Natto Res Cent — Reports. Natto Research Center

Rep Nav Obs Wash — Report of the Naval Observatory [Washington]

Rep Nav Res Lab Prog — Report of Naval Research Laboratory Progress

Rep N Carol Agric Exp Stn — Report of the North Carolina Agricultural Experiment Station

Rep N Carol Agric Ext Serv — Report. North Carolina Agricultural Extension Service

Rep N Carol For Ass — Report of the North Carolina Forestry Association

Rep N Carol Geol Econ Surv — Report of the North Carolina Geological and Economic Survey

Rep N Carol Sanat Treat Tuberc — Report of the North Carolina Sanatorium for the Treatment of Tuberculosis

Rep N Carol St Coll Sch Agric — Report of the North Carolina State College School of Agriculture

Rep N Carol Wildl Resour Commn — Report. North Carolina Wildlife Resources Commission

Rep N Cent St Ent Conf — Report of the North Central States Entomologists' Conference

Rep N Dak Agric Exp Stn — Report of the North Dakota Agricultural Experiment Station

Rep NEast Forest Exp Stn New Haven — Report. Northeastern Forest Experiment Station. New Haven, Connecticut

Rep NEast Forest Exp Stn Upper Darby — Report. Northeastern Forest Experiment Station. Upper Darby

Rep Neb Agric Exp Stn — Report. Nebraska Agricultural Experiment Station

Rep Neb St Bd Agric — Report. Nebraska State Board of Agriculture

Rep Ned Scheepsstudiecent TNO — Report. Nederlands Scheepsstudiecentrum TNO

Rep Nene River Bd — Report. Nene River Board [Oundle]

Rep N Engl Assoc Chem Teach — Report. New England Association of Chemistry Teachers

Rep N Engl Inst Min Mech Engrs — Report. North of England Institute of Mining and Mechanical Engineers

Rep Neth Indian Civ Med Serv — Reports. Netherlands-Indian Civil Medical Service

Rep Neurol Inst NY — Report of the Neurological Institute of New York

Rep Nevada Bur Mines Geol — Report. Nevada Bureau of Mines and Geology

Rep Nev Agric Exp Stn — Report. Nevada Agricultural Experiment Station

Rep Nev Bur Mines — Report. Nevada Bureau of Mines

Rep Nev Bur Mines Geol — Report. Nevada Bureau of Mines and Geology

Rep Nev St Apiary Commn — Report. Nevada State Apiary Commission

Rep Nev St Dep Agric — Report. Nevada State Department of Agriculture

Rep New Brunsw Dep Lds Mines — Report. New Brunswick Department of Lands and Mines

Rep Newfoundland Miner Dev Div — Report. Newfoundland. Mineral Development Division

Rep Newfoundld Dep Agric — Report of the Newfoundland Department of Agriculture

Rep Newfoundld Dep Mar Fish — Report from the Newfoundland Department of Marine and Fisheries

Rep Newfoundld Dep Nat Resour — Report. Newfoundland Department of Natural Resources

Rep Newfoundld Fishery Res Lab — Report. Newfoundland Fishery Research Lab

Rep Newfoundld Forest Prot Ass — Report. Newfoundland Forest Protection Association

Rep New Hamps Agric Exp Stn — Report of the New Hampshire Agricultural Experiment Station

Rep New Hamps Fish Game Dep — Report. New Hampshire Fish and Game Department

Rep New Hamps For Commn — Report of the New Hampshire Forestry Commission

Rep New Hebrides Geol Surv — Report. New Hebrides Geological Survey

Rep New Jers Agric Coll Exp Stn — Report. New Jersey Agricultural College Experimental Station

Rep New Jers Dep Agric — Report of the New Jersey Department of Agriculture

Rep New Jers Dep Conserv Dev — Report of the New Jersey Department of Conservation and Development

Rep New Jers Dep Hlth — Report of the New Jersey Department of Health

Rep New Jers Fish Surv — Report. New Jersey Fisheries Survey

Rep New Jers Geol Surv — Report of the New Jersey Geological Survey

Rep New Jers St Agric Exp Stn — Report. New Jersey State Agricultural Experiment Station

Rep New Mex Agric Exp Stn — Report of the New Mexico Agricultural Experiment Station

Rep New Mex Bur Mines Miner Resour — Report. New Mexico Bureau of Mines and Mineral Resources

Rep Niigata Agric Exp Stn — Report. Niigata Agricultural Experiment Station

Rep Niigata Food Res Inst — Report. Niigata Food Research Institute

Rep NIM — Report NIM

Rep Nizamiah Obs — Report. Nizamiah Observatory [Hyderabad]

Rep NJ St Agric Exp Stat — Report. New Jersey State Agricultural Experiment Station

Rep N La Exp Stn — Report. North Louisiana Experiment Station

Rep N Lond Nat Hist Soc — Report. North London Natural History Society

Rep N Manchur Plague Prev Serv — Report. North Manchurian Plague Prevention Service

Rep Noda Inst Scient Res — Report of the Noda Institute for Scientific Research

Rep Noda Inst Sci Res — Report. Noda Institute for Scientific Research

Rep Non Conventl Tech Inf Syst Curr Use — Report. Non-Conventional Technical Information Systems in Current Use [Washington]

Rep Non Metall Miner Invest Br Columb — Report on Non-Metallic Mineral Investigations. British Columbia Department of Mines

Rep Nordita — Report Nordita. Nordisk Organisation for Teoretisk Atomfysik

Rep Nord PAH Proj — Report. Nordic PAH [Polycyclic Aromatic Hydrocarbons] Project

Rep Norfolk Agric Stn — Report. Norfolk Agricultural Station

Rep Norman Lockyer Obs — Report. Norman Lockyer Observatory

Rep Northeast Corn Impr Conf — Report. Northeastern Corn Improvement Conference

Rep Northumb Tyneside River Bd — Report. Northumberland and Tyneside River Board

Rep Norw Fishery Mar Invest — Report on Norwegian Fishery and Marine Investigations

Rep Norw Fish Mar Invest Rep Technol Res — Reports on Norwegian Fishery and Marine Investigation. Reports on Technological Research

Rep Norw For Res Inst — Reports. Norwegian Forest Research Institute

Rep Norw Inst Seaweed Res — Report. Norwegian Institute of Seaweed Research. Norsk Institut for Tang- og Tareforskning

Rep Notes Publ Hlth Labs Cairo — Report and Notes of the Public Health Laboratories (Cairo)

Rep Notif Dis Can — Report of Notifiable Diseases. Canada

Rep Nottingham Univ Sch Agr — Report. Nottingham University. School of Agriculture

Rep Nott Nat Sci Fld Club — Report. Nottingham Natural Science Field Club and Trent Valley Bird Watchers

Rep Nov — Reportorium Novum

Rep Nova Scotia Dep Agric — Report of the Nova Scotia Department of Agriculture

Rep Nova Scotia Dep Mines Energy — Report. Nova Scotia Department of Mines and Energy

Rep Nova Scotia Dep Nat Resour — Report. Nova Scotia Department of Natural Resources

Rep Nova Scotia Fruit Grow Ass — Report. Nova Scotia Fruit Growers Association

Rep Nova Scotia Pwr Commn — Report. Nova Scotia Power Commission

Rep Nova Scotia Res Fdn — Report. Nova Scotia Research Foundation

Rep Nova Scotia Soil Surv — Report. Nova Scotia Soil Survey

Rep NRL Prog — Report of NRL [Naval Research Laboratory] Progress

Rep N Scotl Coll Agric — Report of the North of Scotland College of Agriculture

Rep N Scotl Hort Arboric Ass — Report of the North of Scotland Horticultural and Arboricultural Association

Rep N Scotl Hydro Elect Bd — Report of the North of Scotland Hydro-Electric Board

Rep NS Dep Mines — Report. Nova Scotia Department of Mines

Rep N Sea Fish Invest Comm — Report of the North Sea Fisheries Investigations Committee

Rep NSW St Nutr Comm — Report. New South Wales State Nutrition Committee

Rep Nth Coke Res Comm — Report. Northern Coke Research Committee [Newcastle]

Rep Nth Cties Anim Dis Res Fund — Report of the Northern Counties Animal Diseases Research Fund [Newcastle]

Rep Nth Ire Fire Auth — Report. Northern Ireland Fire Authority

Rep Nth Ire Tuberc Auth — Report. Northern Ireland Tuberculosis Authority

Rep Nth Rocky Mount Forest Exp Stn — Report. Northern Rocky Mountain Forest Experiment Station

Rep Nuffield Fdn — Report of the Nuffield Foundation

Rep Numer Comput Bur Tokyo — Report. Numerical Computation Bureau (Tokyo)

Rep Nutr Lab Carnegie Instn Wash — Report of the Nutrition Laboratory. Carnegie Institution of Washington

Rep Nutr S Afr — Report. Nutrition in South Africa

Rep NW Exp Stn Crookston — Report. Northwest Experiment Station (Crookston, Minnesota)

Rep NW Terr Yukon Brch Dep Interior — Report of the North West Territories and Yukon Branch. Department of the Interior

Rep NY Acad Med — Report. New York Academy of Medicine

Rep NY Bot Gdn — Report of the New York Botanical Garden

Rep NY Cy Met Obs — Report of the New York City Meteorological Observatory

Rep NY Skin Cancer Hosp — Report. New York Skin and Cancer Hospital

Rep NY St Agric Exp Stn — Report of the New York State Agricultural Experiment Station

Rep NY State Vet Coll Cornell Univ — Report. New York State Veterinary College at Cornell University

Rep NY St Bd Hlth — Report. New York State Board of Health

Rep NY St Bot — Report of the New York State Botanist

Rep NY St Coll Agric Cornell — Report of the New York State College of Agriculture at Cornell University Agricultural Experiment Station

Rep NY St Coll For — Report. New York State College of Forestry

Rep NY St Conserv Dep — Report of the New York State Conservation Department

Rep NY St Dep Agric Mkts — Report. New York State Department of Agriculture and Markets

Rep NY St Dep Fms — Report of the New York State Department of Farms

Rep NY St Dep Hlth — Report of the New York State Department of Health

Rep NY St Div Wat Pwr Control — Report. New York State Division of Water Power and Control

Rep NY St Inst Study Malig Dis — Report. New York State Institute for the Study of Malignant Disease

Rep NY St Mus Nat Hist — Report. New York State Museum of Natural History

Rep NY St Mus Sci Div — Report of the New York State Museum. Science Division

Rep NY St Vet Coll — Report. New York State Veterinary College. Cornell University

Rep NY Zool Soc — Report of the New York Zoological Society

Rep NZ Dairy Bd — Report of the New Zealand Dairy Board

Rep NZ Dairy Res Inst — Report of the New Zealand Dairy Research Institute

Rep NZ Dep Sci Ind Res Chem Div — Report. New Zealand. Department of Scientific and Industrial Research. Chemistry Division

Rep NZ Dep Sci Ind Res Dom Lab — Report. New Zealand. Department of Scientific and Industrial Research. DominionLaboratory

Rep NZ Ecol Soc — Report. New Zealand Ecological Society

Rep NZ Energy Res Dev Comm — Report. New Zealand Energy Research and Development Committee

Rep NZ Geogr Soc — Report. New Zealand Geographical Society

Rep NZ Geol Surv — Report. New Zealand Geological Survey

Rep NZGS — Report. New Zealand Geological Survey

Rep NZ Inst Hort — Report. New Zealand Institute of Horticulture

Rep NZ Leath Res Ass — Report. New Zealand Leather Research Association

Rep NZ Orn Soc — Report of the New Zealand Ornithological Society

Rep NZ Sci Cong — Report. New Zealand Science Congress

Rep NZ Stand Inst Coun — Report of the New Zealand Standards Institute Council

Rep NZ St Forest Serv — Report. New Zealand State Forest Service

Rep NZ Wheat Res Inst — Report of the New Zealand Wheat Research Institute

Repo — Reporter. A Fortnightly of Facts and Ideas

Rep Oak Ridge Inst Nucl Stud — Report. Oak Ridge Institute of Nuclear Studies

Rep Obs Comm Falmouth — Report of the Observatory Committee. Falmouth Observatory

Rep Obs Dep Maurit — Report. Observatory Department. Mauritius

Rep Obs Dep Natn Phys Lab — Report of the Observatory Department. National Physical Laboratory. Teddington [*London*]

Rep Observatories Synd Camb — Report of the Observatories Syndicate (Cambridge)

Rep Obsns Invest Atmos Pollut — Report on Observations. Investigation of Atmospheric Pollution. Department of Scientific and Industrial Research (London)

Rep Obsns Sug Beet Trials E Suffolk — Report and Observations on Sugar Beet Trials, etc. East Suffolk County Council

Rep Obs Okla Univ — Reprints. Observatory of Oklahoma University [*Norman*]

Rep Obs Synd Camb — Report of the Observatory Syndicate (Cambridge)

Rep Occur Insect Fungus Pests — Report on the Occurrence of Insect and Fungus Pests on Plants and Crops. Board of Agriculture and Fisheries [*London*]

Rep Oceanic Dep Univ Lpool — Report of the Oceanic Department of the University of Liverpool

Rep Oceanogr Inst Fla St Univ — Report. Oceanographic Institute. Florida State University

Rep Oceanogr Invest Fusan — Report of the Oceanographical Investigations. Government Fishery Experimental Station (Fusan)

Rep Oceanogr Invest Tokai Reg Fish Res Lab — Report. Oceanographic Investigations. Tokai Regional Fisheries Research Laboratory

Rep Oceanogr Obsns Nagasaki — Report of Oceanographical Observations (Nagasaki)

Rep OEEC Halden Boil Heavy Wat React Proj — Report. O.E.E.C. Halden Boiling Heavy Water Reactor Project

Rep OEEC High Temp React Proj Dragon — Report. O.E.E.C. High Temperature Reactor Project Dragon

Rep Off Exp Stns Wash — Report. Office of Experiment Stations (Washington)

Rep Off Rd Inq Wash — Report of the Office of Road Inquiry (Washington)

Rep Offrs Comm Geol Soc Am — Report of the Officers and Committees. Geological Society of America

Rep Off Seed Test Stn Engl Wales — Report of the Official Seed Testing Station for England and Wales

Rep Ohara Inst Agr Biol — Report. Ohara Institute of Agricultural Biology

Rep Ohara Inst Agric Biol — Report. Ohara Institute of Agricultural Biology

Rep Ohara Inst Agric Res — Report of the Ohara Institute for Agricultural Research

Rep Ohio Agric Exp Stn — Report of the Ohio Agricultural Experiment Station

Rep Ohio Conf Sewage Treat — Report. Ohio Conference on Sewage Treatment

Rep Ohio Conf Wat Purif — Report of the Ohio Conference on Water Purification

Rep Ohio Div Mines — Report of the Ohio Division of Mines

Rep Ohio St Acad Sci — Report. Ohio State Academy of Sciences

Rep Ohio St Univ Engng Exp Stn — Report. Ohio State University Engineering Experiment Station

Rep Ohio Tuberc Hlth Ass — Report. Ohio Tuberculosis and Health Association

Rep Oil Colour Chem Ass — Report of the Oil and Colour Chemists' Association

Rep Oil Crops Invest Pullman — Report on Oil Crops Investigations. Washington Agricultural Experiment Station (Pullman)

Rep Oil Palm Res Stn Nigeria — Report. Oil Palm Research Station. Nigeria

Rep Okla Agric Exp Stn — Report. Oklahoma Agricultural Experiment Station

Rep Okla Fish Res Lab — Report. Oklahoma Fisheries Research Laboratory

Rep Ont Agric Coll Exp Fm — Report of the Ontario Agricultural College and Experimental Farm

Rep Ont Agric Exp Un — Report. Ontario Agricultural and Experimental Union

Rep Ontario Geol Surv — Report. Ontario Geological Survey

Rep Ontario Soil Crop Improv Ass — Report of the Ontario Soil and Crop Improvement Association

Rep Ont Dep Agric — Report. Ontario Department of Agriculture

Rep Ont Dep Mines — Reports. Ontario Department of Mines

Rep Ont Geol Surv — Report. Ontario Geological Survey

Rep Ont Minist Environ — Report. Ontario Ministry of the Environment

Rep Ont Res Fdn — Report. Ontario Research Foundation

Rep Ont Vet Coll — Report. Ontario Veterinary College

Rep Open Hearth Comm Iron Steel Ind Res Coun — Report of the Open-Hearth Committee. Iron and Steel Industrial Research Council

Rep Ophthal Sect Dep Publ Hlth Egypt — Report on the Ophthalmic Section. Department of Public Health. Egypt

Rep Ops Dep Forests Papua — Report of the Operations of the Department of Forests. Papua and New Guinea

Rep Ops Fish Game Dep S Aust — Report of the Operations of the Fisheries and Game Department. South Australia

Rep Ops Fish Res Inst Seattle — Report of Operations. Fisheries Research Institute. University of Washington (Seattle)

Rep Ore Dep Agric — Report of the Oregon Department of Agriculture

Rep Ore Dress Lab CSIRO Aust — Report. Ore-Dressing Laboratory. C.S.I.R.O. Australia

Rep Ore Forest Prod Lab — Report. Oregon Forest Products Laboratory

Rep Ore Forest Res Cent — Report. Oregon Forest Research Centre

Rep Ore For Res Lab — Report. Oregon State University. Forest Research Laboratory

Rep Oreg Agric Exp Stat — Report. Oregon Agricultural Experiment Station

Rep Oreg Wheat Comm — Report. Oregon Wheat Commission

Rep Ore St Bd For — Report of the Oregon State Board of Forestry

Rep Ore St Hort Soc — Report. Oregon State Horticultural Society

Rep Orient Cann Inst — Report. Oriental Canning Institute

Rep Orient Hosp Beirut — Report of the Orient Hospital (Beirut)

Rep Orn Harrogate — Report for Ornithology of the Harrogate and District Naturalist and Scientific Society

Rep ORO US Dep Energy — Report ORO [*Oak Ridge Operations Office*] US Department of Energy

Reporte A Serv Coop Inter Am Agric — Reporte Anual. Servicio Cooperativo Inter-Americano di Agricultura

Reporte Biol Inst Pesca Pacif — Reporte Biologico. Instituto de Pesca del Pacifico [*Guayames, Mexico*]

Reporte Biol Sonora — Reporte Biologico (Sonora)

Reporter Aust Inst of Crim Qrtly — Reporter. Australian Institute of Criminology. Quarterly

Report of Invest Wash Div Mines Geol — Report of Investigations. Washington Division of Mines and Geology

Reportorio — Reportorio Anual de Legislacion

Reportr D — Reporter Dispatch

Reports Inst High Speed Mech Tohoku Univ — Reports. Institute of High Speed Mechanics. Tohoku University

Reports Res Inst Appl Mech Kyushu Univ — Reports. Research Institute for Applied Mechanics. Kyushu University

Report TNO Div Nutr Food Res TNO — Report. TNO. Division for Nutrition and Food Research TNO

Rep Osaka City Inst Hyg — Report. Osaka City Institute of Hygiene

Rep Osaka City Inst Public Health Environ Sci — Report. Osaka City Institute of Public Health and EnvironmentalSciences

Rep Osaka Ind Res Inst — Report. Osaka Industrial Research Institute

Rep Osaka Munic Hyg Lab — Report. Osaka Municipal Hygienic Laboratory

Rep Osaka Munic Inst Domest Sci — Report. Osaka Municipal Institute for Domestic Science

Rep Osaka Prefect Ind Res Inst — Reports. Osaka Prefectural Industrial Research Institute

Repos Trab Lab Patol Vet Lisb — Repositorio de Trabalhos do Laboratorio de Patologia Veterinaria (Lisboa)

Repos Trab LNIV Port Lab Nac Inves Vet — Repositorio de Trabalhos do LNIV-Portugal. Laboratorio Nacional de InvestigacaoVeterinaria

Rep Otago Univ Mus — Report of the Otago University Museum

Rep Ottawa River Forest Prot Ass — Report. Ottawa River Forest Protective Association

Rep Oundle Sch Nat Hist Soc — Report of the Oundle School Natural History Society

Rep Ouse Cam Fishery Distr — Report. Ouse and Cam Fishery District

Rep Ovaltine Res Labs — Report. Ovaltine Research Laboratories

Rep Overseas Div Inst Geol Sci — Report. Overseas Division. Institute of Geological Sciences

Rep Overseas Geol Survs — Report of the Overseas Geological Surveys [*London*]

Rep Oxf Orn Soc — Report of the Oxford Ornithological Society on the Birds of Oxfordshire, Berkshire, and Buckinghamshire

Rep Oxfsh Nat Hist Soc — Report. Oxfordshire Natural History Society and Field Club

Rep Oxf Univ Explor Club — Report. Oxford University Exploration Club

Rep Oxon Archaeol Soc — Report of the Oxfordshire Archaeological Society

R E Pp — Papers on Subjects Connected with the Duties of the Corps of Royal Engineers

REPP — Review of Existential Psychology and Psychiatry

Rep Pa Agric Exp Stn — Report. Pennsylvania Agricultural Experiment Station

Rep Pa Bur Mines — Report of the Pennsylvania Bureau of Mines

Rep Pacif Mar Fish Commn — Report. Pacific Marine Fisheries Commission [*Portland*]

Rep Pacif Nav Lab Esquimalt — Report. Pacific Naval Laboratory. Esquimalt

Rep Pacif NW Forest Exp Stn — Report. Pacific Northwest Forest Experiment Station and Range Experiment Station [*Portland*]

Rep Pacif Sci Bd — Report. Pacific Science Board

Rep Pa Dep Agric — Report of the Pennsylvania Department of Agriculture

Rep Pa Dep Forests Wat — Report of the Pennsylvania Department of Forests and Waters

Rep Pa Dep Hlth — Report of the Pennsylvania Department of Health

Rep Pa Dep Mines — Report of the Pennsylvania Department of Mines

Rep Pakist Ass Advmt Sci — Report. Pakistan Association for the Advancement of Science

Rep Pakist Cent Cott Comm — Report. Pakistan Central Cotton Committee

Rep Pakist Coun Scient Ind Res — Report of the Pakistan Council of Scientific and Industrial Research

Rep Pakist Forest Coll Res Inst — Report. Pakistan Forest College and Research Institute

Rep Palaeontogr Soc — Report of the Palaeontographical Society

Rep Palur Agric Res Stns — Report. Palur Agricultural Research Stations

Rep Panama Canal Hlth Dep — Report of the Panama Canal Health Department

Rep Pan Am Sanit Bur — Report. Pan-American Sanitary Bureau

Rep Pap E Angl Inst Agric — Report and Papers. East Anglian Institute of Agriculture

Rep Pap Northamptonshire Antiq Soc — Reports and Papers. Northamptonshire Antiquarian Society

Rep Pap Stanford Electron Labs — Reports and Papers Published. Stanford Electronics Laboratories

Rep Pap Test Comm Pap Mkrs Ass — Report of the Paper Testing Committee. Paper Makers' Association

Rep Parasite Serv Imp Agric Bur — Report on the Parasite Service. Imperial Agricultural Bureau

Rep Partabgarh Agric Stn — Report of the Partabgarh Agricultural Station of the United Provinces of Agra and Oudh

Rep PAS — Repertoire de Prehistoire et d'Archeologie de la Suisse

Rep Pasteur Inst India — Report of the Pasteur Institute of India

Rep Pasteur Inst Sth India — Report. Pasteur Institute of Southern India

Rep Pasteur Inst Vietnam — Report. Pasteur Institute. Vietnam

Rep Past Res NEast US — Report of Pasture Research in the North Eastern United States

Rep Pat Des Trade Mark Cases Lond — Report of Patent, Design, and Trade Mark Cases. Patent Office (London)

Rep Path Div Rubb Res Inst Malaya — Report. Pathological Division of the Rubber Research Institute of Malaya

Rep Path Lab Lunacy Dep NSW — Report from the Pathological Laboratory of the Lunacy Department. New South Wales

Rep Path Labs Cy Lond Hosp Dis Heart Lungs — Report of the Pathological Laboratories. City of London Hospital for Diseases of the Heart and Longs

Rep Pat Off India — Report. Patent Office. India

Rep Pat Off Japan — Report. Patent Office. Japan

Rep Pattambi Agric Res Stn — Report. Pattambi Agricultural Research Station

Rep Pattukkottai Agric Res Stn — Report. Pattukkottai Agricultural Research Station

Rep Peabody Inst — Report of the Peabody Institute

Rep Peabody Mus — Report of the Peabody Museum of American Archaeology and Ethnology

Rep Pea Grow Res Org — Report. Pea Growing Research Organisation

Rep Pea Improv Wk Wash Agric Exp Stn — Report of Pea Improvement Work. Washington. Agricultural Experiment Station

Rep Pembr Bird Prot Soc — Report. Pembrokeshire Bird Protection Society

Rep Penrose Res Lab Zool Soc Philad — Report of the Penrose Research Laboratory. Zoological Society of Philadelphia

Rep Perm Fld Exp Roseworthy Agric Coll — Report on the Permanent Field Experiments. Roseworthy Agricultural College. South Australia

Rep Pest Infest Res Bd — Report of the Pest Infestation Research Board [*London*]

Rep Peterboro Nat Hist Scient Archaeol Soc — Report of the Peterborough Natural History, Scientific, and Archaeological Society

Rep Pharmac Labs Pharm Soc Gt Br — Report. Pharmacological Laboratories. Pharmaceutical Society of Great Britain

Rep Pharm Soc Egypt — Report of the Pharmaceutical Society of Egypt

Rep Phil — Reports on Philosophy

Rep Philipp For Bur — Report. Philippine Forestry Bureau

Rep Philipp Sug Ass Res Bur — Report. Philippine Sugar Association Research Bureau

Rep Philipp Weath Bur — Report. Philippine Weather Bureau

Rep Phys Dep Minist Publ Wks Egypt — Report of the Physical Department. Ministry of Public Works. Egypt

Rep Phys Dep Natn Phys Lab — Report on the Physics Department. National Physical Laboratory

Rep Phys Metall Sect CSIRO Aust — Report. Physical Metallurgy Section. C.S.I.R.O. Australia

Rep Plankton Kobe — Report on Plankton. Kobe Marine Laboratory

Rep Plann Conf Strategy Virus Manage Potato II — Report. Planning Conference on the Strategy for Virus Management in Potatoes. II

Rep Plann Dev Div US Civ Aeronaut Auth — Report of the Planning and Development Division. U.S. Civil Aeronautics Authority

Rep Plast Trop — Report on Plastics in the Tropics. Ministry of Supply [*London*]

Rep Pl Breed Inst — Report. Plant Breeding Institute [*Cambridge*]

Rep Pl Breed Sect Egypt — Report. Plant Breeding Section. Ministry of Agriculture. Egypt

Rep Pl Breed Sta Univ Coll Aberystwyth — Report. Plant Breeding Station of University College (Aberystwyth, Wales)

Rep Pl Introd Gdns Panama — Report. Plant Introduction Gardens. Canal Zone, Panama

Rep Pl Path Bermuda — Report of the Plant Pathologist. Bermuda

Rep Pl Path Lab Harpenden — Report. Plant Pathology Laboratory. Harpenden

Rep Pl Prot Sect Cyprus — Report. Plant Protection Section. Department of Agriculture. Cyprus

Rep Pl Res Comm NZ — Report to the Plant Research Committee. Agronomy Section. Department of Agriculture. N.Z

Rep Plrs Ass Malaya — Report. Planters' Association of Malaya

Rep Pollut Control Commn Wash St — Report. Pollution Control Commission (Washington State)

Rep Pomol Fruit Grow Soc Queb — Report of the Pomological and Fruit Growing Society of Quebec

Rep Pomol Stn Coonoor Burliar Fruit Stns — Report of the Pomological Station at Connoor and Burliar and Kallar Fruit Stations

Rep Popul-Fam Plann — Reports on Population-Family Planning

Rep Poult Div Exp Fms Serv Can — Report. Poultry Division. Experimental Farms Service. Department of Agriculture. Canada

Rep Prat — Repertoire Pratique du Droit Belge

Rep Prat Dr B — Repertoire Pratique du Droit Belge

Rep Prefect Ind Res Inst (Shizuoka) — Reports. Prefectural Industrial Research Institute (Shizuoka)

Rep Prep Commn Int Atom Energy Ag — Report of the Preparatory Commission. International Atomic Energy Agency

Rep Pres Hawaii Sug Plrs Ass — Report of the President. Hawaiian Sugar Planters' Association

Rep Pres Nat Res Counc Can — Report. President. National Research Council. Canada

Rep Pre Stress Concr — Report on Pre-stressed Concrete. Institution of Structural Engineers

Rep Preval Pl Dis Can — Report on the Prevalence of Plant Diseases in the Dominion of Canada

Rep Prickly Pear Ld Commn Qd — Report of the Prickly-Pear Land Commission. Queensland

Rep P Rico Fed Agric Exp Stn — Report. Porto Rico Federal Agricultural Experiment Station. Mayaguez

Rep P Rico Insul Agric Exp Stn — Report. Porto Rico Insular Agricultural Experiment Station

Rep P Rico Sug Prod Ass Exp Stn — Report. Porto Rico Sugar Producers' Association Experiment Station

Rep Princ Chem Lond — Report of the Principal Chemist (London)

Rep Princeton Univ Exped Patagonia — Report. Princeton University Expeditions to Patagonia

Rep Princ Med Offr Tanganyika — Report of the Principal Medical Officer and Senior Sanitary Officer. Tanganyika Territory

Rep Princ Miner Surv Ceylon — Report of the Principal Mineral Surveyor. Ceylon

Rep Prisons Dep Fish Scheme Gold Cst — Report of the Prisons Department Fisheries Scheme. Fisheries Division. Gold Coast

Rep Proc Acts Sea Fish Lond — Report of Proceedings under Acts relating to Sea Fisheries (London)

Rep Proc Am Min Congr — Report of Proceedings. American Mining Congress

Rep Proc Am Pap Pulp Ass — Report of Proceedings. American Paper and Pulp Association

Rep Proc Am Rly Mast Mech Ass — Report of Proceedings of the American Railway Master Mechanics' Association

Rep Proc Am Soc Sanit Engng — Report of Proceedings. American Society of Sanitary Engineering

Rep Proc Am WatWks Ass — Report of Proceedings. American Waterworks Association

Rep Proc Annu Conf Int Iron Steel Inst — Report of Proceedings. Annual Conference. International Iron and SteelInstitute

Rep Proc Annu Conv Am Electroplat Soc — Report of Proceedings. Annual Convention. American Electroplaters'Society

Rep Proc Annu Conv Natl Pecan Assoc — Report. Proceedings. Annual Convention. National Pecan Association

Rep Proc Ass Gas Engrs Mgrs UK — Report of Proceedings. Associations of Gas Engineers and Managers of the United Kingdom

Rep Proc Assoc Shellfish Comm — Report. Proceedings. Association of Shellfish Commissioners

Rep Proc Atlant Deep WatWays Ass — Report of Proceedings. Atlantic Deeper Waterways Association

Rep Proc Aust For Conf — Report of the Proceedings of the Australian Forestry Conference

Rep Proc Barrow Nat Fld Club — Report and Proceedings of the Barrow Naturalists' Field Club

Rep Proc Belfast Nat Hist Philos Soc — Reports and Proceedings. Belfast Natural History and PhilosophicalSociety

Rep Proc Belf Nat Fld Club — Report and Proceedings of the Belfast Naturalists' Field Club

Rep Proc Bldg Congr — Report of Proceedings. Building Congress

Rep Proc Br Commonw Scient Conf — Report of Proceedings. British Commonwealth Scientific Conference

Rep Proc Br Pharm Conf — Report of Proceedings. British Pharmaceutical Conference

Rep Proc Br Soc Anim Prod — Report of Proceedings. British Society of Animal Production

Rep Proc Cocoa Conf — Report and Proceedings Cocoa Conference

Rep Proc Emp Conf Surv Offrs — Report of Proceedings. Empire Conference of Survey Officers

Rep Proc Ent Meet Pusa — Report of Proceedings of Entomological Meetings at Pusa

Rep Proc Fertil Feed Stuffs Act Ire — Report of Proceedings under the Fertilisers and Feeding Stuffs Act. Department of Agriculture. Ireland

Rep Proc Imp Agric Bur Conf — Report of Proceedings. Imperial Agricultural Bureaux Conference

Rep Proc Indiana Engng Soc — Report and Proceedings. Indiana Engineering Society

Rep Proc Instn Fire Engrs — Report and Proceedings. Institution of Fire Engineers</PHR> %

Rep Proc Int Ass Met Atmos Phys — Report of Proceedings. International Association of Meteorology and Atmospheric Physics

Rep Proc Int Assoc Ice Cream Manuf — Report of Proceedings. International Association of Ice Cream Manufacturers

Rep Proc Int Coun Scient Un — Report of Proceedings of the International Council of Scientific Unions

Rep Proc Int Res Coun — Report of Proceedings. International Research Council

Rep Proc Lincoln Engng Soc — Report and Proceedings of the Lincoln Engineering Society

Rep Proc Maize Conf Kenya — Report of Proceedings. Maize Conference. Kenya Colony

Rep Proc Manchr Fld Nat Archaeol Soc — Report and Proceedings of the Manchester Field Naturalists' and Archaeologists' Society

Rep Proc Mersey Aquar Soc — Report and Proceedings. Merseyside Aquarium Society

Rep Proc Nat Archaeol Circle Littlehampton — Report of Proceedings. Nature and Archaeology Circle (Littlehampton)

Rep Proc Natl Assoc Ice Cream Manuf — Report. Proceedings. National Association of Ice Cream Manufacturers

Rep Proc Natn Conf Infant Mort — Report of Proceedings. National Conference on Infantile Mortality [London]

Rep Proc Nat Sci Archaeol Soc Littlehampton — Report of Proceedings. Natural Science and Archaeological Society (Littlehampton)

Rep Proc N Nut Growers Assoc — Report. Proceedings. Northern Nut Growers Association

Rep Proc Norwich Sci Gossip Club — Report of Proceedings of the Norwich Science Gossip Club

Rep Proc ORAU IEA (Oak Ridge Assoc Univ Inst Energy Anal) — Report and Proceedings. ORAU/IEA (Oak Ridge Associated Universities.Institute for Energy Analysis)

Rep Proc Qd Cane Grow Ass — Report of Proceedings. Queensland Cane Growers' Association

Rep Proc R Agric Soc Vict — Report of the Proceedings of the Royal Agricultural Society of Victoria

Rep Proc Reading Lit Scient Soc — Report and Proceedings. Reading Literary and Scientific Society

Rep Proc Sale Fd Drugs Acts Lond — Report of Proceedings under the Sale of Food and Drugs Acts. Board of Agriculture [London]

Rep Proc Salm Freshwat Fish Acts — Report of Proceedings under the Salmon and Freshwater Fisheries Acts [London]

Rep Proc S Dak Engng Soc — Report and Proceedings. South Dakota Engineering Society

Rep Proc SW Soil Wat Conserv Conf — Report of Proceedings of the Southwest Soil and Water Conservation Conference [Stillwater]

Rep Proc Teign Nat Fld Club — Report of Proceedings of the Teign Naturalists' Field Club

Rep Proc Trienn Conf Dep Agric Un S Afr — Report of Proceedings. Triennial Conference. Department of Agriculture. Union of South Africa

Rep Proc W Canad Soc Hort — Report. Proceedings. Western Canadian Society for Horticulture

Rep Proc West Can Irrig Ass — Report of Proceedings. Western Canada Irrigation Association

Rep Proc West Can Soc Hort — Report of Proceedings. Western Canadian Society of Horticulture

Rep Proc West Nut Grow Ass — Report and Proceedings. Western Nut Gowers Association [Oregon]

Rep Prod Div Milk Mktg Bd — Report of the Production Division. Milk Marketing Board [Thames Ditton]

Rep Prod Insp Serv West Reg Nigeria — Report. Produce Inspection Service of the Western Region of Nigeria

Rep Prod Prec Metals US — Report upon the Production of the Precious Metals in the United State

Rep Prog Agric Exp Stn Univ Me — Report of Progress. Agricultural Experiment Station. University of Maine

Rep Prog Agric India — Report on the Progress of Agriculture in India

Rep Prog Agric Sci Tokyo — Report of Progress in Agricultural Sciences. Science Council of Japan (Tokyo)

Rep Prog Ala St Geol Surv — Report of Progress. Alabama State Geological Survey

Rep Prog Appl Chem — Report of the Progress of Applied Chemistry [London]

Rep Prog Appl Chem — Reports on the Progress of Applied Chemistry

Rep Prog Asthma Res Coun — Report of Progress. Asthma Research Council [London]

Rep Prog Chem — Report on the Progress of Chemistry [London]

Rep Prog Civ Aviat — Report on the Progress of Civil Aviation [London]

Rep Prog Discovery Comm Invest — Report on the Progress of the Discovery Committee's Investigations [London]

Rep Prog Forage Crops Res Okla Agric Exp Stn — Report of Progress in Forage Crops Research. Oklahoma Agricultural Experiment Station

Rep Prog Indiana Div Geol — Report of Progress. Indiana Division of Geology

Rep Prog Indiana Geol Surv — Report of Progress. Indiana. Geological Survey

Rep Prog Kans Agric Exp Stn Kans State Coll Agric Appl Sci — Report of Progress. Kansas Agricultural Experiment Station. Kansas State College of Agriculture and Applied Science

Rep Prog Ordn Surv — Report of the Progress of the Ordnance Survey [London]

Rep Prog Phys — Reports on Progress in Physics

Rep Prog Polym Phys (Jpn) — Reports on Progress in Polymer Physics (Japan)

Rep Prog Prod Insp Serv Nth Reg Nigeria — Report on the Progress of the Produce Inspection Service. Northern Region of Nigeria

Rep Progr Appl Chem — Reports on the Progress of Applied Chemistry

Rep Progr Chem — Report on the Progress of Chemistry

Rep Progr Kans Agr Exp Sta — Report of Progress. Kansas Agricultural Experiment Station

Rep Prog Kansas Agric Exp Stn — Report of Progress. Kansas Agricultural Experiment Station

Rep Progr Phys — Reports on Progress in Physics

Rep Prog Rubb Technol — Report on the Progress of Rubber Technology [London]

Rep Prog Stream Meas Can — Report of Progress on Stream Measurements. Department of the Interior. Canada

Rep Prog Tob Res Bd Sth Rhod — Report of Progress. Tobacco Research Board of Southern Rhodesia

Rep Proj LA Agr Exp Sta Dept Agron — Report of Projects. Louisiana Agricultural Experiment Station. Department of Agronomy

Rep Proj La Agric Exp Stn Dep Agron — Report of Projects. Louisiana Agricultural Experiment Station. Department of Agronomy

Rep Propag Dep Int Vereen Rubb Cult Ned Indie — Report of the Propaganda Department. Internationale Vereeniging voor de Rubber-Cultuur in Nederlandsch-Indie

Rep Prot Wood Stockh — Report on the Protection of Wood from Decay, Noxious Animals, and Fire (Stockholm)

Rep Provancher Soc Nat Hist Can — Report of the Provancher Society of Natural History of Canada

Rep Prov Bd Hlth Br Columb — Report of the Provincial Board of Health. British Columbia

Rep Prov Bd Hlth Ontario — Report. Provincial Board of Health. Ontario

Rep Prov Dep Fish Br Columb — Report. Provincial Department of Fisheries. British Columbia

Rep Prov Game Commn Br Columb — Report of the Provincial Game Commission. Province of British Columbia

Rep Prov Game Commnr Br Columb — Report of the Provincial Game Commissioner. Province of British Columbia

Rep Prov Game Ward Br Columb — Report of the Provincial Game Warden. Province of British Columbia

Rep Prov Mus Nat Hist Anthrop Br Columb — Report of the Provincial Museum of Natural History and Anthropology. Province of British Columbia

Rep Prov NS Dep Mines — Report. Province of Nova Scotia Department of Mines

Rep Prov NS Dep Mines Energy — Report. Province of Nova Scotia Department of Mines and Energy

Rep Pr Ph — Reports on Progress in Physics

Rep Pr Phys — Reports on Progress in Physics

Rep Psychol Lab Univ Sth Calif — Report from the Psychological Laboratory. University of Southern California

Rep Psycho Ther Soc — Report of the Psycho-Therapeutic Society [London]

Rep Publ Hlth Adm Burma — Report on the Public Health Administration of Burma

Rep Publ Hlth Comm Ind — Report. Public Health Commissioner, India

Rep Publ Hlth Comm LCC — Report of the Public Health Committee. London County Council

Rep Publ Hlth Commnr India — Report. Public Health Commissioner. India

Rep Publ Hlth Comm NY Acad Med — Report. Public Health Committee of the New York Academy of Medicine

Rep Publ Hlth Dep Cy Lond — Report of the Public Health Department. City of London

Rep Publ Hlth Dep Edinb — Report of the Public Health Department. Edinburgh

Rep Publ Hlth Educ Comm Am Med Ass — Report of Public Health Education Committee. American Medical Association

Rep Publ Hlth Fed Rhod Nyasald — Report on Public Health. Federation of Rhodesia and Nyasaland

Rep Publ Hlth Gibraltar — Report on Public Health. Gibraltar

Rep Publ Hlth Med Subj Lond — Report on Public Health and Medical Subjects. Ministry of Health (London)</PHR> %

Rep Publ Hlth Nova Scotia — Report of the Public Health of Nova Scotia

Rep Publ Hlth Sect R Coll Nurs — Report. Public Health Section. Royal College of Nursing [London]

Rep Publ Hlth Sth Rhod — Report on the Public Health of Southern Rhodesia

Rep Public Gdns Plantns Jamaica — Report Public Gardens and Plantations. Kingston, Jamaica

Rep Public Health Med Subj (Lond) — Reports on Public Health and Medical Subjects (London)

Rep Publ Libr Mus S Aust — Report of the Public Library and Museum of South Australia

Rep Publ Mus Milwaukee — Report of the Public Museum. Milwaukee

Rep Publ Sch Explor Soc — Report. Public Schools Exploring Society [Oxford]

Rep Publ Wks Dep Fed Rhod Nyasald — Report. Public Works Department. Federation of Rhodesia and Nyasaland

Rep Pulp Eval Comm Pap Mkrs Ass — Report of the Pulp Evaluation Committee. Paper Makers' Association

Rep Punjab Irrig Res Inst — Report. Punjab Irrigation Research Institute

Rep Punjab Vet Coll — Report. Punjab Veterinary College and Civil Veterinary Department

Rep Pure Rivers Soc — Report. Pure Rivers Society

Rep Pyrethrum Bd Kenya — Report. Pyrethrum Board of Kenya

Rep Qd Acclim Soc — Report of the Queensland Acclimatisation Society

Rep Qd Inst Med Res — Report of the Queensland Institute for Medical Research

Rep Qd Radium Inst — Report of the Queensland Radium Institute

Rep Quarant Wkg Party Eur Pl Prot Org — Report. Quarantine Working Party. European Plant Protection Organization

Rep Quebec Soc Protect Pl — Report. Quebec Society for the Protection of Plants

Rep Quebec Soc Prot Plant — Report. Quebec Society for the Protection of Plants

Rep Queb Soc Prot Pl — Report of the Quebec Society for the Protection of Plants from Insects and Fungus Diseases

Rep Queb Streams Commn — Report. Quebec Streams Commission

Rep Queensland Geol Surv — Report. Queensland Geological Survey

Rep Que Soc Prot Plants — Report. Quebec Society for the Protection of Plants

REPR — Reports on Polar Research. Berichte zur Polarforschung

Rep Rabb Destruct Coun NZ — Report of the Rabbit Destruction Council of New Zealand

Rep R Acad Med Ire — Report. Royal Academy of Medicine in Ireland

Rep R Adelaide Hosp — Report. Royal Adelaide Hospital

Rep Radiat Chem Res Inst Tokyo — Report of the Radiation Chemistry Research Institute (Tokyo)

Rep Radiat Chem Res Inst Tokyo Univ — Reports. Radiation Chemistry Research Institute. Tokyo University

Rep Radiat Obs Tokyo — Report of Radiation Observation. Central Meteorological Observatory of Japan (Tokyo)

Rep Radiochem Cent — Report. Radiochemical Centre [Amersham]

Rep Radio Div US Dep Commerce — Report. Radio Division. United States Department of Commerce

Rep Radio Res Bd Aust — Report. Radio Research Board. Australia

Rep Radio Res Bd Lond — Report of the Radio Research Board. Department of Scientific and Industrial Research [London]

Rep Radio Res Japan — Report of Radio Research in Japan

Rep Radio Res Wks Japan — Report of Radio Researches and Works in Japan

Rep Radiother Cancer Geneva — Report of Radiotherapy in Cancer (Geneva)

Rep Radiother Univ Coll Hosp Lond — Report on Radiotherapy. University College Hospital (London)

Rep Radium Treat Univ Coll Hosp Lond — Report of Radium Treatment. University College Hospital (London)

Rep R Agric Coll Swed Ser A — Reports. Royal Agricultural College of Sweden. Series A

Rep Rain Making Jpn — Report of Rain-Making in Japan

Rep R Aircr Establ — Report. Royal Aircraft Establishment. Farnborough

Rep R Alfred Obs — Report of the Royal Alfred Observatory. Mauritius

Repr Alumin Dev Ass — Reprints. Aluminium Development Association [London]

Rep Ray Soc — Report of the Ray Society [London]

Rep R Berks Hosp — Report. Royal Berkshire Hospital

Rep R Bot Gdns Edinb — Report of the Royal Botanic Gardens. Edinburgh

Rep R Bot Gdns Peradeniya — Report of the Royal Botanic Gardens. Peradeniya, Ceylon

Rep R Bot Gdns Trin — Report. Royal Botanic Gardens. Trinidad

Rep R Botl Gdns Calcutta — Report of the Royal Botanical Gardens. Calcutta

Repr BRA — Reprint. Bee Research Association

Repr Bull Amer Math Soc — Reprints from the Bulletin of the American Mathematical Society

Repr Bull Bk R — Reprint Bulletin. Book Reviews

Repr Bull Fac Agric Mie Univ — Reprints from Bulletins. Faculty of Agriculture. Mie University

Repr Bur Engng Res Univ Tex — Reprints. Bureau of Engineering Research. University of Texas

Repr Camb Obs — Reprints. Cambridge Observatories

Rep R Can Inst — Report of the Royal Canadian Institute

Repr Carter Obs — Reprints. Carter Observatory [Wellington, New Zealand]

Repr Chem Dep Univ Bgham — Reprints. Chemistry Department. University of Birmingham

Rep R Coll Nurs — Report. Royal College of Nursing [London]

Rep R Coll Obstet Gynaec — Report. Royal College of Obstetricians and Gynaecologists [London]

Rep R Coll Sci Technol Glasg — Report. Royal College of Science and Technology. Glasgow

Rep R Coll Surg — Report. Royal College of Surgeons

Rep R Coll Surg Ire — Report. Royal College of Surgeons in Ireland

Repr Colon Termite Res Unit — Reprints. Colonial Termite Research Unit [London]

Rep R Commn Arsen Poison — Report. Royal Commission on Arsenical Poisoning

Rep R Commn Energy Can — Report. Royal Commission on Energy. Canada

Rep R Commn Sewage Disp — Report of the Royal Commission on Sewage Disposal [London]

Rep R Commn Tuberc — Report of the Royal Commission on Tuberculosis [London]

Rep R Commn Vacc — Report of the Royal Commission on Vaccination [London]

Repr Commonw Bur Hort Plantn Crops — Reprints. Commonwealth Bureau of Horticulture and Plantation Crops

Repr Commonw Sol Obs Canberra — Reprints from the Commonwealth Solar Observatory (Canberra)

Repr Cornell Univ Engng Exp Stn — Reprints. Cornell University Engineering Experiment Station

Rep R Cornwall Polytech Soc — Report of the Royal Cornwall Polytechnic Society

Repr Daubeny Lab — Reprints. Daubeny Laboratory [Oxford]

Rep R Dent Hosp — Report of the Royal Dental Hospital [London]

Repr Div Forest Prod CSIR Aust — Reprints. Division of Forest Products. Council for Scientific and Industrial Research. Australia [Melbourne]

Repr Dom Obs Ottawa — Reprints. Dominion Observatory (Ottawa)

Rep Rd Res Bd — Report. Road Research Board [London]

Rep Rd Res Lab Minist Transp — Report. Road Research Laboratory. Ministry of Transport

Rep Rds Japan Rd Ass — Report on Roads. Japan Road Association

Rep React Cent (Ned) — Report. Reactor Centrum (Nederlandse)

Rep Reading Path Soc — Report of the Reading Pathological Society

Rep Rec Clin Stud Squibb Clin — Report of Recent Clinical Studies. Squibb Clinic

Rep Reclam Serv Can — Report of the Reclamation Service of Canada

Rep Recommend Comm Natn Weed Comm West Sect Can — Report. Recommendations Committee. National Weed Committee. Western Section. Canada

Rep Reelfoot Lake Biol Stn — Report. Reelfoot Lake Biology Station of the Tennessee Academy of Science [Nashville]

Rep Reelfoot Lake Biol Stn Tenn Acad Sci — Report. Reelfoot Lake Biological Station. Tennessee Academy of Science

Rep Ref Bk Mid Somers Nat Soc — Report and Reference Book. Mid-Somerset Naturalist Society

Rep Reg Past Lab Armidale — Report. Regional Pastoral Laboratory. Armidale, N.S.W. (Armidale)

Rep Reg Res Cent ICTA (Trinidad) — Report. Regional Research Centre of the British Caribbean. Imperial College of Tropical Agriculture (Trinidad)

Rep Reg Res Lab CSIR India — Report. Regional Research Laboratory. C.S.I.R. India

Rep Reg Surv Copperbelt Nth Rhod — Report. Regional Survey of the Copperbelt. Northern Rhodesia

Rep Reg Swine Breed Lab US — Report. Regional Swine Breeding Laboratory. United States Department of Agriculture

Rep Reindeer Coun UK — Report. Reindeer Council of the United Kingdom

Rep Reinf Concr Ass — Report. Reinforced Concrete Association [London]

Rep Rel — Repertoire de Reliefs Grecs et Romains

Repr Eng Exp Stn Oreg State Coll — Reprint. Engineering Experiment Station. Oregon State College

Repr Engng Exp Stn Ga Inst Technol — Reprints. Engineering Experiment Station. Georgia Institute of Technology [Atlanta]

Rep Repr Scient Pap Saranac Lab Study Tuberc — Report and Reprints of Scientific Papers. Saranac Laboratory for the Study of Tuberculosis

Rep Repr Sci Pap Saranac Lab Study Tuberc — Report and Reprints of Scientific Papers. Saranac Laboratory for the Study of Tuberculosis

Rep Res Advis Dep SEast Agric Coll Wye — Report. Research and Advisory Department South-Eastern Agricultural College (Wye, Kent)

Rep Res Advis Wk Agric Econ Aberyst — Report on Research and Advisory Work in Agricultural Economics (Aberystwyth)

Rep Res Ass Br Rubb Mfrs — Report. Research Association of British Rubber Manufacturers

Rep Res Cent Assoc Am Railroads — Report. Research Center. Association of American Railroads

Rep Res Cent Ion Beam Technol Hosei Univ — Report. Research Center of Ion Beam Technology. Hosei University

Rep Res Cent Ion Beam Technol Hosei Univ Suppl — Report. Research Center of Ion Beam Technology. Hosei University.Supplement

Rep Res Comm Applic Artif Radioact Isotopes Japan — Report of the Research Committee on the Application of Artificial Radioactive Isotopes in Japan

Rep Res Comm Instn Civ Engrs — Report of the Research Committee. Institution of Civil Engineers [London]

Rep Res Comm Inst Weld — Report of the Research Committee. Institute of Welding

Rep Res Comm North Cent Weed Control Conf — Report. Research Committee. North Central Weed Control Conference

Rep Res Coun Alberta — Report of the Research Council of Alberta

Rep Res Coun Br Whiting Fdn — Report. Research Council. British Whiting Foundation

Rep Res Counc Alberta — Report. Research Council of Alberta

Rep Res Coun DSIR — Report of the Research Council. D.S.I.R. [London]

Rep Res Coun Israel — Report. Research Council of Israel

Rep Res Coun Ont — Report. Research Council of Ontario

Rep Res Def Soc — Report. Research Defence Society [London]

Rep Res Dep Agric Can — Report on Research. Department of Agriculture. Canada

Rep Res Dep Ass Am Portl Cem Mfrs — Report of the Research Department. Association of American Portland Cement Manufacturers

Rep Res Dep Br Sulph Ammon Fed — Report of the Research Department. British Sulphate of Ammonia Federation

Rep Res Dep Cold Wkg Steel Sheffld Univ — Report. Research Department for the Cold Working of Steel and other Ferrous Metals. Sheffield University

Rep Res Dep Combust Appl Mkrs Ass — Report of the Research Department. Combustion Appliance Makers' Association

Rep Res Dep Indian Coff Bd — Report. Research Department. Indian Coffee Board

Rep Res Deps Coll Pharm Soc — Report of the Research Departments. College of the Pharmaceutical Society [London]

Rep Res Dep Sug Mfrs Ass Jamaica — Report. Research Department. Sugar Manufacturers' Association. Jamaica

Rep Res Dept Kyushu Electr Power Co Inc — Report. Research Department. Kyushu Electric Power Company, Incorporated

Rep Res Dev Comm Timb Dev Ass — Report of the Research and Development Committee. Timber Development Association [London]

Rep Res Div Coll Engng NY Univ — Report. Research Division. College of Engineering. New York University

Rep Res Div Minist Agric Sudan — Report of the Research Division. Ministry of Agriculture. Sudan

Rep Researches Elect Commun Lab Tokyo — Report of the Researches of the Electrical Communication Laboratory. Ministry of Telecommunication (Tokyo)

Rep Res Econ Agric Ext Brchs Straits Settl — Report of the Research. Economic and Agricultural Extension Branches. Department of Agriculture. Straits Settlements and Federated Malay States

Rep Res Educ Div Minist Agric Fish Lond — Report. Research and Education Division. Ministry of Agriculture and Fisheries (London)

Represent Mind — Representation and Mind

Rep Res Exp Wk Dep Agric Hyderabad — Report of Research and Experimental Work of the Department of Agriculture (Hyderabad-Deccan)

Rep Res Fdn Ohio St Univ — Report. Research Foundation. Ohio State University

Rep Res Grantees Minist Educ (Jpn) — Reports on Researches by Grantees. Ministry of Education (Japan)

Rep Res Inst Agric Tokyo — Report. Research Institute on Agriculture (Tokyo)

Rep Res Inst Appl Mech — Reports. Research Institute for Applied Mechanics

Rep Res Inst Appl Mech Kyushu Univ — Reports. Research Institute for Applied Mechanics. Kyushu University

Rep Res Inst Basic Sci Chungnam Nat Univ — Reports. Research Institute of Basic Sciences. Chungnam NationalUniversity

Rep Res Inst Brew — Report. Research Institute of Brewing

Rep Res Inst Ceram Tokyo Inst Technol — Reports. Research Institute of Ceramics. Tokyo Institute of Technology

Rep Res Inst Chem Spectrosc Chungnam Natl Univ — Reports. Research Institute of Chemical Spectroscopy. Chungnam NationalUniversity

Rep Res Inst Dent Mater Tokyo Med Dent Univ — Report. Research Institute of Dental Materials. Tokyo Medical andDental University

Rep Res Inst Elect Commun Tohoku Univ — Report of the Research Institute of Electrical Communication. Tohoku University

Rep Res Inst Electr Commun Tohoku Univ — Reports. Research Institute of Electrical Communication. Tohoku University

Rep Res Inst Endem Dis Hosp Cairo — Report. Research Institute and Endemic Diseases Hospital (Cairo)

Rep Res Inst Envir Med Nagoya Univ — Report. Research Institute of Environmental Medicine. Nagoya University

Rep Res Inst Gunze Silk Manuf Co Ltd — Reports. Research Institute. Gunze Silk Manufacturing Co. Ltd.

Rep Res Inst Ind Saf — Reports. Research Institute of Industrial Safety

Rep Res Inst Ind Sci Kyushu Univ — Reports. Research Institute of Industrial Science. Kyushu University

Rep Res Inst Nat Resour Min Coll Akita Univ — Report. Research Institute of Natural Resources. Mining College. AkitaUniversity

Rep Res Inst Nat Sci — Report. Research Institute of Natural Sciences

Rep Res Inst Nat Sci Chungnam Natl Univ — Reports. Research Institute of Natural Sciences. Chungnam National University

Rep Res Inst Phys Chem Chungnam Natl Univ — Reports. Research Institute of Physics and Chemistry. Chungnam NationalUniversity

Rep Res Inst Publ Hlth Engng TNO — Report. Research Institute for Public Health Engineering T.N.O

Rep Res Inst Sci Ind Kyushu Univ — Reports. Research Institute of Science and Industry. Kyushu University

Rep Res Inst Sci Technol Nihon Univ — Report. Research Institute of Science and Technology. Nihon University

Rep Res Inst Stanford — Report of the Research Institute. Stanford

Rep Res Inst Strength and Fract Mater — Reports. Research Institute for Strength and Fracture of Materials

Rep Res Inst Strength Fract Mater Tohoku Univ — Reports. Research Institute for Strength and Fracture of Materials. Tohoku University

Rep Res Inst Strength Fracture Mater Tohoku Univ (Sendai) — Reports. Research Institute for Strength and Fracture of Materials. Tohoku University (Sendai)

Rep Res Inst Technol Nihon Univ — Report. Research Institute of Technology. Nihon University

Rep Res Inst Tuberc Lepr Tohoku Univ — Report of the Research Institute for Tuberculosis and Leprosy. Tohoku University

Rep Res Inst Underground Resour Min Coll Akita Univ — Report. Research Institute of Underground Resources. Mining College. Akita University

Rep Res Invest Univ Melb — Report of Research and Investigation. University of Melbourne

Rep Res Kagawa-Ken Meizen Jr Coll — Reports of Research. Kagawa-Ken Meizen Junior College

Rep Res Lab Asahi Glass Co Ltd — Report. Research Laboratory. Asahi Glass Company Limited

Rep Res Lab Electron Chalmers Univ Technol — Report from the Research Laboratory of Electronics. Chalmers University of Technology

Rep Res Lab Electron MIT — Report. Research Laboratory of Electronics. Massachusetts Institute of Technology

Rep Res Lab Eng Mater Tokyo Inst Technol — Report. Research Laboratory of Engineering Materials. Tokyo Institute of Technology

Rep Res Lab Hydrotherm Chem (Kochi Jpn) — Reports. Research Laboratory of Hydrothermal Chemistry (Kochi, Japan)

Rep Res Lab Imp Iron Works (Jpn) — Report. Research Laboratory. Imperial Iron Works (Japan)

Rep Res Lab Japan Mar Prod Co — Report of Research Laboratory of Japan Marine Products Company

Rep Res Lab Kirin Brew Co — Report. Research Laboratories of Kirin Brewery Company

Rep Res Lab Kirin Brewery Co Ltd — Report. Research Laboratories of Kirin Brewery Company Limited

Rep Res Lab Nippon Seitetsu Yawata Steel Works — Report. Research Laboratory. Nippon Seitetsu. Yawata Steel Works

Rep Res Lab Nippon Suisan Co — Reports. Research Laboratory. Nippon Suisan Co.

Rep Res Lab Precis Mach Electron Tokyo — Report of the Research Laboratory of Precision Machinery and Electronics (Tokyo)

Rep Res Lab Shimizu Constr Co Ltd — Reports. Research Laboratory of Shimizu Construction Company Limited

Rep Res Labs Kirin Brew Co — Report of the Research Laboratories of Kirin Brewery Co

Rep Res Labs Natn Cann Ass Wash — Report of the Research Laboratories. National Canners Association (Washington)

Rep Res Lab Snow Brand Milk Prod Co — Reports. Research Laboratory. Snow Brand Milk Products Company

Rep Res Lab Surf Sci Okayama Univ — Reports. Research Laboratory for Surface Science. Okayama University

Rep Res Lab Tohoku Electr Power Co Ltd — Report. Research Laboratory. Tohoku Electric Power Company Limited

Rep Res Matsuyama Shinonome Jr Coll — Reports of Research. Matsuyama Shinonome Junior College

Rep Res Med Allied Probl Natn Coal Bd — Report. Research on Medical and Allied Problems. National Coal Board

Rep Res Mishimagakuen Women's Jr Sr Coll — Reports. Researches. Mishimagakuen Women's Junior and Senior College

Rep Res Nippon Inst Technol — Report of Researches. Nippon Institute of Technology

Rep Resour Dev Commn Arkans — Report. Resources and Development Commission. Arkansas

Rep Resour Res Inst (Kawaguchi) — Report. Resource Research Institute (Kawaguchi)

Rep Res Progr Ill Agr Exp Sta — Report. Research Progress at the Illinois Agricultural Experiment Station

Rep Res Proj Dis Ornam Pl — Report. Research Project for Diseases of Ornamental Plants (Victorian Plant Research Institute)

Rep Res Standard Comm Instn Auto Engrs — Report. Research and Standardization Committee of the Institution of Automobile Engineers [London]

Rep Res Sub Comm Gas Invest Comm Instn Gas Engrs — Report of the Research Sub-Committee of the Gas Investigation Committee. Institution of Gas Engineers [London]

Rep Result Obsns Fernley Met Obs — Report and Result of Observations. Fernley Meteorological Observatory [Southport]

Rep Results Bacteriol Chem Biol Exam London Waters — Report on the Results of the Bacteriological, Chemical, and BiologicalExamination of the London Waters

Rep Results Chem Bact Exam Lond Wat — Report on the Results of the Chemical and Bacteriological Examination of the London Waters

Rep Results Met Obsns Guernsey — Report on the Results. Meteorological Observations. Guernsey

Rep Results Radiother Cancer Uter Cervix — Report on the Results of Radiotherapy in Cancer of the Uterine Cervix [Stockholm]

Rep Results Treat Carcinoma Uterus — Report on the Results of Treatment in Carcinoma of the Uterus [Stockholm]

Rep Res Wk Bd Agric Fish Plaice N Sea — Report on Research Work. Board of Agriculture and Fisheries in Relation to the Plaice Fisheries in the North Sea

Rep Res Wk Deps Min Fuel Technol Univ Sheffld — Report on Research Work. Departments of Mining and Fuel Technology. University of Sheffield

Rep Res Wk Div Surg Harv Med Sch — Report of Research Work. Division of Surgery. Harvard Medical School

Rep Res Wk Scient Dep Natn Coal Bd — Report of the Research Work of the Scientific Department. National Coal Board [London]

Rep Res Wk SugCane Agric Br W Indies Sug Ass — Report on Research Work on Sugarcane Agriculture. British West Indies Sugar Association, Inc.

Rep Res Worcester Found Exp Biol — Report of Research. Worcester Foundation for Experimental Biology

Repr Flower Astr Obs — Reprints. Flower Astronomical Observatory. University of Pennsylvania

Repr For Prod (Aust) — Reprint. Division of Forest Products (Melbourne, Australia)

Rep R Free Hosp Sch Med — Report. Royal Free Hospital School of Medicine [London]

Repr Geophys Inst Zagr — Reprints. Geophysical Institute. University of Zagreb

Repr Goethe Link Obs — Reprints. Goethe Link Observatory. University of Indiana [Bloomington]

Repr Hannah Dairy Res Inst — Reprints. Hannah Dairy Research Institute [Glasgow]

Rep Rheum Dis — Reports on Rheumatic Diseases

Rep Rheum Dis Ser 2 Pract Probl — Reports on Rheumatic Diseases. Series 2. Practical Problems

Rep Rheum Dis Ser 2 Top Rev — Reports on Rheumatic Diseases. Series 2. Topical Reviews

Rep Rhinoc Beetle Erad Bd Fiji — Report. Rhinoceros Beetle Eradication Board. Fiji

Rep Rhod Chamb Mines — Report. Rhodesia Chamber of Mines

Rep Rhode Isl Agric Exp Stn — Report of the Rhode Island Agricultural Experiment Station

Rep Rhode Isl Bd Purif Wat — Report of the Rhode Island Board of Purification of Waters

Rep Rhode Isl Commnr For — Report of the Rhode Island Commissioner of Forestry

Rep Rhode Isl Commnr Inld Fish — Report. Rhode Island Commissioner of Inland Fisheries

Rep Rhode Isl Dep Agric Conserv — Report. Rhode Island Department of Agriculture and Conservation

Rep Rhode Isl Dep Publ Hlth — Report. Rhode Island Department of Public Health

Rep Rhode Isl Div Fish Game — Report. Rhode Island Division of Fish and Game

Rep Rhode Isl Off Forests Pks — Report. Rhode Island Office of Forests and Parks

Rep Rhode Isl St Bd Agric — Report of the Rhode Island State Board of Agriculture

Rep Rhod Mus — Report. Rhodesia Museum

Rep Rhod Scient Ass — Report of the Rhodesia Scientific Association

Rep R Hort Soc — Report. Royal Horticultural Society [London]

Rep Ribble Bd Conserv — Report. Ribble Board of Conservators [Southport]

Rep Rice Res Inst Cuttack — Report. Rice Research Institute (Cuttack)

Rep Rice Res Offr Burma — Report of the Rice Research Officer. Burma

Rep Rice Res Stn Ambasamudram — Report of the Rice Research Station. Ambasamudram

Rep Rice Substn Buchireddipalem — Report of the Rice Substation. Buchireddipalem

Repr Ill Univ Engng Exp Stn — Reprints. Illinois University Engineering Experiment Station [Urbana]

Repr Inst Atmos Phys Univ Ariz — Reprints. Institute of Atmospheric Physics. University of Arizona [Tucson]

Rep R Inst Br Archit — Report. Royal Institute of British Architects [London]

Rep R Inst Chem — Report. Royal Institute of Chemistry [*London*]

Rep R Instn S Wales — Report. Royal Institution of South Wales

Rep R Inst Publ Hlth Hyg — Report. Royal Institute of Public Health and Hygiene [*London*]

Rep R Inst Sci Bombay — Report. Royal Institute of Science (Bombay)

Repr Inst Theor Astrophys — Reprints. Institute of Theoretical Astrophysics [*Blindern*]

Reprint Bull Bk R — Reprint Bulletin. Book Reviews

Reprint Bull Dep Engng Res N Carol St Coll — Reprint Bulletin. Department of Engineering Research. North Carolina State College

Reprint Circ Ser Natn Res Coun Wash — Reprint and Circular Series of the National Research Council (Washington)

Reprint Rep Coun Pharm Chem Am Med Ass — Reprint of the Report of the Council on Pharmacy and Chemistry. American Medical Association

Reprint Ser Dep Engng Res Univ Mich — Reprint Series. Department of Engineering Research. University of Michigan [*Ann Arbor*]

Reprint Ser Engng Exp Stn La St Univ — Reprint Series. Engineering Experiment Station. Louisiana State University and Agricultural and Mechanical College

Reprint Ser Engng Exp Stn Ore Agric Coll — Reprint Series. Engineering Experiment Station. Oregon Agricultural College [*Corvallis*]

Reprint Ser Engng Exp Stn Ore St Coll — Reprint Series. Engineering Experiment Station. Oregon State College [*Corvallis*]

Reprint Ser Engng Exp Stn Univ Ill — Reprint Series. Engineering Experiment Station. University of Illinois [*Urbana*]

Reprint Ser Geol Surv Ohio — Reprint Series. Geological Survey of Ohio

Reprint Ser Steamship Hist Soc Am — Reprint Series. Steamship Historical Society of America [*Salem*]

Reprint Ser Univ Wis Engng Exp Stn — Reprint Series. University of Wisconsin Engineering Experiment Station [*Madison*]

Reprint Ser Va Agric Exp Stn — Reprint Series. Virginia Agricultural Experiment Station of the Virginia Polytechnic Institute

Repr Ist Naz Elettroacust O M Corbino — Reprints. Istituto Nazionale di Elettroacustica O. M. Corbino [*Roma*]

Repr Ist Naz Ultracust O M Corbino — Reprints. Istituto Nazionale di Ultracustica O. M. Corbino

Rep River Res Inst W Beng — Report. River Research Institute. West Bengal

Rep Rivers Dep Manchr — Report of the Rivers Department. Manchester

Rep R Jersey Agric Hort Soc — Report. Royal Jersey Agricultural and Horticultural Society [*Jersey*]

Repr Kans State Univ Kans Eng Exp Stn — Reprint. Kansas State University. Kansas Engineering Experiment Station

Rep Rly Accid Gt Br — Report on Railway Accidents which Occurred on the Railways of Great Britain

Rep Rly Canal Commn — Report of the Railway and Canal Commission [*London*]

Rep Rly Tech Res Inst Tokyo — Report. Railway Technical Research Institute (Tokyo)

Rep Rly Test Res Cent New Delhi — Report of the Railway Testing and Research Centre [*New Delhi*]

Repr McMath Hulbert Obs — Reprints. McMath-Hulbert Observatory [*Ann Arbor*]

Repr Mont St Bur Mines Geol — Reprints. Montana State Bureau of Mines and Geology

Repr Mt Wilson Palomar Obs — Reprints. Mount Wilson and Palomar Observatories [*Pasadena*]

Rep R Natn Hosp Rheum Dis — Report. Royal National Hospital for Rheumatic Diseases [*Bath*]

Repr Natn Obs Athens — Reprints. National Observatory of Athens

Rep R Nav Bird Watch Soc — Report of the Royal Naval Bird Watching Society

Repr NZ For Serv — Reprint. New Zealand Forest Service

Rep R NZ Soc Hlth Wom Child — Report. Royal New Zealand Society for the Health of Women and Children

Repr Obs Astr Univ Wrocl — Reprints. Obserwatorium Astronomiczne Uniwersytetu Wroclawskiego im. B. Bieruta

Repr Obs Astr Warsz — Reprints. Obserwatoryum Astronomiczne Warszawskie

Repr Obs Univ St Andrews — Reprints from the Observatory. University of St. Andrews

Reprocess Newsl — Reprocessing Newsletter

Rep Rockefeller Fdn — Report. Rockefeller Foundation

Rep Rockefeller Sanit Commn — Report. Rockefeller Sanitary Commission [*Washington*]

Rep Rock Found — Report. Rockefeller Foundation

Rep Rocky Mount Forest Range Exp Stn — Report. Rocky Mountains Forest and Range Experiment Station

Reprod Contracept — Reproduction and Contraception

Reprod Domest Anim — Reproduction in Domestic Animals

Reprod Engr — Reproduction Engineer [*Ann Arbor*]

Reprod Fert — Reproduction Fertility and Development

Reprod Fertil Dev — Reproduction, Fertility, and Development

Reprod Growth Dev — Reproduction, Growth, and Development

Reprod Health Matters — Reproductive Health Matters

Reprod Immunol — Reproductive Immunology

Reprodn Paper News Bull — Reproduction Paper News. Bulletin

Reprodn Rev — Reproductions Review and Methods

Reprod Nutr Dev — Reproduction, Nutrition, Developpement

Reprod Perinat Med — Reproductive and Perinatal Medicine

Reprod Physiol Fish — Reproductive Physiology of Fish

Reprod Rev — Reproductions Review

Reprod Tox — Reproductive Toxicology

Reprod Toxicol — Reproductive Toxicology

Reproduc Campech Campeche — Reproduccion Campechano (Campeche, Mexico)

Reproduccio — Reproduccion

Reproduction Eng — Reproduction Engineering

Reprographics Q — Reprographics Quarterly

Reprography Newsl — Reprography Newsletter

Reprogr Q — Reprographics Quarterly

Rep Rontgen Soc — Report of the Rontgen Society

Rep R Ont Mus Zool Palaeont — Report. Royal Ontario Museum of Zoology and Palaeontology

Rep Rose Lake Wildl Exp Stn — Report. Rose Lake Wildlife Experiment Station [*Rose Lake, British Columbia*]

Rep Rosewarne Exp Stn — Report. Rosewarne Experimental Station and Elbridge Sub-Station [*Camborne*]

Rep Ross Conf Med Res — Report. Ross Conference on Medical Research

Rep Ross Conf Obstet Res — Report. Ross Conference on Obstetric Research

Rep Ross Conf Pediatr Res — Report. Ross Conference on Pediatric Research

Rep Ross Inst Hosp Trop Dis — Report. Ross Institute and Hospital for Tropical Diseases [*London*]

Rep Ross Inst Ind Advis Comm — Report. Ross Institute Industrial Advisory Committee

Rep Ross Inst Trop Hyg India Pakist Brch — Report. Ross Institute of Tropical Hygiene. India and Pakistan Branch

Rep Ross Obst Res Conf — Report. Ross Obstetric Research Conference [*Columbus*]

Rep Ross Pediatr Res Conf — Report. Ross Pediatric Research Conference

Rep Rothamsted Exp Sta — Report. Rothamsted Experimental Station

Rep Rothamsted Exp Stn — Report. Rothamsted Experimental Station

Rep Rowett Inst — Report. Rowett Institute

Rep Roy Soc Van Diemens Land — Report. Royal Society of Van Diemen's Land

Repr Pap Dep Anat Univ Calif — Reprints of Papers from the Department of Anatomy of the University of California [*Berkeley*]

Repr Publ Hlth Rep Wash — Reprints from the Public Health Repots (Washington)

Repr Purdue Univ Engng Exp Stn — Reprints. Purdue University Engineering Experiment Station [*Lafayette*]

Repr Radcliffe Obs — Reprints. Radcliffe Observatory [*Pretoria*]

Repr Radio Astr Stn Univ Helsinki — Reprints. Radio Astronomy Station. University of Helskinki

Repr Res SP — Representative Research in Social Psychology

Repr Riverview Coll Obs — Reprints. Riverview College Observatory [*Riverview, N.S.W.*]

Rep RRL GB Dep Sci Ind Res Road Res Lab — Report RRL. Great Britain Department of Scientific and Industrial Research. Road Research Laboratory

Repr Rothamsted Exp Stn — Reprints. Rothamsted Experimental Station

Repr Rowett Res Inst — Reprints. Rowett Research Institute [*Glasgow*]

Rep R Soc Promot Hlth — Report. Royal Society for the Promotion of Health [*London*]

Rep R Soc Prot Birds — Report of the Royal Society for the Protection of Birds [*London*]

Rep R Soc Vict — Report of the Royal Society of Victoria

Rep R Swed Acad Agric Sci Sect — Report. Royal Swedish Academy of Agriculture. Scientific Section

Rep R Tech Coll Glasg — Report of the Royal Technical College. Glasgow

Repr Technol Lab Indian Cent Cott Comm — Reprints. Technological Laboratory. Indian Central Cotton Committee [*Bombay*]

Repr Tokyo Astr Obs — Reprints. Tokyo Astronomical Observatory

Rep Rubb Chem Div El Du Pont — Report. Rubber Chemicals Division. E. I. Du Pont de Nemours & Co

Rep Rubb Chem ICI — Report on Rubber Chemicals. Imperial Chemicals Industries, Ltd [*London*]

Rep Rubb Res Inst Ceylon — Report. Rubber Research Institute of Ceylon

Rep Rubb Res Inst Malaya — Report. Rubber Research Institute of Malaya

Rep Rubb Tech Dev — Report. Rubber Technical Developments [*London*]

Rep Rugby Sch Nat Hist Soc — Report of the Rugby School Natural History Society

Rep Rugby School Nat Hist Soc — Report. Rugby School Natural History Society

Repr Unit Exp Agron Agric Res Coun — Reprints. Unit of Experimental Agronomy. Agricultural Research Council

Repr Univ Br Columb Biol Sci — Reprints. University of British Columbia. Biological Sciences [*Vancouver*]

Repr Univ Br Columb Phys Sci — Reprints. University of British Columbia. Physical Sciences [*Vancouver*]

Repr Univ Inst Agric West Aust — Reprints. University Institute of Agriculture. Western Australia

Repr Univ Pretoria — Reprints. University of Pretoria

Rep Rur Inds Bur — Report. Rural Industries Bureau [*London*]

Rep Rur Wat Supplies Soil Conserv Bd Sudan — Report. Rural Water Supplies and Soil Conservation Board of the Sudan Government

Repr US Nav Obs — Reprints. United States Naval Observatory [*Washington D.C.*]

Rep Rutland Archaeol Nat Hist Soc — Report of the Rutland Archaeological and Natural History Society

Repr Var Star Sect RNZ Astr Soc — Reprints. Variable Star Section. Royal New Zealand Astronomical Society [*Wellington*]

Repr Warner & Swasey Obs — Reprints. Warner and Swasey Observatory [*Cleveland*]

Repr Wash Univ Engng Exp Stn — Reprints. Washington University Engineering Experiment Station [*Seattle*]

Rep R Welsh Agric Soc — Report. Royal Welsh Agricultural Society

Repr Wis Eng Exp Stn — Reprint. Wisconsin Engineering Experiment Station

Repr Wye Agric Coll — Reprints. Wye Agricultural College

Repr Yale Columb Sth Stn Mt Strombo — Reprints. Yale-Columbia Southern Station. Mount Strombo [*New Haven*]

Rep Ryojun Coll Eng — Reports. Ryojun College of Engineering

Rep Ryojun Coll Engng — Report. Ryojun College of Engineering

Rep R Zool Soc Ire — Report of the Royal Zoological Society of Ireland

REPS — Regional Economic Projections Series

REPS — Revista de Estudios Politicos

REPSA — Revista de Psicoanalisis

Rep SA Ass Adv Sci — Report. South African Association for the Advancement of Science

Rep SAAS Staatl Amt Atomsicherh Strahlenschutz DDR — Report-SAAS. Staatliches Amt fuer Atomsicherheit und Strahlenschutz der DDR

Rep Sado Mar Biol Stn Niigata Univ — Report. Sado Marine Biological Station. Niigata University

Rep Saf Mines Res — Report on Safety-in-Mines Research [*London*]

Rep Saf Mines Res Bd — Report of the Safety-in-Mines Research Board [*London*]

Rep Saf Mines Res Establ (GB) — Report. Safety in Mines Research Establishment (Great Britain)

Rep Saf Plann Div Aeronaut Brch US — Report. Safety and Planning Division. Aeronautics Branch. U.S. Department of Commerce

Rep S Afr Ass Adv Sci — Report. South African Association for the Advancement of Science

Rep S Afr Assoc Adv Sci — Report. South African Association for the Advancement of Science

Rep S Afr Inst Med Res — Report. South African Institute for Medical Research

Rep Saghalien Cent Exp Stn — Report. Saghalien Central Experiment Station

Rep Saitama Inst Environ Pollut — Report. Saitama Institute of Environmental Pollution

Rep Saitama Prefect Brew Inst — Report. Saitama Prefectural Brewery Institute

Rep Salm Freshwat Fish Commn Tasm — Report. Salmon and Freshwater Fisheries Commission. Tasmania

Rep Salm Freshwat Fish Lond — Report on Salmon and Freshwater Fisheries. Ministry of Agriculture and Fisheries (London)

Rep Samalkot Agric Res Stn — Report. Samalkot Agricultural Research Station

Rep Sanit Meas India — Report on Sanitary Measures in India [*London*]

Rep Santa Barbara Bot Gdn — Report. Santa Barbara Botanic Garden

Rep Sapporo Brch For Exp Stn — Report of the Sapporo Branch Forestry Experiment Station

Rep Saskatchewan Energy Mines — Report. Saskatchewan Energy and Mines

Rep Sask Cancer Commn — Report. Saskatchewan Cancer Commission

Rep Sask Dep Agric — Report of the Saskatchewan Department of Agriculture

Rep Sask Dep Highw Transpn — Report. Saskatchewan Department of Highways and Transportation

Rep Sask Dep Miner Resour — Report. Saskatchewan Department of Mineral Resources

Rep Sask Dep Nat Resour — Report. Saskatchewan Department of Natural Resources

Rep Sask Dep Publ Wks — Report. Saskatchewan Department of Public Works

Rep Sask Dep Reconstr Rehabil — Report. Saskatchewan Department of Reconstruction and Rehabilitation

Rep Sask Res Counc — Report. Saskatchewan Research Council

Rep Sask Res Counc Geol Div — Report. Saskatchewan Research Council. Geology Division

Rep Sask Soil Surv — Report. Saskatchewan Soil Survey

Rep Savilian Prof Astr Oxf — Report of the Savilian Professor of Astronomy to the Visitors of the University Observatory (Oxford)

Rep SCAT — Report SCAT

Rep Sch Agric Kings Coll Newcastle — Report. School of Agriculture. King's College. Newcastle upon Tyne

Rep Sch Agric Macdonald Coll — Report. School of Agriculture. Macdonald College

Rep Sch Agric Potchefstroom — Report. School of Agriculture. Potchefstroom

Rep Sch Agric Univ Nott — Report of the School of Agriculture. University of Nottingham

Rep Sch Agric Univ Nottingham — Report. School of Agriculture. University of Nottingham

Rep Sch Agric Univ Sydney — Report. School of Agriculture. University of Sydney

Rep Sch Hyg Univ Toronto — Report. School of Hygiene. University of Toronto

Rep Sch Trop Med P Rico — Report. School of Tropical Medicine. Porto Rico

Rep Sci Advis Bd Natn Res Coun Wash — Report of the Science Advisory Board of the National Research Council [*Washington*]

Rep Sci Coun Japan — Report. Science Council of Japan

Rep Scient Advis Bd Indian Res Fund Ass — Report. Scientific Advisory Board. Indian Research Fund Association [*New Delhi*]

Rep Scient Advis Comm Med Adm Invest Edinb — Report of the Scientific Advisory Committee on Medical Administration and Investigation (Edinburgh)

Rep Scient Adviser Publ Hlth Dep LCC — Report of the Scientific Adviser. Public Health Department. London County Council

Rep Scient Dep Indian Tea Ass — Report. Scientific Department. Indian Tea Association [*Calcutta*]

Rep Scient Dep Overseas Fd Corp Tanganyika — Report. Scientific Department. Overseas Food Corporation. Tanganyika

Rep Scient Dep Tea Sect Un Plrs Ass Sth India — Report. Scientific Department. Tea Section. United Planters Association of Southern India

Rep Scient Dir Nutr Fdn Inc — Report of the Scientific Director. Nutrition Foundation, Inc [*New York*]

Rep Scient Exped Manchoukuo — Report of the Scientific Expedition to Manchoukuo

Rep Scient Ind Res Coun Alberta — Report of the Scientific and Industrial Research Council of Alberta

Rep Scient Inf Serv Eur Org Nucl Res — Report. Scientific Information Service. European Organization for Nuclear Research

Rep Scient Invest Imp Bur Fish Tokyo — Report. Scientific Investigations. Imperial Bureau of Fisheries (Tokyo)

Rep Scient Invest Micronesia — Report on the Scientific Investigations in Micronesia [*Washington*]

Rep Scient Invest Northumb Sea Fish Comm — Report on the Scientific Investations. Northumberland Sea Fisheries Committee

Rep Scient Police Res Inst Tokyo — Report. Scientific Police Research Institute (Tokyo)

Rep Scient Res Comm Sudan — Report. Scientific Research Committee. Sudan

Rep Scient Res Inst Tokyo — Report of the Scientific Research Institute (Tokyo)

Rep Scient Results Michael Sars N Atlant Deep Sea Exped — Report on the Scientific Results of the Michael Sars North Atlantic Deep Sea Expedition [*Bergen*]

Rep Scient Results Norw Exped Nova Zemlya — Report of the Scientific Results of the Norwegian Expedition to Novaya Zemlya [*Kristiania*]

Rep Scient Results Scott Natn Antarct Exped — Report on Scientific Results. Scottish National Antarctic Expedition

Rep Scient Wks Osaka Univ — Report of Scientific Works. Faculty of Science. Osaka University

Rep Scient Wk Surg Staff Wom Hosp St NY — Report on the Scientific Work of the Surgical Staff of the Women's Hospital of the State of New York

Rep Sci Ind Forum — Report. Science and Industry Forum. Australian Academy of Science

Rep Sci Indust Forum — Report. Science and Industry Forum. Australian Academy of Science

Rep Sci Indust Forum Aust Acad Sci — Report. Science and Industry Forum. Australian Academy of Science

Rep Sci Living — Reports of the Science of Living

Rep Sci Mus Lond — Report on the Science Museum and on the Geological Survey and Museum of Practical Geology (London)

Rep Sci Res Inst — Reports. Scientific Research Institute

Rep Sci Res Inst Tokyo — Reports. Scientific Research Institute. Tokyo

Rep Sci Servant Agric — Report. Science-Servant of Agriculture

Rep Sci Serv Dep Agric Can — Report of the Science Service. Department of Agriculture. Canada

Rep Sci Serv Lab Lond Ont — Report. Science Service Laboratory (London, Ontario)

Rep Sci Sess Jpn Dent Assoc — Reports. Scientific Session. Japan Dental Association

Rep Scott Advis Comm Rivers Pollut Prev — Report. Scottish Advisory Committee on Rivers' Pollution Prevention

Rep Scott Agric Org Soc — Report of the Scottish Agricultural Organization Society Ltd

Rep Scott Bd Hlth — Report of the Scottish Board of Health

Rep Scott Beekprs Ass — Report. Scottish Beekeepers Association

Rep Scott Fld Stud Ass — Report. Scottish Field Studies Association

Rep Scott Hort Res Inst — Report. Scottish Horticultural Research Institute

Rep Scott Mar Biol Ass — Report of the Scottish Marine Biological Association

Rep Scott Pl Breed Stn — Report. Scottish Plant Breeding Station

Rep Scott Seaweed Res Ass — Report. Scottish Seaweed Research Association

Rep Scott Soc Res Pl Breed — Report. Scottish Society for Research in Plant Breeding

Rep Scripps Instn Oceanogr — Report. Scripps Institution of Oceanography

Rep SC Water Resour Comm — Report. South Carolina Water Resources Commission

Rep Sea Fish Inst Ser B (Gdynia Pol) — Reports. Sea Fisheries Institute. Series B. Fishing Technique and Fishery Technology (Gdynia, Poland)

Rep Sea Fish Lond — Report on Sea Fisheries (London)

Rep Sea Inld Fish Eire — Report on the Sea and Inland Fisheries. Fisheries Branch. Eire

Rep Sea Inld Fish Ire — Report on the Sea and Inland Fisheries of Ireland

Rep Sea Inld Fish Nth Ire — Report on the Sea and Inland Fisheries of Northern Ireland

Rep Seale Hayne Agric Coll — Report of the Seale Hayne Agricultural College

Rep Seas Crops East Beng Assam — Report on the Seasons and Crops. Eastern Bengal and Assam

Rep Secr Agric — Report. Secretary of Agriculture

Rep Secr Fed Minist Agric Fed Rhod Nyasald — Report. Secretary of the Federal Ministry of Agriculture. Federation of Rhodesia and Nyasaland

Rep Secr Mines Lond — Report of the Secretary for Mines (London)

Rep Secr Mines Sth Rhod — Report of the Secretary for Mines. Southern Rhodesia

Rep Secr Mines Tasm — Report of the Secretary for Mines. Tasmania

Rep Seed Test Pl Regist Stn Scotl — Report on the Seed Testing and Plant Registration Station for Scotland

Rep Seismogr Stn Woodbridge Hill — Report of the Seismograph Station. Woodbridge Hill, Guildford

Rep Selborne Soc Whitgift Sch — Report. Selborne Society. Whitgift School [*Croydon*]

Rep Selsk Ind Tek Forsk Nor Tek Hoegsk — Report. Selskapet for Industriell og Teknisk Forskning ved NorgesTekniske Hoegskole

Rep Sendai Munic Inst Public Health — Report. Sendai Municipal Institute of Public Health

Rep Sendai Public Health Cent — Report. Sendai Public Health Center

Rep Ser Ark Agr Exp Sta — Report Series. Arkansas Agricultural Experiment Station

Rep Ser Ark Agric Exp Stn — Report Series. Arkansas Agricultural Experiment Station

Rep Ser Arkansas Agric Exp Stn — Report Series. Arkansas Agricultural Experiment Station

Rep Ser Chem Univ Oulu — Report Series in Chemistry. University of Oulu

Rep Ser Geol Surv Irel — Report Series. Geological Survey of Ireland

Rep Ser Inland Waters Branch (Can) — Report Series. Inland Waters Branch (Canada)

Rep Ser Inland Waters Dir (Can) — Report Series. Inland Waters Directorate (Canada)

Rep Ser Phys Univ Helsinki — Report Series in Physics. University of Helsinki

Rep Ser Theoret Phys — Report Series in Theoretical Physics

Rep Ser Univ Inst Phys — Report Series. University of Oslo. Institute of Physics

Rep Ser Univ Oslo Dep Phys — Report Series. University of Oslo. Department of Physics

Rep Sess Gen Fish Counc Mediterr — Report of the Session. General Fisheries Council for the Mediterranean

Rep S Francisco Cancer Surv — Report. San Francisco Cancer Survey

Rep Shiga Prefect Inst Public Health — Report. Shiga Prefectural Institute of Public Health

Rep Shiga Prefect Inst Public Health Environ Sci — Report. Shiga Prefectural Institute of Public Health and EnvironmentalScience

Rep Shikoku Eng Assoc — Report. Shikoku Engineering Association

Rep Shimane Prefect Inst Public Health Environ Sci — Report. Shimane Prefectural Institute of Public Health andEnvironmental Science

Rep Shinshu-Miso Res Inst — Reports. Shinshu-Miso Research Institute

Rep Ship Res Inst (Tokyo) — Report. Ship Research Institute (Tokyo)

Rep Shizuoka Citrus Exp Sta — Report. Shizuoka Citrus Experiment Station/ Shizuoka-Ken Kankitsu Shikenjo Hokoku

Rep Shizuoka Ind Technol Cent — Reports. Shizuoka Industrial Technology Center

Rep Shizuoka Prefect Hamamatsu Text Ind Res Inst — Reports. Shizuoka Prefectural Hamamatsu Textile Industrial Research Institute

Rep Shizuoka Prefect Ind Res Inst — Reports. Shizuoka Prefectural Industrial Research Institute

Rep Shizuoka Prefect Ind Technol Cent — Reports. Shizuoka Prefectural Industrial Technology Center

Rep Silk Sci Res Inst — Reports. Silk Science Research Institute

Rep SIPRE — Report SIPRE

Rep (Sixth) Conf Int Ass Quatern Res — Report. Sixth Conference. International Association on Quaternary Research

Rep Smithson Instn — Report. Smithsonian Institution

Rep Soc Friends St Georges — Report of the Society of Friends of St. George's

Rep Soc Hist Germ Maryld — Reports. Society for the History of German in Maryland

Rep Soc Lib St — Society of Libyan Studies. Annual Report

Rep Soc Naut Res — Report. Society for Nautical Research

Rep Soc Res City Futu — Report of the Social Research on the City of Futu

Rep Sol Energy Stud CSIRO — Report. Solar Energy Studies. Commonwealth Scientific and Industrial Research Organisation

Rep South Conf Geront — Report. Southern Conference on Gerontology

Rep South Corn Impr Conf — Report. Southern Corn Improvement Conference

Rep Spec Res Natl Inst Environ Stud (Jpn) — Report of Special Research. National Institute for EnvironmentalStudies (Japan)

Rep Spec Res Proj Natl Inst Environ Stud (Jpn) — Report. Special Research Project. National Institute for Environmental Studies (Japan)

Rep S Pedro Citrus Path Lab — Report of the San Pedro Citrus Pathological Laboratory

Rep Sproul Obs — Reprints. Sproul Observatory. Swarthmore College

Rep Staatl Amtes Atomsicherh Strahlenschutz DDR — Report des Staatlichen Amtes fuer Atomsicherheit und Strahlenschutz derDDR

Rep Staat Zent Strahlenschutz DDR — Report. Staatliche Zentrale fuer Strahlenschutz der DDR

Rep St Andrews Inst Clin Res — Report of the Saint Andrew's Institute for Clinical Research

Rep Stanford Univ John A Blume Earthquake Eng Cent — Report. Stanford University. John A. Blume Earthquake Engineering Center

Rep Stat Appl Res UJSE — Reports of Statistical Application Research. Union of Japanese Scientists and Engineers

Rep Stat Appl Res Union Jpn Sci Eng — Reports of Statistical Application Research. Union of Japanese Scientists and Engineers

Rep State Bd Health Iowa — Report. State Board of Health of Iowa

Rep State Biol Surv Kans — Reports. State Biological Survey of Kansas

Rep State Energy Comm WA — Report. State Energy Commission of Western Australia

Rep Statist Appl Res Un Japan Sci Engrs — Reports of Statistical Application Research. Union of Japanese Scientists and Engineers

Rep St Bartholomews Hosp — Reports of St. Bartholomew's Hospital

Rep Steno Mem Hosp Nord Insulinlab — Reports. Steno Memorial Hospital and the Nordisk Insulinlaboratorium

Rep Sticht CONCAWE — Report. Stichting CONCAWE

Rep Stiftelsen Sven Skeppsforsk — Report. Stiftelsen Svensk Skeppsforskning

Rep St Maurice Forest Prot Ass — Report. Saint Maurice Forest Protective Association

Rep St Thom Hosp — Report. St. Thomas' Hospital [*London*]

Rep Stud GESAMP — Reports and Studies. GESAMP (Joint Group of Experts on the ScientificAspects of Marine Pollution)

Rep Stud Tokyo Coll Domest Sci — Reports of Studies. Tokyo College of Domestic Science

Rep Stud Upland Farming Kawatabi Farm Tohoku Univ — Report of the Studies on Upland Farming in Kawatabi Farm. Tohoku University

Rep Sugar Exp Sta (Taiwan) — Report. Sugar Experimental Station (Taiwan)

Rep Suginami Ward Inst Public Health Res — Report. Suginami Ward Institute of Public Health Research

Rep Surg-Gen US Army — Report. Surgeon-General. United States Army

Rep Surg Gen US Navy — Report. Surgeon General. United States Navy

Rep Surv Thirty-Two NSW River Valleys — Report. Survey of Thirty-Two New South Wales River Valleys

Rep Swed Acad Eng Sci Finl — Report. Swedish Academy of Engineering Sciences in Finland

Rep Swed Deep Sea Exped 1947-1948 — Reports. Swedish Deep-Sea Expedition, 1947-1948

Rep Swed Univ Agric Sci Dep Agric Eng — Report. Swedish University of Agricultural Sciences. Department of AgriculturalEngineering

Rep Swed Univ Agric Sci Dep Farm Build — Report. Swedish University of Agricultural Sciences. Department of Farm Buildings

Rep Swed Univ Agric Sci Dep For Prod — Report. Swedish University of Agricultural Sciences. Department of Forest Products

Rep Swed Univ Agric Sci Dep Plant Husb — Report. Swedish University of Agricultural Sciences. Department ofPlant Husbandry

Rep Swed Univ Agric Sci Dep Radiobiol — Report. Swedish University of Agricultural Sciences. Department ofRadiobiology

Rep Swed Univ Agric Sci Dep Radioecol — Report. Swedish Univeristy of Agricultural Sciences. Department of Radioecology

Rep Swed Weed Conf — Reports. Swedish Weed Conference

Rep Swed Wood Preserv Inst — Report. Swedish Wood Preservation Institute

Rep Symp Brookhaven Natl Lab Biol Dep — Report of Symposium. Brookhaven National Laboratory. BiologyDepartment

Rep Taiwan Sugar Exp Stn — Report. Taiwan Sugar Experiment Station

Rep Taiwan Sugar Res Inst — Report. Taiwan Sugar Research Institute

Rep Tech Coll Hosei Univ (Tokyo) — Report. Technical College. Hosei University (Tokyo)

Rep Technol Cent Nagasaki — Reports of Technology Center of Nagasaki

Rep Technol Iwate Univ — Report on Technology. Iwate University

Rep Technol Res Norw Fish Ind — Reports on Technological Research Concerning Norwegian Fish Industry

Rep Tech Res Cent Finl Biotech Lab — Report. Technical Research Centre of Finland. Biotechnical Laboratory

Rep Tech Res Cent Finl Food Res Lab — Report. Technical Research Centre of Finland. Food Research Laboratory

Rep Tech Res Cent Finl Fuel Lubr Res Lab — Report. Technical Research Centre of Finland. Fuel Lubricant Research Laboratory

Rep Tech Res Cent Finl Met Lab — Report. Technical Research Centre of Finland. Metals Laboratory

Rep Tech Res Cent Finl React Lab — Report. Technical Research Centre of Finland. Reactor Laboratory

Rep Tech Res Inst Ohbayashi Corp — Report. Technical Research Institute. Ohbayashi Corporation

Rep Tech Res Inst Taisei Corp — Reports. Technical Research Institute. Taisei Corporation

Rep Teleph Eng — Reports on Telephone Engineering

Rep Tenn Agric Exp Stat — Report. Tennessee Agricultural Experiment Station

Rep Tex Agric Exp Stn — Report. Texas Agricultural Experiment Station

Rep Tex Dep Water Resour — Report. Texas Department of Water Resources

Rep Text Res Inst Saitama Prefect — Reports. Textile Research Institute. Saitama Prefecture

Rep Tex Water Dev Board — Report. Texas Water Development Board

Rep TKKVB Helsinki Univ Technol Lab Mater Process Powder Met — Report TKK-V-B. Helsinki University of Technology. Laboratory of Materials Processing and Powder Metallurgy

Rep TKK V B Helsinki Univ Technol Lab Metall — Report TKK-V-B. Helsinki University of Technology. Laboratory of Metallurgy

Rep TKKV Helsinki Univ Technol Inst Process Metall — Report TKK-V. Helsinki University of Technology. Institution ofProcess Metallurgy

Rep Tob Res Inst (Taiwan) — Annual Report. Tobacco Research Institute (Taiwan)

Rep Tob Res Inst Taiwan Tob Wine Monop Bur — Report. Tobacco Research Institute. Taiwan Tobacco and Wine Monopoly Bureau

Rep Tochigi Prefect Hyg Inst — Report. Tochigi Prefectural Hygienic Institute

Rep Tohoku Br Crop Sci Soc Jap — Report. Tohoku Branch. Crop Science Society of Japan

Rep Tokai Br Crop Sci Soc Jap — Report. Tokai Branch. Crop Science Society of Japan

Rep Tokoname Ceram Res Inst Aichi Prefect Gov — Reports. Tokoname Ceramic Research Institute. Aichi PrefecturalGovernment

Rep Tokushima Agr Exp Sta — Report. Tokushima Agricultural Experiment Station

Rep Tokushima Food Res Inst — Report. Tokushima Food Research Institute

Rep Tokushima Prefect Ind Res Inst — Report. Tokushima Prefectural Industrial Research Institute

Rep Tokyo Imp Ind Res Inst Lab — Reports. Tokyo Imperial Industrial Research Institute Laboratory

Rep Tokyo Ind Res Inst Lab — Reports. Tokyo Industrial Research Institute Laboratory

Rep Tokyo Ind Test Lab — Reports. Tokyo Industrial Testing Laboratory

Rep Tokyo Industr Res Inst — Report. Tokyo Industrial Research Institute

Rep Tokyo Metrop Ind Res Inst — Reports. Tokyo Metropolitan Industrial Research Institute

Rep Tokyo Metrop Ind Tech Inst — Report. Tokyo Metropolitan Industrial Technic Institute

Rep Tokyo Metrop Res Lab Public Health — Reports. Tokyo Metropolitan Research Laboratory of Public Health

Rep Tokyo-to Lab Med Sci — Report. Tokyo-to Laboratories for Medical Sciences

Rep Tokyo Univ Fish — Report. Tokyo University. Fisheries

Rep Tottori Mycol Inst — Reports. Tottori Mycological Institute

Rep Toyoda Phys Chem Res Inst — Report. Toyoda Physical and Chemical Research Institute

Rep Toyo Jr Coll Food Technol Toyo Inst Food Technol — Reports. Toyo Junior College of Food Technology and Toyo Institute ofFood Technology

Rept Progr Appl — Reports on the Progress of Applied Chemistry

Rept Progr Phys — Reports on Progress in Physics

Rept Progr Polymer Phys (Japan) — Reports on Progress in Polymer Physics (Japan)

Rep Train Inst Eng Teach Kyoto Univ — Report. Training Institute for Engineering Teachers. Kyoto University

Rep Trans Cardiff Naturalists Soc — Report and Transactions. Cardiff Naturalists' Society

Rep Trans (Devonshire) — Report and Transactions (Devonshire)

Rep Trans Devonshire Ass — Reports and Transactions. Devonshire Association for the Advancement of Science, Literature, and Art

Rep Trans E Kent Sci Soc — Reports and Transactions. East Kent Scientific and Natural History Society

Rep Transp Tech Res Inst (Tokyo) — Report. Transportation Technical Research Institute (Tokyo)

Rep Trans Soc Guernesiaise — Report and Transactions. Societe Guernesiaise

Rept Statist Appl Res — Report on Statistical Applications Research

Rep Tuberc Res Inst Kyoto Univ — Reports. Tuberculosis Research Institute. Kyoto University

Repub — Republic

Repubb Ital Minist Agri For Collana Verde — Repubblica Italiana Ministero dell'Agricoltura e delle Foreste Collana Verde

Repub Cote Ivoire Dir Mines Geol Bull — Republique de Cote d'Ivoire. Direction des Mines et de la Geologie. Bulletin

Repub Fed Cameroun Bull Dir Mines Geol — Republique Federale du Cameroun. Bulletin. Direction des Mines etde la Geologie

Repub Malagasy Ann Geol Madagascar — Republique Malagasy. Annales Geologiques de Madagascar

Repub Malagasy Doc Bur Geol — Republique Malagasy. Documentation du Bureau Geologique

Repub Malgache Doc Bur Geol — Republique Malgache. Documentation du Bureau Geologique

Repub Malgache Rapp Annu Serv Geol — Republique Malgache. Rapport Annuel du Service Geologique

Repub Philipp Dep Agric Nat Resour Bur Mines Inf Circ — Republic of the Philippines. Department of Agriculture and Natural Resources. Bureau of Mines. Information Circular

Repub Philipp Dep Agric Nat Resour Bur Mines Rep Invest — Republic of the Philippines. Department of Agriculture and NaturalResources. Bureau of Mines. Report of Investigation

Repub Pop Rom Com Geol Stud Teh Econ — Republica Populara Romina. Comitetul Geologic. Studii Tehnice siEconomice

Repub Rwandaise Bull Serv Geol — Republique Rwandaise. Bulletin du Service Geologique

Repub S Afr At Energy Board Rep PEL — Republic of South Africa. Atomic Energy Board. Report PEL

Repub S Afr At Energy Board Rep PER — Republic of South Africa. Atomic Energy Board. Report PER

Repub S Afr Dep Agric Tech Serv Bull — Republic of South Africa. Department of Agricultural TechnicalServices. Bulletin

Repub S Afr Dep Agric Tech Serv Entomol Mem — Republic of South Africa. Department of Agricultural Technical Services. Entomology Memoirs

Repub S Afr Dep Agric Tech Serv Sci Bull — Republic of South Africa. Department of Agricultural Technical Services. Science Bulletin

Repub S Afr Dep Agric Tech Serv Tech Commun — Republic of South Africa. Department of Agricultural Technical Services. Technical Communication

Repub S Afr Dep Mines Geol Surv Explan Sheets — Republic of South Africa. Department of Mines. Geological Survey.Explanation of Sheets

Repub S Afr Dep Mines Geol Surv Mem — Republic of South Africa. Department of Mines. Geological Survey. Memoir

Repub S Afr Dep Mynwese Geol Opname Ann Geol Opname — Republiek van Suid-Afrika. Departement van Mynwese. Geologiese Opname.Annale van die Geologiese Opname

Repub S Afr Dep Mynwese Geol Opname Handb — Republiek van Suid-Afrika. Departement van Mynwese. Geologiese Opname.Handbook

Repub S Afr Dep Mynwese Geol Opname Toeligting Blaaie — Republiek van Suid-Afrika. Departement van Mynwese. Geologiese Opname.Toeligting van Blaaie

Repub S Afr Geol Opname Bull — Republiek van Suid-Afrika. Geologiese Opname. Bulletin

Repub S Afr Geol Opname Handb — Republiek van Suid-Afrika. Geologiese Opname. Handboek

Repub S Afr Geol Surv Handb — Republic of South Africa. Geological Survey. Handbook

Repub S Afr Geol Surv Mem — Republic of South Africa. Geological Survey. Memoir

Repub Soc Rom Com Geol Stud Teh Econ — Republica Socialista Romania. Comitetul Geologic. Studii Tehnice siEconomice

Repub Venezuela Bol Acad Cienc Fis Mat Natur — Republica de Venezuela. Boletin. Academia de Ciencias Fisicas, Matematicas, y Naturales

Repub Venezuela Bol Acad Ci Fis Mat Natur — Republica de Venezuela. Boletin. Academia de Ciencias Fisicas, Matematicas, y Naturales

Repub Zavod Zast Prir Prir Muz Titogradu Glas — Republicki Zavod za Zastitu Prirode i Prirodnjacki Muzej u Titogradu.Glasnik

Rep Univ Alaska Inst Mar Sci — Report. University of Alaska. Institute of Marine Science

Rep Univ Calif Berkeley Sanit Eng Res Lab — Report. University of California, Berkeley. Sanitary Engineering Research Laboratory

Rep Univ Calif Davis Calif Water Resour Cent — Report. University of California, Davis. California Water Resources Center

Rep Univ Calif Water Resour Cent Universitywide — Report. University of California. Water Resources Center.Universitywide

Rep Univ Copenhagen Phys Lab — Report. University of Copenhagen. Physics Laboratory

Rep Univ Electro-Comm — Reports. University of Electro-Communications

Rep Univ Electro-Commun — Reports. University of Electro-Communications

Rep Univ Leeds Cent Comput Stud — Report. University of Leeds. Centre for Computer Studies

Rep Univ Leeds Dep Comput Stud — Report. University of Leeds. Department of Computer Studies

Rep Univ Melbourne Dep Electr Eng — Report. University of Melbourne. Department of Electrical Engineering

Rep Univ Natal Wattle Res Inst — Report. University of Natal. Wattle Research Institute

Rep Univ NSW Water Res Lab — Report. University of New South Wales. Water Research Laboratory

Rep Univ Oslo Dep Phys — Report. University of Oslo. Department of Physics

Rep Univ Oulu Dep Phys — Report. University of Oulu. Department of Physics

Rep Univ Oxford Dep Eng Sci — Report. University of Oxford. Department of Engineering Science

Rep Univ Rhod Inst Min Res — Report. University of Rhodesia. Institute of Mining Research

Rep Univ Tokyo Inst Space Aeronaut Sci — Report. University of Tokyo. Institute of Space and AeronauticalScience

Rep Univ Waikato Antarct Res Unit — Report. University of Waikato. Antarctic Research Unit

Rep Univ Wis Eng Exp Stn — Report. University of Wisconsin. Engineering Experiment Station

Rep Univ Zimbabwe Inst Min Res — Report. University of Zimbabwe. Institute of Mining Research

Rep USA Mar Biol Inst Kochi Univ — Reports. USA Marine Biological Institute. Kochi University

Rep USA Mar Biol Stn — Reports. USA Marine Biological Station

Rep US Dep Agric For Pest Manage Methods Appl Group — Report. US Department of Agriculture. Forest Pest Management. Methods Application Group

Rep US Dep Agric For Serv Coop For Pest Manage North Reg — Report. US Department of Agriculture. Forest Service. Cooperative Forestry and Pest Management. Northern Region

Rep US Dep Agric For Serv North Reg State Priv For — Report. United States Department of Agriculture Forest Service. Northern Region. State and Private Forestry

Rep Vases — Repertoire des Vases Peints Grecs et Etrusques

Rep Va St Ent — Report of the Virginia State Entomologist [*Blacksburg*]

Rep Va St Hort Soc — Report of the Virginia State Horticultural Society [*Winchester*]

Rep Vet Lab Inst Agric (South Korea) — Report. Veterinary Laboratory. Institute of Agriculture (South Korea)

Rep Victoria Univ Wellington Chem Dep — Report. Victoria University of Wellington. Chemistry Department

Rep V I Lenin All Union Acad Agric Sci — Reports. V. I. Lenin All-Union Academy of Agricultural Sciences

Rep Virus Res Inst Entebbe — Report. Virus Research Institute. Entebbe

Rep Vitic Res Stn Oxted — Report from the Viticultural Research Station. Oxted, Surrey

Rep VT Wood Prod Conf — Report. Vermont Wood Products Conference

Rep Wadi Fara Agric Res Stn — Report Wadi Far'a Agricultural Research Station

Rep W Afr Cacao Res Inst — Report. West African Cacao Research Institute [*Tafo*]

Rep W Afr Cocoa Res Inst — Report. West African Cocoa Research Institute. Tafo [*London*]

Rep W Afr Inst Oil Palm Res — Report. West African Institute for Oil Palm Research [*Benin City*]

Rep W Afr Inst Trypan Res — Report. West African Institute for Trypanosomiasis Research [*Kaduna, Zaria*]

Rep W Afr Maize Rust Res Unit — Report. West African Maize Rust Research Unit [*Ibadan*]

Rep W Afr Rice Res Stn — Report. West African Rice Research Station. Rokupr [*Freetown*]

Rep W Afr Stored Prod Res Unit — Report. West African Stored Products Research Unit [*Lagos*]

Rep W Afr Timb Borer Res Unit — Report of the West African Timber Borer Research Unit. Kumasi [*Princes Risborough*]

Rep Waite Agric Res Inst — Report. Waite Agricultural Research Institute

Rep Walter & Eliza Hall Inst Res Path Med — Report. Walter and Eliza Hall Institute of Reseach in Pathology and Medicine [*Melbourne*]

Rep Ward Ron Devlei Bird Sanct — Report of the Warden of the Ron Devlei Bird Sanctuary [*Capetown*]

Rep Warren Spring Lab — Report of the Warren Spring Laboratory. Stevenage [*London*]

Rep Warwick Nat Hist Soc — Report. Warwick Natural History Society

Rep Wash Agric Exp Stn — Report. Washington Agircultural Experiment Station [*Pullman*]

Rep Wash Forest Fire Ass — Report. Washington Forest Fire Association

Rep Wash Geol Surv — Report of the Washington Geological Survey [*Olympia*]

Rep Wash State Highw Dep Res Program — Report. Washington State Highway Department. Research Program

Rep Wash St Dep Fish — Report. Washington State Department of Fisheries [*Seattle*]

Rep Wash St Dep For — Report of the Washington State Department of Forestry [*Olympia*]

Rep Wash Univ Engng Exp Stn — Report. Washington University Engineering Experiment Station [*Seattle*]

Rep Wat Conserv Irrig Commn NSW — Report. Waster Conservation and Irrigation Commission. New South Wales [*Sydney*]

Rep Wat Dev Dep Tanganyika — Report. Water Development Department. Tanganyika [*Dar-es-Salaam*]

Rep Wat Dev Dep Uganda — Report. Water Development Department. Uganda [*Entebbe*]

Rep Wat Dev Irrig Dep Nth Rhod — Report. Water Development and Irrigation Department. Northern Rhodesia [*Lusaka*]

Rep Water Res Found Aust — Report. Water Research Foundation of Australia

Rep Water Res Found Aust Ltd — Report. Water Research Foundation of Australia Limited

Rep Water Res Lab NSW Univ — Report. Water Research Laboratory. University of New South Wales

Rep Water Resour Res Inst Univ NC — Report. Water Resources Research Institute. University of North Carolina

Rep Water Resour Surv — Report. Water Resources Survey. Tasmania

Rep Wat Res Fdn — Report. Water Research Foundation of Australia

Rep Wat Res Fdn Aust — Report. Water Research Foundation of Australia

Rep Wat Res Lab NSW Univ — Report. Water Research Laboratory. University of New South Wales

Rep Watson Bot Exch Club — Report of the Watson Botanical Exchange Club [*York*]

Rep Wat Supply Dep Ghana — Report. Water Supply Department. Ghana [*Accra*]

Rep Wat Supply Dep Gold Cst — Report. Water Supply Department. Gold Coast [*Accra*]

Rep Wat Supply Irrig Dep Cyprus — Report. Water Supply and Irrigation Department. Cyprus [*Nicosia*]

Rep Watt Comm Energy — Report. Watt Committee on Energy

Rep Wattle Res Inst Univ Natal — Report. Wattle Research Institute. University of Natal [*Pietermaritzburg*]

Rep W Cent Exp Stn Morris — Report of the West Central Experiment Station. Morris [*St. Paul, Minnesota*]

Rep Wear Tees River Bd — Report. Wear and Tees River Board [*Darlington*]

Rep Weath Bur Un S Afr — Report. Weather Bureau. Union of South Africa [*Pretoria*]

Rep Weath Cairo — Report on the Weather (Cairo)

Rep Weath Div USAAF — Report. Weather Division. U.S.A.A.F [*Washington*]

Rep Weath St River Cairo — Report on the Weather and State of the River (Cairo)

Rep Weizmann Inst Sci — Report. Weizmann Institute of Science [*Rehovoth*]

Rep Weld Res Coun — Report of the Welding Research Council [*London*]

Rep Welland River Bd — Report. Welland River Board [*Spalding*]

Rep Wellcome Research Lab — Report. Wellcome Research Laboratories

Rep Wellcome Res Lab — Report. Wellcome Research Laboratories

Rep Wellcome Res Lab — Report. Wellcome Research Laboratories at the Gordon Memorial College

Rep Wellcome Trop Research Lab — Report. Wellcome Tropical Research Laboratories

Rep Wellcome Trop Res Labs — Report of the Wellcome Tropical Research Laboratories [*Khartoum*]

Rep Wellington Coll Nat Sci Soc — Report of the Wellington College Natural Science Society [*Wellington*]

Rep Welsh Agric Org Soc — Report. Welsh Agricultural Organization Society [*Aberystwyth*]

Rep Welsh Plant Breed Stn (Aberystwyth Wales) — Report. Welsh Plant Breeding Station (Aberystwyth, Wales)

Rep Welsh Pl Breed Stn — Report. Welsh Plant Breeding Station

Rep Welsh Soils Discuss Grp — Report. Welsh Soils Discussion Group

Rep West Wash Exp Stn — Report. Western Washington Experiment Station [*Puyallup*]

Rep West Wheat Conf — Report. Western Wheat Conference [*Pullman*]

Rep Wheat Qual Conf — Report. Wheat Quality Conference

Rep White Sea Biol Stn State Univ Moscow — Reports. White Sea Biological Station. State University of Moscow

Rep Wildfowl Trust — Report. Wildfowl Trust [*London*]

Rep Wildl Brch NZ — Report. Wildlife Branch. Department of Internal Affairs. New Zealand [*Wellington*]

Rep Wildl Surv Sect CSIRO Aust — Report. Wildlife Survey Section. C.S.I.R.O. Australia [*Melbourne*]

Rep Winchester Coll Nat Hist Soc — Report of Winchester College Natural History Society

Rep Wis Agric Exp Stn — Report of the Wisconsin Agricultural Experiment Station [*Madison*]

Rep Wk Agric Res Insts UK — Report on the Work of Agricultural Research Institutes in the United Kingdom [*London*]

Rep Wk Army Tumour Regist — Report on the Work of the Army Tumour Registry. Royal Army Medical College [*London*]

Rep Wk Ent Sect Minist Agric Egypt — Report on the Work of the Entomological Section. Ministry of Agriculture. Egypt [*Cairo*]

Rep Wkg Adm Govt Gdns Allahabad — Report on the Working and Administration of the Government Gardens (Allahabad)

Rep Wkg Microbiol Sect King Inst Prev Med — Report on the Working of the Microbiological Section of the King Institute of Preventive Medicine. Madras

Rep Wkg Party Fertil FAO — Report. Working Party on Fertilizers. F.A.O. (Food and Agriculture Organization of the United Nations) [*Rome*]

Rep Wkg Party Rice Breed FAO — Report. Working Party in Rice Breeding. F.A.O. (Food and Agriculture Organization of the United Nations)

Rep Wkg Pasteur Inst Burma — Report of the Working of the Pasteur Institute of the Union of Burma and Government Bacteriological Laboratory [*Rangoon*]

Rep Wk Ld Div Minist Agric Lond — Report on the Work of the Land Division. Ministry of Agriculture (London)

Rep Wk Med Res Endow Act Aust — Report upon the Work done under the Medical Research Endowment Act. Australia [*Melbourne*]

Rep Wk Min Res Lab Bgham Univ — Report on the Work of the Mining Research Laboratory. Birmingham University

Rep Wk Radium Inst — Report of the Work of the Radium Institute [*London*]

Rep Wk Saito Ho-on Kai — Report of Work. Saito Ho-on Kai [*Sendai*]

Rep Wld Met Org — Report of the World Meteorological Organisation [*Geneva*]

Rep Wld Pwr Conf — Report. World Power Conference [*London*]

Rep Woburn Agric Exp Stn — Report of the Woburn Agricultural Experiment Station [*London*]

Rep Woburn Exp Fruit Fm — Report of the Woburn Experimental Fruit Farm [*London*]

Rep Wood Saccharif Discuss Comm — Report. Wood Saccharification Discussion Committee

Rep Woods Forests Dep S Aust — Report. Woods and Forests Department. South Australia [*Adelaide*]

Rep Woods Hole Oceanogr Instn — Report. Woods Hole Oceanographic Institution

Rep Wool Inds Res Ass — Report. Wool Industries Research Association [*Leeds*]

Rep Wool Res Labs CSIRO Aust — Report. Wool Research Laboratories. C.S.I.R.O. Australia [*Melbourne*]

Rep Wool Res Organ NZ — Report. Wool Research Organisation of New Zealand

Rep World Aff — Report on World Affairs

Rep World Congr Agr Res — Report. World Congress on Agricultural Research

Rep World Fertil Surv — Reports on the World Fertility Survey

Rep W Pakist Forest Dep — Report. West Pakistan Forest Department

Rep W Riding Yorks Rivers Bd — Report. West Riding of Yorkshire Rivers Board [*Wakefield*]

Rep W Scot Agr Coll Econ Dept — Report. West of Scotland Agricultural College. Economics Department

Rep W Scotl Agric Coll — Report of the West of Scotland Agricultural College [*Glasgow*]

Rep WS Undersea Med Soc — Report WS. Undersea Medical Society

Rep W Sussex River Bd — Report. West Sussex River Board [*Chichester*]

Rep W Va Agric Exp Stn — Report. West Virginia Agricultural Experiment Station [*Morgantown*]

Rep W Va Conserv Commn — Report. West Virginia Conservation Commission [*Charleston*]

Rep W Va Dep Mines — Report of the West Virginia Department of Mines [*Charleston*]

Rep W Va Geol Surv — Report. West Virginia Geological Survey

Rep W Wales Fld Soc — Report. West Wales Field Society [*Haverfordwest*]

Rep Wye Agric Coll — Report. Wye Agricultural College

Rep Wye Bd Conserv — Report. Wye Board of Conservators [*Chepstow*]

Rep Wye Coll — Report. Wye College [*Ashford*]

Rep Wye Coll Dep Hop Res — Report. Wye College. Department of Hop Research

Rep Wye River Bd — Report. Wye River Board [*Hereford*]

Rep Wyo Agric Exp Stn — Report of the Wyoming Agricultural Experiment Station [*Laramie*]

Rep Wyo Game Fish Commn — Report. Wyoming Game and Fish Commission [*Cheyenne*]

Rep Yakima Cty Hort Dep — Report of the Yakima County Horticultural Department

Rep Yamagata Prefect Inst Public Health — Report. Yamagata Prefectural Institute of Public Health

Rep Yamanashi Ind Technol Cent — Report. Yamanashi Industrial Technology Center

Rep Yamanouchi Cent Res Lab — Report. Yamanouchi Central Research Laboratories

REPYB — Research Policy

Rep Yb Essex Cty Fmrs Un — Report and Year Book. Essex County Farmers' Union [*Chelmsford*]

Rep Yb Soc Prev Relief Cancer — Report and Yearbook. Society for the Prevention and Relief of Cancer [*London*]

Rep Yellow Fever Commn W Afr — Report of the Yellow Fever Commission. West Africa [*London*]

Rep Yerkes Obs — Report. Yerkes Observatory of the University of Chicago

Rep Yeungnam Univ Inst Ind Technol — Report. Yeungnam University. Institute of Industrial Technology

Rep Yeungnam Univ Inst Nat Prod — Report. Yeungnam University. Institute of Natural Products

Rep Yorks Fish Distr — Report. Yorkshire Fishery District [*Hull*]

Rep Yorks Nat Sci Ass — Report. Yorkshire Natural Science Association [*York*]

Rep Yorks Nat Un — Report. Yorkshire Naturalists' Union [*Leeds*]

Rep Yorks Phil Soc — Report of the Yorkshire Philosophical Society [*York*]

Rep Yorks River Bd — Report. Yorkshire River Board [*Leeds*]

Rep Yr Dublin Univ Coll Agr Dept — Report of the Year. Dublin University College. Agricultural Department

Rep Zinc Dev Ass — Report of the Zinc Development Association [*Oxford*]

Rep Zion Org Inst Agric Nat Hist Agric Exp Stn — Report of the Zionist Organisation Institute of Agriculture and Natural History Agricultural Experiment Station [*Tel-Aviv*]

Rep Zool Gdns Gizeh — Report. Zoological Gardens. Gizeh

Rep Zool Serv Egypt — Report of the Zoological Service. Ministry of Public Works. Egypt [*Cairo*]

Rep Zool Soc Lond — Report of the Zoological Society of London

Rep Zool Soc Philad — Report of the Zoological Society of Philadelphia

Rep Zool Soc Scotl — Report of the Zoological Society of Scotland [*Edinburgh*]

Rep Zool Surv India — Report. Zoological Survey of India [*Calcutta*]

REQUEL — Revue d'Entomologie du Quebec

RER — Radio Expenditure Report

RER — Real Estate Review

ReR — Records and Recording

RER — Review of Educational Research

RER — Revue des Etudes Rabelaisiennes

RER — Revue des Etudes Roumaines

RERA — Reclamation Era

RERA — RERA: Official Monthly Journal. Radio and Electrical Retailers' Association of New South Wales

RERAA — Reclamation Era

RERIC Int Energ J — RERIC International Energy Journal

Rer Nat Scr Graec Min — Rerum Naturalium Scriptores Graeci Minores

RERo — Revue des Etudes Roumaines

RE Roum — Revue des Etudes Roumaines

RERTD — Regelungstechnik. RT

RES — Recent Economic Developments

ReS — Reinare en Espana

ReS — Religion et Societes

RES — Repertoire d'Epigraphie Semitique

Res — Researcher

Res — Resurrection

RES — Review of Economics and Statistics

RES — Review of English Studies

RES — Revue de l'Enseignement Superieur

RES — Revue des Etudes Semitiques

RES — Revue des Etudes Semitiques et Babyloniaca

RES — Revue des Etudes Slaves

Res Abstr Highw Res Bd Wash — Research Abstracts. Highway Research Board. National Research Council (Washington)

Res Abstr Natn Advis Comm Aeronaut — Research Abstracts. National Advisory Committee for Aeronautics [*Washington*]

Res Abstr Reclassif Not Nat Advis Comm Aeronaut (US) — Research Abstracts and Reclassification Notice. National AdvisoryCommittee for Aeronautics (United States)

Res Abstr Rep Agric Dep St Lucia — Research Abstract Report of the Agricultural Department of St. Lucia [*Castries*]

Res Abstrs Newsl — Research Abstracts and Newsletter

Res/Accel — Research/Accelerators

Res Achiev Sh US Dep Agric — Research Achievement Sheet. United States Department of Agriculture [*Washington*]

Res Act Fac Sci Engrg Tokyo Denki Univ — Research Activities. Faculty of Science and Engineering of Tokyo Denki University

Res Act For Comm (Victoria Aust) — Research Activity. Forests Commission (Victoria, Australia)

Res Activ Sch Engng Ore St Univ — Research Activities of the School of Engineering. Oregon State University

RESAD — Revista Saude

Res Adv Alcohol Drug Probl — Research Advances in Alcohol and Drug Problems

Res Adv Compositae — Research Advances in the Compositae

Res African Lit — Research in African Literatures

Res Afric Lit — Research in African Literatures

Res Afr Lit — Research in African Literatures

Res Afr Literatures — Research in African Literatures

Res Aging — Research on Aging

Res Agric N Dak — Research in Agriculture. North Dakota

Res & Dev — Research and Development

Res & Eq J — Reserved and Equity Judgements

Res & Eq Jud — Reserved and Equity Judgements

Res & Eq Judg — A'Beckett's Reserved Judgements

Res & Eq Judgm — Reserved and Equity Judgements

Res & Farm — Research and Farming

Res & Invt — Research and Invention

Res Annu Nihon Nosan Kogyo — Research Annual. Nihon Nosan Kogyo

Res Appl Ind — Research Applied in Industry

Res Appl Industr — Research Applied in Industry

Res Appl Natl Needs Rep NSF/RA (US) — Research Applied to National Needs. Report. NSF/RA [*National Science Foundation/Research Applied*] (United States)

Res Appl Technol Symp Mined-Land Reclam Pap — Research and Applied Technology Symposium on Mined-Land Reclamation. Papers

Res Ass — Research Association. Department of Scientific and Industrial Research [*London*]

Res Assoc Br Paint Colour Varn Manuf Bull — Research Association of British Paint, Colour, and Varnish Manufacturers. Bulletin

RESB — Revue des ETudes Semitiques et Babyloniaca

Res Bib — Research Service Bibliographies

Res Biblphies Sheffld Cy Libr — Research Bibliographies. Sheffield City Libraries

Res Biol — Res Biologicae [*Torino*]

Res Bk — Reserve Bank Bulletin

Res Bk NZ — Reserve Bank of New Zealand. Bulletin

Res Brch Pap For Commn — Research Branch Papers. Forestry Commission [*London*]

Res Brch Rep Can Dep Agric — Research Branch Report. Canada Department of Agriculture

Res Briefs — Research Briefs

Res Briefs Fish Commn Ore — Research Briefs. Fish Commission of Oregon [*Portland*]

Res Briefs Fish Comm Oreg — Research Briefs. Fish Commission of Oregon

Res Briefs Sch For Resour PA St Univ — Research Briefs. School of Forest Resources. Pennsylvania State University

Res Bul CERI — Research Bulletin. Central Education Research Institute

Res Bull — Res Bulletin [*Ridgefield, Connecticut*]

Res Bull Agr Home Econ Exp Sta Iowa State Coll — Research Bulletin. Agricultural and Home Economics Experiment Station. Iowa State College

Res Bull Agric Exp Sta Kung Chu Ling Manchoukuo — Research Bulletin. Agricultural Experiment Station. Kung-chu-ling, Manchoukuo/Man Chu Kuo Litsi Kung Chu Ling. Noji Shikenjo Kenkyu Jiho

Res Bull Agric Exp Stn (Ga) — Research Bulletin. Agricultural Experiment Stations (Georgia)

Res Bull Agric Exp Stn (Iowa) — Research Bulletin. Agricultural Experiment Station (Iowa)

Res Bull Agric Exp Stn Kung Chu Ling — Research Bulletin of the Agricultural Experiment Station. Kung-chu-ling [*Manchuria*]

Res Bull Agric Exp Stn Univ Idaho — Research Bulletin. Agricultural Experiment Station. University of Idaho

Res Bull Agric Exp Stn Univ Nebr — Research Bulletin. Agricultural Experiment Station. University of Nebraska

Res Bull Agric Exp Stn Univ Wis — Research Bulletin. Agricultural Experiment Station. College of Agriculture. University of Wisconsin

Res Bull Agric Home Econ Exp Stn (Iowa) — Research Bulletin. Agricultural and Home Economics Experiment Station (Iowa)

Res Bull Aichi-Ken Agric Res Cent — Research Bulletin. Aichi-Ken Agricultural Research Center

Res Bull Aichi-Ken Agric Res Cent Ser A — Research Bulletin. Aichi-Ken Agricultural Research Center. Series A.Food Crop

Res Bull Aichi-Ken Agric Res Cent Ser B — Research Bulletin. Aichi-Ken Agricultural Research Center. Series B. Horticulture

Res Bull Aichi-Ken Agric Res Cent Ser B Hortic — Research Bulletin. Aichi-Ken Agricultural Research Center. Series B. Horticulture

Res Bull Aichi-Ken Agric Res Cent Ser C — Research Bulletin. Aichi-Ken Agricultural Research Center. Series C.Poultry

Res Bull Aichi-Ken Agric Res Cent Ser D — Research Bulletin. Aichi-Ken Agricultural Research Center. Series D.Sericulture

Res Bull Aichi-Ken Agric Res Cent Ser E — Research Bulletin. Aichi-Ken Agricultural Research Center. Series E. Animal Industry

Res Bull Am Petrol Inst — Research Bulletin. American Petroleum Institute [*New York*]

Res Bull BCSIR Lab (Chittagong) — Research Bulletin. BCSIR [(*Bangladesh Council of Scientific and Industrial Research*)] Laboratories (Chittagong)

Res Bull Birla Archaeol Cult Res Inst — Research Bulletin. Birla Archaeological and Cultural Research Institute

Res Bull Br Cast Iron Res Ass — Research Bulletin of the British Cast Iron Research Association [*Birmingham*]

Res Bull Bunda Coll Agric Univ Malawi — Research Bulletin. Bunda College of Agriculture. University of Malawi

Res Bull Cem Res Inst India — Research Bulletin. Cement Research Institue of India

Res Bull Cent Arabic Documn Univ Ibadan — Research Bulletin. Centre for Arabic Documentation (Ibadan)

Res Bull Centre Arabic Doc Ibadan — Research Bulletin. Centre of Arabic Documentation. University of Ibadan

Res Bull Chiba Zootech Exp Stn — Research Bulletin. Chiba Zootechnical Experiment Station

Res Bull CIMMYT — Research Bulletin. Centro Internacional de Mejoramiento de Maiz y Trigo

Res Bull Coll Agric Alberta Univ — Research Bulletin. College of Agriculture. Alberta University

Res Bull Coll Agric Univ Idaho — Research Bulletin. College of Agriculture. University of Idaho

Res Bull Coll Exp Forests Hokkaido Univ — Research Bulletin of the College Experimental Forests. College of Agriculture. Hokkaido University [*Sapporo*]

Res Bull Coll Exp For Hokkaido Univ — Research Bulletins. College Experiment Forests. Hokkaido University

Res Bull Coll Expt Forest Hokkaido Univ — Research Bulletins. College Experiment Forests. Hokkaido University

Res Bull Coll Gen Educ Nagoya Univ Nat Sci Psychol — Research Bulletin. College of General Education. Nagoya University. Natural Sciences and Psychology

Res Bull Colo Greenhouse Grow Assoc — Research Bulletin. Colorado Greenhouse Growers Association

Res Bull Dep Agric Br Columb — Research Bulletin. Department of Agriculture. British Columbia [*Victoria*]

Res Bull Dep Agric Econ Univ Sydney — Research Bulletin. Department of Agricultural Economics. University of Sydney

Res Bull Dep Agric Tasm — Research Bulletin. Department of Agriculture. Tasmania [*Hobart*]

Res Bull Dep Sea Shore Fish Me — Research Bulletin. Department of Sea and Shore Fisheries. Maine [*Augusta*]

Res Bull Div Fish Res Newfoundld — Research Bulletin. Division of Fishery Research. Department of Natural Resources. Newfoundland [*St. Johns*]

Res Bull Div Forest Res Ndola — Research Bulletin. Division of Forest Research. Forest Department. Ndola

Res Bull East Panjab Univ — Research Bulletin. East Panjab University

Res Bull Egypt Sugar Distill Co Sugar Cane Dep — Research Bulletin. Egyptian Sugar and Distillation Company. Sugar-CaneDepartment

Res Bull Electr Power Dev Co Ltd — Research Bulletin. Electric Power Development Company Limited

Res Bull E Panjab Univ — Research Bulletin of the East Panjab University [*Hoshiarpur*]

Res Bull Exp For Hokkaido Univ — Research Bulletin. College Experiment Forests. Hokkaido University

Res Bull Fac Agr Gifu Univ — Research Bulletin. Faculty of Agriculture. Gifu University

Res Bull Fac Agric Ain Shams Univ — Research Bulletin. Faculty of Agriculture. Ain Shams University

Res Bull Fac Agric Gifu-Ken Prefect Univ — Research Bulletin. Faculty of Agriculture. Gifu-Ken Prefectural University

Res Bull Fac Agric Gifu Univ — Research Bulletin. Faculty of Agriculture. Gifu University

Res Bull Fac Ed Oita Univ — Research Bulletin. Faculty of Education. Oita University

Res Bull Fac Educ Oita Univ Nat Sci — Research Bulletin. Faculty of Education. Oita University. Natural Science

Res Bull Fac Lib Arts Oita Univ — Research Bulletin. Faculty of Liberal Arts. Oita University

Res Bull For Dep Kenya — Research Bulletin. Forestry Department. Kenya [*Nairobi*]

Res Bull Forest Exp Sta — Research Bulletin. Forest Experiment Station/Ryukyu Seifu, Keizai-Kyoku Ringyo Shikenjo/Ryukyu Government. Economics Department. Forest Experiment Station

Res Bull For Res Lab Oreg State Univ — Research Bulletin. Forest Research Laboratory. Oregon State University

Res Bull Fukien Agric For Exp Stn — Research Bulletin. Fukien Agricultural and Forestry Experiment Station

Res Bull Ga Agric Exp Stn — Research Bulletin. Georgia Agricultural Experiment Stations

Res Bull Gangweon Natl Univ — Research Bulletin. Gangweon National University

Res Bull Gas Prod Res Comm Am Gas Ass — Research Bulletin. Gas Production Research Committee. American Gas Association [*New York*]

Res Bull Geol Mineral Inst Tokyo Univ Educ — Research Bulletin. Geological and Mineralogical Institute. TokyoUniversity of Education

Res Bull Geol Miner Inst Tokyo Univ — Research Bulletin of the Geological and Mineralogical Institute. Tokyo University

Res Bull Gifu Imp Coll Agr — Research Bulletin. Gifu Imperial College of Agriculture

Res Bull Gifu Imp Coll Agric — Research Bulletin. Gifu Imperial College of Agriculture

Res Bull Gifu Univ Fac Agric — Research Bulletin. Gifu University. Faculty of Agriculture

Res Bull Gov Print Bur — Research Bulletin. Government Printing Bureau

Res Bull Hawaii Agric Exp Stn — Research Bulletin. Hawaii Agricultural Experiment Station

Res Bull Hiroshima Inst Technol — Research Bulletin. Hiroshima Institute of Technology

Res Bull Hokkaido Nat Agr Exp Sta — Research Bulletin. Hokkaido National Agricultural Experiment Station

Res Bull Hokkaido Natl Agric Exp Stn — Research Bulletin. Hokkaido National Agricultural Experiment Station

Res Bull Hokkaido Natn Agric Exp Stn — Research Bulletin. Hokkaido National Agricultural Experiment Station

Res Bull Idaho Agric Exp Stn — Research Bulletin. Idaho Agricultural Experiment Station

Res Bull Iida Women's Jr Coll — Research Bulletin. Iida Women's Junior College

Res Bull Imp Hort Exp Stn Okitsu — Research Bulletin. Imperial Horticultural Experiment Station (Okitsu)

Res Bull Indiana Agr Exp Sta — Research Bulletin. Indiana Agricultural Experiment Station

Res Bull Inst Study Worship & Relig Archit — Research Bulletin. The Institute for the Study of Worship and Religious Architecture

Res Bull Int Cent Impr Maize Wheat — Research Bulletin. International Center for the Improvement of Maize and Wheat

Res Bull Iowa Agric Exp Stn — Research Bulletin. Iowa Agricultural Experiment Station

Res Bull Iowa Agric Home Econ Exp Stn — Research Bulletin. Iowa Agricultural and Home Economics Experiment Station

Res Bull Iowa State Univ Sci Technol Agric Home Econ Exp Stn — Research Bulletin. Iowa State University of Science and Technology.Agriculture and Home Economics Experiment Station

Res Bull Iowa St Univ Agric Home Econ Exp Stn — Research Bulletin. Iowa State University Agricultural and Home Economics Experiment Station

Res Bull Iwate Ind Res Inst — Research Bulletin of the Iwate Industrial Research Institute

Res Bull Kangweon Natl Univ — Research Bulletin. Kangweon National University

Res Bull Korean Soc Anim Sci — Research Bulletin. Korean Society of Animal Science

Res Bull Marathwada Agric Univ — Research Bulletin. Marathwada Agricultural University

Res Bull Mass Agric Exp Stn — Research Bulletin. Massachusetts Agricultural Experiment Station

Res Bull Matsumoto Dent Coll Gen Educ — Research Bulletin. Matsumoto Dental College. General Education

Res Bull Meguro Parasitol Mus — Research Bulletin. Meguro Parasitological Museum

Res Bull Meisei Univ — Research Bulletin. Meisei University

Res Bull Meisei Univ Phys Sci Eng — Research Bulletin. Meisei University. Physical Sciences and Engineering

Res Bull Missouri Agric Exp Stn — Research Bulletin. Missouri Agricultural Experiment Station

Res Bull MO Agric Exp Sta — Research Bulletin. Missouri Agricultural Experiment Station

Res Bull Mo Agric Exp Stn — Research Bulletin. Missouri Agricultural Experiment Station

Res Bull Nat Hist Parks Site Branch — Research Bulletin. National Historic Parks and Site Branch

Res Bull Neb Agric Exp Stn — Research Bulletin. Nebraska Agricultural Experiment Station

Res Bull Nebr Agric Exp Stn — Research Bulletin. Nebraska Agricultural Experiment Station

Res Bull NJ Zinc Co — Research Bulletin. New Jersey Zinc Company

Res Bull Obihiro Univ Ser I — Research Bulletin. Obihiro University. Series I

Res Bull Obihiro Zootech Univ — Research Bulletin. Obihiro Zootechnical University. Series I

Res Bull Obihiro Zootech Univ Ser I — Research Bulletin. Obihiro Zootechnical University. Series I

Res Bull Ohio Agric Exp Stn — Research Bulletin. Ohio Agricultural Experiment Station

Res Bull Ohio Agric Res Dev Cent — Research Bulletin. Ohio Agricultural Research and Development Center

Res Bull Ohio Agric Res Dev Center — Research Bulletin. Ohio Agricultural Research and Development Center

Res Bull Ohio Agric Res Developm Cent — Research Bulletin. Ohio Agricultural Research and Development Center

Res Bull Oita Res Stn Agric Util Hotspring — Research Bulletin. Oita Research Station for Agricultural Utilizationof Hotspring

Res Bull Ore Agric Exp Stn — Research Bulletin. Oregon Agricultural Experiment Station [Corvallis]

Res Bull Ore For Res Lab — Research Bulletin. Oregon State University. Forest Research Laboratory

Res Bull Ore St Bd For — Research Bulletin. Oregon State Board of Forestry [Salem]

Res Bull Pa Dep Forests Wat — Research Bulletin. Pennsylvania Department of Forests and Waters [Harrisburg]

Res Bull Pak CSIR Lab (Rajshahi) — Research Bulletin. Pakistan Council of Scientific and IndustrialResearch Laboratories (Rajshahi)

Res Bull Panjab Univ — Research Bulletin. Panjab University

Res Bull Panjab Univ NS — Research Bulletin. Panjab University. New Series

Res Bull Panjab Univ Sci — Research Bulletin. Panjab University. Science

Res Bull PCSIR Lab — Research Bulletin. PCSIR [Pakistan Council of Scientific and Industrial Research] Laboratories

Res Bull PCSIR Lab (Rajshahi) — Research Bulletin. PCSIR [Pakistan Council of Scientific and Industrial Research] Laboratories (Rajshahi)

Res Bull Perusahaan Negara Bio Farma — Research Bulletin. Perusahaan Negara Bio Farma

Res Bull Plant Prot Serv (Jap) — Research Bulletin. Plant Protection Service (Japan)

Res Bull Plant Prot Serv (Jpn) — Research Bulletin. Plant Protection Service (Japan)

Res Bull Pl Protect Serv Japan — Research Bulletin of Plant Protection Service (Japan) / Shokubutso Bolkisho Chosa Kenkyu Hokoku

Res Bull PN Bio Farma — Research Bulletin. PN [Perusahaan Negara] Bio Farma

Res Bull P Rico Univ Agric Exp Stn — Research Bulletin. Porto Rico University Agricultural Experiment Station [Rio Piedras]

Res Bull Print Bur Minist Finance — Research Bulletin. Printing Bureau. Ministry of Finance

Res Bull Printing Bur (Tokyo) — Research Bulletin. Printing Bureau. Ministry of Finance (Tokyo)

Res Bull Purdue Univ Agr Exp Sta — Research Bulletin. Purdue University. Agricultural Experiment Station

Res Bull Purdue Univ Agric Exp Stn — Research Bulletin. Purdue University. Agricultural Experiment Station

Res Bull Purdue Univ Engng Exp Stn — Research Bulletin. Purdue University Engineering Experiment Station [Lafayette]

Res Bull Reg Eng Coll (Warangal) — Research Bulletin. Regional Engineering College (Warangal)

Res Bull Saitama Agr Exp Sta — Research Bulletin. Saitama Agricultural Experiment Station

Res Bull Saitama Agric Exp Stn — Research Bulletin. Saitama Agricultural Experiment Station

Res Bull Saito Ho On Kai Mus — Research Bulletin. Saito Ho-on Kai Museum [Sendai]

Res Bull Saugur Univ Phys Soc — Research Bulletin of the Saugur University Physical Society

Res Bull Sch Engng Toronto Univ — Research Bulletin. School of Engineering. Toronto University

Res Bull Sims Woodhead Meml Lab — Research Bulletin. Sims Woodhead Memorial Laboratory [Papworth]

Res Bull Sisal Exp Stn Ngomeni — Research Bulletin. Sisal Experimental Station. Ngomeni

Res Bull State Univ Oklahoma — Research Bulletin. State University of Oklahoma

Res Bull St Fish NSW — Research Bulletin. State Fisheries. New South Wales [Sydney]

Res Bull Sugar-Cane Dep Egypt Sugar Distill Co — Research Bulletin. Sugar-Cane Department. Egyptian Sugar andDistillation Company

Res Bull Tokushima Bunri Univ — Research Bulletin. Tokushima Bunri University

Res Bull Toyama Prefect Coll Technol — Research Bulletin. Toyama Prefectural College of Technology

Res Bull Univ Calcutta — Research Bulletin. University of Calcutta

Res Bull Univ Farm Hokkaido Univ — Research Bulletin. University Farm. Hokkaido University

Res Bull Univ For Tokyo Univ Agric Technol — Research Bulletin of the University Forests. Tokyo University of Agriculture and Technology

Res Bull Univ Ga Coll Agric Exp Stn — Research Bulletin. University of Georgia. College of Agriculture Experiment Stations

Res Bull Univ GA Exp Stn — Research Bulletin. University of Georgia. Experiment Stations

Res Bull Univ Idaho Agric Exp Stn — Research Bulletin. University of Idaho. Agricultural Experiment Station

Res Bull Univ MO Coll Agr Exp Sta — Research Bulletin. University of Missouri. College of Agriculture. Experiment Station

Res Bull Univ Neb — Research Bulletin. University of Nebraska [Lincoln]

Res Bull Univ Nebr Coll Agr Home Econ Agr Exp Sta — Research Bulletin. University of Nebraska. College of Agriculture and Home Economics. Agricultural Experiment Station

Res Bull Univ Nebr Lincoln Agric Exp Stn — Research Bulletin. University of Nebraska-Lincoln. AgriculturalExperiment Station

Res Bull Univ Okla — Research Bulletin. University of Oklahoma [Norman]

Res Bull Univ Wis Madison Coll Agric Life Sci Res Div — Research Bulletin. University of Wisconsin-Madison. College ofAgricultural and Life Sciences. Research Division

Res Bull Univ Wis Madison Res Div Coll Agric Life Sci — Research Bulletin. University of Wisconsin-Madison. Research Division. College of Agricultural and Life Sciences

Res Bull Wash State Univ Agric Res Cent — Research Bulletin. Washington State University. Agricultural Research Center

Res Bull Wash St Dep Fish — Research Bulletin. Washington State Department of Fisheries [Seattle]

Res Bull West Scotl Agric Coll — Research Bulletin. West of Scotland Agricultural College

Res Bull Wis Agr Exp Sta — Research Bulletin. Wisconsin Agricultural Experiment Station

Res Bull Wis Agric Exp Stn — Research Bulletin. Wisconsin Agricultural Experiment Station

Res Bull W Scotl Coll Agric — Research Bulletin. West of Scotland College of Agriculture

Res Bull W Va Engng Exp Stn — Research Bulletin. West Virginia Engineering Experiment Station

Res Bul NIER — Research Bulletin. National Institute for Educational Research

Res Bul RICEC — Research Bulletin. Research Institute of Comparative Education and Culture

Res Bull Soviet Union — Research Bulletin on the Soviet Union. American Russian Institute for Cultural Relations with the Soviet Union

Res Bus Econ Pub Pol — Research in Business Economics and Public Policy

Res Cent Ion Beam Technol Hosei Univ Rep Suppl — Research Center of Ion Beam Technology. Hosei University. Report. Supplement

R Esc Est Penitenciarios — Revista. Escuela de Estudios Penitenciarios. Publicacion Oficial de la Direccion General de Prisiones

Res Chem In — Research on Chemical Intermediates

Res Chem Intermed — Research on Chemical Intermediates

Res Chem Kinet — Research in Chemical Kinetics

Res Chron — Research Chronicle. Royal Musical Association

Res Circ For Commn — Research Circular. Forestry Commission [London]

Res Circ Ohio Agric Exp Stn — Research Circular. Ohio Agricultural Experiment Station

Res Circ Ohio Agric Res Dev Cent — Research Circular. Ohio Agricultural Research and Development Center

Res Circ Ohio Agr Res Develop Cent — Research Circular. Ohio Agricultural Research and Development Center

Res Circ Pa Dep Forests Wat — Research Circular. Pennsylvania Department of Forests and Waters [Harrisburg]

Res Circ Wash State Univ Agric Res Cent — Research Circular. Washington State University. Agricultural ResearchCenter

Res Clin Forums — Research and Clinical Forums

Res Clin L — Research in Clinic and Laboratory

Res Clin Lab — Research in Clinic and Laboratory

Res Clin Stud Headache — Research and.Clinical Studies in Headache

Res Coat — Research for Coatings

Res Comm C P — Research Communications in Chemical Pathology and Pharmacology

Res Comments Evans Res Dev Corp — Research Comments. Evans Research and Development Corporation [New York]

Res Comments Facts Trend Evans Res Dev Corp — Research Comments, Facts, and Trends. Evans Research and Development Corporation [New York]

Res Commun Alcohol Subst Abuse — Research Communications in Alcohol and Substances of Abuse

Res Commun Biochem Cell & Mol Biol — Research Communications in Biochemistry and Cell and Molecular Biology

Res Commun Biol Psychol Psychiatr — Research Communications in Biological Psychology and Psychiatry

Res Commun Chem Pathol Pharmacol — Research Communications in Chemical Pathology and Pharmacology

Res Commun Gas Coun — Research Communications. Gas Council [London]

Res Commun Inst Ferment (Osaka) — Research Communications. Institute for Fermentation (Osaka)

Res Commun Mol Pathol Pharmacol — Research Communications in Molecular Pathology and Pharmacology

Res Commun Pharmacol Toxicol — Research Communications in Pharmacology and Toxicology

Res Commun Psychol Psychiatry Behav — Research Communications in Psychology, Psychiatry, and Behavior

Res Communs Chem Path Pharmac — Research Communications in Chemical Pathology and Pharmacology

Res Commun Subst Abuse — Research Communications in Substances of Abuse

Res Conf Rep Bldg Res Advis Bd Wash — Research Conference Report. Building Research Advisory Board (Washington)

Res Confs Govrs Br E Afr Terr — Research Conferences. Governors of British East African Territories [Nairobi]

Res Constructs Peaceful Uses Nucl Energy — Research Constructs on Peaceful Uses of Nuclear Energy

Res Corresp — Research Correspondence

Res Counc Alberta Bull — Research Council of Alberta. Bulletin

Res Counc Alberta (Can) Inform Ser — Research Council of Alberta (Canada). Information Series

Res Counc Alberta Econ Geol Rep — Research Council of Alberta. Economic Geology Report

Res Counc Alberta Geol Div Bull — Research Council of Alberta. Geological Division. Bulletin

Res Counc Alberta Geol Div Mem — Research Council of Alberta. Geological Division. Memoir

Res Counc Alberta Geol Div Rep — Research Council of Alberta. Geological Division. Report

Res Counc Alberta Inf Ser — Research Council of Alberta. Information Series

Res Counc Alberta Mimeogr Circ — Research Council of Alberta. Mimeographed Circular

Res Counc Alberta Mimeogr Ser — Research Council of Alberta. Mimeographed Series

Res Counc Alberta Rep — Research Council of Alberta. Report

Res Counc Isr Annu Rep — Research Council of Israel. Annual Report

Rescue Archaeol Hampshire — Rescue Archaeology in Hampshire

R Escuela Def Nac — Revista. Escuela de Defensa Nacional

Res Def Soc — Research Defence Society [London]

Res Dep Fuel Abstr Combust Appl Mkrs Ass — Research Department Fuel Abstracts. Combustion Appliance Makers' Association [London]

Res Dep Rep Furn Dev Coun — Research Department Report. Furniture Development Council [London]

Res Dep Rep Post Off Res Cent (UK) — Research Department Report. Post Office Research Centre (United Kingdom)

Res Des — Research and Design

Res Dev — Research/Development

Res Dev Agric — Research and Development in Agriculture

Res Dev Assoc Mil Food Packag Syst Act Rep — Research and Development Associates for Military Food and Packaging Systems. Activities Report

Res Dev Assoc Mil Food Packag Syst Act Rep R & D Assoc — Research and Development Associates for Military Food and PackagingSystems. Activities Report. R and D Associates

Res Dev Bull Nth Alumin Co — Research and Development Bulletin. Northern Aluminium Company Ltd [Banbury]

Res Dev Bull Portland Cem Assoc — Research and Development Bulletin. Portland Cement Association

Res Dev Disabil — Research in Developmental Disabilities

Res/Develop — Research/Development

Res Developm Pap For Comm (Lond) — Research and Development Paper. Forestry Commission (London)

Res Dev Fruit Veg Cann Quick Freez Res Ass — Research and Development. Fruit and Vegetable Canning and Quick Freezing Research Association [Chipping Campden]

Res Dev Ind — Research and Development for Industry

Res Dev Lab Portland Cem Assoc Res Dep Bull — Research and Development Laboratories. Portland Cement Association. Research Department Bulletin

Res Dev News Wat Inf Cent Albertson — Research and Development News. Water Information Center, Inc (Abbertson, L.I.)

Res Dev Non Mech Electr Power Sources — Research and Development.in Non-Mechanical Electrical Power Sources

Res Dev Pap For Comm (GB) — Research and Development Paper. Forestry Commission (Great Britain)

Res Dev Pap UK For Comm — Research and Development Paper. United Kingdom Forestry Commission

Res Dev Rep Br Libr — Research and Development Reports. British Library

Res Dev Rep Monsanto Res Corp Mound Lab — Research and Development Report. Monsanto Research Corp. Mound Laboratory

Res Dev Rep US Atom Energy Commn — Research and Development Report. United States Atomic Energy Commission

Res Dev Rep US Dep Inter Off Coal Res — Research and Development Report. United States Department of the Interior.Office of Coal Research

Res Dev Rep US Off Coal Res — Research and Development Report. United States Office of Coal Research

Res Dev Rep US Pat Off — Research and Development Reports. United States Patent Office [Washington]

Res Dev Rev Mitsubishi Chem — Research and Development Review. Mitsubishi Chemical

Res Dev Rev Mitsubishi Kasei Corp — Research and Development Review. Mitsubishi Kasei Corporation

Res Dev Tech Rep ECOM US Army Electron Command — Research and Development Technical Report ECOM. United States ArmyElectronics Command

Res Dev Tech Rep US Army Electron Command — Research and Development Technical Report. United States ArmyElectronics Command

Res Discl — Research Disclosure

Res Disclosure — Research Disclosure

Res Div Bull Va Polytech Inst State Univ — Research Division Bulletin. Virginia Polytechnic Institute and State University

Res Div Rep Va Polytech Inst State Univ — Research Division Report. Virginia Polytechnic Institute and State University

Res Domest Int Agribusiness Manage — Research in Domestic and International Agribusiness Management

Res Drug Actions Interact — Research on Drug Actions and Interactions

RESE — Reseaux

Research B — Research Bulletin. Centre of Arabic Documentation

Research Bul — Liberal Party of Australia. New South Wales Division. Research Bulletin

Research Council Alberta Bull — Research Council of Alberta. Bulletin

Research Council Alberta Rept — Research Council of Alberta. Report

Researches Biochem Johnston Lab — Researches in Biochemistry. Johnston Laboratory. University of Liverpool

Researches Dep Terr Magn Carnegie Instn Wash — Researches of the Department of Terrestrial Magnetism. Carnegie Institution of Washington

Researches Electrotech Lab Japan — Researches. Electrotechnical Laboratory. Ministry of Communications. Japan

Researches Ess Oils Aust Flora — Researches on Essential Oils of the Australian Flora [Sydney]

Researches Inoc Dep St Marys Hosp Paddington — Researches from the Inoculation Department. St. Mary's Hospital. Paddington

Researches Mellon Inst — Researches of the Mellon Institute [Pittsburg]

Researches Popul Ecol Kyoto Univ — Researches on Population Ecology. Kyoto University

Researches Snow Ice Meguro — Researches on Snow and Ice (Meguro)

Researches Urol Brady Urol Inst — Researches in Urology. Collected Reprints from the Brady Urological Institute [Baltimore]

Researches Wards Labs Lond Hosp — Researches from the Wards and Laboratories of the London Hospital

Research F — Research Film

Research in Ed — Research in Education

Research Mgt — Research Management

Research R — Research Review. Institute of African Studies

Research Stud Pullman — Research Studies. Washington State University (Pullman, Washington)

RESEB — Resources in Education

Res Econ Anthrop — Research in Economic Anthropology

Res Econ Anthropol — Research in Economic Anthropology

Res Econ Hist — Research in Economic History

Res Educ — Research in Education

ResEduc — Resources in Education

RESEE — Revue des Etudes Sud-Est Europeennes

Res Electrotech Lab — Researches. Electrotechnical Laboratory

Res Electrotech Lab (Tokyo) — Researches. Electrotechnical Laboratory (Tokyo)

RESem — Revue des Etudes Semitiques

Resena Met Obs Met Magn Habana — Resena Meteorologica. Observatorio Meteorologico y Magnetico (Habana)

Resen Cient R Soc Esp Hist Nat — Resenas Cientificas de la Real Sociedad Espanola de Historia Natural [Madrid]

Resen Clin Cient — Resenha Clinico-Cientifica

Res Eng — Research Engineer

Res Eng Des — Research in Engineering Design

Res Eng Jeonbug Natl Univ — Research of Engineering. Jeonbug National University

Res Engng Datamation — Research and Engineering-Datamation [Chicago]

Res Engr — Research Engineer. Georgia Institute of Technology Engineering Experiment Station [Atlanta]

Res Eng Res Inst Ind Technol Jeonbug Natl Univ — Research of Engineering. Research Institute of Industrial Technology. Jeonbug National University

Resen Med — Resenha Medica [Rio de Janeiro]

Resen Vet — Resenha Veterinaria [Rio de Janeiro]

Res Environ Disruption Interdiscip Coop — Research on Environmental Disruption toward Interdisciplinary Cooperation

Reserve Bank Australia Statis Bul — Reserve Bank of Australia. Statistical Bulletin

Reserve Bank India B — Reserve Bank of India. Bulletin

Reserve Bank NZ Bul — Reserve Bank of New Zealand. Bulletin

Res Essent Oils Aust Flora — Researches on Essential Oils of the Australian Flora

Res Esst Oils Aust Flora — Researches on Essential Oils of the Australian Flora

Res Establ Risoe Rep Risoe-M (Den) — Research Establishment Risoe. Report. Risoe-M (Denmark)

Res Establ Risoe Risoe Rep (Den) — Research Establishment Risoe. Risoe Report (Denmark)

Res Exp Econ — Research in Experimental Economics

Res Exp Math — Research and Exposition in Mathematics

Res Exp Med — Research in Experimental Medicine

Res Exp Med (Berlin) — Research in Experimental Medicine (Berlin)

Res Exp Rec Minist Agric North Irel — Research and Experimental Record. Ministry of Agriculture. Northern Ireland

Res Exp Rec Minist Agric (Nth Ire) — Research and Experimental Record. Ministry of Agriculture. Northern Ireland)

Res Ext Ser Hawaii Inst Trop Agric Hum Resour — Research Extension Series. Hawaii Institute of Tropical Agriculture andHuman Resources

Res Farmers — Research for Farmers

Res Farming — Research and Farming

Res Farming (NC Agric Exp Stn) — Research and Farming (North Carolina Agricultural Experiment Station)

Res Farming NC Agric Res Serv — Research and Farming. North Carolina Agricultural Research Service

RESFDJ — Rivista Europea per le Scienze Mediche e Farmacologiche

Res Fem Res — Resources for Feminist Research

Res Film — Research Film

Res Find Smok Abused Subst — Research Findings on Smoking of Abused Substances

Res Fish Annu Rep Coll Fish Univ Wash — Research in Fisheries. Annual Report. College of Fisheries. University of Washington

Res Fish Annu Rep Sch Fish Univ Wash — Research in Fisheries. Annual Report. School of Fisheries. University of Washington

Res Fish (Seattle) — Research in Fisheries (Seattle)

Res Fmg — Research and Farming. North Carolina Agricultural Experiment Station [Raleigh]

Res Fmrs — Research for Farmers. Department of Agriculture. Canada [Ottawa]

Res Food Sci — Research in Food Science

Res Food Sci Nutr — Research in Food Science and Nutrition

Res Forest Prod Madison — Research in Forest Products. Annual Report. Forest Products Laboratory (Madison, Wisconsin)

Res Front Fertil Regul — Research Frontiers in Fertility Regulation

Res Future Res Pap — Resources for the Future Research Paper

Res Futures — Research Futures

RESFV — Renaissance Editions. San Fernando Valley State College

Res Grp News Elect Steel Fndrs Res Grp — Research Group News. Electric Steel Founders' Research Group [Chicago]

Res Health Econ — Research in Health Economics

Res High Educ Abstr — Research into Higher Education. Abstracts

Res Higher Educ — Research in Higher Education

RESHUS — Reseau Documentaire en Sciences Humaines de la Sante

Resid Group Care & Treat — Residential Group Care and Treatment

Resid Staff Physician — Resident and Staff Physician

Residual Eff Abused Drugs Behav — Residual Effects of Abused Drugs on Behavior

Residual Gases Electron Tubes Proc Int Conf — Residual Gases in Electron Tubes. Proceedings. International Conference

Residuals Trace Elem Iron Steel Int Conf — Residuals and Trace Elements in Iron and Steel. International Conference

Residue Rev — Residue Reviews

Residues Effluents Process Environ Consid Proc Int Symp — Residues and Effluents. Processing and Environmental Considerations. Proceedings. International Symposium

Res Ill Text Edn — Research Illustrated. Textile Edition. E. F. Houghton and Co. [Philadelphia]

Res Immunochem Immunobiol — Research in Immunochemistry and Immunobiology

Res Immunol — Research in Immunology

Res Ind — Research and Industry

Res Indicat Petrol — Resumos Indicativos do Petroleo

Res Ind Lond — Research for Industry (London)

Res Ind (New Delhi) — Research and Industry (New Delhi)

Res Ind Stanford — Research for Industry. Stanford Research Institute [Stanford, California]

Res Indus — Research and Industry

Resin Reptr — Resinous Reporter [Philadelphia]

Resin Rev — Resin Review

Resin Rev (Philadelphia) — Resin Review (Philadelphia)

Resin Rev (Richmond Engl) — Resin Review (Richmond, England)

Resins Drying Oils Varn Paints — Resins, Drying Oils, Varnishes, and Paints [Cambridge]

Resins Rubb Plast Yb — Resins, Rubbers, and Plastics Yearbook [New York]

Res Inst Analysis — Research Institute Analysis. Research Institute of America [New York]

Res Inst Appl Electr Hokkaido Univ Monogr Ser — Research Institute of Appled Electricity. Hokkaido University. Monograph Series

Res Inst Appl Mech Kyushu Univ Report — Research Institute for Applied Mechanics. Kyushu University. Reports

Res Inst Fund Information Sci Res Rep — Research Institute of Fundamental Information Science. Research Report

Res Inst Fund Inform Sci Res Rep — Kyushu University. Research Institute of Fundamental Information Science. Research Report

Res Inst Ind Technol Chungnam Natl Univ Rep — Research Institute of Industrial Technology. Chungnam NationalUniversity. Report

Res Inst Ind Technol Chungnam Univ — Research Institute of Industrial Technology. Chungnam University

Res Inst Mem Linen Ind Res Ass — Research Institute Memoirs. Linen Industry Research Association [Belfast]

Res Inst Nedri As (Hveragerdi Icel) Rep — Research Institute Nedri As (Hveragerdi, Iceland). Report

Res Inst Phys Annu Rep (Swed) — Research Institute of Physics. Annual Report (Sweden)

Res Inst Sumatra Plant Assoc Bull — Research Institute. Sumatra Planters Association. Bulletin

Res Inst Sumatra Plant Assoc Commun Rubber Ser — Research Institute. Sumatra Planters Association. Communications.Rubber Series

Res Int — Residential Interiors

Res Intell News — Research and Intelligence News

Res Invent — Research and Invention [Columbus, Ohio]

Resist Arteries Struct Funct Proc Int Symp — Resistance Arteries. Structure and Function. Proceedings. International Symposium on Resistance Arteries

Resistencia (Ser Econ e Gestao) — Resistencia (Serie de Economia e Gestao)

Resist Furnace — Resistance Furnace. Electric Resistance Furnace [London]

Res J — Research Journal

RESJA — RES. Journal of the Reticuloendothelial Society

Res J Agric Anim Sci (Karnal India) — Research Journal of Agriculture and Animal Sciences (Karnal, India)

Res J Aleppo Univ Basic Sci Ser — Research Journal. Aleppo University. Basic Sciences Series

Res J Chem Environ — Research Journal of Chemistry and Environment

Res J Dir Gen Higher Educ Indones — Research Journal. Directorate General of Higher Education. Indonesia

Res J Dir Higher Educ (Indones) — Research Journal. Directorate of Higher Education (Indonesia)

Res J Fac Agric Andalas Univ — Research Journal. Faculty of Agriculture. Andalas University

Res J Fac Sci Kashmir Univ — Research Journal. Faculty of Science. Kashmir University

Res J Hindi Sci Acad — Research Journal. Hindi Science Academy

Res J Kanpur Agr Coll — Research Journal. Kanpur Agricultural College

Res J Living Sci — Research Journal of Living Science

Res J Mahatma Phule Agric Univ — Research Journal. Mahatma Phule Agricultural University

Res J Philo Soc Sci — Research Journal of Philosophy and Social Sciences

Res J Phys Educ — Research Journal of Physical Education

RES J Reticuloendothel Soc — RES. Journal of the Reticuloendothelial Society

Res J Sci — Research Journal of Sciences

Res J Sci Devi Ahilya Vishwavidyalaya Indore — Research Journal. Science. Devi Ahilya Vishwavidyalaya. Indore

Res J Sci Univ Indore — Research Journal: Science. University of Indore

Res Jud — Res Judicatae

Res J Univ Wyo Agric Exp Stn — Research Journal. University of Wyoming. Agricultural Experiment Station

Res J Water — Research Journal. Water Pollution Control Federation

Res J Water Pollut Control Fed — Research Journal. Water Pollution Control Federation

Res J West Mindanao State Univ Univ Res Cent — Research Journal. Western Mindanao State University. University Research Center

RESL — Revue des Etudes Slaves

Res Lab Bull Gen Elect Co — Research Laboratory Bulletin. General Electric Company

Res Lab Commun Sci Univ Electro-Commun Annu Rep — Research Laboratory of Communication Science. University of Electro-Communications. Annual Report

Res Lab Eng Mater Tokyo Inst Technol Rep — Research Laboratory of Engineering Materials. Tokyo Institute of Technology. Report

Res Lab Gen Mot Corp Res Publ — Research Laboratories. General Motors Corporation. Research Publication

Res Lab Notes West Pine Ass — Research Laboratory Notes. Western Pine Association [Portland, Oregon]

Res Lab Portland Cem Assoc Bull — Research Laboratories. Portland Cement Association. Bulletin

Res Lab Precis Mach Electron — Research Laboratory Precision Machinery and Electronics

Res Lab Publs Br Thomson Houston — Research Laboratory Publications. British Thomson-Houston Company [Rugby]

Res Lab Publs Heat Vent Res Coun — Research Laboratory Publications. Heating and Ventilating Research Council [Bracknell]

Res Lab Rec — Research Laboratory Record

Res L & Econ — Research in Law and Economics

Res L and Soc — Research in Law and Sociology

RESlaves — Revue des Etudes Slaves

Res L Deviance and Soc Control — Research in Law, Deviance, and Social Control

Res Leafl For Res Inst NZ For Serv — Research Leaflet. Forest Research Institute. New Zealand Forest Service

Res Leafl Fruit Veg Cann Quick Freez Res Ass — Research Leaflet. Fruit and Vegetable Canning and Quick Freezing Research Association [Chipping Campden]

Res Leafl New Zealand Forest Res Inst — Research Leaflet. New Zealand Forest Research Institute

Res Leafl Oreg For Prod Lab — Research Leaflet. Oregon Forest Products Laboratory

Res Leafl Ore St Coll Sch For — Research Leaflet. Oregon State College School of Forestry [Corvallis]

Res Leafl Sav For Res Sta — Research Leaflet. Savanna Forestry Research Station

Res Lecture Notes Math — Research and Lecture Notes in Mathematics

Res Lecture Notes Math Complex Anal Geom — Research and Lecture Notes in Mathematics. Complex Analysis and Geometry

Res Lett Atmos Electr — Research Letters on Atmospheric Electricity

Res Libnship — Research in Librarianship

Res Librarianship — Research in Librarianship

Res Life Sci — Research in Life Sciences
Res Life Sci Maine Life Sci Agric Exp Stn — Research in the Life Sciences. Maine Life Sciences and Agriculture Experiment Station
Res Lit — Respublica Literaria
RESMA — Research Management
Res Manag — Research Management
Res Management — Research Management
Res Math — Research in Mathematics
Res McGill — Research McGill
Res Meas Approv — Research - Measurement - Approval
Res Mech — Res Mechanica
Res Mech Lett — Res Mechanica Letters
Res Med Edinb — Res Medica. Royal Medical Society (Edinburgh)
Res Med Roma — Res Medicae (Roma)
Res Melanes — Research in Melanesia
Res Mem Emp Cott Grow Corp — Research Memoirs. Empire Cotton Growing Corporation [London]
Res Mem Lond Sch Trop Med — Research Memoirs of the London School of Tropical Medicine [London]
Res Memo Ass Scient Wkrs S Aust — Research Memoranda. Association of Scientific Workers of South Australia [Adelaide]
Res Memo Int Inst Appl Syst Anal — Research Memorandum. International Institute for Applied Systems Analysis
Res Memo Res Ass Br Rubb Mfrs — Research Memoranda. Research Association of British Rubber Manufacturers [Croydon]
Res Memor Int Inst Appl Syst Anal — Research Memorandum. International Institute for Applied Systems Analysis
Res Memo T Moriya Meml Semin Aerodyn — Research Memoranda. T. Moriya Memorial Seminar for Aerodynamics. Tokyo University
Res Meth Neurochem — Research Methods in Neurochemistry
Res Methods Neurochem — Research Methods in Neurochemistry
Res Mgmt — Research Management [New York]</PHR> %
Res Mgt — Research Management
Res Microb — Research in Microbiology
Res Microbiol — Research in Microbiology
Res Mol Biol — Research in Molecular Biology
Res Monogr Br Non Ferr Metals Res Ass — Research Monographs. British Non-Ferrous Metals Research Associaton [London]
Res Monogr Cell Tissue Physiol — Research Monographs in Cell and Tissue Physiology
Res Monogr Immunol — Research Monographs in Immunology
Res Monogr Natl Inst Alcohol Abuse Alcohol — Research Monograph. National Institute on Alcohol Abuse and Alcoholism
Res Monogr Ser Natl Inst Drug Abuse (US) — Research Monograph Series. National Institute on Drug Abuse (United States)
Res Monogr Tex A & M Univ Tex Agric Exp Stn — Research Monograph. Texas A and M University. Texas AgriculturalExperiment Station
Res Natl Mus (Bloemfontein) — Researches. National Museum (Bloemfontein)
RESND — Resources and Energy
Res News Bull Natn Inst Ind Psychol — Research News Bulletin. National Institute of Industrial Psychology [London]
Res Newsl Br Columb Ind Scient Res Coun — Research Newsletter. British Columbia Industrial and Scientific Research Council [Vancouver]
Res Newsl Calif Spray Chem Corp — Research Newsletter. California Spray-Chemical Corporation
Res Newsl Coll Gen Practnrs — Research Newsletter. College of General Practitioners [London]
Res News Off Res Adm Univ Mich (Ann Arbor) — Research News. Office of Research Administration. University of Michigan (Ann Arbor)
Res News SEast Forest Exp Stn — Research News. Southeastern Forest Experiment Station [Ashville, North Carolina]
Res Nondestr Eval — Research in Nondestructive Evaluation
Res Norw Agric — Research in Norwegian Agriculture
Res Note BC For Serv — Research Notes. British Columbia Forest Service
Res Note Bur For (Philippines) — Research Note. Bureau of Forestry (Philippines)
Res Note Colo Coll For Nat Resour — Research Note. Colorado State University. College of Forestry and Natural Resources
Res Note Div For Res (Zambia) — Research Note. Division of Forest Research (Zambia)
Res Note Fac For Univ BC — Research Note. Faculty of Forestry. University of British Columbia
Res Note For Comm NSW — Research Note. Forestry Commission of New South Wales
Res Note For Mgmt Res Ore For Res Lab — Research Note. Forest Management Research. Oregon State University. Forest Research Laboratory
Res Note FPL For Prod Lab — Research Note FPL. Forest Products Laboratory
Res Note FPL US Dep Agric For Serv For Prod Lab — Research Note FPL. US Department of Agriculture. Forest Service. Forest Products Laboratory
Res Note Int US Dep Agric For Serv Intermt Res Stn — Research Note INT. US Department of Agriculture. Forest Service. Intermountain Research Station
Res Note NB Res Prod Counc — Research Note. New Brunswick Research and Productivity Council
Res Note N Cent Forest Exp Stn US Dep Agric — Research Note. North Central Forest Experiment Station. US Department of Agriculture
Res Note NC US For Serv — Research Note NC. US Forest Service
Res Note NE RN US Dep Agric For Serv Northeast For Exp Stn — Research Note NE-RN. US Department of Agriculture. Forest Service. NortheasternForest Experiment Station
Res Note NE US Dep Agric For Serv — Research Note NE. US Department of Agriculture. Forest Service
Res Note Oreg State Univ Sch For For Res Lab — Research Notes. Oregon State University. School of Forestry. Forest Research Laboratory
Res Note Pacif SW For Exp Stn — Research Note. Pacific Southwest Forest and Range Experiment Station. US Department of Agriculture

Res Note Prov BC Minist For — Research Note. Province of British Columbia. Ministry of Forests
Res Note Qd For Serv — Research Notes. Queensland Forest Service
Res Note Res Prod Counc (NB) — Research Note. Research and Productivity Council (New Brunswick)
Res Note RM US Dep Agric For Serv Rocky Mt For Range Exp Stn — Research Note RM. US Department of Agriculture. Forest Service. Rocky Mountain Forest and Range Experiment Station
Res Notes Artif Intell — Research Notes in Artificial Intelligence
Res Notes Br Columb Forest Serv — Research Notes. British Columbia Forest Service [Victoria]
Res Notes Cansapscal Forest Res Stn — Research Notes. Cansapscal Forest Research Station [Quebec]
Res Notes Cem Concr Ass — Research Notes. Cement and Concrete Association [London]
Res Notes Colo Sch For Range Mgmt — Research Notes. Colorado School of Forestry and Range Management [Fort Collins]
Res Notes Dep Geogr Univ Coll Ibadan — Research Notes. Department of Geography. University College. Ibadan
Res Notes Dep Linguistics — Research Notes. Department of Linguistics and Nigerian Languages
Res Notes Div Forest Mgmt NSW — Research Notes. Division of Forest Management. Forestry Commission. N.S.W.
Res Note SE US Dep Agric For Serv Southeast For Exp Stn — Research Note SE. US Department of Agriculture. Forest Service. Southeastern Forest Experiment Station
Res Notes Fac For Univ Br Columb — Research Notes. Faculty of Forestry. University of British Columbia [Vancouver]
Res Notes Forest Exp Stn Ore St Coll — Research Notes. Forest Experiment Station. Oregon State College [Corvallis]
Res Notes Forest Lds Res Cent — Research Notes. Forest Lands Research Center [Corvallis]
Res Notes Forest Prod Labs Can — Research Notes. Forest Product Laboratories. Canada
Res Notes Forest Res Div Ore St Coll — Research Notes. Forest Research Division. Oregon State College [Corvallis]
Res Notes Forest Res Div Philipp — Research Notes. Forest Research Division. Bureau of Forestry. Department of Agriculture and Natural Resources. Philippines [Manila]
Res Notes For Inst Nanking — Research Notes. Forestry Institute (Nanking)
Res Notes in Math — Research Notes in Mathematics
Res Notes Memoranda Appl Geom Post-RAAG — Research Notes and Memoranda of Applied Geometry in Post-RAAG
Res Notes NSW For Comm — New South Wales. Forestry Commission. Research Notes
Res Notes NWest Comm Coord Res — Research Notes. Northwestern Committee on Co-ordinated Research [Ontario]
Res Notes Ore St Bd For — Research Notes. Oregon State Board of Forestry [Salem]
Res Note SO US Dep Agric For Serv South For Exp Stn — Research Note SO. US Department of Agriculture. Forest Service. Southern ForestExperiment Station
Res Notes Pacif NW Forest Range Exp Stn — Research Notes. Pacific Northwest Forest and Range Experiment Station [Portland, Oregon]
Res Notes Pap NEast Forest Exp Stn — Research Notes and Papers. Northeastern Forest Experimental Station
Res Notes Pulp Pap Res Inst Can — Research Notes. Pulp and Paper Research Institute of Canada [Montreal]
Res Notes Qd Dep For — Research Notes. Queensland Department of Forestry
Res Notes Qd Forest Serv — Research Notes. Queensland Forest Service [Brisbane]
Res Notes Rocky Mount Forest Range Exp Stn — Research Notes. Rocky Mountain Forest and Range Experiment Station [Fort Collins, Colorado]
Res Notes Sch For Fla Univ — Research Notes. School of Forestry. Florida University [Gainsville]
Res Notes SEast Forest Exp Stn — Research Notes. Southeastern Forest Experiment Station [Asheville]
Res Notes Ser Dep Agric Can — Research Notes Series. Department of Agriculture. Canada [Ottawa]
Res Notes Ser Ent Div Can — Research Notes Series. Entomology Division. Department of Agriculture. Canada [Ottawa]
Res Notes Ser Sci Serv Can — Research Notes Series. Science Service. Canada [Ottawa]
Res Notes Shellac Res Bur Brooklyn — Research Notes. Shellac Research Bureau (Brooklyn)
Res Notes SWest Forest Exp Stn — Research Notes. Southwestern Forest Experiment Station [Tucson]
Res Notes Tex Forest Serv — Research Notes. Texas Forest Service [College Station]
Res Notes Theoret Comput Sci — Research Notes in Theoretical Computer Science
Res Notes UBC Forest Club — Research Notes. UBC Forest Club. University of British Columbia [Vancouver]
Res Note Tex For Serv — Research Note. Texas Forest Service
Res Note UBC For Club — Research Notes. University of British Columbia. Forest Club
Res Note Univ Tex Austin Bur Econ Geol — Research Note. University of Texas at Austin. Bureau of Economic Geology
Res Not Ford For Cent — Research Note. Ford Forestry Center
RESNS — Review of English Studies. New Series
Res Nurs Health — Research in Nursing and Health
Res Nurs Hlth — Research in Nursing and Health
RESO — Resources Bulletin. Man and Resources Conference Program
Resoc Adun Soc Med Chir Bologna — Resoconti delle Adunanze della Societa Medico-Chirurgica di Bologna

Resoc Lav Assemb Ord Sanit Prov Campobasso — Resoconti dei Lavori dell'Assemblea dell'Ordine dei Sanitari della Provincia di Campobasso

Resoconti Assoc Min Sarda — Resoconti. Associazione Mineraria Sarda

Resoconti Riun Assoc Min Sarda — Resoconti delle Riunioni dell'Associazione Mineraria Sarda

Resoconti Sedute Assoc Min Sarda — Resoconti delle Sedute dell'Associazione Mineraria Sarda

Resoc Sed Ass Miner Sarda — Resoconti delle Sedute dell'Associazione Mineraria Sarda [*Iglesias*]

Resoc Sez Ent Soc Adriat Sci Nat Trieste — Resoconti della Sezione Entomologica della Societa Adriatica di Scienze Naturali in Trieste

Reson — Resonances

RESORS — Remote Sensing On-Line Retrieval System

Resour Am L — Resources for American Literary Study

Resour and Energy — Resources and Energy

Resour Atlas Univ Nebr Lincoln Conserv Surv Div — Resource Atlas. University of Nebraska-Lincoln. Conservation and SurveyDivsion

Resour Biomed Res Educ — Resources for Biomedical Research and Education

Resour Biosphere (USSR) — Resources of the Biosphere (USSR)

Resour Book Publ — Resources for Book Publishers

Resour Bull FPL US Dep Agric For Serv For Prod Lab — Resource Bulletin FPL. US Department of Agriculture. Forest Service. Forest Products Laboratory

Resour Bull RM US Dep Agric Rocky Mt For Range Exp Stn — Resource Bulletin RM. US Department of Agriculture. Rocky Mountain Forest and Range Experiment Station

Resour Bull SE US Dep Agric For Serv Southeast For Exp Stn — Resource Bulletin SE. US Department of Agriculture. Forest Service. Southeastern Forest Experiment Station

Resource Ind Ser Forest Res Coun Ga — Resource-Industry Series. Forest Research Council. Georgia

Resources Conserv — Resources and Conservation

Resources Pol — Resources Policy

Resour Conserv — Resources and Conservation

Resour Conserv Recycl — Resources, Conservation, and Recycling

Resour Dev Rep Ala Coop Ext Serv Auburn Univ — Resource Development Report. Alabama Cooperative Extension Service. Auburn University

Resour Educ — Resources in Education

Resour Energy — Resources and Energy

Resour Energy Econ — Resource and Energy Economics

Resour Environ Biotechnol — Resource and Environmental Biotechnology

Resour Geol — Resource Geology

Resour Ind — Resources Industry

Resour Manage and Optimiz — Resource Management and Optimization

Resour Manage Optim — Resource Management and Optimization

Resour Manage Optimization — Resource Management and Optimization

Resour Manage Ser W Va Univ Coll Agric For Agric Exp Stn — Resource Management Series. West Virginia University. College of Agriculture and Forestry. Agricultural Experiment Station. Division of Resource Management

Resour Policy — Resources Policy

Resour Recovery Conserv — Resource Recovery and Conservation

Resour Recovery Energy Rev — Resource Recovery and Energy Review

Resour Rep Coop Ext Univ Wis — Resource Report. Cooperative Extension. University of Wisconsin

Resour Sharing and Libr Networks — Resource Sharing and Library Networks

Resour Study Rep Chesapeake Biol Lab — Resources Study Report. Chesapeake Biological Laboratory

Resour Survs Dep Natn Dev Aust — Resources Surveys. Department of National Development. Australia [*Canberra*]

Resour Tenn — Resources of Tennessee. Geological Survey [*Nashville*]

Res Outlook — Research Outlook

ResP — Research and Progress

REsp — Revista de Espana

Res Pam (Div For Res Zambia) — Research Pamphlet (Division of Forest Research, Zambia)

Res Pam For Res Inst (Kepong) — Research Pamphlet. Forest Research Institute (Kepong)

Res Pamph Forest Res Inst Fed Malaya — Research Pamphlet. Forest Research Institute Federation of Malaya [*Kepong*]

Res Pamphl For Res Inst (Malaya) — Research Pamphlet. Forest Research Institute (Malaya)

R Espan De Crimin — Revista Espanola de Criminologie

R Espan De Med Y Cir — Revista Espanola de Medicina y Cirugia

R Espan Derecho Canonico — Revista Espanola de Derecho Canonico

R Espan Derecho Int — Revista Espanola de Derecho Internacional

R Espan Pedag — Revista Espanola de Pedagogia. CSIC (Consejo Superior de Investigaciones Cientificas)

R Espan Seguros — Revista Espanola de Seguros

R Espan Teol — Revista Espanola de Teologia. CSIC (Consejo Superior de Investigaciones Cientificas)

Res Pap Benzole Prod — Research Papers. Benzole Producers Ltd [*London*]

Res Pap Br Ceram Res Ass — Research Papers. British Ceramic Research Association [*Stoke-on-Trent*]

Res Pap Dep For (Qd) — Research Paper. Department of Forestry (Queensland)

Res Pap Dep For (Queensl) — Research Paper. Department of Forestry (Queensland)

Res Pap Dep Geogr Univ Chicago — Research Papers. Department of Geography. University of Chicago

Res Pap Div Bldg Res Can — Research Papers. Division of Building Research. National Research Council. Canada [*Ottawa*]

Res Paper Horace Lamb Centre Oceanogr Res — Research Paper. Horace Lamb Centre for Oceanographical Research. Flinders University

Res Pap Fac For Univ BC — Research Paper. Faculty of Forestry. University of British Columbia

Res Pap For Dep (West Aust) — Research Paper. Forests Department (Western Australia)

Res Pap Forests Dep (West Aust) — Research Paper. Forests Department (Western Australia)

Res Pap (Forest Ser) Fed Dep Forest Res (Niger) — Research Paper (Forest Series). Federal Department of Forest Research (Nigeria)

Res Pap For Res Lab Oreg State Univ — Research Paper. Forest Research Laboratory. Oregon State University

Res Pap FPL For Prod Lab (US) — Research Paper FPL. Forest Products Laboratory (US)

Res Pap FPL US Dep Agric For Serv For Prod Lab — Research Paper FPL. US Department of Agriculture. Forest Service. Forest Products Laboratory

Res Pap GA For Res Coun — Research Paper. Georgia Forest Research Council

Res Pap Geogr Univ Newcastle — Research Papers in Geography. University of Newcastle

Res Pap Helsinki Univ Technol — Research Papers. Helsinki University of Technology

Res Pap Horace Lamb Centre Oceanogrl Res — Research Paper. Horace Lamb Centre for Oceanographical Research. Flinders University

Res Pap Intermount Forest Range Exp Stn — Research Papers. Intermountain Forest and Range Experiment Station

Res Pap INT US Dep Agric For Serv Intermt Res Stn — Research Paper INT. US Department of Agriculture. Forest Service. IntermountainResearch Station

Res Pap John Tracy Clin — Research Papers. John Tracy Clinic. University of South California [*Los Angeles*]

Res Pap Math Dep Univ Edinb — Research Papers. Mathematical Department. University of Edinburgh

Res Pap Math Dep Univ St Andrews — Research Papers. Mathematical Department. University of St. Andrews

Res Pap Natl Build Stud — Research Paper. National Building Studies

Res Pap Natn Bldg Stud — Research Papers. National Building Studies. Building Research Station [*Watford*]

Res Pap NC US Dep Agric For Serv North Cent For Exp Stn — Research Paper NC. US Department of Agriculture. Forest Service. North Central Forest Experiment Station

Res Pap NE US Dep Agric For Serv Northeast For Exp Stn — Research Paper NE. US Department of Agriculture. Forest Service. Northeastern Forest Experiment Station

Res Pap Ore For Res Lab — Research Paper. Oregon State University. Forest Research Laboratory

Res Pap Oreg State Univ For Res Lab — Research Paper. Oregon State University. Forest Research Lab

Res Pap Pacif NW Forest Range Exp Stn — Research Papers. Pacific Northwest Forest and Range Experiment Station [*Portland, Oregon*]

Res Pap Pa St Forest Sch — Research Papers. Pennsylvania State Forest School

Res Pap Phys Educ — Research Papers in Physical Education

Res Pap PNW (Pac Northwest For Range Exp Stn) — Research Paper PNW (Pacific Northwest Forest and Range Experiment Station)

Res Pap PNW US Dep Agric For Serv Pac Northwest Res Stn — Research Paper PNW. US Department of Agriculture. Forest Service. Pacific Northwest Research Station

Res Pap PNW US For Serv — Research Paper PNW [*Pacific Northwest Forest and Range Experiment Station*] . US Forest Service

Res Pap Resour Future — Research Paper. Resources for the Future

Res Pap RM US Dep Agric For Serv Rocky Mt For Range Exp Stn — Research Paper RM. US Department of Agriculture. Forest Service. Rocky MountainForest and Range Experiment Station

Res Pap Sav For Res Sta — Research Paper. Savanna Forestry Research Station

Res Pap Sch For Resour PA St Univ — Research Paper. School of Forest Resources. Pennsylvania State University

Res Pap Sch Sci Ore St Coll — Research Papers. School of Science. Oregon State College [*Corvallis*]

Res Pap Ser Int Rice Res Inst — Research Paper Series. International Rice Research Institute

Res Pap Snow Ice Permafrost Res Establ — Research Papers. Snow, Ice, and Permafrost Research Establishment

Res Pap SO US Dep Agric For Serv South For Exp Stn — Research Paper SO. US Department of Agriculture. Forest Service. Southern Forest Experiment Station

Res Pap Tob Mfrs Stand Comm — Research Papers. Tobacco Manufacturers' Standing Committee [*London*]

Res Pap Tob Res Counc — Research Paper. Tobacco Research Council

Res Pap US Forest Serv Lake St Forest Exp Stn — Research Paper. United States Forest Service. Lake States Forest Experiment Station

Res Pap US Natn Bur Stand — Research Papers. United States National Bureau of Standards [*Washington*]

Res Pap US Nav Postgrad Sch — Research Papers. United States Naval Postgraduate School [*Monterey*]

Res Pap US Weath Bur — Research Papers. United States Weather Bureau [*Washington*]

Res Pap (West Aust) For Dep — Research Paper (Western Australia). Forests Department

Res Parapsychol — Research in Parapsychology

Res Past Clim Contin Drift Taipei — Research on the Past Climate and Continental Drift. National Taiwan University [*Taipei*]

Res Pat Trade Marks — Research, Patents, and Trade Marks [*New York*]

Resp C — Respiratory Care

Resp Care — Respiratory Care

RESPD — Revue d'Epidemiologie et de Sante Publique

R Esp Der Int — Revista Espanola de Derecho Internacional

R Especialid — Revista de Especialidades

Res Perspect — Research Perspectives

Res Phenomenol — Research in Phenomenology

Res Phil Technol — Research in Philosophy and Technology

Res Photobiol Proc Int Congr — Research in Photobiology. Proceedings. International Congress onPhotobiology

REspir — Revista de Espiritualidad

Respiration Suppl — Respiration. Supplement
Respir Care — Respiratory Care
Respir Care Clin N Am — Respiratory Care Clinics of North America
Respir Circ — Respiration and Circulation
Respir Med — Respiratory Medicine
Respir Mol Med — Repiratory Molecular Medicine
Respir Physiol — Respiration Physiology
Respir Res — Respiration Research
Respir Technol — Respiratory Technology
Respir Ther — Respiratory Therapy
Resp Konf Anal Khim Tezisy Dokl — Respublikanskaya Konferentsiya po Analiticheskoi Khimii. TezisyDokladov
Resp Konf Elektrokhim Lit SSR — Respublikanskaya Konferentsiya Elektrokhimikov Litovskoi SSR
Resp Konf Fiziol Biokhim — Respublikanskaya Konferentsiya Fiziologov i Biokhimikov
REspL — Revista Espanola de Linguistica
Resp Med — Respiratory Medicine
Resp Nauchno Proizvod Konf Zashch Rast Kaz — Respublikanskaya Nauchno-Proizvodstvennaya Konferentsiya po Zashchite Rastenii v Kazakhstane
Resp Nauchno Tekh Konf Molodykh Uch Pererab Nefti Neftekhim — Respublikanskaya Nauchno-Tekhnicheskaya Konferentsiya Molodykh Uchenykh po Pererabotke Nefti i Neftekhimii
Resp Nauchno Tekh Konf Neftekhim — Respublikanskaya Nauchno-Tekhnicheskaya Konferentsiya po Neftekhimii
Resp Nauchno Tekh Konf Povysh Eff Proizvod Uluchsheniya Kach — Respublikanskaya Nauchno-Tekhnicheskaya Konferentsiya Povyshenie Effektivnosti Proizvodstva i Uluchsheniya Kachestva Elektroferrosplavov
Resp Nauchn Semin Vliyanie Vys Davleniya Veshchestvo — Respublikanskii Nauchnyi Seminar Vliyanie Vysokogo Davleniya na Veshchestvo
Res Pol — Research Policy
Res Polit Econ — Research in Political Economy
Response Nerv Syst Ioniz Radiat Proc Int Symp — Response of the Nervous System to Ionizing Radiation. Proceedings. International Symposium
R Esp Opinion Publica — Revista Espanola de la Opinion Publica
R Esp Opin Publ — Revista Espanola de la Opinion Publica
Res Populat Ecol — Researches on Population Ecology. Society of Population Ecology
Res Popul Ecol — Researches on Population Ecology
Res Popul Ecol (Kyoto) — Researches on Population Ecology (Kyoto)
Resp Physl — Respiration Physiology
Res Pract Challenge Appl Congr — Research into Practice. The Challenge of Application. Congress
Res Pract Forensic Med — Research and Practice in Forensic Medicine
Res Preview — Research Previews
Res Prod Coun NB Res Note — Research and Productivity Council. New Brunswick. Research Note.
Res Prog — Research and Progress
Res Prog Graphic Arts Tech Found — Research Progress. Graphic Arts Technical Foundation
Res Prog Ill Agric Exp Stn — Research Progress at the Illinois Agricultural Experiment Station
Res Prog Lithogr Tech Found — Research Progress. Lithographic Technical Foundation
Res Progm Ind Dev Forest Prod Res Inst Philipp — Research Programme for Industrial Development. Forest Products Research Institute. Philippines [Manila]
Res Prog Org-Biol Med Chem — Research Progress in Organic-Biological and Medicinal Chemistry
Res Program Rep Wash State Highw Dep — Research Program Report. Washington State Highway Department
Res Prog Rep Indiana Agric Exp Stn — Research Progress Report. Indiana. Agricultural Experiment Station
Res Prog Rep Purdue Univ Agric Exp Stn — Research Progress Report. Purdue University. Agricultural Experiment Station
Res Prog Rep Tokai-Kinki Natn Agric Exp Stn — Research Progress Report. Tokai-Kinki National Agricultural Experiment Station
Res Prog Rep UK At Energy Res Establ Health Phys Med Div — Research Progress Report. United Kingdom Atomic Energy Research Establishment. Health Physics and Medical Division
Res Prog Rep West Soc Weed Sci — Research Progress Report. Western Society of Weed Science
Res Progr Rep Indiana Agr Exp Sta — Research Progress Report. Indiana Agricultural Experiment Station
Res Progr Rep Purdue Agric Exp Sta — Research Progress Report. Purdue University. Agricultural Experiment Station
Res Progr Rep Purdue Univ Agr Exp Sta — Research Progress Report. Purdue University. Agricultural Experiment Station
Res Progr Rep Tokai-Kinki Nat Agr Exp Sta — Research Progress Report. Tokai-Kinki National Agricultural Experiment Station
Res Progr Rep Tokai Kinki Natl Agric Exp Sta — Research Progress Report. Tokai-Kinki National Agricultural Experiment Station/Norin-Sho Tokai Kinki Nogyo Shikenjo Kenkyu Sokuho
Res Progr Rep West Weed Control Conf — Research Progress Report. Western Weed Control Conference
Res Proj Am Inst Chem Engrs — Research Project. American Institute of Chemical Engineers [New York]
Res Proj Rep Graphic Arts Tech Found — Research Project Report. Graphic Arts Technical Foundation
Res Proj Ser Dep Agric Victoria — Research Project Series. Department of Agriculture (Victoria)
Res Proj Ser Victoria Dep Agric — Victoria. Department of Agriculture. Research Project Series
Res Prostaglandins — Research in Prostaglandins
Res Protozool — Research in Protozoology

Resp Sb Nauchn Tr Yarosl Gos Pedagog Inst im KD Ushinskogo — Respublikanskii Sbornik Nauchnykh Trudov. Yaroslavskii Gosudarstvennyi Pedagogicheskii Institut imeni K.D. Ushinskogo
Resp Shk Semin Spektrosk Mol Krist — Respublikanskaya Shkola-Seminar Spektroskopiya Molekul i Kristallov
Resp Soveshch Neorg Khim — Respublikanskoe Soveshchanie po Neorganicheskoi Khimii
REspT — Revista Espanola de Teologia
Resp Technol — Respiratory Technology
Resp Ther — Respiratory Therapy
Res Publ — Res Publica
Res Publ Assoc Res Nerv Ment Dis — Research Publications Association for Research in Nervous and Mental Disease
Res Publ Gen Mot Corp Res Lab — Research Publication. General Motors Corporation. Research Laboratories
Res Publ Geogr — Resource Publications in Geography
Res Publ Ill Inst Technol — Research Publications. Illinois Institute of Technology
Res Publ Inst Hist Arabic Sci — Research Publications of the Institute for the History of Arabic Science
Res Publ Kan Agric Exp Stn — Research Publication. Kansas Agricultural Experiment Station
Res Publ Punjab Irrig Res Inst — Research Publication. Punjab Irrigation Research Institute
Res Publs Ass Res Nerv Ment Dis — Research Publications. Association for Research in Nervous and Mental Diseases [New York]
Res Publs Cent Irrig Hydrodyn Res Stn Poona — Research Publications. Central Irrigation and Hydrodynamic Research Station [Poona]
Res Publs Cent Wat Pwr Irrig Navig Res Stn Poona — Research Publications. Central Waterpower, Irrigation, and Navigation Research Station. Poona [New Delhi]
Res Publs Cent Wat Pwr Res Stn Poona — Research Publications. Central Water and Power Research Station. Poona [New Delhi]
Res Publs Coll Phys Sci Sch Mines Univ Durham — Research Publications. College of Physical Sciences. University School of Mines. University of Durham
Res Publs Dep Min Engng Univ Durham — Research Publications. Department of Mining Engineering. University School of Mines. University of Durham
Res Publs Hirakud Dam Proj — Research Publications. Hirakud Dam Project
Res Publs Ill Inst Technol — Research Publications. Illinois Institute of Technology [Chicago]
Res Publs Indian WatWays Exp Stn Poona — Research Publications. Indian Waterways Experiment Station. Poona [New Delhi]
Res Publs Irrig Pwr Res Inst Amritsar — Research Publications. Irrigation and Power Research Institute. Amritsar
Res Publs Polytech Inst Brooklyn — Research Publications. Polytechnic Institute of Brooklyn
Res Publs Punjab Irrig Res Inst — Research Publications. Punjab Irrigation Research Institute [Lahore]
Res Publs Sch Mines Kings Coll Newcastle — Research Publications. School of Mines. King's College. Newcastle
Res Publs Univ Hawaii — Research Publications. University of Hawaii [Honolulu]
Res Publs Univ Minn — Research Publications of the University of Minnesota [Minneapolis]
Res Q — Research Quarterly
Res Q (AAHPER) — Research Quarterly. American Association for Health, Physical Education, and Recreation
Res Q Am Alliance Health Phys Educ Recreat — Research Quarterly. American Alliance for Health, Physical Education, and Recreation
Res Q Am Ass Hlth Phys Educ — Research Quarterly of the American Association for Health, Physical Education, and Recreation [Washington]
Res Q Am Assoc Health Phys Educ Recreat — Research Quarterly. American Association for Health, Physical Education, and Recreation
Res Q Am Assoc Health Phys Educ Recreation — Research Quarterly. American Association for Health, Physical Education, and Recreation
Res Q Exercise Sport — Research Quarterly for Exercise and Sport
Res Q Exerc Sport — Research Quarterly for Exercise and Sport
Res Q Ont Hydro — Research Quarterly. Ontario Hydro
Res Quart — Research Quarterly
ReSR — Recherches de Science Religieuse
Res R — Research in Review
Res Rap Atlant Sea Run Salm Commn Me — Research Report. Atlantic Sea Run Salmon Commission of the State of Maine [Augusta]
Resrce Recv — Resource Recovery Update
Res React Proc UN Int Conf Peaceful Uses At Energy — Research Reactors. Proceedings. United Nations International Conference. Peaceful Uses of Atomic Energy
Res Rec Malawi For Res Inst — Research Record. Malawi Forest Research Institute
Res Relat Child — Research Relating to Children
Res Rep — Research Reporter
Res Rep AGARD — Research Report. AGARD. Advisory Group for Aeronautical Research and Development [Paris]
Res Rep Agric Exp Stn Mich St Univ — Research Report. Agricultural Experiment Station. Michigan State University
Res Rep Agric Exp Stn Univ Wisc — Research Report. Agricultural Experiment Station. University of Wisconsin
Res Rep Agric Exp Stn Utah St Univ — Research Report. Agricultural Experiment Station. Utah State University
Res Rep Agric Sci Technol Inst Agric Sci Technol Chungnam Nat — Research Reports. Agricultural Science and Technology. Institute of Agricultural Science and Technology. Chungnam National University
Res Rep Akita Natl Coll Technol — Research Reports. Akita National College of Technology
Res Rep Akita Tech Coll — Research Reports. Akita Technical College
Res Rep Alumin Dev Ass — Research Report. Aluminium Development Association [London]

Res Rep Am Gas Ass Labs — Research Report. American Gas Association Laboratories [*Cleveland*]

Res Rep Anan Coll Technol — Research Reports. Anan College of Technology

Res Rep Anan Tech College — Research Reports. Anan Technical College

Res Rep Ariake Natl Coll Technol — Research Reports. Ariake National College of Technology

Res Rep Ariake Tech Coll — Research Reports. Ariake Technical College

Res Rep Ashikaga Inst Technol — Research Reports. Ashikaga Institute of Technology

Res Rep At Energy Control Board — Research Report. Atomic Energy Control Board

Res Rep Autom Control Lab Fac Eng Nagoya Univ — Research Reports. Automatic Control Laboratory. Faculty of Engineering. Nagoya University

Res Rep Biomass Convers Program — Research Report. Biomass Conversion Program

Res Rep Biotech Fac Univ Edvard Kardelj (Ljublj) Vet Issue — Research Reports. Biotechnical Faculty. University of Edvard Kardelj (Ljubljana). Veterinary Issue

Res Rep Biotech Fac Univ Ljublj Agric Issue — Research Reports. Biotechnical Faculty. University of Ljubljana. Agricultural Issue

Res Rep Br Boot Shoe Res Ass — Research Report. British Boot. Shoe and Allied Trades Research Association [*Kettering*]

Res Rep Br Intern Combust Engine Res Ass — Research Report. British Internal Combustion Engine Research Association [*Slough*]

Res Rep Br Non Ferr Metals Res Ass — Research Report. British Non-Ferrous Metals Research Association [*London*]

Res Rep Can Dept Agr Nat Weed Comm West Sect — Research Report. Canada Department of Agriculture. National Weed Committee. Western Section

Res Rep Cem Concr Ass — Research Report. Cement and Concrete Association [*London*]

Res Rep Cent Highw Res Univ Tex Austin — Research Report. Center for Highway Research. University of Texas at Austin

Res Rep Cent Ops Res MIT — Research Report. Centre for Operations Research. Massachusetts Institute of Technology [*Cambridge*]

Res Rep City Guilds Coll — Research Report of the City and Guilds College [*London*]

Res Rep Cocoon Test Stn Wakayama Prefect — Research Reports. Cocoon Testing Station of Wakayama Prefecture

Res Rep Coff Res Stn Lyamungu — Research Report. Coffee Research Station Lyamungu

Res Rep Coll Agric Korea Univ — Research Reports. College of Agriculture. Korea University

Res Rep Coll Agric Univ Wis — Research Report. Experiment Station. College of Agriculture. University of Wisconsin

Res Rep Coll Agric Vet Med Nihon Univ — Research Reports. College of Agriculture and Veterinary Medicine. Nihon University

Res Rep Coll Eng Busan Natl Univ — Research Report. College of Engineering. Busan National University

Res Rep Conn Storrs Agric Res Stn — Research Report. Connecticut. Storrs Agricultural Research Station

Res Rep Counc Br Archaeol — Research Report. Council for British Archaeology

Res Rep CRR Timber Res Dev Assoc High Wycombe Engl — Research Report C/RR. Timber Research and Development Association. High Wycombe, England

Res Rep CSIR — Research Report. Council for Scientific and Industrial Research

Res Rep Czech Acad Sci Inst Plasma Phys — Research Report. Czechoslovak Academy of Sciences. Institute of Plasma Physics

Res Rep DAE LA St Univ Agric Exp Stn — Research Report. Department of Agricultural Economics and Agri-Business. Louisiana State University and Agricultural Experiment Station

Res Rep David Taylor Model Basin Hydromech Lab — Research Report. David Taylor Model Basin Hydromechanical Laboratory

Res Rep Dep Civ Engng Univ Sydney — Research Report. Department of Civil Engineering. University of Sydney

Res Rep Dep Crop Sci NC State Univ — Research Report. Department of Crop Science. North Carolina State University. Agricultural Experiment Station

Res Rep Dep Elect Engng Univ Toronto — Research Report. Department of Electrical Engineering. University of Toronto

Res Rep Dep Electl Engng Melb Univ — Research Report. Department of Electrical Engineering. University of Melbourne

Res Rep Dep Electr Eng Melb Univ — Research Report. Department of Electrical Engineering. University of Melbourne

Res Rep Dep Fld Crops N Carol St Coll — Research Report. Department of Field Crops. North Carolina State College [*Raleigh*]

Res Rep Dep Hort Univ Nott — Research Report. Department of Horticulture. University of Nottingham [*Sutton Bonington*]

Res Rep Div Appl Org Chem CSIRO — Research Report. Division of Applied Organic Chemistry. Commonwealth Scientificand Industrial Research Organisation

Res Rep Div Forest Res Toronto — Research Report. Division of Forest Research. Department of Lands and Forests (Toronto)

Res Rep East Sect Nat Weed Comm Can — Research Report. Eastern Section. National Weed Committee of Canada

Res Rep Electron Gen Res Inst — Research Report. Electronics General Research Institute

Res Rep Ent Lab Kamloops — Research Report. Entomology Laboratory. Kamloops, British Columbia

Res Rep Ent Res Inst Biol Control — Research Report. Entomology Research Institute for Biological Control [*Belleville, Ontario*]

Res Rep ESPRIT Proj — Research Reports ESPRIT. Project

Res Rep Ext Serv Inst Agric Sci Pullman — Research Report. Extension Service. Institute of Agricultural Sciences (Pullman)

Res Rep Fac Biotech Univ Ljublj Vet Issue — Research Reports. Faculty of Biotechnics. University of Ljubljana. Veterinary Issue

Res Rep Fac Eng Gifu Univ — Research Report. Faculty of Engineering. Gifu University

Res Rep Fac Eng Kagoshima Univ — Research Reports. Faculty of Engineering. Kagoshima University

Res Rep Fac Eng Kinki Univ — Research Reports. Faculty of Engineering. Kinki University

Res Rep Fac Eng Meiji Univ — Research Reports. Faculty of Engineering. Meiji University

Res Rep Fac Eng Mie Univ — Research Reports. Faculty of Engineering. Mie University

Res Rep Fac Eng Nagoya Univ — Research Reports. Faculty of Engineering. Nagoya University

Res Rep Fac Engng Gifu Univ — Research Report of the Faculty of Engineering. Gifu Prefectural University

Res Rep Fac Engng Meiji Univ — Research Report of the Faculty of Engineering. Meiji University [*Tokyo*]

Res Rep Fac Eng Niigata Univ — Research Report. Faculty of Engineering. Niigata University

Res Rep Fac Engrg Tokyo Denki Univ — Research Reports. Faculty of Engineering. Tokyo Denki University

Res Rep Fac Eng Tokyo Denki Univ — Research Reports. Faculty of Engineering. Tokyo Denki University

Res Rep Fac Eng Toyo Univ — Research Reports. Faculty of Engineering. Toyo University

Res Rep Fac Sci and Technol Meijyo Univ — Research Reports. Faculty of Science and Technology. Meijyo University

Res Rep Fac Sci Kyushu Univ — Research Report. Faculty of Science. Kyushu University [*Fukuoka*]

Res Rep Fac Technol Chiba Univ — Research Reports. Faculty of Technology. Chiba University

Res Rep Fac Text Seric Shinshu Univ — Research Reports. Faculty of Textiles and Sericulture. Shinshu University

Res Rep Fish Comm Oreg — Research Reports. Fish Commission of Oregon

Res Rep Fish Wildl Serv (US) — Research Report. Fish and Wildlife Service (United States)

Res Rep Fla Agric Exp Stn — Research Report. Florida Agricultural Experiment Station

Res Rep Fla Sch For — Research Report. University of Florida. School of Forestry

Res Rep Flinders Inst Atmos Mar Sci — Research Report. Flinders Institute of Atmospheric and Marine Sciences. Flinders University

Res Rep Fm Econ Res Serv US — Research Report. Farm Economics Research Service. U.S. Department of Agriculture

Res Rep Food Ind Res Dev Inst (Taiwan) — Research Report. Food Industry Research and Development Institute (Taiwan)

Res Rep For Prod Util Lab Miss St Univ — Research Report. Forest Products Utilization Laboratory. Mississippi State University

Res Rep For Res Inst — Research Reports. Forest Research Institute

Res Rep Fuel Res Inst (Jpn) — Research Reports. Fuel Research Institute (Japan)

Res Rep Fukui Tech Coll Nat Sci Eng — Research Reports. Fukui Technical College. Natural Science and Engineering

Res Rep Fukuoka Agr Exp Sta — Research Report. Fukuoka Agricultural Experiment Station

Res Rep Fukuoka Agric Exp Stn — Research Report. Fukuoka Agricultural Experiment Station

Res Rep Fukushima Tech Coll — Research Reports. Fukushima Technical College

Res Rep Fu Min Geogr Inst Econ Dev — Research Report of the Fu-Min Geographical Institute of Economic Development [*Taipei*]

Res Rep GA Agr Exp Sta — Research Report. Georgia Agricultural Experiment Station

Res Rep Ga Agric Exp Stn — Research Report. Georgia. Agricultural Experiment Stations

Res Rep Gen Educ Course Fac Eng Toyo Univ — Research Reports. General Education Course. Faculty of Engineering. Toyo University

Res Rep Geogr Lab Univ West Aust — Research Report of the Geographical Laboratory. University of Western Australia [*Nedlands*]

Res Rep Hakodate Tech Coll — Research Reports. Hakodate Technical College

Res Rep Hanyang Res Inst Ind Sci — Research Reports. Hanyang Research Institute of Industrial Sciences

Res Rep Hawaii Agric Exp Stn — Research Report. Hawaii Agricultural Experiment Station

Res Rep Helsinki Univ Technol Lab Phys — Research Report. Helsinki University of Technology. Laboratory of Physics

Res Rep Highw Res Bd Wash — Research Report. Highway Research Board (Washington)

Res Rep Hokkaido Natl Agric Exp Stn — Research Report. Hokkaido National Agricultural Experiment Station

Res Rep Huang Hai Chem Ind Res Inst — Research Report. Huang Hai Chemical Industry Research Institute

Res Rep Hunter Valley Res Fdn — Research Report. Hunter Valley Research Foundation

Res Rep Hunter Valley Res Found — Research Report. Hunter Valley Research Foundation

Res Rep Hyogo Agric Coll — Research Report. Hyogo Agricultural College / Hyogo Nogyo Tanki Daigaku Kenkyu Shuroku

Res Rep Ibaraki Tech Coll — Research Reports. Ibaraki Technical College

Res Rep Ikutoku Tech Univ Part B — Research Reports. Ikutoku Technical University. Part B. Science and Technology

Res Rep Inf Sci Electr Eng Kyushu Univ — Research Reports on Information Science and Electrical Engineering of Kyushu University

Res Rep Inst Agric Geogr Taipei — Research Report of the Institute of Agricultural Geography (Taipei)

Res Rep Inst Anim Genet — Research Report. Institute of Animal Genetics

Res Rep Inst Forest Genet Suwon — Research Report. Institute of Forest Genetics. Forest Experiment Station. Suwon, Korea

Res Rep Inst For Genet — Research Report. Institute of Forest Genetics

Res Rep Inst For Genet (Korea) — Research Report. Institute of Forest Genetics (Suwon, Korea)

Res Rep Inst For Genet (Suwon) Imop Sihomjang — Research Report. Institute of Forest Genetics (Suwon). Imop Sihomjang

Res Rep Inst Industr Res (Nigeria) — Research Report. Federal Institute of Industrial Research (Lagos, Nigeria)

Res Rep Inst Inform Sci Tech Tokyo Denki Univ — Tokyo Denki University. Institute of Information Science and Technology. Research Reports

Res Rep Inst Inf Sci and Technol Tokyo Denki Univ — Research Reports. Institute of Information Science and Technology. Tokyo Denki University

Res Rep Inst Plasma Phys Nagoya Univ — Research Report. Institute of Plasma Physics. Nagoya University

Res Rep Inst Radio Phys Electron Calcutta — Research Report. Institute of Radio Physics and Electronics. University of Calcutta

Res Rep Inst Statist Math Tokyo — Research Report of the Institute of Statistical Mathematics (Tokyo)

Res Rep Int Food Policy Res Inst — Research Report. International Food Policy Research Institute

Res Rep Int Inst Appl Syst Anal — Research Report. International Institute for Applied Systems Analysis

Res Rep IPPCZ Czech Acad Sci Inst Plasma Phys — Research Report IPPCZ. Czechoslovak Academy of Sciences. Institute of Plasma Physics

Res Rep Kagawa Ken Fishery Exp Stn — Research Report of the Kagawa-ken Fishery Experiment Station

Res Rep Kagoshima Tech Coll — Research Reports. Kagoshima Technical College

Res Rep Kasetsart Univ — Research Reports. Kasetsart University

Res Rep Kitakyushu Tech Coll — Research Report. Kitakyushu Technical College

Res Rep Kochi Univ — Research Reports. Kochi University/Kochi Daigaku Gakujutsu Kenkyu Hokoku

Res Rep Kochi Univ Agric Sci — Research Reports. Kochi University. Agricultural Science

Res Rep Kochi Univ Nat Sci — Research Reports. Kochi University. Natural Science

Res Rep Kogakuin Univ — Research Reports. Kogakuin University

Res Rep Korea Min Agr Forest Office Rural Develop — Research Reports. Republic of Korea Ministry of Agriculture and Forestry. Office of Rural Development

Res Rep Kurume Tech Coll — Research Reports. Kurume Technical College

Res Rep Kushiro Tech College — Research Reports. Kushiro Technical College

Res Rep Lab Exp Limnol Ont — Research Report. Laboratory for Experimental Limnology. Ontario

Res Rep Lab Nucl Sci Tohoku Univ — Research Report. Laboratory of Nuclear Science. Tohoku University

Res Rep Lab Nucl Sci Tohoku Univ Suppl — Research Report. Laboratory of Nuclear Science. Tohoku University. Supplement

Res Rep MAFES — Research Report. MAFES

Res Rep Maizuru Coll Technol — Research Reports. Maizuru College of Technology

Res Rep Maizuru Tech Coll — Research Reports. Maizuru Technical College

Res Rep Mar Res Lab SW Afr — Research Report. Marine Research Laboratory. South West Africa [Windhoek]

Res Rep Matsue Coll Technol Nat Sci Eng — Research Reports. Matsue College of Technology, Natural Science, and Engineering

Res Rep Matsue Tech Coll — Research Reports. Matsue Technical College

Res Rep Metrop Wat Bd — Research Report. Metropolitan Water Board [London]

Res Rep Mich State Univ Agric Exp Stn — Research Report. Michigan State University. Agricultural Experiment Station

Res Rep Mich State Univ Agric Exp Stn East Lansing — Research Report. Michigan State University. Agricultural Experiment Station. East Lansing

Res Rep Microbiol Res Inst Can — Research Report. Microbiology Research Institute. Department of Agriculture. Canada [Ottawa]

Res Rep Mines Branch Can — Research Report. Mines Branch, Canada

Res Rep Mines Brch Can — Research Report. Mines Branch. Department of Mines and Technical Surveys. Canada [Ottawa]

Res Rep Miss Agric For Exp Stn — Research Report. Mississippi Agricultural and Forestry Experiment Station

Res Rep Miyagi Natl Coll Technol — Research Reports. Miyagi National College of Technology

Res Rep Miyagi Tech College — Research Reports. Miyagi Technical College

Res Rep Miyakonojo Natl Coll Technol — Research Report. Miyakonojo National College of Technology

Res Rep Miyakonojo Tech Coll — Research Report. Miyakonojo Technical College

Res Rep Mont Agric Exp Stn — Research Report. Montana Agricultural Experiment Station

Res Rep Nagano State Lab Food Technol — Research Report. Nagano State Laboratory of Food Technology

Res Rep Nagano Tech Coll — Research Report. Nagano Technical College

Res Rep Nagaoka College Tech — Research Reports of Nagaoka College of Technology

Res Rep Nagaoka Coll Technol — Research Reports. Nagaoka College of Technology

Res Rep Nagaoka Tech Coll — Research Reports. Nagaoka Technical College

Res Rep Nagoya Ind Sci Res Inst — Research Reports. Nagoya Industrial Science Research Institute

Res Rep Nagoya Munic Ind Res Inst — Research Reports. Nagoya Municipal Industrial Research Institute

Res Rep Nagoya Univ Inst Plasma Phys — Research Report. Nagoya University. Institute of Plasma Physics

Res Rep Nara Natl Coll Technol — Research Reports. Nara National College of Technology

Res Rep Nara Tech Coll — Research Reports. Nara Technical College

Res Rep Natl Geogr Soc — Research Reports. National Geographic Society

Res Rep Natl Inst Environ Stud Jpn — Research Report. National Institute for Environmental Studies. Japan

Res Rep Natl Inst Nutr — Research Report. National Institute of Nutrition

Res Rep Natl Res Inst Met J — Research Report. National Research Institute for Metals (Japan)

Res Rep Natl Res Inst Mother Child Warsaw — Research Reports. National Research Institute of Mother and Child (Warsaw)

Res Rep Natn Bldg Res Inst Un S Afr — Research Report. National Building Research Institute. C.S.I.R. Union of South Africa [Pretoria]

Res Rep Natn Weed Comm East Sect Can — Research Report. National Weed Committee. Eastern Section. Canada [Quebec]

Res Rep Natn Weed Comm West Sect Can — Research Report. National Weed Committee. Western Section. Canada

Res Rep Nat Sci Council Math Res Center — Research Reports. National Science Council. Mathematics Research Center

Res Rep NC Agr Exp Sta Dept Crop Sci — Research Report. North Carolina Agricultural Experiment Station. Department of Crop Science

Res Rep NC Agr Exp Sta Dept Field Crops — Research Report. North Carolina Agricultural Experiment Station. Department of Field Crops

Res Rep N Cent Weed Contr Conf — Research Report. North Central Weed Control Conference

Res Rep N Cent Weed Control Conf — Research Report. North Central Weed Control Conference

Res Rep NC State Univ Dep Crop Sci — Research Report. North Carolina State University. Department of Crop Science

Res Rep N Dak Agr Exp Sta — Research Report. North Dakota Agricultural Experiment Station

Res Rep New Mex Agric Exp Stn — Research Report. New Mexico Agricultural Experiment Station

Res Rep NH Agric Exp Stn — Research Report. New Hampshire Agricultural Experiment Station

Res Rep NIFS PROC Ser — Research Report. NIFS (National Institute for Fusion Science). PROC Series

Res Rep Niger Fed Inst Ind Res — Research Report. Nigeria. Federal Institute of Industrial Research

Res Rep NM Agric Exp Stn — Research Report. New Mexico. Agricultural Experiment Station

Res Rep N Mex Agr Exp Sta — Research Report. New Mexico Agricultural Experiment Station

Res Rep Norfolk Agr Exp Sta — Research Report. Norfolk Agricultural Experiment Station

Res Rep North Cent Weed Control Conf — Research Report. North Central Weed Control Conference

Res Rep Nth Cent Weed Control Conf — Research Report. North Central Weed Control Conference

Res Rep Numazu Tech Coll — Research Reports. Numazu Technical College

Res Rep Office Rur Dev Minist Agric For (Korea) — Research Reports. Office of Rural Development. Ministry of Agriculture and Forestry (Suwon, South Korea)

Res Rep Off Rural Dev Agric Eng Farm Manage & Seric (Suweon) — Research Reports. Office of Rural Development. Agricultural Engineering, Farm Management, and Sericulture (Suweon)

Res Rep Off Rural Dev Crop (Suwon) — Research Reports. Office of Rural Development. Crop (Suwon, South Korea)

Res Rep Off Rural Dev Hortic Agric Eng (Korea Repub) — Research Reports. Office of Rural Development. Horticulture and Agricultural Engineering (Korea Republic)

Res Rep Off Rural Dev Hortic (Suwon) — Research Reports. Office of Rural Development. Horticulture (Suwon, South Korea)

Res Rep Off Rural Dev Livest & Vet (Suweon) — Research Reports. Office of Rural Development. Livestock and Veterinary (Suweon)

Res Rep Off Rural Dev Livest (Korea Republic) — Research Reports. Office of Rural Development. Livestock (Korea Republic)

Res Rep Off Rural Dev Livest Seric (Suwon) — Research Reports. Office of Rural Development. Livestock, Sericulture (Suwon, South Korea)

Res Rep Off Rural Dev Livest (Suwon) — Research Reports. Office of Rural Development. Livestock (Suwon, South Korea)

Res Rep Off Rural Dev Plant Environ (Suwon) — Research Reports. Office of Rural Development. Plant Environment (Suwon, SouthKorea)

Res Rep Off Rural Dev Seric-Vet (Suwon) — Research Reports. Office of Rural Development. Sericulture-Veterinary (Suwon, South Korea)

Res Rep Off Rural Dev (Suwon) — Research Reports. Office of Rural Development (Suwon, South Korea)

Res Rep Off Rural Dev Suwon Korea — Research Reports. Office of Rural Development (Suwon, Korea)

Res Rep Off Rural Dev (Suwon) Livestock — Research Reports. Office of Rural Development (Suwon, South Korea). Livestock

Res Rep Off Rural Dev Vet Seric (Korea Republic) — Research Reports. Office of Rural Development. Veterinary and Sericulture (Korea Republic)

Res Rep Off Rural Dev Vet (Suwon) — Research Reports. Office of Rural Development. Veterinary (Suwon, SouthKorea)

Res Rep Oklahoma Agric Exp St — Oklahoma. Agricultural Experiment Station. Research Report

Res Rep Ont Minist Environ Res Branch — Research Report. Ontario Ministry of the Environment. Research Branch

Res Rep Ore St Univ Forest Res Lab — Research Report. Oregon State University. Forest Research Laboratory

Res Reports Fac Engng Meiji Univ — Research Reports. Faculty of Engineering. Meiji University

Res Rep Osaka Munic Inst Domest Sci — Research Report. Osaka Municipal Institute for Domestic Science

Res Rep Oyama Natl Coll Technol — Research Reports. Oyama National College of Technology

Res Rep Oyama Tech Coll — Research Reports. Oyama Technical College

Res Rep P Agric Exp Stn Okla State Univ — Research Report P. Agricultural Experiment Station. Oklahoma State University
Res Rep Pestic Res Inst Can — Research Report. Pesticide Research Institute. Department of Agriculture. Canada
Res Rep Phys — Research Reports in Physics
Res Rep Pl Sci Crop Husb Dubl — Research Report. Plant Sciences and Crop Husbandry (Dublin)
Res Rep P Okla Agric Exp Stn — Research Report P. Oklahoma Agricultural Experiment Station
Res Rep Pollut Control Branch Toronto — Research Report. Pollution Control Branch (Toronto)
Res Rep Raw Silk Test — Research Reports. Raw Silk Testing
Res Rep R Coll Sci — Research Report. Royal College of Science [London]
Res Rep R Coll Sci Technol Glasg — Research Report. Royal College of Science and Technology. Glasgow
Res Rep Res Ass Br Rubb Mfrs — Research Report. Research Association of British Rubber Manufacturers [Croydon]
Res Rep Res Inst Ind Saf — Research Report. Research Institute of Industrial Safety
Res Rep Res Lab Gunze Silk Manuf Co Ltd — Research Reports. Research Laboratory. Gunze Silk Manufacturing Company, Limited
Res Rep Res Lab St Jean — Research Report. Research Laboratory. St. Jean, Quebec
Res Rep Res Program Abatement Munic Pollut Provis Can Ont Ag — Research Report. Research Program for the Abatement of Municipal Pollution under Provisions of the Canada-Ontario Agreement on Great Lakes Water Quality
Res Reprod — Research in Reproduction
Res Rep R Sch Mines — Research Report. Royal School of Mines [London]
Res Rep R Tech Coll Glasg — Research Report. Royal Technical College. Glasgow
Res Rep Rural Dev Adm — Research Reports. Rural Development Administration
Res Rep Rural Dev Adm (Suweon) — Research Reports. Rural Development Administration (Suweon)
Res Rep Saf Mines Res Bd — Research Report. Safety-in-Mines Research Board (Establishment) [London]
Res Rep Saf Mines Res Establ GB — Research Report. Safety in Mines Research Establishment (Great Britain)
Res Rep Sasebo Coll Technol — Research Reports. Sasebo College of Technology
Res Rep Sasebo Tech Coll — Research Reports. Sasebo Technical College
Res Rep Sch Aviat Med Brooks Air Force Base — Research Report. School of Aviation Medicine. Brooks Air Force Base [Texas]
Res Rep Sch Civ Engng Syd Univ — Research Report. School of Civil Engineering. University of Sydney
Res Rep Sch For Fla Univ — Research Report. School of Forestry. Florida University [Gainesville]
Res Rep Scient Dep Natn Coal Bd — Research Report. Scientific Department. National Coal Board [London]
Res Rep Ser Ala Agric Exp Stn Auburn Univ — Research Report Series. Alabama Agricultural Experiment Station. Auburn University
Res Rep Ser Brock Univ Dep Geol Sci — Research Report Series. Brock University Department of Geological Sciences
Res Rep Ser Univ Queensl Dep Civ Eng — Research Report Series. University of Queensland. Department of Civil Engineering
Res Rep Shibaura Inst Technol — Research Reports. Shibaura Institute of Technology
Res Rep Silk Cond Houses — Research Reports. Silk Conditioning Houses
Res Rep Snow Ice Permafrost Res Establ — Research Report. Snow, Ice, and Permafrost Research Establishment [Wilmette]
Res Rep Storrs Agric Exp Stn — Research Report. Storrs Agricultural Experiment Station
Res Rep Struct Clay Prod Res Fdn — Research Report. Structural Clay Products Research Foundation [Chicago]
Res Rep Suzuka Univ Med Sci Technol — Research Reports of Suzuka University of Medical Science and Technology
Res Rep SWest Forest Range Exp Stn — Research Report. Southwestern Forest and Range Experiment Station [Tucson]
Res Rep Taiwan Sugar Exp Stn — Research Report. Taiwan Sugar Experiment Station
Res Rep Tech Res Cent Finl — Research Reports. Technical Research Centre of Finland
Res Rep Tex Engng Exp Stn — Research Report. Texas Engineering Experiment Station [College Station]
Res Rep Timb Dev Ass — Research Report. Timber Development Association [London]
Res Rep Timber Dev Assoc (London) — Research Report. Timber Development Association (London)
Res Rep Timb Res Developm Ass — Research Report. Timber Research and Development Association
Res Rep Tokyo Denki Univ — Research Reports. Tokyo Denki University
Res Rep Tokyo Elect Engng Coll — Research Report of the Tokyo Electrical Engineering College
Res Rep Tokyo Electr Eng Coll — Research Reports. Tokyo Electrical Engineering College
Res Rep Tokyo Electr Engrg College — Research Reports. Tokyo Electrical Engineering College
Res Rep Tokyo Electrical Engrg College — Research Reports. Tokyo Electrical Engineering College
Res Rep Tokyo Natl Tech Coll — Research Reports. Tokyo National Technical College
Res Rep Toyama Natl Coll Technol — Research Reports. Toyama National College of Technology
Res Rep Tsuruoka Tech Coll — Research Reports. Tsuruoka Technical College
Res Rep Ube Tech Coll — Research Reports. Ube Technical College

Res Rep Univ Arkansas Eng Exp Stn — Research Report. University of Arkansas. Engineering Experiment Station
Res Rep Univ Fla Sch For Resour Conserv — Research Report. University of Florida. School of Forest Resources and Conservation
Res Rep Univ GA Coll Agric Exp Stn — Research Report. University of Georgia. College of Agriculture. Experiment Stations
Res Rep Univ Ill Urbana Champaign Water Resour Cent — Research Report. University of Illinois at Urbana-Champaign. Water Resources Center
Res Rep Univ Leeds Dep Comput Stud — Research Report. University of Leeds. Department of Computer Studies
Res Rep Univ Melbourne Dep Electr Eng — Research Report. University of Melbourne. Department of Electrical Engineering
Res Rep Univ Sydney Sch Civ Min Eng — Research Report. University of Sydney. School of Civil and Mining Engineering
Res Rep Univ Tex Austin Cent Highw Res — Research Report. University of Texas at Austin. Center for Highway Research
Res Rep Univ Wis Coll Agric Life Sci Res Div — Research Report. University of Wisconsin. College of Agricultural and Life Sciences. Research Division
Res Rep Univ Wis Eng Exp Stn — Research Report. University of Wisconsin. Engineering Experiment Station
Res Rep US Army Eng Waterw Exp Stn — Research Report. US Army Engineers. Waterways Experiment Station
Res Rep US Army Mater Command Cold Reg Res Engng Lab — Research Report. United States Army Material Command. Cold Regions Research andEngineering Laboratory
Res Rep US Bur Sport Fish Wildl — Research Report. United States Bureau of Sport Fisheries and Wildlife
Res Rep US Fish Wildl Serv — Research Report. United States Fish and Wildlife Service
Res Rep US Natn Ind Conf Bd — Research Report. United States National Industrial Conference Board [Boston]
Res Rep VA Agr Exp Sta — Research Report. Virginia Agricultural Experiment Station
Res Rep Va Agric Exp Stn — Research Report. Virginia Agricultural Experiment Station [Blacksburg]
Res Rep Vet Issue — Research Reports. Veterinary Issue
Res Rep Vt Agric Exp Stn — Research Report. Vermont Agricultural Experiment Station
Res Rep Wash Res Labs Natn Cann Ass — Research Report. Washington Research Laboratories. National Canners Association [Washington]
Res Rep WatWays Exp Stn Vicksburg — Research Report. Waterways Experiment Station. Vicksburg
Res Rep Weath Radar Res MIT — Research Report. Weather Radar Research. Massachusetts Institute of Technology
Res Rep West Pine Ass — Research Report. Western Pine Association [Portland]
Res Rep West Sect Nat Weed Comm Can — Research Report. Western Section. National Weed Committee of Canada
Res Rep West Sect Weed Comm Can — Research Report. Western Section. Weed Committee (Canada)
Res Rep Winnipeg Manitoba Res Sta — Research Report. Winnipeg, Manitoba Research Station
Res Rep Wis Agr Exp Sta — Research Report. Wisconsin Agricultural Experiment Station
Res Rep Yonago Tech Coll — Research Reports. Yonago Technical College
Res Results Dig — Research Results Digest
ResRev — Research Review
Res Rev Aust CSIRO Div Chem Technol — Research Review. Australia. Commonwealth Scientific and Industrial Research Organization. Division of Chemical Technology
Res Rev Biochem — Research Reviews in Biochemistry
Res Rev Bur Hort Plantat Crops — Research Review. Commonwealth Bureau of Horticulture and Plantation Crops
Res Rev Calcutta — Research and Review (Calcutta)
Res Rev Can Res Stn (Agassiz BC) — Research Review. Canada Research Station. (Agassiz, British Columbia)
Res Rev Chung-Buk Natl Univ — Research Review. Chung-Buk National University
Res Rev CSIRO Aust — Research Review. C.S.I.R.O. Australia [Melbourne]
Res Rev CSIRO Div Chem Technol — Australia. Commonwealth Scientific and Industrial Research Organisation. Division of Chemical Technology. Research Review
Res Rev CSIR Un S Afr — Research Review. C.S.I.R. Union of South Africa
Res Rev Div Chem Technol CSIRO — Research Review. Division of Chemical Technology. Commonwealth Scientific and Industrial Research Organisation
Res Rev Florida State Univ Bull — Research in Review. Florida State University. Bulletin
Res Rev Immunol — Research Reviews in Immunology
Res Rev Inst Afr Stud — Research Review. Institute of African Studies. University of Ghana
Res Rev Kyungpook Univ — Research Review. Kyungpook University
Res Rev Mass Agric Exp Stn — Research in Review. Massachusetts Agricultural Experiment Station [Amherst]
Res Rev Med — Research Reviews in Medicine
Res Rev Neurosci — Research Reviews in Neuroscience
Res Rev (Off Aerosp Res) — Research Review (Office of Aerospace Research)
Res Rev Off Nav Res US — Research Reviews. Office of Naval Research (United States)
Res Rev Pharmacol — Research Reviews in Pharmacology
Res Revs Bowman Gray Sch Med — Research and Reviews. Bowman Gray School of Medicine. West Forest College [Salem]
Res Revs Off Nav Res — Research Reviews. Office of Naval Research [Washington]
Res Rhode Isl Agric Exp Stn — Research. Rhode Island Agricultural Experiment Station [Kingston]
Res Rural Sociol Dev — Research in Rural Sociology and Development

Res Ser AEI — Research Series. A.E.I. Associated Electrical Industries [*Manchester*]

Res Ser Am Geogr Soc — Research Series. American Geographical Society [*New York*]

Res Ser Appl Geogr New Engl Univ — Research Series in Applied Geography. University of New England

Res Ser Asph Inst NY — Research Series. Asphalt Institute (New York)

Res Ser Bull Dep Agric Tasm — Research Series Bulletin. Department of Agriculture. Tasmania [*Hobart*]

Res Ser Dep Geogr Kings Coll Durham — Research Series. Department of Geography. King's College. Durham

Res Ser Fowlers Gap Arid Zone Res Stn — Research Series. Fowlers Gap Arid Zone Research Station. University of New England

Res Ser ICAR — Research Series ICAR. Indian Council of Agricultural Research

Res Ser Purdue Univ Engng Exp Stn — Research Series. Purdue University Engineering Experiment Station [*Lafayette*]

Res Sociol Knowl — Research in Sociology of Knowledge

Res Sociol Knowl Sci Art — Research in Sociology of Knowledge, Sciences, and Art

Res Stat Note — Research and Statistics Note. Social Security Administration. Office of Research and Statistics

Res Stat Note Health Care Financ Adm Off Policy Plann Res — Research and Statistics Note. Health Care Financing Administration. Office of Policy, Planning, and Research

Res Steroids — Research on Steroids

Res Stud — Research Studies

Res Students Rep Furn Dev Coun — Research Student's Report. Furniture Development Council [*London*]

Res Stud Med Hist — Research Studies in Medical History. Wellcome. Historical Medical Museum [*London*]

Res Stud Pierce Fdn — Research Studies. Pierce Foundation [*New York*]

Res Stud State Coll Wash — Research Studies. State College of Washington

Res Stud State Univ Wash — Research Studies. State University of Washington

Res Stud Udaipur Univ Coll Agr — Research Studies. Udaipur University. College of Agriculture

Res Stud Wash State Univ — Research Studies. Washington State University

Res Stud Wash St Univ — Research Studies. Washington State University [*Pullman*]

Res Study Rep Envir Prot Res Div Wash — Research Study Report. Environmental Protection Research Division (Washington)

Res Sum Ohio Agr Res Develop Cent — Research Summary. Ohio Agricultural Research and Development Center

Res Surf Forces Proc Conf — Research in Surface Forces. Proceedings. Conference

Res Surf Forces Rep Conf — Research in Surface Forces. Reports Presented. Conference

Res T — Ressurection (Toulouse)

RESt — Review of English Studies

R Est — Revue de l'Est

R Est — Rivista di Estetica

RESTA — Revue de Stomatologie [*Later, Revue de Stomatologie et de Chirurgie Maxillo-Faciale*]

R Est Agrosociales — Revista de Estudios Agro-Sociales. Instituto de Estudios Agro-Sociales. Ministerio de Agricultura

RESTAT — Review of Economics and Statistics

Restau & Inst — Restaurants and Institutions

Restau Bus — Restaurant Business

Restaurant Bus — Restaurant Business

Restaurant Manage — Restaurant Management

Restaurants Inst — Restaurants and Institutions

Restaur Bus — Restaurant Business and Economic Research

Restaurnt B — Restaurant Business

Rest Carlino — Resto del Carlino

RESTD — Real Estate Today

Res Teach Engl — Research in the Teaching of English

Res Tech Instrum — Research Techniques and Instrumentation

Res Technol Man — Research Technology Management

Res Technol Manage — Research. Technology Management

Res Technol Technol — Research Technology and Technology

R Est Extremenos — Revista de Estudios Extremenos. Publicacion. Institucion de Servicios Culturales de la Diputacion Provincial de Badajoz

R Esthet — Revue d'Esthetique

Rest Inst — Restaurants and Institutions

R Est LJ — Real Estate Law Journal

Res Today — Research Today

Res Topics Physiol — Research Topics in Physiology

Res Top Physiol — Research Topics in Physiology

Restoration Q — Restoration Quarterly

Restorative Dent — Restorative Dentistry

Restor Eigh — Restoration and Eighteenth Century Theatre Research

Restor Neurol Neurosci — Restorative Neurology and Neuroscience

R Est Penales — Revista de Estudios Penales. Universidad de Valladolid

R Est Pol — Revista de Estudios Politicos. Suplemento de Politica Social

Rest Q — Restoration Quarterly

Res Trends — Research Trends

Res Trends Cornell Aeronaut Lab — Research Trends. Cornell Aeronautical Laboratory [*Buffalo*]

Res Trends Phys — Research Trends in Physics

Restr Mgt — Restaurant Management

Restrnt H — Restaurant Hospitality

Restr Rep — Restaurant Reporter

R E Stud — Review of Economic Studies

R Estud Agro-Soc — Revista de Estudios Agro-Sociales

R Estud Penitenciarios — Revista de Estudios Penitenciarios

R Estud Pol — Revista de Estudios Politicos

R Estud Polit — Revista de Estudios Politicos

R Estud Sindic — Revista de Estudios Sindicales

R Estud Soc — Revista de Estudios Sociales

R Estud Vida Loc — Revista de Estudios de la Vida Local

R Estud Vida Local — Revista de Estudios de la Vida Local

R Est Vida Local — Revista de Estudios de la Vida Local

RESUB — Resources

RESUDU — Records. Western Australian Museum. Supplement

Resultados Camp Int Inst Esp Oceanogr — Resultados de las Campanas Internacionales. Instituto Espanol de Oceanografia

Resultados Obscoes Met Guine — Resultados das Observacoes Meteorologicas. Guine [*Bissan*]

Resultados Obscoes Met Loanda — Resultados das Observacoes Meteorologicas. Loanda

Resultados Obscoes Met Macau — Resultados das Observacoes Meteorologicas de Macau

Resultados Obs Nac Argent Cordoba — Resultados del Observatorio Nacional Argentino en Cordoba [*Buenos Aires*]

Resultados Obsnes Obs Astr Univ Nac La Plata — Resultados de las Observaciones. Observatorio Astronomico. Universidad Nacional de La Plata

Resultate Beob Grund U Donauwass Staende Wien — Resultate der Beobachtungen ueber die Grund- u. Donauwasserstaende, dann ueber die Niederschlagsmengen in Wien

Resultate Forstverw Reg Bez Duesseldorf — Resultate der Forstverwaltung im Regierungs-Bezirk Duesseldorf

Resultate Forstverw Reg Bez Frankf A O — Resultate der Forstverwaltung im Regierungs-Bezirk Frankfurt an der Oder

Resultate Forstverw Reg Bez Wiesbaden — Resultate der Forstverwaltung im Regierungs-Bezirk Wiesbaden

Resultate Magn Beob Helsingf — Resultate Magnetischer Beobachtungen. Meteorologiska Centralanstalt. Helsingfors

Resultate Math — Resultate der Mathematik

Resultate Met Beob Dt Hollaend Schiff Eingradfelder Nordatland Oz — Resultate Meteorologischer Beobachtungen von Deutschen u. Hollaendischen Schiffen fuer Eingradfelder des Nordatlantischen Ozeans

Resultater Int Hafsforsk — Resultater af den Internationella Hafsforskningens

Resultate Sternw Met Seism Magn Beob Krakau — Resultate der an der Sternwarte Angestellten Meteorologischen Seismologischen und Magnetischen Beobachtungen (Krakau)

Resultats — Resultats Statistiques du Poitou-Charentes

Result Exped Cient — Resultados Expediciones Cientificas

Result Exped Cient Buque Oceanogr "Cornide de Saavedra" — Resultados Expediciones Cientificas del Buque Oceanografico "Cornide de Saavedra"

Result Scient Camp Calypso — Resultats Scientifiques des Campagnes de la Calypso [*Paris*]

Result Scient Explor Hydrobiol Lac Tanganika — Resultats Scientifiques de l'Exploration Hydrobiologique du Lac Tanganika

Result Scient Voyage Indes Orient Neerl — Resultats Scientifiques du Voyage aux Indes Orientales Neerlandaises [*Bruxelles*]

Results Exps Dom Exp Substn Delhi Ont — Results of Experiments. Dominion Experiment Substation. Delhi [*Ontario*]

Results Exps Dom Range Exp Stn Manyberries — Results of Experiments. Dominion Range Experiment Station. Manyberries [*Ottawa*]

Results Exps Exp Stn Harrow Ont — Results of Experiments. Experimental Station. Harrow (Ontario)

Results Exps Exp Stn Saanichton — Results of Experiments. Experimental Station. Saanichton

Results Exps Exp Substn Regina — Results of Experiments. Experimental Substation. Regina [*Saskatchewan*]

Results Fld Exps Dep Agric Zanzibar — Results of Field Experiments. Department of Agriculture. Zanzibar

Results Fld Exps Rothamsted Exp Stn — Results of Field Experiments. Rothamsted Experimental Station [*Harpenden*]

Results Geophys Sol Obsns Stonyhurst — Results of Geophysical and Solar Observations (Stonyhurst)

Results IGY Mex — Results of the I.G.Y. in Mexico

Results Int Latit Serv — Results of the International Latitude Service [*Mizusawa*]

Results Magnl Met Obsns R Alfred Obs Maurit — Results of the Magnetical and Meteorological Observations Made at the Royal Alfred Observatory. Mauritius

Results Magnl Met Obsns R Obs Greenw — Results of the Magnetical and Meteorological Observations Made at the Royal Observatory. Greenwich [*London*]

Results Magn Obsns Auroral Obs Tromso — Results of Magnetic Observations. Auroral Observatory at Tromso

Results Magn Obsns Cst Geod Surv Wash — Results of Magnetic Observations Made by the Coast and Geodetic Survey (Washington)

Results Magn Obsns HM Ships — Results of Magnetic Observations Received from H.M. Ships [*London*]

Results Magn Obsns Magn Obs Cape Tn — Results of Magnetic Observations Made at the Magnetic Observatory. University of Cape Town

Results Magn Obsns R Greenwich Obs — Results of the Magnetic Observations Made at the Royal Greenwich Observatory

Results Magn Stn Dombas — Results from the Magnetic Station at Dombas

Results Math — Results in Mathematics

Results Met Obsns NSW — Results of Meteorological Observations Made in New South Wales [*Sydney*]

Results Met Obsns Radcliffe Obs — Results of Meteorological Observations Made at the Radcliffe Observatory [*Oxford*]

Results Met Obsns Totland Bay — Results of Meteorological Observations. Totland Bay

Results Met Seism Magn Obsns Toronto — Results of Meteorological, Seismological, and Magnetic Observations (Toronto)

Results Norw Scient Exped Tristan da Cunha — Results of the Norwegian Scientific Expedition to Tristan da Cunha, 1937-38 [*Oslo*]

Results Norw Sci Exped Tristan Da Cunha 1937-1938 — Results of the Norwegian Scientific Expedition to Tristan Da Cunha 1937-1938

Results Obsns Can Magn Obs Agincourt Meanook — Results of Observations at the Canadian Magnetical Observatories. Agincourt and Meanook [Ottawa]

Results Obsns Met Terr Magn Melb Obs — Results of Observations in Meteorology and Terrestrial Magnetism. Melbourne Observatory [Melbourne]

Results Perspect Part Phys Recontres Phys Vallee Aoste — Results and Perspectives in Particle Physics. Recontres de Physique de la Vallee d'Aoste

Results Probl Cell Differ — Results and Problems in Cell Differentiation

Results Rain River Evap Obsns NSW — Results of Rain, River, and Evaporation Observations Made in New South Wales [Sydney]

Results Rec Exps Wales NAAS — Results of Some Recent Experiments in Wales. National Agricultural Advisory Service. Wales [Aberystwyth]

Results Res Agric Exp Stn Univ Ky — Results of Research. Agricultural Experiment Station. University of Kentucky

Results Res Annu Rep Univ KY Agr Exp Sta — Results of Research. Annual Report. University of Kentucky. Agricultural Experiment Station

Results Saxmundham Exp Stn — Results. Saxmundham Experimental Station

Results Tree Ring Invest — Results of Tree-Ring Investigations

Result Voyage SY Belgica — Resultats du Voyage du S.Y. Belgica en 1897-99. Expedition Antarctique Belge [Bruxelles]

Resumaro Genet Citol Tokyo — Resumaro Genetika kaj Citologia (Tokyo)

Resume A Obsns Met Noumea — Resume Annuel des Observations Meteorologiques Effectuees a Noumea. Nouvelle Caledonie

Resume Clim Cameroun — Resume Climatologique du Cameroun [Douala]

Resume Clim Casablanca — Resume Climatologique (Casablanca)

Resume Clim Tunis — Resume Climatologique (Tunis)

Resume Commun Microsc Can — Resume des Communications. Societe de Microscopie du Canada

Resume CRA Inst Geod Finl — Resume du Compte Rendu Annuel de l'Institut Geodesique de Finlande [Helsingissa]

Resume Discuss Tables Rondes Congr Int Protozool — Resume des Discussions des Tables Rondes. Congres International de Protozoologie

Resume Mem Soc Vaud Sci Nat — Resume des Memoires, Envoyes, au Concours Ouvert Par la Societe Vaudoise des Sciences Naturelles

Resume Mens Inst Natn Met Vars — Resume Mensuel. Institut National Meteorologique (Varsovie)

Resume Mens Temp Alger — Resume Mensuel du Temps en Algerie

Resume Mens Temps AEF — Resume Mensuel du Temps en A.E.F [Brazzaville]

Resume Mens Temps Cameroun — Resume Mensuel du Temps au Cameroun [Douala]

Resume Mens Temps Djibouti — Resume Mensuel du Temps (Djibouti)

Resume Mens Temps Fr — Resume Mensuel du Temps en France. Meteorologie Nationale

Resume Mens Temps Grpe Antilles Guyane — Resume Mensuel du Temps du Groupe Antilles-Guyane

Resume Mens Temps Indochine Viet Nam — Resume Mensuel du Temps en Indochine (Viet-Nam) [Saigon]

Resume Mens Temps Madagascar — Resume Mensuel du Temps a Madagascar [Tananarive]

Resume Mens Temps Maroc — Resume Mensuel du Temps au Maroc [Casablanca]

Resume Mens Temps Nouv Caledonie — Resume Mensuel du Temps. Nouvelle Caledonie et Dependences [Noumea]

Resume Mens Temps Reun — Resume Mensuel du Temps a la Reunion [Tananarive]

Resume Mens Temps Tunis — Resume Mensuel du Temps. Tunis

Resume Met Aerodr Khalde — Resume Meteorologique. Aerodrome de Khalde [Beyrouth]

Resume Met Annee Geneve Gr St Bernard — Resume Meteorologique de l'Annee pour Geneve et la Grand St.-Bernard [Geneve]

Resume Met A Obs Magn Met Lu Kia Pang — Resume Meteorologique Annuel. Observatoire Magnetique et Meteorologique. Lu-Kia-Pang

Resumen Activid Serv Shell Agric — Resumen de Actividades. Servicio Shell para el Agricultor [Cagua]

Resumen Agric — Resumen de Agricultura [Barcelona]

Resumen A Obsnes Met S Sebastian — Resumen Anual de las Observaciones Meteorologicas (San Sebastian)

Resumen Boln Mens Obs Astr Met Quito — Resumen del Boletin Mensual del Observatorio Astronomico y Meteorologico de Quito

Resumen Boln Met Obs Geofis Cartuja — Resumen del Boletin Meteorologico. Observatorio Geofisico. Cartuja [Granada]

Resumenes Aeronaut Int — Resumenes Aeronauticos Internacionales [Madrid]

Resumenes Fac Odont Univ Habana — Resumenes de la Facultad de Odontologia. Universidad de la Habana

Resumenes Invest INP-CIP — Resumenes de Investigacion. INP-CIP

Resumen Estac Cent Met Habana — Resumen. Estacion Central Meteorologica (Habana)

Resumen Labores Lab Fis Cosm La Paz — Resumen de Labores. Laboratorio de Fisica Cosmica. Universidad Mayor de San Andres (La Paz)

Resumen Mens Carta Tiempo B Aires — Resumen Mensual de la Carta del Tiempo (Buenos Aires)

Resumen Mens Obs Cent Tacubaya — Resumen Mensual del Observatorio Central Tacubaya

Resumen Mens Obsnes Estac Fuerza Aerea Nac — Resumen Mensual de las Observaciones Efectuadas por las Estaciones de la Fuerza Aerea Nacional [Santiago de Chile]

Resumen Mens Obsnes Met Lima — Resumen Mensual de las Abbreviaciones Meteorologicas (Lima)

Resumen Mens Obsnes Met Obs Igueldo — Resumen Mensual de las Observaciones Meteorologicas. Observatorio de Igueldo

Resumen Mens Serv Met Mex — Resumen Mensual. Servicio Meteorologico Mexicano [Tacubaya]

Resumen Mens Tiempo B Aires — Resumen Mensual del Tiempo (Buenos Aires)

Resumen Obsnes Estac Serv Met Esp — Resumen de las Observaciones Efectuades en las Estaciones del Servicio Meteorologico Espanol [Madrid]

Resumen Obsnes Met Caracas — Resumen de las Observaciones Meteorologicas (Caracas)

Resumen Obsnes Met Obs Estac Ecuad — Resumen de las Observaciones Meteorologicas en el Observatorio y Estaciones de la Republica del Ecuador [Quito]

Resumen Obsnes Met Obs Fabra — Resumen de las Observaciones Meteorologicas del Observatorio Fabra [Barcelona]

Resumen Obsnes Met Obs S Calixto — Resumen de las Observaciones Meteorologicas. Observatorio San Calixto [La Paz]

Resumen Obsnes Pluviom Soc Met Urug — Resumen de las Observaciones Pluviometricas. Sociedad Meteorologica Uruguaya [Montevideo]

Resumen Obsnes Serv Met Repub Dominica — Resumen de las Observaciones. Servicio Meteorologico de la Republica Dominica

Resumen Obsnes Termopluviom Xalapa — Resumen de Observaciones Termopluviometricas (Xalapa)

Resumen Sism Provis Obs Geofis Cartuja — Resumen Sismico Provisional. Observatorio Geofisico de Cartuja [Granada]

Resume Obsns Commn Met Puy De Dome — Resume des Observations. Commission Meteorologique du Puy-de-Dome [Clermont-Ferrand]

Resume Obsns Magn Obs Geophys St Maur — Resume des Observations Magnetiques. Observatoire Geophysique de Saint-Maur

Resume Obsns Met Luganville — Resume des Observations Meteorologiques Effectuees a Luganville. Pentecote et Norsup. Nouvelles Hebrides [Noumea]

Resume Obsns Met Obs St Louis — Resume des Observations Meteorologiques. Observatoire St. Louis (Jersey)

Resume Obsns Met Strasb — Resume des Observations Meteorologiques. Strasbourg

Resume Obsns Mois Serv Met Afr Occid Fr — Resume des Observations du Mois. Service Meteorologique de l'Afrique Occidentale Francais

Resume Obsns Mouvem Nuages Serv Met Acores — Resume des Observations du Mouvement des Nuages. Service Meteorologique des Acores

Resume Obsns Serv Met Acores — Resume d'Observations. Service Meteorologique des Acores [Lisbonne]

Resume Obsns Stn Met Mota Uta — Resume des Observations Effectuees a la Station Meteorologique de Mota-Uta [Iles Wallis]

Resume Obsns Stn Met Port Au Prince — Resume des Observations. Station Meteorologique. Port-au-Prince

Resumes Commun Conf Int Phys Chim Miner Amiante — Resumes des Communications. Conference Internationale sur la Physique et la Chimie des Mineraux d'Amiante

Resumes Conf Commun Symp Int Jets Mol — Resumes des Conferences et Communications. Symposium International sur les JetsMoleculaires

Resume Serv Hydrom Bassin Seine — Resume. Service Hydrometrique du Bassin de la Seine [Paris]

Resumes Met Soc Astr Met Port Au Prince — Resumes Meteorologiques. Societe Astronomique et Meteorologique (Port-au-Prince)

Resumo Malar Doenc Trop — Resumo de Malariologia e Doencas Tropicais [Rio de Janeiro]

Resumo Mens Obscoes Clim Loanda — Resumo Mensal das Observacoes Climatologicas. Loanda

Resumo Mens Obscoes Met Beira — Resumo Mensal das Observacoes Meteorologicas na Beira

Resumo Mens Obscoes Met Estac Contin Arquip Madeira — Resumo Mensal das Observacoes Meteorologicas feitas nas Estacoes do Continente e dos Arquipelagos da Madeira e Cabo Verde [Lisboa]

Resumo Mens Obscoes Met Obs Cent Met Infante D Luis — Resumo Mensal das Observacoes Meteorologicas. Observatorio Central Meteorologico Infante D. Luis [Lisboa]

Resumo Mens Obscoes Met Postos Lourenco Marques — Resumo Mensal das Observacoes Meteorologicas nos Postos em Lourenco Marques

Resumo Mens Obscoes Met Postos Prov Angola — Resumo Mensal das Observacoes Meteorologicas nos Postos de 1 e 2 Ordem da Provincia de Angola [Loanda]

Resumo Mens Obscoes Met Postos Prov Mocamb — Resumo Mensal das Observacoes Meteorologicas nos Postos da Provincia de Mocambique

Resumo Met Aeronaut S Tome — Resumo Meteorologico para a Aeronautica (Sao Tome e Principe)

Resumo Obscoes Obs Serra Do Pilar — Resumo das Observacoes. Observatorio da Serra do Pilar [Coimbra]

Resumo Obscoes Postos Territ Beira — Resumo das Observacoes nos Postos do Territorio (Beira)

Resumos Indicativos Ind Pet — Resumos Indicativos da Industria de Petroleo

Resumos Met Aeronaut Guine — Resumos Meteorologicos para a Aeronautica. Servico Meteorologico da Guine

Resumos Met Aeronaut Lisb — Resumos Meteorologicos para a Aeronautica. Servico Meteorologico National (Lisboa)

Resumptio Genet — Resumptio Genetica

Res Univ Fla — Research at the University of Florida

Resur Biosfery — Resursy Biosfery

Res Vet Sci — Research in Veterinary Science

Res Virol — Research in Virology

Res Voc Educ — Resources in Vocational Education

Res Vol Surrey Archaeol Soc — Research Volumes. Surrey Archaeological Society

Res Wis — Research in Wisconsin. A Technical Digest of Research Results in Fish, Forest, and Game Management [Madison]

Res Wk Agric Exp Stn Univ Ill — Research Work. Agricultural Experiment Station. University of Illinois

Res Wks Georgian Beekeep Res Stn (Tbilisi) — Research Works. Georgian Beekeeping Research Station (Tbilisi)

Res Wk Swed — Research Work Published in Sweden [Stockholm]

Res Work Pap Inst Eduardo Torroja Constr Cem — Research Working Papers. Instituto Eduardo Torroja de la Construccion y del Cemento

Res Works Grad Sch Dong A Univ — Research Works of the Graduate School. Dong-A University
RET — Revista Espanola de Teologia
Retail Chem — Retail Chemist [*London*]
Retail Dist Mgmt — Retail and Distribution Management
Retailer of Q — Retailer of Queensland
Retail Packag — Retail Packaging
Retail Pkg — Retail Packaging
Retail Tenn — Retailing in Tennessee
R Et Anc — Revue des Etudes Anciennes
R Et Arm — Revue des Etudes Armeniennes
R Et Comp Est-Ouest — Revue d'Etudes Comparatives Est-Ouest
R Et Coop — Revue des Etudes Cooperatives
RETD — Recueil d'Etudes Theologiques et Dogmatiques
R Et Gr — Revue des Etudes Grecques
REth — Revue d'Ethnographie
R Ethnol — Review of Ethnology
Reticuloendothel Soc J — Reticuloendothelial Society. Journal
Reticuloendothel Struct Funct Proc Int Symp — Reticuloendothelial Structure and Function. Proceedings. International Symposium
Retina Found Inst Biol Med Sci Monogr Conf — Retina Foundation. Institute of Biological and Medical Sciences. Monographs andConferences
Retinoids & Lipid Soluble Vitam Clin Pract — Retinoids and Lipid-Soluble Vitamins in Clinical Practice
Ret Liv — Retirement Living
RETNA — Reactor Technology
Ret News — Retail News
R Etnografie Folclor — Revista de Etnografie si Folclor
RETP — Revue d'Ethnographie et des Traditions Populaires
R Et Rab — Revue des Etudes Rabelaisiennes
Retros — Retrospective Review
Retrosp Biblfia Geol Pol — Retrospektywna Bibliografia Geologiczna Polski [*Warszawa*]
Retrosp Med — Retrospect of Medicine [*London*]
Retrosp Med Pharm — Retrospect of Medicine and Pharmacy [*Philadelphia*]
RetS — Revue des Etudes Slaves
RETS Dig — RETS [*Research Engineering Technical Services*] Digest
Ret Serv Lab Rep — Retail/Services Labor Report
R Et Sud-Est Europ — Revue des Etudes Sud-Est Europeennes
RETUA — Revue de Tuberculose
R Etud Byzantines — Revue des Etudes Byzantines
R Etud Coops — Revue des Etudes Cooperatives
R Etud Grecques — Revue des Etudes Grecques
R Etud Islamiques — Revue des Etudes Islamiques
R Etud Juives — Revue des Etudes Juives
RETVE5 — Revue d'Ecologie; la Terre et la Vie
RETXEB — Reviews in Environmental Toxicology
REU — AREUEA [*American Real Estate and Urban Economics Association*] Journal
REU — Revista de Estudios Universitarios
Reuleaux Mitt — Reuleaux-Mitteilungen und Archiv fuer Getriebetechnik [*Berlin*]
REUMA — Reumatismo
Reumatismo Suppl — Reumatismo. Supplement
Reum Pol — Reumatologia Polska [*Warszawa*]
Reun A Acad Estomat Peru — Reunion Anual. Academia de Estomatologia del Peru [*Lima*]
Reun Annu Sci Terre (Programme Resumes) — Reunion Annuelle des Sciences de la Terre (Programme et Resumes)
Reun Anu Arroz An — Reuniao Anual do Arroz. Anais
Reun A Soc Bras Genet — Reuniao Anual. Sociedade Brasileira de Genetica
Reun Com Int Perm Carte Photogr Ciel — Reunion du Comite International Permanent pour l'Execution de la Carte Photographique du Ciel [*Paris*]
Reun Com Reg Cent Ouest Geol Commn Coop Tech Afr S Sahara — Reunion. Comite Regional Centre-Ouest pour la Geologie. Commission de Cooperation Technique en Afrique au Sud du Sahara
Reun Com Reg E Cent Geol Commn Coop Tech Afr S Sahara — Reunion. Comite Regional Est-Central pour la Geologie. Commission de Cooperation Technique en Afrique au Sud du Sahara
Reun Com Reg S Geol Commn Coop Tech Afr S Sahara — Reunion. Comite Regional Sud pour la Geologie. Commission de Cooperation Technique en Afrique au Sud du Sahara
Reun Com Scient Int Rech Trypan — Reunion. Comite Scientifique International de Recherches sur les Trypanosomiases
Reun Cult Arroz An — Reuniao da Cultura do Arroz. Anais
Reun Endocrinol Lang Fr Rapp — Reunion des Endocrinologistes de Langue Francaise. Rapports
Reun Grupo Esp Trab Cuat — Reunion. Grupo Espanol de Trabajo del Cuaternario
Reun Grupo Trab Cuat — Reunion del Grupo de Trabajo del Cuaternario
Reunion Latinoam Prod Anim — Reunion Latinoamericana de Produccion Animal
Reunion Soc Argent Pathol Regional N — Reunion de Sociedad Argentina de Pathologia Regional del Norte
Reun Latinoamer Fitotec Actas — Reunion Latinoamericana de Fitotecnia. Actas
Reun Mat Apl Comput Cient — Reunioes em Matematica Aplicada e Computacao Cientifica
Reun Nac Cuat Medios Semiaridos — Reunion Nacional el Cuaternario en Medios Semiaridos
Reun Nac Soc Argent Cienc Nat — Reunion Nacional de la Sociedad Argentina de Ciencias Naturales [*Buenos Aires*]
Reun Prod Mar Explot Pesq — Reunion sobre Produccion Marina y Explotacion Pesquera
Reun Prod Pesq Actas — Reunion sobre Productividad y Pesquerias. Actas
Reun Product Pesq — Reunion sobre Productividad y Pesquerias [*Barcelona*]
Reuns Etude Cent Natn Coord Etud Rech Nutr Aliment — Reunions d'Etude. Centre National de Coordination des Etudes et Recherches sur la Nutrition et l'Alimentation [*Paris*]

Reun Soc Argent Patol Reg N — Reunion de la Sociedad Argentina de Patologia Regional del Norte [*Buenos Aires*]
Reun Soc B A Dept — Reunion des Societes des Beaux-Arts des Departements
Reun Soc Chim Phys — Reunion. Societe de Chimie Physique
Reun Soc Fr Phys — Reunion. Societe Francaise de Physique [*Paris*]
Reuns Scient Soc Med Aix Les Bains — Reunions Scientifiques. Societe Medicale d'Aix-les-Bains
Reun Trab Fis Energ Intermed — Reuniao de Trabalho sobre Fisica de Energias Intermediarias
Reun Trab Fis Nucl Bras An — Reuniao de Trabalho sobre Fisica Nuclear no Brasil. Anais
REur — Revue Europeenne
R Eur A — Religions de l'Europe Ancienne
REURD — Reuse/Recycle
R Europ Sci Soc — Revue Europeenne des Sciences Sociales. Cahiers Vilfredo Pareto
Rev — Review
Rev — Revue. Litterature, Histoire, Arts, et Sciences des Deux Mondes
Rev 19e Siecle — Revue du 19e Siecle
RevA — Revista de Archivos, Bibliotecas, y Museos
Rev A — Revue A
Rev A — Revue Archeologique
RevA — Revue d'Allemagne
RevA — Revue de l'Albigeois
Rev A — Revue de l'Art
RevAA — Revue Anglo-Americaine
RevAAM — Revue de l'Art Ancien et Moderne
Rev A Anc & Mod — Revue de l'Art Ancien et Moderne
Rev A & Letras — Revista de Artes y Letras
Rev A & Oficios — Revista de Arte y Oficios
Rev A Asiat — Revue des Arts Asiatiques
Rev ABIA/SAPRO — Revista. ABIA/SAPRO
RevAC — Revue de l'Art Chretien
Rev Acad Bras Letr Rio — Revista da Academia Brasileira de Letras (Rio de Janeiro)
Rev Acad Canaria Cienc — Revista de la Academia Canaria de Ciencias
Rev Acad Cienc Exactas Fis Quim Nat Madrid — Revista. Academia de Ciencias Exactas, Fisico-Quimicas, y Naturales de Madrid
Rev Acad Cienc Exactas Fis-Quim Nat Zaragoza — Revista. Academia de Ciencias Exactas, Fisico-Quimicas, y Naturales de Zaragoza
Rev Acad Cienc Exactas Fix Nat Madrid — Revista. Academia de Ciencias Exactas, Fisicas, y Naturales de Madrid
Rev Acad Cienc (Zaragoza) — Revista. Academia de Ciencias (Zaragoza)
Rev Acad Cienc Zaragoza 2 — Revista. Academia de Ciencias Exactas, Fisico-Quimicas, y Naturales de Zaragoza. Serie 2
Rev Acad Ci Zaragoza — Revista. Academia de Ciencias Exactas, Fisico-Quimicas, y Naturales de Zaragoza
Rev Acad Col Cien Exact Fis Nat Bogota — Revista. Academia Colombiana de Ciencias Exactas, Fisicas, y Naturales (Bogota)
Rev Acad Colomb Cienc Exactas Fis Nat — Revista. Academia Colombiana de Ciencias Exactas Fisicas y Naturales
Rev Acad Colombiana Cienc Exact Fis Natur — Revista. Academia Colombiana de Ciencias Exactas, Fisicas, y Naturales
Rev Acad Costarricense Hist S Jose — Revista. Academia Costarricense de Historia (San Jose, Costa Rica)
Rev Acad Galega Cienc — Revista. Academia Galega de Ciencias
Rev Acad Geogr Hist S Jose — Revista. Academia de Geographia and Historia de Costa Rica (San Jose)
Rev Acad Inscr & B Lett — Revue de l'Academie des Inscriptions et Belles-Lettres
Rev Acad Letr Bahia Salvador — Revista da Academia de Letras da Bahia (Salvador, Brazil)
Rev Acad Letr Rio — Revista das Academias de Letras (Rio de Janeiro)
Rev Acad Nat Sci Philad — Review. Academy of Natural Sciences of Philadelphia
Rev Acad Paulista Letr S Paulo — Revista da Academia Paulista de Letras (Sao Paulo)
Rev Acc Tr — Revue des Accidents du Travail
Rev A Chret — Revue de l'Art Chretien
Rev Acoust — Revue d'Acoustique
Rev Activ Natn Res Coun Can — Review of Activities. National Resarch Council. Canada [*Ottawa*]
Rev Activ William Hooper Fdn Fish Res Lab — Review of the Activities. William Hooper Foundation Fisheries Research Laboratory
Rev Act Metallges — Review of Activities. Metallgesellschaft
Rev Act Metallges AG — Review of Activities. Metallgesellschaft AG
Rev Act Sci — Revue de 'Activite Scientifique
Rev Actual Estomatol Esp — Revista de Actualidad Estomatologica Espanola
Rev A Dec — Revue des Arts Decoratifs
Rev ADM — Revista ADM (Asociacion Dental Mexicana)
Rev Adm — Revue de l'Administration et du Droit Administratif
Rev Admin Munici Rio — Revista de Administracao Municipal. Rio de Janeiro
Rev Admin Publ BA — Revista de Administracion Publica. Instituto de la Superintendencia de Administracion Publica (Buenos Aires)
Rev Admin Publ Madrid — Revista de Administracion Publica (Madrid)
Rev Admin Publ Mex — Revista de Administracion Publica (Mexico)
Rev Admin S Paulo — Revista de Administracao. Universidade de Sao Paulo
Rev Adm Nac Agua (Argent) — Revista. Administracion Nacional del Agua (Argentina)
Rev Aeronaut — Revista de Aeronautica
Rev Aeronaut Res Coun — Review. Aeronautical Research Council [*London*]
Rev Afr — Revue Africaine
Rev Afr Polit Economy — Review of African Political Economy
Rev Afr Strat — Revue Africaine de Strategie
RevAg — Revue de l'Agenais et des Anciennes Provinces de Sud-Ouest
Rev Agr — Revue de l'Agriculture
Rev Agr (Brussels) — Revue de l'Agriculture (Brussels)

Rev Agr France — Revue Agricole de France
Rev Agr Ganad Hav — Revista de Agricultura y Ganaderia. Departamento de Agricultura (La Habana)
Rev Agri — Revista de Agricultura
Rev Agric (Bogota) — Revista Agricola (Bogota)
Rev Agric (Bruss) — Revue de l'Agriculture (Brussels)
Rev Agric (Ciudad Trujillo) — Revista de Agricultura (Ciudad Trujillo)
Rev Agric Econ Hokkaido Univ — Review of Agricultural Economics. Hokkaido University
Rev Agric Egypt — Revue Agricole Egyptienne
Rev Agric Fr — Revue des Agriculteurs de France
Rev Agric Fr Agric Prat — Revue des Agriculteurs de France et l'Agriculture Pratique
Rev Agric Haiti — Revue Agricole d'Haiti
Rev Agric (Havana) — Revista de Agricultura (Havana)
Rev Agric Ile Maurice — Revue Agricole de l'Ile Maurice
Rev Agric Ind Comer PR — Revista de Agricultura. Industria y Comercio de Puerto Rico
Rev Agricola (Chicago) — Revista Agricola (Chicago)
Rev Agrico Port Au Prince — Revue Agricole d'Haiti (Port-au-Prince)
Rev Agric Ops India — Review of Agricultural Operations in India [Calcutta]
Rev Agric (Piracicaba) — Revista de Agricultura (Piracicaba)
Rev Agric Piracicaba Braz — Revista de Agricultura (Piracicaba, Brazil)
Rev Agric (Piracicaba) (S Paulo) — Revista de Agricultura (Piracicaba) (Estado de Sao Paulo)
Rev Agric (PR) — Revista de Agricultura (Puerto Rico)
Rev Agric (Recife) — Revista de Agricultura (Recife)
Rev Agric Res — Review of Agricultural Research
Rev Agric (San Jacinto Mex) — Revista Agricola (San Jacinto, Mexico)
Rev Agric (Sao Paulo) — Revista de Agricultura (Sao Paulo)
Rev Agric St Domingo — Revista de Agricultura (Santo Domingo)
Rev Agric Sucr Ile Maurice — Revue Agricole et Sucriere de l'Ile Maurice
Rev Agricultura — Revista de Agricultura
Rev Agr (Mocambique) — Revista Agricola (Mocambique)
Rev Agrol Bot Kivu — Revue Agrologique et Botanique du Kivu
Rev Agron — Revista Agronomica
Rev Agron Can — Revue Agronomique Canadienne
Rev Agron (Lisb) — Revista Agronomica (Lisbon)
Rev Agron Louvain — Revue Agronomique (Louvain)
Rev Agron Noroeste Argent — Revista Agronomica del Noroeste Argentino
Rev Agroquim Tecnol Aliment — Revista de Agroquimica y Tecnologia de Alimentos
Rev Agr (Piracicaba) — Revista de Agricultura (Piracicaba)
Rev Agustiniana — Revista Agustiniana
Rev Air Liq — Revue l'Air Liquide
Rev Aisthesis — Revista Aisthesis. Revista Chilena de Investigaciones Esteticas
RevAL — Revue de l'Amerique Latine
Rev Alcool — Revue de l'Alcoolisme
Rev Alerg Mex — Revista Alergia Mexico
Rev Alger — Revue Algerienne/Societe des Beaux-Arts
Rev Algol — Revue Algologique
Rev Aliment — Revista Alimentar
Rev Aliment Anim — Revue de l'Alimentation Animale
Rev Allergy — Review of Allergy and Applied Immunology
Rev Allergy Appl Immun — Review of Allergy and Applied Immunology [Minneapolis]
Rev Allergy Appl Immunol — Review of Allergy and Applied Immunology
Rev Alliance Franc — Revue de l'Alliance Francaise
Rev Alloc Fam — Revues des Allocations Familiales
Rev Alsace — Revue d'Alsace
Rev Alteneo Paraguayo — Revista del Alteneo Paraguayo
Rev Alum — Revue de l'Aluminum
Rev Alum Ses Appl — Revue de l'Aluminum et de Ses Applications
RevAm — Revista de America
RevAm — Revue des Amateurs
Rev AMB — Revista da AMB (Associacao Medica Brasileira)
Rev Am Chem Res — Review of American Chemical Research [Easton, Pennsylvania]
Rev Amer Hist — Reviews in American History
Rev Amerique Latine — Revue de l'Amerique Latine
Rev Amersham Corp — Review. Amersham Corporation
Rev Ameublement — Revue de l'Ameublement
Rev Am Hist — Reviews in American History
Rev AMMG — Revista da AMMG (Associacao Medica de Minas Gerais)
Rev AMRIGS — Revista. AMRIGS
Rev Am Soc Met — Review. American Society for Metals
Rev Am Soc Metals — Review. American Society for Metals [Cleveland]
Rev Am Soc Steel Treat — Review. American Society for Steel Treating [Cleveland]
Rev Anal Chem — Reviews in Analytical Chemistry
Rev Anal Chem Euroanal — Reviews on Analytical Chemistry. Euroanalysis
Rev Anal Educ Paris — Revista Analitica de Educacion (Paris)
Rev Anal Numer Teoria Aproximatiei — Revista de Analiza Numerica si Teoria Aproximatiei
Rev Anal Numer Theor Approx — Revue d'Analyse Numerique et de la Theorie de l'Approximation
Rev Anal Numer Theorie Approximation — Revue d'Analyse Numerique et de la Theorie de l'Approximation
Rev Anat Embryol Cell Biol — Reviews of Anatomy, Embryology, and Cell Biology
Rev Anat Morphol Exp — Revues d'Anatomie et de Morphologie Experimentale
Rev Anc Etud Inst Tech Roubaisien — Revue des Anciens Etudiants de l'Institut Technique Roubaisien
Rev And — Revista Andina
Rev & Bol Acad N BA — Revista e Boletim da Academia Nacional de Belas Artes
Rev & Expositor — Review and Expositor

Rev and Expositor — Review and Expositor
Rev Andina — Revista Andina
Rev Ang-Am — Revue Anglo-Americaine
Rev Anglo Am — Revue Anglo-Americaine
Rev Annu Chimiother Physiatr Cancer — Revue Annuelle de Chimiotherapie et de Physiatrie du Cancer
Rev Annu Chimiother Prophyl Cancer — Revue Annuelle de Chimiotherapie et de Prophylaxie du Cancer
Rev Annu Physiatr Prophyl Cancer — Revue Annuelle de Physiatrie et de Prophylaxie du Cancer
Rev Annu Soc Odontostomatol Nordest — Revue Annuelle. Societe Odonto-Stomatologique du Nord-Est
Rev Anorg Chem Paris — Revue fuer Anorganische Chemie (Paris)
Rev Anthr — Revue Anthropologique
Rev Anthr — Revue d'Anthropologie
Rev Anthrop — Revue Anthropologique. Ecole d'Anthropologie
Rev Anthropol — Revue Anthropologique
Rev Anthropol (Paris) — Revue Anthropologique (Paris)
Rev Antrop Arqueol Bogota — Revista de Antropologia y Arqueologia (Bogota)
Rev Antropol — Revista de Antropologia
Rev Antropol (Sao Paulo) — Revista de Antropologia (Sao Paulo)
Rev Antrop Sao Paulo — Revista de Antropologia (Sao Paulo)
Rev Antrop S Paulo — Revista de Antropologia. Universidade de Sao Paulo
Rev Antwerp — Revue Antwerpen
Rev Apollo — Revue Apollo
Rev Appl Elect — Revue des Applications de l'Electricite
Rev Appl Ent — Review of Applied Entomology
Rev Appl Entomol Ser A — Review of Applied Entomology. Series A. Agricultural
Rev Appl Entomol Ser B — Review of Applied Entomology. Series B. Medical and Veterinary
Rev Appl Mycol — Review of Applied Mycology
Rev Aquat Sci — Reviews in Aquatic Sciences
Rev Arachnol — Revue Arachnologique
Rev Aragon — Revista de Aragon
Rev Arch — Revue Archeologique
Rev Arch Bibl Mus — Revista de Archivos, Bibliotecas, y Museos
Rev Arch Bibl Nac Tegucigalpa — Revista. Archivo y Biblioteca Nacionales (Tegucigalpa)
Rev Arch ECE — Revue Archeologique de l'Est et du Centre-Est
Rev Archeol — Revue Archeologique
Rev Archeoloques & Historiens A Louvain — Revue des Archeologues et Historiens d'Art de Louvain
Rev Archeol Ouest — Revue Archeologique de l'Ouest
Rev Archeol Picardie — Revue Archeologique de Picardie
Rev Arch Est et Centre Est — Revue Archeologique de l'Est et du Centre-Est
Rev Arch Hist Cuzco — Revista. Archivo Historico del Cuzco (Cuzco, Peru)
Rev Archit — Revue Architecture
Rev Arch Ital Biol — Revue. Archives Italiennes de Biologie
Rev Archit & Trav Pub — Revue de l'Architecture et des Travaux Publics
Rev Archit Sci Unit Univ Queensl — Review. Architectural Science Unit. University of Queensland
Rev Archivos — Revista de Archivos, Bibliotecas y Museos
Rev Arch Nac Bogota — Revista. Archivo Nacional (Bogota)
Rev Arch Nac Lima — Revista. Archivo Nacional (Lima)
Rev Arch Nac S Jose — Revista de los Archivos Nacionales (San Jose, Costa Rica)
Rev Arch Narbonn — Revue Archeologique de Narbonnaise
Rev Archv N Peru — Revista del Archivo Nacional del Peru
Rev Archvs Bib & Mus — Revista de Archivos, Bibliotecas, y Museos
Rev Arg Der Intern BA — Revista Argentina de Derecho Internacional (Buenos Aires)
Rev Argent Agron — Revista Argentina de Agronomia
Rev Argent Alerg — Revista Argentina de Alergia
Rev Argent Alergia — Revista Argentina de Alergia
Rev Argent Anest — Revista Argentina de Anestesia y Analgesia
Rev Argent Anestesiol — Revista Argentina de Anestesiologia
Rev Argent Angiol — Revista Argentina de Angiologia
Rev Argent Cancerol — Revista Argentina de Cancerologia
Rev Argent Cardiol — Revista Argentina de Cardiologia
Rev Argent Cir — Revista Argentina de Cirugia
Rev Argent Dermatol — Revista Argentina de Dermatologia
Rev Argent Endocrinol Metab — Revista Argentina de Endocrinologia y Metabolismo
Rev Argent Grasas Aceites — Revista Argentina de Grasas y Aceites
Rev Argent Implantol Estomatol — Revista Argentina de Implantologia Estomatologica
Rev Argent Microbiol — Revista Argentina de Microbiologia
Rev Argent Neurol — Revista Argentina de Neurologia, Psiquiatria, y Medicina Legal
Rev Argent Neurol Psiquiat y Med Leg — Revista Argentina de Neurologia, Psiquiatria, y Medicina Legal
Rev Argent Norteam Cienc Med — Revista Argentino-Norteamericana de Ciencias Medicas
Rev Argent Pueric Neonatol — Revista Argentina de Puericultura y Neonatologia
Rev Argent Quim Ind — Revista Argentina de Quimica e Industrias
Rev Argent Radiol — Revista Argentina de Radiologia
Rev Argent Reum — Revista Argentina de Reumatologia
Rev Argent Reumatol — Revista Argentina de Reumatologia
Rev Argent Tuberc Enferm Pulm — Revista Argentina de Tuberculosis y Enfermedades Pulmonares
Rev Argent Tuberc Enferm Pulm Salud Publica — Revista Argentina de Tuberculosis, Enfermedades, Pulmonares, y Salud Publica
Rev Argent Urol Nefrol — Revista Argentina de Urologia y Nefrologia
Rev Argonne Natl Lab US — Reviews. Argonne National Laboratory (United States)

Rev Arg Psicol — Revista Argentina de Psicologia
Rev Arh — Revista Arhivelor
Rev Arhiv — Revista Arhivelor
Rev Armee Belge — Revue de l'Armee Belge
Rev Armoric Med Chir — Revue Armoricaine de Medecine, Chirurgie
Rev Arqueol Amer — Revista de Arqueologia Americana
Rev Arqueol Belem — Revista de Arqueologia (Belem)
Rev Arqueol Etnol Hav — Revista de Arqueologia y Etnologia. Junta Nacional de Arqueologia (La Habana)
Rev Arqueol [*Lisbon*] — Revista Arqueologica [*Lisbon*]
Rev Arqueol [*Madrid*] — Revista de Arqueologia [*Madrid*]
Rev Arquit [*Arg*] — Revista de Arquitectura [*Argentina*]
Rev Arquit [*Lisbon*] — Revista de Arquitectura [*Lisbon*]
Rev Arquiv Munici S Paulo — Revista do Arquivo Municipal (Sao Paulo)
Rev Art — Revue de l'Art
Rev Art Anc — Revue de l'Art Ancien et Moderne
RevArte — Revista de Arte
Rev Arts — Revue des Arts. Musees de France
Rev Arvore — Revista Arvore
Rev A Santiago — Revista de Arte [*Santiago*]
Rev A Sevill — Revista de Arte Sevillano
Rev Asoc Argent Criad Cerdos — Revista. Asociacion Argentina Criadores de Cerdos
Rev Asoc Argent Dietol — Revista. Asociacion Argentina de Dietologia
Rev Asoc Argent Microbiol — Revista. Asociacion Argentina de Microbiologia
Rev Asoc Argent Mineral Petrol Sedimentol — Revista. Asociacion Argentina de Mineralogia, Petrologia, y Sedimentologia
Rev Asoc Argent Nutr Dietol — Revista. Asociacion Argentina de Nutricion y Dietologia
Rev Asoc Argent Quim Tec Ind Cuero — Revista. Asociacion Argentina de los Quimicos y Tecnicos de la Industria del Cuero
Rev Asoc Bioquim Argent — Revista. Asociacion Bioquimica Argentina
Rev Asoc Cienc Nat Litoral — Revista. Asociacion de Ciencias Naturales del Litoral
Rev Asoc Dent Mex — Revista. Asociacion Dental Mexicana
Rev Asoc Esp Ferm Hosp — Revista. Asociacion Espanola de Farmaceuticos de Hospitales
Rev Asoc Farm Mex — Revista. Asociacion Farmaceutica Mexicana
Rev Asoc Geol Argent — Revista. Asociacion Geologica Argentina
Rev Asoc Ing Agron — Revista. Asociacion de Ingenieros Agronomos
Rev Asoc Med Argent — Revista. Asociacion Medica Argentina
Rev Asoc Med Cuen — Revista. Asociacion Medica de Cuenca
Rev Asoc Med Mex — Revista. Asociacion Medica Mexicana
Rev Asoc Mex Enferm — Revista. Asociacion Mexicana de Enfermeras
Rev Asoc Odontol Argent — Revista. Asociacion Odontologica Argentina
Rev Asoc Odontol Costa Rica — Revista. Asociacion Odontologica de Costa Rica
Rev Asoc Prof Hosp Nac Odontol — Revista. Asociacion de Profesionales. Hospital Nacional de Odontologia
Rev Asoc Rural Urug — Revista. Asociacion Rural del Uruguay
Rev Asoc Rural Uruguay — Revista. Asociacion Rural del Uruguay
Rev Assoc Fr Tech Pet — Revue. Association Francaise des Techniciens du Petrole
Rev Assoc Jur Dem — Revue. Association des Juristes Democrates
Rev Assoc Med Bras — Revista. Associacao Medica Brasileira
Rev Assoc Med Minas Gerais — Revista. Associacao Medica de Minas Gerais
Rev Assoc Med Rio Grande Do Sul — Revista. Associacao Medica do Rio Grande Do Sul
Rev Assoc Med Rio Grande Sul — Revista da Associacao Medica do Rio Grande do Sul
Rev Assoc Natl Agron Haitiens — Revue. Association Nationale des Agronomes Haitiens
Rev Assoc Paul Cir Dent — Revista. Associacao Paulista de Cirurgioes Dentistas
Rev Assoc Paul Cir Dent Reg Aracatuba — Revista. Associacao Paulista de Cirurgioes Dentistas Regional de Aracatuba
Rev Assoc Paul Med — Revista. Associacao Paulista de Medicina
Rev Assoc Prev Pollut Atmos — Revue. Association pour la Prevention de la Pollution Atmospherique
Rev Assoc Psychiatres Can — Revue. Association des Psychiatres du Canada
Rev Assoc Tech Ind Papet — Revue. Association Technique de l'Industrie Papetiere
Rev Ass Resp — Revue des Assurances et des Responsabilites
Rev Ass Terr — Revue Generale des Assurances Terrestres
Rev Assyriol — Revue d'Assyriologie
Rev Assyriol — Revue d'Assyriologie et d'Archeologie Orientale
Rev Astron — Revista Astronomica
Rev Asturiana Cien Med — Revista Asturiana de Ciencias Medicas
Rev Ateneo Argent Odontol — Revista del Ateneo Argentino de Odontologia
Rev Ateneo Catedra Tec Oper Dent — Revista. Ateneo de la Catedra de Tecnica de Operatoria Dental
Rev Atheroscler — Revue de l'Atherosclerose
Rev Atheroscler Arteriopathies Peripher — Revue de l'Atherosclerose et des Arteriopathies Peripheriques
Rev Atheroscler Arteriopathies Peripheriques — Revue de l'Atherosclerose et des Arteriopathies Peripheriques
Rev At Ind — Review of Atomic Industries
Rev ATIP — Revue ATIP
Rev Atual Indig — Revista de Atualidade Indigena
Rev AUPELF — Revue de l'AUPELF. Association des Universites Partiellement ou Entierement de Langue Francaise
Rev Aust Timb Supply — Review of Australian Timber Supply [*Canberra*]
Rev Autom — Revista de Automatica
Rev Auvergne — Revue d'Auvergne
Rev Avic — Revista Avicultura
Rev Azucar — Revista Azucarera
RevB — Revista (Barcelona)

Rev B — Revue Belge de Philologie et d'Histoire
RevB — Revue Biblique
Rev Bact Protozool Gen Parasit — Review of Bacteriology, Protozoology, and General Parasitology [*London*]
Rev Bago — Revista Bago
RevBAM — Revista. Biblioteca, Archivo, y Museo del Ayuntamiento de Madrid
Rev B A [*Madrid*] — Revista de Bellas Artes [*Madrid*]
Rev BA [*Mexico*] — Revista de Bellas Artes [*Mexico*]
Rev Banco Repub Bogota — Revista. Banco de la Republica (Bogota)
Rev Bank London South Am — Review. Bank of London and South America
Rev Bank NSW — Review. Bank of New South Wales
Rev Banque — Revue de la Banque
Rev Bar — Revue du Barreau
Rev Barreau Que — Revue. Barreau de Quebec
Rev Base Metal Condit — Review of Base Metal Conditions. British Metal Corporation [*London*]
Rev Bas Poitou — Revue du Bas-Poitou
Rev Belg Arch — Revue Belge d'Archeologie et d'Histoire de l'Art
Rev Belge — Revue Belge
Rev Belge — Revue Belge de Philologie et d'Histoire
Rev Belge A & Hist — Revue Belge d'Art et d'Histoire
Rev Belge Archeol & Hist A — Revue Belge d'Archeologie et d'Histoire de l'Art
Rev Belge Archeol & Hist A Belge Tijdschr Outhdknde & Kstgesc — Revue Belge d'Archeologie et d'Histoire de l'Art/Belge Tijdschrift voor Oudheidkunde en Kustgeschiedenis
Rev Belge de Droit Internat — Revue Belge de Droit International
Rev Belge de Num — Revue Belge de Numismatique et de Sigillographie
Rev Belge de Phil et d'Hist — Revue Belge de Philologie et d'Histoire
Rev Belge de Philologie et d Hist — Revue Belge de Philologie et d'Histoire
Rev Belge Dr Int'l — Revue Belge de Droit International
Rev Belge du C — Revue Belge du Cinema
Rev Belge Hist Mil — Revue Belge d'Histoire Militaire
Rev Belge Hist Milit — Revue Belge d'Histoire Militaire
Rev Belge Homoeopath — Revue Belge d'Homoeopathie
Rev Belge Ind Verrieres — Revue Belge des Industries Verrieres
Rev Belge Ind Verrieres Ceram Emaill — Revue Belge des Industries Verrieres. Ceramiques et de l'Emaillerie
Rev Belge Matieres Plast — Revue Belge des Matieres Plastiques
Rev Belge Med Dent — Revue Belge de Medecine Dentaire
Rev Belge Numi — Revue Belge de Numismatique
Rev Belge Pathol Med Exp — Revue Belge de Pathologie et de Medecine Experimentale
Rev Belge Phil Hist — Revue Belge de Philologie et d'Histoire
Rev Belge Philol — Revue Belge de Philologie et d'Histoire
Rev Belge Philol Hist — Revue Belge de Philologie et d'Histoire
Rev Belge Sci Med — Revue Belge des Sciences Medicales
Rev Belge Stat Inf et Rech Oper — Revue Belge de Statistique, d'Informatique, et de Recherche Operationnelle
Rev Belge Transp — Revue Belge des Transports
Rev Belgique — Revue de Belgique
Rev Belg Num — Revue Belge de Numismatique et de Sigillographie
Rev Belg Pathol Med Exp — Revue Belge de Pathologie et de Medecine Experimentale
Rev Belg Philol Hist — Revue Belge de Philologie et d'Histoire
Rev Bel Ph — Revue Belge de Philologie et d'Histoire
Rev Ben — Revue Benedictine
Rev Bened — Revue Benedictine
Rev Benedictine — Revue Benedictine
Rev Benzole Technol — Review of Benzole Technology [*London*]
Rev Bib — Revista Biblica
Rev Bib — Revista Bibliotecilor
Rev Bib — Revue Biblique
Rev Bibl — Revue des Bibliotheques
Rev Bibl — Revue Biblique
Rev Bibliof — Revista Bibliofila
Rev Bibliogr Complement Ann Sci Nat — Revue Bibliographique pour Servir de Complement aux Annales des Sciences Naturelles
Rev Bibliogr Cubana Hav — Revista Bibliografica Cubana (La Habana)
Rev Biblioth — Revue des Bibliotheques
Rev Bibl Nac BA — Revista. Biblioteca Nacional (Buenos Aires)
Rev Bibl Nac Guat — Revista. Biblioteca Nacional (Guatemala)
Rev Bibl Nac Hav — Revista. Biblioteca Nacional (La Habana)
Rev Bibl Nac S Salvador — Revista. Biblioteca Nacional (San Salvador)
Rev Bib N — Revista de la Biblioteca Nacional
Rev Bib N — Revista de la Bibliotheque Nationale
Rev Bib N Jose Marti — Revista de la Biblioteca Nacional Jose Marti
Rev Bib N [*Lisbon*] — Revista da Biblioteca National [*Lisbon*]
Rev Bib Paroiss & Faits Relig Prov Eccles Avignon — Revue des Bibliotheques Paroissiales et des Faits Religieux de la Province Ecclesiastique d'Avignon
Rev Bigott — Revista Bigott
Rev Bimes Cubana Hav — Revista Bimestre Cubana. Sociedad Economica de Amigos del Pais (La Habana)
Rev Biochem Toxicol — Reviews in Biochemical Toxicology
Rev Biol Acad Rep Pop Roumaine — Revue de Biologie. Academie de la Republique Populaire Roumaine
Rev Biol (Buchar) — Revue de Biologie (Bucharest)
Rev Biol For Limnol — Revista de Biologia Forestal y Limnologia
Rev Biol (Lisb) — Revista de Biologia (Lisbon)
Rev Biol Lisbon — Revista de Biologia (Lisbon)
Rev Biol Mar — Revista de Biologia Marina
Rev Biol Med Nucl — Revista de Biologia y Medicina Nuclear
Rev Biol Oral — Revista de Biologia Oral
Rev Biol Res Aging — Review of Biological Research in Aging
Rev Biol Trop — Revista de Biologia Tropical
Rev Biol Univ Oviedo — Revista de Biologia. Universidad de Oviedo

Rev Biol Urug — Revista de Biologia del Uruguay
Rev Bio-Math — Revue de Bio-Mathematique
Rev Blanche — Revue Blanche
Rev Bleue — Revue Politique et Litteraire. Revue Bleue
Rev Bl Pol — Review of Black Political Economy
Rev Bl Polit Lit — Revue Bleue Politique et Litteraire
RevBM — Revue Belge de Musicologie
RevBN — Revista de Bibliografia Nacional
Rev Bois Appl — Revue du Bois et de Ses Applications
Rev Bolivar Bogota — Revista Bolivariana. Sociedad Bolivariana de Colombia (Bogota)
Rev Boliv Quim — Revista Boliviana de Quimica
Rev Bolsa Cereal — Revista. Bolsa de Cereales
Rev Bolsa Comer Rosario — Revista. Bolsa de Comercio de Rosario
Rev Bot Appl Agric Colon — Revue de Botanique Appliquee et d'Agriculture Coloniale
Rev Bot Appl Agric Trop — Revue de Botanique Appliquee et d'Agriculture Tropicale
Rev Bot Appl Agric Trop Suppl — Revue de Botanique Appliquee et d'Agriculture Tropicale. Supplement
Rev Bot Appl Agr Trop — Revue de Botanique Appliquee et d'Agriculture Tropicale
Rev Bot Recueil Mens — Revue Botanique. Recueil Mensuel
Rev Bourgogne — Revue de Bourgogne
Rev Bourguignonne Ens Sup — Revue Bourguignonne de l'Enseignement Superieur
Rev Bra Ec — Revista Brasileira de Economia
Rev Bras Anal Clin — Revista Brasileira de Analises Clinicas
Rev Bras Anestesiol — Revista Brasileira de Anestesiologia
Rev Bras Armazenamento — Revista Brasileira de Armazenamento
Rev Bras Biol — Revista Brasileira de Biologia
Rev Bras Bot — Revista Brasileira de Botanica
Rev Bras Cancerol — Revista Brasileira de Cancerologia
Rev Bras Cardiovasc — Revista Brasileira Cardiovascular
Rev Bras Chim — Revista Brasileira de Chimica
Rev Bras Chim (Sao Paulo) — Revista Brasileira de Chimica (Sao Paulo)
Rev Bras Cienc Solo — Revista Brasileira de Ciencia do Solo
Rev Bras Cien Soc Belo Horizonte — Revista Brasileira de Ciencias Sociais. Faculdade de Ciencias Economicas. Universidade Federal do Minas Gerais (Belo Horizonte, Brazil)
Rev Bras Cir — Revista Brasileira de Cirurgia
Rev Bras Cirurg — Revista Brasileira de Cirurgia
Rev Bras Clin Ter — Revista Brasileira de Clinica e Terapeutica
Rev Bras Defic Ment — Revista Brasileira de Deficiencia Mental
Rev Bras Econ Rio — Revista Brasileira de Economia. Organo do Instituto Brasileiro de Economia (Riode Janeiro)
Rev Bras Enferm — Revista Brasileira de Enfermagem
Rev Bras Eng — Revista Brasileira de Engenharia
Rev Bras Eng Cad Eng Quim — Revista Brasileira de Engenharia. Caderno de Engenharia Quimica
Rev Bras Eng Quim — Revista Brasileira de Engenharia Quimica
Rev Bras Ent — Revista Brasileira de Entomologia
Rev Bras Entomol — Revista Brasileira de Entomologia
Rev Bras Estat — Revista Brasileira de Estatistica
Rev Bras Estud Pedag Rio — Revista Brasileira de Estudos Pedagogicos. Instituto Nacional de Estudos Pedagogicos (Rio de Janeiro)
Rev Bras Estud Pol Belo Horizonte — Revista Brasileira de Estudos Politicos (Belo Horizonte, Brazil)
Rev Bras Farm — Revista Brasileira de Farmacia
Rev Bras Farmacogn — Revista Brasileira de Farmacognosia
Rev Bras Filos S Paulo — Revista Brasileira de Filosofia. Instituto Brasileiro de Filosofia (Sao Paulo)
Rev Bras Fis — Revista Brasileira de Fisica
Rev Bras Fisiol Veg — Revista Brasileira de Fisiologia Vegetal
Rev Bras Folk Rio — Revista Brasileira de Folclore (Rio de Janeiro)
Rev Bras Frutic — Revista Brasileira de Fruticultura
Rev Bras Gastroenterol — Revista Brasileira de Gastroenterologia
Rev Bras Genet — Revista Brasileira de Genetica
Rev Bras Geocienc — Revista Brasileira de Geociencias
Rev Bras Geogr — Revista Brasileira de Geografia
Rev Bras Ginecol Obstet — Revista Brasileira de Ginecologia e Obstetricia
Rev Brasil Geogr — Revista Brasileira de Geografia
Rev Brasil Quim — Revista Brasileira de Quimica
Rev Bras Leprol — Revista Brasileira de Leprologia
Rev Bras Malariol Doencas Trop — Revista Brasileira de Malariologia e Doencas Tropicais
Rev Bras Malariol Doencas Trop Publ Avulsas — Revista Brasileira de Malariologia e Doencas Tropicais. Publicacoes Avulsas
Rev Bras Mandioca — Revista Brasileira de Mandioca
Rev Bras Med — Revista Brasileira de Medicina
Rev Bras Med Farm — Revista Brasileira de Medicina e Farmacia
Rev Bras Munici Rio — Revista Brasileira dos Municipios. Conselho Nacional de Estatistica. Organo da Associacao Brasileira dos Municipios (Rio de Janeiro)
Rev Bras Odont — Revista Brasileira de Odontologia
Rev Bras Odontol — Revista Brasileira de Odontologia
Rev Bras Oftalmol — Revista Brasileira de Oftalmologia
Rev Bras Otorrinolaringol — Revista Brasileira de Otorrinolaringologia
Rev Bras Patol Clin — Revista Brasileira de Patologia Clinica
Rev Bras Pesqui Med Biol — Revista Brasileira de Pesquisas Medicas e Biologicas
Rev Bras Pol Intern Rio — Revista Brasileira de Politica Internacional (Rio de Janeiro)
Rev Bras Psiquiatr — Revista Brasileira de Psiquiatria
Rev Bras Quim — Revista Brasileira de Quimica. Ciencia and Industria
Rev Bras Quim (Sao Paulo) — Revista Brasileira de Quimica (Sao Paulo)

Rev Bras Reprod Anim — Revista Brasileira de Reproducao Animal
Rev Bras Reum — Revista Brasileira de Reumatologia
Rev Bras Reumatol — Revista Brasileira de Reumatologia
Rev Bras Rio — Revista Brasileira (Rio de Janeiro)
Rev Brass Boissons — Revue de la Brasserie et des Boissons
Rev Bras S Paulo — Revista Brasiliense (Sao Paulo)
Rev Bras Tecnol — Revista Brasileira de Tecnologia
Rev Bras Tuberc Doencas Torac — Revista Brasileira de Tuberculose e Doencas Toracicas
Rev Bras Zool — Revista Brasileira de Zoologia
Rev Bras Zootec — Revista Brasileira de Zootecnia
Rev Bretagne & Vendee — Revue de Bretagne et de Vendee
Rev Bretonne Bot Pure Appl — Revue Bretonne de Botanique Pure et Appliquee
Rev Brown Boveri — Revue Brown Boveri
Rev Brown Boveri Cie — Revue Brown Boveri et Cie
Rev Bryol Lichenol — Revue Bryologique et Lichenologique
Rev B Sec Soc — Revue Belge de Securite Sociale
Rev Bulb Exps Kirton Exp Husb Fm — Review of Bulb Experiments. Kirton Experimental Husbandry Farm. Boston [London]
Rev Bulg Geol Soc — Review. Bulgarian Geological Society
Rev Bull Calcutta Math Soc — Review Bulletin. Calcutta Mathematical Society
Rev Bus Econ Res — Review of Business and Economic Research
RevC — Revista Camoniana
RevC — Revista Cubana
RevC — Revue Catholique (Louvain)
Rev C Abo PR — Revista. Colegio de Abogados de Puerto Rico
Rev C Abo PR — Revista de Derecho. Colegio de Abogados de Puerto Rico
Rev Cafe Col Bogota — Revista Cafetera de Colombia. Federacion Nacional de Cafeteros (Bogota)
Rev Cafe Port — Revista do Cafe Portugues
Rev Cafetalera (Guatem) — Revista Cafetalera (Guatemala)
Rev Cafetera Colomb — Revista Cafetera de Colombia
Rev Caja Jubil Pension Monte — Revista. Caja de Jubilaciones y Pensiones de la Industria y Comercio (Montevideo)
Rev Can — Revue Canadienne
Rev Canad Biol — Revue Canadienne de Biologie
Rev Canadienne Geographie — Revue Canadienne de Geographie
Rev Can Anthropol — Revue Canadienne d'Anthropologie
Rev Can Bio — Revue Canadienne de Biologie
Rev Can Biochim Biol Cell — Revue Canadienne de Biochimie et Biologie Cellulaire
Rev Can Biol — Revue Canadienne de Biologie
Rev Can Biol Exp — Revue Canadienne de Biologie Experimentale
Rev Can Biol Suppl — Revue Canadienne de Biologie. Supplement
Rev Can D Fam — Revue Canadienne de Droit Familial
Rev Can Dr Com — Revue Canadienne de Droit Communautaire
Rev Can Econ Publique Coop Can J Public Coop Econ — Revue Canadienne d'Economie Publique et Cooperative. Canadian Journal of Publicand Cooperative Economy
Rev Can Gen Elcotr — Revue Canadienne de Genie Electrique
Rev Can Geotech — Revue Canadienne de Geotechnique
Rev Can Hyg Publique — Revue Canadienne d'Hygiene Publique
Rev Can Med Comp — Revue Canadienne de Medecine Comparee
Rev Can Phytopathol — Revue Canadienne de Phytopathologie
Rev Can Phytotechnie — Revue Canadienne de Phytotechnie
Rev Can Psychol — Revue Canadienne de Psychologie
Rev Can Rech Vet — Revue Canadienne de Recherche Veterinaire
Rev Can Sante Publique — Revue Canadienne de Sante Publique
Rev Can Sci Comport — Revue Canadienne des Sciences du Comportement
Rev Can Sci Comportement — Revue Canadienne des Sciences du Comportement
Rev Can Sci Sol — Revue Canadienne de la Science du Sol
Rev Can Zootech — Revue Canadienne de Zootechnie
Rev Cart BA — Revista Cartografica. Instituto Panamericano de Geografia e Historia (Buenos Aires)
Rev CASL — Revista CASL (Centro Academico Sarmento Leite)
Rev Castell — Revista Castellana
Rev Catarinense Odontol — Revista Catarinense de Odontologia
Rev Celt — Revue Celtique
Rev Celtique — Revue Celtique
Rev CENIC Cienc Biol — Revista CENIC [Centro Nacional de Investigaciones Cientificas]. Ciencias Biologicas
Rev CENIC Cienc Fis — Revista CENIC [Centro Nacional de Investigaciones Cientificas]. Ciencias Fisicas
Rev Cent Acad Sarmento Leite — Revista. Centro Academico Sarmento Leite
Rev Cent Cienc Biomed Univ Fed Santa Maria — Revista. Centro de Ciencias Biomedicas. Universidade Federal de Santa Maria
Rev Cent Cienc Biomed Univ Fed St Maria — Revista. Centro de Ciencias Biomedicas. Universidade Federal de Santa Maria
Rev Cent Cienc Rurais — Revista. Centro de Ciencias Rurais
Rev Cent Cienc Rurais Univ Fed St Maria — Revista. Centro de Ciencias Rurais. Universidade Federal de Santa Maria
Rev Cent Cienc Saude — Revista. Centro de Ciencias da Saude
Rev Cent Cienc Saude Univ Fed St Maria — Revista. Centro de Ciencias da Saude. Universidade Federal de Santa Maria
Rev Cent Cient Luis Pasteur — Revista. Centro Cientifico Luis Pasteur
Rev Cent Cult Sci (Pelotas Braz) — Revista. Centro de Cultura Scientifica (Pelotas, Brazil)
Rev Cent Ed — Revista. Centro de Estudios Educativos
Rev Cent Estud Cabo Verde Ser Cienc Biol — Revista. Centro de Estudos de Cabo Verde. Serie de Ciencias Biologicas
Rev Cent Estud Farm Bioquim — Revista del Centro Estudiantes de Farmacia y Bioquimica
Rev Cent Ing Prov Buenos Aires — Revista. Centro de Ingenieros. Provincia de Buenos Aires

Rev Cent Letr Curitiba — Revista do Centro de Letras (Curitiba, Brazil)
Rev Cent Nac Patol Anim — Revista. Centro Nacional de Patologia Animal
Rev Cent Quim Ind Buenos Aires — Revista del Centro de Quimicos Industriales. Buenos Aires
Rev Centr Estud Med Vet — Revista. Centro de Estudiantes de Medicina Veterinaria
Rev Centroam Nutr Cienc Aliment — Revista Centroamericana de Nutricion y Ciencias de Alimentos
Rev Centro Cienc Biomed Univ Fed Uberlandia — Revista do Centro de Ciencias Biomedicas da Universidade Federal de Uberlandia
Rev Centro Estud Agronom y Vet Univ Buenos Aires — Revista. Centro de Estudiantes de Agronomia y Veterinaria. Universidad de Buenos Aires
Rev Cent Tech Fonderie Assoc Tech Fonderie — Revue. Centre Technique. Fonderie et de l'Association Technique de Fonderie
Rev Ceres — Revista Ceres
Rev CETHEDEC — Revue. Centre d'Etudes Theoriques de la Detection et des Communications
Rev CETHEDEC Cahier — Revue. Centre d'Etudes Theoriques de la Detection et des Communications. Cahier
Rev C Genie Civil Constr — Revue C. Genie Civil. Construction
Rev Champagne & Brie — Revue de Champagne et de Brie
Rev Chapingo — Revista Chapingo
Rev Chem Biol Coord Cent — Review. Chemical-Biological Coordination Center [*Washington*]
Rev Chem En — Reviews in Chemical Engineering
Rev Chem Eng — Reviews in Chemical Engineering
Rev Chem Intermed — Reviews of Chemical Intermediates
Rev Chicano-Riquena — Revista Chicano-Riquena
Rev Chil Anest — Revista Chilena de Anestesia
Rev Chil Antrop — Revista Chilena de Antropologia
Rev Chil Educ Fisic Santiago — Revista Chilena de Educacion Fisica. Instituto de Educacion Fisica y Tenica. Universidad de Chile (Santiago)
Rev Chilena Hist Y Geog — Revista Chilena de Historia y Geografia. Sociedad Chilena de Historia
Rev Chilena Ing — Revista Chilena de Ingenieria
Rev Chil Entomol — Revista Chilena de Entomologia
Rev Chil Hig Med Prev — Revista Chilena de Higiene y Medicina Preventiva
Rev Chil Hist Geogr Santiago — Revista Chilena de Historia y Geografia. Sociedad Chilena de Historia y Geografia (Santiago)
Rev Chil Hist Nat — Revista Chilena de Historia Natural
Rev Chil Ing — Revista Chilena de Ingenieria
Rev Chil Neuro Psiquiatr — Revista Chilena de Neuro-Psiquiatria
Rev Chil Obstet Ginecol — Revista Chilena de Obstetricia y Ginecologia
Rev Chil Ortop Traum — Revista Chilena de Ortopedia y Traumatologia
Rev Chil Pediatr — Revista Chilena de Pediatria
Rev Chil Tecnol Med — Revista Chilena de Tecnologia Medica
Rev Chil Urol — Revista Chilena de Urologia
Rev Chim — Revista de Chimie
Rev Chim Acad Repub Pop Roum — Revue de Chimie. Academie de la Republique Populaire Roumaine
Rev Chim (Bucharest) — Revista de Chimie (Bucharest)
Rev Chim Bucharest Supl — Revista de Chimie (Bucharest). Supliment
Rev Chim Ind — Revista de Chimica Industrial
Rev Chim Mi — Revue de Chimie Minerale
Rev Chim Miner — Revue de Chimie Minerale
Rev Chim Pharm Mil — Revista de Chimica e Pharmacia Militar
Rev Chim Pura Appl — Revista de Chimica Pura e Applicada
Rev Chim Zagreb — Revue Chimique (Zagreb)
Rev Chir — Revista de Chirurgie. Stomatologie
Rev Chir Oncol Radiol ORL Oftalmol Stomatol — Revista de Chirurgie, Oncologie, Radiologie, ORL, Oftalmologie, Stomatologie
Rev Chir Oncol Radiol ORL Oftalmol Stomatol Oncol — Revista de Chirurgie, Oncologie, Radiologie, ORL, Oftalmologie, Stomatologie. Oncologia
Rev Chir Oncol Radiol ORL Oftalmol Stomatol Radiol — Revista de Chirurgie, Oncologie, Radiologie, ORL, Oftalmologie, Stomatologie. Radiologia
Rev Chir Oncol Radiol ORL Oftalmol Stomatol Ser Chir — Revista de Chirurgie, Oncologie, Radiologie, ORL, Oftalmologie, Stomatologie. Seria Chirurgie
Rev Chir Oncol Radiol ORL Oftalmol Stomatol Ser Oncol — Revista de Chirurgie, Oncologie, Radiologie, ORL, Oftalmologie, Stomatologie. Seria Oncologie
Rev Chir Oncol Radiol ORL Oftalmol Stomatol Ser Radiol — Revista de Chirurgie, Oncologie, Radiologie, ORL, Oftalmologie, Stomatologie. Seria Radiologie
Rev Chir Oncol Radiol ORL Oftalmol Stomatol Ser Stomatol — Revista de Chirurgie, Oncologie, Radiologie, ORL, Oftalmologie, Stomatologie. Seria Stomatologie
Rev Chir Or — Revue de Chirurgie Orthopedique et Reparatrice de l'Appareil Moteur
Rev Chir Orthop — Revue de Chirurgie Orthopedique et Reparatrice de l'Appareil Moteur
Rev Chir Orthop Reparatrice Appar Mot — Revue de Chirurgie Orthopedique et Reparatrice de l'Appareil Moteur
Rev Cianc Sociais — Revista de Ciancias Sociais
Rev Ci Biol — Revista de Ciencias Biologicas
Rev Cie Gen Electr — Review of Compagnie Generale d'Electricite
Rev Cienc — Revista de Ciencias
Rev Cienc Agrar — Revista de Ciencias Agrarias
Rev Cienc Agron — Revista de Ciencias Agronomicas
Rev Cienc Agron Ser A — Revista de Ciencias Agronomicas. Serie A
Rev Cienc Agron Ser B — Revista de Ciencias Agronomicas. Serie B
Rev Cienc & Tecnol — Revista de Ciencia & Tecnologia
Rev Cienc Apl — Revista de Ciencia Aplicada
Rev Cienc Apl (Madrid) — Revista de Ciencias Aplicadas (Madrid)
Rev Cienc Biol — Revista de Ciencias Biologicas
Rev Cienc Biol (Belem) — Revista de Ciencias Biologicas (Belem)

Rev Cienc Biol (Havana) — Revista de Ciencias Biologicas (Havana)
Rev Cienc Biol Ser A — Revista de Ciencias Biologicas. Serie A
Rev Cienc Biol Ser A (Lourenco Marques) — Revista de Ciencias Biologicas. Serie A (Lourenco Marques)
Rev Cienc Biol Ser B — Revista de Ciencias Biologicas. Serie B
Rev Cienc Biol Ser B (Lourenco Marques) — Revista de Ciencias Biologicas. Serie B (Lourenco Marques)
Rev Cienc Biomed — Revista de Ciencias Biomedicas
Rev Cienc Farm — Revista de Ciencias Farmaceuticas
Rev Cienc Farm (Araraquara Braz) — Revista de Ciencias Farmaceuticas (Araraquara, Brazil)
Rev Cienc Farm Sao Paulo — Revista de Ciencias Farmaceuticas (Sao Paulo)
Rev Cienc Geol Ser A — Revista de Ciencias Geologicas. Serie A
Rev Cienc Mat Univ Lourenco Marques — Revista de Ciencias Matematicas. Universidade de Lourenco Marques
Rev Cienc Med (Havana) — Revista de Ciencias Medicas (Havana)
Rev Cienc Med (Lourenco Marques) — Revista de Ciencias Medicas. Serie A (Lourenco Marques)
Rev Cienc Med Ser A (Lourenco Marques) — Revista de Ciencias Medicas. Serie A (Lourenco Marques)
Rev Cienc Med Ser B (Lourenco Marques) — Revista de Ciencias Medicas. Serie B (Lourenco Marques)
Rev Cienc Psicol Neurol (Lima) — Revista de Ciencias Psicologicas y Neurologicas (Lima)
Rev Cienc Quim — Revista de Ciencias Quimicas
Rev Cienc Univ Nac Mayor San Marcos — Revista de Ciencias. Universidad Nacional Mayor de San Marcos
Rev Cienc Univ Oviedo — Revista de Ciencias. Universidad de Oviedo
Rev Cienc Vet — Revista de Ciencias Veterinarias
Rev Cienc Vet Lisbon — Revista de Ciencias Veterinarias (Lisbon)
Rev Cien Econ — Revista de Ciencias Economicas
Rev Cien Econ BA — Revista de Ciencias Economicas (Buenos Aires)
Rev Cien Jur S Jose — Revista de Ciencias Juridicas (San Jose, Costa Rica)
Rev Cien Jur Soc Sante Fe — Revista de Ciencias Juridicas y Sociales (Santa Fe, Argentina)
Rev Cien Jur Soc S Jose — Revista de Ciencias Juridico-Sociales (San Jose, Costa Rica)
Rev Cien Lima — Revista de Ciencias (Lima)
Rev Cien Penal Santiago — Revista de Ciencias Penales (Santiago)
Rev Cien Soc Rio Piedras — Revista de Ciencias Sociales (Rio Piedras)
Rev Cient — Revista Cientifica
Rev Cient CASL — Revista Cientifica. CASL
Rev Cient Cent Invest Cient — Revista Cientifica. Centro de Investigaciones Cientificas
Rev Cient Invest Mus Hist Nat San Rafael (Mendoza) — Revista Cientifica de Investigaciones del Museo de Historia Natural de San Rafael (Mendoza)
Rev Cient Univ Auton Tomas Frias — Revista Cientifica. Universidad Autonoma Tomas Frias
Rev Cient Univ Boliv Tomas Frias — Revista Cientifica. Universidad Boliviana Tomas Frias
Rev Cien Vet — Revista de Ciencias Veterinarias
Rev Ci (Lima) — Revista de Ciencias (Lima)
Rev Ci Mat Univ Lourenco Marques — Revista de Ciencias Matematicas. Universidade de Lourenco Marques
Rev Ci Mat Univ Lourenco Marques Ser A — Revista de Ciencias Matematicas. Universidade de Lourenco Marques. Serie A
Rev Cinema — Revue du Cinema/Image et Son. Ecran
Rev Cir — Revista de Cirugia
Rev Circ Argent Odontol — Revista. Circulo Argentino de Odontologia
Rev Circ Eng Mil — Revista. Circulo de Engenharia Militar
Rev Circ Odontol Cordoba — Revista del Circulo Odontologico de Cordoba
Rev Circ Odontol Sur — Revista. Circulo Odontologico del Sur
Rev Cir (Mex) — Revista de Cirugia (Mexico)
Rev Cirug — Revista de Cirugia
Rev Cir Urug — Revista de Cirugia del Uruguay
Rev Citobiol — Revista Citobiologica
Rev Clasica — Revista Clasica
Rev Clin — Revista Clinica
Rev Clin Basic Pharm — Reviews in Clinical and Basic Pharmacology
Rev Clin Basic Pharmacol — Reviews in Clinical and Basic Pharmacology
Rev Clin Esp — Revista Clinica Espanola
Rev Clin Esp Eur Med — Revista Clinica Espanola. Europa Medica
Rev Clin Exp Hematol — Reviews in Clinical and Experimental Hematology
Rev Clin Inst Matern (Lisb) — Revista Clinica. Instituto Maternal (Lisbon)
Rev Clin Med — Revista de Clinica Medica
Rev Clin Pharmacol Pharmacokinet — Review of Clinical Pharmacology and Pharmacokinetics
Rev Clin Pharmacol Pharmacokinet Ind Ed — Review of Clinical Pharmacology and Pharmacokinetics. International Edition
Rev Clin Sao Paulo — Revista Clinica de Sao Paulo
Rev Clin Stomat — Review of Clinical Stomatology [*New York*]
Rev Coal Tar Technol — Review of Coal Tar Technology [*Gomersal*]
Rev Coat Corros — Reviews on Coatings and Corrosion
Rev Col Abogad Caracas — Revista. Colegio de Abogados del Distrito Federal (Caracas)
Rev Col Abogad Hav — Revista. Colegio de Abogados (La Habana)
Rev Col Abogad Rosario — Revista. Colegio de Abogados (Rosario, Argentina)
Rev Col Abogad S Jose — Revista. Colegio de Abogados Francisco Echeverria Garcia (San Jose, Costa Rica)
Rev Col Antrop Bogota — Revista Colombiana de Antropologia (Bogota)
Rev Col Boyaca Tunja — Revista. Colegio de Boyaca (Tunja, Colombia)
Rev Col Estomatol Guatem — Revista. Colegio Estomatologico de Guatemala
Rev Col Farm Nac — Revista de Colegios de Farmaceuticos Nacionales
Rev Col Folk Bogota — Revista Colombiana de Folklore (Bogota)
Rev Col Ing Caracas — Revista. Colegio de Ingenieros de Venezuela (Caracas)

Rev Col Ing Venez — Revista. Colegio de Ingenieros de Venezuela
Rev Coll Plasma Phys — Reviews from College on Plasma Physics
Rev Col Mayor Nues Sra Rosario Bogota — Revista. Colegio Mayor de Nuestra Senora del Rosario (Bogota)
Rev Col Med Guatem — Revista. Colegio Medico de Guatemala
Rev Col Nac Enferm — Revista. Colegio Nacional de Enfermeras
Rev Col Nac V Rocafuerte Guayaquil — Revista. Colegio Nacional Vicente Rocafuerte (Guayaquil)
Rev Colomb Antrop — Revista Colombiana de Antropologia
Rev Colomb Antropol — Revista Colombiana de Antropologia
Rev Colomb Cienc Quimico-Farm — Revista Colombiana de Ciencias Quimico-Farmaceuticas
Rev Colomb Entomol — Revista Colombiana de Entomologia
Rev Colomb Fis — Revista Colombiana de Fisica
Rev Colomb Flclor — Revista Colombiana de Folclor
Rev Colombiana Estadist — Revista Colombiana Estadistica
Rev Colombiana Mat — Revista Colombiana de Matematicas
Rev Colomb Obstet Ginecol — Revista Colombiana de Obstetricia y Ginecologia
Rev Colomb Pediatr Pueric — Revista Colombiana de Pediatria y Puericultura
Rev Colomb Quim — Revista Colombiana de Quimica
Rev Color — Revue Coloristique
Rev Col Quim Ing Quim Costa Rica — Revista. Colegio de Quimicos e Ingenieros Quimicos de Costa Rica
Rev Col Quim PR — Revista. Colegio de Quimicos de Puerto Rico
Rev Columb Cienc Quim Farm — Revista Columbiana de Ciencias Quimico-Farmaceuticas
Rev COMALFI — Revista COMALFI
Rev Combust Liq — Revue des Combustibles Liquides
Rev Comique — Revue Comique
Rev Comm — Revue Communale
Rev Commer — Revue Commerce
Rev Commer Ind Text — Revue du Commerce et de l'Industrie Textile
Rev Comminges — Revue de Comminges
Rev Compos Mater Av — Revue des Composites et des Materiaux Avances
Rev Comput Chem — Reviews in Computational Chemistry
Rev Comunic BA — Revista de Comunicaciones (Buenos Aires)
Rev Confed Med Panam — Revista. Confederacion Medica Panamericana
Rev Conserve — Revue de la Conserve
Rev Conserve Aliment Mod — Revue de la Conserve. Alimentation Moderne
Rev Conserve Fr Outre-Mer — Revue de la Conserve de France et d'Outre-Mer
Rev Conserve Fr Union Fr — Revue de la Conserve de France et de l'Union Francaise
Rev Conserv Pens Centroam Managua — Revista Conservadora del Pensamiento Centroamericano (Managua)
Rev Consor Cent Agr Manabi — Revista. Consorcio de Centros Agricolas de Manabi
Rev Cons Rectores Univ Chilenas — Revista. Consejo de Rectores. Universidades Chilenas
Rev Constr Mater Constr — Revista Constructiilor si a Materialelor de Constructii
Rev Contemp — Revue Contemporaine
Rev Contemp Pharmacother — Reviews in Contemporary Pharmacotherapy
Rev Cont L — Review of Contemporary Law
Rev Coree — Revue de Coree
Rev Coroz — Revista de Coroziune
Rev Corps Sante Armees — Revue des Corps de Sante des Armees
Rev Corps Sante Armees Terre Mer Air — Revue des Corps de Sante des Armees. Terre, Mer, Air
Rev Corps Sante Mil — Revue du Corps de Sante Militaire
Rev Correos Telegr BA — Revista de Correos y Telegrafos (Buenos Aires)
Rev Corros Inhib Sci Technol Vol 2 Pap Corros 96 Symp — Reviews on Corrosions Inhibitor Science and Technology. Vol. 2. Papers presented at the Corrosion/96 Symposium
Rev Corros Prot Mater — Revista de Corrosao e Proteccao de Materiais
Rev Costarric Cienc Med — Revista Costarricense de Ciencias Medicas
Rev Cours Conf — Revue des Cours et Conferences
Rev Cours Sci France Etranger — Revue des Cours Scientifiques de la France et de l'Etranger
Rev Cr — Revista Cristiana
Rev Cr — Revue Critique d'Histoire et de Litterature
Rev CREA (Asoc Argent Consorcios Reg Exp Agric) — Revista. CREA (Asociacion Argentina de Consorcios Regionales de ExperimentacionAgricola)
Rev Cresterea Anim — Revista de Cresterea Animalelor
Rev Criad — Revista dos Criadores
Rev Criadores — Revista dos Criadores
Rev Crit — Revue Critique de Legislation et de Jurisprudence de Canada
Rev Crit de Droit Internat Prive — Revue Critique de Droit International Prive
Rev Crit de Jurispr Belge — Revue Critique de Jurisprudence Belge
Rev Crit de Legis et Jur — Revue Critique de Legislation et de Jurisprudence
Rev Crit des Idees et des Livr — Revue Critique des Idees et des Livres
Rev Crit des Idees et des Livres — Revue Critique des Idees et des Livres
Rev Crit des Id et des Livr — Revue Critique des Idees et des Livres
Rev Crit des Id et des Livres — Revue Critique des Idees et des Livres
Rev Crit Hispamer — Revista Critica Hispanoamericana
Rev Crit Jur B — Revue Critique de Jurisprudence Belge
Rev Crit L — Revista de Critica Literaria Latinoamericana
Rev C Tijdschr Civ Tech Genie Civ — Revue C. Tijdschrift Civiele Techniek. Genie Civil
RevCu — Revista Cubana
Rev Cuba Hig Epidemiol — Revista Cubana de Higiene y Epidemiologia
Rev Cubana — Revista Cubana
Rev Cubana Cardiol — Revista Cubana de Cardiologia
Rev Cubana Cienc Agric — Revista Cubana de Ciencia Agricola
Rev Cubana Cienc Agric Engl Ed — Revista Cubana de Ciencia Agricola. English Edition
Rev Cubana Cienc Avic — Revista Cubana de Ciencia Avicola

Rev Cubana Cienc Vet — Revista Cubana de Ciencias Veterinarias
Rev Cubana Cir — Revista Cubana de Cirugia
Rev Cubana de Derecho — Revista Cubana de Derecho
Rev Cubana Der — Revista Cubana de Derecho
Rev Cubana Enferm — Revista Cubana de Enfermeria
Rev Cubana Estomatol — Revista Cubana de Estomatologia
Rev Cubana Farm — Revista Cubana de Farmacia
Rev Cubana Fis — Revista Cubana de Fisica
Rev Cubana Hig Epidemiol — Revista Cubana de Higiene y Epidemiologia
Rev Cubana Invest Biomed — Revista Cubana de Investigaciones Biomedicas
Rev Cubana Invest Pesq — Revista Cubana de Investigaciones Pesqueras
Rev Cubana Lab Clin — Revista Cubana de Laboratorio Clinico
Rev Cubana Med — Revista Cubana de Medicina
Rev Cubana Med Trop — Revista Cubana de Medicina Tropical
Rev Cubana Oftal — Revista Cubana de Oftalmologia
Rev Cubana Pediatr — Revista Cubana de Pediatria
Rev Cubana Quim — Revista Cubana de Quimica
Rev Cubana Reprod Anim — Revista Cubana de Reproduccion Animal
Rev Cubana Tuber — Revista Cubana de Tuberculosis
Rev Cuban Cienc Social — Revista Cubana de Ciencias Sociales
Rev Cub Cienc Vet — Revista Cubana de Ciencias Veterinarias
Rev Cult — Revista de Cultura
Rev Cult — Revolucion y Cultura
Rev Cult Bras — Revista de Cultura Brasilena
Rev Cult [Macau] — Revista de Cultura [Macau]
Rev Cult Rio — Revista de Cultura (Rio de Janeiro)
Rev Current Activities Tech Ed — Review of Current Activities in Technical Education
Rev Curr Lit Paint Colour Varn Allied Ind — Review of Current Literature Relating to the Paint, Colour, Varnish, and AlliedIndustries
Rev Curr Lit Res Ass Br Paint Colour Varn Mfrs — Review of Current Literature. Research Association of British Paint, Colour, and Varnish Manufacturers [Teddington]
Rev Cytobiol — Revue Cytobiologique
Rev Cytol Biol Veg — Revue de Cytologie et de Biologie Vegetales
Rev Cytol Biol Veg Bot — Revue de Cytologie et de Biologie Vegetales -La Botaniste
Rev Cytol Cytophysiol Veg — Revue de Cytologie et de Cytophysiologie Vegetales
Rev Czech Med — Review of Czechoslovak Medicine
RevD — Revista de Derecho y Ciencias Politicas
RevD — Revue Dominicaine
Rev d'Acoustique — Revue d'Acoustique
Rev da Fac de Direito (Lisbon) — Revista. Faculdade de Direito. Universidade de Lisboa (Lisbon)
Rev d'Anthropol — Revue d'Anthropologie
Rev d Assyr — Revue d'Assyriologie
Rev d'Assyr — Revue d'Assyriologie et d'Archeologie Orientale
Rev Data Res Dev Natn Sci Fdn — Review of Data on Research and Development. National Science Foundation [Washington]
Rev Data Sci Resour — Reviews of Data on Science Resources
Rev Data Sci Resour Natl Sci Found — Reviews of Data on Science Resources. National Sciences Foundation
Rev d Caucho — Revista del Caucho
Rev de Archit — Revue de l'Architecture
Rev de Arquit — Revista de Arquitectura
Rev Debrecen — Revue de Debrecen
Rev de Derecho Esp y Amer — Revista de Derecho Espanol y Americano
Rev de Derecho Internac y Cienc Diplom — Revista de Derecho Internacional y Ciencias Diplomaticas
Rev de Derecho Jurispr y Cienc Soc — Revista de Derecho, Jurisprudencia, y Ciencias Sociales y Gaceta de los Tribunales
Rev de Derecho Publ — Revista de Derecho Publico. Universidad de Chile. Escuela de Derecho
Rev de Derecho y Cienc Polit — Revista de Derecho y Ciencias Politicas. Organo de la Facultad de Derecho. Universidad Nacional Mayor de San Marcos
Rev de Direito Adm (Coimbra) — Revista de Direito Administrativo (Coimbra)
Rev de Direito Adm (Rio De Janeiro) — Revista de Direito Administrativo (Rio De Janeiro),
Rev de Dr Int'l de Sci Dip et Pol — Revue de Droit International de Sciences Diplomatiques et Politiques
Rev de Droit — Revue de Droit. Universite de Sherbrooke
Rev de Droit Canonique — Revue de Droit Canonique
Rev de Droit Compare — Revue de Droit International et de Droit Compare
Rev de Droit Contemp — Revue de Droit Contemporain
Rev de Droit Hong — Revue de Droit Hongrois
Rev de Droit Internat de Sci Diplom — Revue de Droit International de Sciences Diplomatiques et Politiques
Rev de Droit Internat et de Droit Compare — Revue de Droit International et de Droit Compare
Rev de Droit Penal et de Criminologie — Revue de Droit Penal et de Criminologie
Rev de Droit Penal Mil et de Droit de la Guerre — Revue de Droit Penal Militaire et de Droit de la Guerre
Rev de Droit Unif — Revue de Droit Uniforme
Rev de Droit Uniforme — Revue de Droit Uniforme
Rev de Est Extremenos — Revista de Estudios Extremenos. Revista Historica, Literaria, y Artistica
Rev de Fac de Direito (Sao Paulo) — Revista. Faculdade de Direito. Universidade de Sao Paulo
Rev Defense Nat — Revue de Defense Nationale
Rev Def Natl — Revue de Defense Nationale
Rev Deform Behav Mater — Reviews on the Deformation Behavior of Materials
Rev d'Egypt — Revue d'Egyptologie
Rev de Jur — Revue de Jurisprudence
Rev De La Corse — Revue de la Corse, Ancienne et Moderne

Rev de l'Adm — Revue de l'Administration et du Droit Administratif de la Belgique
Rev de la Fac de Derecho (Caraboba) — Revista. Facultad de Derecho. Universidad de Caraboba
Rev de la Fac de Derecho (Caracas) — Revista. Facultad de Derecho. Universidad Catolica Andres Bello (Caracas)
Rev de la Fac de Derecho de Mex — Revista. Facultad de Derecho de Mexico
Rev de la Fac de Derecho y Cienc Soc — Revista. Facultad de Derecho y Ciencias Sociales
Rev de Leg — Revue de Legislation et de Jurisprudence
Rev de Legis — Revue de Legislation
Rev del Inst de Derecho Comparado — Revista. Instituto de Derecho Comparado
Rev de Lit Comp — Revue de Litterature Comparee
Rev de l'Or Chret — Revue de l'Orient Chretien
Rev de Med (Rosario) — Revista de Medicina (Rosario)
Rev de Med (S Paulo) — Revista de Medicina (Sao Paulo)
Rev Dent Chil — Revista Dental de Chile
Rev Dent Child — Review of Dentistry for Children
Rev Dent Chile — Revista Dental de Chile
Rev Dent Liban — Revue Dentaire Libanaise
Rev Dent (San Salv) — Revista Dental (San Salvador)
Rev Dent (St Domingo) — Revista Dental (Santo Domingo)
Rev de Paris — Revue de Paris
Rev Dep Nac Prod Anim Braz — Revista do Departamento Nacional da Produccao Animal. Brazil
Rev Dep Quim Univ Nac Colomb — Revista. Departamento de Quimica. Universidad Nacional de Colombia
Rev Dept Hist Med — Revista del Departamento de Historia Medieval
Rev Der Cien Pol Lima — Revista de Derecho y Ciencias Politicas (Lima)
Rev Der Cien Soc Quito — Revista de Derecho y Ciencias Sociales (Quito)
Rev Der Espanol Am Madrid — Revista de Derecho Espanol y Americano (Madrid)
Rev Der Intern Cien Diplom Rosario — Revista de Derecho Internacional y Ciencias Diplomaticas (Rosario, Argentina)
Rev Der Intern Hav — Revista de Derecho Internacional (La Habana)
Rev Deriv Cana Azucar — Revista sobre los Derivados de la Cana de Azucar
Rev Der Juris Admin Monte — Revista de Derecho (Montevideo)
Rev Der La Paz — Revista de Derecho (La Paz, Bolivia)
Rev Der Legis Caracas — Revista de Derecho y Legislacion (Caracas)
Rev Der Penal BA — Revista de Derecho Penal (Buenos Aires)
Rev Der Quito — Revista de Derecho (Quito)
Rev Der Soc Ecuat Quito — Revista de Derecho Social Ecuatoriano (Quito)
Rev des A — Revue des Arts
Rev de Sci Criminelle et de Droit Penal Compare — Revue de Science Criminelle et de Droit Penal Compare
Rev des Cours et Conf — Revue des Cours et Conferences
Rev des Droits de l'Homme — Revue des Droits de l'Homme. Droit International et Droit Compare
Rev des Et Histor — Revue des Etudes Historiques
Rev des Et Historiques — Revue des Etudes Historiques
Rev des Et It — Revue des Etudes Italiennes
Rev des Et Ital — Revue des Etudes Italiennes
Rev des Etudes Histor — Revue des Etudes Historiques
Rev des Etudes Historiques — Revue des Etudes Historiques
Rev des Questions Histor — Revue des Questions Historiques
Rev de Stomat — Revue de Stomatologie
Rev Deux Mondes — Revue des Deux Mondes
Rev Dev Somalild — Review of Development. Somaliland [*Hargeisa*]
Rev d Hist de l Eglise de France — Revue d'Histoire de l'Eglise de France
Rev d Hist Diplom — Revue d'Histoire Diplomatique
Rev d Hist et de Philos Religieuses — Revue d'Histoire et de Philosophie Religieuses
Rev D Hist Litt Relig — Revue d'Histoire et de Littetature Religieuses
Rev d Histoire Mod et Cont — Revue d'Histoire Moderne et Contemporaine
Rev Diagn Biol — Revista de Diagnostico Biologico
Rev Dialectologia & Trad Pop — Revista de Dialectologia y Tradiciones Populares
Rev Diners — Revista Diners
Rev Direit Publ Cien Pol Rio — Revista de Direito Publico e Ciencia Politica (Rio de Janeiro)
Rev Dir Gen Geol Minas (Ecuador) — Revista. Direccion General de Geologia y Minas (Ecuador)
Rev Doc — Revue de la Documentation
Rev Dom Cult C Trujillo — Revista Dominicana de Cultura (Ciudad Trujillo)
Rev d'Optique — Revue d'Optique
Rev Doyma Inmunol — Revista Doyma de Inmunologia
Rev D P — Revista de Derecho Puertorriqueno
Rev DPR — Revista de Derecho Puertorriqueno
Rev Dr Belge — Revue de Droit Belge
Rev Dr Comp — Revue. Institut Belge de Droit Compare
Rev Dr Contemp — Revue de Droit Contemporain ou des Juristes Democrates
Rev Dr Fam — Revue de Droit Familial
Rev Dr Intern et Dr Comp — Revue de Droit International et de Droit Compare
Rev Dr Min — Revue de Droit Minier
Rev Droit Intern Legisl Compar — Revue de Droit International et de Legislation Comparee
Rev Droit Int'l Moyen-Orient — Revue de Droit International pour le Moyen-Orient
Rev Droit Penal Militaire et Dr de la Guerre — Revue de Droit Penal Militaire et de Droit de la Guerre
Rev Droit Public Sci Polit — Revue du Droit Public et de la Science Politique en France et a l'Etranger
Rev Droit Publ Sci Poli France Et Etranger — Revue du Droit Public et de la Science Politique en France et a l'Etranger
Rev Droit U Sher — Revue de Droit. Universite de Sherbrooke
Rev Drome — Revue Dromoise
Rev Dr Pen — Revue de Droit Penal et de Criminologie
Rev Dr Soc — Revue de Droit Social

Rev Drug Metabol Drug Interact — Reviews on Drug Metabolism and Drug Interactions
Rev du B — Revue. Barreau de la Province de Quebec
Rev du Dr — Revue du Droit
Rev du Droit Publ et de la Sci Polit en France — Revue du Droit Public et de la Science Politique en France et a l'Etranger
Rev du Marche Commun — Revue du Marche Commun
Rev du Moyen-Age Latin — Revue du Moyen-Age Latin
Rev du Nord — Revue du Nord
Rev du Not — Revue du Notariat
Rev du Notariat — Revue du Notariat
Rev du Siezieme Siecle — Revue du Seizieme Siecle
RevE — Revista de Educacion
RevE — Revue d'Esthetique
Rev E — Revue E. Electricite, Electrotechnique Generale, Courants Forts, et Applications
Reveal Antiq — Revealing Antiquity
Rev East Med Sci — Review of Eastern Medical Sciences
Rev Eaux Forets — Revue des Eaux et Forets
Rev Eccl — Revue d'Histoire Ecclesiastique
Rev Ecles — Revista Eclesiastica
Rev Ecles Bras Petropolis — Revista Eclesiastica Brasileira (Petropolis, Brazil)
Rev Ecol Biol Sol — Revue d'Ecologie et de Biologie du Sol
Rev Ecol BS — Revue d'Ecologie et de Biologie du Sol
Rev Ecol Terre Vie — Revue d'Ecologie; la Terre et la Vie
Rev Econ — Revue Economique
Rev Econ Co — Review of the Economic Conditions in Italy
Rev Econ Cont Mex — Revista de Economia Continental (Mexico)
Rev Econ Cordoba — Revista de Economia (Cordoba)
Rev Econ Estad Cordoba — Revista de Economia y Estadistica (Cordoba, Argentina)
Rev Econ Fr — Revue Economique Francaise
Rev Econ Latinoam Caracas — Revista de Economia Latinoamericana (Caracas)
Rev Econ Mex — Revista de Economia (Mexico)
Rev Econom Statist — Review of Economics and Statistics
Rev Econom Stud — Review of Economic Studies
Rev Economy Emplyment — Review of the Economy and Employment
Rev Econ Polit — Revue d'Economie Politique
Rev Econ S — Review of Economic Studies
Rev Econ Soc — Revue Economique et Sociale
Rev Econ S Salvador — Revista de Economia de El Salvador
Rev Econ St — Review of Economics and Statistics
Rev Econ Stat — Review of Economics and Statistics
Rev Econ Stat — Review of Economic Statistics
Rev Econ Statist — Review of Economics and Statistics
Rev Econ Stud — Review of Economic Studies
Rev Ecuat Educ Quito — Revista Ecuatoriana de Educacion (Quito)
Rev Ecuat Entomol Parasitol — Revista Ecuatoriana de Entomologia y Parasitologia
Rev Ecuat Ent Parasit — Revista Ecuatoriana de Entomologia y Parasitologia
Rev Ecuat Hig Med — Revista Ecuatoriana de Higiene y Medicina Tropical
Rev Ecuat Hig Med Trop — Revista Ecuatoriana de Higiene y Medicina Tropical
Rev Ecuat Med Cienc Biol — Revista Ecuatoriana de Medicina y Ciencias Biologicas
Rev Ecuat Pediatr — Revista Ecuatoriana de Pediatria
Rev Ed — Revista de Educacion
Rev Educ Asuncion — Revista de Educacion (Asuncion)
Rev Educational Res — Review of Educational Research
Rev Educ C Trujillo S Domingo — Revista de Educacion (Ciudad Trujillo, Santo Domingo)
Rev Educ La Plata — Revista de Educacion (La Plata, Argentina)
Rev Educ Publ Rio — Revista de Educacao (Rio de Janeiro)
Rev Educ Re — Review of Educational Research
Rev Educ Res — Review of Educational Research
Rev Educ Santiago — Revista de Educacion (Santiago)
Rev EEG Neurophysiol Clin — Revue d'EEG et de Neurophysiologie Clinique de Langue Francaise
Rev E Elec Electrotech Gen — Revue E. Electricite, Electrotechnique Generale, Courants Forts, et Applications
RevEG — Revista de Educacion (Guatemala)
Rev Eg — Revue d'Egyptologie
Rev Egypt — Revue d'Egyptologie
Rev Egypt de Droit Internat — Revue Egyptienne de Droit International
Rev Egypt Geol — Review of Egyptian Geology
Rev Egyptol — Revue d'Egyptologie
Rev Egyptol — Revue Egyptologique
Rev EIE — Revue des Etudes Indo-Europeennes
Rev El Comm — Review. Electrical Communication Laboratory
Rev Elec Commun Lab (Tokyo) — Review. Electrical Communication Laboratory (Tokyo)
Rev Elect Commun Lab Tokyo — Review. Electrical Communication Laboratory. Nippon Telegraph and Telephone Public Corporation (Tokyo)
Rev Electr — Revista Electricidade
Rev Electr & Mec — Revue d'Electricite et de Mecanique
Rev Electr Commun Lab — Review. Electrical Communication Laboratory
Rev Electr Commun Lab (Tokyo) — Review. Electrical Communication Laboratory (Tokyo)
Rev Electr Electron — Revue de l'Electricite et de l'Electronique
Rev Electr Mecan — Revue d'Electricite et de Mecanique
Rev Electrochim Electrometall — Revue d'Electrochimie et d'Electrometallurgie
Rev Electroencephalogr Neurophysiol Clin — Revue d'Electroencephalographie et de Neurophysiologie Clinique
Rev Electrotec — Revista Electrotecnica
Rev Electrotec (Buenos Aires) — Revista Electrotecnica (Buenos Aires)
Rev Electrotech Energ — Revue d'Electrotechnique et d'Energetique

Rev Electrotech Energ Acad Repub Pop Roum — Revue Electrotechnique et Energetique. Academie de la Republique Populaire Roumaine

Rev Electrotech Energ Ser A — Revue d'Electrotechnique et d'Energetique. Serie A. Electrotechnique, Electroenergetique et Energetique Generale

Rev Electrotech Energ Ser B — Revue d'Electrotechnique et d'Energetique. Serie B. Thermoenergetique et Utilisation Energetique des Combustibles

Rev Elevage — Revue de l'Elevage. Betail et Basse Cour

Rev Elev Med Vet Pays Trop — Revue d'Elevage et de Medecine Veterinaire des Pays Tropicaux

Rev El Mecan — Revue d'Electricite et de Mecanique

Rev Empresas Publicas Medellin — Revista Empresas Publicas de Medellin

RevEn — Revue Encyclopedique

Rev Enc — Revue Encyclopedique

Rev Enc Archit — Revue d'Encyclopedie d'Architecture

Rev Endocr Relat Cancer — Reviews on Endocrine-Related Cancer

Rev Endocr Relat Cancer Suppl — Reviews on Endocrine-Related Cancer. Supplement

Rev Energ — Revue de l'Energie

Rev Energ At — Revista de Energia Atomica

Rev Energ At — Revue of Energie Atomique

Rev Energie — Revue de l'Energie

Rev Energ Primaire — Revue de l'Energie Primaire

Rev Enferm (Lisboa) — Revista de Enfermagem (Lisboa)

Rev Enferm Nov Dimens — Revista Enfermagem em Novas Dimensoes

Rev Engen Rio — Revista de Engenharia do Estado da Guanabara (Rio de Janeiro)

Rev Eng Geol — Reviews in Engineering Geology

Rev Eng Lit — Review of English Literature

Rev Engl St — Review of English Studies

Rev Engl Stu — Review of English Studies

Rev Engl Stud — Review of English Studies

Rev Eng Mackenzie — Revista de Engenharia Mackenzie

Rev Enr — Revue de l'Enregistrement et des Douanes

Rev Ens Phil — Revue de l'Enseignement Philosophique

Rev Ens Sup — Revue de l'Enseignement Superieur

Rev Entomol — Revue Entomologique

Rev Entomol Mocambique — Revista de Entomologia de Mocambique

Rev Entomol Mocambique Supl — Revista de Entomologia de Mocambique. Suplemento

Rev Entomol Que — Revue d'Entomologie du Quebec

Rev Entomol (Rio De J) — Revista de Entomologia (Rio De Janeiro)

Rev Entomol URSS — Revue d'Entomologie de l'URSS

Rev Environ Contam Toxicol — Reviews of Environmental Contamination and Toxicology

Rev Environ Health — Reviews on Environmental Health

Rev Environ Toxicol — Reviews in Environmental Toxicology

RevEp — Revue de l'Epoque

Rev Ep — Revue Epigraphique

Rev Epidem — Revue d'Epidemiologie, Medecine Sociale, et Sante Publique [*Later, Revue d'Epidemiologie et de Sante Publique*]

Rev Epidemiol Med Soc Sante Publique — Revue d'Epidemiologie, Medecine Sociale, et Sante Publique [*Later, Revue d'Epidemiologie et de Sante Publique*]

Rev Epidemiol Sante Publique — Revue d'Epidemiologie et de Sante Publique

RevEpigr — Revue Epigraphique

RevER — Revue des Etudes Roumaines

Rev Esc Agron Vet Univ Fed Parana — Revista. Escola de Agronomia e Veterinaria. Universidade Federal do Parana

Rev Esc Agron Vet Univ Rio Grande Do Sul (Porto Alegre) — Revista. Escola de Agronomia e Veterinaria da Universidade do Rio Grande Do Sul(Porto Alegre)

Rev Esc Enferm USP — Revista. Escola de Enfermagem. Universidade de Sao Paulo

Rev Esc Minas — Revista. Escola de Minas

Rev Esc Odontol Tucuman — Revista. Escuela de Odontologia. Universidad Nacional de Tucuman. Facultad de Medicina

Rev Escola Belas Art Pernam Recife — Revista da Escola de Belas Artes de Pernambuco (Recife, Brazil)

Rev Escuela Contab Econ Adm Monterrey — Revista. Escuela de Contabilidad, Economia, y Administracion. Instituto Tecnologico y de Estudios Superiores (Monterrey, Mexico)

Rev Escuela Militar Chorillos — Revista. Escuela Militar (Chorillos, Peru)

Rev Esp A — Revista Espanola de Arte

Rev Espana — Revista de Espana

Rev Esp Anest — Revista Espanola de Anestesiologia

Rev Esp Anestesiol — Revista Espanola de Anestesiologia

Rev Esp Anestesiol Reanim — Revista Espanola de Anestesiologia y Reanimacion

Rev Espan Fisiol — Revista Espanola de Fisiologia

Rev Espanola Micropaleontologia — Revista Espanola de Micropaleontologia

Rev Esp Antrop Amer — Revista Espanola de Antropologia Americana

Rev Esp Antropol Amer — Revista Espanola de Antropologia Americana

Rev Esp Cardiol — Revista Espanola de Cardiologia

Rev Esp Cienc Tecnol Aliment — Revista Espanola de Ciencia y Tecnologia de Alimentos

Rev Esp de Derecho Canonico — Revista Espanola de Derecho Canonico

Rev Esp de Derecho Internac — Revista Espanola de Derecho Internacional

Rev Esp de Derecho Mil — Revista Espanola de Derecho Militar

Rev Esp Der Can — Revista Espanola de Derecho Canonico

Rev Esp Doc Cient — Revista Espanola de Documentacion Cientifica

Rev Espec — Revista de Especialidades

Rev Esp Electron — Revista Espanola de Electronica

Rev Esp Endodoncia — Revista Espanola de Endodoncia

Rev Esp Enferm Apar Dig — Revista Espanola de las Enfermedades del Aparato Digestivo

Rev Esp Enferm Apar Dig Nutr — Revista Espanola de las Enfermedades del Aparato Digestivo y de la Nutricion

Rev Esp Estomatol — Revista Espanola de Estomatologia

Rev Esp Fis — Revista Espanola de Fisiologia

Rev Esp Fisiol — Revista Espanola de Fisiologia

Rev Esp Fisiol Suppl — Revista Espanola de Fisiologia. Supplement

Rev Esp Lech — Revista Espanola do Lecheria

Rev Esp Med Cirug Guerra — Revista Espanola de Medicina y Cirugia de Guerra

Rev Esp Micropaleontol — Revista Espanola de Micropaleontologia

Rev Esp Obstet Ginecol — Revista Espanola de Obstetricia y Ginecologia

Rev Esp Obstet Ginecol Supl — Revista Espanola de Obstetricia y Ginecologia. Suplemento

Rev Esp Oncol — Revista Espanola de Oncologia

Rev Esp Oto Neu Oft — Revista Espanola de Oto-Neuro-Oftalmologia y Neurocirugia

Rev Esp Oto-Neuro-Oftalmol Neurocir — Revista Espanola de Oto-Neuro-Oftalmologia y Neurocirugia

Rev Esp Parad — Revista Espanola de Paradoncia

Rev Esp Pediatr — Revista Espanola de Pediatria

Rev Esp Reum Enferm Osteoartic — Revista Espanola de Reumatismo y Enfermedades Osteoarticulares

Rev Esp Tuber Arch Nac Enferm Torax — Revista Espanola de Tuberculosis y Archivos Nacionales de Enfermedades del Torax

Rev Esp Tuberc — Revista Espanola de Tuberculosis

Rev Est — Revue de l'Est

Rev Estad Geogr — Revista de Estadistica y Geografia

Rev Esth — Revue d'Esthetique

Rev Esthet — Revue d'Esthetique

Rev Est His — Revista de Estudios Hispanicos

Rev Estud Extrem — Revista de Estudios Extremenos

Rev Estud Extremenos — Revista de Estudios Extremenos

Rev Estud Gerais Univ Mocambique Ser 3 Cienc Med — Revista de Estudos Gerais Universitarios de Mocambique. Serie 3. Ciencias Medicas

Rev Estud Jur Pol Soc Sucre — Revista de Estudios Juridicos, Politicos, y Sociales (Sucre, Bolivia)

Rev Estud Music Mendoza — Revista de Estudios Musicales (Mendoza, Argentina)

Rev Estud Pol Madrid — Revista de Estudios Politicos (Madrid)

Rev Estud Teatro BA — Revista de Estudios de Teatro (Buenos Aires)

Rev Estud Yucat Merida — Revista de Estudios Yucatecos (Merida, Yucatan)

Rev ET — Revista Espanola de Teologia

Rev Et Anc — Revue des Etudes Anciennes

Rev Et Armen — Revue des Etudes Armeniennes

Rev Et Byzant — Revue des Etudes Byzantines

Rev Et Gr — Revue des Etudes Grecques

Rev Et Grec — Revue des Etudes Grecques

Rev Et Hist — Revue des Etudes Historiques

Rev Ethn — Revue d'Ethnographie

Rev Ethnog & Sociol — Review of Ethnography and Sociology

Rev Ethnog & Trad Pop — Revue d'Ethnographie et des Traditions Populaires

Rev Ethnol & Sociol — Revue d'Ethnologie et de Sociologie

Rev Ethnol Quebec — Revue d'Ethnologie du Quebec

Rev Et Ind — Revue des Etudes Indo-Europeennes

Rev Et Islam — Revue des Etudes Islamiques

Rev Et Juiv — Revue des Etudes Juives

Rev Et Lat — Revue des Etudes Latines

Rev Etnogr Folcl — Revista de Etnografie si Folclor

Revet Prot — Revetement et Protection [*Bruxelles*]

Rev Et Rabelais — Revue des Etudes Rabelaisiennes

Rev Et Roum — Revue des Etudes Roumaines

Rev Et SE Eur — Revue des Etudes Sud-Est Europeennes

Rev Et Slav — Revue des Etudes Slaves

Revet Sols — Revetement de Sols [*Paris*]

Revet Sols Murs — Revetements de Sols et Murs [*Paris*]

Rev Etud Anc — Revue des Etudes Anciennes

Rev Etud Armen — Revue des Etudes Armeniennes

Rev Etud Augustin — Revue des Etudes Augustiniennes

Rev Etud Byz — Revue des Etudes Byzantines

Rev Etud Byzant — Revue des Etudes Byzantines

Rev Etud Calamites Geneva — Revue Pour l'Etude des Calamites (Geneva)

Rev Etud Comp Est Ouest — Revue d'Etudes Comparatives Est-Ouest

Rev Etud Coop — Revue des Etudes Cooperatives

Rev Etud Georg & Caucas — Revue des Etudes Georgiennes et Caucasiennes

Rev Etud Gr — Revue des Etudes Grecques

Rev Etud Grec — Revue des Etudes Grecques

Rev Etud Islam — Revue des Etudes Islamiques

Rev Etud It — Revue des Etudes Italiennes

Rev Etud Ital — Revue des Etudes Italiennes

Rev Etud Juives — Revue des Etudes Juives

Rev Etud Juives — Revue des Etudes Juives et Historia Judaica

Rev Etud Lat — Revue des Etudes Latines

Rev Etud Napoleoniennes — Revue des Etudes Napoleoniennes

Rev Etud Slav — Revue des Etudes Slaves

Rev Etud Sud Est Eur — Revue des Etudes Sud-Est Europeennes

Rev Eur — Revue Europeenne

Rev Eur Endocrinol — Revue Europeenne d'Endocrinologie

Rev Eur Etud Clin Biol — Revue Europeenne d'Etudes Cliniques et Biologiques

Rev Eur Farm Hosp — Revista Europa de Farmacia de Hospital

Rev Eur Odontoestomatol — Revista Europea de Odonto-Estomatologia

Rev Europeenne Elem Finis — Revue Europeenne des Elements Finis

Rev Europ Papiers Cartons Complexes — Revue Europeenne des Papiers Cartons-Complexes

Rev Eur Pomme Terre — Revue Europeenne de la Pomme de Terre

Rev Eur Sci Med Pharmacol — Revue Europeenne pour les Sciences Medicales et Pharmacologiques

Rev Exam Mater Budapest — Review for the Examination of Materials (Budapest)

Rev Excel Disput Prov Cuenca — Revista de la Excelentisima Diputacion Provincial de Cuenca

Rev Exist Psychol Psychiat — Review of Existential Psychology and Psychiatry

Rev Exist Psych Psychiat — Review of Existential Psychology and Psychiatry

RevExp — Review and Expositor

Rev Exp Agrar — Revista de Extension Agraria

Rev Extr — Revue de l'Extradition

RevF — Revista de Filosofia (Madrid)

Rev F — Revue Fiscale

RevF — Revue Francaise

Rev Fac Agrar Minist Educ Univ Nac Cuyo (Mendoza) — Revista. Facultad de Ciencias Agrarias. Ministerio de Educacion. Universidad Nacional de Cuyo (Mendoza)

Rev Fac Agric Ege Univ — Review. Faculty of Agriculture. Ege University

Rev Fac Agric Univ Cent Venez — Revista. Facultad de Agricultura. Universidad Central de Venezuela

Rev Fac Agron Alcance (Maracay) — Revista. Facultad de Agronomia Alcance (Maracay)

Rev Fac Agron La Plata — Revista. Facultad de Agronomia. Universidad Nacional de La Plata (La Plata, Argentina)

Rev Fac Agron (Maracay) — Revista. Facultad de Agronomia (Maracay)

Rev Fac Agron Monte — Revista. Facultad de Agronomia. Universidad de la Republica (Montevideo)

Rev Fac Agron Univ Cent Venez — Revista. Facultad de Agronomia. Universidad Central de Venezuela

Rev Fac Agron Univ Cent Venezuela — Revista. Facultad de Agronomia. Universidad Central de Venezuela

Rev Fac Agron Univ Fed Rio Grande Sul — Revista. Faculdade de Agronomia. Universidade Federal do Rio Grande Do Sul

Rev Fac Agron Univ Nac La Plata — Revista. Facultad de Agronomia. Universidad Nacional de La Plata

Rev Fac Agron Univ Repub (Montevideo) — Revista. Facultad de Agronomia. Universidad de la Republica (Montevideo)

Rev Fac Agron Vet (Buenos Aires) — Revista. Facultad de Agronomia y Veterinaria (Buenos Aires)

Rev Fac Agron Vet Univ B Aires — Revista. Facultad de Agronomia y Veterinaria. Universidad de Buenos Aires

Rev Fac Agron Vet Univ Buenos Aires — Revista. Facultad de Agronomia y Veterinaria. Universidad de Buenos Aires

Rev Fac Agron Vet Univ Rio Grande Do Sul — Revista. Faculdade de Agronomia e Veterinaria. Universidade do Rio GrandeDo Sul

Rev Fac Agron Vet Univ Rio Grande Sul — Revista. Faculdade de Agronomia e Veterinaria. Universidade do Rio Grande Do Sul

Rev Fac Agron (Zulia Venez) Univ — Revista. Facultad de Agronomia (Zulia, Venezuela). Universidad

Rev Fac Arquit Monte — Revista. Facultad de Arquitectura. Universidad de la Republica (Montevideo)

Rev Fac Cienc 2a Ser A Cienc Mat — Revista. Faculdade de Ciencias. Universidade de Lisboa. 2a Serie A. Ciencias Matematicas

Rev Fac Cienc Agrar Minist Educ Univ Nac Cuyo (Mendoza) — Revista. Facultad de Ciencias Agrarias. Ministerio de Educacion. Universidad Nacional de Cuyo (Mendoza)

Rev Fac Cienc Agrar Univ Nac Cuyo — Revista. Facultad de Ciencias Agrarias. Universidad Nacional de Cuyo

Rev Fac Cienc Agr Univ Nac Cuyo — Revista. Facultad de Ciencias Agrarias. Universidad Nacional de Cuyo

Rev Fac Cienc Exactas Nat Agrimensura Univ Nac Nordeste — Revista. Facultad de Ciencias Exactas y Naturales y Agrimensura. Universidad Nacional del Nordeste

Rev Fac Cienc Exactas Quim Nat Univ Moron — Revista de la Facultad de Ciencias Exactas, Quimicas y Naturales de la Universidad de Moron

Rev Fac Cienc Farm (Araraquara) — Revista. Faculdade de Ciencias Farmaceuticas (Araraquara)

Rev Fac Cienc Farm Univ Estadual Paul Julio de Mesquita Filh — Revista. Facultdade de Ciencias Farmaceuticas. Universidade Estadual Paulista Julio de Mesquita Filho

Rev Fac Cienc Med Buenos Aires — Revista. Facultad de Ciencias Medicas de Buenos Aires

Rev Fac Cienc Med Cordoba — Revista. Facultad de Ciencias Medicas de Cordoba

Rev Fac Cienc Med Univ Catol Parana — Revista. Faculdade de Ciencias Medicas. Universidade Catolica do Parana

Rev Fac Cienc Med Univ Cent Ecuador — Revista. Facultad de Ciencias Medicas. Universidad Central del Ecuador

Rev Fac Cienc Med Univ Nac Cordoba — Revista. Facultad de Ciencias Medicas. Universidad Nacional de Cordoba

Rev Fac Cienc Med Univ Nac Cuyo — Revista. Facultad de Ciencias Medicas. Universidad Nacional de Cuyo

Rev Fac Cienc Med Univ Nac Litoral Rosario — Revista. Facultad de Ciencias Medicas. Universidad Nacional del Litoral Rosario

Rev Fac Cienc Med Univ Nac Rosario — Revista. Facultad de Ciencias Medicas. Universidad Nacional de Rosario

Rev Fac Cienc Nat Salta Univ Nac Tucuman — Revista. Facultad de Ciencias Naturales de Salta. Universidad Nacional de Tucuman

Rev Fac Cienc Quim Univ Nac La Plata — Revista. Facultad de Ciencias Quimicas. Universidad Nacional de La Plata

Rev Fac Cienc Univ Coimbra — Revista. Faculdade de Ciencias. Universidade de Coimbra

Rev Fac Cienc Univ Lisboa B — Revista. Faculdade de Ciencias. Universidade de Lisboa. Serie B. Ciencias Fisico-Quimicas

Rev Fac Cienc Univ Lisboa Ser B — Revista. Faculdade de Ciencias. Universidade de Lisboa. Serie B. Ciencias Fisico-Quimicas

Rev Fac Cienc Univ Lisboa Ser C — Revista. Faculdade de Ciencias. Universidade de Lisboa. Serie C. Ciencias Naturais

Rev Fac Cienc Univ Lisb Ser C Cienc Nat — Revista. Faculdade de Ciencias. Universidade de Lisboa. Serie C. Ciencias Naturais

Rev Fac Cienc Univ Oviedo — Revista. Facultad de Ciencias. Universidad de Oviedo

Rev Fac Cienc Univ Oviedo Ser Biol — Revista. Facultad de Ciencias. Universidad de Oviedo. Serie Biologia

Rev Fac Cienc Vet — Revista. Facultad de Ciencias Veterinarias

Rev Fac Cienc Vet La Plata — Revista. Facultad de Ciencias Veterinarias de La Plata

Rev Fac Cien Econ Admin Monte — Revista. Facultad de Ciencias Economicas y de Administracion. Universidad de laRepublica (Montevideo)

Rev Fac Cien Econ BA — Revista. Facultad de Ciencias Economicas. Universidad Nacional de Buenos Aires

Rev Fac Cien Econ Cochabamba — Revista. Facultad de Ciencias Economicas. Universidad Mayor de San Simon (Cochabamba, Bolivia)

Rev Fac Cien Econ Comer Lima — Revista. Facultad de Ciencias Economicas y Comerciales. Universidad Mayor de San Marcos (Lima)

Rev Fac Cien Econ Comer Pol Rosario — Revista. Facultad de Ciencias Economicas, Comerciales, y Politicas. UniversidadNacional del Litoral (Rosario, Argentina)

Rev Fac Cien Econ Cordoba — Revista. Facultad de Ciencias Economicas. Universidad de Cordoba (Cordoba, Argentina)

Rev Fac Cien Econ Lima — Revista. Facultad de Ciencias Economicas. Universidad Mayor de San Marcos (Lima)

Rev Fac Cien Exact Fis Nat Cordoba — Revista. Facultad de Ciencias Exactas, Fisicas, y Naturales (Cordoba, Argentina)

Rev Fac Cien Jur Soc Guat — Revista. Facultad de Ciencias Juridicas y Sociales. Universidad de San Carlos (Guatemala)

Rev Fac Cien Med Univ Nac Cordoba — Revista. Facultad de Ciencias Medicas. Universidad Nacional de Cordoba

Rev Fac Der Caracas — Revista. Facultad de Derecho. Universidad Central de Venezuela (Caracas)

Rev Fac Der Cien Soc Monte — Revista. Facultad de Derecho y Ciencias Sociales. Universidad de la Republica (Montevideo)

Rev Fac Der Maracaibo — Revista. Facultad de Derecho. Universidad del Zulia (Maracaibo)

Rev Fac Der Mex — Revista. Facultad de Derecho. Universidad Nacional Autonoma de Mexico

Rev Fac Direit S Paulo — Revista da Faculdade de Direito. Universidade de Sao Paulo

Rev Fac Educ Univ Catol Lima — Revista. Facultad de Educacion. Universidad Catolica del Peru (Lima)

Rev Fac Eng Univ Porto — Revista. Faculdade de Engenharia. Universidade do Porto

Rev Fac Farm Bioquim Univ Cent Ecuador — Revista. Facultad de Farmacia y Bioquimica. Universidad Central del Ecuador

Rev Fac Farm Bioquim Univ Fed St Maria — Revista. Faculdade de Farmacia e Bioquimica. Universidade Federal de Santa Maria

Rev Fac Farm Bioquim Univ Nac Mayor San Marcos — Revista. Facultad de Farmacia y Bioquimica. Universidad Nacional Mayor de San Marcos

Rev Fac Farm Bioquim Univ Nac Mayor San Marcos (Lima) — Revista. Facultad de Farmacia y Bioquimica. Universidad Nacional Mayor de San Marcos (Lima)

Rev Fac Farm Bioquim Univ Sao Paulo — Revista. Faculdade de Farmacia e Bioquimica. Universidade de Sao Paulo

Rev Fac Farm Odontol Araraquara — Revista. Faculdade de Farmacia e Odontologia de Araraquara

Rev Fac Farm Odontol Ribeirao Preto — Revista. Faculdade de Farmacia e Odontologia de Ribeirao Preto

Rev Fac Farm Odontol Ribeirao Preto Univ Sao Paulo — Revista da Faculdade de Farmacia e Odontologia de Ribeirao Preto. Universidade de Sao Paulo

Rev Fac Farm St Maria Univ Rio Grande Sul — Revista. Faculdade de Farmacia de Santa Maria. Universidade do Rio Grande do Sul

Rev Fac Farm Univ Cent Venez — Revista. Facultad de Farmacia. Universidad Central de Venezuela

Rev Fac Farm Univ Los Andes — Revista. Facultad de Farmacia. Universidad de Los Andes

Rev Fac Human Cien Monte — Revista. Facultad de Humanidades y Ciencias. Universidad de la Republica (Montevideo)

Rev Fac Humanid Cienc Univ Repub Montevideo — Revista. Facultad de Humanidades y Ciencias. Universidad de la Republica, Montevideo

Rev Fac Ing Agron Univ Cent Venez — Revista. Facultad de Ingenieria Agronomica. Universidad Central de Venezuela

Rev Fac Ing Quim Univ Nac Litoral — Revista. Facultad de Ingenieria Quimica. Universidad Nacional del Litoral

Rev Fac Ing Univ Cent Venez — Revista de la Facultad de Ingenieria. Universidad Central de Venezuela

Rev Fac Med (Maracaibo) — Revista. Facultad de Medicina (Maracaibo)

Rev Fac Med (Mex) — Revista. Facultad de Medicina (Mexico)

Rev Fac Med (Mexico City) — Revista. Facultad de Medicina (Mexico City)

Rev Fac Med (Tucuman) — Revista. Facultad de Medicina (Tucuman)

Rev Fac Med UNAM — Revista. Facultad de Medicina UNAM

Rev Fac Med Univ Fed Ceara — Revista. Faculdade de Medicina. Universidade Federal do Ceara

Rev Fac Med Univ Fed Santa Maria — Revista. Faculdade de Medicina. Universidade Federal de Santa Maria

Rev Fac Med Univ Nac Bogota — Revista. Facultad de Medicina. Universidad Nacional. Bogota

Rev Fac Med Univ Nac Colomb (Bogota) — Revista. Facultad de Medicina. Universidad Nacional de Colombia (Bogota)

Rev Fac Med Vet Teheran — Revue. Faculte de Medecine Veterinaire de Teheran

Rev Fac Med Vet Univ Nac Mayor San Marcos — Revista. Facultad de Medicina Veterinaria. Universidad Nacional Mayor de San Marcos

Rev Fac Med Vet Univ Sao Paulo — Revista. Faculdade de Medicina Veterinaria. Universidade de Sao Paulo

Rev Fac Med Vet Zootec (Bogota) — Revista. Facultad de Medicina, Veterinaria, y Zootecnia (Bogota)

Rev Fac Med Vet Zootec Univ Nac Colomb — Revista. Facultad de Medicina Veterinaria y de Zootecnia. Universidad Nacional de Colombia

Rev Fac Med Vet Zootec Univ San Carlos — Revista. Facultad de Medicina, Veterinaria, y Zootecnia. Universidad de San Carlos

Rev Fac Med Vet Zootec Univ Sao Paulo — Revista. Faculdade de Medicina Veterinaria e Zootecnia. Universidade de Sao Paulo

Rev Fac Med Vet Zoot Univ Nac Colomb — Revista. Facultad de Medicina, Veterinaria, y Zootecnia. Universidad Nacional de Colombia

Rev Fac Nac Agron (Medellin) — Revista. Facultad Nacional de Agronomia (Medellin)

Rev Fac Nac Agron (Medellin Colomb) — Revista. Facultad Nacional de Agronomia (Medellin, Colombia)

Rev Fac Nac Agron Univ Antioquia — Revista. Facultad Nacional de Agronomia. Universidad de Antioquia

Rev Fac Nac Agron Univ Nac (Colombia) — Revista. Facultad Nacional de Agronomia. Universidad Nacional (Colombia)

Rev Fac Odontol Aracatuba — Revista. Faculdade de Odontologia de Aracatuba

Rev Fac Odontol Araraquara — Revista. Faculdade de Odontologia de Araraquara

Rev Fac Odontol (P Alegre) — Revista. Faculdade de Odontologia (Porto Alegre)

Rev Fac Odontol Pernambuco — Revista. Faculdade de Odontologia de Pernambuco

Rev Fac Odontol Port Alegre — Revista. Faculdade de Odontologia de Port Alegre

Rev Fac Odontol Ribeirao Preto — Revista. Faculdade de Odontologia de Ribeirao Preto

Rev Fac Odontol Ribeirao Preto Univ Sao Paulo — Revista. Faculdade de Odontologia de Ribeirao Preto. Universidade de Sao Paulo

Rev Fac Odontol Sao Jose Dos Campos — Revista. Faculdade de Odontologia de Sao Jose Dos Campos

Rev Fac Odontol Sao Paulo — Revista. Faculdade de Odontologia. Universidade de Sao Paulo

Rev Fac Odontol Tucuman — Revista. Facultad de Odontologia. Universidad Nacional de Tucuman

Rev Fac Odontol Univ Chile — Revista de La Facultad de Odontologia. Universidad de Chile

Rev Fac Odontol Univ Fed Bahia — Revista. Faculdade de Odontologia. Universidade Federal da Bahia

Rev Fac Odontol Univ Nac Colomb — Revista. Facultade de Odontologia. Universidad Nacional de Colombia

Rev Fac Odontol Univ Nac (Cordoba) — Revista de la Facultad de Odontologia (Cordoba)

Rev Fac Odontol Univ Sao Paulo — Revista. Faculdade de Odontologia. Universidade de Sao Paulo

Rev Fac Quim Farm Univ Cent Ecuador — Revista. Facultad de Quimica y Farmacia. Universidad Central del Ecuador

Rev Fac Quim Ind Agric Univ Nac Litoral — Revista. Facultad de Quimica Industrial y Agricola. Universidad Nacional del Litoral

Rev Fac Quim Univ Nac Mayor San Marcos — Revista. Facultad de Quimica. Universidad Nacional Mayor de San Marcos

Rev Fac Sci Econ Univ Istanbul — Revue. Faculte des Sciences Economiques de l'Universite d'Istanbul

Rev Fac Sci For Univ Istanbul — Revue. Faculte des Sciences Forestieres. Universite d'Istanbul

Rev Fac Sci Univ Istanbul — Revue. Faculte des Sciences. Universite d'Istanbul

Rev Fac Sci Univ Istanbul C — Revue. Faculte des Sciences. Universite d'Istanbul. Serie C

Rev Fac Sci Univ Istanbul Ser A — Revue. Faculte des Sciences. Universite d'Istanbul. Serie A. Mathematiques Pures et Appliquees

Rev Fac Sci Univ Istanbul Ser B — Revue. Faculte des Sciences. Universite d'Istanbul. Serie B. Sciences Naturelles

Rev Fac Sci Univ Istanbul Ser B Sci Nat — Revue. Faculte des Sciences. Universite d'Istanbul. Serie B. Sciences Naturelles

Rev Fac Sci Univ Istanbul Ser C — Review. Faculty of Science. University of Istanbul. Series C

Rev Faculdade Odontol Fzl — Revista da Faculdade de Odontologia da Fzl

Rev Faculdade Odontol Lins — Revista da Faculdade de Odontologia de Lins

Rev Fac Vet Univ Teheran — Revue. Faculte Veterinaire. Universite de Teheran

Rev Faill — Revue des Faillites, Concordats, et Liquidations

Rev Farmacol Clin Exp — Revista de Farmacologia Clinica y Experimental

Rev Farm Bahia — Revista Farmaceutica da Bahia

Rev Farm (B Aires) — Revista Farmaceutica (Buenos Aires)

Rev Farm Bioquim — Revista de Farmacia e Bioquimica

Rev Farm Bioquim Amazonia — Revista de Farmacia e Bioquimica da Amazonia

Rev Farm Bioquim Belo Horizonte Braz — Revista de Farmacia e Bioquimica (Belo Horizonte, Brazil)

Rev Farm Bioquim (Lima) — Revista de Farmacia y Bioquimica (Lima)

Rev Farm Bioquim Univ Sao Paulo — Revista de Farmacia e Bioquimica. Universidade de Sao Paulo

Rev Farm (Bucharest) — Revista Farmaciei (Bucharest)

Rev Farm Buenos Aires — Revista Farmaceutica (Buenos Aires)

Rev Farm Cuba — Revista Farmaceutica de Cuba

Rev Farm Odontol — Revista de Farmacia e Odontologia

Rev Farm Peru — Revista Farmaceutica Peruana

Rev Farm PR — Revista Farmaceutica de Puerto Rico

Rev Farm Quim — Revista de Farmacia y Quimica

Rev F de C — Revue des Fonds de Commerce

Rev Fd Technol — Review in Food Technology

RevFE — Revue Francaise de l'Elite

RevFed — Revue Federaliste

Rev Fed Am Health Syst — Review. Federation of American Health Systems

Rev Fed Am Hosp — Review. Federation of American Hospitals

Rev Fed Doct Cienc Filos Let (Havana) — Revista. Federacion de Doctors en Ciencias y en Filosofia y Letras (Havana)

Rev Fed Fr Soc Sci Nat — Revue. Federation Francaise des Societes de Sciences Naturelles

Rev Fed Odontol Colomb — Revista. Federacion Odontologica Colombiana

Rev Fed Odontol Ecuat — Revista. Federacion Odontologica Ecuatoriana

Rev Ferment Ind Aliment — Revue des Fermentations et des Industries Alimentaires

Rev Fett Harz Ind — Revue ueber die Fett- und Harz-Industrie

Rev F Gy Ob — Revue Francaise de Gynecologie et d'Obstetrique

Rev Filip Med Farm — Revista Filipina de Medicina y Farmacia

Rev Filol Esp — Revista de Filologia Espanola

Rev Filol Istr Cl — Revista di Filologia e di Isturzione Classica

Rev Filos Mex — Revista de Filosofia. Escuela Nacional Preparatoria (Mexico)

Rev Filosof (Argentina) — Revista de Filosofia (Argentina)

Rev Filosof Costa Rica — Revista de Filosofia. Universidad de Costa Rica

Rev Filosof (Mexico) — Revista de Filosofia (Mexico)

Rev Filosof (Spain) — Revista de Filosofia (Spain)

Rev Filos S Jose — Revista de Filosofia. Universidad de Costa Rica (San Jose, Costa Rica)

Rev Filoz — Revista de Filozofie

Rev Financ Bursatil Min — Revista Financiera. Bursatil y Minera

Rev Financ Salitre Minas — Revista Financiera. Salitre y Minas

Rev Finan Publ Rio — Revista de Financas Publicas (Rio de Janeiro)

Rev Fis — Revista de Fisica

Rev Fisc — Revue Fiscale

Rev Fish Sci — Reviews in Fisheries Science

Rev Fis Quim Eng — Revista de Fisica, Quimica, e Engenharia

Rev Fis Quim Eng Ser A — Revista de Fisica, Quimica, e Engenharia. Serie A

Rev FITCE — Revue FITCE

Rev Fiz Chim — Revista de Fizica si Chimie

Rev Fiz Chim Ser A — Revista de Fizica si Chimie. Seria A

Rev Fiz Chim Ser B — Revista de Fizica si Chimie. Seria B

Rev Fiziol Norm Patol — Revista de Fiziologie Normala si Patologica

Rev Flora Med — Revista da Flora Medicinai

Rev Foie — Revue du Foie

Rev Fomen Caracas — Revista de Fomento (Caracas)

Rev Fonderie Mod — Revue de Fonderie Moderne

Rev Food Sci Technol — Reviews in Food Science and Technology

Rev Food Sci Technol (Mysore) — Reviews in Food Sciences and Technology (Mysore)

Rev Food Technol — Reviews in Food Technology

Rev Food Technol (Mysore) — Reviews in Food Technology (Mysore)

Rev Forest Adm Br India — Review of Forest Administration in British India [Calcutta]

Rev Forest Adm Burma — Review of Forest Administration in Burma [Rangoon]

Rev Forest Adm Unit Prov — Review of Forest Administration in the United Provinces [Naini Tal]

Rev Forest Serv Invest US — Review of Forest Service Investigations. Bureau of Forestry. United States Department of Agriculture [Washington]

Rev Forest Venezolana — Revista Forestal Venezolana

Rev For Franc — Revue Forestiere Francaise

Rev For Fr (Nancy) — Revue Forestiere Francaise (Nancy)

Rev Foro Lima — Revista del Foro (Lima)

Rev For Peru — Revista Forestal del Peru

Rev Fort Argent — Revista Forestal Argentina

Rev Fortschr Naturwiss — Revue der Fortschritte der Naturwissenschaften in Theoretischer und PraktischerBeziehung

Rev For Venez — Revista Forestal Venezolana

Rev Fot — Revue Fotografie

RevFP — Revue Francaise de la Psychanalyse

Rev Fr — Revolution Francaise

Rev Fr — Revue Francaise

Rev Fr Alle — Revue Francaise d'Allergologie [Later, Revue Francaise d'Allergologie et d'Immunologie Clinique]

Rev Fr Allerg — Revue Francaise d'Allergie

Rev Fr Allergol — Revue Francaise d'Allergologie

Rev Fr Allergol Immunol Clin — Revue Francaise d'Allergologie et d'Immunologie Clinique

Rev Franc Agr — Revue Francais de l'Agriculture

Rev Francaise Automat Inform Rech Oper Ser Bleue — Revue Francaise d'Automatique, d'Informatique, et de Recherche Operationnelle. Serie Bleue

Rev Francaise Automat Inform Rech Oper Ser Jaune — Revue Francaise d'Automatique, d'Informatique, et de Recherche Operationnelle. Serie Jaune

Rev Francaise Automat Inform Rech Oper Ser Rouge Anal Numer — Revue Francaise d'Automatique, d'Informatique, et de Recherche Operationnelle. Serie Rouge. Analyse Numerique

Rev Francaise Automat Inform Rech Oper Ser Verte — Revue Francaise d'Automatique, d'Informatique, et de Recherche Operationnelle. Serie Verte

Rev Franc de Droit Aer — Revue Francaise de Droit Aerien

Rev France — Revue de la France

Rev Franc Herald Sigillogr — Revue Francaise d'Heraldique et de Sigillographie

Rev Franc Hist Outre-Mer — Revue Francaise d'Histoire d'Outre-Mer

Rev Franc Phot — Revue Francaise de Photographie

Rev Franc Sci Polit — Revue Francaise de Science Politique

Rev Fr Astronaut — Revue Francaise d'Astronautique

Rev Fr Aut Inf Rech Oper Anal Num — Revue Francaise d'Automatique, d'Informatique, et de Recherche Operationnelle. Serie Analyse Numerique

Rev Fr Autom Inf Rech Oper — Revue Francaise d'Automatique, d'Informatique, et de Recherche Operationnelle

Rev Fr Autom Inf Rech Oper Anal — Revue Francaise d'Automatique, d'Informatique, et de Recherche Operationelle. Analyse Numerique

Rev Fr Corps Gras — Revue Francaise des Corps Gras

Rev Fr de C — Revue Francaise de Communication

Rev Fr Dommage Corpor — Revue Francaise du Dommage Corporel

Rev Fr Electr — Revue Francaise de l'Electricite

Rev Fr Elite Eur — Revue Francaise de l'Elite Europeenne

Rev Fr Endocrinol — Revue Francaise d'Endocrinologie
Rev Fr Endocrinol Clin Nutr Metab — Revue Francaise d'Endocrinologie Clinique, Nutrition, et Metabolisme
Rev Fr Energ — Revue Francaise de l'Energie
Rev Fr Entomol — Revue Francaise d'Entomologie
Rev Fr Entomol Nouv Ser — Revue Francaise d'Entomologie. Nouvelle Serie
Rev Fr Etr Colon — Revue Francaise de l'Etranger et des Colonies
Rev Fr Etud Clin Biol — Revue Francaise d'Etudes Cliniques et Biologiques
Rev Fr Geotech — Revue Francaise de Geotechnique
Rev Fr Gerontol — Revue Francaise de Gerontologie
Rev Fr Gynecol Obstet — Revue Francaise de Gynecologie et d'Obstetrique
Rev Fr Hist — Revue Francaise d'Histoire d'Outre-Mer
Rev Fr Hist Livre — Revue Francaise d'Histoire du Livre
Rev Fr Hist OM — Revue Francaise d'Histoire d'Outre Mer
Rev Fr Hist Outre Mer — Revue Francaise d'Histoire d'Outre Mer
Rev Fr Inf and Rech Oper — Revue Francaise d'Informatique et de Recherche Operationnelle
Rev Frio — Revista del Frio
Rev Fr Mal Respir — Revue Francaise des Maladies Respiratoires
Rev Fr Mec — Revue Francaise de Mecanique
Rev Fr Mkt — Revue Francaise du Marketing
Rev Fr Odonto Stomatol (Paris) — Revue Francaise d'Odonto-Stomatologie (Paris)
Rev Fr Oenol — Revue Francaise d'Oenologit
Rev Fr Pedagog — Revue Francaise de Pedagogie
Rev Fr Pediatr — Revue Francaise de Pediatrie
Rev Fr Photogr Cinematogr — Revue Francaise de Photographie et de Cinematographie
Rev Fr Prothes Dent — Revue Francaise des Prothesistes Dentaires
Rev Fr Psychanal — Revue Francaise de Psychanalyse
Rev Fr Sci Eau — Revue Francaise des Sciences de l'Eau
Rev Fr Sci Polit — Revue Francaise de Science Politique
Rev Fr Sc P — Revue Francaise de Science Politique
Rev Fr Soc — Revue Francaise de Sociologie
Rev Fr Sociol — Revue Francaise de Sociologie
Rev Fr Tel — Revue Francaise des Telecommunications
Rev Fr Trait Inf — Revue Francaise de Traitement de l'Information
Rev Fr Tran — Revue Francaise de Transfusion [*Later, Revue Francaise de Transfusion et Immuno-Hematologie*]
Rev Fr Transfus — Revue Francaise de Transfusion [*Later, Revue Francaise de Transfusion et Immuno-Hematologie*]
Rev Fr Transfus Immuno-Hematol — Revue Francaise de Transfusion et Immuno-Hematologie
Rev Fuerzas Armadas Venez — Revista de las Fuerzas Armadas de Venezuela
Rev Fundatiilor Regale — Revista Fundatiilor Regale
Rev Fund Serv Saude Publica (Braz) — Revista da Fundacao Servicos de Saude Publica (Brazil)
Rev Fund SESP — Revista. Fundacao Servicos de Saude Publica
Rev Fund SESP (Braz) — Revista. Fundacao Servicos de Saude Publica (Brazil)
RevG — Revista de Guatemala
Rev Garcia da Orta — Revista de Garcia da Orta
Rev Gastroent — Review of Gastroenterology [*New York*]
Rev Gastroenterol — Review of Gastroenterology
Rev Gastroenterol Mex — Revista de Gastroenterologia de Mexico
Rev Gastroenterol Peru — Revista de Gastroenterologia del Peru
Rev Gaucha Enferm — Revista Gaucha de Enfermagem
Rev Gaucha Odontol — Revista Gaucha de Odontologia
Rev Gemmol AFG — Revue de Gemmologie. Association Francaise de Gemmologie
Rev Gen Agron — Revue Generale Agronomique
Rev Gen Archit — Revue Generale de l'Architecture
Rev Gen Ass et Resp — Revue Generale des Assurances et des Responsabilites
Rev Gen Assoc Turk Chem Sect B — Review. General Association of Turkish Chemists. Section B
Rev Gen Ass Terr — Revue Generale des Assurances Terrestres
Rev Gen Assur Terr — Revue Generale des Assurances Terrestres
Rev Gen Biog & Necrol — Revue Generale Biographique et Necrologique
Rev Gen Bot — Revue Generale de Botanique
Rev Gen Caoutch — Revue Generale du Caoutchouc
Rev Gen Caoutchouc — Revue Generale du Caoutchouc/Institut Francais du Caoutchouc
Rev Gen Caoutch Plast — Revue Generale des Caoutchoucs et Plastiques
Rev Gen Caoutch Plast Ed Plast — Revue Generale des Caoutchoucs et Plastiques. Edition Plastiques
Rev Gen Chem Fer — Revue Generale des Chemins de Fer
Rev Gen Chemins de Fer — Revue Generale des Chemins de Fer
Rev Gen Chemins Fer — Revue Generale des Chemins de Fer
Rev Gen Chim Pure Appl — Revue Generale de Chimie Pure et Appliquee
Rev Gen Clin et Therap — Revue Generale de Clinique et de Therapeutique
Rev Gen Clin Ther J Prat — Revue Generale de Clinique et de Therapeutique. Journal des Praticiens
Rev Gen Colloides — Revue Generale des Colloides
Rev Gen Colloides Suppl — Revue Generale des Colloides. Supplement
Rev Gen de Droit — Revue Generale de Droit
Rev Gen de Legis y Jurispr — Revista General de Legislacion y Jurisprudencia
Rev Gen Droit — Revue Generale de Droit
Rev Geneal Lat S Paulo — Revista Genealogica Latina (Sao Paulo)
Rev Gen Elec — Revue Generale de l'Electricite
Rev Gen Electr — Revue Generale de l'Electricite
Rev Gen Ens Sourds Muets — Revue Generale de l'Enseignement des Sourds Muets
Rev Generale de Droit — Revue Generale de Droit
Rev Generale Thermique — Revue de Generale de Thermique
Rev Gener Hebdom Industr Nation — Revue Generale Hebdomadaire de l'Industrie Nationale

Rev Geneve — Revue de Geneve
Rev Gen Froid — Revue Generale du Froid
Rev Gen Gaz — Revue Generale du Gaz
Rev Gen Ind Text — Revue Generale de l'Industrie Textile
Rev Gen Lait — Revue Generale de Lait
Rev Gen Mar — Revista General de Marina
Rev Gen Matieres Color Blanchiment Teint Impress Apprets — Revue Generale des Matieres Colorantes du Blanchiment de la Teinture de l'Impression et des Apprets
Rev Gen Matieres Plast — Revue Generale des Matieres Plastiques
Rev Gen Matieres Plast Suppl — Revue Generale des Matieres Plastiques. Supplement
Rev Gen Mec — Revue Generale de Mecanique
Rev Gen Mec Electr — Revue Generale de Mecanique. Electricite
Rev Gen Med Vet (Toulouse) — Revue Generale de Medecine Veterinaire (Toulouse)
Rev Gen Meet Cem Assoc Jpn — Review of General Meeting. Cement Association of Japan
Rev Gen Meet Tech Sess Cem Assoc Jpn — Review of General Meeting. Technical Session. Cement Association of Japan
Rev Gen Nucl — Revue Generale Nucleaire
Rev Gen Sci — Revue Generale des Sciences
Rev Gen Sci Appl — Revue Generale des Sciences Appliquees
Rev Gen Sci Pures Appl — Revue Generale des Sciences Pures et Appliquees
Rev Gen Sci Pures Appl Bull Assoc Fr Av Sci — Revue Generale des Sciences Pures et Appliquees et Bulletin de l'Association Francaise pour l'Avancement des Sciences
Rev Gen Sci Pures Appl Bull Soc Philomath — Revue Generale des Sciences Pures et Appliquees et Bulletin de la Societe Philomathique
Rev Gen Sc Pures et Appliq — Revue Generale des Sciences Pures et Appliquees
Rev Gen Tech — Revue Generale des Techniques
Rev Gen Teint Impress Blanchiment Appret — Revue Generale de Teinture, Impression, Blanchiment, Appret
Rev Gen Text Chim — Revue Generale de tous Textiles Chimiques
Rev Gen Therm — Revue Generale de Thermique
Rev Geodesia La Plata — Revista de Geodesia (La Plata)
Rev Geofis — Revista de Geofisica
Rev Geog — Revista Geografica
Rev Geog E — Revue Geographique de l'Est
Rev Geog Pays Medit — Revue Geographique des Pays Mediterraneens
Rev Geog Ph — Revue de Geographie Physique et de Geologie Dynamique
Rev Geogr — Revue Geographique. Extrait de la Revue Maritime et Coloniale
Rev Geogr Alpine — Revue de Geographie Alpine
Rev Geogr Am BA — Revista Geografica Americana (Buenos Aires)
Rev Geographie Alpine — Revue de Geographie Alpine
Rev Geographie Montreal — Revue de Geographie de Montreal
Rev Geogr Barranquilla — Revista Geografica/Instituto de Investigacion Etnologica (Barranquilla)
Rev Geogr Chile Santiago — Revista Geografica de Chile Terra Australis (Santiago)
Rev Geogr Hav — Revista Geografica (La Habana)
Rev Geogr Inst Univ Istanb — Review of the Geographical Institute of the University of Istanbul
Rev Geogr Maroc — Revue de Geographie du Maroc
Rev Geogr Merida — Revista Geografica (Merida, Venezuela)
Rev Geogr Phys Geol Dyn — Revue de Geographie Physique et de Geologie Dynamique
Rev Geogr Phys Geol Dynam — Revue de Geographie Physique et de Geologie Dynamique
Rev Geogr Pyrenees Sud-Ouest — Revue Geographique des Pyrenees et du Sud-Ouest
Rev Geogr Rio — Revista Geografica (Rio de Janeiro)
Rev Geol Chile — Revista Geologica de Chile
Rev Geol Connected Sci — Review of Geology and the Connected Sciences
Rev Geol Dyn Geogr Phys — Revue de Geologie Dynamique et de Geographie Physique
Rev Geol Minas Ecuador Dir Gen Geol Minas — Revista de Geologia y Minas. Ecuador. Direccion General de Geologia y Minas
Rev Geologia — Revista de Geologia
Rev Geomorphol Dyn — Revue de Geomorphologie Dynamique
Rev Geophys — Reviews of Geophysics [*Later, Reviews of Geophysics and Space Physics*]
Rev Geophys — Reviews of Geophysics and Space Physics
Rev Geophys and Space Phys — Reviews of Geophysics and Space Physics
Rev Geophysics — Reviews of Geophysics [*Later, Reviews of Geophysics and Space Physics*]
Rev Geophys Space Phys — Reviews of Geophysics and Space Physics
Rev Ger — Revista de Gerona
Rev Geriatr — Revue de Geriatrie
Rev Germ — Revue Germanique
Rev Gerona — Revista de Gerona
Rev Gerontol Expression Fr — Revue de Gerontologie d'Expression Francaise
Rev Ghana Law — Review of Ghana Law
Rev Ginecol Obstet — Revista de Ginecologia e d'Obstetricia
Rev Goiana Med — Revista Goiana de Medicina
Rev Gospod Agr Stat (Bucharest) — Revista Gospodariilor Agricole de Stat (Bucharest)
Rev G Therm — Revue Generale de Thermique
Rev Guad — Revue Guadeloupeenne
Rev Guadalupe — Revista de Guadalupe
Rev Guatem Estomatol — Revista Guatemalteca de Estomatologia
Rev Guat Guat — Revista de Guatemala (Guatemala)
Rev Guim — Revista de Guimaraes
Rev Guimaraes — Revista de Guimaraes

Rev Guimaraes — Revista de Guimaraes. Publicacao da Sodiedade Martins Sarmento

Rev Gynae et Chir Abd — Revue de Gynaecologie et de Chirurgie Abdominale

Rev Gynecol Obstet — Revista de Gynecologia e d'Obstetricia

RevH — Revista de Historia

RevH — Revista de Historia de America

RevH — Revista de la Habana

REVHA — Reviews on Environmental Health

Rev Habana Hav — Revista de La Habana (La Habana)

Rev Hac Caracas — Revista de Hacienda (Caracas)

Rev Hac Lima — Revista de Hacienda (Lima)

Rev Hac Mex — Revista de Hacienda (Mexico)

Rev Haute Auvergne — Revue de la Haute Auvergne. Societe des Sciences et Arts

Rev Hautes Temp Refract — Revue des Hautes Temperatures et des Refractaires

Rev H Dr — Revue d'Histoire du Droit

Rev Hebd Laryngol Otol Rhinol — Revue Hebdomadaire de Laryngologie, d'Otologie, et de Rhinologie

Rev Hebdomadaire — Revue Hebdomadaire

Rev HE Fr — Revue d'Histoire de l'Eglise de France

Rev Hell Dr Int — Revue Hellenique de Droit International

Rev Hellen de Droit Internat — Revue Hellenique de Droit International

Rev Hellenique de Dr Int'l — Revue Hellenique de Droit International

Rev Hemat — Revue d'Hematologie

Rev Hematol — Revue d'Hematologie

Rev Hematol Westbury NY — Reviews of Hematology (Westbury, New York)

Rev Heteroat Chem — Reviews on Heteroatom Chemistry

Rev HF Electron Telecommun — Revue HF, Electronique, Telecommunications

Rev Hidrocarburos Minas — Revista de Hidrocarburos y Minas

Rev High Pressure Sci Technol — Review of High Pressure Science and Technology

Rev High-Temp Mater — Reviews on High-Temperature Materials

Rev Hig Med Esc — Revista de Higiene y Medicina Escolares

Rev Hig Sanid Pecu — Revista de Higiene y Sanidad Pecuarias

Rev Hig y San Pecuarias — Revista de Higiene y Sanidad Pecuarias

Rev Hig y San Vet (Madrid) — Revista de Higiene y Sanidad Veterinaria (Madrid)

Rev His A F — Revue d'Histoire de l'Amerique Francaise

Rev Hisp — Revue Hispanique

Rev Hispan — Revista Hispanica Moderna

Rev Hisp Mod — Revista Hispanica Moderna

RevHist — Revista de Historia

Rev Hist — Revue Historique

Rev Hist A — Revue de l'Histoire de l'Art

Rev Hist Am — Revista de Historia de America

Rev Hist Am — Revue d'Histoire de l'Amerique Francaise

Rev Hist Am Arg — Revista de Historia Americana y Argentina (Mendoza, Argentina)

Rev Hist Amer Fr — Revue d'Histoire de l'Amerique Francaise

Rev Hist Am Fr — Revue d'Histoire de l'Amerique Francaise

Rev Hist Am Mex — Revista de Historia de America (Mexico)

Rev Hist & Archeol — Revue d'Histoire et d'Archeologie

Rev Hist & Geneal Esp — Revista de Historia y de Genealogia Espanola

Rev Hist & Litt Languedoc — Revue Historique et Litteraire du Languedoc

Rev Hist & Philos — Revue d'Histoire et de la Philosophie

Rev Hist Ardenn — Revue Historique Ardennaise

Rev Hist Armee — Revue Historique de l'Armee

Rev Hist Armees — Revue Historique des Armees

Rev Hist BA — Revista de Historia (Buenos Aires)

Rev Hist Bordeaux & Dept Gironde — Revue Historique de Bordeaux et du Departement de la Gironde

Rev Hist Bordeaux Dep Gironde — Revue Historique de Bordeaux et du Departement de la Gironde

Rev Hist Canaria — Revista de Historia Canaria

Rev Hist Caracas — Revista de Historia (Caracas)

Rev Hist Col — Revue de l'Histoire des Colonies

Rev Hist Colon — Revue d'Histoire des Colonies

Rev Hist Colon Fr — Revue de l'Histoire des Colonies Francaises

Rev Hist Comp — Revue d'Histoire Comparee

Rev Hist Crit Lit Centroam — Revista Historico. Critica de Literatura Centroamericana

Rev Hist de Droit Fr et Etr — Revue Historique de Droit Francais et Etranger

Rev Hist Deux Guerre Mond — Revue d'Histoire de la Deuxieme Guerre Mondiale

Rev Hist Di — Revue d'Histoire Diplomatique

Rev Hist Dipl — Revue d'Histoire Diplomatique

Rev Hist Diplomat — Revue d'Histoire Diplomatique

Rev Hist Doctr Econ — Revue d'Histoire des Doctrines Economiques

Rev Hist Dr — Revue d'Histoire du Droit

Rev Hist Dr — Revue Historique de Droit Francais et Etranger

Rev Hist Dr Fr et Etrang — Revue d'Histoire du Droit Francais et Etranger

Rev Hist Droit — Revue d'Histoire du Droit

Rev Hist Droit Franc Etr — Revue Historique de Droit Francais et Etranger

Rev Hist Eccl — Revue d'Histoire Ecclesiastique

Rev Hist Eccles — Revue d'Histoire Ecclesiastique

Rev Hist Econ Soc — Revue d'Histoire Economique et Sociale

Rev Hist Econ Social — Revue d'Histoire Economique et Sociale

Rev Hist Eglise France — Revue d'Histoire de l'Eglise de France

Rev Hist et Archeol du Maine — Revue Historique et Archeologique du Maine

Rev Hist Idea Quito — Revista de Historia de las Ideas (Quito)

Rev Hist Inde Fr — Revue Historique de l'Inde Francaise

Rev Hist L — Revue d'Histoire Litteraire de la France

Rev Hist Lima — Revista Historica (Lima)

Rev Hist Litt — Revue d'Histoire Litteraire de la France

Rev Hist Litt Fr — Revue d'Histoire Litteraire de la France

Rev Hist Litt France — Revue d'Histoire Litteraire de la France

Rev Hist M — Revue d'Histoire Moderne et Contemporaine

Rev Hist Maghrebine — Revue d'Histoire Maghrebine

Rev Hist Med Hebr — Revue d'Histoire de la Medecine Hebraique

Rev Hist Med Hebraique — Revue d'Histoire de la Medecine Hebraique

Rev Hist Med Hebraique — Revue d'Histoire de la Medecine Hebraique / Societe de la Medecine Hebraique

Rev Hist Mendoza — Revista de Historia (Mendoza)

Rev Hist Mil — Revista de Historia Militar

Rev Hist Missions — Revue d'Histoire des Missions

Rev Hist Mod — Revue d'Histoire Moderne

Rev Hist Mod & Contemp — Revue d'Histoire Moderne et Contemporaine

Rev Hist Mod Cont — Revue d'Histoire Moderne et Contemporaine

Rev Hist Mod Contemp — Revue d'Histoire Moderne et Contemporaine

Rev Hist Moderne — Revue d'Histoire Moderne. Societe d'Histoire Moderne

Rev Hist Monte — Revista Historica (Montevideo)

Rev Hist Nat Appliq — Revue d'Histoire Naturelle Appliquee

Rev Hist Nobil — Revue Historique Nobiliaire

Rev Histoire Math — Revue d'Histoire des Mathematiques

Rev Histoire Sci — Revue d'Histoire des Sciences

Rev Histoire Sci Appl — Revue d'Histoire des Sciences et de Leurs Applications

Rev Histor — Revue Historique

Rev Hist Pasto — Revista de Historia (Pasto, Colombia)

Rev Hist Ph — Revue d'Histoire et de Philosophie Religieuses

Rev Hist Pharm — Revue d'Histoire de la Pharmacie

Rev Hist Philos Relig — Revue d'Histoire et de Philosophie Religieuse

Rev Hist R — Revue de l'Histoire des Religions

Rev Hist Rel — Revue d'Histoire des Religions

Rev Hist Relig — Revue de l'Histoire des Religions

Rev Hist Religions — Revue de l'Histoire des Religions

Rev Hist Sci — Revue d'Histoire des Sciences

Rev Hist Sci Applic — Revue d'Histoire des Sciences et de Leurs Applications

Rev Hist Sci Leurs Appl — Revue d'Histoire des Sciences et de Leurs Applications

Rev Hist S Juan — Revista de Historia (San Juan, Argentina)

Rev Hist S Paulo — Revista de Historia (Sao Paulo)

Rev Hist Spirit — Revue d'Histoire de la Spiritualite

Rev Hist Textes — Revue d'Histoire des Textes

Rev Hist Th — Revue d'Histoire du Theatre

Rev Hist Theat — Revue d'Histoire du Theatre

Rev Hist Vaudoise — Revue Historique Vaudoise

Rev Hist Versailles — Revue de l'Histoire de Versailles

RevHL — Revista de Historia. La Laguna de Tenerife

RevHL — Revista de Historia (Lisbon)

RevHM — Revue Hommes et Mondes

Rev Hong Metall — Revue Hongroise de Metallurgie

Rev Hong Mines Metall Mines — Revue Hongroise de Mines et Metallurgie. Mines

Rev Hort — Revue Horticole

Rev Hort Belge Etrangere — Revue de l'Horticulture Belge et Etrangere

Rev Hortic — Revue Horticole

Rev Hortic (Paris) — Revue Horticole (Paris)

Rev Hortic Suisse — Revue Horticole Suisse

Rev Hortic Vitic — Revista de Horticultura si Viticultura

Rev Hort Viticult — Revista de Horticultura si Viticultura

Rev Hosp Clin Fac Med Univ Sao Paulo — Revista. Hospital das Clinicas. Faculdade de Medicina. Universidade deSao Paulo

Rev Hosp Clin Fac Med Univ Sao Paulo Supl — Revista. Hospital das Clinicas. Faculdade de Medicina. Universidade de Sao Paulo. Suplemento

Rev Hosp Clin Sao Paulo — Revista. Hospital das Clinicas. Faculdade de Medicina. Universidade de SaoPaulo

Rev Hosp Nino (Lima) — Revista. Hospital del Nino (Lima)

Rev Hosp Ninos (B Aires) — Revista. Hospital de Ninos (Buenos Aires)

Rev Hosp Psiquiatr Habana — Revista. Hospital Psiquiatrico de la Habana

Rev Hosp San Juan De Dios (Bogota) — Revista. Hospital de San Juan de Dios (Bogota)

Rev Hosp S Juan — Revista. Hospital de San Juan de Dios

Rev H Philos — Revue d'Histoire et de Philosophie Religieuse

RevHS — Revista de Historia (Sao Paulo)

Rev H Text — Revue d'Histoire des Textes

Rev Huis — Revue des Huissiers

Rev Human Cordoba — Revista de Humanidades (Cordoba, Argentina)

Rev Hydraul — Revue d'Hydraulique

Rev Hydrobiol Trop — Revue d'Hydrobiologie Tropicale

Rev Hyg — Revue d'Hygiene

Rev Hyg (Ankara) — Revue d'Hygiene (Ankara)

Rev Hyg et Med Prevent — Revue d'Hygiene et de Medecine Preventive

Rev Hyg Med Infant Ann Polyclin H de Rothschild — Revue d'Hygiene et de Medecine Infantiles et Annales de la Polyclinique H. de Rothschild

Rev Hyg Med Prev — Revue d'Hygiene et de Medecine Preventive

Rev Hyg Med Sc Univ — Revue d'Hygiene et Medecine Scolaire et Universitaire

Rev Hyg Med Soc — Revue d'Hygiene et de Medecine Sociale

Rev Hyg Police Sanit — Revue d'Hygiene et de Police Sanitaire

Rev Hyg Prof — Revue de l'Hygiene Professionnelle

Rev Hyg Trav — Revue d'Hygiene du Travail

RevI — Revista de Indias

Rev/I — Revista/Review Interamericana

RevIb — Revista Iberoamericana

Rev Iber Endocr — Revista Iberica de Endocrinologia

Rev Iber Endocrinol — Revista Iberica de Endocrinologia

Rev Iber Micol — Revista Iberica de Micologia

Rev Iberoam — Revista Iberoamericana

Rev Iberoam Corros Prot — Revista Iberoamericana de Corrosion y Proteccion

Rev Iberoam Educ Quim — Revista Iberoamericana de Educacion Quimica

Rev Iberoam Lit Monte — Revista Iberoamericana de Literatura (Montevideo)

Rev Iberoam Ortod — Revista Ibero-Americana de Ortodoncia

Rev Iberoam Segur Soc — Revista Iberoamericana de Seguridad Social

Rev Iber Parasitol — Revista Iberica de Parasitologia

Rev IBPT Curitiba — Revista IBPT [*Instituto de Biologia e Pesquisas Tecnologicas*]. Curitiba
Rev IBYS — Revista. IBYS
Rev ICA — Revista ICA
Rev ICAITI — Revista ICAITI (Instituto Centroamericano de Investigacion y Tecnologia Industrial)
Rev ICIDCA — Revista. ICIDCA
Rev Ideas Estet — Revista de Ideas Esteticas
Rev IDIEM — Revista. IDIEM
RevIE — Revista de Ideas Esteticas
Review — Weekly Review
Review Coal Util Coun — Review. Journal of the Coal Utilisation Council [*London*]
Review Ethnol — Review of Ethnology
Review Inst Nucl Power Oper — Review. Institute of Nuclear Power Operations
Rev I F Pet — Revue. Institut Francais du Petrole
Rev Ig — Revista. Igiena, Bacteriologie, Virusologie, Parazitologie, Epidemiologie, Pneumoftiziologie
Rev Ig Bacteriol Virusol Parazitol Epidemiol Pneumoftiziol — Revista. Igiena, Bacteriologie, Virusologie, Parazitologie, Epidemiologie, Pneumoftiziologie
Rev Ig Bacteriol Virusol Parazitol Epidemiol Pneumoftiziol I — Revista de Igiena, Bacteriologie, Virusologie, Parazitologie, Epidemiologie, Pneumoftiziologie. Igiena
Rev Ig Soc — Revista de Igiena Sociala
Rev Illus — Revue Illustree
RevIMA — Review of Indonesian and Malayan Affairs
Rev Imagem — Revista da Imagem
Rev IMESC (Inst Med Soc Criminol Sao Paulo) — Revista. IMESC (Instituto de Medicina Social e de Criminologia de Sao Paulo)
Rev Imigr Coloniz Rio — Revista de Imigracao e Colonizacao (Rio de Janeiro)
Rev Immunoassay Technol — Reviews on Immunoassay Technology
Rev Immunogenet — Reviews in Immunogenetics
Rev Immunol — Revue d'Immunologie
Rev Immunol Ther Antimicrob — Revue d'Immunologie et de Therapie Antimicrobienne
Rev Immunopharmacol Symp — Reviews. Immunopharmacology Symposium
Rev Income Wealth — Review of Income and Wealth
RevInd — Revue Indo-Chinoise
Rev Ind — Revue Industrielle
Rev Ind Agr — Revista de Industria Agricola
Rev Ind Agric (Tucuman) — Revista Industrial y Agricola (Tucuman)
Rev Ind Aliment Prod Anim — Revista Industriei Alimentare. Produse Animale
Rev Ind Aliment Prod Veg — Revista Industriei Alimentare. Produse Vegetale
Rev Ind Anim — Revista de Industria Animal
Rev Ind Chim — Revue Hebdomadaire des Industries Chimiques
Rev Ind Elec — Revue Hebdomadaire de l'Industrie Electrique et Electronique
Rev Indep — Revue Independante
Rev Ind Fabril — Revista Industrial y Fabril
Rev Indias — Revista de Indias
Rev Indias — Revista de las Indias
Rev Indias Bogota — Revista de las Indias (Bogota)
Rev Indias Madrid — Revista de Indias (Madrid)
Rev Ind Miner — Revue de l'Industrie Minerale
Rev Ind Miner Mines — Revue de l'Industrie Minerale. Mines
Rev Indon & Malay Affairs — Review of Indonesian and Malaysian Affairs
Rev Indon & Malay Affairs — Review of Indonesian and Malayan Affairs
Rev Indones Malay Aff — Review of Indonesian and Malayan Affairs
Rev Ind S Paulo — Revista Industrial de Sao Paulo
Rev Ind Text — Revista de la Industria Textil
Rev Ind Text Eur — Revue de l'Industrie Textile Europeenne
Rev Indus Agri Tucuman — Revista Industrial y Agricola de Tucuman (Tucuman, Argentina)
Rev Industr — Revue Industrielle
Rev Industr Agric (Tucuman) — Revista Industrial y Agricola (Tucuman)
Rev Inf & Autom — Revista de Informatica y Automatica
Rev Inf Bull Leag Red Cross Socs — Review and Information Bulletin of the League of Red Cross Societies [*Geneva*]
Rev Infect Dis — Review of Infectious Diseases
Rev Infirm — Revue de l'Infirmiere
Rev Infirm Infirm Aux Que — Revue des Infirmieres et Infirmiers Auxiliaires du Quebec
Rev Inf Legis — Revista de Informacao Legislativa
Rev Inf Med — Revue d'Informatique Medicale
Rev Inform Automat — Revista de Informatica y Automatica
Rev Inform Legis Brasilia — Revista de Informacao Legislativa (Brasilia)
Rev Inform Munici BA — Revista de Informacion Municipal (Buenos Aires)
Rev Infrared Millimeter Waves — Reviews of Infrared and Millimeter Waves
Rev Ing — Revue des Ingenieurs des Ecoles Nationales Superieures des Mines
Rev Ing (Buenos Aires) — Revista de Ingenieria (Buenos Aires)
Rev Ingenieur Berlin — Revisions-Ingenieur und Gewerbe-Anwalt (Berlin)
Rev Ing Hidraul Mex — Revista Ingenieria Hidraulica en Mexico
Rev Ing Ind — Revista de Ingenieria Industrial
Rev Ing (Montevideo) — Revista de Ingenieria (Montevideo)
Rev Ing (Montreal) — Revue de l'Ingenierie (Montreal)
Rev Ing Quim — Revista de Ingenieria Quimica
Rev Ingr — Universidad Catolica Argentina. Facultad de Ciencias Fisicomatematicas e Ingenieria. Revista da Ingenieria
Rev In Haut — Revue Internationale des Hautes Temperatures et des Refractaires
Rev Inorg Chem — Reviews in Inorganic Chemistry
Rev Inst Adolfo Lutz — Revista. Instituto Adolfo Lutz
Rev Inst Agr Catalan San Isidro — Revista. Instituto Agricola Catalan de San Isidro
Rev Inst Am Arte Cuzco — Revista. Instituto Americano de Arte (Cuzco, Peru)
Rev Inst Antibiot (Recife) — Revista. Instituto de Antibioticos. Universidade Federal de Pernambuco (Recife)

Rev Inst Antibiot Univ Fed Pernambuco — Revista. Instituto de Antibioticos. Universidade Federal de Pernambuco
Rev Inst Antibiot Univ Fed Pernambuco Recife — Revista do Instituto de Antibioticos. Universidade Federal de Pernambuco (Recife)
Rev Inst Antibiot Univ Recife — Revista. Instituto de Antibioticos. Universidade do Recife
Rev Inst Antrop Cordoba — Revista. Instituto de Antropologia. (Cordoba, Argentina)
Rev Inst Antropol — Revista del Instituto de Antropologia
Rev Inst Antropol Univ Cordoba — Revista. Instituto de Antropologia. Universidad Nacional de Cordoba
Rev Inst Antrop Tucuman — Revista. Instituto de Antropologia. Universidad Nacional de Tucuman (Tucuman, Argentina)
Rev Inst Arqueol Cuzco — Revista del Instituto Arqueologico del Cuzco
Rev Inst Bacteriol Buenos Aires — Revista. Instituto Bacteriologica. Buenos Aires
Rev Inst Bacteriol Dep Nac Hig (Argent) — Revista. Instituto Bacteriologico. Departamento Nacional de Higiene (Argentina)
Rev Inst Bacteriol Dr Carlos G Malbran — Revista. Instituto Bacteriologico Dr. Carlos G. Malbran
Rev Inst Bacteriol Malbran — Revista. Instituto Bacteriologico Malbran
Rev Inst Biol Pesquis Tecnol Curitiba — Revista. Instituto de Biologia e Pesquisas Tecnologicas. Curitiba
Rev Inst B Lett Arab — Revue de l'Institut des Belles-Lettres Arabes
Rev Inst Bras Estad Unidos Rio — Revista do Instituto Brasil-Estados Unidos (Rio de Janeiro)
Rev Inst Ceara Fortaleza — Revista do Instituto do Ceara (Fortaleza, Brazil)
Rev Inst Centroam Invest Tecnol Ind — Revista. Instituto Centroamericano de Investigacion y Tecnologia Industrial
Rev Inst Colomb Agropecu — Revista. Instituto Colombiano Agropecuario
Rev Inst Cult Puertorriq S Juan — Revista. Instituto de Cultura Puertorriquena (San Juan, Puerto Rico)
Rev Inst Cult Puertorriquena — Revista del Instituto de Cultura Puertorriquena
Rev Inst Defensa Cafe S Jose — Revista. Instituto de Defensa del Cafe de Costa Rica (San Jose, Costa Rica)
Rev Inst Der Trab Invest Soc Quito — Revista. Instituto de Derecho del Trabajo y de Investigaciones Sociales (Quito)
Rev Inst Est Isl — Revista. Instituto de Estudios Islamicos
Rev Inst Estud Alicant — Revista del Instituto de Estudios Alicantinos
Rev Inst Estud Brasil — Revista do Instituto de Estudios Brasileiros
Rev Inst Estud Super Monte — Revista. Instituto de Estudios Superiores (Montevideo)
Rev Inst Etnol Nac Bogota — Revista. Instituto Etnologico Nacional (Bogota)
Rev Inst Franc Petrol — Revue. Institut Francais du Petrole
Rev Inst Fr Pet — Revue. Institut Francais du Petrole
Rev Inst Fr Pet — Revue. Institut Francais du Petrole et Annales des Combustibles Liquides[*Later, Revue. Institut Francais du Petrole*]
Rev Inst Fr Pet Ann Combust Liq — Revue. Institut Francais du Petrole et Annales des Combustibles Liquides [*Later, Revue. Institut Francais du Petrole*]
Rev Inst Geogr Geol (Sao Paulo) — Revista. Instituto Geografico e Geologico (Sao Paulo)
Rev Inst Geol Min Univ Nac Tucuman — Revista. Instituto de Geologia y Mineria. Universidad Nacional de Tucuman
Rev Inst Geol Univ Nac Auton Mex — Revista. Instituto de Geologia. Universidad Nacional Autonoma de Mexico
Rev Inst Hist Der BA — Revista. Instituto de Historia del Derecho. Universidad Nacional de Buenos Aires
Rev Inst Hist Geogr Aracaju — Revista. Instituto Historico e Geografico de Sergipe (Aracaju, Brazil)
Rev Inst Hist Geogr Bras — Revista. Instituto Historico e Geografico Brasileiro
Rev Inst Hist Geogr S Paulo — Revista. Instituto Historico e Geografico de Sao Paulo
Rev Inst Hyg Mines — Revue. Institut d'Hygiene des Mines
Rev Inst Hyg Mines (Hasselt) — Revue. Institut d'Hygiene des Mines (Hasselt)
Rev Inst Invest Econ Rosario — Revista. Instituto de Investigaciones Economicas (Rosario, Argentina)
Rev Inst Invest Ensayes Mater — Revista del Instituto de Investigaciones y Ensayes de Materiales
Rev Inst Invest Hist Univ T Frias Potosi — Revista. Instituto de Investigaciones Historicas. Universidad Tomas Frias (Potosi, Bolivia)
Rev Inst Invest Med — Revista. Instituto de Investigaciones Medicas
Rev Inst Invest Tecnol (Bogota) — Revista. Instituto de Investigaciones Tecnologicas (Bogota)
Rev Inst Laticinios Candido Tostes — Revista. Instituto de Laticinios Candido Tostes
Rev Inst Malbran — Revista. Instituto Malbran
Rev Inst Med Leg Estado Guanabara — Revista. Instituto Medico-Legal do Estado da Guanabara
Rev Inst Med Trop Sao Paulo — Revista. Instituto de Medicina Tropical de Sao Paulo
Rev Inst Mex Ing Quim — Revista del Instituto Mexicano de Ingenieros Quimicos
Rev Inst Mex Ing Quim Supl — Revista del Instituto Mexicano de Ingenieros Quimicos. Suplemento
Rev Inst Mex Pet — Revista. Instituto Mexicano del Petroleo
Rev Inst Mex Petrol — Revista. Instituto Mexicano del Petroleo
Rev Inst Munic Bot (B Aires) — Revista. Instituto Municipal de Botanica (Buenos Aires)
Rev Inst Nac Gen Frco Menendez S Salvador — Revista. Instituto Nacional General Francisco Menendez (San Salvador)
Rev Inst Nac Geol Min (Argent) — Revista. Instituto Nacional de Geologia y Mineria (Argentina)
Rev Inst Nac Hig — Revista. Instituto Nacional de Higiene
Rev Inst Nacl Cancerol (Mex) — Revista. Instituto Nacional de Cancerologia (Mexico)
Rev Inst Nac Med Leg Colomb — Revista del Instituto Nacional de Medicina Legal de Colombia

Rev Inst Nac Med Leg Colombia — Revista. Instituto Nacional de Medicina Legal de Colombia

Rev Inst Nac Tradicion BA — Revista. Instituto Nacional de la Tradicion (Buenos Aires)

Rev Inst Napoleon — Revue. Institut Napoleon

Rev Inst N Cult — Revista del Instituto Nacional de Cultura

Rev Instn Motor Engrs — Review. Institution of Motor Engineers [*London*]

Rev Inst Paraguaya — Revista del Instituto Paraguayano

Rev Inst Pasteur Lyon — Revue. Institut Pasteur de Lyon

Rev Inst Pedag Nac Caracas — Revista. Instituto Pedagogico Nacional (Caracas)

Rev Inst Rech Agron Bulg — Revue. Instituts de Recherches Agronomiques en Bulgarie

Rev Inst Rech Sci Minist Agric Bulg — Revue. Instituts de Recherches Scientifiques aupres du Ministere de l'Agriculture (Bulgaria)

Rev Inst Salubr Enferm Trop — Revista. Instituto de Salubridad y Enfermedades Tropicales

Rev Inst Salubr Enferm Trop Mexico City — Revista. Instituto de Salubridad y Enfermedades Tropicales. Mexico City

Rev Inst Sociol — Revue. Institut de Sociologie

Rev Inst Sociol Boliv Sucre — Revista. Instituto de Sociologia. Boliviana (Sucre)

Rev Inst Sociol Brussels — Revista de l'Institut de Sociologie (Brussels)

Rev Inst Tec Admin Trab Mex — Revista. Instituto Tenico Administrativo del Trabajo (Mexico)

Rev Inst Tech Roubaisien — Revue Institut Technique Roubaisien

Rev Int — Revista Internacional

Rev Int A & Curiosite — Revue Internationale de l'Art et de la Curiosite

Rev Int Aff — Review of International Affairs

Rev Int Agric — Revista International de Agricultura

Rev Int Appl Gaz — Revue Internationale des Applications du Gaz

Rev Int Biol Prog — Review. International Biological Programme

Rev Int Bois — Revue Internationale du Bois

Rev Int Bois Mater Premieres Veg — Revue Internationale du Bois et des Materieres Premieres Vegetales

Rev Int Bois Matieres Premieres Prod Ind Origine Veg — Revue Internationale du Bois et des Matieres Premieres et Produits Industriels d'Origine Vegetale

Rev Int Bot Appl Agric Trop — Revue Internationale de Botanique Appliquee et d'Agriculture Tropicale

Rev Int Brass Malt — Revue Internationale de Brasserie et de Malterie

Rev Int Choc — Revue Internationale de la Chocolaterie

Rev Int Commission of Jurists — Review. International Commission of Jurists

Rev Int Conc — Revue Internationale de la Concurrence

Rev Int Contam Ambiental — Revista Internacional de Contaminacion Ambiental

Rev Int Coop — Review of International Cooperation

Rev Int Crim — Revue Internationale du Criminalistique

Rev Int Criminol Police Tech — Revue Internationale de Criminologie et de Police Technique

Rev Int Doc — Revue Internationale de la Documentation

Rev Integr Temas Mat — Revista Integracion. Temas de Matematicas

Rev Int Ens — Revue Internationale de l'Enseignement

Rev Interam Educ Bogota — Revista Interamericana de Educacion (Bogota)

Rev Interamer Cienc Soc — Revista Interamericana de Ciencias Sociales

Rev Interam Min Publ S Paulo — Revista Interamericana do Ministerio Publico (Sao Paulo)

Rev Interam Radiol — Revista Interamericana de Radiologia

Rev Inter B — Revista Interamericana de Bibliografia

Rev Interchem Corp — Review. Interchemical Corporation [*New York*]

Rev Internac Metod Numer Calc Disen Ingr — Revista Internacional de Metodos Numericos para Calculo y Diseno en Ingenieria

Rev Internac y Diplom — Revista Internacional y Diplomatica. Publicacion Mensual

Rev Internat de Droit Compare — Revue Internationale de Droit Compare. Continuation du Bulletin de la Societe de Legislation Comparee

Rev Internat de Droit Penal — Revue Internationale de Droit Penal. Bulletin de l'Association Internationale de Droit Penal

Rev Internat Droits Antiquite — Revue Internationale des Droits de l'Antiquite

Rev Internat Franc du Droit des Gens — Revue Internationale Francaise du Droit des Gens

Rev Internat Hist Milit — Revue Internationale d'Histoire Militaire

Rev Internat Hist Polit Constitut — Revue Internationale d'Histoire Politique et Constitutionelle

Rev Internat Onomast — Revue Internationale d'Onomastique

Rev Internat Philos — Revue Internationale de Philosophie

Rev Internat Sci Adm — Revue Internationale des Sciences Administratives

Rev Intern Crim et Pol Tech — Revue Internationale de Criminologie et de Police Technique

Rev Intern Def Soc — Revue Internationale de Defense Sociale

Rev Intern Dr Ant — Revue Internationale des Droits de l'Antiquite

Rev Intern Dr Comp — Revue Internationale de Droit Compare

Rev Intern Dr Pen — Revue Internationale de Droit Penal

Rev Intern Enseign — Revue Internationale de l'Enseignement

Rev Intern Not — Revue Internationale du Notariat

Rev Intern Pol Crim — Revue Internationale de Police Criminelle

Rev Intern Sc Adm — Revue Internationale des Sciences Administratives

Rev Intern Trab — Revista Internacional del Trabajo

Rev Intern Trav — Revue Internationale du Travail

Rev Int Falsif — Revue Internationale des Falsifications

Rev Int Falsif Anal Matieres Aliment — Revue Internationale des Falsifications et d'Analyse des Matieres Alimentaires

Rev Int Hautes Temp et Refract — Revue Internationale des Hautes Temperatures et des Refractaires

Rev Int Hautes Temp Refract — Revue Internationale des Hautes Temperatures et des Refractaires

Rev Int Heliotech — Revue Internationale d'Heliotechnique

Rev Int Hepatol — Revue Internationale d'Hepatologie

Rev Int Hist Banque — Revue Internationale d'Histoire de la Banque

Rev Int Hist Milit — Revue Internationale de l'Histoire Militaire

Rev Int Hist Psychiat — Revue Internationale d'Histoire de la Psychiatrie

Rev Int Ind Agric — Revue Internationale des Industries Agricoles

Rev Int Ind Min Metall Electrotherm Electrochim — Revue Internationale des Industries Minieres, Metallurgiques, Electrothermiques, et Electrochimiques

Rev Int'l Comm Jurists — Review. International Commission of Jurists

Rev Int'l des Droits de l'Antiquite — Revue Internationale des Droits de l'Antiquite

Rev Int'l Dr Auteur — Revue Internationale du Droit d'Auteur

Rev Int'l Droit Comp — Revue Internationale de Droit Compare

Rev Int'l Dr Penal — Revue Internationale de Droit Penal

Rev Int Mus — Revue Internationale de Musique

Rev Int Oceanogr Med — Revue Internationale d'Oceanographie Medicale

Rev Int Pediatr — Revue Internationale de Pediatrie

Rev Int Ph — Revue Internationale de Philosophie

Rev Int Pharm — Revue Internationale de Pharmacie

Rev Int Phil — Revue Internationale de Philosophie

Rev Int Philos — Revue Internationale de Philosophie

Rev Int Prod Colon Mater Colon — Revue Internationale des Produits Coloniaux et du Materiel Colonial

Rev Int Prod Trop Mater Trop — Revue Internationale des Produits Tropicaux et du Materiel Tropical

Rev Int Psy — Revue Internationale de Psychologie Appliquee

Rev Int Rech Readapt — Revue Internationale de Recherches en Readaptation

Rev Int Renseign Agric — Revue Internationale de Renseignements Agricoles

Rev Int Sc — Revista Internazionale di Scienze Economiche e Commerciali

Rev Int Sci — Revue International des Sciences

Rev Int Serv Sante Armees — Revue Internationale des Services de Sante des Armees de Terre, de Mer, et de l'Air

Rev Int Serv Sante Armees Terre Mer Air — Revue Internationale des Services de Sante des Armees de Terre, de Mer, et de l'Air

Rev Int Soja — Revue Internationale du Soja

Rev Int Tab — Revue Internationale des Tabacs

Rev Int Trach — Revue Internationale du Trachome

Rev Int Trach Pathol Oculaire Trop Subtrop Sante Publique — Revue Internationale du Trachome et de Pathologie Oculaire Tropicale et Subtropicale et de Sante Publique

Rev Int Trach Pathol Ocul Trop Subtrop — Revue Internationale du Trachome et de Pathologie Oculaire Tropicale et Subtropicale

Rev Int Trach Pathol Ocul Trop Subtrop Sante Publique — Revue Internationale de Trachome et de Pathologie Oculaire Tropicale et Subtropicale et de Sante Publique

Rev Inv Cli — Revista de Investigacion Clinica

Rev Invest — Revista de Investigacion

Rev Invest Agr — Revista de Investigaciones Agricolas

Rev Invest Agric — Revista de Investigaciones Agricolas

Rev Invest Agropec Ser — Revista de Investigaciones Agropecuarias. Serie

Rev Invest Agropecuar Ser 2 — Revista de Investigaciones Agropecuarias. Serie 2. Biologia y Produccion Vegetal

Rev Invest Agropecu Ser 5 — Revista de Investigaciones Agropecuarias. Serie 5. Patologia Vegetal

Rev Invest Agropecu Ser 1 — Revista de Investigaciones Agropecuarias. Serie 1. Biologia y Produccion Animal

Rev Invest Agropecu Ser 1 Biol Prod Anim — Revista de Investigaciones Agropecuarias. Serie 1. Biologia y Produccion Animal

Rev Invest Agropecu Ser 2 Biol Prod Veg — Revista de Investigaciones Agropecuarias. Serie 2. Biologia y Produccion Vegetal

Rev Invest Agropecu Ser 3 — Revista de Investigaciones Agropecuarias. Serie 3. Clima y Suelo

Rev Invest Agropecu Ser 3 Clima Suelo — Revista de Investigaciones Agropecuarias. Serie 3. Clima y Suelo

Rev Invest Agropecu Ser 4 — Revista de Investigaciones Agropecuarias. Serie 4. Patologia Animal

Rev Invest Agropecu Ser 4 Patol Anim — Revista de Investigaciones Agropecuarias. Serie 4. Patologia Animal

Rev Invest Agropecu Ser 5 Patol Veg — Revista de Investigaciones Agropecuarias. Serie 5. Patologia Vegetal

Rev Invest Agropecu Ser 6 — Revista de Investigaciones Agropecuarias. Serie 6. Economia y Administracion Rural

Rev Invest Clin — Revista de Investigacion Clinica

Rev Invest Desarrollo Pesq — Revista de Investigacion y Desarrollo Pesquero

Rev Invest For — Revista de Investigaciones Forestales

Rev Invest Ganad — Revista de Investigaciones Ganaderas

Rev Invest Inst Nac Pesca — Revista de Investigaciones. Instituto Nacional de la Pesca

Rev Invest Mar — Revista de Investigaciones Marinas

Rev Invest Salud Publica — Revista de Investigacion en Salud Publica

Rev Invest Univ Guadalajara (Mex) — Revista de Investigacion. Universidad de Guadalajara (Mexico)

Rev Ion — Revista Ion

RevIP — Revue Internationale de la Philosophie

Rev I Psych — Revue Internationale de Psychologie Appliquee

Rev Irb Rio — Revista do IRB [*Instituto de Resseguros do Brasil*] Ministerio da Industria e Comercio (Rio de Janeiro)

Rev IRE — Revue. IRE

Rev Iron Steel Lit — Review of Iron and Steel Literature [*Pittsburgh*]

Rev Irrig India — Review of Irrigation in India [*Simla*]

Revision Hist Tucuman — Revision Historica (Tucuman, Argentina)

Revisionsing Gewerbeanw — Revisionsingenieur und Gewerbeanwalt [*Berlin*]

Rev I Soc — Revue. Institut de Sociologie

Revisorbl — Revisorbladet

Rev Ist — Revista de Istorie

Revista ABM — Revista de Archivos, Bibliotecas, y Museos

Revista Acad Ci Exact Zaragoza — Revista de Academia de Ciencias Exactas, Fisico-Quimicas y Naturales de Zaragoza

Revista Agric Cochabamba — Revista de Agricultura/Universidad Autonoma Simon Bolivar. Escuela Superior de Agronomia (Cochabamba)

Revista Agric Comercio Panama — Revista de Agricultura y Comercio/Panama. Ministerio de Agricultura y Comercio

Revista Agric Cub — Revista de Agricultura Cubana

Revista Agric Ganad Asuncion Minist Agric — Revista de Agricultura y Ganaderia/Paraguay. Ministerio de Agricultura

Revista Agric Ganad Buenos Aires — Revista de Agricultura y Ganaderia (Buenos Aires)

Revista Agric Ganad Nicarag — Revista de Agricultura y Ganaderia Nicaraguense/Liberia Moderna

Revista Agric Guatemala City — Revista Agricola (Guatemala City)

Revista Agric Piracicaba — Revista de Agricultura (Piracicaba)

Revista Agric Puerto Rico — Revista de Agricultura de Puerto Rico

Revista Agric Santiago — Revista de Agricultura (Santiago)

Revista Agric Sao Paulo — Revista Agricola (Sao Paulo)

Revista Agric Trop Mexico City — Revista de Agricultura Tropical/Review of Tropical Agriculture (Mexico City)

Revista Agric Veterin Olinda — Revista Agricolo-Veterinaria (Olinda)

Revista Agron Lisbon — Revista Agronomica/Sociedade de Sciencias Agronomicas de Portugal (Lisbon)

Revista Agropecu — Revista Agropecuaria

Revista Agroquim Tecnol Aliment — Revista de Agroquimica y Tecnologia de Alimentos/Instituto de Quimica

Revista Asoc Med Argent — Revista. Asociacion Medica Argentina

Revista Biol Trop — Revista de Biologia Tropical/Universidad Nacional

Revista Brasil Geogr — Revista Brasileira de Geografia/Conselho Nacional de Geografia. Instituto Brasileiro de Geografia e Estatistica

Revista Caball — Revista de Caballeria

Revista Cafe — Revista del Cafe

Revista Centro Estud Doct Ci Nat — Revista. Centro de Estudiantes del Doctorado en Ciencias Naturales

Revista Centro Nac Agric — Revista del Centro Nacional de Agricultura

Revista CF — Revista Colombiana de Folclor

Revista Chilena Hist Nat — Revista Chilena de Historia Natural

Revista Ci Buenos Aires — Revista Cientifica/Instituto Cientifico Argentina (Buenos Aires)

Revista Ci Letras — Revista de Ciencias i Letras

Revista Ci Lit Mexico — Revista Cientifica y Literaria de Mexico

Revista Ci Nat Madrid — Revista di Ciencias Naturales de Madrid

Revista Cons Oceanogr Ibero Amer — Revista del Consejo Oceanografico Ibero-Americana

Revista Esp Biol — Revista Espanola de Biologia

Revista Fac Agron Univ Nac La Plata — Revista. Facultad de Agronomia. Universidad Nacional de La Plata

Revista Fac Agron Univ Rio Grande Do Sul — Revista da Faculdade de Agronomia e Veterinaria da Universidade do Rio Grande do Sul

Revista Fac Ci Univ Lisboa Ser 2 C Ci Nat — Revista da Faculdade de Ciencias, Universidade de Lisboa. Ser. 2. C. Ciencias Naturais

Revista Fac Nac Agron Medellin Univ Antioquia — Revista. Facultad Nacional de Agronomia. Medellin Universidad de Antioquia

Revista Farm — Revista Farmaceutica/Associacion Farmaceutica y Bioquimica Argentina

Revista Filol Esp — Revista de Filologia Espanola

Revista Fomento — Revista de Fomento/Venezuela. Ministerio del Fomento

Revista Forest Chilena — Revista Forestal Chilena

Revista Geogr Mexico City — Revista Geografica [*Instituto Panamericano de Geografia i Historia*] (Mexico City)

Revista Guimaraes — Revista de Guimaraes

Revista Inst Agric Catalan San Isidro — Revista. Instituto Agricola Catalan de San Isidro/Servicio Sindical de Alta Cultura Agricola

Revista Inst Antibiot — Revista do Instituto de Antibioticos/Universidade de Recife

Revista Inst Defensa Cafe — Revista. Instituto de Defensa del Cafe

Revista Inst Nac Cafe — Revista. Instituto Nacional del Cafe

Revista Inst Nac Invest Ci Nat Ci Bot — Revista del Instituto Nacional de Investigacion de las Ciencias Naturales Anexoal Museo Argentino de Ciencias Naturales Bernardino Rivadavia. Ciencias Botanicas

Revista Inst Nac Invest Ci Nat Ci Geol — Revista. Instituto Nacional de Investigacion de las Ciencias Naturales Anexo. Museo Argentino de Ciencias Naturales Bernardino Rivadavia. Ciencias Geologicas

Revista Interamer Bibliogr — Revista Interamericana de Bibliografia/Pan American Union

Revista Invest Agric — Revista de Investigaciones Agricolas

Revista Invest Forest — Revista de Investigaciones Forestales/Argentina. Administracion Nacional de Bosques

Revista Invest Salud Publica — Revista de Investigacion en Salud Publica

Revista Litt — Revist Litteraria. Periodico de Litteratura, Philosophia, Viagem, Eciencias e Bellas Artes

Revista Med Latino Amer — Revista Medica Latino-Americana

Revista Med Militar Oporto — Revista de Medicina Militar (Oporto)

Revista Med Uruguay — Revista Medica del Uruguay

Revista Mex — Revista Mexicana. Periodico Cientifico y Literario

Revista Minist Agric — Revista. Ministerio de Agricultura

Revista Mus La Plata Secc Bot — Revista del Museo de La Plata. Seccion Botanica

Revista Oto Laringol Sao Paulo — Revista Oto-Laringologica de Sao Paulo

Revista Paul Med — Revista Paulista de Medicina

Revista Progr Ci Exact — Revista de los Progresos de las Ciencias Exactas, Fisicas, y Naturales

Revista Soc Agron Para — Revista. Sociedade dos Agronomos e Veterinarios do Para

Revista Soc Mex Hist Nat — Revista de la Sociedad Mexicana de Historia Natural

Revista Soc Quim Mexico — Revista. Sociedad Quimica de Mexico

Revista Sudamer Morfol — Revista Sudamericana de Morfologia

Revista Trimensal Hist Geogr — Revista Trimensal de Historia e Geografia/Jornal. Instituto Historico, Geografico, e Ethnografico do Brazil

Revista Univ Costa Rica — Revista. Universidad de Costa Rica

Revista Uruguaya Dermatol Sifilogr — Revista Uruguaya de Dermatologia y Sifilografia

Revista Vinic Agric — Revista Vinicola y de Agricultura

Rev It Mus — Revista Italiana di Musicologia

Rev Ivoirienne de Droit — Revue Ivoirienne de Droit

Rev Japan Cem Engng Ass — Review. Japan Cement Engineering Association [*Tokyo*]

Rev Jard — Revue des Jardins

Rev Jard Bot Nac — Revista. Jardin Botanico Nacional

Rev Javer Bogota — Revista Javeriana (Bogota)

Rev J de P — Revue des Justices de Paix

Rev Jeumont-Schneider — Revue Jeumont-Schneider

Rev JFF — Revue Juridique, Fiscale, et Financiere

Rev J Phil Soc Sci — Review Journal of Philosophy and Social Science

Rev Junt Estud Hist Mendoza — Revista. Junta de Estudios Historicos (Mendoza, Argentina)

Rev Junt Hist Letr La Rioja — Revista. Junta de Historia y Letras (La Rioja, Argentina)

Rev Jur — Revista Juridica

Rev Jur Arg BA — Revista Juridica Argentina (Buenos Aires)

Rev Jur BA — Revista Juridica de Buenos Aires

Rev Jur Cochabamba — Revista Juridica (Cochabamba, Bolivia)

Rev Jur Congo — Revue Juridique du Congo Belge

Rev Jur d'Alsace et de Lorraine — Revue Juridique d'Alsace et de Lorraine

Rev Jur de Buenos Aires — Revista Juridica de Buenos Aires

Rev Jur de la Univ de Puerto Rico — Revista Juridica. Universidad de Puerto Rico

Rev Jur del Peru — Revista Juridica del Peru

Rev Jur Dom C Trujillo — Revista Juridica Dominicana (Ciudad, Trujillo)

Rev Jur du Congo — Revue Juridique du Congo

Rev Jur Fisc Fin — Revue Juridique, Fiscale, et Financiere

Rev Juridique de Madagascar — Revue Juridique de Madagascar

Rev Jur Polit Un Fr — Revue Juridique et Politique de l'Union Francaise

Rev Jur Rio Piedras — Revista Juridica (Rio Piedras, Puerto Rico)

Rev Jur Themis — Revue Juridique Themis

Rev Jur Tucuman — Revista Juridica (Tucuman, Argentina)

Rev Jur U Inter PR — Revista Juridica. Universidad Interamericana de Puerto Rico

Rev Jur UPR — Revista Juridica. Universidad de Puerto Rico

Rev Kobe Univ Merc Mar Part 2 — Review. Kobe University of Mercantile Marine. Part 2

Rev Kobe Univ Merc Mar Part 2 Marit Stud Sci Eng — Review. Kobe University of Mercantile Marine. Part 2. Maritime Studies, and Science and Engineering

Rev Kuba Med Trop Parasitol — Revista Kuba de Medicina Tropical y Parasitologia

RevL — Revista de Letras

RevLA — Revista de Letras (Assis)

Rev Lampara — Revista Lampara

Rev Lang R — Revue des Langues Romanes

Rev Lang V — Revue des Langues Vivantes/Tijdschrift voor Levende Talen

Rev Lang Viv — Revue des Langues Vivantes

Rev La Plata — Revista de La Plata

Rev Laryngol Otol Rhinol — Revue de Laryngologie, Otologie, Rhinologie

Rev Laryngol Otol Rhinol (Bord) — Revue de Laryngologie, Otologie, Rhinologie (Bordeaux)

Rev Laryngol Otol Rhino Suppl — Revue de Laryngologie, Otologie, Rhinologie. Supplement

Rev Laser Eng — Review of Laser Engineering

Rev Latam Microbiol — Revista Latinoamericana de Microbiologia

Rev Latam P — Revista Latinoamericana de Psicologia

Rev Latam Patol — Revista Latinoamericana de Patologia

Rev Lat Am Psiquiat — Revista Latinoamericana de Psiquiatria

Rev Latin de Filosof — Revista Latinoamericana de Filosofia

Rev Latinoam Anat Patol — Revista Latinoamericana de Anatomia Patologica

Rev Latinoam Cienc Agric — Revista Latinoamericana de Ciencias Agricolas

Rev Latinoam Cir Plast — Revista Latinoamericana de Cirurgia Plastica

Rev Latinoam Ing Quim Quim Apl — Revista Latinoamericana de Ingenieria Quimica y Quimica Aplicada

Rev Latinoam Microbiol — Revista Latinoamericana de Microbiologia

Rev Latinoam Microbiol Parasitol — Revista Latinoamericana de Microbiologia y Parasitologia [*Later, Revista Latinoamericana de Microbiologia*]

Rev Latinoam Microbiol Supl — Revista Latinoamericana de Microbiologia. Suplemento

Rev Latinoam Patol — Revista Latinoamericana de Patologia

Rev Latinoam Psicol — Revista Latinoamericana de Psicologia

Rev Latinoam Quim — Revista Latinoamericana de Quimica

Rev Latinoam Sider — Revista Latinoamericana de Siderurgia

Rev Latinoam Sociol BA — Revista Latinoamericana de Sociologia (Instituto Di Tella, Buenos Aires)

Rev Leg — Revue de Legislation et de Jurisprudence

Rev Leg — Revue Legale

Rev Legale — Revue Legale

Rev Leg NS — Revue Legale. New Series

Rev Leg (OS) — Revue Legale (Old Series)

Rev Leprol Dermatol Sifilogr — Revista de Leprologia, Dermatologia, y Sifilografia

Rev Leprol Sao Paulo — Revista de Leprologia de Sao Paulo

Rev Lett Mod — Revue des Lettres Modernes

Rev Lettr Mod — Revue des Lettres Modernes

RevLi — Revue Libre

Rev Liberale — Revue Liberale

Rev Ling Rom — Revue de Linguistique Romane

Rev Linguist Philol Compar — Revue de Linguistique et de Philologie Comparee

Rev Lit — Revista de Literatura

Rev Lit — Revue de Litterature Comparee

Rev Lit Arg Iberoam Mendoza — Revista de Literatura Argentina e Iberoamericana (Mendoza, Argentina)

Rev Lit Comp — Revue de Litterature Comparee
Rev Litigation — Review of Litigation
Rev Lit Madrid — Revista de Literatura (Madrid)
Rev Litt & A — Revue Litteraire et Artistique
Rev Litt Comp — Revue de Litterature Comparee
Rev Livro — Revista do Livro
RevLM — Revista de Literaturas Modernas
Rev Lorraine Ill — Revue Lorraine Illustree
Rev Loteria — Revista Loteria
Rev Louvre — Revue du Louvre et des Musees de France
RevLR — Revista do Livro (Rio)
RevLR — Revue de Linguistique Romane
Rev Lyceum Hav — Revista Lyceum (La Habana)
Rev Lyon — Revue du Lyonnais
Rev Lyon Med — Revue Lyonnaise de Medecine
RevM — Revista (Madrid)
Rev M — Revue de la Mecanique
Rev M — Revue M
Rev Mabillon — Revue Mabillon
Rev Macromol Chem — Reviews in Macromolecular Chemistry
Rev Madagascar — Revue de Madagascar
Rev Madeira (Sao Paulo) — Revista da Madeira (Sao Paulo)
Rev Maestro Guat — Revista del Maestro (Guatemala)
Rev Maghrebine Math — Revue Maghrebine de Mathematiques
Rev Maigret — Revue Henri Maigret
Rev Mal Respir — Revue des Maladies Respiratoires
Rev Marina Callao — Revista de Marina (Callao, Peru)
Rev Marit — Revue Maritime
Rev Mark Agric Econ — Review of Marketing and Agricultural Economics
Rev Market Agric Econ — Review of Marketing and Agricultural Economics
Rev Market Agric Econ (Sydney) — Review of Marketing and Agricultural Economics (Sydney)
Rev Market & Ag Econ — Review of Marketing and Agricultural Economics
Rev Marketing Agr Econ — Review of Marketing and Agricultural Economics
Rev Marq Parfum Savonn — Revue des Marques de la Parfumerie et de la Savonnerie
Rev Marques Parfums Fr — Revue des Marques des Parfums de France
Rev Marseille — Revue Marseille
Rev Mat Apl — Revista de Matematicas Aplicadas
Rev Mat Dominicana — Revista Matematica Dominicana
Rev Mater Constr Trav Publics — Revue des Materiaux de Construction et de Travaux Publics
Rev Mater Constr Trav Publics Ed B — Revue des Materiaux de Construction et de Travaux Publics. Edition B. Brique, Tuile, Ceramique
Rev Mat Estatist — Revista de Matematica e Estatistica
Rev Mat Hisp-Amer — Revista Matematica Hispano-Americana
Rev Mat Hisp-Amer 4 — Revista Matematica Hispano-Americana. Serie 4
Rev Math Phys — Reviews in Mathematical Physics
Rev Math Phys — Revue de Mathematiques et de Physique
Rev Math Pures Appl — Revue de Mathematiques Pures et Appliquees
Rev Mat Iberoamericana — Revista Matematica Iberoamericana
Rev Mat Univ Complut Madrid — Revista Matematica de la Universidad Complutense de Madrid
Rev MBLE — Revue MBLE
RevMe — Review of Metaphysics
Rev Mecan — Revue de la Mecanique
Rev Mec Appl — Revue de Mecanique Appliquee
Rev Mec Tijdsch — Revue Mecanique Tijdschrift
Rev Med — Revista de Medicina
Rev Med — Revista Medica
Rev Med — Revista Medicala
Rev Med Accidents Mal Prof — Revue de Medecine des Accidents et des Maladies Professionnelles
Rev Med Accid Mal Prof — Revue de Medecine des Accidents et des Maladies Professionnelles
Rev Med Aero — Revista Medica da Aeronautica
Rev Med Aeronaut — Revista Medica da Aeronautica
Rev Med Aeronaut (Paris) — Revue de Medecine Aeronautique (Paris) [Later, Medecine Aeronautique et Spatial - Medecine Subaquatique et Hyperbare]
Rev Med Aeronaut Spat — Revue de Medecine Aeronautique et Spatiale [Later, Medecine Aeronautique et Spatial - Medecine Subaquatique et Hyperbare]
Rev Med Aeronaut Spat Med Subaquat Hyperbare — Revue de Medecine Aeronautique et Spatiale - Medecine Subaquatique et Hyperbare
Rev Med Aliment — Revista de Medicina y Alimentacion
Rev Med Angola — Revista Medica de Angola
Rev Med ATM — Revista de Medicina. ATM
Rev Med Bahia — Revista Medica de Bahia
Rev Med Bogota — Revista Medica de Bogota
Rev Med Bras — Revista Medica Brasileira
Rev Med Brux — Revue Medicale de Bruxelles
Rev Med Bruxelles — Revue Medicale de Bruxelles
Rev Med Brux Nouv Ser — Revue Medicale de Bruxelles. Nouvelle Serie
Rev Med Chi — Revista Medica de Chile
Rev Med Chil — Revista Medica de Chile
Rev Med Chile — Revista Medica de Chile
Rev Med Chir — Revista Medico-Chirurgicala
Rev Med Chir — Revue Medico-Chirurgicale
Rev Med-Chir (Iasi) — Revue Medico-Chirurgicale (Iasi)
Rev Med-Chir Mal Foie — Revue Medico-Chirurgicale des Maladies du Foie
Rev Med-Chir Mal Foie Rate Pancreas — Revue Medico-Chirurgicale des Maladies du Foie, de la Rate, et du Pancreas
Rev Med-Chir Soc Med Nat din Iasi — Revista Medico-Chirurgicala. Societatii de Medici si Naturalisti din Iasi
Rev Med-Chir Soc Med Nat Iasi — Revista Medico-Chirurgicala. Societatii de Medici si Naturalisti din Iasi

Rev Med Cienc Afines — Revista de Medicina y Ciencias Afines
Rev Med Cir Habana — Revista de Medicina y Cirugia de La Habana
Rev Med Cir Sao Paulo — Revista de Medicina e Cirurgia de Sao Paulo
Rev Med Cirurg Brasil — Revista Medico-Cirurgica do Brasil
Rev Med Cordoba — Revista Medica de Cordoba
Rev Med Costa Rica — Revista Medica de Costa Rica
Rev Med Cubana — Revista Medica Cubana
Rev Med de S Paulo — Revista Medica de Sao Paulo
Rev Med Dijon — Revue Medicale de Dijon
Rev Med d Rosario — Revista Medica del Rosario
Rev Med Est — Revue Medicale de l'Est
Rev Med Estado Guanabara — Revista Medica do Estado da Guanabara
Rev Med Estado Rio De J — Revista Medica do Estado do Rio De Janeiro
Rev Med Estud Gen Navarro — Revista de Medicina del Estudio General de Navarro
Rev Med Exp — Revista de Medicina Experimental
Rev Med Exp (Lima) — Revista de Medicina Experimental (Lima)
Rev Med Fr — Revue Medicale Francaise
Rev Med Galicia — Revista Medica de Galicia
Rev Med (Hanoi) — Revue Medicale (Hanoi)
Rev Med Hondur — Revista Medica Hondurena
Rev Med Hosp Cent Empl (Lima) — Revista Medica. Hospital Central del Empleado (Lima)
Rev Med Hosp Colon — Revista Medica. Hospital Colonia
Rev Med Hosp Colon (Mex) — Revista Medica. Hospital Colonia (Mexico)
Rev Med Hosp Ernesto Dornelles — Revista de Medicina. Hospital Ernesto Dornelles
Rev Med Hosp Esp — Revista Medica. Hospital Espanol
Rev Med Hosp Gen (Mex) — Revista Medica. Hospital General (Mexico)
Rev Med Hosp Gen (Mexico City) — Revista Medica. Hospital General (Mexico City)
Rev Med Hosp Obrero — Revista Medica. Hospital Obrero
Rev Med Hosp Servidores Estado — Revista Medica. Hospital dos Servidores do Estado
Rev Med HSE — Revista Medica. Hospital dos Servidores do Estado
Rev Med Inst Mex Seguro Soc — Revista Medica. Instituto Mexicano del Seguro Social
Rev Med Inst Previdencia Serv Estado Minas Gerais — Revista Medica. Instituto de Previdencia dos Servidores do Estado de Minas Gerais
Rev Med Inst Previdencia Servidores Estado Minas Gerais — Revista Medica. Instituto de Previdencia dos Servidores do Estado de Minas Gerais
Rev Med Interna Med Interna — Revista de Medicina Interna, Neurologie, Psihiatrie, Neurochirurgie, Dermato-Venerologie. Seria Medicina Interna
Rev Med Interna Neurol Psihiatr — Revista de Medicina Interna, Neurologie, Psihiatrie, Neurochirurgie, Dermato-Venerologie. Neurologie, Psihiatrie, Neurochirurgie
Rev Med Interna Neurol Psihiatr Neurochir Dermato — Revista de Medicina-Interna, Neurologie, Psihiatrie, Neurochirurgie, Dermato-Venerologie. Seria Medicina Interna
Rev Med Interna Neurol Psihiatr Neurochir Dermato-Venerol — Revista de Medicina Interna, Neurologie, Psihiatrie, Neurochirurgie, Dermato-Venerologie
Rev Med Interne — Revue de Medecine Interne
Rev Med Int Photo Cinema Telev — Revue Medicale Internationale de Photo, Cinema, Television
Rev Mediterranee — Revue de la Mediterranee
Rev Mediterr Sci Med — Revue Mediterraneenne des Sciences Medicales
Rev Med Juiz de Fora — Revista Medica de Juiz de Fora
Rev Med Leg Colomb — Revista de Medicina Legal de Colombia
Rev Med Liege — Revue Medicale de Liege
Rev Med Liege Suppl — Revue Medicale de Liege. Supplement
Rev Med Limoges — Revue de Medecine de Limoges
Rev Med Limousin — Revue de Medecine du Limousin
Rev Med Louvain — Revue Medicale de Louvain
Rev Med Mil — Revista de Medicina Militar
Rev Med Min — Revue Medicale Miniere
Rev Med Miniere — Revue Medicale Miniere
Rev Med Mocambique — Revista Medica de Mocambique
Rev Med Moyen-Orient — Revue Medicale du Moyen-Orient
Rev Med Nancy — Revue Medicale de Nancy
Rev Med Nav — Revue de Medecine Navale (Metropole et Outre-Mer)
Rev Med Normandes — Revues Medicales Normandes
Rev Med Panama — Revista Medica de Panama
Rev Med Parag — Revista Medica del Paraguay
Rev Med (Paris) — Revue de Medecine (Paris)
Rev Med Paris — Revue Medicale (Paris)
Rev Med Pharmacol — Review of Medical Pharmacology
Rev Med Prev — Revue de Medecine Preventive
Rev Med Psychosomat Psychol Med — Revue de Medecine Psychosomatique et de Psychologie Medicale
Rev Med PUCRS — Revista de Medicina da PUCRS
Rev Med Quir Asoc Med Hosp Rivadavia — Revista Medico-Quirurgica. Asociacion Medica. Hospital Rivadavia
Rev Med-Quir (Buenos Aires) — Revista Medico-Quirurgica (Buenos Aires)
Rev Med Quir Patol Femenina — Revista Medico-Quirurgica de Patologia Femenina
Rev Med Quir Teguelgalpa — Revista Medico-Quirurgica Teguelgalpa
Rev Med Rio Grande Do Sul — Revista de Medicina do Rio Grande Do Sul
Rev Med Rosario — Revista Medica del Rosario
Rev Med (Sao Paulo) — Revista de Medicina (Sao Paulo)
Rev Med Sevilla — Revista Medica de Sevilla
Rev Med Suisse Romande — Revue Medicale de la Suisse Romande
Rev Med (Tirgu-Mures) — Revista Medicala (Tirgu-Mures)
Rev Med Toulouse — Revue de Medecine de Toulouse
Rev Med Toulouse Suppl — Revue de Medecine de Toulouse. Supplement
Rev Med Tours — Revue de Medecine de Tours

Rev Med Tours — Revue Medicale de Tours
Rev Med Trav — Revue de Medecine du Travail
Rev Med Trop — Revista de Medicina Tropical
Rev Med Univ Fed Ceara — Revista de Medicina. Universidade Federal do Ceara
Rev Med Univ Montr — Revue Medicale. Universite de Montreal
Rev Med Univ Navarra — Revista de Medicina. Universidad de Navarra
Rev Med Uruguay — Revista Medica del Uruguay
Rev Med (Valparaiso) — Revista de Medicina (Valparaiso)
Rev Med Veracruz — Revista Medica Veracruzana
Rev Med Vet — Revista de Medicina Veterinaria
Rev Med Vet — Revue de Medecine Veterinaire
Rev Med Vet (B Aires) — Revista de Medicina Veterinaria (Buenos Aires)
Rev Med Vet (Bogota) — Revista de Medicina Veterinaria (Bogota)
Rev Med Vet Escuela Montevideo — Revista de Medicina Veterinaria. Escuela de Montevideo
Rev Med Vet (Montev) — Revista de Medicina Veterinaria (Montevideo)
Rev Med Vet Mycol — Review of Medical and Veterinary Mycology
Rev Med Vet Parasit — Revista de Medicina Veterinaria y Parasitologia
Rev Med Vet Parasitol (Maracay) — Revista de Medicina Veterinaria y Parasitologia (Maracay)
Rev Med Vet (Santiago) — Revista de Medicina Veterinaria (Santiago)
Rev Med Vet (Sao Paulo) — Revista de Medicina Veterinaria (Sao Paulo)
Rev Med Vet (Toulouse) — Revue de Medecine Veterinaire (Toulouse)
Rev Med Virol — Reviews in Medical Virology
Rev Med y Cirug (Caracas) — Revista de Medicina y Cirugia (Caracas)
Rev Med y Cirug Habana — Revista de Medicina y Cirugia de La Habana
Rev Med Yucatan — Revista Medica de Yucatan
Rev Mens Asoc Rural Urug — Revista Mensual. Asociacion Rural del Uruguay
Rev Mens Blanchissage Blanchiment Apprets — Revue Mensuelle de Blanchissage, du Blanchiment, et des Apprets
Rev Mens Ecole Anthropol — Revue Mensuelle. Ecole d'Anthropologie de Paris
Rev Mens Mal Enf — Revue Mensuelle des Maladies de l'Enfance
Rev Mens Med Cirug — Revista Mensual de Medicina e Cirugia
Rev Mens Pediat — Revue Mensuelle de Pediatrie
Rev Mens Sui Odont — Revue Mensuelle Suisse d'Odontologie
Rev Mens Suisse Odonto-Stomatol — Revue Mensuelle Suisse d'Odonto-Stomatologie
Rev Metal — Revista de Metalurgia
Rev Metall — Revue de Metallurgie
Rev Metall Cah Inf Tech — Revue de Metallurgie. Cahiers d'Informations Techniques
Rev Metall (Paris) — Revue de Metallurgie (Paris)
Rev Metall (Paris) Part 1 — Revue de Metallurgie (Paris) Part 1. Memoires
Rev Metall (Paris) Part 2 — Revue de Metallurgie (Paris) Part 2. Extraits
Rev Metal (Madrid) — Revista de Metalurgia (Madrid)
Rev Metaph — Review of Metaphysics
Rev Metaph Mor — Revue de Metaphysique et de Morale
Rev Metaph Morale — Revue de Metaphysique et de Morale
Rev Metaphy — Review of Metaphysics
Rev Metaphys Morale — Revue de Metaphysique et de Morale
Rev Meteorol — Revista Meteorologica
Rev Met Lit — Review of Metal Literature
Rev Met (Madrid) — Revista de Metalurgia (Madrid)
Rev Met Mor — Revue de Metaphysique et de Morale
Rev Met (Paris) — Revue de Metallurgie (Paris)
Rev Metrol Prat Leg — Revue de Metrologie Pratique et Legale
Rev Met Technol — Review of Metals Technology
Rev Mex Anestesiol — Revista Mexicana de Anestesiologia
Rev Mex Astron Astrof — Revista Mexicana de Astronomia y Astrofisica
Rev Mex Astron Astrofis — Revista Mexicana de Astronomia y Astrofisica
Rev Mex Astron Astrofis Ser Conf — Revista Mexicana de Astronomia y Astrofisica. Serie de Conferencias
Rev Mex Astron y Astrofis — Revista Mexicana de Astronomia y Astrofisica
Rev Mex Cienc Farm — Revista Mexicana de Ciencias Farmaceuticas
Rev Mex Cienc Med Biol — Revista Mexicana de Ciencias Medicas y Biologicas
Rev Mex Cir Ginecol Cancer — Revista Mexicana de Cirugia, Ginecologia, y Cancer
Rev Mex Cirug Ginec Canc — Revista Mexicana de Cirugia, Ginecologia, y Cancer
Rev Mex Constr — Revista Mexicana de la Construccion
Rev Mex Electr — Revista Mexicana de Electricidad
Rev Mex Estud Antrop Mex — Revista Mexicana de Estudios Antropologicos (Mexico)
Rev Mex Estud Antropol — Revista Mexicana de Estudios Antropologicos
Rev Mex Estud Hist — Revista Mexicana de Estudios Historicos
Rev Mex Fis — Revista Mexicana de Fisica
Rev Mex Fis Supl Ensenanza — Revista Mexicana de Fisica. Suplemento de Ensenanza
Rev Mex Fis Supl Fis Apl — Revista Mexicana de Fisica. Suplemento de Fisica Aplicada
Rev Mex Fis Supl Reactor — Revista Mexicana de Fisica. Suplemento del Reactor
Rev Mex Fitopatol — Revista Mexicana de Fitopatologia
Rev Mex Geogr Mex — Revista Mexicana de Geografia (Mexico)
Rev Mexicana Astronom Astrofis — Revista Mexicana de Astronomia y Astrofisica
Rev Mexicana Fis — Revista Mexicana de Fisica
Rev Mex Ing Arquitec Mex — Revista Mexicana de Ingenieria y Arquitectura (Mexico)
Rev Mex Lab Clin — Revista Mexicana de Laboratorio Clinico
Rev Mex Pediatr — Revista Mexicana de Pediatria
Rev Mex Psiquiat Neurol Med Leg — Revista Mexicana de Psiquiatria, Neurologia, y Medicina Legal
Rev Mex Radiol — Revista Mexicana de Radiologia
Rev Mex Soc — Revista Mexicana de Sociologia
Rev Mex Sociol — Revista Mexicana de Sociologia
Rev Mex Sociol Mex — Revista Mexicana de Sociologia (Mexico)
Rev Mex Trab Mex — Revista Mexicana del Trabajo (Mexico)

Rev Mex Tuberc Apar Respir — Revista Mexicana de Tuberculosis y Aparto Respiratorio
Rev Mex Tuber Enferm Apar Respir — Revista Mexicana de Tuberculosis y Enfermedades del Aparato Respiratorio
Rev Mex Urol — Revista Mexicana de Urologia
Rev Micr El — Revista de Microscopia Electronica
Rev Microbiol — Revista de Microbiologia
Rev Microbiol Appl Agric Hyg Ind — Revue de Microbiologie Appliquee a l'Agriculture, a l'Hygiene, a l'Industrie
Rev Micropal — Revue de Micropaleontologie
Rev Micropaleontol — Revue de Micropaleontologie
Rev Mil — Revista Militar
Rev Milit Gen — Revue Militaire Generale
Rev Milit Suisse — Revue Militaire Suisse
Rev Mil Med Vet — Revista Militar de Medicina Veterinaria
Rev Mil Remonta Vet — Revista Militar de Remonta e Veterinaria
Rev Mil Vet — Revista Militar de Veterinaria
Rev Mil Vet (Rio De Janeiro) — Revista Militar de Veterinaria (Rio De Janeiro)
Rev Min — Revista Mineria
Rev Minas — Revista de Minas
Rev Minas Hidrocarburos — Revista de Minas e Hidrocarburos
Rev Minelor — Revista Minelor
Rev Minelor (Bucharest) — Revista Minelor (Bucharest)
Rev Min Eng — Revista Mineira de Engenharia
Rev Minera BA — Revista Minera (Buenos Aires)
Rev Minera Geol Mineral — Revista Minera, Geologia, y Mineralogia
Rev Minera Geol Mineral BA — Revista Minera, Geologia, y Mineralogia (Buenos Aires)
Rev Mineral — Reviews in Mineralogy
Rev Minera y Petrolera — Revista Minera y Petrolera
Rev Min Geol Mineral — Revista Minera, Geologia, y Mineralogia
Rev Min Jus Caracas — Revista. Ministerio de Justicia (Caracas)
Rev Min Ops S Aust — Review of Mining Operations in South Australia [*Adelaide*]
Rev Mktg Agric Econ (Sydney) — Review of Marketing and Agricultural Economics (Sydney)
Rev M Mec — Revue M - Mecanique
Rev Mnmts Hist — Revue des Monuments Historiques
Rev Mod — Revista Moderna
Rev Mod Astron — Reviews in Modern Astronomy
Rev Modern Phys — Reviews of Modern Physics
Rev Mod Phy Monogr — Reviews of Modern Physics Monographs
Rev Mod Phys — Reviews of Modern Physics
Rev Monde Lat — Revue du Monde Latin
Rev Monde Musul — Revue du Monde Musulman
Rev Monogr Bur Hyg Trop Med Lond — Review Monographs. Bureau of Hygiene and Tropical Medicine (London)
Rev Morpho-Phys Hum — Revue de Morpho-Physiologie Humaine
Rev Moyen A — Revue du Moyen-Age Latin
Rev M Phys — Reviews of Modern Physics
Revm Resp Mezhved Sb — Revmatizm Respublikanskii Mezhvedomstvennyi Sbornik
RevMu — Revue de Musicologie
Rev Mun — Revista Municipal
Rev Munic Eng — Revista Municipal de Engenharia
Rev Munici Engen Rio — Revista Municipal de Engenharia (Rio de Janeiro)
Rev Munici S Jose — Revista Municipal de Costa Rica (San Jose, Costa Rica)
Rev Mus — Revue Musicale
Rev Mus Atlantico Barranquilla — Revista. Museo del Atlantico (Barranquilla, Colombia)
Rev Mus Chilena — Revista Musical Chilena
Rev Mus Hist Nac Santiago — Revista. Museo Historico Nacional de Chile (Santiago)
Rev Mus Hist Nat Mendoza — Revista. Museo de Historia Natural de Mendoza
Rev Mus Hist Quito — Revista. Museo Historico (Quito)
Rev Music — Revue de Musicologie
Rev Musical — Revue Musicale
Rev Music Chilena — Revista Musical Chilena
Rev Music Chil Santiago — Revista Musical Chilena (Santiago)
Rev Mus Inst Arqueol Cuzco — Revista. Museo e Instituto Arqueologico (Cuzco, Peru)
Rev Mus J Castilhos Arquiv Hist P Alegre — Revista. Museo Julio de Castilhos e Arquivo Historico do Rio Grande do Sul (Porto Alegre, Brazil)
Rev Mus Juan Manuel Blanes — Revista del Museo Juan Manuel Blanes
Rev Mus La Plata — Revista. Museo de La Plata
Rev Mus La Plata Antrop — Revista del Museo de La Plata Seccion Antropologia
Rev Mus La Plata Secc Antropol — Revista. Museo de La Plata. Seccion Antropologia
Rev Mus La Plata Secc Bot — Revista. Museo de La Plata. Seccion Botanica
Rev Mus La Plata Secc Geol — Revista. Museo de La Plata. Seccion Geologia
Rev Mus La Plata Secc Paleontol — Revista. Museo de La Plata. Seccion Paleontologia
Rev Mus La Plata Secc Zool — Revista. Museo de La Plata. Seccion Zoologia
Rev Mus N — Revista del Museo Nacional
Rev Mus Nac Antrop Arqueol Lima — Revista. Museo Nacional de Antropologia y Arqueologia (Lima)
Rev Mus Nac Lima — Revista. Museo Nacional (Lima)
Rev Mus N Antropol & Arqueol — Revista del Museo Nacional de Antropologia y Arqueologia
Rev Mus Paulista — Revista do Museo Paulista
Rev Mus Paulista S Paulo — Revista do Museu Paulista (Sao Paulo)
Rev Mus Prov Neuquen — Revista del Museo Provincial de Neuquen
Rev Muz — Revista Muzeelor
Rev Muz — Revista Muzeelor si Monumentelor
Rev Muz & Mnmt Ser Mnmt Ist & A — Revista Muzeelor si Monumentelor. Seria Monumente Istorice si de Arta

Rev Muz M Mon — Revista Muzeelor si Monumentelor. Seria Monumente Istorice si Arta

Rev Muz M Muz — Revista Muzeelor si Monumentelor. Seria Muzee

Rev Muz Monum Muz — Revista Muzeelor si Monumentelor. Seria Muzee

Rev Mycol — Revue de Mycologie

Rev Mycol (Paris) — Revue de Mycologie (Paris)

Rev Mycol (Paris) Suppl Colon — Revue de Mycologie. Supplement Colonial (Paris)

RevN — Revista. Biblioteca Nacional Jose Marti

Rev N — Revue du Nord

RevN — Revue Nouvelle

RevN — Revue Nouvelle [*Tournai*]

Rev Nac Agr — Revista Nacional de Agricultura

Rev Nac Agric (Bogota) — Revista Nacional de Agricultura (Bogota)

Rev Nac Cult Caracas — Revista Nacional de Cultura (Caracas)

Rev Nac Hosp — Revista Nacional de Hospitales

Rev Nac Monte — Revista Nacional (Montevideo)

Rev N Arquit — Revista Nacional de Arquitectura

Rev Nat — Revue Nationale

Rev Nat Lit — Review of National Literatures

Rev Natn Fdrs Ass Chicago — Review. National Founders' Association [*Chicago*]

Rev Natn Metal Trades Ass Chicago — Review. National Metal Trades Association [*Chicago*]

Rev Natn Res Coun Can — Review. National Research Council. Canada [*Ottawa*]

Rev Nat Res Counc Can — Review. National Research Council of Canada

Rev N Cult — Revista Nacional de Cultura

Rev Nema — Revue de Nematologie

Rev Nematol — Revue de Nematologie

Rev N Etrangere Pol Sci & Litt — Revue Nationale Etrangere, Politique, Scientifique, et Litteraire

Rev Neurol — Revista de Neurologia

Rev Neurol — Revue Neurologique

Rev Neurol B Aires — Revista Neurologica de Buenos Aires

Rev Neurol Buenos Aires — Revista Neurologica de Buenos Aires

Rev Neurol Clin (Madrid) — Revista de Neurologia Clinica (Madrid)

Rev Neurol (Paris) — Revue Neurologique (Paris)

Rev Neurol Psychiat — Review of Neurology and Psychiatry [*Edinburgh*]

Rev Neurops — Revue de Neuropsychiatrie Infantile et d'Hygiene Mentale de l'Enfance

Rev Neuro-Psiquiatr — Revista de Neuro-Psiquiatria

Rev Neuropsychiatr Infant — Revue de Neuropsychiatrie Infantile et d'Hygiene Mentale de l'Enfance

Rev Neuropsychiatr Infant Hyg Ment Enfance — Revue de Neuropsychiatrie Infantile et d'Hygiene Mentale de l'Enfance

Rev Neurosci — Reviews of Neuroscience

Rev New Energ Technol — Review of New Energy Technology

Rev Newsl Dep Psychiat MacGill Univ — Review and Newsletter. Department of Psychiatry and the Department of Sociology and Anthropology. MacGill University [*Montreal*]

Rev Nickel — Revue du Nickel

Rev Noire — Revue Noire

Rev Nord — Revue du Nord

Rev Nordestina Biol — Revista Nordestina de Biologia

Rev Not — Revue du Notariat

Rev Not — Revue Pratique du Notariat Belge

Rev Notariat — Revue du Notariat

Rev Nouv — Revue Nouvelle

Rev Nucl Azuay Casa Cult Ecuat Cuenca — Revista del Nucleo del Azuay de la Casa de la Cultura Ecuatoriana (Cuenca)

Rev Nucl Guayas Casa Cult Ecuat Guayaquil — Revista del Nucleo Guayas. Casa de la Cultura Ecuatoriana (Guayaquil)

RevNum — Revue Numismatique

Rev Num Arg — Revista Numismatica Argentina

Rev Numi — Revue Numismatique

Rev Numi Belge — Revue de la Numismatique Belge

Rev Numism — Revue Numismatique

Rev Nutr Anim — Revista de Nutricion Animal

Rev Oak Ridge Natl Lab (US) — Review. Oak Ridge National Laboratory (United States)

Rev Obras Pub — Revista de Obras Publicas

Rev Obras Publicas — Revista de Obras Publicas

Rev Obras Sanit Nac (Argent) — Revista de Obras Sanitarias de la Nacion (Argentina)

Rev Obras Sanit Nac (B Aires) — Revista de Obras Sanitarias de la Nacion (Buenos Aires)

Rev Obstet Ginecol Venez — Revista de Obstetricia y Ginecologia de Venezuela

Rev Oc — Revista de Occidente

Rev Occidente — Revista de Occidente

Rev Occident Musulman & Medit — Revue de l'Occident Musulman et de la Mediterranee

Rev O Chr — Revue de l'Orient Chretien

Rev Ocrotirea Mediului Inconjurator Nat Terr Nat — Revista Ocrotirea Mediului Inconjurator Natura. Terra Natura

Rev Oculomot Res — Reviews of Oculomotor Research

Rev Odontoestomatol — Revista Odonto-Estomatologica

Rev Odontoimplantol — Revue Odonto-Implantologique

Rev Odontol Circ Odontol Parag — Revista Odontologica. Circulo de Odontologos del Paraguay

Rev Odontol Concepcion — Revista Odontologica de Concepcion

Rev Odontol (Cordoba) — Revista Odontologica (Cordoba)

Rev Odontol Costa Rica — Revista Odontologica de Costa Rica

Rev Odontol Ecuat — Revista Odontologica Ecuatoriana

Rev Odontol Parana — Revista Odontologica do Parana

Rev Odontol PR — Revista Odontologica de Puerto Rico

Rev Odontol PR (Santurce) — Revista Odontologica de Puerto Rico (Santurce)

Rev Odontol St Catarina — Revista de Odontologia. Universidade Federal de Santa Catarina

Rev Odontol UNESP (Univ Estadual Paul) — Revista de Odontologia da UNESP (Universidade Estadual Paulista)

Rev Odonto Stomatol — Revue d'Odonto-Stomatologie

Rev Odonto-Stomatol (Bord) — Revue d'Odonto-Stomatologie (Bordeaux)

Rev Odonto-Stomatol Midi Fr — Revue d'Odonto-Stomatologie du Midi de la France

Rev Odontostomatol Nordest — Revue Odonto-Stomatologique du Nord-Est

Rev Odonto-Stomatol (Paris) — Revue d'Odonto-Stomatologie (Paris)

Rev Of Fed Med Ecuador — Revista Oficial. Federacion Medica del Ecuador

Rev of Ghana L — Review of Ghana Law

Rev of Politics — Review of Politics

Rev Oka — Revue d'Oka

Revol 1848 — Revolution de 1848

Revol & Cult — Revolucion y Cultura

Revol Surrealiste — Revolution Surrealiste

Revolution Franc — Revolution Francaise. Societe de l'Histoire de la Revolution Francaise

Revol Wld — Revolutionary World

Revol World — Revolutionary World

Rev Opt — Revue d'Optique Theorique et Instrumentale

Rev Opt Theor Instrum — Revue d'Optique Theorique et Instrumentale

Rev Or Chr — Revue de l'Orient Chretien

Rev Orl — Revista de Otorrinolaringologia

Rev Or Lat — Revue de l'Orient Latin

Rev Orthod — Review of Orthodontia [*New York*]

Rev Orthop Dento-Faciale — Revue d'Orthopedie Dento-Faciale

Rev Ortop Traumatol Latinoam — Revista de Ortopedia y Traumatologia Latinoamericana

Rev Oto-Neuro-Oftalmol Cir Neurol Sud-Am — Revista de Oto-Neuro-Oftalmologica y de Cirugia Neurologica Sud-Americana

Rev Oto-Neuro-Ophtalmol — Revue d'Oto-Neuro-Ophtalmologie

Rev Oto-Neuro-Ophtalmol (Paris) — Revue d'Oto-Neuro-Ophtalmologie (Paris)

Rev Otorrinolaringol — Revista de Otorrinolaringologia

RevP — Revista del Pacifico

RevP — Revolution Proletarienne. Revue Syndicaliste Revolutionnaire

RevPac — Revue du Pacifique

Rev Padurilor — Revista Padurilor

Rev Padurilor Ind Lemnului Celul Hirtie Ind Lemnului — Revista Padurilor-Industria Lemnului. Celuloza si Hirtie. Industria Lemnului

Rev Padurilor Ind Lemnului Celul Hirtie Silvic Exploatarea — Revista Padurilor-Industria Lemnului. Celuloza si Hirtie. Silvicultura si Exploatarea Padurilor

Rev Padurilor-Ind Lemnului Ser Ind Lemnului — Revista Padurilor-Industria Lemnului. Seria Industria Lemnului

Rev Padurilor-Ind Lemnului Ser Silvic Exploatarea Padurilor — Revista Padurilor-Industria Lemnului. Seria Silvicultura si Exploatarea Padurilor

Rev Padurilor Ind Lemnului Ser Silvic Exploat Padurilor — Revista Padurilor-Industria Lemnului. Seria Silvicultura si Exploatarea Padurilor

Rev Padurilor Silvic Exploat Padurilor — Revista Padurilor. Silvicultura si Exploatarea Padurilor

Rev Palaeobot Palynol — Review of Palaeobotany and Palynology

Rev Palaeobot Palynology — Review of Palaeobotany and Palynology

Rev Palae P — Review of Palaeobotany and Palynology

Rev Palais Decouv — Revue du Palais de la Decouverte

Rev Paleobiol — Revue de Paleobiologie

Rev Palud Med Trop — Revue du Paludisme et de Medecine Tropicale

Rev Paraguaya Sociol Asuncion — Revista Paraguaya de Sociologia (Asuncion)

Rev Paris — Revue de Paris

Rev Part Mater — Reviews in Particulate Materials

Rev Path Comp — Revue de Pathologie Comparee

Rev Path Gen Physiol Clin — Revue de Pathologie Generale et de Physiologie Clinique

Rev Pathol Comp — Revue de Pathologie Comparee

Rev Pathol Comp Hyg Gen — Revue de Pathologie Comparee et Hygiene Generale

Rev Pathol Comp Med Exp — Revue de Pathologie Comparee et de Medecine Experimentale

Rev Pathol Gen Comp — Revue de Pathologie Generale et Comparee

Rev Pathol Gen Physiol Clin — Revue de Pathologie Generale et de Physiologie Clinique

Rev Pathol Veg Entomol Agr France — Revue de Pathologie Vegetale et d'Entomologie Agricole de France

Rev Pathol Veg Entomol Agric Fr — Revue de Pathologie Vegetale et d'Entomologie Agricole de France

Rev Path Veg et Entom Agric — Revue de Pathologie Vegetale et d'Entomologie Agricole

Rev Patrim Hist Artist Nac Rio — Revista do Patrimonio Historico e Artistico Nacional (Rio de Janeiro)

Rev Patronato Biol Anim — Revista del Patronato de Biologia Animal

Rev Pau Bearn — Revue de Pau et du Bearn

Rev Paul Endodontia — Revista Paulista de Endodontia

Rev Paul Enferm — Revista Paulista de Enfermagem

Rev Paul Med — Revista Paulista de Medicina

Rev Paul Tisiol Torax — Revista Paulista de Tisiologia e do Torax

Rev Pays Loire — Revue des Pays de la Loire

RevPe — Enseignement Public. Revue Pedagogique

Rev Pedag — Revista de Pedagogia

Rev Pediatr — Revue de Pediatrie

Rev Pediatr Obstet Ginecol — Revista de Pediatrie, Obstetrica, si Ginecologie

Rev Pediatr Obstet Ginecol Pediatr — Revista de Pediatrie, Obstetrica, si Ginecologie. Pediatria

Rev Pediatr Obstet Ginecol Ser Obstet Ginecol — Revista de Pediatrie, Obstetrica, si Ginecologie. Seria Obstetrica si Ginecologie

Rev Pediatr Obstet Ginecol Ser Pediatr — Revista de Pediatrie, Obstetrica, si Ginecologie. Seria Pediatria
Rev Penal Peniten BA — Revista Penal y Penitenciaria (Buenos Aires)
Rev Pensam Centamer — Revista Pensamiento Centroamericano
Rev Per Ent Agric — Revista Peruana de Entomologia Agricola
Rev Per Fis — Revista Peruana de Fisica
Rev Perinat Med — Reviews in Perinatal Medicine
Rev Pernambucana Odontol — Revista Pernambucana de Odontologia
Rev Pernam Dir Penal Crimin — Revista Pernambucana de Direito Penal e Criminologia
Rev Perspect — Review and Perspective
Rev Per Tuberc — Revista Peruana de Tuberculosis y Enfermedades Respiratorias
Rev Peruana Cult Lima — Revista Peruana de Cultura (Lima)
Rev Peru Entomol — Revista Peruana de Entomologia
Rev Peru Entomol Agr — Revista Peruana de Entomologia Agricola
Rev Peru Entomol Agric — Revista Peruana de Entomologia Agricola
Rev Peru Med Trop — Revista Peruana de Medicina Tropical
Rev Peru Salud Publica — Revista Peruana de Salud Publica
Rev Peru Tuberc Enferm Respir — Revista Peruana de Tuberculosis y Enfermedades Respiratorias
Rev Pestic Toxicol — Reviews in Pesticide Toxicology
Rev Petrol Bogota — Revista del Petroleo (Bogota)
Rev Petrol Geol — Review of Petroleum Geology [*Golden, Colorado*]
Rev Petrolifere — Revue Petrolifere
Rev Petrol Technol — Review of Petroleum Technology
Rev Pet Technol (London) — Reviews of Petroleum Technology (London)
RevPF — Revista Portuguesa de Filosofia
Rev Ph — Revue de Philologie, de Litterature, et d'Histoire Anciennes
Rev Pharm — Revue Pharmaceutique
Rev Pharmacol Ter Exp — Revue de Pharmacologie et de Therapeutique Experimentale
Rev Pharm Liban — Revue Pharmaceutique Libanaise
Rev Ph Ch J — Review of Physical Chemistry of Japan
Rev Phil — Revue de Philologie, de Litterature, et d'Histoire Anciennes
Rev Phil — Revue de Philosophie
Rev Phil Fr — Revue Philosophique de la France et de l'Etranger
Rev Phil Fr Etrang — Revue Philosophique de la France et de l'Etranger
Rev Phil Louvain — Revue Philosophique de Louvain
Rev Philol — Revue de Philologie, de Litterature, et d'Histoire Anciennes
Rev Philol Fr Litt — Revue de Philologie Francaise et de Litterature
Rev Philol Litt Hist Ancien — Revue de Philologie, de Litterature et d'Histoire Anciennes
Rev Philom Bordeaux & Sud Ouest — Revue Philomatique de Bordeaux et du Sud-Ouest
Rev Philos — Revue de Philosophie
Rev Philos — Revue Philosophique de Louvain
Rev Philos Fr Etrang — Revue Philosophique de la France et de l'Etranger
Rev Philos Louv — Revue Philosophique de Louvain
Rev Phonet Appl — Revue de Phonetique Appliquee
Rev Phot — Revue de Photographie
Rev Phys — Revue de Physique
Rev Phys Acad Repub Pop Roum — Revue de Physique. Academie de la Republique Populaire Roumaine
Rev Phys Ap — Revue de Physique Appliquee
Rev Phys Appl — Revue de Physique Appliquee
Rev Phys Appl Suppl — Revue de Physique Appliquee. Supplement
Rev Phys Appl (Suppl J Phys) — Revue de Physique Appliquee (Supplement to Journal de Physique)
Rev Phys B — Reviews of Physiology, Biochemistry, and Pharmacology
Rev Phys Chem Jpn — Review of Physical Chemistry of Japan
Rev Physiol — Revue Physiologique
Rev Physiol Biochem Exp Pharmacol — Reviews of Physiology, Biochemistry, and Experimental Pharmacology
Rev Physiol Biochem Pharmacol — Reviews of Physiology, Biochemistry, and Pharmacology
Rev Physiother Chir Rad — Revue de Physiotherapie Chirurgicale et de Radiologie
Rev Phys Technol — Review of Physics in Technology
Rev Phytother — Revue de Phytotherapie
RevPL — Revue Politique et Litteraire. Revue Bleue
Rev Planeacion Desarrollo — Revista de Planeacion y Desarrollo
Rev Plant Path — Review of Plant Pathology
Rev Plant Pathol — Review of Plant Pathology
Rev Plant Prot Res — Review of Plant Protection Research
Rev Plasma Phys — Reviews of Plasma Physics
Rev Plast (Madrid) — Revista de Plasticos (Madrid)
Rev Plast Mod — Revista de Plasticos Modernos
Rev Pneumol Clin — Revue de Pneumologie Clinique
Rev Pol — Review of Politics
Rev Pol — Revista de Estudios Politicos
Rev Pol Acad Sci — Review. Polish Academy of Sciences
Rev Polarogr — Review of Polarography
Rev Polarogr (Jpn) — Review of Polarography (Japan)
Rev Policlin (Caracas) — Revista de la Policlinica (Caracas)
Rev Polit — Review of Politics
Rev Polit — Revue Politique
Rev Politec — Revista Politecnica
Rev Polit et Litt Rev Bleue — Revue Politique et Litteraire. Revue Bleue
Rev Polit Int — Revista de Politica Internacional
Rev Polit Litt — Revue Politique et Litteraire
Rev Polit Parl — Revue Politique et Parlementaire
Rev Pologne — Revue de Pologne
Rev Polym Technol — Reviews in Polymer Technology
Rev Polytech — Revue Polytechnique
Rev Po Quim — Revista Portuguesa de Quimica

Rev Port Bioquim Apl — Revista Portuguesa de Bioquimica Aplicada
Rev Port Cardiol — Revista Portuguesa de Cardiologia
Rev Port Cienc Vet — Revista Portuguesa de Ciencias Veterinarias
Rev Port Estomat — Revista Portuguesa de Estomatologia e Cirurgia Maxilofacial
Rev Port Estomatol Cir Maxilofac — Revista Portuguesa de Estomatologia e Cirurgia Maxilofacial
Rev Port Farm — Revista Portuguesa de Farmacia
Rev Port Filosof — Revista Portuguesa de Filosofia
Rev Port Med — Revista Portuguesa de Medicina
Rev Port Med Milit — Revista Portuguesa de Medicina Militar
Rev Port Obstet — Revista Portuguesa de Obstetricia, Ginecologia, e Cirurgia
Rev Port Pediatr — Revista Portuguesa de Pediatria
Rev Port Pediatr Pueric — Revista Portuguesa de Pediatria e Puericultura
Rev Port Quim — Revista Portuguesa de Quimica
Rev Port Quim (Lisbon) — Revista Portuguesa de Quimica (Lisbon)
Rev Port Zool Biol Geral — Revista Portuguesa de Zoologia e Biologia Geral
Rev Powder Metall Phys Ceram — Reviews on Powder Metallurgy and Physical Ceramics
Rev PR — Revista de Derecho Puertorriqueno
Rev Prat — Revue du Praticien
Rev Prat Biol Appl Clin Ther — Revue Pratique de Biologie Appliquee a la Clinique et a la Therapeutique
Rev Prat Connaiss Med — Revue Pratique des Connaissances Medicales
Rev Prat Controle Ind — Revue Pratique du Controle Industriel
Rev Prat Dr Soc — Revue Pratique de Droit Social
Rev Prat Froid — Revue Pratique du Froid [*Later, Journal RPF*]
Rev Prat Froid Cond Air — Revue Pratique du Froid et du Conditionnement de l'Air [*Later, Journal RPF*]
Rev Prat Mal Pays Chands — Revue Pratique des Maladies des Pays Chands
Rev Prat Not — Revue Pratique du Notariat
Rev Prat Quest Com et Econom — Revue Pratique des Questions Commerciales et Economiques
Rev Prat Soc — Revue Pratique des Societes Civiles et Commerciales
Rev Preh — Revue Prehistorique
Rev Prehist — Revue Prehistorique
Rev Presse Econ Min — Revue de Presse d'Economie Miniere
Rev Prod Chim — Revue des Produits Chimiques
Rev Prod Chim Actual Sci Reunis — Revue des Produits Chimiques et l'Actualite Scientifique Reunis
Rev Prog — Revue du Progres
Rev Prog Color Relat Top — Review of Progress in Coloration and Related Topics
Rev Prog Quant Nondestr Eval — Review of Progress in Quantitative Nondestructive Evaluation
Rev Prot — Revue de la Protection
Rev Prum Obchodu — Revue Prumyslu a Obchodu
RevPs — Revista de Psicoanalisis
Rev Psicol — Revista de Psicologia
Rev Psicol Gen Apl — Revista de Psicologia General y Aplicada
Rev Psihol — Revista de Psihologie
Rev Psiquiat Dinam — Revista de Psiquiatria Dinamica
Rev Psiquiat Psicol Med — Revista de Psiquiatria y Psicologia Medica de Europeo y America Latina
Rev Psiquiatr — Revista de Psiquiatria
Rev Psiquiatr Peru — Revista Psiquiatrica Peruana
Rev Psy App — Revue de Psychologie Appliquee
Rev Psych Appl — Revue de Psychologie Appliquee
Rev Psychiatr Univ Ottawa — Revue de Psychiatrie. Universite d'Ottawa
Rev Psychol Peuples — Revue de Psychologie des Peuples
Rev Pub Dat — Review of Public Data Use
Rev Pub Data Use — Review of Public Data Use
Rev Pubns A — Review of Publications of Art
Rev Pure Appl Chem — Reviews of Pure and Applied Chemistry
Rev Pure Appl Pharmacol Sci — Reviews in Pure and Applied Pharmacological Sciences
Rev Quest Hist — Revue des Questions Historiques
Rev Questions Hist — Revue des Questions Historiques
Rev Questions Sci — Revue des Questions Scientifiques
Rev Quest Sci — Revue des Questions Scientifiques
Rev Quim — Revista Quimica
Rev Quim Farm (Rio De Janeiro) — Revista de Quimica e Farmacia (Rio De Janeiro)
Rev Quim Farm (Santiago) — Revista Quimico-Farmaceutica (Santiago)
Rev Quim Farm (Tegucigalpa) — Revista de Quimica y Farmacia (Tegucigalpa)
Rev Quim Ind (Buenos Aires) — Revista de Quimica Industrial (Buenos Aires)
Rev Quim Ind Ed Cient — Revista de Quimica Industrial. Edicao Cientifica
Rev Quim Ind (Rio De Janeiro) — Revista de Quimica Industrial (Rio De Janeiro)
Rev Quim Indus Rio — Revista de Quimica Industrial (Rio de Janeiro)
Rev Quim Ing Quim — Revista de Quimica e Ingenieria Quimica
Rev Quim Pura Apl — Revista de Quimica Pura e Aplicada
Rev Quim Text — Revista de Quimica Textil
Rev Quirurgica Esp — Revista Quirurgica Espanola
RevQum — Revue de Qumran
RevR — Review of Religion
RevR — Revue Romane
Rev R Acad Cienc Exactas Fis Nat Esp — Revista de la Real Academia de Ciencias Exactas, Fisicas, y Naturales (Espana)
Rev R Acad Cienc Exactas Fis Nat Madr — Revista. Real Academia de Ciencias Exactas, Fisicas, y Naturales de Madrid
Rev R Acad Cienc Exactas Fis Nat Madrid — Revista de la Real Academia de Ciencias Exactas, Fisicas, y Naturales de Madrid
Rev R Acad Farm Barcelona — Revista. Real Academia de Farmacia de Barcelona
Rev R Acad Galega Cienc — Revista. Real Academia Galega de Ciencias
Rev Radical Polit Econ — Review of Radical Political Economics
Rev Radic Polit Econ — Review of Radical Political Economics

Rev Radiochem Cent (Amersham Eng) — Review. Radiochemical Centre (Amersham, England)
Rev Radio Res Lab — Review. Radio Research Laboratories
Rev R Agric Soc Engl — Review. Royal Agricultural Society of England [*London*]
Rev React Species Chem React — Reviews on Reactive Species in Chemical Reactions
Rev Real Acad Cienc Exact Fis Natur Madrid — Real Academia de Ciencias Exactas, Fisicas, y Naturales de Madrid. Revista
Rev Real Acad Ci Exact Fis Natur Madrid — Revista. Real Academia de Ciencias Exactas, Fisicas, y Naturales de Madrid
Rev Rec Prog Reinf Concr Ass — Review of Recent Progress. Reinforced Concrete Association [*London*]
RevRef — Revue Reformee
Rev Reform — Revue Reformee
Rev Rel — Revue d'Histoire des Religions
Rev Relig — Review for Religious
Rev Rel Res — Review of Religious Research
Rev Rep Inf Cent Pol AEC — Review Report Information Center. Polish Atomic Energy Commission
Rev Reprod — Reviews of Reproduction
Rev Repub — Revue Republicaine
Rev Res Vis Arts Educ — Review of Research in Visual Arts Education
Rev Rev — Revue des Revues
Rev Rev (A) — Review of Reviews. Australian Edition
Rev Revolut — Revue de la Revolution
Rev Revs Australas Ed — Review of Reviews. Australasian Edition
Rev Rhum — Revue du Rhumatisme et des Maladies Osteo-Articulaires
Rev Rhum Engl Ed — Revue du Rhumatisme. English Edition
Rev Rhum Mal Osteo-Artic — Revue du Rhumatisme et des Maladies Osteo-Articulaires
Rev River Plate — Review of the River Plate
Rev Ro Bioc — Revue Roumaine de Biochimie
Rev "Roche" Farm — Revista "Roche" de Farmacia
Rev Ro Chim — Revue Roumaine de Chimie
Rev Roman — Revue Romane
Rev Romande Agric Vitic Arboric — Revue Romande d'Agriculture, de Viticulture, et d'Arboriculture
Rev Romande Agr Viticult Arboricult — Revue Romande d'Agriculture, de Viticulture, et d'Arboriculture
Rev Rom Pet — Revista Romana de Petrol
Rev Ro Phys — Revue Roumaine de Physique
Rev Rouen — Revue de Rouen
Rev Roumaine Linguist — Revue Roumaine de Linguistique
Rev Roumaine Math Pures Appl — Revue Roumaine de Mathematiques Pures et Appliquees
Rev Roumaine Phys — Revue Roumaine de Physique
Rev Roumaine Sci Soc — Revue Roumaine des Sciences Sociales. Serie de Sciences Juridiques
Rev Roumaine Sci Tech Mecanique Appl — Revue Roumaine des Sciences Techniques. Serie de Mecanique Appliquee
Rev Roumaine Sci Tech Ser Electrotech Energet — Revue Roumaine des Sciences Techniques. Serie Electrotechnique et Energetique
Rev Roumaine Sci Tech Ser Mec Appl — Revue Roumaine des Sciences Techniques. Serie de Mecanique Appliquee
Rev Roum Biochim — Revue Roumaine de Biochimie
Rev Roum Biol — Revue Roumaine de Biologie
Rev Roum Biol Ser Biol Anim — Revue Roumaine de Biologie. Serie de Biologie Animale
Rev Roum Biol Ser Biol Veg — Revue Roumaine de Biologie. Serie Biologie Vegetale
Rev Roum Biol Ser Bot — Revue Roumaine de Biologie. Serie Botanique
Rev Roum Biol Ser Zool — Revue Roumaine de Biologie. Serie Zoologie
Rev Roum Chim — Revue Roumaine de Chimie
Rev Roum Embryol — Revue Roumaine d'Embryologie
Rev Roum Embryol Cytol Ser Embryol — Revue Roumaine d'Embryologie et de Cytologie. Serie d'Embryologie
Rev Roum Endocrinol — Revue Roumaine d'Endocrinologie
Rev Roum Geol Geophys Geogr Ser Geogr — Revue Roumaine de Geologie, Geophysique, et Geographie. Serie de Geographie
Rev Roum Geol Geophys Geogr Ser Geol — Revue Roumaine de Geologie, Geophysique, et Geographie. Serie de Geologie
Rev Roum Geol Geophys Geogr Ser Geophys — Revue Roumaine de Geologie, Geophysique, et Geographie. Serie de Geophysique
Rev Roum H — Revue Roumaine d'Histoire
Rev Roum Hist — Revue Roumaine d'Histoire
Rev Roum Hist A — Rev Roumaine d'Histoire de l'Art
Rev Roum Inframicrobiol — Revue Roumaine d'Inframicrobiologie
Rev Roum Math Pures Appl — Revue Roumaine de Mathematiques Pures et Appliquees
Rev Roum Med — Revue Roumaine de Medecine
Rev Roum Med Endocrinol — Revue Roumaine de Medecine. Endocrinologie
Rev Roum Med Interne — Revue Roumaine de Medecine Interne [*Later, Revue Roumaine de Medecine. Medecine Interne*]
Rev Roum Med Med Interne — Revue Roumaine de Medecine. Medecine Interne
Rev Roum Med Neurol Psychiatr — Revue Roumaine de Medecine. Neurologie et Psychiatrie
Rev Roum Med Ser Neurol Psychiatr — Revue Roumaine de Medecine. Serie de Neurologie et Psychiatrie
Rev Roum Med Virol — Revue Roumaine de Medecine. Virologie
Rev Roum Metall — Revue Roumaine de Metallurgie
Rev Roum Morphol Embryol — Revue Roumaine de Morphologie et d'Embryologie
Rev Roum Morphol Embryol Physiol Morphol Embryol — Revue Roumaine de Morphologie, d'Embryologie, et de Physiologie. Serie Morphologie et Embryologie

Rev Roum Morphol Embryol Physiol Physiol — Revue Roumaine de Morphologie, d'Embryologie, et de Physiologie. Serie Physiologie
Rev Roum Morphol Physiol — Revue Roumaine de Morphologie et du Physiologie
Rev Roum Neurol — Revue Roumaine de Neurologie [*Later, Revue Roumaine de Medecine. Serie Neurologie et Psychiatrie*]
Rev Roum Neurol Psychiatr — Revue Roumaine de Neurologie et de Psychiatrie [*Later, Revue Roumaine de Medecine. Serie Neurologie et Psychiatrie*]
Rev Roum Phys — Revue Roumaine de Physique
Rev Roum Physiol — Revue Roumaine de Physiologie [*Later, Revue Roumaine de Morphologie, d'Embryologie, et de Physiologie*]
Rev Roum Sci Soc Philos Logique — Revue Roumaine des Sciences Sociales. Serie de Philosophie et de Logique
Rev Roum Sci Tech Mec Appl — Revue Roumaine des Sciences Techniques. Serie de Mecanique Appliquee
Rev Roum Sci Tech Ser Electrotech Energ — Revue Roumaine des Sciences Techniques. Serie Electrotechnique et Energetique
Rev Roum Sci Tech Ser Mec Appl — Revue Roumaine des Sciences Techniques. Serie de Mecanique Appliquee
Rev Roum Sci Tech Ser Met — Revue Roumaine des Sciences Techniques. Serie de Metallurgie
Rev Roum Virol — Revue Roumaine de Virologie
RevRP — Revue Regionaliste des Pyrenees
Rev R Soc Tosc Ortic — Rivista della Reale Societa Toscana di Orticultura
RevS — Revista. Sociedad Bolivariana de Venezuela
RevS — Revue du Siecle
Rev Sagsaywamman — Revista Sagsaywamman
Rev Saintonge & Aunis — Revue de la Saintonge et d'Aunis
Rev Salud Anim — Revista de Salud Animal
Rev Salvador Cien Soc S Salvador — Revista Salvadorena de Ciencias Sociales (San Salvador)
Rev Sanid Aeronaut — Revista de Sanidad de Aeronautica
Rev Sanid Asist Soc Caracas — Revista de Sanidad y Asistencia Social. Ministerio de Sanidad y Asistencia Social (Caracas)
Rev Sanid Fuerzas Policiales — Revista de la Sanidad de las Fuerzas Policiales
Rev Sanid Hig Publica — Revista de Sanidad e Higiene Publica
Rev Sanid Hig Publica (Madr) — Revista de Sanidad e Higiene Publica (Madrid)
Rev Sanid Mil Arg — Revista de Sanidad Militar Argentina
Rev Sanid Mil (Argent) — Revista de la Sanidad Militar (Argentina)
Rev Sanid Polic — Revista de la Sanidad de Policia
Rev Sanit Mil — Revista Sanitaria Militara
Rev Sanit Milit Asuncion — Revista Sanitaria Militar (Asuncion)
Rev San Mil (Buenos Aires) — Revista de la Sanidad Militar (Buenos Aires)
Rev Santiago — Revista Santiago
Rev Sao Paulo Braz Univ Fac Med Vet Zootec — Revista. Sao Paulo Universidade. Faculdade de Medicina Veterinaria e Zootecnia
Rev Saude — Revista Saude
Rev Saude Publica — Revista de Saude Publica
Rev Sc Crim — Revue de Science Criminelle et de Droit Penal Compare
Rev Sch Aviat Med Brooks Air Force Base — Review. School of Aviation Medicine. Brooks Air Force Base [*Texas*]
Rev Sci — Revue Scientifique
Rev Sci Bourbonnais Cent Fr — Revue Scientifique du Bourbonnais et du Centre de la France
Rev Sci Bourbonnais Centr France — Revue Scientifique du Bourbonnais et du Centre de la France
Rev Sci Eau — Revue des Sciences de l'Eau
Rev Sci Ed — Revue des Sciences de l'Education
Rev Scient Instrum — Review of Scientific Instruments [*New York*]
Rev Scient (Paris) — Revue Scientifique (Paris)
Rev Sci Hum — Revue des Sciences Humaines
Rev Sci Humaines — Revue des Sciences Humaines
Rev Sci Industr Breton — Revue Scientifique et Industrielle (Breton, Editor)
Rev Sci Ins — Review of Scientific Instruments
Rev Sci Instr — Review of Scientific Instruments
Rev Sci Instrum — Review of Scientific Instruments
Rev Sci Limousin — La Revue Scientifique du Limousin
Rev Sci Med — Revue des Sciences Medicales
Rev Sci Nat Auvergne — Revue des Sciences Naturelles d'Auvergne
Rev Sci Natur Auvergne — Revue des Sciences Naturelles d'Auvergne
Rev Sci Ph — Revue des Sciences Philosophiques et Theologiques
Rev Sci Philos & Theol — Revue des Sciences Philosophiques et Theologiques
Rev Sci Phil Theol — Revue des Sciences Philosophiques et Theologiques
Rev Sci Pol — Revue des Sciences Politiques
Rev Sci Rel — Revue des Sciences Religieuses
Rev Sci Relig — Revue des Sciences Religieuses
Rev Sci Tech — Revue de Science et Technique
Rev Sci Tech OIE (Off Int Epizoot) — Revue Scientifique et Technique OIE (Office International des Epizooties)
Rev Sc Leg Fin — Revue de Science et de Legislation Financiere
Rev Scot Cult — Review of Scottish Culture
Rev Sc Phil Theol — Revue des Sciences Philosophiques et Theologiques
RevScPhTh — Revue des Sciences Philosophiques et Theologiques
RevScR — Regue des Sciences Religieuses
RevScRel — Revue des Sciences Religieuses
Rev Sec Reg — Review of Securities Regulation
Rev Sec Soc — Revue Belge de Securite Sociale
Rev Senegalaise de Droit — Revue Senegalaise de Droit
Rev Ser Commonw Bur Anim Hlth — Review Series. Commonwealth Bureau of Animal Health [*Weybridge*]
Rev Ser IAEA — Review Series. International Atomic Energy Agency
Rev Ser Int Atom Energy Agency — Review Series. International Atomic Energy Agency
Rev Serv Espec Saude Publica — Revista. Servicio Especial de Saude Publica
Rev Serv Nac Min Geol (Argent) — Revista. Servicio Nacional Minero Geologico (Argentina)

Rev Serv Nac Salud — Revista. Servicio Nacional de Salud
Rev Serv Publ Rio — Revista do Servico Publico (Rio de Janeiro)
Rev Serv Soc S Juan — Revista de Servicio Social (San Juan, Puerto Rico)
Rev SESDA — Revue du SESDA
Rev SESP — Revista. Servicio Especial de Saude Publica
Revs Geophys Space Phys — Reviews of Geophysics and Space Physics
Rev Shell — Revista Shell
Rev Shorthorn — Revista Shorthorn
Rev Sifilogr Leprol Dermatol — Revista de Sifilografia, Leprologia, y Dermatologia
Rev Silicon Germanium Tin Lead Compd — Reviews on Silicon, Germanium, Tin, and Lead Compounds
Rev Sind Estad — Revista Sindical de Estadistica
Rev SNCASO — Revue SNCASO
RevsO — Revista de Occidente
Rev Soc — Revue des Societes
Rev Soc — Revue Pratique des Societes Civiles et Commerciales
Rev Soc Amig Arqueol Monte — Revista. Sociedad Amigos de la Arqueologia (Montevideo)
Rev Soc Amis Mus Armee — Revue de la Societe des Amis du Musee de l'Armee
Rev Soc Argent Biol — Revista. Sociedad Argentina de Biologia
Rev Soc Argent Neurol y Psiquiat — Revista. Sociedad Argentina de Neurologia y Psiquiatria
Rev Soc Biom Hum — Revue. Societe de Biometre Humaine
Rev Soc Bolivar Venez Caracas — Revista. Sociedad Bolivariana de Venezuela (Caracas)
Rev Soc Boliv Hist Nat — Revista. Sociedad Boliviana de Historia Natural
Rev Soc Bras Agron — Revista. Sociedade Brasileira de Agronomia
Rev Soc Bras Med Trop — Revista. Sociedade Brasileira de Medicina Tropical
Rev Soc Bras Quim — Revista. Sociedade Brasileira de Quimica
Rev Soc Bras Zootec — Revista. Sociedade Brasileira de Zootecnia
Rev Soc Cient Parag — Revista. Sociedad Cientifica del Paraguay
Rev Soc Colomb Endocrinol — Revista. Sociedad Colombiana de Endocrinologia
Rev Soc Colomb Ortod — Revista. Sociedad Colombiana de Ortodoncia
Rev Soc Cubana Bot — Revista. Sociedad Cubana de Botanica
Rev Soc Cubana Ing — Revista. Sociedad Cubana de Ingenieros
Rev Soc Cub Hist Med — Revista. Sociedad Cubana de la Historia de Medicina
Rev Soc Ec — Review of Social Economy
Rev Soc Econ — Review of Social Economy
Rev Soc Entomol Argent — Revista. Sociedad Entomologica Argentina
Rev Soc Esp Bioquim Clin Patol Mol — Revista de la Sociedad Espanola de Bioquimica Clinica y Patologia Molecular
Rev Soc Esp Quim Clin — Revista de la Sociedad Espanola de Quimica Clinica
Rev Soc Etud XVIIe Siecle — Revue de la Societe d'Etudes du XVIIe Siecle
Rev Soc Geogr Hist Tegucigalpa — Revista. Sociedad de Geografia e Historia de Honduras (Tegucigalpa)
Rev Soc Geol Argent — Revista. Sociedad Geologica Argentina
Rev Soc Hait Hist Geogr Geol Port Au Prince — Revue. Societe Haitienne d'Histoire, de Geographie, et de Geologie (Port-au-Prince)
Rev Soc Hist Geogr Haiti — Revue. Societe d'Histoire et de Geographie d'Haiti
Rev Soc Hist Geogr Port Au Prince — Revue. Societe d'Histoire et Geographie d'Haiti (Port-au-Prince)
Rev Soc Hist Theatre — Revue. Societe d'Histoire du Theatre
Rev Social — Revue Socialiste
Rev Sociale — Revue Sociale
Rev Socialiste — Revue Socialiste
Rev Soc L — Review of Socialist Law
Rev Soc Lun Int — Revista. Sociedad Lunar Internacional
Rev Soc Malacol Carlos Torre — Revista. Sociedad Malacologica Carlos de la Torre
Rev Soc Martins Sarmento — Revue de la Societe Martins Sarmento
Rev Soc Med Argent — Revista. Sociedad Medica Argentina
Rev Soc Med Cir Sao Jose Rio Preto — Revista. Sociedade de Medicina e Cirurgia de Sao Jose Do Rio Preto
Rev Soc Med Int — Revista. Sociedad de Medicina Interna
Rev Soc Med Int y Soc Tisiol — Revista. Sociedad de Medicina Interna y Sociedad de Tisiologia
Rev Soc Med Vet (Buenos Aires) — Revista. Sociedad de Medicina Veterinaria (Buenos Aires)
Rev Soc Med Vet Chile — Revista. Sociedad de Medicina Veterinaria de Chile
Rev Soc Mex Hig — Revista. Sociedad Mexicana de Higiene
Rev Soc Mex Hist Nat — Revista. Sociedad Mexicana de Historia Natural
Rev Soc Mex Hist Natur — Revista. Sociedad Mexicana de Historia Natural
Rev Soc Mex Lepid AC — Revista. Sociedad Mexicana de Lepidopterologia. AC
Rev Soc Mex Lepidopterol AC — Revista. Sociedad Mexicana de Lepidopterologia. AC
Rev Soc Nucl Esp — Revista de la Sociedad Nuclear Espanola
Rev Soc Obstet Ginec — Revista. Sociedad de Obstetricia y Ginecologia de Buenos Aires
Rev Soc Odontol La Plata — Revista de la Sociedad Odontologica de la Plata
Rev Soc Pediat — Revista. Sociedad de Pediatria
Rev Soc Pediatr Litoral — Revista. Sociedad de Pediatria del Litoral
Rev Soc Peru Endocrinol — Revista. Sociedad Peruana de Endocrinologia
Rev Soc Quim Mex — Revista. Sociedad Quimica de Mexico
Rev Soc R Belge Ing Ind — Revue. Societe Royale Belge des Ingenieurs et des Industriels
Rev Soc Rural Rosario — Revista. Sociedad Rural de Rosario
Rev Soc Sav — Revue des Societes Savantes
Rev Soc Savantes France Etranger — Revue des Societe Savantes de la France et de l'Etranger
Rev Soc Savantes Haute Normandie — Revue des Societes Savantes de Haute-Normandie
Rev Soc Sci Hyg Aliment Aliment Ration Homme — Revue. Societe Scientifique d'Hygiene Alimentaire et de l'Alimentation Rationnelle de l'Homme
Rev Soc Telecommun Engrs — Review. Society of Telecommunication Engineers [London]

Rev Soc Venez Cardiol — Revista. Sociedad Venezolana de Cardiologia
Rev Soc Venez Hist Med — Revista. Sociedad Venezolana de Historia de la Medicina
Rev Soc Venez Quim — Revista. Sociedad Venezolana de Quimica
Rev Soldadura — Revista de Soldadura
Rev Solid State Sci — Reviews of Solid State Science
Rev Soudre Lastijdschrift — Revue de la Soudure/Lastijdschrift
Rev Soudure — Revue de la Soudure/Lastijdschrift
Rev Soudure Autogene — Revue de la Soudure Autogene
Rev Soudure/Lastijdschrift — Revue de la Soudure/Lastijdschrift
Rev Sov Med — Review of Soviet Medicine
Rev Sov Med Sci — Review of Soviet Medical Sciences
Rev SPAHN — Revista do Servico do Patrimonio Historico e Artistico Nacional
Rev Sport Leisure — Review of Sport and Leisure
RevSR — Revue des Sciences Religieuses
Rev Stat Ap — Revue de Statistique Appliquee
Rev Statist Appl — Revue de Statistique Appliquee
Rev Stiint "V Adamachi" — Revista Stiintifica "V. Adamachi"
Rev Stomat — Revue de Stomatologie [Later, Revue de Stomatologie et de Chirurgie Maxillo-Faciale]
Rev Stomatol — Revue de Stomatologie [Later, Revue de Stomatologie et de Chirurgie Maxillo-Faciale]
Rev Stomatol Chir Maxillo-Fac — Revue de Stomatologie et de Chirurgie Maxillo-Faciale
Rev Stomato-Odontol Nord Fr — Revue Stomato-Odontologique du Nord de la France
Rev Stud Orient — Revista di Studi Orientali
Rev Sudam Bot — Revista Sudamericana de Botanica
Rev Sud-Am Cien Med — Revista Sud-Americana de Ciencias Medicas
Rev Sud-Am Endocrin — Revista Sud-Americana de Endocrinologia
Rev Sud-Am Endocrinol Immunol Quimioter — Revista Sud-Americana de Endocrinologia, Immunologia, y Quimioterapia
Rev Sudam Morfol — Revista Sudamericana de Morfologia
Rev Suis Num — Revue Suisse de Numismatique
Rev Suisse Agric — Revue Suisse d'Agriculture
Rev Suisse Cathol — Revue de la Suisse Catholique
Rev Suisse Dr Int'l Concurrence — Revue Suisse du Droit International de la Concurrence
Rev Suisse Gynecol Obstet — Revue Suisse de Gynecologie et d'Obstetrique
Rev Suisse Gynecol Obstet Suppl — Revue Suisse de Gynecologie et d'Obstetrique. Supplementum
Rev Suisse Hydrol — Revue Suisse d'Hydrologie
Rev Suisse Med Prax — Revue Suisse de Medecine. Praxis
Rev Suisse Med Sport — Revue Suisse de Medecine des Sports
Rev Suisse Med Sports — Revue Suisse de Medecine des Sports
Rev Suisse Num — Revue Suisse de Numismatique
Rev Suisse Numi — Revue Suisse de Numismatique
Rev Suisse Pathol Gen Bact — Revue Suisse de Pathologie Generale et de Bacteriologie
Rev Suisse Psychol Pure Appl — Revue Suisse de Psychologie Pure et Appliquee
Rev Suisse Tuberc Pneum — Revue Suisse de la Tuberculose et de Pneumonologie
Rev Suisse Vitic Arboric — Revue Suisse de Viticulture et Arboriculture
Rev Suisse Vitic Arboric Hortic — Revue Suisse de Viticulture et Arboriculture. Horticulture
Rev Suisse Zool — Revue Suisse de Zoologie
Rev Summa — Revista Summa
Rev Surg — Review of Surgery
Rev Syn — Revue de Synthese
Rev Syniatrica — Revista Syniatrica
Rev Synthese — Revue de Synthese
Rev Synthese Hist — Revue de Synthese Historique
RevT — Revue du Tarn
RevtA — Revista del Archivo Central
Revta Acad Cienc Exact Fis Quim Nat Zaragoza — Revista de la Academia de Ciencias Exactas, Fisico-Quimicas y Naturales de Zaragoza
Revta Acad Colomb Cienc Exact Fis Nat — Revista de la Academia Colombiana de Ciencias Exactas, Fisicas y Naturales [Bogota]
Revta Adm Nac Agua B Aires — Revista de la Administracion Nacional del Agua [Buenos Aires]
Revta Aeronaut — Revista de Aeronautica [Madrid]
Revta Agric Badajoz — Revista Agricola (Badajoz)
Revta Agric Bogota — Revista Agricola (Bogota)
Revta Agric Comerc Ind Panama — Revista de Agricultura, Comercio, a Industria (Panama)
Revta Agric Guatem — Revista Agricola (Guatemala)
Revta Agric (Habana) — Revista de Agricultura (Habana)
Revta Agric Ind Comerc B Aires — Revista de Agricultura, Industria, y Comercio [Buenos Aires]
Revta Agric Ind Comml Min Rio De J — Revista Agricola, Industrial e Commercial Mineira (Rio de Janeiro)
Revta Agric Madr — Revista Agricola (Madrid)
Revta Agric Pernamb — Revista de Agricultura (Pernambuco)
Revta Agric (Piracicaba) — Revista de Agricultura (Piracicaba)
Revta Agric Porto — Revista Agricola (Porto)
Revta Agric P Rico — Revista de Agricultura de Puerto Rico [San Juan]
Revta Agric Santiago — Revista de Agricultura (Santiago)
Revta Agric S Jacinto — Revista Agricola (San Jacinto, Mexico)
Revta Agric S Jose — Revista de Agricultura (San Jose, Costa Rica)
Revta Agric S Paulo — Revista de Agricultura (Sao Paulo)
Revta Agric Trop Mex — Revista de Agricultura Tropical (Mexico)
Revta Agric Trop S Salvador — Revista de Agricultura Tropical (San Salvador)
Revta Agric Trujillo — Revista de Agricultura (Trujillo)

Revta Agric Univ Cochabamba — Revista de Agricultura. Universidad Autonoma de Cochabamba

Revta Agric Vet Olinda — Revista Agricolo-Veterinaria (Olinda, Brazil)

Revta Agron Lisb — Revista Agronomica (Lisboa)

Revta Agron NE Argent — Revista Agronomica del Noroeste Argentino

Revta Agron Porto Alegre — Revista Agronomica (Porto Alegre)

Revta Agrup Odont B Aires — Revista de la Agrupacion Odontologica de la Capital Federal (Buenos Aires)

Revta Algod Est S Paulo — Revista do Algodao do Estado de Sao Paulo

Revta Aliment — Revista Alimentar. Quimica Industrial [Rio de Janeiro]

Revta Am Farm Hosp — Revista Americana de Farmacia y Hospitales [New York]

Revta Amig Flora Bras — Revista dos Amigos da Flora Brasileira [Sao Paulo]

Revta Angiol — Revista de Angiologia [Buenos Aires]

Revta Antrop Bolivia — Revista de Antropologia de Bolivia [La Paz]

Revta Antrop S Paulo — Revista de Antropologia (Sao Paulo)

Revta Ar — Revista do Ar [Lisboa]

Revta Archit — Revista de Architectura [Rio de Janeiro]

Revta Archos Bibltcas Mus Madr — Revista de Archivos, Bibliotecas, y Museos (Madrid)

Revta Argent Agron — Revista Argentina de Agronomia [Buenos Aires]

Revta Argent Alerg — Revista Argentina de Alergia [Buenos Aires]

Revta Argent Anest Analg — Revista Argentina de Anestesia y Analgesia [Buenos Aires]

Revta Argent Bot — Revista Argentina de Botanica [La Plata]

Revta Argent Cardiol — Revista Argentina de Cardiologia [Buenos Aires]

Revta Argent Defus Anest Gen Odont — Revista Argentina para la Defusion de la Anestesia General en Odontologia [Buenos Aires]

Revta Argent Derm Sif — Revista Argentina de Dermato-Sifilogia [Buenos Aires]

Revta Argent Endocr Metab — Revista Argentina de Endocrinologia y Metabolismo [Buenos Aires]

Revta Argent Ent — Revista Argentina de Entomologia [Buenos Aires]

Revta Argent Frio — Revista Argentina del Frio [Buenos Aires]

Revta Argent Hist Med — Revista Argentina de Historia de la Medicina [Buenos Aires]

Revta Argent Leprol — Revista Argentino de Leprologia [Buenos Aires]

Revta Argent Neurol Psiquiat — Revista Argentina de Neurologia y Psiquiatria [Rosario]

Revta Argent Neurol Psiquiat Med Leg — Revista Argentina de Neurologia, Psiquiatria, y Medicina Legal [Buenos Aires]

Revta Argent Norteam Cienc Med — Revista Argentino-Norteamericana de Ciencias Medicas [Buenos Aires]

Revta Argent Oto Rino Lar — Revista Argentina de Oto-Rino-Laringologia [Buenos Aires]

Revta Argent Paleont Antrop Ameghinia — Revista Argentina de Paleontologia y Antropologia Ameghinia [Buenos Aires]

Revta Argent Quim Ind — Revista Argentina de Quimica e Industria [Buenos Aires]

Revta Argent Radiol — Revista Argentina de Radiologia [Buenos Aires]

Revta Argent Reum — Revista Argentina de Reumatologia [Buenos Aires]

Revta Argent Tuberc — Revista Argentina de Tuberculosis y Enfermedades Pulmonares [Buenos Aires]

Revta Argent Urol — Revista Argentina de Urologia [Buenos Aires]

Revta Argent Zoogeogr — Revista Argentina de Zoogeografia [Buenos Aires]

Revta Arquit — Revista de Arquitectura [Buenos Aires]

Revta Arte Sci — Revista de Arte e Sciencia [Rio de Janeiro]

Revta Asoc Argent Criad Cerdos — Revista de la Asociacion Argentina Criadores de Cerdos

Revta Asoc Argent Derm Sif — Revista de la Asociacion Argentina de Dermatologia y Sifilologia [Buenos Aires]

Revta Asoc Argent Diet — Revista de la Asociacion Argentina de Dietologia [Buenos Aires]

Revta Asoc Argent Nutr Diet — Revista de la Asociacion Argentina de Nutricion et Dietologia [Buenos Aires]

Revta Asoc Arquit Barcelona — Revista de la Asociacion de Arquitectos [Barcelona]

Revta Asoc Bioquim Argent — Revista de la Asociacion Bioquimica Argentina [Buenos Aires]

Revta Asoc Esc Quim Farm Quito — Revista de la Asociacion de la Escuela de Quimica y Farmacia (Quito)

Revta Asoc Gen Conduct Lucr Publ Rom — Revista Asociatiei Generale a Conductorilor de Lucrari Publice din Romania [Bucuresti]

Revta Asoc Geol Argent — Revista de la Asociacion Geologica Argentina [Buenos Aires]

Revta Asoc Ing Agron Montev — Revista de la Asociacion de Ingenieros Agronomos (Montevideo)

Revta Asoc Ing Urug — Revista de la Asociacion de Ingenieros del Uruguay [Montevideo]

Revta Asoc Med Argent — Revista de la Asociacion Medica Argentina [Buenos Aires]

Revta Asoc Med Cuenca — Revista de la Asociacion Medica de Cuenca

Revta Asoc Med Farm Cuba — Revista de la Asociacion Medico-Farmaceutica de la Isla de Cuba [Habana]

Revta Asoc Med Mex — Revista. Asociacion Medica Mexicana

Revta Asoc Med Prov Yauli — Revista de la Asociacion Medica de la Provincia de Yauli [La Oroya, Peru]

Revta Asoc Med Trujillo — Revista de la Asociacion Medica de Trujillo

Revta Asoc Odont Argent — Revista. Asociacion Odontologica Argentina [Buenos Aires]

Revta Asoc Odont Cuba — Revista de la Asociacion Odontologica del Cuba [Habana]

Revta Asoc Odont Peru — Revista de la Asociacion Odontologica del Peru [Lima]

Revta Asoc Odont Urug — Revista de la Asociacion Odontologica Uruguaya [Montevideo]

Revta Asoc Prof Policlin Ezeiza — Revista de la Asociacion de Profesionales del Policlino Ezeiza [Buenos Aires]

Revta Ass Bras Farm — Revista da Associacao Brasileira de Farmaceuticos Pharmaceuticos [Rio de Janeiro]

Revta Ass Engenh Civ Port — Revista da Associacao dos Engenheiros Civis Portuguezes [Lisboa]

Revta Ass Med Bras — Revista da Associacao Medica Brasileira [Sao Paulo]

Revta Ass Med Minas Gerais — Revista da Associacao Medica de Minas Gerais [Belo Horizonte]

Revta Ass Med Rio Grande Do Sul — Revista da Associacao Medica do Rio Grande do Sul

Revta Ass Paul Cirurg Dent — Revista da Associacao Paulista de Cirugioes Dentistas [Sao Paulo]

Revta Ass Paul Med — Revista da Associacao Paulista de Medicina [Sao Paulo]

Revta Astr B Aires — Revista Astronomica (Buenos Aires)

Revta Aten Hosp Ital Cordoba — Revista Ateneo Hospital Italiano (Cordoba)

Revta Auto — Revista Automobila [Bucuresti]

Rev Tabacs Hellen — Revue des Tabacs Helleniques

Revta Bago — Revista Bago [Buenos Aires]

Revta Bahiana Odont — Revista Bahiana de Odontologia [Bahia]

Revta Balear Cienc Med — Revista Balear de Ciencias Medicas [Palma]

Revta Barcelon Enferm Oido Garg Nariz — Revista Barcelonesa de Enfermedades de Oido, Garganta y Nariz [Barcelona]

Revta Biol — Revista de Biologia

Revta Biol For Limnol — Revista de Biologia Forestal y Limnologia [Madrid]

Revta Biol Hyg — Revista de Biologia e Hygiene [Sao Paulo]

Revta Biol Lisb — Revista de Biologia. Revista Brasileira e Portuguesa de Biologia em Geral (Lisboa)

Revta Biol Lourenco Marq — Revista de Biologia. Lourenco Marques

Revta Biol Mar — Revista de Biologia Marina [Valparaiso]

Revta Biol Trop — Revista de Biologia Tropical

Revta Boie — Revista Boie [Manila]

Revta Bolsa Cereales — Revista de la Bolsa de Cereales

Revta Bras Anest — Revista Brasileira de Anestesiologia [Rio de Janeiro]

Revta Bras Biol — Revista Brasileira de Biologia

Revta Bras Cancer — Revista Brasileira de Cancerologia [Rio de Janeiro]

Revta Bras Chim — Revista Brasileira de Chimica [Rio de Janeiro]

Revta Bras Chim Sci Ind — Revista Brasileira de Chimica Sciencia e Industria [Sao Paulo]

Revta Bras Cirurg — Revista Brasileira de Cirurgia [Rio de Janeiro]

Revta Bras Engenh — Revista Brasileira de Engenharia [Rio de Janeiro]

Revta Bras Ent — Revista Brasileira de Entomologia

Revta Bras Estatist — Revista Brasileira de Estatistica [Rio de Janeiro]

Revta Brasil Mala Do Trop — Revista Brasileira de Malariologia e Doencas Tropicais

Revta Brasil Polit Int — Revista Brasileira de Politica Internacional

Revta Bras Leprol — Revista Brasileira de Leprologia [Sao Paulo]

Revta Bras Malar Doenc Trop — Revista Brasileira de Malariologia e Doencas Tropicais [Rio de Janeiro]

Revta Bras Med — Revista Brasileira de Medicina [Rio de Janeiro]

Revta Bras Microbiol — Revista Brasileira de Microbiologia [Rio de Janeiro]

Revta Bras Odont — Revista Brasileira de Odontologia [Rio de Janeiro]

Revta Bras Oftal — Revista Brasileira de Oftalmologia [Rio de Janeiro]

Revta Bras Orthop Traum — Revista Brasileira de Orthopedia y Traumatologia [Rio de Janeiro]

Revta Bras Oto Rino Lar — Revista Brasileira de Oto-Rino-Laringologia [Sao Paulo]

Revta Bras Pesquisas Med Biol — Revista Brasileira de Pesquisas Medicas e Biologicas

Revta Bras Plast — Revista Brasileira de Plasticos [Rio de Janeiro]

Revta Bras Reum — Revista Brasileira de Reumatologia [Rio de Janeiro]

Revta Bras Saude Ment — Revista Brasileira de Saude Mental [Rio de Janeiro]

Revta Bras Tuberc Doenc Torac — Revista Brasileira de Tuberculose e Doencas Toracicas [Rio de Janeiro]

Revta Cafe Port — Revista do Cafe Portugues

Revta Cafet Colomb — Revista Cafetera de Colombia [Bogota]

Revta Cafet Guatem — Revista Cafetalera (Guatemala)

Revta Calculo Autom Clbern — Revista de Calculo Automatico y Cibernetico [Madrid]

Revta Cam Agric Balear — Revista de la Camara Agricola Balear [Palma de Mallorca]

Revta Capit Argent Col Int Ciruj — Revista del Capitulo Argentino del Colegio Internacional de Cirujanos [Buenos Aires]

Revta Cent Estud Agron B Aires — Revista. Centro de Estudiantes de Agronomia (Buenos Aires)

Revta Cent Estud Doct Cienc Nat B Aires — Revista del Centro de Estudiantes del Doctorado en Ciencias Naturales (Buenos Aires)

Revta Cent Estud Med B Aires — Revista del Centro Estudiantes de Medicina (Buenos Aires)

Revta Cent Estud Med Quito — Revista del Centro de Estudiantes de Medicina (Quito)

Revta Cent Estud Med Vet B Aires — Revista del Centro Estudiantes de Medicina Veterinaria (Buenos Aires)

Revta Cent Estud Odont B Aires — Revista del Centro Estudiantes de Odontologia (Buenos Aires)

Revta Cent Ind Agric Santiago — Revista del Centro Industrial y Agricola (Santiago de Chile)

Revta Cent Med Torreon — Revista del Centro Medico de Torreon

Revta Cent Sci Letr Artes Campinas — Revista do Centro de Sciencias, Letras, e Artes de Campinas

Revta Ceres — Revista Ceres [Vicosa]

Revta Chil Anest — Revista Chilena de Anestesia [Santiago]

Revta Chil Angiol — Revista Chilena de Angiologia [Santiago]

Revta Chil Ent — Revista Chilena de Entomologia

Revta Chil Hig — Revista Chilena de Higiene [Santiago de Chile]

Revta Chil Hig Med Prev — Revista Chilena de Higiene y Medicina Preventiva [Santiago]

Revta Chil Hist Geogr — Revista Chilena de Historia y Geografia [*Santiago de Chile*]
Revta Chil Hist Nat — Revista Chilena de Historia Natural [*Santiago*]
Revta Chil Neuro Psiquiat — Revista Chilena de Neuro-Psiquiatria [*Santiago*]
Revta Chil Ortop Traum — Revista Chilena de Ortopedia y Traumatologia [*Santiago*]
Revta Chil Urol — Revista Chilena de Urologia [*Santiago*]
Revta Chim — Revista de Chimie [*Bucuresti*]
Revta Chim Pura Appl — Revista de Chimica Pura e Applicada [*Lisboa*]
Revta Chir — Revista de Chirurgie [*Bucuresti*]
Revta Cienc Artes Lit Tarragona — Revista de Ciencias, Artes, y Literatura (Tarragona)
Revta Cienc Biol — Revista de Ciencias Biologicas [*Cochabamba*]
Revta Ciencia Apl — Revista de Ciencia Aplicada [*Madrid*]
Revta Ciencia Vet — Revista de Ciencia Veterinaria [*Madrid*]
Revta Cienc Lima — Revista de Ciencias (Lima, Peru)
Revta Cienc Med B Aires — Revista de Ciencias Medicas (Buenos Aires)
Revta Cienc Med Barcelona — Revista de Ciencias Medicas de Barcelona
Revta Cienc Med Esc Med Milit Mex — Revista de Ciencias Medicas de la Escuela Medico-Militar (Mexico)
Revta Cienc Med Habana — Revista de Ciencias Medicas (Habana)
Revta Cienc Social — Revista de Ciencias Sociales
Revta Cienc Vet — Revista de Ciencias Veterinarias [*Lisboa*]
Revta Cient Acad Cienc Habana — Revista Cientifica. Academia de Ciencias
Revta Cient Inst Cient Argent — Revista Cientifica. Instituto Cientifico Argentino [*Buenos Aires*]
Revta Cient Invest Mus Hist Nat S Rafael — Revista Cientifica de Investigaciones del Museo de Historia Natural de San Rafael [*Mendoza*]
Revta Cient Univ Cent Venez — Revista Cientifica de la Universidad Central de Venezuela [*Caracas*]
Revta Circulo Med Argent — Revista del Circulo Medico Argentino [*Buenos Aires*]
Revta Circulo Med Cordoba — Revista del Circulo Medico de Cordoba
Revta Circulo Odont Argent — Revista del Circulo Odontologico Argentino y Centro Estudiantes de Odontologia [*Buenos Aires*]
Revta Circulo Odont B Aires — Revista del Circulo Odontologico de Buenos Aires [*Buenos Aires*]
Revta Circulo Odont Cordoba — Revista del Circulo Odontologico de Cordoba
Revta Circulo Odont Oeste — Revista del Circulo Odontologico del Oeste [*Buenos Aires*]
Revta Circulo Odont Rosario — Revista del Circulo Odontologico de Rosario
Revta Circulo Odont Santafes — Revista del Circulo Odontologico Santafesino [*Santa Fe*]
Revta Circulo Odont Tucuman — Revista del Circulo Odontologico de Tucuman
Revta Cirug B Aires — Revista de Cirugia (Buenos Aires)
Revta Cirug Barcelona — Revista de Cirugia de Barcelona
Revta Cirug Hosp Juarez — Revista de Cirugia. Hospital Juarez [*Mexico*]
Revta Cirug Mes — Revista de Cirugia (Mexico)
Revta Cirug Oral Maxilo Fac — Revista de Cirugia Oral Maxilo-Facial y Endodoncia [*Lima*]
Revta Cirurg Dent — Revista o Cirurgiao Dentista [*Rio de Janeiro*]
Revta Cirurg S Paulo — Revista de Cirurgie de Sao Paulo
Revta Citric — Revista Citricola [*Sao Paulo*]
Revta Clin Esp — Revista Clinica Espanola [*Madrid*]
Revta Clin Inst Matern Lisb — Revista Clinica do Instituto Maternal (Lisboa)
Revta Clin Luis Razetti — Revisto de la Clinica Luis Razetti [*Caracas*]
Revta Clin Madr — Revista Clinica de Madrid
Revta Clin Medellin — Revista Clinica (Medellin, Colombia)
Revta Clin Med Montev — Revista de Clinica Medica. Facultad de Medicina y Centro de Investigaciones Clinicas del Ministerio de Salud Publica (Montevideo)
Revta Clin S Paulo — Revista Clinica de Sao Paulo
Revta Clins Rio De J — Revista das Clinicas (Rio de Janeiro)
Revta Club Engenh Rio De J — Revista do Club e de Engenharia (Rio de Janeiro)
Revta Col Farm Caracas — Revista de Colegio Farmaceutico (Caracas)
Revta Col Farm Habana — Revista de Colegio Farmaceutico de la Habana
Revta Col Farms Nac Rosario — Revista de Colegio de Farmaceuticos Nacionales (Rosario)
Revta Col Ing Venez — Revista del Colegio de Ingenieros de Venezuela [*Caracas*]
Revta Col M B Aires — Revista de Colegio de Medicos (Buenos Aires)
Revta Col Med Castellon De La Plana — Revista del Colegio Medico (Castellon de la Plana)
Revta Col Med Est Merida — Revista del Colegio de Medicos del Estado Merida
Revta Col Med Guatem — Revista Colegio Medico de Guatemala
Revta Col Med Habana — Revista del Colegio Medico (Habana)
Revta Col Nac Vicente Rocafuerte — Revista del Colegio Nacional Vicente Rocafuerte [*Guayaquil*]
Revta Colomb Antrop — Revista Colombiana de Antropologia [*Bogota*]
Revta Colomb Biol Crim — Revista Colombiana de Biologia Criminal [*Bogota*]
Revta Colomb Cancer — Revista Colombiana de Cancerologia [*Bogota*]
Revta Colomb Leprol — Revista Colombiana de Leprologia [*Bogota*]
Revta Colomb Obstet Ginec — Revista Colombiana de Obstetricia y Ginecologia [*Bogota*]
Revta Colomb Pediat Pueric — Revista Colombiana de Pediatria y Puericultura [*Bogota*]
Revta Colomb Quim — Revista Colombiana de Quimica [*Bogota*]
Revta Colon Agric La Paz — Revista de Colonizacion y Agricultura (La Paz)
Revta Combate Lepra — Revista de Combate Lepra [*Rio de Janeiro*]
Revta Confed Med Panam — Revista de la Confederacion Medica Panamericana [*La Habana*]
Revta Conf Sanit Nac Venez — Revista de la Conferencia Sanitaria Nacional. Estados Unidos de Venezuela [*Caracas*]
Revta Cons Oceanogr Ib Am — Revista del Consejo Oceanografico Ibero-Americano [*Madrid*]
Revta Constr Agrimens — Revista de Construcciones y Agrimensura [*Habana*]
Revta Constr Mater Constr — Revista Constructiilor si a Materialelor de Constructii
Revta Cub Azuc Alcoh — Revista Cubana de Azucar y Alcohol [*Habana*]

Revta Cub Cardiol — Revista Cubana de Cardiologia [*Habana*]
Revta Cub Gastroent — Revista Cubana de Gastroenterologia [*Habana*]
Revta Cub Lab Clin — Revista Cubana de Laboratorio Clinico [*Habana*]
Revta Cub Obstet Ginec — Revista Cubana de Obstetricia y Ginecologia [*Habana*]
Revta Cub Oftal Oto Rino Lar — Revista Cubana de Oftalmologia y Oto-Rino-Laringologia [*Habana*]
Revta Cub Oto Neuro Oftal — Revista Cubana de Oto-Neuro-Oftalmiatria [*Habana*]
Revta Cub Pediat — Revista Cubana de Pediatria [*Habana*]
Revta Cub Terap — Revista Cubana de Terapeutica [*Habana*]
Revta Cub Tuberc — Revista Cubana de Tuberculosis [*Habana*]
Revta Curs Fac Med Bahia — Revista dos Cursos da Faculdade de Medicina da Bahia [*Rio de Janeiro*]
Revta Dent Chile — Revista Dental de Chile [*Santiago de Chile*]
Revta Dent Ciud Trujillo — Revista Dental (Ciudad Trujillo)
Revta Dent Guatem — Revista Dental (Guatemala)
Revta Dent Habana — Revista Dental (Habana)
Revta Dent Int — Revista Dental Internacional [*Pittsburg*]
Revta Dent Montev — Revista Dental (Montevideo)
Revta Dent P Rico — Revista Dental de Puerto Rico
Revta Derm Argent — Revista Dermatologica Argentina [*Buenos Aires*]
Revta Diagn Biol — Revista de Diagnostico Biologico [*Madrid*]
Revta Diagn Trat Fis — Revista de Diagnostica y Tratamiento Fisicos [*Barcelona*]
Revta Dir Engenh Rio De J — Revista da Directoria de Engenharia [*Rio de Janeiro*]
Revta Divulg Agric Ecuad — Revista de Divulgacion Agricola. Ecuador [*Quito*]
Revta Ecuat Enferm Torac — Revista Ecuatoriana de Enfermedades del Torac [*Guayaquil*]
Revta Ecuat Ent Parasit — Revista Ecuatoriana de Entomologia y Parasitologia [*Quito*]
Revta Ecuat Hig Med Trop — Revista Ecuatoriana de Higiene y Medicina Tropical [*Guayaquil*]
Revta Ecuat Pediat — Revista Ecuatoriana de Pediatria [*Guayaquil*]
Revta Ecuat Pediat Pueric — Revista Ecuatoriana de Pediatria y Puericultura [*Quito*]
Revta Electrotec — Revista Electrotecnica [*Buenos Aires*]
Revta Engenh Est Guanabara — Revista de Engenharia do Estado da Guanabara
Revta Engenh Milit — Revista de Engenharia Militar [*Lisboa*]
Revta Ent Mocamb — Revista de Entomologia de Mocambique [*Lourenco Marques*]
Revta Ent (Rio De J) — Revista de Entomologia (Rio De Janeiro)
Revta Esc Agron Vet Porto Alegre — Revista da Escola de Agronomia e Veterinaria (Porto Alegre)
Revta Esc Mec B Aires — Revista del Escuela de Mecanica del Ejercito Teniente Coronel Fray Luis Beltran (Buenos Aires)
Revta Esc Prat Agric Evora — Revista da Escola Pratica de Agricultura de Evora
Revta Esc Sup Colon Lisb — Revista da Escola Superior Colonial (Lisboa)
Revta Esp Am Lar Otol Rinol — Revista Espanola y Americana de Laringologia, Otologia, y Rinologia [*Madrid*]
Revta Esp Anest — Revista Espanola de Anestesiologia [*Madrid*]
Revta Esp Biol — Revista Espanola de Biologia
Revta Esp Cardiol — Revista Espanola de Cardiologia [*Madrid, Barcelona*]
Revta Esp Cirug Traum Ortop — Revista Espanola de Cirugia, Traumatologia y Ortopedia [*Valencia*]
Revta Esp Cirug Urol — Revista Espanola de Cirugia y Urologia [*Madrid*]
Revta Esp Derm Sif — Revista Espanola de Dermatologia y Sifilografia [*Madrid*]
Revta Espec Asoc Med Argent — Revista de Especialidades. Asociacion Medica Argentina [*Buenos Aires*]
Revta Espec Med — Revista de Especialidades Medicas [*Madrid*]
Revta Esp Electrol Radiol Med — Revista Espanola de Electrologia y Radiologia Medicas [*Valencia*]
Revta Esp Electron — Revista Espanola de Electronica [*Barcelona*]
Revta Esp Enferm Apar Dig Nutr — Revista Espanola de la Enfermedades del Aparato Digestivo y de la Nutricion [*Madrid*]
Revta Esp Estomat — Revista Espanola de Estomatologia [*Barcelona, Madrid*]
Revta Esp Farmac Terap — Revista Espanola de Farmacologia y Terapeutica [*Madrid*]
Revta Esp Fisiol — Revista Espanola de Fisiologia
Revta Esp Lar Otol Rinol — Revista Espanola de Laringologia, Otologia, y Rinologia [*Madrid*]
Revta Esp Lech — Revista Espanola do Lecheria [*Madrid*]
Revta Esp Med Cirug — Revista Espanola de Medicina y Cirugia [*Barcelona*]
Revta Esp Med Cirug Guerra — Revista Espanola de Medicina y Cirugia de Guerra [*Valladolid*]
Revta Esp Neuropsiquiat Infant — Revista Espanola de Neuropsiquiatria Infantil [*Sevilla*]
Revta Esp Obstet Ginec Madr — Revista Espanola de Obstetricia y Ginecologia (Madrid)
Revta Esp Obstet Ginec Valencia — Revista Espanola de Obstetricia y Ginecologia (Valencia)
Revta Esp Oncol — Revista Espanola de Oncologia [*Madrid*]
Revta Esp Oto Neuro Oftal Neurocirug — Revista Espanola de Oto-Neuro-Oftalmologia y Neurocirugia [*Valencia*]
Revta Esp Pediat — Revista Espanola de Pediatria [*Zaragoza*]
Revta Esp Reum Enferm Osteoartic — Revista Espanola de Reumatismo y Enfermedades Osteoarticulares
Revta Esp Tuberc — Revista Espanola de Tuberculosis y Archivos Nacionales de Enfermedades del Torax [*Madrid*]
Revta Esp Urol Derm — Revista Espanola de Urologia y Dermatologia [*Madrid*]
Revta Estadist Mex — Revista de Estadistica (Mexico)
Revta Estomat Cuba — Revista Estomatologica de Cuba [*Habana*]
Revta Estr Ferro Agric Pecu — Revista das Estradas de Ferro, Agricultura e Pecuaria [*Rio de Janeiro*]
Revta Estud Agro Soc — Revista de Estudios Agro-Sociales [*Madrid*]
Revta Estud Ing — Revista de Estudios de Engenieria [*Caracas*]

Revta Etnol Arqueol Ling S Salv — Revista de Etnologia, Arqueologia, y Linguistica (San Salvador)

Revta Fac Agric Univ Cent Venez — Revista de la Facultad de Agricultura. Universidad Central de Venezuela [*Maracay*]

Revta Fac Agron Univ Cent Venez — Revista. Facultad de Agronomia. Universidad Central de Venezuela

Revta Fac Agron Univ Nac La Plata — Revista. Facultad de Agronomia y Veterinaria. Universidad Nacional de La Plata

Revta Fac Agron Univ Repub (Urug) — Revista. Facultad de Agronomia. Universidad de la Republica (Uruguay)

Revta Fac Agron Vet Univ B Aires — Revista. Facultad de Agronomia y Veterinaria. Universidad de Buenos Aires

Revta Fac Cienc Agrar Univ Nac Cuyo — Revista. Facultad de Ciencias Agrarias. Universidad Nacional de Cuyo

Revta Fac Cienc Med B Aires — Revista de la Facultad de Ciencias Medicas de Buenos Aires [*Buenos Aires*]

Revta Fac Cienc Med Quito — Revista de la Facultad de Ciencias Medicas, Quito

Revta Fac Cienc Med Univ Cuenca — Revista de la Facultad de Ciencias Medicas de la Universidad de Cuenca

Revta Fac Cienc Med Univ Nac Cordoba — Revista de la Facultad de Ciencias Medicas de la Universidad Nacional de Cordoba

Revta Fac Cienc Quim Farm Univ Nac La Plata — Revista de la Facultad de Ciencias Quimicas. Universidad Nacional de La Plata

Revta Fac Cienc Univ Coimbra — Revista da Faculdade de Ciencias. Universidade de Coimbra

Revta Fac Cienc Univ Nac Lima — Revista. Facultad Ciencias. Universidad Nacional Mayor de San Marcos (Lima)

Revta Fac Cienc Univ Oviedo — Revista de la Facultad de Ciencias. Universidad de Oviedo

Revta Fac Engenh Univ Porto — Revista da Faculdade de Engenharia. Universidade de Porto

Revta Fac Farm Bioquim S Paulo — Revista. Faculdade de Farmacia e Bioquimica. Universidade de Sao Paulo

Revta Fac Farm Bioquim Univ Nac Lima — Revista de la Facultad de Farmacia y Bioquimica. Universidad Nacional Mayor de San Marcos (Lima)

Revta Fac Farm S Maria — Revista da Faculdade de Farmacia de Santa Maria

Revta Fac Hum Cienc Univ Repub Urug — Revista de la Facultad de Humanidades y Ciencias. Universidad de la Republica. Uruguay

Revta Fac Ing Agron Univ Cent Venez — Revista de la Facultad de Ingenieria Agronomica. Universidad Central de Venezuela

Revta Fac Ing Agron Univ Montev — Revista de la Facultad de Ingenieria Agronomica. Universidad de Montevideo

Revta Fac Letr Cienc Univ Habana — Revista de la Facultad de Letras y Ciencias. Universidad de la Habana

Revta Fac Med Tucuman — Revista de la Facultad de Medicina de Tucuman

Revta Fac Med Univ Nac Colomb — Revista de la Facultad de Medicina. Universidad Nacional de Colombia

Revta Fac Med Vet Univ Nac La Plata — Revista de la Facultad de Medicina Veterinaria. Universidad Nacional de La Plata

Revta Fac Med Vet Univ Nac Lima — Revista de la Facultad de Medicina Veterinaria. Universidad Nacional Mayor de San Marcos (Lima)

Revta Fac Med Vet Univ S Paulo — Revista da Faculdade de Medicina Veterinaria. Universidade de Sao Paulo

Revta Fac Med Vet Zootec Univ Nac Colomb — Revista de la Facultad de Medicina Veterinaria y de Zootecnia. Universidad Nacional de Colombia

Revta Fac Nac Agron Medellin — Revista de la Facultad Nacional de Agronomia (Medellin)

Revta Fac Odont Pelotas — Revista da Faculdade de Odontologia de Pelotas

Revta Fac Odont Porte Alegre — Revista da Faculdade de Odontologia de Porte Alegre

Revta Fac Quim Univ Nac Lima — Revista de la Facultad de Quimica. Universidad Nacional Mayor de San Marcos (Lima)

Revta Farm — Revista Farmaciei

Revta Farmac Med Exp — Revista de Farmacologia y Medicina Experimental

Revta Farm Bahia — Revista Farmaceutica de Bahia

Revta Farm B Aires — Revista Farmaceutica (Buenos Aires)

Revta Farm Chil — Revista Farmaceutica Chilena

Revta Farm Cuba — Revista Farmaceutica de Cuba

Revta Farm Goa — Revista Farmaceutica (Goa)

Revta Farm Odont Rio de J — Revista de Farmacia e Odontologia (Rio de Janeiro)

Revta Farm Ouro Preto — Revista Farmaceutica de Ouro Preto

Revta Farm Peru — Revista Farmaceutica Peruana

Revta Farm P Rico — Revista Farmaceutica de Puerto Rico

Revta Farm S Jose — Revista Farmaceutica (San Jose, Costa Rica)

Revta Fed Rur Urug — Revista de la Federacion Rural del Uruguay

Revta Filip Med Farm — Revista Filipina de Medicina y Farmacia

Revta Fil Mendoza Soc Argent Pediat — Revista de la Filial Mendoza de la Sociedad Argentino de Pediatria

Revta Fitopatol — Revista de Fitopatologia [*Madrid*]

Revta Fiziol Norm Patol — Revista de Fiziologie Normala si Patologica

Revta Flor — Revista Florestal [*Rio de Janeiro*]

Revta Flora Med — Revista da Flora Medicinal [*Rio de Janeiro*]

Revta Floresta — Revista Floresta

Revta Fom Caracas — Revista de Fomento (Caracas)

Revta Fontilles — Revista Fontilles

Revta For Argent — Revista Forestal Argentina

Revta For B Aires — Revista Forestal (Buenos Aires)

Revta For Mex — Revista Forestal Mexicana

Revta For Venez — Revista Forestal Venezolana

Revta Frenopat Esp — Revista Frenopatica Espanola

Revta Frio — Revista del Frio

Revta Ganad B Aires — Revista Ganadera (Buenos Aires)

Revta Ganad Habana — Revista Ganadera (Habana)

Revta Ganad Ind Coml Magallanes — Revista Ganadera, Industrial, y Comercial de Magallanes

Revta Ganad S Salv — Revista Ganadera (San Salvador)

Revta Gastroent Mex — Revista de Gastroenterologia de Mexico

Revta Gastroent S Paulo — Revista de Gastroenterologia de Sao Paulo

Revta Gaucha Odont — Revista Gaucha de Odontologia

Revta Geogr Am — Revista Geografica Americana

Revta Geogr Chile — Revista Geografica de Chile

Revta Geogr Colomb — Revista Geografica de Colombia

Revta Geogr Colon Merc — Revista de Geografia Colonial y Mercantil. Real Sociedad Geografica

Revta Geogr Inst Panam Geogr — Revista Geografica del Instituto Panamericano de Geografia

Revta Geriat — Revista de Geriatria

Revta Ginec Obstet Rio de J — Revista de Ginecologia e d'Obstetricia (Rio de Janeiro)

Revta Goiana Med — Revista Goiana de Medicina

Revta Grancolomb Zootec Hig Med Vet — Revista Grancolombiana de Zootecnia, Higiene, y Medicina Veterinaria

Revta Guimaraes — Revista de Guimaraes

Revta Hig Bogota — Revista de Higiene (Bogota)

Revta Hig Fom Pecu — Revista de Higiene y Fomento Pecuario

Revta Hig Sanid Pecu — Revista de Higiene y Sanidad Pecuarias

Revta Hig Saude Publ — Revista de Higiene e Saude Publica

Revta Hig Tuberc — Revista de Higiene y de Tuberculosis

Revta Hist Am — Revista de Historia de America

Revta Homeop — Revista Homeopatica

Revta Homeop Catal — Revista Homeopatica Catalana

Revta Hort — Revista Horticola

Revta Hort Vitic — Revista de Horticultura si Viticultura

Revta Hosp — Revista Hospitalar

Revta Hosp Nino Lima — Revista del Hospital del Nino (Lima)

Revta Hosp Ninos B Aires — Revista del Hospital de Ninos (Buenos Aires)

Revta Hosp Ninos Maracaibo — Revista del Hospital de Ninos de Maracaibo

Revta Hosp Nossa Senh Aparecida S Paulo — Revista do Hospital Nossa Senhora Aparecida (Sao Paulo)

Revta Hosp Psiquiat Habana — Revista del Hospital Psiquiatrico de la Habana

Revta Hosp Samarit Bogota — Revista del Hospital de la Samaritana (Bogota)

Revta Hosp S Juan de Dios Bogota — Revista del Hospital San Juan de Dios (Bogota)

Revta Hosps Mex — Revista de Hospitales (Mexico)

Revta Hosps Montev — Revista de los Hospitales (Montevideo)

Revta Hosp Univ Dr Jose Eleuterio Gonzalez — Revista del Hospital Universitario Dr. Jose Eleuterio Gonzalez

Revta Ib Am Cienc Med — Revista Ibero-Americana de Ciencias Medicas

Revta Iber Endocr — Revista Iberica de Endocrinologia

Revta Iber Parasit — Revista Iberica de Parasitologia

Revta Ig Microbiol Epidem — Revista de Igiena, Microbiologie si Epidemiologie

Revta Ig Soc — Revista de Igiena Sociala

Revta Ilust Zapat — Revista Ilustrada de la Zapateria

Revta Ind Agric (Tucuman) — Revista Industrial y Agricola (Tucuman)

Revta Ind Anim — Revista de Industria Animal

Revta Ind Fabr — Revista Industrial y Fabril

Revta Indias — Revista de Indias

Revta Ind Mex — Revista Industrial. Secretaria de la Economia Nacional (Mexico)

Revta Inds Bogota — Revista de Industrias (Bogota)

Revta Inf Electron — Revista de Informacion Electronica

Revta Inf Farm Sanit — Revista de Informacion Farmaceutica, Sanitaria, y de Aduanas

Revta Infnes Aeronaut — Revista de Informaciones Aeronauticas

Revta Ing Arquit — Revista de Ingenieria y Arquitectura

Revta Ing B Aires — Revista de Ingenieria (Buenos Aires)

Revta Ing La Paz — Revista de Ingenieria (La Paz)

Revta Ing Mex — Revista de Ingenieria (Mexico)

Revta Ing Montev — Revista de Ingenieria (Montevideo)

Revta Ings Milit — Revista de Ingenieros Militares

Revta Insp Ganad Agric Montev — Revista de la Inspeccion de Ganaderia y Agricultura (Montevideo)

Revta Inst Adolfo Lutz — Revista do Instituto Adolfo Lutz

Revta Inst Agric Catal S Isidro — Revista del Instituto Agricola Catalan de San Isidro

Revta Inst Antibiot Univ Recife — Revista do Instituto de Antibioticos. Universidade do Recife

Revta Inst Antrop Univ Nac Tucuman — Revista del Instituto de Antropologia. Universidad Nacional de Tucuman

Revta Inst Archeol Geogr Pernamb — Revista do Instituto Archeologico e Geographico Pernambucano

Revta Inst Bact B Aires — Revista del Instituto Bacteriologico (Buenos Aires)

Revta Inst Bact Chile — Revista del Instituto Bacteriologico de Chile y de la Sociedad Chilena de Microbiologia e Higiene

Revta Inst Bact Dr Carlos G Malbran — Revista del Instituto Bacteriologico Dr Carlos G. Malbran

Revta Inst Biol Argent — Revista del Instituto Biologico Argentino

Revta Inst Biol Pesq Tecnol Curitiba — Revista. Instituto de Biologia e Pesquisas Tecnologicas (Curitiba)

Revta Inst Cafe Est S Paulo — Revista del Instituto de Cafe do Estado de Sao Paulo

Revta Inst Def Cafe C Rica — Revista del Instituto de Defensa del Cafe de Costa Rica

Revta Inst Etnol — Revista. Instituto de Etnologia

Revta Inst Etnol Nac Bogota — Revista del Instituto Etnologico Nacional (Bogota)

Revta Inst Etnol Univ Nac Tucuman — Revista del Instituto de Etnologia. Universidad Nacional de Tucuman

Revta Inst Fis Univ Nac Tucuman Ser A — Revista. Instituto de Fisica. Universidad Nacional de Tucuman. Serie A. Matematicas y Fisica Teorica

Revta Inst Geogr Lima — Revista. Instituto de Geografia. Universidad Nacional Mayor de San Marcos (Lima)

Revta Inst Hist Geogr Bras — Revista do Instituto Historico e Geographico Brasileiro

Revta Inst Invest Doenc Crim La Plata — Revista del Istituto de Investigaciones y Doencias Criminologicas (La Plata)

Revta Interam Psicologia — Revista Interamericana de Psicologia

Revta Invest Agropec (B Aires) — Revista de Investigaciones Agropecuarias (Buenos Aires)

Revta Med Aeronaut — Revista Medica de Aeronautica

Revta Med Aliment Santiago — Revista de Medicina y Alimentacion (Santiago de Chile)

Revta Med Angola — Revista Medica de Angola

Revta Med Arequipa — Revista Medica de Arequipa

Revta Med Bahia — Revista Medica de Bahia

Revta Med Barcelona — Revista Medica de Barcelona

Revta Med Bogota — Revista Medica de Bogota

Revta Med Bras — Revista Medica Brasileira

Revta Med Chile — Revista Medica de Chile

Revta Med Chir Iasi — Revista Medico-Chirurgicala din Iasi

Revta Med Chir Soc Med Nat Iasi — Revista Medico-Chirurgicala a Societatii de Medici si Naturalisti din Iasi

Revta Med Cienc Afin B Aires — Revista de Medicina y Ciencias Afines (Buenos Aires)

Revta Med Cienc Afin Mex — Revista de Medicina y Ciencias Afines (Mexico)

Revta Med Cirug Barcelona — Revista de Medicina y Cirugia (Barcelona)

Revta Med Cirug Barranq — Revista de Medicina y Cirugia (Barranquilla)

Revta Med Cirug Caracas — Revista de Medicina y Cirugia (Caracas)

Revta Med Cirug Farm — Revista de Medicina, Cirugia y Farmacia

Revta Med Cirug Habana — Revista de Medicina y Cirugia de la Habana

Revta Med Cirug Pract — Revista de Medicina y Cirugia Practicas

Revta Med Cirurg Braz — Revista Medico-Cirurgica do Brazil

Revta Med Cirurg Lisb — Revista de Medicina e Cirurgia (Lisboa)

Revta Med Cirurg Milit — Revista Medico-Cirurgica Militar

Revta Med Cirurg S Paulo — Revista de Medicina e Cirurgia de Sao Paulo

Revta Med Colomb — Revista Medica de Colombia

Revta Med Contemp — Revista de Medicina Contemporanea

Revta Med Cordoba — Revista Medica de Cordoba

Revta Med Corrientes — Revista Medica de Corrientes

Revta Med C Rica — Revista Medica de Costa Rica

Revta Med Cub — Revista Medica Cubana

Revta Med Dominic — Revista Medica Dominicana

Revta Med Ejerc Rebelde — Revista Medica del Ejercito Rebelde

Revta Med Esp — Revista Medica Espanola y Boletin de Higiene y Salubridad

Revta Med Est Guanabara — Revista Medica do Estado da Guanabara

Revta Med Estud Gen Navarra — Revista de Medicina del Estudio General de Navarra

Revta Med Exp — Revista de Medicina Experimental

Revta Med Farm — Revista de Medicina y Farmacia

Revta Med Farm Dominic — Revista Medico-Farmaceutica Dominicana

Revta Med Forense Crim — Revista de Medicina Forense y Criminalistica

Revta Med Gallega — Revista Medica Gallega

Revta Med Hondur — Revista Medica Hondurena

Revta Med Hosp Colonia Mex — Revista Medica del Hospital Colonia (Mexico)

Revta Med Hosp Esp B Aires — Revista Medica del Hospital Espanol (Buenos Aires)

Revta Med Hosp Esp Mex — Revista Medica del Hospital Espanol (Mexico)

Revta Med Hosp Gen Mex — Revista Medica del Hospital General (Mexico)

Revta Med Hosp Ital La Plata — Revista Medica del Hospital Italiano de La Plata

Revta Med Hosp Obrero Lima — Revista Medica del Hospital Obrero (Lima)

Revta Med Hyg Milit — Revista de Medicina e Hygiene Militar

Revta Med Iasi — Revista Medicala de Iasi

Revta Med Inst Mex Seguro Soc — Revista Medica del Instituto Mexicano del Seguro Social

Revta Med Iquitos — Revista Medica de Iquitos

Revta Med Juiz De Fora — Revista Medica de Juiz de Fora

Revta Med La Plata — Revista Medica de La Plata

Revta Med Malaga — Revista Medica de Malaga

Revta Med Managua — Revista Medica (Managua)

Revta Med Mex — Revista Medica (Mexico)

Revta Med Milit — Revista de Medicina Militar

Revta Med Munic Rio De J — Revista Medica Municipal (Rio de Janeiro)

Revta Med N Antofagasta — Revista Medica del Norte (Antofagasta)

Revta Med N S Miguel Tucuman — Revista Medica del Norte (San Miguel de Tucuman)

Revta Med Panam — Revista Medica Panamericana

Revta Med Parag — Revista Medica del Paraguay

Revta Med Parana — Revista Medica do Parana

Revta Med Pediat — Revista Mexicana de Pediatria

Revta Med Pernamb — Revista Medica de Pernambuco

Revta Med Peru — Revista Medica Peruana

Revta Med Pinar — Revista de Medicina Pinarena

Revta Med Potos — Revista Medica Potosina

Revta Med Prof — Revista Medico-Profesional

Revta Med Puebla — Revista Medica (Puebla)

Revta Med Quir — Revista Medico-Quirurgica

Revta Med Quir Hosp Ital B Aires — Revista Medico-Quirurgica del Hospital Italiano de Buenos Aires

Revta Med Quir Hosps Bogota — Revista Medico-Quirurgica de los Hospitales (Bogota)

Revta Med Quir Oriente — Revista Medico-Quirurgica de Oriente

Revta Med Quir Patol Fem — Revista Medico-Quirurgica de Patologia Femenina

Revta Med Quito — Revista Medica (Quito)

Revta Med Reus — Revista Medica (Reus)

Revta Med Rio Grande do Sul — Revista de Medicina do Rio Grande do Sul

Revta Med Soc Sanid Benef Munic Habana — Revista Medico-Social de la Sanidad y Beneficencia Municipal (La Habana)

Revta Med Soc Trab Montev — Revista de Medicina Social y del Trabajo (Montevideo)

Revta Med Sul Minas — Revista Medica do Sul de Minas

Revta Med Trop Bogota — Revista de Medicina Tropical (Bogota)

Revta Med Trop Habana — Revista de Medicina Tropical (Habana)

Revta Med Trop Parasit Habana — Revista de Medicina Tropical y Parasitologia, Bacteriologia, Clinica y Laboratorio (Habana)

Revta Med Turgu Mures — Revista Medicala (Turgu Mures)

Revta Med Urug — Revista Medica del Uruguay</PHR> %

Revta Med Valparaiso — Revista de Medicina (Valparaiso)

Revta Med Valparaiso — Revista Medica de Valparaiso

Revta Med Veracruz — Revista Medica Veracruzana

Revta Med Vet B Aires — Revista de Medicina Veterinaria (Buenos Aires)

Revta Med Vet Bogota — Revista de Medicina Veterinaria (Bogota)

Revta Med Vet Parasit (Caracas) — Revista de Medicina Veterinaria y Parasitologia (Caracas)

Revta Med Vet Santiago — Revista de Medicina Veterinaria (Santiago de Chile)

Revta Med Vet Zootec Bogota — Revista de Medicina Veterinaria y de Zootecnia (Bogota)

Revta Med Vet Zootech — Revista de Medicina Veterinara si'de Zootechnie

Revta Med Xalap — Revista Medica Xalapena

Revta Med Yucatan — Revista Medica de Yucatan

Revta Mens BAP — Revista Mensual B.A.P

Revta Mens Cent Farm Urug — Revista Mensual. Centro Farmaceutico del Uruguay

Revta Mens Dir Met Braz — Revista Mensual. Directoria de Meteorologia. Brazil

Revta Mens Esc Agric S Jose — Revista Mensual. Escuela de Agricultura (San Jose, Costa Rica)

Revta Mens Med Cirug Farm Vet — Revista Mensual de Medicina, Cirugia, Farmacia, y Veterinaria

Revta Mens Med Cirug Mex — Revista Mensual de Medicina e Cirugia (Mexico)

Revta Mens Univ Mex — Revista Mensual. Universidad de Mexico

Revta Metal — Revista del Metal

Revta Met Montev — Revista Meteorologica (Montevideo)

Revta Mex Alerg — Revista Mexicana de Alergiologia

Revta Mex Anest — Revista Mexicana de Anestesiologia

Revta Mex Biol — Revista Mexicana de Biologia

Revta Mex Cienc Med Biol — Revista Mexicana de Ciencias Medicas y Biologicas

Revta Mex Cirug Ginec Cancer — Revista Mexicana de Cirugia, Ginecologia, y Cancer

Revta Mex Elect — Revista Mexicana de Electricidad

Revta Mex Estud Antrop — Revista Mexicana de Estudios Antropologicos

Revta Mex Fis — Revista Mexicana de Fisica

Revta Mex Geogr — Revista Mexicana de Geografia

Revta Mex Ing Arquit — Revista Mexicana de Ingenieria y Arquitectura

Revta Mex Med Vet — Revista Mexicana de Medicina Veterinaria

Revta Mex Psiquiat Neurol Med Leg — Revista Mexicana de Psiquiatria, Neurologia, y Medicina Legal

Revta Mex Pueric — Revista Mexicana de Puericultura

Revta Mex Tuberc — Revista Mexicana de Tuberculosis y Enfermedades del Aparato Respiratorio

Revta Milit Remonta Vet — Revista Militar de Remonta e Veterinaria

Revta Min — Revista Minelor

Revta Minas Hidrocarb Caracas — Revista de Minas e Hidrocarburos (Caracas)

Revta Min B Aires — Revista Minera (Buenos Aires)

Revta Min Bolivia — Revista Minera de Bolivia

Revta Min Copiapo — Revista Minera (Copiapo)

Revta Min Engenh — Revista Mineira de Engenharia

Revta Miner Medellin — Revista Mineria (Medellin)

Revta Min Ind Linares — Revista Minera de Industrial (Linares)

Revta Minist Agric Cuba — Revista. Ministerio de Agricultura. Cuba

Revta Minist Colon Agric La Paz — Revista. Ministerio de Colonias y Agricultura (La Paz)

Revta Minist Fom Caracas — Revista. Ministerio de Fomento (Caracas)

Revta Minist Inds Montev — Revista del Ministerio de Industrias (Montevideo)

Revta Minist Obr Publ Fom Bogota — Revista del Ministerio de Obras Publicas y Fomento (Bogota)

Revta Min Lisb — Revista Mineira (Lisboa)

Revta Min Metal Ing — Revista Minera, Metalurgica, y de Ingenieria

Revta Min Santiago — Revista Minera (Santiago de Chile)

Revta Mus Argent Cienc Nat Bernardina Rivadavia Zool — Revista. Museo Argentino de Ciencias Naturales Bernardina Rivadavia. Zoologia

Revta Mus Argent Cienc Nat Bernardino Rivadavia Cienc Bot — Revista del Museo Argentino de Ciencias Naturales Bernardino Rivadavia. Ciencias Botanicas

Revta Mus Argent Cienc Nat Bernardino Rivadavia Cienc Zool — Revista del Museo Argentino de Ciencias Naturales Bernardino Rivadavia. Ciencias Zoologicas

Revta Mus Hist Nat Mendoza — Revista del Museo de Historia Natural de Mendoza

Revta Mus La Plata Antrop — Revista del Museo de La Plata. Seccion Antropologia

Revta Mus La Plata Botan — Revista del Museo de La Plata. Seccion Botanica

Revta Mus La Plata Geol — Revista del Museo de La Plata. Seccion Geologia

Revta Mus La Plata Paleontol — Revista del Museo de La Plata. Seccion Paleontologia

Revta Mus La Plata Zool — Revista del Museo de La Plata. Seccion Zoologia

Revta Mus Munic Cienc Nat Mar Del Plata — Revista del Museo Municipal de Ciencias Naturales y Tradicional de Mar del Plata

Revta Mus Nac Lima — Revista. Museo Nacional (Lima)

Revta Mus Nac Rio de J — Revista do Museu Nacional (Rio de Janeiro)

Revta Mus Paul — Revista. Museu Paulista

Revta Muz Geol Miner Univ Cluj — Revista Muzeului Geologic-Mineralogic al Universitatii din Cluj
Revta Nac Aeronaut — Revista Nacional de Aeronautica
Revta Nac Agric Bogota — Revista Nacional de Agricultura (Bogota)
Revta Nac Arquit Madr — Revista Nacional de Arquitectura (Madrid)
Revta Nac Hosps Caracas — Revista Nacional de Hospitales (Caracas)
Revta Nac Pesca S Paulo — Revista Nacional da Pesca (Sao Paulo)
Revta Natn Agric — Revista Nationala de Agricultura
Revta Nav Odont — Revista Naval de Odontologia
Revta Neurol B Aires — Revista Neurologica de Buenos Aires
Revta Neurol Clin — Revista de Neurologia Clinica
Revta Neurol Psiquiat Hig Ment — Revista de Neurologia, Psiquiatria, e Higiene Mental
Revta Neurol Psychiat S Paulo — Revista de Neurologia e Psychiatria de Sao Paulo
Revta Neuropsiquiat — Revista de Neuro-Psiquiatria
Revta Nutr — Revista de Nutricion
Revta Obr Publ — Revista de Obras Publicas
Revta Obr Publ Minas — Revista de Obras Publicas e Minas
Revta Obr Sanit Nac B Aires — Revista de Obras Sanitarias de la Nacion (Buenos Aires)
Revta Obs Rio De J — Revista do Observatorio do Rio de Janeiro
Revta Obstet — Revista Obstetrica
Revta Obstet Ginec S Paulo — Revista de Obstetricia e Ginecologia de Sao Paulo
Revta Obstet Ginec Venez — Revista de Obstetricia y Ginecologia de Venezuela
Revta Obstet Matr — Revista de Obstetricia para Matronas
Revta Ocrot Sanit RPR — Revista de Ocrotirii a Sanitatii in R.P.R
Revta Odont B Aires — Revista Odontologica. Circulo Odontologico Argentino (Buenos Aires)
Revta Odont Bras — Revista Odontologica Brasileira
Revta Odont Circulo Odont B Aires — Revista Odontologica del Circulo Odontologico (Buenos Aires)
Revta Odont Circulo Odont Parag — Revista Odontologica del Circulo de Odontologos del Paraguay
Revta Odont Concepcion — Revista Odontologica de Concepcion (Concepcion)
Revta Odont Lisb — Revista Odontologica (Lisboa)
Revta Odont Mex — Revista Odontologica de Mexico
Revta Odont Mex — Revista Odontologica (Mexico)
Revta Odont Paraiba — Revista Odontologica da Paraiba
Revta Odont Paul — Revista Odontologica Paulista. Sociedade Odontologica Paulista
Revta Odont Soc Propag Hig Dent Bogota — Revista Odontologia del Sociedad Propagandista de Higiene Dental y de los Intereses Profesionales (Bogota)
Revta Odont Univ S Domingo — Revista Odontologica. Universidad de Santa Domingo
Revta Odont Zulia — Revista Odontologica del Zulia
Revta Of Asoc Empl Farm B Aires — Revista Oficial. Asociacion Empleados de Farmacia (Buenos Aires)
Revta Of Inst Quim Ind Montev — Revista Oficial. Instituto de Quimica Industrial (Montevideo)
Revta Oftal S Paulo — Revista de Oftalmologia (Sao Paulo)
Revta Oftal Venez — Revista Oftalmologica Venezolana
Revta Ortop Traum — Revista de Ortopedia y Traumatologia
Revta Ortop Traum Lat Am — Revista de Ortopedia y Traumatologia Latino-Americano
Revta Oto Lar S Paulo — Revista Oto-Laringologica de Sao Paulo
Revta Oto Neuro Oftal Cirug Neurol Sud Am — Revista Oto-Neuro-Oftalmologica y de Cirugia Neurologica Sud-Americana
Revta Otorinolar — Revista de Otorinolaringologia
Revta Padur — Revista Padurilor
Revta Panam Med Cirug Torax — Revista Panamericana de Medicina y Cirugia del Torax
Revta Parasit Clin Lab — Revista de Parasitologia, Clinica y Laboratorio
Revta Pasteur — Revista Pasteur
Revta Patron Biol Anim — Revista del Patronato de Biologia Animal
Revta Paul Hosp — Revista Paulista de Hospitais
Revta Paul Med — Revista Paulista de Medicina
Revta Peru Ent Agric — Revista Peruana de Entomologia Agricola
Revta Peru Obstet — Revista Peruana de Obstetricia
Revta Peru Otorrinolar Oftal — Revista Peruana de Otorrinolaringologia y Oftalmologia
Revta Peru Patol — Revista Peruana de Patologia
Revta Peru Pediat — Revista Peruana de Pediatria
Revta Peru Radiol — Revista Peruana de Radiologia
Revta Peru Salud Publ — Revista Peruana de Salud Publica
Revta Peru Tuberc Enferm Respir — Revista Peruana de Tuberculosis y Enfermedades Respiratorias
Revta Policl Cara — Revista de la Policlinica Caracas
Revta Port Farm — Revista Portuguesa de Farmacia
Revta Port Med — Revista Portuguesa de Medicina
Revta Port Med Cirurg Prat — Revista Portugueza de Medicina e Cirurgia Praticas
Revta Port Med Milit — Revista Portuguesa de Medicina Militar
Revta Port Obstet Ginec Cirurg — Revista Portuguesa de Obstetricia, Ginecologia, e Cirurgia
Revta Port Pediat Pueric — Revista Portuguesa de Pediatria e Puericultura
Revta Post Telegr Telef — Revista Postala, Telegrafica, si Telefonica
Revta Pract — Revista del Practicante
Revta Prod Minas Geraes — Revista da Produccao (Minas Geraes)
Revta Psicoanal — Revista de Psicoanalisis
Revta Psicol Bogota — Revista de Psicologia (Bogota)
Revta Psicol Gen Apl — Revista de Psicologia General y Aplicada
Revta Psicol Lima — Revista de Psicologia (Lima)
Revta Psicol Norm Patol — Revista de Psicologia Normal e Patologica
Revta Psicol Pedag — Revista de Psicologia y Pedagogia
Revta Psicol Pedag Apl — Revista de Psicologia y Pedagogia Aplicadas

Revta Psihol Buc — Revista de Psihologie (Bucuresti)
Revta Psihol Clug — Revista de Psihologie (Cluj)
Revta Psiquiat Crim — Revista de Psiquiatria y Criminologia
Revta Psiquiat Discip Conex Lima — Revista de Psiquiatria y Disciplinas Conexas (Lima)
Revta Psiquiat Discip Conex Santiago — Revista de Psiquiatria y Disciplinas Conexas (Santiago)
Revta Psiquiat Neurol — Revista de Psiquiatria y Neurologia
Revta Psiquiat Neurol Med Leg — Revista de Psiquiatria, Neurologia, y Medicina Legal
Revta Psiquiat Peru — Revista Psiquiatrica Peruana
Revta Psiquiat Psicol Med Eur Am Lat — Revista de Psiquiatria y Psicologia Medica de Europa y America Latinas
Revta Psiquiat Urug — Revista de Psiquiatria del Uruguay
Revta Publnes Nav B Aires — Revista de Publicaciones Navales. Ministerio de Marina (Buenos Aires)
Revta Quim Farm — Revista de Quimica e Farmacia
Revta Quim Farm — Revista Quimico-Farmaceutica
Revta Quim Ind B Aires — Revista de Quimica Industrial (Buenos Aires)
Revta Quim Ind Rio De J — Revista de Quimica Industrial (Rio de Janeiro)
Revta Quinc Anat Patol Clin Med Quir — Revista Quincenal de Anatomia Patologica y Clinica Medica y Quirurgica
Revta Quir Vias Urin — Revista Quirurgica de la Vias Urinarias
Revta Radiol — Revista de Radiologia
Revta Radiol Fisioter — Revista de Radiologia y Fisioterapia
Rev Tarn — Revue du Tarn
Revta Rom Stomat — Revista Romana de Stomatologia
Revta Rom Urol — Revista Romana de Urologia
Revta Salud Publ Lima — Revista de Salud Publica (Lima)
Revta Sanid Aeronaut — Revista de Sanidad de Aeronautica
Revta Sanid Asist Soc Caracas — Revista de Sanidad y Asistencia Social (Caracas)
Revta Sanid Benef Munic Habana — Revista de Sanidad y Beneficencia Municipal (Habana)
Revta Sanid Gendarm Nac B Aires — Revista de Sanidad de Gendarmeria Nacional (Buenos Aires)
Revta Sanid Guerra — Revista de Sanidad de Guerra
Revta Sanid Hig Publ — Revista de Sanidad e Higiene Publica
Revta Sanid La Plata — Revista de Sanidad (La Plata)
Revta Sanid Milit Argent — Revista de la Sanidad Militar Argentina
Revta Sanid Milit Caracas — Revista de Sanidad Militar (Caracas)
Revta Sanid Milit Habana — Revista de la Sanidad Militar (Habana)
Revta Sanid Milit Lima — Revista de Sanidad Militar (Lima)
Revta Sanid Milit Med Milit Esp — Revista de Sanidad Militar y la Medicina Militar Espanola
Revta Sanid Milit Mex — Revista de Sanidad Militar (Mexico)
Revta Sanid Milit Peru — Revista de Sanidad Militar del Peru
Revta Sanid Milit Santiago — Revista de Sanidad Militar (Santiago de Chile)
Revta Sanid Polic — Revista de la Sanidad de Policia
Revta Sanid Vet — Revista de Sanidad Veterinaria
Revta Sanit — Revista Sanitaria
Revta Sanit Milit — Revista Sanitara Militara
Revta Sci — Revista de Sciencias
Revta Seara Odont Bras — Revista Seara Odontologica Brasileira
Revta Serv Esp Saude Publ Rio De J — Revista do Servico Especial de Saude Publica (Rio de Janeiro)
Revta Serv Nac Salud Santiago — Revista del Servicio Nacional de Salud (Santiago de Chile)
Revta Servs Sanit Demogr Barcelona — Revista de los Servicios Sanitarios y Demograficos de Barcelona
Revta Sif Leprol Derm — Revista de Sifilografia, Leprologia, y Dermatologia
Revta Sind Nac Engenh Aux — Revista. Sindicato Nacional dos Engenheiros Auxiliares, Agentes Tecnicos de Engenharia e Condutores
Revta Sind Nac Ind Quim Madr — Revista del Sindicato Nacional de Industrias Quimicas (Madrid)
Revta Sind Odont Rio De J — Revista do Sindicato dos Odontologistas do Rio de Janeiro
Revta Soc Argent Biol — Revista de la Sociedad Argentina de Biologia
Revta Soc Argent Hemat Hemoterap — Revista de la Sociedad Argentina de Hematologia y Hemoterapia
Revta Soc Argent Neurol Psiquiat — Revista de la Sociedad Argentina de Neurologia y Psiquiatria
Revta Soc Argent Nipiol — Revista de la Sociedad Argentina de Nipiologia
Revta Soc Argent Oftal — Revista de la Sociedad Argentina de Oftalmologia
Revta Soc Argent Otorinolar — Revista de la Sociedad Argentina de Otorinolaringologia
Revta Soc Argent Proct — Revista de la Sociedad Argentina de Proctologia
Revta Soc Argent Radio Electrol — Revista de la Sociedad Argentina de Radio y Electrologia
Revta Soc Argent Tisiol — Revista de la Sociedad Argentina de Tisiologia
Revta Soc Argent Urol — Revista de la Sociedad Argentina de Urologia
Revta Soc Astr Esp Am — Revista de la Sociedad Astronomica de Espana y America
Revta Soc Bras Agron — Revista da Sociedade Brasileira de Agronomia
Revta Soc Brasil Geogr — Revista. Sociedade Brasileira de Geografia
Revta Soc Bras Quim — Revista da Sociedade Brasileira de Quimica
Revta Soc Bras Sci — Revista. Sociedade Brasileira de Sciencias
Revta Soc Chil Urol — Revista de la Sociedad Chilena de Urologia
Revta Soc Cient Parag — Revista de la Sociedad Cientifica del Paraguay
Revta Soc Cirug Bucal Rosario — Revista de la Sociedad de Cirugia Bucal de Rosario
Revta Soc Colomb Cienc Nat — Revista de la Sociedad Colombiana de Ciencias Naturales
Revta Soc Colomb Endocr — Revista de la Sociedad Colombiana de Endocrinologia

Revta Soc Colomb Pediat Pueric — Revista de la Sociedad Colombiana de Pediatria y Puericultura

Revta Soc Cub Bot — Revista de la Sociedad Cubana de Botanica

Revta Soc Cub Cienc Fis Mat — Revista de la Sociedad Cubana de Ciencias Fisicas y Matematicas

Revta Soc Cub Hist Med — Revista de la Sociedad Cubana de Historia de la Medicina

Revta Soc Cub Ing — Revista de la Sociedad Cubana de Ingenieros

Revta Soc Ent Argent — Revista de la Sociedad Entomologica Argentina

Revta Soc Estud Ortod Tweed Mex — Revista de la Sociedad de Estudios de Ortodoncia Tweed de Mexico

Revta Soc Geogr Cuba — Revista de la Sociedad Geografica de Cuba

Revta Soc Geogr Rio Jan — Revista. Sociedade de Geografia do Rio de Janeiro

Revta Soc Geol Argent — Revista de la Sociedad Geologica Argentina

Revta Soc Hig Microbiol B Aires — Revista de la Sociedad de Higiene y Microbiologia (Buenos Aires)

Revta Soc Lun Int — Revista de la Sociedad Lunar Internacional

Revta Soc Malac Carlos de la Torre — Revista de la Sociedad Malacologia Carlos de la Torre

Revta Soc Maranhense Agric — Revista da Sociedade Maranhense de Agricultura

Revta Soc Mat Esp — Revista de la Sociedad Matematica Espanola

Revta Soc Med Quir Magdalena — Revista de la Sociedad Medico-Quirurgica del Magdalena

Revta Soc Med Quir Zulia — Revista de la Sociedad Medico-Quirurgica del Zulia

Revta Soc Med Tapachula — Revista de la Sociedad Medica de Tapachula

Revta Soc Med Vet B Aires — Revista. Sociedad de la Medicina Veterinaria (Buenos Aires)

Revta Soc Med Vet Chile — Revista de la Sociedad de Medicina Veterinaria de Chile

Revta Soc Mex Ent — Revista de la Sociedad Mexicana de Entomologia

Revta Soc Mex Hist Nat — Revista de la Sociedad Mexicana de Historia Natural

Revta Soc Nac Agric Quito — Revista de la Sociedad Nacional de Agriculture (Quito)

Revta Soc Obstet Ginec B Aires — Revista de la Sociedad de Obstetricia y Ginecologia de Buenos Aires (Buenos Aires)

Revta Soc Quim Mex — Revista. Sociedad Quimica de Mexico

Revta Soc Rur Bras — Revista da Sociedade Rural Brasileira

Revta Soc Rur Cordoba — Revista de la Sociedad Rural de Cordoba

Revta Soc Scient S Paulo — Revista da Sociedade Scientifica de Sao Paulo

Revta Soc Venez Hist Med — Revista de la Sociedad Venezolana de Historia de la Medicina

Revta Soc Venez Quim — Revista de la Sociedad Venezolana de Quimica

Revta Stiint Med — Revista Stiintelor Medicale

Revta Stiint V Adamachi — Revista Stiintifica V. Adamachi

Revta Stiint Vet — Revista Stiintelor Veterinare

Revta Sudam Bot — Revista Sudamericana de Botanica

Revta Sudam Endocr Immun Quimioter — Revista Sudamericana de Endocrinologia, Immunologia, y Quimioterapia

Revta Sudam Morf — Revista Sudamericana de Morfologia

Revta Synat — Revista Synatrica

Revta Tec Curitiba — Revista Tecnica (Curitiba)

Revta Tec Minist Obr Publ Venez — Revista Tecnica. Ministerio de Obras Publicas. Venezuela

Revta Tec Planej Hosp — Revista Tecnica de Planejamento Hospitalar

Revta Tec Sulam — Revista Tecnica Sulamericana

Revta Teh AGIR — Revista Tehnica AGIR. Asociatie Generala Inginerilor din Romania

Revta Telecomun — Revista de Telecomunicacion

Revta Telef Argent — Revista Telefonica Argentina

Revta Telegr Electron — Revista Telegrafica Electronica

Revta Terap Peru — Revista Terapeutica Peruana

Revta Text — Revista Textil

Revta Tierr Colon B Aires — Revista de Tierras y Colonizacion (Buenos Aires)

Revta Tisiol Neumon — Revista de Tisiologia y Neumonologia

Revta Tuberc Lima — Revista de Tuberculosis (Lima)

Revta Tuberc Urug — Revista de Tuberculosis del Uruguay

Revta Univ Al I Cuza Inst Politeh Iasi — Revista Universitatii Al. I. Cuza si a Institutului Politehnic din Iasi

Revta Univ Andes — Revista de la Universidad de los Andes

Revta Univ Auton G R Moreno — Revista. Universidad Autonoma Gabriel Rene Moreno

Revta Univ B Aires — Revista de la Universidad de Buenos Aires

Revta Univ C I Parhon Politeh Buc — Revista Universitatii C. I. Parhon si a Politehnicii Bucuresti

Revta Univ Coimbra — Revista da Universidade de Coimbra

Revta Univ Cuzco — Revista Universitaria (Cuzco)

Revta Univ Ind Santander — Revista de la Universidad Industrial de Santander

Revta Univ La Paz — Revista Universitaria (La Paz, Bolivia)

Revta Univ Lima — Revista Universitaria. Universidad Mayor de San Marcos (Lima)

Revta Univ Madr — Revista de la Universidad de Madrid

Revta Univ Mat — Revista Universitara Matematica

Revta Univ Nac Cordoba — Revista de la Universidad Nacional de Cordoba

Revta Univ Nac La Plata — Revista. Universidad Nacional de La Plata

Revta Univ Univ Catol Chile — Revista Universitaria. Universidad Catolica de Chile

Revta Un Mat Argent — Revista de la Union Matematica Argentina

Revta Un Odont Bras — Revista da Uniao Odontologica Brasileira

Revta Urol Recife — Revista de Urologia (Recife)

Revta Urug Geogr — Revista Uruguaya de Geografia

Revta Urug Psicoanal — Revista Uruguaya de Psicoanalisis

Revta Vac Cienc Nat Salta — Revista de la Facultad de Ciencias Naturales de Salta. Universidad Nacional de Tucuman

Revta Valenc Cienc Med — Revista Valenciana de Ciencias Medicas

Revta Venez Sanid Asist Soc — Revista Venezolana de Sanidad y Asistencia Social

Revta Vet Fom Equino — Revista de Veterinaria y Fomento Equino

Revta Vet Milit — Revista de Veterinaria Militar

Revta Vet Venez — Revista Veterinaria Venezolana

Revta Vet Zootech — Revista de Veterinaria e Zootechnia

Revta Vet Zootec Manizales — Revista de Veterinaria y Zootecnia (Manizales)

Revta Viernes Med — Revista del Viernes Medico

Revta Vinic Agric — Revista Vinicola y de Agricultura

Revta Viti Vinic — Revista Viti-Vinicola

Rev Tax Indiv — Review of Taxation of Individuals

Revta YPF — Revista YPF

Revta Zootec — Revista Zootechica

Revta Zootech Vet — Revista de Zootechnica e Veterinaria

Rev Teatro Rio — Revista de Teatro (Rio de Janeiro)

Rev Tec — Revista Tecnica

Rev Tec Col Ing Agron Mex — Revista Tecnica. Colegio de Ingenieros Agronomos de Mexico

Rev Tech Batim Constr Ind — Revue Technique du Batiment et des Constructions Industrielles

Rev Tech Ind Aliment — Revue Technique de l'Industrie Alimentaire

Rev Tech Ind Cuir — Revue Technique des Industries du Cuir

Rev Tech Luxemb — Revue Technique Luxembourgeoise

Rev Techn Ind Cuir — Revue Technique des Industries du Cuir

Rev Tech Thomson CSF — Revue Technique Thomson - CSF

Rev Tec Inst Nac Electron — Revista Tecnica. Instituto Nacional de Electronica

Rev Tec INTEVEP — Revista Tecnica INTEVEP

Rev Tecn Fac Ingr Univ Zulia — Revista Tecnica. Facultad de Ingenieria. Universidad del Zulia

Rev Tecnol Ind — Revista Tecnologico-Industrial

Rev Tecnol Med — Revista de Tecnologia Medica

Rev Tec Sulzer — Revista Tecnica Sulzer

Rev Tec Text Vestido — Revista Tecnica Textil-Vestido

Rev Tec Yacimientos Pet Fiscales Boliv — Revista Tecnica. Yacimientos Petroliferos Fiscales Bolivianos

Rev Tec Zulia Univ — Revista Tecnica. Zulia University

Rev Teilhard de Chardin — Revue Teilhard de Chardin

Rev Telecom — Revista de Telecomunicacion

Rev Telecommun — Revue des Telecommunications

Rev Telecomun (Madrid) — Revista de Telecomunicacion (Madrid)

Rev Telegr Electron — Revista Telegrafica Electronica

Rev Temas Mil — Revista de Temas Militares

Rev Terrington Exp Husb Fm — Review. Terrington Experimental Husbandry Farm

Rev Text (Ghent) — Revue Textilis (Ghent)

Rev Textile Progr — Review of Textile Progress

Rev Text (Paris) — Revue Textile (Paris)

Rev Text Prog — Review of Textile Progress [*Manchester*]

Rev Text Progr — Review of Textile Progress

Rev Text Res Dev — Review of Textile Research and Development. Textile Research Institute [*Princeton*]

Rev Text Tiba — Revue Textile Tiba

RevTh — Revue Theatrale. Revue Internationale du Theatre

Rev Theobroma — Revista Theobroma

Rev Theol Phil — Revue de Theologie et de Philosophie

Rev Theol Philos — Revue de Theologie et de Philosophie

Rev Ther — Revue Therapeutique

Rev Therap — Revue Therapeutique

Rev Therap Bibliogr Med — Revue Therapeutique et Bibliographie Medicale

Rev Therap Med-Chir — Revue de Therapeutique Medico-Chirurgicale

Rev Thomiste — Revue Thomiste

Rev Th Philos — Revue de Theologie et de Philosophie

Revtl — Revista. Instituto de Historia de Derecho Ricardo Levene

Rev Tisiol Neumonol — Revista de Tisiologia y Neumonologia

Rev Tournais — Revue Tournaisienne

Rev Toxicol — Revista de Toxicologia

Rev Toxicol Alicante Spain — Revista de Toxicologia (Alicante, Spain)

Rev Toxicol Amsterdam — Reviews in Toxicology (Amsterdam)

Rev Trab — Revista de Trabajo

Rev Trab Caracas — Revista del Trabajo (Caracas)

Rev Trab S Salvador — Revista de Trabajo (San Salvador)

Rev Trach — Revue du Trachome

Rev Tradit Popul — Revue des Traditions Populaires

Rev Trad Pop — Revue des Traditions Populaires

Rev Transp Telecomun — Revista Transporturilor si Telecomunicatiilor

Rev Trav — Revue du Travail

Rev Trav — Revue du Travail et du Bien-Etre Social

Rev Trav Acad Sci Morales Polit — Revue des Travaux. Academie des Sciences Morales et Politiques et Comptes-Rendus de ses Seances

Rev Trav Inst Peches Marit — Revue des Travaux. Institut des Peches Maritimes

Rev Trav Inst Sci Tech Peches Marit — Revue des Travaux. Institut Scientifique et Technique des PechesMaritimes

Rev Tr Dr Civ — Revue Trimestrielle de Droit Civil

Rev Trimest Can — Revue Trimestrielle Canadienne

Rev Trimestr de Droit Eur — Revue Trimestrielle de Droit Europeen

Rev Trimestr de Jurispr — Revista Trimestral de Jurisprudencia

Rev Trimestrielle Canad — Revue Trimestrielle Canadienne

Rev Trimestrielle Canadienne — Revue Trimestrielle Canadienne

Rev Trop Dis — Review of Tropical Diseases [*Calcutta*]

Rev Troup Colon — Revue des Troupes Coloniales

Rev Tuberc — Revue de Tuberculose

Rev Tuberc Pneumol — Revue de Tuberculose et de Pneumologie [*Later, Revue Francaise des Maladies Respiratoires*]

Rev Tun Droit — Revue Tunisienne de Droit

Rev Tunisienne de Droit — Revue Tunisienne de Droit

Rev Tunis Sci Soc — Revue Tunisienne de Sciences Sociales
Rev Tun Sc Soc — Revue Tunisienne des Sciences Sociales
Rev Turq Hyg Biol Exp — Revue Turque d'Hygiene et de Biologie Experimentale
Rev Turque Hyg Biol Exp — Revue Turque d'Hygiene et de Biologie Experimentale
Rev Tussock Grassl Mt Lands Inst — Review. Tussock Grasslands and Mountain Lands Institute
RevU — Revue Universitaire
RevuB — Revue Belge de Philologie et d'Histoire
Rev U Bruxelles — Revue de l'Universite de Bruxelles
Rev U Coimbra — Revista da Universidade de Coimbra
Rev U Complutense — Revista de la Universidad Complutense
RevudA — Revue d'Allemagne
Rev UDEM — Revista. Universidad de Medellin
RevudHA — Revue d'Histoire de l'Amerique Francaise
RevudHE — Revuc d'Histoire Ecclesiastique
RevudHF — Revue d'Histoire de l'Eglise de France
RevudHM — Revue d'Histoire Moderne et Contemporaine
RevudHP — Revue d'Histoire de la Pharmacie
RevudHV — Revue d'Histoire Vaudoise
RevudI — Revue de l'Institut Napoleon
RevudO — Revue. Universite d'Ottawa
RevudP — Revue de Paris
RevudS — Revue des Etudes Sud-Est Europeenes
RevudT — Revue des Travaux. Academie des Sciences Morales et Publiques
RevuduN — Revue du Nord
Revue Abatt Hyd Aliment Ind Anim — Revue des Abattoirs, d'Hygiene Alimentaire et de l'Industrie Animale
Revue Accid Trav Mal Prof — Revue des Accidents du Travail et des Maladies Professionelles
Revue Acoust — Revue d'Acoustique
Revue Actinol Physiother — Revue d'Actinologie et de Physiotherapie
Revue Aeronaut Exp — Revue de l'Aeronautique Experimentale
Revue Aeronaut Fr — Revue Aeronautique de France
Revue Aeronaut Int — Revue Aeronautique Internationale
Revue Aeronaut Milit — Revue de l'Aeronautique Militaire
Revue Afr Mgmt — Revue Africaine de Management
Revue Agglom Cim — Revue des Agglomeres de Ciment
Revue Ag Phys — Revue des Agents Physiques et de Leurs Applications a la Clinique et a la Therapeutique
Revue Agric Afr N — Revue Agricole de l'Afrique du Nord
Revue Agric (Brux) — Revue de l'Agriculture (Bruxelles)
Revue Agric Guadeloupe — Revue Agricole. Service de l'Agriculture de Guadeloupe
Revue Agric Ile Maurice — Revue Agricole de l'Ile Maurice
Revue Agric Ile Reunion — Revue Agricole de l'Ile de Reunion
Revue Agric Nouv Caled — Revue Agricole de la Nouvelle-Caledonie et Dependances
Revue Agric Puy De Dome — Revue Agricole du Puy-de-Dome
Revue Agricrs Fr — Revue des Agriculteurs de France
Revue Agric Sucr Ile Maurice — Revue Agricole et Sucriere de l'Ile Maurice
Revue Agric Sucr Rhum Antilles Fr — Revue Agricole Sucriere et Rhumiere des Antilles Francaises
Revue Agric Vet Tananarive — Revue Agricole et Veterinaire (Tananarive)
Revue Agric Vitic Afr N — Revue Agricole et Viticole de l'Afrique du Nord
Revue Agrol Bot Kivu — Revue Agrologique et Botanique du Kivu
Revue Agron Colon — Revue d'Agronomie Coloniale
Revue Air Liq — Revue de l'Air Liquide
Revue Alcool — Revue de l'Alcoolisme
Revue Algerienne Sci Juridiques Econ et Polit — Revue Algerienne des Sciences Juridiques, Economiques, et Politiques
Revue Algol — Revue Algologique
Revue Alumin — Revue de l'Aluminium et de ses Applications
Revue Anc Etud Inst Tech Roubais — Revue des Anciens Etudiants. Institut Technique Roubaisen
Revue Anthr — Revue Anthropologique
Revue Anthr — Revue d'Anthropologie
Revue Anthrop — Revue Anthropologique
Revue Applic Elect — Revue des Applications de l'Electricite
Revue Arch Centre — Revue Archeologique du Centre
Revue Archeol — Revue Archeologique
Revue Archs Ital Biol — Revue des Archives Italiennes de Biologie
Revue Arch Syr — Revue Archeologique Syrienne
Revue Ass Gen Chim Ind Text — Revue de l'Association Generale des Chimistes de l'Industrie Textile
Revue Assyriol — Revue d'Assyriologie et d'Archeologie Orientale
Revue Atheroscler — Revue de l'Atherosclerose
Revue Aviat — Revue de l'Aviation
Revue BBC — Revue BBC. Brown Boveri et Cie
Revue Belge Arch et Hist Art — Revue Belge d'Archeologie et d'Histoire de l'Art
Revue Belge Hist Contemporaine — Revue Belge d'Histoire Contemporaine
Revue Belge Inds Verr — Revue Belge des Industries Verrieres
Revue Belge Odont — Revue Belge d'Ontologie
Revue Belge Path Med Exp — Revue Belge de Pathologie et de Medecine Experimentale
Revue Belge Psychol Pedag — Revue Belge de Psychologie et de Pedagogie
Revue Belge Sci Dent — Revue Belge de Science Dentaire
Revue Belge Stomat — Revue Belge de Stomatologie
Revue Belge Transp — Revue Belge des Transports
Revue Belge Tuberc — Revue Belge de la Tuberculose
Revue Belge Urol Derm Syph — Revue Belge d'Urologie et de Dermato-Syphiligraphie
Revue Belg Pueric — Revue Belge de Puericulture
Revue Belg Sci Med — Revue Belge des Sciences Medicales
Revue Bett — Revue de la Betterave

Revue Biblphiq Sci — Revue Bibliographique des Sciences Naturelles Pures et Appliquees
Revue Bimens Obs Univ Sun Yatsen — Revue Bimensuelle. Observatoire de l'Universite Sun Yatsen
Revue Bimens Seric — Revue Bimensuelle de la Sericulture
Revue Biol Buc — Revue de Biologie (Bucarest)
Revue Bleue — Revue Politique et Litteraire. Revue Bleue
Revue Brass — Revue de la Brasserie
Revue Bret Bot — Revue Bretonne de Botanique
Revue Bryol — Revue Bryologique
Revue Bryol Lichen — Revue Bryologique et Lichenologique
Revue Bulg Pediat — Revue Bulgare de Pediatrie
Revue Can Biol — Revue Canadienne de Biologie
Revue Cancer — Revue du Cancer
Revue Can Geogr — Revue Canadienne de Geographie
Revue Carb Fr — Revue des Carburants Francais
Revue CENPA — Revue CENPA (Societe Centrale des Usines a Papiers et Papeteries)
Revue Cent Neuro Psychiat Brux — Revue du Centre Neuro-Psychiatrique (Bruxelles)
Revue Ceram — Revue de Ceramique
Revue Chauff Elect — Revue du Chauffage Electrique
Revue Chim Appl Scient Tech — Revue de Chimie Appliquee, Scientifique Technique
Revue Chim Brux — Revue Chimique (Bruxelles)
Revue Chim Buc — Revue de Chimie (Bucarest)
Revue Chim Ind — Revue de Chimie Industrielle et le Moniteur Scientifique Quesneville Reunis
Revue Chim Zagr — Revue Chimique (Zagreb)
Revue Chir Plast — Revue de Chirurgie Plastique
Revue Chir Struct — Revue de Chirurgie Structive
Revue Chronom — Revue Chronometrique
Revue Cines Electrother — Revue de Cinesie et d'Electrotherapie
Revue Clin Androl Gynec — Revue Clinique d'Andrologie et de Gynecologie
Revue Clin Med Chir Accid Trav — Revue Clinique Medico-Chirurgicale Accidents du Travail
Revue Clin Ther — Revue de Clinique et de Therapeutique
Revue Clin Urol — Revue Clinique d'Urologie
Revue Colon — Revue Coloniale
Revue Colon Belge — Revue Coloniqle Belge
Revue Colon Med Chir — Revue Coloniale de Medecine et de Chirurgie
Revue Combust Liq — Revue des Combustibles Liquides
Revue Com Natn Chasse — Revue du Comite National de la Chasse
Revue Comp Anim — Revue du Comportement Animal
Revue Congol — Revue Congolaise
Revue Congol Batim Ind — Revue Congolaise du Batiment et de l'Industrie
Revue Corps Sante Armees — Revue des Corps de Sante des Armees, Terre, Mer, Air, et du Corps Veterinaire
Revue Corps Sante Milit — Revue du Corps de Sante Militaire
Revuc Corps Vet Armee — Revue du Corps Veterinaire de l'Armee
Revue Couvert Plomb — Revue de la Couverture Plomberie
Revue Crit Med Chir — Revue Critique de Medecine et de Chirurgie
Revue Crit Paleozool — Revue Critique de Paleozoologie
Revue Cult Colon — Revue des Cultures Coloniales
Revue Cytol Biol Veg — Revue de Cytologie et de Biologie Vegetales
Revue Cytol Cytophysiol Veg — Revue de Cytologie et de Cytophysiologie Vegetales
Revue Dent Fr — Revue Dentaire de France
Revue Dent Int Electrol Physiother Cancers Bucc — Revue Dentaire Internationale d'Electrologie et de Physiotherapie des Cancers Buccaux
Revue Dent Liban — Revue Dentaire Libanaise
Revue Deontol — Revue de Deontologie et d'Interets Professionels Medicaux
Revue d'Histoire du Theatre — Publications de la Societe d'Histoire du Theatre. Revue de la Societe d'Histoire du Theatre
Revue d Histoire Litteraire — Revue d'Histoire Litteraire de la France
Revue Diel — Revue de Dietetique
Revue Docum — Revue de la Documentation
Revue Droit Intell Ing Cons — Revue de Droit Intellectuel, l'Ingenieur-Conseil
Revue Droit Pen Crim — Revue de Droit Penal et de Criminologie et Archives Internationales de Medecine Legale
Revue E — Revue E. Societe Belge des Electriciens
Revue Eaux Forets — Revue des Eaux et Forets
Revue Eclair — Revue des Eclairages
Revue Eclect Apic — Revue Eclectic de l'Apiculture
Revue Econ Fr — Revue Economique Francaise Publiee par la Societe de Geographie Commerciale
Revue Econ Ind Technol Mod — Revue d'Economie Industrielle et de Technologie Moderne
Revue Elect — Revue Electrique
Revue Elect Eclair — Revue de l'Electricite et de l'Eclairage
Revue Elect Mecan — Revue d'Electricite et de Mecanique</PHR> %
Revue Electrochim Electrometall — Revue de l'Electrochimie et de l'Electrometallurgie
Revue Electroradiol — Revue Electro-Radiologique
Revue Electrotech Energ — Revue de l'Electrotechnique et d'Energetique
Revue Elev — Revue de l'Elevage. Productions Animales - Productions Fourrageres
Revue Elev Prod Anim Fr — Revue de l'Elevage et des Productions Animales Francaise. Betail et Basse-Cour
Revue Emball — Revue de l'Emballage
Revue Embouteill — Revue de l'Embouteillage et des Industries Connexes
Revue Ent — Revue d'Entomologie
Revue Estud Als Lorr — Revue Estudiantine d'Alsace-Lorraine
Revue Ethnogr Sociol — Revue d'Ethnographie et de Sociologie
Revue Ethnogr Tradit Pop — Revue d'Ethnographie et des Traditions Populaires

Revue Etud Clin Biol — Revue d'Etudes Cliniques et Biologiques
Revue Etud Comp Est Ouest — Revue d'Etudes Comparatives Est-Ouest. Economie, Planification, et Organisation
Revue Etud Coop — Revue des Etudes Cooperatives
Revue Ferment Ind Aliment — Revue des Fermentations et des Industries Alimentaires
Revue Filat Tiss — Revue de la Filature et du Tissage
Revue Film Med Chir — Revue du Film Medical et Chirurgical
Revue Flore Med Vet Pop N Fr — Revue de la Flore Medicinale et Veterinaire Populaire du Nord de la France
Revue Foie — Revue du Foie
Revue For Fr — Revue Forestiere Francaise
Revue Fr Allerg — Revue Francaise d'Allergie
Revue Fr Allergol — Revue Francaise d'Allergologie [*Later,* Revue Francaise d'*Allergologie et d'Immunologie Clinique*]
Revue Fr Allergol Immunol Clin — Revue Francaise d'Allergologie et d'Immunologie Clinique
Revue Franco Roum Ind Petrol — Revue Franco-Roumaine de l'Industrie Petrolifere
Revue Franco Russe Med Biol — Revue Franco-Russe de Medecine et de Biologie
Revue Fr Apic — Revue Francaise d'Apiculture
Revue Fr Astronaut — Revue Francaise d'Astronautique
Revue Fr Constr Auto Aeronaut — Revue Francaise de Construction Automobile et Aeronautique
Revue Fr Cps Gras — Revue Francaise des Corps Gras
Revue Fr d Adm Publique — Revue Francaise d'Administration Publique
Revue Fr Derm Vener — Revue Francaise de Dermatologie et de Venereologie
Revue Fr Diet — Revue Francaise de Dietetique
Revue Fr Endocr — Revue Francaise d'Endocrinologie
Revue Fr Endocr Clin — Revue Francaise d'Endocrinologie Clinique, Nutrition, et Metabolisme
Revue Fr Energ — Revue Francaise de l'Energie
Revue Fr Ent — Revue Francaise d'Entomologie
Revue Fr Etranger Colon — Revue Francaise de l'Etranger et des Colonies. Explorations et Gazette Geographique
Revue Fr Etud Clin Biol — Revue Francaise d'Etudes Cliniques et Biologiques
Revue Fr Etud Polit Afr — Revue Francaise d'Etudes Politiques Africaines
Revue Fr Geront — Revue Francaise de Gerontologie
Revue Fr Gynec Obstet — Revue Francaise de Gynecologie et d'Obstetrique
Revue Fr Hist Outre Mer — Revue Francaise d'Histoire d'Outre-Mer
Revue Fr Hyg Med Scol Univ — Revue Francaise d'Hygiene et Medecine Scolaire et Universitaire
Revue Fr Lepidopt — Revue Francaise de Lepidopterologie
Revue Fr Mammal — Revue Francaise de Mammalogie
Revue Fr Med Chir — Revue Francaise de Medecine et de Chirurgie
Revue Fr Odonto Stomat — Revue Francaise d'Odonto-Stomatologie
Revue Fr Orn Scient Prat — Revue Francaise d'Ornithologie Scientifique et Pratique
Revue Fr Pediat — Revue Francaise de Pediatrie
Revue Fr Photogramm — Revue Francaise de Photogrammetrie
Revue Fr Photogr Cinem — Revue Francaise de Photographie et Cinematographie
Revue Fr Psychoanal — Revue Francaise de Psychoanalyse
Revue Fr Pueric — Revue Francaise de Puericulture
Revue Fr Rech Oper — Revue Francaise de Recherche Operationnelle
Revue Fr Sci Polit — Revue Francaise de Science Politique
Revue Fr Serol Chimiother — Revue Francaise de Serologie et de Chimiotherapie
Revue Fr Sociologie — Revue Francaise de Sociologie
Revue Fr TSF — Revue Francaise de T.S.F
Revue Gen Acet — Revue Generale de l'Acetylene
Revue Gen Aeronaut — Revue Generale de l'Aeronautique
Revue Gen Aeronaut Milit — Revue Generale de l'Aeronautique Militaire
Revue Gen Aeronaut Theor Prat — Revue Generale de l'Aeronautique Theorique et Pratique
Revue Gen Agric Vitic Merid — Revue Generale d'Agriculture et de Viticulture Meridionales
Revue Gen Agron — Revue Generale Agronomique
Revue Gen Air — Revue Generale de l'Air
Revue Gen Applic Ind — Revue Generale des Applications Industrielles
Revue Gen Art Dent — Revue Generale de l'Art Dentaire
Revue Gen Bot — Revue Generale de Botanique
Revue Gen Caoutch — Revue Generale du Caoutchouc
Revue Gen Ceram Verr — Revue Generale de Ceramique, Verrerie, Chaufournerie, Beton, Agglomeres et Materiaux de Construction pour le Batiment, et les Travaux Publics
Revue Gen Chem De Fer Tramw — Revue Generale des Chemins de Fer et des Tramways
Revue Gen Chim Pure Appl — Revue Generale de Chimie Pure et Appliquee
Revue Gen Colloid — Revue Generale des Colloides
Revue Gen Constr Metall Serrur — Revue Generale de la Construction Metallique et de la Serrurerie
Revue Gen Constr Trav Publ — Revue Generale de la Construction et des Travaux Publics
Revue Gen de Droit Int Public — Revue Generale de Droit International Public
Revue Gen Drog Prod Chim — Revue Generale de la Droguerie et des Produits Chimiques
Revue Generale Lettres Arts et Sci Hum — Revue Generale. Lettres, Arts, et Science Humaines
Revue Gen Froid — Revue Generale du Froid
Revue Gen Gaz — Revue Generale du Gaz
Revue Gen Matier Color — Revue Generale des Matieres Colorantes, de la Teinture, de l'Impression et des Apprets
Revue Gen Matier Plast — Revue Generale des Matieres Plastiques
Revue Gen Matier Plast Sect Peint — Revue Generale des Matieres Plastiques. Section Peintures et Vernis

Revue Gen Mec — Revue Generale de Mecanique
Revue Gen Mec Elect — Revue Generale de Mecanique-Electricite
Revue Gen Med Chir Afr N — Revue Generale de Medecine et de Chirurgie de l'Afrique du Nord et des Colonies Francaises
Revue Gen Med Chir Un Fr — Revue Generale de Medecine et de Chirurgie de l'Union Francaise
Revue Gen Med Vet — Revue Generale de Medecine Veterinaire
Revue Gen Ophtal — Revue Generale d'Ophtalmologie
Revue Gen Path Guerre — Revue Generale de Pathologie de Guerre
Revue Gen Path Interne — Revue Generale de Pathologie Interne
Revue Gen Pharm — Revue Generale de Pharmacie
Revue Geogr Maroc — Revue de Geographie du Maroc
Revue Geogr Phys Geol Dyn — Revue de Geographie Physique et de Geologie Dynamique
Revue Geol Dyn Geogr Phys — Revue de Geologie Dynamique et de Geographie Physique
Revue Hist — Revue Historique
Revue Hist 2 Guerre Mondiale — Revue d'Histoire de [*La Deuxieme*] Guerre Mondiale
Revue Hist Econ et Soc — Revue d'Histoire Economique et Sociale
Revue Hist et de Civilisation du Maghreb — Revue d'Histoire et de Civilisation du Maghreb
Revue Hist Mod et Contemporaine — Revue d'Histoire Moderne et Contemporaine
Revue Hist Theatre — Revue d'Histoire du Theatre
Revue Hort Bouches Rhone — Revue Horticole des Bouches du Rhone
Revue Hort Suisse — Revue Horticole Suisse
Revue Hort Vitic Suisse Romande — Revue Horticole et Viticole de la Suisse Romande
Revue Hydrol Comm — Revue d'Hydrologie Commerciale
Revue Hyg — Revue d'Hygiene
Revue Hyg Dent Fr — Revue d'Hygiene Dentaire de France
Revue Hyg Med Chir — Revue d'Hygiene, de Medecine, et de Chirurgie
Revue Hyg Med Infant — Revue d'Hygiene et de Medecine Infantiles et Annales de la Polyclinique H. de Rothschild
Revue Hyg Med Prev — Revue d'Hygiene et de Medecine Preventive
Revue Hyg Med Soc — Revue d'Hygiene et de Medecine Sociale
Revue Hyg Police Sanit — Revue d'Hygiene et de Police Sanitaire
Revue Hyg Prophyl Soc — Revue d'Hygiene et de Prophylaxie Sociales
Revue Hyg Soc Strasb — Revue d'Hygiene Sociale de Strasbourg
Revue Hyg Ther — Revue d'Hygiene Therapeutique
Revue Hyg Ther Ocul — Revue d'Hygiene et de Therapeutique Oculaires
Revue Hypnot — Revue de l'Hypnotisme
Revue Immunol Ther Antimicrob — Revue d'Immunologie et de Therapie Antimicrobienne
Revue Ind — Revue Industrielle
Revue Ind Auto Aeronaut — Revue de l'Industrie Automobile et Aeronautique
Revue Ind Cent — Revue Industrielle du Centre
Revue Ind E — Revue Industrielle de l'Est
Revue Ind Lait — Revue Industrielle du Lait
Revue Ind Miner — Revue de l'Industrie Minerale
Revue Indo Chln — Revue Indo-Chinoise
Revue Inds Batim — Revue des Industries du Batiment
Revue Inds Fr Opt — Revue des Industries Francaises de l'Optique et de la Precision
Revue Inds Livre — Revue des Industries du Livre
Revue Ind Text Belge — Revue de l'Industrie Textile Belge
Revue Ing Index Tech — Revue de l'Ingenieur et Index Technique
Revue Ins Fr Petrole — Revue de l'Institut Francais du Petrole et Annales des Combustibles Liquides
Revue Inst Agric Oka — Revue. Institut Agricole d'Oka
Revue Inst Hyg Mines — Revue. Institut d'Hygiene des Mines
Revue Inst Int Statist — Revue de l'Institut International de Statistique
Revue Inst Sociologie — Revue. Institut de Sociologie
Revue Inst Tech Scient Prothese Appar — Revue de l'Institut Technique et Scientifique de Prothese et d'Appareillage
Revue Int Acupunct — Revue Internationale d'Acupuncture
Revue Int Apic — Revue Internationale d'Apiculture
Revue Int Archit — Revue Internationale d'Architecture
Revue Int Bois — Revue Internationale du Bois
Revue Int Bot Appl Agric Trop — Revue Internationale de Botanique Appliquee et d'Agriculture Tropicale
Revue Int Brass Malt — Revue Internationale de Brasserie et de Malterie
Revue Int Croix Rouge — Revue Internationale de la Croix-Rouge
Revue Int Eclair — Revue Internationale de l'Eclairage
Revue Int Electrother Radiother — Revue Internationale d'Electrotherapie et de Radiotherapie
Revue Int Enfant — Revue Internationale de l'Enfant
Revue Interall Etude Quest Mutiles Guerre — Revue Interalliee pour l'Etude des Questions Interessant les Mutiles de la Guerre
Revue Int Ethnopsychol Norm Path — Revue Internationale d'Ethnopsychologie Normale et Pathologique
Revue Int Falsif Analyse Matier Aliment — Revue Internationale des Falsifications et d'Analyse des Matieres Alimentaires
Revue Int Genet — Revue Internationale de Genetique
Revue Int Hepat — Revue Internationale d'Hepatologie
Revue Int Hyg Publ — Revue Internationale d'Hygiene Publique
Revue Int Hyg Ther Ocul — Revue Internationale d'Hygiene et de Therapeutique Oculaire
Revue Int Inds Agric — Revue Internationale des Industries Agricoles
Revue Int Inds Caoutch — Revue Internationale des Industries du Caoutchouc, Celluloid, Liege et Amiante et leurs Applications
Revue Int Legisl Prot Nat — Revue Internationale de Legislation pour la Protection de la Nature
Revue Int Med Chir — Revue Internationale de Medecine et de Chirurgie

Revue Int Med Prof Soc — Revue Internationale de Medecine Professionelle et Sociale

Revue Int Peche Piscic — Revue Internationale de Peche et de Pisciculture

Revue Int Photogr — Revue Internationale de Photographie

Revue Int Prod Colon — Revue Internationale des Produits Coloniaux

Revue Int Prod Trop — Revue Internationale des Produits Tropicaux

Revue Int Prosth Dent — Revue Internationale de Prosthese Dentaire

Revue Int Servs Sante Armees — Revue Internationale des Services de Sante des Armees de Terre, de Mer, et de l'Air

Revue Int Tabacs — Revue Internationale des Tabacs

Revue Int Ther Pharmac — Revue Internationale de Therapeutique et de Pharmacologie

Revue Int Ther Phys — Revue Internationale de Therapie Physique

Revue Int Tuberc — Revue Internationale de la Tuberculose

Revue Int Vacc — Revue Internationale de la Vaccine

Revue Invent Mod — Revue des Inventions Modernes et des Produits Nouveaux du Commerce et de l'Industrie

Revue Invent Tech — Revue des Inventions Techniques

Revue Iranienne des Relations Int — Revue Iranienne des Relations Internationales

Revue Juridique et Polit Independance et Cooperation — Revue Juridique et Politique, Independance et Cooperation

Revue Juridique Polit et Econ du Maroc Rabat — Revue Juridique Politique et Economique du Maroc (Rabat)

Revue Kinesither — Revue de Kinesitherapie

Revue Lar Otol Rhinol — Revue de Laryngologie, d'Otologie, et de Rhinologie

Revue Lit Comp — Revue de Litterature Comparee

Revue Lux — Revue Trimestrielle d'Etudes Linguistiques, Folkloriques, et Toponymiques (Luxembourg)

Revue Med Afr N — Revue Medicale de l'Afrique du Nord

Revue Med Alger — Revue Medicale d'Alger et Iconographie Medicale Algerienne

Revue Med Biarritz — Revue Medicale de Biarritz

Revue Med Can — Revue Medicale du Canada

Revue Med Cannes — Revue Medicale de Cannes

Revue Med Cent — Revue Medicale du Centre

Revue Med Cent Ouest — Revue Medicale du Centre-Ouest

Revue Med Chir Jassy — Revue Medico-Chirurgicale de Jassy

Revue Med Chir Mal Foie Pancr Rate — Revue Medico-Chirurgicale des Maladies du Foie, du Pancreas, et de la Rate

Revue Med Chir NE — Revue Medico-Chirurgicale du Nord-Est

Revue Med Chir Paris — Revue Medico-Chirurgicale (Paris)

Revue Med E — Revue Medicale de l'Est

Revue Med Egypte — Revue Medicale d'Egypte

Revue Med Fr — Revue Medicale de France

Revue Med Fr — Revue Medicale Francaise

Revue Med Franche Comte — Revue Medicale de la Franche-Comte

Revue Med Fr Colon — Revue Medicale de France et des Colonies

Revue Med Fr Extr Orient — Revue Medicale Francaise d'Extreme-Orient

Revue Med Liege — Revue Medicale de Liege

Revue Med Mt Dore — Revue Medicale de Mont-Dore

Revue Med Nancy — Revue Medicale de Nancy

Revue Med NE — Revue Medicale du Nord-Est

Revue Med Soc — Revue Medico-Sociale

Revue Med Suisse Romande — Revue Medicale de la Suisse Romande

Revue Med Tours — Revue Medicale de Tours

Revue Med Univ — Revue Medicale Universelle

Revue Med Univ Montreal — Revue Medicale. Universite de Montreal

Revue Med Vet — Revue Medicale et Veterinaire

Revue Mens Blanchiss — Revue Mensuelle du Blanchissage, du Blanchiment, et des Apprets

Revue Mens Ec Anthrop Paris — Revue Mensuelle de l'Ecole d'Anthropologie de Paris

Revue Mens Grpmt Avanc Mec Ind — Revue Mensuelle. Groupement pour l'Avancement de la Mecanique Industrielle

Revue Mens Gynec Obstet Pediat — Revue Mensuelle de Gynecologie d'Obstetrique et de Pediatrie

Revue Mens Gynec Obstet Pediat Bordeaux — Revue Mensuelle de Gynecologie, Obstetrique, et Pediatrie de Bordeaux

Revue Mens Mal Enf — Revue Mensuelle des Maladies de l'Enfance, Hygiene, Medecine, Chirurgie, Orthopedie

Revue Mens Mass Gymn Med — Revue Mensuelle de Massage et de Gymnastique Medicale

Revue Mens Med Interne Ther — Revue Mensuelle de Medecine Interne et de Therapeutique

Revue Mens Med Prat — Revue Mensuelle de Medecine Pratique

Revue Mens Obs Tsing Tao — Revue Mensuelle de l'Observatoire, Tsing-Tao

Revue Mens Oeuvre Natn Enf — Revue Mensuelle. Oeuvre National de l'Enfance

Revue Mens Pediat — Revue Mensuelle de Pediatrie

Revue Mens Physiother Prat — Revue Mensuelle de Physiotherapie Pratique pour la Diffusion des Methodes Physiques

Revue Mens Soc Ent Namur — Revue Mensuelle de la Societe Entomologique Namuroise

Revue Metall Buc — Revue de Metallurgie (Bucarest)

Revue Metall Paris — Revue de Metallurgie (Paris)

Revue Metapsych — Revue Metapsychique

Revue Miner Ill — Revue Mineralurgique Illustree

Revue Min Ill — Revue Miniere Illustree

Revue Minist Agric Paris — Revue du Ministre de l'Agriculture (Paris)

Revue Min Metall — Revue Miniere et Metallurgique

Revue Mod Med Chir — Revue Moderne de Medecine et de Chirurgie

Revue Morpho Physiol Hum — Revue de Morpho-Physiologie Humaine

Revue Mycol — Revue de Mycologie [*Paris*]

Revue Mycol — Revue Mycologique [*Toulouse*]

Revue Naut — Revue Nautique

Revue Navig Inter Rhen — Revue de la Navigation Interieure et Rhenane

Revue Nephol — Revue Nephologique

Revue Neurol — Revue Neurologique

Revue Neurol Psychiat Praha — Revue v Neurologii, Psychiatrii, Fysikalni a Diateticke Therapii (Praha)

Revue Neuropsychiat Infant — Revue de Neuropsychiatrie Infantile et d'Hygiene Mentale de l'Enfance

Revue Neuropsychopath Praha — Revue. Neuropsychopathologie, Lekarstvi Socialni, Dedicnost a Eugenika, Therapie (Praha)

Revue Nickel — Revue du Nickel

Revue Normande Physiother — Revue Normande de Physiotherapie, Thermalotherapie et Thalassotherapie

Revue Num — Revue Numismatique

Revue Odont — Revue Odontologique

Revue Odonto Stomat — Revue d'Odonto-Stomatologie

Revue Odont Stomat Maxillo Fac — Revue d'Odontologie et Stomatologie et Maxillo-Faciale

Revue Oka — Revue d'Oka. Agronomie. Medicine. Veterinaire

Revue Opt Theor Instrum — Revue d'Optique Theorique et Instrumentale

Revue Orthop Chir Appar Mot — Revue d'Orthopedie et de Chirurgie de l'Appareil Moteur

Revue OSE — Revue O.S.E. Union des Societes pour la Protection de la Sante des Populations Juives

Revue Ostrec Marit — Revue Ostreicole et Maritime

Revue Oto Neuro Ocul — Revue d'Oto-Neuro-Oculistique

Revue Oto Neuro Ophtal — Revue d'Oto-Neuro-Ophtalmologie

Revue Palud Med Trop — Revue du Paludisme et de Medecine Tropicale

Revue Pap Cartons — Revue des Papiers et Cartons

Revue Papet — Revue de la Papeterie

Revue Paramed Ill — Revue Paramedicale Illustree

Revue Parfum — Revue de la Parfumerie

Revue Path Comp — Revue de Pathologie Comparee

Revue Path Comp Hyg Gen — Revue de Pathologie Comparee et Hygiene Generale

Revue Path Gen Comp — Revue de Pathologie Generale et Comparee

Revue Path Gen Physiol Clin — Revue de Pathologie Generale et de Physiologie Clinique

Revue Path Physiol Trav — Revue de Pathologie et de Physiologie du Travail

Revue Path Veg Ent Agric Fr — Revue de Pathologie Vegetale et d'Entomologie Agricole de France

Revue Period Vulg Sci Nat Prehist Physiophile — Revue Periodique de Vulgarisation des Sciences Naturelles et Prehistoriques de la Physiophile

Revue Petrol — Revue Petroliere

Revue Petrole Buc — Revue du Petrole (Bucarest)

Revue Petrolif — Revue Petrolifere

Revue Pharm — Revue Pharmaceutique

Revue Pharmac Med — Revue de Pharmacologie Medicale

Revue Pharmac Ther Exp — Revue de Pharmacologie et de Therapeutique Experimentale

Revue Pharm Hypod — Revue Pharmaceutique d'Hypodermie

Revue Pharm Liban — Revue Pharmaceutique Libanaise

Revue Philomath Bordeaux — Revue Philomathique de Bordeaux et du Sud-Ouest (Bordeaux)

Revue Phtisiol Med Soc — Revue de Phtisiologie Medico-Sociale

Revue Phys Buc — Revue de Physique (Bucarest)

Revue Phys Chim — Revue de Physique et de Chimie et de Leurs Applications Industrielles

Revue Physiother — Revue de Physiotherapie

Revue Physiother Chir Radiol — Revue de Physiotherapie Chirurgicale et de Radiologie

Revue Phytopagh Appl — Revue de Phytopathologie Appliquee

Revue Phytother — Revue de Phytotherapie

Revue Prat Abatt — Revue Pratique des Abattoirs et de l'Inspection des Viandes et d'Hygiene Publique

Revue Prat Biol Clin Ther — Revue Pratique de Biologie Appliquee a la Clinique et a la Therapeutique

Revue Prat Connaiss Med — Revue Pratique des Connaissances Medicales

Revue Prat Elect — Revue Pratique de l'Electricite

Revue Prat Electro Radiol — Revue Pratique d'Electro-Radiologie

Revue Prat Froid Paris — Revue Pratique du Froid (Paris)

Revue Prat Gynec Obstet Pediat — Revue Pratique de Gynecologie, d'Obstetrique, et de Pediatrie

Revue Prat Hyg Munic Urb Rur — Revue Pratique d'Hygiene Municipale, Urbaine, et Rurale

Revue Prat Inds Metall — Revue Pratique des Industries Metallurgiques

Revue Prat Mal Cutan Syph Vener — Revue Pratique des Maladies Cutanees, Syphilitiques, et Veneriennes

Revue Prat Mal Org Genito Urin — Revue Pratique des Maladies des Organes Genito-Urinaires

Revue Prat Mal Pays Chauds — Revue Pratique des Maladies des Pays Chauds

Revue Pratn — Revue du Praticien

Revue Prat Obstet Gynec — Revue Pratique d'Obstetrique et de Gynecologie

Revue Prat Obstet Pediat — Revue Pratique d'Obstetrique et de Pediatrie

Revue Prat Radiumther — Revue Pratique de Radiumtherapie, Rayonnements, Emanations, Substances Radioactives Diverses

Revue Prat Serrur — Revue Pratique de Serrurerie

Revue Prat Trav Med Abeille Med — Revue Pratique des Travaux de Medecine L'Abeille Medicale

Revue Prehist — Revue Prehistorique

Revue Presse Cent Tech Ind Fond — Revue de Presse. Centre Technique des Industries de la Fonderie

Revue Presse Med Pol — Revue de la Presse Medicale Polonaise

Revue Prod Chim — Revue des Produits Chimiques et l'Actualite-Scientifique Reunies

Revue Psych Exp — Revue de Psychisme Experimental

Revue Psychiat Psychol Exp — Revue de Psychiatrie et de Psychologie Experimentale

Revue Psychol — Revue Psychologique

Revue Psychol Appl — Revue de Psychologie Appliquee

Revue Psychol Clin Ther — Revue de Psychologie Clinique et Therapeutique

Revue Psychother Psychol Appl — Revue de Psychotherapie et de Psychologie Appliquee

Revue PTT Bern — Revue des PTT. Schweizerische Post-, Telegraphen-, und Telephonverwaltung (Bern)

Revue PTT Paris — Revue des PTT. Ministere des Postes, Telegraphes, et Telephones (Paris)

Revue Quest Colon Marit — Revue des Questions Coloniales et Maritimes

Revue Quest Hosp — Revue des Questions Hospitalieres

Revue Quest Scient — Revue des Questions Scientifiques

Revue Radio Revues — Revue des Radio-Revues

Revue Rech Oper — Revue de Recherche Operationnelle

Revue Revues Art Dent — Revue des Revues d'Art Dentaire

Revue Revues Hist Nat — Revue des Revues d'Histoire Naturelle

Revue Revues Litt Scient Hongr — Revue des Revues Litteraires et Scientifiques Hongroises

Revue Rhum Mal Osteo Artic — Revue du Rhumatisme et des Maladies Osteo-Articulaires

Revue Romande Agric Vitic Arboric — Revue Romande d'Agriculture, de Viticulture, et d'Arboriculture

Revue Roulem Billes — Revue des Roulements a Billes

Revue Roumaine d Etud Int — Revue Roumaine d'Etudes Internationales

Revue Roum Biochim — Revue Roumaine de Biochimie

Revue Roum Biol Ser Bot — Revue Roumaine de Biologie. Serie Botanique

Revue Roum Metall — Revue Roumaine de Metallurgie

Revue Rust Med Z — Revue der Russischen Medizinischen Zeitschriften

Revue Savois — Revue Savoisienne. Societe Florimontaine d'Annecy

Revue Savonn Ind Matier Grass — Revue de la Savonnerie et de l'Industrie des Matieres Grasses

Revue Scient Bourbon Cent Fr — Revue Scientifique du Bourbonnais et du Centre de la France

Revue Scient Ind Comm Metaux — Revue Scientifique, Industrielle et Commerciale des Metaux et Alliages, Sauf le Fer et l'Acier

Revue Scient Limousin — Revue Scientifique du Limousin

Revue Scient Montreal — Revue Scientifique (Montreal)

Revue Scient Paris — Revue Scientifique. Revue Rose Illustree (Paris)

Revue Scient Tech Chim Appl — Revue Scientifique et Technique de Chimie Appliquee

Revue Sci Med Buc — Revue des Sciences Medicales (Bucarest)

Revue Sci Med Fr Moyen Orient — Revue de la Science Medicale Francaise du Moyen-Orient

Revue Sci Med Pharm Vet Afr Fr Libre — Revue des Sciences Medicales, Pharmaceutiques, et Veterinaires de l'Afrique Francaise Libre

Revue Sci Nat Auvergne — Revue des Sciences Naturelles d'Auvergne

Revue Sci Oto Rhino Lar Cluj — Revue des Sciences Oto-Rhino-Laryngologiques (Cluj)

Revue Sci Tech Buc — Revue des Sciences Techniques (Bucarest)

Revue Sci Trav — Revue de la Science du Travail: Psychotechnique et Organisation

Revue Sci Zootech — Revue des Sciences Zootechniques

Revues Crit Constantes — Revues Critiques de Constantes

Revues Med Normandes — Revues Medicales Normandes

Revue Soc Biometrie Hum — Revue de la Societe de Biometrie Humaine

Revue Soc Geogr Comm Paris Sect Tunis — Revue de la Societe de Geographie Commerciale de Paris. Section Tunisienne

Revue Soc Geogr Tours — Revue de la Societe de Geographie de Tours

Revue Soc Morphophysiol Hum — Revuede la Societe de la Morphophysiologie Humaine

Revue Soc Scient Hyg Aliment — Revue de la Societe Scientifique d'Hygiene Alimentaire

Revue Soud Elect — Revue de Soudure Electrique

Revue Soud Geneve — Revue de Soudure (Geneve)

Revue Suisse Zool — Revue Suisse de Zoologie

Revue SW — Revue S-W. Materiel Electrique

Revue Ther Clin Tuberc — Revue Therapeutique et Clinique de la Tuberculose

Revue Ther Derm Syph — Revue de Therapeutique Dermatologique et Syphiligraphique

Revue Ther Med Chir — Revue de Therapeutique Medico-Chirurgicale

Revue Ther Meurice — Revue de Therapeutique Meurice

Revue Ther Phys Appl Hyg — Revue de Therapeutique Physique Appliquee et d'Hygiene

Revue Tipogr — Revue Tipographique

Revue Trachome — Revue du Trachome

Revue Transm — Revue des Transmissions

Revue Transm Hydromec — Revue des Transmissions Hydromecaniques

Revue Trav — Revue du Travail

Revue Trav Rech — Revue des Travaux de Recherches

Revue Tuberc — Revue de la Tuberculose et de Pneumologie

Revue Tunis — Revue Tunisienne

Revue Tunisienne Sci Soc — Revue Tunisienne de Sciences Sociales

Revue Tunis Sci Med — Revue Tunisienne de Sciences Medicales

Revue Un Int Tramw — Revue. Union Internationale de Tramways

Revue Un Int Transp Publ — Revue. Union Internationale des Transports Publics

Revue Univ — Revue Universitaire

Revue Univ Brux — Revue de l'Universite de Bruxelles

Revue Univlle Brass Malt — Revue Universelle de la Brasserie et de la Malterie

Revue Univlle Distill — Revue Universelle de la Distillerie

Revue Univlle Mines — Revue Universelle des Mines, de la Metallurgie, de la Mecanique, des Travaux Publics, des Sciences, et des Arts Appliquees a l'Industrie

Revue Univlle Soies — Revue Universelle des Soies et des Soies Artificielles

Revue Univlle Transp Commun — Revue Universelle des Transports et des Communications

Revue Univ Lyon — Revue de l'Universite de Lyon

Revue Ver Soie — Revue du Ver a Soie

Revue Verviet Hist Nat — Revue Vervietoise d'Histoire Naturelle

Revue Vet Constantinpole — Revue Veterinaire (Constantinople)

Revue Vet Milit — Revue Veterinaire Militaire

Revue Vet Toulouse — Revue Veterinaire et Journal de Medecine Veterinaire et de Zootechnie (Toulouse)

Revue Vinic — Revue Vinicole

Revue Vitic — Revue de Viticulture

Revue Vitic Agric Hort Franche Comte — Revue Viticole, Agricole, et Horticole de la Franche-Comte et de la Bourgogne

Revue Zairoise Psychol Pedagogie — Revue Zairoise de Psychologie et de Pedagogie

Revue Zivnost Vlasn — Revue Zivnostenskeho Vlasnietvi

Revue Zool Afr — Revue de Zoologie Africaine

Revue Zool Agric Appl — Revue de Zoologie Agricole et Appliquee

Revue Zool Bot Afr — Revue de Zoologie et de Botanique Africaines

Revue Zootech — Revue de Zootechnie

RevuFE — Revue Francaise d'Etudes Politiques Africaines

RevuFS — Revue Francaise de la Sociologie

RevuFSP — Revue Francaise de Science Politique

RevuH — Revue Historique

RevuHA — Revue Historique de l'Armee

RevuHB — Revue Historique de Bordeaux [et du Departement de la Gironde]

RevUL — Revista. Universidade de Lisboa. Faculdade de Letras

Rev U La Habana — Revista. Universidad de La Habana

Rev ULB — Revue. Universite Libre de Bruxelles

RevULy — Revue de l'Universite de Lyon

Rev U Madrid — Revista de la Universidad de Madrid

Rev U Moncton — Revue de l'Universite de Moncton

Rev Un Affiche Fr — Revue de l'Union de l'Affiche Francaise

Rev Un B — Revue. Universite de Bruxelles

Rev Uni — Revue Universitaire

Rev Uniao Pharm (Sao Paulo) — Revista Uniao Pharmaceutica (Sao Paulo)

Rev Union Indus Arg BA — Revista. Union Industrial Argentina (Buenos Aires)

Rev Union Mat Argent — Revista. Union Matematica Argentina

Rev Union Mat Argent Asoc Fis Argent — Revista. Union Matematica Argentina y Asociacion Fisica Argentina

Rev Univ — Revue Universitaire

Rev Univ Al I Cuza Inst Politeh Iasi — Revista Universitati "Al. I. Cuza" si a Institutului Politehnic din Iasi

Rev Univ Andes Bogota — Revista. Universidad de los Andes (Bogota)

Rev Univ Arequipa — Revista. Universidad de Arequipa (Peru)

Rev Univ BA — Revista. Universidad de Buenos Aires (Buenos Aires)

Rev Univ Brux — Revue. Universite de Bruxelles

Rev Univ Bruxelles — Revue. Universite de Bruxelles

Rev Univ Burundi — Revue. Universite du Burundi

Rev Univ Caldas Manizales — Revista. Universidad de Caldas (Manizales, Colombia)

Rev Univ Catol Lima — Revista. Universidad Catolica del Peru (Lima)

Rev Univ Cato S Paulo — Revista da Universidade Catolica de Sao Paulo

Rev Univ Cauca — Revista. Universidad del Cauca

Rev Univ Cauca Popayan — Revista. Universidad del Cauca (Popayan, Colombia)

Rev Univ C I Parhon Politeh Bucuresti Ser Stiint Nat — Revista Universitatii "C. I. Parhon" si a Politehnicii Bucuresti. Seria Stiintelor Naturii

Rev Univ Coimbra — Revista. Universidade de Coimbra

Rev Univ Cordoba — Revista. Universidad Nacional de Cordoba (Cordoba, Argentina)

Rev Univ Cuzco — Revista Universitaria (Cuzco, Peru)

Rev Universelle — Revue Universelle

Rev Univers Mines Metall Mec — Revue Universelle des Mines, de la Metallurgie, de la Mecanique, des Travaux Publics, des Sciences, et des Arts Appliques a l'Industrie

Rev Univers Min Metall Trav Publ Sci Arts Appl Indus — Revue Universelle des Mines, de la Metallurgie des Travaux Publics, des Sciences et des Arts Appliques a l'Industries

Rev Univ Fed Para Ser II — Revista. Universidade Federal do Para. Serie II

Rev Univ G Rene Moreno Santa Cruz — Revista. Universidad Autonoma Gabriel Rene Moreno (Santa Cruz de la Sierra, Bolivia)

Rev Univ Guadalajara — Revista Universitaria (Guadalajara, Mexico)

Rev Univ Guayaquil Guayaquil — Revista. Universidad de Guayaquil (Guayaquil, Ecuador)

Rev Univ Hond Tegucigalpa — Revista. Universidad (Tegucigalpa)

Rev Univ Ind Santander — Revista. Universidad Industrial de Santander

Rev Univ Ind Santander Invest — Revista. Universidad Industrial de Santander. Investigaciones

Rev Univ Ind Santander Tecnolo — Revista. Universidad Industrial de Santander. Tecnologia

Rev Univ Indus Santander Bucaramanga — Revista. Universidad Industrial de Santander (Bucaramanga, Colombia)

Rev Univl A — Revue Universelle des Arts

Rev Univ La Plata — Revista. Universidad (La Plata, Argentina)

Rev Univl Lisbo — Revista Universal Lisbonense

Rev Univ Los Andes (Bogota) — Revista. Universidad de Los Andes (Bogota)

Rev Univ Madrid — Revista. Universidad de Madrid

Rev Univ Mex — Revista. Universidad de Mexico

Rev Abniv Minas Gerais Belo Horizonte — Revista. Universidade de Minas Gerais (Belo Horizonte, Brazil)

Rev Univ Nac Cordoba — Revista. Universidad Nacional de Cordoba

Rev Univ Nac Tucuman Ser A — Revista. Universidad Nacional de Tucuman. Serie A. Matematica y Fisica Teorica

Rev Univ Natl Zaire Campus Lubumbashi Ser B — Revue. Universite Nationale du Zaire. Campus de Lubumbashi. Serie B. Sciences

Rev Univ Norte (Chile) — Revista. Universidad del Norte (Chile)
Rev Univ Ottawa — Revue. Universite d'Ottawa
Rev Univ Puebla — Revista. Universidad de Puebla
Rev Univ Puno — Revista. Universidad (Puno, Peru)
Rev Univ S Augustin Arequipa — Revista. Universidad Nacional de San Agustin (Arequipa, Peru)
Rev Univ S Jose — Revista. Universidad de Costa Rica (San Jose, Costa Rica)
Rev Univ Sonora Hermosillo — Revista. Universidad de Sonora (Hermosillo, Mexico)
Rev Univ Trujillo — Revista Universitaria (Trujillo, Peru)
Rev Univ Univ Catol Santiago — Revista Universitaria. Universidad Catolica de Chile (Santiago)
Rev Univ Univ Nac Cuzco — Revista Universitaria. Universidad Nacional del Cuzco
Rev Univ Yucatan — Revista. Universidad de Yucatan
Rev Univ Zulia — Revista. Universidad del Zulia
Rev Univ Zulia (Maracaibo) — Revista. Universidad del Zulia (Maracaibo)
Rev Un Mat Argentina — Revista. Union Matematica Argentina
RevUO — Revista de la Universidad de Oviedo
RevuP — Revue Politique et Parlementaire
Rev U Popayan — Revista de la Universidad de Popayan
RevuR — Revue Roumaine d'Histoire
Rev Urol (Caracas) — Revista de Urologia (Caracas)
Rev Urug Est Internac — Revista Uruguaya de Estudios Internacionales
Rev Urug Geogr Monte — Revista Uruguaya de Geografia (Montevideo)
Rev Usem — Revista Usem
Rev US Pat Pest Control — Review of United States Patents Relating to Pest Control [Washington]
RevV — Revue des Vivants. Organe des Generations de la Guerre
Rev Venez Cir — Revista Venezolana de Cirugia
Rev Venez Sanid Asist Soc — Revista Venezolana de Sanidad y Asistencia Social
Rev Venez Urol — Revista Venezolana de Urologia
Rev Ven Filosof — Revista Venezolana de Filosofia
Rev Ver Soie — Revue du Ver a Soie
Rev Vervietoise Hist Nat — Revue Vervietoise d'Histoire Naturelle
Rev Vet Alger Tunis — Revue Veterinaire Algerienne et Tunisienne
Rev Vet Can — Revue Veterinaire Canadienne
Rev Vet Milit — Revista de Veterinaria Militar
Rev Vet Slave — Revue Veterinaire Slave
Rev Vet Venez — Revista Veterinaria Venezolana
Rev Vet Zootec (Manizales) — Revista de Veterinaria y Zootecnia (Manizales)
Rev Viernes Med — Revista del Viernes Medico
Rev Vieux Geneve — Revue du Vieux Geneve
Rev Vitic — Revue de Viticulture
Rev Vivarais — Revue du Vivarais
Rev Voyages — Revue des Voyages
Rev V Tr — Revue des Ventes et Transports
Rev Warren Spring Lab (UK) — Review. Warren Spring Laboratory (United Kingdom)
Rev War Surg Med — Review of War Surgery and Medicine. Surgeon General's Office [Washington]
Rev Weed Sci — Reviews of Weed Science
Rev Whale Fish — Review of the Whale Fishery [New Bedford]
Rev Wk Exp Stns Emp Cott Grow Corp — Review of the Work of the Experiment Stations. Empire Cotton Growing Corporation [London]
Rev Wks Prog Dep Agric Cyprus — Review of Works in Progress. Department of Agriculture. Cyprus [Nicosia]
Rev World — Revolutionary World
Rev X — Revue X
Rev Zair Sci Nucl — Revue Zairoise des Sciences Nucleaires
Rev Zaragoza — Revista de Zaragoza
Rev Zoo Agr — Revue de Zoologie Agricole et de Pathologie Vegetale
Rev Zooiatr — Revista Zooiatria
Rev Zool Afr — Revue de Zoologie Africaine
Rev Zool Agric Appl — Revue de Zoologie Agricole et Appliquee
Rev Zool Agric Pathol Veg — Revue de Zoologie Agricole et de Pathologie Vegetale
Rev Zool Bot Afr — Revue de Zoologie et de Botanique Africaines
Rev Zool Bot Africaines — Revue de Zoologie et de Botanique Africaines
Rev Zootec (B Aires) — Revista Zootecnica (Buenos Aires)
Rev Zooteh Med Vet — Revista de Zootehnie si Medicina Veterinara
REW — Russisch-Etymologisches Woerterbuch
REX — Rechtswissenschaftliche Experten und Gutachter
R EX — Review and Expositor
R Exist Psych Psych — Review of Existential Psychology and Psychiatry
R Exp — Review and Expositor
Rexroth Inf — Rexroth Informationen
Reynolds Alumin Abstr — Reynolds Aluminium Abstracts
Reynolds Alumin Dig — Reynolds Aluminium Digest
Reynolds Metals Tech Advis — Reynolds Metals Technical Advisor
Reyon Synth Zellwolle — Reyon, Synthetica, Zellwolle
Reyon Zellwolle — Reyon, Zellwolle und Andere Chemiefasern
Reyon Zellwolle Andere Chem Fasern — Reyon, Zellwolle, und Andere Chemie Fasern
Reyrolle Parsons Rev — Reyrolle Parsons Review
Reyrolle Rev — Reyrolle Review
Rezanie Instrum — Rezanie i Instrument
Rez Ezhedn Obsled Svobod Atmos Petrogr — Rezul'taty Ezhednevnykh Obsledovanii Svobodnoi Atmosfery. Aerologicheskaya Observatoriya (Petrograd)
Re Zh Khim Neftepererab Polim Mashinostr — Referativnyi Zhurnal. Khimicheskoe. Neftepererabatyuayushchee i Polimerjnoe Mashinostroenie
Rez Nabl Met Obs Univ Kharkov — Rezul'taty Nablyudenii. Meteorologicheskaya Observatoriya Universiteta (Khar'kov)
Rezul't Issled Mezhdunar Geofiz Proektam — Rezul'taty Issledovanyi po Mezhdunarodny Geofizicheskim Proektam

Rez Veg Opyt — Rezul'taty Vegetatsionnykh Opytov
RF — Rapports des Fouilles
RF — Razon y Fabula
RF — Razon y Fe
RF — Regeszeti Fuzetek. Magyar Nemzeti Muzeum
RF — Republique Francaise
RF — Revista de Filologie
RF — Revista de Filozofie
RF — Revista de Folklore [Bogota]
RF — Revista Forense
RF — Revue de France
RF — Revue des Faillites, Concordats, et Liquidations
RF — Revue Fiscale
RF — Revue Francaise
RF — Rivista di Filologia e di Istruzione Classica
RF — Rivista di Filosofia
RF — Romanische Forschungen
RF — Ruch Filozoficzny
RFA — Revista. Facultad de Agronomia
RFA — Revue de la Franco-Ancienne
RFA — Revue de l'Energie
RFAAD — Revue Francaise d'Automatique, d'Informatique, et de Recherche Operationnelle. Serie Automatique
RFACA — Revista. Facultad de Ciencias Agrarias. Universidad Nacional de Cuyo
R Fac Cienc Ec Com — Revista. Facultad de Ciencias Economicas y Comerciales
R Fac Der (Caracas) — Revista. Facultad de Derecho (Caracas)
R Fac Der Mexico — Revista. Facultad de Derecho de Mexico
RFAGB — Riforma Agraria
RFALA — Revue Francaise d'Allergie
RFAND — Revue Francaise d'Automatique, d'Informatique, et de Recherche Operationnelle. Serie Analyse Numerique
RFAPA — Revista. Facultad de Agronomia. Universidad Nacional de La Plata
RFB — Rabobank
RFB — Recent French Books
RFBABQ — Anais. Reuniao de Fitossanitarisatas do Brasil
RFBUB — Revista de Farmacia e Bioquimica. Universidade de Sao Paulo (Brazil)
RFC — Revista da Faculdade de Ciencias
RFC — Revista de Folklore Chileno
RFC — Revista de Folklore (Colombia)
RFC — Rivista di Filologia Classica
RFC — Rivista di Filologia e di Istruzione Classica
RFCA — Revue des Facultes Catholiques d'Angres
RFCC — Revista de Folklore. Organo de la Comision Nacional de Folklore (Colombia)
RF (Cern) — Revista de Filologie (Cernauti)
RFCFDE — Revista. Faculdade de Ciencias Farmaceuticas
RFCh — Revista de Filosofia (Chile)
RFCJP — Revista. Facultad de Ciencias Juridicas Politicas
RFCO — Revue des Facultes Catholiques de l'Ouest
RFCR — Revista de Filosofia. Universidad de Costa Rica
RFCTA — Rassegna di Fisiopatologia Clinica e Terapeutica
RFCVET — Revista. Facultad de Ciencias Veterinarias
RFD — Revista. Federacion de Doctores en Ciencias y en Filosofia y Letras
RFDC — Revista. Facultad de Derecho de Caracas
RFDM — Revista. Facultad de Derecho de Mexico
RFE — Radio Free Europe
R Fe — Razon y Fe
RFE — Revista de Filologia Espanola
RFE — Revista de Filosofia (Espana)
RFE — Revue Francaise d'Entomologie
RFEA — Revista de Filologia Espanola. Anejos
RFEA — Revue Francaise d'Etudes Americaines
RFEC — Revue Francaise de l'Etranger et des Colonies
RFECA — Revue Francaise d'Etudes Cliniques et Biologiques
R Fed Am Hosp — Review. Federation of American Hospitals
RFELB — Radio Fernsehen Elektronik
RFEP — Revista de Filologia Espanola. Publicaciones
RFERB — Radio Free Europe. Research Bulletin
R Fernand Braudel Center — Review. Fernand Braudel Center for the Study of Economies, Historical Systems, and Civilizations
RFEV — Revista. Federacion de Estudiantes de Venezuela
RFF — Rundbrief zur Foerderung der Freundschaft
RFFH — Revista. Facultad de Filosofia y Humanidades
RFFID4 — Canadian Forestry Service. Forest Pest Management Institute. Information Report. FPM-X
RFFL — Revista. Facultad de Filosofia y Letras
RFFLUP — Revista. Faculdade de Filosofia e Letras. Universidade do Parana
RFGND — RoeFo. Fortschritte auf dem Gebiete der Roentgenstrahlen und der Nuklearmedizin
RFH — Revista de Filologia Hispanica
RFHC — Revista. Facultad de Humanidades y Ciencias
RFHL — Revue Francaise d'Histoire du Livre
RFHMA — Repertorium Fontium Historiae Medii Aevi
RFHOM — Revue Francaise d'Histoire d'Outre-Mer
RFHSP — Revista de Filologia e Historia (Sao Paulo)
RFI — Regionalism and the Female Imagination
RFi — Revista de Filosofia
RFI — Revue Fiscale
RFI — Revue Juridique, Fiscale, et Financiere
RFIAAQ — Revue des Fermentations et des Industries Alimentaires
RFIC — Rivista di Filologia e di Istruzione Classica
RFICI — Rivista di Filologia e d'Istruzione Classica
R Fil — Revista de Filosofia
RFil — Rivista di Filologia
RFil — Russkaja Filologija

R Fil Cl — Rivista di Filologia e d'Istruzione Classica
R Fil Ist Cl — Rivista di Filologia e d'Istruzione Classica
RF Illus — RF [*Rockefeller Foundation*] Illustrated
R Filol Esp — Revista de Filologia Espanola
R Filol Espan — Revista de Filologia Espanola. CSIC (Consejo Superior de Investigaciones Cientificas)
RFilos — Rivista di Filosofia
R Filoz — Revista de Filozofie
R Financ — Revue Financiere
R Fins Publicas — Revista de Financas Publicas
RFIOA — Revue Francaise d'Informatique et de Recherche Operationnelle
RFISA — Revista de Fisica
RFJ — Radio Free Jazz
RFK — Reflets et Perspectives de la Vie Economique
RFKUL — Roczniki Filozoficzne. Towarzystwo Naukowe Katolickiego Uniwersytetu Lubelskiego
RFL — Reports of Family Law
RFL — Revista. Faculdade de Letras. Universidade de Lisboa
RFL — Revista. Facultad de Letras
RFL 2d — Reports of Family Law. Second Series
RFLC — Revista. Facultad de Letras y Ciencias. Universidad de la Habana
RFLHG — Review of the Faculty of Language, History, and Geographiy (University of Ankara)
RFLHGA — Revue. Faculte de Langues, d'Histoire, et de Geographie. Universite d'Ankara
RFLL — Revista. Faculdade de Letras. Universidade de Lisboa
RFLUL — Revista. Faculdade de Letras. Universidade de Lisboa
RFM — Razon y Fe (Madrid)
RFM — Review of Futures Markets
RFM — Revista de Filosofia (Madrid)
RFM — Revue Francaise du Marketing
RFMI — Review of the Faculty of Medicine. University of Istanbul
RFMNB — Rein et Foie. Maladies de la Nutrition
RFM Rev Fr Mec — RFM. Revue Francaise de Mecanique
RFN — Rivista di Filosofia Neo-Scolastica
RFNS — Rivista di Filosofia Neo-Scolastica
RFOFD6 — Revista. Faculdade de Odontologia de Araraquara
RFolc — Revista de Folclor
R Fomento Soc — Revista de Fomento Social
R Fom Soc — Revista de Fomento Social
RFor — Romanische Forschungen. Organ fuer Romanische Sprachen, Volks- und Mitteilatein
RFORE9 — Rivista di Frutticoltura e di Ortofloricoltura
R For Franc — Revue Forestiere Francaise
R Format Perm — Revue de la Formation Permanente
RForsch — Romanische Forschungen
RFOSA — Revue Francaise d'Odonto-Stomatologie
RFP — Review Fiction and Poetry
RFP — Reviews for Physicians
RFP — Revista de Filologia Portuguesa
RFP — Rivista Filosofica (Pavia)
RFPRA — Reactor Fuel Processing
RFR — Rassegna di Filosofia (Roma)
RFr — Revolution Francaise
RFr — Revue Francaise
R Fr Affaires Socs — Revue Francaise des Affaires Sociales
RFran — Revue de France
R Franc Adm Publ — Revue Francaise d'Administration Publique
R Franc Aff Soc — Revue Francaise des Affaires Sociales
R Francaise Hist Livre — Revue Francaise d'Histoire du Livre
R Francaise Hist Outre-Mer — Revue Francaise d'Histoire d'Outre-Mer
R Francaise Sci Pol — Revue Francaise de Science Politique
R Francaise Sociol — Revue Francaise de Sociologie
R Franc Comptab — Revue Francaise de Comptabilite
R Franc Dr Aer — Revue Francaise de Droit Aerien
RFrance — Revue de France
R Franc En — Revue Francaise de l'Energie
R Franc Et Amer — Revue Francaise d'Etudes Americaines
R Franc Et Polit Afr — Revue Francaise d'Etudes Politiques Africaines
R Franc Et Polit Medit — Revue Francaise d'Etudes Politiques Mediterraneennes
R Franc Gestion — Revue Francaise de Gestion
R Franc Hist O Mer — Revue Francaise d'Histoire d'Outre-Mer
R Franc Hist Outre-Mer — Revue Francaise d'Histoire d'Outre-Mer
R Franc Mkting — Revue Francaise du Marketing
R Franc Pedag — Revue Francaise de Pedagogie
R Franc Psych — Revue Francaise de Psychoanalyse
R Franc Sci Polit — Revue Francaise de Science Politique
R Franc Soc — Revue Francaise de Sociologie
R Franc Sociol — Revue Francaise de Sociologie
R Fr De Dermat Et De Ven — Revue Francaise de Dermatologie et de Venereologie
R Fr De Psychanal — Revue Francaise de Psychanalyse
R Fr El — Revue Francaise de l'Elite
R Fr Energ — Revue Francaise de l'Energie
R Fr Etud Pol Afr — Revue Francaise d'Etudes Politiques Africaines
R Fr Etud Pol Mediterraneennes — Revue Francaise d'Etudes Politiques Mediterraneennes
RFRG — Revista de Filologie Romanica si Germanica
R Fr Gestion — Revue Francaise de Gestion
RFrign — Rassegna Frignanese
R Fr Marketing — Revue Francaise du Marketing
RFRO — Raumforschung und Raumordnung
RFRR-A — Raumforschung und Raumordnung
R Fr Science Pol — Revue Francaise de Science Politique
R Fr Sociol — Revue Francaise de Sociologie

RFS — Review of Financial Studies
RFS — Revue Francaise de Sociologie
RFSEDN — French Journal of Water Science
RFSFI — Revue de la Faculte des Sciences Forestieres de l'Universite d'Istanbul
RFSHA — Reports. Liberal Arts and Science Faculty. Shizuoka University. Natural Science
RFSO-A — Revue Francaise de Sociologie
RFSP — Revue Francaise de Science Politique
RFSUI — Revue de la Faculte des Sciences de l'Universite d'Istanbul
RFT — Revue Francaise de Transfusion
RFT — Rivista di Filosofia (Torino)
RFTPG — Recueil. Faculte de Theologie Protestante (Geneve)
RFTRA — Revue Francaise de Traitement de l'Information
RFUCR — Revista de Filosofia. Universidad de Costa Rica
RFUSA4 — Clinical Gynecology and Obstetrics
RG — Readers' Guide to Periodical Literature
RG — Recherches Germaniques
RG — Recueil General des Monnaies Grecques d'Asie Mineure
RG — Religion und Geisteskultur
RG — Revista de Guimaraes
RG — Revista Geografica
RG — Revue de Geographie
RG — Revue Generale
RG — Revue Germanique
RG — Romana Gens
RGA — Readers' Guide Abstracts
RGA — Reallexikon der Germanischen Altertumskunde
RGA — Revista Geograhica Americana
R Gabonaise Etud Pols Econs et Juridiques — Revue Gabonaise d'Etudes Politiques. Economiques et Juridiques
RGAC — Revista Geografica de America Central
R Gad — Raina Gadagramata
RGAG — Revue de Geogaphie Alpine (Grenoble)
RGand — Romanica Gandensia
RGAR — Revue Generale des Assurances et des Responsabilites
RGas — Revue de Gascogne
RGB — Revue Generale Belge
RGBelge — Revue Generale Belge
RGBR — Recueil General des Bas-Reliefs de la Gaule Romaine
RGC — Revista de Geografia (Chile)
RGCM — Revista de Geografic Commercial (Madrid)
RGCT — Residential Group Care and Treatment
RGD — Revue de Geomorphologie Dynamique
RGD — Revue Generale de Droit
RGDPD — Revue de Geologie Dynamique et de Geographie Physique
RGE — Revue Geographique de l'Est
RGEFA — Revue Generale du Froid
R Gen — Revue Generale
R Gen — Revue Generale de Droit
R Gen Air Espace — Revue Generale de l'Air et de l'Espace
R Gen Assur Terr — Revue Generale des Assurances Terrestres
R Gen Chem de Fer — Revue Generale des Chemins de Fer
R Gen De Der Y Juris — Revista General de Derecho y Jurisprudencia
R Gen De Dr Int Pub — Revue Generale de Droit International Public
R Gen De Droit Int Pub — Revue Generale de Droit International Public
R Gen De Leg Y Juris — Revista General de Legislacion y Jurisprudencia
R Gen De Med Et De Chir — Revue Generale de Medecine et de Chirurgie de l'Afrique du Nord
R Gen Dr Int Publ — Revue Generale de Droit International Public
R Gener Derecho — Revista General de Derecho
R Gener Legisl Jurisp — Revista General de Legislacion y Jurisprudencia
R Gener Marina — Revista General de Marina
RGeneve — Revue de Geneve
R Gen Sci — Revue Generale des Sciences Pures et Appliquees
R Gen Sci Pures et Ap — Revue Generale des Sciences Pures et Appliquees
R Geog — Revista Geografica
R Geogr Alp — Revue de Geographie Alpine
R Geogr Alpine — Revue de Geographie Alpine
R Geogr Am — Revista Geografica Americana
R Geogr Espan — Revista Geografica Espanola
R Geogr Est — Revue Geographique de l'Est
RGeogrH — Revue de Geographie Humaine et d'Ethnologie
R Geogr Lyon — Revue de Geographie de Lyon
R Geogr Maroc — Revue de Geographie du Maroc
R Geogr Pyrenees — Revue Geographique des Pyrenees et du Sud-Ouest
R Geogr (Rio De Janeiro) — Revista Geografica (Rio De Janeiro)
R Geog Soc Pr — Royal Geographical Society. Proceedings
R Geol Soc Ir J — Royal Geological Society of Ireland. Journal
RGer — Recherches Germaniques
RGF — Roemisch-Germanische Forschungen
RGFII — Romano-Germanskaja Filologija
RGFRD4 — Ghana. Fishery Research Unit. Information Report
RGG — Religion in Geschichte und Gegenwart
R Ghana Law — Review of Ghana Law
RGHSDH — Annual Research Reviews. Regulation of Growth Hormone Secretion
RGI — Relaciones Geograficas de Indias
RGI — Revista Geografica Italiana
RGIRAG — Rivista Generale Italiana di Chirurgia
RGIUI — Review of the Geographical Institute of the University of Istanbul
RGIUIE — Review of the Geographical Institute of the University of Istanbul. International Edition
RGK — Roemisch-Germanisches Korrespondenzblatt
RGKAI — Roemisch-Germanische Kommission des Archaeologischen Instituts
RG KBI — Roemisch-Germanisches Korrespondenzblatt
RGKNA — Rikagaku Kenkyusho Kenkyu Nempo

RG Korr Bl — Roemisch-Germanisches Korrespondenzblatt
RG Korr Blatt — Roemisch-Germanisches Korrespondenzblatt
RGL — Reihe Germanistische Linguistik
RGL — Relgionsgeschichtliches Lesebuch
RGL — Resources Policy
RGL — Review of Ghana Law
RGL — Revue de Geographie de Lyon
R Gle B — Revue Generale Belge
RGM — Revue de Geograhie Marocaine
Rg Mag Th — Rechtsgeleerd Magazijn Themis
RGMG — Recueil General des Mosaiques de la Gaule
RGMNA — Chijil Kwangmul Chosa Yongu Pokoso
RGMSN — Royal Geological and Mining Society of the Netherlands
RGNEB — Review of Compagnie Generale d'Electricite
RGNUD — Revue Generale Nucleaire
RGO — Regulation
RGo — Romanica Gothoburgensia
RGP — Revue de Geographie Physique et de Geologie Dynamique
RGP — Rijks Geschiedkundige Publicaties
RGP — Royal Greek Portrait Coins
RGPGD — Revue de Geographie Physique et de Geologie Dynamique
RGr — Rassegna Gregoriana
RGR — Revista Germanistilor Romani
RGr — Revue Gregorienne
RGRCD — Geothermal Resources Council. Special Report
R Greenwich Obs Bull — Royal Greenwich Observatory. Bulletins
R Gregor — Revue Gregorienne
RGS — Revue Generale des Sciences
RGS — Revue Generale des Sciences Pures et Appliques
RGS — Royal Geographical Society
RGSA — Rassegna Gallaratese di Storia e d'Arte
RGS Austsia SA Br Proc — Royal Geographical Society of Australasia. South Australian Branch. Proceedings
RGSI — Records. Geological Survey of India
RGSIA — Records. Geological Survey of India
RGSL — Rassegna Gregoriana per Gli Studi Liturgici e Pel Canto Sacro
R G Soc Cornwall Tr — Royal Geological Society of Cornwall. Transactions
R G Soc Ireland J — Royal Geological Society of Ireland. Journal
RGSR — Repertoire General des Sciences Religieuses
RGST — Reformationsgeschichtliche Studien und Texte
RGSt — [Entscheidungen des] Reichsgerichts in Strafsachen
RGSWA — Records. Geological Survey of New South Wales
RGT — Religionsgeschichtliche Texte
RGTHA — Revue Generale de Thermique
R Guardia Fin — Rivista della Guardia di Finanza
RGuim — Revista de Guimaraes
R Guimar — Revista de Guimaraes
R Guimaraes — Revista de Guimaraes
RGUMD — Argument
RGVV — Religionsgeschichtliche Versuche und Vorarbeiten
RGZM — Roemisch-Germanische Zentralmuseum (Mainz)
RGZTA — Railway Gazette [Later, Railway Gazette International]
RH — Radical Humanist
RH — Relacoes Humanos [Sao Paulo]
RH — Religious Humanism
RH — Repertorio Historico
RH — Restaurant Hospitality
RH — Revista de Historia
RH — Revue de Hollande
RH — Revue Hebdomadaire
RH — Revue Hispanique
RH — Revue Historique
RH — Rochester History
RH — Roczniki Humanistyczne
RHA — Revista de Historia de America
RHA — Revue Hittite et Asiatique
RHab — Revista Habanera
R Hacienda — Revista de Hacienda
RHAF — Revue d'Histoire de l'Amerique Francaise
RHAM — Revue Historique et Archeologique du Maine
R Hanazono Coll — Review of Hanazono College
RH Ard — Revue Historique Ardennaise
RHAs — Revue Hittite et Asianique
RH Auv — Revue de la Haute Auvergne
RHB — Revue Historique de Bordeaux
RhB — Rheinische Blaetter
RHB — Rheinische Heimatblaetter
RHBNA — Rehabilitation
RH Bord — Revue Historique de Bordeaux et du Departement de la Gironde
RHC — Recueil des Historiens des Croisades
RHC — Revue d'Histoire Comparee
RHC — Revue Historique (Constantinople)
RHCB — Revista Historica Critica y Bibliografica de la Literatura Cubana
RHCF — Revue de l'Histoire des Colonies Francaises
RHCFA — Revista. Hospital das Clinicas. Faculdade de Medicina. Universidade de Sao Paulo
RHCM — Revue d'Histoire et de Civilisation du Maghreb
RHComp — Revue d'Histoire Comparee
RHCR — Revista de Historia
RHCS — Rocznik Historii Czasopismiennictwa Polskiego
RHD — Revue d'Histoire Diplomatique
RHD — Revue d'Histoire du Droit
RHD — Revue Historique de Droit Francais et Etranger
RHDE — Revue d'Histoire des Doctrines Economiques et Sociales
RHDF — Revue Historique de Droit Francais et Etranger

RHDFE — Revue Historique de Droit Francais et Etranger
RHD Fr Etr — Revue Historique de Droit Francais et Etranger
RHDGM — Revue d'Histoire de la Deuxieme Guerre Mondiale
RHDip — Revue d'Histoire Diplomatique
RHDRA — Radiological Health Data and Reports
RHE — Revista de Historia Economica
RHE — Revue d'Histoire Ecclesiastique
RHEA — Research into Higher Education. Abstracts
RHEAA — Rheologica Acta
RHeb — Revue Hebdomadaire
R Hebd — Revue Hebdomadaire
RHEF — Revue d'Histoire de l'Eglise de France
Rhein Aerztekorresp — Rheinische Aerztekorrespondenz
Rhein Baufachztg — Rheinische Baufachzeitung
Rhein Bienenztg — Rheinische Bienenzeitung
Rhein Bll Wohngsw — Rheinische Blaetter fuer Wohnungswesen und Bauberatung
Rhein Chem Retorte — Rhein-Chemie Retorte
Rhein Eisenind — Rheinische Eisenindustrie
Rheingau Weinztg — Rheingauer Weinzeitung
Rheinisches Mus Philol — Rheinisches Museum fuer Philologie
Rheinisches Museum Philol — Rheinisches Museum fuer Philologie
Rheinisch-Westfael Akad Wiss Nat- Ing- Wirtschaftswiss Vort — Rheinisch-Westfaelische Akademie der Wissenschaften Natur-, Ingenieur-, und Wirtschaftswissenschaften. Vortraege
Rheinisch Westfaelische Akad Wiss Natur Ingr Wirtschaftswiss — Rheinisch-Westfaelische Akademie der Wissenschaften. Natur , Ingenieur-, und Wirtschaftswissenschaften
Rheinisch Westfael Z Volkskd — Rheinisch-Westfaelische Zeitschrift fuer Volkskunde
Rhein Kststatten — Rheinische Kunststatten
Rhein Lebensbild — Rheinische Lebensbilder
Rheinl Westphal Sb — Sitzungsberichte der Niederrheinischen Gesellschaft fuer Natur- und Heilkunde zu Bonn
Rheinl Westphal Vh — Verhandlungen des Naturhistorischen Vereins der Preussischen Rheinlande, Westfalens und des Reg.-Bezirks Osnabruek
Rhein Mag Erweit Naturk — Rheinisches Magazin zur Erweiterung der Naturkunde
Rhein Main Forsch — Rhein-Mainische Forschungen
Rhein Mannigfaltigk — Rheinische Mannigfaltigkeiten
Rheinmetall Borsig Mitt — Rheinmetall-Borsig-Mitteilungen
Rheinmetall Borsig Tech Rev — Rheinmetall-Borsig Technical Review
Rhein Mus — Rheinisches Museum
Rhein Mus (Bonn) — Rheinische Landesmuseum (Bonn)
Rhein Museum Philol — Rheinisches Museum fuer Philologie
Rhein Not Z — Rheinpreussen Notariat Zeitschrift
Rhein Philol — Rheinische Philologie
Rheinstahl Tech — Rheinstahl Technik
Rhein Vb — Rheinische Vierteljahresblaetter
Rhein Viert Jbl — Rheinische Vierteljahrsblaetter
Rhein Vjbl — Rheinische Vierteljahrsblaetter
Rhein Vjsbll — Rheinische Vierteljahrsblaetter
Rhein Weinztg — Rheinische Weinzeitung
Rhein-Westfael Akad Wiss Vortr N — Rheinisch-Westfaelische Akademie der Wissenschaften Natur-, Ingenieur-, und Wirtschaftswissenschaften. Vortraege
Rhein Westfael Inst Wirtsch Forsch Mitt — Rheinisch-Westfaelisches Institut fuer Wirtschaftsforschung. Mitteilungen
Rhein Westf Anz Bund Tech Ind Beamt — Rheinisch-Westfaelischer Anzeiger des Bundes der Technisch-Industriellen Beamten
Rhein Z — Rheinische Zeitschrift fuer Zivil- und Prozessrecht des In- und Auslandes
Rhein Zs Zivilr — Rheinische Zeitschrift fuer Zivil- und Zivilprozessrecht
RHel — Romanica Helvetica
R Hell Dr Int — Revue Hellenique de Droit International
Rheol Abstr — Rheology Abstracts
Rheol Act — Rheologica Acta
Rheol Acta — Rheologica Acta
Rhcol Bull — Rheology Bulletin
Rheol Fresh Cem Concr Proc Int Conf — Rheology of Fresh Cement and Concrete. Proceedings. International Conference
Rheol Fundam Polym Process — Rheological Fundamentals of Polymer Processing
Rheol Leafl — Rheology Leaflet
Rheol Mem — Rheological Memoirs
Rheology Ser — Rheology Series
Rheol Ser — Rheology Series
Rheol Texture Food Qual — Rheology and Texture in Food Quality
RHES — Revue d'Histoire Economique et Sociale
Rhet Gr — Rhetores Graeci
Rhet Graec — Rhetores Graeci
Rhet Lat Min — Rhetores Latini Minores
Rheumatol Balneo Allergol — Rheumatologia, Balneologia, Allergologia
Rheumatol Int — Rheumatology International
Rheumatol Phys Med — Rheumatology and Physical Medicine
Rheumatol Rehabil — Rheumatology and Rehabilitation
Rheum Baln Allerg Bpest — Rheumatologia, Balneologia, Allergiologia (Budapest)
Rheum Dis — Rheumatic Diseases
Rheum Int — Rheumatology International
Rheum Rev — Rheumatic Review
Rheydter Jb Gesch Kst & Heimatknd — Rheydter Jahrbuch fuer Geschichte, Kunst, und Heimatkunde
RHF — Revue de l'Histoire de France
RHF — Revue d'Histoire Franciscaine
RHGL — Recueil des Historiens des Gaules et de la France
Rh Gr — Rhetores Graeci
RHI — Revista Historica Iquena [Ica]
RHi — Revue Hispanique

RhI — Rhode Island History
RHiM — Revista Hispanica Moderna
Rhinol Suppl — Rhinology. Supplement
RHis — Revue Historique
RHisp — Revue Hispanique
R Hispan Mod — Revista Hispanica Moderna
R Hist — Revista de Historia
R Hist — Revista Historica. Publicacion del Museo Historico Nacional
R Hist — Revue Historique
RHist — Roczniki Historyczne
R Hist Am — Revista de Historia de America
R Hist America — Revista de Historia de America
R Hist & Philos Rel — Revue d'Histoire et de Philosophie Religieuses
R Hist Arch Soc Ir J — Royal Historical and Archaeological Society of Ireland. Journal
R Hist Ard — Revue Historique Ardennaise
R Hist Bul — Revue Historique. Bulletins Critiques
R Hist Civ Maghreb — Revue d'Histoire et de Civilisation du Maghreb
R Hist D Col Fr — Revue de l'Histoire des Colonies Francaises
R Hist Deuxieme Geurre Mondiale — Revue d'Histoire de la Deuxieme Guerre Mondiale
R Hist Diplom — Revue d'Histoire Diplomatique
R Hist Droit — Revue Historique de Droit Francais et Etranger
R Hist Eccl — Revue d'Histoire Ecclesiastique
R Hist Eccles — Revue d'Histoire Eclesiastique
R Hist Fascisme — Revue d'Histoire du Fascisme
R Hist Litt France — Revue d'Histoire Litteraire de la France
RHistM — Roemische Historische Mitteilungen
R Hist Mem — Revue Historique. Memoires et Etudes
R Hist Mod & Contemp — Revue d'Histoire Moderne et Contemporaine
RHistorique — Revue Historique
R Hist Peru — Revista Historica (Lima, Peru)
R Hist Ph Rel — Revue d'Histoire et de Philosophie Religieuses
R Hist Rel — Revue de l'Histoire des Religions
R Hist Sao Paulo — Revista de Historia (Sao Paulo)
R Hist Sci & Ap — Revue d'Histoire des Sciences et de Leurs Applications
R Hist Soc — Royal Historical Society
R Hist Spiritualite — Revue d'Histoire de la Spiritualite
R Hist Toulouse — Revue Historique de Toulouse
R Hitt As — Revue Hittite et Asianique
RhJbV — Rheinisches Jahrbuch fuer Volkskunde
RHJE — Revue de l'Histoire Juive en Egypte
RHKUL — Roczniki Humanistyczne. Towarzystwo Naukowe Katolickiego Uniwersytetu Lubelskiego
RHL — Revista de Historia. La Laguna de Tenerife
RHL — Revista Historica [Lima]
RHL — Revue d'Histoire Litteraire de la France
Rh Lat Min — Rhetores Latini Minores
RHLB — Revue d'Histoire Litteraire (Bucharest)
RHLE — Revista Critica de Historia y Literatura Espanolas
RHLF — Revue d'Histoire Litteraire de la France
Rh LJ — Rhodesian Law Journal
RHLK — Reihe Hanser Literature-Kommentare
RHLN — Revista da Historia (Lisboa)
RHLP — Revista de Historia Literaria de Portugal
RHLR — Revue d'Histoire et de Litterature Religieuse
RHM — Revista Hispanica Moderna
RHM — Revista Historica (Montevideo)
RHM — Revue d'Histoire Moderne
RHM — Revue Histoire Missions
RhM — Rheinische Merkur
RhM — Rheinisches Museum fuer Philologie
RHM — Roemische Historische Mitteilungen
RhMBl — Rheinische Musikblaetter
RHMC — Revue d'Histoire Moderne et Contemporaine
RHMH — Revue d'Histoire de la Medicine Hebraique
RHMis — Revue d'Histoire des Missions
RH Miss — Revue d'Histoire des Missions
RH Mo — Revue d'Histoire Moderne
RhMP — Rheinisches Museum fuer Philologie
Rh M Ph — Rheinisches Museum fuer Philologie
RHMSA — Revue d'Hygiene et de Medecine Sociale
RHMTA — Rhumatologie
Rh Mus — Rheinisches Museum fuer Philologie
Rh N — Rheinische Neujahrsblaetter
RHNB — Revue Historique, Nobiliaire et Biographique
RHNL — Reindeer Herders Newsletter. Institute of Arctic Biology. University of Alaska
RHODA — Rhodora
Rhod Agric J — Rhodesia Agricultural Journal
Rhod Agric J Tech Handb — Rhodesia Agricultural Journal. Technical Handbook
Rhod Beekeeping — Rhodesian Beekeeping
Rhod Bee News — Rhodesian Bee News
Rhod Bull For Res — Rhodesia. Bulletin of Forestry Research
Rhod Chibero Coll Agric Annu Rep — Rhodesia. Chibero College of Agriculture. Annual Report
Rhod Cotton Res Inst Annu Rep — Rhodesia Cotton Research Institute. Annual Report
Rhod Div Livest Pastures Annu Rep — Rhodesia. Division of Livestock and Pastures. Annual Report
Rhode Isl Agric — Rhode Island Agriculture
Rhode Island — Bulletin. Rhode Island School of Design. Museum Notes
Rhode Island Med J — Rhode Island Medical Journal
Rhode Isl Fish Pamph — Rhode Island Fisheries Pamphlet
Rhode Isl Med J — Rhode Island Medical Journal

Rhod Eng — Rhodesian Engineer
Rhod Engr — Rhodesian Engineer
Rhodesia Ag J — Rhodesia Agricultural Journal
Rhodesia Agric J — Rhodesia Agricultural Journal
Rhodesia Agr J — Rhodesia Agricultural Journal
Rhodesian Agric J — Rhodesian Agricultural Journal
Rhodesian Hist — Rhodesian History
Rhodesian J Agric Res — Rhodesian Journal of Agricultural Research. Agricultural Research Council of Central Africa
Rhodesian J Agr Res — Rhodesian Journal of Agricultural Research
Rhodesian J Econ — Rhodesian Journal of Economics
Rhodesian LJ — Rhodesian Law Journal
Rhodesian Min Jour — Rhodesian Mining Journal
Rhodesian Tobacco J — Rhodesian Tobacco Journal
Rhodesian Tob J — Rhodesian Tobacco Journal
Rhodesia Rlys Bull — Rhodesia Railways Bulletin
Rhodesia Zambia Malawi J Agr Res — Rhodesia, Zambia, and Malawi Journal of Agricultural Research
Rhod Esigodini Agric Inst Annu Rep — Rhodesia. Esigodini Agricultural Institute. Annual Report
Rhodes Livingstone J — Rhodes-Livingstone Journal
Rhodes Livingstone Pap — Rhodes-Livingstone Papers
Rhodes Liv J — Rhodes-Livingstone Journal
Rhodes Sci Assn Proc — Rhodesia Scientific Association. Proceedings
Rhodes Univ Dep Ichthyol Ichthyol Bull — Rhodes University. Department of Ichthyology. Ichthyological Bulletin
Rhodes Univ Dep Ichthyol Occas Pap — Rhodes University. Department of Ichthyology. Occasional Paper
Rhodes Univ J L B Smith Inst Ichthyol Spec Publ — Rhodes University. J. L. B. Smith Institute of Ichthyology. Special Publication
Rhod Fmr — Rhodesian Farmer
Rhod Fmr Yb — Rhodesian Farmer Yearbook
Rhod Geol Surv Bull — Rhodesia. Geological Survey. Bulletin
Rhod Geol Surv Miner Resour Ser — Rhodesia. Geological Survey. Mineral Resources Series
Rhod Geol Surv Short Rep — Rhodesia. Geological Survey. Short Report
Rhod Grassl Res Stn Annu Rep — Rhodesia Grasslands Research Station. Annual Report
Rhod Hist — Rhodesian History
Rhod J Agric Res — Rhodesia Journal of Agricultural Research
Rhod Jl Agric Res — Rhodesian Journal of Agricultural Research
RHJE — Rhodesian Law Journal
Rhod Librn — Rhodesian Librarian
Rhod Lowveld Res Stn Annu Rep — Rhodesia. Lowveld Research Station. Annual Report
Rhod Min Engng — Rhodesian Mining and Engineering
Rhod Min Engng Rev — Rhodesian Mining and Engineering Review
Rhod Min Engng Yb — Rhodesian Mining and Engineering Yearbook
Rhod Minist Agric Dep Res Spec Serv Seed Serv Annu Rep — Rhodesia. Ministry of Agriculture. Department of Research and Specialist Services. Seed Services. Annual Report
Rhod Minist Agric Gatooma Res Stn Annu Rep — Rhodesia. Ministry of Agriculture. Gatooma Research Station. Annual Report
Rhod Minist Agric Grassl Res Stn Annu Rep — Rhodesia. Ministry of Agriculture. Grasslands Research Station. Annual Report
Rhod Min J — Rhodesian Mining Journal
Rhod Nurse — Rhodesian Nurse
Rhodod Camellia Yb — Rhododendron and Camellia Yearbook
Rhododendron Soc Notes — Rhododendron Society Notes
Rhodod Immergrune Laubgeholze Jb — Rhododendron und Immergruene Laubgeholze Jahrbuch
Rhodod Soc Notes — Rhododendron Society Notes
Rhodod Yb Lond — Rhododendron Year Book. Royal Horticultural Society (London)
Rhodod Yb Portland — Rhododendron Year Book. American Rhododendron Society (Portland)
Rhod Pharm J — Rhodesian Pharmaceutical Journal
Rhod Prehist — Rhodesian Prehistory
Rhod Salisbury Res Stn Annu Rep — Rhodesia. Salisbury Research Station. Annual Report
Rhod Sci News — Rhodesia Science News
Rhod Tob — Rhodesian Tobacco
Rhod Zambia Malawi J Agric Res — Rhodesia, Zambia, and Malawi Journal of Agricultural Research
Rhokana Rev — Rhokana Review
Rhone Med — Rhone Medical
RHOSA — Rinsho Hoshasen
R Hospital France — Revue Hospitaliere de France
RHP — Revista de Historia (Pasto)
RHP — Revue d'Histoire de la Philosophie et d'Histoire Generale de la Civilisation
RHPC — Review of Historical Publications Relating to Canada
RHph — Revue d'Histoire de la Philosophie
RHPH — Revue d'Histoire de la Philosophie et d'Histoire Generale de la Civilisation
RHPhC — Revue d'Histoire de la Philosophie et d'Histoire Generale de la Civilisation
RH Phil Rel — Revue d'Histoire et de Philosophie Religieuse
RHPhR — Revue d'Histoire et de Philosophie Religieuses
RHPhRel — Revue d'Histoire et de Philosophie Religieuses
RHPR — Revista de Historia de Puerto Rico
RHPR — Revue d'Histoire et de Philosophie Religieuses
RHPS — Revue d'Hygiene et de Police Sanitaire
RHR — Revue de l'Histoire des Religions
RHRCA — Rehabilitation Record
RH Rel — Revue d'Histoire des Religions
RHS — Revue d'Histoire de la Spiritualite

RHS — Revue d'Histoire des Sciences et de Leurs Applications
RHS — Royal Historical Society. Transactions
RHSA — Revue d'Histoire des Sciences et de Leurs Applications
RHSc — Revue d'Histoire des Sciences et de Leurs Applications
RHSE — Revue Historique du Sud-Est Europeen
RHSEE — Revue Historique du Sud-Est Europeen
RHSP — Revista de Historia (Sao Paulo)
RH Spir — Revue d'Histoire de la Spiritualite
RHSQ — Royal Historical Society of Queensland. Journal
RHSQJ — Royal Historical Society of Queensland. Journal
RHSTr — Royal Historical Society. Transactions
RHT — Revue d'Histoire des Textes
RHT — Revue d'Histoire du Theatre
RHTe — Revue d'Histoire des Textes
RHTKA — Rheinstahl Technik
RHTMA — Reviews on High-Temperature Materials
RHTRB — Revue des Hautes Temperatures et des Refractaires
RHUEA — Rheumatism
RHUL — Revista de Historia. Universidad de La Laguna
RHUL — Roczniki Humanistyczne Uniwersitetu Lubelskiego
RHUMA — Rhumatologie
RHumm — Revista de Humanidades. Publicacion Universitaria
RHV — Revista de Historia (Venezuela)
RHV — Revue de l'Histoire de Versailles et de Seine-et-Oise
RHV — Revue Historique Vaudoise
RhV — Rheinische Vierteljahresblaetter
RhV — Rheinische Vorzeit in Wort und Bild
RhVJ — Rheinische Vierteljahresblaetter
Rhythmes Monde — Rhythmes du Monde
RI — Rassegna Italiana
RI — Regesta Imperii
RI — Religion Indexes
RI — Revista de Indias
RI — Revista de Istorie
RI — Revista de las Indias
RI — Revista Iberoamericana
RI — Revista Insulana. Instituto Cultural de Ponta Delgada
RI — Revue Indochinoise
RI — Revue Internationale
RI — Rhode Island Music Educators Review
RI — Rhode Island Reports
RI — Rice Institute Pamphlet
RI — Risorgimento Italiano
RI — Rivista d'Italia
RI — Rivista Israelitica
RIA — Reallexikon der Indo-Germanischen Altertumskunde
RIA — Revista del Instituto de Antropologia. Universidad Nacional de Cordoba
RIA — Revista Iberoamericana
RIA — Rivista. Istituto Nazionale d'Archeologia e Storia dell'Arte
RIAA — Revista del Instituto Americano de Arte [*Cuzco*]
RIAB — Revista Interamericana de Bibliografia
RI Acts & Resolves — Acts and Resolves of Rhode Island and Providence Plantations
RIADAG — Radovi Instituta za Proucavanje i Suzbijanje Alkoholizma i Drugih Narkomanija uZagrebu
RIAf — Review of International Affairs
RIAF — Revista Pentru Istorie, Arheologie, si Filologie
RI Ag — Rhode Island Agriculture
RI Ag Exp — Rhode Island. Agricultural Experiment Station. Publications
RI Agr — Rhode Island Agriculture. Rhode Island Agricultural Experiment Station
RI Agric — Rhode Island Agriculture
RI Agric Exp Stn Bull — Rhode Island. Agricultural Experiment Station. Bulletin
RI Agric Exp Stn Res Q Rev — Rhode Island. Agricultural Experiment Station. Research Quarterly Review
RIAHG — Revista do Instituto Archeologico, Historico, e Geografico Pernambucano
RIAND — Risk Analysis
RIAR — Revista del Instituto de Antropologia. Universidad Nacional del Litoral (Rosario)
RIA Rev Econ Tech Ind Aliment Eur — RIA. Revue Economique et Technique de l'Industrie Alimentaire Europeenne
RIASA — Revista. Istituto d'Archeologia e Storia dell'Arte
RIASB — Richerche Astronomiche
Riass Agro Met Puglia Lucania — Riassunto Agro-Meteorologico per la Puglia e Lucania
Riass A Ossmi Met Oss Ital — Riassunto Annuale delle Osservazioni Meteorologiche Eseguite Negli Osservatori Italiani
Riass Clim Puglia Lucania — Riassunto Climatico in Puglia e Lucania
Riass Mens Ossni Uff Presagi — Riassunto Mensile delle Osservazioni. Ufficio Presagi. Ministerio dell'Aeronautica
Riass Met Ist Geofis Genova — Riassunto Meteorologico. Istituto Geofisico (Genova)
Riass Oss Met Genova — Riassunto. Osservatorio Meteorologico di Genova
Riass Ossni Met Sondalo — Riassunto delle Osservazioni Meteorologiche. Osservatorio Meteorologico del Villaggio Sanatoriale, Sondalo
Riass Staz Met Milano — Riassunto. Stazione Meteorologica di Milano. Istituto Geofisico Italiano (Milano)
RIAT — Revista del Instituto de Antropologia de Tucuman
RIAUL — Annual Report. Institute of Archaeology. University of London
Riazi J Karachi Math Assoc — Riazi. Journal of Karachi Mathematical Association
RIB — Rendiconto. Accademia della Scienze. Istituto di Bologna
RIB — Review of International Affairs. Politics, Economics, Law, Science, Culture
RIB — Review of International Broadcasting
RIB — Revista de las Indias (Bogota)
RIB — Revista Iberoamericana de Bibliografia
RIB — Revista Interamericana de Bibliografia. Organization of American States

RIB — Revue de l'Instruction Publique en Belgique
Ri B — Rivista Biblica
RIB — Roman Inscriptions of Britain
RIBA J — Royal Institute of British Architects. Journal
RIBA Journal — Journal. Royal Institute of British Architects
Ribarst Jugosl — Ribarstvo Jugoslavije
RIBA Trans — Royal Institute of British Architects Transactions
Ribe Amts Vestre Landboforen Beretn — Ribe Amts Vestre Landboforeningens Beretning
R Iber — Rassegna Iberistica
R Iberoamer Segur Soc — Revista Iberoamericana de Seguridad Social
R Iberoam Seguridad Soc — Revista Iberoamericana de Seguridad Social
RIBJ — Rhode Island Bar Journal
RIBJD — RIBA [*Royal Institute of British Architects*] Journal
RI Bur Industrial Statistics An Rp Nat Res S B — Rhode Island Bureau of Industrial Statistics. Annual Report. Natural Resources Survey. Bulletin
RIB Wuerttemb — Roemischen Inschriften und Bildwerke Wuertembergs
RIC — Repertoire Bibliographique des Institutions Chretiennes
RIC — Review of International Cooperation
RIC — Revista Trimensal do Instituto do Ceara [*Fortaleza*]
RIC — Revue de Droit Intellectuel "l'Ingenieur Conseil"
RIC — Roman Imperial Coinage
Ric & Stud Archv Romani — Ricerche e Studi Negli Archivi Romani
Ric Autom — Ricerche di Automatica
RicBibRel — Ricerche Bibliche e Religiose
Ric Biol Selvaggina — Ricerche di Biologia della Selvaggina
Ric Clin Lab — Ricerca in Clinica e in Laboratorio
Ric Demos — Ricerche Demoscopiche
Ric Distrib Altim Veg Ital — Ricerche sulla Distribuzione Altimetrica della Vegetazione in Italia
Ric Doc Tess — Ricerca e Documentazione Tessile
RICE — Resources in Computer Education
Rice Bull Br Guiana — Rice Bulletin. Department of Agriculture (British Guiana)
Rice Bull Lond — Rice Bulletin (London)
Ric Econ — Ricerche Economiche
Rice Grow Exp Yance Rice Res Stn — Rice Growing Experiments. Yance Rice Research Station
Rice Ind — Rice Industry
Rice Inst P — Rice Institute Pamphlet
Rice Inst Pam — Rice Institute Pamphlet
Rice Inst Pamph — Rice Institute Pamphlets
Rice J — Rice Journal
RiceP — Rice Institute Pamphlets
Ricerca Scient — Ricerca Scientifica
Ricerca Scient Rc — Ricerca Scientifica. Rendiconti
Ricerca Scient Ricostr Memorie — Ricerca Scientifica e Ricostruzione. Memorie
Ricerche Automat — Ricerche di Automatica
Ricerche Mat — Ricerche di Matematica
Ric Esper Ist Poderi Sper Lab Chim Agr Oss Met Firenze — Ricerche ed Esperienze Istitute nei Poderi Sperimentali nel Laboratorio di Chimica Agraria e nell'Osservatorio Meteorologico (Firenze)
Rice Sugar J — Rice and Sugar Journal
Rice Sug Coff J — Rice, Sugar, and Coffee Journal
Rice Sug J — Rice and Sugar Journal
Rice Suppl Grain Bull — Rice Supplement to Grain Bulletin. Commonwealth Economic Committee
Rice Univ Aero-Astronaut Rep — Rice University. Aero-Astronautic Report
Rice Univ Stud — Rice University. Studies
Rice Univ Studies — Rice University. Studies
RiceUS — Rice University. Studies
RicF — Ricerche Filosofiche
Ric Fisiol Chim Biol Staz Zool Napoli — Ricerche di Fisiologia e di Chimica Biologica. Stazione Zoologica di Napoli
Ric Fotom — Ricerche Fotometriche
Ric Geogr Econ Porti Ital — Ricerche di Geografia Economica sui Porti Italiani
RICHD — Reviews in Inorganic Chemistry
Rich Ethnogr Yougosl — Richesses Ethnographiques en Yougoslavie
Richmd T-D — Richmond Times-Dispatch
Richmond Co Hist — Richmond County History
Richmond Cty Hist — Richmond County History
Richmond J Pract — Richmond Journal of Practice
Richmond Louisville Med J — Richmond and Louisville Medical Journal
Richters Annalen — Richters Annalen der Deutschen Geschichte
Ric Ing — Ricerche di Ingegneria
RICJA — Rice Journal
Rickia Arq Bot Estado Sao Paulo Ser Criptogam — Rickia. Arquivos de Botanica do Estado de Sao Paulo. Serie Criptogamica
Rickia Arq Bot Estado Sao Paulo Ser Criptogam Supl — Rickia. Arquivos de Botanica do Estado de Sao Paulo. Serie Criptogamica
Rickia Supl — Rickia. Suplemento
Rickmansworth Hist — Rickmansworth Historian
Ric Lav Ist Bot Univ Pisa — Ricerche e Lavori. Istituto Botanico. Univerista di Pisa
Ric Lg — Richerche Linguistiche
Ric Limnol — Ricerche Limnologiche
RicLing — Ricerche Linguistiche
RicM — Ricerche Musicali
Ric Mat — Ricerche di Matematica
Ric Med — Richerche Medievali
Ric Morf — Ricerche di Morfologia
Ric Morf Idrogr Cars — Ricerche sulla Morfologia e Idrografia Carsica
Ric Morfol — Ricerche di Morfologia
RICOA — Rivista dei Combustibili
Ric Ossni Divulg Fitopat Campan Mezzogiorno — Ricerche, Osservazioni, e Divulgazioni Fitopatologiche per la Campania e il Mezzogiorno
RICP — Revista. Instituto de Cultura Puertorriquena

RICP — Revue de l'Institut Catholique de Paris
Ric Psicol — Ricerche di Psicologia. Laboratorio di Psicologia Sperimentale
RicR — Ricerche Religiose
RicRel — Ricerche Religiose
RICS — Revista Interamericana de Ciencias Sociales [*Washington*]
RICS Abs Rev — RICS [*Royal Institution of Chartered Surveyors*] Abstracts and Review
Ric Sci — Ricerca Scientifica
Ric Sci Parte 1 — Ricerca Scientifica. Parte 1. Rivista
Ric Sci Parte 2 Sez A — Ricerca Scientifica. Parte 2. Rendiconti. Sezione A. Biologica
Ric Sci Parte 2 Sez B — Ricerca Scientifica. Parte 2. Rendiconti. Sezione B. Biologica
Ric Sci Prog Tec — Ricerca Scientifica ed il Progresso Tecnico
Ric Sci Quad — Ricerca Scientifica. Quaderni
Ric Sci Rend Sez B — Ricerca Scientifica. Serie Seconda. Parte II. Rendiconti. Sezione B. Biologica
Ric Sci Ricostr — Ricerca Scientifica e Ricostruzione
Ric Sci Ser 2a Pt 2 Rendiconti Sez B Biol — Ricerca Scientifica. Serie 2a. Parte II. Rendiconti. Sezione B. Biologica
Ric Sci Suppl — Ricerca Scientifica. Supplemento
Ric Sez Sper Zucch Ist Chim Ind — Ricerche della Sezione Sperimentale Zuccheri presso l'Istituto di Chimica Industriale
RicSL — Ricerche Slavistiche
Ric Slav — Ricerche Slavistiche
Ric Slavist — Ricerche Slavistiche
Ric Sper Attiv Spieg — Ricerche Sperimentali e Attivita Spiegata
Ric Sper Dendrom Auxom — Ricerche Sperimentali di Dendrometria e di Auxometria
Ric Sper Ist Fisiol Univ Bologna — Ricerche Sperimentali. Istituto di Fisiologia. Universita di Bologna
Ric Sper Lab Chim Univ Bologna — Ricerche Sperimentali eseguite nel Laboratorio di Chimica della Universita di Bologna
Ric Spettrosc — Ricerche Spettroscopiche
Ric Spettros Lab Astrofis Specola — Ricerche Spettroscopiche. Laboratorio Astrofisico della Specola Vaticana
RicSRel — Ricerche di Storia Religiosa
Ric St (Brindisi) — Ricerche e Studi. Museo Provinciale Francesco Ribezzo (Brindisi)
Ric Stor A — Ricerche di Storia dell'Arte
Ric Stor Pesaro — Ricerca Storica di Pesaro
Ric Stor Relig Roma — Ricerche della Storia Religiosa di Roma
RicStRel — Ricerche di Storia Religiosa
Ric Studi Med Sper — Ricerche e Studi di Medicina Sperimentale
Ric Termotecnica — Ricerche di Termotecnica
Ric Terrazzi Fluv Mar Ital — Ricerche sui Terrazzi Fluviali e Marini d'Italia
Ric Var Spiagge Ital — Ricerche sulle Variazioni delle Spiagge Italiane
Ric Var Stor Clima Ital — Ricerche sulle Variazioni Storiche del Clima Italiano
Ric Zool Appl Caccia — Ricerche di Zoologia Applicata alla Caccia
Ric Zool Appl Caccia Suppl — Ricerche di Zoologia Applicata alla Caccia. Supplemento
Rid — Ridotto
RID — Rivista Italiana del Drama
RID — Rivista Italiana di Dialettologia
RIDA — Revue Internationale des Droits de l'Antiquite
RIDC — Revue Internationale de Droit Compare
RIDD — Rivista Italiana di Drammaturgia. Trimestrale dell'Istituto del Dramma Italiano
R Ideas Estet — Revista de Ideas Esteticas. CSIC (Consejo Superior de Investigaciones Cientificas)
RI Dent J — Rhode Island Dental Journal
RIdeP — Revue Internationale de Philosophie
RIDEQ — Revista Iberoamericana de Educacion Quimica
RI Des Bull — Rhode Island Design Bulletin
RI Dev Counc Geol Bull — Rhode Island Development Council. Geological Bulletin
RI Devel Council Geol Bull Sci Contr — Rhode Island Development Council. Geological Bulletin. Scientific Contribution
Ridgew L & S (Ire) — Ridgeway, Lapp, and Schoales' Irish Term Reports
RIdIMN — RIdIM (Repertoire Internationale d'Iconographie Musicale) Newsletter
RIdM — Rivista Italiana di Musicologia
RIDPE3 — Bulletin of Fisheries Research and Development
RIE — Revista de Ideas Esteticas
RIE — Revue Internationale de l'Enseignement
RIEAA — Rivista di Economia Agraria
RIEB — Revista. Instituto de Estudos Brasileiros
RIEB — Revue Internationale des Etudes Balkaniques
Riech Aromen Kosmet — Riechstoffe, Aromen, Kosmetica
Riechst Aromen — Riechstoffe und Aromen
Riechst Aromen Koerperpflegem — Riechstoffe, Aromen, Koerperpflegemittel [*Later, Riechstoffe, Aromen, Kosmetica*]
Riechstoffe Arom — Riechstoffe und Aromen
Riechstoff Ind Kosmet — Riechstoff-Industrie und Kosmetik
RIEEC — Research Institute for the Education of Exceptional Children
RIEI — Revista. Instituto de Estudios Islamicos
RIEMA — Rapports et Proces-Verbaux des Reunions. Conseil International pour l'Exploration de la Mer
RIEN — Revista del Instituto Etnologico Nacional [*Bogota*]
RIENP — Revue Internationale d'Ethnopsychologie Normale et Pathologique
RIENT — Revista del Instituto de Etnologia de la Universidad Nacional de Tucuman
RIEs — Revista de Ideas Esteticas
RIES — Revue Internationale des Institutions Economiques et Sociales
Riesengebirge Im Wort Bild — Das Riesengebirge im Wort und Bild
RIETDJ — Institut d'Elevage et de Medecine Veterinaire des Pays Tropicaux. Rapport d'Activite
RIEtnN — Revista. Instituto Etnologico Nacional

RIEV — Revista Internacional de Estudios Vascos
RIF — Research in Finance
RIF — Rivista Italiana di Filosofia
RIFAA — Revista Industrial y Fabril
Rif Agr — Riforma Agraria
RIFBAZ — Ching Chi Pu Kuo Li Taiwan Ta Hsueh Ho Pan Yu Yeh Sheng Wu Shih Yen So Yen ChiuPao Kao
RIFD — Rivista Internazionale di Filosofia del Diritto
Rif Lett — Riforma Letteraria
Rif Med — Riforma Medica
Riforma Agrar — Riforma Agraria
Riforma Med — Riforma Medica
RIFPA — Revue. Institut Francais du Petrole et Annales des Combustibles Liquides [*Later, Revue. Institut Francais du Petrole*]
RIFRAF — Institute of Freshwater Research (Drottningholm). Report
RIFSF — Rivista Internazionale di Fonte e Studi della Filosofia
Rif Stomat — Riforma Stomatologica
RIG — Bouwadviseur Opinievormend Beroepstijdschrift voor Adviseurs
RIG — Recueil d'Inscriptions Grecques
RIGAA — Rinsho Ganka
Riga Arb Nf Vr — Arbeiten des Naturforschenden Vereins in Riga
Riga Cor Bl — Correspondenzblatt des Naturforscher-Vereins zu Riga
Riga IndZtg — Rigasche Industriezeitung
Rigaku J — Rigaku Journal
Rigasche Ind Ztg — Rigasche Industrie Zeitung
Rigas Med Inst Zinat Rakstu Krajums — Rigas Medicinas Instituta Zinatnisko Rakstu Krajums
Rigas Politeh Inst Zinat Raksti — Rigas Politehniskais Instituts. Zinatniskie Raksti
Riga Zeitsch F Rechtswiss — Rigasche Zeitschrift fuer Rechtswissenschaft
RIGB — Royal Institution of Great Britain. Proceedings
RI Gen Laws — General Laws of Rhode Island
RIGH — Revista do Instituto Geografico e Historico da Baia
RIGI — Rivista Indo-Greco-Italica di Filologia, Lingua, Antichita
RIGI — Rivista Indo-Greco-Italico
RIGI — Romanskoe i Germanskoe Iazykoznanie
RIGIB — Radovi Instituta za Geolosko-Rudarska Istrazivanja i Ispitivanja Nuklearnih i Drugih Mineralnih Sirovina
RIGPA — Rezul'taty Issledovanyi po Mezhdunarodny Geofizicheskim Proektam
RI Grad Sch Oceanogr Occas Publ — Rhode Island Graduate School of Oceanography. Occasional Publication
RIH — Rhode Island History
RIHAA — Rivers and Harbors
Rihaknonjip Res Inst Appl Sci Kon-Kuk Univ — Rihaknonjip. Research Institute of Applied Science. Kon-Kuk University
RIHG — Revista do Instituto Historico e Geographico Brazileiro
RIHGSP — Revista. Instituto Historico e Geografico de Sao Paulo
RI His S — Rhode Island Historical Society. Collections
RI Hist — Rhode Island History
RI Hist Soc Coll — Rhode Island Historical Society. Collections
RIHPC — Revue Internationale d'Histoire Politique et Constitutionnelle
RIHS — Revista do Instituto Historico e Geographico de Sao Paulo
RIHTA — Revue Internationale des Hautes Temperatures et des Refractaires
RIHYA — Rinsho Hinyokika
RII — Rivista Inguana et Intemelia
RIIA/IA — International Affairs. Royal Institute of International Affairs
RIIA/WT — World Today. Royal Institute of International Affairs
RIIGA — Rivista Italiana d'Igiene
RIISA — Report. Institute of Industrial Science. University of Tokyo
Riista-Kalataloudes Tutkimuslaitos Kalantutkimusosasto Tied — Riista- ja Kalataloudes Tutkimuslaitos Kalantutkimusosasto Tiedonantoja
Riistatiet Julk — Riistatieteellisia Julkaisuja
Riistatiet Julkaisuja — Riistatieteellisia Julkaisuja
R I J — Journal of the Royal Institution of Great Britain
RIJ — Revista de Investigaciones Juridicas
RIJAZ — Radovi Instituta Jugoslavenske Akademije Znanosti i Umjetnosti u Zadru
RIJAZUZ — Radovi Instituta Jugoslavenske Akademije Znanosti i Umjetnosti u Zadru
RI Jew Hist Note — Rhode Island Jewish Historical Notes
RI Jewish Historical Notes — Rhode Island Jewish Historical Notes
RIJG — Recueil des Inscriptions Juridiques Grecques
RIJHN — Rhode Island Jewish Historical Notes
Rijks Geol Dienst Meded Nieuwe Ser (Neth) — Rijks Geologische Dienst. Mededelingen. Nieuwe Serie (Netherlands)
Rijksuniv Utrecht Jaarversl Wet Deel — Rijksuniversiteit Utrecht. Jaarverslag Wetenschappelijk Deel
Rijkswaterstaat Commun — Rijkswaterstaat Communications
Rijkswat St Commun — Rijkswaterstaat Communications
Rijksw Commun — Rijkswaterstaat Communications
RIJU — Riistatieteellisia Julkaisuja. Finnish Game Research
RIK — Regesta Imperii. Die Regesten der Karolinger
RIKAA — Rinsho Kagaku
RIKEB — Rinsho Ketsueki
RIKR — Regesta Imperii. Die Regesten des Kaiserreiches
RIL — Radiology and Imaging Letter
RIL — Recueil des Inscriptions Libyques
RIL — Religion in Life
RIL — Rendiconti. Istituto Lombardo di Scienze e Lettere
RIL — Revista Iberoamericana de Literatura
RIL — Revista sobre Relaciones Industriales y Laborales
RiL — Rivista Lasalliana
RILA — International Repertory of the Literature of Art
RILA — Rassegna Italiana di Linguistica Applicata
RILA — Recueil des Inscriptions en Lineaire A
RILA — Repertoire International de la Litterature de l'Art

RILAN — RILA [*Repertoire International de la Litterature de l'Art / International Repertory of the Literature of Art*] News

RILD — Rivista Italiana di Letteratura Dialettale

RIL di Scienze e Lettere — Rendiconti. Istituto Lombardo di Scienze e Lettere. Classe di Lettere e ScienzeMorali e Politiche

RILL — Rendiconti. Istituto Lombardo di Scienze e Lettere. Classe di Lettere e ScienzeMorali e Storiche

RILLM — Rendiconti. Istituto Lombardo di Scienze e Lettere. Classe di Lettere e ScienzeMorali e Politiche

RILM — Recherches Internationales a la Lumiere du Marxisme

RILM — RILM [*Repertoire International de la Litterature Musicale*] Abstracts of Music Literature

RiLM — Rivista di Letteratura Moderne

RILM Abstr — RILM [*Repertoire International de la Littature Musicale*] Abstracts

RILOB — Recherches Publiees sous la Direction de l'Institut de Lettres Orientales de Beyrouth

RILPG — Rendiconti. Istituto Lombardo di Scienze e Lettere. Parte Generale e Atti Ufficiali

RILSL — Rendiconti. Istituto Lombardo. Classe di Lettere, Scienze Morali, e Storiche

Ril Urne Et — Rilievi delle Urne Etrusche

RIM — Recreation Information Management System

RIM — Relazione Internationale (Milan)

RIM — Research in Marketing

RIM — Rivista Italiana di Musicologia

RIMA — Revue de l'Institut des Manuscrits Arabes

Rimba Indones — Rimba Indonesia

RI Med — Rhode Island Medicine

RI Med J — Rhode Island Medical Journal

Rimed Nuovi — Rimedii Nuovi

Rimini Stor Art Cult — Rimini Storia Arte e Cultura

RIMJA — Rhode Island Medical Journal

RIM Monogr Math — RIM Monographs in Mathematics

RIMPA — Rivista degli Infortuni e delle Malattie Professionali

RIMS — Rivista Internazionale di Musica Sacra

RIn — Revista de las Indias

RIN — Revue Internationale du Notariat

Rin — Rinascimento

Rin — Rinascita

RIN — Rivista Italiana di Numismatica

RIN — Rivista Italiana di Numismatica e Scienze Affini

RINA — Rivista. Istituto Nazionale d'Archeologia e Storia dell'Arte

RINAB — Research Institute Nedri As (Hveragerdi, Iceland). Bulletin

RINASA — Rivista. Istituto Nazionale d'Archeologia e Storia dell'Arte

Rinasc — Rinasciemento

Rinasc Agric — Rinascenza Agricola

Rinascenza Med — Rinascenza Medica

Rinasc Med — Rinascenza Medica

Rin B — Rinascita. Biblioteca

R Income Wealth — Review of Income and Wealth

R Ind — Revista de las Indias

RINDA — Revue Industrielle

Rindertuberk Brucell — Rindertuberkulose und Brucellose

R Indias — Revista de las Indias

R Indigene — Revue Indigene

RIndM — Revista de las Indias (Madrid)

R Indo Mal Aff — Review of Indonesian and Malayan Affairs

R Indones Malay Aff — Review of Indonesian and Malayan Affairs

R Indones Malayan Aff — Review of Indonesian and Malayan Affairs

RINEEK — Rivista Italiana di Nutrizione Parenterale ed Enterale

Rin F — Rinascita (Firenze)

R Info Legis — Revista de Informacao Legislativa

RINGDOC — Pharmaceutical Literature Documentation

Ringing Migr — Ringing and Migration

R Ing Intem — Rivista Ingauna e Intemelia

Ring Int Ornithol Bull — Ring. International Ornithological Bulletin

Ringling Mus A J — Ringling Museum of Art Journal

Rinkj Aa — Ringkjobing Aarbog

Rinnov Agr — Rinnovamento Agrario

Rinnovamento Med — Rinnovamento Medico

Rinnov Econ Agr — Rinnovamento Economico-Agrario

Rinnov Med — Rinnovamento Medico

RINPA — Rivista di Istochimica Normale e Patologica

RINRBM — Berichte aus der Forschungsstelle Nedri As Hveragerdi Island

Rin S — Rinascenza Salentina

Rin S — Rinascita. Supplement

R Ins Soc — Revue. Institut de Sociologie

R Ins (Solv) — Revue. Institut de Sociologie (Solvay)

R Inst Antropol Cordoba — Revista. Instituto de Antropologia. Universidad de Cordoba

R Inst Chem Lect Monogr Rep — Royal Institute of Chemistry. Lectures, Monographs, and Reports

R Inst Chem Lect Ser — Royal Institute of Chemistry. Lecture Series

R Inst Cienc Soc — Revista. Instituto de Ciencias Sociales

R Inst Egip Est Islam — Revista. Instituto Egipcio de Estudios Islamicos

R Inst Est Islam — Revista. Instituto de Estudios Islamicos

R Inst GB Proc — Royal Institution of Great Britain. Proceedings

R Instit Europ — Revista de Instituciones Europeas

R Inst Nav Archit (London) Suppl Pap — Royal Institution of Naval Architects (London). Supplementary Papers

R Inst Nav Archit Q Trans — Royal Institution of Naval Architects [*London*]. Quarterly Transactions

R Inst Nav Archit Suppl Pap — Royal Institution of Naval Architects [*London*]. Supplementary Papers

R Inst Peruano Investigaciones Genealogicas — Revista. Instituto Peruano de Investigaciones Genealogicas

R Inst Pr — Royal Institution of Great Britain. Proceedings

R Inst Public Health Hyg J — Royal Institute of Public Health and Hygiene. Journal

R Inst Sociol — Revue. Institut de Sociologie

RINT — Revista. Instituto Nacional de la Tradicion

R Int Commiss Jurists — Review. International Commission of Jurists

R Int Coop — Review of International Cooperation

R Int Croix Rouge — Revue Internationale de la Croix Rouge

R Int Cr Rouge — Revue Internationale de la Croix Rouge

R Int De Crimin — Revue Internationale de Criminalistique

R Int De Dr Pen — Revue Internationale de Droit Penal

R Int De L Enf — Revue Internationale de l'Enfant

R Int De Soc — Revue Internationale de Sociologie

R Int Dr Comp — Revue Internationale de Droit Compare

R Int Droits Ant — Revue Internationale des Droits de l'Antiquite

R Int Droits Antiquite — Revue Internationale des Droits de l'Antiquite

R Int Dr Penal — Revue Internationale de Droit Penal

RINTDU — Reactive Intermediates

R Integr — Revista de la Integracion

R Integracion — Revista de la Integracion

R Integracion y Desarrollo Centroam — Revista de la Integracion y el Desarrollo de Centroamerica

RInter — Revista/Review Interamericana

R Interam Bibl — Revista Interamericana de Bibliografia

R Interam Bibliog — Revista Interamericana de Bibliografia

R Inter Am Bibliogr — Inter-American Review of Bibliography/Revista Interamericana de Bibliografia

R Interam Cienc Soc — Revista Interamericana de Ciencias Sociales

R Interamer Planif — Revista Interamericana de Planificacion

R Interam Sociol — Revista Interamericana de Sociologia

R Internac Sociol — Revista Internacional de Sociologia

R Internat Affairs — Review of International Affairs

R Internat Hist Banque — Revue Internationale d'Histoire de la Banque

R Internat Rech Urbaine et Reg — Revue Internationale de Recherche Urbaine et Regionale

R Internaz Econ Trasporti — Revista Internazionale del Trasporti

R Internaz Scienze Econ e Commer — Rivista Internazionale di Scienze Economiche e Commerciali

R Internaz Scienze Soc — Rivista Internazionale di Scienze Sociali

R Int Hist Milit — Revue Internationale d'Histoire Militaire

RIntMS — Rivista Internazionale di Musica Sacra

R Int Pol Crim — Revue Internationale de Police Criminelle

R Int Sci Adm — Revue Internationale des Sciences Administratives

R Int Sci Soc — Revue Internationale des Sciences Sociales

R Int Secur Soc — Revue Internationale de la Securite Sociale

R Int Sociol — Revue Internationale de Sociologie

R Int Sociol (Madrid) — Revista Internacional de Sociologia (Madrid)

R Int Sociologia — Revista Internacional de Sociologia. CSIC (Consejo Superior de Investigaciones Cientificas)

R Int Stat — Revue Internationale de Statistique

R Int Trav — Revue Internationale du Travail

RINUA — Rivista di Ingegneria Nucleare

R I Num — Rivista Italiana di Numismatica e Scienze Affini

RIO — Revue Internationale d'Onomastique

RIO — Rivista Italiana di Ornitologia

RIO — Russkoe Istoriceskoe Obscestvo

RIOAL — Revue. International Organization for Ancient Languages Analysis by Computer

Rio De Janeiro Univ Federal Inst Geociencias Bol Geologia — Universidade Federal do Rio De Janeiro. Instituto de Geociencias. Boletim Geologia

RIOE — Research in Ocean Engineering. University Sources and Resources

Rio Grande Do Sul Inst Geocien Mapa Geol — Universidade Federal do Rio Grande do Sul. Instituto de Geociencias. Mapa Geologico da Folha de Morretes

Rio Grande Do Sul Inst Pesqui Zootec Bol Tec — Rio Grande Do Sul. Instituto de Pesquisas Zootecnicas. Boletim Tecnico

Rio Grande Odont — Rio Grande Odontologico

RIOno — Revue Internationale d'Onomastique

Rio Obs Rv — Revista do Observatorio. Publicacao Mensal do Imperial Observatorio do Rio de Janeiro

RIOTE2 — Rivista Italiana di Ortopedia e Traumatologia

R I P — Notice of the Proceedings at the Meetings of the Members of the Royal Institution, with Abstracts of the Discourses Delivered at the Evening Meetings

RIP — Revista del Instituto Paraguayo

RIP — Revista Interamericana de Psicologia

RIP — Revue Internationale de Philosophie

RIP — Rice Institute Pamphlet

RIPB — Revue de l'Instruction Publique en Belgique

RIPC — Rassegna Italiana di Politica e di Cultura

RIPD — RLG [*Research Libraries Group, Inc.*] Research-in-Progress Database

RIPEH — Review of Iranian Political Economy and History

RIPF — Revue de l'Instruction Publique. En France

RIPh — Revue Internationale de Philosophie

RIPIA — Revue Internationale de la Propriete Industrielle et Litteraire

RIPMA — Revue des Travaux. Institut des Peches Maritimes

RIPOAM — Rivista Italiana delle Essenze dei Profumi e delle Piante Officinali Aromi Saponi Cosmetici Aerosol

RI Port Indus Devel Comm Geol Bull Sci Contr — Rhode Island. Port and Industrial Development Commission. Geological Bulletin. Scientific Contribution

RIPSD3 — Annual Report. Institute of Physics. Academia Sinica

RIPTC — Revue Internationale Pierre Teilhard de Chardin

RI Pub Laws — Public Laws of Rhode Island and Providence Plantations

RIR — Revista Interamericana Review

RIR — Revista Istorica Romana

RIRAB — Rivista di Radiologia
R Ir Acad Proc Sect B — Royal Irish Academy. Proceedings. Section B
R Ir Acad Trans — Royal Irish Academy Transactions
R Iranienne Relations Internat — Revue Iranienne des Relations Internationales
R Iran Relat Int — Revue Iranienne des Relations Internationales
RIRED — Revue. IRE
RI Resour — Rhode Island Resources
R Irish Ac Pr — Royal Irish Academy. Proceedings
RIS — Rassegna Italiana di Sociologia
RIS — Rerum Italicarum Scriptores ab Anno Aerae Christianae 500 ad 1500
RIS — Revista Internacional de Sociologia
RIS — Revue. Institut de Sociologie
RIS — Revue Internationale de Sociologie
RIS — Revue Internationale du Socialisme
Ris — Risorgimento
RIS — Rivista Italiana di Sociologia
RiS — Rivista Storica Italiana
RISA — Revue Internationale des Sciences Administratives
RISA — Royal Inscriptions from Sumer and Akkad
RISAA — Rivista Italiana della Saldatura
Risal Balai Penjel Kehut — Risalah Balai Penjelidikan Kehutanan
RISB — Revista del Instituto de Sociologia Boliviana
RISB — Revista International de Sociologia. Instituto Balmes de Sociologia
RISCA — Ricerca Scientifica
RI Sc G — Rivista Italiana per la Scienze Giuridiche
RI Sch Des Bul — Rhode Island School of Design. Bulletin
RISE — Rivista Internazionale di Scienze Economiche e Commerciali
RISE — Rulings Information System, Excise
RISEB8 — Clinical Orthopaedic Surgery
RISG — Rivista Italiana di Scienze Giuridiche
RISHB — Rinsho Shinkeigaku
RISHBH — Clinical Neurology
RISI — Review. International Statistical Institute
RISID — Revista Padurilor-Industria Lemnului. Seria Industria Lemnului
Rising Up — Rising Up Angry
Risk Anal — Risk Analysis
Risk Based Decis Making Water Resour Proc Conf — Risk-Based Decision Making in Water Resources. Proceedings of the Conference
Risk Bk Ser — Risk. Book Series
Risk Manage — Risk Management
Risk Mgmt — Risk Management
Risk Mgt — Risk Management
RiSL — Rossija i Slavjanstvo
R Islamique — Revue des Etudes Islamiques
RISM — Repertoire International des Sources Musicales
Riso — Forsogsanlaeg Riso. Arsberetning
RISO — Revista Internacional de Sociologia
RISoc — Revue. Institut de Sociologie
Risoe Inf — Risoe Information
Risoe Natl Lab Rep Risoe-M (Den) — Risoe National Laboratory. Report Risoe-M (Denmark)
Risoe Natl Lab Rep Risoe R — Risoe National Laboratory. Report. Risoe-R
Risoe Rep (Den) Res Establ Risoe — Risoe Report. (Denmark) Research Establishment Risoe
Riso Rep — Risoe Report
Risorg Graf — Risorgimento Grafico. Rivista Tecnica
Risorgiment — Risorgimento
RISP — Revista del Instituto Sanmartiniano del Peru
RISP — Revue Internationale de Sociologie (Paris)
RISPT — Ross Ice Shelf Project. Technical Reports
RISR — Rassegna d'Informazioni. Istituto di Studi Romani
RiSR — Ricerche di Storia Religiosa
RISRA — Report of Ionosphere and Space Research in Japan
RISS — Revue de l'Institut de Sociologie. Institut de Sociologie Solvay
RISS — Revue Internationale des Sciences Sociales
RISS — Rivista Internazionale di Scienze Sociali e Discipline Ausiliari
RIst — Revista de Istorie
RISTA — Rivista Italiana di Stomatologia
R Istituto Veneto Memorie — Reale Istituto Veneto di Scienze, Lettere, ed Arti. Memorie
R Ist Lomb — Rendiconti. Istituto Lombardo di Scienze e Lettere
R Ist Rom — Revista Istorica Romana
Ri St V — Richtlinien fuer das Strafverfahren
RISULB — Revue. Institut de Sociologie. Universite Libre de Bruxelles
Risv Med — Risveglio Medico
Risv Ostet — Risveglio Ostetrico
Risv Zootec Abruzz — Risveglio Zootecnico Abruzzese
RIT — Revue Internationale du Travail
RIT — Rivista Italiana del Teatro
RIT — Roemischen Inschriften von Tarraco
RITAA — Revue d'Immunologie et de Therapie Antimicrobienne
R Ital Diritto Lav — Rivista Italiana di Diritto del Lavoro
R Ital Econ Demografia e Statis — Rivista Italiana di Economia. Demografia e Statistica
R Italiana Musicol — Rivista Italiana di Musicologia
R Ital Mus — Nuova Rivista Musicale Italiana
R Ital Mus — Rivista Italiana di Musicologia
RiTh — Revue Internationale de Theologie
RITL — Revista de Istorie si Theori Literara
Rit LandbDeild — Rit Landbunaoardeildar, Atvinnudeild Haskolans
RITMB — Rayonnements Ionisants
R It Num — Rivista Italiana di Numismatica e Scienze Affini
Rit Visindafj Isl — Rit Visindafjelags Islendinga
Riun Annu Assoc Elettrot Elettron Ital Rend — Riunione Annuale della Associazione Elettrotecnica ed Elettronica Italiana. Rendiconti

RI Univ Agric Exp Stn Bull — Rhode Island University. Agricultural Experiment Station. Bulletin
RI Univ Div Eng Res Dev Eng Repr — Rhode Island University. Division of Engineering. Research and Development Engineering Reprint
RI Univ Div Eng Res Dev Leafl — Rhode Island University. Division of Engineering. Research and Development Leaflet
RI Univ Eng Exp Stn Bull — Rhode Island University. Engineering Experiment Station. Bulletin
RI Univ Eng Exp Stn Eng Repr — Rhode Island University. Engineering Experiment Station. Engineering Reprint
RI Univ Mar Tech Rep — Rhode Island University. Marine Technical Report
RIUPDJ — US National Institute on Drug Abuse. Research Issues
Riv — Rivarol
Riv A — Rivista d'Arte
Riv A — Rivista dell'Arte
Riv Abruzz Agric Zootec — Rivista Abruzzese di Agricoltura e Zootecnia
Riv AC — Rivista di Archeologia Cristiana
Riv Accad Med Lomb — Rivista dell'Accademia Medica Lombarda
Riv Aeronaut — Rivista Aeronautica
Riv Aeronaut-Astronaut-Missil — Rivista Aeronautica-Astronautica-Missilistica
Riv Aeronaut Astronaut Missil Suppl Tec — Rivista Aeronautica-Astronautica-Missilistica. Supplemento Tecnico
Riv Agric — Rivista di Agricoltura
Riv Agric Comm Ravenna — Rivista Agricola e Commerciale (Ravenna)
Riv Agric Comm Reggio Emilia — Rivista Agricola e Commerciale (Reggio-Emilia)
Riv Agric Ital — Rivista Agricola Italiana
Riv Agric Romana — Rivista Agricola Romana
Riv Agric Subtrop Trop — Rivista di Agricoltura Subtropicale e Tropicale
Riv Agric Zootec — Rivista di Agricoltura e Zootecnia
Riv Agron — Rivista di Agronomia
Riv Agr Polesana — Rivista Agraria Polesana
Riv Agr Subtrop Trop — Rivista di Agricoltura Subtropicale e Tropicale
Riv Agrumic — Rivista di Agrumicoltura
Riv Albania — Rivista d'Albania
Riv Ampelogr — Rivista di Ampelografia
Riv Anat Patol Oncol — Rivista di Anatomia Patologica e di Oncologia
Riv Ant — Rivista di Antropologia
Riv Antr — Rivista di Antropologia
Riv Antrop — Rivista di Antropologia
Riv Antropol — Rivista di Antropologia
Riv Arald — Rivista Araldica
Riv Arch Como — Rivista Archeologia della Provincia e Diocesi di Como
Riv Arch Cr — Rivista di Archeologia Cristiana
Riv Arch Crist — Rivista di Archeologia Cristiana
Riv Archeol — Rivista di Archeologia
Riv Archeol Crist — Rivista di Archeologia Cristiana
Riv Archeol Prov & Ant Dioc Como — Rivista Archeologica della Provincia e Antica Diocesi di Como. Periodico della Societa Archeologica Comense
Riv Archeol Prov Como — Rivista Archeologica della Provincia di Como
Riv Archivi Ital Biol — Rivista degli Archivi Italiani di Biologia
Riv Arte — Rivista d'Arte
Riv Artigl Genio — Rivista d'Artiglieria e Genio
Riv Astr — Rivista di Astronomia e Scienze Affini
Riv Audiol Prat — Rivista di Audiologia Pratica
Riv Aviaz — Rivista dell'Aviazione
Riv B — Rivista Biblica
RivB — Rivista Bibliografica
RivBA — Rivista delle Biblioteche e degli Archivi
Riv Bas Bull — River Basin Bulletin
Riv Bib — Rivista Biblica
RivBibl — Rivista Biblica
Riv Bibl — Rivista delle Biblioteche e degli Archivi
Riv Bibliot — Rivista delle Biblioteche
Riv Biol — Rivista di Biologia
Riv Biol Colon — Rivista di Biologia Coloniale
Riv Biol Gen — Rivista di Biologia Generale
Riv Biol Norm Patol — Rivista di Biologia Normale e Patologica
Riv Biol (Perugia) — Rivista di Biologia (Perugia)
Riv Birr Bibite — Rivista delle Birrerie e delle Bibite
RivC — Rivista Contemporanea
Riv Canapa — Rivista della Canapa
Riv Catasto Serv Tec Erar — Rivista del Catasto e dei Servizi Tecnici Erariali
Riv Cereali — Rivista dei Cereali e Giornale dei Mugnai
Riv Chim Sci Ind — Rivista di Chimica Scientifica e Industriale
Riv Chir (Como) — Rivista di Chirurgia (Como)
Riv Chir Med — Rivista di Chirurgia e Medicina
Riv Chir Napoli — Rivista di Chururgia (Napoli)
Riv Chir Pediat — Rivista di Chirurgia Pediatrica
Riv Civ — Rivista di Diritto Civile
Riv Clin — Rivista Clinica
Riv Clin Bologna — Rivista Clinica di Bologna
Riv Clin Med — Rivista di Clinica Medica
Riv Clin Pediat — Rivista di Clinica Pediatrica
Riv Clin Pediatr — Rivista di Clinica Pediatrica
Riv Clin Tossicol — Rivista di Clinica Tossicologica
Riv Clin Univ Napoli — Rivista Clinica. Universita di Napoli
Riv Col — Rivista Coloniale
Riv Coleott — Rivista di Coleotterologia
Riv Coleott Ital — Rivista Coleotterologica Italiana
Riv Coll Araldica — Rivista del Collegio di Araldica
Riv Colon — Rivista Coloniale. Istituto Coloniale Italiano
Riv Colon Ital — Rivista delle Colonie Italiane
Riv Colon It ('Oltremare') — Rivista delle Colonie Italiane ('Oltremare')
Riv Colore Verniciatura Ind — Rivista del Colore-Verniciatura Industriale
Riv Com — Rivista del Comune

Riv Com Bologna — Rivista del Comune di Bologna
Riv Combust — Rivista dei Combustibili
Riv Combustibili — Rivista dei Combustibili
Riv Com It — Rivista dei Comuni Italiani
Riv Comm — Rivista del Diritto Commerciale e del Diritto Generale delle Obbligazioni
Riv Como — Rivista di Como
Riv Comun — Rivista delle Comunicazioni
Riv Comun Ferrov — Rivista delle Comunicazioni Ferroviarie
Riv Coniglic — Rivista di Coniglicoltura
Riv Coniglicolt — Rivista di Coniglicoltura
Riv Cr — Rivista Cristiana
Riv Crist — Rivista Cristiana
Riv Crit Clin Med — Rivista Critica di Clinica Medica
Riv Crit St — Rivista Critica di Storia della Filosofia
Riv Crit Stor Fil — Rivista Critica di Storia della Filosofia
Riv Crit Stor Filos — Rivista Critica di Storia della Filosofia
Riv Cult Class Med — Rivista di Cultura Classica e Medioevale
Riv Cult Class Mediev — Rivista di Cultura Classica e Medievale
Riv Cult Mar — Rivista di Cultura Marinara
RivDal — Rivista Dalmatica
Riv d'Alb — Rivista d'Albania
Riv d Arch Cristiana — Rivista di Archeologia Cristiana
Riv d Bibl e d Arch — Rivista delle Biblioteche e degli Archivi
Riv di Antr — Rivista di Antropologia
Riv di Cultura Class e Med — Rivista di Cultura Classica e Medioevale
Riv di Diritto Civile — Rivista di Diritto Civile
Riv di Diritto Internaz — Rivista di Diritto Internazionale
Riv di Diritto Internaz e Comparato del Lavoro — Rivista di Diritto Internazionale e Comparato del Lavoro
Riv Dif Soc — Rivista di Difesa Sociale
Riv di LM — Rivista di Letterature Moderne
Riv Dir Agr — Rivista di Diritto Agrario
Riv Dir Civ — Rivista di Diritto Civile
Riv Dir Comm — Rivista del Diritto Commerciale e del Diritto Generale delle Obbligazioni
Riv Dir Europ — Rivista di Diritto Europeo
Riv Dir Finanz — Rivista di Diritto Finanziaro e Scienza delle Finanze
Riv Dir Ind — Rivista di Diritto Industriale
Riv Dir Int — Rivista di Diritto Internazionale
Riv Dir Int e Comp del Lavoro — Rivista di Diritto Internazionale e Comparato del Lavoro
Riv Dir Int'le — Rivista di Diritto Internazionale
Riv Dir Int'le Priv & Proc — Rivista di Diritto Internazionale Privato e Processuale
Riv Dir Proc Civ — Rivista di Diritto e Procedura Civile
Riv Dir Sport — Rivista di Diritto Sportivo
Riv Di Soc — Rivista di Sociologia
Riv d It — Rivista d'Italia
RIVE — Resources in Vocational Education
Riv Ecol — Rivista di Ecologia
Riv Econ Agr — Rivista di Economia Agraria
Riv Emoterap Immunoemat — Rivista di Emoterapia ed Immunoematologia
Riv Emoter Immunoematol — Rivista di Emoterapia ed Immunoematologia
Riveon Lemat — Riveon Lematematika
River Bds Ass Yb — River Boards Association Yearbook [London]
River Gaug — River Gauging. State Rivers and Water Supply Commission
River Plat — Review of the River Plate
Riv Est — Rivista di Estetica
Riv Estimo Agr Genio Rur — Rivista di Estimo Agrario e Genio Rurale
Riv Et — Rivista di Etnografia
Riv Etnogr — Rivista di Etnografia
Riv Eur Sci Med Farmacol — Rivista Europea per le Scienze Mediche e Farmacologiche
Riv Farmacol Ter — Rivista di Farmacologia e Terapia
RivFC — Rivista di Filologia e di Istruzione Classica
Riv Fecond Artif — Rivista della Fecondazione Artificiale
Riv Ferrara — Rivista di Ferrara
RivFil — Rivista di Filologia
Riv Fil — Rivista di Filologia e di Istruzione Classica
Riv Fil — Rivista di Filosofia
Riv Fil Cl — Rivista di Filologia e d'Istruzione Classica
Riv Fil Class — Rivista di Filologia e di Istruzione Classica
Riv Filol — Rivista di Filologia e d'Istruzione Classica
Riv Filol Istruz Classica — Rivista di Filologia e di Istruzione Classica
Riv Filos — Rivista di Filosofia
Riv Filos Neo Scolast — Rivista di Filosofia Neo-Scolastica
Riv Filosof — Rivista di Filosofia
Riv Filosof Neo-Scolas — Rivista di Filosofia Neo-Scolastica
Riv Fin Loc — Rivista della Finanza Locale
Riv Fis Mat Sci Nat — Rivista di Fisica, Matematica, e Scienze Naturali
Riv Fitosanit — Rivista Fitosanitaria
Riv Fot — Rivista Fotografica
Riv Fotogr Ital — Rivista Fotografica Italiana
Riv Freddo — Rivista del Freddo
Riv Frutti — Rivista di Frutticoltura
Riv Fruttic — Rivista di Frutticoltura
Riv Fruttic Ortofloric — Rivista di Frutticoltura e di Ortofloricoltura
Riv Gastro Enterol — Rivista di Gastro-Enterologia
Riv Gen Ital Chir — Rivista Generale Italiana di Chirurgia
Riv Geofis Appl — Rivista di Geofisica Applicata
Riv Geog It — Rivista Geografica Italiana
Riv Geogr Cult Geogr — Rivista di Geografia e Cultura Geografica
Riv Geogr Didatt — Rivista di Geografia Didattica
Riv Geogr Ital — Rivista Geografica Italiana
Riv Geront Geriat — Rivista di Gerontologia e Geriatria

Riv Gerontol Geriatr — Rivista di Gerontologia e Geriatria
Riv Guard Fin — Rivista della Guardia di Finanza
Riv Idrobiol — Rivista di Idrobiologia
Riv Idroclim Talass Terap Fis — Rivista di Idroclimatologia, Talassologia, e Terapia Fisica
Riv Idrol Clim Terap Fis — Rivista di Idrologia, Climatologia, e Terapia Fisica
Riviera Sci — Riviera Scientifique
Riv Ig e San Pubb — Rivista d'Igiene e Sanita Pubblica
RivIGI — Rivista Indo-Greco-Italico di Filologia, Lingua, Antichita
Riv Ig Med Soc — Rivista d'Igiene e Medicina Sociale
Riv Ig Sanita Pubbl — Rivista d'Igiene e Sanita Pubblica
Riv Illus Pop Italia — Rivista Illustrata del Popolo d'Italia
Riv Immun — Rivista di Immunologia e Scienze Affini
Riv Ind — Rivista di Diritto Industriale
Riv Ind Coton — Rivista dell'Industria Cotoniera
Riv Ind Elettroferrov Lav Pubbl — Rivista delle Industrie Elettroferroviarie e dei Lavori Pubblici
Riv Indo Greco It — Rivista Indo-Greco-Italica di Filologia
Riv Indo Greco Ital — Rivista Indo-Greco-Italica [di Filologia, Lingua, Antichita]
Riv Inf — Rivista dell'Informazione
Riv Inf — Rivista dell'Informazione/Information Review
Riv Inf — Rivista di Informatica
Riv Inferm — Rivista dell'Infermiere
Riv Infort Mal Prof — Rivista degli Infortuni e delle Malattie Professionali
Riv Ing — Rivista di Ingegneria
Riv Ing — Rivista Ingauna et Intemelia N.S.
Riv Ing Int — Rivista Inguana et Intemelia
Riv Ing Nucl — Rivista di Ingegneria Nucleare
Riv Ing Sanit — Rivista d'Ingegneria Sanitaria
Riv Inguana — Rivista Ingauna e Intemelia N.S.
Riv Insubra Sci Med — Rivista Insubra di Scienze Mediche
Riv Int — Rivista di Diritto Internazionale
Riv Int Agric — Rivista Internazionale di Agricoltura
Riv Int Clin Terap — Rivista Internazionale di Clinica e Terapia
Riv Int Ec — Rivista Internazionale di Scienze Economiche e Commerciali
Riv Interamer Bibliog — Rivista Interamericana di Bibliografia
Riv Internaz di Filos del Diritto — Rivista Internazionale di Filosofia del Diritto
Riv Internaz Sci Soc — Rivista Internazionale di Scienze Sociali
Riv Intern di Filos del Diritto — Rivista Internazionale di Filosofia del Diritto
Riv Intern Sci Ec Comm — Rivista Internazionale di Scienze Economiche e Commerciali
Riv Intern Sci Soc — Rivista Internazionale di Scienze Sociali
Riv Int Filosof Diritto — Rivista Internazionale di Filosofia del Diritto
Riv Int Filos Polit Soc Dir Comp — Rivista Internazionale di Filosofia Politica e Sociale e di Diritto Comparato
Riv Int Ig Org Opoter — Rivista Internazionale d'Igiene e di Organo-Opoterapia
Riv Int Ing Sanit Urb — Rivista Internazionale di Ingegneria Sanitaria ed Urbanistica
Riv Int Sanita Pubbl — Rivista Internazionale di Sanita Pubblica
Riv Int Sci Econ Com — Rivista Internazionale di Scienze Economiche e Commerciali
Riv Int Sci Soc — Rivista Internazionale di Scienze Sociali
Riv Int Terap Fis — Rivista Internazionale di Terapia Fisica
Riv Ist — Rivista. Istituto Nazionale d'Archeologia e Storia dell'Arte
Rivista Biol — Rivista di Biologia
Rivista Biol Gen — Rivista di Biologia Generale
Rivista Fruttic — Rivista di Frutticultura
Rivista Int Agric — Rivista Internazionale di Agricoltura
Rivista Ital Stomatol Rome — Rivista Italiana di Stomatologia. Rome
Rivista Ital Stomatol Venice — Rivista Italiana di Stomatologia / Associazione Medici Dentisti Italiani. Venice
Rivista Radiol Fis Med — Rivista di Radiologia e Fisica Medica
Riv Ist Arch — Rivista. Reale Istituto d'Archeologia e Storia dell'Arte
Riv Ist Arch e St Arte — Rivista. Istituto Nazionale d'Archeologia e Storia dell'Arte
Rivista Sanit Sicil — Rivista Sanitaria Siciliana
Rivista Soc Tosc Ortic — Rivista. Societa Toscana di Orticultura
Riv Ist N Archeol & Stor A — Rivista dell'Istituto Nazionale d'Archeologia e Storia dell'Arte
Riv Ist N Archeol & Stor Roma — Rivista dell'Istituto Nazionale d'Archeologia e Storia di Roma
Riv Istochim Norm Patol — Rivista di Istochimica Normale e Patologica
Riv Istor Benedettina — Rivista Istorica Benedettina
Riv Ist Sieroter Ital — Rivista dell'Istituto Sieroterapico Italiano
Riv Ist Sieroter Ital — Rivista. Istituto Sieroterapico Italiano
Riv Ist Vaccinogeno Consorzi Prov Antituberc — Rivista. Istituto Vaccinogeno e Consorzi Provinciali Antitubercolari
Riv Ital Aeronaut — Rivista Italiana di Aeronautica
Riv Ital Amm Ec — Rivista Italiana di Amministrazione dell'Economia e Sociologia Industriale
Riv Ital Calzat — Rivista Italiana delle Calzature
Riv Ital Cinetec — Rivista Italiana di Cinetecnica
Riv Ital del Dramma — Rivista Italiana del Dramma
Riv Ital Di Dir Pen — Rivista Italiana di Diritto Penale
Riv Ital Dir Proc Pen — Rivista Italiana di Diritto e Procedura Penale
Riv Ital Dir Soc — Rivista Italiana di Diritto Sociale
Riv Ital Ediliz Lab Pubbl — Rivista Italiana di Edilizia e Lavori Pubblici
Riv Ital Endocr E Neurochir — Rivista Italiana di Endocrino-e Neurochirurgia
Riv Ital Essenze — Rivista Italiana delle Essenze
Riv Ital Essenze Profumi — Rivista Italiana delle Essenze e Profumi
Riv Ital Essenze Profumi Piante Off — Rivista Italiana delle Essenze dei Profumi e delle Piante Officinali
Riv Ital Essenze Profumi Piante Off Aromi Saponi Cosmet — Rivista Italiana delle Essenze dei Profumi e delle Piante Officinali Aromi Saponi Cosmetici
Riv Ital Essenze Profumi Piante Offic Aromi Saponi Cosmet — Rivista Italiana delle Essenze dei Profumi e delle Piante Officinali Aromi Saponi Cosmetici

Riv Ital Essenze Profumi Piante Offic Olii Veg Saponi — Rivista Italiana delle Essenze dei Profumi e delle Piante Officinali Olii Vegetali Saponi
Riv Ital Ge — Rivista Italiana di Geofisica e Scienze Affini
Riv Ital Geofis — Rivista Italiana di Geofisica
Riv Ital Geotec — Rivista Italiana di Geotecnica
Riv Ital Ginec — Rivista Italiana di Ginecologia
Riv Ital Ginecol — Rivista Italiana di Ginecologia
Riv Italia — Rivista d'Italia
Riv Italiana Paleontologia e Stratigrafia — Rivista Italiana di Paleontologia e Stratigrafia
Riv Ital Ig — Rivista Italiana d'Igiene
Riv Ital Med Ig Scu — Rivista Italiana di Medicina e Igiene della Scuola
Riv Ital Metano — Rivista Italiana de Metano
Riv Ital Neuropat Psichiat Elettroter — Rivista Italiana di Neuropatologia, Psichiatria, ed Elettroterapia
Riv Ital Num — Rivista Italiana di Numismatica e Scienze Affini
Riv Ital Nutr Parenter Enterale — Rivista Italiana di Nutrizione Parenterale ed Enterale
Riv Ital Odontotec — Rivista Italiana degli Odontotecnici
Riv Ital Orn — Rivista Italiana di Ornitologia
Riv Ital Ornitol — Rivista Italiana di Ornitologia
Riv Ital Ortop Traum — Rivista Italiana d'Ortopedia e Traumatologia
Riv Ital Ortop Traumatol — Rivista Italiana di Ortopedia e Traumatologia
Riv Ital Ottalm — Rivista Italiana di Ottalmologia
Riv Ital Paleontol Stratigr — Rivista Italiana di Paleontologia e Stratigrafia
Riv Ital per la Sc Giur — Rivista Italiana per la Scienze Giuridiche
Riv Ital Pet — Rivista Italiana del Petrolio
Riv Ital Petrol — Rivista Italiana del Petrolio
Riv Ital Radiol Clin — Rivista Italiana di Radiologia Clinica
Riv Ital Saldatura — Rivista Italiana della Saldatura
Riv Ital Sci Alimenti — Rivista Italiana di Scienza degli Alimenti
Riv Ital Sci Econ — Rivista Italiana di Scienze Economiche
Riv Ital Sci Giur — Rivista Italiana per le Scienze Giuridiche
Riv Ital Sci Nat — Rivista Italiana di Scienze Naturali
Riv Ital Sci Polit — Rivista Italiana di Scienza Politica
Riv Ital Sostanze Grasse — Rivista Italiana delle Sostanze Grasse
Riv Ital Sostanze Grasse Suppl — Rivista Italiana delle Sostanze Grasse. Supplemento
Riv Ital Sost Grasse — Rivista Italiana delle Sostanze Grasse
Riv Ital Statist — Rivista Italiana di Statistica
Riv Ital Stomatol — Rivista Italiana di Stomatologia
Riv Ital Terap — Rivista Italiana di Terapia
Riv Ital Tracoma Patol Ocul Vir Esot — Rivista Italiana del Tracoma e di Patologia Oculare Virale ed Esotica
Riv Ital Trac Patol Ocul Virale Esotica — Rivista Italiana del Tracoma e di Patologia Oculare, Virale, ed Esotica
Riv Ital Tuberc — Rivista Italiana della Tuberculosi
Riv Ital Vulc — Rivista Italiana di Vulcanologia
Riv It Num — Rivista Italiana di Numismatica e Scienze Affini
Riv It Numi — Rivista Italiana della Numismatica
Riv It Scienze Giur — Rivista Italiana per le Scienze Giuridiche
RIVL — Regesten van de Aanwinsten van het Institut voor Vergelijkend Literatuuronderzoek aan de Rijksuniversiteit te Utrecht
RivL — Rivista Letteraria. Licei Classico, Scientifico, Artistico, e Istituto Magistrale
Riv Latte — Rivista del Latte
Riv Let Mod — Rivista di Letteratura Moderne e Comparate
Riv Lett Class — Rivista di Letteratura Classiche
Riv Lett Mod — Rivista di Letteratura Moderne
Riv Lett Mod Comp — Rivista di Letterature Moderne Comparate
Riv Li — Rivista Liturgica
Riv Lig — Rivista di Studi Liguri
Riv Ligure Sci Lett Arti — Rivista Ligure di Scienze, Lettere, ed Arti
Riv Liturg — Rivista Liturgica
Riv Macch Mar Tec Naut — Rivista di Macchine Marine e Tecnica Nautica
Riv Magn — Rivista Magnetica
Riv Malar — Rivista di Malariologia
Riv Malariol — Rivista Malariologia
Riv Mal Infett — Rivista di Malattie Infettive
Riv Maritt — Rivista Marittima
Riv Mat — Rivista di Matematica
Riv Mat Pura Appl — Rivista di Matematica Pura ed Applicata
Riv Mat Sci Econom Social — Rivista di Matematica per le Scienze Economiche e Sociali
Riv Mat Univ Parma — Rivista di Matematica. Universita di Parma
Riv Mat Univ Parma 4 — Rivista di Matematica. Universita di Parma. Serie 4
Riv Mat Univ Parma 5 — Rivista di Matematica della Universita di Parma. Serie 5
Riv Mecc — Rivista di Meccanica
Riv Mecc Agr — Rivista di Meccanica Agraria
Riv Med — Rivista Medica
Riv Med Aer — Rivista di Medicina Aeronautica e Spaziale
Riv Med Aeronaut — Rivista di Medicina Aeronautica e Spaziale
Riv Med Aeronaut Spaz — Rivista di Medicina Aeronautica e Spaziale
Riv Med Bologna — Rivista Medica di Bologna
Riv Med Chir — Rivista di Medicina e Chirurgia
Riv Med Dosim — Rivista di Medicina Dosimetrica
Riv Med Lav Ig Ind — Rivista di Medicina del Lavoro ed Igiene Industriale
Riv Med Leg Giurispr Med — Rivista di Medicina Legale e di Giurisprudenza Medica
Riv Med Leg Legisl Sanit — Rivista di Medicina Legale e Legislazione Sanitaria
Riv Med Milano — Rivista Medica (Milano)
Riv Med Soc Tuberc — Rivista Medico-Sociale della Tuberculosi
Riv Med Vet — Rivista di Medicina Veterinaria
Riv Med Vet Zootec — Rivista di Medicina Veterinaria e Zootecnica
Riv Mens Ass Disegn Capi Assist Tec — Rivista Mensile dell'Associazione fra i Disegnatori, Capi ed Assistenti Tecnici

Riv Mens Citta Venezia — Rivista Mensile della Citta di Venezia
Riv Mens Diffus Cult Chim — Rivista Mensile per la Diffusione della Cultura Chimica
Riv Mens Lega Aer Naz — Rivista Mensile della Lega Aerea Nazionale
Riv Mens Neuropat Psichiat — Rivista Mensile di Neuropatologia e Psichiatria
Riv Mens Pesca Idrobiol — Rivista Mensile di Pesca e Idrobiologia
Riv Mens Psichiat Forense — Rivista Mensile di Psichiatria Forense, Antropologia Criminale e Scienze Affini
Riv Mens Reg Ass Siciliana Mont Sylv — Rivista Mensile della Regionale Associazione La Siciliana pro Montibus et Sylvis
Riv Mens Svizz Odontol Stomatol — Rivista Mensile Svizzera di Odontologia e Stomatologia
Riv Merceol — Rivista di Merceologia
Riv Met Aeronaut — Rivista di Meteorologia Aeronautica
Riv Met Agr — Rivista Meteorico-Agraria
Riv Meteo A — Rivista di Meteorologia Aeronautica
Riv Meteorol Aeronaut — Rivista di Meteorologia Aeronautica
RivMI — Rivista Musicale Italiana
Riv Milano — Rivista di Milano
Riv Milit It — Rivista Militare Italiana
Riv Mineral Cristallogr Ital — Rivista di Mineralogia e Cristallografia Italiana
Riv Mineral Ital — Rivista Mineralogica Italiana
Riv Mineraria Sicil — Rivista Mineraria Siciliana
Riv Miner Cristall Ital — Rivista di Mineralogia e Cristallografia Italiana
Riv Min Sicil — Rivista Mineraria Siciliana
Riv Min Ung — Rivista Mineraria Ungarica
Riv Mus Ital — Rivista Musicale Italiana
Riv Mus Italiana — Rivista Musicale Italiana
Riv Neurobiol — Rivista di Neurobiologia
Riv Neurol — Rivista di Neurologia
Riv Neurol — Rivista Neurologica [Torino]
Riv Neurol Med Chir — Rivista di Neurologia, Medicina, Chirurgia
Riv Neuropat — Rivista Neuropatologica
Riv Neuropsichiat — Rivista de Neuropsichiatria e Scienze Affini
Riv Neuropsichiatr Sci Affini — Rivista di Neuropsichiatria e Scienze Affini
Riv Nipiol — Rivista di Nipiologia
Riv Novita Invenz — Rivista delle Novita e delle Invenzioni
Riv Num — Rivista Italiana di Numismatica e Scienze Affini
Riv Nuovo Cim — Rivista del Nuovo Cimento
Riv Nuovo Cimento — Rivista del Nuovo Cimento
Riv Nuovo Cimento 2 — Rivista del Nuovo Cimento. Serie 2
Riv Nuovo Cimento 3 — Rivista del Nuovo Cimento. Serie 3
Riv Nuovo Cimento Ser 1 — Rivista del Nuovo Cimento. Serie 1
Riv Nuovo Cimento Soc Ital Fis — Rivista del Nuovo Cimento. Societa Italiana di Fisica
Riv Odontoiatr — Rivista di Odontoiatria degli Amici de Brugg
Riv Odontoiatr Amici Brugg — Rivista dI Odontoiatria degli Amici di Brugg
Riv Odont Ortognad — Rivista di Odontoiatria e Ortognadonzia
Riv Odonto Stomat Odontotec — Rivista di Odonto-Stomatologia ed Odontotecnica
Riv Odontostomatol Implantoprotesi — Rivista de Odontostomatologia e Implantoprotesi
Rivol Ind — Rivoluzione Industriale
Rivoluzione Ind — Rivoluzione Industriale
Riv Omeop — Rivista Omeopatica
RIVON (Rijksinst Veldbiol Onderz Natuurbehd) Jaarversl — RIVON (Rijksinstituut voor Veldbiologische Onderzoek ten Behoeve van het Natuurbehoud) Jaarverslag
Riv Org Aziend — Rivista di Organizzazione Aziendale
Riv Ortoflorofruttic Ital — Rivista della Ortoflorofrutticoltura Italiana
Riv Ortop Terap Fis — Rivista di Ortopedia e Terapia Fisica
Riv Osp — Rivista degli Ospedali
Riv Osp Psichiatr — Rivista l'Ospedale Psichiatrico
Riv Osp Roma — Rivista Ospedaliera Roma
Riv Ostet Ginec — Rivista di Ostetricia e Ginecologia
Riv Ostet Ginecol — Rivista di Ostetricia e Ginecologia
Riv Ostet Ginecol (Flor) — Rivista di Ostetricia e Ginecologia (Florence)
Riv Ostet Ginecol Prat — Rivista di Ostetricia e Ginecologia Pratica
Riv Ostet Ginecol Prat Med Perinat — Rivista di Ostetricia e Ginecologia Pratica e di Medicina Perinatale
Riv Ostet Ginec Prat — Rivista di Ostetricia e Ginecologia Pratica
Riv Oto Neuro Oftal — Rivista Oto-Neuro-Oftalmologica
Riv Oto-Neuro-Oftalmol — Rivista Oto-Neuro-Oftalmologica
Riv Oto-Neuro-Oftalmol Radio-Neuro-Chir — Rivista Oto-Neuro-Oftalmologica e Radio-Neuro-Chirurgica
Riv Ottica Mecc Precis — Rivista d'Ottica e Meccanica di Precisione
Riv Paras — Rivsta di Parassitologia
Riv Parassit — Rivista di Parassitologia
Riv Parassitol — Rivista di Parassitologia
Riv Patol Appar Respir — Rivista Patologia dell'Apparato Respiratorio
Riv Patol Clin — Rivista di Patologia e Clinica
Riv Patol Clin Sper — Rivista di Patologia Clinica e Sperimentale
Riv Patol Clin Tuberc — Rivista di Patologia e Clinica della Tuberculosi
Riv Patol Clin Tuberc Pneumol — Rivista di Patologia e Clinica della Tuberculosi e di Pneumologia
Riv Patol Nerv Ment — Rivista di Patologia Nervosa e Mentale
Riv Patol Sper — Rivista di Patologia Sperimentale
Riv Patol Um — Rivista di Patologia Umana
Riv Patol Veg — Rivista di Patologia Vegetale
Riv Patol Veg Padova — Rivista di Patologia Vegetale (Padova)
RivPed — Rivista Pedagogica
Riv Pedag — Rivista Pedagogica
Riv Pediatr Sicil — Rivista Pediatrica Siciliana
Riv Pellagr Ital — Rivista Pellagrologica Italiana

Riv Pen Di Dott Legis E Giuris — Rivista Penale di Dottrina, Legislazione, e Giurisprudenza

Riv Per Lav Accad Sc Lett ed Arti Padova — Rivista Periodica del Lavori. Accademia di Scienze, Lettere, ed Arti di Padova

Riv Per Naut Triest — Rivista. Periodico Nautico (Trieste)

Riv Polit Agr — Rivista di Politica Agraria

Riv Polit Econ — Rivista di Politica Economica

Riv Privat Ind — Rivista delle Privative Industriali

Riv Propr Intell Ind — Rivista della Proprietà Intellettuale ed Industriali

Riv Psicol Norm Patol Appl — Rivista di Psicologia Normale, Patologica e Applicata

Riv Psicopat Neuropsichiat Psicoanal — Rivista di Psicopatologia, Neuropsichiatria, e Psicoanalisi

RivR — Rivista delle Religioni

Riv Radiol — Rivista di Radiologia

Riv Radiol Fis Med — Rivista di Radiologia e Fisica Medica

Riv Reale Ist Archeol & Stor A — Rivista del Reale Istituto d'Archeologia e Storia dell'Arte

Riv Rom — Rivista Romana

Riv Rosmin — Rivista Rosminiana

Riv Rosmin Filos Cult — Rivista Rosminiana di Filosofia e di Cultura

Riv R Soc Ital Ig — Rivista della Reale Società Italiana d'Igiene

Riv Sanit — Rivista Sanitaria

Riv Sanit Sicil — Rivista Sanitaria Siciliana

Riv Sci — Rivista di Scienza

Riv Sci Bot Zool — Rivista delle Scienze Botanica e Zoologica

Riv Scient Lett — Rivista Scientifico-Letteraria

Riv Scient Prat Fisioter Idroter — Rivista Scientifica e Pratica di Fisioterapia, Idroterapia

Riv Scient Prat Mens Ambul Pediat — Rivista Scientifico-Pratica Mensile dell'Ambulatorio Pediatrico

Riv Scienze Preist — Rivista di Scienze Preistoriche

Riv Sci Lett — Rivista di Scienze e Lettere

Riv Sci Preist — Rivista di Scienze Preistoriche

Riv Sci Tecnol Alimenti Nutr Um — Rivista di Scienza e Tecnologia degli Alimenti e di Nutrizione Umana

Riv Sci Tecnol Aliment Nutr Umana — Rivista di Scienza e Tecnologia degli Alimenti e di Nutrizione Umana

Riv Sc Pr — Rivista di Scienze Preistoriche

Riv Semest Stor A — Rivista Semestrale di Storia dell'Arte

Riv Serv Miner — Rivista del Servizio Minerario

Riv Sicil Ostet Ginec Prat — Rivista Siciliana d'Ostetricia e Ginecologia Pratica

Riv Sicil Paleont — Rivista Siciliana di Paleontologia

Riv Sicil Tuberc — Rivista Siciliana della Tubercolosi

Riv Sicil Tuberc Mal Respir — Rivista Siciliana della Tubercolosi e delle Malattie Respiratorie

Riv SO — Rivista degli Studi Orientali

Riv Sociol — Rivista di Sociologia

Riv Soc Ital Sci Aliment — Rivista della Società Italiana di Scienze dell'Alimentazione

Riv Sper Freniat Med Leg Alien — Rivista Sperimentale di Freniatria e Medicina Legale delle Alienazioni Mentali

Riv Sper Freniatr Med Leg Alienazioni Ment — Rivista Sperimentale di Freniatria e Medicina Legale delle Alienazioni Mentali

Riv St Ant — Rivista di Storia Antica

Riv Staz Spermntl Vetro — Rivista della Stazione Sperimentale del Vetro

Riv St Cl — Rivista di Studi Classici

Riv St Fen — Rivista di Studi Fenici

Riv St Lig — Rivista di Studi Liguri

Riv Stn Sper Vetro (Murano Italy) — Rivista della Stazione Sperimentale del Vetro (Murano, Italy)

Riv Stomat — Rivista Stomatologica

Riv St Or — Rivista degli Studi Orientali

Riv Stor — Rivista Storica Italiana

Riv Stor A Archeol Prov Alessandria — Rivista di Storia, Arte, Archeologia della Provincia di Alessandria

Riv Stor Agric — Rivista di Storia dell'Agricoltura

Riv Stor & Lett Relig — Rivista della Storia e Letteratura Religiosa

Riv Stor Ant — Rivista di Storia Antica

Riv Stor Ant — Rivista Storica dell'Antichità

Riv Stor Antica — Rivista di Storia Antica

Riv Stor Chiesa Ital — Rivista di Storia della Chiesa in Italia

Riv Stor Contemp — Rivista di Storia Contemporanea

Riv Stor Crit Sci Med Nat — Rivista di Storia Critica delle Scienze Mediche e Naturali

Riv Stor dell Antichita — Rivista Storica dell'Antichità

Riv Stor Fil — Rivista di Storia della Filosofia

Riv Stor It — Rivista Storica Italiana

Riv Stor Ital — Rivista Storica Italiana

Riv Stor Mant — Rivista Storica Mantovana

Riv Stor Med — Rivista di Storia della Medicina

Riv Stor Sci — Rivista di Storia della Scienza

Riv Stor Sci Med Nat — Rivista di Storia della Scienze Mediche e Naturali

Riv Stor Socialismo — Rivista Storica del Socialismo

Riv Stud Croc — Rivista di Studi Crociani

Riv Stud Croci — Rivista di Studi Crociani

Riv Stud Crociani — Rivista di Studi Crociani

Riv Studi Cl — Rivista di Studi Classici

Riv Studi Politici Int — Rivista di Studi Politici Internazionali

Riv Studi Polit Int — Rivista di Studi Politici Internazionali

Riv Studi Polit Internaz — Rivista di Studi Politici Internazionali

Riv Stud Lig — Rivista di Studi Liguri

RivStudOr — Rivista degli Studi Orientali

Riv Stud Or — Rivista degli Studi Orientali

Riv Stud Orient — Rivista degli Studi Orientali

Riv Stu Lig — Rivista di Studi Liguri

Riv Sulnicolt — Rivista di Suinicoltura

Riv Svizz Apic — Rivista Svizzera di Apicoltura

Riv Svizz Birr — Rivista Svizzera delle Birrerie

Riv Svizz Med Sport — Rivista Svizzera di Medicina dello Sport

Riv Svizz Tuberc Pneumonol — Rivista Svizzera della Tubercolosi e della Pneumonologia

Riv Tec — Rivista Tecnica

Riv Tec Elett — Rivista Tecnica d'Elettricita

Riv Tec Elettr — Rivista Tecnica d'Elettricita

Riv Tec Emiliana — Rivista Tecnica Emiliana

Riv Tec Ferrovie Ital — Rivista Tecnica delle Ferrovie Italiane

Riv Tec Giur Pesca — Rivista Tecnico-Giuridica della Pesca

Riv Tec Sci Arti Appl Ind — Rivista Tecnica delle Scienze, delle Arti Applicate all'Industria

Riv Tec Selenia (Engl Ed) — Rivista Tecnica Selenia (English Edition)

Riv Tec Svizz — Rivista Tecnica Svizzera

Riv Tec Svizzera It — Rivista Tecnica della Svizzera Italiana

Riv Tess — Rivista Tessile

Riv Tess Aracne — Rivista Tessile Aracne

Riv Tess Text — Rivista Tessile-Textilia

Riv Tiflol Prev Cecita — Rivista di Tiflologia e per la Prevenzione della Cecità

Riv Tossicol Sper Clin — Rivista di Tossicologia Sperimentale e Clinica

Riv Trasp — Rivista dei Trasporti

Riv Trim Dir Pubbl — Rivista Trimestrale di Diritto Pubblico

Riv Trimest di Diritto Pubbl — Rivista Trimestrale di Diritto Pubblico

Riv Trimest Odont Prot Dent — Rivista Trimestrale di Odontoiatria e Protesi Dentaria

Riv Tripolit — Rivista della Tripolitana

Riv Tuberc Mal Appar Resp — Rivista della Tuberculosis e delle Malattie dell'Apparato Respiratoria

Riv Tuberc Mal Appar Respir — Rivista della Tubercolosi e delle Malattie dell'Apparato Respiratorio

Riv Tuberc Mal App Resp — Rivista della Tubercolosi e delle Malattie dell'Apparato Respiratorio

Riv Tumori — Rivista Tumori

Riv Ungh Min — Rivista Ungherese di Minieria

Riv Ung Metall — Rivista Ungherese de Metallurgia

Riv Univ Torino — Rivista Universitaria (Torino)

Riv Urol — Rivista Urologica

Riv Veneta Sc Med — Rivista Veneta di Scienze Mediche

Riv Venezia — Rivista di Venezia

Riv Vet — Rivista di Veterinaria

Riv Vitic Enol — Rivista di Viticoltura e di Enologia

Riv Vitic Enol Agr — Rivista di Viticoltura, Enologia, ed Agraria

Riv World — River World

Riv Zoofila Ital — Rivista Zoofila Italiana

Riv Zootec — Rivista di Zootecnia e Veterinaria

Riv Zootec Romagn — Rivista Zootecnica Romagnola

Riv Zootec Vet — Rivista di Zootecnia e Veterinaria

RIW — Review of Income and Wealth

RI Water Res Coordinating Board Geol Bull Hydrol Bull — Rhode Island. Water Resources Coordinating Board. Geological Bulletin. Hydrologic Bulletin

RI Water Resour Board Hydrol Bull — Rhode Island. Water Resources Board. Hydrologic Bulletin

RI Water Resour Cent Annu Rep — Rhode Island. Water Resources Center. Annual Report

RI Water Resour Coord Board Geol Bull — Rhode Island. Water Resources Coordinating Board. Geological Bulletin

RI Water Resour Coordinating Board Geol Bull — Rhode Island. Water Resources Coordinating Board. Geological Bulletin

Riyad Univ Fac Sci Bull — Riyad University. Faculty of Science. Bulletin

Riyad Univ Fac Sci J — Riyad University. Faculty of Science. Journal

Rizh Med Inst Sb Nauchn Rab — Rizhskii Meditsinskii Institut. Sbornik Nauchnykh Rabot

Riz Rizi — Riz et Riziculture

Riz Rizic Cult Vivieres Trop — Riz et Riziculture et Cultures Vivieres Tropicales

Riz Rizicult Cult Vivr Trop — Riz et Riziculture et Cultures Vivrieres Tropicales

Rizsk Inst Inz Grazdan Aviacii — Rizskii Institut Inzenerov Grazdanskoi Aviacii Imeni Leninskogo Komsomola

RJ — A'Beckett's Reserved Judgements

RJ — Reformed Journal

RJ — Revista Javeriana

RJ — Revue de Jurisprudence

RJ — Revue des Jeunes

RJ — Romanistisches Jahrbuch

RJ — Rusky Jazyk

RJa — Romanistisches Jahrbuch

RJAC — Revue Juridique de l'Afrique Centrale

RJaS — Russkij Jazyk v Skole

RJav — Revista Javeriana

R Javer — Revista Javeriana

RJaz — Rusky Jazyk

Rjazansk Gos Ped Inst Ucen Zap — Rjazanskii Gosudarstvennyi Pedagogiceskii Institut. Ucenye Zapiski

RJb — Romanistisches Jahrbuch

RJC — Revue Juridique du Congo

RJCB — Revue Juridique du Congo Belge

RJE — Revue Juridique et Economique du Sud-Ouest

RJEH — Revista de la Junta de Estudios Historicos de Mendoza

R Jeu — Revue des Jeunes

RJFF — Revue Juridique, Fiscale, et Financiere

RJICA — Russian Journal of Inorganic Chemistry

RJL — Revista Juridica Latinoamericana

RJL — Revue Juive de la Lorraine

RJMBA — Roczniki Akademii Medycznej Imienia Juliana Marchlewskiego w Bialymstoku
RJN — Robinson Jeffers Newsletter
RJO — Rapports Judiciaires Officiels de Quebec
RJOQ (BR) — Rapports Judiciaires Officiels de Quebec, Cour du Banc du Roi
RJOQ (CS) — Rapports Judiciaires Officiels de Quebec, Cour Superieure
RJPCA — Russian Journal of Physical Chemistry
RJPUF — Revue Juridique et Politique de l'Union Francaise
RJR — Russkij Jazyk za Rubezom
RJRB — Revue Juridique du Rwanda et du Burundi
RJS — Russkij Jazyk v Skole
RJSCA — Revue Jeumont-Schneider
RJSHDQ — Jugoslovanski Simpozij za Hmeljarstvo Referati
RJT — Revue Juridique Themis
R Jud C — Revue Judiciaire Congolaise
RJUI — Revista Juridica. Universidad Interamericana
R Jur — Revue Juridique
R Jur Afr Cent — Revue Juridique de l'Afrique Centrale
R Jur Cong B — Revue Juridique du Congo Belge
R Jur Environ — Revue Juridique de l'Environnement
R Juridica Cataluna — Revista Juridica de Cataluna
R Juridique — Revue Juridique
R Juridique et Econ Sud-Ouest Ser Econ — Revue Juridique et Economique du Sud-Ouest. Serie Economique
R Juridique et Pol — Revue Juridique et Politique
R Jur Polit — Revue Juridique et Politique. Independance et Cooperation
RJV — Rheinisches Jahrbuch fuer Volkskunde
RJVK — Rheinisches Jahrbuch fuer Volkskunde
RK — Rekishigaku Kenkyu. Journal. Historical Science Society
RK — Religion och Kultur
RK — Religion und Kultus der Roemer
RKANA — Rost Kristallov
R K Bouwbl — RK (Rooms-Katholiek) Bouwblad
RKCLA — Reaction Kinetics and Catalysis Letters
RKCSN — Rospravy Kralovske Ceske Spolecnosti Nauk
RKFJ — Rad Kongresa Folklorista Jugoslavije
RKHLit — Rocznik Komisji Historycznoliterackiej Pan
RKHS — Register. Kentucky Historical Society
RKhT Radiats Khim Tekhnol — RKhT. Radiatsionno-Khimicheskaya Tekhnologiya
RKJ — Rozprawy Komisji Jezykowej Lodzkiego Towarzystwa Naukowego
RKJL — Rozprawy Komisji Jezykowej Lodzkiego Towarzystwa Naukowego
RKJW — Rozprawy Komisji Jezykowej Wroclawskiego Towarzystwa Naukowego
RKKHA — Rikagaku Kenkyusho Hokoku
RKM — Risk Management
RKNKA — Rakuno Kagaku No Kenkyu
RKr — Rakstu Krajums
RKR — Religion und Kultus der Roemer
RKS — Rocket Stories
RKTEA — Rakennusteknikka
Rk Ts B — Rechtskundig Tijdschrift voor Belgie
RKW — Repertorium fuer Kunstwissenschaft
Rk Wkbl — Rechtskundig Weekblad
RKZ — Reformierte Kirchenzeitung
RL — Radio Liberty
RL — Religion in Life
RL — Revista de Letras
RL — Revista de Literatura
RL — Revista Lusitana
RL — Revue de Lille
RL — Revue de Linguistique
RL — Revue Legale
RL — Revue Roumaine de Linguistique
RL — Ricerche Linguistiche
RL — Rivista Letteraria
RL — Ruch Literacki
RL — Russian Literature
RLA — Reallexikon der Assyriologie
RLA — Religious Leaders of America
RLA — Repertorio Latinoamericano
RLA — Revista de Letras. Faculdade de Filosofia, Ciencias, e Letras (Assis)
RLA — Revista Liturgica Argentina
RLAC — Reallexikon fuer Antike und Christentum
RLAE — Resena de Literatura, Arte, y Espectaculo
RLAF — Revista Latino Americana de Filosofia
RLAF — Revue de Legislation Ancienne et Moderne Francaise et Etrangere
RLAL — Latin American Literature and Arts Review
R Lang — Revue de Languedoc
R Lang Rom — Revue des Langues Romanes
RLAQA — Revista Latinoamericana de Quimica
RLaR — Revue des Langues Romanes
Rlat — Revue Latine
RLati — Repertorio Latinoamericano
R Latinoamer Estud Educ — Revista Latinoamericana de Estudios Educativos
R Latinoamer Psicol — Revista Latinoamericana de Psicologia
R Latinoamer Sociol — Revista Latinoamericana de Sociologia
R Latinoam Estud Urbano Reg — Revista Latinoamericana de Estudios Urbano Regionales
RLav — Revue de l'Universite Laval
RLaV — Revue des Langues Vivantes
RLB — Revue Liturgique et Benedictine
RLC — Rassegna Italiana di Lingue e Letteratura Classiche
RLC — Revista Historica-Critica de la Literatura Centro-Americana
RLC — Revue de Litterature Comparee
RLCAA — Railway Locomotives and Cars
RLCAD — Revista Latinoamericana de Ciencias Agricolas

RLCP — Revista Latinoamericana de Cirugia Plastica
RLE — Revista Latinoamericana de Educacion (Educadores)
RLeIt — Rassegna della Letteratura Italiana
R Let — Revista de Letras
R Lett Mod — Revue des Lettres Modernes
R Lex Assyr — Reallexikon der Assyriologie
RLF — Revista Latinoamericana de Filosofia
RLFE — Revista. Laboratorio de Fonetica Experimental
RLFE — Revue des Lettres Francaises et Etrangeres
RLH — Raleigh Lecture on History
RLHAS — Revue de Litterature, Histoire, Arts, et Sciences
RLI — Rassegna della Letteratura Italiana
RLI — Revista de las Indias
RLI — Revista do Livro
RLi — Revue de Linguistique
RLIBD6 — Swedish University of Agricultural Sciences. Department of Farm Buildings. Report
R Libourne — Revue Historique et Archeologique du Libournais
RLIC — Revue des Lois, Decrets, Traites de Commerce. InstitutInternational du Commerce
RLIlle — Revue de Lille
RLing — Revue de Linguistique
R Ling — Revue Roumaine de Linguistique
RLing — Ricerche Linguistiche
RLing — Russian Linguistics
R Li Oe — Roemische Limes in Oesterreich
RLir — Realismo Lirico
RLIR — Revue de Linguistique Romane
RLit — Revista de Literatura
RLit — Russkaja Literatura
RLitC — Readings in Literary Criticism
RLITDQ — Swedish University of Agricultural Sciences. Department of Agricultural Engineering. Report
R Literatura — Revista de Literatura. CSIC (Consejo Superior de Investigaciones Cientificas)
R Litt Comp — Revue de Litterature Comparee
RLiv — Rivista di Livorno
RLJ — Rhodesia Law Journal
RLJ — Rhodesian Law Journal
RLJ — Rhodes-Livingstone Journal
RLJ — Russian Language Journal
RLJS — B.G. Rudolph Lectures in Judaic Studies
RLKBAD — Report. Research Laboratories of Kirin Brewery Company Limited
RLL — Reviews in Leukemia and Lymphoma
RLLO — Revue de Langue et Litterature d'Oc
RLLP — Revue de Langue et Litterature Provencales
RLLProv — Revue de Langue et Litterature Provencales
RLLR — Revue de Louisiane/Louisiana Review
RLM — Revista de Literaturas Modernas
RLM — Revista di Letterature Moderne e Comparate
RLM — Revue des Langues Modernes
RLM — Revue des Lettres Modernes
RLM — Revue Liturgique et Monastique
RLM — Rivista di Letteratura Moderne e Comparate
RLM — Rivista di Letteratura Moderne
RLMBA — Rendiconti. Istituto Lombardo. Accademia di Scienze e Lettere. Sezione B. Scienze Biologiche e Mediche
RLMC — Rivista di Letteratura Moderne e Comparate
RLMF — Revue du Louvre et des Musees de France
RLMo — Rivista di Letterature Moderne
RLMod — Revue des Lettres Modernes
RLMPA — Revista Latinoamericana de Microbiologia y Parasitologia [*Later, Revista Latinoamericana de Microbiologia*]
RLMPB — Proceedings. Reliability and Maintainability Conference
RLNS — Revue Legale. New Series
RLOE — Roemische Limes in Oesterreich
RLORA — Revue de Laryngologie, Otologie, Rhinologie
RLOS — Revue Legale (Old Series)
RLOSA — Revue de Laryngologie, Otologie, Rhinologie. Supplement
R Louvre — Revue du Louvre et des Musees de France
RLP — Revista Latinoamericana de Psicologia
RLPC — Revue de Linguistique et de Philologie Comparee
RLQB — Revue Legale Reports, Queen's Bench
RLR — Revue de Linguistique Romane
RLR — Revue des Langues Romanes
RLR — Riverina Library Review
RLR — Rutgers Law Review
RLRB — Radio Liberty Research Bulletin
RIrd Gaz — Railroad Gazette [*New York*]
RLS — Regional Language Studies
RLS — Revista Latinoamericana de Sociologia
RLSC — Revue Legale Reports, Supreme Court
RLSCA — Research in Life Sciences
R L St — Rackham Literary Studies
RLSTA — Regelungstechnik
RLT — Rassegna di Letteratura Tomistica
RLT — Russian Literature Triquarterly
RLTA — Revista de Linguistica Teorica y Aplicada
RLu — Rassegna Lucchese
RLub — Rocznik Lubelski
RLuc — Rassegna Lucchese
RLux — Revue Trimestrielle d'Etudes Linguistiques, Folkloriques, et Toponymiques (Luxembourg)
RLV — Reallexikon der Vorgeschichte
RLV — Revue des Langues Vivantes

RLW — Rajasthan Law Weekly
Rly — Railway
Rly Age Chicago — Railway Age (Chicago)
Rly Age Gaz — Railway Age Gazette [*Chicago*]
Rly Age Gaz Mech Edn — Railway Age Gazette. Mechanical Edition [*New York*]
Rly Age NY — Railway Age (New York)
Rly Elect Engr — Railway Electrical Engineer [*New York*]
Rly Engng — Railway Engineering Journal
Rly Engng Abstr — Railway Engineering Abstracts
Rly Engng Maint — Railway Engineering and Maintenance [*Chicago*]
Rly Engng Maint Way — Railway Engineering and Maintenance of Way [*Chicago*]
Rly Engng Rev — Railway and Engineering Review [*Chicago*]
Rly Engr — Railway Engineer [*London*]
Rly Gaz — Railway Gazette [*Later, Railway Gazette International*]
Rly J — Railway Journal [*Chicago*]
Rly J Can — Railway Journal of Canada
Rly Loco Engng — Railway and Locomotive Engineering [*New York*]
Rly Locos — Railway Locomotives [*Leamington Spa*]
Rly Locos Cars — Railway Locomotives and Cars [*New York*]
Rly Mach — Railway Machinery [*New York*]
Rly Mag — Railway Magazine
Rly Maint Engr — Railway Maintenance Engineer [*Chicago*]
Rly Mech Elect Engr — Railway Mechanical and Electrical Engineer [*New York*]
Rly Mech Engr — Railway Mechanical Engineer [*New York*]
Rly News — Railway News [*London*]
Rly Res Engng News — Railway Research and Engineering News [*Amsterdam*]
Rly Res News — Railway Research News [*Amsterdam*]
Rly Rev — Railway Review [*Chicago*]
Rly Shipp Mar Wld — Railway and Shipping and Marine World [*Toronto*]
Rly Signal Engr — Railway Signal Engineer [*New York*]
Rly Signall Commun — Railway Signalling and Communications [*New York*]
Rly Steel Top — Railway Steel Topics [*Sheffield*]
Rly Surg — Railway Surgeon [*Chicago*]
Rly Surg J — Railway Surgical Journal [*Chicago*]
Rly Tech Rev — Railway Technical Review [*Darmstadt*]
Rly Times — Railway Times [*London*]
Rly Track Struct — Railway Track and Structures [*Chicago*]
Rly Wld Philad — Railway World (Philadelphia)
Rly Wld Radlett — Railway World (Radlett)
R Lz — Radjans'ke Literaturoznavstvo. Naukovo-Teoretycnyj Zurnal
RM — Journal of Recreational Mathematics
RM — Mitteilungen des Deutschen Archaeologischen Instituts. Roemische Abteilung
RM — Rassegna Monetaria
RM — Rassegna Musicale
RM — Rechtsgeleerd Magazijn
RM — Record Mirror
RM — Rejected MSS and Others
RM — Religionen der Menschheit
RM — Review of Metaphysics
RM — Revista Militar [*Asuncion*]
RM — Revue de la Mediterranee
RM — Revue de Metaphysique et de Morale
RM — Revue Mondiale
RM — Revue Musicale
RM — Rheinisches Museum fuer Philologie
RM — Risk Management
RM — Roemische Mitteilungen
RM — Rowohlts Monographien
RM — Russkaja Mysl'
RMA — Royal Musical Association. Proceedings
RMAAD — Revista Mexicana de Astronomia y Astrofisica
RMab — Revue Mabillon
R Mad — Revue de Madagascar
RMAFA — Revista. Union Matematica Argentina y Asociacion Fisica Argentina
R Maine — Revue Historique et Archeologique du Maine
RMAL — Revue du Moyen-Age Latin
RMAM — Revue du Monde, Ancien et Moderne
R Manche — Revue. Departement de la Manche
RMA Proc — Royal Musical Association. Proceedings
RMar — Revue de Marseille
RMARC — Royal Musical Association. Research Chronicle
R Marche Commun — Revue du Marche Commun
RMARDL — Revista Medico-Quirurgica. Asociacion Medica del Hospital Rivadavia
RMA Res Chron — RMA [*Royal Musical Association*] Research Chronicle
RMA Research — Royal Musical Association. Research Chronicle
RMA Research Chron — RMA [*Royal Musical Association*] Research Chronicle
RMA Res Notes Appl Math — RMA. Research Notes in Applied Mathematics
R Mark Agric Econ — Review of the Marketing and Agricultural Economy
R Marketing & Ag Econ — Review of Marketing and Agricultural Economics
R Marketing and Agric Econ — Review of Marketing and Agricultural Economics
RMA Rubber — RMA [*Rubber Manufacturers Association*] Industry Rubber Report
Rm At — Atti dell' Accademia Pontificia de' Nuovi Lincei (Roma)
RMA Tire — RMA [*Rubber Manufacturers Association*] Tire and Innertube Statistical Report
Rm At N Linc — Atti dell' Accademia Pontificia de' Nuovi Lincei (Roma)
Rm At R Ac — Atti della Reale Accademia dei Lincei (Roma)
RMAZDB — Revista. Museo Argentino de Ciencias Naturales Bernardino Rivadavia e Instituto Nacional de Investigacion de las Ciencias Naturales. Zoologia
RMBC — Revista Brasileira de Mercado de Capitais. Instituto Brasileiro de Mercado de Capitais
RMBI — Canadian Risk Management and Business Insurance
RM BI — Reichministerialblatt
Rm Bll Met — Bullettino Meteorologico dell' Osservatorio del Collegio Romano
RMBRDQ — Revue Medicale de Bruxelles. Nouvelle Serie
RMC — Revista Medica Cubana

RMC — Revista Musical Chilena
RMC — Revue des Materiaux de Construction et de Travaux Publics
RMC — Revue du Marche Commun
RMC — Revue du Monde Catholique
RMC — Revue Maritime et Coloniale
RMCA — Rassegna Musicale Curci Anno
R M Ch — Revista Musical Chilena
RM Chilena — Revista Musical Chilena
RMCLB — Revue Medico-Chirurgicale
Rm Cor Sc — Corrispondenza Scientifica in Roma per l'Avanzamento delle Scienze
RMCPS — Revista Mexicana de Ciencias Politicas y Sociales
RMCT — Research Monographs in Cell and Tissue Physiology
RMD — Roemischen Mosaiken in Deutschland
RMDAB — Revue de Medecine Aeronautique
RMDMDL — Revista Medica de Mocambique
RMDSA — Rivista di Medicina Aeronautica e Spaziale
RME — Railway Age
RME — Rise of Modern Europe. Edited by William L. Langer
RMEA — Revista Mexicana de Estudios Antropologicos y Historicos
RMed — Revue de la Mediterranee
R Med De Barcelona — Revista Medica de Barcelona
R Med De La Suisse Rom — Revue Medicale de la Suisse Romande
R Med Fr Et Etrang — Revue Medicale Francaise et Etrangere
R Medicina Legal — Revista de Medicina Legal
R Medit — Revue de la Mediterranee
R Mediterr — Revue de la Mediterranee
RMEIDE — Revista de Medicina Interna, Neurologie, Psihiatrie, Neurochirurgie, Dermato-Venerologie. Seria Neurologia, Psihiatrie, Neurochirurgie
RMELB — Radio Mentor Electronic
R Melbourne Hosp Clin Rep — Royal Melbourne Hospital. Clinical Reports
RMEMAN — Revue Medicale Miniere
RMEMD — Revue Roumaine de Morphologie, d'Embryologie, et de Physiologie. Serie Morphologie et Embryologie
R Menorca — Revista de Menorca
RMEPD — Revue Roumaine de Morphologie, d'Embryologie, et de Physiologie. Serie Physiologie
RMEPDZ — Romanian Journal of Morphology, Embryology, and Physiology
RMeR — Rivista di Meteorologia (Rome)
RMERA — Rumanian Medical Review
R Mercados — Revista dos Mercados
R Met — Review of Metaphysics
R Meta — Review of Metaphysics
R Metaph Mor — Revue de Metaphysique et de Morale
R Metaphys — Review of Metaphysics
R Mex Agr — Revista del Mexico Agrario
R Mex Ciencias Pols y Socs — Revista Mexicana de Ciencias Politicas y Sociales
R Mexicana De Der Pen — Revista Mexicana de Derecho Penal
R Mexic Scciol — Revista Mexicana de Sociologia
R Mexic Trab — Revista Mexicana del Trabajo
RMF — Research Management. The International Journal of Research Management
R M F C — Recherches sur la Musique Francaise Classique
RMFEB — Revista Mexicana de Fisica. Suplemento de Ensenanza
RMFFA — Raumfahrtforschung
RMFIEK — Revista Mexicana de Fitopatologia
RMFMA — Rock Mechanics
R Mf Ph — Rheinisches Museum fuer Philologie
RMFSA — Revista Mexicana de Fisica. Suplemento del Reactor
RMFZA — Radovi Medicinskogo Fakulteta u Zagrebu
RMG — Revue Militaire Generale
RMG — Russkaya Muzikal'naya Gazeta
RMGCA — Rocky Mountain Association of Geologists. Field Conference
RMGQA — Records Management Quarterly
RMH — Reserve Bank of Malawi. Financial and Economic Review
RMHNC — Revista del Museo Historico Nacional de Chile
RMHPB — Reports on Mathematical Physics
RMI — Rassegna Mensile di Israel
RMI — Research Monographs in Immunology
RMI — Rivista Mensile di Israel
RMI — Rivista Musicale Italiana
RMIA — Revista del Museo e Instituto Arqueologico [*Cuzco*]
RMid — Revue des Universites du Midi
RMIDDJ — Revista de Medicina Interna, Neurologie, Psihiatrie, Neurochirurgie, Dermato-Venerologie. Seria Dermato-Venerologia
RMIIA — Rassegna di Medicina Industriale e di Igiene del Lavoro
RMIIDY — Revista de Medicina Interna, Neurologie, Psihiatrie, Neurochirurgie, Dermato-Venerologie. Seria Medicina Interna
R Mil Coll Can Civ Eng Res Rep — Royal Military College of Canada. Civil Engineering Research Report
RMIMDC — Research Monographs in Immunology
RMIND — Reviews in Mineralogy
RMIs — Rassegna Mensile di Israel
RMJ — Revista del Ministerio de Justicia
RMJC — Revista do Museo Julio de Castilhos e Arquivo Historico do Rio Grande do Sul
RMJMA — Rocky Mountain Journal of Mathematics
RMJSA — Roczniki Akademii Medycznej Imienia Juliana Marchlewskiego w Bialymstoku. Suplement
R Mkting Agric Econ — Review of Marketing and Agricultural Economics
RMKUA — Report. Research Institute for Applied Mechanics (Kyushu University)
RML — Ausfuehrliches Lexikon der Griechischen und Roemischen Mythologie
RML — Review of Metal Literature
RML — Revista Mexicana de Literatura
RML — Revista Municipal. [*Camara Municipal de*] Lisboa
R MI — Revue de Musicologie
RML — Revue du Monde Latin

RML — Revue Medicale de Liege
RML — Riddell Memorial Lectures
RMLMA — Revue MBLE
RMLMDR — Revue de Medecine du Limousin
RMLR — Rocky Mountain Law Review [*Later, University of Colorado. Law Review*]
RMM — Revista Muzeelor
RMM — Revista Muzeelor si Monumentelor
RMM — Revue de Metaphysique et de Morale
RMM — Revue du Monde Musulman
RMMCVG — Revue Mensuelle des Musees et Collections de la Ville de Geneve
RMMFA — Revue Medico-Chirurgicale des Maladies du Foie, de la Rate, et du Pancreas
RMMID — Revue Roumaine de Medecine. Medecine Interne
RMMJA — Rocky Mountain Medical Journal
RMMLR — Rocky Mountain Mineral Law Review
RMMND — Rocky Mountain Mineral Law Newsletter
RMMO — Revue Medicale du Moyen-Orient
RMN — Revista do Museu Nacional [*Rio de Janeiro*]
RMN — Revista. Museo Nacional
RMNac — Revista. Museo Nacional
RMNL — Revista del Museo Nacional [*Lima*]
Rm N Linc At — Atti dell' Accademia Pontificia de' Nuovi Lincei (Roma)
Rm N Linc Mm — Memorie della Pontificia Accademia dei Nuovi Lincei (Roma)
RMNUBP — Research Methods in Neurochemistry
RMNZA — Rudy i Metale Niezelazne
RMOC — Reaction Mechanisms in Organic Chemistry
RMod — Revue Moderne
Rmois — Revue du Mois
R Mo Mu — Revue du Monde Musulman
R Mon — Rassegna Monetaria
RMon — Revue Mondiale
R Mondiale — Revue Mondiale
R Monet — Rassegna Monetaria
R Mons — Revista Monserratena
R Montceau — Revue Periodique de "La Physiophile." Societe d'Etudes des Sciences Naturelles et Historiques de Montceau-Les-Mines
RMP — International Migration
RMP — Revista del Museo de la Plata
RMP — Rheinisches Museum fuer Philologie
RMPaul — Revista. Museu Paulista
RMPIA — Razrabotka Mestorozhdenii Poleznykh Iskopaemykh
RMPPA — Revue de Medecine Psychosomatique et de Psychologie Medicale
RMPR — Revista de Prevencion de Readaptacion Social
RMPS — Revista do Museu Paulista (Sao Paulo)
RMQ — Records Management Quarterly
RMR — Rivista di Malariologia (Rome)
RMR — Rocky Mountain Law Review [*Later, University of Colorado. Law Review*]
RMR — Rocky Mountain Review
RMR — Rocky Mountain Review of Language and Literature
Rm R Ac Linc At — Atti della Reale Accademia dei Lincei (Roma)
Rm R Ac Linc Mm — Atti della Reale Accademia dei Lincei. Memorie della Classe di Scienze Fisiche, Matematiche e Naturali (Roma)
Rm R Ac Linc Rd — Atti della Reale Accademia dei Lincei. Rendiconti (Roma)
Rm R Ac Linc T — Atti della Reale Accademia dei Lincei. Transunti (Roma)
RMREEY — Revue des Maladies Respiratoires
RM Rev Med Estado Guanabara — RM. Revista Medica do Estado da Guanabara
RMRGS — Revista de Medicina do Rio Grande do Sul
RMRHB — Rheumatology and Rehabilitation
RMRMA — Revue M - Mecanique
RMS — Renaissance and Modern Studies
RMS — Revista Mexicana de Sociologia
RMSCA — Rivista Mineraria Siciliana
Rm Sc Cor — Corrispondenza Scientifica in Roma per l'Avanzamento delle Scienze
RMSFA — Revista Mexicana de Fisica. Suplemento de Fisica Aplicada
Rm S It Mm — Memorie di Matematica e di Fisica della Societa Italiana delle Scienze (Napoli, Roma)
RMSM — Revista Mexicana de Sociologia (Mexico City)
RMSoc — Revista Mexicana de Sociologia
Rm Spec Vat Pb — Pubblicazioni della Specola Vaticana (Roma, Torino)
RMSRA — Revue Medicale de la Suisse Romande
RMSSJ — Rocky Mountain Social Science Journal
RMSt — Reading Medieval Studies
RM Suisse — Schweizerische Musikzeitung/Revue Musicale Suisse
RM Suisse Romande — Revue Musicale de Suisse Romande
RMTAA — Rivista di Meteorologia Aeronautica
RM Th — Rechtsgeleerd Magazijn Themis
RMTHD — Recueil de Memoires et Travaux. Societe d'Histoire du Droit et des Institutionsde Anciens Pays de Droit Ecrit
RM Themis — Rechtsgeleerd Magazijn Themis
RMTOB3 — Revue Medicale de Tours
RMTRD — Revue de Medecine du Travail
RMTSA — Revista. Instituto de Medicina Tropical de Sao Paulo
RMTSDH — Texas. Agricultural Experiment Station. Research Monograph
RMu — Revue Musicale
Rm Uff Centr Met A — Annali dell' Ufficio Centrale di Meteorologia Italiana. Ufficio Centrale Meteorologico e Geodinamico Italiano (Roma)
RMUNA — Revista de Medicina. Universidad de Navarra
R Mus — Revue Musicale
R Mus Art Archeol — Revue. Musee d'Art et d'Archeologie
R Mus Chile — Revista Musical Chilena
R Mus de Suisse Romande — Revue Musicale de Suisse Romande
R Musicol — Revue de Musicologie
R Mus Ital — Nuova Rivista Musicale Italiana. Trimestrale di Cultura e Informazione Musicale
R Mus Ital — Rivista Musicale Italiana

R Mus La Plata Antropol — Revista. Museo de La Plata. Seccion Antropologia
R Mus Nac — Revista. Museo Nacional
RMV — Revue de Metrique et de Versification
RMyP — Revue de Mycologie (Paris)
RMZBA — Rudarsko-Metalurski Zbornik
RN — Rada Narodowa
RN — Rassegna Monetaria
RN — Realta Nuova
RN — Registered Nurse
RN — Renaissance News
RN — Review of Nations
RN — Revista Nacional. Literatura, Arte, Ciencia [*Montevideo*]
RN — Revista Notarial
RN — Revue du Nord
RN — Revue Nouvelle
RN — Revue Numismatique
RN — Rough Notes
RNA — Revista del Notariado (Argentina)
RNa — Revue Nationale
RNABC News — RNABC (Registered Nurses Association of British Columbia) News
R Nac Arquitectura — Revista Nacional de Arquitectura
R Nac Cult — Revista Nacional de Cultura. Ministerio de Educacion Nacional
RNAI — Annual Report. National Archives of India
RN and O — Raleigh News and Observer
RNAO News — RNAO (Registered Nurses Association of Ontario) News
RNap — Revue Napoleonienne
RNar — Ragioni Narrative
RNA Rev Nutr Anim — RNA. Revista de Nutricion Animal
R Nat — Revue Nationale
R Nations — Revue des Nations
R Navig Fluv Europ — Revue de la Navigation Fluviale Europeenne
RNaz — Rassegna Nazionale
RNB — Revue Belge de Numismatique
RNBLA — Rivista di Neurobiologia
RNC — Revista Nacional de Cultura
RNCA — Revista Nacional de Cultura (Argentina)
RNCT — Reports of the Working Committees. Northeast Conference on the Teaching of Foreign Languages
RND — Rocznik Naukowo-Dydaktyczny
RNDPD — Roundup
RNEMDX — Revue de Nematologie
RNeosc — Revue Neo-Scolastique de Philosophie
RNeu — Revue Neuchateloise
R Neuve — Revue Neuve
RNF — La Rassegna Nazionale (Florence)
RNGMA — Refiner and Natural Gasoline Manufacturer
RNGYA — Rhinology
RNI — Research Notes (Ibadan)
RNI — Research Policy. A Journal Devoted to Research Policy, Research Management, andPlanning
RN ID — RN Idaho
RNKID — Rikuyo Nainen Kikan
RNL — Retail Newsletter
RNL — Review of National Literatures
RNLAC — Revista Nacional, Literatura, Arte, Ciencia [*Montevideo*]
RNLJ — Rhodesia and Nyasaland Law Journal
R Nlle — Revue Nouvelle
RNM — Revista Nacional (Montevideo)
RN Mag — RN Magazine
RNMTA — Rendiconti di Matematica
RNMVDW — Reports. National Museum of Victoria
RNO — Rough Notes
RNOBDG — Revista Nordestina de Biologia
R Nord — Revue du Nord
RNOUD — Revue Nouvelle
R Nouv — Revue Nouvelle
RNP — Revue Neo-Scolastique de Philosophie
RN Regist Nurse — RN. Registered Nurse
RNRLA — Report of Naval Research Laboratory Progress
RNRVAK — Feddes Repertorium. Specierum Novarum Regni Vegetabilis
RNS — Revue Neo-Scolastique de Philosophie
RNSJA — Rinsho Seijinbyo
RNSP — Revue Neo-Scolastique de Philosophie
RNT — Regensburger Neues Testament
RNT — Revista Nacional de Teatro
RNUCA — Rivista del Nuovo Cimento. Societa Italiana di Fisica
RNum — Rassegna Numismatica
RNum — Revue Numismatique
R Numis Soc Spec Publ — Royal Numismatic Society. Special Publication
RNVSDY — Kongelige Norske Videnskabers Selskab. Museet. Botanisk Avdeling Rapport
RNWSD — Research News
RNZ — Reserve Bank of New Zealand. Bulletin
RNZ — Rhein-Neckar-Zeitung
RNZOD8 — Polish Journal of Animal Science and Technology
RO — Recueil Officiel des Lois et Ordonnances de la Confederation Suisse
RO — Renaissance d'Occident
RO — Revista de Occidente
RO — Revue de l'Orient
RO — Revue Orientale
RO — Rocznik Orientalistyczny
RO — Roemisches Oesterreich. Jahresschrift der Oesterreichischen Gesellschaft fuer Archaeologie
Ro — Romania

ROA — RAS. Rohr-Armatur-Sanitaer-Heizung Informationsblatt fuer den Fachhandel und das Sanitaerfach und Heizungsfach
ROA — Report on the ORT Activities
ROA — Revue Orientale et Africaine
Ro Abr — Rolle's Abridgment
Road Abstr — Road Abstracts
Road A R — Road Apple Review
Road Maps — Economic Road Maps
Road Note Road Res Lab (UK) — Road Note. Road Research Laboratory (United Kingdom)
Road Res Bull — Road Research Bulletin
Road Res Lab (UK) RRL Rep — Road Research Laboratory (United Kingdom). RRL Report
Road Res Monogr — Road Research Monographs
Road Res Notes — Road Research Notes
Road Res Pap — Road Research Papers
Road Res Techn Pap — Road Research Technical Papers
Road Saf — Road Safety
Roads & Bridges — Roads and Bridges
Roads & Constr — Roads and Construction
Roads & Eng Constr — Roads and Engineering Construction
Roads Construct — Roads and Construction
Roads Road Constr — Roads and Road Construction
Roads St — Roads and Streets
Road Transp Aust — Road Transporter of Australia
Road Transp of Aust — Road Transporter of Australia
ROAS — Ritus Orientalium, Coptorum, Syrorum, et Armenorum in Administrandis Sacramentis
RoB — Religion och Bibel
ROB — Review of Business
ROB — Rijksdienst voor het Oudheidkundig Bodemonderzoek
ROB — Robotics Age
Rob Autom Syst — Robotics and Autonomous Systems
Rob Colo — Robinson's Reports
Rob Comput Integr Manuf — Robotics and Computer-Integrated Manufacturing
Robert A Taft Sanit Eng Cent Tech Rep — Robert A. Taft Sanitary Engineering Center. Technical Report
Robert A Taft Water Res Cent Rep — Robert A. Taft Water Research Center. Report
Robert A Welch Found Conf Chem Res Proc — Robert A. Welch Foundation. Conferences on Chemical Research. Proceedings
Robert A Welch Found Res Bull — Robert A. Welch Foundation. Research Bulletin
Robert Morris Associates Bull — Robert Morris Associates. Bulletin
Rob Exp Suppl — Robot Experimenter. Supplement
Rob J An — Journal de l'Anatomie et de la Physiologie Normales et Pathologiques de l'Homme et des Animaux. Robin
Robot Abstr — Robotics Abstracts
Robot Age — Robotics Age
Robot Eng — Robotics Engineering
Robot Exp — Robot Experimenter
Robotic Pat Newsl — Robotic Patents Newsletter
Robotics T — Robotics Today
Robotron Tech Commun — Robotron Technical Communications
Robotron Tech Mitt — Robotron Technische Mitteilungen
Robot Wld — Robotics World
R Obs Ann — Royal Observatory. Annals
R Obs Bull — Royal Observatory. Bulletins
Rob W — Roberts. Wills and Codicils
Rob World — Robotics World
RoC — Records of Civilization
ROc — Revista de Occidente
ROC — Revue de l'Orient Chretien
Rocas Miner — Rocas y Minerales
Rocc — Revista de Occidente
R Occid Musul Mediterr — Revue de l'Occident Musulman et de la Mediterranee
Rocenka Vlastiv Spolecn Jihoceske V Ceskych Budejovicich — Rocenka Vlastivedne Spolecnosti Jihoceske v Ceskych Budejovicich
Roc Gdanski — Rocznik Gdanski
RocH — Rochester History
ROCHA — Roczniki Chemii
Roche Image Med Res — Roche Image of Medicine and Research
Roche Med Image Comment — Roche Medical Image and Commentary
Rochester Acad Sci Proc — Rochester Academy of Science. Proceedings
Rochester Conf Coherence Quantum Opt Proc — Rochester Conference on Coherence and Quantum Optics. Proceedings
Rochester Conf Data Acquis Processing Biol Med Proc — Rochester Conference on Data Acquisition and Processing in Biology and Medicine. Proceedings
Rochester Conf Toxic — Rochester Conference on Toxicity
Rochester Hist — Rochester History
Rochester Hist Soc Pub — Rochester Historical Society Publication Fund Series
Rochester Hist Soc Publ Fund Ser — Rochester Historical Society. Publication Fund Series
Rochester Int Conf Environ Toxic — Rochester International Conference on Environmental Toxicity
Rochester NY Ac Sc P — Proceedings of the Rochester Academy of Sciences (Rochester, New York)
Rochester Univ Lib Bul — University of Rochester. Library Bulletin
Roc Hist Czasopismiennictwa Pol — Rocznik Historii Czasopismiennictwa Polskiego
Roc Hist Sztuki — Rocznik Historii Sztuki
Roch Patr — Rochester Patriot
Roch Phil — Rochester Philharmonic Orchestra. Program Notes
RO Chr — Revue de l'Orient Chretien

Roc Human — Roczniki Humanistyczne
ROCIA — Rozhledy v Chirurgii
Rock Art Res — Art Research Association (AURA) and International Federation of Rock Art Organizations (IFRAO)
Rockefeller Inst Rev — Rockefeller Institute Review
Rocket News Lett — Rocket News Letter
Rocket News Lett J Space Flight — Rocket News Letter and Journal of Space Flight
Rocket Propul Technol — Rocket Propulsion Technology
Rock Form Miner Proc Gen Meet IMA — Rock-Forming Minerals. Proceedings. General Meeting of IMA
Rock Magn Paleogeophys — Rock Magnetism and Paleogeophysics
Rock Mech — Rock Mechanics
Rock Mech Am Northwest Congr Exped Guide — Rock Mechanics. The American Northwest. Congress Expedition Guide
Rock Mech Eng Geol — Rock Mechanics and Engineering Geology
Rock Mech Felsmech Mec Roches — Rock Mechanics/Felsmechanik/Mecanique des Roches
Rock Mech Rock Eng — Rock Mechanics and Rock Engineering
Rock Miner Anal — Rock and Mineral Analysis
Rock Oil Ind — Rock Oil Industry
Rock Prod — Rock Products
Roc Krakow — Rocznik Krakowski
Roc Kruhu Pestovani Dejin Umeni — Rocenka Kruhu pro Pestovani Dejin Umeni
Rocks Miner — Rocks and Minerals
Rocky Mo L R — Rocky Mountain Law Review
Rocky Mountain J Math — Rocky Mountain Journal of Mathematics
Rocky Mountain MJ — Rocky Mountain Medical Journal
Rocky Mount Med J — Rocky Mountain Medical Journal
Rocky Mt Assoc Geol — Rocky Mountain Association of Geologists
Rocky Mt B — Rocky Mountain Business Journal
Rocky Mt Bioeng Symp Proc — Rocky Mountain Bioengineering Symposium. Proceedings
Rocky Mt J Math — Rocky Mountain Journal of Mathematics
Rocky Mt Law Rev — Rocky Mountain Law Review
Rocky Mt L Rev — Rocky Mountain Law Review [Later, University of Colorado. Law Review]
Rocky Mt Med J — Rocky Mountain Medical Journal
Rocky Mt Miner Law Inst Annu Inst Proc — Rocky Mountain Mineral Law Institute. Annual Institute. Proceedings
Rocky Mt Miner L Rev — Rocky Mountain Mineral Law Review
Rocky Mt Min L Inst — Rocky Mountain Mineral Law Institute. Proceedings
Rocky Mt Min L Inst Proc — Rocky Mountain Mineral Law Institute. Proceedings
Rocky Mtn L Rev — Rocky Mountain Law Review [Later, University of Colorado. Law Review]
Rocky Mtn Med J — Rocky Mountain Medical Journal
Rocky Mtn Oil Reporter — Rocky Mountain Oil Reporter
Rocky Mtn Soc Sci J — Rocky Mountain Social Science Journal
Rocky Mt R — Rocky Mountain Review of Language and Literature
Rocky Mt So — Rocky Mountain Social Science Journal
Rocky Mt Soc Sci J — Rocky Mountain Social Science Journal
Rocky Mt Spectrosc Conf Program Abstr — Rocky Mountain Spectroscopy Conference. Program and Abstracts
Rocla Pipes Ltd Tech J — Rocla Pipes Limited. Technical Journal
RocM — Rocky Mountain Social Science Journal
Roc Muz — Rocznik Muzealny
Roc Muz N Warszaw Annu Mus N Varsovie — Rocznik Muzeum Narodowego w Warszawie / Annuaire du Musee National de Varsovie
Roc Muz Toruniu — Rocznik Muzeum w Toruniu
RocO — Rocznik Orientalistyczny
Roc Or — Rocznik Orientalistyczny
Roc Sztuki Slaskiej — Roczniki Sztuki Slaskiej
Roc T Kan — Roczniki Teologiczno-Kanoniczne
Roc Towarzystwa Naukowego Krakow — Rocznik Towarzystwa Naukowego Krakowskiego
Roc Warszaw — Rocznik Warszawski
Rocz Akad Med Bialymst — Roczniki Akademii Medycznej w Bialymstoku
Rocz Akad Med Bialymstoku — Roczniki Akademii Medycznej Imienia Juliana Marchlewskiego w Bialymstoku
Rocz Akad Med Bialymstoku Supl — Roczniki Akademii Medycznej Imienia Juliana Marchlewskiego w Bialymstoku. Suplement
Rocz Akad Med Bialymst Supl — Roczniki Akademii Medycznej w Bialymstoku. Suplement
Rocz Akad Med Im Juliana Marchlewskiego Bialymstoku Supl — Roczniki Akademii Medycznej Imienia Juliana Marchlewskiego w Bialymstoku.Suplement
Rocz Akad Med Juliana Marchlewskiego Bialymstoku — Roczniki Akademii Medycznej Imienia Juliana Marchlewskiego w Bialymstoku
Rocz Akad Med Juliana Marchlewskiego Bialymstoku Supl — Roczniki Akademii Medycznej Imienia Juliana Marchlewskiego w Bialymstoku. Suplement
Rocz Akad Med Poznaniu — Roczniki Akademii Medycznej w Poznaniu
Rocz Akad Nauk Tech Warszawie — Roczniki Akademii Nauk Technicznych w Warszawie
Rocz Akad Roln Poznaniu — Roczniki Akademii Rolniczej w Poznaniu
Rocz Akad Roln Poznaniu Pr Habilitacyjne — Roczniki Akademii Rolniczej w Poznaniu. Prace Habilitacyjne
Rocz Akad Roln Poznaniu Rozpr Nauk — Roczniki Akademii Rolniczej w Poznaniu. Rozprawy Naukowe
Roc Zakladu Narodowego Im Ossolinskich — Rocznik Zakladu Narodowego Imienia Ossolinskich
Rocz Bial — Rocznik Bialostocki
Rocz Bialostocki — Rocznik Bialostocki
Rocz Chem — Roczniki Chemii
Rocz Glebozn — Roczniki Gleboznawcze
RoczH — Roczniki Humanistyczne Katolickiego Uniwersytetu
Rocz Hist — Roczniki Historyczne

Rocz Hum — Roczniki Humanistyczne
Rocz Inst Przem Miesn Tluszczowego — Roczniki Instytutu Przemyslu Miesnego i Tluszczowego
Rocz Inst Przem Mlecz — Roczniki Instytutu Przemyslu Mleczarskiego
Rocz Jeleniogorski — Rocznik Jeleniogorski
Rocz Krakowski — Rocznik Krakowski
Rocz Muz Etnogr — Rocznik Muzeum Etnograficznego w Krakowie
Rocz Muz Narod Warszawie — Rocznik Muzeum Narodowego w Warszawie
Rocz Muz Swiet — Rocznik Muzeum Swietokrzyskiego
Rocz Muz Toruniu — Rocznik Muzeum w Toruniu
Rocz Muz Warsz — Rocznik Muzeum Narodowego w Warszawie
Roczn Akad Roln Poznan — Roczniki Akademii Rolniczej w Poznaniu
Rocz Nauk Akad Med Lodzi — Roczniki Naukowe Akademii Medycznej w Lodzi
Rocz Nauk Akad Roln Poznaniu Rozpr Nauk — Roczniki Naukowe Akademii Rolniczej w Poznaniu. Rozprawy Naukowe
Rocz Nauk Roln — Roczniki Nauk Rolniczych
Rocz Nauk Roln Les — Roczniki Nauk Rolniczych i Lesnych
Rocz Nauk Roln Lesn — Roczniki Nauk Rolniczych i Lesnych
Rocz Nauk Roln Lesn Dodatek — Roczniki Nauk Rolniczych i Lesnych. Dodatek
Rocz Nauk Roln Ser A — Roczniki Nauk Rolniczych. Seria A
Rocz Nauk Roln Ser A — Roczniki Nauk Rolniczych. Seria A. Produkcja Roslinna
Rocz Nauk Roln Ser A Prod Rosl — Roczniki Nauk Rolniczych. Seria A. Produkcja Roslinna
Rocz Nauk Roln Ser B — Roczniki Nauk Rolniczych. Seria B. Zootechniczna
Rocz Nauk Roln Ser B Zootech — Roczniki Nauk Rolniczych. Seria B. Zootechniczna
Rocz Nauk Roln Ser C — Roczniki Nauk Rolniczych. Seria C. Technika Rolnicza
Rocz Nauk Roln Ser C Mech Roln — Roczniki Nauk Rolniczych. Seria C. Mechznizacja Rolnictwa
Rocz Nauk Roln Ser C Tech Roln — Roczniki Nauk Rolniczych. Seria C. Technika Rolnicza
Rocz Nauk Roln Ser D — Roczniki Nauk Rolniczych. Seria D. Monografie
Rocz Nauk Roln Ser D Monogr — Roczniki Nauk Rolniczych. Seria D. Monografie
Rocz Nauk Roln Ser E — Roczniki Nauk Rolniczych. Seria E. Ochrona Roslin
Rocz Nauk Roln Ser E — Roczniki Nauk Rolniczych. Seria E. Weterynarii
Rocz Nauk Roln Ser E 1953-60 — Roczniki Nauk Rolniczych. Seria E. Weterynarii 1953-60
Rocz Nauk Roln Ser E Ochr Rosl — Roczniki Nauk Rolniczych. Seria E. Ochrona Roslin
Rocz Nauk Roln Ser F — Roczniki Nauk Rolniczych. Seria F. Melioracji i Vzytkow Zielonych
Rocz Nauk Roln Ser F Melio Vzytkow Zielonych — Roczniki Nauk Rolniczych. Seria F. Melioracji i Vzytkow Zielonych
Rocz Nauk Roln Ser H — Roczniki Nauk Rolniczych. Seria H. Rybactwo
Rocz Nauk Roln Ser H Rybactwo — Roczniki Nauk Rolniczych. Seria H. Rybactwo
Rocz Nauk Wyzsza Szk Wychow Fiz Gdansku — Roczniki Naukowe. Wyzsza Szkola Wychowania Fizycznego w Gdansku
Rocz Nauk Zootech — Roczniki Naukowe Zootechniki
Rocz Nauk Zootech Monogr Rozpr — Roczniki Naukowe Zootechniki. Monografie i Rozprawy
Rocz Nauk Zootech Pol J Anim Sci Technol — Rocznik Naukowe Zootechniki. Polish Journal of Animal Science and Technology
Roczn Bibl — Rocznik Biblioteczne
Roczn Bibliot Narodowe — Rocznik Bibliotek Narodowe
Roczn Chem — Roczniki Chemii
Roczn Dendrol Polsk Tow Bot — Rocznik Sekcji Dendrologicznej Polskiego Towarzystwa Botanicznego
Roczniki Glebozn — Roczniki Gleboznawcze
Rocznik Nauk Dydakt Prace Mat — Rocznik Naukowo-Dydaktyczny. Prace Matematyczne
Roczn Inst Handlu Wewn — Roczniki Instytutu Handlu Wewnetrznego
Roczn Nauk Roln A — Roczniki Nauk Rolniczych. A. Produkcja Roslinna
Roczn Nauk Roln Lesn — Roczniki Nauk Rolniczych i Lesnych
Roczn Nauk Roln Ser A Rosl — Roczniki Nauk Rolniczych. Seria A. Roslinna
Roczn Panst Zakl Hig — Roczniki Panstwowego Zakladu Higieny
Roczn T Ch AT — Roczniki Teologiczne Chrzescijanskiej Akademii Teologicznej
Roczn Uniw Marie Curie Lubl — Roczniki Uniwersytetu Marie Curie-Sklodowskiej w Lublinie
Roczn Wyz Szk Roln Poznan — Rocznik Wyzszej Szkoly Rolniczej Poznaniu
RoczOr — Rocznik Orientalistyczny
Rocz Orjent — Rocznik Orjentalistyczny
Rocz Panstw Zakl Hig — Roczniki Panstwowego Zakladu Higieny
Rocz Panst Zakl Hig (Warszawa) — Roczniki Panstwowego Zakladu Higieny (Warszawa)
Rocz Pol Tow Geol — Rocznik Polskiego Towarzystwa Geologicznego
Rocz Pomor Akad Med — Roczniki Pomorska Akademia Medyczna Imienia Generala Karola Swierczewskiego w Szczecinie
Rocz Pomor Akad Med Im Gen Karola Swierczewskiego Szczecin — Roczniki Pomorska Akademia Medyczna Imienia Generala Karola Swierczewskiego w Szczecinie
Rocz Pomor Akad Med Szczecinie — Roczniki Pomorskiej Akademii Medycznej Imienia Generala Karola Swierczewskiego wSzczecinie
Rocz Pomor Akad Med Szczecinie Supl — Roczniki Pomorskiej Akademii Medycznej w Szczecinie. Suplement
Rocz Sekc Dendrol Pol Tow Bot — Rocznik Sekcji Dendrologicznej Polskiego Towarzystwa Botanicznego
RoczSl — Rocznik Slawistyczny
Rocz Stat Pow Tar — Rocznik Statystyczny Powiatu Tarnow
Rocz Stat Pow Zot — Rocznik Statystyczny Powiatu Zotow
Rocz Technol Chem Zywn — Rocznik Technologii Chemii Zywnosci
Rocz Uniw Marli Curie Sklodowskiej Dzial A — Roczniki Uniwersytetu Marii Curie-Sklodowskiej. Dzial A. Matematyka
Rocz Uniw Marli Curie Sklodowskiej Dzial B — Roczniki Uniwersytetu Marii Curie-Sklodowskiej. Dzial B. Geografia,Geologia, Mineralogia, i Petrografia

Rocz Uniw Marli Curie Sklodowskiej Dzial C — Roczniki Uniwersytetu Marii Curie-Sklodowskiej. Dzial C. NaukiBiologiczne
Rocz Uniw Marli Curie Sklodowskiej Dzial C Dodatek — Roczniki Uniwersytetu Marii Curie-Sklodowskiej. Dzial C. NaukiBiologiczne. Dodatek
Rocz Uniw Marli Curie Sklodowskiej Dzial D — Roczniki Uniwersytetu Marii Curie-Sklodowskiej. Dzial D. NaukiLekarskie
Rocz Uniw Marli Curie Sklodowskiej Dzial DD — Roczniki Uniwersytetu Marii Curie-Sklodowskiej. Dzial DD. MedycynaWeterynaryjna
Rocz Uniw Marli Curie Sklodowskiej Dzial E — Roczniki Uniwersytetu Marii Curie-Sklodowskiej. Dzial E. Nauki Rolnicze
Rocz Uniw Marli Curie Sklodowskiej Dzial E Dodatek — Roczniki Uniwersytetu Marii Curie-Sklodowskiej. Dzial E. NaukiRolnicze. Dodatek
Rocz Uniw Marij Curi-Sklodowskiej Dzial AA — Roczniki Uniwersytetu Marij Curie-Sklodowskiej. Dzial AA. Fizyka i Chemia
Rocz Wojsk Inst Hig Epidemiol — Rocznik Wojskowego Instytutu Higieny i Epidemiologii
Rocz Wroclaw — Rocznik Wroclawski
Rocz Wyzs Szkoly Roln Poznaniu — Roczniki Wyzszej Szkoly Rolniczej w Poznaniu
Rocz Wyzsz Roln Poznaniu — Roczniki Wyzszej Szkoly Rolniczej w Poznaniu
Rocz Wyzsz Szk Roln Poznaniu Pr Habilitacyjne — Roczniki Wyzszej Szkoly Rolniczej w Poznaniu. Prace Habilitacyjne
Rod and Gun and Canad Silver Fox News — Rod and Gun and Canadian Silver Fox News
Rodds Chem Carbon Comp — Rodd's Chemistry of Carbon Compounds
Rodo Kenky Kenky — Rodoeisei Kenkyujo Kenkyuhokoku
Rodopskii Zbor — Rodopskii Zbornik
RODSB — Revue d'Odonto-Stomatologie
ROE — Review of Economics and Statistics
ROE — Roemisches Oesterreich
RoeFo Fortschr Geb Roentgenstr Nuklearmed — RoeFo. Fortschritte auf dem Gebiete der Roentgenstrahlen und der Nuklearmedizin
RoeHM — Roemische Historische Mitteilungen
Roem Ger Forsch — Roemisch-Germanische Forschungen
Roem Germ F — Roemisch-Germanische Forschungen
Roem Germ Korrbl — Roemisch-Germanisches Korrespondenzblatt
Roem Hist Mitt — Roemische Historische Mitteilungen
Roem Inschr Wuerttemb — Roemischen Inschriften und Bildwerke Wuerttembergs
Roemische Quartalschrift — Roemische Quartalschrift fuer Christliche Altertumskunde und fuer Kirchengeschichte
Roem Jahr Kunstges — Roemisches Jahrbuch fuer Kunstgeschichte
Roem Jb Bib Hertz — Roemisches Jahrbuch der Bibliotheca Hertziana
Roem Jb Kstgesch — Roemisches Jahrbuch fuer Kunstgeschichte
Roem Kaiserl Akad Naturf Auserlesene Med Chir Abh — Der Roemisch Kaiserlichen Akademie der Naturforscher Auserlesene Medicinisch- Chirurgisch-Anatomisch- Chymisch- und Botanische Abhandlungen
Roem Mltt — Mitteilungen. Deutsches Archaeologische Institut. Abteilung Rome
Roem Mitt — Roemische [*Abteilung*] Mitteilungen des Deutschen Archaeologischen Instituts
Roem Oe — Roemisches Oesterreich. Jahresschrift der Oesterreichischen Gesellschaft fuer Archaeologie
Roem Q — Roemische Quartalschrift fuer Christliche Altertumskunde und fuer Kirchengeschichte
Roem Qschr — Roemische Quartalschrift
Roem Q Schr — Roemische Quartalschrift fuer Christliche Altertumskunde und fuer Kirchengeschichte
Roem Qschr Christ Altertknd & Kirchgesch — Roemische Quartalschrift fuer Christliche Altertumskunde und fuer Kirchengeschichte
Roem Qu — Roemische Quartalschrift fuer Christliche Altertumskunde und fuer Kirchengeschichte
Roem Quartschr Christl Altertskde — Roemische Quartalsschrift fuer Christliche Altertumskunde
Roem Quart Schr Christl Altertumskde — Roemische Quartalsschrift fuer Christliche Altertumskunde und Kirchengeschichte
Roem Staatsr — Roemisches Staatsrecht
Roem Strafr — Roemisches Strafrecht
ROEND — Roentgenstrahlen
Roentgen Ber — Roentgen Berichte
Roentgen-Bl — Roentgen-Blaetter
Roentgen Bl — Roentgen-Blaetter. Klinik und Praxis
Roentgen Laboratoriumsprax — Roentgen Laboratoriumspraxis
Roentgenogr Duennschicht Oberflaechencharakt — Roentgenographische Duennschicht- und Oberflaechencharakterisierung
Roentgenprax — Roentgenpraxis
Roentgen Technol — Roentgen Technology. Official Journal of the Indian Association of RadiologicalTechnologists
Roep — Roeping
Roe Q — Roemische Quartalschrift fuer Christliche Altertumskunde und fuer Kirchengeschichte
ROF — Romanische Forschungen
Rofo Fortschr Beg Rontgenstr Neuen Bildgeb Verfahr — Rofo. Fortschritte auf dem Gebiete der Rontgenstrahlen und der Neuen Bildgebenden Verfahren
R of Religion — Review of Religion
RofThPh — Review of Theology and Philosophy
ROGLA — Roczniki Gleboznawcze
Rog Min — Rogers. Mines, Minerals, and Quarries
ROGNA — Rivista di Ostetricia e Ginecologia
RoH — Roumeliotiko Hemerologio
Rohm & Haas Reptr — Rohm and Haas Reporter
Rohm Haas Rep — Rohm and Haas Reporter
ROHRA — Rohre, Rohrleitungsbau, Rohrleitungstransport
Rohre Rohrleitungsbau Rohrleitungstransp — Rohre, Rohrleitungsbau, Rohrleitungstransport
Rohst Landerber — Rohstoffwirtschaftliche Landerberichte

Rohst Umwelt Vort Int Kongr — Rohstoff und Umwelt. Vortraege des Internationalen Kongresses
RoHum — Roczniki Humanistyczne
ROITL — Reports of Interest to Lawyers
ROJ — Romanistisches Jahrbuch
ROKAA — Rodo Kagaku
ROKOA5 — Folia Entomologica Hungarica
ROL — Revue de l'Orient Latin
Rol — Rolet
Role Fert Intensif Agric Prod Proc Congr Int Potash Inst — Role of Fertilization in the Intensification of Agricultural Production. Proceedings. Congress. International Potash Institute
Role Immunol Factors Viral Oncog Processes Int Symp — Role of Immunological Factors in Viral and Oncongenic Processes. International Symposium
Role Membr Secretory Processes Proc Meet Int Conf Biol Membr — Role of Membranes in Secretory Processes. Proceedings. Meeting. International Conference on Biological Membranes
Role Pharmacokinet Prenatal Perinat Toxicol Symp Prenatal De — Role of Pharmacokinetics in Prenatal and Perinatal Toxicology. Symposium on Prenatal Development
Role Phosphodiesterase Inhib Heart Failure Proc Symp — Role of Phosphodiesterase-Inhibitors in Heart Failure. Proceedings. Symposium
Rolf Nevanlinna Inst Res Rep A — Rolf Nevanlinna Institute Research Reports. A
RoLit — Romania Literara
Roll Stone — Rolling Stone
Rol Mikroelem Selsk Khoz Tr Mezhvuz — Rol Mikroelementov v Sel'skom Khozyaistve. Trudy MezhvuzovskogoSoveshchaniya po Mikroelementam
Roln Ochr Srodowiska Czlowieka Mater Konf Nauk — Rolnictwo a Ochrona Srodowiska Czlowieka, Materialy, z KonferencjiNaukowej
Rom — Romania
Rom — Romania. Revue Consacree a l'Etude des Langues et Litteratures Romanes
Roma Econ — Roma Economica
Romagna A & Stor — Romagna Arte e Storia
Romagna Med — Romagna Medica
Roman Bibl — Romanische Bibliothek
Roman Biblioth — Romanische Bibliothek
Romance Philol — Romance Philology
Roman Forsc — Romanische Forschungen
Roman Forsch — Romanische Forschungen
Romania Lit — Romania Literara
Romanian F — Romanian Film
Romanian J Phys — Romanian Journal of Physics
Romanian R — Romanian Review
Romanian Rep Phys — Romanian Reports in Physics
Romania P — Romania during the 1981-1985 Development Plan
Romania Vitic — Romania Viticola
Romanica Gothoburg — Romanica Gothoburgensia
Romanic Rev — Romanic Review
Romanische Forsch — Romanische Forschungen
Romanist Jb — Romanistisches Jahrbuch
Roman Note — Romance Notes
Romanobarbar — Romanobarbarica. Contributi allo Studio dei Rapporti Culturali tra il Mondo Latino e Mondo Barbarico
Roman Phil — Romance Philology
Roman Philol — Romance Philology
Roman R — Romanic Review
Roman Rev — Romanian Review
Roman Rev — Romanic Review
Roman Stud — Romanische Studien
Romant Move — Romantic Movement
Roman Z Lit — Romanistische Zeitschrift fuer Literaturgeschichte
Rom Arch Microbiol Immunol — Romanian Archives of Microbiology and Immunology
Rombach Hochsch Paperback — Rombach Hochschul Paperback
Rom Barb — Romanobarbarica
Rom Bull — Romanian Bulletin
Rom Com Geol Dari Seama Sedin — Romania Comitetul de Stat al Geologiei. Institutul Geologic. Dari de Seama ale Sedintelor
Rom Com Stat Energ Nucl Inst React Nucl Energ Tech Rep IRNE — Romania Comitetul de Stat pentru Energia Nucleara. Institutul deReactori Nucleari Energetici. Technical Report IRNE
Rom Con — Romana Contact. Organe Trimestriel de la Societe d'Archeologie
Rom Cont — Romana Contact
ROME — Resource Organizations and Meetings for Educators
RomF — Romanische Forschungen
Rom Fgn Tr — Romanian Foreign Trade
Rom Forsch — Romanische Forschungen
Rom G — Romanica Gandensia
Rom Germ Korrbl — Roemisch-Germanisches Korrespondenzblatt
Rominshu — Rodo Kankei Minji Saibanreishu
Rom Inst Geol Dari Seama Sedin — Romania Institutul Geologic. Dari de Seama ale Sedintelor
Rom Inst Geol Mem — Romania Institutul Geologic. Memorii
Rom Inst Geol Stud Teh Econ Ser B — Romania Institutul Geologic. Studii Tehnice si Economice. Seria B. Prepararea Minereurilor
Rom Inst Geol Stud Teh Econ Ser D — Romania Institutul Geologic. Studii Tehnice si Economice. Seria D. Prospectiuni Geofizice
Rom Inst Geol Stud Teh Econ Ser E — Romania Institutul Geologic. Studii Tehnice si Economice. Seria E
Rom Inst Geol Stud Teh Econ Ser I — Romania Comitetul de Stat al Geologiei. Institutul Geologic. Studii Tehnice si Economice. Seria I. Mineralogie-Petrografie
Rom Inst Meteorol Hidrol Stud Hidrogeol — Romania Institutul de Meteorologie si Hidrologie. Studii de Hidrogeologie
RomJ — Romanistisches Jahrbuch

Rom J Biophys — Romanian Journal of Biophysics
Rom J Chem — Romanian Journal of Chemistry
Rom J Endocrinol — Romanian Journal of Endocrinology
Rom J Gerontol Geriatr — Romanian Journal of Gerontology and Geriatrics
Rom J Intern Med — Romanian Journal of Internal Medicine
Rom J Med Endocrinol — Romanian Journal of Medicine. Endocrinology
Rom J Med Intern Med — Romanian Journal of Medicine. Internal Medicine
Rom J Med Neurol Psychiatry — Romanian Journal of Medicine. Neurology and Psychiatry
Rom J Med Virol — Romanian Journal of Medicine. Virology
Rom J Morphol — Romanian Journal of Morphology, Embryology, and Physiology. Morphology and Embryology
Rom J Morphol Embryol — Romanian Journal of Morphology and Embryology
Rom J Morphol Embryol Physiol Physiol — Romanian Journal of Morphology, Embryology, and Physiology. Physiology
Rom J Neurol Psychiatry — Romanian Journal of Neurology and Psychiatry
Rom J Physiol — Romanian Journal of Physiology
Rom J Tech Sci Appl Mech — Romanian Journal of Technical Sciences. Applied Mechanics
Rom J Virol — Romanian Journal of Virology
RomLit — Romania Literara
Rom Med Rev — Romanian Medical Review
Rom Mitteilungen — Mitteilungen des Deutschen Archaeologischen Instituts. Roemische Abteilung
RomN — Romance Notes
RoMo — Rowohlts's Monographien
Rom Of Stat Invent Marci Bul Inf Invent Marci — Romania. Oficiul de Stat pentru Inventii si Marci. Buletin de Informarepentru Inventii si Marci
Rom Of Stat Invent Marci Bul Invent Marci — Romania. Oficiul de Stat pentru Inventii si Marci. Buletin pentruInventii si Marci
RomP — Romance Philology
Rom Pat Doc — Romania. Patent Document
RomPh — Romance Philology
Rom Quart — Roemische Quartalschrift fuer Christliche Altertumskunde und fuer Kirchengeschichte
Rom Quartal Schrift — Roemische Quartalschrift fuer Christliche Altertumskunde und fuer Kirchengeschichte
RomR — Romanic Review
Rom Rep Phys — Romanian Reports in Physics
Rom Rev — Romanic Review
RomSl — Romanoslavica
Rom Staatsr — Roemisches Staatsrecht
Rom Strafr — Roemisches Strafrecht
Rom Texte — Romanische Texte
Rom Today — Romania Today
RoN — Romance Notes
Ronal Inst Architects Canada J — Royal Institute of Architects of Canada Journal
Rond Point Port Au Prince — Rond-Point (Port-au-Prince)
RONOA — Revue d'Oto-Neuro-Ophtalmologie
R Onom — Revue Internationale d'Onomastique
R Ont Mus J — Royal Ontario Museum. Journal
R Ont Mus Life Sci Contrib — Royal Ontario Museum. Life Sciences. Contributions
R Ont Mus Life Sci Misc Publ — Royal Ontario Museum. Life Sciences. Miscellaneous Publications
R Ont Mus Life Sci Occas Pap — Royal Ontario Museum. Life Sciences. Occasional Paper
R Ont Mus Zool Paleontol Contrib — Royal Ontario Museum of Zoology and Paleontology. Contributions
Roofing Res Stand Dev — Roofing Research and Standards Development
ROORD3 — Radiologia
Roorkee Univ Res J — Roorkee University. Research Journal
Roosevelt Wild Life Bull — Roosevelt Wild Life Bulletin
Roots Dig — Roots Digest
ROP — Romance Philology
ROPM — Revue. Ordre de Premontre et de Ses Missions
ROPRA — Rock Products
ROPXA — Roentgenpraxis
RoR — Review of Religion
RoR — Revision og Regnskabsvaesen
R Or — Revue de l'Orient, de l'Algerie et des Colonies
RoR — Romanian Review
ROR — Romanic Review
RORD — Research Opportunities in Renaissance Drama
Rororo Sci — Rororo Science
Ros — Rosario
ROSC — Review of Scottish Culture
Rose Annu R Natl Rose Soc — Rose Annual. Royal National Rose Society
Roser U Wunderlich Arch — Archiv fuer Physiologische Heilkunde. Roser, Wunderlich, Griesinger
Rose Techn — Rose Technic. Rose Polytechnic Institute
Roskills Lett China — Roskill's Letter from China
RoSlaw — Rocznik Slawistyczny
ROSMT — Regesta Historico-Diplomatica Ordinis S. Mariae Theutonicorum
ROSMTR — Regesta Historico-Diplomatica Ordinis S. Mariae Theutonicorum. Regesta Privilegiorum
ROSMTT — Regesta Historico-Diplomatica Ordinis S. Mariae Theutonicorum. Index Tabularii Ordinis
RosO — Roseau d'Or. Oeuvres et Chroniques
ROSP — Report on Syndicated Programs
Ross Arkheol — Rossiiskaia Arkheologiia
Ross Conf Med Res Rep — Ross Conference on Medical Research. Report
Ross Conf Pediatr Res Rep — Ross Conference on Pediatric Research. Report
Ross Fiziol Zh I M Sechenova — Rossiiskii Fiziologicheskii Zhurnal imeni I. M. Sechenova
Ross Gastroenterol Zh — Rossiiskii Gastroenterologicheskii Zhurnal

Ross Khim Zh — Rossiiskii Khimicheskii Zhurnal
ROSTA — Roads and Streets
ROSTA Bull — ROSTA [*Victoria. Road Safety and Traffic Authority*] Bulletin
Rost Defekty Met Krist Mater Vses Soveshch — Rost i Defekty Metallicheskikh Kristallov. Materialy VsesoyuznogoSoveshchaniya po Rosty i Nesovershenstvam Metallicheskikh Kristallov
Roster Organ Field Autom Comput Mach — Roster of Organizations in the Field of Automatic Computing Machinery
Rost Krist — Rost Kristallov
Rost Legir Poluprovodn Krist Plenok Mater Vses Simp — Rost i Legirovanie Poluprovodnikovykh Kristallov i Plenok. MaterialyVsesoyuznogo Simpoziuma po Protsessam Rosta i Sinteza PoluprovodnikovykhKristallov i Plenok
Rostl Vyroba — Rostlinna Vyroba
Rostl Vyroba Cesk Akad Zemed Ustav Vedeckotech Inf Zemed — Rostlinna Vyroba-Ceskoslovenska Akademie Zemedelska. Ustav Vedeckotechnickych Informaci pro Zemedelstvi
Rostocker Phys Manuskr — Rostocker Physikalische Manuskripte
Rostock Math Kolloq — Rostocker Mathematisches Kolloquium
Rostov Gidrometeorol Obs Sb Rab — Rostovskaya Gidrometeorologicheskaya Observatoriya. Sbornik Rabot
Rostov Gos Med Inst Sb Nauchn Tr — Rostovskii Gosudarstvennyi Meditsinskii Institut. Sbornik NauchnykhTrudov
Rostov-Na Donu Gos Ped Inst Fiz Mat Fak Ucen Zap — Rostovskii-Na-Donu Gosudarstvennyi Pedagogiceskii Institut. Fiziko-Matematiceskii Fakultet Ucenye Zapiski
Rostov-Na-Donu Gos Univ Ucen Zap — Rostovskii-Na-Donu Gosudarstvennyi Universitet. Ucenyi Zapiski
Rostovye Veshchestva Rost Rast — Rostovye Veshchestva i Rost Rastenii
Rost Ustoich Rast — Rost i Ustoichivost Rastenii
Rost Ustoich Rast Respub Mezhved Sb — Rost i Ustoichivost Rastenii Respublikanskii Mezhvedomstvennyi Sbornik
ROT — Rechtsinformation. Berichte und Dokumente zum Auslaendischen Wirtschafts- und Steuerrecht
ROTAA — Road Tar
ROTAD — Round Table
Rotation Method Crystallogr — Rotation Method in Crystallography
Rotenburger Symp — Rotenburger Symposium
Rotenburg Ferment Symp — Rotenburg Fermentation Symposium
Rotenburg Schr — Rotenburger Schriften
Rothamsted Exp Stn Rep — Rothamsted Experimental Station. Report
Rothamsted Exp Stn Rep Part 1 — Rothamsted Experimental Station. Report. Part 1
Rothamsted Exp Stn Rep Part 2 — Rothamsted Experimental Station. Report. Part 2
Rothmill Q — Rothmill Quarterly
RothsJber — Roths Jahresbericht ueber die Leistungen und Fortschritte auf dem Gebiete des Militaersanitaetswesens
RoTKan — Roczniki Teologiczno-Kanoniczne
Rot N Vh — Nieuwe Verhandelingen van het Bataafsch Genootschap der Proefondervindelijke Wijsbegeerte te Rotterdam
ROTOB — Romania Today
Rotor & W — Rotor and Wing International
Rotterdam Jb — Rotterdamsche Jaarboekje
Rotterdam Nieuwsbl — Rotterdamsche Nieuwsblad
Rouen Ac Tr — Precis Analytique des Travaux de l'Academie des Sciences, Belles-Lettres, et Arts de Rouen
Rouen Bll S Em — Bulletins des Travaux de la Societe Libre d'Emulation de Rouen
Rouen S Sc Bll — Bulletin de la Societe des Amis des Sciences Naturelles de Rouen
Rouen Tr Ac — Precis Analytique des Travaux de l'Academie des Sciences, Belles-Lettres, et Arts de Rouen
ROUHA — Ropa a Uhlie
Roum Arch Microbiol Immunol — Roumanian Archives of Microbiology and Immunology
Roum Biotechnol Lett — Roumanian Biotechnological Letters
Roum I Met A — Annales de l'Institut Meteorologique de Roumanie
Roum J Morphol Embryol — Roumanian Journal of Morphology and Embryology
Round Tab — Round Table
Round Table Semin Int Miner Process Congr — Round Table Seminar. International Mineral Processing Congress
Route Circ Routiere — Route et la Circulation Routiere
Roux Arch Entwicklungsmech Org — Roux Archiv fuer Entwicklungsmechanik der Organismen
Roux Archiv EntwMech Organ — Roux Archiv fuer Entwicklungsmechanik der Organismen
Roux's Arch Dev Biol — Roux's Archives of Developmental Biology
Rovart Lapok — Rovartani Lapok
Rov Koezlem — Rovartani Koezlemenyek
ROVYA — Rostlinna Vyroba
ROW — Romanian Engineering
Rowett Res Inst Annu Rep Stud Anim Nutr Allied Sci — Rowett Research Institute. Annual Report. Studies in Animal Nutrition and Allied Sciences
ROWJ — Records of Oceanographic Works in Japan
ROWJA — Records of Oceanographic Works in Japan
Rowley Hist Soc Pub — Rowley Historical Society. Publications
Rowman & Allanheld Probab Statist Ser — Rowman and Allanheld Probability and Statistics Series
Rowman & Littlefield Probab Statist Ser — Rowman and Littlefield Probability and Statistics Series
Rowohlts Bildmonograph — Rowohlts Bildmonographien
Roy Aeronaut Soc J — Royal Aeronautical Society. Journal
Royal — [*The*] Royal Magazine
Royal Agric Soc England J — Journal. Royal Agricultural Society of England
Royal Anthrop Inst Jour — Royal Anthropological Institute of Great Britain and Ireland. Journal

Royal Anthropol Inst News — Royal Anthropological Institute News
Royal Antiqua Inst News — Royal Antiquarians Institute News
Royal Astron Soc Canada Jour — Royal Astronomical Society of Canada. Journal
Royal Astron Soc Geophys Jour — Royal Astronomical Society. Geophysical Journal
Royal Astron Soc Monthly Notices Geophys Supp — Royal Astronomical Society. Monthly Notices. Geophysical Supplements
Royal Astron Soc Quart Jour — Royal Astronomical Society. Quarterly Journal
Royal Aust Army Ed Corps News — Royal Australian Army. Educational Corps. Newsletter
Royal Aust Chem Inst J & Proc — Royal Australian Chemical Institute. Journal and Proceedings
Royal Aust Chem Inst Proc — Royal Australian Chemical Institute. Proceedings
Royal Aust Hist Soc J — Royal Australian Historical Society. Journal and Proceedings
Royal Aust Hist Soc J & Proc — Royal Australian Historical Society. Journal and Proceedings
Royal Aust Hist Soc J Proc — Royal Australian Historical Society. Journal and Proceedings
Royal Australian Planning Inst Jnl — Royal Australian Planning Institute. Journal
Royal Auto — Revue. Royal Automobile Club de Belgique
Royalauto — Royalauto [*Royal Automobile Club of Victoria*] Journal
Royal Bank Can Mo Letter — Royal Bank of Canada. Monthly Letter
Royal Canad Inst Trans — Royal Canadian Institute. Transactions. University of Toronto
Royal Can Mounted Police Q — Royal Canadian Mounted Police Quarterly
Royal Col Inst Pr — Royal Colonial Institute Proceedings
Royal Econom Soc Prize Monograph — Royal Economics Society Prize Monograph
Royal Empire Soc News — Royal Empire Society. News
Royal Geog Soc Asia SA Branch Proc — Royal Geographical Society of Australasia. South Australian Branch. Proceedings
Royal Hist Soc Q Hist Misc — Royal Historical Society of Queensland. Historical Miscellanea
Royal Hist Soc QJ — Royal Historical Society of Queensland. Journal
Royal Hist Soc Trans — Royal Historical Society. Transactions
Royal Hort Soc J — Royal Horticultural Society. Journal
Royal Incorp Architects Scotland Q — Royal Incorporation of Architects in Scotland. Quarterly
Royal Inst Architects Ireland Yb — Royal Institute of the Architects Ireland Yearbook
Royal Inst of British Archts Trans — Royal Institute of British Architects. Transactions
Royal Microscopical Soc Proc — Royal Microscopical Society. Proceedings
Royal Ontario Mus Div Zoology and Palaeontology Contr — Royal Ontario Museum. Division of Zoology and Palaeontology. Contributions
Royal Ont Mus Archaeol Bul — Royal Ontario Museum of Archaeology. Bulletin. University of Toronto
Royal Ont Mus Archaeol Bull — Royal Ontario Museum of Archaeology. Bulletin
Royal Perth Hospital J — Royal Perth Hospital. Journal
Royal Prince Alfred Hospital J — Royal Prince Alfred Hospital. Journal
Royal Soc Arts Jnl — Royal Society of Arts. Journal
Royal Soc Canada Proc — Royal Society of Canada. Proceedings
Royal Soc Hlth J — Royal Society of Health. Journal
Royal Soc NSW J & Proc — Royal Society of New South Wales. Journal and Proceedings
Royal Soc of Health Jnl — Royal Society of Health. Journal
Royal Soc Q Proc — Royal Society of Queensland. Proceedings
Royal Soc SA Trans — Royal Society of South Australia. Transactions
Royal Soc Tasmania Papers and Proc — Royal Society of Tasmania. Papers and Proceedings
Royal Soc Tas Papers & Proc — Royal Society of Tasmania. Papers and Proceedings
Royal Soc Ulster Architects Yb — Royal Society of Ulster Architects Yearbook and Directory
Royal Soc Vic Proc — Royal Society of Victoria. Proceedings
Royal Soc Victoria Proc — Royal Society of Victoria. Proceedings
Royal Statis Soc J Ser A Gen — Journal. Royal Statistical Society. Series A. General
Royalton R — Royalton Review
Royal Unit Ser Inst Jour — Royal United Service Institution. Journal
Royal Zoological Soc NSW Proc — Royal Zoological Society of New South Wales. Proceedings
Roy Anthropol Inst J — Royal Anthropological Institute of Great Britain and Ireland. Journal
Roy Arch Inst Can J — Royal Architectural Institute of Canada. Journal
Roy Astron Soc Mem — Royal Astronomical Society. Memoirs
Roy Aust Hist J — Royal Australian Historical Society. Journal
Roy Aust Hist Soc J Proc — Royal Australian Historical Society. Journal and Proceedings
Roy Can Inst Trans — Royal Canadian Institute. Transactions
Roy Col Inst Proc — Royal Colonial Institute. Proceedings
Roy Eng J — Royal Engineers Journal
Roy Geog Soc Proc — Royal Geographical Society. Proceedings
Roy His S — Royal Historical Society. Transactions
Roy Hist Soc Qld Hist Misc — Royal Historical Society of Queensland. Historical Miscellanea
Roy Hist Soc Qld J — Royal Historical Society of Queensland. Journal
Roy Hist Soc Tr — Royal Historical Society. Transactions
Roy Hist Soc Trans — Royal Historical Society. Transactions
Roy Hist Soc Vic News — Royal Historical Society of Victoria. Newsletter
Roy Hort Soc J — Royal Horticultural Society. Journal
Roy Inst Brit Arch J — Royal Institute of British Architects. Journal
Roy Inst Nav Architects Quart Trans — Royal Institution of Naval Architects [*London*]. Quarterly Transactions

Roy Inst Ph — Royal Institute of Philosophy. Lectures
Roy Inst Philos Suppl — Royal Institute of Philosophy Supplement
Roy Irish Acad Proc — Royal Irish Academy. Proceedings
Roy Med Chir Soc Glasgow Tr — Royal Medico-Chirurgical Society of Glasgow. Transactions
Roy Meteorol Soc Q J — Royal Meteorological Society. Quarterly Journal
Roy Microscop Soc Proc — Royal Microscopical Society. Proceedings
Roy Micros Soc J — Royal Microscopical Society. Journal
Roy Soc Arts J — Royal Society of Arts. Journal
Roy Soc Can — Royal Society of Canada. Proceedings and Transactions
Roy Soc Can Proc — Royal Society of Canada. Proceedings
Roy Soc Edinb Trans — Royal Society of Edinburgh. Transactions
Roy Soc Hea — Royal Society of Health. Journal
Roy Soc London Proc — Royal Society of London. Proceedings
Roy Soc Lond Philos Trans — Royal Society of London. Philosophical Transactions
Roy Soc Lond Proc — Royal Society of London. Proceedings
Roy Soc NSW J — Royal Society of New South Wales. Journal
Roy Soc NSW J & Proc — Royal Society of New South Wales. Journal and Proceedings
Roy Soc NZ Bull — Royal Society of New Zealand. Bulletin
Roy Soc NZ J — Royal Society of New Zealand. Journal
Roy Soc NZ Proc — Royal Society of New Zealand. Proceedings
Roy Soc NZ Trans — Royal Society of New Zealand. Transactions
Roy Soc NZ Trans Bot — Royal Society of New Zealand. Transactions. Botany
Roy Soc NZ Trans Earth Sci — Royal Society of New Zealand. Transactions. Earth Sciences
Roy Soc NZ Trans Gen — Royal Society of New Zealand. Transactions. General
Roy Soc NZ Trans Geol — Royal Society of New Zealand. Transactions. Geology
Roy Soc NZ Trans Zool — Royal Society of New Zealand. Transactions. Zoology
Roy Soc of Canada Trans — Royal Society of Canada. Proceedings and Transactions
Roy Soc of Edinburgh Trans — Royal Society of Edinburgh. Transactions
Roy Soc of London Philos Trans — Royal Society of London. Philosophical Transactions
Roy Soc of New South Wales Jour and Proc — Royal Society of New South Wales. Journal and Proceedings
Roy Soc Proc — Proceedings. Royal Society
Roy Soc Qld Proc — Royal Society of Queensland. Proceedings
Roy Soc SA Trans — Royal Society of South Australia. Transactions
Roy Soc So Africa Trans — Royal Society of South Africa. Transactions
Roy Soc Tas Papers — Royal Society of Tasmania. Papers and Proceedings
Roy Soc Vic Proc — Royal Society of Victoria. Proceedings
Roy Soc Victoria Proc — Royal Society of Victoria. Proceedings
Roy Soc WA J — Royal Society of Western Australia. Journal
Roy Statist Soc Lecture Note Ser — Royal Statistical Society Lecture Note Series
Roy Stat Soc J — Royal Statistical Society. Journal
Roy Telev Soc J — Royal Television Society. Journal
Roy Town Plan Inst — Royal Town Planning Institute. Journal
Roy United Serv Inst J — Royal United Service Institution. Journal
Roy West Aust Hist Soc J Proc — Royal Western Australian Historical Society. Journal and Proceedings
Roy Zool Soc NSW Proc — Royal Zoological Society of New South Wales. Proceedings
Roz Cesk Akad — Rozpravy Ceskoslovenske Akademie Ved
Rozhl Chir — Rozhledy v Chirurgii
Rozhl Tuberk Nemocech Plicn — Rozhledy v Tuberkulose a v Nemocech Plicnich
Roz Narod Tech Muz Praze — Rozpravy Narodniho Technickeho Muzea v Praze
Rozpr Akad Roln Szczecinie — Rozprawy. Akademia Rolnicza w Szczecinie
Rozpr Akad Umiejetn Wydz Mat Przyr — Rozprawy Akademii Umiejetnosci. Wydzial Matematyczno-Przyrodniczy
Rozpravy CSAV — Rozpravy Ceskoslovenske Akademie Ved
Rozprawy & Sprawozdania Muz N Krakow — Rozprawy i Sprawozdania Muzeum Narodwego w Krakow
Rozprawy Elektrotech — Rozprawy Elektrotechniczne. Polska Akademia Nauk. Instytut Technologii Elektronowej.
Rozprawy Politech Poznan — Rozprawy. Politechnika Poznanska
Rozpr Cesk Akad Rada Tech Ved — Rozpravy Ceskoslovenske Akademie Ved. Rada Technickych Ved
Rozpr Cesk Akad Ved Rada Mat Prir Ved — Rozpravy Ceskoslovenske Akademie Ved. Rada Matematickych a Prirodnich Ved
Rozpr Cesk Akad Ved Rada Tech Ved — Rozpravy Ceskoslovenske Akademie Ved. Rada Technickych Ved
Rozpr Ceske Acad Cisare Frantiska Josefa Vedy Tr 2 Vedy Math — Rozpravy Ceske Akademie Cisare Frantiska Josefa Pro Vedy, Slovesnost a Umeni. Trida 2. Vedy Mathematicke, Prirodni
Rozpr Elektrotech — Rozprawy Elektrotechniczne
Rozpr Gdansk Tow Nauk Wydz 3 — Rozprawy Gdanskie Towarzystwo Naukowe. Wydzial 3. NaukMatematyczno-Przyrodniczych
Rozpr Hydrotech — Rozprawy Hydrotechniczne
Rozpr Inz — Rozprawy Inzynierskie
Rozpr Monogr — Rozprawy Monografie
Rozpr Nauk Szk Gl Gospod Wiejsk Akad Roln Warszawie — Rozprawy Naukowe Szkoly Glownej Gospodarstwa Wiejskiego-AkademiiRolniczej w Warszawie
Rozpr Politech Poznan — Rozprawy. Politechnika Poznanska
Rozpr Politech Rzeszowska Im Ignacego Lukasiewicza — Rozprawy. Politechnika Rzeszowska Imienia Ignacego Lukasiewicza
Rozpr Spraw Inst Badawczy Lasow Panstw — Rozprawy i Sprawozdania. Instytut Badawczy Lasow Panstwowych
Rozpr Spraw Inst Badawczy Lesn — Rozprawy i Sprawozdania. Instytut Badawczy Lesnictwa
Rozpr Statniho Geol Ustavu Cesk Repub — Rozpravy Statniho Geologickeho Ustavu Ceskoslovenske Republiky
Rozpr Ustred Ustavu Geol — Rozpravy Ustredniho Ustavu Geologickeho

Rozpr Wydz 3 Nauk Mat Przyr Gdansk Tow Nauk — Rozprawy Wydzialu 3. Nauk Matematyczno-Przyrodniczych. Gdanskie Towarzystwo Naukowe
Rozpr Wydz Lek Pol Akad Umiejet — Rozprawy Wydzialu Lekarskiego. Polska Akademia Umiejetnosci
Rozpr Wydz Mat Przyr Pol Akad Umiejet Dzial A — Rozprawy Wydzialu Matematyczno-Przyrodniczego. Polska AkademiaUmiejetnosci. Dzial A. Nauki Matematyczno-Fizyczne
Rozpr Wydz Mat Przyr Pol Akad Umiejet Dzial B — Rozprawy Wydzialu Matematyczno-Przyrodniczego. Polska AkademiaUmiejetnosci. Dzial B. Nauki Biologiczne
Rozpr Wydz Nauk Med Pol Akad Nauk — Rozprawy Wydzialu Nauk Medyczynch Polska Akademia Nauk
Rozpr Wyzsza Szk Roln Szczecinie — Rozprawy. Wyzsza Szkola Rolnicza w Szczecinie
RP — Regulatory Peptides
RP — Renaissance Papers
RP — Repertoire de Peintures Grecques et Romaines
RP — Review of Politics
RP — Revista de Portugal
RP — Revue de Paris
RP — Revue de Philologie, de Litterature, et d'Histoire Anciennes
RP — Revue de Phonetique
RP — Revue Philosophique
RP — Rio Piedras
RP — Rivista di Parasitologia
RP — Romance Philology
RPA — British Plastics and Rubber
RPA — Revista Pan-America
RPa — Revue de Paris
RPA — Revue de Phonetique Appliquee
RPA — Revue Pratique d'Apologetique
RPA — RPA [*Royal Prince Alfred Hospital*] Magazine
RPAA — Rendiconti. Pontificia Accademia di Archeologia
R Pac — Revue du Pacifique. Etudes de Litterature Francaise
RPACA — Reports on the Progress of Applied Chemistry
RPACDV — Australia. Commonwealth Scientific and Industrial Research Organisation. Division of Applied Organic Chemistry. Research Report
RPAHS — Report. Proceedings. American Historical Society
RPal — Revue Paladienne
R Palaeobot & Palynol — Review of Palaeobotany and Palynology
RPall — Revue Palladienne
R Pallad — Revue Palladienne
RPAN — Revista de Preistorie si Antichitati Nationale
RP and P — Romanticism Past and Present
R Par — Revue de Paris
RPARA — Rendiconti. Pontificia Accademia Romana di Archologia
R Paraguaya Sociol — Revista Paraguaya de Sociologia
RPAS — Repertoire de Prehistoire et d'Archeologie de la Suisse
RPAS — Review. Polish Academy of Sciences
RPASDB — Reviews in Pure and Applied Pharmacological Sciences
R Pays Est — Revue des Pays de l'Est
RPB — Revue Philomathique de Bordeaux et du Sud-Ouest
RPB — Revue Protestante Belge
Rp B Bk R — Reprint Bulletin. Book Reviews
RPC — Revista del Pensamiento Centroamericano. Consejo Superior de la Empresa Privada
RPCSB — Rivista di Patologia Clinica e Sperimentale
RPD — Radiation Protection Dosimetry
RPD — Review of Public Data Use
RPD & TM — Reports of Patent, Design, and Trade Mark Cases
RPDC — Revue Pratique de Droit Commercial, Financier, et Fiscal
RPDED — Revue du Palais de la Deouverte
RPDQDK — Queensland. Department of Forestry. Research Paper
RPDS — Revista Paraguaya de Sociologia
RPE — Revue d'Etudes Comparatives Est-Ouest
RPE — Rivista di Politica Economica
RPed — Revue Pedagogic
R Penitent De Pologne — Revue Penitentiaire de Pologne
R Penitent Et De Dr Pen — Revue Penitentiaire et de Droit Penal
R Pernambucana Desenvolvimento — Revista Pernambucana de Desenvolvimento
R Peruana Derecho Internac — Revista Peruana de Derecho Internacional
RPF — Revista Portuguesa de Filologia
RPF — Revista Portuguesa de Filosofia
RPF — Revue de la Pensee Francaise
RPFADG — Forests Department of Western Australia. Research Paper
RPFB — Rivista Portuguesa de Filosofia. Supplement Bibliografico
RPFCA — Revue Pratique du Froid et du Conditionnement de l'Air [*Later, Journal RPF*]
RPFE — Revue Philosophique de la France et de l'Etranger
RPFilos — Revista Portuguesa de Filosofia
RPFL — Revue de Philologie Francaise et de Litterature
RPFP — Revue de Philologie Francaise et Provencale
R P Fr — Revue de la Pensee Francaise
RPFUB — Radovi Poljoprivrednog Fakulteta Univerziteta u Sarajevu
RPFWDE — US Fish and Wildlife Service. Resource Publication
RPGA — Revista de Psicologia General Aplicada
RPGPA — Recent Publications on Governmental Problems
RPGR — Repertoire de Peintures Grecques et Romaines
RPH — Revista Portuguesa de Historia
RPH — Revue Belge de Philologie et d'Histoire
RPh — Revue de Philologie
RPh — Revue de Philologie, de Litterature, et d'Histoire Anciennes
RPh — Revue de Philosophie
R Ph — Revue Philosophique de la France et de l'Etranger

RPh — Romance Philology
R Ph F E — Revue Philosophique de la France et de l'Etranger
RPhil — Revue de Philosophie
R Phil — Revue Philosophique de la France et de l'Etranger
R Phil Louvain — Revue Philosophique de Louvain
R Philos — Revue Philosophique
R Philos — Revue Philosophique de la France et de l'Etranger
RPHJ — Royal Perth Hospital. Journal
RPhL — Revue Philosophique de Louvain
RphLH — Revue de Philologie, de Litterature, et d'Histoire Anciennes
R Ph LHA — Revue de Philologie de Litterature et d'Histoire Anciennes
RPHRA — Recent Progress in Hormone Research
RPhs — Revue Philosophique
R Phys Soc Edinb Pr — Royal Physical Society of Edinburgh. Proceedings
R Phys Soc Edinb Proc — Royal Physical Society of Edinburgh. Proceedings
RPI — Rassegna di Politica Internazionale
RPI — Religious Periodicals Index
RPI — Revue Politique Internationale
RPJ — Revue de la Pensee Juive
RPL — Review of the River Plate
RPL — Revisor Politico y Literario
RPL — Revue Philosophique de Louvain
RPL — Revue Politique et Litteraire
RPLAA — Reinforced Plastics
R Plan Desarr (Bogota) — Revista de Planeacion y Desarrollo (Bogota)
R Planeacion y Desarrollo — Revista de Planeacion y Desarrollo
R Plastiq — Revue Generale des Caoutchoucs et Plastiques
RPLH — Revue de Philologie, de Litterature, et d'Histoire Anciennes
RPLHA — Revue de Philologie, de Litterature, et d'Histoire Anciennes. Troisieme Serie
RPLHD — Revista Padurilor-Industria Lemnului. Celuloza si Hirtie. Seria Celuloza si Hirtie
RPLit — Res Publica Litterarum
RP Lit — Res Publica Litterarum. Studies in the Classical Tradition
RPLLD — Revista Padurilor-Industria Lemnului. Celuloza si Hirtie. Seria Industria Lemnului
RPLPA — Reviews of Plasma Physics
Rpm Anal C — Repertorium der Analytischen Chemie fuer Handel, Gewerbe und Oeffentliche Gesundheitspflege
RPMDA — Recenti Progressi in Medicina
RPMDDQ — Malaysia. Ministry of Agriculture and Rural Development. Risalah Penerangan
RPMKA — Rocznik Pomorskiej Akademii Medycznej Imienia Generala Karola Swierczewskiego wSzczecinie
RPMKAA — Annales Academiae Medicae Stetinensis
Rpm Mth — Repertorium der Literarischen Arbeiten aus dem Gebiete der Reinen und Angewandten Mathematik
Rpm Phm — Repertorium fuer die Pharmacie
Rpm Ps — Repertorium der Physik. Enthaltend eine Vollstaendige Zusammenstellung der neuern Fortschritte dieser Wissenschaft
RPMSBZ — Roczniki Pomorska Akademia Medyczna Imienia Generala Karola Swierczewskiego w Szczecinie. Suplement
RPN — Revue Pratique du Notariat
RPNB — Revue Pratique du Notariat Belge
RPO — Religion and Public Order
R Pol — Review of Politics
R Pol Agr — Rivista di Politica Agraria
R Pol Econ Terza Ser — Revista di Politica Economica. Terza Serie
R Pol et Litt — Revue Politique et Litteraire
R Pol et Parlementaire — Revue Politique et Parlementaire
R Pol Internac — Revista de Politica Internacional
R Polish L & Econ — Review of Polish Law and Economics
R Polit — Review of Politics
R Polit et Litt — Revue Politique et Litteraire
R Politics — Review of Politics
R Polit Int — Revue de Politique Internationale
R Polit Int (Madrid) — Revista de Politica Internacional (Madrid)
R Polit Parl — Revue Politique et Parlementaire
R Polit Soc — Revista de Politica Social
R Polon De Leg Civile Et Crim — Revue Polonaise de Legislation Civile et Criminelle
R Pol Soc — Revista de Politica Social
R Porto — Revista. Faculdade de Letras. Serie de Historia. Universidade do Porto
R Portug Hist — Revista Portuguesa de Historia
RPP — Real Property Practice
RPP — Real Property, Probate, and Trust Journal
RPP — Review of Public Personnel Administration
RPP — Revue des Pays de l'Est
RPP — Revue Politique et Parlementaire
RPPA — Revue Politique et Parlementaire
RPPHA — Reports on Progress in Physics
RPPJA — Reports on Progress in Polymer Physics (Japan)
RPPS — Revue du Progres Politique, Social et Litteraire
RPPsy — Revue de Psychokladologie et Psychotheie
RPQEA — Radiophysics and Quantum Electronics
RPR — Real Property Reports
RPR — Reintegro (Puerto Rico)
RPR — Research Project Report
RPR — Review of Philosophy and Religion
RPR — Roemische Privatrecht
RPrag — Romanistica Pragensia
RPrat — Revue Pratique d'Apologetique
R Prat Dr Soc — Revue Pratique de Droit Social
R Pratique Questions Commer et Econs — Revue Pratique des Questions Commerciales et Economiques

R Prehist — Revue Prehistorique
RPRFA — Revue Pratique du Froid [Later, Journal RPF]
RPRGP — Regesta Pontificum Romanorum. Germania Pontificia
RPRIP — Regesta Pontificum Romanorum. Italia Pontificia
RPRODG — Annual Research Reviews. Renal Prostaglandins
R Prop Prob and Tr J — Real Property, Probate, and Trust Journal
RPRRA — Revue de Physique. Academie de la Republique Populaire Roumaine
RPS — Revista de Politica Social
RPS — Revue Pratique des Societes Civiles et Commerciales
RPSHED — Recueil des Publications. Societe Havraise d'Etudes Diverses
R Psicol Gen Apl — Revista de Psicologia General y Aplicada
RPSoc — Revue Pratique des Societes Civiles et Commerciales
RPsP — Revue de Psychologie des Peuples
RPSR — Rivista di Pedagogia e Scienze Religiose
RPS Subj Cat — Royal Photographic Society of Great Britain. Library Catalogue. Part 2. SubjectCatalogue
RPSTA — Rivista di Parassitologia
R Psych — Reading Psychology
RPTEA — Reviews of Petroleum Technology
RPTGA — Rocznik Polskiego Towarzystwa Geologicznego
RPTOW — Rocznik Polskiego Towarzystwa
Rpt Superv Surg Gen Mar Hosp Wash — Report. Supervising Surgeon-General. Marine Hospital (Washington)
RPu — Rassegna Pugliese
R Public Data Use — Review of Public Data Use
RPUSSR — Research Program of the USSR. New York Series
RPVEAF — Revue de Pathologie Vegetale et d'Entomologie Agricole de France
RPW — Reformed and Presbyterian World
Rpyr — Revue des Pyrenees
RPZ — Rada Pomocy Zydom
RPZ — Religionspaedagogische Zeitfragen
RPZDA — Regelungstechnik und Prozess-Datenverarbeitung
RPZHA — Roczniki Panstwowego Zakladu Higieny
RQ — Reference Quarterly
RQ — Renaissance Quarterly
RQ — Restoration Quarterly
RQ — Revue de la Quinzaine
RQ — Revue de Qumran
RQ — Revue des Questions Historiques
RQ — Riverside Quarterly
RQ — Roemische Quartalschrift fuer Christliche Altertumskunde und fuer Kirchengeschichte
RQ — RQ. Reference Quarterly
RQA — Roemische Quartalschrift fuer Christliche Altertumskunde und fuer Kirchengeschichte
RQAHA — Research Quarterly. American Association for Health, Physical Education, and Recreation
RQAK — Roemische Quartalschrift fuer Christliche Altertumskunde und fuer Kirchengeschichte
RQCAK — Roemische Quartalschrift fuer Christliche Altertumskunde und fuer Kirchengeschichte
RQCAKG — Roemische Quartalschrift fuer Christliche Altertumskunde und fuer Kirchengeschichte
R Q Ch A K — Roemische Quartalschrift fuer Christliche Altertumskunde und fuer Kirchengeschichte
RQFA — Review of Quantitative Finance and Accounting
RQH — Revue des Questions Historiques
RQHist — Revue des Questions Historiques
RQIRA — Revista de Quimica Industrial (Rio De Janeiro)
RQK — Roemische Quartalschrift fuer Kirchengeschichte
RQPAA — Revista de Investigaciones Agropecuarias. Serie 4. Patologia Animal
RQS — Religioese Quellenschriften
RQS — Revue des Questions Scientifiques
RQS — Roemische Quartalschrift fuer Christliche Altertumskunde und fuer Kirchengeschichte
RQSc — Revue des Questions Scientifiques
RQu — Revue de Qumran
R Quest Hist — Revue des Questions Historiques
R QUM — Revue de Qumran
RR — Naval Research Reviews
RR — Record Research
RR — Record Review
RR — Records and Recording
RR — Reformed Review
RR — Repertoire de Reliefs Grecs et Romains
RR — Review for Religious
RR — Review of Religion
RR — Review of Reviews
RR — Revue de la Renaissance
RR — Rhetoric Review
RR — Ricerche Religiose
RR — Right Review
RR — Romanic Review
RR — Roman Revolution
RR — Russian Review
RRA — Review of Reviews
RRACD — Ciencia e Cultura (Sao Paulo). Suplemento
R Radical Pol Econ — Review of Radical Political Economics
R Radic Polit Econ — Review of Radical Political Economics
R Rad Pol Econ — Review of Radical Political Economics
RRAEA — Rendiconti. Riunione Annuale. Associazione Elettrotecnica Italiana
RRAL — Rendiconti. Reale Accademia Nazionale dei Lincei
RRALA — Radiochemical and Radioanalytical Letters
RRAM — Roman Rule in Asia Minor to the End of Third Century After Christ
RRBBA — Revue Roumaine de Biologie. Serie Botanique

RRBLB — United States Railroad Retirement Board. Law Bulletin
RRBODI — Brazilian Journal of Botany
RRB Q Rev — RRB [*Railroad Retirement Board*] Quarterly Review
RRB (Railroad Retirement Bd) Q R — RRB (Railroad Retirement Board) Quarterly Review
RRBVD — Revue Roumaine de Biologie. Serie Biologie Vegetale
RRBZA — Revue Roumaine de Biologie. Serie Zoologie
RRC — Coinage of the Roman Republic
RRC — Roman Republican Coinage
RRCGDX — Australia. Commonwealth Scientific and Industrial Research Organisation. Division of Animal Genetics. Research Report
RRCH — Roman Republican Coin Hoards
RRCHA — Revue Roumaine de Chimie
RRCOD — Resource Recovery and Conservation
RRCRB — Recent Results in Cancer Research
RRC (Rep) React Res Cent Kalpakkam — RRC (Report). Reactor Research Centre. Kalpakkam
RRDB — Research Results Data Base
RRDS — Regents Renaissance Drama Series
RRE — Review of Regional Economics and Business
RRE — Revue Russe d'Entomologie
RRef — Revue Reformee
R Regional Econ and Bus — Review of Regional Economics and Business
R Rel — Review for Religious
RRel — Review of Religion
R Relig Res — Review of Religious Research
R Rel Res — Review of Religious Research
Rren — Revue de la Renaissance
RRENA — Revue Roumaine d'Endocrinologie
RRERD — Resource Recovery and Energy Review
RRESA — Rastitel'nye Resursy
R Rest DS — Regents Restoration Drama Series
Rret — Revue Retrospective
RRETA — Reports. Research Institute of Electrical Communication. Tohoku University
RRev — Revue de la Revolution
RRev — Rijecka Revija
RREVA — Residue Reviews
RRFC — Rivista Rosminiana di Filosofia e di Cultura
RRFIA — Radiobiologia, Radioterapia, e Fisica Medica
RRG — Roemische Rechtsgeschichte
RRG — Roemische Religionsgeschichte
RRGA — Revue Roumaine de Geologie, Geophysique, et Geographie. Serie de Geographie
RRGAB — Rendiconti Romani di Gastroenterologia
RRGR — Repertoire de Reliefs Grecs et Romains
RRH — Revue Roumaine d'Histoire
RRHDAC — Reports on Rheumatic Diseases
RRI — Revista/Review Interamericana
R/RIA — Revista/Review Interamericana
RRIC (Rubber Res Inst Ceylon) Bull — RRIC (Rubber Research Institute of Ceylon) Bulletin
RRIL — Rendiconti. Reale Istituto Lombardo di Scienze e Lettere
RRIMA — Revue Roumaine d'Inframicrobiologie
RRIM Technol Ser Rep — RRIM [*Rubber Research Institute of Malaysia*] Technology Series Report
RRIM Train Man Soils Manage Soils Nutr Hevea — RRIM [*Rubber Research Institute of Malaysia*] Training Manual on Soils, Management of Soils, and Nutrition of Hevea
RRIS — Railroad Research Information Service
RRISL Bull — RRISL [*Rubber Research Institute of Sri Lanka*] Bulletin
RRI Sri Lanka Bull — RRISL (Rubber Research Institute of Sri Lanka) Bulletin
RRITA — Report. Research Institute of Science and Technology. Nihon University
R River Plate — Review of the River Plate
RRJaNS — Rodnoj i Russkij Jazyki v Nacional'noj Skole
RRL — Revue Roumaine de Linguistique
RRL Rep (UK) — RRL [*Road Research Laboratory*] Report (UK)
RRLTD — Report. Research Laboratory of Engineering Materials. Tokyo Institute of Technology
RRMIA — Revue Roumaine de Medecine Interne [*Later, Revue Roumaine de Medecine. Medecine Interne*]
RRMPB — Revue Roumaine de Mathematiques Pures et Appliquees
RRMTA — Reactor Materials
RRN — Running Research News
RRNGA — Razvedka i Razrabotka Neftyanykh i Gazovykh Mestorozhdenii
RRNUA — Revue Roumaine de Neurologie [*Later, Revue Roumaine de Medecine. Serie Neurologie et Psychiatrie*]
RRo — Rivista Rosminiana
R Roumaine — Revue Roumaine d'Histoire de l'Art
R Roumaine Hist — Revue Roumaine d'Histoire
R Roumaine Hist Art — Revue Roumaine d'Histoire de l'Art
R Roumaine Sciences Socs Ser Sciences Econs — Revue Roumaine des Sciences Sociales. Serie de Sciences Economiques
R Roumaine Sciences Socs Ser Sciences Juridiques — Revue Roumaine des Sciences Sociales. Serie de Sciences Juridiques
R Roum Et Int — Revue Roumaine d'Etudes Internationales
R Roum Hist — Revue Roumaine d'Histoire
R Roum Sci Soc — Revue Roumaine des Sciences Sociales
R Roum Sci Soc Ser Philos Logique — Revue Roumaine des Sciences Sociales. Serie de Philosophie et de Logique
R Roum Sci Soc Ser Sci Econ — Revue Roumaine des Sciences Sociales. Serie de Sciences Economiques
R Roum Sci Soc Ser Sci Jur — Revue Roumaine des Sciences Sociales. Serie de Sciences Juridiques

R Roum Sci Soc Ser Sociol — Revue Roumaine des Sciences Sociales. Serie de Sociologie
RRP — Reviews of Research and Practice. Institute for Research into Mental and Multiple Handicap
RRP — Revue des Religions (Paris)
RRPE — Union for Radical Review of Radical Political Economics
RRPHA — Revue Roumaine de Physiologie
RRPQA — Revue Roumaine de Physique
RRPRD — RTP. Regelungstechnische Praxis
RRPSDW — Reading Psychology
RRQ — Reading Research Quarterly
RRQ — Romanic Review Quarterly
RRR — Regensbergs Roemische Reihe
RRR — Review of Religions (Rabwah)
RRR — Review of Religious Research
RRREA — Radiation Research Reviews
RRRED — Reclamation and Revegetation Research
R Rs — Review of Reviews
RRStM — Review for Religious (St. Mary's)
RRTCD — Tokyo Denki Daigaku Kenkyu Hokoku
RRUSEO — University of Miami. Rosenstiel School of Marine and Atmospheric Science. Research Review
RRVRA — Revue Roumaine de Virologie
RRWBDG — Report of Research. Worcester Foundation for Experimental Biology
RRWL — Renaissance and Renascences in Western Literature
RS — Mission de Has Shamra
RS — Raccolta Sistematica del Diritto Federale
RS — Realites Secretes
RS — Rechtsstrijd
RS — Recueil Systematique du Droit Federal
RS — Reference Shelf
RS — Reforme Sociale
RS — Religious Studies
RS — Reprint of the Statutes of New Zealand
RS — Research on Steroids
RS — Research Studies
RS — Revista Scientifica
RS — Revue de Synthese
RS — Revue Suisse
RS — Ricerche Slavistiche
RS — Rocznik Slawistyczny
RS — Rolling Stone
RS — Romanische Studien
RS — Roma Sotteranea Cristiana
RS — Rural Society
RS — Rural Sociology
RSA — Report from South Africa
RSA — Revue Internationale des Sciences Administratives
RSA — Rivista di Storia Antica
RSA — Royal Society of Arts. Journal
RSAA — Relaciones de la Sociedad Argentina de Antropologia
RSAA — Revue Suisse d'Art et d'Archeologie
RSAA — Rivista di Storia, Arte Archeologia
RSABA — Revista. Sociedad Argentina de Biologia
RSAC — Recueil des Notices et Memoires. Societe Archeologique de Constantine
RSAC — Recueil des Notices et Memoires. Societe Archeologiques, Historique, et Geographique du Departement de Constantine
R Saintonge — Revue de la Saintonge et de l'Aunis
RSAL — Reports. Research Committee. Society of Antiquaries of London
RSAM — Revista de la Sociedad de los Amigos de la Arqueologia de Montevideo
R San Inst Jnl — Royal Sanitary Institute. Journal
R Sanit Inst J — Royal Sanitary Institute. Journal
RSAP — Regional Science Association. Papers and Proceedings
RSAT — Recueil. Societe de Prehistoire et d'Archeologie de Tebessa
RSAUN — Revista de la Seccion Arqueologica de la Universidad Nacional del Cuzco
RSav — Revue de Savoie
R Sav — Revue Savoisienne
RSB — Revista. Sociedad Bolivariana
RSB — Rivista di Studi Bizantini e Neoellenici
RSB — Rivista Storica Benedettina
RSB — Roller Skating Business Magazine
RSBC — Revised Statutes of British Columbia
R Sb Ekonom Promysl D — Referativnyi Sbornik. Ekonomika Promyslennosti. D. Primenenie Matematiceskih Metodov v Ekonomiceskih Issledovanijah i Planirovanii
RSBKDD — Reports. State Biological Survey of Kansas
RSBN — Rivista di Studi Bizantini e Neoellenici
RS Bodin — Recueil. Societe Jean Bodin pour l'Histoire Comparative des Institutions
RSBTA3 — Rio Grande Do Sul. Departamento Producao Animal. Divisao de Zootecnia. Servico de Experimentacao Zootecnia. Boletim Tecnico
RSBV — Revista. Sociedad Bolivariana de Venezuela
RSC — Railway Systems Control
RSC — Revised Statues of Canada
Rsc — Revue Scientifique (Revue Rose)
RSC — Revue Sociale Catholique
RSC — Rivista di Studi Classici
RSC — Rivista di Studi Crociani
RSC — Roma Sotteranea Cristiana
RSCCDS — Reactivity and Structure Concepts in Organic Chemistry
R Sc Eco — Revue des Sciences Economiques
RScH — Revue des Sciences Humaines
R Sch Mines J — Royal School of Mines. Journal
RSCHS — Record. Scottish Church History Society

R Sc Hum — Revue des Sciences Humaines
R Sci — Revue Scientifique
RSCI — Rivista di Storia della Chiesa in Italia
R Science Fin — Revue de Science Financiere
R Sciences Econs — Revue des Sciences Economiques
R Sci Financ — Revue de Science Financiere
R Sci Hum — Revue des Sciences Humaines
R Sci Instr — Review of Scientific Instruments
R Sci Philos & Theol — Revue des Sciences Philosophiques et Theologiques
R Sci Ph Th — Revue des Sciences Philosophiques et Theologiques
R Sci Pol — Revue des Sciences Politiques
R Sci Preistor — Rivista di Scienze Preistoriche
R Sci Rel — Revue des Sciences Religieuses
R Sci Soc France Est — Revue des Sciences Sociales de la France de l'Est
RSCL — Rivista di Studi Classici
RSCO — Rules of the Supreme Court, Order
R Scolaire — Revue Scolaire
RSCom — Revue Belge des Sciences Commerciales
R Scott Mus Inf Ser Geol — Royal Scottish Museum. Information Series. Geology
RSCP — Revista de la Sociedad Cientifica del Paraguay
RScP — Revue Scientifique (Paris)
RScPhilT — Revue des Sciences Philosophiques et Theologiques
RscPhTh — Revue des Sciences Philosophiques et Theologiques
R Sc Pr — Rivista di Scienze Preistoriche
Rs C Ps S J — Journal of the Russian Chemical Society and of the Physical Society of the Imperial University of St. Petersburg
RSCQAX — Riviera Scientifique
RScR — Revue des Sciences Religieuses
RSCr — Roma Sotterranea Cristiana
RScRel — Revue des Sciences Religieuses
R Sc Relig — Recherches de Science Religieuse
R Sc Relig — Revue des Sciences Religieuses
Rs C S J — Journal of the Russian Chemical Society
RSCST — Rivista Storico-Critica delle Scienze Teologiche
RSCT — Royal Society of Canada. Transactions
RSDB — SCB [*Statistiska Centralbyran*] Regional Statistical Data Base
RSDI — Rivista di Storia del Diritto Italiano
RSE — Rassegna di Studi Etiopici
RSE — Renewable Sources of Energy
RSE — Review of Social Economy
RSE — Revue des Sciences Ecclesiastiques
RSE — Revue des Sciences Economiques
RSE — Revue. Societe d'Etudes et d'Expansion
RSE — Rivista di Storia Economica
RSE — Romanische Studien. Edited by Emil Ebering
RSE — Rutgers Studies in English
RSEA — Revue de Sud-Est Asiatique
R Se As Stud — Review of Southeast Asian Studies
RSEc — Revue des Sciences Ecclesiastiques
RSEc — Revue des Sciences Economiques
R Secur Soc — Revue de la Securite Sociale
RSEEA — Remote Sensing of Environment
RSEH — Revue. Societe des Etudes Historiques
RSEHA — Revue Semitique d'Epigraphie et d'Histoire Ancienne
R Seneg Dr — Revue Senegalaise de Droit
R Servizio Soc — Rivista di Servizio Sociale
RSESC — Revue des Sciences Ecclesiastiques et la Science Catholique Reunies
RSEt — Rassegna di Studi Etiopici
RSF — Rassegna di Scienze Filosofiche
RSF — Rassegna di Studi Francesi
RSF — Revue de Science Financiere
RSF — Rivista Critica di Storia della Filosofia
RSF — Rivista di Storia della Filosofia
RSFB — Revista de Santa Fe y Bogota
RSFFA — Rendiconti. Scuola Internazionale di Fisica "Enrico Fermi"
RSFI — Rivista di Storia della Filosofia
RSFII — Rassegna di Scienze Filosofiche
RSFMA — Rivista Sperimentale di Freniatria e Medicina Legale delle Alienazioni Mentali
RSFPA — Revista de la Sanidad de las Fuerzas Policiales del Peru
RSFR — Rivista di Studi Filosofici e Religiosi
RSFSA — Rendiconti. Seminario della Facolta di Scienze. Universita di Cagliari
RSG — Recueil. Societe de Geographie
RSG — Revue des Sciences Generales et Appliquees
RSGA — Revista de la Sociedad Geografica Argentina
RSGG — Recht und Staat in Geschichte und Gegenwart
RSGPB — Rinsan Shikenjo Geppo
RSGR — Repertoire de la Statuaire Grecque et Romaine
RSh — Revista Shell
RSH — Revue des Sciences Humaines
RSH — Revue de Synthese Historique
RSH — Revue. Societe Historique
RSHC — Research in the Sociology of Health Care
RSHEA — Royal Society of Health. Journal
RSHG — Revue. Societe Haitienne d'Histoire, de Geographie, et de Geologie
RSHKA6 — Bulletin. Forestry and Forest Products Research Institute
RSHNDI — Annual Report. Hokkaido Branch. Forestry and Forest Products Research Institute
RSHum — Revue des Sciences Humaines
RSI — Review of Scientific Instruments
RSI — Rivista Storica Italiana
RSI — Roofing/Siding/Insulation
RSIDA — Research and Industry
R Signals Radar Estabi Newsl Res Rev — Royal Signals and Radar Establishment. Newsletter and Research Review

RSIJA — Journal. Royal College of Surgeons in Ireland
R Sind Estadist — Revista Sindical de Estadist
R Sindical Estadistica — Revista Sindical de Estadistica
RSIR — International Statistical Institute. Review
RSIt — Rivista Storica Italiana
RSITD — Revue Francaise d'Automatique, d'Informatique, et de Recherche Operationnelle. Serie Informatique Theorique
RSJB — Recueils. Societe Jean Bodin
RS KY Agric Exp Stn — RS. Kentucky Agricultural Experiment Station
RSI — Revue des Etudes Slaves
RSL — Ricerche Slavistiche
RSL — Rivista di Sintesi Litteraria
RSL — Rivista di Studi Liguri
RSI — Rocznik Slawistyczny
RSlav — Ricerche Slavistiche
RSlav — Romanoslavica
R S Leg F — Revue de Science et de Legislation Financiere
RSLF — Revue de Science et de Legislation Financiere
RSII — Radovi Slavenskog Instituta
RSLig — Rivista di Studi Liguri
RSLit — Riverside Studies in Literature
RSLMDZ — Swedish University of Agricultural Sciences. Department of Microbiology. Report
RSLR — Rivista di Storia e Letteratura Religiosa
RSLTDM — Swedish University of Agricultural Sciences. Department of Horticultural Science. Report
RSIU — Rocenka Slovanskeho Ustavu v Praze
RSLVDS — Swedish University of Agricultural Sciences. Department of Plant Husbandry. Report
RSM — Rivista Storico-Critica delle Scienze Mediche e Naturali
RSMFA — Rendiconti. Seminario Matematico e Fisico di Milano
RSMJA — Royal School of Mines. Journal
Rs Mod Physics — Reviews of Modern Physics
RSN — Revue Suisse de Numismatique
RSNRV — Repertorium Specierum Novarum Regni Vegetabilis
RSNS — Revista de Sciencias Naturais e Sociais
RSO — Resonans
RSO — Rivista degli Studi Orientali
R Soc — Revue des Societes
RSoc — Revue Socialiste
R Soc Antiq Ir J — Royal Society of Antiquaries of Ireland. Journal
R Soc Can — Royal Society of Canada. Transactions
R Soc Can Proc — Royal Society of Canada. Proceedings
R Soc Can Proc Trans — Royal Society of Canada. Proceedings and Transactions
R Soc Can Spec Publ — Royal Society of Canada. Special Publications
R Soc Can Symp — Royal Society of Canada. Symposium
R Soc Chem Annu Rep Sect A Inorg Chem — Royal Society of Chemistry. Annual Reports. Section A. Inorganic Chemistry
R Soc Chem Annu Rep Sect B — Royal Society of Chemistry. Annual Reports. Section B. Organic Chemistry
R Soc Chem Annu Rep Sect C — Royal Society of Chemistry. Annual Reports. Section C. PhysicalChemistry
R Soc Chem Faraday Discuss — Royal Society of Chemistry. Faraday Discussions
R Soc Chem Faraday Symp — Royal Society of Chemistry. Faraday Symposia
R Soc Chem Spec Publ — Royal Society of Chemistry. Special Publication
R Soc Econ — Review of Social Economy
R Soc Edinb Proc Sect B — Royal Society of Edinburgh. Proceedings. Section B. Biology
R Soc Edinburgh Commun Phys Sci — Royal Society of Edinburgh. Communications. Physical Sciences
R Soc Edinburgh Proc Sect A Math — Royal Society of Edinburgh. Proceedings. Section A. Mathematics
R Soc Edinburgh Proc Sect A Math Phys Sci — Royal Society of Edinburgh. Proceedings. Section A. Mathematical andPhysical Sciences
R Soc Edinburgh Proc Sect B Nat Environ — Royal Society of Edinburgh. Proceedings. Section B. Natural Environment
R Soc Edinburgh Trans — Royal Society of Edinburgh. Transactions
R Soc Edinburgh Trans Earth Sci — Royal Society of Edinburgh. Transactions. Earth Sciences
R Soc Esp Fis Quim Reun Bienal — Real Sociedad Espanola de Fisica y Quimica. Reunion Bienal
R Soc Et Expans — Revue. Societe d'Etudes et d'Expansion
R Soc Health Health Congr Pap — Royal Society for the Promotion of Health. Health Congress. Papers
R Soc Health Health Congr Pap Discuss — Royal Society of Health. Health Congress. Papers for Discussion
R Soc Health J — Royal Society of Health. Journal
R Social Economy — Review of Social Economy
R Sociol — Revija za Sociologiju
R Soc London Proc — Royal Society of London. Proceedings
R Soc London Proc A — Royal Society of London. Proceedings. Series A. Mathematical and Physical Sciences
R Soc London Proc Ser B — Royal Society of London. Proceedings. Series B. Biological Sciences
R Soc Lond Philos Trans — Royal Society of London. Philosophical Transactions
R Soc Lond Philos Trans Ser A — Royal Society of London. Philosophical Transactions. Series A
R Soc Lond Philos Trans Ser B — Royal Society of London. Philosophical Transactions. Series B
R Soc Lond Proc Ser B — Royal Society of London. Proceedings. Series B. Biological Sciences
R Soc Med J — Royal Society of Medicine. Journal
R Soc Med Serv Ltd Int Congr Symp Ser — Royal Society of Medicine Services Limited International Congress andSymposium Series

R Soc NR — Notes and Records. Royal Society of London
R Soc NSW Monogr — Royal Society of New South Wales. Monograph
R Soc NZ Bull — Royal Society of New Zealand. Bulletin
R Soc NZJ — Royal Society of New Zealand. Journal
R Soc NZ Proc — Royal Society of New Zealand. Proceedings
R Soc NZ Trans Proc — Royal Society of New Zealand. Transactions and Proceedings
R Soc Obit N — Obituary Notices. Royal Society of London
R Soc Promot Health J — Royal Society for the Promotion of Health. Journal
R Soc Queensl Proc — Royal Society of Queensland. Proceedings
R Soc S Afr Trans — Royal Society of South Africa. Transactions
R Soc S Aust Trans — Royal Society of South Australia. Transactions
R Soc Tasmania Pap Proc — Royal Society of Tasmania. Papers and Proceedings
R Soc Theory — Review of Social Theory
R Soc Victoria Proc — Royal Society of Victoria. Proceedings
R Soc West Aust J — Royal Society of Western Australia. Journal
RSOHJ — Royal Society of Health. Journal
RSOLB — Research Outlook
RSONA — Revue Stomato-Odontologique du Nord de la France
RS Or — Rivista degli Studi Orientali
RSov — Rassegna Sovietica
R S P — Abstracts of the Papers Printed in the Philosophical Transactions of the Royal Society of London from 1800 to 1843
RSP — Revue des Sciences Politiques
RSP — Rivista di Scienze Preistoriche
RSP — Rivista di Studi Pompeiani
RSPCR — Roma Sotterranea. Le Pitture delle Catacombe Romane
RSPH — Revista do Servico do Patrimonio Historico e Artistico Nacional [Rio de Janeiro]
RSPh — Revue des Sciences Philosophiques et Theologiques
RSPhTh — Revue des Sciences Philosophiques et Theologiques
RSPI — Rivista di Studi Politici Internazionali
RSPMB — Research in the Psychology of Music
RS Pomp — Rivista di Studi Pompeiani
RSPP — Revue Suisse de Psychologie Pure et Appliquee
RsprOLG — Rechtsprechung der Oberlandesgerichte auf dem Gebiete des Zivilrechts
Rs Ps C S J — Journal of the Russian Physico-Chemical Society of the Imperial University of St. Petersburg
RSPT — Revue des Sciences Philosophiques et Theologiques
RSPTA — Recherche Spatiale
RSPUB9 — Journal of Public Health
RSQ — Rhetoric Society. Quarterly
RSR — Rassegna Storica del Risorgimento
RSR — Recherches de Science Religieuse
RSR — Reference Services Review
RSR — Revue des Sciences Religieuses. Universite de Strasbourg
RSR — Rivista di Studi Religiosi
RSR — Roemisches Staatsrecht
RSRel — Revue des Sciences Religieuses. Universite de Strasbourg
RSRE Newsl Res Rev — RSRE [Royal Signals and RADAR Establishment] Newsletter and Research Review
RSRis — Rassegna Storica del Risorgimento
RSROD — Revue Francaise d'Automatique, d'Informatique, et de Recherche Operationnelle. Serie Recherche Operationnelle
RSRPB — Research and the Retarded
RSRS — Revue des Sciences Religieuses
RSRUS — Revue des Sciences Religieuses. Universite de Strasbourg
RSS — Rassegna Storica Salernitana
RSS — Revue de Securite Sociale
RSS — Revue du Seizieme Siecle
RSS — Rivista di Scienze Storiche
RSS — Royal Statistical Society. Journal
RSSAA — Revue Internationale des Services de Sante des Armees de Terre, de Mer, et de l'Air
RSSal — Rassegna Storica Salernitana
RSSCW — Research Studies. State College of Washington
RSSHN — Revue des Societes Svantes de Haute Normandie
RSSI — Radovi Staroslovenskog Instituta
RSSJ — Researches in the Social Sciences on Japan. East Asian Institute. Columbia University
RSSJA — Journal. Royal Statistical Society. Series C. Applied Statistics
RSSLI — Radovi Staroslavenskog Instituta
RSSME3 — Swedish University of Agricultural Sciences. Reports in Forest Ecology and Forest Soils
RSSMN — Rivista di Storia delle Scienze Mediche e Naturali
RSSND — Roessing
RSt — Research Studies
RST — Review of Economic Studies
RST — Revista do Supremo Tribunal
RST — Rivista di Studi Teatrali
RST — Rivista Storica Ticinese
RSt — Rolling Stone
RSt — Romanische Studien
RStA — Rivista di Storia Antica
RStAnt — Rivista di Storia Antica
R Statis Quebec — Revue Statistique du Quebec
R Statist (Bucuresti) — Revista de Statistica (Bucuresti)
R St Biz Neoell — Rivista di Studi Bizantini e Neoellenici
RStCr — Rivista Storico-Critica delle Scienze Teologiche
R St Fen — Rivista di Studi Fenici
R St Lig — Rivista di Studi Liguri
R St March — Rivista di Studi Marchigiani
RSTN — Resource Technology
R St O — Rivista degli Studi Orientali

R Stor Ant — Rivista di Storia Antica
R Stor Ant — Rivista Storica dell'Antichita
R Storia Contemporanea — Rivista di Storia Contemporanea
R Stor Italiana — Rivista Storica Italiana
R St Pomp — Rivista di Studi Pompeiani
R Str — Roemisches Strafrecht
R Stuart Pap — Royal Stuart Papers
RSTUD — Rivista di Scienza e Tecnologia degli Alimenti e di Nutrizione Umana
R Stud — Romanische Studien
R Stud Fen — Rivista di Studi Fenici
R Studi Eur — Rivista di Studi Europei
R Stud Liguri — Rivista di Studi Liguri
R Stud Or — Revista degli Studi Orientali
R St Wi — Recht, Staat, Wirtschaft
RSU — Regional Science and Urban Economics
RSU — Rocenka Slovanskeho Ustavu
RSUED — Regional Science and Urban Economics
R Suisse Zool — Revue Suisse de Zoologie
RSUNAC — Rassegna di Urologia e Nefrologia
RS Univ Ky Agric Exp Stn — RS. University of Kentucky. Agricultural Experiment Station
RSUSEV — Arkansas. Agricultural Experiment Station. Research Series
RSUTA — Reconstruction Surgery and Traumatology
RSV — Relgioese Stimmen der Voelker
RSV — Revista Signos de Valparaiso
RSVR — Roma. Rivista di Studi e di Vita Romana
R Swaziland Soc Sci Technol J — Royal Swaziland Society of Science and Technology. Journal
RSWB — Raumordnung, Stadtebau, Wohnungswesen, Bauwesen
R Swed Acad Eng Sci Proc — Royal Swedish Academy of Engineering Sciences. Proceedings
R Swed Inst Eng Res Proc — Royal Swedish Institute for Engineering Research. Proceedings
RSWSU — Research Studies. Washington State University
RSYCA — Railway Systems Control
R S Yearbook — Yearbook of the Royal Society of London
RSyn — Revue de Synthese
R Synd Suisse — Revue Syndicale Suisse
RSynH — Revue de Synthese Historique
RSZ — Revue Suisse de Zoologie. Annales de la Societe Zoologique Suisse et du Museum d'Histoire Naturelle de Geneve
RSZOA — Revue Suisse de Zoologie
RT — Rabbinische Texte
RT — Radio Times
RT — Reading Teacher
RT — Recherches Theatrales
RT — Rechtskundig Tijdschrift voor Belgie
RT — Recueil des Travaux Relatifs a la Philologie et a l'Archeologie Egyptiennes et Assyriennes
Rt — Regelungstechnik
RT — Religious Theatre
RT — Revista de Turismo [Asuncion]
RT — Revista dos Tribunais
RT — Revue du Travail
RT — Revue Theatrale
RT — Revue Thomiste
RT — Revue Trimestrielle
RT — Revue Tunisienne
RT — Revue Tunisienne des Sciences Medicales
RT — Rough Times [Formerly, Radical Therapist]
RT — Round Table
RT — Royal Tombs of the First Dynasty
RTA — Religious and Theological Abstracts
RTAE — Revue de Theologie et d'Action Evangelique
RTAM — Recherches de Theologie Ancienne et Medievale
R Tarn — Revue du Tarn
RTASM — Revue des Travaux. Academie des Sciences Morales et Politiques
RTASMP — Revue des Travaux et Comptes Rendus. Academie des Sciences Morales et Politiques
RTATD8 — Annual Report. Tokyo University of Agriculture and Technology
R Taxation Individuals — Review of Taxation of Individuals
RTB — Rechtskundig Tijdschrift voor Belgie
RTBCA — Revue Technique du Batiment et des Constructions Industrielles
RTBG — Record and Tape Buyer's Guide
RTBNA — Recueil des Travaux Botaniques Neerlandais
RTC — Recueil Tablettes Chaldeennes
RTC — Revue Trimestrielle Canadienne
RTCHP — Recueil de Travaux. Conference d'Histoire et de Philologie
RTC Met Cl J — RTC [Royal Technical College] Metallurgical Club. Journal
RTCPA — Recueil des Travaux Chimiques des Pays-Bas
RTD — Royal Tombs of the First Dynasty
RTDE — Revue Trimestrielle de Droit Europeen
RTDVA — Rechentechnik-Datenverarbeitung
RTE — Research in the Teaching of English
RTE — Revista de Tecnologia Educativa
RTE — RTE. Radio-TV-Electronics
R Tech Coll Metall Club J — Royal Technical College. Metallurgical Club. Journal
RTECS — Registry of Toxic Effects of Chemical Substances
RTEEA — Revue Roumaine des Sciences Techniques. Serie Electrotechnique et Energetique
RTEID — Revista Tecnica INTEVEP
RTel — Revista Teologica
R Telev Soc J — Royal Television Society. Journal
RTEMB5 — Revista Espanola de Micropaleontologia
RTESB — Radio-TV-Electronic Service [Later, RTE. Radio-TV-Electronic]

RTF — Revue Theologique Francaise
RTFL — Recueil de Travaux. Faculte des Lettres. Universite de Neuchatel
RTFR — Revista de Jurisprudencia do Tribunal Federal de Recursos
RTG — Recherches et Travaux. Universite de Grenoble
RTH — Retail Business. A Monthly Journal Concerned with Consumer Goods Markets, Marketing and Management, and Distribution in the United Kingdom
R Th — Revue de Theologie
RTh — Revue de Theologie et de Philosophie
RTh — Revue Theologique
RTh — Revue Thomiste
R Th A — Recherches de Theologie Ancienne et Medievale
RThAbstr — Religious and Theological Abstracts
RThAM — Recherches de Theologie Ancienne et Medievale
R Theol Louvain — Revue Theologique de Louvain
RThL — Revue Theologique de Louvain
RThom — Revue Thomiste
RThP — Revue Theologique (Paris)
RThPh — Revue de Theologie et de Philosophie
RThQR — Revue de Theologie et de Questions Religieuses
R Th R — Reformed Theological Review
RTI — Review of Taxation of Individuals
RTIA — RTIA. Revue Technique de l'Industrie Alimentaire
RTICBT — Communication. Department of Agricultural Research. Royal Tropical Institute
R Tiers-Monde — Revue Tiers-Monde
RTijd — Rechtskundig Tijdschrift
RTJ — Revista Trimestral de Jurisprudencia
RTK — Roczniki Teologiczno-Kanoniczne
RTKHA — Radiotekhnika (Kharkov)
RTKKUL — Roczniki Teologiczno-Kanoniczne. Katolickiego Uniwersytetu Lubelskiego
RTKL — Roczniki Teologiczno-Kanoniczne. Katolickiego Uniwersytetu Lubelskiego
RTL — Revue Theologique de Louvain
RTLXA — Revue Technique Luxembourgeoise
RTM — Revue des Temps Modernes
RTM — Rivista di Teologia Morale
RTMAA — Revue Roumaine des Sciences Techniques. Serie de Mecanique Appliquee
RTMTA — Revue Roumaine des Sciences Techniques. Serie de Metallurgie
RTN — RTN: Radio Television News
RTNLB — Rationalisierung
RTNT — Roczniki Towarzystwa Naukowego w Toruniu
RTO — Revue de Tourisme
RTODA — Rassegna Trimestrale di Odontoiatria
RTOPS — NASA [*National Aeronautics and Space Administration*] Research and Technology Objectives and Plans Summary
RTor — Rocznik Torunski
RTOSA — Revue de Medecine de Toulouse. Supplement
R Tourisme — Revue de Tourisme
RTP — Review of Theology and Philosophy
RTP — Revue de Theologie et de Philosophie
RTPE — Recueil de Travaux Relatifs a la Philologie et a l'Archeologie Egyptiennes et Assyriennes
RTPh — Revue de Theologie et de Philosophie
RTPhil — Revue de Theologie et de Philosophie
RTPI J — Royal Town Planning Institute. Journal
RTPL — Revue de Theologie et de Philosophie (Lausanne)
RTPM — Revista de Tradiciones Populares (Madrid)
RTP Regelungstech Prax — RTP. Regelungstechnische Praxis
RTR — Reading Test and Reviews
RTR — Reformed Theological Review
RTR — Restoration and Eighteenth Century Theatre Research
RTr — Rivista della Tripolitania
R Trabajo — Revista de Trabajo. Ministerio de Trabajo
R Trab (Madrid) — Revista de Trabajo (Madrid)
R Trav — Revue du Travail
R Trav Acad Sci Mor Polit — Revue des Travaux. Academie des Sciences Morales et Politiques
R Travail Bruxelles — Revue du Travail
R Trav (Bruxelles) — Revue du Travail (Bruxelles)
RT Regelungstech — RT. Regelungstechnik
R Tres — Revue du Tresor
R Tresor — Revue du Tresor
R Trim Dr Com — Revue Trimestrielle de Droit Commercial
R Trim Dr Europ — Revue Trimestrielle de Droit Europeen
R Trim Droit Eur — Revue Trimestrielle de Droit Europeen
R Trim Dr Sanit Soc — Revue Trimestrielle de Droit Sanitaire et Social
RTRPAEA — Recueil des Travaux Relatifs a la Philologie et a l'Archeologie Egyptiennes et Assyriennes
RTRPhAEA — Recueil des Travaux Relatifs a la Philologie et a l'Archeologie Egyptiennes et Assyriennes
RTS — Renaissance Text Series
RTSD LRTS — RTSD [*Resources and Technical Services Division*] Library Resources and Technical Services
RTSFR — Rivista Trimestrale di Studi Filosofici e Religiosi
RTSO — Rocznik Teologiczny Slyska Opolskiego
RTSS — Revue Tunisienne de Sciences Sociales
RTST — Revista de Jurisprudencia do Tribunal Superior do Trabalho
RTSTA — Railway Track and Structures
RTSZA — Revista Tecnica Sulzer
RTT — Research in Text Theory/Untersuchungen zur Text-Theorie
RTTCB — Revue Technique Thomson - CSF
RTTLA — Revista Transporturilor si Telecomunicatiilor
RTTR — Recherches Theatrales, Theater Research
RTUCO — Recherches et Travaux. Universite Catholique de l'Ouest

R Tun — Revue Tunisienne
R Tunis Geogr — Revue Tunisienne de Geographie
R Tunisienne Sciences Socs — Revue Tunisienne de Sciences Sociales
R Tunis Sci Soc — Revue Tunisienne de Sciences Sociales
RTur — Revue de Turcologie
RTVA Rev Tech Vet Aliment — RTVA. Revue Technique Veterinaire de l'Alimentation
RU — Raccolta Ufficiale delle Leggi, Decreti, e Regolamente dellaConfederazione Svizzera
RU — Rajasthan University. Studies. Arts
RU — Religioni dell'Umanita
RU — Revista Universitaria. Universidad Catolica de Chile
RU — Revista Universitaria. Universidad Nacional de Cuzco
RU — Revue Universelle
RU — Revue Universitaire
RU — Zeitschrift fuer die Praxise des Religionsunterrichts
RUA — Revista Universidad de Antioquia
RUAGA — Rubber Age
Ruakura Farm Conf Proc — Ruakura Farmers' Conference. Proceedings
Ruakura Farmers Conf Proc — Ruakura Farmers' Conference. Proceedings
RUB — Revue. Universite de Bruxelles
RuB — Russkoe Bogatstvo
RUBA — Revista. Universidad de Buenos Aires
Rubb Board Bull — Rubber Board. Bulletin
Rubb Chem — Rubber Chemistry and Technology
Rubb Dev — Rubber Developments
Rubber Age (NY) — Rubber Age (New York)
Rubber Age Synth — Rubber Age and Synthetics
Rubber Board Bull (India) — Rubber Board Bulletin (India)
Rubber Bul — Rubber Statistical Bulletin
Rubber Chem & Tech — Rubber Chemistry and Technology
Rubber Chem Technol — Rubber Chemistry and Technology
Rubber Dev — Rubber Developments
Rubber Developm — Rubber Developments. Natural Rubber Producers' Research Association
Rubber Devs — Rubber Developments
Rubber Dev Suppl — Rubber Developments. Supplement
Rubber Devts — Rubber Developments
Rubber Dig (Tokyo) — Rubber Digest (Tokyo)
Rubber Div Symp — Rubber Division Symposia
Rubber Ind — Rubber Industry
Rubber Ind (London) — Rubber Industry (London)
Rubber Ind (NY) — Rubber Industry (New York)
Rubber J — Rubber Journal
Rubber J Int Plast — Rubber Journal and International Plastics
Rubber Plant Conf Souvenir — Rubber Planters' Conference. Souvenir
Rubber Plast — Rubber and Plastics
Rubber Plast Age — Rubber and Plastics Age
Rubber Plast Wkly — Rubber and Plastics Weekly
Rubber Res Inst Ceylon Advis Circ — Rubber Research Institute of Ceylon. Advisory Circular
Rubber Res Inst Ceylon Annu Rep — Rubber Research Institute of Ceylon. Annual Report
Rubber Res Inst Ceylon Annu Rev — Rubber Research Institute of Ceylon. Annual Review
Rubber Res Inst Ceylon Bull — Rubber Research Institute of Ceylon. Bulletin
Rubber Res Inst Ceylon Q Circ — Rubber Research Institute of Ceylon. Quarterly Circular
Rubber Res Inst Ceylon Q J — Rubber Research Institute of Ceylon. Quarterly Journal
Rubber Res Inst Malaya Annu Rep — Rubber Research Institute of Malaya. Annual Report
Rubber Res Inst Malaya Bull — Rubber Research Institute of Malaya. Bulletin
Rubber Res Inst Malaya Circ — Rubber Research Institute of Malaya. Circular
Rubber Res Inst Malaya Plant Bull — Rubber Research Institute of Malaya. Planters' Bulletin
Rubber Res Inst Malaya Plant Man — Rubber Research Institute of Malaya. Planting Manual
Rubber Res Inst Malaya Q J — Rubber Research Institute of Malaya. Quarterly Journal
Rubber Res Inst Malaya Rep — Rubber Research Institute of Malaya. Report
Rubber Res Inst Malays Annu Rep — Rubber Research Institute of Malaysia. Annual Report
Rubber Res Inst Malays J — Rubber Research Institute of Malaysia. Journal
Rubber Res Inst Malays Plant Bull — Rubber Research Institute of Malaysia. Planters' Bulletin
Rubber Res Inst Malays Plant Conf Proc — Rubber Research Institute of Malaysia. Planters' Conference. Proceedings
Rubber Res Inst Malays Technol Ser Rep — Rubber Research Institute of Malaysia. Technology Series Report
Rubber Res Inst Sri Lanka Advis Circ — Rubber Research Institute of Sri Lanka. Advisory Circular
Rubber Res Inst Sri Lanka Annu Rev — Rubber Research Institute of Sri Lanka. Annual Review
Rubber Res Inst Sri Lanka Bull — Rubber Research Institute of Sri Lanka. Bulletin
Rubber Res Inst Sri Lanka J — Rubber Research Institute of Sri Lanka. Journal
Rubber Res Inst Sri Lanka Q J — Rubber Research Institute of Sri Lanka. Quarterly Journal
Rubber Sticht (Delft) Commun — Rubber-Stichting (Delft). Communication
Rubber Technol — Rubber Technology
Rubber Wld — Rubber World
Rubb (India) — Rubber (India)
Rubb J — Rubber Journal and International Plastics
Rubb News — Rubber News
Rubb Plast Age — Rubber and Plastics Age

Rubb Plast Fire Flamm Bull — Rubber and Plastics Fire and Flammability Bulletin
Rubb Plast News — Rubber and Plastics News
Rubb Plast News 2 — Rubber and Plastics News. 2
Rubb Statist Bull — Rubber Statistical Bulletin
Rubb Trends — Rubber Trends
Rubb World — Rubber World
Rubey Vol — Rubey Volume
RuBi — Ruch Biblijny i Liturgiczny
RubN — Rubriques Nouvelles
RubR — Ruban Rouge
RU Brux — Revue. Universite de Bruxelles
RUBruxelles — Revue. Universite de Bruxelles
Rub Trends — Rubber Trends
RUBWA — Rubber World
RUC — Revista. Universidad de Cordoba
RUC — Revista. Universidade de Coimbra
RUC — Revista Universitaria. Universidad Nacinal de Cuzco
RuC — Ruperto-Carola
RUCE — Revista. Universidad Catolica (Ecuador)
RuchBL — Ruch Biblijny i Liturgiczny
Ruch L — Ruch Literacki
RuchM — Ruch Muzyczny
Ruch Muz — Ruch Muzyczny
Ruch Prawn Ekon Socjol — Ruch Prawniczy Ekonomiczny i Socjologiczny
Ruch Prawn I Ekon I Socjol — Ruch Prawniczy i Ekonomiczny i Socjologiczny
RUCM — Revista. Universidad Complutense de Madrid
RUCP — Revista de la Universidad del Cauca (Popayan)
RUCP — Revista. Universidad Catolica del Peru
RUCR — Revista. Universidad de Costa Rica
Rud Geol Metal — Rudarstvo. Geologija i Metalurgija
Rud Glas — Rudarski Glasnik
Rud-Metal Zb — Rudarsko-Metalurski Zbornik
Rud-Met Zb — Rudarsko-Metalurski Zbornik
Rudn Mestorozhd — Rudnye Mestorozhdeniya
Rudodobiv Metal — Rudodobiv i Metalurgiya
Rudodobiv Metal (Sofia) — Rudodobiv i Metalurgiya (Sofia)
Rudodob Metal — Rudodobiv i Metalurgiya
Rudolstaedter Heimath — Rudolstaedter Heimathefte Beitraege zur Heimatkunde des Kreises Rudolstaedt
Rudoobraz Procesi Miner Nakhodisha — Rudoobrazuvatelni Procesi i Mineralni Nakhodisha
RUDVA — Rubber Developments
Rudy Met — Rudy i Metally
Rudy Met Niezelaz — Rudy i Metale Niezelazne
RUE — Rilievi delle Urne Etrusche
RUEAC — Revista. Union de Escritores y Artistas de Cuba
Rueckstands Ber — Rueckstands-Berichte
Ruf D Ostens — Ruf des Ostens
RUFE — Zeitschrift fuer Rundfunk und Fernsehen
Ruff Fin Suc Rep — Howard Ruff's Financial Success Report
RUG — Revista. Universidad de Guayaquil
Rugby NH S Rp — Reports of the Rugby School Natural History Society
RUGED — Rural Georgia
RUGLA — Rudarski Glasnik
RUIMB — Ruimtevaart
RUIS — Revista. Universidad Industrial de Santander
RUISA — Revista. Universidad Industrial de Santander
RuJ — Rusky Jazyk
RUKR — Religion und Kultus der Roemer
RUL — Revista Universal Lisbonense
RUL — Revista. Universidad de La Salle
RUL — Revista Universitaria (Lima)
RUL — Revue. Universite de Lyon
RUL — Revue. Universite Laval
RULau — Revue de l'Universite Laurentienne
RULet — Revista Universitaria de Letras
RuLit — Ruch Literacki
RULP — Revista. Universidad de La Plata
Ru L T — Russian Literature Triquarterly
RUM — Revista. Universidad de Madrid
RUM — Revista. Universidad de Mexico
RUM — Revue des Universites du Midi
RuM — Ruch Muzyczny
RUMa — Revista. Universidad de Madrid
RUMEA — Rudodobiv i Metalurgiya
Rumen Microb Metab Ruminant Dig — Rumen Microbial Metabolism and Ruminant Digestion
RUMG — Revista. Universidade de Minas Gerais
RUMIA — Rundfunktechnische Mitteilungen
RUMMA — Russian Metallurgy
Rum Med Rev — Rumanian Medical Review
RUMRA — Revue Universelle des Mines, de la Metallurgie, de la Mecanique, des Travaux Publics, des Sciences, et des Arts Appliques a l'Industrie
RUM Rev Univers Mines — RUM. Revue Universelle des Mines, de la Metallurgie, de la Mechanique, des Travaux Publics, des Sciences
RUM Rev Univers Mines Metall Mec — RUM (Revue Universelle des Mines, de la Metallurgie, de la Mechanique, des Travaux Publics, des Sciences et des Arts Appliques a l'Industrie)
Rum Sci Abstr — Rumanian Scientific Abstracts
RUMUDA — Reports. USA Marine Biological Institute. Kochi University
RUN — Revista. Universidad Nacional
RUNAA — Revista. Universidad Nacional de Tucuman. Serie A. Matematica y Fisica Teorica
RUnBrux — Revue. Universite de Bruxelles
RUNC — Revista. Universidad Nacional de Cordoba

RUNC — Revista. Universidad Nacional del Centro
Rundfunk & F — Rundfunk und Fernsehen
Rundfunktech Mitt — Rundfunktechnische Mitteilungen
Rundschau Smlg Ger Entsch Frankft — Rundschau. Sammlung Gerichtlicher Entscheidungen aus dem Bezirke des Oberlandesgerichts Frankfurt am Main
Rundsch Dtsch Tech — Rundschau Deutscher Technik
Rundsch F Kommunalbeamte — Rundschau fuer Kommunalbeamte
Rundsch Geol Verw Wiss — Rundschau fuer Geologie und Verwandte Wissenschaften
Rundsch Tech Arb — Rundschau Technischer Arbeit
Rundt Verd — Rundt i Verden
RUNE — Revista. Universidad Nacional (Ecuador)
R Union Ind — Revista de la Union Industrial
RUniv — Revue Universelle
R Univ — Revue Universitaire
R Univ Bruxelles — Revue. Universite de Bruxelles
R Univ Buenos Aires — Revista. Universidad de Buenos Aires
R Univ Burundi — Revue. Universite du Burundi
R Universitaria — Revista Universitaria
R Univ Madrid — Revista. Universidad de Madrid
R Univ Ottawa — Revue. Universite d'Ottawa
R Univ Oviedo — Revista. Universidad de Oviedo
R Univ Universidad Mayor de San Marcos — Revista Universitaria. Universidad Mayor de San Marcos
RUnLav — Revue. Universite Laval
Runn Times — Running Times
Runn World — Runner's World
RUnOtt — Revue. Universite d'Ottawa
RUNP — Revista. Universidad de La Plata
RUO — Revista. Universidad de Oviedo
RUO — Revue. Universite d'Ottawa
RUOt — Revue. Universite d'Ottawa
RU Ottawa — Revue. Universite d'Ottawa
RUOUS — Re-Union ut Omnes Unum Sint
RUOv — Revista. Universidad de Oviedo
RuP — Renaissance und Philosophie
RUP — Revista. Faculdade de Letras. Universidade de Porto
RUPAA — Rubber and Plastics Age
RupC — Rupert-Carola
RUR — Russkaja Rech'
Rur Advis Leafl Edinb Sch Agric — Rural Advisory Leaflet. Edinburgh School of Agriculture
Rur Afr — Rural Africana
RURAL — Abstracts on Rural Development in the Tropics
Rural Am — Rural America
Rural Develop — Rural Development
Rural Dev News — Rural Development News
Rural Dev Perspect RDP — Rural Development Perspectives. RDP
Rural Dev Res Educ — Rural Development. Research and Education
Rural Dev Res Rep US Dep Agric Econ Stat Coop Serv — Rural Development Research Report. United States Department of Agriculture. Economics, Statistics, and Cooperatives Service
Rural Elec N — Rural Electrification News
Rural Enterp — Rural Enterprise
Rural GA — Rural Georgia
Rural Libr — Rural Libraries
Rural Life Res — Rural Life Research
Rural Newsl — Rural Newsletter. Central Coast Agricultural Research and Extension Committee
Rural N Y — Rural New Yorker
Rural Recreat Tour Abstr — Rural Recreation and Tourism Abstracts
Rural Res — Rural Research. Commonwealth Scientific and Industrial Research Organisation
Rural Res CSIRO — Rural Research. Commonwealth Scientific and Industrial Research Organisation
Rural Res CSIRO Q — Rural Research. A CSIRO [*Commonwealth Scientific and Industrial Research Organization*] Quarterly
Rural Socio — Rural Sociology
Rural Sociol — Rural Sociologist
Rural Sociol — Rural Sociology
RURCA — Rural Research
Rur Ind — Rural India
Rur Newsl — Rural Newsletter
Rur Prod — Rural Production
Rur Res — Rural Research
Rur Res CSIRO — Rural Research. Commonwealth Scientific and Industrial Research Organisation
Rur Res CSIRO (Aust) — Rural Research. Commonwealth Scientific and Industrial Research Organisation (Australia)
Rur Sociol — Rural Sociology
R Uruguaya Ciencias Socs — Revista Uruguaya de Ciencias Sociales
RUS — Rice University. Studies
RUS — Rundbrief. Una Sancta
Rus Arkhv — Russkiy Arkhiv
RUSC — Revista Universidad Social Catolica
RUSCA — Rural Sociology
Rus Chr — Russie et Chretiente
RUSE — Rundbrief. Una-Sancta-Einigung
RUSE — Rutgers University. Studies in English
RUSEng — Rajasthan University. Studies in English
RusF — Russkij Fol'klor
RUSh — Revue de l'Universite de Sherbrooke
Rus Hist — Russian History
Rush-Presbyt-St Luke's Med Bull — Rush-Presbyterian-St. Luke's Medical Center. Bulletin

Rush-Presbyt-St Luke's Med Cent Res Rep — Rush-Presbyterian-St. Luke's Medical Center. Research Report
RUSI — Journal. Royal United Services Institute for Defence Studies
Rusk N — Ruskin Newsletter
RusL — Russkaja Literatura
Rus Lang J — Russian Language Journal
Rus Ling — Russian Linguistics
Rus Lit — Russian Literature
Rus Lit Triq — Russian Literature Triquarterly
Rus LT — Russian Literature Triquarterly
RUSNM — Reports. United States National Museum
RusR — Russian Review
RusR — Russkaja Rech'
Rus Re — Russkaja Rech'
Russ Annu Geol Mineral — Russian Annual of Geology and Mineralogy
Russ Arkh Anat Gistol Embriol — Russkii Arkhiv Anatomii, Gistologii, i Embriologii
Russ Astron Kal — Russkii Astronomicheskii Kalendar
Russ Astron Zh — Russkii Astronomicheskii Zhurnal
Russ Bierbrau — Russische Bierbrauer
Russ Cast Prod — Russian Castings Production
Russ Cast Prod Engl Transl — Russian Castings Production (English Translation)
Russ Chem Bull — Russian Chemical Bulletin
Russ Chem Pharm J — Russian Chemico-Pharmaceutical Journal
Russ Chem Rev — Russian Chemical Reviews
Russ Chem Rev (Engl Transl) — Russian Chemical Reviews (English Translation)
Russ Dtsch Nachr Wiss Tech — Russisch-Deutsche Nachrichten fuer Wissenschaft und Technik
Russell-Cotes Mus Bul — Russell-Cotes Art Gallery and Museum. Bulletin
Russ Eng J — Russian Engineering Journal
Russ Eng J (Engl Transl) — Russian Engineering Journal (English Translation)
Russ En J — Russian Engineering Journal
Russ Entomol Obozr — Russkoe Entomologicheskoe Obozrenie
Russ Fiziol Zh Im I M Sechenova — Russkii Fiziologicheskii Zhurnal Imeni I. M. Sechenova
Russ Ger Her Sci Technol — Russian-German Herald of Science and Technology
Russ Ger Vestn Nauki Tekh — Russko-Germanskii Vestnik Nauki i Tekhniki
Russ Hist — Russian History
Russian Acad Sci Dokl Math — Russian Academy of Sciences. Doklady Mathematics
Russian Acad Sci Izv Math — Russian Academy of Sciences. Izvestiya. Mathematics
Russian Acad Sci Sb Math — Russian Academy of Sciences. Sbornik. Mathematics
Russian J Math Phys — Russian Journal of Mathematical Physics
Russian J Numer Anal Math Modelling — Russian Journal of Numerical Analysis and Mathematical Modelling
Russian J Physical Chem — Russian Journal of Physical Chemistry
Russian Math — Russian Mathematics
Russian Math Surveys — Russian Mathematical Surveys
Russian Phys J — Russian Physics Journal
Russian R — Russian Review
Russian Rev — Russian Review
Russie et Chret — Russie et Chretiente
Russ Jahrb Pharm — Russisches Jahrbuch der Pharmacie
Russ J Bioorg Chem Transl of Bioorg Khim — Russian Journal of Bioorganic Chemistry (Translation of Bioorganicheskaya Khimiya)
Russ J Coord Chem Transl of Koord Khim — Russian Journal of Coordination Chemistry (Translation of Koordinatsionnaya Khimiya)
Russ J Dev Biol — Russian Journal of Developmental Biology
Russ J Dev Biol Transl of Ontogenes — Russian Journal of Developmental Biology (Translation of Ontogenes)
Russ J Ecol Transl of Ekologiya Ekaterinburg — Russian Journal of Ecology (Translation of Ekologiya) (Ekaterinburg)
Russ J Electrochem Transl of Elektrokhimiya — Russian Journal of Electrochemistry (Translation of Elektrokhimiya)
Russ J Eng Thermophys — Russian Journal of Engineering Thermophysics
Russ J Exp Landwirtsch — Russisches Journal fuer Experimentelle Landwirtschaft
Russ J Gen Chem — Russian Journal of General Chemistry
Russ J Genet Transl of Genetika Moscow — Russian Journal of Genetics (Translation of Genetika) (Moscow)
Russ J Inorg Chem — Russian Journal of Inorganic Chemistry
Russ J Inorg Chem (Engl Transl) — Russian Journal of Inorganic Chemistry (English Translation)
Russ J Mar Biol Transl of Biol Morya Vladivostok — Russian Journal of Marine Biology (Translation of Biologiya Morya) (Vladivostok)
Russ J Nondestr Test — Russian Journal of Nondestructive Testing
Russ J Numer Anal Math Modell — Russian Journal of Numerical Analysis and Mathematical Modelling
Russ J Org Chem — Russian Journal of Organic Chemistry
Russ J Org Chem Transl of Zh Org Khim — Russian Journal of Organic Chemistry (Translation of Zhurnal Organicheskoi Khimii)
Russ J Phys Chem — Russian Journal of Physical Chemistry
Russ J Phys Chem (Engl Transl) — Russian Journal of Physical Chemistry (English Translation)
Russ J Physiol — Russian Journal of Physiology
Russ J Plant Physiol Transl of Fiziol Rast Moscow — Russian Journal of Plant Physiology (Translation of Fiziologiya Rastenii) (Moscow)
Russkaia L — Russkaia Literatura
Russk Arkh Protist — Russkii Arkhiv Protistologii
Russk Bibliogr Estestv Mat — Russkaja Bibliografija po Estestvoznaniju i Matematike, Sostavlennaja Sostojascim pri Imperatorskoj Akademii Nauk Sankt-Peterburgskim Bjuro Mezdunarodnoj Bibliografii
Russk Bot Zurn — Russkij Botaniceskij Zurnal/Journal Russe de Botanique
Russk Gidrobiol Zurn — Russkij Gidrobiologiceskij Zurnal/Russische Hydrobiologische Zeitschrift

Russk Med — Russkaia Meditsina
Russ-K Min Ges St Petersburg Verh — Russisch-Kaiserliche Mineralogische Gesellschaft zu St. Petersburg. Verhandlungen
Russk Vestnik Dermat — Russkii Vestnik Dermatologii
Russk Zhurnal Trop Med — Russkii Zhurnal Tropicheskoi Meditsiny
Russk Zool Zhurnal — Russkii Zoologicheskii Zhurnal
Russ Lit — Russkaja Literatura
Russ Lit Tr — Russian Literature Triquarterly
Rus Slovo — Russkoye Slovo
Russl Phm Z — Pharmaceutische Zeitschrift fuer Russland
Russ Math Surv — Russian Mathematical Surveys
Russ Met — Russian Metallurgy
Russ Metall — Russian Metallurgy
Russ Metall (Engl Transl) — Russian Metallurgy (English Translation)
Russ Metall Fuels — Russian Metallurgy and Fuels
Russ Metall Min — Russian Metallurgy and Mining
Russ Microelectron — Russian Microelectronics
Russ Microelectron Transl of Mikroelektronika — Russian Microelectronics (Translation of Mikroelektronika)
Russ Pharmacol Toxicol — Russian Pharmacology and Toxicology
Russ Pharmacol Toxicol (Engl Transl) — Russian Pharmacology and Toxicology (English Translation)
Russ Physiol J — Russian Physiological Journal
Russ Phys J — Russian Physics Journal
Russ Pivovar — Russkii Pivovar
Russ Pochvoved — Russkii Pochvoved
Russ Polym News — Russian Polymer News
Russ R — Russian Review
Russ Rev — Russian Review
Russ Rev — Russische Revue
Russ Rev Biol — Russian Review of Biology
Russ Rev Harmondsworth — Russian Review (Harmondsworth)
Russ Ultrason — Russian Ultrasonics
Russ Vinograd — Russkii Vinograd
Russ Vrach — Russkii Vrach
RUSTA — Rustica
Rust Prev Control — Rust Prevention and Control
Rusts Magaz — Magazin fuer die Gesammte Heilkunde (Von J. N. Rust)
Rus Vestnik — Russkiy Vestnik
RUT — Revista. Universidad (Tegucigalpa)
RUT — Revue. Faculte des Lettres. Universite de Teheran
RUT — Rubber Trends
Rut-Cam LJ — Rutgers-Camden Law Journal
Rutgers A Rev — Rutgers Art Review
Rutgers Camden L J — Rutgers-Camden Law Journal
Rutgers Comput and Technol Law J — Rutgers Computer and Technology Law Journal
Rutgers J Comp & L — Rutgers Journal of Computers and the Law
Rutgers J Comput & Law — Rutgers Journal of Computers and the Law
Rutgers J Computers & Law — Rutgers Journal of Computers and the Law
Rutgers J Computer Tech and L — Rutgers Journal of Computers, Technology, and the Law
Rutgers J Comput Technol and Law — Rutgers Journal of Computers, Technology, and the Law
Rutgers Jrnl — Rutgers Computer and Technology Law Journal
Rutgers LJ — Rutgers Law Journal
Rutgers L Rev — Rutgers Law Review
Rutgers State Univ Coll Eng Eng Res Bull — Rutgers State University. College of Engineering. Engineering Research Bulletin
Rutgers State Univ Coll Eng Eng Res Publ — Rutgers State University. College of Engineering. Engineering ResearchPublication
Rutgers UL Rev — Rutgers University. Law Review
Rutgers Univ Annu Res Conf Bur Biol Res — Rutgers University. Annual Research Conference of the Bureau ofBiological Research
Rutgers Univ Bur Biol Res Annu Conf Protein Metab Proc — Rutgers University. Bureau of Biological Research. Annual Conference onProtein Metabolism. Proceedings
Rutgers Univ Bur Biol Res Serol Mus Bull — Rutgers University. Bureau of Biological Research. Serological Museum. Bulletin
Rutgers Univ Bur Eng Res Eng Res Publ — Rutgers University. Bureau of Engineering Research. Engineering Research Publication
Rutgers Univ Bur Miner Res Bull — Rutgers University. Bureau of Mineral Research. Bulletin
Rutgers Univ Coll Eng Eng Res Bull — Rutgers University. College of Engineering. Engineering Research Bulletin
Rutg L Rev — Rutgers Law Review
Rutherford Appleton Lab Rep RAL — Rutherford Appleton Laboratory. Report RAL
Rutherford Appleton Lab Rep RL — Rutherford Appleton Laboratory. Report RL
Rutherford Lab Rep — Rutherford Laboratory. Report
Rutherford Lab Tech Rep RL — Rutherford Laboratory. Technical Report RL
Rut J Comp L — Rutgers Journal of Computers, Technology, and the Law
Rut LJ — Rutgers Law Journal
Rut LR — Rutgers Law Review
RUUC — Revista Universitaria. Universidad Catolica de Chile
RUUP — Revista de la Universidad Catolica del Peru
RUY — Revista. Universidad de Yucatan
RUZ — Revista. Universidad de Zulia
RV — Rassegna Volterrana
RV — Raven
RV — Refuah Veterinarith
RV — Religionsgeschichtliche Volksbuecher
RV — Rheinische Vierteljahresblaetter
RV — RV: Recreational Vehicles
RVA — Red-Figured Vases of Apulia

RVAEA — Rivista Aeronautica
RVAHA — Revue d'Acoustique
R Valenciana Filol — Revista Valenciana de Filologia. Instituto de Literatura y Estudios Filologicos. Institucion Alfonso el Magnanimo
RVAP — Red-Figured Vases of Apulia
Rv Arti — Revue d'Artillerie
RVASA — Revue de l'Atherosclerose
RVB — Rheinische Vierteljahresblaetter
Rv Brazil — Revista Brazileira, Jornal de Sciencias, Lettras, e Artes
RV Bsns — Recreational Vehicle Business
R v B S V — Raad van Beroep. Sociale Verzekering
Rv Bt — Revue de Botanique. Bulletin Mensuel de la Societe Francaise de Botanique
RVBTA — Revue Belge des Transports
RvC — Raad van Commissarissen
RVC — Review of Economic Studies
RVCCB — Reviews on Coatings and Corrosion
Rv Cours Sc — Revue des Cours Scientifiques de la France et de l'Etranger
RVCZA — Revista de Coroziune
RV Dealer — Recreational Vehicle Dealer
RVDSB — Revue Medicale de Liege. Supplement (Belgium)
RVEAAG — Escuela Nacional de Agricultura [Chapingo]. Revista
RVELA — Revista Electrotecnica
RVENA — Rivista di Viticoltura e di Enologia
R Venez Folk — Revista Venezolana de Folklore
R Venezolana Estud Municipales — Revista Venezolana de Estudios Municipales
R Venezolana Folklore — Revista Venezolana de Folklore
R Venezolana Sanidad y Asistencia Soc — Revista Venezolana de Sanidad y Asistencia Social
RVETA5 — Refuah Veterinarith
R Vet Agric Univ Steril Res Inst Annu Rep — Royal Veterinary and Agricultural University. Sterility Research Institute. Annual Report
R Vet Agric Univ Yearb (Copenhagen) — Royal Veterinary and Agricultural University. Yearbook (Copenhagen)
Rv Et Byz — Revue des Etudes Byzantines
RvEx — Review and Expositor
RVF — Revista Valenciana de Filologia
RVF — Revista Venezolana de Filosofia
RVF — Revista Venezolana de Folklore
RVFO — Revista Venezolana de Folklore
RVGA-A — Revue de Geographie Alpine
Rv Gen Bt — Revue Generale de Botanique
Rv Gen Sciences — Revue Generale des Sciences Pures et Appliquees
Rv Gg It — Rivista Geografica Italiana
RVGPA — Reviews of Geophysics [Later, Reviews of Geophysics and Space Physics]
RVIAJ — Royal Victorian Institute of Architects. Journal
Rv It Sc Nt Siena — Rivista Italiana di Scienze Naturali (Siena)
R Vivarais — Revue du Vivarais
RVL — Revue Economique et Sociale (Lausanne)
RVLI — Raksti. Latvijas PSR Zinatnu Akademija. Valodas und Literaturas Instituta
Rv Mar — Revue Maritime et Coloniale
Rv Mar Et Col — Revue Maritime et Coloniale
RVMCA — Rivista di Meccanica
Rv Mn Cr — Rivista di Mineralogia e Cristallografia Italiana
Rv Mt — Rivista di Matematica
Rv Mth — Revue de Mathematiques
RVOMA — Revue Internationale d'Oceanographie Medicale
RVOOA — Rivista Oto-Neuro-Oftalmologica
RVPF — Recherches pour Servir a l'Histoire du Vocabulaire Poetique en Francais
RVPMB — Review of Psychology of Music
RVPTB — Revue Polytechnique
Rv Quest Sc — Revue des Questions Scientifiques, Publiee par la Societe Scientifique de Bruxelles
RVS — Rivista di Vita Spirituale
Rv Sc — Revue Scientifique de la France et de l'Etranger
Rv Sc — Revue Scientifique et Industrielle
Rv Scient — Revue Scientifique
Rv Sc Ind — Rivista Scientifico-Industriale delle Principali Scoperte ed Invenzioni Fatte nelle Scienze e nelle Industrie
RVSMB — Revista Sanitaria Militara
Rv Sper Freniatr — Rivista Sperimentale di Freniatria e di Medicina Legale
Rv Trim Can — Revue Trimestrielle Canadienne
Rv Trim Mcrgr — Revista Trimestral Micrografica. Organo del Laboratorio Histologico de la Facultad de Medicina de Madrid
RVTSA — Research in Veterinary Science
RVU — Revue Economique
RVUHA — Revue HF, Electronique, Telecommunications
Rv Un Mines — Revue Universelle des Mines, de la Metallurgie
RVUXA — Revue X
RVV — Religionsgeschichtliche Versuche und Vorarbeiten
RVV — Romanistische Versuche und Vorarbeiten
RW — Rechtskundig Weekblad
RW — Reformed World
RW — Romanica Wratislavensia
RW — Rough Weather
RW — Runner's World
RW — Russkij Wiestnik
RWAHSJ — Royal Western Australian Historical Society. Journal
RWAMD — Radioactive Waste Management
RWAVA — Rheinisch-Westfaelische Akademie der Wissenschaften Natur-, Ingenieur-, und Wirtschaftswissenschaften. Vortraege
RWB — Relgionswissenschaftliche Bibliothek
RWCNEC — Reports of the Working Committees. Northeast Conference
RWE — Review of World Economics

RWE — REWE Echo. Fachzeitschrift fuer Modernen Handel
R Week — Rechtskundig Weekblad
RWF — Rozprawy Wydzialu Filologicznego Polskiej Akademyi Umiejetnosci
RWFSDH — Reports on the World Fertility Survey
RWGS — Religionswissenschaft der Gegenwart in Selbstdarstellungen
RWK — Relgion, Wissenschaft, Kultur
RWM — Rocznik Wolnej Mysli
RWMEB — Railway Mechanical Engineer
RWP — Reformacja w Polsce
RWR — Romance Writers Report
RWS — Religionswissenschaftliche Studien
RWTK — Rozprawy Wydzialu Teologiczno-Kanonicznego
RWW — Religionswissenschaftliches Woerterbuch
Rwy Age — Railway Age
RWZVK — Rheinisch-Westfaelische Zeitschrift fuer Volkskunde
RYa — Russkii Yazyk v Shkole
Ry Age — Railway Age
Ryan Advis Health Serv Gov Boards — Ryan Advisory for Health Services Governing Boards
Ry & Corp Law J — Railway and Corporation Law Journal
Ry & Corp Law Jour — Railway and Corporation Law Journal
Ryazan Gos Pedagog Inst Uch Zap — Ryazanskii Gosudarstvennyi Pedagogicheskii Institut. Uchenye Zapiski
Ryazan Med Inst Im Akad I P Pavlova Nauchn Tr — Ryazanskii Meditsinskii Institut Imeni Akademika I. P. Pavlova.Nauchnye Trudy
Rybinsk Aviats Tekhnol Inst Sb Tr — Rybinskii Aviatsionnyi Tekhnologicheskii Institut. Sbornik Trudov
Ryb Khoz — Rybnoe Khozyaistvo
Rybn Khoz — Rybnoe Khozyaistvo
Rybn Khoz (Kiev) — Rybnoe Khozyaistvo (Kiev)
Rybn Khoz (Moscow) — Rybnoe Khozyaistvo (Moscow)
Rybn Khoz Resp Mezhved Temat Nauchn Sb — Rybnoe Khozyaistvo Respublikanskii Mezhvedomstvennyi Tematicheskii Nauchnyi Sbornik
Rybn Khoz SSSR — Rybnoe Khozyaistvo SSSR
Rybn Promst Dalnego Vostoka — Rybnaya Promyshlennost' Dal'nego Vostoka
Rybn Prom-St Dal'n Vost — Rybnaya Promyshlennost' Dal'nego Vostoka
Rybokhoz Issled Basseine Balt Morya — Rybokhozyaistvennye Issledovaniya v Basseine Baltiiskogo Morya
Rybokhoz Izuch Vnutr Vodoemov — Rybokhozyaistvennoe Izuchenie Vnutrennikh Vodoemov
RyC — Religion y Cultura
RyC — Revolucion y Cultura
Ry Corp Law Jour — Railway and Corporation Law Journal
Rydge's — Rydge's Business Journal
Rydge's Constr Civ Eng & Min Rev — Rydge's Construction, Civil Engineering, and Mining Review
RYEJA — Royal Engineers Journal
RyF — Razon y Fe
RyFa — Razon y Fabula
RyFab — Razon y Fabula
Ry Gaz Int — Railway Gazette International
RYKHA — Rybnoe Khozyaistvo
RYKOD — Ryutai Kogaku
Ry Loco & Cars — Railway Locomotives and Cars
Ry Mech & Elec Eng — Railway Mechanical and Electrical Engineer
Ry Mech Eng — Railway Mechanical Engineer
Ry Mo — Rythmes du Monde
Ryojun Coll Eng Mem — Ryojun College of Engineering. Memoirs
Ryojun Coll Eng Publ — Ryojun College of Engineering. Publications
RYPAAO — Annals. Royal College of Physicians and Surgeons of Canada
RYPFA — Revista YPF [Yacimientos Petroliferos Fiscales] (Argentina)
Ry R — Railway Review
Ry Surg J — Railway Surgical Journal
Ryth Monde — Rythmes du Monde
Ry Track Struct — Railway Track and Structures
Ryukoku J Humanit Sci — Hyukoku Journal of Humanities and Sciences
Ryukyu Math J — Ryukyu Mathematical Journal
Ryukyu Med J — Ryukyu Medical Journal
RYUSA — Ryusan To Kogyo
RZ — Rada Zydowska
RZ — Radostna Zeme
RZ — Radovi (Filozofski Fakultet-Zadar)
RZ — Referativnyi Zhurnal. Informatika
RZ — Revista Zurita Saragosse
Rz — Roemisches Zivilprozessrecht
R Z Avtomat Telemeh i Vycisl Tehn — Referativnyi Zhurnal. Avtomatika. Telemehanika i Vycislitelnaja Tehnika
RZBLA — Referativnyi Zhurnal. Biologiya
RZE — Chemiefasern/Textil-Industrie. Zeitschrift fuer die Gesamte Textil Industrie
RZEPEV — Russkogo Zapadno-Evropeiskogo Patriarshego Ekzarkhata. Vestnik
RZETA — Rozprawy Elektrotechniczne
R Z Fiz — Referativnyi Zhurnal. Fizika
RZFZA — Referativnyi Zhurnal. Fizika
RZh Avtomat Telemekh i Vychisl Tekhn — Akademiya Nauk SSSR. Institut Nauchnoi Informatsii. Referativnyi Zhurnal. Avtomatika. Telemekhanika i Vychislitel'naya Tekhnika
RZh Mat — Akademiya Nauk SSSR. Institut Nauchnoi Informatsii. Referativnyi Zhurnal. Matematika
RZhMekh — Referativnyi Zhurnal. Mekhanika. Akademiya Nauk SSSR. Institut Nauchnoi Informatsii
RZh Tekhn Kibernet — Akademiya Nauk SSSR. Institut Nauchnoi i Tekhnicheskoi Informatsii. Referativnyi Zhurnal. Tekhnicheskaya Kibernetika
RZINA — Rozprawy Inzynierskie
RZInformat — Referativnyi Zhurnal. Informatika
RZKibernet — Referativnyi Zhurnal. Kibernetika

RZMat — Referativnyi Zhurnal. Matematika
RZMeh — Referativnyi Zhurnal. Mehanika
RZMTA — Referativnyi Zhurnal. Metallurgiya
RZMVA — Revista de Zootechnic si Medicina Veterinara
RZNDA — Razvedka Nedr

RZONA — Razvedka i Okhrana Nedr
RZOOA — Rivista di Zootecnia
RZPR — Roemisches Zivilprozessrecht
RZSF — Radovi Zavoda za Slavensku Filologiju
RZSND — Revue Zairoise des Sciences Nucleaires
RZZP — Rheinische Zeitschrift fuer Zivil- und Prozessrecht des In- und Auslandes

S

S — Seed
S — September
S — Sezatoarea. Revista de Folklor
S — Slavia
S — Sociologus [Berlin]
S — Sokrates
S — Sophia (Naples)
S — Spectator
S — Speculum
S — Sportologue
S — Staatsblad van het Koninkrijk der Nederlanden
S — Studio
S — Survey
S — Symposium
S — Wetboek van Strafrecht
S 8 Fmkr — Super 8 Filmaker
S/40 — Sex Over Forty
Sa — Samtiden
Sa — Sankhya
SA — Science Abstracts
SA — Scientific American
Sa — Senckenbergiana
SA — Sistema
S A — Slovenska Archaeologia
SA — Sociological Abstracts
SA — Sociological Analysis
SA — Something About the Author
SA — South African Law Reports
SA — South Australiana
SA — Sovietskaia Archeologiia
SA — Specialty Advertising Business
SA — Speech Activities
SA — Storia dell'Arte
SA — Studia Albanica
SA — Studi Americani
SA — Studies in Astronautics
SA — Symbolae Arctoae
SAA — Bulletin. Societe d'Archeologie d'Alexandrie
SAA — Schriften der Sektion fuer Altertumswissenschaft
SAA — Schweizer Anglistische Arbeiten
SAA — South Asian Affairs
SAA — Soviet Anthropology and Archaeology
SAA/AA — American Antiquity. Society for American Archaeology
SAAAS — Something About the Author. Autobiography Series
SAAB — South African Archaeological Bulletin
SAAD Dig — SAAD [Society for the Advancement of Anaesthesia in Dentistry] Digest
SA Advertiser (Newspr) — South Australian Advertiser Reports (Newspaper)
SAAFA — Astrometriya i Astrofizika
SAA/HO — Human Organization. Society for Applied Anthropology
SAAJA — Soviet Astronomy
Saalb Jb — Saalburg-Jahrbuch. Bericht des Saalburg-Museums
Saalburg Jahrb — Saalburg Jahrbuch. Saalburg-Museum
SAANAn — Societe Archeologique de l'Arrondissement de Nivelles. Annales
SAA/R — Relaciones. Sociedad Argentina de Antropologia
SA Arch J — SA [South African] Archives Journal
SAAS Bull Biochem Biotechnol — SAAS [Southern Association of Agricultural Scientists] Bulletin. Biochemistry and Biotechnology
Saatgut-Wirt — Saatgut-Wirtschaft
Saatgut-Wirtsch — Saatgut-Wirtschaft
SAAWA — Schweizer Archiv fuer Angewandte Wissenschaft und Technik
Sab — Sabadellum
SAB — Shakespeare Association. Bulletin
SAB — Sitzungsberichte der Bayerischen Akademie der Wissenschaften
SAB — Sitzungsberichte. Deutsche (Preussische) Akademie der Wissenschaften zu Berlin.Philosophisch-Historische Klasse
SAB — South Atlantic Bulletin
SABA — Societe Archeologique de Bruxelles. Annales
Sabah For Rec — Sabah Forest Record
Sabah Soc J — Sabah Society. Journal
SABAM — Bulletin. Societe des Auteurs, Compositeurs, et Editeurs
SA Bank Officials J — South Australian Bank Officials' Journal
Sabchota Med — Sabchota Meditsina
SABCO J — SABCO [Society for the Areas of Biological and Chemical Overlap] Journal
SaBe — Savoir et Beaute

SABKG — Studien zur Altbayerischen Kirchengeschichte
SABNWTR — Science Advisory Board of the Northwest Territories. Report
SABNWTRP — Science Advisory Board of the Northwest Territories. Research Paper
SABNWTWP — Science Advisory Board of the Northwest Territories. Working Paper
SABOA — Sabouraudia
SABOJ — South Australian Bank Officials' Journal
Sabrao Newslett — Sabrao Newsletter
SABRB — Siemens-Albis Berichte
SABS Bull — SABS [South African Bureau of Standards] Bulletin
Sac — Sacris Erudiri. Jaarboek voor Godsdienstwetenschappen
SAC — Studi di Antichita Christiana
SAC — Studies in Ancient Civilization
SAC — Studies in the Age of Chaucer
SAC — Sussex Archaeological Collections
SACCD — Saccharum
Sac D — Sacra Doctrina. Quaderni Periodici di Teologia e di Filosofia
Sac Dot — Sacra Dottrina
SacE — Sacris Erudiri. Jaarboek voor Godsdienstwetenschappen
SACED — South African Journal of Continuing Medical Education
SA Census & Statistics Bul — Australia. Commonwealth Bureau of Census and Statistics. South Australian Office. Bulletin
SA Cereb Palsy J — SA [South African] Cerebral Palsy Journal
SACh — Studies in Analytical Chemistry
Sachs Akad d Wiss Philol-Hist Kl Ber u d Verhandl — Saechsische Akademie der Wissenschaften. Philologisch-Historische Klasse. Berichte ueber die Verhandlungen
Sachverstaend Zeit — Aerztliche Sachverstaendigenzeitung
SACLA — Srpski Arhiv za Celokupno Lekarstvo
Sac M — Sacred Music
SACPB — South African Chemical Processing
SACR — Studies in Anthropology and Comparative Religion
Sacramento Bus — Sacramento Business
Sacramnt B — Sacramento Bee
Sacra Pag — Sacra Pagina
Sacred Mus — Sacred Music
Sacrum Pol Millenn — Sacrum Poloniae Millennium
Sacr Ver — Sacramentarium Veronense
SA Dep Agric Tech Bull — South Australia. Department of Agriculture. Technical Bulletin
SADID4 — Annual Research Reviews. Sphingolipidoses and Allied Disorders
Sadivn Resp Mizhvid Nauk-Temat Zb — Sadivnytstvo Respublikanskyi Mizhvidomchyi Naukovo-Tematychnyi Zbirnik
SaDo — Sacra Doctrina
SADOAJ — Sadovodstvo
Sado Mar Biol Stn Niigata Univ Spec Publ — Sado Marine Biological Station. Niigata University. Special Publication
Sadovod — Sadovodstvo
Sadovod Vinograd Mold — Sadovodstvo i Vinogradarstvo Moldavii
Sadovod Vinograd Moscow — Sadovodstvo i Vinogradarstvo (Moscow)
Sadovod Vinograd (Tashkent) — Sadovodstvo i Vinogradarstvo (Tashkent)
Sadovod Vinograd Vinodel Mold — Sadovodstvo Vinogradarstvo i Vinodelia Moldavii
Sadtler Commer Spectra — Sadtler Commercial Spectra
SAE — Studia et Acta Ecclesiastica
SAE Australas — SAE [Society of Automotive Engineers] Australasia
SAEBA — Soviet Antarctic Expedition. Information Bulletin
Saec — Saeculum
SaechsA — Saechsisches Archiv fuer Deutsches Buergerliches Recht
Saechs Arch Dt Buerg R — Saechsisches Archiv fuer Deutsches Buergerliches Recht und Prozess
Saechs Forschungsinstitut in Leipzig — Saechsische Forschungsinstitut in Leipzig
Saechs Heimatbl — Saechsische Heimatblaetter
Saechs Heimatschutz Mitt Landesvereins Saechs Heimatschutz — Saechsischer Heimatschutz, Landesverein zur Pflege Heimatlicher Natur, Kunst und Bauweise/Mitteilungen des Landesvereins Saechsischer Heimatschutz
Saechs Jahresschr — Saechse Jahresschrift. Jahsesschrift fuer die Vorgeschichte der Saechsisch-Thueringischen Laender
Saeculum — Saeculum. Jahrbuch fuer Universalgeschichte
SA Ed — South Australian Education
SA Ed Gaz — Education Gazette. South Australia Department of Education
SAED Info — SAED [Societe Africaine d'Etudes et de Developpement] Information
SAE Handb — SAE [Society of Automotive Engineers] Handbook
SAE J — SAE [Society of Automotive Engineers] Journal

SAEJA — SAE [*Society of Automotive Engineers*] Journal

SAE J Automot Eng — SAE [*Society of Automotive Engineers*] Journal of Automotive Engineering

SAE Journ — SAE [*Society of Automotive Engineers*] Journal

SAE Meet Pap — Society of Automotive Engineers. Meeting. Papers

SAEND — Save Energy

Saenger Musikanten Z — Saenger- und Musikantenzeitung

SAE Prepr — SAE [*Society of Automotive Engineers*] Preprints

SAE Proc — Society of Automotive Engineers. Proceedings

SAE Prog Technol — SAE [*Society of Automotive Engineers*] Progress in Technology

SAE Q Trans — SAE [*Society of Automotive Engineers*] Quarterly Transactions

SAE Quart Trans — SAE [*Society of Automotive Engineers*] Quarterly Transactions

SAERB — South African Electrical Review

Saertr Livsmedelstek Forskningsinst (Alnarp) — Saertryck. Livsmedelstekniska Forskningsinstitutet (Alnarp)

Saertr Sven Forskningsinst Cem Betong K Tek Hoegsk Stockholm — Saertryck. Svenska Forskningsinstitutet foer Cement och Betong vidKungliga Tekniska Hoegskolan i Stockholm

SAESA — SAE [*Society of Automotive Engineers*] Special Publications

SAE (Soc Automot Eng) Tech Pap — SAE (Society of Automotive Engineers) Technical Papers

SAE Spec Publ — SAE [*Society of Automotive Engineers*] Special Publications

SAETB — SAE [*Society of Automotive Engineers*] Technical Progress Series

SAE Tech Lit Abstr — SAE [*Society of Automotive Engineers*] Technical Literature Abstracts

SAE Tech Lit Abstracts — SAE (Society of Automotive Engineers) Technical Literature Abstracts

SAE Tech Pap — SAE [*Society of Automotive Engineers*]. Technical Papers

SAE Tech Pap Ser — SAE [*Society of Automotive Engineers*]. Technical Paper Series

SAE Tech Prog Ser — SAE [*Society of Automotive Engineers*] Technical Progress Series

SAE Trans — SAE [*Society of Automotive Engineers*] Transactions

Saeugetierkd Mitt — Saeugetierkundliche Mitteilungen

SAF — Studies in American Fiction

Saf Air Ammonia Plants — Safety in Air and Ammonia Plants

Saf Asp Fuel Behav Off Norm Accid Cond Proc CSNI Spec Meet — Safety Aspects of Fuel Behaviour in Off-Normal and Accident Conditions.Proceedings of a CSNI Specialist Meeting

SAFB — Societe Arctique Francaise Bulletin

SAFD — Plastics (Southern Africa)

Saf Dig — Safety Digest

SAFE — Software Abstracts for Engineers

SAFEA — Safety

Safeguarding Am Against Fire — Safeguarding America Against Fire

Safe Manag — Safety Management

Saf Eng — Safety Engineering

Safety Ed — Safety Education

Safety Educ — Safety Education

Safety Eng — Safety Engineering

Safety Maint — Safety Maintenance

Safety Maint & Prod — Safety Maintenance and Production

Safety Man Newsl — Safety Management Newsletter

Safety Surv — Safety Surveyor

Saf Health Pract — Safety and Health Practitioner

Saf Health Welfare — Safety, Health, and Welfare

Saf Hlth Bull — Safety and Health Bulletin

Saf Hyg (Osaka) — Safety and Hygiene (Osaka)

SAFJB — South African Forestry Journal

S Af J Econ — South African Journal of Economics

Saf Maint — Safety Maintenance

Saf Maint Proc — Safety Maintenance and Production

Saf Manage — Safety Management

SAFMem — Societe Nationale des Antiquaires de France. Memoires

Saf Mines — Safety in Mines

Saf Mines Res Establ GB Rep — Safety in Mines Research Establishment. Great Britain. Report

Saf Mines Res Establ (GB) Res Rep — Safety in Mines Research Establishment (Great Britain). Research Report

Saf Mines Res Test Branch GB Res Rep — Safety in Mines Research and Testing Branch. Great Britain. Research Report

Saf News Bull — Safety News Bulletin

Saf Newsl — Safety Newsletter

SAFOAT — South African Avifauna Series. Percy Fitzpatrick Institute of African Ornithology. University of Cape Town

SAFPD — Safety Practitioner

Saf Pract — Safety Practitioner

S Afr Annu Insur Rev — South African Annual Insurance Review

S Afr AR — Annual Economic Report. South African Reserve Bank

S Afr Archaeol Bull — South African Archaeological Bulletin

S Afr Archaeol Soc Goodwin Ser — South African Archaeological Society. Goodwin Series

S Afr Architect — South African Architect

S Afr Archit J — South African Architectural Journal

S Afr Archit Rec — South African Architectural Record

S Afr Arch Ophthalmol — South African Archives of Ophthalmology

S-Afr Argief Oftalmol — Suid-Afrikaanse Argief vir Oftalmologie

S Afr Assoc Adv Sci Spec Publ — South African Association for the Advancement of Science. Special Publication

S Afr Assoc Mar Biol Res Bull — South African Association for Marine Biological Research. Bulletin

S Afr At Energy Board Rep PEL — South Africa. Atomic Energy Board. Report PEL

S Afr At Energy Board Rep PER — South Africa. Atomic Energy Board. Report PER

S Afr Bakery Confect Rev — South African Bakery and Confectionery Review

S Afr Bank — South African Reserve Bank. Quarterly Bulletin

S Afr Bankers J — South African Bankers' Journal

S Afr Bee J — South African Bee Journal

S-Afr Bosbou Tydskr — Suid-Afrikaanse Bosbou Tydskrif

S Afr Build — South African Builder

S Afr Bur Stand Bull — South African Bureau of Standards. Bulletin

S Afr Cancer Bull — South African Cancer Bulletin

S Afr (Cape Good Hope) Dep Nat Conserv Rep — South Africa (Cape Of Good Hope) Department of Nature. Conservation Report

S Afr Chart Account — South African Chartered Accountant

S Afr Chem — South African Chemicals

S Afr Chem Process — South African Chemical Processing

S Afr Citrus J — South African Citrus Journal

S Afr C Mtl S J — Journal of the Chemical and Metallurgical Society of South Africa

S Afr C Mtl S P — Proceedings of the Chemical and Metallurgical Society of South Africa

S Afr Constr World — South African Construction World

S Afr Corros Conf — South African Corrosion Conference

S Afr Corros J — South African Corrosion Journal

S Afr Counc Sci Ind Res Nat Bldg Res Inst Bull — South Africa. Council for Scientific and Industrial Research. National BuildingResearch Institute. Bulletin

S Afr CSIR Air Pollut Group Annu Rep — South Africa CSIR [*Council for Scientific and Industrial Research*] Air Pollution Group. Annual Report

S Afr CSIR Air Pollut Res Group Annu Rep — South Africa CSIR [*Council for Scientific and Industrial Research*] Air Pollution Research Group. Annual Report

S Afr CSIR Air Pollut Res Group Rep APRG — South African Council for Scientific and Industrial Research. Air Pollution Research Group. Report APRG

S Afr CSIR Annu Rep — South Africa CSIR [*Council for Scientific and Industrial Research*] AnnualReport

S Afr CSIR Rep BOU — South African Council for Scientific and Industrial Research. Report Series BOU

S Afr CSIR Res Rep — South Africa CSIR [*Council for Scientific and Industrial Research*] Research Report

S Afr CSIR Spec Rep — South Africa CSIR [*Council for Scientific and Industrial Research*] Special Report

S Afr CSIR Spec Rep WISK — South African Council for Scientific and Industrial Research. Special Report. Series WISK

SAFRD — South African Food Review

S Afr Dent J — South African Dental Journal

S Afr Dep Agric Entomol Mem — South Africa. Department of Agriculture. Entomology Memoir

S Afr Dep Agric Fish Entomol Mem — South Africa. Department of Agriculture and Fisheries. Entomology Memoir

S Afr Dep Agric Fish Tech Commun — South Africa. Department of Agriculture and Fisheries. Technical Communication

S Afr Dep Agric Tech Serv Bot Surv Mem — South Africa. Department of Agricultural Technical Services. Botanical Survey Memoir

S Afr Dep Agric Tech Serv Bull — South Africa. Department of Agricultural Technical Services. Bulletin

S Afr Dep Agric Tech Serv Entomol Mem — South Africa. Department of Agricultural Technical Services. Entomology Memoirs

S Afr Dep Agric Tech Serv Pam — South Africa. Department of Agricultural Technical Services. Pamphlet

S Afr Dep Agric Tech Serv Sci Bull — South Africa. Department of Agricultural Technical Services. Scientific Bulletin

S Afr Dep Agric Tech Serv Tech Commun — South Africa. Department of Agricultural Technical Services. Technical Communication

S Afr Dep Agric Water Supply Entomol Mem — South Africa. Department of Agriculture and Water Supply. Entomology Memoir

S Afr Dep Agric Water Supply Tech Commun — South Africa. Department of Agriculture and Water Supply. Technical Communication

S-Afr Dep Bosbou Jaarversl — Suid-Afrika. Departement van Bosbou Jaarverslag

S Afr Dep For Annu Rep — South Africa. Department of Forestry. Annual Report

S Afr Dep For Bull — South Africa. Department of Forestry. Bulletin

S-Afr Dep Landbou-Teg Dienste Teg Meded — Suid-Afrika. Departement van Landbou-Tegniese Dienste Tegniese Mededeling

S Afr Dep Landbou Visserye Teg Meded — Suid-Afrika. Departement van Landbou Visserye Tegniese Mededeling

S Afr Dep Landbou Viss Teg Meded — Suid-Afrika. Departement van Landbou en Visserye. Tegniese Mededeling

S Afr Dep Mines Coal Surv Mem — South Africa. Department of Mines. Coal Survey Memoir

S Afr Dep Mines Geol Surv Ann Geol Surv — South Africa. Department of Mines. Geological Survey. Annals of theGeological Survey

S Afr Dep Mines Geol Surv Div Geol Surv Mem — South Africa. Department of Mines. Geological Survey Division. Geological Survey Memoirs

S Afr Dep Mines Quart Inform Circ Miner — South Africa. Department of Mines. Quarterly Information Circular. Minerals

S Afr Dep Mynwese Geol Opname Bull — Suid-Afrika. Departement van Mynwese. Geologiese Opname. Bulletin

S Afr Dep Mynwese Geol Opname Mem — Suid-Afrika. Departement van Mynwese. Geologiese Opname. Memoire

S Afr Dig — South African Digest

S Afr Div Sea Fish Annu Rep — South Africa. Division of Sea Fisheries. Annual Report

S Afr Div Sea Fish Fish Bull — South Africa. Division of Sea Fisheries. Fisheries Bulletin

S Afr Div Sea Fish Invest Rep — South Africa. Division of Sea Fisheries. Investigational Report

S Afr Electr Rev — South African Electrical Review

S Afr Electr Rev Eng — South African Electrical Review and Engineer

S Afr Eng — South African Engineer
S Afr Eng Electr Rev — South African Engineer and Electrical Review
S Afr Eng Met Ind Rev — South African Engineer and Metal Industries Review
S Afr Food Rev — South African Food Review
S Afr For J — South African Forestry Journal
S Afr Friesland J — South African Friesland Journal
S Afr Geogr — South African Geographer
S Afr Geogr J — South African Geographical Journal
S Afr Geol Surv Bibliogr Subj Index S Afr Geol — South Africa. Geological Survey. Bibliography and Subject Index of South African Geology
S Afr Geol Surv Bull — South Africa. Department of Mines. Geological Survey. Bulletin
S Afr Geol Surv Explan Sheets — South Africa. Geological Survey. Explanation of Sheets
S Afr Geol Surv Handb — South Africa. Geological Survey. Handbook
S Afr Geol Surv Mem — South Africa. Department of Mines. Geological Survey. Memoir
S Afr Geol Surv Seismol Ser — South Africa. Geological Survey. Seismologic Series
S Afr Geol Surv South-West Afr Ser — South Africa. Geological Survey. South-West Africa Series
S Afr Hist J — South African Historical Journal
S African — South African Patent Document
S African Country Life — South African Country Life
S African J Commun Disorders — South African Journal of Communication Disorders
S African J Nat Hist — South African Journal of Natural History
S African J Psychol — South African Journal of Psychology
S African Lib — South African Libraries
S African Lib Q Bull — South African Library Quarterly Bulletin
S African L J — South African Law Journal
S African L T — South African Law Times
S African Med J — South African Medical Journal
S African M J — South African Medical Journal
S African Rep Sci — South African Report of Science
S African Sugar J — South African Sugar Journal
S Afr Ind Chem — South African Industrial Chemist
S Afr Ind Chem — Suid-Afrikaanse Industriele Chemikus
S Afr Inst Assayers Anal Bull — South African Institute of Assayers and Analysts. Bulletin
S Afr Inst Chem Eng Natl Meet — South African Institution of Chemical Engineers. National Meeting
S Afr Inst Essaieurs Anal Bull — Suid-Afrikaanse Instituut van Essaieurs en Analitici. Bulletin
S Afr Inst Mech Eng J — South African Institution of Mechanical Engineers. Journal
S Afr Inst Med Res Annu Rep — South African Institute for Medical Research. Annual Report
S Afr Inst Med Res Publ — South African Institute for Medical Research. Publications
S Afr Inst Min Metall J — South African Institute of Mining and Metallurgy. Journal
S Afr Inst Seevisserye Ondersoekverslag — Suid-Afrika. Instituut Seevisserye Ondersoekverslag
S Afr Insur Mag — South African Insurance Magazine
S Afr Int — South Africa International
S Afr J Afr Affairs — South African Journal of African Affairs
S Afr J Agric Ext — South African Journal of Agricultural Extension
S Afr J Agric Sci — South African Journal of Agricultural Science
S Afr J Agr Sci — South African Journal of Agricultural Science
S Afr J Anim Sci — South African Journal of Animal Science
S Afr J Anim Sci S Afr Tydskr Veekunde — South African Journal of Animal Science/Suid-Afrikaanse Tydskrif vir Veekunde
S Afr J Antarct Res — South African Journal of Antarctic Research
S Afr J Antarct Res Suppl — South African Journal of Antarctic Research. Supplement
S Afr J Bot — South African Journal of Botany
S Afr J Bus Manage — South African Journal of Business Management
S Afr J Chem — South African Journal of Chemistry
S Afr J Chem/S Afr Tydskr Chem — South African Journal of Chemistry/Suid-Afrikaanse Tydskrif vir Chemie
S Afr J Clin Sci — South African Journal of Clinical Science
S Afr J Comm Disorders — South African Journal of Communication Disorders
S Afr J Commun Disord — South African Journal of Communication Disorders
S Afr J Contin Med Educ — South African Journal of Continuing Medical Education
S Afr J Crim L — South African Journal of Criminal Law and Criminology
S Afr J Crim Law Criminol — South African Journal of Criminal Law and Criminology
S Afr J Cult & A Hist — South African Journal of Culture and Art History
S Afr J Dairy Sci — South African Journal of Dairy Science
S Afr J Dairy Sci Suid Afr Tydskr Suiwelkunde — South African Journal of Dairy Science/Suid-Afrikaanse Tydskrif vir Suiwelkunde
S Afr J Dairy Technol — South African Journal of Dairy Technology
S Afr J Ec — South African Journal of Economics
S Afr J Econ — South African Journal of Economics
S Afr J Educ — South African Journal of Education
S Afr J Enol Vitic — South African Journal for Enology and Viticulture
S Afr Jersey — South African Jersey
S Afr J Ethnol — South African Journal of Ethnology
S Afr J Geol — South African Journal of Geology
S Afr J Hosp Med — South African Journal of Hospital Medicine
S Afr J Ind — South African Journal of Industries
S Afr J Ind Labour Gaz — South African Journal of Industries and Labour Gazette
S Afr J Lab Clin Med — South African Journal of Laboratory and Clinical Medicine
S Afr J Labour Relat — South African Journal of Labour Relations

S Afr J Libr Inf Sci — South African Journal for Librarianship and Information Science
S Afr J Mar Sci — South African Journal of Marine Science
S Afr J Med Lab Technol — South African Journal of Medical Laboratory Technology
S Afr J Med Sci — South African Journal of Medical Sciences
S Afr J Musicology — South African Journal of Musicology
S Afr J Music Therap — South African Journal of Music Therapy
S Afr J Nutr — South African Journal of Nutrition
S Afr J Nutr/S Afr Tydskr Voeding — South African Journal of Nutrition/Suid-Afrikaanse Tydskrif vir Voeding
S Afr J Obstet Gynaecol — South African Journal of Obstetrics and Gynaecology
S Afr J Occup Ther — South African Journal of Occupational Therapy
S Afr J Philos — South African Journal of Philosophy
S Afr J Photogramm Remote Sensing Cartogr — South African Journal of Photogrammetry. Remote Sensing and Cartography
S Afr J Phys — South African Journal of Physics
S Afr J Physiother — South African Journal of Physiotherapy
S Afr J Plant Soil — South African Journal of Plant and Soil
S Afr J Plant Soil S Afr Tydskr Plant Grond — South African Journal of Plant and Soil/Suid-Afrikaanse Tydskrif vir Plant en Grond
S Afr J Psychol — South African Journal of Psychology
S Afr J Radiol — South African Journal of Radiology
S Afr J Sci — South African Journal of Science
S Afr J Sci Suppl — South African Journal of Science. Supplement
S Afr J Sociology — South African Journal of Sociology
S Afr J Sports Med — South African Journal of Sports Medicine
S Afr J Surg — South African Journal of Surgery
S Afr J Surg/S Afr Tydskr Chir — South African Journal of Surgery/Suid-Afrikaanse Tydskrif vir Chirurgie
S Afr J Wildl Res — South African Journal of Wildlife Research
S Afr J Wild Res — South African Journal of Wildlife Research
S Afr J Zool — South African Journal of Zoology
S Afr J Zool S Afr Tydskr Dierkd — South African Journal of Zoology/Suid-Afrikaanse Tydskrif vir Dierkunde
S Afr Kankerbull — Suid-Afrikaanse Kankerbulletin
SAfrL — Studies in African Literature
S Afr Labour Bull — South African Labour Bulletin
S Afr Lapid Mag — South African Lapidary Magazine
S Afr Law J — South African Law Journal
S Afr Libr — South African Libraries
S Afr Librs — South African Libraries
S Afr LJ — South African Law Journal
S Afr LR — South African Law Reports
S Afr Mach Tool Rev — South African Machine Tool Review
S Afr Mater Handl News — South African Materials Handling News
S Afr Mech Eng — South African Mechanical Engineer
S Afr Mech Engr — South African Mechanical Engineer
S Afr Med Equip News — South African Medical Equipment News
S Afr Med J — South African Medical Journal
S Afr Med Post — South African Medical Post
S Afr Med Tim — South African Medical Times
S-Afr Med Tydskr — Suid-Afrikaanse Mediese Tydskrif
S Afr Meg Ing — Suid-Afrikaanse Meganiese Ingenieur
S Afr Min Eng J — South African Mining and Engineering Journal
S Afr Min J — South African Mining Journal
S Afr Min Rev — South African Mining Review
S Afr Min World — South African Mining World
S Afr Mus Ann — South African Museum. Annals
S Afr Mus Assoc Bull — South African Museums Association Bulletin
S Afr Music Teach — South African Music Teacher
S Afr Mus Rep — South African Museum Report
S Afr Nucl Dev Corp Rep — South Africa. Nuclear Development Corporation. Report PER
S Afr Numis J — South African Numismatic Journal
S Afr Nurs J — South African Nursing Journal
S Afr Optom — South African Optometrist
S Afr Outl — South African Outlook
S Afr Outlook — South African Outlook
S Afr Panorama — South African Panorama
S Afr Pat Doc — South Africa. Patent Document
S Afr Pat Trade Marks Off Pat J Incl Trade Marks Des — South Africa. Patent and Trade Marks Office. Patent Journal, Including Trade Marks and Designs
S Afr Pharm J — South African Pharmaceutical Journal
S Afr Ph S T — Transactions of the South African Philosophical Society
S Afr Pneumoconiosis Rev — South African Pneumoconiosis Review
S Afr Poult Bull — South African Poultry Bulletin
S Afr Pract — South African Practitioner
S Afr QJ — South African Quarterly Journal
S Afr Radiogr — South African Radiographer
S Afr Railw — South African Railways
S Afr Rep Secr Water Affairs — South Africa. Report of the Secretary for Water Affairs
S Afr Sci — South African Science
S Afr Sea Fish Branch Invest Rep — South Africa. Sea Fisheries Branch. Investigational Report
S Afr Sea Fish Inst Invest Rep — South Africa. Sea Fisheries Institute. Investigational Report
S Afr Sea Fish Res Inst Invest Rep — South Africa. Sea Fisheries Research Institute. Investigational Report
S Afr Shipp News Fish Ind Rev — South African Shipping News and Fishing Industry Review
S Afr Spectrosc Conf Proc — South African Spectroscopy Conference. Proceedings
S Afr Spektrosk Konf — Suid-Afrikaanse Spektroskopiese Konferensie

S-Afr Spoorwee — Suid-Afrikaanse Spoorwee
S Afr Stat — South African Statistical Journal
S Afr Stat J — South African Statistical Journal
S Afr Sugar Assoc Exp Stn Annu Rep — South African Sugar Association Experiment Station. Annual Report
S Afr Sugar Assoc Exp Stn Bull — South African Sugar Association Experiment Station. Bulletin
S Afr Sugar J — South African Sugar Journal
S Afr Sugar Tehnol Assoc Proc Annu Congr — South African Sugar Technologists' Association. Proceedings. Annual Congress
S Afr Sugar Year Book — South African Sugar Year Book
S Afr Sug J — South African Sugar Journal
S Afr Surv J — South African Survey Journal
S Afr Text — South African Textiles
S Afr Transp — South African Transport
S Afr Treas — South African Treasurer
S Afr Tunnel — South African Tunnelling
S Afr Tunnelling — South African Tunnelling
S-Afr Tydsk Natuurwet Tegnol — Suid-Afrikaanse Tydskrif vir Natuurwetenskap en Tegnologie
S-Afr Tydskr Antarkt Navors — Suid-Afrikaanse Tydskrif vir Antarktiese Navorsing
S-Afr Tydskr Antarkt Navors Suppl — Suid-Afrikaanse Tydskrif vir Antarktiese Navorsing. Supplement
S Afr Tydskr Apteekwese — Suid-Afrikaanse Tydskrif vir Apteekwese
S Afr Tydskr Chem — Suid-Afrikaanse Tydskrif vir Chemie
S-Afr Tydskr Chir — Suid-Afrikaanse Tydskrif vir Chirurgie
S Afr Tydskr Dierkd — Suid-Afrikaanse Tydskrif vir Dierkunde
S Afr Tydskr Fis — Suid-Afrikaanse Tydskrif vir Fisika
S-Afr Tydskr Geneeskd — Suid-Afrikaanse Tydskrif vir Geneeskunde
S Afr Tydskr Geol — Suid-Afrikaanse Tydskrif vir Geologie
S Afr Tydskr Klin Wet — Suid-Afrikaanse Tydskrif vir Kliniese Wetenskap
S Afr Tydskr Kultgesk — Suid-Afrikaanse Tydskrif vir Kultuurgeskiedenis
S-Afr Tydskr Lab Kliniekwerk — Suid-Afrikaanse Tydskrif vir Laboratorium en Kliniekwerk
S-Afr Tydskr Landbouwet — Suid-Afrikaanse Tydskrif vir Landbouwetenskap
S Afr Tydskr Med Lab Tegnol — Suid-Afrikaanse Tydskrif vir Mediese Laboratorium-Tegnologie
S Afr Tydskr Natuurnavors — Suid-Afrikaanse Tydskrif vir Natuurnavorsing
S Afr Tydskr Natuurwet Tegnol — Suid-Afrikaanse Tydskrif vir Natuurwetenskap en Tegnologie
S Afr Tydskr Navors Antarkt — Suid-Afrikaanse Tydskrif vir Navorsing in Antarktika
S-Afr Tydskr Obstet Ginekol — Suid-Afrikaanse Tydskrif vir Obstetrie en Ginekologie
S Afr Tydskr Plant Grond — Suid-Afrikaanse Tydskrif vir Plant en Grond
S Afr Tydskr Plantkd — Suid-Afrikaanse Tydskrif vir Plantkunde
S Afr Tydskr Plantkunde — Suid-Afrikaanse Tydskrif vir Plantkunde
S-Afr Tydskr Radiol — Suid-Afrikaanse Tydskrif vir Radiologie
S-Afr Tydskr Seewetenskap — Suid-Afrikaanse Tydskrif vir Seewetenskap
S Afr Tydskr Suiwelkd — Suid-Afrikaanse Tydskrif vir Suiwelkunde
S-Afr Tydskr Suiweltegnol — Suid-Afrikaanse Tydskrif vir Suiweltegnologie
S-Afr Tydskr Veekd — Suid-Afrikaanse Tydskrif vir Veekunde
S-Afr Tydskr Voeding — Suid-Afrikaanse Tydskrif vir Voeding
S-Afr Tydskr Wet — Suid-Afrikaanse Tydskrif vir Wetenskap
S Afr Tydskr Wysbegeerte — Suid-Afrikaanse Tydskrif vir Wysbegeerte
S Afr Wet Nywerheidnavorsingsraad Jaarversl — Suid-Afrikaanse Wetenskaplike en Nywerheidnavorsingsraad. Jaarverslag
S-Afr Wet Nywerheid-Navorsingsraad Navorsingsversl — Suid-Afrikaanse Wetenskaplike en Nywerheidnavorsingsraad. Navorsingsverslag
S-Afr Wet Nywerheid-Navorsingsraad Spes Versl — Suid-Afrikaanse Wetenskaplike en Nywerheidnavorsingsraad. Spesiale Verslag
S Afr Woltekst Navorsingsinst Jaarversl — Suid-Afrikaanse Woltekstiel-Navorsingsinstituut Jaarverslag
S Afr Woltekst Navorsingsinst Tech Rep — Suid-Afrikaanse Woltekstiel-Navorsingsinstituut. Technical Report
S Afr Wool Text Res Inst Annu Rep — South African Wool and Textile Research Institute. Annual Report
S Afr Wool Text Res Inst Bull — South African Wool and Textile Research Institute. Bulletin
S Afr Wool Text Res Inst Dig — South African Wool Textile Research Institute. Digest
S Afr Wool Text Res Inst SAWTRI Spec Publ — South African Wool and Textile Research Institute. SAWTRI Special Publication
S Afr Wool Text Res Inst Tech Rep — South African Wool and Textile Research Institute. Technical Report
S Afr Yearb Int Law — South African Yearbook of International Law
S Afr YIL — South African Yearbook of International Law
Saf Sci — Safety Science
Saf Sci Abstr — Safety Science Abstracts Journal
Saf Sci Abstr J — Safety Science Abstracts Journal
Saf Ser IAEA — Safety Series. IAEA
Saf Surv — Safety Surveyor
SAFTTA Jnl — SAFTTA [*South African Film and Television Technicians Association*] Journal
Safugetierkd Mitt — Safugetierkundliche Mitteilungen
Sag — Saggiatore
SAG — Stuttgarter Arbeiten zur Germanistik
Saga Bk Viking Soc N Res — Saga-Book. Viking Society for Northern Research
Saga-Book — Saga-Book. Viking Society for Northern Research
SAGA Bull — SAGA [*Sand and Gravel Association Ltd.*] Bulletin
Sagamore Army Mater Res Conf Proc — Sagamore Army Materials Research Conference Proceedings
Saga S — Saga och Sed
Sage Annu R Communic Res — Sage Annual Reviews of Communication Research

Sage Elect Stud Yb — Sage Electoral Studies Yearbook
Sage Fam Stud Abstr — Sage Family Studies Abstracts
Sage Int Yb For Pol Stud — Sage International Yearbook of Foreign Policy Studies
Sage/JIAS — Journal of Interamerican Studies and World Affairs. Sage Publication for the Center for Advanced International Studies. University of Miami
SA Geol Atlas Ser — South Australia. Geological Survey. Atlas Series
SA Geol Surv Bull — South Australia. Geological Survey. Bulletin
SA Geol Surv Geol Atlas 1 Mile Ser — South Australia. Geological Survey. Geological Atlas. 1 Mile Series
SA Geol Surv Rep Invest — South Australia. Geological Survey. Report of Investigations
Sage Pap CP — Sage Professional Papers in Comparative Politics
Sage Pub Admin Abstr — Sage Public Administration Abstracts
Sage Public Adm Abstr — Sage Public Administration Abstracts
Sage Univ Paper Ser Quant Appl Social Sci — Sage University Paper Series on Quantitative Applications in the Social Sciences
Sage Urban Abs — Sage Urban Abstracts
Sage Urban Stud Abstr — Sage Urban Studies Abstracts
Sage Urb Stud Abstr — Sage Urban Studies Abstracts
Sage Yb Polit Publ Pol — Sage Yearbooks in Politics and Public Policy
Sage Yb Women's Pol — Sage Yearbook in Women's Policy Studies
Sagg Fen — Saggi Fenici
Saggi — Saggi e Ricerche di Letteratura Francese
Saggi & Mem Stor A — Saggi e Memorie di Storia dell'Arte
Saggi Sci — Saggi Scientifici
Saggi Sci Filos Natur — Saggi di Scienze e Filosofia Naturale
SAGLBQ — Acta Geographica Lodziensia
Saglik Derg — Saglik Dergisi
SAGMN — Sudhoffs Archiv fuer Geschichte der Medizin und der Naturwissenschaften
SAGN — Sagkeeng News
Sag Ric — Saggi e Ricerche
Sague Med — Saguenay Medical
SAH — Sitzungsberichte. Heidelberg Akademie der Wissenschaften. Philosophisch-Historische Klasse
SAH — Stratford-On-Avon Herald
SAH — Svenska Akademiens Handlingar
Sah de Dem — Sahara de Demain
SAHEA — Sanitaer- und Heizungstechnik
SAHG — Die Sumerischen und Akkadischen Hymnen und Gebete
SAHJ — Society of Architectural Historians. Journal
SAHJ — Society of Automotive Historians. Journal
SAHLBull — Societe d'Art et d'Histoire du le Diocese de Liege. Bulletin
SAHOA — Saiko To Hoan
SA Homes & Gardens — South Australian Homes and Gardens
SAHP — St. Antony's Hall Publications
SAHR — Society for Army Historical Research. Journal
SAHS — Swiss American Historical Society. Newsletter
SAI — Seltene Assyrische Ideogramme
SAI — Statistical Abstracts of Israel
SAI — Studii si Articole de Istorie
SaiA — Saisons d'Alsace
Saibanshu — Saiko Saibansho Saibanshu
SAIBB — Soil Association. Information Bulletin and Advisory Service
SAICDB — Israel. Institute of Field and Garden Crops. Scientific Activities
Said Med J — Said Medical Journal
SAIEDH — Israel. Institute of Agricultural Engineering. Scientific Activities
SAIG — South Australian Industrial Gazette
SAIGA — Saishin Igaku
SAIGB — Sangyo Igaku
SAIHDO — Israel. Institute of Horticulture. Scientific Activities
SAIL Stud Amer Indian Lit — SAIL. Studies in American Indian Literatures
SAIME J — South African Institution of Mechanical Engineers. Journal
Sains Malays — Sains Malaysiana
SA Inst J — South Australian Institutes. Journal
Saint Lawrence Univ Geol Inf and Referral Service Bull — Saint Lawrence University. Geological Information and Referral Service. Bulletin
Saint Louis Univ LJ — St. Louis University. Law Journal
SAIR — South Australian Industrial Reports
Sairaanhoitaja — Sairaanhoitaja Sjuksiterskan
Sairaanh Vuosik — Sairaanhoidon Vuosikirja
SAISDP — Israel. Institute of Animal Science. Scientific Activities
SAIS Rev — SAIS [*School of Advanced International Studies*] Review
Saitama Math J — Saitama Mathematical Journal
SAIT News — SAIT [*South Australian Institute of Teachers*] Newsletter
Sait Not — Saitabi. Noticiario de Historia, Arte, y Arqueologia de Levante
Saito Ho-On Kai Mus Nat Hist Res Bull — Saito Ho-On Kai Museum of Natural History. Research Bulletin
Saito Ho-On Kai Mus Res Bull — Saito Ho-On Kai Museum Research Bulletin
SA/J — Journal. Societe des Americanistes
SaJ — Saalburg-Jahrbuch
SAJ — South African Journal of Economics
SAJAC — South African Journal of Animal Science
SAJAR — South African Journal of Antarctic Research
SAJBDD — Suid-Afrikaanse Tydskrif vir Plantkunde
SAJCD — South African Journal of Chemistry
SAJE — South African Journal of Economics
SA J Educ Res — South Australian Journal of Education Research
SAJER — South Australian Journal of Education Research
SAJH — Studies in American Jewish History
SAJL — Studies in American Jewish Literature
SAJM — South African Journal of Musicology
SAJMA — South African Journal of Medical Sciences
SAJPA — South African Journal of Physiotherapy
SAJPEM — Suid-Afrikaanse Tydskrif vir Wysbegeerte

SAJRA — South African Journal of Radiology

SAJ Res Sport Phys Educ Recreat — SA [*South African*] Journal for Research in Sport. Physical Education and Recreation

SAJSA — South African Journal of Science

SAJSB — South African Journal of Surgery

SAJSEV — Suid-Afrikaanse Tydskrif vir Plant en Grond

SA J Sports Med — SA [*South African*] Journal of Sports Medicine

SAJTA — South African Journal of Medical Laboratory Technology

SAJZD — South African Journal of Zoology

SAK — Sumerischen und Akkadischen Koenigsinschriften

SAKAD — Sangyo To Kankyo

Sakhalin Kompleksn Nauchno Issled Inst Akad Nauk SSSR Tr — Sakhalinskii Kompleksnyi Nauchno-Issledovatel'skii Institut. AkademiyaNauk SSSR. Trudy

Sakharn — Sakharnyi

Sakharth SSR Mecn Akad Gamothvl Centr Srom — Sakharthvelos SSR Mecnierebatha Gamothvlithi Centris Sromebi

Sakharth SSR Mecn Akad Marthw Sistem Inst Srom — Sakharthvelos SSR Mecnierebatha Akademia Marthwis Sistemebis Instituti Sromebi

Sakharth SSR Mecn Akad Math Inst Srom — Sakharthvelos SSR Mecnierebatha Akademia A. Razmadzis Sahelobis Thbilsis Mathematikis Institutis Sromebi

Sakharth SSR Mecn Akad Moambe — Sakharthvelos SSR Mecnierebatha Akademia Moambe

Sakharth SSR Ped Inst Srom Phiz-Math Ser — Sakharthvelos SSR Pedagogiuri Institutebis Sromebi. Phizika-Mathematikis Seria

Sakharthw SSR Mecniereb Akad Moambe — Sakharthwelos SSR Mecnierebatha Akademiis Moambe

SAKHB — Sangyo Anzen Kenkyusho Hokoku

Sakh Prom — Sakharnaya Promyshlennost

Sakh Promst — Sakharnaya Promyshlennost

Sakh Svekla — Sakharnaya Svekla

Sak Ku — Sakrale Kunst

SAKM — Schriftenreihe des Arbeitskreises fuer Evangelische Kirchenmusik

SAKM — Schriftenreihe des Arbeitskreises fuer Kirchenmusik

SAKOD — Sangyo Kogai

Sakura X-Ray Photogr Rev — Sakura X-Ray Photographic Review

SAL — Sales and Marketing Management

Sal — Salesianum

Sal — Salmagundi

SAL — Salmanticensis

SAL — Solar Age. A Magazine of the Sun

SAL — Southwestern American Literature

SAL — Studies in African Linguistics

SALA — Statistical Abstract of Latin America

SA Law Soc Bull — South Australian Law Society. Bulletin

Sal B — Salesianum Biblioteca [*Torino*].

SALB — Studia Albanica

SALCR — South Australian Licensing Court. Reports

Saldat Auto — Saldatura Autogena

SALEA — Sanshi Kenkyu

Sales & Mkt Mgt — Sales and Marketing Management

Sales Mgt — Sales Management [*Later, Sales and Marketing Management*]

Sales TC — Sales Tax Cases

SALIA7 — Ernaehrungswissenschaft

Salisbury Med Bull — Salisbury Medical Bulletin

Salisbury Rev — Salisbury Review

SALit — Studies in American Literature

SA L J — South African Law Journal

Salm — Salmagundi

Salm — Salmanticensis

Salmon Trou Mag — Salmon and Trout Magazine

Salmon Trout Mag — Salmon and Trout Magazine

Sal Ocup — Salud Ocupacional

Sal Publ — Salud Publica

SALR — South African Law Reports

SALR — South Australian Law Reports

SALRA — Schweizer Aluminium Rundschau

SALS — Saint Augustine Lecture Series

SALSSAH — Serials in Australian Libraries: Social Sciences and Humanities

SALSSAH/NRT — Serials in Australian Libraries: Social Sciences and Humanities/ Newly Reported Titles

Sal T — Salesianum (Torino)

SALT — South African Law Times

Salt C R — New Salt Creek Reader

Sal Ter — Sal Terre

Salt Lake Min Rev — Salt Lake Mining Review

Salt Lake M Rv — Salt Lake Mining Review

Salt Lk Tr — Salt Lake City Tribune

Salt Mon (Taipei) — Salt Monthly (Taipei)

Salt Res Ind — Salt Research and Industry

Salt Res Ind J — Salt Research and Industry Journal

Salub Asist Mex — Salubridad y Asistencia (Mexico)

Salub Asist Soc Hav — Salubridad y Asistencia Social (La Habana)

Salud Ocup — Salud Ocupacional

Salud Publica Mex — Salud Publica de Mexico

Salute Italia Med — Salute Italia Medica

Salvav — Salvavidas

Salv Med — Salvador Medico

Salzburg Conf Cereb Vasc Dis — Salzburg Conference on Cerebral Vascular Disease

Salzburger Beitr Paracelsusforsch — Salzburger Beitraege zur Paracelsusforschung

Salzburger Jrbh Phil — Salzburger Jahrbuch fuer Philosophie

Salzburg Gel Unterhalt — Salzburgische Gelehrte Unterhaltungen

Salzburg Haus Nat Ber Abt B Geol-Mineral Samml — Salzburg Haus der Natur. Berichte. Abteilung B. Geologisch-Mineralogische Sammlungen

Salzburg Landes Ztg — Salzburger Landes-Zeitung

Salzburg Musbl — Salzburger Museumsblaetter

Salz St Ang — Salzburger Studien zur Anglistik und Amerikanistik

Sam — Samadhi

SAM — SAM [*Society for Advancement of Management*] Advanced Management Journal

Sam — Samisdat

Sam — Sammlung

S Am — Scientific American

SAm — Sembradores de Amistad

Sam — Serving Advertising in the Midwest [*Later, Adweek*]

SAM — Sitzungsberichte. Bayerische Akademie der Wissenschaften

S Am — South American

SAM — Studies in Applied Mechanics

SAMA — Survey of Adults and Markets of Affluence

SAM Advanced Mgt J — SAM [*Society for Advancement of Management*] Advanced Management Journal

SAM Adv Man — SAM [*Society for Advancement of Management*] Advanced Management Journal

Samark Gos Univ Im Alishera Navoi Tr — Samarkandskii Gosudarstvennyi Universitet Imeni Alishera Navoi. Trudy

Samaru Agric Newsl — Samaru Agricultural Newsletter

Samaru Agr Newslett — Samaru Agricultural Newsletter

Samaru Inst Agric Res Soil Surv Bull — Samaru Institute for Agricultural Research. Soil Survey Bulletin

Samaru Misc Pap — Samaru Miscellaneous Paper

Samaru Res Bull — Samaru Research Bulletin

SA Mast Build — South Australian Master Builder

Sambalpur Univ J Sci Technol — Sambalpur University. Journal of Science and Technology

SAMBHist — Societe des Antiquaires de la Morinie. Bulletin Historique

Sam BN — Samuel Butler Newsletter

Sam Dial — Sammlung Dialog

SAMEA — South African Mechanical Engineer

SAMEB — SA [*South African*] Mining and Engineering Journal

SAMED — South African Medical Literature

Same Day Surg — Same-Day Surgery

Samenvatting Energ Stud Cent — Samenvatting. Energie Studie Centrum

S Amer Explor — South American Explorer

SA Methodist — South Australian Methodist

SAmF — Studies in American Fiction

Samf St Eriks Arsb — Samfundet St Eriks Arsbok

SAmH — Studies in American Humor

SAMH — Studies in Anabaptist and Mennonite History

SAMIDF — Systematic and Applied Microbiology

SA Min Eng J — SA [*South African*] Mining and Engineering Journal

SAMJ — Sami Medica. Journal. Sami Medical Association

SAMJA — South African Medical Journal

Saml — Samlaren

SAML — Studies in American Literature

Saml Roen Uptaeckter Phys — Samling af Roen Och Uptaekter, Gjorde i Senare Tider, Uti Physik, Medecin, Chirurgie, Natural-Historia, Chemie, Hushallning

Samm — Sammlung. Zeitschrift fuer Kultur und Erziehung

SAMM — South American Missionary Magazine, including A Voice for South America, A Voice of Pity for South America

Sammbl Hist Ver Eichstatt — Sammelblatt des Historischen Vereins Eichstatt

Sammbl Hist Ver Ingolstadt — Sammelblatt des Historischen Vereins Ingolstadt

Sammelbl Hist Ver Ingolstadt — Sammelblatt des Historischen Vereins Ingolstadt und Umgebung

Sammel Bl Ingolstadt — Sammelblatt der Historischer Verein Ingolstadt

Sammelh Kurznachr Akad Wiss Goettingen — Sammelheft. Kurznachrichten der Akademie der Wissenschaften inGoettingen

Sammelschriften Paedagog Fak Ostrau — Sammelschriften Paedagogischen Fakultaet in Ostrau

Samml Auserlesener Abh Gebrauche Prakt Aerzte — Sammlung Auserlesener Abhandlungen zum Gebrauche Praktischer Aerzte

Samml Auserlesener Schriften Staats Landw Inhalt — Sammlung Auserlesener Schriften von Staats- und Landwirthschaftlichem Inhalte

Samml Forschungsarb Landwirtsch Fak Belgrader Univ — Sammlung der Forschungsarbeiten der Landwirtschaftlichen Fakultaet.Belgrader Universitaet

Samml Forschungsarb Pap Zellstoffind — Sammlung der Forschungsarbeiten aus der Papier- und Zellstoffindustrie

Samml Geol Fuehrer — Sammlung Geologischer Fuehrer

Samml Goeschen — Sammlung Goeschen

Samml Interessanter Zwekmaessig Abgefasster Reisebeschreib Ju — Sammlung Interessanter und Durchgaengig Zwekmaessig Abgefasster Reisebeschreibungen fuer die Jugend

Samml Kleiner Ausfuehr Verschiedenen Wiss — Sammlung Kleiner Ausfuehrungen aus Verschiedenen Wissenschaften

Samml Neuer Nuetzl Abh Versuche Oekon — Sammlung Neuer und Nuetzlicher Abhandlungen und Versuche aus der Oekonomie, Mechanik und Naturlehre

Samml Nuetzl Angenehmer Gegenstaende Natur-Gesch — Sammlungen Nuetzlicher und Angenehmer Gegenstaende aus Allen Theilen der Natur-Geschichte, Arzneywissenschaft und Haushaltungskunst

Samml Nuetzl Aufs & Nachr Baukst Betreff — Sammlung Nuetzlicher Aufsaetze und Nachrichten die Baukunst Betreffend

Sammlung Kurzer Lehrbuecher d Roman Spr u Lit — Sammlung Kurzer Lehrbuecher der Romanischen Sprachen und Literaturen

Sammlung Wichmann NF — Sammlung Wichmann. Neue Folge

Samml Vergiftungsfaellen — Sammlung von Vergiftungsfaellen

Samml Zwangl Abh Geb Psychiatr Neurol — Sammlung Zwangloser Abhandlungen aus dem Gebiete der Psychiatrie und Neurologie

Samml Zwangloser Abh Dermatol — Sammlung Zwangloser Abhandlungen aus dem Gebiete der Dermatologie, der Syphilidologie und der Krankheiten des Urogenitalapparates

Samoan Pac LJ — Samoan Pacific Law Journal
Samoletnoe Elektrooborud — Samoletnoe Elektrooborudovanie
Samoletostr Tekh Vozdushn Flota — Samoletostroenie i Tekhnika Vozdushnogo Flota
Samoregul Metab Rast Mater Rab Soveshch Kollok — Samoregulyatsiya Metabolizma Rastenii. Materialy RabochegoSoveshchaniya s Kollokviumom po teme Samoregulyatsiya Metabolizma Rastenii
SA Motor — South Australian Motor
Samotsvety Mater Sezda MMA — Samotsvety. Materialy S'ezda MMA
SAMPE J — SAMPE [*Society for the Advancement of Material and Process Engineering*] Journal
SAMPE Q — SAMPE [*Society for the Advancement of Material and Process Engineering*] Quarterly
SAMPE Qtly — SAMPE [*Society for the Advancement of Material and Process Engineering*] Quarterly
Sampling Assaying Precious Met Proc Int Semin — Sampling and Assaying of Precious Metals. Proceedings. International Seminar
SAMQA — SAMPE [*Society for the Advancement of Material and Process Engineering*] Quarterly
SAMRD — South African Machine Tool Review
Samt — Samtiden
SAMUS — South African Journal of Musicology
SA Museum Rec — South Australian Museum. Records
SA Mus Tcr — South Africa Music Teacher
Samv — Samvirke
SAN — Glasnik. Srpska Akademija Nauka i Umetnosti
SAN — SAN: Journal of the Society for Ancient Numismatics
SANAn — Societe Archeologique de Namur. Annales
San Anto E — San Antonio Executive
SA Nat — South Australian Naturalist
SA Naturalist — South Australian Naturalist
SANA Update Newsl — SANA [*Scientists Against Nuclear Arms*] Update Newsletter
SANBB — Sankhya. Series B. Indian Journal of Statistics
San Bernardino County Med Soc Bull — San Bernardino County Medical Society. Bulletin
Sanc Nost — Sanctificatio Nostra
Sandal — Sandalion. Quaderni di Cultura Classica, Cristiana, e Medievale
S & C Bank — Standard and Chartered Review
S & C Spec — Soap/Cosmetics/Chemical Specialties
Sand Dune Res — Sand Dune Research
Sandf (NY) — Sandford's New York Superior Court Reports
S and H Bull — Smoking and Health Bulletin
Sandia Lab Tech Rep SAND — Sandia National Laboratories. Technical Report SAND
Sandia Natl Lab Tech Rep SAND — Sandia National Laboratories. Technical Report SAND
Sandia SN — Sandia Science News
San Diego B — San Diego Business Journal
San Diego Biomed Symp Proc — San Diego Biomedical Symposium. Proceedings
San Diego L Rev — San Diego Law Review
San Diego Soc Nat Hist Mem — San Diego Society of Natural History. Memoirs
San Diego Soc Nat History Occasional Paper Trans — San Diego Society of Natural History. Occasional Papers. Transactions
San Diego Soc Nat History Trans — San Diego Society of Natural History. Transactions
San Diego Soc N H Tr — San Diego Society of Natural History. Transactions
San Diego Symp Biomed Eng Proc — San Diego Symposium for Biomedical Engineering. Proceedings
San Diego U — San Diego Union
San DLR — San Diego Law Review
S & M — Sun and Moon
S & MR — Shire and Municipal Record
S & M Record — Shire and Municipal Record
S & N — Statesman and Nation
Sandoz Bull — Sandoz Bulletin
S & S — School and Society
S & S — Science and Society
S & S — Sight and Sound
S & S — Stars & Stripes
S&S — Strategies and Solutions
S & S — Syntax and Semantics
SAND (Sandia Natl Lab) — SAND (Sandia National Laboratories)
Sands Clays Miner — Sands, Clays, and Minerals
S & T — Sky and Telescope
S & T — Strategy and Tactics
S & W — South and West
SANE — Sources from the Ancient Near East
SANET — Supplement to Ancient Near Eastern Texts
SanF — San Francisco Magazine
San Fernando Val Dent Soc Bull — San Fernando Valley Dental Society. Bulletin
San Fern Val LR — San Fernando Valley Law Review
San Fern VL Rev — San Fernando Valley Law Review
San FLJ — San Francisco Law Journal
San Fran B — San Francisco Business Journal
San Francisco Bus — San Francisco Business
San Francisco Bus Jnl — San Francisco Business Journal
San Francisco Med — San Francisco Medicine
San Francisco Micro Soc Tr — San Francisco Microscopical Society. Transactions
San Francisco Munic Rec — San Francisco Municipal Record
San Francisco Police & Peace Offic J — San Francisco Police and Peace Officers Journal
San Fran Cro — San Francisco Chronicle
San Fran Law Bull — San Francisco Law Bulletin
San Fran LB — San Francisco Law Bulletin

San Fran LJ — San Francisco Law Journal
San Fran Opera — San Francisco Opera Magazine
San Fr LB — San Francisco Law Bulletin
San Fr LJ — San Francisco Law Journal
Sang — Sangre
San Gabriel Val Dent Soc Bull — San Gabriel Valley Dental Society. Bulletin
Sang Natak — Sangeet Natak
SANGruz — Soobscenija Akademiji Nauk Gruzinskoj SSR
SANGT — Soobshcheniia. Akademiia Nauk Gruzinskoi SSR (Tiflis)
SANH — Somerset Archaeology and Natural History
Sanid Aeronaut — Sanidad Aeronautica
Sanid Benef Munic — Sanidad y Beneficiencia Municipal
Sanid Mil — Sanidad Militar
Sanitary & Heat Eng — Sanitary and Heating Engineering
Sanit Eng Pap Colo State Univ — Sanitary Engineering Papers. Colorado State University
Sanit Heiz Tech — Sanitaer- und Heizungstechnik
Sanit Heizungstech (Duesseldorf) — Sanitaer- und Heizungstechnik (Duesseldorf)
Sanit Heizungstechnik — Sanitaer- und Heizungstechnik
Sanit Nytt — Sanitets Nytt Utgitt av Forsvarets Sanitet
Sanit Okh Vodoemov Zagryaz Prom Stochnymi Vodami — Sanitarnaya Okhrana Vodoemov ot Zagryazneniya Promyshlennymi Stochnymi Vodami
Sanit Rec J Munic Eng — Sanitary Record and Journal of Municipal Engineering
Sanit Rec Munic Eng — Sanitary Record and Municipal Engineering
Sanit Tech (Duesseldorf) — Sanitaere Technik (Duesseldorf)
Sanit Tekh — Sanitarnaya Tekhnika
Sanit Tekh Dokl Nauchn Konf Leningr — Sanitarnaya Tekhnika. Doklady Nauchnoi Konferentsii. LeningradskiiInzhenerno-Stroitel'nyi Institut
SANJ — South Australian Numismatic Journal
SANJA — South African Nursing Journal
San Jose Bus — San Jose Business Journal
San Jose M — San Jose Mercury News
San Jose Stud — San Jose Studies
San Juan Rev — San Juan Review
Sanka Fuji — Sanka To Fujinka
Sanken Tech Rep — Sanken Technical Report
Sankhya A — Sankhya. Series A. Indian Journal of Statistics
Sankhya B — Sankhya. Series B. Indian Journal of Statistics
Sankhya C — Sankhya. Series C. Indian Journal of Statistics
Sankhya Indian J Stat Ser B — Sankhya. Series B. Indian Journal of Statistics
Sankhya Ser A — Sankhya. Series A
Sankhya Ser A — Sankhya. Series A. Indian Journal of Statistics
Sankhya Ser B — Sankhya. Series B. Indian Journal of Statistics
SANNA — Schweizer Archiv fuer Neurologie, Neurochirurgie, und Psychiatrie
SANNAW — Archives Suisses de Neurologie, Neurochirurgie, et de Psychiatrie/ Archivio Svizzero di Neurologia, Neurochirurgia, e Psichiatria
SAns — Studia Anselmiana
SANSS — Structure and Nomenclature Search System
SANT — Studien zum Alten und Neuen Testament
S Ant — Suomen Antropologi/Antropologi i Finland
Santa Barbara Mus Nat History Dept Geology Bull — Santa Barbara Museum of Natural History. Department of Geology. Bulletin
Santa Barbara Soc N H B — Santa Barbara Society of Natural History. Bulletin
Santa Clara L — Santa Clara Lawyer
Santa Clara Law — Santa Clara Lawyer
Santa Clara LR — Santa Clara Law Review
Santa Clara L Rev — Santa Clara Law Review
Santa Fe Inst Stud Sci Complexity Lectures — Santa Fe Institute Studies in the Sciences of Complexity. Lectures
Santa Fe Inst Stud Sci Complexity Proc — Santa Fe Institute Studies in the Sciences of Complexity. Proceedings
Sant Cl LR — Santa Clara Law Review
Sante — Sante Mentale au Canada
Sante Publique (Bucur) — Sante Publique. Revue Internationale (Bucuresti)
Sante Secur Soc — Sante Securite Sociale
Santiago De Chile Un A — Anales de la Universidad de Chile (Santiago de Chile)
Santo Domingo Univ Anales Pub — Santo Domingo Universidad. Anales. Publicaciones
Santo Tomas J Med — Santo Tomas Journal of Medicine
SA Nurs J — South African Nursing Journal
SANYD — Sanitets Nytt
SAO — Smithsonian Institution. Astrophysical Observatory
SAO — Studia et Acta Orientalia
SAOAAW — Sbornik Nauchnykh Rabot Arkhangel'skogo Otdeleniya Vsesoyuznogo Nauchnogo Obshchestva Anatomov, Gistologov, i Embriologov
SAOABX — Archivos. Sociedad Americana de Oftalmologia y Optometria
SAOB — Svenska Akademiens Ordbok
SAOC — Studies in Ancient Oriental Civilization. The Oriental Institute of the University of Chicago
Sao Jose dos Campos Fac Odontol Rev — Sao Jose dos Campos. Faculdade de Odontologia. Revista
Sao Paulo Brazil Inst Pesqui Tecnol Bol — Sao Paulo, Brazil. Instituto de Pesquisas Tecnologicas. Boletin
Sao Paulo Inst Agron (Campinas) Bol — Sao Paulo. Instituto Agronomico (Campinas). Boletim
Sao Paulo Inst Agron (Campinas) Bol Tec — Sao Paulo. Instituto Agronomico (Campinas). Boletim Tecnico
Sao Paulo Inst Agron (Campinas) Circ — Sao Paulo. Instituto Agronomico (Campinas). Circular
Sao Paulo Inst Geogr Geol Bol — Sao Paulo. Instituto Geografico e Geologico. Boletim
Sao Paulo Inst Geogr Geol Relat — Sao Paulo. Instituto Geografico e Geologico. Relatorio
Sao Paulo Med — Sao Paulo Medico
Sao Paulo Med J — Sao Paulo Medical Journal

Sao Paulo Univ Inst Geocienc Bol — Sao Paulo. Universidade. Instituto de Geociencias. Boletim

Sao Paulo Univ Inst Geogr Geogr Planejamento — Sao Paulo. Universidade. Instituto de Geografia. Geografia e Planejamento

Sao Paulo Univ Inst Geogr Geomorfol — Sao Paulo. Universidade. Instituto de Geografia. Geomorfologia

Sao Paulo Univ Inst Geogr Ser Teses Monogr — Sao Paulo. Universidade. Instituto de Geografia. Serie Teses e Monografias

SA Ornithol — South Australian Ornithologist

SA Ornithologist — South Australian Ornithologist

Sap — Sapientia

SAP — Sbornik Archivnich Praci

SAP — Skandinavisches Archiv fuer Physiologie

SAP — Sociological Analysis

SAP — Studia Anglica Posnaniensia

SAPAA3 — Escuela Nacional do Agricultura [*Chapingo*]. Serie de Apuntes

SA Parl Deb — South Australia. Parliamentary Debates

SA Parl Parl Deb — South Australia. Parliament. Parliamentary Debates

Sap Dom — Sapienza. Rivista di Filosofia e di Teoogia dei Domenicani d'Italia

SAPEA — Sapere

SAPED — Salt 'n' Pepper

SAPHD — South African Journal of Physics

SAPNA — South African Panorama

SAPO — Societe Agricole, Scientifique, et Litteraire des Pyrenees Orientales. Bulletin

SAPOA — Savremena Poljoprivreda

SAPOAB — Contemporary Agriculture

Sapporo Med J — Sapporo Medical Journal

SAPR — Societe des Amis de Port-Royal

SAPR — South Australian Planning Reports

SAPRA — Sakharnaya Promyshlennost

SAPTA — SAE [*Society of Automotive Engineers*] Progress in Technology

SA Pub Serv R — South Australian Public Service Review

SAQ — South Atlantic Quarterly

SAR — Sociological Analysis

SAR — South Asian Review

SAR — South Australian Industrial Reports

SAR — Studies in the American Renaissance

Sarabhai M Chem Tech News Serv — Sarabhai M. Chemicals. Technical News Service

SA Railways — South Australian Railways Institute. Magazine

SA Railways Institute Mag — South Australian Railways Institute. Magazine

Sarat Gos Med Inst Tr — Saratovskii Gosudarstvennyi Meditsinskii Institut. Trudy

Sarat Nauchno Issled Vet Stn Sb Nauchn Rab — Saratovskaya Nauchno-Issledovatel'skaya Veterinarnaya Stantsiya.Sbornik Nauchnykh Rabot

Sarat Otd Gos Nauchno Issled Inst Ozern Rechn Rybn Khoz Tr — Saratovskoi Otdelenie Gosudarstvennogo Nauchno-Issledovatel'skogoInstituta Ozernogo i Rechnogo Rybnogo Khozyaistva. Trudy

Saratov Gos-Ped Inst Ucen Zap — Saratovskii Gosudarstvennyi-Pedagogiceskii Institut. Ucenye Zapiski

Sarat Politekh Inst Nauchn Tr — Saratovskii Politekhnicheskii Institut. Nauchnye Trudy

Sarat Skh Inst Nauchn Tr — Saratovskii Sel'skokhozyaistvennyi Institut. Nauchnye Trudy

Sarat Skh Inst Sb Nauchn Rab — Saratovskii Sel'skokhozyaistvennyi Institut. Sbornik Nauchnykh Rabot

Sarat Skh Inst Tr — Saratovskii Sel'skokhozyaistvennyi Institut. Trudy

Sarawak Gaz — Sarawak Gazette

SarawakMJ — Sarawak Museum. Journal

Sarawak Mus J — Sarawak Museum. Journal

Sarawak Res Branch Dep Agric Annu Rep — Sarawak. Research Branch. Department of Agriculture. Annual Report

Sarcoidose Rapp Conf Int — Sarcoidose. Rapports. Conference International

Sarcolemma Proc Annu Meet Int Study Group Res Card Metab — Sarcolemma. Proceedings. Annual Meeting. International Study Group for Researchin Cardiac Metabolism

Sardegna Econ — Sardegna Economica

SaRe — Saturday Review

SARE — Southeast Asian Review of English

SARE-A — Saturday Review

SA Regr — South Australian Register

SA Regr (Newspr) — South Australian Register Reports (Newspaper)

SA Res Service Bibliog — South Australia. Public Library. Research Service. Bibliographies

SARev — South Asian Review

SARev — South Atlantic Review

Sar Gaz — Sarawak Gazette

Sarget — Sargetia. Acta Musei Devensis

Sargetia Ser Sci Nat — Sargetia [*Acta Devensis*]. Series Scientia Naturae

S Ariegeoise — Societe Ariegeoise des Sciences, Lettres, et Arts. Bulletin Annuel

Sar Mus J — Sarawak Museum. Journal

Sarot Otd Gos Nauchno-Issled Inst Ozern Rechn Rybn Khoz Tr — Sarotovskoe Otdelenie Gosudarstvennogo Nauchno-Issledovatel'skogo Instituta Ozernogo i Rechnogo Rybnogo Khozyaistva. Trudy

SAR QSAR Environ Res — SAR and QSAR in Environmental Research

Sarthe S BII — Bulletin de la Societe d'Agriculture de la Sarthe

SaS — Slovo a Slovesnost

SAS — Studia Academica Slovaca

SASAE — Supplements. Annales. Service des Antiquites de l'Egypt

SA Sch Post — South Australian School Post

SasH — Saskatchewan History

SASHA — Sanfujinka No Shimpo

SA Shipp News — South African Shipping News and Fishing Industry Review

S Asian Archaeol — South Asian Archaeology

S Asian Rev — South Asian Review

S Asian Stud — South Asian Studies

S Asia R — South Asian Review

S Asia Res — South Asia Research

SASILO — Schriftenreihe. A. Stifer-Institut des Landes Oberoesterreich

Saskatchewan Dept Nat Res Ann Rept Mineral Res Br Misc Paper — Saskatchewan. Department of Natural Resources. Annual Report. Mineral ResourcesBranch. Miscellaneous Paper

Saskatchewan Geol Survey Rept — Saskatchewan Geological Survey. Report

Saskatchewan L Rev — Saskatchewan Law Review

Saskatch Med Quart — Saskatchewan Medical Quarterly

Sask Bar Rev — Saskatchewan Bar Review

Sask BR — Saskatchewan Bar Review

Sask B Rev — Saskatchewan Bar Review

Sask Bul — Saskatchewan Bulletin

Sask Busn — Saskatchewan Business

Sask Dep Miner Resour Geol Sci Br Precambrian Geol Div Rep — Saskatchewan. Department of Mineral Resources. Geological Sciences Branch. Precambrian Geology Division. Report

Sask Dep Miner Resour Pet Natural Gas Reservoir Ann — Saskatchewan. Department of Mineral Resources. Petroleum and Natural Gas Reservoir. Annual

Sask Dep Miner Resour Rep — Saskatchewan. Department of Mineral Resources. Report

Sask Dep Nat Resour Fish Branch Fish Rep — Saskatchewan. Department of Natural Resources. Fisheries Branch. Fisheries Report

Sask Dep Nat Resour Fish Wildl Branch Fish Rep — Saskatchewan. Department of Natural Resources. Fisheries and Wildlife Branch. Fisheries Report

Sask Ed Admin — Saskatchewan Education Administrator

Sask Gaz — Saskatchewan Gazette

Sask Geol Soc Spec Publ — Saskatchewan Geological Society. Special Publication

Sask Hist — Saskatchewan History

Sask Law Rev — Saskatchewan Law Review

Sask Lib For — Saskatchewan Library Forum

Sask Libr — Saskatchewan Library

Sask LR — Saskatchewan Law Review

Sask L Rev — Saskatchewan Law Review

Sask Mus Q — Saskatchewan Museums Quarterly

Sask Power Corp SPC Rep — Saskatchewan Power Corp. SPC Report

Sask (Prov) Dep Miner Resour Rep — Saskatchewan (Province). Department of Mineral Resources. Report

Sask Res Counc Eng Div Rep — Saskatchewan Research Council. Engineering Division. Report

Sask Res Counc Eng Div Rep E — Saskatchewan Research Council. Engineering Division. Report E

Sask Res Counc Geol Div Circ — Saskatchewan Research Council. Geology Division. Circular

Sask Res Counc Geol Div Rep — Saskatchewan Research Council. Geology Division. Report

Sask Res Counc Geol Div Rep G — Saskatchewan Research Council. Geology Division. Report G

Sask Res Counc Phys Div Rep — Saskatchewan Research Council. Physics Division. Report

Sask Res Counc Publ — Saskatchewan Research Council. Publication

Sask Res Counc Rep E — Saskatchewan Research Council. Report E

Sask Res Counc Tech Rep — Saskatchewan Research Council. Technical Report

SASMIRA's Bull — SASMIRA's [*Silk and Art Silk Mills' Research Association*] Bulletin

SASMIRA Tech Dig — SASMIRA [*Silk and Art Silk Mills' Research Association*] Technical Digest

SASNA — South African Shipping News and Fishing Industry Review

SASOP — Sudan. Antiquities Service. Occasional Papers

SASR — South Australian State Reports

SASRAZ — Sbornik Trudov Aspirantov i Molodykh Nauchnykh Sotrudnikov Vsesoyuznyi Nauchno-Issledovatel'skii Institut Rastenievodstva

SASS — South Australian Secrets Summary

SASS — South Australian Social Science

SASSAR — Suid-Afrikaanse Spoorwee/South African Railways

SASTAJ — SASTA [*South Australian Science Teachers Association*] Journal

SA Storekeepers J — South Australian Storekeepers and Grocers Journal

SASW — Studien des Spologetischen Seminars in Wernigerode

SAT — Die Schriften des Alten Testaments in Auswahl Neu Uebersetzt und fuer die Gegenwart Erklaert

Sat — Satellite Science Fiction

SATA — Die Schriften des Alten Testaments in Auswahl Neu Uebersetzt und fuer die Gegenwart Erklaert

SATDB — Sangyo To Denki

SATEA — Soviet Atomic Energy

SA Teachers J — SA [*South Australia*] Teachers' Journal

SA Teach J — South Australian Teachers' Journal

Sateilyturvakeskus Rapp STUK YTO TR — Sateilyturvakeskus. Rapportti STUK-YTO-TR

Satel Dir — Satellite Communications. Satellite Industry Directory

Satell Commun — Satellite Communications

Satellite — Satellite Communications

Satell Symp Congr FIP — Satellite Symposium. Congress. FIP

Satel News — Satellite News

Sat E P — Saturday Evening Post

Sat Eve Post — Saturday Evening Post

SATF — Societe des Anciens Textes Francais

SATh — Studies in Ascetical Theology

SATHA — Schweizer Archiv fuer Tierheilkunde

Satire N — Satire Newsletter

SatireNL — Satire Newsletter

SATKB — Sanitarnaya Tekhnika

S Atlan Bull — South Atlantic Bulletin
S Atlan Q — South Atlantic Quarterly
S Atlantic Q — South Atlantic Quarterly
S Atl Q — South Atlantic Quarterly
S Atl Quart — South Atlantic Quarterly
S Atl Rev — South Atlantic Review
S Atl Urb Stud — South Atlantic Urban Studies
Sat N — Saturday Night
Sat NL — Satire Newsletter
Sat Oklahom — Saturday Oklahoman and Times
Sat Orb Int — Satellite Orbit International
Sat R — Saturday Review
SatR — Saturday Review of Literature
SATRA Bull — SATRA [*Shoe and Allied Trades Research Association*] Bulletin
Sat R Arts — Saturday Review of the Arts
Sat R Ed — Saturday Review of Education
Sat Rev — Saturday Review
Sat Rev Literature — Saturday Review of Literature
Sat R Lit — Saturday Review of Literature
Sat R Of Lit — Saturday Review of Literature
Sat R Sci — Saturday Review of the Sciences
Sat R Soc — Saturday Review of Society
Sat R/World — Saturday Review/World
SATTDF — Suid-Afrikaanse Tydskrif vir Natuurwetenskap en Tegnologie
SATUD — South African Tunnelling
Saturated Heterocycl Chem — Saturated Heterocyclic Chemistry
Saturday Rev — Saturday Review
Saturd Revw — Saturday Review
SA Tydskr Sportgeneeskd — SA [*South African*] Tydskrif van Sportgeneeskunde
SAU — Schriften der Albertus-Universitaet
SAU — Sprawozdania Akademii Umiejetnosci
SAUCB — Soviet Automatic Control
Saudi Arabia Dir Gen Resour Bull — Saudi Arabia. Directorate General of Mineral Resources. Bulletin
Saudi Arabia Dir Gen Miner Resour Geol Map — Saudi Arabia. Directorate General of Mineral Resources. Geologic Map
Saudi Arabia Dir Gen Miner Resour Geol Map GM — Saudi Arabia. Directorate General of Mineral Resources. Geologic Map GM
Saudi Arabia Dir Gen Miner Resour Miner Resour Rep Invest — Saudi Arabia. Directorate General of Mineral Resources. Mineral Resources Report of Investigations
Saudi Arabia Dir Gen Miner Resour Miner Resour Res — Saudi Arabia. Directorate General of Mineral Resources. Mineral Resources Research
Saudi Arabia Proj Rep US Geol Surv — Saudi Arabia Project Report. US Geological Survey
Saudi Med J — Saudi Medical Journal
Saudi Pharm J — Saudi Pharmaceutical Journal
SAUG — Schriften der Albertus-Universitaet. Geisteswissenschaftliche Reihe
Saugar Univ J Part 2 — Saugar University. Journal. Part 2. Science
Saugertierkd Mitt — Saugetierkundliche Mitteilungen
Saugetierkundliche Mitt — Saugetierkundliche Mitteilungen
Saunders Monogr Clin Radiol — Saunders Monographs in Clinical Radiology
Saunders Ser — Saunders Series
S Aus Nat Gal Bul — South Australia. National Gallery. Bulletin
S Aust — South Australiana
S Aust Clinics — South Australian Clinics
S Aust Coal Abstr Bull — South Australian Coal Abstract Bulletin
S Aust Dir Mines Gov Geol Annu Rep — South Australia. Director of Mines and Government Geologist. Annual Report
S Aust Geol Atlas Ser — South Australia. Geological Survey. Atlas Series
S Aust Geol Surv 1:250000 Geol Ser — South Australia. Geological Survey. 1:250,000 Geological Series
S Aust Geol Surv Bull — South Australia. Geological Survey. Bulletin
S Aust Geol Surv Q Geol Notes — South Australia. Geological Survey. Quarterly Geological Notes
S Aust Geol Surv Rep Invest — South Australia. Geological Survey. Report of Investigations
S Aust Golfer — South Australian Golfer
S Austl LR — South Australian Law Reports
S Aust LR — South Australian Law Reports
S Aust Miner Resour Rev — South Australia Mineral Resources Review
S Aust Nat — South Australian Naturalist
S Aust Orn — South Australian Ornithologist
S Aust Ornithol — South Australian Ornithologist
S Australia Geol Surv Rep Invest — South Australia. Geological Survey. Report of Investigations
S Australiana — South Australiana
S Aust Rep Mus Board — South Australia. Report of the Museum Board
S Austrl LR — South Australian Law Reports
S Aust R S T — Transactions and Proceedings and Report of the Royal Society of South Australia
SAUZA — Stroitel'stvo i Arkhitektura Uzbekistana
Sav — Savanna
Sav — Savremenik
SAV — Schweizerisches Archiv fuer Volkskunde
SAV — Slovenska Akademia Vied
Sav Ac Mm — Memoires de la Societe Academique de Savoie
Sav & Loan N — Savings and Loan News
Sav Bank J — Savings Bank Journal
Sav Dev — Savings and Development
Savia Mod — Savia Moderna
Savings Bank J — Savings Bank Journal
Savings Banks Internat — Savings Banks International
SAVK — Schweizerisches Archiv fuer Volkskunde
SAVL — Studien zur Allgemeinen und Vergleichenden Literaturwissenschaft

Sav Loan News — Savings and Loan News
Savng Inst — Savings Institutions
Savremena Poljopr — Savremena Poljoprivreda
Savrem Med — Savremenna Medicina
Savrem Med (Sofia) — Savremenna Meditsina (Sofia)
Savrem Poljopr — Savremena Poljoprivreda
Savrem Poljoprivreda — Savremena Poljoprivreda
SavS — Savannah State College Bulletin
Savv Kn — Savvina Kniga
Sav Zeitschr — Zeitschr der Savigny-Stiftung fuer Rechtsgeschichte. Romanistische Abteilung
SAW — Sitzungsberichte. Akademie der Wissenschaft in Wien
SAW — Sozialistische Arbeitswissenschaft
SA Waterabstr — SA [*South African*] Waterabstracts
SAWB — Sitzungsberichte. Akademie der Wissenschaften zu Berlin
SAWM — Sitzungsberichte. Akademie der Wissenschaften zu Muenchen
SAWPHK — Saechsische Akademie der Wissenschaften zu Leipzig. Philologisch-Historische Klasse
SAWTRI Annu Rep — South African Wool and Textile Research Institute. Annual Report
SAWTRI Bull — SAWTRI [*South African Wool and Textile Research Institute*] Bulletin
SAWTRI Dig — SAWTRI [*South African Wool and Textile Research Institute*] Digest
SAWTRI Spec Publ — SAWTRI [*South African Wool and Textile Research Institute*] Special Publication
SAWTRI Tech Rep — SAWTRI (South African Wool and Textile Research Institute) TechnicalReport
SAWW — Sitzungsberichte. Akademie der Wissenschaft in Wien
SAWWPH — Sitzungsberichte der Akademie der Wissenschaften in Wien. Philosophisch-Historische Klasse
Sawyer's Gas Turbine Int — Sawyer's Gas Turbine International
SaxJ — Saxophone Journal
SaxS — Saxophone Symposium
SAY — Science Fiction Adventures Yearbook
SAYKA — Sovistva Atomnykh Yader
SB — Automotive Engine Rebuilders Association. Service Bulletin
SB — Griechische Grammatik auf der Grundlage von Karl Brugmanns Griechischer Grammatik
SB — Schweizer Buch
SB — Science Books
SB — Science Books and Films
SB — Selmer Bandwagon
SB — Skandinaviska Banken. Quarterly Review [*Later, Skandinaviska Enskilda Banken. Quarterly Review*]
SB — Sociologisch Bulletin
SB — Soncino Blaetter
SB — Soundboard
SB — Sources Bibliques
SB — Sovetskaya Bibliografia
SB — Soviet Biotechnology
SB — Special Bulletin. New York Department of Labor
SB — Sprakliga Bidrag
SB — Studi Baltici
SB — Studi Bizantini
SB — Studies in Bibliography
SBA — Schweizerische Beitraege zur Altertumswissenschaft
SBA — Sitzungsberichte. Bayerische Akademie der Wissenschaften
SBA — Sitzungsberichte der Preussischen Akademie der Wissenschaften zu Berlin
SBA — Standard Chartered Review
SBA — Studies in Biblical Archaeology
SBAG — Schweizer Beitraege zur Allgemeinen Geschichte
SB Agric Exp Stn Univ Nebr — SB. Agricultural Experiment Station. University of Nebraska
SbAk — Sbornik na Balgarskata Akademija na Naukite
Sb Akad Nauk Gruz SSR Inst Neorg Khim Elektrokhim — Sbornik. Akademiya Nauk Gruzinskoi SSR. Institut Neorganicheskoi Khimiii Elektrokhimii
Sb Akad Nauk SSSR — Sbornik Rabot Akademiya Nauk SSSR
Sb Akad (Wien) — Sitzungsberichte der Oesterreichischen Akademie der Wissenschaften. Philosophisch-Historische Klasse (Wien)
S Balc — Studia Balcanica
SBAME — Selected Bibliography of Articles Dealing with the Middle East
SB & F — Science Books and Films
Sb Annot Nauchno Issled Rab Tomsk Politekh Inst — Sbornik Annotatsii Nauchno-Issledovatel'skikh Rabot. TomskiiPolitekhnicheskii Institut
SBAr — Studies in Biblical Archaeology
S Bar J — State Bar Journal of California
SBARMO Bull — SBARMO [*Scientific Ballooning and Radiations Monitoring Organization*] Bulletin
Sb Aspir Rab Kazan Gos Univ Estest Nauki — Sbornik Aspirantskikh Rabot Kazanskii Gosudarstvennyi Universitet Estestvennye Nauki
Sb Aspir Rab Kazan Gos Univ Estest Nauki Biol — Sbornik Aspirantskikh Rabot Kazanskii Gosudarstvennyi Universitet Estestvennye Nauki Biologiya
Sb Aspir Rab Kazan Gos Univ Tochn Nauki Mekh Fiz — Sbornik Aspirantskikh Rabot Kazanskii Gosudarstvennyi Universitet Tochnye NaukiMekhanika Fizika
Sb Aspir Rab Kazan Khim Tekhnol Inst — Sbornik Aspirantskikh Rabot Kazanskii Khimiko Tekhnologicheskii Institut
Sb Aspir Rab Kazan Univ Estestv Nauk — Sbornik Aspirantskikh Rabot Kazanskogo Universiteta Estestvennykh Nauk
Sb Aspir Rab Ufim Neft Nauchno-Issled Inst — Sbornik Aspirantskikh Rabot Ufimskii Neftyanoi Nauchno-Issledovatel'skii Institut
Sb Aspir Rab Voronezh Lesotekh Inst — Sbornik Aspirantskikh Rabot Voronezhskii Lesotekhnicheskii Institut
Sb Aspir Rab Vses Nauchno Issled Inst Zhivotnovod — Sbornik Aspirantskikh Rabot Vsesoyuznyi Nauchno Issledovatel'skii Institut Zhivotnovodstva
SBAW — Sitzungsberichte. Bayerische Akademie der Wissenschaften

SBAWPPH — Sitzungsberichte der Bayerischen Akademie der Wissenschaften. Philosophisch-Philologisch und Historische Klasse

SBAWW — Sitzungsberichte. Akademie der Wissenschaft in Wien

SBB — Sociology Bulletin (Bombay)

SBB — Studies in Bibliography and Booklore

SBB — Stuttgarter Biblische Beitraege

SBBA — Sitzungsberichte der Bayerischen Akademie der Wissenschaften

Sb Bakteriofagiya — Sbornik Bakteriofagiya

SBBAW — Sitzungsberichte. Bayerische Akademie der Wissenschaften

SB Bayer Ak — Sitzungsberichte der Bayerischen Akademie der Wissenschaften

Sb Bayern — Sitzungsberichte der Bayerischen Akademie der Wissenschaften

SB Berl — Sitzungsberichte der Deutsche Akademie der Wissenschaften zu Berlin

SB Berlin — Sitzungsberichte. Deutsche Akademie der Wissenschaften zu Berlin. Klasse fuer Sprachen, Literatur, und Kunst

SBBGA — Studia Universitatis Babes-Bolyai. Series Geologia-Geographia

Sb Biokhim Zerna Akad Nauk SSSR Inst Biokhim A N Bakha — Sbornik. Biokhimiya Zerna. Akademiya Nauk SSSR. Institut Biokhimii Imeni A. N. Bakha

SBBKA — Selbutsu Butsuri Kagaku

SBBL — Studies in Bibliography and Booklore

Sb Bot Rab Beloruss Otd Vses Bot Ova — Sbornik Botanicheskikh Rabot Belorusskogo Otdelenie Vsesoyuznogo Botanicheskogo Obshchestva

Sb Bot Rabot Vses Bot Obshch Beloruss Otd — Sbornik Botanicheskikh Rabot Vsesoyuznogo Botanicheskogo Obshchestva. Belorusskoe Otdelenie

SBBPA — Studia Universitatis Babes-Bolyai. Series Physica

Sb (Brno) — Sbornik Ceskoslovenska Akademie Ved. Archeologicky Ustav (Brno)

Sb Brno — Sbornik. Ceskoslovenska Spolecnosti Archeologicka (Brno)

SBBS — Soncino Books of the Bible Series

SBBud — Sacred Books of the Buddhists

SBBUD — SBARMO [*Scientific Ballooning and Radiations Monitoring Organization*] Bulletin

Sb Bulg Akad Nauk Klon Prir Mat — Sbornik na Bulgarskata Akademiya na Naukite. Klon Prirodo-Matematichen

SBC — Studies in Browning and His Circle

SBCABE — Annual Symposium on Biomathematics and Computer Science in the Life Sciences. Abstracts

SBCBA — Sounding Brass and the Conductor

SBCED — Scientific Bulletin. Canada Centre for Mineral and Energy Technology

Sb Celostatni Prac Konf Anal Chem — Sbornik Celostatni Pracovni Konference Analytickych Chemiku

Sb Cesk Akad Zemed — Sbornik Ceskoslovenske Akademie Zemedelske

Sb Cesk Akad Zemed Ved — Sbornik Ceskoslovenske Akademie Zemedelskych Ved

Sb Cesk Akad Zemed Ved Lesn — Sbornik Ceskoslovenske Akademie Zemedelskych Ved. Lesnictvi

Sb Cesk Akad Zemed Ved Rada A — Sbornik Ceskoslovenske Akademie Zemedelskych Ved. Rada A

Sb Cesk Akad Zemed Ved Rada B — Sbornik Ceskoslovenske Akademie Zemedelskych Ved. Rada B

Sb Cesk Akad Zemed Ved Rostl Vyr — Sbornik Ceskoslovenske Akademie Zemedelskych Ved. Rostlinna Vyroba

Sb Cesk Akad Zemed Ved Rostl Vyroba — Sbornik Ceskoslovenske Akademie Zemedelskych Ved. Rostlinna Vyroba

Sb Cesk Akad Zemed Ved Vet Med — Sbornik Ceskoslovenske Akademie Zemedelskych Ved. Veterinarni Medicina

Sb Cesk Akad Zemed Ved Zivocisna Vyroba — Sbornik Ceskoslovenske Akademie Zemedelskych Ved. Zivocisna Vyroba

Sb Ceske Akad Zemed — Sbornik Ceske Akademie Zemedelske

Sb Chekh Khim Rab — Sbornik Chekhoslovatskikh Khimicheskikh Rabot

Sb Chelyab Politekh Inst — Sbornik Chelyabinskii Politekhnicheskii Institut

Sb Csl Akad Zemed Ved Rostlinna Vyroba — Sbornik Ceskoslovenske Akademie Zemedelskych Ved. Rada C. Rostlinna Vyroba

Sb Csl Akad Zemed Ved Zemed Ekon — Sbornik Ceskoslovenske Akademie Zemedelskych Ved. Rada B. Zemedelska Ekonomika

Sb Csl Akad Zemed Ved Ziv Vyroba — Sbornik Ceskoslovenske Akademie Zemedelskych Ved. Rada E. Zivocisna Vyroba

SBD — Schoolbestuur

SBD — Space Business Daily

SBDAW — Sitzungsberichte. Deutsche Akademie der Wissenschaften zu Berlin. Klasse fuer Sprachen, Literatur, und Kunst

SBDAWB — Sitzungsberichte. Deutsche Akademie der Wissenschaften zu Berlin. Klasse fuer Sprachen, Literatur, und Kunst

SB Deut Akad — Sitzungsberichte der Deutschen Akademie der Wissenschaften zu Berlin

Sb Dokl Gidrotekh Vses Nauchno Issled Inst Gidrotekh — Sbornik Dokladov po Gidrotekhnike. Vsesoyuznyi Nauchno-Issledovatel'skii Institut Gidrotekhniki

Sb Dokl Konf Poverkhn Silam — Sbornik Dokladov Konferentsii po Poverkhnostnym Silam

Sb Dokl Konf Vysokomol Soedin — Sbornik Dokladov Konferentsii po Vysokomolekulyarnym Soedineniyam

Sb Dokl Mezhdunar Sezda Obshch Issled Torfov — Sbornik Dokladov Mezhdunarodnogo S'ezda po Obshchemu IssledovaniyuTorfov

Sb Dokl Mezhvuz Konf Proboyu Dielektr Poluprovodn — Sbornik Dokladov Mezhvuzovskoi Konferentsii po Proboyu Dielektrikov iPoluprovodnikov

Sb Dokl Nats Konf Mladite Nauchni Rab Spets Neft Khim — Sbornik Dokladi. Natsionalna Konferentsiya na Mladite NauchniRabotnitsi i Spetsialisti Neft i Khimiya

Sb Dokl Nats Konf Vodopodgot Voden Rezhim Koroz TETs AETs — Sbornik Dokladi. Natsionalna Konferentsiya po Vodopodgotovka. VodenRezhim i Koroziya v TETs i AETs

Sb Dokl Nauchna Ses Druzh Med Khim — Sbornik Dokladi. Nauchna Sesiya na Druzhestvoto po Meditsinska Khimiya

Sb Dokl Nauchn Konf Molodykh Uch TatNIPIneft — Sbornik Dokladov na Nauchnykh Konferentsiyakh Molodykh UchenykhTatNIPIneft

Sb Dokl Nauchno Metod Konf Probl Prepod VUZ — Sbornik ot Dokladi pred Nauchno-Metodicheska Konferentsiya poProblemite na Prepodavane vuv VUZ

Sb Dokl Nauchno Tekh Soveshch Instrum Stalyam — Sbornik Dokladov Nauchno-Tekhnicheskogo Soveshchaniya poInstrumental'nym Stalyam

Sb Dokl Nauchn Stud Ova Kalinin Gos Pedagog Inst — Sbornik Dokladov Nauchnogo Studencheskogo Obshchestva Kalininskii Gosudarstvennyi Pedagogicheskii Institut

Sb Dokl Otchetnaya Nauchn Konf Biol Otd Inst At Energ — Sbornik Dokladov. Otchetnaya Nauchnaya Konferentsiya BiologicheskogoOtdela. Institut Atomnoi Energii

Sb Dokl Probl Simp Fiz Yadra — Sbornik Dokladov na Problemnom Simpoziume po Fizike Yadra

Sb Dokl Resp Sezda Epidemiol Mikrobiol Infekts Gig — Sbornik Dokladov Respublikanskogo S'ezda Epidemiologov. Mikrobiologov,Infektsionistov, i Gigienistov

Sb Dokl Sib Soveshch Spektrosk — Sbornik Dokladov na Sibirskom Soveshchanii po Spektroskopii

Sb Dokl Vses Akust Konf Fiz Tekh Akust — Sbornik Dokladov. Vsesoyuznaya Akusticheskaya Konferentsiya poFizicheskoi i Tekhnicheskoi Akustike

Sb Dokl Vses Konf Fiziol Biokhim Osn Povysh Prod Skh Zhivotn — Sbornik Dokladov Vsesoyuznoi Konferentsii po Fiziologicheskim iBiokhimicheskim Osnovam Povysheniya Produktivnosti Sel'skokhozyaistvennykhZhivotnykh

Sb Dokl Vses Konf Molodykh Uch Sadovod — Sbornik Dokladov Vsesoyuznoi Konferentsii Molodykh Uchenykh poSadovodstvu

Sb Dokl Vses Nauchn Konf Zhidk Kris Simp Ikh Prakt Primen — Sbornik Dokladov Vsesoyuznoi Nauchnoi Konferentsii po ZhidkimKristallam i Simpoziuma po Ikh Prakticheskomu Primeneniyu

Sb Dokl Vses Semin Prizmennym Beta Spektrom Vopr Ikh Primen — Sbornik Dokladov Vsesoyuznogo Seminara po Prizmennym Beta-Spektrometrami Voprosam Ikh Primeneniya

Sb Dokl Vses Shk Vnutrireakt Metodam Issled — Sbornik Dokladov Vsesoyuznogo Shkoly po Vnutrireaktornym MetodamIssledovanii

Sb Dokl Vses Soveshch Model Optim Katal Protsessov — Sbornik Dokladov na Vsesoyuznom Soveshchanii po Modelirovaniyu iOptimizatsii Kataliticheskikh Protsessov

Sb Donetsk Nauchno Issled Ugoln Inst — Sbornik Donetskii Nauchno-Issledovatel'skii Ugol'nyi Institut

SBdSAdW — Sitzungsberichte der Saechsischen Akademie der Wissenschaften

SBE — Sacred Books of the East

SBE — Semana Biblica Espanola

SBE — Southwest Journal of Business and Economics

S Beekeeper — Southern Beekeeper

SBelEx — Bulletin. Societe Belge d'Etudes et d'Expansion

Sb Ent Odd Nar Mus Praze — Sbornik Entomologickeho Oddeleni Narodniho Musea v Praze

Sber & Abh Flora Dresden — Sitzungsberichte und Abhandlungen der 'Flora' in Dresden

Sber Bayer Akad Wiss — Sitzungsberichte. Bayerische Akademie der Wissenschaften zu Muenchen

Sber Bayer Akad Wiss Philos Hist Kl — Sitzungsberichte der Bayerischen Akademie der Wissenschaften. Philosophische-Historische Klasse

Sber Dt Akad Landwwiss Berl — Sitzungsberichte. Deutsche Akademie der Landwirtschaftswissenschaften zu Berlin

Sber Fin Akad Wiss — Sitzungsberichte der Finnischen Akademie der Wissenschaften

Sber Ges Morph Physiol Muench — Sitzungsberichte. Gesellschaft fuer Morphologie und Physiologie in Muenchen

Sber Ges Naturf Freunde Berl — Sitzungsberichte. Gesellschaft Naturforschender Freunde zu Berlin

Sber Heidelberg Akad Wiss — Sitzungsberichte der Heidelberger Akademie der Wissenschaften

Sber K Boehm Ges Wiss — Sitzungsberichte der Koeniglich Boehmischen Gesellschaft der Wissenschaften

Sber K Preuss Akad Wiss — Sitzungsberichte. Koeniglich-Preussische Akademie der Wissenschaften

Sber Kstgesch Ges — Sitzungsberichte der Kunstgeschichtlichen Gesellschaft

Sber Muenchn Altert Ver — Sitzungsberichte des Muenchner Alterthums-Vereins

Sber Philos Hist Cl Ksr Akad Wiss Wien — Sitzungsberichte der Philosophisch-Historischen Classe der Kaiserlichen Akademie der Wissenschaften Wien

Sber Phys Mediz Soz Erlangen — Sitzungsberichte Physikalischen-Medizinischen Sozietaet zu Erlangen

Sber Preuss Akad Wiss — Sitzungsberichte der Preussischen Akademie der Wissenschaft

Sber Wien Akad — Sitzungsberichte Wiener Akademie

SBEsp — Semana Biblica Espanola

SBF — Science Books and Films

SBF — Senckenbergiana Biologica (Frankfurt-am-Main)

SBF — Studii Biblici Franciscani. Liber Annuus

SBF — Studium Biblicum Franciscanum

Sb Faun Praci Ent Odd Nar Mus Praze — Sbornik Faunistickych Praci Entomologickeho Oddeleni Narodniho Musea v Praze

SBFAW — Sitzungsberichte. Finnische Akademie der Wissenschaften

SBFCMi — Studium Biblicum Franciscanum. Collectio Minor

SBFLA — Studii Biblici Franciscani. Liber Annus

SBFRA — Schriftenreihe. Bundesminister fuer Wissenschaftliche Forschung (Germany). Radionuklide

SBFSDH — Synopses of the British Fauna. New Series

SBG — School Board Gazette

SBGDA — Spisanie na Bulgarskoto Geologichesko Druzhestvo

Sb Geol Pruzkumu Ostrava — Sbornik Geologickeho Pruzkumu Ostrava

Sb Geol Ved Antropozoikum — Sbornik Geologickych Ved. Antropozoikum

Sb Geol Ved Geol — Sbornik Geologickych Ved. Geologie

Sb Geol Ved Hydrogeol Inz Geol — Sbornik Geologickych Ved. Hydrogeologie, Inzenyrska, Geologie

Sb Geol Ved Loziskova Geol — Sbornik Geologickych Ved. Loziskova Geologie

Sb Geol Ved Loziskova Geol Mineral — Sbornik Geologickych Ved. Loziskova Geologie. Mineralogie

Sb Geol Ved Paleontol — Sbornik Geologickych Ved. Paleontologie
Sb Geol Ved Rada A — Sbornik Geologickych Ved. Rada A. Antropozoikum
Sb Geol Ved Rada G — Sbornik Geologickych Ved. Rada G. Geologie
Sb Geol Ved Rada HIG — Sbornik Geologickych Ved. Rada HIG. Hydrogeologie, Inzenyrska Geologie
Sb Geol Ved Rada LG — Sbornik Geologickych Ved. Rada LG. Loziskova Geologie
Sb Geol Ved Rada Loziskova Geol — Sbornik Geologickych Ved. Rada Loziskova Geologie
Sb Geol Ved Rada P — Sbornik Geologickych Ved. Rada P. Paleontologie
Sb Geol Ved Rada P Paleontol — Sbornik Geologickych Ved. Rada P. Paleontologie
Sb Geol Ved Rada TG — Sbornik Geologickych Ved. Rada TG. Technologie, Geochemie
Sb Geol Ved Rada UG — Sbornik Geologickych Ved. Rada UG. Uzita Geofyzika
Sb Geol Ved Rada Uzita Geofyz — Sbornik Geologickych Ved. Rada UG. Uzita Geofyzika
Sb Geol Ved Technol Geochem — Sbornik Geologickych Ved. Technologie, Geochemie
Sb Geol Ved Uzita Geofyz — Sbornik Geologickych Ved. Uzita Geofyzika
Sb Geol Ved Zapadne Karpaty — Sbornik Geologickych Ved. Zapadne Karpaty
SBGGAKOPR — Sitzungsberichte. Gesellschaft fuer Geschichte und Altertumskunde der Ostseeprovinzen Russlands
SBGGAKR — Sitzungsberichte. Gesellschaft fuer Geschichte und Altertumskunde der Ostseeprovinzen Russlands
Sbg J — Saalburg Jahrbuch. Saalburg-Museum
SBGKAT — Godishnik na Sofiiskiya Universitet. Biologicheski Fakultet. Kniga 2. Botanika, Mikrobiologiya, Fiziologiya, i Biokhimiya Rasteniyata
SBGMA — Sitzungsberichte. Gesellschaft zur Befoerderung der Gesamten Naturwissenschaften zu Marburg
SbGNFB — Sitzungsberichte der Gesellschaft der Naturforschenden Freunde. Berlin
Sb Gos Geol Kom ChSR — Sbornik Gosudarstvennogo Geologicheskogo Komiteta ChSR
Sb GPO — Sbornik GPO
Sb Grozn Neft Inst — Sbornik Groznenskii Neftyanoi Institut
SBGU — Sammelbuch Griechischer Urkunden aus Aegypten
SBH — Sacred Books of the Hindus
SBh — Stuttgarter Bibelhefte
SBHAD7 — Social Biology and Human Affairs
SBHAW — Sitzungsberichte. Heidelberg Akademie der Wissenschaft
SBHC — Studies in Browning and His Circle
SBHE — Sacred Books of the Hindus. Extra Volumes
SB Heidelb — Sitzungsberichte der Heidelberger Akademie der Wissenschaften. Philosophisch-Historische Klasse
S B Heidelberg — Sitzungsberichte. Heidelberg Akademie der Wissenschaften. Philosophisch-Historische Klasse
SBHLA — Schweizerische Blaetter fuer Heizung und Lueftung
SBHRAL — Biometrie Humaine
SBHT — Studien en Bijdragen op't Gebiet der Historische Theologie
SBHT — Studies in Burke and His Time
SB-I — Service de Bibliographie sur l'Informatique
SBi — Sources Bibliques
Sb Inf Metod Mater Gos Nauchno Issled Inst Glaznykh Bolezn — Sbornik Informatsionno-Metodicheskikh Materialov. GosudarstvennyiNauchno-Issledovatel'skii Institut Glaznykh Boleznei
Sb Inf Obogashch Briket Uglei — Sbornik Informatsii po Obogashcheniyu i Briketirovaniyu Uglei
Sb Inst Fiz Akad Nauk Gruz SSR — Sbornik. Ordena Trudovogo Krasnogo Znameni Institut Fiziki. Akademiya Nauk Gruzinskoj SSR
Sb Inst Neorg Khim Elektrokhim Akad Nauk Gruz SSR — Sbornik Institut Neorganicheskoi Khimii i Elektrokhimii Akademiya Nauk Gruzinskoi SSR
Sb Issled Rab Bum Tsellyul — Sbornik Issledovatel'skikh Rabot po Bumage i Tsellyuloze
SBiz — Studi Bizantini
Sb "Izme Pochv Okul'turiv Klassifik Diagnostika" — Sbornik "Izmenenie Pochv pri Okul'turivanii, Ikh Klassifikatsiya i Diagnostika"
SBJ — Journal. State Bar of California
SBJ — Sainte Bible Traduite en Francais sous la Direction de l'Ecole Biblique de Jerusalem
SBJ — Saul Bellow Journal
SBJ — Savings Bank Journal
Sb Jihoceskeho Muz Cesk Budejovicich Prir Vedy — Sbornik Jihoceskeho Muzea v Ceskych Budejovicich Prirodni Vedy
SBKAB — Studien und Berichte der Katholischen Akademie in Bayern
Sb Karantinu Rast — Sbornik po Karantinu Rastenii
SBKAW — Sitzungsberichte. Kaiserliche Akademie der Wissenschaften in Wien
SBKAWW — Sitzungsberichte. Kaiserliche Akademie der Wissenschaften in Wien
Sb Khim Tekhnol Inst Praga Protsessy Appar Avtom — Sbornik Khimiko-Tekhnologicheskogo Instituta Praga. Protsessy iApparaty Avtomatizatsiya
Sb Khim Tekhnol Inst Prage Neorg Org Tekhnol — Sbornik Khimiko-Tekhnologicheskogo Instituta v Prage. Neorganicheskayai Organicheskaya Tekhnologiya
Sb Khim Tekhnol Inst Prage Neorg Tekhnol — Sbornik Khimiko-Tekhnologicheskogo Instituta v Prage. NeorganicheskayaTekhnologiya
Sb Khim Tekhnol Inst Prage Org Tekhnol — Sbornik Khimiko-Tekhnologicheskogo Instituta v Prage. OrganicheskayaTekhnologiya
Sb Khim Tekhnol Inst Prage Tekhnol Vody — Sbornik Khimiko-Tekhnologicheskogo Instituta v Prage. Tekhnologiya Vody
SBKK — Schriften der Baltischen Kommission zu Kiel
Sb Klubu Prirodoved Brno — Sbornik Klubu Prirodovedeckeho v Brno
SBKMAL — Sbornik Trudov Byuro Glavnoi Sudebnomeditsinskoi Ekspertizy i Kafedry Sudebnoi Meditsiny Erevanskogo Meditsinskogo Instituta
Sb Kom Fil — Sbornik Filozofickej Fakulty Univerzity Komenskeho
Sb Kratk Soobshch Fiz An SSSR — Sbornik. Kratkie Soobshcheniya po Fizike An SSSR

Sb Kratk Soobshch Fiz AN SSSR Fiz Inst P N Lebedeva — Sbornik Kratkie Soobshcheniya po Fizike. Akademiya Nauk SSSR. Fizicheskii Institut Imeni P. N. Lebedeva
Sb Kratk Soobshch Kazan Univ Bot Pochvoved — Sbornik Kratkikh Soobshchenii Kazanskogo Universiteta Botanika i Pochvovedenie
Sb Kratk Soobshch Kazan Univ Zool — Sbornik Kratkikh Soobshchenii Kazanskogo Universiteta po Zoologii
SBL — Schildersblad. Algemeen Vakblad voor het Schildersbedrijf en Afwerkingsbedrijf
SBL — Studies in Black Literature
SBL — Svenskt Biografiskt Lexikon
SBLEA — Sbornik Lekarsky
SB (Leipzig) — Sitzungsberichte. Saechsische Akademie der Wissenschaften (Leipzig)
Sb Lek — Sbornik Lekarsky
Sb Lekar — Sbornik Lekarsky
Sb Lektsii Mezhdunar Shk Neitr Fiz — Sbornik Lektsii. Mezhdunarodnaya Shkola po Neitronnoi Fizike
Sb Leningr Elektro Mekh Inst — Sbornik Leningradskogo Elektro-Mekhanicheskogo Instituta
Sb Leningr Ind Inst — Sbornik Leningradskogo Industrial'nogo Instituta
Sb Leningr Inst Inzh Zheleznodorozhn Transp — Sbornik Leningradskogo Instituta Inzhenerov Zheleznodorozhnogo Transporta
Sb Leningr Tekst Inst — Sbornik Leningradskogo Tekstil'nogo Instituta
Sb Lesn Khoz Lesokult — Sbornik po Lesnomu Khozyaistvu i Lesokul'turam
SB Lpz — Sitzungsberichte der Saechsischen Akademie der Wissenschaften zu Leipzig. Philologisch-Historische Klasse
SBL Sem Pap — Society of Biblical Literature. Seminar Papers
SBM — Sovetskaia Botanika (Moscow and Leningrad)
SBM — Stuttgarter Biblische Monographien
Sb Masaryk Akad Pr — Sbornik Masarykovy Akademie Prace
Sb Mater Anapskoi Opytn Stn Nauchno Proizvodstvennoi Konf — Sbornik Materialov Anapskoi Opytnoi Stantsii k Nauchno Proizvodstvennoi Konferentsii
Sb Mater Avtom Dispetcher Proizvod Protsessov — Sbornik Materialov po Avtomatizatsii i DispetcherizatsiiProizvodstvennykh Protsessov
Sb Mater Avtom Proizvod Protsessov Dispetcher — Sbornik Materialov po Avtomatizatsii Proizvodstvennykh Protsessov i Dispetcherizatsii
Sb Mater Geol Tsvetn Redk Blagorodn Met — Sbornik Materialov po Geologii Tsvetnykh, Redkikh, i BladorodnykhMetallov
Sb Mater Gorn Delu Obogashch Metall — Sbornik Materialov po Gornomu Delu Obogashcheniyu i Metallurgii
Sb Mater Mezhdunar Kongr Lugovod — Sbornik Materialov Mezhdunarodnogo Kongressa po Lugovodstvu
Sb Mater Nov Tekh Peredovom Opyte Stroit — Sbornik Materialov o Novoi Tekhnike i Peredovom Opyte v Stroitel'stve
Sb Mater Obmenu Opytom Nauchn Inst Udobr Insektofungits — Sbornik Materialov po Obmenu Opytom. Nauchnyi Institut po Udobreniyam iInsektofungitsidam
Sb Mater Permsk Nauchno Issled Ugoln Inst — Sbornik Materialov Permskogo Nauchno-Issledovatel'skogo Ugol'nogoInstituta
Sb Mater Vak Tekh — Sbornik Materialov po Vakuumnoi Tekhnike
SBMEA — Space Biology and Medicine
Sb Mezhdunar Polyarogr Sezda — Sbornik Mezhdunarodnogo Polyarograficheskogo S'ezda
Sb Mezinar Polarogr Sjezdu — Sbornik Mezinarodniho Polarografickeho Sjezdu
Sb Mikroelementy i Produktivn Rast — Sbornik Mikroelementy i Produktivnost Rastenii
SBMMB — Studia Universitatis Babes-Bolyai. Series Mathematica-Mechanica
Sb Mosk Inst Stali — Sbornik Moskovskii Institut Stali
Sb Mosk Inst Stali Splavov — Sbornik Moskovskii Institut Stali Splavov
Sb Mosk Inzh Stroit Inst Im V V Kuibysheva — Sbornik. Moskovskii Inzhenerno-Stroitel'nyi Institut Imeni V. V.Kuibysheva
Sb Muz Antropol Etnogr — Sbornik Muzeja Antropologii i Etnografii
SBN — Scrip. Leader in World Pharmaceutical News
SBN — Studi Bizantini e Neoellenici
SBN — Stuttgarter Beitraege zur Naturkunde
SBN — Subic Bay News
Sb Nar Mus Praze Rada B Prir Vedy — Sbornik Narodniho Muzea v Praze. Rada B: Prirodni Vedy
Sb Nauchni Tr — Sbornik Nauchni Trudove
Sb Nauchni Tr Obogat NIPRORUDA — Sbornik Nauchni Trudove. Obogatyvane. NIPRORUDA
Sb Nauchni Tr Rudodobiv Obogat NIPRORUDA — Sbornik Nauchni Trudove. Rudodobiv i Obogatyvane. NIPRORUDA
Sb Nauchn Metod Tr Yarosl Gos Pedagog Inst Im K D Ushinskogo — Sbornik Nauchnykh i Metodicheskikh Trudov. Yaroslavskii GosudarstvennyiPedagogicheskii Institut Imeni K. D. Ushinskogo
Sb Nauchno Issled Inst Fiz OGU — Sbornik Nauchno-Issledovatel'skogo Instituta Fiziki OGU
Sb Nauchno Issled Inst Gidrometeorol Priborostr — Sbornik Nauchno-Issledovatel'skii Institut Gidrometeorologicheskogo Priborostroeniya
Sb Nauchno Issled Inst Osn Podzemn Sooruzh — Sbornik Nauchno-Issledovatel'skii Institut Osnovanii i Podzemnykh Sooruzhenii
Sb Nauchno Issled Inst Sanit Tekh — Sbornik Nauchno-Issledovatel'skii Institut Sanitarnoi Tekhniki
Sb Nauchno-Issled Rab Adygeisk Oblast Opyt Sta — Sbornik Nauchno-Issledovatel'skikh Rabot Adygeikaya Oblast Opytnaya Stantsiya
Sb Nauchno Issled Rab Arkhang Lesotekh Inst — Sbornik Nauchno-Issledovatel'skikh Rabot Arkhangel'skogoLesotekhnicheskogo Instituta
Sb Nauchno Issled Rab Aspir Altai Skh Inst — Sbornik Nauchno-Issledovatel'skikh Rabot Aspirantov. Altaiskii Sel'skokhozyaistvennyi Institut
Sb Nauchno-Issled Rab Aspir Molodykh Uch Altai Skh Inst — Sbornik Nauchno-Issledovatel'skikh Rabot Aspirantov i Molodykh Uchenykh. Altaiskii Sel'skokhozyaistvennyi Institut

Sb Nauchno-Issled Rab Azovo-Chernomorsk S-Kh Inst — Sbornik Nauchno-Issledovatel'skikh Rabot Azovo-Chernomorskogo Sel'skokhozyaistvennogo Instituta

Sb Nauchno-Issled Rab Gor'k Obl Opytn Stn Zhivotnovod — Sbornik Nauchno-Issledovatel'skikh Rabot Gor'kovskoi Oblastnoi Opytnoi StantsiiZhivotnovodstva

Sb Nauchno Issled Rab Ivanov Tekst Inst — Sbornik Nauchno-Issledovatel'skikh Rabot. Ivanovskii Tekstil'nyiInstitut

Sb Nauchno Issled Rab Kuibyshev Ind Inst — Sbornik Nauchno-Issledovatel'skikh Rabot. Kuibyshevskii Industrial'nyiInstitut

Sb Nauchno Issled Rab Orlov Gos Obl Skh Opytn Stn — Sbornik Nauchno-Issledovatel'skikh Rabot. Orlovskoi GosudarstvennoiOblastnoi Sel'skokhozyaistvennoi Opytnoi Stantsii

Sb Nauchno-Issled Rab Orlov Gos Sel'-Khoz Opyt Sta — Sbornik Nauchno-Issledovatel'skikh Rabot Orlovskoi Gosudarstvennoi Sel'skokhozyaistvennoi Opytnoi Stantsii

Sb Nauchno-Issled Rab Pchel — Sbornik Nauchno-Issledovatel'skikh Rabot po Pchelovodstvu

Sb Nauchno Issled Rab Permsk Skh Inst — Sbornik Nauchno-Issledovatel'skikh Rabot. PermskogoSel'skokhozyaistvennogo Instituta

Sb Nauchno Issled Rab Sev Kavk Zernovoi Inst — Sbornik Nauchno-Issledovatel'skikh Rabot. Severo-Kavkazskii ZernovoiInstitut

Sb Nauchno Issled Rab Tashk Inst Tekst Legk Promst — Sbornik Nauchno-Issledovatel'skikh Rabot. Tashkentskii InstitutTekstil'noi i Legkoi Promyshlennosti

Sb Nauchno Issled Rab Tashk Tekst Inst — Sbornik Nauchno-Issledovatel'skikh Rabot Tashkentskogo Tekstil'nogo Instituta

Sb Nauchno Issled Rab Ulyanovsk Skh Inst — Sbornik Nauchno-Issledovatel'skikh Rabot. Ul'yanovskogoSel'skokhozyaistvennogo Instituta

Sb Nauchno-Issled Rab Vses Nauchno-Issled Inst Tab Makhorki — Sbornik Nauchno-Issledovatel'skikh Rabot Vsesoyuznogo Nauchno-Issledovatel'skogo Instituta Tabaka i Makhorki

Sb Nauchno Issled Tr Mosk Inst Inzh Kommunaln Stroit — Sbornik Nauchno-Issledovatel'skikh Trudov. Moskovskogo InstitutaInzhenerov Kommunal'nogo Stroitel'stva

Sb Nauchno Issled Tr Mosk Tekst Inst — Sbornik Nauchno-Issledovatel'skikh Trudov Moskovskii Tekstil'nyi Institut

Sb Nauchno Issled Tr Tsentr Nauchno Issled Inst Lub Volokon — Sbornik Nauchno-Issledovatel'skikh Trudov. Tsentral'nyiNauchno-Issledovatel'skii Institut Lubyanykh Volokon

Sb Nauchno Metod Statei Fiz — Sbornik Nauchno-Metodicheskikh Statei po Fizike

Sb Nauchno Tekh Inf Vses Inst Gelmintol — Sbornik Nauchno-Tekhnicheskoi Informatsii Vsesoyuznogo InstitutaGel'mintologii

Sb Nauchno Tekh Statei Inst Elektrotekh Akad Nauk Ukr SSR — Sbornik Nauchno-Tekhnicheskoi Statei Instituta Elektrotekhniki.Akademiya Nauk Ukrainskoi SSR

Sb Nauchn Rab Agron Khim Mosk Skh Akad — Sbornik Nauchnykh Rabot po Agronomicheskoi Khimii. MoskovskayaSel'skokhozyaistvennaya Akademiya

Sb Nauchn Rab Akad Kommunaln Khoz Im K D Pamfilova — Sbornik Nauchnykh Rabot. Akademiya Kommunal'nogo Khozyaistva Imeni K D.Pamfilova

Sb Nauchn Rab Akad Nauk B SSR Inst Fiz Org Khim — Sbornik Nauchnykh Rabot. Akademiya Nauk Belorusskoi SSR. InstitutFiziko-Organicheskoi Khimii

Sb Nauchn Rab Akad Nauk B SSR Inst Obshch Neorg Khim — Sbornik Nauchnykh Rabot. Akademiya Nauk Belorusskoi SSR. InstitutObshchei i Neorganicheskoi Khimii

Sb Nauchn Rab Angar Nauchno-Issled Inst Gig Tr Prof Zabol — Sbornik Nauchnykh Rabot Angarskogo Nauchno-Issledovatel'skogo Instituta GigienyTruda i Professional'nykh Zabolevanii

Sb Nauchn Rab Arkhang Obl Sanit Bakteriol Inst — Sbornik Nauchnykh Rabot. Arkhangel'skogo OblastnogoSanitarno-Bakteriologicheskogo Instituta

Sb Nauchn Rab Aspir Kabard Balkar Gos Univ — Sbornik Nauchnykh Rabot Aspirantov Kabardino-Balkarskii Gosudarstvennyi Universitet

Sb Nauchn Rab Aspir Lvov Politekh Inst — Sbornik Nauchnykh Rabot Aspirantov. L'vovskii PolitekhnicheskiiInstitut

Sb Nauchn Rab Aspir Molodykh Sotr Fiz Fak Tadzh Gos Univ — Sbornik Nauchnykh Rabot Aspirantov i Molodykh Sotrudnikov FizicheskogoFakul'teta. Tadzhikskii Gosudarstvennyi Universitet

Sb Nauchn Rab Aspir Voronezh Gos Univ — Sbornik Nauchnykh Rabot Aspirantov Voronezhskogo Gosudarstvennogo Universiteta

Sb Nauchn Rab Aspir Vses Nauchno Issled Inst Khlopkovod — Sbornik Nauchnykh Rabot Aspirantov Vsesoyuznyi Nauchno-Issledovatel'skii Institut Khlopkovodstva

Sb Nauchn Rab Azerb Nauchno Issled Oftalmol Inst — Sbornik Nauchnykh Rabot. Azerbaidzhanskii Nauchno-Issledovatel'skiiOftal'mologicheskii Institut

Sb Nauchn Rab Beloruss Gos Univ — Sbornik Nauchnykh Rabot Belorusskogo Gosudarstvennogo Universiteta

Sb Nauchn Rab Beloruss Lesotekh Inst — Sbornik Nauchnykh Rabot. Belorusskii Lesotekhnicheskii Institut

Sb Nauchn Rab Beloruss Nauchno Issled Inst Lesn Khoz — Sbornik Nauchnykh Rabot. Belorusskii Nauchno-Issledovatel'skii InstitutLesnogo Khozyaistvu

Sb Nauchn Rab Beloruss Nauchno-Issled Kozhnovenerol Inst — Sbornik Nauchnykh Rabot Belorusskogo Nauchno-Issledovatel'skogo Kozhnovenerologicheskogo Instituta

Sb Nauchn Rab Beloruss Otd Vses Bot Ova — Sbornik Nauchnykh Rabot. Belorusskoe Otdelenie VsesoyuznogoBotanicheskogo Obshchestva

Sb Nauchn Rab Beloruss Politekh Inst — Sbornik Nauchnykh Rabot. Belorusskii Politekhnicheskii Institut

Sb Nauchn Rab Beloruss Skh Akad — Sbornik Nauchnykh Rabot. Belorusskaya Sel'skokhozyaistvennaya Akademiya

Sb Nauchn Rab Beloruss Tekhnol Inst — Sbornik Nauchnykh Rabot Belorusskii Tekhnologicheskii Institut

Sb Nauchn Rab Checheno Ingush Nauchno Issled Vet Stn — Sbornik Nauchnykh Rabot Checheno-Ingushskoi Nauchno-Issledovatel'skoi Veterinarnoi Stantsii

Sb Nauchn Rab Chelyab Gos Skh Opytn Stn — Sbornik Nauchnykh Rabot. Chelyabinskaya GosudarstvennayaSel'skokhozyaistvennaya Opytnaya Stantsiya

Sb Nauchn Rab Chernovits Gos Med Inst — Sbornik Nauchnykh Rabot. Chernovitskogo Gosudarstvennogo MeditsinskogoInstituta

Sb Nauchn Rab Chit Gos Med Inst — Sbornik Nauchnykh Rabot. Chitinskii Gosudarstvennyi MeditsinskiiInstitut

Sb Nauchn Rab Dagest Nauchno Issled Vet Inst — Sbornik Nauchnykh Rabot. Dagestanskii Nauchno-Issledovatel'skiiVeterinarnyi Institut

Sb Nauchn Rab Dal'nevost Nauchno Issled Inst Stroit — Sbornik Nauchnykh Rabot Dal'nevostochnyi Nauchno-Issledovatel'skii Institut po Stroitel'stvu

Sb Nauchn Rab Dnepropetr Gos Med Inst — Sbornik Nauchnykh Rabot Dnepropetrovskii Gosudarstvennyi Meditsinskii Institut

Sb Nauchn Rab Dnepropetr Inst Inzh Zheleznodorozhn Transp — Sbornik Nauchnykh Rabot. Dnepropetrovskii Institut InzhenerovZheleznodorozhnogo Transporta

Sb Nauchn Rab Dnepropetr Skh Inst — Sbornik Nauchnykh Rabot. Dnepropetrovskii Sel'skokhozyaistvennyiInstitut

Sb Nauchn Rab Farm Fak Pervyi Mosk Med Inst — Sbornik Nauchnykh Rabot. Farmatsevticheskii Fakul'tet. PervyiMoskovskii Meditsinskii Institut

Sb Nauchn Rab Inst Fiz Org Khim Akad Nauk B SSR — Sbornik Nauchnykh Rabot. Institut Fiziko-Organicheskoi Khimii.Akademiya Nauk Belorusskoi SSR

Sb Nauchn Rab Inst Khim Akad Nauk B SSR — Sbornik Nauchnykh Rabot. Instituta Khimii. Akademiya Nauk BelorusskoiSSR

Sb Nauchn Rab Inst Lesn Khoz Akad Skh Nauk B SSR — Sbornik Nauchnykh Rabot. Instituta Lesnogo Khozyaistva. AkademiyaSel'skokhozyaistvennykh Nauk Belorusskoi SSR

Sb Nauchn Rab Inst Melior Vodn Bolotnogo Khoz Akad Nauk BSSR — Sbornik Nauchnykh Rabot Instituta Melioratsii. Vodnogo i Bolotnogo Khozyaistva.Akademiya Nauk Belorusskoi SSR

Sb Nauchn Rab Inst Metallofiz Akad Nauk Ukr SSR — Sbornik Nauchnykh Rabot. Instituta Metallofiziki. Akademiya NaukUkrainskoi SSR

Sb Nauchn Rab Inst Obshch Neorg Khim Akad Nauk B SSR — Sbornik Nauchnykh Rabot. Instituta Obshchei i Neorganicheskoi Khimii.Akademiya Nauk Belorusskoi SSR

Sb Nauchn Rab Inst Okhr Tr VTsSPS — Sbornik Nauchnykh Rabot. Institutov Okhrany Truda VTsSPS

Sb Nauchn Rab Inst Stroit Arkhit Akad Nauk B SSR — Sbornik Nauchnykh Rabot. Institut Stroitel'stva i Arkhitektury.Akademiya Nauk Belorusskoi SSR

Sb Nauchn Rab Irkutsk Gos Med Inst — Sbornik Nauchnykh Rabot. Irkutskii Gosudarstvennyi MeditsinskiiInstitut

Sb Nauchn Rab Izhevsk Med Inst — Sbornik Nauchnykh Rabot Izhevskii Meditsinskii Institut

Sb Nauchn Rab Kafedry Mikrobiol Kirg Gos Med Inst — Sbornik Nauchnykh Rabot Kafedry Mikrobiologii. KirgizskiiGosudarstvennyi Meditsinskii Institut

Sb Nauchn Rab Kazan Gos Med Inst — Sbornik Nauchnykh Rabot Kazanskogo Gosudarstvennogo Meditsinskogo Instituta

Sb Nauchn Rab Khar'k Gos Med Inst — Sbornik Nauchnykh Rabot Khar'kovskogo Gosudarstvennogo Meditsinskogo Instituta

Sb Nauchn Rab Khar'k Inst Mekh Sots Sel'sk Khoz — Sbornik Nauchnykh Rabot Khar'kovskii Institut Mekhanizatsii SotsialisticheskogoSel'skogo Khozyaistva

Sb Nauchn Rab Khar'k Nauchno-Issled Inst Vaktsin Syvorot — Sbornik Nauchnykh Rabot Khar'kovskogo Nauchno-Issledovatel'skogo Instituta Vaktsin i Syvorotok

Sb Nauchn Rab Kiev Voen Gosp — Sbornik Nauchnykh Rabot Kievskii Voennyi Gospital

Sb Nauchn Rab Kirg Gos Med Inst — Sbornik Nauchnykh Rabot Kirgizskogo Gosudarstvennogo MeditsinskogoInstituta

Sb Nauchn Rab Kirg Med Inst — Sbornik Nauchnykh Rabot Kirgizskii Meditsinskii Institut

Sb Nauchn Rab Kirg Nauchno Issled Inst Okhr Materin Det — Sbornik Nauchnykh Rabot Kirgizskogo Nauchno-Issledovatel'skogo Instituta Okhrany Materinstva i Detstva

Sb Nauchn Rab Kirg Nauchno-Issled Inst Tuberk — Sbornik Nauchnykh Rabot Kirgizskogo Nauchno-Issledovatel'skogo Instituta Tuberkuleza

Sb Nauchn Rab Krasnoyarsk Gos Med Inst — Sbornik Nauchnykh Rabot Krasnoyarskogo Gosudarstvennogo Meditsinskogo Instituta

Sb Nauchn Rab Kurgan Gos S-Kh Inst — Sbornik Nauchnykh Rabot Kurganskii Gosudarstvennyi Sel'skokhozyaistvennyi Institut

Sb Nauchn Rab Kursk Nauchno Issled Vet Stan — Sbornik Nauchnykh Rabot. Kurskaya Nauchno-Issledovatel'skayaVeterinarnaya Stantsiya

Sb Nauchn Rab Kursk Nauchno Proizvod Vet Lab — Sbornik Nauchnykh Rabot. Kurskaya Nauchno-ProizvodstvennayaVeterinarnaya Laboratoriya

Sb Nauchn Rab Kursk Obl Nauchno Proizvod Vet Lab — Sbornik Nauchnykh Rabot. Kurskaya Oblastnaya Nauchno-ProizvodstvennayaVeterinarnaya Laboratoriya

Sb Nauchn Rab Lab Metallofiz Akad Nauk Ukr SSR — Sbornik Nauchnykh Rabot Laboratorii Metallofiziki. Akademiya NaukUkrainskoi SSR

Sb Nauchn Rab Leningr Gos Inst Usoversh Vrachei — Sbornik Nauchnykh Rabot Leningradskii Gosudarstvennyi Institut Usovershenstvovaniya Vrachei

Sb Nauchn Rab Leningr Inst Sov Torg — Sbornik Nauchnykh Rabot Leningradskii Institut Sovetskoi Torgovli

Sb Nauchn Rab Leningr Khim-Farm Inst — Sbornik Nauchnykh Rabot Leningradskogo Khimiko-Farmatsevticheskogo Instituta

Sb Nauchn Rab Leningr Nauchno Issled Inst Antibiot — Sbornik Nauchnykh Rabot Leningradskii Nauchno-Issledovatel'skii Institut Antibiotikov

Sb Nauchn Rab Leningr Vet Inst — Sbornik Nauchnykh Rabot. Leningradskii Veterinarnyi Institut

Sb Nauchn Rab Lesn Khoz — Sbornik Nauchnykh Rabot po Lesnomu Khozyaistvu

Sb Nauchn Rab Lvov Gos Med Inst — Sbornik Nauchnykh Rabot. L'vovskii Gosudarstvennyi MeditsinskiiInstitut

Sb Nauchn Rab Magnitogorsk Gornometall Inst — Sbornik Nauchnykh Rabot. Magnitogorskii Gornometallurgicheskii Institut

Sb Nauchn Rab Med Fak Karlova Univ Gradtse Kralove — Sbornik Nauchnykh Rabot Meditsinskogo Fakul'teta Karlova Universitetav Gradtse Kralove

Sb Nauchn Rab Minsk Gos Med Inst — Sbornik Nauchnykh Rabot Minskogo Gosudarstvennogo Meditsinskogo Instituta

Sb Nauchn Rab Molodykh Uch Chuv Skh Inst — Sbornik Nauchnykh Rabot Molodykh Uchenykh. ChuvashskiiSel'skokhozyaistvennyi Institut

Sb Nauchn Rab Mosk Farm Inst — Sbornik Nauchnykh Rabot Moskovskogo Farmatsevticheskogo Instituta

Sb Nauchn Rab Mosk Gorn Inst Kafedra Khim — Sbornik Nauchnykh Rabot. Moskovskii Gornyi Institut. Kafedra Khimii

Sb Nauchn Rab Mosk Inst Nar Khoz — Sbornik Nauchnykh Rabot. Moskovskii Institut Narodnogo Khozyaistva

Sb Nauchn Rab Mosk Inzh Fiz Inst — Sbornik Nauchnykh Rabot. Moskovskii Inzhenerno-Fizicheskii Institut

Sb Nauchn Rab Murm Olenevodcheskaya Opytn Stn — Sbornik Nauchnykh Rabot Murmanskaya Olenevodcheskaya Opytnaya Stantsiya

Sb Nauchn Rab Nauchno-Issled Inst Sadov Im I V Michurina — Sbornik Nauchnykh Rabot Nauchno-Issledovatel'skogo Instituta Sadov Imeni I. V. Michurina

Sb Nauchn Rab Nauchno Issled Inst Sadovod — Sbornik Nauchnykh Rabot. Nauchno-Issledovatel'skii Institut Sadovodstva

Sb Nauchn Rab Nauchno Issled Inst Stroit Mater (Minsk) — Sbornik Nauchnykh Rabot Nauchno-Issledovatel'skogo InstitutaStroitel'nykh Materialov (Minsk)

Sb Nauchn Rab Novosib Nauchno Issled Vet Stn — Sbornik Nauchnykh Rabot Novosibirskoi Nauchno-Issledovatel'skoi Veterinarnoi Stantsii

Sb Nauchn Rab Omsk Nauchno Issled Vet Inst — Sbornik Nauchnykh Rabot Omskogo Nauchno-Issledovatel'skogoVeterinarnogo Instituta

Sb Nauchn Rab Pchelovod — Sbornik Nauchnykh Rabot Pchelovodstvu

Sb Nauchn Rab Penz Inzh Stroit Inst — Sbornik Nauchnykh Rabot. Penzenskii Inzhenerno-Stroitel'nyi Institut

Sb Nauchn Rab Permsk Gos Med Inst — Sbornik Nauchnykh Rabot. Permskii Gosudarstvennyi Meditsinskii Institut

Sb Nauchn Rab Rizh Med Inst — Sbornik Nauchnykh Rabot Rizhskogo Meditsinskogo Instituta

Sb Nauchn Rab Rostov Gos Med Inst — Sbornik Nauchnykh Rabot. Rostovskii Gosudarstvennyi MeditsinskiiInstitut

Sb Nauchn Rab Rostov Med Inst — Sbornik Nauchnykh Rabot Rostovskogo Meditsinskogo Instituta

Sb Nauchn Rab Ryazan Gos Skh Stn — Sbornik Nauchnykh Rabot. Ryazanskaya GosudarstvennayaSel'skokhozyaistvennaya Stantsiya

Sb Nauchn Rab Ryazan S-Kh Inst — Sbornik Nauchnykh Rabot Ryazanskii Sel'skokhozyaistvennyi Institut

Sb Nauchn Rab Ryazan Skh Inst Im Prof P A Kostycheva — Sbornik Nauchnykh Rabot. Ryazanskii Sel'skokhozyaistvennyi InstitutImeni Prof. P. A. Kostycheva

Sb Nauchn Rab Sarat Inst Giproniigaz — Sbornik Nauchnykh Rabot. Saratovskii Institut Giproniigaz

Sb Nauchn Rab Sarat Med Inst — Sbornik Nauchnykh Rabot Saratovskii Meditsinskii Institut

Sb Nauchn Rab Sarat Nauchno Issled Vet Stn — Sbornik Nauchnykh Rabot. Saratovskaya Nauchno-Issledovatel'skayaVeterinarnaya Stantsiya

Sb Nauchn Rab Sarat Skh Inst — Sbornik Nauchnykh Rabot. Saratovskii Sel'skokhozyaistvennyi Institut

Sb Nauchn Rab Sev Oset Gos Med Inst — Sbornik Nauchnykh Rabot. Severo-Osetinskii Gosudarstvennyi MeditsinskiiInstitut

Sb Nauchn Rab Sib Nauchno Issled Inst Selsk Khoz — Sbornik Nauchnykh Rabot. Sibirskii Nauchno-Issledovatel'skii InstitutSel'skogo Khozyaistva

Sb Nauchn Rab Sib Nauchno Issled Inst Zernogo Khoz — Sbornik Nauchnykh Rabot. Sibirskii Nauchno-Issledovatel'skii InstitutZernogo Khozyaistva

Sb Nauchn Rab Sib Nauchno Issled Vet Inst — Sbornik Nauchnykh Rabot Sibirskogo Nauchno-Issledovatel'skogoVeterinarnogo Instituta

Sb Nauchn Rab SibNIVI — Sbornik Nauchnykh Rabot SibNIVI

Sb Nauchn Rab Sib Zon Nauchno-Issled Vet Inst — Sbornik Nauchnykh Rabot Sibirskogo Zonal'nogo Nauchno-Issledovatel'skogo Veterinarnogo Instituta

Sb Nauchn Rab Stud Aspir Mosk Vet Akad — Sbornik Nauchnykh Rabot Studentov i Aspirantov. MoskovskayaVeterinarnaya Akademiya

Sb Nauchn Rab Stud Donetsk Ind Inst — Sbornik Nauchnykh Rabot Studentov. Donetskii Industrial'nyi Institut

Sb Nauchn Rab Stud Erevan Gos Univ — Sbornik Nauchnykh Rabot Studentov Erevanskii Gosudarstvennyi Universitet

Sb Nauchn Rab Stud Ivanov Gos Med Inst — Sbornik Nauchnykh Rabot Studentov Ivanovskogo Gosudarstvennogo Meditsinskogo Instituta

Sb Nauchn Rab Stud Karelo Fin Gos Univ — Sbornik Nauchnykh Rabot Studentov Karelo-Finskogo Gosudarstvennogo Universiteta

Sb Nauchn Rab Stud Kirg Gos Univ — Sbornik Nauchnykh Rabot Studentov Kirgizskii Gosudarstvennyi Universitet

Sb Nauchn Rab Stud Leningr Gorn Inst — Sbornik Nauchnykh Rabot Studentov Leningradskogo Gornogo Instituta

Sb Nauchn Rab Stud Mosk Vet Akad — Sbornik Nauchnykh Rabot Studentov. Moskovskaya Veterinarnaya Akademiya

Sb Nauchn Rab Stud Petrozavodsk Gos Univ — Sbornik Nauchnykh Rabot Studentov Petrozavodskogo Gosudarstvennogo Universiteta

Sb Nauchn Rab Stud Rostov Gos Univ — Sbornik Nauchnykh Rabot Studentov. Rostovskogo GosudarstvennogoUniversiteta

Sb Nauchn Rab Stud Sarat Zootekh Vet Inst — Sbornik Nauchnykh Rabot Studentov Saratovskii Zootekhnichesko-Veterinarnyi Institut

Sb Nauchn Rab Stud Stalingr S-Kh Inst — Sbornik Nauchnykh Rabot Studentov Stalingradskogo Sel'skokhozyaistvennogo Instituta

Sb Nauchn Rab Sverdl Gos Med Inst — Sbornik Nauchnykh Rabot Sverdlovskogo Gosudarstvennyi MeditsinskiiInstitut

Sb Nauchn Rab Sverdl Med Inst — Sbornik Nauchnykh Rabot Sverdlovskogo Meditsinskogo Instituta

Sb Nauchn Rab Sverdl Otd Vses O-Va Anat Gistol Embriol — Sbornik Nauchnykh Rabot Sverdlovskogo Otdeleniya Vsesoyuznogo Obshchestva Anatomov, Gistologov, i Embriologov

Sb Nauchn Rab Tsentr Bot Sad Akad Nauk BSSR — Sbornik Nauchnykh Rabot. Tsentral'nyi Botanicheskii Sad Akademii NaukBSSR

Sb Nauchn Rab Tsentr Nauchno-Issled Lab Rostov Med Inst — Sbornik Nauchnykh Rabot Tsentral'naya Nauchno-Issledovatel'skaya Laboratoriya Rostov'skogo Meditsinskogo Instituta

Sb Nauchn Rab Ukr Nauchno Issled Inst Sadovod — Sbornik Nauchnykh Rabot Ukrainskii Nauchno-Issledovatel'skii Institut Sadovodstva

Sb Nauchn Rab Vitebsk Gos Med Inst — Sbornik Nauchnykh Rabot Vitebskogo Gosudarstvennogo MeditsinskogoInstituta

Sb Nauchn Rab Vitebsk Med Inst — Sbornik Nauchnykh Rabot Vitebskogo Meditsinskogo Instituta

Sb Nauchn Rab Voen-Med Fak Kuibyshev Med Inst — Sbornik Nauchnykh Rabot Voenno-Meditsinskogo Fakul'teta Kuibyshevskogo Meditsinskogo Instituta

Sb Nauchn Rab Volgogr Gos Med Inst — Sbornik Nauchnykh Rabot Volgogradskoi Gosudarstvennyi Meditsinskii Institut

Sb Nauchn Rab Volgogr Med Inst — Sbornik Nauchnykh Rabot Volgogradskogo Meditsinskogo Instituta

Sb Nauchn Rab Volgogr Obl Klin Boln — Sbornik Nauchnykh Rabot Volgogradskoi Oblastnoi Klinicheskoi Bol'nitsy

Sb Nauchn Rab Volgogr Pedagog Inst — Sbornik Nauchnykh Rabot Volgogradskogo Pedagogicheskogo Instituta

Sb Nauchn Rab Vseross Nauchno Issled Inst Vinograd Vinodel — Sbornik Nauchnykh Rabot. Vserossiiski Nauchno-Issledovatel'skiiInstitut Vinogradarstva i Vinodeliya

Sb Nauchn Rab Vses Nauchno-Issled Inst Lek Rast — Sbornik Nauchnykh Rabot Vsesoyuznyi Nauchno-Issledovatel'skii Institut Lekarstvennykh Rastenii

Sb Nauchn Rab Vses Nauchno Issled Inst Ovtsevod Kozovod — Sbornik Nauchnykh Rabot Vsesoyuznogo Nauchno-Issledovatel'skogoInstituta Ovtsevodstva i Kozovodstva

Sb Nauchn Rab Vses Nauchno-Issled Inst Poligr Promsti — Sbornik Nauchnykh Rabot. Vsesoyuznyi Nauchno-Issledovatel'skogoInstitut Poligraficheskoi Promyshlennosti

Sb Nauchn Rab Vses Nauchno-Issled Inst Sadovod — Sbornik Nauchnykh Rabot Vsesoyuznyi Nauchno-Issledovatel'skii Institut Sadovodstva

Sb Nauchn Rab Vses Nauchno-Issled Inst Zhivotnovod — Sbornik Nauchnykh Rabot Vsesoyuznyi Nauchno-Issledovatel'skii Institut Zhivotnovodstva

Sb Nauchn Rab Vses Zaochn Inst Sov Torg — Sbornik Nauchnykh Rabot. Vsesoyuznyi Zaochnyi Institut SovetskoiTorgovli

Sb Nauchn Rab Yarosl Gorzdravotd — Sbornik Nauchnykh Rabot Yaroslavskogo Gorzdravotdela

Sb Nauchn Rab Yarosl Gorzdravotdela — Sbornik Nauchnykh Rabot Yaroslavskogo Gorzdravotdela

Sb Nauchn Rab Yarosl Med Inst — Sbornik Nauchnykh Rabot Yaroslavskogo Meditsinskogo Instituta

Sb Nauchn Rab Zaochn Inst Sov Torg — Sbornik Nauchnykh Rabot Zaochnyi Institut Sovetskoi Torgovli

Sb Nauchn Rab Zaporozh Gos Inst Usoversh Vrachei — Sbornik Nauchnykh Rabot Zaporozhskogo Gosudarstvennogo InstitutaUsovershenstvovaniya Vrachei

Sb Nauchn Soobshch Dagest Gos Univ Kafedra Khim — Sbornik Nauchnykh Soobshchenii Dagestanskii Gosudarstvennyi Universitet Kafedra Khimii

Sb Nauchn Soobshch Dagest Otd Vses Bot Ova — Sbornik Nauchnykh Soobshchenii Dagestanskogo Otdela Vsesoyuznogo BotanicheskogoObshchestva

Sb Nauchn Soobshch Estest Tekh Nauk Dagest Univ — Sbornik Nauchnykh Soobshchenii Estestvennykh i Tekhnicheskikh Nauk Dagestanskogo Universitet

Sb Nauchn Soobshch Kafedry Arkhit Odess Inzh Stroit Inst — Sbornik Nauchnykh Soobshchenii Kafedry Arkhitektury. OdesskiiInzhenerno-Stroitel'nyi Institut

Sb Nauchn Soobshch Kafedry Org Fizk Khim Dagest Gos Univ — Sbornik Nauchnykh Soobshchenii Kafedry Organicheskoi i Fizkolloidnoi Khimii Dagestanskii Gosudarstvennyi Universitet

Sb Nauchn Soobshch Kafedry Zool Biol Khim Dagest Univ — Sbornik Nauchnykh Soobshchenii Kafedry Zoologii Biologii Khimii Dagestanskogo Universiteta

Sb Nauchn Soobshch Sarat Avtomob Dorozhn Inst — Sbornik Nauchnykh Soobshchenii Saratovskii Avtomobil'no Dorozhnyi Institut

Sb Nauchn Soobshch Sarat Politekh Inst — Sbornik Nauchnykh Soobshchenii. Saratovskii Politekhnicheskii Institut

Sb Nauchn Statei Beloruss Skh Akad — Sbornik Nauchnykh Statei. Belorusskaya Sel'skokhozyaistvennayaAkademiya

Sb Nauchn Statei Inst Bot Akad Nauk Lit SSR — Sbornik Nauchnykh Statei. Institut Botaniki. Akademiya Nauk LitovskoiSSR

Sb Nauchn Statei Khark Inst Inzh Zheleznodorozhn Transp — Sbornik Nauchnykh Statei Khar'kovskogo Instituta InzhenerovZheleznodorozhnogo Transporta

Sb Nauchn Statei Krasnoyarsk Inst Tsvetn Met — Sbornik Nauchnykh Statei. Krasnoyarskii Institut Tsvetnykh Metallov

Sb Nauchn Statei Tashk Inst Inzh Zheleznodorozhn Transp — Sbornik Nauchnykh Statei. Tashkentskii Institut InzhenerovZheleznodorozhnogo Transporta

Sb Nauchn Statei Vinnitsk Gos Med Inst — Sbornik Nauchnykh Statei Vinnitskogo Gosudarstvennogo Meditsinskogo Instituta

Sb Nauchn Stud Ova Geol Fak Mosk Gos Univ — Sbornik Nauchnogo Studencheskogo Obshchestva Geologicheskii Fakul'tet Moskovskii Gosudarstvennyi Universitet

Sb Nauchn Stud Rab Omsk Gos Pedagog Inst — Sbornik Nauchnykh Studencheskikh Rabot Omskii Gosudarstvennyi Pedagogicheskii Institut

Sb Nauchn Stud Rab Sarat Zoovetinst — Sbornik Nauchnykh Studencheskikh Rabot Saratovskogo Zoovetinstituta

Sb Nauchn Tr Akad Nauk B SSR Fiz Tekh Inst — Sbornik Nauchnykh Trudov. Akademiya Nauk Belorusskoi SSR. Fiziko-Tekhnicheskii Institut

Sb Nauchn Tr Akad Nauk SSSR Sib Otd Inst Gidrodin — Sbornik Nauchnykh Trudov. Akademiya Nauk SSSR. Sibirskoe Otdelenie. Institut Gidrodinamiki

Sb Nauchn Tr Andizh Gos Med Inst — Sbornik Nauchnykh Trudov Andizhanskii Gosudarstvennyi Meditsinskii Institut

Sb Nauchn Tr Andizh Med Inst — Sbornik Nauchnykh Trudov Andizhanskogo Meditsinskogo Instituta

Sb Nauchn Tr Arm Gos Pedagog Inst Ser Fiz Mat — Sbornik Nauchnykh Trudov Armyanskii Gosudarstvennyi Pedagogicheskii Institut. Seriya Fiziko-Matematicheskaya

Sb Nauchn Tr Arm Gos Zaochn Pedagog Inst — Sbornik Nauchnykh Trudov Gosudarstvennogo Zaochnogo Pedagogicheskogo Instituta

Sb Nauchn Tr Arm Otd Vses Bot Ova — Sbornik Nauchnykh Trudov Armyanskogo Otdelnykh Vsesoyuznogo Botanicheskoi Obshchestva

Sb Nauchn Tr Arm S-Kh Inst — Sbornik Nauchnykh Trudov Armyanskogo Sel'skokhozyaistvennogo Instituta

Sb Nauchn Tr Azerb Nauchno Issled Inst Gematol Pereliv Krovi — Sbornik Nauchnykh Trudov Azerbaidzhanskogo Nauchno-Issledovatel'skogo InstitutaGematologii i Perelivaniya Krovi

Sb Nauchn Tr Azerb Nauchno-Issled Inst Pereliv Krovi — Sbornik Nauchnykh Trudov Azerbaidzhanskogo Nauchno-Issledovatel'skogo InstitutaPerelivaniya Krovi

Sb Nauchn Tr Azerb Nauchno Issled Inst Perel Krovi — Sbornik Nauchnykh Trudov Azerbaidzhanskogo Nauchno-Issledovatel'skogo InstitutaPerelivaniya Krovi

Sb Nauchn Tr Bashk Gos Med Inst — Sbornik Nauchnykh Trudov Bashkirskogo Gosudarstvennogo Meditsinskogo Instituta

Sb Nauchn Tr Bashk Med Inst — Sbornik Nauchnykh Trudov Bashkirskogo Meditsinskogo Instituta

Sb Nauchn Tr Bashk Nauchno-Issled Trakhomatoznogo Inst — Sbornik Nauchnykh Trudov Bashkirskogo Nauchno-Issledovatel'skogo Trakhomatoznogo Instituta

Sb Nauchn Tr Beloruss Inst Mekh Selsk Khoz — Sbornik Nauchnykh Trudov Belorusskii Institut Mekhanizatsii Sel'skogo Khozyaistva

Sb Nauchn Tr Beloruss Lesotekh Inst — Sbornik Nauchnykh Trudov Belorusskogo Lesotekhnicheskogo Instituta

Sb Nauchn Tr Beloruss Nauchno Issled Inst Pochvoved — Sbornik Nauchnykh Trudov. Belorusskii Nauchno-Issledovatel'skii Institut Pochvovedeniya

Sb Nauchn Tr Beloruss Nauchno-Issled Inst Pochvoved Agrokhim — Sbornik Nauchnykh Trudov Belorusskii Nauchno-Issledovatel'skii Institut Pochvovedeniya i Agrokhimii

Sb Nauchn Tr Beloruss Nauchno-Issled Inst Zemled — Sbornik Nauchnykh Trudov Belorusskii Nauchno-Issledovatel'skii Institut Zemledeliya

Sb Nauchn Tr Beloruss Nauchno Issled Kozhno Venerol Inst — Sbornik Nauchnykh Trudov Belorusskii Nauchno-Issledovatel'skii Kozhno-Venerologicheskii Institut

Sb Nauchn Tr Beloruss Politekh Inst — Sbornik Nauchnykh Trudov Belorusskii Politekhnicheskii Institut

Sb Nauchn Tr Beloruss S-Kh Akad — Sbornik Nauchnykh Trudov Belorusskoi Sel'skokhozyaistvennoi Akademii

Sb Nauchn Tr Chelyab Med Inst — Sbornik Nauchnykh Trudov Chelyabinskogo Meditsinskogo Instituta

Sb Nauchn Tr Chelyab Nauchno Issled Inst Gorn Dela — Sbornik Nauchnykh Trudov Chelyabinskii Nauchno-Issledovatel'skii Institut Gornogo Dela

Sb Nauchn Tr Chelyab Politekh Inst — Sbornik Nauchnykh Trudov Chelyabinskii Politekhnicheskii Institut

Sb Nauchn Tr Chit Gos Med Inst — Sbornik Nauchnykh Trudov Chitinskii Gosudarstvennyi Meditsinskii Institut

Sb Nauchn Tr Chuv Nauchno-Issled Trakhomatoznogo Inst — Sbornik Nauchnykh Trudov Chuvashskogo Nauchno-Issledovatel'skogo Trakhomatoznogo Instituta

Sb Nauchn Tr Dagest Gos Med Inst — Sbornik Nauchnykh Trudov Dagestanskii Gosudarstvennyi Meditsinskii Institut

Sb Nauchn Tr Dagest Nauchno Issled Otd Energ — Sbornik Nauchnykh Trudov. Dagestanskii Nauchno-Issledovatel'skii Otdel Energetiki

Sb Nauchn Tr Dnepropetr Gos Med Inst — Sbornik Nauchnykh Trudov Dnepropetrovskii Gosudarstvennyi Meditsinskii Institut

Sb Nauchn Tr Dnepropetr Inzh Stroit Inst — Sbornik Nauchnykh Trudov Dnepropetrovskii Inzhenerno-Stroitel'nyi Institut

Sb Nauchn Tr Dnepropetr Metall Inst — Sbornik Nauchnykh Trudov. Dnepropetrovskii Metallurgicheskii Institut

Sb Nauchn Tr Donskogo S-Kh Inst — Sbornik Nauchnykh Trudov Donskogo Sel'skokhozyaistvennogo Instituta

Sb Nauchn Tr Donskoi Skh Inst — Sbornik Nauchnykh Trudov. Donskoi Sel'skokhozyaistvennyi Institut

Sb Nauchn Tr Erevan Arm Gos Pedagog Inst Khim — Sbornik Nauchnykh Trudov Erevanskii Armyanskii Gosudarstvennyi PedagogicheskiiInstitut. Khimiya

Sb Nauchn Tr Erevan Politekh Inst — Sbornik Nauchnykh Trudov Erevanskii Politekhnicheskii Institut

Sb Nauchn Tr Est Nauchno-Issled Inst Zemled Melior — Sbornik Nauchnykh Trudov Estonskogo Nauchno-Issledovatel'skogo Instituta Zemledeliya i Melioratsii

Sb Nauchn Tr Est Nauchno Issled Inst Zhivotnovod Vet — Sbornik Nauchnykh Trudov. Estonskii Nauchno-Issledovatel'skii Institut Zhivotnovodstva i Veterinarii

Sb Nauchn Tr Est Nauchno Issled Inst Zhivotnovod Vet im A Mel — Sbornik Nauchnykh Trudov. Estonskii Nauchno-Issledovatel'skii Institut Zhivotnovodstva i Veterinarii im A. Mel'dera

Sb Nauchn Tr Est S-Kh Akad — Sbornik Nauchnykh Trudov Estonskaya Sel'skokhozyaistvennaya Akademiya

Sb Nauchn Tr Fiz Tekh Inst Akad Nauk B SSR — Sbornik Nauchnykh Trudov Fiziko-Tekhnicheskii Institut Akademiya Nauk Belorusskoi SSR

Sb Nauchn Tr Fiz Tekh Inst Nizk Temp Akad Nauk Ukr SSR — Sbornik Nauchnykh Trudov. Fiziko-Tekhnicheskii Institut Nizkikh Temperatur Akademiya Nauk Ukrainskoi SSR

Sb Nauchn Tr Frunz Politekh Inst — Sbornik Nauchnykh Trudov. Frunzenskogo Politekhnicheskogo Instituta

Sb Nauchn Tr Gazov Khromatogr — Sbornik Nauchnykh Trudov po Gazovoi Khromatografii

Sb Nauchn Tr Gidroproekta — Sbornik Nauchnykh Trudov Gidroproekta

Sb Nauchn Tr Gintsvetmeta — Sbornik Nauchnykh Trudov Gintsvetmeta

Sb Nauchn Tr Glavgeologii Uzb SSR Tashk Politekh Inst — Sbornik Nauchnykh Trudov Glavgeologii Uzbekskoi SSR i Tashkentskogo Politekhnicheskogo Instituta

Sb Nauchn Tr Gos Nauchno Issled Inst Elektrodnoi Promsti — Sbornik Nauchnykh Trudov Gosudarstvennyi Nauchno-Issledovatel'skii Institut Elektrodnoi Promyshlennosti

Sb Nauchn Tr Gos Nauchno Issled Inst Keram Promsti — Sbornik Nauchnykh Trudov Gosudarstvennyi Nauchno-Issledovatel'skii Institut Keramicheskoi Promyshlennosti

Sb Nauchn Tr Gos Nauchno Issled Inst Keramzitu — Sbornik Nauchnykh Trudov Gosudarstvennyi Nauchno-Issledovatel'skii Institut poKeramzitu

Sb Nauchn Tr Gos Nauchno Issled Inst Ozern Rechn Rybn Khoz — Sbornik Nauchnykh Trudov. Gosudarstvennyi Nauchno-Isslovatel'skii Institut Ozernogo i Rechnogo Rybnogo Khozyaistva

Sb Nauchn Tr Gos Nauchno-Issled Inst Tsvet Met — Sbornik Nauchnykh Trudov Gosudarstvennogo Nauchno-Issledovatel'skogo Instituta Tsvetnykh Metallov

Sb Nauchn Tr Gos Nauchno Issled Proektn Inst Metall Promsti — Sbornik Nauchnykh Trudov Gosudarstvennyi Nauchno-Issledovatel'skii i ProektnyiInstitut Metallurgicheskoi Promyshlennosti

Sb Nauchn Tr Gos Nauchno Issled Proektn Inst Redkomet Promst — Sbornik Nauchnykh Trudov. Gosudarstvennyi Nauchno-Issledovatel'skii i ProektnyiInstitut Redkometallicheskoi Promyshlennosti

Sb Nauchn Tr Gos Proektn Nauchno Issled Inst Gipronikel — Sbornik Nauchnykh Trudov. Gosudarstvennyi Proektnyi i Nauchno-Issledovatel'skii Institut Gipronikel

Sb Nauchn Tr Gos Vses Nauchno Issled Inst Stroit Mater Konst — Sbornik Nauchnykh Trudov. Gosudarstvennyi Vsesoyuznyi Nauchno-Issledovatel'skiiInstitut Stroitel'nykh Materialov i Konstruktsii VNIIStrom

Sb Nauchn Tr Grodn Skh Inst — Sbornik Nauchnykh Trudov Grodnenskii Sel'skokhozyaistvennyi Institut

Sb Nauchn Tr Grozn Neft Nauchno Issled Inst — Sbornik Nauchnykh Trudov. Groznenskii Neftyanoi Nauchno-Issledovatel'skii Institut

Sb Nauchn Tr Inst Biol Akad Nauk B SSR — Sbornik Nauchnykh Trudov Institut Biologii Akademiya Nauk Belorusskoi SSR

Sb Nauchn Tr Inst Geol Geofiz Akad Nauk Uzb SSR — Sbornik Nauchnykh Trudov Instituta Geologii i Geofiziki Akademii Nauk Uzbekskoi SSR

Sb Nauchn Tr Inst Gorn Dela Krivorozh Fil Akad Nauk Ukr SSR — Sbornik Nauchnykh Trudov. Institut Gornogo Dela Krivorozhskii Filial. Akademiya Nauk Ukrainskoi SSR

Sb Nauchn Tr Inst Gorn Dela Sverdlovsk — Sbornik Nauchnykh Trudov. Institut Gornogo Dela, Sverdlovsk

Sb Nauchn Tr Inst Kurortol Fizioter Yerevan — Sbornik Nauchnykh Trudov Instituta Kurortologii i Fizioterapii. Yerevan

Sb Nauchn Tr Inst Mekhanobrchermet — Sbornik Nauchnykh Trudov Instituta Mekhanobrchermet

Sb Nauchn Tr Inst Melior Vodn Bolotnogo Khoz Akad Nauk BSSR — Sbornik Nauchnykh Trudov Instituta Melioratsii Vodnogo i Bolotnogo Khozyaistva Akademiya Nauk Belorusskoi SSR

Sb Nauchn Tr Inst Metallofiz Akad Ukr SSR — Sbornik Nauchnykh Trudov Instituta Metallofiziki Akademiya Nauk Ukrainskoi SSR

Sb Nauchn Tr Inst Torfa Akad Nauk B SSR — Sbornik Nauchnykh Trudov. Instituta Torfa. Akademiya Nauk Belorusskoi SSR

Sb Nauchn Tr Inst Tsvetn Met — Sbornik Nauchnykh Trudov Institut Tsvetnykh Metallov

Sb Nauchn Tr Inst Tsvetn Met im MI Kalinina — Sbornik Nauchnykh Trudov. Institut Tsvetnykh Metallov imeni M.I. Kalinina

Sb Nauchn Tr Irkutsk Gos Nauchno-Issled Inst Redk Met — Sbornik Nauchnykh Trudov Irkutskii Gosudarstvennyi Nauchno-Issledovatel'skii Institut Redkikh Metallov

Sb Nauchn Tr Irkutsk Inst Epidemiol Mikrobiol — Sbornik Nauchnykh Trudov. Irkutskii Institut Epidemiologii i Mikrobiologii

Sb Nauchn Tr Ivanov Energ Inst — Sbornik Nauchnykh Trudov Ivanovskogo Energeticheskogo Instituta

Sb Nauchn Tr Ivanov Energ Inst im V I Lenina — Sbornik Nauchnnykh Trudov Ivanovskogo Energeticheskogo Instituta imeni V.I. Lenina

Sb Nauchn Tr Ivanov Gos Med Inst — Sbornik Nauchnykh Trudov Ivanovskogo Gosudarstvennogo Meditsinskogo Instituta

Sb Nauchn Tr Ivanov Med Inst — Sbornik Nauchnykh Trudov Ivanovskogo Meditsinskogo Instituta

Sb Nauchn Tr Ivanov S-Kh Inst — Sbornik Nauchnykh Trudov Ivanovskogo Sel'skokhozyaistvennogo Instituta

Sb Nauchn Tr Kafedr Mat Mekh Khim Leningr Inst Tochn Mekh Opt — Sbornik Nauchnykh Trudov Kafedr Matematiki, Mekhaniki, Khimii. Leningradskii Institut Tochnoi Mekhaniki i Optiki

Sb Nauchn Tr Kafedr Met Grafiki Khim Teor Mekh Leningr Inst — Sbornik Nauchnykh Trudov. Kafedr Matematiki. Grafiki, Khimii i Teoreticheskoi Mekhaniki. Leningradskii Institut Tochnoi Mekhaniki i Optiki

Sb Nauchn Tr Kalinin Gos Skh Opyt Stant — Sbornik Nauchnykh Trudov Kalininskaya Gosudarstvennaya Sel'skokhozyaistvennaya Opytnaya Stantsiya

Sb Nauchn Tr Kalinin Gos Skh Opytn Stn — Sbornik Nauchnykh Trudov Kalininskaya Gosudarstvennaya Sel'skokhozyaistvennaya Opytnaya Stantsiya

Sb Nauchn Tr Kamenets Podolsk Skh Inst — Sbornik Nauchnykh Trudov Kamenets-Podol'skogo Sel'skokhozyaistvennogo Instituta

Sb Nauchn Tr Kar'k Gos Med Inst — Sbornik Nauchnykh Trudov Khar'kovskogo Gosudarstvennogo Meditsinskogo Instituta

Sb Nauchn Tr Kazan Aviats Inst — Sbornik Nauchnykh Trudov Kazanskogo Aviatsionnogo Instituta

Sb Nauchn Tr Kazan Gos Med Inst — Sbornik Nauchnykh Trudov. Kazanskii Gosudarstvennyi Meditsinskogo Instituta

Sb Nauchn Tr Kaz Gorno-Metall Inst — Sbornik Nauchnykh Trudov Kazakhskii Gorno-Metallurgicheskii Institut

Sb Nauchn Tr Kaz Politekh Inst — Sbornik Nauchnykh Trudov Kazakhskii Politekhnicheskii Institut

Sb Nauchn Tr Khabar Politekh Inst — Sbornik Nauchnykh Trudov. Khabarovskii Politekhnicheskii Institut

Sb Nauchn Tr Khark Gorn Inst — Sbornik Nauchnykh Trudov. Khar'kovskii Gornyi Institut

Sb Nauchn Tr Khark Inst Inzh Kommunaln Stroit — Sbornik Nauchnykh Trudov. Khar'kovskii Institut Inzhenerov Kommunal'nogo Stroitel'stva

Sb Nauchn Tr Khark Inzh Stroit Inst — Sbornik Nauchnykh Trudov. Khar'kovskii Inzhenerno-Stroitel'nyi Institut

Sb Nauchn Tr Khar'k Med Inst — Sbornik Nauchnykh Trudov Khar'kovskogo Meditsinskogo Instituta

Sb Nauchn Tr Khar'k Skh Inst Im V V Dokuchaeva — Sbornik Nauchnykh Trudov Khar'kovskii Sel'skokhozyaistvennyi Institut Imeni V. V. Dokuchaeva

Sb Nauchn Tr Kiev Inst Inzh Grazhd Aviats — Sbornik Nauchnykh Trudov Kievskogo Instituta Inzhenerov Grazhdanskoi Aviatsii

Sb Nauchn Tr Kiev Inzh Stroit Inst — Sbornik Nauchnykh Trudov Kievskogo Inzhenerno-Stroitel'nogo Instituta

Sb Nauchn Tr Kiev Tekhnol Inst Legk Promsti — Sbornik Nauchnykh Trudov. Kievskii Tekhnologicheskii Institut Legkoi Promyshlennosti

Sb Nauchn Tr Kirg Gos Med Inst — Sbornik Nauchnykh Trudov. Kirgizskii Gosudarstvennyi Meditsinskii Institut

Sb Nauchn Tr Kirg Med Inst — Sbornik Nauchnykh Trudov Kirkizskogo Meditsinskogo Instituta

Sb Nauchn Tr Kirg Nauchno Issled Tekh Inst Pastbishch Kormov — Sbornik Nauchnykh Trudov. Kirgizskii Nauchno-Issledovatel'skii Tekhnologicheskii Institute Pastbishch i Kormov

Sb Nauchn Tr Krasnoyarsk Gos Med Inst — Sbornik Nauchnykh Trudov Krasnoyarskogo Gosudarstvennogo Meditsinskogo Instituta

Sb Nauchn Tr Krivorozh Fil Inst Gorn Dela Akad Nauk Ukr SSR — Sbornik Nauchnykh Trudov Krivorozhskii Filial Instituta Gornogo Dela Akademiya Nauk Ukrainskoi SSR

Sb Nauchn Tr Krivorozh Gornorudn Inst — Sbornik Nauchnykh Trudov Krivorozhskii Gornorudnyi Institut

Sb Nauchn Tr Krym Gos Med Inst — Sbornik Nauchnykh Trudov Krymskogo Gosudarstvennogo Meditsinskogo Instituta

Sb Nauchn Tr Kuibyshev Ind Inst — Sbornik Nauchnykh Trudov Kuibyshevskii Industrial'nyi Institut

Sb Nauchn Tr Kuibyshev Inzh Stroit Inst — Sbornik Nauchnykh Trudov Kuibyshevskii Inzhenerno-Stroitel'nyi Institut

Sb Nauchn Tr Kuibyshev Nauchno Issled Inst Epidemiol Gig — Sbornik Nauchnykh Trudov Kuibyshevskogo Nauchno-Issledovatel'skogo Instituta Epidemiologii i Gigieny

Sb Nauchn Tr Kuibyshev Nauchno Issled Inst Gig — Sbornik Nauchnykh Trudov Kuibyshevskii Nauchno-Issledovatel'skii Institut Gigieny

Sb Nauchn Tr Kuibyshev Nauchno Issled Vet Stn — Sbornik Nauchnykh Trudov Kuibyshevskoi Nauchno-Issledovatel'noi Veterinarnoi Stantsii

Sb Nauchn Tr Kuzbasskii Politekh Inst — Sbornik Nauchnykh Trudov Kuzbasskii Politekhnicheskii Institut

Sb Nauchn Tr Leningr Elektrotekh Inst Inzh Zheleznodorozhn T — Sbornik Nauchnykh Trudov. Leningradskii Elektrotekhnicheskii Institut Inzhenerov Zheleznodorozhnogo Transporta

Sb Nauchn Tr Leningr Elektrotekh Inst Svyazi — Sbornik Nauchnykh Trudov. Leningradskii Elektrotekhnicheskii Institut Svyazi

Sb Nauchn Tr Leningr Farm Inst — Sbornik Nauchnykh Trudov Leningradskii Farmatsevticheskii Institut

Sb Nauchn Tr Leningr Gos Inst Nauchno Issled Proektn Inst Os — Sbornik Nauchnykh Trudov. Leningradskii Gosudarstvennyi Nauchno-Issledovatel'skii i Proektnyi Institut Osnovnoi Khimicheskoi Promyshlennosti

Sb Nauchn Tr Leningr Gos Inst Usoversh Vrachei im SM Kirova — Sbornik Nauchnykh Trudov. Leningradskii Gosudarstvennyi Institut Usovershenstvovaniya Vrachei imeni S.M. Kirova

Sb Nauchn Tr Leningr Inst Sov Torg — Sbornik Nauchnykh Trudov Leningradskii Institut Sovetskoi Torgovli

Sb Nauchn Tr Leningr Inst Tochn Mekh Opt — Sbornik Nauchnykh Trudov Leningradskii Institut Tochnoi Mekhaniki i Optiki

Sb Nauchn Tr Leningr Inst Usoversh Vet Vrachei — Sbornik Nauchnykh Trudov Leningradskogo Instituta Usovershenstvovaniya Veterinarnykh Vrachei

Sb Nauchn Tr Leningr Inst Usoversh Vrachei — Sbornik Nauchnykh Trudov Leningradskii Instituta Usovershenstvovaniya Vrachei

Sb Nauchn Tr Leningr Inzh-Stroit Inst — Sbornik Nauchnykh Trudov Leningradskii Inzhenerno-Stroitel'nyi Institut

Sb Nauchn Tr Leningr Khim Farm Inst — Sbornik Nauchnykh Trudov Leningradskii Khimiko-Farmatsevticheskii Institut

Sb Nauchn Tr Leningr Nauchno Issled Inst Antibiot — Sbornik Nauchnykh Trudov Leningradskii Nauchno-Issledovatel'skii Institut Antibiotikov

Sb Nauchn Tr Leningr Nauchno Issled Inst Lesn Khoz — Sbornik Nauchnykh Trudov Leningradskii Nauchno-Issledovatel'skii Institut Lesnogo Khozyaistva

Sb Nauchn Tr Leningr Nauchno-Issled Inst Pereliv Krovi — Sbornik Nauchnykh Trudov Leningradskogo Nauchno-Issledovatel'skogo Instituta Perelivanya Krovi

Sb Nauchn Tr Leningr Sanit Gig Med Inst — Sbornik Nauchnykh Trudov. Leningradskii Sanitarno-Gigienicheskii Meditsinskii Institut

Sb Nauchn Tr Leningr Vet Inst — Sbornik Nauchnykh Trudov. Leningradskii Veterinarnyi Institut

Sb Nauchn Tr Leningr Voen Mekh Inst — Sbornik Nauchnykh Trudov Leningradskii Voenno-Mekhanicheskii Institut

Sb Nauchn Tr Litov Skh Akad — Sbornik Nauchnykh Trudov. Litovskaya Sel'skokhozyaistvennaya Akademiya

Sb Nauchn Tr Lugansk S-Kh Inst — Sbornik Nauchnykh Trudov Luganskogo Sel'skokhozyaistvennogo Instituta

Sb Nauchn Tr Lvov Gos Med Inst — Sbornik Nauchnykh Trudov. L'vovski Gosudarstvennyi Meditsinskii Institut

Sb Nauchn Tr L'vov Nauchn Ovo Derm Venerol — Sbornik Nauchnykh Trudov L'vovskoe Nauchnoe Obshchestvo Dermato-Venerologov

Sb Nauchn Tr Magnitogorsk Gornometall Inst — Sbornik Nauchnykh Trudov Magnitogorskii Gornometallurgicheskii Institut

Sb Nauchn Tr Magnitogorsk Gorno Metall Inst im G I Nosova Me — Sbornik Nauchnykh Trudov. Magnitogorskii Gorno-Metallurgicheskii Institut imeniG.I. Nosova. Mezhvuzovskii Vypusk

Sb Nauchn Tr Minsk Gos Med Inst — Sbornik Nauchnykh Trudov Minskii Gosudarstvennyi Meditsinskii Institut

Sb Nauchn Tr Mogilev Obl Gos Skh Opytn Stn — Sbornik Nauchnykh Trudov Mogilevskaya Oblastnaya Gosudarstvennaya Sel'skokhozyaistvennaya Opytnaya Stantsiya

Sb Nauchn Tr Morfol Kafedry Bashk Med Inst — Sbornik Nauchnykh Trudov Morfologicheskoi Kafedry Bashkirskogo Meditsinskogo Instituta

Sb Nauchn Tr Mosk Gorn Inst — Sbornik Nauchnykh Trudov Moskovskogo Gornogo Instituta

Sb Nauchn Tr Mosk Inst Inzh Skh Proizvod — Sbornik Nauchnykh Trudov. Moskovskii Institut Inzhenerov Sel'skokhozyaistvennogo Proizvodstva

Sb Nauchn Tr Mosk Inst Khim Mashinostr — Sbornik Nauchnykh Trudov. Moskovskii Institut Khimicheskogo Mashinostroeniya

Sb Nauchn Tr Mosk Inst Stali Splavov — Sbornik Nauchnykh Trudov. Moskovskii Institut Stali i Splavov

Sb Nauchn Tr Mosk Inst Tsvetn Met Zolota — Sbornik Nauchnykh Trudov Moskovskii Institut Tsvetnykh Metallov i Zolota

Sb Nauchn Tr Mosk Nauchno Issled Inst Gig — Sbornik Nauchnykh Trudov. Moskovskii Nauchno-Issledovatel'skii Institut Gigieny

Sb Nauchn Tr Mosk Nauchno Issled Inst Gig Im F F Erismana — Sbornik Nauchnykh Trudov Moskovskii Nauchno-Issledovatel'skii Institut Gigieny Imeni F. F. Erismana

Sb Nauchn Tr Mosk Obl Nauchno Issled Inst Akush Ginekol — Sbornik Nauchnykh Trudov Moskovskogo Oblastnogo Nauchno-Issledovatel'skogo Instituta Akusherstva i Ginekologii

Sb Nauchn Tr Mosk Poligr Inst — Sbornik Nauchnykh Trudov Moskovskii Poligraficheskii Institut

Sb Nauchn Tr Mosk Tekhnol Inst Pishch Promsti — Sbornik Nauchnykh Trudov Moskovskii Tekhnologicheskii Institut Pishchevoi Promyshlennosti

Sb Nauchn Tr Mosk Vet Akad im K I Skryabina — Sbornik Nauchnykh Trudov. Moskovskaya Veterinarnaya Akademiya imeni K.I. Skryabina

Sb Nauchn Tr Nauchno Issled Gornorudn Inst Krivoy Rog USSR — Sbornik Nauchnykh Trudov. Nauchno-Issledovatel'skii Gornorudnyi Institut (Krivoy Rog, USSR)

Sb Nauchn Tr Nauchno Issled Inst Keramzita — Sbornik Nauchnykh Trudov Nauchno-Issledovatel'skogo Instituta Keramzita

Sb Nauchn Tr Nauchno Issled Inst Kurortol Fizioter Yerevan — Sbornik Nauchnykh Trudov. Nauchno-Issledovatel'skogo Instituta Kurortologii i Fizioterapii. Yerevan

Sb Nauchn Tr Nauchno Issled Inst Monomerov Sint Kauch — Sbornik Nauchnykh Trudov. Nauchno-Issledovatel'skii Institut Monomerov dlya Sinteticheskogo Kauchuka

Sb Nauchn Tr Nauchno Issled Inst Onkol (Tbilisi) — Sbornik Nauchnykh Trudov. Nauchno-Issledovatel'skogo Instituta Onkologii (Tbilisi)

Sb Nauchn Tr Nauchno-Issled Inst Pereliv Krovi Arm SSR — Sbornik Nauchnykh Trudov Nauchno-Issledovatel'skogo Instituta Gematologii i Perelivaniya Krovi Armyanskoi SSR

Sb Nauchn Tr Nauchno Issled Inst Rentgenol Radiol Onkol Baku — Sbornik Nauchnykh Trudov. Nauchno Issledovatel'skii Institut Rentgenologii, Radiologii, i Onkologii (Baku)

Sb Nauchn Tr Nauchno Issled Inst Stroit g Tashkente — Sbornik Nauchnykh Trudov. Nauchno-Issledovatel'skii Institut po Stroitel'stvu v g. Tashkente

Sb Nauchn Tr Nauchno Issled Inst Vent Pyleulavlivaniyu Ochis — Sbornik Nauchnykh Trudov. Nauchno-Issledovatel'skii Institut po Ventilyatsii, Pyleulavlivaniyu i Ochistke Vozdukha na Predpriyatiyakh Metallurgicheskoi Promyshlennosti

Sb Nauchn Tr Nauchno Issled Inst Vet Uzb Akad Skh Nauk — Sbornik Nauchnykh Trudov. Nauchno-Issledovatel'skii Institut Veterinarii, Uzbekskaya Akademiya Sel'skokhozyaistvennykh Nauk

Sb Nauchn Tr Nauchno Issled Inst Zemled Echmiadzin Arfmenian — Sbornik Nauchnykh Trudov. Nauchno-Issledovatel'skii Institut Zemledeliya. Echmiadzin. Arfmenian SSR

Sb Nauchn Tr Nauchno-Issled Inst Zemled Echmiadzin (Arm SSR) — Sbornik Nauchnykh Trudov Nauchno-Issledovatel'skii Institut Zemledeliya Echmiadzin (Armenian SSR)

Sb Nauchn Tr Nauchno Issled Kozhno Venerol Inst (Minsk) — Sbornik Nauchnykh Trudov. Nauchno-Issledovatel'skii Kozhno-Venerologicheskii Institut (Minsk)

Sb Nauchn Tr Nauchno Issled Proektn Inst Obogashch Aglom Rud — Sbornik Nauchnykh Trudov. Nauchno-Issledovatel'skii i Proektnyi Institut po Obogashcheniyu i Aglomeratsii Rud Chernykh Metallov

Sb Nauchn Tr Nauchno Issled Proektno Konstr Inst Dobyche Pol — Sbornik Nauchnykh Trudov. Nauchno-Issledovatel'skii i Proektno-Konstruktorskii Institut po Dobyche Poleznykh Iskopaemykh Otkrytym Sposobom

Sb Nauchn Tr Nauchno Tekh Ovo Tsvet Metall Mosk Inst Tsvetn M — Sbornik Nauchnyck Trudov. Nauchno-Tekhnicheskoe Obshchestvo Tsvetnoi Metallurgii i Moskovskii Institut Tsvetnykh Metallov i Zolota

Sb Nauchn Tr NIIKeramzita — Sbornik Nauchnykh Trudov NIIKeramzita

Sb Nauchn Tr Norilsk Vech Ind Inst — Sbornik Nauchnykh Trudov Noril'skogo Vechernego Industrial'nogo Instituta

Sb Nauchn Tr Novocherk Nauchn Issled Inst Elektrovozostr — Sbornik Nauchnykh Trudov. Novocherkasskii Nauchno-Issledovatel'skii Institut Elektrovozostroeniya

Sb Nauchn Tr Odess Inzh Stroit Inst — Sbornik Nauchnykh Trudov. Odesskii Inzhenerno-Stroitel'nyi Institut

Sb Nauchn Tr Odess Skh Instiuta — Sbornik Nauchnykh Trudov Odesskogo Sel'skokhozyaistvennogo Instiuta

Sb Nauchn Tr Permsk Gorn Inst — Sbornik Nauchnykh Trudov Permskii Gornyi Institut

Sb Nauchn Tr Permsk Gos Med Inst — Sbornik Nauchnykh Trudov Permskii Gosudarstvennyi Meditsinskii Institut

Sb Nauchn Tr Permsk Gos Skh Opytn Stn — Sbornik Nauchnykh Trudov Permskaya Gosudarstvennaya Sel'skokhoziaistvennaya Opytnaya Stantsiya

Sb Nauchn Tr Permsk Med Inst — Sbornik Nauchnykh Trudov Permskogo Meditsinskogo Instituta

Sb Nauchn Tr Permsk Politekh Inst — Sbornik Nauchnykh Trudov Permskij Politekhnicheskij Institut

Sb Nauchn Tr Primorsk S-Kh Inst — Sbornik Nauchnykh Trudov Primorskogo Sel'skokhoziaistvennogo Instituta

Sb Nauchn Tr Probl Mikroelektron — Sbornik Nauchnykh Trudov po Problemam Mikroelektroniki

Sb Nauchn Tr Rostov Donu Gos Med Inst — Sbornik Nauchnykh Trudov Rostovskogo-Na-Donu Gosudarstvennogo Meditsinskogo Instituta

Sb Nauchn Tr Rostov Gos Med Inst — Sbornik Nauchnykh Trudov. Rostovskii Gosudarstvennyi Meditsinskii Institut

Sb Nauchn Tr Rostov na Donu Inst Inzh Zheleznodorozhn Transp — Sbornik Nauchnykh Trudov. Rostovskogo-na-Donu Instituta Inzhenerov Zheleznodorozhnogo Transporta

Sb Nauchn Tr Rostov Nauchno-Issled Inst Akad Kommunaln Khoz — Sbornik Nauchnykh Trudov Rostovskii Nauchno-Issledovatel'skii Institut AkademiiKommunal'nogo Khoziaistva

Sb Nauchn Tr Ryazan Med Inst — Sbornik Nauchnykh Trudov Ryazanskogo Meditsinskogo Instituta

Sb Nauchn Tr Ryazan Med Inst im Akad I P Pavlova — Sbornik Nauchnykh Trudov. Ryazanskii Meditsinskii Institut imeni Akademika I.P. Pavlova

Sb Nauchn Tr Ryazan S-Kh Inst — Sbornik Nauchnykh Trudov Ryazanskogo Sel'skokhoziaistvennogo Instituta

Sb Nauchn Tr Samark Gos Med Inst — Sbornik Nauchnykh Trudov Samarkandskogo Gosudarstvennogo Meditsinskogo Instituta

Sb Nauchn Tr Sanit Tekh — Sbornik Nauchnykh Trudov po Sanitarnoi Tekhnike

Sb Nauchn Tr Sarat Med Inst — Sbornik Nauchnykh Trudov Saratovskogo Meditsinskogo Instituta

Sb Nauchn Tr Semipalat Zootekh Vet Inst — Sbornik Nauchnykh Trudov. Semipalatinskii Zootekhnichesko-Veterinarnyi Institut

Sb Nauchn Tr Sev Kavk Gornometall Inst — Sbornik Nauchnykh Trudov Severo-Kavkazskogo Gornometallurgicheskogo Instituta

Sb Nauchn Tr Sev-Oset Gos Med Inst — Sbornik Nauchnykh Trudov Severo-Osetinskii Gosudarstvennyi Meditsinskii Institut

Sb Nauchn Tr Sib Nauchno Issled Inst Geol Geofiz Miner Syrya — Sbornik Nauchnykh Trudov. Sibirskii Nauchno-Issledovatel'skii Institut Geologii, Geofiziki i Mineral'nogo Syr'ya

Sb Nauchn Tr Sochinskoi Nauchno Issled Opytn Stn Subtrop Les — Sbornik Nauchnykh Trudov. Sochinskoi Nauchno-Issledovatel'skoi Opytnoi StantsiiSubtropicheskogo Lesnogo i Lesoparkovogo Khoziaistva

Sb Nauchn Tr Soversh Porod Skh Zhivotn — Sbornik Nauchnykh Trudov Sovershenstvovania Porod Sel'skokhozyaistvennykh Zhivotnykh

Sb Nauchn Tr Sredneaziat Nauchno Issled Proektn Inst Tsvetn — Sbornik Nauchnykh Trudov. Sredneaziatskii Nauchno-Issledovatel'skii i ProektnyiInstitut Tsvetnoi Metallurgii

Sb Nauchn Tr Stalinskii Gos Med Inst — Sbornik Nauchnykh Trudov Stalinskii Gosudarstvennyi Meditsinskii Institut

Sb Nauchn Tr Sverdl Fil Mosk Inst Nar Khoz — Sbornik Nauchnykh Trudov Sverdlovskii Filial Moskovskogo Instituta Narodnogo Khoziaistva

Sb Nauchn Tr Tashk Gos Med Inst — Sbornik Nauchnykh Trudov Tashkentskogo Gosudarstvennogo Meditsinskogo Instituta

Sb Nauchn Tr Tashk Gos Univ — Sbornik Nauchnykh Trudov Tashkentskiy Gosudarstvennyy Universitet

Sb Nauchn Tr Tashk Gos Univ im V I Lenina — Sbornik Nauchnykh Trudov. Tashkentskii Gosudarstvennyi Universitet imeni V.I. Lenina

Sb Nauchn Tr Tashk Inst Inzh Zheleznodorozhn Transp — Sbornik Nauchnykh Trudov. Tashkentskii Institut Inzhenerov Zheleznodorozhnogo Transporta

Sb Nauchn Tr Tashk Politekh Inst — Sbornik Nauchnykh Trudov Tashkentskogo Politekhnicheskogo Instituta

Sb Nauchn Tr Teploobmenu Gidrodin — Sbornik Nauchnykh Trudov po Teploobmenu i Gidrodinamike

Sb Nauchn Tr Tomsk Elektromekh Inst Inzh Zheleznodorozhn Tra — Sbornik Nauchnykh Trudov. Tomskii Elektromekhanicheskii Institut Inzhenerov Zheleznodorozhnogo Transporta

Sb Nauchn Tr Tomsk Inzh Stroit Inst — Sbornik Nauchnykh Trudov Tomskii Inzhenerno-Stroitel'nyi Institut

Sb Nauchn Tr Tsentr Aptechn Nauchno-Issled Inst — Sbornik Nauchnykh Trudov Tsentral'nogo Aptechnogo Nauchno-Issledovatel'skogo Instituta

Sb Nauchn Tr Tsentr Gos Nauchno Issled Inst Tsvetn Met — Sbornik Nauchnykh Trudov. Tsentral'nyi Gosudarstvennyi Nauchno-Issledovatel'skii Institut po Tsvetnym Metallam

Sb Nauchn Tr Tsentr Nauchn Issled Aptechn Inst — Sbornik Nauchnykh Trudov. Tsentral'nyi Nauchno-Issledovatel'skii Aptechnyi Institut

Sb Nauchn Tr Tsentr Nauchno Issled Inst Mekh Obrab Drev — Sbornik Nauchnykh Trudov. Tsentral'nyi Nauchno-Issledovatel'skii Institut Mekhanicheskoi Obrabotki Drevesiny

Sb Nauchn Tr Ukr Inst Usoversh Vrachei — Sbornik Nauchnykh Trudov Ukrainskogo Instituta Usovershenstvovaniy Vrachei

Sb Nauchn Tr Ukr Nauchno Issled Inst Eksp Endokrinol — Sbornik Nauchnykh Trudov. Ukrainskii Nauchno-Issledovatel'skii Institut Eksperimental'noi Endokrinologii

Sb Nauchn Tr Ukr Nauchno-Issled Inst Ogneuporov — Sbornik Nauchnykh Trudov Ukrainskii Nauchno-Issledovatel'skii Institut Ogneuporov

Sb Nauchn Tr Ukr Nauchno Issled Inst Solyanoi Promsti — Sbornik Nauchnykh Trudov Ukrainskii Nauchno-Issledovatel'skii Institut Solyanoi Promyshlennosti

Sb Nauchn Tr Ukr Nauchno-Issled Uglekhim Inst — Sbornik Nauchnykh Trudov Ukrainskii Nauchno-Issledovatel'skii Uglekhimcheskii Institut

Sb Nauchn Tr Ukr Skh Akad — Sbornik Nauchnykh Trudov. Ukrainskaya Sel'skokhozyaistvennaya Akademiya

Sb Nauchn Tr Ural Politekh Inst — Sbornik Nauchnykh Trudov. Ural'skii Politekhnicheskii Institut

Sb Nauchn Tr Uzb Akad Skh Nauk Nauchno Issled Inst Vet — Sbornik Nauchnykh Trudov. Uzbekskaya Akademiya Sel'skokhozyaistvennykh Nauk. Nauchno-Issledovatel'skii Institut Veterinarii

Sb Nauchn Tr Uzb Nauchno Issled Vet Inst — Sbornik Nauchnykh Trudov. Uzbekskii Nauchno-Issledovatel'skii Veterinarnyi Institut

Sb Nauchn Tr Vinnitsk Gos Med Inst — Sbornik Nauchnykh Trudov Vinnitskogo Gosudarstvennogo Meditsinskogo Instituta

Sb Nauchn Tr Vitebsk Gos Med Inst — Sbornik Nauchnykh Trudov Vitebskogo Gosudarstvennogo Meditsinskogo Instituta

Sb Nauchn Tr Vitebsk Med Inst — Sbornik Nauchnykh Trudov Vitebskogo Meditsinskogo Instituta

Sb Nauchn Tr Vladimir Politekh Inst — Sbornik Nauchnykh Trudov. Vladimirskii Politekhnicheskii Institut

Sb Nauchn Tr Vladimir Vech Politekh Inst — Sbornik Nauchnykh Trudov Vladimirskii Vechernii Politekhnicheskii Institut

Sb Nauchn Tr Vladivost Med Inst — Sbornik Nauchnykh Trudov Vladivostokskii Meditsinskii Institut

Sb Nauchn Tr VNII Monokrist — Sbornik Nauchnykh Trudov VNII [*Vsesoyuznyi Nauchno-Issledovatel'skii Institut*] Monokristallov

Sb Nauchn Tr VNIKhFI — Sbornik Nauchnykh Trudov VNIKhFI

Sb Nauchn Tr Voen Med Fak Sarat Medinst — Sbornik Nauchnykh Trudov Voenno-Meditsinskii Fakul'tet Saratovskom Medinstitut

Sb Nauchn Tr Voronezh Inzh Stroit Inst — Sbornik Nauchnykh Trudov Voronezhskii Inzhenerno-Stroitel'nyi Institut

Sb Nauchn Tr Vses Gos Nauchno Issled Proektn Inst Khim Fotog — Sbornik Nauchnykh Trudov. Vsesoyuznogo Gosudarstvennogo Nauchno Issledovatel'skogo i Proektnogo Instituta Khimiko-Fotograficheskoi Promyshlennosti

Sb Nauchn Tr Vses Nauchno-Issled Gorno-Metall Inst Tsvet Met — Sbornik Nauchnykh Trudov Vsesoyuznogo Nauchno-Issledovatel'skogo Gorno-Metallurgiceskogo Instituta Tsvetnykh Metallov

Sb Nauchn Tr Vses Nauchno Issled Gornometall Inst Tsvetn Met — Sbornik Nauchnykh Trudov Vsesoyuznyi Nauchno-Issledovatel'skii Gornometallurgicheskii Institut Tsvetnykh Metallov

Sb Nauchn Tr Vses Nauchno Issled Inst Gidrogeol Inzh Geol — Sbornik Nauchnykh Trudov Vsesoyuznyi Nauchno-Issledovatel'skii Institut Gidrogeologii i Inzhenernoi Geologii

Sb Nauchn Tr Vses Nauchno Issled Inst Legk Tekst Mashinostr — Sbornik Nauchnykh Trudov. Vsesoyuznyi Nauchno-Issledovatel'skii Institut Legkogo i Tekstil'nogo Mashinostroeniya

Sb Nauchn Tr Vses Nauchno Issled Inst Lyuminoforov Osobo Chis — Sbornik Nauchnykh Trudov. Vsesoyuznyi Nauchno-Issledovatel'skii Institut Lyuminoforov i Osobo Chistykh Veshchestv

Sb Nauchn Tr Vses Nauchno Issled Inst Metall Teplotekh — Sbornik Nauchnykh Trudov Vsesoyuznyi Nauchno-Issledovatel'skii Institut Metallurgicheskoi Teplotekhniki

Sb Nauchn Tr Vses Nauchno Issled Inst Miner Syrya — Sbornik Nauchnykh Trudov. Vsesoyuznogo Nauchno-Issledovatel'skogo Instituta Mineral'nogo Syr'ya

Sb Nauchn Tr Vses Nauchno Issled Inst Monokrist Stsintill Mat — Sbornik Nauchnykh Trudov. Vsesoyuznyi Nauchno-Issledovatel'skii Institut Monokristallov. Stsintillyatsionnykh Materialov i Osobo Chistykh Khimicheskikh Veshchestv

Sb Nauchn Tr Vses Nauchno Issled Inst Ogneuporov — Sbornik Nauchnykh Trudov. Vsesoyuznyi Nauchno-Issledovatel'skii Institut Ogneuporov

Sb Nauchn Tr Vses Nauchno Issled Inst Pererab Nefti — Sbornik Nauchnykh Trudov. Vsesoyuznyi Nauchno-Issledovatel'skii Institut po Pererabotke Nefti

Sb Nauchn Tr Vses Nauchno Issled Inst Zhivotnovod — Sbornik Nauchnykh Trudov. Vsesoyuznyi Nauchno-Issledovatel'skii Institut Zhivotnovodstva

Sb Nauchn Tr Vses Nauchno Issled Tekhnol Inst Ptitsevod — Sbornik Nauchnykh Trudov. Vsesoyuznyi Nauchno-Issledovatel'skii i Tekhnologicheskii Institut Ptitsevodstva

Sb Nauchn Tr Vses Neftegazov Nauchno Issled Inst — Sbornik Nauchnykh Trudov Vsesoyuznyi Neftegazovyi Nauchno-Issledovatel'skii Institut

Sb Nauchn Tr Vses Sel Genet Inst — Sbornik Nauchnykh Trudov Vsesoyuznogo Selektsionno-Geneticheskogo Instituta

Sb Nauchn Tr Vses Zaochn Inst Pishch Promsti — Sbornik Nauchnykh Trudov. Vsesoyuznyi Zaochnyi Institut Pishchevoi Promyshlennosti

Sb Nauchn Tr Yarosl Gos Pedagog Inst im K D Ushinskogo — Sbornik Nauchnykh Trudov. Yaroslavskii Gosudarstvennyi Pedagogicheskii Institut imeni K.D. Ushinskogo

Sb Nauchn Tr Yarosl Politekh Inst Ser Kauch Rezina — Sbornik Nauchnykh Trudov. Yaroslavskii Politekhnicheskii Institut. Seriya Kauchuk i Rezina

Sb Nauchn Tr Yarosl Tekhnol Inst — Sbornik Nauchnykh Trudov. Yaroslavskogo Tekhnologicheskogo Instituta

Sb Nauchn Tr Zaochn Inst Sov Torg — Sbornik Nauchnykh Trudov Zaochnyi Institut Sovetskoi Torgovli

Sb Nauchn Tr Zhdan Metall Inst — Sbornik Nauchnykh Trudov Zhdanovskogo Metallurgicheskogo Instituta

Sb Nauchn Tr Zootekh Fak Belotserk Skh Inst — Sbornik Nauchnykh Trudov Zootekhnicheskogo Fakul'teta Belotserkovskii Sel'skokhozyaistvennyi Institut

Sb Nauchn Voen-Med Fak Kuibyshev Med Inst — Sbornik Nauchnykh Rabot Voenno-Meditsinskogo Fakul'teta Kuibyshevskogo Meditsinskogo Instituta

Sb Nauchn Vrachei Kabard Balkarii — Sbornik Nauchnykh Vrachei Kabardino Balkarii

Sb Nauch Tr Beloruss Nauch-Issled Inst Zemled — Sbornik Nauchnykh Trudov Belorusskii Nauchno-Issledovatel'skii Institut Zemledeliya

Sb Nauch Tr Eston Sel'skokhoz Akad — Sbornik Nauchnykh Trudov Estonskoi Sel'skokhozyaistvennoi Akademii

Sb Nauch Trud Eston Nauch Inst Zeml Melior — Sbornik Nauchnykh Trudov Estonskogo Nauchnogo Instituta Zemledeliya i Melioratsii

Sb Nauch Trud Eston Sel'khoz Akad — Sbornik Nauchnykh Trudov Estonskoi Sel'skokhozyaistvennoi Akademii

Sb Nauch Trud Leningr Inst Usoversh Vet Vrach — Sbornik Nauchnykh Trudov Leningradskogo Instituta Usovershenstvovaniya Veterinarnykh Vrachei

Sb Naucn Soobsc Dagestan Gos Univ — Sbornik Naucnyh Soobscenii Dagestanskii Gosudarstvennyi Universitet Imeni V. I. Lenina

Sb Nauc Trud Jaroslav Pedag Inst — Sbornik Naucnyh Trudov Jaroslavskogo Pedagogiceskij Institut

SbNM — Sbornik Narodnihi Muzea v Prave Rada A. Historicky

SbNU — Sbornik za Narodni Umotvorenija i Narodopis

SbNVB — Sitzungsberichte des Naturhistorischen Vereines. Bonn

S Bo — Siegel aus Bogazkoy

SBO — Studia Biblica et Orientalia

SBOAA — Soobshcheniya Byurakanskoi Observatorii Akademiya Nauk Armyanskoi SSR

SbOAW — Sitzungsberichte. Oesterreichische Akademie der Wissenschaften in Wien. Philosophisch-Historische Klasse

SBoc — Studi sul Boccaccio

SB Oe AK — Sitzungsberichte der Oesterreichischen Akademie der Wissenschaften. Philosophisch-Historische Klasse

SBol — Strenna Bolognese

SBONT — Sacred Books of the Old and New Testaments

Sbor Arch Praci — Sbornik Archivnich Praci

Sbor Brno — Sbornik. Ceskoslovenska Spolecnosti Archeologicka

Sbor (Brno) — Sbornik Praci Filosofficke Fakulty Brnenske University (Brno)

Sbor Narod Muz Praze — Sbornik Narodniho Muzea v Praze [*Acta Musei Nationalis Pragae*]. Rada A:Historia

Sborn Biol Geol Ved Pedagog Fak — Sbornik Biologickych a Geologickych Ved Pedagogickych Fakulty

Sborn Ceske Spolecn Zemevedne — Sbornik Ceske Spolecnosti Zemevedne

Sborn Ceskoslov Akad Zemed Ved Rostl Vyroba — Sbornik Ceskoslovenske Akademie Zemedelskych Ved. Ser. Rostlinna Vyroba

Sborn Ceskoslov Spolecn Zemep — Sbornik Ceskoslovenske Spolecnosti Zemepisne

Sborn Geog Top Statisticheskikh Mat Azii Izdaniya Voyenno Uch — Sbornik Geograficheskikh, Topograficheskikh, i Statisticheskikh Materialov po Azii. Izdaniya Voyenno-Uchonnogo Komiteta Glavnogo Shtaba

Sborn Hist — Sbornik Historicky

Sbornik Cesk Ak Ved Arch Ust — Sbornik Ceskoslovenska Akademie Ved. Archeologicky Ustav

Sbornik Cesk Spol Arch — Sbornik. Ceskoslovenska Spolecnosti Archeologicka

Sbornik CSSA — Sbornik. Ceskoslovenska Spolecnosti Archeologicka

SbornikP — Sbornik Praci Filosoficke Fakulty Brnenske University

Sbornik Post Plen Verkh Suda SSSR — Sbornik Postanovlenii Plenuma Verkhovnovo Suda SSSR

Sbornik Praci Brnenske U Rada Hud — Sbornik Praci Filosoficke Fakulty Brnenske University. Rada Hudebnevedna

Sbornik (Praha) — Sbornik Narodnihi Muzea v Prave Rada A. Historicky (Praha)

Sborn Imp Rus Ist Ibshchestva — Sbornik Imperialskogo Russkogo Istoricheskogo Obshchestva

Sborn Krajsk Muz V Trnave — Sbornik Krajskeho Muzea v Trnave. Acta Musei Tyrnaviensis

Sborn Masarykovy Akad Prace — Sbornik Masarykovy Akademie Prace

Sborn Matice Morav — Sbornik Matice Moravske

Sborn Muz Anthropol & Etnog — Sbornik Muzea Anthropologii i Etnografii

Sborn Antrop Etnogr Moscow Leningr — Sbornik Muzeya Antropologii y Etnografii (Moscow, Leningrad)

Sborn Nar Mus V Praze Rada B Prir Vedy — Sbornik Narodniho Musea v Praze. Rada B. Prirodni Vedy (Prirodovedny). Acta Musei Nationalis Pragae. Series B. Historia Naturalis

Sborn N Muz Praze — Sbornik Narodniho Muzea v Praze

Sborn N Tech Muz Praze — Sbornik Narodniho Technickeho Muzea v Praze

Sborn Pedagog Inst V Jihlave — Sbornik Pedagogickeho Institutu v Jihlave

Sborn Pedagog Inst V Kosiciach — Sbornik Pedagogickeho Institutu v Kosiciach

Sborn Pedagog Inst V Presove — Sbornik Pedagogickeho Institutu v Presove

Sborn Prac Filoz Fak Brn U — Sbornik Praci Filozofficke Fakulty Brnenske Univerzity

Sborn Prac Lesn Muz Ve Zvolene — Sbornik Prac Lesnickeho a Drevarskeho Muzea ve Zvolene

Sborn Prir Klubu V Kosiciach — Sbornik Prirodovedeckeho Klubu v Kosiciach

Sborn Prir Prague — Sbornik Prirodovedecky (Prague)

Sborn Rabot Lesn Hoz Vsesojuz Nauc-Issled Inst Lesovod — Sbornik Rabot po Lesnomu Hozjajstvu. Vsesojuznyj Naucno-Issledovat'skij Institut Lesovodstva i Mehanizacii Lesnogo Hozjajstva

Sborn Rabot Vopr Karant Rast — Sbornik Rabot po Voprosam Karantina Rastenij

Sborn Rabot v Pam I M Sadovskago (S Peterburg) — Sbornik Rabot v Pamiat Professora Ivana Mikhailovicha Sadovskago (S Peterburg)

Sborn Radova Vizant Inst — Sbornik Radova Vizantoloskogo Instituta

Sborn Trudov Gosud Irkutsk Univ — Sbornik Trudov Gosudarstvennogo Irkutskogo Universiteta. Recueil de Travaux de l'Universite d'Etat a Irkoutsk. Wissenschaftliche Abhandlungen der Staatsuniversitaet in Irkutsk

Sborn Trudov Profess Prepodav Gosud Irkutsk Univ — Sbornik Trudov Professorov i Prepodavatelej Gosudarstvennogo Irkutskogo Universiteta. Recueil des Travaux des Professeurs. Universite d'Etat a Irkoutsk

Sborn Ved Lesn Ust Vysoke Skoly Zemed — Sbornik Vedeckeho Lesnickeho Ustavu Vysoke Skoly Zemedelske v Praze

Sborn Ved Praci Fak Lesn — Sbornik Vedeckych Praci Fakulty Lesnicke

Sborn Vlastiv Mus V Olomouci — Sbornik Vlastivedneho Musea v Olomouci

Sborn Vychodoslov Muz V Kosiciach — Sbornik Vychodoslovenskeho Muzea v Kosiciach

Sborn Vysoke Skoly Pedagog V Olomouci Prir Vedy — Sbornik Vysoke Skoly Pedagogicke v Olomouci. Prirodni Vedy

Sborn Vysoke Skoly Zemed V Praze — Sbornik Vysoke Skoly Zemedelske v Praze. Acta Universitatis Agriculturae Praha

Sborn Vyssej Pedagog Skoly V Plzni — Sbornik Vyssej Pedagogicke Skoly v Plzni

Sbor Praci Filos Fak — Sbornik Praci Filosoficke Fakulty Brnenske University

Sbor Vlast Prac Podblanicka — Sbornik Vlastivednych Praci z Podblanicka

SB Osterr — Sitzungsberichte der Oesterreichischen Akademie der Wissenschaften. Philosophisch-Historische Klasse

SBOT — Sacred Books of the Old Testament

SBP — Etudes et Expansion

SBP — Shop Procedure Bulletin

Sb Pathofysiol Traveni Vyz — Sbornik pro Pathofysiologii Traveni a Vyzivy

SBPAW — Sitzungsberichte. Kaiserliche Preussische Akademie der Wissenschaften

SBPAWB — Sitzungsberichte. Kaiserliche Preussische Akademie der Wissenschaften (Berlin)

SBPC — Sainte Bible. Louis Pirot et A. Clamer

SBPC Cienc Cult — SBPC Ciencia e Cultura

Sb Pedagog Fak Plzni Chem — Sbornik Pedagogicke Fakulty v Plzni. Chemie

Sb Pedagog Fak Plzni Ser Chem — Sbornik Pedagogicke Fakulty v Plzni. Serie Chemie

Sb Pedagog Fak Presove Univ P J Safarika Kosiciach — Sbornik Pedagogickej Fakulty v Presove Univerzity P.J. Safarika v Kosiciach

SBPI — Southern Baptist Periodical Index

Sb Prac Chem Fak SVST — Sbornik Prac Chemickej Fakulty Slovenskej Vysokej Skoly Technickej

Sb Praci Ped Fak Ostrave Ser A Mat Fyz — Sbornik Praci Pedagogicke Faculty v Ostrave. Series A. Matematika, Fyzika

Sb Praci Ped Fak v Ostrave Ser A — Sbornik Praci Pedagogicke Fakulty v Ostrave. Seria A

Sb Praci Prirodoved Fak Univ Palackeho v Olomouci — Sbornik Praci Prirodovedecke Fakulty University Palackeho v Olomouci

Sb Praci Prirodoved Fak Univ Palackeho v Olomouci Chem — Sbornik Praci Prirodovedecke Fakulty University Palackeho v Olomouci. Obor Chemica

Sb Praci Prirodoved Fak Univ Palackeho v Olomouci Fyz — Sbornik Praci Prirodovedecke Fakulty University Palackeho v Olomouci. Obor Fyzika

Sb Praci Prirodoved Fak Univ Palackeho v Olomouci Mat — Sbornik Praci Prirodovedecke Fakulty University Palackeho v Olomouci. Obor Matematika

Sb Prazhskogo Khim Tekhnol Inst B Neorg Khim Tekhnol — Sbornik Prazhskogo Khimiko-Tekhnologicheskogo Instituta. B. Neorganicheskaya Khimiya i Tekhnologiya

Sb Prazhskogo Khim Tekhnol Inst E Pishch Prod — Sbornik Prazhskogo Khimiko-Tekhnologicheskogo Instituta. E. Pishchevye Produkty

Sb Prazhskogo Khim Tekhnol Inst F Tekhnol Vody Okruzh Sredy — Sbornik Prazhskogo Khimiko-Tekhnologicheskogo Instituta. F. Tekhnologiya Vody iOkruzhayushchei Sredy

Sb Prazhskogo Khim Tekhnol Inst G Mineral — Sbornik Prazhskogo Khimiko-Tekhnologicheskogo Instituta. G. Mineralogiya

Sb Prazhskogo Khim Tekhnol Inst H Anal Khim — Sbornik Prazhskogo Khimiko-Tekhnologicheskogo Instituta. H. Analiticheskaya Khimiya

Sb Prazhskogo Khim Tekhnol Inst J Ekon Upr Khim Prom — Sbornik Prazhskogo Khimiko-Tekhnologicheskogo Instituta. J. Ekonomika i Upravlenie Khimicheskoi Promyshlennost'yu

Sb Prazhskogo Khim Tekhnol Inst K Protsessy Appar — Sbornik Prazhskogo Khimiko-Tekhnologicheskogo Instituta. K. Protsessy i Apparaty

Sb Prazhskogo Khim Tekhnol Inst L Khim Tekhnol Silik — Sbornik Prazhskogo Khimiko-Tekhnologicheskogo Instituta. L. Khimiya i Tekhnologiya Silikatov

Sb Prazhskogo Khim Tekhnol Inst N Fiz Khim — Sbornik Prazhskogo Khimiko-Tekhnologicheskogo Instituta. N. Fizicheskaya Khimiya

Sb Prazhskogo Khim Tekhnol Inst P Fiz Mater Izmer Tekh — Sbornik Prazhskogo Khimiko-Tekhnologicheskogo Instituta. P. Fizika Materialov i Izmeritel'naya Tekhnika

Sb Prazhskogo Khim Tekhnol Inst R Avtom Sist Upr Vychisl Met — Sbornik Prazhskogo Khimiko-Tekhnologicheskogo Instituta. R. Avtomatizirovannye Sistemy Upravleniya i Vychislitel'nye Metody

Sb Prazhskogo Khim Tekhnol Inst Sekts Protsessy Appar — Sbornik Prazhskogo Khimiko Tekhnologicheskogo Instituta Sektsiya. Protsessy i Apparaty

Sb Prazhskogo Khim Tekhnol Inst S Polim Khim Svoistva Perera — Sbornik Prazhskogo Khimiko-Tekhnologicheskogo Instituta. S. Polimery-Khimiya, Svoistva i Pererabotka

Sb Prazhskogo Khim Tekhnol Inst T Uchebno Vospitatelnyi Prot — Sbornik Prazhskogo Khimiko-Tekhnologicheskogo Instituta. T. Uchebno-Vospitatel'nyi Protsess

SBPR Bol — SBPR Boletin

Sb Pr Chemickotechnol Fak SVST — Sbornik Prac Chemickotechnologickej Fakulty SVST

Sb Prednasek Makrotest Celostatni Konf — Sbornik Prednasek Makrotest. Celostatni Konference

Sb Prednasek Prac Vyzk Ustavu Tepelne Tech — Sbornik Prednasek Pracovniku Vyzkumneho Ustavu Tepelne Techniky

Sb Pr Lek Fak Brne — Sbornik Praci Lekarske Fakulty v Brne

Sb Pr Lek Fak Univ P J Safarika Kosiciach — Sbornik Prac Lekarskej Fakulty Univerzity P. J. Safarika v Kosiciach

Sb Provozne Ekon Fak Cesk Budejovicich Zootech Rada — Sbornik Provozne Ekonomicke Fakulty v Ceskych Budejovicich. Zootechnicka Rada

Sb Pr Pedagog Fak Ostrave Rada A — Sbornik Praci Pedagogicke Fakulty v Ostrave. Rada A. Matematika Fizika

Sb Pr Pedagog Fak Ostrave Rada A Mat Fyz — Sbornik Praci Pedagogicke Fakulty v Ostrave. Rada A. Matematika, Fyzika

Sb Pr Pedagog Fak Ostrave Rada A Prir Vedy Mat — Sbornik Praci Pedagogicke Fakulty v Ostrave. Rada A. Prirodni Vedy a Matematika

Sb Pr Pedagog Fak Ostrave Rada E — Sbornik Praci Pedagogicke Fakulty v Ostrave. Rada E

Sb Pr Pedagog Fak Univ J E Purkyne Brne — Sbornik Praci Pedagogicke Fakulty University J.E. Purkyne v Brne

Sb Pr Pedagog Inst Ostrave Prir Vedy Mat — Sbornik Praci Pedagogickeho Instituta i Ostrave Prirodni Vedy a Matematika

Sb Pr Prirodoved Fak Univ Palackeho Olomouci — Sbornik Praci Prirodovedecke Fakulty University Palackeho v Olomouci

Sb Pr Tech Kralovopolske Strojir — Sbornik Praci Techniku Kralovopolske Strojirny

Sb Pr UNIGEO Statni Podnik Ostrava — Sbornik Praci. UNIGEO. Statni Podnik, Ostrava

S B Prussia — Sitzungsberichte der Altertumsgesellschaft Prussia zu Koenigsberg

Sb Pr Ustavu Vyzk Rud (Prague) — Sbornik Praci Ustavu pro Vyzkum Rud (Prague)

Sb Pr UVP — Sbornik Praci UVP

Sb Pr VSD VUD — Sbornik Praci VSD a VUD

Sb Pr Vyzk Chem Vyuziti Uhli Dehtu Ropy — Sbornik Praci z Vyzkumu Chemickeho Vyuziti Uhli. Dehtu a Ropy

Sb Pr Vyzk Ustavu Zelezorudn Dolu Hrudkoven — Sbornik Praci Vyzkumneho Ustavu Zelezorudnych Dolu a Hrudkoven

SBR — School Book Review

SBR — Small Business Report

SBR — Studies in the Bengal Renaissance

Sb Rab Agron Fiz — Sbornik Rabot po Agronomicheskoi Fizike

Sb Rab Ashkhab Gidrometeorol Obs — Sbornik Rabot Ashkhabadskoi Gidrometeorologicheskoi Observatorii

Sb Rab Aspir Krasnodar Gos Pedagog Inst — Sbornik Rabot Aspirantov Krasnodarskogo Gosudarstvennogo Pedagogicheskogo Instituta

Sb Rab Aspir Tadzh Gos Univ — Sbornik Rabot Aspirantov Tadzhikskii Gosudarstvennyi Universitet

Sb Rab Aspir Ukr Nauchno Issled Inst Fiziol Rast — Sbornik Rabot Aspirantov Ukrainskii Nauchno-Issledovatel'skii Institut Fiziologii Rastenii

Sb Rab Aspir Voronezh Gos Univ — Sbornik Rabot Aspirantov Voronezhskogo Gosudarstvennogo Universiteta

Sb Rab Basseinovoi Gidrometeorol Obs Chern Azovskogo Morei — Sbornik Rabot Basseinovoi Gidrometeorologicheskoi Chernogo i Azovskogo Morei

Sb Rab Beloruss Gos Med Inst — Sbornik Rabot Belorusskii Gosudarstvennyi Meditsinskii Institut

Sb Rab Biol Tekh Rybolov Tekhnol — Sbornik Rabot po Biologii. Tekhnike Rybolovstva i Tekhnologii

Sb Rab Buryat Otd Vses Nauchn Ova Anat Gistol Embriol — Sbornik Rabot Buryatskogo Otdel'nogo Vsesoyuznogo Nauchnogo Obshchestva Anatomii, Gistologii, i Embriologii

Sb Rab Chist Prikl Khim — Sbornik Rabot po Chistoi i Prikladnoi Khimii

Sb Rab Chuv Resp Vet Lab — Sbornik Rabot Chuvashskoi Respublikanskoi Veterinarnoi Laboratorii

Sb Rab Gidrol — Sbornik Rabot po Gidrologii

Sb Rab Gidrol Leningr Gos Gidrol Inst — Sbornik Rabot po Gidrologii Leningradskogo Gosudarstvennogo Gidrologicheskogo Instituta

Sb Rab Gor'k Volzh Rybinsk Gidrometeorol Obs — Sbornik Rabot Gor'kovskoi Volzhskoi i Rybinskoi Gidrometeorologicheskikh Observatorii

Sb Rab Gos Inst Prikl Khim — Sbornik Rabot Gosudarstvennyi Institut Prikladnoi Khimii

Sb Rab Ikhtiol Gidrobiol — Sbornik Rabot po Ikhtiologii i Gidrobiologii

Sb Rab Inst Prikl Zol Fitopatol — Sbornik Rabot Instituta Prikladnoi Zoologii i Fitopatologii

Sb Rab Inst Prikl Zool Fitopatol — Sbornik Rabot Instituta Prikladnoi Zoologii i Fitopatologii

Sb Rab Inst Tsitol Akad Nauk SSSR — Sbornik Rabot Instituta Tsitologii Akademii Nauk SSSR

Sb Rab Kafedry Fak Khir Sverdl Med — Sbornik Rabot Kafedry i Fakul'tete Khirurgii Sverdlovskogo Meditsinskogo

Sb Rab Kaz Resp Nauchn Ova Anat Gistol Embriol — Sbornik Rabot Kazakhskogo Respublikanskogo Nauchnogo Obshchestva Anatomov, Gistologov, i Embriologov

Sb Rab Khim Istochnikam Toka — Sbornik Rabot po Khimicheskim Istochnikam Toka

Sb Rab Kursk Gidrometeorol Obs — Sbornik Rabot Kurskoi Gidrometeorologicheskoi Observatorii

Sb Rab Lab Yuzhn Morei Gos Okeanogr Inst — Sbornik Rabot Laboratoriya Yuzhnykh Morei Gosudarstvennyi Okeanograficheskii Institut

Sb Rab Leningr Inst Sov Torg — Sbornik Rabot Leningradskii Institut Sovetskoi Torgovli

Sb Rab Leningr Vet Inst — Sbornik Rabot Leningradskii Veterinarnyi Institut

Sb Rab Lesn Khoz Mold Mold Lesn Opytn Stn — Sbornik Rabot po Lesnomu Khozyaistva Moldavii Moldavskaya Lesnaya Opytnaya Stantsiya

Sb Rab Maslichn Efiromaslichn Kul't — Sbornik Rabot po Maslichnym i Efiromaslichnym Kul'turam

Sb Rab Maslichn Kult — Sbornik Rabot po Maslichnym Kul'turam

Sb Rab Mezhdunar Geofiz Godu — Sbornik Rabot po Mezhdunarodnomu Geofizicheskom Godu

Sb Rab Mikol Algol Akad Kirg SSR — Sbornik Rabot po Mikologii i Al'gologii Akademii Kirgizskoi SSR

Sb Rab Mikol Al'gol Kirg SSR — Sbornik Rabot po Mikologii i Al'gologii Akademii Kirgizskoi SSR

Sb Rab Minsk Med Inst — Sbornik Rabot Minskogo Meditsinskogo Instituta

Sb Rab Molodykh Uch Akad Nauk Mold SSR — Sbornik Rabot Molodykh Uchenykh Akademii Nauk Moldavskoi SSR

Sb Rab Molodykh Uch Gorskogo Skh Inst — Sbornik Rabot Molodykh Uchenykh Gorskogo Sel'skokhozyaistvennogo Instituta

Sb Rab Molodykh Vses Sel Genet Inst — Sbornik Rabot Molodykh Vsesoyuznogo Selektsii Genetiki Instituta

Sb Rab Mosk Lesotekh Inst — Sbornik Rabot Moskovskii Lesotekhnicheskii Institut

Sb Rab Nematodam Skh Rast — Sbornik Rabot po Nematodam Sel'skokhozyaistvennykh Rastenii

Sb Rab Nauch Inst Udobr Insektofungits (Moscow) — Sbornik Rabot Nauchnyi Institut po Udobreniyam i Insektofungitsidam (Moscow)

Sb Rab Pozharno Ispyt Stn — Sbornik Rabot Pozharno Ispytatel'nykh Stantsii

Sb Rab Rostov Gidrometeorol Obs — Sbornik Rabot Rostovskoi Gidrometeorologicheskoi Observatorii

Sb Rab Rybinsk Gidrometeorol Obs — Sbornik Rabot Rybinskoi Gidrometeorologicheskoi Observatorii

Sb Rab Silikozu — Sbornik Rabot po Silikozu

Sb Rab Silikozu Ural Fil Akad Nauk SSSR — Sbornik Rabot po Silikozu Ural'skii Filial Akademii Nauk SSSR

Sb Rab Stud Nauchn Ova Leningr Inst Tochn Mekh Opt — Sbornik Rabot Studencheskogo Nauchnogo Obshchestva. Leningradskii Institut Tochnoi Mekhaniki i Optiki

Sb Rab Sverdl Gos Med Inst — Sbornik Rabot Sverdlovskii Gosudarstvennyi Meditsinskii Institut

Sb Rab Sverdl Med Inst — Sbornik Rabot Sverdlovskogo Meditsinskogo Instituta

Sb Rab Sverdl Nauchno Issled Kozhno Venerol Inst — Sbornik Rabot Sverdlovskii Nauchno-Issledovatel'skii Kozhno Venerologicheskii Institut

Sb Rab Tsentr Muz Pochvoved Im V — Sbornik Rabot Tsentral'nogo Muzeya Pochvovedeniya Imeni V. V. Dokuchaeva

Sb Rab Tsentr Muz Pochvoved Im V V Dokuchaeva — Sbornik Rabot Tsentral'nogo Muzeya Pochvovedeniya Imeni V. V. Dokuchaeva

Sb Rab Tsentr Nauchno Issled Inst Kozh Obuvn Promsti — Sbornik Rabot Tsentral'nyi Nauchno-Issledovatel'skii Institut Kozhevenno Obuvnoi Promyshlennosti

Sb Rab Tsiml Gidrometeorol Obs — Sbornik Rabot Tsimlyanskoi Gidrometeorologicheskoi Observatorii

Sb Rab Ukr Nauchno Issled Inst Ogneuporov — Sbornik Rabot Ukrainskii Nauchno-Issledovatel'skii Institut Ogneuporov

Sb Rab Vologod Nauchno-Issledovat Vet Opytn Stn — Sbornik Rabot Vologodskoi Nauchno-Issledovat' Skoi Veterinarnoi Opytnoi Stantsii

Sb Rab Vopr Proizvod Primen Biol Prep — Sbornik Rabot Voprosov Proizvodstva i Primononiya Biologicheskikh Preparatov

Sb Rab Vses Nauchno Issled Inst Agrolesomelior — Sbornik Rabot Vsesoyuznogo Nauchno-Issledovatel'skogo Instituta Agrolesomelioratsii

Sb Rab Vses Nauchno Issled Inst Okhr Tr — Sbornik Rabot Vsesoyuznyi Nauchno-Issledovatel'skii Institut Okhrany Truda

Sb Rab Vses Nauchno Issled Inst Okhr Tr im SM Kirova — Sbornik Rabot. Vsesoyuznyi Nauchno-Issledovatel'skii Institut Okhrany Truda imeni S. M. Kirova

Sb Rab Vses Nauchno Issled Inst Tsem — Sbornik Rabot. Vsesoyuznyi Nauchno-Issledovatel'skii Institut Tsementov

Sb Rab Vses Zaochn Inst Pishch Promsti — Sbornik Rabot Vsesoyuznyi Zaochnyi Institut Pishchevoi Promyshlennosti

Sb Rab Vychisl Tsentra Mosk Gos Univ — Sbornik Rabot Vychislitel'nogo Tsentral'nogo Moskovskogo Gosudarstvennogo Universiteta

Sb Rab Zashch Lesa Mosk Lesotekh Inst — Sbornik Rabot po Zashchite Lesa. Moskovskii Lesotekhnicheskii Institut

Sb Ref Nauchn Rab Dagest Gos Med Inst — Sbornik Referatov Nauchnykh Rabot. Dagestanskii Gosudarstvennyi Meditsinskii Institut

Sb Ref Nauchn Rab Nauchno Issled Inst Okhr Materin Det — Sbornik Referatov Nauchnykh Rabot. Nauchno-Issledovatel'skii Institut Okhrany Materinstva i Detstva

Sb Ref Nauchn Rab Vses Nauchno Issled Inst Maslodel Syrodeln — Sbornik Referatov Nauchnykh Rabot. Vsesoyuznyi Nauchno-Issledovatel'skii Institut Maslodel'noi i Syrodel'noi Promyshlennosti

Sb Rost Ustoichivost Rast Akad Nauk Ukr SSR Respub Mezhved — Sbornik Rosti i Ustoichivost' Rastenii Akademiya Nauk Ukrainskoi SSR Respublikanskii Mezhvedomstvennyi

Sb Ruk Mater Konsult Stroit — Sbornik Rukovodyashchikh Materialov i Konsul'tatsii po Stroitel'stvu

SBS — Stuttgarter Bibelstudien

Sb SAO VASKhNIL — Sbornik SAO VASKhNil (Sredneaziatskoe Otdelenie Vsesoyuznoi Akademii Sel'skokhozyaistvennykh Nauk imeni Lenina)

SBSAW — Sitzungsberichte. Saechsische Akademie der Wissenschaften (Leipzig). Philologisch-Historische Klasse

SBSAWL — Sitzungsberichte. Saechsische Akademie der Wissenschaften (Leipzig). Philologisch-Historische Klasse

SBSBDV — Symposium. British Society for Developmental Biology

Sb Serv Geol Repub Tchec — Sbornik. Service Geologique. Republique Tchecoslovaque

Sb Severocesk Mus Prir Vedy Sci Nat — Sbornik Severoceskeho Musea Prirodni Vedy Scientiae Naturales

SBSt — Sankt-Benedikt-Stimmen

Sb Statei Aspir Kirg Gos Univ — Sbornik Statei Aspirantov Kirgizskogo Gosudarstvennogo Universiteta

Sb Statei Aspir Kirg Univ Fiz-Mat Estestv Nauk — Sbornik Statei Aspirantov Kirgizskogo Universiteta Fiziko-Matematicheskikh Estestvennykh Nauk

Sb Statei Chelyab Politekh Inst — Sbornik Statei. Chelyabinskii Politekhnicheskii Institut

Sb Statei Daugavpilsskii Pedagog Inst — Sbornik Statei. Daugavpilsskii Pedagogicheskii Institut

Sb Statei Donskoi Skh Inst — Sbornik Statei. Donskoi Sel'skokhozyaistvennyi Institut

Sb Statei Erevan Gos Univ — Sbornik Statei Erevanskii Gosudarstvennyi Universitet

Sb Statei Geol Gidrogeol — Sbornik Statei po Geologii i Gidrogeologii

Sb Statei Geol Inzh Geol — Sbornik Statei po Geologii i Inzhenernoi Geologii

Sb Statei Geol Polezn Iskop Tsentr Kaz — Sbornik Statei po Geologii i Poleznym Iskopaemym Tsentral'nogo Kazakhstana

Sb Statei Gidrogeol Geoterm — Sbornik Statei po Gidrogeologii i Geotermii

Sb Statei Leningr Inst Tochn Mekh Opt — Sbornik Statei Leningradskii Institut Tochnoi Mekhaniki i Optiki

Sb Statei Leningr Tekhnol Inst Tsellyul Bum Promsti — Sbornik Statei Leningradskogo Tekhnologicheskogo Instituta Tsellyulozno-Bumazhnoi Promyshlennosti

Sb Statei Lesn Khoz — Sbornik Statei. Lesnomu Khozyaistvu

Sb Statei Lesn Khoz Lesoekspl — Sbornik Statei po Lesnomu Khozyaistvu i Lesoekspluatatsii

Sb Statei Magnitogorsk Gornometall Inst — Sbornik Statei. Magnitogorskii Gornometallurgicheskii Institut

Sb Statei Makeev Nauchno Issled Inst Bezop Rab Gorn Promsti — Sbornik Statei Makeevskii Nauchno Issledovatel'skii Institut Bezopasnykh Rabot Gornoi Promyshlennosti

Sb Statei Molodykh Nauchn Rab Leningr Inst Vodn Transp — Sbornik Statei Molodykh Nauchnykh Rabotnikov Leningradskii Institut Vodnogo Transporta

Sb Statei Molodykh Nauchn Sotr Leningr Geol Uchrezhd Akad Nauk — Sbornik Statei Molodykh Nauchnykh Sotrudnikov Leningradskikh Geologicheskikh Uchrezhdenii Akademii Nauk SSSR

Sb Statei Mosk Inzh-Fiz Inst — Sbornik Statei Moskovskii Inzhenerno-Fizicheskii Institut

Sb Statei Mosk Vyssh Tekh Uchil im N E Baumana — Sbornik Statei. Moskovskoe Vysshee Tekhnicheskoe Uchilishche imeni N.E. Baumana

Sb Statei Nauchno Issled Inst Org Poluprod Krasitelei — Sbornik Statei Nauchno-Issledovatel'skii Institut Organicheskikh Poluproduktov i Krasitelei

Sb Statei Nauchn Sotr Leningr Geol Uchrezhd Akad Nauk SSSR — Sbornik Statei Nauchnykh Sotrudnikov Leningradskikh Geologicheskikh Uchrezhdenii Akademii Nauk SSSR

Sb Statei Rab Ukr Nauchno Issled Inst Maslozhir Promsti — Sbornik Statei o Rabotakh Ukrainskogo Nauchno Issledovatel'skogo Instituta Maslozhirovoi Promyshlennosti

Sb Statei Rezult Rab Novgorod Gos Skh Opytn Stn — Sbornik Statei po Rezul'tatam Raboty Novgorodskoi Gosudarstvennoi Sel'skokhozyaistvennoi Opytnoi Stantsii

Sb Statei Sverdl Skh Inst — Sbornik Statei. Sverdlovskii Sel'skokhozyaistvennyi Institut

Sb Statei Ural Politekh Inst — Sbornik Statei. Uralskii Politekhnicheskii Institut

Sb Statei Vses Nauchno Issled Inst Khim Reakt — Sbornik Statei Vsesoyuznyi Nauchno-Issledovatel'skii Institut Khimicheskikh Reaktivov

Sb Statei Vses Nauchno Issled Inst Transp Stroit — Sbornik Statei. Vsesoyuznyi Nauchno-Issledovatel'skii Institut Transportnogo Stroitel'stva

Sb Statei Vses Nauchno Issled Konstr Inst Khim Mashinostr — Sbornik Statei. Vsesoyuznyi Nauchno-Issledovatel'skii i Konstruktorskii InstitutKhimicheskogo Mashinostroeniya

Sb Statei Vses Zaochn Politekh Inst — Sbornik Statei. Vsesoyuznogo Zaochnogo Politekhnicheskogo Instituta

Sb Statniho Geol Ustavu Cesk Repub — Sbornik Statniho Geologickeho Ustavu Ceskoslovenski Republiky

Sb Statniho Vyzk Ustavu Tepelne Tech — Sbornik Statniho Vyzkumneho Ustavu Tepelne Techniky

Sb Stat Obsc Chim — Sbornik Statej po Obscej Chimii

Sb Stud Nauchn Issled Rab Arkhang Lesotekh Inst — Sbornik Studencheskikh Nauchno-Issledovatel'skikh Rabot Arkhangel'skii Lesotekhnicheskii Institut

Sb Stud Nauchno Issled Rab Mosk Vet Akad — Sbornik Studencheskikh Nauchno Issledovatel'skikh Rabot Moskovskaya Veterinarnaya Akademiya

Sb Stud Nauchno-Issled Rab Kirg S-Kh Inst — Sbornik Studencheskikh Nauchno-Issledovatel'skikh Rabot Kirgizskogo Sel'skokhozyaistvennogo Instituta

Sb Stud Nauchno Issled Rab Sib Lesotekh Inst — Sbornik Studencheskikh Nauchno-Issledovatel'skikh Rabot. Sibirskii Lesotekhnicheskii Institut

Sb Stud Nauchn Rab Alma-At Zoovet Inst — Sbornik Studencheskikh Nauchnykh Rabot Alma-Atinskogo Zooveterinarnogo Instituta

Sb Stud Nauchn Rab Kabard Balkar Gos Univ — Sbornik Studencheskikh Nauchnykh Rabot Kabardino Balkarskii Gosudarstvennyi Universitet

Sb Stud Nauchn Rab Mosk Skh Akad — Sbornik Studencheskikh Nauchnykh Rabot Moskovskaya Sel'skokhozyaistvennaya Akademiya

Sb Stud Nauchn Rab Odess Gos Univ — Sbornik Studencheskikh Nauchnykh Rabot. Odesskii Gosudarstvennyi Universitet

Sb Stud Nauchn Rab Penz Skh Inst — Sbornik Studencheskikh Nauchnykh Rabot Penzenskii Sel'skokhozyaistvennyi Institut

Sb Stud Nauchn Rab Rostov Gos Univ — Sbornik Studencheskikh Nauchnykh Rabot Rostovskogo Gosudarstvennogo Universiteta

Sb Stud Nauchn Rab Voronezh Gos Univ — Sbornik Studencheskikh Nauchnykh Rabot Voronezhskii Gosudarstvennyi Universitet

Sb Stud Nauchn Tr Erevan Gos Univ — Sbornik Studencheskikh Nauchnykh Trudov Erevanskii Gosudarstvennyi Universitet

Sb Stud Rab Krasnodar Gos Pedagog Inst — Sbornik Studencheskikh Rabot Krasnodarskogo Gosudarstvennogo Pedagogicheskogo Instituta

Sb Stud Rab Mosk Tekhnol Inst Myasn Molochn Promsti — Sbornik Studencheskikh Rabot Moskovskogo Tekhnologicheskogo Instituta Myasnoi iMolochnoi Promyshlennosti

Sb Stud Rab Rostov Gos Univ — Sbornik Studencheskikh Rabot Rostovskogo Gosudarstvennogo Universiteta

Sb Stud Rab Sredneaziat Gos Univ — Sbornik Studencheskikh Rabot Sredneaziatskogo Gosudarstvennogo Universiteta

Sb Stud Rab Uzb Gos Univ — Sbornik Studencheskikh Rabot Uzbekskogo Gosudarstvennogo Universitet

Sb Stud Rab Voronezh Gos Univ — Sbornik Studencheskikh Rabot. Voronezhskii Gosudarstvennyi Universitet

SBT — Sacra Bibbia (Torino)

SBT — Studies in Biblical Theology

SBT — Svensk Botanisk Tidskrift

SBTDA — Sbornik Trudov Vsesoyuznogo Zaochnogo Politekhnicheskogo Instituta

SBTL — Studies in Biblical Theology (London)

Sb Tr Abkhazskii Fil Nauchno Issled Inst Kurortol im I G Kon — Sbornik Trudov. Abkhazskii Filial. Nauchno-Issledovatel'skii Institut Kurortologii imeni I.G. Koniashvili

Sb Tr Agrofiz Nauchno Issled Inst — Sbornik Trudov Agrofizicheskii Nauchno-Issledovatel'skii Institut

Sb Tr Agron Fiz — Sbornik Trudov po Agronomicheskoi Fizike

Sb Tr Alma At Zoovet Seminalat Zoovet Omsk Vet Inst — Sbornik Trudov. Alma-Atinskogo Zooveterinarnogo. Seminalatinskogo Zooveterinarnogo i Omskogo Veterinarnogo Instituta

Sb Tr Altai Gos Med Inst — Sbornik Trudov Altaiskii Gosudarstvennyi Meditsinskii Institut

Sb Tr Andizh Gos Med Inst — Sbornik Trudov Andizhanskii Gosudarstvennyi Meditsinskii Institut

Sb Tr Arkhang Gos Med Inst — Sbornik Trudov Arkhangel'skii Gosudarstvennyi Meditsinskii Institut

Sb Tr Arkhang Med Inst — Sbornik Trudov Arkhangel'skogo Meditsinskogo Instituta

Sb Tr Arm Nauchno Issled Inst Stroit Mater Sooruzh — Sbornik Trudov. Armyanskii Nauchno-Issledovatel'skii Institut Stroitel'nykh Materialov i Sooruzhenii

Sb Tr Arm Nauchno-Issled Lesn Opytn Stn — Sbornik Trudov Armyanskoi Nauchno-Issledovatel'skoi Lesnoi Opytnoi Stantsii

Sb Tr Aspir Molodykh Nauchn Sotr Vses Inst Rastenievod — Sbornik Trudov Aspirantov i Molodykh Nauchnykh Sotrudnikov Vsesoyuznyi Institut Rastenievodstva

Sb Tr Aspir Molodykh Nauchn Sotr Vses Nauchno Issled Inst Ras — Sbornik Trudov Aspirantov i Molodykh Nauchnykh Sotrudnikov. Vsesoyuznyi Nauchno-Issledovatel'skii Institut Rastenievodstva

Sb Tr Aspir Soiskatelei Kirg Gos Univ — Sbornik Trudov. Aspirantov i Soiskatelei Kirgizskogo Gosudarstvennogo Universiteta

Sb Tr Aspir Tadzh Univ Estest Nauk — Sbornik Trudov Aspirantov Tadzhikskogo Universiteta Estestvennykh Nauk

Sb Tr Astrakh Gos S-Kh Opytn Stn — Sbornik Trudov Astrakhanskoi Gosudarstvennoi Sel'skokhozyaistvennoi Opytnoi Stantsii

Sb Tr Astrakh Protivochumn Stn — Sbornik Trudov Astrakhanskoi Protivochumnoi Stantsii

Sb Tr Astrakh Tekh Inst Rybn Promsti Khoz — Sbornik Trudov Astrakhanskogo Tekhnicheskogo Instituta Rybnoi Promyshlennosti i Khozyaistva

Sb Tr Avtom Svarke Flyusom — Sbornik Trudov. Avtomaticheskoi Svarke pod Flyusom

Sb Tr Azerb Gos Inst Usoversh Vrachei — Sbornik Trudov Azerbaidzhanskii Gosudarstvennyi Institut Usovershenstvovaniya Vrachei

Sb Tr Azerb Gos Med Inst — Sbornik Trudov Azerbaidzhanskogo Gosudarstvennogo Meditsinskogo Instituta

Sb Tr Azerb Nauchno-Issled Inst Kurortol Fiz Metod Lech — Sbornik Trudov Azerbaidzhanskogo Nauchno-Issledovatel'skogo Instituta Kurortologii i Fizicheskikh Metodov Lecheniya

Sb Tr Azerb Nauchno Issled Inst Neftepererab Promsti — Sbornik Trudov. Azerbaidzhanskii Nauchno-Issledovatel'skii Institut Neftepererabatyvayushehei Promyshlennosti

Sb Tr Azerb Nauchno Issled Inst Oftalmol — Sbornik Trudov. Azerbaidzhanskii Nauchno-Issledovatel'skii Institut Oftal'mologii

Sb Tr Azerb Nauchno Issled Inst Pererab Nefti — Sbornik Trudov. Azerbaidzhanskii Nauchno-Issledovatel'skii Institut po Pererabotke Nefti

Sb Tr Bashk Gos Zapov — Sbornik Trudov Bashkirskogo Zapovednika

Sb Tr Bashk Skh Inst — Sbornik Trudov Bashkirskogo Sel'skokhozyaistvennogo Instituta

Sb Tr Beloruss Gos Med Inst — Sbornik Trudov Belorusskii Gosudarstvennyi Meditsinskii Institut

Sb Tr Beloruss Inst Mekh Selsk Khoz — Sbornik Trudov. Belorusskii Institut Mekhanizatsii Sel'skogo Khozyaistva

Sb Tr Beloruss Lesotekh Inst — Sbornik Trudov. Belorusskogo Lesotekhnicheskogo Instituta

Sb Tr Bryansk Inst Transp Mashinostr — Sbornik Trudov Bryanskii Institut Transportnogo Mashinostroeniya

Sb Tr Bytovoi Khim — Sbornik Trudov po Bytovoi Khimii

Sb Tr Chelyab Elektrometall Komb — Sbornik Trudov Chelyabinskogo Elektrometallurgicheskogo Kombinata

Sb Tr Chelyabinsk Elektrometal Komb — Sbornik Trudov Chelyabinskogo Elektrometallurgicheskogo Kombinata

Sb Tr Chelyab Politekh Inst — Sbornik Trudov. Chelyabinskii Politekhnicheskii Institut

Sb Tr Dal'nevost Nauchno-Issled Inst Lesn Khoz — Sbornik Trudov Dal'nevostochnyi Nauchno-Issledovatel'skii Institut Lesnogo Khozyaistva

Sb Tr Dnepropetr Inst Inzh Zheleznodorozhn Transp — Sbornik Trudov. Dnepropetrovskii Institut Inzhenerov Zheleznodorozhnogo Transporta

Sb Tr Donetsk Nauchno-Issled Inst Cher Metall — Sbornik Trudov Donetskii Nauchno-Issledovatel'skii Institut Chernoi Metallurgii

Sb Tr Donets Nauchno-Issled Inst Chern Metall — Sbornik Trudov Donetskii Nauchno-Issledovatel'skii Institut Chernoi Metallurgii

Sb Tr Energ Inst im G M Krzhizhanovskogo — Sbornik Trudov. Energeticheskii Institut imeni G.M. Krzhizhanovskogo

Sb Tr Erevan Med Inst — Sbornik Trudov. Erevanskii Meditsinskii Institut

Sb Tr Erevan Politekh Inst — Sbornik Trudov Erevanskogo Politekhnicheskogo Instituta

Sb Tr Geobot Eksped L'vov Univ — Sbornik Trudov Geobotanicheskoi Ekspeditsii L'vovskogo Universiteta

Sb Tr Giproniselprom — Sbornik Trudov. Gipronisel'prom

Sb Tr GIPROSANTEKHPROM — Sbornik Trudov. GIPROSANTEKHPROM

Sb Tr Glavniproekt Energ Inst (USSR) — Sbornik Trudov Glavniproekt Energeticheskii Institut (USSR)

Sb Tr Gork Gos Med Inst im SM Kirova — Sbornik Trudov. Gor'kovskii Gosudarstvennyi Meditsinskii Institut imeni S.M. Kirova

Sb Tr Gor'k Skh Inst — Sbornik Trudov Gor'kovskogo Sel'skokhozyaistvennogo Instituta

Sb Tr Gos Inst Prikl Khim — Sbornik Trudov Gosudarstvennogo Instituta Prikladnoi Khimii

Sb Tr Gos Inst Proekt Zavodov Sanit Tekh Oborudovaniya — Sbornik Trudov Gosudarstvennyi Institut po Proektirovaniyu Zavodov Sanitarno Tekhnicheskogo Oborudovaniya

Sb Tr Gos Inst Usoversh Vrachei Kazani — Sbornik Trudov Gosudarstvennogo Instituta dlya Usovershenstvovaniya Vrachei v Kazani

Sb Tr Gos Nauchno-Issled Energ Inst im G M Krzhizhanovskogo — Sbornik Trudov Gosudarstvennyi Nauchno-Issledovatel'skii Energeticheskii Institut Imeni G. M. Krzhizhanovskogo

Sb Tr Gos Nauchno Issled Inst Kurortol Fizioter (Tbilisi) — Sbornik Trudov. Gosudarstvennyi Nauchno-Issledovatel'skii Institut Kurortologiii Fizioterapii (Tbilisi)

Sb Tr Gos Nauchno Issled Inst Rentgenol Radiol — Sbornik Trudov Gosudarstvennyi Nauchno-Issledovatel'skii Institut Rentgenologii i Radiologii

Sb Tr Gos Nauchno Issled Inst Tsvetn Met — Sbornik Trudov. Gosudarstvennyi Nauchno-Issledovatel'skii Institut Tsvetnykh Metallov

Sb Tr Gos Nauchno Issled Proektn Inst Silik Betona Avtoklavn — Sbornik Trudov. Gosudarstvennyi Nauchno-Issledovatel'skii i Proektnyi Institut Silikatnogo Betona Avtoklavnogo Tverdeniya

Sb Tr Gos Vses Nauchno-Issled Inst Stroit Mater Konstr — Sbornik Trudov Gosudarstvennyi Vsesoyuznyi Nauchno-Issledovatel'skii Institut Stroitel'nykh Materialov i Konstruktsii

Sb Tr Gos Zootekh Vet Inst (Tbilisi) — Sbornik Trudov. Gosudarstvennogo Zootekhnichesko-Veterinarnogo Institut (Tbilisi)

Sb Tr Gruz Zootekh Vet Inst — Sbornik Trudov Gruzinskii Zootekhnichesko Veterinarnyi Institut

Sb Tr Gruz Zootekh-Vet Uchebn-Issled Inst — Sbornik Trudov Gruzinskogo Zootekhnichesko-Veterinarnogo Uchebno-Issledovatel'skogo Instituta

Sb Tr Inst Avtom — Sbornik Trudov. Institut Avtomatiki

Sb Tr Inst Chern Metall Dnepropetrovsk — Sbornik Trudov. Institut Chernoi Metallurgii. Dnepropetrovsk

Sb Tr Inst Eksp Patol Ter Akad Med Nauk SSSR — Sbornik Trudov Instituta Eksperimental'noi Patologii i Terapii Akademii Meditsinskikh Nauk SSSR

Sb Tr Inst Elektrotekh Akad Nauk Ukr SSR — Sbornik Trudov Instituta Elektrotekhniki Akademiya Nauk Ukrainskoi SSR

Sb Tr Inst Epidemiol Gig Arm SSR — Sbornik Trudov Instituta Epidemiologii i Gigieny Armyanskoi SSR

Sb Tr Inst Gidrodin Akad Nauk SSSR Sib Otd — Sbornik Trudov Instituta Gidrodinamiki. Akademiya Nauk SSSR. Sibirskoe Otdelenie

Sb Tr Inst Gorn Dela Akad Nauk Ukr SSR — Sbornik Trudov Instituta Gornogo Dela Akademiya Nauk Ukrainskoi SSR

Sb Tr Inst Kurortol Fizioter Yerevan — Sbornik Trudov Instituta Kurortologii i Fizioterapii Yerevan

Sb Tr Inst Kurortol Fiz Metodov Lech Yerevan — Sbornik Trudov Instituta. Kurortologii i Fizicheskikh Metodov Lecheniya. Yerevan

Sb Tr Inst Mashinoved Avtom Akad Nauk B SSR — Sbornik Trudov Institut Mashinovedeniya i Avtomatizats Akademii Nauk Belorusskoi SSR

Sb Tr Inst Metalloved Fiz Met — Sbornik Trudov. Instituta Metallovedeniya i Fiziki Metallov

Sb Tr Inst Neftekhim Protsessov Akad Nauk Az SSR — Sbornik Trudov Institut Neftekhimicheskikh Protsessov Akademiya Nauk Azerbaidzhanskoi SSR

Sb Tr Inst Okhr Materin Det — Sbornik Trudov Instituta Okhrany Materinstva i Detstva

Sb Tr Inst Stroit Mekh Seismostoikosti Akad Nauk Gruz SSR — Sbornik Trudov Institut Stroitel'noi Mekhaniki i Seismostoikosti Akademiya NaukGruzinskoi SSR

Sb Tr Inst Teploenerg Akad Nauk Ukr SSR — Sbornik Trudov. Institut Teploenergetiki. Akademiya Nauk Ukrainskoi SSR

Sb Tr Inst Urol Akad Med Nauk SSSR — Sbornik Trudov Instituta Urologii Akademii Meditsinskikh Nauk SSSR

Sb Tr Inst Urol Gruz SSR — Sbornik Trudov Instituta Urologii Gruzinskoi SSR

Sb Tr Inst Urol Nefrol Im AP Tsulukidze — Sbornik Trudov. Institut Urologii i Nefrologii imeni A.P. Tsulukidze

Sb Tr Inst Vses Nauchno Issled Inst Prir Gazov — Sbornik Trudov Instituta. Vsesoyuznyi Nauchno-Issledovatel'skii Institut Prirodnykh Gazov

Sb Tr Ivanov Med Inst — Sbornik Trudov Ivanovskogo Meditsinskogo Instituta

Sb Tr Izhevsk Med Inst — Sbornik Trudov Izhevskogo Meditsinskogo Instituta

Sb Tr Kafedra Yad Fiz Radiats Khim Leningr Tekhnol Inst im Le — Sbornik Trudov. Kafedra Yadernoi Fiziki i Radiatsionnoi Khimii. Leningradskii Tekhnologicheskii Institut imeni Lensoveta

Sb Tr Kafedr Fiz Obshch Khim Voronezh Politekh Inst — Sbornik Trudov Kafedr Fizicheskoi i Obshchei Khimii. Voronezhskii Politekhnicheskii Institut

Sb Tr Kafedry Metallorezhushchie Stanki Instrum Voronezh Pol — Sbornik Trudov. Kafedry Metallorezhushchie Stanki i Instrumenty Voronezhskii Politekhnicheskii Institut

Sb Tr Kafedry Mikrobiol Orenb Med Inst — Sbornik Trudov Kafedry Mikrobiologii Orenburgskogo Meditsinskogo Instituta

Sb Tr Kazan Aviats Inst — Sbornik Trudov. Kazanskogo Aviatsionnogo Instituta

Sb Tr Kazan Gos Med Inst — Sbornik Trudov Kazanskii Gosudarstvennyi Meditsinskii Institut

Sb Tr Khabar Inst Inzh Zheleznodorozhn Transp — Sbornik Trudov. Khabarovskii Institut Inzhenerov Zheleznodorozhnogo Transporta

Sb Tr Khabar Politekh Inst — Sbornik Trudov Khabarovskogo Politekhnicheskogo Instituta

Sb Tr Khar'k Avtomob Dorozhn Inst — Sbornik Trudov Khar'kovskogo Avtomobil'no Dorozhnogo Instituta

Sb Tr Khark Eksploatatsionno Mekh Inst Inzh Zheleznodorozhn T — Sbornik Trudov. Khar'kovskii Eksploatatsionno-Mekhanicheskii Institut Inzhenerov Zheleznodorozhnogo Transporta

Sb Tr Khar'k Gidrometeorol Inst — Sbornik Trudov Khar'kovskii Gidrometeorologicheskii Institut

Sb Tr Khark Inst Inzh Zheleznodorozhn Transp — Sbornik Trudov. Khar'kovskogo Instituta Inzhenerov Zheleznodorozhnogo Transporta

Sb Tr Khark Vet Inst — Sbornik Trudov Khar'kovskogo Veterinarnogo Instituta

Sb Tr Khim Tekhnol Inst — Sbornik Trudov. Khimiko-Tekhnologicheskii Institut

Sb Tr Khim Tekhnol Inst Pardubice — Sbornik Trudov. Khimiko-Tekhnologicheskii Institut. Pardubice

Sb Tr Khim Tekhnol Inst Prage Fak Neorg Org Tekhnol — Sbornik Trudov Khimiko-Tekhnologicheskogo Instituta v Prage. Fakul'tety Neorganicheskoi i Organicheskoi Tekhnologii

Sb Tr Kiev Inzh Stroit Inst — Sbornik Trudov Kievskii Inzhenerno-Stroitel'nyi Institut

Sb Tr Kiev Stroit Inst — Sbornik Trudov Kievskii Stroitel'nyi Institut

Sb Tr Kiev Tekhnol Inst Legk Promsti — Sbornik Trudov. Kievskii Tekhnologicheskii Institut Legkoi Promyshlennosti

Sb Tr Kirg Nauchno-Issled Inst Epidemiol Mikrobiol Gig — Sbornik Trudov Kirgizskii Nauchno-Issledovatel'skii Institut Epidemiologii, Mikrobiologii, i Gigieny

Sb Tr Klyuchevskogo Zavoda Ferrosplavov — Sbornik Trudov Klyuchevskogo Zavoda Ferrosplavov

Sb Tr Klyuchevsk Zavoda Ferrosplavov — Sbornik Trudov Klyuchevskogo Zavoda Ferrosplavov

Sb Tr Krasnoyarsk Inst Tsvetn Met — Sbornik Trudov. Krasnoyarskii Institut Tsvetnykh Metallov

Sb Tr Krivorozh Gornorudn Inst — Sbornik Trudov. Krivorozhskii Gornorudnyi Institut

Sb Tr Krym Gos Med Inst — Sbornik Trudov Krymskogo Gosudarstvennogo Meditsinskogo Instituta

Sb Tr Krym Med Inst — Sbornik Trudov Krymskogo Meditsinskogo Instituta

Sb Tr Kursk Gos Med Inst — Sbornik Trudov Kurskii Gosudarstvennyi Meditsinskii Institut

Sb Tr Kursk Med Inst — Sbornik Trudov Kurskogo Meditsinskogo Instituta

Sb Tr Latv Fil Vses Ova Pochvovedov — Sbornik Trudov Latviiskii Filial Vsesoyuznogo Obshchestva Pochvovedov

Sb Tr Latv Nauchno Issled Inst Zhivotnovod Vet — Sbornik Trudov Latviiskogo Nauchno-Issledovatel'skogo Instituta Zhivotnovodstvai Veterinarii

Sb Tr Leningr Elektrotekh Inst Svyazi — Sbornik Trudov. Leningradskii Elektrotekhnicheskii Institut Svyazi

Sb Tr Leningr Gidrometeorol Inst — Sbornik Trudov. Leningradskii Gidrometeorologicheskii Institut

Sb Tr Leningr Gos Inst Usoversh Vrachei — Sbornik Trudov Leningradskii Gosudarstvennyi Institut Usovershenstvaniya Vrachei

Sb Tr Leningr Inst Inzh Zheleznodorozhn Transp — Sbornik Trudov Leningradskii Institut Inzhenerov Zheleznodorozhnogo Transporta

Sb Tr Leningr Inst Inzh Zheleznodorozhn Transp im Akad V N Ob — Sbornik Trudov. Leningradskii Institut Inzhenerov Zheleznodorozhnogo Transportaimeni Akademika V. N. Obraytsova

Sb Tr Leningr Inst Sov Torg — Sbornik Trudov Leningradskii Institut Sovetskoi Torgovli

Sb Tr Leningr Inst Usoversh Vrachei Im S M Kirova — Sbornik Trudov Leningradskii Institut Usovershenstvovaniya Vrachei imeni S. M. Kirova

Sb Tr Leningr Inzh-Stroit Inst — Sbornik Trudov Leningradskii Inzhenerno-Stroitel'nyi Institut

Sb Tr Leningr Mekh Inst — Sbornik Trudov Leningradskii Mekhanicheskii Institut

Sb Tr Leningr Nauchno-Issled Inst Gematol Pereliv Krovi — Sbornik Trudov Leningradskogo Nauchno-Issledovatel'skogo Instituta Gematologii i Perelivaniya Krovi

Sb Tr Leningr Nauchno Issled Inst Vaktsin Syvorotok — Sbornik Trudov Leningradskii Nauchno-Issledovatel'skii Institut Vaktsin i Syvorotok

Sb Tr Leningr Nauchn O-Va Nevropatol Psikhiatr — Sbornik Trudov Leningradskogo Nauchnogo Obshchestva Nevropatologov i Psikhiatrov

Sb Tr Leningr Nauchn Ova Nevropatol Psikhiatrov — Sbornik Trudov Leningradskogo Nauchnogo Obshchestva Nevropatologov i Psikhiatrov

Sb Tr Leningr Tekhnol Inst im Lensoveta Kafedra Tekhnol Neor — Sbornik Trudov. Leningradskii Tekhnologicheskii Institut imeni Lensoveta. Kafedra Tekhnologii Neorganicheskikh Veshchestv

Sb Tr Leningr Tekhnol Inst im Lensoveta Kafedra Yad Fiz Rad — Sbornik Trudov. Leningradskii Tekhnologicheskii Institut imeni Lensoveta. Kafedra Yadernoi Fiziki i Radiatsionnoi Khimii

Sb Tr Lesn Khoz (Kazan) — Sbornik Trudov po Lesnomu Khozyaistvu (Kazan)

Sb Tr Lipetskii Fil Mosk Inst Stali Splavov — Sbornik Trudov. Lipetskii Filial. Moskovskii Institut Stali i Splavov

Sb Tr Med Uchrezhd Mosk Oksko Volzh Vozdravotdela — Sbornik Trudov Meditsinskikh Uchrezhdenii Moskovsko-Oksko-Volzhskogo Vozdravotdela

Sb Tr Mladite Nauchni Rab Stud Plovdivski Univ Paisii Khilend — Sbornik Trudove na Mladite Nauchni Rabotnitsi i Studentite. Plovdivski Universitet Paisii Khilendarski

Sb Tr Mold Nauchno Issled Inst Epidemiol Mikrobiol Gig — Sbornik Trudov Moldavskii Nauchno-Issledovatel'skii Institut Epidemiologii, Mikrobiologii, i Gigieny

Sb Tr Mold Stn Vses Inst Zashch Rast — Sbornik Trudov Moldavskoi Stantsii Vsesoyuznogo Instituta Zashchity Rastenii

Sb Tr Molodykh Nauchn Rab Inst Bot Akad Nauk Gruz SSR — Sbornik Trudov Molodykh Nauchnykh Rabotnikov Institut Botaniki Akademiya Nauk Gruzinskoi SSR

Sb Tr Molodykh Uch Kirg Nauchno Issled Inst Zemled — Sbornik Trudov Molodykh Uchenykh Kirgizskii Nauchno-Issledovatel'skii Institut Zemledeliya

Sb Tr Molodykh Uch Kirg Nauchno Issled Inst Zhivotnovod Vet — Sbornik Trudov. Molodykh Uchenykh. Kirgizskii Nauchno-Issledovatel'skii Institut Zhivotnovodstva i Veterinarii

Sb Tr Molodykh Uch Tomsk Politekh Inst — Sbornik Trudov Molodykh Uchenykh. Tomskii Politekhnicheskii Institut

Sb Tr Molodykh Uch Tselinogr Med Inst — Sbornik Trudov Molodykh Uchenykh Tselinogradskogo Meditsinskogo Instituta

Sb Tr Mosk Inst Stali — Sbornik Trudov Moskovskogo Instituta Stali

Sb Tr Mosk Inst Stali Splavov Lipetskii Fil — Sbornik Trudov. Moskovskii Institut Stali i Splavov. Lipetskii Filial

Sb Tr Mosk Inzh-Stroit Inst Im V V Kuibysheva — Sbornik Trudov Moskovskii Inzhenerno-Stroitel'nyi Institut Imeni V. V. Kuibysheva

Sb Tr Mosk Inzh Stroit Inst — Sbornik Trudov Moskovskii Inzhenerno-Stroitel'nyi Institut

Sb Tr Mosk Nauchno Issled Inst Kosmetol — Sbornik Trudov Moskovskogo Nauchno-Issledovatel'skogo Instituta Kosmetologii

Sb Tr Mosk Poligr Inst — Sbornik Trudov Moskovskii Poligraficheskii Institut

Sb Tr Mosk Skh Akad im K A Timiryazeva — Sbornik Trudov. Moskovskaya Sel'skokhozyaistvennaya Akademiya imeni K.A. Timiryazeva

Sb Tr Mosk Tekhnol Inst — Sbornik Trudov Moskovskii Tekhnologicheskii Institut

Sb Tr Mosk Tekhnol Inst Pishch Promsti — Sbornik Trudov. Moskovskii Tekhnologicheskii Institut Pishchevoi Promyshlennosti

Sb Tr Mosk Vech Metall Inst — Sbornik Trudov Moskovskii Vechernii Metallurgicheskii Institut

Sb Tr Mosk Vyssh Tekh Uchil im NE Baumana — Sbornik Trudov Moskovskogo Vysshego Tekhnicheskogo Uchilishcha imeni N. E. Baumana

Sb Tr Mosk Zaochn Poligr Inst — Sbornik Trudov Moskovskii Zaochnyi Poligraficheskii Institut

Sb Tr MVTU — Sbornik Trudov MVTU

Sb Tr MVTU im NE Baumana — Sbornik Trudov MVTU imeni N. E. Bauman

Sb Tr Nauchn Issled Inst Kurortol Fizioter (Tiflis) — Sbornik Trudov Nauchno-Issledovatel'skii Institut Kurortologii i Fizioterapii (Tiflis)

Sb Tr Nauchn Issled Inst Probl Kursk Magn Anomalii — Sbornik Trudov Nauchno-Issledovatel'skii Institut po Problenam Kurskoi Magnitnoi Anomalii

Sb Tr Nauchno Issled Derm Venerol Inst (Tbilisi) — Sbornik Trudov. Nauchno-Issledovatel'skii Dermato-Venerologicheskii Institut (Tbilisi)

Sb Tr Nauchno Issled Farm Khim Inst Tbilisi — Sbornik Trudov Nauchno-Issledovatel'skogo Farmako-Khimicheskogo Instituta (Tbilisi)

Sb Tr Nauchno Issled Gornorudn Inst Krivoy Rog USSR — Sbornik Trudov. Nauchno-Issledovatel'skii Gornorudnyi Institut (Krivoy Rog, USSR)

Sb Tr Nauchno Issled Inst Akush Ginekol (Tbilisi) — Sbornik Trudov Nauchno-Issledovatel'skii Institut Akusherstva i Ginekologii (Tbilisi)

Sb Tr Nauchno-Issled Inst Eksp Klin Ter — Sbornik Trudov Nauchno-Issledovatel'skii Institut Eksperimental'noi i Klinicheskoi Terapii

Sb Tr Nauchno-Issled Inst Eksp Klin Ter Gruz SSR — Sbornik Trudov Nauchno-Issledovatel'skii Instituta Eksperimental'noi Klinicheskoi Terapii Gruzinskoi SSR

Sb Tr Nauchno-Issled Inst Epidemiol Mikrobiol Gig — Sbornik Trudov Nauchno-Issledovatel'skii Institut Epidemiologii, Mikrobiologii, i Gigieny

Sb Tr Nauchno-Issled Inst Gematol Pereliv Krovi Gruz SSR — Sbornik Trudov Nauchno-Issledovatel'skogo Instituta Gematologii i Perelivaniya Krovi Gruzinskoi SSR

Sb Tr Nauchno Issled Inst Gematol Pereliv Krovi (Tiflis) — Sbornik Trudov Nauchno-Issledovatel'skii Institut Gematologii i Perelivaniya Krovi (Tiflis)

Sb Tr Nauchno-Issled Inst Gig Tr Profzabol Gruz SSR — Sbornik Trudov Nauchno-Issledovatel'skii Institut Gigieny Truda i Profzabolevanii Gruzinskoi SSR

Sb Tr Nauchno Issled Inst Gig Tr Profzabol im NI Makhviladze — Sbornik Trudov. Nauchno-Issledovatel'skii Institut Gigieny Truda i Profzabolevanii imeni N.I. Makhviladze

Sb Tr Nauchno Issled Inst Gig Tr Profzabol (Tiflis) — Sbornik Trudov Nauchno-Issledovatel'skii Institut Gigieny Truda i Profzabolevanii (Tiflis)

Sb Tr Nauchno Issled Inst Kurortol Fizioter Abkhazskii Fil — Sbornik Trudov Nauchno-Issledovatel'skii Institut Kurortologii i Fizioterapii Abkhazskii Filial

Sb Tr Nauchno Issled Inst Kurortol Fizioter (Tbilisi) — Sbornik Trudov. Nauchno-Issledovatel'skii Institut Kurortologii i Fizioterapii (Tbilisi)

Sb Tr Nauchno Issled Inst Kurortol Fizioter Yerevan — Sbornik Trudov. Nauchno-Issledovatel'skogo Instituta Kurortologii i Fizioterapii. Yerevan

Sb Tr Nauchno Issled Inst Med Parazitol Trop Med Gruz SSR — Sbornik Trudov Nauchno-Issledovatel'skogo Instituta Meditsinskoi Parazitologii i Tropicheskoi Meditsiny Gruzinskoi SSR

Sb Tr Nauchno Issled Inst Okhr Materin Det — Sbornik Trudov. Nauchno-Issledovatel'skii Institut Okhrany Materinstva i Detstva

Sb Tr Nauchno Issled Inst Osn Podzemn Sooruzh — Sbornik Trudov. Nauchno-Issledovatel'skii Institut Osnovanii i Podzemnykh Sooruzhenii

Sb Tr Nauchno Issled Inst Pererab Nefti — Sbornik Trudov. Nauchno-Issledovatel'skii Institut po Pererabotke Nefti

Sb Tr Nauchno Issled Inst Probl Kursk Magn Anomalii — Sbornik Trudov. Nauchno-Issledovatel'skii Institut po Problemam Kurskoi Magnitnoi Anomalii

Sb Tr Nauchno Issled Inst Prom Stroit — Sbornik Trudov. Nauchno-Issledovatel'skii Institut Promyshlennogo Stroitel'stva

Sb Tr Nauchno Issled Inst Prom Stroit Ufa — Sbornik Trudov Nauchno-Issledovatel'skii Institut Promyshlennogo Stroitel'stva Ufa

Sb Tr Nauchno-Issled Inst Rentgenol Med Radiol Gruz SSR — Sbornik Trudov Nauchno-Issledovatel'skogo Instituta Rentgenologii i Meditsinskoi Radiologii Gruzinskoi SSR

Sb Tr Nauchno Issled Inst Rentgenol Med Radiol (Tiflis) — Sbornik Trudov Nauchno-Issledovatel'skii Institut Rentgenologii i MeditsinskoiRadiologii (Tiflis)

Sb Tr Nauchno-Issled Inst Rentgenol Med Radio Tbilisi — Sbornik Trudov. Nauchno-Issledovatel'skii Institut Rentgenologii i Meditsinskoi Radiologii (Tbilisi)

Sb Tr Nauchno-Issled Inst Sanit Gig Gruz SSR — Sbornik Trudov Nauchno-Issledovatel'skogo Instituta Sanitarii i Gigieny Gruzinskoi SSR

Sb Tr Nauchno Issled Inst Sanit Gig im GM Natadze — Sbornik Trudov. Nauchno-Issledovatel'skii Institut Sanitarii i Gigieny imeni G.M. Natadze

Sb Tr Nauchno Issled Inst Sanit Tekh — Sbornik Trudov Nauchno-Issledovatel'skii Institut Sanitarnoi Tekhniki

Sb Tr Nauchno Issled Inst Selsk Khoz Tsentr Raionov Necherno — Sbornik Trudov. Nauchno-Issledovatel'skii Institut Sel'skogo Khozyaistva Tsentral'nykh Raionov Nechernozemnoi Zony

Sb Tr Nauchno Issled Inst Sint Spirtov Org Prod — Sbornik Trudov. Nauchno-Issledovatel'skii Institut Sinteticheskikh Spirtov i Organicheskikh Produktov

Sb Tr Nauchno Issled Inst Stroit g Sverdlovske — Sbornik Trudov Nauchno-Issledovatel'skogo Instituta po Stroitel'stvu v g. Sverdlovske

Sb Tr Nauchno Issled Inst Tekh Ekon Issled — Sbornik Trudov. Nauchno-Issledovatel'skii Institut Tekhniko-Ekonomicheskikh Issledovanii

Sb Tr Nauchno-Issled Inst Travmatol Ortoped Gruz SSR — Sbornik Trudov Nauchno-Issledovatel'skogo Instituta Travmatologii i Ortopedii Gruzinskoi SSR

Sb Tr Nauchno Issled Inst Travmatol Ortop Gruz SSR — Sbornik Trudov Nauchno-Issledovatel'skogo Instituta Travmatologii i Ortopedii Gruzinskoi SSR

Sb Tr Nauchno Issled Inst Zashch Rast Arm SSR — Sbornik Trudov Nauchno-Issledovatel'skogo Institut Zashchity Rastenii Armyanskoi SSR

Sb Tr Nauchno Issled Inst Zhelezobeton Izdelii Stroit Nerudn — Sbornik Trudov. Nauchno-Issledovatel'skii Institut Zhelezobetonnykh Izdelii. Stroitel'nykh i Nerudnykh Materialov

Sb Tr Nauchno Issled Khozhno Venerol Inst Gruz SSR — Sbornik Trudov Nauchno-Issledovatel'skogo Khozhno-Venerologicheskogo Instituta Gruzinskoi SSR

Sb Tr Nauchno Issled Kozhno Venerol Inst Tbilisi — Sbornik Trudov. Nauchno-Issledovatel'skii Kozhno-Venerologicheskii Institut (Tbilisi)

Sb Tr Nauchno Issled Proektn Inst Ural Promstroiniiproekt — Sbornik Trudov. Nauchno-Issledovatel'skii i Proektnyi Institut Ural'skii Promstroiniiproekt

Sb Tr Nauchno Issled Tekhnokhim Inst Bytovogo Obsluzhivaniya — Sbornik Trudov. Nauchno-Issledovatel'skogo Tekhnokhimicheskogo Instituta Bytovogo Obsluzhivaniya

Sb Tr Nauchnoizsled Inst Kauch Plastmasova Promst — Sbornik ot Trudove na Nauchnoizsledovatelskiya Institut po Kauchukova i Plastmasova Promishlenost

Sb Tr Nauchno Izsled Inst Okhr Tr — Sbornik Trudove na Nauchno-Izsledovatelskiya Instituta po Okhrana na Truda

Sb Tr Nauchnoizsled Inst Tr Khig Prof Bol — Sbornik Trudov na Nauchnoizsledovatelskiya Instituta po Trudova-Khigienna i Professionalni Bolesti

Sb Tr Nauchnoizsled Inst Tr Khig Prof Boles — Sbornik Trudove na Nauchnoizsledovatelskiya Instituta po Trudova-Khigienna i Profesionalni Bolesti

Sb Tr Nauchno Izsled Onkol Inst (Sofia) — Sbornik Trudov Nauchno-Izsledovatelski Onkologichen Institut (Sofia)

Sb Tr Nauchnoizsled Proekt Inst Rudodobiv Obogat Obogat — Sbornik ot Trudov na Nauchnoizsledovatelskiya i Proektantski Institut za Rudodobiv i Obogatyavane. Obogatyavane

Sb Tr Nauchnoizsled Proekt Inst Rudodobiv Obogat Rudodobiv — Sbornik ot Trudove na Nauchnoizsledovatelskiya i Proektantski Institut za Rudodobiv i Obogatyavane. Rudodobiv

Sb Tr Nauchno Tekh Konf Khabar Politekh Inst — Sbornik Trudov Nauchno-Tekhnicheskoi Konferentsii. Khabarovskii Politekhnicheskii Institut

Sb Tr Nauchno Tekh Obedin GruzNIIstrom — Sbornik Trudov. Nauchno-Tekhnicheskoe Ob'edinenie GruzNIIstrom

Sb Tr Novocherk Politekh Inst im Sergo Ordzhonikidze — Sbornik Trudov Novocherkasskogo Politekhnicheskogo Instituta imeni Sergo Ordzhonikidze

Sb Tr Novoross Gos Proektn Inst Tsem Promsti — Sbornik Trudov. Novorossiiskii Gosudarstvennyi Proektnyi Institut Tsementnoi Promyshlennosti

Sb Tr Novosb Vseross O-Va Otolaringol — Sbornik Trudov Novosibirskogo Otdeleniya Vserossiiskogo Obshchestva Otolaringologov

Sb Tr Novosib Inst Inzh Zheleznodorozhn Transp — Sbornik Trudov. Novosibirskii Institut Inzhenerov Zheleznodorozhnogo Transporta

Sb Tr Novosib Otd Vseross Ova Otolaringol — Sbornik Trudov Novosibirskogo Otdeleniya Vserossiiskogo Obshchestva Otolaringologov

Sb Tr Obshchetekh Kafedr Leningr Tekhnol Inst Kholod Promsti — Sbornik Trudov Obshchetekhnicheskikh Kafedr Leningradskii Tekhnologicheskii Institut Kholodil'noi Promyshlennosti

Sb Tr Odess Inzh Stroit Inst — Sbornik Trudov Odesskii Inzhenerno-Stroitel'nyi Institut

Sb Tr Odess Med Inst — Sbornik Trudov Odesskii Meditsinskii Institut

Sb Tr Orenb Gos Med Inst — Sbornik Trudov Orenburgskogo Gosudarstvennogo Meditsinskogo Instituta

Sb Tr Osvo Terskokumskikh Peskov — Sbornik Trudov Osvoeniyu Terskokumskikh Peskov

Sb Tr Penz Skh Inst — Sbornik Trudov Penzenskogo Sel'skokhozyaistvennogo Instituta

Sb Tr Permsk Gor Psikhiatr Boln — Sbornik Trudov Permskoi Gorodskoi Psikhiatricheskoi Bol'nitsy

Sb Tr Povolzh Lesotekh Inst — Sbornik Trudov Povolzhskogo Lesotekhnicheskogo Instituta

Sb Tr Proektn Nauchno-Issled Inst Ural Promstroiniiproekt — Sbornik Trudov Proektnyi i Nauchno-Issledovatel'skii Institut "Ural'skii Promstroiniiproekt"

Sb Tr Rentgenol — Sbornik Trudov po Rentgenologii

Sb Tr Resp Kostno Tuberk Bol'n Im Lenina — Sbornik Trudov Respubliki Kostno Tuberkuleznaya Bol'nitsa Imeni Lenina

Sb Tr Resp Nauchno-Issled Inst Mestnykh Stroit Mater — Sbornik Trudov Respublikanskii Nauchno-Issledovatel'skii Institut Mestnykh Stroitel'nykh Materialov

Sb Tr Resp Nauchno-Issled Inst Okhr Materin Det — Sbornik Trudov Respublikanskii Nauchno-Issledovatel'skii Institut Okhrany Materinstva Detstva

Sb Tr Rostov na Donu Inst Inzh Zheleznodorozhn Transp — Sbornik Trudov Rostovskogo-na-Donu Instituta Inzhenerov Zheleznodorozhnogo Transporta

Sb Tr Rybinsk Aviats Tekhnol Inst — Sbornik Trudov. Rybinskii Aviatsionnyi Tekhnologicheskii Institut

Sb Tr Samark Med Inst — Sbornik Trudov Samarkandskogo Meditsinskogo Instituta

Sb Tr Sekt Radiobiol Akad Nauk Arm SSR — Sbornik Trudov Sektor Radiobiologii Akademiya Nauk Armyanskoi SSR

Sb Tr Sev Nauchno-Issled Inst Promsti — Sbornik Trudov Severnyi Nauchno-Issledovatel'skii Institut Promyshlennosti

Sb Tr Skh Inst SSR Arm — Sbornik Trudov Sel'skokhozyaistvennogo Instituta SSR Armenii

Sb Tr Sochinskoi Nauchno Issled Opytn Stn Subtrop Lesn Lesopa — Sbornik Trudov Sochinskoi Nauchno-Issledovatel'skoi Opytnoi Stantsii Subtropicheskoyo Lesnogo i Lesoparkovogo Khozyaistva

Sb Tr Stalingr Inst Inzh Gor Khoz — Sbornik Trudov Stalingradskii Institut Inzhenerov Gorodskogo Khozyaistva

Sb Tr Stalingr Opytno Melior Stn — Sbornik Trudov Stalingradskaya Opytno-Meliorativnaya Stantsiya

Sb Tr Stalinskogo Inst Usoversh Vrachei — Sbornik Trudov Stalinskogo Instituta Usovershenstvovaniya Vrachei

Sb Tr Stavrop Gos Pedagog Inst — Sbornik Trudov Stavropol'skii Gosudarstvennyi Pedagogicheskii Institut

Sb Tr Sud Med Sud Khim — Sbornik Trudov po Sudebnoi Meditsine i Sudebnoi Khimii

Sb Tr Sverdl Gor Klin Bol'n No 1 — Sbornik Trudov Sverdlovskoi Gorodskoi Klinicheskoi Bol'nitsy No. 1

Sb Tr Sverdl Gos Med Inst — Sbornik Trudov. Sverdlovskogo Gosudarstvennogo Meditsinskogo Instituta

Sb Tr Sverdl Nauchno Issled Inst Pererab Drev — Sbornik Trudov Sverdlovskii Nauchno-Issledovatel'skii Institut Pererabotki Drevesiny

Sb Tr Sverdl Nauchno-Issled Inst Stroit — Sbornik Trudov Sverdlovskii Nauchno-Issledovatel'skii Institut po Stroitel'stvu

Sb Tr Tadzh Nauchno-Issled Inst Zemled — Sbornik Trudov Tadzhikskogo Nauchno-Issledovatel'skogo Instituta Zemledeliya

Sb Tr Tashk Inst Inzh Zheleznodorozhn Transp — Sbornik Trudov. Tashkentskii Institut Inzhenerov Zheleznodorozhnogo Transporta

Sb Tr Tbilis Gos Nauchno Issled Inst Stroit Mater — Sbornik Trudov Tbilisskii Gosudarstvennyi Nauchno-Issledovatel'skii Institut Stroitel'nykh Materialov

Sb Tr Tbilis Inst Usoversh Vrachei — Sbornik Trudov Tbilisskogo Instituta Usovershenstvovaniya Vrachei

Sb Tr Tbilis Nauchno Issled Khim Farm Inst — Sbornik Trudov Tbilisskogo Nauchno-Issledovatel'skogo Khimiko-Farmatsevticheskogo Instituta

Sb Tr Tekhnol Khim Pishch Prod — Sbornik Trudov. Tekhnologii i Khimii Pishchevykh Produktov

Sb Tr TEPLOPROEKT — Sbornik Trudov. TEPLOPROEKT

Sb Tr Tsent Nauchno-Issled Inst Chern Metall — Sbornik Trudov Tsentral'nogo Nauchno-Issledovatel'skogo Instituta Chernoj Metallurgii

Sb Tr Tsentr Muz Pochvoved — Sbornik Trudov Tsentral'nyi Muzei Pochvovedeniya

Sb Tr Tsentr Muz Pochvoved im V V Dokuchaeva — Sbornik Trudov. Tsentral'nyi Muzei Pochvovedeniya imeni V.V. Dokuchaeva

Sb Tr Tsentr Nauchno Issled Eksp Proektn Inst Selsk Stroit — Sbornik Trudov. Tsentral'nyi Nauchno-Issledovatel'skii, Eksperimental'nyi i Proektnyi Institut po Sel'skomu Stroitel'stvu

Sb Tr Tsentr Nauchno Issled Inst Bum — Sbornik Trudov Tsentral'nogo Nauchno-Issledovatel'skogo Instituta Bumagi

Sb Tr Tsentr Nauchno-Issled Inst Chern Metall — Sbornik Trudov Tsentral'nogo Nauchno-Issledovatel'skogo Instituta Chernoj Metallurgii

Sb Tr Tsentr Nauchno-Issled Inst Olovyannoi Promsti — Sbornik Trudov Tsentral'nyi Nauchno-Issledovatel'skii Institut Olovyannoi Promyshlennosti

Sb Tr Tsentr Nauchno Issled Inst Tary Upakovki — Sbornik Trudov. Tsentral'nyi Nauchno-Issledovatel'skii Institut Tary i Upakovki

Sb Tr Tsentr Nauchno Issled Lesokhim Inst — Sbornik Trudov. Tsentral'nyi Nauchno-Issledovatel'skii Lesokhimicheskii Institut

Sb Tr Tsentr Nauchno Issled Proektn Inst Lesokhim Promsti — Sbornik Trudov Tsentral'nyi Nauchno-Issledovatel'skii Proektnyi Institut Lesokhiimicheskoi Promyshlennosti

Sb Tr Tskhaltub Fil Nauchno Issled Inst Kurortol Fiz im I G K — Sbornik Trudov. Tskhaltubskii Filial Nauchno-Issledovatel'skogo Instituta Kurortologii i Fizioterapii imeni I.G. Koniashvili

Sb Tr Tskhaltub Fil Nauchno Issled Inst Kurortol Fizioter — Sbornik Trudov Tskhaltubskii Filial Nauchno-Issledovatel'skii Institut Kurortoloogii i Fizioterapii

Sb Tr TsNILKhI — Sbornik Trudov TsNILKhI

Sb Tr Tul Mekh Inst — Sbornik Trudov Tul'skogo Mekhanicheskogo Instituta

Sb Trud Agron Fiz — Sbornik Trudov po Agronomicheskoi Fizike

Sb Trud Moskov Obl Pedag Inst — Sbornik Trudov Moskovskogo Oblastskogo Pedagogiceskij Institut

Sb Trud Nauc-Issled Inst Hudoz Promys — Sbornik Trudov Nauchno-Issledovatel'skogo Instituta Hudozestvennoj Promyshlennosti

Sb Trudov Inst Problem Upravlen — Sbornik Trudov Institut Problem Upravlenina

Sb Trudov Odess Elektrotehn Inst Svjazi — Sbornik Trudov Odesskogo Elektrotehniceskogo Instituta Svjazi Imeni A. S. Popova

Sb Trudov Vsesojuz Zaocn Politehn Inst — Sbornik Trudov Vsesojuznogo Zaocnogo Politehniceskogo Instituta

Sb Trud Vopros Zool Kazansk Gos Pedagog Inst — Sbornik Trudov Vopros Zool Kazanskii Gosudarstvennyi Pedagogicheskii Institut

Sb Trud Zool Muz — Sbornik Trudov Zoologicheskogo Muzeya

Sb Tr Ufim Neft Inst — Sbornik Trudov Ufimskogo Neftyanogo Instituta

Sb Tr Ufim Neft Nauchno Issled Inst — Sbornik Trudov. Ufimskii Neftyanoi Nauchno-Issledovatel'skii Institut

Sb Tr Ukr Nauchno Issled Inst Kozh Obuvn Promsti — Sbornik Trudov. Ukrainskii Nauchno-Issledovatel'skii Institut Kozhevenno-Obuvnoi Promyshlennosti

Sb Tr Ukr Nauchno-Issled Inst Met — Sbornik Trudov Ukrainskij Nauchno-Issledovatel'skij Institut Metallov

Sb Tr Ukr Nauchno Issled Inst Pishch Promsti — Sbornik Trudov Ukrainskii Nauchno-Issledovatel'skii Institut Pishchevoi Promyshlennosti

Sb Tr Ukr Nauchno Issled Inst Poligr — Sbornik Trudov Ukrainskogo Nauchno-Issledovatel'skogo Instituta Poligrafil

Sb Tr Ukr Nauchno Issled Inst Poligr Promsti — Sbornik Trudov Ukrainskogo Nauchno-Issledovatel'skogo Instituta Poligraficheskoi Promyshlennosti

Sb Tr Ukr Nauchno Issled Inst Spets Stalei Splavov Ferrosplav — Sbornik Trudov. Ukrainskii Nauchno-Issledovatel'skii Institut Spetsial'nykh Stalei, Splavov i Ferrosplavov

Sb Tr Ukr Nauchno Issled Inst Tsellyul Bum Promsti — Sbornik Trudov Ukrainskogo Nauchno-Issledovatel'skogo Instituta Tsellyulozno-Bumazhnoi Promyshlennosti

Sb Tr Ukr Nauchno Issled Uglekhim Inst — Sbornik Trudov. Ukrainskii Nauchno-Issledovatel'skii Uglekhimicheskii Institut

Sb Tr Ukr Tsentr Nauchno-Issled Inst Ortop Travmatol — Sbornik Trudov Ukrainskogo Tsentral'nogo Nauchno-Issledovatel'skogo Instituta Ortopedii i Travmatologii

Sb Tr Ulyanovsk Politekh Inst — Sbornik Trudov. Ul'yanovskii Politekhnicheskii Institut

Sb Tr Ural Lesotekh Inst — Sbornik Trudov Ural'skii Lesotekhnicheskii Institut

Sb Tr Ural Nauchno Issled Khim Inst — Sbornik Trudov. Ural'skii Nauchno-Issledovatel'skii Khimicheskii Institut

Sb Tr Uzb Gos Nauchno Issled Inst Kurortol Fizioter — Sbornik Trudov Uzbekskogo Gosudarstvennogo Nauchno-Issledovatel'skogo Instituta Kurortologii i Fizioterapii

Sb Tr Vil'nyus Gos Nauchno Issled Inst Stroit Mater — Sbornik Trudov Vil'nyusskogo Gosudarstvennogo Nauchno-Issledovatel'skogo Instituta Stroitel'nykh Materialov

Sb Tr Vissh Med Inst I P Pavlov (Plovdiv Bulg) — Sbornik Trudove na Visshiya Meditsinski Institut I.P. Pavlov (Plovdiv, Bulgaria)

Sb Tr Vitebsk Gos Med Inst — Sbornik Trudov Vitebskogo Gosudarstvennogo Meditsinskogo Instituta

Sb Tr Vladivost Nauchno Issled Inst Epidemiol Mikrobiol Gig — Sbornik Trudov Vladivostokskogo Nauchno-Issledovatel'skogo Instituta Epidemiologii, Mikrobiologii, i Gigieny

Sb Tr VNIIB — Sbornik Trudov VNIIB

Sb Tr VNIIstrom — Sbornik Trudov. VNIIstrom

Sb Tr VNIKhFI — Sbornik Trudov VNIKhFI (Vsesoiuznyi Nauchno-Issledovatel'skii Khimiko-Farmatsevticheskii Institut)

Sb Tr Volgogr Nauchno Issled Inst Neft Gazov Promsti — Sbornik Trudov. Volgogradskii Nauchno-Issledovatel'skii Institut Neftyanoi i Gazovoi Promyshlennosti

Sb Tr Voronezh Gos Med Inst — Sbornik Trudov. Voronezhskii Gosudarstvennyi Meditsinskii Institut

Sb Tr Voronezh Inzh Stroit Inst — Sbornik Trudov Voronezhskogo Inzhenerno-Stroitel'nogo Instituta

Sb Tr Voronezh Otd Vses Khim Ova — Sbornik Trudov Voronezhskogo Otdeleniya Vsesoyuznogo Khimicheskogo Obshchestva

Sb Tr Voronezh S-Kh — Sbornik Trudov Voronezhskogo Sel'skokhozyaistvennogo Instituta

Sb Tr Voronezh S-Kh Inst — Sbornik Trudov Voronezhskogo Sel'skokhozyaistvennogo Instituta

Sb Tr Vost Sib Kraev Nauchno Issled Inst Epidemiol Mikrobiol — Sbornik Trudov Vostochno-Sibirskogo Kraevogo Nauchno-Issledovatel'skogo Instituta Epidemiologii i Mikrobiologii

Sb Tr Vrachei Dorogi — Sbornik Trudov Vrachei Dorogi

Sb Tr Vrachei Pribalt Zhelezn — Sbornik Trudov Vrachei Pribaltiiskogo Zheleznodorozhliya

Sb Tr Vses Inst Rastenievod — Sbornik Trudov Vsesoyuznyi Institut Rastenievodstva

Sb Tr Vses Inst Zashch Rast — Sbornik Trudov Vsesoyuznogo Instituta Zashchity Rastenii

Sb Tr Vses Nauchno-Issled Eksp-Konstr Inst Tary Upakovki — Sbornik Trudov Vsesoyuznyi Nauchno-Issledovatel'skii i Eksperimental'no-Konstruktorskii Institut Tary i Upakovki

Sb Tr Vses Nauchno Issled Gornometall Inst Tsvetn Met — Sbornik Trudov. Vsesoyuznyi Nauchno-Issledovatel'skii Gornometallurgicheskii Institut Tsvetnykh Metallov

Sb Tr Vses Nauchno-Issled Inst Bolezn Ptits — Sbornik Trudov Vsesoyuznogo Nauchno-Issledovatel'skogo Instituta po Boleznyam Ptits

Sb Tr Vses Nauchno Issled Inst Derevoobrab Promsti — Sbornik Trudov Vsesoyuznyi Nauchno-Issledovatel'skii Institut Derevoobrabatyvayuushchei Promyshlennosti

Sb Tr Vses Nauchno-Issled Inst Gidroliza Rastit Mater — Sbornik Trudov Vsesoyuznyi Nauchno-Issledovatel'skii Institut Gidroliza Rastitel'nykh Materialov

Sb Tr Vses Nauchno Issled Inst Gidrotekh Sanit Tekh Rab — Sbornik Trudov. Vsesoyuznyi Nauchno-Issledovatel'skii Institut Gidrotekhnicheskikh i Sanitarno-Tekhnicheskikh Rabot

Sb Tr Vses Nauchno Issled Inst "Goznaka" — Sbornik Trudov Vsesoyuznyi Nauchno-Issledovatel'skii Institut "Goznaka"

Sb Tr Vses Nauchno Issled Inst Mash Proizvod Sint Volokon — Sbornik Trudov. Vsesoyuznyi Nauchno-Issledovatel'skii Institut Mashin dlya Proizvodstva Sinteticheskikh Volokon

Sb Tr Vses Nauchno-Issled Inst Nerudn Stroit Mater Gidromekh — Sbornik Trudov. Vsesoyuznyi Nauchno-Issledovatel'skii Institut Nerudnykh Stroitel'nykh Materialov i Gidromekhanizatsii

Sb Tr Vses Nauchno-Issled Inst Nov Stroit Mater — Sbornik Trudov Vsesoyuznyi Nauchno-Issledovatel'skii Institut Novykh Stroitel'nykh Materialov

Sb Tr Vses Nauchno Issled Inst Sint Kauch im S V Lebedeva — Sbornik Trudov. Vsesoyuznyi Nauchno-Issledovatel'skii Institut Sinteticheskogo Kauchuka imeni S.V. Lebedeva

Sb Tr Vses Nauchno-Issled Inst Stroit Mater Konstr — Sbornik Trudov Vsesoyuznyi Nauchno-Issledovatel'skii Institut Stroitel'nykh Materialov i Konstruktsii

Sb Tr Vses Nauchno-Issled Inst Tsellyul Bum Promsti — Sbornik Trudov Vsesoyuznogo Nauchno-Issledovatel'skogo Instituta Tsellyulozno- Bumazhnoi Promyshlennosti

Sb Tr Vses Nauchno Issled Inst Tsvetn Met — Sbornik Trudov Vsesoyuznogo Nauchno-Issledovatel'skogo Instituta Tsvetnykh Metallov

Sb Tr Vses Nauchno Issled Inst Tverd Splavov — Sbornik Trudov Vsesoyuznyi Nauchno-Issledovatel'skii Institut Tverdykh Splavov

Sb Tr Vses Nauchno Issled Khim Farm Inst — Sbornik Trudov Vsesoyuznogo Nauchno-Issledovatel'skogo Khimiko-Farmatsevticheskogo Instituta

Sb Tr Vses Nauchno-Issled Proekt Inst Titana — Sbornik Trudov Vsesoyuznyi Nauchno-Issledovatel'skii i Proektnyi Institut Titana

Sb Tr Vses Nauchno Issled Proektn Inst TEPLOPROEKT — Sbornik Trudov. Vsesoyuznyi Nauchno-Issledovatel'skii i Proektnyi Institut TEPLOPROEKT

Sb Tr Vses Nauchno-Issled Proektn Inst Teplotekh Sooruzh — Sbornik Trudov Vsesoyuznyi Nauchno-Issledovatel'skii i Proektnyi Institut po Teplotekhnicheskim Sooruzheniyam

Sb Tr Vses Nauchno Issled Proektn Inst Titana — Sbornik Trudov Vsesoyuznyi Nauchno-Issledovatel'skii i Proektnyi Institut Titana

Sb Tr Vses Nauchno Issled Proektn Inst Tugoplavkikh Met Tver — Sbornik Trudov. Vsesoyuznyi Nauchno-Issledovatel'skii i Proektnyi Institut Tugoplavkikh Metallov i Tverdykh Splavov

Sb Tr Vses Nauchno Issled Proektn Inst Vtorichnym Met — Sbornik Trudov. Vsesoyuznyi Nauchno-Issledovatel'skii i Proektnyi Institut po Vtorichnym Metallam

Sb Tr Vses Nauchno Issled Proektno Konstr Inst Polim Stroit M — Sbornik Trudov. Vsesoyuznyi Nauchno-Issledovatel'skii i Proektno-Konstruktorskii Institut Polimernykh Stroitel'nykh Materialov

Sb Tr Vses Nauchno Issled Proektno Konstr Inst Yuvelirnoi Pr — Sbornik Trudov. Vsesoyuznyi Nauchno-Issledovatel'skii i Proektno-Konstruktorskii Institut Yuvelirnoi Promyshlennosti

Sb Tr Vses Neft Nauchno Issled Inst — Sbornik Trudov. Vsesoyuznyi Neftyanoi Nauchno-Issledovatel'skii Institut

Sb Tr Vses Proektn Nauchno Issled Inst Giproniselprom — Sbornik Trudov. Vsesoyuznyi Proektnyi i Nauchno-Issledovatel'skii Institut Giproniselprom

Sb Tr Vses Zaochn Energ Inst — Sbornik Trudov. Vsesoyuznyi Zaochnyi Energeticheskii Institut

Sb Tr Vses Zaochn Inzh Stroit Inst — Sbornik Trudov Vsesoyuznyi Zaochnyi Inzhenerno-Stroitel'nyi Institut

Sb Tr Vses Zaochn Politekh Inst — Sbornik Trudov Vsesoyuznogo Zaochnogo Politekhnicheskogo Instituta

Sb Tr Yuzhn Nauchno Issled Inst Prom Stroit — Sbornik Trudov Yuzknyi Nauchno-Issledovatel'skii Institut Promyshlennogo Stroitel'stva

Sb Tr Zool Muz MGU — Sbornik Trudov. Zoologicheskogo Muzeya MGU

Sb Tr Zool Muz Mosk Univ — Sbornik Trudov Zoologicheskogo Muzeya Moskovskogo Universiteta

Sb Tsentr Geol Inst ChSSR — Sbornik Tsentral'nogo Geologicheskogo Instituta ChSSR

Sb Tsentr Nauchno Issled Inst Tekhnol Mashinostr — Sbornik Tsentral'nyi Nauchno-Issledovatel'skii Institut Tekhnologii i Mashinostroeniya

SBU — Mois Economique et Financier

SBU — Svenskt Bibliskt Uppslagsverk

SBU — Symbolae Biblicae Upsalienses

Sb Uch Zap Aspir Latv Nauchno Issled Inst Zemled — Sbornik Uchenykh Zapisok Aspirantov. Latviiskii Nauchno-Issledovatel'skii Institut Zemledeliya

Sb UNIGEO Statni Podnik Ostrava — Sbornik. UNIGEO, Statni Podnik, Ostrava

SBUPAC — Symbolae Botanicae Upsalienses

Sb Ural Politekh Inst — Sbornik. Ural'skii Politekhnicheskii Institut

Sb Ustavu Nerostych Surovin Kutne Hore — Sbornik Ustavu Nerostych Surovin v Kutne Hore

Sb Ustavu Vyzk Vyz Lidu Praze — Sbornik Ustavu pro Vyzkum Vyzivy Lidu v Praze

Sb Ustav Vedeckotech Inf Genet Slechteni — Sbornik Ustav Vedeckotechnickych Informaci Genetika a Slechteni

Sb Ustav Vedeckotech Inf Melior — Sbornik Ustav Vedeckotechnickych Informaci. Rada Meliorace

Sb Ustav Vedeckotech Inf Zemed Genet Slechteni — Sbornik Ustav Vedeckotechnickych Informaci pro Zemedelstvi, Genetika, a Slechteni

Sb Ustav Vedeckotech Inf Zemed Melior — Sbornik Ustav Vedeckotechnickych Informaci pro Zemedelstvi Rada Meliorace

Sb Ustred Ustavu Geol — Sbornik Ustredniho Ustavu Geologickeho

Sb Ustred Ustavu Geol Oddil Geol — Sbornik Ustredniho Ustavu Geologickeho. Oddil Geologicky

Sb UVTI Genet Slechteni — Sbornik UVTI [Ustav Vedeckotechnickych Informaci] Genetika a Slechteni

Sb UVTI Melior — Sbornik UVTI [Ustav Vedeckotechnickych Informaci] Meliorace

Sb UVTI Ochr Rostl — Sbornik UVTI [Ustav Vedeckotechnickych Informaci] Ochrana Rostlin

Sb UVTI (Ustav Vedeckotech Inf) Zahradnictvi — Sbornik UVTI (Ustav Vedeckotechnickych Informaci) Zahradnictvi

Sb UVTIZ Genet Slechteni — Sbornik UVTIZ [Ustav Vedeckotechnickych Informaci Pro Zemedelstvi]. Genetika a Slechteni

Sb UVTIZ Melior — Sbornik UVTIZ [Ustav Vedeckotechnickych Informaci Pro Zemedelstvi] Meliorace

Sb UVTIZ Potravin Vedy — Sbornik UVTIZ (Ustav Vedeckotechnickych Informaci Pro Zemedelstvi). Potravinarske Vedy

Sb UVTIZ (Ustav Vedeckotech Inf Zemed) Ochr Rostl — Sbornik UVTIZ (Ustav Vedeckotechnickych Informaci pro Zemedelstvi) Ochrana Rostlin

Sb Uzb Gos Nauchno Issled Inst Kurortol Fizioter — Sbornik Uzbekskogo Gosudarstvennogo Nauchno-Issledovatel'skogo Instituta Kurortologii i Fizioterapii

SbV — Sbornik Velehradsky. Archeologicky Spolek Stary Velehrad se Sidlem na Velehrade

SBV — Schweizer Buecherverzeichnis

Sb Ved Lesn Ustav Vys Sk Zemed Praze — Sbornik Vedeckeho Lesnickeho Ustavu Vysoke Skoly Zemedelske v Praze

Sb Ved Odb Praci — Sbornik Vedeckych a Odbornych Praci. Vysoke Uceni Technicke v Brne. Fakulta Stavebni

Sb Ved Praci Ustred Statniho Ust Praze — Sbornik Vedeckych Praci Ustredniho Statniho Ustavu v Praze

Sb Ved Praci Vyzk Ustav Vyz Zvirat — Sbornik Vedeckych Praci-Vyzkumny Ustav Vyzivy Zvirat

Sb Ved Pr Lek Fak Karlovy Univerzity Hradci Kralove — Sbornik Vedeckych Praci Lekarske Fakulty Karlovy Univerzity v Hradci Kralove

Sb Ved Pr Lek Fak Karlovy Univerzity Hradci Kralove Supl — Sbornik Vedeckych Praci Lekarske Fakulty Karlovy Univerzity v Hradci Kralove. Supplementum

Sb Ved Pr Lek Fak Karlovy Univ Hradci Kralove — Sbornik Vedeckych Praci Lekarske Fakulty Karlovy University v Hradci Kralove

Sb Ved Pr Lek Fak Karlovy Univ Hradci Kralove Suppl — Sbornik Vedeckych Praci Lekarske Fakulty Karlovy University v Hradci Kralove. Supplementum

Sb Ved Pr Lek Fak Univ Karlovy Hradci Kralove — Sbornik Vedeckych Praci Lekarske Fakulty Karlovy University v Hradci Kralove

Sb Ved Pr Stavebnej Fak Slov Vys Sk Tech Bratislave — Sbornik Vedeckych Prac Stavebnej Fakulty Slovenskej Vysokej Skoly Technickej v Bratislave

Sb Ved Pr VLVDU Hradci Kralove — Sbornik Vedeckych Praci VLVDU [Vojenskeho Lekarskeho Vyzkumneho a Doskolovaciho Ustavu] v Hradci Kralove

Sb Ved Pr Vys Banske Ostrave Rada Hutn — Sbornik Vedeckych Praci Vysoke Skoly Banske v Ostrave. Rada Hutnicka

Sb Ved Pr Vysk Ustavu Vyz Zvirat Pohorelice — Sbornik Vedeckych Praci Vyzkumneho Ustavu Vyzivy Zvirat Pohorelice

Sb Ved Pr Vys Sk Banske Ostrave — Sbornik Vedeckych Praci Vysoke Skoly Banske v Ostrave

Sb Ved Pr Vys Sk Banske Ostrave Rada Horn-Geol — Sbornik Vedeckych Praci Vysoke Skoly Banske v Ostrave. Rada Hornicko-Geologicka

Sb Ved Pr Vys Sk Banske Ostrave Rada Hutn — Sbornik Vedeckych Praci Vysoke Skoly Banske v Ostrave. Rada Hutnicka

Sb Ved Pr Vys Sk Banske Ostrave Rada Strojnicka — Sbornik Vedeckych Praci Vysoke Skoly Banske v Ostrave. Rada Strojnicka

Sb Ved Pr Vys Sk Banske Tech Univ Ostrava Rada Horn Geol — Sbornik Vedeckych Praci Vysoke Skoly Banske-Technicke Univerzity Ostrava. Rada Hornicko-Geologicka

Sb Ved Pr Vys Sk Banske Tech Univ Ostrava Rada Hutn — Sbornik Vedeckych Praci Vysoke Skoly Banske-Technicke Univerzity Ostrava. Rada Hutnicka

Sb Ved Pr Vys Sk Bransk Ostrave — Sbornik Vedeckych Praci Vysoke Skoly Banske v Ostrave

Sb Ved Pr Vys Sk Chemickotechnol Pardubice — Sbornik Vedeckych Praci. Vysoka Skola Chemickotechnologicka Pardubice

Sb Ved Pr Vys Sk Chem-Technol (Pardubice) — Sbornik Vedeckych Praci. Vysoka Skola Chemickotechnologicka (Pardubice)

Sb Ved Pr Vys Sk Tech Kosiciach — Sbornik Vedeckych Prac Vysokej Skoly Technickej v Kosiciach

SBVG — Schaffhauser Beitraege zur Vaterlaendischen Geschichte

SBVH — Schwaebische Blaetter fuer Volksbildung und Heimatpflege

Sb VIZRa — Sbornik VIZR'a

Sb "Vop Issled Izpol'z Pochv Moldavii" — Sbornik "Voprosy Issledovaniya i Izpol'zovaniya Pochv Moldavii"

SBVS — Saga-Book. Viking Society for Northern Research

Sb Vses Inst Zashch Rast — Sbornik Vsesoyuznogo Instituta Zashchity Rastenii

Sb Vses Sov Nauchno-Tekh Obshchestv Kom Korroz Zashch Met — Sbornik Vsesoyuznyi Sovet Nauchno-Tekhnickeskikh Obshchestv. Komitet po Korrozii Zashchite Metallov

Sb Vynalezu — Sbirka Vynalezu

Sb Vys Chem Technol Praze Ekon Rizeni Chem Prum — Sbornik Vysoke Skoly Chemicko-Technologicke v Praze. Ekonomika a Rizeni Chemickeho Prumyslu

Sb Vysk Pr Odboru Celul Pap — Sbornik Vyskumnych Prac z Odboru Celulozy a Papiera

Sb Vysk Pr Odboru Pap Celul — Sbornik Vyskumnych Prac z Odboru Papiera a Celulozy

Sb Vysk Pr Ustavu Vysk Rud Prague — Sbornik Vyzkumnych Praci Ustavu pro Vyzkum Rud. Prague

Sb Vysk Sk Chem-Technol Praze (Oddil) Chem Inz — Sbornik Vysoke Skoly Chemicko-Technologicke v Praze (Oddil). Chemicke Inzenyrstvi

Sb Vysk Sk Chem-Technol Praze (Oddil) Chem Inz Autom — Sbornik Vysoke Skoly Chemicko-Technologicke v Praze (Oddil). Chemicke Inzenyrstvi a Automatizace

Sb Vysk Sk Chem Technol Praze (Oddil) K — Sbornik Vysoke Skoly Chemicko-Technologicke v Praze (Oddil). K

Sb Vysoke Uceni Tech v Brne — Sbornik Vysokeho Uceni Technickeho v Brne

Sb Vys Sk Chem-Technol Praze — Sbornik Vysoke Skoly Chemicko-Technologicke v Praze

Sb Vys Sk Chem Technol Praze A — Sbornik Vysoke Skoly Chemicko-Technologicke v Praze. A. Zpravy o Cinnosti a Jine Celoskolske Publikace

Sb Vys Sk Chem Technol Praze Anal Chem — Sbornik Vysoke Skoly Chemicko-Technologicke v Praze. Analyticka Chemie

Sb Vys Sk Chem Technol Praze Anorg Chem Technol — Sbornik Vysoke Skoly Chemicko-Technologicke v Praze. Anorganicka Chemie a Technologie

Sb Vys Sk Chem Technol Praze Anorg Org Technol — Sbornik Vysoke Skoly Chemicko-Technologicke v Praze. Anorganicka a Organicka Technologie

Sb Vys Sk Chem Technol Praze Anorg Technol — Sbornik Vysoke Skoly Chemicko-Technologicke v Praze. Anorganicka Technologie

Sb Vys Sk Chem Technol Praze B Anorg Chem Technol — Sbornik Vysoke Skoly Chemicko-Technologicke v Praze. B. Anorganicka Chemie a Technologie

Sb Vys Sk Chem Technol Praze Chem Inz — Sbornik Vysoke Skoly Chemicko-Technologicke v Praze. Chemicke Inzenyrstvi

Sb Vys Sk Chem Technol Praze Chem Inz Autom — Sbornik Vysoke Skoly Chemicko-Technologicke v Praze. Chemicke Inzenyrstvi a Automatizace

Sb Vys Sk Chem Technol Praze Chem Technol Silik — Sbornik Vysoke Skoly Chemicko-Technologicke v Praze. Chemie a Technologie Silikatu

Sb Vys Sk Chem Technol Praze C Org Chem Technol — Sbornik Vysoke Skoly Chemicko-Technologicke v Praze. C. Organicka Chemie a Technologie

Sb Vys Sk Chem Technol Praze D Technol Paliv — Sbornik Vysoke Skoly Chemicko-Technologicke v Praze. D. Technologie Paliv

Sb Vys Sk Chem Technol Praze Ekon Rizeni Chem Prum — Sbornik Vysoke Skoly Chemicko-Technologicke v Praze. Ekonimika a Rizeni Chemickeho Prumyslu

Sb Vys Sk Chem Technol Praze E Potraviny — Sbornik Vysoke Skoly Chemicko-Technologicke v Praze. Rada E. Potraviny

Sb Vys Sk Chem Technol Praze F Technol Vody Prostredi — Sbornik Vysoke Skoly Chemicko-Technologicke v Praze. Rada F. Technologie Vody aProstredi

Sb Vys Sk Chem Technol Praze Fys Chem — Sbornik Vysoke Skoly Chemicko-Technologicke v Praze. Fysikalni Chemie

Sb Vys Sk Chem Technol Praze Fyz Mater Merici Tech — Sbornik Vysoke Skoly Chemicko-Technologicke v Praze. Fyzika Materialu a Merici Technika

Sb Vys Sk Chem Technol Praze G Miner — Sbornik Vysoke Skoly Chemicko-Technologicke v Praze. G. Mineralogie

Sb Vys Sk Chem Technol Praze H Anal Chem — Sbornik Vysoke Skoly Chemicko-Technologicke v Praze. H. Analyticka Chemie

Sb Vys Sk Chem Technol Praze J Ekon Rizeni Chem Prum — Sbornik Vysoke Skoly Chemicko-Technologicke v Praze. J. Ekonomika a Rizeni Chemickeho Prumyslu

Sb Vys Sk Chem Technol Praze K Chem Inz — Sbornik Vysoke Skoly Chemicko-Technologicke v Praze. K. Chemicke Inzenyrstvi

Sb Vys Sk Chem Technol Praze L Chem Technol Silik — Sbornik Vysoke Skoly Chemicko-Technologicke v Praze. L. Chemie a Technologie Silikatu.

Sb Vys Sk Chem Technol Praze Mineral — Sbornik Vysoke Skoly Chemicko-Technologicke v Praze. Mineralogie

Sb Vys Sk Chem Technol Praze N Fys Chem — Sbornik Vysoke Skoly Chemicko-Technologicke v Praze. N. Fysikalni Chemie

Sb Vys Sk Chem Technol Praze (Oddil) Fak Anorg Technol — Sbornik Vysoke Skoly Chemicko-Technologicke v Praze (Oddil). Fakulty Anorganicke a Organicke Technologie

Sb Vys Sk Chem Technol Praze (Oddil) Fak Potravin Technol — Sbornik Vysoke Skoly Chemicko-Technologicke v Praze (Oddil). Fakulty Poetravinarske Technologie

Sb Vys Sk Chem-Technol Praze (Oddil) Fak Technol Paliv Vody — Sbornik Vysoke Skoly Chemicko-Technologicke v Praze (Oddil). Fakulty Technologie Paliv a Vody

Sb Vys Sk Chem Technol Praze Oddil Mineral — Sbornik Vysoke Skoly Chemicko-Technologicke v Praze. Oddil Mineralogie

Sb Vys Sk Chem Technol Praze Oddil Technol Vody — Sbornik Vysoke Skoly Chemicko-Technologicke v Praze. Oddil Technologie Vody

Sb Vys Sk Chem Technol Praze Org Chem Technol — Sbornik Vysoke Skoly Chemicko-Technologicke v Praze. Organicka Chemie a Technologie

Sb Vys Sk Chem Technol Praze Org Technol — Sbornik Vysoke Skoly Chemicko-Technologicke v Praze. Organicka Technologie

Sb Vys Sk Chem Technol Praze P Fyz Mater Merici Tech — Sbornik Vysoke Skoly Chemicko-Technologicke v Praze. P. Fyzika Materialu a Merici Technika

Sb Vys Sk Chem Technol Praze Polym Chem Vlastnosti Zprac — Sbornik Vysoke Skoly Chemicko-Technologicke v Praze. Polymery-Chemie, Vlastnosti a Zpracovani

Sb Vys Sk Chem Technol Praze Potravin Technol — Sbornik Vysoke Skoly Chemicko-Technologicke v Praze. Potravinarska Technologie

Sb Vys Sk Chem Technol Praze Potraviny — Sbornik Vysoke Skoly Chemicko-Technologicke v Praze. Potraviny

Sb Vys Sk Chem-Technol Praze Rada B — Sbornik Vysoke Skoly Chemicko-Technologicke v Praze. Rada B. Anorganicka Chemiea Technologie

Sb Vys Sk Chem Technol Praze Rada H — Sbornik Vysoke Skoly Chemicko-Technologicke v Praze. Rada H

Sb Vys Sk Chem Technol Praze S Polym Chem Vlastnosti Zprac — Sbornik Vysoke Skoly Chemicko-Technologicke v Praze. S. Polymery-Chemie, Vlastnosti a Zpracovani

Sb Vys Sk Chem Technol Praze Technol Paliv — Sbornik Vysoke Skoly Chemicko-Technologicke v Praze. Technologie Paliv

Sb Vys Sk Chem-Technol Praze Technol Vody — Sbornik Vysoke Skoly Chemicko-Technologicke v Praze. Technologie Vody

Sb Vys Sk Chem Technol Praze Technol Vody Prostredi — Sbornik Vysoke Skoly Chemicko-Technologicke v Praze. Technologie Vody a Prostredi

Sb Vys Sk Chem Technol Praze T Vychovne Vzdelavaci Proces — Sbornik Vysoke Skoly Chemicko-Technologicke v Praze. T. Vychovne-Vzdelavaci Proces

Sb Vys Sk Chem Technol Praze Vychovne Vzdelavaci Proces — Sbornik Vysoke Skoly Chemicko-Technologicke v Praze. Vychovne-Vzdelavaci Proces

Sb Vys Sk Chem-Technol Pr Potraviny — Sbornik Vysoke Skoly Chemicko-Technologicke v Praze. Potraviny

Sb Vys Skola Chem-Technol Fak Potrav Technol — Sbornik Vysoka Skola Chemicko-Technologicka. Fakulta Potravinarske Technologie

Sb Vys Skoly Polnohospod Nitre Prevadzkovo-Ekon Fak — Sbornik Vysokej Skoly Polnohospodarskej v Nitre Prevadzkovo-Ekonomicka Fakulta

Sb Vys Skoly Zemed Brne Rada A — Sbornik Vysoke Skoly Zemedelske v Brne. Rada A

Sb Vys Skoly Zemed Brne Rada B — Sbornik Vysoke Skoly Zemedelske v Brne. Rada B

Sb Vys Skoly Zemed Praze — Sbornik Vysoke Skoly Zemedelske v Praze

Sb Vys Sk Zemed Brne — Sbornik Vysoke Skoly Zemedelske v Brne

Sb Vys Sk Zemed Brne Rada A — Sbornik Vysoke Skoly Zemedelske v Brne. Rada A. Spisy Fakulty Agronomicke

Sb Vys Sk Zemed Brne Rada C — Sbornik Vysoke Skoly Zemedelske v Brne. Rada C. Spisy Fakulty Lesnicke

Sb Vys Sk Zemed Brne Rada C Spisy Fak Lesn — Sbornik Vysoke Skoly Zemedelske v Brne. Rada C. Spisy Fakulty Lesnicke

Sb Vys Sk Zemed Lesn Brne Rada B — Sbornik Vysoke Skoly Zemedelske a Lesnicke v Brne. Rada B. Spisy Fakulty Veterinarni

Sb Vys Sk Zemed Lesn Brne Rada C — Sbornik Vysoke Skoly Zemedelske a Lesnicke v Brne. Rada C. Spisy Fakulty Lesnicke

Sb Vys Sk Zemed Lesn Fak Brne B Spisy Fak Vet — Sbornik Vysoke Skoly Zemedelske a Lesnicke Fakulty v Brne. Rada B. Spisy Fakulty Veterinarni

Sb Vys Sk Zemed Lesn Fak Brne Rada C Spisy — Sbornik Vysoke Skoly Zemedelske a Lesnicke Fakulty v Brne. Rada C. Spisy Fakulty Lesnicke

Sb Vys Sk Zemed Lesn Fak Brne Rada C Spisy Fak Lesn — Sbornik Vysoke Skoly Zemedelske a Lesnicke Fakulty v Brne. Rada C. Spisy Fakulty Lesnicke

Sb Vys Sk Zemed Praze — Sbornik Vysoke Skoly Zemedelske v Praze

Sb Vys Sk Zemed Praze Fak Agron — Sbornik Vysoke Skoly Zemedelske v Praze. Fakulta Agronomicka

Sb Vys Sk Zemed Praze Fak Agron Rada A — Sbornik Vysoke Skoly Zemedelske v Praze. Fakulta Agronomicka. Rada A. RostlinnaVyroba

Sb Vys Sk Zemed Praze Fak Agron Rada AC — Sbornik Vysoke Skoly Zemedelske v Praze. Fakulta Agronomicka. Rada A-C. Rostlinna Vyroba-Zemedelske Meliorace a Stavby

Sb Vys Sk Zemed Praze Fak Agron Rada B — Sbornik Vysoke Skoly Zemedelske v Praze. Fakulta Agronomicka. Rada B. ZivocisnaVyroba

Sb Vys Sk Zemed Praze Provozne Ekon Fak Ceskych Budejovicich — Sbornik Vysoke Skoly Zemedelske v Praze. Provozne Ekonomicke Fakulty v Ceskych Budejovicich. Rada Biologicka

Sb Vys Sk Zemed v Brne A — Sbornik Vysoke Skoly Zemedelske v Brne. Rada A

Sb Vys Uceni Tech Brne — Sbornik Vysokeho Uceni Technickeho v Brne

Sb Vys Zemed Lesn Fak Brne B Spisy Fak Vet — Sbornik Vysoke Skoly Zemedelske a Lesnicke Fakulty v Brne. Rada B. Spisy Fakulty Veterinarni

Sb VZPI — Sbornik Statej Vsesojuznogo Zaocnogo Politechniceskogo Instituta

SBW — Sitzungsberichte der Wiener Akademie der Wissenschaften

SBW — Studien der Bibliothek Warburg

SBWA — Sammlung Bibliothekswissenschaftlicher Arbeiten

SbWAk — Sitzungsberichte. Wiener Akademie

SBWFA — Schriftenreihe. Bundesminister fuer Wissenschaftliche Forschung (Germany). Strahlenschutz

S B Wien — Sitzungsberichte. Oesterreichische Akademie der Wissenschaften in Wien

SB Wiener AK — Sitzungsberichte der Oesterreichischen Akademie der Wissenschaften. Philosophisch-Historische Klasse (Wien)

SBZ Sanit Heiz Klimatech — SBZ Sanitaer-, Heizungs-, und Klimatechnik

SC — MARDATA [Maritime Data Network] Ship Casualty Library

Sc — Nederlandse Staatscourant

Sc — Science

SC — Science and Culture

SC — Science and Society

Sc — Scientia

Sc — Scientia. Organo Internazionale di Sintesi Scientifica

Sc — Scriptorium

SC — Scuola Cattolica

SC — Shakespearean Criticism

SC — Social Casework

SC — Social Compass

SC — Socialist Commentary

SC — Soil Conservation

SC — Sources Chretiennes

SC — South Carolina Musician

SC — South Carolina Reports

SC — Stendhal Club

SC — Stratigraphie Comparee et Chronologie de l'Asie Occidentale

SC — Studia Catholica

SC — Studia Celtica

SC — Studi Colombiani

SC — Studii Clasice

SC — Suisse Contemporaine

SCA — Sarcofagi Cristiani Antichi

Sca — Scandia

Sca — Scandinavica

SCA — Science Fiction Classics Annual

ScA — Sciences de l'Art

SCA — Smithsonian Contributions to Anthropology

SCA — Smithsonian Contributions to Astrophysics

SCA — Studies in Christian Antiquity

SCA — Survey of Current Business

Sc Abs — Science Abstracts. Physics and Electrical Engineering

SC Acad Sci Bull — South Carolina Academy of Science. Bulletin

SC Acts — Acts and Joint Resolutions. South Carolina

Sc Advocate — Science Advocate

SC Ag Dept — South Carolina. Department of Agriculture, Commerce, and Industries. Publications

SC Ag Exp — South Carolina. Agricultural Experiment Station. Publications

SC Agric Exp Stn Bull — South Carolina. Agricultural Experiment Station. Bulletin

SC Agric Exp Stn Circ — South Carolina. Agricultural Experiment Station. Circular

SC Agric Exp Stn SB — South Carolina Agricultural Experiment Station. Bulletin SB

SC Agric Exp Stn Tech Bull — South Carolina. Agricultural Experiment Station. Technical Bulletin

SC Agr Res — South Carolina Agricultural Research

S Cal Ac Sc B — Southern California Academy of Sciences. Bulletin

SCALE — Supreme Court Almanac

S Calif Crops — Southern California Crops

S Calif Law Rev — Southern California Law Review

S Calif L R — Southern California Law Review

S California Quart — Southern California Quarterly

S Cal Law R — Southern California Law Review

S Cal L Rev — Southern California Law Review

S Cal R — Selections from the Calcutta Review

S CA LR — Southern California Law Review

Sc Am — Scientific American

SCAMA — Scientific American

Sc Am Sup — Scientific American. Supplement

Scan — Scandinavian Studies

Scan — Scandinavica

Scan Aud — Scandinavian Audiology

Scand — Scandinavica

Scand Actuar J — Scandinavian Actuarial Journal

Scand Audiol — Scandinavian Audiology

Scand Audiol Suppl — Scandinavian Audiology. Supplement

Scand Brew Rev — Scandinavian Brewers' Review

Scand Corros Congr Proc — Scandinavian Corrosion Congress. Proceedings

Scand Ec Hist Rev — Scandinavian Economic History Review

Scand Econ Hist Rev — Scandinavian Economic History Review

Scand Energy — Scandinavian Energy

Scandinavian Econ Hist R — Scandinavian Economic History Review

Scandinavian Publ Libr Q — Scandinavian Public Library Quarterly

Scandinavian R — Scandinavian Review

Scandinavian Stud And Notes — Scandinavian Studies and Notes. Society for the Advancement of Scandinavian Studies

Scandinav J Clin Lab Invest — Scandinavian Journal of Clinical and Laboratory Investigation

Scandinav J Econ — Scandinavian Journal of Economics

Scandinav J Gastroent — Scandinavian Journal of Gastroenterology

Scandinav J Haemat — Scandinavian Journal of Haematology

Scandinav J Resp Dis — Scandinavian Journal of Respiratory Diseases

Scand J Behav Ther — Scandinavian Journal of Behaviour Therapy

Scand J Clin Lab Inv — Scandinavian Journal of Clinical and Laboratory Investigation

Scand J Clin Lab Invest — Scandinavian Journal of Clinical and Laboratory Investigation

Scand J Clin Lab Invest Suppl — Scandinavian Journal of Clinical and Laboratory Investigation. Supplement

Scand J Dent Res — Scandinavian Journal of Dental Research

Scand J Des Hist — Scandinavian Journal of Design History
Scand J Econ — Scandinavian Journal of Economics
Scand J For Res — Scandinavian Journal of Forest Research
Scand J Gastroenterol — Scandinavian Journal of Gastroenterology
Scand J Gastroenterol Suppl — Scandinavian Journal of Gastroenterology. Supplement
Scand J Haematol — Scandinavian Journal of Haematology
Scand J Haematol Suppl — Scandinavian Journal of Haematology. Supplement
Scand J Haematol Suppl Ser Haematol — Scandinavian Journal of Haematology. Supplement. Series Haematological
Scand J Immunol — Scandinavian Journal of Immunology
Scand J Immunol Suppl — Scandinavian Journal of Immunology. Supplement
Scand J Infect Dis — Scandinavian Journal of Infectious Diseases
Scand J Infect Dis Suppl — Scandinavian Journal of Infectious Diseases. Supplement
Scand J Med Sci Sports — Scandinavian Journal of Medicine and Science in Sports
Scand J Metall — Scandinavian Journal of Metallurgy
Scand J Plast Reconstr Surg — Scandinavian Journal of Plastic and Reconstructive Surgery
Scand J Plast Reconstr Surg Hand Surg — Scandinavian Journal of Plastic and Reconstructive Surgery and Hand Surgery
Scand J Plast Reconstr Surg Hand Surg Suppl — Scandinavian Journal of Plastic and Reconstructive Surgery and Hand Surgery. Supplementum
Scand J Plast Reconstr Surg Suppl — Scandinavian Journal of Plastic and Reconstructive Surgery. Supplement
Scand J Plast Recon Surg — Scandinavian Journal of Plastic and Reconstructive Surgery
Scand J Plst Reconstr Hand Surg — Scnadinavian Journal of Plastic and Reconstructive and Hand Surgery
Scand J Prim Health Care — Scandinavian Journal of Primary Health Care
Scand J Prim Health Care Suppl — Scandinavian Journal of Primary Health Care. Supplement
Scand J Psychol — Scandinavian Journal of Psychology
Scand J Rehabil Med — Scandinavian Journal of Rehabilitation Medicine
Scand J Rehabil Med Suppl — Scandinavian Journal of Rehabilitation Medicine. Supplement
Scand J Rehab Med — Scandinavian Journal of Rehabilitation Medicine
Scand J Respir Dis — Scandinavian Journal of Respiratory Diseases
Scand J Respir Dis Suppl — Scandinavian Journal of Respiratory Diseases. Supplement
Scand J Rheumatol — Scandinavian Journal of Rheumatology
Scand J Rheumatol Suppl — Scandinavian Journal of Rheumatology. Supplement
Scand J Soc Med — Scandinavian Journal of Social Medicine
Scand J Soc Med Suppl — Scandinavian Journal of Social Medicine. Supplement
Scand J St — Scandinavian Journal of Statistics
Scand J Statist — Scandinavian Journal of Statistics. Theory and Applications
Scand J Stat Theory and Appl — Scandinavian Journal of Statistics. Theory and Applications
Scand J Thorac Cardiovasc Surg — Scandinavian Journal of Thoracic and Cardiovascular Surgery
Scand J Thorac Cardiovasc Surg Suppl — Scandinavian Journal of Thoracic and Cardiovascular Surgery. Supplement
Scand J Urol Nephrol — Scandinavian Journal of Urology and Nephrology
Scand J Urol Nephrol Suppl — Scandinavian Journal of Urology and Nephrology. Supplement
Scand J Work Envir Hlth — Scandinavian Journal of Work Environment and Health
Scand J Work Environ Health — Scandinavian Journal of Work Environment and Health
Scand Laundry Dry Clean J — Scandinavian Laundry and Dry Cleaning Journal
Scand Oil-Gas Mag — Scandinavian Oil-Gas Magazine
Scand Paint Printing Ink Res Inst Rept — Scandinavian Paint and Printing Ink Research Institute. Reports
Scand Polit St — Scandinavian Political Studies
Scand Polit Stud — Scandinavian Political Studies
Scand Pol Stud — Scandinavian Political Studies
Scand Public Lib Q — Scandinavian Public Library Quarterly
Scand Publ Libr Q — Scandinavian Public Library Quarterly
Scand R — Scandinavian Review
Scand Refrig — Scandinavian Refrigeration
Scand Stud — Scandinavian Studies
Scand Stud in L — Scandinavian Studies in Law
Scand Stud Law — Scandinavian Studies in Law
Scand Stud No — Scandinavian Studies and Notes
Scand Symp Surf Chem — Scandinavian Symposium on Surface Chemistry
Scand Yb — Scandinavian Yearbook
Scan Ec Hist Rev — Scandinavian Economic History Review
Scan Electron Microsc — Scanning Electron Microscopy
Scan J Gast — Scandinavian Journal of Gastroenterology
SCAN J Med & Sci Sport — Scandinavian Journal of Medicine & Science in Sports
Scan J Sports Sci — Scandinavian Journal of Sports Sciences
Scan J Stat — Scandinavian Journal of Statistics. Theory and Applications
SCanL — Studies in Canadian Literature
Scanning Electron Microsc — Scanning Electron Microscopy
Scanning Microsc — Scanning Microscopy
Scanning Microsc Suppl — Scanning Microscopy. Supplement
Scanning Tunneling Microsc — Scanning Tunneling Microscopy
SCANP — Scandinavian Periodicals Index in Economics and Business
Scan Pub Lib — Scandinavian Public Library Quarterly
Scan R — Scandinavian Review
Scan Refrig — Scandinavian Refrigeration
Scan Soc Forensic Odontol Newsl — Scandinavian Society of Forensic Odontology. Newsletter
SCAR — Scandinavian Review

Scarborough Dist Archaeol Soc Res Rep — Scarborough District Archaeological Society. Research Reports
Sc As Trinidad Pr — Scientific Association of Trinidad. Proceedings
SCathol — Studia Catholica
SCAUA — Scientific Australian
SCauc — Studia Caucasica
Sc Azione — Scuola in Azione
SCB — South Central Bulletin
SCB — Standard of California Oil Bulletin
SCB — Studii si Cercetari de Bibliologie
SCB — Survey of Current Business
S C B Assn Tr — South Carolina Bar Association. Transactions
SCBO — Scriptorum Classicorum Bibliotheca Oxoniensia
SCBOA — Studii si Cercetari de Biologie. Seria Botanica
SCBUB — Sierra Club. Bulletin
SCBUB8 — Sierra Club. Bulletin
SCBZA — Studii si Cercetari de Biologie. Seria Zoologie
ScC — Science and Culture. Calcutta
SCC — Science Fiction Chronicle
SCC — Studies in Comparative Communism
SCC — Studies in Creative Criticism
Sc Cath — Science Catholique
ScCatt — Scuola Cattolica
SCCBS — Science Council of Canada. Background Study
SCCJ — Supreme Court of Canada Judgements
Sc Code Ann (Law Co-Op) — Code of Laws of South Carolina Annotated (Lawyers Co-Op)
SC Code Regs — Code of Laws of South Carolina Annotated. Code of Regulations
Sc Conspectus — Science Conspectus
SCCR — Science Council of Canada. Report
SCC Spec — Soap/Cosmetics/Chemical Specialties
SCCSS — Science Council of Canada. Special Study
SCCWRP TR — SCCWRP (Southern California Coastal Water Research Project). TR
SCDCN — Sanctorum Consiliorum et Decretorum Collection Nova
SC Dent J — South Carolina Dental Journal
SCDI — Science Dimension
SCDIA — Science Digest
Sc Dimension — Science Dimension
SC Div Geol Bull — South Carolina. Division of Geology. Bulletin
SC Div Geol Geol Notes — South Carolina. Division of Geology. Geologic Notes
SC Div Geol Miner Resour Ser — South Carolina. Division of Geology. Mineral Resources Series
SC Div Geol Misc Rep — South Carolina. Division of Geology. Miscellaneous Report
SC Div Geology Mineral Industries Lab Monthly Bull — South Carolina. Division of Geology. Mineral Industries Laboratory. Monthly Bulletin
Sc E — Science et Esprit
ScE — Sciences Ecclesiastiques
SCE — Strukturen Christlicher Existenz
SCE — Swedish Cypress Expedition
SCEAB — Studii si Cercetari de Astronomie
Sc Ec — Sciences Ecclesiastiques
SCECA — Studii si Cercetari de Chimie
ScEccl — Sciences Ecclesiastiques
SCEDA — Studii si Cercetari de Endocrinologie
SCEDSIP Bull — SCEDSIP [Standing Conference on Educational Development Services in Polytechnics] Bulletin
SCEEA — Studii si Cercetari de Energetica si Electrotehnica
SCEFA — Studii si Cercetari de Fizica
Scelta Opusc Interessanti Turin — Scelta di Opuscoli Interessanti Tradotti da Varie Lingue (Turin)
Scen — Scenario
Scena — Scena Illustrata
SCENA — Science and Engineering
Scenic And Hist America — Scenic and Historic America. American Scenic and Historic Preservation Society. Bulletin
Scenic Trips Geol Past — Scenic Trips to the Geologic Past
SC Eq — South Carolina Equity Reports
ScEs — Science et Esprit
SCESBH — Smithsonian Contributions to the Earth Sciences
SCF — Science Fantasy
SCFO — Science Forum
SCFOA — Schiffbauforschung
SCFOB — Science Forum
Sc for People — Science for People
SCFP — Studies in Christian Faith and Practice
SCFR — Seminarios
SCFZA — Studii si Cercetari de Fiziologie
Sc G — Science Gossip
SCG — Syntax of Classical Greek
SC Geol — South Carolina Geology
SCGGA — Studii si Cercetari de Geologie, Geofizica, si Geografie. Seria Geologie
Sc Gg Mg — Scottish Geographical Magazine
SCGOC — Statuta Capitulorum Generalium Ordinis Cisterciensis
SCH — Scherl and Roth Orchestra News
Sch — Scholastik
Sch — School
Sch — Schule
ScH — Scientiarum Historia
SCh — Sources Chretiennes
SCH — Studies in Church History
Sch A — Schwaebisches Archiv
SchA — Schweizer Annalen
Sch Activities — School Activities

Sch Adv Int Stud Rev — School of Advanced International Studies Review

Schaffhauser Beitr Gesch — Schaffhauser Beitraege zur Geschichte

Sch Agric Aberdeen Ann Rep — School of Agriculture. Aberdeen. Annual Report

Sch & Com — School and Community

Sch and Home — School and Home

Sch & Parent — School and Parent

Sch & Soc — School and Society

Sch Arts — School Arts Magazine

Sch Arts M — School Arts Magazine

Schattauer Prax Buech — Schattauer Praxis Buecherei

Schatzkammer — Schatzkammer der Deutschen Sprachlehre. Dichtung und Geschichte

Schau ins Land Jhft Breisgau Geschver — Schau-ins-Land. Jahresheft des Breisgau-Geschichtsvereins

SchAVk — Schweizer Archiv fuer Volkskunde

Sch Bell — School Bell

SchBull — Schweizer Bulletin des Elektrotechnischen Vereins

Sch Coach — Scholastic Coach

Sch Community News — School and Community News

Sch Counsel — School Counselor

Sch Days — School Days

Sch Dent Serv Gaz (NZ) — School Dental Services Gazette (Wellington, New Zealand)

Sch Ed — School and Home Education

Sched Discounts Differentials Serv Charges Applying Wheat — Schedule of Discounts, Differentials, and Service Charges Applying to Wheat

Schede Med — Schede Medievali

Sch (El Ed) — School (Toronto) (Elementary Edition)

Schelling N Z Spec Ps — Neue Zeitschrift fuer Speculative Physik. Schelling

Schelling Z Spec Ps — Zeitschrift fuer Speculative Physik. Schelling

Schenectady Bur Munic Res Bul — Schenectady Bureau of Municipal Research. Bulletin

Sch Eng Bull NC State Univ — School of Engineering. Bulletin. North Carolina State University

Scherer J C — Allgemeines Journal der Chemie. Scherer

Schering Found Workshop — Schering Foundation Workshop

Sch Exec — School Executive

Sch Exec Mag — School Executives Magazine

Sch Executives M — School Executives Magazine

SchF — Schultexte aus Fara

Sch Foodserv J — School Foodservice Journal

Sch Foodserv Res Rev — School Foodservice Research Review

SCHGM — South Carolina Historical and Genealogical Magazine

SCHG/R — Revista Chilena de Historia y Geografia. Sociedad Chilena de Historia y Geografia

Sch Gs N D — Neue Denkschriften der Allgemeinen Schweizerischen Gesellschaft fuer die Gesammten Naturwissenschaften

Sch Gs Vh — Verhandlungen der Schweizerischen Gesellschaft fuer die Gesammten Naturwissenschaften

Sch Guidance W — School Guidance Worker

SChH — Studies in Church History

SCHHA — Schiff und Hafen

Sch Health Rev — School Health Review

SchHJ — Schleswig-Holsteinisches Jahrbuch

Schiffstechnik — Schiffstechnik. Forschungshefte fuer Schiffbau und Schiffsmaschinenbau

Schild Steier — Schild von Steier. Beitraege zur Steierischen Vor- und Fruehgeschichte und Muenzkunde

Schimmelpfeng R — Schimmelpfeng Review

Sch Inq Nurs Pract — Scholarly Inquiry for Nursing Practice

SC His M — South Carolina Historical and Genealogical Magazine

SC Hist & Geneal Mag — South Carolina Historical and Genealogical Magazine

SC Hist Assn Proc — South Carolina Historical Association. Proceedings

SC Hist Mag — South Carolina Historical Magazine

Schizophr Bull — Schizophrenia Bulletin

Schizophr Res — Schizophrenia Research

Schizophr Syndr — Schizophrenic Syndrome

Schizophr Syndr Annu Rev — Schizophrenic Syndrome: An Annual Review

SchJZ — Schweizerische Juristen-Zeitung

SCHK — Studies in Church History. Institute for Dansk Church History. Kobenhaven University

Sch L — Jahresbericht. Schweizerisches Landesmuseum

Sch L — Schweich Lectures of the British Academy

SCHL — Studies in Church History (London)

Schlachtofwes Lebensmittelueberwach — Schlachtofwesen Lebensmittelueberwachung

Schlaegel Eisen Teplice Sanov Czech — Schlaegel und Eisen (Teplice-Sanov, Czechoslovakia)

Sch LBA — Schweich Lectures on Biblical Archaeology

Sch L Bull — School Law Bulletin

Schleif Polier Oberflaechentech — Schleif-, Polier-, und Oberflaechentechnik

Schleif Poliertech (Hoya Weser Ger) — Schleif- und Poliertechnik (Hoya-Weser, Germany)

Schlern Illus Mhft Heimat & Vlksknd — Schlern. Illustrierte Monatshefte fuer Heimat- und Volkskunde

Schlern Schr — Schlern Schriften

Schlernschr — Schlernschriften

Schles Ges Jber — Schlesische Gesellschaft fuer Vaterlaendische Kultur. Jahres-Bericht

Schles Heim — Schlesisches Heim

Schlesiens Vorzeit Bild & Schr — Schlesiens Vorzeit in Bild und Schrift. Zeitschrift des Vereins fuer das Museum Schlesischer Altertuemer

Schles Jb Dt Kulturarb — Schlesisches Jahrbuch fuer Deutsche Kulturarbeit im Gesamtschlesischen Raum

Schles Landw Z — Schlesische Landwirthschaftliche Zeitschrift

Schles Mhft — Schlesische Monatshefte

Schles Provinzialbl — Schlesische Provinzialblaetter

Schles Vorzeit — Schlesiens Vorzeit in Bild und Schrift

Schlesw Holst Anzgn — Schleswig-Holsteinische Anzeigen

Schlesw-Holst Bienenztg — Schleswig-Holsteinisches Bienenzeitung

Schleswig Holsteinisches Aerztebl — Schleswig-Holsteinisches Aerzteblatt

Schleswig Holst Lauenburg Provinzialber — Schleswig-Holstein-Lauenburgische Provinzialberichte

Schleswig Holst Mag — Schleswig-Holsteinisches Magazin der Sammlung Vermischter Schriften zur Aufnahmeder Wissenschaften und Kuenste

Schl Holst Nt Vr Schr — Schriften des Naturwissenschaftlichen Vereins fuer Schleswig-Holstein

Sch Lib — School Librarian

Sch Lib — School Libraries

Sch Lib Assn Calif Bul — School Library Association of California. Bulletin

Sch Lib Aust — School Libraries in Australia

Sch Lib Can — School Libraries in Canada

Sch Lib J — School Library Journal

Sch Lib Med N — School Library-Media News

Sch Libn — School Librarian

Sch Libr — School Libraries

Sch Lib R — School Library Review and Educational Record

Sch Libr Bull — School Library Bulletin

Sch Librn — School Librarian and School Library Review [Later, School Librarian]

Schlief-Poliertech — Schlief- und Poliertechnik

Sch Life — School Life

Schloemilchs Zschr — (Schloemilchs) Zeitschrift feur Mathematik und Physik

Schloemilch Z — Zeitschrift fuer Mathematik und Physik. Schloemilch

Schl Schr — Schlern-Schriften

Sch M — Schweizer Monatshefte

SchM — Schweizer Monatshefte fuer Politik und Kultur

SCHM — South Carolina Historical and Genealogical Magazine

Schmal Z Betriebswirtsch Forsch — Schmalenbachs Zeitschrift [feur Betriebwirtschaftliche] Forschung

Sch Manag — School Management

Sch Manage — School Management Bulletin

Sch Management — School Management

Sch Management Bul — School Management Bulletin

Sch Media Q — School Media Quarterly

Schmerz Narkose Anaesth — Schmerz. Narkose-Anaesthesie

Schm Exp — Schmitthoff. Export Trade

Sch Mgt — School Management

Schmiedebg Arch — Schmiedebergs Archiv

Schmierstoffe Schmierungstech — Schmierstoffe und Schmierungstechnik

Schmierst Schmierungstech — Schmierstoffe und Schmierungstechnik

Schmiertech Tribol — Schmiertechnik und Tribologie

Sch Mines Metall Univ Mo Bull — School of Mines and Metallurgy. University of Missouri. Bulletin

Sch Mines Metall Univ Mo Bull Tech Ser — School of Mines and Metallurgy. University of Missouri. Bulletin. Technical Series

Sch Mines Q — School of Mines Quarterly

Sch Mines Q N Y — School of Mines Quarterly (New York)

Schmollers Jahrb — Schmollers Jahrbuch fuer Gesetzgebung, Verwaltung und Volkswirtschaft im Deutschen Reiche

SchMpBl — Schweizerische Musikpaedagogische Blaetter

Sch Mus — School Music

SchMus — School Musician

SchMus — Schweizerische Musikzeitung und Saengerblatt

Sch Mus Dir Teach — School Musician Director and Teacher

Sch MZ — Schweizerische Musikzeitung

SCHND — Soon Chun Hyang Taehak Nonmunjip

Schneeberger Hb — Schneeberger Heimatbuechlein

Schnell Inf Hydraul & Pneum — Schnell Informationen Hydraulik und Pneumatik

Sch Nf Gs Vh — Verhandlungen der Schweizerischen Gesellschaft fuer die Gesammten Naturwissenschaften

SCHNT — Studia ad Corpus Hellenisticum Novi Testamentl

Schnurpfeils Rev Glass Works — Schnurpfeil's Review for Glass Works

Schoenberg Inst — Arnold Schoenberg Institute. Journal

Schoenburg Gesch Bl — Schoenburgische Geschichtsblaetter

Schol — Scholastik. Vierteljahresschrift fuer Theologie und Philosophie

Scholarly Pub — Scholarly Publishing

Scholar Pub — Scholarly Publishing

Scholastic — Senior Scholastic

Scholastic D — Scholastic Debater

Schol Coach — Scholastic Coach

Schol S — Scholia Satyrica

Schol Teach — Scholastic Teacher

Schol Teach JH/SH Ed — Scholastic Teacher. Junior/Senior High Teacher's Edition

School & Col — School and College

School and Soc — School and Society

School Arts M — School Arts Magazine

School Fam — School Family

School Law Bul (Univ NC) — School Law Bulletin (University of North Carolina)

School Lib — School Libraries

School L Rep Natl Org on Legal Probs in Educ — School Law Reporter. National Organization on Legal Problems inEducation

Schoolmens W Univ PA Proc — Schoolmen's Week. University of Pennsylvania. Proceedings

School Mus — School Musician

School of Advanced Studies Rev — School of Advanced International Studies. Review

School of LR — School of Law. Review. Toronto University

School Organ Manage Abstr — School Organisation and Management Abstracts

School Psych Rev — School Psychology Review

School Rev — School Review. A Journal of Secondary Education

Schopenhauer-Jahr — Schopenhauer-Jahrbuch
Schopenhauer-Jahrb — Schopenhauer-Jahrbuch
Schoppe Faeser Tech Mitt — Schoppe und Faeser. Technische Mitteilungen
Schorns Kstbl — Schorns Kunstblatt
Schott Inf — Schott Information
SchP — Scholarly Publishing
SCHPB — Bulletin et Memoires. Societe des Chirurgiens de Paris
Sch Pharm Bull Ext Serv Pharm Univ Wis Ext Div — School of Pharmacy Bulletin. Extension Services in Pharmacy. University of Wisconsin Extension Division
Sch Pharm Bull Univ Wis Ext Div — School of Pharmacy. Bulletin. University of Wisconsin. Extension Division
Sch Pol Z — Schweizerische Polytechnische Zeitschrift
Sch Proc Wint Sch Biophys Membr Transp — School Proceedings. Winter School on Biophysics of Membrane Transport
Sch Psychol R — School Psychology Review
Sch R — School Review
SchR — Schweizerische Rundschau
Sc HR — Scottish Historical Review
Schrader Journ Botan — Journal fuer die Botanik (H. A. Schrader, Editor)
Schrad Journ Bot — Journal fuer die Botanik (Goettingen) (Edited by H. A. Schrader)
Schr Berl — Schriften. Akademie der Wissenschaften zu Berlin
Schr Bremer Wiss Ges Reihe B — Schriften der Bremer Wissenschaftlichen Gesellschaft. Reihe B
Schr d Bodensee V — Schriften des Vereins fuer Geschichte des Bodensees und Seiner Umgebung
Schr Deut Schiffahrtsmus — Schriften des Deutschen Schiffahrtsmuseums
Schr Dt Archit Mus Frankfurt — Schriften des Deutschen Architektur Museums Frankfurt
Sch Rev — School Review
Schr Forschungszent Juelich Bilateral Semin Int Bur — Schriften des Forschungszentrums Juelich. Bilateral Seminars of the International Bureau
Schr Forschungszent Juelich Lebenswiss Life Sci — Schriften des Forschungszentrums Juelich. Lebenswissenschaften/Life Sciences
Schr Forschungszent Juelich Mater Mater — Schriften des Forschungszentrums Juelich. Materie und Material
Schr Forschungszent Juelich Reihe Energietech Energy Technol — Schriften des Forschungszentrums Juelich. Reihe Energietechnik/Energy Technology
Schr Forschungszent Juelich Reihe Umwelt — Schriften des Forschungszentrums Juelich. Reihe Umwelt
Schr GDMB (Ges Dtsch Metallhuetten Bergleute) — Schriften der GDMB (Gesellschaft Deutscher Metallhuetten- und Bergleute)
Schr Geb Brennst Geol — Schriften aus dem Gebiet der Brennstoff-Geologie
Schr Ges Dtsch Metallhuetten Bergleute — Schriften der Gesellschaft Deutscher Metallhuetten- und Bergleute
Schr Ges Soz Ref — Schriften der Gesellschaft fuer Soziale Reform
Schr Heeresgesch Mus Wien — Schriften des Heeresgeschichtlichen Museums in Wien
Schr Hist Mus Frankfurt Am Main — Schriften des Historischen Museums Frankfurt am Main
Schrift Adam Ries Bundes Annaberg Buchholz — Schriften des Adam-Ries-Bundes Annaberg-Buchholz
Schrift Angew Oekonom — Schriften zur Angewandten Oekonometrie
Schriften Berlin Ges Naturf Freunde — Schriften der Berlinischen Gesellschaft Naturforschender Freunde
Schriften Bot Gart Univ — Acta Horti Botanici Universitatis. Schriften des Botanischen Gartens der Universitaet. Universitaetes Botaniska Darza Rakst
Schriften Duisburg Gel Ges — Schriften der Duisburgischen Gelehrten Gesellschaft
Schriften Freien Vereinigung Freunden Mikroskop — Schriften der Freien Vereinigung von Freunden der Mikroskopie
Schriften Koenigsberger Gel Ges Naturwiss Kl — Schriften der Koenigsberger Gelehrten Gesellschaft. Naturwissenschaftliche Klasse
Schriften Kurfuerstl Deutsch Ges Mannheim — Schriften der Kurfuerstlichen Deutschen Gesellschaft in Mannheim
Schriften Naturf Ges Kopenhagen — Schriften der Naturforschenden Gesellschaft zu Kopenhagen
Schriften Naturf Ges Univ Dorpat — Schriften. Herausgegeben von der Naturforscher-Gesellschaft bei der Universitaet Dorpat
Schriften Naturwiss Vereins Schleswig Holstein — Schriften des Naturwissenschaftlichen Vereins fuer Schleswig-Holstein
Schriftenr — Schriftenreihe fuer die Evangelisch Frau. (Geinhausen, Germany)
Schriftenr Aerztl Fortbild — Schriftenreihe der Aerztlichen Fortbildung
Schriftenr Agrarwiss Fak Univ Kiel — Schriftenreihe. Agrarwissenschaftliche Fakultaet. Universitaet Kiel
Schriftenr Arbeitsschutz — Schriftenreihe Arbeitsschutz
Schriftenr Bauforsch Reihe Tech Organ — Schriftenreihen der Bauforschung. Reihe Technik und Organisation
Schriftenr Bayer Landesamt Wasserwirt — Schriftenreihe. Bayerisches Landesamt fuer Wasserwirtschaft
Schriftenr Bayer Landesapothekerkammer — Schriftenreihe der Bayerischen Landesapothekerkammer
Schriftenr Bundesanst Arbeitsschutz Gefaehrliche Arbeitsst — Schriftenreihe der Bundesanstalt fuer Arbeitsschutz. Gefaehrliche Arbeitsstoffe
Schriftenr Bundesapothekerkammer Wiss Fortbild Gelbe Reihe — Schriftenreihe der Bundesapothekerkammer zur Wissenschaftlichen Fortbildung. Gelbe Reihe
Schriftenr Bundesapothekerkammer Wiss Fortbild Weisse Reihe — Schriftenreihe der Bundesapothekerkammer zur Wissenschaftlichen Fortbildung. Weisse Reihe
Schriftenr Bundesminist Atomfragen Ger Strahlenschutz — Schriftenreihe der Bundesministers fuer Atomfragen (Germany). Strahlenschutz
Schriften Bundesminist Wiss Forsch Forsch Bild — Schriftenreihe. Bundesminister fuer Wissenschaftliche Forschung. Forschung und Bildung

Schriftenr Bundesminist Wiss Forsch (Ger) Radionuklide — Schriftenreihe. Bundesminister fuer Wissenschaftliche Forschung (West Germany).Radionuklide
Schriftenr Bundesminist Wiss Forsch (Ger) Strahlenschutz — Schriftenreihe. Bundesminister fuer Wissenschaftliche Forschung (West Germany) .Strahlenschutz
Schriftenr Bundesminist Wiss Forsch Kernenergierecht — Schriftenreihe. Bundesminister fuer Wissenschaftliche Forschung. Kernenergierecht
Schriftenr Bundesminist Wiss Forsch Strahlenschutz — Schriftenreihe. Bundesminister fuer Wissenschaftliche Forschung. Strahlenschutz
Schriftenr Bundesverb Dtsch Kalkind — Schriftenreihe. Bundesverband der Deutschen Kalkindustrie
Schriftenr Dtsch Atomforums — Schriftenreihe des Deutschen Atomforums
Schriftenr Dtsch Ausschusses Stahlbeton — Schriftenreihe des Deutschen Ausschusses fuer Stahlbeton
Schriftenr Dtsch Ges Atomenerg — Schriftenreihe der Deutschen Gesellschaft fuer Atomenergie
Schriftenr Dtsch Ges Tech Zusammenarb — Schriftenreihe der Deutschen Gesellschaft fuer Technische Zusammenarbeit
Schriftenr Dtsch Phytomed Ges — Schriftenreihe der Deutschen Phytomedizinischen Gesellschaft
Schriftenr Dtsch Verb Wasserwirtsch Kulturbau — Schriftenreihe der Deutschen Verbandes fuer Wasserwirtschaft und Kulturbau
Schriftenr Dtsch Wollforschungsinst Tech Hochsch Aachen — Schriftenreihe der Deutschen Wollforschungsinstitutes. Technische Hochschule Aachen
Schriftenr der Oesterreich Comput Ges — Schriftenreihe der Oesterreichischen Computer Gesellschaft
Schriftenreihe Didaktik Math — Schriftenreihe Didaktik der Mathematik
Schriftenreihe Forstl Bundesversuchsanst Mariabrunn Wien — Schriftenreihe der Forstlichen Bundesversuchsanstalt Mariabrunn in Wien
Schriftenreihe Inst Empirische Wirtschaftsforsch Univ Zuerich — Schriftenreihe des Instituts fuer Empirische Wirtschaftsforschung der Universitaet Zuerich
Schriftenreihe Landwirt Fak Univ Kiel — Schriftenreihe der Landwirtschaftlichen Fakultaet der Universitaet Kiel
Schriftenreihe Math — Schriftenreihe fuer Mathematik
Schriftenreihe Math Inst Grad Univ Muenster 3 Ser — Schriftenreihe des Mathematischen Instituts und des Graduiertenkollegs der Universitaet Muenster. 3. Serie
Schriftenreihe Math Inst Univ Muenster — Schriftenreihe. Mathematisches Institut. Universitaet Muenster
Schriftenreihe Math Inst Univ Muenster 3 Ser — Schriftenreihe des Mathematischen Instituts der Universitaet Muenster. 3. Serie
Schriftenreihe Math Inst Univ Muenster Ser 2 — Schriftenreihe des Mathematischen Instituts der Universitaet Muenster. Serie 2
Schriftenreihe Max Planck Inst Strahlenchem — Schriftenreihe des Max-Planck-Instituts fuer Strahlenchemie
Schriftenreihe Paedagog Hochsch Heidelberg — Schriftenreihe der Paedagogischen Hochschule Heidelberg
Schriftenreihe Rechenzentrum Univ Koeln — Schriftenreihe des Rechenzentrums. Universitaet zu Koeln
Schriftenreihe Univ Regensburg — Schriftenreihe der Universitaet Regensburg
Schriftenreihe Vegetationsk — Schriftenreihe der Vegetationskunde. Bundesanstalt fuer Vegetationskunde, Naturschutz, und Landschaftspflege
Schriftenreihe Wittgenstein Ges — Schriftenreihe der Wittgenstein-Gesellschaft
Schriftenreihe Zentralinst Math Mech — Schriftenreihe. Zentralinstitut fuer Mathematik und Mechanik
Schriftenr Erdwiss Komm Oesterr Akad Wiss — Schriftenreihe der Erdwissenschaftlichen Kommissionen. Oesterreichische Akademie der Wissenschaften
Schriftenr Fachgeb Getreidetechnol — Schriftenreihe aus dem Fachgebiet Getreidetechnologie
Schriftenr Forschungsgem Schweiz Lackfabr — Schriftenreihe. Forschungsgemeinschaft Schweizerischer Lackfabrikanten
Schriftenr Forschungsinst Biol Landwirtsch Nutziere — Schriftenreihe. Forschungsinstitut fuer die Biologie Landwirtschaftlicher Nutziere
Schriftenr Forstl Fak Univ Goettingen — Schriftenreihe. Forstliche Fakultaet. Universitaet Goettingen und Mitteilungen.Niedersaechsische Forstliche Versuchsanstalt
Schriftenr Fraunhofer Inst Atmos Umweltforsch — Schriftenreihe des Fraunhofer - Instituts Atmosphaerische Umweltforschung
Schriftenr GDMB — Schriftenreihe der GDMB
Schriftenr GDMB — Schriftenreihe der GDMB (Gesellschaft Deutscher Metallhuetten- und Bergleute)
Schriftenr Geb Off Gesundheitswes — Schriftenreihe aus dem Gebiete des Oeffentlichen Gesundheitswesens
Schriftenr Intensivmed Notfallmed Anaesthesiol — Schriftenreihe Intensivmedizin, Notfallmedizin, Anaesthesiologie
Schriftenr Int Ges Nahr Vitalst Forsch eV — Schriftenreihe. Internationale Gesellschaft fuer Nahrungs- und Vitalstoff-Forschung eV
Schriftenr ISWW Karlsruhe — Schriftenreihe des ISWW Karlsruhe
Schriftenr Kunstst Forsch — Schriftenreihe Kunststoff-Forschung
Schriftenr Landesanst Immissionisschutz — Schriftenreihe. Landesanstalt fuer Immissionsschutz
Schriftenr Landschaftspflege Naturschutz — Schriftenreihe fuer Landschaftspflege und Naturschutz
Schriftenr Lebensmittelchem Lebensmittelqual — Schriftenreihe. Lebensmittelchemie, Lebensmittelqualitaet
Schriftenr Med Orthop Tech — Schriftenreihe der Medizinisch-Orthopaedischen Technik
Schriftenr Naturwiss Forschungsergeb — Schriftenreihe Naturwissenschaftliche Forschungsergebnisse
Schriftenr Neurol — Schriftenreihe Neurologie
Schriften Neurol-Neurol Ser — Schriftenreihe Neurologie-Neurology Series
Schriftenr Oesterr Wasserwirtschaftsverb — Schriftenreihe. Oesterreichischer Wasserwirtschaftsverband

Schriftenr Otto Graf Inst Univ Stuttgart — Schriftenreihe. Otto-Graf-Institut. Universitaet Stuttgart

Schriftenr Schweissen Schneiden — Schriftenreihe Schweissen und Schneiden

Schriftenr Schweissen Schneiden Ber — Schriftenreihe Schweissen Schneiden. Bericht

Schriftenr Tech Nochsch Wien — Schriftenreihe der Technischen Hochschule in Wien

Schriftenr Theor Prax Med Psychol — Schriftenreihe zur Theorie und Praxis der Medizinischen Psychologie

Schriftenr Vegetationskd — Schriftenreihe fuer Vegetationskunde

Schriftenr Versuchstierkd — Schriftenreihe Versuchstierkunde

Schriftenr Ver Wasser Boden Lufthyg — Schriftenreihe. Verein fuer Wasser, Boden, und Lufthygiene

Schriftenr WAR — Schriftenreihe WAR (Institut fur Wasserversorgung, Abwasserbeseitigung und Raumplanung der Technischen Hochschule Darmstadt)

Schriftenr Wasserforsch — Schriftenreihe Wasserforschung

Schriftenr Wien Int Akad Ganzheitsmed — Schriftenreihe. Wiener Internationale Akademie fuer Ganzheitsmedizin

Schriftenr Z Blut — Schriftenreihe zur Zeitschrift Blut

Schriftenr Zementind — Schriftenreihe der Zementindustrie

Schriftenr Zentralbl Arbeitsmed Arbeitsschtz Prophyl — Schriftenreihe. Zentralblatt fuer Arbeitsmedizin, Arbeitsschutz, und Prophylaxe

Schriften Thuering Landesarbeitsgem Heilpflanzenk Weimar — Schriften der Thueringischen Landesarbeitsgemeinschaft fuer Heilpflanzenkunde und Heilpflanzenbeschaffung Weimar

Schriften Vereins Gesch Baar Donaueschingen — Schriften des Vereins fuer Geschichte und Naturgeschichte der Baar und der Angrenzenden Landestheile in Donaueschingen

Schriften Wirtschaftwiss Forsch — Schriften zur Wirtschaftwissenschaftlichen Forschung

Schriften Wuerttemberg Naturhist Reisevereins — Schriften des Wuertembergischen Naturhistorischen Reisevereins. Enthaltend Reisebeschreibungen und Mittheilungen aus der Natur- und Voelkerkunde

Schrifter Geol Wiss — Schriftenreihe fuer Geologische Wissenschaften

Schrifter GTZ — Schriftenreihe der GTZ (Gesellschaft fuer Technische Zusammenarbeit)

Schrift Naturf Gesellsch Kopenhagen — Schriften. Naturforschende Gesellschaft zu Kopenhagen

Schrifttum Agrarwirt — Schrifttum der Agrarwirtschaft

Schrifttum Bodenkult — Schrifttum der Bodenkultur

Schr Koenigsberg Gelehrten Ges Geistwiss Klasse — Schriften der Koenigsberger Gelehrten Gesellschaft. Geistwissenschaftliche Klasse

Schr Koenigsb Gelehrten Ges Naturwiss Kl — Schriften der Koenigsberger Gelehrten Gesellschaft. Naturwissenschaftliche Klasse

Schr Leningr Wiss Forsch Inst Lebensmittelind — Schriften des Leningrader Wissenschaftlichen Forschungs-Instituts der Lebensmittelindustrie

Schr Math Inst Univ Muenster 2 — Schriftenreihe. Mathematisches Institut. Universitaet Muenster. 2 Serie

Schr Math Inst Univ Muneter — Schriftenreihe. Mathematisches Institut. Universitaet Muenster

Schr Mineral Petrogr Inst Univ Kiel — Schriften aus dem Mineralogisch-Petrographischen Institut der Universitaet Kiel

Schr Naturwiss Ver Schleswig-Holstein — Schriften. Naturwissenschaftlicher Verein fuer Schleswig-Holstein

Schroeder B Zeev — Berigten en Verhandelingen over eenige Onderwerpen des Zeevaarts. Schroeder

Schr Phys Oekon Ges Koenigsbg — Schriften der Physikalisch-Oekonomischen Gesellschaft zu Koenigsberg

Schr Puckler Ges — Schriften der Puckler-Gesellschaft

Schrreihe Bayer Landesgesch — Schriftenreihe zur Bayerischen Landesgeschichte

Schrreihe Forstl Fak Univ Goettingen — Schriftenreihe. Forstliche Fakultaet. Universitaet Goettingen

Schrreihe Inst Staedtebau Raumplan & Raumordnung Tech Hochsch — Schriftenreihe des Institutes fuer Staedtebau, Raumplanung, und Raumordnung. Technische Hochschule Wien

Schrreihe Ratsarchvs Stadt Gorlitz — Schriftenreihe des Ratsarchivs der Stadt Gorlitz

Schrreihe Salzburg Mus Carolino Augusteum — Schriftenreihe des Salzburger Museums Carolino Augusteum

Schr Staatl Ksthalle Karlsruhe — Schriften der Staatlichen Kunsthalle Karlsruhe

Schr Ver Gesch Bodensees & Umgebung — Schriften des Vereins fuer Geschichte des Bodensees und Seiner Umgebung

Schr Ver Gesch Leipz — Schriften des Vereins fuer die Geschichte Leipzigs

Schr Ver Sozialpolit — Schriften des Vereins fuer Sozialpolitik

Schr Ver Verbr Naturwiss Kennt Wien — Schriften. Verein zur Verbreitung Naturwissenschaftlicher Kenntnisse in Wien

SchrVfS — Schriften des Vereins fuer Sozialpolitik

Schr Wiss Forsch Inst Nahrungsmittelind UdSSR — Schriften des Wissenschaftlichen Forschungs-Instituts fuer Nahrungsmittelindustrie der UdSSR

Schr Zent Biochem Forsch Inst Nahr Genussmittelind — Schriften des Zentralen Biochemischen Forschungs-Instituts der Nahrungs- und Genssmittelindustrie

Schr Zent Forsch Inst Lebensmittelchem — Schriften des Zentralen Forschungs-Instituts der Lebensmittelchemie

SCHSA — Soap and Chemical Specialties [*Later, Soap/Cosmetics/Chemical Specialties*]

Sch Sci — School Science

Sch Sci & Math — School Science and Mathematics

Sch Sci Rev — School Science Review

Sch (Sec Ed) — School (Toronto) (Secondary Edition)

Sch Shop — School Shop

Sch St — Schild von Steier. Beitraege zur Steirischen Vor- und Fruehgeschichte und Muenzkunde

Sch Technol — School Technology

Sch Trust — School Trustee

Schumacher As Ab — Astronomische Abhandlungen. Schumacher

Schumacher Jb — Jahrbuch Astronomisches. Schumacher

Schuyl Leg Reg — Schuylkill's Legal Register

SCHVD — Sachverhalte

SchVjKW — Schweizerische Vierteljahrsschrift fuer Kriegswissenschaft

SCHWA — Schweisstechnik Soudure

Schwabens Vergangenheit — Aus Schwabens Vergangenheit

Schwaeb Archv — Schwaebisches Archiv

Schwaeb Gs D — Denkschriften der Schwaebischen Gesellschaft der Aerzte und Naturforscher

Schwaeb Heimat — Schwaebische Heimat

Schwaeb Heimatb — Schwaebisches Heimatbuch

Schwaeb Imkerkal — Schwaebischer Imkerkalender

Schwaeb Merkur — Schwaebischer Merkur

Schwaeb Mus — Schwaebisches Museum

Schwaeb Museum — Schwaebisches Museum

Schw A Neur — Schweizer Archiv fuer Neurologie, Neurochirurgie, und Psychiatrie

SchwArchV — Schweizerisches Archiv fuer Volkskunde

Schwarz Man Int L — Schwarzenberger's Manual of International Law

Schwed Mag Schriften Naturf — Schwedisches Magazin, oder Schriften aus der Naturforschung, Stadt- und Landwirthschaft

Schweigger J — Journal fuer Chemie und Physik. Schweigger

Schweinfurt Heimatbl — Schweinfurter Heimatblaetter

Schweissen Kerntech Vortr Int Kolloq — Schweissen in der Kerntechnik. Vortraege des Internationalen Kolloquiums

Schweiss Prueftech — Schweiss- und Prueftechnik

Schweiss Schneidbrenner — Schweiss- und Schneidbrenner

Schweisstech Konf Vortr — Schweisstechnische Konferenz. Vortraege

Schweisstech Prax — Schweisstechnische Praxis

Schweisstech Soudure (Zurich) — Schweisstechnik Soudure (Zurich)

Schweissung Tech Gase — Schweissung und Technische Gase

Schweiz Aero Rev — Schweizer Aero-Revue

Schweiz Aerzteztg — Schweizerische Aerztezeitung

Schweiz Alum Rundsch — Schweizer Aluminium Rundschau

Schweiz Anst Forstl Versuchswesen Mitt — Schweizerische Anstalt fuer das Forstliche Versuchswesen. Mitteilungen

Schweiz Anst Forstl Versuchswes Mitt — Schweizerische Anstalt fuer das Forstliche Versuchswesen. Mitteilungen

Schweiz Apoth Ztg — Schweizerische Apotheker-Zeitung

Schweiz Apoth Ztg Suppl — Schweizerische Apotheker-Zeitung. Supplement

Schweiz Arch — Schweizer Archiv

Schweiz Arch Angew Wiss Tech — Schweizer Archiv fuer Angewandte Wissenschaft und Technik

Schweiz Arch F Neurol U Psychiat — Schweizer Archiv fuer Neurologie und Psychiatrie

Schweiz Archiv f Volksk — Schweizerisches Archiv fuer Volkskunde

Schweiz Arch Neurol Neurochir Psychiatr — Schweizer Archiv fuer Neurologie, Neurochirurgie, und Psychiatrie

Schweiz Arch Neurol Psychiatr — Schweizer Archiv fuer Neurologie und Psychiatrie

Schweiz Arch Tierh — Schweizer Archiv fuer Tierheilkunde

Schweiz Arch Tierh (Bern) — Schweizerisches Archiv fuer Tierheilkunde und Tierzucht (Bern)

Schweiz Arch Tierheilkd — Schweizer Archiv fuer Tierheilkunde

Schweiz Arch Verkehrswiss und Verkehrspol — Schweizerisches Archiv fuer Verkehrswissenschaft und Verkehrspolitik

Schweiz Arch Volksk — Schweizer Archiv fuer Volkskunde

Schweiz Arch Volkskde — Schweizer Archiv fuer Volkskunde

Schweiz Archv Vlksknd — Schweizerisches Archiv fuer Volkskunde

Schweiz Bauztg — Schweizerische Bauzeitung

Schweiz Beitr Allg Gesch — Schweizer Beitraege zur Allgemeinen Geschichte

Schweiz Beitr Dendrol — Schweizerische Beitrage zur Dendrologie

Schweiz Beitr Musikwiss — Schweizer Beitrage zur Musikwissenschaft

Schweiz Beitr Z Allg Gesch — Schweizer Beitraege zur Allgemeinen Geschichte. Etudes Suisses d'Histoire Generale

Schweiz Bienen-Ztg — Schweizerische Bienen-Zeitung

Schweiz Bl Heiz Lueft — Schweizerische Blaetter fuer Heizung und Lueftung

Schweiz Bll Wirtsch Polit — Schweizerische Blaetter fuer Wirtschafts- und Sozialpolitik

Schweiz Brau-Rundsch — Schweizerische Brauerei-Rundschau

Schweiz Chem Ztg — Schweizerische Chemiker-Zeitung

Schweiz Chem Ztg Tech Ind — Schweizer Chemiker-Zeitung Technik-Industrie

Schweiz Elektrotech Ver Bull — Schweizerischer Elektrotechnischer Verein. Bulletin

Schweiz Elektrotech Z — Schweizerische Elektrotechnische Zeitschrift

Schweizer Archiv Verkehrswiss u -Polit — Schweizerisches Archiv fuer Verkehrswissenschaft und Verkehrspolitik

Schweizer Arch Tierheilk — Schweizer Archiv fuer Tierheilkunde

Schweizer Arch Volksk — Schweizer Archiv fuer Volkskunde

Schweizer Mineralog u Petrog Mitt — Schweizerische Mineralogische und Petrographische Mitteilungen

Schweizer Monatshefte f Polit Wirt Kult — Schweizer Monatshefte fuer Politik, Wirtschaft, Kultur

Schweizer Musikztg — Schweizerische Musikzeitung und Saengerblatt

Schweizer Natschutz — Schweizer Naturschutz

Schweizer Palaeont Abh Mem Suisses Paleontologie — Schweizerische Palaeontologische Abhandlungen. Memoires Suisses de Palaeontologie

Schweizer Z Soziol — Schweizerische Zeitschrift fuer Soziologie

Schweizer Z Volkswirtsch u Statist — Schweizerische Zeitschrift fuer Volkswirtschaft und Statistik

Schweiz Gaertnerzeitung — Schweizerische Gaertnerzeitung

Schweiz Gaertnerztg — Schweizerische Gaertnerzeitung

Schweiz Ges Klin Chem Bull — Schweizerische Gesellschaft fuer Klinische Chemie. Bulletin

Schweiz Handelsztg — Schweizerische Handelszeitung
Schweiz Ing & Archit — Schweizer Ingenieur und Architekt
Schweiz Inst Kstwiss Jber & Jb — Schweizerisches Institut fuer Kunstwissenschaft. Jahresbericht und Jahrbuch
Schweiz Jb f Internat Recht — Schweizerisches Jahrbuch fuer Internationales Recht/Annuaire Suisse de Droit In ternational
Schweiz Juristen Zeit — Schweizerische Juristen-Zeitung
Schweiz Juristenztg — Schweizerische Juristen-Zeitung
Schweiz Lab Z — Schweizerische Laboratoriums-Zeitschrift
Schweiz Landtech — Schweizer Landtechnik
Schweiz Landw Forsch — Schweizerische Landwirtschaftliche Forschung
Schweiz Landwirtsch Forsch — Schweizerische Landwirtschaftliche Forschung
Schweiz Landwirtsch Forsch Rech Agron Suisse — Schweizerische Landwirtschaftliche Forschung/La Recherche Agronomique en Suisse
Schweiz Landwirtsch Monatsh — Schweizerische Landwirtschaftliche Monatshefte
Schweiz Landw Mh — Schweizerische Landwirtschaftliche Monatshefte
Schweiz Landw Z Die Gruene — Schweizerische Landwirtschaftliche Zeitschrift Die Gruene
Schweiz Med Wchnschr — Schweizerische Medizinische Wochenschrift
Schweiz Med Wochenschr — Schweizerische Medizinische Wochenschrift
Schweiz Med Wochenschr Suppl — Schweizerische Medizinische Wochenschrift. Supplementum
Schweiz Med Wschr — Schweizerische Medizinische Wochenschrift
Schweiz Mh — Schweizer Monatshefte
Schweiz Mhefte Pol Wirt Kultur — Schweizer Monatshefte. Zeitschrift fuer Politik, Wirtschaft, Kultur
Schweiz Milchwirtsch Forsch — Schweizerische Milchwirtschaftliche Forschung
Schweiz Milchztg — Schweizerische Milchzeitung
Schweiz Mineral Petrogr Mitt — Schweizerische Mineralogische und Petrographische Mitteilungen
Schweiz Monatsschr Zahnheilkd — Schweizerische Monatsschrift fuer Zahnheilkunde
Schweiz Monatsschr Zahnmed — Schweizerische Monatsschrift fuer Zahnmedizin
Schweiz Monatsschr Zahnmed — Schweizer Monatsschrift fuer Zahnmedizin
Schweiz Monats Zahnheilk — Schweizerische Monatsschrift fuer Zahnheilkunde
Schweiz Mschr Offiz — Schweizerische Monatsschrift fuer Offiziere aller Waffen
Schweiz Muenzbl — Schweizer Muenzblaetter
Schweiz Mus — Schweizerische Musikzeitung
Schweiz Musikztg — Schweizer Musik-Zeitung
Schweiz Naturf Ges Verh — Schweizerische Naturforschende Gesellschaft. Verhandlungen
Schweiz Naturforsch Ges Ber SNG Kernenerg — Schweizerische Naturforschende Gesellschaft. Berichte der SNG zur Kernenergie
Schweiz Naturschutz Prot Nat — Schweizer Naturschutz. Protection de la Nature
Schweiz Palaeontol Abh — Schweizerische Palaeontologische Abhandlungen
Schweiz Palaeontol Abh-Mem Suisse Palaeontol — Schweizerische Palaeontologische Abhandlungen. Memoires Suisses de Palaeontologie
Schweiz Pat Muster Markenbl Ausg A — Schweizerisches Patent-, Muster-, und Markenblatt. Ausgabe A
Schweiz Photorundsch — Schweizerische Photorundschau
Schweiz Photo Ztg — Schweizerische Photo-Zeitung
Schweiz Rdsch — Schweizerische Rundschau
Schweiz Rundschau — Schweizer Rundschau
Schweiz Rundsch Med Prax — Schweizerische Rundschau fuer Medizin Praxis
Schweiz Strahler — Schweizerische Strahler
Schweiz Tech — Schweizerische Technikerzeitung
Schweiz Tech Z — Schweizerische Technische Zeitschrift
Schweiz Text Ztg — Schweizer Textil-Zeitung
Schweiz Theol Zs — Schweizerische Theologische Zeitschrift
Schweiz Tonwaren Ind — Schweizerische Tonwaren-Industrie
Schweiz Ver Atomenerg Bull — Schweizerische Vereinigung fuer Atomenergie. Bulletin
Schweiz Verein Versicherungsmath Mitt — Schweizerische Vereinigung der Versicherungsmathematiker. Mitteilungen
Schweiz Ver Faerbereifachleuten Fachorgan Textilveredl — Schweizerische Verginigung von Faerbereifachleuten Fachorgan fuer Textilveredlung
Schweiz Ver Faerbereifachleuten Lahrgang Textilveredler — Schweizerische Verginigung von Faerbereifachleuten-Lehrgang fuer den Textilveredler
Schweiz Ver F Straf Gefaengniswes U Schutzaufsicht Verh — Schweizerischen Vereins fuer Straf-, Gefaengniswesen, und Schutzaufsicht. Verhandlungen
Schweiz Ver Gas-Wasserfachmaennern Monatsbull — Schweizerische Verein von Gas- und Wasserfachmaennern. Monatsbulletin
Schweiz Ver Lack Farbenchem Bull — Schweizerische Vereinigung der Lack- und Farbenchemiker. Bulletin
Schweiz Ver Sonnenenerg Symp — Schweizerische Vereinigung fuer Sonnenenergie. Symposium
Schweiz Volkskd — Schweizer Volkskunde
Schweiz Weinztg — Schweizerishce Weinzeitung
Schweiz Wochenschr Chem Pharm — Schweizerische Wochenschrift fuer Chemie und Pharmacie
Schweiz Wochenschr Pharm — Schweizerische Wochenschrift fuer Pharmacie
Schweiz Wohnschr Chem u Pharm — Schweizerische Wochenschrift fuer Chemie und Pharmacie
Schweiz Z Allg Path Bakt — Schweizerische Zeitschrift fuer Allgemeine Pathologie und Bakteriologie
Schweiz Z Allg Pathol Bakterol — Schweizerische Zeitschrift fuer Allgemeine Pathologie und Bakteriologie
Schweiz Z Biochem — Schweizerische Zeitschrift fuer Biochemie
Schweiz Zeitsch F Gesundheitspfl — Schweizerische Zeitschrift fuer Gesundheitspflege
Schweiz Zeitsch F Strafr — Schweizerische Zeitschrift fuer Strafrecht
Schweiz Z Forstwes — Schweizerische Zeitschrift fuer Forstwesen
Schweiz Z f Strafrecht — Schweizerische Zeitschrift fuer Strafrecht/Revue Penale Suisse
Schweiz Z Gesch — Schweizerische Zeitschrift fuer Geschichte

Schweiz Z Gynaekol Geburtshilfe — Schweizerische Zeitschrift fuer Gynaekologie und Geburtshilfe
Schweiz Z Gynaekol Geburtshilfe Suppl — Schweizerische Zeitschrift fuer Gynaekologie und Geburtshilfe. Supplementum
Schweiz Z Hydrol — Schweizerische Zeitschrift fuer Hydrologie
Schweiz Z Med Traumatol — Schweizerische Zeitschrift fuer Medizin und Traumatologie
Schweiz Z Obst-u Weinb — Schweizerische Zeitschrift fuer Obst- und Weinbau
Schweiz Z Obst-Weinbau — Schweizerische Zeitschrift fuer Obst- und Weinbau
Schweiz Z Pathol Bakteriol — Schweizerische Zeitschrift fuer Pathologie und Bakteriologie
Schweiz Z Pharm — Schweizerische Zeitschrift fuer Pharmacie
Schweiz Z Pilzk — Schweizerische Zeitschrift fuer Pilzkunde. Bulletin Suisse de Mycologie
Schweiz Z Pilzkd — Schweizerische Zeitschrift fuer Pilzkunde
Schweiz Z Pilzkd Bull Suisse Mycol — Schweizerische Zeitschrift fuer Pilzkunde. Bulletin Suisse de Mycologie
Schweiz Z Psychol Anwend — Schweizerische Zeitschrift fuer Psychologie und Ihre Anwendungen
Schweiz Zs Artill — Schweizerische Zeitschrift fuer Artillerie und Genie
Schweiz Z Sozialversicherung — Schweizerische Zeitschrift fuer Sozialversicherung
Schweiz Z Sportmed — Schweizerische Zeitschrift fuer Sportmedizin
Schweiz Z Tuberk — Schweizerische Zeitschrift fuer Tuberkulose
Schweiz Z Tuberk Pneumonol — Schweizerische Zeitschrift fuer Tuberkulose und Pneumonologie
Schweiz Z Tuberk Pneumonol Suppl — Schweizerische Zeitschrift fuer Tuberkulose und Pneumonologie. Supplementa
Schweiz Z Verkehrswirt — Schweizerische Zeitschrift fuer Verkehrswirtschaft
Schweiz Z Vermess Photogramm Kulturtech — Schweizerische Zeitschrift fuer Vermessung, Photogrammetrie, und Kulturtechnik
Schweiz Z Volkswirt und Statis — Schweizerische Zeitschrift fuer Volkswirtschaft und Statistik
Schwenk — Schwenckfeldiana
Schwest Rev — Schwestern Revue
Schwiez Z Path Bakt — Schweizerische Zeitschrift fuer Pathologie und Bakteriologie
SchwKiZ — Schweizerische Kirchenzeitung
SchwKZ — Schweizerische Kirchenzeitung
Schw Lex — Schweizer Lexikon
SchwM — Schweizer Monatshefte
Schw Mbl — Schweizer Muenzblaetter
Schw Med Wo — Schweizerische Medizinische Wochenschrift
SchwMH — Schweizer Monatshefte
Schw Musikz — Schweizerische Musikzeitung/Revue Musicale Suisse
Schw NR — Schweizerische Numismatische Rundschau
Schw Rd — Schweizerische Rundschau
SchwRundschau — Schweizerische Rundschau
SchwV — Schweizer Volkskunde
Schw Z f Gesch — Schweizerische Zeitschrift fuer Geschichte
Schw Z Gesc — Schweizerische Zeitschrift fuer Geschichte
Schw Z Hydrol — Schweizerische Zeitschrift fuer Hydrologie
Schw Z Pilzk — Schweizerische Zeitschrift fuer Pilzkunde
Schw Z Psyc — Schweizerische Zeitschrift fuer Psychologie und Ihre Anwendungen
Schw Z Psychol — Schweizerische Zeitschrift fuer Psychologie und Ihre Anwendungen
Schw Zs f G — Schweizerische Zeitschrift fuer Geschichte
Schw Z Soz — Schweizerische Zeitschrift fuer Sozialversicherung
Schw Z Sportmed — Schweizerische Zeitschrift fuer Sportmedizin
Schw Zs Tbk — Schweizerische Zeitschrift fuer Tuberkulose
Schw Zs Vermess — Schweizerische Zeitschrift fuer Vermessungswesen
Schw Ztschr Ges — Schweizerische Zeitschrift fuer Geschichte
Schw ZV St — Schweizerische Zeitschrift fuer Volkswirtschaft und Statistik
SchZVermW — Schweizer Zeitschrift fuer Vermessungswesen
SCI — Science
SCI — Science Citation Index
Sci — Scientia. Revista Internazionale di Sintesi Scientifica
Sci — Scientia. Rivista de Tecnica y Cultura
SCI — Scripta Classica Israelica
ScI — Scripta Islandica
SCI — Studii si Cercetari de Istorie
Sci 80 (Eighty) — Science 80 (Eighty)
SciA — Scientific American
SCIA — Studii si Cercetari de Istoria Artei. Seria Arta Plastica
SciAb — Science Abstracts
Sci Abstr — Science Abstracts
Sci Abstr Ch — Science Abstracts of China
Sci Abstr China Biol Sci — Science Abstracts of China. Biological Sciences
Sci Abstr China Chem Chem Technol — Science Abstracts of China. Chemistry and Chemical Technology
Sci Abstr China Math Phys Sci — Science Abstracts of China. Mathematical and Physical Sciences
Sci Abstr China Med — Science Abstracts of China. Medicine
Sci Abstr China Tech Sci — Science Abstracts of China. Technical Sciences
Sci Abstr Sect A — Science Abstracts. Section A
Sci Abstr Sect A Phys Abstr — Science Abstracts. Section A. Physics Abstracts
Sci Abstr Sect B — Science Abstracts. Section B
Sci Abstr Ser C — Science Abstracts. Series C
Sci Act Rev — Scientific Activity Review
SCIADJ — Centro Internacional de Agricultura Tropical [*CIAT*]. Series Seminars
Sci Adv Mater Process Eng Proc — Science of Advanced Materials and Process Engineering. Proceedings
Sci Adv Mater Process Eng Q — Science of Advanced Materials and Process Engineering. Quarterly
Sci Aer Aerotech — Science Aerienne et l'Aerotechnique

Sci Ag — Scientific Agriculture
Sci Agr — Scientific Agriculture
Sci Agric — Science in Agriculture
Sci Agric Bohemoslov — Scientia Agriculturae Bohemoslovaca
Sci Agric Ottawa — Scientific Agriculture (Ottawa)
Sci Agric PA State Univ Agric Exp Stn — Science in Agriculture. Pennsylvania State University. Agricultural Experiment Station
Sci Agric Sin — Scientia Agricultura Sinica
Sci Agric (Taipei) — Scientific Agriculture (Taipei)
Sci Agric (Tokyo) — Science of Agriculture (Tokyo)
Sci Agron Rennes — Sciences Agronomiques Rennes
Sci Alaska Proc Alaskan Sci Conf — Science in Alaska. Proceedings. Alaskan Science Conference
Sci Aliment — Science de l'Alimentation
Sci Aliment — Scienza dell'Alimentazione
Sci Aliments — Sciences des Aliments
Sci Am — Scientific American
Sci Amer — Scientific American
Sci American — Scientific American
Sci Amer Lib Paperback — Scientific American Library Paperback
Sci Amer Monthly — Scientific American Monthly
Sci Am Mo — Scientific American Monthly
Sci Am Monthly — Scientific American Monthly
Sci Am S — Scientific American. Supplement
Sci Am Sci Med — Scientific American Science and Medicine
Sci & Archaeol — Science and Archaeology
Sci & Aust Technol — Science and Australian Technology
Sci & Child — Science and Children
Sci and Cult — Science and Culture
Sci and Eng Rep Def Acad — Scientific and Engineering Reports. Defense Academy
Sci and Eng Rep Natl Def Acad (Jpn) — Scientific and Engineering Reports. National Defense Academy (Japanese)
Sci & Eng Rep Saitama Univ C — Science and Engineering Reports. Saitama University. Series C
Sci and Eng Rep Saitama Univ Ser C — Science and Engineering Reports. Saitama University. Series C
Sci & Scty — Science and Society
Sci & Soc — Science and Society
Sci & Tech — Science and Technology
Sci & Tech Aerosp Reports — Scientific and Technical Aerospace Reports
Sci Ann Fac Phys Mat Aristotelian Univ Thessaloniki — Scientific Annals. Faculty of Physics and Mathematics. Aristotelian University of Thessaloniki
Sci Ann Fac Phys Math Aristotelian Univ Thessaloniki — Scientific Annals. Faculty of Physics and Mathematics. Aristotelian University of Thessaloniki
Sci Ant — Scienze dell'Antichita
Sci Appliance — Science and Appliance
SciArch — Science and Archaeology
Sci Archaeol Symp Archaeol Chem — Science and Archaeology. Symposium on Archaeological Chemistry
Sci Art Min — Science and Art of Mining
Sci Arts Orient — Sciences and Arts (Oriental)
Sci Asahi — Scientific Asahi
Sci Atmos Sin — Scientia Atmospherica Sinica
Sci Aust — Scientific Australian
Sci Aust Technol — Science and Australian Technology
Sci Av — Sciences et Avenir
Sci Avenir — Sciences et Avenir
SCIBA — Studii si Cercetari de Inframicrobiologie
Sci Basis Med — Scientific Basis of Medicine
Sci Basis Nucl Waste Manage — Scientific Basis for Nuclear Waste Management. Proceedings. International Symposium
Sci Basis Nucl Waste Manage Proc Mater Res Soc Annu Meet — Scientific Basis for Nuclear Waste Management. Proceedings. Materials Research Society Annual Meeting
Sci Basis Nucl Waste Manage Symp — Scientific Basis for Nuclear Waste Management. Symposium
Sci Basis Psychiatr — Scientific Basis of Psychiatry
Sci Basis Toxic Assess Proc Symp Sci Basis Toxic Assess — Scientific Basis of Toxicity Assessment. Proceedings. Symposium on the Scientific Basis of Toxicity Assessment
Sci Bas Med Ann Rev — Scientific Basis of Medicine. Annual Review
Sci Biol J — Science of Biology Journal
Sci Biol Ser — Science of Biology Series
Sci Bk — Science Books and Films
Sci Bks — Science Books
Sci Bks & Films — Science Books and Films
Sci Bul — Science Bulletin
Sci Bul — Science Bulletin for Teachers in Secondary Schools
Sci Bull Academ Min Metall (Krakow) Geol — Scientific Bulletins. Academy of Mining and Metallurgy (Krakow). Geology
Sci Bull Acad Min Metall (Krakow) Ceram — Scientific Bulletins. Academy of Mining and Metallurgy (Krakow). Ceramics
Sci Bull Acad Min Metall (Krakow) Electrif Mech Min Metall — Scientific Bulletins. Academy of Mining and Metallurgy (Krakow). Electrification and Mechanization in Mining and Metallurgy
Sci Bull Acad Min Metall Krakow Geol — Scientific Bulletins. Academy of Mining and Metallurgy (Krakow). Geology
Sci Bull Acad Min Metall (Krakow) Math Phys Chem — Scientific Bulletins. Academy of Mining and Metallurgy (Krakow). Mathematics, Physics, Chemistry
Sci Bull Acad Min Metall (Krakow) Metall Foundry Pract — Scientific Bulletins. Academy of Mining and Metallurgy (Krakow). Metallurgy andFoundry Practice
Sci Bull Acad Min Metall (Krakow) Min — Scientific Bulletins. Academy of Mining and Metallurgy (Krakow). Mining

Sci Bull Acad Min Metall (Krakow) Spec Ser — Scientific Bulletins. Academy of Mining and Metallurgy (Krakow). Special Series
Sci Bull Acad Min Metall Krakow Trans — Scientific Bulletins. Academy of Mining and Metallurgy (Krakow). Transaction
Sci Bull Am Sov Sci Soc — Science Bulletin. American-Soviet Science Society
Sci Bull At Energy New Energ Organ — Scientific Bulletin. Atomic Energy and New Energies Organization
Sci Bull At Energy Organ Iran — Scientific Bulletin. Atomic Energy Organization of Iran
Sci Bull Beijing — Science Bulletin (Beijing)
Sci Bull Can Cent Miner Energy Technol — Scientific Bulletin. Canada Centre for Mineral and Energy Technology
Sci Bull Coll Agric Univ Ryukyus Okinawa — Science Bulletin. College of Agriculture. University of Ryukyus. Okinawa
Sci Bull Cotton Res Inst Sindos — Science Bulletin. Cotton Research Institute. Sindos
Sci Bull Dep Agric For Un S Afr — Science Bulletin. Department of Agriculture and Forestry. Union of South Africa
Sci Bull Dep Agric NSW — Science Bulletin. Department of Agriculture. New South Wales
Sci Bull Dept Agr NSW — Science Bulletin. Department of Agriculture. New South Wales
Sci Bull Dept Agr S Afr — Science Bulletin. Department of Agriculture. South Africa
Sci Bull Des Bot Gard Ariz — Science Bulletin. Desert Botanical Garden of Arizona
Sci Bull Fac Agric Kyushu Univ — Science Bulletin. Faculty of Agriculture. Kyushu University
Sci Bull Fac Agric Univ Ryukyus — Science Bulletin. Faculty of Agriculture. University of the Ryukyus/Ryukyu Daigaku Nogakubu Gakujutsu Hokoku
Sci Bull Fac Agr Kyushu Univ — Science Bulletin. Faculty of Agriculture. Kyushu University
Sci Bull Fac Ed Nagasaki Univ — Science Bulletin. Faculty of Education. Nagasaki University
Sci Bull Fac Educ Nagasaki Univ — Science Bulletin. Faculty of Education. Nagasaki University
Sci Bull Fac Lib Arts Educ Nagasaki Univ — Science Bulletin. Faculty of Liberal Arts and Education. Nagasaki University
Sci Bull Natl Chiao Tung Univ — Science Bulletin. National Chiao-Tung University
Sci Bull Natl Sci Dev Board Philipp — Science Bulletin. National Science Development Board (Philippines)
Sci Bull Politeh Univ Bucharest Ser B — Scientific Bulletin. Politehnica. University of Bucharest. Series B. Chemistry and Materials Science
Sci Bull Polytech Inst Bucharest Chem Mater Sci — Scientific Bulletin. Polytechnic Institute of Bucharest. Chemistry and Materials Science
Sci Bull Qatar Univ — Science Bulletin. Qatar University
Sci Bull Repub S Afr Dept Agr Tech Serv — Science Bulletin. Republic of South Africa. Department of Agricultural Technical Services
Sci Bull S Afr Dep Agruc Tech Serv — Science Bulletin. South Africa. Department of Agricultural Technical Services
Sci Bull Sci Found Philipp — Science Bulletin. Science Foundation of the Philippines
Sci Bull Stanislaw Staszic Acad Min Metall Chem — Scientific Bulletins. Stanislaw Staszic Academy of Mining and Metallurgy. Chemistry
Sci Bull Stanislaw Staszic Acad Min Metall Phys — Scientific Bulletins. Stanislaw Staszic Academy of Mining and Metallurgy. Physics
Sci Bull Stanislaw Staszic Univ Min Metall Ceram — Scientific Bulletins. Stanislaw Staszic University of Mining and Metallurgy. Ceramics
Sci Bull Stanislaw Staszic Univ Min Metall Geod — Scientific Bulletins. Stanislaw Staszic University of Mining and Metallurgy. Geodesy
Sci Bull Stanislaw Staszic Univ Min Metall Geol — Scientific Bulletins. Stanislaw Staszic University of Mining and Metallurgy. Geology
Sci Bull Stanislaw Staszic Univ Min Metall Math Phys Chem — Scientific Bulletins. Stanislaw Staszic University of Mining and Metallurgy. Mathematics, Physics, Chemistry
Sci Bull Stanislaw Staszic Univ Min Metall Min — Scientific Bulletins. Stanislaw Staszic University of Mining and Metallurgy. Mining
Sci Bull Stanislaw Staszic Univ Min Metall Sozol Sozotech — Scientific Bulletins. Stanislaw Staszic University of Mining and Metallurgy. Sozology and Sozotechnics
Sci Bull Stanislaw Staszic Univ Min Metall Spec Ser — Scientific Bulletins. Stanislaw Staszic University of Mining and Metallurgy. Special Series
Sci Bull Stanislaw Staszic Univ Min Metall Tech Econ Probl — Scientific Bulletins. Stanislaw Staszic University of Mining and Metallurgy. Technical and Economic Problems
Sci Bull Taipei — Science Bulletin/K'o Hsueeh Hui Pao/Chinese Association for the Advancement of Science (Taipei)
Sci Bull Tech Univ Lodz Phys — Scientific Bulletin. Technical University of Lodz. Physics
Sci Bull Univ Agric Sci — Scientific Bulletin. University of Agricultural Sciences
Sci Bull Univ Kans — Science Bulletin. University of Kansas
Sci Bull Univ Kansas — Science Bulletin. Kansas University
Sci Canadensis — Scientia Canadensis. Journal of the History of Canadien Science, Technology, and Medicine
Sci Ceram — Science of Ceramics
Sci Ceram Interfaces — Science of Ceramic Interfaces
Sci China A — Science in China. Series A. Mathematics, Physics, Astronomy, and Technological Sciences
Sci China B — Science in China. Series B. Chemistry, Life Sciences, and Earth Sciences
Sci China Ser A — Science in China. Series A. Mathematics, Physics, Astronomy, andTechnological Sciences
Sci China Ser A Math Phys Astron — Science in China. Series A. Mathematics, Physics, Astronomy

Sci China Ser A Math Phys Astron & Technol Sci — Science in China. Series A. Mathematics, Physics, Astronomy, and Technological Sciences

Sci China Ser B — Science in China. Series B. Chemistry, Life Sciences, and Earth Sciences

Sci China Ser B Chem — Science in China. Series B. Chemistry

Sci China Ser B Chem Life Sci & Earth Sci — Science in China. Series B. Chemistry, Life Sciences, and Earth Sciences

Sci China Ser C Life Sci — Science in China. Series C. Life Sciences

Sci China Ser D Earth Sci — Science in China. Series D. Earth Sciences

Sci China Ser E — Science in China (Scientia Sinica). Series E

Sci China Ser E Technol Sci — Science in China. Series E. Technological Sciences

Sci Chron — Science Chronicle

Sci Chron (Karachi) — Science Chronicle (Karachi)

Sci Cit Ind — Science Citation Index

Sci Cit Index — Science Citation Index

Sci Comm Probl Environ Rep — Scientific Committee on Problems of the Environment. Report

Sci Comput Program — Science of Computer Programming

Sci Comput Programming — Science of Computer Programming

Sci Concept Found — Science and its Conceptual Foundations

Sci Conf Ges Dtsch Naturforsch Aerzte — Scientific Conference. Gesellschaft Deutscher Naturforscher und Aerzte

Sci Conserv (Tokyo) — Science for Conservation (Tokyo)

Sci Context — Science in Context

Sci Counc Afr Publ — Scientific Council for Africa. Publication

Sci Counc Afr South Sahara Publ — Scientific Council for Africa South of the Sahara. Publication

Sci Counc Jap Annu Rep — Science Council of Japan. Annual Report

Sci Couns — Science Counselor

Sci Counselor — Science Counselor. Quarterly Journal for Teachers of Science in the Catholic High Schools

Sci Crime Detect — Science and Crime Detection

Sci Cult — Science and Culture

Sci Cult (New Delhi) — Science and Culture (New Delhi)

Sci Cult Ser Phys — Science and Culture Series. Physics

SCID-A — Studies in Comparative International Development

Sci Dating Methods — Scientific Dating Methods

Sci Dep Bull United Plant Assoc South India — Scientific Department Bulletin. United Planters' Association of Southern India

Sci Detect Fakery Art — Scientific Detection of Fakery in Art

Sci Dig — Science Digest

Sci Digest — Science Digest

Sci Diliman — Science Diliman

Sci Dimens — Science Dimension

Sci Dimension — Science Dimension

Sci Diss Silesian Univ Katowice — Scientific Dissertations. Silesian Univeristy. Katowice

Sci Drugs (Tokyo) — Science of Drugs (Tokyo)

SCIEA — Science

Sci Earth Geol — Science of the Earth. Geology

Sci Eau — Sciences de l'Eau

Sci Ed — Science and Education

Sci Ed — Science Education

Sci Ed News — Science Education Newsletter

Sci Educ — Science Education

Sci Educ Adm Agric Rev Man ARM-NE — Science and Education Administration. Agricultural Reviews and Manuals. ARM-NE

Sci Educ Adm Agric Rev Man ARM-W — Science and Education Administration. Agricultural Reviews and Manuals. ARM-W

Sci Educ Adm Agric Rev Man West Ser US Dep Agric — Science and Education Administration. Agricultural Reviews and Manuals. WesternSeries. United States Department of Agriculture

Sci Educ Adm North Cent Reg Publ — Science and Education Administration. North Central Region Publication

Sci Educ Tokyo — Science Education/Rika Kyoiku (Tokyo)

Sci Elec — Scientia Electrica

Sci Electr — Scientia Electrica

Science — Science for People

Science and Tech Libs — Science and Technology Libraries

Science Ed — Science Education

Science et Industrie Phot — Science et Industries Photographiques

Science Fiction Stud — Science-Fiction Studies

Science Lib Bibliog Ser — Science Museum Library. Bibliographical Series

Science N L — Science News Letter

Science Prog — Science Progress

Sciences Assoc Fr Av Sci — Sciences. Association Francaise pour l'Avancement des Sciences

Sciences (NY) — Sciences (New York)

Sciences NY Acad Sci — Sciences. New York Academy of Sciences

Sciences Paris — Sciences. Revue de l'Association Francaise pour l'Advancement des Sciences (Paris)

Sciences Pol — Sciences Politiques

Science Suppl — Science. Supplement

Sciencia Med — Sciencia Medica

Sci Eng — Science and Engineering

Sci Eng Ethics — Science and Engineering Ethics

Sci Eng J — Science & Engineering Journal

Sci Eng Rep Saitama Univ — Science and Engineering Reports. Saitama University

Sci Eng Rep Tohoku Gakuin Univ — Science and Engineering Reports of Tohoku Gakuin University

Sci Eng Res Counc Daresbury Lab Rep — Science and Engineering Research Council. Daresbury Laboratory. Report

Sci Eng Rev Doshisha Univ — Science and Engineering Review. Doshisha University

Sci Enseignem Sci — Sciences et l'Enseignement des Sciences

Sci Enseign Sci — Sciences et l'Enseignement des Sciences

Scient Agric — Scientific Agriculture

Scient Am — Scientific American

Scient Amer — Scientific American

Scient Am Suppl — Scientific American. Supplement

Scient Film Rev — Scientific Film Review

Scient Hort — Scientific Horticulture

Scientia Genet — Scientia Genetica

Scientiarum Hist — Scientiarum Historia

Scient Instrum — Scientific Instruments

Scient Mon — Scientific Monthly

Scient Month — Scientific Monthly

Scient Pap Coll Gen Educ Tokyo — Scientific Papers. College of General Education. University of Tokyo

Scient Papers Civil Vet Dept (Madras) — Scientific Papers. Civil Veterinary Department (Madras)

Scient Proc R Dubl Soc — Scientific Proceedings. Royal Dublin Society

Scient Rep Fac Agric Okayama Univ — Scientific Reports. Faculty of Agriculture. Okayama University

Scient Rep Govt Inst Infect Dis Tokyo Imp Univ — Scientific Reports. Government Institute for Infectious Diseases. Tokyo Imperial University

Scient Rep Kyoto Prefect Univ Agric — Scientific Reports. Kyoto Prefectural University. Agriculture

Scient Res (Bangladesh) — Scientific Researches (Bangladesh)

Scient Trans Dubl Soc — Scientific Transactions. Royal Dublin Society

Scient Work — Scientific Worker

Sci Environ — Science and Environment

Scienza Aliment — Scienza dell'Alimentazione

Scienza Tecnol Aliment — Scienza e Tecnologia degli Alimenti

Sci Espr — Science et Esprit

Sci Esprit — Science et Esprit

Sci Eval Workshop Localized Bone Loss Proc — Scientific Evaluation Workshop on Localized Bone Loss. Proceedings

Sci Exp — Science through Experiments

Sci Exploration — Science Exploration

SCIF — Science Forum

Sci Farm — Science for the Farmer

Sci Farm — Scienza del Farmaco

Sci Farmer — Science for the Farmer

Sci Fict Book Rev Index — Science Fiction Book Review Index

Sci Fiction Bk Rev Ind — Science Fiction Book Review Index

Sci Fict St — Science Fiction Studies

Sci Food Agric — Science of Food and Agriculture

Sci For — Science Forum

Sci For Prod — Science of Forest Products

Sci Forum — Science Forum

Sci Found Philipp Sci Bull — Science Foundation. Philippines. Science Bulletin

SCIGA — Society of Chemical Industry (London). Monograph

SCIGB — Sicherheitsingenieur

Sci Genet — Scientia Genetica

Sci Geol Bull — Sciences Geologiques. Bulletin

Sci Geol Bull Inst Geol Univ Louis Pasteur Strasbourg — Sciences Geologiques. Bulletin. Institut de Geologie. Universite Louis Pasteur de Strasbourg

Sci Geol Mem — Sciences Geologiques. Memoires

Sci Geol S — Scientia Geologica Sinica

Sci Geol Sin — Scientia Geologica Sinica

Sci Global Change — Science of Global Change

Sci Gov Rep — Science and Government Report

Sci Govt Rep — Science and Government Report

Sci Hist — Scientiarum Historia

Sci Hort — Scientific Horticulture

Sci Hortic — Scientia Horticulturae

Sci Hortic (Amst) — Scientia Horticulturae (Amsterdam)

Sci Hortic (Canterbury) — Scientific Horticulture (Canterbury)

Sci Hum — Sciences Humaines

Sci Humanisme — Science et Humanisme

Sci Hum Life — Science of Human Life

SCII — Science in Iceland

Sci Icel — Science in Iceland

Sci Ilus — Science Illustrated

Sci Ind — Science and Industry

Sci Ind — Science et Industrie

Sci Ind Bull Roure Bertrand Fils — Scientific and Industrial Bulletin of Roure-Bertrand Fils

Sci Ind Ed Constr Trav Publics — Science et Industrie. Edition Construction et Travaux Publics

Sci Ind Ed Metall Constr Mec Energ — Science et Industrie. Edition Metallurgie. Construction, Mecaniques, Energie

Sci Ind Equip Bull — Scientific and Industrial Equipment Bulletin

Sci Ind Forum Aust Acad Sci Forum Rep — Science and Industry Forum. Australian Academy of Science. Forum Report

Sci Ind (Karachi) — Science and Industry (Karachi)

Sci Ind (Melbourne) — Science and Industry (Melbourne)

Sci Ind (Osaka) — Science and Industry (Osaka)

Sci Ind Paris — Science et Industrie (Paris)

Sci Ind (Philips) — Science and Industry (Philips)

Sci Ind Phot — Science et Industries Photographiques

Sci Ind Photogr — Science et Industries Photographiques

Sci Ind Res Counc Alberta Rep — Scientific and Industrial Research Council of Alberta. Reports

Sci Ind Spat — Sciences et Industries Spatiales

Sci Ind Spatiales Space Res Eng Weltraumforsch Ind — Sciences et Industries Spatiales, Space Research and Engineering, Weltraumforschung und Industrie

Sci Inf News — Science Informations News. National Science Foundation

Sci Inf Notes — Scientific Information Notes

Sci Info N — Scientific Information Notes

Sci in Ind (Lond) — Science in Industry (London)

Sci Ins Contr — Scientific Insect Control

Sci Insect Control (Kyoto) — Scientific Insect Control (Kyoto)

Sci Inst Cereal Res USSR Pap — Scientific Institute of Cereal Research (USSR). Papers

Sci Instr — Scientific Instruments

Sci Instr J Phys E — Scientific Instruments. Journal of Physics. E

Sci Instrum — Journal of Physics. E: Scientific Instruments

Sci Int (Lahore) — Science International (Lahore)

Sci Invest Freshwater Salmon Fish Res Scott Home Dep — Scientific Investigations. Freshwater and Salmon Fisheries Research. Scottish Home Department

Sci Invest Freshw Salmon Fish Res Scott Home Dep — Scientific Investigations. Freshwater and Salmon Fisheries Research. Scottish Home Department

Sci Iran — Scientia Iranica

Sci Isl — Scientia Islandica

Sci Island — Scientia Islandica

Sci J — Science Journal

Sci J (Lond) — Science Journal (London)

Sci J London — Science Journal (London)

Sci Jour — Science Journal

Sci J R Coll Sci — Scientific Journal. Royal College of Science

Sci J Roy Coll Sci — Scientific Journal. Royal College of Science

Sci J Shivaji Univ — Science Journal. Shivaji University

Sci Justice — Science and Justice

Sci Komun — Sciencaj Komunikajoj

SCIL — Small Computers in Libraries

Sciland — Scienceland

Sci Leafl — Science Leaflet

SCILF — Studii si Cercetari de Istorie Literara si Folclor

Sci Life — Science and Life

Sci Light — Science of Light

Sci Living Body — Science of the Living Body

Sci Lubr — Scientific Lubrication

Sci Lubr Liq Fuel — Scientific Lubrication and Liquid Fuel

Sci M — Scientific Monthly

Sci Mac — Science of Machine

Sci Mag Chem Catheder Katerinoslav — Scientific Magazine. Chemical Catheder of Katerinoslav

Sci Mag Metall Catheder Dnepropetrovsk — Scientific Magazine. Metallurgical Catheder at Dnepropetrovsk

Sci Man — Science of Man

Sci Man — Science of Man and Australasian Anthropological Journal

Sci Mar — Scientia Marina

Sci March — Science on the March

Sci Mat — Scienze Matematiche

Sci Mat Loro Insegnamento — Scienze la Matematica e il Loro Insegnamento

Sci Meat Meat Prod — Science of Meat and Meat Products

Sci Mech — Science and Mechanics

Sci Med — Sciences Medicales

Sci Med Ital — Scientia Medica Italica

Sci Med Ital (Engl Ed) — Scientia Medica Italica (English Edition)

Sci Med Man — Science, Medicine, and Man

Sci Med NY — Science and Medicine (New York)

Sci Med Philadelphia — Science and Medicine (Philadelphia)

Sci Meet — Scientific Meetings

Sci Mem Kazan State Univ — Scientific Memoirs. Kazan State University

Sci Mem M Gorkii Univ Molotov — Scientific Memoirs. M. Gor'kii University of Molotov

Sci Mem Off Med Dept Gov India — Scientific Memoirs by Officers of the Medical and Sanitary Department. Government of India

Sci Mem Univ Perm — Scientific Memoirs. University of Perm

Sci Mem Univ Saratov — Scientific Memoirs. University of Saratov

Sci Message — Science Message

Sci Mo — Scientific Monthly

Sci Mon — Scientific Monthly

SCI Monogr — SCI (Society of Chemical Industry. London) Monograph

Sci Monogr Pak Assoc Adv Sci — Scientific Monograph. Pakistan Association for the Advancement of Science

Sci Monogr SM Univ Wyo Agric Exp Stn — Science Monograph SM. University of Wyoming. Agricultural Experiment Station

Sci Monogr Univ Wyo Agric Exp Stn — Science Monograph. University of Wyoming. Agricultural Experiment Station

Sci Monogr Wyo Expl Stn — Science Monograph. Wyoming Experimental Station

Sci Mon Taipei — Science Monthly (Taipei)

Sci Monthly — Scientific Monthly

Sci Mus Lib Bull — Science Museum Library Bulletin

Sci Mus Minn Monogr — Science Museum of Minnesota. Monograph

Sci N — Science News

SCINA — Science and Culture

Sci Nat — Science et Nature

Sci Natur — Science and Nature

Sci Networks Hist Stud — Science Networks. Historical Studies

Sci New Guinea — Science in New Guinea

Sci News — Science News

Sci News (Harmondsworth) — Science News (Harmondsworth)

Sci News Karachi — Science News. National Science Council (Karachi)

Sci News Lett — Science News Letter

Sci News Peking — Science News/Academia Sinica/K'o Hsueeh T'ung Pao (Peking)

Sci News (Washington DC) — Science News (Washington, D.C.)

S C In J — Journal of the Society of Chemical Industry

Sci NL — Science News Letter

Sci Notes Sugar Ind — Scientific Notes on the Sugar Industry

Sci Nourishment — Science of Nourishment

Sci Nova — Scientia Nova

Sci Nuncius Radiophonicus — Scientiarum Nuncius Radiophonicus

Sci Opin — Scientific Opinion

Sci Orient — Scientia Orientalis

Sci Our Time — Scientists of Our Time

Sci Paed Ex — Scientia Paedagogica Experimentalis

Sci Paed Exp — Scientia Paedagogica Experimentalis

Sci Pap Cancer Res Inst Sofia — Scientific Papers. Cancer Research Institute. Sofia

Sci Pap Cent Res Inst Jpn Monop Corp — Scientific Papers. Central Research Institute. Japan Monopoly Corporation

Sci Pap Cent Res Inst Jpn Tob Salt Publ Corp — Scientific Papers. Central Research Institute. Japan Tobacco and Salt Public Corporation

Sci Pap Coll Arts Sci Univ Tokyo — Scientific Papers. College of Arts and Sciences. University of Tokyo

Sci Pap Coll Ed — Scientific Papers. College of General Education

Sci Pap Coll Gen Educ Univ Tokyo — Scientific Papers. College of General Education. University of Tokyo

Sci Pap Coll Gen Educ Univ Tokyo (Biol Part) — Scientific Papers. College of General Education. University of Tokyo (Biological Part)

Sci Paperbacks — Science Paperbacks

Sci Papers College Arts Sci Univ Tokyo — Scientific Papers of the College of Arts and Sciences. University of Tokyo

Sci Papers College Gen Ed Univ Tokyo — Scientific Papers. College of General Education. University of Tokyo

Sci Papers Prague ICT C — Scientific Papers. Prague Institute of Chemical Technology. Part C. Organic Chemistry and Technology

Sci Pap Fac Eng Tokushima Univ — Scientific Papers. Faculty of Engineering. Tokushima University

Sci Pap Fac Eng Univ Tokushima — Scientific Papers. Faculty of Engineering. University of Tokushima

Sci Pap Hokkaido Fish Sci Inst — Scientific Papers. Hokkaido Fisheries Scientific Institution/Hokkaido Sui San Shikenjo Hokoku

Sci Pap Imp Fuel Res Inst (Jpn) — Scientific Papers. Imperial Fuel Research Institute (Japan)

Sci Pap Inst Algol Res Fac Sci Hokkaido Univ — Scientific Papers. Institute of Algological Research. Faculty of Science. Hokkaido University

Sci Pap Inst Build Wroclaw Tech Univ — Scientific Papers. Institute of Building. Wroclaw Technical University

Sci Pap Inst Chem Technol Pardubice — Scientific Papers. Institute of Chemical Technology. Pardubice

Sci Pap Inst Chem Technol (Prague) Chem Eng Autom — Scientific Papers. Institute of Chemical Technology (Prague). Chemical Engineering and Automation

Sci Pap Inst Chem Technol (Prague) Fac Food Ind — Scientific Papers. Institute of Chemical Technology. (Prague). Faculty of Food Industry

Sci Pap Inst Chem Technol Prague Fac Inorg Org Technol — Scientific Papers. Institute of Chemical Technology. (Prague). Faculties of Inorganic and Organic Technology

Sci Pap Inst Chem Technol Prague Fac Technol Fuel Water — Scientific Papers. Institute of Chemical Technology. (Prague). Faculty of Fuel and Water

Sci Pap Inst Chem Technol Prague Inorg Org Technol — Scientific Papers. Institute of Chemical Technology. Prague. Inorganic and Organic Technology

Sci Pap Inst Chem Technol (Prague) Inorg Technol — Scientific Papers. Institute of Chemical Technology. (Prague). Inorganic Technology

Sci Pap Inst Chem Technol Prague Technol Water — Scientific Papers. Institute of Chemical Technology. (Prague). Technology of Water

Sci Pap Inst Electr Mach Syst Wroclaw Tech Univ — Scientific Papers. Institute of Electric Machine Systems. Wroclaw Technical University

Sci Pap Inst Electr Power Eng Wroclaw Tech Univ — Scientific Papers. Institute of Electric Power Engineering. Wroclaw Technical University

Sci Pap Inst Org Phys Chem Wroclaw Tech Univ — Scientific Papers. Institute of Organic and Physical Chemistry. Wroclaw Technical University

Sci Pap Inst Phys and Chem Res — Scientific Papers. Institute of Physical and Chemical Research

Sci Pap Inst Phys Chem Res (Jpn) — Scientific Papers. Institute of Physical and Chemical Research (Japan)

Sci Pap Inst Phys Chem Res (Tokyo) — Scientific Papers. Institute of Physical and Chemical Research (Tokyo)

Sci Pap Jpn Antiq Art Crafts — Scientific Papers on Japanese Antiques and Art Crafts

Sci Pap Osaka Univ — Scientific Papers. Osaka University

Sci Pap Pasteur Inst Vet Res Biol Prod Bucharest — Scientific Papers. Pasteur Institute for Veterinary Research and Biological Products (Bucharest)

Sci Pap Prague Inst Chem Technol Anal Chem — Scientific Papers. Prague Institute of Chemical Technology. Analytical Chemistry

Sci Pap Prague Inst Chem Technol B Inorg Chem Technol — Scientific Papers. Prague Institute of Chemical Technology. B. Inorganic Chemistry and Technology

Sci Pap Prague Inst Chem Technol C Org Chem Technol — Scientific Papers. Prague Institute of Chemical Technology. C. Organic Chemistry and Technology

Sci Pap Prague Inst Chem Technol D Technol Fuel — Scientific Papers. Prague Institute of Chemical Technology. D. Technology of Fuel

Sci Pap Prague Inst Chem Technol E Food — Scientific Papers. Prague Institute of Chemical Technology. E. Food

Sci Pap Prague Inst Chem Technol F Technol Water Environ — Scientific Papers. Prague Institute of Chemical Technology. F. Technology of Water and Enviroment

Sci Pap Prague Inst Chem Technol G Mineral — Scientific Papers. Prague Institute of Chemical Technology. G. Mineralogy

Sci Pap Prague Inst Chem Technol J Econ Manage Chem Ind — Scientific Papers. Prague Institute of Chemical Technology. J. Economics and Management of the Chemical Industry

Sci Pap Prague Inst Chem Technol N Phys Chem — Scientific Papers. Prague Institute of Chemical Technology. N. Physical Chemistry

Sci Pap Prague Inst Chem Technol P Mater Sci Meas Tech — Scientific Papers. Prague Institute of Chemical Technology. P. Material Scienceand Measurement Technique

Sci Pap Prague Inst Chem Technol Sect Chem Eng — Scientific Papers. Prague Institute of Chemical Technology. Section: Chemical Engineering

Sci Pap Prague Inst Chem Technol S Polym Chem Prop Process — Scientific Papers. Prague Institute of Chemical Technology. S. Polymers-Chemistry, Properties, and Processing

Sci Pap Prague Inst Chem Technol T Educ Process — Scientific Papers. Prague Institute of Chemical Technology. T. Educational Process

Sci Pap Univ Chem Technol Pardubice — Scientific Papers. University of Chemical Technology. Pardubice

Sci Pap Univ Chem Technol Prague — Scientific Papers of the University of Chemical Technology Prague

Sci Peche — Science et Peche

Sci Peo — Science for People

Sci Peopl — Science for People

Sci Pest Contr — Scientific Pest Control

Sci Pest Control — Scientific Pest Control

Sci Pest Control (Kyoto) — Scientific Pest Control (Kyoto)

Sci Pharm — Scientia Pharmaceutica

Sci Pharm Biol Lorraine — Sciences Pharmaceutiques et Biologiques de Lorraine

Sci Pharm Proc Congr — Scientiae Pharmaceuticae. Proceedings. Congress of Pharmaceutical Sciences

Sci Photogr Proc Int Colloq — Scientific Photography. Proceedings. International Colloquium

Sci Phys Sci — Scientist of Physical Sciences

Sci Pict — Science Pictorial

SCIPIO — Sales Catalog Index Project Input Online

Sci Pract Clin Med — Science and Practice of Clinical Medicine

Sci Pract Surg — Science and Practice of Surgery

Sci Presentations Annu Meet Am Anim Hosp Assoc — Scientific Presentations. Annual Meeting. American Animal Hospital Association

Sci Press — Scientific Press

Sci Pro — Science Progress

Sci Pro — Scientific Progress

Sci Proc Cardiff Med Soc — Scientific Proceedings. Cardiff Medical Society

Sci Proc Dublin Soc — Scientific Proceedings. Royal Dublin Society

Sci Proc R Dublin Soc — Scientific Proceedings. Royal Dublin Society

Sci Proc R Dublin Soc A — Scientific Proceedings. Royal Dublin Society. Series A

Sci Proc R Dublin Soc New Ser — Scientific Proceedings. Royal Dublin Society. New Series

Sci Proc R Dublin Soc Ser A — Scientific Proceedings. Royal Dublin Society. Series A

Sci Proc R Dublin Soc Ser B — Scientific Proceedings. Royal Dublin Society. Series B

Sci Proc Roy Dublin Soc — Scientific Proceedings. Royal Dublin Society

Sci Proc Roy Dublin Soc Ser B — Scientific Proceedings. Royal Dublin Society. Series B

Sci Prog — Science Progress

Sci Prog Amoy China — Scientific Progress (Amoy, China)

Sci Prog Decouverte — Science Progres Decouverte

Sci Prog (Lond) — Science Progress (London)

Sci Prog (London) — Science Progress (London)

Sci Prog Nat — Science, Progres, la Nature

Sci Prog Nat (Paris) — Science, Progres, la Natur (Paris)

Sci Prog (New Haven) — Science in Progress (New Haven)

Sci Prog Northwood UK — Science Progress (Northwood, United Kingdom)

Sci Prog (Oxf) — Science Progress (Oxford)

Sci Progr — Science Progress

Sci Program — Scientific Programming

Sci Progr Decouverte — Science Progres Decouverte

Sci Psychoanal — Science and Psychoanalysis

Sci Pub Aff Rev — Science and Public Affairs Review

Sci Publ Af — Science and Public Affairs. Bulletin of the Atomic Scientists

Sci Publ For Timber Ind — Scientific Publications of Forestry and Timber Industry

Sci Publ Fuji Photo Film C — Scientific Publications. Fuji Photo Film Company Ltd.

Sci Publ Fuji Photo Film Co Ltd — Scientific Publications. Fuji Photo Film Company Limited

Sci Public Aff Bull At Sci — Science and Public Affairs. Bulletin of the Atomic Scientists

Sci Public Policy — Science and Public Policy

Sci Publ Pan Am Health Organ — Scientific Publication. Pan American Health Organization

Sci Publ Pol — Science and Public Policy

Sci Publ Res Inst Fed Sch Phys Educ Magglingen — Scientific Publication. Research Institute. Federal School of Physical Education. Magglingen

Sci Publ Res Inst Radiol Radiat Hyg — Scientific Publications. Research Institute of Radiology and Radiation Hygiene

Sci Publ Sci Mus Minn — Scientific Publications. Science Museum of Minnesota

Sci Publ Sci Mus (St Paul) — Scientific Publications. Science Museum of Minnesota (St. Paul)

Sci Publ Ser Tea Board India — Scientific Publications Series. Tea Board. India

Sci Publ Univ For Timber Ind — Scientific Publications. University of Forestry and Timber Industry

Sci Pub Pol — Science and Public Policy

Sci Q Natl Univ Peking — Science Quarterly. National University of Peking

Sci R — Science Review

SCIRA — Science Review

S Circular — South Circular

Sci Rec — Science Record

Sci Rec (Chin Ed) — Science Record (Chinese Edition)

Sci Rec Chungking — Science Record/Academia Sinica/K'o Hsueeh Chi Lu (Chungking)

Sci Rec Dunedin — Science Record. Otago University Science Students' Association (Dunedin)

Sci Rec Gorky State Univ — Scientific Records. Gorky State University

Sci Rech — Science et Recherche

Sci Rech Odontostomatol — Science et Recherche Odontostomatologiques

Sci Rec Leningrad Univ — Scientific Records. Leningrad University

Sci Rec (Peking) — Science Record (Peking)

Sci Rec Saratov Univ — Scientific Records. Saratov University

Sci Rec S M Kirov Kaz State Univ — Scientific Records. S. M. Kirov Kazakh State University

Sci Rep — Science Reporter

Sci Rep Agric Coll Norway — Scientific Reports. Agricultural College of Norway

Sci Rep Agric Col Norw — Scientific Reports. Agricultural College of Norway

Sci Rep Agric Exped Cambodia — Scientific Reports. Agricultural Expedition to Cambodia

Sci Rep Agruc Univ Norw — Scientific Reports. Agricultural University of Norway

Sci Rep Azabu Vet Coll — Science Reports. Azabu Veterinary College

Sci Rep Br Antarct Surv — Scientific Reports. British Antarctic Survey

Sci Rep Cent Res Inst Kasauli — Scientific Report. Central Research Institute. Kasauli

Sci Rep Coll Agric Life Sci Res Div Univ Wis — Science Report. College of Agricultural and Life Sciences Research Division. University of Wisconsin

Sci Rep College Gen Ed Osaka Univ — Science Reports. College of General Education. Osaka University

Sci Rep Coll Gen Educ Osaka Univ — Science Reports. College of General Education. Osaka University

Sci Rep Dep Geol Kyushu Univ — Science Reports. Department of Geology. Kyushu University

Sci Rep Ehime Agric Coll — Scientific Reports. Ehime Agricultural College

Sci Rep Ehime Prefect Pap Making Exp Stn — Scientific Report. Ehime Prefecture Paper Making Experiment Station

Sci Rep Fac Agr Ibaraki Univ — Scientific Report. Faculty of Agriculture. Ibaraki University

Sci Rep Fac Agric Ibaraki Univ — Science Reports. Faculty of Agriculture. Ibaraki University

Sci Rep Fac Agric Kobe Univ — Science Reports. Faculty of Agriculture. Kobe University

Sci Rep Fac Agric Meijo Univ — Scientific Reports. Faculty of Agriculture. Meijo University

Sci Rep Fac Agr Okayama Univ — Scientific Report. Faculty of Agriculture. Okayama University

Sci Rep Fac Arts Sci Fukushima Univ — Science Reports. Faculty of Arts and Science. Fukushima University

Sci Rep Fac Ed Gifu Univ Natur Sci — Science Reports. Faculty of Education. Gifu University. Natural Science

Sci Rep Fac Educ Fukushima Univ — Science Reports. Faculty of Education. Fukushima University

Sci Rep Fac Educ Gunma Univ — Science Reports. Faculty of Education. Gunma University

Sci Rep Fac Liberal Art Educ Gifu Univ Natur Sci — Science Report. Faculty of Liberal Arts and Education. Gifu University. NaturalScience

Sci Rep Fac Lit Sci Hirosaki Univ — Science Reports. Faculty of Literature and Science. Hirosaki University

Sci Rep Fac Lit Sci Toyama Univ — Science Reports. Faculty of Literature and Science. Toyama University

Sci Rep Fac Sci Ege Univ — Scientific Reports. Faculty of Science. Ege University

Sci Rep Fac Sci Kyushu Univ Geol — Science Reports. Faculty of Science. Kyushu University. Geology

Sci Rep Gov Inst Infect Dis Tokyo Imp Univ — Scientific Reports. Government Institute for Infectious Diseases. Tokyo Imperial Universtiy

Sci Rep Gunma Univ — Science Reports. Gunma Universtiy

Sci Rep Gunma Univ Nat Sci Ser — Science Report. Gunma University. Natural Science Series/Gunma Daigaku Kiyo. Shizen Kagaku Hen

Sci Rep Hirosaki Univ — Science Reports. Hirosaki University

Sci Rep Hokkaido Fish Exp Stn — Scientific Reports. Hokkaido Fisheries Experimental Station

Sci Rep Hokkaido Salmon Hatchery — Scientific Reports. Hokkaido Salmon Hatchery

Sci Rep Hoyo Univ Agr — Scientific Report. Hoyo University of Agriculture

Sci Rep Hyogo Univ Agr Fac Agr Kobe Univ — Science Reports. Hyogo University of Agriculture and Faculty of Agriculture. Kobe University

Sci Rep Hyogo Univ Agric — Science Reports. Hyogo University of Agriculture

Sci Rep Hyogo Univ Agric Fac Agric Kobe Univ — Science Reports. Hyogo University of Agriculture and Faculty of Agriculture. Kobe University

Sci Rep Hyogo Univ Agric Ser Agric — Science Reports. Hyogo University of Agriculture. Series Agriculture

Sci Rep Hyogo Univ Agric Ser Agric Chem — Science Reports. Hyogo University of Agriculture. Series Agricultural Chemistry

Sci Rep Hyogo Univ Agric Ser Agric Hortic — Science Reports. Hyogo University of Agriculture. Series Agriculture and Horticulture

Sci Rep Hyogo Univ Agric Ser Agric Technol — Science Reports. Hyogo University of Agriculture. Series Agriculture Technology

Sci Rep Hyogo Univ Agric Ser Nat Sci — Science Reports. Hyogo University of Agriculture. Series Natural Science

Sci Rep Hyogo Univ Agric Ser Plant Prot — Science Reports. Hyogo University of Agriculture. Series Plant Protection

Sci Rep Hyogo Univ Agric Ser Zootech Sci — Science Reports. Hyogo University of Agriculture. Series Zootechnical Science

Sci Rep (India) — Science Reporter (India)

Sci Rep Indian Agric Res Inst — Scientific Reports. Indian Agricultural Research Institute

Sci Rep Inst Atmos Environ Res Garmisch Partenkirchen Ger — Scientific Reports. Insitute for Atmospheric Environmental Research (Garmisch-Partenkirchen, Germany)

Sci Rep Int Cancer Res Found — Scientific Report. International Cancer Research Foundation

Sci Rep Inter-Union Comm Geodyn — Scientific Report. Inter-Union Commission on Geodynamics

Sci Rep Ist Super Sanita — Scientific Reports. Istituto Superiore di Sanita

Sci Rep Kagawa Prefect Fish Exp Stn — Scientific Reports. Kagawa Prefectural Fisheries Experimental Station

Sci Rep Kagoshima Univ — Science Reports. Kagoshima University

Sci Rep Kanazawa Univ — Science Reports. Kanazawa University

Sci Rep Kanazawa Univ Biol — Science Reports. Kanazawa University. Biology/Kanazawa Daigaku Rika Hokoku. Seibutsugaku

Sci Rep Kanazawa Univ Part II Biol Geol — Science Reports. Kanazawa University. Part II. Biology and Geology

Sci Rep Karzan State Univ — Scientific Reports. Kazan State Universtiy

Sci Rep Kyoto Prefect Univ Agric — Scientific Reports. Kyoto Prefectural University. Agriculture

Sci Rep Kyoto Prefect Univ Nat Sci Life Sci — Scientific Reports. Kyoto Prefectural University. Natural Science and Life Science

Sci Rep Kyoto Prefect Univ Nat Sci Living Sci Welfare Sci — Scientific Reports. Kyoto Prefectural University. Natural Science, Living Science, and Welfare Science

Sci Rep Kyoto Prefect Univ Natur Sci Living Sci — Kyoto Prefectural University. Scientific Reports. Natural Science and Living Science

Sci Rep Kyoto Pref Univ — Scientific Report. Kyoto Prefectural University

Sci Rep Kyoto Pref Univ Natur Sci Living Sci — Kyoto Prefectural University. Scientific Reports. Natural Science and Living Science

Sci Rep Lab Amphib Biol Hiroshima Univ — Scientific Report. Laboratory for Amphibian Biology. Hiroshima University

Sci Rep Lith Branch All Union Res Inst Butter Cheese Ind USS — Scientifical Reports. Lithuanian Branch of All-Union Research Institute of Butter and Cheese Industries. USSR

Sci Rep Matsuyama Agric Coll — Scientific Reports. Matsuyama Agricultural College

Sci Rep Meiji Seika Kaisha — Scientific Reports. Meiji Seika Kaisha

Sci Rep Miyagi Agr Coll — Scientific Report. Miyagi Agricultural College

Sci Rep Natl Taiwan Univ Acta Geol Taiwan — Science Reports. National Taiwan University. Acta Geologica Taiwanica

Sci Rep Natl Tsing Hua Univ Ser A — Science Reports. National Tsing Hua University. Series A. Mathematical, Physical, and Engineering Sciences

Sci Rep Natl Tsing Hua Univ Ser B Biol Sci — Science Reports of National Tsing Hua University. Series B. Biological and Psychological Sciences/Kuo Li Ch'ing-Hua Ta Hsueeh Li K'o Pao Kao

Sci Rep Natl Tsing Hua Univ Ser C — Science Reports. National Tsing Hua University. Series C. Geological, Geographical, and Meteorological Sciences

Sci Rep Natl Univ Peking — Science Reports. National University of Peking

Sci Rep Niigata Univ Ser A — Science Reports. Niigata University. Series A. Mathematics

Sci Rep Niigata Univ Ser B — Science Reports. Niigata University. Series B. Physics

Sci Rep Niigata Univ Ser C — Science Reports. Niigata University. Series C. Chemistry

Sci Rep Niigata Univ Ser D Biol — Science Reports. Niigata University. Series D. Biology

Sci Rep Niigata Univ Ser E — Science Reports. Niigata University. Series E. Geology and Mineralogy

Sci Rep Niigata Univ Ser F Geol Mineral — Science Reports. Niigata University. Series F. Geology and Mineralogy

Sci Rep Osaka Univ — Science Reports. Osaka University

Sci Rep Res Inst Engrg Kanagawa Univ — Science Reports. Kanagawa University. Research Institute for Engineering

Sci Rep Res Inst Theor Phys Hiroshima Univ — Scientific Reports. Research Institute for Theoretical Physics. Hiroshima University

Sci Rep Res Inst Tohoku Univ — Science Reports. Research Institutes. Tohoku University

Sci Rep Res Inst Tohoku Univ A — Science Reports. Research Institutes. Tohoku University. Series A. Physics, Chemistry, and Metallurgy

Sci Rep Res Inst Tohoku Univ Med — Science Reports. Research Institutes. Tohoku University. Series C. Medicine

Sci Rep Res Inst Tohoku Univ Ser A — Science Reports. Research Institutes. Tohoku University. Series A. Physics, Chemistry, and Metallurgy

Sci Rep Res Inst Tohoku Univ Ser B — Science Reports. Research Institutes. Tohoku University. Series B. Technology

Sci Rep Res Inst Tohoku Univ Ser B Rep Inst High Speed Mech — Science Reports. Research Institutes. Tohoku University. Series B. Technology. Reports. Institute of High Speed Mechanics

Sci Rep Res Inst Tohoku Univ Ser C — Science Reports. Research Institutes. Tohoku University. Series C. Medicine

Sci Rep Res Inst Tohoku Univ Ser C Med — Science Reports. Research Institutes. Tohoku University. Series C. Medicine

Sci Rep Res Inst Tohoku Univ Ser D — Science Reports. Research Institutes. Tohoku University. Series D

Sci Rep Res Inst Tohoku Univ Ser D Agric — Science Reports. Research Institutes. Tohoku University. Series D. Agriculture

Sci Rep Saikyo Univ Agric — Scientific Reports. Saikyo University. Agriculture

Sci Rep Saitama Univ Ser A — Science Reports. Saitama University. Series A. Mathematics, Physics, and Chemistry

Sci Rep Saitama Univ Ser B — Scientific Reports. Saitama University. Series B

Sci Rep Saitama Univ Ser B Biol Earth Sci — Science Reports. Saitama University. Series B. Biology and Earth Sciences

Sci Rep S Coll N Coll Osaka Univ — Science Reports of South College and North College of Osaka University/Osaka Daigaku Nanko, Hokko Rika Hokoku

Sci Rep Shiga Agric Coll — Scientific Reports. Shiga Agricultural College

Sci Rep Shiga Agric Exp Sta — Scientific Reports of Shiga Agricultural Experiment Station/Shiga-Ken Nogyo Shikenjo Kenkyu Hokoku

Sci Rep Shiga Agric Exp Stn — Scientific Reports. Shiga Agricultural Experiment Station

Sci Rep Shiga Pref Jr Coll — Scientific Report. Shiga Prefectural Junior College

Sci Rep Shimabara Volcano Obs Fac Sci Kyushu Univ — Science Reports. Shimabara Volcano Observatory. Faculty of Science. Kyushu University

Sci Rep Shima Marinel — Science Report. Shima Marineland

Sci Rep Soc Res Phys Chem — Science Reports. Society for the Research of Physics Chemistry

Sci Rep Soc Res Theor Chem — Science Reports. Society for the Research of Theoretical Chemistry

Sci Rep Tohoku Imp Univ Ser 1 — Science Reports. Tohoku Imperial University. Series 1. Mathematics, Physics, Chemistry

Sci Rep Tohoku Imp Univ Ser 3 — Science Reports. Tohoku Imperial University. Series 3. Mineralogy, Petrology, Economic Geology

Sci Rep Tohoku Imp Univ Ser 4 — Science Reports. Tohoku Imperial University. Series 4. Biology

Sci Rep Tohoku Univ — Science Reports. Tohoku University

Sci Rep Tohoku Univ 8th Series — Science Reports. Tohoku University. Eighth Series

Sci Rep Tohoku Univ A — Science Reports. Tohoku University. Series A

Sci Rep Tohoku Univ Eighth Ser Phys and Astron — Science Reports. Tohoku University. Eighth Series. Physics and Astronomy

Sci Rep Tohoku Univ Fifth Ser — Science Reports. Tohoku University. Fifth Series

Sci Rep Tohoku Univ Fifth Ser Geophys — Science Reports. Tohoku University. Fifth Series. Geophysics

Sci Rep Tohoku Univ First Ser — Science Reports. Tohoku University. First Series

Sci Rep Tohoku Univ Fourth Ser (Biol) — Science Reports. Tohoku University. Fourth Series. Biology

Sci Rep Tohoku Univ I — Science Reports. Tohoku University. First Series

Sci Rep Tohoku Univ Second Ser (Geol) — Science Reports. Tohoku University. Second Series. Geology

Sci Rep Tohoku Univ Ser 2 — Science Reports. Tohoku University. Series 2. Geology

Sci Rep Tohoku Univ Ser 5 — Science Reports. Tohoku University. Fifth Series. Geophysics

Sci Rep Tohoku Univ Ser 8 — Science Reports. Tohoku University. Series 8. Physics and Astronomy

Sci Rep Tohoku Univ Ser IV — Scientific Report. Tohoku University. Series IV. Biology

Sci Rep Tohoku Univ Seventh Ser — Science Reports. Tohoku University. Seventh Series

Sci Rep Tohoku Univ Third Ser — Science Reports. Tohoku University. Third Series. Mineralogy, Petrology, and Economic Geology

Sci Rep Toho Rayon Co Ltd — Scientific Reports. Toho Rayon Company, Limited

Sci Rep Tokyo Bunrika Daigaku Sect A — Science Reports. Tokyo Bunrika Daigaku. Section A. Mathematics, Physics, Chemistry

Sci Rep Tokyo Bunrika Daigaku Sect B — Science Reports. Tokyo Bunrika Daigaku. Section B

Sci Rep Tokyo Bunrika Daigaku Sect C — Science Reports. Tokyo Bunrika Daigaku. Section C

Sci Rep Tokyo Kyoiku Daigaku Sect A — Science Reports. Tokyo Kyoiku Daigaku. Section A

Sci Rep Tokyo Kyoiku Daigaku Sect B — Science Reports. Tokyo Kyoiku Daigaku. Section B

Sci Rep Tokyo Kyoiku Daigaku Sect C — Science Reports. Tokyo Kyoiku Daigaku. Section C

Sci Rep Tokyo Univ Educ Sect A — Science Reports. Tokyo University of Education. Section A

Sci Rep Tokyo Univ Educ Sect B — Science Reports. Tokyo University of Education. Section B

Sci Rep Tokyo Univ Educ Sect C — Science Reports. Tokyo University of Education. Section C

Sci Rep Tokyo Univ Let Sci Sect A — Science Reports. Tokyo University of Literature and Science. Section A. Mathematics, Physics, Chemistry

Sci Rep Tokyo Univ Let Sci Sect C — Science Reports. Tokyo University of Literature and Science. Section C. Geology

Sci Rep Tokyo Woman's Christian College — Science Reports. Tokyo Woman's Christian College

Sci Rep Tokyo Woman's Christian Univ — Tokyo Woman's Christian University. Science Reports

Sci Rep Toyo Rayon Co — Scientific Reports. Toyo Rayon Co., Ltd.

Sci Rep Toyo Soda Manuf Co Ltd — Scientific Reports. Toyo Soda Manufacturing Company, Limited

Sci Rep Univ Agric Sci Godollo Hung — Scientific Reports. University of Agricultural Sciences. Godollo, Hungary

Sci Rep Univ Chekiang — Science Reports. University of Chekiang

Sci Rep Whales Res Inst (Tokyo) — Scientific Reports. Whales Research Institute (Tokyo)

Sci Rep Yamaguchi Univ — Science Reports. Yamaguchi University

Sci Rep Yerevan Phys Inst — Scientific Report. Yerevan Physics Institute

Sci Rep Yokohama Natl Univ I — Science Reports. Yokohama National University. Section I. Mathematics, Physics,and Chemistry

Sci Rep Yokohama Natl Univ Sect I — Science Reports. Yokohama National University. Section I. Mathematics, Physics,and Chemistry

Sci Rep Yokohama Natl Univ Sect II Biol Geol — Science Reports. Yokohama National University. Section II. Biology and Geology

Sci Rep Yokohama Natl Univ Sect II Biol Geol Sci — Science Reports. Yokohama National University. Section II. Biological and Geological Sciences

Sci Rep Yokohama Nat Univ Sect 2 — Science Reports. Yokohama National University. Section 2. Biological and Geological Sciences

Sci Rep Yokohama Nat Univ Sect I — Science Reports. Yokohama National University. Section I. Mathematics and Physics

Sci Rep Yokohama Nat Univ Sect I Math Phys Chem — Science Reports of the Yokohama National University. Section I. Mathematics, Physics, Chemistry

Sci Rep Yokosuka City Mus — Science Report. Yokosuka City Museum

Sci Rep Yokosuka City Mus Nat Sci — Science Report. Yokosuka City Museum. Natural Sciences

Sci Rep Yokosuka Cy Mus — Science Report. Yokosuka City Museum

Sci Res — Scientific Researches

Sci Res Abstr — Science Research Abstracts

Sci Res Abstr A — Science Research Abstracts. Part A. Superconductivity,Magnetohydrodynamics, and Plasmas. Theoretical Physics

Sci Res Abstr J — Science Research Abstracts Journal

Sci Res Abstr J B — Science Research Abstracts Journal. Part B. Laser and Electro-OpticReviews, Quantum Electronics, and Unconventional Energy Sources

Sci Res Abstr J Part A — Science Research Abstracts Journal. Part A. Super Conductivity, Magnetohydrodynamics and Plasmas, Theoretical Physics

Sci Res Abstr J Part B — Science Research Abstracts Journal. Part B. Laser and Electro-Optic Reviews, Quantam Electronics, and Unconventional Energy

Sci Res Br Univ Coll — Scientific Research in British Universities and Colleges

Sci Res Counc Jam J — Scientific Research Council of Jamaica. Journal

Sci Res (Dacca) — Scientific Research (Dacca)

Sci Res (Dacca, Bangladesh) — Scientific Researches (Dacca, Bangladesh)

Sci Res Natl Sci Ed — Scientific Research. Natural Science Edition

Sci Res News — Science Research News

Sci Res News (Kanpur) — Science Research News (Kanpur)

Sci Res (NY) — Scientific Research (New York)

Sci Resour Lett — Science Resource Letter

Sci Rev — Scienca Revuo

Sci Rev — Science Review

Sci Rev — Scientific Review

Sci Rev (Belgrade) — Scienca Revuo (Belgrade)

Sci Rev Calcutta — Science Review (Calcutta)

Sci Rev Civ Eng — Scientific Review of Civil Engineering

Sci Rev Civilis Sci — Sciences. Revue de la Civilisation Scientifique

Sci Rev Fr Sci Tech — Sciences. Revue Francaise des Sciences et des Techniques

Sci Rev Int Sci Asoc Esperantista — Scienca Revuo. Internacia Scienca Asocio Esperantista

Sci Rev (Manila) — Science Review (Manila)

Sci Rev (Neth) — Scienca Revuo (Netherlands)

Sci Roll Mag Syst Notes — Scientific Roll and Magazine of Systematized Notes

Sci Roll Mag Syst Notes Bot Sect Bact — Scientific Roll and Magazine of Systematized Notes. Botanical Section. Bacteria

Sci Rondo — Scienca Rondo

Sci R Toh A — Science Reports. Research Institutes. Tohoku University. Series A. Physics, Chemistry, and Metallurgy

SCIS — Social Change in Sweden

Sci S Afr — Scientific South Africa

Sci Sect Can Pharm J — Scientific Section. Canadian Pharmaceutical Journal

Sci Ser Inland Waters Branch Can — Scientific Series. Inland Waters Branch. Canada

Sci Ser Inland Waters Dir (Can) — Scientific Series. Inland Waters Directorate (Canada)

Sci Ser Inland Waters Lands Dir (Can) — Scientific Series. Inland Waters/Lands Directorate (Canada)

Sci Serves Farm — Science Serves Your Farm

Sci Silvae — Scientia Silvae

Sci Silvae (Beijing) — Scientia Silvae (Beijing)

Sci Silvae Sin — Scientia Silvae Sinica

Sci Sin — Scientia Sinica

Sci Sin B — Scientia Sinica. Series B. Chemical, Biological, Agricultural, Medical, and Earth Sciences

Sci Sin Chin Ed — Scientia Sinica (Chinese Edition)

Sci Sin Engl Ed — Scientia Sinica (English Edition)

Sci Sinica — Scientia Sinica

Sci Sinica Ser A — Scientia Sinica. Series A. Mathematical, Physical, Astronomical, and Technical Sciences

Sci Sinica Ser B — Scientia Sinica. Series B. Chemical, Biological, Agricultural, Medical, and Earth Sciences

Sci Sinica Suppl — Scientia Sinica. Supplement

Sci Sin Ser A (Engl Ed) — Scientia Sinica. Series A. Mathematical, Physical, Astronomical, andTechnical Sciences (English Edition)

Sci Sin Ser B Chem Biol Agric Med & Earth Sci — Scientia Sinica. Series B. Chemical, Biological, Agricultural, Medical, and Earth Sciences

Sci Sin Ser B (Engl Ed) — Scientia Sinica. Series B. Chemical, Biological, Agricultural, Medical,and Earth Sciences (English Edition)

Sci Sinter — Science of Sintering

Sci Sintering — Science of Sintering

Sci Sintering Proc Round Table Conf Sintering — Science of Sintering. New Directions for Materials Processing and Microstructural Control. Proceedings. Round Table Conference on Sintering

Sci Soc — Science and Society

Sci Soc — Sciences Sociales

Sci Sociale — Science Sociale

Sci Soc Moscou — Sciences Sociales. Academie des Sciences de L'URSS (Moscou)

Sci Soc Thailand J — Science Society of Thailand. Journal

Sci Soft X Rays — Science with Soft X-Rays

Sci Sol — Science du Sol

Sci Spectra — Science Spectra

Sci Sports — Science and Sports

SCI/SR — Shakaichosa-Kenkyusho Consumer Index Summary Report

Sci STKE — Science's STKE (Signal Transduction Knowledge Environment)

Sci Stud — Science Studies

Sci Stud London — Science Studies (London)

Sci Stud St Bonaventure Univ — Science Studies. St. Bonaventure University

SCIT — Science Teacher

Sci Teach — Science Teacher

Sci Teach (New Delhi) — Science Teacher (New Delhi)

Sci Teach News — Science Teachers News

Sci Tec — Scienza e Tecnica

Sci Tech — Science and Australian Technology

Sci Tech — Science and Technology

Sci Tech Aerosp Rep — Scientific and Technical Aerospace Reports

Sci Tech Armement — Sciences et Techniques de l'Armement

Sci Tech Armement Meml Artillerie Fr — Sciences et Techniques de l'Armement. Memorial de l'Artillerie Francaise

Sci Tech Caoutch — Science et Technique du Caoutchouc

Sci Tech Commun Int Congr Glass — Scientific and Technical Communications. International Congress on Glass

Sci Tech Conf Electrost Ind ELSTAT 80 — Scientific-Technical Conference Electrostatics in Industry. ELSTAT-80

Sci Tech Conf Glass Fine Ceram — Scientific-Technical Conference Glass and Fine Ceramics

Sci Tech Eau — Sciences et Techniques de l'Eau

Sci Tech Froid — Science et Technique du Froid

Sci Tech Human Values — Science, Technology, and Human Values

Sci Tech Inf CRIAC — Sciences, Techniques, Informations CRIAC

Sci Tech Inf Process — Scientific and Technical Information Processing

Sci Tech Inf Process (Engl Transl) — Scientific and Technical Information Processing (English Translation)

Sci Tech Inf Process (Eng Transl Nauchno-Tekh Inf Ser I) — Scientific and Technical Information Processing (English Translation of Nauchno-Tekhnicheskaya Informatsiya Seriya I)

Sci Techn Aerospace Rep — Scientific and Technical Aerospace Reports

Sci Tech News — Science and Technology News

Sci Technol — Science and Technology

Sci Technol — Sciences and Technologies. Korea University

Sci Technol Aliment — Science et Technologie Alimentaire

Sci Technol Aliment London — Science and Technologie Alimentaire (London)

Sci Technol China — Science and Technology in China

Sci Technol Dim — Science and Technology Dimensions

Sci Technol Eng Sian China — Science and Technology. Engineering (Sian, China)

Sci Technol Environ Prot — Science and Technology of Environmental Protection

Sci Technol Humanities — Science/Technology and the Humanities

Sci Technol Hum Val — Science, Technology, and Human Values

Sci Technol Japan — Science and Technology in Japan

Sci Technol Jpn — Science and Technology of Japan

Sci Technol Korea Univ — Sciences and Technologies. Korea University

Sci Technol Libr — Science and Technology Libraries

Sci Technol Med — Science and Technology. Medicine

Sci Technol Membr Sep — Science and Technology of Membrane Separation

Sci Technol Nanostruct Magn Mater — Science and Technology of Nanostructured Magnetic Materials

Sci Technol (NY) — Science and Technology (New York)

Sci Technol Phys Sci Sian China — Science and Technology. Physical Sciences (Sian, China)

Sci Technol Quart — Science and Technology Quarterly

Sci Technol Rev — Science and Technology Review

Sci Technol Rev Agron Anim Sci Ser — Science and Technology Review. Agronomic and Animal Sciences Series

Sci Technol (San Diego) — Science and Technology (San Diego)

Sci Technol (Seoul) — Science and Technologies (Seoul)

Sci Technol Ser — Science Technology Series

Sci Technol (Surrey Hills Aust) — Science and Technology (Surrey Hills, Australia)

Sci Technol Thin Film Supercond 2 Proc Conf — Science and Technology of Thin Film Superconductors 2. Proceedings. Conference on the Science and Technology of Thin Film Superconductors

Sci Technol Weld Joining — Science and Technology of Welding and Joining

Sci Technol Zirconia — Science and Technology of Zirconia

Sci Tech (Paris) — Sciences et Techniques (Paris)

Sci Tech Persp — Sciences et Techniques en Perspective

Sci Tech Perspect — Sciences et Techniques en Perspective

Sci Tech Pharm — Sciences et Techniques Pharmaceutiques

Sci Tech Prat Pharm — Sciences Techniques et Pratiques Pharmaceutiques

Sci Tech Prat Pharm STP Pharma — Sciences Techniques et Pratiques Pharmaceutiques. S.T.P. Pharma

Sci Tech Rep Min Coll Akita Univ — Scientific and Technical Reports. Mining College. Akita University

Sci Tech Rep Soap Deterg Assoc — Scientific and Technical Report. Soap and Detergent Association

Sci Tech Surv Br Food Manuf Ind Res Assoc — Scientific and Technical Surveys. British Food Manufacturing Industries Research Association

Sci Tec Latt-Casearia — Scienza e Tecnica Lattiero-Casearia

Sci Tecnol Alimenti — Scienza e Tecnologia degli Alimenti

Sci Terre — Sciences de la Terre

Sci Terre Inf Geol — Sciences de la Terre. Informatique Geologique

Sci Terre Mem — Sciences de la Terre. Memoires

Sci Today (Bombay) — Science Today (Bombay)

Sci Tools — Science Tools

Sci Total Environ — Science of the Total Environment

Sci Tree Top — Scientific Tree Topics

Sci USSR — Science in USSR

SCIV — Studii si Cercetari de Istorie Veche [Later, Studii si Cercetari de Istorie Veche si Arheologie]

SCIVA — Studii si Cercetari de Istorie Veche si Arheologie

Sci Vet Med Comp — Sciences Veterinaires Medecine Comparee
Sci Vie — Science et Vie
Sci Works Agric Acad Sofia Ser Plant Grow — Scientific Works. Agricultural Academy. Sofia. Series. Plant Growing
Sci Works Agric Coll Bucharest Ser A — Scientific Works. Agricultural College Nicolae Balcescu. Bucharest. Bucharest. Seria A. Agronomy
Sci Works Agron Inst Nicolae Balcescu Bucharest Ser C — Scientific Works. Agronomic Institute Nicolae Balcescu. Bucharest. Series C. Zootechny and Veterinary Science
Sci Works Cancer Res Inst Sofia — Scientific Works. Cancer Research Institute (Sofia)
Sci Works Cann Res Inst Plovdiv — Scientific Works. Canning Research Institute (Plovdiv)
Sci Works For Res Inst (Zvolen) — Scientific Works. Forest Research Institute (Zvolen)
Sci Works Higher Inst Agric Sofia Agric Fac Ser Plant Grow — Scientific Works. Higher Institute of Agriculture. Sofia. Agricultural Faculty.Series. Plant Growing
Sci Works Higher Inst Agric Zootech Fac — Scientific Works. Higher Institute of Agriculture G. Dimitrov. Zootechnical Faculty
Sci Works Higher Inst Vet Med Sofia — Scientific Works. Higher Institute of Veterinary Medicine (Sofia)
Sci Works Higher Inst Zootech Vet Med Vet Med Stara Zagora — Scientific Works. Higher Institute of Zootechnics and Veterinary Medicine. Faculty of Veterinary Medicine. Stara Zagora
Sci Works Higher Med Inst Pleven — Scientific Works. Higher Medical Institute. Pleven
Sci Works High Med Inst Pleven — Scientific Works. Higher Medical Institute of Pleven
Sci Works Med Univ Pleven — Scientific Works of the Medical University of Pleven
Sci Works Postgrad Med Inst (Sofia) — Scientific Works. Postgraduate Medical Institute (Sofia)
Sci Works Poult Sci Poult Res Inst — Scientific Works. Poultry Science. Poultry Research Institute
Sci Works Res Inst Anim Prod Nitra — Scientific Works. Research Institute of Animal Production at Nitra
Sci Works Res Inst Epidemiol Microbiol (Sofia) — Scientific Works. Research Institute of Epidemiology and Microbiology (Sofia)
Sci Works Res Inst Plant Prod Piestany — Scientific Works. Research Institute of Plant Production at Piestany
Sci World — Scholastic Science World
Sci World — Scientific World
Sci World Chunking Nanking — Scientific World. Natural Science Society of China/K'o Hsueeh Shih Chieh. ChungHua Tsu Jao K'o Hsueeh She (Chungking and Nanking)
Sci Yearb Vet Fac (Thessalonica) — Scientific Yearbook. Veterinary Faculty (Thessalonica)
SC J — Nebraska Supreme Court Journal
ScJ — Scottish Journal of Political Economy
Sc J — Scripta Judaica
SCJ — Siberian Chemistry Journal
SCJ — Sixteenth Century Journal
SCJ — Southern Communication Journal
SC J — Supreme Court Journal
SCJ — Sydney Cinema Journal
S C Jap — Studia Celtica Japonica
Sc J Cl Inv — Scandinavian Journal of Clinical and Laboratory Investigation
Sc J Dent R — Scandinavian Journal of Dental Research
Sc J Gastr — Scandinavian Journal of Gastroenterology
Sc J Haemat — Scandinavian Journal of Haematology
Sc J Hist — Scandinavian Journal of History
Sc J Immun — Scandinavian Journal of Immunology
Sc J In Dis — Scandinavian Journal of Infectious Diseases
Sc J Plast — Scandinavian Journal of Plastic and Reconstructive Surgery
Sc J Psycho — Scandinavian Journal of Psychology
Sc J Re Med — Scandinavian Journal of Rehabilitation Medicine
Sc J Resp D — Scandinavian Journal of Respiratory Diseases
Sc J Rheum — Scandinavian Journal of Rheumatology
Sc J S Med — Scandinavian Journal of Social Medicine
ScJTh — Scottish Journal of Theology
Sc J Thor C — Scandinavian Journal of Thoracic and Cardiovascular Surgery
SCJUA — Science Journal Incorporating Discovery
Sc J Urol N — Scandinavian Journal of Urology and Nephrology
SCK — Smithsonian Contributions to Knowledge
SCL — Santa Clara Lawyer
SCL — Sather Classical Lectures
SCL — Southern California Law Review
SCL — Stendhal Club
SCL — Studies in Canadian Literature
SCL — Studii si Cercetari Lingvistice
Scl & Lbr Bul — Social and Labour Bulletin
SClas — Studii Clasice
SCLE — Society and Leisure
SC Libn — South Carolina Librarian
SCLing — Siouan and Caddoan Linguistics
S Clin North America — Surgical Clinics of North America
Sc LJ — Scottish Law Journal and Sheriff Court Record
Sc L J — Scottish Literary Journal
SCLJ — South Carolina Law Journal
SC LM — Scottish Law Magazine and Sheriff Court Reporter
Scl Problems — Social Problems
SC L Q — South Carolina Law Quarterly
SCLR — Santa Clara Law Review
Sc LR — Scottish Law Review and Sheriff Court Reports
SC LR — South Carolina Law Review
SCLRA — School Review

SC L Rev — South Carolina Law Review
SCLSA — Scandinavian Journal of Clinical and Laboratory Investigation. Supplement
Scl Sci Q — Social Science Quarterly
Scl Sec Bul — Social Security Bulletin
Sc LT — Scots Law Times
SCM — School Musician. Director and Teacher
ScM — Scripta Mathematica
SCM — Sussex County Magazine
SCMAA — Studii si Cercetari de Mecanica Aplicata
SC Mar Resour Cent Tech Rep — South Carolina. Marine Resources Center. Technical Report
SCMB — Seaby's Coin and Medal Bulletin
Sc Mcr S P & T — Proceedings and Transactions of the Scottish Microscopical Society
Sc Met S J — Journal of the Scottish Meteorological Society
SCMM — Selections from China Mainland Magazines
SCMP — South China Morning Post
SCMPBN — South China Morning Post (Business News)
SCMQ — Swarthmore College Monographs on Quaker History
SCN — Seventeenth-Century News
SCN — Studii si Cercetari de Numismatica
SCNCA — Sciences
SCNEB — Science News
SCNL — Seventeenth-Century News Letter
SC Num — Studii si Cercetari de Numismatica
SC Nurs — South Carolina Nursing
SCO — Studi Classici e Orientali
ScoGaelS — Scottish Gaelic Studies
ScoGS — Scottish Gaelic Studies
SCOLAG Bull — Scottish Legal Action Group. Bulletin
Scone & Upper Hunter Hist Soc J — Scone and Upper Hunter Historical Society. Journal
S Cont — Suisse Contemporaine
ScoS — Scottish Studies
SCOSA — Sadtler Commercial Spectra
Scot A & Lett — Scottish Art and Letters
Scot A Forum — Scottish Archaeological Forum
Scot Agr — Scottish Agriculture
Scot AL — Scottish Art and Letters
Scot Antiqua — Scottish Antiquary
Scot Archaeol Forum — Scottish Archaeological Forum
Scot A Rev — Scottish Art Review
Scot Art R — Scottish Art Review
Scot Art Rev — Scottish Art Review
Scot Edu St — Scottish Educational Studies
Scot Geog M — Scottish Geographical Magazine
Scot Geogr Mag — Scottish Geographical Magazine
Scot Geogr Mg — Scottish Geographical Magazine
Scot Georg Soc Bull — Scottish Georgian Society Bulletin
Scot GM — Scottish Geographical Magazine
Scot His R — Scottish Historical Review
Scot Hist R — Scottish Historical Review
Scot Hist Rev — Scottish Historical Review
Scot Hist Riv — Scottish Historical Review
Scotl — Scottish International
Scot J Geol — Scottish Journal of Geology
Scot J PE — Scottish Journal of Physical Education
Scot J Pol Econ — Scottish Journal of Political Economy
Scot J Poli — Scottish Journal of Political Economy
Scot J Rel — Scottish Journal of Religious Studies
Scot J Rel St — Scottish Journal of Religious Studies
ScotJt — Scottish Journal of Theology
Scot J Th — Scottish Journal of Theology
Scot J Theo — Scottish Journal of Theology
ScotL — Scottish Language
Scot Law J — Scottish Law Journal
Scotl Dep Agric Fish Mar Res — Scotland Department of Agriculture and Fisheries. Marine Research
Scotl Dep Agric Fish Tech Bull — Scotland Department of Agriculture and Fisheries. Technical Bulletin
Scot Lit J — Scottish Literary Journal
Scot LJ — Scottish Law Journal and Sheriff Court Record
Scot LM — Scottish Law Magazine and Sheriff Court Reporter
Scot L Mag — Scottish Law Magazine
Scot Local Hist — Scottish Local History
Scot L R — Scottish Law Review
Scot L Rev — Scottish Law Review
Scot LT — Scots Law Times
Scot Med J — Scottish Medical Journal
ScotP — Scottish Periodical
Scot Pott Hist Rev — Scottish Pottery Historical Review
Scot Pott Stud — Scottish Pottery Studies
Scot R — Scottish Review
Scot Rev — Scottish Review
Scots L T — Scots Law Times
Scots LTR — Scots Law Times Reports
Scots Mag — Scots Magazine
Scotsman Mag — Scotsman Magazine
Scots Philos Monograph Ser — Scots Philosophical Monograph Series
Scot Stud — Scottish Studies
Scott Agric — Scottish Agriculture
Scott Art Rev — Scottish Art Review
Scott Australas — Scottish Australasian
Scott Bankers Mag — Scottish Bankers Magazine

Scott Bee J — Scottish Bee Journal
Scott Beekeep — Scottish Beekeeper
Scott Beekpr — Scottish Beekeeper
Scott Birds — Scottish Birds
Scott Birds J Scott Ornithol Club — Scottish Birds. Journal. Scottish Ornithologists' Club
Scott Bot Rev — Scottish Botanical Review
Scott Econ Bull — Scottish Economic Bulletin
Scott Econ Soc Hist — Scottish Economic and Social History
Scott Educ Rev — Scottish Educational Review
Scott Elect Engr — Scottish Electrical Engineer
Scott Field — Scottish Field
Scott Fish Bull — Scottish Fisheries Bulletin
Scott Fish Res Rep — Scottish Fisheries Research Report
Scott Fmr — Scottish Farmer and Farming World
Scott For — Scottish Forestry
Scott For J — Scottish Forestry Journal
Scott Genealog — Scottish Genealogist
Scott Geog Mag — Scottish Geographical Magazine. Royal Scottish Geographical Society
Scott Geogr Mag — Scottish Geographical Magazine
Scott Hist Rev — Scottish Historical Review
Scott Hortic Res Inst Annu Rep — Scottish Horticultural Research Institute. Annual Report
Scott Ind Hist — Scottish Industrial History
Scottish Art R — Scottish Art Review
Scottish Bankers M — Scottish Bankers Magazine
Scottish Econ Bul — Scottish Economic Bulletin
Scottish Ednl J — Scottish Educational Journal
Scottish Ednl Studies — Scottish Educational Studies
Scottish Geog Mag — Scottish Geographical Magazine
Scottish Geogr Mag — Scottish Geographical Magazine
Scottish Georgian Soc Bull — Scottish Georgian Society. Bulletin
Scottish J Pol Economy — Scottish Journal of Political Economy
Scottish Mus — Scottish Music and Drama
Scott J Adult Educ — Scottish Journal of Adult Education
Scott J Agric — Scottish Journal of Agriculture
Scott J Geol — Scottish Journal of Geology
Scott J Polit Econ — Scottish Journal of Political Economy
Scott J Theology — Scottish Journal of Theology
Scott Jur — Scottish Jurist
Scott Labour Hist Soc J — Scottish Labour History Society Journal
Scott Lang — Scottish Language
Scott Life-Boat — Scottish Life-Boat
Scott Lit J — Scottish Literary Journal
Scott Mar Biol Assoc Annu Rep — Scottish Marine Biological Association. Annual Report
Scott Marxist — Scottish Marxist
Scott Med — Scottish Medicine
Scott Med J — Scottish Medical Journal
Scott Med Surg J — Scottish Medical and Surgical Journal
Scott Mountaineering Club J — Scottish Mountaineering Club Journal
Scott Nat — Scottish Naturalist
Scott Naturalist Perth — Scottish Naturalist (Perth)
Scott Opera N — Scottish Opera News
Scott R — Scottish Review
Scott Rep — Scott Report
Scott Rev — Scottish Review
Scott S — Scottish Studies
Scott Stud — Scottish Studies
Scotts Turfgrass Res Conf Proc — Scotts Turfgrass Research Conference. Proceedings
Scott Trade Union Rev — Scottish Trade Union Review
Scott Tradit — Scottish Tradition
Scott Univ Summer Sch — Scottish Universities Summer School
Scott Univ Summer Sch Phys Proc — Scottish Universities Summer School in Physics. Proceedings
Scott Wildl — Scottish Wildlife
Scouting in NSW — Scouting in New South Wales
SCP — Scoops
SCP — Segundo Congresso Pedagogico
SCP — Studies in Classical Philology
Sc Paed — Scientia Paedagogica
Sc Parliament — Science in Parliament
SCPGB — Revista. Sociedad Cientifica del Paraguay
SCPH — San Carlos Publications. Humanities
SCPR — San Carlos Publications. Religion
SCPRA — Science Progress
SCPYB — Social Policy
SCR — Canada. Supreme Court Reports
Sc R — Science Religieuse
Scr — Scrinium
Scr — Scriptorium
SCR — Scrutiny
SCR — South Carolina Review
SCR — Soviet Cybernetics Review
SCR — Standard Chartered Review
SCR — Stanford Campus Report
SCR — Stock Car Racing
S Cr — Strumenti Critici
SCR — Studies in Comparative Religion
SCR — Supreme Court Reports
SCRAM Energy Bull — SCRAM [Scottish Campaign to Resist the Atomic Menace] Energy Bulletin
Scr & Civilta — Scrittura e Civilta

SCraneN — Stephen Crane Newsletter
Scr B — Scripture Bulletin
Scr Bull — Scripture Bulletin
Scr Byz — Scriptores Byzantini
Scr Demolinguist — Scritti Demolinguistici
SCRE — Scandinavian Review
SCREB — Scientific Research
Screen Ed — Screen Education
Screen Ed Notes — Screen Education Notes
SC Reg — South Carolina State Register
SC Research Plan Devel Board Bull — South Carolina Research Planning and Development Board. Bulletin
SC Resour Cent Tech Rep — South Carolina. Marine Resources Center. Technical Report
Scr Ethnol Suppl — Scripta Ethnologica. Supplementa
Scr Fac Sci Nat Univ Purkynianae Bru Biol — Scripta Facultatis Scientiarum Naturalium Universita J. E. Purkyne Brunensis. Biiologia
Scr Fac Sci Nat Univ Purkynianae Brun — Scripta Facultatis Scientiarum Naturalium Universitatis Purkynianae Brunensis
Scr Fac Sci Nat Univ Purkynianae Brunensis Geol — Scripta Facultatis Scientiarum Naturalium Universitatis Purkynianae Brunensis. Geologia
Scr Fac Sci Nat Univ Purkynianae Brunensis Phys — Scripta Facultatis Scientiarum Naturalium Universitatis Purkynianae Brunensis. Physica
Scr Geobot — Scripta Geobotanica
Scr Geogr — Scripta Geographica
Scr Geol — Scripta Geologica
Scr Geol (Leiden) — Scripta Geologica (Leiden)
ScrH — Scripta Hierosolymitana
Scr Hie — Scripta Hierosolymitana
ScrHier — Scripta Hierosolymitana
Scr Hieros — Scripta Hierosolymitana. Publications of the Hebrew University. Jerusalem
ScrHierosol — Scripta Hierosolymitana
Scr Hierosolymitana — Scripta Hierosolymitana
Scr Hierosolymitana Publ Heb Univ (Jerus) — Scripta Hierosolymitana. Publications of the Hebrew University (Jerusalem)
SCRI — Suplemento de Cuadernos de Ruedo Iberico
Scrib — Scribner's Monthly
Scrib Com — Scribner's Commentator
Scrib M — Scribner's Magazine
Scribners — Scribner's Magazine
Scribners Mag — Scribner's Magazine
Scribn Mag — Scribner's Magazine
Scr I Donn — Scripta Instituti Donneriana Aboensis
Scri Geol — Scripta Geologica
Scrin Hist — Scrinium Historiale
Scrinia Flor Sel — Scrinia Florae Selectae
Scrin Theol — Scrinium Theologicum. Contributi di Scienze Religiose
Scrip — Scriptorium
Scrip — Scripture
Scrip Metal — Scripta Metallurgica
Scripps Inst Oceanogr Bull — Scripps Institution of Oceanography. Bulletin
Scripps Inst Oceanogr Contrib — Scripps Institution of Oceanography. Contributions
Script — Scriptorium
Script — Scripture
Scripta Bot — Scripta Botanica
Scripta Bot Mus Transsilv — Scripta Botanica Musei Transsilvanici
Scripta Comput Sci Appl Math — Scripta. Computer Science and Applied Mathematics
Scripta Fac Sci Natur UJEP Brunensis Biol — Scripta Facultatis Scientiarum Naturalium Universita J. E. Purkyne Brunensis. Biologia
Scripta Fac Sci Natur UJEP Brunensis Chem — Scripta Facultatis Scientiarum Naturalium Universita J. E. Purkyne Brunensis. Chemia
Scripta Fac Sci Natur UJEP Brunensis Geol — Scripta Facultatis Scientiarum Naturalium Universita J. E. Purkyne Brunensis. Geologia
Scripta Fac Sci Natur UJEP Brunensis Math — Scripta Facultatis Scientiarum Naturalium Universita J. E. Purkyne Brunensis. Mathematica
Scripta Fac Sci Natur UJEP Brunensis Phys — Scripta Facultatis Scientiarum Naturalium Universita J. E. Purkyne Brunensis. Physica
Scripta Fac Sci Natur Univ Purk Brun — Scripta Facultatis Scientiarum Naturalium Universitatis Purkynianae Brunensis
Scripta Math — Scripta Mathematica
Scripta Medit — Scripta Mediterranea
Script B — Scripture Bulletin
Script Eccl Hisp Lat — Scriptores Ecclesiastici Hispano-Latini Veteris et Medii Aevi
Script Hier — Scripta Hierosolymitana
Script Lat Hib — Scriptores Latini Hiberniae
Script Metr — Metrologicorum Scriptorum Reliquiae
Script Rer Myth Lat Tr Rom Nup Rep — Scriptores Rerum Mythicarum Latini Tres Romae Nuper Reperti
ScrJud — Scripta Judaica
SCR (L) — Supreme Court Reports (Law)
Scr LT — Scranton Law Times
Scr Mater — Scripta Materialia
Scr Math — Scripta Mathematica
Scr Med (Brno) — Scripta Medica (Brno)
Scr Med Fac Med Univ Brun Masaryk — Scripta Medica. Facultatis Medicae Universitatis Brunensis Masarykianae
Scr Med Fac Med Univ Brun Olomuc — Scripta Medica. Facultatum Medicinae. Universitatum Brunensis et Olomucencis
Scr Med Fac Med Univ Brun Purkynianae — Scripta Medica Facultatis Medicae Universitatis Brunensis Purkynianae
Scr Met — Scripta Metallurgica
Scr Metall — Scripta Metallurgica

Scr Metall Mater — Scripta Metallurgica et Materialia
Scr Minora — Scripta Minora-Regiae Societatis Humaniorum Litterarum Lundensis
Scr Mon — Scritti Monastici
SCR (NS) (NSW) — Supreme Court Reports (New Series) (New South Wales)
SCR (NSW) — Supreme Court Reports (New South Wales)
SCR (NSW) Eq — Supreme Court Reports (Equity) (New South Wales)
Scr Ostet Ginecol — Scritti Ostetrici e Ginecologici
SCRPA — Science Reporter
SCR (Q) — Queensland. Supreme Court. Reports
Scr Sci Med — Scripta Scientifica Medica
Scr Sci Med Annu Sci Pap — Scripta Scientifica Medica. Annual Scientific Papers
Scr Th — Scripta Theologica
ScrTheol — Scripta Theologica
Scr Varia Pontif Acad Sci — Scripta Varia. Pontificia Academia Scientiarum
Scr Vict — Scriptorium Victoriense
ScS — Scandinavian Studies and Notes
ScS — Scottish Studies
SCS — Studies of Church and State
SCS — Suspect Chemicals Sourcebook
SCSA — Sbornik. Ceskoslovenska Spolecnosti Archeologicka
Sc S Arts T — Transactions of the Royal Scottish Society of Arts
ScSat — Scholia Satyrica
SCSCA — Schweissen und Schneiden
SCSCD7 — Smithsonian Contributions to the Marine Sciences
SCS Cluj — Studii si Cercetari Stiintifice. Filiala Cluj. Academia Republicii Populare Romine
SCSFI — Studii si Cercetari Stiintifice. Filologie (Iasi)
ScSl — Scandoslavica
SCSLA — Science du Sol
ScSo — Science and Society
Sc Soc San Antonio B — Scientific Society of San Antonio. Bulletin
SCSPR — Symposium. Conference on Science, Philosophy, and Religion in their Relation tothe Democratic Way of Life
ScSt — Scandinavian Studies
SC State Dev Board Bull — South Carolina. State Development Board. Bulletin
SC State Dev Board Div Geol Misc Rep — South Carolina. State Development Board. Division of Geology. Miscellaneous Report
SC State Devel Board Div Geology Bull Geol Notes — South Carolina State Development Board. Division of Geology. Bulletin. GeologicNotes
Sc St I — Studii si Cercetari Stiintifice
Sc St N — Scandinavian Studies and Notes
Sc Stud — Scandinavian Studies
Sc Stud L — Scandinavian Studies in Law
Sc Stud Law — Scandinavian Studies in Law
SCSZ — Sbornik Ceskoslovenske Spolecnosti Zemepisne
S Ct Bull (CCH) — United States Supreme Court Bulletin (Commerce Clearing House)
SCTCA — Schweisstechnik
SCTE — Science of the Total Environment
SCTHA — Ssu Ch'uan Ta Hsueh Hsueh Pao - Tzu Jan K'o Hsueh
SCTNC — Sources Chretiennes. Serie Annexe des Textes Non-Chretiens
SCTOA — Science Tools
Sc Total Env — Science of the Total Environment
S Ct Rev — Supreme Court Review
SCTTB — Schmiertechnik und Tribologie
SCTYB — Science Today (Bombay)
SCU — Schweizer Buchhandel
ScUB — Scandinavian University Books
Scu Citta — Scuola e Citta
SCUL — Soundings. University of California. Library
Sculp Int — Sculpture International
Sculp Mag — Sculpture Magazine
Sculpt R — Sculpture Review
SC Univ Pubs Phys Sci Bull — South Carolina University. Publications. Physical Sciences Bulletin
Scuola Dir — Scuola e Diritto
Scuola Pen Uman — Scuola Penale Umanista
Scuola Pos — Scuola Positiva. Rivista di Criminologia e Diritto Criminale
Scuol C — Scuola Cattolica. Rivista di Scienze Religiose
Scu Salern — Scuola Salernitana
SCVIA — Science et Vie
SCW — Schoenwereld. Vakblad voor de Schoenlederbranche
SCW — Schriften zur Caritaswissenschaft
SC Water Resour Comm Rep — South Carolina. Water Resources Commission. Report
SCWFA — Schip en Werf
SCWIA — South Carolina Wildlife
SC Wildl — South Carolina Wildlife
SCZ — Schweizerische Chor Zeitung
ScZ — Schweizerische Zeitschrift fuer Geschichte
SCZFA — Schweizerische Zeitschrift fuer Forstwesen
SD — Sammlung Dalp
SD — Sammlung Dieterich
SD — Scientific Detective Monthly
SD — South Dakota Musician
SD — South Dakota Reports
SD — Space Digest
Sd — Sprachdienst
SD — Sprache und Dichtung
SD — Storm Data
SD — Studia Delitschiana
SD — Studia et Documenta ad Iura Orientis Antiqui Pertinentia
SD — Studi Danteschi
SD — Studi e Documenti di Storia e Diritto

SD 4H Doings SD State Univ Coop Ext Serv — South Dakota 4-H Doings. South Dakota State University. Cooperative Extension Service
SD Admin R — Administrative Rules of South Dakota
SD Ag Exp — South Dakota. Agricultural Experiment Station. Publications
SD Agric Exp Stn Bull — South Dakota. Agricultural Experiment Station. Bulletin
SD Agric Exp Stn Circ — South Dakota. Agricultural Experiment Station. Circular
SD Agric Exp Stn Tech Bull — South Dakota. Agricultural Experiment Station. Technical Bulletin
SDAHS — Studies. Dutch Archaeological and Historical Society
S Dak Acad Sci Proc — South Dakota Academy of Science. Proceedings
S Dak Agr Expt Sta Tech Bull — South Dakota. Agricultural Experiment Station. Technical Bulletin
S Dak Bus R — South Dakota Business Review
S Dak Farm Home Res — South Dakota Farm and Home Research
S Dak Geol Surv Bull — South Dakota. Geological Survey. Bulletin
S Dak Geol Surv Circ — South Dakota. Geological Survey. Circular
S Dak Geol Survey Oil and Gas Inv Map Rept Inv — South Dakota. Geological Survey. Oil and Gas Investigations Map. Report of Investigation
S Dak His R — South Dakota Historical Review
S Dak His S — South Dakota State Historical Society. Collections
S Dak HR — South Dakota Historical Review
S Dak J Med — South Dakota Journal of Medicine
S Dak J Med Pharm — South Dakota Journal of Medicine and Pharmacy
S Dak Lib Bull — South Dakota Library Bulletin
S Dak Libr Bull — South Dakota Library Bulletin
S Dak Rev — South Dakota Review
S Dak Sch Mines B — South Dakota. School of Mines. Bulletin
S Dak State Geologist Bienn Rept — South Dakota State Geologist. Biennial Report
S Dak State Univ Coop Ext Serv — South Dakota State University. Cooperative Extension Service
SDAW — Sitzungsberichte. Deutsche Akademie der Wissenschaften zu Berlin
SDAWB — Sitzungsberichte. Deutsche Akademie der Wissenschaften zu Berlin
SDAWG — Sitzungsberichte der Deutschen Akademie der Wissenschaften zu Berlin. Klasse fuer Gesellschaftswissenschaften
SDB — South Dakota Business Review
SDB — Supplement au Dictionnaire de la Bible
SD Bird Notes — South Dakota Bird Notes
S D B J — South Dakota Bar Journal
SDB Jo — South Dakota Bar Journal
SD Black Hills Eng — South Dakota Black Hills Engineer
SDC Mag — Systems Development Corporation Magazine
SD Codified Laws Ann — South Dakota Codified Laws Annotated
SDCU — Studia Doctrinae Christianae Upsaliensia
SD DHIA News SD State Univ Coop Ext Serv — South Dakota DHIA News. South Dakota State University. Cooperative Extension Service
SDDIDP — Survey of Digestive Diseases
SDD-NU — Summaries of Doctoral Dissertations. Northwestern University
SDDRA — Showa Densen Denran Rebyu
SDDUW — Summaries of Doctoral Dissertations. University of Wisconsin
Sdelovaci Tech — Sdelovaci Technika
SDERDN — Seminars in Dermatology
SdF — Semaine de France
SDF — Standard Drug File
SDF — Studia et Documenta Franciscana
SD Farm Home Res — South Dakota Farm and Home Research
SD Farm Home Res SD Agric Exp Stn — South Dakota Farm and Home Research. South Dakota Agricultural Experiment Station
SDFL — Fund and Wagnalls' Standard Dictionary of Folklore
SDFRA — Reports. Faculty of Science. Shizuoka University
SDG — Schriften. Droste-Gesellschaft
SdG — Studii de Gramatica
SD Geol Nat Hist Surv Misc Invest — South Dakota. Geological and Natural History Survey. Miscellaneous Investigations
SD Geol Surv Bull — South Dakota. Geological Survey. Bulletin
SD Geol Surv Misc Invest — South Dakota. Geological Survey. Miscellaneous Investigations
SD Geol Surv Rep Invest — South Dakota. Geological Survey. Report of Investigations
SD Geol Surv Spec Rep — South Dakota. Geological Survey. Special Report
SDGRA — Report of Investigations. South Dakota Geological Survey
SDGSTh — Studien zur Dogmengeschichte und Systematischen Theologie
SDH — Slavistische Drukken en Herdrukken
SDHI — Studia et Documenta Historiae et Iuris
SD Hist — South Dakota History
SDHR — South Dakota Historical Review
SDi — Slovenske. Revue Dramatickych Umeni
SDIM — System for Documentation and Information in Metallurgy
SDIO — Studia et Documenta ad Iura Orientis
SDIOA — Studia et Documenta ad Iura Orientis Antiqui Pertinenta
SDIOAP — Studia et Documenta ad Iura Orientis Antiqui Pertinenta
SDISDC — Sexuality and Disability
SDJEG — Subsidia Diplomatica ad Selecta Juris Ecclesiastici Germaniae
SD J Med — South Dakota Journal of Medicine
SD J Med Pharm — South Dakota Journal of Medicine and Pharmacy
SDK — Si De Ka Quarterly
SDKF — Sueddeutsche Kirchenfuehrer
SDKG — Studien zur Deutschen Kunstgeschichte
SDKK — Studia z Dziejow Kosciola Katolickiego
SDKOD — Saitama Daigaku Kiyo. Kogakubu
SDKSB — Saitama Daigaku Kiyo. Shizenkagaku-Hen
SDL — Schriften zur Deutschen Literatur
SD Laws — Laws of South Dakota
SD LR — South Dakota Law Review
SD L Rev — South Dakota Law Review

SDM — Scripta et Documenta. Abadia de Montserrat
SdM — Siglo de las Misiones
SdM — Spectacle du Monde
SDMAA — Stroitel'nye i Dorozhnye Mashiny
SDMEA — South Dakota Journal of Medicine
SdMh — Sueddeutsche Monatshefte
SDMM — Scripta et Documenta. Abadia de Montserrat. Monastica
SDN — Satellite Data Network
SDN — Service Dealer's Newsletter
SDNIA — Saga Daigaku Nogaku Iho
SDNID7 — Bulletin. Faculty of Agriculture. Saga University
SD Nurse — South Dakota Nurse
SDO — Serra Dor
SDO — Studia et Documenta Orientalia
SDOG — Sendschrift. Deutsche Orient-Gesellschaft
SDPFE — Select Documents of the Principates of the Flavian Emperors
SDPI — Schriften des Deutschen Palaestina-Instituts
SDR — Sezione Demografia e Razza
SDR — South Dakota Review
SDR — Succession Duties Reports
SDRDDC — Survey of Drug Research in Immunologic Disease
SD Reg — South Dakota Register
SDRSA — Shimane Daigaku Ronshu: Shizen Kagaku
SDS — Sydsvenska Dagbladet Snaellposten
SD Sch Mines Bull — South Dakota. School of Mines. Bulletin
SDSD — Studi e Documenti di Storia e Diritto
SD State Coll Agric Exp Stn Circ — South Dakota State College. Agricultural Experiment Station. Circular
SD State Coll Agric Exp Stn Tech Bull — South Dakota State College. Agricultural Experiment Station. Technical Bulletin
SD State Geol Spec Rep — South Dakota. State Geologist. Special Report
SD State Geol Surv Misc Invest — South Dakota. State Geological Survey. Miscellaneous Investigations
SD State Geol Surv Rep Invest — South Dakota. State Geological Survey. Report of Investigations
SD State Geol Surv Spec Rep — South Dakota. State Geological Survey. Special Report
SD State Univ Agric Exp Stn Bull — South Dakota State University. Agricultural Experiment Station. Bulletin
SD St BJ — South Dakota State Bar Journal
SDTGA — Staedtetag
Sdt Ztg — Sueddeutsche Zeitung
S Dv — Sprache und Datenverarbeitung
SD Water Resour Comm Rep Invest — South Dakota. Water Resources Commission. Report of Investigations
SDXKDT — Shanxi University Journal. Natural Science Edition
S Dyers Col J — Journal of the Society of Dyers and Colourists
SDZ — Srpski Dijalektoloski Zbornik
SD Zb — Srpski Dijalektoloski Zbornik
SE — Sacris Erudiri. Jaarboek voor Godsdienstwetenschappen
SE — Sciences Ecclesiastiques
Se — Semeia
Se — Seminar
Se — Semiotica
SE — Siempre
SE — Slovenski Etnograf
SE — Social Education
SE — Sovetskaja Estonija
SE — Sovetskaja Etnografija
SE — Studia Estetyczne
SE — Studia Evangelica
SE — Studies in English
SE — Studi Etruschi
SE — Sunday Express
Sea — Sankt Eriks Arsbok
SEA — Schriftenreihe der Evangelischen Akademie
SEA — Studies in Economic Analysis
SEA — Studies in Educational Administration
SEA — Studies in English and American
SEA — Svensk Exegetisk Arsbok
SeAA — Southeast Asian Archives
Seabys Coin & Medal Bull — Seabys Coin and Medal Bulletin
Seabys Coin Bull — Seaby's Coin and Medal Bulletin
SEADAG — Southeast Asia Development Advisory Group Papers
SEAE — Sociedad Espanola de Antropologia, Etnografia, y Prehistoria
Sea Fish Res Stn (Haifa) Bull — Sea Fisheries Research Station (Haifa). Bulletin
Seafood Bus — Seafood Business
Seafood Export J — Seafood Export Journal
Seafood Merch — Seafood Merchandising
Sea Front — Sea Frontiers
Sea Grant Coll Tech Rep Univ Wis — Sea Grant College Technical Report. University of Wisconsin
Sea Grant Pub Ind — Sea Grant Publications Index
Sea Grant Tech Rep Univ Wis Sea Grant Program — Sea Grant Technical Report. University of Wisconsin. Sea Grant Program
SEAH — Schriftenreihe der Evangelischen Akademie Hamburg
SEAIQ — Southeast Asia. An International Quarterly
SEAISI Q — SEAISI (South East Asia Iron and Steel Institute) Quarterly
SEAJS — Southeast Asian Journal of Sociology
SEAJT — South East Asia Journal of Theology
SEAM — Sociology and Economic Aspects of Medicine
Seamens J — Seamen's Journal
Seanad Deb — Seanad Debates
Sean Ard — Seanchas Ardmhaca
SEAN Bull — SEAN [Scientific Event Alert Network] Bulletin

Seance Pub Ann Acad Pharm — Seance Publique Annuelle. Academie de Pharmacie
Seances Publiques Soc Amateurs Sci Lille — Seances Publiques. Societe des Amateurs des Sciences, de l'Agriculture, et desArts de Lille
Seances Trav Acad Sc Moral — Seances et Travaux. Academie des Sciences Morales et Politiques
Seanc Soc Belge Biol — Seances. Societe Belge de Biologie
Seanc Soc Fr Phys — Seances. Societe Francaise de Physique
SE & FBR — Science Fiction and Fantasy Book Review
Sean O Cas — Sean O'Casey Review
SeAP — Southeast Asian Perspectives
SEAPA — Society of Petroleum Engineers. American Institute of Mining, Metallurgical, and Petroleum Engineers. Papers
Sea Pwr A — Almanac of Seapower
SeAQ — Southeast Asia Quarterly
Seara Med — Seara Medica
Seara Med Neurocir — Seara Medica Neurocirurgica
SE Archaeol — Southeastern Archaeology
Search Agric — Search: Agriculture
Search Agric Ent (Ithaca NY) — Search Agriculture. Entomology (Ithaca, New York)
Search Agric (Geneva NY) — Search Agriculture (Geneva, New York)
Search Agric NY State Agric Exp Stn (Ithaca) — Search Agriculture. New York State Agricultural Experiment Station (Ithaca)
Search and Seizure L Rep — Search and Seizure Law Report
Search Hum Ecol — Search. Human Ecology
Search Together — Searching Together
SEARMG Newsl — SEARMG [Southeast Asian Research Materials Group] Newsletter
Sears Found Marine Research Mem — Sears Foundation for Marine Research. Memoir
SEARW — Studienhefte der Evangelischen Akademie Rheinland-Westfalen
SEAS — Seasons. Federation of Ontario Naturalists
Se As Aff — Southeast Asian Affairs
Se As Chron — Southeast Asia Chronicle
SE Asia — Southeast Asia Chronicle
SE Asia — Southeastern Asia
SE Asia Dig — South East Asia Digest
SE Asia J Th — Southeast Asia Journal of Theology
SE Asia J Trop Med Pub Health — Southeast Asian Journal of Tropical Medicine and Public Health
SE Asian Stud — Southeast Asian Studies
Se As Iron Steel Inst Q — Southeast Asia Iron and Steel Institute Quarterly
Se As J Soc Sci — Southeast Asian Journal of Social Science
Se As J Theo — South East Asia Journal of Theology
S E As R — South East Asian Review
Seas Sci — Seasoning Science
S E As Stud — South East Asian Studies
SEATA — Sea Technology
Sea Technol — Sea Technology
SEATO Med Res Monogr — Southeast Asia Treaty Organization. Medical Research Monograph
Seatrade BR — Seatrade Business Review
Seatrade S — Fuel Economy. A Seatrade Study
Seatrade We — Seatrade Week
Seattl Bsn — Seattle Business
(Seattle) Q — Quarterly Review (Seattle)
Seattle Sym — Seattle Symphony Orchestra. Program Notes
Seattle T — Seattle Times
Sea View Hosp Bull — Sea View Hospital. Bulletin
Sea Water Convers Lab Rep — Sea Water Conversion Laboratory Report
Seaway Rev — Seaway Review
Sea Yrbk — Seatrade North American Yearbook
SEB — Software Engineering Bibliographic Database
SEB — Statistische Studien (Brussels)
SEBAn — Societe d'Emulation de Bruges. Annales
SEB/EB — Economic Botany. New York Botanical Garden for the Society for Economic Botany
SEB Symp — Symposia. Society for Experimental Biology
SEBUA — Seibutsu Butsuri
SeC — Scuola e Cultura del Mondo
SEC — SEC: Bi-Monthly Magazine for Employees of the State Electricity Commission of Victoria
Se C — Second Coming
SEC — Secretary
SEC — Social and Economic Commentaries on Classical Texts
SEC — Societe de l'Ecole des Chartes
SEC Accounting R CCH — SEC [Securities and Exchange Commission] Accounting Rules. Commerce Clearing House
SECAe — Studien zur Erforschung des Christlichen Aegyptens
Sec & Fed Corp L Rep — Securities and Federal Corporate Law Report
SEC Bull — SEC [Securities and Exchange Commission] Bulletin
SECC — Studies in Eighteenth-Century Culture
Seccion A — Seccion de Arte
Sec City — Second City
Sec D & M — Security Distributing and Marketing
Sec Demo — Secular Democracy
Sec Ed — Secondary Education
Sechenov J Physiol USSR — Sechenov Journal of Physiology of the USSR
Sechenov Physiol J — Sechenov Physiological Journal
Sechenov Physiol J USSR — Sechenov. Physiological Journal of the USSR
Sechenov Physiol J USSR Suppl — Sechenov Physiology Journal of the USSR. Supplement
Sec Ind Digest — Secondary Industries Digest
Sec Ind R — Securities Industry Review

SECJA — Southern Economic Journal
Sec L Rev — Securities Law Review
SECM — Societa dell'Esplorazione Commerciale di Milano
SEC Mag — SEC Magazine: Journal of the State Electricity Commission of Victoria
SECMem — Societe d'Emulation de Cambrai. Memoires
Sec Mgmt — Security Management
Sec Mgt — Security Management
SEC Mon Stat Rev — SEC [US Securities and Exchange Commission] Monthly Statistical Review
SECN — Bulletins et Memoires. Societe d'Emulation des Cotes-du-Nord
SECN — Sex Education Coalition News
SECN — Supplements to Electroencephalography and Clinical Neurophysiology
SEC News — SEC [US Securities and Exchange Commission] News Digest
SECOLAS A — SECOLAS [Southeastern Conference on Latin American Studies] Annals
SECOLAS/SELA — South Eastern Latin Americanist. Southeastern Conference on Latin American Studies
SE Coll Rev — Southeastern College Art Conference Review
SECOLR — SECOL [Southeastern Conference on Linguistics] Review
Secondary Teach — Secondary Teacher
Second Cent — Second Century
Second Cycle Univ Ecoles Ing — Second Cycle des Universites et Ecoles d'Ingenieurs
Second Forms Hypertens Int Symp Nephrol — Secondary Forms of Hypertension. Current Diagnosis and Management. International Symposium of Nephrology
Second Ion Mass Spectrom Proc Int Conf — Secondary Ion Mass Spectrometry. Proceedings. International Conference on Secondary Ion Mass Spectrometry
Second Line Agents Treat Rheum Dis — Second-Line Agents in the Treatment of Rheumatic Diseases
Second Opin Health Care Issues — Second Opinions of Health Care Issues
S Econ J — Southern Economic Journal
Sec Reg & L Rep — Securities Regulation and Law Reports
Sec Reg & L Rep BNA — Securities Regulation and Law Report. Bureau of National Affairs
Sec Reg & Trans — Securities Regulations and Transfer Report
Sec Reg Guide P-H — Securities Regulation Guide. Prentice-Hall
Sec Reg LJ — Securities Regulation Law Journal
Secretion Its Control Annu Symp — Secretion and Its Control. Annual Symposium
Secr Ind Comer Bol (Argent) — Secretaria de Industria y Comercio. Boletin (Argentina)
Secr Pap Int Wheat Counc — Secretariat Papers. International Wheat Council
Sec Syst Dig — Security Systems Digest
SECTDQ — Centro Internacional de Agricultura Tropical [CIAT]. Series EE
Sec Teach — Secondary Teacher
Sec Teacher — Secondary Teacher
Sect Romandes Club Alpin Suisse — Sections Romandes du Club Alpin Suisse
Secure Commun Syst Int Conf — Secure Communication Systems. International Conference
Security Surv — Security Surveyor
Secur Manage — Security Management
Secur Med Trav — Securite et Medecine du Travail
Secur R Law — Securities Regulation Law Journal
Sec Wave — Second Wave
Sec World — Security World
SED — Survey of English Dialects
SED — Sylloge Excerptorum e Dissertationibus ad Gradum Doctoris in Sacra Theologia
SEDA — Side Effects of Drugs. Annual
Sedalia N H Soc B — Sedalia Natural History Society. Bulletin
SEDES — Societe d'Editions d'Enseignement Superieur
Sed Geol — Sedimentary Geology
Sediment Ge — Sedimentary Geology
Sediment Geol — Sedimentary Geology
Sedimentol — Sedimentology
Sedimentol Pedol — Sedimentologia e Pedologia
SEDS — State Energy Data System
SEE — Studien zur Evangelischen Ethik
SEE — Studies in Educational Evaluation
SEEC — Series Episcoporum Ecclesiae Catholicae
Seed and Nursery Tr — Seed and Nursery Trader
Seed Bull — Seed Bulletin
Seed Gard Merch — Seed and Garden Merchandising
Seedlings Hort — Seedlings and Horticulture/Shubyo to Engei
Seed Res — Seed Research
Seed Res (New Delhi) — Seed Research (New Delhi)
Seed Sci Tech — Seed Science and Technology
Seed Sci Techn — Seed Science and Technology
Seed Sci Technol — Seed Science and Technology
Seed Technol Trop Pap Natl Seed Symp — Seed Technology in the Tropics. Papers. National Seed Symposium
Seed Trade Rev — Seed Trade Review
SEEE — Studies in Electrical and Electronic Engineering
SEEI — Selected Essays. English Institute
SEEJ — Slavic and East European Journal
Seel — Seelsorger
Seels — Seelsorger
Seeman Journ Bot — Journal of Botany, British and Foreign (London)
SEER — Slavonic and East European Review
SEERB — South African Engineer and Electrical Review
SEES — Slavic and East European Studies
SE Eur — Southeastern Europe
Sef — Sefarad
SEF — Supermarketing
SEFDAO — Side Effects of Drugs

SEFP — Studies in Eucharistic Faith and Practice
Seg — Segismundo
SEG — Supplementum Epigraphicum Graecum
SEGEA — Orthopaedic Surgery
Seguranca Desenvolv — Seguranca e Desenvolvimento. ADESG
Segur Soc BA — Seguridad Social (Buenos Aires)
Segur Soc Mex — Seguridad Social (Mexico)
SEGW — Studien der Evangelischen Geistlichen Wirtembergs
SEH — Social and Economic History of the Hellenistic World
SEH — Southern Economic Journal
SEHHW — Social and Economic History of the Hellenistic World
SEHL — Scriptores Ecclesiastici Hispano-Latini Veteris et Medii Aevi
SEHR — Scandinavian Economic History Review
SEHRE — Social and Economic History of the Roman Empire
SEI — Shorter Encyclopaedia of Islam
SEIB — Statistical and Economic Information Bulletin for Africa
SEIE — Solvent Extraction and Ion Exchange
Seifen Fachbl — Seifen Fachblatt
Seifen Ole — Seifen, Oele, Fette, Waechse
Seifensieder Ztg — Seifensieder-Zeitung
Seifensieder Ztg Allg Oel Fett Ztg — Seifensieder-Zeitung in Gemeinschaft auf Kriegsdauer mit Allgemeine Oel- und Fett-Zeitung
Seifensieder Ztg Beibl Chem Tech Fabr — Seifensieder-Zeitung. Beiblatt. Chemisch-Technische Fabrikant
Seifens Zt — Seifensieder-Zeitung
SEIGA — Seishin Igaku
Sei-i-Kai Med J — Sei-i-Kwai Medical Journal
SEIJAN — Congenital Anomalies
SEIJD — Seijinbyo
Seikag — Seikagaku
Seik Ziho — Seiken Ziho. Report of the Kihara Institute for Biological Research
SEIR — Solar Energy Intelligence Report
Seish Iga — Seishin Igaku
Seish Shink Zass — Seishin Shinkeigaku Zasshi
Seism Instrum — Seismic Instruments
Seismol and Geol — Seismology and Geology
Seismol Bull — Seismological Bulletin
Seismol Invest — Seismological Investigations. British Association for the Advancement of Science
Seismolog Soc Am Bull — Seismology Society of America. Bulletin
Seismol Ser Earth Phys Branch — Seismological Series of the Earth Physics Branch
Seismol Ser Geol Surv (S Afr) — Seismologic Series. Geological Survey (South Africa)
Seismol Serv Can Seismol Ser — Seismological Service of Canada. Seismological Series
Seismol Soc Am Bul — Seismological Society of America. Bulletin
Seismostoikost Sooruzh — Seismostoikost Sooruzhenii
Seism Prib Instrum Sredstva Seism Nabl — Seismichiskie Pribory. Instrumental'naye Sredstva Seismicheskikh Nablyudenll
SEI Socio Econ Inf Ohio State Univ Coop Exp Serv — SEI (Socio-Economic Information) Ohio State University. Cooperative Extension Service
SEITA Ann Dir Etud Equip Sect 2 — SEITA [Service d'Exploitation Industrielle des Tabacs et des Allumettes] Annales de la Direction des Etudes de l'Equipement. Section 2
SEITA Annls — Service d'Exploitation Industrielle des Tabacs et des Allumettes. Annales de laDirection des Etudes de l'Equipement
SEJ — Australian Stock Exchange Journal
SEJ — Security Pacific National Bank. Quarterly Economic Report
SEJ — Southern Economic Journal
SEJG — Sacris Erudiri. Jaarboek voor Godsdienstwetenschappen
SEJI — State Education Journal Index
Sejtosztodas Farmakol — Sejtosztodas Farmakologiaja
Sek San Fuji Sor — Sekai San Fujinka Soran. Survey of World Obstetrics and Gynaecology
SeL — Storia e Letteratura
SEL — Studies in English Literature
Sel Annu Rev Anal Sci — Selected Annual Reviews of the Analytical Sciences
Sel Bibliogr Algae — Selected Bibliography on Algae
Sel Bibliogr Middle East Geol — Selected Bibliography of Middle East Geology
Sel Cancer Ther — Selective Cancer Therapeutics
Sel Chim — Selecta Chimica
Sel Chim Tintoria — Selezione Chimica Tintoria
Seld Mar Cl — Selden's Mare Clausum
Seld Soc Yrbk — Selden Society Yearbook
Sele A — Sele Arte
Selec Ed R — Selections from the Edinburgh Review
Selecta Math NS — Selecta Mathematica. New Series
Selecta Math Soviet — Selecta Mathematica Sovietica
Selecta Statist Canadiana — Selecta Statistica Canadiana
Select Bibliogr Algae — Selected Bibliography on Algae. Nova Scotia Research Foundation
Select Canc — Selective Cancer Therapeutics
Selected Reports — Selected Reports in Ethnomusicology
Selected Water Resources Abstr — Selected Water Resources Abstracts
Select J — Select Journal
Select Papers Italian Phys — Selected Papers of Italian Physicists
Selec Water Resources Abstr — Selected Water Resources Abstracts
Selek Semenovod — Selektsiya i Semenovodstvo
Selekts Semenov — Selektsiya i Semenovodstvo
Sel Electrode Rev — Selective Electrode Reviews
Selenium Tellurium Abstr — Selenium and Tellurium Abstracts
SelEnv — Selected References on Environmental Quality
Selez Tec Molit — Selezione di Tecnica Molitoria

Self Organ Emerging Prop Learn — Self-Organization, Emerging Properties, and Learning
Self Rel — Self-Reliance
SE Libn — Southeastern Librarian
SELID — Serials Librarian
SELit — Studies in English Literature
SELJ — Studies in English Literature (Japan)
Sel'Khoz Beloruss — Sel'skoe Khozyaistvo Belorussii
Sel'-Khoz Biol — Sel'skokhozyaistvennaya Biologiya
Sel Khoz Kazakh — Sel'skoe Khozyaistvo Kazakstana
Sel'Khoz Kirgizii — Sel'skoe Khozyaistvo Kirgizii
Sel'Khoz Povol — Sel'skoe Khozyaistvo Povolzh'ya
Sel'Khoz Sev Kavkaz — Sel'skoe Khozyaistvo Severnogo Kavkaza
Sel'Khoz Sev-Zapad Zony — Sel'skoe Khozyaistvo Severo-Zapadnoi Zony
Sel Khoz Sev Zap Zony — Sel'skoe Khozyaistvo Severo-Zapadnoi Zony
Sel'Khoz Sib — Sel'skoe Khozyaistvo Sibiri
Sel Khoz Tadzhik — Sel'skoe Khozyaistvo Tadzhikistana
Sel'Khoz Tadzhikistana — Sel'skoe Khozyaistvo Tadzhikistana
Sel Khoz Tatarii — Sel'skoe Khozyaistvo Tatarii
Sel Khoz Turkmen — Sel'skoe Khozyaistvo Turkmenistana
SELL — Studies in English Literature and Language
Sel Lecture Math — Selected Lectures in Mathematics. American Mathematicas Society
Sellowia Anais Bot — Sellowia. Anais Botanicos do Herbario Barbosa Rodriques
Sel Math Sov — Selecta Mathematica Sovietica
Sel Med — Selecciones Medicas
Sel Nasinnitstvo — Selektsiya i Nasinnitstvo
Sel Neurotoxic — Selective Neurotoxicity
Sel Odontol (Sao Paulo) — Selecoes Odontologicas (Sao Paulo)
Sel Org Transform — Selective Organic Transformations
Sel Pap — Select Papyri
Sel Pap Am Chem Soc Symp Plast Deform Plym — Selected Papers Presented. American Chemical Society Symposium on Plastic Deformation of Polymers
Sel Pap Annu Gas Meas Inst — Selected Papers. Heart of America Annual Gas Measurement Institute
Sel Pap Annu Pipeline Oper Maint Inst — Selected Papers. Heart of America Annual Pipeline Operation and Maintenance Institute
Sel Pap Carle Clin Carle Found — Selected Papers. Carle Clinic and Carle Foundation
Sel Pap Conf Exp Med Surg Primates — Selected Papers. Conference on Experimental Medicine and Surgery in Primates
Sel Pap EC&M China — Selected Papers of EC&M (Engineering Chemistry and Metallurgy)
Sel Pap Eng Chem Metall China — Selected Papers of Engineering Chemistry and Metallurgy (China)
Sel Pap Environ Isr — Selected Papers on the Environment in Israel
Sel Pap Heart Am Annu Gas Compressor Inst — Selected Papers. Heart of America Annual Gas Compressor Institute
Sel Pap Heart Am Annu Gas Meas Inst — Selected Papers. Heart of America Annual Gas Measurement Institute
Sel Pap Inst Human Nutr Prague — Selected Papers. Institute of Human Nutrition in Prague
Sel Pap Int Astronaut Congr — Selected Papers. International Astronautical Congress
Sel Pap Isr Environ Prot Service — Selected Papers. Israel. Environmental Protection Service
Sel Pap Nucl Eng Sci Congr — Selected Papers. Nuclear Engineering and Science Congress
Sel Philip Period Index — Selected Philippine Periodical Index
Sel PRC Mag — Selections from People's Republic of China Magazines
Sel Rand Abstr — Selected Rand Abstracts
Sel Rast Akklim Semenovod — Selektsiya Rastenii Akklimatizatsiya i Semenovodstvo
Sel Sci Pap Ist Super Sanita — Selected Scientific Papers. Istituto Superiore di Sanita
Sel Sci Pap Shanghai Chiao Tung Univ — Selected Scientific Papers. Shanghai Chiao Tung University
Sel Sci Pap Shanghai Jiao Tong Univ — Selected Scientific Papers. Shanghai Jiao Tong University
Sel Semenovod (Kiev) — Selektsiya i Semenovodstvo (Kiev)
Sel Semenovod (Mosc) — Selektsiya i Semenovodstvo (Moscow)
Sel Semenovod Resp Mezhved Temat Sb — Selektsiya i Semenovodstvo Respublikanskii Mezhvedomstvennyi Tematicheskii Sborrnik
Selsk Ind Tek Forsk Nor Tek Hoegsk Rep — Selskapet for Industriell og Teknisk Forskning ved Norges TeknishkiHoegskole. Report
Sel'sk Khoz — Sel'skoe Khozyaistvo
Sel'sk Khoz Kaz — Sel'skoe Khozyaistvo Kazakhstana
Sel'sk Khoz Kirg — Sel'skoe Khozyaistvo Kirgizii
Sel'sk Khoz Mold — Sel'skoe Khozyaistvo Moldavii
Sel'sk Khoz Podmoskov'ya — Sel'skoe Khozyaistvo Podmoskov'ya
Sel'sk Khoz Povolzh'ya — Sel'skoe Khozyaistvo Povolzh'ya
Sel'sk Khoz Rubezhom Rastenievod — Sel'skoe Khozyaistvo za Rubezhom. Rastenievodstvo
Sel'sk Khoz Sev Zapadn Zony — Sel'skoe Khozyaistvo Severo-Zapadnoi Zony
Sel'sk Khoz Tadzh — Sel'skoe Khozyaistvo Tadzhikistana
Sel'sk Khoz Tatar — Sel'skoe Khozyaistvo Tatarii
Sel'sk Khoz Tatarii — Sel'skoe Khozyaistvo Tatarii
Sel'sk Khoz Turkm — Sel'skoe Khozyaistvo Turkmenistana
Sel'skokhoz Biol — Sel'skokhozyaistvennaya Biologiya
Sel'skokhoz Proizv Nechernozem Zony — Sel'skokhozyaistvennoe Proizvodstvo Nechernozemnoi Zony
Sel'skokhoz Proizv Povol — Sel'skokhozyaistvennoe Proizvodstvo Povolzh'ya
Sel'skokhoz Proizv Sev Kavkaza TSCHO — Sel'skokhozyaistvennoe Proizvodstvo Severnogo Kavkaza i TSCHO

Sel'skokhoz Proizv Sib Dal'nego Vostoka — Sel'skokhozyaistvennoe Proizvodstvo Sibiri i Dal'nego Vostoka
Sel'skokhoz Proizv Urala — Sel'skokhozyaistvennoe Proizvodstvo Urala
Selskostop Misul — Selskostopanska Misul
Selskostop Nauka — Selskostopanska Nauka
Selskostop Tekh — Selskostopanska Tekhnika
Sel Sortoizuch Agrotekh Plodovykh Yagodnykh Kul't — Selektsiya, Sortoizuchenie, Agrotekhnika Plodovykh i Yagodnykh Kul'tur
Sel Statist Can — Selecta Statistica Canadiana
Sel Tec Molitoria — Selezione di Tecnica Molitoria
Sel Tekhnol Vozdelyvaniya Efirnomaslichn Kul't — Selektsiya i Tekhnologiya Vozdelyvaniya Efirnomaslichnykh Kul'tur
Seltene Met — Seltene Metalle
Sel Teol — Selecciones de Teologia
Sel Top Electron Syst — Selected Topics in Electronics and Systems
Sel Top Liq Cryst Res — Selected Topics in Liquid Crystal Research
Sel Top Mod Phys — Selected Topics in Modern Physics
Sel Top Solid State Phys — Selected Topics in Solid State Physics
Sel Top Solid State Theor Phys Proc Lat Am Sch Phys — Selected Topics in Solid State and Theoretical Physics. Proceedings. Latin American School of Physics
Sel Vet Ist Zooprofil Sper Lomb Emilia — Selezione Veterinaria-Istituto Zooprofilattico Sperimentale della Lombardia e dell'Emilia
Sel Water Res Abstr — Selected Water Resources Abstracts
Sel Water Resour Abstr — Selected Water Resources Abstracts
SEM — Bulletin et Memoires. Societe d'Emulation de Montbeliard
SEM — Security Management
Sem — Semaine dans le Monde
Sem — Semana
Sem — Seminar
Sem — Seminario Conciliar
Sem — Semiotica
Sem — Semitica
SEM — Sovetskaia Etnografiia (Moscow and Leningrad)
S-EM — Suck-Egg Mule
Semaine Med — Semaine Medicale
Semaine Vet — Semaine Veterinaire
Sem Anal — Seminaire d'Analyse
Sem Anal Convexe — Seminaire d'Analyse Convexe
Sem Anal Moderne — Seminaire d'Analyse Moderne
Semana Med — Semana Medica
Semanario — Semanario Judicial de la Federacion
Semanario Agric Artes — Semanario de Agricultura y Artes
Sem Arghiriade — Seminar Arghiriade
Sem Arth Rh — Seminars in Arthritis and Rheumatism
SemBEsp — Semana Biblica Espanola
Sem Bibl Esp — Semana Biblica Espanola
Sem Constructeurs — Semaine des Constructeurs
SEM/E — Ethnos. Statens Etnografiska Museum
Semen Elette — Sementi Elette
Sem Hematol — Seminars in Hematology
Sem Hop — Semaine des Hopitaux
Sem Hop Inf — Semaine des Hopitaux. Informations
Sem Hop Paris — Semaine des Hopitaux de Paris
Sem Hop Paris Suppl Arch Anat Pathol — Semaine des Hopitaux de Paris. Supplement. Archives d'Anatomie Pathologique
Sem Hop Paris Suppl Med Monde — Semaine des Hopitaux de Paris. Supplement. Medecine dans le Monde
Sem Hop Paris Suppl Pathol Biol — Semaine des Hopitaux de Paris. Supplement. Pathologie et Biologie
Sem Hop Paris Suppl Sem Med Prof Med Soc — Semaine des Hopitaux de Paris. Supplement. Semaine Medicale Professionnelle et Medico-Sociale
Sem Hop Suppl Ann Chir Plast — Semaine des Hopitaux. Supplement. Annales de Chirurgie Plastique
Sem Hop Suppl Sem Ther — Semaine des Hopitaux. Supplement. Semaine Therapeutique
Sem Hop Suppl Ther — Semaine des Hopitaux. Supplement. Therapeutique
Sem Hop The — Semaine des Hopitaux. Therapeutique
Sem Hop Ther — Semaine des Hopitaux. Therapeutique
Semi-Annu Prog Rep Tokai Works — Semi-Annual Progress Report. Tokai Works
Semicond and Insul — Semiconductors and Insulators
Semicond Insul — Semiconductors and Insulators
Semicond Int — Semiconductor International
Semicond Interfaces Microstruct — Semiconductor Interfaces and Microstructures
Semicond Optoelectron — Semiconductor Optoelectronics
Semicond Photonics Technol — Semiconductor Photonics and Technology
Semicond Prod — Semiconductor Production
Semicond Prod — Semiconductor Products
Semicond Prod and Solid State Technol — Semiconductor Products and Solid State Technology [*Later, Solid State Technology*]
Semicond Pure Water Chem Conf — Semiconductor Pure Water and Chemicals Conference
Semicond Sci Technol — Semiconductor Science and Technology
Semicond Semimet — Semiconductors and Semimetals
Semicond Silicon Int Symp Mat Pap — Semiconductor Silicon. International Symposium on Silicon Materials Science andTechnology. Papers
Semicond Silicon Pap Int Symp Silicon Mater Sci Technol — Semiconductor Silicon. Papers Presented. International Symposium on Silicon Materials Science and Technology
Semicond Wafer Bonding Sci Technol Appl — Semiconductor Wafer Bonding. Science, Technology, and Applications
SEMIKON — Seminare/Konferenzen
Semimagn Semicond Diluted Magn Semicond — Semimagnetic Semiconductors and Diluted Magnetic Semiconductors
Semin A Aragon — Seminario del Arte Aragones

Semin Amibiasis — Seminario sobre Amibiasis
Semin Anesth — Seminars in Anesthesia
Semin Anesth Perioper Med Pain — Seminars in Anesthesia, Perioperative Medicine, and Pain
Semin Arte Aragones — Seminario de Arte Aragones
Semin Arthritis Rheum — Seminars in Arthritis and Rheumatism
Seminary Q — Seminary Quarterly
Semin At Spectrochem — Seminar on Atomic Spectrochemistry
Semin Biol Fac Med Chir Univ Cattol Sacro Cuore — Seminari Biologici. Facolta di Medicina e Chirurgia. UniversitaCattolica del Sacro Cuore
Semin Biomass Energy City Farm Ind — Seminar on Biomass Energy for City, Farm, and Industry
Semin Cancer Biol — Seminars in Cancer Biology
Semin Cell Biol — Seminars in Cell Biology
Semin Cell Dev Biol — Seminars in Cell and Developmental Biology
Semin Chim Etat Solide — Seminaires de Chimie de l'Etat Solide
Semin Clin Neuropsychiatry — Seminars in Clinical Neuropsychiatry
Semin Dermatol — Seminars in Dermatology
Semin Dev Biol — Seminars in Developmental Biology
Semin Diagn Pathol — Seminars in Diagnostic Pathology
Semin Dial — Seminars in Dialysis
Semin Drug Treat — Seminars in Drug Treatment
Semin Electrochem — Seminar on Electrochemistry
Semin Enseign INSERM — Seminaire d'Enseignement. INSERM
Semin Enson Odontopediatr — Seminario de Ensenanza de la Odontopediatria
Semin Estratigrafia — Seminarios de Estratigrafia
Semin Estud Galegos — Seminario de Estudos Galegos
Semin Eval Contam Ambiental — Seminario sobre Evaluacion de la Contaminacion Ambiental
Semin Fam Med — Seminars in Family Medicine
Sem Infect Dis — Seminars in Infectious Disease
Semin Fiz Tekhnol Vopr Kibern — Seminar. Fiziko-Tekhnologicheskie Voprosy Kibernetiki
Semin Gastrointest Dis — Seminars in Gastrointestinal Disease
Semin Hear — Seminars in Hearing
Semin Hematol — Seminars in Hematology
Semin Immunol — Seminars in Immunology
Semin Infect Dis — Seminars in Infectious Disease
Semin Interno Explor Geol Min — Seminario Interno sobre Exploracion Geologico-Minera
Semin Interventional Radiol — Seminars in Interventional Radiology
Semin Khim Tekh Primen Khal'kogenidov — Seminar po Khimii i Tekhnicheskomu Primeneniyu Khal'kogenidov
Semin Kondakov — Seminarium Kondakovianum
Semin Kraev Zadacham Tr — Seminar po Kraevym Zadacham. Trudy
Semin Liver Dis — Seminars in Liver Diseases
Semin Mar Radioecol — Seminar on Marine Radioecology
Semin Mat Fis Univ Modena Atti — Seminario Matematico e Fisico. Universita di Modena. Atti
Semin Med — Seminario Medico
Semin Migr Relat Soc Health Probl Pap — Seminar on Migration and Related Social and Health Problems in New Zealand and the Pacific. Papers
Semin Musculoskelet Radiol — Seminars in Musculoskeletal Radiology
Semin Neonatol — Seminars in Neonatology
Semin Nephrol — Seminars in Nephrology
Semin Neurol — Seminars in Neurology
Semin Neurosci — Seminars in Neuroscience
Semin Nucl Med — Seminars in Nuclear Medicine
Semin Nutr — Seminars in Nutrition
Semin Oncol — Seminars in Oncology
Semin Oncol Nurs — Seminars in Oncology Nursing
Semin Orthod — Seminars in Orthodontics
Semin Pap La Trobe Univ Sch Agri — Seminar Paper. La Trobe University. School of Agriculture
Semin Pediatr Neurol — Seminars in Pediatric Neurology
Semin Pediatr Surg — Seminars in Pediatric Surgery
Semin Perinatol — Seminars in Perinatology
Semin Perinatol (NY) — Seminars in Perinatology (New York)
Semin Pint Esp — Seminario Pintoresco Espanol
Semin Plansee — Seminaire Plansee
Semin Pokroky Vyrobe Pouziti Lepidiel Drevopriem Zb Ref — Seminar Pokroky vo Vyrobe a Pouziti Lepidiel v Drevopriemysle. ZbornikReferatov
Semin Probl Upr Raspred Sist Podvizhnym Vozdelstv Mater — Seminar po Problemam Upravleniya Raspredelennymi Sistemami s PodvizhnymVozdeistviem. Materialy
Semin Psychiatry — Seminars in Psychiatry
Semin R & D Bioenerg CR — Seminaire R & D Bioenergetique. Compte Rendu
Semin Reprod Endocrinol — Seminars in Reproductive Endocrinology
Semin Reprod Med — Seminars in Reproductive Medicine
Semin Respir Infect — Seminars in Respiratory Infections
Semin Respir Med — Seminars in Respiratory Medicine
Semin Roentgenol — Seminars in Roentgenology
Semin Ser Soc Exp Biol — Seminar Series. Society for Experimental Biology
Semin Speech Lang — Seminars in Speech and Language
Semin Sp Lang Hear — Seminars Speech, Language, Hearing
Sem Inst Prikl Mat Annotac Dokladov — Seminar Instituta Prikladnoi Matematiki. Annotacii Dokladov
Semin Surg Oncol — Seminars in Surgical Oncology
Semin Technol INSERM — Seminaire Technologique. INSERM
Semin Theor Phys — Seminar on Theoretical Physics
Semin Thorac Cardiovasc Surg — Seminars in Thoracic and Cardiovascular Surgery
Semin Thorac Cardiovasc Surg Pediatr Card Surg Annu — Seminars in Thoracic and Cardiovascular Surgery. Pediatric Cardiac Surgery Annual
Semin Thromb Hemost — Seminars in Thrombosis and Hemostasis

Semin Thromb Hemostas — Seminars in Thrombosis and Hemostasis
Semin Thromb Hemostasis — Seminars in Thrombosis and Hemostasis
Semin Ultrasound — Seminars in Ultrasound [Later, Seminars in Ultrasound, CT, and MR]
Semin Ultrasound CT MR — Seminars in Ultrasound, CT, and MR
Semin Univ Singapore Chem Dep — Seminar. University of Singapore. Chemistry Department
Semin Urol — Seminars in Urology
Semin Urol Oncol — Seminars in Urologic Oncology
Semin Vasc Surg — Seminars in Vascular Surgery
Semin Vet Med Surg Small Anim — Seminars in Veterinary Medicine and Surgery. Small Animal
Sem'ja Sk — Sem'ja Skola
Sem Jur — Semaine Juridique
SEMKA — Semento Kogyo
Sem Kond — Seminarium Kondakovianum
Sem Kondakov — Annaly Instituta imeni N.P. Kondakova
SemL — Semaine Litteraire
Sem Lothar Combin — Seminaire Lotharingien de Combinatoire
Sem Math — Seminars in Mathematics
Sem Math Luxembourg — Seminaire de Mathematique de Luxembourg
Sem Math Sci — Seminar on Mathematical Sciences
Sem Math Sup — Seminaire de Mathematiques Superieures
Sem Math Superieures — Seminaire de Mathematiques Superieures
Sem Math V A Steklov — Seminars in Mathematics. V. A. Steklov Mathematical Instituto
Sem Med — Semaine Medicale
Sem Med — Semana Medica
Sem Med Esp — Semana Medica Espanola
Sem Med Mex — Semana Medica de Mexico
Sem Med Prof Med Soc — Semaine Medicale Professionnelle et Medico-Sociale
SemMo — Semaine dans le Monde
Sem Nephrol — Seminars in Nephrology
Sem Nota — Seminaro Nota
Semper Nutritionssympo — Semper Nutritionssymposium
Semper Symp — Semper Symposium
Sem Prof Med Soc — Semaine Professionnelle et Medico-Sociale
SemRC — Semaine a Radio-Canada
Sem Roentg — Seminars in Roentgenology
Sem S — Semiotic Scene
Sem Ser Math Algebra — Seminar Series in Mathematics. Algebra
Sem Ser Math Anal — Seminar Series in Mathematics. Analysis
SEMSM — Statens Etnografiska Museum (Riksmuseets Etnografiska Avdelning), Smaerre Meddelanden [Stockholm]
Sem St — Semitistische Studien
SEMT — Science, Engineering, Medicine, and Technology
SEMTD8 — Special Topics in Endocrinology and Metabolism
Sem Ther — Semaine Therapeutique
Se Mulli (New Phys) — Se Mulli (New Physics)
Sem Ultrasound — Seminars in Ultrasound
Sem Vitivinic — Semana Vitivinicola
SeN — Seara Nova
SENAAL — Agricultural Science
S E Naturalist — South Eastern Naturalist
Senckb Nf Gs B — Bericht ueber die Senckenbergische Naturforschende Gesellschaft in Frankfurt am Main
Senckenb Biol — Senckenbergiana Biologica
Senckenberg Biol — Senckenbergiana Biologica
Senckenbergiana Biol — Senckenbergiana Biologica
Senckenbergiana Marit — Senckenbergiana Maritima
Senckenbergiana Mitt Naturf — Senckenbergiana. Wissenschaftliche Mitteilungen der Senckenbergischen Naturforschenden Gesellschaft
Senckenbergische Nat Ges Frankfurt Ber — Senckenbergische Naturforschende Gesellschaft in Frankfurt Am Main. Bericht
Senckenberglschen Naturf Gesell Senckenberg-Buch — Senckenbergischen Naturforschenden Gesellschaft Senckenberg-Buch
Senckenberg Marit — Senckenbergiana Maritima
Senckenb Lethaea — Senckenbergiana Lethaea
Senckenb Marit — Senckenbergiana Maritima
Senckenb Naturforsch Ges Abh — Senckenbergische Naturforschende Gesellschaft. Abhandlungen
S en D — Socialisme en Democratie
Sendai Astron Rap — Sendai Astronomiaj Raportoj
Sendai Symp Acoustoelectron — Sendai Symposium on Acoustoelectronics
Senegal Cent Rech Oceanogr Dakar-Thiaroye Arch — Senegal. Centre de Recherches Oceanographiques de Dakar-Thiaroye. Archive
Senegal Cent Rech Oceanogr Dakar-Thiaroye Doc Sci — Senegal. Centre de Recherches Oceanographiques de Dakar-Thiaroye. Document Scientifique
Senegal Dir Mines Geol Bull — Senegal. Direction des Mines et de la Geologie. Bulletin
SEngL — Studies in English Literature
SENPD — Senpaku
Sen R — Seneca Review
Senri Ethnol Stud — Senri Ethnological Studies
S en S — Schip en Schade
Sens Actuators A Phys — Sensors and Actuators. A. Physical
Sens Actuators B Chem — Sensors and Actuators. B. Chemical
Sens and Actuators — Sensors and Actuators
SENSB — Sense Processes
Sens C — Sens Chretien
Sen Schol — Senior Scholastic
Sens Controlling Motion — Sensing and Controlling Motion. Vestibular and Sensorimotor Function
SENSD — Studies in Environmental Science

Sens Fusion IV Control Paradigms Data Struct — Sensor Fusion IV. Control Paradigms and Data Structures
Sens Fusion V — Sensor Fusion V
Sensibilizirovannaya Fluorests Smesej Parov Met — Sensibilizirovannaya Fluorestsentsiya Smesej Parov Metallov
Sensing — Remote Sensing
Sens Nerves Neuropept Gastroenterol — Sensory Nerves and Neuropeptides in Gastroenterology
Sensor Rev — Sensor Review
Sens Peterborough NH — Sensors (Peterborough, NH)
Sens Process — Sensory Processes
Sens Recept Signal Transduction — Sensory Receptors and Signal Transduction
Sens Rev — Sensor Review
Sens Sens Syst Guid Navig II — Sensors and Sensor Systems for Guidance and Navigation II
Sens Sist — Sensornye Sistemy
Sens Technol Anwend Vortr Fachtag — Sensoren. Technologie und Anwendung. Vortraege der Fachtagung
Sens Transduction — Sensory Transduction
Sens Update — Sensors Update
SEO — Scriptorum Ecclestiasticorum Opuscula
SeO — Serra d'Or
Seoul J Med — Seoul Journal of Medicine
Seoul Natl Univ Coll Agric Bull — Seoul National University. College of Agriculture. Bulletin
Seoul Natl Univ Eng Rep — Seoul National University. Engineering Reports
Seoul Nat Univ Econ R — Seoul National University. Economic Review
Seoul Nat Univ Eng Rep — Seoul National University Engineering Report
Seoul Nat Univ Fac Pap Bio Agric Ser — Seoul National University. Faculty Papers. Biology and Agriculture Series
Seoul Nat Univ Fac Pap Biol Agric Ser E — Seoul National University Faculty Papers. Biology and Agriculture. Series E
Seoul Nat Univ Fac Pap Med Pharm Ser — Seoul National University. Faculty Papers. Medicine and Pharmacy Series
Seoul Nat Univ Fac Pap Sci Technol Ser — Seoul National University. Faculty Papers. Science and Technology Series
Seoul Nat Univ J Agric Sci — Seoul National University. Journal of Agricultural Sciences
Seoul University J Pharm Sci — Seoul University. Journal of Pharmaceutical Sciences
Seoul Univ Fac Pap Ser C — Seoul University. Faculty Papers. Series C. Science and Technology
Seoul Univ Fac Pap Ser D — Seoul University. Faculty Papers. Series D. Medicine and Pharmacy
Seoul Univ Fac Pap Ser E — Seoul University. Faculty Papers. Series E. Biology and Agriculture
Seoul Univ J Biol Agric Ser B — Seoul University. Journal. Series B. Biology and Agriculture
Seoul Univ J Biol Agr Ser B — Seoul University. Journal. Series B. Biology and Agriculture
Seoul Univ J Biol Ser — Seoul University Journal. Biology and Agriculture Series/ Seoul Taehak-Kyo Nonmun-Jip Soengnong-Kae
Seoul Univ J Med Pharm Ser C — Seoul University. Journal. Series C. Medicine and Pharmacy
Seoul Univ J Nat Sci — Seoul University. Journal. Series A. Natural Science
Seoul Univ J Nat Sci Ser A — Seoul University. Journal. Series A. Natural Science
Seoul Univ J Nat Sci Ser B — Seoul University. Journal. Series B. Natural Science
Seoul Univ J Nat Sci Ser C — Seoul University. Journal. Series C. Natural Science
Seoul Univ J Pharm Sci — Seoul University. Journal of Pharmaceutical Sciences
Seoul Univ J Sci Technol Ser A — Seoul University. Journal. Series A. Science and Technology
SEP — Saturday Evening Post
SEP — Secretaria de Educacion Publica
SEP — Survey of Eastern Palestine
Separation Sci Tech — Separation Science and Technology
Separ Sci — Separation Science [*Later, Separation Science and Technology*]
SEPGB — Studien der Evangelisch-Protestantischen Geistlichen des Grossherzogtums Baden
Sep Hydrogen Isot Symp Jt Conf — Separation of Hydrogen Isotopes. Symposium. Joint Conference. Chemical Institute of Canada and the American Chemical Society
Sep Immed Chromatogr Journ Int Etude — Separation Immediate et Chromatographie. Journees Internationalesd'Etude
SEPM Core Workshop — Society of Economic Paleontologists and Mineralogists. Core Workshop
SEPM Short Course — SEPM [*Society of Economic Paleontologists and Mineralogists*] Short Course
SEPM (Soc Econ Paleontol Miner) Field Trip Guideb — SEPM (Society of Economic Paleontologists and Mineralogists) Field Trip Guidebook
SEPP — Seppyo. Journal. Japanese Society of Snow and Ice
Sep Purif — Separation and Purification
Sep Purif M — Separation and Purification Methods
Sep Purif Methods — Separation and Purification Methods
Sep Purif Technol — Separation and Purification Technology
SEPR — Studies in Ethics and the Philosophy of Religion
SEPRD — Sensory Processes
SEPS — Socio-Economic Planning Sciences
SEPS-B — Socio-Economic Planning Sciences
Sep Sci — Separation Science [*Later, Separation Science and Technology*]
Sep Sci Suppl — Separation Science. Supplement
Sep Sci Technol — Separation Science and Technology
Sept Arb — Septuaginta Arbeiten
Sep Technol — Separations Technology
Sep Technol Pro Eng Found Conf — Separation Technology. Proceedings. Engineering FoundationConference

Septent — Septentrion. Revue Archeologique Trimestrielle
Sept St — Septuaginta Studien
SEQ — String Education Quarterly
Sequential Anal — Sequential Analysis
SeR — Science et Religion
SER — Semaine d'Ethnologie Religieuse
Ser — Serapeum
Ser — Service
SeR — Sewanee Review
SeR — Studi e Ricerche
SERAA — Seramikkusu
Ser Adv Math Appl Sci — Series on Advances in Mathematics for Applied Sciences
Ser Adv Statist Mech — Series on Advances in Statistical Mechanics
Ser Algebra — Series in Algebra
Ser Appl Math — Series on Applied Mathematics
Ser Approx Decompos — Series in Approximations and Decompositions
Ser Astrom Astrofiz — Seriya Astrometriya i Astrofizika
Ser Astron Uniw Adama Mickiewicza Poznaniu — Seria Astronomia. Uniwersytet Imeni Adama Mickiewicza w Poznaniu
Serb Acad Sci Arts Bull — Serbian Academy of Sciences and Arts. Bulletin
Serb Acad Sci Arts Glas — Serbian Academy of Sciences and Arts. Glas
Serb Acad Sci Arts Monogr Dep Sci — Serbian Academy of Sciences and Arts. Monographs. Department of Sciences
Serb Acad Sci Arts Sep Ed Dep Nat Math Sci — Serbian Academy of Sciences and Arts. Separate Editions. Department of Natural and Mathematical Sciences
Serb Arch Gen Med — Serbian Archives of General Medicine
Serb Arch Med — Serbian Archives of Medicine
Serb Bull — Serbian Bulletin
Serb Chem Soc J — Serbian Chemical Society. Journal
Serbian Acad Sci and Arts Monogr Dep Tech Sci — Serbian Academy of Sciences and Arts. Monographs. Department of Technical Sciences
Ser Bibliogr — Serie Bibliografica
Ser Bibliogr INTA (Pergamino) — Serie Bibliografica. Instituto Nacional de Tecnologia Agropecuaria (Pergamino, Argentina)
Ser Biol Monogr Programa Reg Desarrollo Cient Tecnol — Serie de Biologia. Monografia. Programa Regional de DesarrolloCientifico y Tecnologico
Ser Biol Monogr Programa Reg Desenvolvimento Cient Tecnol — Serie de Biologia. Monografia. Programa Regional de DesenvolvimentoCientifico e Tecnologico
Ser Biol Programa Reg Desarrollo Cient Tecnol — Serie de Biologia. Programa Regional de Desarrollo Cientifico yTecnologico
Ser Biol Uniw Adama Mickiewicza Poznaniu — Seria Biologia. Uniwersytet Imeni Adama Mickiewicza w Poznaniu
Ser Biophys Biocybern — Series on Biophysics and Biocybernetics
Ser Cana Azucar — Serie Cana de Azucar
Ser Cent Estud Cient Santiago — Series of the Centro de Estudios Cientificos de Santiago
Ser Chem Uniw Adama Mickiewicza Poznaniu — Seria Chemia. Uniwersytet Imeni Adama Mickiewicza w Poznaniu
Ser Chim Univ Timisoara — Serie Chimie. Universitatea din Timisoara
Ser Chim Univ Timisoara Fac Chim Biol Geogr — Serie Chimie. Universitatea din Timisoara. Facultatea de Chimie-Biologie-Geografie
Ser Comput Methods Mech Thermal Sci — Series in Computational Methods in Mechanics and Thermal Sciences
Ser Comput Sci — Series in Computer Science
Ser Conf Union Math Internat — Serie des Conferences. Union Mathematique Internationale
Ser Defects Cryst Solids — Series Defects in Crystalline Solids
Serdica Math J — Serdica. Mathematical Journal
Ser Didact Univ Nac Tucuman Fac Agronom Zooteh — Serie Didactica. Universidad Nacional de Tucuman. Facultad de Agronomia y Zootecnia
Ser Dir Condens Matter Phys — Series on Directions in Condensed Matter Physics
Ser Div Ind Chem CSIRO — Serial. Division of Industrial Chemistry. Commonwealth Scientific and Industrial Research Oganisation
Ser Divulg Agron Angolana — Serie Divulgacao. Agronomia Angolana
Ser Divulg Projeto Desenvolvimento Pesqui Florestal — Serie Divulgacao. Projeto de Desenvolvimento e Pesquisa Florestal
SeRe — Sewanee Review
Ser Eksp Med (Riga) — Seriya Eksperimental'naya Meditsina (Riga)
Ser Emp — Service Employee
Serengeti Res Inst Annu Rep — Serengeti Research Institute. Annual Report
Ser Entomol (The Hague) — Series Entomologica (The Hague)
Ser Espec Sup Desenvolvimento Nordeste Div Geol (Braz) — Serie Especial. Superintendencia do Desenvolvimento do Nordeste.Divisao de Geologia (Brazil)
Ser Filoz Logika — Seria Filozofia i Logika
Ser Fis Monogr Programa Reg Desarrollo Cient Tecnol — Serie de Fisica. Monografia. Programa Regional de Desarrollo Cientificoy Tecnologico
Ser Fis Monogr Programa Reg Desenvolvimento Cient Tecnol — Serie de Fisica. Monografia. Programa Regional de DesenvolvimentoCientifico e Tecnologico
Ser Fis Programa Reg Desarrollo Cient Tecnol — Serie de Fisica. Programa Regional de Desarrollo Cientifico yTecnologico
Ser Fiz Uniw Im Adama Mickiewicza Poznaniu — Seria Fizyka. Uniwersytet Imienia Adama Mickiewicza w Poznaniu
Ser Food Mater Sci — Series in Food Material Science
Ser Geol Acad Cienc Cuba Inst Geol — Serie Geologica. Academia de Ciencias de Cuba. Instituto de Geologia
Ser Geol Econ (Braz) Sup Desenvolvimento Nordeste Div Geol — Serie Geologia Economica (Brazil). Superintendencia do Desenvolvimento do Nordeste. Divisao de Geologia
Ser Geol Espec (Braz) Supt Desenvolvimento Nordeste Div Geol — Serie Geologia Especial (Brazil). Superintendencia do Desenvolvimento doNordeste. Divisao de Geologia

Ser Haematol — Series Haematologica
Ser Handb Mod Psych — Serial Handbook of Modern Psychiatry
Ser Hum — Series in the Humanities
Serials BLL — Serials in the British Lending Library
Serials Libn — Serials Librarian
Serials Libr — Serials Librarian
Serials R — Serials Review
Sericult Res — Sericultural Research
Serie Bibliogr Temat — Serie Bibliografia Tematica
Ser Inf Conf Cursos Reun Interam Inst Agric Sci — Serie Informes de Conferencias. Cursos y Reuniones-Inter-American Institute of Agricultural Sciences
SERIX — Swedish Environmental Research Index
Ser Knots Everything — Series on Knots and Everything
Ser L — Serie Linguistica
Ser Lib — Serials Librarian
Ser Libr — Serials Librarian
SERL Rep — SERL [*Sanitary Engineering Research Laboratory*] Report
SERM — Syncrude Environmental Research Monograph
Ser Mat — Seria Matematyka
Ser Mat Fis — Serie di Matematica e Fisica
Ser Math Biol Med — Series in Mathematical Biology and Medicine
Ser Metallofiz — Seriya Metallofizika
Ser Modern Appl Math — Series in Modern Applied Mathematics
Ser Modern Condensed Matter Phys — Series in Modern Condensed Matter Physics
Ser Mol Biol — Seriya Molekulyarnaya Biologiya
Ser Monogr Gen Physiol — Series of Monographs on General Physiology
Ser Monogr Inst Zootec — Serie Monografias. Instituto de Zootecnia
Ser Multivariate Anal — Series on Multivariate Analysis
Ser Mycol — Series on Mycology
Ser Nonlinear Opt — Series in Nonlinear Optics
Ser Notes Rech Fond Univ Luxemb — Serie Notes de Recherche. Fondation Universitaire Luxembourgeoise
Ser Number Theory — Series in Number Theory
Ser Obz Mezhdunar Agentstvo At Energ — Seriya Obzorov. Mezhdunarodnoe Agentstvo po Atomnoi Energii
Serol Mus Bull — Serological Museum Bulletin
Serono Clin Colloq Reprod Proc — Serono Clinical Colloquia on Reproduction. Proceedings
Serono Symp Proc — Serono Symposia. Proceedings
Serono Symp Publ Raven Press — Serono Symposia Publications from Raven Press
Serono Symp Ser Adv Exp Med — Serono Symposia Series Advances in Experimental Medicine
Ser Optim — Series on Optimization
Ser Opt Photonics — Series in Optics and Photonics
Serotonin Mol Biol Recept Funct Eff — Serotonin. Molecular Biology, Receptors, and Functional Effects
SERP — Studies in the History and Art of the Eastern Provinces of the Roman Empire
Ser Paedopsychiatr — Series Paedopsychiatrica
Ser Pap Tech Univ Den Inst Hydrodyn Hydraul Eng — Series Papers. Technical University of Denmark. Institute of Hydrodynamics and Hydraulic Engineering
Ser Piper — Serie Piper
Ser Poeyana Inst Biol Acad Cienc Cuba — Serie Poeyana. Instituto de Biologia. Academia de Ciencias de Cuba
Ser Poeyana Inst Zool Acad Cienc Cuba — Serie Poeyana. Instituto de Zoologia. Academia de Ciencias de Cuba
Ser Publ Geogr — Serial Publications in Geography
Ser Publ US Northeast Reg Plant Introd Stn — Serial Publication. United States Northeast Regional Plant Introduction Station
Ser Pure Math — Series in Pure Mathematics
Ser Quim Monogr Programa Reg Desarrollo Cient Tecnol — Serie de Quimica. Monografia. Programa Regional de DesarrolloCientifico y Tecnologico
Ser Quim Monogr Programa Reg Desenvolvimento Cient Tecnol — Serie de Quimica. Monografia. Programa Regional de DesenvolvimentoCientifico e Tecnologico
Ser Quim Programa Reg Desarrollo Cient Tecnol — Serie de Quimica. Programa Regional de Desarrollo Cientifico yTecnologico
Ser R — Serials Review
Serra Or — Serra d'Or
SerrC — Serraika Chronika
Ser Real Anal — Series in Real Analysis
Ser Res Publ Assoc Res Nerv Ment Dis — Series of Research Publications. Association for Research in Nervousand Mental Disease
Ser Rev — Serials Review
Ser Sci — Serie Scientifica
Ser Semicond Sci Technol — Series on Semiconductor Science and Technology
Ser SI — Serial Slants
Ser Slants Chicago — Serial Slants (Chicago)
Ser Soviet East European Math — Series on Soviet and East European Mathematics
Ser Theoret Appl Mech — Series in Theoretical and Applied Mechanics
SERT J — SERT [*Society of Electronic and Radio Technicians*] Journal
Ser Univ — Serie Universitaria
Ser Univ Fund Juan March — Serie Universitaria. Fundacion "Juan March"
Ser Univ Math — Series on University Mathematics
Serv — Service: A Review of Agricultural and Chemical Progress
Serv Can Faune Cah Biol — Service Canadien de la Faune. Cahiers de Biologie
Serv Carte Geol Alsace Lorraine Bull — Service de la Carte Geologique d'Alsace et de Lorraine. Bulletin
Serv Cent Prot Rayonnement Ionis (Fr) Rapp Act — Service Central de Protection Contre les Rayonnements Ionisants (France). Rapport d'Activite

Serv Esp Saude Publica Rev (Brazil) — Servico Especial de Saude Publica. Revista (Brazil)
Serv Farm Ranch Home — Serving Farm, Ranch, and Home. Quarterly. University of Nebraska. College of Agriculture and Home Economics. Agricultural Experiment Station
Serv Fom Min Lab DGGM Estud Notas Trab — Servico de Fomento Mineiro e Laboratorio da DGGM. Estudos. Notas eTrabalhos
Serv For Invest Exper Trab — Servicio Forestal de Investigaciones y Experiencias. Trabajos
Serv Geol Bolivia Bol — Servicio Geologico de Bolivia. Boletin
Serv Geol Ital Mem Descr Carta Geol Ital — Servizio Geologico d'Italia Memorie Descrittive della Carta Geologica d'Italia
Serv Geol Pol Inst Geol Pol Bull — Service Geologique de Pologne. Institut Geologique de Pologne. Bulletin
Serv Geol Port Mem — Servicos Geologics de Portugal. Memoria
Service Soc — Service Social
Servico Soc de Comer Bol Bibl — Servico Social de Comercio. Boletim Bibliografico
Servico Soc e Soc — Servico Social e Sociedade
Serv Nac Min Geol (Argent) Rev — Servicio Nacional Minero Geologico (Argentina). Revista
Serv Shell Agric Ser A — Servicio Shell para el Agricultor. Serie A
Serv Shell Agr Ser A — Servicio Shell para el Agricultor. Serie A. Informe
Serv Soc (Bruxelles) — Service Social (Bruxelles)
Serv Soc Lima — Servicio Social (Lima)
Serv Soc Monde — Service Social dans le Monde
Serv Soc (Quebec) — Service Social (Quebec)
Serv Soc Santiago — Servicio Social (Santiago)
Serv Soc S Paulo — Servico Social (Sao Paulo)
Serv Stn Merch — Service Station Merchandising
Serv World — Service World International
Ser Work Organ — Series on Work and Organization
SES — Schriften far Ekonomik un Statistik
SEs — Science et Esprit
SES — Social and Economic Studies
SES — Sophia English Studies
SES — Studies in Environmental Science
SES — Syro-Egyptian Society. Original Papers
SESA Pap — SESA [*Society for Experimental Stress Analysis*] Papers
SESEA — Schriften der Evangelischen Studiengemeinschaft der Evangelischen Akademien
Ses Inaug R Acad Farm Barcelona — Sesion Inaugural. Real Academia de Farmacia de Barcelona
SeSL — Studi e Saggi Linguistici
SESM — Sovetskaia Etnografiia. Sbornik (Moscow)
Ses Nauk Inst Ochr Rosl Mater — Sesja Naukowa Instytutu Ochrony Roslin. Materialy
SES Rep CSIRO Sol Energy Stud — SES Report. Solar Energy Studies Unit. Commonwealth Scientific and Industrial Research Organisation
Sess Cas — Session Cases. Court of Session
Sess Cas J — Session Cases. High Court of Justiciary
Sess Com Int Poids Mes Com Consult Thermom — Session. Comite International des Poids et Mesures. Comite Consultatifde Thermometrie
Sess Etud Bienn Phys Nucl CR — Session d'Etudes Biennale de Physique Nucleaire. Comptes-Rendus
Sess Pap Am Min Congr Coal Conv — Session Papers. American Mining Congress Coal Convention
Sess Pap CC — Central Criminal Court Cases, Sessions Papers
Sess Pap Parl Dominion Canada — Sessional Papers of the Parliament of the Dominion of Canada
Sess Pap RIBA — Sessional Papers of the Royal Institute of British Architects
Sess Pubbliche Ateneo Veneto — Sessioni Pubbliche dell' Ateneo Veneto
SEST — Studien zur Evangelischen Sozialtheologie und Sozialethhik
SET — Semana Espanola de Teologia
SET — Studies in English (University of Texas)
SeT — Studi e Testi
SEt — Studi Etruschi
Seta Artif — Seta Artificiale
Set Hall Leg J — Seton Hall Legislative Journal
Set H LR — Seton Hall Law Review
SEtI — Serie Etudes sur l'Islam
SET Manpower Comments — Scientific Engineering. Technical Manpower Comments
SEtn — Sovetskaja Etnografija
Seto Mar Biol Lab Publ — Seto Marine Biological Laboratory. Publications
Seton Hall Leg J — Seton Hall Legislative Journal
Seton Hall L Rev — Seton Hall Law Review
Settim Med — Settimana Medica
Settim Osp — Settimana Ospitaliera
Sett Studio Cent It Stud Alto Med — Settimane di Studio del Centro Italiano di Studi sull'Alto Medioevo
SETU — Sumerian Economic Texts from the Third Ur Dynasty
Set Valued Anal — Set-Valued Analysis
SEU — Dynamik im Handel
SEU — Studia Ethnographica Upsaliensa
Seu Chuan Ta Hsueh Pao Tzu Jan Ko Hsueh — Acta Scientiarum Naturalium Universitatis Szechuanensis/Seu ch'uan Ta Hsueh Hsueh Pao, Tzu Jan K'o Hsueh
SEV — Annuaire. Societe d'Emulation de la Vendee
Sevcenko Ges Wiss — Sevcenko Gesellschaft der Wissenschaften
Sevcenko Soc Sci Sect Chim Biol Med — Sevcenko Societe Scientifique. Section de Chimie, de Biologie, et deMedecine
Sev Cent N — Seventeenth-Century News
Seven Ct N — Seventeenth-Century News
Seventh-Day Adventist Period Index — Seventh-Day Adventist Periodical Index

Severni Morava — Severni Morava Vastivedny Sbornik
Sev Oset Gos Med Inst Sb Nauchn Tr — Severo-Osetinskii Gosudarstvennyi Meditsinskii Institut. SbornikNauchnykh Trudov
Sev-Oset Gos Pedagog Inst Uch Zap — Severo-Osetinskii Gosudarstvennyi Pedagogicheskii Institut. Uchenye Zapiski
SEVPEN — Service d'Edition et de Vente des Publications de l'Education Nationale
Sev-Vost Kompleks Nauch-Issled Inst Akad Nauk SSSR Sib Otd — Severo-Vostochnyy Kompleksnyy Nauchno-Issledovatel'skiy Institut Akademiya NaukSSSR Sibirskoye Otdeleniye
Sev Vost Petrogr Soveshch — Severo-Vostochnoe Petrograficheskoe Soveshchanie
Sev Zapad Evr Chasti SSSR — Severo-Zapad Evropeiskoi Chasti SSSR
Sev Zapadn Zaochn Politekh Inst Tr — Severo-Zapadnyi Zaochnyi Politekhnicheskii Institut Trudy
Sew — Sewanee Review
Sewage Effluent Water Resour Symp Rep Proc — Sewage Effluent as a Water Resource. Symposium. Report of Proceedings
Sewage Ind Waste Eng — Sewage and Industrial Waste Engineering
Sewage Ind Wastes — Sewage and Industrial Wastes
Sewage Purif Land Drain Water River Eng — Sewage Purification. Land Drainage. Water and River Engineering
Sewage Works Eng Munic Sanit — Sewage Works Engineering and Municipal Sanitation
Sewage Works J — Sewage Works Journal
Sewanee R — Sewanee Review
Sewanee Rev — Sewanee Review
Sewan R — Sewanee Review
Sew R — Sewanee Review
Sew Rev — Sewanee Review
Sex — Sextant
Sex Disabil — Sexuality and Disability
Sex Plant R — Sexual Plant Reproduction
Sex Plant Reprod — Sexual Plant Reproduction
Sex Scien — Working Papers on Sex, Science, and Culture
SexST — Sextant-Signes du Temps
Sex Transm Dis — Sexually-Transmitted Diseases
Seybold Rep Off Systems — Seybold Report on Office Systems
Seybold Rep Prof Comp — Seybold Report on Professional Computing
Seychelles Dep Agric Annu Rep — Seychelles Department of Agriculture. Annual Report
SEZ — Seifen, Oele, Fette, Waechse. Die Internationale Fachzeitschrift
Sez Clin Eur Assoc Int Gerontol Congr — Sezione Clinica Europea. Associazione Internazionale diGerontologia. Congresso
Sezd Arm Fiziol Ova — S'ezd Armyanskogo Fiziologicheskogo Obshchestva
Sezd Biokhim Lit SSR — S'ezd Biokhimikov Litovskoi SSR
Sezd Dermatol Venerol BSSR — S'ezd Dermatologov i Venerologov BSSR
Sezd Farm Kaz — S'ezd Farmatsevtov Kazakhstana
Sezd Farm Ukr SSR — S'ezd Farmatsevtov Ukrainskoi SSR
Sezd Mikrobiol Ukr — S'ezd Mikrobiologov Ukrainy
Sezd Vses Fiziol Ova Im I P Pavlova — S'ezd Vsesoyuznogo Fiziologicheskogo Obshchestva Imeni I. P. Pavlova
SEzik — Sapostavitelno Ezikoznanie
SF — Sbornik Filologicky
SF — Science Fiction
SF — Security Forecast
SF — Social Forces
SF — Socialisticki Front
SF — Soils and Fertilizers
Sf — Sprachforum
SF — Stray Feathers. Ornithological Journal
SF — Studia Fennica
SF — Studia Filozoficzne
SF — Studia Friburgensia
SF — Studi Francesi
SF — Suedostforschungen. Internationale Zeitschrift fuer Geschichte, Kultur, und Landeskunde Suedosteuropas
SFA — Science Fiction Adventures
SFAB — Science Fiction Adventures
SFAC — Science Fiction Adventure Classics
SFAD — Science Fiction Adventures
SFANA2 — Sheepfarming Annual
SF & R — Scholars' Facsimiles and Reprints
SFAW — Sitzungsberichte der Finnischen Akademie der Wissenschaften
SFB — Sbornik Filosoficke Fakulty v Bratislave
SFB — Science Fantasy
SFB — Sugarcane Farmers Bulletin
SFBAEMN — San Francisco Bay Area Early Music News
SF Bay — San Francisco Bay Guardian
SF Bay Gdn — San Francisco Bay Guardian
SFC — San Francisco Chronicle
SFC — San Francisco Examiner and Chronicle
SFC — Science Fiction Adventure Classics
SFC — SF Commentary
SFC — Sweden Now
SFCAe — Studien zur Erforschung des Christlichen Aegyptens
SFCHD — Solid Fuel Chemistry
SFCRAO — Collection of Papers Presented at the Annual Symposium on Fundamental Cancer Research
SFCTDX — Centro Internacional de Agricultura Tropical [*CIAT*]. Series FE
SFD — Science Fiction Digest
SFD — Sound and Vibration
SFDH — Schriften des Freien Deutschen Hochstifts
SFDY — Studies by Members of the French Department. Yale University. Department of French
SFE — Studies in Financial Economics

SFECAG — Figlina. Societe Francaise d'Etude de la Ceramique Antique en Gaule
SFELT — Societe Francaise d'Editions Litteraires et Techniques
SFen — Studia Fennica
S Fernando Obs Mar A — Anales del Instituto y Observatorio de Marina de San Fernando
SF Examiner — San Francisco Examiner
SFFAAM — Fauna Fennica
SFFBU — Sbornik Praci Filosoficke Fakulty Brnenske University
SFFF — Societas pro Fauna et Flora Fennica
SFFFM — Societas pro Fauna et Flora Fennica. Memoranda
SFFUK — Sbornik Filozofickej Fakulty Univerzity Komenskeho. Philologica
SFFUP — Sbornik Filozofickej Fakulty Univerzity P. J. Safarika v Presove
SFG — SF Greats
SFG — Spanische Forschungen. Gorresgesellschaft
SFGG — Spanische Forschungen der Goerresgesellschaft
SFH — Serie de Fuentes Historicas. Instituto de Antropologia e Historia. Universidad Central de Venezuela
SFH — SF Horizons
SFHE — Series Facultatis Historiae Ecclesiasticae
SFI — SF Impulse
SFI — Statistiques Financieres Internationales
SFI — Studi di Filogia Italiana
SFIB — SFI [*Sport Fishing Institute*] Bulletin
SFic — Science Fiction
S Fict R — Science Fiction Review
SFil — Studime Filologjike
SFIQ — Science Fiction Quarterly
SFIS — Stanford French and Italian Studies
SFJC — Series Facultatis Juris Canonici
SFK — Periodiekenparade
Sf K — Samfundets Krav
SFKGA — Sprechsaal fuer Keramik, Glas, Email, Silikate
SFL — Studies in French Literature
SFLJ — San Francisco Law Journal
S Florist Nurseryman — Southern Florist and Nurseryman
SFLR — University of San Francisco. Law Review
SFM — Science Fiction Monthly
SFM — Series Facultatis Missiologicae
SFM — Studi di Filologia Moderna
SFM — Symposia. Fondation Merieux
SFMA — Studien zu den Fundmuenzen der Antike
SFMV — Studien und Forschungen zur Menschen-und Voelkerkunde
SFN — Sammlung Franzoesischer Neudrucke
SFN — SFRA Newsletter
SFNL — Shakespeare on Film Newsletter
SFNYA — Southern Florist and Nurseryman
SFOK — Schriftenreihe des Studienausschusses der EKU fuer Fragen der Orthodoxen Kirche
SFORD — Sozialistische Forstwirtschaft
SFP — Science Fiction Plus
SfP — Science for People
SFPE Technol Rep — SFPE [*Society of Fire Protection Engineers*] Technology Report
SFPS — Studia z Filologii Polskiej i Slowianskiej
SFQ — Science Fiction Quarterly
SFQ — Southern Folklore Quarterly
SFR — San Francisco Review
SFR — Science Fiction Review
SFR — Stanford French Review
S Fr — Studi Francesi
SFR — Studii de Filologia Romanza
SFran — Studi Francescani
SFRB — San Francisco Review of Books
SF Rev Bks — San Francisco Review of Books
SFrL — Studies in French Literature
SFRM — Science Fiction Review. Monthly
SFrQ — San Francisco Quarterly
SFRSAY — Food Research Institute. Studies
SFRT — Science Fiction and Fantasy RoundTable
SFS — Science Fiction Stories
SFS — Science Fiction Studies
SFS — Science for Schools
SFS — Spicilegii Friburgensis Subsidia
SFSL — Science Fiction. Review of Speculative Literature
SFSLA — Sbornik Trudov po Agronomicheskoi Fizike
SFSMD — Studia Francisci Scholten Memoriae Dicata
SFSS — Svenska Fornskriftsaellskapets Skrifter
SFST — Science Fiction Studies
SFSt — Swiss-French Studies
SFSUA — Studia Forestalia Suecica
SFSV — Svenska Forfattare Utgivna av Svenska Vitterhetssamfundet
SF Sym — San Francisco Symphony. Program Notes
SFT — Series Facultatis Theologicae
SFT — Sheffield Morning Telegraph
SFT — Soviet and Eastern European Foreign Trade
SFT — Studi di Filologia Todeska
SFTB — Science Fiction Times
SFThL — Schriften der Finnischen Theologischen Literaturgesellschaft
SFUJA — Steam and Fuel Users' Journal
SFUK — Sbornik Filozofickej Fakulty Univerzity Komenskeho
SFUPD — Synthetic Fuels Update
SFUS — Sbornik Filozofickej Fakulty Univerzity P. J. Safarika
SFUS — Sovetskoe Finno-Ugrovedenie/Soviet Fenno-Ugric Studies
SFVK — Svenska Folkskolans Vaenner. Kalender
SFY — Science Fiction Yearbook

SG — Sammlung Goeschen
SG — Siculorum Gymnasium
SG — Sinte Geertruydtsbronne
SG — Sintesis Geografica
SG — Socialistische Gids
SG — Sprach der Gegenwart
SG — Studi Genuensi
SG — Studi Germanici
SG — Studi Goriziani
SG — Studium Generale
SG — Sydney Gazette
SGA J — SGA [*Society of Gastrointestinal Assistants*] Journal
SGAK — Studien zur Germanistik, Anglistik und Komparatistik
SGAOR — Sitzungsberichte. Gesellschaft fuer Geschichte und Altertumskunde der Ostseeprovinzen Russlands
SGB — Schlesische Geschichtsblaetter (Breslau)
SGB — Studien und Mitteilungen zur Geschichte des Benediktiner-Ordens
SGBIA — Symposia Genetica et Biologica Italica
SGCL — Studies in General and Comparative Literature
SGD — Solar-Geophysical Data
SGDG — Studia op Godsdienstig, Wetenschappelijk en Letterkundig Gebied
SGDI — Sammlung der Griechischen Dialekinschriften
SGE — Soobshcheniia Gosudarstvennogo Ermitazha
SGEGA — Studia Geophysica et Geodaetica
SGen — Studium Generale
SGer — Studia Germanica
S Ger S — Stanford German Studies
SGF — Sozialgeschichtliche Forschungen
SGF — Stockholmer Germanistische Forschungen
SGFMV — Sammendrag af Groenlands Fangstilister MV
SGF Publ — SGF [*Sveriges Gummitekniska Foerening*] Publicerande
SGFWJ — Schriften der Gesellschaft zur Foerderung der Wissenschaft des Judentums
SGG — Studia Germanica Gandensia
SGGAOPR — Sitzungsberichte. Gesellschaft fuer Geschichte und Altertumskunde der Ostseeprovinzen Russlands
SGGT — Svenskt Gudstjaenstliv
SGH — Generale Maatschappij van Belgie. Informatieblad
SGh — Studia Ghisleriana
SGHLA — Stadt- und Gebaeudetechnik
SGI — Studi di Grammatica Italiana
SGJ — Sunday Gleaner (Jamaica)
SGK — Schriften der Koenigsberger Gelehrten Gesellschaft Geisteswissenschaftliche Klasse
SGK — Shinagaku Kenkyu
SGKA — Studien zur Geschichte und Kultur des Altertums
SGKAE — Studien zur Geschichte und Kultur des Altertums. Ergaenzungsband
SGKIO — Studien zur Geschichte und Kultur des Islamischen Orients
SGKL — Stimme der Gemeinde zum Kirchlichen Leben
SGKMT — Studien zur Geschichte der Katholischen Moraltheologie
SGL — Spiegel
SGL — Studies in German Literature
SGL/B — Boletin. Sociedad Geografica de Lima
SGLF — Symposia. Giovanni Lorenzini Foundation
SGLG — Sammlung Griechischer und Lateinischer Grammatiker
SGLG — Studien zur Griechischen und Lateinischen Grammatik
SGLI — Societe Geographique de Liege. Bulletin
SGLL — Studies in the Germanic Languages and Literatures
SGLSA — Stomatoloski Glasnik Srbije
SGM — Schachtgraeber von Mykenae
SGM — Scottish Geographical Magazine
SGMH — Study Group. Institute for Research into Mental and Multiple Handicap
SGMII — Soobshcheniia Gosudarstvennyi Muzei Izobrazitel'nykh Iskusstv imeni A.S. Pushkina
SGN — Simulation Gaming News
SGNAD — Shoni Geka Naika
SGNET — Sea Grant Network
SGNP — Studien zur Geschichte des Neueren Protestantismus
SGNPQ — Studien zur Geschichte des Neueren Protestantismus. Quellenhefte
SGNRA — Surgical Neurology
SGo — Studi Goriziani
SGOBA — Surgery, Gynecology, and Obstetrics
SGOE — Studien zur Geschichte Osteuropas
SGoldoniani — Studi Goldoniani
SGor — Studi Goriziani
SGPS — Structure and Growth of Philosophic Systems from Plato to Spinoza
SGR — Science and Government Report
SGR — Studien zu den Grundlagen der Reformation
SGr — Studii de Gramatica
SGram — Studii de Gramatica
S Gravenh I Ing Ts — Tijdschrift van het Koninklijk Instituut van Ingenieurs. 's Gravenhage
S Gravenh I Ing Vh — Verhandelingen van het Koninklijk Instituut van Ingenieurs. 's Gravenhage
SGRT — Soviet Geography. Review and Translations
SGS — Scottish Gaelic Studies
SGS — Studii Graeca Stockholmiensis
SGSG — Studi Gregoriani per la Storia di Gregorio VII
SGSHA — Shigen Gijutsu Shikenjo Hokoku
SGSLM — Seances Generales. Societe des Lettres, Sciences, et Arts et d'Agriculture
SGSRDC — Selye's Guide to Stress Research
SGSt — Seckauer Geschichtliche Studien
SGSYB — Stadler Genetics Symposia
SGT — Schriften. Gesellschaft fuer Theatergeschichte

SGTADY — University of Southern California. Institute for Marine and Coastal Studies. Sea Grant Technical Report Series
SGTID — Sawyer's Gas Turbine International
SGTK — Studien zur Geschichte der Theologie und Kirche
Sgtl — Sightlines
SGTPA — Sbornik Trudov Nauchno-Issledovatel'skii Institut Gigieny Truda i Profzabolevanii Imeni N. I. Makhviladze
SGU — Studia Germanistica Upsaliensia
SGU — Studia Graeca Upsaliensia
SGV — Summlung Gemeinverstaendlicher Vortraege und Schriften aus dem Gebiet der Theologie und Religionsgeschichte
SGVGA — Sbornik Geologickych Ved. Geologie
SGVLA — Sbornik Geologickych Ved. Loziskova Geologie
SGVS — Summlung Gemeinverstaendlicher Vortraege und Schriften aus dem Gebiet der Theologie und Religionsgeschichte
SGVUA — Sbornik Geologickych Ved. Uzita Geofyzika
SGym — Siculorum Gymnasium
SGZAB — Sanyo Gijutsu Zasshi
SH — Seckauer Hefte
SH — Semantische Hefte
Sh — Shadforth's Reserved Judgements
Sh — Shakti
SH — Shih-ta Hsueeh-pao
Sh — Shiso
S H — Slovenska Hudba
SH — South Third World Magazine
SH — Speighel Historiael van de Bond van Gentse Germanisten
SH — Sprache der Hethiter
SH — Studia Hellenistica
SH — Studia Hibernica
SH — Subsidia Hagiographica
SH — Sun-Herald
SH — Sydney Herald
SHA — Sitzungsberichte. Heidelberg Akademie der Wissenschaft
SHA — Sun-Herald (Australia)
Shaanxi Med J — Shaanxi Medical Journal
SHAF — Societe de l'Histoire de l'Art Francais
SHAGAn — Societe d'Histoire et d'Archeologie de Gand. Annales
SHAGBull — Societe d'Histoire et d'Archeologie de Gand. Bulletin
SHAGL — Schriften des Hessischen Amts fuer Geschichtliche Landeskunde
Shakes Jah — Shakespeare-Jahrbuch
Shakespeare-Jahrb — Shakespeare-Jahrbuch
Shakespeare Q — Shakespeare Quarterly
Shakespeare S — Shakespeare Survey
Shakespeare Surv — Shakespeare Survey
Shakes Q — Shakespeare Quarterly
Shakes Surv — Shakespeare Survey
Shakhtnoe Stroit — Shakhtnoe Stroitel'stvo
Shak-Jahrb — Shakespeare-Jahrbuch
ShakS — Shakespeare Studies
Shale Ctry — Shale Country
Shale Rev — Shale Review
SHALPub — Societe Historique et Archeologique dans le Duche de Limbourg. Publications
Shambhala Occas Pap Inst Tib Stud — Shambhala Occasional Papers of the Institute of Tibetan Studies
Shane Q — Shane Quarterly
Shanghai Chem Ind — Shanghai Chemical Industry
Shanghai Educ Rev — Shanghai Educational Review/Chung-Hua Chiao Yue Chieh
Shanghai Environ Sci — Shanghai Environmental Sciences
Shanghai Iron Steel Res Inst Tech Rep — Shanghai Iron and Steel Research Institute. Technical Report
Shanghai Mus Bull — Shanghai Museum Bulletin
Shantung Med J — Shantung Medical Journal
Shantung Univ J — Shantung University Journal / Shan Tung Ta Hsueeh Pao
Shanxi A Med Rev — Shanxi-A Medicina Revuo
Shanxi Med J — Shanxi Medical Journal
Shanxi Med Pharm J — Shanxi Medical and Pharmaceutical Journal
Shanxi Univ J Nat Sci Ed — Shanxi University. Journal. Natural Science Edition
Sharpe — Sharpe's London Magazine
Sharpes Lond M — Sharpe's London Magazine
Sharp Tech J — Sharp Technical Journal
SHA Senlis — Comptes-Rendus et Memoires. Societe d'Histoire et d'Archeologie de Senlis
SHAssocPub — Southern History Association. Publications
SHATAn — Societe Historique et Archeologique de Tournai. Annales
SHAW — Sitzungsberichte. Heidelberg Akademie der Wissenschaft
ShawB — Shaw Bulletin
SHAWPH — Sitzungsberichte der Heidelberger Akademie der Wissenschaften. Philosophisch-Historische Klasse
Shaw R — Shaw Review
Shaw Rev — Shaw Review
S Hb — Saechsische Heimatblaetter
Shchorichnyk Ukrayins'ke Bot Tov — Shchorichnyk Ukrayins'ke Botanichne Tovarystvo
SHCS — Springer Series on Health Care and Society
SHCSR — Spicilegium Historicum Congregationis Smi Redemptoris
SHCT — Studies in the History of Christian Thought
SHE — Studia Historico-Ecclesiastica
SHECD — Solar Heating and Cooling
Sheep Beef Farm Surv — Sheep and Beef Farm Survey
Sheepfarm Annu — Sheepfarming Annual
Sheepfarming Annu — Sheepfarming Annual
Sheepfarming Annu Massey Agr Coll — Sheepfarming Annual. Massey Agricultural College

Sheep Goat Handb — Sheep and Goat Handbook
Sheep Goat Wool Mohair — Sheep and Goat. Wool and Mohair
Sheet Met Ind — Sheet Metal Industries
Sheet Met Platework News — Sheet Metal and Plateworking News
Sheffield Univ Fuel Soc J — Sheffield University. Fuel Society. Journal
Sheffield Univ Geol Soc J — Sheffield University. Geological Society. Journal
SHEH — Stanford Honors Essays in the Humanities
S Heim — Schones Heim
S Heimat — Schoenere Heimat
Shelf Life Foods Beverages Proc Int Flavor Conf — Shelf Life of Foods and Beverages. Proceedings. InternationalFlavor Conference
Shell — Revista Shell
Shell Agric — Shell in Agriculture
Shell Aviat News — Shell Aviation News
Shell Bitum Rev — Shell Bitumin Review
Shell Devel Co Explor and Production Research Div Pub — Shell Development Company. Exploration and Production Research Division. Publication
Shellfish — Shellfish. Market Review and Outlook
Shell House J — Shell House Journal
Shell J — Shell Journal
Shell Mag — Shell Magazine
Shell Polym — Shell Polymers
Shell Trin — Shell Trinidad
Shelter — Shelterforce
Shen — Shenandoah
Shepard Commem Vol Pap Mar Geol — Shepard Commemorative Volume. Papers on Marine Geology
Sherst Delo — Sherstyanoe Delo
SHEU — Studia Historico-Ecclesiastica Upsaliensia
SHF — Societe de l'Histoire de France
SHFABull — Societe de l'Histoire de France. Annuaire Bulletin
SHG — Subsidia Hagiographica
SHGAB8 — Siriraj Hospital Gazette
SHGED — Shoni Geka
SHGNA — Shigen
SHH — Studia Historica Academiae Scientiarum Hungaricae
SHHPB — Shu-Hsueh Hsueh-Pao
SHib — Studia Hibernica
Shield — Shield Civil Service News
SHIGD4 — Japanese Journal of Psychosomatic Medicine
Shikoku Acta Med — Shikoku Acta Medica
Shikoku Agric Res — Shikoku Agricultural Research
Shikoku Agr Res — Shikoku Agricultural Research
Shikoku Dent Res — Shikoku Dental Research
Shikoku J Clin Chem — Shikoku Journal of Clinical Chemistry
Shikoku Med J — Shikoku Medical Journal
Shilling Mag — Shilling Magazine
Shimadzu Rev — Shimadzu Review
Shimane J Med Sci — Shimane Journal of Medical Science
Shinagawa Refract Tech Rep — Shinagawa Refractories Technical Report
Shinagawa Tech Rep — Shinagawa Technical Report
Shinbun — Horitsu Shinbun
Shinko Electr J — Shinko Electric Journal
Shinshu Hort — Shinshu Horticulture/Nagano Horticultural Society
Shinshu Med J — Shinshu Medical Journal
Shinshu Univ Fac Sci J — Shinshu University. Faculty of Science. Journal
Ship Abstr — Ship Abstracts
Ship and Boat — Ship and Boat International
Ship & Boat Int — Ship and Boat International
Shipbldg Mar Engng Int — Shipbuilding and Marine Engineering International
Shipbldg Shipp Rec — Shipbuilding and Shipping Record
Ship Boat — Ship and Boat
Shipbuild & Mar Engng Int — Shipbuilding and Marine Engineering International
Shipbuild Mar Engine Build — Shipbuilder and Marine Engine Builder
Shipbuild Mar Eng Int — Shipbuilding and Marine Engineering International
Shipbuild Rep — Shipbuilding and Repair
Shipcare Marit Manage — Shipcare and Maritime Management
Ship Com Aviation — Shipping, Commerce, and Aviation of Australia
Shipping Reg P & F — Shipping Regulation. Pike and Fischer
Shipping Statis — Shipping Statistics
Shipping Statis and Econ — Shipping Statistics and Economics
Shipp Weekly — Shipping Weekly
Shipp Wld Shipbldr — Shipping World and Shipbuilder
Shipp World & Shipb — Shipping World and Shipbuilder
Shipp World & Shipbuild — Shipping World and Shipbuilder
Ship Res Inst (Tokyo) Pap — Ship Research Institute (Tokyo). Papers
Shire & Munic R — Shire and Municipal Record
Shire & Munic Rec — Shire and Municipal Record
Shire Munic Rec — Shire and Municipal Record
Shirley Inst Bull — Shirley Institute. Bulletin
Shirley Inst Mem — Shirley Institute. Memoirs
Shirley Inst Publ — Shirley Institute Publication
S Hist — Studia Historica. Acta Societatis Historiae Ouluensis
S Hist — Studime Historike
Shivaji Univ J — Shivaji University. Journal
Shivaji Univ Sci J — Shivaji University. Science Journal
Shiva Math Ser — Shiva Mathematics Series
Shizenshi-Kenkyu Occas Pap Osaka Mus Nat Hist — Shizenshi-Kenkyu Occasional Papers. Osaka Museum of Natural History
Shizuoka Univ Fac Sci Rep — Skizuoka University Faculty of Science. Reports
SHJ — Scripta Hierosolymitana (Jerusalem)
Sh-J — Shakespeare-Jahrbuch
Sh-Jb — Shakespeare-Jahrbuch
SHJMD — Soon Chun Hyang Journal of Medicine
ShJW — Shakespeare-Jahrbuch (Weimar)

SHK — Shock
SHKBA — Schriftenreihe der Historischen Komission bei der Bayerischen Akademie der Wissenschaften
SHKBDX — Saito Ho-On Kai Museum of Natural History. Research Bulletin
SHKEA5 — Japanese Journal of Psychology
SHKKA — Shika Kiso Igakkai Zasshi
SHL — Amsterdam Studies in the Theory and History of Linguistic Science
SHL-3 — Amsterdam Studies in the Theory and History of Linguistic Science. Series III. Studies in the History of Linguistics
Sh Metal Inds — Sheet Metal Industries
SHMH — Societe d'Histoire et du Musee d'Huningue et du Canton de Huningue. Bulletin
SHMRD — Shire and Municipal Record
ShN — Shakespeare Newsletter
SHNAD — Shoni Naika
Shock Cir Homeostasis Trans Conf — Shock and Circulatory Homeostasis. Transactions of the Conference
Shock Vib Bull — Shock and Vibration Bulletin
Shock Vib Dig — Shock and Vibration Digest
Shock Waves Condens Matter Proc Am Phys Soc Top Conf — Shock Waves in Condensed Matter. Proceedings. American PhysicalSociety Topical Conference on Shock Waves in Condensed Matter
Shoe Leather Rep — Shoe and Leather Reporter
Shokubai Suppl — Shokubai. Supplement
Shokubutsu Boeki Plant Prot — Shokubutsu Boeki/Plant Protection
Shokubutsu Bunrui Chiri — Acta Phytotaxonomica et Geobotanica/Shokubutsu Bunrui Chiri
S Home Gard — Southern Home and Garden
SHOND — Shoni No Noshinkei
Short Course Handb Mineral Assoc Can — Short Course Handbook. Mineralogical Association of Canada
Short Course Notes Mineral Soc Am — Short Course Notes. Mineralogical Society of America
Short Course Ser Mineral Assoc Can — Short Course Series. Mineralogical Association of Canada
Short Rep Rhod Geol Surv — Short Report. Rhodesia Geological Survey
Short Rep South Rhod Geol Surv — Short Report. Southern Rhodesia Geological Survey
Short Wave Mag — Short Wave Magazine
Showa Wire and Cable Rev — Showa Wire and Cable Review
Showa Wire Cable Rev — Showa Wire and Cable Review
Show-Me — Show-Me News and Views
Show Me Lib — Show-Me Libraries
ShP — Shakespeare Pictorial
SHP — Starohrvatska Prosvjeta. Muzej Hrvatskih Starina Jugoslovenske Akademij e Znanosti i Umjetnosti
Shp — Starship. The Magazine about Science Fiction
SHPA — Shelf Paper. Alaska Outer Continental Shelf Office
SHPHUJ — Scripta Hierosolymitana. Publications of the Hebrew University (Jerusalem)
Sh Q — Shakespeare Quarterly
SHQ — Southwestern Historical Quarterly
SHR — Hotel Revue. Wochenzeitung fuer Hotellerie und Tourismus
SHR — Scottish Historical Review
ShR — Shakespeare Review
SHR — Southern Humanities Review
SHR — Studies in the History of Religions
Shrop Mag — Shropshire Magazine
SHRTA — Scientia Horticulturae (Amsterdam)
ShS — Shakespeare Survey
SHSJ — Subsidia ad Historiam SJ
SHSPB — Soviet Hydrology. Selected Papers
ShStud — Shakespeare Studies
SHT — Historisk Tidskrift utgivet av Svensk Historisk Foerening
SHT — Recycling
SHT — Shetland Times
SHT — Studies in Historical Theology
SHT — Svensk Humanistisk Tidsskrift
SHUJA — Shujutsu
SHum — Studies in the Humanities
S Hum Rev — Southern Humanities Review
Shuttle — Shuttle, Spindle, and Dyepot
Shuttle Spin and Dye — Shuttle, Spindle, and Dyepot
SHVE — Sammelblatt der Historischer Verein Eichstatt
SHVF — Sammelblatt der Historischer Verein Freising
SHVI — Sammelblatt der Historischer Verein Ingolstadt
SHVL — Skrifter Utgivna av Humanistiska Vetenskapssamfundet i Lund
SHVU — Skrifter Utgivna av Humanistiska Vetenskapssamfundet i Uppsala
SHWPA — Sheng Wu Hua Hsueh Yu Sheng Wu Wu Li Hsueh Pao
SHZAA — Shoyakugaku Zasshi
SHZAAY — Japanese Journal of Pharmacognosy
SI — Savings Institutions
SI — Scuola Italiana
SI — Signo-Revista para el Dialogo
SI — Sing Out
SI — Sistema
SI — Sociologia Internationalis
SI — Spettatore Italiano
SI — Sports Illustrated
SI — Statutory Instruments
SI — Studia Islamica
SI — Studii Italiene
SI — Svizzera Italiana
SIA — Special Interest Automobiles
SIA — Studia Instituti Anthropos

SIAC — Studies in Automation and Control
SIA J — SIA [*Societe des Ingenieurs de l'Automobile*] Journal
SIAJ — SIAJ: Singapore Institute of Architects. Journal
SIAM AMS Proc — SIAM [*Society for Industrial and Applied Mathematics*]-AMS Proceedings
Siamese Vet Assoc J — Siamese Veterinary Association. Journal
SIAM J Algebraic and Discrete Methods — SIAM [*Society for Industrial and Applied Mathematics*] Journal on Algebraic and Discrete Methods
SIAM J Algebraic Discrete Methods — SIAM [*Society for Industrial and Applied Mathematics*] Journal on Algebraic and Discrete Methods
SIAM J A Ma — SIAM [*Society for Industrial and Applied Mathematics*] Journal on AppliedMathematics
SIAM J Appl Math — SIAM [*Society for Industrial and Applied Mathematics*] Journal on Applied Mathematics
SIAM J App Math — SIAM [*Society for Industrial and Applied Mathematics*] Journal on AppliedMathematics
SIAM J Comput — SIAM [*Society for Industrial and Applied Mathematics*] Journal on Computing
SIAM J Cont — SIAM [*Society for Industrial and Applied Mathematics*] Journal on Control
SIAM J Control — SIAM [*Society for Industrial and Applied Mathematics*] Journal on Control
SIAM J Control and Optimiz — SIAM [*Society for Industrial and Applied Mathematics*] Journal on Control and Optimization
SIAM J Control Optim — SIAM [*Society for Industrial and Applied Mathematics*] Journal on Control and Optimization
SIAM J Control Optimization — SIAM [*Society for Industrial and Applied Mathematics*] Journal on Control and Optimization
SIAM J Discrete Math — SIAM Journal on Discrete Mathematics
SIAM J Math — SIAM [*Society for Industrial and Applied Mathematics*] Journal on Mathematical Analysis
SIAM J Math Anal — SIAM [*Society for Industrial and Applied Mathematics*] Journal on Mathematical Analysis
SIAM J Matrix Anal Appl — SIAM Journal on Matrix Analysis and Applications
SIAM J Num — SIAM [*Society for Industrial and Applied Mathematics*] Journal on Numerical Analysis
SIAM J Numer Anal — SIAM [*Society for Industrial and Applied Mathematics*] Journal on Numerical Analysis
SIAM J Optim — SIAM Journal on Optimization
SIAM J Sci and Stat Comput — SIAM [*Society for Industrial and Applied Mathematics*] Journal on Scientific and Statistical Computing
SIAM J Sci Stat Comput — SIAM [*Society for Industrial and Applied Mathematics*] Journal on Scientific and Statistical Computing
SIAM J Sci Statist Comput — SIAM [*Society for Industrial and Applied Mathematics*] Journal on Scientific and Statistical Computing
SIAM R — SIAM [*Society for Industrial and Applied Mathematics*] Review
SIAM Rev — SIAM [*Society for Industrial and Applied Mathematics*] Review
SIAM Sci Bull — SIAM [*Society for Industrial and Applied Mathematics*] Science Bulletin
SIAM (Soc Ind Appl Math) SIMS (SIAM Inst Math Soc) Conf Ser — SIAM (Society for Industrial and Applied Mathematics) SIMS (SIAM Institute for Mathematics and Society) Conference Series
Siam Soc Newslett — Siam Society Newsletter
SIAM Stud Appl Math — SIAM [*Society for Industrial and Applied Mathematics*] Studies in Applied Mathematics
SIAM Studies in Appl Math — SIAM [*Society for Industrial and Applied Mathematics*] Studies in Applied Mathematics
Si & So — Sight and Sound
SIAP — SIAP. Revista de la Sociedad Interamericana de Planificacion
SIA Surf Interface Anal — SIA. Surface and Interface Analysis
SIB — Studii de Istorie Banatului
Sib Biol Zh — Sibirskii Biologicheskii Zhurnal
Sib Chem J — Siberian Chemistry Journal
Sib Chem J Engl Transl — Siberian Chemistry Journal. English Translation
SIBE — Studies in Bayesian Econometrics
Sibelius — Sibelius-Mitteilungen
Siberian Adv Math — Siberian Advances in Mathematics
Siberian J Comput Math — Siberian Journal of Computer Mathematics
Siberian J Differential Equations — Siberian Journal of Differential Equations
Siberian Math J — Siberian Mathematical Journal
Siberian School Algebra Logic — Siberian School of Algebra and Logic
Siberian Wld — Siberian World
Sib Fiz Tekh Zh — Sibirskii Fiziko-Tekhnicheskii Zhurnal
Sib Geogr Sb — Sibirskii Geograficheskii Sbornik
Sibirsk Mat Z — Sibirskii Matematiceskii Zurnal
Sibirsk Mat Zh — Akademiya Nauk SSSR. Sibirskoe Otdelenie. Sibirskii Matematicheskii Zhurnal
Sibirsk Vrach Viedom — Sibirskiia Vrachebnyia Viedomosti
Sib J Biol — Siberian Journal of Biology
Sib J Chem — Siberian Journal of Chemistry
Sib Khim Zh — Sibirskii Khimicheskii Zhurnal
Sib Math J — Siberian Mathematical Journal
Sib Mat Zh — Sibirskij Matematickij Zhurnal
Sib Nauchno Issled Inst Energ Tr — Sibirskii Nauchno-Issledovatel'skii Institut Energetiki. Trudy
Sib Nauchno Issled Inst Geol Geofiz Miner Syrya Tr — Sibirskii Nauchno-Issledovatel'skii Institut Geologii. Geofiziki iMineral'nogo Syr'ya. Trudy
Sib Nauchno Issled Inst Khim Selsk Khoz Nauchno Tekh Byull — Sibirskii Nauchno-Issledovatel'skii Institut Khimizatsii Sel'skogoKhozyaistva. Nauchno-Tekhnicheskii Byulleten
Sibri — Sibrium. Collana di Studi e Documentazioni
SIBS — Semiconductor Industry and Business Survey
Sib Teplofiz Semin — Sibirskii Teplofizicheskii Seminar
Sib Vest Sel'Khoz Nauki — Siberskii Vestnik Sel'skokhozyaistvennoi Nauki
SIC — Studies in Inorganic Chemistry

SIC — Systeme Informatique pour la Conjoncture
Sic A — Sicilia Archeologica
SICAB — Sichere Arbeit
Sic Arch — Sicilia Archeologica
SicG — Siculorum Gymnasium
Sic Gym — Siculorum Gymnasium
Sic Gymn — Siculorum Gymnasium
Sich Arb — Sichere Arbeit
Sich Arch — Sicilia Archeologica
SICHD — Sicherheit
SICHEJ — Studies in Inorganic Chemistry
Sicherh Chem Umwelt — Sicherheit in Chemie und Umwelt. Zeitschrift zum Handbuch derGefaehrlichen Gueter
Sicherheit — Wirtschaftsschutz und Sicherheitstechnik
Sicherheit Chem Umwelt — Sicherheit in Chemie und Umwelt
Sicherheitspol Heute — Sicherheitspolitik Heute
Sicil Art ed Arch — Sicilia Artistica ed Archeologica
Sicilia Arch — Sicilia Archaeologica. Rassegna Periodica di Studi, Notizie e Documentazione
Sicilia Archeol — Sicilia Archeologica. Rassegna Periodica di Studi, Notizie, e Documentazione
Sicil Med — Sicilia Medica
Sicil Sanit — Sicilia Sanitaria
SICJA — Siberian Chemistry Journal
SICMAU — International Congress for Microbiology. Symposia
S Icon — Studies in Iconography
SICSA — Sicher Ist Sicher
Sic Sac — Sicilia Sacra
SICSW — Schriften des Instituts fuer Christliche Sozialwissenschaften
Siculorum Gym — Siculorum Gymnasium
Sicurezza Ig Ind — Sicurezza e l'Igiene nell'Industria
SICV — Sylloge Inscriptionum Christianarum Veterum Musei Vaticani
SID — ICP [*International Computer Programs*] Software Information Database
SIDA — Scripta Instituti Donneriani Aboensis
Sida Contrib Bot — Sida Contributions to Botany
Side Eff Drugs — Side Effects of Drugs
Side Eff Drugs Annu — Side Effects of Drugs. Annual
Si De Ka Q — Si-De-Ka Quarterly
Sider Latinoam — Siderurgia Latinoamericana
SID J — SID [*Society for Information Display*] Journal
SIDL — Schriften des Institutum Delitzschianum zu Leipzig
Sid Mess — Sidereal Messenger
SIDT — Studies. Institutum Divi Thomae
SIDZD — Saitama Ika Daigaku Zasshi
SIE — Sovetskaia Istoricheskaia Entsiklopediia
SIE — Studies in International Economics
SIE — Suicide Information and Education
SIEBA7 — Sieboldia Acta Biologica
Siebel Tech Rev — Siebel Technical Review
Siebenburg Arch — Siebenbuergisches Archiv
Siebenburg Quartalschr — Siebenbuergische Quartalschrift
Siebenburg Vjschr — Siebenburgische Vierteljahresschrift. Korrespondenzblatt des Vereins fuer Siebenburgische Landeskunde
Sieboldia Acta Biol — Sieboldia Acta Biologica
Sieb Vjschr — Siebenbuergische Vierteljahresschrift
SiEc — Siecle Eclate
Siedlungswasserwirtsch Kolloq — Siedlungswasserwirtschaftliches Kolloquium
Siemens-Albis Ber — Siemens-Albis Berichte
Siemens Compon — Siemens Components
Siemens Components (Engl Ed) — Siemens Components (English Edition)
Siemens Electron Components Bull — Siemens Electronic Components Bulletin
Siemens Energietech — Siemens Energietechnik
Siemens Forsch Entwickl — Siemens Forschungs- und Entwicklungsberichte. Research and Development Reports
Siemens Forsch Entwicklungsber — Siemens Forschungs- und Entwicklungsberichte
Siemens Forsch Entwicklungsber Res Dev Rep — Siemens Forschungs- und Entwicklungsberichte. Research and Development Reports
Siemens Forsch- und Entwicklungsber — Siemens Forschungs- und Entwicklungsberichte
Siemens Power Eng — Siemens Power Engineering
Siemens Res Dev Rep — Siemens Research and Development Reports
Siemens Res Dev Repts — Siemens Research and Development Reports
Siemens Rev — Siemens Review
Siemens-Z — Siemens-Zeitschrift
Siena At Ac — Atti dell' Accademia delle Scienze di Siena detta de' Fisio-Critici
SIEND — Saiensu
Sierra — Sierra Club. Bulletin
Sierra Club B — Sierra Club. Bulletin
Sierra Club Bul — Sierra Club Bulletin
Sierra Club Bull — Sierra Club. Bulletin
Sierra Ed News — Sierra Educational News
Sierra Educ N — Sierra Educational News
Sierra L Bull Rel — Sierra Leone Bulletin of Religion
Sierra Leone Agric Div Minist Agric Nat Resour Rep — Sierra Leone Agricultural Division. Ministry of Agriculture and Natural Resources. Report
Sierra Leone Fish Div Tech Pap — Sierra Leone Fisheries Division. Technical Paper
Sierra Leone Geogr J — Sierra Leone Geographical Journal
Sierra Leone Lang R — Sierra Leone Language Review
Sierra Leone Lang Rev — Sierra Leone Language Review
Sierra Leone LR — Law Reports, Sierra Leone Series
Sierra Leone L Rec — Law Recorder (Sierra Leone)
Sierra Leone Rep Geol Surv Div — Sierra Leone. Report on the Geological Survey Division

Sierra Leone Stud — Sierra Leone Studies
Sierra Leone Trade J — Sierra Leone Trade Journal
SIF — Studi Internazionali di Filosofia
SIFC — Studi Italiani di Filologia Classica
SIFEA — Silva Fennica
SIFJ — Saskatchewan Indian Federated College. Journal
SIG — Service d'Information Geologique du Bureau de Recherches Geologiques, Geophysiques, et Minieres
Sig — Sigma. Revue du Centre d'Etudes Linguistiques d'Aix Montpellier
SIG — Signs
SIG — Sylloge Inscriptionum Graecarum
SIG — Three Sigma Market Newspaper Audiences
SIGAB — Saigai Igaku
SIGEA — Silvae Genetica
Sight & S — Sight and Sound
Sight-Sav R — Sight-Saving Review
Sight-Sav Rev — Sight-Saving Review
SIGIR Forum — SIGIR Forum (ACM Special Interest Group on Information Retrieval)
SIGLE — System for Information on Grey Literature in Europe
SIGLH — Schriften des Instituts fuer Geschichtliche Landeskunde von Hessen-Nassau
Siglo Med — Siglo Medico
Siglo Mis — Siglo de las Misiones
Sigma Ser Appl Math — Sigma Series in Applied Mathematics
Sigma Ser Pure Math — Sigma Series in Pure Mathematics
Sigma Xi Q — Sigma Xi Quarterly
SIGMOD Rec — SIGMOD Record (ACM Special Interest Group on Management of Data)
Signalmans J — Signalman's Journal
Signal Mol Behav — Signal Molecules and Behaviour
Signalpo — Signalposten
Signal Process — Signal Processing
Signal Process Digit Filtering — Signal Processing and Digital Filtering
Signal Process Image Commun — Signal Processing. Image Communication
Sign Lang Stud — Sign Language Studies
Signs J Women Cult Soc — Signs; Journal of Women in Culture and Society
Sig T — Signes du Temps
Sigurnost Rudn — Sigurnost u Rudnicima
SIGZA — Showa Igakkai Zasshi
SIH — Studies in the Humanities
SIHED — Sanitaer-Installateur und Heizungsbauer
SIINA — Silicates Industriels
SIJ — Silliman Journal
SIJ — Small Industry Journal
SIJB — Schriften des Instituts Judaicum in Berlin
SIJD — Schriften des Institutum Judaicum in Delitzschianum
SIJL — Schriften des Institutum Judaicum in Leipzig
SIK — Studi Italici (Kyoto)
SiK — Sztuka i Krytyka
Sikh R — Sikh Review
Sikh Rev — Sikh Review
SIK Publ — SIK [Svenska Institutet foer Konserveringsforskning] Publikation
SIK Rapp — SIK [Svenska Institutet foer Konserveringsforskning] Rapport
SIKS — Schriften des Instituts fuer Kultur- und Sozialforschung
SIKTA — Silikaty
SIL — Studies in Linguistics
SILAD — Siderurgia Latinoamericana
Silent Pic — Silent Picture
Siles Antiq — Silesia Antiqua
SILICA — System for International Literature Information on Ceramics and Glass
Silicates Indus — Silicates Industriels
Silic Conf Proc — Silicate Conference. Proceedings
Silic Ind — Silicates Industriels
Silicon Carbide Proc Int Conf — Silicon Carbide. Proceedings. International Conference on Silicon Carbide
Silicon Chem Ind Int Conf — Silicon for Chemical Industry. International Conference
Silicon Mol Beam Epitaxy Symp — Silicon Molecular Beam Epitaxy. Symposium
Silik — Silikaty
Silikatzs — Silikat-Zeitschrift
Silik J — Silikat Journal
Silik Z — Silikat-Zeitschrift
Silk Artif Silk Mercury — Silk and Artificial Silk Mercury
Silk Dig Wkly — Silk Digest Weekly
Silk J — Silk Journal
Silk J Rayon World — Silk Journal and Rayon World
Silk Rayon Dig — Silk and Rayon Digest
Silk Rayon Ind India — Silk and Rayon Industries of India
Silk Road A & Archaeol — Silk Road Art and Archaeology
Silkworm Inf Bull — Silkworm Information Bulletin
Silliman J — American Journal of Science and Arts. Silliman
Silliman J — Silliman Journal
Sillimans J Sci — Silliman's Journal of Science
S Ill ULJ — Southern Illinois University. Law Journal
SILOP — Studies in Linguistics. Occasional Papers
Silpakorn U J — Silpakorn University Journal
SILTA — Studi Italiani di Linguistica Teorica ed Applicata
Silumine Fiz — Silumine Fizika
Silvaecult Trop Subtrop — Silvaecultura Tropica et Subtropica
Silvae Gen — Silvae Genetica
Silvae Genet — Silvae Genetica
Silva Fenn — Silva Fennica
Silver Inst Lett — Silver Institute Letter
Silver Soc J — Silver Society Journal

Silvic Sao Paulo — Silvicultura em Sao Paulo
Silv Notes Ont Dep Lds For — Silvicultural Notes. Ontario Department of Lands and Forests
Silv Res Note (Tanz) — Silviculture Research Note (Tanzania)
Silv Trop Sub — Silvaecura Tropica et Subtropica
Sim — Simoun. Revue Litteraire Bimestrielle
SIM — Studia Instituti Missiologici
SiM — Studies in Music
SIMA — Studies in Mediterranean Archaeology
SIMArsbok — Svenska Israels-Missionens Arsbok
SIME — Studies in Mechanical Engineering
SIMG — Sammelbaende. Internationale Musik Gesellschaft
SIMJA — Singapore Medical Journal
SIMM — Studies in Indo-Muslim Mysticism
Simon's Town Hist Soc — Simon's Town Historical Society
SIMPA — Rendiconti. Societa Italiana di Mineralogia e Petrologia
Simp Biodeterior Clim Lucr — Simpozion de Biodeteriorare si Climatizare. Lucrarile
Simp Bras Eletroquim Eletroanal — Simposio Brasileiro de Eletroquimica e Eletroanalitica
Simp Ferment — Simposio de Fermentacao
Simp Hig Ind — Simposium de Higiene Industrial
Simp Hig Ind Trab — Simposium de Higiene Industrial. Trabajos
Simpler Nerv Syst — Simpler Nervous Systems
Simplicity Mag — Simplicity Magazine
Simp Otlalennoi Gibrid Rast — Simpozium po Otlalennoi Gibridizatsii Rastenii
Simp Panam Farmacol Ter — Simposio Panamericano de Farmacologia y Terapeutica
Simp Ravnovesnoi Din Strukt Biopolim — Simpozium po Ravnovesnoi Dinamike Struktury Biopolimerov
Simp Reg Geol — Simposio Regional de Geologia
SIMRDU — Survey of Immunologic Research
SIMS — Schriftenreihe des Instituts fuer Missionarische Seelsorge
SiMS — Studier i Modern Sprakvetenskap
SIMUA — Simulation
Simul and Games — Simulation and Games
Simulat & Games — Simulation and Games
Simulat Gam — Simulation and Games
Simulations Councils Proc — Simulations Councils. Proceedings
Simul Counc Proc Ser — Simulation Councils. Proceedings Series
Simul Games Learn — Simulation/Games for Learning
Simul Today — Simulation Today
Sin — Phi Mu Alpha Sinfonian
SIN — Scientific Information Notes
SiN — Sin Nombre
Sin — Sinologica
Sinai Hosp J — Sinai Hospital. Journal
SIND — Saskatchewan Indian
S Ind Archaeol — South Indian Archaeology
Sindar Rep — Sindar Reporter
S Ind Art Archaeol Ser — South Indian Art and Archaeological Series
SINDB — Science and Industry
S Ind Stud — Southern Indian Studies
Sind Univ J Ed — Sind University Journal of Education
Sind Univ Res J Sci Ser — Sind University Research Journal. Science Series
Sinema — Andere Sinema
S in Eng — Studies in English
Sinet Ethiop J Sci — Sinet: An Ethiopian Journal of Science
Sinfonian Mag — Sinfonian Magazine
SINFUB — Skrifter Utgitt. Instituttet foer Nordisk Filologi. Universitetet i Bergen
Singapore Bus — Singapore Business
Singapore Dent J — Singapore Dental Journal
Singapore ICCS Conf Proc — Singapore ICCS. Conference Proceedings
Singapore J Obstet Gynaecol — Singapore Journal of Obstetrics and Gynaecology
Singapore J Phy — Singapore Journal of Physics
Singapore J Primary Ind — Singapore Journal of Primary Industries
Singapore J Trop Geogr — Singapore Journal of Tropical Geography
Singapore Lib — Singapore Libraries
Singapore L Rev — Singapore Law Review
Singapore Med J — Singapore Medical Journal
Singapore MJ — Singapore Medical Journal
Singapore Nat Acad Sci J — Singapore National Academy of Science. Journal
Singapore Natl Inst Chem Bull — Singapore National Institute of Chemistry. Bulletin
Singapore Soc Microbiol Congr — Singapore Society for Microbiology. Congress
Singapore Statist Bull — Singapore Statistical Bulletin
Sing J Ob Gyn — Singapore Journal of Obstetrics and Gynecology
Sing J Trop Geo — Singapore Journal of Tropical Geography
Sing Kir — Singende Kirche
Single Cryst Prop — Single Crystal Properties
Single Electron Tunneling Mesosc Devices Proc Int Conf SQUID — Single-Electron Tunneling and Mesoscopic Devices. Proceedings. International Conference SQUID
Sing LR — Singapore Law Review
Sing Med J — Singapore Medical Journal
Sing Pub Health B — Singapore Public Health Bulletin
Sing Shipbuild Rep Dir — Singapore Shipbuilding and Repairing Directory
Sing Stat B — Singapore Statistical Bulletin
Sing YB — Singapore Year Book
Sinister — Sinister Wisdom
Sin N — Sin Nombre
SIN Newsl — SIN [Schweizerisches Institut fuer Nuklearforschung] Newsletter
Sino-Am Rels — Sino-American Relations

Sino Jpn J Allergol Immunol — Sino-Japanese Journal of Allergology and Immunology

Sinop Odontol — Sinopse de Odontologia

S in Ph — Studies in Philology

SINSU — Skrifter Utgivna. Institutionen foer Nordiska Sprak Vid. Uppsala Universitet

SINSUU — Skrifter Utgivna. Institutionen foer Nordiska Sprak Vid. Uppsala Universitet

Sint Almazy — Sinteticheskie Almazy

Sint Anal Strukt Org Soedin — Sintez, Analiz, i Struktura Organicheskikh Soedinenii

Sint Delenie Tr Sov Am Semin — Sintez-Delenie. Trudy Sovetsko-Amerikanskogo Seminara

SINTEF Rep — SINTEF [Selskapet for Industriell og Teknisk Forskning Ved Norges Tekniske Hoegskole] Report

Sintering Proc Int Symp Sci Technol Sintering — Sintering. Proceedings. International Symposium on the Science and Technology of Sintering

Sintering Proc Powder Metall Conf Exhib — Sintering. Proceedings. Powder Metallurgy Conference and Exhibition

Sintesi Econ — Sintesi Economica

Sint Fiz-Khim Polim — Sintez i Fiziko-Khimiya Polimerov

Sint Geterotsikl Soedin — Sintezy Geterotsiklicheskikh Soedinenii

Sint Issled Eff Khim Dobovok Polim Mater — Sintez i Issledovanie Effektivnosti Khimikatov-Dobavok dlyaPolimernykh Materialov

Sint Issled Eff Khim Polim Mater — Sintez i Issledovanie Effektivnosti Khimikatov dlya PolimernykhMaterialov

Sint Issled Katal Neftekhim — Sintez i Issledovanie Katalizatorov Neftekhimii

Sint Issled Svoistv Kompleksn Soedin — Sintez i Issledovanie Svoistv Kompleksnykh Soedinenii

Sint Kauch — Sinteticheskii Kauchuk

Sint Khim Prevrashch Polim — Sintez i Khimicheskie Prevrashcheniya Polimerov

Sint Mater Med — Sinteticheskie Materialy v Meditsine

Sint Org Soedin — Sintezy Organicheskikh Soedinenij

Sint Pol Econ Soc Rio — Sintese Politica, Economica, Social (Rio de Janeiro)

SIO — Sylloge Inscriptionum Oscarum

SIOBA — Sbornik Informatsii po Obogashcheniyu i Briketirovaniyu Uglei

SIOSR — Studien aus dem Institut fuer Ost- und Suedslawische Relgions- und Kirchenkundeder Humboldt-Universitaet

Sip — Sipario

SIP — Studia Islamica (Paris)

SIP — Subject Index to Periodicals

SIPAAP — Escuela Nacional de Agricultura [Chapingo]. Serie de Investigaciones

SIPL — Studies in Philippine Linguistics

SIPN — Security Industry and Product News

SIPO — Soobshcheniia Imperatorskovo Pravoslavnovo Palestinskovo Obshchestva

SIQR — Studies: An Irish Quarterly Review of Letters, Philosophy, and Science

SIR — Studies in Romanticism

SIRA Abstr Rev — SIRA Abstracts and Reviews

Sirag — Sirag. Amsagir Grakanut ean ew Aruesdi

SIREA — SIAM [Society for Industrial and Applied Mathematics] Review

SIRIO — Sbornik Imperatorskogo Russkogo Istoricheskogo Obshchestva

Siriraj Hosp Gaz — Siriraj Hospital Gazette

SIRIS — Sylloge Inscriptionum Religionis Isiacae et Serapicae

Sirpur Ind J — Sirpur Industries Journal

SIRRBJ — Institutionen foer Skogsforyngring Rapporter och Uppsatser

SIS — Schriften des Instituts fuer Sozialforschung

SIs — Scripta Islandica

SIS — Sino-Indian Studies

SIS — Studies in Islam Series

SIs — Studi Ispanici

Sisal Mex — Sisal Mexicano

Sisal Rev — Sisal Review

SISCIS — Subject Index to Sources of Comparative International Statistics

SISIMS — Say It So It Makes Sense

SIsI — Studia Islamica

SIS News — Society for Iranian Studies. Newsletter

SISRBO — Institutionen foer Skogszoologi Rapporter och Uppsatser

Sist Avtom Nauchn Issled — Sistemy Avtomatisatsii Nauchnykh Issledovanii

Sist e Autom — Sistemi e Automazione

Sistema — Sistema Revista de Ciencias Sociales

Sistem Metod Sovrem Nauka — Sistemnyj Metod i Sovremennaja Nauka

Sisters — Sisters Today

Sist Nerv — Sistema Nervoso

Sistole Rev Urug Cardiol — Sistole. Revista Uruguaya de Cardiologia

Sist Zametki Mater Gerb Krylova Tomsk Gosud Univ Kujbyseva — Sistematiceskie Zametki po Materialam Gerbarii Imeni P. N. Krylova Pri Tomskom Gosudarstvennom Universitete Imeni V. V. Kujbyseva

Sit — Situazione. Cultura e Poesia

Sites & Mnmts — Sites et Monuments. Bulletin de la Societe pour la Protection des Paysages et de l'Esthetique Generale de la France

Site Sel Hdbk — Site Selection Handbook

SITKA — Silikattechnik

Situatia Daunatorilor Anim Pl Cult — Situatia Daunatorilor Animali ai Plantelor Cultivate

Sitz Akad Wis Wien — Sitzungsberichte der Oesterreichischen Akademie der Wissenschafte. Philosophisch-Historische Klasse (Wien)

Sitz Arbeitskreises Rastermikrosk Materialpruef — Sitzung des Arbeitskreises Rastermikroskopie in der Materialpruefung

Sitz Bay Akad Wis — Sitzungsberichte der Bayerischen Akademie der Wissenschaften

Sitz Ber Bayer Akad Wiss — Sitzungsberichte der Bayerischen Akademie der Wissenschaften

Sitz Ber Finn Akad Wiss — Sitzungsberichte der Finnischen Akademie der Wissenschaften

Sitzber Oesterr Akad Wiss Math — Sitzungsberichte. Oesterreichische Akademie der Wissenschafte. Mathematisch-Naturwissenschaftliche Klasse. Abteilung 2. Mathematik, Astron Physik, Meteorologieund Technik

Sitzb Heidelb Akad — Sitzungsberichte der Heidelberger Akademie der Wissenschaften. Philosophisch-Historische Klasse

Sitzgb Berlin — Sitzungsberichte der Deutschen Akademie der Wissenschaften zu Berlin

Sitzgsber Ges Natf Frde Berlin — Sitzungsberichte der Gesellschaft der Naturforschenden Freunde. Berlin

Sitzgsberr Abh Natf Ges Isis — Sitzungsberichte und Abhandlungen der Naturforschenden Gesellschaft Isis. Dresden

Sitzgsberr Altertsges Prussia — Sitzungsberichte der Altertumsgesellschaft Prussia

Sitzgsberr Bayer Akad Wiss — Sitzungsberichte der Bayerischen Akademie der Wissenschaften. Muenchen

Sitzgsberr Ges Befoerd Ges Natwiss — Sitzungsberichte der Gesellschaft zur Befoerderung der Gesamten Naturwissenschaft. Marburg

Sitzgsberr Natf Ges Rostock — Sitzungsberichte der Naturforschenden Gesellschaft. Rostock

Sitzgsberr Preuss Akad Wiss — Sitzungsberichte der Preussischen Akademie der Wissenschaft

Sitzungber Saechs Akad Wiss (Leipzig) Math-Natur Kl — Sitzungsberichte. Saechsische Akademie der Wissenschaften (Leipzig). Mathematisch-Naturwissenschaftliche Klasse

Sitzungsber Abh Naturf Ges Rostock — Sitzungsberichte und Abhandlungen der Naturforschenden Gesellschaft zu Rostock

Sitzungsber Abh Naturforsch Ges Rostock — Sitzungsberichte und Abhandlungen der Naturforschenden Gesellschaft zuRostock

Sitzungsber Akad Wiss Berlin — Sitzungsberichte der Akademie der Wissenschaften in Berlin

Sitzungsber Akad Wiss DDR — Sitzungsberichte der Akademie der Wissenschaften der DDR

Sitzungsber Akad Wiss DDR Math Naturwiss Tech — Sitzungsberichte. Akademie der Wissenschaften der DDR. Mathematik-Naturwissenschaften-Technik

Sitzungsber Akad Wiss DDR Math-Naturwiss-Tech Jahrgang 1977 — Sitzungsberichte. Akademie der Wissenschaften der DDR. Mathematik-Naturwissenschaften-Technik. Jahrgang 1977

Sitzungsber Akad Wiss DDR Math-Naturwiss Tech Jahrgang 1979 — Sitzungsberichte. Akademie der Wissenschaften der DDR. Mathematik-Naturwissenschaften-Technik. Jahrgang 1979

Sitzungsber Akad Wiss Wien Math Naturwiss Kl Abt 2A — Sitzungsberichte. Akademie der Wissenschaften in Wien. Mathematisch-Naturwissenschaftliche Klasse. Abteilung 2A. Mathematik, Astronomie, Physik,Meteorologie, und Technik

Sitzungsber Akad Wiss Wien Math Naturwiss Kl Abt 2B — Sitzungsberichte. Akademie der Wissenschaften in Wien. Mathematisch-Naturwissenschaftliche Klasse. Abteilung 2B. Chemie

Sitzungsber Akad Wiss Wien Math Naturwiss Kl Abt 3 — Sitzungsberichte. Akademie der Wissenschaften in Wien. Mathematisch-Naturwissenschaftliche Klasse. Abteilung 3. Anatomie und Physiologie desMenschen und der Tiere sowie Theoretische Medizin

Sitzungsber Bayer Akad Wiss — Sitzungsberichte der Bayerischen Akademie der Wissenschaften

Sitzungsber Bayer Akad Wiss Math — Sitzungsberichte der Bayerische Akademie der Wissenschaften. Mathematisch-Naturwissenschaftliche Klasse

Sitzungsber Bayer Akad Wiss Math-Naturwiss Kl — Sitzungsberichte. Bayerische Akademie der Wissenschaften. Mathematisch-Naturwissenschaftliche Klasse

Sitzungsber Berl Ges Naturforsch Freunde — Sitzungsberichte. Berlinische Gesellschaft Naturforschender Freunde

Sitzungsber Bern Bot Ges — Sitzungsberichte der Bernischen Botanischen Gesellschaft

Sitzungsber d Akadem d Wiss — Sitzungsberichte. Akademie der Wissenschaften

Sitzungsber Deut Akad Landwirt Wiss Berlin — Sitzungsberichte. Deutsche Akademie der Landwirtschaftswissenschaften zu Berlin

Sitzungsber Deut Akad Wiss Berlin Kl Math Phys Tech — Sitzungsberichte. Deutsche Akademie der Wissenschaften zu Berlin. Klasse fuer Mathematik, Physik, und Technik

Sitzungsber Deutsch Akad Wiss Berlin Kl Landw Wiss — Sitzungsberichte der Deutschen Akademie der Wissenschaften zu Berlin. Klasse fuer Landwirtschaftliche Wissenschaften

Sitzungsber Dtsch Akad Landwirtschaftswiss Berlin — Sitzungsberichte. Deutsche Akademie der Landwirtschaftswissenschaftenzu Berlin

Sitzungsber Dtsch Akad Wiss Berlin Kl Chem Geol Biol — Sitzungsberichte.Deutsche Akademie der Wissenschaften zu Berlin.Klasse fuer Chemie, Geologie, und Biologie

Sitzungsber Dtsch Akad Wiss Berlin Kl Gesellschaftswiss — Sitzungsberichte. Deutsche Akademie der Wissenschaften zu Berlin.Klasse fuer Gesellschaftswissenschaften

Sitzungsber Dtsch Akad Wiss Berlin Kl Math Allg Naturwiss — Sitzungsberichte. Deutsche Akademie der Wissenschaften zu Berlin.Klasse fuer Mathematik und Allgemeine Naturwissenschaften

Sitzungsber Dtsch Akad Wiss Berlin Kl Math Phys Tech — Sitzungsberichte. Deutsche Akademie der Wissenschaften zu Berlin.Klasse fuer Mathematik, Physik, und Technik

Sitzungsber Dtsch Akad Wiss Berlin Kl Med — Sitzungsberichte. Deutsche Akademie der Wissenschaften zu Berlin.Klasse fuer Medizin

Sitzungsber Dtsch Akad Wiss Berlin Kl Tech Wiss — Sitzungsberichte. Deutsche Akademie der Wissenschaften zu Berlin.Klasse fuer Technische Wissenschaften

Sitzungsber Dtsch Akad Wiss Berlin Math Naturwiss Kl — Sitzungsberichte. Deutsche Akademie der Wissenschaften zu Berlin.Mathematisch-Naturwissenschaftliche Klasse

Sitzungsber Finn Akad Wiss — Sitzungsberichte. Finnische Akademie der Wissenschaften

Sitzungsber Gel Estn Ges — Sitzungsberichte der Gelehrten Estnischen Gesellschaft

Sitzungsber Ges Befoerd Gesamten Naturwiss Marburg — Sitzungsberichte. Gesellschaft zur Befoerderung der GesamtenNaturwissenschaften zu Marburg

Sitzungsber Ges Befoerd Ges Naturwiss Marburg — Sitzungsberichte. Gesellschaft zur Befoerderung der Gesamten Naturwissenschaften zu Marburg

Sitzungsber Ges Naturforsch Freunde Berlin — Sitzungsberichte. Gesellschaft Naturforschender Freunde zu Berlin

Sitzungsber Ges Natur Heilk Dresden — Sitzungsberichte der Gesellschaft fuer Natur- und Heilkunde zu Dresden

Sitzungsber Heidelb Akad Wiss Math-Natur Kl — Sitzungsberichte. Heidelberg Akademie der Wissenschaften. Mathematisch-Naturwissenschaftliche Klasse

Sitzungsber Heidelb Akad Wiss Naturwiss Kl — Sitzungsberichte. Heidelberg Akademie der Wissenschaften. Mathematisch-Naturwissenschaftliche Klasse

Sitzungsber Heidelberger Akad Wiss Math Naturwiss Kl — Sitzungsberichte der Heidelberger Akademie der Wissenschaften. Mathematisch-Naturwissenschaftliche Klasse

Sitzungsber Heidelberger Akad Wiss Stiftung Heinrich Lanz Mat — Sitzungsberichte der Heidelberger Akademie der Wissenschaften. Stiftung Heinrich Lanz. Mathematisch-Naturwissenschaftliche Klasse

Sitzungsber Kaiserl Akad Wiss Math Naturwiss Cl — Sitzungsberichte der Kaiserlichen Akademie der Wissenschaften. Mathematisch-Naturwissenschaftliche Classe

Sitzungsber K Preuss Akad Wiss — Sitzungsberichte. Koeniglich-Preussische Akademie derWissenschaften

Sitzungsber Math Naturwiss Abt Bayer Akad Wiss Muenchen — Sitzungsberichte der Mathematisch-Naturwissenschaftlichen Abteilung der Bayerischen Akademie der Wissenschaften zu Muenchen

Sitzungsber Math Naturwiss Aerztl Sekt — Sitzungsberichte der Mathematisch-Naturwissenschaftlich-Aerztlichen Sektion/Ukrainische Sevcenko-Gesellschaft der Wissenschaften in Lemberg

Sitzungsber Math Naturwiss Kl — Sitzungsberichte der Mathematisch-Naturwissenschaftlichen Klasse

Sitzungsber Math Naturwiss Kl Bayer Akad Wiss — Sitzungsberichte der Mathematisch-Naturwissenschaftlichen Klasse derBayerischen Akademie der Wissenschaften

Sitzungsber Math Phys Kl Bayer Akad Wiss Muenchen — Sitzungsberichte der Mathematisch-Physikalischen Klasse der BayerischenAkademie der Wissenschaften zu Muenchen

Sitzungsber Mitt Braunschw Wiss Ges — Sitzungsberichte und Mitteilungen der Braunschweigischen Wissenschaftlichen Gesellschaft

Sitzungsber Naturf Ges Leipzig — Sitzungsberichte der Naturforschenden-Gesellschaft zu Leipzig

Sitzungsber Naturf Ges Univ Dorpat — Sitzungsberichte der Naturforscher-Gesellschaft bei der Universitaet Dorpat

Sitzungsber Naturforsch Ges Dorpat — Sitzungsberichte der Naturforscher-Gesellschaft zu Dorpat

Sitzungsber Naturforsch Ges Rostock — Sitzungsberichte der Naturforschenden Gesellschaft zu Rostock

Sitzungsber Naturforsch Ges Univ Dorpat — Sitzungsberichte der Naturforscher-Gesellschaft bei der UniversitaetDorpat

Sitzungsber Naturforsch Ges Univ Jurjeff — Sitzungsberichte der Naturforscher-Gesellschaft bei der UniversitaetJurjeff

Sitzungsber Naturforsch Ges Univ Tartu — Sitzungsberichte der Naturforscher-Gesellschaft bei der UniversitaetTartu

Sitzungsber Naturhist Vereins Preuss Rheinl — Sitzungsberichte, Herausgegeben vom Naturhistorischen Verein der Preussischen Rheinlande und Westfalens

Sitzungsber Oesterr Akad Wiss Math Naturwiss Kl Abt — Sitzungsberichte. Oesterreichische Akademie der Wissenschaften.Mathematisch-Naturwissenschaftliche Klasse. Abteilung 1. Biologie, Mineralogie,Erdkunde, und Verwandte Wissenschaften

Sitzungsber Oesterr Akad Wiss Math Naturwiss Kl Abt 2a — Sitzungsberichte. Oesterreichische Akademie der Wissenschaften. Mathematisch-Naturwissenschaftliche Klasse. Abteilung 2a. Mathematik, Astronomie, Physik, Meteorologie, und Technik

Sitzungsber Oesterr Akad Wiss Math Naturwiss Kl Abt 2b — Sitzungsberichte. Oesterreichische Akademie der Wissenschaften. Mathematisch-Naturwissenschaftliche Klasse. Abteilung 2b. Chemie

Sitzungsber Oesterr Akad Wiss Math-Naturwiss Kl Abt II — Sitzungsberichte. Oesterreichische Akademie der Wissenschaften. Mathematisch-Naturwissenschaftliche Klasse. Abteilung II. Mathematik, Astronomie, Physik, Meteorologie, und Technik

Sitzungsber Ophthalmol Ges — Sitzungsberichte der Ophthalmologischen Gesellschaft

Sitzungsber Phys Med Soc Erlangen — Sitzungsberichte der Physikalisch-Medicinischen Societaet zu Erlangen

Sitzungsber Plenums Kl Akad Wiss DDR — Sitzungsberichte des Plenums und der Klassen der Akademie der Wissenschaften der DDR

Sitzungsber Preuss Akad Wiss — Sitzungsberichte. Preussische Akademie der Wissenschaften

Sitzungsber Preuss Akad Wiss Phys Math Kl — Sitzungsberichte der Preussischen Akademie der Wissenschaften. Physikalisch-Mathematische Klasse

Sitzungsber Prussia — Sitzungsberichte der Altertumsgesellschaft Prussia zu Koenigsberg

Sitzungsber Saechs Akad Wiss Leipzig Math Naturwiss Kl — Sitzungsberichte der Saechsischen Akademie der Wissenschaften zu Leipzig. Mathematisch-Naturwissenschaftliche Klasse

Sitzungsber Saechs Akas Wiss Leipzig Math Natur Kl — Sitzungsberichte der Saechsischen Akademie der Wissenschaften zu Leipzig. Mathematisch-Naturwissenschaftliche Klasse

Sitzungsber Weltkongr Psychiatr — Sitzungsberichte. Welkongress der Psychiatrie

Sitzungsber Wiss Ges Johann Wolfgang Goethe Univ Frankfurt — Sitzungsberichte der Wissenschaftlichen Gesellschaft an der Johann Wolfgang Goethe-Universitaet Frankfurt am Main

Sitzungsb Gesellsch Naturf Fr Berlin — Sitzungsberichte der Gesellschaft Naturforschender Freunde zu Berlin

Sitzungsb Heidelberger Akad Wiss Math Natur Kl — Sitzungsberichte der Heidelberger Akademie der Wissenschaften. Mathematisch-Naturwissenschaftliche Klasse

SIV — South Italian Vase Painting

SIV — Vierteljahrshefte zur Wirtschaftsforschung

SIVP — South Italian Vase Painting

SIX — Sigma

Six — Sixties

Six Cent J — Sixteenth Century Journal

Six Ct J — Sixteenth Century Journal

Sixteen Cent J — Sixteenth Century Journal

Sixteenth Cent J — Sixteenth Century Journal

Sixth Gener Comput Tech Ser — Sixth-Generation Computer Technology Series

SiZ — Studies in Zionism

SIZSA — Sapporo Igaku Zasshi

SJ — Saalburg-Jahrbuch

SJ — Saxophone Journal

SJ — Schmoller's Jahrbuch

SJ — Semaine Judiciaire

SJ — Shakespeare-Jahrbuch

SJ — Silliman Journal

SJ — Simulation Journal

SJ — Slovensky Jazyk

SJ — Solicitors' Journal

SJ — Staden-Jahrbuch [Sao Paulo]

SJ — Studia Judaica

SJA — Southwestern Journal of Anthropology

SJAEA — Soviet Journal of Atomic Energy

Sjaek — Sjaek'len

SJAnth — Southwestern Journal of Anthropology

SJb — Staden-Jahrbuch

SJB — Surinaams Juristenblad

SJB — Zeitschrift fuer Wirtschaftswissenschaften und Sozialwissenschaften

SJBCD5 — Soviet Journal of Bioorganic Chemistry

SJbMw — Schweizerisches Jahrbuch fuer Musikwissenschaft

SJCCA — Stroke

SJCLA — Scandinavian Journal of Clinical and Laboratory Investigation

SJCOA — SIAM [Society for Industrial and Applied Mathematics] Journal on Control

SJCOD — SIAM [Society for Industrial and Applied Mathematics] Journal on Control and Optimization

SJCT — SJC Today. Sheldon Jackson College

SJDBA — Soviet Journal of Developmental Biology

SJE — Swedish Journal of Economics

SJECA — Soviet Journal of Ecology

SJER — Scandinavian Journal of Educational Research

SJESNP — Scandinavian Joint Expedition to Sudanese Nubia Publications

SJF — Japanese Finance and Industry

SJFMA — Soviet Journal of Non-Ferrous Metals

SJFRE3 — Scandinavian Journal of Forest Research

SJFT — Svenska Jerusalems-Foereningens Tidskrift

SJFTD8 — Sudan Journal of Food Science and Technology

SJG — Schmollers Jahrbuch fuer Gesetzgebung, Verwaltung, und Volkswirtschaft im Deutschen Reich

SJGHA — Sumitomo Jukikai Giho

SJGRA — Scandinavian Journal of Gastroenterology

SJH — Shakespeare-Jahrbuch (Heidelberg)

SJHAA — Scandinavian Journal of Haematology

SJI — Studien aus dem C. G. Jung-Institut

SJL — Semitic Journal of Linguistics

SJL — Slovensky Jazyk a Literatura v Skole

SJL — Southwest Journal of Linguistics

SJLA — Studies in Judaism in Late Antiquity

SJLR — St. John's Law Review

SJM — Saint James Magazine

SJMAA — SIAM [Society for Industrial and Applied Mathematics] Journal on Mathematical Analysis

SJMED — South African Journal of Hospital Medicine

SJMN — San Jose Mercury News

SJMPT — Sammlung Jurisprudenz, Medizin, Philosophie, Theologie

SJMS — Speculum

SJMSE7 — Suid-Afrikaanse Tydskrif vir Seewetenskap

SJNAA — SIAM [Society for Industrial and Applied Mathematics] Journal on Numerical Analysis

SJNCA — Soviet Journal of Nuclear Physics

SJNTA — Soviet Journal of Nondestructive Testing

SJNY — Studies in Judaica (New York)

SJO — Jahrbuch. Deutsche Shakespeare-Gesellschaft Ost

Sjoehist Arsb — Sjoehistorisk Arsbok

SJOTB — Soviet Journal of Optical Technology

SJP — Salzburger Jahrbuch fuer Philosophie und Psychologie

SJP — Scottish Journal of Political Economy

SJP — Southern Journal of Philosophy

SJPE — Scottish Journal of Political Economy

SJPh — Southwestern Journal of Philosophy

S J Phil — Southern Journal of Philosophy

SJ Philos — Southern Journal of Philosophy

SJPNA — Soviet Journal of Particles and Nuclei

SJPRB — Scandinavian Journal of Plastic and Reconstructive Surgery

SJPSDL — Suid-Afrikaanse Tydskrif vir Sielkunde

SJPYA — Scandinavian Journal of Psychology

SJR — Social Justice Review
SJR — Textile Month
SJRDA — Scandinavian Journal of Respiratory Diseases
SJS — San Jose Studies
SJS — San Juan Star
SJSCDM — Shimane Journal of Medical Science
SJSUD — Science Journal. Shivaji University
SJT — Scottish Journal of Theology
SJT — Southwestern Journal of Theology
SJTCA — Scandinavian Journal of Thoracic and Cardiovascular Surgery
SJTGD5 — Singapore Journal of Tropical Geography
SJTh — Scottish Journal of Theology
SJThOP — Scottish Journal of Theology. Occasional Papers
SJUNA — Scandinavian Journal of Urology and Nephrology
SJUS — St. John's University Studies
SJUST — St. John's University Studies. Theological Series
SJV — Kyoto University. Jimbun Kagaku Kenkyu-sho. Silver Jubilee Volume
SjV — Sirp ja Vasar
SJW — Shakespeare-Jahrbuch (Weimar)
SJ(Weimar) — Shakespeare-Jahrbuch (Weimar)
SJZ — Schweizerische Juristen-Zeitung
SK — Annaly Instituta imeni N.P. Kondakova
SK — Schriften zur Katechetik
SK — Seminarium Kondakovianum
SK — Sovetskii Kollektsioner
SKA — Skandinaviska Enskilda Banken. Quarterly Review
SKA — Svenska Kyrkans Arsbok
Skand — Skandinavistik
Skand Arch Physiol — Skandinavisches Archiv fuer Physiologie
Skand Bank — Skandinaviska Enskilda Banken
Skand Ensk Bank Quart R — Skandinaviska Enskilda Banken. Quarterly Review
Skandia Int Symp — Skandia International Symposia
Skandinavis — Skandinavistik
Skandinaviska Enskilda Banken Q R — Skandinaviska Enskilda Banken. Quarterly Review
Skand Manadsskr Textilind — Skandinavisk Manadsskrift foer Textilindustri
Skand Numis — Skandinavisk Numismatik
Skand Sborn — Skandinavsky Sbornik
Skand Tidskr Faerg Lack — Skandinavisk Tidskrift foer Faerg och Lack
Skand Tidskr Textilind — Skandinavisk Tidskrift foer Textilindustri
Skand Vet Tidskr — Skandinavisk Veterinaertidskrift foer Bakteriologi, Patologi, samt Koettoch Mjoelkhygien
Skanes Naturskyddsfoeren Arsberaett — Skanes Naturskyddsfoerenings Arsberaettelse
Skat Mag — Skating Magazine
Skat Over — Skattepolitisk Oversigt
SKAW — Sitzungsberichte der Kaiserlichen Akademie der Wissenschaften. Philosophisch-Historische Klasse
SKAW — Sitzungsberichte der Kaiserlichen Akademie der Wissenschaften
SKAWW — Sitzungsberichte. Kaiserliche Akademie der Wissenschaften in Wien
SKB — Salzburger Kirchenblatt
SKBF KBS Tek Repp — SKBF / KBS Teknisk Rapport
SKBGD — Sangyo Kogai Boshi Gijutsu
SKBGW — Sitzungsberichte der Koeniglichen Boehmischen Gesellschaft der Wissenschaften. Mathematisch-Naturwissenschaftliche Classe
SKBK — Studien zur Katholischen Bistums- und Klostergesehichte
SKB Tech Rep — SKB (Svensk Kaernbraenslehantering) Technical Report
Sk Chem Kerntegnol Ref — Skool vir Chemie in Kerntegnologie. Referate
SKD — Svenska Dagbladet
SKDGQ — Sammlung Ausgewaehlter Kirchen- und Dogmengeschichtlichen Quellenschriften
SKEIA — Sanshi Kagaku Kenkyusho Iho
Skeletal Radiol — Skeletal Radiology
SKENAN — Ecological Review
SkFi — Skandinavskaga Filologija
SKF Psychiatr Rep — SK and F [Smith, Kline, and French] Psychiatric Reporter
SKG — Schriften. Koenigsberger Gelehrten-Gesellschaft
SKG — Srpski Knjizevni Glasnik
SKGG — Schriften der Koenigsberger Gelehrten Gesellschaft. Geisteswissenschaftliche Klasse
SKGG — Schriften. Koenigsberger Gelehrten-Gesellschaft
SKGGD — Sammlung Kurzer Grammatiken Germanischer Dialekte
SKGI — Srpski Knjizevni Glasnik
SKGND — Sanup Kwahak Gisul Yeonguso Nonmunjip
SKGNS — Studien zur Kirchengeschichte Niedersachsens
SKGS — Schriften der Koenigsberger Gelehrten Gesellschaft. Sonderreihe
SKGSA — Sekiyu Gakkaishi
SKGSW — Studien und Mitteilungen aus dem Kirchengeschichtlichen Seminar der Theologischen Fakultaet der Universitaet Wien
SKH — Sociaal Kompas. Tijdschrift voor Sociologie, Sociographie, Sociale Psychologie, en Statistiek (The Hague)
SKH — Staatsblad van het Koninkrijk der Nederlanden
SKH — Svenska Kyrkans Historia
S-Kh Biol — Sel'skokhozyaistvennaya Biologiya
SKHF — Skrifter Utgivna av Kyrkohistoriska Foereningen
SKHFS — Skrifter Utgivna av Kyrkohistoriska Foereningen. Svenska Synodalakter
Skh Ispolz Pochv Trop Subtrop — Sel'skokhozyaistvennoe Ispol'zovanie Pochv Tropikov i Subtropikov
Skh Ispolz Stochnykh Vod — Sel'skokhozyaistvennoe Ispol'zovanie Stochnykh Vod
Skh Proizvod Nechernozemn Zony — Sel'skokhozyaistvennoe Proizvodstvo Nechernozemnoi Zony
Skh Proizvod Povolzhya — Sel'skokhozyaistvennoe Proizvodstvo Povolzh'ya
S-Kh Proizvod Urala — Sel'skokhozyaistvennoe Proizvodstvo Urala
Ş-Kh Rub Rastenievod — Sel'skokhozyaistvo za Rubezhom Rastenievodstvo

SKHVL — Skrifter Utgivna av Kungliga Humanistiska Vetenskapssamfundet i Lund
SkHVSU — Skrifter Utgivna. Humanistiska Vetenskapssamfundet i Uppsala
Skhy T — Skolehygiejnisk Tidsskrift
Skillings' Min Rev — Skillings' Mining Review
Skil Mining — Skillings' Mining Review
Skin Diver Mag — Skin Diver Magazine
Skin Drug Appl Eval Environ Hazards OHOLO Biol Conf — Skin. Drug Application and Evaluation of Environmental Hazards. OHOLO Biological Conference
Skinners Silk Rayon Rec — Skinner's Silk and Rayon Record
Skin Pharmacol — Skin Pharmacology
Skin Pharmacol Appl Skin Physiol — Skin Pharmacology and Applied Skin Physiology
Skin Res — Skin Research
Skin Res Technol — Skin Research and Technology
Skin Therapy Lett — Skin Therapy Letter
SKK — Selskoe Khoziaistvo Kazakhstana
SKK — Sydslesvigsk Kirkekalender
SKKA — Staat und Kirche in Katalonien und Aragon
SKKEA — Sklar a Keramik
SKKG — Studien zur Koelner Kirchengeschichte
SKKNAJ — Annual Report. Sankyo Research Laboratories
SKKOA — Shin Kinzoku Kogyo
SKL — Salmonsens Konversationsleksikon
Sklar Keram — Sklar a Keramik
Sklarske Rozhl — Sklarcko Rozhledy
S Kl V — Sammlung Klinischer Vortraege
SKM — Schweizerische Kreditanstalt. Bulletin
SKMRA — Skillings' Mining Review
SKNEA7 — Annual Report. Shionogi Research Laboratory
Sk Nf F — Forhandlingar vid det af Skandinaviska Naturforskare och Lakare hallna Mote
SKNSAF — Advances in Neurological Sciences
SKNSB — Shokuhin Shosha
Sk Nt Mot F — Forhandlingar vid det af Skandinaviska Naturforskare och Lakare hallna Mote
Skoda Concern Nucl Power Plants Div Inf Cent Rep — Skoda-Concern. Nuclear Power Plants Division. Information Centre. Report
Skoda Rev — Skoda Review
Skoda Works Nucl Power Constr Div Inf Cent Rep ZJE — Skoda Works. Nuclear Power Construction Division. Information Centre. Report ZJE
Sk Odsh — Det Skonne Odsherred
Skog — Skogen
Skogshoegsk Inst Skogstek Rapp Uppsats Res Notes — Skogshoegskolan, Institutionen foer Skogsteknik, Rapporter och Uppsatser. Research Notes
Skogs-Lantbruksakad Tidskr — Skogs- och Lantbruksakademiens Tidskrift
Skogstradsforadling Inst Skogsforbattring — Skogstradsforadling-Institutet foer Skogsforbattring
SKOKAU — Sbornik Nauchnykh Rabot Kafedry Otorinolaringologii Kishinevskogo Meditsinskogo Instituta Moldavskogo Nauchnogo Otorinolaringologicheskogo Obshchestva
Skole Samf — Skole og Samfund
Skolps — Skolepsykologi
S Kond — Annaly Instituta imeni N.P. Kondakova
SKPA — Sitzungsberichte der Koenigliche Preussischen Akademie der Wissenschaften
SKPanKr — Sprawozdania z Posiedzen Komisji Pan. Oddzial w Krakowie
SKP J — S-K-P (Schoenheitspflege-Kosmetik-Parfumerie) Journal
SKPTA — Skipsteknikk
SKR — Antiken Sarkophagreliefs
SKRA — Staatskirchenrechtliche Abhandlungen
SKRAD — Skeletal Radiology
Skr Finl Adelsfoerb — Skrifter utgivet av Finlands Adelsfoerbund
SKRG — Schriften zur Kirchen- und Rechtsgeschichte
Skrifter Trondheim — Skrifter K. Norske Videnskabers Selskab
Skriftserie Roskilde Universitetsblbl — Skriftserie. Roskilde Universitetsbibliotek
Skript Math Statist — Skripten zur Mathematischen Statistik
Skriv O R — Almanak. Skriv- og Rejse-Kalender for det ar Efter Kristi Fodsel
Skr K Nor Vidensk Selsk — Skrifter. Kongelige Norske Videnskabers Selskab
Skr Lund — Skrifter av Vetenskaps-Societeten i Lund
Skr Lund — Skrifter Utgivna. Vetenskaps-Societeten i Lund
Skr Mineral Paleontol Geol Inst — Skrifter fran Mineralogisk och Paleontologisk-Geologiska Institutionerna
Skr Naturhist Selsk — Skrifter af Naturhistorie-Selskabet
Skr Naturh Selsk Kiobenhavn — Skrivteraf Naturhistorie Selskabet Kiobenhavn
Skr Naturskyddsaerenden — Skrifter i Naturskyddsaerenden/Svenska Vetenskapsakademien
Skr Nor Geol Unders — Skrifter. Norges Geologiske Undersoekelse
Skr Nor Polarinst — Skrifter. Norsk Polarinstitutt
Skr Norske Vid-Akad Oslo I — Skrifter Utgitt. Norske Videnskaps-Akademi i Oslo. I. Matematisk-Naturvidenskapelig Klasse
Skr Nor Vidensk Akad Kl 1 Mat Naturvidensk Kl — Skrifter Uutgitt av det Norske Videnskaps-Akademi. Klasse 1. Matematisk-Naturvidenskapelig Klasse
Skr Nor Vidensk-Akad Oslo I — Skrifter Utgitt. Norske Videnskaps-Akademi i Oslo. I. Matematisk-Naturvidenskapelig Klasse
Skr Nor Vidensk-Akad Oslo I Mat-Naturvidensk Kl — Skrifter. Norske Videnskaps-Akademi i Oslo. I. Matematisk-Naturvidenskapelig Klasse
Skroty Zgloszonych Pr Ogolnopol Semin Mieszanie — Skroty Zgloszonych Prac. Ogolnopolskie Seminarium na temat Mieszanie
Skr Sjoehist Samf — Skrifter utgivet av Sjoehistoriska Samfundet
Skr Szk Gl Gospod Wiejsk-Akad Roln Warszawie Ogrod — Skrypty Szkoly Glownej Gospodarstwa Wiejskiego-Akademii Rolniczej w Warszawie. Ogrodnictwo
Skr Udgivet Univ Zool Mus (Kbh) — Skrifter Udgivet. Universitetets Zoologiske Museum (Kobenhavn)

Skr Uppsala — Skrifter Utgivna av Kungliga Humanist. Vetenskaps-Samfundet i Uppsala

Skr Videnskabsselsk Kristiania — Skrifter udg af Videnskabsselskabet i Kristiania

Skr Vidensk Selsk Kristiania Mat Naturvidensk Kl — Skrifter Utgitt av Videnskabs-Selskabet i Kristiania. Matematisk-Naturvidenskabelig Klasse

Skrypty Uczel — Skrypty Uczelniane

Skrypty Univ Slaskiego — Skrypty Uniwersytetu Slaskiego

SKS — Skrifter som udi det Kiobenhavnske Selskab

SKS — Suomalainen Kirjallisuuden Seura

SKSA — Schriftenreihe der Katholischen Sozialakademie

SkSb — Skandinavskij Sbornik

SKSODV — Neurology. Series One. Neural Mechanisms of Movement

SK Stand Kach — SK. Standarti i Kachestvo

SKT — Svensk Kemisk Tidskrift

SKTEA — Sky and Telescope

SKTFM — Schriftenreihe der Katholisch-Theologischen Fakultaet der Johannes-Gutenberg-Universitaet in Mainz

SKTSW — Schriftenreihe der Kirchlich-Theologischen Soziataet in Wuerttemberg

SKU — Schriften zur Katechetischen Unterweisung

SKU — Selskoe Khoziaistvo Uzbekistana

Skvb — Historisk Aarbog for Skive og Omegn

Skvb — Skivelbogen

SKVSAL — Sbornik Trudov Khar'kovskogo Nauchno-Issledovatel'skogo Instituta Vaktsin i Syvorotok Imeni Mechnikov

SKWKA — Sanop Kwa Kisul

Sky — Skywriting

Sky & Tel — Sky and Telescope

Sky and Telesc — Sky and Telescope

Skylab Sol Workshop Monogr — Skylab Solar Workshop. Monograph

SKYOA — Shikizai Kyokaishi

Skyscraper Mgt — Skyscraper Management

Sky Telesc — Sky and Telescope

SKZ — Schweizerische Kirchenzeitung

SL — MARDATA [*Maritime Data Network*] Ship Library

Sl — Slavia

SL — Slavica

Sl — Slovo. Casopis Staroslavenskog Instituta

SL — Southern Lumberman

SL — Soviet Life

SL — Soviet Literature

SL — Special Libraries

SL — Spectator (London)

SL — Sprache und Literatur

SL — Storia e Litteratura

SL — Studia Linguistica

SL — Studies in Linguistics

SL — Sumerisches Lexikon

SL — Svenska Landsmal och Svenskt Folkliv

Sla — Slavia

SIA — Slavia Antiqua

SIA — Slovenska Archeologia

SLA — Studien der Luther-Akademie

SLA — Studies in Linguistic Analysis

SLA — Svenska Linne-Sallskapet Arsskrift

SLA Adv & Mkt Div Bul — Special Libraries Association. Advertising and Marketing Division. Bulletin

SLA Alabama Chap Bul — Special Libraries Association. Alabama Chapter. Bulletin

SLA Biol Sci Div Reminder — Special Libraries Association. Biological Sciences Division. Reminder

Slaboproudy Obz — Slaboproudy Obzor

SLA Bus & Fin Div Bul — Special Libraries Association. Business and Financial Division. Bulletin

SLAC — Studies in Latin American Culture

SLA Fin Div Bul — Special Libraries Association. Financial Division. Bulletin

SLAG — Schriften der Luther-Agricola-Gesellschaft in Finnland

SLA GA Chap Bul — Special Libraries Association. Georgia Chapter. Bulletin

SLA Geog & Map Div Bul — Special Libraries Association. Geography and Map Division. Bulletin

SLA Geog and Map Div Bull — Special Libraries Association. Geography and Map Division. Bulletin

SLA Ind Chap Slant — Special Libraries Association. Indiana Chapter. Slant

SLAIP — Special Lectures. Aquinas Institute of Philosophy and Theology

SlaK — Slaski Kwartalnik Historyczny Sobota

SLA Metals Div News — Special Libraries Association. Metals Division. News

SLA Mich Chap Bul — Special Libraries Association. Michigan Chapter. Bulletin

SLA Montreal Chap Bul — Special Libraries Association. Montreal Chapter. Bulletin

SLA Museum Div Bul — Special Libraries Association. Museum Division. Bulletin

SLA News — SLA [*Scottish Library Association*] News

S Lang — Studies in Language

SlAnt — Slavia Antiqua

SLANTN — SLANT [*School Library Association of the Northern Territory*] News

Slants Khim Prom-St — Slantsevaya i Khimicheskaya Promyshlennost

SLAPC — Studies in Latin American Popular Culture

SLA Picture Div Picturescope — Special Libraries Association. Picture Division. Picturescope

SLA Pittsburgh Chap Bul — Special Libraries Association. Pittsburgh Chapter. Bulletin

SlaR — Slavic Review

SLARD — Saskatchewan Law Review

SLA Sci-Tech News — Special Libraries Association. Science-Technology Division. News

Slaski Kwar Hist Sobotka — Slaski Kwartalnik Historyczny Sobotka

Slask STHT — Slaskie Studia Historyczno-Teologiczne

SLATA — Secondary Learning Assistance Teachers' Association. Newsletter

SLA Texas Chap Bul — Special Libraries Association. Texas Chapter. Bulletin

SLA Toronto Chap Bul — Special Libraries Association. Toronto Chapter. Bulletin

SLatU — Studia Latina Upsaliensia

Slav — Slavia

SlavA — Slavia Antiqua

Slav & E Eur Rev — Slavonic and East European Review

Slav Ant — Slavia Antiqua

Slav Antiq — Slavia Antiqua

Slav Beitr — Slavistische Beitraege

Slav East Eur Rev — Slavonic and East European Review

Slav E Eur — Slavic and East European Journal

Slav Euro Educ Rev — Slavic and European Education Review

SlavF — Slavjanskaja Filologija

Slav Goth — Slavica Gothoburgensia

Slav Helv — Slavica Helvetica

Slavia Ant — Slavia Antiqua

Slavic & E Eur J — Slavic and East European Journal

Slavic E Eu — Slavic and East European Journal

Slavic R — Slavic Review

Slavic Rev — Slavic Review

Slav Lund — Slavica Lundensia

SlavO — Slavica Othiniensia

Slav Occ — Slavia Occidentalis

Slavon & E Eur R — Slavonic and East European Review

Slavon E Eu — Slavonic and East European Review

Slavonic & E Eur R — Slavonic and East European Review

Slavonic East Eur Rev — Slavonic and East European Review

Slavonic/EER — Slavonic and East European Review

Slavonic R — Slavonic Review

SlavonR — Slavonic Review

Slav Or — Slavia Orientalis

SlavP — Slavica Pragensia

SlavR — Slavic Review

Slav R — Slavische Rundschau

SlavR — Slavisticna Revija

SLAVR — Slavonic Review

Slav Rdsch — Slavische Rundschau

SlavRev — Slavisticna Revija

SlavS — Slavica Slovaca

Slav S — Slavisticki Studii

SLA Western NY Chap Bul — Special Libraries Association. Western New York Chapter. Bulletin

S Lawyer — Southern Lawyer

SLB — Schaulade. Unabhaengiges Internationales Fachblatt fuer Porzellan, Keramik, Glas, Geschenkartikel, und Hausrat

SLB — Studia ad Tabulas Cuneiformes Collectas a de Liagre Boehl Pertinentia

SLBEDP — Suicide and Life-Threatening Behavior

SLBR — Sierra Leona Bulletin of Religion

SL Council Phila & Vicinity Bul — Special Libraries Council of Philadelphia and Vicinity. Bulletin

SLCS — Studies in Language. Companion Series

SLD — Studia Litteraria (University of Debrecen)

SIE — Slavonic and East European Review

SLED — Software Life Cycle Empirical Database

Sleep NY — Sleep (New York)

Sleep Res Online — Sleep Research Online

Sleep Sick Bureau Bull — Sleeping Sickness Bureau. Bulletin

SLESP — Suplemento Literario do Estado de Sao Paulo

Sleszky Num — Sleszky Numismatik

SLet — Sestante Letterario

SLEVA — Slevarenstvi

SLF — Skrifter Utgivna av Svenska Litteratursaellskapet i Finland

SLF — Svenska Litteratursaellskapet i Finland

SLFA — Svensklaerarfoereningens Arsskrift

SLFU — Skrifter Utgivna. Genom Landsmals-och Folk-Minnesarkivet i Uppsala

SLG — Schriftenreihe der Luther-Gesellschaft

SLG — Scottish Law Gazette

SLG — Studia Linguistica Germanica

SLG — Supplementum Lyricis Graecis

SLH — Scriptores Latini Hiberniae

SLI — Special Libraries

SLI — Studi di Litteratura Ispano-Americana

SLI — Studies in the Literary Imagination

SLI — Studi Linguistici Italiani

SLIC — School Libraries in Canada

SLif — Slovjans'ke Literaturoznavstvo i Fol'klorystyka

S Life Home Gard Mag — Southern Life. Home and Garden Magazine

S Lincolnshire Archaeol — South Lincolnshire Archaeology

SLIS — Special Lectures. Institute of Spirituality

SLit — Slovenska Literatura

SLit — Studies in Literature

SLitI — Studies in the Literary Imagination

S Lit J — Southern Literary Journal

Slitok Svoistva Stali Tr Konf Fiz Khim Osn Proizvod Stali — Slitok i Svoistva Stali. Trudy Konferentsii po Fiziko-Khimicheskim Osnovam Proizvodstva Stali

S Liv — Southern Living

SLJ — School Library Journal

SLJ — Scottish Law Journal

SLJ — Singapore Library Journal

SLJ — Southern Literary Journal

SLJ — Southwestern Law Journal

SLJ — Straits Law Journal

SLJR — Sudan Law Journal and Reports

SLK — Schwerpunkte Linguistik und Kommunikationswissenschaft

SLKW — Schwerpunkte Linguistik und Kommunikationswissenschaft
SLL — Skrifter Utgivna. Genom Landsmalsarkivet i Lund
SLL — Studies in Language Learning
SLLR — Sierra Leone Language Review
SLM — Sales and Marketing Management
SLM — Sealift Magazine
SLM — Sharpe's London Magazine
SLM — Southern Literary Messenger
SlMov — Sloc'jans'ke Movoznavstvo
SLMQ — School Library Media Quarterly
SLN — Sinclair Lewis Newsletter
SLN/ALN — Archivos Latinoamericanos de Nutricion. Organo Oficial. Sociedad Latinoamericano de Nutricion
SLO — Slavia Orientalis
Sloan — Sloan Management Review
Sloan Manag — Sloan Management Review
Sloan Manage Rev — Sloan Management Review
Sloan Mgmt Rev — Sloan Management Review
Sloan Mgt R — Sloan Management Review
Sloans Archit Rev & Bldrs J — Sloan's Architectural Review and Builders' Journal
SLOc — Slavia Occidentalis
SLOcc — Slavia Occidentalis
Slo L — Slovo Lektora
SloM — Slovak Music
SLoP — Slovancky Prehled
SLOR — Slavia Orientalis
Slov A — Slovenska Archeologia
Slov Acad Sci Arts J Stefan Inst Phys Rep — Slovenian Academy of Sciences and Arts. J Stefan. Institute of Physics. Reports
Slov Akad Vied Ustav Exp Farmakol Zb Pr — Slovenska Akademia Vied. Ustav Experimentalnej Farmakologie. Zbornik Prac
Slov Akad Znan Umet Razred Prirodosl Vede Dela — Slovenska Akademija Znanosti in Umetnosti. Razred za Prirodoslovne Vede. Dela
Slovak Geol Mag — Slovak Geological Magazine
Slovak Mus — Slovak Musik
Slov Arch — Slovenska Archeologia
Slov Archeol — Slovenska Archeologia
Slov Ceb — Slovenski Cebelar
Slovenska Arch — Slovenska Archeologia
Slovenska Hud — Slovenska Hudba
Slov Etnogr — Slovenski Etnograf
SlovH — Slovenska Hudba
Slov Hud — Slovenska Hudba
Slov Kybern Spol Slov Akad Vied Symp — Slovenska Kyberneticka Spolocnost pri Slovenskej Akademii Vied. Sympozium
Slov Lesne Drev Hospod — Slovenske Lesne a Drevarske Hospodarstvo
Slov Lit — Slovenska Literatura
SlovN — Slovensky Narodopis
Slov Narod — Slovensky Narodopis
Slov Num — Slovenska Numizmatika
Slov Numiz — Slovenska Numizmatika
SlovP — Slovensky Pohl'ady
Slov Preh — Slovansky Prehled
SlovS — Slovene Studies
Slov Vys Sk Tech Bratislave Zb Ved Konf SVST — Slovenska Vysoka Skola Technicka v Bratislave. Zbornik Vedeckej Konferencie SVST
Slow Dyn Condens Matter Proc Tohwa Univ Int Symp — Slow Dynamics in Condensed Matter. Proceedings. Tohwa University International Symposium
Slow Learn — Slow Learning Child
Slow Learn Child — Slow Learning Child
SLOZA — Slaboproudy Obzor
Slozhnye Elektromagn Polya Elektr Tsepi — Slozhnye Elektromagnitnye Polya i Elektricheskie Tsepi
SLP — Serie Linguistica Peruana
SLP — Slovansky Prehled
SLP — Slovensky Pohl'ady
SLP — Slovensky Porocevalec
SLPo — Slovensky Pohl'ady
SLPoh — Slovensky Pohl'ady
SLPr — Slavica Pragensia
SLPR — Slavistic Printings and Reprintings
SLPRB — Steroids and Lipids Research
SLPT — Sammlung von Lehrbuechern der Praktischen Theologie in Gedraengter Darstellung
SLQ — Saint Louis Quarterly
SLR — Scottish Law Review and Sheriff Court Reports
SLR — Slager. Vakblad voor de Vleesspecialist
SLR — Slavische Rundschau
SLR — Slavisticna Revija
SLR — Slavonic and East European Review
SlR — Slavonic Review
SLR — Southern Law Review
SLR — Stanford Law Review
SLR — Sydney Law Review
SLRAAA — Sprache und Literatur. Regensburger Arbeiten zur Anglistik und Amerikanistik
SLRec — Slovenska Rec
SL Rev — Scottish Law Review and Sheriff Court Reports
SLRev — Slavonic and East European Review
SLRev — Slavonic Review
SLRJ — St. Louis University. Research Journal. Graduate School of Arts and Sciences
SlRund — Slavische Rundschau
SLS — Annual Report. Society for Libyan Studies
SLS — Sign Language Studies

SLS — Studia Latina Stockholmiensis
SLS — Svenska Lakartidningen (Stockholm)
SLSA — Svenska Linne-Sallskapet Arsskrift
SlSb — Slezsky Sbornik
SLSc — Studies in the Linguistic Sciences
SLSF — Svenska Landsmal och Svenskt Folkliv
SLSp — Slovensky Spisovatel
SLSS — State and Local Statistical Sources
SLSt — Sierra Leona Studies
SLT — Scots Law Times
SLT — Slavorum Litterae Theologicae
SLT — Svensk Litteraturtidskrift
SLTerm — Slavjanska Lingvisticna Terminologija
SLTh — Slavorum Litterae Theologicae
SLT (Lyon Ct) — Scots Law Times (Lyon Court Reports)
SLTM — Storia delle Letteratura di Tutto il Mondo
SLT (Notes) — Scots Law Times (Notes of Recent Decisions)
SLT (Sh Ct) — Scots Law Times Sheriff Court Reports
SLU — Spil. Een Progressief Onafhankelijk Maandblad voor Zelfstandigen en Werknemers in het Middenbedrijf en Kleinbedrijf
SLU — Studii de Literatura Universala
SLU — Svenska Litteraursaellskapet i Uppsala
Sludge Mag — Sludge Magazine
Sludge Manage Ser — Sludge Management Series
SLULJ — St. Louis University. Law Journal
SLUMA — Southern Lumberman
Slup Prace Mat Przyr Mat Fiz — Slupskie Prace Matematyczno-Przyrodnicze Matematyka. Fizyka
SLURJ — St. Louis University. Research Journal
Sl UVAN — Slavistica. Praci Institutu Slov'janoznavstva Ukrajins'koji Vil'noji Akademiji Nauk
SLWFA — Schweizerische Landwirtschaftliche Forschung
SLY — Slijtersvakblad. Vakblad voor de Drankenbranche
SLZ Schweiz Lab Z — SLZ. Schweizerische Laboratoriums-Zeitschrift
SM — MARDATA [*Maritime Data Network*] Ship Movement Library
SM — Sacred Music
Sm — Saeculum
SM — Sales and Marketing Management
SM — Sales Management [*Later, Sales and Marketing Management*]
SM — Sammlung Metzler
SM — Schweizer Muenzblaetter
SM — Scientific Monthly
SM — Scripta Minora
SM — Scripta Minores
Sm — Smena
Sm — Smithsonian
SM — Sociaal Maandblad
SM — Soma
SM — Sound Management
SM — Speech Monographs
SM — Sports Medicine
S M — Studia Musicologica. Academiae Scientiarum Hungaricae
SM — Studi Medievali
SM — Summer
SM — Sydney Mail
SM — Symposium
SMA — Sociaal Maandblad Arbeid
SMA — Southern Marketing Association. Proceedings
SMA — Stavanger Museums Arbok
S M (A) — Studies in Music (Australia)
SMA — Syrie et Monde Arabe
SMAE — Sbornik Muzeja Antropologii i Etnografii
SMAGD — Solaire 1 Magazine
SMAH — Scriptoria Medii Aevi Helvetica
Small Bus — Small Business Reporter
Small Bus Bull — Small Business Bulletin
Small Bus Comp — Small Business Computers Magazine
Small Bus Comput — Small Business Computers
Small Bus Comput News — Small Business Computer News
Small Business — Small Business Report
Small Bus Reporter — Small Business Reporter
Small Bus Rev — Small Business Review
Small Bus Rt — Small Business Report
Small Comput Libr — Small Computers in Libraries
Small Fatigue Cracks Proc Eng Found Int Conf Workshop — Small Fatigue Cracks. Proceedings. Engineering Foundation International Conference/Workshop
Small Gr B — Small Group Behavior
Small Group Behav — Small Group Behavior
Small Mamm Newsl — Small Mammal Newsletters
Small Pr — Small Press Review
Small Press Rev — Small Press Review
Small Ruminant Res — Small Ruminant Research
Small Rural Hosp Rep — Small and Rural Hospital Report
Small-Scale Master Bldr — Small-Scale Master Builder
Small Sch For — Small School Forum
Small Stock Mag — Small Stock Magazine
Small Sys — Small Systems World
Small Sys Soft — Small Systems Software
Small Syst Software — Small Systems Software
Small Syst World — Small Systems World
SMAN — Studi e Materiali di Archeologia e Numismatica
Smarandache Funct Jnl — Smarandache Function Journal
Smarandache Notions J — Smarandache Notions Journal
SM Arch — SM [*Solid Mechanics*] Archives

SM Arch — Solid Mechanics Archives
Smart Mater Struct — Smart Materials and Structures
Smaskrift Landbruksdep Opplysningstjenesten — Smaskrift-Norway. Landbruksdepartementet. Opplysningstjenesten
SMATA — Studia Mathematica
SMB — Schweizer Muenzblaetter
SMBC — Studien und Mitteilungen aus dem Benediktiner- und dem Cistercienser-Orden
SMBCO — Studien und Mitteilungen aus dem Benediktiner- und dem Cistercienser-Orden
SMBCOZ — Studien und Mitteilungen aus dem Benediktiner- und dem Cistercienser-Orden
SMBD — Stat'i Materialy po Bolgarskoj Dialektologii
SMBO — Studien und Mitteilungen aus dem Benedictiner und Cistercienser-Orden
SMC — Sales and Marketing Management in Canada
SMC — Smithsonian Miscellaneous Collections
SMC — Studies in Medieval Culture
SMCPA — Simulation Councils. Proceedings Series
SMCRD8 — Saunders Monographs in Clinical Radiology
SMCT — Soldier's Manual of Common Tasks
SMD — Sacramentum Mundi
SMDL — Stoff- und Motivgeschichte der Deutschen Literatur
SMDTB — School Musician. Director and Teacher
SME — Sacramentum Mundi
SME — Showme
SME — Studies in Monetary Economics
SMe — Studi Medievali
SMEA — Studi Micenei ed Egeo-Anatolici
SMEC Mag — SMEC [*Snowy Mountains Engineering Corporation*] Magazine
SME Collect Pap — Society of Manufacturing Engineers. Collective Papers
SME Creative Mfg Semin Tech Pap — Society of Manufacturing Engineers. Creative Manufacturing Seminars. Technical Papers
SMed — Studi Medievali
S Med & Surgery — Southern Medicine and Surgery
S Med J Nashville — Southern Medical Journal (Nashville)
Smelter Process Gas Handl Treat Proc Int Symp — Smelter Process Gas Handling and Treatment. Proceedings. International Symposium
SME SPE Int Solution Min Symp — SME-SPE International Solution Mining Symposium
SME Tech Pap — Society of Manufacturing Engineers. Technical Paper
SME Tech Pap Rep MSR — SME Technical Report (Series) MSR
SME Tech Pap Ser AD — SME [*Society of Manufacturing Engineers*] Technical Paper. Series AD. Assembly Division
SME Tech Pap Ser CM — SME Technical Paper (Series) CM
SME Tech Pap Ser EE — Society of Manufacturing Engineers. Technical Paper. Series EE (Electrical Engineering)
SME Tech Pap Ser EM — Society of Manufacturing Engineers. Technical Paper. Series EM (Engineering Materials)
SME Tech Pap Ser FC — Society of Manufacturing Engineers. Technical Paper. Series FC (Finishing and Coating)
SME Tech Pap Ser IQ — SME [*Society of Manufacturing Engineers*] Technical Paper. Series IQ
SME Tech Pap Ser MF — Society of Manufacturing Engineers. Technical Paper. Series MF (Material Forming)
SME Tech Pap Ser MM — SME Technical Paper (Series) MM
SME Tech Pap Ser MR — Society of Manufacturing Engineers. Technical Paper. Series MR (Material Removal)
SME Tech Pap Ser MRR — SME (Society of Manufacturing Engineers) Technical Paper. Series MRR
SME Tech Pap Ser MS — SME [*Society of Manufacturing Engineers*] Technical Paper. Series MS
SME Tech Pap Ser TE — SME (Society of Manufacturing Engineers) Technical Paper. Series TE
SME Tech Pap Ser TER — SME Technical Report (Series) TER
SME West Metal Tool Expos Conf Tech Pap — Society of Manufacturing Engineers. Western Metal and Tool Exposition and Conference. Technical Papers
SMF — Skrifter Utgivna. Modernsmalslararnas Forening
Sm F — Small Farm
SMG — Schweizerische Musikforschende Gesellschaft. Mitteilungsblatt
SMGB — Studien und Mitteilungen zur Geschichte des Benediktiner-Ordens und Seiner Zweige
SMGBE — Studien und Mitteilungen zur Geschichte des Benediktinerordens und Seiner Zweige. Ergaenzungsheft
SMGBOZ — Studien und Mitteilungen zur Geschichte des Benediktiner-Ordens und Seiner Zweige
SMGH — Schriften der Monumenta Germaniae Historica
SMGP — Studien und Materialien zur Geschichte der Philosophie
SMGV — Schriftenreihe des Mennonitischen Geschichtsvereins
SMH — Speelgoed en Hobby. Vakblad voor de Speelgoedbranche
SMH — Studies in Medieval History
SMH — Sydney Morning Herald
SMH (Newspr) (NSW) — Sydney Morning Herald Reports (Newspaper) (New South Wales)
SMHR — Smoking and Health Reporter
SMHVL — Scripta Minora Humanistaka Vetenskapssamfundet i Lund
SMIA — Studies in Mathematics and Its Applications
SMID — Studies in Mycenaean Inscriptions and Dialect
SMIJA — South African Mining and Engineering Journal
SMIL — Statistical Methods in Linguistics
SMIM — Studii si Materiale de Istorie Medie
SMIM — Studii si Materiale de Muzeografie si Istorie Militara
SMiss — Studia Missionalia
Smith — Smithsonian
Smith Coll — Smith College. Studies in Social Work

Smith Coll Mus A Bull — Smith College Museum of Art Bulletin
Smith Coll Mus Bul — Smith College. Museum of Art. Bulletin
Smith Coll Stud In Hist — Smith College Studies in History
Smith Coll Stud Mod Lang — Smith College Studies in Modern Languages
Smith Coll Stud Social Work — Smith College. Studies in Social Work
Smith Col Stud Soc Wk — Smith College Studies in Social Work
Smith Kline French Res Symp New Horiz Ther — Smith, Kline, and French. Research Symposium on New Horizons in Therapeutics
Smiths Blood Dis Infancy Child — Smith's Blood Diseases of Infancy and Childhood [*monograph*]
Smiths Ct — Smithsonian Contributions to Knowledge
Smiths I Asps Obs A — Annals of the Astrophysical Observatory of the Smithsonian Institution
Smiths Misc Col — Smithsonian Miscellaneous Collections
Smithson Ann Flight — Smithsonian Annals of Flight
Smithson Contr Bot — Smithsonian Contributions to Botany
Smithson Contrib Anthropol — Smithsonian Contributions to Anthropology
Smithson Contrib Astrophys — Smithsonian Contributions to Astrophysics
Smithson Contrib Bot — Smithsonian Contributions to Botany
Smithson Contrib Earth Sci — Smithsonian Contributions to the Earth Sciences
Smithson Contrib Earth Sciences — Smithsonian Contributions to the Earth Sciences
Smithson Contrib Knowl — Smithsonian Contributions to Knowledge
Smithson Contrib Mar Sci — Smithsonian Contributions to the Marine Sciences
Smithson Contrib Paleobiol — Smithsonian Contributions to Paleobiology
Smithson Contrib Zool — Smithsonian Contributions to Zoology
Smithson Contr Zool — Smithsonian Contributions to Zoology
Smithsonian Inst Misc Col — Smithsonian Institution Miscellaneous Collection
Smithsonian Inst Misc Coll — Smithsonian Instition Miscellaneous Collection
Smithsonian Inst Rep — Smithsonian Institution. Annual Report
Smithsonian Misc Coll — Smithsonian Miscellaneous Collections. Smithsonian Institution
Smithsonian Stud Amer A — Smithsonian Studies in American Art
Smithson Inst Annu Rep — Smithsonian Institution. Annual Report
Smithson Inst Cent Short-Lived Phenom Annu Rep Rev Events — Smithsonian Institution. Center for Short-Lived Phenomena. Annual Report and Review of Events
Smithson Inst Contr — Smithsonian Institution. Contributions
Smithson Inst Publ Contrib Knowl — Smithsonian Institution Publications. Contributions to Knowledge
Smithson Inst Publ Misc Collect — Smithsonian Institution Publications. Miscellaneous Collections
Smithson Inst Rpt — Smithsonian Institution. Report
Smithson Misc Colins — Smithsonian Miscellaneous Collections
Smithson Misc Collect — Smithsonian Miscellaneous Collections
Smithson Misc Colln — Smithsonian Miscellaneous Collections
Smithson Miscell Coll — Smithsonian Miscellaneous Collection
Smithson Rep — Smithsonian Institution. Annual Report
Smithson Rept — Smithsonian Institution. Reports
Smithson Year — Smithsonian Year
Smiths Rp — Annual Report of the Board of Regents of the Smithsonian Institution
SMIU — Studies by Members of the Istanbul University English Department
SMIZD — Sei Marianna Ika Daigaku Zasshi
SMJ — Sarawak Museum. Journal
SMJ — Siberian Mathematical Journal
S M J — Southern Medical Journal
SMJ — Strategic Management Journal
SMJMA — SIAM [*Society for Industrial and Applied Mathematics*] Journal on Applied Mathematics
SMJOA — Southern Medical Journal
SMK — Somogyi Muzeumok Koezlemenyei
SMKHDI — Science Report. Shima Marineland
SMKRA — Stroitel'naya Mekhanika i Raschet Sooruzheniy
SML — Seagoer Magazine (London)
SML — Statistical Methods in Linguistics
SML — Stimmen aus Maria-Laach
SMLAA — Smokeless Air
Smlbde Intern Musikges — Sammelbaende der Internationalen Musikgesellschaft
SMLF — Skrifter Utgivna. Modernsmalslararnas Forening
Smlg Entsch Oberst Ldsger Bayern — Sammlung der Entscheidungen des Bayerischen Obersten Landesgerichts
Smlg Kirchenr Abh — Sammlung Kirchrechtlicher Abhandlungen
Smlg Zwangl Abh Aughlkde — Sammlung Zwangloser Abhandlungen aus dem Gebiete der Augenheilkunde
SM Lit — Studies in Mystical Literature
SMLJ — St. Mary's Law Journal
SMLS — Schowalter Memorial Lecture Series
SMLV — Studi Mediolatini e Volgari
SMM — Simmons Study of Media and Markets
SMMART — Society for Mass Media and Resource Technology. Journal
SMME — Studies in Mathematical and Managerial Economics
SMMIM — Studii si Materiale de Muzeografie si Istorie Militara
SMMRT Journal — Society for Mass Media and Resource Technology. Journal
SM Muz — Studii si Materiale de Muzeografie si Istorie Militara
SMN — Studia Musicologica Norvegica
SMNSA — Soviet Mining Science
Smolensk Gos Ped Inst Ucen Zap — Smolenskii Gosudarstvennyi Pedagogiceskii Institut. Ucenye Zapiski
SMon — Studia Monastica
SMpB — Schweizerische Musikpaedagogische Blaetter
Sm Pd — Small Pond
SMPKA — Sempaku
SMPM — Schweizerische Mineralogische und Petrographische Mitteilungen
Sm Pr R — Small Press Review
SMPT — Sammlung Medizin, Philosophie, Theologie

SMPTA — Schweizerische Mineralogische und Petrographische Mitteilungen
SMPTE J — Society of Motion Picture and Television Engineers. Journal
SMQ — School Media Quarterly
SMR — Sloan Management Review
SMR — Studia Montis Regii
SMRE Rep — SMRE [*Safety in Mines Research Establishment*] Report
SMRL — Studies in Medieval and Renaissance Latin Language and Literature
SMRRA — Report. Saskatchewan Department of Mineral Resources
SMRT — Studies in Medieval and Reformation Thought
SMRVA — Sloan Management Review
SMS — Startling Mystery Stories
SMS — Studier i Modern Sprakvetenskap
SMS — Syro-Mesopotamian Studies
SMSA — Saggi e Memorie di Storia dell'Arte
SMSNA — Smithsonian
SMSpr — Studier i Modern Sprakvetenskap
SMSR — Studi e Materiali di Storia della Religioni
SMSRAH — Institutionen foer Skoglig Matematisk Statistik Rapporter och Uppsatser
SMS Report — Socioeconomic Monitoring System Report
SMSS — Studies in Management Science and Systems
SMSt — Saugetierkundliche Mitteilungen (Stuttgart)
SMT — Studies in Modern Thermodynamics
SMT — Successful Meetings
SMT — Svensk Missionstidskrift
SMTEBI — Entomologische Abhandlungen
SMTFBL — Faunistische Abhandlungen
SMTLB — Strength of Materials
SMTM — Studii si Materiale. Muzeul Judetean
SMTSDS — Annual Research Reviews. Somatostatin
SMTS Journal — Saskatchewan Mathematics Teachers' Society. Journal
SMu — Sacred Music
SMU — Studia Missionalia Upsaliensia
SMus — Studia Musicologica
SMV — Studi Mediolatini e Volgari
SMVMA — Sbornik Trudov Moskovskii Vechernii Metallurgicheskii Institut
S Mw — Studien zur Musikwissenschaft
SMW — Studies in Ministry and Worship
SMWOA — Schweizerische Medizinische Wochenschrift
SMy — Studia Mystica
SMYA — Suomen Muinaismuistoyhdistyksen Aikakauskirija
SMYRAD — Smithsonian Year
S Mz — Schweizerische Musikzeitung/Revue Musicale Suisse
SMZHA — Sibirskii Matematiceskii Zurnal
SN — Saturday Night
SN — Schirmer News
SN — Science News
SN — Shakespeare Newsletter
SN — Sin Nombre
SN — Slovensky Narodopis
SN — Sovetskaja Nauka
SN — Sporting News
SN — Studia Neophilologica
SN — Studie Neotestamentica
SNA — Shakespeariana
SNa — Sot la Nape
SNAG — Short Notes on Alaskan Geology. Alaska Department of Natural Resources. Geologic Report
SNA Nursery Res J South Nurserymen's Assoc — SNA Nursery Research Journal. Southern Nurserymen's Association
SND — Scottish National Dictionary
SNDL — Studienausgaben zur Neueren Deutschen Literatur
SNDR — Shimane Daigaku Ronshu: Jinbun Kagaku
SNDSB — Sonderschule
SNEIA — Sbornik Nauchnykh Trudov Ivanovskogo Energeticheskogo Instituta
SNERA — Statistica Neerlandica
S New — Sidney Newsletter
SNF — Selskab foer Nordisk Filologi Arsberetning
SNF — Studier i Nordisk Filologi
SNG — Sylloge Nummorum Graecarum
SNGRA — Sangre
SNI — Staatsblad Nederlands-Indie
SNIC Bull — SNIC [*Singapore National Institute of Chemistry*] Bulletin
SNL — Satire Newsletter
SNL — Science News Letter
SNL — Shakespeare Newsletter
SNLN — Saskatchewan Native Library Services Newsletter
SNM — Sbornik Narodniho Muzea
SNMAD — Southwest Bulletin
SNMPAM — Acta Musei Nationalis Pragae. Series B. Historia Naturalis
SNNG — Schakels Nederlands Nieuw Guinea
SNNSB3 — Food Irradiation
SNNTS — Studies in the Novel. North Texas State University
SNoF — Studier i Nordisk Filologi
SNov — Seara Nova
S Nov — Studi Novecenteschi
SNovel — Studies in the Novel
Snow Revel — Snow Revelry
SNP — Studia Neophilologica
SNPh — Studia Neophilologica
SNQ — Scottish Notes and Queries
SNQ — Sussex Notes and Queries
SNR — Revue Suisse de Numismatique
SNR — Schweizerische Numismatische Rundschau
SNR — Sudan Notes and Records
SNRA — Sbornik Nauchnykh Rabot Aspirantov

SNRK — Studencheskie Nauchn'ie Rabot'i Kazakhskogo Un-Ta
SNS — Slovo na Storozi
SNS — Spanish Economic News Service
SNS — Studie Neotestamentica. Subsidia
SNSS — Skrifter Utgivna. Namnden foer Svensk Sprakvard
SNT — Sbornik Nauchnykh Trudov. Armianskii Zaochnyi Pedagogicheskii Institut
SNT — Schriften des Neuen Testaments
SNT — Supplements. Novum Testamentum
SNTCDL — INTA [*Instituto Nacional de Tecnologia Agropecuaria*] Estacion Experimental Agropecuaria Concordia. Serie Notas Tecnicas
SNTSB — Studiorum Novi Testamenti Societas. Bulletin
SNTSMS — Studiorum Novi Testamenti Societas. Monograph Series
SNUCD — Software Newsletter
SNVA — Skrifter Utgitt av det Norske Videnskaps-Akademi i Oslo. Historisk-Filosofisk Klasse
SNVAO — Skrifter Utgitt. Det Norske Videnskaps-Akademi i Oslo
SNVAOHF — Skrifter Utgitt av det Norske Videnskaps-Akademi i Oslo. Historisk-Filosofisk Klasse
SNVKB — Sbornik Nauchnykh Rabot Voenno-Meditsinskogo Fakul'teta Kuibyshevskogo Meditsinskogo Instituta
SNVO — Skrifter. Norske Videnskaps-Akademi i Oslo
SNW — Schip en Werf. Tijdschrift Gewijd aan Scheepsbouw en Werktuigbouw, Elektrotechniek, Scheepvaart, en Aanverwante Vakken
SNWT — Snowshoe. Newsletter. NWT [*Northwest Territories, Canada*] Library Association
SNWTH — Source for NWT [*Northwest Territory*] History. Prince of Wales Northern Heritage Centre
SNZM — Schriftenreihe der Neuen Zeitschrift fuer Missionswissenschaft
SO — MARDATA [*Maritime Data Network*] Ships-on-Order Library
SO — Santiago
SO — Sibirskie Ogni
SO — Sing Out!
SO — Slavia Occidentalis
So — Societa
So — Sojourner
So — Sokrates
So — Sophia: Studies in Western Civilization and the Cultural Interaction of East and West
So — Soundings
SO — Statutes of Ontario
SO — Studia Oliveriana
SO — Studia Orientalia
SO — Symbolae Osloenses
SOA — Sammlung Orientalistischer Arbeiten
SOA — Society of Arts. Journal
So A — Sonderjyske Arboger
SOA — Svenska Orientsallskapets Arsbok
SOA — Sydsvenska Ortnamns-Saellskapets Arsskrift
So Aa — Sonderjydske Aarboger
SoAB — South Atlantic Bulletin
So Africa — Southern Africa
So African Assn Adv Sci Rpt — South African Association for the Advancement of Science. Report
So African J Sci — South African Journal of Science
So African L — South African Law Reports
So African LJ — South African Law Journal
So African Med Rec — South African Medical Record
So African Outl — South African Outlook
So African Philos Soc Trans — South African Philosophical Society. Transactions
So African Q — South African Quarterly
So African Ry M — South African Railway. Magazine
So Afr LJ — South African Law Journal
So Afr LR — South African Law Reports
So Afr LT — South African Law Times
SoAfrStJ — South African Statistical Journal
SOAGD — Solar Age
SOAIAG — Annales Medicinae Militaris Fenniae
SoAM — Sovetskaia Arkheologiia. Akademiia Nauk SSSR. Institut Antropologii, Arkheologii, i Etnografii (Moscow)
SOAMB — Soviet Applied Mechanics
SoANGr — Soobscenija Akademiji Nauk Gruzinskoj SSR
Soap & Chem Spec — Soap and Chemical Specialties [*Later, Soap/Cosmetics/Chemical Specialties*]
Soap & San Chem — Soap and Sanitary Chemicals
Soap Chem Spec — Soap and Chemical Specialties [*Later, Soap/Cosmetics/Chemical Specialties*]
Soap Cosmet — Soap/Cosmetics/Chemical Specialties
Soap/Cosmet/Chem Spec — Soap/Cosmetics/Chemical Specialities
Soap Deterg Assoc Sci Tech Rep — Soap and Detergent Association. Scientific and Technical Report
Soap Gaz Perfum — Soap Gazette and Perfumer
Soap Perfum Cosmet — Soap, Perfumery, and Cosmetics
Soap Perfum Cosmet Trade Rev — Soap, Perfumery Cosmetic Trade Review
Soap Perfum Cosmet Yearb Buyers Guide — Soap, Perfumery, and Cosmetics. Yearbook and Buyers' Guide
Soap Prf Cos — Soap, Perfumery, and Cosmetics
Soap Sanit Chem — Soap and Sanitary Chemicals
Soaps Deterg Toiletries Rev — Soaps, Detergents, and Toiletries Review
Soap Trade Perfum Rev — Soap Trade and Perfumery Review
Soap Trade Rev — Soap Trade Review
SO Ar — Suedostdeutsches Archiv
So AS — Somersetshire Archaeological and Natural History Society. Proceedings [*Later, Somerset Archaeology and Natural History*]
So Asia — South Asia
So Asia Anthro — South Asian Anthropologist

So Asia Bul — South Asian Bulletin
So Asia Q — South Asia Quarterly
So Asia Rev — South Asian Review
So Asia Stud — South Asian Studies
SOAS JLCR — School of Oriental and African Studies. Jordan Lectures in Comparative Religion
So Assn Q — Southern Association Quarterly
SOAS ULLOS — School of Oriental and African Studies. University of London. London. Oriental Series
So Atlan Bul — South Atlantic Bulletin
So Atlan Q — South Atlantic Quarterly
So Atlan Quar — South Atlantic Quarterly
So Atl Q — South Atlantic Quarterly
So Atl Quar — South Atlantic Quarterly
So Aus Bul — National Gallery of South Australia. Bulletin
So Aus LR — South Australian Law Reports
So Aust LR — South Australian Law Reports
So Austr L — South Australian Law Reports
So Austr St — South Australian State Reports
SOAW — Sitzungsberichte. Oesterreichische Akademie der Wissenschaften in Wien. Philosophisch-Historische Klasse
SOB — Sintesi dell'Oriente e della Bibbia
So Bench Bar R — Southern Bench and Bar Review
SOBIA — Social Biology
So Biv — Southern Bivouac
So Bivouac — Southern Bivouac
So Bod — Sounding Board
Sobre Deriv Cana Azucar — Sobre los Derivados de la Cana de Azucar
Sobr Kn Spets Nauchn Proizvedenyi Politekh Inst Brno — Sobranie Knig Spetsial'nykh i Nauchnykh Proizvedenyi Politekhnicheskogo Instituta v Brno
Sobr Spets Nauchn Sochinenii Politekh Inst Brno B — Sobranie Spetsial'nykh i Nauchnykh Sochinenii Politekhnicheskogo Instituta v g.Brno. B
Sobr Spets Nauchn Sochinenii Politekh Inst g Brno A — Sobranie Spetsial'nykh i Nauchnykh Sochinenii Politekhnicheskogo Instituta. Brno. A
SOC — Soap, Perfumery, and Cosmetics
Soc — Societas
Soc — Society
SOC — Sociologia
Soc — Sociologia [Sao Paulo]
Soc — Sociologus
SOC — Standard Oiler (California)
SOC — Studia Orientalia Christiana
SOC — Studies in Organic Chemistry
Soc A — Sociological Abstracts
SocAb — Sociological Abstracts
Soc Act — Social Action
Soc Act & L — Social Action and the Law
Soc Action — Social Action. Council for Social Action [New York]
Soc Actuar Trans — Society of Actuaries. Transactions
Soc Adriat Sci Boll — Societa Adriatica di Scienze. Bollettino
Soc Adv Electrochem Sci Technol Trans — Society for the Advancement of Electrochemical Science and Technology. Transactions
Soc Adv Mater Process Eng Natl SAMPE Symp Exhib — Society for the Advancement of Material and Process Engineering. National SAMPESymposium and Exhibition
SOCAe — Studia Orientalia Christiana. Aegyptiaca
Soc Aerosp Mater Process Eng Natl Symp Exhib — Society of Aerospace Material and Process Engineers National Symposium and Exhibit
Soc African J — Societe des Africanistes. Journal
Soc Agric Alger Bull — Societe des Agricultures d'Algerie. Bulletin
So Cal Acad Sci Bul — Southern California Academy of Sciences. Bulletin
So Cal Bsn — Southern California Business
So Cal Hist Soc Pub — Historical Society of Southern California. Annual Publications
So Calif L Rev — Southern California Law Review
So Calif Q — Southern California Quarterly
So Calif Quar — Southern California Quarterly
So Cal Law Rev — Southern California Law Review
So Cal LR — Southern California Law Review
Soc Alp Giulie Comm Grotte Eugenio Boegan Atti Mem — Societa Alpina delle Giulie. Club Alpino Italiano. Sezione di Trieste. Commissione Grotte "Eugenio Boegan." Atti e Memorie
Soc Alt — Social Alternatives
Soc Altern — Social Alternatives
Soc Alternatives — Social Alternatives
Soc Am Cienc Hortic Reg Trop Congr Anu — Sociedad Americana de Ciencias Horticolas. Region Tropical. Congreso Anual
Soc Amer J — Societe des Americanistes de Paris. Journal
Soc Amer Paris Jour — Societe des Americanistes de Paris. Journal
Soc Am For — Society of American Foresters. Proceedings
Soc Amis Port Royal — Societe des Amis de Port-Royal
Soc Amis Sci Lett Poznan Bull Ser B — Societe des Amis des Sciences et des Lettres de Poznan. Bulletin. Serie B. Sciences Mathematiques et Naturelles
Soc Amis Sci Poznan Trav Sect Sci Math Nat — Societe des Amis des Sciences de Poznan. Travaux. Section des Sciences Mathematiques et Naturelles
Soc An — Sociological Analysis
Soc Anal — Sociological Analysis
Soc Anal Chem Monogr — Society for Analytical Chemistry. Monograph
Soc Anarc — Social Anarchism
Soc Anat De Paris Bul — Societe Anatomique de Paris
Soc & Econ Stud — Social and Economic Studies
Soc and Econ Studs — Social and Economic Studies
Soc & Ind R — Social and Industrial Review
Soc and Leisure — Society and Leisure
Soc & Sci Res — Sociology and Social Research

Soc Anthro Peas — Social Anthropology of Peasantry
Soc Anthropol Paris Bull Mem — Societe d'Anthropologie de Paris. Bulletins et Memoires
Soc Antiescl De France Bul — Societe Antiesclavagiste de France. Bulletin
Soc Appl Bacteriol Symp Ser — Society for Applied Bacteriology. Symposium Series
Soc Appl Bacteriol Tech Ser — Society for Applied Bacteriology. Technical Series
Soc Appl Microbiol Symp Ser — Society for Applied Microbiology Symposium Series
Soc Appl Spectrosc Bull — Society for Applied Spectroscopy. Bulletin
So Ca R — South Carolina Review
Soc Arbeid — Socialt Arbeid
So Car BJ — South Carolina Business Journal
Soc Archeol & Hist Limousin Bul — Societe Archeologique et Historique du Limousin. Bulletin
Soc Archeol Bordeaux — Societe Archeologique de Bordeaux
Soc Archeol Chatillon — Societe Archeologique du Chatillonnais
Soc Arch Hist J — Society of Architectural Historians. Journal
Soc Arch Hist Poitou Arch — Societe des Archives Historiques du Poitou. Archives
Soc Archit Hist J — Society of Architectural Historians. Journal
Soc Archtl Historians Jnl — Society of Architectural Historians. Journal
Soc Areas Biol Chem Overlap J — Society for the Areas of Biological and Chemical Overlap. Journal
Soc Argent Cancerol Bol Trab — Sociedad Argentina de Cancerologia. Boletines y Trabajos
Soc Argent Cir Jornadas Quir — Sociedad Argentina de Cirujanos Jornadas Quirurgicas
So Car Hist Assoc Proc — South Carolina Historical Association. Proceedings
So Car Hist Mag — South Carolina Historical and Genealogical Magazine
So Car LJ — South Carolina Law Journal
So Car LQ — South Carolina Law Quarterly
So Car L Rev — South Carolina Law Review
So Car Med Assn Trans — South Carolina Medical Association. Transactions
Soc Army Hist Research Jour — Society for Army Historical Research. Journal
Soc Arts J — Society of Arts. Journal
Soc Astron Ital Mem — Societa Astronomica Italiana. Memorie
Soc Auto Eng J — Society of Automotive Engineers. Journal
Soc Automob Eng Trans — Society of Automobile Engineers. Transactions
Soc Automot Eng Jpn Rev — Society of Automotive Engineers of Japan. Review
Soc Automot Eng Prepr — Society of Automotive Engineers. Preprint
Soc Automot Eng Proc P — Society of Automotive Engineers. Proceedings P
Soc Automot Eng Q Trans — Society of Automotive Engineers. Quarterly Transactions
Soc Automot Eng SAE Tech Pap Ser — Society of Automotive Engineers. SAE Technical Paper Series
Soc Automot Eng Spec Publ SP — Society of Automotive Engineers. Special Publication SP
Soc Automot Eng Tech Pap Ser — Society of Automotive Engineers. Technical Paper Series
Soc Automot Eng Trans — Society of Automotive Engineers. Transactions
Soc B — Sociologisch Bulletin
SocB — Sociologus. Beiheft
SoCB — South Central Bulletin
Soc Banque Suisse Bul — Societe de Banque Suisse. Bulletin
Soc Behav Pers — Social Behavior and Personality
Soc Behav Sci — Social and Behavioral Sciences
Soc Beh Per — Social Behavior and Personality
Soc Belge De Geog Bul — Societe Belge de Geographie. Bulletin
Soc Belge d'Etudes Geog Bull — Societe Belge d'Etudes Geographiques. Bulletin
Soc Belge D Etudes Hist Et Sci Bul — Societe Belge d'Etudes Historiques et Scientifiques. Bulletin
Soc Belge Etude Pet Ses Deriv Succedanes Ann — Societe Belge pour l'Etude du Petrole, de Ses Derives et Succedanes. Annales
Soc Belge G B — Societe Belge de Geologie. Bulletin
Soc Belge Geol Bull — Societe Belge de Geologie. Bulletin
Soc Bibliog Nat Hist J — Society for the Bibliography of Natural History. Journal
Soc Biol — Social Biology
Soc Biol Hum Aff — Social Biology and Human Affairs
Soc Biol Santiago de Chile Bol — Sociedad de Biologia de Santiago de Chile. Boletin
Soc Bot France B — Societe Botanique de France. Bulletin
Soc Bot Fr Mem — Societe Botanique de France. Memoires
Soc Bot Geneve Trav — Societe Botanique de Geneve. Travaux
Soc Bot Mexico Bol — Sociedad Botanica de Mexico. Boletin
Soc Bras Nematol Publ — Sociedade Brasileira de Nematologia. Publicacao
Soc Bras Progr Cienc Simp — Sociedade Brasileira para o Progresso da Ciencia. Simposios
Soc Bras Zootec Rev — Sociedade Brasileira de Zootecnia. Revista
Soc Brotheriana Bol — Sociedade Brotheriana. Boletim
Soc Bul — Sociological Bulletin
SOCC — Studia Orientalia Christiana. Collectanea
Soc Casework — Social Casework
Soc Catalana Biol Colloq — Societat Catalana de Biologia. Colloquis
Soc Catalana Pediatr Butll — Societat Catalana de Pediatria. Butlleti
Soc Cear Agron Bol — Sociedade Cearense de Agronomia. Boletim
Soccer J — Soccer Journal
Soccer M — Soccer Monthly
Soc Chem Ind J — Society of Chemical Industry. Journal
Soc Chem Ind (Lond) Monogr — Society of Chemical Industry (London). Monograph
Soc Chem Ind London Chem Eng Group Proc — Society of Chemical Industry. London Chemical Engineering Group. Proceedings
Soc Chem Ind Monogr — Society of Chemical Industry Monograph

Soc Chem Ind Victoria Proc — Society of Chemical Industry of Victoria. Proceedings

Soc Chim Fr Bull — Societe Chimique de France. Bulletin

Soc Chim Phys Int Meet Proc — Societe de Chimie Physique. International Meeting. Proceedings

Soc Chim Phys Proc Int Meet — Societe de Chimie Physique. Proceedings. International Meeting

Soc Chim Tunis J — Societe Chimique de Tunisie. Journal

Soc Choice Welf — Social Choice and Welfare

Soc Cienc Nat La Salle Mem — Sociedad de Ciencias Naturales La Salle. Memoria

Soc Cient Ant Alz Mem — Sociedad Cientifica "Antonio Alzate." Memorias y Revista

Soc Cient Parag Rev — Sociedad Cientifica del Paraguay. Revista

Soc Ci Lit Campeche — Sociedad Cientifica y Literaria de Campeche

Soc Cir Buenos Aires Bol Trab — Sociedad de Cirugia de Buenos Aires. Boletines y Trabajos

Soc Cognit — Social Cognition

SOC Coll — Studia Orientalia Christiana. Collectanea

Soc Colomb Control Malezas Fisiol Veg Rev — Sociedad Colombiana de Control de Malezas y Fisiologia Vegetal. Revista

Soc Colomb Quim Farm Bol — Sociedad Colombiana de Quimicos Farmaceuticos. Boletin

Soc Commer Potasses Azote Doc Tech SCPA — Societe Commerciale des Potasses et de l'Azote. Document Technique de la SCPA

Soc Comp — Social Compass

Soc Compass — Social Compass

Soc Con — Social Concept

Soc Cubana Historia Nat Mem — Sociedad Cubana de Historia Natural. Memorias

Soc Cubana Ingenieros Rev — Sociedad Cubana de Ingenieros. Revista

Soc Cubana Ing Rv — Sociedad Cubana de Ingenieros. Revista

SOCD — Studia Orientalia Christiana. Aegyptiaca. Documenti

Soc Dairy Technol J — Journal. Society of Dairy Technology

Soc D Amer De Paris J — Societe des Americanistes de Paris. Journal

Soc d Americanistes J — Societe des Americanistes de Paris. Journal

Soc D Anthropol De Brux Bul — Societe d'Anthropologie de Bruxelles. Bulletin

Soc D Anthropol De Paris Bul — Societe d'Anthropologie de Paris. Bulletin

Soc De Biol Compt Rend — Societe de Biologie. Comptes Rendus

Soc De Biol Paris Comptes Rendus — Societe de Biologie. Comptes-Rendus (Paris)

Soc Def — Social Defence

Soc De Leg Comp Bul — Societe de Legislation Comparee. Bulletin

Soc De Obst Y Ginec Bol — Sociedad de Obstetrica y Ginecologia de Buenos Aires. Boletin

Soc de Statist de Paris J — Societe de Statistique de Paris. Journal

Soc d'Etudes Sc d'Angers B — Societe d'Etudes Scientifiques d'Angers. Bulletin

Soc Dev — Social Development

Soc Dev Biol Symp — Society for Developmental Biology. Symposium

Soc Die Cast Eng Int Die Cast Expos Congr — Society of Die Casting Engineers International Die Casting Exposition and Congress

Soc Dir Roma — Societa e Diritto di Roma

Soc D Rech Congol Bul — Societe des Recherches Congolaises. Bulletin

Soc Dyers & Col J — Society of Dyers and Colourists. Journal

Soc Dyn — Social Dynamics

Soc Dynamics — Social Dynamics

Soc Econ — Social Economist

Soc Econ Admin — Social and Economic Administration

Soc Econ Bot Proc Annu Meet — Society for Economic Botany. Proceedings. Annual Meeting

Soc Econ Paleontol Mineral Pac Sect Guideb — Society of Economic Paleontologists and Mineralogists. Pacific Section. Guidebooks

Soc Econ Paleontol Mineral Paleontol Monogr — Society of Economic Paleontologists and Mineralogists. Paleontological Monograph

Soc Econ Paleontol Mineral Permian Basin Sect Publ — Society of Economic Paleontologists and Mineralogists. Permian Basin Section. Publication

Soc Econ Paleontol Mineral Repr Ser — Society of Economic Paleontologists and Mineralogists. Reprint Series

Soc Econ Paleontol Mineral Spec Publ — Society of Economic Paleontologists and Mineralogists. Special Publication

Soc Econ Paleontologists and Mineralogists Special Pub — Society of Economic Paleontologists and Mineralogists. Special Publication

Soc Econ Paleontologists and Mineralogists Spec Pub — Society of Economic Paleontologists and Mineralogists. Special Publication

Soc-Econ Plan Sci — Socio-Economic Planning Sciences

Soc Econ Rev — Socialist Economic Review

Soc Econ Stud — Social and Economic Studies

Soc Econ Wetgeving — Social Economisch Wetgeving. Tijdschrift voor Europees en Economisch Recht

Soc Ed — Social Education

Soc Educ — Social Education

Soc Ekon Integrace — Socialisticka Ekonomicka Integrace

Soc Encour Ind Natl Bull — Societe d'Encouragement pour l'Industrie Nationale. Bulletin

Soc Eng (London) J — Society of Engineers (London). Journal

Soc Eng London J Trans — Society of Engineers (London). Journal and Transactions

Soc Eng Sci Annu Meet — Society of Engineering Science. Annual Meeting

Soc Entomol Bras An — Sociedade Entomologica do Brasil. Anais

Soc Entomol Que Ann — Societe Entomologique du Quebec. Annales

Soc Espan Hist Nat Bol Secc Geol — Sociedad Espanola de Historia Natural. Boletin. Seccion Geologica

Soc Espanola H N An — Sociedad Espanola de Historia Natural. Anales

Soc Esp Quim Clin Rev — Sociedad Espanola de Quimica Clinica. Revista

Soc Etud et Expansion R — Societe d'Etudes et d'Expansion. Revue

Soc Etud Indochinoises Bul — Societe des Etudes Indochinoises. Bulletin

Soc Etud Iran & A Persan — Societe des Etudes Iraniennes et de l'Art Persan

Soc Exp Biol Semin Ser — Society for Experimental Biology. Seminar Series

Soc Explor Geophys Annu Int Meet Abstr — Society of Exploration Geophysicists. Annual International Meeting. Abstracts

Soc Exp Stress Anal Pap — Society for Experimental Stress Analysis. Papers

Soc Exp Stress Anal Proc — Society for Experimental Stress Analysis. Proceedings

Soc Fauna Flora Fenn Flora Fenn — Societas pro Fauna et Flora Fennica. Flora Fennica

Soc Fauna Flora Fenn Memo — Societatis pro Fauna et Flora Fennica. Memoranda

Soc Folk Arts Preserv Newsl — Society for Folk Arts Preservation. Newsletter

Soc Forces — Social Forces

Soc for Exp Biol Symp — Society for Experimental Biology. Symposia

Soc Fr Allergol Journ Natl — Societe Francaise d'Allergologie. Journees Nationales

Soc Francaise Mineralogie et Cristallographie Bull — Societe Francaise de Mineralogie et de Cristallographie. Bulletin

Soc Franc Miner B — Societe Francaise de Mineralogie. Bulletin

Soc Fr Anesth Analg Reanim — Societe Francaise d'Anesthesie. d'Analgesie et de Reanimation

Soc Fr Biol Clin Monogr Annu — Societe Francaise de Biologie Clinique. Monographie Annuelle

Soc Fr Ceram Bull — Societe Francaise de Ceramique. Bulletin

Soc Fr De Dermat Et De Syphil Bul — Societe Francaise de Dermatologie et de Syphilographie. Bulletin

Soc Fr Dermatol Syphiligr Bull — Societe Francaise de Dermatologie et de Syphiligraphie. Bulletin

Soc Fr D Hist De La Med Bul — Societe Francaise d'Histoire de la Medecine. Bulletin

Soc Fr Gynecol C R — Societe Francaise de Gynecologie. Comptes Rendus

Soc Fribourgeoise Sc Nat B Mem — Societe Fribourgeoise des Sciences Naturelles. Bulletin. Memoires

Soc Fr Microbiol Sect Microbiol Ind Biotechnol Colloq — Societe Francaise de Microbiologie. Section de Microbiologie Industrielle et deBiotechnologie. Colloque

Soc Fr Mineral Cristallogr Bull — Societe Francaise de Mineralogie et de Cristallographie. Bulletin

Soc F TV Arts J — Society of Film and Television Arts. Journal

Soc G Belgique An — Societe Geologique de Belgique. Annales

Soc Gen Microbiol Spec Publ — Society for General Microbiology. Special Publications

Soc Gen Microbiol Symp — Society for General Microbiology Symposium

Soc Gen Physiol Ser — Society of General Physiologists. Series

Soc Geo A Oran — Bulletin Trimestriel. Societe de Geographie et d'Archeologie de la Province d'Oran

Soc Geog Fenniae Acta Geog — Societas Geographica Fenniae. Acta Geographica

Soc Geog Liege Bul — Societe Geographique de Liege. Bulletin

Soc Geog Lima Bol — Sociedad Geografica de Lima. Boletin

Soc Geog Mex B — Sociedad de Geografia y Estadistica de la Republica Mexicana. Boletin

Soc Geog (Paris) B — Societe de Geographie (Paris). Bulletin

Soc Geog Que B — Societe de Geographie de Quebec. Bulletin

Soc Geog Quebec Bul — Societe de Geographie de Quebec. Bulletin

Soc Geogr Bol (Madrid) — Sociedad Geografica. Boletin (Madrid)

Soc Geol Appl Miner Deposits Spec Publ — Society for Geology Applied to Mineral Deposits. Special Publication

Soc Geol Belg Ann — Societe Geologique de Belgique. Annales

Soc Geol Belg Bull — Societe Geologique de Belgique. Bulletin

Soc Geol Belgique Annales — Societe Geologique de Belgique. Annales

Soc Geol Boliv Bol — Sociedad Geologica Boliviana. Boletin

Soc Geol et Mineralog Bretagne Bull — Societe Geologique et Mineralogique de Bretagne. Bulletin

Soc Geol France Bull — Societe Geologique de France. Bulletin

Soc Geol Fr Bull — Societe Geologique de France. Bulletin

Soc Geol Fr Mem — Societe Geologique de France. Memoires

Soc Geol Fr Mem Hors Ser — Societe Geologique de France. Memoire Hors Serie

Soc Geol Ital Boll — Societa Geologica Italiana. Bollettino

Soc Geol Ital Mem — Societa Geologica Italiana. Memorie

Soc Geol Mex Bol — Sociedad Geologica Mexicana. Boletin

Soc Geol Mexicana Bol — Sociedad Geologica Mexicana. Boletin

Soc Geol Mineral Bretagne Bull — Societe Geologique et Mineralogique de Bretagne. Bulletin

Soc Geol Nord Ann — Societe Geologique du Nord. Annales

Soc Geol Normandie Bull — Societe Geologique de Normandie. Bulletin

Soc Geol Peru Bol — Sociedad Geologica del Peru. Boletin

Soc Geol Port Bol — Sociedade Geologica de Portugal. Boletim

Soc G France B Mem — Societe Geologique de France. Bulletin. Memoires

Soc G Italiana B — Societa Geologica Italiana. Bollettino

Soc Glass Technology Jour — Society of Glass Technology. Journal

Soc G Mex B — Sociedad Geologica Mexicana. Boletin

Soc G Nord An Mem — Societe Geologique du Nord. Annales. Memoires

Soc G Normandie B — Societe Geologique de Normandie. Bulletin

SocH — Social History

Soc Haitienne Histoire Geographie Geologie Revue — Societe Haitienne d'Histoire de Geographie et de Geologie. Revue

Soc Hist — Social History

Soc Hist de France — Societe de l'Histoire de France

Soc Hist France — Societe de l'Histoire de France

Soc Hist Germans In Maryland Rep — Society for the History of the Germans in Maryland. Annual Report

Soc Hist/Hist Soc — Social History/Histoire Sociale

So C Hist Mag — South Carolina Historical Magazine

Soc Hist Nat Afr Nord Bull — Societe d'Histoire Naturelle de l'Afrique du Nord. Bulletin
Soc Hist Nat Toulouse Bull — Societe d'Histoire Naturelle de Toulouse. Bulletin
Soc Hongroise Geog Abrege B — Societe Hongroise de Geographie. Abrege du Bulletin
Soc Hydrotech Fr C R Journ Hydraul — Societe Hydrotechnique de France. Compte Rendu des Journees de l'Hydraulique
Soc Hygiene — Social Hygiene
Soc Hyg N — Social Hygiene News
Social Analys — Social Analysis
Social and Econ Admin — Social and Economic Administration
Social & Econ Stud — Social and Economic Studies
Social Biol — Social Biology
Social Case — Social Casework
Social Comp — Social Compass
Social Droit Slav — Sociologie et Droit Slaves
Social Ec A — Social and Economic Administration
Social Econ — Social and Economic Studies
Social Educ — Social Education
Social en Democr — Socialisme en Democratie
Social Forc — Social Forces
Social Ind — Social Indicators Research
Social Indicators Res — Social Indicators Research
Socialist Kmet Gos — Socialisticno Kmetifstvo in Gosudarstvo
Socialist Plodoovoscn Hoz — Socialisticeskoe Plodoovoscnoe Hozjajstvo
Socialist R London — Socialist Review (London)
Socialist Wkr — Socialist Worker
Social Netwks — Social Networks
Social Pol — Social Policy
Social Policy Admin — Social Policy and Administration
Social Prax — Social Praxis
Social Prob — Social Problems
Social Psy — Social Psychiatry
Social Psychol Q — Social Psychology Quarterly
Social R — Socialist Review
Social R — Socialni Revue
Social Regist — Socialist Register
Social Res — Social Research
Social Revol — Socialist Revolution
Social Sci — Social Science Quarterly
Social Sci — Social Scientist
Social Scie — Social Science
Social Science J (Fort Collins) — Social Science Journal (Fort Collins)
Social Science Q — Social Science Quarterly
Social Sci Inf — Social Science Information
Social Sci Q — Social Science Quarterly
Social Sc M — Social Science and Medicine
Social Sec — Social Security Bulletin
Social Security Bul — Social Security Bulletin
Social Se R — Social Service Review
Social Service R — Social Service Review
Social Service Rev — Social Service Review. University of Chicago
Social Services Abs — Social Services Abstracts
Social Services J — Social Services Journal
Social St S — Social Studies of Science
Social Stud — Social Studies
Social Theor Pract — Social Theory and Practice
Social Trud — Socialisticeskij Trud
Social Wk Today — Social Work Today
Social Yugosl Theory Pract — Socialism in Yugoslav Theory and Practice
Societe d'Etudes et d'Expansion Revue — Societe d'Etudes et d'Expansion. Revue
Soc Imp Nat Moscou B — Societe Imperiale des Naturalistes de Moscou. Bulletin
Soc Ind Appl Math Am Math Soc Proc — Society for Industrial and Applied Mathematics-American Mathematical Society Proceedings
Soc Ind Appl Math J Appl Math — Society for Industrial and Applied Mathematics. Journal on Applied Mathematics
Soc Ind Appl Math J Ser A — Society for Industrial and Applied Mathematics. Journal. Series A. Control
Soc Ind Appl Math Rev — Society for Industrial and Applied Mathematics. Review
Soc Indep Prof Earth Sci Bull — Society of Independent Professional Earth Scientists. Bulletin
Soc Indiana Pioneers Yr Bk — Society of Indiana Pioneers. Year Book
Soc Indicators Res — Social Indicators Research
Soc Indicat Res — Social Indicators Research
Soc Indic Res — Social Indicators Research
Soc Ind Min B C R Men — Societe de l'Industrie Minerale. Bulletin. Comptes Rendus Mensuels des Reunions
Soc Ind Mulhouse Bull — Societe Industrielle de Mulhouse. Bulletin
Soc Ind Res — Social Indicators Research
Soc Inf Disp J — Society for Information Display. Journal
Soc Ing Archit Torino Atti Rass Tec — Societa degli Ingegneri e degli Architetti in Torino. Atti e Rassegna Tecnica
Soc Ing Automob J — Societe des Ingenieurs de l'Automobile. Journal
Soc Ing Civ Fr Bull — Societe des Ingenieurs Civils de France. Bulletin
Soc Ing Civ Fr Mem ICF — Societe des Ingenieurs Civils de France. Memoires ICF
Soc Ing Civils France Mem — Societe des Ingenieurs Civils de France. Memoires
Soc Insects — Social Insects
Soc Int Etude Corps Gras Actes Congr Mond — Societe Internationale pour l'Etude des Corps Gras. Actes du Congres Mondial
Soc Int Hist Pharm Publ — Societe Internationale d'Histoire de la Pharmacie. Publications
Soc Int Microbiol Sez Ital Boll — Societa Internazionale di Microbiologia. Sezione Italiana. Bollettino
Soc Int Pedod J — Societe Internationale de Pedodontie. Journal

Socio-Econ — Socio-Economic Planning Sciences
Socioecon Issues Health — Socioeconomic Issues of Health
Socioecon Newsletter — Socioeconomic Newsletter
Socio-Econ Planning Sciences — Socio-Economic Planning Sciences
Socio-Econ Plann Sci — Socio-Economic Planning Sciences
Socioecon Rep — Socioeconomic Report. California Medical Association
Sociol — Sociologus
Sociol — Sociology
Sociol Abstr — Sociological Abstracts
Sociol Anal — Sociological Analysis
Sociol Anal Theory — Sociological Analysis and Theory
Sociol & Social Res — Sociology and Social Research
Sociol & Soc Res — Sociology and Social Research
Sociol B — Sociological Bulletin (New Delhi)
Sociol B (Bombay) — Sociological Bulletin (Bombay)
Sociol Bull — Sociological Bulletin
Sociol Cas — Sociologicky Casopis
Sociol Contemp — Sociologie Contemporaine
Sociol Educ — Sociology of Education
Sociol Educ Abstr — Sociology of Education Abstracts
Sociol et Soc — Sociologie et Societes
Sociol Focu — Sociological Focus
Sociol Fors — Sociologisk Forskning
Sociol Gids — Sociologische Gids
Sociol Health Illn — Sociology of Health and Illness
Sociol Health Illness — Sociology of Health and Illness
Socioling Newsl — Sociolinguistics Newsletter
Sociol Inq — Sociological Inquiry
Sociol Inquiry — Sociological Inquiry
Sociol Int (Berlin) — Sociologia Internationalis (Berlin)
Sociol Issled (Moskva) — Sociologiceskie Issledovanija (Moskva)
Sociol Issled (Sverdlovsk) — Sociologiceskie Issledovanija (Sverdlovsk)
Sociol Lav — Sociologia del Lavoro
Sociol Law — Sociology of Law
Sociol Leis Sports Abstr — Sociology of Leisure and Sport Abstracts
Sociol Meddel — Sociologiske Meddelelser
Sociol Meth — Sociological Methods and Research
Sociol Methods & Res — Sociological Methods and Research
Sociol Neer — Sociologia Neerlandica
Sociol of Ed — Sociology of Education
Sociological R — Sociological Review
Sociologicka R — Sociologicka Revue
Sociologus — Sociologus Zeitschrift fuer Empirische Soziologie, Sozialpsychologische, und Ethnologische Forschung
Sociol Org — Sociologia dell'Organizzazione
Sociol Q — Sociological Quarterly
Sociol Quart — Sociological Quarterly
Sociol R — Sociological Review
Sociol Rev — Sociological Review
Sociol Rev Monogr — Sociological Review. Monograph
Sociol R Mg — Sociological Review. Monograph
Sociol R NS — Sociological Review. New Series
Sociol Rur — Sociologia Ruralis
Sociol Ruralis — Sociologia Ruralis
Sociol Rural Life Minn Univ Agric Ext Serv — Sociology of Rural Life. Minnesota University. Agricultural Extension Service
Sociol Sela — Sociologija Sela
Sociol Soc — Sociology and Social Research
Sociol Soci — Sociologie et Societes
Sociol Soc Res — Sociology and Social Research
Sociol Symp — Sociological Symposium
Sociol Theory — Sociological Theory
Sociol Trav — Sociologie du Travail
Sociol Wk Occupat — Sociology of Work and Occupations
Sociol W Oc — Sociology of Work and Occupations
Sociol Work Occ — Sociology of Work and Occupations
Sociol World — Sociological World
Sociol Yb Relig Britain — Sociological Yearbook of Religion in Britain
Sociom — Sociometry
Socio Meth — Sociological Methodology
Socio R — Sociological Review
Socio-Tech B — Social-Technological Bulletin
Soc Ital Buiatria Atti — Societa' Italiana di Buiatria. Atti
Soc Ital Fis Atti Conf — Societa Italiana di Fisica. Atti di Conferenze
Soc Ital Fis Lett Nuovo Cimento — Societa Italiana di Fisica. Lettere al Nuovo Cimento
Soc Italiana Sc Nat Milano Atti — Societa Italiana di Scienze Naturali in Milano. Atti
Soc Ital Prog Sci Atti Riun — Societa Italiana per il Progresso delle Scienze. Atti della Riunione
Soc Ital Prog Sci Sci Tec — Societa Italiana per il Progresso delle Scienze. Scienze e Tecnica
Soc Ital Sci Aliment Riv — Societa Italiana di Scienza dell'Alimentazione. Rivista
Soc Ital Sci Farm Doc — Societa Italiana di Scienze Farmaceutiche Documento
Soc Ital Sci Nat Mus Civ Stor Nat Milano Atti — Societa Italiana di Scienze Naturali e Museo Civico di Storia Naturale di Milano. Atti
Soc Ital Sci Nat Mus Civ Stor Nat Milano Mem — Societa Italiana di Scienze Naturali e Museo Civico di Storia Naturale di Milano. Memorie
Soc J — Soccer Journal
Soc Jus R — Social Justice Review
SocJust — Social Justice Review
Socker Handl 2 — Socker. Handlingar 2. Communications from the Swedish Sugar Corporation
Socker Handli — Socker Handlingar
Soc Lab Bull — Social and Labour Bulletin

Soc Languedoc Geogr — Societe Languedocienne de Geographie

Soc Languedocienne Geogr Bull — Societe Languedocienne de Geographie. Bulletin

SOCLD — Solar Cells

Soc Leather Technol Chem S Afr Sect Conv — Society of Leather Technologists and Chemists (South African Section). Convention

Soc Leather Trades Chem Proc Annu Conv — Society of Leather Trades Chemists. Proceedings. Annual Convention

Soc Ligustica Sc Nat Geog Atti — Societa Ligustica di Scienze Naturali e Geografiche. Atti

Soc l'Industrie Minerale Cong Cent — Societe de l'Industrie Minerale. Congres du Centenaire

So Clinic — Southern Clinic

Soc Linn Bord Bull — Societe Linneenne de Bordeaux. Bulletin

Soc Linneenne Normandie Bull — Societe Linneenne de Normandie. Bulletin

Soc Linn Lyon Bull — Societe Linneenne de Lyon. Bulletin Mensuel

Soc Maandbl Arb — Sociaal Maandblad Arbeid

Soc Malac Belgique An — Societe Malacologique de Belgique. Annales

Soc Malacologica Rev — Sociedad Malacologica. Revista

Soc Malawi J — Society of Malawi. Journal

Soc Manuf Eng Assoc Finish Processes Tech Pap Ser FC — Society of Manufacturing Engineers. Association for Finishing Processes. Technical Paper. Series FC

Soc Manuf Eng Tech Pap AD — Society of Manufacturing Engineers. Technical Paper. AD

Soc Manuf Eng Tech Pap MR — Society of Manufacturing Engineers. Technical Paper. MR

Soc Manuf Eng Tech Pap Ser AD — Society of Manufacturing Engineers. Technical Paper. Series AD (Assembly Division)

Soc Manuf Eng Tech Pap Ser EE — Society of Manufacturing Engineers. Technical Paper. Series EE (Electrical Engineering)

Soc Manuf Eng Tech Pap Ser EM — Society of Manufacturing Engineers. Technical Paper. Series EM (Engineering Materials)

Soc Manuf Eng Tech Pap Ser FC — Society of Manufacturing Engineers. Technical Paper. Series FC (Finishing and Coating)

Soc Manuf Eng Tech Pap Ser IQ — Society of Manufacturing Engineers. Technical Paper. Series IQ (Inspection and Quality)

Soc Manuf Eng Tech Pap Ser MF — Society of Manufacturing Engineers. Technical Paper. Series MF (Material Forming)

Soc Manuf Eng Tech Pap Ser MR — Society of Manufacturing Engineers. Technical Paper. Series MR (Material Removal)

Soc Manuf Eng Tech Pap Ser MS — Society of Manufacturing Engineers. Technical Paper. Series MS

Soc Manuf Eng Tech Pap Ser TE — Society of Manufacturing Engineers. Technical Paper. Series TE

Soc Mass Media Resour Technol J — Society for Mass Media and Resource Technology. Journal

Soc Mass Media Res Tech Jnl — Society of Mass Media and Resource Technology. Journal

Soc Mbl — Sociaal Maandblad

Soc Mean Leg Con — Social Meaning of Legal Concepts

Soc Med Afr Noire Lang Fr Bull — Societe Medicale d'Afrique Noire de Langue Francaise. Bulletin

Soc Med Chir Cremona Boll — Societa Medico-Chirurgica di Cremona. Bollettino

Soc Med-Chir Hop Form Sanit Armees — Societe Medico-Chirurgicale des Hopitaux et Formations Sanitaires des Armees

Soc Med Chir Modena Boll — Societa Medico-Chirurgica di Modena. Bollettino

Soc Med De Charleroi Bul — Societe Medicale de Charleroi. Bulletin

Soc Med Havn Collect — Societatis Medicae Havniensis Collectanea

Soc Med Lazzaro Spallanzani Boll — Societa Medica Lazzaro Spallanzani. Bollettino

Soc Med Mil Franc Bull — Societe de Medecine Militaire Francaise. Bulletin

Soc Med Tidskr — Social-Medicinsk Tidskrift

Soc Meth — Sociological Methodology

Soc Mex Geog Estadistica B — Sociedad Mexicana de Geografia y Estadistica. Boletin

Soc Mexicana Geografia y Estadistica Bol — Sociedad Mexicana de Geografia y Estadistica. Boletin

Soc Mexicana Historia Nat Rev — Sociedad Mexicana de Historia Natural. Revista

Soc Mex Lepidopterol Bol Inf — Sociedad Mexicana de Lepidopterologia. Boletin Informativo

Soc Mex Oftalmol An — Sociedad Mexicana de Oftalmologia. Anales

Soc Micros Can Bull — Societe de Microscopie du Canada. Bulletin

Soc Microsc Can Resume Commun — Societe de Microscopie du Canada. Resume des Communications

Soc Min Eng AIME Annu Uranium Semin — Society of Mining Engineers of AIME [*American Institute of Mining, Metallurgical, and Petroleum Engineers*] Annual Uranium Seminar

Soc Min Eng AIME Trans — Society of Mining Engineers of AIME [*American Institute of Mining, Metallurgical, and Petroleum Engineers*]. Transactions

Soc Min Eng Trans — Society of Mining Engineers. Transactions

Soc Miner France — Societe Mineralogique de France. Bulletin

Soc Mining Engineers AIME Trans — Society of Mining Engineers of AIME [*American Institute of Mining, Metallurgical, and Petroleum Engineers*]. Transactions

Soc Motion Pict Telev Eng J — Society of Motion Picture and Television Engineers. Journal

SocN — Sociolinguistics Newsletter

Soc Natl Elf Aquitaine Prod Bull Cent Rech Explor Prod Elf A — Societe Nationale Elf-Aquitaine (Production). Bulletin des Centres de Recherches Exploration-Production Elf-Aquitaine

Soc Nat Luxemb Bull — Societe des Naturalistes Luxembourgeois. Bulletin

Soc Nat Napoli Boll — Societa dei Naturalisti in Napoli. Bollettino

Soc Nat Pet Aquitaine Bull Cent Rech Pau — Societe Nationale des Petroles d'Aquitaine. Bulletin de Centres de Recherches de Pau

Soc Nat Resour — Society and Natural Resources

Soc Nav Architects Mar Eng Tech Res Bull — Society of Naval Architects and Marine Engineers. Technical and Research Bulletin

Soc Nav Architects Mar Eng Trans — Society of Naval Architects and Marine Engineers of New York. Transactions

Soc Nav Archit Mar Eng Trans — Society of Naval Architects and Marine Engineers. Transactions

Soc Nematol Spec Publ — Society of Nematologists. Special Publication

Soc Neuchat De Geog Bul — Societe Neuchateloise de Geographie. Bulletin

Soc Neuchatel Geogr Bull — Societe Neuchateloise de Geographie. Bulletin

Soc Neurosci Abstr — Society for Neuroscience. Abstracts

Soc Neurosci Symp — Society for Neuroscience. Symposia

Soc Nouv — Societe Nouvelle

Soc Nucl Can Congr Annu C R — Societe Nucleaire Canadienne. Congres Annuel. Comptes Rendus

Soc Nucl Med Southeast Chapter Contin Educ Lect — Society of Nuclear Medicine. Southeastern Chapter. Continuing Education Lectures

Soc Num Mexico Bol — Sociedad Numismatica de Mexico. Boletin

Soc Nurs Hist Gaz — Society for Nursing History. Gazette

Soc Occup Medicine J — Society of Occupational Medicine. Journal

Soc Occup Med Trans — Society of Occupational Medicine. Transactions

Soc Ocean J — Societe des Oceanistes. Journal

SOCOEE — Social Cognition

Soc of Archtl Historians Newsletter — Society of Architectural Historians. Newsletter

Soc of Ed — Sociology of Education

Soc Ophtalmol Fr Bull — Societes d'Ophtalmologie de France. Bulletin

Soc Oto Rhino Laryngol Lat Conv — Societas Oto-Rhino-Laryngologica Latina. Conventus

Socp — Socialpaedagogen

Soc Paleontol Ital Boll — Societa Paleontologica Italiana. Bollettino

Soc Pathol Exot Bul — Societe de Pathologie Exotique. Bulletin

Soc Pathol Exot Bull — Societe de Pathologie Exotique. Bulletin

Soc Peloritana Sci Fis Mat Nat Atti — Societa Peloritana di Scienze Fisiche. Matematiche e Naturali. Atti

Soc Perspect — Social Perspectives

Soc Pet E J — Society of Petroleum Engineers. American Institute of Mining, Metallurgical, and Petroleum Engineers. Journal

Soc Pet Eng AIME Improv Oil Recovery Field Rep — Society of Petroleum Engineers. American Institute of Mining, Metallurgical, and Petroleum Engineers. Improved Oil Recovery Field Reports

Soc Pet Eng AIME J — Society of Petroleum Engineers. American Institute of Mining, Metallurgical, and Petroleum Engineers. Journal

Soc Pet Eng AIME Pap — Society of Petroleum Engineers. American Institute of Mining, Metallurgical, and Petroleum Engineers. Papers

Soc Pet Eng AIME Pap SPE — Society of Petroleum Engineers of AIME. Paper SPE

Soc Pet Eng AIME Trans — Society of Petroleum Engineers. American Institute of Mining, Metallurgical, and Petroleum Engineers. Transactions

Soc Pet Eng Form Eval — Society of Petroleum Engineers. Formation Evaluation

Soc Pet Eng J — Society of Petroleum Engineers. American Institute of Mining, Metallurgical, and Petroleum Engineers. Journal

Soc Pet Eng Prod Eng — Society of Petroleum Engineers. Production Engineering

Soc Pet Eng Reservoir Eng — Society of Petroleum Engineers. Reservoir Engineering

Soc Pet Engr J — Society of Petroleum Engineers. American Institute of Mining, Metallurgical, and Petroleum Engineers. Journal

Soc Pet Engrs J — Society of Petroleum Engineers. American Institute of Mining, Metallurgical, and Petroleum Engineers. Journal

Soc Petrol Eng J — Society of Petroleum Engineers. American Institute of Mining, Metallurgical, and Petroleum Engineers. Journal

Soc Petrol Eng Trans — Society of Petroleum Engineers. American Institute of Mining, Metallurgical, and Petroleum Engineers. Transactions

Soc Petroleum Engineers AIME Trans — Society of Petroleum Engineers. American Institute of Mining, Metallurgical, and Petroleum Engineers. Transactions

Soc Petroleum Engineers Jour — Society of Petroleum Engineers. American Institute of Mining, Metallurgical, and Petroleum Engineers. Journal

Soc Petroleum Engrs Jol — Society of Petroleum Engineers. Journal

Soc Pharmacol Environ Pathol Bull — Society of Pharmacological and Environmental Pathologists. Bulletin

Soc Pharmacol Hung Conf — Societas Pharmacologica Hungarica. Conferentia

Soc Pharm Lille Bull — Societe de Pharmacie de Lille. Bulletin

Soc Pharm Lyon Bull Trav — Societe de Pharmacie de Lyon. Bulletin des Travaux

Soc Pharm Montpellier Trav — Societe de Pharmacie de Montpellier. Travaux

Soc Phot Instr Eng Newsletter — Society of Photographic Instrumentation Engineers. Newsletter

Soc Photogr Instrum Eng J — Society of Photographic Instrumentation Engineers. Journal

Soc Photogr Instrum Eng Newsl — Society of Photographic Instrumentation Engineers. Newsletter

Soc Photogr Sci Eng Annu Conf Semin Qual Control Summ Pap — Society of Photographic Scientists and Engineers. Annual Conference and Seminaron Quality Control. Summaries of Papers

Soc Photogr Sci Eng News — Society of Photographic Scientists and Engineers. News

Soc Photo Opt Instrum Eng Annu Tech Symp Proc — Society of Photo-Optical Instrumentation Engineers. Annual Technical Symposium.Proceedings

Soc Photo Opt Instrum Eng J — Society of Photo-Optical Instrumentation Engineers. Journal

Soc Photo-Opt Instrum Eng Proc — Society of Photo-Optical Instrumentation Engineers. Proceedings

Soc Phys Hist Nat Geneve C R Seances — Societe de Physique et d'Histoire Naturelle de Geneve. Compte Rendu des Seances

Soc Physique et Histoire Nat Geneve Compte Rendu — Societe de Physique et d'Histoire Naturelle de Geneve. Compte Rendu des Seances

Soc Plan Policy Dev Abstr — Social Planning, Policy, and Development Abstracts

Soc Plant Ind — Socialist Plant Industry

Soc Plant Prot North Jpn Spec Rep — Society of Plant Protection of North Japan. Special Report

Soc Plast Eng Annu Tech Conf — Society of Plastics Engineers. Annual Technical Conference

Soc Plast Eng Div Tech Conf Tech Pap — Society of Plastics Engineers. Divisional Technical Conference. Technical Papers

Soc Plast Eng Eur Reg Tech Conf Plast Process — Society of Plastics Engineers European Regional Technical Conference. Plastics and Processing

Soc Plast Eng J — Society of Plastics Engineers. Journal

Soc Plast Eng Natl Tech Conf — Society of Plastics Engineers. National Technical Conference

Soc Plast Eng Natl Tech Conf High Perform Plast Prepr — Society of Plastic Engineers. National Technical Conference. High Performance Plastics. Preprints

Soc Plast Eng Pac Tech Conf Tech Pap — Society of Plastics Engineers. Pacific Technical Conference. Technical Papers

Soc Plast Eng Tech Pap — Society of Plastics Engineers. Technical Papers

Soc Plast Eng Trans — Society of Plastics Engineers. Transactions

Soc Plast Eng Vinyl Plast Div Lect Notes Div Tech Conf — Society of Plastics Engineers. Vinyl Plastics Division. Lecture Notes. DivisionTechnical Conference

Soc Plast Ind Can CanPlast — Society of the Plastics Industry of Canada. CanPlast

Soc Plast Ind Cell Plast Div Annu Conf — Society of the Plastics Industry. Cellular Plastics Division. Annual Conference

Soc Plast Ind Cell Plast Div Annu Tech Conf — Society of the Plastics Industry. Cellular Plastics Division. Annual Technical Conference

Soc Plast Ind Natl Plast Conf Proc — Society of the Plastics Industry. National Plastics Conference Proceedings

Soc Plast Ind Polyurethane Div Proc SPI Annu Tech Mark Conf — Society of the Plastics Industry. Polyurethane Division. Proceedings. SPI Annual Technical/Marketing Conference

Soc Plast Ind Struct Foam Conf Proc — Society of the Plastics Industry. Structural Foam Conference. Proceedings

Soc Plast Ind Urethane Div Proc Annu Tech Conf — Society of the Plastics Industry. Urethane Division. Proceedings. Annual Technical Conference

Soc Pol — Social Policy

Soc Policy — Social Policy

Soc-Polit Soc-Ekon Probl Razvit Social Obsc — Social'no-Politiceskie i Social'no-Ekonomiceskie Problemy Razvitogo Socialisticeskogo Obscestva

Soc Port Cardiol Bol — Sociedade Portuguesa de Cardiologia. Boletim

Soc Port Quim Bol — Sociedade Portuguesa de Quimica. Boletim

Soc pour l Et des Lang Rom — Societe pour l'Etude des Langues Romanes

Soc Pr — Social Progress

Soc Prax — Social Praxis

Soc Praxis — Social Praxis

Soc Prehist Francais Bull — Societe Prehistorique Francaise. Bulletin

Soc Prehist Francaise Bul — Societe Prehistorique Francaise. Bulletin

Soc Prehist Fr Bull — Societe Prehistorique Francaise. Bulletin

Soc Prehist Fr Bull Soc Prehist Fr — Societe Prehistorique Francaise. Bulletin de la Societe Prehistorique Francaise

Soc Prob — Social Problems

Soc Probl — Social Problems

Soc Probl Nauc-Tehn Revol — Social'nye Problemy Naucno-Tehniceskogo Revoljucii

Soc Prof Well Log Anal Annu Logging Symp Trans — Society of Professional Well Log Analysts. Annual Logging Symposium. Transactions

Soc Promotion Agr Sc Pr — Society for the Promotion of Agricultural Science. Proceedings of the Annual Meeting

Soc Psichol Filos — Social'naja Psichologija i Filosofija

Soc Psychiatry — Social Psychiatry

Soc Psychol — Social Psychology

Soc Psychol Q — Social Psychology Quarterly

Soc Psych Q — Social Psychology Quarterly

Soc Psych Res Proc — Society for Psychical Research. Proceedings

Soc Pure Appl Nat Sci J — Society for Pure and Applied Natural Sciences. Journal

SocQ — Social Science Quarterly

Soc Que Prot Plant Rapp — Societe de Quebec pour la Protection des Plantes. Rapport

Soc Quim Mexico Rev — Sociedad Quimica de Mexico. Revista

Soc R — Socialist Review

Socr — Socialradgiveren

Soc R — Social Research

Soc R — Sociological Review

SoCR — South Carolina Review

Soc Radiol Prot J — Society for Radiological Protection. Journal

Soc R Belge Electr Bull — Societe Royale Belge des Electriciens. Bulletin

Soc R Belge Ing Ind Bull — Societe Royale Belge des Ingenieurs et des Industriels. Bulletin

Soc R Belge Ing Ind Mem — Societe Royale Belge des Ingenieurs et des Industriels. Memoires

Soc R Belge Ing Ind Publ Ser A — Societe Royale Belge des Ingenieurs et des Industriels. Publications. Serie A. Bulletin

Soc R Belge Ing Ind Publ Ser B — Societe Royale Belge des Ingenieurs et des Industriels. Publications. Serie B. Memoires

Soc R Bot Belg Mem — Societe Royale de Botanique de Belgique. Memoires

Soc R di Nap Accad di Archeol Atti — Societa Reale di Napoli. Accademia di Archeologia, Lettere, e Belle Arti. Atti

Soc R di Nap Accad di Sci Mor e Pol Atti — Societa Reale di Napoli. Accademia di Scienze Morali e Politiche. Atti

Soc R di Napoli Accad di Archeol Atti — Societa Reale di Napoli. Accademia di Archeologia, Lettere, e Belle Arti. Atti

Soc R di Napoli Accad d Sci Fis e Mat Atti — Societa Reale di Napoli. Accademia delle Scienze, Fisiche, e Matematiche. Atti

Soc Reconstr Sci — Socialist Reconstruction and Science

Soc Regis — Socialist Register

Soc Rehabil Rec — Social and Rehabilitation Record

Soc Rel — Sociological Religiosa

Soc Ren Stud Occas Pas — Society for Renaissance Studies. Occasional Papers

Soc Repr Dessins Maitres — Societe de Reproduction des Dessins de Maitres

Soc Res — Social Research

Soc Res — Social Reserve

Soc Res Child Devel Monogr — Society for Research in Child Development. Monographs

Soc Research Administrators J — Journal. Society of Research Administrators

Soc Resp — Social Responsibility

SOC Rev — Sean O'Casey Review

Soc Rev — Socialist Review

Soc Revol — Socialist Revolution

Soc Rheol Trans — Society of Rheology. Transactions

Soc Royale Archeol Belgique — Societe Royale d'Archeologie de Belgique

Soc Royale Econ Pol Belgique Seance — Societe Royale d'Economie Politique de Belgique. Seances

Soc Royale Vieux Liege Feuil Archeol — Societe Royale du Vieux Liege. Feuillers Archeologiques

Soc Roy Belge de Geog B — Societe Royale Belge de Geographie. Bulletin

Soc Roy Belge De Geog Bul — Societe Royale Belge de Geographie. Bulletin

Soc Roy Econ Polit Belgique — Societe Royale d'Economie Politique de Belgique

Soc Rural Argent An — Sociedad Rural Argentina. Anales

SocS — Social Studies

Soc Sci — Social Sciences

Soc Sci A & Lett Hainaut Mem & Pubns — Societe des Sciences, des Arts, et des Lettres du Hainaut. Memoires et Publications

Soc Sci and Med — Social Science and Medicine

Soc Sci & Med Part A Med Psychol & Med Sociol — Social Science and Medicine. Part A. Medical Psychology and Medical Sociology

Soc Sci & Med Part A Med Sociol — Social Science and Medicine. Part A. Medical Sociology

Soc Sci & Med Part B Med Anthropol — Social Science and Medicine. Part B. Medical Anthropology

Soc Sci & Med Part C Med Econ — Social Science and Medicine. Part C. Medical Economics

Soc Sci & Med Part D Med Geogr — Social Science and Medicine. Part D. Medical Geography

Soc Sci & Med Part E Med Psychol — Social Science and Medicine. Part E. Medical Psychology

Soc Sci & Med Part F Med & Soc Ethics — Social Science and Medicine. Part F. Medical and Social Ethics

Soc Sci Basse Alsace Bull Mens — Societe des Sciences, Agriculture, et Arts de la Basse-Alsace/Gesellschaft zur Befoerderung der Wissenschaften, des Ackerbaues und der Kuenste im Unter-Elsass.Bulletin Mensuel

Soc Sci Bull — Social Science Bulletin

Soc Sci Can — Social Sciences in Canada

Soc Sci Citation Index — Social Science Citation Index

Soc Sci De Sao Paulo R — Sociedad Scientifica de Sao Paulo. Revista

Soc Sciences — Social Sciences

Soc Scien Mex Mex — Social Sciences in Mexico (Mexico)

Soc Scientist — Social Scientist

Soc Sci Fenn Arsb-Vuosik — Societas Scientiarum Fennicae. Arsbok-Vuosikirja

Soc Sci Fenn Commentat Biol — Societas Scientiarum Fennica. Commentationes Biologicae

Soc Sci Fenn Commentat Phys-Math — Societas Scientiarum Fennica. Commentationes Physico-Mathematicae

Soc Sci Fenn Comment Phys-Math — Societas Scientiarum Fennica. Commentationes Physico-Mathematicae

Soc Sci Fennica Arsb — Societas Scientiarum Fennica. Arsbok

Soc Sci Fennica Commentationes Phys-Math — Societas Scientiarum Fennica. Commentationes Physico-Mathematicae

Soc Sci Hist — Social Science History

Soc Sci Humanit Index — Social Sciences and Humanities Index

Soc Sci Ind — Social Sciences Index

Soc Sci Index — Social Sciences Index

Soc Sci Inf — Social Science Information

Soc Sci Inform — Social Science Information

Soc Sci Inf Stud — Social Science Information Studies

Soc Sci Isl Greinar — Societas Scientiarum Islandica. Greinar

Soc Sci J — Social Science Journal

Soc Sci J Fort Collins — Social Science Journal (Fort Collins)

Soc Sci J Seoul — Social Science Journal (Seoul)

Soc Sci Lett Lodz Bull Cl 4 — Societe des Sciences et des Lettres de Lodz. Bulletin. Classe 4. Sciences Medicales

Soc Sci Lettres & Arts Pau Bul — Societe des Sciences, Lettres, et Arts. Pau Bulletin

Soc Sci Lodz Acta Chim — Societatis Scientiarum Lodziensis. Acta Chimica

Soc Sci Med — Social Science and Medicine

Soc Sci Med A — Social Science and Medicine. Part A. Medical Sociology

Soc Sci Med B — Social Science and Medicine. Part B. Medical Anthropology

Soc Sci Med C — Social Science and Medicine. Part C. Medical Economics

Soc Sci Med D — Social Science and Medicine. Part D. Medical Geography

Soc Sci Med Grand Duche Luxemb Bull — Societe des Sciences Medicales du Grand-Duche de Luxembourg. Bulletin

Soc Sci Medic — Social Science and Medicine

Soc Sci Med (Med Anthropol) — Social Science and Medicine (Medical Anthropology)

Soc Sci Med Med Econ — Social Science and Medicine. Part C. Medical Economics

Soc Sci Med (Med Geogr) — Social Science and Medicine (Medical Geography)

Soc Sci Med (Med Psychol Med Sociol) — Social Science and Medicine (Medical Psychology and Medical Sociology)

Soc Sci Micro Rev — Social Science Micro Review

Soc Sci Monographs — Social Science Monographs

Soc Sci Nat Croat Period Math Phys Astron — Societas Scientiarum Naturalium Croatica. Periodicum Mathematico-Physicum et Astronomicum

Soc Sci Nat Grand Duche Luxembourg — Societe des Sciences Naturelles. Grand-Duche de Luxembourg

Soc Sci Nat Misc Entomol — Societe des Sciences Naturelles Miscellanea Entomologia

Soc Sci Nat Ouest Fr Bull — Societe des Sciences Naturelles de l'Ouest de la France. Bulletin

Soc Sci Nat Phys Maroc Bull — Societe des Sciences Naturelles et Physiques du Maroc. Bulletin

Soc Sci Nat Phys Maroc C R Seances Mens — Societe des Sciences Naturelles et Physiques du Maroc. Comptes Rendus des Seances Mensuelles

Soc Sci Nat Phys Maroc Trav Sect Pedol — Societe des Sciences Naturelles et Physiques du Maroc. Travaux. Section de Pedologie

Soc Sci NL — Social Science Newsletter

Soc Sci Q — Social Science Quarterly

Soc Sci Quart — Social Science Quarterly

Soc Sci R — Social Science Review

Soc Sci Res — Social Science Research

Soc Sci Res Council Bull — Social Science Research Council. Bulletin

Soc Sci Rev — Social Science Review

Soc Sci Stetin Wydz Nauk Lek Pr — Societas Scientiarum Stetinensis. Wydzial Nauk Lekarskich. Prace

Soc Sci (Winfield) — Social Science (Winfield)

Soc Sc Nat Neuchatel B — Societe des Sciences Naturelles de Neuchatel. Bulletin

Soc Sec Bull — Social Security Bulletin

Soc Sec Handb — Social Security Handbook

Soc Sec Rep — Social Security Reporter

Soc Secur Bull Annu Stat Suppl — Social Security Bulletin. Annual Statistical Supplement

Soc Serbe Geographie Mem — Societe Serbe de Geographie. Memoires

Soc Ser Rev — Social Service Review

Soc Serv — Social Service

Soc Serv Del Syst — Social Service Delivery Systems

Soc Serv J — Social Services Journal

Soc Serv Q — Social Service Quarterly

Soc Serv R — Social Service Review

Soc Serv Rev — Social Service Review

Soc Serv R London — Social Service Review (London)

Soc Sismol Ital Boll — Societa Sismologica Italiana. Bollettino

Soc Soc Hist Med Bull — Society for the Social History of Medicine. Bulletin

Soc Social Hist Med Bull — Society for the Social History of Medicine Bulletin

Soc Soc Res — Sociology and Social Research

Soc Soil Sci Fert Technol Taiwan Newsl — Society of Soil Scientists and Fertilizer Technologists of Taiwan. Newsletter

Soc Soil Sci Hung Assoc Agric Sci Soil Biol Sect Proc Meet — Society for Soil Science. Hungarian Association of Agricultural Sciences. Soil Biology Section. Proceedings. Meeting

Soc Sport J — Sociology of Sport Journal

Soc St — Social Studies

Soc Stat — Social Statistics

Soc Statist Paris J — Societe de Statistique de Paris. Journal

Soc Stiinte Geol Repub Soc Rom Bul — Societatea de Stiinte Geologice din Republica Socialista Romania. Buletinul

Soc Stor — Societa e Storia

Soc Stud — Social Studies

Soc Stud Archit Canada Sel Pap — Society for the Study of Architecture in Canada. Selected Papers

Soc Stud Hum Biol Symp — Society for the Study of Human Biology. Symposia

Soc Studies — Social Studies

Soc Stud Sci — Social Studies of Science

Soc Stud St Louis — Social Studies of St. Louis

Soc Study Amphib Reptiles Herpetol Circ — Society for the Study of Amphibians and Reptiles. Herpetological Circular

Soc Study Inborn Errors Metab Proc Symp — Society for the Study of Inborn Errors of Metabolism. Proceedings of the Symposium

Soc Study Reprod Annu Meet Abstr — Society for the Study of Reproduction. Annual Meeting. Abstracts

Soc Suisse Chim Clin Bull — Societe Suisse de Chimie Clinique. Bulletin

Soc Sur — Social Survey

Soc Surv — Social Survey

Soc Survey — Social Survey

Soc Svizz Chim Clin Bull — Societa Svizzera di Chimica Clinica. Bulletin

Soc T — Socialt Tidsskrift

Soct — Societas

SoctH — Societe d'Histoire et d'Archeologie de Molsheim

Soc Theory — Sociological Theory

Soc Theory & Pract — Social Theory and Practice

Soc Thought — Social Thought

Soc Thr — Socialist Theory and Practice

Soc Toscana Sci Nat Atti Mem Ser A — Societa Toscana di Scienze Naturali. Atti. Memorie. Serie A

Soc Tr — Socialisticeskij Trud

Soc Trav — Sociologie du Travail

Soc Travail — Sociologie du Travail

Soc Trends — Social Trends

Soc Tss — Social Tidsskrift

Soc Vac Coaters Annu Tech Conf Proc — Society of Vacuum Coaters. Annual Technical Conference Proceedings

Soc Vac Coaters Proc Annu Conf — Society of Vacuum Coaters. Proceedings. Annual Conference

Soc Vac Coaters Proc Annu Tech Conf — Society of Vacuum Coaters. Proceedings. Annual Technical Conference

Soc Vaudoise Sci Nat Bull — Societe Vaudoise des Sciences Naturelles. Bulletin

Soc Vector Ecol Bull — Society of Vector Ecologists. Bulletin

Soc Venez Cienc Nat Bol — Sociedad Venezolana de Ciencias Naturales. Boletin

Soc Venez Espeleol Bol — Sociedad Venezolana de Espeleologia. Boletin

Soc Venezolana Ciencias Natur Bol — Sociedad Venezolana de Ciencias Naturales. Boletin

Soc Ven Sci Nat Lav — Societa Veneziana di Scienze Naturali Lavori

Soc W — Social Work

Soc Welfare — Social Welfare

Soc Welf Bul — Social Welfare Bulletin

Soc Welf Soc Plan Policy Soc Dev — Social Welfare. Social Planning/Policy and Social Development

Soc Welf Toronto — Social Welfare (Toronto)

Soc Wetensch — Sociale Wetenschappen

Soc Wk (Albany) — Social Work (Albany)

Soc Wk Tech — Social Work Technique

Soc Wk Yrbk — Social Work Yearbook

Soc Work — Social Work

Soc Work Health Care — Social Work in Health Care

Soc Work Lect — Social Work Lectures

Soc Workr — Socialist Worker

Soc Work Res Abstr — Social Work Research and Abstracts

Soc Work Today — Social Work Today

SOCYA — Society

Soc Zemed — Socialisticke Zemedelstvi

Soc Zemes Ukis — Socialistinis Zemes Ukis

Soc Zemjod — Socijalisticko Zemjodelstvo

Soc Zool France B — Societe Zoologique de France. Bulletin

Soc Zool Fr Bull — Societe Zoologique de France. Bulletin

SOD — Socialisme en Democratie

Sod — Sodobnost

SODA — Suedostdeutsches Archiv

SODAA — Solnechnye Dannye

So Dak B Jo — South Dakota Bar Journal

So Dak Hist — South Dakota History

So Dak Hist Coll — South Dakota Historical Collections

So Dak L Rev — South Dakota Law Review

So Dakota Lib Bul — South Dakota Library Bulletin

So Dak R — South Dakota Review

Sodankyla Rep — Sodankyla Report

Soderzh Mikroelem Pochvakh Ukr SSR — Soderzhanie Mikroelementov v Pochvakh Ukrainskoi SSR

Sodium Calcium Exch Proc Int Conf — Sodium-Calcium Exchange. Proceedings. International Conference

Sodium Pump Recent Dev Soc Gen Physiol Annu Symp — Sodium Pump. Recent Developments. Society of General Physiologists Annual Symposium

Sodium Pump Struct Mech Regul Soc Gen Physiol Annu Symp — Sodium Pump. Structure, Mechanism, and Regulation. Society of General Physiologists Annual Symposium

Sod Thom — Sodalitas Thomistica

SOE — Socio-Economic Planning Sciences

SOE — Soft Drinks Trade Journal

SOeA — Schriften des Oekumenischen Archivs

S Oe AW — Sitzungsberichte der Oesterreichischen Akademie der Wissenschaften. Philosophisch-Historische Klasse

SOeAWPH — Sitzungsberichte der Oesterreichischen Akademie der Wissenschaften. Philosophisch-Historische Klasse

SOECA — Soviet Electrochemistry

So Econ J — Southern Economic Journal

Soedin Perem Sostava — Soedineniya Peremennogo Sostava

So Educ Report — Southern Education Report

SOEEA — Soviet Electrical Engineering

SOeKIK — Schriften des Oesterreichischen Kultur-Instituts Kairo

SOEMD — Solar Energy Materials

SOeMZ — Streffleurs Oesterreichische Militaerische Zeitschrift

SOEND — Solar Engineering

SOeR — Studien des Oekumenischen Rates

Soester Z — Soester Zeitschrift

Soest Z — Soester Zeitschrift

So Expose — Southern Exposure

SoF — Samtid och Framtid

SOF — Soldier of Fortune

SOF — Suedost-Forschungen

SOF — Suedostforschungen. Internationale Zeitschrift fuer Geschichte, Kultur, und Landeskunde Suedosteuropas

Sofia Univ Geol-Geogr Fak God Kn 2 Geogr — Sofia Universitet. Geologo-Geografski Fakultet. Godishnik. Kniga 2. Geografiya

Sofia Univ Geol-Geogr Fak God Kniga 1 Geol — Sofia Universitet. Geologo-Geografski Fakultet. Godishnik. Kniga 1. Geologiya

Sofia Vissh Minno Geol Inst God — Sofia Vissh Minno-Geolozhki Institut. Godishnik

Sofii Univ Kliment Okhridski Biol Fak God — Sofiiski Universitet Kliment Okhridski. Biologicheski Fakultet. Godishnik

Sofii Univ Kliment Okhridski Fak Mat Mekh God — Sofiiski Universitet Kliment Okhridski. Fakultet po Matematika i Mekhanika. Godishnik

Sofii Univ Kliment Okhridski Fiz Fak God — Sofiiski Universitet Kliment Okhridski. Fizicheski Fakultet. Godishnik

Sofii Univ Kliment Okhridski Khim Fak God — Sofiiski Universitet Kliment Okhridski. Khimicheski Fakultet. Godishnik

Sofii Univ Mat Fak God — Sofiiskii Universitet. Matematicheski Fakultet. Godishnik

So Fla BJ — South Florida Business Journal

SOFMA — Soviet Fluid Mechanics
SOFOA — Social Forces
So Folklore Q — Southern Folklore Quarterly
SOFT — Australian Software Locator
Soft Eng — IEEE. Transactions on Software Engineering
Soft Eng Notes — Software Engineering Notes
Soft News — Software News
Software — Software: Practice and Experience
Software Dev Chem 4 Proc Workshop Comput Chem — Software Development in Chemistry 4. Proceedings. Workshop Computers in Chemistry
Software Dev Chem 5 Proc Workshop Comput Chem — Software Development in Chemistry 5. Proceedings. Workshop. Computers in Chemistry
Software Dig Rat Newsl — Software Digest Ratings Newsletter
Software Eng J — Software Engineering Journal
Software Eng Telecommun Switching Syst Int Conf — Software Engineering for Telecommunication Switching Systems. International Conference
Software Entwickl Chem 1 Proc Workshops Comput Chem — Software-Entwicklung in der Chemie 1. Proceedings des Workshops Computer in der Chemie
Software Entwickl Chem 2 Proc Workshops Comput Chem — Software-Entwicklung in der Chemie 2. Proceedings des Workshops Computer in derChemie
Software Environ Tools — Software, Environments, and Tools
Software N — Software News
Software Pract and Exper — Software: Practice and Experience
Software Pract Exper — Software: Practice and Experience
Software Pub Rep — Software Publishing Report
Software Rev — Software Review
Software Test Verif Reliab — Software Testing Verification and Reliability
Software Tools Commun — Software Tools Communications
Softw Healthc — Software in Healthcare
Softw Newsl — Software Newsletter
Soft World — Software World
Sof Vr — Sofijskij Vremennik
SOFW J — SOFW Journal. Cosmetics, Detergents, Specialties
SOGEA — Southeastern Geology
SOGEB — Soviet Genetics
Sog Iga — Sogo Igaku
SoGM — Sovetskaia Geologia (Moscow)
Sogo Hog — Sogo Hogaku
Sogo Ky Kenk Kiyo — Sogo Kyodo Kenkyusho Kiyo
Sog Rinsh — Sogo Rinsho
Sog Shik Nenpo — Sogo Shikensho Nenpo
Sohag Pure Appl Sci Bull — Sohag Pure and Applied Science Bulletin
SOHED — Sowjetunion Heute
SOHID — Sohioan
So His S — Southern Historical Society
So Hist Assn Publ — Southern Historical Association. Publications
So Hist Pap — Southern Historical Society. Papers
So Hist Soc Pap — Southern Historical Society. Papers
SoHR — Southern Humanities Review
SoiA — Soirees d'Anvers
SOIFA — Soils and Fertilizers
Soil and Water Conser News — Soil and Water Conservation News
Soil and Water Conserv Jour — Soil and Water Conservation Journal
Soil Assoc Inf Bull Advis Serv — Soil Association. Information Bulletin and Advisory Service
Soil Biochem — Soil Biochemistry
Soil Biol — Soil Biology
Soil Biol and Biochem — Soil Biology and Biochemistry
Soil Biol B — Soil Biology and Biochemistry
Soil Biol Biochem — Soil Biology and Biochemistry
Soil Biol Microbiol — Soil Biology and Microbiology
Soil Biol Sect Soc Soil Sci Hung Assoc Agric Sci Proc Meet — Soil Biology Section. Society for Soil Science. Hungarian Association of Agricultural Sciences. Proceedings. Meeting
Soil Bull Natl Geol Surv China — Soil Bulletin. National Geological Survey of China
Soil Bur Bull NZ — Soil Bureau Bulletin (New Zealand)
Soil Chem Phys Sci — Soil, Chemical, and Physical Sciences
Soil Compon — Soil Components
Soil Cond Proc Symp — Soil Conditioners. Proceedings. Symposium
Soil Cons — Soil Conservation
Soil Conser — Soil Conservation
Soil Conserv — Soil Conservation
Soil Conserv Soc Am Proc Annu Meet — Soil Conservation Society of America. Proceedings. Annual Meeting
Soil Conserv US Soil Conserv Serv — Soil Conservation. United States Soil Conservation Service
Soil Cons Serv NSW J — Soil Conservation Service of New South Wales. Journal
Soil Crop Sci Soc Fla Proc — Soil and Crop Science Society of Florida. Proceedings
Soil Cryog — Soil Cryogenesis
Soil Dyn Earthquake Eng — Soil Dynamics and Earthquake Engineering
Soil Environ — Soil and Environment
Soil Fert — Soils and Fertilizers
Soil Fertil — Soils and Fertilizers
Soil Fert Newsl — Soil and Fertilizer Newsletter
Soil Fert Taiwan — Soils and Fertilizers in Taiwan
Soil Ld-Use Surv Br Caribb — Soil and Land-Use Surveys of the British Caribbean
Soilless Cult — Soilless Culture
So Ill LJ — Southern Illinois University. Law Journal
So Ill ULJ — Southern Illinois University. Law Journal
Soil Mech Found Eng — Soil Mechanics and Foundation Engineering

Soil Mech Found Eng (Engl Transl) — Soil Mechanics and Foundation Engineering (English Translation)
Soil Mech Found Engng — Soil Mechanics and Foundation Engineering
Soil Mech Found Eng Proc Reg Conf Afr — Soil Mechanics and Foundation Engineering. Proceedings. Regional Conference for Africa
Soil Mech Found Eng Reg Conf Afr Proc — Soil Mechanics and Foundation Engineering. Regional Conference for Africa. Proceedings
Soil Micromorphol Proc Int Work Meet — Soil Micromorphology. Proceedings. International Working-Meeting on Soil Micromorphology
Soil Microsc Proc Int Work Meet Soil Micromorphol — Soil Microscopy. Proceedings. International Working-Meeting on Soil Micromorphology
Soil Nitrogen Fert Pollut Proc Rep Res Coord Meet — Soil Nitrogen as Fertilizer or Pollutant. Proceedings and Report. Research Coordination Meeting
Soil Phys West Sib — Soil Physics of Western Siberia
Soil Plant — Soil and Plant
Soil Plant Food Tokyo — Soil and Plant Food (Tokyo)
Soil Publ — Soil Publication. Commonwealth Scientific and Industrial Research Organisation
Soil Publ CSIRO — Soil Publication. Commonwealth Scientific and Industrial Research Organisation
Soil Res — Soil Research
Soil Res Inst Kumasi Ghana Tech Rep — Soil Research Institute (Kumasi, Ghana). Technical Report
Soil Res Suppl — Soil Research. Supplement
Soil Restor — Soil Restoration
Soils Bull — Soils Bulletin
Soils Bull FAO — Soils Bulletin. Food and Agriculture Organization
Soil Sci — Soil Science
Soil Sci Agrochem — Soil Science and Agrochemistry
Soil Sci Agrochem Ecol — Soil Science, Agrochemistry, and Ecology
Soil Sci Agrochem Plant Prot — Soil Science, Agrochemistry, and Plant Protection
Soil Sci Agron — Soil Science and Agronomy
Soil Sci Annu Warsaw — Soil Science Annual (Warsaw)
Soil Sci Plant Nutr — Soil Science and Plant Nutrition
Soil Sci Plant Nutr (Tokyo) — Soil Science and Plant Nutrition (Tokyo)
Soil Sci Pl Nutr — Soil Science and Plant Nutrition
Soil Sci So — Soil Science Society of America. Proceedings
Soil Sci Soc Am Book Ser — Soil Science Society of America. Book Series
Soil Sci Soc America Proc — Soil Science Society of America. Proceedings
Soil Sci Soc Am J — Soil Science Society of America. Journal
Soil Sci Soc Am Proc — Soil Science Society of America. Proceedings
Soil Sci Soc Fla Proc — Soil Science Society of Florida. Proceedings
Soil Ser Dep Soil Sci Minnesota Univ — Minnesota University. Department of Soil Science. Soil Series
Soil Ser Minn Univ Agr Ext Serv — Soil Series. Minnesota University. Agriculture Extension Service
Soils Fert — Soils and Fertilizers
Soils Fert Commonw Bur Soil Sci — Soils and Fertilizers. Commonwealth Bureau of Soil Science
Soils Fertil — Soils and Fertilizers
Soils Fertil Taiwan — Soils and Fertilizers in Taiwan
Soils Fert Taiwan — Soils and Fertilizers in Taiwan
Soils Found — Soils and Foundations
Soils Land Use Ser Div Soils CSIRO — Soils and Land Use Series. Division of Soils. Commonwealth Scientific and Industrial Research Organisation
Soils Ld Use Ser Div Soils CSIRO — Soils and Land Use Series. Division of Soils. Commonwealth Scientific and Industrial Research Organisation
Soils Q — Soils Quarterly
Soils Quart — Soils Quarterly. Geological Survey of China
Soils Rep Manitoba Soil Surv — Soils Report. Manitoba Soil Survey
Soil Surv Bull Samaru — Soil Survey Bulletin. Samaru Institute for Agricultural Research
Soil Surv Horiz — Soil Survey Horizons
Soil Surv Invest Rep — Soil Survey Investigations. Report
Soil Surv Pap Neth Soil Surv Inst — Soil Survey Papers. Netherlands Soil Survey Institute
Soil Surv Tech Monogr UK — Soil Survey Technical Monograph (United Kingdom)
Soil Technol — Soil Technology
Soil Test Plant Anal (Revis Ed) — Soil Testing and Plant Analysis (Revised Edition)
Soil Tillage Res — Soil and Tillage Research
Soil Use Manage — Soil Use and Management
Soil Water Conserv News US Dep Agric Soil Conserv Serv — Soil and Water Conservation News. US Department of Agriculture. Soil Conservation Service
Soins Cardiol — Soins. Cardiologie
Soins Chir — Soins. Chirurgie
Soins Chir Gen Spec — Soins. Chirurgie Generale et Specialisee
Soins Gynecol Obstet Pueric Pediatr — Soins. Gynecologie, Obstetrique, Puericulture, Pediatrie
Soins Gynecol Obst Pueric — Soins. Gynecologie, Obstetrique, Puericulture
Soins Pathol Trop — Soins. Pathologie Tropicale
Soins Psychiatr — Soins. Psychiatrie
SoirB — Soir [*Brussels daily*]
Soirees Paris — Soirees de Paris
SoJA — Soviet Jewish Affairs
SO Jb — Suedosteuropa-Jahrbuch
SoJP — Southern Journal of Philosophy
Sojuzot Zdruzenijata Farm Farm Teh SR Maked Bilt — Sojuzot na Zdruzenijata na Farmacevtite i Farmacevtskite Tehnicari na SR Makedonija. Bilten
Sok — Sokrates
SoK — Sovetskii Kazakhstan
SOK — Sprog og Kultur
SOKAB — Sosei To Kako
Sokhrannost Radiog Argona Gorn Porodakh — Sokhrannost Radiogennogo Argona v Gornykh Porodakh

Sokolovskoe Magnetitovoe Mestorozhd Geol Razved Perspekt — Sokolovskoe Magnetitovoe Mestorozhdenie. Geologiya, Razvedka, Perspektivy

Sol — Solaria

Sol — Solicitor

Sol — Solidarity

So L — Sowjetliteratur. Eine Monatsschrift

Sol Act — Solar Activity

Sol Age — Solar Age

Solaire 1 Mag — Solaire 1 Magazine

Solar 1985 — Solar Energy Employment and Requirements, 1978-1985

Solar E D — Solar Energy Digest

Solar En D — Solar Energy Digest

Solar Energ — Solar Energy

Solar Intel — Solar Energy Intelligence Report

Solar L Rep — Solar Law Reporter

Solar Mag — Solar Magazine

Solar Phys — Solar Physics

Solar Syst Res — Solar System Research

Solartherm Kraftwerke Waerme Stromerzeug Tag — Solarthermische Kraftwerke zur Waerme- und Stromerzeugung. Tagung

So Law R — Southern Law Review

Solb — Sollerodbogen

Sol Cells — Solar Cells

Soldering Surf Mount Technol — Soldering and Surface Mount Technology

Solder Mech — Solder Mechanics. A State of the Art Assessment

Sol Energ Mater Sol Cells — Solar Energy Materials and Solar Cells

Sol Energy — Solar Energy

Sol Energy Eng — Solar Energy Engineering

Sol Energy Intell Rep — Solar Energy Intelligence Report

Sol Energy Intel Rep — Solar Energy Intelligence Report

Sol Energy Mater — Solar Energy Materials

Sol Energy Mater Sol Cells — Solar Energy Materials and Solar Cells

Sol Energy Prog Aust NZ — Solar Energy Progress in Australia and New Zealand

Sol Energy R & D Eur Community Ser D — Solar Energy R & D in the European Community. Series D. Photochemical, Photoelectrochemical, and Photobiological Processes

Sol Energy R & D Eur Community Ser E Energy Biomass — Solar Energy R and D [Research and Development] in the European Community. Series E. Energy from Biomass

Sol Energy Res Dev Rep — Solar Energy Research and Development Report

Sol Energy Res Inst Tech Rep SERI CP — Solar Energy Research Institute. Technical Report SERI/CP

Sol Energy Res Inst Tech Rep SERI TP — Solar Energy Research Institute. Technical Report SERI/TP

Sol Energy Res Inst Tech Rep SERI TR — Solar Energy Research Institute. Technical Report SERI/TR

Sol Energy Res Rep Univ Queensl — Solar Energy Research Report. University of Queensland

Sol Energy Seoul — Solar Energy (Seoul)

Sol Energy Update — Solar Energy Update

Sol Energy Util — Solar Energy Utilization

Sol Eng — Solar Engineering

Sol Eng Mag — Solar Engineering Magazine

Sol Flare Magnetohydrodyn — Solar Flare Magnetohydrodynamics

Sol Flares Monogr Skylab Sol Workshop — Solar Flares. Monograph from Skylab Solar Workshop

Sol Gamma X EUV Radiat — Solar Gamma-, X-, and EUV Radiation

Sol Gel Sci Technol — Sol-Gel Science and Technology

Sol Heat Cool — Solar Heating and Cooling

SOLI — Soviet Life

Solic — Solicitor

Solicitors' J — Solicitors' Journal

Solic J — Solicitors' Journal

Solic Q — Solicitor's Quarterly

SOLID — Solar Life

Solidar Racional S Jose — Solidarismo y Racionalizacion (San Jose, Costa Rica)

Solid Earth Sci Libr — Solid Earth Sciences Library

Solid Freeform Fabr Symp Proc — Solid Freeform Fabrication Symposium Proceedings

Solid Fuel Chem — Solid Fuel Chemistry

Solid Fuel Chem (Engl Transl) — Solid Fuel Chemistry (English Translation)

Solidif Microgravity — Solidification and Microgravity

Solid Mech Appl — Solid Mechanics and its Applications

Solid Mech Arch — Solid Mechanics Archives

Solid Mech Its Appl — Solid Mechanics and Its Applications

Solid St Abstr — Solid State Abstracts

Solid Stat — Solid State Technology

Solid State Abstr — Solid State Abstracts

Solid State Abstr J — Solid State Abstracts Journal

Solid State Chem Sens — Solid State Chemical Sensors

Solid State Commun — Solid State Communications

Solid State Devices Invited Pap ESSDERC — Solid State Devices. Invited Papers presented at the ESSDERC (European Solid State Device Research Conference)

Solid State Devices Pap Eur Semicond Device Res Conf — Solid State Devices. Papers. European Semiconductor Device Research Conference

Solid State Devices Proc Eur Conf — Solid State Devices. Proceedings. European Conference

Solid-State Electron — Solid-State Electronics

Solid State J — Solid State Journal

Solid State Nucl Magn Reson — Solid State Nuclear Magnetic Resonance

Solid State Nucl Track Detect Proc Int Conf — Solid State Nuclear Track Detectors. Proceedings. International Conference

Solid State Phys — Solid State Physics

Solid State Phys Chem — Solid State Physics and Chemistry

Solid State Phys (New York) — Solid State Physics. Advances in Research and Applications (New York)

Solid State Phys Nucl Phys Part Phys Lat Am Sch Phys — Solid State Physics, Nuclear Physics, and Particle Physics. Latin American School of Physics

Solid State Phys Simon Fraser Univ Lect — Solid State Physics. The Simon Fraser University Lectures

Solid State Phys Suppl — Solid State Physics. Supplement

Solid State Phys (Tokyo) — Solid State Physics (Tokyo)

Solid State Surf Sci — Solid State Surface Science

Solid State Technol — Solid State Technology

Solid St Commun — Solid State Communications

Solid Waste Bull — Solid Waste Bulletin

Solid Waste Manage Branch Rep EPS Can Environ Prot Serv — Solid Waste Management Branch Report EPS (Canada. Environmental Protection Service)

Solid Waste Man Newsl — Solid Waste Management Newsletter

Solid Wastes Manage — Solid Wastes Management

Solid Wastes Manage Refuse Removal J — Solid Wastes Management/Refuse Removal Journal [Later, World Wastes]

Solid Wastes Mgmt — Solid Wastes Management [Later, World Wastes]

Solid Waste Syst — Solid Waste Systems

Solid WM — Solid Wastes Management [Later, World Wastes]

Sol Ind Ind — Solar Industry Index

SOLINEWS — Southeastern Library Network. Newsletter

SOLIS — Sozialwissenschaftliches Literaturinformationssystem

So Lit J — Southern Literary Journal

So Lit Mess — Southern Literary Messenger

SOliv — Studia Oliveriana

Sol J — Solicitors' Journal

So LJ — Southern Law Journal and Reporter

SoLJ — Southern Literary Journal

Sol J & R — Solicitors' Journal and Reporter

Sol Jo (Eng) — Solicitors' Journal (England)

Sol Law Rep — Solar Law Reporter

Sol Life — Solar Life

Sol Man Cl Gaz — Solicitor's Managing Clerks' Gazette

SOLMD — Solar Magazine

Soln Akt — Solnechnaya Aktivnost

Soln Dannye — Solnechnye Dannye

Sol News Int — Solar News International

Solo Cent Acad "Luiz De Queiroz" Univ Sao Paulo — Solo Centro Academico "Luiz De Queiroz." Universidade de Sao Paulo

Sol Phys — Solar Physics

Sol Q — Solicitor Quarterly

So Q — Solicitor's Quarterly

So LQ — Southern Law Quarterly

SOLQA — Sociological Quarterly

So LR — Southern Law Review

SOL Rev — School of Law. Review

So L Rev — Southern Law Review

So L Rev NS — Southern Law Review, New Series

So LRNS — Southern Law Review, New Series

Sols Afr — Sols Africains

Sol St Comm — Solid State Communications

Sol-St Elec — Solid-State Electronics

Sol St Tech — Solid State Technology

Sol Syst Res — Solar System Research

Sol Syst Res (Engl Transl) — Solar System Research (English Translation)

So LT — Southern Law Times

SOLTA — Sotsialisticheskiy Trud

Sol Terr Environ Res Jpn — Solar Terrestrial Environmental Research in Japan

Sol Therm Components — Solar Thermal Components

Sol Therm Energy Util — Solar Thermal Energy Utilization

Sol Therm Heat Cool — Solar Thermal Heating and Cooling

Sol Therm Power Gener — Solar Thermal Power Generation

Sol Therm Rep — Solar Thermal Report

Sol Times — Solar Times

SOLUB — Aqueous Solubility Database

Solubility Data Ser — Solubility Data Series

Solvation Phenom Symp Repr — Solvation Phenomena. Symposium Reprints

Solvent Ext — Solvent Extraction and Ion Exchange

Solvent Extr Chem Met Proc Int Conf — Solvent Extraction Chemistry of Metals. Proceedings. International Conference

Solvent Extr Ion Exch — Solvent Extraction and Ion Exchange

Solvent Extr Res Dev Jpn — Solvent Extraction Research and Development (Japan)

Solvent Extr Res Proc Int Conf Solvent Extr Chem — Solvent Extraction Research. Proceedings. International Conference on Solvent Extraction Chemistry

Solvent Extr Rev — Solvent Extraction Reviews

Solvents Symp Ind — Solvents Symposium for Industry

Solvent Substitution Annu Int Workshop Solvent Substitution — Solvent Substitution. Annual International Workshop on Solvent Substitution

Sol World Congr Proc Bienn Congr Int Sol Energy Soc — Solar World Congress. Proceedings. Biennial Congress. International Solar Energy Society

SOM — Lundberg Survey Share of Market

SOM — Sociaal Maandblad Arbeid. Tijdschrift voor Sociaal Recht en Sociaal Geleid

Som — Somerset Legal Journal

So M — Sonderjydsk Maanedsskrift

So M — Southern Magazine

So M — Sovetskaja Muzyka

SOMA — Soobscenija Otdela Machanizacii i Avtomatizacii Informacionnych Rabot

Som A Natur Hist — Somerset Archaeology and Natural History

Somat Cell Mol Genet — Somatic Cell and Molecular Genetics

Somatic Cell Genet — Somatic Cell Genetics

Somatic Cell Mol Genet — Somatic Cell and Molecular Genetics

Somatosens Mot Res — Somatosensory and Motor Research
Somatosens Res — Somatosensory Research
SOMBA — Southern Medical Bulletin
Som Cell G — Somatic Cell Genetics
SOMDA — Southwestern Medicine
SOMEA — Sovetskaya Meditsina
So Med Assn J — Southern Medical Association. Journal
So Med J — Southern Medical Journal
So Med Rpts — Southern Medical Reports
Some Math Quest Biol — Some Mathematical Questions in Biology
Some Pioneers Ind Hyg — Some Pioneers of Industrial Hygiene
Someraj Univ Kursoj Kursotekstoj — Someraj Universitataj Kursoj. Kursotekstoj
Somerset Archaeol Natur Hist — Somerset Archaeology and Natural History
Somerset Arch Nat Hist — Somerset Archaeology and Natural History
Somerset Industrial Archaeology Soc Jnl — Somerset Industrial Archaeology Society. Journal
Somerset Levels Pap — Somerset Levels Papers
Somerset LJ — Somerset Legal Journal
Some Spec Aspects Nutr — Some Special Aspects of Nutrition
Some Theor Probl Catal Res Rep Sov Jpn Semin Catal — Some Theoretical Problems of Catalysis. Research Reports. Soviet-Japanese Seminar on Catalysis
SOMIA8 — Sbornik Nauchnykh Rabot Moldavskogo Otdeleniya Vsesoyuznogo Nauchnogo Obshchestva Mikrobiologov, Epidemiologov, i Infektsionistov
Som Leg J (PA) — Somerset Legal Journal
Som LJ — Somerset Legal Journal
SoMM — Sovetskaia Meditsina (Moscow)
Somogyi MK — Somogyi Muzeumok Koezlemenyei
Somogyi Muesz Sz — Somogyi Mueszaki Szemle
SOMSA — Soviet Materials Science
Som S P — Somersetshire Archaeological and Natural History Society's Proceedings
SOMZ — Streffleurs Oesterreiche Militaerische Zeitschrift
SON — Slovenske Odborne Nazvoslovie
Son — Sonus
Soncino BI — Soncino-Blaetter
Sonderb Fortschr Phys — Sonderband der Fortschritte der Physik
Sonderb Naturwiss Ver Hamb — Sonderbaende des Naturwissenschaftlichen Vereins in Hamburg
Sonderb Prakt Metallogr — Sonderbaende der Praktischen Metallographie
Sonderb Strahlenther — Sonderbaende zur Strahlentherapie
Sonderb Z Strahlenther Onkol — Sonderband. Der Zeitschrift Strahlentherapie und Onkologie
Sonderdr Internist Welt — Sonderdruck aus Internistische Welt
Sonderdruck Schr Ver Gesch Bodensees & Umgebung — Sonderdruck aus den Schriften des Vereins fuer Geschichte des Bodensees und Seiner Umgebung
Sonderh Bayer Landw Jb — Sonderhefte. Bayerisches Landwirtschaftliches Jahrbuch
Sonderhefte zum Allgemein Statist Arch — Sonderhefte zum Allgemeinen Statistischen Archiv
Sonderh Landw Forsch — Sonderheft zur Zeitschrift "Landwirtschaftliche Forschung"
Sonderh Z PflKrankh PflPath PflSchutz — Sonderheft. Zeitschrift fuer Pflanzenkrankheiten, Pflanzenpathologie, und Pflanzenschutz
Sonderjydsk M-Skr — Sonderjydsk Manedsskrift
Sonenergie — Sonnenenergie und Waermepumpe
Song Hits Mag — Song Hits Magazine
Songklanakarin J Sci Technol — Songklanakarin Journal of Science and Technology
Songwriter — Songwriter Magazine
Songwriters R — Songwriter's Review
SONKA — Shonika
Sonneck S — Sonneck Society Bulletin for American Music
Sonnenenerg — Sonnenenergie
Sonnenenerg Waermepumpe — Sonnenenergie und Waermepumpe
SQnoM — Studia Ononmastica Monacensia
So NQ — Somerset Notes and Queries
Son Spec — Sonorum Speculum
SONWD — Sonnenenergie und Waermepumpe
Soob A N Gruz SSR — Soobshcheniia Akademii Nauk Gruzinskoi SSR
Soob Erm — Soobshcheniia Gosudarstvennogo Ermitazha
Soob Ermit — Soobscenija Gosudarstvennogo Ordena Lenina Ermitaza
Soob Ermit — Soobshcheniya Gosudarstvennogo Ermitazha
Soob G Ermitazh — Soobshcheniia Gosudarstvennogo Ermitazha
Soob G Muz Izob Isk Pushkin — Soobshcheniia Gosudarstvennyi Muzei Izobrazitel'nykh Iskusstv Imeni A. S. Pushkina
Soob Gos Erm — Soobshcheniia Gosudarstvennogo Ermitazha
Soob Gruz — Soobshcheniya Akademii Nauk Gruzinskoi SSR
Soob Kherson Muz — Soobshcheniia Khersonnesskogo Muzeia
Soob Pus — Soobshcheniia Gosudarstvennyi Muzei Izobrazitel'nykh Iskusstv imeni A.S. Pushkina
Soobsc Bjuro Castn Rasteniev Ucen Komiteta Minist Zemland — Soobscenija Bjuro po Castnomu Rastenievodstvu Ucenago Komieteta Ministerstva Zemledelija
Soobsc Dalnevost Fil Komarova Akad Nauk SSSR — Soobscenija Dal'nevostocnogo Filiala Imeni V. L. Komarova Akademii Nauk SSSR
Soobscenija Akad Nauk Gruz SSR — Soobscenija Akademiji Nauk Gruzinskoj SSR
Soobsc Gosud Russk Muz — Soobscenija Gosudarstvennogo Russkogo Muzeja
Soobsc Muz Isk Nar Vostoka — Soobscenija Muzeja Iskusstva Narodov Vostoka
Soobsc Vycisl Mat — Soobscenija po Vychislitel noi Matematike
Soobshch Akad Nauk Gruz — Soobshcheniya Akademii Nauk Gruzii
Soobshch Akad Nauk Gruzii — Akademiya Nauk Gruzii. Soobshcheniya
Soobshch Akad Nauk Gruzin SSR — Soobshcheniya Akademiya Nauk Gruzinskoi SSR

Soobshch Akad Nauk Gruz SSSR — Soobshcheniya Akademiya Nauk Gruzinskoi SSSR
Soobshch Byurakan Obs Akad Nauk Arm SSR — Soobshcheniya Byurakanskoi Observatorii Akademiya Nauk Armyanskoi SSR
Soobshch Chuv Zon Agrokhim Lab — Soobshcheniya Chuvashskoi Zonal'noi Agrokhimicheskoi Laboratorii
Soobshch Dalnevost Fil Akad Nauk SSSR — Soobshcheniya Dal'nevostochnogo Filiala Akademii Nauk SSSR
Soobshch Dal'Nevost Fil Sib Otd Aka Nauk SSSR — Soobshcheniya Dal'Nevostochnogo Filiala Sibirskogo Otdela Akademii Nauk SSSR
Soobshcheniya Gosudarstvennogo Rus Muz — Soobshcheniya Gosudarstvennogo Russkogo Muzeya
Soobshcheniya Inst Istor Iskusstv AN SSSR — Soobshcheniya Instituta Istorii Iskusstv Akademii Nauk SSSR
Soobshcheniya Respub Istor Kraevedcheskogo Muz Tadzhik SSR — Soobshcheniya Respublikanskogo Istoriko-Kraevedcheskogo Muzeya Tadzhikskoy SSR
Soobshch Gos Astron Inst Mosk Gos Univ — Soobshcheniya Gosudarstvennogo Astronomicheskogo Instituta. Moskovskii Gosudarstvennyi Universitet
Soobshch Gos Soyuz Inst Proekt Predpr Koksokhim Promsti — Soobshcheniya Gosudarstvennogo Soyuznogo Instituta po Proektirovaniyu Predpriyatii Koksokhimicheskoi Promyshlennosti
Soobshch Gos Vses Inst Proekt Predpr Koksokhim Promsti SSSR — Soobshcheniya Gosudarstvennogo Vsesoyuznogo Instituta po Proektirovaniyu Predpriyatii Koksokhimicheskoi Promyshlennosti
Soobshch Gruz Fil Akad Nauk SSSR — Soobshcheniya Gruzinskogo Filiala Akademii Nauk SSSR
Soobshch Inst Agrokhim Probl Gidroponiki Akad Nauk Arm SSR — Soobshcheniya Instituta Agrokhimicheskikh Problem i Gidroponiki Akademiya NaukArmyanskoi SSR
Soobshch Inst Lesa Akad Nauk SSSR — Soobshcheniya Instituta Lesa Akademii Nauk SSSR
SoobshchIPPO — Soobshcheniia Imperialnovo Pravoslavnovo Palestinskavo Obshchestva
Soobshch Issled Inst Sel Rastenievod G Shopronkhorpach — Soobshcheniya Issledovatel'skogo Instituta po Selektsii i Rastenievodstvu. G. Shopronkhorpach
Soobshch Lab Agrokhim Akad Nauk Arm SSR — Soobshcheniya Laboratorii Agrokhimii. Akademiya Nauk Armyanskoi SSR
Soobshch Lab Lesoved Akad Nauk SSSR — Soobshcheniya Laboratorii Lesovedeniya. Akademiya Nauk SSSR
Soobshch Leningr Inst Met — Soobshcheniya Leningradskogo Instituta Metallov
Soobshch Mosk Otd Vses Bot Ova — Soobshcheniya Moskovskogo Otdeleniya Vsesoyuznogo Botanicheskogo Obshchestva
Soobshch Nauchno Issled Inst Elektron Promsti KHIKI Budapest — Soobshcheniya Nauchno-Issledovatel'skogo Instituta Elektronnoi Promyshlennosti KHIKI (Budapest)
Soobshch Nauchno Issled Inst Lesn Khoz Budapest — Soobshcheniya Nauchno-Issledovatel'skogo Instituta Lesnogo Khozyaistva. Budapest
Soobshch Nauchno Issled Rab Kiev Politekh Inst — Soobshcheniya o Nauchno-Issledovatel'skoi Rabote Kievski Politekhnicheskii Institut
Soobshch Nauchno Tekh Rab Nauchn Inst Udobr Insektofungits — Soobshcheniya o Nauchno-Tekhnicheskikh Rabotakh. Nauchnyi Institut Udobrenii i Insektofungitsidov
Soobshch Ob'edin Inst Yad Issled (Dubna) — Soobshcheniya Ob'edinennogo Instituta Yadernykh Issledovanii (Dubna)
Soobshch Obshch Lab Agrokhim Akad Nauk Armyan SSR — Soobshcheniya Obshchestvoi Laboratorii Agrokhimii Akademii Nauk Armyanskoi SSR
Soobshch Rab Mezhduved Postoyan Kom Zhelezu Akad Nauk SSSR — Soobshcheniya o Rabotakh Mezhduvedomstvennoi Postoyannoi Komissii po Zhelezu. Akademiya Nauk SSSR
Soobshch Sakhalin Fil Akad Nauk SSSR — Soobshcheniya Sakhalinskogo Filiala Akademii Nauk SSSR
Soobshch Shemakh Astrofiz Obs Akad Nauk Az SSR — Soobshcheniya Shemakhinskoi Astrofizicheskoi Observatorii. Akademiya Nauk Azerbaidzhanskoi SSR
Soobshch Shemakhinskoi Astrofiz Obs Akad Nauk Azerb SSR — Soobshcheskoi Shemakhinskoi Astrofizicheskoi Observatorii Akademiya Nauk Azerbaidzhan SSR
Soobshch Tadzh Fil Akad Nauk SSSR — Soobshcheniya Tadzhikskogo Filiala Akademii Nauk SSSR
Soobshch Tsentr Inst Fiz Issled Budapest — Soobshcheniya Tsentral'nogo Instituta Fizicheskikh Issledovanii. Budapest
Soobshch Tsentr Inst Met Leningrad — Soobshcheniya Tsentral'nogo Instituta Metallov. Leningrad
Soobshch Vses Inst Met — Soobshcheniya Vsesoyuznogo Instituta Metallov
Soochow J Hum — Soochow Journal of Humanities
Soochow J Lit Soc Stud — Soochow Journal of Literature and Social Studies
Soochow J Math — Soochow Journal of Mathematics
Soochow J Math Natur Sci — Soochow Journal of Mathematical and Natural Sciences [Later, Soochow Journal of Mathematics]
Soon Chun Hyang J Med — Soon Chun Hyang Journal of Medicine
Sootnoshenie Magmat Metamorf Genezise Ul'trabazitov — Sootnoshenie Magmatizma i Metamorfizma v Genezise Ul'trabazitov
SOP — Scriptores Ordinis Praedicatorum
So P — Sovjetskaja Pecat'
SOPAA — Soviet Physics. Acoustics
Soph — Sophia
Sophia Econ R — Sophia Economic Review
Sophia Int Rev — Sophia International Review
Sophia:T — Sophia: Studies in Western Civilization and the Cultural Interaction of East and West (Tokyo)
SOPJA — Soviet Physics Journal
SOPLA — Soviet Plastics
SOPODA — Social Planning/Policy and Development Abstracts
SOPPA — Soviet Plant Physiology

Sopr Archeol Sassari Quad — Soprintendenza Archeologica, Sassari. Quaderni
Sopr Mater Kaunas Politekh Inst Tr Nauchno Tekh Konf — Soprotivlenie Materialov. Kaunasskii Politekhnicheskii Institut. Trudy Nauchno-Tekhicheskoi Konferentsii
Sopr Mater Teor Sooruzh — Soprotivlenie Materialov i Teoriya Sooruzhenii
Sopr Mater Tepl Energ Tr Yubileinoi Nauchno Tekh Konf — Soprotivlenie Materialov i Teplovaya Energetika. Trudy Yubileinoi Nauchno-Tekhnicheskoi Konferentsii
Soproni Musz Egy Karok Banyamern Foldmeromern Karok Kozl — Soproni Muszaki Egyetemi Karok. Banyamernoki es Foldmeromernoki Karok Kozlemenyei
SOPUA — Soviet Physics. Uspekhi
SoQ — Southern Quarterly
So Q — Southern Quarterly Review
So Q R — Southern Quarterly Review
SOR — Serie Orientale Roma
SOr — Sources Orientales
So R — Southern Review
SoR — Southern Review: An Australian Journal of Literary Studies
SOR — Statutory Orders and Regulations of Canada
S Or — Studia Orientalia
S Or A — Sammlung Orientalistischer Arbeiten
SoRA — Southern Review (Adelaide, Australia)
So R A — Southern Review: An Australian Journal of Literary Studies
Sor Ark — Sovetskaia Arkheologiia
Sor Bl — Medlemsblad for Soransk Samfund
S O Rev — Sean O'Casey Review
So R NS — Southern Review: New Series
Sort — Sortileges
SOrth — Stimme der Orthodoxie
So Ruralist — Southern Ruralist
SoS — Saga och Sed
SOS — Semitic and Oriental Studies
S o S — Sprak och Stil
SOS — Symbolae Osloenses. Supplement
SoS — Syn og Segn
SOS — Systems, Objectives, Solutions
Sos Aikakausk — Sosiaalinen Aikakauskirja
SOSB — Scriptores Ordinis S. Benedicti
So School News — Southern School News
Sosh — Soshioloji
S Osl — Symbolae Osloenses
S Oslo — Symbolae Osloenses
So St — Southern Studies
Sostav Str Osad Form — Sostav i Stroenie Osadochnykh Formatsii
Sostdt Forsch — Suedostdeutsche Forschungen
Sostoyanie Zadachi Sov Litol Dokl Zased Vses Litol Soveshch — Sostoyanie i Zadachi Sovetskoi Litologii. Doklady na Zasedaniyakh Vsesoyuznogo Litologicheskogo Soveshchaniya
SoT — Sloejd och Ton
Sota — South Atlantic Quarterly
SotA — South Australiana
Sotahist Seuran Julk — Sotahistoriallisen Seuran Julkaisuja
SotC — Southern California Quarterly
SOTCA — Soudage et Techniques Connexes
So Tex LJ — Southern Texas Law Journal
SOTIB — Sotsialisticheskaya Industriya
SOTID — Solar Times
Sotilaslaak Aikak — Sotilaslaaketieteellinen Aikakauslehti
SotS — Southern Speech Journal
Sotsial Rekonstr Gorodov — Sotsialisticheskuyu Rekonstruktsiyu Gorodov
Sots Pollum — Sotsialistik Pollumajandus
Sots Rastenievod — Sotsialisticheskoe Rastenievodstvo
Sots Sel'Khoz Azerb — Sotsialisticheskoe Sel'skoe Khozyaistvo Azerbaidzhana
Sots Sel'Khoz Uzbek — Sotsialisticheskoe Sel'skoe Khozyaistvo Uzbekistana
Sots Selsk Khoz — Sotsialisticheskoe Sel'skoe Khozyaistvo
Sots Sel'sk Khoz Azerb — Sotsialisticheskoe Sel'skoe Khozyaistvo Azerbaidzhana
Sots Sel'sk Khoz Uzb — Sotsialisticheskoe Sel'skoe Khozyaistvo Uzbekistana
Sots Trud — Sotsialisticheskiy Trud
Sots Tvarinnit — Sotsialistichne Tvarinnitstvo
Sots Tvarynnytstvo — Sotsialistychne Tvarynnytstvo
Sots Zak — Sotsialisticheskaya Zakonnost
Sots Zhivotnovod — Sotsialisticheskoe Zhivotnovodstvo
SOU — South. The Third World Magazine
Sou Aus LR — South Australian Law Reports
Soubor Pr Ustavu Vyzk Vyz Lidu Praze — Soubor Praci Ustavu pro Vyzkum Vyzivy Lidu v Praze
Soudage Fusion Faisceau Electrons — Soudage et Fusion par Faisceau d'Electrons. Colloque International
Soudage Monde — Soudage dans le Monde
Soudage Tech Connexes — Soudage et Techniques Connexes
Soud Lek — Soudni Lekarstvi
Soudni Lek — Soudni Lekarstvi
Soudure Tech Connexes — Soudure et Techniques Connexes
SouH — Southwestern Historical Quarterly
Soul Il — Soul Illustrated
So U LR — Southern University Law Review
So U L Rev — Southern University Law Review
Soun — Soundings
Sound — Soundings
Sound & Vib — Sound and Vibration
Sound Brass — Sounding Brass and the Conductor
Sound (Can) — Sound (Canada)
Sound Vib — Sound and Vibration
Sound Vis Broadc — Sound and Vision Broadcasting

So Univ L Rev — Southern University Law Review
SouQ — Southern Quarterly
SOUR — Sourdough Journal. Alaska Library Association
SouR — Southern Review
Source Notes Hist A — Source. Notes in the History of Art
Sources and Stud Hist Arabic-Islamic Sci Hist of Math Ser — Sources and Studies in the History of Arabic-Islamic Science. History of Mathematics Series
Sources Chr — Sources Chretiennes
Sources Hist Math Phys Sci — Sources in the History of Mathematics and Physical Sciences
Sources in Hist of Math and Phys Sci — Sources in the History of Mathematics and Physical Sciences
Sources Sci — Sources of Science
Sources Stud Hist Arabic-Islamic Sci Hist of Tech Ser — Sources and Studies in the History of Arabic-Islamic Science. History of Technology Series
Sources Stud Hist Arabic Math — Sources and Studies in the History of Arabic Mathematics
SOUTB — Statens Offentliga Utredningar
South Afr Archaeol B — South African Archaeological Bulletin
South Afr Arch B — South African Archaeological Bulletin
South Afr Geogr J — South African Geographical Journal
South African J African Affairs — South African Journal of African Affairs
South African J Econ — South African Journal of Economics
South African Labour Bul — South African Labour Bulletin
South African Med J — South African Medical Journal
South African Med Rec — South African Medical Record
South African Min Eng Jour — South African Mining and Engineering Journal
South African MJ — South African Medical Journal
South African Statist J — South African Statistical Journal
South Afr Int Quart — South Africa International Quarterly
South Afr J Afr Aff — South African Journal of African Affairs
South Afr J Econ — South African Journal of Economics
South Afr J Sci — South African Journal of Science
South Afr J Surg — South African Journal of Surgery
South Afr Law J — South African Law Journal
South Afr LJ — South African Law Journal
South Afr Text — Southern Africa Textiles
South Am J Bio-Sci — South American Journal of Bio-Sciences
South Am J Med — South American Journal of Medicine
South Ariz Guideb — Southern Arizona Guidebook
South As Dig Reg Writ — South Asian Digest of Regional Writing
South Asian R — South Asian Review
South Asian Stud — South Asian Studies
South Asia Pap — South Asia Papers
South Assoc Agric Sci Bull Biochem Biotechnol — Southern Association of Agriculture Scientists Bulletin Biochemistry and Biotechnology
South As Stud — South Asian Studies
South As Surv — South Asian Survey
South Atlan Q — South Atlantic Quarterly
South Atlantic Quart — South Atlantic Quarterly
South Atl Bull — South Atlantic Bulletin
South Atl Q — South Atlantic Quarterly
South Aus LR — South Australian Law Reports
South Aust Dep Agric Fish Agron Branch Rep — South Australia. Department of Agriculture and Fisheries. Agronomy Branch. Report
South Aust Dep Agric Fish Agron Bran Rep — South Australia. Department of Agriculture and Fisheries. Agronomy Branch. Report
South Aust Dep Mines Energy Miner Resour Rev — South Australia. Department of Mines and Energy. Mineral Resources Review
South Aust Dep Mines Miner Resour Rev — South Australia. Department of Mines. Mineral Resources Review
South Aust Geol Surv 1:250000 Geol Ser — South Australia. Geological Survey. 1:250,000 Geological Series
South Aust Geol Surv Bull — South Australia. Geological Survey. Bulletin
South Aust Geol Surv Q Geol Notes — South Australia. Geological Survey. Quarterly Geological Notes
South Aust Geol Surv Rep Invest — South Australia. Geological Survey. Report of Investigations
South Aust Mot — South Australian Motor
South Aust Nat — South Australian Naturalist
South Aust Orn — South Australian Ornithologist
South Aust Rep Mus Board — South Australia. Report of the Museum Board
South Bap Per Ind — Southern Baptist Periodical Index
South Baptist Period Index — Southern Baptist Periodical Index
South Birds — Southern Birds
South Braz J Chem — Southern Brazilian Journal of Chemistry
South Bus — Southern Business
South Calif Coastal Water Res Proj Annu Rep — Southern California Coastal Water Research Project. Annual Report
South Calif Coastal Water Res Proj Bienn Rep — Southern California Coastal Water Research Project. Biennial Report
South Calif L Rev — Southern California Law Review
South Calif Q — Southern California Quarterly
South Cal Law Rev — Southern California Law Review
South Canner Packer — Southern Canner and Packer
South Cant J — South Canterbury Journal
South Carbonator Bottler — Southern Carbonator and Bottler
South Carolina Acad Sci Bull — South Carolina Academy of Science. Bulletin
South Carolina Div Geology Geol Notes — South Carolina. Division of Geology. Geologic Notes
South Carolina Div Geology Misc Rept — South Carolina. Division of Geology. Miscellaneous Report
South Carolina L Rev — South Carolina Law Review
South Car R — South Carolina Review
South Chem — Southern Chemist

South Chem Ind — Southern Chemical Industry
South China J Agric Sci — South China Journal of Agricultural Science
South Conf Gerontol Rep — Southern Conference on Gerontology. Report
South Coop Ser Bull — Southern Cooperative Series Bulletin
South Corn Impr Conf Rep — Southern Corn Improvement Conference. Report
South Dairy Prod J — Southern Dairy Products Journal
South Dak L Rev — South Dakota Law Review
South Dakota Agric Exp Sta Agron Dept Pam — South Dakota Agricultural Experiment Station. Agronomy Department Pamphlet
South Dakota Agric Exp Sta Pl Pathol Dept Pam — South Dakota Agricultural Experiment Station. Plant Pathology Department Pamphlet
South Dakota Geol Survey Guidebook — South Dakota. Geological Survey. Guidebook
South Dakota Geol Survey Rept Inv — South Dakota. Geological Survey. Report of Investigations
South Dakota Geol Survey Spec Rept — South Dakota. Geological Survey. Special Report
South Dakota Geol Survey Water Resources Rept — South Dakota Geological Survey and South Dakota Water Resources Commission. Water Resources Report
South Dakota L Rev — South Dakota Law Review
Southeast Asia Bldg Materials & Equipment — Southeast Asia Building Materials and Equipment
South East Asia Iron Steel Inst Q — South East Asia Iron and Steel Institute. Quarterly
Southeast Asia J Theol — Southeast Asia Journal of Theology
Southeast Asian Conf Soil Eng Proc — Southeast Asian Conference on Soil Engineering. Proceedings
Southeast Asian Fish Dev Cent Aquacult Dep Q Res Rep — Southeast Asian Fisheries Development Center. Aquaculture Department. QuarterlyResearch Report
Southeast Asian J Soc Sci — Southeast Asian Journal of Social Science
Southeast Asian J Trop Med Public Health — Southeast Asian Journal of Tropical Medicine and Public Health
South East Asian Pac Congr Clin Biochem — South East Asian and Pacific Congress of Clinical Biochemistry
South East Asian Stud — South East Asian Studies
Southeast Asia Pet Explor Soc Proc — Southeast Asia Petroleum Exploration Society. Proceedings
Southeast Conf Appl Sol Energy Proc — Southeast Conference on Application of Solar Energy. Proceedings
Southeastcon Reg 3 (Three) Conf Proc — Southeastcon Region 3 (Three) Conference Proceedings
Southeast Drug J — Southeastern Drug Journal
Southeastern Geology Spec Pub — Southeastern Geology. Special Publication
Southeast Geogr — Southeastern Geographer
Southeast Geol — Southeastern Geology
Southeast Geol Soc Field Conf Guideb — Southeastern Geological Society. Field Conference Guidebook
Southeast Geol Spec Publ — Southeastern Geology. Special Publication
Southeast Reg Conf Kraft Mill Process Prod Eng — Southeast Regional Conference. Kraft Mill Process and ProductEngineering
Southeast Reg Water Resour Symp Proc — Southeast Region Water Resources Symposium. Proceedings
Southeast Semin Therm Sci — Southeastern Seminar on Thermal Sciences
Southeast Semin Therm Sci Proc — Southeastern Seminar on Thermal Sciences. Proceedings
South Econ — Southern Economist
South Econ J — Southern Economic Journal
South Econ Jour — Southern Economic Journal
Southern Calif Acad Sci Bull — Southern California Academy of Sciences. Bulletin
Southern Econ J — Southern Economic Journal
Southern Folklore Q — Southern Folklore Quarterly
Southern H R — Southern Humanities Review
Southern Hum R — Southern Humanities Review
Southern J Med Phys Sc — Southern Journal of the Medical and Physical Sciences
Southern J Phil — Southern Journal of Philosophy
Southern Lit J — Southern Literary Journal
Southern P R — Southern Poetry Review
Southern Pulp Paper Mfr — Southern Pulp and Paper Manufacturer
Southern R — Southern Review
Southern Rev — Southern Review
South Exposure — Southern Exposure
South Fem — Southern Feminist
South Fisherman — Southern Fisherman
South Florist Nurseryman — Southern Florist and Nurseryman
South Folk — Southern Folklore
South Folkl Q — Southern Folklore Quarterly
South Folkl Quart — Southern Folklore Quarterly
South Folk Q — Southern Folklore Quarterly
South Folk Quart Gainesville — Southern Folklore Quarterly (Gainesville, Florida)
South Food Process — Southern Food Processor
South Gen Pract Med Surg — Southern General Practitioner of Medicine and Surgery
South Hist Assoc Publ — Southern Historical Association. Publications
South Hist Soc Papers — Southern Historical Society. Papers
South Hort — Southern Horticulture
South Hortic — Southern Horticulture
South Hosp — Southern Hospitals
South Hum Rev — Southern Humanities Review
South Ill Lab Trib — Southern Illinois Labor Tribune
South Ill ULJ — Southern Illinois University. Law Journal
South Indian Hortic — Southern Indian Horticulture
South Ind St — Southern Indian Studies

South J Agric Econ — Southern Journal of Agricultural Economics
South J Agric Econ South Agric Econ Assoc — Southern Journal of Agricultural Economics. Southern Agricultural Economics Association
South J Appl For — Southern Journal of Applied Forestry
South Jewel — Southern Jeweler
South Law J — Southern Law Journal
South Law J & Rep — Southern Law Journal and Reporter
South Law Rev — Southern Law Review
South Law Rev NS — Southern Law Review, New Series
South Lit J — Southern Literary Journal
South Liv — Southern Living
South LJ — Southern Law Journal
South LJ & Rep — Southern Law Journal and Reporter
South L Rev — Southern Law Review
South L Rev NS — Southern Law Review, New Series
South Lumberman — Southern Lumberman
South M — South Magazine
South Med — Southern Medicine
South Med Bull — Southern Medical Bulletin
South Med J — Southern Medical Journal
South Med Surg — Southern Medicine and Surgery
South Methodist Univ Inst Stud Earth Man Rep — Southern Methodist University. Institute for the Study of Earth and Man. Reports of Investigations
South MJ — Southern Medical Journal
South Pac — South Pacific
South Pac Bull — South Pacific Bulletin
South Pac Comm Handb — South Pacific Commission. Handbook
South Pac Comm Tech Pap — Southern Pacific Commission. Technical Paper
South Pacific B — South Pacific Bulletin
South Pacific Bul — South Pacific Bulletin
South Pacific J Ed — South Pacific Journal of Education
South Pac J Nat Sci — South Pacific Journal of Natural Science
South Pac J Teach Educ — South Pacific Journal of Teacher Education
South Pac Mar Geol Notes — South Pacific Marine Geological Notes
South Petrochem Ind Corp Ind Eng Train Bull — Southern Petrochemical Industries Corp. Industrial Engineering and Training Bulletin
South Pharm J — Southern Pharmaceutical Journal
South Plast Chem — Southern Plastics and Chemicals
South Power Ind — Southern Power and Industry
South Power J — Southern Power Journal
South Pract — Southern Practitioner
South Pulp Pap — Southern Pulp and Paper
South Pulp Pap J — Southern Pulp and Paper Journal
South Pulp Pap Manuf — Southern Pulp and Paper Manufacturer
South Q — Southern Quarterly
South Quar — Southern Quarterly Review
South Quart — Southern Quarterly
South Queensl Conf — Southern Queensland Conference
South R — South Carolina Review
South R — Southern Review
South Rag — Southern Rag
South Reg Beef Cow Calf Handb Agric Ext Serv NC State Univ — Southern Regional Beef Cow-Calf Handbook. Agricultural Extension Service. NorthCarolina State University
South Res Inst Bull — Southern Research Institute. Bulletin
South Rhod Geol Surv Bull — Southern Rhodesia. Geological Survey. Bulletin
South Rhod Geol Surv Short Rep — Southern Rhodesia. Geological Survey. Short Report
South Seedsman — Southern Seedsman
South Speech Comm J — Southern Speech Communication Journal
South Stars — Southern Stars
South States Assoc Comm Agric Other Agric Work Proc — Southern States Association of Commissioners of Agriculture and Other Agricultural Workers. Proceedings
South Stud — Southern Studies
South Surg — Southern Surgeon
South Texas Geol Soc Bull — South Texas Geological Society. Bulletin
South Texas LJ — South Texas Law Journal
South Text Bull — Southern Textile Bulletin
South UL Rev — Southern University Law Review
Southw Agric Sci — Southwest Agricultural Science/Hsi Nan Nung Yeh K'o Hsueeh
South Weed Sci Soc Proc — Southern Weed Science Society. Proceedings
Southwest Afr Ann — Southwest Africa Annual
South West Afr Sci Soc J — South West Africa Scientific Society. Journal
Southwest Bull — Southwest Bulletin
Southwest Bus and Econ R — Southwest Business and Economic Review
Southwest Entomol — Southwestern Entomologist
Southwest Entomol Suppl — Southwestern Entomologist. Supplement
Southwestern As Petroleum G B — Southwestern Association of Petroleum Geologists. Bulletin
Southwestern J Anthr — Southwestern Journal of Anthropology
Southwestern LA Jour — Southwestern Louisiana Journal
Southwestern LJ — Southwestern Law Journal
Southwestern R Mgt and Econ — Southwestern Review of Management and Economics
Southwestern UL Rev — Southwestern University. Law Review
Southwestern Univ L Rev — Southwestern University. Law Review
Southwest Hist Q — Southwestern Historical Quarterly
Southwest Hist Quart — Southwestern Historical Quarterly
Southwest IEEE Conf Exhib Rec — Southwestern IEEE [*Institute of Electrical and Electronics Engineers*] Conference and Exhibition. Record
Southwest J — Southwest Journal
Southwest J Anthropol — Southwestern Journal of Anthropology

Southwest Jour Anthrop Albuquerque — Southwest Journal of Anthropology (Albuquerque, NM; Santa Fe, NM)

Southwest J Phil — Southwestern Journal of Philosophy

Southwest J Pure Appl Math — Southwest Journal of Pure and Applied Mathematics

Southwest Med — Southwestern Medicine

Southwest Miller — Southwestern Miller

Southwest Mus Paper — Southwest Museum. Papers

Southwest Nat — Southwestern Naturalist

Southwest Pet Short Course Proc Annu Meet — Southwestern Petroleum Short Course. Proceedings of the Annual Meeting

Southwest Reg Conf Astron Astrophys Proc — Southwest Regional Conference for Astronomy and Astrophysics.Proceedings

Southwest Rev — Southwest Review

Southwest Soc Sci Quart — Southwestern Social Science Quarterly

Southwest Tex Water Works J — Southwest and Texas Water Works Journal

Southwest UL Rev — Southwestern University. Law Review

Southwest Vet — Southwestern Veterinarian

Southwest Water Works J — Southwest Water Works Journal

Southw His Q — Southwestern Historical Quarterly

Southw Hist Quar — Southwestern Historical Quarterly

Southw Hist Quart — Southwestern Historical Quarterly

Southw J Anthrop — Southwestern Journal of Anthropology

Southw J Anthropol — Southwestern Journal of Anthropology. University of New Mexico

Southw Jnl Philos — Southwestern Journal of Philosophy

SouthWJTh — Southwestern Journal of Theology

Southw LJ — Southwestern Law Journal

Southw LJ — Southwestern Law Journal and Reporter

Southw Lore — Southwestern Lore

Southw Pol and Soc Sci Q — Southwestern Political and Social Science Quarterly

Southw Pol Sci Quar — Southwest Political Science Quarterly

Southw Pol Social Sci Assn Proc — Southwestern Political and Social Science Association. Proceedings

Southw Rev — Southwest Review

Southw Sci Bull — Southwest Science Bulletin

Southw Soc Sci Quar — Southwestern Social Science Quarterly

Sov A — Sovetskaia Arkheologiia

Sov Aeronaut — Soviet Aeronautics

Sov Agric Biol Part 1 Plant Biol — Soviet Agricultural Biology. Part 1. Plant Biology

Sov Agric Biol Part 2 Anim Biol — Soviet Agricultural Biology. Part 2. Animal Biology

Sov Agric Sci — Soviet Agricultural Sciences

Sov Agron — Sovetskaya Agronomiya

Sov Am Konf Kosmokhim Luny Planet Tr — Sovetsko-Amerikanskaya Konferentsiya po Kosmokhimii Luny i Planet.Trudy

Sov Am Semin Sint Delenie Tr — Sovetsko-Amerikanskii Seminar Sintez-Delenie. Trudy

Sov Am Simp Khim Zagryaz Morsk Sredy Tr — Sovetsko-Amerikanskii Simpozium po Khimicheskomu Zagryazneniyu MorskoiSredy. Trudy

Sov Am Simp Razrushenie Kompoz Mater — Sovetsko-Amerikanskii Simpozium Razrushenie Kompozitnykh Materialov

Sov Am Simp Teor Rasseyan Sveta Kondens Sredakh — Sovetsko-Amerikanskii Simpozium po Teorii Rasseyaniya Sveta vKondensirovannykh Sredakh

Sov Am Simp Teor Vopr Vodn Toksikol — Sovetsko-Amerikanskii Simpozium Teoreticheskie Voprosy VochnoiToksikologii

Sov Am Simp Vsestoronnemu Anal Okruzh Sredy Tr — Sovetsko-Amerikanskii Simpozium po Vsestoronnemu AnalizuOkruzhayushchei Sredy. Trudy

Sov Am Symp Compr Anal Environ — Soviet-American Symposium on the Comprehensive Analysis of theEnvironment

Sov Am Symp Theory Light Scattering Solids — Soviet-American Symposium on the Theory of Light Scattering in Solids

Sov Antarct Exped Inf Bull — Soviet Antarctic Expedition. Information Bulletin

Sov Antarct Exped Inf Bull (Engl Transl) — Soviet Antarctic Expedition. Information Bulletin (English Translation)

Sov Antarct Exped Inform Bull — Soviet Antarctic Expedition. Information Bulletin

Sov Antarkt Eksped Inf Byull — Sovetskaya Antarkticheskaya Ekspeditsiya. Informatsionnyi Byulleten

Sov Antarkt Eksped Inform Byull — Sovetskaya Antarkticheskaya Ekspeditsiya. Informatsionnyi Byulleten

Sov Anthr A — Soviet Anthropology and Archeology

Sov Anthro Arch — Soviet Anthropology and Archeology

Sov Appl Mech — Soviet Applied Mechanics

Sov Appl Mech (Engl Transl) — Soviet Applied Mechanics (English Translation)

Sov Arch — Sovetskaja Archeologija

Sov Arh — Sovetskaya Arkheologiia

Sov Arh — Sovetskie Arhivi

Sov Arkh — Sovetskie Arkhivy

Sov Arkheol — Sovetskaya Arkheologiya

Sov Arkhit — Sovetskaya Arkhitektura

Sov Astron — Soviet Astronomy

Sov Astron (Engl Transl) — Soviet Astronomy (English Translation)

Sov Astron Lett — Soviet Astronomy. Letters

Sov Astron Lett (Engl Transl) — Soviet Astronomy. Letters (English Translation)

Sov At Energy — Soviet Atomic Energy

Sov At Energy (Engl Transl) — Soviet Atomic Energy (English Translation)

Sov At En R — Soviet Atomic Energy (USSR)

Sov Atom Energy — Soviet Atomic Energy

Sov Automat Contr — Soviet Automatic Control

Sov Autom Control — Soviet Automatic Control

Sov Autom Control (Engl Transl) — Soviet Automatic Control (English Translation)

Sov Bibliog — Sovetskaya Bibliografia

Sov Bibliotekov — Sovetskaia Bibliotekovedenie

Sov Biotechnol — Soviet Biotechnology

Sov Bolg Simp Issled Fiz Khim Svoistv Prir Tseolitov Tr — Sovetsko-Bolgarskii Simpozium po Issledovaniyu Fiziko-KhimicheskikhSvoistv Prirodnykh Tseolitov. Trudy

Sov Bot — Sovetskaya Botanika

Sov Bus Trade — Soviet Business and Trade

Sov Chem Ind — Soviet Chemical Industry

Sov Chem Ind (Engl Transl) — Soviet Chemical Industry (English Translation)

Sov Cybern Rev — Soviet Cybernetics Review

Sov Dek Isk — Sovetskoye Dekorativnoye Iskusstvo

SOVEA — Southwestern Veterinarian

Sov East Eur China Bus Trade — Soviet-Eastern Europe-China Business and Trade

Sov East Europ For Trade — Soviet and Eastern European Foreign Trade

Sov Educ — Soviet Education

Sov E E For — Soviet and Eastern European Foreign Trade

Sov Elco Eng — Soviet Electrical Engineering

Sov Electr Eng — Soviet Electrical Engineering

Sov Electr Eng (Engl Transl) — Soviet Electrical Engineering (English Translation)

Sov Electrochem — Soviet Electrochemistry

Sov Electrochem (Engl Transl) — Soviet Electrochemistry (English Translation)

Sov Eng J — Soviet Engineering Journal

Sov Engng Res — Soviet Engineering Research

Sov Eng Res — Soviet Engineering Research

Soversh Agrotekh Priemov Ukhodu Sadom Fiziol Osn Povysh Ego — Sovershenstvovanie Agrotekhnicheskikh Priemov po Ukhodu za Sadom iFiziologicheskie Osnovy Povysheniya Ego Produktivnosti

Soversh Konstr Povysh Eff Trakt Avtomob Mater Zon Konf — Sovershenstvovanie Konstruktsii i Povyshenie Effektivnosti Traktorov iAvtomobilei. Materialy Zonal'noi Konferentsii

Soversh Metodov Razrab Rudn Mestorozhd — Sovershenstvovanie Metodov Razrabotki Rudnykh Mestorozhdenii

Soversh Porod Skh Zhivotn — Sovershenstvovanie Porod Sel'skokhozyaistvennykh Zhivotnykh

Soversh Protsessov Obrab Met Rezaniem — Sovershenstvovanie Protsessov Obrabotki Metallov Rezaniem

Soversh Tekhnol Avtom Stalepalavil'n Protsessov — Sovershenstvovanie Tekhnologii i Avtomatizatsii Staleplavil'nykhProtsessov

Soversh Tekhnol Kontrolya Proizvod Stalnoi Emal Posudy — Sovershenstvovanie Tekhnologii i Kontrolya Proizvodstva Stal'noiEmalirovannoi Posudy

Soversh Tekhnol Pererab Khim Volokon — Sovershenstvovanie Tekhnologii Pererabotki Khimicheskikh Volokon

Soversh Tekh Tekhnol Proizvod Kozhi Obuvi Dubilnykh Ekstr — Sovershenstvovanie Tekhniki i Tekhnologii Proizvodstva Kozhi, Obuvi, iDubil'nykh Ekstraktov

Soveshch Diagn Vysokotemp Plazmy Tezisy Dokl — Soveshchanie po Diagnostike Vysokotemperaturnoi Plazmy. Tezisy Dokladov

Soveshch Din Eff Rasseyan Rentgenovskikh Luchei Elektronov — Soveshchanie po Dinamicheskim Effektam Rasseyaniya RentgenovskikhLuchei i Elektronov

Soveshch Geol Boksitovykh Mestorozhd Proyavlenii Sredn Azii — Soveshchanie po Geologii Boksitovykh Mestorozhdenii i ProyavleniiSrednei Azii. Doklady

Soveshch Khim Prakt Primen Kremniiorg Soedin — Soveshchanie po Khimii i Prakticeskomu PrimeneniyuKremniiorganicheskikh Soedinenii

Soveshch Kinet Mekh Khim Reakts Tverd Tele — Soveshchanie po Kinetike i Mekhanizmu Khimicheskikh Reaktsii v TverdomTele

Soveshch Poluch Profilirovannykh Krist Izdelii Sposobom Step — Soveshchanie po Polucheniyu Profilirovannykh Kristallov i IzdeliiSposobom Stepanova i Ikh Primeneniyu v Narodnom Khozyaistve

Soveshch Semin Sovrem Probl Metod Prepod Kristallokhim — Soveshchanie-Seminar po Sovremennym Problemam i Metodike PrepodavaniyaKristallokhimii

Soveshch Spektrosk Akt Krist — Soveshchanie po Spektroskopii Aktivirovannykh Kristallov

Soveshch Teor Liteinykh Protsessov — Soveshchanie po Teorli Lltelnykh Protsessov

Soveshch Vopr Izuch Endog Mestorozhd Sredn Azii Tezisy Dokl — Soveshchanie po Voprosam Izucheniya Endogennykh Mestorozhdenii SredneiAzii. Tezisy Dokladov

Soveshch Vyazkosti Zhidk Kolloidn Rastvorov Dokl — Soveshchanie po Vyazkosti Zhidkostei i Kolloidnykh Rastvorov. Doklady

Soveshch Yad Spektrosk Strukt At Yadra Tezisy Dokl — Soveshchanie po Yadernoi Spektroskopii i Strukture Atomnogo Yadra.Tezisy Dokladov

Soveshch Yad Spektrosk Teor Yadra Tezisy Dokl — Soveshchanie po Yadernoi Spektroskopii i Teorii Yadra. Tezisy Dokladov

SovEt — Sovetskaya Etnografija

Sovet Etnogr — Sovetskaya Etnografiya

Sovet Geol — Sovetskaya Geologiya

Sovet Geologiya — Sovetskaya Geologiya

Sov Ethnogr — Sovetskaia Etnografiia

Sovet Muz — Sovetskaya Muzyka

SovEtn — Sovetskaya Etnografija

Sov Etnogr — Sovetskaja Etnografija

Sov Etnogr — Sovetskaya Etnografia

Sov Etnog Sborn Statey — Sovetskaya Etnografiya. Sbornik Statyey

Sovetskaja Arch — Sovetskaia Arkheologiia

Sovetskaja M — Sovetskaya Muzyka

Sovetskoe Bibl — Sovetskoe Bibliotekovedenie

Sovetsk Subtrop Sukhumi — Sovetskie Subtropiki/Soviet Subtropics (Sukhumi)

Sov Export — Soviet Export

Sov Farm — Sovetskaya Farmatsiya

Sov Film — Soviet Film

Sov Finno-Ugroved — Sovetskoje Finno-Ugrovedenie

Sov Flour Milling Baking — Soviet Flour Milling and Baking

Sov Fluid Mech (Engl Transl) — Soviet Fluid Mechanics (English Translation)

Sov Foto — Sovetskoe Foto

Sov Fr Semin Mat Model Katal Protsessov Reakt — Sovetsko-Frantsuzskii Seminar po Matematicheskomu ModelirovaniyuKataliticheskikh Protsessov i Reaktorov

SovFU — Sovetskoje Finno-Ugrovedenie

Sov Genet — Soviet Genetics

Sov Genet (Engl Transl) — Soviet Genetics (English Translation)

Sov Genet (Engl Transl Genetika) — Soviet Genetics (English Translation of Genetika)

Sov Geogr — Soviet Geography. Review and Translations

Sov Geogr R — Soviet Geography. Review and Translations

Sov Geol — Sovetskaya Geologiya

Sov Geol and Geophys — Soviet Geology and Geophysics

Sov Geol Geophys — Soviet Geology and Geophysics

Sov Geol Geophys (Engl Transl) — Soviet Geology and Geophysics (English Translation)

Sov Gold Min Ind — Soviet Gold Mining Industry

Sov Gos i Pravo — Sovetskoe Gosudarstvo i Pravo

Sov Gos Pravo — Sovetskoe Gosudarstvo i Pravo

Sov Graf — Sovetskaya Grafika

SovH — Sovetish Heymland

Sov Health Prot Turkomen — Soviet Health Protection in Turkomen

Sov Hydrol — Soviet Hydrology. Selected Papers

Sov Hydrol Sel Pap — Soviet Hydrology. Selected Papers

SOVIA — Sound and Vibration

Soviet Aeronaut — Soviet Aeronautics

Soviet Agric Sci — Soviet Agricultural Science

Soviet and Eastern Eur For Trade — Soviet and Eastern European Foreign Trade

Soviet Appl Mech — Soviet Applied Mechanics

Soviet Astronom — Soviet Astronomy

Soviet Automat Control — Soviet Automatic Control

Soviet Chem Ind — Soviet Chemical Industry

Soviet Ed — Soviet Education

Soviet F — Soviet Film

Soviet Genet — Soviet Genetics

Soviet J Automat Inform Sci — Soviet Journal of Automation and Information Sciences

Soviet J Comm Tech Electron — Soviet Journal of Communications, Technology, and Electronics

Soviet J Comput Systems Sci — Soviet Journal of Computer and Systems Sciences

Soviet J Contemporary Math Anal — Soviet Journal of Contemporary Mathematical Analysis

Soviet J Ecol — Soviet Journal of Ecology

Soviet J Nuclear Phys — American Institute of Physics. Soviet Journal of Nuclear Physics

Soviet J Numer Anal Math Modelling — Soviet Journal of Numerical Analysis and Mathematical Modelling

Soviet J Particles and Nuclei — Soviet Journal of Particles and Nuclei

Soviet L & Govt — Soviet Law and Government

Soviet Law and Govt — Soviet Law and Government

Soviet Lit — Soviet Literature

Soviet Math Dokl — Soviet Mathematics. Doklady

Soviet Math (Iz VUZ) — Soviet Mathematics (Izvestija Vyssih Ucebnyh Zavedenii. Matematika)

Soviet Mat Sci Rev — Soviet Materials Science Reviews

Soviet Phys Acoust — Soviet Physics. Acoustics

Soviet Phys Collection — Soviet Physics. Collection

Soviet Phys Cryst — Soviet Physics. Crystallography

Soviet Physics Acoust — Soviet Physics. Acoustics

Soviet Physics Dokl — Soviet Physics. Doklady

Soviet Physics J — Soviet Physics Journal

Soviet Phys J — Soviet Physics Journal

Soviet Phys JETP — Soviet Physics. JETP

Soviet Phys Usp — Soviet Physics. Uspeki

Soviet Phys Uspekhi — Soviet Physics. Uspekhi

Soviet Plant Physiol — Soviet Plant Physiology

Soviet Pl Physiol — Soviet Plant Physiology

Soviet Rev — Soviet Review

Soviet Sci Rev Sect C Math Phys Rev — Soviet Scientific Reviews. Section C. Mathematical Physics Reviews

Soviet Sociol — Soviet Sociology

Soviet Soil Sci — Soviet Soil Science

Soviet Stud — Soviet Studies

Soviet Stud Phil — Soviet Studies in Philosophy

Soviet Union R — Soviet Union Review

Sov Indian Semin Catal — Soviet-Indian Seminar on Catalysis

Sov India Rubber — Soviet India Rubber

Sov Indiiskii Simp Khim Prir Soedin Tezisy Dokl — Sovetsko-Indiiskii Simpozium po Khimii Prirodnykh Soedinenii. TezisyDokladov

Sov Instrum & Control J — Soviet Journal of Instrumentation and Control

Sov Instrum Control J (Engl Transl) — Soviet Instrumentation and Control Journal (English Translation)

Sov Isk — Sovetskoe Iskusstvo

Sov Isk — Sovetskoye Iskusstvoznanije. Sbornik Statyey

Sovistva At Yader — Sovistva Atomnykh Yader

Sov Ital Symp Macromol Funct Cell — Soviet-Italian Symposium on Macromolecules in the Functioning Cell

Sov Iust — Sovetskaya Iustitsiya

Sovj — Sovjetunionen

SovJa — Sovetska Jazykoveda

Sov J At — Soviet Journal of Atomic Energy

Sov J At Energy — Soviet Journal of Atomic Energy

Sov J Bioorganic Chem — Soviet Journal of Bioorganic Chemistry

Sov J Bioorg Chem (Engl Transl) — Soviet Journal of Bioorganic Chemistry (English Translation of Bioorganicheskaya Khimiya)

Sov J Bioorg Chem (Engl Transl Bioorg Khim) — Soviet Journal of Bioorganic Chemistry (English Translation of Bioorganicheskaya Khimiya)

Sov J Coord Chem (Engl Transl) — Soviet Journal of Coordination Chemistry (English Translation)

Sov J Coord Chem (Engl Transl Koord Khim) — Soviet Journal of Coordination Chemistry (English Translation of Koordinatsionnaya Khimiya)

Sov J Dev Biol (Engl Transl) — Soviet Journal of Developmental Biology (English Translation)

Sov J Dev Biol (Engl Transl Ontogenez) — Soviet Journal of Developmental Biology (English Translation of Ontogenez)

Sov J Ecol — Soviet Journal of Ecology

Sov J Ecol (Engl Transl) — Soviet Journal of Ecology (English Translation)

Sov J Ecol (Engl Transl Ekologiya) — Soviet Journal of Ecology (English Translation of Ekologiya)

Sov Jew Aff — Soviet Jewish Affairs

Sov Jew Affairs — Soviet Jewish Affairs

Sov J Glass Phys and Chem — Soviet Journal of Glass Physics and Chemistry

Sov J Glass Phys Chem — Soviet Journal of Glass Physics and Chemistry

Sov J Glass Phys Chem (Engl Transl) — Soviet Journal of Glass Physics and Chemistry (English Translation)

Sov J Instrum Control — Soviet Journal of Instrumentation and Control

Sov J Instrum Control (Engl Transl) — Soviet Journal of Instrumentation and Control (English Translation)

Sov J Low Temp Phys — Soviet Journal of Low Temperature Physics

Sov J Low Temp Phys (Engl Transl) — Soviet Journal of Low Temperature Physics (English Translation)

Sov J Mar Biol — Soviet Journal of Marine Biology

Sov J Mar Biol (Engl Transl) — Soviet Journal of Marine Biology (English Translation)

Sov J Mar Biol (Engl Transl Biol Morya) — Soviet Journal of Marine Biology (English Translation of Biologiya Morya)

Sov J Nondestr Test — Soviet Journal of Nondestructive Testing

Sov J Nondestr Test (Engl Transl) — Soviet Journal of Nondestructive Testing (English Translation)

Sov J Nondestruct Test — Soviet Journal of Nondestructive Testing

Sov J Non-Ferrous Met — Soviet Journal of Non-Ferrous Metals

Sov J Nucl Phys — Soviet Journal of Nuclear Physics

Sov J Nucl Phys (Engl Transl) — Soviet Journal of Nuclear Physics (English Translation)

Sov J Nuc R — Soviet Journal of Nuclear Physics (USSR)

Sov J Opt Technol — Soviet Journal of Optical Technology

Sov J Opt Technol (Engl Transl) — Soviet Journal of Optical Technology (English Translation)

Sov J Part Nucl — Soviet Journal of Particles and Nuclei

Sov J Part Nucl (Engl Transl) — Soviet Journal of Particles and Nuclei (English Translation)

Sov J Plasma Phys — Soviet Journal of Plasma Physics

Sov J Plasma Phys (Engl Transl) — Soviet Journal of Plasma Physics (English Translation)

Sov J Quant Electron — Soviet Journal of Quantum Electronics

Sov J Quantum Electron — Soviet Journal of Quantum Electronics

Sov J Quantum Electron (Engl Transl) — Soviet Journal of Quantum Electronics (English Translation)

Sov Kauch — Sovetskii Kauchuk

Sov Khir — Sovetskaya Khirurgiya

Sov Khlopok — Sovetskii Khlopok

Sov Kino Fotoprom — Sovetskaya Kino-Fotopromyshlennost

Sov Kino Fotopromst — Sovetskaya Kino-Fotopromyshlennost

SovKniga — Sovetskaya Kniga

Sov Kotloturbostr — Sovetskoe Kotloturbostroenie

Sov Krasnyi Krest — Soveti Krasnyi Krest

Sov Kult — Sovetskaya Kul'tura

SovL — Soviet Literature

SOVLA — Sovetskaya Latvija

Sov Law & Govt — Soviet Law and Government

Sov Law Gov — Soviet Law and Government

Sov Law Gvt — Soviet Law and Government

Sov Life — Soviet Life

Sov Lit — Soviet Literature

Sov M — Sovetskaya Muzyka

Sov Mater Sci — Soviet Materials Science

Sov Mater Sci (Engl Transl) — Soviet Materials Science (English Translation of Fiziko-Khimicheskaya MekhanikaMaterialov)

Sov Math — Soviet Mathematics

Sov Math (Engl Transl) — Soviet Mathematics (English Translation)

Sov Med — Sovetskaya Meditsina

Sovmestnaya Sov-Mong Nauchno-Issled Geol Eksped — Sovmestnaya Sovetsko-Mongol'skaya Nauchno-Issledovatel'skaya Geologicheskaya Ekspeditsiya

Sovmestnaya Sov-Mong Nauchno-Issled Geol Eksped Tr — Sovmestnaya Sovetsko-Mongol'skaya Nauchno-Issledovatel'skaya Geologicheskaya Ekspeditsiya Trudy

Sov Metall — Sovetskaya Metallurgiya

Sov Meteorol and Hydrol — Soviet Meteorology and Hydrology

Sov Meteorol Hydrol — Soviet Meteorology and Hydrology

Sov Meteorol Hydrol (Engl Transl) — Soviet Meteorology and Hydrology (English Translation)

Sov Microelectron — Soviet Microelectronics

Sov Min Sci — Soviet Mining Science

Sov Min Sci (Engl Transl) — Soviet Mining Science (English Translation)

Sov Ml Rev — Soviet Military Review

Sov Mukomole Khlebopech — Sovetskoe Mukomol'e i Khlebopechenie

Sov Muz — Sovetskiy Muzey

Sov Nauka — Sovetskaya Nauka
Sov Neurol Psychiatry — Soviet Neurology and Psychiatry
Sov Neur R — Soviet Neurology and Psychiatry (USSR)
Sov Nevropatol Psikhiatr Psikhogig — Sovetskaya Nevropatologiya, Psikhiatriya, i Psikhogigiena
Sov Non-Ferrous Met Res — Soviet Non-Ferrous Metals Research
Sov Non-Ferrous Met Res (Engl Transl) — Soviet Non-Ferrous Metals Research (English Translation)
Sov Oceanogr — Soviet Oceanography
Sov Pedag — Soviet Pedagogy
Sov Pediatr — Sovetskaya Pediatriya
Sov Ph Ac R — Soviet Physics. Acoustics (USSR)
Sov Pharm — Soviet Pharmacy
Sov Ph Se R — Soviet Physics. Semiconductors (USSR)
Sov Phys Acoust — Soviet Physics. Acoustics
Sov Phys Acoust (Engl Transl) — Soviet Physics. Acoustics (English Translation)
Sov Phys Collect — Soviet Physics. Collection
Sov Phys Collect (Engl Transl) — Soviet Physics. Collection (English Translation)
Sov Phys Coll (Engl Transl) — Soviet Physics. Collection (English Translation)
Sov Phys Cryst — Soviet Physics. Crystallography
Sov Phys Crystallogr — Soviet Physics. Crystallography
Sov Phys Crystallogr (Engl Transl) — Soviet Physics. Crystallography (English Translation)
Sov Phys Dokl — Soviet Physics. Doklady
Sov Phys Dokl (Engl Transl) — Soviet Physics. Doklady (English Translation)
Sov Physicians J — Soviet Physicians' Journal
Sov Phys J — Soviet Physics Journal
Sov Phys J (Engl Transl) — Soviet Physics Journal (English Translation)
Sov Phys JETP — Soviet Physics. JETP
Sov Phys Lebedev Inst Rep — Soviet Physics. Lebedev Institute Reports
Sov Phys Lebedev Inst Rep (Engl Transl) — Soviet Physics. Lebedev Institute Reports (English Translation)
Sov Phys Semicond — Soviet Physics. Semiconductors
Sov Phys Semicond (Engl Transl) — Soviet Physics. Semiconductors (English Translation)
Sov Phys Solid State — Soviet Physics. Solid State
Sov Phys Solid State (Engl Transl) — Soviet Physics. Solid State (English Translation)
Sov Phys Sol St — Soviet Physics. Solid State Physics
Sov Phys Tech Phys — Soviet Physics. Technical Physics
Sov Phys Tech Phys (Engl Transl) — Soviet Physics. Technical Physics (English Translation)
Sov Phys Tech Phys Lett — Soviet Physics. Technical Physics. Letters
Sov Phys T P — Soviet Physics. Technical Physics
Sov Phys Usp — Soviet Physics. Uspekhi
Sov Phys Uspekhi — Soviet Physics. Uspekhi
Sov Phys Usp (Engl Transl) — Soviet Physics. Uspekhi (English Translation)
Sov Plant Ind Rec — Soviet Plant Industry Record
Sov Plant Physiol — Soviet Plant Physiology
Sov Plant Physiol (Engl Transl) — Soviet Plant Physiology (English Translation)
Sov Plant Physiol (Engl Transl Fiziol Rast) — Soviet Plant Physiology (English Translation of Fiziologiya Rastenii)
Sov Plast — Soviet Plastics
Sov Plast (Engl Transl) — Soviet Plastics (English Translation)
Sov Powder Metall and Met Ceram — Soviet Powder Metallurgy and Metal Ceramics
Sov Powder Metall Met Ceram — Soviet Powder Metallurgy and Metal Ceramics
Sov Powder Metall Met Ceram (Engl Transl) — Soviet Powder Metallurgy and Metal Ceramics (English Translation)
Sov Powder Met Metal Ceram — Soviet Powder Metallurgy and Metal Ceramics
Sov Power Eng — Soviet Power Engineering
Sov Power Eng (Engl Transl) — Soviet Power Engineering (English Translation of Elektricheskie Stantsii)
Sov Prog Chem — Soviet Progress in Chemistry
Sov Prog Chem (Engl Transl) — Soviet Progress in Chemistry (English Translation)
Sov Psikhonevrol — Sovetskaya Psikhonevrologiya
Sov Psychol — Soviet Psychology
Sov Psychoneurol — Soviet Psychoneurology
Sov Psyco R — Soviet Psychology (USSR)
Sov Public Health — Soviet Public Health
Sov Public Health (Engl Transl) — Soviet Public Health (English Translation)
SovR — Soviet Review
Sov Radiochem — Soviet Radiochemistry
Sov Radiochem (Engl Transl) — Soviet Radiochemistry (English Translation)
Sov Radio Eng — Soviet Radio Engineering
Sov Radiophys — Soviet Radiophysics
Sov Radiophys (Engl Transl) — Soviet Radiophysics (English Translation of Izvestiya Vysshikh Uchebnykh Zavedenii Radiofizika)
Sovrem Biokhim Morfol Probl Soedin Tkani Mater Vses Soveshch — Sovremennye Biokhimicheskie i Morfologicheskie Problemy Soedinitel'noiTkani. Materialy Vsesoyuznogo Soveshchaniya po Soedinitel'noi Tkani
Sovrem Dannye Lech Primen Vitam Rab Vses Soveshch — Sovremennye Dannye po Lechebnomu Primeneniyu Vitaminov. RabotyDolozhennye na Vsesoyuznom Soveshchani po Vitaminam
Sovremennaya Arkhit — Sovremennaya Arkhitektura
Sovrem Metody Issled — Sovremennye Metody Issledovaniya
Sovrem Metody Issled Khim Lignina Mater Vses Semin — Sovremennye Metody Issledovaniya v Khimii Lignina, po MaterialamVsesoyuznogo Seminara
Sovrem Metody YaMR EPR Khim Tverd Tela Mater Vses Koord — Sovremennye Metody YaMR [Yadernyi Magnitnyi Rezonans] EPR v Khimii Tverdogo Tela. Materialy Vsesoyuznogo Koordinatsionnogo Soveshchaniya
Sovrem Probl Deyat Str Tsentr Nervn Sist — Sovremennye Problemy Deyatel'nosti i Stroeniya Tsentral'noe Nervnoi Sistemy
Sovrem Probl Fiz Khim — Sovremnnye Problemy Fizicheskoi Khimii

Sovrem Probl Gastroenterol — Sovremennye Problemy Gastroenterologii
Sovrem Probl Gastroenterol Resp Mezhved Sb — Sovremennye Problemy Gastroenterologii Respublikanskii Mezhvedomstvennyi-Sbornik
Sovrem Probl Gematol Pereliv Krovi — Sovremennye Problemy Gematologii i Perelivaniya Krovi
Sovrem Probl Onkol — Sovremennye Problemy Onkologii
Sovrem Probl Organ Khim — Sovremennye Problemy Organicheskoi Khimii
Sovrem Probl Org Khim — Sovremennye Problemy Organicheskoi Khimii
Sovrem Probl Otolaringol Resp Mezhved Sb — Sovremennye Problemy Otolaringologii Respublikanskoi Mezhvedomstvennyi Sbornik
Sovrem Probl Otorinolaringol — Sovremennye Problemy Otorinolaringologii
Sovrem Probl Radiobiol — Sovremennye Problemy Radiobiologii
Sovrem Probl Teor Prikl Mekh Tr Vses Sezda Teor Prikl Mekh — Sovremennye Problemy Teoreticheskoi i Prikladnoi Mekhaniki. TrudyVsesoyuznogo Sezda po Teoreticheskoi i Prikladnoi Mekhanike
Sovrem Psikhonevrol — Sovremennaya Psikhonevrologiya
Sovrem Psikhotropnye Sredstva — Sovremennye Psikhotropnye Sredstva
Sovrem Vopr Endokrinol — Sovremennye Voprosy Endokrinologii
Sovrem Vopr Sud Med Ekspertnoi Prak — Sovremennye Voprosy Sudebnoi Meditsiny i Ekspertnoi Praktiki
Sovrem Zadachi Tochn Naukakh — Sovremennye Zadachi v Tochnykh Naukakh
Sov Res High Energy Fission — Soviet Research in High Energy Fission
Sov Res Nucl Phys — Soviet Research in Nuclear Physics
Sov Res Nucl Solid State Phys — Soviet Research in Nuclear and Solid State Physics
Sov Res Phys — Soviet Research in Physics
Sov Rubber Technol — Soviet Rubber Technology
Sov Rubber Technol (Engl Transl) — Soviet Rubber Technology (English Translation)
SovS — Soviet Studies
SovS — Soviet Survey
Sov Sakhar — Sovetskii Sakhar
Sov Sci — Soviet Science
Sov Sci (Engl Transl) — Soviet Science (English Translation)
Sov Sci Rev — Soviet Science Review
Sov Sci Rev Sect A — Soviet Scientific Reviews. Section A. Physics Reviews
Sov Sci Rev Sect B — Soviet Scientific Reviews. Section B. Chemistry Reviews
Sov Sci Rev Sect D Biol Rev — Soviet Scientific Reviews. Section D. Biology Reviews
Sov Sci Rev Sect E — Soviet Scientific Reviews. Section E. Astrophysics and Space PhysicsReviews
Sov Shakhtior — Sovetskii Shakhtior
Sovshch Belku Sb Dokl Konf Vysokomol Soedin — Soveshchanie po Belku Sbornik Dokladov Konferentsii poVysokomolekulyarnym Soedineniyam
Sov Shvedskaya Kompleksn Eksped Balt More — Sovetsko-Shvedskaya Kompleksnaya Ekspeditsiya v Baltiiskom More
SovSlav — Sovetskoe Slavjanovedenie
Sov Soc — Soviet Sociology
Sov Sociol — Soviet Sociology
Sov Soil Sci — Soviet Soil Science
Sov Soil Sci (Engl Transl) — Soviet Soil Science (English Translation of Pochvovedenie)
Sov Soil Sci (Engl Transl Pochvovedenie) — Soviet Soil Science (English Translation of Pochvovedenie)
Sov Soil Sci Suppl — Soviet Soil Science. Supplement
Sov Stat & Dec — Soviet Statutes and Decisions
Sov St Hist — Soviet Studies in History
Sov St Lit — Soviet Studies in Literature
Sov Stomatol — Sovetskaya Stomatologiya
Sov St Phil — Soviet Studies in Philosophy
Sov Stud — Soviet Studies
Sov Stud Hist — Soviet Studies in History
Sov Subtrop (Moscow) — Sovetskie Subtropiki (Moscow)
Sov Subtrop (Sukhumi USSR) — Sovetskie Subtropiki (Sukhumi, USSR)
Sov Sudostr — Sovetskoe Sudostroenie
Sov Sugar — Soviet Sugar
Sov Swed Symp Pollut Balt — Soviet-Swedish Symposium on the Pollution of the Baltic
SovT — Sovetskaja Tjurkologija
Sov Technol Rev Sect A Energy Rev — Soviet Technology Reviews. Section A. Energy Reviews
Sov Technol Rev Sect B Therm Phys Rev — Soviet Technology Reviews. Section B. Thermal Physics Reviews
Sov Tech Phys Lett — Soviet Technical Physics. Letters
Sov Tech Phys Lett (Engl Transl) — Soviet Technical Physics. Letters (English Translation)
Sov Tjurkolog — Sovetskaja Tjurkologija
Sov Torg — Sovetskaya Torgovlya
Sov T P Lett — Soviet Technical Physics. Letters
Sov Union — Soviet Union
Sov Un Un Sov — Soviet Union / Union Sovietique
Sov Veda Chem — Sovetska Veda. Chemie
Sov Vestn Oftalmol — Sovetskii Vestnik Oftal'mologii
Sov Vestn Venerol Dermatol — Sovetskii Vestnik Venerologii i Dermatologii
Sov Vet — Sovetskaya Veterinariya
SovVo — Sovetskoje Vostokovedenie
Sov Vost Sb — Sovetskoe Vostokovedenie. Sbornik
Sov Vrach Gaz — Sovetskaya Vrachebnaya Gazeta
Sov Vrach Zh — Sovetskii Vrachebnyi Zhurnal
Sov Yaponskii Semin Katal Sb Dokl — Sovetsko-Yaponskii Seminar po Katalizu. Sbornik Dokladov
Sov Yaponskii Simp Izuch Str Kory Verkhn Mantii Zony — Sovetsko-Yaponskii Simpozium po Izucheniyu Stroeniya Kory i VerkhneiMantii Zony Perekhoda ot Aziatskogo Kontinenta k Tikhomu Okeanu

Sov Yaponskii Simp Izuch Str Zemnoi Kory Verkhn Mantii Zony — Sovetsko-Yaponskii Simpozium po Izucheniyu Stroeniya Zemnoi Kory iVerkhnei Mantii Zony Perekhoda ot Aziatskogo Kontinenta k Tikhomu Okeanu
Sov Zdravookhr — Sovetskoe Zdravookhranenie
Sov Zdravookhr Kirg — Sovetskoe Zdravookhranenie Kirgizii
Sov Zdravookhr Turkm — Sovetskoe Zdravookhranenie Turkmenii
Sov Zhenshchina — Sovetskaya Zhenshchina
Sov Zhivopis — Sovetskaya Zhivopis'
Sov Zolotopromst — Sovetskaya Zolotopromyshlennost
Sov Zootekh — Sovetskaya Zootekhniya
So West LJ — Southwestern Law Journal
Sow Geol — Sowjet Geologie
Sowjetruss Aerztl Z — Sowjetrussische Aerztliche Zeitschrift
Sowjetstud — Sowjetstudien
Sowjetw Ges — Sowjetwissenschaft Gesellschaft
Sowjetwiss — Sowjetwissenschaft
Sow Kautsch — Sowjet Kautschuk
Sow Metall — Sowjet Metallurgie
So Work — Southern Workman
So Workm — Southern Workman
So Workman — Southern Workman
Sow Pharm — Sowjet Pharmazie
SoWS — Southern Writers Series
Soybean Dig — Soybean Digest
Soybean Genet Newsl US Dep Agric Agric Res Serv — Soybean Genetics Newsletter. US Department of Agriculture. Agricultural Research Service
Soy Protein Prev Atheroscler Proc Int Symp — Soy Protein in the Prevention of Atherosclerosis. Proceedings. International Symposium
SoZ — Sovremennye Zapiski
Soz Arbeit — Soziale Arbeit
Soz Berufsarbeit — Soziale Berufsarbeit
SOZDA — Sovetskoe Zdravookhranenie
SozEp Ber — SozEp-Berichte
Soz Forstwirtsch — Sozialistische Forstwirtschaft
Soz Fortsch — Sozialer Fortschrift
Soz Fortschritt — Sozialer Fortschritt
Sozialdemokr Pressedienst — Sozialdemokratische Pressedienst
Sozial Forstw — Sozialistische Forstwirtschaft
Sozialist Akad — Sozialistische Akademiker
Sozialistische Arbeitswiss — Sozialistische Arbeitswissenschaft
Sozialistische Finwirt — Sozialistische Finanzwirtschaft
Sozialist Mhft — Sozialistische Monatshefte
Sozialmed Paedagog Jugendkd — Sozialmedizinische und Paedagogische Jugendkunde
Sozial Polit — Sozialistische Politik
Soziol Jb — Soziologisches Jahrbuch
Soz Kommun — Sozialisation und Kommunikation
Soz Kultur — Soziale Kultur
Soz Landwirtsch Usb — Sozialistische Landwirtschaft von Usbekistan
SozM — Sozialistische Monatshefte
Soz- Praeventivmed — Sozial- und Praeventivmedizin
Soz Praxis — Soziale Praxis
SozRev — Soziale Revue
Soz Sicherheit — Soziale Sicherheit
Soz und Wirtpol MSpiegel — Sozial- und Wirtschaftspolitischer Monatsspiegel aus Zeitungen und Zeitschriften
Soz Welt — Soziale Welt
Soz Wiederaufbau Wiss — Sozialistischer Wiederaufbau und Wissenschaft
Soz Wiss Jb Polit — Sozialwissenschaftliches Jahrbuch fuer Politik
SP — Scholarly Publishing
SP — Select Papyri
SP — Slovansky Prehled
SP — Socialismo y Participacion
SP — Soundpost
SP — Sovetskaya Pedagogika
SP — Space Propulsion
Sp — Spectator
Sp — Speculum
Sp — Sphere
Sp — Spomenik. Srpska Akademija Nauka i Umjetnosti
SP — Spring
Sp — Sputnik
SP — Studia Papyrologica
SP — Studia Patristica
SP — Studies in Philology
SP — Suisse Primitive
SP — Sumatra Post
SPA — Dagblad Scheepvaart
SPA — Science and Public Affairs. Bulletin of the Atomic Scientists
SPA — Sitzungsberichte. Preussische Akademie der Wissenschaften
SPA — Soviet Periodical Abstracts. Asia, Aftica, Latin America
SPAA — Sage Public Administration Abstracts
SPAA — Spicilegium Pontificii Athenaei Antoniani
SPAAAX — Memoires Suisses de Paleontologie
SPAAAX — Memorie Svizzere di Paleontologia
S Pac — South Pacific
SPACA — Spectrochimica Acta
S Pac Comm Ann Rep — South Pacific Commission. Annual Report
S Pac Comm Occ Pap — South Pacific Commission. Occasional Paper
SPACD8 — Israel. Agricultural Research Organization. Special Publication
SPACDocRap — Societe Paleontologique et Archeologique de l'Arrondissement Judicaire de Charleroi. Documents et Rapports
Space/Aeronaut — Space/Aeronautics
Space Biol Aerosp Med — Space Biology and Aerospace Medicine
Space Biol Med (Engl Transl) — Space Biology and Medicine (English Translation)

Space Cit — Space City News
Space Comm — Space Commerce Bulletin
Space Congr — Space Congress
Space Congr Proc — Space Congress. Proceedings
Spacecr Mater Space Environ Eur Symp Proc — Spacecraft Materials in Space Environment. European Symposium. Proceedings
Space Des — Space Design
Space Econ — Space Economics
Space Electrochem Res Technol Proc Conf — Space Electrochemical Research and Technology. Proceedings. Conference
Space Ind — Space Industrialization
Space Life Sci — Space Life Sciences
Space Marke — Space Markets
Space Res — Space Research
Space Res Bulg — Space Research in Bulgaria
Space Res Eng — Space Research and Engineering
Space Sci Instrum — Space Science Instrumentation
Space Sci R — Space Science Reviews
Space Sci Rev — Space Science Reviews
Space Simul Proc Symp — Space Simulation. Proceedings of a Symposium
Space Sol Power Rev — Space Solar Power Review
Space Stn Autom — Space Station Automation
Space Stn Present Future Proc Int Astronaut Congr — Space Stations Present and Future. Proceedings. InternationalAstronautical Congress
Space Technol — Space Technology
Space Wld — Space World
S Pacific — South Pacific
S Pacific Bull — South Pacific Bulletin
SPAEA — Space/Aeronautics
SPAFA — Sports Afield
Spain Cent Nac Aliment Nutr Bol — Spain. Centro Nacional de Alimentacion y Nutricion. Boletin
Spain Estac Cent Ecol Bol — Spain. Estacion Centro de Ecologia. Boletin
Spain Inst Geol Min Bol Geol Min — Spain. Instituto Geologico y Minero. Boletin Geologico y Minero
Spain Inst Geol Min Mem — Spain. Instituto Geologico y Minero. Memorias
Spain Junta Energ Nucl Rep — Spain. Junta de Energia Nuclear. Report
Spain Junta Energ Nucl Rep JEN — Spain. Junta de Energia Nuclear. Report JEN
Spain Pat Doc — Spain. Patent Document
Spain Regist Prop Ind Bol Of Prop Ind — Spain. Registro de la Propiedad Industrial. Boletin Oficial de laPropiedad Industrial
SPA Jnl — School of Planning and Architecture. Journal
SpAk — Spisanie na Bulgarskata Akademiya na Naukite
SPAN — South Pacific Association for Commonwealth Literature and Language Studies. Newsletter
Span — Spanish (Patent Document)
SPAN — SPAN. Shell Public Health and Agricultural News
SPAN — SPAN: State Planning Authority News
SPAN Prog Agric — SPAN [*Shell Public Health and Agricultural News*] Progress in Agriculture
SPap — Studia Papyrologica
Spar — Sparekassen
SPARD — Sparkasse
SPAR J Eng Technol — SPAR Journal of Engineering and Technology
Sparkasse — Zeitschrift des Deutschen Sparkassen
Spark's Am Biog — Spark's Library of American Biography
SPARMO Bull — SPARMO [*Solar Particles and Radiation Monitoring Organization*] Bulletin
SPat — Studia Patavina
S Patriot — Southern Patriot
Spat Vis — Spatial Vision
Spat Vision — Spatial Vision
SPAW — Sitzungsberichte. Preussische Akademie der Wissenschaften
Spawanie Ciecie Met — Spawanie i Ciecie Metali
SPAWPH — Sitzungsberichte der Preussischen Akademie der Wissenschaften. Philosophisch-Historische Klasse
SPAZD9 — Agronomy Society of New Zealand. Special Publication
Spazio & Soc — Spazio e Societa
SpB — Sprakliga Bidrag
SPB — Studia Patristica et Byzantina
SPB — Studia Post-Biblica
SpBA — Spisanie na Bulgarskata Akademiya na Naukite
SPBAA — Spisanie na Bulgarskata Akademiya na Naukite
Sp BAN — Spisanie na Bulgarskata Akademiia na Naukite i Izkustvata
SpBAN — Spisanie na Bulgarskata Akademiya na Naukite
SPBSES — Special Publications Series. British Ecological Society
SPBUA — SPARMO [*Solid Particles and Radiation Monitoring Organization*] Bulletin
SPC — IEEE. Spectrum
SpC — Sponsa Christi
SPC — Studia Philosophiae Christianae
SPCEBA — Universidade de Sao Paulo. Faculdade de Filosofia, Ciencias, e Letras. Boletim. Antropologia
SPCEBE — Universidade de Sao Paulo. Faculdade de Filosofia, Ciencias, e Letras. Boletim. Etnografia e Tupi-Guarani
SPC Handb — SPC [*South Pacific Commission*] Handbook
SPCHB — Soviet Progress in Chemistry
SPCHDX — Carnegie Museum of Natural History. Special Publication
SPCHN — Sbirka Pramenu Ceskeho Hnuti Nabozenskeho ve XIV. a XV. Stoleti
SPCIC — Studiorum Paulinorum Congressus Internationalis Catholicus
SPCPB — Space Science Reviews
SPCQB — SPC [*South Pacific Commission*] Quarterly Bulletin
SPC Quart Bull — SPC [*South Pacific Commission*] Quarterly Bulletin
SPC Rep Sask Power Corp — SPC Report. Saskatchewan Power Corp.
SPCSDW — Commonwealth Bureau of Soils. Special Publication
SPC Soap Perfum Cosmet — SPC. Soap, Perfumery, and Cosmetics

SPCT — Studi e Problemi di Critica Testuale
SPC Tech Pap — SPC [*South Pacific Commission*] Technical Paper
SPD — Standard Periodical Data Base
SPDN — Screen Printing and Display News
SPDVB — Science Progres Decouverte
SPE — Special Libraries
Spe — Speculum. Journal of Medieval Studies
SPe — Spettatore Italiano
SPE — Studies in Philosophy and Education
SPE — Studies in Public Economics
SPE — Suriname Post
SPE Adv Technol Ser — SPE (Society of Petroleum Engineers) Advanced Technology Series
Spec — Spectator
Spec — Spectrum
Spec — Speculation
Spec — Speculum
SPECA — Spectrum
Spec Aspects Nucl En Isot Appl Proc Int Conf Peace Use At En — Special Aspects of Nuclear Energy and Isotope Applications.Proceedings. International Conference on the Peaceful Uses of Atomic Energy
Spec Bull Aichiken Agric Res Cent — Special Bulletin. Aichi-ken Agricultural Research Center
Spec Bull Coll Agric Utsunomiya Univ — Special Bulletin. College of Agriculture. Utsunomiya University
Spec Bull Coll Agr Utsunomiya Univ — Special Bulletin. College of Agriculture. Utsunomiya University
Spec Bull Dep Agric S Aust — Special Bulletin. Department of Agriculture. South Australia
Spec Bull Dep Agric South Aust — Special Bulletin. Department of Agriculture. South Australia
Spec Bull First Agron Div Tokai-Kinki Natl Agric Exp Stn — Special Bulletin. First Agronomy Division. Tokai-Kinki National Agricultural Experiment Station
Spec Bull Fukui Agric Exp Stn — Special Bulletin. Fukui Agricultural Experiment Station
Spec Bull Fukuoka Agric Res Cent — Special Bulletin. Fukuoka Agricultural Research Center
Spec Bull Hortic Stn Tokai Kinki Agric Exp Stn — Special Bulletin. Horticultural Station. Tokai Kinki AgriculturalExperiment Station
Spec Bull Mich Agric Exp Stn — Special Bulletin. Michigan Agricultural Experiment Station
Spec Bull Mich State Univ Agr Exp Sta — Special Bulletin. Michigan State University. Agricultural Experiment Station
Spec Bull Okayama Agr Exp Sta — Special Bulletin. Okayama Agricultural Experiment Station
Spec Bull Okayama Prefect Agric Exp Stn — Special Bulletin. Okayama Prefectural Agricultural Experiment Station
Spec Bull Rehovot Nat Univ Inst Agr — Special Bulletin. Rehovot. National and University Institute of Agriculture
Spec Bull Taiwan For Res Inst — Special Bulletin. Taiwan Forestry Research Institute
Spec Bull Tottori Agric Exp Stn — Special Bulletin. Tottori Agricultural Experiment Station
Spec Bull Univ Ga Coop Ext Serv — Special Bulletin. University of Georgia. Cooperative Extension Service
Spec Care Dentist — Special Care in Dentistry
Spec Ceram — Special Ceramics
Spec Chem — Specialty Chemicals
Spec Chem Oil Ind Proc Lect Ser — Special Chemicals in the Oil Industry. Proceedings. Lecture Series
Spec Circ Mass Ext Serv — Special Circular. Massachusetts Extension Service
Spec Circ Ohio Agr Exp Sta — Special Circular. Ohio Agricultural Experiment Station
Spec Circ Ohio Agric Res Dev Cent — Special Circular. Ohio Agricultural Research and Development Center
Spec Circ PA State Univ Coll-Agric Ext Serv — Special Circular. Pennsylvania State University. College of Agriculture. Extension Service
Spec Circ Univ Wis Coll Agr Ext Serv — Special Circular. University of Wisconsin. College of Agriculture. Extension Service
Spec Collect — Special Collections
Spec Colloq Ampere Appl Reson Methods Solid State Physics — Specialized Colloque Ampere. Application of Resonance Methods in Solid State Physics
Spec Conf Atmos Deposition Proc — Specialty Conference on Atmospheric Deposition. Proceedings
Spec Conf Contin Monit Stationary Air Pollut Sources Proc — Specialty Conference on Continuous Monitoring of Stationary AirPollution Sources. Proceedings
Spec Conf Control Specific Toxic Pollut Proc — Specialty Conference on Control of Specific Toxic Pollutants. Proceedings
Spec Conf Control Technol Agric Air Pollut — Specialty Conference on Control Technology for Agricultural AirPollutants
Spec Conf Dredging Its Environ Eff Proc — Specialty Conference on Dredging and Its Environmental Effects. Proceedings
Spec Conf Emiss Factors Inventories Proc — Specialty Conference on Emission Factors and Inventories. Proceedings
Spec Conf Emiss Inventories Air Qual Manage — Specialty Conference on Emission Inventories and Air Quality Management
Spec Conf Long Term Maint Clean Air Stand Proc — Specialty Conference on Long Term Maintenance of Clean Air Standards. Proceedings
Spec Conf Meas Monit Non Criter Toxic Contam Air — Specialty Conference on Measurement and Monitoring of Non-Criteria,Toxic Contaminants in Air
Spec Conf Ozone Oxid Interact Total Environ Proc — Specialty Conference on Ozone/Oxidants. Interactions with the Total Environment. Proceedings
Spec Conf Qual Assur Air Pollut Meas Proc — Specialty Conference on Quality Assurance in Air Pollution Measurement.Proceedings

Spec Conf Resid Wood Coal Combust Proc — Specialty Conference on Residential Wood and Coal Combustion. Proceedings
Spec Conf Tech Basis Size Specific Part Stand Proc — Specialty Conference on the Technical Basis for a Size SpecificParticulate Standard. Proceedings
Spec Conf Toxic Subst Air Environ Proc — Specialty Conference on Toxic Substances in the Air Environment.Proceedings
Spec Conf User Fabric Filtr Equip Proc — Specialty Conference on the User and Fabric Filtration Equipment.Proceedings
Spec Conf View Visibility Regul Sci Proc — Specialty Conference on View and Visibility. Regulatory and Scientific. Proceedings
Spec Conf Waste Treat Disposal Aspects Combust Air Pollut — Specialty Conference on Waste Treatment and Disposal Aspects.Combustion and Air Pollution Control Processes
Spec Contrib Geophys Inst Kyoto Univ — Special Contributions. Geophysical Institute. Kyoto University
Spec Contrib Inst Geophys Nat Cent Univ (Taiwan) — Special Contributions. Institute of Geophysics. National Central University (Taiwan)
Spec Contrib Inst Geophys Natl Cent Univ (Miaoli Taiwan) — Special Contributions. Institute of Geophysics. National Central University (Miaoli, Taiwan)
Spec Courses Fd Ind — Specialist Courses for the Food Industry
Spec Courses Food Ind — Specialist Courses for the Food Industry
SPECD — Spectrum
Spec Discuss Faraday Soc — Special Discussions. Faraday Society
Spec Econ Ser Maine Geol Surv — Special Economic Series. Maine Geological Survey
Spec Ed Counc News — Special Education Council. Newsletter
Spec Ed Inst Geol Hydrogeol Geophys Geotech Res — Special Edition. Institute for Geological, Hydrogeological, Geophysical, and Geotechnical Research
Spec Educ — Special Education
Spec Educ — Special Education. Forward Trends
Spec Educ Bull — Special Education Bulletin
Spec Educ Can — Special Education in Canada
Spec Educ Forward Trends — Special Education. Forward Trends
Spec Eng — Specifying Engineer
Spec Environ Rep — Special Environmental Report
Spec Environ Rep WMO — Special Environmental Report. World Meteorological Organization
Special Bull Forest Prod Lab — Special Bulletin. Forest Products Laboratory
Special Bull Hort Sta Tokai Kinki Agric Exp Sta — Special Bulletin. Horticultural Station. Tokai Kinki Agricultural Experiment Station/Tokai Kinki Nogyo Shikenjo Engei-Bu Tokubetsu Hokoku
Special Bull Tokai Kinki Natl Agric Exp Sta — Special Bulletin. Tokai-Kinki National Agricultural Experiment Station/Norin-Sho Tokai Kinki Nogyo Shikenjo Tokubetsu Hokoku
Special Bull Univ Minnesota Agric Exten Div — Special Bulletin. University of Minnesota. Agricultural Extension Division
Special Ed — Special Education
Special Ed — Special Education in Canada
Specialised Nat Councils' M (Egypt) — Specialised National Councils' Magazine (Egypt)
Special Issue Sylvic Educ — Special Issue. Sylviculture and Education. Taiwan Forest Experiment Station/LinYeh T'ui Kuang Tsuan K'an
Speciality Chem — Speciality Chemicals
Special Lib — Special Libraries
Special Pap Geol Soc Amer — Special Papers. Geological Society of America
Special Pap Ohio State Acad Sci — Special Papers. Ohio State Academy of Sciences
Special Publ British Columbia Prov Mus Nat Hist — Special Publications. British Columbia Provincial Museum of Natural History andAnthropology
Special Publ Indo Pacific Fish Council — Special Publications. Indo-Pacific Fisheries Council
Special Publ Limnol Soc Amer — Special Publication. Limnological Society of America
Special Publ Natl Agric Res Bur — Special Publication. National Agricultural Research Bureau/Shih Yeh Pu Chung Yang Nung Yeh Shih Yen So K'an Mu Lu
Special Rep Imp Agric Exp Sta — Special Report. Imperial Agricultural Experiment Station/Noji Shikenjo Tokubetsu Hokoku
Special Rep Ser Med Research Com (London) — Special Report Series. Medical Research Committee (London)
Special Res Bull N China Agric Sci Res Inst — Special Research Bulletin. North China Agricultural Science Research Institute/Hua Pei Nung Yeh K'o Hsueh Yen Chiu So. Yen Chu Tsuan K'an
Special Sch Bul (NT) — Special Schools Bulletin (Northern Territory)
Special Sch Bul (Qld) — Special Schools Bulletin (Queensland Department of Education)
Special Topics Supercomput — Special Topics in Supercomputing
Specif Eng — Specifying Engineer
Specif Engr — Specifying Engineer
Spec Int — Specialties International
Spec Issue Bot Mag — Special Issue. Botanical Magazine
Spec Issue Plant Cell Physiol — Special Issue of Plant and Cell Physiology
Spec Issues Artificial Intelligence — Special Issues of Artificial Intelligence
Spec Law Dig Health Care Mon — Specialty Law Digest. Health Care Monthly
Spec Liaison Rep Commonw Geol Liaison Off — Special Liaison Report. Commonwealth Geological Liaison Office
Spec Libr — Special Libraries
Spec Libr Ass Toronto Chapter Bull — Special Libraries Association. Toronto Chapter. Bulletin
Spec Librs — Special Libraries
Spec Meet Int Combust Inst — Specialists Meeting. International Combustion Institute
Spec Pap Cent Precambrian Res Univ Adelaide — Special Paper. Centre for Precambrian Research. University of Adelaide

Spec Pap Dep Nat Resour (Qd) — Special Papers. Department of Natural Resources (Queensland)

Spec Pap Dep Nat Resour Que — Special Paper. Department of Natural Resources. Quebec

Spec Pap Geol Ass Can — Special Paper. Geological Association of Canada

Spec Pap Geol Assoc Can — Special Paper. Geological Association of Canada

Spec Pap Geol Soc Am — Special Paper. Geological Society of America

Spec Pap Palaeontol — Special Papers in Palaeontology

Spec Pap State Ore Dep Geol Min Ind — Special Paper. State of Oregon Department of Geology and MineralIndustries

Spec Pap Univ Adelaide Cent Precambrian Res — Special Paper. University of Adelaide. Centre for Precambrian Research

Spec Pap Univ Adelaide Cent Prec Res — Special Paper. University of Adelaide. Centre for Precambrian Research

Spec Period Rep Alicyclic Chem — Specialist Periodical Reports. Alicyclic Chemistry

Spec Period Rep Aliphatic Chem — Specialist Periodical Reports. Aliphatic Chemistry

Spec Period Rep Aliphatic Relat Nat Prod Chem — Specialist Periodical Reports. Aliphatic and Related Natural Product Chemistry

Spec Period Rep Alkaloids — Specialist Periodical Reports. Alkaloids

Spec Period Rep Amino-Acids Peptides Proteins — Specialist Periodical Reports. Amino-Acids, Peptides, and Proteins

Spec Period Rep Amino-Acids Pept Proteins — Specialist Periodical Reports. Amino-Acids, Peptides, and Proteins

Spec Period Rep Arom Heteroaromat Chem — Specialist Periodical Reports. Aromatic and Heteroaromatic Chemistry

Spec Period Rep Biosynth — Specialist Periodical Reports. Biosynthesis

Spec Period Rep Carbohydr Chem — Specialist Periodical Reports. Carbohydrate Chemistry

Spec Period Rep Catal — Specialist Periodical Reports. Catalysis

Spec Period Rep Chem Phys Solids Their Surf — Specialist Periodical Reports. Chemical Physics of Solids and TheirSurfaces

Spec Period Rep Chem Thermodyn — Specialist Periodical Reports. Chemical Thermodynamics

Spec Period Rep Colloid Sci — Specialist Periodical Reports. Colloid Science

Spec Period Rep Dielectr Relat Mol Processes — Specialist Periodical Reports. Dielectric and Related Molecular Processes

Spec Period Rep Electrochem — Specialist Periodical Reports. Electrochemistry

Spec Period Rep Electron Spin Reson — Specialist Periodical Reports. Electron Spin Resonance

Spec Period Rep Electron Struct Magn Inorg Compd — Specialist Periodical Reports. Electronic Structure and Magnetism ofInorganic Compounds

Spec Period Rep Environ Chem — Specialist Periodical Reports. Environmental Chemistry

Spec Period Rep Fluorocarbon Relat Chem — Specialist Periodical Reports. Fluorocarbon and Related Chemistry

Spec Period Rep Foreign Compd Metab Mamm — Specialist Periodical Reports. Foreign Compound Metabolism in Mammals

Spec Period Rep Gas Kinet Energy Transfer — Specialist Periodical Reports. Gas Kinetics and Energy Transfer

Spec Period Rep Gen Synth Methods — Specialist Periodical Reports. General and Synthetic Methods

Spec Period Rep Heterocycl Chem — Specialist Periodical Reports. Heterocyclic Chemistry

Spec Period Rep Inorg Biochem — Specialist Periodical Reports. Inorganic Biochemistry

Spec Period Rep Inorg Chem Main Group Elem — Specialist Periodical Reports. Inorganic Chemistry of the Main-GroupElements

Spec Period Rep Inorg Chem Transition Elem — Specialist Periodical Reports. Inorganic Chemistry of the Transition Elements

Spec Period Rep Inorg React Mech — Specialist Periodical Reports. Inorganic Reaction Mechanisms

Spec Period Rep Macromol Chem — Specialist Periodical Reports. Macromolecular Chemistry

Spec Period Rep Mass Spectrom — Specialist Periodical Reports. Mass Spectrometry

Spec Period Rep Mol Struct Diffr Methods — Specialist Periodical Reports. Molecular Structure by Diffraction Methods

Spec Period Rep Nucl Magn Resonance — Specialist Periodical Reports. Nuclear Magnetic Resonance

Spec Period Rep Organomet Chem — Specialist Periodical Reports. Organometallic Chemistry

Spec Period Rep Organophosphorus Chem — Specialist Periodical Reports. Organophosphorus Chemistry

Spec Period Rep Org Compd Sulphur Selenium Tellurium — Specialist Periodical Reports. Organic Compounds of Sulphur, Selenium, and Tellurium

Spec Period Rep Photochem — Specialist Periodical Reports. Photochemistry

Spec Period Rep Radiochem — Specialist Periodical Reports. Radiochemistry

Spec Period Rep React Kinet — Specialist Periodical Reports. Reaction Kinetics

Spec Period Rep Saturated Heterocycl Chem — Specialist Periodical Reports. Saturated Heterocyclic Chemistry

Spec Period Rep Spectrosc Prop Inorg Organomet Compd — Specialist Periodical Reports. Spectroscopic Properties of Inorganic and Organometallic Compounds

Spec Period Rep Stat Mech — Specialist Periodical Reports. Statistical Mechanics

Spec Period Rep Surf Defect Prop Solids — Specialist Periodical Reports. Surface and Defect Properties of Solids

Spec Period Rep Terpenoids Steroids — Specialist Periodical Reports. Terpenoids and Steroids

Spec Period Rep Theor Chem — Specialist Periodical Reports. Theoretical Chemistry

Spec Prog News — Special Programmes News

Spec Pub Agric Res Org — Special Publication. Agricultural Research Organization

Spec Publ Acad Nat Sci Phila — Special Publication. Academy of Natural Sciences. Philadelphia

Spec Publ Agric Res Organ Volcani Cent (Bet Dagan) — Special Publication. Agricultural Research Organization. VolcaniCenter (Bet Dagan)

Spec Publ Agron Soc NZ — Special Publication. Agronomy Society of New Zealand

Spec Publ Am Concr Inst — Special Publication. American Concrete Institute

Spec Publ Am Littoral Soc — Special Publication. American Littoral Society

Spec Publ Am Soc Agron — Special Publication. American Society of Agronomy

Spec Publ Am Soc Mammal — Special Publication. American Society of Mammalogists

Spec Publ ARLCD SP US Army Armament Res Dev Command Large — Special Publication ARLCD-SP. US Army Armament Research and DevelopmentCommand. Large Caliber Weapon System Laboratory

Spec Publ Assoc Explor Geochem — Special Publication. Association of Exploration Geochemists

Spec Publ Aust Conserv Fdn — Special Publication. Australian Conservation Foundation

Spec Publ Aust Conserv Found — Special Publication. Australian Conservation Foundation

Spec Publ BCRA Br Carbonization Res Assoc — Special Publication. BCRA. British Carbonization Research Associaton

Spec Publ Biochem Soc London — Special Publication. Biochemical Society of London

Spec Publ Br Carbonization Res Assoc — Special Publication. British Carbonization Research Association

Spec Publ Br Ceram Res Assoc — Special Publication. British Ceramics Research Association

Spec Publ Br Ecol Soc — Special Publication. British Ecological Society

Spec Publ Bur Mines Geol (Mont) — Special Publication. Bureau of Mines and Geology (Montana)

Spec Publ Chem Soc — Special Publication. Chemical Society

Spec Publ Chicago Acad Sci — Special Publications. Chicago Academy of Science

Spec Publ Coll Agric Natl Taiwan Univ — Special Publication. College of Agriculture. National Taiwan University

Spec Publ Coll Agr Nat Taiwan U — Special Publications. College of Agriculture. National Taiwan University

Spec Publ Coll Earth Miner Sci Pa State Univ — Special Publication. College of Earth and Mineral Sciences.Pennsylvania State University

Spec Publ Colo Geol Surv — Special Publication. Colorado Geological Survey

Spec Publ Colorado Geol Surv — Special Publication. Colorado Geological Survey

Spec Publ Commonw Bur Soils — Special Publication. Commonwealth Bureau of Soils

Spec Publ Counc Agric Sci Technol — Special Publication. Council for Agricultural Science and Technology

Spec Publ Cushman Found Foraminiferal Res — Special Publication. Cushman Foundation for Foraminiferal Research

Spec Publ Ecol Soc Am — Special Publication. Ecological Society of America

Spec Publ Entomol Soc Am — Special Publication. Entomological Society of America

Spec Publ Fla Bur Geol — Special Publication. Florida Bureau of Geology

Spec Publ Forintek Can Corp East Lab — Special Publication. Forintek Canada Corporation. Eastern Laboratory

Spec Publ Geochem Soc — Special Publication. Geochemical Society

Spec Publ Geol Soc Aust — Special Publication. Geological Society of Australia

Spec Publ Geol Soc London — Special Publication. Geological Society of London

Spec Publ Geol Soc S Afr — Special Publication. Geological Society of South Africa

Spec Publ Geol Soc Zimbabwe — Special Publication. Geological Society of Zimbabwe

Spec Publ Geol Surv Indones — Special Publication. Geological Survey of Indonesia

Spec Publ Geol Surv S Afr — Special Publications. Geological Survey of South Africa

Spec Publ IEEE Power Eng Soc — Special Publication. IEEE Power Engineering Society

Spec Publ Int Assoc Sedimentol — Special Publication. International Association of Sedimentologists

Spec Publ Int Fert Dev Cent — Special Publication. International Fertilizer Development Center

Spec Publ (Isr) Agric Res Org — Special Publication (Israel). Agricultural Research Organization

Spec Publ KY Geol Surv — Special Publication. Kentucky Geological Survey

Spec Publ Montana Bur Mines Geol — Special Publication. Montana Bureau of Mines and Geology

Spec Publ Mont Bur Mines Geol — Special Publication. Montana Bureau of Mines and Geology

Spec Publ Mus Tex Tech Univ — Special Publications. Museum. Texas Tech University

Spec Publ Natl Bur Stand US — Special Publication. United States National Bureau of Standards

Spec Publ NC Dep Nat Econ Resour Geol Miner Resour Sect — Special Publication. North Carolina Department of Natural and EconomicResources. Geology and Mineral Resources Section

Spec Publ NC Geol Miner Resour Sect — Special Publication. North Carolina. Geology and Mineral Resources Section

Spec Publ NM Geol Soc — Special Publication. New Mexico Geological Society

Spec Publ Pa State Univ Coll Earth Min Sci — Special Publication. Pennsylvania State University. College of Earthand Mineral Sciences

Spec Publ R Numis Soc — Special Publication. Royal Numismatic Society

Spec Publ Roy Soc Canada — Special Publication. Royal Society of Canada

Spec Publ R Soc Chem — Special Publication. Royal Society of Chemistry

Spec Publ Sado Mar Biol Stn Niigata Univ — Special Publication. Sado Marine Biological Station. Niigata University

Spec Publ S Afr Assoc Adv Sci — Special Publication. South African Association for the Advancement of Science

Spec Publs Am Ass Econ Ent — Special Publications. American Association of Economic Entomology

Spec Publ Sask Geol Soc — Special Publication. Saskatchewan Geological Society

Spec Publ SEPM Soc Sediment Geol — Special Publication. SEPM (Society for Sedimentary Geology)

Spec Publ Ser Br Ecol Soc — Special Publications Series. British Ecological Society

Spec Publ Ser Geol Surv India — Special Publication Series. Geological Survey of India

Spec Publ Ser Int Atl Salmon Found — Special Publication Series. International Atlantic Salmon Foundation

Spec Publ Ser Minn Geol Surv — Special Publication Series. Minnesota Geological Survey

Spec Publ Ser Soil Sci Soc Amer — Special Publication Series. Soil Science Society of America

Spec Publ Seto Mar Biol Lab Ser IV — Special Publications. Seto Marine Biological Laboratory. Series IV

Spec Publ Soc Econ Paleontol Mineral — Special Publication. Society of Economic Paleontologists and Mineralogists

Spec Publ Soc Gen Microbiol — Special Publications. Society for General Microbiology

Spec Publ Soc Geol Appl Miner Deposits — Special Publication. Society for Geology Applied to Mineral Deposits

Spec Publ South Aust Dep Mines Energy — Special Publication. South Australia Department of Mines and Energy

Spec Publ Univ NM Inst Meteorit — Special Publication. University of New Mexico. Institute of Meteoritics

Spec Publ UNM Inst Meteorit — Special Publication. UNM [*University of New Mexico*] Institute of Meteoritics

Spec Publ US Bur Mines — Special Publications. United States Bureau of Mines

Spec Publ US Natn Bur Stand — Special Publications. United States National Bureau of Standards

Spec Publ Volcani Cent (Bet Dagan) — Special Publication. Volcani Center (Bet Dagan)

Spec Publ West Aust Mus — Special Publication. Western Australian Museum

Spec Publ World Maric Soc — Special Publication. World Mariculture Society

Spec Pub R Soc Tasm — Royal Society of Tasmania. Special Publications

Spec Ref Briefs Natl Agric Libr US — Special Reference Briefs. National Agricultural Library (US)

Spec Rep Agric Exp Stn Coop Ext Serv Univ Arkansas — Special Report. Agricultural Experiment Station. Cooperative Extension Service. University of Arkansas

Spec Rep Agric Exp Stn Oreg State Univ — Special Report. Agricultural Experiment Station. Oregon State University

Spec Rep Alaska Div Geol Geophys Surv — Special Report. Alaska Division of Geological and Geophysical Surveys

Spec Rep Alaska Div Mines Geol — Special Report. Alaska. Division of Mines and Geology

Spec Rep APL/JHU SR Johns Hopkins Univ Appl Phys Lab — Special Report. APL/JHU SR. Johns Hopkins University. Applied Physics Laboratory

Spec Rep Arctic Inst N Am — Special Report. Arctic Institute of North America

Spec Rep Ark Agr Exp Sta — Special Report. Arkansas Agricultural Experiment Station

Spec Rep Ark Agric Exp Stn — Special Report. Arkansas Agricultural Experiment Station

Spec Rep Arkansas Agric Exp Stn — Special Report. Arkansas Agricultural Experiment Station

Spec Rep Br Inst Radiol — Special Report. British Institute of Radiology

Spec Rep Br J Radiol — Special Report. British Journal of Radiology

Spec Rep Calif Div Mines Geol — Special Report. California Division of Mines and Geology

Spec Rep Colo Dep Game Fish Parks — Special Report. Colorado Department of Game, Fish, and Parks

Spec Rep Colo Div Game Fish Parks — Special Report. Colorado Division of Game, Fish, and Parks

Spec Rep Colo Div Wildl — Special Report. Colorado Division of Wildlife

Spec Rep Commonw Exp Bldg Stn — Special Report. Commonwealth Experimental Building Station

Spec Rep Electr Power Res Inst EPRI AF — Special Report. Electric Power Research Institute. EPRI AF

Spec Rep Electr Power Res Inst EPRI EA — Special Report. Electric Power Research Institute. EPRI EA

Spec Rep Electr Power Res Inst EPRI EL — Special Report. Electric Power Research Institute. EPRI EL

Spec Rep Electr Power Res Inst EPRI EM — Special Report. Electric Power Research Institute. EPRI EM

Spec Rep Electr Power Res Inst EPRI ER (Palo Alto, Calif) — Special Report. Electric Power Research Institute. EPRI ER (Palo Alto, California)

Spec Rep Electr Power Res Inst EPRI FP (Palo Alto, Calif) — Special Report. Electric Power Research Institute. EPRI FP (Palo Alto, California)

Spec Rep Electr Power Res Inst EPRI NP — Special Report. Electric Power Research Institute. EPRI NP

Spec Rep Electr Power Res Inst EPRI SR — Special Report. Electric Power Research Institute. EPRI SR

Spec Rep EPRI SR Electr Power Res Inst (Palo Alto Calif) — Special Report. Electric Power Research Institute. EPRI SR (Palo Alto, California)

Spec Rep Fulmer Res Inst — Special Report. Fulmer Research Institute

Spec Rep GB For Prod Res — Special Report. Great Britain Forest Products Research

Spec Rep Geol Soc Lond — Special Reports. Geological Society of London

Spec Rep Geol Surv Jpn — Special Report. Geological Survey of Japan

Spec Rep Great Lakes Res Div Univ Mich — Special Report. Great Lakes Research Division. University of Michigan

Spec Rep ICSU Comm Data Sci Technol — Special Report. International Council of Scientific Unions. Committee on Data for Science and Technology

Spec Rep Indiana Geol Surv — Special Report. Indiana Geological Survey

Spec Rep Int Congr Reprogr Inf — Specialists Reports. International Congress on Reprography and Information

Spec Rep Iowa State Univ Coop Ext Serv — Special Report. Iowa State University. Cooperative Extension Service

Spec Rep Iron Steel Inst Jpn — Special Report. Iron and Steel Institute of Japan

Spec Rep Johns Hopkins Univ Appl Phys Lab — Special Report. Johns Hopkins University. Applied Physics Laboratory

Spec Rep Miner Resour GB — Special Reports on the Mineral Resources of Great Britain

Spec Rep Mo Agric Exp Stn — Special Report. Missouri. Agricultural Experiment Station

Spec Rep Natl Inst Anim Ind — Special Report. National Institute of Animal Industry

Spec Rep Nat Res Counc Highw Res Board — Special Report. National Research Council. Highway Research Board

Spec Rep Nat Res Counc Transp Res Board — Special Report. National Research Council. Transportation Research Board

Spec Rep Nat Timber Res Inst CSIR(SA) — Special Report. National Timber Research Institute. Council for Scientific and Industrial Research (South Africa)

Spec Rep NCASI Nat Counc Pap Ind Air Stream Improv — Special Report. NCASI. National Council of the Paper Industry for Air and Stream Improvement

Spec Rep Nebr Agr Exp Sta — Special Report. Nebraska Agricultural Experiment Station

Spec Rep NJ Div Water Resour — Special Report. New Jersey Division of Water Resources

Spec Rep NY State Agric Exp Stn (Geneva) — Special Report. New York State Agricultural Experiment Station (Geneva)

Spec Rep Oreg For Prod Lab — Special Report. Oregon Forest Products Laboratory

Spec Rep (Oregon) Agric Exp Stn — Special Report (Oregon). Agricultural Experiment Station

Spec Rep Oreg State Coll Agr Exp Sta — Special Report. Oregon State College Agricultural Experiment Station

Spec Rep Packag Inst — Special Report. Packaging Institute

Spec Rep Robert Wood Johnson Foundation — Special Report. Robert Wood Johnson Foundation

Spec Rep S Afr CSIR — Special Report. South African Council for Scientific and Industrial Research

Spec Rep SD Geol Surv — Special Report. South Dakota Geological Survey

Spec Rep Ser Indian Counc Med Res — Special Report Series. Indian Council of Medical Research

Spec Rep Ser Med Res Counc (UK) — Special Report Series. Medical Research Council (United Kingdom)

Spec Rep Ser Nat Open Hearth Steel Comm Iron Steel Div Met — Special Report Series. National Open Hearth Steel Committee. Iron and Steel Division. Metals Branch. American Institute of Mining, Metallurgical, and Petroleum Engineers

Spec Rep Soc Plant Prot North Jpn — Special Report. Society of Plant Protection of North Japan

Spec Rep Univ Ill Urbana Champaign Water Resour Cent — Special Report. University of Illinois at Urbana-Champaign. Water Resources Center

Spec Rep Univ Minn Agr Ext Serv — Special Report. University of Minnesota. Agricultural Extension Service

Spec Rep Univ MO Coll Agr Exp Sta — Special Report. University of Missouri. College of Agriculture. Experiment Station

Spec Rep Univ MO Columbia Agric Exp Stn — Special Report. University of Missouri, Columbia. Agricultural Experiment Station

Spec Rep Univ Wis Milwaukee Cent Great Lakes Stud — Special Report. University of Wisconsin, Milwaukee. Center for Great Lakes Studies

Spec Rep Wood Res Lab VA Polyt Inst — Special Report. Wood Research Laboratory. Virginia Polytechnic Institute

Spec Sci Rep FL Dep Nat Resour Mar Res Lab — Special Scientific Report. Florida Department of Natural Resources. Marine Research Laboratory

Spec Sci Rep Wildlife US Fish Wildlife Serv — Special Scientific Report. Wildlife. United States Fish and Wildlife Service

Spec Sci Rep Wildl US Fish Wildl Serv — Special Scientific Report. Wildlife. US Fish and Wildlife Service

Spec Ser Fla Dep Agric — Special Series. Florida Department of Agriculture

Spec Ser Int Assoc Volcanol Chem Earths Inter — Special Series. International Association of Volcanology and Chemistry of the Earth's Interior

Spec Sess Cotton Dust Proc — Special Session on Cotton Dust. Proceedings

Spec Sess Cotton Dust Res Proc — Special Session on Cotton Dust Research. Proceedings

Spec Steel — Special Steel

Spec Steels Rev — Special Steels Review

Spec Steels Tech Rev (Sheffield) — Special Steels Technical Review (Sheffield)

Spec Steel (Tokyo) — Special Steel (Tokyo)

Spec Stud Utah Geol Miner Surv — Special Studies. Utah Geological and Mineral Survey

Spec Symp Am Soc Limnol Oceanogr — Special Symposia. American Society of Limnology and Oceanography

Spec Symp Nat Radiat Environ — Special Symposium on Natural Radiation Environment

Spect — Spectateur

Spect — Spectator

Spect Act A — Spectrochimica Acta. Part A. Molecular Spectroscopy

Spect Act B — Spectrochimica Acta. Part B. Atomic Spectroscopy

Spectateur Milit — Spectateur Militaire

Spec Tech Assoc Publ — Special Technical Association. Publication

Spec Tech Assoc Publ TAPPI — Special Technical Association Publication. TAPPI

Spec Tech Publs Am Soc Test Mater — Special Technical Publications. American Society for Testing Materials
Spect Lett — Spectroscopy Letters
Spec Top Endocrinol Metab — Special Topics in Endocrinology and Metabolism
Spectr — Spectroscopy
Spectra Anal — Spectra Analyse
Spectra Anthro Prog — Spectra of Anthropological Progress
Spectra Biol — Spectra Biologie
Spectral Evol Galaxies Proc Workshop Adv Sch Astron Ettore — Spectral Evolution of Galaxies. Proceedings. Workshop. Advanced Schoolof Astronomy of the "Ettore Majorana" Centre for Scientific Culture
Spectral Line Shapes Proc Int Conf — Spectral Line Shapes. Proceedings. International Conference
Spec Transp Plann Practice — Specialized Transportation Planning and Practice
Spectra Phys Laser Tech Bull — Spectra-Physics Laser Technical Bulletin
Spectrochim Acta — Spectrochimica Acta
Spectrochim Acta A — Spectrochimica Acta. Part A. Molecular Spectroscopy
Spectrochim Acta B — Spectrochimica Acta. Part B. Atomic Spectroscopy
Spectrochim Acta Part A — Spectrochimica Acta. Part A. Molecular Spectroscopy
Spectrochim Acta Part A Mol Spectrosc — Spectrochimica Acta. Part A. Molecular Spectroscopy
Spectrochim Acta Part B — Spectrochimica Acta. Part B. Atomic Spectroscopy
Spectrochim Acta Part B At Spectrosc — Spectrochimica Acta. Part B. Atomic Spectroscopy
Spectrochim Acta Rev — Spectrochimica Acta Reviews
Spectrochim Acta Suppl — Spectrochimica Acta. Supplement
Spectrom Tech — Spectrometric Techniques
Spectrosc Adv Mater — Spectroscopy of Advanced Materials
Spectrosc Biol Mol — Spectroscopy of Biological Molecules
Spectrosc Charact Tech Semicond Technol — Spectroscopic Characterization Techniques for Semiconductor Technology
Spectrosc Eur — Spectroscopy Europe
Spectrosc Int J — Spectroscopy. International Journal
Spectrosc Lett — Spectroscopy Letters
Spectrosc Mol — Spectroscopia Molecular
Spectrosc Sci Ind — Spectroscopy in Science and Industry
Spectrosc Semicond — Spectroscopy of Semiconductors
Spectrosc Spectral Anal (Beijing) — Spectroscopy and Spectral Analysis (Beijing)
Spectrosc World — Spectroscopy World
Spectros Prop Inorg Organomet Compd — Spectroscopic Properties of Inorganic and Organometallic Compounds
Spectrum Int — Spectrum International
Specu — Speculum
Speculations Sci and Technol — Speculations in Science and Technology
Speculations Sci Technol — Speculations in Science and Technology (Complete Edition)
Specul Sci Technol — Speculations in Science and Technology
Spec Vol Can Inst Min Metall — Special Volume. Canadian Institute of Mining and Metallurgy
Spec Vol Ont Geol Surv — Special Volume. Ontario Geological Survey
SPEDA — Special Education
Sped Newsl — Special Education Newsletter
SPE Drill Completion — SPE [*Society of Petroleum Engineers*] Drilling and Completion
SPEE — Studies in Production and Engineering Economics
Speech Commun — Speech Communication
Speech Commun Abstr — Speech Communication Abstracts
Speech Found Am Publ — Speech Foundation of America. Publication
Speech Mon — Speech Monographs
Speech Monogr — Speech Monographs
Speech Pathol Ther — Speech Pathology and Therapy
Speech Teac — Speech Teacher
Speech Technol — Speech Technology
SPEER — Scientists and Professional Engineers Employment Registry
SPE Form Eval — SPE [*Society of Petroleum Engineers*] Formation Evaluation
SPEJ — Society of Petroleum Engineers. American Institute of Mining, Metallurgical, and Petroleum Engineers. Journal
SPE J — SPE [*Society of Plastics Engineers*] Journal
SPEJA — SPE [*Society of Plastics Engineers*] Journal
SPEJ Soc Pet Eng J — SPEJ. Society of Petroleum Engineers [*of AIME*] Journal
Spektr Anal Geol Geokhim Mater Sib Soveshch Spektrosk — Spektral'nyi Analiz v Geologii i Geokhimii. Materialy SibirskogoSoveshchaniya po Spektroskopii
Spektr Elektrofotom Radiolokatsionnye Issled Polyarn Siyanii — Spektral'nye Elektrofotometricheskie i Radiolokatsionnye IssledovaniyaPolyarnykh Siyanii i Svecheniya Nochnogo Neba
Spektrokhim Vnutri Mezhmol Vzaimodeistvii — Spektrokhimiya Vnutri- i Mezhmolekulyarnykh Vzaimodeistvii
Spektrometertag Vortr — Spektrometertagung. Vortraege
Spektrosk Derg — Spektroskopi Dergisi
Spektrosk Gazorazryadnoi Plazmy — Spektroskopiya Gazorazryadnoi Plazmy
Spektrosk Krist Dokl Soveshch Spektrosk Akt Krist — Spektroskopiya Kristallov. Doklady Soveshchaniya po SpektroskopiiAktivirovannykh Kristallov
Spektrosk Krist Mater Simp — Spektroskopiya Kristallov. Materialy Simpoziuma po SpektroskopiiKristallov
Spektrosk Krist Mater Simp Spektrosk Krist Akt Ionami — Spektroskopiya Kristallov. Materialy Simpoziuma po SpektroskopiiKristallov Aktivirovannnykh Ionami Redkozemel'nykh i Perekhodnykh Metallov
Spektrosk Mol Krist Mater Resp Shk Semin — Spektroskopiya Molekul i Kristallov. Materialy RespublikanskoiShkoly-Seminara
Spektroskop Tr Sib Soveshch — Spektroskopiya. Metody i Prilozheniya. Trudy Sibirskogo Soveshchaniyapo Spektroskopii
Spektrosk Svetorasseivayushchikh Sred Dokl Vses Soveshch — Spektroskopiya Svetorasseivayushchikh Sred. Doklady na VsesoyuznomSoveshchanii
Spektrum Wiss — Spektrum der Wissenschaft

Spekulation Erfahrung Abt II Unters — Spekulation und Erfahrung. Abteilung II. Untersuchungen
SPELD Info — SPELD [*Societe de Promotion a l'Etranger du Livre de Droit*] Information
Speleol Abstr — Speleological Abstracts
Speleol Biul Speleoklubu Warsz — Speleologia Biuletyn Speleoklubu Warszawskiego
SPE Monogr Ser — SPE Monograph Series (Society of Petroleum Engineers of AIME)
SPEND — Specifying Engineer
Spenser St — Spenser Studies
SPE Prod Eng — SPE [*Society of Petroleum Engineers*] Production Engineering
SPE Prod Facil — SPE (Society of Petroleum Engineers) Production and Facilities
SPERA — Sperimentale
Sper Arch Biol Norm Patol — Sperimentale. Archivio di Biologia Normale e Patologica
SPERE6 — Sbornik Provozne Ekonomicke Fakulty v Ceskych Budejovicich. Zootechnicka Rada
SPE Reg Tech Conf Tech Pap — SPE [*Society of Plastics Engineers*] Regional Technical Conference. Technical Papers
SPE Repr Ser — Society of Petroleum Engineers. American Institute of Mining, Metallurgical, and Petroleum Engineers. Reprint Series
Spe Rep Ser Ohio Agr Exp Sta — Special Report Series. Ohio Agricultural Experiment Station
SPE Reservoir Eng — SPE [*Society of Petroleum Engineers*] Reservoir Engineering
SPE Reservoir Eval Eng — SPE (Society of Petroleum Engineers) Reservoir Evaluation and Engineering
Sperim — Sperimentale. Giornale Critico di Medicina e Chirurgia
Sperimentale Arch Biol Norm e Patol — Sperimentale. Archivio di Biologia Normale e Patologica
Sperimentale Sez Chim Biol — Sperimentale. Sezione di Chimica Biologica
Sperry Technol — Sperry Technology
SPES — Studies in Philology. Extra Series
SPE Soc Pet Eng AIME Publ — SPE. Society of Petroleum Engineers of AIME [*American Institute of Mining, Metallurgical, and Petroleum Engineers*] Publications
SPE Tech Pap — SPE [*Society of Plastics Engineers*] Technical Papers
Spet It Mm — Memorie della Societa degli Spettroscopisti Italiana, Raccolte e Pubblicate per Cura del Prof. P. Tacchini
SPetr — Studi Petrarcheschi
SPE Trans — SPE [*Society of Plastics Engineers*] Transactions
Spets Stali Splavy — Spetsial'nye Stali Splavy
Spettatore Int — Spettatore Internazionale
Spettatore M — Spettatore Musicale
SPEX — Sozialwissenschaftliche Experten und Gutachter
Spez Aspekte Abwassertech Siedlungswasserwirtsch Kolloq — Spezielle Aspekte der Abwassertechnik. Siedlungswasserwirtschaftliches Kolloquium
Spez Ber Forschungszent Juelich — Spezielle Berichte. Forschungszentrum Juelich
Spez Ber Keraforschungsanlage Juelich — Spezielle Berichte der Keraforschungsanlage Juelich
SPF — Space Science Fiction Magazine
Spf — Sprachforum
SPF — Standard Pesticide File
SPFA — Bulletin. Societe des Professeurs Francais en Amerique
SPFB — Sbornik Pedagogicke Fakulty v Brne
SPFB — Sbornik Praci Filosoficke Fakulty Brnenske University
SPFBE — Sbornik Praci Filosoficke Fakulty Brnenske University
Spfdr — Springfielder
SPFFBU — Sbornik Praci Filosoficke Fakulty Brnenske University
SPFLA — Spaceflight
SPFO — Sbornik Pedagogicke Fakulty (Ostrava)
SPFOL — Sbornik Pedagogicke Fakulty (Olomouci)
SPFTM — Scripta Professorum Facultatis Theologicae Marianum
SPG — Studia Philosophica Gandensia
SPGAP — Studien zur Problemgeschichte der Antiken und Mittelalterlichen Philosophie
SPGCA — Survey of Progress in Chemistry
SPGKA — Senpaku Gijutsu Kenkyujo Hokoku
SPGL — Studien zur Poetik und Geschichte der Literatur
SPH — Social Process in Hawaii
SPh — Studiea Phonetica
SPh — Studies in Philology
SPH — Studies in Presbyterian History
SPHCA — Soviet Physics. Crystallography
SPHDA — Soviet Physics. Doklady
Sp Her — Sports Heritage
Sphere Mag — Sphere Magazine
Spheroid Cult Cancer Res — Spheroid Culture in Cancer Research
Sp Hist — Spiegel Historiael. Maandblad voor Geschiedenis en Archaeologie
SPHJA — Soviet Physics. JETP
SPhNC — Studies in Philology. University of North Carolina
SPhon — Studia Phonologica
SPHP — Studies in Philosophy and the History of Philosophy
SPhP — Symbolae Philologorum Posnaniensium
SPHQ — Swedish Pioneer Historical Quarterly
S Ph S — Studia Philologica Salmanticensia
SPhTh — Sciences Philosophiques et Theologiques
SPI — School Psychology International
SPI Annu Struct Foam Conf Proc — SPI [*Society of the Plastics Industry*] Annual Structural Foam Conference.Proceedings
SPI Annu Tech Conf — SPI [*Society of the Plastics Industry*] Annual Technical Conference

SPI Annu Urethane Div Tech Conf Proc — SPI [*Society of the Plastics Industry*] Annual Urethane Division Technical Conference. Proceedings

SPIB — Scripta Pontificii Instituti Biblici

SPIBB — Sbornik Pedagogickeho Institutu v Banskej Bystrici

S Picen — Studia Picena

SPIC Ind Eng Train Bull — SPIC [*Southern Petrochemical Industries Corp.*] Industrial Engineering andTraining Bulletin

Spic Rom — Spicilegium Romanum

SPIE Annu Tech Symp Proc — SPIE [*Society of Photo-Optical Instrumentation Engineers*] Annual Technical Symposium. Proceedings

SPIEC — Proceedings. Society of Photo-Optical Instrumentation Engineers

Spiegel Hist — Spiegel Historical

Spiegel Jb Propylaen Verlags — Spiegel. Jahrbuch des Propylaen-Verlags

Spiegel Let — Spiegel der Letteren

SPIE Int Soc Opt Eng Proc — SPIE [*Society of Photo-Optical Instrumentation Engineers*] International Society for Optical Engineering. Proceedings

SPIE J — SPIE [*Society of Photo-Optical Instrumentation Engineers*] Journal

SPIE Journal — Society of Photographic Instrumentation Engineers. Journal

SPIE Newsl — SPIE [*Society of Photo-Optical Instrumentation Engineers*] Newsletter

SPIE Proc — SPIE [*Society of Photo-Optical Instrumentation Engineers*] Proceedings

SPIE Semin Proc — SPIE [*Society of Photo-Optical Instrumentation Engineers*] Seminar Proceedings

SPIE Vol — SPIE [*Society of Photo-Optical Instrumentation Engineers*] Volume

SPIF — School Practices Information File

SPIFDN — International Commission for the Northwest Atlantic Fisheries. Selected Papers

SPIG — Sbornik Praci Pedagogickeho Institutu v Gottwaldove

SPIG Invited Lect — SPIG [*Symposium on Physics of Ionized Gases*] Invited Lectures

SpiH — Spiegel Historiael

SPI Int Cell Plast Conf Proc — SPI [*Society of the Plastics Industry*] International Cellular Plastics Conference. Proceedings

SPI Int Tech Mark Conf — SPI [*Society of the Plastics Industry*] International Technical/Marketing Conference

SPILA — Sports Illustrated

SPILB — Spiegel

Spill Sci Technol Bull — Spill Science and Technology Bulletin. Oils, Chemicals, Land, Marine

SPIMD — Siauliu Pedagoginio Instituto Mokslo Darbai

SPIN — Sbornik Pedagogickeho Institutu v Nitre

SPIN — Searchable Physics Information Notices

Spin Isospin Nucl Interact Proc Int Conf — Spin and Isospin in Nuclear Interactions. Proceedings. International Conference

Spinks Numi Circ — Spinks Numismatic Circular

Spinner Weber Textilveredl — Spinner, Weber, Textilveredlung

SPIO — Sbornik Praci Pedagogickeho Institutu v Ostrave

SPIOL — Sbornik Pedagogickeho Institutu v Olomouci

SPIP — Sbornik Pedagogickeho Institutu v Plzni

SPIPA — Scientific Papers. Institute of Physical and Chemical Research

SPIPL — Sbornik Pedagogickeho Institutu v Plzni

SPIR — Search Program for Infrared Spectra

Spir — Spiritualitas

SPI Reinf Plast Compos Inst Annu Conf Proc — SPI [*Society of the Plastics Industry*] Reinforced Plastics/Composites Institute. Annual Conference. Proceedings

Spirit — Spirit That Moves Us

Spirit Ind (Moscow) — Spiritus-Industrie (Moscow)

Spirit Mis — Spirit of Missions

Spirit Pilg — Spirit of the Pilgrims

Spirit Verkauf — Spirituosen-Verkauf

Spir Life — Spiritual Life

Spirt Likero Vodochn Promst Nauchno Tekh Ref Sb — Spirtovaya i Likero-Vodochnaya Promyshlennost. Nauchno-TekhnicheskiiReferativnyi Sbornik

Spir Tod — Spirituality Today

Spirto Vodochn Promst — Spirto-Vodochnaya Promyshlennost

Spirt Prom-St' — Spirtovaya Promyshlennost'

Spis Bulg Akad Nauk — Spisanie na Bulgarskata Akademiya na Naukite

Spis Bulg Geol Druzh — Spisanie na Bulgarskoto Geologichesko Druzhestvo

Spis Bulg Geol Druzhu — Spisania na Bulgarsoto Geologichesko Druzhestvo

Spis Nauchno-Issled Inst Minist Zemed Gorite — Spisanie na Nauchno-Issledovatelskite Instituti pri Ministerstvata na Zemedelete i Gorite

Spis Nauchnoizsled Inst Minist Zemed (Bulg) — Spisanie na Nauchnoizsledovatelskite Instituti pri Ministerstvoto na Zemedelieto (Bulgaria)

Spisok Rast Gerb Fl SSSR Bot Inst Vsesojuzn Akad Nauk — Spisok Rastenij Gerbarija Flory SSSR Izdavaemogo Botaniceskim Institutom Vsesojuznogo Akademii Nauk. Schedae ad Herbarium Florae URSS ab Instituto Botanico Academiae Scientiarum URSS Editum

SPI Struct Foam Conf Proc — SPI [*Society of the Plastics Industry*] Structural Foam Conference. Proceedings

Spisy Lek Fak J E Purkyne Brne — Spisy Lekarske Fakulty Univerzity J. E. Purkyne v Brne

Spisy Lek Fak Masaryk Univ (Brno) — Spisy Lekarske Fakulty Mesarykovy University (Brno)

Spisy Lek Fak Univ J E Purkyne Brne — Spisy Lekarske Fakulty University J. E. Purkyne v Brne

Spisy Pedagog Fak Ostrave — Spisy Pedagogicke Fakulty v Ostrave

Spisy Prir Fak Univ Brne — Spisy Prirodovedecke Fakulty Universita v Brne

Spisy Prirodoved Fak Univ Brne — Spisy Prirodovedecke Fakulty Universita v Brne

Spisy Prirodoved Fak Univ JE Purkyne Brne — Spisy Prirodovedecke Fakulty University J. E. Purkyne v Brne

Spisy Priroved Fak Univ J E Purkyne Brne — Spisy Prirodovedecke Fakulty University J. E. Purkyne v Brne

Spisy Vydavane Prirodoved Fak Massarykovy Univ — Spisy Vydavane Prirodovedeckou Fakultou Massarykovy University

Spis Zemed Izpit Inst Bulg — Spisanie na Zemedelskite Izpitatelni Instituti v Bulgariya

Spis Zemed Opitni Inst Bulg — Spisanie na Zemedelskite Opitni Instituti v Bulgariya

SPIU — Sbornik Praci Pedagogickeho Institutu, Usti Nad Labem

Spixiana Suppl (Muench) — Spixiana. Supplement (Muenchen)

Spixiana Z Zool — Spixiana. Zeitschrift fuer Zoologie

SPJ — Schlesisches Priesterjahrbuch

SPJSEY — South Pacific Journal of Natural Science

SPJUA2 — Sechenov Physiological Journal of the USSR

SPK — Schriften zur Paedagogik und Katechetik

SPKYB — Shih P'in Kung Yeh

SpL — Spiegel der Letteren

SPL — Studie a Prace Linguisticke

Splavy Redk Met — Splavy Redkikh Metallov

Splavy Redk Tugoplavkikh Met Osobymi Fiz Svoistvami Rab Vses — Splavy Redkikh i Tugoplavkikh Metallov s Osobymi FizicheskimiSvoistvami. Raboty Dolozhennye na Vsesoyuznom Soveshchanii po Splavam RedkiMetallov

SPLEB — Spectroscopy Letters

SPLEE2 — Studies in Plant Ecology

SPLi — Studia Pastristica et Liturgica

Sp Lib — Special Libraries

SPLID — SpeciaList

SPLK — Studie Prazskeho Linguistickeho Krouzku

SPLSA — Space Life Sciences

SPM — Sacrum Polonia Millenium

SPM — Salud Publica de Mexico

SPM — South Pacific Mail

SpM — Spectateur Militaire

Sp M — Spicilegio Moderno

SPM — Supervisory Management

SPMCA — Soviet Powder Metallurgy and Metal Ceramics

SPMGA — Speech Monographs

Sp Miss — Spirit of Missions

Sp Mon — Speech Monographs

SPMXA — Salud Publica de Mexico

SPN — School Product News

SP Nev Agric Exp Stn Coll Agric Univ Nev Reno — SP. Nevada Agricultural Experiment Station. College of Agriculture. University of Nevada-Reno

SPo — Sao Paulo. Revista do Arquivo Municipal

SPO — Spotlight

SPOA — Soviet Panorama

SPOFOR — Sportwissenschaftliche Forschungsprojekte

Sp o K — Sprog og Kultur

Spokane Bs — Spokane Business Examiner

SPol — Storia e Politica

Spold Kwartal Nauk — Spoldzielczy Kwartalnik Naukomy

Spolia Zeylan — Spolia Zeylanica

Spolia Zool Mus Haun — Spolia Zoologica Musei Hauniensis

SPOLIT — Sportliteratur

Spomenik SAN — Spomenik. Srpska Akademija Nauka i Umjetnosti

SpomSAN — Spomenik Srpske Akademije Nauka

Spom SANU — Spomenik. Srpska Akademija Nauka i Umjetnosti

Spondee Rev — Spondee Review

Spongia Cm Md — Commentarii di Medicina. Spongia

Spore Res — Spore Research

Sportarzt Sportmed — Sportarzt Sportmedizin

Sport es Testn — Sport es Testneveles

Sport Fish Abstr — Sport Fisheries Abstracts

Sport Fit Ind — Sport and Fitness Index

Sport Leis — Sport and Leisure

Sport Market Q — Sport Marketing Quarterly

Sportmed Aufgaben Bedeutung Menschen Unserer Zeit Dsch Sport — Sportmedizin. Aufgaben und Bedeutung fuer den Menschen in Unserer Zeit.Deutscher Sportaerztekongress

Sport Med J — Sport-Medical Journal

Sportnomed Objave — Sportnomedicinske Objave

Sport Rec — Sport and Recreation

Sport Rec Ind — Sport and Recreation Index

Sportrev Wien Fremdenbl — Sportrevue des Wiener Fremdenblatts

Sports and Ath — Sports and Athletes

Sport Sci Rev — Sport Science Review

Sports Hist Bull — Sports History Bulletin

Sports Ill — Sports Illustrated

Sports Illus — Sports Illustrated

Sports Med — Sports Medicine

Sports Med (Auckland) — Sports Medicine (Auckland)

Sports Med Train & Rehab — Sports Medicine, Training, and Rehabilitation

Sports 'n Spokes — Sports 'n Spokes Magazine

Sports Nutr News — Sports-Nutrition News

Sport Sociol Bul — Sport Sociology Bulletin

Sports Ret — Sports Retailer

Sports Turf Bull — Sports Turf Bulletin

Sportverletz Sportschaden — Sportverletzung Sportschaden

Sporulation Germination Proc Int Spore Conf — Sporulation and Germination. Proceedings. International SporeConference

Sposoby Zap Inf Besserebr Nositelyakh — Sposoby Zapisi Informatsii na Besserebryanykh Nositelyakh

Sposoby Zapisi Inf Besserebryanykh Nositelyakh — Sposoby Zapisi Informatsii na Besserebryanykh Nositelyakh

SPP — Studien zur Palaeographie und Papyruskunde

SPP — Symposium de Prehistoria de la Peninsula Iberica

SPPGA — Society of Economic Paleontologists and Mineralogists. Pacific Section. Guidebooks
SPPLB — Science and Public Policy
SPPMA — Southern Pulp and Paper Manufacturer
SPR — Slavistic Printings and Reprintings
SPR — Southern Poetry Review
Spr — Sprache
SPR — Studien zur Philosophie und Religion
Sprache Tech Zeit — Sprache im Technischen Zeitalter
Sprache und Datenverarb — Sprache und Datenverarbeitung
Sprague's J ME His — Sprague's Journal of Maine History
Sprakvetensk Sallsk i Uppsala Forhandl — Sprakvetenskapliga Sallskapets i Uppsala Foerhandlingar
SPRAM — Sao Paulo. Revista do Arquivo Municipal
Spraw — Sprawozdania
Spraw A — Sprawozdania Archeologiczne
Spraw Archeol — Sprawozdania Archeologiczne
Spraw Komis Fizjogr — Sprawozdanie Komisji Fizjograficznej
Spraw Kom Jez AU — Sprawozdania z Posiedzen Komisji Jezykowej Akademii Umiejetnosci
Spraw Opolskie Tow Przyj Nauk Wydz Nauk Med — Sprawozdania Opolskie Towarzystwo Przyjaciol Nauk. Wydzial Nauk Medycznych
Sprawozdania & Rozprawy Muz N Krakow — Sprawozdania i Rozprawy Muzeum Narodwego w Krakowie
Sprawozdania Czynnosci Posiedzen Pol Akad Umiejetnosci — Sprawozdania z Czynnosci i Posiedzen Polskiej Akademii Umiejetnosci
Sprawozdania Kom Hist Sztuki — Sprawozdania Komisji Historii Sztuki
Sprawozdania Kom Nauk PAN — Sprawozdania z Posiedzen Komisji Naukowych. Polskiej Akademii Nauk
Sprawozdania Posiedzen Kom Naukowych Pol Akad Nauk Krakowie — Sprawozdania w Posiedzen Komisji Naukowych Polaskiej Akademii Nauk w Krakowie
Spraw Panstw Inst Geol — Sprawozdania Panstwowego Instytutu Geologicznego
Spraw Posied Tow Nauk Warsz — Sprawozdania z Posiedzen Towarzystwa Naukowego Warszawskiego
Spraw Poznan Tow Przyj Nauk — Sprawozdania Poznanskiego Towarzystwa Przyjaciol Nauk
Spraw Pr Dzialu Chem Panstw Zakl Hig — Sprawozdania z Prac Dzialu Chemji Panstwowego Zakladu Higjeny
Spraw Pr Panstw Inst Farm — Sprawozdania z Prac Panstwowego Instytutu Farmaceutycznego
Spraw Pr Pol Tow Fiz — Sprawozdania i Prace Polskiego Towarzystwa Fizycznego
Spraw TNW — Sprawozdania z Posiedzen Towarzystwa Naukowego Warszawskiego
Spraw Tow Nauk Lwowie — Sprawozdania Towarzystwa Naukowego we Lwowie
Spraw Tow Nauk Toruniu — Sprawozdania Towarzystwa Naukowego w Toruniu
Spraw Wroclaw Tow Nauk — Sprawozdania Wroclawskiego Towarzystwa Naukowego
Spraw Wroclaw Tow Nauk Ser A — Sprawozdania Wroclawskiego Towarzystwa Naukowego. Seria A
Spraw Wroclaw Tow Nauk Ser B — Sprawozdania Wroclawskiego Towarzystwa Naukowego. Seria B
SprB — Sprakliga Bidrag
Sprechsaal Keram Glas Baust — Sprechsall fuer Keramik, Glas, Baustoffe
Sprechsaal Keram Glas Email — Sprechsall fuer Keramik-Glas-Email
Sprechsaal Keram Glas Email Silik Beil — Sprechsall fuer Keramik, Glas, Email, Silikate. Beilage
Sprechsaal Keram Glas Silik — Sprechsall fuer Keramik, Glas, Email, Silikate
Sprechsaal Keram Glas Verw Ind — Sprechsall fuer Keramik, Glas, und Verwandte Industrie
Sprenger Inst Rap — Sprenger Instituut. Rapporten
SPRF — Societe de Publications Romanes et Francaises
Springer Comput Sci — Springer Computer Science
Springer Lehrbuch Math — Springer Lehrbuch Mathematik
Springer Proc Phys — Springer Proceedings in Physics
Springer Semin Immunopathol — Springer Seminars in Immunopathology
Springer Ser Biophys — Springer Series in Biophysics
Springer Ser Chem Phys — Springer Series in Chemical Physics
Springer Ser Comput Math — Springer Series in Computational Mathematics
Springer Ser Comput Mech — Springer Series in Computational Mechanics
Springer Ser Comput Phys — Springer Series in Computational Physics
Springer Ser Electron Photonics — Springer Series in Electronics and Photonics
Springer Ser Electrophys — Springer Series in Electrophysics
Springer Ser Health Care Soc — Springer Series on Health Care and Society
Springer Ser Inform Sci — Springer Series in Information Sciences
Springer Ser Mater Sci — Springer Series in Materials Science
Springer Ser Nonlinear Dynamics — Springer Series in Nonlinear Dynamics
Springer Ser Nuclear Particle Phys — Springer Series in Nuclear and Particle Physics
Springer Ser Oper Res — Springer Series in Operations Research
Springer Ser Optical Sci — Springer Series in Optical Sciences
Springer Ser Opt Sci — Springer Series in Optical Sciences
Springer Ser Solid-State Sci — Springer Series in Solid-State Sciences
Springer Ser Soviet Math — Springer Series in Soviet Mathematics
Springer Ser Statist — Springer Series in Statistics
Springer Ser Statist Perspect Statist — Springer Series in Statistics. Perspectives in Statistics
Springer Ser Statist Probab Appl — Springer Series in Statistics. Probability and its Applications
Springer Ser Surf Sci — Springer Series in Surface Sciences
Springer Ser Synergetics — Springer Series in Synergetics
Springer Ser Wave Phenomena — Springer Series on Wave Phenomena
Springer Study Ed — Springer Study Edition
Springer Texts Electrical Engrg — Springer Texts in Electrical Engineering
Springer Texts Statist — Springer Texts in Statistics

Springer Tracts Modern Phys — Springer Tracts in Modern Physics
Springer Tracts Mod Phys — Springer Tracts in Modern Physics
Springer Tracts Nat Philos — Springer Tracts in Natural Philosophy
Springfield Sun Un & Repub — Springfield Sunday Union and Republican
Spr i Nord — Sprog i Norden
SprKJ — Sprawozdania z Posiedzen Komisji Jezykowej Towarzystwa Naukowego Warszawskiego
SprKUL — Sprawozdania z Czynnosci Wydawniczej i Posiedzen Naukowych Oraz Kronika Towarzystwa Naukowego Katolockiego Uniwersytetu Lubelskiego
SprLTN — Sprawozdania z Czynnosci i Posiedzen Lodzkiego Towarzystwa Naukowego
Spr Miedzyn — Sprawy Miedzynarodowe
Spr Miedzynar — Sprawy Miedzynarodowe
SPROE — Software Protection
Sprogf Aa — Sprogforeningens Aarsberetning
SprPAUm — Sprawozdania z Czynnosci i Posiedzen Polskiej Akademii Umiejetnosci
SprPTPN — Sprawozdania Poznanskiego Towarzystwa Przyjaciol Nauk
SprSUF — Sprakvetenskapliga Sallskapets i Uppsala Foerhandlingar
SprTNW — Sprawozdania z Posiedzen Towarzystwa Naukowego Warszawskiego
SprTT — Sprawozdania Towarzystwa Naukowego w Toruniu
SprV — Sprachkunst (Vienna)
Sprwoz (Warszawa) — Sprawozdania PMA [*Panstwowe Museum Archeologiczne*] (Warszawa)
SPS — Salzburger Patristische Studien
SPS — Space Stories
SPS — Specimina Philologiae Slavicae
SPS — Stratford Papers on Shakespeare
SPSBDR — Special Publications. Seto Marine Biological Laboratory. Series IV
SPSDC — Surface and Defect Properties of Solids
SPSEA — Soviet Physics. Semiconductors
SPSEE3 — Special Publication. South Australia Department of Mines and Energy
SPSMDQ — Special Publications. Society for General Microbiology
SPsp — Sprachspiegel. Schweizerische Zeitschrift fuer die Deutsche Muttersprache
SPSPCY — Specialist Periodical Reports. Spectroscopic Properties of Inorganic and Organometallic Compounds
SPSRA — Space Science Reviews
SPSU — Serial Publications of the Soviet Union, 1939-1957. A Bibliographic Checklist
SPSU — Studia Philologiae Scandinavicae Upsaliensia
S Psy — Social Psychology Quarterly
SPT — Openbaar Vervoer
SPT — Space Travel
SpT — Speech Teacher
SPT — Studies in Patristic Thought
SPTC — Studies in Physical and Theoretical Chemistry
SPTCDZ — Studies in Physical and Theoretical Chemistry
SPTN — Spill Technology Newsletter
SPTPA — Soviet Physics. Technical Physics
SPTPN — Sprawozdania Poznanskiego Towarzystwa Przyjaciol Nauk
SPU — Statutes of Practical Utility
Spud — Spudasmata
Spurenelem Symp — Spurenelement-Symposium der Karl-Marx-Universitaet Leipzig und der Friedrich-Schiller-Universitaet Jena
Spurenelem Symp Arsen — Spurenelement-Symposium. Arsen
Spurenelem Symp Nickel — Spurenelement-Symposium. Nickel
SPUTA — Scientific Papers. College of General Education. University of Tokyo
SPV — Space Adventures
SPVIEU — Spatial Vision
Spvry Mgt — Supervisory Management
SPW — Shipping World and Shipbuilder
SPW — Spaceway Science Fiction
SPWLA Logging Symp Trans — SPWLA [*Society of Professional Well Log Analysts*] Logging Symposium. Transactions
SPWVSRA — Selected Papers. West Virginia Shakespeare and Renaissance Association
SQ — Shakespeare Quarterly
SQ — Sociological Quarterly
SQ — Southern Quarterly
SQAW — Schriften und Quellen der Alten Welt
SQF — Socialist Thought and Practice
SQLW — Sinclair QL World
SQR — State Reports (Queensland)
SQS — Sammlung Ausgewaehlter Kirchen- und Dogmengeschichtlicher Quellenschriften
Squaring Inf Circle ICSTI Symp Proc — Squaring the Information Circle. ICSTI (International Council for Scientific and Technical Information) Symposium Proceedings
S Quart — Southern Quarterly
Squibb Abstr Bull — Squibb Abstract Bulletin
SR — New South Wales State Reports
SR — Saturday Review
SR — Schweizerische Rundschau
SR — Sciences Religieuses
SR — Sewanee Review
SR — Slave River Journal
SR — Slavic Review
SR — Slavonic Review
SR — Slovenska Rec
SR — Smithsonian Report
SR — Social Research
SR — Sociologia Religiosa
SR — Sociological Review
SR — Songwriter's Review
SR — Southern Review

SR — Southwest Review
SR — Sovjetskaja Rossija
SR — Statistical Reporter
SR — Statutory Regulations
SR — Stereo Review
SR — Studia Rosenthaliana
SR — Studies and Reports. Ben-Zvi Institute
SR — Studies in Religion
SR — Studies in Romanticism
SR — Studies in the Renaissance
SR — Studi Romagnoli
SR — Studi Romani. Istituto di Studi Romani
SR — Systematische Sammlung des Bundesrechts
SRA — Journal. Society of Research Administrators
SRA — Saturday Review of the Arts
SRA — Seatrade
SRA — Sillar-Revista Catolica de Cultura
SRA — Syria. Revue d'Art Oriental et d'Archeologie
SRAeDG — Schriften des Reichsinstituts fuer Aeltere Deutsche Geschichtskunde
SRA-J Soc R — SRA - Journal of the Society of Research Administrators
SR Arts — Saturday Review of the Arts
Sr Autobahn — Strasse und Autobahn
Sravn Elektrokardiol Mater Mezhdunar Simp — Sravnitel'naya Elektrokardiologiya. Materialy Mezhdunarodnogo Simpoziuma
SRAZ — Studia Romanica et Anglica Zagrabiensia
SRB — Senales-Buenos Aieres
SRBUD — Space Research in Bulgaria
SRC — Studies in Religion: A Canadian Journal
SRC — Studies in Religion and Culture
SRCA — Studies in Religion and Culture. American Religion Series
SRCAe — Studien zur Erforschung des Christlichen Aegyptens
SRCM — Speculum Religionis. Presented to Claude G. Montefiore
SRC Publ — SRC [Saskatchewan Research Council] Publication
SRC Rep — SRC [Saskatchewan Research Council] Report
SRCS — Sustancia. Revista de Cultura Superior
SRCT — Studiorum Romanicorum Collectio Turicensis
SRC Tech Rep — SRC [Saskatchewan Research Council] Technical Report
S Rd — Schweizerische Rundschau
SRDC Ser South Rural Dev Cent — SRDC Series. Southern Rural Development Center
SRDDD — Solar Energy R and D in the European Community. Series D
SRDRD — Solar Energy Research and Development Report
SRE — Saturday Review of Education
SRe — Science Review
SRE — Scripta Recenter Edita
SRE — Statistical Reporter
Sreden Med Rab — Sreden Meditsinski Rabotnik
Sred Med Rab — Sreden Medicinski Rabotnik
Sredneaziat Nauchno Issled Inst Geol Miner Syrya Uch Zap — Sredneaziatskii Nauchno-Issledovatel'skii Institut Geologii i Mineral'nogo Syr'ya. Uchenye Zapiski
Sredneaziat Otd Vses Akad Skh Nauk Sb — Sredneaziatskoe Otdelenie Vsesoyuznoi Akademii Sel'skokhozyaistvennykh Nauk. Sbornik
SREH — Sammlung Romanischer Elementar- und Handbuecher. II. Reihe Literarhistorische Elementarbuecher
S Rel Sc Rel — Studies in Religion/Sciences Religieuses
SRen — Studies in the Renaissance
SREND7 — Science Research News
SRetA — Studia Romanica et Anglica Zagrabiensia
SRev — Sayers Review
SRev — School Review
Srev — Sewanee Review
SRev — Slavic Review
SRev — Southwest Review
S Rev (Adel) — Southern Review (Adelaide)
S Rev (Baton) — Southern Review (Baton Rouge)
S Rev Lit — Saturday Review of Literature
S Rev Pub Adm — Southern Review of Public Administration
SRF — Scaenicorum Romanorum Fragmenta
SRFCEE — Fox Chase Cancer Center. Scientific Report
SRG — Schriften. Raabe-Gesellschaft
SRg — Studies in Religion
SRGG — Studien zur Relgion, Geschichte, und Geisteswissenschaften
SRGI — Selections. Records of the Government of India
SRH — Scriptores Rerum Hungaricarum
SRHE Bull — Society for Research into Higher Education. Bulletin
SRHE Newsl — Society for Research into Higher Education. Newsletter
S Rhodesia Geol Surv Bull — Southern Rhodesia. Geological Survey. Bulletin
SRI — British Steel
SRI — Statistical Reference Index
SRI — Sveriges Runinskrifter
SRICDS — Inter-American Tropical Tuna Commission. Special Report
SRIELA — Selected Reports: Publication of the Institute of Ethnomusicology of the University of California at Los Angeles
SRIIA — Silk and Rayon Industries of India
SRI J — SRI [Stanford Research Institute] Journal
SRIKMT — Soobshcheniya Respublikanskogo Istoriko-Kraevedceskogo Muzeia Tadzhikskoi SSR
SRIL — Studi e Richerche. Istituto di Latino
Sri Lan J Hum — Sri Lanka Journal of Humanities
Sri Lanka Assoc Adv Sci Proc Annu Sess — Sri Lanka Association for the Advancement of Science. Proceedings of the AnnualSession
Sri Lanka Fish Res Stn Bull — Sri Lanka. Fisheries Research Station. Bulletin
Sri Lanka For — Sri Lanka Forester

Sri Lanka Geol Surv Dep Econ Bull — Sri Lanka. Geological Survey Department. Economic Bulletin
Sri Lanka J Human — Sri Lanka Journal of the Humanities
Sri Lanka Lab Gaz — Sri Lanka Labour Gazette
SriLJH — Sri Lanka Journal of the Humanities
SRIM — Selected Research in Microfiche
SRI Pestic Res Bull — SRI [Stanford Research Institute] Pesticide Research Bulletin
SRISS — Scientia. Rivista Internazionale di Sintesi Scientifica
SRJKAK — Annual Report. Sado Marine Biological Station. Niigata University
SRL — HRIN [Human Resource Information Network] Special Reports Library
SRL — Saturday Review of Literature
SRL — Saturday Review of Politics, Literature, Science, and Art (London)
SRL — Securities Regulation Law Journal
SRL — Studies in Romance Languages
SRLF — Saggi e Ricerche di Letteratura Francese
SRLing — Studia Romanica et Linguistica
SRLP — Schriften zur Rechtslehre und Politik
SRLR — Securities Regulation and Law Reports
SRLUDT — Scientific Report. Laboratory for Amphibian Biology. Hiroshima University
SRMBDB — Marine Sciences Research Center [Stony Brook]. Special Report
SRMG — Paradoxographoi. Scriptores Rerum Mirabilium Graeci
SRMSDS — Montana. Forest and Conservation Experiment Station. Study Report
SRN — Saturn Science Fiction and Fantasy
SRN — Souvenir Nieuws
SRNB — Sociology. Reviews of New Books
SR (NSW) — State Reports (New South Wales)
SR (NSW) B & P — State Reports (New South Wales). Bankruptcy and Probate
SR (NSW) Eq — State Reports (New South Wales). Equity
Sr Nurse — Senior Nurse
SRO — Shakespearean Research Opportunities
SRO — Statutory Rules and Orders
SRo — Studi Romani
SRom — Studi Romani
SRP — Scriptores Rerum Prussicarum
SRP — Studia Rossica Posnaniensia
Srp Akad Nauka Umet Od Prir-Mat Nauka (Glas) — Srpska Akademija Nauka i Umetnosti Odeljenje Prirodno-Matematickikh Nauka (Glas)
Srp Akad Nauka Umet Od Teh Nauka Glas — Srpska Akademija Nauka i Umetnosti. Odeljenje Tehnickih Nauka. Glas
Srp Akad Nauka Umet Posebna Izdan Od Prir Mat Nauka — Srpska Akademija Nauka i Umetnosti Posebna Izdanja Odeljenje Prirodno-Matematickikh Nauka
Srp Arh Celok Lek — Srpski Arhiv za Celokupno Lekarstvo
Srp Arkh Tselok Lek — Srpski Arkhiv za Tselokupno Lekarstvo
SRPK — Schriften zur Religionspaedagogik und Kerygmatik
SRPO — Soobchtcheniia Russkago Palestinskago Obchtshestva
SRPR — Surtsey Research Progress Report
SRPS — Schriften zur Religionspaedagogik und Seelsorge
SRPSK — Schriften zur Religionspaedagogik und Seelsorge. Klassiker der Seelsorge und Seelenfuehrung
Srpsko Hem Drus Bull — Srpsko Hemiskog Drustvo. Bulletin
SRQ — State Reports (Queensland)
SRR — Schuh Kurier. Das Wirtschaftmagazin der Schuhbranche
SRR — State Regulation Report. Toxics
SRR — Studi Religiosi (Roma)
SRRA — Sage Race Relations Abstracts
SRRDS — Sacrae Romanae Rotae Decisiones seu Sententiae
SRREEC — Institute of Soil Science. Academia Sinica. Soil Research Report
SRRG — Studien zur Rechts-und Relgionsgeschichte
SRS — Salzburg Renaissance Studies
SRS — Social and Rehabilitation Service. Publications
SRS — Sociological Review (Staffordshire, England)
SRS — Strange Stories
SRSC — Saturday Review of the Sciences
Sr Sch — Senior Scholastic
Sr Schol — Senior Scholastic
SR-Sci — Saturday Review of the Sciences
Sr Sci — Senior Science
SR Sci Technol Inf — SR Science and Technology Information
SRSD — Saturday Review of Society
SRSI — Sikh Religious Studies Information
SRSIB — Salt Research and Industry
SRSMA — Scriptores Rerum Suecicarum Medii Aevi
SRSO — Saturday Review of Society
SR-Soc — Saturday Review of Society
SRSRDL — Soviet Scientific Reviews. Section D. Biology Reviews
SRSUE — Studies in Regional Science and Urban Economics
SRT — Skrifter fra Reformationstiden
SRTG-A — Science Reports. Tohoku University. Seventh Series. Geography
SRTS — Skrifter fran Reformationstiden. Uppsala
SRTUAW — Acta Geologica Taiwanica
SRu — Studi Rumeni
SRUEA — Structural Engineer
SRUTA — Soviet Rubber Technology
SRv — Southwest Review
SRVK — Studien zur Religioesen Volkskunde
SRVSB — Saturday Review of the Sciences
SRW — Saturday Review/World
SR (WA) — State Reports (Western Australia)
SRW Nachr — SRW [Siemens-Reiniger-Werke] Nachricht
SR/World — Saturday Review/World
SRWSDA — World Fertility Survey. Scientific Reports
SRZ — Studia Romanica Zagrabiensia
SS — Heinrich Schliemanns Sammlung Trojanische Altertuemer

SS — Scandinavian Studies
SS — Schip en Schade
SS — School and Society
SS — Science and Society
SS — Senior Scholastic
SS — Shakespeare Survey
SS — Sight and Sound
SS — Slovo a Slovesnost
SS — Smokeshop
SS — Social Studies
SS — Sociological Studies
SS — Sound and Sense
SS — Startling Stories
SS — Studia Serdicensia
SS — Studi Sardi
SS — Studi Semitici
SS — Studi Storici
SS — Sugar Series
SS — Syn og Segn
SSA — Social Science Abstracts
SSA — Social Security Administration
SSA — Social Security Administration. Publications
SSAA — Salzburger Studien zur Anglistik und Amerikanistik
SSAAAK — Studi Sassaresi. Sezione 3. Annali della Facolta di Agraria dell'Universita di Sassari
SSA/B — Bulletin. Societe Suisse des Americanistes
SSAB — Selective Soviet Annotated Bibliographies
SSAC — Studi Storici per l'Antichita Classica
SSAC — Sussidi allo Studio della Antichita Cristiana
SSACI — Studi Storici per l'Antichita Classica
SSAD — Starinar Srpskog Arkeoloskog Drustva
SSAEA — Safety Series. IAEA
SSAL — Scientific Serials in Australian Libraries
SSAL Suppt — SSAL [Scientific Serials in Australian Libraries] Supplement
SSAM — Settimade di Studio. Centro Italiano di Studi sull'Alto Medioevo
SSAOA — Soobshcheniya Shemakhinskoi Astrofizicheskoi Observatorii Akademiya Nauk Azerbaidzhanskoi SSR
SSAOI — Sacra Scriptura Antiquitatibus Orientalibus Illustrata
SSAPD — Symposium on Salt. Proceedings
SSar — Studi Sardi
SSARB — Sassar
S Sard — Studi Sardi
SSASH — Studia Slavica. Academiae Scientiarum Hungaricae
SSAW — Sitzungsberichte der Saechischen Akademie der Wissenschaften zu Leipzig. Philologisch-Historische Klasse
SSAWL — Sitzungsberichte. Saechsische Akademie der Wissenschaften (Leipzig). Philologisch-Historische Klasse
SSAWPH — Sitzungsberichte der Saechsischen Akademie der Wissenschaften zu Leipzig. Philosophisch-Historische Klasse
SSB — Reserve Bank of Australia. Statistical Bulletin
SSb — Skandinavskij Sbornik
SSB — Social Security Bulletin
SSB — Societe des Sciences, Lettres, et Arts de Bayonne. Bulletin
SSB — Sonneck Society Bulletin
SSB — Strenna Storica Bolognese
SSBLA — Sel'skokhozyaistvennaya Biologiya
SSBSEF — Scientia Sinica. Series B. Chemical, Biological, Agricultural, Medical, and Earth Sciences
SSC — Short Story Criticism
SSC — Signos. Estudios de Lengua y Literatura (Chile)
SSCA — Stockholm Studies in Classical Archaeology
SSCES — Stanford Studies in the Civilizations of Eastern Asia
SSCI — Social Sciences Citation Index
SSCISAM — Settimane di Studio del Centro Italiano di Studi sull'Alto Medioevo
SSCJ — Southern Speech Communication Journal
SSCR — Stockholm Studies in Comparative Religion
SSCRA — School Science Review
SSCSDJ — SIAM [Society for Industrial and Applied Mathematics] SIMS Conference Series
SSDPW — Schriftenreihe des Sudetendeutschen Priesterwerkes Koenigstein
SSE — North-Holland Series in Systems Science and Engineering
SSE — Serie Socio-Economica. Centro de Investigaciones Sociales [Bogota]
SSE — Sibirskaia Sovetskaia Entsiklopediia
SSE — Strangest Stories Ever Told
SSe — Studi Secenteschi
SSEA — Schriften der Studiengemeinschaft der Evangelischen Akademien
SSEL — Stockholm Studies in English Literature
SSELER — Salzburg Studies in English Literature. Elizabethan and Renaissance
SSELRR — Salzburg Studies in English Literature. Romantic Reassessment
SSEng — Sydney Studies in English
SSept — Studia Septentrionalia
SSF — Studies in Short Fiction
SSF — Super Science Fiction
SSF CHL — Societas Scientiarum Fennicae. Commentationes Humanarum Litterarum
SSFS — Samlingar Utgivna av Svenska Fornskriftssallskapet (Stockholm)
SSG — Schriften. Theodor-Storm-Gesellschaft
SSGED — Seikei-Saigai Geka
SSGIO — Studien zur Sprache, Geschichte, und Kultur des Islamischen Orients
SSGL — Studies in Slavic and General Linguistics
SSGMB — Sbornik Nauchnogo Studencheskogo Obshchestva Geologicheskii Fakul'tet Moskovskii Gosudarstvennyi Universitet
SSG/RGI — Rivista Geografica Italiana. Societa di Studi Geografici e Coloniali
SSGS — Stanford Studies in Germanics and Slavics
SSGVK — Schriften der Schweizerischen Gesellschaft fuer Volkskunde

SSGW — Sitzungsberichte. Saechsische Gesellschaft der Wissenschaften (Leipzig)
SSH — Site Selection Handbook
SSH — Skytteanska Samfundets Handlinger
SSH — Social Sciences and Humanities Index
SSH — Studia Slavica. Academiae Scientiarum Hungaricae
SSH — Studies in Society and History
SSHJ — Sources and Studies for the History of the Jesuits
SSHT — Slaskie Studie Historyczno-Teologiczne
SSHum — Social Sciences and Humanities Index
SSI — Short Story International
SSI — Social Science Information
SSIE — Smithsonian Science Information Exchange
SSI/ISS — Social Science Information/Information sur les Sciences Sociales
SSINA — Scientia Sinica
SSIOD — Solid State Ionics
SSIP — Secondary Students Information Press
SSIR — Skrifter Utgivna av Svenska Institutet i Rom
SSISO — Studi Semitici. Istituto di Studi Orientale. Universita degli Studi
SSJ — Southern Speech Journal
SSJM — United States Embassy. Summary of Selected Japanese Magazines
SSK — Schriftenreihe zur Sektenkunde
SSK — Sudan Silva (Khartoum)
SSKG — Schriften der Saechsischen Kommission fuer Geschichte
SSKGQ — Schoeninghs Sammlung Kirchengeschichtlicher Quellen und Darstellungen
SSKHF — Skrifter. Svenska Kyrkohistoriska Foereningen
SSKSF — Skriftserie. Sverige Kyrkliga Studiefoerbund
SSL — Scandoslavica
SSL — Spicilegium Sacrum Lovaniensis
SSL — Studi e Saggi Linguistici
SSL — Studies in Scottish Literature
SSL — Studies in Semitic Languages and Linguistics
SSLA — Sefar Ha-Sana Lihude Ameriqah
SSlav — Studia Slavica. Academiae Scientiarum Hungaricae
SSlav — Symbolae Slavicae
SSLF — Skrifter Utgivna. Svenska Litteratursallskapet i Finland
SSLI — Studies in Semitic Languages and Linguistics
SS Lit — Soviet Studies in Literature
SSLL — Stanford Studies in Language and Literature
SSLP — Scritti di Storia Letteraria e Politica
SSLSN — Skrifter Utgivna. Svenska Litteratursallskapet Studier i Nordisk Filologi
SSIU — Studia Slavica Upsaliensia
SSM — School Science and Mathematics
SSM — Seguridad Social Mexicana
SSM — Social Science Monographs
SSM — Space Science Fiction Magazine
SSM — Studies in Statistical Mechanics
SSMHA — Studia Scientiarum Mathematicarum Hungarica
SSML — Smith College Studies in Modern Languages
SSMLN — Society for the Study of Midwestern Literature. Newsletter
SSMOA — Scriptura Sacra et Monumenta Orientis Antiqui
SSMP — Stockholm Studies in Modern Philology
SSMSDZ — Social Science and Medicine. Part A. Medical Psychology and Medical Sociology
SSM Tech Rep — SSM Technical Report
SSMU — Studies. Southern Methodist University
SSN — Scandinavian Studies and Notes
SSN — Soil Science (New Brunswick, New Jersey and Baltimore)
SSN — Sonneck Society Newsletter
SSN — Studia Semitica Neerlandica
SSNY — Science and Society (New York)
SSO — Schweizerische Monatsschrift fuer Zahnheilkunde
SSO — Srednee Spetsial'noe Obrazovanie
SSO — Studia Semitica et Orientalia
SSO — Studier fra Sprog- og Oldtidsforskning
SSOED3 — Southwestern Entomologist. Supplement
SSOPK — Schriften der Synodalkommission fuer Ostpreussische Kirchengeschichte
SSORD — Software Review
SSOSM — Studi Storici dell'Ordine dei Servi de Maria
SSP — Selected Topics in Solid State Physics
SSP — Studi della Scuola Papirologica
SSPAV — Studi e Documenti per la Storia del Palazzo Apostolico Vaticano
SSPC Coat Eval Durability Conf — SSPC Coating Evaluation and Durability Conference
SSPDPT — Salzburg Studies. Poetic Drama and Poetic Theory
S Speech Commun J — Southern Speech Communication Journal
SSPh — Salzburger Studien zur Philosophie
SSPHA — Solid State Physics
SSpir — Sources de Spiritualite
SSpJ — Southern Speech Journal
SSPR — Space Solar Power Review
SSQ — Social Science Quarterly
SSQTA — Social Science Quarterly
SSR — SIA [Semiconductor Industry Association] Statistical Review
SSR — Social Security Reporter
SSR — Social Security Rulings
SSR — Sociology and Social Research
SSR — Studi e Materiali di Storia della Religioni
SSR — Studi Romani. Istituto di Studi Romani
SSRC — Social Service Review (Chicago)
SSRC Newsl — SSRC [Social Science Research Council] Newsletter
SSREA — Sight-Saving Review
SSRH — Scriptores Rerum Hungaricarum
SSRL — Stockholm Studies in Russian Literature
SSRWA — Soviet Science Review

SSS — Semitic Study Series
SSS — Super Science Stories
SSSA Spec Publ — SSSA [*Soil Science Society of America*] Special Publication
SSSA Spec Publ Ser — SSSA [*Soil Science Society of America*] Special Publication Series
SSSC — Studies in Surface Science and Catalysis
SSSCA — Soviet Soil Science
SSSCAE — Soviet Soil Science
SSSCD — Social Studies of Science
SSSEAK — Studi Sassaresi. Sezione 2. Archivio Bimestrale di Scienze Mediche e Naturali
SSSJD — Soil Science Society of America. Journal
SSS Journal — State Shipping Service of Western Australia. Journal
SSSKH — Samlingar och Studier till Svenska Kyrkans Historia
SSSP — Stockholm Studies in Scandinavian Philology
SSSQ — Southwestern Social Science Quarterly
SSSR — Southwestern Social Science Review
SSSYDF — Synergetics
SSt — Saechsische Staatszeitung
SST — Science Stories
SST — Shakespeare Studies (Tokyo)
SSt — Sowjet Studien
SSt — Spenser Studies
SST — Studies in Sacred Theology
SSTh — Studien zur Systematischen Theologie
SSTJA — Solid State Journal
SSTRD — Special Steels Technical Review
SST Sver Skogsvaardsfoerb Tidskr — SST. Sveriges Skogsvaardsfoerbunds Tidskrift
SStud — Shakespeare Studies
SSU — Studia Semitica Upsaliensia
SSUF — Sprakvetenskapliga Sallskapets i Uppsala Foerhandlingar
SSUR — Springfield Sunday Union and Republican
SsvOA — Sydsvenska Ortnamns-Saellskapets Arsskrift
SSW — Sunday Star [*Washington newspaper*]
SSz — Soproni Szemle
SSZBA — Sbornik Vysoke Skoly Zemedelske v Brne. Rada B
ST — Journal of Structural Engineering
ST — Science Teacher
ST — Signes du Temps
ST — Slovo a Tvar
ST — Speech Teacher
St — Star
ST — Statsoekonomisk Tidsskrift
ST — Stereo
St — Stereo Review
ST — Storm
ST — Strad
St — Strand
St — Strannik: Dukhovnyi, Ucheno-Literaturnyi Zhurnal
ST — Studia Taiwanica
ST — Studia Theologica
St — Studies
ST — Studi e Testi
ST — Studi e Testi. Biblioteca Apostolica Vaticana
St — Studi Storici
ST — Studi Tassiani
St — Studium
ST — Sunday Telegraph
ST — Sunday Times
ST — Svensk Tidskrift
StA — Raccolta di Studi Critici Dedicata ad Alessandro d'Ancona
Sta — Stampa [*newspaper*]
StA — Steuer-Archiv
STA — Strange Adventures
St A — Studia Archaeologica
StA — Studia Archaeologica
StA — Studi Anselmiana
STA — Sunday Telegraph (Australia)
STA — Syrie et Monde Arabe. Etude Mensuelle Economique, Politique, et Statistique
STAACT J — STAACT [*Science Teachers Association of the Australian Capital Territory*]Journal
Staatl Amt Atomsicherh Strahlenschutz DDR Rep — Staatliches Amt fuer Atomsicherheit und Strahlenschutz der DDR. Report
Staatl Materialpruefungsanst Univ Stuttgart Tech Wiss Ber — Staatliche Materialpruefungsanstalt an der Universitaet Stuttgart. Technisch-Wissenschaftliche Berichte
Staatl Tech Forschungsanst Finnl Publ — Staatliche Technische Forschungsanstalt. Finnland. Publikation
Staatl Zent Strahlenschutz DDR Rep — Staatliche Zentrale fuer Strahlenschutz der DDR. Report
Staatsanz Baden-Wuerttemb — Staatsanzeiger fuer Baden-Wuerttemberg
Staatsanz Rheinl-Pfalz — Staatsanzeiger fuer Rheinland-Pfalz
Staatsbl — Belgisch Staatsblad
Staatsbl K Ned — Staatsblad van het Koninkrijk der Nederlanden
Staatsbl Koninkrijk Ned — Staatsblad van het Koninkrijk der Nederlanden
Staatsbuerger-Beil Bayer Staatsztg — Staatsbuerger-Beilage der Bayerischen Staatszeitung
Staatsbuergerl Mag — Staatsbuergerliches Magazin
Staatsinst Angew Bot Hamburg Jahresber — Staatsinstitut fuer Angewandte Botanik. Hamburg. Jahresbericht
Staat und Wirt in Hessen — Staat und Wirtschaft in Hessen
Staat u Recht — Staat und Recht

Stability Control Theory Methods Appl — Stability and Control. Theory, Methods, and Applications
Stable Isot Proc Int Conf — Stable Isotopes. Proceedings. International Conference
Stab Solidif Hazard Radioact Mixed Wastes — Stabilization and Solidification of Hazardous, Radioactive, and Mixed Wastes
Sta Bull Oreg State Coll Agr Exp Sta — Station Bulletin. Oregon State College. Agricultural Experiment Station
Sta Bull Univ Minn Agr Exp Sta — Station Bulletin. University of Minnesota. Agricultural Experiment Station
StAC — Studi di Antichita Cristiana
Sta Circ Wash Agr Exp Sta — Station Circular. Washington Agricultural Experiment Station
Stadel Jb — Stadel-Jahrbuch
Staden-Jb — Staden-Jahrbuch
Stader Jb — Stader Jahrbuch
Stadler Genet Symp — Stadler Genetics Symposia
Stadler Genet Symp Ser — Stadler Genetics Symposia Series
Stadler Symp — Stadler Symposia
Stadtbauwelt Beitr Neuord Stadt & Land — Stadtbauwelt. Beitraege zur Neuordnung von Stadt und Land
Stadt- Gebaeudetech — Stadt- und Gebaeudetechnik
Stadt-LB — Stadt- und Landesbibliothek
Stadt-UB — Stadt- und Universitaetsbibliothek
Stadt (Wien) — Informationsdienst der Stadt (Wien)
Stad Z — Stadion. Zeitschrift fuer Geschichte des Sports und der Koerperkultur
Staedel Jb — Staedel-Jahrbuch
St Aeg — Studia Aegyptiaca
STAEKU — Schriftenreihe des Theologischen Ausschusses der Evangelischen Kirche der Union
Staff J (University of Reading) — Staff Journal (University of Reading)
Staffordshire Archaeol — Staffordshire Archaeology
Staff Pap — Staff Papers
Staff Pap P Minn Univ Dep Agric Appl Econ — Staff Paper P. Minnesota University. Department of Agricultural and Applied Economics
Staff Pap Univ Fla Food Resour Econ Dep Inst Food Agric Sci — Staff Paper. University of Florida. Food and Resource Economics Department. Institute of Food and Agricultural Sciences
Staff Pap Univ Florida Food Resour Econ Dep — Staff Paper. University of Florida. Food and Resources Economics Department
Staffs Hist — Staffordshire History
Stage Biochim Rapp Sci — Stage de Biochimie. Rapport Scientifique
St A H — Studies in American Humor
STAHA — Stahlbau
Stahlbau Rundsch — Stahlbau Rundschau
Stahlbau Tech — Stahlbau-Technik
Stahlbau Tech Wirtsch — Stahlbau in Technik und Wirtschaft
Stahl Eisen — Stahl und Eisen
Stahl Eisen Beih — Stahl und Eisen. Beihefte
Stahlla Misc Pap — Stahlla Miscellaneous Papers
Stainless Steel Ind — Stainless Steel Industry
Stainl Steel — Stainless Steel
Stain Tech — Stain Technology
Stain Technol — Stain Technology
Stako Porculan Keram — Staklo, Porculan, Keramika
Staleplavil'n Proizvod — Staleplavil'noe Proizvodstvo
Staleplavil'n Proizvod (Moscow) — Staleplavil'noe Proizvodstvo (Moscow)
Stal Nemet Vklyucheniya — Stal'e Nemetallicheskie Vklyucheniya
STAL Sci Tech Anim Lab — STAL. Sciences et Techniques de l'Animal de Laboratoire
St Altaeg Kul — Studien zur Altaegyptischen Kultur
STAM — Statistics in Medicine
St Am Renaissance — Studies in the American Renaissance
Standard Chartered R — Standard Chartered Review
Stand Ass Aust Aust Stand — Standards Association of Australia. Australian Standard
Stand Ass Aust Commercial Stand — Standards Association of Australia. Commercial Standard
Stand Ass Aust Miscell Pub — Standards Association of Australia. Miscellaneous Publication
Stand Bank — Standard Bank Review
Stand Chartered Rev — Standard and Chartered Review
Stand Chart Rev — Standard Chartered Review
Standesa — Standesamt
Standesztg Dtsch Apoth — Standeszeitung Deutscher Apotheker
Stand Fed Tax Rep CCH — Standard Federal Tax Reports. Commerce Clearing House
Stand Kach — Standarty i Kachestvo
Stand Kach (Sofia) — Standarti i Kachestvo (Sofia)
Stand Leist Agrikulturchem Agrarbiol Forsch — Stand und Leistung Agrikulturchemischer und Agrarbiologischer Forschung
Stand Methods Clin Chem — Standard Methods of Clinical Chemistry
Stand Methods Exam Dairy Prod — Standard Methods for the Examination of Dairy Products
Stand News — Standardization News
Stand Obraztsy Chern Metall — Standartnye Obraztsy v Chernoi Metallurgii
Stand Philip Per Ind — Standard Philippine Periodicals Index
Stand Phys Fitness Tests Magglinger Symp — Standardization of Physical Fitness Tests. Magglinger Symposium
Stand Qual — Standardisierung und Qualitaet
St Andrews Stud Hist Scot Archit & Des — St. Andrews Studies in the History of Scottish Architecture and Design
St Andrew Univ Sociol R — St. Andrew's University. Sociological Review
Stan Env't Ann — Stanford Environmental Law Annual
Stanf J Int — Stanford Journal of International Studies

Stanford Fr — Stanford French Review
Stanford French Rev — Stanford French Review
Stanford Ichthyol Bull — Stanford Ichthyological Bulletin
Stanford It Rev — Stanford Italian Review
Stanford J Internat Law — Stanford Journal of International Law
Stanford J Internat Studies — Stanford Journal of International Studies
Stanford J Int'l Stud — Stanford Journal of International Studies
Stanford J Int Stud — Stanford Journal of International Studies
Stanford La — Stanford Law Review
Stanford Law R — Stanford Law Review
Stanford Law Rev — Stanford Law Review
Stanford Lit Rev — Stanford Literature Review
Stanford L Rev — Stanford Law Review
Stanford M Bull — Stanford Medical Bulletin
Stanford Med Bull — Stanford Medical Bulletin
Stanford Mus — Stanford Museum
Stanford Research Inst Jour — Stanford Research Institute. Journal
Stanford Res Inst Pestic Res Bull — Stanford Research Institute. Pesticide Research Bulletin
Stanford Stud Geol — Stanford Studies in Geology
Stanford Stud Med Sci — Stanford Studies in Medical Sciences
Stanford Stud Psychol — Stanford Studies in Psychology
Stanford Univ Dep Civ Eng Tech Rep — Stanford University. Department of Civil Engineering. Technical Report
Stanford Univ Dep Mech Eng Tech Rep — Stanford University. Department of Mechanical Engineering. Technical Report
Stanford Univ Publ Geol — Stanford University Publications in the Geological Sciences
Stanford Univ Publ Geol Sci — Stanford University. Publications in the Geological Sciences
Stanford Univ Publ Univ Ser Biol Sci — Stanford University. Publications. University Series. Biological Sciences
Stanford Univ Publ Univ Ser Eng — Stanford University. Publications. University Series. Engineering
Stanford Univ Publ Univ Ser Geol Sci — Stanford University Publications. University Series. Geological Sciences
Stanford Univ Publ Univ Ser Math Astron — Stanford University. Publications. University Series. Mathematics and Astronomy
Stanford Univ Publ Univ Ser Med Sci — Stanford University. Publications. University Series. Medical Sciences
Stan J Intl L — Stanford Journal of International Law
Stan J Intl St — Stanford Journal of International Studies
Stan J Int'l Stud — Stanford Journal of International Studies
Stanki i Instrum — Stanki i Instrument
Stanki Rezhushchie Instrum — Stanki i Rezhushchie Instrumenty
Stan Law — Stanford Lawyer
Stan LR — Stanford Law Review
Stan L Rev — Stanford Law Review
Sta Note For Exp Sta (Idaho) — Station Note. Forest, Wildlife, and Range Experiment Station (Moscow, Idaho)
St Ans — Studia Anselmiana
St Ant — Studia Antoniana
StANT — Studien zum Alten und Neuen Testament
St Anth — St. Anthony Messenger
St Antonys Pap — St. Antony's Papers
Sta Pap For Exp Sta (Idaho) — Station Paper. Forest, Wildlife, and Range Experiment Station (Moscow, Idaho)
Stapp Car Crash Conf Proc — Stapp Car Crash Conference. Proceedings
STAR — Scientific and Technical Aerospace Reports
St A R — St. Andrews Review
Star — Starinar. Organ Arheoloskog Instituta Srpska Akademija Nauk
Star — Starship. The Magazine about Science Fiction
STAR — Stock Technical Analysis Reports
St Arab — Studia Arabica
Starch Hydrolysis Prod — Starch Hydrolysis Products
Starchroom Laundry J — Starchroom Laundry Journal
STARD — Starch/Staerke
STA Rept Abstr — Scientific and Technical Aerospace Reports Abstract
St Arist — Studia Aristotelica
STARR — Scientific and Technical Annual Reference Review
STARS — Simmons Teen-Age Research Study
STASD — Stainless Steel
Sta Sper Maiscolt (Bergamo) — Stazione Sperimentale di Maiscoltura (Bergamo)
STAT — Soumalaisen Tiedeakatemian Toimituksia
Stat — Stat. Bulletin of the Wisconsin Nurses' Association
Stat — United States Statutes at Large
Stat Ab (NZ) — Monthly Abstract of Statistics (New Zealand)
Stat Abs — Statistical Abstract. United States
Stat Bull — Statistical Bulletin. Metropolitan Life Insurance Company
Stat Bull Metrop Insur Co — Statistical Bulletin. Metropolitan Insurance Companies
Stat Bull Metrop Life Found — Statistical Bulletin. Metropolitan Life Foundation
Stat Bull Metrop Life Insur Co — Statistical Bulletin. Metropolitan Life Insurance Company
Stat Bull Metropol Life Ins Co — Statistical Bulletin. Metropolitan Life Insurance Company
Stat Bull US Farm Credit Admin Econ Anal Div — Statistical Bulletin. United States Farm Credit Administration. EconomicAnalysis Division
STATCAN — Statistics Canada Catalogue Online
State Agric Coll Agric Exp Sta Bull — State Agricultural College Agricultural Experiment Station Bulletin
State Agric Coll Oreg Eng Exp Stn Circ — State Agricultural College of Oregon. Engineering Experiment Station. Circular
State and Local Govt R — State and Local Government Review
State Bank Ind Mon Rev — State Bank of India Monthly Review
State Conn Health Bull — State of Connecticut Health Bulletin

State Court J — State Court Journal
State Dept Bull — United States State Department. Bulletin
State Fish Chief Secr Dep NSW Res Bull — State Fisheries Chief. Secretary's Department. New South Wales. Research Bulletin
State Geol Nat Hist Surv Conn Rep Invest — State Geological and Natural History Survey of Connecticut. Report of Investigation
State Geologists Jour — State Geologists Journal
State Geol Surv Kans Bull — State Geological Survey of Kansas. Bulletin
State Gov — State Government
State Govt — State Government
State Govt News — State Government News
State Hist Soc Wis Proc — State Historical Society of Wisconsin. Proceedings
State Hortic Assoc PA Proc — State Horticultural Association of Pennsylvania. Proceedings
State Hosp Q — State Hospital Quarterly
StateHSocNDColl — State Historical Society of North Dakota Collections
State Ill Div State Geol Surv Bull — State of Illinois. Division of the State Geological Survey. Bulletin
State Ill State Water Surv Div Circ — State of Illinois. State Water Survey Division. Circular
State Inst Tech Res Finl Publ — State Institute for Technical Research. Finland. Publication
State Inst Tech Res Finl Rep — State Institute for Technical Research. Finland. Report
State Inst Tech Res Finl Rep Ser 2 — State Institute for Technical Research. Finland. Report. Series 2. Metals
State Inst Tech Res Finl Rep Ser 3 — State Institute for Technical Research. Finland. Report. Series 3. Building
State Inst Tob Invest USSR Bull — State Institute for Tobacco Investigations. USSR. Bulletins
State Legis — State Legislatures
State Libn — State Librarian
State Libr — State Librarian
State Loc and Urb L Newsl — State, Local, and Urban Law Newsletter
State Locl & Urb L Newsl — State, Local, and Urban Law Newsletter
State Miner Profiles US Bur Mines — State Mineral Profiles. United States Bureau of Mines
State Mont Bur Mines Geol Mem — State of Montana. Bureau of Mines and Geology. Memoir
Staten Island As Pr — Staten Island Association of Arts and Sciences. Proceedings
Staten Island Inst Arts Sci Proc — Staten Island Institute of Arts and Sciences. Proceedings
Statens Husdjursfoers Swed Saertr Foerhandsmedd — Statens Husdjursfoersoek. Sweden. Saertryck och Foerhandsmeddelande
Statens Inst Byggnadsforsk Handl (Trans) — Statens Institut foer Byggnadsforskning. Handlingar (Translations)
Statens Inst Byggnadsforsk Natl Swedish Bldg Res Doc — Statens Institut foer Byggnadsforskning. National Swedish Building Research Document
Statens Lantbrukskem Kontrollanst Medd — Statens Lantbrukskemiska Kontrollanstalt. Meddelande
Statens Lantbrukskem Lab Medd — Statens Lantbrukskemiska Laboratorium. Meddelande
Statens Levnedsmiddelinst Publ — Statens Levnedsmiddelinstitut. Publikation
Statens Naturvetensk Forskningsraad Ecol Bull — Statens Naturvetenskapliga Forskningsraad. Ecological Bulletins
Statens Naturvetensk Forskningsrad Ekologikomm Bull — Statens Naturvetenskapliga Forskningsrad Ekologikommitter Bulletin
Statens Offentliga Utredn — Statens Offentliga Utredningar
Statens Provingsanst (Stockholm) Cirk — Statens Provningsanstalt (Stockholm). Cirkulaer
Statens Provingsanst (Stockholm) Medd — Statens Provningsanstalt (Stockholm). Meddelande
Statens Skadedyrlab Arsberet — Statens Skadedyrlaboratorium Arsberetning
Statens Tek Forskningsanst Finl Ber — Statens Tekniska Forskningsanstalt. Finland. Bericht
Statens Tek Forskningscent Forskningsrapp — Statens Tekniska Forskningscentral. Forskningsrapporter
Statens Tek Forskningscent Textillab Medd — Statens Tekniska Forskningscentral. Textillaboratoriet. Meddelande
Statens Vaeginst (Swed) Medd — Statens Baeginstitut (Sweden). Meddelande
Statens Vaeginst (Swed) Rapp — Statens Vaeginstitut (Sweden). Rapport
Statens Vaextskyddsanst Flygbl — Statens Vaextskyddansanstalt. Flygblad
Statens Vaxtskyddsanst Medd — Statens Vaxtskyddsanstalt Meddelanden
State Nurse Legis Q — State Nursing Legislation. Quarterly
State-of-the-Art Odor Control Technol — State-of-the-Art of Odor Control Technology
State of the Art Rev Occup Med — State of the Art Reviews. Occupational Medicine
State-of-the-Art Symp Energy Mater — State-of-the-Art Symposium on Energy and Materials
State Plann and Environ Comm Tech Bull — State Planning and Environment Commission. Technical Bulletin
State Rep NH Agric Exp Stn — State Report. New Hampshire Agricultural Experiment Station
State Res — State Research
State Sci Res Inst Tob Makhorka Ind USSR — State Scientific Research Institute for the Tobacco and Makhorka Industry. USSR
State Sel State To State Ion Mol React Dyn — State-Selected and State-to-State Ion-Molecule Reaction Dynamics
State Tax Guide CCH — State Tax Guide. Commerce Clearing House
State Univ Coll For Syracuse Univ Tech Publ — State University College of Forestry. Syracuse University. Technical Publication

State Univ NY Mar Sci Res Cent (Stony Brook) Tech Rep Ser — State University of New York. Marine Sciences Research Center (Stony Brook). Technical Report Series

State Vet J — State Veterinary Journal

State Wash Dep Fish Res Div Inf Bkl — State of Washington. Department of Fisheries. Research Division. Information Booklet

State Wash Dep Fish Res Div Inf Booklet — State of Washington. Department of Fisheries. Research Division. Information Booklet

Stat Gen — Statuta Generalia de Religiosa, Clericali, Apostolica Institutione

Static Electrif Invited Contrib Pap Conf — Static Electrification. Invited and Contributed Papers from the Conference

Static Electrif Proc Conf — Static Electrification. Proceedings. Conference

STATINF — Statistical Information System

Stat Instrum (Lond) — Statutory Instrument (London)

Statis — Statistiques

Statis Affaires Socs — Statistiques des Affaires Sociales

Statis Agric — Statistique Agricole

Statis and Econ Info Bul Africa — Statistical and Economic Information Bulletin for Africa

STATIS-BUND — Statistical Information System of the Federal Republic

Statis Enseignements — Statistiques des Enseignements

Statis et Etud Fins (Ser Bleue) — Statistiques et Etudes Financieres (Serie Bleue)

Statis et Etud Fins (Ser Orange) — Statistiques et Etudes Financieres (Serie Orange)

Statis et Etud Fins (Ser Rouge) — Statistiques et Etudes Financieres (Serie Rouge)

Statis et Etud Midi Pyrenees — Statistiques et Etudes Midi-Pyrenees

Statis Judiciaires — Statistiques Judiciaires

Statis Mhefte Rheinland-Pfalz — Statistische Monatshefte Rheinland-Pfalz

Statis Nachr (Austria) NF — Statistische Nachrichten (Austria). Neue Folge

Statis Neerl — Statistica Neerlandica

Statis Reporter — Statistical Reporter

Statist Abstr US — Statistical Abstract. United States

Statist Anal Donnees — Statistique et Analyse des Donnees. Bulletin de l'Association des StatisticiensUniversitaires

Statist Bull USDA — Statistical Bulletin. United States Department of Agriculture

Statist Canad Consumpt Prodn Invent Rubb — Statistics Canada. Consumption. Production Inventories of Rubber and Other Selected Sections

Statist Comput — Statistics and Computing

Statist Decisions Econom — Statistique et Decisions Economiques

Statist Distributions Sci Work — Statistical Distributions in Scientific Work

Statist Ecology Ser — Statistical Ecology Series

Statist Econ Normande — Statistiques pour l'Economie Normande

Statist et Develop Loire — Statistique et Developpement Pays de la Loire

Statist Et Finance Et Econ (Ser Orange) — Statistiques et Etudes Financieres. Etudes Economiques (Serie Orange)

Statist Et Financ (Ser Bleue) — Statistiques et Etudes Financieres (Serie Bleue)

Statist Et Financ (Ser Rouge) — Statistiques et Etudes Financieres (Serie Rouge)

Statist Et Midi-Pyrenees — Statistiques et Etudes Midi-Pyrenees

Statist Foreign Trade B — Statistics of Foreign Trade. Series B. Annual. Tables by Reporting Countries

Statist Hefte — Statistische Hefte

Statistical Register of SA — Statistical Register of South Australia

Statistical Register of WA — Statistical Register of Western Australia

Statist i Elektron-Vycisl Tehn v Ekonom — Statistika i Elektronno-Vycislitel'naja Tehnika v Ekonomike Naucno-Issledovatel'skii Institut po Proektirovanija Vycislitel'nyh Centrov i Sistem Ekonomiceskoi Informacii CSU SSSR

Statist Jb Dt Staedte — Statistisches Jahrbuch Deutscher Staedte

Statist M L — Statistical Methods in Linguistics

Statist Model Decis Sci — Statistical Modeling and Decision Science

Statist Neerlandica — Statistica Neerlandica

Statist Newslett Abstr — Statistical Newsletter and Abstracts. Indian Council of Agricultural Research

Statist Oboz — Statisticheskoe Obozrenie

Statist Paper — Statistics of Paper

Statist Papers — Statistical Papers

Statist Probab Lett — Statistics and Probability Letters

Statist Problems Control — Statistical Problems of Control

Statist R (Beograd) — Statisticka Revija (Beograd)

Statist Sect Pap For Comm (Lond) — Statistics Section Paper. Forestry Commission (London)

Statist Sinica — Statistica Sinica

Statist Soc J — Statistical Society Journal

Statist Theory Method Abstracts — Statistical Theory and Method Abstracts

Statist Trav Suppl B Mens — Statistiques du Travail. Supplement au Bulletin Mensuel

Statiszt Szle — Statisztikai Szemle

Stat Jahr — Statistisches Jahrbuch fuer die Bundesrepublik Deutschland

Stat Japan — Statistics on Japanese Industries 1982

Stat LR — Statute Law Review

Stat Mech — Statistical Mechanics

Stat Med — Statistics in Medicine

Stat Methods Med Res — Statistical Methods in Medical Research

Stat Nachrichtentheorie Ihre Anwend Vortr Int Semin — Statistische Nachrichtentheorie und Ihre Anwendungen. Vortraege Gehlten auf demInternationalen Seminar

STAT News — Science Teachers Association of Tasmania. Newsletter

Stat News Lett (New Delhi) — Statistical News Letter (New Delhi)

Statni Tech Knih Praze Vymena Zkusenosti — Statni Technicka Knihovna v Praze. Vymena Zkusenosti

Statni Vyzk Ustav Sklarsky Kradec Kralove Inf Prehl — Statni Vyzkumny Ustav Sklarsky. Kradec Kralove. Informativni Prehled

Statni Vyzk Ustav Stavbu Stroju Praha Behovice Tech Prirucky — Statni Vyzkumny Ustav pro Stavbu Stroju. Praha-Behovice. Technicke Prirucky

Stat Notes Health Plann — Statistical Notes for Health Planners

Statns Forsoegsmejeri Beret — Statens Forsoegsmejeri. Beretning

Stato Prospett Appl Ind Radiaz Nucl Congr Nucl — Stato e Prospettive delle Applicazioni Industriali delle Radiazioni Nucleari. Congresso Nucleare

Stato Soc — Stato Sociale

Stat R & O N Ir — Statutory Rules and Orders of Northern Ireland

Stat Rep — Statistical Reporter

Stat Rep Pollen Mold Comm Am Acad Allergy — Statistical Report. Pollen and Mold Committee. American Academy of Allergy

Stat Rev Wld Oil Ind — Statistical Review of the World Oil Industry

Stat Rptr — Statistical Reporter

Stat Social Inq Soc Ir J — Statistical and Social Inquiry Society of Ireland. Journal

Statsokon Tss — Statsoekonomisk Tidsskrift

Stat Sum Can Gas Assoc — Statistical Summary. Canadian Gas Association

Stat Suppl Eng Min J — Statistical Supplement to the Engineering and Mining Journal

Statsvet Ts — Statsvetenskaplig Tidskrift

Stat Textb Monogr — Statistics Textbooks and Monographs

Stat Theor Meth Abstr — Statistical Theory and Method Abstracts

Stat Theory Method Abstr — Statistical Theory and Method Abstracts

Stat Tidskr — Statistisk Tidskrift

Stat Tidskrift — Statistick Tidskrift

Statusber Dtsch Kaelte Klimatech Ver — Statusbericht des Deutschen Kaelte- und Klimatechnischen Vereins

Status Differ Ther Cancer — Status of Differentiation Therapy in Cancer

Stat Use Radiat Jpn — Statistics on the Use of Radiation in Japan

Status Future Dev Study Transp Prop — Status and Future Developments in the Study of Transport Properties

Status Perspect Nucl Energy Fission Fusion — Status and Perspectives of Nuclear Energy. Fission and Fusion

Statute L Rev — Statute Law Review

Statutory Invent Regist — Statutory Invention Registration

Statyba Archit — Statyba ir Architektura

Staubforschungsinst Hauptverb Gewerbl Berufsgenoss STF Rep — Staubforschungsinstitut des Hauptverbandes der Gewerblichen Berufsgenossenschaften. STF-Report

Staub J — Staub Journal

Staub-Reinhalt Luft — Staub, Reinhaltung der Luft

St Autobahn — Strasse und Autobahn

STAV — Studi sulla Tradizione Aristotelica nel Veneto

STAVA — Stavivo

Stavby Jadrovej Energ — Stavby Jadrovej Energetiky

Stavebnicky Cas — Stavebnicky Casopis

Stavrop Skh Inst Nauchn Tr — Stavropol'skii Sel'skokhozyaistvennyi Institut. Nauchnye Trudy

Stavrop Skh Inst Tr — Stavropol'skii Sel'skokhozyaistvennyi Institut. Trudy

StB — Stenografische Berichte. Fuenf Hauptversammlungen. Verband der Deutschen Juden

Stb — Steuerberater

StB — Studi sul Boccaccio

St Barbara Mus Nat Hist Contrib Sci — Santa Barbara Museum of Natural History. Contributions in Science

St Bar Rev — State Bar Review

St Ber G — Steuerberatungsgesetz

StBFranc — Studii Biblici Franciscani

StBFranc LA — Studii Biblici Franciscani. Liber Annuus

STBGA — Structure and Bonding

STBIB — Studia Biophysica

St Bibl Theol — Studies in Biblical Theology

St Bi Franc — Studium Biblicum Franciscanum Liber Annuus

St Biophys — Studia Biophysica

St Biz — Rivista di Studi Bizantini e Neoellenici

StBiz — Studi Bizantini e Neoellenici

Stb Jb — Steuerberater-Jahrbuch

Stbk — Stadtbaukunst

Stbl — Staatsblad van het Koninkrijk der Nederlanden

St Bl — Steuer und Zollblatt fuer Berlin

St Bl Nds — Steuerblatt fuer das Land Niedersachsen

St Bl Schl H — Steuerblatt fuer das Land Schleswig-Holstein

StBM — Stuttgarter Biblische Monographien

St Bonaventure Sci Stud — St. Bonaventure Science Studies

StBoT — Studien zu den Bogazkoey-Texten

St BRD — Statistik der Bundesrepublik Deutschland

StBSt — Stuttgarter Bibelstudien

STBT — Straits Times. Business Times

St BT — Studien zu den Bogaskoey-Texten

STC — Sales Tax Cases

STC — Simon's Tax Cases

StC — Studia Catholica

StC — Studia Celtica

STC — Studies in Twentieth Century

St Can Lit — Studies in Canadian Literature

St Cart — Studia Cartesiana

St Catt — Studi Cattolici

StCau — Studia Caucasica

St Cerc Mat Fiz — Studii si Cercetari de Matematica si Fizica

StCILF — Studii si Cercetari de Istorie Literara si Folclor

St C Istor — Studii si Cercetari de Istorie Artei

St C Istor — Studii si Cercetari de Istoria Artei. Seria Arta Plastica

St C Istor — Studii si Cercetari de Istorie Veche si Arheologie

St Cl — Studii Clasice

StCL — Studii si Cercetari Lingvistice

St Clas — Studii Clasice

St Class Or — Studia Classica et Orientalia

StClOr — Studi Classici e Orientali

St C Num — Studii si Cercetari de Numismatica

St Com — Studii si Comunicari. Istorie, Stintele Naturii
St Com — Studii si Comunicari. Muzeul Brukenthal
St Comp Int Devel — Studies in Comparative International Development
St Cons — Studies in Conservation
St Copt — Studi Copti
StCrN — Stephen Crane Newsletter
Stcrt — Nederlandse Staatscourant
St CS — Studies in Contemporary Satire
StCSF — Studii si Cercetari Stiintifice. Filologie
St Ct J — State Court Journal
StD — Romance Studies Presented to William Norton Dey
STD — Sports Trainers Digest
STD — Standaard. Dagblad voor Staatkundige, Matschappelijke, en Economische Belangen
Std — Studia
StD — Studi Danteschi
StD — Studies and Documents
STD — Training and Development Journal
STD Abstr Bib — Sexually Transmitted Diseases. Abstracts and Bibliography
St Del — Studia Delitzschiana
St Dem — Studia Demograficzne
STDHA — Staedtehygiene
St di Filol Mod — Studi di Filologia Moderna
STDJ — Studies on the Texts of the Desert of Judah
St DKG — Studien zur Deutschen Kunstgeschichte
STDNA — ASTM [*American Society for Testing and Materials*] Standardization News
Std Obraztsy Chern Metall — Standartnye Obraztsy v Chernoi Metallurgii
St Doc — Studia et Documenta Historiae et Iuris
St Doc Hist Iur — Studia et Documenta Historiae et Iuris
St DR — Statistik des Deutschen Reichs
STD Stat Let — Sexually Transmitted Disease Statistical Letter
St Dziej Kosc Kat — Studia z Dziejow Kosciola Katolickiego
STE — Stahl und Eisen. Zeitschrift fuer Technik und Wissenschaft der Herstellung und Verarbeitung von Eisen und Stahl
Ste — Steaua
St E — Studienreihe Englisch
StE — Studies in Honor of A. Marshall Elliott
StE — Studi Etruschi
STEADG — Sciences et Techniques de l'Eau
Steads R — Stead's Review
Steam and Heat Eng — Steam and Heating Engineer
Steam Eng — Steam Engineer
Steam Fuel Users J — Steam and Fuel Users' Journal
Steam Heat Eng — Steam and Heating Engineer
Steam Heat Engr — Steam and Heating Engineer
Steam Plant Eng — Steam Plant Engineering
Steam Pwr — Steam Power
Steamusers Fuel Users J — Steamusers' and Fuel Users' Journal
St Ebla — Studi Eblaiti
Stechert-Hafner Bk News — Stechert-Hafner Book News
STEDA — Steroids
Stedebouw & Vlkshuisvest — Stedebouw en Volkshuisvesting
Ste Doc di Stor e di Diritto — Studi e Documenti di Storia e Diritto
Steel Am — Steel and America
Steel Cast Res Trade Assoc Annu Conf — Steel Castings Research and Trade Association. Annual Conference
Steel Cast Res Trade Assoc Monogr — Steel Castings Research and Trade Association. Monograph
Steel Const — Steel Construction
Steel Constr — Steel Construction
Steel Fabric J — Steel Fabrication Journal
Steel Fabr J — Steel Fabrication Journal
Steel Founders' Res J — Steel Founders' Research Journal
Steel Furn Mon — Steel Furnace Monthly
Steel Horiz — Steel Horizons
Steel Ind — World Steel Industry. Into and Out of the 1990's
Steel Ind Energy Crisis Proc C C Furnas Meml Conf — Steel Industry and the Energy Crisis. Proceedings. C. C. Furnas Memorial Conference
Steel Ind Environ Proc CC Furnas Meml Conf — Steel Industry and the Environment. Proceedings. C.C. Furnas Memorial Conference
Steel Ind Jpn Annu — Steel Industry of Japan Annual
Steel Int — Steel International
Steelmaking Conf Proc — Steelmaking Conference Proceedings
Steelmaking Proc — Steelmaking Proceedings
Steel Mater Technol — Steel and Materials Technology
Steel Met Int — Steels and Metals International
Steel Met Mag — Steel and Metals Magazine
Steel Process — Steel Processing
Steel Process Convers — Steel Processing and Conversion
Steel Res — Steel Research
Steel Rev — Steel Review
Steel Stat — Steel Statistics for Europe
Steel Stat Q — Quarterly Bulletin of Steel Statistics for Europe
Steel Times Int — Steel Times International
Steel USSR — Steel in the USSR
Steenbock Symp — Steenbock Symposium
Steenstr — Steenstrupia
STEIA — Stahl und Eisen
Steiermaerk Z — Steiermaerkische Zeitschrift
Steierm Ggn Mont Vr B — Bericht des Geognostisch-Montanistischen Vereines fuer Steiermark
Steierm Mt — Mittheilungen des Naturwissenschaftlichen Vereins fuer Steiermark
Steinbeck M — Steinbeck Monograph Series
Steinbeck Q — Steinbeck Quarterly

SteinbQ — Steinbeck Quarterly
Steine Erdengewinnung Dtschl Vortr Fachtag — Steine- und Erdengewinnung in Deutschland. Vortraege der Fachtagung
Steiner Tb — Rudolf Steiner Taschenbuchausgaben
Steinind Steinstrassenbau — Steinindustrie und Steinstrassenbau
Stein-Ind Strassenbau — Stein-Industrie und -Strassenbau
Steinkohlenbergbauver Kurznachr — Steinkohlenbergbauverein Kurznachrichten
SteiQ — Steinbeck Quarterly
Steirische Beitr Hydrogeol — Steirische Beitraege zur Hydrogeologie
Steirisch Imkerbote — Steirischer Imkerbote
St Ek — Studiea Ekonomiczne
Steklo & Ker — Steklo i Keramika
Stekloemal Emal Met — Stekloemal i Emalirovanie Metallov
Steklo i Keram — Steklo i Keramika
Steklo Inf Byull Vses Nauchno Issled Inst Stekla — Steklo. Informatsionnyi Byulleten Vsesoyuznogo Nauchno-Issledovatel'skogo Instituta Stekla
Steklo Keram — Steklo i Keramika
Stekloobraznoe Sostoyanie Katal Krist Stekla — Stekloobraznoe Sostoyanie. Katalizirovannaya Kristallizatsiya Stekla
Stekloobraznoe Sostoyanie Tr Vses Soveshch — Stekloobraznoe Sostoyanie. Trudy Vsesoyuznogo Soveshchaniya
Stekloplast Steklovolokno Obz Inv — Stekloplastiki i Steklovolokno. Obzornaya Informatsiya
Steklo Sitally Silik — Steklo, Sitally, i Silikaty
Steklo Sitally Silik Mater — Steklo, Sitally, i Silikatnye Materialy
Steklo Tr Gos Nauchno Issled Inst Stekla — Steklo. Trudy Gosudarstvennogo Nauchno-Issledovatel'skogo Instituta Stekla
Steklov Math Inst Preprint — V. A. Steklov Mathematical Institute Preprint
Stekolnaya Keram Promst — Stekol'naya i Keramicheskaya Promyshlennost
Stekol'naya Prom-St — Stekol'naya Promyshlennost
STEL — Sunday Telegraph
STELB — Stereo Review
STELDF — Science and Technology Libraries
Stellar Atmos Classical Models — Stellar Atmospheres. Beyond Classical Models
Stellar Evol Lect Summer Inst Astron Astrophys — Stellar Evolution. Based on Lectures Given at the Summer Institute for Astronomy and Astrophysics
Stellenbosse Stud — Stellenbosse Student
STEM — Science and Technology Employment
SteM — Studi e Materiali di Archeologia e Numismatica
St e Mat — Studi e Materiali di Storia della Religioni
St e Mat Stor Rel — Studi e Materiali de Storia delle Religioni
STEN — Societa Tipografico Editrice Nazionale
St Enc — Study Encounter
Sten Cath — Stenoniana Catholica
Stendhal Cl — Stendhal Club
St Engl Lit — Studies in English Literature
Stenton — Stenton. Rolls of the Justices in Eyre
Stenton G — Rolls of the Justices in Eyre for Gloucestershire, Worcestershire, and Staffordshire
Stenton Y — Rolls of the Justices in Eyre in Yorkshire
STeol — Studii Teologice
Stephen F Austin State Coll Sch For Bull — Stephen F. Austin State College. School of Forestry. Bulletin
STER — Sterna
Stereo — Stereo Review
Stereochem Fundam Methods — Stereochemistry. Fundamentals and Methods
Stereochem Organomet Inorg Compd — Stereochemistry of Organometallic and Inorganic Compounds
Stereol Iugosl — Stereologia Iugoslavica
Stereo R — Stereo Review
Stereosel Synth Nat Prod Proc Workshop Conf Hoechst — Stereoselective Synthesis of Natural Products. Proceedings. Workshop ConferenceHoechst
Stereosel Synth Part A — Stereoselective Synthesis. Part A
Stereosel Synth Part B — Stereoselective Synthesis. Part B
Stereotactic Funct Neurosurg — Stereotactic and Functional Neurosurgery
St Eriks Ab — Sankt Eriks Arsbok
Steril Med Prod Prod Int Kilmer Meml Conf — Sterilization of Medical Products. Proceedings. International Kilmer Memorial Conference on the Sterilization of Medical Products
Steroid Horm — Steroid Hormones
Steroids Lipids Res — Steroids and Lipids Research
Steroids Neuronal Act — Steroids and Neuronal Activity
Steroids Suppl — Steroids. Supplement
STES Newsl — STES [*Seasonal Thermal Energy Storage*] Newsletter
St Et Bll S In Mn — Bulletin de la Societe de l'Industrie Minerale. St. Etienne
Stethoscope Va Med Gaz — Stethoscope and Virginia Medical Gazette
StEtr — Studi Etruschi
St Et S In Mn Bll — Bulletin de la Societe de l'Industrie Minerale. St. Etienne
Stetson L Rev — Stetson Law Review
Stett E Ztg — Entomologische Zeitung. Herausg. v. d. Entomologischen Vereine zu Stettin
Stettin Ent Ztg — Stettiner Entomologische Zeitung
Stettin Genanz — Stettiner Generalanzeiger
STEUA — Steuerungstechnik
Steuer u Wirtsch — Steuer und Wirtschaft
StEv — Studia Evangelica
Stevens Ind — Stevens Indicator
Stevens Inst Technol (Hoboken NJ) Davidson Lab Rep — Stevens Institute of Technology (Hoboken, New Jersey). Davidson Laboratory. Report
Stew Dig — Stewart's Digest of Decisions of Law and Equity
S Texas LJ — South Texas Law Journal
S Tex LJ — South Texas Law Journal
STF — Soviet Studies. A Quarterly Journal on the USSR and Eastern Europe
STF — Strange Fantasy
STF — Studi e Testi Francescani

StF — Studi Filosofici
STFG — Schriften und Vortraege im Rahmen der Theologischen Fakultaet der Universitaet Graz
StFil — Studia Filozoficzne
St Fil — Studi Filosofici
St Fil Cl — Studi Italiani di Filologia Classica
StFK — Studies in Honor of Frederick Klaeber
STFM — Societe des Textes Francais Modernes
St Form Sp — Studies in Formative Spirituality
St For Note Calif Div For — State Forest Notes. California Division of Forestry
STFPA — Strahlenschutz in Forschung und Praxis
StFr — Studi Francescani
St Fr B — Studi Francescani. Firenze. Biblioteca
STF Rep — STF [Staubforschungsinstitut] Report
St Fr T — Studi Francesi. Torino
St Furrow — Straight Furrow
STG — State Government
STG — Studien. Tijdschrift voor Godsdienst. Wetenschap en Letteren. s'Hertogenbosch
StG — Studi Germanici
StG — Studium Generale
STG — Sydney Tourist Guide
StGAK — Studien zur Germanistik, Anglistik und Komparatistik
St Gal B — Bericht ueber die Thaetigkeit der St. Gallischen Naturwissenschaftlichen Gesellschaft
StGB — Studies Aangeboden Aan. Gerard Brom
STGEA — Studium Generale
St Gen — Studium Generale. Zeitschrift fuer die Einheit der Wissenschaften in Zusammenhang ihrer Begriffsbildung und Forschungsmethoden
St Genuensi — Studi Genuensi
St Ghis — Studia Ghisleriana
St Ghis LFH — Studia Ghisleriana. Studi Letterari-Filosofici-Historici
StGKA — Studien zur Geschichte und Kultur des Altertums
STGL — Studien zur Theologie des Geistlichen Lebens
STGMA — Studien und Texte zur Geistesgeschichte des Mittelalters
StGR — French Mind. Studies in Honor of Gustave Rudler
Stgr — Studia Grammatica
St Gra — Studia Gratiana
St Gr I — Studi di Grammatica Italiana
St Griech Lat Gramtk — Curtius' Studien zur Griechischen und Lateinischen Grammatik
St GS — Studien zur Germania Sacra
St G St — Sankt-Gabrieler Studien
StGThK — Studien zur Geschichte der Theologie und der Kirche
STGZM — Sbornik Trudov Gosudarstvennogo Zoologicheskogo Muzeia
STh — Studia Theologica
Sth Afr — Southern Africa
STH Ber — STH (Institut fuer Strahlenhygiene) Berichte
STHEA — Steam and Heating Engineer
StHefte — Statistische Hefte
St Hell — Studia Hellenistica
StHG — Seventeenth Century Studies Presented to Sir Herbert Grierson
St Hib — Studia Hibernica
STHJC — Studia et Textus Historiae Juris Canonici
S Th KAB — Schriften des Theologischen Konvents Augsburgischen Bekenntnisses
Sthn Afr Fam Pract — Southern African Family Practice
Sthn Afr Text — Southern Africa Textiles
Sthn Birds — Southern Birds
STHP — Shih-Ta Hsueh-Pao
STHPD — Shih-Ta Hsueh-Pao
STHRD — Solar Thermal Report
Sth Rev — Southern Review
SThU — Schweizerische Theologische Umschau
St Hum — Studies in the Humanities
STHV — Science, Technology, and Human Values
Sthwest J Anthrop — Southwestern Journal of Anthropology
SThZ — Schweizerische Theologische Zeitschrift
StI — Studia Islandica
StI — Studies: An Irish Quarterly Review of Letters, Philosophy, and Science
StI — Studi Ispanici
StI — Studi Italiani
Sticht Bosbouwproefsta "Dorschkamp" Ber — Stichting Bosbouwproefstation "De Dorschkamp." Berichten
Sticht Bosbouwproefsta "Dorschkamp" Korte Meded — Stichting Bosbouwproefstation "De Dorschkamp." Korte Mededelingen
Sticht Bosbouwproefsta "Dorschkamp" Uitv Versl — Stichting Bosbouwproefstation "De Dorschkamp." Uitvoerige Verslagen
Sticht Bosbouwproefstn "De Dorschkamp" Korte Meded — Stichting Bosbouwproefstation "De Dorschkamp." Korte Mededeling
Sticht Coord Cult Onderz Broodgraan Jaarb — Stichting voor Coordinate van Cultuur en Onderzoek van Broodgraan Jaarboekje
Sticht Energieonderz Cent Ned ECN Rep — Stichting Energieonderzoek Centrum Nederland. ECN Report
Sticht Energieonderz Cent Ned Rep — Stichting Energieonderzoek Centrum Nederland. Report
Sticht Fundam Onderz Mater Jaarb — Stichting voor Fundamenteel Onderzoek der Materie. Jaarboek
Sticht Inst Kernphys Onderz Jaarb — Stichting Instituut voor Kernphysisch Onderzoek. Jaarboek
Sticht Inst Pluimveeonderz Het Spelderholt Jaarversl — Stichting Instituut voor Pluimveeonderzoek "Het Spelderholt" Jaarverslag
Sticht Inst Pluimveeonderz Spelderholt Jaarversl — Stichting Instituut voor Pluimveeonderzoek "Het Spelderholt" Jaarverslag
STI Database — Software Tool Information Database
StIF — Studi Italiani di Filologia Classica

Stiftelsens Aabo Akad Forskningsinst Medd — Stiftelsens foer Aabo Akademi Forskningsinstitut. Meddelanden
Stifter Jb — Stifter-Jahrbuch
Stift Hamburg Ku Samml — Erwerbungen. Stiftung zur Foerderung der Hamburgischen Kunstsammlungen
St I I — Studien zur Indologie und Iranistik
STIIBO — Sbornik Trudov Nauchno-Issledovatel'skogo Instituta Travmatologii i Ortopedii Gruzinskoi SSR
Stiinta Sol — Stiinta Solului
Stiinte Tehnol Ailment — Stiinte si Tehnologii Alimentare
Stikstof Engl Ed — Stikstonf (English Edition)
StIL — Studi. Istituto Linguistico
S Times — Sunday Times
Stimme D Orthodoxie — Stimme der Orthodoxie
Stimmen D Zeit — Stimmen der Zeit
Stimme Pfalz — Stimme der Pfalz
Stimm Zeit — Stimmen der Zeit
Stimul Newsl — Stimulation Newsletter
STINA — Stanki i Instrument
St Inst — Stair's Institutes
StIR — Stanford Italian Review
Stirling E N — Stirling Engine Newsletter
STISA — Sbornik Nauchnykh Trudov Tomskii Inzhenerno-Stroitel'nyi Institut
StIsl — Studia Islandica
StIslam — Studia Islamica
Sti Solului — Stiinta Solului
StIsp — Studi Ispanici
St It — Studi Italiani di Filologia Classica
StIt — Studi Italici
St Ital — Studi Italiani di Filologia Classica
St It Fil — Studi Italiani di Filologia Classica
StJ — Stader Jahrbuch. Stader Geschichts- und Heimatverein
StJ — Steel Today and Tomorrow
StJ — Stettiner Jahrbuch
St Jamess Eve Post — St. James's Evening Post
StJb — Stifter-Jahrbuch
STJCA — Strojnicky Casopis
St J LR — St. John's Law Review
St Johns L R — St John's Law Review [Brooklyn]
St John's L Rev — St. John's Law Review
StJud — Studia Judaica. Forschungen zur Wissenschaft des Judentums
STJVA — Strojniski Vestnik
STK — Svensk Teologisk Kvartalskrift
STKAB — Standarty i Kachestvo
StkIt — Stuekultur. Naturen og Hjemmet
STKMBC — Mammalogical Informations
STKMBC — Saugetierkundliche Mitteilungen
STKRA — Steklo i Keramika
STKv — Svensk Teologisk Kvartalskrift
STL — Startling Stories
St L — Student Lawyer
StL — Studia Linguistica
STL — Studia Theologica Lundensia
STL — Studies in Logic and the Foundations of Mathematics
StL — Studies on the Left
STL — Sunday Times (London)
St Lawrence Cty Coop Ext News — St. Lawrence County Cooperative Extension News
STLE Tribol Trans — STLE Tribology Transactions
StLF — Studi di Letteratura Francese
StLi — Studia Linguistica
StLI — Studi di Letteratura Ispano-Americana
StLing — Studies in Linguistics
St Lit — Studia Liturgica
S T L J — South Texas Law Journal
STLJD — South Texas Law Journal
St L J Th — St. Luke's Journal of Theology
St L M — Studien zur Literatur der Moderne
St Lngst — Statistical Methods in Linguistics
StLo — Studia Logica
StLog — Studia Logica
St Lol Fal — Stiftsbog og Landemode-Akt for Lolland-Falsters Stift
St Lou Com — St. Louis Commerce
St Louis Ac T — Transactions of the Academy of Science of St. Louis
St Louis B — St. Louis Business Journal
St Louis Commer — St. Louis Commerce
St Louis Drug — St. Louis Druggist
St Louis Lab Trib — St. Louis Labor Tribune
St Louis Law R — St. Louis Law Review
St Louis Law Rev — St. Louis Law Review. Washington University Law School
St Louis L R — St. Louis Law Review
St Louis L Rev — St. Louis Law Review
St Louis Metropol Med — St. Louis Metropolitan Medicine
St Louis Mus Bul — St. Louis City Art Museum. Bulletin
St Louis Pub Lib Mthly Bull — St. Louis Public Library Monthly Bulletin
St Louis T Ac — Transactions of the Academy of Science of St. Louis
St Louis U L J — St. Louis University. Law Journal
St Louis Univ B — St. Louis University. Bulletin
St Louis Univ Public Law Forum — St. Louis University. Public Law Forum
St Louis U Res J — St. Louis University. Research Journal
St Lou Mgr — St. Louis Manager
St Lou Pos — St. Louis Post-Dispatch
St Lou ULJ — St. Louis University. Law Journal
St L P — Studia Linguistica et Philologica

STL-QPSR — Speech Transmission Laboratory. Royal Institute of Technology. Stockholm. Quarterly Progress and Status Reports

STLTA — Steel Times

StLU — Studii de Literatura Universala

St LU Intra L Rev — St. Louis University. Intramural Law Review

St Luke J — St. Luke's Journal of Theology

St Luke's Hosp Gaz — St. Luke's Hospital Gazette

St LU LJ — St. Louis University. Law Journal

STM — Standard Test Methods Bulletins

StM — Studia Monastica

StM — Studi e Materiali di Storia delle Religioni

StM — Studien zur Musikwissenschaft

StM — Studi Medievali

STMA — Statistical Theory and Method Abstracts

St Magreb — Studi Magrebini

St Marianna Med J — St. Marianna Medical Journal

St Mark R — St. Mark's Review

St Mark Rev — St. Mark's Review

St Marks R — St. Mark's Review

St Marks Rev — St. Mark's Review

St Mary's L J — St. Mary's Law Journal

St Mat An — Studi e Materiali di Archeologia e Numismatica

St Mater Stor Relig — Studi e Materiali de Storia delle Religioni

St Mat (Ploiesti) — Studii si Materiale Privitoare la Trecutul Istorie al Judetului. Prahova, Istorie, Etnografie (Ploiesti)

StMBC — Studien und Mitteilungen aus dem Benediktiner- und dem Cistercienser-Orden

StMBCO — Studien und Mitteilungen aus dem Benediktiner- und dem Cistercienserorden

StMed — Studia Mediewistyczne

St Med — Studi Medievali

S T Mf — Svensk Tidskrift foer Musikforskning

STMGA — Salmon and Trout Magazine

STMGA3 — Salmon and Trout Magazine

StMGB — Studien und Mitteilungen zur Geschichte des Benediktiner-Ordens

St Mis — Studia Missionalia

St Misc — Studi Miscellanei, Seminario di Archeologia e Storia dell'Arte Greca e Romana dell'Universita di Roma

St Misc Rom — Studi Miscellanei. Seminario di Archeologia e Storia dell'Arte Greca e Romana

St Mitt Gesch Benediktorden — Studien und Mitteilungen zur Geschichte des Benediktineordens

STMLA — Stomatologia

St M LJ — St. Mary's Law Journal

StMon — Studia Monastica

St MS — Steinbeck Monograph Series

StMSR — Studi e Materiali di Storia delle Religioni

STMTA — Stomatologica

STMYA — Stomatologiya

St Myst — Studia Mystica

STN — Staff Papers

St N — St. Nicholas

StN — Studia Neotestamentica

St Nat Reg Hist Pl — State and National Registers of Historic Places

Stn Biol Mar Grande Riviere Que Rapp Annu — Station de Biologie Marine. Grande Riviere, Quebec. Rapport Annuel

Stn Bull Agric Exp Stn Univ Minn — Station Bulletin. Minnesota Agricultural Experiment Station

Stn Bull Dep Agri Econ Agric Exp Stn Purdue Univ — Station Bulletin. Department of Agricultural Economics. Agricultural ExperimentStation. Purdue University

Stn Bull Minn Agric Exp Stn — Station Bulletin. Minnesota. Agricultural Experiment Station

Stn Bull Nebr Agric Exp Stn — Station Bulletin. Nebraska. Agricultural Experiment Station

Stn Bull New Hamps Agric Exp Stn — Station Bulletin. Agricultural Experiment Station. University of New Hampshire

Stn Bull Ore Agric Exp Stn — Station Bulletin. Oregon Agricultural Experiment Station

Stn Bull Purdue Univ Agric Exp Stn — Station Bulletin. Purdue University. Agricultural Experiment Station

Stn Bull Univ Minn Agric Exp Stn — Station Bulletin. Univerity of Minnesota. Agricultural Experiment Station

Stn Cent Apic Sericic Lucr Stiint — Statiunea Centrala de Apicultura si Sericicultura. Lucrari Stiintifice

Stn Chim Agrar Sper Torino Annu — Stazione Chimico-Agraria Sperimentale di Torino. Annuario

Stn Circ Ore Agric Exp Stn — Station Circular. Oregon Agricultural Experiment Station

Stn Circ Purdue Univ Agric Exp Stn — Station Circular. Purdue University. Agricultural Experiment Station

STNEA — Sterne

StNeerla — Statistica Neerlandica

St Neophil — Studia Neophilologica

StNF — Studier i Nordisk Filologi

Stn Fed Essais Agric (Lausanne) Publ — Stations Federales d'Essais Agricoles (Lausanne). Publication

Stng T — Stenografisk Tidsskrift

Stn L — Stanford Law Review

STNLB — Stimulation Newsletter

Stn Note Univ Idaho For Wildl Range Exp Stn — Station Note. University of Idaho. Forest, Wildlife, and Range Experiment Station

Stn Patol Veg Rome Boll — Stazione di Patologia Vegetale. Rome. Bollettino

Stn Rep Hort Res Stn (Tatura) — Station Report. Horticultural Research Station (Tatura)

Stns Circ Wash Agric Exp Stns — Stations Circular. Washington Agricultural Experiment Stations

Stn Sper Agrar Ital — Stazione Sperimentali Agrarie Italiane

Stn Sper Granic Sicil Catania Pubbl — Stazione Sperimentale di Granicoltura per la Sicilia-Catania. Pubblicazione

Stn Sper Vetro Riv (Murano Italy) — Stazione Sperimentale del Vetro. Revista (Murano, Italy)

Stn Sper Vitic Enol (Conegliano Italy) Annu — Stazione Sperimentale di Viticoltura e di Enologia (Conegliano, Italy). Annuario

STNT — Sprawozdania Towarzystwa Naukowego w Toruniu

StNT — Studien zum Neuen Testament

Stn Tech Bull Ore Agric Exp Stn — Station Technical Bulletin. Oregon Agricultural Experiment Station

STNWA — Sci-Tech News

STNYA — Science and Technology

Stn Zool Napoli Pubbl — Stazione Zoologica di Napoli. Pubblicazioni

StO — Stimmen des Orients

Sto — Stoberiet

StO — Studia Oliveriana

StOA — Studies on Asia

STOAA — Stomatologiya

STOCD — Software Tools Communications

Stochastic Model — Stochastic Modeling

Stochastic Model Ser — Stochastic Modeling Series

Stochastic Processes Appl — Stochastic Processes and Their Applications

Stochastics Monogr — Stochastics Monographs

Stochastics Stochastics Rep — Stochastics and Stochastics Reports

Stoch Processes Appl — Stochastic Processes and Their Applications

Stockh Ac Hndl — Kongliga Svenska Vetenskaps-Akademiens Handlingar (Stockholm)

Stockh Ak Hndl Bh — Bihang till Kongliga Svenska Vetenskaps-Akademiens Handlingar (Stockholm)

Stockh Bh Ak Hndl — Bihang till Kongliga Svenska Vetenskaps-Akademiens Handlingar (Stockholm)

Stockh Contrib Geol — Stockholm Contributions in Geology

Stockh Gl For F — Geologiska Foreningens i Stockholm Forhandlingar

Stockh Ofv — Ofversigt af Kongl. Vetenskaps-Akademiens Forhandlingar (Stockholm)

Stockholm Contrib Geol — Stockholm Contributions in Geology

Stockholm Papers Hist Philos Tech — Stockholm Papers in History and Philosophy of Technology

Stockholms Hist Biblioth — Stockholms Historiska Bibliothek

Stockholm Tek Hogsk Avh — Stockholm. Tekniska Hogskolan. Avhandling

Stockholm Tek Hogsk Handl — Stockholm. Tekniska Hogskolan. Handlingar

Stockh Vt Ak Lefn — Lefnadsteckningar ofver Kongl. Svenska Vetenskaps Akademien. Ledamoter (Stockholm)

StocProc — Stochastic Processes and Their Applications

St Offenbach — Studien und Forschungen. Stadt- und Landkreis Offenbach Am Main

St o H — Stads- og Havneingenioren

St Oliv — Studia Oliveriana

Stomach Dis Curr Status Proc Int Congr — Stomach Diseases. Current Status. Proceedings. International Congress on Stomach Diseases

Stomach Endocr Organ Proc Eric K Fernstroem Symp — Stomach as an Endocrine Organ. Proceedings. Eric K. Fernstroem Symposium

Stomach Intest — Stomach and Intestine

S Tomas Nurs J — Santo Tomas Nursing Journal

Stomatol DDR — Stomatologie der DDR

Stomatol Glas Srb — Stomatoloski Glasnik Srbije

Stomatol Hung — Stomatologia Hungarica

Stomatol Mediterr — Stomatologia Mediterranea

Stomatol Vjesn — Stomatoloski Vjesnik

Stomatol Zpr — Stomatologicke Zpracy

STONE4 — Strahlentherapie und Onkologie

Stone And Webster Jour — Stone and Webster Journal

Stone C — Stone Country

Stone D — Stone Drum

Stone Ind — Stone Industries

Stony — Stony Hills

STOP — Software Theft Opposition Project

Stop Pregl — Stopanski Pregled

St Or — Studia Orientalia

StOr — Studia Orientalia. Edidit Societas Orientalis Fennica

Storage Handl Distrib — Storage Handling Distribution

Stor A It — Storia dell'Arte Italiana. Dal Medioevo al Quattrocento

Stor & Civ — Storia e Civilta

Stor Archit — Storia dell'Architettura

Stor Art — Storia dell'Arte

Stor Arte — Storia dell'Arte

Stor Brescia — Storia di Brescia

StOrChrColl — Studia Orientalia Christiana. Collectanea

Stor Citta — Storia della Citta

Stor Crit Psicol — Storia e Critica della Psicologia

Stor Cult Ven — Storia della Cultura Veneta

Stor Ebr It — Storia dell'Ebraismo in Italia. Sezione Toscana

Storefront — Storefront Classroom

Stor Hand Dist — Storage, Handling and Distribution

Storia e Lett — Storia e Litteratura

Storia e Polit — Storia e Politica

Storia Sci — Storia della Scienza

Stor Polit Internaz — Storia e Politica Internazionale

Stor Urb — Storia dell'Urbanistica

Stor Urb — Storia Urbana

Stotz-Kontakt-Roemmler Nachr — Stotz-Kontakt-Roemmler Nachrichten

Stove Mounters — Stove Mounters and Range Workers Journal [*Detroit*]

STP — NAVAS [*Nederlandse Aannemersvereniging van Afbouwen Stukadoorswerken*] 77
STP — North-Holland Studies in Theoretical Poetics
StP — Strassburger Post
StP — Studia Palmyrenskie
StP — Studia Patristica
StP — Studi Petrarcheschi
StPa — Studia Patristica
St Pal — Studia Palmyrenskie
StPapyr — Studia Papyrologica
StPatrist — Studia Patristica
St Paul Med J — St. Paul Medical Journal
St Pauls Rev Sci — St. Paul's Review of Science
St PB — Studia Patristica et Byzantina
StPB — Studia Post-Biblica
St P Brook — Staff Papers. Brookings Institution
St Pet Ac Mm — Memoires de l'Academie Imperiale des Sciences de St. Petersbourg
St Pet Ac Sc Mm — Bulletin Scientifique Publie par l'Academie Imperiale des Sciences de St. Petersbourg
St Pet Ac Sc Mm — Memoires de l'Academie Imperiale des Sciences de St. Petersbourg
St Pet Ac Sc Mm Rs — Memoirs of the Imperial Academy of Science (St. Petersberg)
St Pet Ac Sc N Acta — Nova Acta Academiae Scientiarum Imperialis Petropolitanae
St Pet Bll Ac Sc — Bulletin Scientifique Publie par l'Academie Imperiale des Sciences de St. Petersbourg
St Petersb Med Wchnschr — St. Petersburger Medizinische Wochenschrift
St Petersburger Med Wochenschr — Sankt-Petersburger Medicinsche Wochenschrift
St Petersburg Math J — St. Petersburg Mathematical Journal
St Peters Newspap — St. Peter's Newspaper
STPGA — Steel Processing
STPHB — Springer Tracts in Modern Physics
St Phil — Studia Philosophica
St Philon — Studia Philonica
StPO — Strafprozessordnung
St Pohl — Studia Pohl. Pontificio Istituto Biblico
STP Pharma Prat — STP (Sciences Techniques et Pratiques Pharmaceutiques) Pharma Pratiques
STP Pharma Sci — STP (Sciences Techniques et Pratiques Pharmaceutiques) Pharma Sciences
STPSA — Studia Psychologica
StQ — Steinbeck Quarterly
StR — Roemisches Staatsrecht
STR — Soul-Taehakkyo Ronmunjip. Inmun-Sahoe-Kwahak
STR — Star Science Fiction
STR — Stereo Review
Str — Strad
Str — Strophes
StR — Studia Romanica
StR — Studie o Rukopisech
StR — Studies Presented to R. L. Graeme Ritchie
StR — Studi Religiosi
StR — Studi Romagnoli
StR — Studi Romani. Rivista di Archeologia e Storia
STr — Studi Trentini
STr — Studi Trentini di Scienze Storiche
STRAA — Strahlentherapie
Straalsaekerhetscent Rapp STUK A — Straalsaekerhetscentralen. Rapport STUK-A
Straalsaekerhetsinst Rapp STL A — Straalsaekerhetsinstitutet. Rapport STL-A
STRAB — Strain
Strafrechtl Abh — Strafrechtliche Abhandlungen
Strahlenschutz Forsch Prax — Strahlenschutz in Forschung und Praxis
Strahlenschutz Prax — Strahlenschutz Praxis
Strahlenthe — Strahlentherapie
Strahlenther Onkol — Strahlentherapie und Onkologie
Strahlenther Sonderb — Strahlentherapie. Sonderbaende
Strahltech Vortr Posterbeitr Int Konf Strahltech — Strahltechnik. Vortraege und Posterbeitraege der Internationalen Konferenz Strahltechnik
Straits Times A — Straits Times Annual
Strait Times Ann — Straits Times Annual
Stralsund Mag — Stralsundisches Magazin, Oder Sammlungen Auserlesener Neuigkeiten, zur Aufnahmeder Naturlehre, Arzneywissenschaft, und Haushaltungskunst
Strand — Strand Magazine
Strand (Lond) — Strand Magazine (London)
Strand Mag — Strand Magazine
Strand (NY) — Strand Magazine (New York)
Strarohrv Prosvj — Starohrvatska Prosvjeta. Muzej Hrvatskih Starina Jugoslovenske Akademij e Znanosti i Umjetnosti
Strasb J S Sc — Journal de la Societe des Sciences, Agriculture et Arts, du Departement du Bas-Rhin (Strasbourg)
Strasb Med — Strasbourg Medical
Strasb Mm S H Nt — Memoires de la Societe des Sciences Naturelles de Strasbourg
Strassburg Muenster Bl — Strassburger Muenster-Blatt
Strateg Anal — Strategic Analysis
Strategic Dig — Strategic Digest
Strategic Plann Energy Environ — Strategic Planning for Energy and the Environment
Strategic R — Strategic Review
Strategies Phys Mapp — Strategies for Physical Mapping

Strateg Manage J — Strategic Management Journal
Strateg Plan Energy Manage — Strategic Planning and Energy Management
Stratford Pap — Stratford Papers
Stratford Upon Avon Pap — Stratford-Upon-Avon Papers
Strathclyde Bioeng Semin — Strathclyde Bioengineering Seminars
Strathclyde Educ — Strathclyde Education
Strat R — Strategic Review
Strat Rev — Strategic Review
Strat Svy — Strategic Survey
Strauss — Internationale Richard-Strauss-Gesellschaft. Mitteilungen
Str Autobahn — Strasse und Autobahn
Straw Oppor Innovations Pap Straw Conf — Straw. Opportunities and Innovations. Papers. Straw Conference
STRC — Scientific and Technical Research Centres in Australia
Stredocesky Sborn Hist — Stredocesky Sbornik Historicky
StRel/ScRel — Studies in Religion/Sciences Religieuses
Strem Chem — Strem Chemiker
St Ren — Studies in the Renaissance
Streng and H — Strength and Health
Strength & Con — Strength and Conditioning
Strength Mater — Strength of Materials
Strength Met Alloys Proc Int Conf — Strength of Metals and Alloys. Proceedings. International Conference on Strength of Metals and Alloys
Strenna Piacent — Strenna Piacentina
Strenna Romanisti — Strenna dei Romanisti
Strenna Stor Bologn — Stronna Storica Bolognese
Strenna Stor Bolognese — Strenna Storica Bolognese
St Rep (NSW) — State Reports (New South Wales)
Stressforsk Rapp — Stressforsknings Rapporter
Stress Induced Phenom Met Int Workshop — Stress-Induced Phenomena in Metallization. International Workshop
Streven — Katholiek Cultureel Tijdschrift Streven
Str Fiz Svoistva Veshchestva Zhidk Sostoyanii Mater Soveshch — Stroenie i Fizicheskie Svoistva Veshchestva v Zhidkom Sostoyanii. Materialy Soveshchaniya
STRHA — Staub, Reinhaltung der Luft
Stri — Strings
St Ric Lat — Studi e Ricerche. Istituto di Latino. Universita di Genova
Strides Med — Strides of Medicine
St Riv Wat Supply Comm Tech Bull — Victoria. State Rivers and Water Supply Commission. Technical Bulletin
STRJA — Strojirenstvi
STRKA — Staerke
STR M — Strand Magazine
STRND — Sternenbote
StRo — Studi Romani
Stroemungsmech Stroemungsmasch — Stroemungsmechanik und Stroemungsmaschinen
Stroezh Funkts Mozuka — Stroezh i Funktsii na Mozuka
Stroit Alyum Konstr — Stroitel'nye Alyuminlevye Konstruktsii
Stroit Arkhit — Stroitel'stvo i Arkhitektura
Stroit Arkhit Leningrada — Stroitel'stvo i Arkhitektura Leningrada
Stroit Arkhit Sredn Azii — Stroitel'stvo i Arkhitektura Srednei Azii
Stroit Arkhit Uzb — Stroitel'stvo i Arkhitektura Uzbekistana
Stroit Dorog — Stroitel'stvo Dorog
Stroit Dorozhn Mash — Stroitel'nye i Dorozhnye Mashiny
Stroitelstvo & Arkhit Leningrada — Stroitel'stvo i Arkhitektura Leningrada
Stroitelstvo & Arkhit Moskvy — Stroitel'stvo i Arkhitektura Moskvy
Stroitelstvo & Arkhit Uzbekistana — Stroitel'stvo i Arkhitektura Uzbekistana
Stroit Keram — Stroitel'naya Keramika
Stroit Konstr — Stroitel'nye Konstruktsii
Stroit Konstr Alyum Splavov — Stroitel'nye Konstruktsii iz Alyuminievkh Splavov
Stroit Mater — Stroitel'nye Materialy
Stroit Mater (1929-32) — Stroitel'nye Materialy (1929-32)
Stroit Mater (1933-38) — Stroitel'nye Materialy (1932-38)
Stroit Mater Betony — Stroitel'nye Materialy i Betony
Stroit Mater Detali Izdeliya — Stroitel'nye Materialy. Detali i Izdeliya
Stroit Mater Ikh Proizvod — Stroitel'nye Materialy i Ikh Proizvodstvo
Stroit Mater Izdeliya Konstr — Stroitel'nye Materialy. Izdeliya i Konstruktsii
Stroit Mater Izdeliya Sanit Tekh — Stroitel'nye Materialy. Izdeliya i Sanitarnaya Tekhnika
Stroit Mater Khim Dokl Nauchn Konf Leningr Inzh Stroit Inst — Stroitel'nye Materialy i Khimiya. Doklady Nauchnoi Konferentsii Leningradskogo Inzhenerno-Stroitel'nogo Instituta
Stroit Mater Konstr — Stroitel'nye Materialy i Konstruktsii
Stroit Mater Silik Prom-St — Stroitelni Materiali i Silikatna Promishlenost
Stroit Mekh Raschet Sooruz — Stroitel'naya Mekhanika i Raschet Sooruzheniy
Stroit Predpr Neft Promsti — Stroitel'stvo Predpriyatii Neftyanoi Promyshlennosti
Stroit Promst — Stroitel'naya Promyshlennost
Stroit Truboprovodov — Stroitel'stvo Truboprovodov
Strojir Vyroba — Strojirenska Vyroba
Strojnicky Cas — Strojnicky Casopis
Strojniski Vestn — Strojniski Vestnik
Stroj Vest — Strojniski Vestnik
Stroke Suppl — Stroke. Supplement
StRom — Studia Romanica
StRom — Studies in Romanticism
St Rom — Studi Romani
St Romagnoli — Studi Romagnoli
St Romani — Studi Romani. Istituto di Studi Romani
Stromprax — Strompraxis
St R (Q) — State Reports (Queensland)
St R (Qd) — State Reports (Queensland)
St R (Queensl) — State Reports (Queensland)

Str Svoistva Primen Beta Diketonatov Met Mater Vses Semin — Stroenie, Svoistva, i Primenenie B (Beta)-Diketonatov Metallov. Materialy Vsesoyuznogo Seminara

Str Svoistva Primen Metallidov Mater Simp — Stroenie, Svoistva, i Primenenie Metallidov. Materialy Simpoziuma

Str Tiefbau — Strassen- und Tiefbau

Strucna Izd JUGOMA — Strucna Izdanja JUGOMA

Strucna Izd Jugosl Drus Primjenu Goriva Maziva — Strucna Izdanja Jugoslavenskog Drustvo za Primjenu Goriva i Maziva

Struc Rev — Structuralist Review

Struct Act Enzymes Fed Eur Biochem Soc Symp — Structure and Activity of Enzymes. Federation of European Biochemical Societies Symposium

Struct Anal — Structural Analysis

Struct Antigens — Structure of Antigens [*monograph*]

Struct Biol Membr — Structure of Biological Membranes

Struct Bonding — Structure and Bonding

Struct Bonding Berlin — Structure and Bonding (Berlin)

Struct Chem — Structural Chemistry

Struct Chem Part B — Structure and Chemistry. Part B

Struct Concr — Structural Concrete

Struct Conform Amphiphilic Membr Proc Int Workshop — Structure and Conformation of Amphiphilic Membranes. Proceedings. International Workshop

Struct Des Tall Build — Structural Design of Tall Buildings

Struct Energ React Chem Ser — Structure Energetics and Reactivity in Chemistry Series

Struct Eng — Structural Engineer

Struct Eng Earthquake Eng — Structural Engineering/Earthquake Engineering

Struct Engnr — Structural Engineer. Parts A and B

Struct Eng Pract Anal Des Man — Structural Engineering Practice. Analysis, Design, Management

Struct Engr — Structural Engineer

Struct Eng Rev — Structural Engineering Review

Struct Foam Conf Proc — Structural Foam Conference. Proceedings

Struct Funct Brain — Structure and Functions of the Brain

Struct Funct Proc Conversation Discip Biomol Stereodyn — Structure and Function. Proceedings. Conversation in the Discipline Biomolecular Stereodynamics

Struct Glass — Structure of Glass

Struct Mater Note Aust Aeronaut Res Lab — Australia. Department of Supply. Aeronautical Research Laboratories. Structuresand Materials Note

Struct Mater Rep Aust Aeronaut Res Lab — Australia. Aeronautical Research Laboratories. Structures and Materials Report

Struct Mech Opt Syst — Structural Mechanics of Optical Systems

Struct Mech React Technol — Structural Mechanics in Reactor Technology

Struct Note Aust Aeronaut Res Lab — Australia. Aeronautical Research Laboratories. Structures Note

Struct Phase Stab Alloys — Structural and Phase Stability of Alloys

Struct Rep — Structure Reports

Struct Rep Aust Aeronaut Res Lab — Australia. Aeronautical Research Laboratories. Structures Report

Struct Rep Dep Archit Sci Syd Univ — Structures Report. Department of Architectural Science. University of Sydney

Struct Rev — Structuralist Review

Struct Saf — Structural Safety

Struct Sens Control — Structures Sensing and Control

Struct Surf Proc Int Conf — Structure of Surfaces. Proceedings. International Conference on the Structure of Surfaces

Struct Surv — Structural Survey

Structural Engin — Structural Engineer

Strukt Funkts Fermentov — Struktura i Funktsiya Fermentov

Strukt Modif Khlopk Tsellyul — Struktura i Modifikatsiya Khlopkovoi Tsellyulozy

Strukt Org Soedin Mekh Reakts — Struktura Organicheskikh Soedinenii i Mekhanizmy Reaktsii

Strukt Rol Vody Zhivom Org — Struktura i Rol Vody v Zhivom Organizme

Strukt Svoistva Krist — Struktura i Svoistva Kristallov

Strukt Svoistva Litykh Splavov — Struktura i Svoistva Litykh Splavov

Strukt Svoistva Mono Polikrist Mater — Struktura i Svoistva Mono- i Polikristallicheskikh Materialov

Strukt Svoistva Tverd Tel — Struktura i Svoistva Tverdykh Tel

Strukturn i Mat Lingvistika — Strukturnaja i Matematiceskaja Lingvistika

Strum Crit — Strumenti Critici

Strum una Nuova Cultur Guida e Manual — Strumenti per una Nuova Cultura. Guida e Manuali

Str Verkehr — Strasse und Verkehr

STS — Scottish Text Society

STS — Stirring Science Stories

StS — Studia Slavica

StSa — Studi Salentini

St Salent — Studi Salentini

St Sar — Studi Sardi

St Sard — Studi Sardi

STSBDL — Studi Trentini di Scienze Naturali. Acta Biologica

StSec — Studi Secenteschi

St Sem — Studia Semitica Neerlandica

StSem — Studi Semitici

StSemNeerl — Studia Semitica Neerlandica

STSGD2 — Studi Trentini di Scienze Naturali. Acta Geologica

Stsintill Org Lyuminofory — Stsintillyatory i Organicheskie Lyuminofory

Stsintill Stsintill Mater Mater Koord Soveshch — Stsintillyatory i Stsintillyatsionnye Materialy. Materialy Koordinatsionnogo Soveshchaniya po Stsintillyatoram

StSl — Studia Slavica

StSLL — Studies in Semitic Languages and Linguistics

STSODQ — Annual Report. Natural Products Research Institute. Seoul National University

St Sp Ag It — Stazioni Sperimentali Agrare Italiane

STSS — Studi Trentini di Scienze Storiche

St St A — Studi Storici per l'Antichita Classica

Ststcian — Statistician

St Stor Rel — Studi Storico-Religioso

StSV — Staat und Selbstverwaltung

St Syst Theol — Studien zur Systematischen Theologie

STT — Science Stories

STT — Strange Tales of Mystery and Terror

St T — Studi e Testi. Biblioteca Apostolica Vaticana

StT — Studi Tassiani

STT — Svensk Traevaru- och Pappersmassetidning

St Tax Cas CCH — State Tax Cases. Commerce Clearing House

St Tax Cas Rep CCH — State Tax Cases Reports. Commerce Clearing House

St Tax Rep CCH — State Tax Reports. Commerce Clearing House

STTBA — Strassen- und Tiefbau

StTCL — Studies in Twentieth-Century Literature

StTd — Stockholm Tidningen [*newspaper*]

STTEA — Stain Technology

StTeol — Studii Teologice

StTEstmatn — Statistical Theory of Estimation

STTF — Sanskrittexte aus den Turfanfunden

StTh — Studia Theologica

StTheol — Studia Teologica

StThL — Studia Theologica Lundensia. Skrifter Utgivna av Teologiska Fakulteten i Lund

St Thom Hosp Rp — St. Thomas's Hospital Reports

STTH Sci Technol Hum — STTH. Science, Technology and the Humanities

StThVars — Studia Theologica Varsaviensia

St Tomas J Med — Santo Tomas Journal of Medicine

St Tomas Nurs J — Santo Tomas Nursing Journal

STTRA — Stroitel'stvo Truboprovodov

St Twen Ct — Studies in Twentieth-Century Literature

STU — Schweizerische Theologische Umschau

Stu — Studia

Stu — Studies

STU — Studies on International Relations

Stu — Studium

StU — Studi Urbinati di Storia, Filosofia, et Letteratura

Stu Cer Fiz — Studii si Cercetari de Fizica

Stu Co — Studia Comitatensia. Tanulmanyok Pest Magye Muzeumalbad

Stud — Student and Intellectual Observer of Science, Literature, and Art

Stud — Studien

Stud — Studies

Stud — Studies: An Irish Quarterly Review of Letters, Philosophy, and Science

Stud 18th Cent — Studies in the Eighteenth Century. Papers Presented. David Nichol Smith Memorial Seminar. Canberra

Stud Account — Studies in Accountancy

Stud Achtzehn Jahrh — Studien zum Achtzehnten Jahrhundert

Stud Acta Orient — Studia et Acta Orientalia

StudActOr — Studia et Acta Orientalia

Stud Adv Math — Studies in Advanced Mathematics

StudAeg — Studia Aegyptiaca

Stud Aegyp — Studia Aegyptiaca

Stud Afr Linguist — Studies in African Linguistics

Stud Afr Linguistics — Studies in African Linguistics

Stud Age Chaucer — Studies in the Age of Chaucer

Stud Ag Econ — Stanford University Food Research Institute Studies in Agricultural Economics, Trade, and Development

Stud Alb — Studia Albanica

Stud Alban — Studia Albanica

Stud Albornot — Studia Albornotiana

Stud Algebra Anwendungen — Studien zur Algebra und Ihre Anwendungen

Stud Aliment Apa — Studii de Alimentari cu Apa

Stud Altaegyp Kult — Studien zur Altaegyptischen Kultur

Stud Am Fic — Studies in American Fiction

Stud & Arheol — Studii si Arheologie

Stud & Bibliog An Bib Stat & Lib Civ Cremona — Studi e Bibliografie degli Annali della Biblioteca Statale e Libreria Civica di Cremona

Stud & Cerc Biblio — Studii si Cercetari de Bibliologie

Stud & Cercet Calcul Econ & Cibern Econ — Studii si Cercetari de Calcul Economic si Cibernetica Economica

Stud & Cercet Doc — Studii si Cercetari de Documentare

Stud & Cerc Istor A — Studii si Cercetari de Istoria Artei

Stud & Cerc Istor A Ser A Plast — Studii si Cercetari de Istoria Artei. Seria Arta Plastica

Stud & Cerc Istor A Ser Teat Muzic Cinema — Studii si Cercetari de Istoria Artei. Seria Teatro, Muzica, Cinematografie

Stud & Cerc Istor Veche — Studii si Cercetari de Istorie Veche

Stud & Contrib Ist Archeol & Stor A U Bari — Studi e Contributi dell'Istituto di Archeologia e Storia dell'Arte dell'Universita di Bari

Stud & Crit It A — Study and Criticism of Italian Art

Stud & Doc Archit — Studi e Documenti di Architettura

Stud & Doc His Jur — Studia et Documenta Historiae et Juris

Stud & Doc Stor & Dir — Studi e Documenti per la Storia e Diritto

Stud & Doc Stor Pal Apostol Vatic — Studi e Documenti per la Storia del Palazzo Apostolico Vaticano

Stud & Intel Obs — Student and Intellectual Observer

Stud & Mat Dziejow Nauki Pol — Studia i Materialy z Dziejow Nauki Polskie

Stud & Mat Hist Kult Mat — Studia i Materialy z Historii Kultury Materialnej

Stud & Mat Teor & Hist Archit & Urb — Studia i Materialy do Teorii i Historii Architektury i Urbanistyki

Stud & Mitt Gesch Benediktiner-Ordens & Zweige — Studien und Mitteilungen zur Geschichte des Benediktiner-Ordens und Seiner Zweige

Stud & Prob Crit Test — Studi e Problemi di Critica Testuale

Stud & Skiz Gemaldeknd — Studien und Skizzen zur Gemaldekunde

Stud & Szkice Dziejow Sztuki & Cywiliz — Studia i Szkice z Dziejow Sztuki i Cywilizacji

Stud Angew Wirtschaftsforsch Statist — Studien zur Angewandten Wirtschaftsforschung und Statistik

Stud Anselm — Studia Anselmiana

Stud Anthrop — Studies in Anthropology

Stud Anthropol Visual Communic — Studies in the Anthropology of Visual Communication

Stud Appl M — Studies in Applied Mathematics

Stud Appl Math — Studies in Applied Mathematics

Stud Appl Mech — Studies in Applied Mechanics

Stud Arch — Studia Archaeologica

Stud Archeol Ustavu Cesko Akad Brne — Studie Archeologickeho Ustavu Ceskoslovenske Akademie ved v Brne

Stud Art Ed — Studies in Art Education

Stud Art Educ — Studies in Art Education

Stud A Urbin — Studi Artistici Urbinati

Stud Auslandskde — Studien zur Auslandskunde

Stud Automat Control — Studies in Automation and Control

Stud Bal — Studia Balcanica

Stud Bank Fin — Studies in Banking and Finance

Stud Bayesian Econometrics — Studies in Bayesian Econometrics

Stud Bayesian Econometrics Statist — Studies in Bayesian Econometrics and Statistics

Stud Bibl — Studii Biblici Franciscani. Liber Annus

Stud Bibliog — Virginia University. Bibliographical Society. Studies in Bibliography

Stud Bibliog & Bklore — Studies in Bibliography and Booklore

Stud Biol — Studies in Biology

Stud Biol Acad Sci Hung — Studia Biologica. Academiae Scientiarum Hungaricae

Stud Biol Hung — Studia Biologica Hungarica

Stud Biophy — Studia Biophysica

Stud Biophys — Studia Biophysica

Stud Bitontini — Studi Bitontini

Stud Biz Neoellenici — Studi Bizantini e Neoellenici

Stud Black Lit — Studies in Black Literature

Stud Boccaccio — Studi sul Boccaccio

Stud Bot — Studia Botanica

Stud Bot Cech — Studia Botanica Cechoslavaca

Stud Bot Hung — Studia Botanica Hungarica

Stud Brain Funct — Studies in Brain Function

Stud Br His — Studies in British History and Culture

Stud Broadcast — Studies of Broadcasting

Stud Brown — Studies in Browning and His Circle

StudBT — Studia Biblica et Theologica

Stud Burke — Studies in Burke and his Times

Stud Burke Time — Studies in Burke and His Time

Stud Byz — Rivista di Studi Bizantini e Neoellenici

Stud Can — Studia Canonica

Stud Cartesiana — Studia Cartesiana

StudCath — Studia Catholica

Stud Caucasia — Studia Caucasia

Stud Celt — Studia Celtica

Stud Cent & E Asian Relig — Studies in Central and East Asian Religions

Stud Cerc Buzan — Studii si Cercetari de Istorie Buzoiana

Stud Cerc Docum — Studii si Cercetari de Documentare

Stud Cerc Econom — Studii si Cercetari Economice

Stud Cercet Agron — Studii si Cercetari de Agronomie

Stud Cercet Agron Acad Rep Pop Romine Fil (Cluj) — Studii si Cercetari de Agronomie. Academia Republicii Populare Romine Filiala (Cluj)

Stud Cercet Antrop — Studii si Cercetari de Antropologie

Stud Cercet Antropol — Studii si Cercetari de Antropologie

Stud Cercetari Istoria Artei — Studii si Cercetari de Istoria Artei

Stud Cercet Astron — Studii si Cercetari de Astronomie

Stud Cercet Biochim — Studii si Cercetari de Biochimie

Stud Cercet Biol — Studii si Cercetari de Biologie

Stud Cercet Biol Acad Rep Pop Romine Fil (Cluj) — Studii si Cercetari de Biologie. Academia Republicii Populare Romine Filiala (Cluj)

Stud Cercet Biol Acad Rep Pop Romine Ser Biol Veg — Studii si Cercetari de Biologie. Academia Republicii Populare Romine. Seria Biologi Vegetala

Stud Cercet Biol Bucharest — Studii si Cercetari de Biologie. Etudes et Recherches de Biologie (Bucharest)

Stud Cercet Biol Cluj — Studii si Cercetari de Biologie (Cluj)

Stud Cercet Biol Ser Biol Anim — Studii si Cercetari de Biologie. Seria Biologie Animala

Stud Cercet Biol Ser Biol Veg — Studii si Cercetari de Biologie. Seria Biologie Vegetala

Stud Cercet Biol Ser Bot — Studii si Cercetari de Biologie. Seria Botanica

Stud Cercet Biol Ser Zool — Studii si Cercetari de Biologie. Seria Zoologie

Stud Cercet Chim — Studii si Cercetari de Chimie

Stud Cercet Chim (Cluj) — Studii si Cercetari de Chimie (Cluj)

Stud Cercet Doc Bibliologie — Studii si Cercetari de Documentare si Bibliologie

Stud Cercet Embriol Citol Ser Embriol — Studii si Cercetari de Embriologie si Citologie. Seria Embriologie

Stud Cercet Endocrinol — Studii si Cercetari de Endocrinologie

Stud Cercet Energ — Studii si Cercetari de Energetica

Stud Cercet Energ Electroteh — Studii si Cercetari de Energetica si Electrotehnica

Stud Cercet Energ Ser A — Studii si Cercetari de Energetica. Seria A. Energetica Generala si Electroenergetica

Stud Cercet Energ Ser B — Studii si Cercetari de Energetica. Seria B. Termoenergetica si Utilizarea Energetica a Combustibililor

Stud Cercet Fiz — Studii si Cercetari de Fizica

Stud Cercet Fiziol — Studii si Cercetari de Fiziologie

Stud Cercet Geofiz — Studii si Cercetari de Geofizica

Stud Cercet Geol Geofiz Geogr — Studii si Cercetari de Geologie, Geofizica, Geografie. Seria Geofizica

Stud Cercet Geol Geofiz Geogr Geofiz — Studii si Cercetari de Geologie, Geofizica, Geografie. Geofizica

Stud Cercet Geol Geofiz Geogr Geol — Studii si Cercetari de Geologie, Geofizica, Geografie. Geologie

Stud Cercet Geol Geofiz Geogr Ser Geofiz — Studii si Cercetari de Geologie, Geofizica, si Geografie. Seria Geofizica

Stud Cercet Geol Geofiz Geogr Ser Geogr — Studii si Cercetari de Geologie, Geofizica, si Geografie. Seria Geografie

Stud Cercet Geol Geofiz Geogr Ser Geol — Studii si Cercetari de Geologie, Geofizica, si Geografie. Seria Geologie

Stud Cercet Geol Geogr — Studii si Cercetari de Geologie-Geografie

Stud Cercet Ig Sanat Publica — Studii si Cercetari de Igiena si Sanatate Publica

Stud Cercet Inframicrobiol — Studii si Cercetari de Inframicrobiologie

Stud Cercet Inframicrobiol Microbiol Parazitol — Studii si Cercetari de Inframicrobiologie, Microbiologie, si Parazitologie

Stud Cercet Inst Cercet Piscic — Studii si Cercetari. Institutul de Cercetari Piscicole

Stud Cercet Inst Cercet Proiect Piscic — Studii si Cercetari. Institutul de Cercetari si Proiectari Piscicole

Stud Cercet Inst Meteorol Hidrol Hidrol — Studii si Cercetari. Institutul de Meteorologie si Hidrologie. Hidrologie

Stud Cercet Inst Meteorol Hidrol Partea 1 — Studii si Cercetari. Institutul de Meteorologie si Hidrologie. Partea 1. Meteorologie

Stud Cercet Inst Meteorol Hidrol Partea 2 — Studii si Cercetari. Institutul de Meteorologie si Hidrologie. Partea 2. Hidrologie

Stud Cercet Ist Veche Arheol — Studii si Cercetari de Istorie Veche si Arheologie

Stud Cercet Mat Fiz — Studii si Cercetari de Matematica si Fizica

Stud Cercet Mec Apl — Studii si Cercetari de Mecanica Aplicata

Stud Cercet Med — Studii si Cercetari de Medicina

Stud Cercet Med (Cluj) — Studii si Cercetari de Medicina (Cluj)

Stud Cercet Med Interna — Studii si Cercetari de Medicina Interna

Stud Cercet Metal — Studii si Cercetari de Metalurgie

Stud Cercet Metal Comun Stiint — Studii si Cercetari de Metalurgie. Comunicari Stiintifice

Stud Cercet Neurol — Studii si Cercetari de Neurologie

Stud Cercet Piscic Inst Cercet Proiect Aliment — Studii si Cercetari Piscicole. Institutul de Cercetari si Proiectari Alimentare

Stud Cercet Silvic — Studii si Cercetari de Silvicultura

Stud Cercet Silvic Inst Cercet Amenajari Silvice — Studii si Cercetari de Silvicultura. Institutul de Cercetari si Amenajari Silvice

Stud Cercet Stiint Fil Cluj Acad Repub Pop Rom — Studii si Cercetari Stiintifice. Filiala Cluj. Academia Republicii Populare Romine

Stud Cercet Stiint Fil Cluj Acad Repub Pop Rom Ser 2 — Studii si Cercetari Stiintifice. Filiala Cluj. Academia Republicii Populare Romine. Seria 2. Stiinte Biologice, Agricole, si Medicale

Stud Cercet Stiint Fil Iasi Acad Repub Pop Rom — Studii si Cercetari Stiintifice. Filiala Iasi. Academia Republicii Populare Romine

Stud Cercet Stiint Fil Iasi Acad Repub Pop Rom Chimie — Studii si Cercetari Stiintifice. Filiala Iasi. Academia Republicii Populare Romine. Chimie

Stud Cercet Stiint Fil Iasi Acad Repub Pop Rom Med — Studii si Cercetari Stiintifice. Filiala Iasi. Academia Republicii Populare Romine. Medicina

Stud Cercet Stiint Fil Iasi Acad Repub Pop Rom Ser 2 — Studii si Cercetari Stiintifice. Filiala Iasi. Academia Republicii Populare Romine. Seria 2. Stiinte Biologice, Medicale, si Agricole

Stud Cercet Virusol — Studii si Cercetari de Virusologie

Stud Cerc Fiz — Studii si Cercetari de Fizica

Stud Cerc Inst Cerc For (Industr Lemn) — Studii si Cercetari. Institutul de Cercetari Forestiere (Industrializarea Lemnului)

Stud Cerc Inst Cerc For (Mec Lucr For) — Studii si Cercetari. Institutul de Cercetari Forestiere (Mecanizarea LucrarilorForestiere)

Stud Cerc Inst Cerc For (Silv) — Studii si Cercetari. Institutul de Cercetari Forestiere (Silvicultura)

Stud Cerc Ist Veche — Studii si Cercetari de Istorie Veche si di Archeologie

Stud Cerc Mat — Studii si Cercetari Matematice

Stud Cerc Mec Apl — Studii si Cercetari de Mecanica Aplicata

Stud Cerc Num — Studii si Cercetari de Numismatica

Stud Chem — Studia Chemica

Stud Chemother Inst Med Res — Studies. Chemotherapeutic Institute for Medical Research

Stud Chem Univ Salamanca — Studia Chemica. Universidad de Salamanca

Stud Ch G P — Studies in Chinese Government and Politics

Stud Christ — Studi di Antichita Cristiana

Stud Church Hist — Studies in Church History. American Society of Church History

Stud Citrol — Studia Citrologica. Kankitsu Kenkyu. Tanaka Citrus Experiment Station

Stud Cl — Studii Clasice

Stud Claramontana — Studia Claramontana

StudClas — Studii Clasice

Stud Class — Studies of Classical India

Stud Class & Orient — Studi Classici ed Orientali

Stud Classe Or — Studi Classici e Orientali

Stud Classification Data Anal Knowledge Organ — Studies in Classification, Data Analysis, and Knowledge Organization

Stud Cl Orient — Studi Classici e Orientali

Stud Colombiani — Studi Colombiani. Publicazioni del Civico Istituto Colombiano

Stud Com Co — Studies in Comparative Communism

Stud Comeniana & Hist — Studia Comeniana et Historica

Stud Com I D — Studies in Comparative International Development

Stud Comitat — Studia Comitatensia

Stud Com L G — Studies in Comparative Local Government

Stud Comm R — Studies in Communism, Revisionism, and Revolution

Stud Comp Com — Studies in Comparative Communism

Stud Comp Commun — Studies in Comparative Communism

Stud Comp Communism — Studies in Comparative Communism
Stud Com Pest — Studia Comitatensia. Tanulmanyok Pest Magye Muzeumalbad
Stud Comp Int Dev — Studies in Comparative International Development
Stud Comp Int Develop — Studies in Comparative International Development
Stud Comp R — Studies in Comparative Religion
Stud Comp Relig — Studies in Comparative Religion
Stud Comp Religion — Studies in Comparative Religion
Stud Comput Math — Studies in Computational Mathematics
Stud Comput Sci Artif Intell — Studies in Computer Science and Artificial Intelligence
Stud Comun (Brukenthal) — Studii si Comunicari (Brukenthal)
Stud Comun (Pitesti) — Studii si Comunicari (Pitesti)
Stud Comun (Satu Mare) — Studii si Comunicari (Satu Mare)
Stud Conserv — Studies in Conservation
Stud Cosmic Ray — Studies of Cosmic Ray
Stud Cult Anthrop — Studies in Cultural Anthropology
Stud Demogr — Studia Demograficzne
Stud Design Educ Craft Technol — Studies in Design Education, Craft, and Technology
Stud Develop — Middle East Technical University. Studies in Development
Stud Developing Countries — Studies on the Developing Countries
Stud Develop Special Issue — Studies in Development. Special Issue. Middle East Technical University
Stud Dipl — Studia Diplomatica
Stud Diplom — Studia Diplomatica
Stud Doc Hist et Iuris — Studia et Documenta Historiae et Iuris
Stud Doc Hist Iur — Studia et Documenta Historiae et Iuris
Stud Docum Asian Docum — Studies and Documents. Asian Documentation and Research Center
Stud Dt Kstgesch — Studien zur Deutschen Kunstgeschichte
Stud Dynam Econom Sci — Studies in Dynamical Economic Science
Stud Dziejow Rzemiola & Przemyslu — Studia z Dziejow Rzemiola i Przemyslu
Stud Dziejow Sztuki Polsce — Studia do Dziejow Sztuki w Polsce
Stud Dziejow Wawelu — Studia do Dziejow Wawelu
Stud East Sib State Univ — Studies. East Siberian State University
Stud Ecol — Studies in Ecology
Stud Econ — Studi Economici
Stud Econom Theory — Studies in Economic Theory
Stud Ed — Studies in Education
Stud Educ Adults — Studies in the Education of Adults
Stud Egyptol — Studies in Egyptology
Stud Eight — Studies in Eighteenth-Century Culture
Stud Eighteenth-Century Cult — Studies in Eighteenth-Century Culture
Stud Electr Electron Eng — Studies in Electrical and Electronic Engineering
Stud Emigr — Studi Emigrazione
Stud Empir Econom — Studies in Empirical Economics
Stud Engl L — Studies in English Literature, 1500-1900
Stud Engl Lit — Studies in English Literature
Stud Engl Phil — Studien zur Englischen Philologie
Stud Engl (T) — Studies in English Literature (Tokyo)
Student Adv — Student Advocate
Studente Vet — Studente Veterinario
Student Law — Student Lawyer
Student Law J — Student Lawyer Journal
Student L Rev — Student Law Review
Student Musicol — Student Musicologists at Minnesota
Stud Entomol — Studia Entomologica
Student Q J Instn Elec Engrs — Institution of Electrical Engineers. Student Quarterly Journal
Students'ky Nauk Pratsi Kyyv Derzh Unyv — Students'ky Naukovi Pratsi Kyyivs'kyyi Derzhavnyyi Unyversytet
Stud Environ Sci — Studies in Environmental Science
Stud Environ Sci (Hiroshima) — Studies in Environmental Science (Hiroshima)
Stud Epurarea Apelor — Studii de Epurarea Apelor
Stud Estet — Studia Estetyczne
Stud et Doca Iura Or Ant Pert — Studia et Documenta ad Iura Orientis Antiqui Pertinentia
Stud Ethnog — Studia Ethnographica
Stud Ethnol Zagreb — Studia Ethnologica (Zagreb)
Stud Ethnomethodol — Studies in Ethnomethodology
Stud Etno Antrop Sociol — Studi Etno-Antropologici e Sociologici
Stud Etr — Studi Etruschi
Stud Etrus — Studi Etruschi
Stud Europ Soc — Studies in European Society
Stud Family Plann — Studies in Family Planning
Stud Fam Pl — Studies in Family Planning
Stud Fam Plann — Studies in Family Planning
Stud Fauna Curacao Other Caribb Isl — Studies on the Fauna of Curacao and Other Caribbean Islands
Stud Fauna Suriname Other Guyanas — Studies of the Fauna of Suriname and Other Guyanas
Stud Fenn — Studia Fennica
Stud Filol — Studime Filologjike
Stud Filol Ital — Studia di Filologia Italiana
Stud Finans — Studia Finansowe
Stud Form Spir — Studies in Formative Spirituality
Stud For Suec — Studia Forestalia Suecica
Stud For Suec (Skogshogsk) — Studia Forestalia Suecica (Skogshogskolan)
Stud Fort Ant — Studien zum Fortwirken der Antike
Stud Found Methodol Philos Sci — Studies in the Foundations, Methodology, and Philosophy of Science
Stud Fr — Studi Francesi
Stud Fran — Studi Francesi
Stud Francescani — Studi Francescani
Stud Francesi — Studi Francesi

Stud Fuzziness — Studies in Fuzziness
Stud Gen — Studium Generale
Stud Genet — Studies in Genetics
Stud Genuensi — Studi Genuensi
Stud Geogr — Studies in Geography
Stud Geogr Cesk Akad Ved Geogr Ustav (Brno) — Studia Geographica. Ceskoslovenska Akademie Ved. Geograficky Ustav (Brno)
Stud Geol Mineral Inst Tokyo Univ Educ — Studies from the Geological and Mineralogical Institute. Tokyo University of Education
Stud Geol Pol — Studia Geologica Polonica
Stud Geol Salamanca — Studia Geologica. Universidad de Salamanca
Stud Geol (Tulsa Okla) — Studies in Geology (Tulsa, Oklahoma)
Stud Geol Univ Salamanca — Studia Geologica. Universidad de Salamanca
Stud Geomorphol Carpatho-Balcanica — Studia Geomorphologica Carpatho-Balcanica
Stud Geoph — Studia Geophysica et Geodaetica
Stud Geophys Geod — Studia Geophysica et Geodaetica
Stud Geophys Geod (Cesk Akad Ved) — Studia Geophysica et Geodaetica (Ceskosloven-Akademie Ved)
Stud Geotech — Studia Geotechnica. Politechnika Wroclawaka
Stud Geotech Mech — Studia Geotechnica et Mechanica
Stud Geoteh Fund Constr Hidroteh — Studii de Geotekhnica. Fundatii si Constructii Hidrotehnice
Stud Gesch Akad Wiss DDR — Studien zur Geschichte der Akademie der Wissenschaften der Deutsche Demokratische Republik
Stud Gesch Kult Alt — Studien zur Geschichte und Kultur des Altertums
Stud Gregoriani — Studi Gregoriani
Stud H Art — Studies in the History of Art
Stud Helminthol — Studia Helminthologica
Stud Hib — Studia Hibernica
Stud Hierosolym — Studia Hierosolymitana
Stud High Educ — Studies in Higher Education
Stud High Energy Phys — Studies in High Energy Physics
Stud High Temp Supercond — Studies of High Temperature Superconductors. Advances in Research andApplications
Stud Hist — Studime Historike
Stud Hist & Soc — Studies in History and Society
Stud Hist Art — Studies in the History of Art
Stud Hist Biol — Studies in History of Biology
Stud Hist Math Phys Sci — Studies in the History of Mathematics and Physical Sciences
Stud Hist Med — Studies in History of Medicine
Stud Hist Modern Sci — Studies in the History of Modern Science
Stud Hist P — Studies in History and Philosophy of Science
Stud Hist Philos Sci — Studies in History and Philosophy of Science
Stud Hist Philos Sci B Stud Hist Philos Modern Phys — Studies in History and Philosophy of Science. B. Studies in History and Philosophy of Modern Physics
Stud Hist Phil Sci — Studies in History and Philosophy of Science
Stud Hum Ecol — Studies in Human Ecology
Studia Alban — Studia Albanica
Studia Automat — Studia z Automatiki
Studia Automat Inform — Studia z Automatyki i Informatyki
Studia Can — Studia Canonica
Studia Ent — Studia Entomologica
Studia Forest Suecica — Studia Forestalia Suecica
Studia For Suec — Studia Forestalia Suecica
Studia Geotech Mech — Studia Geotechnica et Mechanica
Studia I — Studia Iranica
Studia Leibnitiana Suppl — Studia Leibnitiana. Supplementa
Studi Am — Studi Americani
Studia M — Studia Missionalia
Studia Math — Studia Mathematica
Studia Math/Math Lehrbuecher — Studia Mathematica/Mathematische Lehrbuecher
Studia Math/Math Lehrbuecher Taschenbuch — Studia Mathematica/Mathematische Lehrbuecher. Taschenbuch
Studia Mission — Studia Missionalia
Studia Mus — Studia Musicologica
Studia Mus Nor — Studia Musicologica Norvegica
Studia Neophil — Studia Neophilologica
Studia Sci Math Hungar — Studia Scientiarum Mathematicarum Hungarica
Studia Ser Math — Studia. Series Mathematica
Studia Univ Bab Bol — Studia Universitatis Babes-Bolyai
Studia Univ Babes-Bolyai Math — Universitatis Babes-Bolyai. Studia. Series Mathematica
Studia Univ Babes-Bolyai Ser Math-Mech — Studia Universitatis Babes-Bolyai. Series Mathematica-Mechanica
Studia Univ Babes-Bolyai Ser Phys — Studia Universitatis Babes-Bolyai. Series Physica
Studia Zool R Scient Univ Hung Budapest — Studia Zoologica Regiae Scientiarum Universitatis Hungaricae Budapestensis
Studi Balt — Studi Baltici
Studi Balt NS — Studi Baltici. N.S. Rom
Studi Bizant Neoell — Studi Bizantini e Neoellenici
Studi Classe Orient — Studi Classici e Orientali
Studi Cl Orient — Studi Classici e Orientali
Stud Iconog — Studies in Iconography
Studiecent TNO Scheepsbouw Navig Commun — Studiecentrum TNO [*Toegepast Natuurwetenschappelijk Onderzoek*] voor Scheepsbouw en Navigatie. Communication
Studicent TNO Scheepsbouw Navig Rep — Studiecentrum TNO [*Toegepast Natuurwetenschappelijk Onderzoek*] voor Scheepsbouw en Navigatie. Report
Studi Econ — Studi d'Economia
Studi Econ (Cagliari) — Studi di Economia (Cagliari)

Studi Econ E Giurid Univ Cagliari — Studi Economici e Giuridici. Universita di Cagliari

Studi Econ (Naples) — Studi Economici (Naples)

Studi Emigr — Studi Emigrazione

Studienb Naturwiss Tech — Studienbuecher Naturwissenschaft und Technik

Studiengruppe Systemforsch Heidelberg Ber — Studiengruppe fuer Systemforschung. Heidelberg. Bericht

Studienmater Weiterbild Med Tech Assist — Studienmaterial zur Weiterbildung Medizinisch-Technischer Assistenten

Studienreihe Inform — Studienreihe Informatik

Studienskripten zur Soziol — Studienskripten zur Soziologie

Studien und Mitteilungen — Studien und Mitteilungen aus dem Benediktiner- und dem Cistercienser-Orden

Studies — Studies in Political Economy

Studies Appl Math — Studies in Applied Mathematics

Studies App Math — Studies in Applied Mathematics

Studies Conserv — Studies in Conservation

Studies Econ Analysis — Studies in Economic Analysis

Studies Hum — Studies in the Humanities

Studies in Art Ed — Studies in Art Education

Studies in Aust Bibliog — Studies in Australian Bibliography

Studies in Can Lit — Studies in Canadian Literature

Studies in Lit a Philol — Studies in Literature and Philology

Studies Internat Relations (Warsaw) — Studies on International Relations (Warsaw)

Studies L & Econ Develop — Studies in Law and Economic Development

Studies Mus — Studies in Music

Studies of Bcasting — Studies of Broadcasting

Studies Parasitol and Gen Zool — Studies in Parasitology and General Zoology

Studies Philol — Studies in Philology

Studies Pol Economy — Studies in Political Economy

Studies Zool Lab Univ Nebr — Studies. Zoological Laboratory. University of Nebraska

Studi Filol Mod — Studi di Filologia Moderna

Studi Franc — Studi Francesi

Studii Cerc Biol — Studii si Cercetari de Biologie

Studii Cerc Biol Biol Anim — Studii si Cercetari de Biologie. Seria Biologie Animala

Studii Cerc Biol Zool — Studii si Cercetari de Biologie. Seria Zoologie

Studii Cercet Chim — Studii si Cercetari de Chimie

Studii Cercet Econ — Studii si Cercetari Economice

Studii Cerc Geol Geofiz Geogr — Studii si Cercetari de Geologie, Geofizica, si Geografie. Seria Geografie

Studii Cerc Stiint Iasi Biol Stiint Agric — Studii si Cercetari Stiintifice. Filiala Iasi. Academia RPR. [*Republicii Populare Romine*]. Biologice si Stiinte Agricole

Studi Ital di Fil Cl — Studi Italiani di Filologia Classica

Studi Ital Filol Cl — Studi Italiani di Filologia Classica

StudiItalFilol Class — Studi Italiani di Filologia Classica

Studii Teh Econ Inst Geol Rom — Studii Tehnice si Economice. Institutului Geologic al Romaniei. Stiinta Solulul

Studi It Filol Class — Studi Italiani di Filologia Classica

Studijni Inform Lesnictyi — Studijni Informace. Lesnictyi

Studi M — Studi Musicali

Studi Materiali di Arche Num — Studi e Materiali di Archeologia e Numismatica

Studi Mat St Religioni — Studi e Materiale di Storia delle Religioni

Studi Med — Studi Medievali

Studi Med Chir Sport — Studi de Medicina e Chirurgia dello Sport

Studi Mediev — Studi Medievali

Studi Mus — Studi Musicali

Stud in Comp Local Govt — Studies in Comparative Local Government

Stud in Contin Educ — Studies in Continuing Education

Stud Indo-As Art Cult — Studies in Indo-Asian Art and Culture

Stud Inf Rostl Vyroba Ustav Vedeckotech Inf Zemed — Studijni Informace. Rostlinna Vyroba. Ustav Vedeckotechnickych Informaci pro Zemedelstvi

Stud Inf Ustav Vedeckotech Inf Zemed Rostl Vyroba — Studijni Informace. Ustav Vedeckotechnickych Informaci pro Zemedelstvi. Rostlinna Vyroba

Stud Inorg Chem — Studies in Inorganic Chemistry

Stud In Philol — Studies in Philology. University of North Carolina

Stud In Relat — Studies in International Relations

Stud Inst Divi Thomae — Studies. Institutum Divi Thomae

Stud Inst Hortic Kyoto Univ — Studies from the Institute of Horticulture. Kyoto University

Stud Inst Med Chem Univ Szeged — Studies from the Institute of Medical Chemistry. University of Szeged

Stud Inst Med Res (Malaya) — Studies. Institute for Medical Research (Malaya)

Stud Int — Studio International

Stud Intellectual Precocity — Studies of Intellectual Precocity

Stud Intell Obs — Student and Intellectual Observer

Stud Interface Sci — Studies in Interface Science

Stud in the Novel — Studies in the Novel

Stud Int Relat — Studies on International Relations

Studio — Studio International

Studiol — Studio International

Studio Int — Studio International

Studio Intl — Studio International

Stud Iran — Studia Iranica

Studi Ric Div Geomineraria Com Naz Ric Nucl — Studi e Ricerche. Divisione Geomineraria. Comitato Nazionale per le Ricerche Nucleari

Studi Ric Ist Mineral Petrogr Univ Pavia — Studi e Ricerche. Istituto di Mineralogia e Petrografia. Universita di Pavia

Studi Ric Univ Naz Somala Fac Agrar — Studi e Ricerche. Universita Nazionale Somala. Facolta di Agraria

Stud Irish Q Rev Lett Philos & Sci — Studies. An Irish Quarterly Review of Letters, Philosophy, and Science

Studi Sassar — Studi Sassaresi

Studi Sassaresi Sez 2 Arch Bimest Sci Med Nat — Studi Sassaresi. Sezione 2. Archivio Bimestrale di Scienze Mediche e Naturali

Studi Sassar Sez 1 — Studi Sassaresi. Sezione 1

Studi Sassar Sez 2 — Studi Sassaresi. Sezione 2. Archivio Bimestrale di Scienze Mediche e Naturali

Studi Sassar Sez 3 — Studi Sassaresi. Sezione 3. Annali della Facolta di Agraria dell Universita di Sassari

Studi Sassar Sez 3 — Studi Sassaresi. Sezione 3. Annali. Facolta di Agraria. Universita di Sassari

Studi Sassar Sez III Ann Fac Agrar Univ Sassari — Studi Sassaresi. Sezione III. Annali. Facolta di Agraria. Universita di Sassari

Stud Islam — Studia Islamica

Stud Islam — Studies in Islamic Art

Stud Islamica — Studia Islamica

Studi Sociol — Studi di Sociologia

Studi Stor — Studi Storici Instituto Gramisci Editor

Studi Stor — Studi Storici per l'Antichita Classica

Stud Istoria Artei — Studii si Cercetari de Istoria Artei

Stud Istoria Artei — Studii si Cercetari de Istoria Artei. Seria Arta Plastica

Stud It — Studi Italiani

Stud It — Studi Italiani di Filologia Classica

Stud Ital Filol Class — Studi Italiana di Filologia Classica

Studi Teh Econ Inst Geol Rom — Studii Tehnice si Economice. Institutului Geologic al Romaniei

Studi Trentini Cl 2 — Studi Trentini. Classe 2. Scienze Naturali ed Economiche

Studi Trentini Sci Nat — Studi Trentini di Scienze Naturali

Studi Trentini Sci Nat Acta Biol — Studi Trentini di Scienze Naturali. Acta Biologica

Studi Trentini Sci Nat Acta Geol — Studi Trentini di Scienze Naturali. Acta Geologica

Studi Trentini Sci Nat Sez A — Studi Trentini di Scienze Naturali. Sezione A. Biologica

Studi Trentini Sci Nat Sez B Biol — Studi Trentini di Scienze Naturali. Sezione B. Biologica

Studi Urbinati Fac Farm — Studi Urbinati. Facolta di Farmacia

Studi Urbinati NSB — Studi Urbinati di Storia, Filosofia, e Letteratura. Nuova Serie B

Stud J Dis — Studies in Joint Disease

Stud J Inst Electron and Telecommun Eng — Students' Journal. Institution of Electronics and Telecommunication Engineers

Stud J Inst Electron Telecommun Eng — Students' Journal. Institution of Electronics and Telecommunication Engineers

Stud Jud & Late Ant — Studies in Judaism and Late Antiquity

Stud Jugendzahn A — Student und Jugendzahnarzt

Stud Kst 19 Jhts — Studien zur Kunst des 19. Jahrhunderts

Stud Kulturkunde — Studien zur Kulturkunde

Stud Laboris Salutis — Studia Laboris et Salutis

Stud Labour Hist — Studies in Labour History

Stud Lang — Studies in Language. International Journal

Stud Lang C — Studies in Language. Companion Series

Stud Lang Ling — Studies in Language and Linguistics

Stud Lat Amer Pop Cult — Studies in Latin American Popular Culture

Stud Latin Amer Pop Cult — Studies in Latin American Popular Culture

Stud Latin Am Rev — Studies in Latin American Revolution

Stud Learn Sci — Studies in the Learning Sciences

Stud Left — Studies on the Left

Stud Leibn — Studia Leibnitiana

Stud Leibnit — Studia Leibnitiana

Stud Leibnitiana — Studia Leibnitiana

Stud Lib Man — Studies in Library Management

Stud Ling — Studia Linguistica

Stud Ling — Studies in Linguistics

Stud Ling Friul — Studi Linguistici Friulani

Stud Ling Lang Learn — Studies in Linguistics and Languages Learning

Stud Ling Sci — Studies in the Linguistic Sciences

Stud Linguist Philos — Studies in Linguistics and Philosophy

Stud Lit — Studia Liturgica

Stud Lit Im — Studies in the Literary Imagination

Stud Lit Imag — Studies in the Literary Imagination

Stud Liturg — Studia Liturgica

Stud Log — Studia Logica

Stud Logic Comput — Studies in Logic and Computation

Stud Logic Foundations Math — Studies in Logic and the Foundations of Mathematics

Stud Logic Lang Inform — Studies in Logic, Language, and Information

Stud Logic Sci — Studies in the Logic of Science

Stud M — Studies in Music

Stud Maceratesi — Studi Maceratesi

Stud Mag — Studi Magrebini

Stud Magr — Studi Magrebini

Stud Management Sci — Studies in the Management Sciences

Stud Management Sci Systems — Studies in Management Science and Systems

Stud Mar Sin — Studia Marina Sinica

Stud Mater Dziej Nauk Pol Ser A — Studia i Materialy z Dziejow Nauki Polskiej. Seria A. Historia Nauk Spolecznych

Stud Mater Dziej Nauk Pol Ser B — Studia i Materialy z Dziejow Nauki Polskiej. Seria B. Historia Nauk Biologicznych i Medycznych

Stud Mater Dziej Nauk Pol Ser C — Studia i Materialy z Dziejow Nauki Polskiej. Seria C. Historia Nauk Matematycznych, Fizykochemicznych i Geoloiczno-geograficznych

Stud Mater Dziej Nauk Pol Ser D — Studia i Materialy z Dziejow Nauki Polskiej. Seria D. Historia Techniki i Nauk Technicznych

Stud Mater Dziej Nauk Pol Ser E — Studia i Materialy z Dziejow Nauki Polskiej. Seria E. Zagadnienia Ogolne

Stud Mater Dziejow Nauki Pol Ser D — Studia i Materialy z Dziejow Nauki Polskiej. Seria D. Historia Techniki i Nauk Technicznych
Stud Materialien Geschichte Philos — Studien und Materialien zur Geschichte der Philosophie
Stud Mater Oceanol Pol Akad Nauk Kom Badan Morza — Studia i Materialy Oceanologiczne. Polska Akademia Nauk. Komitet Badan Morza
Stud Mater Weiterbild Med Tech Laborassistenten — Studien-Material zur Weiterbildung Medizinisch-Technischer Laborassistenten
Stud Math — Studia Mathematica
Stud Math Appl — Studies in Mathematics and Its Applications
Stud Math Ed Ser — Studies in Mathematics Education Series
Stud Math Managerial Econom — Studies in Mathematical and Managerial Economics
Stud Math Phys — Studies in Mathematical Physics
Stud Math Think Learn — Studies in Mathematical Thinking and Learning
Stud Mat Ist Medie — Studii si Materiale de Istorie Medie
Stud Mat Muz Ist Mil — Studii si Materiale de Muzeografie si Istorie Militara
Stud Mat Muz (Tirgu Mures) — Studii si Materiale Muzeul Judetean (Tirgu-Mures, Romania)
Stud Mat Stor Rel — Studi e Materiali di Storia della Religioni
Stud Mat (Suceava) — Studii si Materiale Muzeul Judetean (Suceava, Romania)
Stud Mechlin — Studia Mechliniensia
Stud Med — Student Medicine
Stud Med — Studi Medievali
Stud Med & Ren Hist — Studies in Medieval and Renaissance History
Stud Med Chem — Studies in Medicinal Chemistry
Stud Med Chir Sport — Studi di Medicina e Chirurgia dello Sport
Stud Med Cult — Studies in Medieval Culture
Stud Med Geogr — Studies in Medical Geography
Stud Mediev — Studies in Medieval Culture
Stud Mediev — Studi Medievali
Stud Medievali — Studi Medievali
Stud Medieval Renaiss Hist — Studies in Medieval and Renaissance History
Stud Mediew — Studia Mediewistyczne
Stud Medit Archaeol — Studies in Mediterranean Archaeology
Stud Medizingesch Neunzehnten Jahrhunderts — Studien zur Medizingeschichte des Neunzehnten Jahrhunderts
Stud Med Szeged — Studia Medica Szegedinensia
Stud Med Szegedinensia — Studia Medica Szegedinensia
Stud Merid — Studi Meridionali. Rivista Trimestrale di Studi sull'Italia Centro-Meridionale
Stud Micenei & Egeo Anatol — Studi Micenei ed Egeo-Anatolici
Stud Microbiol — Studia Microbiologica
Stud Microbiol — Studies in Microbiology
Stud Minora Fac Philos U Brunensis — Studi Minora Facultatis Philosophicae Universitatis Brunensis
Stud Misc — Studi Miscellanei
Stud Miss — Studia Missionalia
Stud Mitt Bened Cisterc — Studien und Mitteilungen aus dem Benediktiner- und dem Cistercienser-Orden
Stud Mitt Gesch Benediktinerorden — Studien und Mitteilungen zur Geschichte des Benediktiner-Ordens und Seiner Zweige
Stud Modern Thermodynamics — Studies in Modern Thermodynamics
StudMon — Studia Monastica
Stud Monographs Phys — Student Monographs in Physics
Stud Monzesi — Studi Monzesi
Stud Musicol — Studia Musicologica
Stud Musicol Norvegica — Studia Musicologica Norvegica
Stud Muz — Studia Muzealne
Stud Muzicol — Studii de Muzicologie
Stud MW — Studien zur Musikwissenschaft
Stud Mycol — Studies in Mycology
Stud Myst — Studia Mystica
Stud Nakamura Gakuin Univ — Studies. Nakamura Gakuin University
Stud Nat Pol Akad Nauk Zakl Ochr Przyr Ser A — Studia Naturae. Polska Akademia Nauk, Zaklad Ochrony Przyrody. Seria A. Wydawnictwa Naukowe
Stud Nat Prod Chem — Studies in Natural Products Chemistry
Stud Nat Sci — Studies in the Natural Sciences
Stud Nat Sci NY — Studies in the Natural Sciences (New York)
Stud Nat Sci (Portales NM) — Studies in Natural Sciences (Portales, New Mexico)
Stud Nat Ser A — Studia Naturae. Seria A. Wydawnictwa Naukowe
Stud Nauchno Issled Rab Sib Tekhnol Inst — Studencheskie Nauchno-Issledovatel'skie Raboty. Sibirskii Tekhnologicheskii Institut
Stud Nauchn Rab Novocherk Politekh Inst — Studencheskie Nauchnye Raboty. Novocherkasskii Politekhnicheskii Institut
Stud Nauchn Rab Univ Druzhby Nar — Studencheskie Nauchnye Raboty. Universitet Druzhby Narodov
Stud Nauk Polit — Studia Nauk Politycznych
Stud Nauk Pr Kiiv Derzh Univ — Students'ki Naukovi Pratsi Kiivs'kii Derzhavnii Universitet
Stud Nauk Rob Kiiv Derzh Univ — Students'ki Naukovi Roboty. Kiivs'kii Derzhavnii Universitet
Stud Ned Hist Inst Rome — Studien van het Nederlands Historisch Instituut te Rome
Stud Neoph — Studia Neophilologica
Stud Neophilol — Studia Neophilologica
StudNeot — Studia Neotestamentica
Stud Neotrop Fauna — Studies on the Neotropical Fauna [Later, Studies on the Neotropical Fauna and Environment]
Stud Neotrop Fauna Environ — Studies on the Neotropical Fauna and Environment
Stud Neuro Anat — Studies in Neuro-Anatomy
Stud Neurosci — Studies in Neuroscience
Stud Niger Lang — Studies in Nigerian Languages

Stud Nonlinear Phenom Life Sci — Studies of Nonlinear Phenomena in Life Science
Stud No Phil — Studies and Notes in Philology and Literature
Stud Novel — Studies in the Novel
StudNT — Studien zum Neuen Testament
Stud Nurs Man — Studies in Nursing Management
Stud Oliveriana — Studi Oliveriana
Stud Onomast Monacensia — Studia Onomastica Monacensia
StudOr — Studia Orientalia
Stud Org Chem Amsterdam — Studies in Organic Chemistry (Amsterdam)
Stud Orient — Studia Orientalia
Stud Ostasiat Schrkst — Studien zur Ostasiatischen Schriftkunst
Stud Ov — Studium Ovetense
Stud Pac Lang Cult — Studies in Pacific Languages and Cultures in Honour of Bruce Biggs
Stud Paint (Osaka) — Studies in Paint (Osaka)
StudPal — Studien zur Palaeographie und Papyruskunde
Stud Palmyr — Studia Palmyrenskie
StudPap — Studia Papyrologica
Stud Papyrol — Studia Papyrologica
Stud Pat — Studia Patavina. Rivista di Scienze Religiose
Stud Patr — Studia Patristica
Stud (Pavia) — Studi nelle Scienze Giuridiche e Sociali (Pavia)
Stud Person Psychol — Studies in Personnel Psychology
Stud Pers P — Studies in Personnel Psychology
Stud Pers Psych — Studies in Personnel Psychology
Stud Pharm — Student Pharmacist
Stud Phil — Studia Philosophica
Stud Phil — Studies in Philology
Stud Phil & Ed — Studies in Philosophy and Education
Stud Phil Christ — Studia Philosophiae Christiane
Stud Phil E — Studies in Philosophy and Education
Stud Phil H — Studies in Philosophy and the History of Philosophy
Stud Phil Hist Phil — Studies in Philosophy and the History of Philosophy
Stud Phil Ling — Studies in Philippine Linguistics
Stud Philol — Studies in Philology
Stud Philol ChapelH — Studies in Philology (Chapel Hill)
Stud Philos — Studies in Philosophy
Stud Philos & Educ — Studies in Philosophy and Education
Stud Philos Med — Studies in Philosophy of Medicine
Stud Phil (Switzerland) — Studia Philosophica (Switzerland)
Stud Phoenicia — Studia Phoenicia
Stud Phonet — Studia Phonetica
Stud Phonol — Studia Phonologica
Stud Phys Anthrop — Studies in Physical Anthropology
Stud Phys Anthropol — Studies in Physical Anthropology
Stud Phys Theor Chem — Studies in Physical and Theoretical Chemistry
Stud Phys Theoret Chem — Studies in Physical and Theoretical Chemistry
Stud Pic — Studia Picena
Stud Picena — Studia Picena
Stud Piemont — Studi Piemontesi
Stud Plant Ecol — Studies in Plant Ecology
Stud Plant Sci — Studies in Plant Science
Stud Pneumol Phtiseol Cech — Studia Pneumologica et Phtiseologica Cechoslovaca
Stud Poet Ges Lit — Studien zur Poetik und Geschichte der Literatur
Stud Polym Sci — Studies in Polymer Science
Stud Pomorskie — Studia Pomorskie
Stud Pont — Studia Pontica
Stud Praehist — Studia Praehistorica
Stud Prawno-Ekon — Studia Prawno-Ekonomiczne
Stud Pr Cr — Studi e Problemi di Critica Testuale
Stud Probab Optim Statist — Studies in Probability, Optimization, and Statistics
Stud Prod Engrg Econom — Studies in Production and Engineering Economics
Stud Profertil Ser — Studies in Profertility Series
Stud Proof Theory Lecture Notes — Studies in Proof Theory. Lecture Notes
Stud Proof Theory Monographs — Studies in Proof Theory. Monographs
Stud Prot Epurarea Apelor — Studii de Protectia si Epurarea Apelor
Stud Psych — Studia Psychologica
Stud Psycho — Studia Psychologica
Stud Psychol — Studia Psychologiczne
Stud Psychol (Bratisl) — Studia Psychologica (Bratislava)
Stud Psychol Psychiat Cath Univ Amer — Studies in Psychology and Psychiatry. Catholic University of America
Stud Pub Com — Studies in Public Communication
Stud Q J Inst Electr Eng — Students Quarterly Journal. Institution of Electrical Engineers
Stud QJ Inst El Eng — Students Quarterly Journal. Institution of Electrical Engineers
Stud Radiat Eff Ser A — Studies in Radiation Effects. Series A. Physical and Chemical
Stud Radiat Eff Solids — Studies in Radiation Effects in Solids
Stud Regional Sci Urban Econom — Studies in Regional Science and Urban Economics
Stud Rel — Studies in Religion
Stud Relig — Studies in Religion
Stud Ren — Studia Renesansowe
Stud Ren — Studies in the Renaissance
Stud Renaiss — Studies in the Renaissance
Stud Renaissance — Studies in the Renaissance
Stud Rep Hydrol IAHS - UNESCO — Studies and Reports in Hydrology. International Association of Hydrological Sciences - United Nations Educational, Scientific, and Cultural Organization
Stud Rep U Indust A & Textile Fibres — Study Report of the University of Industrial Arts and Textile Fibres

Stud Res Inst Meteorol Hydrol Part 2 — Studies and Research. Institute of Meteorology and Hydrology. Part 2. Hydrology

Stud Rev Univ Atl (Barranquilla Colomb) — Studia. Revista. Universidad del Atlantico. (Barranquilla, Colombia)

Stud Ric Div Geomineraria Com Naz Ric Nucl — Studi e Ricerche. Divisione Geomineraria. Comitato Nazionale per le Ricerche Nucleari

Stud Ric Ist Mineral Petrogr Univ Pavia — Studi e Ricerche. Istituto di Mineralogia e Petrografia. Universita di Pavia

StudRom — Studi Romani

StudRom — Studi Romanzi

Stud Romagn — Studi Romagnoli

Stud Roman — Studies in Romanticism

Stud Romani — Studi Ronami

Stud Romant — Studies in Romanticism

Stud Romanticism — Studies in Romanticism

Stud Rsch — Studentische Rundschau

Stud Sachsforsch — Studien zur Sachsenforschung

StudSal — Studi Salentini

StudSard — Studi Sardi

Stud S Asian Cult — Studies in South Asian Culture

Stud Sassar Sez 1 — Studi Sassaresi. Sezione 1

Stud Sci Educ — Studies in Science Education

Stud Sci Giur Soc — Studi delle Scienze Giuridiche e Sociali

Stud Sci Math Hung — Studia Scientiarum Mathematicarum Hungarica

Stud Sc Lit — Studies in Scottish Literature

Stud Scott Lit — Studies in Scottish Literature

Stud Secent — Studi Secenteschi

Stud Seicent — Studi Seicenteschi

StudSemNeerl — Studia Semitica Neerlandica

Stud Serv Rev — Student Services Review

Stud Settecento Romano — Studi sul Settecento Romano

Stud Sh Fic — Studies in Short Fiction

Stud Short Fict — Studies in Short Fiction

Stud Short Fiction — Studies in Short Fiction

Stud Sociol — Studi di Sociologia

Stud Socjol — Studia Socjologiczne

Stud Soc Li — Studies in Social Life

Stud Soc Pol — Studia Socjologiczno-Polityczne

Stud Soc Sci Torun Sect A — Studia Societatis Scientiarum Torunensis. Sectio A. Mathematica-Physica

Stud Soc Sci Torun Sect B — Studia Societatis Scientiarum Torunensis. Sectio B (Chemie)

Stud Soc Sci Torun Sect C (Geogr Geol) — Studia Societatis Scientiarum Torunensis. Sectio C (Geographia et Geologia)

Stud Soc Sci Torun Sect D (Bot) — Studia Societatis Scientiarum Torunensis. Sectio D (Botanica)

Stud Soc Sci Torun Sect E (Zool) — Studia Societatis Scientiarum Torunensis. Sectio E (Zoologia)

Stud Soc Sci Torun Sect F — Studia Societatis Scientiarum Torunensis. Sectio F (Astronomia)

Stud Soc Sci Torun Sect G (Physiol) — Studia Societatis Scientiarum Torunensis. Sectio G (Physiologia)

Stud Soc Wk — Studies on Social Work

Stud Solid Phys Chem — Studies on Solid State Physics and Chemistry

Stud Soviet Union — Studies on the Soviet Union

Stud Sov Th — Studies in Soviet Thought

Stud Sov Thought — Studies in Soviet Thought

Stud Spelaeol — Studies in Spelaeology

Stud Speleol — Studies in Speleology

Stud Speleology — Studies in Speleology

Stud Sprogforskn — Studier fra Sprog- og Oldtidsforskning

Stud Sprog Og Oldtidsforskn — Studier fra Sprog- og Oldtidsforskning

Stud Statist Mech — Studies in Statistical Mechanics

Stud Stat Mech — Studies in Statistical Mechanics

Stud Stn Fish Res Board Can — Studies. Stations of the Fisheries Research Board of Canada

Stud Stobi — Studies in the Antiquities of Stobi

Stud Stor — Studia Storia

Stud Stor — Studi Storici

Stud Stor — Studi Storici per l'Antichita Classica

Stud Stor A — Studi di Storia delle Arti

Stud Stor A U Genova Ist Stor A — Studi di Storia delle Arti. Universita di Genova. Istituto di Storia dell'Arte

Stud Storic — Studi Storici

Stud Stor Ordine Servi Maria — Studi Storici sull'Ordine dei Servi di Maria

Stud Stor Veron — Studi Storici Veronesi

Stud Surf Sci Catal — Studies in Surface Science and Catalysis

Studsvik Rep — Studsvik Report

Stud TC — Studies in the Twentieth Century

Stud Tea — Study of Tea/Chagyo Gijutsu Kenkyu. Tea Research Station. Ministry of Agriculture and Forestry

Stud Teh Econ Inst Geol Rom — Studii Tehnice si Economice Institutului Geologic al Romaniei

Stud Teh Econ Inst Geol (Rom) Ser A — Studii Tehnice si Economice. Institutul Geologic (Romania). Seria A. Prospectiuni si Explorari Geologice

Stud Teh Econ Inst Geol (Rom) Ser B — Studii Tehnice si Economice. Institutul Geologic (Romania). Seria B. Chimie

Stud Teh Econ Inst Geol (Rom) Ser C — Studii Tehnice si Economice. Institutul Geologic (Romania). Seria C. Pedologie

Stud Teh Econ Inst Geol (Rom) Ser D — Studii Tehnice si Economice. Institutul Geologic (Romania). Seria D. Prospectiuni Geofizice

Stud Teh Econ Inst Geol (Rom) Ser E — Studii Tehnice si Economice. Institutul Geologic (Romania). Seria E. Hidrogeologie

Stud Teh Econ Inst Geol (Rom) Ser F — Studii Tehnice si Economice. Institutul Geologic (Romania). Seria F. Geologie Tehnice

Stud Teh Econ Inst Geol Ser E — Studii Tehnice si Economice. Institutul Geologic (Romania). Seria E. Hidrogeologie

Stud Teh Econ Inst Geol Ser I — Studii Tehnice si Economice. Institutul Geologic (Romania). Seria I. Mineralogie-Petrografie

Stud Teh Econ Ser A Inst Geol Geofiz Bucharest — Studii Tehnice si Economice. Seria A. Prospectiuni si Explorari Geologice Institul de Geologie si Geolizica. Bucharest

Stud Teh Econ Ser B Inst Geol Geofiz Bucharest — Studii Tehnice si Economice. Seria B. Chimie. Institutul de Geologie si Geofizica. Bucharest

Stud Teh Econ Ser C Inst Geol Rom — Studii Tehnice si Economice. Seria C. Pedologie. Institutul Geologic. Romania

Stud Teh Econ Ser D Inst Geol Geofiz (Bucharest) — Studii Tehnice si Economice. Seria D. Prospectiuni Geofizice. Institutul de Geologie si Geofizica (Bucharest)

Stud Teh Econ Ser E Inst Geol Geofiz — Studii Tehnice si Economice. Seria E. Hidrogeologie. Institutul de Geologie si Geofizica

Stud Teol — Studii Teologice

Stud Test — Studi e Testi. Biblioteca Apostolica Vaticana

Stud Texte Geistesgesch Mittelalt — Studien und Texte zur Geistesgeschichte des Mittelalters

Stud Texte Phys — Studien-Texte. Physik

Stud Textile Hist — Studies in Textile History

Stud Text Math — Studien-Text. Mathematik

Stud Th — Studia Theologica

Stud Theol — Studia Theologica

Stud Third World Soc — Studies In Third World Societies

Stud Tokugawa Inst — Studies. Tokugawa Institute

Stud Tour Rep Dep Prim Ind (Queensl) — Study Tour Report. Department of Primary Industries (Queensland)

Stud Trade Unionists — Studies for Trade Unionists

Stud Trent — Studi Trentini di Scienze Storiche

Stud Trentini Sci Stor — Studi Trentini di Scienze Storiche

Stud Trevi — Studi Trevisani

Stud Trop Oceanogr Inst Mar Sci Univ Miami — Studies in Tropical Oceanography. Institute of Marine Science. University of Miami

Stud Trop Oceanogr (Miami) — Studies in Tropical Oceanography (Miami)

Stud Uch Zap Erevan Gos Univ — Studencheskie Uchenye Zapiski. Erevanskii Gosudarstvennyi Universitet

Stud Univ Babes-Bolyai Biol — Studia Universitatis Babes-Bolyai. Series Biologia

Stud Univ Babes-Bolyai Chem — Studia Universitatis Babes-Bolyai. Series Chemia

Stud Univ Babes-Bolyai Geol-Geogr — Studia Universitatis Babes-Bolyai. Series Geologia-Geographia

Stud Univ Babes-Bolyai Math — Studia Universitatis Babes-Bolyai. Series Mathematica

Stud Univ Babes-Bolyai Phys — Studia Universitatis Babes-Bolyai. Series Physica

Stud Univ Babes-Bolyai Ser Biol — Studia Universitatis Babes-Bolyai. Series Biologia

Stud Univ Babes-Bolyai Ser Chem — Studia Universitatis Babes-Bolyai. Series Chemia

Stud Univ Babes-Bolyai Ser Geol-Minerol — Studia Universitatis Babes-Bolyai. Series Geologia-Minerologia

Stud Univ Babes-Bolyai Ser Math-Phys — Studia Universitatis Babes-Bolyai. Series Mathematica-Physica

Stud Univ Babes-Bolyai Ser Phys — Studia Universitatis Babes-Bolyai. Series Physica

Stud Urb — Studi Urbinati di Storia, Filosofia, e Letteratura

Stud Urbin Sci Giur Polit & Econ — Studi Urbinati di Scienze, Giuridiche, Politiche, ed Economiche

Stud Urbin Stor Filos & Lett — Studi Urbinati di Storia, Filosofia, e Letteratura

Stud Urb (Ser A) — Studi Urbinati di Scienze Giuridiche ed Economiche (Ser. A)

Stud Urb St — Studi Urbinati di Storia, Filosofia, e Letteratura

Stud US Hist Cult — Studies in US History and Culture

Stud Vac Ultraviolet X Ray Processes — Studies of Vacuum Ultraviolet and X-Ray Processes

Stud Ven — Studi Veneziani

Stud Venez — Studi Veneziani

Stud Veneziani — Studi Veneziani

Stud Vers Anthropos Schriftenreihe — Studien und Versuche. Eine Anthroposophische Schriftenreihe

Stud Vis Com — Studies in Visual Communication

Stud Vis Communic — Studies in Visual Communication

Stud Voltaire — Studies on Voltaire and the Eighteenth Century

Stud Voltaire 18th Cent — Studies on Voltaire and the Eighteenth Century

Stud Voltaire & 18th C — Studies on Voltaire and the Eighteenth Century

Stud Voltaire Eighteenth Century — Studies on Voltaire and the Eighteenth Century

Stud VT Geol — Studies in Vermont Geology

Stud VUB — Studies en Voordrachten. Faculteit der Rechtsgeleerdheid VUB

Stud W — Student World

Stud Warb Inst — Studies of the Warburg Institute

Stud Wiss Soz Bildungsgesch Math — Studien zur Wissenschafts-, Sozial-, und Bildungsgeschichte der Mathematik

Stud Women Abstr — Studies on Women Abstracts

Study Elem Particles — Study of Elementary Particles

Study of Soc — Study of Society

Study Tea — Study of Tea

Stud Zrodloznawcze — Studia Zrodloznawcze. Commentationes

StudzumAuNT — Studien zum Alten und Neuen Testament

Stud Zvesti — Studijne Zvesti Archeologickeho Ustavu Slovenskej Akademie v Nitra

Stuekult — Stuekulturer

StuiHS — Studies in History and Society

StuiR — Studies in the Renaissance

St u Komm V — Staats und Kommunalverwaltung

Stu Mon — Studia Monastica
StUmwNT — Studien zur Umwelt des Neuen Testament
St und T z Geistesgesch des MA — Studien und Texte zur Geistesgeschichte des Mittelalters
St UNT — Studien zur Umwelt des Neuen Testament
STUOA — Sbornik Nauchnykh Trudov Ukrainskii Nauchno-Issledovatel'skii Institut Ogneuporov
St u P — Studium und Praxis
Stu Pat — Studia Patavina
Stu Prob & St — Studies in Probability and Statistics
St u R — Staat und Recht
StuR — Studii. Revista de Istorie
St Urbin — Studi Urbinati
Sturg BL — Sturgeon. Bankrupt Acts
Sturgeon A Electr — Annals of Electricity, Magnetism, and Chemistry. And Guardian of Experimental Science. Sturgeon
Stu Ros — Studia Rosenthaliana
Stu Sl — Studia Slavica
StuSta — Studia Staropolskie
StuTC — Studies in the Twentieth Century
Stutt Beitr Naturk — Stuttgarter Beitraege zur Naturkunde
Stuttgarter Beitraege — Stuttgarter Beitraege zur Geschichte und Politik
Stuttgarter Beitr Naturk — Stuttgarter Beitraege zur Naturkunde aus dem Staatlichen Museum fuer Naturkundein Stuttgart
Stuttgarter Geogr Stud — Stuttgarter Geographische Studien
Stuttgart Ztg — Stuttgarter Zeitung
Stuttg Beitr Naturkd — Stuttgarter Beitraege zur Naturkunde
Stuttg Beitr Naturkd Ser A (Biol) — Stuttgarter Beitraege zur Naturkunde. Serie A (Biologie)
Stuttg Beitr Naturkd Ser B (Geol Palaeontol) — Stuttgarter Beitraege zur Naturkunde. Serie B (Geologie und Palaeontologie)
Stuttg Beitr Naturk Ser C Allg Aufsaetze — Stuttgarter Beitraege zur Naturkunde. Serie C. Allgemeinverstaendliche Aufsaetze
Stuttg Geogr Stud — Stuttgarter Geographische Studien
Stu VA — Stuart's Lower Canada Vice-Admiralty Reports
St u W — Steuer und Wirtschaft
STUWA — Sterne und Weltraum
St u Wi — Steuer und Wirtschaft
StV — Studies on Voltaire and the Eighteenth Century
Stva — Stvaranje
STV Bull — STV [*Schweizerischer Technischer Verband*] Bulletin
STVCA — Stavebnicky Casopis
St Vd VUB — Studies en Voordrachten. VUB
St VF — Stoicorum Veterum Fragmenta
STVFB — Samoletostroenie i Tekhnika Vozdushnogo Flota
St VG — Straphenverkehrsgesetz
St Vj — Statistische Vierteljahrsschrift
St VK — Studien und Voelkerkunde
StVladSemQ — St. Vladimir's Seminary. Quarterly
St Vl Th Q — Saint Vladimir's Theological Quarterly
St VO — Strafvollstreckungsordnung
St VO — Strassenverkehrsordnung
St Vollstr O — Strafvollstreckungsordnung
St VZO — Strassenverkehrszulassungsordnung
St W — Steuer und Wirtschaft
Stw — Stimmwart
ST Yill — Sanat Tarihi Yilligi
Styr Tek Utveckling Inf Energitek — Styrelsen foer Teknisk Utveckling Informerar om Energiteknik
STZ — Schweizerische Technische Zeitschrift
STZ — Sprache im Technischen Zeitalter
St ZA — Steuer-Zentralarchiv
STZED — Stimmen der Zeit
Stz Probl Gesch — Studien zur Problemgeschichte der Antiken und Mittelalterlichen Philosophie
SU — Samostijna Ukraina
SU — Schriften des Urchristentums
SU — Signos Universitarios
SU — Studi Urbinati
Su — Sumarstvo
Su — Sundhedsbladet
SUAGDL — Sulphur in Agriculture
Suara Ekon — Suara Ekonomi
Suara Univ — Suara Universiti
SUB — Scandinavian University Books
SUBB — Studia Universitatis Babes-Bolyai. Series Philologia
SUBBA — Studia Universitatis Babes-Bolyai. Series Biologia
SUBBP — Studia Universitatis Babes-Bolyai. Series Philologia
SUBCA — Studia Universitatis Babes-Bolyai. Series Chemia
Sub-Cell Bi — Sub-Cellular Biochemistry
Sub-Cell Biochem — Sub-Cellular Biochemistry
Sub Ind Child Mag — Subject Index to Children's Magazines
Subj Index Child Mag — Subject Index to Children's Magazines
Subj Index Period — Subject Index to Periodicals
Subj Index Sel Period Lit — Subject Index to Select Periodical Literature
Subj of Day — Subject of the Day
Sub Life — Suburban Life
SUBMD — Studia Universitatis Babes-Bolyai. Series Mathematica
Submol Glass Chem Phys — Submolecular Glass Chemistry and Physics
Subnucl Ser — Subnuclear Series
SubP — Subsidia 'Pataphysica
SUBPA — Studia Universitatis Babes-Bolyai. Series Mathematica-Physica
SUBPDJ — Annual Research Reviews. Substance P
SubS — Sub-stance. A Review of Theory and Literary Criticism
Subser Optical Sci Engrg — Subseries on Optical Science and Engineering

Subs Hag — Subsidia Hagiographica
Subsidia Med — Subsidia Medica
Subst Alcohol Actions Misuse — Substance and Alcohol Actions/Misuse
Subst Use Misuse — Substance Use and Misuse
Sub Torg — Sovetskaya Torgovlya
Subtrop Kul't — Subtropicheskie Kul'tury
Subtrop Kul't Min Sel'Khoz SSSR — Subtropicheskie Kul'tury. Ministerstvo Sel'skogo Khozyaistva SSSR
SUC — Saggi di Umanismo Cristiano
Success Farm — Successful Farming
Success Farming — Successful Farming
Success Farm South — Successful Farming in the South
Successful F — Successful Farming
Success M — Success Magazine
Success Mtg — Successful Meetings
SUCEC — Setting Up a Company in the European Community
Suc Farm — Successful Farming
Sucr Belg Sugar Ind Abstr — Sucrerie Belge and Sugar Industry Abstracts
Su Ct Rev — Supreme Court Review
SuD — Sprache und Dichtung
SUD — Sudestasie. Magazine d'Information
SUDAM — Editorial Sudamericana, BA
Sudan Agric J — Sudan Agricultural Journal
Sudan Eng Soc J — Sudan Engineering Society. Journal
Sudan Geol Surv Dep Bull — Sudan. Geological Survey Department. Bulletin
Sudan J Econ and Social Studies — Sudan Journal of Economic and Social Studies
Sudan J Econ Soc Stud — Sudan Journal of Economic and Social Studies
Sudan J Food Sci Technol — Sudan Journal of Food Science and Technology
Sudan J Vet Sci Anim Husb — Sudan Journal of Veterinary Science and Animal Husbandry
Sudan LJ & Rep — Sudan Law Journal and Reports
Sudan Notes — Sudan Notes and Records
Sudan Notes Rec — Sudan Notes and Records
Sudan Soc — Sudan Society
Sudebno-Med Ekspert — Sudebno-Meditsinskaya Ekspertiza
SUDENE Bol Recur Nat — SUDENE [*Superintendencia do Desenvolvimento do Nordeste*] Boletim do Recursos Naturais
Sudh Arch — Sudhoffs Archiv
Sudhoffs Arch — Sudhoffs Archiv fuer Geschichte der Medizin und der Naturwissenschaften
Sudhoffs Arch — Sudhoffs Archiv. Zeitschrift fuer Wissenschaftsgeschichte
Sudhoffs Arch Beih — Sudhoffs Archiv. Zeitschrift fuer Wissenschaftsgeschichte Beihefte
Sudhoffs Arch Gesch Med Naturwiss — Sudhoffs Archiv fuer Geschichte der Medizin und der Naturwissenschaften
Sudhoffs Archv Ges Mediz & Natwiss — Sudhoffs Archiv fuer Geschichte der Medizin und der Naturwissenschaften
Sudhoffs Arch Z Wissenschaftsgesch — Sudhoffs Archiv. Zeitschrift fuer Wissenschaftsgeschichte
Sudhoffs Arch Z Wissenschaftsgesch Beih — Sudhoffs Archiv. Zeitschrift fuer Wissenschaftsgeschichte. Beihefte
Sud Inform Econ Provence-Cote D'Azur-Corse — Sud. Information Economique Provence-Cote D'Azur-Corse
Sud Med Chir — Sud Medical et Chirurgical
Sud-Med Ekspert — Sudebno-Meditsinskaya Ekspertiza
Sud Med Ekspert Krim Sluzhbe Sledstviya — Sudebno-Meditsinskaya Ekspertiza i Kriminalistika na Sluzhbe Sledstviya
Sud Med J — Sudan Medical Journal
SuedA — Suedostdeutsches Archiv
Sueddt Ap Zt — Sueddeutsche Apothekerzeitung
Sueddt Mh — Sueddeutsche Monatshefte
Sueddtsch Ztg — Sueddeutsche Zeitung
Sueddt Tonindustrieztg — Sueddeutsche Tonindustrie- und Bauzeitung
SuedoA — Suedostdeutsches Archiv
Suedostdt Arch — Suedostdeutsches Archiv
Suedostdt Forsch — Suedostdeutsche Forschungen
Suedostdt Semesterbl — Suedostdeutsche Semesterblaetter
Suedostdt Vjbl — Suedostdeutsche Vierteljahresblaetter. Suedostdeutsche Heimatblaetter
Suedost Eur Jb — Suedosteuropa-Jahrbuch
Suedosteur Jb — Suedosteuropa-Jahrbuch
Suedosteur Mitt — Suedosteuropa Mitteilungen
Suedost F — Suedost-Forschungen
Suedost Forsch — Suedostforschungen
Suedost-Forsch — Suedost-Forschungen. Internationale Zeitschrift fuer Geschichte, Kultur, und Landeskunde Sued-Osteuropas
Suedwestdt Imker — Suedwestdeutscher Imker
Suelos Ecuat — Suelos Ecuatoriales
SuF — Sinn und Form
Suffolk Transnatl LJ — Suffolk Transnational Law Journal
Suffolk U L Rev — Suffolk University. Law Review
Suffolk Univ L Rev — Suffolk University. Law Review
Suff Trans LJ — Suffolk Transnational Law Journal
Suff U LR — Suffolk University. Law Review
SuG — Sprache und Gemeinschaft
Sugaku — Sugaku. Mathematical Society of Japan
Sugar — Sugar y Azucar
Sugarbeet Grow — Sugarbeet Grower
Sugar Beet J — Sugar Beet Journal
Sugar Beet Rev — Sugar Beet Review and British Beet Grower
Sugar Bul — Sugar Bulletin
Sugar Bull — Sugar Bulletin
Sugarcane Breed Newsl — Sugarcane Breeders' Newsletter
Sugarcane Var Tests Fla — Sugarcane Variety Tests in Florida

Sugar Ind Abstr — Sugar Industry Abstracts
Sugar J — Sugar Journal
Sugar Mol — Sugar Molecule
Sugar Path News — Sugarcane Pathologists Newsletter
Sugar Process Res Conf Proc — Sugar Processing Research Conference. Proceedings
Sugar Technol Rev — Sugar Technology Reviews
Sug Azuc — Sugar y Azucar
Sug Azucar — Sugar y Azucar
Sug B — Sugar Bulletin
Sug J — Sugar Journal
SUGMAW — Glas. Srpska Akademija Nauka i Umetnosti Odeljenje Medicinskih Nauka
Suhrkamp Taschenbuch Wiss — Suhrkamp Taschenbuch Wissenschaft
SUHS — Susitna Hydro Studies
SuiC — Suisse Contemporaine
SUICA — Soul Uitae Chapchi
Suicide Life Threat Behav — Suicide and Life-Threatening Behavior
Suicide Life Threatening Behav — Suicide and Life Threatening Behavior
Suid-Afrikaanse Tydskr Natuurwetenskap Tegnol — Suid-Afrikaanse Tydskrif vir Natuurwetenskap en Tegnologie
Suid Afr Tyd Geneesk — Suid-Afrikaanse Tydskrif vir Geneeskunde
Suid-Afr Tydskr Geneesk — Suid-Afrikaanse Tydskrif vir Geneeskunde
Suid-Afr Tydskr Landbouwetenskap — Suid-Afrikaanse Tydskrif vir Landbouwetenskap
Suid-Afr Tydskr Sielkd — Suid-Afrikaanse Tydskrif vir Sielkunde
SUK — Sumitomo Bank Review
SUKGA — Sumitomo Kikai Giho
SUKUA — Subtropicheskie Kul'tury
SUL — Per lo Studio e l'Uso del Latino
SuL — Sprache und Literatur
SULAAL — Surinam Agriculture
Sulchgau Altertver Jgabe — Sulchgauer Altertumsverein. Jahresgabe
Sulfuric Acid Ind — Sulfuric Acid and Industry
SULI — Skrifter Utgivna av Litteraturvetenskapliga Institutionen Vid. Uppsala Universitet
Sulphur Agric — Sulphur in Agriculture
Sulphur Inst J — Sulphur Institute. Journal
Su LR — Suffolk University. Law Review
SUL Rev — Southern University Law Review
Sulu Stud — Sulu Studies
Sulzer Tech Rev — Sulzer Technical Review
Sulz Tech Rev — Sulzer Technical Review
Sum — Sumer. A Journal of Archaeology and History in Iraq
SUMA — Sued-und-Mittelamerika
Sumatra Res B — Sumatra Research Bulletin
Sumitomo — Sumitomo Bank Review
Sumitomo Bank R — Sumitomo Bank Review
Sumitomo Bull Ind Health — Sumitomo Bulletin of Industrial Health
Sumitomo Elec Tech Rev — Sumitomo Electric Technical Review
Sumitomo Electr Rev — Sumitomo Electric Review
Sumitomo Electr Tech Rev — Sumitomo Electric Technical Review
Sumitomo Light Metal Tech Rep — Sumitomo Light Metal Technical Reports
Sumitomo Light Met Tech Rep — Sumitomo Light Metal Technical Reports
Sumitomo Mach — Sumitomo Machinery
Sumitomo Met — Sumitomo Metals
Sumitomo Q — Sumitomo Quarterly
Sum List — Sumarski List
Summa A — Summa Artis
Summa Phytopathol — Summa Phytopathologica
Summ Dec — Summary Decisions
Summer Comput Simul Conf Proc — Summer Computer Simulation Conference. Proceedings
Summer Inst Part Phys Proc — Summer Institute on Particle Physics. Proceedings
Summit Mag — Summit Magazine
Summ Pap Aust Ceram Conf — Summaries of Papers. Australian Ceramic Conference
Summ Proc Aust Conf Nucl Tech Anal — Australian Conference on Nuclear Techniques of Analysis. Summary of Proceedings
Summ Proc West Cotton Prod Conf — Summary of Proceedings. Western Cotton Production Conference
Summ Prog Geol Surv Div (Nigeria) — Summary of Progress. Geological Survey Division (Nigeria)
Summ Rep Electrotech Lab — Summary Reports. Electrotechnical Laboratory
Summ World Broadcasts Part 1 — Summary of World Broadcasts. Part 1. The USSR Weekly Economic Report
Summ World Broadcasts Part 2 — Summary of World Broadcasts. Part 2. Eastern Europe Weekly Economic Report
Summ World Broadcasts Part 3 — Summary of World Broadcasts. Part 3. The Middle East, Africa, and Latin AmericaWeekly Economic Report
Sum Proc Soil Sci Soc NC — Summary of Proceedings. Soil Science Society of North Carolina
Sum Rep Electrotech Lab (Tokyo Japan) — Summaries of Reports. Electrotechnical Laboratory (Tokyo, Japan)
SuMW — Surveying and Mapping (Washington, D.C.)
Sun A Q — Sun Art Quarterly
Sund — Sundhedsplejen
Sunday M — Sunday Magazine
Sunday Times Colour Sect — Sunday Times Colour Section
Sunday Times Mag — Sunday Times Magazine
Sun Demo & Ch — Sunday Democrat and Chronicle
S und I — Sprache und Information
Sun Diamond Grow — Sun-Diamond Grower
Sund M — Sunday Magazine
Sun Gaz-Ma — Sunday Gazette-Mail

Sung Kyun Kwan Univ J — Sung Kyun Kwan University. Journal
Sung Stud Newsl — Sung Studies Newsletter
Sun M — Sun and Moon
Sun News Pict — Sun News-Pictorial
Sun Oklahom — Sunday Oklahoman
Sunset Boul — Sunset Boulevard
Sunset Mag — Sunset Magazine
Sunshine St Agric Res Rep — Sunshine State Agricultural Research Report
Sunshine State Agric Res Rep — Sunshine State Agricultural Research Report
Sunshine State Agr Res Rep — Sunshine State Agricultural Research Report. Florida University Agricultural Experiment Station
SUNT — Studien zur Umwelt des Neuen Testament
SunT — Sunday Times
SunTe — Sunday Telegraph [London newspaper]
Sun Times — Sunday Times
SunTM — Sunday Times Magazine
Sun Wld — Sun World
Sun Work Br — Sun at Work in Britain
Sunyatsenia — Sunyatsenia. Journal. Botanical Institute. College of Agriculture. Sun Yatsen University
SUNY Ser Anc Greek Philos — SUNY Series in Ancient Greek Philosophy
SUNY Ser Logic Lang — SUNY Series in Logic and Language
SUNY Ser Philos — SUNY Series in Philosophy
SUNY Ser Sci Tech Soc — SUNY Series in Science, Technology, and Society
Suom Antrop — Suomen Antropologi
Suom Elainlaakarli — Suomen Elainlaakarilehti
Suomen Aikakauskirija — Suomen Muinaismuistoyhdistyksen Aikakauskirja
Suomen Elainlaakril Fin Veterinartidskr — Suomen Elainlaakarilehti. Finsk Veterinartidskrift
Suomen Hist Scusa — Suomen Historiallinen Scusa
Suomen Kem A B — Suomen Kemistilehti A, B
Suomen Kemistil A — Suomen Kemistilehti A
Suomen Maataloust Seura Maataloust Aikakausk — Suomen Maataloustieteellinen Seura. Maataloustieteellinen Aikakauskirj
Suomen Maataloust Seuran Julk — Suomen Maataloustieteellisen Seuran Julkaisuja
Suomen M Vuosikirja — Suomen Musukin Vuosikirja
Suom Hammaslaakarilehti — Suomen Hammaslaakarilehti
Suom Hammaslaak Toim — Suomen Hammaslaakariseuran Toimituksia
Suom Hammaslaak Toimi — Suomen Hammaslaakariseuran Toimituksia
Suom Hist Laeht — Suomen Historian Laehteitae. Finnische Geschichtsquellen
Suom Hyonteistiet Aikak — Suomen Hyonteistieteellinen Aikakauskirja
Suom Kalatalous — Suomen Kalatalous
Suom Kemistil A — Suomen Kemistilehti A
Suom Kemistil B — Suomen Kemistilehti B
Suom Kemistiseuran Tied — Suomen Kemistiseuran Tiedonantoja
Suom Kemistis Tied — Suomen Kemistiseuran Tiedonantoja
Suom Kirj Seuran Toim — Suomen Kirjallinen Seuran Toimituksia. Abhandlungen der Finnischen Literarischen Gesellschaft
Suom Kirkkohist Seuran Toim — Suomen Kirkkohistoriallinen Seuran Toimituksia. Abhandlungen der Finnischen Kirchengeschichtlichen Gesellschaft
Suom Laakaril — Suomen Laakarilehti
Suom Maataloustiet Seuran Julk — Suomen Maataloustieteellisen Seuran Julkaisuja
Suom Maatal Seur Julk — Suomen Maataloustieteellisen Seuran Julkaisuja
Suom Mus — Suomen Museo
Suom Naishammaslaak Julk — Suomen Naishammaslaakarit Ryhma Julkaisu
Suom Pank Tal Tutk Lait Julk — Suomen Pankin Taloustieteellisen Tutkimuslaitoksen Julkaisuja
Suom Psykiatr — Suomalaista Psykiatriaa
Suom Tiedeaka Toim — Suomalaisen Tiedeakatemian Toimituksia
SUP — Spisy University J. E. Purkyne
SUP — Supervision
Sup Ct Hist Socy YB — Supreme Court Historical Society. Yearbook
Sup Ct J — Supreme Court Journal
Sup Ct L Rev — Supreme Court Law Review
Sup Ct MR — Supreme Court Monthly Review
Sup Ct Res — Supreme Court Researcher
Sup Ct Rev — Supreme Court Review
Super Bsns — Supermarket Business
Superclean Rotor Steels Workshop Proc — Superclean Rotor Steels. Workshop Proceedings
Supercomput Chem Debis Workshop — Supercomputer and Chemistry. Debis Workshop
Supercomput Chem IABG Workshop — Supercomputer and Chemistry. IABG (Industrieanlangen-Betriebsgesellscha ft) Workshop
Supercond Appl Proc Annu Conf — Superconductivity and Applications. Proceedings. Annual Conference on Superconductivity and Applications
Supercond Ceram Winter Meet Low Temp Phys — Superconducting Ceramics. Winter Meeting on Low Temperature Physics
Supercond Cryoelectron Proc Symp — Superconductivity and Cryoelectronics. Proceedings. Symposium on Superconductivity and Cryoelectronics
Supercond Its Appl — Superconductivity and Its Applications
Supercond Proc Ital Natl Sch Condens Matter Phys — Superconductivity. Proceedings. Italian National School on Condensed Matter Physics
Supercond Res Dev — Superconductivity. Research and Development
Supercond Rev — Superconductivity Review
Supercond Sci Technol — Superconductor Science and Technology
Superlattices Microstruct — Superlattices and Microstructures
Superlatt M — Superlattices and Microstructures
Supermagnets Hard Magn Mater — Supermagnets. Hard Magnetic Materials
Supermark Retail — Supermarket and Retailer
Super Mgt — Supervisory Management
Supermkt — Supermarketing
Supermkt Bus — Supermarket Business

Super News — Supermarket News
Superphosphat-Mitt — Superphosphat-Mitteilungen
Superplast Aerosp Proc Symp — Superplasticity in Aerospace. Proceedings. Symposium
Superplast Met Ceram Intermet Symp — Superplasticity in Metals, Ceramics, and Intermetallics. Symposium
Superv Manage — Supervisory Management
Superv Nurse — Supervisor Nurse
Supery Manage — Supervisory Management
Supl Antrop Asuncion — Suplemento Antropologico (Asuncion)
Supl Antropol — Suplemento Antropologico
Suplemento Valencia — Suplemento de Valencia
Supl Lit Panama America — Suplemento Literario Panama America
Supp Com — Supplementum Comicum. Commoediae Graecae Fragmenta Post Editiones Kockianam et Kaibelianam
Supp Epigr — Supplementum Epigraphicum Graecum
Suppl Acta Agric Scand — Acta Agriculturae Scandinavica. Supplementum
Suppl Acta Univ Carol Biol — Supplementum. Acta Universitatis Carolinae. Biologica
Suppl Agrokem Talajt — Supplementum. Agrokemia es Talajtan
Suppl Annls Agric Fenn — Annales Agriculturae Fenniae. Supplementum
Suppl Annls Gembloux — Supplement. Annales de Gembloux
Suppl Annls Inst Pasteur (Paris) — Supplement. Annales de l'Institut Pasteur (Paris)
Suppl Bull Mens Soc Cent Architectes — Supplement au Bulletin Mensuel de la Societe Centrale des Architectes
Suppl Certif Eng — Supplement. Certificated Engineer
Suppl Collect Sci Works Charles Univ Fac Med Hradec Kralove — Supplement to Collection of Scientific Works. Charles University Faculty of Medicine. Hradec Kralove
Suppl Com — Supplementum Comicum. Commoediae Graecae Fragmenta Post Editiones Kockianam et Kaibelianam
Suppl Epigr Gr — Supplementum Epigraphicum Graecum
Suppl Eur J Neurosci — Supplement. European Journal of Neuroscience
Suppl For Rep (Sixth) Discuss Meet (Edinb) — Supplement to Forestry. Report of the Sixth Discussion Meeting (Edinburgh)
Suppl Geophys — Supplement. Geophysics
Suppl Israel J Bot — Supplement. Israel Journal of Botany
Suppl J Phys Soc Jap — Supplement. Journal of the Physical Society of Japan
Suppl LC Subj Head — Supplement. LC [*United States Library of Congress*] Subject Headings
Suppl Naeringsforsk — Supplement till Naeringsforskning
Suppl Nord Jordbrforsk — Nordisk Jordbrugsforskning. Supplement
Suppl Papers Roy Geogr Soc — Supplementary Papers. Royal Geographical Society
Suppl Prog Theor Phys — Supplement. Progress of Theoretical Physics
Suppl Ric Biol Selvaggina — Supplemento alle Ricerche di Biologia della Selvaggina
Suppl Ric Sci — Supplemento a la Ricerca Scientifica
Suppl Sb Ved Pr Lek Fak Univ Karlovy (Hradci Kralove) — Supplementum. Sborniku Vedeckych Praci Lekarske Fakulty University Karlovy (Hradci Kralove)
Suppl Social Econ Stud — Supplement to Social and Economic Studies
Suppl Southwest Entomol — Supplement. Southwestern Entomologist
Supplta Ent — Supplementa Entomologica
Sup Pop Sci Mo — Supplement. Popular Science Monthly
Support Care Cancer — Supportive Care in Cancer
Supp Pr T P — Supplement. Progress of Theoretical Physics
Supramol Archit — Supramolecular Architecture
Supramol Chem — Supramolecular Chemistry
Supramol Sci — Supramolecular Science
Supr Court — Supreme Court Review
Supr Ct LR — Supreme Court Law Review
Supreme Court LR — Supreme Court Law Review
Supreme Court Rev — Supreme Court Review
Sup Stud — Superior Student
SUPUSLL — Stanford University. Publications. University Series. Languages and Literatures
Supvry Mgmt — Supervisory Management
Sur — Revista Sur
SUR — Survey of Current Affairs
SURAB — Surgery Annual
Surface Sci — Surface Science
Surface Techn — Surface Technology
Surfacing J — Surfacing Journal
Surfactant Sci Ser — Surfactant Science Series
Surf Anal Methods Mater Sci — Surface Analysis Methods in Materials Science
Surf and Interface Anal — Surface and Interface Analysis
Surf Coat — Surface Coatings
Surf Coat Aust — Surface Coatings Australia
Surf Coat Int — Surface Coatings International
Surf Coat Technol — Surface and Coatings Technology
Surf Colloid Sci — Surface and Colloid Science
Surf Defect Prop Solids — Surface and Defect Properties of Solids
Surf Eng — Surface Engineering
Surf Interface Anal — Surface and Interface Analysis
Surf Interfaces — Surfaces and Interfaces
Surf J — Surfacing Journal
Surf Min Law — Surface Mining Law
Surf Min Reclam Symp — Surface Mining and Reclamation Symposia
Surf Modif Technol 4 Proc Int Conf — Surface Modification Technologies 4. Proceedings. International Conference
Surf Mount Technol — Surface Mount Technology
Surf Res Proc Pol Semin Exoelectron Emiss Relat Phenom — Surface Research. Proceedings. Polish Seminar on Exoelectron Emission and Related Phenomena

Surf Rev Lett — Surface Review and Letters
Surf Sci — Surface Science
Surf Sci Proc Lat Am Symp Surf Phys — Surface Science. Lectures on Basic Concepts and Applications. Proceedings. Latin American Symposium on Surface Physics
Surf Sci R — Surface Science Reports
Surf Sci Rep — Surface Science Reports
Surf Sci Spectra — Surface Science Spectra
Surf Sci Tainan Taiwan — Surface Science (Tainan, Taiwan)
Surf Tech — Surface Technology
Surf Technol — Surface Technology
Surf Warf — Surface Warfare
Surf X Ray Neutron Scattering Proc Int Conf — Surface X-Ray and Neutron Scattering. Proceedings. International Conference
Surg Annu — Surgery Annual
SURGAZ — Surgery
Surg Bus — Surgical Business
Surg Clin N Am — Surgical Clinics of North America
Surg Clin N Amer — Surgical Clinics of North America
Surg Clin North Am — Surgical Clinics of North America
Surg Cl NA — Surgical Clinics of North America
Surg Endosc — Surgical Endoscopy
Surg Forum — Surgical Forum
Surg Gastroenterol — Surgical Gastroenterology
Surg Gynec and Obst — Surgery, Gynecology, and Obstetrics
Surg Gynecol Obstet — Surgery, Gynecology, and Obstetrics
Surg Gyn Ob — Surgery, Gynecology, and Obstetrics
Surgical — Surgical Business
Surg Ital — Surgery in Italy
Surg Laparosc Endosc — Surgical Laparoscopy and Endoscopy
Surg Neurol — Surgical Neurology
Surg Oncol — Surgical Oncology
Surg Oncol Clin N Am — Surgical Oncology Clinics of North America
Surg Radiol Anat — Surgical and Radiologic Anatomy
Surg Technol — Surgical Technologist
Surg Ther — Surgical Therapy
Surg Today — Surgery Today
Surimi Technol — Surimi Technology
Surinaam — Surinaamse Landbouw
Surinam Agric — Surinam Agriculture
Sur Landb — Surinaamse Landbouw
SurM — Surrealisme Meme
SuRo — Suisse Romande. Revue de Litterature, d'Art, et de Musique
Surowce Miner — Surowce Mineralne
Surrealisme Serv Revol — Surrealisme au Service de la Revolution
Surrey AC — Surrey Archaeological Collections
Surrey Archaeol Col — Surrey Archaeological Collections
Surrey Archaeol Collect — Surrey Archaeological Collections
Surrey Arch Coll — Surrey Archaeological Collections
Surry A Coll — Surrey Archaeological Collections
Surtees Soc — Surtees Society
Surtsey Res Prog Rep — Surtsey Research Progress Report
Surv — Survival
Surv & Excav — Survey and Excavation
Surv & Map — Surveying and Mapping
Surv Anesthesiol — Survey of Anesthesiology
Surv Biol Prog — Survey of Biological Progress
Surv Bus — Survey of Business
Surv Cur Bus — Survey of Current Business
Surv Curr Affairs — Survey of Current Affairs
Surv Curr Bus — Survey of Current Business
Surv Curr Busin — Survey of Current Business
Surv Dig Dis — Survey of Digestive Diseases
Surv Drug Res Immunol Dis — Survey of Drug Research in Immunologic Disease
Surv Econ Cond Afr — Survey of Economic Conditions in Africa
Surv Econ Cond Jap — Survey of Economic Conditions in Japan
Surveill Technol II — Surveillance Technologies II
Survey Bus (Univ Tenn) — Survey of Business (University of Tennessee)
Survey Cur Bus — Survey of Current Business
Survey Current Bus — Survey of Current Business
Survey G — Survey Graphic
Surveying Tech — Surveying Technician
Survey Progr Chem — Survey of Progress in Chemistry
Surveys Appl Math — Surveys in Applied Mathematics
Surveys Math Indust — Surveys on Mathematics for Industry
Surveys Reference Works Math — Surveys and Reference Works in Mathematics
Surv Graph — Survey Graphic
Surv Graphic — Survey Graphic
Surv High Energy Phys — Surveys in High Energy Physics
Surv Immunol Res — Survey of Immunologic Research
Surv Immun Res — Survey of Immunologic Research
Survival Int Rev — Survival International Review
Surv-Local Gov Technol — Surveyor-Local Government Technology
Surv Mapp — Surveying and Mapping
Surv Munic Cty Eng — Surveyor and Municipal and County Engineer
Surv Notes Utah Geol Miner Surv — Survey Notes. Utah Geological and Mineral Survey
Surv Ophthalmol — Survey of Ophthalmology
Surv Pap Horace Lamb Centre Oceanogr Res — Survey Paper. Horace Lamb Centre for Oceanographical Research. Flinders University of South Australia
Surv Prog Chem — Survey of Progress in Chemistry
Surv Synth Pathol Res — Survey and Synthesis of Pathology Research
SUS — Schriften der Universitaet des Saarlandes
SUS — Stromata
SUS — Studi Urbinati di Storia, Filosofia, e Letteratura

SUS — Suesswaren. Die Fachzeitschrift der Suesswaren Industrie. Produktion, Verpackung, Verkauf

SUS — Suspense

SUS — Susquehanna University. Studies

Sus — Susreti

SUSA — Sage Urban Studies Abstracts

SUSF — Samlingar Utgivna av Svenska Fornskriftssallskapet

SUSFL — Studi Urbinati di Storia, Filosofia, e Letteratura

SUSFS — Samlingar Utgivna av Svenska Fornskrift-Sallskapet

Sus Leg Chron — Susquehanna Legal Chronicle

Susq LC — Susquehanna Leading Chronicle

Susq L Chron — Susquehanna Legal Chronicle

Susq Legal Chron — Susquehanna Legal Chronicle

Susq Leg Chron — Susquehanna Legal Chronicle

Susquehanna Leg Chron (PA) — Susquehanna Legal Chronicle

SUSRA — Steel in the USSR

SUSRD8 — Sbornik UVTIZ [*Ustav Vedeckotechnickych Informaci pro Zemedelstvi*] Ochrana Rostlin

Sussex AC — Sussex Archaeological Collections

Sussex A Coll — Sussex Archaeological Collections

Sussex Anthro — Sussex Anthropologist

Sussex Anthrop — Sussex Anthropology

Sussex Archaeol Col — Sussex Archaeological Collections

Sussex Arch Coll — Sussex Archaeological Collections

Sussex Arch Coll — Sussex Archaeological Collections Relating to the Antiquities of the County

Sussex Essays In Anthrop — Sussex Essays In Anthropology

Sussex Indust Hist — Sussex Industrial History

SuSu — Suomalainen Suomi

SuSuomi — Suomalainen Suomi

SuSuV — Suomalainen Suomi. Kulttuuripolittinen Aikakauskirja/Valvoja

SUTD — Soviet Union Today

Suth WR — Sutherland's Weekly Reporter, Calcutta

Suth WR Mis — Sutherland's Weekly Reports, Miscellaneous Appeals

SUVA — Suvaguuq. Pauktuutit. Inuit Women's Association of Canada. Newsletter

SUVO — Student Voice

Suvrem Med — Suvremenna Meditsina

Suvrem Probl Endokrinol — Suvremenni Problemi na Endokrinologiyata

SUVSL — Skrifter Utgivna. Vetenskaps-Societeten i Lund

SV — Schweizer Volkskunde

SV — Scuola e Vita

SV — Seven

SV — Siebenbuergische Vierteljahrsschrift

SV — Slovesna Veda

S/V — Sound and Vibration

SV — Sovetskaia Vostokovedenie

SV — Sovetskoe Vostokovedenie

SV — Srednie Veka. Sbornik

SV — Suvaguq. Pond Inlet

SVABB — Schweizerische Vereinigung fuer Atomenergie. Bulletin

SVACB — Sbornik Vysoke Skoly Chemicko-Technologicke v Praze. Anorganicka Chemie a Technologie

Sv Aeroplan Ab SAAB Tech Notes — Svenska Aeroplan Aktiebolaget [*Linkoping, Sweden*]. SAAB Technical Notes

SVAPA — Svarochnoe Proizvodstvo

Svarka Vzryvom Svoistva Svarnykh Soedin — Svarka Vzryvom i Svoistva Svarnykh Soedinenii

Svar Proizvod — Svarochnoe Proizvodstvo

SVBSA — Sivilt Beredskap

SVBUA — Shock and Vibration Bulletin

SVCIA — Soviet Chemical Industry

SVD — Soviet Export. Soviet Foreign Trade Bimonthly

SvD — Svenska Dagbladet

SVDI — Serie de Vocabularios y Diccionarios Indigenas

SvEA — Svensk Exegetisk Arsbok

SVEC — Studies on Voltaire and the Eighteenth Century

Sved Zemed — Svedeniya po Zemedelieto

Sven Bot Tidskr — Svensk Botanisk Tidskrift

Sven Bryggarefoeren Manadsbl — Svenska Bryggarefoereningens Manadsblad

Sven Bryggeritidskr — Svensk Bryggeritidskrift

SvenD — Svenska Dagbladed [*newspaper*]

Sven Ex Ars — Svensk Exegetisk Arsbok

Sven Faerg Tek Tidskr — Svensk Faerg-Teknisk Tidskrift

Sven Farm Tidskr — Svensk Farmaceutisk Tidskrift

Sven Farm Tidskr Sci Ed — Svensk Farmaceutisk Tidskrift. Scientific Edition

Sven Foerfattningssaml — Svensk Foerfattningssamling

Sven Forskningsinst Cem Betong K Tek Hoegsk Stockholm Handl — Svenska Forskningsinstitutet foer Cement och Betong vid Kungliga Tekniska Hoegskolan i Stockholm. Handlingar

Sven Forskningsinst Cem Betong K Tek Hoegsk Stockholm Medd — Svenska Forskningsinstitutet foer Cement och Betong vid Kungliga Tekniska Hoegskolan i Stockholm. Meddelanden

Sven Forskningsinst Cem Betong K Tek Hoegsk Stockholm Saertr — Svenska Forskningsinstitutet foer Cement och Betong vid Kungliga Tekniska Hoegskolan i Stockholm. Saertryck

Sven Forskningsinst Cem Betong K Tek Hoegsk Stockholm Utredn — Svenska Forskningsinstitutet foer Cement och Betong vid Kungliga Tekniska Hoegskolan i Stockholm. Utredningar

Sven Forskningsinst Cem Betong K Tek Hogsk — Svenska Forskningsinstitutet foer Cement och Betong vid Kungliga i Stockholm. Meddelanden Tekniska Hoegskolan

Sven Fotogr Tidskr — Svensk Fotografisk Tidskrift

Sven Frotidn — Svensk Froetidning

Sven Gasfoeren Manadsbl — Svenska Gasfoereningens Manadsblad

Sven Gasverksfoeren Aarsb — Svenska Gasverksfoereningens Aarsbok

Sven Hydrogr Biol Komm Skr Ny Ser Biol — Svenska Hydrografisk-Biologiska Kommissionens Skrifter. Ny Serie. Biologi

Sven Inst Konserveringsforsk Publ — Svenska Institutet foer Konserveringsforskning. Publikation

Sven Kem Tidskr — Svensk Kemisk Tidskrift

Sven Kraftverksfoeren Publ — Svenska Kraftverksfoereningens Publikationer

Sven Kraftverksfoeren Publ Medd — Svenska Kraftverksfoereningens Publikationer Meddelande

Sven Laekaresaellsk Foerh — Svenska Laekaresaellskapets Foerhandlingar

Sven Laekartidn — Svenska Laekartidningen

Sven Linne-SallskArsskr — Svenska Linne-Sallskapet Arsskrift

Sven Mejeriernas Riksfoeren Produkttek Avd Medd — Svenska Mejeriernas Riksfoerening. Produkttekniska Avdelningen. Meddelande

Sven Mejeritidn — Svenska Mejeritidningen

Sven Mosskulturfoeren Tidskr — Svenska Mosskulturfoereningens Tidskrift

Sven Naturvetensk — Svensk Naturvetenskap

Sven Papperfoeraedlingstidskr — Svensk Pappersfoeraedlingstidskrift

Sven Pappersmassetidn — Svensk Pappersmassetidning

Sven Papperstidn — Svensk Papperstidning

Svenska Fornm Tidskr — Svenska Fornminnesfoerningens. Tidskrift

Svenska Humanist Tidskr — Svenska Humanistisk Tidskrift

Svenska Lakare Sallsk Arsberatt — Svenska Lakare-Sallskapet. Arsberattelse

Svenska Linnesallsk Arssk — Svenska Linnesallskapets Arsskrift

Svenska Mosskulturfoen Tidskr — Svenska Mosskulturforeningens Tidskrift

Svensk Artill Tidskr — Svensk Artillerie Tidskrift

Svenska Turistfoeren Arsskr — Svenska Turistfoereningens Arsskrift

Svensk Bot Tidskr — Svensk Botanisk Tidskrift

Svensk Dagbladet — Svenska Dagbladet

Svensk Forskinst Istanbul Meddel — Svenska Forskningsinstitutet i Istanbul. Meddelanden

Svensk Froetidn — Svensk Froetidning

Svensk Geog Arsbok — Svensk Geografisk Arsbok

Svensk Juristtidn — Svensk Juristtidning

Svensk Kem Tidskr — Svensk Kemisk Tidskrift

Svensk Linne Sallsk Arsskr — Svenska Linne Sallskapets Arsskrift

Svensk Litt — Svensk Litteraturtidskrift

Svensk Littsallsk Finland — Svenska Litteratursallskapet i Finland

Sven Skogsvardsforen Tidskr — Svenska Skogsvardsforeningens Tidskrift

Svensk Orientsallskapets Ab — Svenska Orientsallskapets Arsbok

Svensk Papperstidn — Svensk Papperstidning

SvenskPapr — Svensk Papperstidning

Svensk T — Svensk Tidskrift

Svensk Teol Kvartalskr — Svensk Teologisk Kvartalskrift

Svensk Tid — Svensk Tidskrift foer Musikforskning

Svensk Tidskr Musikforsk — Svensk Tidskrift foer Musikforskning

Svenskt MHistoriskt — Svenskt Musikhistoriskt Arkiv. Bulletin

Svensk Travarutidn — Svensk Traevaru- och Pappersmassetidning

Svensk Vet-Tidskr — Svensk Veterinaertidskrift

Svens Pap T — Svensk Papperstidning Tidskrift

Sven Tandlaek Tidskr — Svensk Tandlaekare Tidskrift

Sven Tandlakareforb Tidn — Svensk Tandlaekareforbunds Tidning

Sven Tandlak Tidskr — Svensk Tandlaekare Tidskrift

Sven Tids M — Svensk Tidskrift foer Musikforskning

Sven Traevaru-Tidn — Svensk Traevaru-Tidning

Sven Vaextskyddskonf — Svenska Vaextskyddskonferensen

Sven Vall Mosskulturfoeren Medd — Svenska Vall- och Mosskulturfoereningens Meddelanden

Sven Vattenkraftfoeren Publ — Svenska Vattenkraftforeningens Publikationer

Sven Veterinartidn — Svensk Veterinaertidning

Sverdlovsk God Ped Inst Naucn Trudy — Sverdlovskii Gosudarstvennyi Pedagogiceskii Institut. Naucnyi Trudy

Sverdlovsk Gos Ped Inst Ucen Zap — Sverdlovskii Gosudarstvennyi Pedagogiceskii Institut. Ucenye Zapiski

Sver Geol Unders Arsb — Sveriges Geologiska Undersoekning. Arsbok

Sver Geol Unders Arsb Ser C Avh Uppsatser — Sveriges Geologiska Undersoekning. Arsbok. Serie C. Avhandlingar och Uppsatser

Sver Gummitek Foren Publ — Sveriges Gummitekniska Foerening. Publicerande

Sveriges Geol Unders Ser C — Sveriges Geologiska Undersoekning. Arsbok. Serie C. Avhandlingar och Uppsatser

Sveriges Pomol Foren Arsskr — Sveriges Pomologiska Forenings Arsskrift

Sveriges Riksbank Q R — Sveriges Riksbank. Quarterly Review

Sveriges Skogsvforb Tidskr — Sveriges Skogsvfoerbunds Tidskrift

Sveriges Utsaedesfoer Tidskr — Sveriges Utsaedesfoereningens Tidskrift

Sverige Tyskl — Sverige-Tyskland

Sverkhprovodimost Fiz Khim Tekh — Sverkhprovodimost. Fizika, Khimiya, Tekhnika

Sverkhprovodimost Issled Razrab — Sverkhprovodimost. Issledovaniya i Razrabotki

Sverkhtverd Mater — Sverkhtverdye Materialy

Sver Lantbruksuniv Inst Arbetsmetod Tek Rapp — Sveriges Lantbruksuniversitet Institutionen foer Arbetsmetodik och Teknik. Rapport

Sver Lantbruksuniv Inst Biom Skogsindelning Rapp — Sveriges Lantbruksuniversitet Institutionen foer Biometri och Skogsindelning. Rapport

Sver Lantbruksuniv Inst Husdjursforadling Sjukdomsgenet Rapp — Sveriges Lantbruksuniversitet Institutionen foer Husdjursforadling och Sjukdomsgenetik. Rapport

Sver Lantbruksuniv Inst Lantbrukets Byggnadstek Rapp — Sveriges Lantbruksuniversitet Institutionen foer Lantbrukets Byggnadsteknik. Rapport

Sver Lantbruksuniv Inst Lantbruksteknik Rapp — Sveriges Lantbruksuniversitet Institutionen foer Lantbruksteknik. Rapport

Sver Lantbruksuniv Inst Mikrobiol Rapp — Sveriges Lantbruksuniversitet Institutionen foer Mikrobiologi. Rapport

Sver Lantbruksuniv Inst Radiobiol Rapp — Sveriges Lantbruksuniversitet Institutionen foer Radiobiologi. Rapport

Sver Lantbruksuniv Inst Tradgardsvetensk Rapp — Sveriges Lantbruksuniversitet Institutionen foer Tradgardsvetenskap. Rapport

Sver Lantbruksuniv Inst Vaxtodling Rapp — Sveriges Lantbruksuniversitet Institutionen foer Vaxtodling. Rapport

Sver Lantbruksuniv Konsulentavd Rapp Landskap — Sveriges Lantbruksuniversitet Konsulentavdelningens Rapporter Landskap

Sver Lantbruksuniv Rapp Skogsekol Skoglig Marklara — Sveriges Lantbruksuniversitet Rapporter i Skogsekologi och Skoglig Marklara

Sver Lantbruksuniv Vaxtskyddsrapp Avh — Sveriges Lantbruksuniversitet Vaxtskyddsrapporter Avhandlingar

Sver Lantbruksuniv Vaxtskyddsrapp Jordbruk — Sveriges Lantbruksuniversitet Vaxtskyddsrapporter Jordbruk

Sver Lantbruksuniv Vaxtskyddsrapp Tradg — Sveriges Lantbruksuniversitet Vaxtskyddsrapporter Tradgard

Sver Mekanforb Mekanresult — Sveriges Mekanforbund, Mekanresultat

Sver Nat — Sveriges Natur

Sver Nat Arsb — Sveriges Natur Arsbok

Sver Off Stat Bergshantering — Sveriges Officiella Statistik Bergshantering. Statistika Centralbyran

Sver Pomol Foeren Arsskr — Sveriges Pomologiska Foerening Arsskrift

Sver Skogsvaardsfoerb Tidskr — Sveriges Skogsvaardsfoerbunds Tidskrift

Sver Skogsvardsfoerbunds Tidskr — Sveriges Skogsvardsfoerbunds Tidskrift

Sver Skogsvardsforb Tidskr — Sveriges Skogsvardsfoerbunds Tidskrift

Sver Tandlakarforb Tidn — Sveriges Tandlakarforbund Tidning

Svertyvayushchaya Sist Krovi Akush Ginekol — Svertyvayushchaya Sistema Krovi v Akusherstve i Ginekologii

Sver Utsadesforen Tidskr — Sveriges Utsaedesfoerenings Tidskrift

Sver Utsaedesfoer Tidskr — Sveriges Utsaedesfoerenings Tidskrift

Sveske Fiz Nauka — Sveske Fizicikih Nauka

Sveske Fiz Nauka Ser A — Sveske Fizicikih Nauka. Series A. Conferences

Svetotekh — Svetotekhnika

Svetotekhnika Svetotekh Kom Akad Nauk SSSR — Svetotekhnika. Svetotekhnicheskaya Komissiya Akademii Nauk SSSR

Svetsaren Dtsch Ausg — Svetsaren. Deutsche Ausgabe

Svetsaren Ed Fr — Svetsaren. Edition Francaise

Svetsaren Weld Rev — Svetsaren: A Welding Review

SvExAb — Svensk Exegetisk Arsbok

SvExArsb — Svensk Exegetisk Arsbok

SVF — Stoicorum Veterum Fragmenta

Sv Farm Tid — Svensk Farmaceutisk Tidskrift

SVF Fachorgan Textilveredl — SVF [*Svetstekniska Foereningen*] Fachorgan fuer Textilveredlung

SvFFT — Svenska Fornminnes-Foereningen Tidskrift

SVG — Gids voor Personeelsbeleid. Arbeidsvraagstukken en Sociale Verzekering

SVGLA — Sovetskaya Geologiya

SVGU — Sveriges Geologiska Undersoekning

SVI — Sveriges Riksbank. Quarterly Review

SvI — Svizzera Italiana

Svinovod — Svinovodstvo

SVJ — Sovetska Veda. Jazykoveda

SvJerTs — Svenska Jerusalems-Foereningens Tidskrift

Sv Kraftverksforen Publ — Svenska Kraftverksfoereningens Publikationer

SVKTA — Strassenverkehrstechnik

SVL — Studien zur Vergleichenden Literaturgeschichte

SVLAA — Svenska Laekartidningen

SVLKAO — Collection of Scientific Works. Faculty of Medicine. Charles University (HradecKralove)

SvLm — Svenska Landsmal och Svenskt Folkliv

SvM — Svensk Missionstidskrift

SVMCD8 — Sciences Veterinaires Medecine Comparee

SVNAB — Svensk Naturvetenskap

Svoista Veshchestv Str Mol — Svoistva Veshchestv i Stroenie Molekul

Svojstva At Yader — Svojstva Atomnykh Yader

SVPIA — Surface and Vacuum Physics Index

SVPP/A — Archivos Venezolanas de Puericultura y Pediatria. Sociedad Venezolana de Puericultura y Pediatria

SVPVA — Sbornik Vedeckych Praci. Vysoka Skola Chemickotechnologicka (Pardubice)

SVRBAR — Sbornik Vysoka Skola Zemedelska v Praze Provozne Ekonomicke Fakulty v Ceskych Budejovicich Biologicka Rada

SVRDA — Soviet Radiochemistry

SVS — Saga-Book. Viking Society for Northern Research

SvS — Schild von Steier. Beitraege zur Steirischen Vor- und Fruehgeschichte und Muenzkunde

SVS — Statistica Neerlandica

SVSHA — Sovetskii Shakhtior

SVSHKG — Schriften. Verein fuer Schleswig-Holsteinische Kirchengeschichte

SVSL — Skrifter Utgivna. Vetenskaps-Societeten i Lund

S V Sound Vib — S V. Sound and Vibration

SVSPO — Sbornik Vysoke Skoly Pedagogicke v Olomouci

SVSPO(JL) — Sbornik Vysoke Skoly Pedagogicke v Olomouci. Jazyka a Literatura

SVSPP — Sbornik Vysoke Skoly Pedagogicke v Praze. Jazyka a Literatura

SVSQ — St. Vladimir's Seminary Quarterly

SVSThR — Sammlung Gemeinverstaendlicher Vortraege und Schriften aus dem Gebiet der Theologie und der Religionsgeschichte

SVT — Supplements. Vetus Testamentum

SvT — Svenska Texter

SvT — Svensk Tidskrift

SVTFDI — Sugarcane Variety Tests in Florida

SvTK — Svensk Teologisk Kvartalskrift

SvTKv — Svensk Teologisk Kvartalskrift

SVTP — Studia in Veteris Testamenti Pseudepigrapha

SVTQ — St. Vladimir's Theological Quarterly

Sv Trav Pap — Svensk Traevaru- och Pappersmassetidning

SvTs — Svensk Tidskrift

SVUOJ — Sri Venkateswara University. Oriental Journal

Svy Sports — Survey on Sports Attendance

SW — Science Wonder Stories

SW — Siewernij Wiestnik

SW — Slavic Word

SW — Smith's Weekly

SW — Socialist Worker

SW — Social Work

SW — South and West

SW — Southern Workman

SW — Southwestern Musician - Texas Music Educator

SW — South Western Reporter

SW — Strafwetboek

SWA — Sitzungsberichte. Wiener Akademie

SWA — Southwest Art

SwAL — Southwestern American Literature

SWANS — State Wildlife Advisory News Service

Swansea Coll Fac Ed J — University College of Swansea. Collegiate Faculty of Education. Journal

Swarajya A — Swarajya. Annual Number

SWAW — Sitzungsberichte. Wiener Akademie der Wissenschaften

Swaziland Annu Rep Geol Surv Mines Dep — Swaziland. Annual Report. Geological Survey and Mines Department

Swaziland Geol Surv Mines Dep Annu Rep — Swaziland. Geological Survey and Mines Department. Annual Report

Swaziland Natn Cent Yb — Swaziland National Centre Yearbook

SWB — Stichting Weg. Bulletin

SWBAA — Schweizerische Bauzeitung

SWBRD — Sun at Work in Britain

SWC — Social Work and Christianity

SWE — Southwestern Evangel

Swed Am TN — Swedish American Trade News

Swed Bud — Swedish Budget

Swed Dent J — Swedish Dental Journal

Swed Dent J (Suppl) — Swedish Dental Journal (Supplement)

Swed Environ Res Inst Rep B — Swedish Environmental Research Institute. Report B

Swed Foersvarets Forskningsanst FOA Rep — Sweden. Foersvarets Forskningsanstalt. FOA Report

Swed Geol Unders Ser Ae Geol Kartbl 1:50000 — Sweden. Geologiska Undersoekning. Serie Ae. Geologiska Kartblad i Skala 1:50,000

Swed Geol Unders Ser C — Sweden. Geologiska Undersoekning. Serie C

Swed Geol Unders Ser Ca Avh Uppsatser — Sweden. Geologiska Undersoekning. Serie Ca. Avhandlingar och Uppsatser

Swed Geotech Inst Proc — Swedish Geotechnical Institute. Proceedings

Swed Geotech Inst Rep — Swedish Geotechnical Institute. Report

Swed Inst Agric Eng Circ — Swedish Institute of Agricultural Engineering. Circular

SWEDIS — Swedish Drug Information System

Swedish Am Hist Bul — Swedish-American Historical Bulletin. Swedish Historical Society of America

Swedish Aust & Swedish NZ Trade J — Swedish-Australian and Swedish-New Zealand Trade Journal

Swedish Deep-Sea Expedition Repts — Swedish Deep-Sea Expedition. Reports

Swedish Ec — Swedish Economy

Swedish Econ — Swedish Economy

Swedish Hist Soc Yearbook — Swedish Historical Society. Yearbook

Swedish J Econ — Swedish Journal of Economics

Swed J Agric Res — Swedish Journal of Agricultural Research

Swed J Econ — Swedish Journal of Economics

Swed Pap J — Swedish Paper Journal

Swed State Shipbuild Exp Tank Report — Swedish State Shipbuilding Experiment Tank. Report

Swed Univ Agric Sci Dep Agric Eng Rep — Swedish University of Agricultural Sciences. Department of Agricultural Engineering. Report

Swed Univ Agric Sci Dep Farm Build Rep — Swedish University of Agricultural Sciences. Department of Farm Buildings. Report

Swed Univ Agric Sci Dep Hortic Sci Rep — Swedish University of Agricultural Sciences. Department of Horticultural Science. Report

Swed Univ Agric Sci Dep Microbiol Rep — Swedish University of Agricultural Sciences. Department of Microbiology. Report

Swed Univ Agric Sci Dep Plant Husb Rep — Swedish University of Agricultural Sciences. Department of Plant Husbandry. Report

Swed Univ Agric Sci Rep For Ecol For Soils — Swedish University of Agricultural Sciences. Reports in Forest Ecology and Forest Soils

Swed Water Air Pollut Res Inst Publ B — Swedish Water and Air Pollution Research Institute. Publication B

Swed Weed Conf Rep — Swedish Weed Conference. Reports

Swed Wildl Res (Viltrevy) — Swedish Wildlife Research (Viltrevy)

SWEHO — Scandinavian Journal of Work Environment and Health

SWEIA — Studies in Wind Engineering and Industrial Aerodynamics

SWE Mag — SWE Magazine</PHR> %

SW Entomol — Southwestern Entomology

SweP — Swedish Pioneer Historical Quarterly

SWest Entomologist — Southwestern Entomologist

SWest Nat — Southwestern Naturalist

SWF — Southwest Folklore

SWG — Saeculum Westgeschichte

SWGH — Schriften. Strassburger Wissenschaftliche Gesellschaft in Heidelberg

SWH — Sociale Wetenschappen

SWHC — Social Work in Health Care

SW Hist Q — Southwestern Historical Quarterly

SWHQ — Southwestern Historical Quarterly

SWI — Service World International

SWI — Studies. Warburg Institute

S W I E P — Proceedings and Transactions of the South Wales Institute of Engineers
Swim — Swim Magazine
Swimm Tech — Swimming Technique
Swimm World Jun Swimm — Swimming World and Junior Swimmer
Swim Wld — Swimming World and Junior Swimmer
Swine Day Univ Calif — Swine Day. University of California
Swine Rep Univ Hawaii Coop Ext Serv — Swine Report. University of Hawaii. Cooperative Extension Service
Swiss Credit Bank Bul — Swiss Credit Banking Bulletin
Swiss J Hydrol — Swiss Journal of Hydrology
Swiss Mater — Swiss Materials
Swiss Med Wkly — Swiss Medical Weekly
Swiss News — Swiss Economic News
Swiss Plast — Swiss Plastics
Swiss Rev World Aff — Swiss Review of World Affairs
Swiss R Wld Aff — Swiss Review of World Affairs
Swiss Sem — Swiss Seminars
Swiss Surg — Swiss Surgery
Swiss Surg Suppl — Swiss Surgery. Supplement
SWJ — Sir William Jones. Bicentenary of His Birth Commemoraration Volume 1746-1946
SWJA — Southwestern Journal of Anthropology
SW J Anthrop — Southwestern Journal of Anthropology
SW J Anthropol — Southwestern Journal of Anthropology
SW J Phil — Southwestern Journal of Philosophy
Sw J T — Southwestern Journal of Theology
SW J Th — Southwestern Journal of Theology
SWKA — Schriften der Wiener Katholischen Akademie
SWKGR — Sammlung Wissenschaftlicher Kommentare zu Griechischen und Roemischen Schriftstellen
SW Law J — Southwestern Law Journal
Sw Legal Found Inst on Oil and Gas L and Tax — Southwestern Legal Foundation. Institution on Oil and Gas Law and Taxation
SW L J — Southwestern Law Journal
SWL Rev — Southwestern Law Review
SWMCA — Schweizer Maschinenmarkt
Sw Med — Southwestern Medicine
SWMGA — Solid Wastes Management [Later, World Wastes]
SWML — Southwest Museum Leaflets (Los Angeles)
SWMP — Southwest Museum Papers (Los Angeles)
SW Musician — Southwestern Musician
SWNAA — Southwestern Naturalist
SWNS — Sprawozdanie z Prac Naukowych Wydzialu Nauk Spolecznych Pan
S Workm — Southern Workmen
SWP — Survey of Western Palestine
SW Pacific — South West Pacific
SW Phil Stud — Southwest Philosophical Studies
SW Pol Sci Q — Southwestern Political Science Quarterly
SWPR — Swedish Polar Research
SwR — Sewanee Review
SWR — Southwest Review
SWRA — Selected Water Resources Abstracts
SWRA — Social Work Research and Abstracts
S W R I Rp — Annual Report of the Council of the Royal Institution of South Wales, with Appendix of Original Papers on Scientific Subjects
SWRVDT — Swedish Wildlife Research Viltrevy
SWS — Southwestern Studies
SWS — Southwest Writers Series
SWSJ — Son of WSFA Journal
SW Social Sci Q — Southwestern Social Science Quarterly
Sw Soc Sci Q — Southwestern Social Science Quarterly [Austin]
Sw St Prob & Parole Conf Proc — Southwestern States Probation and Parole Conference. Proceedings
SW St (UTEP) — Southwestern Studies (University of Texas, El Paso)
SWTED — Solar Waerme Technik
SWTN — Sprawozdania Wroclawskiego Towarzystwa Naukowego
Sw U LR — Southwestern University. Law Review
Sw U L Rev — Southwestern University. Law Review
SW Vet — Southwestern Veterinarian
SWW — Hotels and Restaurants International
SWWG — Social Work with Groups
SWY — Swedish Economy
SWZBA — Schweizer Buch
SXD — Notes et Etudes Documentaires
SXI — Singapore Business
SXSKA — Sakura X-Rei Shashin Kenkyu
SXX — Secolul XX
SY — Sociology
SY — Symposium
SY — Synopsis
SY — Synthesis
Sy — Syria. Revue d'Art Oriental et d'Archeologie
SyB — Synthese. An International Journal Devoted to Present-Day Cultural and Scientific Life (Bussum)
SyBU — Symbolae Biblicae Upsalienses
Sydeur Inf — Sydeuropa Information
Syd Inst Crim Proc — University of Sydney Faculty of Law. Proceedings of the Institute of Criminology
Syd Jaycee — Sydney Jaycee
Syd Jewish News — Sydney Jewish News
Syd Law R — Sydney Law Review
Syd LR — Sydney Law Review
Syd L Rev — Sydney Law Review
Syd Morning Her — Sydney Morning Herald

Syd Morning Herald — Sydney Morning Herald
Sydney GCN — Sydney Gay Community News
Sydney Law R — Sydney Law Review
Sydney Law Rev — Sydney Law Review
Sydney L Rev — Sydney Law Review
Sydney Q Mag — Sydney Quarterly Magazine
Sydney Univ Med J — Sydney University. Medical Journal
Sydney Univ Sch Civ Eng Res Rep — Sydney University. School of Civil Engineering. Research Report
Sydney Water Bd J — Sydney Water Board. Journal
Sydowia Ann Mycol — Sydowia. Annales Mycologici
Sydowia Ann Mycolog Beih — Sydowia. Annales Mycologici. Beihefte
Syd Stud — Sydney Studies in English
Sydsven Medicinhist — Sydsvenska Medicinhistoriska Saellskapets Arsskrift
Sydsvenska Ortnamns-Sallsk Arsskr — Sydsvenska Ortnamns-Saellskapets Arsskrift
Syd Univ Ag Economics Res Bul — University of Sydney. Department of Agricultural Economics. Research Bulletin
Syd Univ Civ Engng Schl Res Rep — University of Sydney. School of Civil Engineering. Research Report
Syd Univ Dep Agric Econ Mimeo Rep — University of Sydney. Department of Agricultural Economics. Mimeographed Report
Syd Univ Gaz — Sydney University. Gazette
Syd Univ Med J — Sydney University. Medical Journal
Syd Univ Post Grad Comm Med Bul — University of Sydney. Postgraduate Committee in Medicine. Bulletin
Syd Univ Post Grad Comm Med Oration — University of Sydney. Postgraduate Committee in Medicine. Annual Postgraduate Oration
Syd Univ Sch Agric Rep — University of Sydney. School of Agriculture. Report
Syd Wat Bd J — Sydney Water Board. Journal
Syd Water Bd J — Sydney Water Board. Journal
Syd Water Board J — Sydney Water Board. Journal
SYENDM — Systematic Entomology
SYES — Syesis
Sygek Bl — Sygekasse-Bladet
Sygek T — Sygekasse-Tidende
Sy J Int L — Syracuse Journal of International Law and Commerce
Syl — Syllogos. Journal de la Societe Philologique Grecque de Constantinople
Syll — Sylloge Inscriptionum Graecarum
SYLL — Syllogeus
Syll Inscr Gr — Sylloge Inscriptionum Graecarum
Sy LR — Syracuse Law Review
Sylvatrop Philipp For Res J — Sylvatrop. The Philippine Forest Research Journal
Sylwan Lvov — Sylwan (Lvov, Galicia)
Sym — Symphony
SyM — Symphony Magazine
Sym — Symposium
SYMBA — Symbioses
Symb Bot Ups — Symbolae Botanicae Upsalienses
Symbolae Oslo — Symbolae Osloenses
Symbolae Philol Posn — Symbolae Philologorum Posnaniensium
Symbol Comput Artificial Intelligence — Symbolic Computation. Artificial Intelligence
Symbol Numer Comput Ser — Symbolic and Numeric Computation Series
SymbOsl — Symbolae Osloenses
Symb Oslo — Symbolae Osloenses
SYMCA — Symposium (International) on Combustion. Proceedings
SYMED — Synthetic Metals
Sym Mag — Symphony Magazine
Sym Met Mg — Symons's Monthly Meteorological Magazine
Symmetry Cult Sci — Symmetry. Culture and Science
Sym News — Symphony News
Symp — Symposium. A Critical Review
SYMPA — Symposia on Theoretical Physics and Mathematics
Symp A1 High Temp Supercond Thin Films — Symposium A1 on High Temperature Superconductor Thin Films
Symp A2 Solid State Ionics — Symposium A2 on Solid State Ionics
Symp A3 Non Stoichiom Semicond — Symposium A3 on Non-Stoichiometry in Semiconductors
Symp A4 Compos Mater — Symposium A4 on Composite Materials
Symp Abnorm Subsurf Pressure Proc — Symposium on Abnormal Subsurface Pressure. Proceedings
Symp Adv Oxid Processes Treat Contam Water Air — Symposium on Advanced Oxidation Processes for the Treatment of Contaminated Water and Air
Symp Anal Steroids — Symposium on the Analysis of Steroids
Symp Angiol Sanitoriana — Symposia Angiologica Sanitoriana
Symp Biol Hung — Symposia Biologica Hungarica
Symp Braz Gold — Symposium Brazil Gold
Symp Br Ecol Soc — Symposium. British Ecological Society
Symp Br Soc Dev Biol — Symposium. British Society for Developmental Biology
Symp Br Soc Parasitol — Symposia. British Society for Parasitology
Symp Cell Biol — Symposia for Cell Biology
Symp Cell Model Membr Interact — Symposium on Cell and Model Membrane Interactions
Symp Charact Adv Mater — Symposium on the Characterization of Advanced Materials
Symp Chem Modif Surf — Symposium on Chemically Modified Surfaces
Symp Chem Nat Prod Symp Pap — Symposium on the Chemistry of Natural Products. Symposium Papers
Symp Coal Manag Tech Pap — Symposium on Coal Management Techniques. Papers
Symp Coal Mine Drain Res Pap — Symposium on Coal Mine Drainage Research. Papers
Symp Coal Prep Pap — Symposium on Coal Preparation. Papers
Symp Coal Util Pap — Symposium on Coal Utilization. Papers

Symp Dev Appl Intense Pulsed Part Beams — Symposium on Development and Applications of Intense Pulsed Particle Beams

Symp Ecol Res Humid Trop Vegtn — Symposium on Ecological Research in Humid Tropics Vegetation

Symp Electron Ionic Prop Silver Halides — Symposium on Electronic and Ionic Properties of Silver Halides. Common Trends with Photocatalysis

Symp Eng Appl Mech — Symposium on Engineering Applications of Mechanics

Symp Eng Geol Soils Eng Proc — Symposium on Engineering Geology and Soils Engineering. Proceedings

Symp Faraday Soc — Symposia. Faraday Society

Symp Foods — Symposium of Foods

Symp Freq Control Proc — Symposium on Frequency Control. Proceedings

Symp Fundam Cancer Res — Symposium on Fundamental Cancer Research

Symp Fundam Cancer Res Collect Pap — Symposium on Fundamental Cancer Research. Collections of Papers

Symp Genet Biol Ital — Symposia Genetica et Biologica Italica

Symp Genet Breed Wheat Proc — Symposium on Genetics and Breeding of Wheat. Proceedings

Symp Giovanni Lorenzini Found — Symposia of the Giovanni Lorenzini Foundation

Symp Int Combust — Symposium (International) on Combustion

Symp (Int) Combust Proc — Symposium (International) on Combustion. Proceedings

Symp Int Soc Cell Biol — Symposia. International Society for Cell Biology

Symp Int Union Biol Sci Proc — Symposium. International Union of Biological Sciences. Proceedings

Symp Maize Prod Southeast Asia — Symposium on Maize Production in Southeast Asia

Symp Med Hoechst — Symposia Medica Hoechst

Symp Microb Drug Resist — Symposium on Microbial Drug Resistance

Symp Mine Prep Plant Refuse Disposal Pap — Symposium on Mine and Preparation Plant Refuse Disposal. Papers

Symp Moessbauer Eff Methodol Proc — Symposium on Moessbauer Effect Methodology. Proceedings

Symp Mol Basis Neurol Disord Their Treat — Symposium of Molecular Basis of Neurological Disorders and Their Treatment

Symp Natl Phys Lab (UK) — Symposium. National Physical Laboratory (United Kingdom)

Symp Neurosci — Symposia in Neuroscience

Symp Nondestr Eval Mater Prop Adv Mater — Symposium on Nondestructive Evaluation and Material Properties of Advanced Materials

Symp Nucleic Acids Chem — Symposium on Nucleic Acids Chemistry

Symp Ocul Ther — Symposium on Ocular Therapy

Symp Oral Sens Percept — Symposium on Oral Sensation and Perception

Sympos Gaussiana — Symposia Gaussiana

Symposium — Symposium: A Quarterly Journal in Modern Foreign Literatures

Sympos Math — Symposia Mathematica

Sympos Univ Upsaliensis Annum Quingentesimum Celebrantis — Symposia Universitatis Upsaliensis Annum Quingentesimum Celebrantis

Symp Pap Symp Chem Nat Prod — Symposium Papers. Symposium on the Chemistry of Natural Products

Symp Particleboard Proc — Symposium on Particleboard. Proceedings

Symp Part Surf Detect Adhes Removal — Symposium on Particles on Surfaces. Detection, Adhesion, and Removal

Symp Pharmacol Ther Toxicol Group — Symposium. Pharmacology, Therapeutics, and Toxicology Group. International Association for Dental Research

Symp Photovoltaische Solarenerg — Symposium Photovoltaische Solarenergie

Symp Plasma Sci Mater — Symposium on Plasma Science for Materials

Symp Preh — Symposium de Prehistoria de la Peninsula Iberica

Symp Priv Invest Abroad — Symposium. Private Investors Abroad

Symp Proc Br Crop Prot Counc — Symposium Proceedings. British Crop Protection Council

Symp Protein Soc — Symposium. Protein Society

Symp Pyrrolizidine Senecio Alka — Symposium on Pyrrolizidine Senecio Alkaloids. Toxicity

Symp Regul Enzyme Act Synth Norm Neoplast Tissues Proc — Symposium on Regulation of Enzyme Activity and Syntheses in Normal and Neoplastic Tissues. Proceedings

Symp R Entomol Soc Lond — Symposia. Royal Entomological Society of London

Symp R Entomol Soc London — Symposia. Royal Entomological Society of London

Symp Salivary Gland — Symposium for the Salivary Gland

Symp Ser Australas Inst Min Metall — Symposia Series. Australasian Institute of Mining and Metallurgy

Symp Ser Br Mycol Soc — Symposium Series. British Mycological Society

Symp Ser Immunobiol Stand — Symposia Series in Immunobiological Standardization

Symp Ser Inst Fuel (London) — Symposium Series. Institute of Fuel (London)

Symp Ser Soc Appl Bacteriol — Symposium Series. Society for Applied Bacteriology

Symp Soc Dev Biol — Symposia. Society for Developmental Biology

Symp Soc Exp Biol — Symposia. Society for Experimental Biology

Symp Soc Gen Microbiol — Symposium. Society for General Microbiology

Symp Soc Study Dev Growth — Symposium. Society for the Study of Development and Growth

Symp Soc Study Hum Biol — Symposia. Society for the Study of Human Biology

Symp Soc Study Inborn Errors Metab — Symposium. Society for the Study of Inborn Errors of Metabolism

Symp Space Nucl Power Syst — Symposium on Space Nuclear Power Systems

Symp Supercond Cryoelectron — Symposium on Superconductivity and Cryoelectronics

Symp Surf Min Reclam Pap — Symposium on Surface Mining and Reclamation. Papers

Symp Surf Phenom Enhanced Oil Recovery — Symposium on Surface Phenomena in Enhanced Oil Recovery

Symp Swed Nutr Found — Symposia. Swedish Nutrition Foundation

Symp Theor Phys Math — Symposia on Theoretical Physics and Mathematics

Symp Thermophys Prop Proc — Symposium on Thermophysical Properties. Proceedings

Symp Therm Solarenerg — Symposium Thermische Solarenergie

Symp Turbul Liq Proc — Symposium on Turbulence in Liquids. Proceedings

Symp Underground Min Pap — Symposium on Underground Mining. Papers

Symp Waste Manage Proc — Symposium on Waste Management. Proceedings

Symp Zool Soc Lond — Symposia. Zoological Society of London

SyN — Symphony News

Syn — Syntheses

Synax Eccl CP — Synaxarium Ecclesiae Constantinopolitanae

SynB — Syntheses (Brussels)

Synchrotron Radiat Dyn Phenom Int Meet Phys Chem — Synchrotron Radiation and Dynamic Phenomena. International Meeting of Physical Chemistry

Syn Commun — Synthetic Communications

Syn CP — Synaxarium Ecclesiae Constantinopolitanae

SYNED — Synerjy

SYNEE7 — Symposia in Neuroscience

SYNG — Synergy. Syncrude Canada

Syn Hist L — Synthese Historical Library

Syn Inorg Met-Org Chem — Synthesis in Inorganic and Metal-Organic Chemistry [Later, Synthesis and Reactivity in Inorganic and Metalorganic Chemistry]

Syn/LB — Synagogue/Liberal Judaism

Synop Br Fauna New Ser — Synopses of the British Fauna. New Series

Synopsis R — Synopsis Revue

Synopsis Swedish Bldg Res — Synopsis of Swedish Building Research

Syn Or — Synodicon Oriental ou Recueil des Synodes Nestoriens

Syn Org — Synthetische Methoden der Organischen Chemie

Syn Reac In — Synthesis and Reactivity in Inorganic and Metalorganic Chemistry

Syn Reactiv Inorg Metal Org C — Synthesis and Reactivity in Inorganic and Metalorganic Chemistry

Synth — Synthese

Synth — Syntheses. An International Quarterly for the Logical and Psychological Study of the Foundations of the Sciences

Synth Aperture Radar — Synthetic Aperture Radar

Synth Appl Isot Labelled Compd 1991 Proc Int Symp — Synthesis and Applications of Isotopically Labelled Compounds 1991. Proceedings. International Symposium

Synth Chem Agrochem III — Synthesis and Chemistry of Agrochemicals III

Synth Commun — Synthetic Communications

Synthese Hist Lib — Synthese Historical Library

Synthese Language Lib — Synthese Language Library

Synthese Lib — Synthese Library

Synthesis (C) — Synthesis (Cambridge)

Synth Fuels — Synthetic Fuels

Synth Fuels Update — Synthetic Fuels Update

Synth Libr — Synthese Library

Synth Lubr — Synthetic Lubrication

Synth Met — Synthetic Metals

Synth Methods Org Chem Yearb — Synthetic Methods of Organic Chemistry Yearbook

Synth Oligonucleotides Probl Front Pract Appl — Synthetic Oligonucleotides. Problems and Frontiers of Practical Application

Synth Pipeline Gas Symp Proc — Synthetic Pipeline Gas Symposium. Proceedings

Synth React Inorg Metorg Chem — Synthesis and Reactivity in Inorganic and Metalorganic Chemistry

Synth Rubber — Synthetic Rubber

Synth Rubber Ind (Lanzhou People's Repub China) — Synthetic Rubber Industry (Lanzhou, People's Republic of China)

Sy Os — Symbolae Osloenses

Sy Osl — Symbolae Osloenses

Syoyak Zass — Syoyakugaku Zasshi. Japanese Journal of Pharmacognosy

Sypl — Sygeplejersken

Syr — Syria. Revue d'Art Oriental et d'Archeologie

Syrac Law R — Syracuse Law Review

Syracuse HA — Syracuse Herald-America and Post-Standard

Syracuse HJ — Syracuse Herald Journal

Syracuse Int'l L & Com — Syracuse Journal of International Law and Commerce

Syracuse J Int'l L — Syracuse Journal of International Law

Syracuse L Rev — Syracuse Law Review

Syrian J Stomatol — Syrian Journal of Stomatology

Syria R — Syria. Revue d'Art Oriental et d'Archeologie

Syr J Intl — Syracuse Journal of International Law and Commerce

Syr J Intl L & Com — Syracuse Journal of International Law and Commerce

Syr LR — Syracuse Law Review

Syr Mesop St — Syro-Mesopotamian Studies

Sy S — Syn og Segn. Norsk-Tidsskrift

Sys and Soft — Systems and Software

Sys Proced — Systems and Procedures

Syst — Systems

Syst & Control — Systems and Control

Syst and Control Lett — Systems and Control Letters

Syst Appl Microbiol — Systematic and Applied Microbiology

Syst Ascomycetum — Systema Ascomycetum

Syst Assoc Publ — Systematics Association. Publication

Syst Assoc Spec Vol — Systematics Association. Special Volume

Syst Ass Spec Vol — Systematics Association. Special Volume

Syst Autoimmun — Systemic Autoimmunity

Syst Biol — Systematic Biology

Syst Bot — Systematic Botany

Syst-Comput-Controls — Systems-Computers-Controls

Syst Comput Jpn — Systems and Computers in Japan
Syst de Pensee en Afr Noire — Systemes de Pensee en Afrique Noire
Systematics Assoc Pub — Systematics Association. Publication
Systems Anal Modelling Simulation — Systems Analysis Modelling Simulation
Systems & Proc J — Systems and Procedures Journal
Systems-Comput-Controls — Systems-Computers-Controls
Systems Comput Japan — Systems and Computers in Japan
Systems Control Found Appl — Systems and Control. Foundations and Applications
Systems Control Inform — Systems, Control, and Information
Systems Control Lett — Systems and Control Letters
Systems Engrg Ser — Systems Engineering Series
Systems Sci — Systems Science
Systems Sci Math Sci — Systems Science and Mathematical Sciences
Systems Theory Res — Systems Theory Research
Syst Entomol — Systematic Entomology
Syst Fast Ionic Transp — Systems with Fast Ionic Transport
Syst Int — Systems International
Syst Logiques — Systemes Logiques
Syst Objectives Solutions — Systems, Objectives, Solutions
Syst Parasitol — Systematic Parasitology
Syst Pensee Afr Noire — Systames de Pensee en Afrique Noire
Syst Program Ser — Systems Programming Series
Syst Sci — Systems Science
Syst Technol — Systems Technology
Syst Theory Res — Systems Theory Research
Syst Zool — Systematic Zoology
Sys User — Systems User
SYUBAT — Science Reports. Yokohama National University. Section II. Biology and Geology
Syvrem Med — Syvremenna Meditsina
SZ — Schweizerische Zeitschrift fuer Volkswirtschaft und Statistik
SZ — Sekspirovskij Zbornik
SZ — Shigaku Zasshi
SZ — Sovremennye Zapiski
SZ — Stimmen der Zeit
SZ — Sueddeutsche Zeitung
Sz — Szazadok
SZ — Zeitschrift der Savigny-Stiftung fuer Rechtsgeschichte. Romanistische Abteilung
Szakszerv Szle — Szakszervezeti Szemle
Szamki Koezlem — Szamki Koezlemenyek
Szamki Tanulmanyok — Szamitogepalkalmazasi Kutato Intezet. Tanulmanyok
Szamvit Uegyviteltech — Szamvitel es Ugyviteltechnika
SZAUSAV — Studijne Zvesti Archeologickeho Ustavu Slovenskej Akademie v Nitra
Szaz — Szazadok
SZC — Studia Zrodloznawcze. Commentationes
SZCC — Spolia Zeylanica (Colombo, Ceylon)
SZCSAV — Annual Review of the Schizophrenic Syndrome

Szczecin Tow Nauk Wydz Nauk Przyr Roln — Szczecinskie Towarzystwo Naukowe Wydzial Nauk Przyrodniczo Rolniczych
S Zd — Sovetskoe Zdravoochranenie
SZDKA — Sovetskoe Zdravookhranenie Kirgizii
SzDL — Studien zur Deutschen Literatur
Szechuan Forests — Szechuan Forests/Ssu Chuan Chih Sheng Lin. Szechuan Reconstruction Department
S Zek — Sociale Zekerheidsgids
Szekszardi ME — Szekszardi Beri Balogh Adam Muzeum Evkonyve
SzEP — Studien zur Englischen Philologie
Szeph — Szephalom
SZF — Schweizerische Zeitschrift fuer Forstwesen
SZG — Schweizerische Zeitschrift fuer Geschichte
SZHYA — Schweizerische Zeitschrift fuer Hydrologie
Szigma Mat-Koezgazdasagi Folyoirat — Szigma. Matematikal-Koezgazdasagi Folyoirat
SZK — Studien zur Kulturkunde
Szk Gl Gospod Wiejsk Akad Roln Warszawie Zesz Nauk Ogrod — Szkola Glowna Gospodarstwa Wiejskiego - Akademia Rolnicza w Warszawie. Zeszyty Naukowe. Ogrodnictwo
Szk Gl Gospod Wiejsk Akad Roln Warszawie Zesz Nauk Roln — Szkola Glowna Gospodarstwa Wiejskiego - Akademia Rolnicza w Warszawie. Zeszyty Naukowe. Rolnictwo
Szk Gl Gospod Wiejsk Akad Roln Warszawie Zesz Nauk Zootech — Szkola Glowna Gospodarstwa Wiejskiego - Akademia Rolnicza w Warszawie. Zeszyty Naukowe. Zootechnika
Szk Gl Gospod Wiejsk Akd Roln Warszawie Zesz Nauk Weter — Szkola Glowna Gospodarstwa Wiejskiego - Akademia Rolnicza w Warszawie. Zeszyty Naukowe. Weterynaria
SZKKB — Shimizu Kensetsu Kenkyusho-Ho
Szklo & Cer — Szklo i Keramika
Szklo Ceram — Szklo i Ceramika
Szklo i Ceram — Szklo i Ceramika
SzL — Schriften zur Literatur
SZL — Spielzeug. Internationales Fachblatt fuer Spielmittel, Hobby- und Modellbau-Artikel, Christbaumschmuck, Fest- und Scherzartikel, Rohstoffe, Halbteile, Werkzeuge, Maschinen, und Verpackung
SZLGD — Sozialgerichtsbarkeit
SZM — Sovetskoe Zdravoukhranenie (Moscow)
SzNU — Sbornik za Narodni Umotvorenija
Szoeloesz Borasz Gazd Lap — Szoeloeszeti, Boraszati, es Gazdasagi Lap
Szolesz Boraszat — Szoleszet es Boraszat
Szov Arch — Sovetskaia Arkheologiia
SZPAA — Schweizerische Zeitschrift fuer Psychologie und Ihre Anwendungen
SZPMA — Sozial- und Praeventivmedizin
SZPMAA — Medecine Sociale et Preventive
SZS — Schweizerische Zeitschrift fuer Sozialversicherung
SZ Str R — Schweizerische Zeitschrift fuer Strafrecht
SzT — Schriften zur Theaterwissenschaft
SZTZA — Schweizerische Technische Zeitschrift
Sz VMK — Szegedi Varosi Muzeum Kiadvanyai

T

T — Bibliotheca Scriptorum Graecorum et Romanorum Teubneriana
T — Indisch Tijdschrift van het Recht
T — Teatar
T — Teatr
T — Teuthonista
T — Texana
T — Theatre
T — Themis. Verzameling van Bijdragen tot de Kennis van het PubliekenPrivaatrecht
T — Theology
T — Time
T — Times
T — Tractatenblad van het Koninkrijk der Nederlanden
T — Tradicao
T — Traditio
T — Tribus. Jahrbuch des Linden-Museums
T — Tuermer
T — Turin
T — Twentieth Century Verse
Ta — Talabriga
TA — Technology Assessment Database
TA — Television/Radio Age
TA — Teologinen Aikakauskirja
TA — Theatre Annual
TA — Theatre Arts
TA — Tijdschrift voor Armwezen, Maatschappelijke Hulp en Kinderbescherming
TA — Times of the Americas
TA — Traduction Automatique
TA — Trierisches Archiv
TA — Tropical Agriculture/Journal of the Imperial College of Agriculture. Trinidad, British West Indies
TAA — Transactions and Proceedings. American Philological Association
TAAGA — Transactions. American Association of Genito-Urinary Surgeons
Taal Tong — Taal en Tongval
TAAOA — Transactions. American Academy of Ophthalmology and Oto-Laryngology
TAAPA — Transactions. Association of American Physicians
T Aardrijkskundig Genoot — Tijdschrift van het Kon. Nederlandsche Aardrijkskundig Genootschap
TAB — Tabaktueel Magazine
Tab — Tablet. A Weekly Newspaper and Review
TAB — Technical Abstract Bulletin
Tabak Forsch — Tabak-Forschung
Tabakpfl Ost — Tabakpflanzer Oesterreichs
Tabakw Rdsch — Tabakwirtschaftliche Rundschau
Tabak Ztg — Tabak-Zeitung
Tab Defix — Defixionum Tebellae Atticae
Tabel Divers Serv Met Angola — Tabelas Diversas. Servico Meteorologico de Angola
Tabellen Intens SonnStrahl N U MittEur — Tabellen der Intensitaet der Sonnenstrahlung in Mitteleuropa Nord- und Mitteleuropa
Tabell Reiseber Met Schiffstageb — Tabellarische Reiseberichte nach den Meteorologischen Schiffstagebuechern
Tabell Zusammenst Hauptergebn Schweiz Hydrom Beob — Tabellarische Zusammenstellung der Hauptergebnisse der Schweizerischen Hydrometrischen Beobachtungen
Tabl A Const Donnees Num Chim Phys Technol — Tables Annuelles de Constantes et Donnees Numeriques de Chimie, de Physique, et de Technologie
Tabl Const Donnees Num — Tables de Constantes et Donnees Numeriques
Table Gov Order — Table of Government Orders
TableR — La Table Ronde
Tabl Mens Freq Obsns Serv Met Belgr — Tables Mensuelles de Frequence des Observations. Service Meteorologique. Belgrade
Tabl Thescs Fac Med Univ Paris — Tables des Theses Soutenues Devant la Faculte de Medecine. Universite de Paris
Tablx Mens Freq Inst Met Tchec — Tableaux Mensuels de Frequence. Institut Meteorologique Tchecoslavaque
Tablx Mens Freq Sect Met Buc — Tableaux Mensuels de Frequence. Section Meteorologique (Bucuresti)
Tablx Mens Freq Serv Met Acores — Tableaux Mensuels de Frequence. Service Meteorologique des Acores
Tablx Mens Freq Serv Met Aeronaut Danem — Tableaux Mensuels de Frequence. Service Meteorologique Aeronautique du Danemark
Tablx Pluies Tunis — Tableaux des Pluies (Tunis)</PHR> %
Tab Prom SSSR — Tabachnaya Promyshlennost' SSSR
TabR — La Table Ronde

TABS — Theological Abstracting and Bibliographical Services
TAB Tyres Access Batt — TAB. Tyres, Accessories, Batteries
Tabulae Biol — Tabulae Biologicae
Tabul Biol — Tabulae Biologicae
TAC — [The] Alien Critic
TAC — Turrialba (Costa Rica)
TACC — [The] Australian Comic Collector
Tactical Infrared Syst — Tactical Infrared Systems
Tactical Missile Aerodyn Gen Top — Tactical Missile Aerodynamics. General Topics
Tactical Missile Aerodyn Predict Methodol — Tactical Missile Aerodynamics. Prediction Methodology
TACUDC — Tests of Agrochemicals and Cultivars
TAD — [The] Armchair Detective
TAD — Tax Advisor
TAD — Turk Arkeoloji Dergisi
TAD J — Technical Aid to the Disabled Journal
Tadzik Gos Univ Trudy Meh-Mat Fak — Tadzikskii Gosudarstvennyi Universitet Imeni V. I. Lenina. Trudy Mehaniko-Matematiceskogo Fakulteta
Tadzik Gos Univ Ucen Zap — Tadzikskii Gosudarstvennyi Universitet Imeni V. I. Lenina. Ucenye Zapiski. Trudy Fiziko-Matematiceskogo Fakulteta. Serija Matematiceskaja
Tadzik S-H Inst Trudy — Tadzikskii Sel'skohozjaistvennyi Institut i Tadzikskii Gosudarstvennyi Universitet. Trudy
TAE — Trabalhos de Antropologia e Etnologia
TAE — Tropical Agriculture
TAeB — Tuebinger Aegyptologische Beitraege
TAEDA Newsl — TAEDA [Technology Assessment of Energy Development in Appalachia] Newsletter
Taegl Notizenbl Theilnehmer Versamml Naturf Aerzte Bonn — Taegliches Notizenblatt fuer die Theilnehmer an der Versammlung der Naturforscher und Aerzte zu Bonn
Taegl Rdsch — Taegliche Rundschau
Taegl Synopt WettKart Nordatlant Ozean — Taegliche Synoptische Wetterkarten fuer den Nordatlantischen Ozean
Taegl WettBer Bpest — Taegliche Wetterberichte (Budapest)
Taegl WettBer Dt Seew — Taeglicher Wetterbericht. Deutsche Seewarte
Taegl WettBer Dt WettDienst — Taeglicher Wetterbericht des Deutschen Wetterdienstes
Taegl Wettber Dt WettDienst US Zone — Taeglicher Wetterbericht des Deutschen Wetterdienstes in der U.S. Zone
Taegl WettBer Kuest U Schiffbeob Dt WettDienst — Taeglicher Wetterbericht, Kuesten- und Schiffbeobachtungen. Deutscher Wetterdienst
TAES — Transactions. American Ethnological Society
TaetBer ArbGem Foerd Futterb — Taetigkeitsbericht. Arbeitsgemeinschaft zur Foerderung des Futterbaues
TaetBer Bundesanst PflSchutz — Taetigkeitsbericht. Bundesanstalt fuer Pflanzenschutz
TaetBer Bundesanst QualForsch Pfl Erzeug — Taetigkeitsbericht. Bundesanstalt fuer Qualitaetsforschung Pflanzlicher Erzeugnisse
TaetBer Eidg Kommn Stud Hagelbild — Taetigkeitsbericht. Eidgenoessische Kommission zum Studium der Hagelbildung und Hagelabwehr
TaetBer Eidg Sternw — Taetigkeitsbericht der Eidgenoessischen Sternwarte
TaetBer Grossvers Bekaempf Hagels Magadinoebene — Taetigkeitsbericht. Grossversuch zur Bekaempfung des Hagels auf der Magadinoebene
TaetBer Inst GewHyg — Taetigkeitsbericht des Instituts fuer Gewerbehygiene
TaetBer Inst Lebensmitt Technol — Taetigkeitsbericht des Instituts fuer Lebensmitteltechnologie
TaetBer Landw Chem BundesversAnst Linz — Taetigkeitsbericht. Landwirtschaftlich-Chemische Bundesversuchsanstalt in Linz
TaetBer Landw Chem VerStn Dublany — Taetigkeitsbericht der Landwirtschaftlich-Chemischen Versuchsstation zu Dublany
TaetBer Maehr Landesmus — Taetigkeitsbericht des Maehrischen Landesmuseums
TaetBer Naturf Ges Baselland — Taetigkeitsbericht der Naturforschenden Gesellschaft. Baselland
TaetBer Oest Gartenb Ges — Taetigkeitsbericht der Oesterreichischen Gartenbau-Gesellschaft
TaetBer ReichsforschGes Wirt Bau U WohnWes — Taetigkeitsbericht der Reichsforschungsgesellschaft fuer Wirtschaftlichkeit in Bau- und Wohnungswesen
TaetBer Verein Schweiz Vers U VermittStell Saatkartoff — Taetigkeitsbericht der Vereinigung Schweizerischer Versuchs- und Vermittlungsstellen fuer Saatkartoffeln
TaetBer Wiss Anst Brauind — Taetigkeitsbericht der Wissenschaftlichen Anstalten fuer Brauindustrie

Taet Geol Verein Oberschles — Taetigkeit der Geologischen Vereinigung Oberschlesiens
TaetigkBer MusGes Teplitz — Taetigkeitsbericht der Museumsgesellschaft Teplitz
Taet Phys Tech Reichsanst — Taetigkeit der Physikalisch-Technischen Reichsanstalt
Taet Schweiz Forschlnst Hochgebirgsklima Tuberk — Taetigkeit des Schweizerischen Forschungsinstituts fuer Hochgebirgsklima und Tuberkulose
Taf — Tafelronde
TAFEQ — TAFE [*New South Wales Department of Technical and Further Education*] Quarterly
TAFN — Trabalhos da Associacao de Filosofia Natural
TAFR — Tableaux Analytiques de la Faune de l'URSS
TAFSA — Transactions. American Fisheries Society
TAFSD — Technical Report. AFWAL-TR. United States Air Force Wright Aeronautical Laboratories
Tag — Tagoro
TAG — Tijdschrift Aardrijkskundig Genootschap
TagBer Chem Ges DDR — Tagungsberichte. Chemische Gesellschaft in der Deutschen Demokratischen Republik
Tagber Dt Akad Landw-Wiss Berl — Tagungsberichte. Deutsche Akademie der Landwirtschaftswissenschaften zu Berlin
TagBer Int Kolloq Hochsch Elektrotech Ilmenau — Tagungsberichte. Internationales Kolloquium. Hochschule fuer Elektrotechnik Ilmenau
TagBer Phys Ges DDR — Tagungsberichte. Physikalische Gesellschaft in der Deutschen Demokratischen Republik
TAGLA — Tropical Agriculture
Tag Muellerei-Technol Ber — Tagung ueber die Muellerei-Technologie. Bericht
Tag Oest Ges Roentgenk — Tagung der Oesterreichischen Gesellschaft fuer Roentgenkunde und Strahlenforschung
Tagsber Fortschr Natur Heilk Abth Bot — Tagsberichte ueber die Fortschritte der Natur- und Heilkunde. Abtheilung fuer Botanik
TAGUA — Transactions. American Geophysical Union
Tagungsber Akad Landwirtschaftswiss — Tagungsbericht. Akademie der Landwirtschaftswissenschaften
Tagungsber Akad Landwirtschaftswiss DDR — Tagungsbericht. Akademie der Landwirtschaftswissenschaften der Deutschen Demokratischen Republik
Tagungsber Akad Landwirtschaftswiss Dtsch Demokr Repub — Tagungsbericht. Akademie der Landwirtschaftswissenschaften der Deutschen Demokratischen Republik
Tagungsber Deut Akad Landwirt Wiss Berlin — Tagungsberichte. Deutsche Akademie der Landwirtschaftswissenschaften zu Berlin
Tagungsber Dtsch Wiss Ges Erdoel Erdgas Kohle — Tagungsbericht. Deutsche Wissenschaftliche Gesellschaft fuer Erdoel, Erdgas, und Kohle
Tagungsber Ges Inn Med DDR — Tagungsbericht. Gesellschaft fuer Innere Medizin der DDR
Tagungsber Jahrestag Kerntech — Tagungsbericht. Jahrestagung Kerntechnik
Tagungsber Siemens Prozessrechn Anwenderkreises SAK Jahrestag — Tagungsbericht des Siemens Prozessrechner Anwenderkreises (SAK) Jahrestagung
Tagungsvortr Fachtag Amorphe Nanodispersive Schichsyst — Tagungsvortraege. Fachtagung Amorphe und Nanodispersive Schichsysteme
TAH — [*The*] American Hispanist
TAHCD — Taehan Ankwa Hakhoe Chapchi
TAHFDQ — Allan Hancock Foundation. Technical Reports
TAI — T. A. Informations [*Formerly, Traduction Automatique*]
TAI — Tax Management International Journal
Taidehist Tutkimuksia Ksthist Stud — Taidehistoriallisia Tutkimuksia/ Konsthistoriska Studier
TAIILI — Trudy Abkhazskogo Instituta Iazyka, Literatury i Istorii
TAik — Teologinen Aikakauskirja. Teologisk Tidskrift
Taikab Kogyo — Taikabutsu Kogyo
Taikomoji Branduoline Fiz — Taikomoji Branduoline Fizika
TA Inf — Traduction Automatique Informations
Tait — Tait's Edinburgh Magazine
Taiwan Agric Bimon — Taiwan Agriculture Bimonthly
Taiwan Agric Q — Taiwan Agriculture Quarterly
Taiwan Agr Res J — Taiwan Agricultural Research Journal
Taiwan Eng — Taiwan Engineering
Taiwan Environ Sanit — Taiwan Environmental Sanitation
Taiwan Fish Res Inst Fish Cult Rep — Taiwan. Fisheries Research Institute. Fish Culture. Report
Taiwan Fish Res Inst Lab Biol Rep — Taiwan. Fisheries Research Institute. Laboratory of Biology. Report
Taiwan Fish Res Inst Lab Fish Biol Rep — Taiwan. Fisheries Research Institute. Laboratory of Fishery Biology. Report
Taiwan Fish Yb — Taiwan Fisheries Yearbook
Taiwan Forests — Taiwan Forests/Taiwan Shen Lin
Taiwan J Th — Taiwan Journal of Theology
Taiwan J Vet Med Anim Husb — Taiwan Journal of Veterinary Medicine and Animal Husbandry
Taiwan Sugar Exp Stn Annu Rep — Taiwan. Sugar Experiment Station. Annual Report
Taiwan Sugar Exp Stn Res Rep — Taiwan. Sugar Experiment Station. Research Report
Taiwan Sugar Res Inst Annu Rep — Taiwan. Sugar Research Institute. Annual Report
Taiwan Tig Kizi — Taiwan Tigaku Kizi
Taiwan Trade Mo — Taiwan Trade Monthly
Taiw Ind — Taiwan Industrial Panorama
Taiw Stat — Taiwan Statistical Data Book
Taiw Svy — Monthly Economic Survey. Taiwan
TAK — Tonan Ajia Kenkyu
TAKAAN — Japanese Journal of Physical Fitness and Sports Medicine
TAKC — Taking Care. Newsletter of the Center for Consumer Health Education
TAKEAZ — Japanese Journal of Physical Education

TAKEAZ — Research Journal of Physical Education
Takenaka Tech Res Rep — Takenaka Technical Research Report
TAL — Taiwan Industrial Panorama
Tal — Taliesin
Tal — Talisman
TAL — Taxation for Lawyers
TALIA — Transactions. Association of Life Insurance Medical Directors of America
TALIS — Topics in Australasian Library and Information Studies
TallerC — Taller (Santiago, Cuba)
Tallinna Tehnikaulik Toim — Tallinna Tehnikaulikooli Toimetised
Tallinna Tehn Juur Riikl Katsek Teat — Tallinna Tehnikumi Juures Asuva Riikline Katsekoja Teated
Tallinna TehUlik Toim Ser A — Tallinna Tehnikaulikooli Toimetused. Series A
Tallinna TehUlik Toim Ser B — Tallinna Tehnikaulikooli Toimetused. Series B
Tallin Polueteh Inst Toim — Tallinna Poluetehnilise Instituudi Toimetised
Tall Oil Ind — Tall Oil in Industry
Tall Timbers Res Stn Misc Publ — Tall Timbers Research Station. Miscellaneous Publication
Talouselam — Talouselama
TAm — [*The*] Americas: A Quarterly Review of Inter-American Cultural History
TaM — Tarybine Mokykla
TAM — Taxes. The Tax Magazine
TAM — (The) Americas
TAM — Theatre Arts Magazine
TAM — Theatre Arts Monthly
TAM — Tituli Asiae Minoris
Tamarack R — Tamarack Review
Tamarind Pap — Tamarind Papers
TamC — Tamil Culture
T Am Fish S — Transactions. American Fisheries Society
T Am Geophy — Transactions. American Geophysical Union
Tamil Cult — Tamil Culture
Tamil Nadu Ed — Tamil Nadu Education
Tamil Nadu J Coop — Tamil Nadu Journal of Co-operation
Tamkang J Management Sci — Tamkang Journal of Management Sciences
Tamkang J Math — Tamkang Journal of Mathematics
Tamkang R — Tamkang Review
Tamkang Rev — Tamkang Review
TamkR — Tamkang Review
T Am Math S — Transactions. American Mathematical Society
Tamm Hankk Kasvinjalost Siemenjulk — Tammisto Hankkijan Kasvin-Jalostuslaitos Siemenjulkaisu
T Am Micros — Transactions. American Microscopical Society
T Am Nucl S — Transactions. American Nuclear Society
Tampa Bay — Tampa Bay Business
Tampa Tr & Ti — Tampa Tribune and Times
Tampa Trib — Tampa Tribune
TAMPD — TAPPI [*Technical Association of the Pulp and Paper Industry*] Annual Meeting. Proceedings
T Am Phil S — Transactions. American Philosophical Society
TamR — Tamarack Review
TAMS — Transactions. American Microscopical Society
TAMSA — Transactions. American Microscopical Society
T Am S Art — Transactions. American Society for Artificial Internal Organs
TAMSJ — TAMS [*Token and Medal Society*] Journal
Tamsui Oxford Coll Lecture Notes Ser — Tamsui Oxford College. Lecture Notes Series
Tamsui Oxford J Management Sci — Tamsui Oxford Journal of Management Sciences
TAMTA — Transactions. American Mathematical Society
TAN — Tax Administrators News
TANAA — Transactions. American Neurological Association
TANAz — Trudy. Akademiia Nauk Azerbaidzhanskoi SSR
T Anc Monum — Ancient Monuments Society. Transactions
Tanc QW — Tancred. Quo Warranto
T & C — Technology and Culture
T & C — Town & Country
T&C — Town and Country
T & CJ — Town and Country Journal
T & F Coaches Rev — Track and Field Coaches Review
T and F Q Rev — Track and Field Quarterly Review
Tandheelk CorrespBl Ned Ind — Tandheelkundig Correspondentieblad van Nedelandsch-Indie
Tandlaegernes Tidsskr — Tandlaegernes Nye Tidsskrift
T & R — Travaux et Recherches. Federation Tarnaise de Speleo-Archeologie
T & R Bull — T and R Bulletin [*London*]
T & T — Time and Tide
T & T — Tools and Tillage
Tanganyika Notes & Rec — Tanganyika Notes and Records
Tang Notes — Tanganyika Notes and Records
TANi — Recueil de Jurisprudence des Tribunaux de l'Arrondissement de Nivelles
Taniguchi Symp Brain Sci — Taniguchi Symposia on Brain Sciences
TANK — Trudy. Akademiia Nauk Kazakhskoi SSR
Tank Bulk Marit Manage — Tanker and Bulker Maritime Management
Tanker Bulk Carr — Tanker and Bulk Carrier
Tanker Bulker Int — Tanker and Bulker International
Tankstn Garagenbetr — Tankstation und Garagenbetrieb
Tan Lect HV — Tanner Lectures on Human Values
TANN — Taqrimiut Nipingat News
TANR — Academie Nationale de Rheims. Travaux
TANSA — Transactions. American Nuclear Society
TANTa — Trudy. Akademiia Nauk Tadzhikskoi SSR
Tanulmanyok Magy Tud Akad Szamitastech es Autom Kut Intez — Tanulmanyok Magyar Tudomanyos Akademia Szamitastechnikai es Automatizalasi Kutato Intezet

Tanulmanyok MTA Szamitastechn Automat Kutato Int (Budapest) — Tanulmanyok. MTA [*Magyar Tudomanyos Akademia*] Szamitastechnikai es Automatizalasi Kutato Intezet (Budapest)

Tanzania Miner Resour Power Annu Rep Geol Surv Div — Tanzania. Ministry of Industries. Mineral Resources and Power. Annual Report of the Geological Survey Division

Tanzania Notes Recs — Tanzania Notes and Records

Tanzania Rec Geol Surv Tanganyika — Tanzania. Records of the Geological Survey of Tanganyika

Tanzania Silvic Res Note — Tanzania Silviculture Research Note

Tanzania Silvic Res Stn Tech Note (New Ser) — Tanzania. Silviculture Research Station. Technical Note (New Series)

TAP — Tabaksplant. Maandblad voor de Sigaren, Sigaretten, en Tabakshandel en Industrie

TAPA — Transactions and Proceedings. American Philological Association

Tap Chi Toan Hoc — Tap Chi Toan Hoc. Progress of Mathematical Sciences

Tap Chi Toan Hoc J Math — Tap Chi Toan Hoc. Journal of Mathematics

TAPHA — Transactions. American Philological Association

TAPhA — Transactions and Proceedings. American Philological Association

TA Philos Soc — Transactions. American Philosophical Society

TAPhS — Transactions. American Philosophical Society

TAPI — Trudy. Azerbaidzhanskii Politekhnicheskii Institut

TAPPI — TAPPI [*Technical Association of the Pulp and Paper Industry*] Journal

TAPPI Alkaline Pulping Conf Prepr — TAPPI [*Technical Association of the Pulp and Paper Industry*] Alkaline Pulping Conference Preprint

TAPPI Annu Meet Prepr — TAPPI [*Technical Association of the Pulp and Paper Industry*] Annual Meeting. Preprint

TAPPI Annu Meet Proc — TAPPI [*Technical Association of the Pulp and Paper Industry*] Annual Meeting. Proceedings

TAPPI Bibl — TAPPI [*Technical Association of the Pulp and Paper Industry*] Bibliography of Pulp and Paper Manufacture

TAPPI Bull — TAPPI (Technical Association of the Pulp and Paper Industry) Bulletin

TAPPI Coat Conf Prepr — TAPPI [*Technical Association of the Pulp and Paper Industry*] Coating Conference. Preprint

TAPPI Data Sh — TAPPI (Technical Association of the Pulp and Paper Industry) Data Sheets

TAPPI Environ Conf Proc — TAPPI [*Technical Association of the Pulp and Paper Industry*] Environmental Conference. Proceedings

TAPPI For Biol Wood Chem Conf Conf Pap — TAPPI [*Technical Association of the Pulp and Paper Industry*] Forest Biology - Wood Chemistry Conference. Conference Papers

Tappi J — Tappi Journal

TAPPI J Tech Assoc Pulp Paper Ind — TAPPI. Journal of the Technical Association of the Pulp and Paper Industry

TAPPI Monogr Ser — TAPPI [*Technical Association of the Pulp and Paper Industry*] Monograph Series

TAPPI Papermakers Conf Pap — TAPPI [*Technical Association of the Pulp and Paper Industry*] Papermakers Conference. Papers

TAPPI Papermakers Conf Proc — TAPPI [*Technical Association of the Pulp and Paper Industry*] Papermakers Conference. Proceedings

TAPPI Rout Control Meth — TAPPI (Technical Association of the Pulp and Paper Industry) Routine Control Methods

TAPPI Spec Biblphy Ser — TAPPI (Technical Association of the Pulp and Paper Industry) Special Bibliography Series

TAPPI Special Rept — TAPPI [*Technical Association of the Pulp and Paper Industry*] Special Reports

TAPPI Spec Tech Assoc Publ — TAPPI [*Technical Association of the Pulp and Paper Industry*] Special Technical Association. Publication

Tapp M & Ch — Tapp on Maintenance and Champerty

TAPS — Transactions. American Philosophical Society

TAQK — Taqralik

TAQL — Taqralik

TAQO — Tawow. Canadian Indian Cultural Magazine

TAR — Tara. Schweizerische Fachzeitschrift fuer Moderne Verpackung

TAR — Tax Advance Rulings

TAr — Theater Arts

TAR — Tijdschrift ter Beoefening van het Administratief Recht

Tarb — Tarbiz. Quarterly for Jewish Studies

Tar Bak Orm Gen Mud Yay — Tarim Bakanligi. Orman Genel Mudurlugu Yayinlarindan

Targeted Diagn Ther — Targeted Diagnosis and Therapy

Targeted Diagn Ther Ser — Targeted Diagnosis and Therapy Series

Target Mark — Target Marketing

Targets Backgrounds Discrim — Targets, Backgrounds, and Discrimination

Targets Heterocycl Syst — Targets in Heterocyclic Systems. Chemistry and Properties

Tarib Derg — Tarib Dergisi

Tarl — Tarleton Term Reports

Tarl Term R — Tarleton Term Reports

Tarsad Szle — Tarsadalmi Szemle

Tarsadtud Kozl — Tarsadalomtudomanyi Kozlemenyek

TARSD — Tropical Agriculture Research Series

TArts — Theater Arts

Tartu Riikliku Ulik Toim — Tartu Riikliku Ulikooli Toimetised

Tartu Riiki Ul Toimetised — Tartu Riikliku Uelikooli Toimetised

Tartu Uelik Juures Oleva Loodusuur Seltsi Kirjatoeoed — Tartu Uelikooli Juures Oleva Loodusuurijate Seltsi Kirjatoeoed. Schriften Herausgegeben von der Naturforscher-Gesellschaft bei der Universitaet Tartu

Tartu Ulik Toim — Tartu Ulikooli Toimetised

Tartu Ul Toimetised — Tartu Ulikooli Toimetised. Uchenye Zapiski Tartuskogo Universiteta. Acta et Commentationes Universitatis Tartuensis

TARU Research Note — New South Wales. Traffic Accident Research Unit. TARU Research Note

TARW — Tibet-Archiv fuer Religionswissenschaft

TASA — Teaching Atypical Students in Alberta

TASA — Technical Advisory Service for Attorneys

T ASAE — Transactions. ASAE

Tas Arch — Tasmanian Architect

Tas Architect — Tasmanian Architect

TASB — Texas Archaeological Society. Bulletin

TASB — Transactions. Asiatic Society of Bengal

Tas Bldg App R — Tasmanian Building Appeal Reports

Tas Build — Tasmanian Builder

Taschenb Gartenbesitz Blumenfr — Taschenbuch fuer Gartenbesitzer und fuer Blumenfreunde

Taschenb Kuechen Landwirthschaftsfr — Taschenbuch fuer Kuechen-, Garten-, Blumen-, und Landwirthschaftsfreunde

Taschenbuecher Grundstud Math — Taschenbuecher fuer das Grundstudium Mathematik

Taschenkalend Natur Gartenfr — Taschenkalender fuer Natur- und Gartenfreunde

Tas Dep Agric Bull — Bulletin. Department of Agriculture (Tasmania)

Tas Div Bul — Institution of Engineers of Australia. Tasmania Division. Bulletin

Tas Ed — Tasmanian Education

Tas Ed Gaz — Tasmanian Education Gazette

Tas Ed Rec — Educational Record. Tasmania Education Department

Tas Educ — Tasmanian Education

Tas Fish — Tasmanian Fisheries Research

Tas Fruitgrower and Farmer — Tasmanian Fruitgrower and Farmer

Tas Geol Surv Geol Atlas 1 Mile Ser — Tasmanian Geological Survey. Geological Atlas. 1 Mile Series

Tas Govt Gaz — Tasmanian Government Gazette

Tas Hist Research Assoc Papers & Proc — Tasmanian Historical Research Association. Papers and Proceedings

Tas Hotel R — Tasmanian Hotel Review

Tas Ind — Tasmanian Industry

TASJ — Transactions. Asiatic Society of Japan

Tas J Ag — Tasmanian Journal of Agriculture

Tas J Agric — Tasmanian Journal of Agriculture

Tas J Ed — Tasmanian Journal of Education

Taskent Gos Ped Inst Ucen Zap — Taskentskii Gosudarstvennyi Pedagogiceskii Institut Imeni Nizami Ucenye Zapiski

Taskent Gos Univ Buharsk Ped Inst Naucn Trudy — Taskentskii Gosudarstvennyi Universitet Buharskii Pedagogiceskii Institut Naucnye Trudy

Taskent Gos Univ Naucn Trudy — Taskentskii Gosudarstvennyi Universitet Imeni V. I. Lenina Naucnye Trudy

Taskent Gos Univ Sb Naucn Trudov — Taskentskii Gosudarstvennyi Universitet Sbornik Naucnyh Trudov

Taskent Inst Inz Zeleznodoroz Transporta Trudy — Taskentskii Institut Inzenerov Zeleznodoroznogo Transporta Trudy

Taskent Inst Narod Hoz Naucn Zap — Taskentskii Institut Narodnogo Hozjaistva Naucnye Zapiski

Taskent Inst Narod Hoz Naucn Zap Mat v Prilozen — Taskentskii Institut Narodnogo Hozjaistva Naucnye Zapiski. Matematika v Prilozenijah

Taskent Politehn Inst Naucn Trudy — Taskentskii Politehniceskii Institut Naucnye Trudy. Novaja Serija

Taskent Politehn Inst Naucn Trudy NS — Taskentskii Politehniceskii Institut Naucnye Trudy. Novaja Serija

Tasks Veg Sci — Tasks for Vegetation Science

Tas Lab & Ind Bul — Tasmania. Department of Labour and Industry. Bulletin

Tas LR — Tasmanian Law Reports

Tas L Rev — University of Tasmania. Law Review

Tasm — Tasmanian State Reports

Tasmania Build J — Tasmanian Building Journal

Tasmania Dep Agric Annu Rep — Tasmania. Department of Agriculture. Annual Report

Tasmania Dep Mines Geol Atlas 1:250000 Ser SK — Tasmania. Department of Mines. Geological Atlas. 1:250,000 Series SK

Tasmania Dep Mines Geol Surv Bull — Tasmania. Department of Mines. Geological Survey. Bulletin

Tasmania Dep Mines Geol Surv Rec — Tasmania. Department of Mines. Geological Survey. Record

Tasmania Dep Mines Geol Surv Rep — Tasmania. Department of Mines. Geological Survey. Report

Tasmania Dep Mines Tech Rep — Tasmania. Department of Mines. Technical Report

Tasmania Dep Mines Underground Water Supply Pap — Tasmania. Department of Mines. Underground Water Supply Paper

Tasmania For Comm Bull — Tasmania. Forestry Commission. Bulletin

Tasmania Geol Surv Bull — Tasmania. Geological Survey. Bulletin

Tasmania Geol Surv Explanatory Rep — Tasmania. Geological Survey. Explanatory Report

Tasmania Geol Surv Explan Rep Geol Atlas 1 Mile Ser — Tasmania. Geological Survey. Explanatory Report. Geological Atlas. 1 Mile Series

Tasmania Geol Surv Rec — Tasmania. Geological Survey. Record

Tasmania Geol Surv Rep — Tasmania. Geological Survey. Report

Tasmania Geol Surv Underground Water Supply Pap — Tasmania. Geological Survey. Underground Water Supply Paper

Tasmania Inland Fish Comm Rep — Tasmania. Inland Fisheries Commission. Report

Tasmania LR — University of Tasmania. Law Review

Tasmania Mines Dep Bull — Tasmania. Department of Mines. Bulletin

Tasmanian Dep Agric Insect Pest Surv — Tasmanian Department of Agriculture. Insect Pest Survey

Tasmanian Dep Agric Pamp — Tasmanian Department of Agriculture. Pamphlet

Tasmanian Fish Res — Tasmanian Fisheries Research

Tasmanian Fis Res — Tasmanian Fisheries Research

Tasmanian For Comm Bull — Tasmanian Forestry Commission. Bulletin

Tasmanian J Agr — Tasmanian Journal of Agriculture

Tasmanian J Agric — Tasmanian Journal of Agriculture

Tasmanian U L Rev — Tasmanian University. Law Review
Tasmanian Univ L Rev — Tasmanian University. Law Review
Tasmania Parl Dir Mines Annu Rep — Tasmania. Parliament. Director of Mines. Annual Report
Tasm Dep Agric Bull — Tasmania. Department of Agriculture. Bulletin
Tasm Dep Agric Res Bull — Tasmania. Department of Agriculture. Research Bulletin
Tasm Fmr — Tasmanian Farmer
Tasm Fruitgr Fmr — Tasmanian Fruitgrower and Farmer
Tasm Fruitgrow Fmr — Tasmanian Fruitgrower and Farmer
Tasm Geol Surv Bull — Tasmania. Geological Survey. Bulletin
Tasm Geol Surv Geol Atlas 1 Mile Ser — Tasmania. Geological Survey. Geological Atlas. 1 Mile Series
Tasm Geol Surv Undergr Wat Supply Pap — Tasmania. Geological Survey. Underground Water Supply Paper
Tasm Hist Res Ass Pap Proc — Tasmanian Historical Research Association. Papers and Proceedings
Tasm J Agr — Tasmanian Journal of Agriculture
Tasm J Agric — Tasmanian Journal of Agriculture
Tasm Nat — Tasmanian Naturalist
Tas Motor Trade & Transport J — Tasmanian Motor Trade and Transport Journal
Tasm R S M Not — Monthly Notices of Papers and Proceedings of the Royal Society of Tasmania
Tasm R S P — Monthly Notices of Papers and Proceedings of the Royal Society of Tasmania
Tasm SR — Tasmanian State Reports
Tasm St R — Tasmanian State Reports
Tasm UL Rev — Tasmanian University. Law Review
Tasm Univ Law Rev — University of Tasmania. Law Review
Tas Nat — Tasmanian Naturalist
Tas News — Tasmanian Motor News
Tas News — Tasmanian News Reports
Tas Nurse — Tasmanian Nurse
TASP — Texas Archaeological Society. Papers
Tas R — Tasmanian Reports
Tas R — Tasmanian State Reports
Tas S R — Tasmanian State Reports
Tas Teach — Tasmanian Teacher
Tas Teacher — Tasmanian Teacher
Tas Trader — Tasmanian Trader and Successful Independent
Tas Tramp — Tasmanian Tramp
Tas Univ Gaz — University of Tasmania. Gazette
Tas Univ Law R — University of Tasmania. Law Review
Tas Univ Law Rev — University of Tasmania. Law Review
Tas Univ L Rev — Tasmanian University. Law Review
Tat — Tatwelt
TAT — Treating Abuse Today
Tatabanyai Szenbanyak Musz Kozgazdasagi Kozl — Tatabanyai Szenbanyak Muszaki Kozgazdasagi Kozlemenyei
Tata Inst Fund Res Lectures on Math and Phys — Tata Institute of Fundamental Research. Lectures on Mathematics and Physics
Tata Inst Fund Res Studies in Math — Tata Institute of Fundamental Research. Studies in Mathematics
Tatar Neft — Tatarskaya Neft
Tate Gal Biennial Rep — Tate Gallery Biennial Report
TATEJ — Tasmanian Association for the Teaching of English. Journal
Tatigkeitsber Bundesanst Geowiss Rohst — Taetigkeitsbericht. Bundesanstalt fuer Geowissenschaften und Rohstoffe
Tatigkeitsber Geol Landsamt Nordrhein-Westfal — Taetigkeitsbericht. Geologisches Landesamt Nordrhein-Westfalen
Tatigkeitsber Niedersach Landsamt Bodenforsch — Taetigkeitsbericht. Niedersachsisches Landesamt fuer Bodenforschung
Tatra Mt Math Publ — Tatra Mountains Mathematical Publications
Tatslil — Tatslil [The Chord]. Forum for Music Research and Bibliography
Tatsuta Tech Rev — Tatsuta Technical Review
Tatung J — Tatung Journal
TAUPDJ — Trends in Autonomic Pharmacology
TAUTDV — Texas A & M University. Sea Grant College. TAMU-SG
TAVO — Tuebinger Atlas der Vorderorients
Tax — Taxandria
Tax — Taxation
TAX — Taxation for Accountants
Tax Ad — Tax Advisor
Tax Adm'rs News — Tax Administrators News
Tax Adv — Tax Advisor
Tax Aust — Taxation in Australia
Tax Conf — Tax Conference
Tax Coun Q — Tax Counselor's Quarterly
Tax Ct Mem Dec CCH — Tax Court Memorandum Decisions. Commerce Clearing House
Tax Ct Mem Dec P-H — Tax Court Memorandum Decisions. Prentice-Hall
Tax Ct Rep CCH — Tax Court Reports. Commerce Clearing House
Tax Ct Rep Dec P-H — Tax Court Reported Decisions. Prentice-Hall
Tax Dig — Tax Digest
Taxes — Tax Magazine
Tax Exec — Tax Executive
Tax-Exempt Org P-H — Tax-Exempt Organizations. Prentice-Hall
Tax Expend — Tax Expenditures. Budget Control Options and 5-Year Projections for Fiscal Years 1983-1987
Tax Fin and Est Pl — Tax, Financial, and Estate Planning for the Owner of a Closely Held Corporation
Tax for Law — Taxation for Lawyers
Tax in Aust — Taxation in Australia
Tax Law — Tax Lawyer
Tax Law R — Tax Law Review

Tax LR — Tax Law Review
Tax L Rev — Tax Law Review
Tax Mag — Tax Magazine
Tax Management Int'l — Tax Management International Journal
Tax Mo (Manila) — Tax Monthly (Manila)
Taxn in Aust — Taxation in Australia
Taxon Index — Taxonomic Index
Taxpayers Bul — Taxpayers' Bulletin
Tax Pl Rev — Tax Planning Review
Tax R — Tax Review
Tax Rev — Tax Review
Taylor Sc Mm — Scientific Memoirs, selected from the Transactions of Foreign Academies and Learned Societies and from Foreign Journals. Taylor
Taylor Soc Bul — Taylor Society. Bulletin
TAZ — Tabak Zeitung. Fachorgan der Tabakwirtschaft
TAzerbPI — Trudy Azerbaidzhanskogo Gosudarstvennogo Pedagogicheskogo Instituta
TB — Automotive Engine Rebuilders Association. Technical Bulletin
TB — Tempo Brasileiro
TB — Theologische Blaetter
TB — Thrill Book
TB — Tijdschrift voor Bestuurswetenschappen en Publiek Recht
TB — Topographical Bibliography of Ancient Egyptian Hieroglyphic Texts, Reliefs, andPaintings
TB — Tvorba
TB — Tyndale Bulletin
TB Agric Exp Stn SD State Univ — Technical Bulletin. Agricultural Experiment Station. South Dakota State University
TBB — Trolleybus Bulletin
TBBFA — Trudy Buryatskogo Instituta Estestvennykh Nauk Buryatskii Filial Sibirskoe Otdelenie Akademiya Nauk SSSR
TBBSA — Transactions. British Bryological Society
TBD — Turk Biologi i Dergisi
TBE — Texas Business Executive
TBE — Trade Opportunities in Taiwan
TBE Bull — TBE Bulletin. Israel Mining Industries Laboratories
TBE Class — Timber Bulletin for Europe. Classification and Definitions of Forest Products
T Best — Tijdschrift voor Bestuurswetenschappen
T Best Publ R — Tijdschrift voor Bestuurswetenschappen en Publiek Recht
TBG — Tijdschrift Bataviasch Genootschap
TBGAS — Transactions. Bristol and Gloucestershire Archaeological Society
TBGKW — Tijdschrift van het Bataviaasch Genootschap van Kunsten en Wetenschappen
TBGS — Transactions. Bombay Geographical Society
TBGU — Trudy Belorusskogo Gosudarstvennogo Universiteta
TBH — TourBase Hotel-/Unterkunftsdaten
TBI — Ink and Print
T Bi — Tidsskrift for Biavl
T Bi — Tidsskrift for Biavlerforening
TBI — Training
TBIAN — Trudy Botanicheskogo Instituta Akademii Nauk SSR
TBIK — Trudy Botanicheskogo Instituta Kazakhskoi SSR
Tbilis A Razmadzis Saxel Mat Inst Shromebi — T'bilisis A. Razmadzis Saxelobis Mat'ematikis Institutis Shromebi
Tbilis Gos Univ Inst Prikl Mat Tr — Tbilisskii Gosudarstvennyi Universitet Institut Prikladnoi Matematiki Trudy
Tbilisis Univ Sromebi — Stalinis Sacheolobis Tbilisis Universitatis Sromebi
Tbiliss Gos Univ Inst Prikl Mat Trudy — Tbilisskii Gosudarstvennyi Universitet Institut Prikladnoi Matematiki Trudy
TBK — Toyo Bungaku Kenkyu
TBKK — Toyo Bunka Kenyusho Kiyo
TBKZA — Trudy Instituta Botaniki Akademiya Nauk Kazakhskoi SSR
TBM — Tijdschrift voor Milieu en Recht
TBMS — Transactions of the British Mycological Society
TBMSDT — Mississippi. Agricultural and Forestry Experiment Station. Technical Bulletin
TBN — Thailand Business
TBNNA — Trudy Bashkirskii Nauchno-Issledovatel'skii Institut po Pererabotke Nefti
TBO — TourBase Orstdaten
TBP — Tijdschrift voor Bestuurswetenschappen en Publiek Recht
TBR — New York Times Book Review
TBR — Three Banks Review
TBRD — Taxation Board of Review Decisions
TBRD — Taxation Board of Review Decisions. New Series
TBRD (NS) — Taxation Board of Review Decisions (New Series)
T Br Mycol — Transactions. British Mycological Society
TBSL — Transactions. Bibliographical Society. London
TBSS — Trudy Botanicheskogo Sada v Sukhumi
TBT — Trends in Biotechnology
TBU — Hong Kong Enterprise
TBurNII — Trudy Burjatskogo Kompleksnogo Naucno-Issledovatel'skogo Instituta
TBVG — Thurgauische Beitraege zur Vaterlaendischen Geschichte
TBW — [The] Business World
TC — Chronicle (Toowoomba)
TC — Journal of Technical Topics in Civil Engineering
TC — Reports of Tax Cases
TC — Tablettes Cappadociennes
TC — Tamil Culture
TC — Telecommunications Counselor
TC — TeleCommuting Report
TC — Texto Critico
TC — Theory of Computation Series
TC — Tituli Camirenses
TC — Trierische Chronik

TC — Twentieth Century
TC — Tworczosc
TCA — [The] Canadian Amateur
TCA — Thermochimica Acta
TCAA — Transactions. Connecticut Academy of Arts and Sciences
TCAAS — Transactions and Collections. American Antiquarian Society
TCAAS — Transactions. Connecticut Academy of Arts and Sciences
TCA Man — TCA [Tissue Culture Association] Manual
T Camir — Tituli Camirenses
TCANAQ — Commonwealth Bureau of Animal Nutrition. Technical Communication
TCAus — Twentieth Century (Australia)
TCBAAQ — Commonwealth Bureau of Animal Breeding and Genetics. Technical Communication
TCBS — Transactions. Cambridge Bibliographical Society
TCC — Tamil Culture (Colombo, Ceylon)
TCC — Theory of Culture Change
TCCND5 — Commonwealth Bureau of Nutrition. Technical Communication
TCCOB — Textile Chemist and Colorist
TCC Tech Bull — TCC (Telegraph Condenser Co.) Technical Bulletin [London]
TCD — Turk Cografya Dergisi/Review of the Association of Turkish Geographers, Ankara
TCD Ann Bull — Friends. Library of Trinity College. Dublin. Annual Bulletin
TCEA — Theoretical Chemical Engineering Abstracts
TCEBA — Tribune. CEBEDEAU
TCEL — Thought Currents in English Literature
TCF — Twentieth Century Fiction
TCGCB — Transactions. Caribbean Geological Conference
TCGE-G — Technika Hronika (Greece)
TCGI — Terzo Congresso Geografico Italiano. Saggio di Paleogeografia
TCH — Technovation
TCh — Temoignage Chretien
TCH — Trade Channel
TCHHC — Ti Ch'iu Hua Hsueh
TCHMA — Technika v Chemii
TCHPAX — Acta Geologica Sinica
Tchr Coll Rec — Teachers College Record
T Christ Wet — Tydskrif vir Christelike Wetenskap
TCI — Twentieth Century Interpretations
TCITA — Transactions. Chalmers University of Technology
TCJ — Town and Country Journal
TCJAA — Telecommunication Journal of Australia
TCJOA — Telecommunication Journal
TCKHA — Ti Chih Ko Hsueh
TCL — Textes Cuneiformes. Musee du Louvre. Departement des Antiquites Orientales et de la Ceramique Antique
TCL — Twentieth Century Literature
TCLC — Travaux. Cercle Linguistique de Copenhague
TCLC — Twentienth Century Literary Criticism
TCLP — Travaux. Cercle Linguistique de Prague
TCM — Teratogenesis, Carcinogenesis, and Mutagenesis
TCM — Textil-Mitteilungen. Unabhangige Textil Zeitung fuer Handel und Industrie
TCM — Trade and Commerce
TCM — Twentieth Century Monthly
TCMDBN — Handelinge. Kollege van Geneeskunde van Suid-Afrika
TCMTA — Technometrics
TCMUA — Telecommunications
TCMUD8 — Teratogenesis, Carcinogenesis, and Mutagenesis
TCMUE9 — Topics in Chemical Mutagenesis
TCN — Trolley Coach News
TCNOA — Technology
TCNPEX — Bulletin. Taichung District Agricultural Improvement Station
TCNRS — Transactions. Canadian Numismatic Research Society
TCNSB — Technos
T Coach — Track Coach
TCORA — Teacher's College Record
T C Peirce — Transactions. Charles S. Peirce Society
TCPLA — Town and Country Planning
TCQ — Tax Counselor's Quarterly
TCR — Teacher's College Record
TCR — Technology Review
TCREA — Telecommunications and Radio Engineering
T Crit — Texto Critico
TCRUA — Technische Rundschau
TCS — Temperature Controlled Storage and Distribution
TCS — Texts from Cuneiform Sources
TCS — Transportation Costing Service
TCS — Twentieth Century Studies
T C Ser Soil Conserv Auth (Vic) — T C Series. Soil Conservation Authority (Victoria)
T C Ser Soil Conserv Auth (Vict) — T C Series. Soil Conservation Authority (Victoria)
TCSM — Transactions. Colonial Society of Massachusetts
Tctbl — Tractatenblad
TCTOA — Tectonophysics
TCV — Twentieth Century Views
TCW — Today's Christian Woman
TCWA — Transactions. Cumberland and Westmorland Antiquarian and ArchaeologicalSociety
TCWSA — T'ai-Wan Huan Ching Wei Sheng
TD — Theatre Documentation
TD — Theology Digest
TD — Tundra Drums
TDA — Tombs of the Double Axes and Associated Group
TDA Bull — Timber Development Association. Bulletin
TDA Des Sh — T.D.A. (Timber Development Association) Design Sheet

TDA Statist Yb Timb — T.D.A. (Timber Development Association) Statistical Yearbook of Timber
TDA Yb Timb Statist — T.D.A. (Timber Development Association) Yearbook of Timber Statistics
TDAZA — Tautsaimnieciba Derigie Augi
TDC — [The] Developing Child
TDC — Treasury Department Circular
TDED — Istanbul Universitesi Edegiyat Fakultesi Turk Dili ve Edebiyati Dergisi
TDG — Tradiciones de Guatemala
TdH — Terre des Hommes
Tdhv — Tidehverv
TDHYA — Tohoku Daigaku Hisuiyoeki Kagaku Kenkyusho Hokoku
TDJ — Training and Development Journal
TDJKA — Tokyo Daigaku Jishin Kenkyusho Iho
TDK — Toyo Daigaku Kiyo
TDKF — Fahrzeugtestdatenbank
TDKIB — Tokai Daigaku Kiyo Kogakubu
TDKNAF — Annual Report. Takeda Research Laboratories
Tdlb — Tandlaegebladet
TDLBAI — Deutsche Akademie der Landwirtschaftwissenschaften zu Berlin. Tagungsberichte
TDMOD — Therapeutic Drug Monitoring
TDN — Tendances de la Conjoncture. Graphiques Mensuels
TdN — Tijdschrift der Notarissen
TDNLA — Trudy Universiteta Druzhby Narodov
TDoAx — Tombs of the Double Axes and Associated Group
TDOD — Training and Development Organizations Directory
Tdpl — Tandplejen
TDR — Drama Review [Formerly, Tulane Drama Review]
TDR — Technology Review
TDR — Thailand Development Report
TDR — Tulane Drama Review
TDRCAH — Contributions. Institute of Geology and Paleontology. Tohoku University
TDSKB — Reports. Research Institute for Strength and Fracture of Materials. Tohoku University
TDUKA — Tokyo Daigaku Uchu Koku Kenkyusho Hokoku
TDYKA — Tokushima Daigaku Yakugaku Kenkyu Nempo
TDYKA8 — Annual Reports. Faculty of Pharmaceutical Sciences. Tokushima University
TE — Journal of Transportation Engineering
TE — Teacher Education
Te — Teatr
Te — Teatro. Mensile dello Spettacolo e delle Arti
Te — Tempo
TE — Teologia Espiritual
TE — Tetlit Tribune
TE — Tiger's Eye
TE — Today's Education
TE — Transportation Engineer Magazine
TE — Travaux. Musee d'Etat de l'Ermitage
TE — Trimestre Economico
TE — Trudy Gosudarstvennogo Ermitazha
TEA — Tea and Coffee Trade Journal
Tea — Tea Boards of Kenya, Uganda, and Tanganyika. Journal
TEA — Tijdschrift voor Entomologie (Amsterdam)
Tea & Coff — Tea and Coffee Trade Journal
Teach — Teacher
Teach Adults — Teaching Adults
Teach Aids News — Teaching Aids News
Teach Col J — Teachers College Journal
Teach Coll Rec — Teacher's College Record
Teach Col R — Teacher's College Record
Teach Col Rec — Teachers College Record
Teach Deaf — Teacher of the Deaf
Teach Dist — Teaching at a Distance
Teach Ed — Teacher Education
Teach Educ — Teacher Education
Teach Eng — Teaching of English
Teach Engl — Teaching of English
Teach Engl Deaf — Teaching English to the Deaf
Teacher Ed — Teacher Education in New Countries
Teacher Librn — Teacher-Librarian
Teachers Coll Rec — Teachers College Record. Columbia University
Teachers J — Teachers' Journal
Teach Excep Child — Teaching Exceptional Children
Teach Feedback — Teacher Feedback
Teach Guild NSW Proc — Teachers Guild of New South Wales. Proceedings
Teach Hist — Teaching History
Teaching Elem PE — Teaching Elementary Physical Education
Teaching Engl — Teaching of English
Teaching High Sch PE — Teaching High School Physical Education
Teaching Mid Sch PE — Teaching Middle School Physical Education
Teaching Mus — Teaching Music
Teaching Polit Sci — Teaching Political Science
Teach J — Teachers' Journal
Teach J and Abst — Teachers' Journal and Abstract
Teach J Spec Educ — Teachers' Journal of Special Education
Teach J Vic — Teachers' Journal (Victorian Teachers Union)
Teach Learn — Teaching and Learning
Teach Learn Med — Teaching and Learning in Medicine
Teach Lib — Teacher-Librarian
Teach Lond Kids — Teaching London Kids
Teach Math — Teaching Mathematics
Teach Meth Page — Teaching Methods Page
Teach News Birm — Teaching News. University of Birmingham

Teach Newsl — Teaching Newsletter
Teach Phil — Teaching Philosophy
Teach Pol S — Teaching Political Science
Teach Pol Sci — Teaching Political Science
Teach Sanit Bull — Teachers' Sanitary Bulletin [*Lansing*]
Teach Socio — Teaching Sociology
Teach Sociol — Teaching Sociology
Teach Today — Teacher Today
Teach Train — Teaching and Training
Teach W — Teacher's World
Tea East Afr — Tea in East Africa
Tea Lib — Teacher-Librarian
TEAL Occ Pap — Teachers of English as an Additional Language. Occasional Papers
TE & M — Telephone Engineer and Management
TEAPA — Technikas Apskats
Tea Q — Tea Quarterly
TEARA — Terapevticheskii Arkhiv
Tea Res Assoc Annu Sci Rep — Tea Research Association. Annual Scientific Report
Tea Res Inst Ceylon Annu Rep — Tea Research Institute of Ceylon. Annual Report
Tea Res Inst Sri Lanka Tech Rep — Tea Research Institute of Sri Lanka. Technical Report
Tea Res J — Tea Research Journal
Tea Res J Kyoto — Tea Research Journal. Kyoto/Kyoto-fu Chagyo Kenkyusho Gyomu Hokokusho
Tea Rubb Mail — Tea and Rubber Mail
TEAS — Twayne's English Author Series
TEAT — Obras de Teatro Estrenadas en Espana
Teaterarb — Teaterarbejde
Tebiwa J Idaho Mus Nat Hist — Tebiwa Journal. Idaho Museum of Natural History
Tebiwa Misc Pap Idaho State Univ Mus Nat Hist — Tebiwa Miscellaneous Papers. Idaho State University. Museum of Natural History
TEC — Telecommunications Policy
TEC — Transport Environment Circulation
TecAd Int J Technol Adv — TecAd. International Journal of Technology Advances
Tec Agr — Tecnica Agricola
Tec Agric (Catania) — Tecnica Agricola (Catania)
Tec Agric Madr — Tecnica Agricola (Madrid)
Tec Auto Avia — Tecnica del Automovil en Avia
Tec Autom — Tecniche dell'Automazione
Tec Azuc — Tecnica Azucarera
TECC — Texas Educational Computer Courseware Database
Tec Cult Sobreir — Tecnica Cultural dos Sobreiras. Junta Nacional da Cortica
Tec Econ Bahia Banca — Tecnica y Economia. Instituto Tecnologico del Sul (Bahia Banca)
TECED — Techniques de l'Energie
Tec Frio — Tecnica del Frio
Tech — Technology
Tech Abh Wiss — Technische Abhandlungen aus Wissenschaft und Praxis
Tech Abstr Am Petrol Inst — Technical Abstracts. American Petroleum Institute
Tech Abstr Bristol Eng Div — Technical Abstracts. Bristol Engine Division
Tech Abstr Bristol Siddeley Eng — Technical Abstracts. Bristol Siddeley Engines
Tech Abstr Bull — Technical Abstract Bulletin
Tech Abstr Bull ASTIA — Technical Abstract Bulletin. Armed Services Technical Information Agency (ASTIA)
Tech Abstr Bull High Duty Alloys — Technical Abstract Bulletin. High Duty Alloys
Tech Abstr Linoleum Res Coun — Technical Abstracts. Linoleum Research Council [*London*]
Tech Abstr Pap Mkrs Ass Gt Br Ire — Technical Abstracts. Paper Makers' Association of Great Britain and Ireland
Tech Abstr Wash — Technical Abstracts (Washington)
Tech Advis Anim Ind — Technical Adviser on Animal Industries [*Salisbury, Rhodesia*]
Tech Adv Shikoku Agric — Technical Advances in Shikoku Agriculture
Tech Agri — Technique Agricole
Tech & Archit — Techniques and Architecture
Tech & Archit [Paris] — Techniques et Architecture [*Paris*]
Tech & Cult — Technology and Culture
Tech & Culture — Technology and Culture
Tech Anz Bpest — Technischer Anzeiger (Budapest)
Tech Anz Masch Dampf U MotBetr — Technischer Anzeiger fuer Maschinen-, Dampf-, und Motorenbetriebe
Tech Appl Pet — Techniques et Applications du Petrole
Tech Apskats — Technikas Apskats
Tech Assistentin — Technische Assistentin
Tech Assn Pa — Technical Association Papers
Tech Bau — Technik am Bau
Tech Behav Neural Sci — Techniques in the Behavioral and Neural Sciences
Tech Belge Prothese Dent — Technicien Belge en Prothese Dentaire
Tech Ber Heinrich-Hertz Inst (Berlin-Charlottenburg) — Technischer Bericht. Heinrich-Hertz Institut (Berlin-Charlottenburg)
Tech Ber Sticht Nederl Graan-Cent — Technisch Bericht. Stichting Nederlands Graan-Centrum
Tech Bibliogr Birmingham Public Lib — Technical Bibliographies. Birmingham Public Libraries
Tech Bibliogr Ser Birmingham Cent Lib — Technical Bibliographies Series. Birmingham Central Libraries
Tech Biochem Biophys Morphol — Techniques of Biochemical and Biophysical Morphology
Tech Bkguide — Technical Bookguide [*London*]
Tech Bk Rev — Technical Book Review [*London*]
Tech Bk Rev Index NY — Technical Book Review Index (New York)
Tech Bk Rev Index Pittsb — Technical Book Review Index (Pittsburgh)

Tech Bks Print — Technical Books in Print [*London*]
Tech Bookl Br Geon — Technical Booklets. British Geon [*London*]
Tech Bul Dep Agric (Malaysia) — Technical Bulletin. Department of Agriculture (Malaysia)
Tech Bull Agric Exp Stn Ore St Univ — Technical Bulletin. Agricultural Experiment Station. Oregon State University
Tech Bull Agric Exp Stn Univ Ariz — Technical Bulletin. Arizona Agricultural Experiment Station. University of Arizona
Tech Bull Agric Exp Stn Wash St — Technical Bulletin. Agricultural Experiment Station. Washington State Instituteof Agricultural Sciences
Tech Bull Agric Res Inst — Technical Bulletin. Agricultural Research Institute
Tech Bull Agric Res Inst (Cyprus) — Technical Bulletin. Agricultural Research Institute (Cyprus)
Tech Bull Amersham Buchler — Technisches Bulletin - Amerisham Buchler
Tech Bull Am Refract Inst — Technical Bulletin. American Refractories Institute
Tech Bull Anim Ind Agric Branch NT — Technical Bulletin. Animal Industry and Agricultural Branch. Department of the Northern Territory
Tech Bull Anim Ind Agric Br NT — Technical Bulletin. Animal Industry and Agriculture Branch. Northern Territory
Tech Bull Ariz Agr Exp Sta — Technical Bulletin. Arizona Agricultural Experiment Station
Tech Bull Ariz Agric Exp Stn — Technical Bulletin. Arizona Agricultural Experiment Station
Tech Bull Armour Chem Div — Technical Bulletin. Armour Chemical Division
Tech Bull At Energy Organ Iran — Technical Bulletin. Atomic Energy Organization of Iran
Tech Bull Aust Soc Dairy Technol — Technical Bulletin. Australian Society of Dairy Technology
Tech Bull Autom Teleph Elect Co — Technical Bulletin. Automatic Telephone and Electric Company [*London*]
Tech Bull Baker Castor Oil Co — Technical Bulletin. Baker Castor Oil Co [*New York*]
Tech Bull Banana Res Adv Comm — Technical Bulletin. Banana Research Advisory Committee
Tech Bull Br Celanese — Technical Bulletin. British Celanese
Tech Bull Br Columb Res Coun — Technical Bulletin. British Columbia Research Council
Tech Bull Bur Ent Chekiang Prov — Technical Bulletin. Bureau of Entomology of Chekiang Province
Tech Bull Bur Fish Philipp Isl — Technical Bulletin. Bureau of Fisheries. Philippine Islands
Tech Bull Bur For Philipp Isl — Technical Bulletin. Bureau of Forestry. Philippine Islands
Tech Bull Bur Ships US — Technical Bulletin. Bureau of Ships. United States Navy Department
Tech Bull Can Inland Waters Dir — Technical Bulletin. Canada Inland Waters Directorate
Tech Bull Can Res Inst Laund — Technical Bulletin. Canadian Research Institute of Launderers and Cleaners
Tech Bull Carwin Co — Technical Bulletin. Carwin Company
Tech Bull Cent Fd Technol Res Inst — Technical Bulletin. Central Food Technological Research Institute [*Mysore*]
Tech Bull Coal Util Coun — Technical Bulletin. Coal Utilisation Council [*London*]
Tech Bull Coll Agric Bangalore — Technical Bulletin. College of Agriculture. Bangalore
Tech Bull Coll Agric Univ Philipp — Technical Bulletin. College of Agriculture. University of the Philippines
Tech Bull Coll Engng Archit Pa St Univ — Technical Bulletin. College of Engineering and Architecture. Pennsylvania State University
Tech Bull Colo Agric Exp Stn — Technical Bulletin. Colorado Agricultural Experiment Station
Tech Bull Colo Dep Game Fish — Technical Bulletin. Colorado Department of Game and Fish
Tech Bull Colo State Univ Agr Exp Sta — Technical Bulletin. Colorado State University. Agricultural Experiment Station
Tech Bull Commonwealth Inst Biol Contr — Technical Bulletin. Commonwealth Institute of Biological Control
Tech Bull Commonw Inst Biol Control — Technical Bulletin. Commonwealth Institute of Biological Control
Tech Bull Comm Tidal Hydraul — Technical Bulletin. Committee on Tidal Hydraulics. United States Corps of Engineers
Tech Bull Corros Proof Prod — Technical Bulletin. Corrosion Proof Products
Tech Bull Cott Bur Egypt — Technical Bulletin. Cotton Bureau. Egypt
Tech Bull Cyprus Agr Res Inst — Technical Bulletin. Cyprus Agricultural Research Institute
Tech Bull Cyprus Dep Agric — Technical Bulletin. Cyprus Department of Agriculture
Tech Bull Dan Gov Inst Seed Pathol Developing Countries — Technical Bulletin from the Danish Government Institute of Seed Pathology for Developing Countries
Tech Bull Dep Agric Can — Technical Bulletin. Department of Agriculture. Canada
Tech Bull Dep Agric Commerce Philipp Isl — Technical Bulletin. Department of Agriculture and Commerce. Philippine Islands
Tech Bull Dep Agric East Reg Nigeria — Technical Bulletin. Department of Agriculture. Eastern Region. Nigeria
Tech Bull Dep Agric Fish Siam — Technical Bulletin. Department of Agriculture and Fisheries. Siam
Tech Bull Dep Agric NSW — New South Wales. Department of Agriculture. Technical Bulletin
Tech Bull Dep Agric S Aust — Technical Bulletin. Department of Agriculture. South Australia
Tech Bull Dep Agric Vict — Technical Bulletin. Department of Agriculture. Victoria
Tech Bull Dep Agric West Aust — Technical Bulletin. Department of Agriculture. Western Australia

Tech Bull Dep Hort Univ Reading — Technical Bulletin. Department of Horticulture. University of Reading

Tech Bull Dep Publ Lds Qd — Technical Bulletin. Department of Public Lands. Queensland

Tech Bull Div Game Mgmt Ill — Technical Bulletin. Division of Game Management. Illinois State Department of Conservation

Tech Bull Edinb E Scotl Coll Agric — Technical Bulletin. Edinburgh and East of Scotland College of Agriculture

Tech Bull Exp For Natl Taiwan Univ — Technical Bulletin. Experimental Forest of National Taiwan University

Tech Bull Exp For Taiwan Univ — Technical Bulletin. Experimental Forest. National Taiwan University

Tech Bull Fac Agric Chiba Univ — Technical Bulletin. Faculty of Agriculture. Chiba University

Tech Bull Fac Agric Kagawa Univ — Technical Bulletin. Faculty of Agriculture. Kagawa University

Tech Bull Fac Agric Univ Coll Ibadan — Technical Bulletin. Faculty of Agriculture. University College. Ibadan

Tech Bull Fac Agric Univ Ghana — Technical Bulletin. Faculty of Agriculture. University of Ghana

Tech Bull Fac Agr Kagawa Univ — Technical Bulletin. Faculty of Agriculture. Kagawa University

Tech Bull Fac Hort Chiba Univ — Technical Bulletin. Faculty of Horticulture. Chiba University

Tech Bull Fac Hortic Chiba Univ — Technical Bulletin. Faculty of Horticulture. Chiba University

Tech Bull Fed Hous Adm — Technical Bulletin. Federal Housing Administration [*Washington*]

Tech Bull Ferro Enam Corp — Technical Bulletin. Ferro Enamel Corporation

Tech Bull Fine Chem Div Am Cyanamid Co — Technical Bulletin. Fine Chemicals Division. American Cyanamid Company

Tech Bull Fla Agric Exp Stn — Technical Bulletin. Florida Agricultural Experiment Station

Tech Bull Fla Game Fresh Wat Fish Commn — Technical Bulletin. Florida Game and Fresh Water Fish Commission

Tech Bull For Brch Sask — Technical Bulletin. Forestry Branch. Saskatchewan

Tech Bull Ford For Cent — Technical Bulletin. Ford Forestry Center. Michigan College of Mining and Technology

Tech Bull Forest Prod Lab Kaiting — Technical Bulletin. Forest Products Laboratory. Kaiting

Tech Bull Fruit Veg Cann Quick Freez Res Ass — Technical Bulletin. Fruit and Vegetable Canning and Quick Freezing Research Association [*Chipping Campden*]

Tech Bull Fukien Prov Coll Agric — Technical Bulletin. Fukien Provincial College of Agriculture

Tech Bull Furn Dev Coun — Technical Bulletin. Furniture Development Council [*London*]

Tech Bull Furn Ind Res Ass — Technical Bulletin. Furniture Industry Research Association

Tech Bull GA Agr Exp Sta — Technical Bulletin. Georgia Agricultural Experiment Stations. University of Georgia. College of Agriculture

Tech Bull Ga Agric Exp Stns — Technical Bulletin. Georgia Agricultural Experiment Stations

Tech Bull Goodmans Inds — Technical Bulletin. Goodmans Industries, Ltd. [*Chicago*]

Tech Bull Gt Brit Min Agr Fish Food — Technical Bulletin. Great Britain Ministry of Agiculture, Fisheries, and Food

Tech Bull Harper Adams Agr Coll — Technical Bulletin. Harper Adams Agricultural College

Tech Bull Harper Adams Agric Coll — Technical Bulletin Harper Adams Agricultural College

Tech Bull Hatch Agric Exp Stn — Technical Bulletin. Hatch Agricultural Experiment Station

Tech Bull Hawaii Agric Exp Stn — Technical Bulletin. Hawaii Agricultural Experiment Station

Tech Bull Hawaii Agric Exp Stn Univ Hawaii — Technical Bulletin. Hawaii Agricultural Experiment Station. University of Hawaii

Tech Bull Hokkaido Agric Exp Stn — Technical Bulletin. Hokkaido Agricultural Experiment Station

Tech Bull ICI Plast — Technical Bulletin. I.C.I.Plastics-Limited

Tech Bull Ill Dep Conserv — Technical Bulletin. Illinois Department of Conservation

Tech Bull Inst Ld Wat Mgmt Res — Technical Bulletin. Institute for Land and Water Management Research

Tech Bull Kagawa Agr Coll — Technical Bulletin. Kagawa Agricultural College

Tech Bull Kans Agr Exp Sta — Technical Bulletin. Kansas Agricultural Experiment Station

Tech Bull Kans Agric Exp Stn — Technical Bulletin. Kansas Agricultural Experiment Station

Tech Bull Land Resour Div Dir Overseas Surv — Technical Bulletin. Land Resources Division. Directorate of Overseas Surveys

Tech Bull Life Sci Agric Exp Stn (Maine) — Technical Bulletin. Life Sciences and Agriculture Experiment Station (Maine)

Tech Bull Life Sci Agric Exp Stn Univ Maine — Technical Bulletin. Life Sciences and Agriculture Experiment Station. University of Maine at Orono

Tech Bull Mich State Univ Agr Exp Sta — Technical Bulletin. Michigan State University. Agricultural Experiment Station

Tech Bull Mich St Coll Agric Exp Stn — Technical Bulletin. Michigan State College. Agricultural Experiment Station

Tech Bull Mines Brch Can — Technical Bulletin. Mines Branch. Department of Mines and Technical Surveys. Canada

Tech Bull Minist Agric E Niger — Technical Bulletin. Ministry of Agriculture of Eastern Nigeria

Tech Bull Minist Agric Fish Fd — Technical Bulletin. Ministry of Agriculture, Fisheries, and Food

Tech Bull Minist Agric Fish Food (GB) — Technical Bulletin. Ministry of Agriculture, Fisheries, and Food (Great Britain)

Tech Bull Minist Agric Nth Ire — Technical Bulletin. Ministry of Agriculture. Northern Ireland

Tech Bull Minn Agric Exp Sta — Technical Bulletin. University of Minnesota. Agricultural Experiment Station

Tech Bull Minn Agric Exp Stn — Technical Bulletin. Minnesota Agricultural Experiment Station

Tech Bull Minn Dep Conserv Div Fish Game — Technical Bulletin. Minnesota Department of Conservation. Division of Fish and Game

Tech Bull Miss Agr Exp Sta — Technical Bulletin. Mississippi Agricultural Experiment Station

Tech Bull Miss Agric For Exp Stn — Technical Bulletin. Mississippi Agricultural and Forestry Experiment Station

Tech Bull Miyagi Prefect Agr Exp Sta — Technical Bulletin. Miyagi Prefectural Agricultural Experiment Station

Tech Bull Mont Agr Exp Sta — Technical Bulletin. Montana Agricultural Experiment Station

Tech Bull Mont Fish Game Commn — Technical Bulletin. Montana Fish and Game Commission

Tech Bull Natn Aniline Div Allied Chem Corp — Technical Bulletin. National Aniline Division. Allied Chemical and Dye Corporation [*New York*]

Tech Bull Natn Coun Stream Dev Pulp Pap Inds — Technical Bulletin. National Council for Stream Development of the Pulp, Paper, and Paperboard Industries [*New York*]

Tech Bull Natn Fmrs Un — Technical Bulletin. National Farmers' Union [*London*]

Tech Bull NC Agr Exp Sta — Technical Bulletin. North Carolina Agricultural Experiment Station

Tech Bull NC Agric Exp Sta — Technical Bulletin. North Carolina Agricultural Experiment Station

Tech Bull N Carol Agric Exp Stn — Technical Bulletin. North Carolina Agricultural Experiment Station

Tech Bull N Carol St Coll Agric Exp Stn — Technical Bulletin. North Carolina State College. Agricultural Experiment Station

Tech Bull N Carol St Univ Agric Exp Stn — Technical Bulletin. North Carolina State University. Agricultural Experiment Station

Tech Bull Okla State Univ Agr Exp Sta — Technical Bulletin. Oklahoma State University. Agricultural Experiment Station

Tech Bull Ore Agric Exp Stn — Technical Bulletin. Oregon Agricultural Experiment Station

Tech Bull Oreg State Coll Agr Exp Sta — Technical Bulletin. Oregon State College. Agricultural Experiment Station

Tech Bull Oreg State Univ Agric Exp Stn — Technical Bulletin. Oregon State University. Agricultural Experiment Station

Tech Bull Pine Inst Am — Technical Bulletin of the Pine Institute of America

Tech Bull Pollut Control Commn Wash St — Technical Bulletin. Pollution Control Commission. Washington State

Tech Bull Pwr Crane Shovel Ass — Technical Bulletin. Power Crane and Shovel Association [*New York*]

Tech Bull Radio Electron Compon Mfrs Fed — Technical Bulletin. Radio and Electronics Component Manufacturers' Federation [*London*]

Tech Bull Regist Med Technol — Technical Bulletin. Registry of Medical Technologists

Tech Bull Rhodesia Agric J — Technical Bulletin. Rhodesia Agricultural Journal

Tech Bull SC Agric Exp Stn — Technical Bulletin. South Carolina Agricultural Experiment Station

Tech Bull Sch Mines Metall Univ Mo — Technical Bulletin. School of Mines and Metallurgy. University of Missouri

Tech Bull S Dak Agr Exp Sta — Technical Bulletin. South Dakota Agricultural Experiment Station

Tech Bull S Dak Agric Exp Stn — Technical Bulletin. South Dakota Agricultural Experiment Station

Tech Bull S Dak Dep Game — Technical Bulletin. South Dakota Department of Game, Fish, and Parks

Tech Bull S Dak St Ent — Technical Bulletin. South Dakota State Entomologist

Tech Bull Shell Chem — Technical Bulletin. Shell Chemicals [*London*]

Tech Bull Sindar Corp — Technical Bulletin. Sindar Corporation [*New York*]

Tech Bull Soils Sect Dep Agric Vict — Technical Bulletin. Soils Section. Department of Agriculture. Victoria [*Melbourne*]

Tech Bull St Rivers Wat Supply Commn Vict — Technical Bulletin. State Rivers and Water Supply Commission. Victoria [*Melbourne*]

Tech Bull Sug Manufact Ass — Technical Bulletin. Sugar Manufacturers' Association

Tech Bull Sulphur Inst — Technical Bulletin. Sulphur Institute

Tech Bull Taiwan Agric Res Inst — Technical Bulletin. Taiwan Agricultural Research Institute

Tech Bull Taiwan Fertil Co — Technical Bulletin. Taiwan Fertilizer Company

Tech Bull Taiwan Sug Exp Stn — Technical Bulletin of the Taiwan Sugar Experiment Station

Tech Bull TARC (Trop Agric Res Cent) — Technical Bulletin. TARC (Tropical Agriculture Research Center)

Tech Bull Teleph Mfg Co — Technical Bulletin. Telephone Manufacturing Company [*London*]

Tech Bull Tex Eng Exp Stn — Technical Bulletin. Texas Engineering Experiment Station

Tech Bull Tokushima Bunri Univ — Technical Bulletin. Tokushima Bunri University

Tech Bull Trop Agric Res Cent — Technical Bulletin. Tropical Agriculture Research Center

Tech Bull UAR Minist Agric Agrar Reform — Technical Bulletin. United Arab Republic Ministry of Agriculture and Agrarian Reform

Tech Bull Univ Maine Life Sci Agric Exp Stn — Technical Bulletin. University of Maine. Life Sciences and Agriculture Experiment Station

Tech Bull Univ Minn Agr Exp Sta — Technical Bulletin. University of Minnesota. Agricultural Experiment Station

Tech Bull Univ Nev Agr Exp Sta — Technical Bulletin. University of Nevada. Agricultural Experiment Station

Tech Bull Univ Philippines Coll Agr — Technical Bulletin. University of the Philippines. College of Agriculture

Tech Bull Urban Ld Inst — Technical Bulletin. Urban Land Institute

Tech Bull US Cst Geod Surv — Technical Bulletin. United States Coast and Geodetic Survey

Tech Bull USDA — Technical Bulletin. United States Department of Agriculture

Tech Bull US Dep Agric — Technical Bulletin. United States Department of Agriculture

Tech Bull US Dep Agric Agric Res Serv — Technical Bulletin. United States Department of Agriculture. Agricultural Research Service

Tech Bull US For Serv — Technical Bulletin. United States Forest Service

Tech Bull US Govt Print Off — Technical Bulletin. United States Government Printing Office

Tech Bull US Hous Home Finance Ag — Technical Bulletin. United States Housing and Home Finance Agency

Tech Bull VA Agr Exp Sta — Technical Bulletin. Virginia Agricultural Experiment Station

Tech Bull Va Agric Exp Stn — Technical Bulletin. Virginia Agricultural Experiment Station

Tech Bull Veterans Adm — Technical Bulletin. Veterans' Administration

Tech Bull Vic Ctry Rd Bd — Technical Bulletin. Victoria Country Roads Board

Tech Bull W Afr Cocoa Res Inst — Technical Bulletin. West African Cocoa Research Institute

Tech Bull W Afr Timb Borer Res Unit — Technical Bulletin. West African Timber Borer Research Unit

Tech Bull Wash Agr Exp Sta — Technical Bulletin. Washington Agricultural Experiment Station

Tech Bull Wash Agric Exp Stn — Technical Bulletin. Washington Agricultural Experiment Station

Tech Bull Wash State Univ Coll Agric Res Cent — Technical Bulletin. Washington State University. College of Agriculture. Research Center

Tech Bull W Cst Lumb Mfrs Ass — Technical Bulletin. West Coast Lumber Manufacturers' Association

Tech Bull West Aust Dep Agric — Technical Bulletin. Western Australian Department of Agriculture

Tech Bull West Pine Ass — Technical Bulletin. Western Pine Association

Tech Bull Wis Conserv Dep — Technical Bulletin. Wisconsin Conservation Department

Tech Bull W Va Conserv Dep — Technical Bulletin. West Virginia Conservation Department

Tech Bull W Va Engng Exp Stn — Technical Bulletin. West Virginia Engineering Experiment Station

Tech Bul VIUS Agric Exp Stn — Technical Bulletin. Virgin Islands of the United States Agricultural Experiment Station

Tech CEM — Techniques CEM

Tech Ceram Int — Technical Ceramics International

Tech Chem Jb — Technisch-Chemisches Jahrbuch

Tech Chem (Prague) — Technika v Chemii (Prague)

Tech Chron — Technika Chronika

Tech Cinem — Technical Cinematography

Tech Circ Br Fd Mfg Ind Res Ass — Technical Circular. British Food Manufacturing Industries Research Association

Tech Circ Br Sulph Ammon Fed — Technical Circular. British Sulphate of Ammonia Federation

Tech Circ Dyestuffs Div ICI — Technical Circular. Dyestuffs Division. I.C.I (Imperial Chemical Industries)

Tech Circ ICI — Technical Circular. Imperial Chemical Industries [*London*]

Tech Circ Maurit Sug Ind Res Inst — Technical Circular. Mauritius Sugar Industry Research Institute

Tech Circ Met Brch Dep Agric Can — Technical Circular. Meteorological Branch. Department of Agriculture. Canada

Tech Circ Met Div Dep Transp Can — Technical Circular. Meteorological Division. Department of Transport. Canada

Tech Commun — Technical Communications

Tech Commun Bur Sugar Exp Stn (Queensl) — Technical Communication. Bureau of Sugar Experiment Stations (Queensland)

Tech Commun Bur Sug Exp Stns (Qd) — Technical Communication. Bureau of Sugar Experiment Stations (Queensland)

Tech Commun Central Inform Libr Edit Sect CSIRO — Technical Communication. Central Information, Library, and Editorial Section. Commonwealth Scientific and Industrial Research Organisation

Tech Commun CILES CSIRO — Technical Communication. Central Information, Library, and Editorial Section. Commonwealth Scientific and Industrial Research Organisation

Tech Commun CSIRO (Aust) — Technical Communication. Minerals Research Laboratories. Commonwealth Scientific and Industrial Research Organisation (Australia)

Tech Commun CSIRO Div Mineral — Australia. Commonwealth Scientific and Industrial Research Organisation. Division of Mineralogy. Technical Communication

Tech Commun CSIRO Div Miner Chem — Australia. Commonwealth Scientific and Industrial Research Organisation. Division of Mineral Chemistry. Technical Communication

Tech Commun CSIRO Inst Earth Resour — CSIRO [*Commonwealth Scientific and Industrial Research Organisation*] Institute of Earth Resources. Technical Communication

Tech Commun CSIRO Miner Res Lab — CSIRO [*Commonwealth Scientific and Industrial Research Organisation*] Minerals Research Laboratories. Technical Communication

Tech Commun Dept Agr Tech Serv Repub S Afr — Technical Communication. Department of Agricultural Technical Services. Republic of South Africa

Tech Commun Div Miner Chem CSIRO — Technical Communication. Division of Mineral Chemistry. Commonwealth Scientificand Industrial Research Organisation

Tech Commun Div Miner CSIRO — Technical Communication. Division of Mineralogy. Commonwealth Scientific and Industrial Research Organisation

Tech Commun For Bur (Oxf) — Technical Communication. Commonwealth Forestry Bureau (Oxford)

Tech Commun Geochem Prospect Res Cent — Technical Communications. Geochemical Prospecting Research Centre. Imperial College of Science and Technology [*London*]

Tech Commun Grassld Res Stn — Technical Communications. Grassland Research Station

Tech Commun Imp Bur Anim Breed Genet — Technical Communications. Imperial Bureau of Animal Breeding and Genetics [*Edinburgh*]

Tech Commun Imp Bur Anim Nutr — Technical Communications. Imperial Bureau of Animal Nutrition [*Aberdeen*]

Tech Commun Imp Bur Dairy Sci — Technical Communications. Imperial Bureau of Dairy Science [*Shinfield*]

Tech Commun Imp Bur Fruit Prod — Technical Communications. Imperial Bureau of Fruit Production [*East Malling*]

Tech Commun Imp Bur Hort Plantn Crops — Technical Communications. Imperial Bureau of Horticulture and Plantation Crops [*East Malling*]

Tech Commun Miner Res Lab CSIRO — Technical Communication. Minerals Research Laboratories. Commonwealth Scientific and Industrial Research Organisation

Tech Commun R Sch Mines — Technical Communications. Royal School of Mines

Tech Commun S Afr Dep Agric Fish — Technical Communication. South Africa Department of Agriculture and Fisheries

Tech Commun S Afr Dep Agric Tech Serv — Technical Communications. South Africa Department of Agricultural Technical Services

Tech Commun Woodld Ecol Unit CSIRO — Technical Communication. Woodland Ecology Unit. Commonwealth Scientific and Industrial Research Organisation

Tech Conf Proc Irrig Assoc — Technical Conference Proceedings. Irrigation Association

Tech Counc Cold Reg Eng Monogr — Technical Council on Cold Regions Engineering Monograph

Tech Cybern USSR — Technical Cybernetics USSR

Tech Data Bull Am Inst Steel Constr — Technical Data Bulletin. American Institute of Steel Construction

Tech Data Dig — Technical Data Digest

Tech Data Digest — Technical Data Digest

Tech Data Dig US Air Cps — Technical Data Digest. United States Air Corps

Tech Data Foote Miner Co — Technical Data. Foote Mineral Co

Tech Data Natn Aniline Div Allied Chem Corp — Technical Data. National Aniline Division. Allied Chemical Corporation [*New York*]

Tech Data Publs Br Insul Callenders Cables — Technical Data Publications. British Insulated Callender's Cables

Tech Des Mater — Technical Design and Materials

Tech Dev Note US Civ Aeronaut Auth — Technical Development Note. United States Civil Aeronautics Authority

Tech Dev Rep US Civ Aeronaut Adm — Technical Development Report. United States Civil Aeronautics Administration

Tech Dev Rep US Civ Aeronaut Auth — Technical Development Report. United States Civil Aeronautics Authority

Tech Dev Rep US Fed Aviat Ag — Technical Development Report. United States Federal Aviation Agency

Tech Diagn Pathol — Techniques in Diagnostic Pathology

Tech Dig — Technical Digest

Tech Dig Br Agric Off — Technical Digest. British Agricultural office

Tech Dig GaAs IC Symp — Technical Digest. GaAs IC Symposium (Gallium Arsenide Integrated Circuit)

Tech Dig Int Electron Devices Meet — Technical Digest. International Electron Devices Meeting

Tech Dig Int Vac Microelectron Conf — Technical Digest. International Vacuum Microelectronics Conference

Tech Dig Symp Opt Fiber Meas — Technical Digest. Symposium on Optical Fiber Measurements

Tech Doc FAO Plant Prot Comm Southeast Asia Pac Reg — Technical Document. Food and Agriculture Organization of the United Nations. Plant Protection Committee for the South East Asia and Pacific Region

Tech Eau — Technique de l'Eau et de l'Assainissement

Tech Econ Publ Tatabanyai Szenbanyak — Technical-Economical Publication. Tatabanyai Szenbanyak

Tech Econ Stud Inst Geol Geophys Ser I — Technical and Economical Studies. Institute of Geology and Geophysics. Series I. Mineralogy-Petrology

Tech Educ — Technical Education

Tech Educ Abstr — Technical Education Abstracts

Tech Educ Yrbk — Technician Education Yearbook

Tech EisenbZ — Technische Eisenbahnzeitschrift

Tech Electrochem — Techniques of Electrochemistry

Tech Electron Son Telev — Techniques Electroniques - Son - Television

Tech Energ — Techniques de l'Energie

Tech Energie — Techniques de l'Energie

Tech Energ (Paris) — Techniques de l'Energie (Paris)

Tech Engng News — Tech Engineering News

Tech Environ — Technology and Environment

Tech Equip Rep Forest Serv US — Technical Equipment Report. Forest Service. United States Department of Agriculture

Tech Erzieh — Technische Erziehung. Deutscher Ausschuss fuer Technisches Schulwesen

Tech et Sci Inf — Technique et Science Informatiques

Tech Folder Br Geon — Technical Folder. British Geon

Tech Fore — Technology Forecasts and Technology Surveys

Tech Forum Soc Vac Coaters — Technical Forum. Society of Vacuum Coaters

Tech Gaz NSW — Technical Gazette of New South Wales

Tech Gem — Technische Gemeinschaft

Tech GemBl StrBau Landesplan — Technisches Gemeindeblatt fuer Strassenbau, Landesplanung, Siedlungswesen, Staedtbau, Wasserversorgung und Entwaesserung

Tech Gemeentebl — Technisch Gemeenteblad [Amsterdam]

Tech Gemein — Technische Gemeinschaft

Tech Gemeindebl — Technisches Gemeindeblatt

Tech GenAnz Oberschles IndBez — Technischer Generalanzeiger fuer den Oberschlesischen Industriebezirk

Tech Gesch — Technik-Geschichte

Tech Gids Ziekenhuis Instelling — Technische Gids voor Ziekenhuis en Instelling

Tech Gospod Morsk — Technika i Gospodarka Morska

Tech Handb Gas Coun — Technical Handbook. Gas Council [London]

Tech Handel — Technische Handel

Tech Hausmitt Blaupunkt — Technische Hausmitteilungen Blaupunkt

Tech Hausmitt NWdt Rundf — Technische Hausmitteilungen. Nordwestdeutscher Rundfunk

Tech Heute — Technik Heute

Tech Hochsch Ilmenau Wiss Z — Technische Hochschule Ilmenau. Wissenschaftliche Zeitschrift

Tech Hochsch Koethen Wiss Z — Technische Hochschule Koethen. Wissenschaftliche Zeitschrift

Tech Hochsch Leipzig Wiss Z — Technische Hochschule Leipzig. Wissenschaftliche Zeitschrift

Tech Hogesch Delft Afd Werktuigbouwkd (Rep) WTHD — Technische Hogeschool Delft. Afdeling der Werktuigbouwkunde (Report) WTHD

Tech Illus — Technology Illustrated

Tech-Index Plasmaphys Forsch Fusionreakt — Technik-Index ueber Plasmaphysikalische Forschung und Fusionsreaktoren

Tech Ind Korr — Technisch-Industrielle Korrespondenz

Tech Inf GRW — Technische Information GRW

Tech Inf MCSD — Technical Information M.C.S.D. Miscellaneous Chemical Service Department. I.C.I (Imperial Chemical Industries)

Tech Inf Monel Metal Nickel Alloys Bull — Technical Information. Monel Metal and Nickel Alloys Bulletins [New York]

Tech Info Service — Technical Information Service

Tech Inf Polym Chem Serv Dept ICI — Technical Information. Polymer and Chemical Service Department. Imperial Chemical Industries

Tech Inf Rubb Serv Dep ICI — Technical Information. Rubber Service Department. I.C.I (Imperial Chemical Industries)

Tech Inf Ser For Ag Japan — Technical Information Series. Forestry Agency. Japan

Tech Inf Ser Natn Bldgs Org — Technical Information Series. National Buildings Organisation [New Delhi]

Tech Inf Sh Br Resin Prod — Technical Information Sheet. British Resin Products

Tech Inf Sh Fire Prot Ass — Technical Information Sheet. Fire Protection Association [London]

Tech Inf Sh Pirelli General Cable Wks — Technical Information Sheet. Pirelli-General Cable Works [Southampton]

Tech Inf Sh UKAEA — Technical Information Sheet. United Kingdom Atomic Energy Authority

Tech Ing Genie Chim — Techniques de l'Ingenieur. Genie Chimique

Tech Instructor Soc Lic Aircr Engrs — Technical Instructor of the Society of Licensed Aircraft Engineers [London]

Tech Instruct Pakist Met Serv — Technical Instructions. Pakistan Meteorological Service

Tech Instruct PO Engng Dep — Technical Instructions. Post Office Engineering Department [London]

Tech Instrum Bull — Technical Instrument Bulletin [London]

Tech J — Technical Journal [London]

Tech Jahrb — Technica Jahrbuch

Tech J Ankara Nucl Res Cent — Technical Journal. Ankara Nuclear Research Center

Tech J Ankara Nucl Res Train Cent — Technical Journal. Ankara Nuclear Research and Training Center

Tech Jber Allg Elekt Ges — Technischer Jahresbericht. Allgemeine Elektricitaets Gesellschaft

Tech Jber Berufsgenoss Feinmech Elektrotech — Technischer Jahresbericht. Berufsgenossenschaft der Feinmechanik und Elektrotechnik

Tech J Brush Grp — Technical Journal of the Brush Group [London]

Tech J Japan Broadc Corp — Technical Journal. Japan Broadcasting Corporation

Tech J Jap Broadcast Corp — Technical Journal. Japan Broadcasting Corporation

Tech J Jpn Broadcast Corp — Technical Journal. Japan Broadcasting Corporation

Tech Knih — Technicka Knihovna

Tech Knihovna — Technicka Knihovna

Tech Kurir — Technikai Kurir

Tech Lab Cent Res Inst Electr Power Ind Rep — Technical Laboratory. Central Research Institute of the Electrical Power Industry. Report

Tech Landwirt — Technik und Landwirtschaft. Landtechnischer Ratgeber

Tech Leafl Timb Dev Ass — Technical Leaflet. Timber Development Association [London]

Tech Lect Surv Dep Egypt — Technical Lectures. Survey Department. Egypt

Tech Lett Natn Lumb Mfrs Ass Chicago — Technical Letter. National Lumber Manufacturers' Association (Chicago)_

Tech Life Sci Biochem — Techniques in the Life Sciences. Biochemistry

Tech Lit — Technical Literature [New York]

Tech Lit Summ ICI — Technical Literature Summary. Imperial Chemical Industries [London]

Tech Lotnicza Astronaut — Technika Lotnicza i Astronautyczna

Tech Maandbl Gemeenterein — Technisch Maandblad voor Gemeentereiniging, Vervoerwezen en Ontsmetting [Amsterdam]

Tech Mag — Technicky Magazin

Tech Mag Berl — Technisches Magazin (Berlin)

Tech Man Br Geon — Technical Manual. British Geon

Tech Man Br Resin Prod — Technical Manual. British Resin Products

Tech Manpower — Technical Manpower

Tech Man Yb Am Ass Text Chem Color — Technical Manual and Year Book. American Association of Textile Chemists and Colorists

Tech Mar Environ Sci — Techniques in Marine Environmental Sciences

Tech Mbl Gasverw — Technische Monatsblaetter fuer Gasverwendung

Tech Meas Med — Techniques of Measurement in Medicine

Tech Mech Thermo Dynam Berl — Technische Mechanik und Thermo-Dynamik (Berlin)

Tech Meded PBN — Technische Mededeelingen van P.B.N. Polytechnisch Bureau Nederland

Tech Mem Calif Inst Technol Jet Propul Lab — Technical Memorandum. California Institute of Technology. Jet Propulsion Laboratory

Tech Memo Ass Comm Soil Snow Mech Can — Technical Memoranda. Associate Committee on Soil and Snow Mechanics. National Research Council. Canada

Tech Memo Beach Eros Bd US — Technical Memoranda. Beach Erosion Board. United States Army

Tech Memo Br Non Ferr Metals Res Ass — Technical Memoranda. British Non-Ferrous Metals Research Association

Tech Memo Bur Reclam — Technical Memoranda. Bureau of Reclamation [Washington]

Tech Memo Daresbury Lab — Technical Memorandum. Daresbury Laboratory

Tech Memo Daresbury Nucl Phys Lab — Technical Memorandum. Daresbury Nuclear Physics Laboratory

Tech Memo Davidson Lab Stevens Inst Technol — Technical Memoranda. Davidson Laboratory. Stevens Institute of Technology [Hoboken]

Tech Memo Def Stand Labs Maribyrnong — Technical Memoranda. Defence Standards Laboratories. Maribyrnong

Tech Memo Dep Hlth Scotl — Technical Memoranda. Department of Health for Scotland

Tech Memo Div Appl Geomech CSIRO — Technical Memorandum. Division of Applied Geomechanics. Commonwealth Scientificand Industrial Research Organisation

Tech Memo Div Land Use Res CSIRO — Technical Memorandum. Division of Land Use Research. Commonwealth Scientific and Industrial Research Organisation

Tech Memo Div Wildl Res CSIRO — Technical Memorandum. Division of Wildlife Research. Commonwealth Scientific and Industrial Research Organisation

Tech Memo E Afr Met Dep — Technical Memoranda. East African Meteorological Department

Tech Memo Exp Tow Tank Stevens Inst Technol — Technical Memoranda. Experimental Towing Tank. Stevens Institute of Technology [Hoboken]

Tech Memo Fruit Veg Cann Quick Freez Res Ass — Technical Memoranda. Fruit and Vegetable Canning and Quick Freezing Research Association [Chipping Camden]

Tech Memo Hirakud Dam Proj — Technical Memoranda. Hirakud Dam Project

Tech Memo Inst Weld — Technical Memoranda. Institute of Welding [London]

Tech Memo Jet Propul Lab Calif Inst Technol — Technical Memorandum. Jet Propulsion Laboratory. California Institute of Technology

Tech Memo Jt Numer Weath Predict Unit US — Technical Memoranda. Joint Numerical Weather Prediction Unit. United States Weather Bureau and Air Force

Tech Memo Natn Advis Comm Aeronaut Wash — Technical Memoranda. National Advisory Committee for Aeronautics [Washington]

Tech Memo Natn Inst Agric Engng — Technical Memoranda. National Institute of Agricultural Engineering [Silsoe]

Tech Memo Pea Grow Res Org — Technical Memoranda. Pea Growing Research Organization [Yaxley]

Tech Memor Plant Protection Ltd — Technical Memoranda. Plant Protection Limited

Tech Memo Sandia Corp — Technical Memoranda. Sandia Corporation [Albuquerque]

Tech Mess ATM — Technisches Messen ATM

Tech Mess-TM — Techinsches Messen-TM

Tech Methods Polym Eval — Techniques and Methods of Polymer Evaluation

Tech Meun — Technique Meuniere

Tech Mitt — Technische Mitteilungen

Tech Mitt AEG-Telefunken — Technische Mitteilungen AEG- [Allgemeine Elektrizitaets-Gesellschaft] Telefunken

Tech Mitteil Krupp Forschungsber — Technische Mitteilungen Krupp. Forschungsberichte

Tech Mitteil Krupp Werksber — Technische Mitteilungen Krupp. Werksberichte

Tech Mitt (Essen) — Technische Mitteilungen (Essen)

Tech Mitt InstrumWes Dt WettDienst — Technische Mitteilungen des Instrumentenwesens des Deutschen Wetterdienstes

Tech Mitt Krupp — Technische Mitteilungen Krupp

Tech Mitt Krupp Forschungsber — Technische Mitteilungen Krupp. Forschungsberichte

Tech Mitt Krupp Werksber — Technische Mitteilungen Krupp. Werksberichte

Tech Mitt Malerei — Technische Mitteilungen fuer Malerei

Tech Mitt MaschSetz IG Druck Pap — Technische Mitteilungen fuer die Maschinensetzer in der IG Druck und Papier

Tech Mitt Nachr Ver Rhein Westf BezVer Dt Chem — Technische Mitteilungen und Nachrichten der Vereine. Rheinisch-Westfaelischer Bezirksverein Deutscher Chemiker

Tech Mitt Nassau Hess — Technische Mitteilungen aus Nassau und Hessen

Tech Mitt Orenstein Koppel Luebeck MaschBau — Technische Mitteilungen. Orenstein-Koppel und Luebecker Maschinenbau

Tech Mitt Post Telegr U TelephVerw — Technische Mitteilungen. Post-, Telegraphen-, und Telephonverwaltung

Tech Mitt PTT — Technische Mitteilungen PTT

Tech Mitt RFZ — Technische Mitteilungen. RFZ

Tech Mitt RoentgBetr — Technische Mitteilungen fuer Roentgenbetriebe

Tech Mitt Schoppe U Faeser — Technische Mitteilungen. Schoppe und Faeser

Tech Mitt Tech Dienst Mineraloel ZentVerb — Technische Mitteilungen. Technischer Dienst, Mineraloel-Zentralverband

Tech Mod — Technique Moderne
Tech Motoryzacyjna — Technika Motoryzacyjna
Tech Nachr Elberfeld — Technische Nachrichten (Elberfeld)
Tech Nachr Mix U Genest — Technische Nachrichten. Mix und Genest
Techn Agric Int — Technique Agricole Internationale
Techn Archit — Techniques et Architecture
Tech Naturw Zeit — Technisch-Naturwissenschaftliche Zeit
Techn Ber Lorenz — Technische Berichte der C. Lorenz
Techn Bull Dept Agric — Technical Bulletin. Department of Agriculture
Techn Bull Forests Prod Lab — Technical Bulletin. Forests Products Laboratory. National Bureau of Industrial Research/Ching Chi Pu Chung Yang Kung Yeh Shih Yen So Mu To'ai Shih Yen Kuan Chuan Pao
Techn Bull Reg Med Technol — Technical Bulletin. Registry of Medical Technologists
Techn Chron — Technika Chronika
Techn Cult — Techniques et Culture
Techn Cult — Technology and Culture
Tech Neuh — Technische Neuheiten
Tech News — Technical News
Tech News Bull Metrop Vickers Elect Co — Technical News Bulletin. Metropolitan-Vickers Electrical Co
Tech News Bull Natn Bur Stand — Technical News Bulletin. National Bureau of Standards [*Washington*]
Tech News Bull Res Dep AEI — Technical News Bulletin. Research Department. Associated Electrical Industries [*Manchester*]
Tech Newslett For Prod Res Inst (Ghana) — Technical Newsletter. Forest Products Research Institute (Kumasi, Ghana)
Tech Newsl Natn Paint Vern Lacq Ass — Technical Newsletter. National Paint, Varnish, and Lacquer Association [*Washington*]
Tech News Serv Sarabhai M Chem — Technical News Service. Sarabhai M. Chemicals
Techn Gemeindebl — Technisches Gemeindeblatt
Techn Hosp — Techniques Hospitalieres, Medico-Sociales, et Sanitaires
Technica Hosp — Technica Hospitaliaria [*Caracas*]
Technical J — Technical Journal
Technic Int — Technic International
Techn Ind Rd — Technische und Industrielle Rundschau
Technion Isr Inst Technol Dep Chem Eng Rep CE — Technion-Israel Institute of Technology. Department of Chemical Engineering. Report CE
Technique Atlanta — Technique. Georgia School of Technology (Atlanta)
Technique Beckenham — Technique. A Journal of Instrument Engineering (Beckenham)
Technique Montreal — Technique. Revue Industrielle (Montreal)
Techniques Phys — Techniques of Physics
Techniview Prod Effic — Techniview and Production Efficiency
Techn Lab — Techniques de Laboratoire
Technmcs — Technometrics
Techn Mitt Krupp — Technische Mitteilungen Krupp
Techn Mitt Krupp Forschungsber — Technische Mitteilungen Krupp. Forschungsberichte
Techn Mitt Krupp Werksber — Technische Mitteilungen Krupp. Werksberichte
Techn Mod — Technique Moderne
Techn Nessen TN — Technisches Nessen-TN
Technol — Technology
Technol Adhes Sealing Xiangfan Peoples Repub China — Technology on Adhesion and Sealing (Xiangfan, People's Republic of China)
Technol Bull Pakist Cent Cott Comm — Technological Bulletin. Pakistan Central Cotton Committee
Technol Chim — Tecnologia Chimica
Technol Circ Indian Cent Cott Comm — Technological Circular. Indian Central Cotton Committee
Technol Conserv — Technology and Conservation
Technol Cul — Technology and Culture
Technol Cult — Technology and Culture
Technol Dev Rep EPS (Can Environ Prot Serv) — Technology Development Report EPS (Canada Environmental Protection Service)
Technol Educ — Technology in Education
Technol For — Technological Forecasting and Social Change
Technol Forecast — Technological Forecasting [*Later, Technological Forecasting and Social Change*]
Technol Forecast and Soc Change — Technological Forecasting and Social Change
Technol Forecasting — Technological Forecasting
Technol Forecasting Soc Change — Technological Forecasting and Social Change
Technol Gesch — Technologische Geschichte
Technol Health Care — Technology and Health Care
Technol Imprim — Technologie de l'Imprimerie
Technol Index Plasmaphys Res Fusion React — Technology Index for Plasmaphysics Research and Fusion Reactors
Technol Inf (Sapporo) — Technology and Information (Sapporo)
Technol Innovantes Epur Eaux — Technologies Innovantes en Epuration des Eaux
Technol Ir — Technology Ireland
Technol Ireland — Technology Ireland
Technol Japan — Science and Technology of Japan
Technol J Natl Sci Dev Board (Philip) — Technology Journal. National Science Development Board (Philippines)
Technol Lap — Technologiai Lapok
Technol Leafl ICCC — Technological Leaflet I.C.C.C. Indian Central Cotton Committee
Technol Mono — Technological Monographs
Technol Monogr Dyestuffs Div ICI — Technological Monographs. Dyestuffs Division. Imperial Chemical Industries

Technol-Nachr Manage Inf — Technologie-Nachrichten. Management-Informationen
Technol-Nachr Programm-Inf — Technologie-Nachrichten Programm-Informationen
Technol-Nachr Sonderdienst-Programme — Technologie-Nachrichten Sonderdienst-Programme
Technol News — Technology News. Bureau of Mines
Technol News Bur Mines — Technology News. Bureau of Mines
Technologie Chem Pap U Zellstoff Fabr — Technologie und Chemie der Papier- und Zellstoff-Fabrikation
Technolog Pap Div Forest Prod CSIRO — Technological Paper. Division of Forest Products. Commonwealth Scientific and Industrial Research Organisation
Technol Pap Div Forest Prod CSIRO — Technological Paper. Division of Forest Products. Commonwealth Scientific and Industrial Research Organisation
Technol Pap Forest Prod Lab Div Appl Chem CSIRO — Technological Paper. Forest Products Laboratory. Division of Applied Chemistry.Commonwealth Scientific and Industrial Research Organisation
Technol Pap Forest Prod Lab Div Bldg Res CSIRO — Technological Paper. Forest Products Laboratory. Division of Building Research.Commonwealth Scientific and Industrial Research Organisation
Technol Pap For Prod Lab Div Appl Chem CSIRO — Technological Paper. Forest Products Laboratory. Division of Applied Chemistry.Commonwealth Scientific and Industrial Research Organisation
Technol Pap For Prod Lab Div Build Res CSIRO — Technological Paper. Forest Products Laboratory. Division of Building Research.Commonwealth Scientific and Industrial Research Organisation
Technol Programs Radioact Waste Manage Environ Restor — Technology and Programs for Radioactive Waste Management and Environmental Restoration
Technol Q Proc Soc Arts MIT — Technology Quarterly and Proceedings of the Society of Arts. Massachusetts Institute of Technology
Technol R — Technology Review
Technol Rep Dep Fish Wash — Technological Report. Department of Fisheries. Washington
Technol Rep Iwate Univ — Technology Reports. Iwate University
Technol Rep Kansai Univ — Technology Reports. Kansai University
Technol Rep Kyushu Univ — Technology Reports. Kyushu University
Technol Rep Osaka Univ — Technology Reports. Osaka University
Technol Rep Seikei Univ — Technology Reports. Seikei University
Technol Rep Tohoku Univ — Technology Reports. Tohoku University
Technol Rep Tohoku Univ (Jpn) — Technology Reports. Tohoku University (Japan)
Technol Rep Yamaguchi Univ — Technology Reports. Yamaguchi University
Technol Respir — Technologie Respiratoire
Technol Rev — Technology Review
Technol Rev Chonnam Natl Univ — Technological Review. Chonnam National University
Technol Sci Chung Ang Univ — Technologies and Sciences. Chung-Ang University
Technol Soc — Technology and Society
Technol Soc — Technology in Society
Technol (Syd) — Technology (Sydney)
Technol Use Lignite — Technology and Use of Lignite. Proceedings of a Symposium
Technol Utiliz Prog Rep — Technology Utilization Program Report
Technomet — Technometrics
Tech Normung — Technische Normung
Tech Note Aust Def Stand Lab — Technical Note. Australia Defence Standards Laboratories
Tech Note Aust Mater Res Lab — Technical Note. Australia. Materials Research Laboratory
Tech Note Brick Manuf Assoc NSW — Technical Note. Brick Manufacturers Association of New South Wales
Tech Note Brick Mf Assoc NSW — Technical Note. Brick Manufacturers Association of New South Wales
Tech Note Charles Kolling Res Lab — Technical Note. Charles Kolling Research Laboratory. Department of Mechanical Engineering. University of Sydney
Tech Note Def Stand Lab Aust — Australia. Defence Standards Laboratories. Technical Note
Tech Note Dep For Res (Nigeria) — Technical Note. Department of Forest Research (Nigeria)
Tech Note E Afr Agric For Res Organ — Technical Note. East African Agriculture and Forestry Research Organization
Tech Note For Dep (Brit Solomon Islands Protect) — Technical Note. Forestry Department (British Solomon Islands Protectorate)
Tech Note For Dep (Kenya) — Technical Note. Forest Department (Nairobi, Kenya)
Tech Note For Dep (Uganda) — Technical Note. Forest Department (Uganda)
Tech Note For Prod Res Ind Dev Comm (Philipp) — Technical Note. Forest Products Research and Industries Development Commission (Philippines)
Tech Note For Prod Res Inst (Ghana) — Technical Note. Forest Products Research Institute (Ghana)
Tech Note For Timb Bur — Technical Note. Bureau of Forestry and Timber
Tech Note Harbour Tech Res Inst Minist Transp (Jpn) — Technical Note. Port and Harbour Technical Research Institute. Ministry of Transportation (Japan)
Tech Note Mater Res Lab Aust — Australia. Materials Research Laboratories. Technical Note
Tech Note Oji Inst For Tree Impr — Technical Note. Oji Institute for Forest Tree Improvement
Tech Note Quetico-Sup Wild Res Cent — Technical Note. Quetico-Superior Wilderness Research Center
Tech Note Res Inst Ind Saf — Technical Note. Research Institute of Industrial Safety
Tech Notes Allegheny Forest Exp Stn — Technical Notes. Allegheny Forest Experiment Station
Tech Notes Br Geon — Technical Notes. British Geon [*London*]
Tech Notes Brick Tile Constr — Technical Notes on Brick and Tile Construction

Tech Notes Br Resin Prod — Technical Notes. British Resin Products

Tech Notes Br W Afr Met Servs — Technical Notes. British West African Meteorological Services

Tech Notes Calif Forest Range Exp Stn — Technical Notes. California Forest and Range Experiment Station

Tech Notes Cent St Forest Exp Stn — Technical Notes. Central States Forest Experiment Station

Tech Notes Clay Prod — Technical Notes on Clay Products

Tech Notes Def Stand Labs Maribyrnong — Technical Notes. Defence Standards Laboratories. Maribyrnong

Tech Notes Dep For Relat TVA — Technical Notes. Department of Forestry Relations. Tennessee Valley Authority

Tech Notes Div Wood Technol NSW For Commn — Technical Notes. Division of Wood Technology. Now South Wales Forestry Commission

Tech Notes For Commn — Technical Notes. Forestry Commission [*London*]

Tech Notes For Commn NSW — Technical Notes. Forestry Commission of New South Wales

Tech Notes For Comm NSW — Technical Notes. Forestry Commission of New South Wales

Tech Notes For Dep Me Univ — Technical Notes. Forestry Department. Maine University

Tech Notes Forest Dep Kenya — Technical Notes. Forest Department. Kenya

Tech Notes Forest Dep Tanganyika — Technical Notes. Forest Department. Tanganyika

Tech Notes Forest Dep Uganda — Technical Notes. Forest Department. Uganda

Tech Notes Forest Prod Res Inst Philipp Isl — Technical Notes. Forest Products Research Institute. Philippine Islands

Tech Notes Forest Res Cent Juneau — Technical Notes. Forest Research Center (Juneau)

Tech Notes Forest Res Div Can — Technical Notes. Forest Research Division. Forestry Branch. Canada

Tech Notes Heat Vent Res Ass — Technical Notes. Heating and Ventilating Research Association

Tech Notes IBEC Res Inst — Technical Notes. IBEC Research Institute

Tech Notes Ind Grp Dep Atom Energy Minist Supply — Technical Notes. Industrial Group. Department of Atomic Energy

Tech Notes Ind Grp UKAEA — Technical Notes. Industrial Group. United Kingdom Atomic Energy Authority

Tech Notes India Met Dep — Technical Notes. India Meteorological Department

Tech Notes Indian Lac Res Instn — Technical Notes. Indian Lac Research Institute

Tech Notes Intell Sect Coal Tar Res Ass — Technical Notes. Intelligence Section. Coal Tar Research Association

Tech Notes Lab Anim Bur — Technical Notes of the Laboratory Animals Bureau [*London*]

Tech Notes Lake St Forest Exp Stn — Technical Notes. Lake States Forest Experimental Station [*St. Paul, Minnesota*]

Tech Notes Mechd Fmg — Technical Notes on Mechanized Farming [*Oxford*]

Tech Notes Met Off Bermuda — Technical Notes of the Meteorological Office. Bermuda

Tech Notes Met Off Cyprus — Technical Notes of the Meteorological Office. Cyprus

Tech Notes Met Serv Eire — Technical Notes. Meteorological Service. Eire

Tech Notes Minist Agric Fish Fd — Technical Notes. Ministry of Agriculture, Fisheries, and Food [*London*]

Tech Notes Natn Advis Comm Aeronaut Wash — Technical Notes. National Advisory Committee for Aeronautics (Washington)

Tech Notes Nat Rubb Dev Bd — Technical Notes. Natural Rubber Development Board

Tech Notes NEast Forest Exp Stn — Technical Notes. Northeastern Forest Experiment Station [*Philadelphia*]

Tech Notes New Jers Div Forests Pks — Technical Notes. New Jersey Division of Forests and Parks

Tech Notes NSW For Comm Div Wood Technol — New South Wales. Forestry Commission. Division of Wood Technology. Technical Notes

Tech Notes NZ Met Serv — Technical Notes. New Zealand Meteorological Service

Tech Notes Oji Inst Forest Tree Improv — Technical Notes. Oji Institute for Forest Tree Improvement

Tech Note Sol Energy Stud CSIRO — Technical Note. Solar Energy Studies. Commonwealth Scientific and Industrial Research Organisation

Tech Notes Pap Minist Wks Plann — Technical Notes and Papers. Ministry of Works and Planning [*London*]

Tech Notes Quetico Super Wildern Res Cent — Technical Notes. Quetico-Superior Wilderness Research Center [*Ely, Minnesota*]

Tech Notes R Aircr Establ — Technical Notes. Royal Aircraft Establishment [*Farnborough*]

Tech Notes Res Ass Br Rubb Mfrs — Technical Notes. Research Association of British Rubber Manufacturers

Tech Notes R Obs Hong Kong — Technical Notes. Royal Observatory. Hong Kong

Tech Notes Rubber Ind — Technical Notes for the Rubber Industry

Tech Notes Rubb Ind — Technical Notes for the Rubber Industry

Tech Notes SAAF Met Sect — Technical Notes. S.A.A.F. (South African Air Force) Meteorological Section

Tech Notes SEast Forest Exp Stn — Technical Notes. Southeastern Forest Experiment Station [*Ashville*]

Tech Notes Silvic Sect Forest Div Tanganyika — Technical Notes. Silviculture Section. Forest Division. Ministry of Lands, Forests, and Wildlife. Tanganyika

Tech Notes Train Cent Exp Aerodyn Rhode St Genese — Technical Notes. Training Centre for Experimental Aerodynamics (Rhode-Saint-Genese)

Tech Notes Univ Wash Engng Exp Stn — Technical Notes. University of Washington Engineering Experiment Station

Tech Notes US Forest Prod Lab — Technical Notes. United States Forest Products Laboratory [*Madison*]

Tech Notes US Weath Bur — Technical Notes. United States Weather Bureau

Tech Notes Util Div Forest Dep Tanganyika — Technical Notes. Utilization Division. Forest Department. Tanganyika

Tech Notes Wildl Res Lab Denver — Technical Notes. Wildlife Research Laboratory (Denver)

Tech Notes Wld Met Org — Technical Notes. World Meteorological Organization [*Geneva*]

Tech Notes Zinc Dev Ass — Technical Notes. Zinc Development Association [*London*]

Techn Pap Div Pl Industr CSIRO — Technical Papers. Division of Plant Industry. C.S.I.R.O.

Techn Pharm — Technique Pharmaceutique

Techn Rd — Technische Rundschau

Techn Rep Brit El All Ind Res Ass — Technical Report. British Electrical and Allied Industries Research Association

Techn Rep Ser Wld Hlth Org — Technical Report Series. World Health Organisation

Techn Rep Tohoku — Technology Reports. Tohoku Imperial University

Techn Rundschau — Technische Rundschau

Techn Sci Munic — Techniques et Sciences Municipales

Techn Soc — Technology and Society

Techn Ueberw — Technische Ueberwachung

Techn u Industr — Technik und Industrie und Schweizerische Chemiker-Zeitung

Techn Wirtschaftl Zeitung Mitteleurop Landw — Technisch-Wirtschaftliche Zeitung fuer die Mitteleuropaeische Landwirtschaft

Tech Obzor Slov — Technicky Obzor Slovensky

Tech Order Forest Dep Kenya — Technical Order. Forest Department. Kenya

Tec Hosp — Tecnica Hospitalaria

Tech Pamph E Afr Ind Res Org Bd — Technical Pamphlets. East African Industrial Research Organization (Board)

Tech Pamph Forest Dep Cyprus — Technical Pamphlets. Forest Department. Cyprus

Tech Pamph Sci Mus Lond — Technical Pamphlets. Science Museum (London)

Tech Pamph Wkmen PO Engng Dep — Technical Pamphlets for Workmen. Post Office Engineering Department [*London*]

Tech Pap Addr Tech Ass Pulp Pap Ind — Technical Papers and Addresses. Technical Association of the Pulp and Paper Industry [*New York*]

Tech Pap Agric Exp Stn (P Rico) — Technical Paper. Agricultural Experiment Station (Puerto Rico)

Tech Pap Alumin Res Labs Pittsb — Technical Papers of the Aluminium Research Laboratories. Aluminium Company of America (Pittsburgh)

Tech Pap Am Cyanamid Co — Technical Papers. American Cyanamid Co

Tech Pap Amer Pulpw Ass — Technical Papers. American Pulpwood Association

Tech Pap Am Rocket Soc — Technical Papers. American Rocket Society

Tech Pap Anim Res Lab CSIRO — Technical Paper. Animal Research Laboratories. Commonwealth Scientific and Industrial Research Organisation

Tech Pap Anim Res Labs CSIRO — Technical Paper. Animal Research Laboratories. Commonwealth Scientific and Industrial Research Organization

Tech Pap Arct Inst N Am — Technical Papers. Arctic Institute of North America

Tech Pap Atmos Pollut Res Comm — Technical Papers. Atmospheric Pollution Research Committee [*London*]

Tech Pap (Aust) CSIRO Div Appl Geomech — Technical Paper. (Australia) Commonwealth Scientific and Industrial Research Organisation. Division of Applied Geomechanics

Tech Pap (Aust) CSIRO Div Mineragraphic Invest — Technical Paper. (Australia) Commonwealth Scientific and Industrial Research Organisation. Division of Mineragraphic Investigation

Tech Pap Aust Water Resour Coun — Technical Paper. Australian Water Resources Council

Tech Pap Aust Wat Resour Coun — Technical Paper. Australian Water Resources Council

Tech Pap Bldg Res DSIR — Technical Papers. Building Research. Department of Scientific and Industrial Research [*London*]

Tech Pap Br Coke Res Ass — Technical Papers. British Coke Research Association

Tech Pap Bur Mines Wash — Technical Papers. Bureau of Mines [*Washington*]

Tech Pap Calif Agric Exp Stn — Technical Papers. California Agricultural Experiment Station

Tech Pap Calif Dep Agric — Technical Papers. California Department of Agriculture

Tech Pap Calif Forest Range Exp Stn — Technical Papers. California Forest and Range Experiment Station

Tech Pap Canad Pulp Pap Ass — Technical Paper. Canadian Pulp and Paper Association

Tech Pap Can Diam Drill Ass — Technical Papers. Canadian Diamond Drilling Association

Tech Pap Cent St Forest Exp Stn — Technical Papers. Central States Forest Experiment Station [*Columbus*]

Tech Pap Chem Res Labs CSIRO Aust — Technical Papers. Chemical Research Laboratories. C.S.I.R.O. Australia

Tech Pap Clim Div Philipp Isl — Technical Papers. Climatological Division. Philippine Islands Weather Bureau

Tech Pap Commonw For Inst — Technical Papers. Commonwealth Forestry Institute [*Oxford*]

Tech Pap Coop Stud Sect US Weath Bur — Technical Papers. Cooperative Studies Section. United States Weather Bureau and Bureau of Reclamation

Tech Pap Dep For (Qd) — Technical Paper. Department of Forestry (Queensland)

Tech Pap Dep For (Queensl) — Technical Paper. Department of Forestry (Queensland)

Tech Pap Dep For Un S Afr — Technical Papers. Department of Forestry. Union of South Africa [*Pretoria*]

Tech Pap Div Anim Hlth Prod CSIRO Aust — Technical Papers. Division of Animal Health and Production. C.S.I.R.O. Australia

Tech Pap Div Appl Chem CSIRO — Technical Paper. Division of Applied Chemistry. Commonwealth Scientific and Industrial Research Organisation

Tech Pap Div Appl Geomech CSIRO — Technical Paper. Division of Applied Geomechanics. Commonwealth Scientific and Industrial Research Organisation

Tech Pap Div Appl Miner CSIRO — Technical Paper. Division of Applied Mineralogy. Commonwealth Scientific and Industrial Research Organisation

Tech Pap Div Appl Org Chem CSIRO — Technical Paper. Division of Applied Organic Chemistry. Commonwealth Scientificand Industrial Research Organisation

Tech Pap Div Atmosph Phys CSIRO — Technical Paper. Division of Atmospheric Physics. Commonwealth Scientific and Industrial Research Organisation

Tech Pap Div Atmos Phys CSIRO — Technical Paper. Division of Atmospheric Physics. Commonwealth Scientific and Industrial Research Organisation

Tech Pap Div Bldg Res Can — Technical Papers. Division of Building Research. National Research Council. Canada

Tech Pap Div Bldg Res CSIRO — Technical Paper. Division of Building Research. Commonwealth Scientific and Industrial Research Organisation

Tech Pap Div Build Res CSIRO — Technical Paper. Division of Building Research. Commonwealth Scientific and Industrial Research Organisation

Tech Pap Div Chem Technol CSIRO — Technical Paper. Division of Chemical Technology. Commonwealth Scientific and Industrial Research Organisation

Tech Pap Div Ent CSIRO — Technical Paper. Division of Entomology. Commonwealth Scientific and IndustrialResearch Organisation

Tech Pap Div Fd Preserv CSIRO — Technical Paper. Division of Food Preservation. Commonwealth Scientific and Industrial Research Organisation

Tech Pap Div Fd Preserv Transp CSIRO Aust — Technical Papers. Division of Food Preservation and Transport. C.S.I.R.O. Australia

Tech Pap Div Fd Res CSIRO — Technical Paper. Division of Food Research. Commonwealth Scientific and Industrial Research Organisation

Tech Pap Div Fd Res CSIRO (Aust) — Technical Paper. Division of Food Research. Commonwealth Scientific and Industrial Research Organisation (Australia)

Tech Pap Div Fish Oceanogr CSIRO — Technical Paper. Division of Fisheries and Oceanography. Commonwealth Scientific and Industrial Research Organisation

Tech Pap Div Food Res CSIRO — Technical Paper. Division of Food Research. Commonwealth Scientific and Industrial Research Organisation

Tech Pap Div Forest Prod CSIRO Aust — Technical Papers. Division of Forest Products. C.S.I.R.O. Australia

Tech Pap Div Ind Chem CSIRO Aust — Technical Papers. Division of Industrial Chemistry. C.S.I.R.O. Australia

Tech Pap Div Land Resour Manage CSIRO — Technical Paper. Division of Land Resources Management. Commonwealth Scientificand Industrial Research Organisation

Tech Pap Div Land Use Res CSIRO — Technical Paper. Division of Land Use Research. Commonwealth Scientific and Industrial Research Organisation

Tech Pap Div Ld Res CSIRO — Technical Paper. Division of Land Research. Commonwealth Scientific and Industrial Research Organisation

Tech Pap Div Ld Res Reg Surv CSIRO (Aust) — Technical Papers. Division of Land Research and Regional Survey. Commonwealth Scientific and Industrial Research Organisation (Australia)

Tech Pap Div Ld Use Res CSIRO — Technical Paper. Division of Land Use Research. Commonwealth Scientific and Industrial Research Organisation

Tech Pap Div Math Stat CSIRO — Technical Paper. Division of Mathematics and Statistics. Commonwealth Scientific and Industrial Research Organisation

Tech Pap Div Math Statist CSIRO — Technical Paper. Division of Mathematical Statistics. Commonwealth Scientific and Industrial Research Organisation

Tech Pap Div Mat Statist CSIRO — Technical Paper. Division of Mathematical Statistics. Commonwealth Scientific and Industrial Research Organisation

Tech Pap Div Meteorol Phys CSIRO — Technical Paper. Division of Meteorological Physics. Commonwealth Scientific and Industrial Research Organisation

Tech Pap Div Met Phys CSIRO — Technical Paper. Division of Meteorological Physics. Commonwealth Scientific and Industrial Research Organisation

Tech Pap Div Metrol CSIRO Aust — Technical Papers. Division of Metrology. C.S.I.R.O. Australia

Tech Pap Div Plant Ind CSIRO — Technical Paper. Division of Plant Industry. Commonwealth Scientific and Industrial Research Organisation

Tech Pap Div Pl Ind CSIRO — Technical Paper. Division of Plant Industry. Commonwealth Scientific and Industrial Research Organisation

Tech Pap Div Pl Ind CSIRO (Aust) — Technical Papers. Division of Plant Industry. Commonwealth Scientific and Industrial Research Organisation (Australia)

Tech Pap Div Soil Mechanics CSIRO — Technical Paper. Division of Soil Mechanics. Commonwealth Scientific and Industrial Research Organisation

Tech Pap Div Soils CSIRO — Technical Paper. Division of Soils. Commonwealth Scientific and Industrial Research Organisation

Tech Pap Div Tech Conf Soc Plast Eng — Technical Papers. Divisional Technical Conference. Society of Plastics Engineers

Tech Pap Div Trop Agron CSIRO — Technical Paper. Division of Tropical Agronomy. Commonwealth Scientific and Industrial Research Organisation

Tech Pap Div Trop Crops Pastures CSIRO — Technical Paper. Division of Tropical Crops and Pastures. Commonwealth Scientific and Industrial Research Organisation

Tech Pap Div Trop Pastures CSIRO — Technical Paper. Division of Tropical Pastures. Commonwealth Scientific and Industrial Research Organisation

Tech Pap Div Wildl Res CSIRO — Technical Paper. Division of Wildlife Research. Commonwealth Scientific and Industrial Research Organisation

Tech Pap Ethyl Corp — Technical Papers. Ethyl Corporation

Tech Pap Exp Stn Pineapple Prod Coop Ass Hawaii — Technical Papers of the Experiment Station of the Pineapple Producers' Co-operative Association (University of Hawaii)

Tech Pap For Comm NSW — Technical Paper. Forestry Commission of New South Wales

Tech Pap Forest Serv US — Technical Papers. Forest Service. United States Department of Agriculture [Berkeley]

Tech Pap For Res Inst NZ For Serv — Technical Paper. Forest Research Institute. New Zealand Forest Service

Tech Pap Fuel Res DSIR — Technical Papers. Fuel Research. Department of Scientific and Industrial Research [London]

Tech Pap Gt Lakes Res Inst — Technical Papers. Great Lakes Research Institute. University of Michigan

Tech Pap Hydrol — Technical Papers in Hydrology

Tech Pap IEEE ASME Jt Railroad Conf — Technical Papers. IEEE/ASME Joint Railroad Conference

Tech Pap Illum Res DSIR — Technical Papers. Illumination Research. Department of Scientific and Industrial Research [London]

Tech Pap Imp For Inst — Technical Papers. Imperial Forestry Institute [Oxford]

Tech Pap Indo Pacif Fish Coun — Technical Papers. Indo-Pacific Fisheries Council [Bangkok]

Tech Pap Inst Pet — Technical Papers. Institute of Petroleum

Tech Pap Intersoc Energy Convers Eng Conf — Technical Papers. Intersociety Energy Conversion Engineering Conference

Tech Pap Iowa Geol Surv — Technical Papers. Iowa Geological Survey

Tech Pap Irrig Brch Unit Prov — Technical Papers. Irrigation Branch. United Provinces Department of Public Works

Tech Pap Irrig Res Stns CSIRO Aust — Technical Papers. Irrigation Research Stations. C.S.I.R.O. Australia

Tech Pap La St Dep Conserv — Technical Papers. Louisiana State Department of Conservation

Tech Pap Lond Shellac Res Bur — Technical Papers. London Shellac Research Bureau

Tech Pap Lubric Res DSIR — Technical Papers. Lubrication Research. Department of Scientific and Industrial Research [London]

Tech Pap Mines Brch Can — Technical Papers. Mines Branch. Department of Mines and Technical Surveys. Canada

Tech Pap Minn Univ Engng Exp Stn — Technical Papers. Minnesota University Engineering Experiment Station

Tech Pap Natl Meas Lab CSIRO — Technical Paper. National Measurement Laboratory. Commonwealth Scientific and Industrial Research Organisation

Tech Pap Natn Bldg Stud DSIR — Technical Papers. National Building Studies. Building Research Station. D.S.I.R. (Department of Scientific and Industrial Research) [Watford]

Tech Pap Natn Geogr Soc — Technical Papers. National Geographic Society

Tech Pap Natn Stand Lab CSIRO — Technical Paper. National Standards Laboratory. Commonwealth Scientific and Industrial Research Organisation

Tech Pap NY State Dep Environ Conserv — Technical Paper. New York State Department of Environmental Conservation

Tech Pap Pa Engng Exp Stn — Technical Papers. Pennsylvania Engineering Experiment Station

Tech Pap Queensl Dep For — Technical Paper. Queensland Department of Forestry

Tech Pap Reg Tech Conf Soc Plast Eng — Technical Papers. Regional Technical Conference. Society of Plastics Engineers

Tech Pap Res Ass Br Paint Colour Varn Mfrs — Technical Papers. Research Association of British Paint, Colour, and Varnish Manufacturers [London]

Tech Pap Rly Bd India — Technical Papers. Railway Board. India

Tech Pap Shellac Res Bur Brooklyn — Technical Papers. Shellac Research Bureau. Polytechnic Institute of Brooklyn

Tech Pap SME Ser EE — Technical Paper. Society of Manufacturing Engineers. Series EE (Electrical Engineering)

Tech Pap Soc Manuf Eng Ser AD — Technical Paper. Society of Manufacturing Engineers. Series AD (Assembly Division)

Tech Pap Soc Manuf Eng Ser EE — Technical Paper. Society of Manufacturing Engineers. Series EE (Electrical Engineering)

Tech Pap Soc Manuf Eng Ser EM — Technical Paper. Society of Manufacturing Engineers. Series EM (Engineering Materials)

Tech Pap Soc Manuf Eng Ser FC — Technical Paper. Society of Manufacturing Engineers. Series FC (Finishing and Coating)

Tech Pap Soc Manuf Eng Ser IQ — Technical Paper. Society of Manufacturing Engineers. Series IQ (Inspection and Quality)

Tech Pap Soc Manuf Eng Ser MF — Technical Paper. Society of Manufacturing Engineers. Series MF (Material Forming)

Tech Pap Soc Manuf Eng Ser MR — Technical Paper. Society of Manufacturing Engineers. Series MR (Material Removal)

Tech Pap Soc Plast Engrs — Technical Papers. Society of Plastics Engineers [Greenwich, Connecticut]

Tech Pap S Pacific Commn — Technical Papers. South Pacific Commission [Noumea]

Tech Pap St Anthony Falls Hydraul Lab — Technical Papers. St Anthony Falls Hydraulic Laboratory

Tech Pap Surv India — Technical Papers. Survey of India

Tech Pap Tex Sect Am Soc Civ Engrs — Technical Papers of the Texas Section. American Society of Civil Engineers

Tech Pap Third Weath Grp Air Def Command Forec Cent — Technical Papers. Third Weather Group. Air Defence Command Forecast Center

Tech Pap Tin Res Inst — Technical Papers. Tin Research Institute

Tech Pap Univ PR Agr Exp Sta — Technical Paper. University of Puerto Rico. Agricultural Experiment Station

Tech Pap US Dairy Sect — Technical Papers. United States Dairy Section

Tech Pap US Weath Bur — Technical Papers. United States Weather Bureau

Tech Pap War Off — Technical Papers. War Office [London]

Tech Pap Wash St Agric Exp Stn — Technical Papers. Washington State Agricultural Experiment Station [Pullman]

Tech Pap Wool Text Res Labs Aust — Technical Papers. Wool Textile Research Laboratories. Australia

Tech Pet — Techniques du Petrole

Tech Phot — Technical Photography

Tech Photo — Technical Photography

Tech Phys Einzeldarst — Technische Physik in Einzeldarstellungen

Tech-Phys Monogr — Technisch-Physikalische Monographien

Tech Phys Ser — Techniques of Physics Series

Tech Phys USSR — Technical Physics of the USSR

Tech Poszukiwan — Technika Poszukiwan

Tech Poszukiwan Geol — Technika Poszukiwan Geologicznych

Tech Poszukiwan Geol Geosynoptyka Geoterm — Technika Poszukiwan Geologicznych, Geosynoptyka, i Geotermia

Tech Pr — Technika Prace

Tech Prat Agr — Technique et Pratique Agricoles

Tech Prepr Am Soc Lubr Eng — Technical Preprints. American Society of Lubrication Engineers

Tech Probl Natn Def — Technical Problems Affecting National Defense. National Inventors Council [*Washington*]

Tech Proc A Conv Am Electropl Soc — Technical Proceedings. Annual Convention of the American Electroplaters Society

Tech Proc A Conv Master Brew Ass Am — Technical Proceedings. Annual Convention of the Master Brewers' Association of America

Tech Proc A Meet Fed Paint Varn Prod Clubs — Technical Proceedings. Annual Meetings. Federation of Paint and Varnish Production Clubs

Tech Prog News Cape Asbestos Co — Technical Progress News. Cape Asbestos Co

Tech Prog Rep Engng Ind Exp Stn Univ Fla — Technical Progress Report. Engineering and Industrial Experiment Station. University of Florida

Tech Prog Rep Hawaii Agric Exp Stn — Technical Progress Report. Hawaii Agricultural Experiment Station

Tech Prog Rep Ship Struct Comm — Technical Progress Report. Ship Structure Committee [*Washington*]

Tech Prog Rep US Bur Mines — Technical Progress Report. United States Bureau of Mines

Tech Prog Rev US Atom Energy Commn — Technical Progress Review. United States Atomic Energy Commission

Tech Progr Rep Hawaii Agr Exp Sta — Technical Progress Report. Hawaii Agricultural Experiment Station. University of Hawaii

Tech Prog Sylvania Elect Prod — Technical Progress. Sylvania Electric Products

Tech Protein Chem 2 Pap Annu Symp Protein Soc — Techniques in Protein Chemistry 2. Papers. Annual Symposium. Protein Society

Tech Protein Chem 3 Pap Annu Symp Protein Soc — Techniques in Protein Chemistry 3. Papers. Annual Symposium. Protein Society

Tech Publ Aust Soc Dairy Technol — Australian Society of Dairy Technology. Technical Publication

Tech Publ Div Wood Technol For Comm NSW — Technical Publication. Division of Wood Technology. Forestry Commission of New South Wales

Tech Publ NY St Coll For — Technical Publication. New York State University. College of Forestry

Tech Publ R8-TP US Dep Agric For Serv South Reg — Technical Publication R8-TP. US Department of Agriculture. Forest Service. Southern Region

Tech Publs — Technical Publications

Tech Publs Am Inst Min Metall Engrs — Technical Publications. American Institute of Mining and Metallurgical Engineers

Tech Publs Anglo Am Caribb Commn — Technical Publications. Anglo-American Caribbean Commission and the Caribbean Commission

Tech Publs Announc NASA — Technical Publications Announcements. National Aeronautics and Space Administration [*Washington*]

Tech Publs Aust Soc Dairy Technol — Technical Publications. Australian Society of Dairy Technology

Tech Publs Bell Teleph Syst — Technical Publications. Bell Telephone System [*New York*]

Tech Publs Br Elect All Ind Res Ass — Technical Publications. British Electrical and Allied Industries Research Association

Tech Publs Br Elect Dev Ass — Technical Publications. British Electrical Development Association

Tech Publs Canterbury Agric Coll — Technical Publications. Canterbury Agricultural College [*Christchurch*]

Tech Publs Dep Agric (Vict) — Technical Publications. Department of Agriculture (Victoria)

Tech Publs Div Wood Technol NSW For Comm — Technical Publications. Division of Wood Technology. New South Wales Forestry Commission

Tech Publs Edinb E Scotl Coll Agric — Technical Publications. Edinburgh and East of Scotland College of Agriculture

Tech Publs Feedwater Spec Co — Technical Publications. Feedwater Specialists Co

Tech Publs Forest Serv Br Columb — Technical Publications. Forest Service. British Columbia

Tech Publs Int Tin Res Dev Coun — Technical Publications. International Tin Research and Development Council [*London*]

Tech Publs Joseph Crosfield & Sons — Technical Publications. Joseph Crosfield & Sons [*Warrington*]

Tech Publs Lead Inds Dev Ass — Technical Publications. Lead Industries Development Association [*London*]

Tech Publs NSW For Comm Div Wood Technol — Technical Publications. New South Wales Forestry Commission. Division of Wood Technology

Tech Publs NY St Coll For — Technical Publications. New York State University. College of Forestry

Tech Publs Prices Bromborough — Technical Publications. Price's, Bromborough

Tech Publs R Dutch Shell Grp — Technical Publications. Royal Dutch/Shell Group

Tech Publs Soil Conserv Serv — Technical Publications. Soil Conservation Service [*Washington*]

Tech Publs Stand Oil Co — Technical Publications. Standard Oil Company, New Jersey and Affiliated Companies

Tech Publ State Biol Surv Kans — Technical Publication. State Biological Survey of Kansas

Tech Publ State Univ Coll For Syracuse Univ — Technical Publication. State University College of Forestry. Syracuse University

Tech Publs Trig Surv Un S Afr — Technical Publications. Trigonometrical Survey. Union of South Africa

Tech Publs Wallace & Tiernan — Technical Publications. Wallace and Tiernan [*London*]

Tech Q — Technology Quarterly and Proceedings. Society of Arts

Techq Aeronaut — Technique Aeronautique

Techq Agric — Technique Agricole

Techq Agric — Technique et Agriculture [*Paris*]

Techq Agric Int — Technique Agricole Internationale [*Rome*]

Techq Appl — Technique Appliquee [*Paris*]

Techq Applic Flamme Oxyacet — Technique des Applications de la Flamme Oxyacetylinique [*Bruxelles*]

Techq Auto Aer — Technique Automobile et Aerienne [*Paris*]

Techq Chal — Technique de la Chaleur et Autres Formes d'Energie

Techq Chaussure — Technique Chaussure [*Paris*]

Techq Chir — Technique Chirurgicale [*Paris*]

Techq Cinem — Technique Cinematographique [*Paris*]

Techq Eau Assain — Technique de l'Eau et de l'Assainissement [*Bruxelles*]

Techq Engrais — Technique des Engrais [*Paris*]

Techq Explos — Technique des Explosifs [*Paris*]

Techq Human — Technique Humanisme [*Liege*]

Techq Inds Mec — Technique des Industries Mecaniques [*Paris*]

Techq Lait — Technique Laitiere

Tech Q Mast Brew Assoc Am — Technical Quarterly. Master Brewers Association of the Americas

Techq Mod — Technique Moderne [*Paris*]

Techq Pharm — Technique Pharmaceutique [*Paris*]

Techq Pratn — Technique du Practicien [*Paris*]

Techq Prof Radio — Technique Professionelle Radio [*Paris*]

Techq Rout — Technique Routiere [*Bruxelles*]

Techqs Anim — Techniques Animales

Techq Sanit Munic — Technique Sanitaire et Municipale [*Paris*]

Techqs Applic Petrole — Techniques et Applications du Petrole et Autres Energies [*Paris*]

Techqs Archit — Techniques et Architecture [*Paris*]

Techqs Barnes Engng Co — Techniques. Barnes Engineering Co. [*Stamford*]

Techqs CEM — Techniques CEM. Cie Electro-Mecanique [*Paris*]

Techq Sci Aeronaut — Technique et Sciences Aeronautiques [*Paris*]

Techqs Civil — Techniques et Civilisations [*St. Germain-en-Laye*]

Techqs Emball — Techniques d'Emballage [*Paris*]

Techqs Hosp — Techniques Hospitalieres, Medico-Sociales et Sanitaires

Techqs Memo Br Weld Res Ass — Techniques and Memoranda. British Welding Research Association

Techqs Mond — Techniques Mondiales

Techq Soud Decoup — Technique de la Soudure et du Decoupage [*Bruxelles*]

Techqs Pl Maint Engng — Techniques of Plant Maintenance and Engineering [*New York*]

Techqs Sci Munic — Techniques et Sciences Municipales [*Paris*]

Techq Trav — Technique des Travaux

Tech Quart Master Brew Ass Amer — Technical Quarterly. Master Brewers Association of America

Tech R — Technology Review

Tech Radia & Telew — Technika Radia i Telewizji

Tech Ratg — Technische Ratgeber

Tech Rdsch Anz MaschBau — Technische Rundschau und Anzeiger fuer Maschinenbau, Elektrotechnik, Bergbau, und Verkehrswesen

Tech Rdsch Berl — Technische Rundschau. Wochenschrift des Berliner Tageblatts

Tech Rdsch (Bern) — Technische Rundschau (Bern)

Tech Rdsch Licht Kraft U WassVersorg — Technische Rundschau fuer die Licht-, Kraft-, und Wasserversorgung

Tech Rec Emerg Scient Res Bur Eire — Technical Records. Emergency Scientific Research Bureau. Eire

Tech Rec Explos Supply — Technical Records of Explosives Supply [*London*]

Tech Refrig Air Cond — Technics of Refrigeration and Air Conditioning

Tech Regul Wld Met Org — Technical Regulations. World Meteorological Organisation [*Geneva*]

Tech Release Amer Pulpw Ass — Technical Release. American Pulpwood Association

Tech Rep Advis Comm Aeronaut — Technical Report of the Advisory Committee for Aeronautics [*London*]

Tech Rep Aeronaut Res Comm — Technical Report. Aeronautical Research Committee [*London*]

Tech Rep Aeronaut Res Coun — Technical Report. Aeronautical Research Council [*London*]

Tech Rep AFAPL TR Air Force Aero Propul Lab (US) — Technical Report. AFAPL-TR. Air Force Aero Propulsion Laboratory (United States)

Tech Rep AFFDL TR Air Force Flight Dyn Lab (US) — Technical Report. AFFDL-TR. Air Force Flight Dynamics Laboratory (United States)

Tech Rep AFML TR Air Force Mater Lab (US) — Technical Report. AFML-TR. Air Force Materials Laboratory (United States)

Tech Rep AFWAL-TR US Air Force Wright Aeronaut Lab — Technical Report. AFWAL-TR. United States Air Force Wright Aeronautical Laboratories

Tech Rep Agric Chem Branch (Queensl) — Technical Report. Agricultural Chemistry Branch (Queensland)

Tech Rep Agric Eng Res Stn Min Agric For Ser F — Technical Report. Agricultural Engineering Research Station. Ministry of Agriculture and Forestry. Series F. General

Tech Rep Agric Ld Serv — Technical Report. Agricultural Land Service. Ministry of Agriculture, Fisheries, and Food [*London*]

Tech Rep Agric Ld Serv Minist Agric Fish Fd — Technical Report. Agricultural Land Service. Ministry of Agriculture, Fisheries, and Food

Tech Rep Air Force Camb Res Cent — Technical Report. Air Force Cambridge Research Center (Cambridge, Massachusetts)

Tech Rep Air Pollut Yokohama-Kawasaki Ind Area — Technical Report on Air Pollution in Yokohama-Kawasaki Industrial Area

Tech Rep Air Weath Serv — Technical Report. Air Weather Service [*Washington*]

Tech Rep Ala St Mine Exp Stn — Technical Report. Alabama State Mine Experiment Station

Tech Rep Arct Constr Frost Eff Lab — Technical Report. Arctic Construction and Frost Effects Laboratory

Tech Rep Aust Weapons Res Establ — Technical Report. Australia Weapons Research Establishment

Tech Rep Bitum Coal Res Wash — Technical Report. Bituminous Coal Research (Washington)

Tech Rep Br Elect All Ind Res Ass — Technical Report. British Electrical and Allied Industries Research Association

Tech Rep Br Eng Boil Elect Insur Co — Technical Report. British Engine, Boiler, and Electrical Insurance Co., Ltd.

Tech Rep Bur Aeronaut Res Chengtu — Technical Report. Bureau of Aeronautical Research (Chengtu)

Tech Rep Bur Highw Traff Yale — Technical Report. Bureau of Highway Traffic. Yale University

Tech Rep Bur Met — Technical Report. Bureau of Meteorology

Tech Rep Bur Meteorol — Technical Report. Bureau of Meteorology

Tech Rep Cent Analysis Elect Engng Dep MIT — Technical Report. Center of Analysis. Electrical Engineering Department. Massachusetts Institute of Technology

Tech Rep Cent Bd Irrig India — Technical Report. Central Board of Irrigation and Power. India

Tech Rep Cent Fish Dep Pakist — Technical Report. Central Fisheries Department. Pakistan

Tech Rep Cent Res Inst Electr Power Ind — Technical Report. Central Research Institute of the Electrical Power Industry

Tech Rep Cent Res Water Resour Univ Tex Austin — Technical Report. Center for Research in Water Resources. University of Texas at Austin

Tech Rep Chesapeake Bay Inst — Technical Report. Chesapeake Bay Institute [Baltimore]

Tech Rep Constr Eng Res Lab — Technical Report. Construction Engineering Research Laboratory

Tech Rep Counc Cent Lab Res Counc — Technical Report. Council for the Central Laboratory of the Research Councils

Tech Rep Cstl Stud Inst La St Univ — Technical Report. Coastal Studies Institute. Louisiana State University

Tech Rep Dep Agric Ceylon — Technical Report. Department of Agriculture. Ceylon

Tech Rep Dep Agric FMS — Technical Report. Department of Agriculture. Federated Malay States

Tech Rep Dep Ind Med Yale — Technical Report. Department of Industrial Medicine. Yale University

Tech Rep Dep Mines NSW — Technical Report. Department of Mines. New South Wales

Tech Rep Dep Mines Tas — Technical Report. Department of Mines. Tasmania

Tech Rep Dep Mines Tasm — Technical Report. Department of Mines. Tasmania

Tech Rep Dep Oceanogr Agric Mech Coll Tex — Technical Report. Department of Oceanography. Agricultural and Mechanical College of Texas

Tech Rep Dep Oceanogr Univ Wash — Technical Report. Department of Oceanography. University of Washington

Tech Rep Dep Psychol Stanford Univ — Technical Report. Department of Psychology. Stanford University

Tech Rep Dep Soil Ld Use Surv Ghana — Technical Report. Department of Soil and Land-Use Survey. Ghana

Tech Rep Desert Locust Control Organ East Afr — Technical Report. Desert Locust Control Organization for Eastern Africa

Tech Rep Div Appl Geomech CSIRO — Technical Report. Division of Applied Geomechanics. Commonwealth Scientific andIndustrial Research Organisation

Tech Rep Div Ind Res Wash St Inst Technol — Technical Report. Division of Industrial Research. Washington State Institute of Technology

Tech Rep Div Mech Eng CSIRO — Technical Report. Division of Mechanical Engineering. Commonwealth Scientific and Industrial Research Organisation

Tech Rep Div Mech Engng CSIRO — Technical Report. Division of Mechanical Engineering. Commonwealth Scientific and Industrial Research Organisation

Tech Rep Div Soil Mech CSIRO — Technical Report. Division of Soil Mechanics. Commonwealth Scientific and Industrial Research Organisation

Tech Rep ECETOC — Technical Report. ECETOC (European Chemical Industry Ecology and Toxicology Centre)

Tech Rep Edwards Street Lab Yale — Technical Report. Edwards Street Laboratory. Yale University

Tech Rep EMI Electron — Technical Report. E.M.I. Electronics [Hayes]

Tech Rep Engng Res Inst Kyoto — Technical Report of the Engineering Research Institute. Kyoto University

Tech Rep Eng Res Inst Kyoto Univ — Technical Reports. Engineering Research Institute. Kyoto University

Tech Rep Fac For Univ Toronto — Technical Report. Faculty of Forestry. University of Toronto

Tech Rep For Eng Res Inst Can — Technical Report. Forest Engineering Research Institute of Canada

Tech Rep Grassld Res Inst — Technical Report. Grassland Research Institute

Tech Rep Hydraul Brch Minist Wks Kenya — Technical Report. Hydraulic Branch. Ministry of Works. Kenya

Tech Rep Hydrogr Off Wash — Technical Report. Hydrographic Office. United States Navy (Washington)

Tech Rep Indian Coun Agric Res — Technical Report. Indian Council of Agricultural Research

Tech Rep Inst At Energy Kyoto Univ — Technical Reports. Institute of Atomic Energy. Kyoto University

Tech Rep Inst Atom Energy Kyoto Univ — Technical Reports. Institute of Atomic Energy. Kyoto University

Tech Rep Inst Engng Res Univ Calif — Technical Report. Institute of Engineering Research. University of California [Berkeley]

Tech Rep Inst Printed Circuits — Technical Report. Institute of Printed Circuits

Tech Rep Inst Seaweed Res — Technical Report. Institute of Seaweed Research [Musselburgh]

Tech Rep Inst Sol Terr Res Univ Colo — Technical Report. Institute for Solar-Terrestial Research. High Altitude Observatory of the University of Colorado

Tech Rep Iowa Highw Commn — Technical Report. Iowa Highway Commission

Tech Rep Iron Steel Ind Res Coun — Technical Report. Iron and Steel Industrial Research Council [London]

Tech Rep ISSP (Inst Solid State Phys) Ser A — Technical Report. ISSP (Institute for Solid State Physics). Series A

Tech Rep Jet Propul Lab Calif Inst Technol — Technical Report. Jet Propulsion Laboratory. California Institute of Technology

Tech Rep JSS Proj — Technical Report. JSS [Japanese, Swiss, Swedish] Project

Tech Rep Kansai Univ — Technology Reports. Kansai University

Tech Rep Lab Insul Res MIT — Technical Report. Laboratory for Insulation Research. Massachusetts Institute of Technology

Tech Rep Lab Nucl Sci Engng MIT — Technical Report. Laboratory for Nuclear Science and Engineering. Massachusetts Institute of Technology

Tech Rep Met Clim Arid Reg — Technical Report on the Meteorology and Climatology of Arid Regions. Institute of Atmospheric Physics. University of Arizona [Tucson]

Tech Rep Met Lamont Geol Obs — Technical Report on Meteorology. Lamont Geological Observatory [Palisades]

Tech Rep Miami Conserv Distr — Technical Report. Miami Conservancy District [Dayton, Ohio]

Tech Rep Minist Mines Tasm — Technical Report. Ministry of Mines. Tasmania

Tech Rep Munit Supply Bd Aust — Technical Report. Munitions Supply Board. Australia

Tech Rep Nanyang Univ Coll Grad Stud Inst Nat Sci — Technical Report. Nanyang University. College of Graduate Studies. Institute ofNatural Sciences

Tech Rep Narragansett Mar Lab — Technical Report. Narragansett Marine Laboratory. University of Rhode Island

Tech Rep Natl Space Dev Agency Jpn — Technical Report. National Space Development Agency of Japan

Tech Rep New Mex St Engr — Technical Report. New Mexico State Engineeer

Tech Rep Nisshin Steel Co Ltd — Technical Report. Nisshin Steel Company Limited

Tech Rep Off Nav Res (USA) — Technical Report. Office of Naval Research (USA)

Tech Reports Osaka Univ — Technology Reports. Osaka University

Tech Rep Osaka Univ — Technology Reports. Osaka University

Tech Rep R2 US Dep Agric For Serv For Pest Manage — Technical Report R2. US Department of Agriculture. Forest Service. Forest Pest Management

Tech Rep Reg Res Sta (Samaru) — Technical Report. Regional Research Station (Samaru)

Tech Rep Res Org Ships Compos Mfrs — Technical Report. Research Organization of Ships' Compositions Manufacturers [London]

Tech Repr Graver Water Cond Co — Technical Reprint. Graver Water Conditioning Company

Tech Rep S Afr Wool Text Res Inst — Technical Report. South African Wool Textile Research Institute

Tech Rep Sch Fish Univ Wash — Technical Report. School of Fisheries. University of Washington

Tech Rep Sch For N Carol St Coll — Technical Report. School of Forestry. North Carolina State College of Agriculture and Engineering

Tech Rep Sch For Resour NC St Univ — Technical Report. School of Forest Resources. North Carolina State University

Tech Rep Ser ARL/TR Aust Radiat Lab — Australia. Australian Radiation Laboratory. Technical Report Series ARL/TR

Tech Rep Ser Carcinog Nat Cancer Inst (US) — Technical Report Series: Carcinogenesis. National Cancer Institute (United States)

Tech Rep Ser Int Atom Energy Ag — Technical Reports Series. International Atomic Energy Agency

Tech Rep Ser Victoria Dep Agric — Victoria. Department of Agriculture. Technical Report Series

Tech Rep Ser Wld Hlth Org — Technical Report Series. World Health Organisation

Tech Rep Ship Struct Comm — Technical Report. Ship Structure Committee [Washington]

Tech Rep Snow Ice Permafrost Res Establ — Technical Report. Snow, Ice, and Permafrost Research Establishment [Wilmette]

Tech Rep Soil Res Inst Ghana Acad Sci — Technical Report. Soil Research Institute. Ghana Academy of Sciences

Tech Rep Solid St Molec Theory Grp MIT — Technical Report. Solid State and Molecular Theory Group. Massachusetts Institute of Technology

Tech Rep Sumitomo Met Ind Ltd — Technical Reports. Sumitomo Metal Industries Ltd

Tech Rep Sumitomo Spec Met — Technical Report of Sumitomo Special Metals

Tech Rep Surv India — Technical Report. Survey of India

Tech Rep Syst Am Soc Met — Technical Report System. American Society for Metals

Tech Rep Syst ASM — Technical Report System. American Society for Metals

Tech Rep Tasmania Dep Mines — Tasmania. Department of Mines. Technical Report

Tech Rep Tasm Dep Mines — Technical Report. Tasmania Department of Mines

Tech Rep Tex Forest Serv — Technical Report. Texas Forest Service

Tech Rep Tex For Serv — Technical Report. Texas Forest Service

Tech Rep Toyo Kohan Co Ltd — Technical Reports. Toyo Kohan Company Limited

Tech Rep TVA — Technical Report. Tennessee Valley Authority [Washington]

Tech Rep Univ Chicago — Technical Report. University of Chicago

Tech Rep Univ Tex Austin Cent Res Water Resour — Technical Report. University of Texas at Austin. Center for Research in Water Resources

Tech Rep US Army Beach Eros Bd — Technical Report. United States Army Beach Erosion Board

Tech Rep US Army Eng Waterw Exp Stn — Technical Report. United States Army Engineers. Waterways Experiment Station

Tech Rep US Army Signal Res Dev Lab — Technical Report. United States Army Signal Research and Development Laboratory [Fort Monmouth]

Tech Rep US Nav Postgrad Sch — Technical Report. United States Naval Postgraduate School

Tech Rep Water Resour Res Cent Hawaii Univ — Technical Report. Hawaii University. Water Resource Research Center

Tech Rep Woods Hole Oceanogr Instn — Technical Report. Woods Hole Oceanographic Institution

Tech Rep Yale Sch For — Technical Report. Yale University. School of Forestry

Tech Res Bull Soc Nav Archit Mar Engrs — Technical and Research Bulletin. Society of Naval Architects and Marine Engineers

Tech Res Cent Finland Electr and Nucl Technol Publ — Technical Research Centre of Finland. Electrical and Nuclear Technology Publication

Tech Res Cent Finland Mater and Process Technol Publ — Technical Research Centre of Finland. Materials and Processing Technology Publication

Tech Res Cent Finl Build Technol Community Dev Publ — Technical Research Centre of Finland. Building Technology and Community Development Publication

Tech Res Cent Finl Electr Nucl Technol Publ — Technical Research Centre of Finland. Electrical and Nuclear Technology Publication

Tech Res Cent Finl Gen Div Publ — Technical Research Centre of Finland. General Division Publication

Tech Res Cent Finl Mater Process Technol Publ — Technical Research Centre of Finland. Materials and Processing Technology Publication

Tech Res Cent Finl Publ — Technical Research Centre of Finland. Publications

Tech Res Cent Finl Res Rep — Technical Research Centre of Finland. Research Reports

Tech Res Rep Res Inst Ind Sci Technol — Technical Research Report. Research Institute of Industrial Science and Technology

Tech Rev — Technology Review

Tech Rev B and K — Technical Review (BRUEL and KJAER)

Tech Rev Mitsubishi Heavy-Ind (Jpn Ed) — Technical Review. Mitsubishi Heavy Industries (Japanese Edition)

Tech Rev Mitsubishi Heavy Ind Ltd — Technical Review. Mitsubishi Heavy Industries Ltd.

Tech Rev Sumitomo Heavy Ind Ltd — Technical Review. Sumitomo Heavy Industries Limited

Tech Rev War Off — Technical Review. War Office

Tech Routiere — Technique Routiere

Tech Rundsch — Technische Rundschau

Tech Rundsch Allg Ind Handelsz — Technische Rundschau und Allgemeine Industrie- und Handelszeitung

Tech Rundsch Sulzer — Technische Rundschau Sulzer

Tech Schulfach — Technik als Schulfach

Tech Sci Adv Electron — Technical Sciences. Advances in Electronics

Tech Sci Aeronaut Spat — Technique et Science Aeronautiques et Spatiales

Tech Sci Munic — Techniques et Sciences Municipales

Tech Sci Munic Eau — Techniques et Sciences Municipales/l'Eau

Tech Semin Chem Spills — Technical Seminar on Chemical Spills

Tech Ser Bur Ent US — Technical Series. Bureau of Entomology. United States Department of Agriculture

Tech Ser Fla Dep Nat Resour Mar Res Lab — Technical Series. Florida Department of Natural Resources. Marine Research Laboratory

Tech Ser Fla St Bd Conserv — Technical Series. Florida State Board of Conservation

Tech Ser Instn Fire Engrs — Technical Series. Institution of Fire Engineers [Edinburgh]

Tech Ser Mar Lab Univ Miami — Technical Series. Marine Laboratory. University of Miami

Tech Ser Natn Tuberc Ass NY — Technical Series. National Tuberculosis Association (New York)

Tech Ser Ohio Agric Exp Stn — Technical Series. Ohio Agricultural Experiment Station

Tech Ser Sch Mines Metall Univ Mo — Technical Series. School of Mines and Metallurgy. University of Missouri

Tech Ser Soc Appl Bacteriol — Technical Series. Society for Applied Bacteriology

Tech Serv Bull Borax Consol — Technical Service Bulletin. Borax Consolidated, Ltd

Tech Serv Bull Paisley Prod — Technical Service Bulletin. Paisley Products [Chicago]

Tech Serv Bull Vinyl Prod — Technical Service Bulletin. Vinyl Products [Carshalton]

Tech Serv Circ Natn Aniline Div Allied Chem Corp — Technical Service Circular. National Aniline Division. Allied Chemical Corporation [New York]

Tech Serv Memo — Technical Service Memorandum. Technical Service Library [London]

Tech Serv Newsl — Technical Services Newsletter

Tech Serv Rep Vinyl Prod — Technical Service Report. Vinyl Products [Carshalton]

Tech Skoda — Technika Skoda

Tech Smarownicza — Technika Smarownicza

Tech Smarownicza Trybol — Technika Smarownicza. Trybologia

Tech Soc Pacific Coast Tr — Technical Society of the Pacific Coast. Transactions

Tech Spec Offrs Rep Dep Agric Tanganyika — Technical and Specialist Officers' Reports. Department of Agriculture. Tanganyika

Tech Stand Aust — Technical Standards. Standards Association of Australia

Tech Statist Rev Dep Publ Wks Commun Philipp Isl — Technical-Statistical Review. Department of Public Works and Communications. Philippine Islands

Tech Stochastiques — Techniques Stochastiques

Tech Stud — Technical Studies

Tech Stud Common Exp Bldg Stn — Technical Studies. Commonwealth Experimental Building Station

Tech Stud Commonw Exp Bldg Stn — Technical Studies. Commonwealth Experimental Building Station

Tech Stud Field F A — Technical Studies in the Field of Fine Arts

Tech Studien — Technische Studien

Tech Summ Gulf St Mar Fish Commn — Technical Summary. Gulf States Marine Fisheries Commission

Tech Suppl Inst Civ Def — Technical Supplement. Institute of Civil Defence [London]

Tech Suppl Ltg Serv Bur — Technical Supplement. Lighting Service Bureau [London]

Tech Suppl Rev Foreign Press — Technical Supplement to the Review of the Foreign Press. War Office [London]

Tech Surv Copp Dev Ass — Technical Survey. Copper Development Association [London]

Tech Surv Res Div Comm Fire Prev Engng Stand — Technical Survey. Research Division. Committee on Fire Prevention and Engineering Standards. National Board of Fire Underwriters [New York]

Tech Szem — Technikatoerteneti Szemle

Tech Tag Rhein Westf Steinkohlenbergb — Technische Tagung des Rheinisch-Westfaelischen Steinkohlenbergbaus

Tech Teach — Technical Teacher

Tech Tijdschr — Technisch Tijdschrift [Utrecht]

Tech Timber Guide — Technical Timber Guide

Tech Timb Guide — Technical Timber Guide

Tech Times — Technology Transfer Times

Tech Tips Online — Technical Tips Online

Tech Top Va Polytech Inst — Technical Topics. Virginia Polytechnic Institute

Tech Trans Bull — Technical Translation Bulletin

Tech Transl — Technical Translations

Tech Transl Natn Res Coun Can — Technical Translations. National Research Council of Canada

Tech Transl Off Tech Servs — Technical Translations. Office of Technical Services. United States Department of Commerce

Tech Trav — Techniques des Travaux

Tech Trav (Liege) — Technique des Travaux (Liege)

Tech Tworczego Myslenia — Techniki Tworczego Myslenia

Tech Ueberwach — Technische Ueberwachung

Tech Ueberwach Duesseldorf — Technische Ueberwachung (Duesseldorf)

Tech Ueberwach Essen — Technische Ueberwachung (Essen)

Tech Ueberwach Kleinausg — Technische Ueberwachung. Kleinausgabe

Tech Ueberwach Muench — Technische Ueberwachung (Muenchen)

Tech Umweltschutz — Technik und Umweltschutz

Tech Univ Chemnitz Wiss Z — Technische Universitaet Chemnitz. Wissenschaftliche Zeitschrift

Tech Univ Chemnitz Zwickau Wiss Z — Technische Universitaet Chemnitz-Zwickau. Wissenschaftliche Zeitschrift

Tech Univ Karl Marx Stadt Wiss Tag — Technische Universitaet Karl-Marx-Stadt. Wissenschaftliche Tagungen

Tech Univ Karl Marx Stadt Wiss Z — Technische Universitaet Karl-Marx-Stadt. Wissenschaftliche Zeitschrift

Tech Univ Muenchen Jahrb — Technische Universitaet Muenchen. Jahrbuch

Tech Univ Zvolene Drev Fak Zb Ved Pr — Technicka Univerzita vo Zvolene. Drevarska Fakulta. Zbornik Vedeckych Prac

Tech Urol — Techniques in Urology

Tech Vakbl Noord Scheepsb — Technisch Vakblad voor de Noordelijke Scheepsbouw

Tech Vakbl Waschind — Technisch Vakblad voor de Waschindustrie

Tech Vortr Abh — Technische Vortraege und Abhandlungen

Tech W — Technical World

Tech W — Technology Week

Tech Wet Tijdschr — Technisch-Wetenschappelijk Tijdschrift. Vlamse Ingenieursvereniging

Tech Wet Tijdschr Ing Tijd — Technisch Wetenschappelijk Tijdschrift en Ingenieurs Tijdingen

Tech Wildl Bull Game Mgmt Div Wis — Technical Wildlife Bulletin. Game Management Division. Wisconsin Conservation Department

Tech Wirt Ber Reichskohlenkommr — Technisch-Wirtschaftliche Berichte der Reichskohlenkommissar

Tech-Wiss Abh Osram-Ges — Technisch-Wissenschaftliche Abhandlungen der Osram-Gesellschaft

Tech Wiss Abh ZentInst Schweisstech DDR — Technisch-Wissenschaftliche Abhandlungen. Zentralinstitut fuer Schweisstechnik der Deutschen Demokratischen Republik

Tech Wiss Ber August Thyssen Huette — Technische und Wissenschaftliche Berichte. August Thyssen-Huette

Tech Wiss Ber Osram — Technisch-Wissenschaftliche Berichte Osram G.m.b.H. Kommanditgesellschaft

Tech Wiss Schnell Inf Kohlenind DDR — Technisch-Wissenschaftliche Schnell-Informationen fuer die Kohlenindustrie der Deutschen Demokratischen Republik

Tech Wiss Schriftenr ATV — Technisch-Wissenschaftliche Schriftenreihe der ATV

Tech Wiss Veroeff Zahnradfabr Friedrichshafen — Technisch-Wissenschaftliche Veroeffentlichungen. Zahnradfabrik Friedrichshafen

Tech Wk — Technology Week

Tech Wlok — Technik Wlokienniczy

Tech World — Technical World Magazine

Tech Writ Rev — Technical Writing Review [Boston]

Tech Yb — Technical Year-Book [London]

Tech Yb Natn Ass Poult Pack — Technical Year Book. National Association of Poultry Packers

Tech Zentbl Berg Huett U MaschBau — Technisches Zentralblatt fuer Berg-, Huetten-, und Maschinenbau

Tech Zentralbl — Technisches Zentralblatt

Tech Z Riga — Techniskais Zurnals (Riga)

Tech ZSchau Berl — Technische Zeitschriftenschau (Berlin)

Tech ZSchau Wicht Z HochbWes — Technische Zeitschriftenschau der Wichtigsten Zeitschriften des Hochbauwesens

Tech Ztg — Technische Zeitung

Tech Zukunft — Techniken der Zukunft

TECIB — Technic International

Tec Ind — Tecnica e Industria

Tec Ind (Madrid) — Tecnica Industrial (Madrid)

Tec Ital — Tecnica Italiana

TECLA — Tecnica (Lisbon)

Tec Latte — Tecnica del Latte
Tec Lav — Tecnica del Lavoro
Tec Metal — Tecnica Metalurgica
Tec Met (Barcelona) — Tecnica Metalurgica (Barcelona)
Tec Mit K F — Technische Mitteilungen Krupp. Forschungsberichte
Tec Mit K W — Technische Mitteilungen Krupp. Werksberichte
Tec Molit — Tecnica Molitoria
Tecnica Ital — Tecnica Italiana
Tecnica Lisb — Tecnica. Rivista de Engenharia (Lisboa)
Tecnico Metall — Tecnico Metallurgico
Tecn Ital — Tecnica Italiana
Tecnol Aliment — Tecnologia Alimentaria
Tecnol Aliment Mexico City — Tecnologia de Alimentos (Mexico City)
Tecnol Bras — Tecnologia Brasileira
Tecnol Cienc Educ — Tecnologia, Ciencia, Educacion
Tecnol Elettr — Tecnologie Elettriche
Tecnol Miner — Tecnologia Mineral
Tecnopolim Resine — Tecnopolimeri e Resine
Tec Off — Tecnica d'Officina
Tec Org — Tecnica ed Organizzazione
Tec Osp — Tecnica Ospedaliera
TECPD — TAPPI [*Technical Association of the Pulp and Paper Industry*] Environmental Conference. Proceedings
Tec Pecuar Mex — Tecnica Pecuaria en Mexico
Tec Pecu Mex — Tecnica Pecuaria en Mexico
Tec R — Technology Review
Tec Regul & Mando Autom — Tecnica de la Regulacion y Mando Automatico
Tec Ricostr — Tecnica e Ricostruzione
Tec Sint Spec Org — Tecniche e Sintesi Speciali Organiche
Tectonophys — Tectonophysics
TED — Electrical Distributor
TED — Tenders Electronic Daily
T Ed — Theological Educator
TED — Tuerk Etnografya Dergisi
Tedavi Klin Lab Derg — Tedavi Klinigi ve Laboratuvari Dergisi
TEDGA — Technical Digest
TEE — [*The*] Entrepreneurial Economy
TEE — Teologia Espiritual (Ecuador)
TEE — Tex-Textilis. Technisch Wetenschappelijk Maandblad voor de Benelux Textielindustrie
TeEA — Terres et Eaux (Algiers)
Teer Bitum — Teer und Bitumen
Tee Sq Tape — Tee-Square and Tape. David Rowell & Co.
TEES Tech Bull — TEES [*Texas Engineering Experiment Station*] Technical Bulletin
TEF — Telex Africa
TEFL/TESL Newsl — TEFL [*Teaching English as a Foreign Language*]/TESL Newsletter
TEFO — Technological Forecasting and Social Change
TEFO Verksamh — TEFO Verksamheten. Svenska Textilforskningsinstitutet
TEG — Tijdschrift voor Economische en Sociale Geografie
Tegen De Tuberc — Tegen de Tuberculose
Teg Meded S Afr Dep Landbou Viss — Tegniese Mededeling. Suid Afrika Departement van Landbou en Visserye
TEGNA — Tegnikon
TEGTA — Technische Gemeinschaft
Teg Tek — Teg och Teknik
TeH — Tennessee Historical Quarterly
TEH — Topics in Environmental Health
TEHBA — Tehnika (Belgrade)
Teher Forsch — Teheraner Forschungen. Deutsches Archaeologisches Institut. Abteilung Teheran
Teh Fiz — Tehnicka Fizika
Teh Hron — Tehnika Hronika. Tehnikon Epimeleterion tes 'Ellados en Athenais
Teh Hronika — Tehnika Hronika
Tehnol Fak Novom Sadu Zb Rad — Tehnoloski Fakultet u Novom Sadu. Zbornik Radova
Teh Noua — Tehnica Noua
Teh Pertan — Tehnik Pertanian
Teh Pollum — Tehnika Pollumajanduses
Teh Pregl — Tehnicki Pregled
Teh Rud Geol Metal — Tehnika Rudarstvo Geologiya i Metalurgija
Teh Tootmine — Tehnika ja Tootmine
Teh Ulik Toim — Tehnika-Ulikool Toimetused
TEICA — Transactions. Engineering Institute of Canada
TEIGA — Teishin Igaku
Teilhard Rev — Teilhard Review
Teilhard St — Teilhard Studies
Teint Apprets — Teinture et Apprets
Teint Nett — Teinture et Nettoyage
Teint Prat — Teinturier Pratique
TEIRD — Technology Ireland
Teiss — Teisser's Court of Appeal. Parish of Orleans Reports
TEJIA — Transport Engineer
Tejipari Kut Kozl — Tejipari Kutatasi Kozlemenyek
TEJPA — Tejipar
TeK — Text und Kontext
Tek Aikak — Teknillinen Aikakauslehti
Teka Kom Hist Sztuki — Teka Komisji Historii Sztuki
Teka Kom Urb & Archit Pol Akad Nauk — Teka Komisji Urbanistyki i Architektury Polskiej Akademii Nauk
Teka Kons — Teka Konserwatorska
Tek Bul Petkim Petrokimya A S Arastirma Mudurlugu — Teknik Bulten. Petkim Petrokimya A. S. Arastirma Mudurlugu
Tekel Enst Raporl — Tekel Enstituleri Raporlari

Tekel Inst Mudur Yayinl — Tekel Instituler Mudurlugu Yayinlari
Tekel Tutun Enst Raporl — Tekel Tutun Enstitusu Raporlari
Tek Foren Tidsskr Kbh — Tekniske Forenings Tidsskrift (Kjobenhavn)
Tek For Finl Forh — Tekniska Foreningens i Finland Forhandlingar
Tek For Finl Tidskr — Tekniska Foreningens i Finland Tidskrift
Tek Forum — Tekniskt Forum
TEKHA — Teoreticheskaya i Eksperimental'naya Khimiya
Tekh Biblfch Byull — Tekhniko-Bibliograficheskii Byulleten'. Vseukrainskaya Assotsiatsiya Inzhenerov
Tekh Delo Sof — Tekhnichesko Delo (Sofiya)
Tekh Dokl Gidrol — Tekhnicheskie Doklady po Gidrologii
Tekh Ekon Izv Tatabanyai Szenbanyak — Tekhnichesko Ekonomicheskie Izvestiya Tatabanyai Szenbanyak
Tekh Ekon Vest — Tekhniko-Ekonomicheskii Vestnik
Tekh Estetika — Tekhnicheskaya Estetika
Tekh Gorn — Tekhnika Gornyaku
Tekh Inf Sov Nar Khoz Kuibyshev Ekon Adm Raiona — Tekhnicheskaya Informatsiya. Sovet Narodnogo Khozyaistva Kuibyshevskogo Ekonomicheskogo Administrativnogo Raiona
Tekh Kibern — Tekhnicheskaya Kibernetika
Tekh Kino i Telev — Tekhnika Kino i Televideniya
Tekh Kino Telev — Tekhnika Kino i Televideniya
Tekh Kniga — Tekhnicheskaya Kniga
Tekh Mir — Tekhnicheskii Mir
Tekh Mis'l — Tekhnicheska Mis'l
Tekh Misul — Tekhnicheska Misul
Tekh Molodezhi — Tekhnika Molodezhi
Tekh Nauka — Tekhnika i Nauka
Tekhnika Metall — Tekhnika i Metallist
Tekhnika Molod — Tekhnika Molodezhi
Tekhnika Proizv — Tekhnika i Proizvodstvo
Tekhnika Prom — Tekhnika i Promyshlennost'
Tekhnika Prom Khoz — Tekhnika i Promyshlennoe Khozyaistvo
Tekhnika Prom Torg — Tekhnika, Promyshlennost' i Torgovlya
Tekhnika Radio Slab Toka — Tekhnika Radio i Slabogo Toka
Tekhnika Sel Khoz Mosk — Tekhnika v Sel'skom Khozyaistve (Moskva)
Tekhnika Sel Khoz S Peterb — Tekhnika i Sel'skoe Khozyaistvo (S. Peterburg)
Tekhnika Snabzh Krasn Armii — Tekhnika i Snabzhenie Krasnoi Armii
Tekhnika Stroit Prom — Tekhnika, Stroitel'stvo i Promyshlennost'
Tekhnika Vozdukh — Tekhnika Vozdukhoplavaniya
Tekhnika Vozdush Flota — Tekhnika Vozdushnogo Flota
Tekhnika Zhelez Dorog — Tekhnika Zheleznykh Dorog
Tekhnika Zhizn — Tekhnika i Zhizn'
Tekhnol Avtom Mashinostr — Tekhnologiya i Avtomatizatsiya Mashinostroeniya
Tekhnol Legk Splavov — Tekhnologiya Legkikh Splavov
Tekhnol Mashinostr (Moscow) — Tekhnologiya Mashinostroeniya (Moscow)
Tekhnol Mater — Tekhnologiya Materialov
Tekhnol Neorg Veshchestv — Tekhnologiya Neorganicheskikh Veshchestv
Tekhnol Organ Mekh Liteinogo Proizvod — Tekhnologiya, Organizatsiya, i Mekhanizatsiya Liteinogo Proizvodstva
Tekhnol Organ Proizvod — Tekhnologiya i Organizatsiya Proizvodstva
Tekhnol Proizvod Sukhikh Diagn Pitatel'nykh Sred — Tekhnologiya Proizvodstva Sukhikh Diagnosticheskikh Pitatel'nykh Sred
Tekhnol Stroit Proizvod — Tekhnologiya Stroitel'nogo Proizvodstva
Tekhnol Ugol Mashinost — Tekhnologiya Ugol'nogo Mashinostroeniya. Informatsionnyi Byulleten'
Tekh Obraz — Tekhnicheskoe Obrazovanie
Tek Hoegsk Handl — Tekniska Hoegskolan Handlingar
Tek Hogsk Helsingfors Vetensk Publ — Tekniska Hoegskolan i Helsingfors Vetenskapliga Publikationer
Tekh Prom Vest — Tekhniko-Promyshlennyi Vestnik
Tekh Sel'Khoz — Tekhnika v Sel'skom Khozyaistve
Tekhsov MTS — Tekhsovety MTS
Tekh Usloviya Metody Opred Vrednykh Veshchestv Vozdukhe — Tekhnicheskie Usloviya na Metody Opredeleniya Vrednykh Veshchestv v Vozdukhe
Tekh Vooruzhenie — Tekhnika i Vooruzhenie
Tekh Vozdushn Flota — Tekhnika Vozdushnogo Flota
Tekh Zhelezn Dorog — Tekhnika Zheleznykh Dorog
Tek Inf — Teknisk Information
TEKKA — Tekkokai
Tek Kem Aikak — Teknillisen Kemian Aikakauslehti
Tek Korkeak Opetus — Teknillinen Korkeakoulu Opetusohjelma
Tek Lovsaml — Teknisk Lovsamling
Tek Maailma — Tekniikan Maailma
Tek Medd — Tekniska Meddelanden
Tek Medd Husholdningsraad Den — Tekniske Meddelelser. Husholdningsraad (Denmark)
Tek Meddn Svenska Plastfor — Tekniska Meddelanden. Svenska Plastforeningen
Tek Meddn UndersRapp Svenska CemFor — Tekniska Meddelanden och Undersokningsrapporter. Svenska Cementforeningen
Tekn Forsknstift Skogsarb — Teknik Forskningsstiftelsen Skogsarbeten
Teknik Alla — Teknik for Alla
Teknill Kem Aikak — Teknillisen Kemian Aikakausilehti
Teknill Korkeak Vuos — Teknillinen Korkeakoulu Vuosikertomus
Tekn Kino Televid — Tekhnika Kino i Televideniya
Tekn + Milj — Teknik + Miljo
Teknol Avtom Mashinostr — Tekhnologiya i Avtomatizatsiya Mashinostroeniya
Tekn Skt — Teknisk Skoletidende
Tekn Tss Textil O Beklaedn — Teknisk Tidsskrift for Textil og Beklaedning
TEKSA — Tekhnika (Sofia)
Tek Samf Hand — Tekniska Samfundets Handlingar
Tek Skr Stockh — Tekniska Skrifter (Stockholm)
Tekstil Prom — Tekstil'naya Promyshlennost
Tekst Ind — Tekstilna Industrija
Tekst Izd Sof — Tekstilno Izdanie (Sofiya)

Tekst Prom (Moscow) — Tekstil'naya Promyshlennost (Moscow)
Tekst Prom (Sofia) — Tekstilna Promishlennost (Sofia)
Tekst Prom-St — Tekstil'naya Promyshlennost
TEKTA — Tekstil
Tek Tidskr — Teknisk Tidskrift
Tek Tidsskr Kbh — Teknisk Tidsskrift (Kjobenhavn)
Tek Tidsskr Text Beklaednlng — Teknisk Tidsskrift for Textil og Beklaedning
Tektonika Sib — Tektonika Sibiri
Tek Ukebl — Teknisk Ukeblad
Tek Vetensk Forsk — Teknisk Vetenskaplig Forskning
Tek Yay Kavak Arast Enst (Izmit) — Teknik Yayinlar. Kavakcihk Arastirma Enstitusu (Izmit, Turkey)
TEL — Telegraaf
Tel Aviv J Inst A — Tel Aviv. Journal of the Tel Aviv University Institute of Archaeology
Tel Aviv U Inst Archaeol J — Tel Aviv University Institute of Archaeology. Journal
Telcom Rep — Telcom Report
TELEA — Tetrahedron Letters
Telecom — Telecommunications
Telecom Aust Res Q — Telecom Australia Research Quarterly
Telecom J — Telecommunication Journal of Australia
Telecom J Aust — Telecommunication Journal of Australia
Telecomm — Telecommunications
Telecomm Abstr — Telecommunications Abstracts
Telecomm J — Telecommunication Journal
Tclcoomm J Aust — Telecommunication Journal of Australia
Telecom ML — Telecom Market Letter
Telecomm Po — Telecommunications Policy
Telecomm Prod — Telecommunication Products and Technology
Telecomms — Telecommunications
Telecommun and Radio Eng Part 1 — Telecommunications and Radio Engineering. Part 1. Telecommunications
Telecommun and Radio Eng Part 2 — Telecommunications and Radio Engineering. Part 2. Radio Engineering
Telecommunications Am Ed — Telecommunications (Americas Edition)
Telecommunications Int Ed — Telecommunications (International Edition)
Telecommun J — Telecommunication Journal
Telecommun J Aust — Telecommunication Journal of Australia
Telecommun J (Engl Ed) — Telecommunication Journal (English Edition)
Telecommun J Geneva — Telecommunication Journal. International Telecommunication Union (Geneva)
Telecommun Policy — Telecommunications Policy
Telecommun Radio Eng — Telecommunications and Radio Engineering
Telecommun Radio Eng (USSR) Part 1 — Telecommunications and Radio Engineering. Part 1. Telecommunications (USSR)
Telecommun Radio Eng (USSR) Part 2 — Telecommunications and Radio Engineering (USSR). Part 2. Radio Engineering
Telecommut Rep — Telecommuting Report
Telecom Rep Engl Ed — Telecom Report (English Edition)
Tele (Engl Ed) — Tele (English Edition)
Telefon Rep — Telefon Report
Telef Rep — Telefon Report
Telefunken-Ztg — Telefunken-Zeitung
Telegen Abstr — Telegen Abstracts
Telegen Ann Rev — Telegen Annual Review
Telegen Doc Sourceb — Telegen Document Sourcebook
Telegr & Telef — Telegraaf en Telefoon
Telegr Chron — Telegraph Chronicle
Telegr Fernspr Funk U Fernseh Tech — Telegraphen-, Fernsprech-, Funk-, und Fernseh-Technik
Telegr Hilos — Telegrafia sin Hilos
Telegrm Sism Oss Ximen — Telegrammi Sismologici. Osservatorio Ximeniano
Telegr Praxis — Telegraphen-Praxis
Telegr Telef Provod — Telegrafiya i Telefoniya bez Provodov
Telegr Teleph Age — Telegraph and Telephone Age
Telegr Teleph J — Telegraph and Telephone Journal
Telegr u Fernsprechtechn — Telegraphen- und Fernsprechtechnik
Telegr Weath Rep NZ — Telegraphic Weather Reports. New Zealand
Telegr Wld — Telegraph World
Tel E J — Journal of the Society of Telegraph Engineers
Telekkon Szakl — Telekkonyvi Szaklap
Telekkon Tanacs — Telekkonyvi Tanacsado
Telematics Inf — Telematics and Informatics
Telemktg — Telemarketing
Tele News — Telephone News
Teleph Bull Cincinn — Telephone Bulletin (Cincinnati)
Teleph Bull New Haven — Telephone Bulletin (New Haven, Connecticut)
Teleph Eng & Manage — Telephone Engineer and Management
Teleph Engr — Telephone Engineer
Teleph Engr Mgmt — Telephone Engineer and Management
Teleph Mag — Telephone Magazine
Teleph News Detroit — Telephone News (Detroit)
Teleph News Philad — Telephone News (Philadelphia)
Telephone — Telephone Engineer and Management
Teleph Rev Lond — Telephone Review (London)
Teleph Rev NY — Telephone Review (New York)
Teleph Top — Telephone Topics
Teleph Wld — Telephone World
Tele (Swed Ed) — Tele (Swedish Edition)
Telesys J — Telesystems Journal
Telet — Teleteknik
Tele-Tech & Electronic Ind — Tele-Tech and Electronic Industries
Teleteknik Engl Ed — Teleteknik. English Edition
Telettra Rev — Telettra Review
Teletype Print Telegr Syst — Teletype Printing Telegraph Systems

Teletypesetter Bull — Teletypesetter Bulletin
Telev A Rep Tokyo — Television Annual Report. Institute of Television of Japan (Tokyo)
Telev Eng — Television Engineering
Telev Engng — Television Engineering
Telev Fr — Television Francaise
Television JR Telev Soc — Television. Journal of the Royal Television Society
Telev Ital — Televisione Italiana
Telev J — Television Journal
Telev News — Television News
Telev Prat — Television Pratique
Telev Quart — Television Quarterly
Telev/Radio Age — Television/Radio Age
Telev Short Wave Wld — Television and Short-Wave World
Telhan Patrica Oilseeds J — Telhan Patrica/Oilseeds Journal
Tel J — Telegraphic Journal and Electrical Review
TELLA — Tellus
Tellus Ser A — Tellus. Series A. Dynamic Meteorology and Oceanography
Tellus Ser A Dyn Meteorol Oceanogr — Tellus. Series A. Dynamic Meteorology and Oceanography
Tellus Ser B — Tellus. Series B. Chemical and Physical Meteorology
Tellus Ser B Chem Phys Meteorol — Tellus. Series B. Chemical and Physical Meteorology
TelQ — Tel Quel
Tel Rad E R — Telecommunications and Radio Engineering (USSR)
Tel Vaani — Tolugu Vaani
Tel Vr Z — Zeitschrift des Deutsch-Oesterreichischen Telegraphen-Vereins. Herausg. in dessen Auftrage von der K. Preuss. Telegraphen-Direction
TEM — Exporter. Malta's Monthly Export Journal
TeM — O Tempo e o Modo
Tem — Temoins
Tem — Tempo
Tem — Tempore
Tem — Temps Modernes
Temas Bibliotec Caracas — Temas Biblioteconomicos (Caracas)
Temas Econ Caracas — Temas Economicos (Caracas)
Temas Leprol — Temas de Leprologia
Temas Odont — Temas Odontologicos
Temas Odontol — Temas Odontologicos
Temas Quim — Temas de Quimica
Temas Quim Bibliogr Quim Argent — Temas de Quimica y Bibliografia Quimica Argentina
Temas Socs — Temas Sociales
Temas Soc S Jose — Temas Sociales (San Jose, Costa Rica)
Temat Sb Inst Fiziol Biofiz Rast Akad Nauk Tadzh SSR — Tematicheskii Sbornik Institut Fiziologii i Biofiziki Rastenii. Akademiya Nauk Tadzhikskoi SSR
Temat Sb Nauc Trud Alma-Atin Semipalatin Zoovet Inst — Tematicheskii Sbornik Nauchnykh Trudov Alma-Atinskogo i Semipalatinskogo Zooveterinarnykh Institutov
Temat Sb Otd Fiziol Biofiz Rast Akad Nauk Tadzh SSR — Tematicheskii Sbornik Otdel Fiziologii i Biofiziki Rastenii Akademiya Nauk Tadzhikskoi SSR
Temat Sb Rab Gel'mintol Skh Zhivotn — Tematicheskii Sbornik Rabot po Gel'mintologii Sel'skokhozyaistvennykh Zhivotnykh
Temat Sb Vses Nauchno Issled Inst Gidrogeol Inzh Geol — Tematicheskii Sbornik Vsesoyuznogo Nauchno-Issledovatel'skogo Instituta Gidrogeologii Inzhenerskoi Geologii
Temat Sb Vses Neftegazov Nauchno Issled Inst — Tematicheskii Sbornik Vsesoyuznyi Neftegazovyi Nauchno-Issledovatel'skii Institut
TemC — Temoignage Chretien
Tem Chr — Temoignage Chretien
TEMIA — Technische Mitteilungen
TemM — Temps Meles
TEMOA — Tecnica Molitoria
Temoi — Temoignages
Temp Bar — Temple Bar
Temp Japan — Temperature of Japan
Temple Dent Rev — Temple Dental Review
Temple Law — Temple Law Quarterly
Temple L Quart — Temple Law Quarterly
Temple Newsam Coutry House Stud — Temple Newsam Country House Studies
Temp L Q — Temple Law Quarterly
Temps Mod — Temps Modernes
Temps Nouv — Temps Nouveaux
Temps Present — Temps Present. Revue de Langue Francaise pour la Defense des Interets Vitaux de la France et ses Colonies
Temps Present Rev Mens Litt & A — Temps Present. Revue Mensuelle de Litterature et d'Art
Temp Univ LQ — Temple University. Law Quarterly
Ten — Tennessee Reports
TENCA — Traffic Engineering and Control
Tend — Tendances. Cahiers de Documentation
Tendances Conjonct — Tendances de la Conjoncture
Tendances Polit Act Dom — Tendances et Politiques Actuelles dans le Domaine de l'Habitation de la Construction et de la Planification
TEng — Teaching English
Ten Mag — Tennis Magazine
Tenn — Tennessee Reports
Tenn Admin Reg — Tennessee Administrative Register
Tenn Ag Exp — Tennessee. Agricultural Experiment Station. Publications
Tenn Agric Exp Stn Annu Rep — Tennessee. Agricultural Experiment Station. Annual Report
Tenn Agric Exp Stn Bull — Tennessee. Agricultural Experiment Station. Bulletin
Tenn Agric Exp Stn Farm Econ Bull — Tennessee. Agricultural Experiment Station. Farm Economics Bulletin
Tenn Anthrop — Tennessee Anthropologist

Tenn Anthrop Ass Newsl — Tennessee Anthropological Association Newsletter
Tenn Apiculture — Tennessee Apiculture
Tenn App — Tennessee Appeals
Tenn App Bull — Tennessee Appellate Bulletin
Tenn Bar Assn Proc — Tennessee Bar Association. Proceedings
Tenn Bar J — Tennessee Bar Journal
Tenn BJ — Tennessee Bar Journal
Tenn Code Ann — Tennessee Code Annotated
Tenn Comp R & Regs — Official Compilation Rules and Regulations of the State of Tennessee
Tenn Conservationist — Tennessee Conservationist
Tenn Crim App — Tennessee Criminal Appeals Reports
Tenn Dep Conserv Div Geol Bull — Tennessee. Department of Conservation. Division of Geology. Bulletin
Tenn Dep Conserv Div Geol Inf Circ — Tennessee. Department of Conservation. Division of Geology. Information Circular
Tenn Dept Labor Ann Rept — Tennessee. Department of Labor. Annual Report
Tenn Div Geol Bull — Tennessee. Division of Geology. Bulletin
Tenn Div Geol Environ Geol Ser — Tennessee. Division of Geology. Environmental Geology Series
Tenn Div Geol Inf Circ — Tennessee. Division of Geology. Information Circular
Tenn Div Geol Inform Circ — Tennessee. Division of Geology. Information Circular
Tenn Div Geol Rep Invest — Tennessee. Division of Geology. Report of Investigations
Tenn Div Water Resour Water Resour Ser — Tennessee. Division of Water Resources. Water Resources Series
Tenn Eng — Tennessee Engineer
Tennessee Acad Sci Jour — Tennessee Academy of Science. Journal
Tennessee Div Geology Geol Map — Tennessee. Division of Geology. Geologic Map
Tennessee Div Geology Rept Inv — Tennessee. Division of Geology. Report of Investigations
Tennessees Bus — Tennessee's Business
Tenn Farm & Home Sci — Tennessee Farm and Home Science
Tenn Farm Home Sci Prog Rep Tenn Agric Exp Stn — Tennessee Farm and Home Science. Progress Report. Tennessee Agricultural Experiment Station
Tenn Farm Home Sci Progr Rep — Tennessee Farm and Home Science. Progress Report. University of Tennessee. Agricultural Experiment Station
Tenn Fm Home Sci Prog Rep — Tennessee Farm and Home Science. Progress Report
Tenn Folk S — Tennessee Folklore Society. Bulletin
Tenn G S Res Tenn B — Tennessee State Geological Survey. Resources of Tennessee. Bulletin
Tenn His M — Tennessee Historical Magazine
Tenn Hist M — Tennessee Historical Magazine
Tenn Hist Mag — Tennessee Magazine of History
Tenn Hist Q — Tennessee Historical Quarterly
Tenn Law Rev — Tennessee Law Review
Tenn Libn — Tennessee Librarian
Tenn Libr — Tennessee Librarian
Tenn Librn — Tennessee Librarian
Tenn L R — Tennessee Law Review
Tenn L Rev — Tennessee Law Review
Tenn Mag — Tennessee Magazine
Tenn Med Assoc J — Tennessee Medical Association Journal
Tenn Priv Acts — Private Acts of the State of Tennessee
Tenn Pub Acts — Public Acts of the State of Tennessee
Tenn St Bd Health B Rp — Tennessee State Board of Health. Bulletin. Report
Tenn Surv Bus — Tennessee Survey of Business
Tenn Univ Eng Exp Sta Bull — Tennessee University. Engineering Experiment Station. Bulletin
Tenn Univ Water Resour Res Cent Res Rep — Tennessee University. Water Resources Research Center. Research Report
Tenn Val Auth Chem Eng Bul — Tennessee Valley Authority. Chemical Engineering Bulletin
Tenn Val Auth Natl Fert Dev Cent Bull Y — Tennessee Valley Authority. National Fertilizer Development Center. Bulletin Y
Tenn Val Auth Tech Mon — Tennessee Valley Authority. Technical Monographs
Tenn Val Auth Tech Rep — Tennessee Valley Authority. Technical Reports
Tenn Valley Perspect — Tennessee Valley Perspective
Tenn Wildl — Tennessee Wildlife
Tensai Kenkyu Hokoku Suppl — Tensai Kenkyu Hokoku. Supplement
Tenside — Tenside-Detergents
Tenside-Deterg — Tenside-Detergents
Tensile Test — Tensile Testing
Teolisuuden Keskuslab Tied — Teolisuuden Keskuslaboratorion Tiedonantoja
Teollis Tiedottaa — Teollisuuslitto Tiedottaa
Teol Vida — Teologia y Vida
Teor & Eksp Khim — Teoreticheskaya i Eksperimental'naya Khimiya
Teor Ehlektrotekh — Teoreticheskaya Ehlektrotekhnika
Teor Eksp Biofiz — Teoreticheskaya i Eksperimental'naya Biofizica
Teoret Elektrotekhn — L'vovskii Gosudarstvennyi Universitet. Teoreticheskaya Elektrotekhnika
Teoret i Prikladna Meh — Teoreticna i Prikladna Mehanika Harkivs'kii Derzavnii Universitet Imeni O. M. Gor'kogo
Teoret i Prikl Mekh — Belorusskii Politekhnicheski Institut. Teoreticheskaya i Prikladnaya Mekhanika
Teoret i Priloz Meh — Teoreticna i Prilozna Mehanika
Teoret Mat Fiz — Teoreticskaja i Matematiceskaja Fizika
Teoret Prikl Mat — Teoreticna i Prikladna Matematika
Teoret Priloz Meh — B'lgarska Akademija na Naukite. Teoreticna i Prilozna Mehanika
Teor Funktsii Funktsional Anal i Prilozhen — Khar'kovskii Ordena Trudovogo Krasnogo Znameni Gosudarstvennyi Universitet Imeni A. M. Gor'kogo Teoriya Funktsii Funktsional'nyi Analiz i Ikh Prilozheniya

Teoria NS — Teoria. Nuova Serie
Teorie Praxe Telesne Vych Sportu — Teorie a Praxe Telesne Vychovy a Sportu
Teor i Mat Fiz — Teoreticheskaya i Matematicheskaya Fizika
Teor Imovir ta Mat Statist — Teoriya Imovirnostei ta Matematichna Statistika
Teor Konecn Avtomatov i Prilozen — Institut Elektroniki i Vycislitel'noi Tehniki. Akademija Nauk Latviiskoi SSR. Teorija Konecnyh. Avtomatov i Ee Prilozenja
Teor Mat Fiz — Teoreticheskaya i Matematicheskaya Fizika
Teor Metod — Teorie a Metoda
Teor Osn Khim Tekhnol — Teoreticheskie Osnovy Khimicheskoi Tekhnologii
Teor Prakt — Teoriya Praktika
Teor Prakt Fiz Kul't — Teoriya i Praktika Fizicheskoi Kul'tury
Teor Prakt Katal Reakts Khim Polim — Teoriya i Praktika Kataliticheskikh Reaktsii i Khimii Polimerov
Teor Prakt Metall — Teoriya i Praktika Metallurgii (Chelyabinsk)
Teor Prakt Metall (Chelyabinsk) — Teoriya i Praktika Metallurgii (Chelyabinsk)
Teor Prakt Metall (Dnepropetrovsk) — Teoriya i Praktika Metallurgii (Dnepropetrovsk)
Teor Prakt Podgot Koksovaniya Uglei — Teoriya i Praktika Podgotovki i Koksovaniya Uglei
Teor Prakt Stomatol — Teoriya i Praktika Stomatologii
Teor Prakt Szhiganiya Gaza — Teoriya i Praktika Szhiganiya Gaza
Teor Prakt Vopr Mikrobiol Epidemiol — Teoreticheskie i Prakticheskie Voprosy Mikrobiologii i Epidemiologii
Teor Prakt Vopr Mikrobiol Epidemiol Resp Mezhved Sb — Teoreticheskie i Prakticheskie Voprosy Mikrobiologii i Epidemiologii Respublikanskii Mezhvedomstvennyi Sbornik
Teor Prakt Vopr Vaktsinno Syvorot Dela — Teoreticheskie i Prakticheskie Voprosy Vaktsinno Syvorotochnogo Dela
Teor Prilozh Mekh — Teoreticna i Prilozhna Mekhanika
Teor Primen Meh — Jugoslovensko Drustvo za Mehaniku. Teorijska i Primenjena Mehanika
Teor Rozvoje Vedy — Teorie Rozvoje Vedy
Teor Verojatn Mat Stat — Teoriya Verojatnostei i Matematicheskaya Statistika
Teor Verojatnost i Mat Statist — Teorija Verojatnostei i Matematiceskaja Statistika
Teor Veroya — Teoriya Veroyatnostei i Ee Primeneniya
Teor Veroyatn i Primen — Teoriya Veroyatnostei i Ee Primeneniya
Teor Veroyatn Primen — Teoriya Veroyatnostei i Ee Primeneniya
Teor Veroyat Primen — Teoriya Veroyatnostei i Ee Primeneniya
Teor Vopr Obrab Pochv — Teoreticheskie Voprosy Obrabotki Pochv
Tepl Naprazh Elem Konstr — Teplovye Napryazheniya v Elementakh Konstruktsii
Teploehnerg — Teploehnergetika
Teploenergetika Akad Nauk SSSR Energ Inst — Teploenergetika Akademiya Nauk SSSR. Energeticheskii Institut
Teplofiz Aeromekh — Teplofizika i Aeromekhanika
Teplofiz Kharakt Veshchestv — Teplofizicheskie Kharakteristiki Veshchestv
Teplofiz Optim Tepl Protsessov — Teplofizika i Optimizatsiya Teplovykh Protsessov
Teplofiz Svoistva Veshchestv — Teplofizicheskie Svoistva Veshchestv
Teplofiz Svoistva Veshchestv Mater — Teplofizicheskie Svoistva Veshchestv i Materialov
Teplofiz Teplotekh — Teplofizika i Teplotekhnika
Teplofiz Vys Temp — Teplofizika Vysokikh Temperatur
Teploprovodnost Diffuz — Teploprovodnost i Diffuziya
Teplosi Khoz — Teplosilovoc Khozyaistvo
Teplosil Khoz — Teplosilovoe Khozyaistvo
Teplotekh Probl Pryamogo Preobraz Energ — Teplotekhnicheskie Problemy Pryamogo Preobrazovaniya Energii
TePr — Temps Present
TER — Telecommunications Electronic Reviews
TeR — Te Reo
TERAA — Terapia
Terap Antibiot Chemioter — Terapia, Antibiotica, e Chemioterapia
Terap Arkh — Terapevticheskii Arkhiv
Terap Contemp — Terapia Contemporanea
Terap Ezhem — Terapevticheskii Ezhemesyachnik
Terap Ital — Terapia Italiana
Terap Med Tumori — Terapia Medica dei Tumori
Terap Mod — Terapia Moderna
Terap Obozr — Terapevticheskoe Obozrenie
Ter Arkh — Terapevticheskii Arkhiv
Teratog Carcinog Mutagen — Teratogenesis, Carcinogenesis, and Mutagenesis
Teratogenesis Carcinog Mutagen — Teratogenesis, Carcinogenesis, and Mutagenesis
TEREA — Technology Review
Ter Forma — Ter es Forma
Terkep Kozl — Terkepeszeti Kozlony
TERMA — Termotecnica
Termeloeszoevet Tanacsadoja — Termeloeszoevetkezetek Tanacsadoja
Termeszet Allatt Vadasz Foly — Termeszet Allattani es Vadaszati Folyoirat
Termeszetr Fuz — Termeszetrajzi Fuzetek
Termeszet Tarsad — Termeszet es Tarsadalom
Termeszettud Elem — Termeszettudomanyok Elemei
Termeszettud Fuez — Termeszettudomanyi Fuezetek
Termeszettud Koezloeny — Termeszettudomanyi Koezloeny
Term Gazd Mest Esm Tara — Termeszet, Gazdasagi, es Mestersegi Esmeretek Tara
Termobarogeokhim Mineraloobraz Protsessov — Termobarogeokhimiya Mineraloobrazuyushchikh Protsessov
Term Obrab Chern Metall — Termicheskaya Obrabotka Chernykh Metallov. Vsesoyuznoe Nauchnoe Inzhenerno-Tekhnicheskoe Obshchestvo Metallurgov
Term Obrab Fiz Met — Termicheskaya Obrabotka i Fizika Metallov
Termodin Fiz Kinet Strukturoobra Svoista Chuguna Stali — Termodinamika i Fizicheskaya Kinetika Strukturoobrazovaniya i Svoistva Chuguna i Stali
Termodin Fiz Kinet Strukturoobraz Stali Chugune — Termodinamika i Fizicheskaya Kinetika Strukturoobrazovaniya v Stali i Chugune

Termodin Fiz Kinet Strukturoobraz Svoistva Chuguna Stali — Termodinamika i Fizicheskaya Kinetika Strukturoobrazovaniya i Svoistva Chugunai Stali

Termoprochn Mater Konstr Elem — Termoprochnost Materialov i Konstruktivnykh Elementov

Termotecnica Suppl — Termotecnica. Supplemento

Ter Ortop Stomatol — Terapevticheskaya i Ortopedicheskaya Stomatologiva

Terra Amer — Terra America

Terrae Incog — Terrae Incognitae

Terra Lav — Terra e Lavoro

Terramycine Infs — Terramycine Informations

Terra Port — Terra Portuguesa. Revista Ilustrada de Arqueologia, Artistica, e Etnografia

Terra Sole — Terra e Sole

Terra Trent — Terra Trontina

Terr Behav Pestic — Terrestrial Behavior of Pesticides

Terre Maroc — Terre Marocaine

Terre Meth — Terre et Methode

Terres Australes Antarct Fr — Terres Australes et Antarctiques Francaises

Terres Eaux — Terres et Eaux

Terre Vaud — Terre Vaudoise. Journal Agricole

Terre Vie — Terre et la Vie

Terre Vie Rev Ecol Appl — Terre et la Vie. Revue d'Ecologie Appliquee

Ter Rev Med — Terapeutica. Revista de Medicina

Terr Incog — Terrae Incognitae. The Annals of the Society for the History of Discoveries

Territ — Torritorian

Terr LJ — Territory Law Journal

Terr Mag — Terrestrial Magnetism and Atmospheric Electricity

Terr Magn — Terrestrial Magnetism and Atmospheric Electricity

Terr Magn Atmos Elect — Terrestrial Magnetism and Atmospheric Electricity

Terr Magn Atmos Electr — Terrestrial Magnetism and Atmospheric Electricity

Terror — Terrorism

Ter Stomatol — Terapevticheskaya Stomatologiya

Tertiary Res Spec Pap — Tertiary Research Special Papers

TERU — Teruletrendezes

Terv Kirj — Terveyden Kirjasia

Terylene Tech Inf Notes — Terylene Technical Information Notes

Tes — Tesaur

TES — Textiles Suisses. Revue de l'Industrie Suisse des Textiles d'Habillement

TES — Times Educational Supplement

TESDA — Tenside [Later, Tenside-Detergents]

TeSE — Texas Studies in English

TESG — Tijdschrift voor Economische en Sociale Geografie

TESG-A — Tijdschrift voor Economische en Sociale Geografie

Tesis Mus La Plata — Tesis del Museo de La Plata

TESL — Transactions. Ethnological Society (London)

Tesla Electron — Tesla Electronics

Tesla Electron Q Rev Czech Electron Telecommun — Tesla Electronics. Quarterly Review of Czechoslovak Electronics and Telecommunications

TESL Can J — TESL [Teaching English as a Second Language] Canada Journal

TESOB — Terra e Sole

TESOL Newsl — TESOL (Teachers of English to Speakers of Other Languages) Newsletter

TESOLQ — TESOL [Teachers of English to Speakers of Other Languages] Quarterly

TESOL Quart — TESOL [Teachers of English to Speakers of Other Languages] Quarterly

Tesoro Sacro M — Tesoro Sacro-Musical

Tess Nuovi — Tessili Nuovi

Test AGN Paradigm — Testing the AGN Paradigm

Test Eng Manage — Test Engineering and Management

Test Eval IR Detect Arrays II — Test and Evaluation of IR Detectors and Arrays II

Test Instrum Controls — Testing, Instruments, and Controls

Test Leafl Shirley Inst — Test Leaflets. Shirley Institute

Test Memo Mines Dep — Testing Memoranda. Mines Department

Test Memor Timb Res Developm Ass — Test Memorandum. Timber Research and Development Association

Test Polym — Testing of Polymers

Test Rec Timb Res Developm Ass — Test Record. Timber Research and Development Association

Test Rep Forest Exp Sta Ryukyu Gov — Testing Report. Forestry Experiment Station. Ryukyu Government/Ryukyu Seifu Keizai Kyoku Ringyo Shikenjo Kenkyu Hokoku

Test Rep Ship Lab Can — Test Report. Ship Laboratory. National Research Laboratories. Canada

Test Room Obsns Ringsdorff Carb — Test Room Observations. Ringsdorff Carbons

Tests Agrochem Cult — Tests of Agrochemicals and Cultivars

Tests Agrochem Cultiv — Tests of Agrochemicals and Cultivars

Test Top — Testing Topics

TeT — Taal en Tongval

TETHB — Tethys

Tethys Suppl — Tethys. Supplement

TETRA — Tetrahedron

Tetrabromoeth Bull — Tetrabromoethane Bulletin

Tetrahedr L — Tetrahedron Letters

Tetrahedron Lett — Tetrahedron Letters

Tetrahedron Suppl — Tetrahedron. Supplement

Tetsu Hagan — Tetsu To Hagane Journal. Iron and Steel Institute of Japan

Tetsu To Hagane Abstr — Tetsu-to-Hagane Abstracts. Iron and Steel Institute of Japan

TETYC — Teaching English in the Two-Year College

TEU — Ter Elfder Ure

Teubner — Bibliotheca Scriptorum Graecorum et Romanorum Teubneriana

Teubner Arch Math — Teubner-Archiv zur Mathematik

Teubner Skr Math Stochastik — Teubner Skripten zur Mathematischen Stochastik

Teubner Skr Numer — Teubner Skripten zur Numerik

Teubner Studienbuech Inform — Teubner Studienbuecher Informatik

Teubner Studienbuech Math — Teubner Studienbuecher Mathematik

Teubner Studienbuech Phys — Teubner Studienbuecher Physik

Teubner Studienskr — Teubner Studienskripten

Teubner Texte Phys — Teubner-Texte zur Physik

Teubner-Texte zur Math — Teubner-Texte zur Mathematik

Teut — Teuthonista

Teuth — Teuthonista

TEW Tech Ber — TEW [Technische Edelstahlwerke] Technische Berichte

TEX — Revue Francaise des Telecommunications

Tex — Texas Reports

Tex A & M Univ Dep Civ Eng Rep — Texas A & M University. Department of Civil Engineering. Report

Tex A & M Univ Sea Grant Coll TAMU-SG — Texas A & M University Sea Grant College. TAMU-SG

Tex A & M Univ Syst Tex Agric Ext Serv Fish Dis Diagn Lab — Texas A & M University System. Texas Agricultural Extension Service. Fish Disease Diagnostic Laboratory

Tex A & M Univ Tex Eng Exp Stn Tech Bull — Texas A & M University. Texas Engineering Experiment Station. Technical Bulletin

Tex Admin Code — Texas Administrative Code

Tex Ag Exp — Texas. Agricultural Experiment Station. Publications

Tex Agric Exp Stn Bull — Texas. Agricultural Experiment Station. Bulletin

Tex Agric Exp Stn Leafl — Texas. Agricultural Experiment Station. Leaflet

Tex Agric Exp Stn Misc Publ — Texas. Agricultural Experiment Station. Miscellaneous Publication

Tex Agric Exp Stn Prog Rep — Texas. Agricultural Experiment Station. Progress Report

Tex Agric Exp Stn Res Monogr — Texas. Agricultural Experiment Station. Research Monograph

Tex Agric Exp Stn Tech Monogr — Texas. Agricultural Experiment Station. Technical Monograph

Tex Agric Ext Serv Fish Dis Diagn Lab — Texas. Agricultural Extension Service. Fish Disease Diagnostic Laboratory

Tex Agric Prog — Texas Agricultural Progress

Tex Agric Prog Tex Agric Exp Stn — Texas Agricultural Progress. Texas Agricultural Experiment Station

Tex Agr Progr — Texas Agricultural Progress

Tex A M Univ Oceanogr Stud — Texas A & M University. Oceanographic Studies

Tex A M Univ Syst Tex Agric Ext Serv Fish Dis Diagn Lab FDDL — Texas A & M University System. Texas Agricultural Extension Service. Fish Disease Diagnostic Laboratory. FDDL

Tex App — Texas Appeals Reports

Tex Applic Notes — Texas Application Notes. Texas Instruments

Texas Acad of Sci Trans — Texas Academy of Sciences. Transactions

Texas Ac Sc T — Transactions of the Texas Academy of Science

Texas Agric Exp Sta Techn Monogr — Texas Agricultural Experiment Station. Technical Monograph

Texas AM Univ IUCCP Annu Symp — Texas A and M University. IUCCP Annual Symposium

Texas AM Univ IUCCP Annu Symp Appl Enzyme Biotechnol — Texas A and M University. IUCCP Annual Symposium on Applications of Enzyme Biotechnology

Texas Archaeol And Paleontol Soc Bul — Texas Archaeological and Paleontological Society. Bulletin

Texas Archeol Paleont Soc Bull — Texas Archeological and Paleontological Society. Bulletin

Texas BJ — Texas Bar Journal

Texas Board of Water Engineers Bull — Texas. Board of Water Engineers. Bulletin

Texas Bus — Texas Business

Texas Bus Rev — Texas Business Review

Texas Cour Rec Med — Texas Courier Record of Medicine

Texas Dental Jour — Texas Dental Journal. Texas State Dental Society

Texas Eng Expt Sta Research Rept — Texas. Engineering Experiment Station. Research Report

Texas Engrg Experiment Station Monograph Ser — Texas Engineering Experiment Station Monograph Series

Texas Finite Elem Ser — Texas Finite Element Series

Texas Folk Lore Soc Publ — Texas Folk-lore Society. Publications

Texas Hist Assn Q — Texas Historical Association. Quarterly

Texas Internat L Forum — Texas International Law Forum

Texas Internat LJ — Texas International Law Journal

Texas Int'l LF — Texas International Law Forum

Texas Int'l LJ — Texas International Law Journal

Texas Jour Sci — Texas Journal of Science

Texas J Sci — Texas Journal of Science

Texas Law Rev — Texas Law Review. University of Texas

Texas L Rev — Texas Law Review

Texas Med — Texas Medicine

Texas Med Assn Trans — Texas Medical Association. Transactions

Texas Memorial Mus Pearce-Sellards Ser — Texas Memorial Museum. Pearce-Sellards Series

Texas MJ — Texas Medical Journal

Texas Mo — Texas Monthly

Texas Nurs — Texas Nursing

Texas Oil Jour — Texas Oil Journal

Texas Petroleum Research Comm Bull — Texas Petroleum Research Committee. Bulletin

Texas Rep Biol Med — Texas Reports on Biology and Medicine

Texas South UL Rev — Texas Southern University. Law Review

Texas State J Med — Texas State Journal of Medicine

Texas Stud in Lit & Lang — Texas Studies in Literature and Language

Texas Tech L Rev — Texas Tech Law Review

Texas Tech Univ Math Ser — Texas Tech University Mathematics Series
Texas Univ Austin Bur Econ Geology Geol Circ — Texas University at Austin. Bureau of Economic Geology. Geological Circular
Texas Univ Austin Bur Econ Geology Geol Quad Map — University of Texas at Austin. Bureau of Economic Geology. Geologic Quadrangle Map
Texas Univ Austin Bur Econ Geology Guidebook — Texas University at Austin. Bureau of Economic Geology. Guidebook
Texas Univ Austin Bur Econ Geology Rept Inv — University of Texas at Austin. Bureau of Economic Geology. Report of Investigations
Texas Univ Pub Bur Econ Geology Mineral Res Circ Rept Inv — Texas University. Publication. Bureau of Economic Geology. Mineral Resource Circular. Report of Investigations
Texas Water Devel Board Rept — Texas. Water Development Board. Report
Tex Bank Rec — Texas Bankers Record
Tex B Assn Proc — Texas Bar Association. Proceedings
Tex B J — Texas Bar Journal
Tex Board Water Eng Bull — Texas. Board of Water Engineers. Bulletin
Tex Board Water Eng Chem Compos Tex Surf Waters — Texas. Board of Water Engineers. Chemical Composition of Texas Surface Waters
Tex Bus Corp Act Ann (Vernon) — Texas Business Corporation Act Annotated (Vernon)
Tex Bus Exec — Texas Business Executive
Tex Busin Rev — Texas Business Review
Tex Bus R — Texas Business Review
Tex Bus Rev — Texas Business Review
Tex Cancer Bull — Texas Cancer Bulletin
Tex Civ App — Texas Civil Appeals Reports
Tex Civ Cas — Texas Court of Appeals Decisions. Civil Cases
Tex Coach — Texas Coach
Tex Code An (Vernon) — Texas Codes Annotated (Vernon)
Tex Code Crim Proc Ann (Vernon) — Texas Code of Criminal Procedure Annotated (Vernon)
Tex Cour Rec Med — Texas Courier-Record of Medicine
Tex Crim — Texas Criminal Reports
Tex Cur Bib Ind — Texas Current Bibliography and Index
Tex Dent Assist Assoc Bull — Texas Dental Assistants Association. Bulletin
Tex Dent J — Texas Dental Journal
Tex Energy — Texas Energy
Tex Energy Miner Resour — Texas Energy and Mineral Resources
Tex Eng Exp Stn Bull — Texas. Engineering Experiment Station. Bulletin
Tex Eng Exp Stn News — Texas. Engineering Experiment Station. News
Tex Eng Exp Stn Res Rep — Texas. Engineering Experiment Station. Research Report
Tex Engng Exp Stn News — Texas Engineering Experiment Station News
Tex Engr — Texas Engineer
Tex For Pap — Texas Forestry Paper
Tex Game Fish — Texas Game and Fish
Tex Gen Laws — General and Special Laws of the State of Texas
Tex Geogr Mag — Texas Geographic Magazine
Tex G S Rp Prog — Texas. Geological Survey. Report of Progress
Tex Heart Inst J — Texas Heart Institute. Journal
Tex Highw — Texas Highways
Tex His Q — Texas State Historical Association. Quarterly
Tex Hist Assoc Q — Texas State Historical Association. Quarterly
Tex Hlth Mag — Texas Health Magazine
Tex Hosp — Texas Hospitals
Tex Hospitals — Texas Hospitals
Tex Ins Code Ann (Vernon) — Texas Insurance Code Annotated (Vernon)
Tex Inst — Texas Institutes
Tex Int L Forum — Texas International Law Forum
Tex Int L J — Texas International Law Journal
Tex Intl LJ — Texas International Law Journal
Tex J — Texas Journal
Tex J Pharm — Texas Journal of Pharmacy
Tex J Sci — Texas Journal of Science
Tex J Sci Spec Publ — Texas Journal of Science. Special Publication
Tex La Petrol Rec — Texas-Louisiana Petroleum Record
Tex Law Rev — Texas Law Review
Tex Lib — Texas Libraries
Tex Lib J — Texas Library Journal
Tex Libr — Texas Libraries
Tex LJ — Texas Law Journal
Tex L R — Texas Law Review
Tex L Rev — Texas Law Review
Tex Med — Texas Medicine
Tex Mem Mus Misc Pap — Texas Memorial Museum. Miscellaneous Papers
Tex Mo — Texas Monthly
Tex Munic — Texas Municipalities
Tex Nurs — Texas Nursing
Tex Nutr Conf Proc — Texas Nutrition Conference. Proceedings
Tex Outl — Texas Outlook
Tex Parks Wildl — Texas Parks Wildlife
Tex Pharm — Texas Pharmacy
Tex Prob Code Ann (Vernon) — Texas Probate Code Annotated (Vernon)
Tex Q — Texas Quarterly
Tex Quart — Texas Quarterly
Tex R Civ P Ann (Vernon) — Texas Rules of Civil Procedure Annotated (Vernon)
Tex Reg — Texas Register
Tex Rep Bio — Texas Reports on Biology and Medicine
Tex Rep Biol Med — Texas Reports on Biology and Medicine
Tex Rep Bio Med — Texas Report on Biological Medicine
Tex Res — Textile Research
Tex Res J — Textile Research Journal
Tex Rev — Texas Review

Tex Rev Civ Stat Ann (Vernon) — Texas Revised Civil Statutes Annotated (Vernon)
Tex Rly J — Texas Railway Journal
Texrope V Belt Guide — Texrope V-Belt Guide
Tex Sess Law Serv (Vernon) — Texas Session Law Service (Vernon)
Tex So Intra L Rev — Texas Southern Intramural Law Review
Tex So LR — Texas Southern Law Review
Tex So U L Rev — Texas Southern University. Law Review
Tex State Hist Assoc Quar — Texas State Historical Association. Quarterly
Tex St J Med — Texas State Journal of Medicine
Tex Stk Fm Irrig — Texas Stock Farm and Irrigation
Tex St Lit — Texas Studies in Literature and Language
Tex Stud Lit & Lang — Texas Studies in Literature and Language
Tex SUL Rev — Texas Southern University. Law Review
Tex Sup Ct J — Texas Supreme Court Journal
Tex Symp Relativ Astrophys Cosmol — Texas Symposium on Relativistic Astrophysics and Cosmology
TEXTA — Technical Extracts of Traffic
Text Abstr — Textile Abstracts
Text Adv News — Textile Advance News
Text Age — Textile Age
Text Am — Textile American
Text Anal Bull Serv TABS — Textile Analysis Bulletin Service. TABS
Text Argus — Textile Argus
Text Asia — Textile Asia
TextB — Melliands Textil-Berichte
Text Beklaedning — Textil og Beklaedning
Text Belge Revue — Textile-Belge-Revue
TextBer Wiss Ind Hand — Textilberichte ueber Wissenschaft, Industrie und Handel
Text Betr (Poessneck Ger) — Textil-Betrich (Poessneck, Germany)
Text Blue Bk — Textile Blue Book
Textbooks Math Sci — Textbooks in Mathematical Sciences
Text Bull — Textile Bulletin
Text Chem — Textil a Chemia
TextChem Color — Textilchemiker und Colorist
Text Chem Color — Textile Chemist and Colorist
Textchem Erfind — Textilchemische Erfindungen
TextChem U Kolor — Textilchemiker und -Kolorist
Text Chim — Textiles Chimiques
Text Color — Textile Colorist
Text Color Convert — Textile Colorist and Converter
Text Color Converter — Textile Colorist and Converter
Text Colour Wld — Textile Colouring World and Bleaching and Finishing Review
Text Cordage Q — Textile and Cordage Quarterly
Text Cord Q — Textile and Cordage Quarterly
Text Dig — Textile Digest
Text Dyer Printer — Textile Dyer and Printer
Tex Tech LR — Texas Tech Law Review
Tex Tech L Rev — Texas Tech Law Review
Text Econ — Textile Economist
Texte Didakt Math — Texte zur Didaktik der Mathematik
Texte Kritisch Psych — Texte zur Kritischen Psychologie
TexteM — Texte Metzler
Texte Math Naturwiss Forsch Lehre — Texte zur Mathematisch-Naturwissenschaftlichen Forschung und Lehre
Texte Mem Ass Med Lang Fr Am N — Texte des Memoires. Association des Medecins de Langue Francaise de l'Amerique du Nord
Text Engr — Textile Engineer
Texte Rapp C R Debats Un Int Peril Vener — Texte des Rapports et Compte Rendu des Debats. Assemblee Generale. Union Internationale Contre le Peril Venerien
Textes et Doc (Bruxelles) — Textes et Documents (Bruxelles)
Textes Math — Textes Mathematiques
Text Export — Textile Exporter
Tex-Text — Tex-Textilis
Text Faerberei Ztg — Textil und Faerberei-Zeitung
Text Faserstofftech — Textil und Faserstofftechnik
Text Forsch — Textil-Forschung
Text Hist — Textile History
Text Horiz — Textile Horizons
Text Horizons — Textile Horizons
Text I Ind — Textile Institute and Industry
Textilchem Color — Textilchemiker und Colorist
Textile Hist — Textile History
Textile Ind — Textile Industries
Textile Inst — Textile Institute and Industry
Textile Inst Ind — Textile Institute and Industry
Textile J Aust — Textile Journal of Australia
Textile Jl — Textile Research Journal
Textile Mfr — Textile Manufacturer
Textile Mus J — Textile Museum Journal
Textile Progr — Textile Progress
Textile Res J — Textile Research Journal
Textile Technol Dig — Textile Technology Digest
Textil Ind — Textile Industries
Textil Konfekt — Textil och Konfektion
Textil Mnth — Textile Month
Textil Prax — Textil Praxis International
Textil Rent — Textile Rental
Textil Rep — America's Textiles Reporter/Bulletin Edition
Textilvered — Textilveredelung
Textil-W — Textil-Wirtschaft
Textil Wld — Textile World
Textil Wld — Textile World Buyer's Guide/Fact File

Text Ind — Textile Industries
Text Ind Dyegest Sthn Afr — Textile Industries Dyegest Southern Africa
Text Ind Export — Textile Industry and Exporter
Text Ind Exporter — Textile Industry and Exporter
Text Ind (Moenchen Gladbach Ger) — Textil-Industrie (Moenchen Gladbach, Germany)
Text Ind (Munich) — Textil-Industrie (Munich)
Text Inds — Textile Industries
Text Inds Fibr — Textile Industries and Fibres
Text Ind Sthn Afr — Textile Industries Southern Africa
Text Ind (Zurich) — Textil-Industrie (Zurich)
Text Inf Users Coun Proc Meet — Textile Information Users Council. Proceedings of the Meeting
Text Inst Ann Rep — Textile Institute. Annual Report
Text Inst Ind — Textile Institute and Industry
Text J Aust — Textile Journal of Australia
Text Konfekt — Textil och Konfektion
Text Krit — Text und Kritik
Text Mag — Textile Magazine
Text Manuf J — Textile Manufacturer's Journal
Text Mercury Int — Textile Mercury International
Text Metod Mat — Textos de Metodos Matematicos
Text Mfr — Textile Manufacturer
Text Mitt — Textil-Mitteilungen
Text MJ — Textile Museum Journal
Text Mon — Textile Month
Text Mus J — Textile Museum Journal
Text Obz — Textilni Obzor
Text Organon — Textile Organon
Textos Mat Ser B — Textos de Matematica. Serie B
Textos Univ — Textos Universitarios
Text Pat Newsl — Textile Patents Newsletter
Text-Prax — Textil-Praxis [*Later, Textil Praxis International*]
Text Prax Int — Textil Praxis International
Text Prog — Textile Progress
Text Q — Textile Quarterly
Text Qual Control Pap — Textile Quality Control Papers
Tex Transp Res — Texas Transportation Researcher
Text Raw Mater — Textile Raw Materials
Text Rdsch — Textil-Rundschau
Text Rec — Textile Recorder
Text Rec A — Textile Recorder Annual
Text Rec Bk Yr — Textile Recorder Book of the Year
Text Rec Yb — Textile Recorder Year Book
Text Rent — Textile Rental
Text Res — Textile Research
Text Res J — Textile Research Journal
Text Rev Boston — Textile Review (Boston)
Text Rev Manchr — Textile Review (Manchester)
Text Rev Osaka — Textile Review (Osaka)
Text Ring — Textil-Ring
Text Rundsch — Textil-Rundschau
Texts Appl Math — Texts in Applied Mathematics
Text Sci Taichung — Textile Science (Taichung)
Texts Comput Mech — Texts on Computational Mechanics
Texts Monographs Comput Sci — Texts and Monographs in Computer Science
Texts Monographs Phys — Texts and Monographs in Physics
Texts Monogr Symbol Comput — Texts and Monographs in Symbolic Computation
Texts Read Math — Texts and Readings in Mathematics
Texts Statist Sci Ser — Texts in Statistical Science Series
Text Tech Dig — Textile Technology Digest
Text Technol Dig — Textile Technology Digest
Text U FaerbZtg — Textil- und Faerbereizeitung
Text U Faserstofftech — Textil- und Faserstofftechnik
Texture Cryst Solids — Texture of Crystalline Solids
Textures and Microstruct — Textures and Microstructures
Textures Microstruct — Textures and Microstructures
Text Wkly — Textile Weekly
Text Wld — Textile World
Text Wld J — Textile World Journal
Text Wld Rec — Textile World Record
Text World — Textile World
Text World J — Textile World Journal
Text World R — Textile World Record
Text Yb — Textile Year-Book
Tex Univ B Min S B — Texas University. Bulletin. Mineral Survey Bulletin
Tex Univ Bur Econ Geol Geol Circ — Texas University. Bureau of Economic Geology. Geological Circular
Tex Univ Bur Econ Geol Miner Resour Circ — Texas University. Bureau of Economic Geology. Mineral Resource Circular
Tex Univ Bur Econ Geol Publ — Texas University. Bureau of Economic Geology. Publication
Tex Univ Bur Econ Geol Rep Invest — Texas University. Bureau of Economic Geology. Report of Investigations
Tex Univ Bur Econ Geol Res Note — Texas University. Bureau of Economic Geology. Research Note
Tex Univ Bur Eng Res Circ — Texas University. Bureau of Engineering Research. Circular
Tex Univ Cent Res Water Resour Tech Rep — Texas University. Center for Research in Water Resources. Technical Report
Tex Univ Publ — Texas University. Publication
Tex Vet Bull — Texas Veterinary Bulletin
TE (XVIII) — Textos y Estudios del Siglo XVIII
Tex Water Comm Bull — Texas Water Commission. Bulletin

Tex Water Comm Circ — Texas Water Commission. Circular
Tex Water Comm Mem Rep — Texas Water Commission. Memorandum Report
Tex Water Dev Board Rep — Texas. Water Development Board. Report
TeZ — Texte und Zeichen
Tez Doklad Nauch Konf Zootech Sek — Tezisy Dokladov Nauchnoi Konferentsii. Zootekhnicheskaya Sektsiya
Tezhka Prom — Tezhka Promishlenost
Tezisy Dokl Vses Nauchno Metod Konf Vet Patoloanat — Tezisy Dokladov Vsesoyuznoi Nauchno-Metodicheskoi Konferentsii Veterinarnykh Patologoanatomov
TF — Textes Francais. Collection des Universites de France. Publiees sous les Auspices de l'Association Guillaume Bude
TF — Tierra Firme
TF — Tijdschrift voor Filosofie
TF — Transformation
TFA — Taxation for Accountants
TFAT — Technology for Alaskan Transportation
TFB — Travaux. Brussels. Universite. Faculte de Philosophie et Lettres
TF Byz Ng Phil — Texte und Forschungen zur Byzantinisch-Neugriechischen Philologie
TFHSA — Tennessee Farm and Home Science
T Fjk — Tidsskrift for Fjerkraeavlerforening
TfK — Tidskrift foer Konstvetinskap
TFKVA — Teplofizicheskie Kharakteristiki Veshchestv
TFM — Societe des Textes Francais Modernes
TFM — Textes Francais Modernes
TFMSA — Transactions. Free Museum of Science and Art. University of Pennsylvania
TFORA — Tekniskt Forum
TFR — Technological Forecasting and Social Change. An International Journal
T Fro — Tidsskrift for Froavl
TFS — Technological Forecasting and Social Change
TFSB — Tennessee Folklore Society. Bulletin
TFSCB — Technological Forecasting and Social Change
TFSOA — Transactions. Faraday Society
TFSOA4 — Faraday Society. Transactions
TFSP — Texas Folklore Society. Publications
TFST — Thin Films Science and Technology
TFTTA — Teplofizika i Teplotekhnika
TFW — Tokyo Financial Wire
TFWBKEL — Theologische Forschung Wissenschaftliche Beitraege zur Kirchlichevangelischen Lehre
TFZ — Telefunken-Zeitschrift
TG — Technisch Gemeenteblad. Officieel Orgaan van de Bond van Hoofden vanGemeentewerken en van de Hinderweten Bouwtoezichtvereniging
TG — Theologie und Glaube
TG — Therapeutic Gazette
TG — Tijdschrift voor Gemeenterecht
TG — Tijdschrift voor Geschiedenis. Land en Volkenkunde
TG — Toho Gakuho
TG — TV Guide
TGA — Trade with Greece (Athens)
TGA — Tuebinger Germanistische Arbeiten
TGAJA8 — TGA [*Toilet Goods Association*] Cosmetic Journal
TGANA — Tsitologiya i Genetika
TGA (Toilet Goods Assoc) Cosmet J — TGA (Toilet Goods Association) Cosmetic Journal
TGCGA — Transactions. Gulf Coast Association of Geological Societies
T Gd — Tidsskrift for Gedeavlsforeninger
TGDR — Tokyo Gailkokugo Daigaku Ronshu
T Geesteswet — Tydskrif vir Geesteswetenskappe
TGegw — Theologie der Gegenwart
TGEOD — Technika Poszukiwan Geologicznych
T Gesch — Tijdschrift voor Geschiedenis
TGF — Tijdschrift Gemeente-Financien
TGF — Tijdschrift voor Geschiedenis en Folklore
TGF — Tragicorum Graecorum Fragmenta
TGGL-B — Travaux Geographique de Liege (Belgium)
TGI — Instellingen
TGI — Target Group Index
TGIM — Trudy Gosudarstvennogo Istoriceskogo Muzeja
TGKHA — Takenaka Gijutsu Kenkyu Hokoku
TGKZA — Trudy Instituta Geologicheskikh Nauk Akademiya Nauk Kazakhskoi SSR
T Gl — Theologie und Glaube
TGL — Thesaurus Graecae Linguae
TGLV — Tijdschrift voor Geschiedenis. Land en Volkenkunde
TGM — Theatre Guild Magazine
TGMEA — Tropical and Geographical Medicine
TGorPI — Trudy Goriiskogo Gosudarstvennogo Pedagogicheskogo Instituta
TGO Tijdschr Ther Geneesmiddel Onder — TGO. Tijdschrift voor Therapie, Geneesmiddel, en Onderzoek
TGP — Tasmanian Government Publications
TGPIA — Trudy Gruzinskii Politekhnicheskii Institut Imeni V. I. Lenina
TGR — Tohoku Gakuin Daigaku Ronshu
T Gr F — Tragicorum Graecorum Fragmenta
TGSDA — Tulsa Geological Society. Digest
TGSG — Transactions. Gaelic Society of Glasgow
TGSI — Transactions. Gaelic Society of Inverness
TGT — German Tribune
TGUBA — Bulletin. Tokyo Gakugei University
TGUOS — Transactions. Glasgow University Oriental Society
TGW — Theologie der Gegenwart
TGZIA — Technische Gids voor Ziekenhuis en Instelling
TH — Teaching History
TH — Teki Historyczne

TH — Terre Humaine
Th — Theatre
Th — Themis. Verzameling van Bijdragen tot de Kennis van het PubliekenPrivaatrecht
Th — Theologia
Th — Theology
Th — Things
TH — Thoth
Th — Thought
TH — Tiroler Heimat. Jahrbuch fuer Geschichte und Volkskunde de Tirois
TH — Today's Health
ThA — Theatre Annual
ThA — Theatre Arts
(Thai) Bus R — Business Review (Thailand)
Thai J Agric Sci — Thai Journal of Agricultural Science
Thai J Dev Adm — Thai Journal of Development Administration
Thai J Nurs — Thai Journal of Nursing
Thai J Surg — Thai Journal of Surgery
Thailand Dep Miner Resour Ground Water Bull — Thailand. Department of Mineral Resources. Ground Water Bulletin
Thailand Dep Miner Resour Rep Invest — Thailand. Department of Mineral Resources. Report of Investigation
Thailheimer's Synth Methods of Org Chem Yearb — Thailheimer's Synthetic Methods of Organic Chemistry Yearbook
Thail Plant Prot Serv Tech Bull — Thailand Plant Protection Service. Technical Bulletin
Thai Natl Sci Pap Fauna Ser — Thai National Scientific Papers. Fauna Series
Thai Nurses Assoc J — Thai Nurses Association Journal
Thai Sci Bull — Thai Science Bulletin
Thalassia Jugosl — Thalassia Jugoslavica
ThAM — Theatre Arts Magazine
ThAMo — Theatre Arts Monthly
ThAn — Theatre Annual
Th & Ph — Theologie und Philosophie
Tharandter Forstl Jahrb — Tharandter Forstliches Jahrbuch
Tharandt Forstl Jb — Tharandter Forstliches Jahrbuch
Thar Forstl Jb — Tharandter Forstliches Jahrbuch
ThArts — Theatre Arts
THAT — Theologisches Handwoerterbuch zum Alten Testament
Thatigkeitsber Naturf Ges Baselland — Thatigkeitsbericht der Naturforschenden Gesellschaft Baselland
ThAu — Theatre Aujourd'hui
Th Aust — Theatre Australia
ThB — Theatre de Belgique
ThB — Theologische Blaetter
THB — Today's Housing Briefs
THB — Trierer Heimatbuch
Th Ber — Theologische Berichte
Thbilis Sahelmc Univ Gamoqeneb Math Inst Srom — Thbilisis Sahelmcipho Universiteti Gamoqenebithi Mathematikis Instituti. Sromebi
Thbilis Univ Srom — Thbilisis Universitetis. Phizika-Mathematikisa de Sabunebismetqvelo Mecnierebani. Sromebi
Thbilis Univ Srom A — Thbilisis Universitetis. Phizika-Mathematikisa de Sabunebismetqvelo Mecnierebani. Sromebi. A
T Hbl — Tiroler Heimatblaetter
THbl — Trierische Heimatblaetter
THC — Topics in Health Care Financing
THCF — Topics in Health Care Financing
THCHDM — Specialist Periodical Reports. Theoretical Chemistry
ThD — Theology Digest
Th d G — Therapie der Gegenwart
ThDig — Theology Digest
THEA — Theata
Theat A — Theatre Arts
Theat Ann — Theatre Annual
Theat C — Theatre Crafts
Theat Craft — Theatre Crafts
Theat Europe — Theatre en Europe
Theat Heute — Theater Heute
Theat J — Theatre Journal
Theat Note — Theatre Notebook
Theat Ntbk — Theatre Notebook
Theat Q — Theatre Quarterly
Theat Quart — Theatre Quarterly
Theatre Arts M — Theatre Arts Magazine
Theatre/Drama Abstr — Theatre/Drama Abstracts
Theatre J — Theatre Journal
Theatre M — Theatre Magazine
Theatre Notebk — Theatre Notebook
Theatre Pol — Theatre en Pologne - Theatre in Poland
Theatre Q — Theatre Quarterly
Theatre Res Int — Theatre Research International
Theatre S — Theatre Studies
Theatre S — Theatre Survey
Theat Res I — Theatre Research International
Theat Stud — Theatre Studies
Theat Surv — Theatre Survey
Theat Surv Amer J Theat Hist — Theatre Survey. The American Journal of Theatre History
Theat Zeit — Theater der Zeit
Theb Ostr — Theban Ostraca
Th Ed — Theological Education
T Heden Rom-Holl Reg — Tydskrif vir Hedendaagse Romeins-Hollandse Reg
Th Educ — Theological Education
ThEE — Theskeutike kai Ethike Enkyklopaideia

THE J — THE [*Technological Horizons in Education*] Journal
THE Jrnl — THE [*Technological Horizons in Education*] Journal
Them — La Themis
Them — Themelios
Themis — Rechtsgeleerd Magazijn Themis
Themis — Revue Juridique Themis
Themis (Den Haag) — Themis. Verzameling van Bijdragen tot de Kennis van het PubliekenPrivaatrecht (Den Haag)
Themis (Zwolle) — Rechtsgeleerd Magazijn Themis (Zwolle)
Theo — Theologie (Paris)
Theo — Theoria
Theo & Lit J — Theological and Literary Journal
Theo Ecl — Theological Eclectic
Theokr — Theokratia
Theol — Theologia
Theol — Theology
Theol Akad — Theologische Akademie
Theol & Rel Ind — Theological and Religious Index
Theol Dgst — Theology Digest
Theol Evang — Theologia Evangelica
Theol Geg — Theologie der Gegenwart
Theol Gl — Theologie und Glaube
Theol Jb — Theologisches Jahrbuch
Theol Jber — Theologischer Jahresbericht
Theol Litbl — Theologisches Literaturblatt
Theol Literaturzeitung — Theologische Literaturzeitung
Theol Lit Z — Theologische Literaturzeitung
Theol Lit Ztg — Theologische Literaturzeitung
Theol Ltbl — Theologisches Literaturblatt
Theol LZ — Theologische Literaturzeitung
Theol Markings — Theological Markings
Theol Phil — Theologie und Philosophie
Theol Pract — Theologia Practica
Theol Prakt Quart Schr — Theologisch-Praktische Quartalschrift
Theol Prakt Quartschr — Theologisch-Praktische Quartalschrift
Theol Pr Q Schr — Theologisch-Praktische Quartalschrift
Theol Pr Qu Schr — Theologisch-Praktische Quartalschrift
Theol Quart — Theologische Quartalschrift
Theol Quartschr — Theologische Quartalschrift
Theol Quart-Schrift — Theologische Quartalschrift
Theol R — Theologische Revue
Theol Rdsch — Theologische Rundschau
Theol Relig Index — Theological and Religious Index
Theol Rev — Theologische Revue
Theol Rsch — Theologische Rundschau
Theol Ru — Theologische Rundschau
Theol St — Theological Studies
Theol St — Theologische Studien
Theol Stds — Theological Studies
Theol St Krit — Theologische Studien und Kritiken
Theol Stud — Theological Studies
Theol Szle — Theologiai Szemle
Theol Tijdschr — Theologische Tijdschrift
Theol Today — Theology Today
Theol Via — Theologia Viatorum
Theol WB — Theologisches Woerterbuch zum Alten Testament
Theol Z — Theologische Zeitschrift
Theol Zeitbl — Theologisches Zeitblatt
Theol Zs — Theologische Zeitschrift
Theo Mo — Theological Monthly
Theophrastus Contrib Adv Stud Geol — Theophrastus' Contributions to Advanced Studies in Geology
Theo R — Theological Review
Theor Adv Study Inst Elem Part Phys — Theoretical Advanced Study Institute in Elementary Particle Physics
Theor A Gen — Theoretical and Applied Genetics
Theor and Math Phys — Theoretical and Mathematical Physics
Theor Appl Fract Mech — Theoretical and Applied Fracture Mechanics
Theor Appl Gen — Theoretical and Applied Genetics
Theor Appl Genet — Theoretical and Applied Genetics
Theor Appl Mech (Sofia) — Theoretical and Applied Mechanics (Sofia)
Theor Biochem Mol Biophys — Theoretical Biochemistry and Molecular Biophysics
Theor Chem — Theoretical Chemistry
Theor Chem Adv Perspect — Theoretical Chemistry. Advances and Perspectives
Theor Chem Eng Abstr — Theoretical Chemical Engineering Abstracts
Theor Chem Engng Abstr — Theoretical Chemical Engineering Abstracts
Theor Chem (NY) — Theoretical Chemistry (New York)
Theor Chem Period Chem Biol — Theoretical Chemistry. Periodicities in Chemistry and Biology
Theor Chim — Theoretica Chimica Acta
Theor Chim Acta — Theoretica Chimica Acta
Theor Comput Chem — Theoretical and Computational Chemistry
Theor Comput Fluid Dyn — Theoretical and Computational Fluid Dynamics
Theor Comput Models Org Chem — Theoretical and Computational Models for Organic Chemistry
Theor Comput Sci — Theoretical Computer Science
Theor Decis — Theory and Decision
Theo Repos — Theological Repository
Theoret and Math Phys — Theoretical and Mathematical Physics
Theoret Appl Fracture Mech — Theoretical and Applied Fracture Mechanics
Theoret Appl Genet — Theoretical and Applied Genetics
Theoret Appl Mech — Theoretical and Applied Mechanics
Theoret Chem — Theoretical Chemistry
Theoret Chim Acta — Theoretica Chimica Acta

Theoret Comput Sci — Theoretical Computer Science
Theoret Grundlagen Automat Steuerung — Theoretische Grundlagen der Automatischen Steuerung
Theoret Linguist — Theoretical Linguistics
Theoret Papers — Theoretic Papers
Theoret Phys Text Exerc Books — Theoretical Physics. Text and Exercise Books
Theoret Population Biol — Theoretical Population Biology
Theoret Population Biology — Theoretical Population Biology
Theor Exp Biol — Theoretical and Experimental Biology
Theor Exp Biophys — Theoretical and Experimental Biophysics
Theor Exp Chem — Theoretical and Experimental Chemistry
Theor Exper Chem — Theoretical and Experimental Chemistry
Theor Exp Methoden Regelunstech — Theoretische und Experimentelle Methoden der Regelungstechnik
Theor Foundations Chem Engng — Theoretical Foundations of Chemical Engineering
Theor Found Chem Eng — Theoretical Foundations of Chemical Engineering
Theor Found Chem Eng Transl of Teor Osn Khim Tekhnol — Theoretical Foundations of Chemical Engineering (Translation of Teoreticheskie Osnovy Khimicheskoi Tekhnologii)
Theoria Hist Sci — Theoria et Historia Scientiarum
Theorie et Polit — Theorie et Politique
Theorie Prax — Theorie und Praxis. Fachblatt fuer Maschinenbau und Elektrotechnik
Theorie Prax Med — Theorie und Praxis in der Medizin
Theor Klin Med Einzeldarst — Theoretische und Klinische Medizin in Einzeldarstellungen
Theor Klin Med Einzeldarstell — Theoretische und Klinische Medizin in Einzeldarstellungen
Theor Math — Theoretical and Mathematical Physics
Theor Math Phys — Theoretical and Mathematical Physics
Theor Med — Theoretical Medicine
Theor Phys Semin Trondheim — Theoretical Physics Seminar in Trondheim</PHR> %
Theor Pop B — Theoretical Population Biology
Theor Popul Biol — Theoretical Population Biology
Theor Probability Appl — Theory of Probability and Its Applications
Theor Theor — Theoria to Theory
Theor Treat Large Mol Their Interact — Theoretical Treatment of Large Molecules and Their Interactions
Theory and Soc — Theory and Society
Theory Appl Categ — Theory and Applications of Categories
Theory Appl Transp Porous Media — Theory and Applications of Transport in Porous Media
Theory Biosci — Theory in Biosciences
Theory Decis Lib — Theory and Decision Library
Theory Decis Lib Ser B Math Statist Methods — Theory and Decision Library. Series B. Mathematical and Statistical Methods
Theory Decis Lib Ser D Syst Theory Knowledge Engrg Probl Solv — Theory and Decision Library. Series D. System Theory, Knowledge Engineering, and Problem Solving
Theory Exp Exobiol — Theory and Experiment in Exobiology
Theory Probab and Appl — Theory of Probability and Its Applications
Theory Probab Appl — Theory of Probability and Its Applications
Theory Probab Applic — Theory of Probability and its Applications
Theory Probability and Math Statist — Theory of Probability and Mathematical Statistics
Theory Probab Math Statist — Theory of Probability and Mathematical Statistics
Theory Sci Dev — Theory of Science Development
Theory Soc — Theory and Society
Theosophy in Aust — Theosophy in Australia
Theos Q — Theosophical Quarterly
Theo Today — Theology Today
Ther Ag Phys Nat — Therapeutique par les Agents Physiques et Naturels
Therap — Therapie
Therap Alm Beck — G. Becks Therapeutischer Almanach
Therapeutic Ed — Therapeutic Education
Therapeut Leistgg Jahr — Therapeutischen Leistungen des Jahres. Ein Jahrbuch fuer Praktische Aerzte
Therap Gegenw — Therapie der Gegenwart
Therap Halbmonatsh — Therapeutische Halbmonatshefte
Ther Apher — Therapeutic Apheresis
Therap Hung — Therapia Hungarica
Therapia Hung — Therapia Hungarica
Therapie Gegenw — Therapie der Gegenwart
Therapie Prax Tokyo — Therapie in der Praxis (Tokyo)
Therapie Prax Wien — Therapie und Praxis (Wien)
Therapie Taegl Prax — Therapie der Taeglichen Praxis
Therap Monatsh Vet-Med — Therapeutische Monatshefte fuer Veterinaermedizin
Therap Umschau — Therapeutische Umschau und Medizinische Bibliographie
Ther Bakt Infekt Kinderklin — Therapie Bakterieller Infektionen in der Kinderklinik
Ther Ber — Therapeutische Berichte
Ther Contemp — Therapeutique Contemporaine
Ther Dent — Therapeutique Dentaire
Ther Diagn New Vaccines Interferon Treat Plasma Proteins — Therapeutics, Diagnostics, New Vaccines, Interferon Treatment, and Plasma Proteins
Ther Drug Monit — Therapeutic Drug Monitoring
Ther Gaz — Therapeutic Gazette
Ther Ggw — Therapie der Gegenwart
Ther Halbmonatsh — Therapeutische Halbmonatshefte
Ther Hung — Therapia Hungarica
Ther Immunol — Therapeutic Immunology
Therm — Thermonews
Therm Abstr — Thermal Abstracts

Therm Conduct — Thermal Conductivity. Proceedings of the International Thermal Conductivity Conference
Ther Med Actual — Therapeutiques Medicales d'Actualite
Therm Eng — Thermal Engineering
Therm Engng — Thermal Engineering
Therm Engr — Thermal Engineering
Therm Eng (USSR) — Thermal Engineering (USSR)
Therm Fluid Dyn — Thermo- and Fluid Dynamics
Ther Mh — Therapeutische Monatshefte
Ther Mh VetMed — Therapeutische Monatshefte fuer Veterinaermedizin
Therm Nucl Power — Thermal and Nuclear Power
THERMO — Thermodynamic Property Values Database
Thermoc Act — Thermochimica Acta
Thermochem Bull — Thermochem Bulletin
Thermochim Acta — Thermochimica Acta
Thermoelect Abstr — Thermoelectricity Abstracts. United States Naval Research Laboratory
Ther Mon — Therapeutic Monthly
Ther Monatsh — Therapeutische Monatshefte
Thermophilic Bact — Thermophilic Bacteria
Therm Plasma Appl Mater Metall Process Proc Int Symp — Thermal Plasma Applications in Materials and Metallurgical Processing. Proceedings. International Symposium
Therm Power Conf Proc — Thermal Power Conference. Proceedings
Therm Power Gener — Thermal Power Generation
Therm Sci Eng — Thermal Science and Engineering
Therm Spray Coat Proc Natl Therm Spray Conf — Thermal Spray Coatings. Properties, Processes, and Applications. Proceedings. National Thermal Spray Conference
Therm Spray Int Adv Coat Technol Proc Int Therm Spray Conf — Thermal Spray. International Advances in Coatings Technology. Proceedings. International Thermal Spray Conference
Therm Struct Mater High Speed Flight — Thermal Structures and Materials for High-Speed Flight
Ther Nervensys — Therapie ueber das Nervensystem
Ther Nervensyst — Therapie ueber das Nervensystem
Ther Neuh — Therapeutische Neuheiten
Ther News — Therapeutic News
Ther Notes Detroit — Therapeutic Notes (Detroit)
Ther Notes Lond — Therapeutic Notes. Parke, Davis, & Co. (London)
Ther Nova — Therapeutica Nova
Ther Prat — Therapeutique Pratique
Ther Probl Today — Therapeutic Problems of Today
Ther Prog — Therapeutic Progress
Ther Rdsch — Therapeutische Rundschau
Ther Rec — Therapeutic Record
Ther Recreation J — Therapeutic Recreation Journal
Ther Recr J — Therapeutic Recreation Journal
Ther Rev — Therapeutic Review
Ther R J — Therapeutic Recreation Journal
Ther Sem Hop — Therapeutique. Semaine des Hopitaux
Ther Umsch — Therapeutische Umschau
Ther Umsch Med Biblphie — Therapeutische Umschau und Medizinische Bibliographie
Ther Zentbl — Therapeutisches Zentralblatt
Thes — Thesaurus
THES — Theses of Economics and Business in Finland
THES — Times Higher Education Supplement
THESA N — Teachers of Home Economics Specialist Association. Newsletter
Theses Cathol Med Coll — Theses. Catholic Medical College
Theses Cathol Med Coll (Seoul) — Theses. Catholic Medical College (Seoul)
Theses Collect Chonnam Univ Chonnam Univ — Theses Collection of Chonnam University. Chonnam University
Theses Collect Incheon Jr Coll — Theses Collection. Incheon Junior College
Theses Collect Kyungnam Ind Jr Coll — Theses Collection. Kyungnam Industrial Junior College
Theses Collect Kyungnam Univ — Theses Collection. Kyungnam University
Theses Collect Sookmyung Women's Univ — Theses Collection. Sookmyung Women's University
Theses Collect Yeungnam Univ — Theses Collection. Yeungnam University
Theses Collect Yeungnam Univ Nat Sci — Theses Collection. Yeungnam University. Natural Sciences
Theses Doct Ing Univ Dakar Ser Sci Nat — Theses de Docteur-Ingenieur. Universite de Dakar. Serie Sciences Naturelles
Theses Zool — Theses Zoologicae
Thes Fac Sci Dr Univ Lyon — Theses Presentees a la Faculte des Sciences pour Obtenir le Grade de Docteur es-Sciences de l'Universite. Lyon
Thes Fac Sci Univ Geneve — Theses. Faculte des Sciences. Universite de Geneve
Thes Fac Sci Univ Strasb — Theses. Faculte des Sciences. Universite de Strasbourg
Thesis — Thesis Eleven
Thesis Theo Cassettes — Thesis Theological Cassettes
Thes Li L — Thesaurus Linguae Latinae
Thes Lin Lat — Thesaurus Linguae Latinae
ThesLL — Thesaurus Linguae Latinae
Thes Ser Univ Wash — Theses Series of the University of Washington
Theta NR — Theta News Release
T Heth — Text der Hethiter
Th Ex H — Theologische Existenz Heute
ThF — Theologische Forschung
ThF — Theosophical Forum
Th F Jb — Tharandter Forstliches Jahrbuch
ThG — Theologie der Gegenwart
ThG — Theologie und Glaube

Th G — Therapie der Gegenwart
Th G — Thesaurus Graecae Linguae
THGEA — Therapie der Gegenwart
Th Gl — Theologie und Glaube
Th Gr L — Thesaurus Graecae Linguae
ThH — Theater Heute
THHP — Tung-Hai Hsueh-Pao
Thieles Bauztg — Thieles Bauzeitung
Thiemig-Taschenb — Thiemig-Taschenbuecher
Thiemig Tb — Thiemig-Taschenbuecher
Thieraerzt Mitth (Carlsruhe) — Thieraerztliche Mittheilungen (Carlsruhe)
Thiermed Rundschau — Thiermedicinische Rundschau
THIJDO — Texas Heart Institute. Journal
Thin Films Emerging Appl — Thin Films for Emerging Applications
Thin Films Stresses Mech Prop Symp — Thin Films. Stresses and Mechanical
    Properties. Symposium
Things Chem — Things Chemical
Things Tech — Things Technical. Technical Supply Co
Thin Sol Fi — Thin Solid Films
Thin Walled Struct — Thin-Walled Structures
Third Wld — Third World
Third Wld — Third World Forum
Third Wld Agric — Third World Agriculture
Third Wld Quart — Third World Quarterly
Third World Planning R — Third World Planning Review
Third World Q — Third World Quarterly
Third World Soc — Third World Socialists
Thirties Soc Jnl — Thirties Society. Journal
Thirty-Three/33 Mag Met Prod Ind — Thirty-Three/33. Magazine of the Metals
    Producing Industry
This Formica Wld — This Formica World. Formica Company
This Mag — This Magazine Is about Schools [Later, This Magazine: Education,
    Culture, Politics]
This Month Am Med — This Month in American Medicine
ThJ — Theologische Jahrbuecher
Th Jb — Theologisches Jahrbuch
THJCS — Tsing Hua Journal of Chinese Studies
THJUA — Thalassia Jugoslavica
ThKJ — Thueringer Kirchliches Jahrbuch
THKSA — Taiki Hoshano Kansoku Seiseki
ThL — Theologisches Literaturblatt
ThLB — Theologisches Literaturblatt
ThLBl — Theologisches Literaturblatt
THLC — Transactions. Historical and Literary Committee. American Philosophical
    Society
Th Life — Theology and Life
Th Lit — Theologische Literaturzeitung
Th Lit Z — Theologische Literaturzeitung
ThLL — Thesaurus Linguae Latinae
Th (Lond) — Theology (London)
ThLZ — Theologische Literaturzeitung
THM — Textos Hispanicos Modernos
Thm — Thomist
THM — Tien Hsia Monthly
THM — Topics in Health Care Materials Management
Th Markings — Theological Markings
Th M S — Thomas Mann-Studien
ThN — Theatre Newsletter
Th Nb — Theatre Notebook. A Quarterly of Notes and Research
Tho — Thought. A Review of Culture and Idea
Thol Ed — Theological Educator
Thom — Thomist
Thomas Say Found — Thomas Say Foundation
Thomas Say Found Monogr — Thomas Say Foundation. Monographs
Thomayerova Sbirka Predn Rozpr Oboru Lek — Thomayerova Sbirka Prednasek
    a Rozprav z Oboru Lekarskeho
Thom BBS — Thompson. Benefit Building Societies
Thomond Arch Soc Fld Cl — Thomond Archaeological Society and Field Club
Thompson Yates and Johnston Lab Rep — Thompson, Yates, and Johnston
    Laboratories Reports
Thompson Yates Johnston Labs Rep — Thompson Yates and Johnston
    Laboratories Report
Thompson Yates Lab Rep — Thompson-Yates Laboratories Reports
Thomsen Chem Co Bull — Thomsen Chemical Co. Bulletin
Thomson A Ph — Annals of Philosophy. Or, Magazine of Chemistry, Mineralogy,
    Mechanics, Natural History, Agriculture, and the Arts. Thomson
Thomson Rc — Records of General Science. R. D. and Thos. Thomson
Thomson's Process Chem Eng — Thomson's Process and Chemical Engineering
Thor — Thorax
Thorac Cardiovasc Surg — Thoracic and Cardiovascular Surgeon
Thorax Chir — Thoraxchirurgie und Vaskulaere Chirurgie
Thoraxchir Vask Chir — Thoraxchirurgie und Vaskulaere Chirurgie
Thoreau JQ — Thoreau Journal Quarterly
Thoreau Q — Thoreau Quarterly
Thorntons J — Thornton's Journal
Thoroton Soc Rec Ser — Thoroton Society. Record Series
Thoth Res — Thoth Research Journal
Thou — Thought. Fordham University Quarterly
Thou Econ — Thoughts on Economics
ThP — Theatre Populaire. Revue Trimestrielle d'Information sur le Theatre
ThP — Theosophical Path
ThPM — Theologisch-Praktische Monatsschrift
Th P Q — Theologisch-Praktische Quartalschrift
Th Pract — Theologia Practica
Th Pr Ma St — Theory of Probability and Mathematical Statistics

Th Prob Ap — Theory of Probability and Its Applications
ThPrQSchr — Theologisch-Praktische Quartalschrift
THQ — Tennessee Historical Quarterly
ThQ — Theatre Quarterly
ThQ — Theologische Quartalschrift
ThQ — Tuebinger Theologische Quartalschrift
ThQR — Theological Quarterly Review
Th QS — Theologische Quartalschrift
ThR — Theatre Research
ThR — Theological Review
ThR — Theologische Revue
ThR — Theologische Rundschau
THR — Thrust. Journal for Employment and Training Professionals
THR — Travaux d'Humanisme et Renaissance
THRAP — Tasmanian Historical Research Association. Papers and Proceedings
Th Rd — Theologische Rundschau
Th Rdsch — Theologische Rundschau
Th Rdschau — Theologische Rundschau
Threads Mag — Threads Magazine
Three Bank — Three Banks Review
Three Banks R — Three Banks Review
Three Banks Rev — Three Banks Review
Three Forks — Three Forks of Muddy Creek
Three R Int — Three R International
TH Rep Eindhoven Univ Technol Dep Electr Eng — TH-Report-Eindhoven
    University of Technology. Department of Electrical Engineering
Thresherm Rev Can — Thresherman's Review of Canada
Thresherm Rev St Joseph — Threshermen's Review (St. Joseph, Michigan)
ThRev — Theologische Revue
Th RI — Theatre Research International
Th Ri Po — Three Rivers Poetry Journal
ThRNF — Theologische Rundschau. Neue Folge
Thromb Diat — Thrombosis et Diathesis Haemorrhagica
Thromb Diath Haemorrh — Thrombosis et Diathesis Haemorrhagica
Thromb Diath Haemorrh Suppl — Thrombosis et Diathesis Haemorrhagica.
    Supplementum
Thromb Haemost — Thrombosis and Haemostasis
Thromb Haemostas — Thrombosis and Haemostasis
Thromb Res — Thrombosis Research
Thromb Res Suppl — Thrombosis Research. Supplement
Throop Inst Bull — Throop Institute Bulletin
Th Rsch — Theologische Rundschau
ThRu — Theologische Rundschau
THRU — Thrust
Th Rv — Theologische Revue
Thr Wld Q — Third World Quarterly
THS — Textes pour l'Histoire Sacree
ThS — Theatre Survey
ThS — Theological Studies
ThS — Theologische Studien und Kritiken
THS — Times Health Supplement
THSC — Transactions. Honourable Society of Cymmrodorion
ThSK — Theologische Studien und Kritiken
THSRB — Tufts Health Science Review
ThSt — Theological Studies
Th St — Theologische Studien
Th St B — Theologische Studien. Karl Barth
ThStKr — Theologische Studien und Kritiken
ThStW — Theologische Studien aus Wuerttemberg
ThT — Theologisch Tijdschrift
Th T — Theology Today
THTAD — Thiemig-Taschenbuecher
Th Today — Theology Today
Thueringens Merkwuerdigk Natur — Thueringens Merkwuerdigkeiten aus dem
    Gebiete der Natur, der Kunst, des Menschenlebens
Thuering Saechs Zs Gesch — Thueringisch-Saechsische Zeitschrift fuer
    Geschichte und Kunst
Thuer Landw Ztg — Thueringer Landwirtschaftliche Zeitung
Thuer Mbl — Thueringer Monatsblaetter. Verbandszeitschrift des Thueringer
    Waldvereins
Thuer Saechs Zs Gesch — Thueringisch-Saechsische Zeitschrift fuer Geschichte
    und Kunst
ThuGl — Theologie und Glaube
Thule Int Symp — Thule International Symposia
Thunderstorm Elect Rep — Thunderstorm Electricity Reports. Institute of Mining
    and Technology
Thune Meddr — Thune Meddelelser
Thurgau Beitr Vaterland Gesch — Thurgauische Beitraege zur Vaterlaendischen
    Geschichte
Thurg B — Thurgauische Beitraege zur Vaterlaendischen Geschichte
Thur Marsh LJ — Thurgood Marshall Law Journal
Thurn & Taxis Stud — Thurn und Taxis-Studien
T Hush — Tidsskrift for Husholnding
ThV — Theologia Viatorum. Jahrbuch der Kirchlichen Hochschule
ThV — Theologische Versuche
ThViat — Theologia Viatorum. Jahrbuch der Kirchlichen Hochschule
Th W — Theologisches Woerterbuch zum Neuen Testament
Th WAT — Theologisches Woerterbuch zum Alten Testament
Th Wiss — Theologische Wissenschaft
THY — Thomas Hardy Yearbook
Thy — Thyrse. Revue d'Art et de Litterature
THYMD — Thymus
Thyr V — Thyras Vold
Thyssen Edelstahl Tech Ber — Thyssen Edelstahl Technische Berichte

Thyssen Forsch Ber Forsch Betr — Thyssen Forschung. Berichte aus Forschung und Betrieb
Thyssen Tech Ber — Thyssen Technische Berichte
Th Z — Theater der Zeit
ThZ — Theologische Zeitschrift
THZOEN — Theses Zoologicae
ThZSchw — Theologische Zeitschrift aus der Schweiz
TI — Technical Information for Industry
TI — Timarit Pjooreknisfelags Islendinga 1957
Ti — Timberman. An International Lumber Journal
TI — Tobacco Intelligence
TI — Tobacco International
TI — Turbine Intelligence
TIA — Taxation in Australia
TIA — Times of India Annual
TIA — Tin International
TIAC — Techniques and Instrumentation in Analytical Chemistry
Tianjin J Oncol — Tianjin Journal of Oncology
Tianjin Med J — Tianjin Medical Journal
TIAS — Treaties and Other International Acts Series
TIB — Tabula Imperii Byzantini
Tib Duny — Tib Dunyasi
Tibetan R — Tibetan Review
Tibet J — Tibet Journal
Tibet News Rev — Tibet News Review
Tibet Soc B — Tibet Society. Bulletin
T I Br Geog — Transactions. Institute of British Geographers
TIBS — Trabajos del Instituto Bernadino de Sahagun de Antropologia y Etnologia
TIBS — Trends in Biochemical Sciences
TIC — International Financial Law Review
T I Chem En — Transactions. Institution of Chemical Engineers and the Chemical Engineer
TICL — Topics in Culture Learning
TICOA — Testing, Instruments, and Controls
TICOJ — Transactions. International Conference of Orientalists in Japan
TID — Technical Information Document
Tidal Obsns Cent Met Obs Japan — Tidal Observations. Central Meteorological Observatory of Japan
Tidal Publs Ottawa — Tidal Publications. Canadian Hydrographic (and Map) Service (Ottawa)
Tidal Stream Tabl Indones Archipel — Tidal Stream Tables. Indonesian Archipelago
Tidal Tabl Indian Ocean — Tidal-Tables of the Indian Ocean. Office of the Geodetic and Research Branch. Survey of India
Tid Dok — Tidskrift foer Dokumentation
Tide Tabl Wash — Tide Tables. United States Coast and Geodetic Survey (Washington)
Tidewtr VA — Tidewater Virginian
Tidn Byggnadskonst — Tidning foer Byggnadskonst
Tidn Fjaderfaskot Biskot — Tidning for Fjaderfaskotseln och Biskotsel
Tidn Mjolkhushalln — Tidning for Mjolkhushallning
Tid Nord Retsmed Psykiat — Tidende for Nordisk Retsmedicin og Psykiatri
TID Rep — T.I.D. Reports. Atomic Energy Commission [*Oak Ridge*]
Tids F Retsvidensk — Tidsskrift for Retsvidenskab
Tid Sk — Tidens Skole
Tidsk Dokum — Tidskrift foer Dokumentation
Tidskr Abnormsk Finl — Tidskrift for Abnormskolorna i Finland
Tidskr Dok — Tidskrift foer Dokumentation
Tidskr Hushallningssaellsk Skogsvardsstyr Gaevleborgs Laen — Tidskrift foer Hushallningssaellskapet och Skogsvardsstyrelsen i Gaevleborgs Laen
Tidskr Kstvet — Tidskrift fuer Konstvetenskap
Tidskr Landtm — Tidskrift for Landtman
Tidskr Lantm — Tidskrift for Lantman
Tidskr Lantmaen Andelsfolk — Tidskrift foer Lantmaen och Andelsfolk
Tidskr Lantmaen Andelsfolk — Tidskrift foer Lantmaen och Andelsfolk
Tidskr Ljuskult — Tidskrift tor Ljuskultur
Tidskr Mask — Tidskrift for Maskinister
Tidskr Mask Loko Finl — Tidskrift for Maskinister och Lokomotivman i Finland
Tidskr Mil Halsov — Tidskrift i Militar Halsovard
Tidskr Norske Utskiftningsv — Tidsskrift for det Norske Utskiftningsvaesen
Tidskr Prakt Bygkst & Mek — Tidskrift for Praktisk Byggnadskonst och Mekanik
Tidskr Sjov — Tidskrift i Sjovasendet
Tidskr Sjukvardspedagog — Tidskrift foer Sjukvardspedagoger
Tidskr Skogbruk — Tidskrift foer Skogbruk
Tidskr Skog Lantbruksakad — Tidskrift. Skogs- och Lantbruksakademien
Tidskr Skogshushalln — Tidskrift for Skogshushallning
Tidskr Snabbrakn — Tidskrift for Snabbrakning
Tidskr Sver Sjukskot — Tidskrift foer Sveriges Sjukskoterskor
Tidskr Sver Skogvardsforb — Tidskrift Sveriges Skogsvardsforbund
Tidskr Sver Utsadesforen — Tidskrift. Sveriges Utsaedesfoereningen
Tidskr Varme- Vent- Sanitetstek — Tidskrift foer Varme-, Ventilations-, och Sanitetsteknik
Tids Samfun — Tidsskrift foer Samfunnsforskning
Tidssk Kjemi Bergves Metall — Tidsskrift foer Kjemi. Bergvesen og Metallurgi
Tidsskr Abnormv — Tidsskrift for Abnormvaesenet
Tidsskr Bergv — Tidsskrift for Bergvaesen
Tidsskr Biavl — Tidsskrift foer Biavl
Tidsskr Biskjot — Tidsskrift for Biskjotsel. Tvedestrand & Porsgrund
Tidsskr Froavl — Tidsskrift foer Froavl
Tidsskr Hermetikind — Tidsskrift foer Hermetikindustri
Tidsskr Kemi — Tidsskrift foer Kemi
Tidsskr Kemi Farm Ter — Tidsskrift foer Kemi. Farmaci og Terapi
Tidsskr Kjemi Bergv — Tidsskrift foer Kjemi og Bergvesen
Tidsskr Kjemi Bergves — Tidsskrift foer Kjemi og Bergvesen
Tidsskr Kjemi Bergvesen Met — Tidsskrift foer Kjemi. Bergvesen og Metallurgi

Tidsskr Landokon — Tidsskrift foer Landokonomi
Tidsskr Litt Krit — Tidsskrift for Litteratur og Kritik
Tidsskr Maskinv — Tidsskrift for Maskinvaesen
Tidsskr Nord Retsmed Psykiat — Tidsskrift for Nordisk Retsmedicin og Psykiatri
Tidsskr Nor Laegeforen — Tidsskrift foer den Norske Laegeforening
Tidsskr Nor Landbruk — Tidsskrift foer det Norske Landbruk
Tidsskr Norske Laegeforen — Tidsskrift foer den Norske Laegeforening
Tidsskr Norske Landbr — Tidsskrift for det Norske Landbruk
Tidsskr Norske Landbruk — Tidsskrift foer det Norske Landbruk
Tidsskr Opmaal Og Matrikulsv — Tidsskrift for Opmaalings- og Matrikulsvaesen
Tidsskr PapInd — Tidsskrift for Papirindustri
Tidsskr Papirind — Tidsskrift foer Papirindustri
Tidsskr Plant — Tidsskrift foer Planteavl
Tidsskr Planteavl — Tidsskrift foer Planteavl
Tidsskr Plavl — Tidsskrift foer Planteavl
Tidsskr Prakt Med — Tidsskrift for Praktisk Medicin
Tidsskr Prakt Tandlaeg — Tidsskrift foer Praktiserende Tandlaeger
Tidsskr Samfunnsforskning — Tidsskrift foer Samfunnsforskning
Tidsskr Skogbr — Tidsskrift foer Skogbruk
Tidsskr Skogbruk — Tidsskrift foer Skogbruk
Tidsskr Skovv — Tidsskrift for Skovvaesen
Tidsskr Smaabr — Tidsskrift for Smaabruk
Tidsskr Sov — Tidsskrift for Sovaesen
Tidsskr SundhPleje — Tidsskrift for Sundhedspleje
Tidsskr Sygepl — Tidsskrift foer Sygeplejersker
Tidsskr Sygepleje — Tidsskrift for Sygepleje
Tidsskr Textiltek — Tidsskrift foer Textilteknik
Tidsskr TextTek — Tidsskrift for Textilteknik
Tidsskr Vet — Tidsskrift for Veterinaerer
Tidsskr Vindelekt — Tidsskrift for Vindelektricitet
Tid Stem — Tidens Stemme
Tid Tann — Tidens Tann
TIDU News Lett — T.I.D.U. (Technical Information and Documents Unit) News Letter
TIE — Travaux et Memoires de l'Institut d'Ethnologie
TIEAN — Trudy Instituta Etnografii Akademii Nauk SSSR
Tiedemanns Zschr — Zeitschrift fuer Physiologie (Fr. Tiedemann und G. R. Treviranus, Editors)
Tied Metsateho — Tiedotus Metsateho
Tiedon Hydrogr Toim — Tiedonantoja Hydrografise Toimista
Tied Valt Tekn Tutkimusl — Tiedotus. Valtion Teknillinen Tutkimuslaitos
Tied Valt Tek Tutkimuskeskus Poltto Voiteluainelab — Tiedonanto-Valtion Teknillinen Tutkimuskeskus, Poltto-, ja Voiteluainelaboratorio
TIEED — Transactions. Institute of Electronics and Communication Engineers of Japan. Section E (English)
Tiefb Berufsgenoss — Tiefbau-Berufsgenossenschaft
TIE-IN — Technology Information Exchange-Innovation Network
Tien Hsia Mthly — Tien Hsia Monthly
Tieraerztl Arch Sudetenl — Tieraerztliches Archiv fuer die Sudetenlaender
Tieraerztl Ber — Tieraerztlicher Bericht
Tieraerztl Mitt — Tieraerztliche Mitteilungen
Tieraerztl Prax — Tieraerztliche Praxis
Tieraerztl Rd — Tieraerztliche Rundschau
Tieraerztl Rdsch — Tieraerztliche Rundschau
Tieraerztl Rundsch — Tieraerztliche Rundschau
Tieraerztl Rundschau — Tieraerztliche Rundschau
Tieraerztl Umsch — Tieraerztliche Umschau
Tieraerztl Z — Tieraerztliche Zeitschrift
Tieraerztl ZentAnz — Tieraerztlicher Zentralanzeiger
Tieraerztl Zentbl — Tieraerztliches Zentralblatt
Tierarztl Prax Suppl — Tierarztliche Praxis. Supplement
Tierernaehr Fuetter — Tierernaehrung und Fuetterung
Tierernaehr Tierz — Tierernaehrung und Tierzucht
Tier Erzeu — Viehbestand und Tierische Erzeugung Land und Forstwirtschaft Fischerei
Tierphysiol Tierernaehr Futtermittelk — Tierphysiologie, Tierernaehrung, und Futtermittelkunde
Tierra y Soc — Tierra y Sociedad
Tier U NatPhotogr — Tier- und Naturphotographie
Tieteel Tutk — Tietyeellisiae Tutkimuksia
Tiet Julk Helsingin Tek Korkeakoulu — Tieteellisia Julkaisuja. Helsingin Teknillinen Korkeakoulu
TIEtn — Trudy Instituta Etnografii Imeni N. N. Miklucho Maklaja Akademija Nauk SSSR
TIF — Travaux de l'Institut Francais d'Etudes Andines
TIF — Treaties in Force. US State Department
TIFA — Tourist Information Facts and Abstracts
TIFO — Technische Informationen
TiG — Tijdschrift voor Geschiednis
TIGAN — Trudy Instituta Geologii Akademii Nauk SSSR
TIGC — Topics in Inorganic and General Chemistry
TIGRB — Technische Information GRW
TIGS — Transactions. Inverness Gaelic Society
TIGZD — Teikyo Igaku Zasshi
TiH — Tiroler Heimat
Tihanyi Biol Kutatointezetenek Evkoen — Tihanyi Biologiai Kutatointezetenek Evkoenyve
TIIAE — Trudy Instituta Istorii, Archeologii, i Etnografii
TIIAEK — Trudy Instituta Istorii. Arkheologii i Etnografii. Akademiia Nauk Kazakhskoi SSR
TIIAET — Trudy Instituta Istorii. Arkheologii i Etnografii. Akademiia Nauk Turkmenskoi SSR
TIIAz — Trudy Instituta Istorii. Akademiia Nauk Azerbaidzhanskoi SSR
TIIK — Trudy Instituta Istorii. Akademiia Nauk Kirghizskoi SSR
TIJa — Trudy Instituta Jazykoznanija

Tijd — Onze Tijd
Tijd — Tijdspiegel (The Hague)
Tijd Ec Soc — Tijdschrift voor Economische en Sociale Geografie
Tijd Ec Soc Geogr — Tijdschrift voor Economische en Sociale Geografie
Tijd Ent — Tijdschrift voor Entomologie
Tijd Filos — Tijdschrift voor Filosofie
Tijd Gesch — Tijdschrift voor Geschiedenis
Tijd Ind TLV — Tijdschrift voor Indische Taal-, Land-, en Volkenkunde
Tijd ITL — Tijdschrift van het Institut voor Toegepaste Linguistiek
Tijd Kindergeneeskd — Tijdschrift voor Kindergeneeskunde
Tijd Logop Audiol — Tijdschrift voor Logopedie en Audiologie
Tijd Ned T — Tijdschrift voor Nederlandsche Taal- en Letterkunde
Tijd Phil — Tijdschrift voor Philosophie
Tijd Psych — Tijdschrift voor Psychiatrie
Tijd R Gesch — Tijdschrift voor Rechtsgeschiedenis
Tijdsch Centr Nijv Comite Belg — Tijdschrift van het Centraal Nijverheidscomite van Belgie
Tijdschr Archit & Beeld Kst — Tijdschrift voor Architectuur en Beeldende Kunst
Tijdschr Batav Genootsch Kunst — Tijdschrift van het Bataviaasch Genootschap van Kunsten en Wetenschappen
Tijdschr Bestuursw — Tijdschrift voor Bestuurswetenschappen
Tijdschr Boomteeltk — Tijdschrift over Boomteeltkunde, Bloementeelt, en Moeshovenierderij
Tijdschr Boomteeltk BloemTeelt Moeshov — Tijdschrift over Boomteeltkunde, Bloementeelt en Moeshovenierderij
Tijdschr Brussel Gesch — Tijdschrift voor Brusselse Geschiedenis
Tijdschr Diergeneesk — Tijdschrift voor Diergeneeskunde. Gravenhage
Tijdschr Diergeneeskd — Tijdschrift voor Diergeneeskunde
Tijdschr Diergeneeskd Q Engl Issue — Tijdschrift voor Diergeneeskunde. Quarterly English Issue
Tijdschr d Ktg — Tijdschrift der Kantongerechten
Tijdschr Econ Geogr — Tijdschrift voor Economische Geographie
Tijdschr Econ Soc Geogr — Tijdschrift voor Economische en Sociale Geografie
Tijdschr Econ Social Geogr — Tijdschrift voor Economische en Sociale Geographie
Tijdschr Ent — Tijdschrift voor Entomologie
Tijdschr Entomol — Tijdschrift voor Entomologie
Tijdschr Filosof — Tijdschrift voor Filosofie
Tijdschr Gastroent — Tijdschrift voor Gastroenterologie
Tijdschr Gastro-Enterol — Tijdschrift voor Gastro-Enterologie
Tijdschr Gemeent — Tijdschrift voor Gemeenten
Tijdschr Gemeentekrediet Belgie — Tijdschrift van het Gemeentekrediet van Belgie
Tijdschr Geneeskd — Tijdschrift voor Geneeskunde
Tijdschr Gerontol Geriatr — Tijdschrift voor Gerontologie en Geriatrie
Tijdschr Gesch — Tijdschrift voor Geschiedenis
Tijdschr Gesch & Fiklore — Tijdschrift voor Geschiedenis en Folklore
Tijdschr Gesch Geneesk Natuurwetensch Wisk Tech — Tijdschrift voor de Geschiedenis der Geneeskunde, Natuurwetenschappen, Wiskunde en Techniek
Tijdschr Geschied Natuurwet Wiskd Tec — Tijdschrift voor Geschiedenis Natuurwetenschap Wiskundig. Techniek
Tijdschr Graf — Tijdschrift Grafick
Tijdschrift Aardr Genootschap — Tijdschrift der Aardrijkskundige Genootschap
Tijdschrift Taal & Lett — Tijdschrift voor Taal en Letteren
Tijdschrift V Gesch — Tijdschrift voor Geschiedenis
Tijdschrift voor Econ en Soc Geog — Tijdschrift voor Economische en Sociale Geografie
Tijdschr Indische Taal Land En Volkenk — Tijdschrift voor Indische Taal-, Land-, en Volkenkunde
Tijdschr Ind Taal Land & Vlknknd — Tijdschrift voor Indische Taal, Land- en Volkenkunde Uitgegeven door het (Koninklijk) Bataviaasch Genootschap van Kunsten en Wetenschappen
Tijdschr Ind Taal- Land- en Volkenkunde — Tijdschrift voor Indische Taal-, Land-, en Volkenkunde
Tijdschr Inland Geneesk — Tijdschrift voor Inlandsche Geneeskundigen
Tijdschr Kadaster Landmeetk — Tijdschrift voor Kadaster en Landmeetkunde
Tijdschr Kindergeneeskd — Tijdschrift voor Kindergeneeskunde
Tijdschr Klei Glas Keram — Tijdschrift voor Klei, Glas en Keramiek
Tijdschr K Ned Heidemaatsch — Tijdschrift der Koninklijke Nederlandsche Heidemaatschappij
Tijdschr Land Tuinb Boschkult — Tijdschrift voor Land- en Tuinbouw en Boschkultuur
Tijdschr Lev Talen — Tijdschrift voor Levende Talen
Tijdschr Maatsch Nijv — Tijdschrift der Maatschappij van Nijverheid
Tijdschr Med Analyst — Tijdschrift voor Medische Analysten
Tijdschr Microbiol GezondhLeer — Tijdschrift voor Microbiologie en Gezondheidsleer, Vergelijkende en Tropische Geneeskunde, Parasitaire en Infectieziekten
Tijdschr Ned Aar Genoot — Tijdschrift van het (Koninklijk) Nederlandsch Aardrijkskundig Genootschap
Tijdschr Ned Dierkd Ver — Tijdschrift der Nederlandsche Dierkundige Vereniging
Tijdschr Ned Dierk Vereen — Tijdschrift der Nederlandsche Dierkundige Vereeniging
Tijdschr Ned Elektron- & Radiogenoot — Tijdschrift van het Nederlands Elektronica- en Radiogenootschap
Tijdschr Nederld Aardrijkskd Genootsch — Tijdschrift van het Nederlandsch Aardrijkskundig Genootschap
Tijdschr Ned Heidemaatsch — Tijdschrift der Nederlandsche Heidemaatschappij
Tijdschr Ned Indie — Tijdschrift voor Nederlandsch-Indie
Tijdschr Ned Radiogenoot — Tijdschrift van het Nederlandsch Radiogenootschap
Tijdschr Ned Taalen Lettk — Tijdschrift voor Nederlandsche. Taalen Letterkunde
Tijdschr Ned TL — Tijdschrift voor Nederlandsche Taal- en Letterkunde
Tijdschr Ned Ver Klin Chem — Tijdschrift van de Nederlandse Vereniging voor Klinische Chemie

Tijdschr Nijv Landb Ned Indie — Tijdschrift voor Nijverheid en Landbouw in Nederlandsch-Indie
Tijdschr Not — Tijdschrift voor Notarissen
Tijdschr OngevallGeneesk — Tijdschrift voor Ongevallengeneeskunde
Tijdschr Oppervlaktetech Mater — Tijdschrift voor Oppervlaktetechnieken van Materialen
Tijdschr Oppervlakte Tech Metal — Tijdschrift voor Oppervlakte Technieken van Metalen
Tijdschr Ov — Tijdschriftenoverzicht
Tijdschr Parapsychol — Tijdschrift voor Parapsychologie
Tijdschr Phys Ther Hyg — Tijdschrift voor Physische Therapie en Hygiene
Tijdschr Plantenz — Tijdschrift voor Plantenziekten
Tijdschr Plantenziekten — Tijdschrift voor Plantenziekten
Tijdschr PlZiekt — Tijdschrift over Plantenziekten
Tijdschr Polit — Tijdschrift voor Politicologie
Tijdschr Polit — Tijdschrift voor Politiek
Tijdschr Prakt Verlosk — Tijdschrift voor Praktische Verloskunde
Tijdschr Primaire Energ — Tijdschrift Primaire Energie
Tijdschr Radiotech — Tijdschrift voor Radiotechniek
Tijdschr Soc Geneesk — Tijdschrift voor Sociale Geneeskunde
Tijdschr Soc Geneeskd — Tijdschrift voor Sociale Geneeskunde
Tijdschr Soc Hyg Openb GezondhRegel — Tijdschrift voor Sociale Hygiene en Openbaare Gezondheidsregeling
Tijdschr Soc Wetensch — Tijdschrift voor Sociale Wetenschappen
Tijdschr Strafrecht — Tijdschrift voor Strafrecht
Tijdschr Stud Verlichting — Tijdschrift voor Studie. Verlichting
Tijdschr Tandheelk — Tijdschrift voor Tandheelkunde
Tijdschr Ther Geneesmiddel Onderz — Tijdschrift voor Therapie, Geneesmiddel, en Onderzoek
Tijdschr Tuinb Groningen — Tijdschrift voor Tuinbouw (Groningen)
Tijdschr Veeartsenijk — Tijdschrift voor Veeartsenijkunde
Tijdschr Veeartsenijk en Veeteelt — Tijdschrift voor Veeartsenijkunde en Veeteelt
Tijdschr Verkeerstech — Tijdschrift voor Verkeerstechniek
Tijdschr Volkshuisv Stedeb — Tijdschrift voor Volkshuisvesting en Stedebouw
Tijdschr Vreder — Tijdschrift van de Vrederechters, Plaatsvervangers, Officieren van hetOpenbaar Ministerie en Griffiers
Tijdschr Werktuigk — Tijdschrift voor de Werktuigkunde
Tijdschr Ziekenverpl — Tijdschrift voor Ziekenverpleging
Tijdschr Zwakzinnenzorg — Tijdschrift voor Zwakzinnigenzorg
Tijds Econ — Tijdschrift voor Economie
Tijds Econ Manag — Tijdschrift voor Economic Management
Tijds Gem Recht — Tijdschrift voor Gemeenterecht
Tijds Not — Tijdschrift voor Notarissen
Tijd Soc Wet — Tijdschrift voor Sociale Wetenschappen
Tijds Priv — Tijdschrift voor Privaatrecht
Tijds Pr Recht — Tijdschrift voor Privaatrecht
Tijds Soc Wetensch — Tijdschrift voor Sociale Wetenschappen
Tijds v Bestuursw — Tijdschrift voor Bestuurswetenschappen
Tijd Vlaam Chem Ver — Tijdingen. Vlaamse Chemische Vereniging
Tijeret Malar — Tijeretazos sobre Malaria
Tijkschr Elektrotech — Tijdschrift voor Elektrotechniek. 's Gravenhage
TIKKB8 — Trudy Nauchno-Issledovatel'skogo Instituta Kartofel'nogo Khozyaistva
Til — Tilskueren
TIL — Travaux. Institut de Linguistique
TILAS — Travaux. Institut d'Etudes Latino-Americaines. Universite de Strasbourg
TILAS — Travaux. Institute d'Estudes Iboriques et Latino-Americaines
Tilgate Tech Bull — Tilgate Technical Bulletin
TIM — Time
Tim — Timehri. Journal of the Royal Agricultural and Commercial Society of British Guiana
TIM — Trends in Microbiology
Timarit Hjukrunarfel Isl — Timarit Hjukrunarfelags Islands
Timarit Verkfraedingafelags Is — Timarit Verkfraedingafelags Islands
Timars Rdsch Ind Tech — Timars Rundschau ueber Industrie und Technik
Timb & Plyw Ann — Timber and Plywood Annual
Timb Bull Eur — Timber Bulletin for Europe
Timb Bull Europe FAO — Timber Bulletin for Europe. Food and Agricultural Organization
Timb Can — Timber in Canada
Timb Detail Sh NSW — Timber Detail Sheets. New South Wales Forestry Commission
Timb Econ Bull — Timber Economy Bulletin
Timber B — Timber Bulletin for Europe
Timber BAR — Timber Bulletin for Europe. Annual Forest Products Market Review
Timber BFS — Timber Bulletin for Europe. Forest Fire Statistics
Timber B (Hu) — Timber Bulletin for Europe. Forest and Forest Products Country Profile (Hungary)
Timber B Pr — Timber Bulletin for Europe. Monthly Prices for Forest Products. Supplement
Timber BWP — Timber Bulletin for Europe. Survey of the Wood-Based Panels Industries
Timber Dev Assoc Inf Bull A/IB — Timber Development Association. Information Bulletin A/IB
Timber Dev Assoc Inf Bull B/IB — Timber Development Association. Information Bulletin B/IB
Timber Dev Assoc Inf Bull G/IB — Timber Development Association. Information Bulletin G/IB
Timber Dev Assoc Res Rep C/RR — Timber Development Association. Research Report C/RR
Timber Res Dev Assoc Res Rep C/RR — Timber Research and Development Association. Research Report C/RR
Timber Sit — Analysis of the Timber Situation in the United States 1952-2030
Timber Supp Rev — Timber Supply Review
Timber Technol — Timber Technology

Timber Trades J — Timber Trades Journal and Woodworking Machinery [*Later,* *Timber Trades Journal and Wood Processing*]

Timb Grower — Timber Grower

Timb Grow Q Rev — Timber Growers' Quarterly Review

Timb Leafl For Dep (Brit Solomon Islands Protect) — Timber Leaflet. Forestry Department (British Solomon Islands Protectorate)

Timb Leafl For Dep (Kenya) — Timber Leaflet. Forest Department (Nairobi, Kenya)

Timb Leafl For Dep (Uganda) — Timber Leaflet. Forest Department (Uganda)

Timb Pres Assoc Aust — Timber Preservers' Association of Australia. Pamphlet

Timb Statist Rev — Timber Statistical Review

Timb Technol — Timber Technology

Timb Technol Mach Woodwkg — Timber Technology and Machine Woodworking

Timb Times — Timber Times

Timb Top — Timber Topics

Timb Trade Leafl Kepong — Timber Trade Leaflets (Kepong)

Timb Trade Lect — Timber Trade Lectures

Timb Trades J — Timber Trades Journal

Timb Trades J Wood Process — Timber Trades Journal and Wood Processing

Timb Tr J — Timber Trades Journal

TIMEA — Transactions. Institute of Marine Engineers

Time (Can) — Time (Canada)

Timely Turf Top — Timely Turf Topics

Time Myst — Time and its Mysteries

Time-Picay — Times-Picayune

Timepieces Q — Timepieces Quarterly

Times Br Colon Rev — Times British Colonies Review

Times Br Col R — Times British Colonies Review

Times Ednl Supp — Times Educational Supplement

Times Ed Sup — Times Educational Supplement

Times Educ Supp — Times Educational Supplement

Times Higher Ed Supp — Times Higher Education Supplement

Times Higher Educ Supp — Times Higher Education Supplement

Times Higher Educ Suppl — Times Higher Education Supplement

Times Ind A — Times of India Annual

Times L — Times Literary Supplement

Times Lit Supp — Times Literary Supplement

Times Lit Suppl — Times Literary Supplement

Times (Lond) — Times (London)

Times L Suppl — TLS. Times Literary Supplement

Times Rev Ind — Times Review of Industry

Times R Ind — Times Review of Industry

Times R Ind & Tech — Times Review of Industry and Technology

Times Sci Rev — Times Science Review

Times Trib — Times Tribune

Time Study Engr — Time Study Engineer

TIMFA — Transactions. Institute of Metal Finishing

Timiryazev Chten — Timiryazevskie Chteniya

Timisoara Inst Politeh Traian Vuia Bul Stiint Teh Ser Chim — Timisoara. Institutul Politehnic "Traian Vuia." Buletinul Stiintific si Tehnic.Seria Chimie

Timisoara Med — Timisoara Medicala

TIN — Ebanewsletter. Daily Economic and Political News Indicators from Turkey

Tinbergen Inst Res Ser — Tinbergen Institute Research Series

Tin Box Can Mfr — Tin Box and Can Manufacturer

Tin Copp Wld — Tin and Copper World

T Ind — Tidsskrift for Industri

Tindal Vh Zeewezen — Verhandelingen en Berigten Betrekellelijk het Zeewezen en de Zeewartkunde. Tindal en Swart

Tingo Maria Peru Est Exp Agric Bol — Tingo Maria, Peru. Estacion Experimental Agricola. Boletin

Tin Int — Tin International

Tin Inter — Tin International

Tin Intern — Tin International

TINKER — Timber Information Keyword Retrieval

Tin Lond — Tin (London)

Tin Print Box Mkr — Tin-Printer and Box Maker

Tin Printer Box Mkr — Tin-Printer and Box Maker and the Canning Industry

Tin Res Inst (Greenford Engl) Publ — Tin Research Institute (Greenford, England). Publication

TINS — Trends in Neurosciences

Tinsley — Tinsley's Magazine

TINS Trends Neurosci — TINS. Trends in Neurosciences

Tintor Ind — Tintoreria Industrial

Tin Uses — Tin and Its Uses

Tin Wld Statist — Tin World Statistics

TIOAN — Trudy Instituta Oceanologii. Akademiia Nauk SSSR

TIOCL — Transactions. International Oriental Congress (London)

TIOKA — Trudy Instituta Okeanologii Akademiya Nauk SSSR

TIOOA — Transactions. Indiana Academy of Ophthalmology and Otolaryngology

Ti O Sa Odsher — Ting og Sager fra Odsherred

TIP — Tests in Print

TIP — Theory into Practice

Tip Fak Mecm — Tip Fakultesi Mecmuasi. Istanbul Universitesi

TIPGA — Trudy Instituta Prikladnoi Geofiziki

TIPRO Rep — TIPRO [*Texas Independent Producers and Royalty Owners Association*] Reporter

TIR — Tabula Imperii Romani

Tir — Tirade

Tirada Interna Inst Suelos Agrotec — Tirada Interna. Instituto de Suelos y Agrotecnia

Tirad Aparte Obs Astr Univ Nac Cordoba — Tiradas Aparte. Observatorio Astronomico. Universidad Nacional de Cordoba

Tir A Pt Inst Astr Univ Brux — Tires a Part. Institut d'Astronomie de l'Universite de Bruxelles

Tiraspol Gos Ped Inst Ucen Zap — Tiraspol'skii Gosudarstvennyi Pedagogiceskii Institut Imeni T. G. Sevcenko. Ucenyi Zapiski

Tire Batt Access News — Tire, Battery, and Accessory News

Tire Dealr — Modern Tire Dealer

Tire Rebldrs News — Tire Rebuilders News

Tire Rev — Tire Review

Tire Rev D — Tire Review. 1986 Sourcebook and Directory

Tire Sci Technol — Tire Science and Technology

Tire TBA Rev — Tire and TBA Review

Tire Trade J — Tire Trade Journal

Tire Tread Tidings — Tire and Treading Tidings

Tire Wld — Tire World

TirJ — Tiroler Jahrbuch

TIRJa — Trudy Instituto Russkogo Jazyka

Tiroler Landw Blaett — Tiroler Landwirthschaftliche Blaetter

T Iron St I — Transactions. Iron and Steel Institute of Japan

TIRS — Travaux. Institut de Recherches Sahariennes

TIRVB — Toronto University. Institute for Aerospace Studies. UTIAS Review

TIS — AutEx Trading Information System

TIS — Times

TIS — Tops in Science Fiction

TISCO — TISCO [*Tata Iron & Steel Company*] Technical Journal

TISCO Rev — TISCO [*Tata Iron & Steel Company*] Review

Tishreen Univ J Stud Sci Res — Tishreen University Journal for Studies and Scientific Research

Tisiol Pneumol — Tisiologia-Pneumologia

T I Sjoevas — Tidskrift I Sjoevaesendet

TIS Rep — I.I.S. (Technical Information Service, National Research Council, Canada) Report

Tissue Anti — Tissue Antigens

Tissue Cult Biblphy — Tissue Culture Bibliography

Tissue Eng — Tissue Engineering

Tissue React — Tissue Reactions

Titan Abstr Bull — Titanium Abstract Bulletin

Titan Engng Bull — Titanium Engineering Bulletin

Titanium Prod Appl Proc Tech Program Int Conf — Titanium. Products and Applications. Proceedings. Technical Program. International Conference

Tit Calymn — Tituli Calymnii

Tit Cam — Tituli Camirenses

TI Tech Inf Ind — TI. Technical Information for Industry

TIT J Lif — TIT [*Tower International Technomedical*] Journal of Life Sciences

TIT J Life Sci — TIT [*Tower International Technomedical*] Journal of Life Sciences

TITL — Tijdschrift van het Institut voor Toegepaste Linguistiek

TITLA — Tecnica Italiana

Titles Diss Univ Camb — Titles of Dissertations approved for the Ph.D., M.Sc., and M.Litt. degrees in the University of Cambridge

Titles Pap Publ DSIR — Titles of Papers Published. D.S.I.R

TITLV — Tijdschrift voor Indische Taal-, Land-, en Volkenkunde

TITUS — Textile Information Treatment Users' Service

TIW — Today's Insurance Woman

TIYADG — Tianjin Medical Journal

TIZ — Tonindustrie-Zeitung und Keramische Rundschau. Zentralblatt fuer das Gesamtgebjet der Steine und Erden

TIZ Int — TIZ [*Tonindustrie-Zeitung*] International

TIZ Int Mag Powder Bulk — TIZ International Magazine for Powder and Bulk

TIZ Int Powder Bulk Mag — TIZ International Powder and Bulk Magazine

TIZ Int Pulver & Schuettgut Verfahrenstech — TIZ International Pulver und Schuettgut. Verfahrenstechnik

TIZPK — Trudy Instituta Zoologii i Parazitologii. Akademiia Nauk Kirghizskoi SSR

TIZRG — Trudy Instituta Zashchity Rastenii, Akademiia Nauk Gruzinskoi SSR

TJ — Theatre Journal

TJ — Theologischer Jahresbericht

TJ — Today's Japan

TJ — Tolkien Journal

TJ — Tribune Juive

TJ — Trier Jahresberichte

TJ — Trinity Journal

TJ — Tuba Journal

TJA — Focus Japan

TJA — Telecommunication Journal of Australia

TJADA — Teratology

TJak — Trudy Instituta Jazyka, Literatury, i Istorii

T Jap I Met — Transactions. Japan Institute of Metals

TJASA — Transactions. Japan Society for Aeronautical and Space Sciences

TJB — Theologischer Jahresbericht

T J Br Cer — Transactions and Journal. British Ceramic Society

T Jdm — Tidsskrift for Jordemodre

TJEMA — Tohoku Journal of Experimental Medicine

TJEMD — Tokai Journal of Experimental and Clinical Medicine

TJHC — Theology. Journal of Historic Christianity

TJHPA — T'u Jang Hsueh Pao

TJHPAE — Acta Pedologica Sinica

TJI — Tabak Journal International

TJIDA — Tokyo Jikeikai Ika Daigaku Zasshi

TJIZA — Tokyo Joshi Ika Daigaku Zasshi

TJL — Jonxis Lectures

TJPDA — Turkish Journal of Pediatrics

TJQ — Thoreau Journal Quarterly

TJR — Tenri Journal of Religion

TJS — Timber Trades Journal and Woodworking Machinery

TJSCA — Texas Journal of Science

TJSUDJ — Thai Journal of Surgery

Tjumen Gos Ped Inst Ucen Zap — Ministerstvo Prosvescenija RSFSR Tjumenskii Gosudarstvennyi Pedagogiceskii Institut. Ucenye Zapiski

TK — Tekawennake. Six Nations. New Credit Reporter

TK — Tetzugaku-Kenkyu

TK — Text und Kritik

TK — Tijdschrift voor het Kadaster in Nederlandsch-Indie
TKA — Trudy Kierskoi Dukhovnoi Akademii
TKar — Trudy Karel'skogo Filiala Akademii Nauk SSSR
TKB — Taphikos Kyklos B ton Mykenon
TKBRAS — Transactions. Korean Branch. Royal Asiatic Society
TKDA — Trudy Kievskoi Dukhovnoi Akademii
TKESB — Tekhnicheskaya Estetika
TKFN — Telkwa Foundation. Newsletter
TKGJA — Taisei Kensetsu Gijutsu Kenkyusho-Ho
Tk J — Tamkang Journal
TKKSA — Trudy Khar'kovskogo Sel'skokhozyaistvennogo Instituta
TKKTA — Trudy po Khimii i Khimicheskoi Tekhnologii
TKL — Tijdschrift voor Kadaster en Landmeetkunde
TKMEB — Theoretische und Klinische Medizin in Einzeldarstellungen
TKMSB — Tekhnicheska Misul
T Kn — Tidsskrift for Kaninavlerforening
TKN — Tijdschrift. Koninklijk Nederlandsch Aardrijkskundig Genootschap
TKN — Tractatenblad van het Koninkrijk der Nederlanden
TKNGMP — Tijdschrift. Koninklijk Nederlandsch Genootschap voor Munt en Penningkunde
TKNKB — Tekniikka
TKO — Technieuws Tokio. Korte Berichten op Technisch Wetenschappelijk Gebied
TKP — Taschenbuch fuer Kommunalpolitiker
TkR — Tamkang Review
TKRAS — Transactions. Korean Branch. Royal Asiatic Society
TKrasPI — Trudy Krasnodarskogo Gosudarstvennogo Pedagogicheskogo Instituta
TKSBB — Tektonika Sibiri
TKSGA — Trudy Koordinatsionnykh Soveshchanyi po Gidrotekhnike
TKSGB — Tektonika i Stratigrafiya
TKST — Tukisiviksat
TKTEA — Tekhnika Kino i Televideniya
TKUAA — Trudy Kuibyshevskii Aviatsionnyi Institut
T Kungl Krigsvet Akad — Tidskrift. Kungliga Krigsvetenskaps-Akademien
TKutPI — Trudy Kutaisskogo Gosudarstvennogo Pedagogiceskogo Instituta
TKZRA — Taika Zairyo
TL — Terra Lusa
TL — Theologische Literaturzeitung
TL — Theologisches Literaturblatt
TL — Theoretical Linguistics
TL — Trident (London)
TL — Troquel
TL — Trybuna Literacka
TLA — Tax Lawyer
TLAP — Prace Komisji Jezykowej Polskiej Akademii Umiejetnosci. Travaux de la Commission Linguistique de l'Academie Polonaise des Sciences et des Lettres
Tlargi Yb — Tlargi Yearbook
T Lawyr — Tax Lawyer
TLB — Theologisches Literaturblatt
TLBI — Theologisches Literaturblatt
TLCOA — Telecommunications
TLD — [*The*] Living Daylights
TLDB — Transportation Legislative Data Base
TLE — Testimonia Linguae Etruscae
T Le — Tidsskrift for Legemsovelser
TLEPA — Trudy Laboratorii Elektromagnitnykh Polei Radiochastot Instituta Gigieny Truda i Professional'nykh Zabolevanii Akademii Meditsinskikh Nauk SSSR
T Letterkd — Tydskrif vir Letterkunde
TLF — Textes Litteraires Francais
T Lg — Travaux de Linguistique
TLIB — Transportation Library
TLIG — Tasmanian Legal Information Guide
TLit — Taller Literario
TLit — Theologische Literaturzeitung
TLJ — Transportation Law Journal
TLK — Teaching London Kids
TLL — Thesaurus Linguae Latinae
TLL — Totius Latinitatis Lexicon
TLL — Travaux de Linguistique et de Litterature
TLLS — Travaux de Linguistique et de Litterature (Strasbourg)
TLMMDD — Malaysia. Ministry of Agriculture. Technical Leaflet
TLNDA — Telonde
T Lo — Tidsskrift for Landokonomi
TLOE — Trudy. Leningradskoe Obshchestvo Estestvoispytatelei, Otdeleni Geologii i Mineralogii
TLOP — [*The*] Language of Poetry
TLP — Travaux Linguistiques de Prague
TLQ — Temple Law Quarterly
TLQ — Travaux de Linguistique Quantitative
TLQue — Travaux de Linguistique Quebecoise
TLR — Tanzania Gazette Law Reports
TLR — Tasmanian Law Reports
TLR — Tax Law Review
TLR — Tulane Law Review
TLS — Times Literary Supplement
TLSAP — Wydawnictwa Slaskie Polskiej Akademii Umiejetnosci. Prace Jezykowe. Publications Silesiennes. Academie Polonaise des Sciences et des Lettres. Travaux Linguistiques
TLSM — Talouselama
TLT — Travancore Law Times
TLTC — Ta-Lu Tsa-Chih
TLTL — Teaching Language through Literature
T Lwyr — Tax Lawyer
TLYYA4 — Co-Operative Bulletin. Taiwan Forestry Research Institute
TLZ — Theologische Literaturzeitung
TM — National Income Tax Magazine

TM — Tax Magazine
TM — Temps Modernes
TM — Tennessee Musician
TM — Textus Minores
TM — Theatre Magazine
Tm — Time
TM — Tlalocan: A Journal of Source Materials on the Native Cultures of Mexico
TM — Toelichting-Meijers
Tm — Tomorrow
TM — Tour du Monde
TM — Tourism Management
TM — Traffic Management
TM — Travaux et Memoires. Centre de Recherche d'Histoire et de Civilisation Byzantines
TM — Turkiyat Mecmuasi
TM — Tygodnik Morski
TMA — [*The*] Money Advocate
TMA — Top Management Abstracts
TMA — Traffic Management
TMAGD — Tennessee Magazine
TMAMAP — Ezhegodnik Instituta Eksperimental'noi Meditsiny Akademii Meditsinskikh Nauk SSSR
TMATB — Technische Mitteilungen AEG- [*Allgemeine Elektrizitaets-Gesellschaft*] Telefunken
TMB — Iemootsies
TMC — Revue Tiers-Monde
TMC — Transition Metal Chemistry
TMC — Tribuna Medica
TMCHD — Transition Metal Chemistry
TMCIA — Temperature. Its Measurement and Control in Science and Industry
TMC News Lett — T.M.C. (Telephone Manufacturing Co.) News Letter
TMC Tech J — T.M.C. (Telephone Manufacturing Co.) Technical Journal
TMFL — Lille. Universite. Travaux et Memoires des Facultes de Lille
TMFZA — Teoreticheskaya i Matematicheskaya Fizika
TMGR — Traite des Monnaies Grecques et Romaines
TMH — Texas Military History
TMI — Tax Management International Journal
TMIA — Trudy Muzeia Istorii Azerbaidzhana
TMIEB — Trudy Moskovskii Institut Elektronnogo Mashinostroeniya
TMIG — [*The*] Marketing Information Guide
TMIV — Trudy Moskovskogo Instituta Vostokovedeniia Akademii Nauk SSSR/ Proceedings of the Moscow Oriental Institute of the Academy of Sciences USSR
TMJ — Trade Marks Journal
TMK — Technische Mitteilungen Krupp
TMKFA — Technische Mitteilungen Krupp. Forschungsberichte
TMKWA — Technische Mitteilungen Krupp. Werksberichte
TML — Lille. Universite. Travaux et Memoires. Droit-Lettres
TMLPS — Transactions. Manchester Literary and Philosophical Society
TMM — Technocrat. A Monthly Review of Japanese Technology and Industry
TMM — The Mines Magazine
TMMM — Textes et Monuments Figures Relalifs aus Mysteres de Mithra
TMNP — [*The*] Mystery Readers Newsletter
TMo — O Tempo e o Modo
Tmod — Temps Modernes
TMorNII — Trudy Mordovskogo Nauchno-Issledovatel'skogo Instituta Jazyka, Literatury, Istorii, i Ekonomiki
TMPM Tschermaks Mineral Petrogr Mitt — TMPM. Tschermaks Mineralogische und Petrographische Mitteilungen
TMPTA — Technische Mitteilungen PTT
TMR — Trade-Mark Reporter
TM Rep — Trade-Mark Reporter
TMRK — Canadian Trade Marks
TMRKH — Tromura. Tromsoe Museum Rapportserie. Kulturhistorie
TMRN — [*The*] Mystery Readers Newsletter
TMRNV — Tromura. Tromsoe Museum Rapportserie. Naturvitenskap
TMRSDT — Tropical Medicine Research Studies Series
TMS — Tlalocan: A Journal of Source Materials on the Native Cultures of Mexico
TMSAA — Transactions. Metallurgical Society of AIME
T Msk — Tidsskrift for Maskinvaesen
TMS Northeast Reg Symp — TMS Northeast Regional Symposium
TMT — Toxic Materials Transport
TMT — Tudomanyos es Muszaki Tajekoztatas
TMV — Fitz-Gerald, J. D. and Pauline Taylor, eds. Todd Memorial Volumes. Columbia University Press
TMV — Todd Memorial Volumes
TMW — Textile Museum (Washington, D.C.)
TMW — Tijdschrift voor Maatschappelijk Werk
TMW — Welzijnsweekblad
TMWP — Textile Museum (Washington, D.C.) Papers
TMWR — Tax Management Weekly Report
TMZ — Textile Magazine. Vakblad voor de Handel in Textiel, Kleding, en Woningtextiel
TN — Talking Newspaper News
TN — Theatre Notebook
TN — Tijdschrift voor Notarissen
Tn — Time (New York)
TN — Tin News
TN — Title News
TN — Top of the News
TN — Travel News
TNA — Tidsskrift foer Norron Arkeologi
TNAEA — Teplovye Napryazheniya v Elementakh Konstruktsii
TNAG — Tijdschrift van het Nederlandsch Aardrijkskundig Genootschap
TNAN — Texas Numismatic Association. News

TNBMD — Bureau of Mines. Technology News
TNCSDT — North Carolina. Agricultural Research Service. Technical Bulletin
Tn Ctry Plann — Town and Country Planning
TND — Transnational Data Report. Information Politics and Regulation
Tnd Hotel — Trends in the Hotel-Motel Industry
TNDNA — Tokyo Nogyo Daigaku Nogaku Shuho
TNDNAG — Journal of Agricultural Science. Tokyo Nogyo Daigaku
TNDSA — Trends
TNEMBJ — Annals. Research Institute of Epidemiology and Microbiology
TNHCA — Taehan Naekwa Hakhoe Chapchi
TNI — Tijdschrift van Nederlandsch-Indie
TNI — Tin News. Accurate Information on World Tin Production, Prices, Marketing Developments, and New Uses and Applications
TNIPI — Trudy Nauchno-Issledovatelskogo Protivochumnogo Instituta Kavkaza i Zakavkazia
TNIzam — Trudy Instituta Literatury i Jazyka Imeni Nizami
TNKPB — Trudy Nauchno-Issledovatel'skogo Instituta Kraevoi Patologii
TNKUL — Towarzystwo Naukowe Katolickiego Uniwersytet Lubelskiego
TNKULWP — Towarzystwo Naukowe Katolickiego Uniwersytet Lubelskiego. Wyklady i Przemowienia
TN L — Tennessee Law Review
TNLAAH — Tidsskrift foer den Norske Laegeforening
TN LR — Tennessee Law Review
TNLRA — Tennessee Law Review
TNN — TermNet News
T N Nachr — T N Nachrichten
TNNIA — Trudy Groznenskogo Neftyanogo Nauchno-Issledovatel'skogo Instituta
TNO Div Nutr Food Res TNO Rep — TNO [Nederlands Centrale Organisatie voor Toegepast-Natuurwetenschappelijk Onderzoek] Division for Nutrition and Food Research TNO. Report
TNO Proj — TNO [Nederlands Centrale Organisatie voor Toegepast-Natuurwetenschappelijk Onderzoek] Project
TNOSA — Tunnels et Ouvrages Souterrains
T Not — Tijdschrift voor Notarissen
Tn Plann Rev — Town Planning Review
TNR — [The] New Republic
TNR — Tanzania Notes and Records
TNS — Telecommunications Network Services
TNS — Timber Trade Review
TNSCDR — TINS. Trends in Neurosciences
TNSKA — Tohoku Nogyo Shikenjo Kenkyu Hokoku
TNSRA — Tensor
TN Stud Lit — Tennessee Studies in Literature
TNSX — Taniisix. Aleutian Regional School District
TNT — Tax Notes Today
TNT — Towarzystwo Naukowe w Toruniu
TNT — Transportation News Ticker
TNT-FF — Towarzystwo Naukowe w Toruniu. Prace Wydziau Filologiczno-Filosoficznego
TNTL — Tijdschrift voor Nederlandsche Taal- en Letterkunde
TNUVAN — Trudy Novokuznetskogo Gosudarstvennogo Instituta Usovershenstvovaniya Vrachei
TNVF — Tijdschrift voor het Notarisambt. Venduwezen en Fiscaal Recht
TNW — Tijdschrift van den Nederlandschen Werkloosheidsraad
TNW — Towarzystwo Naukowe Warszawskie
T NY Ac Sci — Transactions. New York Academy of Sciences
TNYAS — Transactions. New York Academy of Sciences
TO — Take One
TO — Theban Ostraca
TO — Tijdschrift voor Overheidsadministratie. Weekblad voor het OpenbaarBestuur
TO — Tobacco Observer
TO — Townsman
TOA — Tijdschrift voor Openbaar Bestuur
TOAMGE — Trudy Otdela Istorii Iskusstva i Kul'tury Antichnogo Mira Gosudarstvennogo Ermitazha
TOAP — Prace Komisji Orientalistycznej Polskiej Akademii Umiejetnosci. Travaux de la Commission Orientaliste de l'Academie Polonaise des Sciences et des Lettres
Tob — Tobacco
TOBAA8 — Tobacco
Tob Abstr — Tobacco Abstracts
Tob Abstracts — Tobacco Abstracts
Tobacco — Tobacco International
Tobacco J — Tobacco Journal
Tob Control — Tobacco Control
Tob Int (NY) — Tobacco International (New York)
Tob Leaf — Tobacco Leaf
Tob Manuf Standing Comm Res Pap — Tobacco Manufacturers' Standing Committee. Research Papers
Tob News — Tobacco News
Tob Rec — Tobacco Record
Tob Rep — Tobacco Report
Tob Res — Tobacco Research
Tob Res Board Rhod Bull — Tobacco Research Board of Rhodesia. Bulletin
Tob Res Counc Res Pap — Tobacco Research Council. Research Paper
Tob Sci — Tobacco Science
Tob Situat — Tobacco Situation
Tob Statist — Tobacco Statistics
Tob Wld Lond — Tobacco World (London)
Tob Wld Philad — Tobacco World (Philadelphia)
Tochn Mekh Mash — Tochnost' Mekhanizmov i Mashin
Tocklai Exp Stn Advis Bull — Tocklai Experimental Station. Advisory Bulletin
Tocklai Exp Stn Advis Leafl — Tocklai Experimental Station. Advisory Leaflet
Tocn i Nadezn Kibernet Sistem — Tocnost i Nadeznost Kiberneticeskih Sistem
Tocqueville Rev — Tocqueville Review / Revue Tocqueville

TOCS — Oriental Ceramic Society. Transactions
Toda Educ — Today's Education
Today — Today for Tomorrow
Today & Tomorrow Educ — Today and Tomorrow in Education
Today Min — Today's Ministry
Todays Chiro — Today's Chiropractic
Today's Ed — Today's Education
Todays Educ — Today's Education
Todays Exec — Today's Executive
Today's Fmkr — Today's Filmmaker
Todays Hlth — Today's Health
Todays Nurs Home — Today's Nursing Home
Today's Sec — Today's Secretary
Todays VD Vener Dis Control Probl — Today's VD. Venereal Disease Control Problem
Today Technol — Today Technology
Tod Cath Teach — Today's Catholic Teacher
Tod Parish — Today's Parish
TODrL — Trudy Otdela Drevnerusskoj Literatury
TOELA — Toute l'Electronique
Toertenelmi Regeszeti Ertes — Toertenelmi es Regeszeti Ertesitoe
Toert Szle — Toertenelmi Szemle
TOF — Tales of the Frightened
TOF — Today's Office
TOGAD2 — Topics in Gastroenterology
(Togo) Plan — Fourth Plan of Economic and Social Development. Summary 1981-1985 (Togo)
Toh J Ex Me — Tohoku Journal of Experimental Medicine
Tohoku Agric — Tohoku Agriculture/Tohoku Nogyo
Tohoku Agr Res — Tohoku Agricultural Research
Tohoku Geophys J Sci Rep Tohoku Univ Fifth Ser — Tohoku Geophysical Journal. Science Reports of the Tohoku University. Fifth Series
Tohoku Imp Univ Technol Rep — Tohoku Imperial University Technology Reports
Tohoku J Agric Res — Tohoku Journal of Agricultural Research
Tohoku J Agr Res — Tohoku Journal of Agricultural Research
Tohoku J Exp Med — Tohoku Journal of Experimental Medicine
Tohoku Math — Tohoku Mathematical Journal
Tohoku Math J — Tohoku Mathematical Journal
Tohoku Math J 2 — Tohoku Mathematical Journal. Second Series
Tohoku Math Publ — Tohoku Mathematical Publications
Tohoku Med J — Tohoku Medical Journal
Tohoku Psychol Fol — Tohoku Psychologica Folia
Tohoku Psychol Folia — Tohoku Psychologica Folia
Tohoku Univ Inst Agric Res Rep — Tohoku University. Institute for Agricultural Research. Reports
Tohoku Univ Sci Rep Ser 2 — Tohoku University. Science Reports. Series 2. Geology
Tohoku Univ Sci Rep Ser 3 — Tohoku University. Science Reports. Series 3. Mineralogy, Petrology, and Economic Geology
Tohoku Univ Sci Rep Ser 5 — Tohoku University. Science Reports. Series 5
Tohoku Univ Sci Repts Geology — Tohoku University. Science Reports. Geology
Toid Eesti NSV Geol Alalt — Toid Eesti NSV Geoloiigia Alalt
Toim Eesti NSV Tead Akad Fuus Mat — Toimetised. Eesti NSV Teaduste Akadeemia. Fuusika. Matemaatika
TOK — Toeristenkampioen
Tokai J Exp Clin Med — Tokai Journal of Experimental and Clinical Medicine
Tokai-Kinki Natl Agric Exp Stn Res Prog Rep — Tokai-Kinki National Agricultural Experiment Station. Research Progress Report
Tokai Technol J — Tokai Technological Journal
Tokai Univ Fac Eng Proc — Tokai University. Faculty of Engineering. Proceedings
Tok Coll Sc J — Journal of the College of Science. Imperial University, Japan. Tokio, Japan
Tok Gl S Gl Mg — Geological Magazine. Geological Society of Tokyo
Tok Gl S J — Journal of the Geological Society of Tokyo
Tokoginecol Prac — Toko-Ginecologia Practica
Toko-Ginecol Pract — Toko-Ginecologia Practica
Toko Ginec Pract — Toko-Ginecologia Practia
TOKSA — Tokushuko
Toksikol Nov Prom Khim Veshchestv — Toksikologiya Novykh Promyshlennykh Khimicheskikh Veshchestv
TOKTA — Teoreticheskie Osnovy Khimicheskoi Tekhnologii
Tok Un Mm — Memoirs of the Science Department. University of Tokio, Japan
Tokushima J Exp Med — Tokushima Journal of Experimental Medicine
Tokyo Astr Bull — Tokyo Astronomical Bulletin
Tokyo Astron Bull — Tokyo Astronomical Bulletin
Tokyo Astron Bull Ser II — Tokyo Astronomical Bulletin. Series II
Tokyo Astron Obs Kiso Inf Bull — Tokyo Astronomical Observatory. Kiso Information Bulletin
Tokyo Astron Obs Rep — Tokyo Astronomical Observatory. Report
Tokyo Astron Obs Time and Latitude Bull — Tokyo Astronomical Observatory. Time and Latitude Bulletins
Tokyo Bk Dev Centre Newsl — Tokyo Book Development Centre. Newsletter
Tokyo Conf Adv Catal Sci Technol — Tokyo Conference on Advanced Catalytic Science and Technology
Tokyo Elect Rev — Tokyo Electrical Review
Tokyo Fin R — Tokyo Financial Review
Tokyo Inst Technol Bull — Tokyo Institute of Technology. Bulletin
Tokyo Jikeika Med J — Tokyo Jikeika Medical Journal
Tokyo J Math — Tokyo Journal of Mathematics
Tokyo J Med Sci — Tokyo Journal of Medical Sciences
Tokyo Kyoiku Daigaku Sci Rep Sec C — Tokyo Kyoiku Daigaku. Science Reports. Section C. Geology, Mineralogy, and Geography
Tokyo Med J — Tokyo Medical Journal
Tokyo Med News — Tokyo Medical News

Tokyo Metrop Isot Cent Annu Rep — Tokyo Metropolitan Isotope Centre. Annual Report

Tokyo Metrop Res Inst Environ Prot Annu Rep Engl Transl — Tokyo Metropolitan Research Institute for Environmental Protection. Annual Report. English Translation

Tokyo Metrop Univ Geogr Rep — Tokyo Metropolitan University. Geographical Reports

Tokyo Munic News — Tokyo Municipal News

Tokyo Natl Sci Mus Bull — Tokyo National Science Museum. Bulletin

Tokyo Tanabe Q — Tokyo Tanabe Quarterly

Tokyo Tungsten Co Ltd Tech Rev — Tokyo Tungsten Co., Ltd. Technical Review

Tokyo Univ Coll Gen Educ Sci Pap — Tokyo University. College of General Education. Scientific Papers

Tokyo Univ Earthquake Research Inst Bull — Tokyo University. Earthquake Research Institute. Bulletin

Tokyo Univ Fac Eng J Ser B — Tokyo University. Faculty of Engineering. Journal. Series B

Tokyo Univ Faculty Sci Jour — Tokyo University. Faculty of Science. Journal

Toledo L Rev — University of Toledo. Law Review

Toledo Mus N — Toledo Museum of Art. Museum News

Toledo Univ Inst Silicate Research Inf Circ — Toledo University. Institute of Silicate Research. Information Circular

Toll Ex — Toller on Executors

Tol LR — University of Toledo. Law Review

To LR — University of Toledo. Law Review

Tolva — Tolva. Revista del Trigo. Harina y del Pan

Tolvmandsbl — Tolvmandsbladet

TOM — Tijdschrift voor Oude Muziek

Tom — Tomorrow. A Review of Literature

Tomsk Gos Pedagog Inst Uch Zap — Tomskii Gosudarstvennyi Pedagogicheskii Institut. Uchenye Zapiski

Tomsk Gos Univ Ucen Zap — Tomskii Gosudarstvennyi Universitet Imeni V. V. Kuibyseva. Ucenye Zapiski

TONGA — Trudy Nauchno-Issledovatel'skogo Instituta Onkologii Gruzinskoi SSR

TONGE — Trudy Otdela Numismatiki Gosudarstvennogo Ermitazha

Tonind Zeitung — Tonindustrie-Zeitung

Tonind-Ztg Keram Rundsch — Tonindustrie-Zeitung und Keramische Rundschau

TONT — Toronto Native Times

TOO — La Tour de l'Orle d'Or

TOOIS — Transactions on Office Information Systems

Tool & Mfg Eng — Tool and Manufacturing Engineer

Tool and Prod — Tooling and Production

Tool Die J — Tool and Die Journal

Tool Eng — Tool Engineer

Tool Engr Tokyo — Tool Engineer (Tokyo)

Tooling P — Tooling and Production

Tooling Prod — Tooling and Production

Tool Mfg Eng — Tool and Manufacturing Engineer

Tool Mfg Engr — Tool and Manufacturing Engineer

Toolmkr Precis Engr — Toolmaker and Precision Engineer

Tool Prod — Tooling and Production

Tools — Tools and Tillage

Tools Equip — Tools and Equipment

Toonug Kusim Eesti NSV Polevkov — Toonugieeni Kusimusi Eesti NSV Polevkovitoostuses. Eesti NSV Teaduste Akadeemia

TOP — Trinity Occasional Papers

Top Allerg Clin Immun — Topics in Allergy and Clinical Immunology

Top Antibiot Chem — Topics in Antibiotic Chemistry

Top Appl Phys — Topics in Applied Physics

Top Astrophys Space Phys — Topics in Astrophysics and Space Physics

Top Autom Chem Anal — Topics in Automatic Chemical Analysis

Top Bioelectrochem Bioenerg — Topics in Bioelectrochemistry and Bioenergetics

Top Catal — Topics in Catalysis

Top Chem Eng — Topics in Chemical Engineering

Top Chem Mutagen — Topics in Chemical Mutagenesis

Top Clin Nurs — Topics in Clinical Nursing

Top Clin Nutr — Topics in Clinical Nutrition

Top Conf Res Trends Nonlinear Relativ Eff Plasmas — Topical Conference on Research Trends in Nonlinear and Relativistic Effects in Plasmas

Top Curr Chem — Topics in Current Chemistry

Top Curr Phys — Topics in Current Physics

Top Emerg Med — Topics in Emergency Medicine

Top Environ Health — Topics in Environmental Health

Top Enzyme Ferment Biotechnol — Topics in Enzyme and Fermentation Biotechnology

Top F Elem Chem — Topics in F-Element Chemistry

Top Fluoresc Spectrosc — Topics in Fluorescence Spectroscopy

Top Gastroenterol — Topics in Gastroenterology

Top Geobiol — Topics in Geobiology

Top Geriatr — Topics in Geriatrics

Top Health Care Financ — Topics in Health Care Financing

Top Health Rec Manage — Topics in Health Record Management

Top Heterocycl Syst Synth React Prop — Topics in Heterocyclic Systems. Synthesis, Reactions, and Properties

Top Horm Chem — Topics in Hormone Chemistry

Top Hosp Pharm Manage — Topics in Hospital Pharmacy Management

T Ophth Soc — Transactions. Ophthalmological Societies of the United Kingdom

Top Hum Genet — Topics in Human Genetics

TOPICS — Transcripts of Parlibns Information Classification System

Topics Appl Phys — Topics in Applied Physics

Topics Clin Nurs — Topics in Clinical Nursing

Topics Current Phys — Topics in Current Physics

Topics Discrete Math — Topics in Discrete Mathematics

Topics Engrg — Topics in Engineering

Topics in Comput Math — Topics in Computer Mathematics

Topics Inform Systems — Topics in Information Systems

Top Inclusion Sci — Topics in Inclusion Science

Top Infect Dis — Topics in Infectious Diseases

Top Issues Glass — Topical Issues in Glass

Top Lipid Chem — Topics in Lipid Chemistry

Topliv Delo — Toplivnoe Delo

Top Magn Reson Imaging — Topics in Magnetic Resonance Imaging

Top Manage Abstr — Top Management Abstracts

Top Mass Spectrom — Topics in Mass Spectrometry

Top Math Phys — Topics in Mathematical Physics

Top Med Chem — Topics in Medicinal Chemistry

Top Meet New Horiz Radiat Prot Shielding — Topical Meeting on New Horizons in Radiation Protection and Shielding

Top Mol Med — Topics in Molecular Medicine

Top Mol Organ Eng — Topics in Molecular Organization and Engineering

Top Mol Pharmacol — Topics in Molecular Pharmacology

Top Mol Struct Biol — Topics in Molecular and Structural Biology

Top Neurochem Neuropharmacol — Topics in Neurochemistry and Neuropharmacology

Top News — Top of the News

Top Ocular Pharmacol Toxicol — Topics in Ocular Pharmacology and Toxicology

Topogr Geod Zh — Topograficheskii i Geodezicheskii Zhurnal

Topogr Instruct US Geol Surv — Topographic Instruction of the United States Geological Survey

Topogr Niederoest — Topographie von Niederoesterreich

Topogr Zytol Neurosekretorischer Syst — Topographie und Zytologie Neurosekretorischer Systeme

Topol Methods Nonlinear Anal — Topological Methods in Nonlinear Analysis

Topology Appl — Topology and Its Applications

Topology Proc — Topology Proceedings

Top Paediatr — Topics in Paediatrics

Top Perinat Med — Topics in Perinatal Medicine

Top Pharm Sci — Topics in Pharmaceutical Sciences

Top Phosphorus Chem — Topics in Phosphorus Chemistry

Top Photosynth — Topics in Photosynthesis

Top Phys Chem — Topics in Physical Chemistry

Top Probl Psychiat — Topical Problems of Psychiatry

Top Probl Psychiatry Neurol — Topical Problems in Psychiatry and Neurology

Top Probl Psychother — Topical Problems of Psychotherapy

TOPRA — Tooling and Production

Top Rep NB Miner Resour Branch — Topical Report. New Brunswick Mineral Resources Branch

Top Rev Haematol — Topical Reviews in Haematology

Topsfield Hist Soc Coll — Topsfield Historical Society. Collections

Top Stereochem — Topics in Stereochemistry

Top Sulfur Chem — Topics in Sulfur Chemistry

Top Ther — Topical Therapy

Top Therap — Topics in Therapeutics

Top Vaccine Adjuvant Res — Topics in Vaccine Adjuvant Research

Tor — Torre

Tor Ac Mm — Memorie della Reale Accademia delle Scienze di Torino

Tor Ac Sc At — Atti della Reale Accademia delle Scienze di Torino

Tor Ac Sc Mm — Memorie della Reale Accademia delle Scienze di Torino

Tor At Ac Sc — Atti della Reale Accademia delle Scienze di Torino

TOREA — Toshiba Review

Torf Delo — Torfyanoe Delo

Torfnachrichten Forsch Werbestelle Torf — Torfnachrichten der Forschungs- und Werbestelle fuer Torf

Torf Prom — Torfyanaya Promyshlennost'

Torf Promst — Torfyanaya Promyshlennost

Torf Zh — Torf Zhurnal

Tori Bull Ornithol Soc Jpn — Tori. Bulletin of the Ornithological Society of Japan

Torino Univ Ist Geol Pub — Torino Universita. Istituto Geologico. Pubblicazioni

Tor Lav Sc Fis Mt — Notizia Storica dei Lavori fatti dalla Classe di Scienze Fisiche e Matematiche della Reale Accademia delle Scienze (Torino)

Tor Life — Toronto Life

Tor Mm Ac — Memorie della Reale Accademia delle Scienze di Torino

Toronto Gen Met Regist — Toronto General Meteorological Register

Toronto U Faculty L Rev — Toronto University. Faculty Law Review

Toronto Univ Dep Mech Eng Tech Publ Ser — Toronto University. Department of Mechanical Engineering. Technical Publication Series

Toronto Univ Inst Aerosp Stud UTIAS Rep — Toronto University. Institute for Aerospace Studies. UTIAS Report

Toronto Univ Inst Aerosp Stud UTIAS Rev — Toronto University. Institute for Aerospace Studies. UTIAS Review

Toronto Univ Inst Aerosp Stud UTIAS Tech Note — Toronto University. Institute for Aerospace Studies. UTIAS Technical Note

Toronto Univ Qtr — Toronto University Quarterly

Toronto Univ Studies G S — Toronto University Studies. Geological Series

TORPA — Torfyanaya Promyshlennost

Torreia Nueva Ser — Torreia Nueva Serie

Torrey Bot Club Bull — Torrey Botanical Club. Bulletin

Torry Advis Note — Torry Advisory Note. Torry Research Station

Torry Leafl — Torry Leaflets. Torry Research Station

Torry Mem — Torry Memoirs. Torry Research Station

Torry Misc Pap — Torry Miscellaneous Papers. Torry Research Station

Torry Res — Torry Research

Torry Res Handl Preserv Fish — Torry Research on the Handling and Preservation of Fish and Fish Products

Torry Res Stn (Aberdeen Scotl) Annu Rep — Torry Research Station (Aberdeen, Scotland). Annual Report

Torry Res Stn Annu Rep Handl Preserv Fish Fish Prod — Torry Research Station. Annual Report on the Handling and Preservation of Fish and Fish Products

Torry Spec Rep — Torry Special Reports. Torry Research Station

Torry Tech Pap — Torry Technical Paper. Torry Research Station
Tortolini A — Annali di Scienze Matematiche e Fisiche. Tortolini
TOS — Texas Ornithological Society. Bulletin
TOSCA — Tobacco Science
Toshiba Rev — Toshiba Review
Toshiba Rev (Int Ed) — Toshiba Review (International Edition)
Tosh-Kai — Toshokan-Kai
Tosh Kenk — Toshokan Kenkyu
Tosh Zass — Toshokan Zasshi
TOT — Tales of Tomorrow
Total Inf — Total Information
Tot Lat Lexikon — Totius Latinitatis Lexicon
Toul Ac Sc BII — Bulletin de l'Academie des Sciences, Inscriptions et Belles, Lettres de Toulouse
Toul Ac Sc Mm — Memoires de l'Academie des Sciences, Inscriptions et Belles-Lettres de Toulouse
Toul Fac Sc A — Annales de la Faculte des Sciences de Toulouse pour les Sciences Mathematiques et les Sciences Physiques
Toul Mm Ac — Memoires de l'Academie des Sciences, Inscriptions et Belles-Lettres de Toulouse
Toul Mm Ac Sc — Memoires de l'Academie des Sciences, Inscriptions et Belles-Lettres de Toulouse
Toulouse Med — Toulouse Medical
Toul S H Nt BII — Bulletin de la Societe d'Histoire Naturelle de Toulouse
Toul S Sc BII — Bulletin de la Societe des Sciences Physiques et Naturelles de Toulouse
Touraine Med — Touraine Medicale
Tourbe Philos — Tourbe Philosophique
TourF — Tour de Feu. Revue Internationaliste de Creation Poetique
Tourism Aust — Tourism Australia
Tourism Engl — Tourism in England
Tourism Intell Q — Tourism Intelligence Quarterly
Tour Monde — Tour du Monde
TourSJ — Tour Saint-Jacques
Tours Symp Nucl Phys — Tours Symposium on Nuclear Physics
Toute Electron — Toute l'Electronique
Toute Radio — Toute la Radio et Radio Constructeur
Tov — Tovaris
Tovar Poshir Polit Nauk Znan Ukr SSR — Tovaristvo dlya Poshirennya Politichnikh i Naukovikh Znan Ukrains'koi SSR
TOW — Tales of Wonder
TOW — The Oil Weekly
TOWA — The Oil Weekly. World Oil Atlas
Tower Hamlets Local Trade Dev — Tower Hamlets Local Trade Development
Town & Country Plan — Town and Country Planning
Town Cntry Plann — Town and Country Planning
Town Ctry Plan — Town and Country Planning
Town Ctry Plann — Town and Country Planning
Town Plan Inst J — Town Planning Institute. Journal
Town Planning R — Town Planning Review
Town Plann Inst J — Town Planning Institute. Journal
Town Plann Q — Town Planning Quarterly
Town Plann Rev — Town Planning Review
Town Plann Today — Town Planning Today
Town Plan R — Town Planning Review
Townsville Nat — Townsville Naturalist
Tox Appl Ph — Toxicology and Applied Pharmacology
TOXIA — Toxicon
Toxic Appl Pharmac — Toxicology and Applied Pharmacology
Toxic Assess — Toxicity Assessment
Toxic Hazard Waste Disposal — Toxic and Hazardous Waste Disposal
Toxicity Assess — Toxicity Assessment
Toxic Model — Toxicology Modeling
Toxicol & Ecotoxicol News Rev — Toxicology and Ecotoxicology News/Reviews
Toxicol Annu — Toxicology Annual
Toxicol Appl Pharmacol — Toxicology and Applied Pharmacology
Toxicol Appl Pharmacol Suppl — Toxicology and Applied Pharmacology. Supplement
Toxicol Ecotoxicol News — Toxicology and Ecotoxicology News
Toxicol Ecotoxicol News Rev — Toxicology and Ecotoxicology News/Reviews
Toxicol Environ Chem — Toxicological and Environmental Chemistry
Toxicol Environ Chem Rev — Toxicological and Environmental Chemistry Reviews
Toxicol Eur Res — Toxicological European Research
Toxicol Ind Health — Toxicology and Industrial Health
Toxicol Lett — Toxicology Letters
Toxicol Lett (Amst) — Toxicology Letters (Amsterdam)
Toxicol Methods — Toxicology Methods
Toxicol Model — Toxicology Modeling
Toxicol Pathol — Toxicologic Pathology
Toxicol Risk Assess — Toxicology and Risk Assessment. Principles, Methods, and Applications [*monograph*]
Toxicol Sci — Toxicological Sciences
Toxicol Vitr — Toxicology in Vitro
Toxic Subst J — Toxic Substances Journal
Toxic Subst Mech — Toxic Substance Mechanisms
TOXLIST — Toxic Regulatory Listings
Toyo Bunka Kenkyu Kiyo — Toyo Bunka Kenkyusho Kiyo
Toyo Junior Coll Food Technol Toyo Inst Food Technol Res Rep — Toyo Junior College of Food Technology and Toyo Institute of Food Technology. Research Report
Toyo Ongaku — Toyo Ongaku Kenkyu
Toyota Conf — Toyota Conference
Toyota Eng — Toyota Engineering
Toyota Tech Rev — Toyota Technical Review
TP — Tempo Presente

TP — Temps Present
TP — Terzo Programma
TP — Thought Patterns
TP — Tijdschrift voor de Politie
TP — Tijdschrift voor Philosophie
TP — Topics in Photosynthesis
TP — T'oung Pao
TP — Trabajos de Prehistoria
TPA — T'oung Pao. Archives
TPAEDP — Topics in Paediatrics
TP & LGG — Town Planning and Local Government Guide
TPAPA — Transactions and Proceedings. American Philological Association
TP A Ph A — Transactions and Proceedings. American Philological Association
TPB — Tennessee Philological Bulletin
TPC — Trade Practices Cases
TPCCA — Topics in Current Chemistry
TPCD — Trade Practices Commission. Decisions and Determinations
TPCDD — Trade Practices Commission. Decisions and Determinations
TPCWDL — Colorado. Division of Wildlife. Technical Publication
TPEMA — Telephone Engineer and Management
TPEMDZ — Topics in Perinatal Medicine
TPer — Tetradi Perevodcika
TPETA — Techniques du Petrole
TPG — Town Planning and Local Government Guide
TPH — Telephony
TPh — Tijdschrift voor Philosophie
TPhS — Transactions. Philological Society
TPhS — Transactions. Philological Society
TPHSDY — Trends in Pharmacological Sciences
TPhSO — Transactions. Philological Society. Oxford
TPIAN — Trudy Paleontologicheskogo Instituta. Akademiia Nauk SSSR
TPIPAR — Trudy Tsentral'nogo Nauchno-Issledovatel'skogo i Proektno-Konstruktorskogo Instituta Profilaktiki Pnevmokoniozov i Tekhniki Bezopasnosti
TPIRA — Trudy Gosudarstvennyi Institut po Proektirovaniyu i Issledovatel'skim Rabotam v Neftedobyvayushchei Promyshlennosti
TPI Rep Trop Prod Inst — TPI Report. Tropical Products Institute
TPI Text Prax Int — TPI Textil Praxis International
TPJ — Tennessee Poetry Journal
TPJSL — Transactions and Proceedings. Japan Society (London)
T Pla — Tidsskrift for Planteavl
TPLAAV — Tidsskrift foer Planteavl
TPLGG — Town Planning and Local Government Guide
TPLOA — Teploenergetika
TPLQ-A — Town Planning Quarterly
TPLR-A — Town Planning Review
TPM — Tubular Products Manual
TPMAD5 — Tropical Pest Management
TPMGA — Teoriya i Praktika Metallurgii
TPMXA — Tecnica Pecuaria en Mexico
TPNF — Tijdschrift voor Privaatrecht, Notariaat, en Fiscaalrecht
TPNO — Tree Planters' Notes
TPNPAI — Trudy Polyarnogo Nauchno-Issledovatel'skogo i Proektnogo Instituta Morskogo Rybnogo Khozyaistva i Okeanografii
TPO — Nederlands Transport
TPow — Tygodnik Powszechny
TPPADK — Trends and Perspectives in Parasitology
TPPha — Transactions. College of Physicians of Philadelphia
TPPYA — Topical Problems of Psychotherapy
TPPYAL — Aktuelle Fragen der Psychotherapie
T P Q — Theologisch-Praktische Quartalschrift
TPQS — Theologisch-Praktische Quartalschrift
TPR — Telecommunications Product Review
TPr — Tempo Presente
T Pr — Temps Present
TPR — Three Penny Review
TPR — Tijdschrift voor Privaatrecht
TPrLJ — Thiels Preussische Landwirtschaftliche Jahrbuecher
TPRRD — Technik-Index ueber Plasmaphysikalische Forschung und Fusionsreaktoren
TPRS — Trade Practices Reporting Service
TPRSL — Transactions and Proceedings. Royal Society of Literature
TPrzPI — Trudy Przeval'skogo Pedagogiceskogo Instituta
TPS — [*The*] Pope Speaks
TPS — Theologie Pastorale et Spiritualite
TPS — Transactions. Philological Society
TPSB — Thomas Paine Society. Bulletin
TPSFA — Tohoku Psychologica Folia
TPSL — Transactions. Philological Society of London
TPSM — Tepatshimuwin. Journal d'Information des Attikamekes et des Montagnais
TPSRS — Theologie Pastorale et Spiritualite. Recherches et Syntheses
TQ — Texas Quarterly
TQ — Theatre Quarterly
TQ — Theologische Quartalschrift
TQ — Toronto Quarterly
TQ — Tri-Quarterly
TQAGA — Technique Agricole
TQE — Technique de l'Eau et de l'Assainissement
TQM Mag — TQM Magazine
TQS — Theologische Quartalschrift
TR — Table Ronde
TR — Technical Reporter
TR — Technology Review
TR — Theatre Research
TR — Theologische Revue
TR — Theologische Rundschau

TR — Tibetan Review
TR — Tijdschrift voor Rechtsgeschiedenis
TR — Tobacco Reporter
TR — Tradicion [*Lima*]
TR — Transatlantic Review
TR — Transportation Science
TR — Triad
Tr — Tribune
Tr — Trivium
Tr — Y Traethodydd
Tr 1 Pervogo Mosk Med Inst — Trudy 1 Pervogo Moskovskogo Meditsinskogo Instituta
TRA — Television/Radio Age
TRA — Toward Revolutionary Art
Tra — Tracker
TrA — Traduction Automatique
TRA — Training
Tr A Am Physicians — Transactions. Association of American Physicians
Trab 5 Cong Med Latino-Am — Trabajos Presentados al Quinto Congreso Medico Latino-Americano
Trab Actas Congr Boliv Ing — Trabajos Presentados y Actas. Congreso Bolivariano de Ingenieria
Trabajos Estadist — Trabajos de Estadistica
Trabajos Estadist Investigacion Oper — Trabajos de Estadistica y de Investigacion Operativa
Trabajos Investigacion Oper — Trabajos Investigacion Operativa
Trab Antrop Etnol — Trabalhos. Sociedade Portuguesa de Antropologia e Etnologia
Trab Antropol Etnol — Trabalhos de Antropologia e Etnologia
Trab Astr Geod Inst Geogr Milit B Aires — Trabajos Astronomicos y Geodesicos. Instituto Geografico Militar (Buenos Aires)
Trab Cat Hist Crit Med Univ Madr — Trabajos. Catedra de Historia Critica de la Medicina. Universidad de Madrid
Trab Cent Bot Junta Invest Ultramar — Trabalhos. Centro de Botanica. Junta de Investigacoes do Ultramar
Trab Cient Univ Cordoba — Trabajos Cientificos de la Universidad de Cordoba
Trab Compostelanos Biol — Trabajos Compostelanos de Biologia
Trab Comunic La Plata — Trabajos y Comunicaciones (La Plata, Argentina)
Trab Dep Bot Fisiol Veg Univ Madrid — Trabajos. Departamento de Botanica y Fisiologia Vegetal. Universidad de Madrid
Trab Dep Mat — Trabalhos do Departamento de Matematica
TrabEsta — Trabajos de Estadistica
Trab Estac Agric Exp Leon — Trabajos. Estacion Agricola Experimental de Leon
Trab Estadistica — Trabajos de Estadistica y de Investigacion
Trab Geol — Trabajos de Geologia
Trab Geol Oviedo Univ Fac Cienc — Trabajos de Geologia. Oviedo Universidad. Facultad de Ciencias
Trabhs Acad Sci Lisb — Trabalhos da Academia de Sciencias de Lisboa
Trabhs Anat Cirurg Exp Univ Oporto — Trabalhos de Anatomia e Cirurgia Experimental. Faculdade de Medicina. Universidade de Oporto
Trabhs Cent Bot Jta Invest Ultramar — Trabalhos do Centro de Botanico da Junta de Investigacoes do Ultramar
Trabhs Cent Invest Cient Algod Lourenco Marq — Trabalhos do Centro de Investigacao Cientifica Algodoeira (Lourenco Marques)
Trabhs Inst Biol Mar Oceanogr Univ Recife — Trabalhos do Instituto de Biologia Maritima e Oceanografia. Universidade de Recife
Trabhs Inst Bot Dr Goncalo Sampaio — Trabalhos do Instituto de Botanica Dr. Goncalo Sampaio
Trabhs Inst Bot Fac Cienc Lisb — Trabalhos do Instituto Botanico da Faculdade de Ciencias de Lisboa
Trab Inst Bernardino Sahagun — Trabajos. Instituto Bernardino de Sahagun
Trab Inst Bernardino Sahagun Antrop Etnol — Trabajos del Instituto Bernardino de Sahagun de Antropologia y Etnologia
Trab Inst Biol Anim Madr — Trabajos del Instituto de Biologia Animal (Madrid)
Trab Inst Cajal Invest Biol — Trabajos. Instituto Cajal de Investigaciones Biologicas
Trab Inst Econ Prod Ganad Ebro — Trabajos. Instituto de Economia y Producciones Ganaderas del Ebro
Trab Inst Esp Entomol — Trabajos. Instituto Espanol de Entomologia
Trab Inst Esp Oceanogr — Trabajos. Instituto Espanol de Oceanografia
Trab Inst Fisiol Fac Med Univ Lisboa — Trabajos. Instituto de Fisiologia. Faculdade de Medicina. Universidade do Lisboa
Trab Inst Nac Cienc Med (Madrid) — Trabajos. Instituto Nacional de Ciencias Medicas (Madrid)
Trab Inst Oceanogr Univ Recife — Trabalhos. Instituto Oceanografico. Universidade do Recife
Trab Investigacao 79 — Trabalhos de Investigacao 79
Trab Investigacao 80 — Trabalhos de Investigacao 80
Trab Lab Anat Microsc Madr — Trabajos del Laboratorio de Anatomia Microscopica. Junta para Amplicacion de Estudios y Investigaciones Cientificas (Madrid)
Trab Lab Bioquim Quim Apl Inst Alonso Barba — Trabajo. Laboratorio de Bioquimica y Quimica Aplicada. Instituto "Alonso Barba"
Trab Lab Cat Parasit Patol Trop Madr — Trabajos del Laboratorio de la Catedra de Parasitologia y de Patologia Tropical (Madrid)
Trab Lab Fisiol Cerebr Madr — Trabajos del Laboratorio de Fisiologia Cerebral. Junta para Ampliacion de Estudios y Investigaciones Cientificas (Madrid)
Trab Lab Histopat Madr — Trabajos del Laboratorio de Histopatologia. Junta para Ampliacion de Estudios y Investigaciones Cientificas (Madrid)
Trab Lab Invest Biol Univ Madrid — Trabajos del Laboratorio de Investigaciones Biologicas de la Universidad de Madrid
Trab Lab Invest Bioquim Univ Zaragoza — Trabajos del Laboratorio de Investigaciones Bioquimicas de la Universidad de Zaragoza
Trab Lab Invest Fis Madr — Trabajos del Laboratorio de Investigaciones Fisicas. Instituto Nacional de Ciencias Fisico-Naturales (Madrid)

Trab Lab Zool Univ Chile — Trabajos del Laboratorio de Zoologia. Universidad de Chile
Trab Mat — Trabajos de Matematica
Trab Mems Soc Nac Cirug Habana — Trabajos y Memorias. Sociedad Nacional de Cirugia (Habana)
Trab Mus Bot Univ Nac Cordoba — Trabajos del Museo Botanico. Universidad Nacional de Cordoba
Trab Mus Cienc Nat Barcelona — Trabajos del Museo de Ciencias Naturales de Barcelona
Trab Mus Coml Venez — Trabajos del Museo Comercial de Venezuela
Trab Mus Zool Barcelona — Trabajos del Museo de Zoologia (Barcelona)
Trab Obs Igueldo — Trabajos del Observatorio de Igueldo
Trab Oceanogr Univ Fed Pernambuco — Trabalhos Oceanograficos. Universidade Federal de Pernambuco
Trab Pesqui Inst Nutr Univ Bras — Trabalhos e Pesquisas. Instituto de Nutricao. Universidade do Brasil
Trab Preh — Trabajos de Prehistoria
Trab Prev Soc Mex — Trabajo y Prevision Social (Mexico)
Trab Pr Hist — Trabajos de Prehistoria
Trab Publnes Inst Nac Nutr B Aires — Trabajos y Publicaciones. Instituto Nacional de la Nutricion (Buenos Aires)
Trab Segur Soc Rio — Trabalho e Seguro Social (Rio de Janeiro)
Trab Sem Mat Argent — Trabajos del Seminario Matematico Argentino
Trab Soc Obstet Ginec Cordoba — Trabajos de la Sociedad de Obstetricia y Ginecologia de Cordoba
Trab Y Conf — Trabajos y Conferencias. Seminario de Estudios Americanistas Facultad de Filosofia y Letras
TRAC — DTIC [*Defense Technical Information Center*] Technical Awareness Circular
TRAC — Travaux et Conferences. Universite Libre de Bruxelles. Faculte de Droit
TrAC — Trends in Analytical Chemistry
Trace — TRACE. Travaux et Recherches dans les Ameriques du Centre
Trace Anal — Trace Analysis
Trace Elem Electrolytes — Trace Elements and Electrolytes
Trace Elem Med — Trace Elements in Medicine
Trace Elem Sci — Trace Elements Science
Trace Met Anal Speciation — Trace Metal Analysis and Speciation
Trace Met Environ — Trace Metals in the Environment
Trace Met Metab Tokyo — Trace Metal Metabolism (Tokyo)
Tracer Elem Rep — Tracer Elements Reports. Commonwealth X-Ray and Radium Laboratory. C.S.I.R.O. Australia
Tracers Exogram Oil Gas Rev — Tracer's Exogram and Oil and Gas Review
Trace Subst Environ Health — Trace Substances in Environmental Health
Trace Subst Environ Health Proc Univ Mo Annu Conf — Trace Substances in Environmental Health. Proceedings. University of Missouri. Annual Conference
Track Field Q Rev — Track and Field Quarterly Review
Track Tech — Track Technique
Tract Fld Bk — Tractor Field Book
Tract Fmg — Tractor Farming
Tract Fm Mach Surv — Tractor and Farm Machinery Survey
Tract Gas Eng Rev — Tractor and Gas Engine Review
Tractn Elect — Traction Electrique
Tractn Nouv — Traction Nouvelle
Tractn Transm — Traction and Transmission
Tractors Mach — Tractors and Machinery. Department of Agricultural Engineering. University of Illinois College of Agriculture
TrAC Trends Anal Chem Pers Ed — TrAC. Trends in Analytical Chemistry (Personal Edition)
Tracts Comput — Tracts for Computers. University College
Tract Sel Khozmashiny — Tractory i Sel Khozmashiny
Tracts Math Nat Sci — Tracts in Mathematics and Natural Science
Tract Trail — Tractor and Trailer
Tract Wld — Tractor World
T Rad — Tidsskrift for Radio
T Rad — Tidsskrift for Radio og Fjernsyn
Trad — Traditio
Trad Dep Exploit Util Bois Univ Laval — Traduction. Departement d'Exploitation et Utilisation des Bois. Universite Laval
Trade and Commer — Trade and Commerce
Trade and Ind — Trade and Industry
Trade Cas CCH — Trade Cases. Commerce Clearing House
Trade Commod Mark Summaries C Exports — Trade by Commodities. Market Summaries. Series C. Exports
Trade Commod Mark Summaries C Imports — Trade by Commodities. Market Summaries. Series C. Imports
Trade D — Trade Digest
Trade Develop — Trade and Development
Trade Dig — Trade Digest
Trade Ind — Trade and Industry
Trade Ind Bul — Trade and Industry Bulletin
Trade Ind Index — Trade and Industry Index
Trademark Bull — Bulletin. United States Trademark Association Series
Trademark Bull (NS) — Trademark Bulletin. United States Trademark Association (New Series)
Trade-Mark Rep — Trade-Mark Reporter
Trademark Rptr — Trademark Reporter
Trade Mks J — Trade Marks Journal
Trade News N — Trade News North
Trade R — Trade Review. Swedish Chamber of Commerce for Australia
Trade Reg Rep CCH — Trade Regulation Reporter. Commerce Clearing House
Trade Reg Rev — Trade Regulation Review
Trades Union D — Trades Union Digest
Tra Devel Aust — Training and Development in Australia
Trad Greec — Trade with Greece
Traditional Kent Bldgs — Traditional Kent Buildings

Trad Mus — Traditional Music
Trad Mus Yrbk — Yearbook for Traditional Music
TRADSTAT — World Trade Statistics Database
Trad Textes Persans — Traductions de Textes Persans
Traducc Estac Exp Agric Lima — Traduccion. Estacion Experimental Agricola (Lima)
Traduct Autom — Traduction Automatique
Traduit Russe Biol — Traduit du Russe. Biologie
Traduit Russe Math — Traduit du Russe. Mathematiques
Traduit Russe Phys — Traduit du Russe. Physique
Trad Un Dig — Trades Union Digest
TRAEA — Technical Report Series. IAEA
Trae O Ind — Trae og Industri
Traff Dig — Traffic Digest
Traff Educ — Traffic Education
Traff Engng — Traffic Engineering
Traff Engng Control — Traffic Engineering and Control
Traffic Dig Rev — Traffic Digest and Review
Traffic Eng — Traffic Engineering
Traffic Eng & Control — Traffic Engineering and Control
Traffic Eng Contr — Traffic Engineering and Control
Traffic Manage — Traffic Management
Traffic Q — Traffic Quarterly
Traffic Qly — Traffic Quarterly
Traffic Saf — Traffic Safety
Traffic Saf Ann Rep — Traffic Safety Annual Report
Traffic Saf Res Rev — Traffic Safety Research Review
Traff Q — Traffic Quarterly
Traf o Tekn — Trafik og Teknik
Traf Tek — Trafik og Teknik
TRAGB — Trudy po Radiatsionnoi Gigiene Leningradskii Nauchno-Issledovatel'skii Institut Radiatsionnoi Gigieny
Trag Graec Frag — Tragicorum Graecorum Fragmenta
TRAIB — Trudy Astrofizicheskogo Instituta Akademiya Nauk Kazakhskoi SSR
TrAIEE — Transactions. American Institution of Electrical Engineers
Train — Training
Train Agric Rural Dev — Training for Agriculture and Rural Development
Train & Devel J — Training and Development Journal
Train Dev Aust — Training and Development in Australia
Train Dev J — Training and Development Journal
Training & Dev J — Training and Development Journal
Train Off — Training Officer
Train Pap US Weath Bur — Training Papers. United States Weather Bureau
Train Sch B — Training School Bulletin
Trains Ill — Trains Illustrated
Traite — Traite des Monnaies Grecques et Romaines
Traite Anat Veg — Traite d'Anatomie Vegetale
Traite Nouvelles Tech — Traite des Nouvelles Technologies
Trait Surf — Traitements de Surface
Trait Therm — Traitement Thermique
Tr Akad Med Nauk SSSR — Trudy Akademii Meditsinskikh Nauk SSSR
Tr Akad Nauk Gruz SSR Inst Sist Upr — Trudy Akademii Nauk Gruzinskoi SSR Institut Sistem Upravleniya
Tr Akad Nauk Kaz SSR Inst Mikrobiol Virusol — Trudy Akademiia Nauk Kazakhskoi SSR Institut Mikrobiologii i Virusologii
Tr Akad Nauk Latv SSR Inst Mikrobiol — Trudy Akademii Nauk Latviiskoi SSR Institut Mikrobiologii
Tr Akad Nauk Litov SSR Inst Biol — Trudy Akademii Nauk Litovskoi SSR Institut Biologii
Tr Akad Nauk Lit SSR Ser V — Trudy Akademii Nauk Litovskoi SSR. Seriya V
Tr Akad Nauk Lit SSR Ser V Biol Nauki — Trudy Akademii Nauk Litovskoi SSR. Seriya V. Biologicheskie Nauki
Tr Akad Nauk SSSR Inst Biol Vnutr Vod — Trudy Akademiia Nauk SSSR Institut Biologii Vnutrennikh Vod
Tr Akad Nauk SSSR Karel Fil — Trudy Akademii Nauk SSSR Karel'skii Filial
Tr Akad Nauk SSSR Sibirsk Otd Biol Inst — Trudy Akademiia Nauk SSSR Sibirskoe Otdelenie. Biologicheskii Institut
Tr Akad Nauk Tadzh SSR — Trudy Akademii Nauk Tadzhikskoi SSR
Tr Akad Nauk Turkm SSR — Trudy Akademii Nauk Turkmenskoi SSR
Tr Akad Neft Promsti — Trudy Akademii Neftyanoi Promyslennosti
Tr Akad Stroit Arkhit SSSR Zapadno Sib Fil — Trudy Akademiya Stroitel'stva i Arkhitektury SSSR Zapadno-Sibirskii Filial
Trakemi PappTek — Trakemi och Pappersteknik
Trak Sel'khozmashiny — Traktory i Sel'khozmashiny
Trakt Landmasch — Traktor und die Landmaschine
Trakt Sel'khozmash — Traktory i Sel'khozmashiny
Tr Alma At Gos Med Inst — Trudy Alma Atinskii Gosudarstvennyi Meditsinskii Institut
Tr Alma-At Med Inst — Trudy Alma-Atinskogo Meditsinskogo Instituta
Tr Alma At Nauchno Issled Proektn Inst Stroit Mater — Trudy Alma-Atinskogo Nauchno-Issledovatel'skogo i Proektnogo Instituta Stroitel'nykh Materialov
Tr Alma-At Zoovet Inst — Trudy Alma-Atinskogo Zooveterinarnogo Instituta
Tr Altai Gorno Metall Nauchno Issled Inst Akad Nauk Kaz SSR — Trudy Altaiskogo Gorno-Metallurgicheskogo Nauchno-Issledovatel'skogo Instituta Akademiya Nauk Kazakhskoi SSR
Tr Altai Politekh Inst — Trudy Altaiskogo Politekhnicheskogo Instituta
Tr Altai Skh Inst — Trudy Altaiskogo Sel'skokhozyaistvennogo Instituta
Tr Am Acad Ophth — Transactions. American Academy of Ophthalmology and Otolaryngology
Tr Am Ass Genito-Urin Surg — Transactions. American Association of Genito-Urinary Surgeons
Tr Am Fish Soc — Transactions. American Fisheries Society
TRAMIT — Especialidades Farmaceuticas en Tramite de Registro
Tr Am Micr Soc — Transactions. American Microscopical Society
Tr Am Neurol A — Transactions. American Neurological Association

Tr Am Ophth Soc — Transactions. American Ophthalmological Society
Tr Am Soc Artific Int Organs — Transactions. American Society for Artificial Internal Organs
Tr Am Soc Trop Med — Transactions. American Society of Tropical Medicine
Tr Amur Skh Opytn Stn — Trudy Amurskoi Sel'skokhozyaistvennoi Opytnoi Stantsii
Tramw Rly Wld — Tramway and Railway World
TRANA — Transfusion
Tr and Est — Trusts and Estates
Tr Angarsk Fil Irkutsk Politekh Inst — Trudy Angarskogo Filiala Irkutskogo Politekhnicheskogo Instituta
Trans — Transactions. Institute of Professional Engineers
Trans — Transition
Trans 8th Int Congr Soil Sci — Transactions. 8th International Congress of Soil Science
Trans AACE — Transactions. American Association of Cost Engineers
Trans A Anthrac Conf Lehigh Univ — Transactons of the Annual Anthracite Conference of Lehigh University
Trans Acad Sci St Louis — Transactions. Academy of Science of St. Louis
Trans A Conf Malar Fld Wkrs — Transactions of the Annual Conference of Malaria Field Workers. United States Public Health Service
Trans A Conf St Territ Hlth Offrs — Transactions of the Annual Conference of State and Territorial Health Officers with the United States Health and Marine Hospital Services
Trans Act — Transactions. American Philological Association
Transact Am Phil Ass — Transactions and Proceedings. American Philological Association
Transact Cumb Ant — Transactions. Cumberland and Westmorland Antiquarian and Archaeological Society
Transact Dumfries — Transactions. Dumfriesshire and Galloway Natural History and Antiquarian Society
Transact Essex — Essex Archaeology and History. The Transactions of the Essex Archaeological Society
Transact Lond — Transactions. London and Middlesex Archaeological Society
Transact Proceed Amer Philol Assoc — Transactions and Proceedings. American Philological Association
Transact Roy Soc Canada — Transactions. Royal Society of Canada
Trans Act Soc Aust & NZ — Transactions. Actuarial Society of Australia and New Zealand
Transact South Stafford — Transactions. South Staffordshire Archaeological and Historical Society
Trans Actuar Soc S Afr — Transactions. Actuarial Society of South Africa
Transact Worc — Transactions. Worcestershire Archaeological Society
Transafr J Hist — Transafrican Journal of History
Trans Agric Engng Soc (Tokyo) — Transactions. Agricultural Engineering Society (Tokyo)
Trans AIChE — Transactions. AIChE
Trans AIME Metall Soc — Transactions. AIME [*American Institute of Mining, Metallurgical, and Petroleum Engineers*] Metallurgical Society
Trans Albany Inst — Transactions. Albany Institute
Trans Alkali Subcommn Int Soc Soil Sci — Transactions of the Alkali Subcommission. International Society of Soil Science
Trans All-India Inst Ment Health — Transactions. All-India Institute of Mental Health
Trans All India Inst Ment Hlth — Transactions of the All-India Institute of Mental Health
Trans All Union Sci Res Inst Confect Ind — Transactions. All-Union Scientific Research Institute of the Confectionery Industry
Trans All Union Sci Res Inst Veg Oils Margarine — Transactions. All-Union Scientific Research Institute for Vegetable Oils and Margarine
Trans Am Acad Ophthalmol Oto-Laryngol — Transactions. American Academy of Ophthalmology and Oto-Laryngology
Trans Am Acad Ophthal Oto Lar — Transactions of the American Academy of Ophthalmology and Oto-Laryngology
Trans Am Acad Pediat — Transactions of the American Academy of Pediatrics
Trans Am Acad Rly Surg — Transactions. American Academy of Railway Surgeons
Trans Am Ass Cereal Chem — Transactions of the American Association of Cereal Chemists
Trans Am Ass Dent Edit — Transactions. American Association of Dental Editors
Trans Am Ass Genito Urin Surg — Transactions of the American Association of Genito-Urinary Surgeons
Trans Am Ass Obstet Gynec — Transactions of the American Association of Obstetricians and Gynecologists
Trans Am Ass Obstet Gynec Abdom Surg — Transactions of the American Association of Obstetricians, Gynaecologists, and Abdominal Surgeons
Trans Am Assoc Cost Eng — Transactions. American Association of Cost Engineers
Trans Am Assoc Genito-Urin Surg — Transactions. American Association of Genito-Urinary Surgeons
Trans Am Assoc Obstet Gynecol — Transactions. American Association of Obstetricians and Gynecologists
Trans Am Assoc Obstet Gynecol Abdom Surg — Transactions. American Association of Obstetricians, Gynecologists, and Abdominal Surgeons
Trans Am Ass Study Goiter — Transactions of the American Association for the Study of Goiter
Trans Am Ass Study Prev Infant Mort — Transactions of the American Association for the Study and Prevention of Infant Mortality
Trans Am Brass Fndrs Ass — Transactions of the American Brass Founders' Association
Trans Am Brew Inst — Transactions. American Brewing Institute
Trans Am Broncho-Esophagol Assoc — Transactions. American Broncho-Esophagological Association
Trans Am Broncho Esoph Ass — Transactions of the American Broncho-Esophagolic Association
Trans Am Ceram Soc — Transactions. American Ceramic Society

Trans Am Child Hlth Ass — Transactions of the American Child Health Association

Trans Am Child Hyg Ass — Transactions of the American Child Hygiene Association

Trans Am Clin Clim Ass — Transactions of the American Clinical and Climatological Association

Trans Am Clin Climatol Assoc — Transactions. American Clinical and Climatological Association

Trans Am Coll Cardiol — Transactions. American College of Cardiology

Trans Am Crystallogr Assoc — Transactions. American Crystallographic Association

Trans Am Dent Ass — Transactions of the American Dental Association

Trans Am Dent Soc Eur — Transactions of the American Dental Society of Europe

Trans Am Derm Ass — Transactions of the American Dermatological Association

Trans Am Electrochem Soc — Transactions of the American Electrochemical Society

Trans Am Electroch Soc — Transactions. American Electrochemical Society

Trans Am Electro Ther Ass — Transactions of the American Electro-Therapeutic Association

Trans Am Entomol Soc (Phila) — Transactions. American Entomological Society (Philadelphia)

Trans Am Ent Soc — Transactions. American Entomological Society

Trans Amer Acad Ophthalmol Otolaryngol — Transactions. American Academy of Ophthalmology and Otolaryngology

Trans Amer Ass Cereal Chem — Transactions. American Association of Cereal Chemists

Trans Amer Electro-Chem Soc — Transactions. American Electrochemical Society

Trans Amer Foundrymen's Soc — Transactions. American Foundrymen's Society

Trans Amer Geophys Union — Transactions. American Geophysical Union

Trans Amer Lar Rhinol Otol Soc — Transactions of the American Laryngological, Rhinological, and Otological Society

Trans Amer Math Soc — Transactions. American Mathematical Society

Trans Amer Med Assoc — Transactions. American Medical Association

Trans Amer Microscop Soc — Transactions. American Microscopical Society

Trans Amer Nucl Soc — Transactions. American Nuclear Society

Trans Amer Phil Ass — Transactions. American Philological Association

Trans Amer Philol Assoc — Transactions. American Philological Association

Trans Am Fisheries Soc — Transactions. American Fisheries Society

Trans Am Fish Soc — Transactions. American Fisheries Society

Trans Am Fndrym Ass — Transactions of the American Foundrymen's Association

Trans Am Fndrym Ass Bull Sect — Transactions. American Foundrymen's Association. Bulletin Section

Trans Am Foundrymen's Assoc Q — Transactions. American Foundrymen's Association [*Later, American Foundrymen's Society*]. Quarterly

Trans Am Geophys Union — Transactions. American Geophysical Union

Trans Am Goiter Assoc — Transactions. American Goiter Association

Trans Am Gynecol Soc — Transactions. American Gynecological Society

Trans Am Inst Chem Eng — Transactions. American Institute of Chemical Engineers

Trans Am Inst Chem Engrs — Transactions of the American Institute of Chemical Engineers

Trans Am Inst Elect Engrs — Transactions of the American Institute of Electrical Engineers

Trans Am Inst Elect Engrs Mon — Transactions of the American Institute of Electrical Engineers. Monthly

Trans Am Inst Electr Eng — Transactions. American Institute of Electrical Engineers

Trans Am Inst Electr Eng Part 1 — Transactions. American Institute of Electrical Engineers. Part 1. Communicationand Electronics

Trans Am Inst Electr Eng Part 2 — Transactions. American Institute of Electrical Engineers. Part 2. Applications and Industry

Trans Am Inst Electr Eng Part 3 — Transactions. American Institute of Electrical Engineers. Part 3. Power Apparatus and Systems

Trans Am Inst Homoeop — Transactions of the American Institute of Homoeopathy

Trans Am Inst Ind Eng — Transactions. American Institute of Industrial Engineers

Trans Am Inst Metals — Transactions. American Institute of Metals

Trans Am Inst Min Eng — Transactions. American Institute of Mining Engineers

Trans Am Inst Min Metall Eng — Transactions. American Institute of Mining and Metallurgical Engineers

Trans Am Inst Min Metall Engn — Transactions. American Institute of Mining and Metallurgical Engineers

Trans Am Inst Min Metall Pet Eng — Transactions. American Institute of Mining, Metallurgical, and Petroleum Engineers

Trans Am Math Soc — Transactions. American Mathematical Society

Trans Am Microsc Soc — Transactions. American Microscopical Society

Trans Am Neurol Assoc — Transactions. American Neurological Association

Trans Am Nucl Soc — Transactions. American Nuclear Society

Trans Am Nucl Soc Suppl — Transactions. American Nuclear Society. Supplement

Trans Am Ophthalmol Soc — Transactions. American Ophthalmological Society

Trans Am Otol Soc — Transactions. American Otological Society

Trans Am Philos Soc — Transactions. American Philosophical Society

Trans Am Phil Soc — Transactions of the American Philosophical Society

Trans Am Proctol Soc — Transactions of the American Proctologic Society

Trans Am Res Free Acc Masons — Transactions. American Lodge of Research Free and Accepted Masons

Trans Am Roentg Ray Soc — Transactions of the American Roentgen Ray Society

Trans Am Soc Agric Eng Gen Ed — Transactions. American Society of Agricultural Engineers. General Edition

Trans Am Soc Agric Engrs — Transactions. American Society of Agricultural Engineers

Trans Am Soc Agric Engrs Gen Edn — Transactions. American Society of Agricultural Engineers. General Edition

Trans Am Soc Artif Internal Organs — Transactions. American Society for Artificial Internal Organs

Trans Am Soc Artif Intern Organs — Transactions. American Society for Artificial Internal Organs

Trans Am Soc Art Int Org — Transactions. American Society for Artificial Internal Organs

Trans Am Soc Civ Eng — Transactions. American Society of Civil Engineers

Trans Am Soc Civ Engrs — Transactions of the American Society of Civil Engineers

Trans Am Soc Heat Air-Cond Eng — Transactions. American Society of Heating and Air-Conditioning Engineers

Trans Am Soc Heat Air Condit Engrs — Transactions of the American Society of Heating and Air-Conditioning Engineers

Trans Am Soc Heat Refrig Air Condit Engrs — Transactions of the American Society of Heating, Refrigerating, and Air-Conditioning Engineers

Trans Am Soc Heat Vent Engrs — Transactions of the American Society of Heating and Ventilating Engineers

Trans Am Soc Lubric Engrs — Transactions of the American Society of Lubrication Engineers

Trans Am Soc Mech Engrs — Transactions of the American Society of Mechanical Engineers

Trans Am Soc Met — Transactions. American Society for Metals

Trans Am Soc Metals — Transactions. American Society for Metals

Trans Am Soc Ophthalmol Otolaryngol Allergy — Transactions. American Society of Ophthalmologic and Otolaryngologic Allergy

Trans Am Soc Refrig Engrs — Transactions of the American Society of Refrigerating Engineers

Trans Am Soc Steel Treat — Transactions. American Society for Steel Treating

Trans Am Soc Trop Med — Transactions of the American Society of Tropical Medicine

Trans Am Surg Ass — Transactions of the American Surgical Association

Trans Am Ther Soc — Transactions. American Therapeutic Society

Trans Am Urol Ass — Transactions of the American Urological Association

Trans Am Urol Ass N Cent Brch — Transactions of the American Urological Association. North Central Branch

Trans Am Urol Assoc — Transactions. American Urological Association

Trans Am Urol Ass S Cent Brch — Transactions of the American Urological Association. South Central Branch

Trans Am Urol Ass SEast Brch — Transactions of the American Urological Association. Southeastern Branch (afterwards Section)

Trans Am Urol Ass SWest Brch — Transactions of the American Urological Association. Southwestern Branch

Trans Am Urol Ass West Brch — Transactions of the American Urological Association. Western Branch

Trans Ancient Monuments Soc — Transactions. Ancient Monuments Society

Trans and J Br Ceram Soc — Transactions and Journal. British Ceramic Society

Trans Anglesea Antiq Soc Fld Club — Transactions of the Anglesea Antiquarian Society and Field Club

Trans Anglesey Antiq Soc — Transactions. Anglesey Antiquarian Society and Field Club

Trans Anglesey Antiq Soc Fld Club — Transactions. Anglesey Antiquarian Society and Field Club

Trans Ann Anthracite Conf Lehigh Univ — Transactions. Annual Anthracite Conference of Lehigh University

Trans Ann Meet Am Laryngol Assoc — Transactions. Annual Meeting. American Laryngological Association

Trans Annu Conf Can Nucl Soc — Transactions. Annual Conference. Canadian Nuclear Society

Trans Annu Meet Allen O Whipple Surg Soc — Transactions. Annual Meeting. Allen O. Whipple Surgical Society

Trans Annu Meet Soc Biomater Inf Biomater Symp — Transactions of the Annual Meeting of the Society for Biomaterials in Conjunction with the International Biomaterials Symposium

Trans Annu Tech Conf Am Soc Qual Control — Transactions. Annual Technical Conference. American Society for Quality Control

Trans Annu Tech Conf ASQC — Transactions. Annual Technical Conference. American Society for Quality Control

Trans Annu Tech Conf Soc Vac Coaters — Transactions. Annual Technical Conference. Society of Vacuum Coaters

Trans APA — Transactions. American Philological Association

Trans A Ph A — Transactions. American Philological Association

Trans Architect Archaeol Soc Durham Northumberland — Transactions. Architectural and Archaeological Society of Durham and Northumberland

Trans Architect Inst Jpn — Transactions. Architectural Institute of Japan

Trans Archit Inst Japan — Transactions. Architectural Institute of Japan

Trans A Rep Lond Derm Soc — Transactions and Annual Report of the London Dermatological Society

Trans A Rep Lpool Geogr Soc — Transactions and Annual Report of the Liverpool Geographical Society

Trans A Rep Manchr Microsc Soc — Transactions and Annual Report. Manchester Microscopical Society

Trans A Rep N Staffs Fld Club — Transactions and Annual Report. North Staffordshire Field Club

Trans A Rep St Johns Hosp Derm Soc Lond — Transactions and Annual Report of the St. John's Hospital Dermatological Society (London)

Trans Ariz Med Assoc — Transactions of the Arizona Medical Association

Trans ASAE — Transactions. ASAE

Trans Ashmolean Soc — Transactions. Ashmolean Society

Trans Asia Oceania Reg Congr Endocr — Transactions. Asia and Oceania Regional Congress of Endocrinology

Trans Asiat Soc Japan — Transactions. Asiatic Society of Japan

Trans ASME — Transactions. American Society of Mechanical Engineers

Trans ASME J Appl Mech — Transactions. American Society of Mechanical Engineers. Journal of Applied Mechanics

Trans ASME J Biomech Eng — Transactions. ASME [*American Society of Mechanical Engineers*] Series K. Journal of Biomechanical Engineering

Trans ASME J Biomech Engng — Transactions. American Society of Mechanical Engineers. Journal of Biomechanical Engineering

Trans ASME J Dyn Syst Meas & Control — Transactions. American Society of Mechanical Engineers. Journal of Dynamic Systems Measurement and Control

Trans ASME J Energy Resour Technol — Transactions. American Society of Mechanical Engineers. Journal of Energy Resources Technology

Trans ASME J Eng Gas Turbines Power — Transactions. ASME [*American Society of Mechanical Engineers*] Journal of Engineering for Gas Turbines and Power

Trans ASME J Eng Ind — Transactions. ASME [*American Society of Mechanical Engineers*] Series B. Journal of Engineering for Industry

Trans ASME J Eng Mater and Technol — Transactions. ASME [*American Society of Mechanical Engineers*] Series H. Journal of Engineering Materials and Technology

Trans ASME J Engng Ind — Transactions. American Society of Mechanical Engineers. Journal of Engineering for Industry

Trans ASME J Engng Mater & Technol — Transactions. American Society of Mechanical Engineers. Journal of Engineering Materials and Technology

Trans ASME J Engng Power — Transactions. American Society of Mechanical Engineers. Journal of Engineering for Power

Trans ASME J Eng Power — Transactions. ASME [*American Society of Mechanical Engineers*] Series A. Journal of Engineering for Power

Trans ASME J Fluids Eng — Transactions. ASME [*American Society of Mechanical Engineers*] Series I. Journal of Fluids Engineering

Trans ASME J Fluids Engng — Transactions. American Society of Mechanical Engineers. Journal of Fluids Engineering

Trans ASME J Heat Transfer — Transactions. American Society of Mechanical Engineers. Journal of Heat Transfer

Trans ASME J Lubr Technol — Transactions. American Society of Mechanical Engineers. Journal of Lubrication Technology

Trans ASME J Mech Des — Transactions. American Society of Mechanical Engineers. Journal of Mechanical Design

Trans ASME J Pressure Vessel Technol — Transactions. American Society of Mechanical Engineers. Journal of Pressure Vessel Technology

Trans ASME J Sol Energy Eng — Transactions. ASME [*American Society of Mechanical Engineers*] Journal of Solar Energy Engineering

Trans ASME J Sol Energy Engng — Transactions. American Society of Mechanical Engineers. Journal of Solar EnergyEngineering

Trans ASME J Tribol — Transactions. ASME [*American Society of Mechanical Engineers*] Journal of Tribology

Trans ASME Ser A — Transactions. ASME [*American Society of Mechanical Engineers*] Series A. Journal of Engineering for Power

Trans ASME Ser A J Eng Power — Transactions. ASME [*American Society of Mechanical Engineers*] Series A. Journal of Engineering for Power

Trans ASME Ser B — Transactions. ASME [*American Society of Mechanical Engineers*] Series B. Journal of Engineering for Industry

Trans ASME Ser B J Eng Ind — Transactions. ASME [*American Society of Mechanical Engineers*] Series B. Journal of Engineering for Industry

Trans ASME Ser C — Transactions. ASME [*American Society of Mechanical Engineers*] Series C. Journal of Heat Transfer

Trans ASME Ser C J Heat Transfer — Transactions. ASME [*American Society of Mechanical Engineers*] Series C. Journal of Heat Transfer

Trans ASME Ser D — Transactions. ASME [*American Society of Mechanical Engineers*] Series D

Trans ASME Ser E — Transactions. ASME [*American Society of Mechanical Engineers*] Series E. Journal of Applied Mechanics

Trans ASME Ser E J Appl Mech — Transactions. ASME [*American Society of Mechanical Engineers*] Series E. Journal of Applied Mechanics

Trans ASME Ser F — Transactions. ASME [*American Society of Mechanical Engineers*] Series F. Journal of Lubrication Technology

Trans ASME Ser F J Lubr Technol — Transactions. ASME [*American Society of Mechanical Engineers*] Series F. Journal of Lubrication Technology

Trans ASME Ser G — Transactions. ASME [*American Society of Mechanical Engineers*] Series G. Journal of Dynamic Systems. Measurement and Control

Trans ASME Ser G J Dynamic Systems — Transactions. ASME [*American Society of Mechanical Engineers*] Series G. Journal of Dynamic Systems. Measurement and Control

Trans ASME Ser G J Dynamic Systems Measurement and Control — Transactions. ASME [*American Society of Mechanical Engineers*] Series G. Journal of Dynamic Systems. Measurement and Control

Trans ASME Ser G J Dyn Syst Meas and Control — Transactions. ASME [*American Society of Mechanical Engineers*] Series G. Journal of Dynamic Systems. Measurement and Control

Trans ASME Ser H — Transactions. ASME [*American Society of Mechanical Engineers*] Series H. Journal of Engineering Materials and Technology

Trans ASME Ser H J Eng Mater and Technol — Transactions. ASME [*American Society of Mechanical Engineers*] Series H. Journal of Engineering Materials and Technology

Trans ASME Ser I — Transactions. ASME [*American Society of Mechanical Engineers*] Series I. Journal of Fluids Engineering

Trans ASME Ser I J Fluids Eng — Transactions. ASME [*American Society of Mechanical Engineers*] Series I. Journal of Fluids Engineering

Trans ASME Ser J J Pressure Vessel Technol — Transactions. ASME [*American Society of Mechanical Engineers*] Series J. Journal of Pressure Vessel Technology

Trans ASME Ser K — Transactions. ASME [*American Society of Mechanical Engineers*] Series K

Trans ASME Ser K J Biomech Eng — Transactions. ASME [*American Society of Mechanical Engineers*] Series K. Journal of Biomechanical Engineering

Trans Ass Am Med Coll — Transactions of the Association of American Medical Colleges

Trans Ass Am Physns — Transactions of the Association of American Physicians

Trans Ass Civ Engrs Cornell Univ — Transactions of the Association of Civil Engineers. Cornell University

Trans Ass Elect Ltg Engrs New Engl — Transactions of the Association of Electric Lighting Engineers of New England

Trans Assoc Am Physicians — Transactions. Association of American Physicians

Trans Assoc Ind Med Off — Transactions. Association of Industrial Medical Officers

Trans Assoc Life Ins Med Dir Am — Transactions. Association of Life Insurance Medical Directors of America

Transatl R — Transatlantic Review

Transatom Bull — Transatom Bulletin [*Brussels*]

Trans Aust Coll Ophthalmol — Transactions. Australian College of Ophthalmologists

Trans B'ham Warwks Arch Soc — Transactions. Birmingham and Warwickshire Archaeological Society

Trans Biochem Soc — Transactions. Biochemical Society

Trans Birmingham Arch Soc — Transactions. Birmingham and Warwickshire Archaeological Society

Trans Birmingham Midl Inst Sci Soc — Transactions. Birmingham and Midland Institute Scientific Society

Trans Birmingham Warwickshire Archaeol Soc — Transactions. Birmingham and Warwickshire Archaeological Society

Trans Bose Res Inst — Transactions. Bose Research Institute

Trans Bose Res Inst (Calcutta) — Transactions. Bose Research Institute (Calcutta)

Trans Bot Soc Edinb — Transactions and Proceedings. Botanical Society of Edinburgh

Trans Br Bryol Soc — Transactions. British Bryological Society

Trans Br Ceram Soc — Transactions. British Ceramic Society

Trans Brecknock Soc — Transactions of the Brecknock Society and Record of the Brecknock Museum

Trans Br Homoeop Soc — Transactions of the British Homoeopathic Society

Trans Br Hosp Ass — Transactions of the British Hospitals Association

Trans Brist Glouces Arch Soc — Transactions. Bristol and Gloucestershire Archaeological Society

Trans Brist Gloucest Archaeol Soc — Transactions. Bristol and Gloucestershire Archaeological Society

Trans Bristol and Glos AS — Transactions. Bristol and Gloucestershire Archaeological Society

Trans Bristol Gloucestershire Archaeol Soc — Transactions. Bristol and Gloucestershire Archaeological Society

Trans Bristol Gloucestershire Arch Soc — Transactions. Bristol and Gloucestershire Archaeological Society

Trans Brit Mycol Soc — Transactions. British Mycological Society

Trans Brit Soc Hist Pharm — Transactions. British Society for the History of Pharmacy

Trans Br Jr Gas Ass — Transactions. British Junior Gas Associations

Trans Br Lar Rhinol Otol Ass — Transactions of the British Laryngological, Rhinological, and Otological Association

Trans Br Mycol Soc — Transactions. British Mycological Society

Trans Br Orthop Soc — Transactions of the British Orthopedic Society

Trans Br Proctol Soc — Transactions. British Proctological Society

Trans Br Soc Dent Surg — Transactions of the British Society of Dental Surgeons

Trans Br Soc Hist Pharm — Transactions. British Society for the History of Pharmacy

Trans Br Soc Study Orthod — Transactions. British Society for the Study of Orthodontics

Trans Buchan Club — Transactions of the Buchan Club

Trans Burnley Lit Scient Soc — Transactions of the Burnley Literary and Scientific Society

Trans Burton On Trent Nat Hist Archaeol Soc — Transactions of the Burton-on-Trent Natural History and Archaeological Society

Trans Butesh Nat Hist Soc — Transactions of the Buteshire Natural History Society

Trans Caernarvonshire Hist Soc — Transactions. Caernarvonshire Historical Society

Trans Calcutta Med Soc — Transactions. Calcutta Medical Society

Trans Calif St Agric Soc — Transactions of the California State Agricultural Society

Trans Camb Phil Soc — Transactions of the Cambridge Philosophical Society

Trans Cambridge Philos Soc — Transactions. Cambridge Philosophical Society

Trans Can Ass Prev Tuberc — Transactions of the Canadian Association for the Prevention of Tuberculosis

Trans Can Dent Ass — Transactions of the Canadian Dental Association

Trans Can Hosp Coun — Transactions of the Canadian Hospital Council

Trans Can Inst Mining Soc NS — Transactions. Canadian Institute of Mining and Metallurgy and Mining Society of Nova Scotia

Trans Can Inst Min Metall — Transactions. Canadian Institute of Mining and Metallurgy and Mining Society of Nova Scotia

Trans Can Inst Min Metall Min Soc NS — Transactions. Canadian Institute of Mining and Metallurgy and Mining Society ofNova Scotia

Trans Can Min Inst — Transactions. Canadian Mining Institute

Trans Can Nucl Soc — Transactions. Canadian Nuclear Society

Trans Can Ophthal Soc — Transactions of the Canadian Ophthalmological Society

Trans Can Soc Civ Engrs — Transactions of the Canadian Society of Civil Engineers

Trans Can Soc Mech Eng — Transactions. Canadian Society of Mechanical Engineers

Trans Can Soc Mech Engrs — Transactions. Canadian Society of Mechanical Engineers

Trans Can Soc Study Dis Child — Transactions of the Canadian Society for the Study of Diseases of Children

Trans Caradoc Severn Vall Fld Club — Transactions. Caradoc and Severn Valley Field Club

Trans Cardiff Nat Soc — Transactions. Cardiff Naturalists Society

Trans Cardiff Natur Soc — Transactions. Cardiff Naturalists Society

Trans Carlisle Nat Hist Soc — Transactions of the Carlisle Natural History Society

Trans Carmarthenshire Antiq Soc — Transactions. Carmarthenshire Antiquarian Society and Field Club

Trans Cave Res Group GB — Transactions. Cave Research Group of Great Britain

Trans Cave Res Grp Gt Br — Transactions of the Cave Research Group of Great Britain

Trans Cedewain Fld Club — Transactions of the Cedewain Field Club

Trans Cent Sci Res Inst Confect Ind — Transactions. Central Scientific Research Institute of the Confectionery Industry

Trans Cent St Pediat Soc — Transactions. Central States Pediatric Society

Trans Ceram Soc — Transactions of the Ceramic Society

Trans Ceylon Coll — Transactions. Ceylon College of Physicians

Trans Chalmers Univ Technol (Gothenburg) — Transactions. Chalmers University of Technology (Gothenburg)

Trans Chart Inst Pat Ag — Transactions of the Chartered Institute of Patent Agents

Trans Chem Div Am Soc Qual Control — Transactions. Chemical Division. American Society for Quality Control

Trans China Pulp Pap — Transactions of China Pulp and Paper

Trans Chin Assoc Adv Sci — Transactions. Chinese Association for the Advancement of Science

Trans Chosen Nat Hist Soc — Transactions. Chosen Natural History Society/ Chosen Hakubutsu Gakkai Kaiho

Trans Citrus Eng Conf — Transactions. Citrus Engineering Conference

Trans Clin Soc Manchr — Transactions. Clinical Society of Manchester

Trans Clin Soc Univ Mich — Transactions of the Clinical Society of the University of Michigan

Trans Coll Med S Afr — Transactions. College of Medicine of South Africa

Trans Coll Physicians Philadelphia — Transactions. College of Physicians of Philadelphia

Trans Coll Physns S Afr — Transactions of the College of Physicians of South Africa, College of Surgeons of South Africa, College of Obstetricians and Gynecologists of South Africa

Trans Colls Physns Surg Gynaec S Afr — Transactions of the Colleges of Physicians, Surgeons, and Gynaecologists of South Africa

Trans Colo St Med Soc — Transactions of the Colorado State Medical Society

Trans Com Bul Asia Asia Pac — Transport and Communications Bulletin of Asia and the Pacific

Trans Concr Inst Chicago — Transactions of the Concrete Institute (Chicago)

Trans Conf Chemother Tuberc — Transactions. Conference on the Chemotherapy of Tuberculosis

Trans Conf Cold Inj — Transactions. Conference on Cold Injury

Trans Conf Genet — Transactions. Conference on Genetics

Trans Conf Glaucoma — Transactions. Conference on Glaucoma

Trans Conf Group Processes — Transactions. Conference on Group Processes

Trans Conf Group Soc Adm Hist — Transactions. Conference Group for Social and Administrative History

Trans Conf Neuropharmacol — Transactions. Conference on Neuropharmacology

Trans Conf Physiol Prematurity — Transactions. Conference on Physiology of Prematurity

Trans Conf Polysaccharides Biol — Transactions. Conference on Polysaccharides in Biology

Trans Congr Am Physns Surg — Transactions of the Congress of American Physicians and Surgeons

Trans Conn Acad Arts Sci — Transactions. Connecticut Academy of Arts and Sciences

Trans Connecticut Acad Arts Sci — Transactions. Connecticut Academy of Arts and Sciences

Trans Corn Inst Eng — Transactions. Cornish Institute of Engineers

Trans Corn Inst Engrs — Transactions. Cornish Institute of Engineers

Trans Corn Inst Min Mech Metall Engrs — Transactions of the Cornish Institute of Mining, Mechanical, and Metallurgical Engineers

Trans Cremat Soc Engl — Transactions of the Cremation Society of England

Transcr Proc US Live Stk Sanit Ass — Transcript of Proceedings. United States Live Stock Sanitary Association [Chicago]

Trans C S Peirce Soc — Transactions. Charles S. Peirce Society

Trans C S Peirce Soc — Transactions. C. S. Peirce Society

Transcult Psychiat Res — Transcultural Psychiatric Research Review

Trans Cumberland Westmorland Antiq Archaeol Soc N Ser — Transactions. Cumberland and Westmorland Antiquarian and Archaeological Society. New Series

Trans Denbighshire Hist Soc — Transactions. Denbighshire Historical Society

Trans Desert Bighorn Counc — Transactions. Desert Bighorn Council

Transducer Technol — Transducer Technology

Trans Dumfries and Galloway NH and AS — Transactions. Dumfriesshire and Galloway Natural History and Antiquarian Society

Trans Dumfries Galloway Nat Hist Antiq Soc — Transactions. Dumfriesshire and Galloway Natural History and Antiquarian Society

Trans Dumfriesshire Galloway Natur Hist Antiq Soc — Transactions. Dumfriesshire and Galloway Natural History and Antiquarian Society

Trans Dumfriesshire Galloway Natur Hist Ant Soc — Transactions. Dumfriesshire and Galloway Natural History and Antiquarian Society

Trans Dynam Dev — Transactions. Dynamics of Development

Trans East Lothian Antiq Field Nat Soc — Transactions. East Lothian Antiquarian and Field Naturalists' Society

Trans Econ & Oper Anal — Transport Economics and Operational Analysis

Trans Edinb Fld Nat Microsc Soc — Transactions of the Edinburgh Field Naturalists' and Microscopical Society

Trans Edinb Geol Soc — Transactions. Edinburgh Geological Society

Trans Edinb Obstet Soc — Transactions of the Edinburgh Obstetrical Society

Trans Edinburgh Geol Soc — Transactions. Edinburgh Geological Society

Trans Electrochem Soc — Transactions. Electrochemical Society

Trans Electr Supply Auth Eng Inst NZ — Transactions. Electric Supply Authority Engineers' Institute of New Zealand, Inc.

Trans Electr Supply Eng Inst — Transactions. Annual Conference. Electric Supply Authority Engineers' Institute of New Zealand, Inc.

Trans Elect Supply Auth Engrs Ass NZ — Transactions. Electric Supply Authority. Engineers' Association of New Zealand

Trans E Lothian Antiq Fld Natur Soc — Transactions. East Lothian Antiquarian and Field Naturalists' Society

Trans Eng Inst Can — Transactions. Engineering Institute of Canada

Trans Engl Ceram Circle — Transactions. English Ceramic Circle

Trans Engl Ceram Soc — Transactions. English Ceramic Society

Trans Engl Jr Gas Ass — Transactions of the English Junior Gas Associations

Trans Engng Ass Ceylon — Transactions of the Engineering Association of Ceylon

Trans Engng Ass Malaya — Transactions of the Engineering Association of Malaya

Trans Engng Ass S — Transactions. Engineering Association of the South

Trans Engng Inst Can — Transactions of the Engineering Institute of Canada

Trans Engng Soc Sch Pract Sci Toronto — Transactions of the Engineering Society of the School of Practical Science (Toronto)

Trans Engng Soc Univ Toronto — Transactions of the Engineering Society. University of Toronto

Trans Ent Soc Japan — Transactions of the Entomological Society of Japan

Trans Essex Arch Soc — Essex Archaeology and History. Transactions. Essex Archaeological Society

Trans Essex Arch Soc — Transactions. Essex Archaeological Society

Trans Essex Field Club — Transactions. Essex Field Club

Trans Est Agric Acad — Transactions. Estonian Agricultural Academy

Trans Eur Orthod Soc — Transactions. European Orthodontic Society

Trans Fac Hortic Chiba Univ — Transactions. Faculty of Horticulture. Chiba University

Trans Farady Soc — Transactions. Faraday Society

Trans Fed-Prov Wildl Conf — Transactions. Federal-Provincial Wildlife Conference

Transform Bois — Transformateur du Bois [Anvers]

Transform Groups — Transformation Groups

Transform (Papeterie) — Transformation (Supplement to La Papeterie)

Transform Plast — Transformations des Plastiques [Paris]

Trans Free Mus Sci Art Philad — Transactions of the Free Museum of Science and Art (Philadelphia)

Trans Fuel Soc Univ Sheff — Transactions. Fuel Society. University of Sheffield

Transfus Clin Biol — Transfusion Clnique et Biologique

Transfus Med — Transfusion Medicine

Transfus Med Rev — Transfusion Medicine Reviews

Transgenic Res — Transgenic Research

Trans Geogr Soc Queb — Transactions. Geographical Society of Quebec

Trans Geol Phys Soc — Transactions of the Geological Physics Society

Trans Geol Soc Glasg — Transactions. Geological Society of Glasgow

Trans Geol Soc S Afr — Transactions. Geological Society of South Africa

Trans Georgia State Agric Soc — Transactions. Georgia State Agricultural Society

Trans Geotherm Resour Counc — Transactions. Geothermal Resources Council

Trans Glasg Obstet Gynaec Soc — Transactions of the Glasgow Obstetrical and Gynaecological Society

Trans Glasg Odont Soc — Transactions of the Glasgow Odontological Society

Trans Glasgow Univ Orient Soc — Transactions. Glasgow University Oriental Society

Trans Glasg Path Clin Soc — Transactions of the Glasgow Pathological and Clinical Society

Trans Grant Coll Med Soc — Transactions of the Grant College Medical Society

Trans Greenwich Lewisham Antiq Soc — Transactions. Greenwich and Lewisham Antiquarian Society

Trans Guinness Res Lab — Transactions of the Guinness Research Laboratory

Trans Gulf Coast Ass Geol Soc — Transactions. Gulf Coast Association of Geological Societies

Trans Gulf Coast Assoc Geol Soc — Transactions. Gulf Coast Association of Geological Societies

Trans Gulf Coast Mol Biol Conf — Transactions. Gulf Coast Molecular Biology Conference

Trans Gulf Cst Ass Geol Socs — Transactions of the Gulf-Coast Association of Geological Societies

Trans Gynaec Soc Boston — Transactions of the Gynaecological Society of Boston

Trans Halifax Antiq Society — Transactions. Halifax Antiquarian Society

Trans Hamps Eng Soc — Transactions of the Hampshire Entomological Society

Trans Hawaii Territ Med Ass — Transactions. Hawaii Territorial Medical Association

Trans Hawick Archaeol Soc — Transactions. Hawick Archaeological Society

Trans Hertfordshire Nat Hist Field Club — Transactions. Hertfordshire Natural History Society and Field Club

Trans Hertfordshire Nat Hist Soc Field Club — Transactions. Hertfordshire Natural History Society and Field Club

Trans Herts Nat Hist Soc Fld Club — Transactions of the Hertfordshire Natural History Society and Field Club

Trans Highl Agric Soc Scotl — Transactions. Highland and Agricultural Society of Scotland

Trans Highld Agric Soc Springfield — Transactions of the Highland Agricultural Society (Springfield, Massachusetts)

Trans Hist Soc Ghana — Transactions. Historical Society of Ghana

Trans Hist Soc Lancashire Cheshire — Transactions. Historic Society of Lancashire and Cheshire

Trans Homoeop Med Soc St Pa — Transactions of the Homoeopathic Medical Society of the State of Pennsylvania

Trans Huddersf Engng Soc — Transactions. Huddersfield Engineering Society

Trans Hull Geol Soc — Transactions of the Hull Geological Society

Trans Hull Sci Club — Transactions. Hull Scientific and Field Naturalists' Club

Trans Hull Scient Fld Nat Club — Transactions of the Hull Scientific and Field Naturalists' Club

Trans Hunter Archaeol Soc — Transactions. Hunter Archaeological Society

Trans Hunterian Soc — Transactions of the Hunterian Society

Trans Hunter Soc — Transactions. Hunterian Society

Trans ILA — Transactions. International Law Association

Trans Illinois State Acad Sci — Illinois State Academy of Science. Transactions

Trans Ill St Acad Sci — Transactions. Illinois State Academy of Science

Trans Ill State Acad Sci — Transactions. Illinois State Academy of Science

Trans Ill State Hortic Soc — Transactions. Illinois State Horticultural Society

Trans Ill State Hortic Soc Ill Fruit Counc — Transactions. Illinois State Horticultural Society and the Illinois Fruit Council

Trans Ill St Dent Soc — Transactions of the Illinois State Dental Society

Trans Ill St Hort Soc — Transactions. Illinois State Horticultural Society

Trans Illum Engng Soc Lond — Transactions of the Illuminating Engineering Society (London)

Trans Illum Engng Soc NY — Transactions of the Illuminating Engineering Society (New York)

Trans Illum Eng Soc — Transactions. Illuminating Engineering Society

Trans I Mar E — Transactions. Institute of Marine Engineers

Trans Indiana Acad Ophthalmol Otolaryngol — Transactions. Indiana Academy of Ophthalmology and Otolaryngology

Trans Indiana Hort Soc — Transactions. Indiana Horticultural Society

Trans Indian Ceram Soc — Transactions. Indian Ceramic Society

Trans Indian Inst Chem Eng — Transactions. Indian Institute of Chemical Engineers

Trans Indian Inst Met — Transactions. Indian Institute of Metals

Trans Indian Inst Metals — Transactions. Indian Institute of Metals

Trans Indian Soc Desert Technol Univ Cent Desert Stud — Transactions. Indian Society of Desert Technology and University Centre of Desert Studies

Trans Ind Inst Chem Eng — Transactions. Indian Institute of Chemical Engineers

Trans Inform Process Soc Japan — Transactions. Information Processing Society of Japan

Trans Inf Process Soc Jpn — Transactions. Information Processing Society of Japan

Trans Inst Act Aust & NZ — Transactions. Institute of Actuaries of Australia and New Zealand

Trans Inst Br Geogr New Ser — Transactions. Institute of British Geographers. New Series

Trans Inst Brit Geogr — Transactions. Institute of British Geographers

Trans Inst Chem Eng — Transactions. Institution of Chemical Engineers

Trans Inst Chem Eng (London) — Transactions. Institution of Chemical Engineers (London)

Trans Inst Chem Engrs — Transactions. Institution of Chemical Engineers

Trans Inst Civ Eng Ir — Transactions. Institution of Civil Engineers of Ireland

Trans Inst Diesel Gas Turbine Eng — Transactions of the Institution of Diesel and Gas Turbine Engineers

Trans Inst Electr Eng Jap — Transactions. Institute of Electrical Engineers of Japan

Trans Inst Electr Eng Jap Overseas Ed — Transactions. Institute of Electrical Engineers of Japan. Overseas Edition

Trans Inst Electr Eng Jpn — Transactions. Institute of Electrical Engineers of Japan

Trans Inst Electr Eng Jpn B — Transactions. Institute of Electrical Engineers of Japan. Part B

Trans Inst Electr Eng Jpn C — Transactions. Institute of Electrical Engineers of Japan. Part C

Trans Inst Electr Eng Jpn Part A — Transactions. Institute of Electrical Engineers of Japan. Part A

Trans Inst Electr Eng Jpn Part B — Transactions. Institute of Electrical Engineers of Japan. Part B

Trans Inst Electr Eng Jpn Part C — Transactions. Institute of Electrical Engineers of Japan. Part C

Trans Inst Electr Eng Jpn Sect E — Transactions. Institute of Electrical Engineers of Japan. Section E

Trans Inst Electron & Commun Eng Jap A — Transactions. Institute of Electronics and Communication Engineers of Japan. Part A

Trans Inst Electron & Commun Eng Jap B — Transactions. Institute of Electronics and Communication Engineers of Japan. Part B

Trans Inst Electron & Commun Eng Jap C — Transactions. Institute of Electronics and Communication Engineers of Japan. Part C

Trans Inst Electron & Commun Eng Jap D — Transactions. Institute of Electronics and Communication Engineers of Japan. Part D

Trans Inst Electron and Commun Eng Jpn Part A — Transactions. Institute of Electronics and Communication Engineers of Japan. Part A

Trans Inst Electron and Commun Eng Jpn Part B — Transactions. Institute of Electronics and Communication Engineers of Japan. Part B

Trans Inst Electron and Commun Eng Jpn Part C — Transactions. Institute of Electronics and Communication Engineers of Japan. Part C

Trans Inst Electron and Commun Eng Jpn Part D — Transactions. Institute of Electronics and Communication Engineers of Japan. Part D

Trans Inst Electron and Commun Eng Jpn Sect E — Transactions. Institute of Electronics and Communication Engineers of Japan. Section E

Trans Inst Electron Commun Eng Jap Sect J Part A — Transactions. Institute of Electronics and Communication Engineers of Japan. Section J. Part A

Trans Inst Electron Commun Eng Jap Sect J Part C — Transactions. Institute of Electronics and Communication Engineers of Japan. Section J. Part C

Trans Inst Electron Commun Eng Jap Sect J Part D — Transactions. Institute of Electronics and Communication Engineers of Japan. Section J [*Japanese*] Part D

Trans Inst Electron Commun Eng Jpn — Transactions. Institute of Electronics and Communication Engineers of Japan. Section E

Trans Inst Electron Commun Eng Jpn Part B — Transactions. Institute of Electronics and Communication Engineers of Japan. Part B

Trans Inst Electron Commun Eng Jpn Sect E (Engl) — Transactions. Institute of Electronics and Communication Engineers of Japan. Section E (English)

Trans Inst Electron Inf Commun — Transactions. Institute of Electronics, Information, and Communication Engineers. Section E

Trans Inst Electron Inf Commun Eng Sect E — Transactions. Institute of Electronics, Information, and Communications Engineers. Section E. English

Trans Inst Eng Aust — Transactions. Institution of Engineers of Australia

Trans Inst Eng Aust Civ Eng — Transactions. Institution of Engineers of Australia. Civil Engineering

Trans Inst Eng Aust Electr Eng — Transactions. Institution of Engineers of Australia. Electrical Engineering

Trans Inst Eng Aust Mech Eng — Transactions. Institution of Engineers of Australia. Mechanical Engineering

Trans Inst Eng Aust Multi Discip — Transactions. Institute of Engineers. Australia. Multi-Disciplinary Engineering

Trans Inst Engrs Aust Civ Engng — Transactions. Institution of Engineers of Australia. Civil Engineering

Trans Inst Engrs Aust Mech Engng — Transactions. Institution of Engineers of Australia. Mechanical Engineering

Trans Inst Eng Shipbuilders Scot — Transactions. Institution of Engineers and Shipbuilders in Scotland

Trans Inst Gas Eng — Transactions. Institution of Gas Engineers

Trans Inst Mar Eng — Transactions. Institute of Marine Engineers

Trans Inst Mar Eng Conf Pap — Transactions. Institute of Marine Engineers. Conference Papers

Trans Inst Mar Engrs — Transactions. Institute of Marine Engineers

Trans Inst Mar Eng Ser C — Transactions. Institute of Marine Engineers. Series C

Trans Inst Mar Eng Tech Meet Pap — Transactions. Institute of Marine Engineers. Technical Meeting Papers

Trans Inst Marine Eng — Transactions. Institute of Marine Engineers

Trans Inst Meas & Control — Transactions. Institute of Measurement and Control

Trans Inst Meas Control — Transactions. Institute of Measurement and Control

Trans Inst Measmt Control — Transactions. Institute of Measurement and Control

Trans Inst Metal Finish — Transactions of the Institute of Metal Finishing

Trans Inst Met Finish — Transactions. Institute of Metal Finishing

Trans Inst Min Eng — Transactions. Institution of Mining Engineers

Trans Inst Mining Met Sect A — Transactions. Institution of Mining and Metallurgy. Section A. Mining Industry

Trans Inst Mining Met Sect B — Transactions. Institution of Mining and Metallurgy. Section B. Applied Earth Science

Trans Inst Mining Met Sect C — Transactions. Institution of Mining and Metallurgy. Section C

Trans Inst Min Metall — Transactions. Institution of Mining and Metallurgy

Trans Inst Min Metall (Ostrava) Min Geol Ser — Transactions. Institute of Mining and Metallurgy (Ostrava). Mining and Geological Series

Trans Inst Min Metall Sec A — Transactions. Institution of Mining and Metallurgy. Section A. Mining Industry

Trans Inst Min Metall Sec B — Transactions. Institution of Mining and Metallurgy. Section B. Applied Earth Science

Trans Inst Min Metall Sec C — Transactions. Institution of Mining and Metallurgy. Section C

Trans Inst Min Metall Sect A Min Ind — Transactions. Institution of Mining and Metallurgy. Section A. Mining Industry

Trans Inst Min Metall Sect B Appl Earth Sci — Transactions. Institution of Mining and Metallurgy. Section B. Applied Earth Science

Trans Inst Min Metall Sect C Miner Process Extr Metall — Transactions of the Institution of Mining and Metallurgy. Section C. Mineral Processing and Extractive Metallurgy

Trans Inst Min Surv — Transactions of the Institute of Mining Surveyors

Trans Instn Chem Engrs — Transactions. Institution of Chemical Engineers

Trans Instn E Shipb Scot — Transactions. Institution of Engineers and Shipbuilders in Scotland

Trans Instn Min Metall — Transactions. Institution of Mining and Metallurgy

Trans Instn Nav Archit — Transactions of the Institution of Naval Architects

Trans Instn Rubb Ind Japan — Transactions of the Institution of the Rubber Industry of Japan

Trans Instn Wat Engrs — Transactions of the Institution of Water Engineers

Trans Inst Plast Ind — Transactions. Institute of the Plastics Industry

Trans Inst Prof Eng — Transactions. Institution of Professional Engineers of New Zealand

Trans Inst Prof Eng NZ — Transactions. Institution of Professional Engineers. New Zealand Civil Engineering Section

Trans Inst Prof Eng NZ Civ Eng Sect — Transactions. Institution of Professional Engineers of New Zealand. Civil Engineering Section

Trans Inst Prof Eng NZ Electr Mech Chem Eng Sect — Transactions. Institution of Professional Engineers of New Zealand. Electrical/Mechanical/Chemical Engineering Section

Trans Inst Prof Eng NZ EMCh — Transactions. Institution of Professional Engineers of New Zealand. Electrical/Mechanical/Chemical Engineering Section

Trans Inst Pure Chem Reagents (Moscow) — Transactions. Institute of Pure Chemical Reagents (Moscow)

Trans Inst Rubber Ind — Transactions. Institution of the Rubber Industry

Trans Inst Systems Control Inform Engrs — Transactions. Institute of Systems, Control, and Information Engineers

Trans Inst Water Eng — Transactions. Institution of Water Engineers

Trans Inst Weld (London) — Transactions. Institute of Welding (London)

Trans Int Assoc Math and Comput Simulation — Transactions. International Association for Mathematics and Computers in Simulation

Trans Int Astron Union — Transactions. International Astronomical Union

Trans Int Astr Un — Transactions of the International Astronomical Union

Trans Int Ceram Congr — Transactions. International Ceramic Congress

Trans Int Coll Surg — Transactions of the International College of Surgeons

Trans Int Conf Endod — Transactions. International Conference on Endodontics

Trans Int Conf Oral Surg — Transactions. International Conference on Oral Surgery

Trans Int Conf Or Ja — Transactions. International Conference of Orientalists in Japan

Trans Int Conf Soil Sci — Transactions. International Conference of Soil Science

Trans Int Congr Agr Eng — Transactions. International Congress of Agricultural Engineering

Trans Int Congr Agric Engng — Transactions. International Congress for Agricultural Engineering

Trans Int Congr Enlightenment — Transactions. International Congress on the Enlightenment

Trans Int Congr Entomol — Transactions. International Congress of Entomology

Trans Int Congr Soil Sci — Transactions. International Congress of Soil Science

Trans Inter Soc Cytol Coun — Transactions. Inter-Society Cytology Council

Trans Intl — Journal pour le Transport International

Trans Intnl — Journal pour le Transport International

Trans Int Soc Geotherm Eng — Transactions. International Society for Geothermal Engineering

Trans Int Soc Plast Surg — Transactions of the International Society of Plastic Surgeons

Trans Int Un Co Op Sol Res — Transactions of the International Union for Cooperation in Solar Research

Trans Int Un Tuberc — Transactions. International Union against Tuberculosis

Trans Inverness Scient Soc Fld Club — Transactions of the Inverness Scientific Society and Field Club

Trans Iowa State Hortic Soc — Transactions. Iowa State Horticultural Society

Trans Iowa St Hort Soc — Transactions. Iowa State Horticultural Society

Trans Iowa St Med Soc — Transactions of the Iowa State Medical Society

Trans Ir For Soc — Transactions of the Irish Forestry Society

Trans Iron Steel Inst Jap — Transactions. Iron and Steel Institute of Japan

Trans Iron Steel Inst Jpn — Transactions. Iron and Steel Institute of Japan

Trans Iron Steel Soc — Transactions of the Iron and Steel Society

Trans Iron Steel Soc AIME — Transactions of the Iron and Steel Society of AIME

Transistor Infs — Transistor Informations [*Paris*]

Transistor Res Bull — Transistor Research Bulletin [*Washington*]

Transition Met Chem — Transition Metal Chemistry

Transition Met Coord Chem — Transition Metal Coordination Chemistry

Transition Met Nucl Magn Reson — Transition Metal Nuclear Magnetic Resonance

Transit J — Transit Journal

Transit J News — Transit Journal News [*New York*]

Transit L Rev — Transit Law Review

Transit Met Chem (Weinheim Ger) — Transition Metal Chemistry (Weinheim, Germany)

Transit Packag — Transit Packaging

Trans Japan Acad — Transactions of the Japan Academy

Trans Japan Inst Metals — Transactions. Japan Institute of Metals

Trans Japan Soc Aeronaut Engng — Transactions of Japan Society of Aeronautical Engineering

Trans Japan Soc Aeronaut Space Sci — Transactions of Japan Society for Aeronautical and Space Sciences

Trans Japan Soc Civ Engrs — Transactions. Japan Society of Civil Engineers

Trans Japan Soc Compos Mater — Transactions. Japan Society for Composite Materials

Trans Japan Soc Mech Engrs — Transactions of the Japan Society of Mechanical Engineers

Trans Japan Soc Mech Engrs Ser B — Transactions. Japan Society of Mechanical Engineers. Series B

Trans Japan Soc Mech Engrs Ser C — Transactions. Japan Society of Mechanical Engineers. Series C

Trans Jap Inst Met — Transactions. Japan Institute of Metals

Trans Jap Inst Metals — Transactions. Japan Institute of Metals

Trans Jap Path Soc — Transactions of the Japanese Pathological Society

Trans Jap Soc Aeronaut Space Sci — Transactions. Japan Society for Aeronautical and Space Sciences

Trans Jap Soc Mech Eng — Transactions. Japan Society of Mechanical Engineers

Trans Jap Weld Soc — Transactions. Japan Welding Society

Trans J Br Ceram Soc — Transactions and Journal. British Ceramic Society

Trans J Brit Ceram Soc — Transactions and Journal. British Ceramic Society

Trans J Eastbourne Nat Hist Soc — Transactions and Journal of the Eastbourne Natural History Society

Trans J Plast Inst — Transactions and Journal. Plastics Institute

Trans Jpn Inst Met — Transactions. Japan Institute of Metals

Trans Jpn Inst Met Suppl — Transactions. Japan Institute of Metals. Supplement

Trans Jpn Pathol Soc — Transactions. Japanese Pathological Society

Trans Jpn Soc Aeronaut and Space Sci — Transactions. Japan Society for Aeronautical and Space Sciences

Trans Jpn Soc Aeronaut Space Sci — Transactions. Japan Society for Aeronautical and Space Sciences

Trans Jpn Soc Civ Eng — Transactions. Japan Society of Civil Engineers

Trans Jpn Soc Compos Mater — Transactions. Japan Society for Composite Materials

Trans Jpn Soc Irrig Drain Reclam Eng — Transactions. Japanese Society of Irrigation Drainage and Reclamation Engineering

Trans Jpn Soc Mech Eng Ser B — Transactions. Japan Society of Mechanical Engineers. Series B

Trans Jpn Weld Soc — Transactions. Japan Welding Society

Trans J Proc Dumfries Galloway Nat Hist Antiq Soc — Transactions and Journal of the Proceedings of the Dumfriesshire & Galloway Natural History and Antiquarian Society

Trans Jr Engng Soc Gt West Rly — Transactions. Junior Engineering Society. Great Western Railway Mechanics' Institution

Trans Jt Mtg Comm Int Soc Soil Sci — Transactions. Joint Meeting of Commissions. International Society of Soil Science

Trans JWRI — Transactions. JWRI

Trans K Acad Sci — Transactions. Kentucky Academy of Science

Trans Kans Acad Sci — Transactions. Kansas Academy of Science

Trans Kansai Ent Soc — Transactions. Kansai Entomological Society

Trans Kans Engng Soc — Transactions of the Kansas Engineering Society

Transkei Dev Rev — Transkei Development Review

Trans Kent Fld Club — Transactions of the Kent Field Club

Trans Kentucky State Hort Soc — Transactions. Kentucky State Horticultural Society

Trans Kinki Coleopt Soc — Transactions of the Kinki Coleopterological Society

Trans Kolar Gold Fld Min Metall Soc — Transactions of the Kolar Gold Field Mining and Metallurgical Society

Trans Koll Geneeskd S-Afr — Transaksies: Kollege van Geneeskunde van Suid-Afrika

Trans Korea Brch R Asiat Soc — Transactions of the Korea Branch of the Royal Asiatic Society

Trans Korean Inst Electr Eng — Transactions. Korean Institute of Electrical Engineers

Trans Korean Soc Mech Eng — Transactions. Korean Society of Mechanical Engineers

Trans KY Acad Sci — Transactions. Kentucky Academy of Science

Trans Kyoto Ent Soc — Transactions. Kyoto Entomological Society

Trans Ky St Hort Soc — Transactions of the Kentucky State Horticultural Society

Trans Ky St Med Soc — Transactions of the Kentucky State Medical Society

Trans Lackawanna Cty Med Soc — Transactions of the Lackawanna County Medical Society

Transl Aeronaut Res Labs Aust — Translations. Aeronautical Research Laboratories formerly Aeronautical Laboratory. C.S.I.R.O. Australia [*Melbourne*]

Trans Lancashire Cheshire Antiq Soc — Transactions. Lancashire and Cheshire Antiquarian Society

Trans Lancs and Chesh Antiq Soc — Transactions. Lancashire and Cheshire Antiquarian Society

Transl Arct Constr Frost Eff Lab — Translations. Arctic Construction and Frost Effects Laboratory

Trans La St Med Soc — Transactions of the Louisiana State Medical Society

Trans Latv Branch All Union Soc Soil Sci — Transactions. Latvian Branch. All-Union Society of Soil Science

Transl Beltone Inst Hear Res — Translations. Beltone Institute for Hearing Research

Transl Br Coke Res Ass — Translations. British Coke Research Association [*London*]

Transl Commonw Sci Industr Res Organ (Aust) — Translation. Commonwealth Scientific and Industrial Research Organisation (CSIRO) (Australia)

Transl David Taylor Model Basin — Translations. David Taylor Model Basin. US Navy Department [*Washington*]

Transld Contents Lists Russ Period — Translated Contents Lists of Russian Periodicals

Transl Def Res Bd Can — Translations. Defence Research Board. Canada [*Ottawa*]

Transl Dep Fish For (Can) — Translation. Department of Fisheries and Forestry (Ottawa, Canada)

Trans Leeds Geol Assoc — Transactions. Leeds Geological Association

Trans Leicestershire Archaeol Hist Soc — Transactions. Leicestershire Archaeological and Historical Society

Transl Explos Res Dev Establ — Translations. Explosives Research and Development Establishment [*Waltham Abbey*]

Transl Fac For Univ BC — Translation. Faculty of Forestry. University of British Columbia

Transl For Comm (Lond) — Translation. Forestry Commission (London)

Transl Fulmer Res Inst — Translations. Fulmer Research Institute [*Stoke Poges*]

Transl Hydrogr Off Wash — Translations. Hydrographic Office (Washington)

Trans Lich S Staffs Arch Hist Soc — Transactions. Lichfield and South Staffordshire Archaeological and Historical Society

Trans Linc — Transunti. Accademia Nazionale dei Lincei

Trans Lincei — Transunti. Accademia Nazionale dei Lincei

Transl Ind Grp UKAEA — Translations. Industrial Group. United Kingdom Atomic Energy Authority [*Risley*]

Trans Linn Soc Lond — Transactions. Linnean Society of London

Trans Linn Soc London Bot — Transactions. Linnean Society of London. Botany

Trans Linn Soc NY — Transactions. Linnaean Society of New York

Trans Liverpool Eng Soc — Transactions. Liverpool Engineering Society

Trans Liverpool Naut Soc — Transactions. Liverpool Nautical Society

Trans LJ — Transportation Law Journal

Transl Libr Commonw Bur Past Forage Crops — Translations Filed in the Library and Available on Loan. Commonwealth Bureau of Pastures and Forage Crops [*Aberystwyth*]

Transl Math Monographs — Translations of Mathematical Monographs

Transl Natn Inst Agric Engng — Translations. National Institute of Agricultural Engineering [*Silsoc*]

Trans Lond Middx Archaeol Soc — Transactions. London and Middlesex Archaeological Society

Trans London Middlesex Archaeol Soc — Transactions. London and Middlesex Archaeological Society

Trans London M'sex Arch — Transactions. London and Middlesex Archaeological Society

Trans London Msex Arch Soc — Transactions. London and Middlesex Archaeological Society

Trans Lpool Astr Soc — Transactions. Liverpool Astronomical Society

Trans Lpool Engng Soc — Transactions of the Liverpool Engineering Society

Transl Reg-Index — Translations Register-Index

Transl Rev — Translation Review

Transl Russ Game Rep — Translations of Russian Game Reports

Transl Ser Math Engrg — Translations Series in Mathematics and Engineering

Transl Snow Ice Permafrost Res Establ — Translations. Snow, Ice, and Permafrost Research Establishment [*Wilmette*]

Transl Soviet Agr US Joint Publ Res Serv — Translations on Soviet Agriculture. United States Joint Publications Research Service

Transl Tech Inf Bur — Translations. Technical Information Bureau. Ministry of Supply [*London*]

Transl Tech Inf Libr Servs — Translations. Technical Information and Library Services. Ministry of Aviation [*London*]

Transl Timb Dev Ass Res Labs — Translations. Timber Development Association Research Laboratories [*High Wycombe*]

Transl US For Prod Lab (Madison) — Translation. United States Forest Products Laboratory (Madison)

Trans Manchester Assoc Eng — Transactions. Manchester Association of Engineers

Trans Manchr Med Soc — Transactions. Manchester Medical Society

Trans Manchr Odont Soc — Transactions of the Manchester Odontological Society

Trans Manchr Statist Soc — Transactions of the Manchester Statistical Society

Transm & Distrib — Transmission and Distribution

Trans Manitoba Hist Scient Soc — Transactions. Manitoba Historical and Scientific Society

Trans Mass Hort Soc — Transactions. Massachusetts Horticultural Society

Trans Mass Med Leg Soc — Transactions of the Massachusetts Medico-Legal Society

Trans Mater Res Soc Jpn — Transactions. Materials Research Society of Japan

Trans Math Monographs — Translations of Mathematical Monographs. American Mathematical Society

Trans Md Acad Sci — Transactions of the Maryland Academy of Science

Transm Distrib — Transmission and Distribution

Trans Med — Transactions Medicales. Journal de Medecine Pratique

Trans Med Ass Cent NY — Transactions of the Medical Association of Central New York

Trans Med Ass Ga — Transactions of the Medical Association of Georgia

Trans Med Ass St Ala — Transactions of the Medical Association of the State of Alabama

Trans Med Ass St Mo — Transactions of the Medical Association of the State of Missouri

Trans Med Chir Fac Md — Transactions of the Medical and Chirurgical Faculty of Maryland

Trans Med Chir Soc Edinb — Transactions of the Medico-Chirurgical Society of Edinburgh

Trans Med Coll Reun Calcutta — Transactions of the Medical College Reunion (Calcutta)

Trans Med Leg Soc Lond — Transactions of the Medico-Legal Society (London)

Trans Med Soc Cy Hosp Alumni St Louis — Transactions of the Medical Society of City Hospital Alumni (St. Louis, Missouri)

Trans Med Soc Distr Columbia — Transactions of the Medical Society of the District of Columbia

Trans Med Soc Hawaii — Transactions of the Medical Society of Hawaii

Trans Med Soc Lond — Transactions. Medical Society of London

Trans Med Soc London — Transactions. Medical Society of London

Trans Med Soc St Calif — Transactions of the Medical Society of the State of California

Trans Med Soc St N Carol — Transactions of the Medical Society of the State of North Carolina

Trans Med Soc St New Jers — Transactions of the Medical Society of the State of New Jersey

Trans Med Soc St NY — Transactions of the Medical Society of the State of New York

Trans Med Soc St Va — Transactions of the Medical Society of the State of Virginia

Trans Meet Commns II & IV Int Soc Soil Sci — Transactions. Meeting of Commissions II and IV. International Society of Soil Science

Trans Meeting Jap Forest Soc — Transactions. Meeting. Japanese Forestry Society

Trans Me Med Ass — Transactions of the Maine Medical Association

Trans Me St Pomol Soc — Transactions of the Maine State Pomological Society

Trans Metall Soc AIME — Transactions. Metallurgical Society of AIME

Trans Metall Soc AIME (Am Inst Min Metall Pet Eng) — Transactions. Metallurgical Society of AIME (American Institute of Mining, Metallurgical, and Petroleum Engineers)

Trans Met Finish Assoc India — Transactions. Metal Finishers' Association of India

Trans Met Heat Treat — Transactions of Metal Heat Treatment

Trans Midl Inst Min Engrs — Transactions of the Midland Institute of Mining Engineers

Trans Midl Jr Gas Engng Soc — Transactions. Midland Junior Gas Engineering Society

Trans Min Geol Metall Inst India — Transactions. Mining, Geological, and Metallurgical Institute of India

Trans Mining Geol Met Inst India — Transactions. Mining, Geological, and Metallurgical Institute of India

Trans Min Instn Scotl — Transactions of the Mining Institution of Scotland

Trans Min Metall Alumni Ass Kyoto — Transactions of the Mining and Metallurgical Alumni Association (Kyoto)

Trans Min Metall Alumni Assoc — Transactions. Mining and Metallurgical Alumni Association

Trans Min Metall Assoc (Kyoto) — Transactions. Mining and Metallurgical Association (Kyoto)

Trans Minn St Med Soc — Transactions of the Minnesota State Medical Society

Trans Miss St Med Ass — Transactions of the Mississippi State Medical Association

Trans Miss Vall Med Ass — Transactions of the Mississippi Valley Medical Association

Trans MO Acad Sci — Transactions. Missouri Academy of Science

Trans MO Acad Scie — Transactions. Missouri Academy of Science

Trans Modular Soc — Transactions of the Modular Society

Trans Monumental Brass Soc — Transactions. Monumental Brass Society

Trans Morris C Res Counc — Transactions. Morris County Research Council

Trans Mosc Math Soc — Transactions. Moscow Mathematical Society

Trans Moscow Math Soc — Transactions. Moscow Mathematical Society

Trans Mycol Soc Jap — Transactions. Mycological Society of Japan

Trans Mycol Soc Japan — Transactions. Mycological Society of Japan

Trans Mycol Soc Jpn — Transactions. Mycological Society of Japan

Trans N Amer Wildlife Conf — Transactions. North American Wildlife and Natural Resources Conference

Trans N Am Wildl Conf — Transactions of the North American Wildlife Conference

Trans N Am Wildl Nat Resour Conf — Transactions. North American Wildlife and Natural Resources Conference

Trans Nat Hist Northumberl Durham Newcastle Upon Tyne — Transactions. Natural History Society of Northumberland, Durham, and Newcastle-Upon-Tyne

Trans Nat Hist Soc Formosa — Transactions. Natural History Society of Formosa

Trans Nat Hist Soc Glasgow — Transactions. Natural History Society of Glasgow

Trans Nat Hist Soc Northumberl Durham Newcastle-Upon-Tyne — Transactions. Natural History Society of Northumberland, Durham, and Newcastle-Upon-Tyne [Later, Natural History Society of Northumbria. Transactions]

Trans Nat Hist Soc Northumbria — Transactions. Natural History Society of Northumbria

Transnational Data Rep — Transnational Data Report

Transnatl Data Rep — Transnational Data Report

Trans Natl Inst Sci India — Transactions. National Institute of Sciences. India

Trans Natl Res Inst Met — Transactions. National Research Institute for Metals

Trans Natl Res Inst Met (Tokyo) — Transactions. National Research Institute for Metals (Tokyo)

Trans Natl Saf Congr — Transactions. National Safety Congress

Trans Natn Ass US Pens Exam Surg — Transactions of the National Association of United States Pension Examining Surgeons

Trans Natn Chrysanth Soc — Transactions of the National Chrysanthemum Society

Trans Natn Dent Ass Chicago — Transactions of the National Dental Association (Chicago)

Trans Natn Game Conf NY — Transactions of the National Game Conference (New York)

Trans Natn Inst Sci India — Transactions of the National Institute of Sciences of India

Trans Natn Saf Congr Chicago — Transactions of the National Safety Congress (Chicago)

Trans Natn Tuberc Ass NY — Transactions. National Tuberculosis Association (New York)

Trans Nat Res Inst Metals (Tokyo) — Transactions. National Research Institute for Metals (Tokyo)

Trans Nat Vac Symp — Transactions. National Vacuum Symposium

Trans Nebr Acad Sci — Transactions. Nebraska Academy of Sciences

Trans Nebr Acad Sci Affiliated Soc — Transactions. Nebraska Academy of Sciences and Affiliated Societies

Trans Neb St Med Soc — Transactions of the Nebraska State Medical Society

Trans NEC Instn E Ship — Transactions. North East Coast Institution of Engineers and Shipbuilders

Trans NE Cst Instn Engrs Shipbldrs — Transactions. North East Coast Institution of Engineers and Shipbuilders

Trans N Engl Inst Min Mech Engrs — Transactions. North of England Institute of Mining and Mechanical Engineers

Trans N Engl Obstet Gynaec Soc — Transactions of the North of England Obstetrical and Gynaecological Society

Trans N Engl Odont Soc — Transactions of the North of England Odontological Society

Trans Newbury Dist Fld Club — Transactions. Newbury District Field Club

Trans Newcomen Soc — Transactions. Newcomen Society

Trans Newcomen Soc Study His Eng Technol — Transactions. Newcomen Society for the Study of the History of Engineering and Technology

Trans New Engl Cott Mfrs Ass — Transactions. New England Cotton Manufacturers' Association

Trans New Engl Obstet Gynecol Soc — Transactions. New England Obstetrical and Gynecological Society

Trans New Engl Obstet Gynec Soc — Transactions of the New England Obstetrical and Gynecological Society

Trans New Engl Surg Soc — Transactions. New England Surgical Society

Trans New Hamps Hort Soc — Transactions of the New Hampshire Horticultural Society

Trans New Hamps Med Soc — Transactions of the New Hampshire Medical Society

Trans NE Wildl Confs — Transactions of the Northeast Wildlife Conferences

Trans New Jers Obstet Gynec Soc — Transactions of the New Jersey Obstetrical and Gynecological Society

Trans New Orleans Acad Ophthalmol — Transactions. New Orleans Academy of Ophthalmology

Trans News — Transport News

Trans New York Acad Sci — Transactions. New York Academy of Sciences

Trans New York Acad Sci Ser II — Transactions. New York Academy of Sciences. Series II

Trans NJ Obstet Gynecol Soc — Transactions. New Jersey Obstetrical and Gynecological Society

Trans Nonferrous Met Soc China — Transactions of Nonferrous Metals Society of China

Trans North Am Wildl Conf — Transactions. North American Wildlife Conference

Trans North Am Wildl Nat Res Conf — Transactions. North American Wildlife and Natural Resources Conference

Trans North Am Wildl Nat Resour Conf — Transactions. North American Wildlife and Natural Resources Conference

Trans North East Coast Inst Eng Shipbuild — Transactions. North East Coast Institution of Engineers and Shipbuilders

Trans Northeast Sect Wildl Soc — Transactions of the Northeast Section. Wildlife Society

Trans N Staffs Ceram Soc — Transactions of the North Staffordshire Ceramic Society

Trans Ny Acad Med — Transactions of the New York Academy of Medicine

Trans NY Acad Sci — Transactions. New York Academy of Sciences

Trans NY Elect Soc — Transactions of the New York Electrical Society

Trans NY Inst Stomat — Transactions of the New York Institute of Stomatology

Trans NY New Engl Ass Rly Surg — Transactions of the New York and New England Association of Railway Surgeons

Trans NY Obstet Soc — Transactions of the New York Obstetrical Society

Trans NY Odont Soc — Transactions of the New York Odontological Society
Trans NY Surg Soc — Transactions of the New York Surgical Society
Trans NZ Inst — Transactions of the New Zealand Institute
Trans NZ Inst Eng — Transactions. New Zealand Institution of Engineers, Incorporated
Trans NZ Inst Eng CE — Transactions. New Zealand Institution of Engineers, Incorporated. Civil Engineering Section
Trans NZ Inst Eng EMCh — Transactions. New Zealand Institution of Engineers, Incorporated. Electrical/Mechanical/Chemical Engineering Section
Trans NZ Inst Eng Inc Civ Eng Sect — Transactions. New Zealand Institution of Engineers, Incorporated. Civil Engineering Section
Trans NZ Inst Eng Inc Electr Mech Chem Eng Sect — Transactions. New Zealand Institution of Engineers, Incorporated. Electrical/Mechanical/Chemical Engineering Section
Trans Obstet Soc Lond — Transactions of the Obstetrical Society of London
Trans Odonto Chir Soc Edinb — Transactions of the Odonto-Chirurgical Society of Edinburgh
Trans Odont Soc Gt Br — Transactions of the Odontological Society of Great Britain
Trans Ohio Homoeop Med Soc — Transactions of the Ohio Homoeopathic Medical Society
Trans Ohio St Ecl Med Ass — Transactions of the Ohio State Eclectic Medical Association
Trans Ohio St Med Ass — Transactions of the Ohio State Medical Association
Trans Ophthalmol Soc Aust — Transactions. Ophthalmological Society of Australia
Trans Ophthalmol Soc NZ — Transactions. Ophthalmological Society of New Zealand
Trans Ophthalmol Soc UK — Transactions. Ophthalmological Societies of the United Kingdom
Trans Ophthal Soc Aust — Transactions. Ophthalmological Society of Australia
Trans Ophthal Soc Ceylon — Transactions of the Ophthalmological Society of Ceylon
Trans Ophthal Soc NZ — Transactions of the Ophthalmological Society of New Zealand
Trans Ophthal Soc S Afr — Transactions of the Ophthalmological Society of South Africa
Trans Ophthal Soc UK — Transactions of the Ophthalmological Society of the United Kingdom
Trans Opt Soc — Transactions. Optical Society
Trans Oswestry Offa Fld Club — Transactions. Oswestry Offa Field Club
Trans Otol Soc UK — Transactions of the Otological Society of the United Kingdom
Trans Ottawa Lit Scient Soc — Transactions of the Ottawa Literary and Scientific Society
Trans Oxf Univ Jr Scient Club — Transactions of the Oxford University Junior Scientific Club
Transp — Transporter
Trans PA Acad Ophthalmol Otolaryngol — Transactions. Pennsylvania Academy of Ophthalmology and Otolaryngology
Trans-Pac — Trans-Pacific
Trans Pac Coast Obstet Gynecol Soc — Transactions. Pacific Coast Obstetrical and Gynecological Society
Trans Pac Coast Oto-Ophthalmol Soc — Transactions. Pacific Coast Oto-Ophthalmological Society
Trans Pac Coast Oto-Ophthalmol Soc Annu Meet — Transactions. Pacific Coast Oto-Ophthalmological Society. Annual Meeting
Transp Age — Transport Age [London]
Trans Papers (L) Brit G — Institute of British Geographers (Liverpool). Transactions and Papers
Trans Pap Inst Brit Geogr — Transactions and Papers. Institute of British Geographers
Transp Aust — Transport Australia
Transp Commun Bull — Transport and Communication Bulletin [Melbourne]
Transp Commun Rev — Transport and Communication Review
Trans Peirce Soc — Transactions. Charles S. Peirce Society
Transp Eng — Transportation Engineering
Transp Eng J ASCE — Transportation Engineering Journal. ASCE
Transp Engng — Transportation Engineering [Formerly, Traffic Engineering]
Transp Engng J Proc ASCE — Transportation Engineering Journal. Proceedings of the American Society of Civil Engineers
Transp Engr — Transport Engineer
Trans Peninsula Hortic Soc — Transactions. Peninsula Horticultural Society
Transp En J — Transportation Engineering Journal. ASCE
Trans Persp — Transnational Perspectives
Trans Philad Pediat Soc — Transactions of the Philadelphia Pediatric Society
Trans Philological Soc — Transactions. Philological Society
Trans Philol Soc — Transactions. Philological Society
Trans Philos Soc New South Wales — Transactions. Philosophical Society of New South Wales
Trans Phil Soc — Transactions. Philological Society
Transp His — Transportation History
Transp Hist — Transport History
Transp J — Transportation Journal
Transp J — Transport Journal
Transp J of Aust — Transport Journal of Australia
Transp Khranenie Nefti Nefteprod — Transport i Khranenie Nefti i Nefteproduktov
Transplan P — Transplantation Proceedings
Transplan R — Transplantation Reviews
Transplant — Transplantation
Transplant Bull — Transplantation Bulletin
Transplant Clin Immunol — Transplantation and Clinical Immunology
Transplant Immunol Clin — Transplantation et Immunologie Clinique
Transplant Int — Transplant International
Transplantn Bull — Transplantation Bulletin [Great Falls, Salt Lake City, Baltimore]
Transplantn Proc — Transplantation Proceedings
Transplant Proc — Transplantation Proceedings

Transplant Proc Suppl — Transplantation Proceedings. Supplement
Transplant Rev — Transplantation Reviews
Transplant Sci — Transplantation Science
Transplant Soc Int Cong Proc — Transplantation Society. International Congress. Proceedings
Trans Plast Inst Aust NSW Sect — Transactions. Plastics Institute of Australia. New South Wales Section
Trans Plast Inst Lond — Transactions of the Plastics Institute (London)
Transpl Immunol — Transplant Immunology
Transpl Infect Dis — Transplant Infectious Disease
Transpl Int — Transplant International
Transp L J — Transportation Law Journal
Trans Plumstead Distr Nat Hist Soc — Transactions of the Plumstead & District Natural History Society
Trans Plymouth Distr Fld Club — Transactions of the Plymouth and District Field Club
Transp Manage — Transport Management
Transp-Med Vesti — Transportno-Meditsinski Vesti
Transp News — Transport News of New Zealand
Transp News Dig — Transport News Digest
Transpn News — Transportation News. Goodyear Tyre and Rubber Co. [Wolverhampton]
Transpn Ser Cps Engrs US Army — Transportation Series. Corps of Engineers. United States Army [Washington]
Transpn Top — Transportation Topics. Railway Association of Canada
Transpn Wld — Transportation World [New York]
Transport and Communications Bul Asia and Pacific — Transport and Communications Bulletin for Asia and the Pacific
Transportat — Transportation
Transportation J — Transportation Journal
Transportation Plann Tech — Transportation Planning and Technology
Transportation Q — Transportation Quarterly
Transportation Res — Transportation Research
Transportation Res Part A — Transportation Research. Part A. General
Transportation Res Part B — Transportation Research. Part B. Methodological
Transportation Sci — Operations Research Society of America. Transportation Science Section. Transportation Science
Transport D — Transport Digest
Transport Theory Statist Phys — Transport Theory and Statistical Physics
Trans Powder Metall Assoc India — Transactions. Powder Metallurgy Association of India
Transp Plan and Technol — Transport Planning and Technology
Transp Plann Tech — Transportation Planning and Technology
Transp Plann Technol — Transportation Planning and Technology
Transp Policy Decision Making — Transport Policy and Decision Making
Transp Porous Media — Transport in Porous Media
Transp Processes Eng — Transport Processes in Engineering
Transp Q — Transportation Quarterly
Trans Prague Conf Inf Theory — Transactions. Prague Conference on Information Theory, Statistical Decision Functions, Random Processes
Transp Res — Transportation Research
Transp Res Abstr — Transportation Research Abstracts
Transp Res Board Spec Rep — Transportation Research Board. Special Report
Transp Res Board Transp Res Rec — Transportation Research Board. Transportation Research Record
Transp Res News — Transportation Research News
Transp Res Part A — Transportation Research. Part A. General
Transp Res Part A Gen — Transportation Research. Part A. General
Transp Res Part A Policy Pract — Transportation Research. Part A. Policy and Practice
Transp Res Part B — Transportation Research. Part B. Methodological
Transp Res Rec — Transportation Research Record
Transp Revs — Transport Reviews
Trans Princeton Conf Cerebrovasc Dis — Transactions. Princeton Conference on Cerebrovascular Diseases
Transp Road Res Lab (GB) TRRL Rep — Transport and Road Research Laboratory (Great Britain). TRRL Report
Trans Proc Amer Philol Ass — Transactions and Proceedings. American Philological Association
Trans Proc Birmingham Arch Soc — Transactions and Proceedings. Birmingham Archaeological Society
Trans Proc Bot Soc Edinb — Transactions and Proceedings. Botanical Society of Edinburgh
Trans Proc Bot Soc Edinburgh — Transactions and Proceedings. Botanical Society Edinburgh
Trans Proc Bot Soc Pa — Transactions and Proceedings of the Botanical Society of Pennsylvania
Trans Proc Calif Ass Nurserym — Transactions and Proceedings. California Association of Nurserymen
Trans Proc Fiji Soc — Transactions and Proceedings of the Fiji Society
Trans Proc Fiji Soc Sci Ind — Transactions and Proceedings. Fiji Society of Science and Industry
Trans Proc Geogr Soc Pacif — Transactions and Proceedings of the Geographical Society of the Pacific
Trans Proc Geol Soc S Afr — Transactions and Proceedings. Geological Society of South Africa
Trans Proc Japan Soc — Transactions and Proceedings of the Japan Society
Trans Proc Lpool Bot Soc — Transactions and Proceedings. Liverpool Botanical Society
Trans Proc Natal Scient Soc — Transactions and Proceedings of the Natal Scientific Society
Trans Proc Natn Soc Sci Durban — Transactions and Proceedings of the National Society of Science at Durban
Trans Proc NZ Inst — Transactions and Proceedings of the New Zealand Institute

Trans Proc Palaeontol Soc Jap — Transactions and Proceedings. Palaeontological Society of Japan

Trans Proc Palaeontol Soc Japan New Ser — Transactions and Proceedings. Palaeontological Society of Japan. New Series

Trans Proc Palaeontol Soc Jpn New Ser — Transactions and Proceedings. Palaeontological Society of Japan. New Series

Trans Proc Palaeont Soc Japan — Transactions and Proceedings of the Palaeontological Society of Japan

Trans Proc Perthshire Soc Natur Sci — Transactions and Proceedings. Perthshire Society of Natural Science

Trans Proc Perthsh Soc Nat Sci — Transactions and Proceedings of the Perthshire Society of Natural Science

Trans Proc Philos Inst Victoria — Transactions and Proceedings. Philosophical Institute of Victoria

Trans Proc R Geogr Soc Australas Vict Brch — Transactions and Proceedings of the Royal Geographical Society of Australasia. Victorian Branch

Trans Proc R Soc NZ — Transactions and Proceedings of the Royal Society of New Zealand

Trans Proc R Soc South Aust — Transactions and Proceedings. Royal Society of South Australia

Trans Proc S Lond Ent Nat Hist Soc — Transactions and Proceedings of the South London Entomological and Natural History Society

Trans Proc Torquay Natur Hist Soc — Transactions and Proceedings. Torquay Natural History Society

Trans Prov Med Assoc — Transactions. Provincial Medical and Surgical Association

Transp Sci — Transportation Science

Transps Mod — Transports Modernes [*Paris*]

Transp Stroit — Transportnoe Stroitel'stvo

Transp Theo — Transport Theory and Statistical Physics

Transp Theory Stat Phys — Transport Theory and Statistical Physics

Transp Th St P — Transport Theory and Statistical Physics

Transp Traffic — Transport and Traffic

Trans Q Am Soc Met — Transactions Quarterly. American Society for Metals

Trans R — Transatlantic Review

Trans R Acad Med Ire — Transactions of the Royal Academy of Medicine in Ireland [*Dublin*]

Trans Radnorshire Soc — Transactions. Radnorshire Society

Trans R Aeronaut Soc Gt Br — Transactions of the Royal Aeronautical Society of Great Britain [*London*]

Trans R Astr Soc Can — Transactions. Royal Astronomical Society of Canada [*Toronto*]

Trans R Caled Hort Soc — Transactions of the Royal Caledonian Horticultural Society [*Edinburgh*]

Trans R Can Inst — Transactions. Royal Canadian Institute

Trans R Engl Arboric Soc — Transactions of the Royal English Arboricultural Society [*Newcastle*]

Trans R Entomol Soc Lond — Transactions. Royal Entomological Society of London

Trans R Ent Soc Lond — Transactions. Royal Entomological Society of London

Trans Rep Lpool Med Instn — Transactions and Report of the Liverpool Medical Institution

Trans Res A — Transportation Research. Part A. General

Trans Res Abstr — Transportation Research Abstracts

Trans Res B — Transportation Research. Part B. Methodological

Trans Res Part B Methodol — Transportation Research. Part B. Methodological

Trans R Geogr Soc Australas Qd Brch — Transactions of the Royal Geographical Society of Australasia. Queensland Branch [*Brisbane*]

Trans R Geol Soc (Corn) — Transactions. Royal Geological Society (Cornwall)

Trans R Highl Agric Soc Scotl — Transactions. Royal Highland and Agricultural Society of Scotland

Trans Rhode Isl Med Soc — Transactions of the Rhode Island Medical Society [*Providence*]

Trans Rhod Sci Assoc — Transactions. Rhodesia Scientific Association

Trans RINA — Transactions. Royal Institution of Naval Architects

Trans R Inst Nav Arch — Transactions. Royal Institute of Naval Architects

Trans R Instn Naval Archit — Quarterly Transactions. Royal Institution of Naval Architects

Trans R Microsc Soc — Transactions. Royal Microscopical Society

Trans Rochdale Lit Scient Soc — Transactions of the Rochdale Literary and Scientific Society

Trans Royal Soc Can Sect 1 Sect 2 and Sect 3 — Transactions. Royal Society of Canada. Section 1, Section 2, and Section 3

Trans Royal Soc Trop Med Hyg — Transactions of the Royal Society of Tropical Medicine and Hygiene

Trans Roy Geol Soc Cornwall — Transactions. Royal Geological Society of Cornwall

Trans Roy Hist Soc — Transactions. Royal Historical Society

Trans Roy Inst Technol (Stockholm) — Transactions. Royal Institute of Technology (Stockholm)

Trans Roy Inst Tech (Stockholm) — Transactions. Royal Institute of Technology (Stockholm)

Trans Roy Soc Canada — Transactions. Royal Society of Canada

Trans Roy Soc Canada 4 — Transactions. Royal Society of Canada. Chemical, Mathematical, and Physical Sciences. Fourth Series

Trans Roy Soc Edinburgh — Transactions. Royal Society of Edinburgh

Trans Roy Soc NZ Bot — Transactions. Royal Society of New Zealand. Botany

Trans Roy Soc S Aust — Royal Society of South Australia. Transactions

Trans Roy Soc South Africa — Transactions. Royal Society of South Africa

Trans Roy Soc Trop Med Hyg — Transactions. Royal Society of Tropical Medicine and Hygiene

Trans R Sch Dent (Stockh Umea) — Transactions. Royal Schools of Dentistry (Stockholm and Umea)

Trans R Soc Arts — Transactions. Royal Society of Arts

Trans R Soc Can — Transactions. Royal Society of Canada

Trans R Soc Can Mem Soc R Can — Transactions. Royal Society of Canada/ Memoires. Societe Royale du Canada

Trans R Soc Can Sect 3 — Transactions. Royal Society of Canada. Section 3. Chemical, Mathematical, and Physical Sciences

Trans R Soc Can Sect 4 — Transaction. Royal Society of Canada. Section 4. Geological Sciences Including Mineralogy

Trans R Soc Can Sect 5 — Transactions. Royal Society of Canada. Section 5. Biological Sciences

Trans R Soc Can Sect 1 2 3 — Transactions. Royal Society of Canada. Section 1, Section 2, and Section 3

Trans R Soc Edinb — Transactions. Royal Society of Edinburgh

Trans R Soc Edinb Earth Sci — Transactions. Royal Society of Edinburgh. Earth Sciences

Trans R Soc Edinburgh — Transactions. Royal Society of Edinburgh

Trans R Soc Edinburgh Earth Sci — Transactions. Royal Society of Edinburgh. Earth Sciences

Trans R Soc Lit — Transactions. Royal Society of Literature of the United Kingdom

Trans R Soc NZ — Transactions. Royal Society of New Zealand

Trans R Soc NZ Biol Sci — Transactions. Royal Society of New Zealand. Biological Science

Trans R Soc NZ Bot — Transactions. Royal Society of New Zealand. Botany

Trans R Soc NZ Earth Sci — Transactions. Royal Society of New Zealand. Earth Science

Trans R Soc NZ Gen — Transactions. Royal Society of New Zealand. General

Trans R Soc NZ Geol — Transactions. Royal Society of New Zealand. Geology

Trans R Soc NZ Zool — Transactions. Royal Society of New Zealand. Zoology

Trans R Soc S Afr — Transactions. Royal Society of South Africa

Trans R Soc S Aust — Transactions. Royal Society of South Australia

Trans R Soc South Aust — Transactions. Royal Society of South Australia

Trans R Soc Trop Med Hyg — Transactions. Royal Society of Tropical Medicine and Hygiene

Trans R Soc Vict — Transactions of the Royal Society of Victoria [*Melbourne*]

Trans Russ Inst Appl Chem — Transactions. Russian Institute of Applied Chemistry

Trans R Welsh Agric Soc — Transactions of the Royal Welsh Agricultural Society [*Wrexham*]

Trans SAEST — Transactions. SAEST

Trans S Afr Inst Civ Eng — Transactions. South African Institution of Civil Engineers

Trans S Afr Inst Elec Eng — Transactions. South African Institute of Electrical Engineers

Trans S Afr Inst Elect Engrs — Transactions of the South African Institute of Electrical Engineers [*Johannesburg*]

Trans S Afr Inst Electr Eng — Transactions. South African Institute of Electrical Engineers

Trans S Afr Instn Civ Engrs — Transactions of the South African Institution of Civil Engineers [*Johannesburg*]

Trans San Diego Soc Nat Hist — Transactions. San Diego Society of Natural History

Trans SBA — Transactions. Society of Biblical Archaeology

Trans Sci — Transportation Science

Trans Sci Assoc — Transactions. Scientific Association

Trans Scient Soc R Tech Coll Glasg — Transactions. Scientific Society of the Royal Technical College. Glasgow

Trans Sci Soc China — Transactions. Science Society of China

Trans Scott Engng Stud Ass — Transactions of the Scottish Engineering Students Association [*Glasgow*]

Trans Scott Hort Ass — Transactions of the Scottish Horticultural Association [*Edinburgh*]

Trans Scott Min Stud Fed — Transactions of the Scottish Mining Students Federation [*Edinburgh*]

Trans Scott Nat Hist Soc — Transactions of the Scottish Natural History Society [*Edinburgh*]

Trans Sect Cutan Med Surg Am Med Ass — Transactions of the Section on Cutaneous Medicine and Surgery of the American Medical Association [*Chicago*]

Trans Sect Derm Syph Am Med Ass — Transactions of the Section on Dermatology and Syphilology of the American Medical Association [*Chicago*]

Trans Sect Dis Child Am Med Ass — Transactions of the Section on Diseases of Children of the American Medical Association [*Chicago*]

Trans Sect Gastroent Proctol Am Med Ass — Transactions of the Section on Gastroenterology and Proctology of the American Medical Association [*Chicago*]

Trans Sect Genito Urin Dis Am Med Ass — Transactions of the Section on Genito-Urinary Diseases of the American Medical Association [*Chicago*]

Trans Sect Gynec Coll Physns Philad — Transactions of the Section on Gynecology of the College of Physicians of Philadelphia

Trans Sect Hosps Am Med Ass — Transactions of the Section on Hospitals of the American Medical Association [*Chicago*]

Trans Sect Lar Otol Rhinol Am Med Ass — Transactions of the Section on Laryngology, Otology, and Rhinology of the American Medical Association [*Chicago*]

Trans Sect Nerv Ment Dis Am Med Ass — Transactions of the Section on Nervous and Mental Diseases of the American Medical Association [*Chicago*]

Trans Sect Obstet Gynec Abdom Surg Am Med Ass — Transactions of the Section on Obstetrics. Gynecology and Abdominal Surgery of the American Medical Association [*Chicago*]

Trans Sect Ophthal Am Med Ass — Transactions of the Section on Ophthalmology of the American Medical Association [*Chicago*]

Trans SHASE — Transactions. Society of Heating, Air Conditioning, and Sanitary Engineers

Trans SHASE Japan — Transactions. SHASE [*Society of Heating, Air Conditioning, and Sanitary Engineers*] (Japan)

Trans Shikoku Entomol Soc — Transactions. Shikoku Entomological Society

Trans Shikoku Ent Soc — Transactions. Shikoku Entomological Society

Trans Shrops Archaeol Nat Hist Soc — Transactions of the Shropshire Archaeological and Natural History Society [*Shrewsbury*]
Trans Shropshire Archaeol Soc — Transactions. Shropshire Archaeological Society
Trans Shropshire A S — Transactions. Shropshire Archaeological and Natural History Society
Trans Sigenkag Kenk — Transactions of the Sigenkagaku Kenkyusyo [*Tokyo*]
Trans SMPE — Transactions. Society of Motion Picture Engineers
Trans Soc Adv Electrochem Sci Technol — Transactions. Society for Advancement of Electrochemical Science and Technology
Trans Soc Alumni Bellevue Hosp NY — Transactions. Society of Alumni of Bellevue Hospital. New York
Trans Soc Alumni Charity Hosp NY — Transactions of the Society of the Alumni of Charity Hospital. New York
Trans Soc Alumni Sloane Hosp Wom — Transactions. Society of the Alumni of the Sloane Hospital for Women [*New York*]
Trans Soc Anaesth — Transactions of the Society of Anaesthetists [*London*]
Trans Soc Bibl Arch — Transactions. Society of Biblical Archaeology
Trans Soc Br Ent — Transactions. Society for British Entomology
Trans Soc Br Entomol — Transactions. Society for British Entomology
Trans Soc Comput Simul — Transactions of the Society for Computer Simulation
Trans Soc Heat Air Cond Sanit Eng Jpn — Transactions. Society of Heating, Air Conditioning, and Sanitary Engineers of Japan
Trans Soc Ill Eng — Transactions. Illuminating Engineering Society
Trans Soc Ind Med Offrs — Transactions of the Society of Industrial Medical Officers [*London*]
Trans Soc Instr Control Eng — Transactions. Society of Instrument and Control Engineers
Trans Soc Instrum and Control Eng — Transactions. Society of Instrument and Control Engineers
Trans Soc Instrum & Control Engrs (Japan) — Transactions. Society of Instrument and Control Engineers (Japan)
Trans Soc Instrum Control Eng — Transactions. Society of Instrument and Control Engineers
Trans Soc Instrum Technol — Transactions. Society of Instrument Technology
Trans Soc Mech Engrs Japan — Transactions of the Society of Mechanical Engineers of Japan [*Tokyo*]
Trans Soc Med Offrs Hlth Ceylon — Transactions of the Society of Medical Officers of Health of Ceylon [*Colombo*]
Trans Soc Min Eng — Transactions. Society of Mining Engineers, Inc.
Trans Soc Min Eng AIME — Transactions. Society of Mining Engineers. AIME
Trans Soc Min Engrs AIME — Transactions. Society of Mining Engineers. AIME
Trans Soc Min Metall Explor — Transactions. Society for Mining, Metallurgy, and Exploration, Inc.
Trans Soc Motion Pict Eng — Transactions. Society of Motion Picture Engineers
Trans Soc Motion Pict Engrs Wash — Transactions. Society of Motion Picture Engineers (Washington)
Trans Soc Mot Pict Eng — Transactions. Society of Motion Picture Engineers
Trans Soc NAME — Transactions. Society of Naval Architects and Marine Engineers
Trans Soc Naval Architects Mar Eng — Transactions. Society of Naval Architects and Marine Engineers
Trans Soc Nav Archit Mar Eng — Transactions. Society of Naval Architects and Marine Engineers
Trans Soc Nav Archit Mar Engrs NY — Transactions of the Society of Naval Architects and Marine Engineers (New York)
Trans Soc Occup Med — Transactions. Society of Occupational Medicine
Trans Soc Pathol Jpn — Transactiones Societatis Pathologicae Japonicae
Trans Soc Pet Eng AIME — Transactions. Society of Petroleum Engineers of AIME
Trans Soc Petrol Geophys — Transactions of the Society of Petroleum Geophysicists [*Houston, Texas*]
Trans Soc Rheol — Transactions. Society of Rheology
Trans Soc State New York Promot Agric — Transactions. Society. Instituted in the State of New-York, for the Promotion of Agriculture, Arts, and Manufactures
Trans Southwest Fed Geol Soc — Transactions. Southwestern Federation of Geological Societies
Trans SPWLA Annu Log Symp — Transactions. SPWLA [*Society of Professional Well Log Analysts*] Annual Logging Symposium
Trans S Staffordshire Archaeol Hist Soc — Transactions. South Staffordshire Archaeological and Historical Society
Trans S Staffs Archaeol Hist Soc — Transactions. South Staffordshire Archaeological and Historical Society
Trans S Staffs Arch Hist Soc — Transactions. South Staffordshire Archaeological and Historical Society
Trans State Inst Appl Chem — Transactions. State Institute of Applied Chemistry
Trans Sth Surg Ass — Transactions of the Southern Surgical Association [*Nashville*]
Trans Stirling Nat Hist Archaeol Soc — Transactions of the Stirling Natural History and Archaeological Society
Trans St John's Hosp Dermatol Soc — Transactions. St. John's Hospital Dermatological Society
Trans Stud Coll Physicians Phila — Transactions and Studies. College of Physicians of Philadelphia
Trans Stud Coll Physns Philad — Transactions and Studies of the College of Physicians of Philadelphia
Trans Suffolk Natur Soc — Transactions. Suffolk Naturalists' Society
Trans Symp Carl Neuberg Soc — Carl Neuberg Society for International Scientific Relations. Transactions of the Symposium
Trans Tallinn Tech Univ — Transactions of Tallinn Technical University
Trans Tech Sect Can Pulp and Pap Assoc — Transactions. Technical Section. Canadian Pulp and Paper Association
Trans Tech Sect Can Pulp Pap Assoc — Transactions. Technical Section. Canadian Pulp and Paper Association
Trans Tenn Acad Sci — Transactions of the Tennessee Academy of Science [*Nashville*]

Trans Tenn St Med Ass — Transactions of the Tennessee State Medical Association [*Nashville*]
Trans Territ Med Soc Hawaii — Transactions. Territorial Medical Society of Hawaii [*Honolulu*]
Trans Tex Acad Sci — Transactions of the Texas Academy of Science [*Austin*]
Trans Tex St Med Ass — Transactions of the Texas State Medical Association [*Fort Worth*]
Trans Ther Soc Lond — Transactions of the Therapeutical Society of London
Trans Thoroton Soc Nottinghamshire — Transaction. Thoroton Society of Nottinghamshire
Trans Thoroton Soc Notts — Transactions. Thoroton Society of Nottinghamshire
Trans Tianjin Univ — Transactions of Tianjin University
Trans Tokyo Univ Fish — Transactions. Tokyo University of Fisheries
Trans Tottori Soc Agric Sci — Transactions. Tottori Society of Agricultural Sciences
Trans Tottori Soc Agr Sci — Transactions. Tottori Society of Agricultural Science
Trans Tuberc Soc Scotl — Transactions. Tuberculosis Society of Scotland
Trans Udgivet Dan Ing — Transactions. Udgivet af Dansk Ingenioeren
Trans Ulster Med Soc — Transactions of the Ulster Medical Society [*Belfast*]
Trans Univ Cent Desert Stud (Jodhpur India) — Transactions. University Centre of Desert Studies (Jodhpur, India)
Trans Utah Acad Sci — Transactions. Utah Academy of Sciences
Transvaal Agric J — Transvaal Agricultural Journal
Transvaal Med J — Transvaal Medical Journal
Transvaal Mus Bull — Transvaal Museum. Bulletin
Transvaal Mus Mem — Transvaal Museum. Memoirs
Transvaal Mus Monogr — Transvaal Museum. Monograph
Transvaal Mus Rep — Transvaal Museum. Report
Transvaal Nat Conserv Div Annu Rep — Transvaal Nature Conservation Division. Annual Report
Trans Vac Symp — Transactions. Vacuum Symposium
Transv Agric J — Transvaal Agricultural Journal [*Pretoria*]
Transv Gdnr — Transvaal Gardener [*Johannesburg*]
Transv Med J — Transvaal Medical Journal [*Durban*]
Transv Mus Mem — Transvaal Museum Memoirs [*Pretoria*]
Transv Obs Circ — Transvaal Observatory Circular [*Johannesburg*]
Trans Wagner Free Inst Sci Philadelphia — Transactions. Wagner Free Institute of Science of Philadelphia
Trans Westermarck Soc — Transactions of the Westermarck Society
Trans West Sect Am Urol Assoc — Transactions. Western Section of the American Urological Association
Trans West Sect Wildl Soc — Transactions. Western Section. Wildlife Society
Trans West Surg Ass — Transactions. Western Surgical Association
Trans Wigan Distr Min Tech Coll Stud Ass — Transactions. Wigan and District Mining and Technical College Past and Present Mining Students' Association [*Wigan*]
Trans Wis Acad Sci — Transactions. Wisconsin Academy of Sciences, Arts, and Letters
Trans Wis Acad Sci Arts Lett — Transactions. Wisconsin Academy of Sciences, Arts, and Letters
Trans Wisc Acad Sci — Transactions. Wisconsin Academy of Sciences, Arts, and Letters
Trans Wisconsin Acad Sci — Transactions. Wisconsin Academy of Sciences, Arts, and Letters
Trans Wisconsin Acad Sci Arts Lett — Transactions. Wisconsin Academy of Science, Arts, and Letters
Trans Woolhope Nat Fld Club — Transactions of the Woolhope Naturalists' Field Club
Trans Woolhope Naturalists — Transactions. Woolhope Naturalists' Field Club
Trans Woolhope Natur Field Club — Transactions. Woolhope Naturalists' Field Club
Trans Woolhope Natur Fld Club — Transactions. Woolhope Naturalists' Field Club
Trans Worc Arch Soc — Transactions. Worcestershire Archaeological Society
Trans Worc Arc Soc — Transactions. Worcestershire Archaeological Society
Trans Worcestershire Archaeol Soc 3 Ser — Transactions. Worcestershire Archaeological Society. Series 3
Trans Worcs Arch Soc — Transaction. Worcestershire Archaeological Society
Trans Worcs Arc Soc — Transactions. Worcestershire Archaeological Society
Trans Worcs Nat Club — Transactions of the Worcestershire Naturalists' Club [*Worcester*]
Trans World Energy Conf — Transactions. World Energy Conference
Trans Yb Engng Soc Univ Toronto — Transactions and Yearbook of the Engineering Society of the University of Toronto
Transylvania J Med — Transylvania Journal of Medicine
Trans Yorks Agric Soc — Transactions of the Yorkshire Agricultural Society [*Leeds*]
Trans Yorks Nat Un — Transactions of the Yorkshire Naturalists' Union [*Leeds*]
Trans Zimbabwe Sci Assoc — Transactions. Zimbabwe Scientific Association
Trans Zimb Sci Ass — Transactions of the Zimbabwe Scientific Association
Trans Zimb Sci Assoc — Transactions. Zimbabwe Scientific Association
Trans Zool Soc Lond — Transactions. Zoological Society of London
Tran USA — Transportation USA
TrAPhA — Transactions. American Philological Assocation
Tr A Ph A — Transactions and Proceedings. American Philological Association
TRAQA — Traffic Quarterly
Tr Arkhang Lesotekh Inst — Trudy Arkhangel'skogo Lesotekhnicheskogo Instituta
Tr Arkt Antarkt Nauchno-Issled Inst — Trudy Arkticheskogo i Antarkticheskogo Nauchno-Issledovatel'skogo Instituta
Tr Arm Geol Upr — Trudy Armyanskogo Geologicheskogo Upravleniya
Tr Arm Inst Stroim Sooruzh — Trudy Armyanskogo Instituta Stroimaterialov i Soozuzhenii
Tr Arm Nauchno Issled Inst Gidrotekh Melior — Trudy Armyanskogo Nauchno-Issledovatel'skogo Instituta Gidrotekhnniki i Melioratsii
Tr Arm Nauchno Issled Inst Vinograd Vinodel Plodovod — Trudy Armyanskogo Nauchno-Issledovatel'skogo Instituta Vinogradarstva Vinodeliya i Plodovodstva

Tr Arm Nauchno-Issled Inst Zhivotnovod Vet — Trudy Armyanskogo Nauchno-Issledovatel'skogo Instituta Zhivotnovodstva i Veterinarii

Tr Arm Nauchno-Issled Vet Inst — Trudy Armyanskogo Nauchno-Issledovatel'skogo Veterinarnogo Instituta

Tr Arm Protivochumn Stn — Trudy Armyanskoi Protivochumnoi Stantsii

TRASA — Traktory i Sel'khozmashiny

Trasf Sangue — Trasfusione del Sangue [Roma]

Trasfus Sangue — Trasfusione del Sangue

Tr Ashkhab Nauchno Issled Inst Epidemiol Gig — Trudy Ashkhabadskogo Nauchno-Issledovatel'skogo Instituta Epidemiologii i Gigieny

Trasp — Trasporti. Rivista di Politica, Economia, e Tecnica

Trasp Ind Tec Prod — Trasporti Industriali nella Tecnica della Produzione [Milano]

Trasp Mecc Pesat — Trasporti Meccanici e Pesatura [Milano]

Trasp Pubbl — Trasporti Pubblici

Tr Astrakh Gos Med Inst — Trudy Astrakhanskogo Gosudarstvennogo Meditinskogo Instituta

Tr Astrakh Gos Zapov — Trudy Astrakhanskogo Gosudarstvennogo Zapovednika

Tr Astrakh Tekh Inst Rybn Promsti Khoz — Trudy Astrakhanskogo Tekhnicheskogo Instituta Rybnoi Promyshlennosti i Khozyaistva

Tr Astrofiz Inst Akad Nauk Kaz SSR — Trudy Astrofizicheskogo Instituta Akademiya Nauk Kazakhskoi SSR

Tr Atl Nauchno-Issled Inst Ryb Khoz Okeanogr — Trudy Atlanticheskii Nauchno-Issledovatel'skii Institut Rybnogo Khozyaistva i Okeanografii

Tratt Met — Trattamenti dei Metalli

Tr At Zoovet Inst — Trudy Alma-Atinskogo Instituta

Traumatol — Traumatology

Trav — Travailleur

Trav — Travel

Trav — Travel/Holiday

Trav — Travelling

TRAVA — Travaux

Trav Acad Natn Reims — Travaux de l'Academie Nationale de Reims

Trav Act Pop — Travaux de l'Action Populaire

Trav A Hop Urol Chir Urin — Travaux Annuels de l'Hopital d'Urologie et de Chirurgie Urinaire [Paris]

Travail Agric — Travail Agricole [Rome]

Travail Hum — Travail Humain [Paris]

Travailleur Can — Travailleur Canadien

Travail Metall — Travailleur de la Metallurgie [Paris]

Travail Meth — Travail et Methodes [Paris]

Travail Secur — Travail et Securite [Paris]

Travail Transform Nickel — Travail de Transformation du Nickel et de ses Alliages non Ferreux [Paris]

Trav Algol — Travaux Algologiques [Paris]

Trav Alphabet — Travail de l'Alphabetisation

Trav Assembl Sanit Dep Seine Inf — Travaux des Assemblees Sanitaires. Departement de la Seine-Inferieure [Rouen]

Trav Ass Inst Marey — Travaux de l'Association de l'Institut Marey [Paris]

Trav Ass Int Geod — Travaux. Association Internationale de Geodesie. Union Geodesique et Geophysique Internationale [Paris]

Trav Ass Magn Elect Terr — Travaux. Association de Magnetisme et d'Electricite Terrestres. Union Geodesique et Geophysique Internationale

Trav Ass Nat Vall Loing — Travaux de l'Association des Naturalistes de la Vallee du Loing [Moret-sur-Loing]

Trav Assoc H Capitant — Travaux. Association Henri Capitant

Trav Astr Geod Suisse — Travaux Astronomiques et Geodesiques Executes en Suisse [Berne]

Travaux Centre Rech Semiol — Travaux du Centre de Recherches Semiologiques

Travaux Inst Etud Lat Am Univ Strasbourg — Travaux de l'Institut d'Etudes Latino-Americaines de l'Universite de Strasbourg

Travaux Inst Fran Etud Andines Paris — Travaux de l'Institut Francais d'Etudes Andines (Paris)

Travaux Log — Travaux de Logique

Travaux Rech — Travaux et Recherches

Travaux Sem Anal Convexe — Travaux. Seminaire d'Analyse Convexe

Trav Biol Inst JB Carnoy — Travaux Biologiques de l'Institut J.B. Carnoy [Louvain]

Trav Bur Geol — Travaux du Bureau Geologique

Trav Bur Geol Madagascar — Travaux. Bureau Geologique, Service Geologique de Madagascar et Dependances [Tananarive]

Trav Bur Int Etal Phys Chim — Travaux du Bureau International des Etalons Physico-Chimiques [Paris]

Trav CCI — Travaux de la CCI

Trav Cent Estud Microsc Fac Farm Univ Porto — Travaux. Centro de Estudos Microscopicos. Faculdade de Farmacia. Universidade do Porto

Trav Cent Etude Eaux Brux — Travaux du Centre d'Etude des Eaux (Bruxelles)

Trav Cent Rech Etudes Oceanogr — Travaux. Centre de Recherches et d'Etudes Oceanographiques

Trav Cent Rech Etud Oceanogr — Travaux du Centre de Recherches et d'Etudes Oceanographiques [Paris]

Trav Cent Rech Sahar — Travaux du Centre de Recherches Sahariennes

Trav Centr Rech Etudes Oceanogr — Travaux du Centre de Recherches et d'Etudes Oceanographiques

Trav Cerc Etud Aerotech — Travaux du Cercle d'Etudes Aerotechniques [Paris]

Trav Cerc Geogr Liege — Travaux. Cercle de Geographes Liegeois [Liege]

Trav C Et — Travaux. Comite d'Etudes et de Legislation de la Federation des Notaires de Belgique

Trav Chim Aliment Hyg — Travaux de Chimie Alimentaire et d'Hygiene

Trav Chim Bull Int Acad Pol — Travaux Chimiques parus au Bulletin International de l'Academie Polonaise [Cracovie]

Trav Clin Chir Hosp Salpetriere — Travaux de la Clinique Chirurgicale, Hospice de la Salpetriere

Trav Clin Mal Cutan Syph Strasb — Travaux de la Clinique des Maladies Cutanees et Syphilitiques (Strasbourg)

Trav Com All Hyg Soc Fr — Travaux du Comite. Alliance d'Hygiene Sociale de France. Comite de l'Herault [Montpellier]

Trav Com Int Etude Bauxites Alumine Alum — Travaux. Comite International pour l'Etude des Bauxites, de l'Alumine, et de l'Aluminium

Trav Com Int Etude Bauxites Oxydes Hydroxydes Alum — Travaux. Comite International pour l'Etude des Bauxites, des Oxydes, et des Hydroxydes d'Aluminium

Trav Communaux — Travaux Communaux

Trav Conf Brux — Travaux et Conferences. Faculte de Droit de Bruxelles

Trav C Ph R — Travaux de Linguistique et de Litterature. Centre de Philologie et de Litteratures Romanes. Universite de Strasbourg

Trav Doc Geogr Trop — Travaux et Documents de Geographie Tropicale

Trav Doc ORSTOM — Travaux et Documents. ORSTOM

Trav et Jours — Travaux et Jours

Trav et Meth — Travail et Methodes

Trav et Rech — Travaux et Recherches

Trav et Soc — Travail et Societe

Trav Geogr Tcheq — Travaux Geographiques Tcheques

Trav Geol Com Publs Siles Acad Pol Sci Lett — Travaux Geologiques du Comite des Publications Silesiennes. Academie Polonaise des Sciences et des Lettres [Krakow]

Trav Geophys (Prague) — Travaux Geophysiques (Prague)

Trav/Holiday — Travel/Holiday

Trav Hum — Travail Humain

Trav Humain — Travail Humain

Trav Hum Ren — Travaux d'Humanisme et Renaissance

Trav Inst Anat Sect Anthrop Ec Sup Med Indochine — Travaux de l'Institut Anatomique. Section Anthropologique. Ecole Superieure de Medecine de l'Indochine [Hanoi]

Trav Inst Biol Gen Zool Univ Montreal — Travaux de l'Institut de Biologie Generale et de Zoologie de l'Universite de Montreal

Trav Inst Bot Leo Errera — Travaux de l'Institut Botanique Leo Errera [Bruxelles]

Trav Inst Bot Univ Lausanne — Travaux de l'Institut de Botanique de l'Universite de Lausanne [Lausanne]

Trav Inst Bot Univ Montpellier — Travaux de l'Institut de Botanique de l'Universite de Montpellier

Trav Inst Bot Univ Neuchatel — Travaux de l'Institute Botanique de l'Universite de Neuchatel

Trav Inst Bunge — Travaux de l'Institut Bunge [Anvers]

Trav Inst Chim Biol Univ Strasb — Travaux de l'Institut de Chimie Biologique de l'Universite de Strasbourg

Trav Inst Ed V Beneden Univ Liege — Travaux de l'Institut Ed. van Beneden. Universite de Liege

Trav Inst Franc Et And — Travaux. Institut Francais d'Etudes Andines

Trav Inst Franc Et Andines — Travaux. Institut Francais d'Etudes Andines

Trav Inst Franc Etudes Andines — Travaux de l'Institut Francais d'Etudes Andines

Trav Inst Fr Etud And — Travaux de l'Institut Francais d'Etudes Andines

Trav Inst Fr Etud Andines — Travaux de l'Institut Francais d'Etudes Andines [Paris, Lima]

Trav Inst Geol Anthropol Prehist Fac Sci Poitiers — Travaux. Institut de Geologie et d'Anthropologie Prehistorique. Faculte des Sciences de Poitiers

Trav Inst Geol Jura — Travaux de l'Institut de la Geologie du Jura [Besancon]

Trav Inst Histol Embryol Univ Porto — Travaux de l'Institut d'Histologie et d'Embryologie de l'Universite de Porto

Trav Inst Hydrol Met Vars — Travaux de l'Institut Hydrologique et Meteorologique (Varsovie)

Trav Inst Hyg Publ Et Tchec — Travaux de l'Institut d'Hygiene Publique de l'Etat Tchecoslovaque [Prague]

Trav Inst L — Travaux. Institut de Linguistique de Lund

Trav Inst Med Super — Travaux. Institut Medical Superieur

Trav Inst Met Phys Globe Alger — Travaux de l'Institut de Meteorologie et de Physique du Globe de l'Algerie

Trav Inst Pharm A Gilkinet Univ Liege — Travaux de l'Institut de Pharmacie A. Gilkinet. Universite de Liege

Trav Inst Physiol Gen Univ Strasb — Travaux de l'Institut de Physiologie Generale de l'Universite de Strasbourg

Trav Inst Rech Cardiol Royat — Travaux de l'Institut de Recherches Cardiologiques de Royat

Trav Inst Rech Sahar — Travaux. Institut de Recherches Sahariennes

Trav Inst Sci Cherifien Fac Sci Rabat Ser Gen — Travaux. Institut Scientifique Cherifien et Faculte des Sciences de Rabat. Serie Generale

Trav Inst Sci Cherifien Fac Sci Ser Sci Phys — Travaux. Institut Scientifique Cherifien et Faculte des Sciences. Serie: Sciences Physiques

Trav Inst Sci Cherifien Fac Sci Ser Zool — Travaux. Institut Scientifique Cherifien et Faculte des Sciences. Serie Zoologie

Trav Inst Sci Cherifien Ser Bot — Travaux. Institut Scientifique Cherifien. Serie Botanique

Trav Inst Sci Cherifien Ser Bot Biol Veg — Travaux. Institut Scientifique Cherifien. Serie Botanique et Biologique Vegetale

Trav Inst Sci Cherifien Ser Geol Geogr Phys — Travaux. Institut Scientifique Cherifien. Serie Geologie et Geographie Physique

Trav Inst Sci Cherifien Ser Sci Phys — Travaux. Institut Scientifique Cherifien. Serie Sciences Physiques

Trav Inst Sci Cherifien Ser Zool — Travaux. Institut Scientifique Cherifien. Serie Zoologique

Trav Inst Serol Buc — Travaux de l'Institut Serologique (Bucarest)

Trav Inst Speleo "Emile Racovitza" — Travaux. Institut de Speleologie "Emile Racovitza"

Trav Inst Ther Univ Brux — Travaux de l'Institut de Therapeutique de l'Universite Libre de Bruxelles

Trav Inst Zool Univ Montpellier — Travaux de l'Institut de Zoologie de l'Universite de Montpellier et de la Station Zoologique de Cette [Montpellier]

Trav Inst Zool Univ Montreal — Travaux de l'Institut de Zoologie de l'Universite de Montreal

Trav Jeunes Sci — Travaux des Jeunes Scientifiques

Trav Lab Anat Fac Med Alger — Travaux du Laboratoire d'Anatomie de la Faculte de Medecine d'Alger

Trav Lab Anat Histol Comp Sorbonne — Travaux du Laboratoire d'Anatomie et d'Histologie Comparees de la Sorbonne [Paris]

Trav Lab Anthropol Prehist Ethnol Pays Mediterr Occid — Travaux. Laboratoire d'Anthropologie de Prehistoire et d'Ethnologie des Paysde la Mediterranee Occidentale

Trav Lab Anthrop Pays Medit Occid — Travaux du Laboratoire ?d'Anthropologie de Prehistoire et ?d'Ethnologie des Pays de la Mediterranee Occidentale

Trav Lab Arago — Travaux du Laboratoire Arago [Banyuls-sur-Mer]

Trav Lab Biol Veg Sorbonne — Travaux du Laboratoire de Biologie Vegetale de la Sorbonne [Paris]

Trav Lab Bot Gen Appl Univ Alger — Travaux du Laboratoire de Botanique Generale et Appliquee de l'Universite d'Alger [Alger]

Trav Lab Bot Syst Phytogeogr Univ Brux — Travaux du Laboratoire de Botanique Systematique et de Phytogeographie de l'Universite Libre de Bruxelles [Bruxelles]

Trav Lab Bot Univ Cath Angers — Travaux du Laboratoire de Botanique de l'Universite Catholique d'Angers

Trav Lab Cent Elect Paris — Travaux du Laboratoire Central d'Electricite. Societe Internationale des Electriciens (Paris)

Trav Lab Chim Gen Louvain — Travaux du Laboratoire de Chimie Generale de Louvain

Trav Lab For Toulouse — Travaux. Laboratoire Forestier de Toulouse

Trav Lab For Toulouse Tome I Artic Divers — Travaux. Laboratoire Forestier de Toulouse. Tome I. Articles Divers

Trav Lab For Toulouse Tome II Etud Dendrol — Travaux. Laboratoire Forestier de Toulouse. Tome II. Etudes Dendrologiques

Trav Lab For Toulouse Tome V Geogr For Monde — Travaux. Laboratoire Forestier de Toulouse. Tome V. Geographie Forestier du Monde

Trav Lab For Univ Toulouse — Travaux. Laboratoire Forestier. Universite de Toulouse

Trav Lab Geol Ec Norm Super (Paris) — Travaux. Laboratoire de Geologie. Ecole Normale Superieure (Paris)

Trav Lab Geol Fac Sci Grenoble — Travaux. Laboratoire de Geologie. Faculte des Sciences de Grenoble

Trav Lab Geol Fac Sci Grenoble Mem — Travaux. Laboratoire de Geologie. Faculte des Sciences de Grenoble. Memoires

Trav Lab Geol Fac Sci Lyon — Travaux. Laboratoire de Geologie. Faculte des Sciences de Lyon

Trav Lab Geol Fac Sci Univ Bordeaux — Travaux. Laboratoire de Geologie. Faculte des Sciences. Universite de Bordeaux

Trav Lab Geol Fac Sci Univ Grenoble — Travaux de Laboratoire de Geologie de la Faculte des Sciences de l'Universite de Grenoble

Trav Lab Geol Hist Paleontol Cent St Charles Univ Provence — Travaux. Laboratoire de Geologie Historique et de Paleontologie. Centre Saint Charles. Universite de Provence

Trav Lab Hydrobiol Piscic Univ Grenoble — Travaux. Laboratoire d'Hydrobiologie et de Pisciculture. Universite de Grenoble

Trav Lab Hydrogeol Geochim Fac Sci Univ Bordeaux — Travaux. Laboratoire d'Hydrogeologie Geochimie. Faculte des Sciences Universitede Bordeaux

Trav Lab Inst Rocha Cabral — Travaux du Laboratoire. Institut Rocha Cabral [Lisbonne]

Trav Lab Leon Fredericq — Travaux du Laboratoire de Leon Fredericq. Institut de Physiologie de l'Universite de Liege

Trav Lab Matiere Med Paris — Travaux du Laboratoire de Matiere Medicale de l'Ecole Superieure de Pharmacie de Paris

Trav Lab Matiere Med Pharm Galenique Fac Pharm (Paris) — Travaux. Laboratoires de Matiere Medicale et de Pharmacie Galenique. Faculte dePharmacie (Paris)

Trav Lab Med Exp Paris — Travaux du Laboratoire de Medecine Experimentale (Paris)

Trav Lab Med Leopoldville — Travaux du Laboratoire Medicale de Leopoldville [Bruxelles]

Trav Lab Microbiol Fac Pharm Nancy — Travaux. Laboratoire de Microbiologie. Faculte de Pharmacie de Nancy

Trav Lab Miner Fac Sci Nancy — Travaux du Laboratoire de Mineralogie de la Faculte des Sciences de Nancy et de la Station Zoologique de Cette

Trav Lab Mus Hist Nat St Servan — Travaux du Laboratoire du Museum d'Histoire Naturelle de Saint-Servan

Trav Lab Physiol Inst Solvay — Travaux du Laboratoire de Physiologie. Institut de Physiologie. Instituts Solvay [Bruxelles]

Trav Lab Physiol Univ Geneve — Travaux du Laboratoire de Physiologie de l'Universite de Geneve

Trav Lab Physiol Univ Louvain — Travaux du Laboratoire de Physiologie de l'Universite de Louvain

Trav Lab Physiol Univ Turin — Travaux du Laboratoire de Physiologie de l'Universite de Turin

Trav Lab Piscic Univ Grenoble — Travaux du Laboratoire de Pisciculture de l'Universite de Grenoble

Trav Lab Psychol Clin Salpetriere — Travaux du Laboratoire de Psychologie de la Clinique a la Salpetriere [Paris]

Trav Lab Scient Int Mt Rosa — Travaux du Laboratoire Scientifique International du Mont Rosa [Turin]

Trav Labs Matiere Med Pharm Galen Univ Paris — Travaux des Laboratoires de Matiere Medicale et de Pharmacie Galenique. Universite de Paris

Trav Labs Soc Scient Stn Zool Arcachon — Travaux des Laboratoires de la Societe Scientifique et Station Zoologique d'Arcachon [Bordeaux]

Trav Lab Ther Exp Univ Geneve — Travaux du Laboratoire de Therapeutique Experimentale de l'Universite de Geneve

Trav Lab Zool Biol Anim Montpellier — Travaux du Laboratoire de Zoologie et Biologie Animale (Montpellier)

Trav Lab Zool Stn Aquic Grimaldi Dijon — Travaux du Laboratoire de Zoologie et de la Station Aquicole Grimaldi de la Faculte des Sciences de Dijon

Trav Linguist Litt — Travaux de Linguistique et de Litterature

Trav LJ — Travancore Law Journal

Trav Lorient — Travaux. Societe Lorientaise d'Archeologie

Travl Wkly — Travel Weekly

Trav Mem — Travaux et Memoires. Centre de Recherche d'Histoire et Civilisation Byzantine

Trav Mem Bur Int Poids Mes — Travaux et Memoires. Bureau International des Poids et Mesures

Trav Mem Inst Biol Anim Univ Sarre — Travaux et Memoires de l'Institut de Biologie Animale de l'Universite de la Sarre [Concarneau]

Trav Mem Inst Ethnol Paris — Travaux et Memoires de l'Institut d'Ethnologie (Paris)

Trav Mem Soc Ramond — Travaux et Memoires Publies par la Societe Ramond [Bagneres de Bigorre]

Trav Mem Univ Lille — Travaux et Memoires de l'Universite de Lille

Trav Met Deform — Travail des Metaux par Deformation

Trav Mus Bot Acad Sci Russ — Travaux du Musee Botanique de l'Academie Imperiale des Sciences de St.-Petersbourg

Trav Mus Georgie — Travaux du Museum de Georgie [Tiflis]

Trav Mus Hist Nat "Gr Antipa" — Travaux. Museum d'Histoire Naturelle "Grigore Antipa"

Trav Mus Hist Nat "Grigore Antipa" — Travaux. Museum d'Histoire Naturelle "Grigore Antipa"

Trav Mycol Tchec — Travaux Mycologiques Tchecoslovaques [Prague]

Trav Nat Vall Loing — Travaux des Naturalistes de la Vallee du Loing [Moret-sur-Loing]

Trav Neurol Chir — Travaux de Neurologie Chirurgicale [Paris]

Trav Not Acad Agric Fr — Travaux et Notices. Academie d'Agriculture de France [Paris]

Trav Notices Acad Agric France — Travaux et Notices de l'Academie d'Agriculture de France

Trav Obs Astr Alger — Travaux de l'Observatoire Astronomique d'Alger

Trav Obs Lyon — Travaux de l'Observatoire de Lyon

Trav Obs Magn Swider — Travaux. Observatoire Magnetique, Swider [Warszawa]

Trav Obs Marseille — Travaux de l'Observatoire de Marseille

Trav Obs Pic Du Midi — Travaux de l'Observatoire du Pic-du-Midi

Trav Off Natn Matier Prem Veg Drog — Travaux de l'Office National des Matieres Premieres Vegetales pour la Droguerie, la Pharmacie, la Distillerie et la Parfumerie [Paris]

Trav Off Natn Propr Ind — Travaux de l'Office National de la Propriete Industrielle [Paris]

Trav Orig Serv Def Veg Rabat — Travaux Originaux. Service de la Defense des Vegetaux [Rabat]

Trav Pech Que — Travaux sur les Pecheries du Quebec

Trav Peint — Travaux de Peinture

Trav Quebec — Travail Quebec

Trav Rech Haut Comite Et Inform Alcool — Travaux et Recherches. Haut Comite d'Etude et d'Information sur l'Alcoolisme

Trav Sci Cent Rech Sci Proj Ind Vini (Sofia) — Travaux Scientifiques. Centre de Recherches Scientifiques et de Projections de l'Industrie Vinicole (Sofia)

Trav Sci Chercheurs Serv Sante Armees — Travaux Scientifiques. Chercheurs du Service de Sante des Armees

Trav Scient Obs Met Dyn Paris — Travaux Scientifiques de l'Observatoire de Meteorologie Dynamique (Paris)

Trav Scient Univ Rennes — Travaux Scientifiques de l'Universite de Rennes

Trav Sci Parc Natl Vanoise — Travaux Scientifiques. Parc National de la Vanoise

Trav Sect Geod UGGI — Travaux de la Section Geodesie de l'Union Geodesique et Geophysique Internationale

Trav Sect Geol Cab St Petersb — Travaux de la Section Geologique du Cabinet de Sa Majeste (St.-Petersbourg)

Trav Sect Magn Elect Terr UGGI — Travaux de la Section de Magnetisme et d'Electricite Terrestres. Union Geodesique et Geophysique Internationale

Trav Sect Pedol Soc Sci Nat Maroc — Travaux de la Section de Pedologie de la Societe des Sciences Naturelles du Maroc [Rabat]

Trav Sect Scient Tech Inst Fr Pondichery — Travaux. Section Scientifique et Technique. Institut Francais de Pondichery

Trav Sect Sci Tech Inst Franc Pondichery — Travaux. Section Scientifique et Technique. Institut Francais de Pondichery

Trav Sect Sci Tech Inst Fr Pondichery — Travaux. Section Scientifique et Technique. Institut Francais de Pondichery

Trav Secur — Travail et Securite

Trav Sem Geogr Univ Liege — Travaux du Seminaire Geographique de l'Universite de Liege

Trav Serv Geol Pol — Travaux du Service Geologique de la Pologne [Varsovie]

Trav Serv Oceanogr Pech Indoch — Travaux du Service Oceanographique des Peches de l'Indochine

Trav Serv Scient Pech Marit Paris — Travaux du Service Scientifique des Peches Maritimes (Paris)

Trav Serv Univ Chir Prof L Deloyers — Travaux du Service. Universitaire de Chirurgie du Prof. L. Deloyers. Hopital de Saint-Pierre [Bruxelles]

Trav Soc Bot Geneve — Travaux. Societe Botanique de Geneve

Trav Soc Chim Biol — Travaux de la Societe de Chimie Biologique [Paris]

Trav Soc Emul Dep Jura — Travaux de la Societe d'Emulation du Departement du Jura

Trav Soc Pharm Montp — Travaux. Societe de Pharmacie de Montpellier

Trav Soc Pharm Montpellier — Travaux. Societe de Pharmacie de Montpellier

Trav Soc Sci Lettres Wroclaw — Travaux. Societe des Sciences et des Lettres de Wroclaw

Trav Soc Sci Phys Chim Univ Kharkow — Travaux de la Societe des Sciences Physico-Chimiques a l'Universite de Kharkow

Trav Sta Rech Groenendaal — Travaux. Station de Recherches des Eaux et Forets. Groenendaal-Hoeilaart

Trav Stn Biol Marit Lisb — Travaux de la Station de Biologie Maritime de Lisbonne [Paris]

Trav Stn Biol Roscoff — Travaux de la Station Biologique de Roscoff [Paris]

Trav Stn Biol Sete — Travaux de la Station Biologique de Sete

Trav Stn Rech Groenendael — Travaux de la Station de Recherches des Eaux et Forets de Groenendael-Hoeilaart

Trav Stn Rech Lacust Thonon — Travaux de la Station de Recherches Lacustres de Thonon

Trav Stns Agron Paris — Travaux Effectues par les Stations Agronomiques. Institut National de la Recherche Agronomique (Paris)

Trav Stn Zool Marit Agigea — Travaux de la Station Zoologique Maritime d'Agigea

Trav Stn Zool Russe Villefranche — Travaux de la Station Zoologique Russe de Villefranche sur Mer [Paris]

Trav Stn Zool Wimereux — Travaux de la Station Zoologique de Wimereaux [Paris]

Trav-Syndicalisme Bibl — Travail-Syndicalisme. Bibliographie

Tr Avtom Svarke Flyusom — Trudy po Avtomaticheskoi Svarke pod Flyusom

Tray Leg Max — Trayner's Latin Maxims and Phrases

Traz Elett — Trazione Elettrica [Roma]

Tr Azerb Gos Nauchno Issled Proektn Inst Neft Promsti — Trudy Azerbaidzhanskii Gosudarstvennyi Nauchno-Issledovatel'skii i Proektnyi Institut Neftyanoi Promyshlennosti

Tr Azerb Gos Pedagog Inst — Trudy Azerbaidzhanskogo Gosudarstvennogo Pedagogicheskogo Instituta

Tr Azerb Gos Univ Ser Khim — Trudy Azerbaidzhanskogo Gosudarstvennogo Universiteta. Seriya Khimicheskaya

Tr Azerb Ind Inst — Trudy Azerbaidzhanskogo Industrial'nogo Instituta

Tr Azerb Inst Nefti Khim — Trudy Azerbaidzhanskogo Instituta Nefti i Khimii

Tr Azerb Nauchno Issled Inst Buren Neft Gazov Skvazhin — Trudy Azerbaidzhanskogo Nauchno-Issledovatel'skogo Instituta po Bureniyu Neftyanykh i Gazovykh Skvazhin

Tr Azerb Nauchno Issled Inst Energ — Trudy Azerbaidzhanskogo Nauchno-Issledovatel'skogo Instituta Energetiki

Tr Azerb Nauchno-Issled Inst Gig Tr Prof Zabol — Trudy Azerbaidzhanskogo Nauchno-Issledovatel'skogo Instituta Gigieny Truda i Professional'nykh Zabolevaniya

Tr Azerb Nauchno-Issled Inst Lesn Khoz Agrolesomelior — Trudy Azerbaidzhanskogo Nauchno-Issledovatel'skogo Instituta Lesnogo Khozyaistva i Agrolesomelioratsii

Tr Azerb Nauchno-Issled Inst Med Parazitol Trop Med — Trudy Azerbaidzhanskogo Nauchno-Issledovatel'skogo Instituta Meditsinskoi Parazitologii i Trophicheskoi Meditsiny

Tr Azerb Nauchno Issled Inst Ovoshchevod — Trudy Azerbaidzhanskogo Nauchno-Issledovatel'skogo Instituta Ovoshchevodstva

Tr Azerb Nauchno Issled Inst Virusol Mikrobiol Gig — Trudy Azerbaidzhanskogo Nauchno-Issledovatel'skogo Instituta Virusologii Mikrobiologii i Gigieny

Tr Azerb Nauchno Issled Inst Zemled — Trudy Azerbaidzhanskogo Nauchno-Issledovatel'skogo Instituta Zemledeliya

Tr Azerb Nauchno Issled Vet Inst — Trudy Azerbaidzhanskogo Nauchno-Issledovatel'skogo Veterinarnogo Instituta

Tr Azerb Nauchno Issled Vet Opytn Stn — Trudy Azerbaidzhanskoi Nauchno-Issledovatel'skoi Veterinarnoi Opytnoi Stantsii

Tr Azerb Neft Nauchno Issled Inst — Trudy Azerbaidzhanskogo Neftyanogo Nauchno-Issledovatel'skogo Instituta

Tr Azerb Otd Tsentr Nauchno Issled Inst Osetr Khoz — Trudy Azerbaidzhanskogo Otdeleniya Tsentral'nogo Nauchno-Issledovatel'skogo Instituta Osetrovgo Khozyaistva

Tr Azerb Politekh Inst — Trudy Azerbaidzhanskogo Politekhnicheskogo Instituta

Tr Azerb Skh Inst — Trudy Azerbaidzhanskogo Sel'skokhozyaistvennogo Instituta

Tr Azerb Vet Nauchno Issled Inst — Trudy Azerbaidzhanskogo Veterinarnogo Nauchno-Issledovatel'skogo Instituta

Tr Azovsko Chernomorsk Nauchn Rybokhoz Stn — Trudy Azovsko-Chernomorskoi Nauchnoi Rybokhozyaistvennoi Stantsii

Tr Azovskogo Nauchno Issled Inst Rybn Khoz — Trudy Azovskogo Nauchno-Issledovatel'skogo Instituta Rybnogo Khozyaistva

TRB — Tennyson Research Bulletin

Trb — Tractatenblad

Tr Baik Limnol Stn Akad Nauk SSSR Vost Sib Fil — Trudy Baikal'skoi Limnologicheskoi Stantsii Akademiya Nauk SSSR Vostochno-Sibirskii Filial

Tr Bakinsk Nauohno-Issled Inst Travmatol Ortop — Trudy Bakinskogo Nauchno-Issledovatel'skogo Instituta Travmatologii Ortopedii

Tr Bakinskogo Nauchno Issled Inst Travmatol Ortop — Trudy Bakinskogo Nauchno-Issledovatel'skogo Instituta Travmatologii Ortopedii

Tr Balt Nauchno Issled Inst Rybn Khoz — Trudy Baltiiskogo Nauchno-Issledovatel'skogo Instituta Rybnogo Khozyaistva

Tr Bashk Gos Nauchno Issled Proektn Inst Neft Promsti — Trudy Bashkirskii Gosudarstvennyi Nauchno-Issledovatel'skii i Proektnyi Institut Neftyanoi Promyshlennosti

Tr Bashk Gos Zapov — Trudy Bashkirskogo Gosudarstvennogo Zapovednika

Tr Bashk Nauchno-Issled Inst Pererab Nefti — Trudy Bashkirskii Nauchno-Issledovatel'skii Institut po Pererabotke Nefti

Tr Bashk Nauchno Issled Inst Sel'sk Khoz — Trudy Bashkirskogo Nauchno-Issledovatel'skogo Instituta Sel'skogo Khozyaistva

Tr Bashk Nauchno Issled Inst Stroit — Trudy Bashkirskii Nauchno-Issledovatel'skii Institut po Stroitel'stvu

Tr Bashk S-Kh Inst — Trudy Bashkirskogo Sel'skokhozyaistvennogo Instituta

Tr Batum Bot Sada Akad Nauk Gruz SSR — Trudy Batumskogo Botanicheskogo Sada Akademii Nauk Gruzinskoi SSR

Tr Belgorod Gos Skh Opytn Stn — Trudy Belgorodskoi Gosudarstvennoi Sel'skokhozyaistvennoi Opytnoi Stantsii

Tr Belgorod Tekhnol Inst Stroit — Trudy Belgorodskogo Tekhnologicheskogo Instituta Stroitel'nyhmaterialov

Tr Belomorsk Biol Stn Mosk Gos Univ — Trudy Belomorskoi Biologicheskoi Stantsii Moskovskogo Gosudarstvennogo Universiteta

Tr Beloruss Nauchno-Issled Inst Melior Vodn Khoz — Trudy Belorusskogo Nauchno-Issledovatel'skogo Instituta Melioratsii i Vodnogo Khozyaistva

Tr Beloruss Nauchno-Issled Inst Pishch Promsti — Trudy Belorusskogo Nauchno-Issledovatel'skogo Instituta Pishchevoi Promyshlennosti

Tr Beloruss Nauchno Issled Inst Pochvoved — Trudy Belorusskii Nauchno-Issledovatel'skii Institut Pochvovedenii

Tr Beloruss Nauchno Issled Inst Promsti Prodovol Tovarov — Trudy Belorusskii Nauchno-Issledovatel'skii Institut Promyshlennosti Prodovol'stvennykh Tovarov

Tr Beloruss Nauchno Issled Inst Rybn Khoz — Trudy Belorusskogo Nauchno-Issledovatel'skogo Instituta Rybnogo Khozyaistva

Tr Beloruss Nauchno Issled Inst Zhivotnovod — Trudy Belorusskii Nauchno-Issledovatel'skii Institut Zhivotnovodstva

Tr Beloruss Naucno-Issled Inst Pishch Prom-Sti — Trudy Belorusskogo Nauchno-Issledovatel'skogo Instituta Pishchevoi Promyshlennosti

Tr Beloruss Sel'skokhoz Akad — Trudy Belorusskoi Sel'skokhozyaistvennoi Akademii

Tr Beloruss Skh Akad — Trudy Belorusskoi Sel'skokhozyaistvennoi Akademii

Tr Berdyanskii Opytn Neftemaslozavod — Trudy Berdyanskii Opytnyi Neftemaslozavod

TRBIDM — Trends in Biotechnology

Tr Biogeokhim Lab Akad Nauk SSSR — Trudy Biogeokhimicheskoi Laboratorii Akademiya Nauk SSSR

Tr Biol Inst Akad Nauk SSSR Sib Otd — Trudy Biologicheskogo Instituta Akademiya Nauk SSSR Sibirskoe Otdelenie

Tr Biol Inst Zapadno-Sib Fil Akad Nauk SSSR — Trudy Biologicheskogo Instituta Zapadno-Sibirskogo Filiala Akademii Nauk SSSR

Tr Biol Nauchno Issled Inst Biol Stn Permsk Gos Univ — Trudy Biologicheskogo Nauchno-Issledovatel'skogo Instituta i Biologicheskoi Stantsii pri Permskom Gosudarstvennom Universitete

Tr Biol Nauchno Issled Inst Molotov Gos Univ — Trudy Biologicheskogo Nauchno-Issledovatel'skogo Instituta pri Molotovskom Gosudarstvennom Universitete

Tr Biol Pochv Inst Dalnevost Nauchn Tsentr Akad Nauk SSSR — Trudy Biologo-Pochvennogo Instituta Dal'nevostochnyi Nauchnyi Tsentr Akademiya Nauk SSSR

Tr Biol Stn Borok Akad Nauk SSSR — Trudy Biologicheskoi Stantsii "Borok" Akademiya Nauk SSSR

Trbl — Tractatenblad

Tr Blagoveshch Gos Med Inst — Trudy Blagoveshchenskogo Gosudarstvennogo Meditsinskogo Instituta

Tr Blagoveshch Skh Inst — Trudy Blagoveshchenskogo Sel'skokhozyaistvennogo Instituta

TRBMA — Texas Reports on Biology and Medicine

Tr Bot Inst Akad Nauk SSSR — Trudy Botanicheskogo Instituta Akademii Nauk SSSR

Tr Bot Inst Akad Nauk SSSR Ser 4 — Trudy Botanicheskogo Instituta Akademii Nauk SSSR. Seriya 4

Tr Bot Inst Akad Nauk SSSR Ser 5 — Trudy Botanicheskogo Instituta Akademiya Nauk SSSR. Seriya 5. Rastitel'noe Syr'ye

Tr Bot Inst Akad Nauk SSSR Ser 6 — Trudy Botanicheskogo Instituta Akademiya Nauk SSSR. Seriya 6. Introduktsiya Rastenii i Zelenoe

Tr Bot Inst Akad Nauk Tadzhikskoi SSR — Trudy Botanicheskogo Instituta Akademii Nauk Tadzhikskoi SSR

Tr Bot Inst Akad Nauk Tadzh SSR — Trudy Botanicheskogo Instituta Akademiya Nauk Tadzhikskoi SSR

Tr Bot Inst Azerb Fil Akad Nauk SSSR — Trudy Botanicheskogo Instituta Azerbaidzhanskii Filial Akademii Nauk SSSR

Tr Bot Inst V L Komarova Akad Nauk SSSR Ser VII — Trudy Botanicheskogo Instituta Imeni V. L. Komarova Akademiya Nauk SSSR. Seriya VII

Tr Bot Sada Akad Nauk Ukr SSR — Trudy Botanicheskogo Sada Akademii Nauk Ukrainskoi SSR

Tr Bot Sada Tashk Akad Nauk Uzb SSR — Trudy Botanicheskogo Sada v Tashkente Akademii Nauk Uzbekskoi SSR

Tr Bot Sada Tashkente Akad Nauk Uzb SSR — Trudy Botanicheskogo Sada v Tashkente Akademii Nauk Uzbekskoi SSR

Tr Bot Sada Zapadn-Sib Fil Akad Nauk SSSR — Trudy Botanicheskogo Sada Zapadno-Sibirskogo Filiala Akademii Nauk SSSR

Tr Bot Sadov Akad Nauk Kaz SSR — Trudy Botanicheskikh Sadov Akademii Nauk Kazakhskoi SSR

Tr Bristol — Transactions. Bristol and Gloucestershire Archaeological Society

Tr Bryansko Lesokhoz Inst — Trudy Bryanskogo Lesokhozyaistvennogo Instituta

Tr Bukhar Obl Opytn Skh Stn — Trudy Bukharskoi Oblastnoi Opytnoi Sel'skokhozyaistvennoi Stantsii

Tr Burat Inst Estest Nauk Buryat Fil Sib Otd Akad Nauk SSSR — Trudy Buryatskogo Instituta Estestvennykh Nauk. Buryatskii Filial. Sibirskoe Otdelenie. Akademiya Nauk SSSR

Tr Buryat-Mong Nauchno-Issled Vet Opytn Stn — Trudy Buryat-Mongol'skoi Nauchno-Issledovatel'skoi Veterinarnoi Opytnoi Stantsii

Tr Buryat Mong Zoovet Inst — Trudy Buryat-Mongol'skogo Zooveterinarnogo Instituta

Tr Buryat S-Kh Inst — Trudy Buryatskogo Sel'skokhozyaistvennogo Instituta

Tr Buryat Zoovet Inst — Trudy Buryatskogo Zooveterinarnogo Instituta

TrC — Trabajos y Comunicaciones

TrCH — Transactions. Congregational Historical Society

Tr Chelyab Gos Pedagog Inst — Trudy Chelyabinskii Gosudarstvennyi Pedagogicheskii Institut

Tr Chelyab Inst Mekh Elektrif Selsk Khoz — Trudy Chelyabinskogo Instituta Mekhanizatsii i Elektrifikatsii Sel'skogo Khozyaistva

Tr Chelyab Politekh Inst — Trudy Chelyabinskii Politekhnicheskii Institut

Tr Chernomorsk Biol Stan Varna — Trudove na Chernomorskata Biologichna Stantsiya v Varna

Tr Chimkent Obl Skh Opytn Stn Kaz SSR — Trudy Chimkentskoi Oblastnoi Sel'skokhozyaistvennoi Opytnoi Stantsii. Kazakhskaya SSR

Tr Chuv Skh Inst — Trudy Chuvashskogo Sel'skokhozyaistvennogo Instituta

Tr Chuv Skh Opytn Stn — Trudy Chuvashskoi Sel'skokhozyaistvennoi Opytnoi Stantsii

TRCI — Thought

TRCO — Trade and Commerce

Tr Coll Physicians Phila — Transactions and Studies. College of Physicians of Philadelphia

Tr Conf ULB — Travaux et Conferences. Universite Libre de Bruxelles

TRCRA — Tobacco Research Council. Research Paper

Tr Cumb — Transactions. Cumberland and Westmorland Antiquarian and Archaeological Society

TrCW — Transactions. Cumberland and Westmorland Antiquarian and Archaeological Society

Tr Dagest Gos Pedagog Inst — Trudy Dagestanskogo Gosudarstvennogo Pedagogicheskogo Instituta

Tr Dagest Gos Pedagog Inst Estestv-Geogr Fak — Trudy Dagestanskogo Gosudarstvennogo Pedagogicheskogo Instituta Estestvenno-Geograficheskii Fakul'tet

Tr Dagest S-Kh Inst — Trudy Dagestanskogo Sel'skokhozyaistvennogo Instituta

Tr Dalnevost Fil Akad Nauk SSSR Ser Geol — Trudy Dal'nevostochnogo Filiala Akademii Nauk SSSR. Seriya Geologicheskaya

Tr Dalnevost Fil Akad Nauk SSSR Ser Khim — Trudy Dal'nevostochnogo Filiala Akademii Nauk SSSR. Seriya Khimicheskaya

Tr Dalnevost Geol Razved Tresta — Trudy Dal'nevostochnogo Geologo-Razvedochnogo Tresta

Tr Dal'nevost Gos Med Inst — Trudy Dal'nevostochnogo Gosudarstvennogo Meditsinskogo Instituta

Tr Dalnevost Gos Univ — Trudy Dal'nevostochnogo Gosudarstvennogo Universiteta

Tr Dalnevost Gos Univ Ser 4 — Trudy Dal'nevostochnogo Gosudarstvennogo Universiteta. Seriya 4. Lesnye Nauki

Tr Dalnevost Gos Univ Ser 5 — Trudy Dal'nevostochnogo Gosudarstvennogo Universiteta. Seriya 5. Sel'skoe Khozyaistvo

Tr Dalnevost Gos Univ Ser 7 — Trudy Dal'nevostochnogo Gosudarstvennogo Universiteta. Seriya 7. Fizika i Khimiya

Tr Dalnevost Gos Univ Ser 8 — Trudy Dal'nevostochnogo Gosudarstvennogo Universiteta. Seriya 8. Biologiya

Tr Dalnevost Gos Univ Ser 11 — Trudy Dal'nevostochnogo Gosudarstvennogo Universiteta. Seriya 11. Geologiya

Tr Dalnevost Gos Univ Ser 12 — Trudy Dal'nevostochnogo Gosudarstvennogo Universiteta. Seriya 12. Gornoe Delo

Tr Dalnevost Gos Univ Ser 13 — Trudy Dal'nevostochnogo Gosudarstvennogo Universiteta. Seriya 13. Tekhnika

Tr Dalnevost Gos Univ Ser 15 — Trudy Dal'nevostochnogo Gosudarstvennogo Universiteta. Seriya 15. Matematika

Tr Dalnevost Kraev Nauchno Issled Inst — Trudy Dal'nevostochnogo Kraevogo Nauchno-Issledovatel'skogo Instituta

Tr Dalnevost Nauchno Issled Gidrometeorol Inst — Trudy Dal'nevostochnogo Nauchno-Issledovatel'skogo Gidrometeorologicheskogo Instituta

Tr Dalnevost Nauchno Issled Vet Inst — Trudy Dal'nevostochnogo Nauchno-Issledovatel'skogo Veterinarnogo Instituta

Tr Dalnevost Politekh Inst — Trudy Dal'nevostochnogo Politekhnicheskogo Instituta

Tr Dalnevost Tekh Inst Rybn Promsti Khoz — Trudy Dal'nevostochnogo Tekhnicheskogo Instituta Rybnoi Promyshlennosti i Khozyaistva

Tr Darvinsk Gos Zapov — Trudy Darvinskogo Gosudarstvennogo Zapovednika

TRDCBC — Datum Collection. Tokai Regional Fisheries Research Laboratory

TRDIA — Transmission and Distribution

Tr Din Raz — Trudy po Dinamike Razvitiya

Tr Dnepropetr Inst Inzh Zheleznodorozhn Transp — Trudy Dnepropetrovskogo Instituta Inzhenerov Zheleznodorozhnogo Transporta

Tr Dnepropetr Khim Tekhnol Inst — Trudy Dnepropetrovskogo Khimiko-Tekhnologicheskogo Instituta

Tr Dnepropetr S-Kh Inst — Trudy Dnepropetrovskogo Sel'skokhozyaistvennogo Instituta

Tr Donbasskaya Nauchno Issled Lab — Trudy Donbasskaya Nauchno-Issledovatel'skaya Laboratoriya

Tr Donetsk Gos Med Inst — Trudy Donetskogo Gosudarstvennogo Meditsinskogo Instituta

Tr Donetsk Ind Inst — Trudy Donetskogo Industrial'nogo Instituta

Tr Donetsk Politekh Inst Ser Fiz Mat — Trudy Donetskogo Politekhnicheskogo Instituta. Seriya Fiziko-Matematicheskaya

Tr Donetsk Politekh Inst Ser Khim Tekhnol — Trudy Donetskogo Politekhnicheskogo Instituta. Seriya Khimiko-Tekhnologicheskaya

Tr Donetsk Politekh Inst Ser Metall — Trudy Donetskogo Politekhnicheskogo Instituta. Seriya Metallurgicheskaya

Tr Donetsk Politekh Inst Ser Stroit — Trudy Donetskogo Politekhnicheskogo Instituta. Seriya Stroitel'naya

TRE — Trusts and Estates

TREA & A — [The] Real Estate Appraiser and Analyst

Treaarsexped Christian Xs Ld — Treaarsexpeditionen til Christian den X's Land, 1931-34. Reports [Kobenhavn]

Treas Hum Inherit — Treasure of Human Inheritance

Treat Fract — Treatment of Fractures. Report of the Committee on Fractures of the American Surgical Association [Philadelphia]

Treat Garb — Treatment of Garbage [Chicago]

Treatise Anal Chem — Treatise on Analytical Chemistry

Treatise Mater Sci Technol — Treatise on Materials Science and Technology

Treatise Neth Exp Stn Util Straw — Treatise of the Netherlands Experiment Station for the Utilization of Straw [Groningen]

Treatises Sect Med Sci Pol Acad Sci — Treatises of the Section of Medical Sciences. Polish Academy of Sciences

Treat Mater Sci Technol — Treatise on Materials Science and Technology

Treat Servs Bull Can — Treatment Services Bulletin. Department of Veterans Affairs. Canada [Ottawa]

Treat Use Sewage Sludge Liq Agric Wastes Proc Symp — Treatment and Use of Sewage Sludge and Liquid Agricultural Wastes. Proceedings.Symposium

Treballs Inst Bot Barc — Treballs. Institut Botanic de Barcelona

Treb Inst Catal Hist Nat — Treballs de la Institucio Catalana d'Historia Natural [Barcelona]

Treb Serv Tec Palud — Treballs del Servei Tecnic del Paludisme [Barcelona]

Treb Soc Biol Barcelona — Treballs de la Societat de Biologia de Barcelona

Tr Ecol Evo — Trends in Ecology and Evolution

Tree Crops J — Tree Crops Journal

Tree Farm Proc — Trees on Farms. Proceedings of a Seminar on Economic and Technical Aspects of Commercial Plantations. Agro-Forestry and Shelter Belts on Farms

Tree Physiol — Tree Physiology

Tree Plant Notes — Tree Planters' Notes

Tree Plant Notes US Dep Agric For Serv — Tree Planters' Notes. US Department of Agriculture. Forest Service

Tree Plant Notes US For Serv — Tree Planter's Notes. United States Forest Service

Tree Pl Notes — Tree Planters' Notes. US Forest Service

Tree Plrs Notes Wash — Tree Planters' Notes. Forest Service (Washington)

Tree Preserv Bull — Tree Preservation Bulletin. National Park Service [Washington]

Tree-Ring Bull — Tree-Ring Bulletin

Trees Fruits Flowers Minn — Trees, Fruits, and Flowers of Minnesota. Minnesota State Horticultural Society [Minneapolis]

Trees Life — Trees and Life [Southampton]

Trees Mag — Trees Magazine

Trees Nat Resour — Trees and Natural Resources

Trees S Afr — Trees in South Africa

Trees Struct Funct — Trees. Structure and Function

Trees Victoria's Resour — Trees and Victoria's Resources

T Regswet — Tydskrif vir Regswetenskap

TRE JI — T.R.E. (Telecommunications Research Establishment) Journal

TREKA — Technical Reports. Engineering Research Institute. Kyoto University

Tr Eksp Nauchno Issled Inst Metallorezhushchikh Stankov — Trudy Eksperimental'nyi Nauchno-Issledovatel'skii Institut Metallorezhushchikh Stankov

Tr Elem Med — Trace Elements in Medicine

TRENA — Tokyo Toritsu Eisei Kenkyusho Kenkyu Nempo

Trencsen Megy TermTud Tars Evk — Trencsen Megyei Termeszettudomanyi Tarsulat Evokonyvei [Trencsen]

TREND — Transportation Research News

Trend Card — Trends in Cardiovascular Medicine

Trend Eng — Trends in Engineering

Trend Engng Univ Wash — Trend in Engineering at the University of Washington [Seattle]

Trend Eng Univ Wash — Trends in Engineering. University of Washington

Trend Prognosticke Inf — Trend Prognosticke Informace

Trends Anal Chem — Trends in Analytical Chemistry

Trends Analyt Chem — Trends in Analytical Chemistry

Trends and Perspect Signal Process — Trends and Perspectives in Signal Processing

Trends Auton Pharmacol — Trends in Autonomic Pharmacology

Trends Biochem Sci — Trends in Biochemical Sciences

Trends Biochem Sci (Pers Ed) — Trends in Biochemical Sciences (Personal Edition)

Trends Biochem Sci (Ref Ed) — Trends in Biochemical Sciences (Reference Edition)

Trends Biomembr Bioenerg — Trends in Biobmembranes and Bioenergetics

Trends Biot — Trends in Biotechnology

Trends Biotechnol — Trends in Biotechnology

Trends Cancer Mortal Ind Countries — Trends in Cancer Morality in Industrial Countries

Trends Carbohydr Chem — Trends in Carbohydrate Chemistry

Trends Cardiovasc Med — Trends in Cardiovascular Medicine

Trends Cell Biol — Trends in Cell Biology

Trends Chem Eng — Trends in Chemical Engineering

Trends Colloid Interface Sci — Trends in Colloid and Interface Science

Trends Comp Biochem & Physiol — Trends in Comparative Biochemistry and Physiology

Trends Corros Res — Trends in Corrosion Research

Trends Ed — Trends in Education

Trends Educ — Trends in Education

Trends Endocrinol Metab — Trends in Endocrinology and Metabolism

Trends Fluoresc — Trends in Fluorescence

Trends Food Sci Technol — Trends in Food Science and Technology

Trends Gen — Trends in Genetics

Trends Genet — Trends in Genetics

Trends Glycoscience Glycotechnol — Trends in Glycoscience and Glycotechnology

Trends Haematol — Trends in Haematology

Trends Hist — Trends in History

Trends Immunol — Trends in Immunology

Trends in Ed — Trends in Education

Trends in Teach Ed — Trends in Teacher Education

Trends Linguist Stud Monogr — Trends in Linguistics. Studies and Monographs

Trends Microbiol — Trends in Microbiology

Trends Mol Med — Trends in Molecular Medicine

Trends Neurosci — Trends in Neurosciences

Trends Opt — Trends in Optics. Research, Developments, and Applications

Trends Organomet Chem — Trends in Organometallic Chemistry

Trends Parasitol — Trends in Parasitology

Trends Perspect Parasitol — Trends and Perspectives in Parasitology

Trends Pharmacol Sci — Trends in Pharmacological Sciences

Trends Plant Sci — Trends in Plant Science

Trends Polym Sci Cambridge UK — Trends in Polymer Science (Cambridge, United Kingdom)

Trends Polym Sci Trivandrum India — Trends in Polymer Science (Trivandrum, India)

Trends Sci Res — Trends in Scientific Research

Trends Tech Contemp Dent Lab — Trends and Techniques in the Contemporary Dental Laboratory

Trends Vac Sci Technol — Trends in Vacuum Science and Technology

Tr Energ Inst Akad Nauk Az SSR — Trudy Energeticheskogo Instituta Akademiya Nauk Azerbaidzhanskoi SSR

Tr Energ Inst Az SSR — Trudy Energeticheskogo Instituta Azerbaidzhanskoi SSR

Tr Energ Inst Im I G Es'mana Akad Nauk Azerb SSR — Trudy Energeticheskogo Instituta Imeni I. G. Es'mana Akademiya Nauk Azerbaidzhanskoi SSR

Trenie Iznos Mash — Trenie i Iznos v Mashinakh [*Moskva*]

Trent LJ — Trent Law Journal

Tr Entom Soc London — Transactions. Entomological Society of London

Tr Erevan Gos Inst Usoversh Vrachei — Trudy Erevanskogo Gosudarstvennogo Instituta Usovershenstvovaniya Vrachei

Tr Erevan Med Inst — Trudy Erevanskogo Meditsinskogo Instituta

Tr Erevan Zootekh Vet Inst — Trudy Erevanskogo Zootekhnichesko-Veterinarnogo Instituta

Tr Erevan Zoovet Inst — Trudy Erevanskogo Zooveterinarnogo Instituta

TRES — Transactions of the Royal Entomological Society of London

Tr Estestvennonauchn Inst Molotov Gos Univ — Trudy Estestvennonauchnogo Instituta pri Molotovskom Gosudarstvennom Universitete

Tr Estestvennonauchn Inst Permsk Gos Univ — Trudy Estestvennonauchnogo Instituta pri Permskom Gosudarstvennom Universitete

Tr Estestv Inst Permsk Gos Univ Radiospektrosk — Trudy Estestvennonauchnogo Instituta pri Permskom Gosudarstvennom Universitete Imeni A. M. Gor'kogo Radiospektroskopiy

Tretol Maint News — Tretol Maintenance News [*London*]

TRev — Theologische Revue

T Rev — Translation Review

TRF — Tragicorum Romanorum Fragmenta

TRFA — Trustees for Alaska. Newsletter

Tr Ferg Politekh Inst — Trudy Ferganskogo Politekhnicheskogo Instituta

Tr (Fifteenth) Internat Cong Hyg and Demog — Transactions. Fifteenth International Congress on Hygiene and Demography

Tr Fiz Inst Akad Nauk SSSR — Trudy Fizicheskogo Instituta Imeni P. N. Lebedeva Akademiya Nauk SSSR

Tr Fiz Inst Im Lebedeva — Trudy Ordena Lenina Fizicheskogo Instituta Imeni P. N. Lebedeva

Tr Fiz Inst Im P N Lebedeva Akad Nauk SSSR — Trudy Fizicheskogo Instituta Imeni P. N. Lebedeva Akademiya Nauk SSSR

Tr Fiziol Biokhim Rast — Trudy po Fiziologii i Biokhimii Rastenii

Tr Fiziol Lab Akad Nauk SSSR — Trudy Fiziologicheskoi Laboratorii Akademii Nauk SSSR

Tr Fiziol Patol Zhen — Trudy Fiziologicheskoi Patologii Zhenshchiny

Tr Fiz Mosk Gorn Inst — Trudy po Fizike Moskovskii Gornyi Institut

Tr Fiz Poluprovodn — Trudy po Fizike Poluprovodnikov

Tr Fiz Tekh Inst Akad Nauk Turkm SSR — Trudy Fiziko-Tekhnicheskogo Instituta Akademiya Nauk Turkmenskoi SSR

Tr Frunz Politekh Inst — Trudy Frunzenskogo Politekhnicheskogo Instituta

Tr FTIAN — Trudy FTIAN (Fiziko-Tekhnologicheskii Institut Akademii Nauk)

TRG — Tijdschrift voor Rechtsgeschiedenis

TRG — Travail et Methodes. Revue des Nouvelles au Service de l'Entreprise

TrG — Tribune de Geneve [*Geneva daily*]

TRGEE2 — Trends in Genetics

Tr Gelmintol Lab — Trudy Gel'mintologicheskoi Laboratorii

Tr Gel'mintol Lab Akad Nauk SSSR — Trudy Gel'mintologicheskaya Laboratoriya Akademiya Nauk SSSR

Tr Geofiz Inst Akad Nauk SSSR — Trudy Geofizicheskogo Instituta Akademiya Nauk SSSR

Tr Geol Bulg Ser Geokhm Mineral Petrogr — Trudove Vurkhu Geologiyata na Bulgariya. Seriya Geokhimaya Mineralogiya i Petrografiya

Tr Geol Bulg Ser Inzh Geol Khidrogeol — Trudove Vurkhu Geologiyata na Bulgariya. Seriya Inzhenerna Geologiya i Khidrogeologiya

Tr Geol Bulg Ser Paleonto — Trudove Vurkhu Geologiyata na Bulgariya. Seriya Paleontologiya

Tr Geol Inst Akad Nauk Gruz SSR — Trudy Geologicheskogo Instituta Akademiya Nauk Gruzinskoi SSR

Tr Geol Inst Akad Nauk Gruz SSR Geol Ser — Trudy Geologicheskogo Instituta Akademiya Nauk Gruzinskoi SSR. GeologicheskayaSeriya

Tr Geol Inst Akad Nauk Gruz SSR Mineral Petrogr Ser — Trudy Geologicheskogo Instituta Akademiya Nauk Gruzinskoi SSR. Mineralogo-Petrograficheskaya Seriya

Tr Geol Inst Akad Nauk SSSR — Trudy Geologicheskogo Instituta Akademiya Nauk SSSR

Tr Geol Inst (Kazan) — Trudy Geologicheskogo Instituta (Kazan)

Tr Geol Zavod Soc Repub Makedonija — Trudovei na Geoloskiot Zavod na Socijalisticka Republika Makedonija

Tr Geom Semin — Trudy Geometriceskogo Seminara

T RGesch — Tijdschrift voor Rechtsgeschiedenis

Tr GIAP — Trudy GIAP

Tr Gidrometeorol Nauchno-Issled Tsentr SSSR — Trudy Gidrometeorologicheskii Nauchno-Issledovatel'skii Tsentral'nogo SSSR

Tr "Giprotsement" — Trudy "Giprotsement"

TRGLA — Triangle

TrGlasgUOrS — Transactions. Glasgow University Oriental Society

Tr Glav Bot Sada — Trudy Glavnogo Botanicheskogo Sada

Tr Glavgeologii (GI Upr Geol Okhr Nedr) Uzb SSR — Trudy Glavgeologii (Glavnoe Upravlenie Geologii i Okhrany Nedr) Uzbekskoi SSR

TRGLB — Triangle

Tr Gl Bot Sada — Trudy Glavnogo Botanicheskogo Sada

Tr Gl Bot Sada Akad Nauk SSSR — Trudy Glavnogo Botanicheskogo Sada Akademiya Nauk SSSR

Tr Gl Geofiz Obs — Trudy Glavnoi Geofizicheskoi Observatorii

Tr Gl Geo Obs — Trudy Glavnoi Geofizicheskoi Observatorii

Tr Golovn Nauchno-Issled Inst Tsem Mashinostr — Trudy Golovnoi Nauchno-Issledovatel'skii Institut Tsementnogo Mashinostroeniya

Tr Goriiskogo Gos Pedagog Inst — Trudy Goriiskogo Gosudarstvennogo Pedagogicheskogo Instituta

Tr Gor'k Golovn Skh Inst — Trudy Gor'kovskii Golovnoi Sel'skokhozyaistvennyi Institut

Tr Gor'k Gos Med Inst — Trudy Gor'kovskogo Gosudarstvennogo Meditsinskogo Instituta

Tr Gor'k Gos Nauchno Issled Inst Gig Tr Profbolezn — Trudy Gor'kovskii Gosudarstvennyi Nauchno-Issledovatel'skii Institut Gigieny Truda i Profboleznei

Tr Gork Gos Pedagog Inst — Trudy Gor'kovskogo Gosudarstvennogo Pedagogicheskogo Instituta

Tr Gork Inst Inzh Vodn Transp — Trudy Gor'kovskogo Instituta Inzhenerov Vodnogo Transporta

Tr Gork Inzh Stroit Inst — Trudy Gor'kovskogo Inzhenero-Stroitel'nogo Instituta

Tr Gork Nauchno Issled Pediatr Inst — Trudy Gor'kovskogo Nauchno-Issledovatel'skogo Pediatricheskogo Instituta

Tr Gor'k Nauchno-Issled Vet Opytn Stn — Trudy Gor'kovskoi Nauchno-Issledovatel'skoi Veterinarnoi Opytnoi Stantsii

Tr Gork Politekh Inst — Trudy Gor'kovskogo Politekhnicheskogo Instituta

Tr Gor'k S-Kh Inst — Trudy Gor'kovskogo Sel'skokhozyaistvennogo Instituta

Tr Gorno Geol Inst Akad Nauk SSSR Ural Fil — Trudy Gorno-Geologicheskogo Instituta Akademiya Nauk SSSR Ural'skii Filial

Tr Gorno Geol Inst Akad Nauk SSSR Zapadno Sib Fil — Trudy Gorno-Geologicheskogo Instituta Akademiya Nauk SSSR Zapadno-Sibirskii Filial

Tr Gos Astron Inst Im Shternberga — Trudy Gosudarstvennogo Astronomicheskogo Instituta Imeni P. K. Shternberga

Tr Gos Astron Inst Mosk Gos Univ — Trudy Gosudarstvennogo Astronomicheskogo Instituta Moskovskii Gosudarstvennyi Universitet

Tr Gos Dorozhn Proektno Izyskatel'skII Nauchno Issled Inst — Trudy Gosudarstvennyi Dorozhnyi Proektno-Izyskatel'skii i Nauchno-Issledovatel'skii Institut

Tr Gos Gidrol Inst — Trudy Gosudarstvennogo Gidrologicheskogo Instituta

Tr Gos Inst Prikl Khim — Trudy Gosudarstvennyi Institut Prikladnoi Khimii

Tr Gos Inst Proekt Issled Rab Neftedobyvayushchei Prom-Sti — Trudy Gosudarstvennyi Institut po Proektirovaniyu i Issledovatel'skim Rabotam vNeftedobyvayushchei Promyshlennosti

Tr Gos Inst Usoversh Vrachei I M Lenina — Trudy Gosudarstvennogo Instituta Usovershenstvovaniya Vrachei I. M. Lenina

Tr Gos Issled Elektrokeram Inst — Trudy Gosudarstvennogo Issledovatel'skogo Elektrokeramicheskogo Instituta

Tr Gos Issled Keram Inst — Trudy Gosudarstvennogo Issledovatel'skogo Keramicheskogo Instituta

Tr Gos Makeev Nauchno-Issled Inst Bezop Rab Gorn Prom-Sti — Trudy Gosudarstvennyi Makeevski Nauchno-Issledovatel'skii Institut po Bezopasnosti Rabot v Gornoi Promyshlennosti

Tr Gos Nauchno Eksp Inst Grazhdanskikh Prom Inzh Sooruzh — Trudy Gosudarstvennogo Nauchno-Eksperimental'nogo Instituta Grazhdanskikh Promyshlennykh i Inzhenernykh Sooruzhenii

Tr Gos Nauchno Issled Elektrokeram Inst — Trudy Gosudarstvennogo Nauchno-Issledovatel'skogo Elektrokeramicheskogo Instituta

Tr Gos Nauchno-Issled Inst Gornokhim Syr — Trudy Gosudarstvennogo Nauchno-Issledovatel'skogo Instituta Gornokhimicheskogo Syr'ya

Tr Gos Nauchno-Issled Inst Gornokhim Syr'ya — Trudy Gosudarstvennogo Nauchno-Issledovatel'skogo Instituta Gornokhimicheskogo Syr'ya

Tr Gos Nauchno Issled Inst Keram Promsti — Trudy Gosudarstvennogo Nauchno-Issledovatel'skogo Instituta Keramicheskoi Promyshlennosti

Tr Gos Nauchno Issled Inst Khim Promsti — Trudy Gosudarstvennogo Nauchno-Issledovatel'skogo Instituta Khimicheskoi Promyshlennosti

Tr Gos Nauchno-Issled Inst Prom Sanit Ochistke Gazov — Trudy Gosudarstvennogo Nauchno-Issledovatel'skogo Instituta po Promyshlennoi i Sanitarnoi Ochistke Gazov

Tr Gos Nauchno Issled Inst Psikhiatrii — Trudy Gosudarstvennogo Nauchno-Issledovatel'skogo Instituta Psikhiatrii

Tr Gos Nauchno-Issled Inst Stroit Keram — Trudy Gosudarstvennyi Nauchno-Issledovatel'skii Institut Stroitel'noi Keramiki

Tr Gos Nauchno-Issled Inst Ukha Gorla Nosa — Trudy Gosudarstvennogo Nauchno-Issledovatel'skogo Instituta Ukha Gorla i Nosa

Tr Gos Nauchno-Issled Keram Inst — Trudy Gosudarstvennogo Nauchno-Issledovatel'skogo Keramicheskogo Instituta

Tr Gos Nauchno-Issled Proekt Inst Splavov Obrab Tsvet Met — Trudy Gosudarstvennyi Nauchno-Issledovatel'skii i Proektnyi Institut Splavov i Obrabotki Tsvetnykh Metallov

Tr Gos Nauchno Issled Proektn Inst "Gipromorneft" — Trudy Gosudarstvennogo Nauchno-Issledovatel'skogo i Proektnogo Instituta "Gipromorneft"

Tr Gos Nauchno-Issled Proektn Inst Splavov Obrab Tsvetn Met — Trudy Gosudarstvennyj Nauchno-Issledovatel'skij i Proektnyj Institut Splavov iObrabotki Tsvetnykh Metallov

Tr Gos Nauchno Issled Rentgeno Radiol Inst — Trudy Gosudarstvennyi Nauchno-Issledovatel'skii Rentgeno-Radiologicheskii Institut

Tr Gos Nauchno-Kontrol'n Inst Vet Prep — Trudy Gosudarstvennogo Nauchno-Kontrol'nogo Instituta Veterinarnykh Preparatov

Tr Gos Nikitskii Bot Sad — Trudy Gosudarstvennyi Nikitskii Botanicheskii Sad

Tr Gos Okeanogr Inst — Trudy Gosudarstvennogo Okeanograficheskogo Instituta

Tr Gos Opt Inst — Trudy Gosudarstvennogo Opticheskogo Instituta

Tr Gos Proektno Issled Inst Vostokgiprogaz — Trudy Gosudarstvennyi Proektno-Issledovatel'skii Institut "Vostokgiprogaz"

Tr Gos Proektno Konstr Nauchno Issled Inst Morsk Transp — Trudy Gosudarstvennyi Proektno-Konstruktorskii i Nauchno-Issledovatel'skii Institut Morskogo Transporta

Tr Gos Soyuzn Nauchno Issled Trakt Inst — Trudy Gosudarstvennyi Soyuznyi-Nauchno-Issledovatel'skii Traktornyi Institut

Tr Gos Tsentr Nauchno Issled Inst Tekhnol Organ Proizvod — Trudy Gosudarstvennyi Tsentral'yni Nauchno-Issledovatel'skii Institut Tekhnologii i Organizatsii Proizvodstva

Tr Gos Vses Dorozhn Nauchno Issled Inst — Trudy Gosudarstvennyi Vsesoyuznyi Dorozhnyi Nauchno-Issledovatel'skii Institut

Tr Gos Vses Inst Proekt Nauchno-Issled Rab Giprotsement — Trudy Gosudarstvennogo Vsesoyuznogo Instituta po Proektirovaniyu i Nauchno-Issledovatel'skim Rabotam "Giprotsement"

Tr Gos Vses Inst Proekt Nauchno-Issled Rab Tsem Promsti — Trudy Gosudarstvennogo Vsesoyuznyi Instituta po Proektirovaniyu i Nauchno-Issledovatel'skim Rabotam v Tsementnoi Promyshlennosti

Tr Gos Vses Proektn Nauchno-Issled Inst Tsem Prom-Sti — Trudy Gosudarstvennyi Vsesoyuznyi Proektnyi i Nauchno-Issledovatel'skii Institut Tsementnoi Promyshlennosti

Tr Grozn Neft Inst — Trudy Groznenskii Neftyanoi Institut

Tr Gruz Nauchno-Issled Inst Energ — Trudy Gruzinskogo Nauchno-Issledovatel'skogo Instituta Energetiki

Tr Gruz Nauchno-Issled Inst Gidrotekh Melior — Trudy Gruzinskogo Nauchno-Issledovatel'skogo Instituta Gidrotekhniki i Melioratsii

Tr Gruz Politekh Inst — Trudy Gruzinskogo Politekhnicheskogo Instituta

Tr Gruz S-Kh Inst — Trudy Gruzinskogo Sel'skokhozyaistvennogo Instituta

TRHADS — Topical Reviews in Haematology

Tr Hist Soc Ghana — Transactions. Historical Society of Ghana

TrHS — Transactions. Historical and Scientific Society of Manitoba

TRHS — Transactions. Royal Historical Society

TRHUA — Travail Humain

TRI — Toxic Chemical Release Inventory

Tri — Triangle of Mu Phi Epsilon

Tri — Tribuna

Trial Diplomacy J — Trial Diplomacy Journal

Trial Dpl J — Trial Diplomacy Journal

Trial Ed Mater Adv Sch — Trial Educational Materials for Advanced Schools

Trial Law G — Trial Lawyer's Guide

Trial Law Guide — Trial Lawyer's Guide

Trial Law Q — Trial Lawyers Quarterly

Trib Agric — Tribune Agricole [*Lannemezan*]

Trib CEBEDEAU — Tribune. CEBEDEAU

Trib Farm (Curitiba) — Tribuna Farmaceutica (Curitiba)

Trib Hort Brux — Tribune Horticole (Bruxelles)

Trib Intl — Tribology International

Trib Med Milano — Tribuna Medica (Milano)

Trib Med Paris — Tribune Medicale (Paris)

Trib Med Rio De J — Tribuna Medica (Rio de Janeiro)

Trib Med Santiago — Tribuna Medica (Santiago de Chile)

Trib Mus — Tribune Musical

Trib Odont B Aires — Tribuna Odontologica (Buenos Aires)

Trib Odontol — Tribuna Odontologica

Tribol Int — Tribology International

Tribol Lett — Tribology Letters

Tribol Lubrificazione — Tribologia e Lubrificazione

Tribol Met Cutting Grinding Pap Jt IMechE IOP Meet — Tribology in Metal Cutting and Grinding. Papers. Joint IMechE/IOP Meeting

Tribol Model Mech Des — Tribological Modeling for Mechanical Designers

Tribologia & Lubr — Tribologia e Lubrificazione

Tribology — Tribology International

Tribology Int — Tribology International

Tribol Schmierungstech — Tribologie und Schmierungstechnik

Tribuna Postale — Tribuna Postale e delle Telecomunicazioni

Tribune Hort — Tribune Horticole. Societe Royale Linneenne de Bruxelles

Tric — Tricycle

Tricontinental Bull — Tricontinental Bulletin

Tricot Revue — Tricotage Revue [*Enschede*]

Trienn Rep Agric Stn Larkana — Triennial Report of the Agricultural Station. Larkana [*Poona*]

Trienn Rep Biochem Standard Lab Calcutta — Triennial Report. Biochemical Standardisation Laboratory (Calcutta)

Trienn Rep Bot Div DSIR NZ — Triennial Report. Botany Division. D.S.I.R. New Zealand [*Wellington*]

Trienn Rep Exp Agric Stns Unit Prov — Triennial Report of Experiments Carried out on the Various Agricultural Stations of the United Provinces [*Allahabad*]

Trienn Rep Exp Wk Agric Stn Landhi — Triennial Report of the Experimental Work of the Agricultural Station. Landhi

Trienn Rep Exp Wk Mirpurkhas Agric Stn — Triennial Report of the Experimental Work of the Mirpurkhas Agricultural Station

Trienn Rep Exp Wk Sukkur Agric Stn — Triennial Report on the Experimental Work of the Sukkur Agricultural Station

Trienn Rep Hosps Disp Cent Prov Berar — Triennial Report on Hospitals and Dispensaries in the Central Provinces and Berar [*Nagpur*]

Trienn Rep Nth Niger Minist Agric — Triennial Report of the Northern Nigerian Ministry of Agriculture [*Zaria*]

Trienn Rep Pl Chem Div NZDSIR — Triennial Report. Plant Chemistry Division. New Zealand Department of Scientific and Industrial Research [*Wellington*]

Trient Ann Soc Alpin Trid — Societa degli Alpinisti Tridentini. Annuario

Trier Archiv — Trierisches Archiv

TriererThZ — Trierer Theologische Zeitschrift

TriererZ — Trierer Zeitschrift fuer Geschichte und Kunst des Trierer Landes und Seiner Nachbargebiete

Trierer Zeitschr — Trierer Zeitschrift fuer Geschichte und Kunst des Trierer Landes und Seiner Nachbargebiete

Trierer Z Gesch Kunst — Trierer Zeitschrift fuer Geschichte und Kunst des Trierer Landes und Seiner Nachbargebiete

Trierer Ztschr — Trier Zeitschrift fuer Geschichte und Kunst des Trierer Landes und Seiner Nachbargebiete

TrierThZ — Trierer Theologische Zeitschrift

Trieste Notes in Phys — Trieste Notes in Physics

Trim — Trimestre

Trim Econ — Trimestre Economico

Trim Econ Mex — El Trimestre Economico (Mexico)

Trimes Econ — Trimestre Economico

Trim Estadis Quito — El Trimestre Estadistico del Ecuador (Quito)

Tri Mon Weath Data Burma — Tri-Monthly Weather Data. Burma Meteorological Department [*Rangoon*]

Trim Pol — Trimestre Politico

Tr Indiana Med Soc — Transactions. Indiana State Medical Society

TRI Newsl — Textile Research Institute. Newletter

Trinidad Tobago Min Petrol Mines Mon Bull — Trinidad and Tobago. Ministry of Petroleum and Mines. Monthly Bulletin

Trinity J — Trinity Journal

Trinity Sem R — Trinity Seminary Review

Trinkwasser-Verord — Trinkwasser-Verordnung

Tr Inst Biol Akad Nauk Latv SSR — Trudy Institut Biologii Akademiya Nauk Latviiskoi SSR

Tr Inst Biol Akad Nauk SSSR Ural Fil — Trudy Instituta Biologii Akademiya Nauk SSSR Ural'skii Filial

Tr Inst Biol Akad Nauk Turkm SSR — Trudy Instituta Biologii Akademii Nauk Turkmenskoi SSR

Tr Inst Biol Bashk Univ — Trudy Instituta Biologii Bashkirskogo Universiteta

Tr Inst Biol Ural Fil Akad Nauk SSSR — Trudy Instituta Biologii Ural'skogo Filiala Akademii Nauk SSSR

Tr Inst Biol Vnutr Vod Akad Nauk SSSR — Trudy Instituta Biologii Vnutrennikh Vod Akademii Nauk SSSR

Tr Inst Biol Yakutsk Fil Sib Otd Akad Nauk SSSR — Trudy Instituta Biologii Yakutskii Filial Sibirskogo Otdeleniya Akademii Nauk SSSR

Tr Inst Bot Akad Nauk Azerb SSR — Trudy Instituta Botaniki Akademiya Nauk Azerbaidzhanskoi SSR

Tr Inst Bot Akad Nauk Kazakh SSR — Trudy Instituta Botaniki Akademiya Nauk Kazakhskoi SSR

Tr Inst Bot Akad Nauk Kaz SSR — Trudy Instituta Botaniki Akademii Nauk Kazakhskoi SSR

Tr Inst Chist Khim Reakt — Trudy Instituta Chistykh Khimicheskikh Reaktivov

Tr Inst Ehkol Rast Zhivotn — Trudy Instituta Ehkologii Rastenij i Zhivotnykh

Tr Inst Ehlektrokhim Akad Nauk SSSR Ural Fil — Trudy Instituta Ehlektrokhimii Akademiya Nauk SSSR Ural'skij Filial

Tr Inst Ehlektrokhim Ural Nauch Tsentr Akad Nauk SSSR — Trudy Instituta Ehlektrokhimii Ural'skij Nauchnyj Tsentr Akademiya Nauk SSSR

Tr Inst Ekol Rast Zhivotn — Trudy Instituta Ekologii Rastenii i Zhivotnykh

Tr Inst Ekol Rast Zhivotn Ural Fil Akad Nauk SSSR — Trudy Instituta Ekologii Rastenii i Zhivotnykh Ural'skogo Filiala Akademii Nauk SSSR

Tr Inst Ekol Rast Zhivotn Ural Nauchn Tsentr Akad Nauk SSSR — Trudy Instituta Ekologii Rastenii i Zhivotnykh Ural'skii Nauchnyi Tsentr Akademiya Nauk SSSR

Tr Inst Eksp Biol Akad Nauk Kaz SSR — Trudy Instituta Eksperimental'noi Biologii Akademiya Nauk Kazakhskoi SSR

Tr Inst Eksper Biol Akad Nauk Eston SSR — Trudy Instituta Eksperimental'noi Biologii Akademiya Nauk Estonskoi SSR

Tr Inst Eksp Klin Khir Gematol — Trudy Instituta Eksperimental'noi i Klinicheskoi Khirurgii i Gematologii

Tr Inst Eksp Klin Med Akad Nauk Latv SSR — Trudy Instituta Eksperimental'noi i Klinicheskoi Meditsiny Akademii Nauk Latviiskoi SSR

Tr Inst Eksp Klin Onkol Akad Med Nauk SSSR — Trudy Instituta Eksperimental'noi Klinicheskoi Onkologii Akademiya Meditsinskikh Nauk SSSR

Tr Inst Eksp Med Akad Med Nauk SSR — Trudy Instituta Eksperimental'noi Meditsiny Akademii Meditsinskikh Nauk SSR

Tr Inst Eksp Med Akad Nauk Latv SSR — Trudy Instituta Eksperimental'noi Meditsiny Akademii Nauk Latviiskoi SSR

Tr Inst Eksp Med Akad Nauk Lit SSR — Trudy Instituta Eksperimental'noi Meditsiny Akademii Nauk Litovskoi SSR

Tr Inst Eksp Meteorol — Trudy Institut Eksperimental'noi Meteorologii

Tr Inst Eksp Meteorol Ser Zagryaz Prir Sred — Trudy Instituta Eksperimental'noi Meteorologii. Seriya Zagryaznenie Prirodnykh Sred

Tr Inst Elektrokhim Ural Nauchn Tsentr Akad Nauk SSSR — Trudy Instituta Elektrokhimii Ural'skii Nauchnyi Tsentr Akademiya Nauk SSSR

Tr Inst Energ Akad Nauk BSSR — Trudy Instituta Energetiki Akademiya Nauk Belorusskoi SSR

Tr Inst Epidemiol Mikrobiol (Frunze) — Trudy Instituta Epidemiologii i Mikrobiologii (Frunze)

Tr Inst Fiz Akad Nauk Azerb SSR — Trudy Instituta Fiziki Akademiya Nauk Azerbaidzhanskoi SSR

Tr Inst Fiz Akad Nauk Est SSR — Trudy Instituta Fiziki Akademii Nauk Estonskoi SSR

Tr Inst Fiz Akad Nauk Gruz SSR — Trudy Instituta Fiziki Akademiya Nauk Gruzinskoi SSR

Tr Inst Fiz Astron Akad Nauk Ehst SSR — Trudy Instituta Fiziki i Astronomii Akademiya Nauk Ehstonskoj SSR

Tr Inst Fiziol Akad Nauk Gruz SSR — Trudy Instituta Fiziologii Akademiya Nauk Gruzinskoi SSR

Tr Inst Fiziol Akad Nauk Kaz SSR — Trudy Instituta Fiziologii Akademiya Nauk Kazakhskoi SSR

Tr Inst Fiziol Akad Nauk SSSR — Trudy Instituta Fiziologii Akademii Nauk SSSR

Tr Inst Fiziol Im I P Pavlova Akad Nauk SSSR — Trudy Instituta Fiziologii Imeni I. P. Pavlova Akademii Nauk SSSR

Tr Inst Fiziol Im I P Pavlova Akad SSSR — Trudy Instituta Fiziologii Imeni I. P. Pavlova Akademii Nauk SSSR

Tr Inst Fiziol Rast Im K A Timiryazeva — Trudy Instituta Fiziologii Rastenii Imeni K. A. Timiryazeva

Tr Inst Fiz Met Ural Nauchn Tsent Akad SSSR — Trudy Instituta Fiziki Metallov Ural'skogo Nauchnogo Tsentra Akademiya Nauk SSSR

Tr Inst Fiz Vys Ehnerg — Trudy Instituta Fiziki Vysokikh Ehnergij

Tr Inst Fiz Vys Energ Akad Nauk Kaz SSR — Trudy Instituta Fiziki Vysokikh Energii Akademiya Nauk Kazakhskoi SSR

Tr Inst Fiz Zemli Akad Nauk SSSR — Trudy Instituta Fiziki Zemli Akademiya Nauk SSSR

Tr Inst Genet Akad Nauk SSSR — Trudy Instituta Genetiki Akademii Nauk SSSR

Tr Inst Genet Sel Akad Nauk Az SSR — Trudy Instituta Genetiki i Selektsii Akademii Nauk Azerbaidzhanskoi SSR

Tr Inst Geofiz Akad Nauk Gruz SSR — Trudy Instituta Geofiziki Akademiya Nauk Gruzinskoi SSR

Tr Inst Geogr Akad Nauk SSSR — Trudy Instituta Geografii Akademii Nauk SSSR

Tr Inst Geol Akad Nauk Est SSR — Trudy Instituta Geologii Akademiya Nauk Estonskoi SSR

Tr Inst Geol Akad Nauk Tadzh SSR — Trudy Instituta Geologii Akademiya Nauk Tadzhikskoi SSR

Tr Inst Geol Arkt — Trudy Instituta Geologii Arktiki

Tr Inst Geol Geofiz Akad Nauk SSSR Sib Otd — Trudy Instituta Geologii i Geofiziki Akademiya Nauk SSSR Sibirskoe Otdelenie

Tr Inst Geol Geofiz Novosibirsk — Trudy Instituta Geologii i Geofiziki (Novosibirsk)

Tr Inst Geol Korisnikh Koplain Akad Nauk Ukr RSR — Trudy Institut Geologii Korl Korisnikh Koplain Akademiya Nauk Ukrains'koi RSR

Tr Inst Geol Nauk Akad Nauk Kaz SSR — Trudy Instituta Geologicheskikh Nauk Akademiya Nauk Kazakhskoi SSR

Tr Inst Geol Ross Akad Nauk Ural Otd Komi Nauchn Tsentr — Trudy Instituta Geologii. Rossiiskaya Akademiya Nauk. Ural'skoe Otdelenie. Komi Nauchnyi Tsentr

Tr Inst "Gipproninemetallorud" — Trudy Instituta "Gipproninemetallorud"

Tr Inst Goryuch Iskop (Moscow) — Trudy Instituta Goryuchikh Iskopaemykh (Moscow)

Tr Inst Im Pastera — Trudy. Instituta Imeni Pastera

Tr Inst Istor Estestvozn Tekh Akad Nauk SSSR — Trudy Instituta Istorii Estestvoznaniya i Tekhniki Akademiya Nauk SSSR

Tr Inst Khig Okhr Tr Prof Zabol — Trudove na Instituta po Khigiona. Okhrana na Truda i Profesionalni Zabolyavaniya

Tr Inst Khim Akad Nauk Kirg SSR — Trudy Instituta Khimii Akademiya Nauk Kirgizskoi SSR

Tr Inst Khim Akad Nauk SSSR Ural Fil — Trudy Instituta Khimii Akademiya Nauk SSSR Ural'skii Filial

Tr Inst Khim Akad Nauk Tadzh SSR — Trudy Instituta Khimii Akademiya Nauk Tadzhikskoi SSR

Tr Inst Khim Akad Nauk Turkm SSR — Trudy Instituta Khimii Akademiya Nauk Turkmenskoi SSR

Tr Inst Khim Akad Nauk Uzb SSR — Trudy Instituta Khimii Akademiya Nauk Uzbekskoi SSR

Tr Inst Khim Metall Akad Nauk SSSR Ural Fil — Trudy Instituta Khimii i Metallurgii Akademiya Nauk SSSR Ural'skii Filial

Tr Inst Khim Nauk Akad Nauk Kaz SSR — Trudy Instituta Khimicheskikh Nauk Akademiya Nauk Kazakhskoi SSR

Tr Inst Khim Nefti Prir Solei Akad Nauk Kaz SSR — Trudy Instituta Khimii Nefti i Prirodnykh Solei Akademiya Nauk Kazakhskoi SSSR

Tr Inst Khim Ural Nauchn Tsentr Akad Nauk SSSR — Trudy Instituta Khimii Ural'skii Nauchnyi Tsentr Akademiya Nauk SSSR

Tr Inst Klin Eksp Kardiol — Trudy Instituta Klinicheskoi i Eksperimental'noi Kardiologii

Tr Inst Klin Eksp Kardiol Akad Nauk Gruz SSR — Trudy Instituta Klinicheskoi i Eksperimental'noi Kardiologii Akademiya Nauk Gruzinskoi SSR

Tr Inst Klin Eksp Khir Akad Nauk Kaz SSR — Trudy Instituta Klinicheskoi i Eksperimental'noi Khirurgii Akademii Nauk Kazakhskoi SSR

Tr Inst Klin Eksp Nevrol Gruz SSR — Trudy Instituta Klinicheskoi i Eksperimental'noi Nevrologii Gruzinskoi SSR

Tr Inst Kom Stand Mer Izmer Prib Sov Minist SSSR — Trudy Institutov Komiteta Standartov Mer i Izmeritel'nykh Priborov pri Sovete Ministrov SSSR

Tr Inst Kraev Eksp Med Akad Nauk Uzb SSR — Trudy Instituta Kraevoi Eksperimental'noi Meditsiny Akademiya Nauk Uzbekskoi SSR

Tr Inst Kraev Med Akad Nauk Kirg SSR — Trudy Instituta Kraevoi Meditsiny Akademii Nauk Kirgizskoi SSR

Tr Inst Kraev Patol Akad Nauk Kaz SSR — Trudy Instituta Kraevoi Patologii Akademii Nauk Kazakhskoi SSR

Tr Inst Kristallogr Akad Nauk SSSR — Trudy Instituta Kristallografii Akademiya Nauk SSSR

Tr Inst Lesa Akad Nauk Gruzin SSR — Trudy Instituta Lesa Akademiya Nauk Gruzinskoi SSR

Tr Inst Lesa Akad Nauk Gruz SSR — Trudy Instituta Lesa Akademii Nauk Gruzinskoi SSR

Tr Inst Lesa Akad Nauk SSSR — Trudy Instituta Lesa Akademii Nauk SSSR

Tr Inst Lesa Drev Akad Nauk SSSR Sib Otd — Trudy Instituta Lesa i Drevesiny Akademiya Nauk SSSR Sibirskoe Otdelenie

Tr Inst Lesokhoz Probl Khim Drev Akad Nauk Latv SSR — Trudy Instituta Lesokhozyaistvennykh Problem i Khimii Drevesiny Akademiya NaukLatviiskoi SSR

Tr Inst Malyarii Med Parazitol — Trudy Instituta Malyarii i Meditsinskoi Parazitologii

Tr Inst Mat Mekh Akad Nauk Az SSR — Trudy Instituta Matematiki i Mekhaniki Akademii Nauk Azerbajdzhanskoj SSR

Tr Inst Mekh Obrab Polezn Iskop — Trudy Instituta Mekhanicheskoi Obrabotki Poleznykh Iskopaemykh

Tr Inst Melior Vodn Bolotnogo Khoz Akad Nauk B SSR — Trudy Instituta Melioratsii Vodnogo i Bolotnogo Khozyaistva Akademiya Nauk Belorusskoi SSR

Tr Inst Merzlotoved Akad Nauk SSSR — Trudy Instituta Merzlotovedeniya Akademiya Nauk SSSR

Tr Inst Metall Akad Nauk SSSR — Trudy Instituta Metallurgii Akademiya Nauk SSSR

Tr Inst Metall Akad Nauk SSSR Ural Nauchn Tsentr — Trudy Instituta Metallurgii Akademiya Nauk SSSR Ural'skii Nauchnyi Tsentr

Tr Inst Metall Im A A Baikova Akad Nauk SSSR — Trudy Instituta Metallurgii Imeni A. A. Baikova Akademiya Nauk SSSR

Tr Inst Metall Obogashch Akad Nauk Kaz SSR — Trudy Instituta Metallurgii i Obogashcheniya Akademiya Nauk Kazakhskoi SSR

Tr Inst Metallofiz Metall Akad Nauk SSSR Ural Fil — Trudy Instituta Metallofiziki Metallurgii Akademiya Nauk SSSR Ural'skii Filial

Tr Inst Metall (Sverdlovsk) — Trudy Instituta Metallurgii (Sverdlovsk)

Tr Inst Met (Leningrad) — Trudy Instituta Metallov (Leningrad)

Tr Inst Mikrobiol Akad Nauk Latv SSR — Trudy Instituta Mikrobiologii Akademii Nauk Latviiskoi SSR

Tr Inst Mikrobiol Akad Nauk SSSR — Trudy Instituta Mikrobiologii Akademii Nauk SSSR

Tr Inst Mikrobiol Virusol Akad Nauk Kaz SSR — Trudy Instituta Mikrobiologii i Virusologii Akademii Nauk Kazakhskoi SSR

Tr Inst Morfol Zhivotn Akad Nauk SSSR — Trudy Instituta Morfologii Zhivotnykh Akademii Nauk SSSR

Tr Inst Mosk Inst Tonkoi Khim Tekhnol — Trudy Instituta Moskovskii Institut Tonkoi Khimicheskoi Tekhnologii

Tr Inst Nefti Akad Nauk Az SSR — Trudy Instituta Nefti Akademiya Nauk Azerbaidzhanskoi SSR

Tr Inst Nefti Akad Nauk Kaz SSR — Trudy Instituta Nefti Akademiya Nauk Kazakhoskoi SSR

Tr Inst Nefti Akad Nauk SSSR — Trudy Instituta Nefti Akademiya Nauk SSSR

Tr Inst Norm Patol Fiziol Akad Mod Nauk SSSR — Trudy Instituta Normal'noi i Patologicheskoi Fiziologii Akademii MeditsinskikhNauk SSSR

Tr Inst Nov Lub Syrya — Trudy Instituta Novogo Lubyanogo Syr'ya

Tr Inst Obogashch Tverd Goryuch Iskop — Trudy Instituta Obogashcheniya Tverdykh Goryuchikh Iskopaemykh

Tr Inst Obshch Fiz Ross Akad Nauk — Trudy Instituta Obshchei Fiziki. Rossiiskaya Akademiya Nauk

Tr Inst Okeanol Akad Nauk SSSR — Trudy Instituta Okeanologii Akademii Nauk SSSR

Tr Inst Onkol Akad Med Nauk SSSR — Trudy Instituta Onkologii Akademii Meditsinskikh Nauk SSSR

Tr Inst Org Katal Elektrokhim Akad Nauk Kaz SSR — Trudy Instituta Organicheskogo Kataliza i Elektrokhimii Akademiya Nauk Kazakhskoi SSR

Tr Inst Pastera — Trudy Instituta Imeni Pastera

Tr Inst Pochvoved Agrokhim Akad Nauk Az SSR — Trudy Instituta Pochvovedeniya i Agrokhimii Akademii Nauk Azerbaidzhanskoi SSR

Tr Inst Pochvoved Agrokhim AN UzSSR — Trudy Instituta Pochvovedeniya i Agrokhimii Akademiya Nauk UzSSR

Tr Inst Pochvoved Akad Nauk Gruz SSR — Trudy Instituta Pochvovedeniya Akademii Nauk Gruzinskoi SSR

Tr Inst Pochvoved Akad Nauk Kaz SSR — Trudy Instituta Pochvovedeniya Akademii Nauk Kazakhskoi SSR

Tr Inst Pochvoved (Tashkent) — Trudy Instituta Pochvovedeniya (Tashkent)

Tr Inst Polevod Akad Nauk Gruz SSR — Trudy Instituta Polevodstva Akademii Nauk Gruzinskoi SSR

Tr Inst Polio Virusn Entsefalitov Akad Med Nauk SSSR — Trudy Instituta Poliomielita i Virusnykh Entsefalitov Akademii Meditsinskikh Nauk SSSR

Tr Inst Prikl Geofiz — Trudy Instituta Prikladnoi Geofiziki

Tr Inst Prikl Khim Elektrokhim Akad Nauk Gruz SSR — Trudy Instituta Prikladnoi Khimii i Elektrokhimii Akademiya Nauk Gruzinskoi SSR

Tr Inst Proektn Nauchno-Issled Inst Ural Promstroiniiproekt — Trudy Instituta Proektnyi i Nauchno-Issledovatel'skii Institut Ural'skii Promstroiniiproekt

Tr Inst Razrab Neft Gazov Mestorozhd Akad Nauk Az SSR — Trudy Instituta Razrabotki Neftyanykh i Gazovykh Mestorozhdenii Akademiya NaukAzerbaidzhanskoi SSR

Tr Inst Sadovod Vinograd Vinodel Gruz SSR — Trudy Instituta Sadovodstva Vinogradarstva i Vinodeliya Gruzinskoi SSR

Tr Inst Sadovod Vinograd Vinodel (Tiflis) — Trudy Instituta Sadovodstva Vinogradarstva i Vinodeliya (Tiflis)

Tr Inst Sel Semenovod Khlop (Tashkent) — Trudy Instituta Selektsii i Semenovodstva Khlopchatnika (Tashkent)

Tr Inst Sist Upr Akad Nauk Gruz SSR — Trudy Institut Sistem Upravleniya Akademiya Nauk Gruzinskoj SSR

Tr Inst Stroit Dela Akad Nauk Gruz SSR — Trudy Instituta Stroitel'nogo Dela Akademiya Nauk Gruzinskoi SSR

Tr Inst Stroit Mater Miner Proiskhozhd Stekla — Trudy Instituta Stroitel'nykh Materialov Mineral'nogo Proiskhozhdeniya i Stekla

Tr Inst Stroit Mekh Seismostoikosti Akad Nauk Gruz SSR — Trudy Instituta Stroitel'noi Mekhaniki i Seismostoikosti Akademiya Nauk Gruzinskoi SSR

Tr Inst Stroit Stroimat Akad Nauk Kazakhskoi SSR — Trudy Instituta Stroitel'stva i Stroimaterialov Akademiya Nauk Kazakhskoi SSR

Tr Inst Teor Astron — Trudy Instituta Teoreticoeskoi Astronomii

Tr Inst Teor Geofiz Akad Nauk SSSR — Trudy Instituta Teoreticheskoi Geofiziki Akademiya Nauk SSSR

Tr Inst Torfa Akad Nauk B SSR — Trudy Instituta Torfa Akademiya Nauk Belorusskoi SSR

Tr Inst Tuberk Akad Med Nauk SSSR — Trudy Instituta Tuberkuleza Akademii Meditsinskikh Nauk SSSR

Tr Inst Vinograd Vinodel Akad Nauk Arm SSR — Trudy Instituta Vinogradarstva i Vinodeliya Akademii Nauk Armyanskoi SSR

Tr Inst Vinograd Vinodel Akad Nauk Gruz SSR — Trudy Instituta Vinogradarstva i Vinodeliya Akademii Nauk Gruzinskoi SSR

Tr Inst Vses Nauchno-Issled Inst Tsellyul Bum Prom-Sti — Trudy Instituta. Vsesoyuznyi Nauchno-Issledovatel'skii Institut Tsellyulozno-Bumazhnoi Promyshlennosti

Tr Inst Vulkanol Akad Nauk SSSR Sib Otd — Trudy Instituta Vulkanologii Akademii Nauk SSSR Sibirskoe Otdelenie

Tr Inst Vyssh Nervn Deya Akad Nauk SSSR Fiziol — Trudy Instituta Vysshei Nervnoi Deyatel'nosti Akademii Nauk SSSR. Seriya Fiziologicheskaya

Tr Inst Vyssh Nervn Deyat Akad Nauk SSSR Ser Fiziol — Trudy Instituta Vysshei Nervnoi Deyatel'nosti Akademii Nauk SSSR. Seriya Fiziologicheskaya

Tr Inst Vyssh Nervn Deyat Ser Fiziol — Trudy Instituta Vysshei Nervnoi Deyatel'nosti. Seriya Fiziologicheskaya

Tr Inst Vyssh Nervn Deyat Ser Patofiziol — Trudy Instituta Vysshei Nervnoi Deyatel'nosti. Seriya Patofiziologicheskaya

Tr Inst Yad Fiz Akad Nauk Kaz SSR — Trudy Instituta Yadernoi Fiziki Akademiya Nauk Kazakhskoi SSR

Tr Inst Zasch Rast (Tiflis) — Trudy Instituta Zashchity Rastenii (Tiflis)

Tr Inst Zashch Rast Akad Nauk Gruz SSR — Trudy Instituta Zashchity Rastenii Akademii Nauk Gruzinskoi SSR

Tr Inst Zashch Rast (Tiflis) — Trudy Instituta Zashchity Rastenii (Tiflis)

Tr Inst Zemled Akad Nauk Azerb SSR — Trudy Instituta Zemledeliya Akademiya Nauk Azerbaidzhanskoi SSR

Tr Inst Zemled Kaz Fil Akad Nauk SSSR — Trudy Instituta Zemledeliya Kazakhskogo Filiala Akademii Nauk SSSR

Tr Inst Zemled (Leningrad) Razdel 3 — Trudy Instituta Zemledeliya (Leningrad). Razdel 3. Pochvovedenie

Tr Inst Zhivotnovod Akad Nauk Turkm SSR — Trudy Instituta Zhivotnovodstva Akademii Nauk Turkmenskoi SSR

Tr Inst Zhivotnovod Dagest Fili Akad Nauk SSSR — Trudy Instituta Zhivotnovodstva Dagestanskogo Filiala Akademii Nauk SSSR

Tr Inst Zhivotnovod Minist Skh Uzb SSR — Trudy Instituta Zhivotnovodstva Ministerstvo Sel'skokhozyaistva Uzbekistanskoi SSR

Tr Inst Zhivotnovod (Tashkent) — Trudy Instituta Zhivotnovodstva (Tashkent)

Tr Inst Zool Akad Nauk Az SSR — Trudy Instituta Zoologii Akademii Nauk Azerbaidzhanskoi SSR

Tr Inst Zool Akad Nauk Gruz SSR — Trudy Instituta Zoologii Akademii Nauk Gruzinskoi SSR

Tr Inst Zool Akad Nauk Kazakh SSR — Trudy Instituta Zoologii Akademii Nauk Kazakhskoi SSR

Tr Inst Zool Akad Nauk Kaz SSR — Trudy Instituta Zoologii Akademii Nauk Kazakhskoi SSR

Tr Inst Zool Akad Nauk Ukr SSR — Trudy Instituta Zoologii Akademii Nauk Ukrainskoi SSR

Tr Inst Zool Biol (Kiev) — Trudy Instytutu Zoolohiyi ta Biolohiyi (Kiev)

Tr Inst Zool Parazitol Akad Nauk Tadzh SSR — Trudy Instituta Zoologii i Parazitologii Akademiya Nauk Tadzhikskoi SSR

Tr Inst Zool Parazitol Akad Nauk Uzb SSR — Trudy Instituta Zoologii i Parazitologii Akademii Nauk Uzbekskoi SSR

Tr Inst Zool Parazitol Akad Tadzh SSR — Trudy Instituta Zoologii i Parazitologii Akademiya Nauk Tadzhikskoi SSR

Tr Inst Zool Parazitol Kirg Fil Akad Nauk SSR — Trudy Instituta Zoologii i Parazitologii Kirgizskogo Filiala Akademii Nauk SSR

Trin Tob For — Trinidad and Tobago Forester

TriQ — Tri-Quarterly

Tri-Quar — Tri-Quarterly

TriQuart — Tri-Quarterly

Tr IREA — Trudy IREA

Tr Irkutsk Gorometall Inst — Trudy Irkutskogo Gornometallurgicheskogo Instituta

Tr Irkutsk Gos Univ — Trudy Irkutskogo Gosudarstvennogo Universiteta

Tr Irkutsk Inst Nar Khoz — Trudy Irkutskogo Instituta Narodnogo Khozyaistva

Tr Irkutsk Nauchno Issled Inst Epidemiol Mikrobiol — Trudy Irkutsk Nauchno-Issledovatel'skogo Instituta Epidemiologii i Mikrobiologii

Tr Irkutsk Politekh Inst — Trudy Irkutskogo Politekhnicheskogo Instituta

TRIS — Transportation Research Information Service

Tri State Med J (Greensburo NC) — Tri-State Medical Journal (Greensburo, North Carolina)

Tri State Med J (Shreveport LA) — Tri-State Medical Journal (Shreveport, Louisiana)

Tri St Dent J — Tri-State Dental Journal [Keobuk]

Tri St Fm News — Tri-State Farm News and Oil Journal [Toledo]

Tri St Med J — Tri-State Medical Journal [Shreveport]

Tri St M J — Tri-State Medical Journal

Tri St Poult J — Tri-State Poultry Journal [Memphis]

Triv — Trivium

Tr Ivanov Khim Tekhnol Inst — Trudy Ivanovskogo Khimiko-Tekhnologicheskogo Instituta

Tr Ivanov Med Inst — Trudy Ivanovskogo Meditsinskogo Instituta

Tr Ivanov Skh Inst — Trudy Ivanovskogo Sel'skokhozyaistvennogo Instituta

TRIYA — Trade and Industry

Tr Izhevsk Med Inst — Trudy Izhevskogo Meditsinskogo Instituta

Tr Izhevsk Otd Vses Fiziol Ova — Trudy Izhevskogo Otdeleniya Vsesoyuznogo Fiziologicheskogo Obshchestva

Tr Izhevsk Skh Inst — Trudy Izhevskogo Sel'skokhoziastvennogo Instituta

Tr Izuch Radiya Radioakt Rud — Trudy po Izucheniyu Radiya i Radioaktivnykh Rud

Tr Japan Path Soc — Transactions. Japanese Pathological Society

TRJaVUZ — Trudy Kafedry Russkogo Jazyka Vuzov Vostocnoj Sibiri i Dal'nego Vostoka

Tr Judge J — Trial Judges' Journal

TRJWD — Transactions. JWRI

Tr Kafedry Avtomob Trakt Vses Zaochn Mashinostroit Inst — Trudy Kafedry Avtomobili i Traktory Vsesoyuznyi Zaochnyi Mashinostroitel'nyi Institut

Tr Kafedry Gosp Khir Lech Fak Sarat Med Inst — Trudy Kafedry Gospital'noi Khirugii i Lechebnogo Fakul'teta Saratovskogo Meditsinskogo Instituta

Tr Kafedry Kozhnykh Vener Bolezn Tashk — Trudy Kafedry Kozhnykh i Venericheskikh Boleznei Tashkentskii Meditsinskii Institut

Tr Kafedry Kozhnykh Vener Bolezn Tashk Med Inst — Trudy Kafedry Kozhnykh i Venericheskikh Boleznei Tashkentskii Meditsinskii Institut

Tr Kafedry Norm Anat Sarat Gos Med Inst — Trudy Kafedry Normal'noi Anatomii Saratovskogo Gosudarstvennogo Meditsinskogo Instituta

Tr Kafedry Oper Khir Topogr Anat Tbilis Gos Med Inst — Trudy Kafedry Operativnoi Khirurgii i Topograficheskoi Anatomii Tbilisskogo Gosudarstvennogo Meditsinskogo Instituta

Tr Kafedry Pochvoved Biol Poch Fak Kaz Gos Univ — Trudy Kafedry Pochvovedeniya Biologo-Pochvennogo Fakul'teta Kazakhskii Gosudarstvennyi Universitet

Tr Kafedry Pochvoved Biol Pochv Fak Kaz Gos Univ — Trudy Kafedry Pochvovedeniya Biologo-Pochvennogo Fakul'teta Kazakhskii Gosudarstvennyi Universitet

Tr Kafedry Teor Eksp Fiz Kaliningr Gos Univ — Trudy Kafedry Teoreticheskoi i Eksperimental'noi Fiziki Kaliningradskii Gosudarstvennyi Universitet

Tr Kalinin Gos Med Inst — Trudy Kalininskogo Gosudarstvennogo Meditsinskogo Instituta

Tr Kaliningr Nauchno Issled Vet Stn — Trudy Kaliningradskoi Nauchno-Issledovatel'skoi Veterinarnoi Stantsii

Tr Kaliningr Tekh Inst Rybn Promsti Khoz — Trudy Kaliningradskogo Tekhnicheskogo Instituta Rybnoi Promyshlennosti i Khozyaistva

Tr Kalinin Politekh Inst — Trudy Kalininskii Politekhnicheskii Institut

Tr Kalinin Torf Inst — Trudy Kalininskogo Torfyanogo Instituta

Tr Kaluzhskoi Gos Obl Skh Opytn Stn — Trudy Kaluzhskoi Gosudarstvennoi Oblastnoi Sel'skokhozyaistvennoi Opytnoi Stantsii

Tr Kamenetsk Podolsk Skh Inst — Trudy Kamenetsk-Podolskogo Sel'skokhozyaistvennogo Instituta

Tr Kamenets Podol'sk Skh Inst — Trudy Kamenets-Podol'skogo Sel'skokhozyaistvennogo Instituta

Tr Kandalakshskogo Gos Zapov — Trudy Kandalakshskogo Gosudarstvennogo Zapovednika

Tr Kansas Acad Sc — Transactions. Kansas Academy of Science

Tr Karagandin Bot Sada — Trudy Karagandinskogo Botanicheskogo Sada

Tr Karel Fil Akad Nauk SSSR — Trudy Karel'skogo Filiala Akademii Nauk SSSR

Tr Karelo-Fin Uchit Inst — Trudy Karelo-Finskogo Uchitel'skogo Instituta

Tr Karel Otd Gos Nauchno Issled Inst Ozern Rechn Rybn Khoz — Trudy Karel'skogo Otdeleniya Gosudarstvennogo Nauchno-Issledovatel'skogo Instituta Ozernogo i Rechnogo Rybnogo Khozyaistva

Tr Kasp Nauchno Issled Inst Rybn Khoz — Trudy Kaspiiskii Nauchno-Issledovatel'skii Institut Rybnogo Khozyaistva

Tr Kaunas Gos Med Inst — Trudy Kaunasskogo Gosudarstvennogo Meditsinskogo Instituta

Tr Kavk Inst Miner Syrya — Trudy Kavkazskogo Instituta Mineral'nogo Syr'ya

Tr Kazan Aviats Inst — Trudy KAI. Kazanskij Ordena Trudovogo Krasnogo Znameni Aviatsionnyj Institut Imeni A. N. Tupoleva

Tr Kazan Aviats Inst Ser Khim — Trudy Kazanskogo Aviatsionogo Instituta. Seriya Khimicheskaya

Tr Kazan Fil Akad Nauk SSSR Ser Geol Nauk — Trudy Kazanskogo Filiala Akademii Nauk SSSR. Seriya Geologicheskikh Nauk

Tr Kazan Fil Akad Nauk SSSR Ser Khim Nauk — Trudy Kazanskogo Filiala Akademii Nauk SSSR. Seriya Khimicheskikh Nauk

Tr Kazan Gor Astron Obs — Trudy Kazanskoi Gorodskoi Astronomicheskoi Observatorii

Tr Kazan Gos Inst Usoversh Vrachei — Trudy Kazanskogo Gosudarstvennogo Instituta Usovershenstvovaniya Vrachei

Tr Kazan Inst Usoversh Vrachei Im V I Lenina — Trudy Kazanskogo Instituta Usovershenstvovaniya Vrachei Imeni V. I. Lenina

Tr Kazan Inzh Stroit Inst — Trudy Kazanskogo Inzhenerno-Stroitel'nogo Instituta

Tr Kazan Khim Tekhnol Inst — Trudy Kazanskogo Khimiko-Tekhnologicheskogo Instituta

Tr Kazan Med Inst — Trudy Kazanskogo Meditsinskogo Instituta

Tr Kazan Nauchno-Inst Onkol Radiol — Trudy Kazanskogo Nauchno-Issledovatel'skogo Instituta Onkologii i Radiologii

Tr Kazan Nauchno-Issled Inst Onkol Radiol — Trudy Kazanskogo Nauchno-Issledovatel'skogo Instituta Onkologii i Radiologii

Tr Kazan Nauchno-Issled Inst Travmatol Ortop — Trudy Kazanskogo Nauchno-Issledovatel'skogo Instituta Travmatologii i Ortopedii

Tr Kazan Nauchno Issled Vet Inst — Trudy Kazanskogo Nauchno-Issledovatel'skogo Veterinarnogo Instituta

Tr Kazan S-Kh Inst — Trudy Kazanskogo Sel'skokhozyaistvennogo Instituta

Tr Kaz Fil Akad Stroit Arkhit SSSR — Trudy Kazakhskogo Filiala Akademiya Stroitel'stva i Arkhitektury SSSR

Tr Kaz Gos Pedagog Inst — Trudy Kazanskii Gosudarstvennyi Pedagogicheskii Institut

Tr Kaz Gos Skh Inst — Trudy Kazakhskogo Gosudarstvennogo Sel'skokhozyaistvennogo Instituta

Tr Kaz Inst Epidemiol Mikrobiol Gig — Trudy Kazakhskii Institut Epidemiologii Mikrobiologii Gigieny

Tr Kaz Inst Klin Eksp Khir Akad Med Nauk SSSR — Trudy Kazakhskogo Instituta Klinicheskoi i Eksperimental'noi Khirurgii Akademiya Meditsinskikh Nauk SSSR

Tr Kaz Inst Klin Ekst Khir — Trudy Kazakhskogo Instituta Klinicheskoi i Eksperimental'noi Khirurgii

Tr Kaz Inst Usoversh Vrachei Im V I Lenina — Trudy Kazakhskogo Instituta Usovershenstvovaniya Vrachei Imeni V. I. Lenina

Tr Kaz Nauchno-Issled Gidrometeorol Inst — Trudy Kazakhskogo Nauchno-Issledovatel'skogo Gidrometeorologicheskogo Instituta

Tr Kaz Nauchno Issled Inst Glaznykh Bolezn — Trudy Kazakhskogo Nauchno-Issledovatel'skogo Instituta Glaznykh Boleznei

Tr Kaz Nauchno-Issled Inst Lesn Khoz — Trudy Kazakhskogo Nauchno-Issledovatel'skogo Instituta Lesnogo Khozyaistva

Tr Kaz Nauchno-Issled Inst Lesn Khoz Agrolesomelior — Trudy Kazakhskogo Nauchno-Issledovatel'skogo Instituta Lesnogo Khozyaistva i Agrolesomelioratsii

Tr Kaz Nauchno Issled Inst Miner Syrya — Trudy Kazakhskogo Nauchno-Issledovatel'skogo Instituta Mineral'nogo Syr'ya

Tr Kaz Nauchno-Issled Inst Onkol Radiol — Trudy Kazakhskogo Nauchno-Issledovatel'skogo Instituta Onkologii i Radiologii

Tr Kaz Nauchno-Issled Inst Tuberk — Trudy Kazakhskogo Nauchno-Issledovatel'skogo Instituta Tuberkuleza

Tr Kaz Nauchno Issled Inst Vodn Khoz — Trudy Kazakhskogo Nauchno-Issledovatel'skogo Instituta Vodnogo Khozyaistva

Tr Kaz Nauchno Issled Inst Zashch Rast — Trudy Kazakhskogo Nauchno-Issledovatel'skogo Instituta Zashchity Rastenii

Tr Kaz Nauchno Issled Inst Zemled — Trudy Kazakhskogo Nauchno-Issledovatel'skogo Instituta Zemledeliya

Tr Kaz Nauchno-Issled Kozhno Venerol Inst — Trudy Kazakhskogo Nauchno-Issledovatel'skogo Kozhno-Venerologicheskogo Instituta

Tr Kaz Nauchno-Issled Vet Inst — Trudy Kazakhskogo Nauchno-Issledovatel'skogo Veterinarnogo Instituta

Tr Kaz Opytn Stn Pchelovod — Trudy Kazakhskoi Opytnoi Stantsii Pchelovodstva

Tr Kaz Politekh Inst — Trudy Kazakhskogo Politekhnicheskogo Instituta

Tr Kaz S-Kh Inst — Trudy Kazakhskogo Sel'skokhozyaistvennogo Instituta

Tr Kaz S-Kh Inst Ser Agron — Trudy Kazakhskogo Sel'skokhozyaistvennogo Instituta. Seriya Agronomii

Tr **Kemer Gos Skh Opytn Stn** — Trudy Kemerovskoi Gosudarstvennoi Sel'skokhozyaistvennoi Opytnoi Stantsii

Tr **Kemer Obl Gos S-Kh Opytn Stn** — Trudy Kemerovskoi Oblastnoi Gosudarstvennoi Sel'skokhozyaistvennoi Opytnoi Stantsii

Tr **Kerch Ikhtiol Lab** — Trudy Kerchenskoi Ikhtiologicheskoi Laboratorii

Tr **Kerch Nauchn Rybokhoz Stn** — Trudy Kerchenskoi Nauchnoi Rybokhozyaistvennoi Stantsii

Tr **Khabar Inst Inzh Zheleznodorozhn Transp** — Trudy Khabarovskogo Instituta Inzhenerov Zheleznodorozhnogo Transporta

Tr **Khabar Med Inst** — Trudy Khabarovskogo Meditsinskogo Instituta

Tr **Khabar Politekh Inst** — Trudy Khabarobskogo Politekhnicheskogo Instituta

Tr **Khark Aviats Inst** — Trudy Khar'kovskogo Aviatsionnogo Instituta

Tr **Khar'k Avtodorozhn Inst** — Trudy Khar'kovskogo Avtodorozhnogo Instituta

Tr **Khar'k Avtomob Dorozhn Inst** — Trudy Khar'kovskogo Avtomobil'no-Dorozhnogo Instituta

Tr **Khark Avtomob Dorozhnogo Instituta** — Trudy Khar'kovskogo Avtomobil'no-Dorozhnogo Instituta

Tr **Khar'k Farm Inst** — Trudy Khar'kovskogo Farmatsevticheskogo Instituta

Tr **Khark Gos Farm Inst** — Trudy Khar'kovskogo Gosudarstvennogo Farmatsevticheskogo Instituta

Tr **Khar'k Gos Med Inst** — Trudy Khar'kovskii Gosudarstvennyi Meditsinskii Institut

Tr **Khark Inst Gorn Mashinostr Avtom Vychisl Tekh** — Trudy Khar'kovskogo Instituta Gornogo Mashinostroeniya. Avtomatiki i Vychislitel'noi Tekhniki

Tr **Khark Inst Inzh Zheleznodorozhn Transp** — Trudy Khar'kovskogo Instituta Inzhenerov Zheleznodorozhnogo Transporta

Tr **Khark Inzh Ekon Inst** — Trudy Khar'kovskogo Inzhenerno-Ekonomicheskogo Instituta

Tr **Khark Khim Tekhnol Inst** — Trudy Khar'kovskogo Khimiko-Tekhnologicheskogo Instituta

Tr **Khar'k Med Inst** — Trudy Khar'kovskogo Meditsinskogo Instituta

Tr **Khark Nauchno Issled Khim Farm Inst** — Trudy Khar'kovskogo Nauchno-Issledovatel'skogo Khimiko-Farmatsevticheskogo Instituta

Tr **Khar'kov Med Inst** — Trudy Khar'kovskogo Meditsinskogo Instituta

Tr **Khark Politekh Inst** — Trudy Khar'kovskogo Politekhnicheskogo Instituta

Tr **Khar'k S-Kh Inst** — Trudy Khar'kovskogo Sel'skokhozyaistvennogo Instituta

Tr **Khar'k Skh Inst Im V V Dokuchaeva** — Trudy Khar'kovskii Sel'skokhozyaistvennyi Institut Imeni V. V. Dokuchaeva

Tr **Khim Inst Im L Ya Karpova** — Trudy Khimicheskogo Instituta Imeni L. Ya. Karpova

Tr **Khim Khim Tekhnol** — Trudy po Khimii i Khimicheskoi Tekhnologii

Tr **Khim-Metall Inst Akad Nauk Kaz SSR** — Trudy Khimiko-Metallurgicheskogo Instituta Akademiya Nauk Kazakhskoj SSR

Tr **Khim Metall Inst Akad Nauk SSSR Sib Otd** — Trudy Khimiko-Metallurgicheskogo Instituta Akademiya Nauk SSSR Sibirskoe Otdelenie

Tr **Khim Prir Soedin** — Trudy po Khimii Prirodnykh Soedinenii

Tr **Kiev Gor Obl Nauchn Ova Dermatol** — Trudy Kievskogo Gorodskogo Oblastnogo Nauchnogo Obshchestva Dermatologii

Tr **Kiev Politekh Inst** — Trudy Kievskogo Politekhnicheskogo Instituta

Tr **Kiev Tekhnol Inst Pishch Promsti** — Trudy Kievskogo Tekhnologicheskogo Instituta Pishchevoi Promyshlennosti

Tr **Kiev Vet Inst** — Trudy Kievskogo Veterinarnogo Instituta

Tr **Kirg Gos Med Inst** — Trudy Kirgizskogo Gosudarstvennogo Meditsinskogo Instituta

Tr **Kirg Gos Univ Ser Fiz Nauk** — Trudy Kirgizskogo Gosudarstvennogo Universiteta. Seriya Fizicheskikh Nauk

Tr **Kirg Inst Epidemiol Mikrobiol Gig** — Trudy Kirgizskogo Instituta Epidemiologii, Mikrobiologii, i Gigieny

Tr **Kirgiz Nauch Issled Inst Zemled** — Trudy Kirgizskogo Nauchno-Issledovatel'skogo Instituta Zemledeliya

Tr **Kirg Lesn Opytn Stn** — Trudy Kirgizskoi Lesnoi Opytnoi Stantsii

Tr **Kirg Nauchno-Issled Inst Onkol Radiol** — Trudy Kirgizskogo Nauchno-Issledovatel'skoi Instituta Onkologii i Radiologii

Tr **Kirg Nauchno-Issled Inst Pochvoved** — Trudy Kirgizskogo Nauchno-Issledovatel'skogo Instituta Pochvovedeniya

Tr **Kirg Nauchno Issled Inst Zemled** — Trudy Kirgizskogo Nauchno-Issledovatel'skogo Instituta Zemledeliya

Tr **Kirg Nauchno-Issled Inst Zhivotnovod** — Trudy Kirgizskogo Nauchno-Issledovatel'skogo Instituta Zhivotnovodstva

Tr **Kirg Nauchno-Issled Inst Zhivotnovod Vet** — Trudy Kirgizskogo Nauchno-Issledovatel'skogo Instituta Zhivotnovodstva i Veterinarii

Tr **Kirg Opytno-Sel Stn Sakh Svekle** — Trudy Kirgizskoi Opytno-Selektsionnoi Stantsii po Sakharnoi Svekle

Tr **Kirg Opytn Stn Khlopkovod** — Trudy Kirgizskoi Opytnoi Stantsii Khlopkovodstva

Tr **Kirg S-Kh Inst** — Trudy Kirgizskogo Sel'skokhozyaistvennogo Instituta

Tr **Kirg Skh Inst Ser Agron** — Trudy Kirgizskogo Sel'skokhozyaistvennogo Seriya Agronomii

Tr **Kirg Univ Ser Biol Nauk** — Trudy Kirgizskogo Universiteta Seriya Biologicheskikh Nauk

Tr **Kirov Obl Nauchno Issled Inst Kraeved** — Trudy Kirovskogo Oblastnogo Nauchno-Issledovatel'skogo Instituta Kraevedeniya

Tr **Kirov Otd Vses Fiziol Ova** — Trudy Kirovskogo Otdeleniya Vsesoyuznogo Fiziologicheskogo Obshchestva

Tr **Kirov S-Kh Inst** — Trudy Kirovskogo Sel'skokhozyaistvennogo Instituta

Tr **Kishinev Gos Med Inst** — Trudy Kishinevskogo Gosudarstvennogo Meditsinskogo Instituta

Tr **Kishinev Politekh Inst** — Trudy Kishinevskii Politekhnicheskii Institut

Tr **Kishinev S-Kh Inst** — Trudy Kishinevskogo Sel'skokhozyaistvennogo Instituta

Tr **Kishinev S-Kh Inst Im M V Frunze** — Trudy Kishinevskii Sel'skokhozyaistvennyi Institut Imeni M. V. Frunze

Tr **Klin Nervn Boleznei Mosk Obl Nauchno-Issled Klin Inst** — Trudy Kliniki Nervnykh Boleznei Moskovskogo Oblastnogo Nauchno-Issledovatel'skogo Klinicheskogo Instituta

Tr **Klin Otd Nauchno Issled Inst Gig Tr Profzabol** — Trudy Klinicheskogo Otdeleniya Nauchno-Issledovatel'skogo Instituta Gigieny Truda i Profzabolevanii

Tr **Kolomenskogo Fil Vses Zaochn Politekh Inst** — Trudy Kolomenskogo Filiala Vsesoyuznogo Zaochnogo Politekhnicheskogo Instituta

Tr **Kom Anal Khim Akad Nauk SSSR** — Trudy Komissii po Analiticheskoi Khimii Akademiya Nauk SSSR

Tr **Kom Borbe s Korroz Met Akad Nauk SSSR** — Trudy Komissii po Bor'be s Korroziei Metallov Akademiya Nauk SSSR

Tr **Komi Fil Akad Nauk SSSR** — Trudy Komi Filiala Akademii Nauk SSSR

Tr **Komi Nauchn Tsentra UrO Ross Akad Nauk** — Trudy Komi Nauchnogo Tsentra UrO Rossiiskoi Akademii Nauk

Tr **Kom Irrig Akad Nauk SSSR** — Trudy Komissii po Irrigatsii Akademiya Nauk SSSR

Tr **Kom Okhr Prir Ural Fil Akad Nauk SSSR** — Trudy Komissii po Okhrane Prirody Ural'skogo Filiala Akademii Nauk SSSR

Tr **Kom Pirom Vses Nauchno Issled Inst Metrol** — Trudy Komissii po Pirometrii Vsesoyuznyi Nauchno-Issledovatel'skii Institut Metrologii

Tr **Kompleksn Eksped Dnepropetr Univ** — Trudy Kompleksnoi Ekspeditsii Dnepropetrovskogo Universiteta

Tr **Kompleksn Eksped Sarat Univ Izuch Volgogr Sarat Vodokhran** — Trudy Kompleksnoi Ekspeditsii Saratovskogo Universiteta po Izucheniyu Volgogradskogo i Saratovskogo Vodokhranilishch

Tr **Kompleksn Yuzhn Geol Eksped Akad Nauk SSSR** — Trudy Kompleksnoi Yuzhnoi Geologicheskoi Ekspeditsii. Akademiya Nauk SSSR

Tr **Kom Spektros Akad Nauk SSSR** — Trudy Komissii po Spektroskopii Akademiya Nauk SSSR

Tr **Koord Soveshch Gidrotekh** — Trudy Koordinatsionnykh Soveshchanyi po Gidrotekhnike

Tr **Kostrom Skh Inst** — Trudy Kostromskogo Sel'skokhozyaistvennogo Instituta "Karavaevo"

Tr **Kranoyarsk Nauchno Issled Inst Selsk Khoz** — Trudy Krasnoyarskogo Nauchno-Issledovatel'skogo Instituta Sel'skogo Khozyaistva

Tr **Krasnodar Fil Vses Neftegazov Nauchno Issled Inst** — Trudy Krasnodarskii Filial Vsesoyuznogo Neftegazovogo Nauchno-Issledovatel'skogo Instituta

Tr **Krasnodar Gos Pedagog Inst** — Trudy Krasnodarskogo Gosudarstvennogo Pedagogicheskogo Instituta

Tr **Krasnodar Inst Pishch Promsti** — Trudy Krasnodarskogo Instituta Pishchevoi Promyshlennosti

Tr **Krasnodar Nauchno-Issled Inst Pishch Promsti** — Trudy Krasnodarskogo Nauchno-Issledovatel'skogo Instituta Pischevoi Promyshlennosti

Tr **Krasnodar Nauchno-Issled Inst Selsk Khoz** — Trudy Krasnodarskogo Nauchno-Issledovatel'skogo Instituta Sel'skogog Khozyaistva

Tr **Krasnodar Politekh Inst** — Trudy Krasnodarskogo Politekhnicheskogo Instituta

Tr **Krasnoyarsk Gos Med Inst** — Trudy Krasnoyarskogo Gosudarstvennogo Meditsinskogo Instituta

Tr **Krasnoyarsk Med Inst** — Trudy Krasnoyarskogo Meditsinskogo Instituta

Tr **Krasnoyarsk Nauchno Issled Inst Sel'sk Khoz** — Trudy Krasnoyarskogo Nauchno-Issledovatel'skogo Instituta Sel'skogo Khozyaistva

Tr **Krasnoyarsk S-Kh Inst** — Trudy Krasnoyarskogo Sel'skokhozyaistvennogo Instituta

Tr **Krym Fil Akad Nauk Ukr SSR** — Trudy Krymskogo Filiala Akademiya Nauk Ukrainskoi SSR

Tr **Krym Gos Med Inst** — Trudy Krymskogo Gosudarstvennogo Meditsinskogo Instituta

Tr **Krym Gos Med Inst Im I V Stalina** — Trudy Krymskogo Gosudarstvennogo Meditsinskogo Instituta Imeni I. V. Stalina

Tr **Krym Gos Skh Opytn Stn** — Trudy Krymskoi Gosudarstvennoi Sel'skokhozyaistvennoi Opytnoi Stantsii

Tr **Krym Gosud Sel'skokhoz Opyt Sta** — Trudy Krymskoi Gosudarstvennoi Sel'skokhozyaistvennoi Opytnoi Stantsii

Tr **Krym Med Inst** — Trudy Krymskogo Meditsinskogo Instituta

Tr **Krym Obl Gos Skh Opytn Stn** — Trudy Krymskoi Oblastnoi Gosudarstvennoi Sel'skokhozyaistvennoi Opytnoi Stantsii

Tr **Krym Opytno Sel Stn VIR** — Trudy Krymskoi Opytno Selektsionnoi Stantsii VIR

Tr **Krym Skh Inst** — Trudy Krymskogo Sel'skokhozyaistvennogo Instituta

Tr **Krym S-Kh Inst Im M I Kalinina** — Trudy Krymskogo Sel'skokhozyaistvennogo Instituta Imeni M. I. Kalinina

TRKUA — Technology Reports. Kansal University

Tr **Kuban Otd Vses Ova Genet Sel** — Trudy Kubanskoe Otdelenie Vsesoyuznogo Obshchestva Genetikovi Selektsionerov

Tr **Kuban S-Kh Inst** — Trudy Kubanskogo Sel'skokhozyaistvennogo Instituta

Tr **Kuibyshev Aviats Inst** — Trudy Kuibyshevskii Aviatsionnyi Institut

Tr **Kuibyshev Gos Nauchno-Issled Inst Neft Prom-Sti** — Trudy Kuibyshevskii Gosudarstvennyi Nauchno-Issledovatel'skii Institut Neftyanoi Promyshlennosti

Tr **Kuibyshev Inzh-Stroit Inst** — Trudy Kuibyshevskii Inzhenerno-Stroitel'nyi Institut

Tr **Kuibyshev Med Inst** — Trudy Kuibyshevskii Meditsinskii Instituta

Tr **Kuibyshev Nauchno-Issled Inst Neft Promsti** — Trudy Kuibyshevskii Nauchno-Issledovatel'skii Institut Neftyanoi Promyshlennosti

Tr **Kuibyshev S-Kh Inst** — Trudy Kuibyshevskogo Sel'skokhozyaistvennogo Instituta

Tr **Kurgan Mashinostroit Inst** — Trudy Kurganskogo Mashinostroitel'nogo Instituta

Tr **Kurortol** — Trudy po Kurortologii

Tr **Kursk Med Inst** — Trudy Kurskogo Meditsinskogo Instituta

Tr **Kutais Skh Inst** — Trudy Kutaisskogo Sel'skokhozyaistvennogo Instituta

TrL — Tribune de Lausanne [*newspaper*]

Tr **Lab Biokhim Fiziol Zhivotn Inst Biol Akad Nauk Latv SSR** — Trudy Laboratorii Biokhimii i Fiziologii Zhivotnykh Instituta Biologii Akademiya Nauk Latviiskoi SSR

Tr **Lab Eksp Biol Mosk Zooparka** — Trudy Laboratorii Eksperimental'noi Biologii Moskovskogo Zooparka

Tr **Lab Evol Ekol Fiziol Akad Nauk SSSR Inst Fiziol Rast** — Trudy Laboratorii Evolyutsionnoi i Ekologicheskoi Fiziologii Akademiya Nauk SSSR Institut Fiziologii Rastenii

Tr **Lab Fiziol Zhivotn Inst Biol Akad Nauk Lit SSR** — Trudy Laboratorii Fiziologii Zhivotnykh Instituta Biologii Akademii Nauk Litovskoi SSR

Tr **Lab Geol Dokembr Akad Nauk SSSR** — Trudy Laboratorii Geologii Dokembriya Akademiya Nauk SSSR

Tr Lab Geol Uglya Akad Nauk SSSR — Trudy Laboratorii Geologii Uglya Akademiya Nauk SSSR

Tr Lab Gidrogeol Probl Akad Nauk SSSR — Trudy Laboratorii Gidrogeologicheskikh Problem Akademiya Nauk SSSR

Tr Lab Izuch Belka Akad Nauk SSSR — Trudy Laboratorii po Izucheniyu Belka Akademiya Nauk SSSR

Tr Lab Lesoved Akad Nauk SSSR — Trudy Laboratorii Lesovedeniya Akademiya Nauk SSSR

Tr Lab Ozeroved Leningr Gos Univ — Trudy Laboratorii Ozerovedeniya Leningradskii Gosudarstvennyi Universitet

Tr Lab Sapropelevykh Otlozh Akad Nauk SSSR — Trudy Laboratorii Sapropelevykh Otlozhenii Akademiya Nauk SSSR

Tr Lab Vulkanol Akad Nauk SSSR — Trudy Laboratorii Vulkanologii Akademiya Nauk SSSR

Tr Latviiskogo Nauchno-Issled Inst Zhivotnovod Vet — Trudy Latviiskogo Nauchno-Issledovatel'skogo Instituta Zhivotnovodstva i Veterinarii

Tr Latv Inst Eksp Klin Med Akad Med Nauk SSSR — Trudy Latviiskogo Instituta Eksperimental'noi i Klinicheskoi Meditsiny AkademiiMeditsinskikh Nauk SSSR

Tr Latv Nauchno Issled Inst Gidrotekh Melior — Trudy Latviiskogo Nauchno-Issledovatel'skogo Instituta Gidrotekhniki i Melioratsii

Tr Latv Nauchno-Issled Inst Zhivotnovod Vet — Trudy Latviiskogo Nauchno-Issledovatel'skogo Instituta Zhivotnovodstva i Veterinarii

Tr Latv Sel'kh Akad — Trudy Latviiskaia Sel'skokhoziaistvennaia Akademiia

Tr Latv S-Kh Akad — Trudy Latviiskoi Sel'skokhozyaistvennoi Akademiia

Tr Law Guide — Trial Lawyer's Guide

Tr Law Q — Trial Lawyers Quarterly

Tr Legochn Patol Inst Eksp Klin Med Est SSR — Trudy po Legochnoi Patologii Institut Eksperimental'noi i Klinicheskoi Meditsiny Estonskoi SSR

Tr Leningrad Tekhnol Inst Tsellyul-Bumazh Prom — Trudy Leningradskogo Tekhnologicheskogo Instituta Tsellyulozno-Bumazhnoi Promyshlennosti

Tr Leningr Elektrotekh Inst Svyazi — Trudy Leningradskii Elektrotekhnicheskii Institut Svyazi

Tr Leningr Geol Upr — Trudy Leningradskogo Geologicheskogo Upravleniya

Tr Leningr Gidrometeorol Inst — Trudy Leningradskii Gidrometeorologicheskii Institut

Tr Leningr Gos Nauchno Issled Inst Travmatol Ortop — Trudy Leningradskogo Gosudarstvennogo Nauchno-Issledovatel'skogo Instituta Travmatologii i Ortopedii

Tr Leningr Ind Inst — Trudy Leningradskii Industrial'nogo Instituta

Tr Leningr Inst Epidemiol Mikrobiol — Trudy Leningradskogo Instituta Epidemiologii i Mikrobiologii

Tr Leningr Inst Inzh Kommunal'n Stroit — Trudy Leningradskii Institut Inzhenerov Kommunal'nogo Stroitel'stva

Tr Leningr Inst Inzh Zheleznodorozhn Transp — Trudy Leningradskii Institut Inzhenerov Zheleznodorozhnogo Transporta

Tr Leningr Inst Kinoinzh — Trudy Leningradskogo Instituta Kinoinzhenerov

Tr Leningr Inst Sov Torg — Trudy Leningradskii Institut Sovetskoi Torgovli

Tr Leningr Inst Tochn Mekh Opt — Trudy Leningradskii Institut Tochnoi Mekhaniki i Optiki

Tr Leningr Inst Usoversh Vrachei — Trudy Leningradskogo Instituta Usovershenstvovaniya Vrachei

Tr Leningr Inst Vaktsin Syvorotok — Trudy Leningradskogo Instituta Vaktsin i Syvorotok

Tr Leningr Inst Vodn Transp — Trudy Leningradskogo Instituta Vodnogo Transporta

Tr Leningr Inzh Ekon Inst — Trudy Leningradskogo Inzhenerno-Ekonomicheskogo Instituta

Tr Leningr Inzh Ekon Inst Im Pal'miro Tol'yatti — Trudy Leningradskii Inzhenerno-Ekonomicheskii Institut Imeni Pal'miro Tol'yatti

Tr Leningr Khim-Farm Inst — Trudy Leningradskogo Khimiko-Farmatsevticheskogo Instituta

Tr Leningr Khim Tekhnol Inst — Trudy Leningradskogo Khimiko-Tekhnologicheskogo Instituta

Tr Leningr Korablestroit Inst — Trudy Leningradskogo Korablestroitel'nogo Instituta

Tr Leningr Korablestroit'nogo Inst — Trudy Leningradskogo Korablestroitel'nogo Instituta

Tr Leningr Lesotekh Akad — Trudy Leningradskoi Lesotekhnicheskoi Akademii

Tr Leningr Med Inst — Trudy Leningradskogo Meditsinskogo Instituta

Tr Leningr Mekh Tekhnol Inst Kholod Promsti — Trudy Leningradskogo Mekhaniko-Tekhnologicheskogo Instituta Kholodil'noi Promyshlennosti

Tr Leningr Met Zavod — Trudy Leningradskii Metallicheskii Zavod

Tr Leningr Nauchno-Issled Inst Antibiot — Trudy Leningradskogo Nauchno-Issledovatel'skogo Instituta Antibiotiki

Tr Leningr Nauchno-Issled Inst Epidemiol Mikrobiol — Trudy Leningradskogo Nauchno-Issledovatel'skogo Instituta Epidemiologii i Mikrobiologii

Tr Leningr Nauchno Issled Inst Neirokhir — Trudy Leningradskogo Nauchno-Issledovatel'skogo Instituta Neirokhirurgii

Tr Leningr Nauchno Issled Inst Radiats Gig — Trudy Leningradskogo Nauchno-Issledovatel'skogo Instituta Radiatsii i Gigieny

Tr Leningr Nauchno Issled Inst Tuberk — Trudy Leningradskogo Nauchno-Issledovatel'skogo Instituta Tuberkuleza

Tr Leningr Nauchno Issled Inst Vaktsin Syvorotok — Trudy Leningradskii Nauchno-Issledovatel'skii Institut Vaktsin i Syvorotok

Tr Leningr Nauchno-Issled Konstr Inst Khim Mashinostr — Trudy Leningradskii Nauchno-Issledovatel'skii i Konstruktorskii Institut Khimicheskogo Mashinostroeniya

Tr Leningr Nauchno Issled Psikhonevrol Inst — Trudy Leningradskogo Nauchno-Issledovatel'skogo Psikhonevrologisheskogo Instituta

Tr Leningr Nauchno Ova Patologoanat — Trudy Leningradskogo Nauchnogo Obshchestva Patologoanatomov

Tr Leningr Ova Anat Gistol Embriol — Trudy Leningradskogo Obshchestva Anatomov, Gistologov, i Embriologov

Tr Leningr O-Va Estestvoispyt — Trudy Leningradskogo Obshchestva Estestvoispytatelei

Tr Leningr Pediatr Med Inst — Trudy Leningradskogo Pediatricheskogo Meditsinskogo Instituta

Tr Leningr Politekh Inst — Trudy Leningradskogo Politekhnicheskogo Instituta Imeni M. I. Kalinina

Tr Leningr Politekh Inst Im M I Kalinina — Trudy Leningradskogo Politekhnicheskogo Instituta Imeni M. I. Kalinina

Tr Leningr Sanit-Gig Med Inst — Trudy Leningradskogo Sanitarno-Gigienicheskogo Meditsinskogo Instituta

Tr Leningr Tekhnol Inst Im Lensoveta — Trudy Leningradskogo Tekhnologicheskogo Instituta Imeni Lensoveta

Tr Leningr Tekhnol Inst Kholod Prom-St' — Trudy Leningradskogo Tekhnologicheskogo Instituta Kholodil'noi Promyshlennosti

Tr Leningr Tekhnol Inst Pishch Prom-Sti — Trudy Leningradskogo Tekhnologicheskogo Instituta Pishchevoi Promyshlennosti

Tr Leningr Tekhnol Inst Tsellyul Bum Promsti — Trudy Leningradskogo Tekhnologicheskogo Instituta Tsellyulozno-Bumazhnoi Promyshlennosti

Tr Leningr Teknol Inst — Trudy Leningradskogo Tekhnologicheskogo Instituta

Tr Leningr Tekst Inst — Trudy Leningradskogo Tekstil'nogo Instituta

Tr Leningr Tsentr Gos Travmatol Inst — Trudy Leningradskogo Tsentral'nogo Gosudarstvennogo Travmatologicheskogo Instituta

Tr Leningr Voen Mekh Inst — Trudy Leningradskii Voenno-Mekhanicheskii Institut

Tr Lesotekh Akad — Trudy Lesotekhnicheskoi Akademii

TRLGA — Translog

Tr Limnol Inst Sib Otd Akad Nauk SSSR — Trudy Limnologicheskogo Instituta Siberskogo Otdeleniya. Akademii Nauk SSSR

Tr Litov Inst Eksp Klin Med Akad Med Nauk SSSR — Trudy Litovskogo Instituta Eksperimental'noi i Klinicheskoi Meditsiny Akademii Meditsinskikh Nauk SSSR

Tr Litov Inst Eksp Med Akad Med Nauk SSSR — Trudy Litovskogo Instituta Eksperimental'noi Meditsiny Akademii Meditsinskikh Nauk SSSR

Tr Litov Nauchno Issled Geologorazves Inst — Trudy Litovskogo Nauchno-Issledovatel'skogo Geologorazvedochnogo Instituta

Tr Litov Nauchno Issled Inst Lesn Khoz — Trudy Litovskogo Nauchno-Issledovatel'skogo Instituta Lesnogo Khozyaistva

Tr Litov Nauchno Issled Inst Vet — Trudy Litovskogo Nauchno-Issledovatel'skogo Instituta Veterinarii

Tr LNIIA — Trudy LNIIA

Tr Lugansk S-Kh Inst — Trudy Luganskogo Sel'skokhozyaistvennoi Instituta

TRM — Telecommunications Regulatory Monitor

TRM — Topics in Health Record Management

Tr M — Traditional Music

TrM — Travaux et Memoires. Centre de Recherche d'Histoire et de Civilisation Byzantines

Tr Magadan Zon Nauchno Issled Inst Selsk Khoz Sev Vostoka — Trudy Magadanskogo Zonal'nogo Nauchno-Issledovatel'skogo Instituta Sel'skogo Khozyaistva Severo-Vostoka

Tr Marii Gos Pedagog Inst — Trudy Mariiskii Gosudarstvennyi Pedagogicheskii Institut

Tr Mater Donetsk Med Inst — Trudy i Materialy Donetskii Meditsinskii Institut

Tr Mater Donetsk Nauchno Issled Inst Fiziol Tr — Trudy i Materialy Donetskii Nauchno-Issledovatel'skii Institut Fiziologii Truda

Tr Mater Leningr Inst Organ Okhr Tr — Trudy i Materialy Leningradskii Institut Organizatsii i Okhrany Truda

Tr Mater Nauchno Issled Inst Fiziol Tr (Stalino) — Trudy i Materialy Nauchno-Issledovatel'skii Institut Fiziologii Truda (Stalino)

Tr Mater Pervogo Ukr Inst Rab Med — Trudy i Materialy Pervogo Ukrainskogo Instituta Rabochei Meditsiny

Tr Mater Ukr Gos Inst Patol Gig Tr — Trudy i Materialy Ukrainskogo Gosudarstvennogo Instituta Patologii i Gigieny Truda

Tr Mater Ukr Gos Inst Rab Med — Trudy i Materialy Ukrainskogo Gosudarstvennogo Instituta Rabochei Meditsiny

Tr Mater Ukr Tsentr Inst Gig Tr Profzabol — Trudy i Materialy Ukrainskii Tsentral'nyi Institut Gigieny Truda i Profzabolevanii

Tr Mat Inst Akad Nauk SSSR — Trudy Matematicheskogo Instituta Akademiya Nauk SSSR

TRMCA — Transition Metal Chemistry

TRMEA — Trattamenti dei Metalli

Tr Med and Phys Soc Bombay — Transactions. Medical and Physical Society of Bombay

Tr Mem — Travaux et Memoires. Centre de Recherche d'Histoire et de Civilisation Byzantines

Tr Metrol Inst SSSR — Trudy Metrologiceskih Institutov SSSR

Tr Mezhdunar Konf Fiz Vys Energ — Trudy Mezhdunarodnaya Konferentsiya po Fizike Vysokikh Energii

Tr Mezhdunar Simp Geterog Katal — Trudy Mezhdunarodnogo Simpoziuma po Geterogennomu Katalizu

Tr Mezhdunar Simp Tsitoekol — Trudy Mezhdunarodnogo Simpoziuma po Tsitoekologii

Tr MFTI Ser "Obshch Mol Fiz" — Trudy Moskovskogo Fiziko-Tekhnicheskogo Instituta. Seriya "Obshchaya i Molekulyarnaya Fizika"

Tr Mineral Inst Akad Nauk SSSR — Trudy Mineralogicheskogo Instituta Akademiya Nauk SSSR

Tr Mineral Muz Akad Nauk SSSR — Trudy Mineralogicheskogo Muzeya Akademiya Nauk SSSR

Tr Minniya Nauchnoizsled Proekto Konstr Inst — Trudove na Minniya Nauchnoizsledovatelski i Proektno Konstruktorski Institut

Tr Minsk Gos Med Inst — Trudy Minskogo Gosudarstvennogo Meditsinskogo Instituta

Tr Moldav Nauch Issled Inst Orosh Zemled Ovoshchev — Trudy Moldavskogo Nauchno-Issledovatel'skogo Instituta Oroshaemogo Zemledeliya i Ovoshchevodstva

Tr Mold Nauchno Issled Inst Epidemiol Mikrobiol Gig — Trudy Moldavskii Nauchno-Issledovatel'skii Institut Epidemiologii, Mikrobiologii, i Gigieny

Tr Mold Nauchno Issled Inst Gig Epidemiol — Trudy Moldavskii Nauchno-Issledovatel'skii Institut Gigieny i Epidemiologii

Tr Mold Nauchno Issled Inst Oroshaemogo Zemled Ovoshchevod — Trudy Moldavskogo Nauchno-Issledovatel'skogo Instituta Oroshaemogo Zemledeliya i Ovoshchevodstva

Tr Mold Nauchno-Issled Inst Orosh Zemled Ovoshchevod — Trudy Moldavskogo Nauchno-Issledovatel'skogo Instituta Oroshaemogo Zemledeliya i Ovoshchevodstva

Tr Mold Nauchno Issled Inst Pishch Promsti — Trudy Moldavskogo Nauchno-Issledovatel'skogo Instituta Pishchevoi Promyshlennosti

Tr Mold Nauchno Issled Inst Tuberk — Trudy Moldavskogo Nauchno-Issledovatel'nogo Instituta Tuberkuleza

Tr Mold Nauchno Issled Inst Zhivotnovod Vet — Trudy Moldavskii Nauchno-Issledovatel'skii Institut Zhivotnovodstva i Veterinarii

Tr Molodykh Uch Dagest Nauchno Issled Inst Selsk Khoz — Trudy Molodykh Uchenykh Dagestanskii Nauchno-Issledovatel'skii Institut Sel'skogo Khozyaistva

Tr Molodykh Uch Spets Chuv Skh Inst — Trudy Molodykh Uchenykh Spetsial'nogo Chuvashskogo Sel'skokhozyaistvennogo Instituta

Tr Molodykh Uch Ukr Skh Akad — Trudy Molodykh Uchenykh Ukrainskoi Sel'skokhozyaistvennoi Akademii

Tr Molodykh Uch Yakutsk Univ — Trudy Molodykh Uchenykh Yakutskogo Universiteta

Tr Molotov Gos Med Inst — Trudy Molotovskogo Gosudarstvennogo Meditsinskogo Instituta

Tr Mord Gos Zapovednika Im P G Smirovicha — Trudy Mordovskogo Gosudarstvennogo Zapovednika Imeni P. G. Smirovicha

Tr Morsk Biol Stn Stalin — Trudove na Morskata Biologichna Stantsiya v Stalin

Tr Morsk Gidrofiz Inst Akad Nauk Ukr SSR — Trudy Morskogo Gidrofizicheskogo Instituta Akademiya Nauk Ukrainskoj SSR

Tr Morsk Rybn Inst Ser A (Gdynia Pol) — Trudy Morskogo Rybnogo Instituta. Seriya A. Okeanografiya i Promyslovaya Ikhtiologiya (Gdynia, Poland)

Tr Morsk Rybn Inst Ser B (Gdynia Pol) — Trudy Morskogo Rybnogo Instituta. Seriya B (Gdynia, Poland)

Tr Mosk Aviats Inst Im S Ordzhonikidze Sb Statei — Trudy Moskovskij Aviatsionnyj Institut Imeni S. Ordzhonikidze Sbornik Statei

Tr Mosk Aviats Tekhnol Inst — Trudy Moskovskij Aviatsionnyj Tekhnologicheskij Institut

Tr Mosk Avtomob Dorozhn Inst — Trudy Moskovskogo Avtomobil'no Dorozhnogo Instituta

Tr Mosk Ehnerg Inst — Trudy Moskovskogo Ordena Lenina Ehnergiticheskogo Instituta

Tr Mosk Energ Inst — Trudy Moskovskogo Energeticheskogo Instituta

Tr Mosk Energ Inst Fiz — Trudy Moskovskogo Energeticheskogo Instituta Fizika

Tr Mosk Fiz Tekh Inst — Trudy Moskovskii Fiziko-Tekhnicheskii Institut

Tr Mosk Fiz Tekh Inst Ser "Obshch Mol Fiz" — Trudy Moskovskogo Fiziko-Tekhnicheskogo Instituta. Seriya "Obshchaya i Molekulyarnaya Fizika"

Tr Mosk Geol Razved Inst — Trudy Moskovskogo Geologo-Razvedochnogo Instituta

Tr Mosk Geol Upr — Trudy Moskovskogo Geologicheskogo Upravlenie

Tr Mosk Gor Bakteriol Inst — Trudy Moskovskii Gorodskoi Bakteriologicheskii Institut

Tr Mosk Gor Inst Epidemiol Bakteriol — Trudy Moskovskii Gorodskoi Institut Epidemiologii i Bakteriologii

Tr Mosk Gor Nauchno Issled Inst Epidemiol Bakteriol — Trudy Moskovskii Gorodskoi Nauchno-Issledovatel'skii Institut Epidemiologii i Bakteriologii

Tr Mosk Gor Nauchno Issled Inst Skoroi Pomoshchi — Trudy Moskovskogo Gorodskogo Nauchno-Issledovatel'skogo Instituta Skoroi Promoshchi

Tr Mosk Gorn Inst — Trudy Moskovskogo Gornogo Instituta

Tr Mosk Inst Elektron Mashinostr — Trudy Moskovskii Institut Elektronnogo Mashinostroeniya

Tr Mosk Inst Epidemiol Mikrobiol Gig — Trudy Moskovskii Institut Epidemiologii, Mikrobiologii, i Gigieny

Tr Mosk Inst Inzh Gor Stroit — Trudy Moskovskogo Instituta Inzhenerov Gorodskogo Stroitel'stva

Tr Mosk Inst Inzh Zheleznodorozhn Transp — Trudy Moskovskogo Instituta Inzhenerov Zheleznodorozhnogo Transporta

Tr Mosk Inst Khim Mashinostr — Trudy Moskovskogo Instituta Khimicheskogo Mashinostroeniya

Tr Mosk Inst Nar Khoz — Trudy Moskovskogo Instituta Narodnogo Khozyaistva

Tr Mosk Inst Neftekhim Gazov Prom-Sti Im I M Gubkina — Trudy Moskovskii Institut Neftekhimicheskoi i Gazovoi Promyshlennosti Imeni I. M. Gubkina

Tr Mosk Inst Neftekhim Gaz Promsti — Trudy Moskovskii Institut Neftekhimicheskoi i Gazovoi Promyshlennosti

Tr Mosk Inst Radiotekh Elektron Avtom — Trudy Moskovskogo Instituta Radiotekhniki, Elektroniki, i Avtomatiki

Tr Mosk Inst Tonkoi Khim Tekhnol — Trudy Moskovskogo Instituta Tonkoi Khimicheskoi Tekhnologii

Tr Mosk Inzh Ekon Inst — Trudy Moskovskogo Inzhenerno-Ekonomicheskogo Instituta

Tr Mosk Khim-Tekhnol Inst — Trudy Moskovskogo Khimiko-Tekhnologicheskogo Instituta Imeni D. I. Mendeleeva

Tr Mosk Mat O-Va — Trudy Moskovskogo Matematicheskogo Obshchestva

Tr Mosk Med Stomatol Inst — Trudy Moskovskogo Meditsinskogo Stomatologichesko Instituta

Tr Mosk Nauchno-Issled Inst Epidemiol Mikrobiol — Trudy Moskovskogo Nauchno-Issledovatel'skogo Instituta Epidemiologii i Mikrobiologii

Tr Mosk Nauchno Issled Inst Epidemiol Mikrobiol Gig — Trudy Moskovskii Nauchno-Issledovatel'skii Institut Epidemiologii, Mikrobiologii, i Gigieny

Tr Mosk Nauchno-Issled Inst Psikhiatr — Trudy Moskovskogo Nauchno-Issledovatel'skogo Instituta Psikhiatrii

Tr Mosk Nauchno-Issled Inst Ukha Gorla Nosa — Trudy Moskovskogo Nauchno-Issledovatel'skogo Instituta Ukha Gorla i Nosa

Tr Mosk Nauchno Issled Inst Virusn Prep — Trudy Moskovskii Nauchno-Issledovatel'skii Institut Virusnykh Preparatov

Tr Mosk Neft Inst — Trudy Moskovskii Neftyanoi Institut

Tr Mosk Obl Nauchno Issled Klin Inst Prakt Nevropatol — Trudy Moskovskogo Oblastnogo Nauchno-Issledovatel'skogo Klinicheskogo InstitutaPrakticheskoi Nevropatologii

Tr Mosk Obshch Ispyt Prir Otedel Biol — Trudy Moskovskoe Obshchestvo Ispytatelei Prirody Otedel Biologicheskii

Tr Mosk O-Va Ispyt Prir — Trudy Moskovskogo Obshchestva Ispytatelei Prirody

Tr Mosk O-Va Ispyt Prir Otd Biol — Trudy Moskovskogo Obshchestva Ispytatelei Prirody Otdel Biologicheskii

Tr Mosk Radiotekh Elektron Avtomat — Trudy Moskovskogo Instituta Radiotekhniki, Elektroniki, i Avtomatiki

Tr Mosk Tekh Inst Rybn Prom-Sti Khoz — Trudy Moskovskogo Tekhnologicheskogo Instituta Rybnoi Promyshlennosti i Khozyaistva

Tr Mosk Tekhnol Inst Myasn Molochn Prom-Sti — Trudy Moskovskogo Tekhnologicheskogo Instituta Myasnol Molochnol Promyshlennosti

Tr Mosk Tekhnol Inst Pishch Promsti — Trudy. Moskovskii Tekhnologicheskii Institut Pishchevoi Promyshlennosti

Tr Mosk Torf Inst — Trudy Moskovskogo Torfyanogo Instituta

Tr Mosk Vet Akad — Trudy Moskovskoi Veterinarnoi Akademii

Tr Mosk Vyssh Tekh Uchil — Trudy Moskovskogo Vysshego Tekhnicheskogo Uchilishcha

TRMPDU — University of Maryland. Sea Grant Program. Technical Report

Tr Murm Biol Stn — Trudy Murmanskoi Biologicheskoi Stantsii

Tr Murm Morsk Biol Inst — Trudy Murmanskogo Morskogo Biologicheskogo Instituta

TrN — Tribune des Nations [*newspaper*]

Tr Nakhich Kompleksn Zon Opytn Stn — Trudy Nakhichevanskoi Kompleksnoi Zonal'noi Opytnoi Stantsii

Tr Nakhich Kompleksn Zon Stn — Trudy Nakhichevanskaya Kompleksnaya Zonal'naya Stantsiya

Tr Nauch Issled Inst Klopkovod (Tashkent) — Trudy Nauchno-Issledovatel'skii Institut po Khlopkovodstvu (Tashkent)

Tr Nauchn Konf Stalinskogo Gos Pedagog Inst — Trudy Nauchnoi Konferentsii Stalinskogo Gosudarstvennogo Pedagogicheskogo Instituta

Tr Nauchn Korresp Inst Stroit Dela Akad Nauk Gruz SSR — Trudy Nauchnykh Korrespondentov Instituta Stroitel'nogo Dela Akademiya Nauk Gruzinskoi SSR

Tr Nauchno Issled Dizeln Inst — Trudy Nauchno-Issledovatel'skogo Dizel'nogo Instituta

Tr Nauchno-Issled Gidrometerol Inst (Alma-Ata) — Trudy Nauchno-Issledovatel'skogo Gidrometeorologicheskogo Instituta (Alma-Ata)

Tr Nauchno-Issled Inst Betona Zhelezobetona — Trudy Nauchno-Issledovatel'skogo Instituta Betona i Zhelezobetona

Tr Nauchno Issled Inst Biol Biofiz Tomsk Gos Univ — Trudy Nauchno-Issledovatel'skogo Instituta Biologii i Biofiziki pri Tomskom Gosudarstvennom Universitete

Tr Nauchno-Issled Inst Biol Khar'k Gos Univ — Trudy Nauchno-Issledovatel'skogo Instituta Biologii Khar'kovskogo Gosudarstvennogo Universiteta

Tr Nauchno-Issled Inst Dobyche Pererab Slantsev — Trudy Nauchno-Issledovatel'skogo Instituta po Dobyche i Pererabotke Slantsev

Tr Nauchno-Issled Inst Eksp Klin Ter Gruz SSR — Trudy Nauchno-Issledovatel'skogo Instituta Eksperimental'noi i Klinicheskoi Terapii Gruzinskoi SSR

Tr Nauchno-Issled Inst Epidemiol Mikrobiol — Trudy Nauchno-Issledovatel'skogo Instituta Epidemiologii i Mikrobiologii

Tr Nauchno Issled Inst Fiziol — Trudy Nauchno-Issledovatel'skogo Instituta Fiziologii

Tr Nauchno-Issled Inst Fiziol Patol Zhen — Trudy Nauchno-Issledovatel'skogo Instituta Fiziologii i Patologii Zhenshchiny

Tr Nauchno-Issled Inst Geol Arktiki — Trudy Nauchno-Issledovatel'skogo Instituta Geologii Arktiki

Tr Nauchno Issled Inst Geol Mineral — Trudy Nauchno-Issledovatel'skogo Instituta Geologii i Mineralogii

Tr Nauchno Issled Inst Gidrometeorol Priborostr — Trudy Nauchno-Issledovatel'skii Institut Gidrometeorologicheskogo Priborostroeniya

Tr Nauchno Issled Inst Gig Vodn Transp — Trudy Nauchno-Issledovatel'skogo Instituta Gigieny Vodnoi Transportatsii

Tr Nauchno Issled Inst Kabeln Prom — Trudy Nauchno-Issledovatel'skogo Instituta Kabel'noi Promyshlennosti

Tr Nauchno Issled Inst Kamnya Silik — Trudy Nauchno-Issledovatel'skogo Instituta Kamnya i Silikatov

Tr Nauchno-Issled Inst Kartofel'n Khoz — Trudy Nauchno-Issledovatel'skogo Instituta Kartofel'nogo Khozyaistva

Tr Nauchno-Issled Inst Kartofel'nogo Khoz — Trudy Nauchno-Issledovatel'skogo Instituta Kartofel'nogo Khozyaistva

Tr Nauchno-Issled Inst Klin Eksp Khir — Trudy Nauchno-Issledovatel'skogo Instituta Klinicheskoi i Eksperimental'noi Khirurgii

Tr Nauchno-Issled Inst Kraev Patol (Alma-Ata) — Trudy Nauchno-Issledovatel'skogo Instituta Kraevoi Patologii (Alma-Ata)

Tr Nauchno-Issled Inst Legk Met — Trudy Nauchno-Issledovatel'skogo Instituta Legkikh Metallov

Tr Nauchno-Issled Inst Med Parazitol Trop Med Gruz SSR — Trudy Nauchno-Issledovatel'skogo Instituta Meditsinskoi Parazitologii i Tropicheskoi Meditsiny Gruzinskoi SSR

Tr Nauchno-Issled Inst Mekh Rybn Promsti — Trudy Nauchno-Issledovatel'skogo Instituta Mekhanizatsii Rybnoi Promyshlennosti

Tr Nauchno Issled Inst Mestnoi Topl Promsti — Trudy Nauchno-Issledovatel'skogo Instituta Mestnoi i Toplivnoi Promyshlennosti

Tr Nauchno Issled Inst Minist Radiotekh Promsti SSSR — Trudy Nauchno-Issledovatel'skogo Instituta Ministerstvo Radiotekhnicheskoi Promyshlennosti SSSR

Tr Nauchno Issled Inst Neftekhim Proizvod — Trudy Nauchno-Issledovatel'skii Institut Neftekhimicheskikh Proizvodstv

Tr Nauchno Issled Inst Okhr Tr Prof Zabol — Trudy Nauchno-Issledovatel'skogo Instituta Okhrany Truda i Professional'nykh Zabolevanii

Tr Nauchno-Issled Inst Onkol Gruz SSR — Trudy Nauchno-Issledovatel'skogo Instituta Onkologii Gruzinskoi SSR

Tr Nauchno Issled Inst Onkol (Tiflis) — Trudy Nauchno-Issledovatel'skii Institut Onkologii (Tiflis)

Tr Nauchno Issled Inst Osnovnoi Khim — Trudy Nauchno-Issledovatel'skogo Instituta Osnovnoi Khimii

Tr Nauchno Issled Inst Pishch Promsti — Trudy Nauchno-Issledovatel'skogo Instituta Pishchevoi Promyshlennosti

Tr Nauchno Issled Inst Pochvoved Agrokhim Melior (Tiflis) — Trudy Nauchno-Issledovatel'skogo Instituta Pochvovedeniya Agrokhimii i Melioratsii (Tiflis)

Tr Nauchno Issled Inst Pochvoved Agrokhim Yerevan — Trudy Nauchno-Issledovatel'skogo Instituta Pochvovedeniya i Agrokhimii Yerevan

Tr Nauchno Issled Inst Pochvoved Tadzh SSR — Trudy Nauchno-Issledovatel'skogo Instituta Pochvovedeniya Tadzhikskoi SSR

Tr Nauchno-Issled Inst Profil Pnevmokoniozov — Trudy Nauchno-Issledovatel'skogo Instituta Profilaktiki i Pnevmokoniozov

Tr Nauchno-Issled Inst Rentgenol Radiol Onkol Az SSR — Trudy Nauchno-Issledovatel'skogo Instituta Rentgenologii Radiologii i OnkologiiAzerbaidzhanskoi SSR

Tr Nauchno Issled Inst Rezin Promsti — Trudy Nauchno-Issledovatel'skogo Instituta Rezinovoi Promyshlennosti

Tr Nauchno Issled Inst Rybn Khoz (Riga) — Trudy Nauchno-Issledovatel'skogo Instituta Rybnogo Khozyaistva (Riga)

Tr Nauchno Issled Inst Sadovod Vinograd Vinodel (Tashkent) — Trudy Nauchno-Issledovatel'skogo Instituta Sadovodstva. Vinogradarstva i Vinodeliya (Tashkent)

Tr Nauchno-Issled Inst Sel'sk Khoz Krainego Sev — Trudy Nauchno Issledovatel'skogo Instituta Sel'skogo Khozyaistva Krainego Severa

Tr Nauchno Issled Inst Shinnoi Promsti — Trudy Nauchno-Issledovatel'skogo Instituta Shinnoi Promyshlennosti

Tr Nauchno Issled Inst Sin Spirtov Org Prod — Trudy Nauchno-Issledovatel'skii Institut Sinteticheskikh Spirtov i Organicheskikh Produktov

Tr Nauchno-Issled Inst Slantsev — Trudy Nauchno-Issledovatel'skogo Instituta Slantsev

Tr Nauchno Issled Inst Teploenerg Priborostr — Trudy Nauchno-Issledovatel'skii Institut Teploenergeticheskogo Priborostroeniya

Tr Nauchno Issled Inst Transp Khraneniyu Nefti Nefteprod — Trudy Nauchno-Issledovatel'skii Institut po Transportu i Khraneniyu Nefti i Nefteproduktov

Tr Nauchno Issled Inst Tuberk — Trudy Nauchno-Issledovatel'skogo Instituta Tuberkuleza

Tr Nauchno-Issled Inst Udobr Insektofungits — Trudy Nauchno-Issledovatel'skii Institut po Udobreniyam i Insektofungitsidam

Tr Nauchno Issled Inst Virusol Mikrobiol Gig — Trudy Nauchno-Issledovatel'skogo Instituta Virusologii Mikrobiologii Gigieny

Tr Nauchno Issled Inst Zashch Rast Uzb SSR — Trudy Nauchno-Issledovatel'skogo Instituta Zashchity Rastenii Uzbekskoi SSR

Tr Nauchno Issled Inst Zhivotnovod (Tashkent) — Trudy Nauchno-Issledovatel'skogo Instituta Zhivotnovodstva (Tashkent)

Tr Nauchno Issled Inst Zhivotnovod Uzb Akad Skh Nauk — Trudy Nauchno-Issledovatel'skogo Instituta Zhivotnovodstva. Uzbekskaya Akademiya Sel'skokhozyaistvennykh Nauk

Tr Nauchno Issled Khim Inst Mosk Univ — Trudy Nauchno-Issledovatel'skogo Khimicheskogo Instituta Moskovskii Universitet

Tr Nauchno Issled Konstr Inst Mekh Rybn Prom-Sti — Trudy Nauchno-Issledovatel'skogo i Konstruktorskogo Instituta Mekhanizatsii Rybnoi Promyshlennosti

Tr Nauchno Issled Lab Geol Zarub Stran — Trudy Nauchno-Issledovatel'skaya Laboratoriya Geologii Zarubezhnykh Stran

Tr Nauchno Issled Proektn Inst Mekh Obrab Polezn Iskop — Trudy Nauchno-Issledovatel'skii i Proektnyi Institut Mekhanicheskoi Obrabotki Poleznykh Iskopaemykh

Tr Nauchno Issled Protivochumn Inst Kavk Zakavk — Trudy Nauchno-Issledovatel'skogo Protivochumnogo Instituta Kavkaza i Zakavkaz'ya

Tr Nauchno Issled Sekt Mosk Fil Inst "Orgenergostroi" — Trudy Nauchno-Issledovatel'skogo Sektora Moskovskogo Filiala Instituta "Orgenergostroi"

Tr Nauchno Issled Sel'sk Khoz Krainego Sev — Trudy Nauchno-Issledovatel'skogo Instituta Sel'skogo Khozyaistva Krainego Severa

Tr Nauchno Issled Tekhnokhim Inst Bytovogo Obsluzhivaniya — Trudy Nauchno-Issledovatel'skogo Tekhnokhimicheskogo Instituta Bytovogo Obsluzhivaniya

Tr Nauchno Issled Vet Inst Tadzh SSR — Trudy Nauchno-Issledovatel'skogo Veterinarnogo Instituta Tadzhikskoi SSR

Tr Nauchnoizsled Inst Cherna Metal — Trudove na Nauchnoizsledovatelskiya Institut po Cherna Metallurgiya

Tr Nauchnoizsled Inst Epidemio Mikrobiol — Trudove na Nauchnoizsledovatelskiya Instituta po Epidemiologiya i Mikrobiologiya

Tr Nauchnoizsled Inst Farm — Trudove na Nauchnoizsledovatelskiya Instituta po Farmatsiya

Tr Nauchnoizsled Inst Okhr Tr Prof Zabol — Trudove na Nauchnoizsledovatelskiya Instituta po Okhrana na Truda i Profesionalnite Zabolyavaniya

Tr Nauchnoizsled Inst Stroit Mater (Sofia) — Trudove na Nauchnoizsledovatelskiya Instituta po Stroitelni Materiali (Sofia)

Tr Nauchnoizsled Inst Tekst Promst (Sofia) — Trudove na Nauchnoizsledovatelskiya Instituta po Tekstilna Promishlenost (Sofia)

Tr Nauchnoizsled Inst Vodosnabdyavane Kanaliz Sanit Tekh — Trudove na Nauchnoizsledovatelskiya Institut po Vodosnabdyavane. Kanalizatsiya i Sanitarna Tekhnika

Tr Nauchnoizsled Khim Farm Inst — Trudove na Nauchnoizsledovatelskiya Khimiko-Farmatsevtichen Institut

Tr Nauchnoizsled Proektokonstr Tekhnol Inst Tekst Promst — Trudove na Nauchnoizsledovatelskiya. Proektokonstruktorski i Tekhnologicheski Institut po Tekstilna Promishlenost

Tr Nauchno Khim Farm Inst — Trudy Nauchnogo Khimiko Farmatsevtecheskogo Instituta

Tr Nauchno Proizvod Konf Agron Buryat Zoovet Inst — Trudy Nauchno-Proizvodstvennoi Konferentsii po Agronomii Buryatskii Zooveterinarnyi Institut

Tr Nauchno-Tekh Konf Leningr Elek-Tekh Inst Svyazi — Trudy Nauchno-Tekhnicheskoi Konferentsii Leningradskogo Elektro-Tekhnicheskogo Instituta Svyazi

Tr Nauchno Tekh Konf Leningr Elektrotekh Inst Svyazi — Trudy Nauchno-Tekhnicheskoi Konferentsii Leningradskogo Elektrotekhnicheskogo Instituta Svyazi

Tr Nauchno Tekh Ova Chern Metall — Trudy Nauchno-Tekhnicheskogo Obshchestva Chernoi Metallurgii

Tr Nauchn Ova Stud Erevan Gos Univ — Trudy Nauchnogo Obshchestva Studentov Erevanskii Gosudarstvennyi Universitet

Tr Nauchn Stud Ova Gork Politekh Inst — Trudy Nauchnogo Studencheskogo Obshchestva Gor'kovskii Politekhnicheskii Institut

Tr New York Acad Sc — Transactions. New York Academy of Sciences

TRNF — Theologische Rundschau. Neue Folge

TRNGA — Traffic Engineering

Tr NII Metrol Vyssh Uchebn Zaved — Trudy NII [*Nauchno-Issledovatel'skogo Instituta*] Metrologii Vysshikh Uchebnykh Zavedeniy

Tr Nikitsk Bot Sada — Trudy Nikitskogo Botanicheskogo Sada

Tr Nikolaev Korablestroit Inst — Trudy Nikolaevskogo Korablestroitel'nogo Instituta

Tr NIRMMI — Trudy NIRMMI

Tr Nizhnednepr Nauchno-Issled Stn Obleseniyu Peskov — Trudy Nizhnedneprovskoi Nauchno-Issledovatel'skoi Stantsii po Obleseniyu Peskov

Tr Nizhnevolzh Nauchno Issled Inst Geol Geofiz — Trudy Nizhnevolzhskogo Nauchno-Issledovatel'skogo Instituta Geologii i Geofiziki

TRNJA — Transportation Journal

Tr Norilsk Vech Ind Inst — Trudy Noril'skogo Vechernego Industrial'nogo Instituta

Tr Nov Appar Metod — Trudy po Novoi Apparature i Metodikam

Tr Novocherkassk Politekh Inst — Trudy Novocherkasskogo Politekhnicheskogo Instituta

Tr Novocherk Inzh Melior Inst — Trudy Novocherkasskogo Inzhenerno-Meliorativnogo Instituta

Tr Novocherk Politekh Inst — Trudy Novocherkasskogo Politekhnicheskogo Instituta

Tr Novocherk Vet Inst — Trudy Novocherkasskogo Veterinarnogo Instituta

Tr Novocherk Zootekh Vet Inst — Trudy Novocherkasskogo Zootekhnichesko-Veterinarnogo Instituta

Tr Novokuz Gos Inst Usoversh Vrach — Trudy Novokuznetskogo Gosudarstvennogo Instituta Usovershenstvovaniya Vrachei

Tr Novokuz Gos Inst Usoversh Vrachei — Trudy Novokuznetskogo Gosudarstvennogo Instituta Usovershenstvovaniya Vrachei

Tr Novokuz Gos Pedagog Inst — Trudy Novokuznetskogo Gosudarstvennogo Pedagogicheskogo Instituta

Tr Novosib Gos Med Inst — Trudy Novosibirskogo Gosudarstvennogo Meditsinskogo Instituta

Tr Novosib Inst Inzh Zheleznodorozhn Transp — Trudy Novosibirskogo Instituta Inzhenerov Zheleznodorozhnogo Transporta

Tr Novosib Inzh Stroit Inst — Trudy Novosibirskogo Inzhenerno-Stroitel'nogo Instituta

Tr Novosib Skh Inst — Trudy Novosibirskogo Sel'skokhozyaistvennogo Instituta

Tr Nurse — Trained Nurse

Tro — Table Ronde

Tr Obedin Semin Gidrotekh Vodokhoz Stroit — Trudy Ob'edinennogo Seminara po Gidrotekhnicheskomu i Vodokhozyaistvennomu Stroitel'stvu

Trockeneis Mitt — Trockeneis-Mitteilungen [*Wien*]

Tr Odess Gidrometeorol Inst — Trudy Odesskogo Gidrometeorologicheskogo Instituta

Tr Odess Nauchno-Issled Inst Epidemiol Mikrobiol — Trudy Odesskogo Nauchno-Issledovatel'skogo Instituta Epidemiologii i Mikrobiologii

Tr Odess S-Kh Inst — Trudy Odesskogo Sel'skokhozyaistvennogo Instituta

Tr Odess Tekhnol Inst — Trudy Odesskogo Tekhnologicheskogo Instituta

Tr Odess Tekhnol Inst Konservn Promsti — Trudy Odesskogo Tekhnologicheskogo Instituta Konservnoi Promyshlennosti

Tr Odess Tekhnol Inst Pishch Kholod Promsti — Trudy Odesskogo Tekhnologicheskogo Instituta Pishchevoi i Kholodil'noi Promyshlennosti

TROEA — Tekko Rodo Eisei

Tr Okeanog Kom Akad Nauk SSSR — Trudy Okeanograficheskoi Komissii. Akademiya Nauk SSSR

TRom — Tribuna Romaniei

Trommsdorff J Phm — Journal der Pharmacie fuer Aerzte und Apotheker

Trommsdorff N J Phm — Neues Journal der Pharmacie fuer Aerzte, Apotheker, und Chemisten. Trommsdorff

Tr Omsk Gos Nauchno-Issled Inst Epidemiol Mikrobiol Gig — Trudy Omskogo Gosudarstvennogo Nauchno-Issledovatel'skogo Instituta Epidemiologii Mikrobiologii i Gigieny

Tr Omsk Inst Molochn Khoz Omsk Zon Stn Molochn Khoz — Trudy Omskogo Instituta Molochnogo Khozyaistva i Omskoi Zonal'noi Stantsii po Molochnomu Khozyaistvu

Tr Omsk Med Inst Im M I Kalinina — Trudy Omskogo Meditsinskogo Instituta Imeni M. I. Kalinina

Tromso Mus Arsberetn — Tromso Museums Arsberetning

Tromso Mus Arsberetning — Tromso Museums Arsberetning

Tromso Mus Arsh — Tromso Museums Arshefter

Tromso Mus Skr — Tromsoe Museum. Skrifter

Trop Abstr — Tropical Abstracts

Trop Agr — Tropical Agriculture

Trop Agr (Ceylon) — Tropical Agriculturist (Ceylon)

Trop Agric — Tropical Agriculture

Trop Agric Ceylon — Tropical Agriculturist. Ceylon [*Agricultural Society Journal*]

Trop Agric (Colombo) — Tropical Agriculturist (Colombo)

Trop Agri (Ceylon) — Tropical Agriculturist (Ceylon)

Trop Agric Mag Ceylon Agric Soc — Tropical Agriculturist and Magazine of the Ceylon Agricultural Society [*Peradeniya*]

Trop Agric Manila — Tropical Agriculture (Manila)

Trop Agric Res Ser — Tropical Agriculture Research Series

Trop Agric Res Ser (Japan) — Tropical Agriculture Research Series (Japan)

Trop Agricst Mag Ceylon Agric Soc — Tropical Agriculturist and Magazine. Ceylon Agricultural Society

Trop Agri [Guildford England] — Tropical Agriculture [Guildford, England]

Trop Agri (Trinidad) — Tropical Agriculture (Trinidad)

Trop Agron Tech Memo Aust CSIRO Div Trop Crops Pastures — Australia. Commonwealth Scientific and Industrial Research Organisation. Division of Tropical Crops and Pastures. Tropical Agronomy. Technical Memorandum

Trop Anim Health Prod — Tropical Animal Health and Production

Trop Anim Prod — Tropical Animal Production

TROPB — Tropenlandwirt

Trop Bldg Stud — Tropical Building Studies. Building Research Station [London]

Trop Build Res Notes Div Build Res CSIRO — Tropical Building Research Notes. Division of Building Research. Commonwealth Scientific and Industrial Research Organisation

Trop Cyclones — Tropical Cyclones. Climatological Division. Weather Bureau. Philippines [Manila]

Trop Dent J — Tropical Dental Journal

Trop Dis Bull — Tropical Diseases Bulletin

Trop Doc — Tropical Doctor

Trop Doct — Tropical Doctor

Trop Ecol — Tropical Ecology

Tropenhyg SchrReihe — Tropenhygienische Schriftenreihe [Stuttgart]

Tropenlandwirt (Germany FR) — Tropenlandwirtschaft (Germany, Federal Republic)

Tropenmed P — Tropenmedizin und Parasitologie

Tropenmed Parasitol — Tropenmedizin und Parasitologie

Tropenpflanzer Beih — Tropenpflanzer. Beiheft

Trop Fd Nutr — Tropical Food and Nutrition [Suva]

Trop F H — Tropical Fish Hobbyist

Trop Fish Hobby — Tropical Fish Hobbyist [New York]

Trop Forest Notes — Tropical Forest Notes. Tropical Forest Research Center [Rio Piedras]

Trop For Notes — Tropical Forest Notes

Trop Gas — Tropical Gastroenteral

Trop Gastroenterol — Tropical Gastroenterology

Trop Geogr Med — Tropical and Geographical Medicine

Trop Geo Me — Tropical and Geographical Medicine

Trop Geo Med — Tropical Geographical Medicine

Trop Grain Leg Bul — Tropical Grain and Legume Bulletin

Trop Grain Legume Bull — Tropical Grain Legume Bulletin

Trop Grassl — Tropical Grasslands

Trop Grasslands — Tropical Grasslands

Trop Grasslds — Tropical Grasslands

Trophoblast Res — Trophoblast Research

Tropical Ag — Tropical Agriculturist

Trop Life — Tropical Life

Trop Man — Tropical Man

Trop Med — Tropical Medicine

Trop Med Hyg News — Tropical Medicine and Hygiene News

Trop Med Int Health — Tropical Medicine and International Health

Trop Med News — Tropical Medicine News [Bethesda]

Trop Med Parasitol — Tropical Medicine and Parasitology

Trop Med Res Stud Ser — Tropical Medicine Research Studies Series

Trop Med Vet Mosk — Tropicheskaya Meditsina i Veterinariya (Moskva)

Trop Natuur — Tropische Natuur. Nederlandsch-Indische Natuurhistorische Vereeniging [Weltevreden]

Trop Pest Bull — Tropical Pest Bulletin

Trop Pestic Res Inst Annu Rep — Tropical Pesticides Research Institute. Annual Report

Trop Pestic Res Inst Misc Rep — Tropical Pesticides Research Institute. Miscellaneous Report

Trop Pest Manage — Tropical Pest Management

Trop Pest Mgmt — Tropical Pest Management

Trop Prod Inst Crop Prod Dig — Tropical Products Institute. Crop and Product Digest

Trop Prod Inst Rep — Tropical Products Institute. Report

Trop Prod Q — Tropical Products Quarterly [London]

Trop Sci — Tropical Science

Trop Sci Cent Occas Pap (San Jose Costa Rica) — Tropical Science Center. Occasional Paper (San Jose, Costa Rica)

Trop Ser Yale Univ Sch For — Tropical Series. Yale University School of Forestry [New Haven]

Trop Silvic — Tropical Silviculture [Rome]

Trop Stored Prod Inf — Tropical Stored Products Information

Trop Stored Prod Inform — Tropical Stored Products Information

Trop Stor Prod Infor — Tropical Stored Products Information

Trop Subtrop Pflwelt — Tropische und Subtropische Pflanzenwelt

Trop Top — Tropic Topics [Loma Linda, California]

Trop Vet — Tropical Veterinarian

Trop Vet Bull — Tropical Veterinary Bulletin

Trop Vet Med Curr Issues Perspect — Tropical Veterinary Medicine. Current Issues and Perspectives

Trop Wd — Tropical Woods

Trop Woods — Tropical Woods

Trop Woods Yale Univ Sch For — Tropical Woods. Yale University School of Forestry

Tr Opytn Stn Plodovod Akad Nauk Gruz SSR — Trudy Opytnoi Stantsii Plodovodstva Akademii Nauk Gruzinskoi SSR

Trop Zool — Tropical Zoology

Tr Orenb Gos Med Inst — Trudy Orenburgskogo Gosudarstvennogo Meditsinskogo Instituta

Tr Orenb Nauchno Issled Inst Molochno Myasn Skotovod — Trudy Orenburgskii Nauchno-Issledovatel'skii Instituta Molochno-Myasnogo Skotovodstva

Tr Orenb Obl Otd Vseross-Nauchn O-Va Ter — Trudy Orenburgskogo Oblastnogo Otdeleniya Vserossiiskogonauchnogo Obshchestva Terapevtov

Tr Orenb Otd Vses Fiziol Ova — Trudy Orenburgskogo Otdeleniya Vsesoyuznogo Fiziologicheskogo Obshchestva

Tr Orenb Otd Vses Ova Fiziol — Trudy Orenburgskogo Otdeleniya Vsesoyuznogo Obshchestva Fiziologov

Tr Orenb Otd Vses Ova Fiziol Biokhim Farmakol — Trudy Orenburgskogo Otdeleniya Vsesoyuznogo Obshchestva Fiziologov, Biokhimikov, i Farmakologov

Tr Orenb Skh Inst — Trudy Orenburgskogo Sel'skokhozyaistvennogo Instituta

TROSA — Tropical Science

Tr Otd Fiziol Biofiz Rast Akad Nauk Tadzh SSR — Trudy Otdel Fiziologii i Biofiziki Rastenii Akademiya Nauk Tadzhikskoi SSR

Tr Otd Geol Buryat Fil Sib Otd Akad Nauk SSSR — Trudy Otdela Geologii Buryatskii Filial Sibirskoe Otdelenie Akademiya Nauk SSSR

Tr Otd Gorn Dela Metall Akad Nauk Kirg SSR — Trudy Otdela Gornogo Dela i Metallurgii Akademiya Nauk Kirgizskoi SSR

Tr Otd Pochvoved Akad Nauk Kirg SSR — Trudy Otdela Pochvovedeniya Akademiya Nauk Kirgizskoi SSR

Tr Otd Pochvoved Dagest Fil Akad Nauk SSSR — Trudy Otdela Pochvovedeniya Dagestanskogo Filiala. Akademii Nauk SSSR

Trouser — Trouser Press

Trout Salm — Trout and Salmon [Peterborough, London]

Tr O-Va Fiziol Azerb — Trudy Obshchestva Fiziologov Azerbaidzhana

T Roy Ent S — Transactions. Royal Entomological Society of London

T Roy Soc C — Transactions. Royal Society of Canada

TRP — Translantic Review (Paris)

TRP — Transportation Proceedings

TRP — Trefpunt

Tr Pacific Coast Oto-Ophth Soc — Transactions. Pacific Coast Oto-Ophthalmological Society

Tr Paleontol Inst Akad Nauk SSSR — Trudy Paleontologicheskogo Instituta Akademiya Nauk SSSR

Tr Path Soc London — Transactions. Pathological Society of London

TRPC — Tradicion. Revista Peruana de Cultura

Tr Pechoro Ilychskogo Gos Zapov — Trudy Pechoro-Ilychskogo Gosudarstvennogo Zapovednika

Tr Permsk Biol Nauchno Issled Inst — Trudy Permskogo Biologicheskogo Nauchno-Issledovatel'skogo Instituta

Tr Permsk Farm Inst — Trudy Permskogo Farmatseuticheskogo Instituta

Tr Permsk Gos Med Inst — Trudy Permskii Gosudarstvennyi Meditsinskii Institut

Tr Permsk Gos Nauchno-Issled Proektn Inst Neft Prom-Sti — Trudy Permskij Gosudarstvennyj Nauchno-Issledovatel'skij i Proektnyj Institut Neftyanoj Promyshlennosti

Tr Permsk Gos Skh Inst — Trudy Permskogo Gosudarstvennogo Sel'skokhozyaistvennogo Instituta

Tr Permsk Nauchno Issled Inst Vaktsin Syvorotok — Trudy Permskogo Nauchno-Issledovatel'skogo Instituta Vaktsin i Syvorotok

Tr Permsk S-Kh Inst — Trudy Permskogo Sel'skohozyaistvennogo Instituta

Tr Perv Mosk Med Inst Im I M Sechenova — Trudy Pervogo Moskovskogo Meditsinskogo Instituta Imeni I. M. Sechenova

Tr Pervogo Mosk Pedagog Inst — Trudy Pervogo Moskovskogo Pedagogicheskogo Instituta

Tr Petergof Biol Inst Leningr Gos Univ — Trudy Petergofskogo Biologicheskogo Instituta. Leningradskii Gosudarstvennyi Universitet

Tr Petergof Estest Nauchn Inst — Trudy Petergofskogo Estestvenno-Nauchnogo Instituta

Tr Petrogr Inst Akad Nauk SSSR — Trudy Petrograficheskogo Instituta. Akademiya Nauk SSSR

TRPLA — Transplantation

Tr Plodoovoshchn Inst — Trudy Plodoovoshchnogo Instituta

Tr Plodoovoshchn Inst Im I V Michurina — Trudy Plodovoshchnogo Instituta Imeni I. V. Michurina

Tr Plodovo-Yagodnogo Inst Im Akad R R Shredera — Trudy Plodovo-Yagodnogo Instituta Imeni Akademika R. R. Shredera

TRPNA2 — Trudy Rostovskogo Gosudarstvennogo Nauchno-Issledovatel'skogo Protivochumnogo Instituta Narkomzdrava SSSR

Tr Poch Inst V V Dokuchaeva Akad Nauk SSSR — Trudy Pochvennogo Instituta Imeni V. V. Dokuchaeva Akademiya Nauk SSSR

Tr Pochv Inst Im V V Dokuchaeva Akad Nauk SSSR — Trudy Pochvennogo Instituta Imeni V. V. Dokuchaeva Akademii Nauk SSSR

Tr Polyar Nauchno-Issled Proekt Inst Morsk Ryb Khoz Okeanogr — Trudy Polyarnyi Nauchno-Issledovatel'skii i Proektnyi Institut Morskogo RybnogoKhozyaistva i Okeanografii

TRPPA — Transplantation Proceedings

TRPRB — Transplantation Reviews

Tr Prik Bot Genet Sel Ser 10 — Trudy po Prikladnoi Botanike. Genetike i Selektsii. Seriya 10. Dendrologiya i Dekorativnoe Sadovodstvo

Tr Prikl Bot Genet Sel — Trudy po Prikladnoi Botanike Genetike i Selektsii

Tr Prikl Bot Genet Selek — Trudy po Prikladnoi Botanike Genetike i Selektsii

Tr Prikl Bot Genet Sel Ser 1 — Trudy po Prikladnoi Botanike. Genetike i Selektsii. Seriya 1. Sistematika, Geografia, i Ekologia Rastenii

Tr Prikl Bot Genet Sel Ser 2 — Trudy po Prikladnoi Botanike. Genetike i Selektsii. Seriya 2. Genetika, Seleksiya, i Tsitologiya Rastenii

Tr Prikl Bot Genet Sel Ser 3 — Trudy po Prikladnoi Botanike. Genetike i Selektsii. Seriya 3. Fiziologiya, Biokhimiya, i Anatomiya Rastenii

Tr Prikl Bot Genet Sel Ser 4 — Trudy po Prikladnoi Botanike. Genetike i Selektsii. Seriya 4. Semenovedenie i Semennoi Kontrol

Tr Prikl Bot Genet Sel Ser 5 — Trudy po Prikladnoi Botanike. Genetike i Selektsii. Seriya 5. Zernovye Kul'tury

Tr Prikl Bot Genet Sel Ser 6 — Trudy po Prikladnoi Botanike. Genetike i Selektsii. Seriya 6. Ovoshchnye Kul'tury

Tr Prikl Bot Genet Sel Ser 9 — Trudy po Prikladnoi Botanike. Genetike i Selektsii. Seriya 9. Tekhnicheskie Kul'tury

Tr Prikl Bot Genet Sel Ser 11 — Trudy po Prikladnoi Botanike. Genetike i Selektsii. Seriya 11. Novye Kul'tury i Voprosy Introduktsii

Tr Prikl Bot Genet Sel Ser 13 — Trudy po Prikladnoi Botanike. Genetike i Selektsii. Seriya 13. Regeraty i Bibliografia

Tr Prikl Bot Genet Sel Ser 14 — Trudy po Prikladnoi Botanike. Genetike i Selektsii. Seriya 14. Osvoenie Pustyn

Tr Prikl Bot Genet Sel Ser 15 — Trudy po Prikladnoi Botanike. Genetike i Selektsii. Seriya 15. Severnoe (Pripolyarnoe) Zemledelie

Tr Prikl Bot Genet Sel Ser A — Trudy po Prikladnoi Botanike. Genetike i Selektsii. Seriya A. Sotsialisticheskoe

Tr Primorsk S-Kh Inst — Trudy Primorskogo Sel'skokhozyaistvennogo Instituta

Tr Priokso Terrasnogo Gos Zapov — Trudy Priokso-Terrasnogo Gosudarstvennogo Zapovednika

Tr Probl Lab Khim Vysokomol Soedin Voronezh Gos Univ — Trudy Problemnoi Laboratorii Khimii Vysokomolekulyarnykh Soedinenii. Voronezhskii Gosudarstvennyi Universitet

Tr Probl Lab Osad Form Osad Rud Tashk Gos Univ — Trudy Problemnoi Laboratorii Osadochnykh Formatsii i Osadochnykh Rud Tashkentskii Gosudarstvennyi Universitet

Tr Probl Lab Silik Mater Konstr Voronezh Inzh Stroit Inst — Trudy Problemnoi Laboratorii Silikatnykh Materialov i Konstruktsii VoronezhskiiInzhenerno-Stroitel'nyi Institut

Tr Probl Temat Soveshch Akad Nauk SSSR Zool Inst — Trudy Problemnykh i Tematicheskikh Soveshchanii Akademiya Nauk SSSR Zoologicheskii Institut

Tr Proizvod Nauchno-Issled Inst Inzh Izyskaniyam Stroit — Trudy Proizvodstvennyi i Nauchno-Issledovatel'skii Institut po Inzhenernym Izyskaniyam v Stroitel'stve

Tr Pskov Obl Gos Skh Opytn Stn — Trudy Pskovskoi Oblastnoi Gosudarstvennoi Sel'skokhozyaistvennoi Opytnoi Stantsii

Tr Pushkin Nauchno-Issled Lab Razvedeniya S-Kh Zhivotn — Trudy Pushkinskoi Nauchno-Issledovatel'skoi Laboratorii Razvedeniya Sel'skokhozyaistvennykh Zhivotnykh

TRQUD — Transportation Quarterly

TRR — [*The*] Rohmer Review

Tr Radiat Gig Leningr Nauchno-Issled Inst Radiats Gig — Trudy po Radiatsionnoi Gigiene Leningradskii Nauchno-Issledovatel'skii Institut Radiatsionnoi Gigieny

Tr Radiats Gig — Trudy po Radiatsionnoi Gigiene

Tr Radiats Gig Leningr Nauchno-Issled Inst Radiats Gig — Trudy po Radiatsionnoi Gigiene Leningradskii Nauchno-Issledovatel'skij Institut Radiatsionnoj Gigieny

Tr Radievogo Inst Akad Nauk SSSR — Trudy Radievogo Instituta Akademiya Nauk SSSR

Tr Radiotekh Inst — Trudy Radiotekhnicheskogo Instituta

Tr Radiotekh Inst Akad Nauk SSSR — Trudy Radiotekhnicheskogo Instituta Akademiya Nauk SSSR

TRRB — Transportation Research Board. Special Report

TRRE — Transportation Research Record

TRREB — Transportation Research

TRRED — Transportation Research Record

Tr Resp Inst Epidemiol Mikrobiol — Trudove na Respublikanskiya Instituta po Epidemiologiya i Mikrobiologiya

Tr Resp Opytn Stn Kartofeln Ovoshchn Khoz Kaz SSR — Trudy Respublikanski Opytnoi Stantsii Kartofel'nogo i Ovoshchnogo KhozyaistvaKazakhskaya SSR

Tr Resp Ova Ftiziatrov Nauchno Issled Inst Tuberk Kaz SSR — Trudy Respublikanskogo Obshchestva Ftiziatrov Nauchno-Issledovatel'skogo Instituta Tuberkuleza Kazakhskoi SSR

Tr Resp Stn Zashch Rast — Trudy Respublikanskoi Stantsii Zashchity Rastenii

TRRFDP — Israel. Agricultural Research Organization. Division of Forestry. Triennial Report of Research

TRRIA — Translations Register-Index

Tr Rizh Inst Inzh Grazhdanskoi Aviats — Trudy Rizhskogo Instituta Inzhenerov Grazhdanskoi Aviatsii

Tr Rizh Nauchno Issled Inst Travmatol Ortop — Trudy Rizhskii Nauchno-Issledovatel'skii Institut Travmatologii i Ortopedii

TRRL Lab Rep — TRRL [*Transport and Road Research Laboratory*] Laboratory Report

TRRL Rep — TRRL [*Transport and Road Research Laboratory*] Report

TRRL Suppl Rep — TRRL [*Transport and Road Research Laboratory*] Supplementary Report

Tr Ross Inst Prikl Khim — Trudy Rossiiskogo Instituta Prikladnoi Khimii

Tr Rostov Na Donu Inst Inzh Zheleznodorozhn Transp — Trudy Rostovskogo-Na-Donu Instituta Inzhenerov Zheleznodorozhnogo Transporta

Tr Rostov-Na-Donu Inzh Stroit Inst — Trudy Rostovskii-Na-Donu Inzhenerno Stroitel'nyi Institut

Tr Roy Soc Edinb — Transactions. Royal Society of Edinburgh

Tr Roy Soc Trop Med Hyg — Transactions. Royal Society of Tropical Medicine and Hygiene

TrRS — Transactions. Royal Society of Canada

TRRS — Transport and Road Research Laboratory. Supplementary Report

Tr Ryazan Med Inst — Trudy Ryazanskogo Meditsinskogo Instituta

Tr Ryazan Radiotekh Inst — Trudy Ryazanskogo Radiotekhnicheskogo Instituta

TRS — Theologische Rundschau

TRS — Toronto. University. Romance Series

TRS — Transportation Research

TRSAA — Transaction. Royal Society of South Africa

Tr Sakhalin Obl Stn Zashch Rast — Trudy Sakhalinskaya Oblastnaya Stantsiya Zashchity Rastenii

Tr Samark Gos Univ — Trudy Samarkandskogo Gosudarstvennogo Universiteta

Tr Samar Skh Inst — Trudy Samarskogo Sel'skokhozyaistvennogo Instituta

Tr Sarat Avtomob Dorozhn Inst — Trudy Saratovskogo Avtomobil'no-Dorozhnogo Instituta

Tr Sarat Inst Mekh Selsk Khoz — Trudy Saratovskogo Instituta Mekhanizatsii Sel'skogo Khozyaistva

Tr Sarat Med Inst — Trudy Saratovskogo Meditsinskogo Instituta

Tr Sarat Nauchno Issled Vet Stn — Trudy Saratovskoi Nauchno-Issledovatel'skogo Veterinarnoi Stantsii

Tr Sarat Otd Vses Nauchno Issled Inst Ozern Rechn Rybn Khoz — Trudy Saratovskogo Otdeleniya Vsesoyuznogo Nauchno-Issledovatel'skogo InstitutaOzernogo i Rechnogo Rybn Khoz

Tr Sarat Ova Estestvoispyt Lyubit Estestvozn — Trudy Saratovskogo Obshchestva Estestvoispytatelei i Lyubitelei Estestvoznaniya

Tr Sarat S-Kh Inst — Trudy Saratovskogo Sel'skokhozyaistvennogo Instituta

Tr Sarat Zootekh Vet Inst — Trudy Saratovskogo Zootekhnicheskogo Veterinarnogo Instituta

Tr Sary Chelekskogo Gos Zap — Trudy Sary Chelekskogo Gosudarstvennogo Zapovednikia

TRSC — Transactions. Royal Society of Canada

TRSCA — Transactions. Royal Society of Canada

TRSCB — Transportation Science

Tr Sch Bul — Training School Bulletin

TRSE — Transactions of Royal Society of Edinburgh

Tr Sekt Astrobot Akad Nauk Kazakh SSR — Trudy Sektora Astrobotaniki Akademiya Nauk Kazakhskoi SSR

Tr Sekt Astrobot Akad Nauk Kaz SSR — Trudy Sektora Astrobotaniki Akademiya Nauk Kazakhskoi SSR

Tr Sekt Energ Azerb Fil Akad Nauk SSSR — Trudy Sektora Energetiki Azerbaidzhanskogo Filiala Akademii Nauk SSSR

Tr Sekt Fiziol Akad Nauk Az SSR — Trudy Sektora Fiziologii Akademiya Nauk Azerbaidzhanskoi SSR

Tr Sekt Fiziol Zhivotn Inst Biol Akad Nauk Latv SSR — Trudy Sektora Fiziologii Zhivotnykh Instituta Biologii Akademiya Nauk Latviiskoi SSR

Tr Sel Agrotekh Zashch Rast — Trudy po Selektsii Agrotekhnike i Zashchite Rastenii

Tr Semin "Bionika Mat Model Biol" — Trudy Seminara "Bionika i Matematicheskoe Modelirovanie v Biologii"

Tr Semin Zharostoikim Mater — Trudy Seminara po Zharostoikim Materialam

Tr Semipalat Med Inst — Trudy Semipalatinskogo Meditsinskogo Instituta

Tr Semipalat Zoovet Inst — Trudy Semipalatinskogo Zooveterinarnogo Instituta

Tr Sess Kom Opred Absol Vozrasta Geol Form Akad Nauk SSSR — Trudy Sessii Komissii po Opredeleniyu Absolyutnogo Vozrasta Geologicheskikh Formatsii Akademiya Nauk SSSR

Tr Sevansk Gidrobiol Stn — Trudy Sevanskoi Gidrobiologicheskoi Stantsii

Tr Sevastop Biol Stn Akad Nauk Ukr SSR — Trudy Sevastopol'skoi Biologicheskoi Stantsii Akademiya Nauk Ukrainskoi SSR

Tr Sevastop Biol Stn Im A D Kovalenskogo Akad Nauk Ukr SSR — Trudy Sevastopol'skoi Biologicheskoi Stantsii Imeni A. D. Kovalenskogo AkademiiNauk Ukrainskoi SSR

Tr Severokavkazskogo Gornometall Inst — Trudy Severokavkazskogo Gornometallurgicheskogo Instituta

Tr Sev Kavk Gornometall Inst — Trudy Severo-Kavkazskogo Gornometallurgicheskogo Instituta

Tr Sev Nauchno Issled Inst Gidrotekh Melior — Trudy Severnyi Nauchno-Issledovatel'skii Institut Gidrotekhniki i Melioratsii

Tr Sev-Oset Med Inst — Trudy Severo-Osetinskogo Meditsinskogo Instituta

Tr Sev-Oset S-Kh Inst — Trudy Severo-Osetinskogo Sel'skokhozyaistvennogo Instituta

Tr Sev Vost Kompleksn Inst Dalnevost Tsentr Akad Nauk SSSR — Trudy Severo-Vostochnogo Kompleksnogo Instituta Dal'nevostochnyi Tsentr Akademiya Nauk SSSR

Tr Sev Zapadn Nauchno Issled Inst Sel'sk Khoz — Trudy Severo. Zapadnogo Nauchno-Issledovatel'skogo Instituta Sel'skogo Khozyaistva

Tr Sev Zapadn Zaochn Politekh Inst — Trudy. Severo-Zapadnyi Zaochnyi Politekhnicheskii Institut

Tr Sib Fiz Tekh Inst Tomsk Gos Univ — Trudy Sibirskogo Fiziko-Tekhnicheskogo Instituta pri Tomskom Gosudarstvennom Universitete

Tr Sib Gos Nauchno Issled Inst Metrol — Trudy Sibirskii Gosudarstvennyi Nauchno-Issledovatel'skii Institut Metrologii

Tr Sib Lesotekh Inst — Trudy Sibirskogo Lesotekhnicheskogo Instituta

Tr Sib Metall Inst — Trudy Sibirskogo Metallurgicheskogo Instituta

Tr Sib Nauch-Issled Inst Zhivotn — Trudy Sibirskogo Nauchno-Issledovatel'skogo Instituta Zhivotnovodstva

Tr Sib Nauchno-Issled Inst Energ — Trudy Sibirskogo Nauchno-Issledovatel'skogo Instituta Energetiki

Tr Sib Nauchno-Issled Inst Geol Geofiz Miner Syr'ya — Trudy Sibirskogo Nauchno-Issledovatel'skogo Instituta Geologii, Geofiziki, i Mineral'nogo Syr'ya

Tr Sib Nauchno Issled Inst Lesn Promsti — Trudy Sibirskii Nauchno-Issledovatel'skii Institut Lesnoi Promyshlennosti

Tr Sib Otd Gos Nauchno-Issled Inst Ozern Rechn Rybn Khoz — Trudy Sibirskogo Otdela Gosudarstvennogo Nauchno-Issledovatel'skogo Instituta Ozernogo i Rechnogo Rybnogo Khozyaistva

Tr Sib Tekhnol Inst — Trudy Sibirskogo Tekhnologicheskogo Instituta

Tr Sikhote-Alinsk Gos Zapov — Trudy Sikhote-Alinskogo Gosudarstvennogo Zapovednika

TrsJH — Transafrican Journal of History

Tr Skh Samarkanskogo Inst — Trudy Sel'skokhozyaistvennogo Samarkanskogo Instituta

TRSL — Transactions. Royal Society of Literature

TRSLA — TRW Space Log

Tr Smolensk Gos Med Inst — Trudy Smolenskogo Gosudarstvennogo Meditsinskogo Instituta

Tr Smolensk Nauchno Issled Vet Stn — Trudy Smolenskoi Nauchno-Issledovatel'skoi Veterinarnoi Stantsii

TRSN — Transition

Tr Soc Trop Med and Hyg (London) — Transactions. Society of Tropical Medicine and Hygiene (London)

Tr Solyanoi Lab Vses Inst Galurgii Akad Nauk SSSR — Trudy Solyanoi Laboratorii Vsesoyuznyi Institut Galurgii Akademiya Nauk SSSR

Tr Sov Antarkt Eksped — Trudy Sovetskoi Antarkticheskoi Ekspeditsii

Tr Soveshch Ikhtiol Kom Akad Nauk SSSR — Trudy Soveshchanii Ikhtiologicheskoi Komissii Akademii Nauk SSSR

Tr Soveshch Morfogen Rast — Trudy Soveshchanii po Morfogenezu Rastenii

Tr Soveshch Poliploidiya Selek Akad Nauk SSSR — Trudy Soveshchaniya Poliploidiya i Selektsiya Akademiya Nauk SSSR

Tr Sovmestnaya Sov Mong Nauchno Issled Geol Eksped — Trudy Sovmestnaya Sovetsko-Mongol'skaya Nauchno-Issledovatel'skaya Geologicheskaya Ekspeditsiya

Tr Sov Sekts Mezhdunar Assots Pochvovedov — Trudy Sovetskoi Sektsii Mezhdunarodnoi Assotsiatsii Pochvovedov

Tr Soyuzn Geologopoisk Kontora — Trudy Soyuznaya Geologopoiskovaya Kontora

Tr Soyuznogo Nauchno-Issled Inst Priborostr — Trudy Soyuznogo Nauchno-Issledovatel'skogo Instituta Priborostroeniya

Tr Soyuzn Trest Razved Burovykh Rab — Trudy Soyuznyi Trest Razvedochno-Burovykh Rabot

Tr Sredneaziat Gos Univ — Trudy Sredneaziatskogo Gosudarstvennogo Universiteta

Tr Sredneaziat Gos Univ Ser 6 — Trudy Sredneaziatskogo Gosudarstvennogo Universiteta. Seriya 6. Khimiya

Tr Sredneaziat Gos Univ Ser 7a — Trudy Sredneaziatskogo Gosudarstvennogo Universiteta. Seriya 7a. Geologiya

Tr Sredneaziat Gos Univ Ser 7d — Trudy Sredneaziatskogo Gosudarstvennogo Universiteta. Seriya 7d. Pochvovedenie

Tr Sredneaziat Gos Univ Ser 8a — Trudy Sredneaziatskogo Gosudarstvennogo Universiteta. Seriya 8a. Zoologiya

Tr Sredneaziat Gos Univ Ser 8b — Trudy Sredneaziatskogo Gosudarstvennogo Universiteta. Seriya 8b. Botanika

Tr Sredneaziat Gos Univ Ser 9 — Trudy Sredneaziatskogo Gosudarstvennogo Universiteta. Seriya 9. Meditsina

Tr Sredneaziat Gos Univ Ser 10 — Trudy Sredneaziatskogo Gosudarstvennogo Universiteta. Seriya 10. Sel'skoe Khozyaistvo

Tr Sredneaziat Gos Univ Ser 11 — Trudy Sredneaziatskogo Gosudarstvennogo Universiteta. Seriya 11. Tekhnika

Tr Sredneaziat Gos Univ Ser 13 — Trudy Sredneaziatskogo Gosudarstvennogo Universiteta. Seriya 13. Varia

Tr Sredneaziat Nauchno Issled Gidrometeorol Institut — Trudy Sredneaziat Nauchno-Issledovatel'skii Gidrometeorologicheskii Institut

Tr Sredneaziat Nauchno Issled Inst Geol Miner Syrya — Trudy Sredneaziatskii Nauchno-Issledovatel'skii Institut Geologii i Mineral'nogo Syr'ya

Tr Sredneaziat Nauchno Issled Inst Irrig — Trudy Sredneaziatskogo Nauchno-Issledovatel'skogo Instituta Irrigatsii

Tr Sredneaziat Nauchno Issled Inst Lesn Khoz — Trudy Sredneaziatskogo Nauchno-Issledovatel'skogo Instituta Lesnogo Khozyaistva

Tr Sredne-Aziat Nauchno-Issled Protivochumn Inst — Trudy Sredne-Aziatskogo Nauchno-Issledovatel'skogo Protivochumnogo Instituta

Tr Sredne Volzh Skh Inst — Trudy Sredne-Volzhskogo Sel'skokhozyaistvennogo Instituta

T Rs S Afr — Transactions. Royal Society of South Africa

TRSTA — Transactions. Royal Society of Tropical Medicine and Hygiene

Tr Stalinab Astron Obs — Trudy Stalinabadskoi Astronomicheskoi Observatorii

Tr Stalinab Gos Med Inst — Trudy Stalinabadskogo Gosudarstvennogo Meditsinskogo Instituta

Tr Stalingr S-Kh Inst — Trudy Stalingradskogo Sel'skokhozyaistvennogo Instituta

Tr Stalinskogo Gos Med Inst — Trudy Stalinskogo Gosudarstvennogo Meditsinskogo Instituta

Tr Stalinskogo Gos Pedagog Inst — Trudy Stalinskogo Gosudarstvennogo Pedagogicheskogo Instituta

Tr Stavrop Kraev Nauchno-Issled Vet Stn — Trudy Stavropol'skoi Kraevoi Nauchno-Issledovatel'skoi Veterinarnoi Stantsii

Tr Stavrop Nauchno Issled Inst Selsk Khoz — Trudy Stavropol'skogo Nauchno-Issledovatel'skogo Instituta Sel'skogo Khozyaistva

Tr Stavropol Sel'skokhoz Inst — Trudy Stavropol'skogo Sel'skokhozyaistvennogo Instituta

Tr Stavrop S-Kh Inst — Trudy Stavropol'skogo Sel'skokhozyaistvennogo Instituta

TRSTM — Transactions. Royal Society of Tropical Medicine and Hygiene

TRSTMH — Transactions of the Royal Society of Tropical Medicine and Hygiene

Tr Stomatol Lit SSR — Trudy Stomatologov Litovskoi SSR

T Rs Trop M — Transactions. Royal Society of Tropical Medicine and Hygiene

Tr Stud Nauchno Tekh Ova Mosk Vyssh Tekh Uchil — Trudy Studencheskogo Nauchno-Tekhnicheskogo Obshchestva Moskovskoe Vysshe Tekhnicheskoe Uchilishche

Tr Stud Nauchn Ova Azerb Gos Med Inst — Trudy Studencheskogo Nauchnogo Obshchestva Azerbaidzhanskii Gosudarstvennyi Meditsinskii Institut

Tr Stud Nauchn Ova Khark Politekh Inst — Trudy Studencheskogo Nauchnogo Obshchestva Khar'kovskii Politekhnicheskii Institut

Tr Sukhum Bot Sada — Trudy Sukhumskogo Botanicheskogo Sada

Tr Sukhum Opytn Stn Efiromaslichn Kult — Trudy Sukhumskoi Opytnoi Stantsii Efiromaslichnykh Kultur

Tr Sverdl Gorn Inst — Trudy Sverdlovskogo Gornogo Instituta

Tr Sverdl Gos Med Inst — Trudy Sverdlovskogo Gosudarstvennogo Meditsinskogo Instituta

Tr Sverdl Med Inst — Trudy Sverdlovskogo Meditsinskogo Instituta

Tr Sverdl Nauchno Issled Inst Lesn Promsti — Trudy Sverdlovskii Nauchno-Issledovatel'skii Institut Lesnoi Promyshlennosti

Tr Sverdl Nauchno Issled Vet Stn — Trudy Sverdlovskoi Nauchno-Issledovatel'skoi Veterinarnoi Stantsii

Tr Sverdl Skh Inst — Trudy Sverdlovskogo Sel'skokhozyaistvennogo Instituta

Tr SZPI — Trudy SZPI

Tr Tadzh Astron Obs — Trudy Tadzhikskoi Astronomicheskoi Observatorii

Tr Tadzh Gos Med Inst — Trudy Tadzhikskogo Gosudarstvennogo Meditsinskogo Instituta

Tr Tadzh Med Inst — Trudy Tadzhikskogo Meditsinskogo Instituta

Tr Tadzh Nauchno Issled Inst Pochvoved — Trudy Tadzhikskogo Nauchno-Issledovatel'skogo Instituta Pochvovedeniya

Tr Tadzh Nauchno Issled Inst Selsk Khoz — Trudy Tadzhikskogo Nauchno-Issledovatel'skogo Instituta Sel'skogo Khozyaistva

Tr Tadzh Nauchno-Issled Inst Zemled — Trudy Tadzhikskogo Nauchno-Issledovatel'skogo Instituta Zemledeliya

Tr Tadzh Politekh Inst — Trudy Tadzhikskogo Politekhnicheskogo Instituta

Tr Taganrog Radiotekh Inst — Trudy Taganrogskogo Radiotekhnicheskogo Instituta

Tr Tallin Pedagog Inst — Trudy Tallinskogo Pedagogicheskogo Instituta

Tr Tallin Politekh Inst — Trudy Tallinskogo Politekhnicheskogo Instituta

Tr Tallin Politekh Inst Ser A — Trudy Tallinskogo Politekhnicheskogo Instituta. Seriya A

Tr Tallin Tekh Univ — Trudy Tallinskogo Tekhnicheskogo Universiteta

Tr Tambov Inst Khim Mashinostr — Trudy Tambovskogo Instituta Khimicheskogo Mashinostroeniya

Tr Tashk Farm Inst — Trudy Tashkentskogo Farmatsevticheskogo Instituta

Tr Tashk Gos Univ — Trudy Tashkentskogo Gosudarstvennogo Universiteta Imeni V. I. Lenina

Tr Tashk Gos Univ Im V I Lenina — Trudy Tashkentskogo Gosudarstvennogo Universiteta Imeni V. I. Lenina

Tr Tashk Inst Inzh Irrig Mekh Selsk Khoz — Trudy Tashkentskogo Instituta Inzhenerov Irrigatsii i Mekhanizatsii Sel'skogo Khozyaistva

Tr Tashk Inst Inzh Zh Zheleznodorozhn Transp — Trudy Tashkentskogo Instituta Inzhenerov Zheleznodorozhnogo Transporta

Tr Tashk Nauchno Issled Inst Vaktsin Syvorotok — Trudy Tashkentskogo Nauchno-Issledovatel'skogo Instituta Vaktsin i Syvorotok

Tr Tashk Politekh Inst — Trudy Tashkentskogo Politekhnicheskogo Instituta

Tr Tashk S-Kh Inst — Trudy Tashkentskogo Sel'skokhozyaistvennogo Instituta

Tr Tatar Gos Nauchno Issled Proektn Inst Neft Promsti — Trudy Tatarskii Gosudarstvennyi Nauchno-Issledovatel'skii i Proektnyi Institut Neftyanoi Promyshlennosti

Tr Tatar Nauchno Issled Inst Selsk Khoz — Trudy Tatarskii Nauchno-Issledovatel'skii Institut Sel'skogo Khozyaistva

Tr Tatar Neft Nauchno Issled Inst — Trudy Tatarskii Neftyanoi Nauchno-Issledovatel'skii Institut

Tr Tatar Otd Gos Nauchno Issled Inst Ozern Rechn Rybn Khoz — Trudy Tatarskogo Otdeleniya Gosudarstvennogo Nauchno-Issledovatel'skogo Instituta Ozernogo i Rechnogo Rybnogo Khozyaistva

Tr Tatar Resp Mezhved Sb — Trudy Tatarskii Respublikanskii Mezhvedomstvennyi Sbornik

Tr Tatar Resp Skh Opytn Stn — Trudy Tatarskoi Respublikanskoi Sel'skokhozyaistvennoi Opytnoi Stantsii

Tr Tatar Respub Gosud Sel'skokhoz Opyt Sta — Trudy Tatarskoi Respublikanskoi Gosudarstvennoi Sel'skokhozyaistvennoi Opytnoi Stantsii

Tr Tbilis Bot Inst Akad Nauk Gruz SSR — Trudy Tbilisskogo Botanicheskogo Instituta Akademiya Nauk Gruzinskoi SSR

Tr Tbilis Gos Med Inst — Trudy Tbilisskogo Gosudarstvennogo Meditsinskogo Instituta

Tr Tbilis Gos Pedagog Inst — Trudy Tbilisskogo Gosudarstvennogo Pedagogiceskogo Instituta Imeni A. S. Pushkina

Tr Tbilis Gos Univ — Trudy Tbilisskogo Gosudarstvennogo Universiteta

Tr Tbilis Gos Univ Im Stalina — Trudy Tbilisskogo Gosudarstvennogo Universiteta Imeni Stalina

Tr Tbilis Gos Univ Inst Prikl Mat — Trudy Tbilisskii Gosudarstvennyi Universitet Institut Prikladnoi Matematiki

Tr Tbilis Inst Lesa — Trudy Tbilisskogo Instituta Lesa

Tr Tbilis Inst Poliklin Funkts Nervn Zabol — Trudy Tbilisskogo Instituta i Polikliniki Funktsional'nykh Nervnykh Zabolevanii

Tr Tbilis Inst Usoversh Vrachei — Trudy Tbilisskogo Instituta Usovershenstvovaniya Vrachei

Tr Tbilis Mat Inst — Trudy Tbilisskogo Ordena Trudovogo Krasnogo Znameni Matematicheskogo Instituta

Tr Tbilis Nauchno-Issled Gidrometeorol Inst — Trudy Tbilisskogo Nauchno-Issledovatel'skogo Gidrometeorologicheskogo Instituta

Tr Tbilis Nauchno Issled Inst Priborostr Sredstv Avtom — Trudy Tbilisskogo Nauchno-Issledovatel'skogo Instituta Priborostroeniya i Sredstv Avtomatizatsii

Tr Tbilissk Bot Inst — Trudy Tbilisskogo Botanicheskogo Instituta

Tr Tekhnol Inst Pishch Promsti (Kiev) — Trudy Tekhnologicheskogo Instituta Pishchevoi Promyshlennosti (Kiev)

Tr Teor Polya — Trudy po Teorii Polya

Tr Ternop Gos Med Inst — Trudy Ternopol'skii Gosudarstvennyi Meditsinskii Institut

TrTh — Travail Theatral

TRTHB — Traitement Thermique

Tr Tom Nauchno Issled Inst Kabeln Promsti — Trudy Tomskogo Nauchno-Issledovatel'skogo Instituta Kabel'noi Promyshlennosti

Tr Tomsk Gos Univ — Trudy Tomskogo Gosudarstvennogo Universiteta

Tr Tomsk Gos Univ Im V V Kuibysheva — Trudy Tomskogo Gosudarstvennogo Universiteta Imeni V. V. Kuibysheva

Tr Tomsk Gos Univ Ser Khim — Trudy Tomskogo Gosudarstvennogo Universiteta Imeni V. V. Kuibysheva. Seriya Khimicheskaya

Tr Tomsk Inst Radioehlektron Ehlektron Tekh — Trudy Tomsk Instituta Radioehlektroniki i Ehlektronnoj Tekhniki

Tr Tomsk Med Inst — Trudy Tomskogo Meditsinskogo Instituta

Tr Tomsk Nauchno-Issled Inst Kabel'n Promsti — Trudy Tomskogo Nauchno-Issledovatel'skogo Instituta Kabel'noi Promyshlennosti

Tr Tomsk Nauchno-Issled Inst Vaksiny Syvorotok — Trudy Tomskogo Nauchno-Issledovatel'skogo Instituta Vaktsiny i Syvorotok

Tr Transp Energ Inst Akad Nauk SSSR Sib Otd — Trudy Transportno-Energeticheskogo Instituta Akademiya Nauk SSSR Sibirskoe Otdelenie

Tr Troitsk Vet Inst — Trudy Troitskogo Veterinarnogo Instituta

Tr Tselinograd Sel'skokhoz Inst — Trudy Tselinogradskogo Sel'skokhozyaistvennogo Instituta

Tr Tselinogr Gos Med Inst — Trudy Tselinogradskii Gosudarstvennyi Meditsinskii Institut

Tr Tselinogr Med Inst — Trudy Tselinogradskogo Meditsinskogo Instituta

Tr Tselinogr S-Kh Inst — Trudy Tselinogradskogo Sel'skokhozyaistvennogo Instituta

Tr Tsent Aerol Obs — Trudy Tsentral'noi Aerologicheskoi Observatorii

Tr Tsent Nauchno-Issled Gornorazved Inst — Trudy Tsentral'nyi Nauchno-Issledovatel'skii Gornorazvedochnyi Institut

Tr Tsent Nauchno-Issled Inst Tekhnol Mashinostr — Trudy Tsentral'nyi Nauchno-Issledovatel'skii Institut Tekhnologii i Mashinostroeniya

Tr Tsent Nauchno-Issled Proekt-Konst Kotloturbinnogo Inst — Trudy Tsentral'nogo Nauchno-Issledovatel'skogo i Proektno-Konstruktorskogo Kotloturbinnogo Instituta

Tr Tsentr Aerol Obs — Trudy Tsentral'noi Aerologicheskoi Observatorii

Tr Tsentr Aptechn Nauchno-Issled Inst — Trudy Tsentral'nogo Aptechnogo Nauchno-Issledovatel'skogo Instituta

Tr Tsentr Chernozemn Gos Zapov — Trudy Tsentral'nogo Chernozemnogo Gosudarstvennogo Zapovednika

Tr Tsentr Genet Lab I V Michurina — Trudy Tsentral'noi Genetiki Laboratorii I. V. Michurina

Tr Tsentr Genet Lab Vses Akad Skh Nauk — Trudy Tsentral'noi Geneticheskoi Laboratorii Vsesoyuznaya Akademiya Sel'skokhozyaistvennykh Nauk

Tr Tsentr Inst Prognozov — Trudy Tsentral'nogo Instituta Prognozov

Tr Tsentr Inst Travmatol Ortop — Trudy Tsentral'nogo Instituta Travmatologii i Ortopedii

Tr Tsentr Inst Usoversh Vrachei — Trudy Tsentral'nogo Instituta Usovershenstvovaniya Vrachei

Tr Tsentr Kaz Geol Upr — Trudy Tsentral'no-Kazakhstanskogo Geologicheskogo Upravleniya

Tr Tsentr Kom Vodookhr — Trudy Tsentral'nogo Komiteta Vodookhraneniya

Tr Tsentr Nauchno Issled Avtomob Avtomot Inst — Trudy Tsentral'nyi Nauchno-Issledovatel'skii Avtomobil'nyi i Avtomotornyi Institut

Tr Tsentr Nauchno-Issled Dezinfekts Inst — Trudy Tsentral'nogo Nauchno-Issledovatel'skogo Dezinfektsionnogo Instituta

Tr Tsentr Nauchno Issled Dizeln Inst — Trudy Tsentral'nogo Nauchno-Issledovatel'skogo Dizel'nogo Instituta

Tr Tsentr Nauchno-Issled Gornorazved Inst — Trudy Tsentral'nyj Nauchno-Issledovatel'skij Gornorazvedochnyj Institut

Tr Tsentr Nauchno Issled Inst Faner Mebeli — Trudy Tsentral'nogo Nauchno-Issledovatel'skogo Instituta Fanery i Mebeli

Tr Tsentr Nauchno Issled Inst Khim Pishch Sredstv — Trudy Tsentral'nogo Nauchno-Issledovatel'skogo Instituta Khimii Pishchevykh Sredstv

Tr Tsentr Nauchno Issled Inst Konditer Promsti — Trudy Tsentral'nogo Nauchno-Issledovatel'skogo Instituta Konditerskoi Promyshlennosti

Tr Tsentr Nauchno Issled Inst Krakhmalo Patochn Promsti — Trudy Tsentral'nyi Nauchno-Issledovatel'skii Institut Krakhmalo-Patochnoi Promyshlennosti

Tr Tsentr Nauchno Issled Inst Kurortol Fizioter — Trudy Tsentral'nogo Nauchno-Issledovatel'skogo Instituta Kurortologii i Fizioterapii

Tr Tsentr Nauchno Issled Inst Osetr Khoz Nauk SSR — Trudy Tsentral'nogo Nauchno-Issledovatel'skogo Instituta Osetrovogo KhozyaistvaNauk SSR

Tr Tsentr Nauchno Issled Inst Rentgenol Radiol — Trudy Tsentral'nogo Nauchno-Issledovatel'skogo Instituta Rentgenologii i Radiologii

Tr Tsentr Nauchno Issled Inst Sakh Promsti Moscow — Trudy Tsentral'nogo Nauchno-Issledovatel'skogo Instituta Sakharnoi Promyshlennosti Moscow

Tr Tsentr Nauchno-Issled Inst Spirt Likero-Vodochn Prom-Sti — Trudy Tsentral'nogo Nauchno-Issledovatel'skogo Instituta Spirtovoi i Likero-Vodochnoi Promyshlennosti

Tr Tsentr Nauchno Issled Inst Stroit Konstr — Trudy Tsentral'nyi Nauchno-Issledovatel'skii Institut Stroitel'nykh Konstruktsii

Tr Tsentr Nauchno Issled Inst Tekhnol Sudostr — Trudy Tsentral'nyi Nauchno-Issledovatel'skii Institut Tekhnologii Sudostroeniya

Tr Tsentr Nauchno Issled Inst Tuberk — Trudy Tsentral'nogo Nauchno-Issledovatel'skogo Instituta Tuberkuleza

Tr Tsentr Nauchno Issled Lab Novosib Med Inst — Trudy Tsentral'noi Nauchno-Issledovatel'skoi Laboratorii Novosibirskogo Meditsinskogo Instituta

Tr Tsentr Nauchno Issled Morsk Flota — Trudy Tsentral'nyi Nauchno-Issledovatel'skii Institut Morskogo Flota

Tr Tsentr Nauchno Issled Proektno Konstr Kotloturbinnyi Inst — Trudy Tsentral'nyi Nauchno-Issledovatel'skii i Proektno-Konstruktorskii Kotloturbinnyi Institut

Tr Tsentr Nauchno-Issled Rentgeno-Radiol Inst — Trudy Tsentral'nogo Nauchno-Issledovatel'skogo Rentgeno-Radiologicheskogo Instituta

Tr Tsentr Nauchno Issled Stn Skh Ispol'z Stochnykh Vod — Trudy Tsentral'noi Nauchno-Issledovatel'skoi Stantsii po Sel'skokhozyaistvennomu Ispol'zovaniyu Stochnykh Vod

Tr Tsentr Nauchnoizsled Inst Ribovud Varna Bulg Akad Nauk — Trudove na Tsentralniya Nauchnoizsledovatelski Institut po Ribovudstvo i Ribolov. Varna. Bulgarska Akademiya na Naukite

Tr Tsentr Sib Bot Sada — Trudy Tsentral'nogo Sibirskogo Botanicheskogo Sada

Tr Tul Gos Skh Opytn Stn — Trudy Tul'skoi Gosudarstvennoi Sel'skokhozyaistvennoi Opytnoi Stantsii

Tr Tul Mekh Inst — Trudy Tul'skogo Mekhanicheskogo Instituta

Tr Turkm Bot Sada Akad Nauk Turkm SSR — Trudy Turkmenskogo Botanicheskogo Sada Akademii Nauk Turkmenskoi SSR

Tr Turkm Fil Vses Neft Nauchno Issled Inst — Trudy Turkmenskogo Filiala Vsesoyuznogo Neftyanogo Nauchno-Issledovatel'skogo Instituta

Tr Turkm Gos Med Inst — Trudy Turkmenskogo Gosudarstvennogo Meditsinskogo Instituta

Tr Turkm Nauchno-Issled Inst Kozhynykh Bolezn — Trudy Turkmenskogo Nauchno-Issledovatel'skogo Instituta Kozhynykh Boleznei

Tr Turkm Nauchno Issled Trakhomatoznogo Inst — Trudy Turkmenskogo Nauchno-Issledovatel'skogo Trakhomatoznogo Instituta

Tr Turkm Politekh Inst — Trudy Turkmenskogo Politekhnicheskogo Instituta

Tr Turkm Skh Inst — Trudy Turkmenskogo Sel'skokhozyaistvennogo Instituta

Tr Turkm S-Kh Inst Im M Kalinina — Trudy Turkmenskogo Sel'skokhozyaistvennogo Instituta Imeni M. I. Kalinina

Tr Turk Nauchno Issled Inst Kozhynykh Bolezn — Trudy Turkmenskogo Nauchno-Issledovatel'skogo Instituta Kozhynykh Boleznei

Tr Tuvinskoi Gos Skh Opytn Stn — Trudy Tuvinskoi Gosudarstvennoi Sel'skokhozyaistvennoi Opytnoi Stantsii

T Rtv — Tidsskrift for Rettsvitenskap

Tr Tyazan Radiotekh Inst — Trudy Tyazanskogo Radiotekhnicheskogo Instituta

Tr Tyumen Ind Inst — Trudy Tyumenskogo Industrial'nogo Instituta

Tr Tyumen Otd Vses Nauchn Ova Anat Gistol Embriol — Trudy Tyumenskogo Otdeleniya Vsesoyuznogo Nauchnogo Obshchestva Anatomov, Gistologov, i Embriologov

Tr Tyumenskogo Ind Inst — Trudy Tyumenskogo Industrial'nogo Instituta

Tru — Tagesrundschau

TRu — Theologische Rundschau

TRU — Trouw

Trubn Proizvod Urala — Trubnoe Proizvodstvo Urala

Truck & Bus Trans — Truck and Bus Transportation

Truck & Bus Transp — Truck and Bus Transportation

Truck Bus Transpn — Truck and Bus Transportation

Truck Off-Highw Ind — Truck and Off-Highway Industries

Truck Top — Truck Topics. Goodrich Rubber Co. [Kitchener, Ontario]

Trud Antrop Tartu — Trudy po Antropologii (Tartu)

Trud Bulg Prir Druzh — Trudove na Bulgarskoto Prirodoispitatelno Druzhestvo [Sofiya]

Trud Chernomorsk Biol Sta Varna — Trudove ot Chernomorskata Biologichna Stantsiya v gr. Varna

Trud Erm — Trudy Gosudarstvennogo Ermitazha

Trud Etnogr Inst Sof — Trudove na Etnografiskiya Institut, Bulgarska Akademiya na Naukite (Sofiya)

Trud Geol Bulg — Trudove Vurkhu Geologiyata na Bulgariya [Sofiya]

Trud Geol Zav Skopje — Trudovi. Geoloski Zavod na NR Makedonija (Skopje)

Trud Inst Nar Zdrave — Trudove na Institutite za Narodno Zdrave (Sofiya)

Trud Inst Zhivot Sof — Trudove na Instituta za Zhivotnovodstvo (Sofiya)

Trud Inst Zool Sof — Trudove na Instituta po Zoologiya, Bulgarska Akademiya na Naukite (Sofiya)

Trud Inzh Stroit Fak Vissh Inst Nar Stop Stalin — Trudove na Inzhenerno-Stroitelna Fakultet, Vissh Institut za Narodno Stopanstvo (Stalin)

Trud Inzh Tekh — Trud Inzhenera i Tekhnika [S. Peterburg]

Trud Ist Muz — Trudy Gosudarstvennogo Istoricheskogo Muzeiia

Trud Mikrobiol Inst Sof — Trudove. Mikrobiologicheski Institut (Sofiya)

Trud Morsk Biol Sta Stalin — Trudove na Morskata Biologichna Stantsiya v Stalin

Trud Nauchnoizsled Inst Ribarst Ribna Prom — Trudove. Nauchnoizsledovatelski Institut po Ribarstvo i Ribna Promishlenost [Varna]

Trud Planin Prir Sta — Trudove. Planinska Prirodonauchna Stantsiya [Vitosha]

Trud (Tbil) — Trudy Instituta Istorii. Akademiia nauk Gruzinskoi SSR (Tbilisi)

Trud Tomsk — Trudy. Tomsk. Universitet

Trud Viss Ikonom Inst Karl Marks-Sofia — Trudove. Vissija Ikonomiceski Institut Karl Marks-Sofija

Trudy Akad Med Nauk SSSR — Trudy Akademii Meditsinskikh Nauk SSSR [Moskva]

Trudy Akad Nauk Azerb SSR — Trudy Akademii Nauk Azerbaidzhanskoi SSR [Baku]

Trudy Akad Nauk Litovsk SSR Ser B — Trudy. Akademii Nauk Litovskoi SSR. Seriya B.

Trudy Akad Nauk Litov SSR — Trudy Akademii Nauk Litovskoi SSR

Trudy Akad Nauk Litov SSR Ser A Obsc Nauki — Trudy Akademii Nauk Litovskoj SSR. Serija A. Obscestvennye Nauki

Trudy Akad Nauk Litov SSR Ser B — Trudy Akademii Nauk Litovskoi SSR. Serija B

Trudy Akad Nauk Tadzh SSR — Trudy Akademii Nauk Tadzhikskoi SSR [Stalinabad]

Trudy Akad Nauk Turkmen SSR — Trudy Akademii Nauk Turkmenskoi SSR

Trudy Akkavak Opyt Orosit Sta — Trudy Akkavakskoi Opytno-Orositel'noi Stantsii

Trudy Akush Ginek Obshch Mosk Univ — Trudy Akushersko-Ginekologicheskago Obshchestva pri Moskovskom Universitete [Moskva]

Trudy Akust Kom — Trudy Akusticheskoi Komisii. Akademiya Nauk SSSR [Moskva]

Trudy (Alma-Ata) — Trudy Instituta Istorii, Arkheologii i Etnografii. Akademiia nauk Kasachskoi SSR (Alma-Ata)

Trudy Alma Atin Bot Sada — Trudy Alma-Atinskogo Botanicheskogo Sada. Akademiya Nauk Kazakhskoi SSR [Alma-Ata]

Trudy Alma Atin Zoovet Inst — Trudy Alma-Atinskogo Zooveterinarnogo Instituta [Alma-Ata]

Trudy Altai Politehn Inst — Trudy Altaiskii Politehniceskii Institut Imeni I. I. Polizunova

Trudy Altaisk Gornometall Nauchno Issled Inst — Trudy Altaiskogo Gornometallurgicheskogo Nauchno-Issledovatel'skogo Instituta. Akademiya nauk Kazakhskoi SSR [Alma-Ata]

Trudy Altaisk Gos Zapov — Trudy Altaiskogo Gosudarstvennogo Zapovednika [Moskva]

Trudy Altaisk Politehn Inst — Trudy Altaiskii Politehniceskii Institut Imeni I. I. Polizunova

Trudy Altaisk Sel'khoz Inst — Trudy Altaiskogo Sel'skokhozyaistvennogo Instituta

Trudy Altajsk Politehn Inst — Trudy Altajskogo Politehniceskogo Instituta

Trudy Anapsk Opyt Sta Vinogr Vinod — Trudy Anapskoi Opytnoi Stantsii po Vinogradarstvu i Vinodeliyu

Trudy Andizhan Ped Inst — Trudy Andizhanskii Gosudarstvennyi Pedagogicheskii Institut

Trudy A N Tadzh — Trudy Akademiia Nauk Tadzhikskoi SSR

Trudy Antrop Obshch Imp Voenno Med Akad — Trudy Antropologicheskago Obshchestva pri Imperatorskoi Voenno-Meditsinskoi Akademii [S. Peterburg]

Trudy Aralo Kasp Kompleks Eksped — Trudy Aralo-Kaspiiskoi Kompleksnoi Ekspeditsii. Akademiya Nauk SSSR [Moskva]

Trudy Arh — Trudy Arhiva

Trudy Arhangel Lesotehn Inst — Trudy Arhangel'skogo Lesotehniceskogo Instituta Imeni V. V. Kuibysheva

Trudy Arkh Akad Nauk SSSR — Trudy Arkhiva Akademii Nauk SSSR [Moskva]

Trudy Arkhangel Lesotekh Inst — Trudy Arkhangel'skogo Lesotekhnicheskogo Instituta

Trudy Arkhangel Lesotekh Inst Im V V Kuibysheva — Trudy Arkhangel'skogo Ordena Trudovogo Kraskogo Znameni Lesotekhnicheskogo Instituta Imeni V. V. Kuibysheva

Trudy Arkt Antarkt Nauchno Issled Inst — Trudy Arkticheskogo i Antarkticheskogo Nauchno-Issledovatel'skogo Instituta [Leningrad]

Trudy Arkt Nauchno Issled Inst — Trudy Arkticheskogo Nauchno-Issledovatel'skogo Instituta [Leningrad]

Trudy Armyansk Fil Akad Nauk SSSR — Trudy Armyanskogo Filiala Akademii Nauk SSSR [Erevan]

Trudy Armyansk Geol Uprav — Trudy Armyanskogo Geologicheskogo Upravleniya. Ministerstvo Geologii i Okhrany Nedr SSSR

Trudy Armyansk Nauchno-Issled Inst Gidrotekh Melior — Trudy Armyanskogo Nauchno-Issledovatel'skogo Instituta Gidrotekhniki i Melioratsii [Erevan]

Trudy Armyansk Nauchno-Issled Inst Vinograd Vinodel Plodov — Trudy Armyanskogo Nauchno-Issledovatel'skogo Instituta Vinogradarstva Vinodeliya i Plodovodstva

Trudy Armyansk Nauchno-Issled Inst Zhivot Vet — Trudy Armyanskogo Nauchno-Issledovatel'skogo Instituta Zhivotnovodstva i Veterinarii

Trudy Armyansk Nauchno-Issled Vet Inst — Trudy Armyanskogo Nauchno-Issledovatel'skogo Veterinarnogo Instituta

Trudy Aspirantov Gruzin Sel'-Khoz Inst — Trudy Aspirantov Gruzinskogo Sel'skokhozyaistvennogo Instituta

Trudy Astrakh Gos Med Inst — Trudy Astrakhanskogo Gosudarstvennogo Meditsinskogo Instituta im. A. B. Lunacharskogo [Astrakhan]

Trudy Astrakh Ikhtiol Lab — Trudy Astrakhanskoi Ikhtiologicheskoi Laboratorii pri Upravlenii Kaspiisko-Volzhskikh Rybnykh i Tyulen'ikh Promyslov [Astrakhan]

Trudy Astrakh Nauch Rybokhoz Sta — Trudy Astrakhanskoi Nauchnoi Rybokhozyaistvennoi Stantsii [Astrakhan]

Trudy Astr Obs Imp Kazan Univ — Trudy Astronomicheskoi Observatorii Imperatorskago Kazanskago Universiteta

Trudy Astr Obs Kharkov Gos Univ — Trudy Astronomicheskoi Observatorii Khar'kovskogo Gosudarstvennogo Universiteta [Kharkov]

Trudy Astr Obs Leningr Gos Univ — Trudy Astronomicheskoi Observatorii Leningradskogo Gosudarstvennogo Universiteta [Leningrad]

Trudy Astr Obs Odes Univ — Trudy Astronomichnoyi Observatoriyi Odes'koho Universyteta [Odessa]

Trudy Astr Obs Petrogr Univ — Trudy Astronomicheskoi Observatorii Petrogradskago Universiteta [Petrograd]

Trudy Astrofiz Inst Alma Ata — Trudy Astrofizicheskogo Instituta. Akademiya Nauk Kazakhskoi SSR (Alma-Ata)

Trudy Astr Sekt Inst Fiz Riga — Trudy Astronomicheskogo Sektora Instituta Fiziki. Akademiya Nauk Latviiskoi SSR (Riga)

Trudy Avtom Svarke Flyus — Trudy po Avtomaticheskoi Svarke pod Flyusom [Kiev]

Trudy Azerbajdzansk Opytn Sta — Trudy Azerbajdzanskogo Opytnoj Stancii

Trudy Azerbajdzansk Stancii Vsesojuzn Inst Zasc Rast — Trudy Azerbajdzanskoj Stancii Vsesojuznogo Instituta Zascity Rastenij

Trudy Azerb Fil Akad Nauk SSSR — Trudy Azerbaidzhanskogo Filial. Akademii Nauk SSSR [Baku]

Trudy Azerb Inst Mikrobiol Epidem — Trudy Azerbaidzhanskogo Instituta Mikrobiologii i Epidemiologii [Baku]

Trudy Azerb Inst Nefti Khim — Trudy Azerbaidzhanskogo Instituta Nefti i Khimii [Baku]

Trudy Azerb Nauchno-Issled Inst Gidrotekh Melior — Trudy Azerbaidzhanskogo Nauchno-Issledovatel'skogo Instituta Gidrotekhniki i Melioratsii

Trudy Azerb Nauchno-Issled Inst Zhivot — Trudy Azerbaidzhanskogo Nauchno-Issledovatel'skogo Instituta Zhivotnovodstva

Trudy Azerb Vet Inst — Trudy Azerbaidzhanskogo Nauchno-Issledovatel'skogo Veterinarnogo Instituta

Trudy Bashkir Fil Akad Nauk SSSR — Trudy Bashkirskogo Filiala Akademii Nauk SSSR [Ufa]

Trudy Bashkir Nauch Inst Sel Khoz — Trudy Bashkirskogo Nauchnogo Instituta Sel'skogo Khozyaistva

Trudy Bashkir Nauchno Issled Inst Pererab Nefti — Trudy Bashkirskogo Nauchno-Issledovatel'skogo Instituta po Pererabotke Nefti

Trudy Bashkir Sel Khoz Inst — Trudy Bashkirskogo Sel'skokhozyaistvennogo Instituta [Ufa]

Trudy Baskir S-H Inst — Trudy Bashkirskogo Sel'skokhozyaistvennogo Instituta

Trudy Belaruski Sel Haspad Inst — Trudy Belaruski Sel'ska-Haspadarchy Instytut [Gorki]

Trudy Belorussk Gos Univ — Trudy Belorusskogo Gosudarstvennogo Universiteta v g. Minske

Trudy Belorussk Nauchno Issled Inst Melior Vod Khoz — Trudy Belorusskogo Nauchno-Issledovatel'skogo Instituta Melioratsii i Vodnogo Khozyaistva

Trudy Belorussk Nauchno Issled Inst Pishch Prom — Trudy Belorusskogo Nauchno-Issledovatel'skogo Instituta Pishchevoi Promyshlennosti

Trudy Belorussk Nauchno-Issled Inst Pochv — Trudy Belorusskogo Nauchno-Issledovatel'skogo Instituta Pochvovedeniya

Trudy Belorussk Sel'-Khoz Akad — Trudy Belorusskoi Sel'skokhozyaistvennoi Akademii

Trudy Belotserk Selekts Sta — Trudy Belotserkovskoi Selektsionnoi Stantsii [Bila-Tserkva]

Trudy Bessarab Obshch Estest — Trudy Bessarabskago Obshchestva Estestvoispytatelei i Lyubitelei Estestvoznaniya [Kishinev]

Trudy Biogeokhim Lab — Trudy Biogeokhimicheskoi Laboratorii. Akademiya Nauk SSSR [Leningrad]

Trudy Biol Fak Tomsk Gosud Univ — Trudy Biologiceskogo Fakul'teta Tomskogo Gosudarstvennogo Universiteta. Wissenschaftliche Berichte der Biologischen Fakultat der Tomsker Staats-Universitaet

Trudy Biol Fak Tomsk Gos Univ — Trudy Biologicheskogo Fakul'teta Tomskogo Gosudarstvennogo Universiteta [Tomsk]

Trudy Biol Inst Erevan — Trudy Biologicheskogo Instituta. Armyanskii Filial, Akademiya Nauk SSSR (Erevan)

Trudy Biol Inst Frunze — Trudy Biologicheskogo Instituta. Akademiya Nauk Kirgizskoi SSR [Frunze]

Trudy Biol Inst Sib Otd Akad Nauk SSSR — Trudy Biologicheskogo Instituta Sibirskoe Otdelenie Akademiya Nauk SSSR

Trudy Biol Inst Zapad Sib Fil Akad Nauk SSSR — Trudy Biologicheskogo Instituta. Zapadno-Sibirskii Filial. Akademiya Nauk SSSR [Novosibirsk]

Trudy Biol Nauchno Issled Inst Perm Gos Univ — Trudy Biologicheskogo Nauchno-Issledovatel'skogo Instituta i Biologicheskoi Stantsii pri Permskom Gosudarstvennom Universitete [Perm]

Trudy Biol Nauchno Issled Inst Tomsk Gos Univ — Trudy Biologicheskogo Nauchno-Issledovatel'skogo Instituta Tomskogo Gosudarstvennogo Universiteta [Tomsk]

Trudy Biol Nauchno Issl Inst Permsk Gosud Univ — Trudy Biologiceskogo Nauono-Issledovatel'skogo Instituta pri Permskom Gosudarstvennom Universitete. Travaux de l'Institut des Recherches Biologiques de Perm

Trudy Biol Sta Borok — Trudy Biologicheskoi Stantsii Borok. Akademiya Nauk SSSR [Moskva]

Trudy Biol Sta Ozere Naroch — Trudy Biologicheskoi Stantsii na Ozere Naroch'. Belorusskii Gosudarstvennyi Universitet im. V.I. Lenina [Minsk]

Trudy Bjuro Mikol Ucen Komiteta Glavn Upravl Zemleustr — Trudy Bjuro po Mikologii i Fitopatologii Ucenago Komiteta Glavnago Upravlenija Zemleustrojstva i Zemledelija

Trudy Blagoveshch Gos Med Inst — Trudy Blagoveshchenskogo Gosudarstvennogo Meditsinskogo Instituta

Trudy Borodinskoj Presnovodn Biol Stancii Karelii — Trudy Borodinskoj Presnovodnoj Biologiceskoj Stancii v Karelii. Berichte der Akademiker Borodin Biologischen Suesswasser Station

Trudy Bot Inst Akad Nauk SSSR Ser 4 Eksper Bot — Trudy Botaniceskogo Instituta Akademii Nauk SSSR. Ser. 4. Eksperimental'naja Botanika. Acta Instituti Botanici Academiae Scientiarum URPSS. Botanica Experimentalis

Trudy Bot Inst Akad Nauk SSSR Ser VI — Trudy Botaniceskij Institut Akademiya Nauk SSSR. Serija VI

Trudy Bot Inst Baku — Trudy Botanicheskogo Instituta. Azerbaidzhanskogo Filiala. Akademii Nauk SSSR (Baku)

Trudy Bot Inst Erevan — Trudy Botanicheskogo Instituta. Akademiya Nauk Armyanskoi SSR (Erevan)

Trudy Bot Inst Erevan — Trudy Botanicheskogo Instituta. Armyanskogo Filiaia. Akademii Nauk SSSR (Erevan)

Trudy Bot Inst Komarova — Trudy Botaniceskogo Instituta imeni Akademika V. L. Komarova

Trudy Bot Inst Tbilisi — Trudy Botanicheskogo Instituta. Akademiya Nauk Gruzinskoi SSR (Tbilisi)

Trudy Bot Inst Tiflis — Trudy Botaniceskogo Instituta (Tiflis)

Trudy Bot Sada Akad Nauk SSSR — Trudy Botaniceskogo Sada Akademii Nauk SSSR. Acta Horti Botanici Academiae Scientiarum Ante Petropolitani

Trudy Bot Sada Erevan — Trudy Botanicheskogo Sada (Erevan)

Trudy Bot Sada Kiev — Trudy Botanicheskogo Sada. Akademiya Nauk Ukrainskoi SSR (Kiev)

Trudy Bot Sada Mosk Gos Univ — Trudy Botanicheskogo Sada Moskovskogo Gosudarstvennogo Universiteta [Moskva]

Trudy Bot Sada Moskovsk Ordena Lenina Gosud Univ Lomonosova — Trudy Botaniceskogo Sada. Moskovskij Ordena Lenina Gosudarstvennyj Universitet imeni M. V. Lomonosova

Trudy Bot Sada Novosibirsk — Trudy Botanicheskogo Sada. Zapadnosibirskii Filial. Akademiya Nauk SSSR (Novosibirsk)

Trudy Bot Sadu Akad Nauk Ukrajinsk RSR — Trudy Botanicnogo Sadu Akademii Nauk Ukrajins'koji RSR

Trudy Briansk Lesokhoz Inst — Trudy Brianskogo Lesokhozyaistvennogo Instituta

Trudy Burjat Inst Obsc Nauk — Trudy Burjatskogo Instituta Obscestvennyh Nauk

Trudy Buryat Mongol Nauchno-Issled Vet Opyt Sta — Trudy Buryat-Mongol'skoi Nauchno-Issledovatel'skoi Veterinarnoi Opytnoi Stantsii

Trudy Buryat Mongol Zoovet Inst — Trudy Buryat-Mongol'skogo Zooveterinarnogo Instituta

Trudy Buryatsk Sel'khoz Inst — Trudy Buryatskogo Sel'skokhozyaistvennogo Instituta

Trudy Byuro Ent — Trudy Byuro po Entomologii [S. Peterburg]

Trudy Byuro Evgen — Trudy Byuro po Evgenike [Leningrad]

Trudy Byuro Genet — Trudy Byuro po Genetike [Leningrad]

Trudy Byuro Koltsev — Trudy Byuro Kol'tsevaniya [Moskva]

Trudy Byuro Metall Teplotekh Konstr — Trudy Byuro Metallurgicheskikh i Teplotekhnicheskikh Konstruktsii [Moskva]

Trudy Byuro Mikol Fitopat — Trudy Byuro po Mikologii i Fitopatologii [Petrograd]

Trudy Byuro Prikl Bot — Trudy Byuro po Prikladnoi Botanike [S. Peterburg]

Trudy Chelyabinsk Inst Mekhaniz Elektrif Sel Khoz — Trudy Chelyabinskogo Instituta Mekhanizatsii i Elektrifikatsii Sel'skogo Khozyaistva [Chelyabinsk]

Trudy Chelyabinsk Med Inst — Trudy Chelyabinskogo Meditsinskogo Instituta [Chelyabinsk]

Trudy CNIIKA — Trudy Gosudarstvennyi Vsesojuznyi Central'nyi Naucno-Issledovatel'skii Institut Kompleksnoi Avtomatizacii

Trudy Dagest Nauchno-Issled Inst Sel Khoz — Trudy Dagestanskogo Nauchno-Issledovatel'skogo Instituta Sel'skogo Khozyaistva

Trudy Dalnevost Fil Akad Nauk SSSR Ser Bot — Trudy Dal'nevostocnogo Filiala Akademii Nauk SSSR. Serija Botaniceskaja

Trudy Dalnevost Lesotekh Inst — Trudy Dal'nevostochnogo Lesotekhnicheskogo Instituta [Vladivostok]

Trudy Dalnevost Nauchno Issled Gidromet Inst — Trudy Dal'nevostochnogo Nauchno-Issledovatel'skogo Gidrometeorologicheskogo Instituta

Trudy Dalnevost Otd Akad Nauk SSSR — Trudy Dal'nevostochnogo Otdeleniya. Akademii Nauk SSSR

Trudy Dalnevost Politekh Inst — Trudy Dal'nevostochnogo Politekhnicheskogo Institute

Trudy Detskosel Akklim Sta — Trudy Detskosel'skoi Akklimatizatsionnoi Stantsii [Leningrad]

Trudy Din Razv — Trudy po Dinamike Razvitiya [Moskva]

Trudy Dnepropetr Inst Inzh Zheleznodorozh Transp — Trudy Dnepropetrovskogo Instituta Inzhenerov Zheleznodorozhnogo Transporta [*Dnepropetrovsk*]

Trudy Dnepropetr Khim Tekhnol Inst — Trudy Dnepropetrovskogo Khimiko-Tekhnologicheskogo Instituta [*Dnepropetrovsk*]

Trudy Dnepropetr Sel Khoz Inst — Trudy Dnepropetrovskogo Sel'skokhozyaistvennogo Instituta

Trudy Dnyprov Biol Sta — Trudy. Dnyprovs'ka Biolohichna Stantsiya [*Kyyiv*]

Trudy Doneck Politehn Inst — Trudy Doneckogo Politehniceskogo Instituta

Trudy Don Otd Imp Russk Tekh Obshch — Trudy Donskago Otdeleniya Imperatorskago Russkago Tekhnicheskago Obshchestva [*Rostov-na-Donu*]

Trudy Don Zonal'Inst Sel'Khoz — Trudy Donskago Zonal'nogo Instituta Sel'skogo Khozyaistva

Trudy Dreif Sta Sev Polyus — Trudy. Dreifuyushchei Stantsii Severnyi Polyus [*Moskva*]

Trudy Eksped Pamir Eksped 1928 — Trudy Ekspeditsii. Pamirskaya Ekspeditsiya 1928 [*Leningrad*]

Trudy Eksp Inst Silik — Trudy Gosudarstvennogo Eksperimental'nogo Instituta Silikatov [*Moskva*]

Trudy Endokr Lab Mosk — Trudy Endokrinologicheskoi Laboratorii. Institut Zhivotnovodstva [*Moskva*]

Trudy Energ Inst IG Esmana — Trudy Energeticheskogo Instituta im. I. G. Es'mana. Akademiya Nauk Azerbaidzhanskoi SSR [*Baku*]

Trudy Erevan Med Inst — Trudy Erevanskogo Meditsinskogo Instituta [*Erevan*]

Trudy Erevan Zoovet Inst — Trudy Erevanskogo Zooveterinarnogo Instituta [*Erevan*]

Trudy Ermit — Trudy Gosudarstvennogo Ermitazha

Trudy Estest Istor Ekon Obsled Kabardy — Trudy po Estestvenno-Istoricheskomu i Ekonomicheskomu Obsledovaniyu Kabardy [*Voronezh*]

Trudy Estest Istor Muz G Zardabi — Trudy Estestvenno-Istoricheskogo Muzeya im. G. Zardabi. Akademiya Nauk Azerbaidzhanskoi SSR [*Baku*]

Trudy Estest Istor Muz Simferopol — Trudy Estestvenno-Istoricheskago Muzeya (Simferopol)

Trudy Estestv Istoric Muz Tavricesk Gub Zemstva — Trudy Estestvenno-Istoriceskago Muzeja Tavriceskago Gubernskago Zemstva

Trudy Fak Terap Klin Imp Mosk Univ — Trudy Fakul'tetskoi Terapevticheskoi Kliniki Imperatorskago Moskovskago Universiteta [*Moskva*]

Trudy Fak Terap Klin Prof SV Levashova Imp Novo Ross Univ — Trudy Fakul'tetskoi Terapevticheskoi Kliniki Professora S. V. Levashova pri Imperatorskom Novo-Rossiiskom Universitete [*Odessa*]

Trudy Fedchenk Melior Opyt Sta — Trudy Fedchenkovskoi Meliorativnoi Opytnoi Stantsii [*Fedchenko*]

Trudy Fiz Inst Lebedev — Trudy Fizicheskogo Instituta Imeni P. N. Lebedeva

Trudy Fiz Inst PN Lebedeva — Trudy Fizicheskogo Instituta imeni P.N. Lebedeva. Akademiya Nauk SSR [*Moskva, Leningrad*]

Trudy Fiziol Inst Imp Mosk Univ — Trudy Fiziologicheskago Instituta Imperatorskago Moskovskago Universiteta [*Moskva*]

Trudy Fiz Khim Sek Obshch Opyt Nauk Kharkov — Trudy Fiziko-Khimicheskoi Sektsii Obshchestva Opytnykh Nauk [*Khar'kov*]

Trudy Fiz Mat Vidd Vseukr Akad Nauk — Trudy Fizychno-Matematychnoho Viddilu. Vseukrayins'ka Akademiya Nauk [*Kyyivi*]

Trudy Fiz Med Obshch Imp Mosk Univ — Trudy Fiziko-Meditsinskago Obshchestva pri Imperatorskom Moskovskom Universitete [*Moskva*]

Trudy Fiz Tekh Inst Ashkhabad — Trudy Fiziko-Tekhnicheskogo Instituta. Akademiya Nauk Turkmenskoi SSR [*Ashkhabad*]

Trudy Frunze Politehn Inst — Trudy Frunzenskogo Politehniceskogo Instituta

Trudy Geobot Obsl Pastb SSR Azerbajdzana Ser A Zimn Pastb — Trudy po Geobotaniceskomu Obsledovaniju Pastbisc SSR Azerbajdzana. Serija A. Zimnie Pastbisca

Trudy Geogr Fak Kirgiz Univ — Trudy Geograficheskogo Fakul'teta Kirgizskogo Universiteta

Trudy Geogr Otd Kom Izuch Estest Sil Ross — Trudy Geograficheskogo Otdela Komissii po Izucheniyu Estestvennykh Sil Rossii [*Leningrad*]

Trudy Geol Inst Frunze — Trudy Geologicheskogo Instituta. Akademiya Nauk Kirgizskoi SSR (Frunze)

Trudy Geol Inst Kazan Fil — Trudy Geologicheskogo Instituta. Kazanskii Filial. Akademiya Nauk SSSR [*Moskva*]

Trudy Geol Inst Leningr — Trudy Geologicheskogo Instituta. Akademiya Nauk SSSR (Leningrad, Moskva)

Trudy Geol Inst Tbilisi — Trudy Geologicheskogo Instituta. Akademiya Nauk Gruzinskoi SSR (Tbilisi)

Trudy Geol Kom — Trudy Geologicheskago Komiteta [*S. Peterburg*]

Trudy Geol Miner Muz — Trudy Geologicheskago i Mineralogicheskago Muzeya imeni Petra Velikago Imperatorskoi Akademii Nauk [*S. Peterburg*]

Trudy Geol Muz — Trudy Geologicheskogo Muzeya Akademii Nauk SSR [*Leningrad*]

Trudy Geol Razv Byuro Gaz Mestorozh — Trudy Geologo-Razvedochnogo Byuro Gazovykh Mestorozhdenii [*Moskva, Leningrad*]

Trudy Geometr Sem — Trudy Geometriceskogo Seminara

Trudy Geomorf Inst — Trudy Geomorfologicheskogo Instituta. Akademiya Nauk SSSR [*Moskva, Leningrad*]

Trudy Geom Sem Kazan Univ — Trudy Geometriceskogo Seminara Kazanskii Universitet

Trudy G Ermitazh — Trudy Gosudarstvennogo Ermitazha

Trudy Gidrav Lab — Trudy Gidravlicheskoi Laboratorii. Vsesoyuznyi Nauchno-Issledovatel'skii Institut Vodosnabzheniya, Kanalizatsii, Gidrotekhnicheskikh Sooruzhenii i Inzhenernoi Gidrogeologii

Trudy Gidrobiol Sta Glubok Ozere — Trudy Gidrobiologicheskoi Stantsii na Glubokom Ozere [*Glubokoe*]

Trudy Gidrobiol Stanciji — Trudy Gidrobiologicnoji Stanciji. Travaux de la Station Hydrobiologique

Trudy Glav Astr Obs Pulkove — Trudy Glavnoi Astronomicheskoi Observatorii v Pulkove

Trudy Glav Bot Sada Leningr — Trudy Glavnogo Botanicheskogo Sada. Akademiya Nauk SSSR (Leningrad)

Trudy Glav Bot Sada Petrogr — Trudy Glavnogo Botanicheskogo Sada (Petrograd)

Trudy Glav Geofiz Obs — Trudy Glavnoi Geofizicheskoi Observatorii Imeni A. I. Voeikova

Trudy Glav Geofiz Obs A I Voeikova — Trudy Glavnoi Geofizicheskoi Observatorii imeni A. I. Voeikova [*Leningrad, Moskva*]

Trudy Glav Geol Razv Uprav VSNKh — Trudy Glavnogo Geologo-Razvedochnogo Upravleniya V.S.N.Kh. SSSR [*Leningrad*]

Trudy Glav Ross Astrofiz Obs — Trudy Glavnoi Rossiiskoi Astrofizicheskoi Observatorii [*Moskva*]

Trudy Gorets Opyt Sta Moloch Kohz — Trudy Goretskoi Zonal'noi Opytnoi Stantsii Molochnogo Khozyaistva [*Gorki*]

Trudy Gorets Sel Khoz Opyt Sta — Trudy Goretskoi Sel'Skokhozyaistvennoi Opytnoi Stantsii [*Gory-Gorki*]

Trudy Gorkov Gos Med Inst — Trudy Gor'kovskogo Gosudarstvennogo Meditsinskogo Instituta [*Gor'kii*]

Trudy Gorkov Inst Inzh Vod Transp — Trudy Gor'kovskogo Instituta Inzhenerov Vodnogo Transporta [*Moskva*]

Trudy Gorkov Nauchno Issled Vet Opyt Sta — Trudy Gor'kovskoi Nauchno-Issledovatel'skoi Veterinarnoi Opytnoi Stantsii [*Gor'kii*]

Trudy Gor'kov Politehn Inst — Trudy Gor'kovskogo Politehniceskii Institut

Trudy Gor'kov Sel'-Khoz Inst — Trudy Gor'kovskogo Sel'skokhozyaistvennogo Instituta

Trudy Gork Politekh Inst Khim Tekhnol Silik Fak — Trudy Gor'kovskogo Politekhnicheskogo Instituta im. A. A. Zhdanoba. Khimiko-Tekhnologicheskii i Silikatnyi Fakultety [*Gor'kii*]

Trudy Gorno Geol Inst Novosibirsk — Trudy Gorno-Geologicheskogo Instituta. Zapadno-Sibirskii Filial. Akademiya Nauk SSSR (Novosibirsk)

Trudy Gorno Geol Inst Ural Fil — Trudy Gorno-Geologicheskogo Instituta. Ural'skii Filial. Akademiya Nauk SSSR

Trudy Gornotaezh Sta Vladiv — Trudy Gornotaezhnoi Stantsii (Vladivostok)

Trudy Gorsk Sel'-Khoz Inst — Trudy Gorskogo Sel'skokhozyaistvennogo Instituta

Trudy Gos Astr Inst Shternberga — Trudy Gosudarstvennogo Astronomicheskogo Instituta im. P.K. Shternberga [*Moskva*]

Trudy Gos Astrofiz Inst — Trudy Gosudarstvennogo Astrofizicheskogo Instituta [*Moskva*]

Trudy Gos Gidrobiol Inst — Trudy Gosudarstvennogo Gidrobiologicheskogo Instituta [*Leningrad*]

Trudy Gos Gidrol Inst — Trudy Gosudarstvennogo Gidrologicheskogo Instituta

Trudy Gos Inst Eksp Vet — Trudy Gosudarstvennogo Instituta Eksperimental'noi Veterinarii [*Moskva*]

Trudy Gos Inst Med Znan — Trudy Gosudarstvennogo Instituta Meditsinskikh Znanii [*Leningrad*]

Trudy Gos Inst Prikl Khim — Trudy Gosudarstvennogo Instituta Prikladnoi Khimii [*Leningrad*]

Trudy Gos Inst Tabakov — Trudy Gosudarstvennogo Instituta Tabakovedeniya [*Krasnodar*]

Trudy Gos Issled Elektrokeram Inst — Trudy Gosudarstvennogo Issledovatel'skogo Elektrokeramicheskogo Instituta [*Leningrad*]

Trudy Gos Nauchno Kontrol Inst Vet Prep — Trudy Gosudarstvennogo Nauchno-Kontrolnogo Instituta Veterinarnykh Preparatov

Trudy Gos Nikit Bot Sada — Trudy Gosudarstvennogo Nikitskogo Botanicheskogo Sada [*Yalta*]

Trudy Gos Okeanogr Inst — Trudy Gosudarstvennogo Okeanograficheskogo Instituta [*Moskva*]

Trudy Gos Opt Inst — Trudy Gosudarstvennogo Opticheskogo Instituta [*Leningrad*]

Trudy Gosp Khir Klin SP Fedorova — Trudy Gospital'noi Khirurgicheskoi Kliniki S.P. Fedorova [*S. Peterburg*]

Trudy Gos Soyuz Nauchno Issled Inst Radioveshch Prima Akust — Trudy Gosudarstvennogo Soyuznogo Nauchno-Issledovatel'skogo Instituta Radioveshchatel'nogo Priema i Akustiki [*Leningrad*]

Trudy Gosudarstvennoy Pub Bib M E Saltykova Shchedrina — Trudy Gosudarstvennoy Publichnoy Biblioteki M. E. Saltykova-Shchedrina

Trudy Gosud Dalnevost Univ Ser 13 Tehn — Trudy Gosudarstvennogo Dal'nevostocnogo Universiteta. Ser. 13. Tehnika/Memoiresde l'Universite d'Etat a l'Extreme Orient. Technique/Publications. Far-Eastern State University/ Veroeffentlichungen der Staatlichen Universitaet des Fernen Ostens

Trudy Gosud Nikitsk Bot Sada — Trudy. Gosudarstvennogo Nikitskogo Botaniceskogo Sada. Arbeiten aus dem Botanischen Garten Nikita, Jalta, Krim

Trudy Gos Vses Inst Proekt Nauchno Issled Rab Tsem Prom — Trudy Gosudarstvennogo Vsesoyuznogo Instituta po Proektirovaniyu i Nauchno-Issledovatel'skim Rabotam Tsementnoi Promyshlennosti [*Leningrad*]

Trudy Gos Vses Issled Proekt Inst Giprovostokneft — Trudy Gosudarstvennogo Vsesoyuznogo Issledovatel'skogo i Proektnogo Instituta Giprovostokneft [*Kuibyshev*]

Trudy Gos Vses Nauchno Issled Inst Tsem Prom — Trudy Gosudarstvennogo Vsesoyuznogo Nauchno-Issledovatel'skogo Instituta Tsementnoi Promyshlennosti

Trudy Grodn Sel Khoz Inst — Trudy Grodnenskogo Sel'skokhozyaistvennogo Instituta

Trudy Grozn Neft Nauchno Issled Inst — Trudy Groznenskogo Neftyanogo Nauchno-Issledovatel'skogo Instituta

Trudy Gruz Nauchno Issled Inst Gidrotekh Melior — Trudy Gruzinskogo Nauchno-Issledovatel'skogo Instituta Gidrotekhniki i Melioratsii

Trudy Gruz Nauchno-Issled Pishch Prom — Trudy Gruzinskii Nauchno-Issledovatel'skii Institut Pishchevoi Promyshlennosti

Trudy Gruz Politeh Inst — Trudy Gruzinskogo Politehniceskogo Instituta im V.I. Lenina

Trudy Gruz Sel'-Khoz Inst — Trudy Gruzinskogo Sel'skokhozyaistvennogo Instituta Imeni L. P. Beriya

Trudy Hydrobiol Sta Kyyiv — Trudy Hidrobiolohichnoy Stantsiyi. Akademiya Nauk URSR (Kyyiv)

Trudy Ikhtiol Lab Uprav Kasp Volzh Ryb Tuyl Promys — Trudy Ikhtiologicheskoi Laboratorii Upravleniya Kaspiisko-Volzhskikh Rybnykh i Tyulen'ikh Promyslov [*Astrakhan*]

Trudy Ilmensk Gos Zapov — Trudy Il'menskogo Gosudarstvennogo Zapovednika [*Moskva*]

Trudy Imp Kazan Univ — Trudy Imperatorskago Kazanskago Universiteta [*Kazan*]

Trudy Imp Obshch Sudokh — Trudy Imperatorskago Obshchestva Sudokhodstva [*S. Peterburg*]

Trudy Imp S Peterb Bot Sada — Trudy Imperatorskago S. Peterburgskago Botanicheskago Sada [*S. Peterburg*]

Trudy Imp S Peterb Obshch Estest — Trudy Imperatorskago S. Peterburgskago Obshchestva Estestvoispytatelei [*S. Peterburg*]

Trudy Imp S Peterburgsk Obsc Estestvoisp Vyp 2 Otd Bot — Trudy Imperatorskago S.-Peterburgskago Obscestva Estestvoispytatelej. Vypusk 2.Otdelenie Botaniki. Travaux de la Societe des Naturalistes de Saint-Petersbourg. Section de Botanique

Trudy Inst Agrokhim Pochv Baku — Trudy Instituta Agrokhimii i Pochvovedenlya. Akademiya Nauk Azerbaidzhanskoi SSR (Baku)

Trudy Inst Antiseism Stroit Ashkhabad — Trudy Instituta Antiseismicheskogo Stroitel'stva Akademiya Nauk Turkmenskoi SSR (Ashkhabad)

Trudy Inst Astrofiz Stalinabad — Trudy Instituta Astrofiziki. Akademiya Nauk Tadzhikskoi SSR (Stalinabad)

Trudy Inst Biol Akad Nauk SSSR Jakutsk Fil — Trudy Instituta Biologii Akademija Nauk SSSR. Jakutskij Filial

Trudy Inst Biol Ashkhabad — Trudy Instituta Biologii. Akademiya Nauk Turkmenskoi SSR (Ashkhabad)

Trudy Inst Biol Fiz — Trudy Instituta Biologicheskoi Fiziki. Akademiya Nauk SSSR [*Moskva*]

Trudy Inst Biol Riga — Trudy Instituta Biologii. Akademlya Nauk Latviiskoi SSR (Riga)

Trudy Inst Biol Sverdlovsk — Trudy Instituta Biologii. Ural'skii Filial. Akademiya Nauk SSSR (Sverdlovsk)

Trudy Inst Biol Ural Fil (Sverdlovsk) — Trudy Instituta Biologii Ural'skii Filial Akademiya Nauk SSSR (Sverdlovsk)

Trudy Inst Biol Vodokhran — Trudy Instituta Biologii Vodokhranilishch. Akademiya Nauk SSSR [*Moskva*]

Trudy Inst Biol Yakutsk — Trudy Instituta Biologii. Yakutskii Filial. Akademiya Nauk SSSR (Yakutsk)

Trudy Inst Bot (Alma-Ata) — Trudy Instituta Botaniki Akademiya Nauk Kazakhskoi SSR (Alma-Ata)

Trudy Inst Bot Ashkhabad — Trudy Instituta Botaniki (Ashkhabad)

Trudy Inst Bot Baku — Trudy Instituta Botaniki im. V.L. Komarova. Akademiya Nauk Azerbaidzhanskoi SSR (Baku)

Trudy Inst Bot Frunze — Trudy Instituta Botaniki. Akademiya Nauk Kirgizskoi SSR (Frunze)

Trudy Inst Bot Kharkiv — Trudy Instytutu Botaniky (Khar'kiv)

Trudy Inst Bot Rasteniev Frunze — Trudy Instituta Botaniki i Rastenievodstva. Akademiya Nauk Kirgizskoi SSR (Frunze)

Trudy Inst Bot Stalinabad — Trudy Instituta Botaniki. Akademiya Nauk Tadzhikskoi SSR (Stalinabad)

Trudy Inst Budyv Mekh Kyyiv — Trudy Instytutu Budivel'noyi Mekhaniky (Kyyiv)

Trudy Inst Chern Metall Kiev — Trudy Instituta Chernoi Metallurgii Akademiya Nauk Ukrainskoi SSR (Kiev)

Trudy Inst Chist Khim Reakt — Trudy Instituta Chistykh Khimicheskikh Reaktivov [*Moskva*]

Trudy Inst Epidem Bakt Pastera — Trudy Instituta Epidemiologii i Bakteriologii imeni Pastera [*Leningrad*]

Trudy Inst Epidem Mikrobiol Gig Pastera Inst Eksp Med — Trudy Instituta Epidemiologii, Mikrobiologii i Gigieny im. Pastera i Instituta Eksperimental'noi Meditsiny Akademii Meditsinskikh Nauk SSSR [*Leningrad*]

Trudy Inst Epidem Mikrobiol Sanit Tashkent — Trudy Instituta Epidemiologii, Mikrobiologii, i Sanitarii (Tashkent)

Trudy Inst Etnogr — Trudy Instituta Etnografii

Trudy Inst Evol Fiziol Patol Vyssh Nerv Deyat — Trudy Instituta Evolyutsionnoi Fiziologii i Patologii Vysshei Nervnoi Deyatel'nosti im. I.P. Pavlova [*Moskva*]

Trudy Inst Fiz Atmos — Trudy Instituta Fiziki Atmosfery. Akademiya Nauk SSSR [*Moskva*]

Trudy Inst Fiz Geofiz Ashkhabad — Trudy Instituta Fiziki I Geofiziki. Akademiya Nauk Turkmenskoi SSR (Ashkhabad)

Trudy Inst Fiz Geogr — Trudy Instituta Fizicheskoi Geografii. Akademiya Nauk SSSR [*Leningrad*]

Trudy Inst Fiziol Alma Ata — Trudy Instituta Fiziologii. Akademiya Nauk Kazakhskoi SSR (Alma-Ata)

Trudy Inst Fiziol (Baku) — Trudy Instituta Fiziologii Akademiya Nauk Azerbaidzhanskoi SSR (Baku)

Trudy Inst Fiziol I P Pavlova — Trudy Instituta Fiziologii Imeni I. P. Pavlova Akademii Nauk SSSR

Trudy Inst Fiziol Minsk — Trudy Instituta Fiziologii. Akademiya Nauk Belorusskoi SSR (Minsk)

Trudy Inst Fiziol Prof I Beritashvili — Trudy Instituta Fiziologii im. Prof. I. Beritashvili [*Tbilisi*]

Trudy Inst Fiziol Rast — Trudy Instituta Fiziologii Rastenii imeni K.A. Timiryazeva [*Moskva*]

Trudy Inst Fiziol Tbilisi — Trudy Instituta Fiziologii. Akademiya Nauk Gruzinskoi SSR (Tbilisi)

Trudy Inst Fiz Khim — Trudy Instituta Fizicheskoi Khimii. Akademiya Nauk SSSR [*Moskva*]

Trudy Inst Fiz Kiev — Trudy Instituta Fiziki. Akademiya Nauk Ukrainskoi SSR (Kiev)

Trudy Inst Fiz Mat Baku — Trudy Instituta Fiziki i Matematiki. Akademiya Nauk Azerbaidzhanskoi SSR (Baku)

Trudy Inst Fiz Mat Minsk — Trudy Instituta Fiziki i Matematiki. Akademiya Nauk Belorusskoi SSR (Minsk)

Trudy Inst Fiz Metall Sverdlovsk — Trudy Instituta Fiziki Metallov. Ural'skii Filial. Akademiya Nauk SSSR (Sverdlovsk)

Trudy Inst Fiz Tbilisi — Trudy Instituta Fiziki. Akademiya Nauk Gruzinskoi SSR (Tbilisi)

Trudy Inst Fiz Zemli — Trudy Instituta Fiziki Zemli. Akademiya Nauk SSSR [*Moskva*]

Trudy Inst Genet — Trudy Instituta Genetiki Akademiya Nauk SSR

Trudy Inst Genet Selek Baku — Trudy Instituta Genetiki i Selektsii. Akademiya Nauk Azerbaidzhanskoi SSR (Baku)

Trudy Inst Geofiz Tbilisi — Trudy Instituta Geofiziki. Akademiya Nauk Gruzinskoi SSR (Tbilisi)

Trudy Inst Geofiz Ural Fil — Trudy Instituta Geofiziki. Ural'skii Filial. Akademiya Nauk SSSR [*Moskva*]

Trudy Inst Geogr Baku — Trudy Instituta Geografii. Akademiya Nauk Azerbaidzhanskoi SSR (Baku)

Trudy Inst Geogr Leningr — Trudy Instituta Geografii. Akademiya Nauk SSSR (Leningrad)

Trudy Inst Geogr Tbilisi — Trudy Instituta Geografii. Akademiya Nauk Gruzinskoi SSR (Tbilisi)

Trudy Inst Geol Baku — Trudy Instituta Geologii im. Akademika I.M. Gubkina. Akademiya Nauk Azerbaidzhanskoi SSR (Baku)

Trudy Inst Geol Dushanbe — Trudy Instituta Geologii. Akademiya Nauk Tadzhikskoi SSR (Stalinabad, Dushanbe)

Trudy Inst Geol Frunze — Trudy Instituta Geologii. Akademiya Nauk Kirgizskoi SSR (Frunze)

Trudy Inst Geol Geofiz Sib Otd — Trudy Instituta Geologii i Geofiziki. Sibirskoe Otdelenie. Akademiya Nauk SSSR [*Leningrad*]

Trudy Inst Geol Nauk Alma Ata — Trudy Instituta Geologicheskikh Nauk. Akademiya Nauk Kazakhskoi SSR (Alma-Ata)

Trudy Inst Geol Nauk Kiev — Trudy Instituta Geologicheskikh Nauk. Akademiya Nauk Ukrainskoi SSR (Kiev)

Trudy Inst Geol Nauk Minsk — Trudy Instituta Geologicheskikh Nauk. Akademiya Nauk Belorusskoi SSR (Minsk)

Trudy Inst Geol Nauk Mosk — Trudy Instituta Geologicheskikh Nauk. Akademiya Nauk SSSR (Moskva)

Trudy Inst Geol Nauk Ser Stratigr — Trudy Instituta Geologiceskih Nauk. Serija Stratigrafii i Paleontologii. Trudy Instytutu Geologicnyh Nauk

Trudy Inst Geol Polez Iskop Riga — Trudy Instituta Geologii i Poleznykh Iskopaemykh. Akademiya Nauk Latviiskoi SSR (Riga)

Trudy Inst Istor A Bakikhanova — Trudy Instituta Istorii imeni A. Bakikhanova

Trudy Inst Istor & Arkheol Akad Nauk UzSSR — Trudy Instituta Istorii i Arkheologii Akademii Nauk UzSSR

Trudy Inst Istor Arkheol Etnogr Stalinabad — Trudy Instituta Istorii, Arkheologii, i Etnografii. Akademiya Nauk Tadzhikskoi SSR (Stalinabad)

Trudy Inst Istor Estest — Trudy Instituta Istorii Estestvoznaniya. Akademiya Nauk SSSR [*Moskva, Leningrad*]

Trudy Inst Istor Estest Tekh — Trudy Instituta Istorii Estestvoznaniya i Tekhniki. Akademiya Nauk SSSR [*Moskva*]

Trudy Inst Istor Estestvoznan Tehn — Trudy Instituta Istorii Estestvoznanija i Tehniki

Trudy Inst Istorii Estestv Tehn — Trudy Instituta Istorii Estestvoznanija i Tehniki

Trudy Inst Istor Nauki Tekh — Trudy Instituta Istorii Nauki i Tekhniki [*Leningrad*]

Trudy Inst Izuch Prof Bolez — Trudy Instituta po Izucheniyu Professional'nykh Boleznoi imoni V.A. Obukha [*Moskva*]

Trudy Inst Izuch Sev — Trudy Instituta po Izucheniyu Severa [*Moskva*]

Trudy Inst Jaz Lit Ist Komi Fil Akad Nauk SSSR — Trudy Instituta Jazyka, Literatury, i Istorii Komi Filiala Akademii Nauk SSSR

Trudy Inst Khem Kharkiv — Trudy Instytutu Khemiyi (Khar'kiv)

Trudy Inst Khim Baku — Trudy Instituta Khimii. Akademiya Nauk Azerbaidzhanskoi SSR (Baku)

Trudy Inst Khim Dushanbe — Trudy Instituta Khimii. Akademiya Nauk Tadzhikskoi SSR (Dushanbe)

Trudy Inst Khim Frunze — Trudy Instituta Khimii. Akademiya Nauk Kirgizskoi SSR (Frunze)

Trudy Inst Khim Metall Ural Fil — Trudy Instituta Khimii i Metallurgii. Ural'skii Filial. Akademiya Nauk SSSR [*Moskva*]

Trudy Inst Khim Nauk Alma Ata — Trudy Instituta Khimicheskikh Nauk. Akademiya Nauk Kazakhskoi SSR (Alma-Ata)

Trudy Inst Khim Sverdlovsk — Trudy Instituta Khimii. Ural'skii Filial. Akademiya Nauk SSSR (Moskva, Sverdlovsk)

Trudy Inst Khim Tbilisi — Trudy Instituta Khimii. Akademiya Nauk Gruzinskoi SSR (Tbilisi)

Trudy Inst Klin Eksp Kardiol — Trudy Instituta Klinicheskoi i Eksperimental'noi Kardiologii

Trudy Inst Klin Eksp Khir Alma Ata — Trudy Instituta Klinicheskoi i Eksperimental'noi Khirurgii. Akademiya Nauk Kazakhskoi SSR (Alma-Ata)

Trudy Inst Kraev Eksp Med Tashkent — Trudy Instituta Kraevoi Eksperimental'noi Meditsiny. Akademiya Nauk Uzbekskoi SSR (Tashkent)

Trudy Inst Kraev Med Frunze — Trudy Instituta Kraevoi Meditsiny. Akademiya Nauk Kirgizskoi SSR (Frunze)

Trudy Inst Kraev Patol Alma Ata — Trudy Instituta Kraevoi Patologii. Akademiya Nauk Kazakhskoi SSR (Alma-Ata)

Trudy Inst Kristall — Trudy Instituta Kristallografii. Akademiya Nauk SSSR [*Moskva*]

Trudy Inst Lesa Drev Sib Otd — Trudy Instituta Lesa i Drevesiny. Sibirskoe Otdelenie. Akademiya Nauk SSSR

Trudy Inst Lesa Mosk — Trudy Instituta Lesa. Akademiya Nauk SSSR (Moskva, Leningrad)

Trudy Inst Lesa Tbilisi — Trudy Instituta Lesa. Akademiya Nauk Gruzinskoi SSR (Tbilisi)

Trudy Inst Malyar Med Parazit Stalinabad — Trudy Instituta Malyarii i Meditsinskoi Parazitologii (Stalinabad)

Trudy Inst Mashinov Semin Kach Poverkh — Trudy Instituta Mashinovedeniya. Seminar po Kachestvu Poverkhnosti. Akademiya Nauk SSSR [*Moskva*]

Trudy Inst Mashinov Semin Prochn Detal Mash — Trudy Instituta Mashinovedeniya. Seminar po Prochnosti Detalei Mashin. Akademiya Nauk SSSR [*Moskva*]

Trudy Inst Mashinov Semin Teor Mash Mekh — Trudy Instituta Mashinovedeniya. Seminar po Teorii Mashin i Mekhanizmov. Akademiya Nauk SSSR [*Moskva*]

Trudy Inst Mashinov Semin Tochn Mashinost Priborost — Trudy Instituta Mashinovedeniya. Seminar po Tochnosti v Mashinostroenii i Priborostroenii. Akademiya Nauk SSSR [*Moskva*]

Trudy Inst Mat i Meh Ural Naucn Centr Akad Nauk SSSR — Trudy Instituta Matematiki i Mehaniki Ural'skii Naucnyi Centr Akademija Nauk SSSR

Trudy Inst Mat i Mekh Ural Nauchn Tsentr Akad Nauk SSSR — Trudy Instituta Matematiki i Mekhaniki Ural'skii Nauchnyi Tsentr Akademiya Nauk SSSR

Trudy Inst Mat Mekh Tashkent — Trudy Instituta Matematiki i Mekhaniki. Akademiya Nauk Uzbekskoi SSR (Tashkent)

Trudy Inst Mat Novosibirsk — Trudy Institute Matematiki (Novosibirsk)

Trudy Inst Melior Vod Bolot Khoz Minsk — Trudy Instituta Melioratsii Vodnogo i Bolotnogo Khozyaistva. Akademiya Nauk Belorusskoi SSR (Minsk)

Trudy Inst Merzlotov — Trudy Instituta Merzlotovedeniya im. V.A. Obrucheva [*Moskva, Leningrad*]

Trudy Inst Metall A A Baikova — Trudy Instituta Metallurgii im. A.A. Baikova. Akademiya Nauk SSSR

Trudy Inst Metall Obogashch Alma Ata — Trudy Instituta Metallurgii i Obogashcheniya. Akademiya Nauk Kazakhskoi SSR (Alma-Ata)

Trudy Inst Metall Sverdlovsk — Trudy Instituta Metallurgii. Ural'skii Filial. Akademiya Nauk SSSR (Sverdlovsk)

Trudy Inst Mikrobiol Riga — Trudy Instituta Mikrobiologii (Riga)

Trudy Inst Norm Patol Fiziol — Trudy Instituta Normal'noi i Patologicheskoi Fiziologii. Akademiya Meditsinskikh Nauk SSSR

Trudy Inst Nov Lubyan Syrya — Trudy Instituta Novogo Lubyanogo Syr'ya [*Moskva*]

Trudy Inst Okeanol — Trudy Instituta Okeanologii. Akademiya Nauk SSSR [*Moskva*]

Trudy Inst Onkol — Trudy Instituta Onkologii. Akademiya Meditsinskikh Nauk SSSR [*Moskva*]

Trudy Inst Opyt Tabakov — Trudy Instituta Opytnogo Tabakovodstva [*Krasnodar*]

Trudy Inst Paleobiol Tbilisi — Trudy Instituta Paleobiologii. Akademiya Nauk Gruzinskoi SSR (Tbilisi)

Trudy Inst Plodov Vinogr Alma Ata — Trudy Instituta Plodovodstva i Vinogradarstva, Kazakhskaya Akademiya Sel'skokhozyaistvennykh Nauk (Alma-Ata)

Trudy Inst Pochv Agrokhim (Baku) — Trudy Instituta Pochvovedeniya i Agrokhimii Akademiya Nauk Azerbaidzhanskoi SSR (Baku)

Trudy Inst Pochv Alma Ata — Trudy Instituta Pochvovedeniya. Akademiya Nauk Kazakhskoi SSR (Alma-Ata)

Trudy Inst Pochv Geobot Tashkent — Trudy Instituta Pochvovedeniya i Geobotaniki Sredne-Aziatskogo Gosudarstvennogo Universiteta (Tashkent)

Trudy Inst Pochv Melior Irrig Stalinabad — Trudy Instituta Pochvovedeniya, Melioratsii, i Irrigatsii. Akademiya Nauk Tadzhikskoi SSR (Stalinabad)

Trudy Inst Pochv Tbilisi — Trudy Instituta Pochvovedeniya. Akademiya Nauk Gruzinskoi SSR (Tbilisi)

Trudy Inst Polev Tbilisi — Trudy Instituta Polevodstva. Akademiya Nauk Gruzinskoi SSR (Tiblisi)

Trudy Inst Prikl Geofiz — Trudy Instituta Prikladnoi Geofiziki [*Leningrad*]

Trudy Inst Prikl Miner Metall — Trudy Instituta Prikladnoi Mineralogii i Metallurgii [*Moskva*]

Trudy Inst Prom Zdan Sooruzh — Trudy Instituta Promyshlennykh Zdanii i Sooruzhenii. Akademiya Stroitel'stva i Arkhitektury SSSR

Trudy Inst Psikhol Tbilisi — Trudy Instituta Psikhologii. Akademiya Nauk Gruzinskoi SSR (Tbilisi)

Trudy Inst Ryb Khoz Promysl Issled Leningr Otd — Trudy Instituta Rybnogo Khozyaistva i Promyslovykh Issledovanii. Leningradskoe Otdelenie (Leningrad)

Trudy Inst Sadov Dushanbe — Trudy Instituta Sadovodstva. Akademiya Nauk Tadzhikskoi SSR (Dushanbe)

Trudy Inst Seism Stalinabad — Trudy Instituta Seismologii. Akademiya Nauk Tadzhikskoi SSR (Stalinabad)

Trudy Inst Seostsmi Stroit Seism Dushanbe — Trudy Instituta Seismostoikogo Stroitel'stva i Seismologii. Akademiya Nauk Tadzhikskoi SSR (Dushanbe)

Trudy Inst Sev Zern Khoz — Trudy Instituta Severnogo Zernovogo Khozyaistva

Trudy Inst Sistem Upravleniya Akad Nauk Gruzin SSR — Trudy Instituta Sistem Upravleniya Akademiya Nauk Gruzinskoi SSR

Trudy Inst Stroit Dela Tbilisi — Trudy Instituta Stroitel'nogo Dela. Akademiya Nauk Gruzinskoi SSR (Tbilisi)

Trudy Inst Stroit Fiz — Trudy Instituta Stroitel'noi Fiziki. Akademiya Stroitel'stva i Arkhitektury SSSR

Trudy Inst Stroit Konstr — Trudy Instituta Stroitel'nykh Konstruktsii. Akademiya Stroitel'stva i Arkhitektury SSSR

Trudy Inst Stroit Mater Miner Proiskhozhd Stekla — Trudy Instituta Stroitel'nykh Materialov Mineral'nogo Proiskhozhdeniya i Stekla

Trudy Inst Stroit Stroimater Alma Ata — Trudy Instituta Stroitel'stva i Stroimaterialov. Akademiya Nauk Kazakhskoi SSR (Alma-Ata)

Trudy Inst Teor Astr — Trudy Instituta Teoreticheskoi Astronomii. Akademiya Nauk SSSR [*Moskva*]

Trudy Inst Teoret Astronom — Trudy Instituta Teoreticeskoi Astronomii

Trudy Inst Teor Geofiz — Trudy Instituta Teoreticheskoi Geofiziki. Akademiya Nauk SSSR [*Moskva, Leningrad*]

Trudy Inst Teploenerg Kiev — Trudy Instituta Teploenergetiki. Akademiya Nauk URSR (Kiev)

Trudy Inst Toch Mekh Vychisl Tekh — Trudy Instituta Tochnoi Mekhaniki i Vychislitel'noi Tekhniki. Akademiya Nauk SSSR [*Moskva*]

Trudy Inst Torfa Minsk — Trudy Instituta Torfa. Akademiya Nauk Belorusskoi SSR (Minsk)

Trudy Inst Tsitol Gistol Embriol — Trudy Instituta Tsitologii, Gistologii, i Embriologii [*Leningrad*]

Trudy Inst Tuberk — Trudy Instituta Tuberkuleza. Akademiya Meditsinskikh Nauk SSSR [*Moskva*]

Trudy Inst Vinogr Vinod Erevan — Trudy Instituta Vinogradarstva i Vinodeliya. Akademiya Nauk Armyanskoi SSR (Erevan)

Trudy Inst Vsesojuz Zaoc Finans Ekon Inst — Trudy Instituta. Vsesojuznyj Zaocnyj Finasovo-Ekonomiceskij Institut

Trudy Inst Vychisl Mat Akad Nauk Gruzin SSR — Trudy Instituta Vychislitelnoi' Matematiki. Akademiya Nauk Gruzinskoi SSR

Trudy Inst Zeml Baku — Trudy Instituta Zemledeliya. Akademiya Nauk Azerbaidzhanskoi SSR (Baku)

Trudy Inst Zemled Alma Ata — Trudy Instituta Zemledeliya. Kazakhskii Filial. Akademiya Nauk SSSR (Alma-Ata)

Trudy Inst Zeml Leningr — Trudy Instituta Zemledeliya. Razdel 3. Pochvovedenie (Leningrad)

Trudy Inst Zemn Magn Ionosf Rasprost Radiov — Trudy Instituta Zemnogo Magnetizma, Ionosfery i Rasprostraneniya Radiovoln

Trudy Inst Zhivot Ashkhabad — Trudy Instituta Zhivotnovodstva. Akademiya Nauk Turkmenskoi SSR (Ashkhabad)

Trudy Inst Zhivot Dagest Fil — Trudy Instituta Zhivotnovodstva. Dagestanskii Filial. Akademiya Nauk SSSR

Trudy Inst Zhivot Stalinabad — Trudy Instituta Zhivotnovodstva. Akademiya Nauk Tadzhikskoi SSR (Stalinabad)

Trudy Inst Zool Alma Ata — Trudy Instituta Zoologii. Akademiya Nauk Kazakhskoi SSR (Alma-Ata)

Trudy Inst Zool Baku — Trudy Instituta Zoologii. Akademiya Nauk Azerbaidzhanskoi SSR (Baku)

Trudy Inst Zool Biol Kyyiv — Trudy Instytutu Zoolohiyi ta Biolohiyi (Kyyiv)

Trudy Inst Zool Kyyiv — Trudy Instytutu Zoolohiyi. Akademiya Nauk Ukrayins'koyi RSR (Kyyiv)

Trudy Inst Zool Parazit Frunze — Trudy Instituta Zoologii i Parazitologii. Akademiya Nauk Kirgizskoi SSR (Frunze)

Trudy Inst Zool Parazit Stalinabad — Trudy Instituta Zoologii i Parazitologii im. E.N. Pavlovskogo. Akademiya Nauk Tadzhikskoi SSR (Stalinabad)

Trudy Inst Zool Parazit (Tashkent) — Trudy Instituta Zoologii i Parazitologii Akademiya Nauk Uzbekskoi SSR (Tashkent)

Trudy Inst Zool Tbilisi — Trudy Instituta Zoologii. Akademiya Nauk Gruzinskoi SSR (Tbilisi)

Trudy Introd Pitomn Subtrop Kult — Trudy Introdukcionnogo Pitomnika Subtropiceskih Kul'tur

Trudy Irkutsk Byuro Obshch Izuch Sib — Trudy Irkutskogo Byuro Obshchestva Izucheniya Sibiri i eya Proizvoditel'skikh Sil [*Irkutsk*]

Trudy Irkutsk Gos Univ — Trudy Irkutskogo Gosudarstvennogo Universiteta

Trudy Irkutsk Magn Met Obs — Trudy Irkutskoi Magnitnoi i Meteorologicheskoi Observatorii [*Irkutsk*]

Trudy Irkutsk Obshch Estest — Trudy Irkutskogo Obshchestva Estestvoispytatelei [*Irkutsk*]

Trudy Ist-Kraev Muz Mold — Trudy Istoriko-Kraevedcheskogo Muzeia Moldavskoi SSR

Trudy Istor Tekh — Trudy po Istorii Tekhniki [*Moskva*]

Trudy IUTAKE — Trudy Iuzhno-Turkmenistanskoi Arkheologicheskoi Kompleksnoi Ekpeditsii

Trudy Izevsk Sel'skohozjaistv Inst — Trudy Izevskii Sel'skohozjaistvennyi Institut

Trudy Izhevsk Gos Med Inst — Trudy Izhevskogo Gosudarstvennogo Meditsinskogo Instituta [*Izhevsk*]

Trudy Izuch Radiya Radioakt Rud — Trudy po Izucheniyu Radiya i Radioaktivnykh Rud [*Leningrad*]

Trudy Izuch Zapov — Trudy po Izucheniyu Zapovednikov. N.K.I [*Moskva*]

Trudy Kab Antrop Etnol Kyyiv — Trudy Kabinetu Antropolohiyi ta Etnolohiyi (Kyyiv)

Trudy Kabardino-Balkarsk Gos Sel'khoz Opyt Sta — Trudy Kabardino-Balkarskoi Gosudarstvennoi Sel'skokhozyaistvennoi Opytnoi Stantsii

Trudy Kaf Avto Trakt — Trudy Kafedry Avtomobil i Traktory Vsesoyuznogo Zaochnogo Mashinostroitel'nogo Instituta [*Moskva*]

Trudy Kaf Istor Entsikl Med Imp Mosk Univ — Trudy Kafedry Istorii i Entsiklopedii Meditsiny Imperatorskago Moskovskago Universiteta [*Moskva*]

Trudy Kaf Norm Anat Saratov — Trudy Kafedry Normal'noi Anatomii Saratovskogo Gosudarstvennogo Meditsinskogo Instituta (Saratov)

Trudy Kaf Oper Khir Topogr Anat Tbilisi — Trudy Kafedry Operativnoi Khirurgii i Topograficheskoi Anatomii Tbilisskogo Gosudarstvennogo Meditsinskogo Instituta (Tbilisi)

Trudy Kaf Teorii Funkcii i Funkcional Anal Moskov Gos Univ — Moskovskii Gosudarstvennyi Universitet. Mehaniko-Matematiceskii Fakul'tet. Kafedra Teorii Funkcii i Funkcional'nogo Analiza. Trudy

Trudy Kalinin Gos Med Inst — Trudy Kalininskogo Gosudarstvennogo Meditsinskogo Instituta [*Kalinin*]

Trudy Kaliningr Tekh Inst Ryb Prom Khoz — Trudy Kaliningradskogo Tekhnicheskogo Instituta Rybnoi Promyshlennosti i Khozyaistva [*Kaliningrad*]

Trudy Kamchat Vulk Sta — Trudy Kamchatskoi Vulkanologicheskoi Stantsii. Akademiya Nauk SSSR [*Moskva*]

Trudy Karadagsk Biol Stancii — Trudy Karadagskoj Biologiceskoj Stancii

Trudy Karadah Nauch Sta Tl Vyazemskoho — Trudy Karadahs'koyi Nauchnoyi Stantsiyi imeni T.I. Vyazems'koho [*Simferopol*]

Trudy Karagand Bot Sada — Trudy Karagandinskogo Botanicheskogo Sada

Trudy Karagand Gos Med Inst — Trudy Karagandinskii Gosudarstvennyi Meditsinskii Institut

Trudy Karel' Fil Akad Nauk SSSR — Trudy Karel'skogo Filiala Akademii Nauk SSSR

Trudy Karel Nauchno Issled Rybokhoz Sta — Trudy Karel'skoi Nauchno-Issledovatel'skoi Rybokhozyaistvennoi Stantsii [*Leningrad, Petrodarsk*]

Trudy Karelo Finsk Fil Akad Nauk SSSR — Trudy Karelo-Finskogo Filiala Akademii Nauk SSSR

Trudy Kavkaz Gos Zapov — Trudy Kavkazskogo Gosudarstvennogo Zapovednika

Trudy Kavk Obshch Sel Khoz — Trudy Kavkazskago Obshchestva Sel'skago Khozyaistva [*Tiflis*]

Trudy Kazakh Opyt Sta Pchelov — Trudy Kazakhskoi Opytnoi Stantsii Pchelovodstva

Trudy Kazakh Sel'-Khoz Inst — Trudy Kazakhskogo Sel'skokhozyaistvennogo Instituta

Trudy Kazan Aviacion Inst — Trudy Kazanskogo Aviacionnogo Instituta. Matematika i Mehanika

Trudy Kazan Fil Akad Nauk SSSR — Trudy Kazanskogo Filiala. Akademiya Nauk SSSR [*Kazan*]

Trudy Kazan Gorod Astronom Observator — Trudy Kazanskoi Gorodskoi Astronomiceskoi Observatorii

Trudy Kazan Gos Pedagog Inst — Trudy Kazanskogo Gosudarstvennogo Pedagogicheskogo Instituta

Trudy Kazan Khim Tech Inst — Trudy Kazanskogo Khimiko-Tekhnologicheskogo Instituta im. S.M. Kirova [*Kazan*]

Trudy Kazan Nauchno Issled Gidromet Inst — Trudy Kazanskogo Nauchno-Issledovatel'skogo Gidrometeorologicheskogo Instituta [*Kazan*]

Trudy Kazan Obshch Pchelov — Trudy Kazanskago Obshchestva Pchelovodstva [*Kazan*]

Trudy Kazan Sel'-Khoz Inst — Trudy Kazanskogo Sel'skokhozyaistvennogo Instituta

Trudy Kazan S-H Inst — Trudy Kazanskogo Sel'skokhozyaistvennogo Instituta

Trudy Kazan Voenno Sanit Obshch — Trudy Kazanskago Voenno-Sanitarnago Obshchestva [*Kazan*]

Trudy Kemerov Gos Sel Khoz Opyt Sta — Trudy Kemerovskoi Gosudarstvennoi Sel'skokhozyaistvennoi Opytnoi Stantsii

Trudy Kerch Ikhtiol Lab — Trudy Kerchenskoi Ikhtiologicheskoi Laboratorii [*Kerch*]

Trudy Kerch Nauch Rybokhoz Sta — Trudy Kerchenskoi Nauchnoi Rybokhozyaistvennoi Stantsii [*Kerch*]

Trudy Khabarovsk Gos Med Inst — Trudy Khabarovskogo Gosudarstvennogo Meditsinskogo Instituta [*Khabarovsk*]

Trudy Khabarovsk Inst Inzh Zhelezno Dorozh Transp — Trudy Khabarovskogo Instituta Inzhenerov Zhelezno-Dorozhnogo Transporta

Trudy Kharkov Inst Inzh Zhelezno Dorozh Transp — Trudy Khar'kovskogo Instituta Inzhenerov Zhelezno-Dorozhnogo Transporta im. S.M. Kirova

Trudy Kharkov Khim Tekhnol Inst — Trudy Khar'kovskogo Khimiko-Tekhnologicheskogo Instituta imeni S.M. Kirova [*Khar'kov*]

Trudy Kharkov Med Obshch — Trudy Khar'kovskago Meditsinskago Obshchestva [*Khar'kov*]

Trudy Kharkov Opyt Sta Pchelov — Trudy Khar'kovskaya Opytnaya Stantsiya Pchelovodstva

Trudy Kharkov Politekh Inst — Trudy Khar'kovskogo Politekhnicheskogo Instituta im. V.I. Lenina [*Khar'kov*]

Trudy Kharkov Sel'-Khoz Inst — Trudy Khar'kovskogo Sel'skokhozyaistvennogo Instituta

Trudy Khibinsk Geogr Sta Mosk Univ — Trudy Khibinskoi Geograficheskoi Stantsii Moskovskogo Universiteta [*Moskva*]

Trudy Khim Inst Baku — Trudy Khimicheskogo Instituta. Azerbaidzhanskii Filial. Akademiya Nauk SSSR (Baku)

Trudy Khim Inst L Ya Karpova — Trudy Khimicheskogo Instituta imeni L. Ya. Karpova [*Moskva*]

Trudy Khim Metall Inst Novosibirsk — Trudy Khimiko-Metallurgicheskogo Instituta. Sibirskoe Otdelenie. Akademiya Nauk SSSR (Novosibirsk)

Trudy Khorezm Arkheol Etnog Eksped — Trudy Khorezmskoy Arkheologo-Etnograficheskoy Ekspeditsii

Trudy Kiev Khir Obshch — Trudy Kievskago Khirurgicheskago Obshchestva [*Kiev*]

Trudy Kiev Obshch Detsk Vrach — Trudy Kievskago Obshchestva Detskikh Vrachei [*Kiev*]

Trudy Kiev Orn Obshch — Trudy Kievskago Ornitologicheskago Obshchestva [*Kiev*]

Trudy Kiev Sta Borbe Vredit Rast — Trudy Kievskoi Stantsii po Bor'be s Vreditelyami Rastenii pri Yuzhno-Russkom Obshchestve Pooshchrenii Sels'koi Promyshlennosti [*S. Peterburg*]

Trudy Kiev Tekhnol Inst Pishch Prom — Trudy Kievskogo Tekhnologicheskogo Instituta Pishchevoi Promyshlennosti

Trudy Kiev Vet Inst — Trudy Kievskogo Veterinarnogo Instituta [*Kiev*]

Trudy Kiev Voenno Sanit Obshch — Trudy Kievskago Voenno-Sanitarnago Obshchestva [*Kiev*]

Trudy Kirgiz Arkheol Etnog Eksped — Trudy Kirgizskoy Arkheologo-Etnograficheskoy Ekspeditsii

Trudy Kirgiz Gos Med Inst — Trudy Kirgizskogo Gosudarstvennogo Meditsinskogo Instituta [*Frunze*]

Trudy Kirgiz Gos Univ Ser Biol Nauk — Trudy Kirgizskogo Gosudarstvennogo Universiteta. Seriya Biologicheskikh Nauk Zoologiya-Fiziologiya

Trudy Kirgiz Gos Univ Ser Mat Nauk — Trudy Kirgizskogo Gosudarstvennogo Universiteta. Serija Matematiceskikh Nauk

Trudy Kirgiz Kompleks Eksped — Trudy Kirgizkoi Kompleksnoi Ekspeditsii 1932-1933 [*Leningrad, Moskva*]

Trudy Kirgiz Nauchno-Issled Inst Zeml — Trudy Kirgizkogo Nauchno-Issledovatel'skogo Instituta Zemledeliya

Trudy Kirgiz Sel'-Khoz Inst — Trudy Kirgizskogo Sel'skokhozyaistvennogo Instituta

Trudy Kishinev Sel'-Khoz Inst — Trudy Kishinevskogo Sel'skokhozyaistvennogo Instituta

Trudy Kolomen Filiala Vsesojuz Zaocn Politehn Inst — Trudy Kolomenskogo Filiala Vsesojuznyi Zaocnyi Politehniceskii Institut

Trudy Kom Analit Khim — Trudy Komissii po Analiticheskoi Khimii Akademiya Nauk SSSR

Trudy Komi Fil Akad Nauk SSSR — Trudy Komi Filiala Akademii Nauk SSSR

Trudy Komi Filiala Akad Nauk SSSR — Trudy Komi Filiala Akademii Nauk SSSR

Trudy Komiss Izuc Cetvert Perioda — Trudy Komissii po Izuceniju Cetverticnogo Perioda

Trudy Kom Izuch Chetv Perioda — Trudy Komissii po Izucheniyu Chetvertichnogo Perioda. Akademiya Nauk SSSR [*Leningrad*]

Trudy Kompleks Yuzh Geol Eksped — Trudy Kompleksnoi Yuzhnoi Geologicheskoi Ekspeditsii. Akademiya Nauk SSSR

Trudy Konf Pochv Sib Dal'n Vostoka Akad Nauk SSSR — Trudy Konferentsiya Pochvovedov Sibiri i Dal'nego Vostoka Akademiya Nauk SSSR

Trudy Konf Vysokomolek Soed — Trudy. Konferentsiya po Vysokomolekulyarnym Soedineniyam [*Moskva*]

Trudy Kosin Biol Sta — Trudy Kosinskoi Biologicheskoi Stantsii [*Moskva*]

Trudy Kosinsk Biol Stancii Moskovsk Obsc Isp Prir — Trudy Kosinskoj Biologiceskog Stancii Moskovskogo Obscestva Ispytatelej Prirody. Arbeiten der Biologischen Station zu Kossino bei Moskau

Trudy Kostrom Nauch Obshch Izuch Mest Kr — Trudy Kostromskogo Nauchnogo Obshchestva po Izucheniyu Mestnogo Kraya [*Kostroma*]

Trudy Kostrom Sel Khoz Inst — Trudy Kostromskogo Sel'skokhozyaistvennogo Instituta

Trudy Krasnodar Fil Vses Neftegaz Nauchno Issled Inst — Trudy Krasnodarskogo Filiala Vsesoyuznogo Neftegazovogo Nauchno-Issledovatel'skogo Instituta

Trudy Krasnodar Inst Pishch Prom — Trudy Krasnodarskogo Instituta Pishchevoi Promyshlennosti [*Krasnodar*]

Trudy Krasnodar Selek Opyt Sta — Trudy Krasnodarskoi Selektsionno-Opytnoi Stantsii [*Krasnodar*]

Trudy Krasnodar Sel Khoz Inst — Trudy Krasnodarskogo Sel'sko-Khozyaistvennogo Instituta [*Krasnodar*]

Trudy Krim Nauchno Issled Inst — Trudy Krymskogo Nauchno-Issledovatel'skogo Instituta [*Simferopol*]

Trudy Krim Zonal Opyt Sta Vinogr Vinod — Trudy Krymskoi Zonal'noi Opytnoi Stantsii po Vinogradarstvu i Vinodeliyu [*Yalta*]

Trudy Krivorozh Gorno Rud Inst — Trudy Krivorozhskogo Gorno-Rudnogo Instituta [*Moskva*]

Trudy Krym Gos Med Inst — Trudy Krymskogo Gosudarstvennogo Meditsinskogo Instituta

Trudy Kuban Gos Med Inst — Trudy Kubanskogo Gosudarstvennogo Meditsinskogo Instituta imeni Krasnoi Armii [*Krasnodar*]

Trudy Kuban Sel'-Khoz Inst — Trudy Kubanskogo Sel'skokhozyaistvennogo Instituta

Trudy Kuibyshev Aviats Inst — Trudy Kuibyshevskogo Aviatsionnogo Instituta [*Kuibyshev*]

Trudy Kuibyshev Gos Med Inst — Trudy Kuibyshevskogo Gosudarstvennogo Meditsinskogo Instituta

Trudy (Kujbys Aviac) Inst — Trudy (Kujbysevskij Aviacionnyj) Institut

Trudy Kutais Med Obshch — Trudy Kutaiskago Meditsinskago Obshchestva [*Kutais*]

Trudy Kyyiv Astr Obs — Trudy Kyyivs'koyi Astronomichnoyi Observatoriyi [*Kyyiv*]

Trudy Lab Aerometod — Trudy Laboratorii Aerometodov. Akademiya Nauk SSSR [*Moskva*]

Trudy Lab Dvigat — Trudy Laboratorii Dvigatelei. Akademiya Nauk SSSR [*Moskva*]

Trudy Lab Eksp Biol Mosk Zoopk — Trudy Laboratorii Eksperimental'noi Biologii Moskovskogo Zooparka [*Moskva*]

Trudy Lab Eksp Zool Morf Zhivot — Trudy Laboratorii Eksperimental'noi Zoologii i Morfologii Zhivotnykh [*Leningrad*]

Trudy Lab Evol Morf — Trudy Laboratorii Evolyutsionnoi Morfologii [*Leningrad*]

Trudy Lab Fiziol Biokhim Rast — Trudy Laboratorii Fiziologii i Biokhimii Rastenii [*Moskva*]

Trudy Lab Fiziol Zhivot Inst Biol Vilnius — Trudy Laboratorii Fiziologii Zhivotnykh Instituta Biologii. Akademiya Nauk Litovskoi SSR (Vilnius)

Trudy Lab Genet — Trudy Laboratorii po Genetike [*Leningrad, Moskva*]

Trudy Lab Geol Dokembr — Trudy Laboratorii Geologii Dokembriya. Akademiya Nauk SSSR [*Moskva*]

Trudy Lab Geol Uglya — Trudy Laboratorii Geologii Uglya. Akademiya Nauk SSSR [*Moskva*]

Trudy Lab Gidrogeol Probl — Trudy Laboratorii Gidrogeologicheskikh Problem im. F.P. Savarenskogo [*Moskva*]

Trudy Lab Lesov — Trudy Laboratorii Lesovedeniya. Akademiya Nauk SSSR [*Moskva*]

Trudy Lab Muz Mestn Kr — Trudy Laboratorii pri Muzee Mestnago Kraya [*Vyatka*]

Trudy Lab Osnov Rybov — Trudy Laboratorii Osnov Rybovodstva. Akademiya Nauk SSSR [*Moskva*]

Trudy Lab Ozerov — Trudy Laboratorii Ozerovedeniya. Akademiya Nauk SSSR [*Moskva*]

Trudy Lab Sakar Pitom Am Loz — Trudy Laboratorii pri Sakarskom Pitomnike Amerikanskikh Loz [*Tiflis*]

Trudy Lab Sapropel Otlozh — Trudy Laboratorii Sapropelevykh Otlozhenii. Institut Lesa. Akademiya Nauk SSSR [*Moskva*]

Trudy Latv Sel'-Khoz Inst — Trudy Latviiskogo Sel'skokhozyaistvennogo Instituta

Trudy Lekarstv Aromat Rast — Trudy po Lekarstvennym i Aromaticeskim Rastenijam

Trudy Leningrad Tehnolog Inst Holod Promysl — Trudy Leningradskogo Tehnologicheskogo Instituta Holodil'noi Promyslennosti

Trudy Leningr Gidromet Inst — Trudy Leningradskogo Gidrometeorologicheskogo Instituta

Trudy Leningr Inst Kul't — Trudy Leningradskii Institut Kul'tury

Trudy Leningr Obshch Estest — Trudy Leningradskogo Obshchestva Estestvoispytatelei

Trudy Leningr Oftal Nauchno Prakt Inst — Trudy Leningradskogo Oftalmologicheskogo Nauchno-Prakticheskogo Instituta [*Leningrad*]

Trudy Leningr Sanit Gig Med Inst — Trudy Leningradskogo Sanitarno-Gigienicheskogo Meditsinskogo Instituta [*Leningrad*]

Trudy Leningr Tekhnol Inst — Trudy Leningradskogo Tekhnologicheskogo Instituta [*Leningrad*]

Trudy Leningr Tekhnol Inst Kholod Prom — Trudy Leningradskogo Tekhnologicheskogo Instituta Kholodil'noi Promyshlennosti

Trudy Leningr Tekhnol Inst Pishch Prom — Trudy Leningradskogo Tekhnologicheskogo Instituta Pishchevoi Promyshlennosti

Trudy Lesn Opytn Delu Omsk — Trudy po Lesnomu Opytnomu Delu. Mitteilungen aus dem Forstlichen Versuchswesen (Omsk)

Trudy Lesoekon Eksped — Trudy Lesoekonomicheskikh Ekspeditsii [*Moskva*]

Trudy Les Opyt Delu Ross — Trudy po Lesnomu Opytnomu Delu v Rossii [*Leningrad*]

Trudy Les Opyt Delu Ukr — Trudy po Lesnomu Opytnomu Delu Ukrainy

Trudy Lesotekh Akad SM Kirova — Trudy Lesotekhnicheskoi Akademii im. S.M. Kirova [*Leningrad*]

Trudy Limnol Sta Kosine — Trudy Limnologicheskoi Stantsii v Kosine [*Moskva*]

Trudy Lis Dosv Spravi Ukr — Trudy po Lisoviy Dosvidniy Spravi na Ukrayini [*Kyyiv*]

Trudy Litov Nauchno-Issled Inst Zeml — Trudy Litovskogo Nauchno-Issledovatel'skogo Instituta Zemledeliya

Trudy Lnyan Opyt Sta — Trudy Lnyanoi Opytnoi Stantsii [*Moskva*]

Trudy Lomonosov Inst Geokhim Kristallogr Miner — Trudy Lomonosovskogo Instituta Geokhimii, Kristallografii, i Mineralogii [*Leningrad*]

Trudy LPI — Trudy L.P.I. Leningradskii Politekhnicheskii Institut im. M.I. Kalinina [*Leningrad*]

Trudy Lvov Geol Obshch — Trudy L'vovskogo Geologicheskogo Obshchestva

Trudy Mat Inst Steklov — Trudy Matematiceskogo Instituta Imeni V. A. Steklova

Trudy Mat Inst VA Steklova — Trudy Matematicheskogo Instituta imeni V.A. Steklova. Akademiya Nauk SSSR [*Leningrad*]

Trudy Med Biol Genet Nauchno Issled Inst — Trudy Mediko-Biologicheskogo Geneticheskogo Nauchno-Issledovatel'skogo Instituta imeni M. Gor'kogo [*Moskva*]

Trudy Med Khim Lab Imp Tomsk Univ — Trudy Mediko-Khimicheskoi Laboratorii Imperatorskago Tomskago Universiteta [*Tomsk*]

Trudy Med Sel Khoz Seti Vladimir Gub Zemst — Trudy Meteorologicheskoi Sel'sko-Khozyaistvennoi Seti Vladimirskago Gubernskago Zemstva [*Vladimir*]

Trudy Metrolog Inst SSSR — Trudy Metrologiceskih Institutov SSSR

Trudy Met Seti Kharkov Gub Zemst — Trudy Meteorologicheskoi Seti Khar'kovskago Gubernskago Zemstva [*Khar'kov*]

Trudy Met Seti Vost Ross — Trudy Meteorologicheskoi Seti Vostoka Rossii [*Kazan*]

Trudy Mikrobiol Nauchno Issled Inst — Trudy Mikrobiologicheskogo Nauchno-Issledovatel'skogo Instituta [*Moskva*]

Trudy Miner Inst — Trudy Mineralogicheskogo Instituta. Akademiya Nauk SSSR [*Leningrad*]

Trudy Miner Muz — Trudy Mineralogicheskogo Muzeya Akademii Nauk SSSR [*Leningrad, Moskva*]

Trudy Mleev Sad Ogorod Opyt Sta — Trudy Mleevskoi Sadovo-Ogorodnoi Opytnoi Stantsii [*Mleev*]

Trudy Mold Akad Nauk — Trudy Ob'edinennoi Nauchnoi Sessii Moldavskii Filial Akademii Nauk SSR

Trudy Moldav Nauchno Issled Inst Epidem Mikrobiol Gig — Trudy Moldavskogo Nauchno-Issledovatel'skogo Instituta Epidemiologii, Mikrobiologii, i Gigieny [*Kishinev*]

Trudy Moldav Nauchno Issled Inst Sadov Vinogr Vinod — Trudy Moldavskogo Nauchno-Issledovatel'skogo Instituta Sadovodstva, Vinogradarstva, i Vinodeliya [*Kishinev*]

Trudy Mol Ucen Kirigiz Univ — Trudy Molodyh Ucenyh Kirigizskogo Universiteta

Trudy Mongolsk Komiss — Trudy Mongol'skoj Komissii

Trudy Mosk Geol Razv Inst — Trudy Moskovskogo Geologo-Razvedochnogo Instituta im. Ordzhonikidze [*Moskva*]

Trudy Mosk Gorod Bakt Inst — Trudy Moskovskogo Gorodskogo Bakteriologicheskogo Instituta [*Moskva*]

Trudy Mosk Inst Inzh Geod Aerofot Kartogr — Trudy Moskovskogo Instituta Inzhenerov Geodezii, Aerofotos'emki i Kartografii [*Moskva*]

Trudy Mosk Inst Inzh Transp — Trudy Moskovskogo Instituta Inzhenerov Transporta [*Moskva*]

Trudy Mosk Mat Obshch — Trudy Moskovskogo Matematicheskogo Obshchestva [*Moskva*]

Trudy Mosk Neft Inst — Trudy Moskovskogo Neftyanogo Instituta im. I.M. Gubkina [*Moskva*]

Trudy Mosk Obshch Ispyt Prir — Trudy Moskovskogo Obshchestva Ispytatelei Prirody. Otdel Biologicheskii Moskva]

Trudy Mosk Ordena Lenina Aviats Inst — Trudy Moskovskogo Ordena Lenina Aviatsionnogo Instituta im. Sergo Ordzhonikidze [*Moskva*]

Trudy Mosk Ordena Lenina Sel'Khoz Akad — Trudy Moskovskoi Ordena Lenina Sel'sko-Khozyaistvennoi Akademii Imeni K. A. Timiryazeva

Trudy Mosk Otd Vyssh Utverzh Russk Obshch Okhran Nar Zdrav — Trudy Moskovskogo Otdela Vysshago Utverzhdennago Russkago Obshchestva Okhraneniya Narodnago Zdraviya [*Moskva*]

Trudy Moskov Elektrotehn Inst Svjazi — Trudy Moskovskogo Elektrotehniceskogo Instituta Svjazi

Trudy Moskov Inst Inzen Zelezno-Doroz Transporta — Trudy Moskovskogo Instituta Inzenerov Zeleznodoroznogo Transporta

Trudy Moskov Inst Istoriji — Trudy Moskovskogo Instituta Istoriji, Filosofiji, i Literatury

Trudy Moskov Inst Radiotehn Elektron i Avtomat — Trudy Moskovskogo Instituta Radiotekhniki, Elektroniki, i Avtomatiki

Trudy Moskov Mat Obsc — Trudy Moskovskogo Matematiceskogo Obshchestva

Trudy Moskov Mat Obshch — Trudy Moskovskogo Matematicheskogo Obshchestva

Trudy Moskov Orden Lenin Energet Inst — Trudy Moskovskogo Ordena Lenina Energeticeskogo Instituta

Trudy Mosk Tekhnol Inst Myas Moloch Prom — Trudy Moskovskogo Tekhnologicheskogo Instituta Myasnoi i Molochnoi Promyshlennosti [*Moskva*]

Trudy Mosk Tekhnol Inst Ryb Prom Khoz — Trudy Moskovskogo Tekhnologicheskogo Instituta Rybnoi Promyshlennosti i Khozyaistva

Trudy Mosk Terap Obshch — Trudy Moskovskago Terapevticheskogo Obshchestva [*Moskva*]

Trudy Mosk Torf Inst — Trudy Moskovskogo Torfyanogo Instituta [*Moskva*]

Trudy Mosk Transp Ekon Inst — Trudy Moskovskogo Transportno-Ekonomicheskogo Instituta [*Moskva*]

Trudy Mosk Vet Akad — Trudy Moskovskoi Veterinarnoi Akademii [*Moskva*]

Trudy Mosk Zoopk — Trudy Moskovskogo Zooparka [*Moskva*]

Trudy Murgabsk Gidrobiol Sta — Trudy Murgabskoi Gidrobiologicheskoi Stantsii

Trudy Murmansk Biol Inst — Trudy Murmanskogo Biologicheskogo Instituta. Murmanskii Morskoi Biologicheski Institut. Akademiya Nauk SSSR

Trudy Murmansk Biol Sta — Trudy Murmanskoi Biologicheskoi Stantsii. Kol'skii Filial im. S.M. Kirova. Akademiya Nauk SSSR

Trudy Nakhich Kompleks Zonal Opyt Sta — Trudy Nakhichevanskoi Kompleksnoi Zonal'noi Opytnoi Stantsii

Trudy Nauch Inst Ryb Khoz — Trudy Nauchnogo Instituta Rybnogo Khozyaistva [*Moskva*]

Trudy Nauch Inst Selek — Trudy Nauchnogo Instituta Selektsii [*Kiev*]

Trudy Nauch Inst Udobr Insektofung — Trudy Nauchnogo Instituta po Udobreniyam i Insektofungitsidam Imeni Ya. V. Satoilova

Trudy Nauch Khim Farm Inst — Trudy Nauchnogo Khimiko-Farmatsevticheskogo Instituta [*Moskva*]

Trudy Nauch Korresp Inst Stroit Dela Tbilisi — Trudy Nauchnykh Korrespondentov Instituta Stroitel'nogo Dela. Akademiya Nauk Gruzinskoi SSR (Tbilisi)

Trudy Nauchnogo Inst Muz — Trudy Nauchnogo Instituta Muzeyevedeniya

Trudy Nauchno Issled Ikhtiol Inst — Trudy Nauchno-Issledovatel'skogo Ikhtiologicheskogo Instituta [*Leningrad*]

Trudy Nauchno Issled Inst Aeroklim — Trudy Nauchno-Issledovatel'skogo Instituta Aeroklimatologii [*Moskva*]

Trudy Nauchno Issled Inst Mekhaniz Ryb Prom — Trudy Nauchno-Issledovatel'skogo Instituta Mekhanizatsii Rybnoi Promyshlennosti [*Leningrad*]

Trudy Nauchno-Issled Inst Pchelov — Trudy Nauchno-Issledovatel'skogo Instituta Pchelovodstva

Trudy Nauchno Issled Inst Pishch Prom — Trudy Nauchno-Issledovatel'skogo Instituta Pishchevoi Promyshlennosti [*Leningrad*]

Trudy Nauchno Issled Inst Prom — Trudy Nauchno-Issledovatel'skikh Institutov Promyshlennosti [*Moskva*]

Trudy Nauchno-Issled Inst Prud Rybn Khoz — Trudy Nauchno-Issledovatel'skogo Instituta Prudovogo Rybnogo Khozyaistva

Trudy Nauchno Issled Inst Ptitseprom Narkomsnaba SSSR — Trudy Nauchno-Issledovatel'skogo Instituta Ptitsepromyshlennosti Narkomsnaba SSSR [*Moskva*]

Trudy Nauchno Issled Inst Ptitsev — Trudy Nauchno-Issledovatel'skogo Instituta Ptitsevodstva [*Moskva*]

Trudy Nauchno Issled Inst Sel Khoz Krain Sev — Trudy Nauchno-Issledovatel'skogo Instituta Sel'skogo Khozyaistva Krainogo Severa

Trudy Nauchno-Issled Inst Sel'Khoz Severn Zaural'ya — Trudy Nauchno-Issledovatel'skogo Instituta Sel'skogo Khozyaistva Severnogo Zaural'ya

Trudy Nauchno Issled Inst Svinov — Trudy Nauchno-Issledovatel'skogo Instituta Svinovodstva [*Kiev*]

Trudy Nauchno Issled Inst Voronezh Gos Univ — Trudy Nauchno-Issledovatel'skogo Instituta pri Voronezhskom Gosudarstvennom Universitete [*Voronezh*]

Trudy Nauchno Issled Inst Zemn Magn Ionosf Rasprost Radiovoln — Trudy Nauchno-Issledovatel'skogo Instituta Zemnogo Magnetizma, Ionosfery, i Rasprostraneniya Radiovoln [*Leningrad*]

Trudy Nauchno Issled Inst Zool — Trudy Nauchno-Issledovatel'skogo Instituta Zoologii [*Moskva*]

Trudy Nauchno Issled Kaf Metall Gorn Mater Dnepropetr — Trudy Nauchno-Issledovatel'skoi Kafedry Metallurgii i Gornykh Materialov (Dnepropetrovsk)

Trudy Nauchno Issled Khim Inst — Trudy Nauchno-Issledovatel'skogo Khimicheskogo Instituta [*Leningrad*]

Trudy Nauchno Issled Kino Foto Inst — Trudy Nauchno-Issledovatel'skogo Kino-Foto-Instituta [*Moskva*]

Trudy Nauchno Issled Lab Otravl Veshch — Trudy Nauchno-Issledovatel'skoi Laboratorii Otravlyayushchikh Veshchestv [*Leningrad*]

Trudy Nauchno Issled Lab Tary — Trudy Nauchno-Issledovatel'skoi Laboratorii Tary [*Moskva*]

Trudy Nauc-Issled Inst Sociol Kul't — Trudy Nauchno-Issledovatel'skogo Instituta Sociologiceskoj Kul'tury

Trudy Naucno Issl Inst Bot — Trudy Naucno-Issledovatel'skogo Instituta Botaniki. Trudy Naukova-Doslidnogo Instytutu Botaniky

Trudy Neft Geol Razv Inst — Trudy Neftyanogo Geologo-Razvedochnogo Instituta [*Moskva*]

Trudy Nikol Rybov Zav — Trudy Nikol'skago Rybovodnago Zavoda [*Vele*]

Trudy Nizhne Volzh Kraev Muz — Trudy Nizhne-Volzhskogo Kraevogo Muzeya [*Saratov*]

Trudy Novocherk Inzh-Melior Inst — Trudy Novocherkasskogo Inzhenerno-Meliorativnogo Instituta

Trudy Novocherk Politekh Inst — Trudy Novocherkasskogo Politekhnicheskogo Instituta im. S. Ordzhonikidze

Trudy Novocherk Zoovet Vet Inst — Trudy Novocherkasskogo Zooveterinarnogo (afterwards Veterinarnogo Instituta) [*Novocherkassk*]

Trudy Novosib Gos Med Inst — Trudy Novosibirskogo Gosudarstvennogo Meditsinskogo Instituta [*Novosibirsk*]

Trudy Novosib Gos Nauchno Issled Inst Travmat Ortop — Trudy Novosibirskogo Gosudarstvennogo Nauchno-Issledovatel'skogo Instituta Travmatologii i Ortopedii [*Novosibirsk*]

Trudy Novosib Inst Inzh Zhelezno Dorozh Transp — Trudy Novosibirskogo Instituta Inzhenerov Zheleznodorozhnogo Transporta

Trudy Novosib Sel Khoz Nauchno Issled Inst — Trudy Novosibirskogo Sel'skokhozyaistvennogo Nauchno-Issledovatel'skogo Instituta [*Novosibirsk*]

Trudy Obsc Estestvoisp Imp Tomsk Univ — Trudy Obscestva Estestvoispytatelej i Vracej pri Imperatorskom Tomskom Universitete

Trudy Obshch Det Vrach Mosk — Trudy Obshchestva Detskikh Vrachei v Moskve (Moskva)

Trudy Obshch Estest Imp Kazan Univ — Trudy Obshchestva Estestvoispytatelei pri Imperatordkom Kazanskom Universitete Kazan

Trudy Obshch Estest Imp Kharkov Univ — Trudy Obshchestva Estestvoispytatelei pri Imperatorskom Khar'kovskom Universitete [*Khar'kov*]

Trudy Obshch Fiz Khim Nauk Imp Kharkov Univ — Trudy Obscestva Fiziko-Khimicheskikh Nauk pri Imperatorskom Khar'kovskom Universitete

Trudy Obshch Ispyt Prir Imp Kharkov Univ — Trudy Obshchestva Ispytatelei Prirody pri Imperatorskom Khar'kovskom Universitete [*Khar'kov*]

Trudy Obshch Nizhegorod Vrach — Trudy Obshchestva Nizhegorodskikh Vrachei [*Nizhnii-Novgorod*]

Trudy Obshch Obsled Izuch Azerb — Trudy Obshchestva Obsledovaniya i Izucheniya Azerbaidzhana [*Baku*]

Trudy Obshch Patol S Peterb — Trudy Obshchestva Patologov v S. Peterburge [*Khar'kov*]

Trudy Obshch Perm Vrach — Trudy Obshchestva Permskikh Vrachei [*Perm*]

Trudy Obshch Psikhiat S Peterb — Trudy Obshchestva Psikhiatrov (S. Peterburge)

Trudy Obshch Russk Vrach Mosk — Trudy Obshchestva Russkikh Vrachei v Moskve

Trudy Obshch Russk Vrach Odesse — Trudy Obshchestva Russkikh Vrachei v Odesse

Trudy Obshch Sel Khoz Poltava — Trudy Obshchestva Sel'skago Khozyaistva (Poltava)

Trudy Obshch Tul Vrach — Trudy Obshchestva Tul'skikh Vrachei [*Tula*]

Trudy Obshch Voenn Vrach Mosk — Trudy Obshchestva Voennykh Vrachei g. Moskvy

Trudy Obshch Vrach Chernigov Gub — Trudy Obshchestva Vrachei Chernigovskoi Gubernii [*Chernigov*]

Trudy Obshch Vrach Odess Gorod Boln — Trudy Obshchestva Vrachei Odesskoi Gorodskoi Bol'nitsy [*Odessa*]

Trudy Obshch Vrach Rostova Nakhichevani — Trudy Obshchestva Vrachei gg. Rostova i Nakhichevani [*Rostov na Donu*]

Trudy Obshch Zemlev Imp S Peterb Univ — Trudy Obshchestva Zemlevedeniya pri Imperatorskom S. Peterburgskom Universitete

Trudy Obsh Dietsk Vrach Moskve — Trudy Obshchestva Dietskikh Vrachei v Moskve

Trudy Odess Derzh Unlv — Trudy Odesskogo Derzhavnogo Universiteta [*Odessa*]

Trudy Odess Gidromet Inst — Trudy Odesskogo Gidrometeorologicheskogo Instituta [*Odessa*]

Trudy Odess Nauchno Issled Inst Epidem Mikrobiol — Trudy Odesskogo Nauchno-Issledovatel'skogo Instituta Epidemiologii i Mikrobiologii

Trudy Odess Nauchno Issled Inst Stomat — Trudy Odesskogo Nauchno-Issledovatel'skogo Instituta Stomatologii [*Odessa*]

Trudy Odess Otd Obshch Okhr Nar Zdrav — Trudy Odesskago Otdeleniya Russkago Obshchestva Okhraneniya Narodnago Zdraviya

Trudy Odess Sel Khoz Inst — Trudy Odesskogo Sel'skokhozyaistvennogo Instituta

Trudy Odess Tekhnol Inst Pishch Kholod Prom — Trudy Odesskogo Tekhnologicheskogo Instituta Pishchevoi i Kholodil'noi Promyshlennosti [*Odessa*]

Trudy Omsk Vet Inst — Trudy Omskogo Veterinarnogo Instituta

Trudy Omsk Vyss Skoly Milicii — Trudy Omskogo Vyssej Skoly Milicii

Trudy Opytn Lesnic — Trudy Opytnyh Lesnicestv

Trudy Opyt Sta Plodov Tbilisi — Trudy Opytnoi Stantsii Plodovodstva. Akademiya Nauk Gruzinskoi SSR (Tbilisi)

Trudy Osob Kom Issled Kursk Magn Anom — Trudy Osoboi Komissii po Issledovaniyu Kurskoi Magnitnoi Anomalii V.S.N.Kh [*Moskva*]

Trudy Osob Kompleks Eksped Zeml Nov Sel Khoz Osvoen — Trudy Osoboi Kompleksnoi Ekspeditsii po Zemlyam Novogo Sel'skokhozyaistvennogo Osvoeniya

Trudy Otdela Drevnerus Lit Inst Rus Lit Akad Nauk SSR — Trudy Otdela Drevnerusskoy Literatury Instituta Russkoy Literatury Akademii Nauk SSR

Trudy Otd Torg Portov — Trudy Otdela Torgovykh Portov

Trudy Paleont Inst — Trudy Paleontologicheskogo Instituta. Akademiya Nauk SSSR [*Leningrad*]

Trudy Paleozool Inst — Trudy Paleozoologicheskogo Instituta. Akademiya Nauk SSSR [*Leningrad*]

Trudy Pamir Biol Sta — Trudy Pamirskoi Biologicheskoi Stantsii. Botanicheskoi Institut. Akademiya Nauk Tadzhikskoi SSR [*Dushanbe*]

Trudy Parazit Nemat Vyzyv Zabolev — Trudy. Paraziticheskie Nematody i Vyzyvaemye imi Zabolevaniya

Trudy Ped Inst Gruzin SSR Ser Fiz i Mat — Trudy Pedagogiceskih Institutov Gruzinskoj SSR. Serija Fiziki i Matematiki

Trudy Penz Obshch Lyub Estest — Trudy Penzenskago Obshchestva Lyubitelei Estestvoznaniya [*Penza*]

Trudy Perm Med Inst — Trudy Permskogo Meditsinskogo Instituta [*Perm*]

Trudy Perv Mosk Gos Med Inst — Trudy Pervogo Moskovskogo Gosudarstvennogo Meditsinskogo Instituta [*Moskva*]

Trudy Perv Sov Tuberk Inst — Trudy Pervago Sovetskago Tuberkuleznago Instituta

Trudy Petergof Biol Inst — Trudy Petergofskogo Biologicheskogo Instituta [*Petergof*]

Trudy Petergof Estest Nauch Inst — Trudy Petergofskogo Estestvenno-Nauchnogo Instituta [*Petergof*]

Trudy Petergofsk Biol Inst — Trudy Petergofskogo Biologiceskogo Instituta. Travaux de l'Institut Biologique de Peterhof

Trudy Petrogr Inst — Trudy Petrograficheskogo Instituta. Akademiya Nauk SSSR [*Leningrad*]

Trudy Petrogr Obshch Estest — Trudy Petrogradskago Obshchestva Estestvoispytatelei [*Petrograd*]

Trudy Plodov Inst — Trudy Plodovoshchnogo Instituta Imeni I. V. Michurina

Trudy Plodovo Yagod Inst — Trudy Plodovo-Yagodnogo Instituta imeni Akademika R.R. Shredera

Trudy Plov Morsk Nauch Inst — Trudy Plovuchego Morskogo Nauchnogo Instituta [*Moskva*]

Trudy Pochv Bot Eksped Izsled Kolon Raion Aziyat Ross — Trudy Pochvenno-Botanicheskikh Ekspeditsii po Izsledovaniyu Kolonizatsionnykh Raionov Aziyatskoi Rossii

Trudy Pochv Inst — Trudy Pochvennogo Instituta imeni V.V. Dokuchaeva. Akademiya Nauk SSSR

Trudy Poljarn Komiss — Trudy Poljarnoj Komissii

Trudy Poltav Gravim Obs — Trudy Poltavskoi Gravitmetricheskoi Observatorii. Akademiya Nauk Ukrainskoi SSR [*Kiev*]

Trudy Poltav Sel Khoz Opyt Sta — Trudy Poltavskoi Sel'sko-Khozyaistvennoi Opytnoi Stantsii [*Poltava*]

Trudy Polyar Kom — Trudy Polyarnoi Komissii. Akademiya Nauk SSSR [*Moskva, Leningrad*]

Trudy Polyar Nauchno Issled Inst Morsk Ryb Khoz Okeanogr — Trudy Polyarnogo Nauchno-Issledovatel'skogo Instituta Morskogo Rybnogo Khozyaistva i Okeanografii imeni N.M. Knipovicha [*Murmansk*]

Trudy Postoyan Kom Alkog — Trudy Postoyannoi Komissii po Voprosu ob Al'kogolizme [*S. Peterburg*]

Trudy Presnov Biol Sta S Peterb Obshch Estest — Trudy Presnovodnoi Biologicheskoi Stantsii Imperatorskago S. Peterburgskago Obshchestva Estestvoispytatelei [*S. Peterburg*]

Trudy Priamur Otd Imp Russk Geogr Obshch — Trudy Priamurskago Otdela Imperatorskago Russkago Geograficheskago Obshchestva [*Moskva*]

Trudy Pridnepr Met Seti — Trudy Pridneprovskoi Meteorologicheskoi Seti [*Kiev*]

Trudy Prikl Bot Genet Selek — Trudy po Prikladnoi Botanike Genetike i Selektsii

Trudy Prikl Bot Ser 5 Zernov Kult — Trudy po Prikladnoj Botanike, Genetike, i Selekcii. Serija 5. Zernovye Kul'tury/Bulletin of Applied Botany, of Genetics, and Plant-Breeding. Grain Crops

Trudy Prikl Bot Ser 9 Tehn Kult — Trudy po Prikladnoj Botanike, Genetike, i Selekcii. Serija 9. Tehniceskie Kul'tury/Bulletin of Applied Botany, of Genetics, and Plant-Breeding. Technical Plants

Trudy Prikl Bot Ser 15 Probl Severn Rasteniev — Trudy po Prikladnoj Botanike, Genetike, i Selekcii. Serija 15. Problemy Severnogo Rastenievodstva/Bulletin of Applied Botany, Genetics, and Plant-Breeding. Problems of Plant Industry in the Extreme North

Trudy Prikl Ent — Trudy po Prikladnoi Entomologii [*Leningrad*]

Trudy Probl Temat Soveshch Zool Inst — Trudy Problemnykh i Tematicheskikh Soveshchanii. Zoologicheskii Institut. Akademiya Nauk SSSR [*Leningrad, Moskva*]

Trudy Protok Imp Kavk Med Obshch — Trudy i Protokoly Imperatorskago Kavkazskago Meditsinskago Obshchestva [*Tiflis*]

Trudy Protok Zased Russk Khir Obshch — Trudy i Protokoly Zasedanii Russkago Khirurgicheskago Obshchestva im. N.I. Pirogova [*S. Peterburg*]

Trudy Pryr Tekh Vidd Kyyiv — Trudy Pryrodnycho-Tekhnichnoho Viddylu. Vseukrayins'ka Akademiya Nauk [*Kyyiv*]

Trudy Przeval'sk Gos Ped Inst — Trudy Przeval'skogo Gosudarstvennogo Pedagogiceskogo Instituta

Trudy Psikhiat Klin Voronezh — Trudy Psikhiatricheskoi Kliniki (Voronezh)

Trudy Pushkin Nauchno Issled Lab Razv Sel Khoz Zhivot — Trudy Pushkinskoi Nauchno-Issledovatel'skoi Laboratorii Razvedeniya Sel'skokhozyaistvennykh Zhivotnykh

Trudy Radiats Gig Leningr Nauchno-Issled Inst Radiats Gig — Trudy Radiatsii i Gigieny Leningradskogo Nauchno-Issledovatel'skogo Instituta Radiatsii Gigieny

Trudy Radiev Eksped — Trudy Radievoi Ekspeditsii Rossiiskoi Akademii Nauk [*Petrograd*]

Trudy Radiev Inst — Trudy Radievogo Instituta im. V.G. Khlopina. Akademiya Nauk SSSR [*Leningrad*]

Trudy Respubl Stancii Zasc Rast — Trudy Respublikanskoj Stancii Zascity Rastenij

Trudy Rjazan Radiotehn Inst — Trudy Rjazanskogo Radiotehniceskogo Instituta

Trudy Russk Ent Obshch — Trudy Russkogo Entomologicheskogo Obshchestva

Trudy Samarkand Gos Univ — Trudy Samarkandskogo Gosudarstvennogo Unlversiteta Imeni Alisera Navoi

Trudy Samarkand Gos Univ NS — Ministerstvo Vyssego i Srednigo Obrazovanija UzSSR Trudy Samarkandskogo Gosuda rstvennogo Universiteta Imeni A. Navoi Novaja Serija

Trudy Samarkand Univ — Trudy Samarkandskogo Universiteta

Trudy Saratov Fiz Med Obshch — Trudy Saratovskago Fiziko-Meditsinskago Obshchestva [*Saratov*]

Trudy Saratov Inst Meh S-H — Trudy Saratovskogo Instituta Mehanizacii Sel'skogo-Hozjaistva

Trudy Saratov Inst Mekhaniz Sel Khoz — Trudy Saratovskogo Instituta Mekhanizatsii Sel'skogo Khozyaistva [*Saratov*]

Trudy Saratov Med Inst — Trudy Saratovskogo Meditsinskogo Instituta [*Saratov*]

Trudy Saratov Nauchno-Issled Vet Sta — Trudy Saratovskoi Nauchno-Issledovatel'skoi Veterinarnoi Stantsii

Trudy Saratov Sel'-Khoz Inst — Trudy Saratovskogo Sel'skokhozyaistvennogo Instituta

Trudy Saratov Zootekh Vet Inst — Trudy Saratovskogo Zootekhnicheskogo Veterinarnogo Instituta

Trudy Sekt Arkheol Inst Arkheol & Iskznaniya — Trudy Sektsii Arkheologii Instituta Arkheologii i Iskusstvoznaniya

Trudy Sekt Fiziol Baku — Trudy Sektora Fiziologii. Akademiya Nauk Azerbaidzhanskoi SSR (Baku)

Trudy Sekt Geogr Alma Ata — Trudy Sektora Geografii. Akademiya Nauk Kazakhskoi SSR (Alma-Ata)

Trudy Sekt Mat Mekh Alma Ata — Trudy Sektora Matematiki i Mekhaniki. Akademiya Nauk Kazakhskoi SSR (Alma-Ata)

Trudy Sekt Pochv Frunze — Trudy Sektora Pochvovedeniya. Akademiya Nauk Kirgizskoi SSR (Frunze)

Trudy Sekts Mikol Fitopat Russk Bot Obshch — Trudy Sektsii po Mikologii i Fitopatologii Russkogo Botanicheskogo Obshchestva

Trudy Sekts Nauch Razrab Probl Elektrosvarki Elektrotermii — Trudy Sektsii po Nauchnoi Razrabotke Problem Elektrosvarki i Elektrotermii. Akademiya Nauk SSSR [*Moskva*]

Trudy Sekt Vod Khoz Energ Frunze — Trudy Sektora Vodnogo Khozyaistva i Energetiki. Akademiya Nauk Kirgizskoi SSR (Frunze)

Trudy Selek Agrotekh Zashch Rast — Trudy po Selektsii Agrotekhniki i Zashchite Rastenii

Trudy Selekcion Stancii Moskovsk Selskohoz Inst — Trudy Selekcionnoj Stancii pri Moskovskom Sel'skohozjajstvennom Institute. Arbeiten der Versuchsstation fuer Pflanzenzuechtung am Moskauer LandwirtschaftlichenInstitut

Trudy Selek Genet Inst Odessa — Trudy Selektsiino-Genetichnogo Instituta (Odessa)

Trudy Selek Saratov Selek Genet Sta — Trudy po Selektsii Saratovskoi Selektsionno-Geneticheskoi Stantsii [*Saratov*]

Trudy Sel Khoz Akad KA Timiryazeva — Trudy Sel'skokhozyaistvennoi Akademii imeni K.A. Timiryazeva [*Moskva*]

Trudy Sel Khoz Met — Trudy po Sel'skokhozyaistvennoi Meteorologii [*S. Peterburg/Leningrad*]

Trudy Sel Khoz Opyt Uchrezhd Dona Sev Kavk — Trudy Sel'sko-Khozyaistvennykh Opytnykh Uchrezhdenii Dona i Severnogo Kavkaza

Trudy Sem Kraev Zadacham — Trudy Seminara po Kraevym Zadacham

Trudy Sem Mat Fiz Nelinien Koleban — Trudy Seminara po Matematiceskoi Fizike i Nelinienym Kolebanijam

Trudy Sem Petrovsk — Trudy Seminara Imeni I. G. Petrovskogo

Trudy Sem Vektor Tenzor Anal — Trudy Seminara po Vektornomu i Tenzornomu Analizu s ih Prilozenijami k Geometrii. Mehanike i Fizike

Trudy Sev Chernoz Obl Sel Khoz Opyt Sta — Trudy Severo-Chernozemnoi Oblastnoi Sel'skokhozyaistvennoi Opytnoi Stantsii [*Orel*]

Trudy Severo Kavkazsk Inst Zasc Rast — Trudy Severo-Kavkazskogo Instituta Zascity Rastenij/Bulletin. North Caucasian Institute for Plant Protection

Trudy Sev Kavk Ass Nauchno Issled Inst — Trudy Severo-Kavkazskoi Assotsiatsii Nauchno-Issledovatel'skikh Institutov [*Rostov na Donu*]

Trudy Sev Kavk Inst Spets Tekh Kult — Trudy Severo-Kavkazskogo Instituta Spetsial'nykh i Tekhnicheskikh Kul'tur

Trudy Sev Kavk Inst Zashch Rast — Trudy Severo-Kavkazskogo Instituta Zashchity Rastenii [*Rostov*]

Trudy Sev Nauch Inst Ryb Khoz — Trudy Severnogo Nauchnogo Instituta Rybnogo Khozyaistva [*Leningrad*]

Trudy Sev Nauch Issled Inst Gidrotekh Melior — Trudy Severnogo Nauchno-Issledovatel'skogo Instituta Gidrotekhniki i Melioratsii [*Leningrad*]

Trudy Sev Nauchno Issled Inst Moloch Khoz — Trudy Severnogo Nauchno-Issledovatel'skogo Instituta Molochnogo Khozyaistva [*Vologda*]

Trudy Sev Nauchno Prom Eksped — Trudy Severnoi Nauchno-Promyslovoi Ekspeditsii VSNKh [*Petrograd*]

Trudy Sev Oset Sel Khoz Inst — Trudy Severo-Osetinskogo Sel'skokhozyaistvennogo Instituta

Trudy Shatilov Sel Khoz Opyt Sta — Trudy Shatilovskoi Sel'sko-Khozyaistvennoi Opytnoi Stantsii [*Orel*]

Trudy Shirabud Opyt Sel Khoz Sta — Trudy Shirabudinskoi Opytnoi Sel'sko-Khozyaistvennoi Stantsii [*Staraya Bukhara*]

Trudy Sib Avto Dorozh Inst — Trudy Sibirskogo Avtomobil'no-Dorozhnogo Instituta [*Omsk*]

Trudy Sib Fiz Tekh Inst — Trudy Sibirskogo Fiziko-Tekhnicheskogo Instituta [*Tomsk*]

Trudy Sib Ikhtiol Lab — Trudy Sibirskoi Ikhtiologicheskoi Laboratorii

Trudy Sib Inst Sel Khoz Lesov — Trudy Sibirskogo Instituta Sel'skogo Khozyaistva i Lesovodstva [*Omsk*]

Trudy Sibirsk Fiz-Tehn Inst — Trudy Sibirskogo Fiziko-Tehniceskogo Instituta Imeni Akademika V. D. Kuznecova

Trudy SibNIIE — Trudy Sibirskii Nauchno-Issledovatel'skii Institut Energetiki

Trudy Sogdiysko Tadzhikskoy Arkheol Eksped — Trudy Sogdiysko-Tadzhikskoy Arkheologischeskoy Ekspeditsii

Trudy Solikam Sel'-Khoz Opyt Sta — Trudy Solikamskoi Sel'skokhozyaistvennoi Opytnoi Stantsii

Trudy Soveshch Eksp Miner Petrogr — Trudy Soveshchaniya po Eksperimental'noi Mineralogii i Petrografii. Akademiya Nauk SSSR [*Moskva*]

Trudy Soveshch Ikhtiol Kom — Trudy Soveshchanii. Ikhtiologicheskaya Komissiya [*Moskva*]

Trudy Soveshch Teor Litein Prots — Trudy Soveshchaniya po Teorii Litenykh Protsessov. Institut Mashinovedeniya [*Moskva*]

Trudy Soveshch Vopr Kosmog — Trudy Soveshchaniya po Voprosam Kosmogonii. Akademiya Nauk SSSR [*Moskva*]

Trudy Soveta Izuc Prir Resursov Ser Dalne Vost — Trudy Soveta po Izuceniju Prirodnyh Resursov. Serija Dal'ne-Vostocnaja

Trudy Soyuza NIKhl — Trudy Soyuza NIKhl. Vsesoyuznyi Ordena Lenina Nauchno-Issledovatel'skii Institut po Khlopkovodstvu [*Tashkent*]

Trudy S Peterb Obshch Estest — Trudy Sankt-Peterburgskago Obshchestva Estestvoispytatelei

Trudy S Peterburg Mat Obshch — Trudy Sankt-Peterburgskogo Matematicheskogo Obshchestva

Trudy S Peterburgsk Obsc Estestvoisp Otd Bot — Trudy S.-Peterburgskago Obscestva Estestvoispytatelej. Otdelenie Botaniki/Travaux de la Societe des Naturalistes de Saint-Petersbourg. Section de Botanique

Trudy Sravn Anat Inst Mosk Univ — Trudy Sravnitel'no-Anatomiceskago Instituta pri Moskovskom Universitete [*Moskva*]

Trudy Sred Aziat Gos Univ — Trudy Sredne-Aziatskogo Gosudarstvennogo Universiteta

Trudy Sred Aziat Ind Inst Gorn Fak — Trudy Sredne-Aziatskogo Industrial'nogo Instituta. Gornyi Fakultet [*Tashkent*]

Trudy Sred Aziat Inst Zashch Rast — Trudy Sredne-Aziatskogo Issledovatel'skogo Instituta Zashchity Rastenii [*Tashkent*]

Trudy Sred Aziat Nauchno Issled Gidromet Inst — Trudy Sredne-Aziatskogo Nauchno-Issledovatel'skogo Gidrometeorologicheskogo Instituta

Trudy Sred Aziat Nauchno Issled Inst Irrig — Trudy Sredne-Aziatskogo Nauchno-Issledovatel'skogo Instituta Irrigatsii [*Tashkent*]

Trudy Sredne Aziatsk Gosud Univ Ser 8b Bot — Trudy Sredne-Aziatskogo Gosudarstvennogo Universiteta. Serija 8b. Botanika. Acta Universitatis Asiae Mediae. Botanica

Trudy Sredneaziatskogo Gosudarstvennogo U — Trudy Sredneaziatskogo Gosudarstvennogo Universiteta

Trudy Stavropol' Sel'-Khoz Inst — Trudy Stavropol'skogo Sel'skokhozyaistvennogo Instituta

Trudy Sukhum Bot Sada — Trudy Sukhumskogo Botanicheskogo Sada [*Sukhum*]

Trudy Sverdlovsk Gorn Inst — Trudy Sverdlovskogo Gornogo Instituta im. V.V. Vakhrusheva [*Sverdlovsk*]

Trudy Sverdlovsk Sel'-Khoz Inst — Trudy Sverdlovskogo Sel'skokhozyaistvennogo Instituta

Trudy Tadzhik Astr Obs — Trudy Tadzhikskoi Astronomicheskoi Observatorii [*Stalingrad*]

Trudy Tadzhik Bot Sada — Trudy Tadzhikskogo Botanicheskogo Sada

Trudy Tadzhik Fil Akad Nauk SSSR — Trudy Tadzhikskogo Filiala. Akademiya Nauk SSSR [*Moskva*]

Trudy Tadzhik Fil Geogr Obshch SSSR — Trudy Tadzhikskogo Filiala Grograficheskogo Obshchestva SSSR. Akademiya Nauk Tadzhikskoi SSR

Trudy Tadzhik Nauchno-Issled Inst Sel Khoz — Trudy Tadzhikskogo Nauchno-Issledovatel'skogo Instituta Sel'skogo Khozyaistva

Trudy Tadzikistansk Bazy — Trudy Tadzikistanskoj Bazy

Trudy Tadzik Politehn Inst — Trudy Tadzikskogo Politehniceskogo Instituta

Trudy Taganrog Radiotekh Inst — Trudy Taganrogskogo Radiotekhnicheskogo Instituta [*Taganrog*]

Trudy Tallinsk Politehn Inst — Trudy Tallinskogo Politekhnicheskogo Instituta

Trudy Tashkent Astr Fiz Obs — Trudy Tashkentskoi Astronomicheskoi i Fizicheskoi Observatorii [*Tashkent*]

Trudy Tashkent Geofiz Obs — Trudy Tashkentskoi Geofizicheskoi Observatorii [*Tashkent*]

Trudy Tashkent Inst Inzh Irrig Mekhaniz Sel Khoz — Trudy Tashkentskogo Instituta Inzhenerov Irrigatsii i Mekhanizatsii Sel'skogo Khozyaistva [*Tashkent*]

Trudy Tashkent Inst Inzh Zheleznodorozh Transp — Trudy Tashkentskogo Instituta Inzhenerov Zheleznodorozhnogo Transporta [*Tashkent*]

Trudy Tashkent Sel Khoz Inst — Trudy Tashkentskogo Sel'skokhozyaistvennogo Instituta [*Tashkent*]

Trudy Taskent Gos Univ — Trudy Taskentskogo Gosudarstvennogo Universiteta Imeni V. I. Lenina. Matematika

Trudy Tatar Nauchno-Issled Inst Sel'Khoz — Trudy Tatarskii Nauchno-Issledovatel'skii Institut Sel'skogo Khozyaistva

Trudy Tatar Respub Gos Sel-Khoz Opyt Sta — Trudy Tatarskoi Respublikanskoi Gosudarstvennoi Sel'skokhozyaistvennoi Opytnoi Stantsii

Trudy Tbilis Bot Inst — Trudy Tbilisskogo Botanicheskogo Instituta [*Tbilisi*]

Trudy Tbilis Gos Med Inst — Trudy Tbilisskogo Gosudarstvennogo Meditsinskogo Instituta [*Tbilisi*]

Trudy Tbilis Gos Univ — Trudy Tbilisskogo Gosudarstvennogo Universiteta [*Tbilisi*]

Trudy Tbilisk Univ Fiz-Mat Estestv Nauki — Trudy Tbilisskogo Universiteta Fiziko-Matematiceske i Estestvennyi Nauki

Trudy Tbilis Mat Inst — Trudy Tbilisskogo Matematicheskogo Instituta. Akademiya Nauk Gruzinskoi SSR [*Tbilisi*]

Trudy Tbilis Nauchno Issled Gidromet Inst — Trudy Tbilisskogo Nauchno-Issledovatel'skogo Gidrometeorologicheskogo Instituta [*Tbilisi*]

Trudy Tbilissk Bot Sada — Trudy Tbilisskogo Botaniceskogo Sada/Thbilisis Botanikuri Bagis Sromebi/Travauxdu Jardin Botanique du Tibilissi

Trudy Tbiliss Mat Inst Razmadze Akad Nauk Gruzin SSR — Trudy Tbilisskogo Matematiceskogo Instituta Imeni A. M. Razmadze Akademija Nauk Gruzinskoi SSR

Trudy Tbiliss Univ — Trudy Tbilisskogo Universiteta Fiziko-Matematiceskie i Estestvennyi Nauki

Trudy Tbiliss Univ Mat Mekh Astronom — Trudy. Tbilisskii Universitet. Matematika. Mekhanika. Astronomiya

Trudy Tekh Kom Glav Uprav Neoklad Sbor Kazenn Prodazhi Pitei — Trudy Tekhnicheskago Komiteta Glavnago Upravleniya Neokladnykh Sborov i Kazennoi Prodazhi Pitei [*S. Peterburg*]

Trudy Terap Klin Imp Mosk Univ — Trudy Terapevticheskoi Kliniki Imperatorskago Moskovskago Universiteta [*Moskva*]

Trudy Tersk Otd Imp Russk Tekh Obshch — Trudy Terskago Otdeleniya Imperatskago Russkago Tekhnicheskago Obshchestva [*Groznyi*]

Trudy Tikhookean Inst — Trudy Tikhookeanskogo Instituta

Trudy Tikhookean Kom — Trudy Tikhookeanskogo Komiteta. Akademiya Nauk SSSR

Trudy Tomsk Elektromekh Inst Inzh Zheleznodorozh Transp — Trudy Tomskogo Elektromekhanicheskogo Instituta Inzhenerov Zheleznodorozhnogo Transporta [*Tomsk*]

Trudy Tomsk Gosud Univ Kujbyseva Tomsk Gosud Pedagog Inst — Trudy Tomskogo Gosudarstvennogo Universiteta imeni V. V. Kujbyseva i Tomskogo Gosudarstvennogo Pedagogiceskogo Instituta

Trudy Tomsk Gos Univ — Trudy Tomskogo Gosudarstvennogo Universiteta

Trudy Tomsk Med Inst — Trudy Tomskogo Meditsinskogo Instituta [*Tomsk*]

Trudy Tomsk Univ — Trudy Tomskogo Universiteta

Trudy Tsent Chernoz Gos Zapov — Trudy Tsentral'nogo Chernozemnogo Gosudarstvennogo Zapovednika

Trudy Tsent Nauchno Issled Dezinfekt Inst — Trudy Tsentral'nogo Nauchno-Issledovatel'skogo Dezinfektsionnogo Instituta [*Moskva*]

Trudy Tsent Nauchno Issled Inst Sakh Prom — Trudy Tsentral'nogo Nauchno-Issledovatel'skogo Instituta Sakharnoi Promyshlennosti

Trudy Tsent Nauchno Issled Inst Tekst Prom — Trudy Tsentral'nogo Nauchno-Issledovatel'skogo Instituta Tekstil'noi Promyshlennosti [*Moskva*]

Trudy Tsent Nauchno Issled Inst Torf Prom — Trudy Tsentral'nogo Nauchno-Issledovatel'skogo Instituta po Torfyanoi Promyshlennosti [*Moskva*]

Trudy Tsent Nauchno Issled Lab Biol Okhot Promysla — Trudy Tsentral'noi Nauchno-Issledovatel'skoi Laboratorii Biologii Okhotnich'ego Promysla i Tovarovedeniya Zhivotnogo Syr'ya

Trudy Tsent Nauchno Issled Lab Elekt Obrab Mater — Trudy Tsentral'noi Nauchno-Issledovatel'skoi Laboratorii Elektricheskoi Obrabotki Materialov

Trudy Tsent Nauchno Issled Lab Ionif — Trudy Tsentral'noi Nauchno-Issledovatel'skoi Laboratorii Ionifikatsii [*Voronezh*]

Trudy Tsent Nauchno Issled Lesokhim Inst — Trudy Tsentral'nogo Nauchno-Issledovatel'skogo Lesokhimicheskogo Instituta [*Moskva*]

Trudy Tsent Shelkov Sta RSFSR — Trudy Tsentral'noi Shelkovodnoi Stantsii RSFSR [*Moskva*]

Trudy Tsent Sib Bot Sada — Trudy Tsentral'nogo Sibirskogo Botanicheskogo Sada

Trudy Tsent Torf Sta — Trudy Tsentral'noi Torfyanoi Stantsii [*Moskva*]

Trudy Tsent Uprav Prom Razv — Trudy Tsentral'nogo Upravleniya Promyshlennykh Razvedok [*Moskva*]

Trudy Tul Mekh Inst — Trudy Tul'skogo Mekhanicheskogo Instituta [*Tula*]

Trudy Turkestansk Naucn Obsc — Trudy Turkestanskogo Naucnogo Obscestva/ Transactions. Scientific Society of Turkestan

Trudy Turkest Gos Univ — Trudy Turkestanskogo Gosudarstvennogo Universiteta

Trudy Turkest Nauch Obshch — Trudy Turkestanskogo Nauchnogo Obshchestva [*Tashkent*]

Trudy Turkest Selek Sta — Trudy Turkestanskoi Selektsionnoi Stantsii [*Tashkent*]

Trudy Turkmen Gos Bot Sada — Trudy Turkmenskogo Gosudarstvennogo Botanicheskogo Sada [*Stalinabad*]

Trudy Turkmen Gos Med Inst — Trudy Turkmenskogo Gosudarstvennogo Meditsinskogo Instituta [*Ashkhabad*]

Trudy Turkmen Kozhno Vener Inst — Trudy Turkmenskogo Kozhno-Venerologicheskogo Instituta [*Ashkhabad*]

Trudy Turkmen Nauchno Issled Inst Zeml — Trudy Turkmenskogo Nauchno-Issledovatel'skogo Instituta Zemledeliya [*Ashkhabad*]

Trudy Turkmen Nauchno Issled Trakhom Inst — Trudy Turkmenskogo Nauchno-Issledovatel'skogo Trakhomatoznogo Instituta

Trudy Turkmen Sel'Khoz Inst — Trudy Turkmenskogo Sel'sko-Khozyaistvennogo Instituta

Trudy Tuvin Kompleks Eksped — Trudy Tuvinskoi Kompleksnoi Ekspeditsii. Sovet po Izucheniyu Proizvoditel'nykh Sil. Akademiya Nauk SSSR

Trudy Ufim Gub Zemsk Zootekh Kom — Trudy Ufimskoi Gubernskoi Zemskoi Zootekhnicheskoi Komissii [*Ufa*]

Trudy Ufim Nauchno Issled Inst Vaktsin Syvor — Trudy Ufimskogo Nauchno-Issledovatel'skogo Instituta Vaktsin i Syvorotok [*Ufa*]

Trudy Ufim Neft Nauchno Issled Inst — Trudy Ufimskogo Neftyanogo Nauchno-Issledovatel'skogo Instituta

Trudy Ufmsk Aviac Inst — Trudy Ufimskogo Aviacionnogo Instituta

Trudy Ukrajinsk Inst Prykl Bot — Trudy Ukrajins'kogo Instytutu Prykladnoji Botaniky. Arbeiten des Ukralnischen Instituts fuer Angewandte Botanik

Trudy Ukr Gidromet Inst — Trudy Ukrainskogo Gidrometeorologicheskogo Instituta

Trudy Ukr Inst Hruntozn — Trudy Ukrains'kogo Instytutu Hruntoznavstva [*Khar'kiv*]

Trudy Ukr Inst Prykl Bot — Trudy Ukrayins'koho Instytutu Prykladnoyi Botaniky [*Khar'kiv*]

Trudy Ukr Nauchno Issled Geologo Razv Inst — Trudy Ukrainskogo Nauchno-Issledovatel'skogo Geologo-Razvedochnogo Instituta [*Moskva*]

Trudy Ukr Nauchno Issled Gidromet Inst — Trudy Ukrainskogo Nauchno-Issledovatel'skogo Gidrometeorologicheskogo Instituta [*Kiev*]

Trudy Ukr Nauchno Issled Inst Les Khoz Agrolesomelior — Trudy Ukrainskogo Nauchno-Issledovatel'skogo Instituta Lesnogo Khozyaistva i Agrolesomelioratsii

Trudy Ukr Nauchno Issled Inst Metallov — Trudy Ukrainskogo Nauchno-Issledovatel'skogo Instituta Metallov [*Kharkov*]

Trudy Ukr Nauchno Issled Inst Pochv — Trudy Ukrainskogo Nauchno-Issledovatel'skogo Instituta Pochvovedeniya [*Kharkov*]

Trudy Ukr Nauchno Issled Inst Vinogr — Trudy Ukrainskogo Nauchno-Issledovatel'skogo Instituta Vinogradarstva [*Khar'kov*]

Trudy Ukr Nauchno Issled Inst Zern Khoz — Trudy Ukrainskogo Nauchno-Issledovatel'skogo Instituta Zernovogo Khozyaistva [*Khar'kov*]

Trudy Ukr Nauchno Issled Lab Moloch Maslosyr Prom — Trudy Ukrainskoi Nauchno-Issledovatel'skoi Laboratorii, Molochnoi i Maslosyrodel'noi Promyshlennosti [*Kiev*]

Trudy Ukr Nauchno Tekh Obshch Chern Metall — Trudy Ukrainskogo Nauchno-Tekhnicheskogo Obshchestva Chernoi Metallurgii

Trudy Ukr Nauk Dosl Heol Inst — Trudy. Ukrayins'kyi Naukovo-Doslidchyi Heolohichnyi Instytut [*Kyyiv*]

Trudy Ul'yanov Sel'khoz Inst — Trudy Ul'yanovskogo Sel'skokhozyaistvennogo Instituta

Trudy Univ Druzby Narod — Trudy Universiteta Druzhby Narodov Imeni Patrisa Lumumby

Trudy Ural Politehn Inst — Trudy Ural'skogo Politehniceskogo Instituta

Trudy Uzbek Filiala Akad Nauk SSSR — Trudy Uzbekistanskogo Filiala Akademii Nauk SSSR

Trudy Vladimir Uchonoy Arkhv Kom — Trudy Vladimirskoy Uchonoy Arkhivnoy Komissii

Trudy VNIITTI — Trudy Vyshiy Natsional'nyy Institut Iskusstva i Tekhniki

Trudy Volgogr Opytno-Melior Sta — Trudy Volgogradskoi Opytno-Meliorativnoi Stantsii

Trudy Vologod Sel'khoz Inst — Trudy Vologodskogo Sel'skokhozyaistvennogo Instituta

Trudy Voronezh Gos Zapov — Trudy Voronezhskogo Gosudarstvennogo Zapovednika [*Moskva*]

Trudy Voronezh Khim Tekhnol Inst — Trudy Voronezhskogo Khimiko-Tekhnologicheskogo Instituta [*Voronezh*]

Trudy Voronezh Otd Vses Nauchno Issled Inst Prud Ryb Khoz — Trudy Voronezhskogo Otdeleniya Vsesoyuznogo Nauchno-Issledovatel'skogo Instituta Prudovogo Rybnogo Khozyaistva

Trudy Voronezh Sta Borbe Vredit Rast — Trudy Voronezhskoi Stantsii po Bor'be s Vreditelyami Rastenii [*Voronezh*]

Trudy Voronezh Univ — Trudy Voronezhskogo Universiteta

Trudy Voronezh Zoovetinst — Trudy Voronezhskogo Zooveterinarnogo Instituta

Trudy Voroshilov Zootekh Vet Inst — Trudy Voroshilovskogo Zootekhnichesko-Veterinarnogo Instituta [*Pyatigorsk*]

Trudy Vost Kazakh Gos Opyt Sta — Trudy Vostochno-Kazakhstanskaya Gosudarstvennaya Sel'skokhozyaistvennaya Opytnaya Stantsiya

Trudy Vost Sib Fil Akad Nauk SSSR — Trudy Vostochno-Sibirskogo Filiala Akademii Nauk SSSR [*Moskva*]

Trudy Vost Sib Geol Inst — Trudy Vostochno-Sibirskogo Geologicheskogo Instituta. Sibirskoe Otdelenie. Akademiya Nauk SSSR

Trudy Vost Sib Geol Razv Tresta — Trudy Vostochno-Sibirskogo Geologo-Razvedochnogo Tresta

Trudy Vost Sib Gos Univ — Trudy Vostochno-Sibirskogo Gosudarstvennogo Universiteta [*Moskva, Irkutsk*]

Trudy Vost Sibirsk Fil — Trudy Vostocno-Sibirskogo Filiala

Trudy Vost-Sibir Tehnol Inst — Trudy Vostochno-Sibirskogo Tekhnologicheskogo Instituta

Trudy Vost Sib Med Inst — Trudy Vostochno-Sibirskogo Meditsinskogo Instituta [*Irkutsk*]

Trudy Vost Sib Nauch Rybokhoz Sta — Trudy Vostochno-Sibirskoi Nauchnoi Rybokhozyaistvennoi Stantsii [*Krasnoyarsk*]

Trudy Vost Sib Otd Imp Russk Geogr Obshch — Trudy Vostochno-Sibirskago Otdela Imperatorskago Russkago Geograficheskago Obshchestva [*Irkutsk*]

Trudy Vrem Med Obshch Daln Vost — Trudy Vremennago Meditsinskago Obshchestva v Dal'nem Vostoke v g. Kharbine

Trudy Vseross Elektrotekh Sezda — Trudy Vserossiiskogo Elektrotekhnicheskogo S"ezda [*S. Peterburg*]

Trudy Vseross Entomo Fitopat Sezda — Trudy Vserossiiskogo Entomo-Fitopatologicheskogo S"ezda [*S. Peterburg*]

Trudy Vseross Farm Sezda — Trudy Vserossiiskago Farmatsevticheskago S"ezda [*Moskva*]

Trudy Vseross Gidrol Sezda — Trudy Vserossiiskogo Gidrologicheskogo S"ezda [*Leningrad*]

Trudy Vserossiskoy Akad Khudozhestv — Trudy Vserossiskoy Akademii Khudozhestv

Trudy Vseross Nauchno Issled Inst Sakh Svekly — Trudy Vserossiiskogo Nauchno-Issledovatel'skogo Instituta Sakharnoi Svekly i Sakhara [*Ramon'*]

Trudy Vseross Oto Lar Sezda — Trudy Vserossiiskago Oto-laringologicheskogo S"ezda v S. Peterburge

Trudy Vseross Sezda Detsk Vrach — Trudy Vserossiiskago S"ezda Detskikh Vrachei [*S. Peterburg*]

Trudy Vseross Sezda Deyat Geol — Trudy Vserossiiskago S"ezda Deyatelei po Geologii i Razvedochnomu Delu [*S. Peterburg*]

Trudy Vseross Sezda Deyat Klim — Trudy Vserossiiskago S"ezda Deyatelei po Klimatologii, Gidrologii i Bal'neologii [*S. Peterburg*]

Trudy Vseross Sezda Estest Vrach — Trudy Vserossiiskago S"ezda Estestvoispytatelei i Vrachei [*S. Peterburg*]

Trudy Vseross Sezda Ptitsev — Trudy Vserossiiskago S"ezda Ptitsevodov [*Moskva*]

Trudy Vseross Sezda Zool Anat Gistol — Trudy Vserossiiskago S"ezda Zoologov, Anatomov i Gistologov [*Petrograd*]

Trudy Vseross Vet Sezda — Trudy Vserossiiskago Veterinarnago S"ezda [*S. Peterburg*]

Trudy Vses Aerogeol Tresta — Trudy Vsesoyuznogo Aerogeologicheskogo Tresta

Trudy Vses Elektrotekh Ass — Trudy Vsesoyuznoi Elektrotekhnicheskoi Assotsiatsii [*Leningrad, Moskva*]

Trudy Vses Ent Obshch — Trudy Vsesoyuznogo Entomologicheskogo Obshchestva

Trudy Vses Nauchno-Issled Geol Inst — Trudy Vsesoyuznogo Nauchno-Issledovatel'skogo Geologicheskogo Instituta

Trudy Vses Nauchno Issled Geol Razv Neft Inst — Trudy Vsesoyuznogo Nauchno-Issledovatel'skogo Geologo-Razvedochnogo Neftyanogo Instituta

Trudy Vses Nauchno Issled Inst Antibiot — Trudy Vsesoyuznogo Nauchno-Issledovatel'skogo Instituta Antibiotikov [*Moskva*]

Trudy Vses Nauchno Issled Inst Aviats Mater — Trudy Vsesoyuznogo Nauchno-Issledovatel'skogo Instituta Aviatsionnykh Materialov [*Moskva*]

Trudy Vses Nauchno Issled Inst Burov Tekh — Trudy Vsesoyuznogo Nauchno-Issledovatel'skogo Instituta Burovoi Tekhniki

Trudy Vses Nauchno Issled Inst Chai Khoz — Trudy Vsesoyuznogo Nauchno-Issledovatel'skogo Instituta Chainogo Khozyaistva [*Tiflis*]

Trudy Vses Nauchno Issled Inst Konserv Ovoshchesush Prom — Trudy Vsesoyuznogo Nauchno-Issledovatel'skogo Instituta Konservnoi i Ovoshchesushel'noi Promyshlennosti

Trudy Vses Nauchno Issled Inst Korml Sel Khoz Zhivot — Trudy Vsesoyuznogo Nauchno-Issledovatel'skogo Instituta Kormleniya Sel'skokhozyaistvennykh Zhivotnykh [*Moskva*]

Trudy Vses Nauchno Issled Inst Les Khoz — Trudy Vsesoyuznogo Nauchno-Issledovatel'skogo Instituta Lesnogo Khozyaistva [*Putkino, Moskva*]

Trudy Vses Nauchno Issled Inst Makhor Prom — Trudy Vsesoyuznogo Nauchno-Issledovatel'skogo Instituta Makhorochnoi Promyshlennosti [*Kiev*]

Trudy Vses Nauchno Issled Inst Mekhaniz Sel Khoz — Trudy Vsesoyuznogo Nauchno-Issledovatel'skogo Instituta Mekhanizatsii Sel'skogo Khozyaistva

Trudy Vses Nauchno-Issled Inst Metod Tekh Razv — Trudy Vsesoyuznogo Nauchno-Issledovatel'skogo Instituta Metodiki i Tekhniki Razvedki

Trudy Vses Nauchno Issled Inst Metrol — Trudy Vsesoyuznogo Nauchno-Issledovatel'skogo Instituta Metrologii im. D.I. Mendeleeva

Trudy Vses Nauchno Issled Inst Miner Syrya — Trudy Vsesoyuznogo Nauchno-Issledovatel'skogo Instituta Mineral'nogo Syr'ya [*Moskva*]

Trudy Vses Nauchno Issled Inst Moloch Prom — Trudy Vsesoyuznogo Nauchno-Issledovatel'skogo Instituta Molochnoi Promyshlennosti [*Moskva*]

Trudy Vses Nauchno Issled Inst Morsk Ryb Khoz Okeanogr — Trudy Vsesoyuznogo Nauchno-Issledovatel'skogo Instituta Morskogo Rybnogo Khozyaistva i Okeanografii [*Moskva, Leningrad*]

Trudy Vses Nauchno Issled Inst Myas Prom — Trudy Vsesoyuznogo Nauchno-Issledovatel'skogo Instituta Myasnoi Promyshlennosti

Trudy Vses Nauchno Issled Inst Norm Mashinost — Trudy Vsesoyuznogo Nauchno-Issledovatel'skogo Instituta po Normalizatsii v Mashinostroenii [*Moskva*]

Trudy Vses Nauchno Issled Inst Ovchev Kozov — Trudy Vsesoyuznogo Nauchno-Issledovatel'skogo Instituta Ovchevodstva i Kozovodstva [*Pyatigorsk*]

Trudy Vses Nauchno Issled Inst Pererab Ispolzov Topl — Trudy Vsesoyuznogo Nauchno-Issledovatel'skogo Instituta Pererabotki i Ispol'zovaniya Topliva

Trudy Vses Nauchno Issled Inst Pererab Slantsev — Trudy Vsesoyuznogo Nauchno-Issledovatel'skogo Instituta po Pererabotke Slantsev

Trudy Vses Nauchno Issled Inst Pezoopt Miner Syrya — Trudy Vsesoyuznogo Nauchno-Issledovatel'skogo Instituta P'ezooopticheskogo Mineral'nogo Syr'ya

Trudy Vses Nauchno Issled Inst Prir Gazov — Trudy Vsesoyuznogo Nauchno-Issledovatel'skogo Instituta Prirodnykh Gazov

Trudy Vses Nauchno-Issled Inst Sakharn Svekly Sakhara — Trudy Vsesoyuznogo Nauchno-Issledovatel'skogo Instituta Sakharnoi Svekly i Sakhara

Trudy Vses Nauchno Issled Inst Sel Khoz Mikrobiol — Trudy Vsesoyuznogo Nauchno-Issledovatel'skogo Instituta Sel'skokhozyaistvennoi Mikrobiologii [*Leningrad*]

Trudy Vses Nauchno Issled Inst Sint Nat Dush Veshch — Trudy Vsesoyuznogo Nauchno-Issledovatel'skogo Instituta Sinteticheskikh i Natural'nykh Dushistykh Veshchestv

Trudy Vses Nauchno Issled Inst Sol Prom — Trudy Vsesoyuznogo Nauchno-Issledovatel'skogo Instituta Solyanoi Promyshlennosti [*Moskva*]

Trudy Vses Nauchno-Issled Inst Spirt Prom — Trudy Vsesoyuznogo Nauchno-Issledovatel'skogo Instituta Spirtovoi Promyshlennosti [*Moskva*]

Trudy Vses Nauchno Issled Inst Stekla — Trudy Vsesoyuznogo Nauchno-Issledovatel'skogo Instituta Stekla

Trudy Vses Nauchno-Issled Inst Torf Prom — Trudy Vsesoyuznogo Nauchno-Issledovatel'skogo Instituta Torfyanoi Promyshlennosti

Trudy Vses Nauchno-Issled Inst Udobr Agrotekh Agropochv — Trudy Vsesoyuznogo Nauchno-Issledovatel'skogo Instituta Udobrenii Agrotekhnikii Agropochvovedeniya

Trudy Vses Nauchno-Issled Inst Vet Sanit Ektoparazit — Trudy Vsesoyuznogo Nauchno-Issledovatel'skogo Instituta Veterinarnoi Sanitarii i Ektoparazitologii

Trudy Vses Nauchno-Issled Inst Zashch Rast — Trudy Vsesoyuznogo Nauchno-Issledovatel'skogo Instituta Zashchity Rastenii

Trudy Vses Nauchno Issled Inst Zerna — Trudy Vsesoyuznogo Nauchno-Issledovatel'skogo Instituta Zerna i Produktov ego Pererabotki

Trudy Vses Nauchno Issled Inst Zernob Kult — Trudy Vsesoyuznogo Nauchno-Issledovatel'skogo Instituta Zernobobovykh Kul'tur [*Moskva*]

Trudy Vses Nauchno Issled Inst Zheleznodorozh Transp — Trudy Vsesoyuznogo Nauchno-Issledovatel'skogo Instituta Zheleznodorozhnogo Transporta [*Moskva*]

Trudy Vses Neftegaz Nauchno Issled Inst — Trudy Vsesoyuznogo Neftegazovogo Nauchno-Issledovatel'skogo Instituta

Trudy Vses Neft Nauchno Issled Geol Razv Inst — Trudy Vsesoyuznogo Neftyanogo Nauchno-Issledovatel'skogo Geologo-Razvedochnogo Instituta [*Leningrad*]

Trudy Vses Obshch Fiziol Biokhim Farmak — Trudy Vsesoyuznogo Obshchestva Fiziologov, Biokhimikov, i Farmakologov. Akademiya Nauk SSSR

Trudy Vsesojuzn Akad Selsko Hoz Nauk Lenina Ser 17 Borba Vred — Trudy Vsesojuznoj Akademii Sel'sko-Hozjajstvennyh Nauk imeni V. I. Lenina. Serija 17. Bor'ba s Vrediteljami Sel'skohozjajstvennyh Rastenij

Trudy Vsesojuz Nauc-Issled Inst Sov Zakon — Trudy Vsesojuznogo Nauchno-Issledovatel'skogo Instituta Sovetskogo Zakonodatel'stva

Trudy Vsesojuz Nauc-Issled Inst Zascity Rast — Trudy Vsesojuznogo Naucno-Issledovatel'skogo Instituta Zascity Rastenij

Trudy Vsesojuz Naucno-Issled Inst Elektromeh — Trudy Vsesojuznogo Naucno-Issledovatel'skogo Instituta Elektromehaniki

Trudy Vsesojuzn Gidrobiol Obsc — Trudy Vsesojuznogo Gidrobiologiceskogo Obscestva

Trudy Vsesojuzn Sezda Ohr Prir SSSR — Trudy Vsesojuznogo S"ezda po Ohrane Prirody v SSSR

Trudy Vsesojuz Zaocn Energet Inst — Trudy Vsesojuznogo Zaocnogo Energeticeskogo Instituta

Trudy Vses Ordena Lenina Inst Eksp Vet — Trudy Vsesoyuznogo Ordena Lenina Instituta Eksperimental'noi Veterinarii

Trudy Vses Tsent Nauchno Issled Inst Sakh Prom — Trudy Vsesoyuznogo Tsentral'nogo Nauchno-Issledovatel'skogo Instituta Sakharnoi Promyshlennosti [*Moskva*]

Trudy Vses Tsent Sta Ris Khoz — Trudy Vsesoyuznoi Tsentral'noi Stantsii Risovogo Khozyaistva [*Leningrad*]

Trudy Vses Zaoch Energ Inst — Trudy Vsesoyuznogo Zaochnogo Energeticheskogo Instituta [*Moskva*]

Trudy VTI — Trudy Vsesojuznogo Teplotehniceskogo Instituta

Trudy Vychisl Tsentra Tartu Gos Univ — Trudy Vychislitel'nogo Tsentra Tartuskii Gosudarstvennyi Universitet

Trudy Vychisl Tsentra Tartu Univ — Trugy Vychislitel'nogo Tsentra. Tartuskii Universite

Trudy Vycisl Centra Akad Nauk Gruzin SSR — Trudy Vycislitel'nogo Centra Akademija Nauk Gruzinskoi SSR

Trudy Vycisl Centra Tartu Gos Univ — Trudy Vycislitel'nogo Centra Tartuskii Gosudarstvennyi Universitet

Trudy Yuzhno Russk Obshch Pchelov — Trudy Yuzhno-Russkago Obshchestva Pchelovodstva [*Kiev*]

Trudy Yuzhno Turkmen Arkheol Kompleks Eksped — Trudy Yuzhno-Turkmenistanskoi Arkheologicheskoi Kompleksnoi Ekspeditsii

Trudy Yuzhno Turkmen Arkheol Kompleksnoy Eksped — Trudy Yuzhno-Turkmenistanskoy Arkheologicheskoy Kompleksnoy Ekspeditsii

Trudy Zabaikal Obshch Vrach — Trudy Zabaikal'skago Obshchestva Vrachei [*Chita*]

Trudy Zabaikal Otd Imp Russk Geogr Obshch — Trudy Zabaikal'skago Otdeleniya Priamurskago Otdela Imperatskago Russkago Geograficheskago Obshchestva [*Chita*]

Trudy Zakavk Nauch Ass — Trudy Zakavkazskoi Nauchnoi Assotsiatsii [*Tiflis*]

Trudy Zakavk Nauchno Issled Inst Vod Khoz — Trudy Zakavkazskogo Nauchno-Issledovatel'skogo Instituta Vodnogo Khozyaistva [*Tbilisi*]

Trudy Zasc Rast Sibiri — Trudy po Zascite Rastenij Sibiri

Trudy Zashch Rast — Trudy po Zashchite Rastenii [*Leningrad*]

Trudy Zashch Rast Sib — Trudy po Zashchite Rastenii Sibiri [*Novosibirsk*]

Trudy Zashch Rast Vost Sib — Trudy po Zashchite Rastenii Vostochnoi Sibiri [*Irkutsk*]

Trudy Zonal Sta Plodov Khoz Tiflis — Trudy Zonal'noi Stantsii Plodovogo Khozyaistva (Tiflis)

Trudy Zool Inst Baku — Trudy Zoologicheskogo Instituta. Azerbaidzhanskii Filial. Akademiya Nauk SSSR (Baku)

Trudy Zool Inst (Leningr) — Trudy Zoologicheskogo Instituta Akademii Nauk SSSR (Leningrad)

Trudy Zool Inst Tbilisi — Trudy Zoologicheskogo Instituta. Akademiya Nauk Gruzinskoi SSR (Tbilisi)

Trudy Zool Sekt Baku — Trudy Zoologicheskogo Sektora Zakavkazskogo Filiala. Akademiya Nauk SSSR (Baku)

Trudy Zool Sekt Tbilisi — Trudy Zoologicheskogo Sektora Gruzinskogo Otdeleniya Zakavkazskogo Filiala. Akademiya Nauk SSSR [*Tbilisi*]

Tru Est — Trusts and Estates

Tr Ufim Aviats Inst — Trudy Ufimskogo Aviatsionnogo Instituta

Tr Ufim Nauchno-Issled Inst Gig Profzabol — Trudy Ufimskogo Nauchno-Issledovatel'skogo Instituta Gigieny i Profzabolevanii

Tr Ufim Neft Naucho-Issled Inst — Trudy Ufimskii Neftyanoi Nauchno-Issledovatel'skii Institut

TRUGA — Trudy Ukrainskii Nauchno-Issledovatel'skii Geologo-Razvedochnyi Institut

Tr Ukr Gos Nauchno-Issled Inst Prikl Khim — Trudy Ukrainskogo Gosudarstvennogo Nauchno-Issledovatel'skogo Instituta Prikladnoi Khimii

Tr Ukr Inst Eksp Endokrinol — Trudy Ukrainskogo Instituta Eksperimental'noi Endokrinologii

Tr Ukr Nauch-Issled Gidrometeorol Inst — Trudy Ukrainsko Nauchno-Issledovatel'skogo Gidrometeorologicheskogo Instituta

Tr Ukr Nauchno Issled Geol Razved Inst — Trudy Ukrainskii Nauchno-Issledovatel'skii Geologo-Razvedochnyi Institut

Tr Ukr Nauchno-Issled Gidrometeorol Inst — Trudy Ukrainskogo Nauchno-Issledovatel'skogo Gidrometeorologicheskogo Instituta

Tr Ukr Nauchno Issled Inst Klin Med — Trudy Ukrainskogo Nauchno-Issledovatel'skogo Instituta Klinicheskoi Meditsiny

Tr Ukr Nauchno Issled Inst Konservn Promsti — Trudy Ukrainskogo Nauchno-Issledovatel'skogo Instituta Konservnoi Promyshlennosti

Tr Ukr Nauchno Issled Inst Lesn Khoz Agrolesomelior — Trudy Ukrainskogo Nauchno-Issledovatel'skogo Instituta Lesnogo Khozyaista i Agrolesomelioratsii

Tr Ukr Nauchno Issled Inst Pishch Promsti — Trudy Ukrainskii Nauchno-Issledovatel'skii Institut Pishchevoi Promyshlennosti

Tr Ukr Nauchno-Issled Inst Prir Gazov — Trudy Ukrainskii Nauchno-Issledovatel'skii Institut Prirodnykh Gazov

Tr Ukr Nauchno-Issled Inst Rastenievod Sel Genet — Trudy Ukrainskogo Nauchno-Issledovatel'skogo Instituta Rastenievodstva Selektsii i Genetiki

Tr Ukr Nauchno-Issled Inst Spirt Likero Vodochn Promsti — Trudy Ukrainskii Nauchno-Issledovatel'skii Institut Spirtovoi i Likero-Vodochnoi Promyshlennosti

Tr Ukr Nauchno-Issled Inst Zernovogo Khoz — Trudy Ukrainskogo Nauchno-Issledovatel'skogo Instituta Zernovogo Khozyaistva

Tr Ukr Reg Nauchno Issled Inst — Trudy Ukrainskogo Regional'nogo Nauchno-Issledovatel'skogo Instituta

Tr Ul'vanovsk Gos Opytn Stn Zhivotnovod — Trudy Ul'vanovskaya Gosudarstvennaya Opytnaya Stantsiya Zhivotnovodstva

Tr Ulyanovsk Politekh Inst — Trudy Ul'yanovskii Politekhnicheskii Institut

Tr Ul'yanovsk S-Kh Inst — Trudy Ul'yanovskogo Sel'skokhozyaistvennogo Instituta

Tr Ul'yanovsk Skh Opytn Stn — Trudy Ul'yanovskoi Sel'skokhozyaistvennoi Opytnoi Stantsii

Tr Univ Druzhby Nar — Trudy Universiteta Druzhby Narodov

Tr Univ Druzhby Nar Fiz — Trudy Universiteta Druzhby Narodov. Fizika

Tr Univ Druzhby Nar Im Patrisa Lumumby — Trudy Universiteta Druzhby Narodov Imeni Patrisa Lumumby

Tr Univ Druzhby Nar Ser Fiz — Trudy Universiteta Druzhby Narodov Imeni Patrisa Lumumby. Seriya Fizika

Tr Upr Geol Okhr Nedr Sov Minist Kirg SSR — Trudy Upravleniya Geologii i Okhrany Nedr pri Sovete Ministrov Kirgizskoi SSR

Tr Ural Elektromekh Inst Inzh Zheleznodorozhn — Trudy Ural'skogo Elektromekhanicheskogo Instituta Inzhenerov ZheleznodorozhnogoTransporta

Tr Ural Ind Inst — Trudy Ural'skogo Industrial'nogo Instituta

Tr Ural Lesotekh Inst — Trudy Ural'skogo Lesotekhnicheskogo Instituta

Tr Ural Nauchno-Issled Inst Chern Met — Trudy Ural'skogo Nauchno-Issledovatel'skogo Instituta Chernykh Metallov

Tr Ural Nauchno-Issled Inst Sel'sk Khoz — Trudy Ural'skogo Nauchno-Issledovatel'skogo Instituta Sel'skogo Khozyaistva

Tr Ural Nauchno-Issled Khim Inst — Trudy Ural'skogo Nauchno-Issledovatel'skogo Khimicheskogo Instituta

Tr Ural Nauchno-Issled Proekt Inst Mednoi Promsti — Trudy Ural'skii Nauchno-Issledovatel'skii i Proektnyi Institut Mednoi Promyshlennosti

Tr Ural Nauchno-Issled Proektn Inst Mednoi Promsti — Trudy Ural'skii Nauchno-Issledovatel'skii i Proektnyi Institut Mednoi Promyshlennosti

Tr Ural Otd Gos Nauchno-Issled Inst Ozern Rechn Rybn Khoz — Trudy Ural'skogo Otdeleniya Gosudarstvennyi Nauchno-Issledovatel'skii InstitutOzernogo i Rechnogo Rybnogo Khozyaistva

Tr Ural Otd Mosk Ova Ispyt Prir — Trudy Ural'skogo Otdeleniya Moskovskogo Obshchestva Ispytatelei Prirody

Tr Ural Otd Sib Nauchno-Issled Inst Rybn Khoz — Trudy Ural'skogo Otdeleniya Sibirskogo Nauchno-Issledovatel'skogo Instituta Rybnogo Khozyaistva

Tr Ural Politekh Inst — Trudy Ural'skogo Politekhnicheskogo Instituta Imeni S. M. Kirova

Tr Ural Politekh Inst Im S M Kirova — Trudy Ural'skogo Politekhnicheskogo Instituta Imeni S. M. Kirova

Truscon Rev — Truscon Review [*London*]

Trust Bull — Trust Bulletin

Trust Co — Trust Companies Magazine

Trust Co Mag — Trust Companies Magazine

Trust Lett — Trust Letter. American Bankers Association

Trust Newsl — Trust Newsletter

Trust Nletter — Trust Newsletter

Trusts & Es — Trusts and Estates

Trusts & Est — Trusts and Estates

Tr Uzb Geol Upr — Trudy Uzbekskogo Geologicheskogo Upravlenie

Tr Uzb Gos Nauchno-Issled Inst Kurortol Fizioter — Trudy Uzbekskogo Gosudarstvennogo Nauchno-Issledovatel'skogo i Instituta Kurortologii i Fizioterapii

Tr Uzb Inst Malyarii Med Parazitol — Trudy Uzbekistanskogo Instituta Malyarii i Meditsinskoi Parazitologii

Tr Uzb Nauchno-Issled Inst Fizioter Kurortol — Trudy Uzbekistanskogo Nauchno-Issledovatel'skogo Instituta Fizioterapii i Kurortologii

Tr Uzb Nauchno-Issled Inst Ortop Travmatol Prot — Trudy Uzbekistanskogo Nauchno-Issledovatel'skogo Instituta Ortopedii Travmatologii i Protezirovaniya

Tr Uzb Nauchno-Issled Inst Ortop Travmatol Protez — Trudy Uzbekistanskogo Nauchno-Issledovatel'skogo Instituta Ortopedii Travmatologii i Protezirovaniya

Tr Uzb Nauchno-Issled Inst Vet — Trudy Uzbekistanskogo Nauchno-Issledovatel'skogo Instituta Veterinarii

Tr VAMI — Trudy VAMI

TRVED8 — Theory of Science Development

Tr Velikoluk S-Kh Inst — Trudy Velikolukskogo Sel'skokhozyaistvennogo Instituta

Tr Vinnitsk Gos Med Inst — Trudy Vinnitskogo Gosudarstvennogo Meditsinskogo Instituta

Tr Vissh Inst Nar Stop (Varna Bulg) — Trudove na Visshiya Institut za Narodno Stopanstvo "D. Blagoev" (Varna Bulgaria)

Tr Vissh Pedagog Inst (Plovdiv) Mat Fiz Khim Biol — Trudove na Visshiya Pedagogicheski Institut (Plovdiv). Matematika, Fizika, Khimiya, Biologiya

Tr Vladivost Nauchno Issled Inst Epidemiol Mikrobiol Gig — Trudy Vladivostokskogo Nauchno-Issledovatel'skogo Instituta Epidemiologii, Mikrobiologii, i Gigieny

Tr VNIGRI — Trudy VNIGRI

Tr VNIIEI — Trudy VNIIEI

Tr VNII Fiz-Tekh Radiotekh Izmer — Trudy Vsesoyuznyj Nauchno-Issledovatel'skij Institut Fiziko-Tekhnicheskikh i Radiotekhnicheskikh Izmerenij

Tr Volgogr Gos Nauchno-Issled Proektn Inst Neft Promsti — Trudy Volgogradskii Gosudarstvennyi Nauchno-Issledovatel'skii i Proektnyi Institut Neftyanoi Promyshlennosti

Tr Volgogr Med Inst — Trudy Volgogradskogo Meditsinskogo Instituta

Tr Volgogr Nauchno-Issled Inst Neft Gazov Promsti — Trudy Volgogradskii Nauchno-Issledovatel'skii Institut Neftyanoi i Gazovoi Promyshlennosti

Tr Volgogr Opytno Melior Stn — Trudy Volgogradskaya Opytno-Meliorativnaya Stantsiya

Tr Volgogr Otd Gos Nauchno-Issled Inst Ozern Rechn Rybn Khoz — Trudy Volgogradskogo Otdeleniya Gosudarstvennogo Nauchno-Issledovatel'skogo Instituta Ozernogo i Rechnogo Rybnogo Khozyaistva

Tr Volgogr S-Kh Inst — Trudy Volgogradskogo Sel'skokhozyaistvennogo Instituta

Tr Vologod Molochn Inst — Trudy Vologodskogo Molochnogo Instituta

Tr Vologod Molochno Khoz Inst — Trudy Vologodskogo Molochno-Khozyaistvennogo Instituta

Tr Volzh Kamskogo Gos Zapov — Trudy Volzhsko-Kamskogo Gosudarstvennogo Zapovednika

Tr Voronezh Gos Med Inst — Trudy Voronezhskii Gosudarstvennyi Meditsinskii Institut

Tr Voronezh Gos Univ — Trudy Voronezhskogo Gosudarstvennogo Universiteta

Tr Voronezh Gos Zapov — Trudy Voronezhskogo Gosudarstvennogo Zapovednika

Tr Voronezh Inzh Stroit Inst — Trudy Voronezhskogo Inzhenerno-Stroitel'nogo Instituta

Tr Voronezh Khim Tekhnol Inst — Trudy Voronezhskogo Khimiko-Tekhnologicheskogo Instituta

Tr Voronezh Med Inst — Trudy Voronezhskogo Meditsinskogo Instituta

Tr Voronezh Nauchno Issled Vet Stn — Trudy Voronezhskoi Nauchno-Issledovatel'skoi Veterinarnoi Stantsii

Tr Voronezh Stn Zashch Rast — Trudy Voronezhskogo Stantsii Zashchity Rastenii

Tr Voronezh Tekhnol Inst — Trudy Voronezhskogo Tekhnologicheskogo Instituta

Tr Voronezh Zoovet Inst — Trudy Voronezhskogo Zooveterinarnogo Instituta

Tr Voroshil Gorno Metall Inst — Trudy Voroshilovskogo Gorno-Metallurgicheskogo Instituta

Tr Voroshilovgr S-Kh Inst — Trudy Voroshilovgradskogo Sel'skokhozyaistvennogo Instituta

Tr Vost Inst Ogneuporov — Trudy Vostochnogo Instituta Ogneuporov

Tr Vost Kaz Gos Skh Opytn Stn — Trudy Vostochno-Kazakhskoi Gosudarstvennoi Sel'skokhozyaistvennoi Opytnoi Stantsii

Tr Vost Nauchno Issled Gornorudn Inst — Trudy Vostochnogo Nauchno-Issledovatel'skogo Gornorudnogo Instituta

Tr Vost-Sib Fil Akad Nauk SSSR — Trudy Vostochno-Sibirskogo Filiala Akademii Nauk SSSR

Tr Vost Sib Geol Inst Akad Nauk SSSR Sib Otd — Trudy Vostochno-Sibirskogo Geologicheskogo Instituta Akademiya Nauk SSSR Sibirskoe Otdelenie

Tr Vost Sib Geol Upr — Trudy Vostochno-Sibirskogo Geologicheskogo Upravleniya

Tr Vost Sib Tekhnol Inst — Trudy Vostochno-Sibirskogo Tekhnologicheskogo Instituta

TRVSA — Travail et Securite

Tr Vseross Konf Khir Flebol — Trudy Vserossiiskoi Konferentsii Khirurgov po Flebologii

Tr Vseross Nauchno Issled Inst Sakh Svekly Sakhara — Trudy Vserossiiskogo Nauchno-Issledovatel'skogo Instituta Sakharnoi Svekly i Sakhara

Tr Vses Aerogeol Tresta — Trudy Vsesoyuznogo Aerogeologicheskogo Tresta

Tr Vses Alyum Magnievyi Inst — Trudy Vsesoyuznyi Alyuminievo-Magnievyi Institut

Tr Vses Elektrotekh Inst — Trudy Vsesoyuznogo Elektrotekhnicheskogo i Instituta

Tr Vses Entomol Obshch — Trudy Vsesoyuznogo Entomologicheskogo Obshchestva

Tr Vses Entomol O-Va — Trudy Vsesoyuznogo Entomologicheskogo Obshchestva

Tr Vses Geol Razved Obedin — Trudy Vsesoyuznogo Geologo-Razvedochnogo Ob'edineniya

Tr Vses Gidrobiol O-Va — Trudy Vsesoyuznogo Gidrobiologicheskogo Obshchestva

Tr Vses Gos Nauchno Issled Proektn Inst Khim Fotogr Promsti — Trudy Vsesoyuznogo Gosudarstvennogo Nauchno-Issledovatel'skogo Proektnogo Instituta Khimiko-Fotograficheskoi Promyshlennosti

Tr Vses Inst Eksp Med — Trudy Vsesoyuznogo Instituta Eksperimental'noi Meditsiny

Tr Vses Inst Eksp Vet — Trudy Vsesoyuznogo Instituta Eksperimental'noi Veterinarii

Tr Vses Inst Gel'mintol — Trudy Vsesoyuznogo Instituta Gel'mintologii

Tr Vses Inst Rastenievod — Trudy Vsesoyuznogo Instituta Rastenievodstva

Tr Vses Inst Rast Prob Pop Vyssh Rast — Trudy Vsesoyuznyi Institut Rastenievodstva Problema Populatsii u Vysshikh Rastenii

Tr Vses Inst Sodovoi Promsti — Trudy Vsesoyuznogo Instituta Sodovoi Promyshlennosti

Tr Vses Inst Zashch Rast — Trudy Vsesoyuznogo Instituta Zashchity Rastenii

Tr Vses Mekh Tekhnol Inst Konservn Promsti — Trudy Vsesoyuznogo Mekhaniko-Tekhnologicheskogo Instituta Konservnoi Promyshlennosti

Tr Vses Nauch-Issled Inst Zashch Rast — Trudy Vsesoyuznogo Nauchno-Issledovatel'skogo Instituta Zashchity Rastenii

Tr Vses Nauch-Issled Inst Lub Kul't — Trudy Vsesoyuznyi Nauchno-Issledovatel'skii Institut Lubyanykh Kul'ture

Tr Vses Nauch-Issled Inst Ptitsevod — Trudy Vsesoyuznogo Nauchno-Issledovatel'skogo Instituta Ptitsevodstva

Tr Vses Nauch-Issled Inst Zerna Prod Ego Pererab — Trudy Vsesoyuznyi Nauchno-Issledovatel'skii Institut Zerna i Produktov Ego Pererabotki

Tr Vses Nauch-Issled Inst Zhivotnovod — Trudy Vsesoyuznyi Nauchno-Issledovatel'skii Institut Zhivotnovodstva

Tr Vses Nauchn Inzh Tekh Ova Metall — Trudy Vsesoyuznogo Nauchno Inzhenerno-Tekhnicheskogo Obshchestva Metallurgov

Tr Vses Nauchn-Issled Inst Spirt Likero-Vodoch Prom — Trudy Vsesoyuznogo Nauchno-Issledovatel'skogo Instituta Spirtovoi i Likero-Vodochnoi Promyshlennosti

Tr Vses Nauchno Issled Alyum Magnievyi Inst — Trudy Vsesoyuznyi Nauchno-Issledovatel'skii Alyuminievo-Magnievyi Institut

Tr Vses Nauchno-Issled Eksp Konstr Inst Prodovol Mashinostr — Trudy Vsesoyuznyi Nauchno-Issledovatel'skii i Eksperimental'no-Konstruktorskii Institut Prodovol'stvennogo Mashinostroeniya

Tr Vses Nauchno-Issled Galurgii — Trudy Vsesoyuznogo Nauchno-Issledovatel'skogo Instituta Galurgii

Tr Vses Nauchno-Issled Geol Inst — Trudy Vsesoyuznogo Nauchno-Issledovatel'skogo Geologicheskogo Instituta

Tr Vses Nauchno Issled Geologorazved Inst — Trudy Vsesoyuznogo Nauchno-Issledovatel'skogo Geologorazvedochnogo Instituta

Tr Vses Nauchno-Issled Geologorazved Neft Inst — Trudy Vsesoyuznyi Nauchno-Issledovatel'skii Geologorazvedochnyi Neftyanoi Instituta

Tr Vses Nauchno-Issled Inst Abrazivov Shlifovaniya — Trudy Vsesoyuznyi Nauchno-Issledovatel'skii Institut Abrazivov i Shlifovaniya

Tr Vses Nauchno-Issled Inst Antibiot — Trudy Vsesoyuznogo Nauchno-Issledovatel'skogo Instituta Antibiotikov

Tr Vses Nauchno-Issled Inst Aviats Mater — Trudy Vsesoyuznogo Nauchno-Issledovatel'skogo Instituta Aviatsionnykh Materialov

Tr Vses Nauchno-Issled Inst Burovoi Tekh — Trudy Vsesoyuznyi Nauchno-Issledovatel'skii Institut Burovoi Tekhniki

Tr Vses Nauchno-Issled Inst Efirnomaslichn Kult — Trudy Vsesoyuznogo Nauchno-Issledovatel'skogo Instituta Efirnomaslichnykh Kul'tur

Tr Vses Nauchno-Issled Inst Elektromekh — Trudy Vsesoyuznogo Nauchno-Issledovatel'skogo Instituta Elektromekhaniki

Tr Vses Nauchno-Issled Inst Elektroterm Oborudovaniya — Trudy Vsesoyuznogo Nauchno-Issledovatel'skogo Instituta Elektrotermicheskogo Oborudovaniya

Tr Vses Nauchno-Issled Inst Fermentn Spirt Promsti — Trudy Vsesoyuznyi Nauchno-Issledovatel'skii Institut Fermentnoi i Spirtovoi Promyshlennosti

Tr Vses Nauchno-Issled Inst Fiziol Biokhim Pitan Skh Zhivotn — Trudy Vsesoyuznogo Nauchno-Issledovatel'skogo Instituta Fiziologii, Biokhimii, i Pitaniya Sel'skokhozyaistvennykh Zhivotnykh

Tr Vses Nauchno-Issled Inst Fiziol Biokhim Skh Zhivotn — Trudy Vsesoyuznogo Nauchno-Issledovatel'skogo Instituta Fiziologii i Biokhimii Sel'skokhozyaistvennykh Zhivotnykh

Tr Vses Nauchno-Issled Inst Galurgii — Trudy Vsesoyuznogo Nauchno-Issledovatel'skogo Instituta Galurgii

Tr Vses Nauchno Issled Inst Geofiz Metodov Razved — Trudy Vsesoyuznyi Nauchno-Issledovatel'skii Institut Geofizicheskikh Metodov Razvedki

Tr Vses Nauchno-Issled Inst G Gidrotekh Melior — Trudy Vsesoyuznogo Nauchno-Issledovatel'skogo Instituta Gidrotekhniki i Melioratsii

Tr Vses Nauchno Issled Inst Gidrogeol Inzh Geol — Trudy Vsesoyuznogo Nauchno-Issledovatel'skogo Instituta Gidrogeologii i Inzhenernoi Geologii

Tr Vses Nauchno-Issled Inst Gidrotekh Melior — Trudy Vsesoyuznogo Nauchno-Issledovatel'skogo Instituta Gidrotekhniki i Melioratsii

Tr Vses Nauchno-Issled Inst Ikusstv Zhidk Topl Gaza — Trudy Vsesoiuznogo Nauchno-Issledovatel'skogo Instituta Iskusstvennogo ZhidkogoTopliva i Gaza

Tr Vses Nauchno Issled Inst Iskusstv Zhidk Topl Gaza — Trudy Vsesoyuznogo Nauchno-Issledovatel'skogo Instituta Iskusstvennogo ZhidkogoTopliva i Gaza

Tr Vses Nauchno Issled Inst Karakulevod — Trudy Vsesoyuznogo Nauchno-Issledovatel'skogo Instituta Karakulevodstva

Tr Vses Nauchno-Issled Inst Khim Pererab Gazov — Trudy Vsesoyuznogo Nauchno-Issledovatel'skogo Instituta Khimicheskoi Pererabotki Gazov

Tr Vses Nauchno-Issled Inst Khim Reakt — Trudy Vsesoyuznogo Nauchno-Issledovatel'skogo Instituta Khimicheskikh Reaktivov

Tr Vses Nauchno-Issled Inst Khlebopek Promsti — Trudy Vsesoyuznyi Nauchno-Issledovatel'skii Institut Khlebopekarnoi Promyshlennosti

Tr Vses Nauchno-Issled Inst Khlopkovod — Trudy Vsesoyuznogo Nauchno-Issledovatel'skogo Instituta Khlopkovodstva

Tr Vses Nauchno-Issled Inst Khlopkovod Nov Raionov — Trudy Vsesoyuznogo Nauchno-Issledovatel'skii Institut Khlopkovodstva Novykh Raionov

Tr Vses Nauchno-Issled Inst Konditer Promsti — Trudy Vsesoyuznogo Nauchno-Issledovatel'skogo Instituta Konditerskoi Promyshlennosti

Tr Vses Nauchno-Issled Inst Konservn Ovoshchesush Promsti — Trudy Vsesoyuznogo Nauchno-Issledovatel'skogo Instituta Konservnoi i Ovoshchesushyl'noi Promyshlennosti

Tr Vses Nauchno-Issled Inst Korml S-Kh Zhivotn — Trudy Vsesoyuznogo Nauchno-Issledovatel'skogo Instituta Kormleniya Sel'skokhozyaistvennykh Zhivotnykh

Tr Vses Nauchno Issled Inst Krakhmaloprod — Trudy Vsesoyuznyi Nauchno-Issledovatel'skii Institut Krakhmaloproduktov

Tr Vses Nauchno-Issled Inst L'na — Trudy Vsesoyuznogo Nauchno-Issledovatel'skogo Instituta L'na

Tr Vses Nauchno-Issled Inst Med Instrum Oborudovaniya — Trudy Vsesoyuznogo Nauchno-Issledovatel'skogo Instituta Meditsinskikh Instrumentov Oborudovaniya

Tr Vses Nauchno-Issled Inst Med Priborostr — Trudy Vsesoyuznogo Nauchno-Issledovatel'skogo Instituta Meditsinskikh Priborostroenii

Tr Vses Nauchno Issled Inst Metod Tekh Razved — Trudy Vsesoyuznogo Nauchno-Issledovatel'skogo Instituta Metodiki i Tekhniki Razvedki

Tr Vses Nauchno-Issled Inst Molochn Prom-St — Trudy Vsesoyuznogo Nauchno-Issledovatel'skogo Instituta Molochnoi Promyshlennost

Tr Vses Nauchno-Issled Inst Morsk Ryb Khoz Okeanogr — Trudy Vsesoyuznogo Nauchno-Issledovatel'skogo Instituta Morskogo Rybnogo Khozyaistva i Okeanografii

Tr Vses Nauchno-Issled Inst Morsk Rybn Khoz Okeanogr — Trudy Vsesoyuznogo Nauchno-Issledovatel'skogo Instituta Morskogo Rybnogo Khozyaistva i Okeanografii

Tr Vses Nauchno-Issled Inst Myasn Prom-St — Trudy Vsesoyuznogo Nauchno-Issledovatel'skogo Instituta Myasnoi Promyshlennost

Tr Vses Nauchno-Issled Inst Pererab Ispol'z Topl — Trudy Vsesoyuznogo Nauchno-Issledovatel'skogo Instituta Pererabotki i Ispol'zovaniya Topliva

Tr Vses Nauchno-Issled Inst Pererab Nefti — Trudy Vsesoyuznyj Nauchno-Issledovatel'skij Institut po Pererabotke Nefti

Tr Vses Nauchno-Issled Inst Pererab Slantsev — Trudy Vsesoyuznogo Nauchno-Issledovatel'skogo Instituta po Pererabotke Slantsev

Tr Vses Nauchno Issled Inst Pivo Bezalkogol'n Promsti — Trudy Vsesoyuznogo Nauchno-Issledovatel'skogo Instituta Pivo-Bezalkogol'noi Promyshlennosti

Tr Vses Nauchno-Issled Inst Pivovar Promsti — Trudy Vsesoyuznyi Nauchno-Issledovatel'skii Institut Pivovarennoi Promyshlennosti

Tr Vses Nauchno-Issled Inst Podzemn Gazif Uglei — Trudy Vsesoyuznyi Nauchno-Issledovatel'skii Institut Podzemnoi Gazifikatsii Uglei

Tr Vses Nauchno-Issled Inst Prir Gazov — Trudy Vsesoyuznyi Nauchno-Issledovatel'skii Institut Prirodnykh Gazov

Tr Vses Nauchno-Issled Inst Prod Brozheniya — Trudy Vsesoyuznyi Nauchno-Issledovatel'skii Institut Produktov Brozheniya

Tr Vses Nauchno Issled Inst Proizvod Pishch Prod Kartofelya — Trudy Vsesoyuznyi Nauchno-Issledovatel'skii Institut po Proizvodstvu Pishchevykh Produktov iz Kartofelya

Tr Vses Nauchno-Issled Inst Prud Rybn Khoz — Trudy Vsesoyuznogo Nauchno-Issledovatel'skogo Instituta Prudovogo Rybnogo Khozaistva

Tr Vses Nauchno-Issled Inst Radiat Tekh — Trudy Vsesoyuznyj Nauchno-Issledovatel'skij Institut Radiatsionnoj Tekhniki

Tr Vses Nauchno-Issled Inst Rastit Masel Margarina — Trudy Vsesoyuznogo Nauchno-Issledovatel'skogo Instituta Rastitel'nykh Masel i Margarina

Tr Vses Nauchno-Issled Inst Sint Nat Dushistykh Veshchestv — Trudy Vsesoyuznogo Nauchno-Issledovatel'skogo Instituta Sinteticheskikh i Natural'nykh Dushistykh Veshchestv

Tr Vses Nauchno Issled Inst Skh Mikrobiol — Trudy Vsesoyuznogo Nauchno-Issledovatel'skogo Instituta Sel'skokhozyaistvennoi Mikrobiologii

Tr Vses Nauchno-Issled Inst Solvanoi Promsti — Trudy Vsesoyuznyi Nauchno-Issledovatel'skii Institut Solvanoi Promyshlennosti

Tr Vses Nauchno-Issled Inst Spirt Prom-Sti — Trudy Vsesoyuznogo Nauchno-Issledovatel'skogo Instituta Spirtovoi Promyshlennosti

Tr Vses Nauchno-Issled Inst Stand Obraztsov Spektr Etalonov — Trudy Vsesoyuznogo Nauchno-Issledovatel'skogo Instituta Standartnykh Obraztsov i Spektral'nykh Etalonov

Tr Vses Nauchno-Issled Inst Steklyannogo Volokna — Trudy Vsesoyuznogo Nauchno-Issledovatel'skogo Instituta Steklyannogo Volokna

Tr Vses Nauchno-Issled Inst Torf Prom-Sti — Trudy Vsesoyuznogo Nauchno-Issledovatel'skogo Instituta Torfyanoi Promyshlennosti

Tr Vses Nauchno-Issled Inst Udobr Agropochvoved — Trudy Vsesoyuznogo Nauchno-Issledovatel'skogo Instituta Udobreniya i Agropochvovedeniya

Tr Vses Nauchno-Issled Inst Vet Sanit — Trudy Vsesoyuznogo Nauchno-Issledovatel'skogo Instituta Veterinarnoi Sanitarii

Tr Vses Nauchno-Issled Inst Vet Sanit Ektoparazitol — Trudy Vsesoyuznogo Nauchno-Issledovatel'skogo Instituta Veterinarnoi Sanitarii i Ektoparazitologii

Tr Vses Nauchno-Issled Inst Yad Geofiz Geokhim — Trudy Vsesoyuznyi Nauchno-Issledovatel'skii Institut Yadernoi Geofiziki i Geokhimii

Tr Vses Nauchno-Issled Inst Zashch Rast — Trudy Vsesoyuznogo Nauchno-Issledovatel'skogo Instituta Zashchity Rastenii

Tr Vses Nauchno-Issled Inst Zerna Prod Pererab — Trudy Vsesoyuznogo Nauchno-Issledovatel'skogo Instituta Zerna i Produktov Ego Pererabotki

Tr Vses Nauchno-Issled Inst Zheleznodorozhn Transp — Trudy Vsesoyuznogo Nauchno-Issledovatel'skogo Instituta Zheleznodorozhnogo Transporta

Tr Vses Nauchno-Issled Inst Zheleznodorzhn — Trudy Vsesoyuznogo Nauchno-Issledovatel'skogo Instituta Zheleznodorozhnogo Transporta

Tr Vses Nauchno Issled Inst Zhirov — Trudy Vsesoyuznyi Nauchno-Issledovatel'skii Institut Zhirov

Tr Vses Nauchno-Issled Inst Zhivotn Syr'ya Pushn — Trudy Vsesoyuznogo Nauchno-Issledovatel'skogo Instituta Zhivotnogo Syr'ya Pushniny

Tr Vses Nauchno-Issled Inst Zolota Redk Met — Trudy Vsesoyuznogo Nauchno-Issledovatel'skogo Instituta Zolota i Redkikh Metallov

Tr Vses Nauchno-Issled Konstr Inst Avtog Mashinostr — Trudy Vsesoyuznogo Nauchno-Issledovatel'skogo i Konstruktorskogo Instituta Avtogennogo Mashinostroeniya

Tr Vses Nauchno Issled Konstr Inst Nauchn Priborostr — Trudy Vsesoyuznyi Nauchno-Issledovatel'skii i Konstruktorskii Institut Nauchnogo Priborostroeniya

Tr Vses Nauchno Issled Proektn Inst Galurgii — Trudy Vsesoyuznogo Nauchno-Issledovatel'skogo i Proektnogo Instituta Galurgii

Tr Vses Nauchno-Issled Proektn Inst Mekh Obrab Polezn Iskop — Trudy Vsesoyuznyi Nauchno-Issledovatel'skii i Proektnyi Institut Mekhanicheskoi Obrabotki Poleznykh Iskopaemykh

Tr Vses Neftegazov Nauchno-Issled Inst — Trudy Vsesoyuznyi Neftegazovyi Nauchno-Issledovatel'skii Institut

Tr Vses Neft Nauchno-Issled Geologorazved Inst — Trudy Vsesoyuznogo Neftyanogo Nauchno-Issledovatel'skogo Geologorazvedochnogo Instituta

Tr Vses Neft Nauchno-Issled Inst Tekh Bezop — Trudy Vsesoyuznyi Neftyanoi Nauchno-Issledovatel'skii Institut po Tekhnike Bezopasnosti

Tr Vses O Genet Sel Kuban Otd — Trudy Vsesoyuznoe Obshchestvo Genetikov i Selektsionerov Kubanskoe Otdelenie

Tr Vses O-Va Fiziol Biokhim Farmakol — Trudy Vsesoyuznogo Obshchestva Fiziologov Biokhimikov i Farmakologov

Tr Vses S-Kh Inst Zaochn Obraz — Trudy Vsesoyuznogo Sel'skokhozyaistvennogo Instituta Zaochnogo Obrazovaniya

Tr Vses Teplotekh Nauchno-Issled Inst — Trudy Vsesoyuznyi Teplotekhnikii Nauchno-Issledovatel'skii Institut

Tr Vses Tsentr Nauchno Issled Inst Zhirov — Trudy Vsesoyuznogo Tsentral'nogo Nauchno-Issledovatel'skogo Instituta Zhirov

Tr Vses Zaochn Energ Inst — Trudy Vsesoyuznogo Zaochnogo Energeticheskogo Instituta

Tr Vses Zaochn Inst Inzh Zheleznodorozhn Transp — Trudy Vsesoyuznyi Zaochnyi Institut Inzhenerov Zheleznodorozhnogo Transporta

Tr Vses Zaochn Inst Pishch Promsti — Trudy Vsesoyuznyi Zaochnyi Institut Pishchevoi Promyshlennosti

TRVTDJ — Tropical Veterinarian

Tr VTI — Trudy VTI

Tr Vtorogo Leningr Med Inst — Trudy Vtorogo Leningradskogo Meditsinskogo Instituta

Tr Vtorogo Mosk Med Inst — Trudy Vtorogo Moskovskogo Meditsinskogo Instituta

Tr Vysokogorn Geofiz Inst — Trudy Vysokogornyj Geofizicheskij Institut

TRWOA — Traffic World

Tr Yakutsk Fil Akad Nauk SSSR Ser Fiz — Trudy Yakutskogo Filiala Akademiya Nauk SSSR Seriya Fizicheskaya

Tr Yakutsk Fil Akad Nauk SSSR Ser Geol — Trudy Yakutskogo Filiala Akademii Nauk SSSR Seriya Geologicheskaya

Tr Yakutsk Nauchno-Issled Inst Selsk Khoz — Trudy Yakutskogo Nauchno-Issledovatel'skogo Instituta Sel'skogo Khozyaistva

Tr Yakutsk Nauchno-Issled Inst Tuberk — Trudy Yakutskogo Nauchno-Issledovatel'skii Instituta Tuberkuleza

Tr Yakutsk Otd Sib Nauchno-Issled Inst Rybn Khoz — Trudy Yakutskogo Otdeleniya Sibirskogo Nauchno-Issledovatel'skogo Instituta Rybnogo Khozyaistva

Tr Yalt Nauchno-Issled Inst Fiz Metodov Lech Med Klimatol — Trudy Yaltinskogo Nauchno-Issledovatel'nogo Instituta Fizicheskikh Metodov Lecheniya i Meditsinskoi Klimatologii

Tr Yarosl Med Inst — Trudy Yaroslavskogo Meditsinskogo Instituta

Tr Yarosl Skh Inst — Trudy Yaroslavskogo Sel'skohozyaistvennogo Instituta

Tryb Spold — Trybuna Spoldzielcza

Trye Jus Filiz — Trye's Jus Filizarii

TrZ — Trierer Zeitschrift

Tr Z — Trierer Zeitschrift fuer Geschichte und Kunst des Trierer Landes und Seiner Nachbargebiete

TrZ — Trivium (Zuerich)

Tr Zakavk Nauchno-Issled Gidrometeorol Inst — Trudy Zakavkazskogo Nauchno-Issledovatel'skogo Gidrometeorologicheskogo Instituta

Tr Zapadno Sib Fil Akad Stroit Arkhit SSSR — Trudy Zapadno-Sibirskii Filial Akademiya Stroitel'stva i Arkhitektury SSSR

Tr Zool Inst Akad Nauk SSSR — Trudy Zoologicheskogo Instituta Akademii Nauk SSSR

Tr Ztschr — Trier Zeitschrift fuer Geschichte und Kunst des Trierer Landes und Seiner Nachbargebiete

TS — Texaco Star

TS — Texts and Studies. Contributions to Biblical and Patristic Literature

TS — Theatre Studies

TS — Theatre Survey

TS — Theological Studies

TS — Tijdschrift voor Skandinanistiek

TS — Tijdschrift voor Strafrecht

TS — Today's Speech

TS — Treaty. US State Department Series

TS — Tribology Series

TS — Tropical Science

TS-3 Bibliograf Informacija — TS-3 Bibliografija Informacija

TS-3 Referativnyi Sb — TS-3 Referativnyi Sbornik

TSA — Teater SA. Quarterly for South African Theater

TSA Bull — Turkish Studies Association Bulletin

TSACA — Transactions. South African Institution of Civil Engineers

TSAEA — Transactions. South African Institute of Electrical Engineers

TSAFA — Traffic Safety

TSamU — Trudy Samarkandskogo Gosudarstvennogo Universiteta Imeni Alisera Navoi

TSB — Theological Studies (Baltimore)

TSB — Thoreau Society. Bulletin

TSb — Tjurkologiceskij Sbornik

TSB — Two Complete Science Adventure Books

TSBA — Transactions. Society of Biblical Archaeology

TSBMD — Tellus. Series B. Chemical and Physical Meteorology

T S Booklet — Thoreau Society. Booklet

TSBS — Trudy. Sevastopolskaia Biologicheskaia Stantsii. Academiia Nauk SSSR

TSBUD — Tennessee Survey of Business

Ts BW P R — Tijdschrift voor Bestuurswetenschappen en Publiek Recht

TSC — Trabajo Social (Chile)

TSCA — Toxic Substances Control Act Chemical Substances Inventory

TSCGD — GRS [*Gesellschaft fuer Reaktorsicherheit*] Translations. Safety Codes and Guides

Tschermaks Mineralog u Petrog Mitt — Tschermaks Mineralogische und Petrographische Mitteilungen

Tschermaks Mineral Petrogr Mitt — Tschermaks Mineralogische und Petrographische Mitteilungen

Tschermaks Miner Petrogr Mitt — Tschermaks Mineralogische und Petrographische Mitteilungen [*Wien*]

Tsch Min Pe — Tschermaks Mineralogische und Petrographische Mitteilungen

TSCPA — Transactions and Studies. College of Physicians of Philadelphia

TSDB — SCB [*Statistiska Centralbyran*] Time Series Data Base

TSDL — Tuebingen Studien zur Deutschen Literatur

TSDTA — Tenside-Detergents

TSE — Texas Studies in English

TSE — Tulane Studies in English

TSE300 — Toronto Stock Exchange 300 Index and Stock Statistics

Tselliul Bum Karton — Tselliuloza, Bumaga, i Karton

Tsem Ego Primen — Tsement i Ego Primenenie

Tsem Kamen Zhelezo — Tsement, Kamen' i Zhelezo [*S. Peterburg*]

Tsem Rastvory Krepleniya Glubokikh Skvazhin — Tsementnye Rastvory dlya Krepleniya Glubokikh Skvazhin

Tsent Ref Med Zh — Tsentral'nyi Referativnyi Meditsinskii Zhurnal [*Moskva*]

Tsentr Nauchno Issled Dizel'n Inst Tr — Tsentral'nyi Nauchno-Issledovatel'skii Dizel'nyi Institut Trudy

Tsentr Nauchno-Issled Inst Bum Sbor Tr — Tsentral'nyi Nauchno-Issledovatel'skii Institut Bumagi Sbornik Trudov

Tsentr Nauchno-Issled Inst Olovyannoi Promsti Nauchny Tr — Tsentral'nyi Nauchno-Issledovatel'skll Institut Olovyannoi Promyshlennosti Nauchnyo Trudy

Tsentr Nauchno-Issled Inst Tekhnol Mashinostr Sb — Tsentral'nyi Nauchno-Issledovatel'skii Institut Tekhnologii i MashinostroeniyaSbornik

Tsentr Ref Med Zh Ser A — Tsentral'nyi Referativnyi Meditsinskii Zhurnal. Seriya A. Biologiya, Teoreticheskie Problemy Meditsiny

Tsentr Ref Med Zh Ser B — Tsentral'nyi Referativnyi Meditsinskii Zhurnal. Seriya B. Vnutrennye Bolezni

Tsentr Ref Med Zh Ser G — Tsentral'nyi Referativnyi Meditsinskii Zhurnal. Seriya G. Mikrobiologiya, Gigiena, i Sanitariya

Tsentr Ref Med Zh Ser V — Tsentral'nyi Referativnyi Meditsinskii Zhurnal. Seriya V. Khirurgiya

Tsetse Reclam A Rep Tanganyika — Tsetse Reclamation Annual Report. Tanganyika Territory [*Dar-es-Salaam*]

TSF — Ten Story Fantasy

TSF — Test Aankoop

TSF — Theological Students Fellowship. Bulletin

TSF Bul — TSF [*Theological Students Fellowship*] Bulletin

TSFMES — Thomas Say Foundation. Monographs

TSFTA — Trudy Sibirskogo Fiziko-Tekhnicheskogo Instituta pri Tomskom Gosudarstvennom Universitete

TSGU — Trudy Sredneaziatskogo Gosudarstvennogo Universiteta

TsGw — Tydskrif vir Geesteswetenskappe

TSH — Tijdschrift voor Sociale Hygiene

TSHIDP — Tsurumi University Dental Journal

TSI — Tax Shelter Insider

TSI — Technology and Science of Informatics

TSIGA — Trudy Sibirskogo Nauchno-Issledovatel'skogo Instituta Geologii, Geofiziki, i Mineral'nogo Syr'ya

Tsinghua Sci Technol — Tsinghua Science and Technology

Tsirk Astr Obs Kharkov Gos Univ — Tsirkulyar Astronomicheskoi Observatorii, Khar'kovskogo Gosudarstvennogo Universiteta [*Khar'kov*]

Tsirk Astr Obs Leningr Gos Univ — Tsirkulyar Astronomicheskoi Observatorii pri Leningradskom Gosudarstvennom Universitete [*Leningrad*]

Tsirk Astr Obs Lvov Gos Univ — Tsirkulyar Astronomicheskoi Observatorii, L'vovskogo Gosudarstvennogo Universiteta [*L'vov*]

Tsirk Glav Astr Obs Pulkove — Tsirkulyar Glavnoi Astronomicheskoi Observatorii v Pulkove

Tsirk Kiev Astr Obs — Tsirkulyar Kievskoi Astronomicheskoi Observatorii [*Kiev*]

Tsirk Shemakh Astrofiz Obs — Tsirkulyar Shemakhinskoi Astrofizicheskoi Observatorii

Tsirk Tadzhik Astr Obs — Tsirkulyar Tadzhikskoi Astronomicheskoi Observatorii [*Stalinabad*]

Tsirk Tashkent Astr — Tsirkulyar Tashkentskoi Astronomicheskoi Observatorii [*Tashkent*]

TsIT — Tijdschrift voor Indische Taal-, Land-, en Volkenkunde

TSITA — Tsitologiya

Tsititiksiny Sovrem Med — Tsititiksiny e Sovremennoi Meditsine

Tsitol — Tsitologiya

Tsitol Genet — Tsitologiya i Genetika

Tsitol Genet Akad Nauk Ukr SSR — Tsitologiya i Genetika. Akademiya Nauk Ukrainsoi SSR

Tsitologiya Genet — Tsitologiya i Genetika

TSJ — Toxic Substances Journal

TSJSN — Transactions. Samuel Johnson Society of the Northwest

TSJSNW — Transactions. Samuel Johnson Society of the Northwest

Ts Jur Foer Finland — Tidskrift Utgiven av Juridiska Foereningen i Finland

TSK — Theologische Studien und Kritiken

Ts Kad en Landmeetk — Tijdschrift voor Kadaster en Landmeetkunde

Ts Kad Lmk — Tijdschrift voor Kadaster en Landmeetkunde

TSKHAY — Bulletin. Freshwater Fisheries Research Laboratory

TSKTA — Toyo Shokuhin Kogyo Tanki Daigaku. Toyo Shokuhin Kenkyusho Kenkyu Hokokusho

TSKZA — Tekhnika v Sel'skom Khozyaistve

TSL — Tennessee Studies in Literature

TSL — Travaux. Classe I de Linguistique, de Litterature, et de Philosophie. Societe des Sciences et des Lettres de Lodz

TS Lang — Typological Studies in Language

TS Lit — Trierer Studien zur Literatur

Ts LJ — Tulsa Law Journal

TSLL — Texas Studies in Literature and Language

TSM — Tesoro Sacro-Musical

TSM — Texte des Spaeten Mittelalters

TSM — Trends. Financieel Economisch Magazine

TSMDAL — Trudy Sverdlovskogo Gosudarstvennogo Meditsinskogo Instituta

TSMRD9 — Canada. Fisheries and Marine Service. Resource Development Branch. Maritimes Region Technical Report. Series Mar-T

Ts Mt Fys — Tidskrift for Matematik och Fysik, Tillegnad den Svenska Elementar-Undervisningen

Ts Mth — Tidskrift for Mathematik

TSMYDU — Thailheimer's Synthetic Methods of Organic Chemistry. Yearbook

TSN — The Sports Network

TsNAG — Tijdschrift. Koninklijk Nederlandsch Aardrijkskundig Genootschap

TSNGA — Trudy. Sredneaziatskii Nauchno-Issledovatel'skii Institut Geologii i Mineral'nogo Syr'ya

Ts N I — Tijdschrift voor Nederlandsch-Indie

TSNL — Travaux de la Societe Imperiale des Naturalistes de St. Petersbourg (Leningrad)

TSNL Index Series — Texas System of Natural Laboratories. Index Series

Ts Not — Tijdschrift voor Notarissen

TSNSDH — US National Oceanic and Atmospheric Administration. Northeast Fisheries Center Sandy Hook Laboratory. Technical Series Report

TsNTL — Tijdschrift voor Nederlandsche Taal- en Letterkunde

TSO — Information Society

T Soc R — Tijdschrift voor Sociaal Recht en van de Arbeidsgerechten

T Soc Rheol — Transactions. Society of Rheology

T Sov — Tidsskrift for Sovaesen

Ts Ovadm — Tijdschrift voor Overheidsadministratie

T Sovaes — Tidsskrift foer Sovaesen

TSP — Tulane Studies in Philosophy

TsPhil — Tijdschrift voor Philosophie

TSPMA — Travaux. Societe de Pharmacie de Montpellier

Ts Ps C — Tidsskrift for Physik og Chemi samt disse Videnskabers Avendelse

TSP Tech Pap — T.S.P. Technical Papers. Aktiebolaget Svenska Kullagerfabriken

TSR — [*The*] Shopper Report

TSR — Technical Services Report

TSR — Tijdschrift voor Sociaal Recht

TSR — Times Saturday Review

TSRA — Tijdschrift voor Sociaal Recht en van de Arbeidsgerechten

TSRLD — TRRL [*Transport and Road Research Laboratory*] Supplementary Report

TSRLL — Tulane Studies in Romance Languages and Literature

TSRVA — Times Science Review

TSSD — Telecommunications Systems and Services Directory

Tss F Racefjerk — Tidsskrift for Racefjerkraeavl

Tss Fri Laererskole — Tidsskriftet Den Frie Laererskole

Tss Jordem — Tidsskrift for Jordemodre

Tss Maskinv — Tidsskrift for Maskinvaesen

Ts Soc R — Tijdschrift voor Sociaal Recht

Tss Polit Okon — Tidsskriftet for Politisk Okonomi

Tss Uddannelsespolit — Tidsskriftet Uddannelsespoltik

TsSV — Tijdschrift voor de Studie van de Verlichting

TST — Textile Science and Technology

TSTIA — Trudy Sibirskogo Tekhnologicheskogo Instituta

TsTK — Tidsskrift for Teologi og Kirke

TSTKA — Tsuchi To Kiso

Tsukuba-Daigaku Shakaigaku J — Tsukuba-Daigaku Shakaigaku Journal

Tsukuba J Math — Tsukuba Journal of Mathematics

Tsukuba Univ Inst Geosci Annu Rep — Tsukuba University. Institute of Geoscience. Annual Report

Tsukumo Earth Sci — Tsukumo Earth Science

Tsurumi Univ Dent J — Tsurumi University. Dental Journal

TsV — Tserkovnye Vedomosti

Tsvet Metal — Tsvetnye Metally

Tsvet Metally Mosk — Tsvetnye Metally (Moskva)

Tsvet Metally NY — Tsvetnye Metally (New York)

Tsvetn Met — Tsvetnye Metally

Tsvetn Metall — Tsvetnaya Metallurgiya

Tsvetn Metall Nauchno Tekh Sb — Tsvetnaya Metallurgiya-Nauchno-Tekhnicheskii Sbornik

Tsvetn Metall (Ordzhonikidze, USSR) — Tsvetnaya Metallurgiya (Ordzhonikidze, USSR)

Tsvtn Metall Nauchno Tekh Byull — Tsvetnaya Metallurgiya-Nauchno-Tekhnicheskii Byulleten

TsVUB — Tijdschrift van de Vrige Universiteit van Brussel

TsVV — Tydskrif vir Volkskunde en Volkstaal

TSW — Prace Wroclawskiego Towarzystwa Naukowego

TSW — Three Banks Review

TsWK — Tydskrif vir Wetenskap en Kuns

TSWL — Tulsa Studies In Women's Literature

TSYK — Tusaayaksat

TSYKDE — Annual Report. Tobacco Research Institute. Taiwan Tobacco and Wine Monopoly Bureau

T Sypl — Tidsskrift for Sygepleje

TSz — Toertenelmi Szemle

TSZGK — Thueringisch-Saechsische Zeitschrift fuer Geschichte und Kunst

TT — Taal en Tongval

TT — Taiga Times '71

Tt — Tatler

TT — Teologisk Tidsskrift

TT — Theologisch Tijdschrift

TT — Theology Today

TT — Theorie en Techniek

TT — Time and Tide

TT — Times

TT — Toertenelmi Tar

TT — Transport

TT — Turk Tarih Arkeologya ve Etnografya Dergisi

TTAE — Turk Tarih. Arkeologya ve Etnografya Dergisi

TTAED — Turk Tarih Arkeologya ve Etnografya Dergisi

TTagPl — Trudy Taganrogskogo Gosudarstvennogo Pedagogiceskogo Instituta

TTAV — TTAV [*Technical Teachers Association of Victoria*] News

TTb — Trudy Tbilisskogo Pedagogiceskogo Instituta

TTCMA — Turk Tip Cemiyeti Mecmuasi

TTD — Textile Technology Digest

TTD — [*The*] Third Degree

TTE — Talks to Teachers of English

TTE — Texpress. Economisch en Technisch Weekblad voor de Textiel en Kledingindustrie en Handel in de Benelux

T Tech — Track Technique Annual
TTEKA — Tokyo Toritsu Eisei Kenkyusho Kenkyu Hokoku
TTele — Tatar Tele Hem Adebijaty
T Textilt — Tidsskrift for Textilteknik
TTG — Travel Trade Gazette UK
TTh — Tijdschrift voor Theologie
T Th Z — Trierer Theologische Zeitschrift
TTI — Tulane Tax Institute
TTIDA — Teknisk Tidskrift
TTIIA — Trudy Tashkentskogo Instituta Inzhenerov Irrigatsii i Mekhanizatsii Sel'skogo Khozyaistva
T Times — These Times
TTIS Publ — TTIS [*Translation and Technical Information Service*] Publication
TTJ — Timber Trades Journal and Wood Processing
TTK — Belleten. Tuerk Tarih Kurumu
TTK — Tuerk Tarih Kurumu Yalinlarinin
TTK — Turk Tarih Kurumu
TTKB — Turk Tarih Kurumu. Belleten
TTK "Belleten" — Turk Tarih Kurumu "Belleten"
TTKi — Tidsskrift for Teologi og Kirke
TTKLAJ — Trudy Turkmenskogo Nauchno-Issledovatel'skogo Instituta Klimatologii Kurortologii i Fizicheskikh Metodov Lecheniya
TTKMA — Trudy Tambovskogo Instituta Khimicheskogo Mashinostroeniya
TTKSA — Tokyo-Toritsu Kogyo Shoreikan Hokoku
TTKY — Turk Tarih Kurumu. Yayinlarindan
TTL — Tijdschrift voor Taal en Letteren
TTLPA — Tekstil'naya Promyshlennost
TTM — Taiwan Trade Monthly
TTMTA — Tungsram Technische Mitteilungen
T Today — Theology Today
T Tokyo U F — Transactions. Tokyo University of Fisheries
TTomU — Trudy Tomskogo Gosudarstvennogo Universiteta
TTP — Tamarind Technical Papers
TTP — Trudy Tallinskogo Politekhnicheskogo Instituta. Seriya B, XX
TTPI — Trudy Tbilisskogo Gosudarstvennogo Pedagogiceskogo Instituta
TTQ — Tuebinger Theologische Quartalschrift
TTQS — Tuebinger Theologische Quartalschrift (Stuttgart)
TTrA — Textes et Traitement Automatique
TTS — Transactions. Thoroton Society
TTSPB — Transport Theory and Statistical Physics
TTT — Teylers Theologisch Tijdschrift
TTT — Trade Token Topics
TTT — TTT - Teatrets Teori og Teknikk
TTUV News — TTUV (Technical Teachers Union of Victoria) News
TTW — Test
TTZ — Trierer Theologische Zeitschrift
TTZED — TIZ. Tonindustrie-Zeitung
TTZGAB — Trudy Respublikanskogo Nauchno-Issledovatel'skogo Instituta Tuberkuleza Ministerstva Zdravookhraneniya Gruzinskoi SSR
TU — Technische Ueberwachung
TU — Texte und Untersuchungen zur Geschichte der Altchristlichen Literatur
TU — This Unrest
TU — Tundra Times
TUAGAT — Tunisie Agricole. Revue Mensuelle Illustree
TUAS — Temple University Aegean Symposium
TUB — Tulane University. Bulletin
TUBA J — TUBA [*Tubists Universal Brotherhood Association*] Journal for Euphonium and Tuba
TUBEA — Tubercle
Tuberc A Dacca — Tuberculosis Annual. East Pakistan Tuberculosis Association (Dacca)
Tuberc Adulte — Tuberculose Adulte [*Paris*]
Tuberc Cancer Paris — Tuberculose et Cancer (Paris)
Tuberc Commonw — Tuberculosis in the Commonwealth. Transactions of the Commonwealth Health and Tuberculosis Conference
Tuberc Doenc Torac — Tuberculose e Doencas Toracicas [*Lisboa*]
Tuberc Res — Tuberculosis Research
Tuberc Respir Dis — Tuberculosis and Respiratory Diseases
Tuberculol Thorac Dis — Tuberculology and Thoracic Diseases
Tuberk Forschungsinst Borstel Jahresber — Tuberkulose Forschungsinstitut Borstel. Jahresbericht
TuberkFuersorgebl Dt ZentKom Bekaempf Tuberk — Tuberkulosefuersorgeblatt des Deutschen Zentralkomitees zur Bekaempfung der Tuberkulose [*Berlin*]
Tuberk Grenzgeb Einzeldarst — Tuberkulose und Ihre Grenzgebiete in Einzeldarstellungen
Tuberk Ihre Grenzgeb Einzeldarst — Tuberkulose und Ihre Grenzgebiete in Einzeldarstellungen
Tuberk Klin — Tuberkuloz Klinigi [*Istanbul*]
Tuberk Kuzd — Tuberkulozis elleni Kuzdelem [*Budapest*]
Tuberk Toraks — Tuberkuloz ve Toraks [*Ankara*]
Tuber Lung Dis — Tubercle and Lung Disease
Tubular Struct — Tubular Structures
TUBWPL — Technische Universitaet Berlin. Arbeitspapiere zur Linguistik/Working Papers inLinguistics
T Ud — Tidsskrift for Udenrigspolitik
TUD — Trudy Universiteta Druzhby Narodov Imeni Patrisa Lumumby
Tud & Musz Tajek — Tudomanyos es Muszaki Tajekoztatas
T Udenrigspolitik — Tidsskrift foer Udenrigspolitik
Tud Ert Agrartud Egy Godollo — Tudomanyos Ertesito-Agrartudomanyi Egyetem Godollo
Tud Ert Agrartud Egy Godollo (Hung) — Tudumanyos Ertesito-Agrartudomanyi Egyetem Godollo (Hungary)
Tud Mezogazd — Tudomany es Mezogazdasag
TUDNL — Trudy Universiteta Druzhby Narodov Imeni Patrisa Lumumby
Tudobetegg Tuberk — Tudobeteggondozas es Tuberkulozis

Tudomanytar Ertek — Tudomanytar. Ertekezerek
Tudom Musz Tajek — Tudomanyos es Muszaki Tajekoztatas
Tud-Szerv Tajekoz — Tudomanyszervezesi Tajekoztato
Tuebingen Bl Albver — Blaetter des Schwaebischen Albvereins (Tuebingen)
Tuebinger Bl — Tuebinger Blaetter
Tuebinger Bl — Tuebinger Blaetter fuer Naturwissenschaften und Arzneikunde
Tuebinger Naturw Abh — Tuebinger Naturwissenschaftliche Abhandlungen
Tuerk AD — Tuerk Arkeoloji Dergisi
Tuerk Ark Derg — Tuerk Arkeoloji Dergisi
Tuerk Ark Dergisi — Tuerk Tarih Arkeologya ve Etnografya Dergisi
Tuerk Et Derg — Tuerk Etnografya Dergisi
Tuerk Z Hyg Exp Biol — Tuerkische Zeitschrift fuer Hygiene und Experimentelle Biologie
Tues Rev — Tuesday Review
TUeV Mitt Mitglieder Tech Ueberwach-Ver Bayern — TUeV [*Technischer Ueberwachungs-Verein*] Mitteilungen fuer die Mitglieder. Technischer Ueberwachungs-Verein Bayern
TUF — Umweltmagazin. Fachzeitschrift fuer Umwelttechnik in Industrie und Kommune
TUFPB — Proceedings. Faculty of Science. Tokai University
Tufs Folia Med — Tufs Folia Medica
Tufts Coll Stud — Tufts College Studies [*Medford*]
Tufts Coll Studies — Tufts College Studies
Tufts Coll Stud Sci Ser — Tufts College Studies. Scientific Series
Tufts Dent Outl — Tufts Dental Outlook [*Boston*]
Tufts Dent Outlook — Tufts Dental Outlook
Tufts Health Sci Rev — Tufts Health Science Review
Tufts Med J — Tufts Medical Journal [*Boston*]
Tufts Univ Diet Nutr Lett — Tufts University Diet and Nutrition Letter
TUGAL — Texte und Untersuchungen zur Geschichte der Altchristlichen Literatur
TU Gazette — University of Tasmania. Gazette
TUGEA — Teknisk Ukeblad
TUGRA — Report of Investigations. University of Texas at Austin. Bureau of Economic Geology
TUH — Review of Economic Conditions
TUI — Tuinderij. Vakblad voor de Intensieve Groenteteelt
TuK — Text und Kritik
TUKMAT — Trudy Ukrainskogo Nauchno-Issledovatel'skogo Instituta Klinicheskoi Meditsiny
Tu L — Tulane Law Review
Tulane Law R — Tulane Law Review
Tulane L R — Tulane Law Review
Tulane L Rev — Tulane Law Review
Tulane St — Tulane Studies in English
Tulane Stud Eng — Tulane Studies in English
Tulane Stud Geol — Tulane Studies in Geology
Tulane Stud Geol Paleontol — Tulane Studies in Geology and Paleontology
Tulane Stud Phil — Tulane Studies in Philosophy
Tulane Stud Zool — Tulane Studies in Zoology
Tulane Stud Zool Bot — Tulane Studies in Zoology and Botany
Tulane U Stud Eng — Tulane University. Studies in English
TU Law R — University of Tasmania. Law Review
Tul Gorn Inst Nauchn Tr — Tul'skii Gornyi Institut Nauchnye Trudy
Tul Gos Pedagog Inst Uch Zap Fiz Tekh Nauk — Tul'skii Gosudarstvennyi Pedagogicheskii Institut Uchenye Zapiski Fiziko-Tekhnicheskie Nauki
Tul Gos Ped Inst Ucen Zap Mat Kaf — Tul'skii Gosudarstvennyi Pedagogiceskii Institut Imeni L. N. Tolstogo Ucenye Zapiski Matematiceskih Kafedr
Tul LR — Tulane Law Review
Tul L Rev — Tulane Law Review
Tu LR — Tulane Law Review
TULS — Tulsa World
TULSA — Petroleum Abstracts
Tulsa Bs C — Tulsa Business Chronicle
Tulsa Geol Soc Dig — Tulsa Geological Society. Digest
Tulsa Geol Soc Digest — Tulsa Geological Society. Digest
Tulsa L J — Tulsa Law Journal
Tulsa Med — Tulsa Medicine
Tul Tax Inst — Tulane Tax Institute
Tul Tidelands Inst — Tulane Mineral and Tidelands Law Institute
TUMEA — Tunisie Medicale
Tumor Biol — Tumor Biology. From Basic Science to Clinical Application
Tumor Diagn — Tumor Diagnostik
Tumor Diagn Ther — Tumor Diagnostik und Therapie
Tumor Res — Tumor Research
Tumor Suppr Genes — Tumor Suppressor Genes
Tumour Biol — Tumour Biology
Tuna Fishg — Tuna Fishing. Investigative Society of Tuna Fishing [*Misaki*]
Tuna Rep — Tuna Report. California Department of Fish and Game
T und K — Text und Kontext
Tuners JL — Tuners' Journal
Tunghai J — Tunghai Journal
Tungsram Tech Mitt — Tungsram Technische Mitteilungen
Tungsten Other Adv Met ULSI Appl 1990 Proc Workshop — Tungsten and Other Advanced Metals for ULSI (Ultra Large Scale Integration) Applications in 1990. Proceedings. Workshop
Tung Wld — Tung World [*Gulfport, Mississippi*]
Tunis Agric — Tunisie Agricole
Tunisie Agr — Tunisie Agricole
Tunisie Agric Rev Mens Illus — Tunisie Agricole. Revue Mensuelle Illustree
Tunisie Econ — Tunisie Economique
Tunis Med — Tunisie Medicale
Tunnelling Underground Space Technol — Tunnelling and Underground Space Technology
Tunnels Ouvrages Souterr — Tunnels et Ouvrages Souterrains
Tunnels Tunnell — Tunnels and Tunnelling

Tunnlg Technol Newsl — Tunneling Technology Newsletter
Tunn Technol Newsl — Tunneling Technology Newsletter
Tunn Tunn — Tunnels and Tunnelling
Tunn Tunnlg — Tunnels and Tunnelling
TUPMA — Trudy Ural'skii Nauchno-Issledovatel'skii i Proektnyi Institut Mednoi Promyshlennosti
Tur — Turistarbogen
TUR — Turkish Economy
Turan Z Osteuropa Vorder & Innerasiat Stud — Turan Zeitschrift fuer Osteuropaische Vorder- und Innerasiatische Studien
Turbomachinery Int — Turbomachinery International
Turbomachinery Intl — Turbomachinery International
Turbomach Int — Turbomachinery International
Turbul Meas Liq Proc Symp — Turbulence Measurements in Liquids. Proceedings of Symposium
Turc — Turcica. Revue d'Etudes Turques
TUREA — Tumor Research
Turf Bull — Turf Bulletin
Turf Cult — Turf Culture
Turf Sport — Turf for Sport
Turin Ac Mm — Memoires de l'Academie Royale des Sciences de Turin
Turing Inst Press Knowledge Engrg Tutor Ser — Turing Institute Press Knowledge Engineering Tutorial Series
Turin Mm Ac — Memoires de l'Academie Royale des Sciences de Turin
Turist Alpinism — Turistasag es Alpinismus
Turk AD — Turk Arkeoloji Dergisi
Turk AEC Ankara Nucl Res Cent Tech J — Turkish Atomic Energy Commission. Ankara Nuclear Research Center. Technical Journal
Turk Antrop Mecm — Turk Antropoloji Mecmuasi [Istanbul]
Turk Ark Derg — Turk Arkeoloji Dergisi
Turk Arkeol Derg — Turk Arkeoloji Dergisi
Turk Biol Derg — Turk Biologi Dergisi
Turk Bitki Koruma Derg — Turkiye Bitki Koruma Dergisi
Turk Bot Derg — Turk Botanik Dergisi
Turk Bull Hyg Exp Biol — Turkish Bulletin of Hygiene and Experimental Biology
Turk Cerrahi Cemiy Mecm — Turk Cerrahi Cemiyeti Mecmuasi
Turk Cerr Cemiy Mecm — Turk Cerrahi Cemiyeti Mecmuasi [Istanbul]
Turk Cogr Derg — Turk Cografya Dergisi [Ankara]
Turk Cumh Jeol Gor — Turkiye Cumhuriyetinde Jeolojik Gorumler [Ankara]
Turk Cumh Tarim Bakan Derg — Turkiye Cumhuriyeti Tarim Bakanligi Dergisi [Ankara]
Turk Distab Cemiy Mecm — Turk Distabibleri Cemiyeti Mecmuasi [Istanbul]
Turk Etnog Derg — Turk Etnografya Dergisi
Turkey Prod — Turkey Producer
Turkeys Yb — Turkeys Year Book
Turk Fiz Dernegi Bul — Turk Fizik Dernegi Bulteni
Turk For Pol Rep — Turkish Foreign Policy Report
Turk Gen Kim Kurumu Derg B — Turkiye Genel Kimyagerler Kurumu Dergisi-B
Turk Hemsire Derg — Turk Hemsireler Dergisi
Turk Hifzissihha Tecr Biol Mecm — Turk Hifzissihha ve Tecrubi Biologi Mecmuasi
Turk Hij Deney Biyol Derg — Turk Hijiyen ve Deneysel Biyoloji Dergisi
Turk Hij Deneysel Biyol Derg — Turk Hijiyen ve Deneysel Biyoloji Dergisi
Turk Hij Tecr Biyol Derg — Turk Hijiyen ve Tecruby Biyoloji Dergisi
Turkish J Math — Turkish Journal of Mathematics
Turk J Agric For — Turkish Journal of Agriculture and Forestry
Turk J Biol — Turkish Journal of Biology
Turk J Bot — Turkish Journal of Botany
Turk J Chem — Turkish Journal of Chemistry
Turk J Earth Sci — Turkish Journal of Earth Sciences
Turk J Eng Environ Sci — Turkish Journal of Engineering and Environmental Sciences
Turk Jeol Kurumu Bul — Turkiye Jeoloji Kurumu Bulteni
Turk Jeomorfologlar Dernegi Yayini — Turkiye Jeomorfologlar Dernegi. Yayini
Turk J Immunol — Turkish Journal of Immunology
Turk J Nucl Sci — Turkish Journal of Nuclear Sciences
Turk J Pediatr — Turkish Journal of Pediatrics
Turk J Phys — Turkish Journal of Physics
Turk Ljiyen Tecruebi Biyol Dergisi — Turk Ljiyen ve Tecruebi Biyoloji Dergisi
Turkmen Gos Univ Ucen Zap — Turkmenskii Gosudarstvennyi Universitet Imeni A. M. Gor'kogo Ucenye Zapiski
Turk Mikrobiyol Cemiy Derg — Turk Mikrobiyoloji Cemiyeti Dergisi
Turk Miner Res Explor Bull — Turkey. Mineral Research and Exploration Institute. Bulletin
Turkm Iskra — Turkmenskaya Iskra
Turk Odont Bult — Turk Odontoloji Bulteni [Istanbul]
Turk Oftal Gaz — Turk Oftalmoloji Gazetesi [Istanbul]
Turkoman Stud — Turkoman Studies
Turk Ortodonti Derg — Turk Ortodonti Dergisi
Turk Publ Adm Annu — Turkish Public Administration Annual
Turk Ship — Turkish Shipping
Turk TAED — Turk Tarih Arkeologya ve Etnografya Dergisi
Turk Tar Derg — Turk Tarih. Arkeologya ve Etnografya Dergisi
Turk Tarih Arkeol Etnogr Derg — Turk Tarih, Arkeologya ve Etnografya Dergisi [Istanbul]
Turk Tib Cemiy Mecm — Turk Tib Cemiyeti Mecmuasi [Istanbul]
Turk Tib Encum Arc — Turkiye Tib Encumeni Arcivi [Istanbul]
Turk Tib Mecm — Turk Tib Mecmuasi [Istanbul]
Turk Tip Akad Mecm — Turkiye Tip Akademisi Mecmuasi
Turk Tip Cemiy Mecm — Turkiye Tip Cemiyeti Mecmuasi
Turk Tip Cem Mecm — Turkiye Tip Cemiyeti Mecmuasi
Turk Tip Dern Derg — Turk Tip Dernegi Dergisi
Turk Tip Encumeni Ars — Turkiye Tip Encumeni Arsivi
Turnbull Libr Rec — Turnbull Library Record
Turner Stud — Turner Studies
Turn Rec — Turnbull Library Record

Turon Yliopiston Julk Sar A-II — Turon Yliopiston Julkaisuja. Sarja A-II
Turquie Kemal — Turquie Kemaliste
TURRA — Turrialba
Turrialba — Turrialba. Revista Interamericana de Ciencias Agricolas
Turrialba Supl — Bibliografico de Turrialba. Suplemento
Turun Hist Yhd Julk — Turun Historiallisen Yhdistyksen Julkaisuja
Turun Yliop Bakt Serol Laitok Julk — Turun Yliopiston Bakteriologis-Serologiselta Laitokselta Julkaisuja [Turku]
Turun Yliop Julk — Turun Yliopiston Julkaisuja
TUSAS — Twayne's United States Authors Series
Tusc — Tusculum Buecher
Tuskegee Agric Exp Stn Bull — Tuskegee Agricultural Experiment Station Bulletin [Tuskegee, Alabama]
Tuskegee Exp — Tuskegee Normal and Industrial Institute. Experiment Station. Publications
TUSLA — Trudy Ukrainskii Nauchno-Issledovatel'skii Institut Spirtovoi i Likero-Vodochnoi Promyshlennosti
TUSQA — Quarterly Bulletin. Faculty of Science. Tehran University
Tussock Grassl Mt Lands Inst Annu Rep — Tussock Grasslands and Mountain Lands Institute. Annual Report
Tutkimuksia Res Rep — Tutkimuksia Research Reports
Tutkimus Tek — Tutkimus ja Tekniikka
TUTNB — Tunneling Technology Newsletter
Tutto Mus — Tutto Musica
TUTUB — Tunnels and Tunnelling
TUU — Trudy Uzbekskogo Universiteta
TUVMAG — Trudy Ufimskogo Nauchno-Issledovatel'skogo Instituta Vaktsin i Syvorotok Imeni I. I. Mechnikova
TuW — Technik und Wirtschaft
TuZ — Texte und Zeichen
Tuzeles Vilag — Tuzeles es Vilagitas [Budapest]
TV — Television
TV — Teologia y Vida
TV — Tev'a Va-Arets
TV — Treji Varti
TV — Tzertovnyia Viedomosti
TVA — Television Age
TVA Bibliogr Tenn Val Auth Tech Libr — TVA Bibliography. Tennessee Valley Authority. Technical Library
TVA Chem Eng Rept — Tennessee Valley Authority. Chemical Engineering Report
Tvaett Ind — Tvaett Industrin
TVAR — Television Advertisers' Report
Tvarinnictvo Ukr — Tvarinnictvo Ukraini
Tvarynnytstvo Ukr — Tvarynnytstvo Ukrainy
TVA Tech Rept — Tennessee Valley Authority. Technical Report
TVBTA — Trudy Vsesoyuznyi Nauchno-Issledovatel'skii Institut Burovoi Tekhniki
TV Commun — TV Communications
TVD — Television Digest
TVD — Travaux sur Voltaire et le Dix-Huitieme Siecle
TVE — Tijdschrift voor Economie
T Ver Nederlandse Mg — Tijdschrift van de Vereeniging voor Nederlandse Muziekgeschiedenis
TVF — Tidskrift foer Teknisk-Vettenskaplig Forskning
TvF — Tijdschrift voor Filosofie
TVF Tek Vetensk Forsk — TVF. Teknisk Vetenskaplig Forskning
TVG — Tijdschrift voor Geschiedenis
TVG — TV Guide
TvG — Tydskrif vir Geesteswetenskappe
TVGO — Trudy Vsesoyuznogo Gidrobiologicheskogo Obshchestva
T vh Not — Tijdschrift voor het Notarisambt
T v h R — Tijdschrift van het Recht
TVI — Tarih Vesikalari (Istanbul)
TVIIJ — Trudy Vojennogo Instituta Inostrannykh Jazykov
TVIIJa — Trudy Vojennogo Instituta Inostrannykh Jazykov
TV Int — Television International
TVL — Tijdschrift voor Liturgei
TvL — Tydskrif vir Letterkunde
Tvl Educ News — Transvaal Educational News
T v M W — Tijdschrift voor Maatschappelijk Werk
TVNMG — Tidschrift van de Vereniging voor Nederlandse Muziek Geschiedenis
T v O — Tijdschrift voor Overheidsadministratie en Openbaar Bestuur
T Volkskd Volkstaal — Tydskrif vir Volkskunde en Volkstaal
TVP — Television and Video Production
TVP — Terre et la Vie. Revue d'Histoire Naturelle (Paris)
TVPED — Tennessee Valley Perspective
T v P N en F — Tijdschrift voor Privaatrecht, Notariaat, en Fiscaalrecht
TVPRA — Teoriya Veroyatnostei i Ee Primeneniya
TV Q — Television Quarterly
T v R — Tijdschrift voor Rechtsgeschiedenis
TV Radio A — Television/Radio Age
TV/Radio Age — Television/Radio Age
TV/Radio Age Int — Television/Radio Age International
TV Radio Engng — TV and Radio Engineering
T Vred — Tijdschrift voor Vrederechters
TVRG — Tijdschrift voor Rechtsgeschiedenis
T v S — Tijdschrift voor Strafrecht
TVS — Tijdschrift voor Volkhuisvesting en Stedebouw, uitgave NederlandsInstituut voor Volkshuisvesting en Stedebouw
T v Sr — Tijdschrift voor Strafrecht
TVT — Tijdschrift voor Theologie
TVUAAG — Trudy Vsesoyuznogo Nauchno-Issledovatel'skogo Instituta Udobrenii Agrotekhniki i Agropochvovedeniya Imeni Gedroitsa
TVUB — Tijdschrift van de Vrige Universiteit van Brussel
TVVS — Tijdschrift voor Vennootschappen, Verenigingen, en Stichtingen
TVXCA — Travaux Communaux

TVYTA — Teplofizika Vysokikh Temperatur
TW — Journal of Technical Writing and Communication
TW — Tapwe
TW — Terre Wallonne
TW — Textil-Wirtschaft
TW — Third World
TW — Thrilling Wonder Stories
TW — Tools and Weapons Illustrated by the Egyptian Collection University College. London
TW — Travel Writer
Tw — Tworczosc
TWA — Tijdschrift voor Sociale Wetenschappen
TWA — Transactions. Wisconsin Academy of Sciences, Arts, and Letters
TWA Met Tech Bull — T.W.A. (Trans World Airlines) Meteorological Technical Bulletin
TWAS — Twayne's World Authors Series
TWBR — Third World Book Review
TwC — Twentieth Century
TwC — Two Cities. La Revue Bilingue de Paris
TWC — [*The*] Wordsworth Circle
TW Dermatol — TW (Therapiewoche) Dermatologie
TWDRA — Report. Texas Water Development Board
TWE — Times Weekly Edition
Tweemandelijksche Tijdschr Lett Kst Wet & Polit — Tweemandelijksche Tijdschrift voor Letteren, Kunst, Wetenschap, en Politiek
Twen Cen — Twentieth Century
Twen Cent — Twentieth Century
Twen Ct Lit — Twentieth Century Literature
Twent Cent — Twentieth Century
Twent Century Lit — Twentieth Century Literature
Twent Cen V — Twentieth Century Views
Twentieth C Archit — Twentieth Century Architecture
Twentieth Cent — Twentieth Century
TWICE — This Week in Consumer Electronics
TWI J — TWI (The Welding Institute) Journal
Twin Res — Twin Research [*Basingstoke*]
T Wisc Ac — Transactions. Wisconsin Academy of Sciences, Arts, and Letters
TWLOA — Technik Wlokienniczy
TWLS — Twayne's World Leaders Series
TWN — Thomas Wolfe Newsletter
TWNT — Theologisches Woerterbuch zum Neuen Testament
TWO — Financial World
Two Bud — Two and a Bud. Tocklai Experimental Station. Indian Tea Association [*Tocklai*]
T Wolfe New — Thomas Wolfe Newsletter
T Wolfe Rev — Thomas Wolfe Review
Two Phase Polym Syst — Two-Phase Polymer Systems
Tworzywa Sztuczne Med — Tworzywa Sztuczne'w Medycynie
Two-Year College Math J — Two-Year College Mathematics Journal
Two-Yr Coll Math J — Two-Year College Mathematics Journal
TWP — Trondheim Workingpapers
TWP — [*The*] Washington Post
TWQ — Third World Quarterly
TWR — Thomas Wolfe Review
TWR — Times Weekly Review
TWS — Thrilling Wonder Stories
TWSUA — Taiwan Sugar
TWT — Ingenieursblad
TWT — Technical Writing Teacher
TWX — Transport en Opslag. Maandblad voor Managers en Medewerkers op het Gebied van Intern Transport, Opslag, Magazijntechniek, en Distributietechniek
TXAPA — Toxicology and Applied Pharmacology
TXB — TextielVisie. Vakblad voor de Textielbranche
TXBRA — Texas Business Review
TX Bus Rev — Texas Business Review
TXCYA — Toxicology
TXE — Tax Executive
TXECB — Toxicological and Environmental Chemistry Reviews
TXHL — Texas Health Letter
TX L — Texas Law Review
TX LJ — Texas Law Journal
TX LR — Texas Law Review
TXLRA — Texas Law Review
TXMDA — Texas Medicine
TxSE — Texas Studies in English
TXV — Texas Business Review

TXV — Textil Revue. Fachblatt fuer Textilhandel, Konfektionsindustrie, und Textilindustrie
TY — Tyler's Quarterly Historical and Genealogical Magazine
Tyazh Mashinost — Tyazheloe Mashinostroenie [*Kharkov*]
Tyazh Mashinostr — Tyazhelie Mashinostroenie
Tyazh Vozd — Tyazhelee Vozdukha [*Kharkov*]
TYC — Texto y Concreto
TYC — Trabajos y Conferencias [*Madrid*]
TyD — Trabajos y Dias
TYDNAP — Annual Report. Tokyo College of Pharmacy
TYDS — Transactions. Yorkshire Dialect Society
Tydskr Aardryksk — Tydskrif vir Aardrykskunde. Universiteit van Stellenbosch [*Stellenbosch*]
Tydskr Dieetkd Huishoudkd — Tydskrif vir Dieetkunde en Huishoudkunde
Tydskr Natuurwet — Tydskrif vir Natuurwetenskappe
Tydskr Natuurwetenskap — Tydskrif vir Natuurwetenskappe. Suid-Afrikaanse Akademie vir Wetenskap en Kuns
Tydskr S-Afr Ver Spraak Gehoorheelkd — Tydskrif van die Suid-Afrikaanse Vereniging vir Spraaken Gehoorheelkunde
Tydskr S-Afr Vet Ver — Tydskrif. Suid-Afrikaanse Veterinere Vereniging
Tydskr Skoon Lug — Tydskrif vir Skoon Lug
Tydskr Tandheelkd Ver S-Afr — Tydskrif. Tandheelkundige Vereniging van Suid-Afrika
Tydskr Wet Kuns — Tydskrif vir Wetenskap en Kuns
Tyg Lek — Tygodnik Lekarski [*Krakow*]
TygP — Tygodnik Powszechny
Tyg Roln Krakow — Tygodnik Rolniczy (Krakow)
Tyg Roln Wilno — Tygodnik Rolniczy (Wilno)
TYI — Turk Yurdu (Istanbul)
TYKNAQ — Annual Report. Tohoku College of Pharmacy
Tyler's — Tyler's Quarterly Historical and Genealogical Magazine
Tyler's Quar — Tyler's Quarterly Historical and Genealogical Magazine
Tylers Quar Hist And Geneal Mag — Tyler's Quarterly Historical and Genealogical Magazine
TyM — Tydskrif vir Maatskaplike Navorsing
TYNAA — Tydskrif vir Natuurwetenskappe
Tyndale Bul — Tyndale Bulletin
Tyndale House Bull — Tyndale House Bulletin
TYO — Tokyo Newsletter
Tyoevaeen Taloudell Tutkimus Katsaus — Tyoevaeen Taloudellinen Tutkimuslaitos Katsaus
Tyo Ihminen — Tyo ja Ihminen
Typ — Typographica
Typesett Mach Engrs J — Typesetting Machine Engineers' Journal [*New York*]
Typhoons China Seas — Typhoons of the China Seas
Typ News — Typewriting News
Typographical J — Typographical Journal
Typogr Circ — Typographical Circular [*Manchester*]
Typogr Mitt — Typograph-Mitteilungen [*Berlin*]
Typogr Monatsbl — Typographische Monatsblaetter
Typoth Bull — Typothetae Bulletin [*Chicago*]
Tyres & Access — Tyres and Accessories
Tyre Wheel Stand — Tyre and Wheel Standards. Society of Motor Manufacturers and Traders [*London*]
TYS — Overzicht van de Economische Ontwikkeling
TZ — Theologische Zeitschrift
TZ — Times of Zambia
TZ — Trierer Zeitschrift
TZ — Trier Zeitschrift fuer Geschichte und Kunst des Trierer Landes und Seiner Nachbargebiete
TZA — Finanzierung, Leasing, Factoring
TZANG — Trudy Zoologicheskogo Sektora Gruzinskogo Otdeleniia Zakavkazskogo Filiala Akademii Nauk SSSR
TZB — Theologische Zeitschrift (Basel)
TZBas — Theologische Zeitschrift (Basel)
TZI — Traditiones. Zbornik Instituta za Slovensko Narodopisje
TZI — Trudy Zoologicheskogo Instituta Akademii Nauk SSSR
TZIAz — Trudy Zoologicheskogo Instituta Akademii Nauk Azerbaidzhanskoi SSR
TZIK — Trudy Zoologicheskogo Instituta Akademii Nauk Kazakhskoi SSR
TZKRA — Tonindustrie-Zeitung und Keramische Rundschau
TZM — Turkiye Ziraat Mecmuasi. Ziraat-Veteriner-Orman/Turkish Agricultural Journal. Agriculture-Veterinary Science-Forestry
TZNSDW — Topographie und Zytologie Neurosekretorischer Systeme
TZ Prakt Metallbearb — TZ fuer Praktische Metallbearbeitung
TZS — Terzake Subsidies
TZS — Transactions of the Zoological Society of London

U

U — Uitgelezen
U — Universitas
UA — Union des Arts
UA — United Asia
UA — Universidad de Antioquia
UA — Universitas. (Argentina)
UA — Ural-Altaische Jahrbuecher
UA — Urban Anthropology
UAA — Universitet i Bergen. Arbok. Historisk-Antikvarisk Rekke
UAB — United Asia (Bombay)
UAC — Universidad de Antioquia (Colombia)
UAC — Universitas Humanistica (Colombia)
UAegAI — Urkunden die Aegyptischen Altertums
UAERA — United States. Air Force. School of Aerospace Medicine. Technical Report
UAFZAG — Contributions. Faculty of Science. University College of Addis Ababa (Ethiopia). Series C. Zoology
UAG — USSR. Academy of Science. Proceedings. Geographical Series
U Agr — Ugeskrift for Agronomer, Hortonomer, Forstkandidater og Licentiater
UAIA — Universidad de Antioquia. Instituto de Antropologia. Boletin [*Medellin*]
UAJ — Ural-Altaische Jahrbuecher
UAJb — Ural-Altaische Jahrbuecher
UALG — Untersuchungen zur Antiken Literatur und Geschichte
UALR LJ — University of Arkansas at Little Rock. Law Journal
UAM — Universidad de Antioquia (Medellin)
UAMGAS — Anales. Instituto de Geologia. Universidad Nacional Autonoma de Mexico
UAMR Trav Newsl — UAMR [*United Association Manufacturers' Representatives*] Travel Newsletter
U & F — Unterricht und Forschung
U&O — Ulm und Oberschwaben. Zeitschrift fuer Geschichte und Kunst
UAnt — Universidad de Antioquia
UAQUA — Urban Affairs Quarterly
UAR Geol Surv Miner Res Dep Pap — United Arab Republic. Geological Survey and Mineral Research Department. Papers
UAR Inst Oceanogr Fish Bull — United Arab Republic. Institute of Oceanography and Fisheries. Bulletin
UARJ Anim Prod — United Arab Republic. Journal of Animal Production
UARJ Bot — United Arab Republic. Journal of Botany
UARJ Chem — United Arab Republic. Journal of Chemistry
UARJ Geol — United Arab Republic. Journal of Geology
UAR J Microbiol — United Arab Republic. Journal of Microbiology
UARJ Pharm Sci — United Arab Republic. Journal of Pharmaceutical Sciences
UAR J Phys — United Arab Republic. Journal of Physics
UARJ Soil Sci — United Arab Republic. Journal of Soil Science
UARJ Vet Sci — United Arab Republic. Journal of Veterinary Science
U Ark Little Rock LJ — University of Arkansas at Little Rock. Law Journal
UAR Minist Agric Agrar Reform Tech Bull — United Arab Republic. Ministry of Agriculture and Agrarian Reform. Technical Bulletin
UAR Minist Agric Tech Bull — United Arab Republic. Ministry of Agriculture. Technical Bulletin
UAR (South Reg) Minist Agric Hydrobiol Dep Notes Mem — United Arab Republic (Southern Region). Ministry of Agriculture. Hydrobiological Department. Notes and Memoirs
UAS — University of Alabama. Studies
UAS — Uralic and Altaic Series. Indiana University. Publications
UAS (Hebbal) Monogr Ser — UAS (Hebbal) Monograph Series
UASSB — University of Arizona Social Science Bulletin
UAVA — Untersuchungen zur Assyriologie und Vorderasiatischen Archaeologie
UB — University Bookman
UB — Urban Buecher
UB — Uttara Bharati
UBA — Universitet i Bergen. Arbok. Historisk-Antikvarisk Rekke
U Baltimore L Rev — University of Baltimore. Law Review
U Balt LR — University of Baltimore. Law Review
U Balt L Rev — University of Baltimore. Law Review
UBC Alumni Chronicle — Alumni Association. University of British Columbia. Chronicle
UBC Legal N — University of British Columbia. Legal Notes
UBC Legal Notes — University of British Columbia. Legal Notes
UBCLN — University of British Columbia. Legal News
UBC LR — University of British Columbia. Law Review
UBC L Rev — University of British Columbia. Law Review
UBCNREP — University of British Columbia. Programme in Natural Resource Economics. Resources Paper
UBEA Forum — United Business Education Association. Forum

U Bergen Ab — Universiteit i Bergen Arbok
UBGI/E — Erkunde. Archiv fuer Wissenschaftliche Geographie. Universitaet Bonn. Geographisches Institut
UBHJ — University of Birmingham. Historical Journal
U Birmingham Hist J — University of Birmingham. Historical Journal
UBJSA — Union of Burma. Journal of Science and Technology
UBKHA — Uspekhi Biologicheskoi Khimii
UBL — UNESCO Bulletin for Libraries
UBLR — University of Baltimore. Law Review
UBLSLJ — University of Botswana, Lesotho, and Swaziland Law Journal
U Brdgprt LR — University of Bridgeport. Law Review
U Bridgeport L Rev — University of Bridgeport. Law Review
U Brit Col L Rev — University of British Columbia. Law Review
U Brit Colum L Rev — University of British Columbia. Law Review
UBS — University of Buffalo. Studies
UBSB — United Bible Societies. Bulletin
UBU — UNESCO [*United Nations Educational, Scientific, and Cultural Organization*] Journal of Information Science, Librarianship, and Archives Administration
UBZHA — Ukrayinski Biokhimichnyi Zhurnal
UC — National Union Catalogue
Uc — Uncanny Stories
UC — UNESCO [*United Nations Educational, Scientific, and Cultural Organization*] Chronicle
UC — Unesco y Cresalc
UCA — Uniform Companies Act
UCASBJ — Agro Sur
UCB — Canadian Union Catalogue of Books
UCB — Universidad Catolica Bolivariana [*Medellin*]
UC/BPC — Boletin de Prehistoria de Chile. Universidad de Chile
UCC — Uniform Commercial Code Law Journal
UCC — University of California. Chronicle
UC/CA — Current Anthropology. University of Chicago
UCCEW — University of Cape Coast. English Department. Workpapers
UCCLJ — Uniform Commercial Code Law Journal
UCD — University of California (Davis). Law Review
UCD LR — University of California (Davis). Law Review
UCD L Rev — UCD [*University of California, Davis*] Law Review
UCDPE — University of California (Davis). Publications in English
UC/EDCC — Economic Development and Cultural Change. University of Chicago
Ucenyje Zapiski Belorusskogo Gosud Univ — Ucenyje Zapiski Belorusskogo Gosudarstvennogo Universiteta
Ucenyje Zapiski Jaroslav — Ucenyje Zapiski Jaroslavskogo Universiteta
Ucenyje Zapiski Leningrad — Ucenyje Zapiski Leningradskogo Gosudarstvennogo Universiteta
Ucenyje Zapiski Leningrad Pedag Inst — Ucenyje Zapiski Leningradskogo Gosudarstvennogo Pedagogiceskogo Instituta
Ucenyje Zapiski Moskov Gosud Pedag Inst — Ucenyje Zapiski Moskovskogo Gosudarstvennogo Pedagogiceskogo Instituta Inostraunych Jazykov
Ucenyje Zapiski Moskva — Ucenyje Zapiski Moskovskogo Gosudarstvennogo Universiteta Imeni Lononosova
Ucenyje Zapiski (Tomsk) — Ucenyje Zapiski Tomskogo Gosudarstvennogo Universiteta Imeni Kujbyseva (Tomsk)
Ucen Zap Azerb Gosud Univ Ser Ist Filos Nauk — Ucenye Zapiski. Azerbajdzanskij Gosudarstvennyj Universitet. Serija Istoriceskih i Filosofskih Nauk
Ucen Zap Azerb Inst Nar Hoz Ser Ekon Nauk — Ucenye Zapiski. Azerbajdzanskij Institut Narodnogo Hozjajstva. Serija Ekonomiceskih Nauk
Ucen Zap Azerb Univ Ser Ist Filos Nauk — Ucenye Zapiski. Azerbajdzanskij Universitet. Serija Istoriceskih i Filosofskih Nauk
Ucen Zap Biol Fak — Ucenye Zapiski Biologiceskogo Fakul'teta
Ucen Zap CAGI — Ucenyi Zapiski Central'nogo Aero-Gidrodinamiceskogo Instituta
Ucen Zap Dal'nevost Univ — Ucenye Zapiski Dal'nevostocnogo Universiteta
Ucen Zap Dusan Gos Pedag Inst — Ucenye Zapiski Dusanbinskogo Gosudarstvennogo Pedagogiceskogo Instituta
Ucen Zap Erevan Gos Univ Estestv Nauki — Ucenye Zapiski Erevanskogo Gosudarstvennogo Universiteta Estestvennye Nauki
Ucen Zap Hakas Nauc-Issled Inst Jaz Lit Ist — Ucenye Zapiski Hakasskogo Naucno-Issledovatel'skogo Instituta Jazyka, Literatury, i Istorii
Ucen Zap Imp Kazansk Univ — Ucenyja Zapiski. Izdavaemyja Imperatorskim Kazanskim Universitetom
Ucen Zap Ivanov Univ — Ucenye Zapiski Ivanovskogo Universitet
Ucen Zap Kaf Obsc Nauk Leningr Filos — Ucenye Zapiski Kafedr Obscestvennykh Nauk Vuzov Leningrada Filosofija
Ucen Zap Kaf Obsc Nauk Vuzov G Leningr Filos — Ucenye Zapiski Kafedr Obscestvennykh Nauk Vuzov Goroda Leningrada Filosofskih

Ucen Zap Kaf Obsc Nauk Vuzov G Leningr Probl Nauc Kommunizma — Ucenye Zapiski Kafedr Obscestvennykh Nauk Vuzov Goroda Leningrada Problemy Naucnogo Kommunizma

Ucen Zap Kalmyk Nauc-Issled Inst Jaz Lit Ist — Ucenye Zapiski Kalmykskogo Naucno-Issledovatel'skogo Instituta Jazyka, Literatury, i Istorii

Ucen Zap Karelo Finsk Gosud Univ — Ucenye Zapiski Karelo-Finskogo Gosudarstvennogo Universiteta

Ucen Zap Karel Ped Inst Ser Fiz-Mat Nauk — Ucenye Zapiski Karel'skii Pedagogiceskii Institut. Serija Fiziko-Matematiceskih Nauk

Ucen Zap Kazan Pedag Inst — Ucenye Zapiski. Kazanskij Pedagogiceskij Institut

Ucen Zap Krasnojarsk Gosud Pedagog Inst — Ucenye Zapiski. Krasnojarskij Gosudarstvennyj Pedagogiceskij Instituta

Ucen Zap Latv Univ — Ucenye Zapiski. Latvijskogo Universiteta

Ucen Zap Lening Pedag Inst — Ucenye Zapiski. Leningradskij Pedagogiceskij Institut

Ucen Zap Molotovsk Gosud Univ Gorkogo — Ucenye Zapiski. Molotovskij Gosudarstvennyj Universitet imeni A. M. Gor'kogo

Ucen Zap Moskov Pedag Inst — Ucenye Zapiski. Moskovskogo Pedagogiceskogo Instituta

Ucen Zap Perm Univ — Ucenye Zapiski Permskogo Universiteta

Ucen Zap Petrozavodsk Gosud Univ Vyp 3 Biol Selskohoz Nauki — Ucenye Zapiski Petrozavodskogo Gosudarstvennogo Universiteta. Vypusk 3. Biologiceskie i Sel'skohozjajstvennye Nauki

Ucen Zap Statist — Ucenyi Zapiski po Statistike Akademija Nauk SSSR Central'nyi Ekonomiko-Matematiceskii Institut

Ucen Zap Tartus Gos Univ Trudy Politekon — Ucenye Zapiski. Tartuskij Gosudarstvennyj Universitet. Trudy po Politekonomii

Ucen Zap Vyss Part Skola CK KPSS — Ucenye Zapiski. Vyssaja Partijnaja Skola pri CK KPSS

U Ceylon LR — University of Ceylon. Law Review

UCH — China Business Review

Uchen Zap Azerb Gos Univ Ser Biol Nauk — Uchenye Zapiski Azerbaidzhanskogo Gosudarstvennogo Universiteta. Seriya Biologicheskikh Nauk

Uchen Zap Azerb Gos Univ Ser Fiz Mat Nauk — Uchenye Zapiski Azerbaidzhanskogo Gosudarstvennogo Universiteta. Seriya Fiziko-Matematicheskikh Nauk

Uchen Zap Dal'nevost Univ — Uchenye Zapiski Dal'nevostochnogo Universiteta

Uchen Zap Gor'kov Gos Pedagog Inst — Uchenye Zapiski Gor'kovskogo Gosudarstvennogo Pedagogicheskogo Instituta

Uchen Zap Gor'kov Gos Univ Ser Biol — Uchenye Zapiski Gor'kovskogo Gosudarstvennogo Universiteta Imeni N. I. Lobachevskogo. Seriya Biologichevskaya

Uchen Zap Gor'k Univ Ser Biol — Uchenye Zapiski Gor'kovskogo Universiteta. Seriya Biologiya

Uchen Zap Kabardino-Balkar Gos Univ — Uchenye Zapiski Kabardino-Balkarskogo Gosudarstvennogo Universiteta

Uchen Zap Kabardino-Balkars Univ — Uchenye Zapiski Kabardino-Balkarskogo Gosudarstvennogo Universiteta

Uchen Zap Kazan Gos Univ — Uchenye Zapiski Kazanskogo Gosudarstvennogo Universiteta

Uchen Zap Kazan Vet Inst — Uchenye Zapiski Kazanskogo Veterinarnogo Instituta

Uchen Zap Kirovabad Ped Inst — Uchenye Zapiski Kirovabadskii Pedagogicheskii Institut

Uchen Zap Kishinev Univ — Uchenye Zapiski Kishinevskii Gosudarstvennyi Universitet

Uchen Zap Kursk Pedagog Inst — Uchenye Zapiski Kurskii Gosudarstvennyi Pedagogicheskii Institut

Uchen Zap Leningr Gos Pedagog Inst Gertsena — Uchenye Zapiski Leningradskogo Gosudarstvennogo Pedagogicheskogo Instituta Gertsena

Uchen Zap Mosk Gos Univ — Uchenye Zapiski Moskovskogo Gosudarstvennogo Universiteta

Uchen Zap Novgorod Golovn Pedagog Inst — Uchenye Zapiski Novgorodskogo Golovnogo Pedagogicheskogo Instituta

Uchen Zap Petrozavodsk Gos Univ — Uchenye Zapiski Petrozavodskogo Gosudarstvennogo Universiteta

Uchen Zap Ryazan Gos Pedagog Inst — Uchenye Zapiski Ryazanskogo Gosudarstvennogo Pedagogicheskogo Instituta

Uchen Zap Sel Khoz Dal'n Vost (Vladivostok) — Uchenye Zapiski Sel'skogo Khozyaistva Dal'nogo Vostoka (Vladivostok)

Uchen Zap Tartu Gos Univ — Uchenye Zapiski Tartuskogo Gosudarstvennogo Universiteta

Uchen Zap TsAGI — Uchenye Zapiski Tsentral'nogo Aero-Gidrodinamicheskogo Instituta (TsAGI)

Uchen Zap Ural Univ — Uchenye Zapiski Ural'skogo Gosudarstvennogo Universiteta Imeni A. M. Gor'kogo

Uchen Zap Yaroslav Gos Pedagog Inst — Uchenye Zapiski Yaroslavskii Gosudarstvennyi Pedagogicheskii Institut

Uchet Finan Kolkhoz Sovkhoz — Uchet i Finansy v Kolkhozakh i Sovkhozakh

U Chicago L Rev — University of Chicago. Law Review

U Chicago Mag — University of Chicago Magazine

U Chi L Rec — University of Chicago. Law School. Record

U Chi L Rev — University of Chicago. Law Review

U Chi L Sch Rec — University of Chicago. Law School. Record

U Chi LS Conf Series — University of Chicago. Law School. Conference Series

U Chi L S Rec — University of Chicago. Law School. Record

Uch Tr Gork Gos Med Inst — Uchenye Trudy Gorkovskogo Gosudarstvennogo Meditsinskogo Instituta

Uch Tr Gor'k Med Inst — Uchenye Trudy Gor'kovskii Meditsinskii Institut

Uch Zap Anat Gistol Embriol Resp Sredn Azil Kaz — Uchenye Zapiski Anatomov Gistologov i Embriologov Respublik Srednei Azii i Kazakhstana

Uch Zap Azerb Gos Inst Usoversh Vrachei — Uchenye Zapiski Azerbaidzhanskii Gosudarstvennyi Institut Usovershenstvovaniya Vrachei

Uch Zap Azerb Gos Uiv Im S M Kirova — Uchenye Zapiski Azerbaidzhan-Gosudarstvennogo Universiteta Imeni S. M. Kirova

Uch Zap Azerb Gos Univ — Uchenye Zapiski Azerbaidzhanskogo Gosudarstvennogo Universiteta

Uch Zap Azerb Gos Univ Im S M Kirova — Uchenye Zapiski Azerbaidzhanskogo Gosudarstvennogo Universiteta Imeni S. M. Kirova

Uch Zap Azerb Gos Univ Ser Biol Nauk — Uchenye Zapiski Azerbaidzhanskogo Gosudarstvennogo Universiteta. Seriya Biologicheskikh Nauk

Uch Zap Azerb Gos Univ Ser Fiz Mat Nauk — Uchenye Zapiski Azerbaidzhanskogo Gosudarstvennogo Universiteta. Seriya Fiziko-Matematicheskikh Nauk

Uch Zap Azerb Gos Univ Ser Geol Geogr Nauk — Uchenye Zapiski Azerbaidzhanskogo Gosudarstvennogo Universiteta. Seriya Geologo-Geograficheskikh Nauk

Uch Zap Azerb Gos Univ Ser Khim Nauk — Uchenye Zapiski Azerbaidzhanskogo Gosudarstvennogo Universiteta Imeni S. M. Kirova. Seriya Khimicheskikh Nauk

Uch Zap Azerb Inst Nefti Khim Ser 9 — Uchenye Zapiski Azerbajdzhanskij Institut Nefti i Khimii. Seriya 9

Uch Zap Azerb Inst Usoversh Vrachei — Uchenye Zapiski Azerbaidzhanskii Institut Usovershenstvovaniya Vrachei

Uch Zap Azerb Med Inst — Uchenye Zapiski Azerbaidzhanskogo Meditsinskogo Instituta

Uch Zap Azerb Med Inst Klin Med — Uchenye Zapiski Azerbaidzhanskogo Meditsinskogo Instituta Klinicheskoi Meditsiny

Uch Zap Azerb Politekh Inst — Uchenye Zapiski Azerbaidzhanskii Politekhnicheskii Institut

Uch Zap Azerb Skh Inst — Uchenye Zapiski Azerbaidzhánskogo Sel'skokhozyaistvennogo Instituta

Uch Zap Azerb Skh Inst Ser Agron — Uchenye Zapiski Azerbaidzhanskogo Sel'skokhozyaistvennogo Instituta. Seriya Agronomii

Uch Zap Azerb S-Kh Inst Ser Vet — Uchenye Zapiski Azerbaidzhanskogo Sel'skokhozyaistvennogo Instituta. Seriya Veterinarii

Uch Zap Azerb Univ Ser Biol Nauk — Uchenye Zapiski Azerbaidzhanskogo Universiteta. Seriya Biologicheskoi Nauki

Uch Zap Bashk Univ — Uchenye Zapiski Bashkirskogo Universiteta

Uch Zap Beloruss Gos Univ — Uchenye Zapiski Belorusskogo Gosudarstvennogo Universiteta

Uch Zap Beloruss Inst Inzh Zheleznodorozhn Transp — Uchenye Zapiski Belorusskii Institut Inzhenerov Zheleznodorozhnogo Transporta

Uch Zap Bel'tskii Pedagog Inst — Uchenye Zapiski Bel'tskii Pedagogicheskii Institut

Uch Zap Biol Fak Kirg Univ — Uchenye Zapiski Biologicheskogo Fakul'teta Kirgizskogo Universiteta

Uch Zap Biol Fak Osnovn Gos Pedagog Inst — Uchenye Zapiski Biologicheskogo Fakul'teta Osnovnogo Gosudarstvennogo Pedagogicheskogo Instituta

Uch Zap Birskogo Gos Pedagog Inst — Uchenye Zapiski Birskogo Gosudarstvennogo Pedagogicheskogo Instituta

Uch Zap Brest Gos Pedagog Inst — Uchenye Zapiski Brestskii Gosudarstvennyi Pedagogicheskii Institut

Uch Zap Brst Gos Pedagog Inst — Uchenye Zapiski Brestskii Gosudarstvennyi Pedagogicheskii Institut

Uch Zap Bukhar Gos Pedagog Inst — Uchenye Zapiski Bukharskii Gosudarstvennyi Pedagogicheskii Institut

Uch Zap Buryat Gos Pedagog Inst — Uchenye Zapiski Buryatskii Gosudarstvennyi Pedagogicheskii Institut

Uch Zap Buryat Mong Pedagog Inst — Uchenye Zapiski Buryat-Mongol'skii Pedagogicheskii Institut

Uch Zap Checheno Ingush Gos Pedagog Inst — Uchenye Zapiski Checheno-Ingushskii Gosudarstvennyi Pedagogicheskii Institut

Uch Zap Chelyab Gos Pedagog Inst — Uchenye Zapiski Chelyabinskogo Gosudarstvennogo Pedagogicheskogo Instituta

Uch Zap Chit Gos Pedagog Inst — Uchenye Zapiski Chitinskii Gosudarstvennyi Pedagogicheskii Institut

Uch Zap Chuv Gos Pedagog Inst — Uchenye Zapiski Chuvashskii Gosudarstvennyi Pedagogicheskii Institut

Uch Zap Dagest Gos Pedagog Inst — Uchenye Zapiski Dagestanskii Gosudarstvennyi Pedagogicheskii Institut

Uch Zap Dagest Gos Univ — Uchenye Zapiski Dagestanskogo Gosudarstvennogo Universiteta

Uch Zap Dal'nevost Gos Univ — Uchenye Zapiski Dal'nevostochnyi Gosudarstvennyi Universitet

Uch Zap Dushanb Gos Pedagog Inst — Uchenye Zapiski Dushanbinskii Gosudarstvennyi Pedagogicheskii Institut

Uch Zap Erevan Gos Univ — Uchenye Zapiski Erevanskii Gosudarstvennyi Universitet

Uch Zap Erevan Univ — Uchenye Zapiski Erevanskii Universitet

Uch Zap Erevan Univ Estestv Nauk — Uchenye Zapiski Erevanskogo Universiteta Estestvennykh Nauk

Uch Zap Gomel Gos Pedagog Inst — Uchenye Zapiski Gomel'skii Gosudarstvennyi Pedagogicheskii Institut

Uch Zap Gomel Gos Pedagog Inst Im V P Chkalova — Uchenye Zapiski Gomel'skogo Gosudarstvennogo Pedagogicheskogo Instituta Imeni V. P. Chkalova

Uch Zap Gor'k Gos Med Inst Im S M Kirova — Uchenye Zapiski Gor'kovskogo Gosudarstvennogo Meditsinskogo Instituta Imeni S. M. Kirova

Uch Zap Gor'k Gos Pedagog Inst — Uchenye Zapiski Gor'kovskogo Gosudarstvennogo Pedagogicheskogo Instituta

Uch Zap Gor'k Gos Pedagog Inst Im A M Gor'kogo — Uchenye Zapiski Gor'kovskogo Gosudarstvennogo Pedagogicheskogo Instituta Imeni A. M. Gor'kogo

Uch Zap Gor'k Gos Univ — Uchenye Zapiski Gor'kovskogo Gosudarstvennogo Universiteta

Uch Zap Gor'k Univ — Uchenye Zapiski Gor'kovskogo Universiteta

Uch Zap Gor'k Univ Ser Biol — Uchenye Zapiski Gor'kovskogo Universiteta. Seriya Biologiya

Uch Zap Gorno-Altai Gos Pedagog Inst — Uchenye Zapiski Gorno-Altaiskogo Gosudarstvennogo Pedagogicheskogo Instituta

Uch Zap Gos Inst Fiz Kul't Im P F Lesgafta — Uchenye Zapiski Gosudarstvennogo Instituta Fizicheskoi Kul'tury Imeni P. F. Lesgafta

Uch Zap Gos Nauchno-Issled Inst Glazn Bolezn Im Gel'Mgol'Tsa — Uchenye Zapiski Gosudarstvennogo Nauchno-Issledovatel'skogo Instituta Glaznykh Boleznei Imeni Gel'Mgol'Tsa

Uch Zap Gos Nauchno-Issled Inst Glaznykh Bolezn — Uchenye Zapiski Gosudarstvennogo Nauchno-Issledovatel'skogo Instituta Glaznykh Boleznei

Uch Zap Gos Pedagog Inst — Uchenye Zapiski Gosudarstvennogo Pedagogicheskogo Instituta Imeni T. G. Shevchenko

Uch Zap Gos Pedagog Inst Im T G Shevchenko — Uchenye Zapiski Gosudarstvennogo Pedagogicheskogo Instituta Imeni T. G. Shevchenko

Uch Zap Grozn Gos Pedagog Inst — Uchenye Zapiski Groznenskogo Gosudarstvennogo Pedagogicheskogo Instituta

Uch Zap Imp Yur'ev Univ — Uchenyya Zapiskik Imperatorokogo Yur'evskago Universiteta

Uch Zap Irkutsk Gos Pedagog Inst — Uchenye Zapiski Irkutskii Gosudarstvennyi Pedagogicheskii Institut

Uch Zap Irkutsk Inst Nar Khoz — Uchenye Zapiski Irkutskii Institut Narodnogo Khozyaistva

Uch Zap Ivanov Gos Pedagog Inst — Uchenye Zapiski Ivanovskogo Gosudarstvennogo Pedagogicheskogo Instituta

Uch Zap Kabard Balkar Gos Univ — Uchenye Zapiski Kabardino-Balkarskii Gosudarstvennyi Universitet

Uch Zap Kabard-Balkar Nauchno-Issled Inst — Uchenye Zapiski Kabardino-Balkarokogo Nauchno-Issledovatel'skogo Instituta

Uch Zap Kabard Gos Pedagog Inst — Uchenye Zapiski Kabardinskogo Gosudarstvennogo Pedagogicheskogo Instituta

Uch Zap Kalinin Gos Pedagog Inst — Uchenye Zapiski Kalininskii Pedagogicheskii Institut

Uch Zap Kaliningr Gos Pedagog Inst — Uchenye Zapiski Gosudarstvennogo Pedagogicheskogo Instituta

Uch Zap Kaliningr Gos Univ — Uchenye Zapiski Kaliningradskii Gosudarstvennyi Universitet

Uch Zap Karagand Gos Med Inst — Uchenye Zapiski Karagandinskii Gosudarstvennyi Meditsinskii Institut

Uch Zap Karagand Med Inst — Uchenye Zapiski Karagandinskogo Meditsinskogo Instituta

Uch Zap Karelo Fin Gos Univ Biol Nauki — Uchenye Zapiski Karelo-Finskogo Gosudarstvennogo Universiteta Biologicheskie Nauki

Uch Zap Karelo Fin Gos Univ Fiz Mat Nauki — Uchenye Zapiski Karelo-Finskogo Gosudarstvennogo Universiteta Fiziko Matematicheskie Nauki

Uch Zap Karelo-Fin Pedagog Inst — Uchenye Zapiski Karelo-Finskogo Pedagogicheskogo Instituta

Uch Zap Karel Pedagog Inst — Uchenye Zapiski Karel'skogo Pedagogicheskogo Instituta

Uch Zap Karsh Gos Pedagog Inst — Uchenye Zapiski Karshinskii Gosudarstvennyi Pedagogicheskii Institut

Uch Zap Kazan Gos Pedagog Inst — Uchenye Zapiski Kazanskii Gosudarstvennyi Pedagogicheskii Institut

Uch Zap Kazan Gos Univ — Uchenye Zapiski Kazanskii Gosudarstvennyi Universitet

Uch Zap Kazan Univ — Uchenye Zapiski Kazanskogo Universiteta

Uch Zap Kazan Vet Inst — Uchenye Zapiski Kazanskogo Veterinarnogo Instituta

Uch Zap Kazan Yuridicheskogo Inst — Uchenye Zapiski Kazanskogo Yuridicheskogo Instituta

Uch Zap Kaz Gos Uiv Im S M Kirova — Uchenye Zapiski Kazakhskogo Gosudarstvennogo Universiteta Imeni S. M. Kirova

Uch Zap Kaz Gos Univ — Uchenye Zapiski Kazakhskii Gosudarstvennyi Universitet

Uch Zap Kemer Gos Pedagog Inst — Uchenye Zapiski Kemerovskogo Gosudarstvennogo Pedagogicheskogo Instituta

Uch Zap Khabar Gos Pedagog Inst — Uchenye Zapiski Khabarovskogo Gosudarstvennogo Pedagogicheskogo Instituta

Uch Zap Khabar Gos Pedagog Inst Biol Khim Nauk — Uchenye Zapiski Khabarovskii Gosudarstvennyi Pedagogicheskii Institut Biologii i Khimicheskikh Nauk

Uch Zap Khabar Gos Pedagog Inst Ser Biol — Uchenye Zapiski Khabarovskii Gosudarstvennyi Pedagogicheskii Institut. Seriya Biologiya

Uch Zap Khabar Gos Pedagog Inst Ser Estestv Nauk — Uchenye Zapiski Khabarovskii Gosudarstvennyi Pedagogicheskii Institut. Seriya Estestvennykh Nauk

Uch Zap Khabar Nauchno-Issled Inst Epidemiol Mikrobiol — Uchenye Zapiski Khabarovskogo Nauchno-Issledovatel'skogo Instituta Epidemiologii i Mikrobiologii

Uch Zap Khar'k Univ Tr Biol Fak Genet Zool — Uchenye Zapiski Khar'kovskogo Universiteta Trudy Biologicheskogo Fakul'teta po Genetlike i Zoologii

Uch Zap Khark Univ Tr Nauchno Issled Inst Biol Biol Fak — Uchenye Zapiski Khar'kovskogo Universiteta Trudy Nauchno-Issledovatel'skogo Instituta Biologii i Biologicheskogo Fakul'teta

Uch Zap Kiev Nauchno-Issled Rentgeno Radiol Onkol Inst — Uchenye Zapiski Kievskogo Nauchno-Issledovatel'skogo Rentgeno Radiologicheskogoi Onkologicheskogo Instituta

Uch Zap Kirg Zhen Pedagog Inst — Uchenye Zapiski Kirgizskii Zhenskii Pedagogicheskii Institut

Uch Zap Kirovab Pedagog Inst — Uchenye Zapiski Kirovabadskii Pedagogicheskii Institut

Uch Zap Kirov Gos Pedagog Inst — Uchenye Zapiski Kirovskogo Gosudarstvennogo Pedagogicheskogo Instituta

Uch Zap Kishinev Gos Univ — Uchenye Zapiski Kishinevskogo Gosudarstvennogo Universiteta

Uch Zap Komsomol'skogo-Na-Amure Gos Pedagog Inst — Uchenye Zapiski Komsomol'skogo-Na-Amure Gosudarstvennogo Pedagogicheskogo Instituta

Uch Zap Kostrom Gos Pedagog Inst — Uchenye Zapiski Kostromskoi Gosudarstvennyi Pedagogicheskii Institut

Uch Zap Kuibyshev Gos Pedagog Inst — Uchenye Zapiski Kuibyshevskogo Gosudarstvennogo Pedagogicheskogo Instituta

Uch Zap Kursk Gos Pedagog Inst — Uchenye Zapiski Kurskogo Gosudarstvennogo Pedagogicheskogo Instituta

Uch Zap Latv Gos Univ — Uchenye Zapiski Latvijskogo Gosudarstvennogo Universiteta Imeni Petra Stuchki

Uch Zap Latv Gos Univ Astron — Uchenye Zapiski Latvijskogo Gosudarstvennogo Universiteta Imeni Petra Stuchki. Astronomiya

Uch Zap Latv Univ — Uchenye Zapiski Latvijskogo Universiteta

Uch Zap Lenigr Gos Univ Ser Fiz Nauk — Uchenye Zapiski Leningradskogo Gosudarstvennogo Universiteta. Seriya Fizicheskikh Nauk

Uch Zap Leninab Gos Pedagog Inst — Uchenye Zapiski Leninabadskogo Gosudarstvennogo Pedagogicheskogo Instituta

Uch Zap Leningr Gos Inst — Uchenye Zapiski Leningradskogo Gosudarstvennogo Instituta

Uch Zap Leningr Gos Pedagog Inst Im A I Gertsena — Uchenye Zapiski Leningradskogo Gosudarstvennogo Pedagogicheskogo Instituta Imeni A. I. Gertsena

Uch Zap Leningr Gos Univ Im A A Zhdanova Ser Biol Nauk — Uchenye Zapiski Leningradskogo Gosudarstvennogo Universiteta Imeni A. A. Zhdanova. Seriya Biologicheskikh Nauk

Uch Zap Leningr Gos Univ Im A A Zhdanova Ser Fiz Nauk — Uchenye Zapiski Leningradskogo Gosudarstvennogo Universiteta Imeni A. A. Zhdanova. Seriya Fizicheskikh Nauk

Uch Zap Leningr Gos Univ Im A A Zhdanova Ser Geogr Nauk — Uchenye Zapiski Leningradskogo Gosudarstvennogo Universiteta Imeni A. A. Zhdanova. Seriya Geograficheskikh Nauk

Uch Zap Leningr Gos Univ Im A A Zhdanova Ser Geol Nauk — Uchenye Zapiski Leningradskogo Gosudarstvennogo Universiteta Imeni A. A. Zhdanova. Seriya Geologicheskikh Nauk

Uch Zap Leningr Gos Univ Ser Biol Nauk — Uchenye Zapiski Leningradskogo Gosudarstvennogo Universiteta. Seriya Biologicheskikh Nauk

Uch Zap Leningr Gos Univ Ser Fiz Geol Nauk — Uchenye Zapiski Leningradskogo Gosudarstvennogo Universiteta. Seriya Fizicheskikh i Geologicheskikh Nauk

Uch Zap Leningr Gos Univ Ser Geogr Nauk — Uchenye Zapiski Leningradskogo Gosudarstvennogo Universiteta. Seriya Geograficheskikh Nauk

Uch Zap Leningr Gos Univ Ser Geol Nauk — Uchenye Zapiski Leningradskogo Gosudarstvennogo Universiteta. Seriya Geologicheskikh Nauk

Uch Zap Leningr Gos Univ Ser Khim Nauk — Uchenye Zapiski Leningradskogo Gosudarstvennogo Universiteta. Seriya Khimicheskikh Nauk

Uch Zap Leningr Gos Univ Ser Mat Nauk — Uchenye Zapiski Leningradskogo Gosudarstvennogo Ordena Lenina Universita Imeni A. A. Zhdanova. Seriya Matematicheskikh Nauk

Uch Zap Marii Gos Pedagog Inst — Uchenye Zapiski Mariiskii Gosudarstvennyi Pedagogicheskii Institut

Uch Zap Michurinsk Gos Pedagog Inst — Uchenye Zapiski Michurinskii Gosudarstvennyi Pedagogicheskii Institut

Uch Zap Mo Gos Univ — Uchenye Zapiski Moskovskii Gosudarstvennyi Universitet

Uch Zap Molotov Gos Univ Im A M Gor'kogo — Uchenye Zapiski Molotovskogo Gosudarstvennogo Universiteta Imeni A. M. Gor'kogo

Uch Zap Mord Gos Univ — Uchenye Zapiski Mordovskii Gosudarstvennyi Universitet

Uch Zap Mord Univ — Uchenye Zapiski Mordovskogo Universiteta

Uch Zap Mosk Gor Pedagog Inst — Uchenye Zapiski Moskovskogo Gorodskogo Pedagogicheskogo Instituta

Uch Zap Mosk Gos Pedagog Inst — Uchenye Zapiski Moskovskii Gosudarstvennyi Pedagogicheskii Institut

Uch Zap Mosk Gos Pedagog Inst Im Lenina — Uchenye Zapiski Moskovskogo Gosudarstvennogo Pedagogicheskogo Instituta Imeni Lenina

Uch Zap Mosk Gos Univ — Uchenye Zapiski Moskovskii Gosudarstvennyi Universitet

Uch Zap Mosk Gos Zaochn Pedagog Inst — Uchenye Zapiski Moskovskii Gosudarstvennyi Zaochnyi Pedagogicheskii Institut

Uch Zap Mosk Inst Tonkoi Khim Tekhnol — Uchenye Zapiski Moskovskogo Instituta Tonkoi Khimicheskoi Tekhnologii

Uch Zap Mosk Nauchno-Issled Inst Gig — Uchenye Zapiski Moskovskii Nauchno-Issledovatel'skii Institut Gigieny

Uch Zap Mosk Nauchno-Issled Inst Glaznym Bolezn — Uchenye Zapiski Moskovskogo Nauchno-Issledovatel'skogo Instituta po Glaznym Boleznam

Uch Zap Mosk Obl Pedagog Inst — Uchenye Zapiski Moskovskogo Oblastnogo Pedagogicheskogo Instituta

Uch Zap Murom Gos Pedagog Inst — Uchenye Zapiski Muromskii Gosudarstvennyi Pedagogichskii Institut

Uch Zap Namanganskii Gos Pedagog Inst — Uchenye Zapiski Namanganskii Gosudarstvennyi Pedagogicheskii Institut

Uch Zap Nauchno Issled Inst Geol Arktiki Reg Geol — Uchenye Zapiski Nauchno-Issledovatel'skogo Instituta Geologii Arktiki Regional'naya Geologiya

Uch Zap Nauchno-Issled Inst Geol Arkt Reg Geol — Uchenye Zapiski Nauchno-Issledovatel'skogo Instituta Geologii Arktiki Regional'naya Geologiya

Uch Zap Nauchno-Issled Inst Izuch Lepry — Uchenye Zapiski Nauchno-Issledovatel'skogo Instituta po Izucheniyu Lepry

Uch Zap Novgorod Golovn Gos Pedagog Inst — Uchenye Zapiski Novgorodskii Golovnoi Gosudarstvennyi Pedagogicheskii Institut

Uch Zap Novgorod Gos Pedagog — Uchenye Zapiski Novgorodskogo Gosudarstvennogo Pedagogicheskogo Instituta

Uch Zap Novgorod Gos Pedagog Inst — Uchenye Zapiski Novgorodskogo Gosudarstvennogo Pedagogicheskogo Instituta

Uch Zap Novosib Inst Sov Koop Torg — Uchenye Zapiski Novosibirskii Institut Sovetskoi Kooperativnoi Torgovli

Uch Zap Novozybkovskii Gos Pedagog Inst — Uchenye Zapiski Novozybkovskii Gosudarstvennyi Pedagogicheskii Institut

Uch Zap Omsk Gos Pedagog Inst — Uchenye Zapiski Omskogo Gosudarstvennogo Pedagogicheskogo Instituta

Uch Zap Orenb Gos Pedagog Inst — Uchenye Zapiski Orenburgskii Gosudarstvennyi Pedagogicheskii Institut

Uch Zap Orenb Otd Vses Nauchn Ova Anat Gistol Embriol — Uchenye Zapiski Orenburgskogo Otdela Vsesoyuznogo Nauchnogo Obshchestva Anatomov, Gistologov, i Embriologov

Uch Zap Orlov Gos Pedagog Inst — Uchenye Zapiski Orlovskogo Gosudarstvennogo Pedagogicheskogo Instituta

Uch Zap Osh Gos Pedagog Inst — Uchenye Zapiski Oshskii Gosudarstvennyi Pedagogicheskii Institut

Uch Zap Penz Gos Pedagog Inst — Uchenye Zapiski Penzenskogo Gosudarstvennogo Pedagogicheskogo Instituta

Uch Zap Penz S-Kh Inst — Uchenye Zapiski Penzenskogo Sel'skokhozyaistvennogo Instituta

Uch Zap Perm Gos Pedagog Inst — Uchenye Zapiski Permskii Gosudarstvennyi Pedagogicheskii Institut

Uch Zap Perm Gos Univ — Uchenye Zapiski Permskij Gosudarstvennyj Universitet Imeni A. M. Gor'kogo

Uch Zap Permsk Gos Pedagog Inst — Uchenye Zapiski Permskogo Gosudarstvennogo Pedagogicheskogo Instituta

Uch Zap Permsk Univ Im A M Gor'korgo — Uchenye Zapiski Permskogo Universiteta Imeni A. M. Gor'kogo

Uch Zap Perm Univ Im A M Gor'kogo — Uchenye Zapiski Permskogo Universiteta Imeni A. M. Gor'kogo

Uch Zap Petropavlovsk Gos Inst — Uchenye Zapiski Petropavlovskogo Gosudarstvennogo Instituta

Uch Zap Petrozavodsk Gos Univ Fiz Mat Nauki — Uchenye Zapiski Petrozavodskogo Gosudarstvennogo Universiteta Fiziko-Matematicheskie Nauki

Uch Zap Petrozavodsk Inst — Uchenye Zapiski Petrozavodskogo Instituta

Uch Zap Petrozavodsk Univ — Uchenye Zapiski Petrozavodskogo Universiteta

Uch Zap Pskov Gos Pedagog Inst — Uchenye Zapiski Pskovskogo Gosudarstvennogo Pedagogicheskogo Instituta

Uch Zap Pskov Pedagog Inst Estestv Nauk — Uchenye Zapiski Pskovskogo Pedagogicheskogo Instituta Estestvennykh Nauk

Uch Zap Pyatigorsk Farm Inst — Uchenye Zapiski Pyatigorskii Farmatsevticheskii Institut

Uch Zap Pyatigorsk Gos Nauchno Issled Balneol Inst — Uchenye Zapiski Pyatigorskii Gosudarstvennyi Nauchno-Issledovatel'skii Bal'neologicheskii Institut

Uch Zap Rizh Politekh Inst — Uchenye Zapiski Rizhskii Politekhnicheskii Institut

Uch Zap Rostov Na Donu Gos Pedagog Inst Fiz Mat Fak — Uchenye Zapiski Rostovskii-Na-Donu Gosudarstvennyi Pedagogicheskii Institut Fiziko-Matematicheskii Fakul'tet

Uch Zap Rostov Na Donu Gos Univ — Uchenye Zapiski Rostovskogo-Na-Donu Gosudarstvennogo Universiteta

Uch Zap Rostov-Na-Donu Univ Im V M Molotova — Uchenye Zapiski Rostovskogo-Na-Donu Universiteta Imeni V. M. Molotova

Uch Zap Rostov Na Donu Univ V M Molotova — Uchenye Zapiski Rostovskogo-Na-Donu Universiteta Imeni V. M. Molotova

Uch Zap Ryazan Gos Pedagog Inst — Uchenye Zapiski Ryazanskogo Gosudarstvennogo Pedagogicheskogo Instituta

Uch Zap Rybinsk Gos Pedagog Inst — Uchenye Zapiski Rybinskii Gosudarstvennyi Pedagogicheskii Institut

Uch Zap Sarat Gos Pedagog Inst — Uchenye Zapiski Saratovskogo Gosudarstvennogo Pedagogicheskogo Instituta

Uch Zap Sarat Gos Univ — Uchenye Zapiski Saratovskogo Gosudarstvennogo Universiteta

Uch Zap Sev Oset Gos Pedagog Inst — Uchenye Zapiski Severo-Osetinskii Gosudarstvennyi Pedagogicheskii Institut

Uch Zap Sev-Oset Gos Pedagog Inst Im K L Khetagurova — Uchenye Zapiski Severo-Osetinskogo Gosudarstvennogo Pedagogicheskogo Instituta Imeni K. L. Khetagurova

Uch Zap Smolensk Gos Pedagog Inst — Uchenye Zapiski Smolenskogo Gosudarstvennogo Pedagogicheskogo Instituta

Uch Zap Sredneaziat Nauchno-Issled Inst Geol Miner Syr'ya — Uchenye Zapiski Sredneaziatskii Nauchno-Issledovatel'skii Institut Geologii i Mineral'nogo Syr'ya

Uch Zap Stavrop Gos Med Inst — Uchenye Zapiski Stavropol'skogo Gosudarstvennogo Meditsinskogo Instituta

Uch Zap Sverdl Gos Pedagog Inst — Uchenye Zapiski Sverdlovskii Gosudarstvennyi Pedagogicheskii Institut

Uch Zap Tadzh Gos Univ — Uchenye Zapiski Tadzhikskogo Gosudarstvennogo Universiteta

Uch Zap Tartu Gos Univ — Uchenye Zapiski Tartuskogo Gosudarstvennogo Universiteta

Uch Zap Tashk Gos Pedagog Inst — Uchenye Zapiski Tashkentskogo Gosudarstvennogo Pedagogicheskogo Instituta

Uch Zap Tashk Vech Pedagog Inst — Uchenye Zapiski Tashkentskii Vechernii Pedagogicheskii Institut

Uch Zap Tirasp Gos Pedagog Inst — Uchenye Zapiski Tiraspol'skii Gosudarstvennyi Pedagogicheskii Institut

Uch Zap Tomsk Gos Pedagog Inst — Uchenye Zapiski Tomskogo Gosudarstvennogo Pedagogicheskogo Instituta

Uch Zap Tomsk Gos Univ — Uchenye Zapiski Tomskogo Gosudarstvennogo Universiteta

Uch Zap TsAGI — Uchenye Zapiski TsAGI

Uch Zap Tsentr Nauchno-Issled Inst Olovyannoi Promsti — Uchenye Zapiski Tsentral'nyi Nauchno-Issledovatel'skii Institut Olovyannoi Promyshlennosti

Uch Zap Tul Gos Pedagog Inst Fiz Tekh Nauki — Uchenye Zapiski Tul'skii Gosudarstvennyi Pedagogicheskii Institut Fiziko-Tekhnicheskie Nauki

Uch Zap Turkm Gos Pedagog Inst Ser Estest Nauk — Uchenye Zapiski Turkmenskii Gosudarstvennyi Pedagogicheskii Institut Seriya Estestvennykh Nauk

Uch Zap Turkm Gos Univ — Uchenye Zapiski Turkmenskogo Gosudarstvennogo Universiteta

Uch Zap Tyumen Gos Pedagog Inst — Uchenye Zapiski Tyumenskogo Gosudarstvennogo Pedagogicheskogo Instituta

Uch Zap Udmurt Gos Pedagog Inst — Uchenye Zapiski Udmurtskogo Gosudarstvennogo Pedagogicheskogo Instituta

Uch Zap Udmurt Pedagog Inst — Uchenye Zapiski Udmurtskogo Pedagogicheskogo Instituta

Uch Zap Ukr Inst Eksp Endokrinol — Uchenye Zapiski Ukrainskii Institut Eksperimental'noi Endokrinologii

Uch Zap Ukr Nauchno Issled Inst Gig Tr Profzabol — Uchenye Zapiski Ukrainskii Nauchno-Issledovatel'skii Institut Gigieny Truda i Profzabolevanii

Uch Zap Ukr Tsentr Inst Gig Tr Profzabol — Uchenye Zapiski Ukrainskii Tsentral'nyi Institut Gigieny Truda i Profzabolevanii

Uch Zap Ul'yanovsk Pedagog Inst — Üchenye Zapiski Ul'yanovskii Pedagogicheskii Institut

Uch Zap Ural Gos Univ — Uchenye Zapiski Ural'skogo Gosudarstvennogo Universiteta

Uch Zap Ural Gos Univ Im A M Gor'kogo — Uchenye Zapiski Ural'skogo Gosudarstvennogo Universiteta Imeni A. M. Gor'kogo

Uch Zap Ussur Gos Pedagog Inst — Uchenye Zapiski Ussuriiskii Gosudarstvennyi Pedagogicheskii Institut

Uch Zap Velikoluk Gos Pedagog Inst — Uchenye Zapiski Velikolukskii Gosudarstvennyi Pedagogicheskii Institut

Uch Zap Vitebsk Gos Pedagog Inst Im S M Kirova — Uchenye Zapiski Vitebskogo Gosudarstvennogo Pedagogicheskogo Instituta Imeni S.M. Kirova

Uch Zap Vitebsk Vet Inst — Uchenye Zapiski Vitebskogo Veterinarnogo Instituta

Uch Zap Vladimir Gos Pedagog Inst Ser Bot — Uchenye Zapiski Vladimirskogo Gosudarstvennogo Pedagogicheskogo Institut. Seriya Botanika

Uch Zap Vladimir Gos Pedagog Inst Ser Fiz — Uchenye Zapiski Vladimirskii Gosudarstvennyi Pedagogicheskii Institut. Seriya Fizika

Uch Zap Vladimir Gos Pedagog Inst Ser Fiziol Rast — Uchenye Zapiski Vladimirskii Gosudarstvennyi Pedagogicheskii Institut. Seriya Fiziologiya Rastenii

Uch Zap Vladimir Gos Pedagog Inst Ser Khim — Uchenye Zapiski Vladimirskii Gosudarstvennyi Pedagogicheskii Institut. Seriya Khimiya

Uch Zap Volgogr Gos Pedagog Inst — Uchenye Zapiski Volgogradskogo Gosudarstvennogo Pedagogicheskogo Instituta

Uch Zap Vologod Gos Pedagog Inst — Uchenye Zapiski Vologodskii Gosudarstvennyi Pedagogicheskii Institut

Uch Zap Vybors Gos Pedagog Inst — Uchenye Zapiski Vyborskii Gosudarstvennyi Pedagogicheskii Institut

Uch Zap Yakutsk Gos Univ — Uchenye Zapiski Yakutskogo Gosudarstvennogo Universiteta

Uch Zap Yakutsk Inst — Uchenye Zapiski Yakutskogo Instituta

Uch Zap Yarosl Gos Pedagog Inst — Uchenye Zapiski Yaroslavskii Gosudarstvennyi Pedagogicheskii Institut

Uch Zap Yarosl Tekhnol Inst — Uchenye Zapiski Yaroslavskogo Tekhnologicheskogo Instituta

UC/IG — Informaciones Geograficas. Universidad de Chile

U Cin LR — University of Cincinnati. Law Review

U Cin L Rev — University of Cincinnati. Law Review

UCL — University of Chicago. Law Review

UCLA-Alaska L Rev — UCLA [*University of California, Los Angeles*]-Alaska Law Review

UCLA Forum Med Sci — UCLA [*University of California, Los Angeles*] Forum in Medical Sciences

UCLA Hist J — UCLA [*University of California at Los Angeles*] Historical Journal

UCLA Intra L Rev — UCLA [*University of California, Los Angeles*] Intramural Law Review

UCLA J Envt'l L & Pol'y — UCLA [*University of California, Los Angeles*] Journal of Environmental Law and Policy

UCLA/JLAL — Journal of Latin American Lore. University of California. Latin American Center

UCLA Law R — UCLA [*University of California, Los Angeles*] Law Review

UCLA Law Rev — University of California at Los Angeles. Law Review

UCLA L Rev — University of California at Los Angeles. Law Review

UCLA Slav S — UCLA [*University of California at Los Angeles*] Slavic Studies

UCLA Symp Mol Cell Biol — UCLA [*University of California, Los Angeles*] Symposia on Molecular and Cellular Biology

UCLA (Univ Calif Los Ang) Symp Mol Cell Biol New Ser — UCLA (University of California at Los Angeles) Symposia on Molecular and Cellular Biology. New Series

UCLA (Univ Cal Los Angeles)-Alaska Law R — UCLA (University of California, Los Angeles)-Alaska Law Review

UCLA (Univ Cal Los Angeles) J Environmental Law and Policy — UCLA (University of California, Los Angeles) Journal of Environmental Law and Policy

UCLA (Univ Cal Los Angeles) Pacific Basin Law J — UCLA (University of California, Los Angeles) Pacific Basin Law Journal

UCLJ — Upper Canada Law Journal

UCLJ (Can) — Upper Canada Law Journal

UCLJ NS — Upper Canada Law Journal, New Series

UCLJ NS (Can) — Upper Canada Law Journal, New Series

UCLJ OS — Canada Law Journal, Old Series

UCLR — University of Ceylon. Law Review

UCLR — University of Chicago. Law Review

UCLR — University of Cincinnati. Law Review

UCLR — University of Colorado. Law Review

UCLy — Universite Catholique (Lyon)

UCMP — Union Catalog of Medical Periodicals

UCMSA — UCLA [*University of California, Los Angeles*] Forum in Medical Sciences

UCN — Unemployment Compensation News

UCNSA/SA — Suplemento Antropologico. Universidad Catolica de Nuestra Senora de la Asuncion

UCOIP — University of Chicago. Oriental Institute. Publications

U Colo LR — University of Colorado. Law Review

U Colo L Rev — University of Colorado. Law Review

U Color L Rev — University of Colorado. Law Review

U Colo Stud — University of Colorado. Studies

UCOM — Union Catalog of Medical Monographs and Multimedia

UCOP — University of Cambridge. Oriental Publications

UCP — UNESCO Courier (Paris)
UCP — University of California Publications in American Archaeology and Ethnology
UCP — University of California. Publications in Classical Philology
UCPA — University of California. Publications in Classical Archaeology
UCPCP — University of California Publications in Classical Philology
UCPCS — University of California Publications in Culture and Society
UCPES — University of California. Publications in English Studies
UCPFS — University of California. Publications in Folklore Studies
UCPG — University of California Publications in Geography
UCPh — Universitas Carolina: Philologica
UCPH — University of California Publications in History
UCPL — University of California. Publications in Linguistics
UCPM — University of California. Publications in Music
UCPMP — University of California. Publications in Modern Philology
UCPMPh — University of California. Publications in Modern Philology
UCPPh — University of California. Publications in Classical Philology
UCPS — Uomini e la Civilita. Collezione di Profili e Sintesi. Scrittori Stranieri
UCPSP — University of California. Publications in Semitic Philology
UCPSPh — University of California. Publications in Semitic Philology
UCQ — University College Quarterly
UCR — University of Ceylon. Review
UCR — University of Cincinnati. Law Review
UC Rep FM Univ Calif Berkeley Dep Mech Eng — UC. Report FM. University of California, Berkeley. Department of Mechanical Engineering
UCrow — Upstart Crow
UCR/RCS — Revista de Ciencias Sociales. Universidad de Costa Rica
UCS — Canadian Union Catalogue of Serials
UC/S — Signs. University of Chicago Press
UCSC — Universite Cattolica del Sacro Cuore
UCSGS — University of Colorado. Studies. General Series
UCSL — University of California. Studies in Linguistics
UCSLL — University of Colorado. Studies. Series in Language and Literature
UCSMP — University of California. Studies in Modern Philology
UCSSA — University of Colorado Studies. Series in Anthropology
UCSSLL — University of Colorado. Studies. Series in Language and Literature
UCTSE — University of Cape Town. Studies in English
Uc Zap Adyg Nauc-Issled Inst Jaz Lit Ist — Ucenye Zapiski Adygejoskogo Naucno-Issledovatel'skogo Instituta Jazyka, Literatury, i Istorii
Uc Zap Bask Univ Filol N — Ucenye Zapiski. Baskirskij Gosudarstvennyj Universitet. Filolog. Nauki
Uc Zap Dal'nevost Univ — Ucenye Zapiski. Dal'nevostocnyj Universitet
Uc Zap Daug Ped Inst — Ucenye Zapiski. Daugavpilskij Pedagogiceskij Institut
Uc Zap IMO — Ucenye Zapiski Institut Mezdunarodnych Otnosenij
Uc Zap Inst Sl Ved — Ucenye Zapiski Instituta Slavjanovedenija
Uc Zap Kar Ped Inst — Ucenye Zapiski Karel'skogo Pedagogiceskogo Instituta
Uc Zap Kaz Univ — Ucenye Zapiski. Kazachskij Universitet
Uc Zap Kis Gos Univ — Ucenye Zapiski. Kisinevskij Gosudarstvennyj Universitet
Uc Zap Leningr Ped Inst Im — Ucenye Zapiski. Leningradskij Pedagogiceskij Institut Imeni Gercena
Uc Zap LGPI — Ucenye Zapiski. Leningradskij Gosudarstvennyj Pedagogiceskij Institut Imeni A. I. Gercena
Uc Zap MGPI — Ucenye Zapiski Moskovskogo Gosudarstvennogo Pedagogiceskogo Instituta Imeni Lenina
Uc Zap Mosk Bibl Inst — Ucenye Zapiski. Moskovskij Bibliotecnyj Institut
Uc Zap Omsk Ped Inst — Ucenye Zapiski. Omskskij Pedagogiceskij Institut
Uc Zap Perm Gos Univ — Ucenye Zapiski Permskij Gosudarstvennyj Universitet
Uc Zap Stavr Med Inst — Ucenye Zapiski. Stavropol'skij Medicinskij Institut
Uc Zap Stavropol Gos Pedag Inst — Ucenye Zapiski. Stavropol'skij Gosudarstvennyj Pedagogiceskij Institut
Uc Zap Tomsk Ped Inst — Ucenye Zapiskij. Tomskij Pedagogiceskij Institut
Uc Zap Tuv Nauc Issle Inst Jaz Lit Ist — Ucenye Zapiski. Tuvinskij Naucno-Issledovatel'skij Institut Jazyka, Literatury, Istorii
UD — Unlisted Drugs
UDA — Universidad de Antioquia
UDA — University Debaters Annual
U Day LR — University of Dayton. Law Review
U Dayton L Rev — University of Dayton. Law Review
U Dbg — Under Dannebrog
Uddan — Uddannelse
Udenrigspolit Skr Ser 15 — Udenrigspolitiske Skrifter. Serie 15
U Det J Urb L — University of Detroit. Journal of Urban Law
U Det L J — University of Detroit. Law Journal
U Det L Rev — University of Detroit. Law Review
U Detroit LJ — University of Detroit. Law Journal
U d K — Universum der Kunst
UDKKB — Utsunomiya Daigaku Kyoikugakubu Kiyo, Dai-2-Bu
UDL — Untersuchungen zur Deutschen Literaturgeschichte
UdLH — Universidad de la Habana
UDM — Universidad de Medellin
Udm T — Udenrigsministeriets Tidsskrift
UDNGA — Utsunomiya Daigaku Nogakubu Gakujutsu Hokoku
Udobr Urozhai — Udobrenie i Urozhai
Udobr Urozhai Kom Khim Nar Khaz SSSR — Udobrenie i Urozhai. Komitet po Khimaisatsii Narodnogo Khozyaistva SSSR
Udobr Urozhai Minist Sel'sk Khoz SSSR — Udobrenie i Urozhai. Ministerstvo Sel'skogo Khozyaistva SSSR
UDQ — University of Denver. Quarterly
UDR — University of Dayton. Review
UDS — Urban Data Service
UDSKD — Udenrigspolitiske Skrifter. Serie 15
U d SSR — Union der Sozialistischen Sowjetrepubliken
UDURA — Udobrenie i Urozhai
UE — United Empire
UE — Universale Economica
UE — Use of English

UEA — United Evangelical Action
Ueber Bestehen Wirken Naturf Ges Bamberg — Ueber das Bestehen und Wirken der Naturforschenden Gesellschaft zu Bamberg
Uebergaenge Texte Stud Handlung Sprache Lebenswelt — Uebergaenge. Texte und Studien zu Handlung, Sprache, und Lebenswelt
Ueber Kst & Altert Rhein & Maingeg — Ueber Kunst und Alterthum in der Rhein- und Maingegenden
Ueber Land & Meer — Ueber Land und Meer
Ueberr Tb — Ueberreuter Taschenbuecher
Uebersee Rdsch — Uebersee Rundschau
Uebers Neuesten Pomol Lit — Uebersicht der Neuesten Pomologischen Literatur
Ue Bg u Tal — Ueber Berg und Tal
UEC — Revista. Universidad Externado de Colombia
UEE — US Commercial Newsletter
UEEBA — Bulletin. Utah Engineering Experiment Station
UEES Report — Utah. Engineering Experiment Station. Report
UEIES — Uppsala English Institute. Essays and Studies
UEJ — University of Edinburgh. Journal
U e L — Uomini e Libri
UEL — Uomini e Libri
UE Law J — University of the East. Law Journal
UELJ — UE [*University of the East*] Law Journal
UEMB — Universitets Etnografiske Museum Bulletin
U Empire — United Empire
UEPEDY — US Environmental Protection Agency. Office of Air and Waste Management. EPA-450
UES — UNISA [*University of South Africa*] English Studies
UESPDE — University of Tasmania. Environmental Studies Working Paper
UF — Ugarit-Forschungen
UF — Ulster Folklife
UFAJ — University Film Association. Journal
UFA Rev Union Fed Coop Agric Suisse — UFA Revue. Union des Federations Cooperatives Agricoles de la Suisse
UFAS — Ur- und Fruehgeschichte Archaeologie der Schweiz
UFAW Courr — UFAW [*Universities Federation for Animal Welfare*] Courrier
UFBTAD — Universidad de la Republica del Uruguay. Facultad de Agronomia. Estacion Experimental de Paysandu Dr. Mario A. Cassinoni. Boletin Tecnico
UFEBB — Bulletin. Faculty of Education. Utsunomiya University
Uffizi Stud & Ric — Uffizi. Studi e Ricerche
UFFT — Upplands Fornminnesfoerenings Tidskrift
Ufim Aviacion Inst Trudy — Ufimskii Aviacionnyi Institut Imeni Ordzonikidze Trudy
UFIZA — Ukrainskii Fizicheskii Zhurnal
UFKT — Universitetsforlagets Kronikktjeneste
U F Laeg — Ugeskrift for Laeger
U Fla LR — University of Florida. Law Review
U Fla L Rev — University of Florida. Law Review
U Florida L Rev — University of Florida. Law Review
UFMH — University of Florida. Monographs. Humanities Series
UFN — Uspechi Fiziceskich Nauk
UFNAA — Uspekhi Fizicheskikh Nauk
UFOAAL — Anales. Facultad de Odontologia. Universidad de la Republica
UFORDAT — Umweltforschungsdatenbank
UFP/EB — Estudos Brasileiros. Universidad Federal do Parana. Setor de Ciencias Humanas. Centro de Estudos Brasileiros
UFT — Finance and Trade Review
UFZ Ber — UFZ [*Umweltforschungszentrum*] Bericht
Ug — Ugaritica
UGA — Untersuchungen zur Geschichte und Altertumskunde Agyptens
UGA — Urgeschichtlicher Anzeiger
Uganda Dep Agric Annu Rep — Uganda. Department of Agriculture. Annual Report
Uganda Dep Agric Mem Res Div Ser II Veg — Uganda. Department of Agriculture. Memoirs of the Research Division. Series II.Vegetation
Uganda For Dep Tech Note — Uganda. Forest Department. Technical Note
UgandaJ — Uganda Journal
Uganda Natl Parks Dir Rep — Uganda National Parks Director's Report
UGAPB — Publication. Utah Geological Association
Ugarit F — Ugarit-Forschungen. Internationales Jahrbuch fuer die Altertumskunde Syrien-Palaestinas
Ugarit Forsch — Ugarit Forschungen
Ugeskr Agron Hortonomer — Ugeskrift foer Agronomer og Hortonomer
Ugeskr Jordbrug — Ugeskrift foer Jordbrug
Ugeskr Laeg — Ugeskrift foer Laeger
Ugeskr Laeger — Ugeskrift for Laeger
Ugeskr Landm — Ugeskrift foer Landmaend
Ugeskr Landmaend — Ugeskrift foer Landmaend
Ugeskr Lg — Ugeskrift for Laeger
Ug F — Ugarit-Forschungen
Ug Fo — Ugarit Forschungen
UGGI Chron — UGGI [*Union Geodesique et Geophysique Internationale*] Chronicle
Ug Hb — Ugaritic Handbook
UGI Bull — UGI [*Union Geographique Internationale*] Bulletin
UgJ — Uganda Journal
UGL — Uitgelezen. Documentatieoverzicht Bibliotheek en Documentatiedienst Ministerie van Sociale Zaken
UGLAA — Ugeskrift foer Laeger
Ugleobogat Oborudovanie — Ugleobogatitel'noe Oborudovanie
UGLJ — University of Ghana. Law Journal
UGM — University of Georgia. Monographs
Ug Man — Ugaritic Manual
Ugol' Ukr — Ugol' Ukrainy
UGOUA — Ugol' Ukrainy
UGTS — Ueberlieferung und Gestaltung. Theophil Spoerri zum Sechzigsten Geburtstag
UH — Ukrainian Herald

UH — Universidad de la Habana

UH — Unsere Heimat. Verein fuer Landeskunde von Niederoesterreich und Wien

U Hart St L — University of Hartford. Studies in Literature

U Hawaii L Rev — University of Hawaii. Law Review

U Haw LR — University of Hawaii. Law Review

UH/ED — Economia y Desarrollo. Universidad de La Habana

Uhli Rudy Geol Pruzkum — Uhli-Rudy-Geologicky Pruzkum

UHQ — Utah Historical Quarterly

UI — Uj Iras

UIA — Union of International Associations. Documents

UIA Int Architect — UIA International Architect

UICC Monogr Ser — UICC [*Union Internationale Contre le Cancer*] Monograph Series

UICC Tech Rep Ser — UICC [*Union Internationale Contre le Cancer*] Technical Report Series

UIEUA — Upravlenie Yadernymi Energeticheskimi Ustanovkami

UILL — University of Illinois. Studies in Language and Literature

U Ill LB — University of Illinois. Law Bulletin

U Ill L Bull — University of Illinois. Law Bulletin

U Ill L F — University of Illinois. Law Forum

U Ill L Forum — University of Illinois. Law Forum

U Ill LR — University of Illinois. Law Review

U Ill L Rev — University of Illinois. Law Review

U Iowa L Rev — University of Iowa. Law Review

UIR/Res Newsl — UIR [*University-Industry Research Program*]/Research Newsletter

UISL — University of Illinois Studies in Language and Literature

Uit — Uitleg

UIT — Unit Investment Trusts

Uitgaben Natuurwet Stud Suriname Ned Antillen — Uitgaben Natuurwetenschappelijke Studichring voor Suriname en de Nederlandse Antillen

Uitgaven Natuurw Studiekring Suriname Curacao — Uitgaven. Natuurwetenschappelijke Studiekring voor Suriname en Curacao

Uitg Natuurwet Studiekring Suriname Ned Antillen — Uitgaven Natuurwetenschappelijke Studiekring voor Suriname en de Nederlandse Antillen

Uitg Natuurwet Werkgroep Ned Antillen (Curacao) — Uitgaven. Natuurwetenschappelijke Werkgroep Nederlandse Antillen (Curacao)

UIT Rep — UIT [*Ulsan Institute of Technology*] Report

Uitvoerige Versl Sticht Bosbouwproefstn De Dorschkamp — Uitvoerige Verslagen van de Stichting Bosbouwproefstation "De Dorschkamp"

Uitvoer Versl Bosbouwproefsta — Uitvoerige Verslagen van de Stichting Bosbouwproefstation "De Dorschkamp"

UJ — Uganda Journal

UJ — Ungarische Jahrbuecher

UJ — Uniwersytet Jagiellonski

UJA — Ulster Journal of Archaeology

U Jb — Ungarische Jahrbuecher

U Jb — Ural-Altaische Jahrbuecher

UJCD Union Jeunes Chir Dent — UJCD. Union des Jeunes Chirurgiens-Dentistes

UJCT Rep — UJCT [*Ulsan Junior College of Technology*] Report

UJDS — Universitetsjubilaeets Danske Samfund

UJE — Universal Jewish Encyclopedia

UJISLAA — UNESCO [*United Nations Educational, Scientific, and Cultural Organization*] Journal of Information Science, Librarianship, and Archives Administration

UJ (SC) — Unreported Judgments (Supreme Court)

UJSC/EA — ECA [*Estudios Centroamericanos*]. Universidade Centroamericana Jose SimeonCanas

UJSC/ECA — Estudios Centroamericanos. Universidade Centroamericana Jose Simeon Canas

UK — Unknown

UK — Unknown Worlds

UK — Unsere Kunstdenkmaeler

U Kan City L Rev — University of Kansas City. Law Review

U Kan LR — University of Kansas. Law Review

U Kan L Rev — University of Kansas. Law Review

U Kans Publ — University of Kansas. Publications. Library Series

UK At Energy Auth At Weapons Res Establ Lib Bibliogr — United Kingdom. Atomic Energy Authority. Atomic Weapons Research Establishment.Library Bibliography

UK At Energy Auth At Weapons Res Establ Rep Ser NR — United Kingdom. Atomic Energy Authority. Atomic Weapons Research Establishment.Report. Series NR

UK At Energy Auth At Weapons Res Establ Rep Ser O — United Kingdom. Atomic Energy Authority. Atomic Weapons Research Establishment.Report. Series O

UK At Energy Auth At Weapons Res Establ Rep Ser R — United Kingdom. Atomic Energy Authority. Atomic Weapons Research Establishment.Report. Series R

UK At Energy Auth Auth Health Saf Branch Mem — United Kingdom. Atomic Energy Authority. Authority Health and Safety Branch. Memorandum

UK At Energy Auth Auth Health Saf Branch Rep — United Kingdom. Atomic Energy Authority. Authority Health and Safety Branch. Report

UK At Energy Auth Culham Lab Rep CLM R — United Kingdom Atomic Energy Authority. Culham Laboratory. Report CLM-R

UK At Energy Auth Dev Eng Group DEG Rep — United Kingdom. Atomic Energy Authority. Development and Engineering Group. DEGReport

UK At Energy Auth Harwell Lab Mem — United Kingdom Atomic Energy Authority. Harwell Laboratory. Memorandum

UK At Energy Auth Harwell Lab Rep — United Kingdom Atomic Energy Authority. Harwell Laboratory. Report

UK At Energy Auth Health Saf Code Auth Code — United Kingdom. Atomic Energy Authority. Health and Safety Code. Authority Code

UK At Energy Auth Ind Group IG Rep — United Kingdom. Atomic Energy Authority. Industrial Group. IG Report

UK At Energy Auth Prod Group PG Rep — United Kingdom. Atomic Energy Authority. Production Group. PG Report

UK At Energy Auth Radiochem Cent Mem — United Kingdom. Atomic Energy Authority. Radiochemical Centre. Memorandum

UK At Energy Auth Radiochem Cent Rep — United Kingdom. Atomic Energy Authority. Radiochemical Centre. Report

UK At Energy Auth React Group Rep — United Kingdom. Atomic Energy Authority. Reactor Group. Report

UK At Energy Auth React Group TRG Rep — United Kingdom. Atomic Energy Authority. Reactor Group. TRG Report

UK At Energy Auth Res Group Culham Lab Rep — United Kingdom. Atomic Energy Authority. Research Group. Culham Laboratory. Report

UK At Energy Auth Res Group Culham Lab Transl — United Kingdom. Atomic Energy Authority. Research Group. Culham Laboratory. Translation

UK At Energy Auth Saf Reliab Dir SRD Rep — United Kingdom. Atomic Energy Authority. Safety and Reliability Directorate. SRD Report

UK At Energy Res Establ Anal Method — United Kingdom. Atomic Energy Research Establishment. Analytical Method

UK At Energy Res Establ Bibliogr — United Kingdom. Atomic Energy Research Establishment. Bibliography

UK At Energy Res Establ Health Phys Med Div Res Prog Rep — United Kingdom. Atomic Energy Research Establishment. Health Physics and Medical Division. Research Progress Report

UK At Energy Res Establ Lect — United Kingdom. Atomic Energy Research Establishment. Lectures

UK At Energy Res Establ Memo — United Kingdom. Atomic Energy Research Establishment. Memorandum

UK At Energy Res Establ Rep — United Kingdom. Atomic Energy Research Establishment. Report

UK At Energy Res Establ Transl — United Kingdom. Atomic Energy Research Establishment. Translation

UKC — University of Kansas City. Review

UK CEED Bull — UK CEED [*Centre for Economic and Environmental Development*] Bulletin

UKCR — University of Kansas City. Review

UKCRv — University of Kansas City. Review

UkI — Ukrains'kyi Istorychnyi Zhurnal

UKIC Occas Pap — United Kingdom Institute for Conservation. Occasional Papers

UK Jt Fire Res Organ Fire Res Tech Pap — United Kingdom. Joint Fire Research Organization. Fire Research Technical Paper

UKLA — Ukalaha

UKLR — University of Kansas. Law Review

UK Miner Stat — United Kingdom Mineral Statistics

UKMJB — Ukrainian Mathematical Journal

UKPG — United Kingdom Press Gazette

UKPHS — University of Kansas. Publications. Humanistic Studies

UKPJA — Ukrainian Physics Journal

Uk Q — Ukranian Quarterly

Ukraine Vergangenh Gegenw — Ukraine in Vergangenheit und Gegenwart

Ukrain Fiz Z — Ukrainskii Fizicheskii Zhurnal

Ukrain Fiz Zh — Akademiya Nauk Ukrainskoi SSR. Otdelenie Fiziki. Ukrainskii Fizicheskii Zhurnal

Ukrain Geometr Sb — Ukrainskii Geometriceskii Sbornik

Ukrain Geom Sb — Ukrainskii Geometriceskii Sbornik

Ukrainian Math J — Ukrainian Mathematical Journal

Ukrainian Q — Ukrainian Quarterly

Ukrain Lit — Ukrains'ka Literatura

Ukrain Mat Z — Ukrainskii Matematicheskii Zhurnal

Ukrain Mat Zh — Akademiya Nauk Ukrainskoi SSR. Institut Matematiki. Ukrainskii Matematicheskii Zhurnal

Ukrain Phys J — Ukrainian Physics Journal

Ukrain Quart — Ukrainian Quarterly

Ukrain Rev — Ukrainian Review

Ukrain Rev London — Ukranian Review (London)

Ukrajinsk Bot Zurn — Ukrajins'kyj Botanicnyj Zurnal/The Ukranian Botanical Review

Ukr Biochim Z — Ukrains'kyj Biochimicnyj Zurnal

Ukr Biokhim — Ukrainskii Biokhimicheski Zhurnal

Ukr Biokhim Zh — Ukrainskij Biokhimicheskij Zhurnal

Ukr Biokhim Zh (1946-1977) — Ukrains'kii Biokhimichnii Zhurnal (1946-1977)

Ukr Bot Z — Ukrains'kyj Botanicnyj Zurnal

Ukr Bot Zh — Ukrayins'kyi Botanichnyi Zhurnal

Ukr Chim Z — Ukrainskij Chimiceskij Zurnal

UK Report — Economic Progress Report (United Kingdom)

Ukr Fiz Z — Ukrains'kyj Fizycnyj Zurnal

Ukr Fiz Zh — Ukrainskii Fizichnii Zhurnal

Ukr Fiz Zh (Kiev) — Ukrayinskoyi Fizicnij Zhurnal (Ukrainian Edition) (Kiev)

Ukr Fiz Zh Russ Ed — Ukrainskii Fizicheskii Zhurnal (Russian Edition)

Ukr Fiz Zh Ukr Ed — Ukrainskii Fizicheskii Zhurnal (Ukrainian Edition)

Ukr Geom Sb — Ukrainskij Geometricheskij Sbornik

Ukrl — Ukrajins'kyj Istoryk

Ukr Ist Zhurnal — Ukrainskyi Istorichnyi Zhurnal

Ukr Ist Zur — Ukrains'kyi Istorychnyi Zhurnal

Ukr J Biochem — Ukrainian Journal of Biochemistry

Ukr J Chem — Ukrainian Journal of Chemistry

UkrK — Ukrajins'ka Knyha

Ukr Khim Zh — Ukrainskii Khimicheskii Zhurnal

UkrM — Ukrajins'ka Mova i Literatura v Skoli

Ukr Math J — Ukrainian Mathematical Journal

Ukr Mat Zh — Ukrainskii Matematicheskii Zhurnal

Ukr Mov — Ukrajins'ke Movnoznavstvo

Ukr Nauchno Issled Inst Eksp Vet Nauchn Tr — Ukrainskii Nauchno-Issledovatel'skii Institut Eksperimental'noi Veterinarii Nauchnye Trudy

Ukr Nauchno Issled Inst Fiziol Rast Nauchn Tr — Ukrainskii Nauchno-Issledovatel'skii Institut Fiziologii Rastenii Nauchnye Trudy

Ukr Nauchno Issled Inst Pishch Promsti Sb Tr — Ukrainskii Nauchno-Issledovatel'skii Institut Pishchevoi Promyshlennosti Sbornik Trudov
Ukr Phys J — Ukrainian Physics Journal
Ukr Poligr Inst Nauchn Zap — Ukrainskii Poligraficheskii Institut Nauchnye Zapiski
Ukr Polim Zh — Ukrains'kii Polimernii Zhurnal
Ukr Polym J — Ukrainian Polymer Journal
Ukr Q — Ukrainian Quarterly
Ukr Quart — Ukrainian Quarterly
UkrR — Ukrainian Review
Ukr Reg Nauchno Issled Inst Tr — Ukrainskii Regional'nyi Nauchno-Issledovatel'skii Institut. Trudy
UkrS — Ukrajins'kyj Samostijnyk
UKSTU Newsl — UKSTU [*United Kingdom Schmidt Telescope Unit*] Newsletter
UKTM — UK Trade Marks
UK Trends — Economic Trends (United Kingdom)
UKVA — Uitgaven der Koninklijke Vlaamse Academie voor Taal- en Letterkunde
UKZHA — Ukrainskii Khimicheskii Zhurnal
UI — Ulisse
ULA — UCLA [*University of California, Los Angeles*] Law Review
Ulam Quart — Ulam Quarterly
ULA/RG — Revista Geografica. Universidad de Los Andes
U LB — Universitaets- und Landesbibliothek
Ulbandus Rev — Ulbandus Review
UlbR — Ulbandus Review
ULB-VUB Inter Univ High Energ Rep — ULB-VUB [*Universite Libre de Bruxelles - Vrije Universiteit Brussel*] Inter-University Institute for High Energies. Report
ULCBAJ — Uchenye Zapiski Leningradskogo Ordena Lenina Gosudarstvennogo Universiteta Imeni A. A. Zhdanova. Seriya Biologicheskikh Nauk
ULCJ — University Law College. Journal. Rajputana University
U Leeds Rev — University of Leeds Review
ULGLAM — Eugenics Laboratory. Memoirs
ULH — Ukrains'ka Literaturna Hazeta
ULH — Universidad de la Habana
ULI — [*The*] Urban Land Institute
U Libre — Universite Libre
ULIDAT — Umweltliteraturdatenbank
ULIG/C — Cahiers de Geographie de Quebec. Universite Laval. Institut de Geographie
ULI Lm Rep — Urban Land Institute. Landmark Report
ULI Res Rep — Urban Land Institute. Research Report
ULI Spe Rep — Urban Land Institute. Special Report
Ul'janovsk Gos Ped Inst Ucen Zap — Ul'janovskii Gosudarstvennyi Pedagogiceskii Institut Imeni I. N. Ul'janova. Ucennyi Zapiski
Ullmanns Enc Tech Chem — Ullmanns Encyklopaedie der Technischen Chemie
ULLOS — University of London. London Oriental Series
Ullst DG — Ullstein Deutsche Geschichte
Ullst Kr — Ullstein-Buecher. Kriminalromane
Ullst Kunst — Ullstein-Kunstgeschichte
U Lm — Ugeskrift for Landmaend
ULM — Union List of Manuscripts
U Lond I Cl — University of London. Institute of Classical Studies. Bulletin
ULPOD — Urban Law and Policy
ULQ — Utah Foreign Language Quarterly
ULR — Uniform Law Review
ULR — Union Labor Report
ULR — Union Law Review
ULR — University Law Review
ULR — University of Leeds. Review
ULR — Utah Law Review
ULRED — UCLA [*University of California, Los Angeles*] Law Review
Ulrich's Q — Ulrich's Quarterly
Ulrich's Qtly — Ulrich's Quarterly
ULS — Ulysses, KS
ULS — Union List of Serials
UL Sci Mag — UL [*University of Liberia*] Science Magazine
ULSPD — Ultrasonics Symposium. Proceedings
ULSSCL — Union List of Scientific Serials in Canadian Libraries
ULSSSHCL — Union List of Serials in the Social Sciences and Humanities Held by Canadian Libraries
Ulster Arch Her Soc — Ulster Architectural Heritage Society
Ulster Folk — Ulster Folklife
Ulster J Arch — Ulster Journal of Archaeology
Ulster J Archaeol — Ulster Journal of Archaeology
Ulster J Archaeol 3 Ser — Ulster Journal of Archaeology. Series 3
Ulster Journal Arch — Ulster Journal of Archaeology
Ulster Med J — Ulster Medical Journal
Ult — Ultima
Ultim Real Mean — Ultimate Reality and Meaning
ULTRA — Ultrasonics
Ultra Low Doses Int Congr — Ultra Low Doses. International Congress on Ultra Low Doses
Ultramicrosc — Ultramicroscopy
Ultraschall Med — Ultraschall in der Medizin
Ultra Sci Phys Sci — Ultra Scientist of Physical Sciences
Ultrasc Med — Ultraschall in der Medizin
Ultrason — Ultrasonics
Ultrason Imaging — Ultrasonic Imaging
Ultrason Int — Ultrasonics International. Conference Proceedings
Ultrason Sonochem — Ultrasonics Sonochemistry
Ultrason Symp Proc — Ultrasonics Symposium. Proceedings
Ultrasound Annu — Ultrasound Annual
Ultrasound Med & Biol — Ultrasound in Medicine and Biology
Ultrasound Med Biol — Ultrasound in Medicine and Biology
Ultrasound Obstet Gynecol — Ultrasound in Obstetrics and Gynecology
Ultrasound Teach Cases — Ultrasound Teaching Cases

Ultrastruct Pathol — Ultrastructural Pathology
Ultrastrukt Plast Neironov — Ul'trastruktura i Plastichnost Neironov
ULTRD — Ultramicroscopy
Ult Real — Ultimate Reality and Meaning
Ul'yanovsk Skh Opytn Stn Tr — Ul'yanovskaya Sel'skokhozyaistvennaya Opytnaya Stantsiya Trudy
ULz — Ukrajins'ke Literaturoznavstvo
UM — Ugaritic Manual
Um — Umschau
UM — Universidad de Mexico
UM — University Microfilms
U Maine L Rev — University of Maine. Law Review
UMANA — Uspekhi Matematicheskikh Nauk
Um & Court & Fashlonable Gaz — Universal Magazine and Court and Fashionable Gazette
Um & Rev — Universal Magazine and Review
UMB — University Museum Bulletin. University of Pennsylvania
UMB — University of Pennsylvania. Museum Bulletin
UMBC Econ R — UMBC Economic Review
UMBP — University Museum. Bulletin (Philadelphia)
UMBS — Publications. University Museum. Babylonian Section. University of Pennsylvania
UMBS — University of Pennsylvania. University Museum. Publications of the Babylonian Section
UMC — Unified Management Corp. Database
UMC — Union Medicale du Canada
UMCAA — Union Medicale du Canada
UMCJA — University of Michigan. Medical Center. Journal
UMCMP — University of Michigan. Contributions in Modern Philology
UMCS — Uniwersytet Marii Curie-Sklodowskiej
UMEA Psychol Rep — UMEA Psychological Reports
UMEA Psychol Reports — UMEA Psychological Reports
Umeleckohist Sborn — Umeleckohistoricky Sbornik
Umform Tech — Umform Technik
UMHS — University of Miami. Hispanic Studies
U Miami LR — University of Miami. Law Review
U Miami L Rev — University of Miami. Law Review
U Mich Bus R — University of Michigan. Business Review
U Mich J Law Reform — University of Michigan. Journal of Law Reform
U Mich J L Ref — University of Michigan. Journal of Law Reform
U MI Columbia Mus Anthropol Annu Rep — University of Missouri-Columbia. Museum of Anthropology. Annual Report
U MI J Law Reform — University of Michigan Journal of Law Reform
U MI Mus A Bull — University of Michigan Museum of Art Bulletin
U MI Pubns Human Pap — University of Michigan Publications. Humanistic Papers
U MI Q Rev — University of Michigan Quarterly Review
U Missouri at KCL Rev — University of Missouri at Kansas City. Law Review
UMJ — Ukrainian Mathematical Journal
Umjet Rij — Umjetnost Rijeci
UMJOA — Ulster Medical Journal
UMKCLR — University of Missouri at Kansas City. Law Review
UMKC L Rev — University of Missouri at Kansas City. Law Review
UM Knowledge & Pleasure — Universal Magazine of Knowledge and Pleasure
UMLER — Universal Machine Language Equipment Register
UMLR — University of Malaya. Law Review
UMLR — University of Miami. Law Review
UMLRB — University of Miami. Law Review
UMLS — Ukrajins'ka Mova i Literatura v Skoli
UMMJ — University of Manitoba. Medical Journal
UMMPA3 — Contributions. Museum of Paleontology. University of Michigan
UMMR — Minnesota Review
UMN — Uspechi Matematiceskich Nauk
U MO B Law Ser — University of Missouri. Bulletin. Law Series
U MO Bull L Ser — University of Missouri. Bulletin. Law Series
U MO-Kansas City L Rev — University of Missouri at Kansas City. Law Review
U MO KCL Rev — University of Missouri at Kansas City. Law Review
U MO L Bull — University of Missouri. Law Bulletin
UMoS — University of Missouri. Studies
UMPAL — University of Minnesota. Pamphlets on American Literature
UMPAW — University of Minnesota. Pamphlets on American Writers
UMPEAL — University of Miami. Publications in English and American Literature
UMPLL — University of Michigan. Publications in Language and Literature
UM Pub — University Microfilms Publications
UMRI Ne — UMRI [*University of Michigan Research Institute*] News
UMR-MEC Conf Energy Resour Proc — UMR-MEC [*University of Missouri, Rolla - Missouri Energy Council*] Conference on Energy Resources. Proceedings
UMS — Ukrajins'ka Mova v Skoli
UMS — University of Maine. Studies
UMS — University of Michigan. Studies
UMS — University of Missouri. Studies
Umsch — Umschau
Umschau — Umschau in Wissenschaft und Technik
Umsch Fortschr Wiss Tech — Umschau ueber die Fortschritte in Wissenschaft und Technik
Umsch Wiss Tech — Umschau in Wissenschaft und Technik
Umsch Wiss und Tech — Umschau in Wissenschaft und Technik
UMSE — University of Mississippi. Studies in English
UMSHS — University of Michigan. Studies. Humanistic Series
UMSOA — Umi To Sora
Ums St G — Umsatzsteuergesetz
Umst G — Umstellungsgesetz
UMT — United Methodist Today
UMTRIS — Urban Mass Transportation Research Information Service
UMTRI (Univ Mich Transportation Research Inst) — UMTRI (University Michigan Transportation Research Institute) Research Review

UMVBA6 — Contributions. Laboratory of Vertebrate Biology. University of Michigan
UMW — Umwelt
Umwelt Inf Bundesminist Innern — Umwelt. Informationen des Bundesministers des Innern zur Umweltplanung und zum Umweltschutz
Umweltmed Forsch Prax — Umweltmedizin in Forschung und Praxis
Umweltpolit Umweltplanung — Umweltpolitik und Umweltplanung
Umwelt-Rep — Umwelt-Report
Umweltschutz Gesundheitstech — Umweltschutz. Gesundheitstechnik
Umweltschutz - Staedtereinig — Umweltschutz - Staedtereinigung
Umwelt Technol Aktuell — Umwelt-Technologie Aktuell
Umwelt Z Biol Stn Wilhelminenberg — Umwelt Zeitschrift der Biologischen Station Wilhelminenberg
UMW J — United Mine Workers. Journal
UMWLA — Umwelt Zeitschrift der Biologischen Station Wilhelminenberg
Umw Planungsrecht — Umwelt- und Planungsrecht
Umw St G — Umwandlungssteuergesetz
UMWTA — Umwelt
UMx — University of Mexico
UMZHA — Ukrainskii Matematicheskii Zhurnal
Unabashed Libn — Unabashed Librarian
UNA Commun — UNA [*Utah Nurses Association*] Communique
UNAGA — Union Agriculture
UNAH/RCE — Revista Centroamericana de Economia. Universidad Nacional Autonoma de Honduras.Programa de Postgrado Centroamericano en Economia y Planificacion
UNAM — Universidad Nacional Autonoma de Mexico
UNAM/RMS — Revista Mexicana de Sociologia. Universidad Nacional Autonoma de Mexico. Instituto de Investigaciones Sociales
UNA Nursing J — UNA Nursing Journal
UNA Nurs J — UNA [*Utah Nurses Association*] Nursing Journal
Un Apic — Union Apicole
UnAr — Universitas-Archiv
UNASA — Unasylva
Unauth Prac News — Unauthorized Practice News
UNB — United Nations Bulletin
UNB — Universidad Nacional (Bogota, Colombia)
Un Bi Soc Bull — United Bible Societies. Bulletin
UNB Law Journal — University of New Brunswick. Law Journal
UNB L J — University of New Brunswick. Law Journal
UNBLSJ — University of New Brunswick. Law School. Journal
UNBT — United Nations "Blue Top"
UN Bul — United Nations Bulletin
UN Bull — United Nations Bulletin
UN/C — Chungara. Universidad del Norte. Departamento de Antropologia
Unc — Uncanny Stories
UnC — Union College Symposium
UNC — Universidad Nacional de Colombia
UNC — Universidad Nacional de Cordoba
UN CCOP Newslett — United Nations Committee for Coordination of Joint Prospecting. Newsletter
UN Chron — United Nations Chronicle
UNCIO — Documents. United Nations Conference on International Organization
Uncle Remuss M — Uncle Remus's Magazine
UNCo — UNESCO [*United Nations Economic, Social, and Cultural Organization*] Courier
UNCOA — UNESCO [*United Nations Educational, Scientific, and Cultural Organization*] Courier
UNCR — University of North Carolina. Record. Research in Progress
UNC/REE — Revista de Economia y Estadistica. Universidad Nacional de Cordoba. Facultad deCiencias Economicas
UNCSCL — University of North Carolina. Studies in Comparative Literature
UNCSGL — University of North Carolina. Studies in Germanic Languages and Literatures
UNCSGLL — University of North Carolina. Studies in Germanic Languages and Literatures
UNCSRL — University of North Carolina. Studies in the Romance Languages and Literatures
UNCSRLL — University of North Carolina. Studies in the Romance Languages and Literatures
Und Child — Understanding the Child
UNDED — Undercurrents
Undercur — Undercurrents
Undergrad For — Undergraduate Forum
Underground Eng — Underground Engineering
Underground Min Symp — Underground Mining Symposia
Underground Water Conf Aust Newsl — Underground Water Conference of Australia. Newsletter
Undergr Wat Supply Pap (Tasm) — Underground Water Supply Papers (Tasmania)
Under Lttr — Underwater Letter
Undersea Biomed Res — Undersea Biomedical Research
Undersea Technol — Undersea Technology
Under Sign — Under the Sign of Pisces/Anais Nin and Her Circle
Understanding Chem React — Understanding Chemical Reactivity
Underst Chem React — Understanding Chemical Reactivity
Underwater Inf Bull — Underwater Information Bulletin
Underwater J — Underwater Journal
Underwater J & Inf Bull — Underwater Journal and Information Bulletin
Underwater J Inf Bull — Underwater Journal and Information Bulletin
Underwater Nat — Underwater Naturalist
Underwater Sci Technol J — Underwater Science and Technology Journal
Underwater Technol — Underwater Technology
Underwater Technol Symp — Underwater Technology Symposium
Underw J Inf Bull — Underwater Journal and Information Bulletin
Underw Nat — Underwater Naturalist

Underwriters Lab Stand — Underwriters Laboratories. Standards
Underwrit Lab Bull Res — Underwriters Laboratories. Bulletin of Research
UN Doc — United Nations Documents
UN Doc E — United Nations Documents. Economic and Social Council
Und-Oder-Nor & Steuerungstech — Und-Oder-Nor und Steuerungstechnik
Und-Oder-Nor Steuerungstech — Und-Oder-Nor und Steuerungstechnik
UNDP/FAO Pakistan Nat For Res Train Proj Rep — UNDP [*United Nations Development Programme*]/FAO Pakistan National Forestry Research and Training Project Report
UNE — Umweltschutzdienst. Informationsdienst fuer Umweltfragen
UNEA — Unearth
UN Econ Comm Asia Far East Water Resour Ser — United Nations Economic Commission for Asia and the Far East. Water Resources Series
UN Econ Comm Eur Comm Agr Prob Work Party Mech Agr AGRI/WP — United Nations Economic Commission for Europe. Committee on Agricultural Problems. Working Party on Mechanization of Agriculture AGRI/WP
UN Econo Comm Asia Far East Miner Resour Develop Ser — United Nations Economic Commission for Asia and the Far East. Mineral Resources Development Series
UN (Educ Sci Cult Organ) Cour — UNESCO (United Nations Educational, Scientific, and Cultural Organization) Courier
Unemployment Ins Statis — Unemployment Insurance Statistics
Unempl Unit Bull Briefing — Unemployment Unit Bulletin and Briefing
UNEP — United Nations Energy Planning
UNESCO B Li — UNESCO [*United Nations Educational, Scientific, and Cultural Organization*] Bulletin for Libraries
UNESCO Bull For Libraries — UNESCO Bulletin for Libraries
UNESCO Bul Lib — UNESCO [*United Nations Educational, Scientific, and Cultural Organization*] Bulletin for Libraries
UNESCO Bull Lib — UNESCO [*United Nations Educational, Scientific, and Cultural Organization*] Bulletin for Libraries
UNESCO Bull Libr — UNESCO [*United Nations Educational, Scientific, and Cultural Organization*] Bulletin for Libraries
UNESCO Cour — UNESCO [*United Nations Educational, Scientific, and Cultural Organization*] Courier
UNESCO Inf Bul — UNESCO Information Bulletin
UNESCO Inf Bul Read Mat — UNESCO Information Bulletin for Reading Materials
UNESCO Inf Circ — Australian National Advisory Committee for UNESCO [*United Nations Educational, Scientific, and Cultural Organization*]. Information Circular
UNESCO/IRE — International Review of Education. United Nations Educational, Scientific, and Cultural Organization. Institute for Education
UNESCO J Infor Sci Lib Arch Admin — UNESCO Journal of Information Science, Librarianship, and Archives Administration
UNESCO J Inf Sci Librarianship and Arch Adm — UNESCO [*United Nations Educational, Scientific, and Cultural Organization*] Journal of Information Science, Librarianship, and Archives Administration
UNESCO J Inf Sci Librsp & Archvs Admin — UNESCO Journal of Information Science, Librarianship, and Archives Administration
UNESCO M — UNESCO Monthly
UNESCO Nat Resour Res — United Nations Educational, Scientific, and Cultural Organization. Natural Resources Research
UNESCO Phil — UNESCO Philippines
UNESCO Reg Cen Bk Dev in Asia — UNESCO Regional Centre for Book Development in Asia
UNESCO Reg Off Ed Asia — UNESCO [*United Nations Education, Scientific, and Cultural Organization*] Regional Office of Education in Asia
UNESCO Tech Pap Mar Sci — UNESCO [*United Nations Educational, Scientific, and Cultural Organization*] Technical Papers in Marine Science
U Newark L Rev — University of Newark. Law Review
U New Brunswick LJ — University of New Brunswick. Law Journal
U New South Wales LJ — University of New South Wales. Law Journal
U New S Wales LJ — University of New South Wales. Law Journal
Unfallchir — Unfallchirurg
UNFAO (Organ) World Soil Resour Rep — United Nations. FAO (Food and Agriculture Organization) World Soil Resources Reports
UNFGA — Unternehmensforschung
UNFKA — Uspekhi Nauchnoi Fotografii
Ung — Ungdomsarbejderen
Ungar Fil L — Ungar Film Library
Ungarische Rundschau — Ungarische Rundschau fuer Historische und Sociale Wissenschaften
Ungarn Jb — Ungarn-Jahrbuch
Ungerer's Bull — Ungerer's Bulletin
Ung Forstwiss Rundsch — Ungarische Forstwissenschaftliche Rundschau
Ung Jb — Ungarische Jahrbuecher
Ung Jhb — Ungarische Jahrbuecher
Ung NW Vr Jb — Abhandlungen aus dem dritten Bande der Jahrbuecher des Ungarischen Naturwissenschaftlichen Vereins zu Pest
Ung Rev — Ungarische Revue
Ung Z Berg Huettenwes Bergbau — Ungarische Zeitschrift fuer Berg und Huettenwesen. Bergbau
UnH — Universidad de la Habana
UnHJ — University of Birmingham Historical Journal
UNHJ — University of Newcastle. Historical Journal
Uni — Universe Science Fiction
UNICIV Rep — UNICIV [*School of Civil Engineering, University of New South Wales*] Report
Unicorn J — Unicorn Journal
UNIDA — Unidia
Unidroit Yb — International Institute for the Unification of Private Law. Yearbook
Unif C Code — Uniform Commercial Code Law Journal
Unif L Conf — Uniform Law Conference
Uniform City Ct Act — New York Uniform City Court Act
Uniform Dist Ct Act — New York Uniform District Court Act
Uniform Just Ct Act — New York Uniform Justice Court Act

UNIHI SEAGRANT MB Univ Hawaii Sea Grant Coll Program — UNIHI-SEAGRANT-MB. University of Hawaii. Sea Grant College Program

Uni Ljubljai Teh Fak Acta Tech Ser Chim — Univerza v Ljubljani. Tehniska Fakulteta. Acta Technica. Series Chimica

UN Int Mtg Oilfield Dev Techniques — United Nations International Meeting on Oilfield Development Techniques

Uni of Q LR — University of Queensland. Law Review

Uni of Tas LR — University of Tasmania. Law Review

Union Agric — Union Agriculture

Union Burma J Life Sci — Union of Burma. Journal of Life Sciences

Union Burma J Sci and Technol — Union of Burma. Journal of Science and Technology

Union Burma J Sci Technol — Union of Burma. Journal of Science and Technology

Union Carbide Met Rev — Union Carbide Metals Review

Union Int Sci Biol Ser A Gen — Union Internationale des Sciences Biologiques. Serie A. Generale

Union Int Sci Biol Ser B Colloq — Union Internationale des Sciences Biologiques. Serie B. Colloques

Union Int Sci Biol Ser C Publ Diverses — Union Internationale des Sciences Biologiques. Serie C. Publications Diverses

Union Lab Rep BNA — Union Labor Report. Bureau of National Affairs

Union Med Can — Union Medicale du Canada

Union Med Mexico — Union Medica de Mexico

Union Med (Paris) — Union Medicale (Paris)

Union Med Santiago — Union Medica. Sociedad del Mismo Nombre (Santiago)

Union Nova Scotia Munic — Union of Nova Scotia Municipalities. Proceedings

Union Oceanogr Fr — Union des Oceanographes de France

Union Pac LDB — Union Pacific Law Department. Bulletin

Union Pharm — Union Pharmaceutique

Union Rec — Union Recorder

Union S Afr Dep Commer Ind Div Fish Invest Rep — Union of South Africa. Department of Commerce and Industries. Division of Fisheries. Investigational Report

Union Soc Fr Hist Nat Bull Trimest — Union des Societes Francaises d'Histoire Naturelle. Bulletin Trimestriel

Union S Q R — Union Seminary. Quarterly Review

Union Tank Car Co Graver Water Cond Div Tech Repr — Union Tank Car Company. Graver Water Conditioning Division. Technical Reprint

Union Univ Q — Union University. Quarterly

UNISA Engl Stud — UNISA [*University of South Africa*] English Studies

UNISA Psychol — UNISA [*University of South Africa*] Psychologia

UNISURV G Rep — UNISURV G Report. School of Surveying. University of New South Wales

UNISURV Rep — UNISURV Report. School of Surveying. University of New South Wales

Unit Aborig Messenger — United Aborigines' Messenger

Unita R — Unitarian Review

UNITAR Prepr or Proc — UNITAR [*United Nations Institute for Training and Research*] Preprints or Proceedings

Unitar Univ Wld — Unitarian Universalist World

Uni-Taschenb — Uni-Taschenbuecher

Unit Asia — United Asia

Unitas Int — Unitas. Revue Internationale

Uni-TB — Uni-Taschenbuecher

United Dent Hosp Syd Inst Dent Res Annu Rep — United Dental Hospital of Sydney. Institute of Dental Research. Annual Report

United Dent Hosp Sydney Inst Dent Res Annu Rep — United Dental Hospital of Sydney. Institute of Dental Research. Annual Report

United Emp — United Empire

United Fresh Fruit Veg Assoc Yearb — United Fresh Fruit and Vegetable Association. Yearbook

United Methodist Period Index — United Methodist Periodical Index

United Plant Assoc South India Sci Dep Bull — United Planters' Association of Southern India. Scientific Department. Bulletin

United Service Q — United Service Quarterly

United Serv Rev — United Services Review

Unit Empire — United Empire. The Royal Colonial Institute. Journal

Unit Stat Cath Hist Soc — United States Catholic Historical Society

Unit Univ Chr — Unitarian Universalist Christian

Univ — Universitas

Univ — Universo

UNIVA — Universitas

Univ Abidjan Dep Geol Ser Doc — Universite d'Abidjan. Departement de Geologie. Serie Documentation

Univ Adelaide Cent Precambrian Res Spec Pap — University of Adelaide. Centre for Precambrian Research. Special Paper

Univ Aff/Aff Univ — University Affairs/Affaires Universitaires

Univ Agric Sci (Bangalore) Curr Res — University of Agricultural Sciences (Bangalore). Current Research

Univ Agric Sci (Bangalore) Misc Ser — University of Agricultural Sciences (Bangalore). Miscellaneous Series

Univ Agric Sci (Bangalore) Res Ser — University of Agricultural Sciences (Bangalore). Research Series

Univ Agric Sci (Hebbal Bangalore) Annu Rep — University of Agricultural Sciences (Hebbal, Bangalore). Annual Report

Univ Agric Sci (Hebbal Bangalore) Ext Ser — University of Agricultural Sciences (Hebbal, Bangalore). Extension Series

Univ Agric Sci (Hebbal Bangalore) Stn Ser — University of Agricultural Sciences (Hebbal, Bangalore). Station Series

Univ Agric Sci (Hebbal Bangalore) Tech Ser — University of Agricultural Sciences (Hebbal, Bangalore). Technical Series

Univ Alaska Agric Exp Stn Bull — University of Alaska. Agricultural Experiment Station. Bulletin

Univ Alaska Inst Mar Sci Rep — University of Alaska. Institute of Marine Science. Report

Univ Alaska IWR (Inst Water Resour) Ser — University of Alaska. IWR (Institute of Water Resources) Series

Univ Alaska Mag — University of Alaska Magazine

Univ Alberta Agric Bull — University of Alberta. Agriculture Bulletin

Univ Alberta Agric For Bull — University of Alberta. Agriculture and Forestry Bulletin

Univ Alberta Dep Civ Eng Struct Eng Rep — University of Alberta. Department of Civil Engineering. Structural Engineering Report

Univ Alberta Fac Agric Bull — University of Alberta. Faculty of Agriculture. Bulletins

Univ Alexandria Fac Eng Bull Chem Eng — University of Alexandria. Faculty of Engineering. Bulletin. Chemical Engineering

Univ Alger Trav Inst Rech Sahariennes — Universite d'Alger. Travaux. Institut de Recherches Sahariennes

Univ Allahabad Stud — University of Allahabad. Studies

Univ Allahabad Stud Biol Sect — University of Allahabad. Studies. Biology Section

Univ Allahabad Stud Bot Sect — University of Allahabad. Studies. Botany Section

Univ Allahabad Stud Chem Sect — University of Allahabad. Studies. Chemistry Section

Univ Allahabad Stud Math Sect — University of Allahabad. Studies. Mathematics Section

Univ Allahabad Stud New Ser — University of Allahabad. Studies. New Series

Univ Allahabad Stud Phys Sect — University of Allahabad. Studies. Physics Sootion

Univ Allahabad Stud Zool Sect — University of Allahabad. Studies. Zoology Section

Univ Ankara Fac Agri Publ — Universite d'Ankara. Faculte de l'Agriculture. Publications

Univ Ankara Fac Sci Commun Ser A — Universite d'Ankara. Faculte des Sciences. Communications. Serie A. Mathematiques, Physique, et Astronomie

Univ Ankara Fac Sci Commun Ser A2 — Universite d'Ankara. Faculte des Sciences. Communications. Serie A2. Physique

Univ Ankara Fac Sci Commun Ser B Chem Chem Eng — Universite d'Ankara. Faculte des Sciences. Communications. Series B. Chemistry and Chemical Engineering

Univ Ankara Fac Sci Commun Ser C — Universite d'Ankara. Faculte des Sciences. Communications. Serie C. Sciences Naturelles

Univ Ankara Yearb Fac Agric — University of Ankara. Yearbook. Faculty of Agriculture

Univ Antioq Medellin — Universidad de Antioquia (Medellin, Colombia)

Univ Antioquia — Universidad de Antioquia

Univ Antioquia Cuad — Universidad de Antioquia Cuadernos

Univ Ariz Coop Ext Serv Bull — University of Arizona. Cooperative Extension Service. Bulletin

Univ Ariz Coop Ext Serv Circ — University of Arizona. Cooperative Extension Service. Circular

Univ Ariz Coop Ext Serv Ser P — University of Arizona. Cooperative Extension Service. Series P

Univ Arizona Agric Exp Sta Bull — University of Arizona. Arizona Agricultural Experiment Station. Bulletin

Univ Arkansas Coll Agric Arkansas Agric Exp Sta Bull — University of Arkansas. College of Agriculture. Arkansas Agricultural Experiment Station. Bulletin

Univ Arkansas Eng Exp Stn Res Rep Ser — University of Arkansas. Engineering Experiment Station. Research Report Series

Univ Arkansas Lecture Notes in Math — University of Arkansas. Lecture Notes in Mathematics

Univ Austral Chile Fac Cienc Agrar Agro Sur — Universidad Austral de Chile. Facultad de Ciencias Agrarias. Agro Sur

Univ Auton Barcelona Col Univ Gerona Secc Cienc An — Universidad Autonoma de Barcelona. Colegio Universitario de Gerona. Seccion de Ciencias. Anales

Univ Auton Potosina Inst Geol Metal Foll Tec — Universidad Autonoma Potosina. Instituto de Geologia y Metalurgia. Folleto Tecnico

Univ Baghdad Nat Hist Res Cent Annu Rep — University of Baghdad. Natural History Research Center. Annual Report

Univ Baghdad Nat Hist Res Cent Publ — University of Baghdad. Natural History Research Center. Publication

Univ Bahia Esc Geol Publ Avulsa — Universidade de Bahia. Escola de Geologia. Publicacao Avulsa

Univ BC Bot Gard Tech Bull — University of British Columbia. Botanical Garden. Technical Bulletin

Univ BC Res For Annu Rep — University of British Columbia. Research Forest. Annual Report

Univ Beograd Publ Elektrotehn Fak Ser Mat Fiz — Univerzitet u Beogradu. Publikacije Elektrotehnickog Fakulteta. Serija Matematika i Fizika

Univ Beograd Tehn Fiz — Univerzitet u Beogradu. Tehnicka Fizika

Univ Beograd Zb Radova Gradevin Fak — Univerzitet u Beogradu. Zbornik Radova Gradevinskog Fakulteta u Beogradu

Univ Bergen Arb Naturv R — Universitetet i Bergen Arbok. Naturvitenskapelig Rekke

Univ Bergen Arbok Med Rekke — Universitetet i Bergen Arbok Medisinsk Rekke

Univ Bergen Arbok Naturvitensk Rekke — Universitetet i Bergen Arbok. Naturvitenskapelig Rekke

Univ Bergen Arsmeld — Universitetet i Bergen Arsmelding

Univ Bergen Med Avh — Universitetet i Bergen Medisinske Avhandlinger

Univ Bergen Skr — Universitetet i Bergen Skrifter

Univ Besancon Ann Sci Biol Veg — Universite de Besancon. Annales Scientifiques. Biologie Vegetale

Univ Birm Hist J — University of Birmingham History Journal

Univ Bonn Phys Inst Tech Rep — Universitaet Bonn. Physikalisches Institut. Technical Report

Univ Botswana Swazil Agric Res Div Annu Rep — University of Botswana and Swaziland. Agricultural Research Division. Annual Report

Univ Botswana Swaziland Agric Res Div Annu Rep — University of Botswana, Swaziland. Agricultural Research Division. Annual Report

Univ Bras Cent Estud Zool Avulso — Universidade do Brasil. Centro de Estudos Zoologicos Avulso

Univ Brasov Lucrari Stiint — Universitatea din Brasov. Lucrari Stiintifice

Univ British Columbia Law R — University of British Columbia. Law Review

Univ Bruxelles Inst Phys Bull — Universite de Bruxelles. Institut de Physique. Bulletin

Univ Buenos Aires Fac Agrom Vet Bol — Universidad de Buenos Aires. Facultad de Agronomia y Veterinaria. Boletin

Univ Buenos Aires Inst Anat Publ — Universidad de Buenos Aires. Instituto de Anatomia. Publicacion

Univ Burundi Rev — Universite du Burundi. Revue

Univ Calicut Zool Monogr — University of Calicut. Zoological Monograph

Univ Calif Agric Exp Sta Rep — University of California Agricultural Experiment Station. Reports

Univ Calif Agric Ext Serv — University of California. Agricultural Extension Service

Univ Calif (Berkeley) Publ Agric Sci — University of California (Berkeley). Publications in Agricultural Sciences

Univ Calif (Berkeley) Publ Bot — University of California (Berkeley). Publications in Botany

Univ Calif (Berkeley) Publ Eng — University of California (Berkeley). Publications in Engineering

Univ Calif (Berkeley) Publ Entomol — University of California (Berkeley). Publications in Entomology

Univ Calif (Berkeley) Publ Health — University of California (Berkeley). Publications in Public Health

Univ Calif (Berkeley) Publ Pharmacol — University of California (Berkeley). Publications in Pharmacology

Univ Calif (Berkeley) Publ Zool — University of California (Berkeley). Publications in Zoology

Univ Calif (Berkeley) Sanit Eng Res Lab Rep — University of California (Berkeley). Sanitary Engineering Research Laboratory. Report

Univ Calif (Berkely) Publ Pathol — University of California (Berkeley). Publications in Pathology

Univ Calif Bull — University of California. Bulletin

Univ Calif Div Agric Sci Bull — University of California. Division of Agricultural Sciences. Bulletin

Univ Calif Div Agric Sci Leafl — University of California. Division of Agricultural Sciences. Leaflet

Univ Calif Lawrence Livermore Lab Rep — University of California. Lawrence Livermore Laboratory. Report

Univ Calif (Los Angeles) Symp Mol Cell Biol — University of California (Los Angeles). Symposia on Molecular and Cellular Biology

Univ California Los Angeles L Rev — University of California at Los Angeles. Law Review

Univ California Publ Internat Rel — University of California. Publications in International Relations

Univ Calif Press Publs Hist — University of California Press. Publications in History

Univ Calif Publ Agric Sci — University of California Publications in Agricultural Sciences

Univ Calif Publ Am Archaeol Ethnol — University of California. Publications in American Archaeology and Ethnology

Univ Calif Publ Bot — University of California. Publications in Botany

Univ Calif Publ Ent — University of California. Publications in Entomology

Univ Calif Publ Entomol — University of California. Publications in Entomology

Univ Calif Publ Geol Sci — University of California. Publications in Geological Sciences

Univ Calif Publications Zool — University of California. Publications in Zoology

Univ Calif Publ Physiol — University of California. Publications in Physiology

Univ Calif Publ Psychol — University of California. Publications in Psychology

Univ Calif Publs Ent — University of California. Publications in Entomology

Univ Calif Publ Zool — University of California. Publications in Zoology

Univ Calif Sea Water Convers Lab Rep — University of California. Sea Water Conversion Laboratory. Report

Univ Calif Univ Los Angeles Publ Biol Sci — University of California. University at Los Angeles. Publications in BiologicalSciences

Univ Calif Univ Los Angeles Publ Math Phys Sci — University of California. University at Los Angeles. Publications in Mathematical and Physical Sciences

Univ Calif Water Resour Cent Contrib — University of California. Water Resources Center. Contribution

Univ Cal Lib Bull — University of California Library Bulletin

Univ Camb Dep Appl Biol Mem Rev Ser — University of Cambridge. Department of Applied Biology. Memoirs. Review Series

Univ Cambridge Dep Eng Rep CUDE/A-Aerodyn — University of Cambridge. Department of Engineering. Report. CUDE [*Cambridge University Department of Engineering*]/A-Aerodynamics

Univ Cambridge Dep Eng Rep CUDE/A-Thermo — University of Cambridge. Department of Engineering. Report. CUDE [*Cambridge University Department of Engineering*]/A-Thermo

Univ Cambridge Dep Eng Rep CUDE/A-Turbo — University of Cambridge. Department of Engineering. Report. CUDE [*Cambridge University Department of Engineering*]/A-Turbo

Univ Cambridge Inst Anim Pathol Rep Dir — University of Cambridge. Institute of Animal Pathology. Report of the Director

Univ Canterbury Publ — University of Canterbury. Publications

Univ Cathol Louvain Fac Sci Agron Lab Biochim Nutr Publ — Universite Catholique de Louvain. Faculte des Sciences Agronomiques. Laboratoire de Biochimie de la Nutrition. Publication

Univ Cathol Louv Inst Agron Mem — Universite Catholique de Louvain. Institut Agronomique. Memoires

Univ Catol Bolivar — Universidad Catolica Bolivariana

Univ Catol Bolivar Medellin — Universidad Catolica Bolivariana (Medellin)

Univ Cent Desert Stud Trans (Jodhpur India) — University Centre of Desert Studies. Transactions (Jodhpur, India)

Univ Cent Venez Inst Mater Modelos Estruct Bol Tec — Universidad Central de Venezuela. Instituto de Materiales y Modelos Estructurales. Boletin Tecnico

Univ Chic — Library of the University of Chicago

Univ Chicago Law Rev — University of Chicago Law Review

Univ Chicago Libr Soc Bull — University of Chicago Library Society Bulletin

Univ Chicago Publ — University of Chicago. Publications

Univ Chicago Rep — University of Chicago. Reports

Univ Chic L — University of Chicago. Law Review

Univ Chic L R — University of Chicago Law Review

Univ Chic M — University of Chicago. Magazine

Univ Chic Rec — University of Chicago. Record

Univ Chile Dep Prod Agric Publ Misc Agric — Universidad de Chile. Departamento de Produccion Agricola. Publicaciones Miscelaneas Agricolas

Univ Chile Fac Agron Dep Sanid Veg Bol Tec — Universidad de Chile. Facultad de Agronomia. Departamento Sanidad Vegetal. Boletin Tecnico

Univ Chile Fac Agron Publ Misc Agric — Universidad de Chile. Facultad de Agronomia. Publicaciones Miscelaneas Agricolas

Univ Chile Fac Cienc Fis Mat An — Universidad de Chile. Facultad de Ciencias Fisicas y Matematicas. Anales

Univ Chile Fac Cienc Fis Mat Inst Geol Publ — Universidad de Chile. Facultad de Ciencias Fisicas y Matematicas. Instituto de Geologia. Publicacion

Univ Chile Fac Cienc For Bol Tec — Universidad de Chile. Facultad de Ciencias Forestales. Boletin Tecnico

Univ Chile Fac Cienc For Manual — Universidad de Chile. Facultad de Ciencias Forestales. Manual

Univ Chile Fac Quim Farm Tesis Quim Farm — Universidad de Chile. Facultad de Quimica y Farmacia. Tesis de Quimicos Farmaceuticos

Univ Chile Inst Invest Ensayes Mater Inf Tec — Universidad de Chile. Instituto de Chile. Instituto de Investigaciones y Ensayes de Materiales. Informe Tecnico

Univ Chitt Stud — University of Chittagong Studies

Univ Cincinnati Med Bul — University of Cincinnati. Medical Bulletin

Univ Cincin Stud — University of Cincinnati. Studies

Univ Cin L R — University of Cincinnati Law Review

Univ Cluj-Napoca Gradina Bot Contrib Bot — Universitatea din Cluj-Napoca Gradina Botanica Contributii Botanice

Univ Col Eng Exp Stn Bull — University of Colorado. Engineering Experiment Station. Bulletin

Univ Coll Dublin Agric Fac Rep — University College of Dublin. Agricultural Faculty. Report

Univ Coll Dublin Fac Gen Agric Res Rep — University College of Dublin. Faculty of General Agriculture. Research Report

Univ Coll Wales (Aberystwyth) Memorandum — University College of Wales (Aberystwyth). Memorandum

Univ Color Stud Ser A — University of Colorado. Studies. Series A. General Series

Univ Color Stud Ser B — University of Colorado. Studies. Series B. Studies in the Humanities

Univ Colo Stud Ser Anthropol — University of Colorado. Studies. Series in Anthropology

Univ Colo Stud Ser Biol — University of Colorado. Studies. Series in Biology

Univ Colo Stud Ser Chem Pharm — University of Colorado. Studies. Series in Chemistry and Pharmacy

Univ Colo Stud Ser D — University of Colorado. Studies. Series D. Physical and Biological Sciences

Univ Colo Stud Ser Earth Sci — University of Colorado. Studies. Series in Earth Sciences

Univ Col Stud — University of Colorado. Studies

Univ Col Stud Ser C — University of Colorado. Studies. Series C. Studies in the Social Sciences

Univ Comeniana Acta Fac Rerum Nat Form Prot Nat — Universitas Comeniana. Acta Facultatis Rerum Naturalium. Formatio et Protectio Naturae

Univ Conn Occas Pap Biol Sci Ser — University of Connecticut. Occasional Papers. Biological Science Series

Univ Craiova An Ser 3 — Universitatea din Craiova. Analele. Seria a/3. Stiinte Agricole

Univ Craiova An Ser Biol Med Stiinte Agric — Universitatea din Craiova. Analele. Seria. Biologie, Medicina, Stiinte Agricole

Univ Craiova An Ser Chim — Universitatea din Craiova. Analele. Seria Chimie

Univ Craiova An Ser Mat Fiz Chim — Universitatea din Craiova. Analele. Seria. Matematica, Fizica-Chimie

Univ Craiova An Ser Mat Fiz Chim Electroteh — Universitatea din Craiova. Analele. Seria. Matematica, Fizica, Chimie, Electrotehnica

Univd — Universidad

Univ Debaters Ann — University Debaters' Annual

Univ Debaters Annual — University Debaters' Annual

Univ de Grenoble Annales n s Sci — Universite de Grenoble. Sciences-Medecine. Annales

Univ Delaware Agric Exp Sta Bull — University of Delaware Agricultural Experiment Station Bulletin

Univ Del Mar Lab Inf Ser Publ — University of Delaware. Marine Laboratories. Information Series Publication

Univ de Nancy Fac d Lettres Annales de l'Est — Universite de Nancy. Faculte des Lettres. Annales de l'Est

Univ Detroit L J — University of Detroit Law Journal

Univ Durban-Westville J — University of Durban-Westville. Journal

Univ Durban-Westville Tydskr — Universiteit van Durban-Westville. Tydskrif

Univ Durham King's Coll Dep Civ Eng Bull — University of Durham. King's College. Department of Civil Engineering. Bulletin

UnivE — Universitas. Quarterly English Language Edition [*Stuttgart*]

Univ Edinb Pfizer Med Monogr — University of Edinburgh. Pfizer Medical Monographs

Univ Edinburgh J — University of Edinburgh. Journal

Univ Emerit Merida — Universitas Emeritensis (Merida, Venezuela)

Univers BA Mex — Universidades Buenos Aires (Mexico)

Universe Nat Hist Ser — Universe Natural History Series
Univers Farm — Universal Farmacia
Universidad — Universidad [de Zaragoza. Revista]
Universitas (Bogota) — Universitas Pontificia Universidad Catolica Javeriana (Bogota)
Universitext Tracts Math — Universitext. Tracts in Mathematics
Universities Q — Universities Quarterly
University of Calif Publ in Mod Philol — University of California Publications in Modern Philology
University of Singapore School of Archre Jnl — University of Singapore. School of Architecture. Journal
University of Southern Calif School of Archre Yearbook — University of Southern California. School of Architecture. Yearbook
Univ Estad Paulista Dep Educ Bol — Universidade Estadual Paulista. Departamento de Educacao. Boletim
Univ Fed Par Cent Estud Port Arq — Universidade Federal do Parana. Centro de Estudos Portugueses. Arquivos
Univ Fed Pernambuco Esc Quim Dep Technol Publ Avulsa — Universidade Federal de Pernambuco. Escola de Quimica. Departamento de Technologia. Publicacao Avulsa
Univ Fed Pernambuco Inst Biocienc Publ Avulsa — Universidade Federal de Pernambuco. Instituto de Biociencias. Publicacao Avulsa
Univ Fed Pernambuco Inst Micol Publ — Universidade Federal de Pernambuco. Instituto de Micologia. Publicacao
Univ Fed Pernambuco Mem Inst Biocienc — Universidade Federal de Pernambuco. Memorias do Instituto de Biociencias
Univ Fed Rio De Janeiro Inst Geocienc Geol Bol — Universidade Federal do Rio De Janeiro. Instituto de Geociencias. Geologia. Boletim
Univ Fed Rio De J Inst Geocienc Bol Geol — Universidade Federal do Rio De Janeiro. Instituto de Geociencias. Boletim Geologia
Univ Fed Rio De J Inst Geocienc Dep Geol Contrib Dida — Universidade Federal do Rio De Janeiro. Instituto de Geociencias. Departamentode Geologia. Contribuicao Didatica
Univ Fed Rio Grande do Sul Fac Med Anais — Universidade Federal do Rio Grande do Sul. Faculdade de Medicina. Anais
Univ Fed Rural Rio Grande Do Sul Dep Zootec Bol Tec — Universidade Federal Rural do Rio Grande Do Sul. Departamento do Zootecnia. Boletin Tecnico
Univ Fed Vicosa Bibl Centr Ser Bibliogr Espec — Universidade Federal de Vicosa. Biblioteca Central. Serie Bibliografias Especializadas
Univ Fed Vicosa Ser Tec Bol — Universidade Federal de Vicosa. Serie Tecnica. Boletin
Univ Ferrara Ann Sez 6 — Universita di Ferrara. Annali. Sezione 6. Fisiologia e Chimica Biologica
Univ Ferrara Mem Geopaleontol — Universita di Ferrara. Memorie Geopaleontologiche
Univ Fla Agric Ext Serv Circ — University of Florida. Agricultural Extension Service. Circular
Univ Fla Coastal Oceanogr Eng Lab Rep UFL COEL TR — University of Florida. Coastal and Oceanographic Engineering Laboratory. Report. UFL/COEL/TR
Univ Fla Contrib Fla St Mus Social Sci — University of Florida. Contributions. Florida State Museum. Social Sciences
Univ Fla Coop Ext Serv Bull — University of Florida. Cooperative Extension Service. Bulletin
Univ Fla Inst Food Agric Sci Annu Res Rep — University of Florida. Institute of Food and Agricultural Sciences. Annual Research Report
Univ Fla Inst Food Agri Sci Publ — University of Florida. Institute of Food and Agricultural Sciences. Publication
Univ Fla Inst Gerontol Ser — University of Florida. Institute of Gerontology Series
Univ Fla Publ Biol Sci Ser — University of Florida. Publications. Biological Science Series
Univ Fla Water Resour Res Cent Publ — University of Florida. Water Resources Research Center. Publication
Univ Fl SSM — University of Florida. Social Sciences Monograph
Univ For — University Forum
Univ For Bois (Sopron) Publ Sci — Universite Forestiere et du Bois (Sopron). Publications Scientifiques
Univ Forst Holzwirtsch (Sopron) Wiss Mitt — Universitaet fuer Forst- und Holzwirtschaft (Sopron). Wissenschaftliche Mitteilungen
Univ For Timber Ind (Sopron) Sci Publ — University of Forestry and Timber Industry (Sopron). Scientific Publications
Univ F Study — University Film Study Center. Newsletter
Univ GA Mar Sci Cent Tech Rep Ser — University of Georgia. Marine Science Center. Technical Report Series
Univ Gaz — University Gazette
Univ Genova Pubbl Ist Mat — Universita di Genova. Pubblicazioni dell'Istituto di Matematica
Univ Geograd Radovi Zavoda za Fiz — Univerzitet u Geogradu Radovi. Zavoda za Fiziku
Univ Ghana Agric Irrig Res Stn (Kpong) Annu Rep — University of Ghana. Agricultural Irrigation Research Station (Kpong). Annual Report
Univ Ghana Agric Res Stn (Kpong) Annu Rep — University of Ghana. Agricultural Research Station (Kpong). Annual Report
Univ Ghana Law J — University of Ghana Law Journal
Univ Ghana Res Rev — University of Ghana. Institute of African Studies Research Review
Univ Habana Hav — Universidad de La Habana (La Habana)
Univ Hawaii Coll Trop Agric Dep Pap — University of Hawaii. College of Tropical Agriculture. Departmental Paper
Univ Hawaii Coop Ext Ser Misc Publ — University of Hawaii. Cooperative Extension Service. Miscellaneous Publication
Univ Hawaii Hawaii Inst Geophys Bienn Rep — University of Hawaii. Hawaii Institute of Geophysics. Biennial Report
Univ Hawaii Hawaii Inst Geophys Rep HIG — University of Hawaii. Hawaii Institute of Geophysics. Report HIG
Univ Hawaii Occas Pap — University of Hawaii. Occasional Papers

Univ Hawaii Quart Bull — University of Hawaii. Quarterly Bulletin
Univ Hawaii Res Publ — University of Hawaii. Research Publications
Univ Hisp An Ser Med — Universidad Hispalense. Anales. Serie Medicina
Univ Hond Tegucigalpa — Universidad de Honduras (Tegucigalpa)
Univ H Sch J — University High School. Journal
Univ Human Rights — Universal Human Rights
Univ Hum Rts — Universal Human Rights
Univ Iagel Acta Math — Universitatis Iagellonicae Acta Mathematica
Univ Iagellon Acta Chim — Universitatis Iagellonicae Acta Chimica
Univ IL Law — University of Illinois. Law Forum
Univ Ill Grad Sc Libr Sci Occas Pap — University of Illinois. Graduate School of Library Science. Occasional Papers
Univ Illinois Agric Exp Sta Bull — University of Illinois Agricultural Experiment Station Bulletin
Univ Ill L Forum — University of Illinois. Law Forum
Univ Ill St Lang Lit — University of Illinois. Studies in Language and Literature
Univ Ill Urbana-Champaign Water Resour Cent Res Rep — University of Illinois at Urbana-Champaign. Water Resources Center. Research Report
Univ Ill Urbana-Champaign Water Resour Cent Spec Rep — University of Illinois at Urbana-Champaign. Water Resources Center. Special Report
Univ Indonesia Inst Man Newsl — University of Indonesia. Institute of Management. Newsletter
Univ Indore Res J Sci — University of Indore. Research Journal. Science
Univ Ind Santander Bol Geol — Universidad Industrial de Santander. Boletin de Geologia
Univ Iowa Monogr Studies in Med — University of Iowa. Monographs. Studies in Medicine
Univ Iowa Stud Nat Hist — University of Iowa. Studies in Natural History
Univ J Busan Natl Univ — University Journal. Busan National University
Univ J Busan Sanup Univ — University Journal. Busan Sanup University
Univ J Nat Sci Ser — University Journal. Natural Sciences Series. Busan National University
Univ Joensuu Publ Sci — University of Joensuu. Publications in Sciences
Univ J of Business — University Journal of Business
Univ Jordan Dirasat — University of Jordan. Dirasat
Univ Jordan Dirasat Ser B — University of Jordan. Dirasat. Series B. Pure and Applied Sciences
Univ Jyvaskyla Stud Sport Phys Educ Health — University of Jyvaskyla. Studies in Sport, Physical Education, and Health
Univ Kansas Sci Bull — University of Kansas. Science Bulletin
Univ Kans Mus Nat Hist Misc Publ — University of Kansas. Museum of Natural History. Miscellaneous Publication
Univ Kans Mus Nat Hist Monogr — University of Kansas. Museum of Natural History. Monograph
Univ Kans Paleontol Contrib Artic — University of Kansas. Paleontological Contributions. Article
Univ Kans Paleontol Contrib Monogr — University of Kansas. Paleontological Contributions. Monograph
Univ Kans Paleontol Contrib Pap — University of Kansas. Paleontological Contributions. Paper
Univ Kans Primary Rec Psychol Publ — University of Kansas. Primary Records in Psychology. Publication
Univ Kans Publ Mus Nat Hist — University of Kansas. Publications. Museum of Natural History
Univ Kans Sci Bull — University of Kansas. Science Bulletin
Univ Kans Sci Bull Suppl — University of Kansas. Science Bulletin. Supplement
Univ KC R — University of Kansas City. Review
Univ K Inst Min Miner Res Tech Rep — University of Kentucky. Institute for Mining and Minerals Research. Technical Report
Univ Kiril Metodij-Skopje Fac Math — Universite Kiril et Metodij-Skopje. Faculte des Mathematiques
Univ Kuwait J Sci — University of Kuwait. Journal. Science
Univ Ky Bur Sch Serv Bul — University of Kentucky. Bureau of School Service. Bulletin
Univ KY Coll Agric Coop Ext Ser Rep — University of Kentucky. College of Agriculture. Cooperative Extension Service. Report
Univ KY Coop Ext Serv 4-H — University of Kentucky. Cooperative Extension Service. 4-H
Univ KY Coop Ext Serv Circ — University of Kentucky. Cooperative Extension Service. Circular
Univ KY Coop Ext Serv Leafl — University of Kentucky. Cooperative Extension Service. Leaflet
Univ KY Coop Ext Serv Misc — University of Kentucky. Cooperative Extension Service. Miscellaneous
Univ KY Eng Exp Stn Bull — University of Kentucky. Engineering Experiment Station. Bulletin
Univ KY Inst Min Miner Res Rep IMMR — University of Kentucky. Institute for Mining and Minerals Research. Report IMMR
Univ KY Inst Min Miner Res Tech Rep IMMR — University of Kentucky. Institute for Mining and Minerals Research. Technical Report. IMMR
Univ KY Off Res Eng Ser Bull — University of Kentucky. Office of Research and Engineering Services. Bulletin
Univ KY Publ Anthropol Archaeol — University of Kentucky. Publications in Anthropology and Archaeology
Univ Laval Dep Exploit Util Bois Note Rech — Universite Laval. Departement d'Exploitation et Utilisation des Bois. Note de Recherches
Univ Laval Dep Exploit Util Bois Note Tech — Universite Laval. Departement d'Exploitation et Utilisation des Bois. Note Technique
Univl Chron — Universal Chronicle
Univ L Coll J — University Law College. Journal. Rajputana University
Univ Lecture Ser — University Lecture Series
Univ Leeds Inst Educ Pap — University of Leeds. Institute of Education. Papers
Univ Leeds Med J — University of Leeds. Medical Journal

Univ Lesn Khoz Derevoobrab Prom-Sti (Sopron) Nauchn Publ — Universitet Lesnogo Khozyaistva i Derevoobrabatyvaoushchei Promyshlennosti (Sopron) Nauchnye Publikatsii

Univ Libre Bogota — Universidad Libre (Bogota)

Univ Libre Bruxelles Inter-Univ Inst High Energ Rep — Universite Libre de Bruxelles. Inter-University Institute for High Energies. Report

Univ Liege Fac Sci Appl Coll Publ — Universite de Liege. Faculte des Sciences Appliques. Collection des Publications

Univl Illus Contemp — Universel. Illustrations Contemporaines

Univl Ilus — Universal Ilustrado

Univ Lisboa Fac Farm Bol — Universidade de Lisboa. Faculdade de Farmacia. Boletim

Univ Lisboa Rev Fac Cienc A 2 — Universidade de Lisboa. Revista da Faculdade de Ciencias. 2. Serie A. Ciencias Matematicas

Univ Lisboa Revista Fac Ci A — Universidade de Lisboa. Revista da Faculdade de Ciencas. 2. Serie A. Ciencias Matematicas

Univ Liverp Rec — University of Liverpool. Recorder

Univ London Galton Lab Univ Coll Eugen Lab Mem — University of London. Galton Laboratory. University College Eugenics Laboratory. Memoirs

Univ Lond Univ Coll Galton Lab Eugen Lab Mem — University of London. University College. Galton Laboratory. Eugenics Laboratory. Memoirs

Univ LR — University Law Review

Univl Rev — Universal Review

Univ L Rev — University Law Review

Univl Spectator — Universal Spectator

Univ Lund Dep Anat Commun — University of Lund. Department of Anatomy. Communications

UnivM — Universite Moderne

Univ M — University Magazine

Univ Madr Fac Vet Publ — Universidad de Madrid. Facultad de Veterinaria. Publicacion

Univ Madrid Bol — Universidad de Madrid. Boletin

Univ Maine Orono Life Sci Agric Exp Stn Annu Rep — University of Maine at Orono. Life Sciences and Agriculture Experiment Station.Annual Report

Univ Maine Orono Life Sci Agric Exp Stn Tech Bull — University of Maine at Orono. Life Sciences and Agriculture Experiment Station.Technical Bulletin

Univ Maine Orono Maine Agric Exp Stn Ann Rep — University of Maine at Orono. Maine Agricultural Experiment Station. Annual Report

Univ Maria Curie-Sklodowsk Ann Sect B — Universitas Maria Curie-Sklodowsk. Annales. Sectio B

Univ Mass Dep Geol Contrib — University of Massachusetts. Department of Geology. Contribution

Univ MD Nat Resour Inst Contrib — University of Maryland. Natural Resources Institute. Contribution

Univ MD Sea Grant Program Tech Rep — University of Maryland. Sea Grant Program. Technical Report

Univ MD Water Resour Res Cent Tech Rep — University of Maryland. Water Resources Research Center. Technical Report

Univ MD Water Resour Res Cent WRRC Spec Rep — University of Maryland. Water Resources Research Center. WRRC Special Report

Univ Med M — University Medical Magazine

Univ Med Rec (London) — Universal Medical Record (London)

Univ Melb Gaz — University of Melbourne. Gazette

Univ Melb Sch For Bull — University of Melbourne. School of Forestry. Bulletin

Univ Mex — Universidad. Mensual de Cultura Popular (Mexico)

Univ Miami Law R — University of Miami. Law Review

Univ Miami Law Rev — University of Miami. Law Review

Univ Miami Rosenstiel Sch Mar Atmos Sci Annu Rep — University of Miami. Rosenstiel School of Marine and Atmospheric Science. Annual Report

Univ Miami Rosenstiel Sch Mar Atmos Sci Res Rev — University of Miami. Rosenstiel School of Marine and Atmospheric Science. Research Review

Univ Miami Sea Grant Program Sea Grant Field Guide Ser — University of Miami. Sea Grant Program. Sea Grant Field Guide Series

Univ Miami Sea Grant Program Sea Grant Tech Bull — University of Miami. Sea Grant Program. Sea Grant Technical Bulletin

Univ Mich (Ann Arbor) Off Res Adm Res News — University of Michigan (Ann Arbor). Office of Research Administration. ResearchNews

Univ Mich Bus R — University of Michigan. Business Review

Univ Mich Bus Rev — University of Michigan. Business Review

Univ Mich Dep Nav Archit Mar Eng Rep — University of Michigan. Department of Naval Architecture and Marine Engineering. Report

Univ Michigan Stud Sci Ser — University of Michigan Studies. Scientific Series

Univ Mich Inst Sci Tech Rep — University of Michigan. Institute of Science and Technology. Report

Univ Mich J Law Reform — University of Michigan. Journal of Law Reform

Univ Mich Med Bull — University of Michigan. Medical Bulletin

Univ Mich Med Cent J — University of Michigan. Medical Center. Journal

Univ Mich Mus Anthropol Tech Rep — University of Michigan. Museum of Anthropology. Technical Reports

Univ Mich Mus Zool Circ — University of Michigan. Museum of Zoology. Circular

Univ Michoac Morelia — Universidad Michoacana (Morelia, Mexico)

Univ Mich Pap Ling — University of Michigan. Papers in Linguistics

Univ Minn Agric Ext Serv Ext Bull — University of Minnesota. Agricultural Extension Service. Extension Bulletin

Univ Minn Agric Ext Serv Ext Folder — University of Minnesota. Agricultural Extension Service. Extension Folder

Univ Minn Agric Ext Serv Ext Pam — University of Minnesota. Agricultural Extension Service. Extension Pamphlet

Univ Minn Agric Ext Serv Misc — University of Minnesota. Agricultural Extension Service. Miscellaneous Publications

Univ Minn Agric Ext Serv Misc Publ — University of Minnesota. Agricultural Extension Service. Miscellaneous Publications

Univ Minn Agric Ext Serv Spec Rep — University of Minnesota. Agricultural Extension Service. Special Report

Univ Minn Bul — University of Minnesota. Bulletin

Univ Minn Contin Med Educ — University of Minnesota. Continuing Medical Education

Univ Minn Med Bull — University of Minnesota. Medical Bulletin

Univ Mississippi Stud Engl — University of Mississippi. Studies in English

Univ Missouri Columbia Mus Anthrop Ann — University of Missouri, Columbia. Museum of Anthropology. Annual

Univ Missouri Stud — University of Missouri. Studies

Univ MO Bull Eng Exp Stn Ser — University of Missouri. Bulletin. Engineering Experiment Station Series

Univ Mo Bul L Ser — University of Missouri Bulletin. Law Series

Univ MO Eng Exp Sta Eng Ser Bull — University of Missouri. Engineering Experiment Station. Engineering Series. Bulletin

Univ Monterrey — Universidad (Monterrey, Mexico)

Univ Montreal Chercheurs — Universite de Montreal. Chercheurs

Univ MO Sch Mines Metall Bull Tech Ser — University of Missouri. School of Mines and Metallurgy. Bulletin. Technical Series

Univ MO Stud — University of Missouri. Studies

Univ Mus B — University Museum. Bulletin

Univ Mus Bull Univ PA — University Museum. Bulletin. University of Pennsylvania

Univ Nac Auton Mex Inst Geol An — Universidad Nacional Autonoma de Mexico. Instituto de Geologia. Anales

Univ Nac Auton Mex Inst Geol Bol — Universidad Nacional Autonoma de Mexico. Instituto de Geologia. Boletin

Univ Nac Auton Mex Inst Geol Paleontol Mex — Universidad Nacional Autonoma de Mexico. Instituto de Geologia. Paleontologica Mexicana

Univ Nac Auton Mex Inst Geol Rev — Universidad Nacional Autonoma de Mexico. Instituto de Geologia. Revista

Univ Nac Col Bogota — Universidad Nacional de Colombia (Bogota)

Univ Nac Cordoba Fac Cienc Med Rev — Universidad Nacional de Cordoba. Facultad de Ciencias Medicas. Revista

Univ Nac Cuyo Fac Cien Agrar Bol Tec — Universidad Nacional de Cuyo. Facultad de Ciencias Agrarias. Boletin Tecnico

Univ Nac Cuyo Fac Cienc Fis-Quim Mat Ses Quim Argent — Universidad Nacional de Cuyo. Facultad de Ciencias Fisico-Quimico Matematicas. Sesiones Quimicas Argentinas

Univ Nac Cuyo Inst Pet Publ — Universidad Nacional de Cuyo. Instituto del Petroleo. Publicacion

Univ Nac de Cuyo Fac Cienc Agrar Bol de Ext — Universidad Nacional de Cuyo. Facultad de Ciencias Agrarias. Boletin de Extension

Univ Nac Eva Peron Fac Cienc Fisicomat Publ Ser 2 — Universidad Nacional de Eva Peron. Facultad de Ciencias Fisicomatematicas. Publicaciones. Serie 2. Revista

Univ Nac La Plata Fac Agron Lab Zool Agric Bol — Universidad Nacional de La Plata. Facultad de Agronomia. Laboratorio de Zoologia Agricola. Boletin

Univ Nac La Plata Fac Cienc Nat Mus Ser Tec Didact — Universidad Nacional de La Plata. Facultad de Ciencias Naturales y Museo. SerieTecnica y Didactica

Univ Nac La Plata Notas Mus Bot — Universidad Nacional de La Plata. Notas del Museo. Botanica

Univ Nac La Plata Notas Mus Geol — Universidad Nacional de La Plata. Notas del Museo. Geologia

Univ Nac La Plata Notas Mus Zool — Universidad Nacional de La Plata. Notas del Museo. Zoologia

Univ Nac La Plata Publ Fac Cienc Fisicomat — Universidad Nacional de La Plata. Publicaciones. Facultad de Ciencias Fisicomatematicas

Univ Nac La Plata Publ Fac Cienc Fisicomat Ser 2 — Universidad Nacional de La Plata. Publicaciones. Facultad de Ciencias Fisicomatematicas. Serie 2. Revista

Univ Nac Tucuman Fac Agron Misc — Universidad Nacional de Tucuman. Facultad de Agronomia. Miscelanea

Univ Nac Tucuman Fac Agron Zootec Bol Divulg — Universidad Nacional de Tucuman. Facultad de Agronomia y Zootecnia. Boletin de Divulgacion

Univ Nac Tucuman Fac Agron Zootec Misc — Universidad Nacional de Tucuman. Facultad de Agronomia y Zootecnia. Miscelanea

Univ Nac Tucuman Fac Agron Zootec Publ Espec — Universidad Nacional de Tucuman. Facultad de Agronomia y Zootecnia. PublicacionEspecial

Univ Nac Tucuman Fac Agron Zootec Ser Didact — Universidad Nacional de Tucuman. Facultad de Agronomia y Zootecnia. Serie Didactica

Univ Nac Tucuman Fund Inst Miguel Lillo Misc — Universidad Nacional de Tucuman. Fundacion e Instituto Miguel Lillo. Miscelanea

Univ Nac Tucuman Inst Fis Publ — Universidad Nacional de Tucuman. Instituto de Fisica. Publicacion

Univ Nac Tucuman Inst Geol Min Rev — Universidad Nacional de Tucuman. Instituto de Geologia y Mineria. Revista

Univ Nac Tucuman Inst Ing Quim Pub — Universidad Nacional de Tucuman. Instituto de Ingenieria Quimica. Publicacion

Univ Nac Tucuman Rev Ser A — Universidad Nacional de Tucuman. Facultad de Ciencias Exactas y Tecnologia. Revista. Serie A. Matematicas y Fisica Teorica

Univ Natal Wattle Res Inst Rep — University of Natal. Wattle Research Institute. Report

Univ NC Ext Bul — University of North Carolina Extension Bulletin

Univ NC N Lett — University of North Carolina News Letter

Univ ND Q J — University of North Dakota Quarterly Journal

Univ Nebr Coll Agric Home Econ Q — University of Nebraska. College of Agriculture and Home Economics. Quarterly

Univ NE Bul — University of New England. Bulletin

Univ N Engl Annu Rep — University of New England. Annual Report

Univ N Engl Explor Soc Aust Rep — University of New England. Exploration Society of Australia. Report

Univ Nev Mackay Sch Mines Geol Min Ser Bull — University of Nevada. Mackay School of Mines. Geological and Mining Series. Bulletin

Univ Nev Max C Fleischmann Coll Agric R — University of Nevada. Max C. Fleischmann College of Agriculture. R Series

Univ Nev Max C Fleischmann Coll Agric Rep — University of Nevada. Max C. Fleischmann College of Agriculture. Report

Univ Nev Max C Fleischmann Coll Agric Ser B — University of Nevada. Max C. Fleischmann College of Agriculture. B Series

Univ Nev Max C Fleischmann Coll Agric T Ser — University of Nevada. Max C. Fleischmann College of Agriculture. T Series

Univ Newcastle Tyne Med Gaz — University of Newcastle Upon Tyne. Medical Gazette

Univ Newcastle Upon Tyne Rep Dove Mar Lab Third Ser — University of Newcastle Upon Tyne. Report of the Dove Marine Laboratory. Third Series

Univ New Eng Bull — University of New England. Bulletin

Univ New Mexico Publ Biol — University of New Mexico. Publication in Biology

Univ News — University News

Univ New South Wales Occas Pap — University of New South Wales. Occasional Papers

Univ NM Bull Biol Ser — University of New Mexico. Bulletin. Biological Series

Univ NM Bull Geol Ser — University of New Mexico. Bulletin. Geological Series

Univ NM Inst Meteorit Spec Publ — University of New Mexico. Institute of Meteoritics. Special Publication

Univ NM Publ Anthropol — University of New Mexico. Publications in Anthropology

Univ NM Publ Biol — University of New Mexico. Publications in Biology

Univ NM Publ Geol — University of New Mexico. Publications in Geology

Univ NM Publ Meteorit — University of New Mexico. Publications in Meteoritics

Univ No Car News Letter — University of North Carolina News Letter

Univ Notre Dame Dep Theol Stud Christ Dem — University of Notre Dame. Department of Theology. Studies in Christian Democracy

Univ Nottingham Dep Agric Hortic Misc Publ — University of Nottingham. Department of Agriculture and Horticulture. Miscellaneous Publication

Univ Nov Sadu Zb Rad Prir Mat Fak Ser Hem — Univerzitet u Novom Sadu Zbornik Radova Prirodno-Matematickog Fakulteta. Serija za Hemiju

Univ NSW LJ — University of New South Wales. Law Journal

Univ NSW Occas Pap — University of New South Wales. Occasional Papers

Univ NSW Q — University of New South Wales. Quarterly

Univ of Brit Columbia L Rev — University of British Columbia. Law Review

Univ of Calif Davis L Rev — University of California at Davis. Law Review

Univ of Calif Publ in English Ling M Ph — University of California. Publications in English, Linguistics, Modern Philology

Univ of Chicago L Rev — University of Chicago. Law Review

Univ of Chi Law Rev — University of Chicago. Law Review

Univ of Cincinnati L Rev — University of Cincinnati. Law Review

Univ of Cinc Law Rev — University of Cincinnati. Law Review

Univ of Colorado L Rev — University of Colorado. Law Review

Univ of Colo Studies — University of Colorado. Studies

Univ of Florida L Rev — University of Florida. Law Review

Univ of Ghana LJ — University of Ghana. Law Journal

Univ of Illinois L Forum — University of Illinois. Law Forum

Univ of Maine Studies — University of Maine. Studies

Univ of Manila L Gaz — University of Manila. Law Gazette

Univ of Miami L Rev — University of Miami. Law Review

Univ of Michigan J of Law Reform — University of Michigan. Journal of Law Reform

Univ of Missouri at Kansas City L Rev — University of Missouri at Kansas City. Law Review

Univ of MO Studies — University of Missouri. Studies

Univ of New Brunswick LJ — University of New Brunswick. Law Journal

Univ of North Carolina Studies — University of North Carolina Studies in Language and Literature

Univ of NSW LJ — University of New South Wales. Law Journal

Univ of PA Pub Pol Econ — University of Pennsylvania. Publications in Political Economy

Univ Of Penn Law Rev — University of Pennsylvania Law Review and American Law Register

Univ Of Penn Mus Jour — University of Pennsylvania. Museum Journal

Univ of Pennsylvania L Rev — University of Pennsylvania. Law Review

Univ of Pittsburgh L Rev — University of Pittsburgh. Law Review

Univ of Queensland LJ — University of Queensland. Law Journal

Univ of Richmond L Rev — University of Richmond. Law Review

Univ of San Fernando Valley L Rev — University of San Fernando Valley. Law Review

Univ of San Francisco L Rev — University of San Francisco. Law Review

Univ of Tas LR — University of Tasmania. Law Review

Univ of Tasmania L Rev — University of Tasmania. Law Review

Univ of Toledo L Rev — University of Toledo. Law Review

Univ of Toronto LJ — University of Toronto. Law Journal

Univ of Tulsa LJ — University of Tulsa. Law Journal

Univ of West Australia L Rev — University of Western Australia. Law Review

Univ of Wisconsin Studies in Lang and Lit — University of Wisconsin Studies in Language and Literature

Univ of Wyoming Publ — University of Wyoming. Publications

Univ Oldsaksaml Arbok (Oslo) — Arbok Universitetets Oldsaksamling (Oslo)

Univ Oldsaksaml Skrifter Oslo — Universitetet Oldsaksamlings Skrifter. Oslo

Univ Orange Free State Publ Ser C — University of the Orange Free State. Publication. Series C

Univ Oriente Inst Oceanogr Bol — Universidad de Oriente. Instituto Oceanografico. Boletin

Univ Oriente Inst Oceanogr Bol Bibliogr — Universidad de Oriente. Instituto Oceanografico. Boletin Bibliografico

Univ Oxford Dept Eng Sci Rep — University of Oxford. Department of Engineering. Science Reports

Univ PA Bull Vet Ext Q — University of Pennsylvania. Bulletin. Veterinary Extension Quarterly

Univ Pa Law R — University of Pennsylvania Law Review

Univ Palermo Ann Fac Econom Commercio — Universita di Palermo. Annali della Facolta di Economia e Commercio

Univ Palermo Ann Fac Econom e Commercio — Universita di Palermo. Annali della Facolta di Economia e Commercio

Univ PA Libr Chron — University of Pennsylvania. Library Chronicle

Univ Pa L R — University of Pennsylvania Law Review

Univ PA Med Bull — University of Pennsylvania. Medical Bulletin

Univ Panama — Universidad (Panama)

Univ Paris Ann — Annales de l'Universite de Paris. Societe des Amis de l'Universite de Paris

Univ Paris Conf Palais Decouverte Ser A — Universite de Paris. Conferences du Palais de la Decouverte. Serie A

Univ Pavia Ist Geol Atti — Universita di Pavia. Istituto Geologico. Atti

Univ Penn Law Rev — University of Pennsylvania. Law Review

UnivPennPub — Publications. University of Pennsylvania

Univ Penn Stud S Asia — University of Pennsylvania Studies on South Asia

Univ Perspect — University Perspectives

Univ Peshawar J — University of Peshawar. Journal

Univ Phil Nat Appl Sci Bull — University of the Philippines. Natural and Applied Science Bulletin

Univ Pittsburgh Bul — University of Pittsburgh. Bulletin

Univ Pittsburgh Ser Philos Sci — University of Pittsburgh Series in the Philosophy of Science

Univ Pontif Bolivariana Publ Trimest — Universidad Pontificia Bolivariana. Publicacion Trimestral

Univ Pontif Bolivar Medellin — Universidad Pontificia Bolivariana (Medellin)

Univ Pontif Bolivar Publ Trimest — Universidad Pontificia Bolivariana. Publicacion Trimestral

Univ Poona Sci Tech J — University of Poona Science and Technology. Journal

Univ Potosi — Universidad (Potosi, Bolivia)

Univ Pretoria Publ Ser 2 — University of Pretoria. Publications. Series 2. Natural Sciences

Univ Q — Universalist Quarterly Review

Univ Q — Universities Quarterly

Univ Qatar Sci Bull — University of Qatar. Science Bulletin

Univ Qd Agric Dep Pap — University of Queensland. Agriculture Department. Papers

Univ Qd Bot Dep Pap — University of Queensland. Botany Department. Papers

Univ Qd Ent Dep Pap — University of Queensland. Entomology Department. Papers

Univ Q Gaz — University of Queensland. Gazette

Univ Q Law J — University of Queensland. Law Journal

Univ Qld Gaz — University of Queensland. Gazette

Univ Qld Law J — University of Queensland. Law Journal

Univ Q LJ — University of Queensland. Law Journal

Univ Quart — Universities Quarterly

Univ Queensl Comput Cent Pap — University of Queensland. Computer Centre. Papers

Univ Queensl Great Barrier Reef Comm Heron Isl Res Stn — University of Queensland. Great Barrier Reef Committee. Heron Island Research Station

Univ Queensl Pap Dep Bot — University of Queensland. Papers. Department of Botany

Univ Queensl Pap Dep Chem — University of Queensland. Papers. Department of Chemistry

Univ Queensl Pap Dep Entomol — University of Queensland. Papers. Department of Entomology

Univ Queensl Pap Dep Geol — University of Queensland. Papers. Department of Geology

Univ Queensl Pap Dep Zool — University of Queensland. Papers. Department of Zoology

Univ Queensl Pap Fac Vet Sci — University of Queensland. Papers. Faculty of Veterinary Science

Univ R — Universal Review

Univ R — University Review

Univ Reading Natl Inst Res Dairy Bienn Rev — University of Reading. National Institute for Research in Dairying. Biennial Reviews

Univ Reading Natl Inst Res Dairy Rep — University of Reading. National Institute for Research in Dairying. Report

Univ Rec — University Record

Univ Repub Fac Agron Bol (Montev) — Universidad de la Republica. Facultad de Agronomia. Boletin (Montevideo)

Univ Repub (Montevideo) Fac Agron Bol — Universidad de la Republica (Montevideo). Facultad de Agronomia. Boletin

Univ Res N — University Research News

Univ Rev — University Review

Univ Rhod Fac Med Res Lect Ser — University of Rhodesia. Faculty of Medicine. Research Lecture Series

Univ RI Mar Publ Ser — University of Rhode Island. Marine Publication Series

Univ Rio Grande Do Sul Esc Geol Avulso — Universidade do Rio Grande Do Sul. Escola de Geologia. Avulso

Univ Rio Grande Do Sul Esc Geol Bol — Universidade do Rio Grande Do Sul. Escola de Geologia. Boletim

Univ Rio Grande Do Sul Esc Geol Notas Estud — Universidade do Rio Grande Do Sul. Escola de Geologia. Notas e Estudos

Univ Rochester Lib Bull — University of Rochester. Library Bulletin

Univ Rochester Libr Bull — University of Rochester. Library Bulletin

Univ Roma Ist Autom Not — Universita di Roma. Istituto di Automatica. Notiziario

Univ Roorkee Res J — University of Roorkee. Research Journal

Univ Rostock Wiss Z Naturwiss Reihe — Universitaet Rostock. Wissenschaftliche Zeitschrift. Naturwissenschaftliche Reihe

Univ Rural Pernambuco Comun Tec — Universidade Rural de Pernambuco. Comunicado Tecnico

Univ Salvador Anal — Universidad del Salvador. Anales

Univ San Carlos Ser D Occ Monogr — University of San Carlos. Series D. Occasional Monographs

Univ Santa Fe — Universidad (Santa Fe, Argentina)

Univ Sao Paulo Esc Politec Geol Metal Bol — Universidade de Sao Paulo. Escola Politecnica, Geologia, e Metalurgia. Boletim

Univ Sao Paulo Esc Super Agric Luiz De Queiroz Bol Tec Cient — Universidade de Sao Paulo. Escola Superior de Agricultura Luiz De Queiroz. Boletim Tecnico Cientifico

Univ Sao Paulo Fac Filos Cienc Let Bol Bot — Universidade de Sao Paulo. Faculdade de Filosofia, Ciencias, e Letras. Boletim.Botanica

Univ Sao Paulo Fac Filos Cienc Let Bol Geol — Universidade de Sao Paulo. Faculdade de Filosofia, Ciencias, e Letras. Boletim.Geologia

Univ Sao Paulo Fac Filos Cienc Let Bol Mineral — Universidade de Sao Paulo. Faculdade de Filosofia, Ciencias, e Letras. Boletim.Mineralogia

Univ Sao Paulo Fac Filos Cienc Let Bol Quim — Universidade de Sao Paulo. Faculdade de Filosofia, Ciencias, e Letras. Boletim.Quimica

Univ Sao Paulo Inst Geocienc Astron Bol — Universidade de Sao Paulo. Instituto de Geociencias e Astronomia. Boletim

Univ Sao Paulo Inst Geocienc Bol IG — Universidade de Sao Paulo. Instituto de Geociencias. Boletim IG

Univ Sao Paulo Inst Geog Sediment Pedol — Universidade de Sao Paulo. Instituto de Geografia. Sedimentologia e Pedologia

Univ S Calif L Lib Bul — University of Southern California. Law Library Bulletin

Univ S Carlos Guat — Universidad de San Carlos (Guatemala)

Univ SC Governmental R — University of South Carolina. Governmental Review

Univ Seoul Collect Theseon Sci Nat — Universitas Seoulensis. Collectio Theseon. Scientia Naturalis. Seoul Taehak-kyoNonmun-jip. Chayon Kwahak

Univ Ser Math — University Series in Mathematics

Univ Ser Modern Engrg — University Series in Modern Engineering

Univ Sevilla Publ Ser Med — Universidad de Sevilla. Publicaciones. Serie Medicina

Univ S Fran Xavier Sucre — Universidad de San Francisco Xavier (Sucre)

Univ Singapore Chin Soc J — University of Singapore. Chinese Society. Journal

Univ S Inst of Crim Proceeding — University of Sydney. Institute of Criminology. Proceedings

Univ Skopje Sumar Fak God Zb — Univerzitet vo Skopje. Sumarski Fakultet. Godisen Zbornik

Univ South Calif Allan Hancock Found — University of Southern California. Allan Hancock Foundation

Univs Q — Universities Quarterly

Univ S Salvador — La Universidad (San Salvador)

Univ Stellenbosch Ann — Universiteit van Stellenbosch. Annale

Univ Strathclyde Annu Rep — University of Strathclyde. Annual Report

Univ Strathclyde Res Rep — University of Strathclyde. Research Report

Univ Stud — University Studies in History and Economics

Univ Stud Hist — University Studies in History

Univ Stud Hist Ec — University Studies in History and Economics

Univ Studies — University Studies in History and Economics

Univ Studies — University Studies in Western Australian History

Univ Studies Math — University Studies in Mathematics

Univ Studi Trieste Fac Econ Commer Ist Merceol Pubbl — Universita degli Studi di Trieste. Facolta di Economia e Commercio. Istituto diMerceologia. Pubblicazione

Univ Studi Trieste Fac Ing Ist Chim App Pubbl — Universita degli Studi di Trieste. Facolta di Ingegneria. Istituto di Chimica Applicata. Pubblicazioni

Univ Studi Trieste Fac Sci Ist Chim Pubbl — Universita degli Studi di Trieste. Facolta di Scienze. Istituto di Chimica. Pubblicazioni

Univ Studi Trieste Fac Sci Ist de Mineral Pubbl — Universita degli Studi di Trieste. Facolta di Scienze. Istituto di Mineralogia.Pubblicazione

Univ Studi Trieste Fac Sci Ist Geol Pubbl — Universita degli Studi di Trieste. Facolta di Scienze. Istituto di Geologia. Pubblicazioni

Univ Studi Trieste Ist Chim Farm Tossicol Pubbl — Universita degli Studi di Trieste. Istituto di Chimica Farmaceutica e Tossicologica. Pubblicazioni

Univ Studi Triest Fac di Sci Ist Geol Pubbl — Universita degli Studi di Trieste. Facolta di Scienze. Istituto di Geologia. Pubblicazioni

Univ Stud Math (Jaipur) — University Studies in Mathematics (Jaipur)

Univ Stud Trieste Fac Farm Ist Chim Farm Tossicol Pubbl — Universita degli Studi di Trieste. Facolta di Farmacia. Istituto di Chimica, Farmaceutica, e Tossicologica. Pubblicazioni

Univ Stud Trieste Fac Farm Ist Tec Farm Pubbl — Universita degli Studi di Trieste. Facolta di Farmacia. Istituto di Tecnica Farmaceutica. Pubblicazioni

Univ Stud Trieste Ist Tec Farm Pubbl — Universita degli Studi di Trieste. Istituto di Tecnica Farmaceutica. Pubblicazioni

Univ Stud Univ Neb — University Studies. University of Nebraska

Univ Sydney Med J — University of Sydney. Medical Journal

Univ Syd Post Grad Ctee Med Bull — University of Sydney. Postgraduate Committee in Medicine. Bulletin

Univ Tarija — Universidad (Tarija, Bolivia)

Univ Tas Gaz — University of Tasmania. Gazette

Univ Tas LR — University of Tasmania. Law Review

Univ Tasmania Environ Stud Occas Pap — University of Tasmania. Environmental Studies. Occasional Paper

Univ Tasmania Environ Stud Work Pap — University of Tasmania. Environmental Studies. Working Paper

Univ Teheran Fac Agron Bull — Universite de Teheran. Faculte d'Agronomie. Bulletin

Univ Tenn Rec — University of Tennessee. Record

Univ Tenn Surv Bus — University of Tennessee. Survey of Business

Univ Tex Austin Bur Econ Geol Handb — University of Texas at Austin. Bureau of Economic Geology. Handbook

Univ Tex Austin Bur Econ Geol Miner Resour Circ — University of Texas at Austin. Bureau of Economic Geology. Mineral Resource Circular

Univ Tex Austin Bur Econ Geol Res Note — University of Texas at Austin. Bureau of Economic Geology. Research Note

Univ Tex Austin Cent Highw Res Res Rep — University of Texas at Austin. Center for Highway Research. Research Report

Univ Tex Austin Cent Res Water Resour Tech Rep — University of Texas at Austin. Center for Research in Water Resources. Technical Report

Univ Tex Bull — University of Texas. Bulletin

Univ Tex Bur Econ Geol Publ — University of Texas. Bureau of Economic Geology. Publication

Univ Tex Bur Econ Geol Rep Invest — University of Texas. Bureau of Economic Geology. Report of Investigations

Univ Tex MD Anderson Symp Fundam Cancer Res — University of Texas. M. D. Anderson Symposium on Fundamental CancerResearch

Univ Timisoara An Stiinte Fiz Chim — Universitatea din Timisoara. Analele. Stiinte Fizice-Chimice

Univ TLR — University of Tasmania. Law Review

Univ Tokyo Comp Cent Rep — University of Tokyo. Computer Center Report

Univ Tokyo Inst Nucl Study INS Rep — University of Tokyo. Institute for Nuclear Study. INS. Report

Univ Tokyo Inst Nucl Study Rep INS J — University of Tokyo. Institute for Nuclear Study. Report. INS-J

Univ Toledo Law R — University of Toledo. Law Review

Univ Tor Dent J — University of Toronto Dental Journal

Univ Toronto Biol Ser — University of Toronto. Biological Series

Univ Toronto Dep Geogr Res Publ — University of Toronto. Department of Geography. Research Publications

Univ Toronto Fac For Tech Rep — University of Toronto. Faculty of Forestry. Technical Report

Univ Toronto Inst Environ Sci Eng Publ EH — University of Toronto. Institute of Environmental Sciences and Engineering. Publication EH

Univ Toronto Inst Environ Stud Publ EH — University of Toronto. Institute for Environmental Studies. Publication EH

Univ Toronto Law J — University of Toronto. Law Journal

Univ Toronto Med J — University of Toronto. Medical Journal

Univ Toronto Q — University of Toronto. Quarterly

Univ Toronto Quart — University of Toronto Quarterly

Univ Toronto Stud Biol Ser — University of Toronto. Studies. Biological Series

Univ Toronto Stud Geol Ser — University of Toronto. Studies. Geological Series

Univ Toronto Stud Pap Chem Lab — University of Toronto. Studies. Papers from the Chemical Laboratories

Univ Toronto Stud Pathol Ser — University of Toronto. Studies. Pathological Series

Univ Toronto Stud Physiol Ser — University of Toronto. Studies. Physiological Series

Univ Toronto Stud Phys Ser — University of Toronto. Studies. Physics Series

Univ Toronto Undergrad Dent J — University of Toronto Undergraduate Dental Journal

Univ Tor Q — University of Toronto. Quarterly

Univ Tripoli Bull Fac Eng — University of Tripoli. Bulletin. Faculty of Engineering

Univ Tsukuba Tech Rep — University of Tsukuba Technical Report

Univ Udaipur Res J — University of Udaipur. Research Journal

Univ Udaipur Res Stud — University of Udaipur. Research Studies

Univ Ulsan Rep Natur Sci Engrg — University of Ulsan. Natural Science and Engineering

Univ Umea Commun Res Unit Proj Rep — University of Umea. Communication Research Unit. Project Report

Univ Umea Dep Math — University of Umea. Department of Mathematics

Univ u Novom Sadu Zb Rad Prirod-Mat Fak — Univerzitet u Novom Sadu. Zbornik Radova Prirodno-Matematickog Fakulteta

Univ u Novom Sadu Zb Rad Prirod Mat Fak Ser Mat — Univerzitet u Novom Sadu. Zbornik Radova Prirodno-Matematickog Fakulteta. Serija za Matemati

Univ Utah Anthropol Pap — University of Utah. Anthropological Papers

Univ Utah Biol Ser — University of Utah. Biological Series

Univ V — University Vision

Univ Va Alumni Bul — University of Virginia Alumni Bulletin

Univ VA News Letter — University of Virginia. News Letter

Univ Va Rec Ext Ser — University of Virginia Record Extension Series

Univ Veracruz Xalapa — Universidad Veracruzana (Xalapa, Mexico)

Univ WA Ann L Rev — University of Western Australia. Annual Law Review

Univ WA Law Rev — University of Western Australia. Law Review

Univ WA L Rev — University of Western Australia. Law Review

Univ Warsaw Dep Radiochem Publ — University of Warsaw. Department of Radiochemistry. Publication

Univ Wash Coll Fish Tech Rep — University of Washington. College of Fisheries. Technical Report

Univ Wash Eng Exp Stn Bull — University of Washington. Engineering Experiment Station. Bulletin

Univ Wash Eng Exp Stn Rep — University of Washington. Engineering Experiment Station. Report

Univ Wash Eng Exp Stn Tech Note — University of Washington. Engineering Experiment Station. Technical Note

Univ Washington Med — University of Washington Medicine

Univ Wash Inst For Prod Contrib — University of Washington. Institute of Forest Products. Contributions

Univ Wash Publ Biol — University of Washington. Publications in Biology

Univ Wash Publ Fish — University of Washington. Publications in Fisheries

Univ Wash Publ Fish New Ser — University of Washington. Publications in Fisheries. New Series

Univ Wash Publ Geol — University of Washington. Publications in Geology

Univ Wash Publ Oceanogr — University of Washington. Publications in Oceanography

Univ Waterloo Biol Ser — University of Waterloo. Biology Series

Univ Waterloo Fac Environ Stud Occas Pap — University of Waterloo. Faculty of Environmental Studies. Occasional Paper

Univ Western Australia Law R — University of Western Australia. Law Review

Univ Western Ontario Series in Philos Sci — University of Western Ontario. Series in Philosophy of Science

Univ West Indies Reg Res Cent Soil Land Use Surv — University of the West Indies. Regional Research Centre. Soil and Land Use Surveys

Univ West Ont Med J — University of Western Ontario. Medical Journal

Univ West Ont Ser Philos Sci — University of Western Ontario. Series in Philosophy in Science

Univ Windsor R — University of Windsor. Review
Univ Wis Coll Agric Life Sci Res Div Bull — University of Wisconsin. College of Agricultural and Life Sciences. Research Division. Bulletin
Univ Wis Coll Agric Life Sci Res Div Res Rep — University of Wisconsin. College of Agricultural and Life Sciences. Research Division. Research Report
Univ Wis Eng Exp Stn Rep — University of Wisconsin. Engineering Experiment Station. Report
Univ Wis-Madison Coll Agric Life Sci Res Div Res Bull — University of Wisconsin-Madison. College of Agricultural and Life Sciences. Research Division. Research Bulletin
Univ Wis Madison Math Res Cent Publ — University of Wisconsin-Madison. Mathematics Research Center. Publication
Univ Wis Milw Field Stn Bull — University of Wisconsin-Milwaukee. Field Stations Bulletin
Univ Wis Sea Grant Coll Tech Rep — University of Wisconsin. Sea Grant College. Technical Report
Univ Wis Sea Grant Program Tech Rep — University of Wisconsin. Sea Grant Program. Technical Report
Univ Wis Water Resour Cent Eutrophication Inf Prog Lit Rev — University of Wisconsin. Water Resources Center. Eutrophication Information Program. Literature Review
Univ Witwatersrand Dep Geogr Environ Stud Occas Pap — University of the Witwatersrand. Department of Geography and Environmental Studies. Occasional Paper
Univ Wyo Publ — University of Wyoming. Publications
Univ Yaounde Fac Sci Ann Ser 3 — Universite de Yaounde. Faculte des Sciences. Annales. Serie 3. Biologie-Biochimie
Uniw Adama Mickiewicza Poznaniu Inst Chem Ser Chem — Uniwersytet Imienia Adama Mickiewicza w Poznaniu. Instytut Chemii. Seria Chemia
Uniw Adama Mickiewicza Poznaniu Ser Astron — Uniwersytet Imienia Adama Mickiewicza w Poznaniu. Seria Astronomia
Uniw Adama Mickiewicza Poznaniu Ser Biol — Uniwersytet Imienia Adama Mickiewicza w Poznaniu. Seria Biologia
Uniw Adama Mickiewicza Poznaniu Ser Chem — Uniwersytet Imienia Adama Mickiewicza w Poznaniu. Seria Chemia
Uniw Adama Mickiewicza w Poznaniu Ser Fiz — Uniwersytet Imienia Adama Mickiewicza w Poznaniu. Seria Fizyka
Uniw Gdanski Wydz Mat Fiz Chem Zesz Nauk Ser Chem — Uniwersytet Gdanski Wydzial Matematyki, Fizyki, Chemii, Zeszyty Naukowe. Seria Chemia
Uniw Lodz Acta Univ Lodz Ser 2 — Uniwersytet Lodzki. Acta Universitatis Lodziensis. Seria 2
Uniw Marii Curie-Sklodowskiej Ann Sect AA — Uniwersytet Marii Curie-Sklodowskiej. Annales. Sectio AA. Physica et Chemia
Uniw Opolski Zesz Nauk Chem — Uniwersytet Opolski. Zeszyty Naukowe. Chemia
Uniw Slaski w Katowicach Prace Nauk — Uniwersytet Slaski w Katowicach. Prace Naukowe
Uniw Slaski w Katowicach Prace Naukowe — Uniwersytet Slaski w Katowicach. Prace Naukowe
Uniw Slaski w Katowicach Prace Naukowe Prace Mat — Uniwersytet Slaski w Katowicach. Prace Naukowe. Prace Matematyczne
Uniw Slaski w Katowicach Prace Nauk-Prace Mat — Uniwersytet Slaski w Katowicach. Prace Naukowe. Prace Matematyczne
UN Juridical YB — United Nations Juridical Year Book
Unk — Unknown Worlds
UNK — Zeitschrift fuer Operations Research
UNL — Umwelt. Forschung, Gestaltung, Schutz
UNL — Universidad Nacional del Litoral
UNL/H — Humanitas. Universidad de Nuevo Leon. Centro de Estudios Humanisticos
UNLP/E — Economica. Universidad Nacional de La Plata. Facultad de Ciencias Economicas. Instituto de Investigaciones Economicas
UNLPM/R — Revista. Museo de La Plata. Universidad Nacional de La Plata. Facultad de Ciencias Naturales y Museo
U NM A Mus Bull — University of New Mexico Art Museum Bulletin
Unman Syst — Unmanned Systems
Un Med Can — Union Medicale du Canada
UNM/JAR — Journal of Anthropological Research. University of New Mexico. Department of Anthropology
UN Mo Bul — Monthly Bulletin of Statistics. United Nations
UN Mo Chron — UN Monthly Chronicle
UN Mon Chron — UN Monthly Chronicle
Unm Ox — Unmuzzled Ox
UNMPA — University of New Mexico Publications in Anthropology
UNN — Unternehmung. Schweizerische Zeitschrift fuer Betriebswirtschaft
Unnumbered Rep US Dep Agric Econ Stat Coop Serv Stat Res Div — Unnumbered Report. United States Department of Agriculture. Economics, Statistics, and Cooperatives Service. Statistical Research Division
UNNUS — Uralic News and Notes from the United States
Un of Gh LJ — University of Ghana. Law Journal
U Notr D St — University of Notre Dame. Studies in the Philosophy of Religion
Unpartizan R — Unpartizan Review
Unpop R — Unpopular Review
Un Prac News — Unauthorized Practice News
UN R — United Nations Review
UN Rev — United Nations Review
UNRP — University of Nottingham. Research Publications
UNRWA — United Nations Relief and Works Administration
UNS — University of Nebraska. Studies
UN Sec Bur Soc Aff Ser K — United Nations Secretariat. Bureau of Social Affairs. Series K
UnSemQR — Union Seminary. Quarterly Review
Unsere Dioz Vergangenheit & Gegenwart — Unsere Diozese in Vergangenheit und Gegenwart
Unsere Heim — Unsere Heimat. Zeitschrift des Vereines fuer Landeskunde von Niederoesterreich und Wien

Unsere Kstdkml — Unsere Kunstdenkmaler
Unsere Welt — Unsere Welt. Illustrierte Monatsschrift zur Foerderung der Naturerkenntnis
Unser Sozial Dorf — Unser Sozialistisches Dorf
Un Serv I J — Journal of the Royal United Service Institution
Un Serv J — Journal of the Royal United Service Institution
Un Serv M — United Service Magazine
Un Serv (Phila) — United Service (Philadelphia)
UNSPD — Underground Space
Unsteady State Processes Catal Proc Int Conf — Unsteady State Processes in Catalysis. Proceedings. International Conference
UNSWLJ — University of New South Wales. Law Journal
UN Symp Dev Use Geotherm Resour Abstr — United Nations Symposium on the Development and Use of Geothermal Resources. Abstracts
UN Symp Dev Use Geotherm Resour Proc — United Nations Symposium on the Development and Use of Geothermal Resources. Proceedings
UnT — Uncanny Tales
UNT — Unitas
UNT — Untersuchungen zum Neuen Testament
UNT — Uppsala Nya Tidning
UNTEA — Undersea Technology
Unternehm — Unternehmung. Schweizerische Zeitschrift fuer Betriebswirtschaft
Unternehmungsfuehrung im Gewerbe — Unternehmungsfuehrung im Gewerbe und Gewerbliche
Unterr Chem — Unterricht Chemie
Unterrichtsbll Math Natwiss — Unterrichtsblaetter fuer Mathematik und Naturwissenschaften
Unters Angebot Nachfrage Miner Rohst — Untersuchungen ueber Angebot und Nachfrage Mineralischer Rohstoffe
Untersuch Natur Menschen — Untersuchungen ueber die Natur des Menschen, der Thiere, und der Pflanzen
UNTP — Universidad de Tucuman. Publications
UNVS-A — Universo
UNW — United Nations World
UNWAL Rev — University of Western Australia. Law Review
UN W Bul — United Nations Weekly Bulletin
UN Wld — United Nations World
UN World — United Nations World
UNWSA — Unterrichtswissenschaft
UNYB — United Nations Year Book
UO — Ukrainica Occidentalia
UO — Ulm-Oberschwaben
U of Col Studies — University of Colorado Studies
U of Detroit LJ — University of Detroit. Law Journal
U of Kansas City L Rev — University of Kansas City. Law Review
U of Kansas L Rev — University of Kansas. Law Review
U of Malaya L Rev — University of Malaya. Law Review
U of MLB — University of Missouri. Law Bulletin
U of Omaha Bull — Night Law School Bulletin. University of Omaha
U of Pitt L Rev — University of Pittsburgh. Law Review
U of PLR — University of Pennsylvania. Law Review
U of PL Rev — University of Pennsylvania. Law Review
U of Queensl LJ — University of Queensland. Law Journal
U of T School of LR — School of Law. Review. Toronto University
U of West Aust L Rev — University of Western Australia. Law Review
U Oldsaksaml Ab — Universitets Oldsaksamling Arbok
UP — Journal of Urban Planning and Development
UP — Paris. Universite. Faculte des Lettres. Bibliotheque
UP — Unge Paedagoger
UP — Uniwersytet Imienia Adama Mickiewicza w Poznaniu
UP — Unterrichtspraxis
UP/A — Apuntes. Universidad del Pacifica. Centro de Investigacion
UPAL — Utrechtse Publikaties voor Algemene Literatuurwetenschap
U PA Law Rev — University of Pennsylvania. Law Review and American Law Register
U PA LR — University of Pennsylvania. Law Review
U PA L Rev — University of Pennsylvania. Law Review
U PA Mus U Mus Bull — University of Pennsylvania Museum. University Museum Bulletin
UPB — Universidad Pontificia Bolivariana
UPCA — Universidade do Parana. Departamento de Antropologia. Comunicacoes Avulsas
UP/CSEC — Cuban Studies/Estudios Cubanos. University of Pittsburg. University Center for International Studies. Center for Latin American Studies
Update — Update on Law-Related Education
Update Clin Immunol — Update. Clinical Immunology
Update Intensive Care Emerg Med — Update in Intensive Care and Emergency Medicine
Update Ser SD Agric Exp Stn — Update Series. South Dakota Agricultural Experiment Station
UP/E — Ethnology. University of Pittsburgh
UP/EA — Estudios Andinos. University of Pittsburgh. Latin American Studies Center
UPGGAZ — Uchenye Zapiski Permskogo Universiteta Imeni A. M. Gor'kogo
UPHR — Up Here
UPHS — Uttar Pradesh Historical Society. Journal
UPHTDE — Annual Research Reviews. Ultrastructural Pathology of Human Tumors
U Pit Law — University of Pittsburgh. Law Review
U Pitt L R — University of Pittsburgh. Law Review
U Pitt L Rev — University of Pittsburgh. Law Review
UP/LAIL — Latin American Indian Literatures. University of Pittsburgh. Department of Hispanic Languages and Literature
UPLT — United Provinces Law Times
UPMB — University of Pennsylvania. Museum Bulletin
UPMFF — University of Pennsylvania. Monographs in Folklore and Folklife
U P News — Unauthorized Practice News

UPortR — University of Portland. Review
UPPIAI — Uchenye Zapiski Permşkogo Gosudarstvennogo Pedagogicheskogo Instituta
Upplands Fornminnesforen Ab — Upplands Fornminnesforenings Arsbok
Upplands Fornminnesforen Tidsk — Upplands Fornminnesforenings Tidskrift
Uppsala U Arsskr — Uppsala Universitets Arsskrift
Uppsala Univ G Inst B — Uppsala University. Geological Institution. Bulletin
Upps Arsskr — Uppsala Universitets Arsskrift
Upps Univ Geol Inst Bull — Uppsala University. Geological Institution. Bulletin
UPr — Ucilisten Pregled
Upravlenie Slozn Sistemami — Upravlenie Sloznymi Sistemami. Rizskii Politehniceskii Institut
Upravlyaemye Sistemy — Upravlyaemye Sistemy Institut Matematiki Institut Kataliza Sibirskogo Otdeleniya Akademii Nauk SSSR
Uprawa Rosl Nawozenie — Uprawa Roslin i Nawozenie
UPR Co — Union Pacific Railroad Company
UPR/CS — Caribbean Studies. University of Puerto Rico. Institute of Caribbean Studies
UP Res Dig — UP [*University of the Philippines*] Research Digest
Uprochnyayushchaya Term Termomekh Obrab Prokata — Uprochnyayushchaya Termicheskaya i Termomekhanicheskaya Obrabotka Prokata
UPR/RCS — Revista de Ciencias Sociales. Universidad de Puerto Rico. Colegio de Ciencias Sociales
Upr Sist Mash — Upravlyayushchie Sistemy i Mashiny
Upr Yad Energ Ustanovkami — Upravlenie Yadernymi Energeticheskimi Ustanovkami
Upsala J Med Sci — Upsala Journal of Medical Sciences
Upsala J Med Sci Suppl — Upsala Journal of Medical Sciences. Supplement
Upsala Lakaref Forh — Upsala Lakareforening Fordhandlingar
Ups Arsk — Upsala Universitets Arsskrift
UPSEELL — University of Pennsylvania. Studies in East European Languages and Literatures
Ups J Med Sci — Upsala Journal of Medical Sciences
Ups J Med Sci Suppl — Upsala Journal of Medical Sciences. Supplement
Ups Lak F — Upsala Lakareforenings Forhandlingar
Ups N Acta S Sc — Nova Acta Regiae Societatis Scientiarum Upsaliensis
Ups S Sc N Acta — Nova Acta Regiae Societatis Scientiarum Upsaliensis
UP/TM — Tiers Monde. Universite de Paris. Institut d'Etude du Developpement Economique et Social
U Puget Sound L Rev — University of Puget Sound. Law Review
UP Vet — UP [*University of the Philippines*] Veterinarian
UPWBA — Uniwersytet Imienia Adama Mickiewicza w Poznaniu. Wydzial Biologii i Nauk o Ziemi. Prace. Seria Geologia
UPZ — Urkunden der Ptolemaeerzeit
UQ — Ukrainian Quarterly
UQ — Umm el-Qura
UQ — Universities Quarterly
UQLJ — University of Queensland. Law Journal
UQP — University of Queensland. Papers
U Qsld P SS — University of Queensland. Papers. Social Sciences
UQTA — Uqaata
U Queens L J — University of Queensland. Law Journal
U Queensl LJ — University of Queensland. Law Journal
U Queens LR — University of Queensland. Law Review
UR — Ukrainian Review
UR — Umjetnost Rijeci
UR — University Review
URAAA — Urania
Ural Altaische Jb — Ural-Altaische Jahrbuecher
Ural Alta Jb — Ural-Altaische Jahrbuecher
Ural Gos Univ Mat Zap — Ural'skii Gosudarstvennyi Universitet Imeni A. M. Gor'kogo Ural'skoe Matematiceskoe Obscestvo Matematiceskie Zapiski
Ural Metall — Ural'skaya Metallurgiya
Ural Politehn Inst Sb — Ural'skii Politehniceskii Institut Imeni S. M. Kirova Sbornik
Ur & Fruehgesch Archaeol Schweiz — Ur- und Fruehgeschichtliche Archaeologie der Schweiz
Uranium Abstr — Uranium Abstracts
Uranium Hexafluoride Handl Int Conf — Uranium Hexafluoride Handling. International Conference
Uranium Min Metall — Uranium Mining and Metallurgy
Uraniun Nucl Energy Proc Int Symp Uranium Inst — Uranium and Nuclear Energy. Proceedings of the International Symposium held by the Uranium Institute
Uran Supply — Uranium Supply and Demand. Perspectives to 1995
URB — University of Riyad. Bulletin. Faculty of Arts
Urb Aff Abstr — Urban Affairs Abstracts
Urb Aff Ann R — Urban Affairs Annual Review
Urb Aff Q — Urban Affairs Quarterly
Urb Aff Quart — Urban Affairs Quarterly
URBAMET — Urbanisme, Amenagement, Equipments et Transports
Urban Abs — Urban Abstracts
Urban Aff Abs — Urban Affairs Abstracts
Urban Affairs Q — Urban Affairs Quarterly
Urban Air Pollut — Urban Air Pollution
Urban Anthr — Urban Anthropology
Urban Anthrop — Urban Anthropology
Urban Can — Urban Canada
Urban Data Service Rept — Urban Data Service Report
Urban Des — Urban Design
Urban Design Intl — Urban Design International
Urban Des Int — Urban Design International
Urban Des Q — Urban Design Quarterly
Urban Ecol — Urban Ecology
Urban Ed — Urban Education
Urban Educ — Urban Education

Urban For — Urban Forum
Urban Hist — Urban History Review
Urban Hist R — Urban History Review
Urban Hist Yearb — Urban History Yearbook
Urban Hlth — Urban Health
Urban Innov Abroad — Urban Innovation Abroad
Urban Inst Policy Res Rep — Urban Institute. Policy and Research Report
Urban L Ann — Urban Law Annual
Urban Law — Urban Lawyer
Urban Law An — Urban Law Annual
Urban Lif C — Urban Life and Culture [*Later, Urban Life*]
Urban R — Urban Review
Urban Rev — Urban Review
Urban Soc C — Urban and Social Change Review
Urban Stud — Urban Studies
Urban Syst — Urban Systems
Urb Anthrop — Urban Anthropology
Urban Transp Abroad — Urban Transportation Abroad
Urb Des Int — Urban Design International
URBE — Urban Ecology
Urb For — Urban Forests
URBH — Urban Health
Urb Hist Rev — Urban History Review
Urb L and P — Urban Law and Policy
Urb L and Poly — Urban Law and Policy
Urb L Ann — Urban Law Annual
Urblaw — Urban Law and Policy
Urb Law — Urban Lawyer
Urb Law Pol — Urban Law and Policy
Urb Life — Urban Life
Urb Life & Cult — Urban Life and Culture [*Later, Urban Life*]
Urb L Rev — Urban Law Review
URBN-A — Urbanisme
Urb Past & Present — Urbanism Past and Present
Urb Rev Puertorriquena Arquit — Urbe Revista Puertorriquena de Arquitectura
URBS-A — Urban Studies
Urb Soc Change R — Urban and Social Change Review
Urb Stud — Urban Studies
Urdmurt i Glazov Ped Inst Ucen Zap — Urdmurtskogo i Glazovskogo Pedagogiceskogo Instituta Ucenye Zapiski
Urdmurt Ped Inst Ucen Zap — Urdmurtskogo Pedagogiceskogo Instituta Ucenye Zapiski
URE — Ukrains'ka Radians'ka Entsyklopediia
URECD — Urban Ecology
Uremia Invest — Uremia Investigation
Urethane — Urethane Plastics and Products
Urethane Plast Prod — Urethane Plastics and Products
Urethanes Technol — Urethanes Technology
URev — University Review
URGAB — Urologe. Ausgabe A
URGYA — Urology
U Rich LR — University of Richmond. Law Review
U Rich L Rev — University of Richmond. Law Review
U Richmond L Rev — University of Richmond. Law Review
URINA — Urologia Internationalis
Urja Oil Gas Int — Urja Oil and Gas International
Urk — Urkunden der Ptolemaeerzeit
Urk — Urkunden des 18. Dynastie. Historisch-Bibliographische Urkunden
URLAA — Urban Land
URLB — University of Rochester. Library Bulletin
URLBB — Urologe. Ausgabe B
URLGA — Urologe
URLH — Urban Renewal and Low Income Housing
URNEA — Urologiya i Nefrologiya
Urner Miner Freund — Urner Mineralien Freund
Ur Nutid Musikliv — Ur Nutidens Musikliv
Urol & Cutan R — Urologic and Cutaneous Review
Urol Ausg A — Urologe. Ausgabe A
Urol Clin North Am — Urologic Clinics of North America
Urol Cutaneous Rev — Urologic and Cutaneous Review
Urol i Nefrol — Urologiya i Nefrologiya
Urol Int — Urologia Internationalis
Urol Intern — Urologia Internationalis
Urol Internat — Urologia Internationalis
Urol Nefrol (Mosk) — Urologiia i Nefrologiia (Moskva)
Urol Nephrol Sz — Urologiai es Nephrologiai Szemle
Urologe — Urologe. Ausgabe A
Urologe A — Urologe. Ausgabe A. Zeitschrift fuer Klinische und Praktische Urologie
Urologe Ausg B — Urologe. Ausgabe B
Urologe B — Urologe. Ausgabe B. Organ des Berufverbandes der Deutschen Urologen
Urol Oncol — Urologic Oncology
Urol Panam — Urologia Panamericana
Urol Pol — Urologia Polska
Urol Radiol — Urologic Radiology
Urol Res — Urological Research
Urol Suppl (Treviso) — Urologia. Supplemento (Treviso)
Urol Surv — Urological Survey
URP — Untersuchungen zur Romanischen Philologie
URPT-A — Urban and Rural Planning Thought
UrR — Urban Review
Ur Schw — Ur-Schweiz
URSR — Ukrains'ka Radjans'ka Socialistyczna Respublika
URSS/AL — America Latina. Academia de Ciencias de la Union de Republicas Sovieticas Socialistas

URSUA — Urological Survey
U Rtv — Ugeskrift for Retsvaesen
URX — Ubersee Rundschau
US — United States Reports
US — Universale Studium
US — University Studies
US — Uusi Suomi
US1 — United States 1 Worksheets
USAEC Rep CONF — US Atomic Energy Commission. Report. CONF
USAEC Rep GJO — United States. Atomic Energy Commission. Report GJO
USAEC Res Dev Rep AEC-TR — US Atomic Energy Commission. Research and Development Report. AEC-TR
USAEC Res Dev Rep ANL — US Atomic Energy Commission. Research and Development Report. ANL
USAEC Res Dev Rep BNL — US Atomic Energy Commission. Research and Development Report. BNL
USAEC Res Dev Rep COO — US Atomic Energy Commission. Research and Development Report. COO
USAEC Res Dev Rep HASL — US Atomic Energy Commission. Research and Development Report. HASL
USAEC Res Dev Rep HW — US Atomic Energy Commission. Research and Development Report. HW
USAEC Res Dev Rep LAMS (LA) — US Atomic Energy Commission. Research and Development Report. LAMS (LA)
USAEC Res Dev Rep LF — US Atomic Energy Commission. Research and Development Report. LF
USAEC Res Dev Rep NYO — US Atomic Energy Commission. Research and Development Report. NYO
USAEC Res Dev Rep ORINS — US Atomic Energy Commission. Research and Development Report. ORINS
USAEC Res Dev Rep ORNL — US Atomic Energy Commission. Research and Development Report. ORNL
USAEC Res Dev Rep ORO — US Atomic Energy Commission. Research and Development Report. ORO
USAEC Res Dev Rep RLO — US Atomic Energy Commission. Research and Development Report. RLO
USAEC Res Dev Rep SCR — US Atomic Energy Commission. Research and Development Report. SCR
USAEC Res Dev Rep TID — US Atomic Energy Commission. Research and Development Report. TID
USAEC Res Dev Rep UCD — US Atomic Energy Commission. Research and Development Report. UCD
USAEC Res Dev Rep UCLA — US Atomic Energy Commission. Research and Development Report. UCLA
USAEC Res Dev Rep UCRL — US Atomic Energy Commission. Research and Development Report. UCRL
USAEC Res Dev Rep UCSF — US Atomic Energy Commission. Research and Development Report. UCSF
USAEC Res Dev Rep UH — US Atomic Energy Commission. Research and Development Report. UH
USAEC Res Dev Rep UR — US Atomic Energy Commission. Research and Development Report. UR
USAEC Res Dev Rep WT — US Atomic Energy Commission. Research and Development Report. WT
USAEC Symp Ser — US Atomic Energy Commission. Symposium Series
US Aeros P — United States Aerospace Industry Profile
US Aerosp Med Res Lab Tech Rep AMRL-TR — United States. Aerospace Medical Research Laboratory. Technical Report. AMRL-TR
US Aerosp Res Lab Rep — United States. Aerospace Research Laboratories. Reports
USAF AFHRL — United States. Air Force. Human Resources Laboratory
USAF NR — United States. Air Force. News Release
USAF Nucl Saf — USAF [*United States Air Force*] Nuclear Safety
Usage Parole — Usage de la Parole
US Agric — United States. Department of Agriculture. Publications
US Agric Mark Serv AMS Series — United States. Agriculture Marketing Service. AMS Series
US Agric Res Serv ARS-NC — US Agricultural Research Service. ARS-NC
US Agric Res Serv ARS-NE — US Agricultural Research Service. ARS-NE
US Agric Res Serv ARS-S — US Agricultural Research Service. ARS-S
US Agric Res Serv ARS-W — US Agricultural Research Service. ARS-W
US Agric Res Serv CA — US Agricultural Research Service. CA
US Agric Res Serv East Reg Res Lab Publ — United States. Agricultural Research Service. Eastern Regional Research Laboratory. Publication
US Agric Res Serv Mark Res Rep — US Agricultural Research Service. Marketing Research Report
US Agric Res Serv North Cent Reg Rep — United States. Agricultural Research Service. North Central Region. Report
US Agric Res Serv Northeast Reg Rep ARS NE — US Agricultural Research Service. Northeastern Region Report. ARS-NE
US Agric Res Serv South Reg Rep — US Agricultural Research Service. Southern Region Report
US Air Force Acad Tech Rep — US Air Force Academy. Technical Report
US Air Force Aeronaut Syst Div Tech Note — United States. Air Force. Aeronautical Systems. Division Technical Note
US Air Force Aeronaut Syst Div Tech Rep — US Air Force. Aeronautical Systems. Division Technical Report
US Air Force Cambridge Res Lab Instrum Pap — United States. Air Force. Cambridge Research Laboratories. Instrumentation Papers
US Air Force Cambridge Res Lab Phy Sci Res Pap — United States. Air Force. Cambridge Research Laboratories. Physical Sciences Research Papers
US Air Force Hum Resour Lab Tech Rep AFHRL-TR — US Air Force. Human Resources Laboratory. Technical Report AFHRL-TR

US Air Force Syst Command Air Force Flight Dyn Lab Tech Rep — United States. Air Force. Systems Command Air Force Flight Dynamics Laboratory.Technical Report
US Air Force Syst Command Air Force Mater Lab Tech Rep AFML — United States. Air Force. Systems Command Air Force Materials Laboratory. Technical Report AFML
US Air Force Syst Command Res Technol Div Tech Doc Rep ASD — United States. Air Force. Systems Command Research and Technology Division. Technical Documentary Report. ASD
US Air Force Tech Doc Rep — United States. Air Force. Technical Documentary Report
US Air Force Tech Doc Rep AFSWC-TDR — US Air Force. Technical Documentary Report. AFSWC-TDR
US Air Force Tech Doc Rep AMRL-TDR — US Air Force. Technical Documentary Report. AMRL-TDR
US Air Force Tech Doc Rep ARL-TDR — US Air Force. Technical Documentary Report. ARL-TDR
US Air Force Tech Doc Rep ASD-TDR — US Air Force. Technical Documentary Report. ASD-TDR
US Air Force Tech Doc Rep RTD-TDR — US Air Force. Technical Documentary Report. RTD-TDR
US Air Force Tech Doc Rep SAM-TDR — US Air Force. Technical Documentary Report. SAM-TDR
US Air Force Tech Doc Rep SEG-TDR — US Air Force. Technical Documentary Report. SEG-TDR
US Air Force WADC Tech Rep — United States. Air Force. Wright Air Development Center. Technical Report
US Air Force Weapons Lab Tech Rep AFWL-TR — United States. Air Force. Weapons Laboratory Technical Report AFWL-TR
US Air Force Wright Air Dev Cent Tech Notes — US Air Force. Wright Air Development Center. Technical Notes
US Air Force Wright Air Dev Cent Tech Rep — US Air Force. Wright Air Development Center. Technical Report
US & Can Av — United States and Canadian Aviation Reports
US & C Avi Rep — United States and Canadian Aviation Reports
US & C Av R — United States and Canadian Aviation Reports
U San Fernando Valley L Rev — University of San Fernando Valley. Law Review
U San Fernando VL Rev — University of San Fernando Valley. Law Review
U San Francisco L Rev — University of San Francisco. Law Review
U San Fran LR — University of San Francisco. Law Review
U San Fran L Rev — University of San Francisco. Law Review
US App (DC) — United States Court of Appeals Reports (District of Columbia)
US-Arab Commer — US-Arab Commerce
US Argonne Nat Lab Biol Med Res Div Semiannu Rep — United States. Argonne National Laboratory. Biological and Medical Research Division. Semiannual Report
US Argonne Natl Lab Rep — US Argonne National Laboratory. Report
US Armed Forces Food Container Inst Libr Bull — United States. Armed Forces Food and Container Institute. Library Bulletin
US Armed Forces Med J — US Armed Forces. Medical Journal
US Armed Forc Med J — United States. Armed Forces Medical Journal
US Army Armament Res Dev Command Tech Rep — US Army. Armament Research and Development Command. Technical Report
US Army Behav Sci Res Lab Tech Res Note — US Army. Behavioral Science Research Laboratory. Technical Research Note
US Army Behav Syst Res Lab Tech Res Note — United States. Army. Behavior and Systems Research Laboratory. Technical Research Note
US Army Behav Syst Res Lab Tech Res Rep — United States. Army. Behavior and Systems Research Laboratory. Technical Research Report
US Army Coastal Eng Res Cent Misc Pap — United States. Army. Coastal Engineering Research Center. Miscellaneous Paper
US Army Coastal Eng Res Cent Tech Memo — US Army. Coastal Engineering Research Center. Technical Memorandum
US Army Corps Eng Cold Reg Res Eng Lab Res Rep — United States. Army Corps of Engineers. Cold Regions Research and Engineering Laboratory [*Hanover, New Hampshire*]. Research Report
US Army Corps Eng Cold Reg Res Eng Lab Tech Rep — United States. Army Corps of Engineers. Cold Regions Research and Engineering Laboratory [*Hanover, New Hampshire*]. Technical Report
US Army Corps Engineers Waterways Expt Sta Misc Paper — United States. Army Corps of Engineers. Waterways Experiment Station. Miscellaneous Paper
US Army Corps Engineers Waterways Expt Sta Tech Rept — United States. Army Corps of Engineers. Waterways Experiment Station. TechnicalReport
US Army Corps of Engineers Comm Tidal Hydraulics Rept — United States. Army Corps of Engineers. Committee on Tidal Hydraulics. Report
US Army Diamond Ord Fuze Lab Tech Rep — US Army. Diamond Ordnance Fuze Laboratories. Technical Report
US Army Diamond Ordnance Fuze Lab Tech Rep — United States. Army. Diamond Ordnance Fuze Laboratories. Technical Report
US Army Eng Waterw Exp Stn Tech Rep — US Army Engineers. Waterways Experiment Station. Technical Report
US Army Med Res Lab Rep — United States. Army. Medical Research Laboratory. Report
US Army Natick Lab Tech Rep Microbiol Ser — US Army. Natick Laboratories. Technical Report. Microbiology Series
USASEW — US Department of Agriculture. Soil Conservation Service. SCS-TP
US Atom Energy Commn Pub — US Atomic Energy Commission. Publication
US Atomic Energy Comm Map Prelim Map — United States. Atomic Energy Commission. Map. Preliminary Map
US Atomic Energy Comm Rept — US Atomic Energy Commission. Report
US Atty Gen Conf Crime Proc — United States Attorney Generals Conference on Crime. Proceedings
USAUD3 — US Air Force Academy. Technical Report
US Auto Ind — Structural Change in the United States Automobile Industry
USB — United States Banker

USB — Uspechi Sovremennoj Biologii

US Banker — United States Banker

US Beach Erosion Board Bull Tech Memo Tech Rept — United States. Beach Erosion Board. Bulletin. Technical Memorandum. Technical Report

USBIA — Uspekhi Sovremennoi Biologii

US Bur Am Ethnology Bull — US Bureau of American Ethnology. Bulletin

US Bur Commer Fish Rep Cal Year — US Bureau of Commercial Fisheries. Report for the Calendar Year

US Bureau Sport Fish Wildl Invest Fish Control — US Bureau of Sport Fisheries and Wildlife. Investigations in Fish Control

USBurEducBul — United States. Bureau of Education. Bulletins

USBurEducCirc — United States. Bureau of Education. Circulars

US Bur Labor Bul — United States. Bureau of Labor Statistics. Bulletins

US Bur Lab Stat Bul — US Bureau of Labor Statistics. Bulletin

US Bur Mines Bull — United States. Bureau of Mines. Bulletin

US Bur Mines Inf Circ — US Bureau of Mines. Information Circular

US Bur Mines Inform Circ — United States. Bureau of Mines. Information Circular

US Bur Mines Miner Yearb — United States. Bureau of Mines. Minerals Yearbook

US Bur Mines New Publ — United States. Bureau of Mines. New Publications Monthly List

US Bur Mines Rep Invest — United States. Bureau of Mines. Report of Investigations

US Bur Mines Rept Inv — US Bureau of Mines. Report of Investigations

US Bur Mines Tech Pa — United States. Bureau of Mines. Technical Paper

US Bur Mines Tech Prog Rep — United States. Bureau of Mines. Technical Progress Report

US Bur Reclam Div Des Dams Br Rep — United States. Department of the Interior. Bureau of Reclamation. Division of Design [*Denver, Colorado*]. Dams Branch Report

US Bur Reclam Eng Monogr — United States. Department of the Interior. Bureau of Reclamation. Engineering Monographs

US Bur Reclam Res Rep — United States. Department of the Interior. Bureau of Reclamation. Research Report

US Bur Reclam Tech Rec Des Constr — United States. Department of the Interior. Bureau of Reclamation. Technical Record of Design and Construction. Dams and Powerplants

US Bur Soils B — US Bureau of Soils. Bulletin

US Bur Sport Fish Wildl Invest Fish Control — United States. Bureau of Sport Fisheries and Wildlife. Investigations in Fish Control

US Bur Sport Fish Wildl Resour Publ — United States. Bureau of Sport Fisheries and Wildlife. Resource Publication

US Bur Sport Fish Wildl Res Rep — US Bureau of Sport Fisheries and Wildlife. Research Report

US Bur Sport Fish Wildl Tech Pap — US Bureau of Sport Fisheries and Wildlife. Technical Papers

US Bur Standards Tech N Bul — US Bureau of Standards. Technical News Bulletin

USCAD — University of Southern California. Abstracts of Dissertations

US Cam — US Camera

US Cath — United States Catholic

US Cath Hist Rec — US Catholic Historical Society. Historical Records and Studies

US Cath Hist Soc Hist Rec — United States Catholic Historical Society. Historical Records

US Cath M — United States Catholic Magazine

US Cath Mag — United States Catholic Magazine

US Cath S — United States Catholic Historical Society. Historical Records and Studies

USCCAN — United States Code Congressional and Administrative News

US Cem Frct — United States Cement Consumption Forecast 1981-86. Market and Economic Research

USCFSTI AD Rep — United States. Clearinghouse for Federal Scientific and Technical Information. AD Reports

USCFSTI PB Rep — United States. Clearinghouse for Federal Scientific and Technical Information. PB Report

USC Govt'l Rev — University of South Carolina. Governmental Review

US Chief Sig Off A Rp — Annual Report of the Chief Signal Officer of the Army to the Secretary of War (US)

US Chil Bur Pub — United States. Children's Bureau. Publications

US China Bus R — US-China Business Review

US Civil Serv Com Ann Rep — US Civil Service Commission. Annual Report

USCM — Usibelli Coal Miner

US Coast and Geod Survey Pub — US Coast and Geodetic Survey. Publication

US Coast Geod Surv Magnetograms Hourly Values MHV — US Department of Commerce. Coast and Geodetic Survey. Magnetograms and Hourly Values MHV

US Coast Geod Sv Bll — United States Coast and Geodetic Survey. Bulletin

US Coast Sv Rp — Reports of the Superintendent of the Coast Survey, showing the Progress of the Survey from Year to Year

US Code Cong & Ad News — United States Code Congressional and Administrative News

US Conf Mayors City Probs — United States Conference of Mayors. City Problems

US Consum Marketing Serv C & MS — US Consumer and Marketing Service. C & MS

USC/SCC — Studies in Comparative Communism. University of Southern California

USDA Agr Econ Rep — US Department of Agriculture. Agricultural Economic Report

USDA Agr Handb — United States. Department of Agriculture. Agricultural Handbook

USDA Bull — United States Department of Agriculture Bulletin

USDA Bur Biol Surv Bull — US Department of Agriculture. Bureau of Biological Survey. Bulletin

USDA Bur Pl Industr Circ — US Department of Agriculture. Bureau of Plant Industry. Circular

USDA Dept Circ — United States Department of Agriculture. Department Circular

USDA Div Forest Bull — United States Department of Agriculture. Division of Forestry Bulletin

USDA Div Veg Pathol Rep Chief Div Veg Pathol — US Department of Agriculture. Division of Vegetable Pathology. Report. Chief ofDivision of Vegetable Pathology

USDA Fert — US Department of Agriculture. Fertilizer Supply

USDA Forest Div Bull — US Department of Agriculture. Forestry Division Bulletin

USDA For Ser Res Bull PNW US Pac Northwest For Range Exp Stn — USDA [*United States Department of Agriculture*]. Forest Service. Resource Bulletin PNW-United States. Pacific Northwest Forest and Range Experiment Station

USDA For Ser Res Pap PSW US Pac Southwest For Range Exp Stn — USDA [*United States Department of Agriculture*]. Forest Service. Research Paper PSW-United States. Pacific Southwest Forest and Range Experiment Station

USDA For Serv Gen Tech Rep INT Intermt For Range Exp Stn — USDA [*United States Department of Agriculture*]. Forest Service. General Technical Report INT-United States. Intermountain Forest and Range Experiment Station

USDA For Serv Gen Tech Rep NC US North Cent For Exp Stn — USDA [*United States Department of Agriculture*]. Forest Service. General Technical Report NC-United States. North Central Forest Experiment Station

USDA For Serv Gen Tech Rep NE NE For Exp Stn — USDA [*United States Department of Agriculture*]. Forest Service. General Technical Report NE-United States. Northeastern Forest Experiment Station

USDA For Serv Gen Tech Rep PSW US Pac Southwest For Exp Stn — USDA [*United States Department of Agriculture*]. Forest Service. General Technical Report PSW-United States. Pacific Southwest Forest and Range ExperimentStation

USDA For Serv Gen Tech Rep SE US Southeast For Exp Stn — USDA [*United States Department of Agriculture*]. Forest Service. General Technical Report SE-United States. Southeastern Forest Experiment Station

USDA For Serv Res Note FPL US For Prod Lab — USDA [*United States Department of Agriculture*]. Forest Service. Research Note FPL-United States. Forest Products Laboratory

USDA For Serv Res Note ITF Inst Trop For — USDA [*United States Department of Agriculture*]. Forest Service. Research Note ITF-United States. Institute of Tropical Forestry

USDA For Serv Res Note NC North Cent For Exp Stn — USDA (US Department of Agriculture) Forest Service Research Note NC. North Central Forest Experiment Station

USDA For Serv Res Note (PNW) — USDA [*United States Department of Agriculture*]. Forest Service. Research Note (Pacific Northwest)

USDA For Serv Res Note PSW US Pac Southwest For Range Exp St — USDA [*United States Department of Agriculture*]. Forest Service. Research Note PSW-United States. Pacific Southwest Forest and Range Experiment Station

USDA For Serv Res Note RM US Rocky Mt For Range Exp Stn — USDA [*United States Department of Agriculture*]. Forest Service. Research Note RM-United States. Rocky Mountain Forest and Range Experiment Station

USDA For Serv Res Note SE US Southeast For Exp Stn — USDA [*United States Department of Agriculture*]. Forest Service. Research Note SE-United States. Southeastern Forest Experiment Station

USDA For Serv Resour Bull NC US North Cent For Exp Stn — USDA [*United States Department of Agriculture*]. Forest Service. Resource Bulletin NC-United States. North Central Forest Experiment Station

USDA For Serv Res Pap INT US Intermt For Range Exp Stn — USDA [*United States Department of Agriculture*]. Forest Service. Research Paper INT-United States. Intermountain Forest and Range Experiment Station

USDA For Serv Res Pap NC US North Cent For Exp Stn — USDA [*United States Department of Agriculture*]. Forest Service. Research Paper NC-United States. North Central Forest Experiment Station

USDA For Serv Res Pap NE US Northeast For Exp Stn — USDA [*United States Department of Agriculture*]. Forest Service. Research Paper NE-United States. Northeastern Forest Experiment Station

USDA For Serv Res Pap (PNW) — USDA [*United States Department of Agriculture*]. Forest Service. Research Paper (Pacific Northwest)

USDA For Serv Res Pap RM US Rocky Mt For Range Exp Stn — USDA [*United States Department of Agriculture*]. Forest Service. Research Paper RM-United States. Rocky Mountain Forest and Range Experiment Station

USDA For Serv Res Pap SO — USDA [*United States Department of Agriculture*]. Forest Service. Research Paper SO

US Daily — United States Daily

USDA Off Exp Sta Exp Sta Rec — US Department of Agriculture. Office of Experiment Stations. Experiment StationRecord

USDA Off Exp Sta Guam Agric Exp Sta Rep — US Department of Agriculture. Office of Experiment Stations. Guam Agricultural Experiment Station. Report

USDA Off Secr Rep — US Department of Agriculture. Office of the Secretary. Report

USDA PA — United States. Department of Agriculture. PA

USDA Prod Res Rep — United States. Department of Agriculture. Production Research Report

USDA Rep Pomol — US Department of Agriculture. Report. Pomologist

US Dep Agric Agric Handb — US Department of Agriculture. Agriculture Handbook

US Dep Agric Agric Inf Bull — US Department of Agriculture. Agriculture Information Bulletin

US Dep Agric Agric Monogr — United States. Department of Agriculture. Agriculture Monograph

US Dep Agric Agric Res Serv ARS Ser — United States. Department of Agriculture. Agricultural Research Service. ARS Series

US Dep Agric Agric Res Serv Rep — United States. Department of Agriculture. Agricultural Research Service. Report

US Dep Agric Agric Res Serv Stat Bull — United States. Department of Agriculture. Agricultural Research Service. Statistical Bulletin

US Dep Agric Bull — United States. Department of Agriculture. Bulletin

US Dep Agric Circ — US Department of Agriculture. Circular

US Dep Agric Conserv Res Rep — US Department of Agriculture. Conservation Research Report

US Dep Agric Farmers' Bull — US Department of Agriculture. Farmers' Bulletin

US Dep Agric For Serv For Prod Lab Rep — United States. Department of Agriculture. Forest Service. Forest Products Laboratory. Report

US Dep Agric For Serv Res Note (PNW) — United States. Department of Agriculture. Forest Service. Research Note (Pacific Northwest)

US Dep Agric For Serv Res Pap NC — United States. Department of Agriculture. Forest Service. Research Note NC

US Dep Agric For Serv Res Pap (PNW) — US Department of Agriculture. Forest Service. Research Paper (Pacific Northwest)

US Dep Agric Home Econ Res Rep — United States. Department of Agriculture. Home Economics Research Report

US Dep Agric Home Gard Bull — US Department of Agriculture. Home and Garden Bulletin

US Dep Agric Index-Cat Med Vet Zool Spec Publ — United States. Department of Agriculture. Index-Catalogue of Medical and Veterinary Zoology. Special Publication

US Dep Agric Index-Cat Med Vet Zool Suppl — United States. Department of Agriculture. Index-Catalogue of Medical and Veterinary Zoology. Supplement

US Dep Agric Leafl — US Department of Agriculture. Leaflet

US Dep Agric Mark Res Rep — United States. Department of Agriculture. Marketing Research Report

US Dep Agric Misc Publ — US Department of Agriculture. Miscellaneous Publications

US Dep Agric Northeast For Exp Stn Stn Pap — United States. Department of Agriculture. Northeastern Forest Experiment Station. Station Paper

US Dep Agric Pat — United States Department of Agriculture Patents

US Dep Agric Plant Inventory — US Department of Agriculture. Plant Inventory

US Dep Agric Prod Res Rep — US Department of Agriculture. Production Research Report

US Dep Agric Res Serv Mark Res Rep — United States. Department of Agriculture. Agricultural Research Service. Marketing Research Report

US Dep Agric Sci Educ Adm Agric Res Man — US Department of Agriculture. Science and Education Administration. Agricultural Research Manual

US Dep Agric Sci Educ Adm Agric Res Results ARR-S — US Department of Agriculture. Science and Education Administration. Agricultural Research Results. ARR-S

US Dep Agric Sci Educ Adm Agric Res Results ARR-W — US Department of Agriculture. Science and Education Administration. Agricultural Research Results. ARR-W

US Dep Agric Sci Educ Adm Bibliogr Lit Agric — US Department of Agriculture. Science and Education Administration. Bibliographies and Literature of Agriculture

US Dep Agric Soil Conserv Ser Soil Surv — United States. Department of Agriculture. Soil Conservation Service. Soil Survey

US Dep Agric Soil Conserv Serv SCS-TP — US Department of Agriculture. Soil Conservation Service. SCS-TP

US Dep Agric Soil Conserv Serv Soil Surv Invest Rep — US Department of Agriculture. Soil Conservation Service. Soil Survey Investigation Report

US Dep Agric Soil Surv — United States. Department of Agriculture. Soil Survey

US Dep Agric Stat Bull — US Department of Agriculture. Statistical Bulletin

US Dep Agric Tech Bull — US Department of Agriculture. Technical Bulletin

US Dep Agric Util Res Rep — United States. Department of Agriculture. Utilization Research Report

US Dep Agric Yearb Agric — US Department of Agriculture. Yearbook of Agriculture

US Dep Commer Natl Bur Stand Tech Note — US Department of Commerce. National Bureau of Standards. Technical Note

US Dep Commer Natl Mar Fish Serv Circ — US Department of Commerce. National Marine Fisheries Service. Circular

US Dep Commer Natl Mar Fish Serv Spec Sci Rep Fish — US Department of Commerce. National Marine Fisheries Service. Special Scientific Report. Fisheries

US Dep Commer Off Tech Serv PB Rep — United States. Department of Commerce. Office of Technical Services. PB Report

US Dep Energy Bartlesville Energy Technol Cent Pet Prod Surv — US Department of Energy. Bartlesville Energy Technology Center. Petroleum Product Surveys

US Dep Energy Bartlesville Energy Technol Cent Publ — US Department of Energy. Bartlesville Energy Technology Center. Publications

US Dep Energy Environ Meas Lab Environ Rep — US Department of Energy. Environmental Measurements Laboratory. Environmental Report

US Dep Energy Indirect Liquefaction Contract Rev Meet — United States. Department of Energy. Indirect Liquefaction Contractors' Review Meeting

US Dep Health Educ Welfare Annu Rep — US Department of Health, Education, and Welfare [*Later, US Department of Health and Human Services*] Annual Report

US Dep Health Educ Welfare DHEW Publ (FDA) — United States. Department of Health, Education, and Welfare. DHEW [*Department of Health, Education, and Welfare*] Publication. (FDA)

US Dep Health Educ Welfare DHEW Publ (NIH) — US Department of Health, Education, and Welfare [*Later, US Department of Health and Human Services*] DHEW Publication (NIH)

US Dep Health Educ Welfare Health Serv Adm Publ HSA — United States. Department of Health, Education, and Welfare. Health Services Administration. Publication HSA

US Dep Health Educ Welfare Natl Inst Ment Health Sci Monogr — US Department of Health, Education, and Welfare. National Institute of Mental Health. Science Monographs

US Dep Health Hum Serv Natl Inst Ment Health Sci Monogr — US Department of Health and Human Services. National Institute of Mental Health. Science Monographs

US Dep Inter Bur Mines New Publ — United States. Department of the Interior. Bureau of Mines. New Publications

US Dep Inter Conserv Yearb — US Department of the Interior. Conservation Yearbook

US Dep Inter Fish Wildl Res Rep — United States. Department of the Interior. Fish and Wildlife Service. Research Report

US Dep Inter MESA Inf Rep — US Department of the Interior. Mining Enforcement and Safety Administration. Informational Report

US Dep Inter Off Libr Serv Bibliogr Ser — United States. Department of the Interior. Office of Library Services. Bibliography Series

US Dep State Bur Public Aff Backgr Notes — United States. Department of State. Bureau of Public Affairs. Background Notes

US Dept Agric Exp St Bul — United States. Department of Agriculture. Experiment Stations. Bulletin

US Dept Agriculture Tech Bull Yearbook — United States. Department of Agriculture. Technical Bulletin. Yearbook

US Dept HEW Publ — US Department of Health, Education, and Welfare [*Later, US Department of Health and Human Services*] Publications

US Dept HHS Publ — US Department of Health and Human Services. Publications

US Dep Transp (Rep) DOT/TST — US Department of Transportation (Report). DOT/TST

USDOE — United States Department of Energy

US Dp Agr B — US Department of Agriculture. Bulletin

US Dp Int — US Department of the Interior. Publication

US Dpt Ag Yearb — Yearbook of the United States Department of Agriculture

USDS — US Department of State Bulletin

USDSB — United States Department of State Bulletin

US Econ P — United States Economic Policies Affecting Industrial Trade

US Econ Rep — US Economic Report

US Econ Res Serv Foreign Agric Econ Rep — US Economic Research Service. Foreign Agricultural Economic Report

US Ec Outlk — US Economic Outlook

Use Engl — Use of English

US Egg — United States Egg and Poultry Magazine

US Energy Res Dev Adm Rep CONF — United States. Energy Research and Development Administration. Report CONF

US Energy Res Dev Adm (Rep) GJO — US Energy Research and Development Administration (Report) GJO

US Environ Prot Agency Control Technol Cent Rep EPA — United States Environmental Protection Agency. Control Technology Center. Report EPA

US Environ Prot Agency Munic Constr Div Rep — United States. Environmental Protection Agency. Municipal Construction Division. Report

US Environ Prot Agency Natl Environ Res Cent Ecol Res Ser — US Environmental Protection Agency. National Environmental Research Center. Ecological Research Series

US Environ Prot Agency Off Air Qual Plann Stand Tech Rep — US Environmental Protection Agency. Office of Air Quality Planning and Standards. Technical Report

US Environ Prot Agency Off Air Waste Manage EPA-450 — US Environmental Protection Agency. Office of Air and Waste Management. EPA-450

US Environ Prot Agency Off Pestic Programs Rep — United States. Environmental Protection Agency. Office of Pesticide Programs. Report

US Environ Prot Agency Off Radiat Programs EPA — US Environmental Protection Agency. Office of Radiation Programs. EPA

US Environ Prot Agency Off Radiat Programs EPA-ORP — US Environmental Protection Agency. Office of Radiation Programs. EPA-ORP

US Environ Prot Agency Off Radiat Programs Tech Rep — United States. Environmental Protection Agency. Office of Radiation Programs. Technical Report

US Environ Prot Agency Off Radiat Programs Tech Rep EPA — U.S. Environmental Protection Agency. Office of Radiation Programs. Technical Report. EPA

US Environ Prot Agency Off Radiat Programs Tech Rep ORP-SID — US Environmental Protection Agency. Office of Radiation Programs. Technical Reports ORP-SID

US Environ Prot Agency Off Res Dev Rep EPA — United States. Environmental Protection Agency. Office of Research and Development. Report EPA

US Environ Prot Agency Off Res Dev Res Rep Ecol Res Ser — US Environmental Protection Agency. Office of Research and Development. Research Reports. Ecological Research Series

US Environ Prot Agency Publ AP Ser — US Environmental Protection Agency. Publication. AP Series

US EPA Ecol Res — US Environmental Protection Agency. Ecological Research

US EPA Envir Health Res — US Environmental Protection Agency. Environmental Health Effects Research

US EPA Envir Monit — United States. Environmental Protection Agency. Environmental Monitoring

US EPA Envir Prot Technol — US Environmental Protection Agency. Environmental Protection Technology

US EPA Socioecon Studies — United States. Environmental Protection Agency. Socioeconomic Environmental Studies

U Serv M — United Service Magazine

US Exec Rep — United States Executive Report

USF — University of Santa Fe

US Fachbuch — U & S [*Urban & Schwarzenberg*] Fachbuch

US Farm — US Farm News

US Fed Pow Com Ann Rep — US Federal Power Commission. Annual Report

US Fed Railroad Adm Rep — US Federal Railroad Administration. Report

US Fish and Wildlife Service Fishery Bull — US Fish and Wildlife Service. Fishery Bulletin

US Fish Com Rp — United States Commission of Fish and Fisheries. Report of the Commissioner

US Fish Wildl Serv Biol Rep — US Fish and Wildlife Service. Biological Report

US Fish Wildl Serv Biol Serv Program FWS-OBS — US Fish and Wildlife Service. Biological Services Program. FWS-OBS

US Fish Wildl Serv Bur Commer Fish Fish Leafl — US Fish and Wildlife Service. Bureau of Commercial Fisheries. Fishery Leaflet

US Fish Wildl Serv Bur Commer Fish Stat Dig — US Fish and Wildlife Service. Bureau of Commercial Fisheries. Statistical Digest

US Fish Wildl Serv Bur Sport Fish Wildl EGL — US Fish and Wildlife Service. Bureau of Sport Fisheries and Wildlife. EGL

US Fish Wildl Serv Circ — US Fish and Wildlife Service. Circular

US Fish Wildl Serv Fish Bull — US Fish and Wildlife Service. Fishery Bulletin

US Fish Wildl Serv Fish Distrib Rep — US Fish and Wildlife Service. Fish Distribution Report

US Fish Wildl Serv Fish Wildl Leafl — US Fish and Wildlife Service. Fish and Wildlife Leaflet

US Fish Wildl Serv FWS-OBS — US Fish and Wildlife Service. Biological Services Program. FWS-OBS

US Fish Wildl Serv Invest Fish Control — US Fish and Wildlife Service. Investigations in Fish Control

US Fish Wildl Serv N Am Fauna — US Fish and Wildlife Service. North American Fauna

US Fish Wildl Serv Resour Publ — US Fish and Wildlife Service. Resource Publication

US Fish Wildl Serv Res Rep — US Fish and Wildlife Service. Research Report

US Fish Wildl Serv Spec Sci Rep Fish — US Fish and Wildlife Service. Special Scientific Report. Fisheries

US Fish Wildl Serv Spec Sci Rep Wildl — US Fish and Wildlife Service. Special Scientific Report. Wildlife

US Fish Wildl Serv Tech Pap — US Fish and Wildlife Service. Technical Papers

US Fish Wildl Serv Wildl Leafl — US Fish and Wildlife Service. Wildlife Leaflet

US Fish Wildl Serv Wildl Res Rep — US Fish and Wildlife Service. Wildlife Research Report

US Fish Wild Serv Fish Bull — US Fish and Wildlife Service. Fishery Bulletin

USFLQ — University of South Florida Language Quarterly

USFLQ — USF Language Quarterly

USFLR — University of San Francisco. Law Review

USF L Rev — University of San Francisco. Law Review

USFOA — Uspekhi Fotoniki

USFODA — US Fish and Wildlife Service. Biological Services Program. FWS-OBS

USFODA — US Fish and Wildlife Service. FWS-OBS

US Food Drug Adm DHEW Publ — United States. Food and Drug Administration. DHEW [*Department of Health, Education, and Welfare*] Publication

US Foreign Agric Serv — US Foreign Agricultural Service

US Forest Serv Agr Hdb — United States. Forest Service. Agriculture Handbooks

US Forest Serv Div Silvics Transl — United States Forest Service. Division of Silvics. Translations

US Forest Serv Res Note — US Forest Service. Research Notes

US Forest Serv Res Paper — US Forest Service. Research Papers

US For Prod Lab Rep — United States. Forest Products Laboratory. Reports

US For Prod Lab Res Note FPL — United States. Forest Products Laboratory. Research Note FPL

US For Prod Lab Tech Notes — United States. Forest Products Laboratory. Technical Notes

US For Serv AIB — US Forest Service. AIB

US For Serv Cent States For Exp Stn Misc Release — United States. Forest Service. Central States Forest Experiment Station. Miscellaneous Release

US For Serv Div State Priv For North Reg Rep — US Forest Service. Division of State and Private Forestry. Northern Region Report

US For Serv For Insect & Dis Leafl — US Forest Service. Forest Insect and Disease Leaflet

US For Serv For Insect & Dis Manage North Reg Rep — US Forest Service. Forest Insect and Disease Management. Northern Region Report

US For Serv For Pest Leafl — US Forest Service. Forest Pest Leaflet

US For Serv For Pest Manage North Reg Rep — US Forest Service. Forest Pest Management. Northern Region Report

US For Serv For Prod Lab Annu Rep — US Forest Service. Forest Products Laboratory. Annual Report

US For Serv For Prod Lab Gen Tech Rep FPL — United States. Forest Service. Forest Products Laboratory. General Technical Report FPL

US For Serv For Resour Rep — United States. Forest Service. Forest Resource Report

US For Serv For Res What's New West — US Forest Service. Forestry Research. What's New in the West

US For Serv Gen Tech Rep INT — US Forest Service. General Technical Report. INT

US For Serv Gen Tech Rep NC — US Forest Service. General Technical Report. NC

US For Serv Gen Tech Rep NE — US Forest Service. General Technical Report. NE

US For Serv Gen Tech Rep PNW — US Forest Service. General Technical Report. PNW

US For Serv Gen Tech Rep PSW — US Forest Service. General Technical Report. PSW

US For Serv Gen Tech Rep RM — US Forest Service. General Technical Report. RM

US For Serv Gen Tech Rep SE — US Forest Service. General Technical Report. SE

US For Serv Gen Tech Rep SO — US Forest Service. General Technical Report. SO

US For Serv Gen Tech Rep WO — US Forest Service. General Technical Report. WO

US For Serv Northeast For Exp Stn Ann Rep — United States. Forest Service. Northeastern Forest Experiment Station. Annual Report

US For Serv Northeast For Exp Stn Annu Rep — US Forest Service. Northeastern Forest Experiment Station. Annual Report

US For Serv Northeast For Exp Stn Stn Pap — United States. Forest Service. Northeastern Forest Experiment Station. Station Paper

US For Serv North Reg Coop For Pest Manage Rep — US Forest Service. Northern Region. Cooperative Forestry and Pest Management Report

US For Serv North Reg For Environ Prot — US Forest Service. Northern Region. Forest Environmental Protection

US For Serv Pac Northwest For Range Experiment Stn Res Notes — United States. Forest Service. Pacific Northwest Forest and Range Experiment Station. Research Notes

US For Serv Pac Northwest For Range Exp Stn Ann Rep — United States. Forest Service. Pacific Northwest Forest and Range Experiment Station. Annual Report

US For Serv Pac Northwest For Range Exp Stn Annu Rep — US Forest Service. Pacific Northwest Forest and Range Experiment Station. Annual Report

US For Serv Pac Northwest For Range Exp Stn Res Pap — United States. Forest Service. Pacific Northwest Forest and Range Experiment Station. Research Paper

US For Serv Pac Northwest For Range Exp Stn Res Pap PNW — US Forest Service. Pacific Northwest Forest and Range Experiment Station. Research Paper PNW

US For Serv Pac Northwest For Range Exp Stn Res Prog — US Forest Service. Pacific Northwest Forest and Range Experiment Station. Research Progress

US For Serv Pac Southwest For Range Exp Stn Misc Pap — United States. Forest Service. Pacific Southwest Forest and Range Experiment Station. Miscellaneous Paper

US For Serv Res Note FPL — US Forest Service. Research Note. FPL

US For Serv Res Note Inst Trop For — United States. Forest Service. Research Note. Institute of Tropical Forestry

US For Serv Res Note INT — US Forest Service. Research Note. INT

US For Serv Res Note Intermt For Range Exp Sta — United States. Forest Service. Research Note. Intermountain Forest and Range Experiment Station

US For Serv Res Note ITF — US Forest Service. Research Note. ITF

US For Serv Res Note NC — US Forest Service. Research Note. NC

US For Serv Res Note NE — US Forest Service. Research Note. NE

US For Serv Res Note Nth Cent For Exp Sta — United States. Forest Service. Research Note. North Central Forest Experiment Station

US For Serv Res Note Ntheast For Exp Sta — United States. Forest Service. Research Note. Northeastern Forest Experiment Station

US For Serv Res Note Nth For Exp Sta — United States. Forest Service. Research Note. Northern Forest Experiment Station

US For Serv Res Note Pacif Nthwest For Range Exp Sta — United States. Forest Service. Research Note. Pacific Northwest Forest and Range Experiment Station

US For Serv Res Note Pacif Sthwest For Range Exp Sta — US Forest Service. Research Note. Pacific Southwest Forest and Range ExperimentStation

US For Serv Res Note PNW — US Forest Service. Research Note. PNW

US For Serv Res Note PSW — US Forest Service. Research Note. PSW

US For Serv Res Note RM — US Forest Service. Research Note. RM

US For Serv Res Note Rocky Mt For Range Exp Sta — US Forest Service. Research Note. Rocky Mountain Forest and Range Experiment Station

US For Serv Res Note SE — US Forest Service. Research Note. SE

US For Serv Res Note SO — US Forest Service. Research Note. SO

US For Serv Res Note Stheast For Exp Sta — US Forest Service. Research Note. Southeastern Forest Experiment Station

US For Serv Res Note Sth For Exp Sta — United States. Forest Service. Research Note. Southern Forest Experiment Station

US For Serv Res Note US For Prod Lab (Madison) — US Forest Service. Research Note. US Forest Products Laboratory (Madison, Wisconsin)

US For Serv Resour Bull INT — US Forest Service. Resource Bulletin. INT

US For Serv Resour Bull NC — US Forest Service. Resource Bulletin. NC

US For Serv Resour Bull NE — US Forest Service. Resource Bulletin. NE

US For Serv Resour Bull PNW — US Forest Service. Resource Bulletin. PNW

US For Serv Resour Bull PSW — US Forest Service. Resource Bulletin. PSW

US For Serv Resour Bull SE — US Forest Service. Resource Bulletin. SE

US For Serv Resour Bull SO — US Forest Service. Resource Bulletin. SO

US For Serv Resource Bull Intermt For Range Exp Sta — United States. Forest Service. Resource Bulletin. Intermountain Forest and Range Experiment Station

US For Serv Resource Bull Nth Cent For Exp Sta — US Forest Service. Resource Bulletin. North Central Forest Experiment Station

US For Serv Resource Bull Ntheast For Exp Sta — US Forest Service. Resource Bulletin. Northeastern Forest Experiment Station

US For Serv Resource Bull Nth For Exp Sta — US Forest Service. Resource Bulletin. Northern Forest Experiment Station

US For Serv Resource Bull Pacif Nthwest For Range Exp Sta — United States. Forest Service. Pacific Northwest Forest and Range Experiment Station. Resource Bulletin

US For Serv Resource Bull Pacif Sthwest For Range Exp Sta — US Forest Service. Resource Bulletin. Pacific Southwest Forest and Range Experiment Station

US For Serv Resource Bull Stheast For Exp Sta — US Forest Service. Resource Bulletin. Southeastern Forest Experiment Station

US For Serv Resource Bull Sth For Exp Sta — US Forest Service. Resource Bulletin. Southern Forest Experiment Station

US For Serv Res Pap FPL — US Forest Service. Research Paper. FPL

US For Serv Res Pap Inst Trop For — US Forest Service. Research Paper. Institute of Tropical Forestry

US For Serv Res Pap INT — US Forest Service. Research Paper. INT

US For Serv Res Pap Intermt For Range Exp Sta — US Forest Service. Research Paper. Intermountain Forest and Range Experiment Station

US For Serv Res Pap ITF — US Forest Service. Research Paper. ITF

US For Serv Res Pap NC — US Forest Service. Research Paper. NC

US For Serv Res Pap NE — US Forest Service. Research Paper. NE

US For Serv Res Pap Nth Cent For Exp Sta — US Forest Service. Research Paper. North Central Forest Experiment Station

US For Serv Res Pap Ntheast For Exp Sta — US Forest Service. Research Paper. Northeastern Forest Experiment Station

US For Serv Res Pap Nth For Exp Sta — United States. Forest Service. Research Paper. Northern Forest Experiment Station

US For Serv Res Pap Pacif Nthwest For Range Exp Sta — US Forest Service. Research Paper. Pacific Northwest Forest and Range Experiment Station

US For Serv Res Pap Pacif Sthwest For Range Exp Sta — US Forest Service. Research Paper. Pacific Southwest Forest and Range Experiment Station

US For Serv Res Pap PNW — US Forest Service. Research Paper. PNW

US For Serv Res Pap PSW — US Forest Service. Research Paper. PSW

US For Serv Res Pap RM — US Forest Service. Research Paper. RM

US For Serv Res Pap Rocky Mt For Range Exp Sta — United States. Forest Service. Research Paper. Rocky Mountain Forest and Range Experiment Station

US For Serv Res Pap SE — US Forest Service. Research Paper. SE

US For Serv Res Pap SO — US Forest Service. Research Paper. SO

US For Serv Res Pap Stheast For Exp Sta — US Forest Service. Research Paper. Southeastern Forest Experiment Station

US For Serv Res Pap Sth For Exp Sta — US Forest Service. Research Paper. Southern Forest Experiment Station

US For Serv Res Pap US For Prod Lab (Madison) — United States. Forest Service. Research Paper. United States Forest Products Laboratory (Madison, Wisconsin)

US For Serv Res Pap WO — US Forest Service. Research Paper. WO

US For Serv Rocky Mount For Range Exp Stn For Sur Release — United States. Forest Service. Rocky Mountain Forest and Range Experiment Station. Forest Survey Release

US For Serv Rocky Mount For Range Exp Stn Res Notes — United States. Forest Service. Rocky Mountain Forest and Range Experiment Station. Research Notes

US For Serv Rocky Mount For Range Exp Stn Stn Pap — United States. Forest Service. Rocky Mountain Forest and Range Experiment Station. Station Paper

US For Serv Southeast For Exp Stn For Surv Release — United States. Forest Service. Southeastern Forest Experiment Station. Forest Survey Release

US For Serv Southeast For Exp Stn Res Notes — United States. Forest Service. Southeastern Forest Experiment Station. ResearchNotes

US For Serv Southeast For Exp Stn Stn Pap — United States. Forest Service. Southeastern Forest Experiment Station. Station Paper

US For Serv South For Exp Stn Annu Rep — US Forest Service. Southern Forest Experiment Station. Annual Report

US For Serv South For Exp Stn For Surv Release — United States. Forest Service. Southern Forest Experiment Station. Forest Survey Release

US For Serv Tech Bull — US Forest Service. Technical Bulletin

US For Serv Tree Plant Notes — US Forest Service. Tree Planters' Notes

USFVL Rev — University of San Fernando Valley. Law Review

USFWSWRR — United States. Fish and Wildlife Service. Wildlife Research Report

USFX — Universidad de San Francisco Xavier [Sucre]

USGA Green Sect Rec — USGA [US Golf Association] Green Section Record

USGA Green Sect Rec US Golf Assoc — USGA Green Section Record. US Golf Association

US Geog G S Rocky Mtn Reg (Powell) — United States Geographical and Geological Survey of the Rocky Mountain Region (Powell)

US Geol S Bul — United States. Geological Survey. Bulletin

US Geol S Professional Pa — United States. Geological Survey. Professional Paper

US Geol Surv Annu Rep — United States. Geological Survey. Annual Report

US Geol Surv Bull — United States. Geological Survey. Bulletin

US Geol Surv Circ — United States. Geological Survey. Circular

US Geol Surv Coal Invest Map — US Geological Survey. Coal Investigations Map

US Geol Survey Bull — United States. Geological Survey. Bulletin

US Geol Survey Circ — US Geological Survey. Circular

US Geol Survey Coal Inv Map — US Geological Survey. Coal Investigations Map

US Geol Survey Geol Quad Map — United States. Geological Survey. Geological Quadrangle Map

US Geol Survey Geol Quadrangle Map — US Geological Survey. Geologic Quadrangle Map

US Geol Survey Geophys Inv Map — US Geological Survey. Geophysical Investigations Map

US Geol Survey Hydrol Inv Atlas — US Geological Survey. Hydrologic Investigations Atlas

US Geol Survey Index Geol Mapping US — US Geological Survey. Index to Geologic Mapping in the United States

US Geol Survey Mineral Inv Field Studies Map — US Geological Survey. Mineral Investigations Field Studies Map

US Geol Survey Mineral Inv Res Map — US Geological Survey. Mineral Investigations Resource Map

US Geol Survey Misc Geol Inv Map — United States. Geological Survey. Miscellaneous Geologic Investigations Map

US Geol Survey Oil and Gas Inv Chart — US Geological Survey. Oil and Gas Investigations Chart

US Geol Survey Oil and Gas Inv Map — United States. Geological Survey. Oil and Gas Investigations Map

US Geol Survey Prof Paper — US Geological Survey. Professional Paper

US Geol Survey Water-Supply Paper — United States. Geological Survey. Water-Supply Paper

US Geol Surv Geol Quadrangle Map — US Geological Survey. Geologic Quadrangle Map

US Geol Surv Geophys Invest Map — US Geological Survey. Geophysical Investigations Map

US Geol Surv Hydrol Invest Atlas — US Geological Survey. Hydrologic Investigations Atlas

US Geol Surv Miner Invest Field Stud Map — United States. Department of the Interior. Geological Survey. Mineral Investigations Field Studies Map

US Geol Surv Misc Field Stud Map — US Geological Survey. Miscellaneous Field Studies Map

US Geol Surv Misc Geol Invest Map — United States. Geological Survey. Miscellaneous Geologic Investigations Map

US Geol Surv Oil Gas Invest Chart — US Geological Survey. Oil and Gas Investigations Chart

US Geol Surv Oil Gas Invest Map — US Geological Survey. Oil and Gas Investigations Map

US Geol Surv Open-File Rep — US Geological Survey. Open-File Report

US Geol Surv Prof Pap — United States. Geological Survey. Professional Paper

US Geol Surv Trace Elem Memo Rep — United States. Geological Survey. Trace Elements Memorandum Report

US Geol Surv Water-Resour Invest — US Geological Survey. Water-Resources Investigations

US Geol Surv Water-Supply Pap — US Geological Survey. Water-Supply Paper

US G Geog S Terr (Hayden) — United States Geological and Geographies Survey of the Territories (Hayden)

US Gl Sv Bll — Bulletin of the United States Geological Survey

US Gl Sv Rp — Annual Report of the United States Geological Survey to the Secretary of the Interior

US Gov Res Dev Rep — US Government Research and Development Reports

US Gov Res Rep — US Government Research Reports

US Govt Paper Spec Std — US Government Paper. Specification Standards

US Govt Res Develop Rept — United States Government Research and Development Reports

US Govt Res Dev Reports — US Government Research and Development Reports

US Govt Res Rept — United States Government Research Report

USGS An Rp PPB W-S P Mon Min Res G Atlas Top Atlas — United States. Geological Survey. Annual Report. Professional Paper. Bulletin. Water-Supply Paper Monograph. Mineral Resources Geology Atlas

USGSB — United States. Geological Survey. Bulletin

USGSC — United States. Geological Survey. Circular

USGSPP — United States. Geological Survey. Professional Paper

USGS Terr — United States Geological Survey of the Territories

US Gym Fed Gym News — United States Gymnastic Federation. Gymnastic News

USHO — US Hydrographic Office

US Hydrog Office Pub — US Hydrographic Office. Publication

USI — Royal United Service Institution of India. Journal

USI — United States Investor

USI — Usine Nouvelle

USIA/PC — Problems of Communism. United States Information Agency

US-IBP Anal Ecosyst Program Interbiome Abstr — US-IBP [International Biological Program] Analyses of Ecosystems Program.Interbiome Abstracts

US-IBP Ecosyst Anal Stud Abstr — US-IBP [International Biological Program] Ecosystem Analysis Studies Abstracts

US-IBP Synth Ser — US-IBP [International Biological Program] Synthesis Series

US Ind Outlk — United States Industrial Outlook

Usine Nouv — Usine Nouvelle

Usine Nouv Ed Suppl — Usine Nouvelle. Edition Supplementaire

Usine Nouv M — Usine Nouvelle. Monthly Edition

Usine Nouv Suppl — Usine Nouvelle. Edition Supplementaire

Using Govt P — Using Government Publications. Volume 2. Finding Statistics and Using Special Techniques

US Inst Text Res Bull — United States Institute for Textile Research. Bulletin

US Interdep Comm Atmos Sci Rep — US Interdepartmental Committee for Atmospheric Sciences. Report

USJ — Uniformed Services Journal

US Joint Publ Res Serv Transl E Eur Agr Forest Food Ind — United States. Joint Publication Research Service. Translations on East European Agriculture, Forestry, and Food Industries

US Jpn Symp Adv Weld Metall — United States-Japan Symposium on Advances in Welding Metallurgy

USKHA — Uspekhi Khimii

Uskor Mosk Inzh-Fiz Inst Sb Statei — Uskoriteli. Moskovskii Inzherno-Fizicheskii Institut. Sbornik Statei

US Law Jour — United States Law Journal

US Law Mag — United States Law Magazine

US Law R — United States Law Review

US Law Rev — United States Law Review

US Lines Paris Rev — United States Lines Paris Review

US Lit Gaz — United States Literary Gazette

USLJ — United States Law Journal

USLL — Utah Studies in Literature and Linguistics

USL Mag — United States Law Magazine

US Long Term — United States Long-Term Review

USLR — United States Law Review

USL Rev — United States Law Review

USLW — United States Law Week

USLW BNA — United States Law Week. Bureau of National Affairs

USM — United Service Magazine

USM — Usine Nouvelle

US Med — US Medicine

USMKA — Uspekhi Mikrobiologii

US Mly Weath Rv — United States of America. Department of Agriculture. Monthly Weather Review and Annual Summary

US Month Law Mag — United States Monthly Law Magazine

US Ms P — Department of the Interior. Proceedings of the United States National Museum

USNASA Conf Publ — United States. National Aeronautics and Space Administration. Conference Publication

US Nation Mus Bul — United States National Museum. Bulletin

US Nation Mus Proc — United States National Museum. Proceedings

US Natl Aeronaut Space Admin Spec Publ — US National Aeronautics and Space Administration. Special Publication

US Natl Bur Stand Handb — US National Bureau of Standards. Handbook

US Natl Bur Stand J Res — United States. National Bureau of Standards. Journal of Research

US Natl Bur Stand J Res Sec A — US National Bureau of Standards. Journal of Research. Section A

US Natl Cancer Inst Carcinog Tech Rep Ser — US National Cancer Institute. Carcinogenesis Technical Report Series

US Natl Clgh Drug Abuse Inf Rep Ser — US National Clearinghouse for Drug Abuse Information. Report Series

US Natl Fert Dev Cent Bull Y — United States National Fertilizer Development Center. Bulletin Y
US Natl Ind Pollut Control Counc Publ — US National Industrial Pollution Control Council. Publications
US Natl Inst Drug Abuse Res Issues — US National Institute on Drug Abuse. Research Issues
US Natl Inst Health Natl Toxicol Program Tech Rep Ser — US National Institutes of Health. National Toxicology Program Technical Report Series
US Natl Inst Health Publ — US National Institutes of Health. Publication
US Natl Lab (Oak Ridge Tenn) Rev — United States National Laboratory (Oak Ridge, Tennessee). Review
US Natl Mar Fish Serv Curr Fish Stat — US National Marine Fisheries Service. Current Fisheries Statistics
US Natl Mar Fish Serv Fish Bull — US National Marine Fisheries Service. Fishery Bulletin
US Natl Mar Fish Serv Fish Facts — US National Marine Fisheries Service. Fishery Facts
US Natl Mar Fish Serv Mar Fish Rev — US National Marine Fisheries Service. Marine Fisheries Review
US Natl Mar Fish Serv Rep Natl Mar Fish Serv — US National Marine Fisheries Service. Report of the National Marine Fisheries Service
US Natl Mar Fish Serv Stat Dig — US National Marine Fisheries Service. Statistical Digest
US Natl Mus Bull — US National Museum. Bulletin
US Natl Mus Bull Proc — United States National Museum. Bulletin. Proceedings
US Natl Oceanic Atmos Adm Environ Data Serv Tech Memo — United States. National Oceanic and Atmospheric Administration. Environmental Data Service. Technical Memorandum
US Natl Oceanic Atmos Adm Key Oceanogr Rec Doc — US National Oceanic and Atmospheric Administration. Key to Oceanographic Records Documentation
US Natl Oceanog Data Center Pub — US National Oceanographic Data Center. Publication
US Natl Park Serv Ecol Serv Bull — US National Park Service. Ecological Services Bulletin
US Natl Park Serv Fauna Natl Parks US Fauna Ser — US National Park Service. Fauna of the National Parks of the United States. Fauna Series
US Natl Park Service Nat History Handb Ser — US National Park Service. Natural History Handbook Series
US Natl Park Serv Natl Cap Reg Sci Rep — US National Park Service. National Capitol Region Scientific Report
US Natl Park Serv Nat Resour Rep — US National Park Service. Natural Resources Report
US Natl Park Serv Occas Pap — US National Park Service. Occasional Paper
US Natl Park Serv Sci Monogr Ser — US National Park Service. Scientific Monograph Series
US Natl Sci Found Res Appl Natl Needs Rep — United States. National Science Foundation. Research Applied to National Needs Report
US Nat Mus Bull — United States National Museum. Bulletin
US Nat Mus Proc — United States National Museum. Proceedings
US Nat Mus Rept — United States National Museum. Reports
US Natn Herb — United States National Herbarium. Contributions
US Nav Aerosp Med Inst (Pensacola) Monogr — US Naval Aerospace Medical Institute (Pensacola). Monograph
US Nav Aerosp Med Inst (Pensacola) NAMI — US Naval Aerospace Medical Institute (Pensacola). NAMI
US Nav Aerosp Med Res Lab (Pensacola) NAMRL — US Naval Aerospace Medical Research Laboratory (Pensacola). NAMRL
US Nav Aerosp Med Res Lab (Pensacola) Spec Rep — US Naval Aerospace Medical Research Laboratory (Pensacola). Special Report
US Nav Air Dev Cent NADC — US Naval Air Development Center. NADC
US Naval Aerospace Med Inst — US Naval Aerospace Medical Institute
US Naval Med Bull — United States Naval Medical Bulletin
US Naval Ordnance Test Sta NAVORD Report — United States. Naval Ordnance Test Station. NAVORD Report
US Naval Res Lab Shock Vib Bull — United States. Naval Research Laboratories. Shock and Vibration Bulletin
US Naval Submar Med Cent Rep — US Naval Submarine Medical Center. Report
US Nav Civ Eng Lab Tech Rep — United States. Department of the Navy. Naval Civil Engineering Laboratory [Port Hueneme, California]. Technical Report
US Nav Inst Proc — US Naval Institute. Proceedings
US Navl Inst Proc — United States Naval Institute. Proceedings
US Navl Med B — US Naval Medical Bulletin
US Nav Med Bull — United States Naval Medical Bulletin
US Nav Med Res Lab Rep — US Naval Medical Research Laboratory. Report
US Nav Oceanogr Off Spec Publ — US Naval Oceanographic Office. Special Publication
US Nav Postgrad Sch Tech Rep/Res Paper — United States. Naval Postgraduate School. Technical Report/Research Paper
US Nav Sch Aviat Med Monogr — US Naval School of Aviation Medicine. Monograph
US Nav Sch Aviat Med Res Rep — US Naval School of Aviation Medicine. Research Report
US Nav Ship Eng Cent Ship Struct Com Rep — United States. Department of the Navy. Naval Ship Engineering Center. Ship Structure Committee. Report
US Nav Ship Res Dev Cent Rep — United States. Naval Ship Research and Development Center. Report
US Nav Submar Med Cent Memo Rep — US Naval Submarine Medical Center. Memorandum Report
US Nav Submar Med Cent Rep — United States. Naval Submarine Medical Center. Report
US Nav Submar Med Res Lab Memo Rep — United States. Naval Submarine Medical Research Laboratory. Memorandum Report
US Nav Submar Med Res Lab Rep — US Naval Submarine Medical Research Laboratory. Report

US Navy Electronics Lab Rept — United States. Navy Electronics Laboratory. Report
US Navy Med — US Navy Medicine
US Navy Med B — United States Navy Medical Bulletin
US News — US News and World Report
US News World R — U.S. News and World Report
US News World Rep — US News and World Report
US N Inst Proc — United States. Naval Institute. Proceedings
USNIP — United States. Naval Institute. Proceedings
US N Mus Bull — United States National Museum Bulletin
USNO ADS — US Naval Observatory Automated Data Service
US North Cent For Exp Stn Res Pap NC — US North Central Forest Experiment Station. Research Paper NC
US NTIS AD Rep — United States. National Technical Information Service. AD Report
US NTIS PB Rep — United States. National Technical Information Service. PB Report
USNWR — US News and World Report
US Oak Ridge Natl Lab Radiat Shield Inf Cent Rep — United States. Oak Ridge National Laboratory. Radiation Shielding Information Center. Report
U So Carol — University of South Carolina. Business and Economic Review
USOE — United States Office of Education. Bulletin
US Office Ed Bul — United States. Office of Education. Bulletin
US Office Ed Circ — United States. Office of Education. Circulars
US Office Ed Pub — United States. Office of Education. Publications
US Office Ed Voc Div Bul — United States. Office of Education. Vocational Division. Bulletin
US Office Saline Water Research and Devel Progress Rept — United States. Office of Saline Water Research and Development. Progress Report
US Off Libr Serv Bibliogr Ser — US Office of Library Service. Bibliography Series
US Off Nav Res Rep ACR — United States. Office of Naval Research. Report ACR
US Off Pub Roads B — US Office of Public Roads. Bulletin
US Off Saline Water Res Dev Prog Rep — United States. Office of Saline Water Research and Development. Progress Report
US Outlook — United States Industrial Outlook
USP — Under the Sign of Pisces
US Pacific RR Expl — US War Department. Pacific Railroad Explorations
US Pac Northwest For Range Exp Stn Res Note PNW — US Pacific Northwest Forest and Range Experiment Station. Research Note PNW
US Pap Maker — United States Paper Maker
US Pat Off Off Gaz US Pat Off Pat — US Patent Office. Official Gazette of the United States Patent Office. Patents
US Pat Q — United States Patent Quarterly
US Pat Quar — United States Patent Quarterly
US Pat Quart — United States Patent Quarterly
US Pat Trademark Off Off Gaz US Pat Trademark Off Pat — US Patent and Trademark Office. Official Gazette of the United States Patent and Trademark Office. Patents
Usp Biol Chim — Uspechi Biologiceskoj Chimii
Usp Biol Khim — Uspekhi Biologicheskoi Khimii
Usp Chim — Uspechi Chimii
Uspehi Fiz Nauk — Akademija Nauk SSSR. Uspehi Fiziceskih Nauk
Uspehi Mat Nauk — Akademija Nauk SSSR i Moskovskoe Matematiceskoe Obscestvo. Uspehi Matematiceskih Nauk
Uspekhi Fiz Nauk — Uspekhi Fizicheskikh Nauk
Uspekhi Mat Nauk — Uspekhi Matematicheskikh Nauk
Usp Fizic N — Uspechi Fiziceskih Nauk
Usp Fiziol Nauk — Uspekhi Fiziologicheskikh Nauk
Usp Fiz Nau — Uspekhi Fizicheskikh Nauk
Usp Fiz Nauk — Uspekhi Fizicheskii Nauk
Usp Foton — Uspekhi Fotoniki
Usp Fotoniki — Uspekhi Fotoniki
US Pharm — US Pharmacist
USPHD5 — US Pharmacist
Usp Kh — Uspekhi Khimii
Usp Khim — Uspekhi Khimii
Usp Khim Fosfororg Seraorg Soedin — Uspekhi Khimii Fosfororganicheskikh i Seraorganicheskikh Soedinenii
Usp Khim Tekhnol Polim — Uspekhi Khimii i Tekhnologii Polimerov
Usp Mat Nauk — Uspekhi Matematicheskikh Nauk
Usp Mikrobiol — Uspekhi Mikrobiologii
Usp Mol Biol — Uspekhi na Molekulyarnata Biologiya
Usp Nauchn Fotogr — Uspekhi Nauchnoi Fotografii
US Polit Sci Doc — United States Political Science Documents
US Posture — United States Military Posture
USPQ BNA — United States Patents Quarterly. Bureau of National Affairs
USP/RA — Revista de Antropologia. Universidade de Sao Paulo. Faculdade de Filosofia, Letras, e Ciencias Humanas e Associacao de Antropologia
USPSD — United States Political Science Documents
Usp Sovrem Biol — Uspekhi Sovremennoi Biologii
Usp Sovrem Genet — Uspekhi Sovremennoi Genetiki
US Publ H Rep — US Public Health Report
US Public Health Serv Public Health Monogr — United States. Public Health Service. Public Health Monograph
US Public Health Serv Radiol Health Data Rep — US Public Health Service. Radiological Health Data and Reports
USQ — United States Quarterly Book Review
USQB — United States Quarterly Book Review
US Q Bk R — United States Quarterly Book Review
USQBL — United States Quarterly Book List
USQBR — United States Quarterly Book Review
USQR — Union Seminary. Quarterly Review
US Quartermaster Food Container Inst Armed Forces Libr Bull — US Quartermaster Food and Container Institute for the Armed Forces. Library Bulletin

USR — Union Seminary. Review

US Res Developm Rep — United States Government Research and Development Reports

USRFP — US Requests for Proposals

US Sci Educ Adm Agric Res Man — US Science and Education Administration. Agricultural Research Manual

USSE — University of Saga. Studies in English

US Sec Ag Rp — Report of the Secretary of Agriculture

US Seed Rep — United States Seed Reporter

US Serv M — United States Service Magazine

USSGA — Uspekhi Sovremennoi Genetiki

US Ship Struct Com Rep — United States. Ship Structure Committee. Report

US Sig Serv Pp — United States of America. War Department. Professional Papers of the Signal Service

US Soil Conserv Service Sedimentation Bull (TP) — United States. Soil Conservation Service. Sedimentation Bulletin (Technical Publication)

US Soil Conserv Serv Soil Surv — US Soil Conservation Service. Soil Survey

USSR Comp Info B — USSR. Union of Composers. Information Bulletin

USSR Computational Math and Math Phys — USSR Computational Mathematics and Mathematical Physics

USSR Comput Math and Math Phys — USSR Computational Mathematics and Mathematical Physics

USSR Comput Math Math Phys — USSR Computational Mathematics and Mathematical Physics

USSR Kom Delam Izobret Otkrytiya Izobret — Union of Soviet Socialist Republics, Komitet po Delam Izobretenii i Otkrytii, Otkrytiya, Izobreteniya

USSR Rep Earth Sci — USSR Report. Earth Sciences

USSR Rep Eng Equip — USSR Report. Engineering Equipment

US Steel News — United States Steel News

US Surg Gen Off Bul — United States. Surgeon-General's Office. Bulletin

UST — Universidad de Santo Tomas

U-Stadtbibliothek — Universitaets- und Stadtbibliothek

US Tariff Comm Rep — United States. Tariff Commission. Reports

US Tariff Comm TC Publ — United States. Tariff Commission. TC Publication

Ustav Jad Fyz Cesk Akad Ved Rep — Ustav Jaderne Fyziky Ceskoslovenska Akademia Ved. Report

Ustav Vedeckotech Inf Sb UVTI Genet Slechteni — Ustav Vedeckotechnickych Informaci. Sbornik UVTI.Genetika a Slechteni

Ustav Vedeckotech Inf Sb UVTI Melior — Ustav Vedeckotechnickych Informaci. Sbornik UVTI.Rada. Meliorace

Ustav Vedeckotech Inf Zemed — Ustav Vedeckotechnickych Informaci pro Zemedelstvi

Ustav Vedeckotech Inf Zemed Sb UVTIZ Melior — Ustav Vedeckotechnickych Informaci pro Zemedelstvi. Sbornik UVTIZ. Rada. Meliorace

Ustav Vedeckotech Inf Zemed Stud Inf Ochr Rostl — Ustav Vedeckotechnickych Informaci pro Zemedelstvi Studijni Informace Ochrana Rostlin

Ustav Vyzk Vyuziti Paliv Monogr — Ustav pro Vyzkum a Vyuziti Paliv Monografie

US Tax Cas CCH — US Tax Cases. Commerce Clearing House

US Tax Rpt — United States Tax Report

US Tb — U & S [*Urban & Schwarzenberg*] Taschenbuecher

USTC Jl BG — United States Tobacco and Candy Journal Buyer's Guide

USTC Jrl — United States Tobacco and Candy Journal

U St G — Umsatzsteuergesetz

USTJ — United States Tobacco Journal

UST J Grad Res — UST. Journal of Graduate Research

U St Rd — Umsatzsteuer-Rundschau

Ust Ved Inf MZLVH Rostl Vyroba — Ustav Vedeckotechnickych Informaci. Ministerstva Zemedelstvi. Lesniho a VodnihoHospodarstvi. Rostlinna Vyroba

Ust Ved Inf MZLVH Stud Inf Pudoz — Ustav Vedeckotechnickych Informaci. MZLVH [*Ministerstva Zemedelstvi. Lesnihoa Vodnlho Hospodarstvi*] Studijni Informace Pudoznalstvi a Meliorace

Ust Ved Inf MZ Rostl Vyroba — Ustav Vedeckotechnickych Informaci. Ministerstva Zemedelstvi. Rostlinna Vyroba

Ust Ved Inf MZVZ Rostl Vyroba — Ustav Vedeckotechnickych Informaci. Ministerstva Zemedelstvi a Vyzivy. Rostlinna Vyroba

USUMS — Utah State University. Monograph Series

USV — Universitas 2000 (Venezuela)

US Vet Bur M Bull — US Veteran's Bureau. Medical Bulletin

US Veterans Adm (W) Dep Med Surg Bull Prosthet Res — United States. Veterans Administration (Washington, DC). Department of Medicineand Surgery. Bulletin of Prosthetics Research

US Veterans Bureau Med Bull — United States. Veterans Bureau. Medical Bulletin

US Veterans Bur Med Bul — United States Veterans' Bureau. Medical Bulletin

USW — Universitaets-Seminar fuer Wirtschaft

US War Dp Chief Eng An Rp — United States. War Department. Chief of Engineers. Annual Report

US Waterw Exp Stn Contract Rep — United States. Waterways Experiment Station. Contract Report

US Waterw Exp Stn Misc Pap — United States. Waterways Experiment Station. Miscellaneous Paper

US Waterw Exp Stn Res Rep — United States. Waterways Experiment Station. Research Report

US Waterw Exp Stn Tech Rep — United States. Waterways Experiment Station. Technical Report

US Waterw Exp Stn (Vicksburg Miss) Misc Pap — United States. Waterways Experiment Station (Vicksburg, Mississippi). Miscellaneous Paper

US Waterw Exp Stn (Vicksburg Miss) Res Rep — United States. Waterways Experiment Station (Vicksburg, Mississippi). Research Report

US Waterw Exp Stn (Vicksburg Miss) Tech Rep — United States. Waterways Experiment Station (Vicksburg, Mississippi). TechnicalReport

US Weath Bur Bll — US Department of Agriculture. Weather Bureau. Bulletin

US Weath Bur Rp — US Department of Agriculture. Weather Bureau. Report of the Chief of the Weather Bureau

US Women's Bur Bul — United States. Women's Bureau. Bulletin

UT — Ugaritic Text

UT — Unser Tsait/Unzer Tsayt

UT — Utah Music Educator

UT — UT - Udenrigsministeriets Tidsskrift

Utah — Utah Reports

Utah Acad Sci Proc — Utah Academy of Sciences, Arts, and Letters. Proceedings

Utah Ac Sc Tr — Utah Academy of Sciences. Transactions

Utah Admin Bull — State of Utah Bulletin

Utah Admin R — Administrative Rules of the State of Utah

Utah Ag Exp — Utah. Agricultural Experiment Station. Publications

Utah Agric Exp Sta Bull — Utah Agricultural College. Agricultural Experiment Station. Bulletin

Utah Agric Exp Stn Bull — Utah. Agricultural Experiment Station. Bulletin

Utah Agric Exp Stn Circ — Utah. Agricultural Experiment Station. Circular

Utah Agric Exp Stn Res Rep — Utah. Agricultural Experiment Station. Research Report

Utah Agric Exp Stn Spec Rep — Utah. Agricultural Experiment Station. Special Report

Utah Agric Exp Stn Utah Resour Ser — Utah. Agricultural Experiment Station. Utah Resources Series

Utah Bar Bull — Utah Bar Bulletin

Utah B Bul — Utah Bar Bulletin

Utah B Bull — Utah Bar Bulletin

Utah BJ — Utah Bar Journal

Utah Bull — State of Utah Bulletin

Utah Code Ann — Utah Code Annotated

Utah Dep Nat Resour Tech Publ — Utah. Department of Natural Resources. Technical Publication

Utah Dep Nat Resour Water Cir — Utah. Department of Natural Resources. Water Circular

Utah Dept Nat Resources Tech Pub — Utah. Department of Natural Resources. Division of Water Rights. Technical Publication

Utah Div Water Resources Coop Inv Rept — Utah. Division of Water Resources. Cooperative Investigations Report

Utah Econ and Bus R — Utah Economic and Business Review

Utah Eng Exp Stn Bull — Utah. Engineering Experiment Station. Bulletin

Utah Farm Home Sci — Utah Farm and Home Science

Utah Geneal And Hist Mag — Utah Genealogical and Historical Magazine. Genealogical Society of Utah

Utah Geol — Utah Geology

Utah Geol and Mineralog Survey Bull — Utah. Geological and Mineralogical Survey. Bulletin

Utah Geol and Mineralog Survey Circ — Utah. Geological and Mineralogical Survey. Circular

Utah Geol and Mineralog Survey Quart Rev — Utah. Geological and Mineralogical Survey. Quarterly Review

Utah Geol and Mineralog Survey Spec Studies — Utah. Geological and Mineralogical Survey. Special Studies

Utah Geol and Mineralog Survey Water Resources Bull — Utah. Geological and Mineralogical Survey. Water Resources Bulletin

Utah Geol Assoc Publ — Utah Geological Association. Publication

Utah Geol Mineral Surv Bull — Utah. Geological and Mineralogical Survey. Bulletin

Utah Geol Mineral Surv Circ — Utah. Geological and Mineralogical Survey. Circular

Utah Geol Mineral Surv Spec Stud — Utah. Geological and Mineralogical Survey. Special Studies

Utah Geol Mineral Surv Water Resour Bull — Utah. Geological and Mineralogical Survey. Water Resources Bulletin

Utah Geol Miner Surv Circ — Utah. Geological and Mineralogical Survey. Circular

Utah Geol Miner Surv Q Rev — Utah. Geological and Mineralogical Survey. Quarterly Review

Utah Geol Miner Surv Surv Notes — Utah. Geological and Mineralogical Survey. Survey Notes

Utah Geol Soc Guidebook to Geology of Utah — Utah Geological Society. Guidebook to the Geology of Utah

Utah Hist Q — Utah Historical Quarterly

Utah Hist Quar — Utah Historical Quarterly

Utah Hist Quart — Utah Historical Quarterly

Utah IC Bull — Utah Industrial Commission. Bulletin

Utah Laws — Laws of Utah

Utah Lib — Utah Libraries

Utah Lib Assn Newsl — Utah Library Association. Newsletter

Utah Libr — Utah Libraries

Utah LR — Utah Law Review

Utah L Rev — Utah Law Review

Utah M — Utah Genealogical and Historical Magazine

Utah Med Bull — Utah Medical Bulletin

Utah Resour Ser Utah Agr Exp Sta — Utah Resources Series. Utah Agricultural Experiment Station

Utah Sci — Utah Science

Utah Sci Utah Agric Exp Stn — Utah Science. Utah Agricultural Experiment Station

Utah State Engineer Bienn Rept Tech Pub — Utah State Engineer. Biennial Report. Technical Publications

Utah State Engineer Inf Bull — Utah State Engineer. Information Bulletin

Utah State Eng Off Basic Data Rep — Utah. State Engineer's Office. Basic Data Report

Utah State Eng Tech Publ — Utah State Engineer. Technical Publication

Utah State Med J — Utah State Medical Journal

Utah State Univ Agric Exp Stn Bull — Utah State University. Agricultural Experiment Station. Bulletin

Utah St B Proc — Utah State Bar. Proceedings

Utah Univ Anthropol Papers Bull — Utah University. Anthropological Papers. Bulletin

Utah Univ Eng Exp Stn Tech Pap — Utah University. Engineering Experiment Station. Technical Paper

Utah Univ Eng Expt Sta Bull — Utah University. Engineering Experiment Station. Bulletin
U Tas LR — University of Tasmania. Law Review
U Tasmania L Rev — University of Tasmania. Law Review
U Tasm L Rev — University of Tasmania. Law Review
UTB — Universitaets-Taschenbuecher
UT BJ — Utah Bar Journal
UTCEU — Universidad de Tucuman. Cuadernos de Extension Universitaria
UTD — Kermisgids
UTDEMS — University of Tulsa. Department of English. Monograph Series
U Tech Umweltmag — U das Technische Umweltmagazin
UTEPDF — University of Tasmania. Environmental Studies Occasional Paper
UTET Boll Ed — UTET [*Unione Tipigrafico-Editrice Torinese*] Bollettino Editoriale
U T Fac L Rev — University of Toronto. Faculty of Law. Review
UT Faculty LR — Faculty of Law Review. University of Toronto
UTFS — University of Toronto. French Series
UtH — Utah Historical Quarterly
UTHS — University of Texas. Hispanic Studies
Utilitas Math — Utilitas Mathematica
Util L Rep CCH — Utilities Law Reports. Commerce Clearing House
Util Rep R8 UR US Dep Agric Forest Serv Coop For — Utilization Report R8-UR. United States Department of Agriculture. Forest Service. Cooperative Forestry
UTLJ — University of Toronto. Law Journal
UTLR — University of Tasmania. Law Review
UT LR — Utah Law Review
UTO — University of Toronto Quarterly
U Toledo Intra LR — University of Toledo. Intramural Law Review
U Toledo L Rev — University of Toledo. Law Review
U Tol Law — University of Toledo. Law Review
U Tol LR — University of Toledo. Law Review
U Tol L Rev — University of Toledo. Law Review
Utopian E — Utopian Eyes
U Tor Fac LR — University of Toronto. Faculty of Law. Review
U Tor Law J — University of Toronto. Law Journal
U Tor LJ — University of Toronto. Law Journal
U Tor L Rev — University of Toronto. School of Law. Review
U Toronto Fac L Rev — University of Toronto. Faculty of Law. Review
U Toronto Faculty L Rev — University of Toronto. Faculty of Law. Review
U Toronto L J — University of Toronto. Law Journal
U Toronto Q — University of Toronto. Quarterly
UTPLF — Universita di Torino. Pubblicazioni della Facolta di Lettere e Filosofia
UTQ — University of Toronto. Quarterly
UTQA — Uutuqtwa. Bristol Bay High School
UT R — University of Tampa. Review
Utr A Ac — Annales Academiae Rheno-Trajectinae. Trajecti ad Rhenum (Utrecht)
Utr Aant Prv Gn — Aanteekeningen van het Verhandelde in de Sectie-Vergaderingen van het Provinciaal Utrechtsch Genootschap van Kunsten en Wetenschappen
Utredn Norsk Tretekn Inst — Utredning. Norsk Treteknisk Institutt
Utr Micropaleontol Bull — Utrecht Micropaleontological Bulletins
Utr Micropaleontol Bull Spec Publ — Utrecht Micropaleontological Bulletins. Special Publication
Utro Ros — Utro Rossu
Utr Oz — Scheilkundige Onderzoekingen, gedaan in het Physiologisch Laboratorium der Utrechtsche Hoogeschool
Utr Prv Gn Aant — Aanteekeningen van het Verhandelde in de Sectie-Vergaderingen van het Provinciaal Utrechtsch Genootschap van Kunsten en Wetenschappen
Utr Scheik Oz — Scheilkundige Onderzoekingen, gedaan in het Physiologisch Laboratorium der Utrechtsche Hoogeschool
UTS — Union Theological Seminary
UTSCB — Utah Science
UTSE — University of Texas. Studies in English
UTSH — University of Tennessee. Studies in the Humanities
Uttar Pradesh Dir Geol Min Monogr — Uttar Pradesh. Directorate of Geology and Mining. Monograph
Uttar Pradesh J Zool — Uttar Pradesh Journal of Zoology
Uttar Pradesh State Dent J — Uttar Pradesh State Dental Journal
UTTBA — Bulletin. International Union Against Tuberculosis
UTVS — Ucebni Texty Vysokych Skol
UUA — Uppsala Universitets Arsskrift
UU/PS — Peasant Studies. University of Utah. Department of History
UUW — Unitarian Universalist World
UU/WPQ — Western Political Quarterly. University of Utah
UVL — Untersuchungen zur Vergleichenden Literatur
UVM — University of Virginia. Magazine
UVMag — University of Virginia. Magazine
UVP Abfallwirtsch Plan Wassertech Semin — UVP in der Abfallwirtschaftlichen Planung. Wassertechnisches Seminar
UV Spectrom Group Bull — UV Spectrometry Group. Bulletin
UW — Us Wurk
UWALR — University of Western Australia. Law Review
UWAL Rev — University of Western Australia. Law Review
U Wash L Rev — University of Washington. Law Review
UW Austl L Rev — University of Western Australia. Law Review
UWCCARG — University of Washington. Contributions. Cloud and Aerosol Research Group
UWCCPGR — University of Washington. Contributions. Cloud Physics Group. Collections from Reprints
UWCETG — University of Washington. Contributions. Energy Transfer Group. Collections from Reprints
UWD — UWD [*Umweltschutz-Dienst*] Informationsdienst fuer Umweltfragen
U West Aust Ann L Rev — University of Western Australia. Annual Law Review
U Western Aust Ann L Rev — University of Western Australia. Annual Law Review
U Western Aust L Rev — University of Western Australia. Law Review

U Western Ont L Rev — University of Western Ontario. Law Review
U West LA L Rev — University of West Los Angeles. Law Review
U West Los Angeles L Rev — University of West Los Angeles. Law Review
UWI/CQ — Caribbean Quarterly. University of the West Indies
UWI/JCH — Journal of Caribbean History. University of the West Indies. Department of History and Caribbean Universities Press
U Windsor L Rev — University of Windsor. Law Review
UWIR — University of Windsor Review
UWI/SES — Social and Economic Studies. University of the West Indies. Institute of Socialand Economic Research
UWLA LR — University of West Los Angeles. Law Review
UWLA L Rev — University of West Los Angeles. Law Review
UWLA Rev — University of West Los Angeles. School of Law. Law Review
UWOL Rev — University of Western Ontario. Law Review
UWOMA6 — University of Western Ontario. Medical Journal
UWO Med J — UWO [*University of Western Ontario*] Medical Journal
UW Ont L Rev — University of Western Ontario. Law Review
UWOPGS — University of Warwick. Occasional Papers in German Studies
UWO (Univ West Ont) Med J — UWO (University of Western Ontario) Medical Journal
UWPA — University of Washington Publications in Anthropology
UWPFAO — University of Washington. Publications in Fisheries. New Series
UWPLL — University of Washington. Publications in Language and Literature
UWR — University of Windsor. Review
UWRFAY — Research in Fisheries. Annual Report. School of Fisheries. University of Washington
UWT — Umschau in Wissenschaft und Technik
UWTCA — Umschau in Wissenschaft und Technik
Uyemury Tech Rep — Uyemura Technical Reports
UY/R — Revista. Universidad de Yucatan
UZ — Unteroffizierzeitung
UZ — Ustredna Zidov
U Zambia LB — University of Zambia. Law Bulletin
UZAPI — Uchenye Zapiski. Alma-Atinskii Pedagogicheskii Institut
UZAstPI — Ucenye Zapiski Astrachanskogo Gosudarstvennogo Pedagogiceskogo Instituta
UZAU — Uchenye Zapiski. Azberbaidzhanskii Universitet
UZAzPI — Ucenye Zapiski Pedagogiceskogo Instituta Jazykov Imeni M. F. Achundova. Serija Filologiceskaja
UZAzU — Ucenye Zapiski Azerbajdzanskogo Gosudarstvennogo Universiteta Imeni S. M. Kirova. Jazyk i Literatura
UZBasU — Ucenye Zapiski Baskirskogo Gosudarstvennogo Universiteta. Serija Filologiceskich Nauk
Uzb Biol Zh — Uzbekskii Biologicheskii Zhurnal
Uzbek Biol Zh — Uzbekskii Biologicheskii Zhurnal
Uzbek Geol Zh — Uzbekskii Geologicheskii Zhurnal
Uzbek Iztim Fanlar — Uzbekiztonda Iztimoii Fanlar
Uzbek Khim Zh — Uzbekskii Khimicheskii Zhurnal
Uzbek Mat Zh — Uzbekskii Matematicheskii Zhurnal
Uzbeksk Biol Zurn — Uzbekskij Biologiceskij Zurnal
Uzb Fiz Zh — Uzbekskii Fizicheskii Zhurnal
Uzb Khim Zh — Uzbekskii Khimicheskii Zhurnal
UZBurPI — Ucenye Zapiski Burjatskogo Gosudarstvennogo Pedagogiceskogo Instituta Imeni Dorzi Banzarova. Istoriko-Filologiceskaja Serija. Ulan-Ude
UZBZA — Uzbekskii Biologiceskii Zhurnal
UZCerepPI — Ucenye Zapiski Cerepoveckogo Gosudarstvennogo Pedagogiceskogo Instituta
UZChabPI — Ucenye Zapiski Chabarovskogo Gosudarstvennogo Pedagogiceskogo Instituta
UZChakNII — Ucenye Zapiski Chakasskogo Naucno-Issledovatel'skogo Instituta Jazyka, Literatury, i Istorii
UZCharU — Ucenye Zapiski Charkovskogo Universiteta Imeni A. M. Gorkogo Trudy Filologiceskogo Fakult'teta
UZCIngPI — Ucenye Zapiski Ceceno-Ingusskogo Pedagogiceskogo Instituta. Serija Filolo Giceskaja
UZCuvNII — Ucenye Zapiski Naucno-Issledovatel'skogo Instituta Jazyka, Literatury, Istorii,i Ekonomiki Pri Sovete Ministrov Cuvasskoj ASSR
UZDag — Ucenye Zapiski Dagestanskogo Filiala Akademii Nauk SSSR. Serija Filologiceskaja
UZDagU — Ucenye Zapiski Dagestanskogo Gosudarstvennogo Universiteta. Serija Filologiceskaja
UZDalU — Ucenye Zapiski Dal'nevostocnogo Universiteta. Serija Filologiceskaja
UZDusPI — Ucenye Zapiski Dusanbinskogo Gosudarstvennogo Pedagogiceskogo Instituta Imeni T. G. Sevcenko Filologiceskaja Serija
UZEIPI — Ucenye Zapiski Elabuzskogo Gosudarstvennogo Pedagogiceskogo Instituta. Serija Istorii i Filologii
UZEnPI — Ucenye Zapiski Enisejskogo Gosudarstvennogo Pedagogiceskogo Instituta Kafedra Russkogo Jazyka
UZErevU — Ucenye Zapiski Erevanskogo Gosudarstvennogo Universiteta. Serija Filologiceskich Nauk
UZEV — Universidad de Zaragosa
UZGIYa — Ucenye Zapiski Gor'kovskii Pedagogicheskii Institut Inostrannykh Yazykov
UZGorPI — Ucenye Zapiski Gor'kovskogo Gosudarstvennogo Pedagogiceskogo Instituta Imeni M.Gor'kogo. Serija Filologiceskaja
UZGorPIIJa — Ucenye Zapiski Gor'kovskogo Pedagogiceskogo Instituta Inostrannych Jazykov
UZGorU — Ucenye Zapiski Gor'kovskogo Universiteta Imeni N. I. Lobacevskogo. Serija Istoriko-Filologiceskaja
UZGPI — Ucenye Zapiski Gor'kovskii Gosudarstvennyi Pedagogicheskii Institut
UZGurPI — Ucenye Zapiski Gur'evskogo Gosudarstvennogo Pedagogiceskogo Instituta. Serija Istoriko-Filologiceskaja
UZGZA — Uzbekskii Geologiceskii Zhurnal
UZII — Ucenye Zapiski Instituta Istorii
UZIIIL — Uchenye Zapiski Instituta Istorii Izayka i Literatury Imena Cadasy

UZIMach — Ucenye Zapiski Instituta Istorii, Jazyka, i Literatury Imeni G. Cadasy. Serija Filologiceskaja. Machackala

UZIMO — Ucenye Zapiski Institut Mezdunarodnych Otnosenij

UZIPI — Ucenye Zapiski Irkutskii Pedagogicheskii Institut

UZIrkutPI — Ucenye Zapiski Irkutskogo Gosudarstvennogo Pedagogiceskogo Instituta Inostrannych Jazykov

UZISL — Ucenye Zapiski Instituta Slavjanovedenija

UZIV — Ucenye Zapiski Instituta Vostokovedenija Akademija Nauk SSSR

UZIVAz — Ucenye Zapiski Instituta Vostokovedenija Akademii Nauk Azerbajdzanskoj SSSR

UZKa — Ucenye Zapiski Kalininskii Gosudarstvennyi Pedagogicheskii Institut

UZKalinPI — Ucenye Zapiski Kalininskogo Pedagogiceskogo Instituta Imeni M. I. Kalinina. Serija Filologiceskaja

UZKalPI — Ucenye Zapiski Kaluzskogo Gosudarstvennogo Pedagogiceskogo Instituta

UZKaragPI — Ucenye Zapiski Karagandinskogo Pedagogiceskogo Instituta Filologiceskie Nauki

UZKarelPI — Ucenye Zapiski Karel'skogo Pedagogiceskogo Instituta

UZKarPI — Ucenye Zapiski Karsinskogo Gosudarstvennogo Pedagogiceskogo Instituta. Filologiceskaja Serija

UZKazanU — Ucenye Zapiski Kazanskogo Universiteta Imeni V. I. Ul'janova'lenina

UZKBI — Ucenye Zapiski Kabardino-Balkarskij Naucno-Issledovatel'skij Institut pri Sovete Ministrov Kbassr

UZKemPI — Ucenye Zapiski Kemerovskogo Gosudarstvennogo Pedagogiceskogo Instituta

UZKGPI — Ucenye Zapiski Kujbysevskogo Gosudarstvennogo Pedagogiceskogo Instituta Imeni V. V. Kujbyseva

UZKi — Ucenye Zapiski Kishinevskii Universitet

UZKirovPI — Ucenye Zapiski Kirovabadskogo Pedagogiceskogo Instituta

UZKisU — Ucenye Zapiski Kisinevskogo Gosudarstvennogo Universiteta

UZKokPI — Ucenye Zapiski Kokandskogo Pedagogiceskogo Instituta Imeni Mukimi. Serija Filologiceskaja

UZKolPI — Ucenye Zapiski Kolomenskogo Gosudarstvennogo Pedagogiceskogo Instituta Istoriko-Filologiceskij Fakul'tet Kafedry Russkogo Jazyka

UZKomPI — Ucenye Zapiski Komi Gosudarstvennogo Pedagogiceskogo Instituta Kafedra Russkogo Jazyka

UZKr — Ucenye Zapiski Krasnodarskii Pedagogicheskii Institut

UZKU — Uchenye Zapiski. Kazakhskii Universitet

UZKujPI — Ucenye Zapiski Kujbysevskogo Gosudarstvennogo Pedagogiceskogo Instituta Imeni V. V. Kujbyseva

UZKVA — Uchenye Zapiski Kazanskogo Veterinarnogo Instituta

UZKZA — Uzbekskii Khimicheskii Zhurnal

UZLa — Ucenye Zapiski Latviiskii Gosudarstvennyi Universitet

UZLenPI — Ucenye Zapiski Leningradskogo Pedagogiceskogo Instituta Imeni S. M. Kirova

UZLGPI — Uchenye Zapiski. Leningradskii Gosudarstvennii Pedagogicheskii Institut imeni A. I. Gercena

UZLPedI — Ucenye Zapiski Leningradskogo Pedagogiceskogo Instituta Imeni A. I. Gercena

UZLPI — Ucenye Zapiski Leningradskogo Pedagogiceskogo Instituta Imeni A. I. Gercena

UZLPI — Uchenye Zapiski. Leningradskii Pedagogiceskii Institut. Istoricheskii Fakultet

UZLU — Ucenye Zapiski Leningradskogo Gosudarstvennogo Ordena Lenina Universiteta ImeniA. A. Zdanova

UZLU-FN — Ucenye Zapiski Leningradskogo Universiteta. Serija Filologiceskikh Nauk

UZI'VovU — Ucenye Zapiski l'Vovskogo Gosudarstvennogo Universiteta

UZMagPI — Ucenye Zapiski Magnitorskogo Gosudarstvennogo Pedagogiceskogo Instituta

UZMIK — Ucenye Zapiski Moskovskii Gosudarstvennyi Institut Kul'tury

UZMKrup — Ucenye Zapiski Moskovskogo Oblastnogo Pedagogiceskogo Instituta Imeni N. K. Krupskoj

UZMOPI — Ucenye Zapiski Moskovski Oblastnoi Pedagogicheskii Institut Imeni N. K. Krupskoi

UZMorU — Ucenye Zapiski Mordovskogo Universiteta. Serija Filologiceskich Nauk

UZMPedI — Ucenye Zapiski Moskovskogo Gosudarstvennogo Pedagogiceskogo Instituta

UZMPI — Ucenye Zapiski Moskovskii Gosudarstvennyi Pedagogicheskii Institut Imeni Lenina

UZMPI — Ucenye Zapiski Moskovskogo Gosudarstvennogo Pedagogiceskogo Instituta Imeni Potemkina

UZMPIIJa — Ucenye Zapiski Moskovskogo Gosudarstvennogo Pedagogiceskogo Instituta Inostrannych Jazykov

UZMU — Ucenye Zapiski Moskovskogo Universiteta

UZNovPI — Ucenye Zapiski Novgorodskogo Gosudarstvennogo Pedagogicesko Instituta Kafedra Russkogo Jazyka

UZOrenPI — Ucenye Zapiski Orenburgskogo Gosudarstvennogo Pedagogiceskogo Instituta Imeni V. P. Ckalova

UZPe — Ucenye Zapiski Penzenskii Pedagogicheskii Institut

UZ Penz — Uchenye Zapiski. Gosudarstvennyi Pedagogicheskii Institut. Penza

UZPer — Ucenye Zapiski Permskii Universitet

UZPerm — Ucenye Zapiski Permskogo Gosudarstvennogo Universiteta Imeni A. M. Gor'kogo

UZ Perm U — Uchenye Zapiski Permskogo Gosudarstvennogo Universiteta

UZPPI — Uchenye Zapiski. Piatigorskii Pedagogicheskii Institut Stavropol

UZPs — Ucenye Zapiski Pskovskii Pedagogicheskii Institut

UZPU — Ucenye Zapiski Petrozavodskogo Universiteta Filologiceskie Nauk

UZRjazPI — Ucenye Zapiski Rjazanskogo Gosudarstvennogo Pedagogiceskogo Instituta

UZRovPI — Ucenye Zapiski Rovenskogo Gosudarstvennogo Pedagogiceskogo Instituta Filologiceskij Fakul'tet

UZSachPI — Ucenye Zapiski Sachtinskogo Gosudarstvennogo Pedagogiceskogo Instituta

UZSarPedI — Ucenye Zapiski Saratovskogo Gosudarstvennogo Pedagogiceskogo Instituta

UZSGU — Ucenye Zapiski Saratovskogo Gosudarstvennogo Universiteta

UZSmolPI — Ucenye Zapiski Smolenskogo Gosudarstvennogo Pedagogiceskogo Instituta

UZSPI — Uchenye Zapiski. Stalinabadskii Pedagogicheskii Institut. Seriia Obshchestvennykh Nauk

UZSterPI — Ucenye Zapiski Sterlitamakskogo Gosudarstvennogo Pedagogiceskogo Instituta. Serija Filologiceskaja

UZTar — Ucenye Zapiski Tartusskii Universitet

UZTarU — Ucenye Zapiski Tartuskogo Gosudarstvennogo Universiteta

UZTasPIIn — Ucenye Zapiski Taskentskogo Pedagogiceskogo Instituta Inostrannych Jazykov

UZTasPINiz — Ucenye Zapiski Taskentskogo Pedagogiceskogo Instituta Imeni Nizami

UZTFA — Uchenye Zapiski Tul'skii Gosudarstvennyi Pedagogicheskii Institut Fiziko-Tekhnicheskie Nauki

UZTI — Ucenye Zapiski Tikhookeanskogo Instituta

UZTI — Uchenye Zapiski. Tuvinskii Nauchno-Issledovatelskii Institut Iazyka, Literatury i Istorii

UZTjPI — Ucenye Zapiski Tjumenskogo Pedagogiceskogo Instituta Kafedra Russkogo Jazyka

UZTomU — Ucenye Zapiski Tomskogo Universiteta Imeni V. V. Kujbyseva

UZToU — Ucenye Zapiski Tomskii Universitet

UZTPI — Ucenye Zapiski Tomskii Gosudarstvennyj Pedagogiceskij Institut

UZTU — Uchenye Zapiski. Turkmenskii Universitet

UZTuvNII — Ucenye Zapiski Tuvinskogo Naucno-Issledovatel'skogo Instituta Jazyka, Literatury, i Istorii

UZUIPI — Ucenye Zapiski Ul'janovskogo Gosudarstvennogo Pedagogiceskogo Instituta Imeni I. N. Ul'janova

UZUPI — Ucenye Zapiski Ural'skogo Pedagogiceskogo i Ucitel'skogo Instituta Imeni Puskina

UZUzPI — Ucenye Zapiski Uzbekskogo Respublikanskogo Pedagogiceskogo Instituta Kafedra Russkogo Jazyka i Literatury

UZVI — Uchenye Zapiski Voennogo Instituta Inostrannych Iazykov

UZVinPI — Ucenye Zapiski Vinnickogo Gosudarstvennogo Pedagogiceskogo Instituta Kafedra Russkogo Jazyka i Literatury

UZVolPI — Ucenye Zapiski Vologodskogo Gosudarstvennogo Pedagogiceskogo Instituta

UZW — Universitas. Zeitschrift fuer Wissenschaft, Kunst, und Literatur

V

V — Valencia
V — Variety
V — Venture
V — Verbo
V — Verordeningenblad
V — Vision
Va — Vasari
VA — Ventana
VA — Vie Africaine
Va — Virginia Reports
VA — Vorderasiatische Abteilung der Staatlichen Museen zu Berlin
VAA — Verhandelingen. Koninklijke Akademie van Wetenschappen te Amsterdam
Vaab Aarb — Vaabenhistoriske Aarboger
Va Acts — Acts of the General Assembly of the Commonwealth of Virginia
VA Ag Dept — Virginia. Department of Agriculture and Immigration. Publications
VA Ag Exp — Virginia Polytechnic Institute. Agricultural Experiment Station. Publications
VA Agric Exp Stn Bull — Virginia. Agricultural Experiment Station. Bulletin
VA Agric Exp Stn Tech Bull — Virginia. Agricultural Experiment Station. Technical Bulletin
VAAHDJ — Virchows Archiv. A. Pathological Anatomy and Histopathology
Va App — Virginia Court of Appeals Reports
VAB — Vorderasiatische Bibliothek
VA BAJ — Virginia Bar Association. Journal
VA Bar News — Virginia Bar News
VABBA — Vestsi Akademii Navuk BSSR. Seryya Biyalagichnykh Navuk
VABFA — Vestsi Akademii Navuk BSSR. Seryya Fizika-Tekhnichnykh Navuk
Vabh — Vabenhuset. Kristendommen og Nutiden
VABPDE — Virchows Archiv. B. Cell Pathology Including Molecular Pathology
Vab T — Vabenhistorisk Tidsskrift
VAC — Vie, Art, Cite. Revue Suisse Romande
VA Cavalcade — Virginia Cavalcade
Vaccine Res — Vaccine Research
Vaccine Res Dev — Vaccine Research and Developments
Vaccines Mod Approaches New Vaccines Incl Prev AIDS Annu Meet — Vaccines. Modern Approaches to New Vaccines Including Prevention of AIDS. Annual Meeting
Vaccines Sex Transm Dis Proc Conf — Vaccines for Sexually Transmitted Diseases. Proceedings. Conference
VACCJ — VACC [*Victorian Automobile Chamber of Commerce*] Journal
Vac Microbalance Tech — Vacuum Microbalance Techniques
Va Code Ann — Code of Virginia Annotated
Vac Struct Intense Fields — Vacuum Structure in Intense Fields
VACUA — Vacuum
Vacuum Chem — Vacuum Chemistry
Vacuum R — Vacuum Review
VA Dent J — Virginia Dental Journal
VA Dept Highways Div Tests Geol Yearbook — Virginia. Department of Highways. Division of Tests. Geological Yearbook
VA Dept Labor and Industry Ann Rept — Virginia. Department of Labor and Industry. Annual Report
VA Div Geol Bull — Virginia. Division of Geology. Bulletin
VA Div Geology Bull Reprint Ser — Virginia. Division of Geology. Bulletin. Reprint Series
VA Div Mineral Res Bull Inf Circ Mineral Res Circ — Virginia. Division of Mineral Resources. Bulletin. Information Circular. Mineral Resources Circular
VA Div Miner Resour Bull — Virginia. Division of Mineral Resources. Bulletin
VA Div Miner Resour Inf Cir — Virginia. Division of Mineral Resources. Information Circular
VA Div Miner Resour Miner Resour Rep — Virginia. Division of Mineral Resources. Mineral Resources Report
VA Div Miner Resour Rep Invest — Virginia. Division of Mineral Resources. Report of Investigations
VAEBAI — Agricultural Experiment Station. University of Vermont. Bulletin
Vaerml Bergsmannafoeren Ann — Vaermlaendska Bergsmannafoereningens Annaler
VAE VA Agric Econ VA Polytech Inst State Univ Coop Ext Serv — VAE. Virginia Agricultural Economics. Virginia Polytechnic Institute and State University. Cooperative Extension Service
Vaextskyddsanst-Notiser — Vaextskyddsanstalt-Notiser
Vaextskyddsrapp Jordbruk — Vaextskyddsrapporter. Jordbruk
VA Farm Econ VA Polytech Inst Agr Ext Serv — Virginia Farm Economics. Virginia Polytechnic Institute. Agricultural ExtensionService
VA Fish Lab Educ Ser — Virginia Fisheries Laboratory. Educational Series
VA Fruit — Virginia Fruit
VAG — Mitteilungen des Vereins fuer Anhaltische Geschichte und Altertumskunde

VAG — Vastgoed
Vaga — Vagabond
VAGAM — Voyage Archeologique en Grece et en Asie Mineure
VA Geol Surv Circ — Virginia. Geological Survey. Circular
VA Geol Survey Bull — Virginia. Geological Survey. Bulletin
VA Geol Surv Repr Ser — Virginia. Geological Survey. Reprint Series
VA GSB — Virginia. Geological Survey. Bulletin
VAHD — Vjesnik za Arheologiju i Historiju Dalmatinsku
VAH Dal — Vjesnik za Arheologiju i Historiju Dalmatinsku
VA Hist Soc Coll — Virginia Historical Society. Collections
VA Horse Ind Yearb — Virginia Horse Industry Yearbook
VA Inst Mar Sci Spec Sci Rep — Virginia Institute of Marine Science. Special Scientific Report
VA J Ed — Virginia Journal of Education
VA J Educ — Virginia Journal of Education
VA J Int L — Virginia Journal of International Law
Va J Int Law — Virginia Journal of International Law
VA J Intl L — Virginia Journal of International Law
VA J Nat Resources L — Virginia Journal of Natural Resources Law
VA J Nat Resour Law — Virginia Journal of Natural Resources Law
VAJODH — Lantbrukshogskolan Vaxtskyddsrapporter Jordbruk
Va Jour Educ — Virginia Journal of Education
VA Jour Sci — Virginia Journal of Science
VA J Sci — Virginia Journal of Science
Vakbl Biol — Vakblad voor Biologen
Vak Forsch Prax — Vakuum in Forschung und Praxis
Vakiflar Derg — Vakiflar Dergisi
Vak Inf — Vakuum Information
Vak Prax — Vakuum in der Praxis
Vakstudie — Fiscale Encyclopedie de Vakstudie
VAKTA — Vakuum-Technik
Vak-Tech — Vakuum-Technik
Vak-Technik — Vakuum-Technik
Vak Tekh Tekhnol — Vakuumnaya Tekhnika i Tekhnologiya
Val — Valeurs
VAL — Valuation
VA L — Virginia Law Review
ValA — Valeurs Actuelles
Valachica — Acta Valachica. Studii si Materiale de Istorie a Culturii
VA Law J — Virginia Law Journal
Va Law J — Virginia Law Journal
VA Law R — Virginia Law Review
Va Law Reg — Virginia Law Register
VA Law Rev — Virginia Law Review
Vale Evesham Hist Soc Res Pap — Vale of Evesham Historical Society. Research Papers
Valenciennes Mm — Memoires de la Societe d'Agriculture, des Sciences et des Arts de l'Arrondissement de Valenciennes
Valenciennes Mm S Ag — Memoires de la Societe d'Agriculture, des Sciences et des Arts de l'Arrondissement de Valenciennes
VA Lib Bul — Virginia Library Bulletin
VA Libn — Virginia Librarian
VA LJ — Virginia Law Journal
Vallalatvez -Szerv — Vallalatvezetes-Vallalatszervezes
VALN — Victorian Adult Literacy News
Valori Plast — Valori Plastici. Rivista d'Arte
Valori Prim — Valori Primordiali
Valparaiso Univ Law R — Valparaiso University. Law Review
Valparaiso Univ L Rev — Valparaiso University. Law Review
VA LR — Virginia Law Review
Va L Reg — Virginia Law Register
VA L Rev — Virginia Law Review
Valsa — Valsalva
Valt Maatalouskoetoiminnan Julk — Valtion Maatalouskoetoiminnan Julkaisuja
Valt Tek Tutkimuskeskus Reaktorilab Tied — Valtion Teknillinen Tutkimuskeskus. Reaktorilaboratorio. Tiedonanto
Valt Tek Tutkimuslaitos Julk — Valtion Teknillinen Tutkimuslaitos. Julkaisu
Valt Tek Tutkimuslaitos Tiedotus Sar 1 Puu — Valtion Teknillinen Tutkimuslaitos. Tiedotus. Sarja 1. Puu
Valt Tek Tutkimuslaitos Tiedotus Sar 2 — Valtion Teknillinen Tutkimuslaitos. Tiedotus. Sarja 2. Metalli
Valt Tek Tutkimuslaitos Tiedotus Sar 4 — Valtion Teknillinen Tutkimuslaitos. Tiedotus. Sarja 4. Kemia
Valt Tek Tutkimuslaitos Tied Sar 2 — Valtion Teknillinen Tutkimuslaitos. Tiedotus. Sarja 2. Metalli

Valt Tek Tutkimuslaitos Tied Sar 3 — Valtion Teknillinen Tutkimuslaitos. Tiedotus. Sarja 3. Rakennus
Valt Tek Tutkimuslaitos Tied Sar I PUU — Valtion Teknillinen Tutkimuslaitos Tiedotus. Sarja I. PUU
Value Eng — Value Engineering
Value Line — Value Line Investment Survey
Val U LR — Valparaiso University. Law Review
Val U L Rev — Valparaiso University. Law Review
Valvo Tech Inf Ind — Valvo Technische Informationen fuer die Industrie
VA L Wk Dicta Comp — Virginia Law Weekly Dicta Compilation
VA M — Virginia Magazine of History and Biography
VA Mag Hist — Virginia Magazine of History and Biography
VA Mag Hist Biog — Virginia Magazine of History and Biography
VA Mag Hist Biogr — Virginia Magazine of History and Biography
VA Med — Virginia Medical
Va Med Mo — Virginia Medical Monthly
VA Med Mon — Virginia Medical Monthly [*Later, Virginia Medical*]
Va Med Q — Virginia Medical Quarterly
Va Med Semi Mo — Virginia Medical Semi-Monthly
VA Miner — Virginia Minerals
Va M M — Virginia Medical Monthly
Va Munic R — Virginia Municipal Review
VAMZ — Vjesnik Arheoloskog Muzeja u Zagrebu
VAN — Vanderbilt Law Review
Van — Vanguard Science Fiction
VAN — Vesti. Akademiia Nauk BSSR
VAN — Vestnik Akademii Nauk SSSR
VAN — Voluntary Action News
VANB — Vesci Akademii Navuk BSSR
Vancoram Rev — Vancoram Review
Vancouver Mag — Vancouver Magazine
Vancouver Op Jnl — Vancouver Opera Journal
Vancouver Stud Cogn Sci — Vancouver Studies in Cognitive Science
V&A Mus Album — Victoria and Albert Museum Album
V&A Mus Bull — Victoria and Albert Museum Bulletin
V&A Mus Yb — Victoria and Albert Museum Yearbook
Vanderbilt J Transnat'l L — Vanderbilt Journal of Transnational Law
Vanderbilt LR — Vanderbilt Law Review
Vanderbilt Univ Abs Theses Bull — Vanderbilt University. Abstracts of Theses. Bulletin
Vanderbilt Univ Q — Vanderbilt University Quarterly
Vander J Transnat Law — Vanderbuilt Journal of Transnational Law
Vander Law — Vanderbilt Law Review
V & G — Vergangenheit und Gegenwart
V & I — Voix et Images. Etudes Quebecoises
Vand Int — Vanderbilt International
Vand J Trans L — Vanderbilt Journal of Transnational Law
Vand J Transnatl L — Vanderbilt Journal of Transnational Law
V & L — Vie et Langage
Vand LR — Vanderbilt Law Review
Vand L Rev — Vanderbilt Law Review
V & P — Votes and Proceedings
Vandtek — Vandteknik
Van Fair — Vanity Fair
Vanguard Newsl — Vanguard Newsletter
VANK — Vestnik Akademii Nauk Kazakhskoi SSR
Van Nostrand Reinhold Electric Comput Sci Engrg Ser — Van Nostrand Reinhold Electrical/Computer Science and Engineering Series
Van Nostrand Reinhold Math Ser — Van Nostrand Reinhold Mathematics Series
VAN SSSR — Vestnik Akademii Nauk SSSR
VANT — Vestnik Akademii Nauk Turkmenskoi SSR
VA Num — Virginia Numismatist
VA Nurse — Virginia Nurse
VA Nurse Q — Virginia Nurse Quarterly [*Later, Virginia Nurse*]
Van Zee Ld — Van Zee tot Land
VAP — Mitteilungen der Vereinigungen von Freunden der Astronomie und Kosmischen Physik
VAPHD — Virchows Archiv. A. Pathological Anatomy and Histology
VA Polytech Inst Bull Eng Expt Sta Ser — Virginia Polytechnic Institute. Bulletin. Engineering Experiment Station Series
VA Polytech Inst Eng Ext Ser Cir — Virginia Polytechnic Institute. Engineering Extension Series. Circular
VA Polytech Inst Res Div Bull — Virginia Polytechnic Institute. Research Division. Bulletin
VA Polytech Inst Res Div Wood Res Wood Constr Lab Bull — Virginia Polytechnic Institute. Research Division. Wood Research and Wood Construction Laboratory [*Blacksburg*]. Bulletin
VA Polytech Inst State Univ Res Div Bull — Virginia Polytechnic Institute and State University. Research Division. Bulletin
VA Polytech Inst State Univ Res Div Monogr — Virginia Polytechnic Institute and State University. Research Division. Monograph
VA Polytech Inst State Univ Res Div Rep — Virginia Polytechnic Institute and State University. Research Division. Report
VA Polytech Inst State Univ Sch For Wildl Resour Publ FWS — Virginia Polytechnic Institute and State University. School of Forestry and Wildlife Resources. Publication FWS
VA Polytech Inst State Univ VA Water Resour Res Cent Bull — Virginia Polytechnic Institute and State University. Virginia Water Resources Research Center. Bulletin
VA Polytech Inst State Univ Water Resour Res Cent Bull — Virginia Polytechnic Institute and State University. Water Resources Research Center. Bulletin
VAPP — Vida e Arte do Povo Portugues
VA Q R — Virginia Quarterly Review
VA Q Rev — Virginia Quarterly Review
Va Quar Rev — Virginia Quarterly Review. University of Virginia

VAR — Variety
VAR — Vorderasiatische Rollsiegel
Var Aegyp — Varia Aegyptiaca
Vara Palsd — Vara Palsdjur
Vard Nord Utveckl Forsk — Vard i Norden. Utveckling och Forskning
Va Regs Reg — Virginia Register of Regulations
Vari — Variegation
Varia Bio-Arch — Varia Bio-Archaeologica
Varian Instrum Appl — Varian Instrument Applications
Varilna Teh — Varilna Tehnika
Various Publ Ser — Various Publications Series
Varme- o Sanit-Tek — Vearme- och Sanitetsteknikern
Var Sci Inst Rebois Tunis — Varietes Scientifiques. Institut de Reboisement de Tunis
Var Spom — Varstvo Spomenikov
Vars S Nt Tr C R Bl — Travaux de la Societe des Naturalistes de Varsovie. Comptes Rendus de la Section Biologique
Vars S Nt Tr C R Ps C — Travaux de la Societe des Naturalistes de Varsovie. Comptes Rendus de la Section de Physique et de Chemie
Vars S Nt Tr Mm — Travaux de la Societe des Naturalistes de Varsovie. Memoires
Varst Spom — Varstvo Spomenikov
VARTA Spez Rep — VARTA Spezial Report
Vartovb — Vartovbogen
VAS — Vorderasiatische Schriftdenkmaeler der Koeniglichen [*or Staatlichen*] Museen zu Berlin
Vasari Soc — Vasari Society
Vasa Suppl — Vasa Supplementum
Vasc Dis — Vascular Diseases
Vasc Surg — Vascular Surgery
VASD — Veroeffentlichungen. Deutsche Akademie fuer Sprache und Dichtung
VaSd — Vorderasiatische Schriftdenkmaeler der Koeniglichen [*or Staatlichen*] Museen zu Berlin
Vasenlisten — Vasenlisten zur Griechischen Heldensage
VA Social Science J — Virginia Social Science Journal
Vasopressin Int Vasopressin Conf — Vasopressin. International Vasopressin Conference
Vassar Bros Inst Tr — Vassar Brothers Institute. Transactions
Va State Lib Bul — Virginia State Library Bulletin
VA State Lib Bull — Virginia State Library. Bulletin
Va St B Assn Proc — Virginia State Bar Association. Proceedings
Va St B Assn Rep — Virginia State Bar Association. Report
Vasterbotten — Vasterbottens Lans Hambygdsforenings Arsbok
Vastergotlands Fornminnesforen Tidskr — Vastergotlands Fornminnesforenings Tidskrift
Vastmanlands Fornminnesforen Arsskr — Vastmanlands Fornminnesforenings Arsskrift
Vasuti Tud Kut Intez Evk — Vasuti Tudomanyos Kutato Intezet Evkoenyve
Vasvarm Muz Term Oszt Evi Jel — Vasvarmegyei Muzeum Termeszetrajzi Osztalyanak evi Jelentese. Annales Musei Comitati Castriferrei. Sectio Historico-Naturalis
VA Tax R — Virginia Tax Review
VA Teach — Virginia Teacher
VATEJ — Victorian Association for the Teaching of English. Journal
Vaterl Blaett Oesterr Kaiserstaat — Vaterlaendische Blaetter fuer den Oesterreichischen Kaiserstaat
Vatican Obs Publ Studi Galileiani — Vatican Observatory Publications. Studi Galileiani
VATISJ — VATIS [*Victorian Association of Teachers in Independent Schools*] Journal
VATRD8 — Sveriges Landbruksuniversitet Vaxtskyddsrapporter Tradgard
VA Truck Exp — Virginia Truck Experiment Station. Publications
Vauc Ac Mm — Memoires de l'Academie de Vaucluse
VA Univ Ph Soc B Sc S — Virginia University. Philosophical Society. Bulletin. Scientific Series
VAV — Veroeffentlichungen zum Archiv fuer Voelkerkunde
VAW — Akademie van Wetenschappen. Amsterdam. Afdeeling Letterkunde. Verhandelingen. Nieuwe Reeks
VA Water Resour Res Cent Bull — Virginia Water Resources Research Center. Bulletin
VA Wildl — Virginia Wildlife
Vaxtekol Stud — Vaxtekologiska Studier
Vaxt-Nar-Nytt — Vaxt-Narings-Nytt
Vaxtodling Inst Vaxtodlingslara Lantbrukshogsk — Vaextodling. Institutionen foer Vaextodlingslara. Lantbrukshoegskolan
Vaxtskyddsnotiser Sver Lantbruksuniver — Vaxtskyddsnotiser. Sveriges Lantbruksuniversitet
Vazduhoplovni Glas — Vazduhoplovni Glasnik
Vb — Verordeningenblad
Vb — Verzekeringsbode
VB — Voks Bulletin
VBA — NIMO [*Nederlands Instituut voor Maatschappelijke Opbouw*] Kroniek. Nieuwsbulletin
VBA — Visva Bharati Annals
VBB — Verordeningenblad Bedrijfsorganisatie
VBB — Visva Bharati Bulletin
VB (B) — Voelkischer Beobachter (Berlin)
Vb Bo — Verordeningenblad Bedrijfsorganisatie
VBBVE6 — Verhandlungen des Berliner Botanischen Vereins
VBelGrN — Vesci Akademii Navuk Belaruskaj SSR. Seryja Gramadskich Navuk
VBGA — Verhandlungen der Berliner Gesellschaft fuer Anthropologie, Ethnologie, und Urgeschichte
VBGAEU — Verhandlungen. Berliner Gesellschaft fuer Anthropologie, Ethnologie, und Urgeschichte
VBGP — Vierzehn Berliner Griechische Papyri
VBKTPS — Vierteljahrschrift fuer Bibelkunde, Talmudische, und Patristische Studien

Vbl — Vakblad
VBL — Vakblad voor de Bloemisterij
Vbl Bedrorg — Verordeningenblad Bedrijfsorganisatie
VB (Mu) — Voelkischer Beobachter (Muenich)
VBN — Victorian Bar News
VBN — Visva Bharati News
VBNIDQ — Vogelkundliche Berichte aus Niedersachsen
VBO — Bouwwereld. Universeel Veertiendaags Vaktijdschrift voor de Bouwnijverheid
VBo — Verordeningenblad Bedrijfsorganisatie
VBQ — Visvabharati Quarterly
VBSFA — Vestsi Akademii Navuk BSSR. Seryya Fizika-Matematychnykh Navuk
VBSKA — Vestsi Akademii Navuk BSSR. Seryya Khimichnykh Navuk
VBST — Vestnik Botanicheskogo Sada (Tbilisi)
VBT — Tabak Plus
VBTPS — Vierteljahrschrift fuer Bibelkunde, Talmudische, und Patristische Studien
VBV — Documentatieblad voor Onderwijs en Wetenschappen
VBVB — Verhandlungen des Botanischen Vereins der Provinz Brandenburg
VBW — Vakbondskrant van Nederland
VBW — Vortraege der Bibliothek Warburg
VC — Verbum Caro
VC — Vigiliae Christianae
VC — Virginia Cavalcade
VCA — Vestnik Ceske Akademie Ved a Umeni
VCA — Vestnik Ceskoslovenske Akademie Ved
VCA — Voice of Chorus America
Vcela Morav — Vcela Moravska
VChr — Vigiliae Christianae
V Christ — Vetera Christianorum
V CJQ — Viewpoints Canadian Jewish Quarterly
VCK — Veckans Affarer
Vc Miss — Voice of Missions
VCSAV — Vestnik Ceskoslovenske Akademie Ved
VCS Bul — VCS [Victorian Computer Society] Bulletin
VcSN — Violincello Society Newsletter
VCT — Vector
VCTA General J — Victorian Commercial Teachers' Association. General Journal
VCV Tijd — VCV (Vlaamse Chemische Vereniging) Tijdingen
Vd — Vaderland
VD — Verbum Domini
VDASD — Veroeffentlichungen. Deutsche Akademie fuer Sprache und Dichtung
VDEFA — VDE [Verband Deutscher Elektrotechniker] Fachberichte
VDE Fachber — VDE [Verband Deutscher Elektrotechniker] Fachberichte
VDEW (Ver Dtsch Elektrizitaetswerke) Informationsdienst — VDEW (Vereinigung Deutscher Elektrizitaetswerke) Informationsdienst (German Federal Republic)
VDF — Vorkaempfer Deutscher Freiheit. Series
VDFAN — Vestnik Dal'nevostochnogo Filiala Akademii Nauk SSSR
VDGIA — Verhandlungen. Deutsche Gesellschaft fuer Innere Medizin
VDGKA — Verhandlungen. Deutsche Gesellschaft fuer Kreislaufforschung
VDGPA — Verhandlungen. Deutsche Gesellschaft fuer Pathologie
VDGRA — Verhandlungen. Deutsche Gesellschaft fuer Rheumatologie
VdGSA — Viola da Gamba Society of America. Journal
VdGSAN — Viola da Gamba Society of America. News
VDGT — Verhandlungen des Deutschen Geographentages
VDI — Vestnik Drevnei Istorii
VDI Ber — VDI [Verein Deutscher Ingenieure] Berichte
V Diem R S Pp — Papers and Proceedings of the Royal Society of Van Diemen's Land
VDIFA — VDI [Verein Deutscher Ingenieure] Forschungsheft
VDI Forsch — VDI (Verein Deutscher Ingenieur) Forschungsheft
VDI Forschungsh — VDI [Verein Deutscher Ingenieure] Forschungsheft
VDI Nachr — Verein Deutscher Ingenieure. Nachrichten
VD Ist — Vestnik Drevnei Istorii
VDI Z — VDI [Verein Deutscher Ingenieure] Zeitschrift
VDI Z Fortschr Ber Reihe 5 — VDI [Verein Deutscher Ingenieure] Zeitschriften. Fortschritt-Berichte. Reihe 5. Grund- und Werkstoffe
VDJT — Verhandlungen des Deutschen Juristentages
VdM — Vie del Mondo
VDNAA — VDI [Verein Deutscher Ingenieure] Nachrichten
VDOG — Wissenschaftliche Veroeffentlichungen der Deutschen Orient-Gesellschaft
VDP — Verhandlungen der Versammlungen Deutscher Philologen und Schulmaenner
VdP — Vie des Peuples
VDP — Von Deutscher Poeterey
VDPh — Verhandlung. Versammlung Deutscher Philologen
VDRG — Verhandlungen der Deutschen Roentgen-Gesellschaft
V Dr Ist — Vestnik Drevnei Istorii
VDS — Veroeffentlichungen. Deutsche Schillergesellschaft
Vds A — Vendsyssel Arbog
Vds Aa — Vendsysselske Aarboger
VDT — Videotex World
VDTIAX — Flemish Veterinary Journal
VDTJ — Voprosy Dialektologii Tjurkskich Jazykov
VDVW — Verhandlungen des Deutschen Wissenschaftlichen Vereins zu Santiago de Chile
VE — Vento Dell'est
VE — Vermont Music Educators News
Ve — Vesey, Senior's, English Chancery Reports
VE — Vestnik Evropy
VE — Vortice
VE — Vox Evangelica
VEAB Ert — VEAB Ertesitoe
VEB — Financieel Ekonomische Tijd
VEB Verlag Tech Mon Tech Rev — VEB [Volkseigener Betrieb] Verlag Technik. Monthly Technical Review

VeC — Vertice (Coimbra)
VECM — Vocational Education Curriculum Materials Database
Vecteur Environ — Vecteur Environnement
Veda Tech Mladezi — Veda a Technika Mladezi
Veda Tech SSSR — Veda a Technika v SSSR
Veda Vyzk Potravin Prum — Veda a Vyzkum v Potravinarskem Prumyslu
Veda Vyzk Prum Sklarskem — Veda a Vyzkum v Prumyslu Sklarskem
Veda Vyzk Prum Text — Veda a Vyzkum v Prumyslu Textilnim
Vedeckovyzk Uhelny Ustav Sb Vyzk Pr — Vedeckovyzkumny Uhelny Ustav Sbornik Vyzkumnych Praci
Ved Inf CSAV — Vedecke Informace CSAV
Ved Kes — Vedanta Kesari
VeDo — Verbum Domini
Ved Prace Ustr Vyzk Ustavu Rost Vyr (Praha) — Vedecke Prace Ustrodniho Vyzkumneho Ustavu Rostlinne Vyroby (Praha)
Ved Prace Vyskum Ust Lesn Hosp Zvolen — Vedecke Prace Vyskumny Ustav Lesneho Hospodarstva v Zvolene
Ved Prace Vysk Ustavu Kukurice Trnave — Vedecke Prace Vyskumneho Ustavu Kukurice v Trnave
Ved Prace Vysk Ustavu Rastlinnej Vyr — Vedecke Prace Vyskumneho Ustavu Rastlinnej Vyroby
Ved Prace Vysk Ustavu Zavlahov Hospod Bratislave — Vedecke Prace Vyskumneho Ustavu Zavlahoveho Hospodarstva v Bratislave
Ved Prace Vysk Ustavu Zivoc Nitre — Vedecke Prace Vyskumneho Ustavu Zivocisnej Vyroby v Nitre
Ved Prace Vyzkum Ust Mellor — Vedecke Prace Vyzkumneho Ustavu Zemedelsko-Lesnickych Melioraci CSAZV [Ceskoslovenska Akademie Zemedelskych Ved] v Praze
Ved Prace Vyzk Ustavu Kraivarsk — Vedecke Prace Vyzkumneho Ustavu Kraivarskeho
Ved Pr Cesk Zemed Muz — Vedecke Prace Ceskoslovenskeho Zemedelskeho Muzea
Ved Pr Hydinarstvo Vysk Ustav Chovu Slachtenia Hydiny — Vedecke Prace Hydinarstvo Vyskumny Ustav Chovu a Slachtenia Hydiny
Ved Pr Lab Podoznalectva Bratisl — Vedecke Prace Laboratoria Podoznalectva v Bratislave
Ved Pr Ustavu Zelinarskeho Olomouci — Vedecke Prace Ustavu Zelinarskeho v Olomouci
Ved Pr Ustr Vyzk Ust Rostl Vyroby Praze-Ruzyni — Vedecke Prace Ustredniho Vyzkumneho Ustavu Rostlinne Vyroby v Praze-Ruzyni
Ved Pr VSCHK (Slatinany) — Vedecke Prace VSCHK [Vyzkumna Stanice pro Chov Koni] (Slatinany)
Ved Pr Vysk Ustav Rastl Vyroby Piestanoch — Vedecke Prace Vyskumneho Ustavu Rastlinnej Vyroby v Piestanoch
Ved Pr Vysk Ustavu Chov Hydiny Ivanka Dunaji — Vedecke Prace Vyskumneho Ustavu pro Chov Hydiny v Ivanka pri Dunaji
Ved Pr Vysk Ustavu Chov Skotu Caz Rapotine — Vedecke Prace Vyskumneho Ustavu pro Chov Skotu Caz v Rapotine
Ved Pr Vysk Ustavu Kukurice Trnave — Vedecke Prace Vyskumneho Ustavu Kukurice v Trnave
Ved Pr Vysk Ustavu Lesn Hospod v Zvolene — Vedecke Prace Vyskumneho Ustavu Lesneho Hospodarstva v Zvolene
Ved Pr Vysk Ustavu Lesn Hospod Zvolen — Vedecke Prace Vyskumneho Ustavu Lesneho Hospodarstva v Zvolene
Ved Pr Vysk Ustavu Luk Pasienkov Banskej Bystrici — Vedecke Prace Vyskumneho Ustavu Luk a Pasienkov v Banskej Bystrici
Ved Pr Vysk Ustavu Ovciar Trencine — Vedecke Prace Vyskumneho Ustavu Ovciarskeho v Trencine
Ved Pr Vysk Ustavu Podoznalectva Vyz Rasti Bratislave — Vedecke Prace Vyskumneho Ustavu Podoznalectva a Vyzivy Rastlin v Bratislave
Ved Pr Vysk Ustavu Podoznalectva Vyz Rastlin Bratisl — Vedecke Prace Vyskumneho Ustavu Podoznalectva a Vyzivy Rastlin v Bratislave
Ved Pr Vysk Ustavu pro Chov Hydiny Ivanka pri Dunaji — Vedecke Prace Vyskumneho Ustavu pro Chov Hydiny v Ivanka pri Dunaji
Ved Pr Vysk Ustavu Rastlinnej Vyroby Piestanoch — Vedecke Prace Vyskumneho Ustavu Rastlinnej Vyroby v Piestanoch
Ved Pr Vysk Ustavu Rastl Vyroby Piestanoch — Vedecke Prace Vyskumneho Ustavu Rastlinnej Vyroby v Piestanoch
Ved Pr Vysk Ustavu Rastl Vyroby Piestanoch Krmoviny — Vedecke Prace Vyskumneho Ustavu Rastlinnej Vyroby v Piestanoch Krmoviny
Ved Pr Vysk Ustavu Zavlahoveho Hospod Bratisl — Vedecke Prace Vyskumneho Ustavu Zavlahoveho Hospodarstva v Bratislave
Ved Pr Vysk Ustavu Zivocisnej Vyroby Nitre — Vedecke Prace Vyskumneho Ustavu Zivocisnej Vyroby v Nitre
Ved Pr Vysk Ustav Zavlahov Hospod — Vedecke Prace Vyskumny Ustavu Zavlahoveho Hospodarstva
Ved Pr Vysk Ustav Zivoc Vyroby Nitre — Vedecke Prace Vyskumneho Ustavu Zivocisnej Vyroby v Nitre
Ved Pr Vysk Ust Rastl Vyroby Piestanoch — Vedecke Prace Ustredniho Vyskumneho Ustavu Rastlinnej Vyroby Piestanoch
Ved Pr Vysk Ust Rastl Vyroby Praze-Ruzyni — Vedecke Prace Ustredniho Vyskumneho Ustavu Rastlinnej Vyroby CSAZV [Ceskoslovenska Akademie Zemedelskych Ved] v Praze-Ruzyni
Ved Pr Vyzk Stanice Chov Koni Slatinany — Vedecke Prace Vyzkumna Stanice pro Chov Koni Slatinany
Ved Pr Vyzk Ustav Melior — Vedecke Prace. Vyzkumny Ustav Melioraci
Ved Pr Vyzk Ustavu Bramborarskeho Havlickove Brode — Vedecke Prace Vyzkumneho Ustavu Bramborarskeho v Havlickove Brode
Ved Pr Vyzk Ustavu Chov Prasat Kostelci Nad Orlice — Vedecke Prace Vyzkumneho Ustavu pro Chov Prasat v Kostelci Nad Orlice
Ved Pr Vyzk Ustavu Chov Skotu Caz Rapotine — Vedecke Prace Vyzkumneho Ustavu pro Chov Skotu Caz v Rapotine
Ved Pr Vyzk Ustavu Krmivarskeho CSAZV Brne — Vedecke Prace Vyzkumneho Ustavu Krmivarskeho CSAZV [Ceskoslovenska Akademie Zemedelskych Ved] v Brne

Ved Pr Vyzk Ustavu Melior Praze — Vedecke Prace Vyzkumneho Ustavu Melioraci v Praze

Ved Pr Vyzk Ustavu Melior Praze Zbraslavi — Vedecke Prace Vyzkumneho Ustavu Melioraci v Praze or Zbraslavi

Ved Pr Vyzk Ustavu Melior Zbraslavi — Vedecke Prace Vyzkumneho Ustavu Melioraci v Zbraslavi

Ved Pr Vyzk Ustavu Obilnarskeho Kromerizi — Vedecke Prace Vyzkumneho Ustavu Obilnarskeho v Kromerizi

Ved Pr Vyzk Ustavu Okrasneho Zahradnictvi Pruhonicich — Vedecke Prace Vyzkumneho Ustavu Okrasneho Zahradnictvi v Pruhonicich

Ved Pr Vyzk Ustavu Ovilnarskeho Kromerizi — Vedecke Prace Vyzkumneho Ustavu Ovilnarskeho v Kromerizi

Ved Pr Vyzk Ustavu Rostl Vyroby Praze Ruzyni — Vedecke Prace Vyzkumnych Ustavu Rostlinne Vyroby v Praze-Ruzyni

Ved Pr Vyzk Ustavu Vcelarskeho Dole Libcic — Vedecke Prace Vyzkumneho Ustavu Vcelarskeho v Dole u Libcic

Ved Pr Vyzk Ustavu Vet CSAZV Brne — Vedecke Prace Vyzkumneho Ustavu Veterinarni CSAZV [*Ceskoslovenska Akademie Zemedelskych Ved*] v Brne

Ved Pr Vyzk Ustavu Vet Lek Brne — Vedecke Prace Vyzkumneho Ustavu Veterinarniho Lekarstvi v Brne

Ved Pr Vyzk Ustavu Zavlahoveho Hospod Bratislave — Vedecke Prace Vyzkumneho Ustavu Zavlahoveho Hospodarstva v Bratislave

Ved Pr Vyzk Ust Vcelar v Dole u Libcic — Vedecke Prace Vyzkumneho Ustavu Vcelarskeho v Dole u Libcic

Ved Svet — Vedecky Svet

Veeartsenijk Blad Nederl-Indie — Veeartsenijkundige Bladen voor Nederlandsch-Indie

Veeteelt Zuivelber — Veeteelt- en Zuivelberichten

VEF Inf Bul — VEF [*Victorian Employers' Federation*] Information Bulletin

Veg Crops Ser Calif Univ Dept Veg Crops — Vegetable Crops Series. California University. Department of Vegetable Crops

Vegetarian Mo — Vegetarian Monthly

Veg Grower — Vegetable Grower

Veg Grow News — Vegetable Growers News

Veg Nutr — Vegetarian Nutrition

Veg Situat TVS US Dep Agric Econ Res Serv — Vegetable Situation. United States Department of Agriculture. Economic Research

Veg Times — Vegetarian Times

Vegyip Kut Intez Kozl — Vegyipari Kutato Intezetek Kozlemenyei

VeH — Vermont History

Veh Environ Tech Pap FISITA Congr — Vehicle and the Environment. Technical Papers. FISITA (Federation Internationale des Societes d'Ingenieurs des Techniques de l'Automobile) Congress

Veh News Ltr — Experimental Vehicle Newsletter

Veh Syst Dyn — Vehicle System Dynamics

Vel — Veroeffentlichungen. Max-Planck-Institut fuer Geschichte

VEJ — DHZ Markt. Vakblad voor de Doe het Zelf Ondernemer

Vej Fr — Vejen Frem

Vejkom Skr — Vejkomiteens Skrifter

Vel — Veltro'

VeL — Vestnik Leningradskogo Universiteta

Vel Lt Trap — Velvet Light Trap

Veltro Riv Civilta It — Veltro. Rivista della Civilta Italiana

VeM — Vestnik Moskovskogo Universiteta

Vema Res Ser — Vema Research Series

Ven — Vendredi. Hebdomadaire Litteraire et Politique

VEN — Venture

VEN — Venture Science Fiction

Ven At — Atti delle Adunanze dell' I. Reale Istituto Veneto di Scienze, Lettere, ed Arti

Ven At Aten — Atti dell' Ateneo Veneto

Ven Aten — Ateneo Veneto. Rivista Mensile di Scienze, Lettere, ed Arti

Ven Aten Esercit — Esercitazioni Scientifiche e Letterarie dell' Ateneo di Venezia

Vend — Vending Times

Vendetta Agric — Vendetta Agricola

Vend Intnl — Vending International

Ven Dis Inf — Venereal Disease Information. US Public Health Service [*Washington, D.C.*]

Ven Esercit Aten — Esercitazioni Scientifiche e Letterarie dell' Ateneo di Venezia

Venez Dir Geol Bol Geol — Venezuela. Direccion de Geologia. Boletin de Geologia

Venez Dir Geol Bol Geol Publ Esp — Venezuela. Direccion de Geologia. Boletin de Geologia. Publicacion Especial

Venezia A — Venezia Arti. Bollettino del Dipartimento di Storia e Critica delle Arti dell'Universita di Venezia

Venezia Stud A & Stor Dir Mus Civ Correr — Venezia. Studi di Arte e Storia a cura della Direzione del Museo Civico Correr

Venez Inst Nac Nutr Publ — Venezuela. Instituto Nacional de Nutricion. Publicacion

Venez Min Minas Hidrocarburos Dir Geol Bol Geol — Venezuela. Ministerio de Minas e Hidrocarburos. Direccion de Geologia. Boletin de Geologia

Venez Mision — Venezuela Misionera

Venez Odontol — Venezuela Odontologica

Venez Univ Cent Esc Geol Minas Lab Petrogr Geoquimica Inf — Venezuela. Universidad Central. Escuela de Geologia y Minas. Laboratorio de Petrografia y Geoquimica. Informe

Venez Up To Date — Venezuela Up-to-Date

Venez UTD — Venezuela Up-to-Date

Vengarskaya Farmakoter — Vengarskaya Farmakoterapiya

Veng Zh Gorn Dela Metall Gorn Delo — Vengerskii Zhurnal Gornogo Dela i Metallurgii. Gornoe Delo

Ven I At — Atti delle Adunanze dell' I. Reale Istituto Veneto di Scienze, Lettere, ed Arti

Ven I Mm — Memorie del Reale Istituto Veneto di Scienze, Lettere, ed Arti

Ven Mm I — Memorie del Reale Istituto Veneto di Scienze, Lettere, ed Arti

Vent — Ventures

Vent Cap Invest — Venture Capital Investment

Vent Forth — Venture Forth

Vent Kond Vozdukha Zdanii — Ventilyatsiya i Konditsionirovanie Vozdukha Zdanii

Vent Kond Vozdukha Zdanii Sooruzh — Ventilyatsiya i Konditsionirovanie Vozdukha Zdanii Sooruzhenii

Vent Ochistka Vozdukha — Ventilyatsiya i Ochistka Vozdukha

Ventr Dev — News from Venture Development Corporation

Vent Shakht Rudn — Ventilyatsiya Shakht i Rudnikov

Venus Jpn J Malacol — Venus: The Japanese Journal of Malacology

VEOFA — Vestnik Oftal'mologii

VEP — Verpakken. Het Vakblad voor de Verpakkende Industrie en Verpakkingsindustrie

VEP — Vida y Espiritualidad (Peru)

V e P — Vita e Pensiero

VEQUD — Veterinary Quarterly

VeR — Verbum (Rio De Janeiro)

VER — Verfkroniek

Ver — Verger. Revue du Spectacle et des Lettres pour la Zone Francaise d'Occupation

Ver — Veritas

Ver — Verri

Ver — Versty

Ver — Vertice. Revista de Cultura e Critica

VER — Verwaltungsfuehrung Organisation Personalwesen

VERAD9 — Veterinary Radiology

Verbandsber Verb Schweiz Abwasser Gewaesserschutzfachleute — Verbandsbericht. Verband Schweizer Abwasser- und Gewaesserschutzfachleute

Verb C — Verbum Caro

Ver Bibl Landes NRW Mitt — Verband der Bibliotheken des Landes Nordrhein-Westfalen. Mitteilungsblatt

Verbindungstech Elektron Vortr Poster Beitr Int Kolloq — Verbindungstechnik in der Elektronik. Vortraege und Poster-Beitraege des Internationalen Kolloquiums

Ver Bl — Verordeningblad voor het Bezette Nederlandse Gebied

Ver Destill Ztg — Vereinigte Destillateur-Zeitungen

Verdi Newsl — Verdi Newsletter

Ver Dtsch Ing Z — Verein Deutscher Ingenieure. Zeitschrift

Ver Dtsch Ing Z Fortschr Ber Reihe 5 — Verein Deutscher Ingenieure. Zeitschriften. Fortschritt-Berichte. Reihe 5. Grund- und Werkstoffe

Vereinigung Schweizer Petroleum-Geologen u Ingenieure Bull — Vereinigung Schweizerischer Petroleum-Geologen und Ingenieure. Bulletin

Vereinte Nationen — Zeitschrift fuer die Vereinten Nationen und Ihre Sonderorganisationen

Vererb U Geschlechtsleb — Vererbung und Geschlechtsleben

Ver Erdk Dresden Mitt — Verein fuer Erdkunde zu Dresden. Mitteilungen

Ver Erdk Leipzig Mitt — Verein fuer Erdkunde zu Leipzig. Mitteilungen

Ver Exploit Proefzuivelboerderij Hoorn Versl — Vereniging tot Exploitatie eener Proefzuivelboerderij te Hoorn. Verslag

Verfahrenstech — Verfahrenstechnik International

Verfahrenstech Chem Apparatebau Semin — Verfahrenstechnik und Chemischer Apparatebau. Seminar

Verfass Recht Uebersee — Verfassung und Recht in Uebersee

Verfassung u Recht Uebersee — Verfassung und Recht in Uebersee

Verfassung u -Wirklichkeit — Verfassung und Verfassungswirklichkeit

Ver f d Gesch Berlins Schr — Verein fuer die Geschichte Berlins. Schriften

Ver f Gesch Dresdens Mitt — Verein fuer Geschichte Dresdens. Mitteilungen

Verfinst TNO Circ — Verfinstituut TNO [*Nederlands Centrale Organisatie voor Toegepast - Natuurwetenschappelijk Onderzoek*] Circulaire

Ver Freunde Naturg Mecklenberg Arch — Verein der Freunde der Naturgeschichte in Mecklenberg. Archiv

Ver Freunden Erdk Leipzig Jber — Verein von Freunden der Erdkunde zu Leipzig. Jahresbericht

Ver f Thuer Gesch u Alt Ztsch — Verein fuer Thueringische Geschichte und Altertumskunde. Zeitschrift

Vergangenh U Gegenw — Vergangenheit und Gegenwart

Verh Afd Natuurkd K Ned Akad Wet Eerste Reeks — Verhandelingen. Afdeling Natuurkunde. Koninklijke Nederlandse Akademie van Wetenschappen. Eerste Reeks

Verh Afd Natuurkd K Ned Akad Wet Tweede Reeks — Verhandelingen. Afdeling Natuurkunde. Koninklijke Nederlandse Akademie van Wetenschappen. Tweede Reeks

Verh Akad Wet Amsterdam Afd Natuurkd — Verhandelingen der Koninklijke Akademie van Wetenschappen te Amsterdam. Afdeeling Natuurkunde

Verh Allg Schweiz Ges Gesammten Naturwiss — Verhandlungen der Allgemeinen Schweizerischen Gesellschaft fuer die Gesammten Naturwissenschaften

Verh Anat Ges — Verhandlungen. Anatomische Gesellschaft

Verhandel Ak Wetensch Amsterd — Verhandelingen van de Akademie van Wetenschapen. Amsterdam

Verhand Hist Ver Niederbayern — Verhandlungen des Historischen Vereins fuer Niederbayern

Verhand Hist Ver Oberpfalz & Regensburg — Verhandlungen des Historischen Vereins fuer Oberpfalz und Regensburg

Verhand Kon Acad Wet Afd Lettknd — Verhandelingen van de Koninklijke Academie voor Wetenschappen, Afdeling Letterkunde

Verhand Kon Inst Taal Land & Vlkenknd — Verhandelingen Koninklijk Instituut voor Taal-, land- en Volkenkunde

Verhand Kon Ned Akad Wet — Verhandelingen der Koninklijke Nederlandse Akademie van Wetenschappen

Verhandl Deutsch Path Gesellsch — Verhandlungen. Deutsche Pathologische Gesellschaft

Verhandl Deutsch Zool Gesellsch — Verhandlungen. Deutsche Zoologische Gesellschaft

Verhandl DPG — Verhandlungen. Deutsche Physikalische Gesellschaft

Verhandl Geol Bundesanstalt — Verhandlungen. Geologische Bundesanstalt

Verhandl Gesellsch Deutsch Naturf u Aerzte — Verhandlungen. Gesellschaft Deutscher Naturforscher und Aerzte

Verhandl Hist Ver Niederbayern — Verhandlungen des Historischen Vereins fuer Niederbayern

Verhandl Naturforsch Ges Basel — Verhandlungen der Naturforschenden Gesellschaft in Basel

Verhandl Naturwiss Ver Hamburg — Verhandlungen des Naturwissenschaftlichen Vereins in Hamburg

Verhandl Naturw Ver Hamburg — Verhandlungen. Naturwissenschaftlicher Verein in Hamburg

Verhandl Naturw Ver Karlsruhe — Verhandlungen. Naturwissenschaftlicher Verein in Karlsruhe

Verhandl Schweiz Naturf Gesellsch — Verhandlungen. Schweizerische Naturforschende Gesellschaft

Verhandlungsber Kolloid-Ges — Verhandlungsberichte. Kolloid-Gesellschaft

Verhand Natforsch Ges Basel — Verhandlungen der Naturforschenden Gesellschaft Basel

Verhand Ver Befoerd Gtnbaues Koen Preuss Staaten — Verhandlungen des Vereins zur Befoerderung des Gartenbaues in den Koeniglichen Preussischen Staaten

Verhand Ver Kst & Altert Ulm & Oberschwaben — Verhandlungen des Vereins fuer Kunst und Altertum in Ulm und Oberschwaben

VerhBer Dt Zool Ges — Verhandlungsbericht. Deutsche Zoologische Gesellschaft

Verh Berl Bot Ver — Verhandlungen des Berliner Botanischen Vereins

Verh Berliner Med Ges — Verhandlungen der Berliner Medicinischen Gesellschaft

Verh Bot Ver Prov Brandenb — Verhandlungen. Botanischer Verein der Provinz Brandenburg

Verh Deutsch Geographentages — Verhandlungen des Deutschen Geographentages

Verh Dt Ges Angew Ent — Verhandlungen. Deutsche Gesellschaft fuer Angewandte Entomologie

Verh Dtsch Ges Angew Entomol — Verhandlungen. Deutsche Gesellschaft fuer Angewandte Entomologie

Verh Dtsch Ges Exp Med — Verhandlungen. Deutsche Gesellschaft fuer Experimentelle Medizin

Verh Dtsch Ges Inn Med — Verhandlungen. Deutsche Gesellschaft fuer Innere Medizin

Verh Dtsch Ges Kreislaufforsch — Verhandlungen. Deutsche Gesellschaft fuer Kreislaufforschung

Verh Dtsch Ges Pathol — Verhandlungen. Deutsche Gesellschaft fuer Pathologie

Verh Dtsch Ges Rheumatol — Verhandlungen. Deutsche Gesellschaft fuer Rheumatologie

Verh Dtsch Ges Verdau Stoffwechselkr — Verhandlungen der Deutschen Gesellschaft fuer Verdauungs- und Stoffwechselkrankheiten

Verh Dtsch Ges Zytol — Verhandlungen der Deutschen Gesellschaft fuer Zytologie

Verh Dtsch Phys Ges — Verhandlungen. Deutsche Physikalische Gesellschaft

Verh Dtsch Zool Ges — Verhandlungen. Deutsche Zoologische Gesellschaft

Verh Dt Zool Ges Bonn — Verhandlungen. Deutsche Zoologische Gesellschaft in Bonn

Verh Dt Zool Ges Erlangen — Verhandlungen. Deutsche Zoologische Gesellschaft in Erlangen

Verh Dt Zool Ges Frankfurt — Verhandlungen. Deutsche Zoologische Gesellschaft in Frankfurt

Verh Dt Zool Ges Goett — Verhandlungen. Deutsche Zoologische Gesellschaft in Goettingen

Verh Dt Zool Ges Graz — Verhandlungen. Deutsche Zoologische Gesellschaft in Graz

Verh Dt Zool Ges Hamburg — Verhandlungen. Deutsche Zoologische Gesellschaft in Hamburg

Verh Dt Zool Ges Jena — Verhandlungen. Deutsche Zoologische Gesellschaft in Jena

Verh Dt Zool Ges (Kiel) — Verhandlungen. Deutsche Zoologische Gesellschaft (Kiel)

Verh Dt Zool Ges (Tuebingen) — Verhandlungen. Deutsche Zoologische Gesellschaft (Tuebingen)

Verh Dt Zool Ges (Wien) — Verhandlungen. Deutsche Zoologische Gesellschaft (Wien)

Verh Dt Zool Ges (Wilhelmshaven) — Verhandlungen. Deutsche Zoologische Gesellschaft (Wilhelmshaven)

Verh Eerste Kl Kon Ned Inst Wetensch Amsterdam — Verhandelingen der Eerste Klasse van het Koninklijk Nederlandsch Instituut van Wetenschappen, Letterkunde, en Schoone Kunsten te Amsterdam

Verh Geol Bundesanst — Verhandlungen. Geologische Bundesanstalt

Verh Geol Bundesanst Bundeslaenderser — Verhandlungen. Geologische Bundesanstalt. Bundeslaenderserie

Verh Ges Deutsch Naturf — Verhandlungen der Gesellschaft Deutscher Naturforscher und Aerzte

Verh Ges Dsch Naturfrsch Aerzte — Verhandlungen. Gesellschaft Deutscher Naturforscher und Aerzte

Verh Ges Oekol — Verhandlungen der Gesellschaft fuer Oekologie

Verh Grossherzogl Bad Landw Vereins Ettlingen — Verhandlungen des Grossherzoglich Badischen Landwirthschaftlichen Vereins zu Ettlingen und Karlsruhe

Verh Hist Nied Bay — Verhandlungen. Historischer Vereine von Niederbayern

Verh Hist Oberpfalz — Verhandlungen. Historischer Vereine von Oberpfalz und Regensburg

Verh Inst Praev Geneeskd — Verhandelingen. Instituut voor Praeventieve Geneeskunde

Verh Int Psychother Kongr — Verhandlungen. Internationaler Psychotherapie Kongress

Verh Int Ver Theor Angew Limnol — Verhandlungen der Internationalen Vereinigung fuer Theoretische und Angewandte Limnologie

Verh K Acad Geneeskd Belg — Verhandelingen. Koninklijke Academie voor Geneeskunde van Belgie

Verh K Acad Wet Lett & Schone Kunsten Belg — Verhandelingen. Koninklijke Academie voor Wetenschappen. Letteren en Schone Kunsten van Belgie

Verh K Acad Wet Lett en Schone Kunsten Belg Kl Wet — Verhandelingen. Koninklijke Academie voor Wetenschappen. Letteren en Schone Kunsten van Belgie. Klasse der Wetenschappen

Verh K Acad Wet Lett Schone Kunsten Belg Kl Wet — Verhandelingen. Koninklijke Academie voor Wetenschappen. Letteren en Schone Kunsten van Belgie. Klasse der Wetenschappen

Verh K Akad Wet Amsterdam Afd Natuurkd — Verhandelingen. Koninklijke Akademie van Wetenschappen te Amsterdam. Afdeeling Natuurkunde

Verh K Akad Wet Amsterdam Afd Natuurkd Sect 2 — Verhandelingen der Koninklijke Akademie van Wetenschappen te Amsterdam. Afdeeling Natuurkunde. Sectie 2

Verh KK Zool Bot Ges Wien — Vorhandlungen der Kaiserlich-Koeniglichen Zoologisch-Botanischen Gesellschaft in Wien

Verh K Ned Akad Wet Afd Natuurkd Eerste Reeks — Verhandelingen. Koninklijke Nederlandse Akademie van Wetenschappen. Afdeling Natuurkunde. Eerste Reeks

Verh K Ned Akad Wet Afd Natuurkd Reeks 1 — Verhandelingen. Koninklijke Nederlandse Akademie van Wetenschappen. Afdeling Natuurkunde. Reeks 1

Verh K Ned Akad Wet Afd Natuurkd Reeks 2 — Verhandelingen. Koninklijke Nederlandse Akademie van Wetenschappen. Afdeling Natuurkunde. Reeks 2

Verh K Ned Akad Wet Afd Natuurkd Tweede Reeks — Verhandelingen. Koninklijke Nederlandse Akademie van Wetenschappen. Afdeling Natuurkunde. Tweede Reeks

Verh K Ned Akad Wetensch Afd Natuurk Reeks 1 — Verhandelingen. Koninklijke Nederlandse Akademie van Wetenschappen. Afdeling Natuurkunde. Reeks 1

Verh K Ned Akad Wetensch Afd Natuurk Reeks 2 — Verhandelingen. Koninklijke Nederlandse Akademie van Wetenschappen. Afdeling Natuurkunde. Reeks 2

Verh K Ned Geol Mijnbouwkd Genoot — Verhandelingen. Koninklijke Nederlands Geologisch Mijnbouwkundig Genootschap

Verh K Ned Geol Mijnbouwkd Genoot Geol Ser — Verhandelingen. Koninklijke Nederlandse Geologisch Mijnbouwkundig Genootschap. Geologische Serie

Verh K Ned Geol Mijnbouwkd Genoot Mijnbouwkd Ser — Verhandelingen. Koninklijke Nederlandse Geologisch Mijnbouwkundig Genootschap. Mijnbouwkundige Serie

Verh Konink Acad Wetensch Belgie — Verhandelingen. Koninklijke Academie voor Wetenschappen. Letteren en Schone Kunsten van Belgie

Verh Kon Nederl Ak Wetensch Afd Lett — Verhandelingen. Koninklijke Nederlandse Akademie van Wetenschappen. Afdeling Letterkunde

Verh K Vlaam Acad Geneesk Belg — Verhandelingen. Koninklijke Vlaamse Academie voor Geneeskunde van Belgie

Verh K Vlaam Acad Geneeskd Belg — Verhandelingen. Koninklijke Vlaamse Academie voor Geneeskunde van Belgie

Verh K Vlaam Acad Wetensch Belg Kl Wetensch — Verhandelingen. Koninklijke Vlaamse Academie voor Wetenschappen, Letteren, en Schone Kunsten van Belgie. Klasse der Wetenschappen

Verh K Vlaam Acad Wet Lett Schone Kunsten Belg Kl Wet — Verhandelingen. Koninklijke Vlaamse Academie voor Wetenschappen, Letteren, en Schone Kunsten van Belgie. Klasse der Wetenschappen

Verh Mecklenburg Naturf Ges — Verhandlungen der Mecklenburgischen Naturforschenden Gesellschaft

Verh Naturforsch Ges Basel — Verhandlungen. Naturforschende Gesellschaft in Basel

Verh Naturforsch Ver Bruenn — Verhandlungen. Naturforschender Verein in Bruenn

Verh Naturhist Med Vereins Heidelberg — Verhandlungen des Naturhistorisch-Medicinischen Vereins zu Heidelberg

Verh Naturhist Vereins Grossherzogth Hessen — Verhandlungen des Naturhistorischen Vereins fuer das Grossherzogthum Hessen undUmgebung

Verh Natur-Med Ver Heidelb — Verhandlungen. Naturhistorisch-Medizinischer Verein zu Heidelberg

Verh Naturwiss Ver Hamb — Verhandlungen des Naturwissenschaftlichen Vereins in Hamburg

Verh Natuur Geneesk Corresp Soc Ver Nederl — Verhandelingen van de Natuur- en Geneeskundige Correspondentie-Societeit in de Vereenigde Nederlanden

Verh Ornithol Ges Bayern — Verhandlungen. Ornithologische Gesellschaft in Bayern

Verh Phys-Med Ges Wuerzb — Verhandlungen. Physikalisch-Medizinische Gesellschaft in Wuerzburg

Verh Phys-Med Ges Wuerzburg — Verhandlungen. Physikalisch-Medizinische Gesellschaft in Wuerzburg

Verh Rijksinst Natuurbeheer — Verhandelingen. Rijksinstituut voor Natuurbeheer

Verh Schriften Oekon Sect Schles Ges Vaterl Cult — Verhandlungen und Schriften der Oekonomischen Section der Schlesischen Gesellschaft fuer Vaterlaendische Cultur

Verh Schweiz Naturf Ges — Verhandlungen. Schweizerische Naturforschende Gesellschaft

Verh Schweiz Naturforsch Ges — Verhandlungen. Schweizerische Naturforschende Gesellschaft

Verh Schweiz Naturforsch Ges Wiss Teil — Verhandlungen. Schweizerische Naturforschende Gesellschaft. Wissenschaftlicher Teil

Verh Vereins Befoerd Gewerbefl — Verhandlungen des Vereins zur Befoerderung des Gewerbefleisses

Verh Vereins Naturwiss Heimatf Hamburg — Verhandlungen des Vereins fuer Naturwissenschaftliche Heimatforschung zu Hamburg

Verh Ver Schweiz Physiol — Verhandlungen. Verein der Schweizer Physiologen

Verh Zeeuwsch Genootsch Wetensch Vlissingen — Verhandelingen Uitgegeven door het Zeeuwsch Genootschap der Wetenschappen te Vlissingen

Verh Zool Bot Ges Oesterr — Verhandlungen der Zoologisch-Botanischen Gesellschaft in Oesterreich

Verh Zool-Bot Ges Wien — Verhandlungen. Zoologisch-Botanische Gesellschaft in Wien

Veritas BA — Veritas (Buenos Aires)

Veritas P Alegre — Veritas (Porto Alegre, Brazil)

Verkehrsmed Grenzgeb — Verkehrsmedizin und Ihre Grenzgebiete
Verkehrsmed Ihre Grenzgeb — Verkehrsmedizin und Ihre Grenzgebiete
VerkF — Verkuendigung und Forschung
Verksamheten Stift Rasforadl Skogstrad — Verksamheten. Stiftelsen foer Rasforadling av Skogstrad
Ver LR — Vermont Law Review
Vermess-Inf — Vermessungs-Informationen
Vermischte Schriften Ackerbauges Tyrol — Vermischte Schriften der Ackerbaugesellschaft in Tyrol
Verm Nox Weeds Destr Board Leafl — Leaflet. Vermin and Noxious Weeds Destruction Board
Verm Nox Weeds Destrn Bd (Melb) Surv — Vermin and Noxious Weeds Destruction Board (Melbourne). Survey
Vermont Agric Exp Sta Misc Publ — Vermont State Agricultural College. Agricultural Experiment Station. Miscellaneous Publication
Vermont Bar Assn — Vermont Bar Association
Vermont Bs — Vermont Business
Vermont Geol Survey Bull — Vermont. Geological Survey. Bulletin
Vermont Hist — Vermont History. Proceedings. Vermont Historical Society
Vermont Lib — Vermont Libraries
Vermont L Rev — Vermont Law Review
Vermont Regist Nurse — Vermont Registered Nurse
Ver Museum Schles Altert — Verein fuer das Museum Schlesischer Altertuemer
Vernacular Architect — Vernacular Architecture
Vernacular Archre — Vernacular Architecture
Vernacular Bldg — Vernacular Building
Vern Archit — Vernacular Architecture
Verniciature Decor — Verniciature e Decorazioni
Veroeff Abt Archit Ksthist Inst U Koln — Veroeffentlichungen der Abteilung Architektur des Kunsthistorischen Instituts der Universitaet zu Koeln
Veroeff Arbeitsgem Forsch Landes Nordrhein Westfalen Abt Natu — Veroeffentlichungen der Arbeitsgemeinschaft fuer Forschung des Landes Nordrhein-Westfalen. Abteilung Naturwissenschaften
Veroeff Aus D Geb D Med Verwalt — Veroeffentlichungen aus dem Gebiete der Medizinal-Verwaltung
Veroeff Bayer Komm Intern Erdmessg — Veroeffentlichungen der Bayerischen Kommission fuer die Internationale Erdmessung
Veroeff Bundesanst Alp Landwirtsch Admont — Veroeffentlichungen. Bundesanstalt fuer Alpine Landwirtschaft in Admont
Veroeff Dtsch Geod Komm Reihe A — Veroeffentlichungen. Deutsche Geodaetiske Kommission. Bayerische Akademie der Wissenschaften. Reihe A
Veroeffentl A D Geb Heeres San Wes — Veroeffentlichungen aus dem Gebiete des Heeressanitaetswesen
Veroeffentl Archenhold Sternwarte — Veroeffentlichungen der Archenhold-Sternwarte
Veroeffentlich Schweizer Gesellsch Medizin Naturwissensch — Veroeffentlichungen. Schweizerische Gesellschaft fuer Geschichte der Medizin und der Naturwissenschaft
Veroeffentlichungen Volkskunde Kulturgesch — Veroeffentlichungen zur Volkskunde und Kulturgeschichte
Veroeffentl Inst Gesch Arabisch Islamischen Wiss Reihe B Abt — Veroeffentlichungen des Institutes fuer Geschichte der Arabisch-Islamischen Wissenschaften. Reihe B. Abteilung Mathematik
Veroeffentl Inst Wiener Kreis — Veroeffentlichungen des Instituts Wiener Kreis
Veroeffentl J-Vet-Ber Beamt Tieraerzte Preuss — Veroeffentlichungen aus den Jahres-Veterinaer-Berichten. Beamtete Tieraerzte Preussen
Veroeffentl Leibniz-Archivs — Veroeffentlichungen. Leibniz-Archiv
Veroeffentl Wiss Photolab — Veroeffentlichungen. Wissenschaftliche Photo-Laboratorien
Veroeff Forstl Bundesversuchsanst Mariabrunn Schoenbrunn Abt — Veroeffentlichungen der Forstlichen Bundesversuchsanstalt Mariabrunn in Schoenbrunn. Abteilung fuer Standortserkundung und -Kartierung
Veroeff Geobot Inst Eidg Tech Hochsch Stift Ruebel Zuer — Veroeffentlichungen. Geobotanisches Institut. Eidgenoessische Technische Hochschule Stiftung Ruebel in Zuerich
Veroeff Geobot Inst Eidg Tech Hochsch Stift Ruebel Zuerich — Veroeffentlichungen. Geobotanisches Institut. Eidgenoessische Technische Hochschule Stiftung Ruebel in Zuerich
Veroeff Geobot Inst Ruebel — Veroeffentlichungen. Geobotanisches Institut Ruebel
Veroeff Gesch Freien & Hansestadt Luebeck — Veroeffentlichungen zur Geschichte der Freien und Hansestadt Luebeck
Veroeff Graph Ges — Veroeffentlichung der Graphischen Gesellschaft
Veroeff Haus Natur Salzburg — Veroeffentlichungen aus dem Haus der Natur in Salzburg
Veroeff Heidelberg Altstadt — Veroeffentlichungen zur Heidelberger Altstadt
Veroeff Hist Komm Hannov — Veroeffentlichungen der Historischen Kommission fuer Hannover
Veroeff Hydrol Abt Dortm Stadtwerke — Veroeffentlichungen der Hydrologischen Abteilung der Dortmunder Stadtwerke
Veroeff Inst Meeresforsch Bremerhaven — Veroeffentlichungen. Institut fuer Meeresforschung in Bremerhaven
Veroeff Inst Meeresforsch Bremerhaven Suppl — Veroeffentlichungen. Institut fuer Meeresforschung in Bremerhaven. Supplement
Veroeff Inst Siedlungswasserwirtsch Abfalltech Univ Hannover — Veroeffentlichungen des Institutes fuer Siedlungswasserwirtschaft und Abfalltechnik der Universitaet Hannover
Veroeff IO (Berl) — Veroeffentlichungen des Instituts fuer Orientforschung der Deutschen Akademie der Wissenschaften (Berlin)
Veroeff Kaiser Wilhelm Inst Silikatforsch Berlin Dahlem — Veroeffentlichungen. Kaiser-Wilhelm-Institut fuer Silikatforschung in Berlin-Dahlem
Veroeff Kultamt Stadt Steyr — Veroeffentlichungen des Kulturamtes der Stadt Steyr
Veroeff Landwirtsch Chem Bundesversuchsanst (Linz) — Veroeffentlichungen. Landwirtschaftlich-Chemische Bundesversuchsanstalt (Linz)

Veroeff Meteorol Dienstes DDR — Veroeffentlichungen. Meteorologischer Dienst. Deutsche Demokratische Republik
Veroeff Meteorl Hydrol Dienstes DDR — Veroeffentlichungen. Meteorologischer und Hydrologischer Dienst. Deutsche Demokratische Republik
Veroeff Militsanitw — Veroeffentlichungen aus dem Gebiete des Militaer-Sanitaetswesens
Veroeff Morphol Pathol — Veroeffentlichungen aus der Morphologischen Pathologie
Veroeff Mus Ferdinandeum — Veroeffentlichungen des Museums Ferdinandeum
Veroeff Mus Ferdinandeum Innsbruck — Veroeffentlichungen des Museums Ferdinandeum in Innsbruck
Veroeff Mus Natur Handelsk Bremen Reihe A Naturwiss — Veroeffentlichungen aus dem Museum fuer Natur, Voelker- und Handelskunde Bremen. Reihe A. Naturwissenschaften
Veroeff Mus (Potsdam) — Veroeffentlichungen des Museums fuer Ur- und Fruehgeschichte (Potsdam)
Veroeff Mus Ur Fruhgesch — Veroeffentlichungen des Museums fuer Ur- und Fruehgeschichte
Veroeff Naturhist Mus (Basel) — Veroeffentlichungen. Naturhistorischer Museum (Basel)
Veroeff Naturh Mus (Wien) — Veroeffentlichungen. Naturhistorischer Museum (Wien)
Veroeff Naturschutz Landschaftspflege Baden Wuerttemb — Veroeffentlichungen fuer Naturschutz und Landschaftspflege in Baden-Wuerttemberg
Veroeff Naturschutz Landschaftspflege Baden-Wuerttemb Beih — Veroeffentlichungen fuer Naturschutz und Landschaftspflege in Baden-Wuerttemberg. Beihefte
Veroeff Niedersaechs Landesverwaltungsamtes Naturschutz Lands — Veroeffentlichungen des Niedersaechsischen Landesverwaltungsamtes. Naturschutz und Landschaftspflege
Veroeff Oe Ur Frueh Gesch — Veroeffentlichungen der Oesterreichischen Arbeitsgemeinschaft fuer Ur- und Fruehgeschichte
Veroeff Pathol — Veroeffentlichungen aus der Pathologie
Veroeff Provinzialmus Halle — Veroeffentlichungen des Provinzialmuseums Halle
Veroeff Reichsgesundheitsamts — Veroeffentlichungen. Reichsgesundheitsamt
Veroeff Reichsmus Vlkerknd Leiden — Veroeffentlichungen des Reichsmuseums fuer Volkerkunde in Leiden
Veroeff Strahlenschutzkomm — Veroeffentlichungen der Strahlenschutzkommission
Veroeff Tiroler Landesmus Ferdinandeum — Veroeffentlichungen des Tiroler Landesmuseum Ferdinandeum
Veroeff Tirol Landesmus Ferdinandeum — Veroeffentlichungen des Tiroler Landesmuseums Ferdinandeum
Veroeff Ueberseemus (Bremen) Reihe A — Veroeffentlichungen. Ueberseemuseum (Bremen). Reihe A
Veroeff Ueberseemus (Bremen) Reihe E Hum Oekol — Veroeffentlichungen. Ueberseemuseum (Bremen). Reihe E. Human-Oekologie
Veroeff Verband Oesterreich Gesch Ver — Veroeffentlichungen des Verbandes des Oesterreichischen Geschichte-Vereins
Veroeff Vorgesch Semin Marburg — Veroeffentlichungen des Vorgeschichtlichen Seminars Marburg
Veroeff Wiss Photo Lab (Wolfen) — Veroeffentlichungen. Wissenschaftliche Photo-Laboratorien (Wolfen)
Veroeff Wiss Zent Lab Photogr Abt AGFA — Veroeffentlichungen. Wissenschaftliches Zentral Laboratorium. Photographische Abteilung AGFA
Veroeff Wuerttemberg Landesstellen Naturschutz Ludwigsburg Tu — Veroeffentlichungen der Wuertt. Landesstellen fuer Naturschutz und Landschaftspflege in Ludwigsburg und Tuebingen
Veroeff Zentinst Kstgesch Munchen — Veroeffentlichungen des Zentralinstituts fuer Kunstgeschichte in Muenchen
Veroeff Zentralinst Phys Erde — Veroeffentlichungen. Zentralinstitut Physik der Erde
Veroeff Zool Staatssamml (Muench) — Veroeffentlichungen. Zoologische Staatssammlung (Muenchen)
Veroeff Zool StSamml (Muench) — Veroeffentlichungen. Zoologische Staatssammlung (Muenchen)
Veroff Inst Agrarmet Univ (Leipzig) — Veroeffentlichungen. Institut fuer Agrarmeteorologie und des Agrarmeteorologischen Observatoriums. Karl Marx-Universitaet (Leipzig)
Veroff Land-Hauswirtsch Auswertungs-Informationsdienst — Veroeffentlichungen. Land- und Hauswirtschaftlicher Auswertungsund Informationsdienst
Verona & Territ — Verona e il suo Territorio
Verona Illus — Verona Illustrata
Verona Mm Ac Ag — Memorie dell' Accademia d'Agricoltura, Scienze e Lettere di Verona
Verona Mm S It — Memorie di Matematica e di Fisica della Societa Italiana delle Scienze (Modena, Verona)
Verona S It Mm — Memorie di Matematica e di Fisica della Societa Italiana delle Scienze (Modena, Verona)
Ver Onderzoek Mnmt — Vereniging Onderzoek Monumentum
Verpack Chemiebetr — Verpackung im Chemiebetrich
Verpack Mag — Verpackungs-Magazin
Verpack-Rundsch — Verpackungs-Rundschau
Verre Bull Inf — Verre. Bulletin d'Information
Verre Silic Ind — Verre et Silicates Industriels
Verres Refract — Verres et Refractaires
Verres Refract Part 1 — Verres et Refractaires. Part 1. Articles Originaux
Verres Refract Part 2 — Verres et Refractaires. Part 2. Documentation
Verre Text Plast Renf — Verre Textile, Plastiques Renforces
Verri — Quaderni del Verri
Verrigtind Kongr S-Afr Genet Ver — Verrigtinge van die Kongres van die Suid-Afrikaanse Genetiese Vereniging

Verrigt Kongr S Afr Genet Ver — Verrigtinge van die Kongres van die Suid-Afrikaanse Genetiese Vereniging

Ver Schweizer Petroleum-Geologen u Ingenieure Bull — Vereinigung Schweizerischer Petroleum-Geologen und Ingenieure. Bulletin

Ver Schweiz Pet-Geol Ing Bull — Vereinigung Schweizerischer Petroleum-Geologen und Ingenieure. Bulletin

Versich U Geldwirts — Versicherung und Geldwirtschaft

Verslag Ver Proeftuin — Verslag van de Vereeniging de Proeftuin

Vers Landbouwkd Onderz — Verslagen van Landbouwkundige Onderzoekingen

Versl & Meded Kon Acad Ned Taal & Lettknd — Verslagen en Mededelingen van de Koninklijke Academie voor Nederlandse Taal- en Letterkunde

Versl & Meded Kon VI Acad Taal & Lettknd — Verslagen en Mededelingen van de Koninklijke Vlaamse Academie voor Taal- en Letterkunde

Versl & Meded Ver Beoef Overijsselsch Regt & Gesch — Verslagen en Mededelingen der Vereeniging tot Beoefening van Overijsselsch Regt en Geschiedenis

Versl En Meded D Kon Akad V Wetensch Afd Natuurk — Verslagen en Mededeelingen der Koninklijke Akademie van Wetenschappen. Afdeeling Natuurkunde

Versl Interprov Proeven Proefstn Akkerbouw Lelystad (Neth) — Verslagen van Interprovinciale Proeven. Proefstation voor de Akkerbouw Lelystad(Netherlands)

Versl Interprov Proeven Proefstn Akkerbouw (Wageningen) — Verslagen van Interprovinciale Proeven. Proefstation voor de Akkerbouw (Wageningen)

Versl Landbouwkd Onderz A — Verslagen van Landbouwkundige Onderzoekingen A. Rijkslandbouwproefstation en Bodemkundig Instituut te Groningen

Versl Landbouwkd Onderz (Agric Res Rep) — Verslagen van Landbouwkundige Onderzoekingen (Agricultural Research Reports)

Versl Landbouwkd Onderz B — Verslagen van Landbouwkundige Onderzoekingen B. Bodemkundig Instituut te Groningen

Versl Landbouwkd Onderz C — Verslagen van Landbouwkundige Onderzoekingen C.Rijkslandbouwproefstation te Hoorn

Versl Landbouwkd Onderz D — Verslagen van Landbouwkundige Onderzoekingen D. Rijksproefstation voor Zaadcontrole te Wageningen

Versl Landbouwkd Onderz E — Verslagen van Landbouwkundige Onderzoekingen E. Rijkslandbouwproefstation voor Veevoederonderzoek te Wageningen

Versl Landbouwkd Onderz F — Verslagen van Landbouwkundige Onderzoekingen F.Rijkslandbouwproefstation te Maastricht

Versl Landbouwkd Onderz G — Verslagen van Landbouwkundige Onderzoekingen G. Onderzoekingen Uitgevoerd in Opdracht van den Algemeenen Nederlandschen Zuivelbond

Versl Landbouwkd Onderz Rijkslandbouwproefstn — Verslagen van Landbouwkundige Onderzoekingen der Rijkslandbouwproefstations

Versl Landbouwkd Onderz — Verslagen van Landbouwkundige Onderzoekingen

Versl Landbouwk Onderz Cent Lanbouwpubl Landbouwdoc — Verslagen van Landbouwkundige Onderzoekingen. Centrum voor Landbouwpublikatien en Landbouwdocumentatie

Versl Landbouwk Onderz Ned — Verslagen van het Landbouwkundig Onderzoek in Nederland

Versl Meded Kon VI Ak Taal & Letterk — Verslagen en Mededeelingen. Koninklijke Vlaamse Akademie voor Taal- en Letterkunde

Versl Meded K Vlaam Acad Taal Lett — Verslagen en Mededeelingen. Koninklijke Vlaamse Academie voor Taal- en Letterkunde

Versl Meded Rijkslandbouwconsul Westelijk Drenthe — Verslagen en Mededeelingen van het Rijkslandbouwconsulentschap Westelijk Drenthe

Versl Tien-Jarenplan Graanonderzoek Sticht Nederl Graan-Cent — Verslagen. Tien-Jarenplan voor Graanonderzoek. Stichting Nederlands Graan-Centrum

Versl Ver Chem Tech Landbouwkd Advis — Verslagen der Vereeniging van Chemisch-Technischen. Landbouwkundig Adviseurs

Verstaendliche Wiss — Verstaendliche Wissenschaft

Versuche Abh Naturf Ges Dantzig — Versuche und Abhandlungen der Naturforschenden Gesellschaft in Dantzig

Versuchsergeb Bundesanst Pflanzenbau Samenpruefung Wien — Versuchsergebnisse der Bundesanstalt fuer Pflanzenbau und Samenpruefung in Wien

Versuchsgrubenges Quartalsh — Versuchsgrubengesellschaft Quartalshefte

Versuchsstn Gaerungsgewerbe Wien Mitt — Versuchsstation fuer das Gaerungsgewerbe in Wien. Mitteilungen

Vertebr Hung — Vertebrata Hungarica

Vertebr Palasiat — Vertebrata Palasiatica

Vertebr Palasiatica — Vertebrata Palasiatica

Vertebr Pest Control Manage Mater — Vertebrate Pest Control and Management Materials

Vert File Ind — Vertical File Index

Vert File Index — Vertical File Index

Verulamium Mus Occas Pap — Verulamium Museum Occasional Papers

Ver Vaterl Naturk Wuerttemberg Jahresh — Verein fuer Vaterlaendische Naturkunde in Wuerttemberg. Jahreshefte

Ver Verbr Naturwiss Kenntnisse Wien Schr — Verein zur Verbreitung Naturwissenschaftlicher Kenntnisse in Wien. Schriften

VerwA — Verwaltungsarchiv

Verwaltung — Zeitschrift fuer Verwaltungswissenschaft

Verwaltungsarch — Verwaltungsarchiv

Verwarm Vent — Verwarming en Ventilatie

Verzam Overdruk Plantenziektenk Dienst (Wageningen) — Verzamelde Overdrukken. Plantenziektenkundige Dienst (Wageningen)

Verzekerings-Arch — Verzekerings-Archief

Verz Gemaldegal Ksthist Mus Wien — Verzeichnis der Gemaldegalerie des Kunsthistorischen Museums. Wien

Verz Mitglieder Dt Archaeol Inst — Verzeichnis der Mitglieder des Deutschen Archaeologischen Institut

VESADE — Elektronmikroskopievereeniging van Suidelike Afrika. Verrigtings

Ves Akad Nauk Kirg SSR — Vestnik Akademii Nauk Kirgizskoi SSR

Vesci Akad Navuk BSSR Ser Fiz-Mat Navuk — Vesci Akademii Navuk BSSR. Seryja Fizika-Matematycnych Navuk

Vesci Ak BSSR — Vesci Akademii Navuk BSSR

Ves Drev Ist — Vestnik Drevnei Istorii

Ves Drev Istor — Vestnik Drevnei Istorii

Vesientutkimuslaitoksen Julk — Vesientutkimuslaitoksen Julkaisuja

Vesn Zavod Geol Geofiz Istraz NR Srb — Vesnik Zavod za Geoloska i Geofizicka Istrazivanja NR Srbije

Vesn Zavod Geol Geofiz Istraz Ser A — Vesnik Zavod za Geoloska i Geofizicka Istrazivanja. Serija A. Geologija

Vesn Zavod Geol Geofiz Istraz Ser C — Vesnik Zavod za Geoloska i Geofizicka Istrazivanja. Serija C. Priminjena Geofizika

Vest Akad Nauk SSSR — Vestnik Akademii Nauk SSSR

Vest Ak Nauk — Vestnik Akademii Nauk SSSR

Vest Ces Akad Zemed — Vestnik Ceskoslovenske Akademie Zemedelske

Vest Csl Fysiat Spol — Vestnik Ceskoslovenske Fysiatricke Spolecnosti

Vest Csl Jedn Reparu — Vestnik Ceskoslovenske Jednoty Reparu

Vest Csl Lek — Vestnik Ceskoslovenskych Lekaru

Vest Csl Mus Spolku Archaeol — Vestnik Ceskoslovenskych Musei a Spolku Archaeologickych

Vest Csl Spol Zool — Vestnik Ceskoslovenske Spolecnosti Zoologicke

Vest Csl Ustr Jedn Velocip — Vestnik Ceskoslovenske Ustredni Jednoty Velocipedistu

Vest Csl Zemed Mus — Vestnik Ceskoslovenskeho Zemedelskeho Museum

Vest Csl Zool Spol — Vestnik Ceskoslovenske Zoologicke Spolecnosti

Vest Csl Zub Tech — Vestnik Ceskoslovenskych Zubnich Techniku

Vest Dal'nevost Fil Akad Nauk SSSR — Vestnik Dal'nevostochnogo Filiala Akademii Nauk SSSR

Vest Derm Vener — Vestnik Dermatologii i Venerologii

Vest Don Otd Imp Obshch Sadov — Vestnik Donskago Otdela Imperatorskago Obshchestva Sadovodstva

Vest Dush Bolez — Vestnik Dushevnykh Boleznei

Vest Edin Gidromet Sluzhby — Vestnik Edinoi Gidrometeorologicheskoi Sluzhby

Vest Eksp Teor Elektrotekh — Vestnik Eksperimental'noi i Teoreticheskoi Elektroteckhniki

Vest Elektroprom — Vestnik Elektropromyshlennosti

Vest Elektrotekh — Vestnik Elektrotekhniki

Vest Endokr — Vestnik Endokrinologii

Vest Farm — Vestnik Farmatsii

Vestf Hjemst — Vestfynsk Hjemstavn

Vest Fiz Kult — Vestnik Fizicheskoi Kul'tury

Vest Fotogr — Vestnik Fotografii

Vest Geol Kom — Vestnik Geologicheskogo Komiteta

Vest Gibrid — Vestnik Gibridizatsii

Vest Glav Uprav Metalloprom — Vestnik Glavnogo Upravleniya Metallopromyshlennosti

Vest Gomeop Med — Vestnik Gomeopaticheskoi Meditsiny

Vest Gos Muz Gruz — Vestnik Gosudarstvennogo Muzeja Gruzii Imeni Akademika S. N. Dzhanashia

Vest Inst Pchelovodstva — Vestnik Institut Pchelovodstva

Vest Inzh Tekh — Vestnik Inzhenerov i Tekhnikov

Vest Irrig — Vestnik Irrigatsii

Vest Ist Mirov Kul't — Vestnik Istorii Mirovoi Kul'tury

Vest Kainsk Obshch Moloch Khoz — Vestnik Kainskago Obshchestva Molochnago Khozyaistva

Vest Khar'k Univ Radiofiz Elektron — Vestnik Khar'kovskogo Universiteta. Radiofizika, Elektronika

Vest Khir — Vestnik Khirurgii

Vest Khir Grekova — Vestnik Khirurgii imeni I. I. Grekova

Vest Khir Pogr Obl — Vestnik Khirurgii i Pogranichnykh Oblastei

Vest Khorol Sel Khoz — Vestnik Khorol'skago Sel'skago Khozyaistva

Vest Klin Sudeb Psikhiat Nevrol — Vestnik Klinicheskoi i Sudebnoi Psikhiatrii i Nevropatologii

Vest Klubu Prir Prostejove — Vestnik Klubu Prirodovedeckeho v Prostejove

Vest Kozhev Obuv Prom — Vestnik Kozhevenno-Obuvnoi Promyshlennosti

Vest Kozhev Prom Torg — Vestnik Kozhevennoi Promyshlennosti i Torgovli

Vest Krolikov — Vestnik Krolikovodstva

Vestland Kstindustmus Ab — Vestlandske Kunstindustrimuseums Arbok

Vest Latv PSR Akad — Vestis Latvijas Pasomju Socialistikas Republikas Zinatu Akademija

Vest Leningr Gos Univ Ser Biol — Vestnik Leningradskogo Gosudarstvennogo Universiteta. Seriya Biologii

Vest Leningr Inst — Vestnik Leningradskogo Instituta

Vest LU — Letopis. Slovenska Akademija Znanosti in Umetnosti v Ljubljani

Vest Mekh Prikl Mat — Vestnik Mekhaniki i Prikladnoi Matematiki

Vest Mikrobiol Epidemiol Parazitol — Vestnik Mikrobiologii, Epidemiologii, i Parazitologii

Vest Mikrobiol Epidem Parazit — Vestnik Mikrobiologii i Epidemiologii i Parazitologii

Vest Minist Prum Repub Csl — Vestnik Ministerstva Prumyslu. Obehodu a Zivnosti Republiky Ceskoslovenske

Vest Minist Verej Zdrav Telesne Vych Repub Csl — Vestnik Ministerstva Verejneho Zdravotnictvi a Telesne Vychovy Republiky Ceskoslovenske

Vest Minist Zemed Repub Csl — Vestnik Ministerstva Zemedelstvi Republiky Ceskoslovenske

Vest Mosk Gorn Akad — Vestnik Moskovskoi Gornoi Akademii

Vest Mosk Gos Univ — Vestnik Moskovskogo Gosudarstvennogo Universiteta

Vest Mosk Gos Univ Ser VI — Vestnik Moskovskogo Gosudarstvennogo Universiteta. Seriya VI

Vest Mosk Inst Biol Pochv — Vestnik Moskovskogo Instituta. Seriya Biologiya, Pochvovedenie

Vest Mosk Inst Geogr — Vestnik Moskovskogo Instituta Geografii

Vest Mosk Univ Ser 15 Vychisl Mat Kibern — Vestnik Moskovskogo Universiteta. Seriya 15. Vychislitel'naya Matematika i Kibernetika

Vest Mosk Univ Ser Biol Pochv Geol Geogr — Vestnik Moskovskogo Universiteta. Seriya Biologii, Pochvovedeniya, Geologii, Geografii

Vest MU — Vestnik Moskovskogo Universiteta

Vest Mylov Zhirov Prom — Vestnik Mylovareniya i Zhirovoi Promyshlennosti

Vestn Akad Med Nauk SSSR — Vestnik Akademii Meditsinskikh Nauk SSSR

Vestn Akad Nauk Beloruss SSR Ser Obsc Nauk — Vestnik Akademii Nauk Belorusskoj SSR. Serija Obscestvennyh Nauk

Vestn Akad Nauk Kazah SSR — Vestnik Akademii Nauk Kazahskoj SSR

Vestn Akad Nauk Kazakh SSR — Vestnik Akademiya Nauk Kazakhskoi SSR

Vestn Akad Nauk Kaz SSR — Vestnik Akademii Nauk Kazakhskoi SSR

Vestn Akad Nauk Resp Kaz — Vestnik Akademii Nauk Respubliki Kazakhstan

Vestn Akad Nauk SSSR — Vestnik Akademii Nauk SSSR

Vestn Akad Nauk Ukr SSR — Vestnik Akademii Nauk Ukrainskoi SSR

Vest Nar Ozdorov — Vestnik Narodnogo Ozdorovleniya

Vest Nar Tech Mus — Vestnik Narodniho Technickeho Musea

Vest Nat Kom Torg Prom — Vestnik Narodnogo Komissariata Torgovli i Promyshlennosti

Vest Nauchno-Issled Inst Pchel — Vestnik Nauchno-Issledovatel'skii Institut Pchelovodstva

Vest Nauch Obshch Tatarov Kazan — Vestnik Nauchnogo Obshchestva Tatarovedeniya (Kazan)

Vestn Beloruss Gos Univ Im VI Lenina Ser 1 — Vestnik Belorusskogo Gosudarstvennogo Universiteta imeni V. I. Lenina, Seriya 1. Fizika, Matematika, Mekhanika

Vestn Beloruss Gos Univ Im VI Lenina Ser 2 — Vestnik Belorusskogo Gosudarstvennogo Universiteta imeni V. I. Lenina, Seriya 2. Khimiya, Biologiya, Geografiya

Vestn Beloruss Gos Univ Ser 1 — Vestnik Belorusskogo Gosudarstvennogo Universiteta. Seriya 1. Matematika, Fizika, Mekhanika

Vestn Beloruss Gos Univ Ser 1 Fiz Mat Inf — Vestnik Belorusskogo Gosudarstvennogo Universiteta. Seriya 1. Fizika, Matematika, Informatika

Vestn Beloruss Gos Univ Ser 1 Fiz Mat Mekh — Vestnik Belorusskogo Gosudarstvennogo Universiteta. Seriya 1. Fizika, Matematika, Mekhanika

Vestn Beloruss Gos Univ Ser 2 Biol Khim Geol Geogr — Vestnik Belorusskogo Gosudarstvennogo Universiteta. Seriya 2. Biologiya, Khimiya, Geologiya, Geografiya

Vestn Beloruss Univ — Vestnik Belorusskogo Universiteta

Vestn Cesk Akad Zemed — Vestnik Ceskoslovenske Akademie Zemedelske

Vestn Cesk Akad Zemed Ved — Vestnik Ceskoslovenske Akademie Zemedelskych Ved

Vestn Cesk Geol Ustavu — Vestnik Ceskeho Geologickeho Ustavu

Vestn Ceskoslov Akad Zemed Ved — Vestnik Ceskoslovenske Akademie Zemedelskych Ved

Vestn Cesk Spol Zool — Vestnik Ceskoslovenske Spolecnosti Zoologicke

Vestn Chkal Otd Vses Khim O-Va Im D I Mendeleeva — Vestnik Chkalovckogo Otdeleniya Vsesoyuznogo Khimicheskogo Obshchestva Imeni D.I. Mendeleeva

Vestn Dermatol Venerol — Vestnik Dermatologii i Venerologii

Vestn Drevnej Istor — Vestnik Drevnej Istorii. Revue d'Histoire Ancienne

Vestn Drevn Ist — Vestnik Drevnei Istorii

Vestn Elektroprom-Sti — Vestnik Elektropromyshlennosti

Vestn Elektrotekh — Vestnik Elektrotekhniki

Vestn Estestv — Vestnik Estestvoznanija. Revue des Sciences Naturelles

Vestn Gos Muz Gruz — Vestnik Gosudarstvennogo Muzeja Gruzii

Vestn Gosud Muz Gruzii — Vestnik Gosudarstvennogo Muzeja Gruzii Imeni Akademika S. N. Dzhanashia

Vestn Gruz Bot Ova — Vestnik Gruzinskogo Botanicheskogo Obshchestva

Vestnik Akad Nauk Kazah SSR — Vestnik Akademii Nauk Kazahskoj SSR

Vestnik Akad Nauk Kazakh SSR — Vestnik Akademii Nauk Kazakhskoi SSR

Vestnik Akad Nauk Respub Kazakhstan — Vestnik. Akademiya Nauk Respubliki Kazakhstan

Vestnik Akad Nauk SSSR — Vestnik Akademii Nauk SSSR

Vestnik Beloruss Gos Univ Ser 1 — Vestnik Belorusskogo Gosudarstvennogo Universiteta Imeni V. I. Lenina. Naucnyi Zurnal. Seriya 1. Matematika, Fizika, Mekhanika

Vestnik Beloruss Gos Univ Ser I Fiz Mat Mekh — Vestnik Belorusskogo Gosudarstvennogo Universiteta imeni V. I. Lenina. Seriya I. Fizika, Matematika, Mekhanika

Vestnik Chelyabinsk Univ Ser 3 Mat Mekh — Vestnik. Chelyabinskii Universitet. Seriya 3. Matematika, Mekhanika

Vestnik Drevney Istor — Vestnik Drevney Istorii

Vestnik Har'kov Gos Univ — Vestnik Har'kovskogo Gosudarstvennogo Universiteta

Vestnik Har'kov Politehn Inst — Vestnik Har'kovskogo Politehniceskogo Instituta

Vestnik Jaroslav Univ — Vestnik Jaroslavskogo Universiteta

Vestnik Karakalpak Fil Akad Nauk UzSSR — Akademija Nauk UzSSR. Karakalpakskii Filial. Vestnik

Vestnik Karakalpak Filiala Akad Nauk Uzbek SSR — Vestnik Karakalpakskogo Filiala Akademii Nauk Uzbekstoy SSR

Vestnik K Ceske Spolec Nauk v Praze Trida Mat Prirod — Vestnik Kralovske Ceske Spolecnosti Nauk v Praze Trida Matematicko Prirodovedecka

Vestnik Khar'kov Gos Univ — Vestnik Khar'kovskogo Gosudarstvennogo Universiteta. Seriya Mekhaniko-Matematicheskaya. Zapiski Mekhaniko-Matematicheskogo Fakul'teta i Khar'kovskogo Matematicheskogo Obshchestva

Vestnik Kharkov Univ — Vestnik. Khar'kovskii Universitet

Vestnik Kiev Politehn Inst Ser Tehn Kibernet — Vestnik Kievskogo Politehniceskogo Instituta. Serija Tehniceskoi Kibernetiki

Vestnik Kiev Univ Model Optim Slozhn Sist — Vestnik Kievskogo Universiteta. Modelirovanie i Optimizatsiya Slozhnykh Sistem

Vestnik Leningrad U — Vestnik Leningradskogo Universiteta

Vestnik Leningrad Univ Fiz Khim — Vestnik Leningradskogo Universiteta. Fizika i Khimiya

Vestnik Leningrad Univ Math — Vestnik Leningrad University. Mathematics

Vestnik Leningrad Univ Mat Mekh Astronom — Vestik Leningradskogo Universiteta. Matematika, Mekhanika, Astronomiya

Vestnik Leningrad Univ Ser Fiz Khim — Vestnik Leningradskogo Universiteta. Seriya Fiziki i Khimii

Vestnik Leningr Gosud Univ — Vestnik Leningradskogo Gosudarstvennogo Universiteta

Vestnik L'vov Politehn Inst — Vestnik L'vovskogo Politehniceskogo Instituta

Vestnik Mikrobiol Epidemiol i Parazitol — Vestnik Mikrobiologii, Epidemiologii, i Parazitologii

Vestnik Mikrobiol i Epidemiol — Vestnik Mikrobiologii i Epidemiologii

Vestnik Moskov Univ Ser III Fiz Astronom — Vestnik Moskovskogo Universiteta. Serija III. Fizika, Astronomija

Vestnik Moskov Univ Ser I Mat Meh — Vestnik Moskovskogo Universiteta. Serija I. Matematika, Mehanika

Vestnik Moskov Univ Ser XV Vycisl Mat Kibernet — Vestnik Moskovskogo Universiteta. Serija XV. Vycislitel'naja Matematika i Kibernetika

Vestnik Mosk Univ Ser Khim — Vestnik Moskovskogo Universiteta. Serija 2. Khimiya

Vestnik Mus Kromerizi — Vestnik Musea v Kromerizi

Vestnik Obsh Vet (S Peterburg) — Vestnik Obshchestvennoi Veterinarii (S. Peterburg)

Vestnik Rentg i Radiol — Vestnik Rentgenologii i Radiologii

Vestnik Ross Akad Nauk — Vestnik. Rossiiskaya Akademiya Nauk. Vestnik

Vestnik Sovrem Vet — Vestnik Sovremennoi Veterinarii

Vestnik S Peterburg Univ Fiz Khim — Vestnik Sankt-Peterburgskogo Universiteta. Fizika. Khimiya

Vestnik S Peterburg Univ Mat Mekh Astronom — Vestnik Sankt-Peterburgskogo Universiteta. Matematika, Mekhanika, Astronomiya

Vestnik Statist — Vestnik Statistiki

Vestnik St Petersburg Univ Math — Vestnik St. Petersburg University. Mathematics

Vestnik Ustredniho Ustavu Geol — Vestnik Ustredniho Ustavu Geologickeho

Vestn Inzh Tekh — Vestnik Inzhenerov i Tekhnikov

Vestn Jaroslav Univ — Vestnik Jaroslavskogo Universiteta

Vestn Kabard Balkar Nauc-Issled Inst — Vestnik Kabardino-Balkarskogo Naucno-Issledovatel'skogo Instituta

Vestn Karakalp Fil Akad — Vestnik Karakalpakskogo Filiala Akademii Nauk Uzbekskoi SSR

Vestn Karakalp Fil Akad Nauk Uzb SSR — Vestnik Karakalpakskogo Filiala Akademii Nauk Uzbekskoi SSR

Vestn Kazahsk Fil Akad Nauk SSSR — Vestnik Kazahskogo Filiala Akademii Nauk SSSR

Vestn Kaz Fil Akad Nauk SSSR — Vestnik Kazakhskogo Filiala Akademii Nauk SSSR

Vestn Khar'k Politekh Inst — Vestnik Khar'kovskogo Politekhnicheskogo Instituta

Vestn Khark Univ — Vestnik Khar'kovskogo Universiteta

Vestn Khar'k Univ Astron — Vestnik Khar'kovskogo Universiteta. Astronomiya

Vestn Khar'k Univ Geol Geogr — Vestnik Khar'kovskogo Universiteta. Geologiya i Geografiya

Vestn Khar'k Univ Ser Biol — Vestnik Khar'kovskogo Universiteta. Seriya Biologicheskaya

Vestn Khar'k Univ Ser Geol — Vestnik Khar'kovskogo Universiteta. Seriya Geologicheskaya

Vestn Khar'k Univ Ser Khim — Vestnik Khar'kovskogo Universiteta. Seriya Khimicheskaya

Vestn Khar'k Univ Vopr Ehlektrokhim — Vestnik Khar'kovskogo Universiteta. Voprosy Ehlektrokhimii

Vestn Khir — Vestnik Khirurgii Imeni I. I. Grekova

Vestn Khir Im I I Grek — Vestnik Khirurgii Imeni I. I. Grekova

Vestn Khir Im I I Grekova — Vestnik Khirurgii Imeni I. I. Grekova

Vestn Kiev Politekh Inst Ser Mashinostr — Vestnik Kievskogo Politekhnicheskogo Instituta. Seriya Mashinostroeniya

Vestn Kiev Politekh Inst Ser Priborostr — Vestnik Kievskogo Politekhnicheskogo Instituta. Seriya Priborostroeniya

Vestn Kiev Politekh Inst Ser Teploenerg — Vestnik Kievskogo Politekhnicheskogo Instituta. Seriya Teploenergetiki

Vestn Kral Ceske Spol Nauk Trida Mat Prirodoved — Vestnik Kralovske Ceske Spolecnosti Nauk Trida Matematicko Prirodovedecka

Vestn La Upr Metallopromsti — Vestnik Lavnogo Upravleniya Metallopromyshlennosti

Vestn Leningradsk Univ Ser Biol Geogr — Vestnik Leningradskogo Universiteta. Serija Biologii, Geografii, i Geologii

Vestn Leningrad Univ Ser Biol — Vestnik Leningradskogo Universiteta. Seriya Biologii

Vestn Leningr Univ — Vestnik Leningradskogo Universiteta

Vestn Leningr Univ Biol — Vestnik Leningradskogo Universiteta. Biologiya

Vestn Leningr Univ Fiz & Khim — Vestnik Leningradskogo Universiteta. Fizika i Khimiya

Vestn Leningr Univ Geol Geogr — Vestnik Leningradskogo Universiteta. Geologiya, Geografiya

Vestn Leningr Univ Ist Jaz Lit — Vestnik Leningradskogo Universiteta. Istorija, Jazyka, i Literatury

Vestn Leningr Univ Mat Mekh Astron — Vestnik Leningradskogo Universiteta. Matematika, Mekhanika, Astronomiya

Vestn Leningr Univ Ser 3 Biol — Vestnik Leningradskogo Universiteta. Seriya 3. Biologiya

Vestn Leningr Univ Ser 4 Fiz Khim — Vestnik Leningradskogo Universiteta. Seriya 4. Fizika, Khimiya

Vestn Leningr Univ Ser 7 Geol Geogr — Vestnik Leningradskogo Universiteta. Seriya 7. Geologiya, Geografiya

Vestn Leningr Univ Ser Ekon Filos Pravo — Vestnik Leningradskogo Universiteta. Serija Ekonomiki, Filosofii, i Pravo

Vestn Leningr Univ Ser Fiz Khim — Vestnik Leningradskogo Universiteta. Seriya Fiziki i Khimii

Vestn Leningr Univ Ser Geol Geogr — Vestnik Leningradskogo Universiteta. Seriya Geologii i Geografii

Vestn Leningr Univ Ser Mat Fiz Khim — Vestnik Leningradskogo Universiteta. Seriya Matematiki, Fiziki, i Khimii

Vestn Leningr Univ Ser Mat Mekh & Astron — Vestnik Leningradskogo Universiteta. Seriya Matematika, Mekhanika, i Astronomiya

Vestn Lening Univ Ser Biol Geogr Geol — Vestnik Leningradskogo Universiteta. Seriya Biologii, Geografii, i Geologii

Vestn L'viv Derzh Univ Ser Fiz — Vestnik L'vivs'kogo Derzhavnogo Universitetu. Seriya Fizichna

Vestn Mashinostr — Vestnik Mashinostroeniya

Vestn Metallopromsti — Vestnik Metallopromyshlennosti

Vestn Minist Nauki Akad Nauk Resp Kaz — Vestnik Ministerstva Nauki-Adademii Nauk Respubliki Kazakhstan

Vestn Minist Zdrav — Vestnik Ministerstva Zdravotnictvi

Vestn Mosk Gos Tekh Univ Ser Mashinostr — Vestnik Moskovskogo Gosudarstvennogo Tekhnicheskogo Universiteta. Seriya Mashinostroenie

Vestn Moskovskogo Univ Fiz-Astron — Vestnik Moskovskogo Universiteta. Seriya Fizika-Astronomiya

Vestn Moskovskogo Univ Khim — Vestnik Moskovskogo Universiteta. Seriya Khimiya

Vestn Moskov Univ Ser 6 — Vestnik Moskovskogo Universiteta. Seriya 6

Vestn Moskov Univ Ser Ekon — Vestnik Moskovskogo Universiteta. Serija Ekonomika

Vestn Moskov Univ Ser Filos — Vestnik Moskovskogo Universiteta. Serija Filosofija

Vestn Moskov Univ Ser Geogr — Vestnik Moskovskogo Universiteta. Serija Geografija

Vestn Moskov Univ Ser Ist — Vestnik Moskovskogo Universiteta. Serija Istorija

Vestn Moskov Univ Ser Pravo — Vestnik Moskovskogo Universiteta. Serija Pravo

Vestn Moskov Univ Teorija Nauc Kommunizma — Vestnik Moskovskogo Universiteta Teorija Naucnogo Kommunizma

Vestn Mosk Univ — Vestnik Moskovskogo Universiteta

Vestn Mosk Univ Biol Pochvoved — Vestnik Moskovskogo Universiteta. Biologiya, Pochvovedenie

Vestn Mosk Univ Fiz Astron — Vestnik Moskovskogo Universiteta. Fizika, Astronomiya

Vestn Mosk Univ Geogr — Vestnik Moskovskogo Universiteta. Geografiya

Vestn Mosk Univ Geol — Vestnik Moskovskogo Universiteta. Geologiya

Vestn Mosk Univ Khim — Vestnik Moskovskogo Universiteta. Khimiya

Vestn Mosk Univ Mat Mekh — Vestnik Moskovskogo Universiteta. Matematika, Mekhanika

Vestn Mosk Univ Ser 1 — Vestnik Moskovskogo Universiteta. Seriya 1. Matematika, Mekhanika

Vestn Mosk Univ Ser 1 Mat Mekh — Vestnik Moskovskogo Universiteta. Seriya 1. Matematika, Mekhanika

Vestn Mosk Univ Ser 2 Khim — Vestnik Moskovskogo Universiteta. Seriya 2. Khimiya

Vestn Mosk Univ Ser 3 — Vestnik Moskovskogo Universiteta. Seriya 3. Fizika, Astronomiya

Vestn Mosk Univ Ser 3 Fiz Astron — Vestnik Moskovskogo Universiteta. Seriya 3. Fizika, Astronomiya

Vestn Mosk Univ Ser 4 Geol — Vestnik Moskovskogo Universiteta. Seriya 4. Geologiya

Vestn Mosk Univ Ser 5 Geogr — Vestnik Moskovskogo Universiteta. Seriya 5. Geografiya

Vestn Mosk Univ Ser 6 Biol Pochvoved — Vestnik Moskovskogo Universiteta. Seriya 6. Biologiya, Pochvovedenie

Vestn Mosk Univ Ser 15 — Vestnik Moskovskogo Universiteta. Seriya 15. Vychislitel'naya Matematika i Kibernetika

Vestn Mosk Univ Ser 15 Vychisl Mat Kibern — Vestnik Moskovskogo Universiteta. Seriya 15. Vychislitel'naya Matematika i Kibernetika

Vestn Mosk Univ Ser 16 Biol — Vestnik Moskovskogo Universiteta. Seriya 16. Biologiya

Vestn Mosk Univ Ser 16 Ser Biol — Vestnik Moskovskogo Universiteta. Seriya 16. Seriya Biologiia

Vestn Mosk Univ Ser 17 Pochvoved — Vestnik Moskovskogo Universiteta. Seriya 17. Pochvovedenie

Vestn Mosk Univ Ser Biol Pochvoved Geol Geogr — Vestnik Moskovskogo Universiteta. Seriya Biologii, Pochvovedeniya, Geologii, Geografii

Vestn Mosk Univ Ser Fiz-Mat Estestv Nauk — Vestnik Moskovskogo Universiteta. Seriya Fiziko-Matematicheskikh i Estestvennykh Nauk

Vestn Mosk Univ Ser II — Vestnik Moskovskogo Universiteta. Nauchnyj Zhurnal. Seriya II. Khimiya

Vestn Mosk Univ Ser Mat Mekh Astron Fiz Khim — Vestnik Moskovskogo Universiteta. Seriya Matematiki, Mekhaniki, Astronomii, Fiziki, Khimii

Vestn Nats Akad Nauk Resp Kaz — Vestnik Natsional'noi Akademii Nauk Respubliki Kazakhstan

Vestn Nauchn Inf Zabaik Fil Geogr Ova SSSR — Vestnik Nauchnoi Informatsii Zabaikal'skogo Filiala Geograficheskogo Obshchestva SSSR

Vestn Nauchno-Issled Inst Gidrobiol (Dnepropetr) — Vestnik Nauchno-Issledovatel'skogo Instituta Gidrobiologii (Dnepropetrovski)

Vestn Obsc Nauk Akad Nauk Arm SSR — Vestnik Obscestvennyh Nauk. Akademija Nauk Armjanskoj SSR

Vestn Oftal'mol — Vestnik Oftal'mologii

Vestn ORL — Vestnik Oto-Rino-Laringologii

Vestn Otorinolaringol — Vestnik Otorinolaringologii

Vestn Protivovozdushnoi Oborony — Vestnik Protivovozdushnoi Oborony

Vestn Rentgenol Radiol — Vestnik Rentgenologii i Radiologii

Vestn Respub Inst Okhr Prir Estestvennonauchn Muz Titograde — Vestnik Respublikanskogo Instituta za Okhranu Prirodyi Estestvennonauchnogo Muzeya v Titograde

Vestn Ross Akad Med Nauk — Vestnik Rossiiskoi Akademii Meditsinskikh Nauk

Vestn Rossijsk Obsc Sadov S Peterburge — Vestnik Rossijskago Obscestva Sadovodstva v S.-Peterburge

Vestn Selsk Hoz Nauki — Vestnik Sel'sko-Hozjajstvennoj Nauki

Vestn Sel'skokhoz Nauki (Alma-Ata) — Vestnik Sel'skokhozyaistvennoi Nauki (Alma-Ata)

Vestn Sel'skokhoz Nauki (Moscow) — Vestnik Sel'skokhozyaistvennoi Nauki (Moscow)

Vestn S-Kh Nauki (Alma-Ata) — Vestnik Sel'skokhozyaistvennoi Nauki (Alma-Ata)

Vestn S-Kh Nauki Kaz — Vestnik Sel'skokhozyaistvennoi Nauki Kazakhstana. Ezhemesiachnyi Nauchnyi Zhurnal

Vestn S-Kh Nauki (Mosc) — Vestnik Sel'skokhozyaistvennoi Nauki (Moscow)

Vestn Slov Kem Drus — Vestnik Slovenskega Kemijskega Drustva

Vestn Sots Rastenievod — Vestnik Sotsialisticheskogo Rastenievodstva

Vestn Stand — Vestnik Standartizatsii

Vestn Statis — Vestnik Statistiki

Vestn Statist — Vestnik Statistiki

Vestn Statniho Geol Ustavu Cesk Repub — Vestnik Statniho Geologickiho Ustavu Ceskoslovenske Republiky

Vestn St Peterb Univ Ser 3 Biol — Vestnik Sankt-Peterburgskogo Universiteta. Seriya 3. Biologiya

Vestn St Peterb Univ Ser 4 Fiz Khim — Vestnik Sankt-Peterburgskogo Universiteta. Seriya 4. Fizika, Khimiya

Vestn St Peterb Univ Ser 7 Geol Geogr — Vestnik Sankt-Peterburgskogo Universiteta. Seriya 7. Geologiya, Geografiya

Vestn Stud Nauchn Ova Kazan Gos Univ Estestv Nauki — Vestnik Studencheskogo Nauchnogo Obshchestva Kazanskii Gosudarstvennyi Universitet Estestvennye Nauki

Vestn Tbilis Bot Sada Akad Nauk Gruz SSR — Vestnik Tbilisskogo Botanicheskogo Sada Akademii Nauk Gruzinskoi SSR

Vestn Tiflissk Bot Sada — Vestnik Tiflisskago Botaniceskago Sada. Moniteur du Jardin Botanique de Tiflis

Vestn Uradu Vynalezy Objevy — Vestnik Uradu pro Vynalezy a Objevy

Vestn Uradu Vynalezy Objevy Cast A Vynalezy — Vestnik Uradu pro Vynalezy a Objevy. Cast A. Vynalezy

Vestn Uradu Vynalezy Objevy Cast B Ochr Znamky Prum Vzory — Vestnik Uradu pro Vynalezy a Objevy. Cast B. Ochranne Znamky. Prumyslovy Vzory

Vestn Uradu Vynalezy Objevy Ochr Znamky Prum Vzory — Vestnik Uradu pro Vynalezy a Objevy. Ochranne Znamky. Prumyslovy Vzory

Vestn Uradu Vynalezy Objevy Vynalezy — Vestnik Uradu pro Vynalezy a Objevy. Vynalezy

Vestn USSR Acad Med Sci — Vestnik. USSR Academy of Medical Science

Vestn Ustred Ustavu Geol — Vestnik Ustredniho Ustavu Geologickeho

Vestn Vyssh Shk — Vestnik Vysshej Shkoly

Vestn Vyzk Ustavu Zemed — Vestnik Vyzkumnych Ustavu Zemedelskych

Vestn Zapadno Sib Geol Upr — Vestnik Zapadno-Sibirskogo Geologicheskogo Upravleniya

Vestn Zapadno Sib i Novosib Geol Upr — Vestnik Zapadno-Sibirskogo i Novosibirskogo Geologicheskikh Upravlenii

Vestn Zashch Rast — Vestnik Zashchity Rastenii

Vestn Zool — Vestnik Zoologii

Vestn Zool Zool Rec — Vestnik Zoologii/Zoological Record

Vest Obshch Gig Sudeb Prakt Med — Vestnik Obshchestvennoi Gigieny, Sudebnoi i Prakticheskoi Meditsiny

Vest Obshch Revnit Voenn Znan — Vestnik Obshchestva Revnitelei Voennykh Znanii

Vest Obshch Sel Khoz Yuzh Ross — Vestnik Imperatorskago Obshchestva Sel'skago Khozyaistva Yuzhnoi Rossii

Vest Obshch Vet — Vestnik Obshchestvennoi Veterinarii

Vest Odb Spol Zveroklest Csl Repub — Vestnik Odborneho Spolku Zveroklestitelu pro Ceskoslovenskou Republiku se Sidlem

Vest Odess Obshch Nadz Parov Kotl — Vestnik Odesskago Obshchestva dlya Nadzora za Parovymi Kotlami

Vest Oftal (Kiev) — Vestnik Oftal'mologii (Kiev)

Vest Oftal (Mosk) — Vestnik Oftal'mologii (Moskva)

Vest Opyt Dela Uprav Opyt Delu Sred Chernoz Obl Nar Kom Zeml — Vestnik Opytnago Dela. Upravlenie po Opytnomu delu Sredne-Chernozemnoi Oblasti nar Kom Zemledeliya

Vest Opyt Fiz — Vestnik Opytnoi Fiziki i Elementarnoi Matematiki

Vest Orlov Obshch Sel Knoz — Vestnik Orlovskago Obshchestva Sel'skago Khozyaistva

Vest Oto-Rino-Lar — Vestnik Otorinolaringologii

Vest Parazit Nemat Vyzyv Zabolev — Vestnik. Paraziticheskie Nematody i Vyzyvaemye imi Zabolevaniya

Vest Penz Obshch Lyub Estest Kraev — Vestnik Penzenskogo Obshchestva Lyubitelei Estestvoznaniya i Kraevedeniya

Vest Podpur Svazu Dilov Prum Ured Brno — Vestnik Podpurneho Svazu Dilovedoucich a Prumyslovych Uredniku (Brno)

Vest Politekh Obshch Imp Tekhnol Uchil — Vestnik Politekhnicheskago Obshchestva Imperatorskago Tekhnologicheskago Uchilishcha

Vest Prikl Bot — Vestnik Prikladnoi Botaniki

Vest Prikl Khim Khim Tekhnol — Vestnik Prikladnoi Khimii i Khimicheskoi Tekhnologii

Vest Prof Tekh Obraz — Vestnik Professional'no-Tekhnicheskogo Obrazovaniya

Vest Prom Torg Transp — Vestnik Promyshlennosti, Torgovli i Transporta

Vest Protivovozd Obor — Vestnik Protivovozdushnoi Oborony

Vest Psikhol Krim Antrop Pedol — Vestnik Psikhologii, Kriminal'noi Antropologii i Pedologii

Vest Put Soobshch — Vestnik Putei Soobshcheniya

Vest Rentg Radiol — Vestnik Rentgenologii i Radiologii

Vest Ross Inostr Pchelov — Vestnik Rossiiskogo i Inostrannogo Pchelovodstva

Vest Russk Flory — Vestnik Russkoi Flory

Vest Russk Obshch Pchelov — Vestnik Russkago Obshchestva Pchelovodstva

Vest Russk Pivov — Vestnik Russkago Pivovareniya

Vest Russk Prikl Ent — Vestnik Russkoi Prikladnoi Entomologii

Vest Ryboprom — Vestnik Rybopromyshlennosti

Vest Sadov Plodov Ogorod — Vestnik Sadovodstva, Plodovodstva i Ogorodnichestva

Vest Sakh Prom — Vestnik Sakharnoi Promyshlennosti

Vest Samoobraz Berl — Vestnik Samoobrazovaniya v Berline

Vest Saratov Otd Imp Russk Tekh Obshch — Vestnik Saratovskago Otdeleniya Imperatorskago Russkago Tekhnicheskago Obshchestva

Vest Sel Khoz — Vestnik Sel'skogo Khozyaistva

Vest Sel Khoz Lit — Vestnik Sel'sko-Khozyaistvennoi Literatury

Vest Sel'-Khoz Nauki (Alma-Ata) Minist Sel Khoz Kazakh SSR — Vestnik Sel'skokhozyaistvennoi Nauki (Alma-Ata). Ministerstvo Sel'skogo Khozyaistva Kazakhskoi SSR

Vest Sel-Khoz Nauki (Mosk) — Vestnik Sel'skokhozyaistvennoi Nauki (Moskva)

Vest Sev Obl Sta Zashch Rast Vredit — Vestnik Severnoi Oblastnoi Stantsii Zashchity Rastenii ot Vreditelei

Vest Sezda Deyat Klim Gidrol Balneol Petra Velikago — Vestnik S'ezda Deyatelei po Klimatologii, Gidrologii i Balneologii v Pamyat' Petra Velikago

Vest SIA — Vestnik SIA

Vestsi Akad Agrar Navuk Belarusi — Vestsi Akademii Agrarnykh Navuk Belarusi

Vestsi Akad Navuk Belarusi Ser Biyal Navuk — Vestsi Akademii Navuk Belarusi. Seryya Biyalagichnykh Navuk

Vestsi Akad Navuk Belarusi Ser Fiz Energ Navuk — Vestsi Akademii Navuk Belarusi. Seryya Fizika-Energetychnykh Navuk

Vestsi Akad Navuk Belarusi Ser Fiz Mat Navuk — Vestsi Akademii Navuk Belarusi. Seryya Fizika-Matematychnykh Navuk

Vestsi Akad Navuk Belarusi Ser Fiz Tech Navuk — Vestsi Akademii Navuk Belarusi. Seryya Fizika-Tekhnichnykh Navuk

Vestsi Akad Navuk Belarusi Ser Khim Navuk — Vestsi Akademii Navuk Belarusi. Seryya Khimichnykh Navuk

Vestsi Akad Navuk BSSR — Vestsi Akademii Navuk Belaruskai SSR

Vestsi Akad Navuk BSSR Khim Navuk — Vestsi Akademii Navuk Belaruskai SSR. Khimichnykh Navuk

Vestsi Akad Navuk BSSR Ser — Vestsi Akademii Navuk Belaruskai SSR. Seriya

Vestsi Akad Navuk BSSR Ser Biyal Navuk — Vestsi Akademii Navuk Belaruskai SSR. Seryya Biyalagichnykh Navuk

Vestsi Akad Navuk BSSR Ser Fiz-Ehnerg Navuk — Vestsi Akademii Navuk BSSR. Seryya Fizika-Ehnergetychnykh Navuk

Vestsi Akad Navuk BSSR Ser Fiz-Mat — Vestsi Akademii Navuk BSSR. Seriya Fizika-Matematicheskikh

Vestsi Akad Navuk BSSR Ser Fiz-Mat Navuk — Vestsi Akademii Navuk BSSR. Seryya Fizika-Matematychnykh Navuk

Vestsi Akad Navuk BSSR Ser Fiz-Tekh Navuk — Vestsi Akademii Navuk BSSR. Seryya Fizika-Tekhnichnykh Navuk

Vestsi Akad Navuk BSSR Ser Gramadskikh Navuk — Vestsi Akademii Navuk BSSR. Seryya Gramadskikh Navuk

Vestsi Akad Navuk BSSR Ser Hramad Navuk — Vestsi Akademii Navuk BSSR. Seryya. Hramadskikh Navuk

Vestsi Akad Navuk BSSR Ser Khim — Vestsi Akademii Navuk BSSR. Seriya Khimicheskikh

Vestsi Akad Navuk BSSR Ser Khim Navuk — Vestsi Akademii Navuk Belaruskai SSR. Seryya Khimichnykh Navuk

Vestsi Akad Navuk BSSR Ser Sel'skagas Navuk — Vestsi Akademii Navuk Belaruskai SSR. Seryya Sel'skagaspadar Navuk

Vestsi Akad Navuk BSSR Ser Selskagaspad Navuk — Vestsi Akademii Navuk BSSR. Seryya Sel'skagaspadarchykh Navuk

Vestsi Belarus Akad Navuk Ser Biyal Navuk — Vestsi Belaruskaya Akademiya Navuk. Seryya Biyalagichnykh Navuk

Vest Sib Inzh — Vestnik Sibirskikh Inzhenerov

Vest Silik Prom — Vestnik Silikatnoi Promyshlennosti

Vestsi Nats Akad Navuk Belarusi Ser Biyal Navuk — Vestsi Natsyyanal'nai Akademii Navuk Belarusi. Seryya Biyalagichnykh Navuk

Vestsi Nats Akad Navuk Belarusi Ser Fiz Mat Navuk — Vestsi Natsyyanal'nai Akademii Navuk Belarusi. Seryya Fizika-Matematychnykh Navuk

Vestsi Nats Akad Navuk Belarusi Ser Fiz Tekh Navuk — Vestsi Natsyyanal'nai Akademii Navuk Belarusi. Seryya Fizika-Tekhnichnykh Navuk

Vestsi Nats Akad Navuk Belarusi Ser Khim Navuk — Vestsi Natsyyanal'nai Akademii Navuk Belarusi. Seryya Khimichnykh Navuk

Vest Sjezdu Ces Prirodozp — Vestnik Sjezdu Ceskych Prirodozpytcu a Lekaru v Praze

Vest Slov Kem Drust — Vestnik Slovenskega Kemijskega Drustva

Vest Sots Rasteniev — Vestnik Sotsialisticheskogo Rastenievodstva

Vest Sov Oto Rino Lar — Vestnik Sovetskoi Oto-Rino-Laringologii

Vest Sovrem Med — Vestnik Sovremennoi Meditsiny

Vest Sovrem Vet — Vestnik Sovremennoi Veterinarii

Vest S Peterb Vrach Obshch Vzaim Pom — Vestnik S. Peterburgskago Vrachebnago Obshchestva Vzaimnoi Pomoshchi

Vest Stavit Podnik Staveb — Vestnik Stavitelu a Podnikatelu Staveb

Vest St Geol Ust Csl Repub — Vestnik Statniho Geologickeho Ustavu Ceskoslovenske Republiky

Vest St Uradu Vynal Norm — Vestnik Statniho Uradu pro Vynalezy a Normalisaci

Vest Sukhum Obshch Sel Khoz — Vestnik Sukhumskago Obshchestva Sel'skago Khozyaistva

Vest Svyazi — Vestnik Svyazi

Vestsyi Akad Navuk BSSR Ser Fyiz-Ehnerg Navuk — Vestsyi Akademhyiyi Navuk BSSR. Seryya Fyizyika-Ehnergetychnykh Navuk

Vestsyi Akad Navuk BSSR Ser Fyiz-Mat Navuk — Vestsyi Akademhyiyi Navuk BSSR. Seryya Fyizyika-Matehmatychnykh Navuk

Vestsyi Akad Navuk BSSR Ser Fyiz-Tehkh Navuk — Vestsyi Akademhyiyi Navuk BSSR. Seryya Fyizyika-Tehkhnyichnykh Navuk

Vestsyi Akad Navuk BSSR Ser Khyim Navuk — Vestsyi Akademhyiyi Navuk BSSR. Seryya Khyimyichnykh Navuk

Vest Tabach Prom — Vestnik Tabachnoi Promyshlennosti

Vest Tech Mus Csl — Vestnik Technickeho Musea Ceskoslovenskeho

Vest Tekh Inf Trakt Sel Khoz Mashinost — Vestnik Tekhnicheskoi Informatsii po Traktornomy i Sel'skokhozyaistvennomy Mashinostroeniyu

Vest Tekhnol Khim — Vestnik Tekhnologii Khimicheskoi i Stroitel'nykh Materialov

Vest Telegr Provod — Vestnik Telegrafii bez Provodov

Vest Terap Tuberk — Vestnik po Terapii Tuberkuleza

Vest Tiflis Bot Sada — Vestnik Tiflisskogo Botanicheskogo Sada

Vest Torf Dela — Vestnik Torfyanago Dela

Vest Torf Dela Sel Khoz Ispol Bolot — Vestnik Torfyanogo Dela i Sel'sko-Khozyaistvennogo Ispol'zovaniya Bolot

Vest Trop Med — Vestnik Tropicheskoi Meditsiny

Vest Ucheta Otchetn — Vestnik Ucheta i Otchetnosti

Vest Uradu Norm — Vestnik Uradu pro Normalizaci

Vest Uradu Pat Vynal — Vestnik Uradu pro Patenty a Vynalezy

Vest Ush Nos Gorl Bolez — Vestnik Ushnykh, Nosovykh i Gorlovykh Boleznei

Vest Ustred Ust Geol — Vestnik Ustredniho Ustavu Geologickeho

Vest Vener Derm — Vestnik Venerologii i Dermatologii

Vest Vinod Ukr — Vestnik Vinodeliya Ukrainy

Vest Vinogr Vinod Vinotorg SSSR — Vestnik Vinogradarstva, Vinodeliya i Vinotorgovli SSSR

Vest Vinokur — Vestnik Vinokureniya

Vest Vodohospod — Vestnik Vodohospodarsky

Vest Vozd Flota — Vestnik Vozdushnogo Flota

Vest Vozdukhopl — Vestnik Vozdukhoplavaniya

Vest Vseross Kozhev Sind — Vestnik Vserossiiskogo Kozhevennogo Sindikata

Vest Vses Geol Razv Upravl — Vestnik Vsesoyuznogo Geologo-Razvedochnogo Upravleniya

Vest Vses Nauchno Issled Inst Drev — Vestnik Vsesoyuznogo Nauchno-Issledovatel'skogo Instituta Drevesiny

Vest Vses Nauchno Issled Inst Zheleznodorozh Transp — Vestnik Vsesoyuznogo Nauchno-Issledovatel'skogo Instituta Zheleznodorozhnogo Transporta

Vest Vyrab Sod Vody Napoju Uhlic — Vestnik Vyrabitelu Sodove Vody a Napoju Uhlicitych

Vest Vyssh Skh — Vestnik Vysshei Shkoly

Vest Yuzhno Russk Zhivot — Vestnik Yuzhno-Russkago Zhivotnovodstva

Vest Zap Sib Geol Razv Tresta — Vestnik Zapadno-Sibirskogo Geologo-Razvedochnogo Tresta

Vest Zaraisk Obshch Sel Khoz — Vestnik Zaraiskago Obshchestva Sel'skago Khozyaistva

Vest Zashch Rast — Vestnik Zashchity Rastenii

Vest Zelez Plavbu — Vestnik pro Zeleznice a Plavbu, Vydavany Ministerstvem Zeleznic

Vest Zemed — Vestnik Zemedelcu

Vest Zemed Obchod Zivnost — Vestnik Zemedelsky, Obchodni a Zivnostensky

Vest Zeml Prom — Vestnik Zemledeliya i Promyshlennosti

Vest Zheleznodorozh Med Sanit — Vestnik Zheleznodorozhnoi Meditsiny i Sanitarii

Vest Zhirov Prom — Vestnik Zhirovoi Promyshlennosti

Vest Zhirov Veshch — Vestnik Zhirovykh Veshchestv

Vest Zhivot — Vestnik Zhivotnovodstva

Vest Znan — Vestnik Znaniya

Vest Zolotonosh Sel Khoz Obshch — Vestnik Zolotonoshskago Sel'sko-Khozyaistvennago Obshchestva

Vest Zoloto Prom Gorn Dela Voobshche — Vestnik Zoloto-Promyshlennosti i Gornago Dela Voobshche

Vest Zool — Vestnik Zoologii

Veszpremi Muzk — Veszprem Megyei Muzeumok Koezlemenyei

Veszpremi Vegyip Egy Tud Ulesszakanak Eloadasai — Veszpremi Vegyipari Egyetem Tudomanyos Ulesszakanak Eloadasai

Veszprem Koezl — Veszprem Megyei Muzeumok Koezlemenyei

Veszprem Megyei Muz — Veszprem Megyei Muzeumok Koezlemenyei

Veszprem Megyei Muz Koezl — Veszprem Megyei Muzeumok Koezlemenyei

Veszprem Megyei Muz Koezlem — Veszprem Megyei Muzeumok Koezlemenyei

Veszprem Mk — Veszprem Megyei Muzeumok Koezlemenyei

Veszprmi Vegyip Egy Kozl — Veszpremi Vegyipari Egyetem Kozlemenyei

Veszpr Vegyip Egy Kozl — Veszpremi Vegyipari Egyetem Kozlemenyei

Vet — Veterinaria

Vet Anesth — Veterinary Anesthesia

Vet Annu — Veterinary Annual

Vet Arh — Veterinarski Arhiv

Vet Bull — Veterinary Bulletin

Vet Bull (London) — Veterinary Bulletin (London)

Vet Bull (Weybridge Eng) — Veterinary Bulletin (Weybridge, England)

Vet Cas — Veterinarsky Casopis

Vet Cas (Kosice) — Veterinarsky Casopis (Kosice)

VetChr — Vetera Christianorum

Vet Christ — Vetera Christianorum

Vet Clin North Am — Veterinary Clinics of North America

Vet Clin North Am Equine Pract — Veterinary Clinics of North America. Equine Practice

Vet Clin North Am Food Anim Pract — Veterinary Clinics of North America. Food Animal Practice

Vet Clin North Am (Large Anim Pract) — Veterinary Clinics of North America (Large Animal Practice)

Vet Clin North Am (Small Anim Pract) — Veterinary Clinics of North America (Small Animal Practice)

Vet Clin Pathol — Veterinary Clinical Pathology

Vet Comp Orthop Tramatol VCOT — Veterinary and Comparative Orthopaedics and Traumatology. VCOT

Vet Dermatol — Veterinary Dermatology

VETDOC — Veterinary Literature Documentation

Vet Econ — Veterinary Economics

Vetensk Arb Fys Org Kemi Inst Allm Org Kemi Stockh — Vetenskapliga Arbeten. Fysikalisk och Organisk Kemi. Institutet for Allman och Organisk Kemi, Stockholms Hogskola

Vetensk Liv — Vetenskapen och Livet

Vetensk Prakt Unders Lappl — Vetenskapliga och Praktiska Undersokningar i Lappland

Vetensk Publ Tek Hoegsk Helsingfors — Vetenskapliga Publikationer. Tekniska Hoegskolan i Helsingfors

Vetensk Soc i Lund Arsbok — Vetenskaps-Societeten i Lund. Aarsbok

Vetera Chr — Vetera Christianorum

Vetera Christ — Vetera Christianorum

Veteran Vint Mag — Veteran and Vintage Magazine

Veterinaria Esp — Veterinaria Espanola

Veterinaria Ital — Veterinaria Italiana

Veterinario Extrem — Veterinario Extremeno

Veterinary Clin North Am Exot Anim Pract — Veterinary Clinics of North America. Exotic Animal Practice
Ve Tes — Vetus Testamentum
Vet Espan — Veterinaria Espanola
Vet Glas — Veterinarski Glasnik
Vet Glasn — Veterinarski Glasnik
Vet Hist — Veterinary History Bulletin. Veterinary History Society
Vet Hist Jb — Veterinaer-Historisches Jahrbuch
Vet Hist Mitt — Veterinaerhistorische Mitteilungen
Vet Hum Toxicol — Veterinary and Human Toxicology
Vet Immunol Immunopathol — Veterinary Immunology and Immunopathology
Vet Insp Annu Inst Vet Insp NSW — Veterinary Inspector Annual. Institute of Veterinary Inspectors of New South Wales
Vet Ital — Veterinaria Italiana
Vet J — Veterinary Journal
Vet J and Ann Comp Path — Veterinary Journal and Annals of Comparative Pathology
Vet J (Bratislava) — Veterinary Journal (Bratislava)
Vet Khron Kherson Gub — Veterinarnaya Khronika Khersonskoi Gubernii
Vet Khron Kursk Gub — Veterinarnaya Khronika Kurskoi Gubernii
Vet Khron Podolsk Gub — Veterinarnaya Khronika Podol'skoi Gubernii
Vet Khron Voronezh Gub — Veterinarnaya Khronika Voronezhskoi Gubernii
Vet Klin Sof — Veterinarna Klinika (Sofiya)
Vet Mag — Veterinary Magazine
Vet Med — Veterinarni Medicina
Vet Med — Veterinary Medicine
Vet Med — Veterinary Medicine and Small Animal Clinician [Later, Veterinary Medicine]
Vet Med & Small Anim Clin — Veterinary Medicine and Small Animal Clinician
Vet Med Nachr — Veterinaer-Medizinische Nachrichten
Vet Med Nachr Bayer Meister Lucius — Veterinaermedizinische Nachrichten Bayer-Meister Lucius
Vet Med Nauki — Veterinarno Meditsinski Nauki
Vet Med Nauki (Sofia) — Veterinarno Meditsinski Nauki (Sofia)
Vet Med (Prague) — Veterinarni Medicina (Prague)
Vet Med (Praha) — Veterinarni Medicina (Praha)
Vet Med Rep — Veterinary Medicine Report
Vet Med Rev — Veterinary Medical Review
Vet Med/SAC — Veterinary Medicine and Small Animal Clinician
Vet Med Sci — Veterinary Medical Science
Vet Med Small Anim Clin — Veterinary Medicine and Small Animal Clinician
Vet Med Sofia — Veterinarna Meditsina (Sofia)
Vet Microbiol — Veterinary Microbiology
Vet Mocambicana — Veterinaria Mocambicana
VETNAL — Veterinariya
Vet News — Veterinary News
Vet Obozr — Veterinarnoe Obozrienie
Vet Ophthalmol — Veterinary Ophthalmology
Vet Paras — Veterinary Parasitology
Vet Parasitol — Veterinary Parasitology
Vet Path — Veterinary Pathology
Vet Pathol — Veterinary Pathology
Vet Pathol (Suppl) — Veterinary Pathology. Supplement
Vet Prof Top Pets Small Anim Prof Top — Veterinary Professional Topics. Pets. Small Animal Professional Topics
Vet Prof Top Swine Swine Prof Top III Univ Coop Ext Serv — Veterinary Professional Topics. Swine. Swine Professional Topics. Illinois University. Cooperative Extension Service
Vet Q — Veterinary Quarterly
Vet QQJ Vet Sci — Veterinary Quarterly. Quarterly Journal of Veterinary Science
Vet Radiol — Veterinary Radiology
Vet Radiol Ultrasound — Veterinary Radiology and Ultrasound
Vet Rec — Veterinary Record
Vet Rec J Br Vet Assoc — Veterinary Record. Journal. British Veterinary Association
Vet Res — Veterinary Research
Vet Res Commun — Veterinary Research Communications
Vet Resp Mezhved Temat Nauchn Sb — Veterinariya Respublikanskii Mezhvedomstvennyi Tematicheskii Nauchnyi Sbornik
Vet Resp Mizhvid Temat Nauk Zb — Veterinariya Respublikanskyu Mizhvidomchyi Tematychnyi Naukovyi Zbirnyk
Vet Rev — Veterinary Review
Vetro Silic — Vetro e Silicati
Vet Sb (Bratislava) — Veterinarsky Sbornik (Bratislava)
Vet Sbirka — Veterinarna Sbirka
Vet Sbir (Sof) — Veterinarna Sbirka (Sofia)
Vet Sb (Sofia) — Veterinarna Sbirka (Sofia)
Vet Sci Commun — Veterinary Science Communications
Vet Sci Sofia — Veterinary Science (Sofia)
Vet Stars — Vets Stars and Stripes for Peace
Vet Surg — Veterinary Surgery
Vet Surgery — Veterinary Surgery
Vet Tec Esp — Veterinaria Tecnica Espanola
Vet Test — Vetus Testamentum
Vet Toled — Veterinaria Toledana
Vet Toxicol — Veterinary Toxicology
Vet Urug — Veterinaria Uruguay
Vetus Test — Vetus Testamentum
VetVaes Kjodkontrollen — Veterinaervaesenet og Kjodkontrollen
Vet Valenc — Veterinaria Valenciana
Vet World — Veterinary World
Vet Zh (Bratislava) — Veterinarnyi Zhurnal (Bratislava)
Vet Zootec — Veterinaria e Zootecnia
Vet Zootec Lima — Veterinaria y Zootecnia
Vet Zootec Rev Peru — Veterinaria y Zootecnia Revista Peruana

Vet Zootec S Domingo — Veterinaria y Zootecnia. Estacion Agronomica de Maina (Santo Domingo)
Veu Catalunya — Veu de Catalunya
VEV — Verre Oosten. Orgaan van de Landenkamers Verre Oosten
VEV Ber — VEV [Vlaams Economisch Verband] Berichten
Vezelinst TNO Delft VI Pam — Vezelinstituut TNO [Nederlands Centrale Organisatie voor Toegepast-Natuurwetenschappelijk Onderzoek] Delft VI Pamflet
Vezetestud — Vezetestudomany
VF — De Vrije Fries
VF — Verkuendigung und Forschung
VF — Vilagirodalmi Figyelo
VF — Voprosy Filologii
VF — Voprosy Filosofii
VFA — Vaestmanlands Fornminnesfoerenings Arsskrift
VFB — Vierteljahrschrift fuer Bibelkunde, Talmudische, und Patristische Studien
VFCBA9 — Forests Commission Victoria. Bulletin
VFDB — VFDB [Vereinigung zur Foerderung des Deutschen Brandschutzes eV] Zeitschrift
VFDB (Ver Foerd Dtch Brandschutzes) Z — VFDB (Vereinigung zur Foerderung des Deutschen Brandschutzes eV) Zeitschrift
VFDB Z — Vereinigung zur Foerderung des Deutschen Brandschutzes. Zeitschrift
VFFM — Vestlandets Forstilige Forsoksstasjon. Meddelelse
VFG — Visual Flight Guide
VFHG — Versammlungen der Freunde des Humanistischen Gymnasiums
VFII — Voprosy Fllologll
VFM — Jahresberichte ueber die Veraenderungen und Fortschritte im Militaerwesen
VFM — Voprosy Filosofii
VFPA — Viking Fund Publications in Anthropology
VFR — Victorian Fiction Research Guides
Vf Sch G — Verfassungsschutzgesetz
VFSSMCQ — Victorian Federation of State Schools Mothers Clubs. Quarterly Review
VFSW — Vierteljahrsschrift fuer Sozial- und Wirtschaftsgeschichte
V f SWG — Vierteljahrsschrift fuer Sozial- und Wirtschaftsgeschichte
V f Z — Vierteljahrshefte fuer Zeitgeschichte
V f ZG — Vierteljahreshefte fuer Zeitgeschichte
VG — Verdens Gang
VG — Voprosy Geografii/Geograficheskoe Obshchestvo SSSR, Moskovskii Filial, Nauchnye Sbornni
VGAnthr — Verhandlungen der Gesellschaft fuer Anthropologie
VGBAW — Verhandlungen der Geologischen Bundesanstalt in Wien
VGB Konf Forsch Kraftwerkstech — VGB-Konferenz Forschung in der Kraftwerkstechnik
VGB Kraftwerkstech — VGB (Vereinigung der Grosskraftwerksbetreiber) Kraftwerkstechnik
Vgbl — Bayerische Vorgeschichtsblaetter
VGE — Verhandlung der Gesellschaft fuer Erdkunde zu Berlin
VGEB — Verhandlungen der Gesellschaft fuer Erdkunde zu Berlin
VGEBA — Verhandlungen. Geologische Bundesanstalt (Austria)
VGH — Vasenlisten zur Griechischen Heldensage
VGH — Verwaltungsgerichtshof
VGIEMTP — Veroeffentlichungen. Grabmann Institut zur Erforschung der Mittelalterlichen Theologie und Philosophie
VGJ — Vorgeschichtliches Jahrbuch
VGL — Schriften des Vereins fuer die Geschichte Leipzigs
VGLKV — Vierteljahrsschrift fuer Geschichte und Landeskunde Vorarlbergs
VGLL — Valstybine Grozines Literaturos Leidykla
VGMG — Vestnik Gosudarstvennogo Muzeia Gruzii Imena S. N. Dzhanashia
VGN — Jahresbericht. Verein fuer Geschichte der Stadt Nuernberg
VGP — Victorian Government Publications
VGQ — Vocational Guidance Quarterly
VGTSA — Voprosy Gigieny Truda v Slantsevoi Promyshlennosti Estonskoi SSR
VH — Vermont History
VHAAH — Vitterhets, Historie- och Antikvitets-Akademiens Handlingar
VHAAM — Vitterhets. Historie och Antiquitets Akademiens Manadsblad
VHB — Van Hanh Bulletin
Vh BAG — Verhandlungen. Berliner Gesellschaft fuer Anthropologie, Ethnologie, und Urgeschichte
Vhdlgg Anthropol Ges — Verhandlungen der Anthropologischen Gesellschaft
Vhdlgg Dt Ges Chir — Verhandlungen der Deutschen Gesellschaft fuer Chirurgie
Vhdlgg Dt Juristtag — Verhandlungen des Deutschen Juristentages
Vhdlgg Dt Physik Ges — Verhandlungen der Deutschen Physikalischen Gesellschaft
Vhdlgg Forstwirte Maehren — Verhandlungen der Forstwirte in Maehren und Schlesien
Vhdlgg Ges Bekaempfg Tuberk — Verhandlungen der Gesellschaft zur Bekaempfung der Tuberkulose
Vhdlgg Ges Kindheilkde — Verhandlungen der Gesellschaft fuer Kinderheilkunde
Vhdlgg Intern Zoolkongr — Verhandlungen des Internationalen Zoologenkongresses
Vhdlgg Nathist Ver Bonn — Verhandlungen des Naturhistorischen Vereins Bonn
Vhdlgg Pathol Ges Wuerzbg — Verhandlungen der Pathologischen Gesellschaft. Wuerzburg
VHEDD8 — Vogelkundliche Hefte Edertal
VHFS — Videnskabernes Selskabs Historisk-Filologiske Skrifter
VHG — Vertragshilfegesetz
VHI — Vies des Hommes Illustres
VHis — Vida Hispanica
VHJ — Victorian Historical Journal
VHM — Victorian Historical Magazine
VHN — Verhandlungen. Historischer Vereine von Niederbayern
VHSG — Vierteljahrsschriftfuer Heraldik, Sphragistik, und Genealogie
VHSKA — Vital and Health Statistics. Series 11
VHVN — Verhandlungen des Historischen Vereins fuer Niederbayern

VHVNB — Verhandlungen. Historischer Verein von Niederbayern
VHVOR — Verhandlungen. Historischer Verein von Oberpfalz und Regensburg
Vi — Viator
VI — Vie Intellectuelle
VI — Viol
VI — Virgin Island Reports
VI — Voprosy Istorii
V Ia — Voprosy Iazykoznaniia. Akademiia Nauk SSSR
VIAL — Vie d'Italia e dell'America Latina
Viata Agric — Viata Agricola
Viata Med — Viata Medicala. Revista a Uniunii Societatelor de Stiinte Medicale din Republica Socialista
Viata Med (Buchar) — Viata Medicala (Bucharest)
Viata Med (Medii Sanit) — Viata Medicala. Revista de Informare Profesionala se Stiintifica a Cadrelor (Medii Sanitare)
Viator Med — Viator. Medieval and Renaissance Studies
Vib Control Microelectron Opt Metrol — Vibration Control in Microelectronics, Optics, and Metrology
Vib Engrg — Vibration Engineering
VIBJ — Virgin Islands Bar Journal
Vibr Spectrosc — Vibrational Spectroscopy
Vib Spectr — Vibrational Spectroscopy
Vib Spectra Struct — Vibrational Spectra and Structure
Vib Spectrosc — Vibrational Spectroscopy
Vib St A — Viborg Stifts Arbog
Vic — Victoire
VIC — Victory Garden
Vic Assn Teach Eng J — Victorian Association for the Teaching of English. Journal
Vic Bar News — Victorian Bar News
Vic CC — County Court Reports (Victoria)
Vic Chamber of Manufactures Econ Serv — Victorian Chamber of Manufactures. Economic Service
Vic Chap News — Victorian Chapter Newsletter
Vic Comm Teach Assn General J — Victorian Commercial Teachers' Association. General Journal
Vic Comput — Vic Computing
Vic Conf Soc Welfare Proc — Victorian Conference of Social Welfare. Proceedings
Vic Creditman — Victorian Creditman
Vic Dairyfarmer — Victorian Dairyfarmer
Vic Dep Agric Tech Bull — Victoria. Department of Agriculture. Technical Bulletin
Vic Ed Gaz — Education Gazette and Teachers Aid (Victoria)
Vic Elec Contractor — Victorian Electrical Contractor
Vic Employers' Federation AR — Victorian Employers' Federation. Annual Report
Vicenza Econ — Vicenza Economica
Vic Fam Alm — Victorian Family Almanac
Vic For Comm Bull — Victoria. Forests Commission. Bulletin
Vic Geogr J — Victorian Geographical Journal
Vic Govt Gaz — Victorian Government Gazette
Vic Hist Mag — Victorian Historical Magazine
Vic Hortic Dig — Victorian Horticultural Digest
Vic Inst Coll News — Victoria Institute of Colleges. Newsletter
Vic Legal Exec — Victorian Legal Executive
Vic LSAJ — Victorian LSA [Limbless Soldiers' Association] Journal
VicN — Victorian Naturalist
Vic Nat — Victorian Naturalist
Vic Naturalist — Victorian Naturalist
VIC News — Victoria Institute of Colleges. Newsletter
VI Code Ann — Virgin Islands Code Annotated
Vic Parl Deb — Victorian Parliamentary Debates
Vic Parl Parl Deb — Victoria. Parliament. Parliamentary Debates
Vic Poultry J — Victorian Poultry Journal
Vic Railways Newsletter — Victorian Railways Newsletter
Vic Resour — Victoria's Resources
Vic Resources — Victoria's Resources
Vic Rev — Victorian Review
VicS — Victorian Studies
Vic Stat Pub — Victorian Statistics Publications
Vict — Victorian Reports
Vict Cancer News — Victorian Cancer News
Vict Co Hist — Victoria History of the Counties of England
Vict Dairyfmr — Victorian Dairyfarmer
Vic Teachers J — Victorian Teachers Journal
Vic Teach J — Victorian Teachers Journal
Vict For Comm Bull — Victoria. Forests Commission. Bulletin
Vict For Comm For Tech Pap — Victoria. Forests Commission. Forestry Technical Paper
Vict For Comm Misc Publ — Victoria. Forests Commission. Miscellaneous Publication
Vict Geogr J — Victorian Geographical Journal
Vict Geol Surv Bull — Victoria. Geological Survey. Bulletin
Vict Geol Surv Mem — Victoria. Geological Survey. Memoirs
Vict Hist Mag — Victorian Historical Magazine
Vict Hort Dig — Victorian Horticultural Digest
Vict I J — Journal of the Transactions of the Victoria Institute, or Philosophical Society of Great Britain
Vict L (Austr) — Victorian Reports (Law)(Australia)
Vict LJ — Victorian Law Journal
Vict LR — Victorian Law Reports
Vict LT — Victorian Law Times
Vict Nat — Victorian Naturalist
Vict Naturalist — Victorian Naturalist
Vict Newsl — Victorian Newsletter
Victoria Country Roads Board Eng Note — Victoria. Country Roads Board. Engineering Note

Victoria Country Roads Board Tech Bull — Victoria. Country Roads Board. Technical Bulletin
Victoria Dep Agric Res Proj Ser — Victoria. Department of Agriculture. Research Project Series
Victoria Dep Agric Tech Bull — Victoria. Department of Agriculture. Technical Bulletin
Victoria Dep Agric Tech Rep Ser — Victoria. Department of Agriculture. Technical Report Series
Victoria Fish Wildl Dep Fish Contrib — Victoria. Fisheries and Wildlife Department. Fisheries Contribution
Victoria Fish Wildl Dep Wildl Contrib — Victoria. Fisheries and Wildlife Department. Wildlife Contribution
Victoria Geol Bull — Victoria. Geological Survey. Bulletin
Victoria Geol Surv Mem — Victoria. Geological Survey. Memoirs
Victoria Inst Tr — Victoria Institute or Philosophical Society of Great Britain. Journal of the Transactions
Victoria Inst (Trinidad) Pr — Victoria Institute (Trinidad). Proceedings
Victoria Mines Dep Annu Rep — Victoria. Mines Department. Annual Report
Victoria Mines Dep Groundwater Invest Program Rep — Victoria. Mines Department. Groundwater Investigation Program. Report
Victoria Minist Conserv Environ Stud Program Proj Rep — Victoria. Ministry for Conservation. Environmental Studies Program. Project Report
Victorian Entomol — Victorian Entomologist
Victorian Hist J — Victorian Historical Journal
Victorian Hist Mag — Victorian Historical Magazine
Victorian Nat — Victorian Naturalist
Victorian Natl Parks Assoc J — Victorian National Parks Association. Journal
Victorian Newslett — Victorian Newsletter
Victorian Period Newslett — Victorian Periodicals Newsletter
Victorian Period Rev — Victorian Periodicals Review
Victorian Railw — Victorian Railways
Victorian Stud — Victorian Studies
Victorian Vet Proc — Victorian Veterinary Proceedings
Victoria's Resour — Victoria's Resources
Victoria State Rivers Water Supply Comm Annu Rep — Victoria. State Rivers and Water Supply Commission. Annual Report
Victoria Univ Antarct Data Ser — Victoria University of Wellington. Antarctic Data Series
Vict Period Newslett — Victorian Periodicals Newsletter
Vict Poet — Victorian Poetry
Vict Poetry — Victorian Poetry
Vict Rep — Victorian Reports
Vict Rep (Adm) — Victorian Reports (Admiralty)
Vict Rep (Austr) — Victorian Reports (Australian)
Vict Rep (Eq) — Victorian Reports (Equity)
Vict Rep (Law) — Victorian Reports (Law)
Vict Res — Victoria's Resources
Vict Resour — Victoria's Resources
Vict Rev — Victorian Review
Vict R S P — Proceedings of the Royal Society of Victoria
Vict R S T — Transactions and Proceedings of the Royal Society of Victoria
Vict Soc Annu — Victorian Society Annual
Vict Soil Conserv Auth TC — Victoria. Soil Conservation Authority. TC Report
Vict Soil Conserv Auth TC Rep — Victoria. Soil Conservation Authority. TC Report
Vict Stud — Victorian Studies
Vict T Ph S — Transactions of the Philosophical Society of Victoria
Vict T R S — Transactions and Proceedings of the Royal Society of Victoria
Vict U C L Rev — Victoria University. College Law Review
Vict UL Rev — Victoria University. Law Review
Vict U of Wellington L Rev — Victoria University of Wellington. Law Review
Vict U Well L Rev — Victoria University of Wellington. Law Review
Vict Vet Proc — Australian Veterinary Association. Victorian Division. Annual General Meeting. Proceedings
Vict Vet Proc — Australian Veterinary Association. Victorian Division. Victorian Veterinary Proceedings
Vic Veg Grower — Victorian Vegetable Grower
Vic Vet Proc — Victorian Veterinary Proceedings
Vic Yrbk — Victoria Yearbook
VID — Vidipress Nieuwsbrief
VID — Vspomogatel'nye Istoricheskie Distsipliny
Vida Agr — Vida Agricola
Vida Agric — Vida Agricola
VidaL — Vida Literaria
Vida Med — Vida Medica
Vida Odontol — Vida Odontologica
Videnskabs-Selsk Christiana Forh — Videnskabs-Selskabet i Christiania. Forhandlingar
Vidensk Akad Avh — Videnskaps-Akademiets Avhandlinger
Vidensk Medd Dan Naturhist Foren — Videnskabelige Meddelelser fra Dansk Naturhistorisk Forening
Vidensk Medd Dan Naturhist Foren Khobenhavn — Videnskabelige Meddelelser fra Dansk Naturhistorisk Forening i Khobenhavn
Video — Video-Tronics
Video Mktg — Video Marketing Newsletter
Video Syst — Video Systems
Video Wld — Video World
Vide Sci Tech Appl — Vide. Science, Technique et Applications
Vide Tech-Appl — Vide. Technique-Applications
Vid Game T — Video Games Today
VIDSL — Veroeffentlichungen. Institut fuer Deutsche Sprache und Literatur. Deutsche Akademie der Wissenschaften zu Berlin
VIDV — Veroeffentlichungen. Institut fuer Deutsche Volkskunde. Deutsche Akademie der Wissenschaften zu Berlin
Vidya B — Vidya. Section B. Sciences
Vidya Bhar — Vidya Bharati

VIE — Vasi Italioli ed Etruschi a Figure Rosse
VIE — Viewpoint
Vie A — Vie des Arts
Vie Acad Acad Sci (Paris) — Vie Academique. Academie des Sciences (Paris)
Vie Agric et Rurale — Vie Agricole et Rurale
Vie Agric Meuse — Vie Agricole de la Meuse
VieC — Vie Catholique en France et a l'Etranger
Vie Camp — Vie a la Campagne
Vie Campagne — Vie a la Campagne
Vie Champagne — Vie en Champagne
Vie Econ (Berne) — Vie Economique (Berne)
Vie et Sciences Econs — Vie et Sciences Economiques
VieF — Vie Francaise
Vie Intell — Vie Intellectuelle
Vie It Am Lat — Vie d'Italia e dell'America Latina
Vie It Mondo — Vie d'Italia e del Mondo
Vie Liege — Vie Liegeoise
Vie Med — Vie Medicale
Vie Med Can Fr — Vie Medicale au Canada Francais
Vie Milie A — Vie et Milieu. Serie A. Biologie Marine
Vie Milie B — Vie et Milieu. Serie B. Oceanographie
Vie Milie C — Vie et Milieu. Serie C. Biologie Terrestre
Vie Milieu Ser A — Vie et Milieu. Serie A. Biologie Marine
Vie Milieu Ser AB Biol Mar Oceanogr — Vie et Milieu. Serie AB. Biologie Marine et Oceanographie
Vie Milieu Ser A Biol Mar — Vie et Milieu. Serie A. Biologie Marine
Vie Milieu Ser B Oceanogr — Vie et Milieu. Serie B. Oceanographie
Vie Milieu Ser C Biol Terr — Vie et Milieu. Serie C. Biologie Terrestre
Vie Mod — Vie Moderne
Vie Mondo — Vie del Mondo
Vie Mus — Vie Musicale
Vie Mus Belge — Vie Musicale Belge
Vienna Circle Coll — Vienna Circle Collection
Vie Paris — Vie Parisienne
Vie Ped — Vie Pedagogique
Vie Pop — Vie Populaire
VIER Bul — Victorian Institute of Educational Research. Bulletin
VIER Bull — Victorian Institute of Educational Research. Bulletin
Vierteljahreschr Gerichtl Med Oeff Sanitaetswes — Vierteljahrschrift fuer Gerichtliche Medizin und Oeffentliches Sanitaetswesen
Vierteljahresschr Schweiz Sanitaetsoffiz — Vierteljahresschrift fuer Schweizerische Sanitaetsoffiziere
Vierteljahressch Wirtschaftsforsch — Vierteljahresschrift Wirtschaftsforschung
Vierteljahrschr Forst Naturk — Vierteljahrschrift fuer Forst-, Jagd- und Naturkunde
Vierteljahrschr Prakt Pharm — Vierteljahrschrift fuer Praktische Pharmazie
Vierteljahrsh Zeitgesch — Vierteljahrshefte fuer Zeitgeschichte
Vierteljahrsschr f Wiss Philos — Vierteljahrsschrift fuer Wissenschaftliche Philosophie und Soziologie
Vierteljahrsschr Naturforsch Ges (Zuer) — Vierteljahrsschrift. Naturforschende Gesellschaft (Zuerich)
Vierteljahrsschr Naturforsch Ges (Zuerich) — Vierteljahrsschrift. Naturforschende Gesellschaft (Zuerich)
Vierteljahrsschr Soz Wirtschgesch — Vierteljahrsschrift fuer Sozial- und Wirtschaftsgeschichte
Viert Naturf Ges Zuerich — Vierteljahrschrift der Naturforschenden Gesellschaft in Zuerich
Vier Zeitg — Vierteljahrshefte fuer Zeitgeschichte
Vie Sci Econ — Vie et Sciences Economiques
Vie Soc — Vie Sociale
Vietnam Chim Acta — Vietnamica Chimica Acta
Vietnam J Math — Vietnam Journal of Mathematics
Viet Stud — Vietnamese Studies
Vie Urb — Vie Urbaine
VieW — Vie Wallonne. Revue Mensuelle et Illustree
Vie Wallonne — La Vie Wallonne. Revue Mensuelle Illustree
View Bot — View from the Bottom
Viewdata — Viewdata and Television User
Vieweg Math Sci Engrs — Vieweg Mathematics for Scientists and Engineers
Vieweg Stud Aufbaukurs Math — Vieweg Studium. Aufbaukurs Mathematik
Vieweg Tracts Pure Appl Phys — Vieweg Tracts in Pure and Applied Physics
Viewpoints Biol — Viewpoints in Biology
Viewpoint Ser Aust Conserv Fdn — Viewpoint Series: Australian Conservation Foundation
Viewpoints Teach & Learn — Viewpoints in Teaching and Learning
Views & R — Views and Reviews
VieZ — Vierteljahrschefte fuer Zeitgeschichte
VIF — Video Information
ViGB — Viewpoints. Georgia Baptist History
Vig C — Vigiliae Christianae
Vig Chr — Vigiliae Christianae
Vig Christ — Vigiliae Christianae
VIGGP — Veroeffentlichungen der Internationalen Gesellschaft fuer Geschichte der Pharmazie
Vigil Chris — Vigiliae Christianae
Vigiliae Christ — Vigiliae Christianae
Viitor Soc — Viitorul Social
VIJ — Vishveshvaranand Indological Journal
Vijes (Zagreb) — Vijesti Muzealaca i Konservatora (Zagreb)
Vik — Viking. Norsk Arkeologisk Selskap
Viking Fund Publ Anthropol — Viking Fund Publication in Anthropology
VIK Mitt — VIK [Vereinigung Industrielle Kraftwirtschaft] Mitteilungen
Vikram Math J — Vikram Mathematical Journal
Vikram Quart Res J Vikram University — Vikram. Quarterly Research Journal of Vikram University

V I Lenin Sakharth Politekh Inst Samecn Srom — V. I. Leninis Sahelobis Sromis Citheli Drosis Ordenosani Sakharthvelos Politekhnikuri Instituti. Samecniero Sromebi
VilFig — Vilagirodalmi Figyeleo
Villa Medici J Voyage — Villa Medici. Journal de Voyage
Villanova L Rev — Villanova Law Review
Vill L Rev — Villanova Law Review
Vilniaus Valstybinis Univ Mokslo Darb — Vilniaus Valstybinis Universitetas Mokslo Darbai
VILTAR — Viltrevy
Vil V — Village Voice
VIM — Voprosy Ikhtiologii (Moscow)
VIMBA — Veroeffentlichungen. Institut fuer Meeresforschung in Bremerhaven
VI (Minsk) — Voprosy Ictorii (Minsk)
VIML — Vestnik Istorii Mirovoi Kultury
VI Moscou — Voprosy Istorii (Moscow)
Vin — Vinduet
Vina Q — Vina Quarterly
Vinar Obz — Vinarsky Obzor
VIndJ — Vishveshvaranand Indological Journal
Vinea Vino Portug Doc Ser 2 Enol — Vinea et Vino Portugaliae Documenta. Ser. II. Enologia. Centro Nacional de Estudos Vitivinicolas
Vineland Hist Mag — Vineland Historical Magazine
Vingt Siecle Feder — Vingtieme Siecle Federaliste
Vinifera Wine Grow J — Vinifera Wine Growers Journal
Vini Ital — Vini d'Italia
Vinodel Vinograd SSSR — Vinodelie i Vinogradarstvo SSSR
Vinograd Plodovod (Budapest) — Vinogradarstvo i Plodovodstvo (Budapest)
Vinograd Vinar (Budapest) — Vinogradarstvo i Vinarstvo (Budapest)
Vinograd Vinodel — Vinogradarstvo i Vinodelie
Vinograd Vinorobstvo — Vinogradarstvo i Vinorobstvo
Vinyls Polym — Vinyls and Polymers
VIO — Veroeffentlichungen. Institut fuer Orientforschung. Deutsche Akademie der Wissenschaften zu Berlin
VIODAWB — Deutsche Akademie der Wissenschaften zu Berlin. Institut fuer Orientforschung. Veroeffentlichungen
Violence Vict — Violence and Victims
VIP — Voix et Images du Pays
ViPe — Vita e Pensiero
ViR — Viata Romaneasca
Vir — Virittaja
VIR — Virtuoso
VIRA — Voprosy Istorii Religii i Ateizma. Sbornik Statei
Viral Gene Tech — Viral Gene Techniques
Viral Immunol — Viral Immunology
VI R & Regs — Virgin Islands Rules and Regulations
VirC — Virginia Cavalcade
Virc Arch A — Virchows Archiv. A. Pathological Anatomy and Histology
Virc Arch B — Virchows Archiv. B. Cell Pathology
VirchA — Virchows Archiv fuer Pathologische Anatomie und Physiologie und fuer Klinische Medizin
Virch Arch — Archiv fuer Pathologische Anatomie und Physiologie und fuer Klinische Medicin. Virchow und Reinhardt
Virchows Arch — Virchows Archiv
Virchows Arch Abt A — Virchows Archiv. Abteilung A. Pathologische Anatomie
Virchows Arch Abt A Pathol Anat — Virchows Archiv. Abteilung A. Pathologische Anatomie
Virchows Arch Abt B — Virchows Archiv. Abteilung B. Zellpathologie
Virchows Arch Abt B Zellpathol — Virchows Archiv. Abteilung B. Zellpathologie
Virchows Arch A Pathol Anat Histol — Virchows Archiv. A. Pathological Anatomy and Histology
Virchows Arch A Pathol Anat Histopathol — Virchows Archiv. A. Pathological Anatomy and Histopathology
Virchows Arch B — Virchows Archiv B. Cell Pathology Including Molecular Pathology
Virchows Arch B Cell Pathol — Virchows Archiv. B. Cell Pathology
Virchows Arch B Cell Pathol Incl Mol Pathol — Virchows Archiv. B. Cell Pathology Including Molecular Pathology
Virchows Archiv F Pathol Anat — Virchow's Archiv fuer Pathologische Anatomie
Virchows Arch Path Anat — Virchows Archiv fuer Pathologische Anatomie
Virchows Arch Pathol Anat Physiol Klin Med — Virchows Archiv fuer Pathologische Anatomie und Physiologie und fuer Klinische Medizin
VIREDF — Virus Research
Virg & Star L — Virginian-Pilot and Ledger-Star
Virginia Div Mineral Rsources Rept Inv — Virginia. Division of Mineral Resources. Report of Investigations
Virginia Jour Sci — Virginia Journal of Science
Virginia J Sci — Virginia Journal of Science
Virginia Law Rev — Virginia Law Review
Virginia Mag Hist Biogr — Virginia Magazine of History and Biography
Virginia Med Month — Virginia Medical Monthly [Later, Virginia Medical]
Virginia Miner — Virginia Minerals
Virginia M Month — Virginia Medical Monthly
Virginia Polytech Inst Research Div Bull — Virginia Polytechnic Institute. Research Division. Bulletin
Virginia Polytech Inst Research Div Mon — Virginia Polytechnic Institute. Research Division. Monograph
Virginia Q R — Virginia Quarterly Review
Virginia Quart Rev — Virginia Quarterly Review
Virginia Res — Virginia Researcher
Virgin Pilo — Virginian-Pilot
Virg J Int'l L — Virginia Journal of International Law
Virg LJ — Virginia Law Journal
Vir LJ — Virginia Law Journal
VirM — Virginia Magazine of History and Biography

Virol — Virology
Virol Abstr — Virology Abstracts
Virol Monogr — Virology Monographs
Vir Q R — Virginia Quarterly Review
VIRS — Veroeffentlichungen. Institut fuer Romanische Sprachwissenschaft. Deutsche Akademie der Wissenschaften zu Berlin
Virtual Lab — Virtual Laboratory
Viruly's Tech Maandbl Wasind — Viruly's Technisch Maandblad voor de Wasindustrie
Virus Res — Virus Research
Virus Res Suppl — Virus Research. Supplement
VIS — Veroeffentlichungen. Institut fuer Slawistik. Deutsche Akademie zu Berlin
Vis — Voprosy Istorii
Vis Aids News — Visual Aids News
Vis Aids Rev — Visual Aids Review
Vis Arts — Visual Arts
Vis Arts Bul — Visual Arts Bulletin
Visbl Lang — Visible Language
VISCA Rev Visayas State Coll Agric — VISCA Review. Visayas State College of Agriculture
Vis Educ — Visual Education
Vi Ser Kunst — Vi Ser pa Kunst
VI Sess Laws — Virgin Islands Session Laws
Vish Indo J — Vishveshvaranand Indological Journal
Vishva Bharati Q — Vishva Bharati Quarterly
Vishvasananda Indol J — Vishvasananda Indological Journal
Vishwa Internat J Graph Theory — Vishwa International Journal of Graph Theory
Visible Lang — Visible Language
Visible Relig — Visible Religion
Vis Ind — Vision Index
Visindafelag Isl Greinar — Visindafelag Islendinga. Greinar
Visindafelag Isl Rit — Visindafelag Islendinga. Rit
Visindafel Isl — Visindafelag Islendinga
Vis Index — Vision Index
Vision Res — Vision Research
Vision Res Suppl — Vision Research. Supplement
Vision Tecnol — Vision Tecnologica
VIsis — Veroeffentlichungen der Naturwissenschaftlichen Gesellschaft Isis. Bautzen
VISI — Veroeffentlichungen. Institut fuer Slawistik. Deutsche Akademie der Wissenschaften zu Berlin
VisL — Visible Language
Visn Akad Nauk Ukr RSR — Visnyk Akademiyi Nauk Ukrayins'koyi RSR
Vis Neurosci — Visual Neuroscience
Visnik Kiiv Univ Ser Mat Meh — Visnik Kiivs'kogo Universitetu. Serija Matematiki ta Mehaniki
Visnik Kiiv Univ Ser Mat Mekh — Visnik Kiivs'kogo Universitetu. Seriya Matematiki ta Mekhaniki
Visnik L'viv Derz Univ Ser Meh-Mat — Visnik L'vivs'kogo Ordena Lenina Derzavogo Universitetu Imeni Ivana Franka. Serija Mehaniko-Matematicna
Visnik L'viv Politehn Inst — Visnik L'vivs'kogo Politehnicnogo Instituu
Visnik Lviv Univ Ser Mekh Mat — Visnik. L'vivs'kii Universitet. Seriya Mekhaniko-Matematichna
Visn Kharkiv Univ Astron — Visnik Kharkivs'kogo Universitetu. Astronomiya
Visn Kharkiv Univ Radiofiz — Visnik Kharkivs'kogo Universitetu. Radiofizika
Visn Kharkiv Univ Radiofiz Elektron — Visnik Kharkivs'kogo Universitetu. Radiofizika i Elektronika
Visn Khark Univ — Visnik Kharkivs'kogo Universitetu
Visn Kiiv Politekh Inst Ser Khim Mashinobuduv Tekhnol — Visnik Kiivs'kogo Politekhnichnogo Instituu. Seriya Khimichnogo Mashinobuduvannya ta Tekhnologii
Visn Kiiv Univ Ser Astron — Visnik Kiivs'kogo Universitetu. Seriya Astronomii
Visn Kiiv Univ Ser Astron Fiz Khim — Visnik Kiivs'kogo Universitetu. Seriya Astronomii, Fiziki, ta Khimii
Visn Kiiv Univ Ser Biol — Visnik Kiivs'kogo Universitetu. Seriya Biologii
Visn Kiiv Univ Ser Fiz — Visnik Kiivs'kogo Universitetu. Seriya Fiziki
Visn Kiiv Univ Ser Fiz Khim — Visnik Kiivs'kogo Universitetu. Seriya Fiziki ta Khimii
Visn Kiiv Univ Ser Geol Geogr — Visnik Kiivs'kogo Universitetu. Seriya Geologii ta Geografii
Visn Kiiv Univ Ser Khim — Visnik Kiivs'kogo Universitetu. Seriya Khimii
Visn Kiyiv Univ Ser Fiz — Visnik Kiyivs'kogo Universitetu. Seriya Fizika
Visn Kyyiv Univ Ser Biol — Visnyk Kyyivs'koho Universytetu. Seriya Biolohiyi
Visn L'viv Derzh Univ Ser Biol — Visnik L'vivs'kogo Derzhavnogo Universitetu. Seriya Biologichna
Visn L'viv Derzh Univ Ser Fiz — Visnik L'vivs'kii Derzhavnii Universitet Imeni Ivana Franka. Seriya Fizichna
Visn L'viv Derzh Univ Ser Geol — Visnik L'vivs'kogo Derzhavnogo Universitetu. Seriya Geologichna
Visn L'viv Derzh Univ Ser Khim — Visnik L'vivs'kogo Derzhavnogo Universitetu Imeni Ivana Franka. Seriya Khimichna
Visn L'viv Univ Ser Biol Heohr — Visnyk L'vivs'koho Universytetu. Seriya Biolohiyi, Heohrafiyi, ta Heolohiyi
Visn L'viv Univ Ser Biol Heohr Heol — Visnyk L'vivs'koho Universytetu. Seriya Biolohiyi, Heohrafiyi, ta Heolohiyi
Visn Sil-Hospod Nauky — Visnyk Sil's'kohospodars'koyi Nauky
Visn Sil's'kohospod Nauki — Visnyk Sil's'kohospodars'koy Nauki
Visn Tsentr Resp Bot Sad Akad Nauk Ukr RSR — Visnik Tsentral'nii Respublikans'kii Botanichnii Sad Akademiya Nauk Ukrains'koiRSR
Visnyk Akad Nauk Ukrain RSR — Visnyk Akademii Nauk Ukrainskoy RSR
Visnyk Akad Nauk Ukr RSR — Visnyk Akademiyi Nauk Ukrayins'koyi RSR
Vissh Inst Arkhit Stroit Sofiya God — Vissh Institut po Arkhitektura i Stroitelstvo-Sofiya. Godishnik
VISSI — Visindafelag Islendinga. Societas Scientiarum Islandica
V Ist — Voprosy Istorii (Moscow)
Vistas Astron — Vistas in Astronomy

Vistas Astronaut — Vistas in Astronautics
Vistas Bot — Vistas in Botany
Vistas Volunt — Vistas for Volunteers
Visti Akad Nauk Ukr RSR — Visti Akademii Nauk Ukrains'koi RSR
Visti Inst Fiz Khim Akad Nauk Ukr RSR — Visti Instituu Fizichnoi Khimii Akademiya Nauk Ukrains'koi RSR
Visti Ukr Nauk Dosl Inst Fiz Khim — Visti Ukrains'kogo Naukovo Doslidchogo Instituu Fizichnoi Khimii
Visti Vseukrajinsk Akad Nauk — Visti Vseukrajins'koji Akademiji Nauk. Procesverbaux de l'Academie des Sciences de l'Ukraine
Visual Aids R — Visual Aids Review
Visual Anthrop — Visual Anthropology
Visual Anthropol Rev — Visual Anthropology Review
Visual Anthrop Rev — Visual Anthropology Review
Visual A Res — Visual Arts Research
Visual Com — Studies in Visual Communication
Visual Comput — Visual Computer
Visual Ed — Visual Education
Visual Inf Process — Visual Information Processing
Visualization Eng Res — Visualization of Engineering Research
Visual Med — Visual Medicine
Visual Sonic Med — Visual Sonic Medicine
VIT — Vital Speeches of the Day
Vita — Vita. Revue Bimensuelle. Confederation de l'Alimentation Belge
Vita A — Vita d'Arte
Vita Hum — Vita Humana
Vita Int — Vita International
Vita Ital — Vita Italiana
Vital C — Vital Christianity
Vital Health Stat 1 — Vital and Health Statistics. Series 1. Programs and Collection Procedures
Vital Health Stat 2 — Vital and Health Statistics. Series 2. Data Evaluation and Methods Research
Vital Health Stat 3 — Vital and Health Statistics. Series 3. Analytical Studies
Vital Health Stat 4 — Vital and Health Statistics. Series 4. Documents and Committee Reports
Vital Health Stat 10 — Vital and Health Statistics. Series 10. Data from the National Health Survey
Vital Health Stat 11 — Vital and Health Statistics. Series 11. Data from the National Health Survey
Vital Health Stat 13 — Vital and Health Statistics. Series 13. Data from the National Health Survey
Vital Health Stat 14 — Vital and Health Statistics. Series 14. Data on National Health Resources
Vital Health Stat 20 — Vital and Health Statistics. Series 20. Data from the National Vital StatisticsSystem
Vital Health Stat 21 — Vital and Health Statistics. Series 21. Data from the National Vital StatisticsSystem
Vital Health Stat 23 — Vital and Health Statistics. Series 23. Data from the National Survey of FamilyGrowth
Vital Health Statist Ser 2 Data Evaluation Methods Res — Vital and Health Statistics. Series 2. Data Evaluation and Methods Research
Vital S HD — Monthly Vital Statistics Report. Hospital Discharge Survey Data
Vital S HI — Monthly Vital Statistics Report. Health Interview Survey
Vital S HS — Monthly Vital Statistics Report. Health Statistics
Vital S MS — Monthly Vital Statistics Report. Advance Report of Final Mortality Statistics. 1981
Vital Speeches — Vital Speeches of the Day
Vital Speeches Day — Vital Speeches of the Day
Vital St A — Monthly Vital Statistics Report. Annual Summary of Births, Deaths, Marriages, and Divorces. 1983
Vital Stat — Monthly Vital Statistics Report. Births, Marriages, Divorces, and Deaths
Vital St N — Monthly Vital Statistics Report. Advance Report of Final Natality Statistics. 1981
Vitalstoffe — Vitalstoffe Zivilisationskrankheiten
Vitalst Zivilisationskr — Vitalstoffe Zivilisationskrankheiten
Vita Math — Vita Mathematica
Vitam D Dig — Vitamin D Digest
Vitam Eksp Klin — Vitaminy v Eksperimente i Klinike
Vitam Horm — Vitamins and Hormones
Vitamin Horm Adv Res Appl — Vitamin and Hormones. Advances in Research and Applications
Vitam K Infancy Int Symp — Vitamin K in Infancy. International Symposium
Vita Mon — Vita Monastica
Vitam Resur Ikh Ispol'z — Vitaminnye Resursy i Ikh Ispol'zovanie
Vitams Horm — Vitamins and Hormones
Vita Veron — Vita Veronese
Vitic Arboric — Viticulture, Arboriculture
Vitic Enol (Budapest) — Viticulture and Enology (Budapest)
Viti-Vinic (Budapest) — Viti-Viniculture (Budapest)
Viv — Vivarium
Vivar — Vivarium. A Journal for Mediaeval Philosophy and the Intellectual Life of the Middle Ages
VIVI — Vivienda
Vivienda Planif — Vivienda y Planificacion
VIVL — Verhandlungen der Internationalen Vereinigung fuer Theoretische und Angewandte Limnologie
VIVTAL — Verhandlungen der Internationalen Vereinigung fuer Theoretische und Angewandte Limnologie
VIY — Visserij. Voorlichtingsblad voor de Nederlandse Visserij
VIZ — Voenno-Istoricheskii Zhurnal
Vizant Vremennik — Vizantijskij Vremennik
Vizan Vrem — Vizantiiskii Vremennik

Vizgazdalkodasi Tud Kut Intez Tanulmanyok Kut Eredmenyek — Vizgazdalkodasi Tudomanyos Kutato Intezet Tanulmanyok es Kutatasi Eredmenyek

Viz Koezl — Vizuegyi Koezlemenyek

ViZoK — Verhandlungen des Internationalen Zoologenkongresses

Vizugyi Kozl — Vizugyi Kozlemenyek

Vizugyi Kozlem — Vizugyi Kozlemenyek

VizV — Vizantiiskii Vremenik

Viz Vrem — Vizantijskij Vremennik

VJ — Vassar Journal of Undergraduate Studies

VJ — Voprosy Jazykoznanija

VJa — Voprosy Jazykoznanija

VJaL — Voprosy Jazyka i Literatury

Vjber — Vierteljahresberichte

Vjes AH Dal — Vjesnik za Arheologiju i Historiju Dalmatinsku

Vjes A Muz Zagreb — Vjesnik Arheoloskog Muzeja u Zagrebu

Vjes Dal — Vjesnik za Arheologiju i Historiju Dalmatinsku

Vjesn Arheol Muz Zagreb — Vjesnik Arheoloskog Muzeja v Zagrebu

Vjesn Bibliot Hrv — Vjesnik Bibliotekara Hrvatske

Vjesnik Arheol & Hist Dalmat — Vjesnik za Arheolgiju i Historiju Dalmatinsku

Vjesnik (Split) — Vjesnik za Arheologiju i Historiju Dalmatinsku (Split)

VJH — Vierteljahrsschrift Herold fuer Heraldik, Sphragistik, und Genealogie

Vjhber Probl Entwickllaend — Vierteljahresberichte Probleme der Entwicklungslaender

Vjhefte Zeitgesch — Vierteljahrshefte fuer Zeitgeschichte

V Jh f Z — Vierteljahrshefte fuer Zeitgeschichte

Vjhh Statist Dt Reich — Vierteljahrshefte zur Statistik des Deutschen Reichs

Vjhschr Soz U Wirtsch Gesch — Vierteljahrsschrift fuer Sozial-und Wirtschaftsgeschichte

Vjh WF — Vierteljahreshefte fuer Wirtschaftsforschung

Vjh Wirtsch-Forsch — Vierteljahreshefte fuer Wirtschaftsforschung

Vjh Zeitg — Vierteljahrshefte fuer Zeitgeschichte

Vjh Zeitgesch — Vierteljahreshefte fuer Zeitgeschichte

V Jh ZG — Vierteljahrshefte fuer Zeitgeschichte

VJLB — Veterans Jewish Legion. Bulletin

VJ Lit — Deutsche Vierteljahrsschrift fuer Literaturwissenschaft und Geistesgeschichte

Vj Nat Ges (Zuer) — Vierteljahrsschrift der Naturforschenden Gesellschaft (Zuerich)

Vj NGZ — Vierteljahrsschrift. Naturforschende Gesellschaft

Vjsch F Wiss Paed — Vierteljahrsschrift fuer Wissenschaftliche Paedagogik

Vjschr Gerichtl Oeff Med — Vierteljahrsschrift fuer Gerichtliche und Oeffentliche Medizin

Vjschr Herald Sphragistik & Geneal — Vierteljahrsschrift fuer Heraldik, Sphragistik, und Genealogie

Vjschr Musikwiss — Vierteljahrsschrift fuer Musikwissenschaft

Vjschr Naturf Ges (Zuerich) — Vierteljahrsschrift. Naturforschende Gesellschaft (Zuerich)

Vjschr Sozialgesch — Vierteljahrsschrift fuer Sozial- und Wirtschaftsgeschichte

Vjschr Soz- und Wirtschaftsgesch — Vierteljahrschrift fuer Sozial- und Wirtschaftsgeschichte

Vjschr Soz U Wirtsch Gesch — Vierteljahrschrift fuer Sozial- und Wirtschaftsgeschichte

Vjschr Wap Siegel & Famknd — Vierteljahresschrift fuer Wappen-, Siegel- und Familienkunde

Vjschr Zahnhlkde — Vierteljahrsschrift fuer Zahnheilkunde

Vjsch Z Statist D Deut Reich — Vierteljahrsschrift zur Statistik des Deutschen Reiches

Vj SR — Vierteljahrsschrift fuer Sozialrecht

VJWPh — Vierteljahrsschrift fuer Wissenschaftliche Philosophie

VjZh — Vierteljahrsschrift fuer Zahnheilkunde

Vk — Vakstudie

VK — Vedanta Kesari

VK — Verbundkatalog Maschinenlesbarer Katalogdaten Deutscher Bibliotheken

VK — Voelkische Kultur

VK — Volkskrant

VK — Vore Kirkegaarde

VKAW — Verhandelingen. Koninklijke Akademie van Wetenschappen

VKC — Tijdschrift voor Vervoerswetenschap

VKCS — Vestnik Kralovske Ceske Spolecnosti Nauk. Trida Filosoficko-Historicko-Jasykospytna

VKCSN — Vestnik Kralovske Ceske Spolecnosti Nauk

VKF — Voprosy Klassicekoj Filologii

VKFLA — Voprosy Kurortologii, Fizioterapii, i Lechebnoi Fizicheskoi Kul'tury

VKG — Vecen'aja Krasnaja Gazeta

VKhark — Visnik Kharkivs'koho Universytetu

VKL — Verhandelingen. Koninklijke Akademie van Wetenschappen. Letterkunde

VKM — Velhagen und Klasings Monatshefte

VKN — Verhandelingen. Koninklijke Akademie van Wetenschappen. Natuurkunde

VKNA — Verhandelingen. Koninklijke Nederlandse Akademie van Wetenschappen. Afdeling Letterkunde

VKNAL — Verhandelingen. Koninklijke Nederlandse Akademie van Wetenschappen. Afdeling Letterkunde

VKNAW — Verhandelingen. Koninklijke Nederlandse Akademie van Wetenschappen

VKR — Volkstum und Kultur der Romanen

VKR — Voprosy Kul'tury Reci

VKS — Vlees en Vleeswaren

VKVAW — Verhandelingen van de Koninklijke Vlaamsche Akademie van Wetenschappen

VKVAWL — Verhandelingen van de Koninklijke Vlaams Akademie voor Wetenschappen, Letteren en Schone Kunsten van Belgie. Klasse der Letteren

VKyjU — Visnyk Kyjivs'koho Universytetu

VL — Deutsche Vierteljahrsschrift fuer Literaturwissenschaft und Geistesgeschichte

VL — Vetenskaps-Societeten i Lund

VL — Vita Latina

VL — Voprosy Literatury

Vl A — Vejle Amts Arbog

VLa — Vie et Langage

Vl Aa — Vejle Amts Aarbog

Vlaam Chem Ver Tijd — Vlaamse Chemische Vereniging. Tijdingen

Vlaams Diergeneeskd Tijdschr — Vlaams Diergeneeskundig Tijdschrift

Vlaams Diergeneesk Tijdschr — Vlaams Diergeneeskundig Tijdschrift

Vladimir Gos Ped Inst Ucen Zap — Vladimirskii Gosudarstvennyi Pedagogiceskii Institut Imeni P. I. Lebedeva-Poljanskogo. Ucenyi Zapiski

Vladimir Vecer Politehn Inst Sb Naucn Trudov — Vladimirskii Vecernyi Politehniceskii Institut. Sbornik Naucnyh Trudov

Vladivost Med Inst Sb Nauchn Tr — Vladivostokskii Meditsinskii Institut. Sbornik Nauohnykh Trudov

Vlakna Text — Vlakna a Textil

V Lang — Visible Language

Vlastivedny Casop — Vlastivedny Casopis

Vlastiv Obzor — Vlastivedny Obzor

Vlastiv Sborn Vychodni Cechy — Vlastivedny Sbornik Vychodni Cecny

VLD — Victorian Licensing Decisions

VLDTA8 — Veldtrust

VLE — Victorian Legal Executive

V Ledeburs Arch — Allgemeines Archiv fuer die Geschichtskunde des Preussischen Staates (V. Ledebur, Editor)

V Lenin Fiz — Vestnik Leningradskogo Universiteta. Seriya Fiziki i Khimii

V Lenin Mek — Vestnik Leningradskogo Universiteta. Seriya Matematiki i Mekhaniki

VLenU — Vestnik Leningradskogo Gosudarstvennogo Universiteta

VLF — Installatie

VLG — Vlaamse Gids

VLIB — Valodas un Literaturas Instituta Biletens

VLIR — Valodas un Literaturas Instituta Raksti

VLit — Voprosy Literatury

Vliyanie Rab Sred Svoistva Mater — Vliyanie Rabochikh Sred na Svoistva Materialov

VLJaTas — Voprosy Literaturovedenija i Jazykoznanija (Taskent)

Vlks Alm Ned Kath — Volks-Almanak voor Nederlandsche Katholieken

Vlkskst & Vlksknd — Volkskunst und Volkskunde

Vl Kstbode — Vlaamsche Kunstbode

VLON — Verwaltungslexikon

VLONAB — Agricultural Research Reports

VLR — Vanderbilt Law Review

VLR — Victorian Law Reports

VLR — Virginia Law Review

VLR (Adm) — Victorian Law Reports (Admiralty)

VLR (E) — Victorian Law Reports (Equity)

VLR (Eq) — Victorian Law Reports (Equity)

VLR (IP & M) — Victorian Law Reports (Insolvency, Probate, and Matrimonial)

VLR (L) — Victorian Law Reports (Law)

VLR (M) — Victorian Law Reports (Mining)

VLR (P & M) — Victorian Law Reports (Probate and Matrimonial)

VLS — Village Voice. Literary Supplement

Vl Sch — Vlaamse School

Vl Stam — Vlaamsche Stam

VLT — Victorian Law Times

VLU — Vestnik Leningradskogo Gosudarstvennogo Universiteta

VLU — Vestnik Leningradskogo Universiteta. Seriya Istorii, Jazyka, i Literatury

Vlugschr Inst Phytopathol — Vlugschriften van het Instituut voor Phytopathologie

VLUist — Vestnik Leningradskogo Gosudarstvennogo Universiteta

VLVH — Veroeffentlichungen des Landesmuseums fuer Vorgeschichte in Halle

VLvivU — Visnyk L'vivs'koho Derzavnoho Universytetu

VLVM — Vlastivedny Vestnik Moravsky

VM — Venezuela Misionera

VM — Verslagen en Mededeelingen

VMAE — Manuel d'Archeologie Egyptienne

VMAN — Vestnik Meditsini. Akademiia Nauk SSSR

VMarJa — Voprosy Marijskogo Jazykoznanija

VMAW — Verslagen en Mededeelingen. Koninklijke Akademie van Wetenschappen

VMB — Vandringar Med Boeker

VMB — Vie Musicale Belge

VMDKA — Voprosy Meditsinskoi Khimii

VMG — Vestnik Gosudarstvennogo Muzeia Gruzii

VMHB — Virginia Magazine of History and Biography

VMI — Meubel. Weekblad voor de Meubelindustrie, Meubelhandel, Woninginrichting, en Toeleveringsbedrijven

VMI — Vertical Markets Information Database

VMJ/BIV — Boletin Indigenista Venezolano. Organo de la Comision Indigenista. Ministerio de Justicia

VMKA — Verslagen en Mededeelingen. Koninklijke Akademie voor Nederlandse Taal- en Letterkunde

VMKH — Vijesti Muzealaca i Konzervatora N.R. Hrvastke

VMKVA — Verslagen en Mededeelingen. Koninklijke Vlaamse Akademie voor Taal- en Letterkunde

VMMK — Veszprem Megyei Muzeumok Koezlemenyei

VMMMA — Vestnik Moskovskogo Universiteta. Seriya 1. Matematika, Mekhanika

VMMOA — Virginia Medical Monthly [*Later, Virginia Medical*]

VMNF — Videnskabelige Meddelelser fra Dansk Naturhistorisk Forening

VMNGM — Veroeffentlichungen der Medizinisch-Naturwissenschaftlichen Gesellschaft. Muenster

VMOGA — Vestnik Moskovskogo Universiteta. Seriya 5. Geografiya

V Mosk Fiz — Vestnik Moskovskogo Universiteta. Seriya Fiziki i Astronomii

V Mosk Mkh — Vestnik Moskovskogo Universiteta. Seriya Matematiki i Mekhaniki

V Mosk U Kh — Vestnik Moskovskogo Universiteta. Seriya Khimiya

VMR Vet Med Rev — VMR. Veterinary Medical Review

VMSDA — Vysokomolekulyarnye Soedineniya

VMSODA — Vie et Milieu. Serie AB. Biologie Marine et Oceanographie

VMU — Vestnik Moskovskogo Gosudarstvennogo Universiteta

VMUBA — Vestnik Moskovskogo Universiteta. Seriya 6. Biologiya, Pochvovedenie

VMUE — Vestnik Moskovskogo Universiteta. Ekonomika, Filosofiia

VMUFA — Vestnik Moskovskogo Universiteta. Seriya 3. Fizika, Astronomiya

VMUGA — Vestnik Moskovskogo Universiteta. Seriya 4. Geologiya

VMUist — Vestnik Moskovskogo Gosudarstvennogo Universiteta

VMUKA — Vestnik Moskovskogo Universiteta. Seriya 2. Khimiya

VMUP — Vie et Milieu. Bulletin du Laboratoire Arago. Universite de Paris

VMUZh — Vestnik Moskovskogo Universiteta Zhurnalistika

VMVB — Veroeffentlichungen aus dem Koeniglichen Museum fuer Voelkerkunde

VMVBORG — Verslagen en Mededeelingen van de Vereeniging tot Beoefening van Overijsselsch Recht en Geschiedenis

VMVL — Veroeffentlichungen des Museums fuer Voelkerkunde zu Leipzig

VMVOVR — Verslagen en Mededeelingen van de Vereeniging tot Uitgaaf van der Bronnen van het Oud-Vaderlandsche Recht

V Mw — Vierteljahrsschrift fuer Musikwissenschaft

VN — Vakstudie-Nieuws

VN — Victorian Newsletter

VN — Vision

VNA — Voprosy Nauchnogo Ateizma

VNAGA2 — Archives Geologiques du Vietnam

VNAW — Verhandelingen der Koninklijke Nederlandse Akademie van Wetenschappen. AfdelingLetterkunde

VNAWAG — Koninklijke Nederlandse Akademie van Wetenschappen. Verhandelingen. Afdeling Natuurkunde. Tweede Reeks

VND — Vprasanja Nasih Dni

Vnesn Torg — Vnesnjaja Torgovlja

VNFH — Vjesnik Narodnog Fronta Hrvatske

VNGB — Verhandlungen der Naturforschenden Gesellschaft. Basel

VNGGA — Verhandelingen. Koninklijke Nederlands Geologisch Mijnbouwkundig Genootschap. Geologische Serie

VNGZ — Verhandlungen der Naturforschenden Gesellschaft (Zuerich)

V Nh F — Videnskabelige Meddelelser fra Dansk Naturhistorisk Forening

Vnitr Lek — Vnitrni Lekarstvi

VNL — Victorian Newsletter

VNL — Vrij Nederland

VNM — Tijdschrift van de Vereeniging voor Nederlandse Muziekgeschiedenis

V Nord M — Vort Nordiske Modersmal

V Nost Eng Mg — Van Nostrand's Engineering Magazine

VNRN — Vladimir Nabokov Research Newletter

VNS — Bondssparbanken

VNVBr — Verhandlungen des Naturforschenden Vereins zu Bruenn

VNZ — Schweizerische Handelskammer in den Niederlanden. Mitteilungen an die Mitglieder

VO — Vesnjani Orbriji

VO — Vocero

VO — Voice

Vo — Voices

VOA — Voorlichter

VOC — VM. Voorlichtingsblad van het Ministerie van Volksgezondheid en Milieuhygiene

Voc Aspect Ed — Vocational Aspect of Education

Vocat Asp Educ — Vocational Aspect of Education

Vocat Guid — Vocational Guidance Quarterly

Vocational Aspect — Vocational Aspect of Education

Vocat Train Bull — Vocational Training. Bulletin

Vocat Training — Vocational Training

VocEd Insider — VocEd Business and Office Insider. Journal of the American Vocational Association

Voc Educ — Vocational Education

Voc Educ M — Vocational Education Magazine

Voc Guidance Bul — Vocational Guidance Bulletin

Voc Guid Q — Vocational Guidance Quarterly

Voc J Ed — VOC Journal of Education

Vod Hospod Ochr Ovzdusi — Vodni Hospodarstvi a Ochrana Osvdusi

Vodn Hospod Rada B — Vodni Hospodarstvi. Rada B

Vodni Hospod — Vodni Hospodarstvi

Vodni Hospod A — Vodni Hospodarstvi. Rada A

Vodni Hospod Rada B — Vodni Hospodarstvi. Rada B

Vodn Resur — Vodnye Resursy

Vodohospod Cas — Vodohospodarsky Casopis

Vodopodgot Ochistka Prom Stokov — Vodopodgotovka i Ochistka Promyshlennykh Stokov

Vodorosli Griby Sib Dal'nego Vostoka — Vodorosli i Griby Sibiri i Dal'nego Vostoka

Vodosnabzh Kanaliz Gidrotekh Sooruzh — Vodosnabzhenie Kanalizatsiya Gidrotekhnicheskie Sooruzheniya

Vodosnabzh Sanit Tekh — Vodosnabzhenie i Sanitarnaya Tekhnika

Vodos Sanit Tekhn — Vodosnabzhenie i Sanitarnaya Tekhnika

Voedingsmiddelen Technol — Voedingsmiddelen Technologie

Voegel Rheinl — Voegel des Rheinlandes

VOEI — Veroeffentlichungen. Osteuropa-Institut

Voen Khim — Voennaya Khimiya

Voen Med Delo — Voenno Meditsinsko Delo

Voen Med Fak Sarat Medinst Sb Nauchn Tr — Voenno-Meditsinskii Fakul'tet pri Saratovskom Medinstitute. Sbornik Nauchnykh Trudov

Voen-Med Zh — Voenno-Meditsinskii Zhurnal

Voenna Tekh — Voenna Tekhnika

Voenno-Ist Zhurnal — Voenno-Istoricheskii Zhurnal

Voenno-Med Zh — Voenno-Meditsinskii Zhurnal

Voenno Med Zhurnal (Leningrad) — Voenno-Meditsinskii Zhurnal (Leningrad)

Voenno-Med Zhurnal (S Peterburg) — Voenno-Meditsinskii Zhurnal (S. Peterburg)

Voen Sanit Delo — Voenno-Sanitarnoe Delo

Voen Vest — Voennyi Vestnik

Voen Znaniya — Voennye Znaniya

Vogelkd Ber Niedersachsen — Vogelkundliche Berichte aus Niedersachsen

Vogelkd Hefte Edertal — Vogelkundliche Hefte Edertal

Vog Liv — Vogue Living

VOH — Grootkeuken. Voedingsblad voor Instellingen en Bedrijven

Vol — Voprosy Istorii

VOIB — Veroeffentlichungen. Abteilung fuer Slavische Sprachen und Literaturen. Osteuropa-Institut [*Slavisches Seminar*]. Freie Universitaet Berlin

Voice — Village Voice

Voice Chorus Am — Voice of Chorus America

Voici — Voici la France de ce Mois

Voigt Mg — Magazin fuer den Neuesten Zustand der Naturkunden, mit Ruecksicht auf die dazu Gehoerigen Huelfswissenschaften. Voigt

VolK — Voprosy Istorii KPSS

VoiN — Voies Nouvelles

VoiP — Voix des Poetes

Voith Forsch Konstr — Voith Forschung und Konstruktion

Voith Res & Constr — Voith Research and Construction

Voix Dent — Voix Dentaire

VOIZD — Voice of Z-39 [*Later, Information Standards Quarterly*]

Vojenskozdrav Knih — Vojenskozdravotnicka Knihovna

Vojen Zdrav Listy — Vojenske Zdravotnicke Listy

Vojnoekon Pregl — Vojnoekonomski Pregled

Vojnosanit Pregl — Vojnosanitetski Pregled

VOK — Volkskrant

VOKK — Visnik Odes'koi Komisii Kraezhavstva. Ukrains'kii Akademii Nauk

VOKKUAN — Vistnyk Odes'koi Komisii Kraezhavstva. Ukrains'kii Akademii Nauk

VOKS — Soviet Union Society for Cultural Relations with Foreign Countries. Weekly NewsBulletin

VOLAD — Voice of the Lakes

Volcani Inst Agric Res Div For Ilanot Leafl — Volcani Institute of Agricultural Research. Division of Forestry. Ilanot Leaflet

Volcani Inst Agric Res Div Sci Publ Pam — Volcani Institute of Agricultural Research. Division of Scientific Publications. Pamphlet

Volcanol Bull Jpn Meterol Agency — Volcanological Meteorological Bulletin. Japan Meteorological Agency

Volcanol Soc Jap Bull — Volcanological Society of Japan. Bulletin

Vol Effort Q — Voluntary Effort Quarterly

Vol Feeding Mgt — Volume Feeding Management

Volgograd Gos Ped Inst Ucen Zap — Volgogradskogo Gosudarstvennogo Pedagogiceskogo Instituta Imeni A. S. Serafimovica Ucenye Zapiski

Vol Homenaje — Volumenes de Homenaje

Volksforsch — Volksforschung

Volksm — Volksmusik

Volksmus — Volksmusik. Zeitschrift fuer das Musikalische Laienschaffen

Volkstum Landschaft — Volkstum und Landschaft. Heimatblaetter der Muensterlaendische Tageszeitung

Volkswirtsch Schriften — Volkswirtschaftliche Schriften

Volk U Reich — Volk und Reich

Volleyball Mag — Volleyball Magazine

Volleyball Tech J — Volleyball Technical Journal

Vologod Gos Ped Inst Ucen Zap — Vologodskii Gosudarstvennyi Pedagogiceskii Institut. Ucenye Zapiski

Vologod I Cerepovec Gos Ped Inst Ucen Zap — Vologodskii Gosudarstvennyi Pedagogiceskii Institut. Cerepoveckii Gosudarstvennyi Pedagogiceskii Institut. Ucenye Zapiski

Vo LR — Villanova Law Review

VolR — Volontes de Ceux de la Resistance

VOLRA — Volta Review

Vol Ret Merch — Volume Retail Merchandising

Volta R — Volta Review

Volt Electr Trade Mon — Volt. Electrical Trade Monthly

Volunt Action — Voluntary Action

Volunt Action Leadersh — Voluntary Action Leadership

Volunt Adm — Volunteer Administration

Volunt Forum Abs — Voluntary Forum Abstracts

Volunt Housing — Voluntary Housing

Volunt Leader — Volunteer Leader

Volz Mat Sb — Volzskii Matematiceskii Sbornik

VON — Vestnik Otdelenija Obscestvennych Nauk. Akademija Nauk Gruzinskoj SSR

VONEA — Voprosy Neirokhirurgii

Von Roll Mitt — Von Roll Mitteilungen

Voorlichting Onderz — Voorlichting en Onderzoek

Vop Bot Akad Nauk Litov SSR Inst Bot — Voprosy Botaniki. Akademiya Nauk Litovskoi SSR. Institut Botaniki

Vop Ekol — Voprosy Ekologii

Vop Erozii Povysh Prod Sklon Zemel' Moldavii — Voprosy Erozii i Povysheniya Produktivnosti Sklonovykh Zemel' Moldavii

Vop Fil — Voprosy Filosofii

Vop Filol — Voprosy Filologii

Vop Filos — Voprosy Filosofii

Vop Genez Krypnomashtabn Kartir Pochv Kazan Univ — Voprosy Genezisa i Krypnomashtabnoi Kartirovanii Pochv Kazanskii Universitet

Vop Geogr Mordovsk ASSR — Voprosy Geografii Mordovskoi ASSR

Vop Iaz — Voprosy Iazykoznaniia. Akademiia Nauk SSSR

VopIst — Voprosy Istorii

Vop Ist Est Tekh — Voprosy Istorii Estestvoznaniia i Tekhniki

Vop Istor — Voprosy Istorii

Vop Med Kh — Voprosy Meditsinskoi Khimii

Vop Mikrobiol Akad Nauk Armyan SSR — Voprosy Mikrobiologii. Akademiya Nauk Armyanskoi SSR

Vop Pitan — Voprosy Pitaniya

Vop Psikhol — Voprosy Psikhologii

Vopr Antrop — Voprosy Antropologii

Vopr Antropol — Voprosy Antropologii

Vopr Arkheol Gruz — Voprosy Arkheologii Gruzii
Vopr At Nauki Tekh Ser Fiz Plazmy Probl Upr Termodad Reakts — Voprosy Atomnoi Nauki i Tekhniki. Seriya Fizika Plazmy i Problemy UpravlyaemykhTermodadernykh Reaktsii
Vopr At Nauki Tekh Ser Fiz Vys Energ At Yadra — Voprosy Atomnoi Nauki i Tekhniki. Seriya Fizika Vysokikh Energii i Atomnogo Yadra
Vopr At Nauki Tekh Ser Obshch Yad Fiz — Voprosy Atomnoi Nauki i Tekhniki. Seriya Obshchaya i Yadernaya Fizika
Vopr At Nauki Tekh Ser Radiats Tekh — Voprosy Atomnoi Nauki i Tekhniki. Seriya Radiatsionnaya Tekhnika
Vopr At Nauki Tekh Ser Yad Konstanty — Voprosy Atomnoi Nauki i Tekhniki. Seriya Yadernye Konstanty
Vopr Bezopasn Ugol'n Shakhtakh — Voprosy Bezopasnosti v Ugol'nykh Shakhtakh
Vopr Biokhim — Voprosy Biokhimii
Vopr Biokhim Mozga — Voprosy Biokhimii Mozga
Vopr Biokhim Nervn Myshechnoi Sist — Voprosy Biokhimii Nervnoi i Myshechnoi Sistem
Vopr Biokhim Nervn Sist — Voprosy Biokhimii Nervnoi Sistemy
Vopr Biol — Voprosy Biologii
Vopr Biol Kraev Med — Voprosy Biologii i Kraevoi Meditsiny
Vopr Biol Semennogo Rezmnozheniya — Voprosy Biologii Semennogo Reszmnozheniya
Vopr Bor'by Silikozom Sib — Voprosy Bor'by s Silikozom v Sibiri
Vopr Bot — Voprosy Botaniki. Essais de Botanique
Vopr Cenoobraz — Voprosy Cenoobrazovanija
Vopr Chetvertechn Geol — Voprosy Chetvertechnoi Geologii
Vopr Din Prochn — Voprosy Dinamiki i Prochnosti
Vopr Din Teor Rasprostr Seism Voln — Voprosy Dinamicheskoi Teorii Rasprostraneniya Seismicjeskikh Voln
Vopr Dozim Zasch Izluch Mosk Inzh Fiz Inst Sb Statei — Voprosy Dozimetrii i Zaschity ot Izluchenii. Moskovskii Inzhenerno Fizicheskii Institut Sbornik Statei
Vopr Dozim Zashch Izluch — Voprosy Dozimetrii i Zashchity ot Izluchenii
Vopr Ekol Biotsenol — Voprosy Ekologii i Biotsenologii
Vopr Ekon — Voprosy Ekonomiki
Vopr Eksp Klin Radiol — Voprosy Eksperimental'noi i Klinicheskoi Radiologii
Vopr Eksp Onkol — Voprosy Eksperimental'noi Onkologii
Vopr Endokrinol Obmena Veshchestv — Voprosy Endokrinologii i Obmena Veshchestv
Vopr Endokrinol Obmena Veshchestv Resp Mezhved Sb — Voprosy Endokrinologii Obmena Veshchestvennyi Respublikanskoi MezhvedomstvennyiSbornik
Vopr Energ — Voprosy Energetiki
Vopr Erozii Povysh Prod Sklonovykh Zemel Mold — Voprosy Erozii i Povysheniya Produktivnosti Sklonovykh Zemel' Moldavii
Vopr Etiol Patog Opukholei — Voprosy Etiologii i Patogeneza Opukholei
Vopr Filos — Voprosy Filosofii
Vopr Fiz Gorn Porod — Voprosy Fiziki Gornykh Porod
Vopr Fiziol Akad Nauk Azerb SSR Sekt Fiziol — Voprosy Fiziologii Akademia Nauk Azerbaidzhanskoi SSR. Sektor Fiziologii
Vopr Fiziol Biokhim Kul't Rast — Voprosy Fiziologii i Biokhimii Kul'turnykh Rastenii
Vopr Fiziol Biokhim Zool Parazitol — Voprosy Fiziologii, Biokhimii, Zoologii, i Parazitologii
Vopr Fiziol Chel Zhivotn — Voprosy Fiziologii Cheloveka i Zhivotnykh
Vopr Fiziol Rast Mikrobiol — Voprosy Fiziologii Rastenii i Mikrobiologii
Vopr Fiz Tverd Tela — Voprosy Fiziki Tverdogo Tela
Vopr Fiz Zasch Reaktorov — Voprosy Fiziki Zashchity Reaktorov
Vopr Fiz Zashch Reakt — Voprosy Fiziki Zashchity Reaktorov
Vopr Fotosint — Voprosy Fotosinteza
Vopr Gazotermodin Energoustanovok — Voprosy Gazotermodinamiki Energoustanovok
Vopr Gematol Pereliv Krovi Krovozamenitelei — Voprosy Gematologii Perelivaniya Krovi i Krovozamenitelei
Vopr Geogr — Voprosy Geografii
Vopr Geogr Dal'nego Vostoka — Voprosy Geografii Dal'nego Vostoka
Vopr Geogr Kaz — Voprosy Geografii Kazakhstana
Vopr Geogr Mordov ASSR — Voprosy Geografii Mordovskoi ASSR
Vopr Geokhim Tipomorfizm Miner — Voprosy Geokhimii i Tipomorfizm Mineralov
Vopr Geol Buren Neft Gazov Skvazhin — Voprosy Geologii i Bureniya Neftyanykh i Gazovykh Skvazhin
Vopr Geol Metallog Kol'sk Poluostrova — Voprosy Geologii i Metallogenii Kol'skogo Poluostrova
Vopr Geol Metod Razved Zolota — Voprosy Geologii i Metodiki Razvedki Zolota
Vopr Geol Mineral Kolsk Poluostrova — Voprosy Geologii i Mineralogii Kol'skogo Poluostrova
Vopr Geol Mineral Rudn Mestorozhd Ukr — Voprosy Geologii i Mineralogii Rudnykh Mestorozhdenii Ukrainy
Vopr Geol Neftegazonsn Uzb — Voprosy Geologii i Neftegazonosnosti Uzbekistana
Vopr Geol Neftenosn Sredn Povolzh'ya — Voprosy Geologii i Neftenosnosti Srednego Povolzh'ya
Vopr Geol Tadzh — Voprosy Geologii Tadzhikistana
Vopr Geol Uzb — Voprosy Geologii Uzbekistana
Vopr Geol Vost Okrainy Russ Platformy Yuzhn Urala — Voprosy Geologii Vostochnoi Okrainy Russkoi Platformy i Yuzhnogo Urala
Vopr Geol Yuzhn Urala Povolzh'ya — Voprosy Geologii Yuzhnogo Urala i Povolzh'ya
Vopr Geomorfol Geol Bashk — Voprosy Geomorfologii i Geologii Bashkirii
Vopr Gerontol Geriatr — Voprosy Gerontologii i Geriatrii
Vopr Gidrodin Teploobmena Kriog Sist — Voprosy Gidrodinamiki i Teploobmena v Kriogennykh Sistemakh
Vopr Gidrogeol Inzh Geol Ukr — Voprosy Gidrogeologii i Inzhenernoi Geologii Ukrainy
Vopr Gidrol — Voprosy Gidrologii

Vopr Gidrotekh — Voprosy Gidrotekhniki
Vopr Gig Pitan — Voprosy Gigieny Pitaniya
Vopr Gig Tr Profpatol Prom Toksikol — Voprosy Gigieny Truda Profpatologii i Promyshlennoi Toksikologii
Vopr Gig Tr Slants Promsti Est SSR — Voprosy Gigieny Truda v Slantsevoi Promyshlennosti Estonskoi SSR
Vopr Ikhtiol — Voprosy Ikhtiologii
Vopr Immunol — Voprosy Immunologii
Vopr Infekts Patol Immunol — Voprosy Infektsionnoi Patologii i Immunologii
Vopr Inf Teor Prakt — Voprosy Informatsionnoi Teorii i Praktiki
Vopr Introd Rast Zelenogo Stroit — Voprosy Introduktsii Rastenii i Zelenogo Stroitel'stva
Vopr Inzh Geol Gruntoved — Voprosy Inzhenernoi Geologii i Gruntovedeniya
Vopr Inzh Seismol — Voprosy Inzhenernoi Seismologii
Vopr Issled Ispol'z Pochv Mold — Voprosy Issledovaniya i Ispol'zovaniya Pochvovedeniya Moldavii
Vopr Issled Lessovykh Gruntov Osn Fundam — Voprosy Issledovaniya Lessovykh Gruntov Osnovanii i Fundamentov
Vopr Ist — Voprosy Istorii
Vopr Ist KPSS — Voprosy Istorii KPSS
Vopr Istor — Voprosy Istorii
Vopr Istor Estestvozn Tekh — Voprosy Istorii Estestvoznaniya i Tekhniki
Vopr Ist Udm — Voprosy Istorii Udmurtii
Vopr Karstoved — Voprosy Karstovedeniya
Vopr Khim Biokhim Sist Soderzh Marganets Polifenoly — Voprosy Khimii i Biokhimii Sistem. Soderzhashchikh Marganets I Pollfenoly
Vopr Khim Khim Tekhnol — Voprosy Khimii i Khimicheskoj Tekhnologii
Vopr Kinet Katal — Voprosy Kinetiki i Kataliza
Vopr Klin Eksp Onkol — Voprosy Klinicheskoi i Eksperimental'noi Onkologii
Vopr Klin Eskp Khir — Voprosy Klinicheskoi i Eksperimental'noi Khirurgii
Vopr Klin Lech Zlokach Novoobraz — Voprosy Kliniki i Lecheniya Zlokachestvennykh Novoobrazovanii
Vopr Klin Med — Voprosy Klinicheskoi Meditsiny
Vopr Kommunal'n Gig — Voprosy Kommunal'noi Gigieny
Vopr Kosmog — Voprosy Kosmogonii
Vopr Kraev Patol Akad Nauk Uzb SSR — Voprosy Kraevoi Patologii Akademii Nauk Uzbekskoi SSR
Vopr Kriog Tekh — Voprosy Kriogennoi Tekhniki
Vopr Kurortol Fizioter (Frunze) — Voprosy Kurortologii i Fizioterapii (Frunze)
Vopr Kurortol Fizioter Lech Fiz Kul't — Voprosy Kurortologii, Fizioterapii, i Lechebnoi Fizicheskoi Kul'tury
Vopr Kurortol Revatol — Voprosy Kurortologii i Revmatologii
Vopr Leikozol — Voprosy Leikozologii
Vopr Leprol Dermatol — Voprosy Leprologii i Dermatologii
Vopr Lesoved — Voprosy Lesovedeniya
Vopr Litol Petrogr — Voprosy Litologii i Petrografii
Vopr Magmat Metamorf — Voprosy Magmatizma i Metamorfizma
Vopr Magmat Metamorfiz — Voprosy Magmatizma i Metamorfizma
Vopr Magn Gidrodin Akad Nauk Latv SSR Inst Fiz — Voprosy Magnitnoi Gidrodinamiki. Akademiya Nauk Latviiskoi SSR. Institut Fiziki
Vopr Med Khim — Voprosy Meditsinskoi Khimii
Vopr Med Khim Akad Med Nauk SSR — Voprosy Meditsinskoi Khimii Akademiya Meditsinskikh Nauk SSSR
Vopr Med Teor Klin Prakt Kurortnogo Lech — Voprosy Meditsinskoi Teorii Klinicheskoi Praktiki i Kurortnogo Lecheniya
Vopr Med Virusol — Voprosy Meditsinskoi Virusologii
Vopr Mekh — Voprosy Mekhanika
Vopr Mekh Real'nogo Tverd Tela — Voprosy Mekhaniki Real'nogo Tverdogo Tela
Vopr Metalloved Korroz Met — Voprosy Metallovedeniya i Korrozii Metallov
Vopr Metod Nauki — Voprosy Metodologii Nauki
Vopr Mikrobiol — Voprosy Mikrobiologii
Vopr Mikrodozim — Voprosy Mikrodozimetrii Ministerstvo Vysshego i Srednego Spetsial'nogo Obrazovaniya SSSR
Vopr Mineral Osad Obraz — Voprosy Mineralogii Osadochnykh Obrazonanii
Vopr Neftekhim — Voprosy Neftekhimii
Vopr Neirokhir — Voprosy Neirokhirurgii
Vopr Obsc Nauk — Voprosy Obscestvennykh Nauk
Vopr Obshch Khim Biokhim — Voprosy Obshchei Khimii i Biokhimii
Vopr Okhr Materin Det — Voprosy Okhrany Materinstva i Detstva
Vopr Onkol — Voprosy Onkologii
Vopr Onkol (Leningr) — Voprosy Onkologii (Leningrad)
Vopr Org Geokhim Gidrogeol Neftegazonosn Basseinov Uzb — Voprosy Organicheskoi Geokhimii i Gidrogeologii Neftegazonosnykh Basseinov Uzbekistana
Voprosy Dinamiki i Procnosti — Rizskii Politehniceskii Institut. Voprosy Dinamiki i Procnosti
Voprosy Filos — Voprosy Filosofii
Voprosy Gidrotekh — Voprosy Gidrotekhniki
Voprosy Informatsion Teorii i Praktiki — Akademiya Nauk SSSR. Vsesoyuznyi Institut Nauchnoi i Tekhnicheskoi Informatsii.Voprosy Informatsionnoi Teorii i Praktiki
Voprosy Istor — Voprosy Istorii
Voprosy Istor Estestvoznan I Tehn — Voprosy Istorii Estestvoznanija i Tehniki
Voprosy Istor Isk — Voprosy Istorii Iskusstva
Voprosy Kibernet (Moscow) — Voprosy Kibernetiki (Moscow)
Voprosy Kibernet (Tashkent) — Voprosy Kibernetiki (Tashkent)
Voprosy Teor Arkhit Kompozitsii — Voprosy Teorii Arkhiturnoy Kompozitsii
Voprosy Teor Sistem Avtomat Upravleniya — Leningradskii Universitet Voprosy Teorii Sistem Avtomaticheskogo Upravleniya
Voprosy Vychisl i Prikl Mat — Akademiya Nauk Uzbekskoi SSR. Trudy Ordena Trudovogo Krasnogo Znameni InstitutaKibernetiki s Vychislitel'nym Tsentrom. Voprosy Vychislitel'noi i Prikladnoi Matematiki
Vopr Patol Krovi Krovoobrashch — Voprosy Patologii Krovi i Krovoobrashcheniya
Vopr Pediatr Ohkr Materin Det — Voprosy Pediatrii i Ohkrany Materinstva i Detstva

Vopr Peredachi Inf — Voprosy Peredachi Informatsii
Vopr Pitan — Voprosy Pitaniya
Vopr Prikl Geokhim — Voprosy Prikladnoi Geokhimii
Vopr Prikl Radiogeol — Voprosy Prikladnoi Radiogeologii
Vopr Prochn Plast Met — Voprosy Prochnosti i Plastichnosti Metallov
Vopr Proekt Sodovykh Zavodov — Voprosy Proekhitovaniya Sodovykh Zavodov
Vopr Proizvod Stali — Voprosy Proizvodstva Stali
Vopr Proizvod Vaktsin Syvorotok — Voprosy Proizvodstva Vaktsin i Syvorotok
Vopr Psikhiat Nevropatol — Voprosy Psikhiatrii i Nevropatologii
Vopr Psikhiatr Nevropatol — Voprosy Psikhiatrii i Nevropatologii
Vopr Psikhol — Voprosy Psikhologii
Vopr Radiobiol — Voprosy Radiobiologii
Vopr Radiobiol Akad Nauk Arm SSR — Voprosy Radiobiologii. Akademiya Nauk Armyanskoi SSR
Vopr Radiobiol Biol Deistviya Tsitostatich Prep — Voprosy Radiobiologii i Biologicheskogo Deistviya Tsitostaticheskikh Preparatov
Vopr Radiobiol Biol Dejstv Tsitostatich Prep — Voprosy Radiobiologii i Biologicheskogo Dejstviya Tsitostaticheskikh Preparatov
Vopr Radiobiol Klin Radiol — Voprosy Radiobiologii i Klinicheskoi Radiologii
Vopr Radiobiol Sb Tr — Voprosy Radiobiologii. Sbornik Trudov
Vopr Radiobiol (Yerevan) — Voprosy Radiobiologii (Yerevan)
Vopr Radioelektron — Voprosy Radioelektroniki
Vopr Ratsion Pitan — Voprosy Ratsional'nogo Pitaniya
Vopr Razved Geofiz — Voprosy Razvedochnoi Geofiziki
Vopr Razvit Gazov Promsti Ukr SSR — Voprosy Razvitiya Gazovoi Promyshlennosti Ukrainskoi SSR
Vopr Razvit Licnosti — Voprosy Razvitija Licnosti
Vopr Reg Geol Metallog Zabaikal'ya — Voprosy Regional'noi Geologii i Metallogenii Zabaikal'ya
Vopr Rentgenol Onkol — Voprosy Rentgenologii i Onkologii
Vopr Revm — Voprosy Revmatizma
Vopr Rud Geofiz — Voprosy Rudnoi Geofiziki
Vopr Rud Geofiz Minist Geol Okhr Nedr SSSR — Voprosy Rudnoi Geofiziki. Ministerstvo Geologii i Okhrany Nedr SSSR
Vopr Rudn Geofiz — Voprosy Rudnoi Geofiziki
Vopr Rudn Radiom — Voprosy Rudnoi Radiometrii
Vopr Rudn Transp — Voprosy Rudichnogo Transporta
Vopr Sel'sk Lesn Khoz Dal'nego Vostoka — Voprosy Sel'skogo i Lesnogo Khozyaistva Dal'nego Vostoka
Vopr Sel'sk Lesn Khoz Dal'n Vost — Voprosy Sel'skogo i Lesnogo Khozyaistva Dal'nego Vostoka
Vopr Sov Finno-Ugroved — Voprosy Sovetskogo Finno-Ugrovedenija
Vopr Stereokhim — Voprosy Stereokhimii
Vopr Strat Takt Marks-Lenin Partij — Voprosy Strategii i Taktiki Marksistsko-Leninskih Partij
Vopr Sudebno-Med Ekspert — Voprosy Sudebno-Meditsinskoi Ekspertizy
Vopr Sud Med Ekspertnoi Prakt — Voprosy Sudebnoi Meditsiny i Ekspertnoi Praktiki
Vopr Tekhnol Obrab Vody Prom Pit'evogo Vodoshnabzh — Voprosy Tekhnologii Obrabotki Vody Promyshlennogo i Pit'evogo Vodosnabzheniya
Vopr Tekhnol Tovaroved Izdelii Legk Promsti — Voprosy Tekhnologii i Tovarovedeniya Izdelii Legkoi Promyshlennosti
Vopr Tekhnol Ulavlivaniya Pererab Prod Koksovaniya — Voprosy Tekhnologii Ulavlivaniya i Pererabotki Produktov Koksovaniya
Vopr Tekh Teplofiz — Voprosy Tekhnicheskoi Teplofiziki
Vopr Teor At Stolknovenii — Voprosy Teorii Atomnykh Stolknovenii
Vopr Teorii Metod Ideol Raboty — Voprosy Teorii i Metodov Ideologiceskoj Raboty
Vopr Teor Plazmy — Voprosy Teorii Plazmy
Vopr Teplofiz Yad Reakt — Voprosy Teplofiziki Yadernykh Reaktorov
Vopr Teploobmena Termodin — Voprosy Teploobmena i Termodinamiki
Vopr Termodin Geterogennykh Sist Teor Poverkhn Yavlenii — Voprosy Termodinamiki Geterogennykh Sistemi Teorii Poverkhnostnykh Yavlenii
Vopr Tuberk (Riga) — Voprosy Tuberkuleza (Riga)
Vopr Urol — Voprosy Urologii
Vopr Vet Virusol — Voprosy Veterinarnoi Virusologii
Vopr Virusol — Voprosy Virusologii
Vopr Vodn Khoz — Voprosy Vodnogo Khozyaistva
Vopr Vychisl Mat Tekh (Tashkent) — Voprosy Vychislitel'noi Matematiki i Tekhniki (Tashkent)
VOPSA — Voprosy Psikhologii
Vop Stat — Voprosy Statistiki
Vop Virus — Voprosy Virusologii
Vop Virusol — Voprosy Virusologii
VOR — Vortex Science Fiction
Vorbereitung Einsatzst Optim Metall Prozesse Vortr Metall Sem — Vorbereitung von Einsatzstoffen zur Optimierung Metallurgischer Prozesse. Vortraege beim Metallurgischen Seminar
Vorgeschichtl Jb — Vorgeschichtliches Jahrbuch fuer die Gesellschaft fuer Vorgeschichtliche Forschung
VORHDW — Voegel des Rheinlandes
VORLA — Vestnik Oto-Rino-Laringologii
Vorles Churpfaelz Phys Oecon Ges — Vorlesungen der Churpfaelzischen Physicalish-Oeconomischen Gesellschaft
Vorlesungen Fachbereich Math Univ Essen — Vorlesungen aus dem Fachbereich Mathematik. Universitaet Essen
Vorlesungen Math — Vorlesungen ueber Mathematik
Vorlesungen Math Inst Giessen — Vorlesungen. Mathematisches Institut Giessen
Vorlesungsmanuskr IFF Ferienkurses — Vorlesungsmanuskripte des IFF (Institut fuer Festkoerperforschung)-Ferienkurses
VornGB — Verhandlungen der Ornithologischen Gesellschaft Bayern
Voronez Gos Univ Trudy Mat Fak — Voronezskii Gosudarstvennyi Universitet Imeni Leninskogo Komsomola. Trudy Matematiceskogo Fakul'teta
Voronez Gos Univ Trudy Naucn Issled Inst Mat VGU — Voronezskii Ordena Lenina Gosudarstvennyi Universitet Imeni Leninskogo Komsomola. Trudy Naucno-Issledovatel'skogo Instituta Matematiki

Voronez Gos Univ Trudy Sem Funkcional Anal — Ministerstvo Vyssego Obrazovanija SSSR Voronezskii Gosudarstvennyi UniversitetTrudy Seminara po Funkcional'nomu Analizu
Voronez Tehn Inst Trudy — Voronezskii Tehnologiceskii Institut. Trudy
Vorsokr — Fragmente der Vorsokratiker
Vortraege Nordrhein Westfaelische Akad Wiss — Vortraege. Nordrhein-Westfaelische Akademie der Wissenschaften
Vortragsveranst Arbeitskreises Rastermikrosk Materialpruef — Vortragsveranstaltung des Arbeitskreises Rastermikroskopie in der Materialpruefung
Vortr Bib Warburg — Vortraege der Bibliothek Warburg
Vortr Gesamtgeb Bot — Vortraege aus dem Gesamtgebiet der Botanik
Vortr Pflanzenz Deut Landwirt Ges Pflanzenzuchtabt — Vortraege fuer Pflanzenzuchter. Deutsche Landwirtschaftliche Gesellschaft Pflanzenzuchtabteilung
Vortr Stud Zent Umweltforsch Westfael Wilhelms Univ — Vortraege und Studien. Zentrum fuer Umweltforschung der Westfaelischen Wilhelms-Universitaet
Vortr VGB Konf Forsch Kraftwerkstech — Vortraege. VGB-Konferenz (Vereinigung der Grosskraftwerksbetreiber) Forschung in der Kraftwerkstechnik
Vortr VGB Konf Kohlevergasung — Vortraege. VGB-Konferenz (Vereinigung der Grosskraftwerksbetreiber) Kohlevergasung
Vort Warb — Vortraege der Bibliothek Warburg
VOSAA — Vox Sanguinis
V Ost Geschichtsv — Veroeffentlichungen. Verband Oesterreichischer Geschichts-Vereine
Vost Neft — Vostochnaya Neft
VOT — Vision of Tomorrow
Vouloir J Action Econ & Soc — Vouloir. Journal d'Action Economique et Sociale
VoW — Voice of the World
Vox Guy — Vox Guyanae
Vox Med — Vox Medica
Vox Sang — Vox Sanguinis
Vox Sanguin — Vox Sanguinis
VoxTh — Vox Theologica
VoxTheol — Vox Theologica
VOYA — Voice of Youth Advocates
Voz — Vozrozhdenie (Paris)
Vozes — Vozes Revista Catolica de Cultura
Voz Farm (Lima) — Voz Farmaceutica (Lima)
VOZNA — Voennye Znaniya
Vozr — Vozrozdenie
VP — Vergessenes Pompeji
VP — Victorian Poetry
VP — Viewpoint
VP — Vita e Pensiero
VP — Voce del Passato
VPA — Verpackung. Schweizerische Fachzeitschrift fuer Verpackung, Technologie, Package Design, Marketing
VPA — Victorian Planning Appeal Decisions
VPARD — Veterinary Parasitology
VPC — Verpackungsberater
VPD — Vremennik Puskinskogo Doma
VPen — Vita e Pensiero
VPIMD — Vilniaus Pedagoginio Instituto Mokslo Darbai
VPITA — Voprosy Pitaniya
VPMLL — Valstybine Politines ir Mokslines Literatu
VPN — Victorian Periodicals Newsletter
VPR — Verpackungs-Rundschau
VPr — Vers et Prose. Recueil de Haute Litterature
VPS — Verhandlungen der Versammlung Deutscher Philologen und Schulmaenner
VPVLBZ — Scientific Works. Forest Research Institute in Zvolen
VPVMA3 — Vedecke Prace Vyzkumneho Ustavu Melioraci v Praze
VPVMA3 — Vedecke Prace Vyzkumneho Ustavu Melioraci v Zbraslavi
VPVZB9 — Scientific Works. Research Institute of Animal Production at Nitra
VPW — Vorarbeiten zum Pommerschen Woerterbuch
VQ — Vermont Quarterly
VQ — Visvabharati Quarterly
VQR — Virginia Quarterly Review
VR — Viata Romaneasca
VR — Victorian Reports
VR — Viera i Razum
VR — Villanova Law Review
VR — Volja Rossii
VR — Vox Romanica
VRA — Vraag en Aanbod voor Techniek, Nijverheid, Bouwvak, en Handel
Vrach Delo — Vrachebnoe Delo
Vrach Gaz — Vrachebnaia Gazeta
VR (Adm) — Victorian Reports (Admiralty)
Vragen D Tijds — Vragen des Tijds
VRARA — Voprosy Radiobiologii. Sbornik Trudov
Vrashchenie i Prilivnye Deform Zemli — Vrashchenie i Prilivnye Deformatsii Zemli
VRB — Verordeningenblad Bedrijfsorganisatie
VRCODX — Veterinary Research Communications
VRDEA — Vrachebnoe Delo
VRE — Venezuelan Economic Review
VR (E) — Victorian Reports (Equity)
Vrednaya Polezn Fauna Bespozvon Mold — Vrednaya i Poleznaya Fauna Bespozvonochnykh Moldavii
Vremennik Gl Palaty Mer Vesov — Vremennik Glavnoi Palaty Mer i Vesov
Vremennik Obshchestva Lyubiteley Rus Knigi — Vremennik Obshchestva Lyubiteley Russkoy Knigi
VR (Eq) — Victorian Reports (Equity)
VR (IE & M) — Victorian Reports (Insolvency, Ecclesiastical, and Matrimonial)
Vrienden Ned Cer Mededbl — Vrienden van de Nederlandse Ceramiek. Mededelingenblad

Vrije Univ Brussel Inter-Univ Inst High Energ Rep — Vrije Universiteit Brussel. Inter-University Institute for High Energies. Report
VRJa — Voprosy Russkogo Jazykoznanija
VRKhD — Vestnik Russkogo (Studencheskogo) Khristianskogo Dvizheniia
VR (L) — Victorian Reports (Law)
VRL — Voprosy Russkoi Literatury. Respublikanskii Mezhvedomstvennyi Nauchnyi Sbornik
VR (Law) — Victorian Law Reports (Law)
VRM — Voyages, Relations, et Memoires Originaux pour Servir a l'Histoire de la Decouverte de l'Amerique [*Paris*]
VR Newsletter — Victorian Railways Newsletter
VRo — Viata Romaneasca
VROA — Verslagen Omtrent's Rijks Oude Archieven
Vrouw & Huis — Vrouw en haar Huis
VRPC — Via. Rivista Mensile di Poesia e Cultura
VRTDC — Viagem. Revista de Turismo, Divulgacao e Cultura
VS — La Vie Spirituelle
VS — Vases Sicyoniens
VS — Verbum Salutis
VS — Victorian Studies
VS — Vida Sobrenatural
VS — Videnskabs Selskapet Skrifter
VS — Vietnamese Studies
VS — Vital Speeches
VS — Voice of Scotland
VS — Vokrug Sveta
VS — Vorderasiatische Schriftdenkmaeler der Koeniglichen Museen zu Berlin
VSA — Mitteilungsblatt. Vereinigung Schweizerischer Angestelltenverbaende
VSA — Violin Society of America. Journal
VSA — Voice for South America [*London*]
VSAJ — Violin Society of America. Newsletter
VSAL — Berichte. Verhandlungen der Saechsischen Akademie der Wissenschaften zu Leipzig
VSAV — Vydavtel'stvo Slovenskej Akademie Vied
VSB — Victorian Studies Bulletin
VSB — Video Source Book
VSB — Vision. The European Business Magazine
V Sch G — Verfassungsschutzgesetz
VSD — Vendredi, Samedi, Dimanche
Vse — Vsesvit
VSEGEI — Vsesojuznyj Naucno-Issledovatel'skij Geologiceskij Institut
Vse Pro Dviz — Vsemirnoe Profsoiuznoe Dvizhenie
Vses Geogr O-Vo Izv — Vsesoyuznoye Geograficheskoye Obshchestvo. Izvestiia
Vses Nauchno Issled Geol Inst Inf Sb — Vsesoyuznyi Nauchno-Issledovatel'skii Geologicheskii Institut. Informatsionnyi Sbornik
Vses Nauchno-Issled Geol Inst Tr — Vsesoyuznyy Nauchno-Issledovatel'skiy Geologicheskiy Institut. Trudy
Vses Nauchno-Issled Geologorazved Neft Inst Tr — Vsesoyuznyy Nauchno-Issledovatel'skiy Geologorazvedochnyi Neftyanoy Institut. Trudy
Vses Nauchno Issled Inst Eksp Vet Im Ya R Kovalenko Byull — Vsesoyuznyi Nauchno-Issledovatel'skii Institut Eksperimental'noi Veterinarii Imeni Ya. R. Kovalenko. Byulleten
Vses Nauchno Issled Inst Geofiz Metodov Razved Tr — Vsesoyuznyi Nauchno-Issledovatel'skii Institut Geofizicheskikh Metodov Razvedki. Trudy
Vses Nauchno Issled Inst Gidrogeol Inzh Geol Tr — Vsesoyuznyi Nauchno-Issledovatel'skii Institut Gidrogeologii i Inzhenernoi Geologii. Trudy
Vses Nauchno Issled Inst Khlopkovod Sb Nauchn Rab Aspir — Vsesoyuznyi Nauchno-Issledovatel'skii Institut Khlopkovodstva. Sbornik Nauchnykh Rabot Aspirantov
Vses Nauchno Issled Inst Konditer Promsti Tr — Vsesoyuznyi Nauchno-Issledovatel'skii Institut Konditerskoi Promyshlennosti. Trudy
Vses Nauchno Issled Inst Solyanoi Promsti Tr — Vsesoyuznyi Nauchno-Issledovatel'skii Institut Solyanoi Promyshlennosti. Trudy
Vses Nauchno Issled Inst Tsellyul Bum Promsti Sb Tr — Vsesoyuznyi Nauchno-Issledovatel'skii Institut Tsellyulozno-Bumazhnoi Promyshlennosti. Sbornik Trudov
Vses Nauchno Issled Inst Zhirov Tr — Vsesoyuznyi Nauchno-Issledovatel'skii Institut Zhirov. Trudy
Vses Nauchno Issled Khim Farm Inst Khim Med — Vsesoyuznyi Nauchno-Issledovatel'skii Khimiko-Farmatsevticheskii Institut. Khimiya i Meditsina
Vses Nauchno Issled Proektn Inst Galurgii Tr — Vsesoyuznyi Nauchno-Issledovatel'skii i Proektnyi Institut Galurgii. Trudy
Vses Nauchno Issled Proektn Inst Mekh Obrab Polezn Iskop Tr — Vsesoyuznyi Nauchno-Issledovatel'skii i Proektnyi Institut Mekhanicheskoi Obrabotki Poleznykh Iskopaemykh. Trudy
Vses Nauchn O-Vo Neirokhir — Vsesoyuznoe Nauchnoe Obshchestvo Neirokhirurgii
Vses Neft Nauchno Issled Geologorazved Inst Tr — Vsesoyuznyi Neftyanoi Nauchno-Issledovatel'skii Geologorazvedochnyi Institut. Trudy
Vsesojuzn Naucno Issl Inst Lekarstv Rast — Vsesojuznyj Naucno-Issledovatel'skij Institut Lekarstvennyh Rastenij
Vsesojuz Zaocn Politehn Inst Sb Trudov — Vsesojuznyi Zaocnyi Politehniceskii Institut. Sbornik Trudov
Vsesoyunaya Nauchno Metod Konf Vet Patologoanat — Vsesoyuznaya Nauchno-Metod Konferentsiya Veterinarnykh Patologoanatomov
Vsesoyuznoe Paleont Obshch Ezhegodnik — Vsesoyuznoe Paleontologicheskoe Obshchestvo Ezhegodnik
Vses Rab Soveshch Primen Kompleksonov Med — Vsesoyuznoe Rabochee Soveshchanie po Primeneniyu Kompleksonov v Meditsine
Vses Simp Fotokhim Protsessam Zemnoi Atmos — Vsesoyuznyi Simpozium po Fotokhimicheskim Protsessam Zemnoi Atmosfery
Vses Soveshch Elektrokhim Org Soedin — Vsesoyuznoe Soveshchanie po Elektrokhimii Organicheskikh Soedinenii
Vses Soveshch Khim Neorg Gidridov — Vsesoyuznoe Soveshchanie po Khimii Neorganicheskikh Gidridov

VSG — Vierteljahrsschrift fuer Sozial- und Wirtschaftsgeschichte
VSH — Vie Economique. Rapports Economiques et de Statistique Sociale
VSI — Vsemirnaja Istorija
VS Ja (M) — Voprosy Slavjanskogo Jazykoznanija (Moskva)
VSL — Metaal en Kunststof
VSL — Vetenskaps-Societeten i Lund
VSLA — Vetenskaps-Societeten i Lund. Aarsbok
VSL Bibs — Research Service Bibliographies. State Library of Victoria
VSlJa — Voprosy Slavjanskogo Jazykoznanija
VSlJa (Lvov) — Voprosy Slavjanskogo Jazykoznanija (Lvov)
VSlJa (Moskva) — Voprosy Slavjanskogo Jazykoznanija (Moskva)
V Sl Jaz — Voprosy Slavjanskogo Jazykoznanija
VSNG — Verhandlungen der Schweizerischen Naturforschenden Gesellschaft
V3O — Handel. Zeitschrift fuer Theorie und Praxis des Innenhandels in der Deutschen Demokratischen Republik
V Soz WG — Vierteljahrsschrift fuer Sozial- und Wirtschaftsgeschichte
VSP — Vital Speeches of the Day
VSpD — Vital Speeches of the Day
VSPP — Vangiya Sahitya Parisat Patrika
VSQ — St. Vladimir's Seminary. Quarterly
VSS — Videnskabs Selskapet Skrifter
VSSF — Videnskabs Selskapet Skrifter. Forhandlingar
VSSR — Vierteljahresschrift fuer Sozialrecht
VSSRBP — Vysoka Skola Zemedelska v Praze Fakulta Provozne Ekonomicka v Ceskych Budejovicich Sbornik Referatu
VS Suppl — Vie Spirituelle. Supplement
VSTCB — Vuoto, Scienza, e Tecnologia
V St DV — Vermoegensteuer- Durchfuehrungsverordnung
V St G — Vermoegensteuergesetz
VStil — Voprosy Stilistiki
VSTKJ — Vesientutkimuslaitoksen Julkaisuja
VStN — Vakstudie-Nieuws
VSU — Vierteljahresschrift fuer Sozial- und Wirtschaftsgeschichte
VSv — Vokrug Sveta
VSVVS — Vereinigung Schweizerischer Versuchs und Vermittlungstellen fuer Saatkartoffeln
VSW — Vierteljahrsschrift fuer Sozial- und Wirtschaftsgeschichte
VSWG — Vierteljahrsschrift fuer Sozial- und Wirtschaftsgeschichte
VSWS — Vierteljahrschrift fuer Sozial- und Wirtschaftsgeschichte
VSystems — Video Systems
VT — Vaulted Tombs of the Mesara
VT — Vermont Reports
VT — Vetus Testamentum
VT — Video Times
VT — Viere i Tzerkov
VTA — Verkeerskunde
VT Admin Proc Bull — Vermont Administrative Procedures Bulletin
VT Admin Proc Comp — Vermont Administrative Procedures Compilation
VT Ag Exp — Vermont. Agricultural Experiment Station. Publications
VT Agric Exp Stn Bull — Vermont. Agricultural Experiment Station. Bulletin
VtB — Verfahrenstechnische Berichte
Vt B Assn Proc — Vermont Bar Association. Proceedings
VTBHA — Vuoriteollisuus/Bergshanteringen
VT Bul — Vermont. Free Public Library Commission and State Library. Bulletin
VTC News — Vocational Training Council. Newsletter
VT Farm & Home Sci — Vermont Farm and Home Science
VT Farm Home Sci — Vermont Farm and Home Science
VTFDA — Ankara Universitesi. Veteriner Fakultesi. Dergisi
VT Geol Sur Econ Geol — Vermont. Geological Survey. Economic Geology
VT Geol Surv Bull — Vermont. Geological Survey. Bulletin
VT Geol Surv Water Resour Dep Environ Geol — Vermont. Geological Survey. Water Resources Department. Environmental Geology
Vt Highw — Vermont Highways
VT His S — Vermont Historical Society. Proceedings
VT Hist — Vermont History
VtHS — Vermont Historical Society. Proceedings
VTL — Vetus Testamentum (Leiden)
Vt Laws — Laws of Vermont
VT Lib — Vermont Libraries
VT L Rev — Vermont Law Review
VTM — Vaulted Tombs of the Mesara
VTMDA — Veterinarni Medicina
VTMIDB — Annual Research Reviews. Vitamin-Trace Mineral-Protein Interactions
VTMRJa — Voprosy Teorii i Metodiki Izucenijy Russkogo Jazyka
VTop — Voprosy Toponomastiki
VTPAI — Victorian Town Planning Appeals Tribunal. Index of Appeals Decisions
VtQ — Vermont Quarterly
VTR — Virginia Tax Review
VT Regist Nurse — Vermont Registered Nurse
VTS — Vetus Testamentum. Supplementum
Vt Stat Ann — Vermont Statutes Annotated
VT St G Rp — Vermont State Geologist. Report
VTSuppl — Vetus Testamentum. Supplementum
VTTJA — Valtion Teknillinen Tutkimuslaitos. Julkaisu
VT Verfahrenstech — VT. Verfahrenstechnik
VTX — Vertex
VU — Vida Universitaria
VU — Voice of Uganda
VU — Vor Ungdom
VUCLR — Victoria University. College Law Review
Vues Econ Aquitaine — Vues sur l'Economie d'Aquitaine
VuF — Verkuendigung und Forschung
VuG — Vergangenheit und Gegenwart
Vuga G — Vuga Gids
Vulkanol Seismol — Vulkanologiya i Seismologiya

VULR — Valparaiso University. Law Review
VULT — Voprosy Uzbekskogo Jazyka i Literatury
VUM — Vuelta (Mexico)
VUMB — Veroeffentlichungen aus dem Uebersee-Museum (Bremen)
VUMD — Vilniaus Valstybinio V. Kapsuko Vardo Universiteto Mokslo Darbai
V/Unq — Voice Unconquered
Vuorit Bergshant — Vuoriteollisuus/Bergshanteringen
Vuoto — Vuoto, Scienza, e Tecnologia
Vuoto Sci Tecnol — Vuoto, Scienza, e Tecnologia
VURB-A — Vie Urbaine
VUSH — Vanderbilt University. Studies in the Humanities
Vutr Boles — Vutreshni Bolesti
VUV Soft X Ray Photoioniz — VUV (Vacuum Ultraviolet) and Soft X-Ray Photoionization
VUWLR — Victoria University of Wellington. Law Review
VUWL Rev — Victoria University of Wellington. Law Review
VV — A Voz da Verdade
VV — Village Voice
VV — Vizantiiskii Vremenik
VV — Volk und Volkstum
VV — Vor Viden
VVa — Vida Vasca
VVAP — Mededelingenblad. Vereniging van Vrieden van het Allard Pierson Museum
VVL — Vee en Vlees. Het Vakblad voor Handelaar en Producent
V Vl Ac — Verhandelingen. Koninklijke Vlaamse Academie voor Wetenschappen, Letteren, en Schone Kunsten van Belgie. Klasse der Letteren
VVM — Vlastivedny Vestnik Moravsky
VVMB — Vesnik Vojnog Muzeja u Beogradu
VVR — Viewdata/Videotex Report
VVS — Vestnik Vysshei Shkoly
VVS — VVS Tidsskrift for Varme, Ventilation, Sanitet
VVS Energi — VVS och Energi
VVS Tidsk Energi VVS Tek — VVS. Tidskrift foer Energi- och VVS-Teknik
VVS Tidsk Energ VVS-Tek — VVS. Tidskrift foer Energi- och VVS [*Vaerme, Ventilation, Sanitet*]-Teknik
VVS Tidskr Vaerme Vent Sanit Kyltetek — VVS. Tidskrift foer Vaerme, Ventilation, Sanitet, och Kylteteknik
VVS Tidskr Varme Vent Sanit — VVS. Tidskrift foer Vaerme, Ventilation, Sanitet
VVTBA — Vaeg- och Vattenbyggaren
VVUU Zpr — VVUU [*Vedeckovyzkumny Uhelny Ustav*] Ostrava-Radvanice Zprava
VW — Vie Wallonne
VWM — Virginia Woolf Miscellany
VWN — Virginia Woolf Newsletter
VWQ — Virginia Woolf Quarterly
Vya — Voprosy Yazykoznaniya
Vyber Inf Organ Vypocetni Tech — Vyber Informaci z Organizacni a Vypocetni Techniky
Vychisl Metody & Program — Vychislitel'nye Metody i Programmirovanie
Vychisl Metody i Programmirovanie — Moskovskii Universitet. Sbornik Rabot Vychislitelnogo Tsentra Moskovskogo Universiteta. Vychislitel'nye Metody i Programmirovanie
Vychisl Metody Progam — Vychislitel'nye Metody i Programmirovanie
Vychisl Prikl Mat — Kievskii Gosudarstvennyi Universitet Mezhvedomstvennyi Nauchnyi Sbornik Vychislitel'naya i Prikladnaya Matematika
Vychisl Seismol — Vychislitel'naya Seismologiya
Vychisl Sist — Vychislitel'nye Sistemy
Vychisl Tekh i Vopr Kibern — Vychislitel'naya Tekhnika i Voprosy Kibernetiki
Vychisl Tekhn i Voprosy Kibernet — Leningradskii Gosudarstvennyi Universitet Vychislitel'nyi Tsentr Moskovskii Gosudarstvennyi Universitet Vychislitel'nyi Tsentr Vychislitel'naya Tekhnika i Voprosy Kibernetiki
Vychisl Tekhn Sistemy Upravlenie — Vychislitel'naya Tekhnika. Sistemy. Upravlenie. Mezhdunarod
Vycisl Mat i Vycisl Tehn (Kharkov) — Vycislitel'naja Matematika i Vycislitel'naja Tehnika (Kharkov)
Vycisl Metody i Programmirovanie — Vychislitel'nye Metody i Programmirovanie. Moskovskii Universitet. Sbornik RabotVycislitel'nogo Centra Moskovskogo Universiteta
Vycisl Prikl Mat (Kiev) — Vycislitel'naja i Prikladnaja Matematika (Kiev)
Vycisl Sistemy — Akademija Nauk SSSR. Sibirskoe Otdelenie. Institut Matematiki. Vycislitel'nye Sistemy. Sbornik Trudov
Vycisl Tehn i Voprosy Kibernet — Vycislitel'naja Tehnika i Voprosy Kibernetiki
Vycisl Tehn v Masinostroen — Akademija Nauk BSSR. Institut Tehniceskoi Kibernetiki. Vycislitel'naja Tehnika v Masinostroenii
Vyestsi Akad Navuk BSSR Syer Biyal Navuk — Vyestsi Akademii Navuk BSSR. Syeryya Biyalagichnykh Navuk

Vyestsi Akad Navuk BSSR Syer Syel' Skahaspad Navuk — Vyestsi Akademii Navuk BSSR. Syeryya Syel' Skahaspadarchukh Navuk
Vyisn Akad Nauk Ukr RSR — Vyisnik Akademyiyi Nauk Ukrayins'koyi RSR
Vyisn Kiyiv Unyiv Ser Astron — Vyisnik Kiyivs'kogo Unyiversitetu. Seryiya Astronomii
Vyisn Kiyiv Unyiv Ser Fyiz — Vyisnik Kiyivs'kogo Unyiversitetu. Seryiya Fyizika
Vyisn L'vyiv Derzh Unyiv Ser Fyiz — Vyisnik L'vyivs'kij Derzhavnij Unyiversitet Imeni I. Franka. Seryiya Fyizichna
Vyisn Syil'skogospod Nauki — Vyisnik Syil'skogospodars'koyi Nauki
VYNAA — Vynalezy
Vynohrad Vynorobstvo — Vynohradarstvo i Vynorobstvo
Vyrocni Zprava Okresniho Archv Olomouci — Vyrocni Zprava Okresniho Archivu v Olomouci
Vyr Zprava Komis Prir Prozk Moravy — Vyrocni Zprava Komise pro Prirodovedecke Prozkoumani Moravy
Vysk Pra Odboru Pap Celul — Vyskumne Prace z Odboru Papiera a Celulozy
Vysk Pr Odboru Pap Celul — Vyskumne Prace z Odboru Papiera a Celulozy
Vyskum Pr Odboru Papiera Celulozy — Vyskumne Prace z Odboru Papiera a Celulozy
Vysk Ustav Lesn Hospod Zvolene Lesn Stud — Vyskumny Ustav Lesneho Hospodarstvavo Zvolene Lesnicke Studie
Vysk Ustav Ovciar Trencine Ved Pr — Vyskumny Ustav Ovciarsky v Trencine. Vedecke Prace
Vysokochist Veshchestva — Vysokochistye Veshchestva
Vysokomol Soed — Vysokomolekulyarnye Soedineniya
Vysokomol Soedin — Vysokomolekulyarnye Soedineniya
Vysokomol Soedin Geterotsepnye Vysokomol Soedin — Vysokomolekulyarnye Soedineniya Geterotsepnye Vysokomolekulyarnye Soedineniya
Vysokomol Soedin Ser A — Vysokomolekulyarnye Soedineniya. Seriya A
Vysokomol Soedin Ser A Ser B — Vysokomolekulyarnye Soedineniya. Seriya A i Seriya B
Vysokomol Soedin Ser B — Vysokomolekulyarnye Soedineniya. Seriya B
Vysokomol Soedin Vses Khim Ovo — Vysokomolekulyarnye Soedineniya Vsesoyuznoe Khimicheskoe Obshchestvo
Vyso Soed A — Vysokomolekulyarnye Soedineniya. Seriya A
Vyso Soed B — Vysokomolekulyarnye Soedineniya. Seriya B
Vyssh Nervn Deyat Norme Patol — Vysshaya Nervnaya Deyatel'nost v Norme i Patologii
Vyssh Uchebn Zaved Izv Geol Razved — Vysshoye Uchebnoye Zavedeniye. Izvestiya Geologiya i Razvedka
Vys Sk Chem Technol Praze Sb E Potraviny — Vysoka Skola Chemicko-Technologicka v Praze. Sbornik. E. Potraviny
Vys Sk Chem-Technol Praze Sb Oddil Chem Inz — Vysoka Skola Chemicko-Technologicka v Praze. Sbornik. Oddil. Chemicke Inzenyrstvi
Vys Sk Dopravna Ziline Pr Stud Ser Strojnicka — Vysoka Skola Dopravna v Ziline. Prace a Studie. Seria Strojnicka
Vys Sk Lesn Drev Zvolene Drev Fak Zb Ved Pr — Vysoka Skola Lesnicka a Drevarska vo Zvolene. Drevarska Fakulta. Zbornik Vedeckych Prac
Vys Sk Zemed Praze Fak Agron Sb Rada A — Vysoka Skola Zemedelska v Praze. Fakulta Agronomicka. Sbornik. Rada A. Rostlinna Vyroba
Vys Sk Zemed Praze Fak Agron Sb Rada A C — Vysoka Skola Zemedelska v Praze. Fakulta Agronomicka. Sbornik. Rada A-C. Rostlinna Vyroba-Zemedelske Meliorace a Stavby
Vys Soed B — Vysokomolekulyarnye Soedineniya. Seriya B
Vytr Boles — Vytreshni Bolesti
Vytvarnia Kult — Vytvarnia Kultura
VyV — Verdad y Vida
VYV — Wegvervoer
Vyzk Ustav Vodohospodar Pr Stud — Vyzkumny Ustav Vodohospodarsky. Prace a Studie
Vyzk Ustav Vodohospod Pr Stud — Vyzkumny Ustav Vodohospodarsky. Prace a Studie
Vyz Lidu — Vyziva Lidu
Vyznach Prisnovod Vodor Ukr RSR — Vyznachnyk Prisnovodnykh Vodorostei Ukrains'koi RSR
Vyz Rodine — Vyziva v Rodine
VyzS — Vyzvol'nyj Sljax
Vyz Zdravie — Vyzica a Zdravie
VZ — Vierteljahrshefte fuer Zeitgeschichte
VZ — Vostocnye Zapiski
V Zashch Mira — V Zashchitu Mira
Vznik Pocatky Slov — Vznik a Pocatky Slovanu
VZP — Verenigde Verzekeringspers. Wekelijks Verschijnend Vakblad voor het Verzekeringswezen in Binnenland en Buitenland
VZRPAS — Veterinaria y Zootecnia Revista Peruana
Vzryvnoe Delo Nauchno-Tekh Gorn O-Vo Sb — Vzryvnoe Delo. Nauchno-Tekhnicheskoe Gornoe Obshchestvo Sbornik

W

W — Wales
W — Weekblad van het Recht
W — Westminster Review
W — Whitehorse Star
W — Winter
W — Wortkunst
W2 — Webster's New International Dictionary. 2nd Edition
W3 — Webster's Third New International Dictionary
WA — Voice of Washington Music
WA — Wanderer
Wa — Warsaw
WA — Weltwirtschaftliches Archiv
WA — West Africa
WA — Wiadomosci Archeologicznne
WA — Wissenschaftliche Annalen
WA — World Affairs
WA — World Affairs Quarterly
WA — World Archaeology
WAA — World Aluminum Abstracts
WAAFLN — Wissenschaftliche Abteilungen der Arbeitsgemeinschaft fuer Forschung des LandesNordrhein-Westfalen
WAAFLNW — Wissenschaftliche Abteilungen der Arbeitsgemeinschaft fuer Forschung des LandesNordrhein-Westfalen
WA Ann LR — University of Western Australia. Annual Law Review
WAAR — Western Australian Arbitration Reports
WA Arb R — Western Australian Arbitration Reports
WA Art Gall Bull — Western Australian Art Gallery. Bulletin
W A'B & W — Webb, A'Beckett, and Williams' Reports
W A'B & W Eq — Webb, A'Beckett, and Williams' Equity Reports
W A'B & W IE & M — Webb, A'Beckett, and Williams' Insolvency, Ecclesiastical, and Matrimonial Reports
W A'B & W Min — Webb, A'Beckett, and Williams' Mining Cases
WAC — Work and Occupations
WAC — World Aeronautical Chart
WAC — Writing Across the Curriculum
WA Craftsman — Western Australian Craftsman
WACRAX — Cocoa Research Institute. Council for Scientific and Industrial Research. Annual Report
Wad — Inventaire Sommaire de la Collection Waddington
WAD — Warta Ekonomi Maritim. Facts and Analysis in Communications, Commerce, and Finance
WAD — World Aviation Directory
WADA — Wissenschaftliche Annalen. Deutsche Akademie
WADC Tech Rept — Wright Air Development Center. Technical Report
Waddington — Inventaire Sommaire de la Collection Waddington
WA Democrat — West Australian Democrat
WADL — Wiener Arbeiten zur Deutschen Literatur
Wadley Med Bull — Wadley Medical Bulletin
Wadsworth & Brooks Cole Math Ser — Wadsworth and Brooks/Cole Mathematics Series
Wadsworth & Brooks Cole Statist Probab Ser — Wadsworth and Brooks/Cole Statistics/Probability Series
Wadsworth Ath Bul — Wadsworth Atheneum. Bulletin
Wadsworth Atheneum & Morgan Mem Bull — Wadsworth Atheneum and Morgan Memorial Bulletin
Wadsworth Atheneum Bull — Wadsworth Atheneum Bulletin
Wadsworth Atheneum News Bull — Wadsworth Atheneum News Bulletin
Wadsworth Math Ser — Wadsworth Mathematics Series
Wadsworth Statist Probab Ser — Wadsworth Statistics/Probability Series
W Adv — Wesleyan Advocate
WAE — Waterkampioen
WA Ed Circ — Education Circular. Education Department of Western Australia
WA Educ News — WA Education News. Education Department of Western Australia
WA Egg Marketing Board Nletter — Western Australia. Egg Marketing Board. Newsletter
WAELD — Wave Electronics
WA Electr Contract — WA [Western Australian] Electrical Contractor
Waerme Kaeltetch — Waerme- und Kaeltetechnik
Waerme- Stoffuebertrag — Waerme- und Stoffuebertragung
Waerme Stoffuebertrag/Thermo Fluid Dyn — Waerme- und Stoffuebertragung/Thermo and Fluid Dynamics
Waermetech — Waermetechnik
Waerme und Stoffuebertrag — Waerme- und Stoffuebertragung
WAERSA — World Agricultural Economics and Rural Sociology Abstracts
WAF — West Africa

Waf & Kostknd — Waffen- und Kostumkunde
Waffen U Kostuemkde — Waffen- und Kostuemkunde
WAFLT Forum — Washington Association of Foreign Language Teachers. Forum
Wa For LR — Wake Forest Law Review
W Afr — West Africa
W Afr Bldr & Architect — West African Builder and Architect
W Africa — West Africa
W African J Biol Chem — West African Journal of Biological Chemistry
W African Rel — West African Religion
W Afr J Arc — West African Journal of Archaeology
W Afr J Archaeol — West African Journal of Archaeology
W Afr J Mod Languages — West African Journal of Modern Languages
W Afr J Sociol Polit Sci — West African Journal of Sociology and Political Science
W Afr Relig — West African Religion
W Afr Rev — West African Review
WA Fruitgrower — Western Australian Fruitgrower
WAG — Welt als Geschichte
WAG — World Agricultural Economics and Rural Sociology Abstracts
WAGB — Winckelmannsprogramm der Archaeologischen Gesellschaft zu Berlin
WAGEA — Waste Age
Wage & Hour Cas BNA — Wage and Hour Cases. Bureau of National Affairs
Wagen Luebeck Jb — Wagen. Ein Luebeckisches Jahrbuch
Wage-Price L & Econ Rev — Wage-Price Law and Economics Review
Wage-Price Law and Econ R — Wage-Price Law and Economics Review
Wage-Pr L — Wage-Price Law and Economics Review
WAGG — Western Australia Government Gazette
Wagga Hist Soc News — Wagga Wagga and District Historical Society. Newsletter
Wagner Free Inst Sci Bull Cards — Wagner Free Institute of Science. Bulletin. Cards
Wagner Free I Sc Tr — Wagner Free Institute of Science [Philadelphia]. Transactions
WA Govt Gaz — Western Australia Government Gazette
WaGS — Welt als Geschichte (Stuttgart)
WAGSO — Wiener Archiv fuer Geschichte des Slawentums und Osteuropas
WAH — Writings on American History
WA Hist Soc J — Western Australian Historical Society. Journal and Proceedings
WAHSJ — Western Australian Historical Society. Journal
WAI — Wall Street Journal. European Edition
WAIG — Western Australian Industrial Gazette
Waikato Univ Antarct Res Unit Rep — Waikato University. Antarctic Research Unit. Reports
WA Ind Gaz — Western Australian Industrial Gazette
WA Indus Gaz — Western Australian Industrial Gazette
W Air Trans — World Air Transport Statistics
WAISER — West African Institute of Social and Economic Research. Proocedings of Annual Conference
WAJE — West African Journal of Education
WAJML — West Africa Journal of Modern Language
Wakayama Med Rep — Wakayama Medical Reports
Wake Forest Intra L Rev — Wake Forest Intramural Law Review
Wake Forest L Rev — Wake Forest Law Review
Wake For L Rev — Wake Forest Law Review
Wake For Univ Dev Nations Monogr Ser Ser II Med Behav Sci — Wake Forest University. Developing Nations Monograph Series. Series II. MedicalBehavioral Science
Waksman Inst Microbiol Rutgers Univ Annu Rep — Waksman Institute of Microbiology. Rutgers University. Annual Report
WAL — Western American Literature
WAL — Wissenschaftliches Archiv fuer Landwirtschaft. Abteilung B. Archiv fuer Tiernaehrung und Tierzucht
WALA News — West African Library Association. News
Walderburg Sch — Walderburger Schriften
Walford's Antiq — Walford's Antiquarian and Bibliographer
Walker Electr Mg — Electrical Magazine. Walker
Walkers Q — Walker's Quarterly
Walking — Walking Magazine
Wallaces F — Wallaces Farmer
Walla Walla Coll Publ — Walla Walla College. Publications
Wallerstein Lab Commun — Wallerstein Laboratories. Communications
Wallerstein Lab Commun Sci Pract Brew — Wallerstein Laboratories. Communications on the Science and Practice of Brewing
Wallraf-Richartz Jahr — Wallraf-Richartz Jahrbuch
Wallraf Richartz Jb — Wallraf-Richartz-Jahrbuch
Wall St J — Wall Street Journal
Wall St J East Ed — Wall Street Journal. Eastern Edition
Wall St J Midwest Ed — Wall Street Journal. Midwest Edition

Wall St Jnl — Wall Street Journal

Wall St J Three Star East Ed — Wall Street Journal. Three Star Eastern Edition

Wall St R Bk — Wall Street Review of Books

Wall Street J Index — Wall Street Journal Index

Wall Str J — Wall Street Journal

Wall St T — Wall Street Transcript

WALMS — West African Language Monograph Series

Walpole Soc — Walpole Society

WALR — University of Western Australia. Law Review

Wa LR — Washington Law Review

WALR — Western Australian Law Reports

Walsh's R — Walsh's American Review

Wal Steve J — Wallace Stevens Journal

Walter Andree Nottbeck Found Sci Rep — Walter and Andree de Nottbeck Foundation. Scientific Reports

Walter Reed Army Med Cent Prog Notes — Walter Reed Army Medical Center. Progress Notes

Walter Reed Gen Hosp Dep Med Prog Notes — Walter Reed General Hospital. Department of Medicine. Progress Notes

Walters A G Bull — Walters Art Gallery Bulletin

Walters J — Walters Art Gallery [*Baltimore*]. Journal

Walt Whit R — Walt Whitman Review

WAM — Wiltshire Archaeological and Natural History Magazine

WAM — Wiltshire Archaeological Magazine [*Later, Wiltshire Archaeological and NaturalHistory Magazine*]

WA Manuf — West Australian Manufacturer

WA Manufacturer — West Australian Manufacturer

WA Mining & Commercial R — West Australian Mining and Commercial Review

WAMOD — Wave Motion

WA Nat — Western Australian Naturalist

WANATCA (West Aust Nut & Tree Crop Assoc) Yearb — WANATCA (West Australian Nut and Tree Crop Association) Yearbook

WA Naturalist — Western Australian Naturalist

W & D — Wort und Dienst

W & G — Wissen und Glauben

W & L — Washington and Lee Law Review

W & L — Women and Literature

W & M — William and Mary Law Review

W and M LR — William and Mary Law Review

W & M L Rev — William and Mary Law Review

W & M Q — William and Mary Quarterly

W and P — Women and Performance

W&R — Wind and the Rain

W & S — Woerter und Sachen

W & W — Wyatt and Webb's Victorian Reports

W & W & A'B — Wyatt, Webb, and A'Beckett's Reports

W & W & A'B (Eq) — Wyatt, Webb, and A'Beckett's Reports (Equity)

W & W & A'B (Min) — Wyatt, Webb, and A'Beckett's Reports (Mining)

W & W (E) — Wyatt and Webb's Reports (Equity)

W & W (Eq) — Wyatt and Webb's Reports (Equity)

W & W (IE & M) — Wyatt and Webb's Reports (Insolvency, Ecclesiastical, and Matrimonial)

W & W (L) — Wyatt and Webb's Reports (Law)

W & W Vict — Wyatt and Webb's Victorian Reports

WA News — West Australian News

WANRDN — Walter and Andree de Nottbeck Foundation. Scientific Reports

WAP (A) — Work and People (Australia)

WA Parent & Cit — Western Australian Parent and Citizen

WA Parent & Citizen — Western Australian Parent and Citizen

WA Parl Deb — Western Australia. Parliamentary Debates

WAPLA — Water, Air, and Soil Pollution

WAPOA — Water Power

WAPRA — Wissenschaftliche Abhandlungen der Physikalische-Technischen Reichsanstalt

WA Primary Princ — WA Primary Principal. West Australian Primary Principals Association

WA Primary Principal — West Australian Primary Principals Association

WAR — Western Australian Reports

WAR — Wisconsin Academy. Review

WAR — World Affairs Report

WARBA — Water Resources Bulletin

Warburg & Courtauld Inst Jnl — Warburg and Courtauld Institute. Journal

Warburg Inst Surveys Texts — Warburg Institute Surveys and Texts

War C — War Cry

W Arch — Western Architect

W Arch — Wiadomosci Archeologicznne

W Arch — World Archaeology

W Architect — Western Architect

W Architect and Engin — Western Architect and Engineer

Ward AW — Ward's Auto World

Wards Auto — Ward's Automotive Reports

Ward's Bull — Ward's Bulletin

Wards Yrbk — Ward's Automotive Yearbook

WARE — Water Research

Warehousing Rev — Warehousing Review

Warehousing Superv Bull — Warehousing Supervisor's Bulletin

War Emerg Proc Inst Mech Eng — War Emergency Proceedings. Institution of Mechanical Engineers

War Hung — War on Hunger

WARMA — Waerme

War Med — War Medicine

War Peace Rep — War/Peace Report

WARR — Water Resources Research

Warsaw Agric Univ SGGW-AR Ann Anim Sci — Warsaw Agricultural University. SGGW-AR [*Szkola Glowna Gospodarstwa Wiejskiego - Akademia Rolnicza*] Annals. Animal Science

Warta Geol — Warta Geologi

Warta Geol (Kuala Lumpur) — Warta Geologi (Kuala Lumpur)

Warwicks Hist — Warwickshire History

WAS — Waste International

WAS — Witchcraft and Sorcery

WAS — Worcester Archaeological Society. Transactions

WAS — World Animal Science

WAS — World Art Series. UNESCO

WASBB — Waerme- und Stoffuebertragung

WascanaR — Wascana Review

Waseda Polit Stud — Waseda Political Studies

Waseda Pol Studies — Waseda Political Studies

Wash — Washington Reports

Wash Acad Sci J — Washington Academy of Sciences. Journal

Wash Acad Sci Jour — Washington Academy of Sciences. Journal

Wash Actions Health — Washington Actions on Health

Wash Admin Code — Washington Administrative Code

Wash Ag Exp — Washington. Agricultural Experiment Station. Publications

Wash Agric Exp Stn Bull — Washington. Agricultural Experiment Station. Bulletin

Wash Agric Exp Stn Cir — Washington. Agricultural Experiment Station. Circular

Wash Agric Exp Stn Stn Circ — Washington. Agricultural Experiment Station. Station Circular

Wash Agric Exp Stn Tech Bull — Washington. Agricultural Experiment Station. Technical Bulletin

Wash and Lee LR — Washington and Lee Law Review

Wash & Lee L Rev — Washington and Lee Law Review

Wash App — Washington Appellate Reports

Wash As Pp For Ephem & Naut Alm — Astronomical Papers Prepared for the use of the American Ephemeris and Nautical Almanac (Washington)

Wash Bsn J — Washington Business Journal

Washburn Coll Lab N H B — Washburn College. Laboratory of Natural History. Bulletin

Washburn L J — Washburn Law Journal

Washburn Obs Pb — Publications of the Washburn Observatory of the University of Wisconsin

Wash Bus L Rpr — Washington Business Law Reporter

Wash Dep Ecol State Water Program Bienn Rep — Washington. Department of Ecology. State Water Program. Biennial Report

Wash Dep Ecol Tech Rep — Washington. Department of Ecology. Technical Report

Wash Dep Ecol Water Supply Bull — Washington. Department of Ecology. Water Supply Bulletin

Wash Dep Fish Annu Rep — Washington. Department of Fisheries. Annual Report

Wash Dep Fish Fish Res Pap — Washington. Department of Fisheries. Fisheries Research Papers

Wash Dep Fish Res Bull — Washington. Department of Fisheries. Research Bulletin

Wash Dep Fish Tech Rep — Washington. Department of Fisheries. Technical Report

Wash Dep Water Resour Water Supply Bull — Washington. Department of Water Resources. Water Supply Bulletin

Wash Div Geol Earth Resour Geol Map — Washington. Division of Geology and Earth Resources. Geologic Map

Wash Div Geol Earth Resour Inf Circ — Washington. Division of Geology and Earth Resources. Information Circular

Wash Div Mines Geol Bull — Washington. Department of Natural Resources. Division of Mines and Geology. Bulletin

Wash Div Mines Geol Inform Circ — Washington. Department of Conservation. Division of Mines and Geology. Information Circular

Wash Div Mines Geol Rep Invest — Washington. Department of Conservation. Division of Mines and Geology. Report of Investigations

Wash Div Mines Min Rep Invest — Washington. Division of Mines and Mining. Report of Investigations

Wash Drug Rev — Washington Drug Review

Wash Fin Rep — Washington Financial Reports

Wash Geol Earth Resour Div Bull — Washington. Department of Natural Resources. Geology and Earth Resources Division. Bulletin

Wash GSB — Washington. Geological Survey. Bulletin

Wash Health Costs Let — Washington Health Costs Letter

Wash His Q — Washington Historical Quarterly

Wash His S — Washington State Historical Society. Publications

Wash Hist Q — Washington Historical Quarterly

Wash Hist Quar — Washington Historical Quarterly. Washington University State Historical Society

Washington Acad Sci Jour — Washington Academy of Sciences. Journal

Washington and Lee L Rev — Washington and Lee Law Review

Washington Dept Water Resources Water Supply Bull — Washington. Department of Water Resources. Water Supply Bulletin

Washington Div Mines and Geology Bull — Washington. Division of Mines and Geology. Bulletin

Washington Div Mines and Geology Geol Map — Washington. Division of Mines and Geology. Geologic Map

Washington Div Mines and Geology Inf Circ — Washington. Division of Mines and Geology. Information Circular

Washington Law Rev — Washington Law Review

Washington L Rev — Washington Law Review

Washington M — Washington Monthly

Washington Quart — Washington Quarterly

Washington Univ L Quart — Washington University. Law Quarterly

Wash Journ Rev — Washington Journalism Review

Wash Land People — Washington's Land and People

Wash Law Re — Washington Law Review

Wash Law Rev — Washington Law Review. University of Washington Law School
Wash Laws — Laws of Washington
Wash Legis Serv (West) — Washington Legislative Service (West)
Wash LR — Washington Law Review
Wash L Rev — Washington Law Review
Wash M — Washington Monthly
Wash Med Ann — Washington Medical Annals
Wash Med Annals — Washington Medical Annals
Wash Mm Nat Ac — Memoirs of the National Academy of Sciences (Washington)
Wash Mon — Washington Monthly
Wash Nat Ac Mm — Memoirs of the National Academy of Sciences (Washington)
Wash News Beat — Washington News Beat
Wash Nurse — Washington Nurse
Wash Ph S Bll — Bulletin of the Philosophical Society of Washington
Wash Post — Washington Post
Wash Prop L Rpr — Washington Property Law Reporter
Wash Public Policy Notes — Washington Public Policy Notes
Wash Q — Washington Quarterly
Wash Rep — Washington Report
Wash Rep Med Health — Washington Report on Medicine and Health
Wash Rev Code — Revised Code of Washington
Wash Rev Code Ann — Revised Code of Washington Annotated
Wash SBA — Washington State Bar Association. Proceedings
Wash Soc Alexandria Bul — Washington Society of Alexandria. Bulletin
Wash State Agric Exp Sta Bull — Washington State Agricultural Experiment Station. Bulletin
Wash State Agric Exp Sta Sta Circ — Washington State Agricultural Experiment Station. Station Circular
Wash State Coll Agric Exp Stn Tech Bull — Washington State College. Washington Agricultural Experiment Station. Instituteof Agricultural Sciences. Technical Bulletin
Wash State Coll Research Studies — Washington State College. Research Studies
Wash State Council Highway Research Eng Soils Manual — Washington State. Council for Highway Research Engineering. Soils Manual
Wash State Dent J — Washington State Dental Journal
Wash State For Prod Inst Bull New Wood Use Ser — Washington State Forest Products Institute. Bulletins. New Wood-Use Series
Wash State Hortic Assoc Proc — Proceedings. Washington State Horticultural Association
Wash State Inst Technol Circ — Washington State Institute of Technology. Circular
Wash State Inst Technology Bull — Washington State Institute of Technology. Bulletin
Wash State Inst Technol Tech Rep — Washington State Institute of Technology. Technical Report
Wash State J Nurs — Washington State Journal of Nursing
Wash State Univ Agric Exp Stn Tech Bull — Washington State University. Agricultural Experiment Station. Institute of Agricultural Sciences. Technical Bulletin
Wash State Univ Agric Res Cent Res Bull — Washington State University. Agricultural Research Center. Research Bulletin
Wash State Univ Coll Agric Res Cent Bull — Washington State University. College of Agriculture. Research Center. Bulletin
Wash State Univ Coll Agric Res Cent Tech Bull — Washington State University. College of Agriculture. Research Center. TechnicalBulletin
Wash State Univ Coll Eng Bull — Washington State University. College of Engineering. Bulletin
Wash State Univ Coll Eng Circ — Washington State University. College of Engineering. Circular
Wash State Univ Coop Ext Serv Ext Bull — Washington State University. Cooperative Extension Service. Extension Bulletin
Wash State Univ Ext Ser Ext Bull — Washington State University. Extension Service. Extension Bulletin
Wash State Univ Ext Serv EM — Washington State University. Extension Service. EM
Wash State Univ Int Symp Particleboard Proc — Washington State University. International Symposium on Particleboard. Proceedings
Wash State Univ Publ Geol Sci — Washington State University. Publications in Geological Sciences
Wash State Univ Symp Particleboard Proc — Washington State University. Symposium on Particleboard. Proceedings
Wash St B Assn Proc — Washington State Bar Association. Proceedings
Wash St G An Rp — Washington State Geologist. Annual Report
Wash St Geneal Hist Rev — Washington State Genealogical and Historical Review
Wash St Reg — Washington State Register
Wash Terr — Washington Territory Reports
Wash U L Q — Washington University. Law Quarterly
Wash UL Rev — Washington University. Law Review
Wash Univ Bull — Washington University. Bulletin
Wash Univ Dent J — Washington University. Dental Journal
Wash Univ Dep Geol Sci Abstr Res — Washington University. Department of Geological Sciences. Abstracts of Research
Wash Univ L Q — Washington University Law Quarterly
Wash Univ Pub G — Washington University. Publications in Geology
Wash Univ Pub Language And Lit — University of Washington Publications in Language and Literature
Wash Univ Pub Soc Sci — University of Washington Publications in Social Sciences
Wash Univ St Hum Ser — Washington University. Studies. Humanistic Series
Wash Univ St Sci Ser — Washington University. Studies. Scientific Series
Wash Univ Studies — Washington University Studies
Wash Univ Stud Lang & Lit — Washington University. Studies. Language and Literature

Wash Univ Stud Sci & Tech — Washington University. Studies. Science and Technology
Wash Univ Stud Sci & Tech NS — Washington University. Studies. Science and Technology. New Series
Wash Univ Stud Social & Philos Sci — Washington University. Studies. Social and Philosophical Sciences
Wash Univ Stud Social & Philos Sci NS — Washington University. Studies. Social and Philosophical Sciences. New Series
Wasmann J Biol — Wasmann Journal of Biology
Wasmuths Mhft Baukst — Wasmuths Monatshefte fuer Baukunst
Wasmuths Mhft Baukst & Staedtebau — Wasmuths Monatshefte fuer Baukunst und Staedtebau
WASP — Water, Air, and Soil Pollution
WASP — Water Spectrum
WASPB — Water Spectrum
Was Polit — Waseda Political Studies
WasR — Wascana Review
Wasser Abfall Eur Essener Tag — Wasser und Abfall in Europa. Essener Tagung
Wasser Abfallwirtsch Duenn Besiedelten Geb Vortr OWWV Semin — Wasser- und Abfallwirtschaft in Duenn Besiedelten Gebieten. Vortraege des OWWV-Seminars
Wasseraufbereit Kleinen Wasserwerken Wassertech Semin — Wasseraufbereitung bei Kleinen Wasserwerken. Wassertechnisches Seminar
Wasser- Energiewirt — Wasser- und Energiewirtschaft
Wasser Luft Betr — Wasser, Luft, und Betrieb
Wasserwirtsch-Wassertech — Wasserwirtschaft-Wassertechnik
Wasserwirt-Wassertech — Wasserwirtschaft-Wassertechnik
W Assn Map Lib Inf Bull — Western Association of Map Libraries. Information Bulletin
Wasswirt Wasstech — Wasserwirtschaft-Wassertechnik
Waste Disposal & Water Manage in Aust — Waste Disposal and Water Management in Australia
Waste Disposal Water Manage Aust — Waste Disposal and Water Management in Australia
Waste Dispos Water Manage Aust — Waste Disposal and Water Management in Australia
Waste Disp Recyc Bull — Waste Disposal and Recycling Bulletin
Waste Manag — Waste Management
Waste Manage — Waste Management
Waste Manage Energ Mater Polym — Waste Management of Energetic Materials and Polymers
Waste Manage Oxford — Waste Management (Oxford). Industrial Hazardous, Radioactive
Waste Manage Pap — Waste Management Paper
Waste Manage Res — Waste Management and Research
Waste Manage Res Tokyo — Waste Management Research (Tokyo)
Waste Manage Tucson Ariz — Waste Management (Tucson, Arizona)
Waste Manag Res — Waste Management & Research
Waste Mgmt Inf Bull — Waste Management Information Bulletin
Waste Mgmt Res — Waste Management Research
Waste Process Transp Storage Disposal Tech Programs Public Ed — Waste Processing, Transportation, Storage, and Disposal. Technical Programs andPublic Education
Waste Resour — Waste and Resource
Wastes Eng — Wastes Engineering
Wastes Mgmt — Wastes Management
WASU — WASU. Journal. West African Students Union of Great Britain
WAT — What Acronym's That
Wat Aust — Water in Australia
Wat Bull — Water Bulletin
WA Teachers J — Western Australian Teachers' Journal
WA Teach J — Western Australian Teachers' Journal
Water Air and Soil Pollut — Water, Air, and Soil Pollution
Water Air Soil Pollut — Water, Air, and Soil Pollution
Water Am Inst Chem Eng — Water. American Institute of Chemical Engineers
Water & Environ Int — Water and Environment International
Water and San — Water and Sanitation
Water & Sewage Works — Water and Sewage Works
Water & Waste Engng — Water and Waste Engineering
Water A S P — Water, Air, and Soil Pollution
Water Biol Syst — Water in Biological Systems
Water E & M — Water Engineering and Management
Water Electrolyte Metab Proc Symp — Water and Electrolyte Metabolism. Proceedings of the Symposium
Water Eng — Water and Wastes Engineering
Water Eng Manage — Water/Engineering and Management
Water Environ Lab Solutions — Water Environment Laboratory Solutions
Water Environ Manage — Water and Environmental Management
Water Environ Res — Water Environment Research
Water Environ Technol — Water Environment and Technology
Waterford SE Ir Arch Soc J — Waterford and South-East of Ireland Archaeological Society. Journal
Water Invest Mich Geol Surv Div — Water Investigation. Michigan Geological Survey Division
Water Law Newsl — Water Law Newsletter
Waterloo Hist Soc Rep — Waterloo Historical Society. Annual Report
Water Manage News — Water Management News
Water Manage Techn Rep Colorado State Univ — Colorado State University. Water Management Technical Report
Water Poll Abstr — Water Pollution Abstracts
Water Poll Cont Fed J — Water Pollution Control Federation. Journal
Water Poll Control Fed J — Water Pollution Control Federation. Journal
Water Pollut Abstr — Water Pollution Abstracts
Water Pollut Contr Fed J — Water Pollution Control Federation. Journal
Water Pollut Control — Water Pollution Control

Water Pollut Control (Don Mills Can) — Water and Pollution Control (Don Mills, Canada)

Water Pollut Control Fed Res J — Water Pollution Control Federation. Research Journal

Water Pollut Control (London) — Water Pollution Control (London)

Water Pollut Control Res Ser — Water Pollution Control Research Series

Water Pollut Modell Meas Predict Pap Int Conf — Water Pollution. Modelling, Measuring, and Prediction. Papers. International Conference

Water Pollut Res Can — Water Pollution Research in Canada

Water Pollut Res J Can — Water Pollution Research Journal of Canada

Water Pollut Res (Stevenage) — Water Pollution Research (Stevenage)

Water Purif Liquid Wastes Treat — Water Purification and Liquid Wastes Treatment

Water Qual Instrum — Water Quality Instrumentation

Water Qual Int — Water Quality International

Water Qual Res J Can — Water Quality Research Journal of Canada

Water Res — Water Research

Water Res Cent Notes Water Res — Water Research Centre. Notes on Water Research

Water Res Found Aust Annu Rep Balance Sheet — Water Research Foundation of Australia Limited. Annual Report and Balance Sheet

Water Res Found Aust Bull — Water Research Foundation of Australia Limited. Bulletin

Water Res Found Aust Lted Ann Rep Balance Sheet — Water Research Foundation of Australia Limited. Annual Report and Balance Sheet

Water Res Found Aust Rep — Water Research Foundation of Australia Limited. Report

Water Res Found of Aust Newsl — Water Research Foundation of Australia Limited. Newsletter

Water Res Inst W Va Univ Inf Rep — Water Research Institute. West Virginia University. Information Report

Water Res J — Water Resource Journal

Water Res News — Water Research News

Water Resour — Water Resources

Water Resour Bull — Water Resources Bulletin

Water Resour Bull Nev Div Water Resour — Water Resources Bulletin. Nevada Division of Water Resources

Water Resour Bull (PR) — Water Resources Bulletin (Puerto Rico)

Water Resources Res — Water Resources Research

Water Resour Circ Arkansas Geol Comm — Water Resources Circular. Arkansas Geological Commission

Water Resour (Engl Transl Vodnye Resursy) — Water Resources (English Translation of Vodnye Resursy)

Water Resour Eng Risk Assess — Water Resources Engineering Risk Assessment

Water Resour Invest — Water Resources Investigations

Water Resour Invest US Geol Surv — Water Resources Investigations. United States Geological Survey

Water Resour J Econ Soc Comm Asia Pac — Water Resources Journal. Economic and Social Commission for Asia and the Pacific

Water Resour Manag Ser — Water Resource Management Series

Water Resour Newsl — Water Resources Newsletter

Water Resour Plann Manage Sav Threatened Resour Search Soluti — Water Resources Planning and Management. Saving a Threatened Resource. In Search of Solutions. Proceedings of the Water Resources Sessions at Water Forum

Water Resour Plann Manage Urban Water Resour — Water Resources Planning and Management and Urban Water Resources

Water Resour Reconnaissance Ser Nev Div Water Resour — Water Resources. Reconnaissance Series. Nevada Division of Water Resources

Water Resour Rep Ariz State Land Dep — Water Resources Report. Arizona State Land Department

Water Resour Rep Ont Minist Environ Water Resour Branch — Water Resources Report. Ontario Ministry of the Environment. Water Resources Branch

Water Resour Res — Water Resources Research

Water Resour Res Cent VA Polytech Inst State Univ Bull — Water Resources Research Center. Virginia Polytechnic Institute and State University. Bulletin

Water Resour Rev Streamflow Ground-Water Cond — Water Resources Review for Streamflow and Ground-Water Conditions

Water Resour Ser Tenn Div Water Resour — Water Resources Series. Tennessee Division of Water Resources

Water Resour Symp — Water Resources Symposium

Water Resour Transl of Vodn Resur — Water Resources (Translation of Vodnye Resursy)

Water Res R — Water Resources Research

Water Reuse Symp Proc — Water Reuse Symposium Proceedings

Water (S Afr) — Water (South Africa)

Water Sanit — Water and Sanitation

Water Sanit Eng — Water and Sanitary Engineer

Water Sci & Technol — Water Science and Technology

Water Sci Rev — Water Science Reviews

Water Sci Technol — Water Science and Technology

Water Sci Technol J Int Assoc Water Pollut Res — Water Science and Technology. Journal. International Association on Water Pollution Research

Water Sci Technol Lib — Water Science and Technology Library

Water Serv — Water Services

Water Sewage Effl — Water, Sewage, and Effluent

Water Supply Manage — Water Supply and Management

Water Supply Pap Geol Surv GB Hydrogeol Rep — Water Supply Papers. Geological Survey of Great Britain. Hydrogeological Report

Water Supply Pap US Geol Surv — Water Supply Paper. United States Geological Survey

Water Treat — Water Treatment

Water Treat Exam — Water Treatment and Examination

Water Waste — Water and Wastes Engineering

Water Wastes Dig — Water and Wastes Digest

Water Wastes Eng — Water and Wastes Engineering

Water Wastes Eng Ind — Water and Wastes Engineering/Industrial

Water Waste Treat — Water and Waste Treatment

Water Waste Treat J — Water Waste Treatment Journal

Water Waste Water Res — Water and Waste Water Research

Water Wastewater Treat Plants Oper Newsl — Water and Wastewater Treatment Plants Operators' Newsletter

Water Water Eng — Water and Water Engineering

Water (WC and IC Staff Journal) — Water (Water Conservation and Irrigation Commission Staff Journal)

Water Well J — Water Well Journal

Water Well Jour — Water Well Journal

Water Works Eng — Water Works Engineering

Water Works Wastes Eng — Water Works and Wastes Engineering

WatPolAb — Water Pollution Abstracts

Wat Pollut Control — Water Pollution Control

Wat Pollut Res J Can — Water Pollution Research Journal of Canada

Wat Pwr — Water Power

WATRA — Water Research

WatResAb — Water Resources Abstracts

Wat Res Fdn Aust Bull — Water Research Foundation of Australia Limited. Bulletin

Wat Res Fdn Rep — Water Research Foundation of Australia Limited. Report

Wat Resour Res — Water Resources Research

Wat Serv — Water Services

Watson House Bull — Watson House Bulletin

WATSTORE — National Water Data Storage and Retrieval System

Wattle Res Inst Univ Natal (S Afr) Rep — Wattle Research Institute. University of Natal (South Africa). Report

Wat Vict — Water in Victoria

Wat Waste Treat — Water and Waste Treatment

Wat Wat Engng — Water and Water Engineering

WAU Law R — University of Western Australia. Law Review

WAULR — Western Australia University. Law Review

WA Univ Gaz — University of Western Australia. Gazette

WA Univ Geog Lab Res Rept — University of Western Australia. Geography Laboratory. Research Report

W Aust For Dep Bull — Western Australia. Forests Department. Bulletin

W Aust Geol Surv 1:250000 Geol Ser — Western Australia. Geological Survey. 1:250,000 Geological Series

W Aust Geol Surv Bull — Western Australia. Geological Survey. Bulletin

W Aust Hist Soc — Western Australian Historical Society. Journal

W Austl — Western Australian Reports

W Austl Ind Gaz — Western Australian Industrial Gazette

W Austl LR — Western Australian Law Reports

W Aust Nat — Western Australian Naturalist

Wave Electron — Wave Electronics

Wavelet Anal Appl — Wavelet Analysis and its Applications

Wave Part Dualism — Wave. Particle Dualism

WAW — Ward's Auto World

WAYED5 — WANATCA [*West Australian Nut and Tree Crop Association*] Yearbook

Wayne LR — Wayne Law Review

Wayne L Rev — Wayne Law Review

Way Suppl — Way. Supplement

WB — Weekblad der Belastingen

WB — Weimarer Beitraege

WB — Wiener Blaetter fuer die Freunde der Antike

Wb — Woerterbuch der Aegyptischen Sprache

WB — Worlds Beyond

WB — Wort und Brauch

WBA — Weekblad voor de Burgerlijke Administratie

WBA — Weekly of Business Aviation

WBANK — Bank of Canada Weekly Financial Statistics

WBC — Bloembollencultuur

WBD — Worlds Beyond

WBE — Weekblad voor Fiscaal Recht

WBEP — Wiener Beitraege zur Englischen Philologie

WBGA — Weekblad voor de Nederlandse Bond van Gemeenteambtenaren

WBI — Washington Beverage Insight

WBIP — Whitaker's Books in Print

WBK — Western Banker

WBKL — Wiener Beitraege zur Kulturgeschichte und Linguistik

W Bl FA — Wiener Blaetter fuer die Freunde der Antike

Wbl v Gembel — Weekblad voor Gemeentebelangen

Wbl voor Fiscaal Recht — Weekblad voor Fiscaal Recht

WbM — Woerterbuch der Mythologie

Wb Myth — Woerterbuch der Mythologie

Wb Mythol — Woerterbuch der Mythologie

WBN — Weekly Book Newsletter

WBN — Wolfenbuetteler Barock-Nachrichten

WBNP — Wood Buffalo National Park. Newsletter

WBOLA — Wasser, Boden, Luft

WBP — Whitaker's Books in Print

WBP — Woodwind World - Brass and Percussion

WBS — Wiener Byzantinistische Studien

WBV — Woningbouwvereniging. Maandblad van de Nationale Woningraad

WBV — Woningraad. Informatiekrant voor Woningcorporaties

WBW — World Business Weekly

W Byz St — Wiener Byzantinistische Studien

WC — Wordsworth Circle

WC — World Christian

WC — World Crops

WC — World Crops. London

WC — Written Communication

WC — Wspolczesnosc
W Can J Ant — West Canadian Journal of Anthropology
WCB — Weekly Criminal Bulletin
WCBD (Vic) — Workers Compensation Board Decisions (Victoria)
WCBD (WA) — Workers Compensation Board Decisions (Western Australia)
WCB (Vic) — Workers Compensation Board Decisions (Victoria)
WCC — Workers' Compensation Cases
WCC — Workmen's Circle Call
WCH — Workshop Conferences Hoechst
Wchnbl K K Gesellsch Aerzte Wien — Wochenblatt. K. K. Gesellschaft der Aerzte in Wien
Wchnschr Ges Heilk — Wochenschrift fuer die Gesamte Heilkunde
Wchnschr Tierh u Viehzucht — Wochenschrift fuer Tierheilkunde und Viehzucht
WCHODW — Workshop Conferences Hoechst
W City — Western City [Los Angeles]
WCJ — White Cloud Journal of American Indian/Alaska Native Mental Health
WCJ — Writing Center Journal
WCJA — Western Canadian Journal of Anthropology
WCJS — World Congress of Jewish Studies
W Class — World in the Classroom
WCLJ — Workmen's Compensation Law Journal
WCLR — Workmen's Compensation Law Review
WCM — Wellesley College Magazine
WCN — World Coin News
WCNL — Winter Cities Newsletter
W Coach Clinic — Women's Coaching Clinic
WCOD — Western Canada Outdoors. Combining The Whooper and Defending All Outdoors
WCoins — World Coins
W Comp Pres Docs — Weekly Compilation of Presidential Documents
WCP — Woman CPA
WCPDD5 — World Crops Production Utilization Description
WCR — West Coast Review
WCR — Workers' Compensation Reports
WCRB — West Coast Review of Books
WCRED — WESCON [Western Electronics Show and Convention] Conference Record
WCR (NSW) — Workers' Compensation Reports (New South Wales)
WCR (Q) — Workers' Compensation Reports (Queensland)
WCR (Qld) — Workers' Compensation Reports (Queensland)
WCR (Qn) — Workers' Compensation Reports (Queensland)
WCR(WA) — Workers' Compensation Reports (Western Australia)
WCS III — Third World Congress of Sociology. Amsterdam, 1956
WCSMLL — Western Canadian Studies in Modern Languages and Literature
WCT — West Coast Travel
WCWN — William Carlos Williams Newsletter
WCWR — William Carlos Williams Review
WD — [The] Weekly Dispatch
WD — Winter's Digest
WD — Wittenberg Door
WD — Woman's Day
Wd — Word
Wd — World
WD — World Development
WD — World Dominion
WD — Writers Digest
WDB — Suedosteuropa. Zeitschrift fuer Gegenwartsforschung
WdB — Weekblad der Belastingen
WDB — Weekblad der Directe Belastingen
WDEFA — Welding Design and Fabrication
WdF — Wege der Forschungen
WDGB — Wuerzburger Diozesangeschichtsblaetter
WDIA — Weekblad der Directe Belastingen, Invoerrechten en Accijnzen
W Dig — New York Weekly Digest
WdL — Welt der Literatur
Wdl — Wirkung der Literatur
WdO — Welt des Orients. Wissenschaftliche Beitraege zur Kunde des Morgenlandes
WDRAA — Welding Research Abroad
WDRKA — Waseda Daigaku Rikogaku Kenkyusho Hokoku
WDRSA — Wood Research
WDSD — Water Data Sources Directory
WdSL — Welt der Slaven
WDT — World Development
Wdt Z Gesch & Kst — Westdeutsche Zeitschrift fuer Geschichte und Kunst
WDWRA — Welding in the World
WDWT — World Dominion and the World Today
WdZ — Westdeutsche Zeitschrift fuer Geschichte und Kunst
WE — Winesburg Eagle
WEA Bul — WEA [Workers Educational Association] Bulletin
Weak Supercond — Weak Superconductivity
Weale Q Pp — Quarterly Papers on Engineering. Weale
Wear Frict Elastomers — Wear and Friction of Elastomers
Wear Mater — Wear of Materials. International Conference on Wear of Materials
Wear Part Proc Leeds Lyon Symp Tribol — Wear Particles. From the Cradle to the Grave. Proceedings. Leeds-Lyon Symposium on Tribology
Weather and Clim — Weather and Climate
Weather C & M — Weather, Crops, and Markets
Weather Dev Res Bull — Weather Development and Research Bulletin
Weather Research Bull — Weather Research Bulletin
Weavers J — Weaver's Journal
WEB — National Westminster Bank. Quarterly Review
WEB — Wealthbuilding
WEBB — Writer's Electronic Bulletin Board
Webb A'B & W — Webb, A'Beckett, and Williams' Reports

Webb A'B & W Eq — Webb, A'Beckett, and Williams' Equity Reports
Webb A'B & W IE & M — Webb, A'Beckett, and Williams' Insolvency, Ecclesiastical, and Matrimonial Reports
Webb A'B & W IP & M — Webb, A'Beckett, and Williams' Insolvency, Probate, and Matrimonial Reports
Webb A'B & W Min — Webb, A'Beckett, and Williams' Mining Cases
Webbia Racc Scr Bot — Webbia; Raccolta di Scritti Botanici
Weber — Descriptive Catalogue of the Collection of Greek Coins Formed by Sir Hermann Weber
Web R — Webster Review
WEC — Whole Earth Catalog
WECAF (West Cent Atl Fish Comm) Stud — WECAF (Western Central Atlantic Fishery Commission) Studies
W Eoon J — Woctorn Economic Journal
WEE — Weerberichten. Informatiebulletin over Windenergie en Zonne-Energie
Weed Abstr — Weed Abstracts
Weed Res — Weed Research
Weed Sci — Weed Science
Weeds Weed Cont — Weeds and Weed Control
Weed Technol J Weed Sci Soc Am — Weed Technology. Journal. Weed Science Society of America
WEEGA — Welding Engineer
Weekbl Priv Not en Reg — Weekblad voor Privaatrecht, Notariaat, en Registratie
Week Cin LB — Weekly Cincinnati Law Bulletin
Week Dig — New York Weekly Digest
Week Dig (NY) — New York Weekly Digest
Week-End R — Australian Week-End Review of Current Books, the Arts, and Entertainments
Week Jur — Weekly Jurist
Week Law & Bk Bull — Weekly Law and Bank Bulletin
Week Law Bull — Weekly Law Bulletin and Ohio Law Journal
Week Law Gaz — Weekly Law Gazette
Week L Gaz — Weekly Law Gazette
Week L Mag — Weekly Law Magazine
Week LR — Weekly Law Reports
Week L Rec — Weekly Law Record
Week L Record — Weekly Law Record
Week LR (Eng) — Weekly Law Reports (England)
Week L Rev — Weekly Law Review
Weekly Bull Calif State Board Health — Weekly Bulletin. California State Board of Health
Weekly Cin Law Bull — Cincinnati Weekly Law Bulletin
Weekly Compilation Presidential Docum — Weekly Compilation of Presidential Documents
Weekly Comp of Pres Doc — Weekly Compilation of Presidential Documents
Weekly Law B — Weekly Law Bulletin
Weekly L Bull — Weekly Law Bulletin
Weekly LR — Weekly Law Reports
Weekly NC — Weekly Notes of Cases
Weekly N L — Weekly News Letter. United States Department of Agriculture
Weekly Observ Roy Dublin Soc — Weekly Observations. Royal Dublin Society
Weekly Underw — Weekly Underwriter
Week No — New South Wales Weekly Notes
Week No — Weekly Notes of Cases
Week No — Weekly Notes of Cases (Law Reports)
Week No Cas — Weekly Notes of Cases
Week No Cas — Weekly Notes of Cases (Law Reports)
Week R — Weekly Reporter
Week R (Eng) — Weekly Reporter (England)
Week Rep — Weekly Reporter
Week Reptr — Weekly Reporter
Week Trans Rep — Weekly Transcript Reports
Week Trans Repts — Weekly Transcript Reports
WEEL — Workplace Environmental Exposure Level
WEESA — Weed Science
WEF — Economic Inquiry
WEG — Wegen
Wege Soz Versicherung — Wege zur Sozialversicherung
Wegleitungen Kstgewmus Zuerich — Wegleitungen des Kunstgewerbemuseums Zuerich
WEH — Hungarian News Agency. Weekly Bulletin
Wehrkd — Wehrkunde
Wehrmed Monatsschr — Wehrmedizinische Monatsschrift
Wehrtech — Wehrtechnik
Wehr und Wirt — Wehr und Wirtschaft
Wehrwiss Rdsch — Wehrwissenschaftliche Rundschau
WEHSA — Work-Environment-Health
WEI — World Energy Industry
Weibulls Arsb — Weibulls Arsbok
Weight Med Leg Gaz — Weightman's Medico-Legal Gazette
Weinbau Kellerwirtsch (Budapest) — Weinbau und Kellerwirtschaft (Budapest)
Wein-Wiss — Wein-Wissenschaft
Weissen Bl — Weissen Blaetter
Weiterbildungszentrum Math Kybernet Rechentech — Weiterbildungszentrum fuer Mathematische Kybernetik und Rechentechnik
Weizmann Mem Lect — Weizmann Memorial Lectures
WEJ — Western Economic Journal
WEJUA — Welding Journal
WEK — Werkgever
WEKLA — Wiadomosci Ekologiczne
WEL — Weltwirtschaftliches Archiv
Weld and Met Fabr — Welding and Metal Fabrication
Weld Des and Fabr — Welding Design and Fabrication
Weld Des Fabr — Welding Design and Fabrication
Weld Dsgn — Welding Design and Fabrication

Weld Eng — Welding Engineer
Weld Fabr Des — Welding Fabrication and Design
Weld Fabrication Design — Welding Fabrication and Design
Weld Fabric Design — Welding Fabrication and Design
Weld Ind — Welding Industry
Welding J — Welding Journal
Welding Rev — Welding Review
Weld Int — Welding International
Weld J — Welding Journal
Weld J (London) — Welding Journal (London)
Weld J (Miami) — Welding Journal (Miami)
Weld J (NY) — Welding Journal (New York)
Weld J Res Suppl — Welding Journal Research. Supplement
Weld Jrl — Welding Journal
Weld Metal Fab — Welding and Metal Fabrication
Weld Metal Fabr — Welding and Metal Fabrication
Weld Met Fabr — Welding and Metal Fabrication
Weld News — Welding News
Weld Prod — Welding Production
Weld Prod Engl Transl — Welding Production (English Translation)
Weld Prod (USSR) — Welding Production (USSR)
Weld Res Abroad — Welding Research Abroad
Weld Res C — Welding Research Council. Bulletin
Weld Res Counc Bull — Welding Research Council. Bulletin
Weld Res Counc Prog Rep — Welding Research Council. Progress Reports
Weld Res Int — Welding Research International
Weld Res (London) — Welding Research (London)
Weld Res (Miami) — Welding Research (Miami)
Weld Res (Miami Fla) — Welding Research (Miami, Florida)
Weld Res News — Welding Research News
Weld Rev — Welding Review
Weld Rev Int — Welding Review International
Weld Rev Redhill UK — Welding Review (Redhill, United Kingdom)
Weld Surf Rev — Welding and Surfacing Reviews
Weld Tech — Welding Technique
Weld Wld — Welding in the World/Le Soudage dans le Monde
Weld World — Welding in the World
Weld World Soudage Monde — Welding in the World/Le Soudage dans le Monde
Weleda Korrespondenzbl Aerzte — Weleda Korrespondenzblaetter fuer Aerzte
Welf — Welfare Magazine
Welfare L Bull — Welfare Law Bulletin
Welfare L News — Welfare Law News
Welf Bul Ill — Welfare Bulletin. Illinois State Department of Public Welfare
Welf Focus — Welfare Focus
Welf Mag — Welfare Magazine
Welf Reptr — Welfare Reporter
WelH — Welsh Historical Review
Well Inventory Ser (Metric Units) Inst Geol Sci — Well Inventory Series (Metric Units). Institute of Geological Sciences
Well Perspect — Wellness Perspectives
Well Serv — Well Servicing
Wells Frgo — Wells Fargo Bank. Business Review
Wellworthy Top — Wellworthy Topics
WELS — Wisconsin English Language Survey
Welsh Bee J — Welsh Bee Journal
Welsh Beekprs' Ass Q Bull — Welsh Beekeepers' Association. Quarterly Bulletin
Welsh Hist — Welsh History Review
Welsh Hist Rev — Welsh History Review
Welsh H R — Welsh History Review
Welsh J Agric — Welsh Journal of Agriculture
Welsh J Educ — Welsh Journal of Education
Welsh M — Welsh Music
Welsh Plant Breed Stn (Aberystwyth) Annu Rep — Welsh Plant Breeding Station (Aberystwyth) Annual Report
Welsh Plant Breed Stn (Aberystwyth) Rep — Welsh Plant Breeding Station (Aberystwyth). Report
Welsh Plant Breed Stn (Aberystwyth) Tech Bull — Welsh Plant Breeding Station (Aberystwyth). Technical Bulletin
Welsh Plant Breed Stn Bull Ser — Welsh Plant Breeding Station. Bulletin Series
Welt Als Gesch — Welt Als Geschichte
Welt d Islam — Welt des Islams
Welt D Orient — Welt des Orients
Welt d Slaven — Welt der Slaven
Welt Gesch — Welt als Geschichte. Eine Zeitschrift fuer Universalgeschichte
Welt Isl — Die Welt des Islam
Weltlit Farbenchem — Weltliteratur der Farbenchemie
Weltraumfahrt Raketentech — Weltraumfahrt und Raketentechnik
Weltwir Arc — Weltwirtschaftliches Archiv
Weltwirt — Weltwirtschaft
Weltwirtschaft Archiv — Weltwirtschaftliches Archiv
Weltwirtsch Archiv — Weltwirtschaftliches Archiv
WelW — Weltwoche
WEM — Western Miner
WEM Newsl — WEM [*World Education Markets, Inc.*] Newsletter
WEMOB — Wehrmedizinische Monatsschrift
Wen — Wending
W Eng J — West of England Journal of Science and Literature
WENMD — Water Engineering and Management
Wenner-Gren Cent Int Symp Ser — Wenner-Gren Center. International Symposium Series
Wenner Gren Int Ser — Wenner-Gren International Series
Wentworth Mag — Wentworth Magazine
WEO — West-Ost-Journal
WEO — World Economic Outlook
WEP — Waseda Economic Papers

WEPRA — Welding Production
WER — Week End Review
Werk — Werk/Archithese
Werk — Werk/Oeuvre
WERKA — Werkstatttechnik
Werk Kstlers — Werk des Kunstlers
Werkstatt Betr — Werkstatt und Betrieb
Werkstattstech Z Ind Fertigung — Werkstatttechnik Zeitschrift fuer Industrielle Fertigung
Werkstatt und Betr — Werkstatt und Betrieb
Werkst Innov — Werkstoff und Innovation
Werkst Korros — Werkstoffe und Korrosion
Werkst u Korrosion — Werkstoffe und Korrossion (Wernheim)
Wernerian N H Soc Mem — Wernerian Natural History Society. Memoirs
Wes CLJ — Westmoreland County Law Journal
Wescon Conf Rec — Wescon Conference Record
WESCON Tech Pap — WESCON [*Western Electronics Show and Convention*] Technical Papers
WesH — West Virginia History
Wesleyan U Alumnus — Wesleyan University Alumnus
Wesley Hist Soc Lect — Wesley Historical Society Lectures
Wesley Th J — Wesleyan Theological Journal
Wesley W Spink Lect Comp Med — Wesley W. Spink Lectures on Comparative Medicine
WesP — Western Pennsylvania Historical Magazine
Wes Res Law Jo — Western Reserve Law Journal
Wes Res Law Jrl — Western Reserve Law Journal
West — Westmoreland County Law Journal
West Afr — West Africa
West Afr Cocoa Res Inst Tech Bull — West African Cocoa Research Institute. Technical Bulletin
West African Farm Food Proc — West African Farming and Food Processing
West African J of Ed — West African Journal of Education
West Afr Inst Oil Palm Res Annu Rep — West African Institute for Oil Palm Research. Annual Report
West Afr J Archaeol — West African Journal of Archaeology
West Afr J Biol Appl Chem — West African Journal of Biological and Applied Chemistry
West Afr J Biol Chem — West African Journal of Biological Chemistry
West Afr J Med — West African Journal of Medicine
West Afr J Pharmacol Drug Res — West African Journal of Pharmacology and Drug Research
West Afr Med J — West African Medical Journal
West Afr Med J Nigerian Pract — West African Medical Journal and Nigerian Practitioner
West Afr Med J Niger Med Dent Pract — West African Medical Journal and Nigerian Medical and Dental Practitioner
West Afr Pharm — West African Pharmacist
West Am Lit — Western American Literature
West Am Sc — West American Scientist
West Assn Map Libs Inf Bul — Western Association of Map Libraries. Information Bulletin
West AULR — Western Australia University. Law Review
West Aust Clin Rep — Western Australian Clinical Reports
West Aust Conf Australas Inst Min Metall — Western Australian Conference. Australasian Institute of Mining and Metallurgy
West Aust Dep Agric Annu Rep — Western Australia. Department of Agriculture. Annual Report
West Aust Dep Fish Fauna Rep — Western Australia. Department of Fisheries and Fauna. Report
West Aust Dep Fish Wildl Rep — Western Australia. Department of Fisheries and Wildlife. Report
West Aust Dep Ind Dev Build Invest — Western Australia. Department of Industrial Development. Building Investment
West Aust Dep Mines Annu Rep — Western Australia. Department of Mines. Annual Report
West Aust Dep Mines Miner Resour West Aust Bull — Western Australia. Department of Mines. Mineral Resources of Western Australia.Bulletin
West Aust Dep Mines Min Resour West Aust Bull — Western Australia. Department of Mines. Mineral Resources of Western Australia.Bulletin
West Aust Dep Mines Rep Gov Mineral Anal Chem — Western Australia. Department of Mines. Report of the Government Mineralogist, Analyst, and Chemist
West Aust Fish — Western Australia Fisheries
West Aust Fish Dep Fish Res Bull — Western Australia. Fisheries Department. Fisheries Research Bulletin
West Aust Geol Surv 1:250000 Geol Ser — Western Australia. Geological Survey. 1:250,000 Geological Series
West Aust Geol Surv Annu Prog Rep — Western Australia. Geological Survey. Annual Progress Report
West Aust Geol Surv Annu Rep — Western Australia. Geological Survey. Annual Report
West Aust Geol Surv Bull — Western Australia. Geological Survey. Bulletin
West Aust Geol Surv Geol Ser Explan Notes — Western Australia. Geological Survey. Geological Series. Explanatory Notes
West Aust Geol Surv Miner Resour Bull — Western Australia. Geological Survey. Mineral Resources Bulletin
West Aust Geol Surv Rep — Western Australia. Geological Survey. Report
West Aust Herb Res Notes — Western Australian Herbarium. Research Notes
West Aust Inst Technol Gaz — Western Australian Institute of Technology. Gazette
West Austl — Western Australian Reports
West Aust L Rev — University of Western Australia. Law Review
West Aust Mar Res Lab Fish Res Bull — Western Australian Marine Research Laboratories. Fisheries Research Bulletin

West Aust Mus Spec Publ — Western Australian Museum. Special Publication
West Aust Nat — Western Australian Naturalist
West Aust Nat Reserve Manage Plan — Western Australian Nature Reserve Management Plan
West Aust Naturalist — Western Australian Naturalist
West Aust Nutgrow Soc Yearb — Western Australian Nutgrowing Society. Yearbook
West Aust Rep Gov Chem Lab — Western Australia. Report. Government Chemical Laboratories
West Austr L — Western Australian Law Reports
West Aust Sch Mines — Western Australian School of Mines
West Aust SWANS — Western Australia SWANS
West Aust SWANS (State Wildl Auth News Serv) — Western Australia SWANS (State Wildlife Authority News Service)
West Aust Wildl Res Cent Wildl Res Bull — Western Australia Wildlife Research Centre. Wildlife Research Bulletin
West Bird Bander — Western Bird Bander
West Birds — Western Birds
West Build — Western Building
West Bus — Western Business
West Canad J Anthropol — Western Canadian Journal of Anthropology
West Can Beekpr — Western Canada Beekeeper
West Can J Anthropol — Western Canadian Journal of Anthropology
West Canner Packer — Western Canner and Packer
West Can Water and Sewage Conf Proc Annu Conv — Western Canada Water and Sewage Conference. Proceedings of the Annual Convention
West Can Water Sewage Conf Pap Annu Conv — Western Canada Water and Sewage Conference. Papers Presented at the Annual Convention
West Chapter Int Shade Tree Conf Proc — Western Chapter. International Shade Tree Conference. Proceedings
West Chem Metall — Western Chemist and Metallurgist
Westchester Co Hist Soc Bul — Westchester County Historical Society. Quarterly Bulletin
Westchester Co Hist Soc Pub — Westchester County Historical Society. Publications
Westchester Co Hist Soc Publ — Westchester County Historical Society. Publications
Westchester Med Bull — Westchester Medical Bulletin
West City — Western City
West Coast R — West Coast Review
West Constr — Western Construction
West Contract — Western Contractor
West Crop Farm Manage N Ed — Western Crops and Farm Management. Northern Edition
West Crop Farm Manage S Ed — Western Crops and Farm Management. Southern Edition
West Dent Soc Bull — Western Dental Society. Bulletin
West Drug — Western Druggist
Westdt Zeitschr — Westdeutsche Zeitschrift fuer Geschichte und Kunst
Westd Zeit — Westdeutsche Zeitschrift fuer Geschichte und Kunst
Westd Zeit Gesch u Kunst — Westdeutsche Zeitschrift fuer Geschichte und Kunst
West Econ Jour — Western Economic Journal
West Elec E — Western Electric Engineer
West Electr Eng — Western Electric Engineer
Westermanns Mhft — Westermanns Monatshefte
Westerm M — Westermanns Monatshefte
Westerm Monatsh — Westermanns Monatshefte
Western Am Lit — Western American Literature
Western Australia Geol Survey Rept — Western Australia. Geological Survey. Report. Government Printer
Western Australia Main Roads Dep Tech Bull — Western Australia. Main Roads Department. Technical Bulletin
Western Bs — Western Business
Western EE — Western Electric Engineer
Western Electric Eng — Western Electric Engineer
Western Eng — Western Engineering
Western Hist Q — Western Historical Quarterly
Western Hum R — Western Humanities Review
Westerm Hum Rev — Western Humanities Review
Western Law Jour — Western Law Journal (Reprint)
Western L Rev — Western Law Review
Western Med — Western Medicine
Western Ont L Rev — Western Ontario Law Review
Westrn Pol Q — Western Political Quarterly
Western Res — Western Reserve Business Review
Western Reserve Hist Soc Tracts — Western Reserve Historical Society. Tracts
Western Res L Rev — Western Reserve Law Review
Western Rv Sc — Western Review of Science and Industry
Western Speleol Inst Bull — Western Speleological Institute. Bulletin
Western Wash Ag Exp B — Western Washington Agricultural Experiment Station. Monthly Bulletin
West Europe Ed — Western European Education
West Europ Polit — West European Politics
West Eur Politics — West European Politics
West-Eur Symp Clin Chem — West-European Symposia on Clinical Chemistry
Westfael Anz — Westfaelischer Anzeiger, oder Vaterlaendisches Archiv zur Befoerderung und Verbreitung des Guten und Nuetzlichen
Westfael Bienenztg — Westfaelische Bienenzeitung
Westfael Forsch — Westfaelische Forschungen
Westfael Lebensbild — Westfaelische Lebensbilder
Westfael Z — Westfaelische Zeitschrift
Westfalen Hft Gesch Kst & Vlksknd — Westfalen. Hefte fuer Geschichte, Kunst, und Volkskunde
West Farmer — Western Farmer
Westf Bienenztg — Westfaelische Bienenzeitung

West Feed — Western Feed
West Feed Seed — Western Feed and Seed
West Fire Jnl — Western Fire Journal
West Folk — Western Folklore
West Folkl — Western Folklore
West Found Vertebr Zool Occas Pap — Western Foundation of Vertebrate Zoology. Occasional Papers
Westfriesch Jb — Westfriesch Jaarboek
West Frozen Foods — Western Frozen Foods
West Fruit Grow — Western Fruit Grower
West Gas — Western Gas
West Grow Ship — Western Grower and Shipper
West Hist Q — Western Historical Quarterly
West Horse — Western Horseman
West HR — Western Humanities Review
West Humanities Rev — Western Humanities Review
West Human Rev — Western Humanities Review
West Hum R — Western Humanities Review
West Hum Rev — Western Humanities Review
West Ind Bull — West Indian Bulletin
West Ind Gids — West-Indische Gids
West Indian Med J — West Indian Medical Journal
West Ind Rev — West Indian Review
Westinghouse Eng — Westinghouse Engineer
Westinghouse Engr — Westinghouse Engineer
West Int Law Bul — West International Law Bulletin
West J Agric Econ — Western Journal of Agricultural Economics
West J Appl For — Western Journal of Applied Forestry
West J Med — Western Journal of Medicine
West J Med Surg — Western Journal of Medicine and Surgery
West J Nurs Res — Western Journal of Nursing Research
West J Surg — Western Journal of Surgery, Obstetrics, and Gynecology
West J Surg Obstet Gynecol — Western Journal of Surgery. Obstetrics and Gynecology
West Law J — Western Law Journal
West Law Jour — Western Law Journal (Reprint)
West Law M — Western Law Monthly
West Law Mo — Western Law Monthly (Reprint)
West Law Month — Western Law Monthly
West Law Rev — Western Law Review
West Leg Obs — Western Legal Observer
West L Gaz — Western Law Gazette
West Lit J — Western Literary Journal
West Livestock J — Western Livestock Journal
West LJ — Western Law Journal
West LJ (Ohio) — Western Law Journal (Ohio)
West LM — Western Law Monthly
West L Mo — Western Law Monthly
West L Month — Western Law Monthly
West Locker — Western Locker
West L Rev — Western Law Review
West LT — Western Law Times
West M — Western Monthly Magazine
Westm — Westminster Review
Westm — Westmoreland County Law Journal
West Mach Steel World — Western Machinery and Steel World
West Malays Geol Surv Dist Mem — West Malaysia. Geological Survey. District Memoir
West Malays Geol Surv Econ Bull — West Malaysia. Geological Survey. Economic Bulletin
West Med — Western Medicine
West Med Med J West — Western Medicine; the Medical Journal of the West
West Met — Western Metals
West Metalwork — Western Metalworking
West Miner — Western Miner
Westmin R — Westminister Review
Westminster Inst Rev — Westminister Institute Review
Westminster Stud Educ — Westminster Studies in Education
Westm LJ — Westmoreland County Law Journal
West Mo R — Western Monthly Review
Westmore Co LJ (PA) — Westmoreland County Law Journal
Westmoreland — Westmoreland County Law Journal
Westmoreland Co LJ — Westmoreland County Law Journal
Westm Th J — Westminster Theological Journal
West Nat — Western Naturalist
West New Engl L Rev — Western New England Law Review
West NY Mg — Western New York Magazine
West Oil Refin — Western Oil Refining
West Oil Rep — Western Oil Reporter
West Ont L Rev — Western Ontario Law Review
West PA Hist Mag — Western Pennsylvania Historical Magazine
West Paint Rev — Western Paint Review
West Pak J Agric Res — West Pakistan Journal of Agricultural Research
West Penn Hist Mag — Western Pennsylvania Historical Magazine
West Penn Hosp Med Bull — Western Pennsylvania Hospital Medical Bulletin
West Pet Refiners Assoc Tech Publ — Western Petroleum Refiners Association. Technical Publication
West Plast — Western Plastics
West Polit Q — Western Political Quarterly
West Polit Quart — Western Political Quarterly
West Pol Q — Western Political Quarterly
West Poult Dis Conf — Western Poultry Disease Conference
Westpreuss Jb — Westpreussen-Jahrbuch
Westpr Geschichtsv Ztsch — Westpreussischer Geschichtsverein. Zeitschrift
West Pulp Pap — Western Pulp and Paper

West R — Western Review
West Reg Ext Publ Co-Op Ext US Dep Ag — Western Region Extension Publication. Cooperative Extension. United States Department of Agriculture
West Reg Pub Colo St Univ Exp Stn — Western Regional Publication. Colorado State University. Experiment Station
West Reg Symp Min Miner Process Wastes — Western Regional Symposium on Mining and Mineral Processing Wastes
West Reserve Law Rev — Western Reserve Law Review
West Res Law Rev — Western Reserve Law Review
West Res L Rev — Western Reserve Law Review
West Resour Conf — Western Resources Conference
West Rev — Westminster Review
West Roads — Western Roads
West Sch Law Dig — Western School Law Digest
West School L Rev — Western School Law Review
West Scot Agric Coll Res Bull — West of Scotland Agricultural College. Research Bulletin
West Scot Iron Steel Inst J — West of Scotland Iron and Steel Institute. Journal
West Scotl Agric Coll Res Bull — West of Scotland Agricultural College. Research Bulletin
West Shade Tree Conf Proc Annu Meet — Western Shade Tree Conference. Proceedings of the Annual Meeting
West Soc Eng J — Western Society of Engineers. Journal
West Soc Malacol Annu Rep — Western Society of Malacologists. Annual Report
West Soc Malacol Occas Pap — Western Society of Malacologists. Occasional Paper
West States Jew Hist Q — Western States Jewish Historical Quarterly
West States Sect Combust Inst Pap — Western States Section. Combustion Institute. Paper
West State UL Rev — Western State University. Law Review
West St U LR — Western State University. Law Review
West St U L Rev — Western State University. Law Review
West Teach — Western Teacher
West Tenn Hist Soc Pap — West Tennessee Historical Society. Papers
West Texas Geol Soc Pub — West Texas Geological Society. Publication
West Tex B — West Texas Business Journal
West Tex Today — Western Texas Today
West Th J — Westminster Theological Journal
WestTJ — Westminster Theological Journal
West Union Tech Rev — Western Union Technical Review
West Va Lib — West Virginia Libraries
West Va L Rev — West Virginia Law Review
West Vet — Western Veterinarian
West Virginia Geol and Econ Survey Basic Data Rept — West Virginia. Geological and Economic Survey. Basic Data Report
West Virginia Geol and Econ Survey Circ — West Virginia. Geological and Economic Survey. Circular
West Virginia Hist — West Virginia History
West Virginia Law Quar — West Virginia Law Quarterly. West Virginia University
West Virginia L Rev — West Virginia Law Review
West Virginia Univ Bus Econ Stud — West Virginia University. Business and Economic Studies
West Vr Jbr — Jahres-Bericht des Westfaelischen Provinzialvereins fuer Wissenschaft und Kunst
West Week (Can) — Western Weekly Notes (Canada)
West Week N — Western Weekly Notes
West Week N (Can) — Western Weekly Notes (Canada)
West Week NS — Western Weekly, New Series
West Week Rep — Western Weekly Reports
West Wildlands — Western Wildlands
Wet Bydraes PU CHO Reeks B Natuurwet — Wetenskaplike Bydraes van die PU [*Potchefstroomse Universiteit*] vir CHO .Reeks B: Natuurwetenskappe
Wetensch Bl — Wetenschappelijke Bladen
Wetenskap Studiereeks — Wetenskaplike Studiereeks
Wet Ground Mica Assoc Inc Tech Bull — Wet Ground Mica Association, Incorporated. Technical Bulletin
Wet Gs Nt B — Berichte der Wetterauischen Gesellschaft fuer die Gesammte Naturkunde zu Hanau
Wetlands Ecol Manage — Wetlands Ecology and Management
Wet Meded KNNV — Wetenschappelijke Mededeling KNNV
Wet Samenleving — Wetenschap en Samenleving
Wett Gesch Bl — Wetterauer Geschichtsblaetter
Wet Tijd — Wetenschappelijke Tijdingen. Vereniging voor Wetenschapp de Gent
Wett Leben — Wetter und Leben
WEU — Ward's Engine Update
Weurman Symp — Weurman Symposium
W Europe Educ — Western European Education
W Eur Policies — West European Policies
W Eur Politics — West European Politics
WEV — World Economy
WEVO — Waehrungsergaenzungsverordnung
WEW — Wasser- und Energiewirtschaft
WeW — Welt und Wort
WeWo — Welt und Wort
WEX — Business Science Experts
Weyerhaeuser Sci Symp — Weyerhaeuser Science Symposium
Weyerhauser For Pap — Weyerhauser Forestry Paper
WEZ — Wiener Entomologische Zeitung
WF — Wege der Forschung, Darmstadt, Wissenschaftliche Buchgesellschaft
WF — Wehrforschung
WF — Western Folklore
WF — Westfaelische Forschungen
WFA — Worlds of Fantasy
WFD — Worldwide Franchise Directory
WFI — World Faiths Insight

WFON — West-Frieslands Oud en Nieuw
WFR — Weekblad voor Fiscaal Recht
WFSUDO — World Fertility Survey. Country Reports
WFS (World Fertil Surv) Comp Stud — WFS (World Fertility Survey) Comparative Studies
WFZ — Wirtschaftswoche
WG — Waehrungsgesetz
Wg — Wandlung
WG — Water Resources News-Clipping Service. General Issue. Water Management Service.Department of the Environment
WG — Welt als Geschichte Zeitschrift fuer Universalgeschichtliche Forschung
WG — Wissenschaft und Gegenwart
WGA — Weekblad voor de Nederlandse Bond van Gemeenteambtenaren
WGB — Weekblad voor Gemeentebelangen. Orgaan van de Vereniging vanNederlandse Gemeenten
WGBI — Wetterauer Geschichtsblaetter
WGCR — West Georgia College. Review
WGI — Nieuwe West-Indische Gids
WGI — Wirtschaftsgeographisches Institut
W Gr — Tijdschrift voor Wetenschappelijke Graphologie
WGW — Wheat Gluten World
WH — Wald und Holz
Whartn Ann — Wharton Annual
Whartn Mag — Wharton Magazine
Wharton — Wharton Magazine
Wharton M — Wharton Magazine
Wharton Mag — Wharton Magazine
Wharton Q — Wharton Quarterly
Whats New — What's New in Advertising and Marketing
Whats New Bldg — What's New in Building
What's New Comput — What's New in Computing
Whats New Crops Soils — What's New in Crops and Soils
Whats New Home Econ — What's New in Home Economics
Whats New in For Res — What's New in Forest Research
Whats New Plant Physiol — What's New in Plant Physiology
WHB — Which
WHB — Wiener Humanistische Blaetter
WH Bl — Wiener Humanistische Blaetter
WHCS — Well History Control System
Wheat Board Gaz — Wheat Board Gazette
Wheat Inform Serv — Wheat Information Service
Wheat Inf Serv — Wheat Information Service
Wheat Situation Bur Agr Econ (Aust) — Wheat Situation. Bureau of Agricultural Economics (Australia)
Wheat Stud Food Res Inst — Wheat Studies. Food Research Institute
WHEE — Wheel Extended
Wheel Ext — Wheel Extended
Where to Find Out More about Educ — Where to Find Out More about Education
Whet — Whetstone
WHG — Wasserhaushaltsgesetz
WHI — World Trade Information
Which Comput — Which Computer
Which Word Process — Which Word Processor
Which Word Process and Off Syst — Which Word Processor and Office System
WHIMSY — Western Humor and Irony Membership. Serial Yearbook
W Hist Q — Western Historical Quarterly
White Met News Lett — White Metal News Letter
Whit Eq Pr — Whitworth. Equity Precedents
Whittier L Rev — Whittier Law Review
Whitt L Rev — Whittier Law Review
WHO — William H. Over Museum. Museum News
WHO Bul — World Health Organization Bulletin
WHOCA — World Health Organization. Chronicle
WHO Chron — WHO [*World Health Organization*] Chronicle
WHO Chronicle — World Health Organization. Chronicle
WHO Environ Health — WHO [*World Health Organization*] Environmental Health
WHO Food Addit Ser — WHO [*World Health Organization*] Food Additives Series
WHO Hist Int Public Health — WHO [*World Health Organization*] History of International Public Health
WHO Int Agency Res Cancer Annu Rep — World Health Organization International Agency for Research on Cancer. Annual Report
WHOI Technical Report — Woods Hole Oceanographic Institution. Technical Report
WHO Libr Ne — WHO [*World Health Organization*] Library News
WHOMAP — FAO [*Food and Agriculture Organization of the United Nations*] NutritionalStudies
WHO Monogr Ser — World Health Organization. Monograph Series
WHO Offset Publ — WHO [*World Health Organization*] Offset Publication
WHOPAY — World Health Organization. Public Health Papers
WHO Pestic Residues Ser — WHO [*World Health Organization*] Pesticide Residues Series
WHO Publ — WHO [*World Health Organization*] Publications
WHO Publ Hlth Pap — WHO [*World Health Organization*] Public Health Papers
WHO Public Health Pap — World Health Organization. Public Health Papers
WHO Public Health Papers — World Health Organization. Public Health Papers
W Hort Rev — Western Horticultural Review
WHO Tech Rep Ser — World Health Organization. Technical Report Series
WHO Tech Rep Sers — World Health Organization. Technical Report Series
WHQ — Western Historical Quarterly
WHR — Welsh History Review
WHR — Western Humanities Review
WHS — Weekly Hansard - Senate
WHS — Works. Richard Hakluyt Society
WHTCA — Wehrtechnik
W Human Rev — Western Humanities Review

WI — Welt des Islams
WI — Wiadomosci
WI — Wiez
WI — Wisconsin School Musician
WI — Wohnungswirtschaftliche Informationen
WI — Wood Industries
WI — Woprosy Istorii
WI — Writing Instructor
WIA — Wirtschaftskonjunktur. Analysen, Perspektiven, Indikatoren
WIAB — Wilderness Alberta
Wiad — Wiadomosci Archeologicznne
Wlad A — Wiadomosci Archeologiczne. Bulletin Archeologique Polonias
Wiad Archeol — Wiadomosci Archeologiczne
Wiad Bot — Wiadomosci Botaniczne
Wiad Chem — Wiadomosci Chemiczne
Wiad Ekol — Wiadomosci Ekologiczne
Wiad Elektrotech — Wiadomosci Elektrotechniczne
Wiad Gorn — Wiadomosci Gornicze
Wiad Hist — Wiadomosci Historyczne
Wiad Hutn — Wiadomosci Hutnicze
Wiad Inst Melior Uzytkow Zielon (Warsaw) — Wiadomosci. Instytut Melioracji i Uzytkow Zielonych (Warsaw)
Wiad Lek — Wiadomosci Lekarskie
Wiad Mat — Wiadomosci Matematyczne
Wiad Melior Lak — Wiadomosci Melioracyjne i Lakarskie
Wiad Melior Lakarsk — Wiadomosci Melioracyjne i Lakarskie
Wiad Meteorol Gospod Wodnej — Wiadomosci Meteorologii i Gospodarki Wodnej
Wiad Mt — Wiadomosci Matematyczne
Wiad Naft — Wiadomosci Naftowe
Wiad Num Arch — Wiadomosci Numizmatyczno-Archeologiczne [*Later, Wiadomosci Numizmatyczne*]
Wiadom Arch — Wiadomosci Archeologicznne
Wiadom Mat — Wiadomosci Matematyczne
Wiadom Mat 2 — Roczniki Polskiego Towarzystwa Matematycznego. Seria II. Wiadomosci Matematyczne
Wiadomosci Numi — Wiadomosci Numizmatyczne
Wiadom Statyst — Wiadomosci Statystyczne
Wiad Parazyt — Wiadomosci Parazytologiczne
Wiad Parazytol — Wiadomosci Parazytologiczne
Wiad Stat — Wiadomosci Statystyczne
Wiad St Hydrol Met — Wiadomosci Sluzby Hydrologicznej i Meteorologicznej
Wiad Telekomun — Wiadomosci Telekomunikacyjne
Wiad Zielarskie — Wiadomosci Zielarskie
WI Archaeologist — Wisconsin Archaeologist
WI Architect — Wisconsin Architect
WIB — West Indian Bulletin
WIB — Wetboek van de Inkomstenbelastingen
WIB — Wetenschapsbeleid
WI Bl — Wirtschaftsrechtliche Informations-Blaetter
WIC — West Indies Chronicle
Wi Ch — Wirtschaftspolitische Chronik
WICHE Publ — Western Interstate Commission for Higher Education. Publications
Wichita Eag — Wichita Eagle-Beacon
WI Comm Circ — West India Committee Circular
Wide World M — Wide World Magazine
Wi Di — Wirtschaftsdienst
W i d Z — Wort in der Zeit
WI Econ — West Indian Economist
Wiederbeleb Organersatz Intensivmed — Wiederbelebung. Organersatz. Intensivmedizin
Wiederg G — Gesetz zur Regelung der Wiedergutmachung Nationalsozialistischen Unrechts fuer Angehoerige des Oeffentlichen Dienstes
Wiederherstellungschir Traumatol — Wiederherstellungschirurgie und Traumatologie
Wien Ak D — Denkschriften der Kaiserlichen Akademie der Wissenschaften. Mathematisch-Naturwissenschaftliche Classe (Wien)
Wien Ak Sb — Sitzungsberichte der Mathematisch-Naturwissenschaftlichen Classe der Kaiserlichen Akademie der Wissenschaften (Wien)
Wien Alm — Almanach der Kaiserlichen Akademie der Wissenschaften (Wien)
Wien Arch Innere Med — Wiener Archiv fuer Innere Medizin
Wien Arch Psychol Psychiat Neurol — Wiener Archiv fuer Psychologie, Psychiatrie, und Neurologie
Wien Beitr — Wiener Beitraege zur Englischen Philologie
Wien Beitr Chir — Wiener Beitraege zur Chirurgie
Wien Beitr Gesch Med — Wiener Beitraege zur Geschichte der Medizin
Wien Beitr Kst & Kultgesch Asiens — Wiener Beitraege zur Kunst- und Kulturgeschichte Asiens
Wien Chem Ztg — Wiener Chemiker Zeitung
Wien D — Denkschriften der Kaiserlichen Akademie der Wissenschaften. Mathematisch-Naturwissenschaftliche Classe (Wien)
Wien Diarium — Wienerisches Diarium
Wien Entom Monatschr — Wiener Entomologische Monatsschrift
Wien Ent Rd — Wiener Entomologische Rundschau
Wiener Arch Gesch Slawentum Osteur — Wiener Archiv fuer Geschichte des Slawentums und Osteuropas
Wiener Bot Z — Wiener Botanische Zeitschrift
Wiener Denkschr — Denkschriften der Oesterreichischen Akademie der Wissenschaften. Philosophisch-Historische Klasse (Wien)
Wiener Ethnohist Bl — Wiener Ethnohistorische Blaetter
Wiener Jahrb Phil — Wiener Jahrbuch fuer Philosophie
Wiener Libr Bull — Wiener Library Bulletin
Wiener Moden Zeitung Z Kunst — Wiener Moden-Zeitung und Zeitschrift fuer Kunst, Schoene Litteratur und Theater
Wiener Slavist Jb — Wiener Slavistisches Jahrbuch
Wiener St — Wiener Studien. Zeitschrift fuer Klassische Philologie

Wiener Stud — Wiener Studien
Wiener Voelkerk Mitt — Wiener Voelkerkundliche Mitteilungen
Wiener Voelkerkundliche Mitt — Wiener Voelkerkundliche Mitteilungen
Wiener Vorl Bl — Wiener Vorlegeblaetter fuer Archaeologische Uebungen
Wiener Z Kde Morgenl — Wiener Zeitschrift fuer die Kunde des Morgenlandes
Wiener Z Kunde Sud — Wiener Zeitschrift fuer die Kunde Suedasiens und Archiv fuer Indische Philosophie
Wiener Z Kunde Suedasiens — Wiener Zeitschrift fuer die Kunde Suedasiens und Archiv fuer Indische Philosophie
Wien Geschb — Wiener Geschichtsbuecher
Wien Geschbl — Wiener Geschichtsblaetter
Wien Geschichtsbl — Wiener Geschichtsblaetter
Wien Jahrb Kunstgesch — Wiener Jahrbuch fuer Kunstgeschichte
Wien Jb Kstgesch — Wiener Jahrbuch fuer Kunstgeschichte
Wien Jb Lit — Wiener Jahrbuecher der Literatur
Wien Jbr Ober Realsch Inn Stadt — Jahresbericht der Oeffentlichen Ober-Realschule in der Innere Stadt (Wien)
Wien Jhft — Wiener Jahreshefte
Wien Klin W — Wiener Klinische Wochenschrift
Wien Klin Wchnschr — Wiener Klinische Wochenschrift
Wien Klin Wochenschr — Wiener Klinische Wochenschrift
Wien Klin Wochenschr Suppl — Wiener Klinische Wochenschrift. Supplementum
Wien Klin Ws — Wiener Klinische Wochenschrift
Wien Landwirtsch Ztg — Wiener Landwirtschaftliche Zeitung
Wien Md Wschr — Wiener Medizinische Wochenschrift
Wien Med Presse — Wiener Medizinische Presse
Wien Med Wchnschr — Wiener Medizinische Wochenschrift
Wien Med Wochenschr — Wiener Medizinische Wochenschrift
Wien Med Wochenschr (Beih) — Wiener Medizinische Wochenschrift (Beihefte)
Wien Med Wochenschr Suppl — Wiener Medizinische Wochenschrift. Supplementum
Wien Med Ws — Wiener Medizinische Wochenschrift
Wien Med Wschr — Wiener Medizinische Wochenschrift
Wien Met Z — Zeitschrift der Oesterreichischen Gesellschaft fuer Meteorologie (Wien)
Wien Mitt Photogr Inhalts — Wiener Mitteilungen Photographischen Inhalts
Wien Mitt Wasser Abwasser Gewaesser — Wiener Mitteilungen. Wasser, Abwaesser, Gewaesser
Wien Naturh Mus Annalen — Wien Naturhistorischer Museum. Annalen
Wien Pharm Wochenschr — Wiener Pharmazeutische Wochenschrift
Wien Phot Bl — Wiener Photographische Blaetter
Wien Pht Cor — Photographische Correspondenz. Organ der Photographischen Gesellschaft in Wien
Wien Praehist Z — Wiener Praehistorische Zeitschrift
Wien Praeh Z — Wiener Praehistorische Zeitschrift
Wien Sb — Sitzungsberichte der Mathematisch-Naturwissenschaftlichen Classe der Kaiserlichen Akademie der Wissenschaften (Wien)
Wien Schr — Schriften des Vereins zur Verbreitung Naturwissenschaftlicher Kenntnisse in Wien
Wien Schr Vr Nw Kennt — Schriften des Vereins zur Verbreitung Naturwissenschaftlicher Kenntnisse in Wien
Wien Slav Jb — Wiener Slavistisches Jahrbuch
Wien Stud — Wiener Studien. Zeitschrift fuer Klassische Philologie
Wien Stud Z Klass Philol — Wiener Studien. Zeitschrift fuer Klassische Philologie
Wien Stud Z Philol & Patristik — Wiener Studien Zeitschrift fuer Philologie und Patristik
Wien Tieraerztl Monatsschr — Wiener Tieraerztliche Monatsschrift
Wien Tieraerztl Mschr — Wiener Tieraerztliche Monatsschrift
Wien Voelkerk Mitt — Wiener Voelkerkundliche Mitteilungen
Wien Vr Nw Kennt Schr — Schriften des Vereins zur Verbreitung Naturwissenschaftlicher Kenntnisse in Wien
Wien Z Gs Aerzte — Zeitschrift der Kaiserlich-Koeniglichen Gesellschaft der Aerzte zu Wien
Wien Z Inn Med Ihre Grenzgeb — Wiener Zeitschrift fuer Innere Medizin und Ihre Grenzgebiete
Wien Z Knd Mrglandes — Wiener Zeitschrift fuer die Kunde des Morgenlandes
Wien Z Knd S & Ostasiens & Archv Ind Philos — Wiener Zeitschrift fuer die Kunde Sued- und Ostasiens und Archiv fuer Indische Philosophie
Wien Z Knd Sudasiens & Archv Ind Philos — Wiener Zeitschrift fuer die Kunde Suedasiens und Archiv fuer Indische Philosophie
Wien Z Kunde Morgenlandes — Wiener Zeitschrift fuer die Kunde des Morgenlandes
Wien Z Kunde Sued Ostasiens — Wiener Zeitschrift fuer die Kunde Sued- und Ostasiens und Archiv fuer Indische Philosophie
Wien Z Met — Zeitschrift der Oesterreichischen Gesellschaft fuer Meteorologie (Wien)
Wien Z Nervenheilkd — Wiener Zeitschrift fuer Nervenheilkunde und deren Grenzgebiete
Wien Z Nervenheilk Grenzgeb — Wiener Zeitschrift fuer Nervenheilkunde und Deren Grenzgebiete
Wien Zs Inn Med — Wiener Zeitschrift fuer Innere Medizin und Ihre Grenzgebiete
Wien Zt — Wiener Zeitung
Wien Ztg — Wiener Zeitung
Wien Zts Morg — Wiener Zeitschrift fuer die Kunde des Morgenlandes
WIERD — Wind Energy Report
WIF — William Faulkner. Materials, Studies, and Criticism
WIF — Worlds of If
WIFO — Wildfowl
WIG — West-Indische Gids
WiG — Wiener Geschichtsblaetter
Wih — Winterthur Portfolio
WIHP — Journal. Wisconsin Association for Health, Physical Education, and Recreation
WIJ — Warburg Institute. Journal

Wijsgerig Perspect Maatsch Wet — Wijsgerig Perspectief op Maatschappij en Wetenschap
Wijsig Perspect — Wijsgerig Perspectief op Maatschappij en Wetenschap
WIK — Deutsches Institut fuer Wirtschaftsforschung. Wochenbericht
Wiko — Wirtschaftskonjunktur
WIL — Wirtschaftliche Lage in der Bundesrepublik Deutschland
WI Law Rev — Wisconsin Law Review
Wild Barfield Heat-Treat J — Wild Barfield Heat-Treatment Journal
Wild Barfield J — Wild Barfield Journal
Wild Camp — Wilderness Camping
Wild Cat — Wild Cat Monthly
Wildenowia Beih — Wildenowia Beiheft
Wilderness Environ Med — Wilderness & Environmental Medicine
Wildfire Stat US Dep Agric For Serv — Wildfire Statistics. United States Department of Agriculture. Forest Service
Wildl Aust — Wildlife in Australia
Wildl Dis — Wildlife Diseases
Wildl Dis Assoc Bull — Wildlife Disease Association. Bulletin
Wildlife — Wildlife in Australia
Wildlife A — Wildlife in Australia
Wildlife Aust — Wildlife in Australia
Wildlife Publ Rev — Wildlife Publications Review
Wildlife R — Wildlife Review
Wild Life Rev — Wild Life Review
Wildl Res — Wildlife Research
Wildl Manage Bull (Ottawa) Ser 1 — Wildlife Management Bulletin (Ottawa). Series 1
Wildl Manage Bull (Ottawa) Ser 2 — Wildlife Management Bulletin (Ottawa). Series 2
Wildl Monogr — Wildlife Monographs
Wildl Res Q — Wildlife Research Quarterly
Wildl Rev — Wildlife Review
Wildl Rev NZ Wildl Serv — Wildlife Review. New Zealand Wildlife Service
Wildl SB — Wildlife Society Bulletin
Wildl Soc Bull — Wildlife Society. Bulletin
Wildl Wildlands Inst Monogr — Wildlife-Wildlands Institute. Monograph
Wildm Int L — Wildman's International Law
Wildm Search — Wildman. Search, Capture, and Prize
Wild Rpm Met — Repertorium fuer Meteorologie, Herausg. von der Kaiserlichen Akademie der Wissenschaften. Wild
Wiley Classics Lib — Wiley Classics Library
Wiley Gauthier Villars Ser Modern Appl Math — Wiley/Gauthier-Villars Series in Modern Applied Mathematics
Wiley Intersci Publ — Wiley-Interscience Publication
Wiley Intersci Ser Discrete Math — Wiley-Interscience Series in Discrete Mathematics
Wiley Intersci Ser Discrete Math Optim — Wiley-Interscience Series in Discrete Mathematics and Optimization
Wiley Intersci Ser Systems Optim — Wiley-Interscience Series in Systems and Optimization
Wiley Lib Newsl — Wiley-Interscience Librarian's Newsletter
Wiley Polym Networks Group Rev Ser — Wiley Polymer Networks Group Review Series
Wiley Prof Comput — Wiley Professional Computing
Wiley Pub Math Statist — Wiley Publication in Mathematical Statistics
Wiley Ser Beam Phys Accel Tech — Wiley Series in Beam Physics and Accelerator Technology
Wiley Ser Comput — Wiley Series in Computing
Wiley Ser Curr Top Reprod Endocrinol — Wiley Series on Current Topics in Reproductive Endocrinology
Wiley Ser New Horiz Oncol — Wiley Series on New Horizons in Oncology
Wiley Ser Nonlinear Sci — Wiley Series in Nonlinear Science
Wiley Ser Numer Methods Engrg — Wiley Series in Numerical Methods in Engineering
Wiley Ser Photosci Photoeng — Wiley Series in Photoscience and Photoengineering
Wiley Ser Probab Math Statist — Wiley Series in Probability and Mathematical Statistics
Wiley Ser Probab Math Statist Appl Probab Statist — Wiley Series in Probability and Mathematical Statistics. Applied Probability and Statistics
Wiley Ser Probab Math Statist Probab Math Statist — Wiley Series in Probability and Mathematical Statistics. Probability and Mathematical Statistics
Wiley Ser Probab Math Statist Tracts Probab Statist — Wiley Series in Probability and Mathematical Statistics. Tracts on Probability and Statistics
Wiley Ser Probab Statist Probab Statist — Wiley Series in Probability and Statistics. Probability and Statistics
Wiley Ser Pure Appl Optics — Wiley Series in Pure and Applied Optics
Wiley Ser Solution Chem — Wiley Series in Solution Chemistry
Wiley Teubner Ser Comput Sci — Wiley-Teubner Series in Computer Science
Wilhelm-Pieck Univ Rostock Wiss Z Math Naturwiss Reihe — Wilhelm-Pieck-Universitaet Rostock. Wissenschaftliche Zeitschrift. Mathematisch-Naturwissenschaftliche Reihe
Wilhelm Pieck Univ Rostock Wiss Z Naturwiss Reihe — Wilhelm-Pieck-Universitaet Rostock. Wissenschaftliche Zeitschrift. Naturwissenschaftliche Reihe
Wilhelm Roux' Arch — Wilhelm Roux' Archiv fuer Entwicklungsmechanik der Organismen [*Later, Roux' Archives of Developmental Biology*]
Wilhelm Roux' Arch Dev Biol — Wilhelm Roux' Archives of Developmental Biology
Wilhelm Roux' Arch Entwicklungsmech Org — Wilhelm Roux' Archiv fuer Entwicklungsmechanik der Organismen [*Later, Roux' Archives of Developmental Biology*]
Wilhelm Roux Arch EntwMech Org — Wilhelm Roux' Archiv fuer Entwicklungsmechanik der Organismen
WILJ — West Indian Law Journal
Wilk Lim — Wilkinson. Limitation of Actions

Willamette L J — Willamette Law Journal
Willamette L Rev — Willamette Law Review
Willc Mun Corp — Willcock's Municipal Corp.
Willdenowia Beih — Willdenowia Beiheft
Willett House Q — Willett House Quarterly
Wille U Macht — Wille und Macht
Wille U Werk — Wille und Werk
William and Mary Bus R — William and Mary Business Review
William and Mary Law R — William and Mary Law Review
William & Mary L Rev — William and Mary Law Review
William & Mary Q — William and Mary Quarterly
William Car — William Carlos Williams Review
William L Hutcheson Mem For Bull — William L. Hutcheson Memorial Forest. Bulletin
William Mary Q — William and Mary College Quarterly
William Mary Quart — William and Mary Quarterly
William Mitchell L Rev — William Mitchell Law Review
William M Q — William and Mary Quarterly
William Roever Lectures Geom — William H. Roever Lectures in Geometry
Willisons Mo — Willison's Monthly
Williston Basin Oil Rev — Williston Basin Oil Review
Will LJ — Willamette Law Journal
Will LR — Willamette Law Review
Wills Est & Tr Serv P-H — Wills, Estates, and Trust Service. Prentice-Hall
WILM — Wildlife Monographs
WILN — Wildlife News
WILPFNSW Branch Monthly Bulletin — WILPF [*Women's International League for Peace and Freedom*]. New South Wales Branch. Monthly Bulletin
Wil Q — Wilson Quarterly
WI LR — Wisconsin Law Review
Wilson — Wilson Quarterly
Wilson B — Wilson Bulletin
Wilson Bul — Wilson Bulletin
Wilson Bull — Wilson Bulletin
Wilson Lib Bul — Wilson Library Bulletin
Wilson Lib Bull — Wilson Library Bulletin
Wilson Libr Bull — Wilson Library Bulletin
Wilson Q — Wilson Quarterly
Wilson Quart — Wilson Quarterly
Wilt A Nat Hist Mag — Wiltshire Archaeological and Natural History Magazine
Wilts Archaeol & Nat Hist Mag — Wiltshire Archaeological and Natural History Magazine
Wilts Arch Natur Hist Mag — Wiltshire Archaeological and Natural History Magazine
Wilts Beekprs Gaz — Wiltshire Beekeepers' Gazette
Wiltshire Archaeol Natur Hist Mag — Wiltshire Archaeological and Natural History Magazine
Wiltshire Arch Mag — Wiltshire Archaeological Magazine [*Later, Wiltshire Archaeological and NaturalHistory Magazine*]
Wiltshire Arch Natur Hist Mag — Wiltshire Archaeological and Natural History Magazine
Wilts Mag — Wiltshire Archaeological and Natural History Magazine
WiM — Wisconsin Magazine of History
WI Mag Hist — Wisconsin Magazine of History
WI Med J — West Indian Medical Journal
Win — Win Magazine
Win — Winter
Winck Progr — Winckelmannsprogramm der Archaeologischen Gesellschaft zu Berlin
Wind — Windmill
Wind Energy Rep — Wind Energy Report
Wind Eng — Wind Engineering
Wind Engng — Wind Engineering
Wind En Rpt — Wind Energy Report
W Indian Dig — West Indian Digest
W Indian Med J — West Indian Medical Journal
W Indian World — West Indian World
Wind Inst Melior Uzytkow Zielonych — Windomosci Instytutu Melioracji i Uzytkow Zielonych
W Ind Med J — West Indian Medical Journal
Wind Muz Ziemi — Windomosci Muzeum Ziemi
Wind O — Windless Orchard
Window Inds — Window Industries
Wind Power Dig — Wind Power Digest
Windsor — Windsor Magazine
Windsor Mag — Windsor Magazine
Windsor R — Windsor Report
Windsor Yearb Access — Windsor Yearbook of Access to Justice
Wind Technol J — Wind Technology Journal
Wine Hdbk — Wine Marketing Handbook
Wine Rev — Wine Review
Wine Vine — Wines and Vines Statistical Issue
Wing — Wing Newsletter
Wings Afr — Wings over Africa
Winnip Clin Q — Winnipeg Clinic. Quarterly
Winter Annu Meet Am Soc Mech Eng — Winter Annual Meeting of the American Society of Mechanical Engineers
Winter Meet Stat Phys — Winter Meeting on Statistical Physics
Winter Simul Conf Proc — Winter Simulation Conference Proceedings
Wintertag — Wintertagung
Winter Tb — Winter's Naturwissenschaftliche Taschenbuecher
Winterthur — Winterthur Portfolio
Winterthur Jb — Winterthur Jahrbuch
Winterthur Port — Winterthur Portfolio
Winthr St M — Winthrop Studies on Major Modern Writers

WIP — Work in Progress
Wi Pr — Wirtschafts-Praxis
WIQUD — Wilson Quarterly
WIR — Western Intelligence Report
Wirbelsacule Forsch Prax — Wirbelsacule in Forschung und Praxis
WIRE — Wildlife Review. British Columbia Ministry of Environment
Wire and Wire Prod — Wire and Wire Products
Wire Ind — Wire Industry
Wire J — Wire Journal
Wire J Int — Wire Journal International
Wireless Eng — Wireless Engineer
Wirel Wld — Wireless World
Wirel World — Wireless World
Wire Prod — Wire and Wire Products
Wire Technol — Wire Technology
WI Rev — West Indian Review
Wire World Int — Wire World International
Wiring Install and Supplies — Wiring Installations and Supplies
Wirkerei Strickerei Tech — Wirkerei und Strickerei Technik
WIRS — Western Illinois Regional Studies
Wirt — Wirtschaftsdienst
Wirtber Lateinam — Wirtschaftsbericht Lateinamerika
WirtBer Lateinam Laender sowie Spanien und Port — Wirtschaftsbericht ueber die Lateinamerikanischen Laender sowie Spanien und Portugal
Wirt Futter — Wirtschaftseigene Futter
Wirt in Za — Wirtschaft in Zahlen
Wirt Pol — Monatsblaetter fuer Freiheitliche Wirtschaftspolitik
Wirt Reihe — Lange Reihen zur Wirtschaftsentwicklung
Wirtschaft — Wirtschafts-Blaetter
Wirtschaftspol Chron — Wirtschaftspolitische Chronik
Wirtschaftswiss — Wirtschaftswissenschaft
Wirtschaftswiss Beitr — Wirtschaftswissenschaftliche Beitraege
Wirtsch-Dienst — Wirtschaftsdienst
Wirtsch Polit Chronik — Wirtschaftspolitische Chronik
Wirtschseig Futter — Wirtschaftseigene Futter
Wirtsch Stat — Wirtschaft und Statistik
Wirtsch u Ges — Wirtschaft und Gesellschaft
Wirtsch u Recht — Wirtschaft und Recht
Wirtsch u Statist — Wirtschaft und Statistik
Wirtsch Verwalt — Wirtschaft und Verwaltung
Wirtsch Wettbewerb — Wirtschaft und Wettbewerb
Wirtsch-Wiss — Wirtschaftswissenschaft
Wirtswoche — Wirtschaftswoche
Wirt und Ges — Wirtschaft und Gesellschaft
Wirt und Investment — Wirtschaft und Investment
Wirt und Recht — Wirtschaft und Recht
Wirt und Sozwiss Inst Mitt — Wirtschafts- und Sozialwissenschaftliches Institut. Mitteilungen
Wirt und Statis — Wirtschaft und Statistik
Wirt und Wettbewerb — Wirtschaft und Wettbewerb
Wirt u Wiss — Wirtschaft und Wissen
Wirt Wiss Inst Mitt — Wirtschaftswissenschaftliches Institut Mitteilungen
Wis — Wisconsin Reports
WIS — World of Islam
Wis Acad of Sci Trans — Wisconsin Academy of Sciences, Arts, and Letters. Transactions
Wis Acad Sci Arts Lett — Wisconsin Academy of Sciences, Arts, and Letters
Wis Acad Sci Arts Letters Trans — Wisconsin Academy of Sciences, Arts, and Letters. Transactions
Wis Acad Sciences Trans — Wisconsin Academy of Sciences, Arts, and Letters. Transactions
Wis Acad Sci Trans — Wisconsin Academy of Sciences, Arts, and Letters. Transactions
Wis Admin Code — Wisconsin Administrative Code
Wis Admin Reg — Wisconsin Administrative Register
Wis Ag Dept — Wisconsin. Department of Agriculture. Publications
Wis Ag Exp — Wisconsin. Agricultural Experiment Station. Publications
Wis Agric Exp Stn Bull — Wisconsin. Agricultural Experiment Station. Bulletin
Wis Agric Exp Stn Res Bull — Wisconsin. Agricultural Experiment Station. Research Bulletin
Wis Agric Exp Stn Res Rep — Wisconsin. Agricultural Experiment Station. Research Report
Wis Agric Exp Stn Spec Bull — Wisconsin. Agricultural Experiment Station. Special Bulletin
Wis Alum M — Wisconsin Alumni Magazine
Wis Arch — Wisconsin Archaeologist
Wis Archeol — Wisconsin Archeologist. Wisconsin Archeological Society
WISB — Wildlife Society. Bulletin
Wis BA Bull — Wisconsin State Bar Association. Bulletin
Wis Badger Bee — Wisconsin's Badger Bee
Wis Bar Bull — Wisconsin State Bar Association. Bulletin
WIS B BULL — Wisconsin Bar Bulletin
Wis B Bulletin — Wisconsin Bar Bulletin
Wis Beekeep — Wisconsin Beekeeping
Wisc Ac T — Transactions of the Wisconsin Academy of Sciences, Arts, and Letters
Wisc Busn — Wisconsin Business
Wisc LB — Wisconsin Library Bulletin
Wisc Lib Bull — Wisconsin Library Bulletin
Wisc LR — Wisconsin Law Review
Wisc Mag Hist — Wisconsin Magazine of History
Wisc Med J — Wisconsin Medical Journal
Wis Coll Agric Life Sci Res Div Res Rep — Wisconsin College of Agricultural and Life Sciences. Research Division. Research Report

Wis Coll Agric Life Sci Res Div Sci Rep Bull — Wisconsin College of Agricultural and Life Sciences. Research Division. ScienceReport Bulletin
Wis Conf Crime Control Proc — Wisconsin Conference on State and Local Organization for Crime Control. Proceedings
Wis Conserv Bull — Wisconsin Conservation Bulletin
Wis Conserv Dep Tech Bull — Wisconsin Conservation Department. Technical Bulletin
Wisconsin Acad Sci Arts and Letters Trans — Wisconsin Academy of Sciences, Arts, and Letters. Transactions
Wisconsin Acad Sci Arts Lett Trans — Wisconsin Academy of Sciences, Arts, and Letters. Transactions
Wisconsin Agric Exp Sta Res Rep — Wisconsin State Agricultural Experiment Station. Research Report
Wisconsin Agric Exp Stn Bull — Wisconsin. Agricultural Experiment Station. Bulletin
Wisconsin Law Rev — Wisconsin Law Review
Wisconsin L Rev — Wisconsin Law Review
Wisconsin Med J — Wisconsin Medical Journal
Wisconsin MJ — Wisconsin Medical Journal
Wisc Stud BJ — Wisconsin Student Bar Journal
Wisc Un Bll Sc — Bulletin of the University of Wisconsin. Science Series
Wis Dent Assoc J — Wisconsin Dental Association. Journal
Wis Dep Nat Resour Publ — Wisconsin. Department of Natural Resources. Publication
Wis Dep Nat Resour Tech Bull — Wisconsin. Department of Natural Resources. Technical Bulletin
Wis Energy Ext Serv Agric-Energy Transp Dig — Wisconsin. Energy Extension Service. Agricultural-Energy Transportation Digest
Wis Eng — Wisconsin Engineer
Wis Eng Exp Stn Repr — Wisconsin. Engineering Experiment Station. Reprint
Wis Engineer — Wisconsin Engineer
WISER — Western Information System for Energy Resources
WiseR — Wiseman Review
Wise Rev — Wiseman Review
Wis Geol Nat Hist Surv Bull — Wisconsin. Geological and Natural History Survey. Bulletin
Wis Geol Survey Bull Inf Circ — Wisconsin. Geological Survey. Bulletin. Information Circular
Wis G S — Wisconsin. Geological and Natural History Survey
Wis G S G Wis B — Wisconsin. Geological Survey. Geology of Wisconsin. Bulletin [*Later, WisconsinGeological and Natural History Survey*]
Wis His Col — Wisconsin State Historical Society. Collections
Wis His Proc — Wisconsin Historical Society. Proceedings
Wis His S Domesday Bk — Wisconsin State Historical Society. Domesday Book
Wis Hist Soc Proc — Wisconsin State Historical Society. Proceedings
Wis Hort — Wisconsin Horticulture
Wis J Ed — Wisconsin Journal of Education
Wis J Educ — Wisconsin Journal of Education
Wis Law R — Wisconsin Law Review
Wis Law Rev — Wisconsin Law Review
Wis Laws — Laws of Wisconsin
Wis Legis Serv — Wisconsin Legislative Service
Wis Leg N — Wisconsin Legal News
Wis Lib Bul — Wisconsin Library Bulletin
Wis LN — Wisconsin Legal News
Wis LR — Wisconsin Law Review
Wis L Rev — Wisconsin Law Review
Wis M — Wisconsin Magazine of History
Wis Mag Hist — Wisconsin Magazine of History
Wis Med J — Wisconsin Medical Journal
Wis M Hist — Wisconsin Magazine of History
Wis M J — Wisconsin Medical Journal
Wis Nat Resour Bull — Wisconsin Natural Resources Bulletin
Wis Natuurk Verh Kon Akad Wetensch Amsterdam — Wis- en Natuurkundige Verhandelingen van de Kon. Akademie van Wetenschappen te Amsterdam
Wis N H Soc B — Wisconsin Natural History Society. Bulletin
WiSo Kurzlehrbuecher Reihe Betriebswirtsch — WiSo-Kurzlehrbuecher. Reihe Betriebswirtschaft
Wis Paper Ind Newsl — Wisconsin Paper Industry. Information Service Newsletter
Wis Pharm — Wisconsin Pharmacist
Wis Pharm Ext Bull — Wisconsin. Pharmacy Extension Bulletin
Wi Spieg — Wirtschaftsspiegel
Wiss 20 Jhd Transdiszip Reflex — Wissenschaft im 20. Jahrhunders. Transdisziplinaere Reflexionen
Wiss Abh Dtsch Akad Landwirtschaftswiss Berlin — Wissenschaftliche Abhandlungen der Deutschen Akademie der Landwirtschaftswissenschaften zu Berlin
Wiss Abh Dtsch Materialpruefungsanst — Wissenschaftliche Abhandlungen der Deutschen Materialpruefungsanstalten
Wiss Abh Phys-Tech Bd Anst — Wissenschaftliche Abhandlungen der Physikalisch-Technischen Bundesanstalt
Wiss Abh Phys-Tech Reichsanst — Wissenschaftliche Abhandlungen der Physikalische-Technischen Reichsanstalt
Wiss Alpenvereinshefte — Wissenschaftliche Alpenvereinshefte
Wiss Ann — Wissenschaftliche Annalen
Wiss Arb Forschungsanst Forstwirtsch Zvolen — Wissenschaftliche Arbeiten der Forschungsanstalt fuer Forstwirtschaft in Zvolen
Wiss Arch Landw Abt A — Wissenschaftliches Archiv fuer Landwirtschaft. Abteilung A. Archiv fuer Pflanzenbau
Wiss Arch Landwirtsch Abt A — Wissenschaftliches Archiv fuer Landwirtschaft. Abteilung A. Archiv fuer Pflanzenbau
Wiss Arch Landwirtsch Abt B — Wissenschaftliches Archiv fuer Landwirtschaft. Abteilung B. Archiv fuer Tierernaehrung und Teirzucht
Wis SBA Bull — Wisconsin State Bar Association. Bulletin
Wiss Beil Dresdn Anz — Wissenschaftliche Beilage des Dresdner Anzeigers

Wiss Beil Jber Gym Bamberg — Wissenschaftliche Beilage zum Jahresbericht des Gymnasiums Bamberg

Wiss Beitr Ingenieurhochsch Koethen — Wissenchaftliche Beitraege. Ingenieurhochschule Koethen

Wiss Beitr Ingenieurhochsch Zwickau — Wissenchaftliche Beitraege. Ingenieurhochschule Zwickau

Wiss Beitr Martin Luther Univ (Halle Wittenberg) — Wissenschaftliche Beitraege. Martin Luther Universitaet (Halle-Wittenberg)

Wiss Beitr Martin Luther Univ (Halle Wittenberg) Reihe M — Wissenschaftliche Beitrage. Martin Luther Universitaet (Halle-Wittenberg). Reihe M

Wiss Beitr Univ (Halle) — Wissenschaftliche Beitrage. Martin Luther Universitaet (Halle-Wittenberg)

Wiss Ber AEG-Telefunken — Wissenschaftliche Berichte AEG-Telefunken

Wiss Ber EM — Wissenschaftliche Berichte EM

Wiss Ber Forschungszent Karlsruhe — Wissenschaftliche Berichte. Forschungszentrum Karlsruhe

Wiss Ber HMFA Braunschweig — Wissenschaftliche Berichte aus der Hochmagnetfeldanlage. Physikalische Institute. Technische Universitaet Braunschweig

Wiss Ber Zentralinst Festkoerperphys Werkstofforsch — Wissenschaftliche Berichte. Zentralinstitut fuer Festkoerperphysik und Werkstofforschung

Wiss Buecherei — Wissenschaftliche Buecherei

Wiss Dienst — Johann-Gottfried-Herder Institut Marburg/Lahn. Wissenschaftlicher Dienst

Wiss Dienst Ostmitteleur — Wissenschaftlicher Dienst fuer Ostmitteleuropa

Wiss Dienst Sudosteuropa — Wissenschaftlicher Dienst Suedosteuropa

Wiss Di Suedost Eur — Wissenschaftlicher Dienst Suedosteuropa

Wissenschaftstheorie- Wissenschaft Philos — Wissenschaftstheorie- Wissenschaft und Philosophie

Wissenschaftstheor Wiss Philos — Wissenschaftstheorie- Wissenschaft und Philosophie

Wissensch Beitr — Wissenschaftliche Beitraege

Wissensch Inform — Wissenschaftliche Information

Wissensch Inform Ber — Wissenschaftliche Informationen und Berichte

Wissensch Meeresuntersuch — Wissenschaftliche Meeresuntersuchungen

Wissensch Sitzungen Stochastik 80 — Wissenschaftliche Sitzungen zur Stochastik 80

Wissensch Sitzungen Stochastik 81 — Wissenschaftliche Sitzungen zur Stochastik 81

Wissensch Sitzungen Stochastik 82 — Wissenschaftliche Sitzungen zur Stochastik 82

Wissensch Taschenbuecher Reihe Math Phys — Wissenschaftliche Taschenbuecher. Reihe Mathematik/Physik

Wissensch Taschenbuecher Reihe Texte Stud — Wissenschaftliche Taschenbuecher. Reihe Texte und Studien

Wiss Forschungsber Naturwiss Reihe — Wissenschaftliche Forschungsberichte. Naturwissenschaftliche Reihe

Wiss Fortschr — Wissenschaft und Fortschritt

Wiss Fortschritt — Wissenschaft und Fortschritt

Wiss Geg — Wissenschaft und Gegenwart

Wiss Konf Ges Dtsch Naturforsch Aerzte — Wissenschaftliche Konferenz. Gesellschaft Deutscher Naturforscher und Aerzte

Wiss Kult — Wissenschaft und Kultur

WisSL — Wisconsin Studies in Literature

Wiss Literaturanz — Wissenschaftlicher Literaturanzeiger

Wiss M Bosn — Wissenschaftliche Mitteilungen des Bosnisch-Herzegowinischen Landesmuseums A. Archaeologie

Wiss Mitt Bosn u Herzeg — Wissenschaftliche Mittheilungen aus Bosnien und der Herzegowina

Wiss Mitt Forst Holzwirtsch — Wissenschaftliche Mitteilungen fuer Forst und Holzwirtschaft

Wiss Mitt Historiker-Ges DDR — Wissenschaftliche Mitteilungen. Historiker-Gesellschaft der DDR

Wiss Mitth Phys Med Soc Erlangen — Wissenschaftliche Mittheilungen der Physicalisch-Medicinischen Societaet zu Erlangen

Wiss Mitt Pharm Forsch Fortbild Inst Oesterr Apoth Ver — Wissenschaftliche Mitteilungen. Pharmazeutisches Forschungs- und Fortbildungs Institut. Oesterreichischer Apotheker-Verein

Wiss Mon ANT — Wissenschaftliche Monographien zum Alten und Neuen Testament

Wiss Prax Ki Ges — Wissenschaft und Praxis in Kirche und Gesellschaft

Wiss Schriftenr Tech Hochsch Karl-Marx-Stadt — Wissenschaftliche Schriftenreihe. Technische Hochschule Karl-Marx-Stadt

Wiss Schr Tech Hochsch Karl Marx Stadt — Wissenschaftliche Schriftenreihe der Technischen Hochschule Karl-Marx-Stadt

Wiss Tag Tech Univ Karl Marx Stadt — Wissenschaftliche Tagungen der Technischen Universitaet Karl-Marx-Stadt

Wiss Taschenb — Wissenschaftliche Taschenbuecher

Wis Stat — Wisconsin Statutes

Wis Stat Ann (West) — West's Wisconsin Statutes Annotated

Wis State Cartogr Off Inf Circ — Wisconsin State Cartographer's Office. Information Circular

Wis State Hist Soc Proc — State Historical Society of Wisconsin. Proceedings

Wis State Hist Soc Pub — State Historical Society of Wisconsin. Publications

Wis St B Assn Bul — Wisconsin State Bar Association. Bulletin

Wis St B Assn Proc — Wisconsin State Bar Association. Proceedings

Wiss-Tech Fortschr Landw — Wissenschaftlich-Technischer Fortschrift fuer die Landwirtschaft

Wiss-Tech Inf VEB Kombinat Automatisierungsanlagenbau — Wissenschaftlich-Technische Informationen des VEB Kombinat Automatisierungsanlagenbau

Wis Stud Contemp Lit — Wisconsin Studies in Contemporary Literature [Later, Contemporary Literature]

Wiss Umwelt — Wissenschaft und Umwelt

Wiss Umwelt ISU — Wissenschaft und Umwelt ISU

Wiss Unt NT — Wissenschaftliche Untersuchungen zum Neuen Testament

Wiss U Weltbild — Wissenschaft und Weltbild

Wiss Veroeff DOG — Wissenschaftliche Veroeffentlichungen der Deutschen Orient-Gesellschaft

Wiss Veroeff Dt Inst Laenderkde — Wissenschaftliche Veroeffentlichungen des Deutschen Instituts fuer Laenderkunde

Wiss Veroeff Siemens-Werken — Wissenschaftliche Veroeffentlichungen aus den Siemens-Werken

Wiss Veroeff Tech Hochsch (Darmstadt) — Wissenschaftliche Veroeffentlichungen. Technische Hochschule (Darmstadt)

Wiss Wb — Wissenschaft und Weltbild

Wiss Weis — Wissenschaft und Weisheit

Wiss Welt — Wissenschaft und Weltbild

Wiss Weltb — Wissenschaft und Weltbild

Wiss Wirtsch Polit — Wissenschaft, Wirtschaft, Politik

Wiss Z — Wissenschaftliche Zeitschrift

WissZ — Wissenschaftliche Zeitung. Humboldt-Universitaet

Wiss Z Bauhaus Univ Weimar — Wissenschaftliche Zeitschrift. Bauhaus-Universitaet Weimar

Wiss Z (Berl) — Wissenschaftliche Zeitschrift. Humboldt-Universitaet (Berlin). Gesellschafts- und Sprachwissenschaftliche Reihe

Wiss Z Berlin — Wissenschaftliche Zeitschrift der Humboldt-Universitaet zu Berlin. Gesellschafts- und Sprachwissenschaftliche Reihe

Wiss Z Brandenburg Landeshochsch — Wissenschaftliche Zeitschrift der Brandenburgischen Landeshochschule

Wiss Z Elektrotech — Wissenschaftliche Zeitschrift der Elektrotechnik

Wiss Z Ernst Moritz Arndt U Greifswald — Wissenschaftliche Zeitschrift der Ernst-Moritz-Arndt-Universitaet Greifswald

Wiss Z Ernst Moritz Arndt Univ — Wissenschaftliche Zeitschrift der Ernst-Moritz-Arndt-Universitaet Greifswald. Mathematisch-Naturwissenschaftliche Reihe

Wiss Z Ernst Moritz Arndt Univ (Greifswald) Math Natur Reihe — Wissenschaftliche Zeitschrift. Ernst-Moritz-Arndt-Universitaet (Greifswald). Mathematisch-Naturwissenschaftliche Reihe

Wiss Z Ernst Moritz Arndt Univ Greifswald Math Naturw Reihe — Wissenschaftliche Zeitschrift. Ernst-Moritz-Arndt-Universitaet (Greifswald). Mathematisch-Naturwissenschaftliche Reihe

Wiss Z Ernst-Moritz-Arndt-Univ Greifsw Math Naturwiss Reihe — Wissenschaftliche Zeitschrift. Ernst-Moritz-Arndt-Universitaet (Greifswald). Mathematisch-Naturwissenschaftliche Reihe

Wiss Z Friedrich Schiller U Jena — Wissenschaftliche Zeitschrift der Friedrich-Schiller-Universitaet Jena

Wiss Z Friedrich Schiller Univ Ges Sprachwiss Reihe — Wissenschaftliche Zeitschrift der Friedrich-Schiller-Universitaet. Gesellschafts- und Sprachwissenschaftliche Reihe

Wiss Z Friedrich Schiller Univ Jena — Wissenschaftliche Zeitschrift der Friedrich-Schiller-Universitaet. Jena. Mathematisch-Naturwissenschaftliche Reihe

Wiss Z Friedrich Schiller Univ Jena — Wissenschaftliche Zeitschrift der Friedrich-Schiller-Universitaet. Jena. Naturwissenschaftliche Reihe

Wiss Z Friedrich-Schiller-Univ (Jena) Math Naturwiss Reihe — Wissenschaftliche Zeitschrift. Friedrich-Schiller-Universitaet (Jena). Mathematisch-Naturwissenschaftliche Reihe

Wiss Z Friedrich Schiller Univ Jena Naturwiss Reihe — Wissenschaftliche Zeitschrift. Friedrich-Schiller-Universitaet Jena. Naturwissenschaftliche Reihe

Wiss Z Greifswald — Wissenschaftliche Zeitschrift der Ernst-Moritz-Arndt-Universitaet Greifswald

Wiss Z Greifswald Ernst Moritz Arndt Univ Math Natur-Reihe — Greifswald Ernst-Moritz-Arndt-Universitaet. Wissenschaftliche Zeitschrift. Mathematisch-Naturwissenschaftliche Reihe

Wiss Z (Halle) — Wissenschaftliche Zeitschrift. Martin-Luther-Universitaet (Halle-Wittenberg)

Wiss Z Hochsch Archit & Bauwsn Weimar — Wissenschaftliche Zeitschrift der Hochschule fuer Architektur und Bauwesen (Weimar)

Wiss Z Hochsch Archit Bauwesen Weimar Univ — Wissenschaftliche Zeitschrift. Hochschule fuer Architektur und Bauwesen Weimar-Universitaet

Wiss Z Hochsch Archit Bauwes (Weimar) — Wissenschaftliche Zeitschrift. Hochschule fuer Architektur und Bauwesen (Weimar)

Wiss Z Hochsch Archit Bauwes Weimar Reihe B — Wissenschaftliche Zeitschrift der Hochschule fuer Architektur und Bauwesen Weimar. Reihe B

Wiss Z Hochsch Bauwes (Cottbus) — Wissenschaftliche Zeitschrift. Hochschule fuer Bauwesen (Cottbus)

Wiss Z Hochsch Bauwes (Leipzig) — Wissenschaftliche Zeitschrift. Hochschule fuer Bauwesen (Leipzig)

Wiss Z Hochsch Bauw (Leipzig) — Wissenschaftliche Zeitschrift. Hochschule fuer Bauwesen (Leipzig)

Wiss Z Hochsch Elektrotech (Ilmenau) — Wissenschaftliche Zeitschrift. Hochschule fuer Elektrotechnik (Ilmenau)

Wiss Z Hochsch Landwirtsch Produktionsgenoss (Meissen) — Wissenschaftliche Zeitschrift. Hochschule fuer Landwirtschaftliche Produktionsgenossenschaften (Meissen)

Wiss Z Hochsch Maschinenbau (Karl Marx-Stadt) — Wissenschaftliche Zeitschrift. Hochschule fuer Maschinenbau (Karl Marx-Stadt)

Wiss Z Hochsch Schwermaschinenbau (Magdeburg) — Wissenschaftliche Zeitschrift. Hochschule fuer Schwermaschinenbau (Magdeburg)

Wiss Z Hochschule — Wissenschaftliche Zeitschrift. Hochschule fuer Oekonomie

Wiss Z Hochsch Oekon Berlin — Wissenschaftliche Zeitschrift der Hochschule fuer Oekonomie Berlin

Wiss Z Hochsch Verkehrswesen (Dresden) — Wissenschaftliche Zeitschrift. Hochschule fuer Verkehrswesen (Dresden)

Wiss Z Hochsch Verkehrswesen Friedrich List (Dresden) — Wissenschaftliche Zeitschrift. Hochschule fuer Verkehrswesen "Friedrich List" (Dresden). Die Anwendung Mathematischer Methoden im Transportund Nachichtenwesen

Wiss Z Humboldt U — Wissenschaftliche Zeitschrift der Humboldt-Universitaet

Wiss Z Humboldt-Univ (Berl) — Wissenschaftliche Zeitschrift. Humboldt-Universitaet (Berlin)

Wiss Z Humboldt-Univ (Berlin) Math-Natur Reihe — Wissenschaftliche Zeitschrift. Humboldt-Universitaet (Berlin). Mathematisch-Naturwissenschaftliche Reihe

Wiss Z Humboldt Univ (Berlin) Math Naturwiss Reihe — Wissenschaftliche Zeitschrift. Humboldt-Universitaet (Berlin). Mathematisch-Naturwissenschaftliche Reihe

Wiss Z Humboldt Univ Berlin Reihe Agrarwiss — Wissenschaftliche Zeitschrift der Humboldt-Universitaet zu Berlin. Reihe Agrarwissenschaften

Wiss Z Humboldt Univ Berl Math — Wissenschaftliche Zeitschrift der Humboldt-Universitaet zu Berlin. Mathematisch- Naturwissenschaftliche Reihe

Wiss Z Humboldt Univ (Berl) Math Naturwiss — Wissenschaftliche Zeitschrift. Humboldt-Universitaet (Berlin). Mathematisch-Naturwissenschaftliche Reihe

Wiss Z Humboldt-Univ (Berl) Math-Naturwiss Reihe — Wissenschaftliche Zeitschrift. Humboldt-Universitaet (Berlin). Mathematisch-Naturwissenschaftliche Reihe

Wiss Z Humboldt Univ Math Naturwiss Reihe — Wissenschaftliche Zeitschrift der Humboldt Universitaet zu Berlin. Mathematisch-Naturwissenschaftliche Reihe

Wiss Z (Jena) — Wissenschaftliche Zeitschrift. Friedrich-Schiller-Universitaet (Jena)

Wiss Z Jena Reihe GS — Wissenschaftliche Zeitschrift der Friedrich-Schiller-Universitaet. Reihe Gesellschaft und Sprachwissenschaften

Wiss Z Karl Marx U Leipzig — Wissenschaftliche Zeitschrift der Karl-Marx-Universitaet Leipzig

Wiss Z Karl-Marx Univ — Wissenschaftliche Zeitschrift. Karl-Marx-Universitaet

Wiss Z Karl Marx Univ Leipzig — Wissenschaftliche Zeitschrift der Karl-Marx-Universitaet Leipzig

Wiss Z Karl-Marx-Univ (Leipzig) Math Natur Reihe — Wissenschaftliche Zeitschrift. Karl-Marx-Universitaet (Leipzig). Mathematisch-Naturwissenschaftliche Reihe

Wiss Z Karl-Marx-Univ (Leipzig) Math-Naturwiss Reihe — Wissenschaftliche Zeitschrift. Karl-Marx-Universitaet (Leipzig). Mathematisch-Naturwissenschaftliche Reihe

Wiss Z Karl-Marx-Univ (Leipz) Math-Naturwiss Reihe — Wissenschaftliche Zeitschrift. Karl-Marx-Universitaet (Leipzig). Mathematisch-Naturwissenschaftliche Reihe

Wiss Z Leipzig — Wissenschaftliche Zeitschrift der Karl-Marx-Universitaet Leipzig. Gesellschafts- und Sprachwissenschaftliche Reihe

Wiss Z Martin Luther U Halle Wittenberg — Wissenschaftliche Zeitschrift der Martin-Luther-Universitaet in Halle-Wittenberg

Wiss Z Martin Luther Univ — Wissenschaftliche Zeitschrift. Martin-Luther-Universitaet (Halle-Wittenberg). Mathematisch-Naturwissenschaftliche Reihe

Wiss Z Martin-Luther-Univ (Halle-Wittenb) — Wissenschaftliche Zeitschrift. Martin-Luther-Universitaet (Halle-Wittenberg)

Wiss Z Martin-Luther-Univ (Halle-Wittenberg) — Wissenschaftliche Zeitschrift. Martin-Luther-Universitaet (Halle-Wittenberg)

Wiss Z Martin-Luther-Univ Halle Wittenberg Math Natur Reihe — Wissenschaftliche Zeitschrift. Martin-Luther-Universitaet (Halle-Wittenberg). Mathematisch-Naturwissenschaftliche Reihe

Wiss Z Math Naturwiss Reihe Halle Univ — Wissenschaftliche Zeitschrift. Mathematisch-Naturwissenschaftliche Reihe. HalleUniversitaet

Wiss Z Paedag Hochsch Potsdam — Wissenschaftliche Zeitschrift der Paedagogischen Hochschule Potsdam. Gesellschafts- und Sprachwissenschaftliche Reihe

Wiss Z Paedagog Hochsch Karl Liebknecht (Potsdam) — Wissenschaftliche Zeitschrift. Paedagogische Hochschule Karl Liebknecht (Potsdam)

Wiss Z Rostock — Wissenschaftliche Zeitschrift. Universitaet Rostock

Wiss Z Zs TH (Dresd) — Wissenschaftliche Zeitschrift. Technische Hochschule (Dresden)

Wiss Z Tech Hochsch Carl Schorlemmer Leuna Merseburg — Wissenschaftliche Zeitschrift der Technischen Hochschule Carl Schorlemmer Leuna-Merseburg

Wiss Z Tech Hochsch Chem Carl Schorlemmer (Leuna-Merseburg) — Wissenschaftliche Zeitschrift. Technische Hochschule fuer Chemie "Carl Schorlemmer" (Leuna-Merseburg)

Wiss Z Tech Hochsch Chem (Leuna-Merseburg) — Wissenschaftliche Zeitschrift. Technische Hochschule fuer Chemie (Leuna-Merseburg)

Wiss Z Tech Hochsch (Dresden) — Wissenschaftliche Zeitschrift. Technische Hochschule (Dresden)

Wiss Z Tech Hochsch (Ilmenau) — Wissenschaftliche Zeitschrift. Technische Hochschule (Ilmenau, West Germany)

Wiss Z Tech Hochsch Karl-Marx-Stadt — Wissenschaftliche Zeitschrift. Technische Hochschule Karl-Marx-Stadt

Wiss Z Tech Hochsch Karl-Marx-Stadt Sonderh — Wissenschaftliche Zeitschrift. Technische Hochschule Karl-Marx-Stadt. Sonderheft

Wiss Z Tech Hochsch Koethen — Wissenschaftliche Zeitschrift. Technische Hochschule Koethen

Wiss Z Tech Hochsch (Leipzig) — Wissenschaftliche Zeitschrift. Technische Hochschule (Leipzig)

Wiss Z Tech Hochsch (Leuna-Merseburg) — Wissenschaftliche Zeitschrift. Technische Hochschule fuer Chemie "Carl Schorlemmer" (Leuna-Merseburg)

Wiss Z Tech Hochsch (Magdeburg) — Wissenschaftliche Zeitschrift. Technische Hochschule Otto Von Guericke (Magdeburg)

Wiss Z Tech Hochsch Otto v Guericke (Magdeburg) — Wissenschaftliche Zeitschrift. Technische Hochschule Otto Von Guericke (Magdeburg)

Wiss Z Tech Hochsch Otto Von Guericke — Wissenschaftliche Zeitschrift. Technische Hochschule Otto Von Guericke

Wiss Z Tech Hochsch Otto von Guericke (Magdeb) — Wissenschaftliche Zeitschrift. Technische Hochschule Otto Von Guericke (Magdeburg)

Wiss Z Tech Hochsch Otto von Guericke (Magdeburg) — Wissenschaftliche Zeitschrift. Technische Hochschule Otto Von Guericke (Magdeburg)

Wiss Z Techn Hochsch Chem (Leuna-Merseburg) — Wissenschaftliche Zeitschrift. Technische Hochschule fuer Chemie (Leuna-Merseburg)

Wiss Z Techn Hochsch (Ilmenau) — Wissenschaftliche Zeitschrift. Technische Hochschule (Ilmenau)

Wiss Z Techn Hochsch Karl-Marx-Stadt — Wissenschaftliche Zeitschrift. Technische Hochschule Karl-Marx-Stadt

Wiss Z Techn Hochsch (Leuna-Merseburg) — Wissenschaftliche Zeitschrift. Technische Hochschule (Leuna-Merseburg)

Wiss Z Techn Univ (Dresden) — Wissenschaftliche Zeitschrift. Technische Universitaet (Dresden)

Wiss Z Tech U Dresden — Wissenschaftliche Zeitschrift der Technischen Universitaet Dresden

Wiss Z Tech Univ Chemnitz — Wissenschaftliche Zeitschrift der Technischen Universitaet Chemnitz

Wiss Z Tech Univ Chemnitz Zwickau — Wissenschaftliche Zeitschrift der Technischen Universitaet Chemnitz-Zwickau

Wiss Z Tech Univ (Dres) — Wissenschaftliche Zeitschrift. Technische Universitaet (Dresden)

Wiss Z Tech Univ (Dresden) — Wissenschaftliche Zeitschrift. Technische Universitaet (Dresden)

Wiss Z Tech Univ Karl Marx Stadt — Wissenschaftliche Zeitschrift der Technischen Universitaet Karl-Marx-Stadt

Wiss Z Tech Univ Magdeburg — Wissenschaftliche Zeitschrift der Technischen Universitaet Otto von Guericke Magdeburg

Wiss Z TH Dresden — Wissenschaftliche Zeitschrift der Technischen Hochschule Dresden

Wiss Z Univ (Greifswald) — Wissenschaftliche Zeitschrift. Ernst-Moritz-Arndt-Universitaet (Greifswald)

Wiss Z Univ (Greifswald) Math-Naturwiss Reihe — Wissenschaftliche Zeitschrift. Ernst-Moritz-Arndt-Universitaet (Greifswald). Mathematisch-Naturwissenschaftliche Reihe

Wiss Z Univ (Halle) — Wissenschaftliche Zeitschrift. Martin-Luther-Universitaet (Halle-Wittenberg)

Wiss Z Univ (Halle-Wittenberg) Math-Naturwiss Reihe — Wissenschaftliche Zeitschrift. Martin-Luther-Universitaet (Halle-Wittenberg). Mathematisch-Naturwissenschaftliche Reihe

Wiss Z Univ (Jena) Math-Naturwiss Reihe — Wissenschaftliche Zeitschrift. Friedrich-Schiller-Universitaet (Jena). Mathematisch-Naturwissenschaftliche Reihe

Wiss Z Univ (Leipzig) Ges-u Sprachwiss R — Wissenschaftliche Zeitschrift. Karl-Marx-Universitaet (Leipzig). Gesellschafts-und Sprachwissenschaftliche Reihe

Wiss Z Univ (Leipzig) Math-Naturwiss Reihe — Wissenschaftliche Zeitschrift. Karl-Marx-Universitaet (Leipzig). Mathematisch-Naturwissenschaftliche Reihe

Wiss Z Univ Rostock Ges- & Sprachwiss Reihe — Wissenschaftliche Zeitschrift. Universitaet Rostock. Gesellschafts- und Sprachwissenschaftliche Reihe

Wiss Z Univ Rostock Ges Sprachwiss Reihe — Wissenschaftliche Zeitschrift. Universitaet Rostock. Gesellschafts- und Sprachwissenschaftliche Reihe

Wiss Z Univ Rostock Ges-Wiss — Wissenschaftliche Zeitschrift. Universitaet Rostock. Gesellschafts- und Wissenschaftliche Reihe

Wiss Z Univ Rostock Math-Natur Reihe — Universitaet Rostock. Wissenschaftliche Zeitschrift. Mathematisch-Naturwissenschaftliche Reihe

Wiss Z Univ Rostock Math Naturwiss — Wissenschaftliche Zeitschrift der Universitaet Rostock. Mathematisch- Naturwissenschaftliche Reihe

Wiss Z Univ Rostock Math Naturwiss Reihe — Wissenschaftliche Zeitschrift. Universitaet Rostock. Mathematisch-Naturwissenschaftliche Reihe

Wiss Z Univ Rostock Naturwiss Reihe — Wissenschaftliche Zeitschrift der Universitaet Rostock. Naturwissenschaftliche Reihe

Wiss Z Univ Rostock Reihe Math — Wissenschaftliche Zeitschrift der Universitaet Rostock. Reihe Mathematik/Naturwissenschaften

Wiss Z Univ Rostock Reihe Math Naturw — Wissenschaftliche Zeitschrift. Universitaet Rostock. Reihe Mathematik und Naturwissenschaften

Wiss Z U Rostock — Wissenschaftliche Zeitschrift der Universitaet Rostock

Wiss Z Wilhelm Pieck Univ Rostock — Wissenschaftliche Zeitschrift der Wilhelm-Pieck-Universitaet Rostock. Naturwissenschaftliche Reihe

Wiss Z Wilhelm-Pieck-Univ Rostock Math Naturwiss Reihe — Wissenschaftliche Zeitschrift der Wilhelm-Pieck-Universitaet Rostock Mathematisch-Naturwissenschaftliche Reihe

Wiss Z Wilhelm-Pieck-Univ Rostock Naturwiss Reihe — Wissenschaftliche Zeitschrift der Wilhelm-Pieck-Universitaet Rostock Naturwissenschaftliche Reihe

Wi St — Wirtschaftswissenschaftliches Studium

WisT — Wisconsin Then and Now

Wistar Inst Symp Monogr — Wistar Institute. Symposium. Monograph

Wi Stat — Wirtschaft und Statistik

Wi St G — Wirtschaftsstratgesetz

Wis U Bul Eng S — Bulletin. University of Wisconsin. Engineering Series

Wis Univ Coll Eng Eng Exp Stn Rep — Wisconsin University. College of Engineering. Engineering Experiment Station. Report

Wis Univ Dept Meteorology Rept Lakes and Streams Inv Comm — Wisconsin University. Department of Meteorology. Report to the Lakes and Streams Investigations Committee

Wis Univ Eng Exp Stn Bull — Wisconsin University. Engineering Experiment Station. Bulletin

Wis Univ Geol Nat Hist Surv Spec Rep — Wisconsin University. Geological and Natural History Survey. Special Report

Wis Univ Geol Natur Hist Surv Inform Circ — Wisconsin University. Geological and Natural History Survey. Information Circular

WisZE — Wissenschaftliche Zeitschrift der Ernst-Moritz-Arndt Universitaet Greifswald

WisZF — Wissenschaftliche Zeitschrift der Friedrich-Schiller Universitaet Jena

WisZH — Wissenschaftliche Zeitschrift der Humboldt Universitaet Berlin

WisZK — Wissenschaftliche Zeitschrift der Karl-Marx Universitaet Leipzig

WisZM — Wissenschaftliche Zeitschrift der Martin Luther Universitaet Halle-Wittenberg

WisZR — Wissenschaftliche Zeitschrift der Universitaet Rostock

WisZT — Wissenschaftliche Zeitschrift der Technische Universitaet Dresden

Wittheit Bremen Jahrb — Wittheit zu Bremen. Jahrbuch

Witt Schlesw-Holst — Witterung in Schleswig-Holstein

Wi u Stat — Wirtschaft und Statistik

WIV — Vakblad voor Textielreiniging

Wi Verw — Wirtschaftsverwaltung

WIW — Wer Informiert Woruber

Wi Wi — Wirtschaftswissenschaft

Wi Wiss — Wirtschaftswissenschaft

WIZ — Wiedza i Zycie
WIZ — Wort in der Zeit
WJ — Western Judean
WJ — Wiener Jahreshefte
WJ — Winterthur Jahrbuch
WJ — Wolfram-Jahrbuch
WJ — World Jewry
WJ — World Justice
WJ — Wuerzburger Jahrbuecher fuer die Altertumswissenschaft
WJA — Wuerzburger Jahrbuecher fuer die Altertumswissenschaft
W Jb — Wolfram-Jahrbuch
W J Barrow Res Lab Publ — W. J. Barrow Research Laboratory. Publication
W Jbb Alt — Wuerzburger Jahrbuecher fuer die Altertumswissenschaft
WJ Bl — Wiener Juristische Blaetter
WJCAR — World Jewish Congress. Annual Report
WJC/AS Bul — World Jewish Congress. Australian Section Bulletin
WJC/BS Rep — World Jewish Congress. British Section Report
WJCIB — World Jewish Congress. Information Bulletin
WJ f Kg — Wiener Jahrbuch fuer Kunstgeschichte
WJh — Wiener Jahreshefte
WJI — Wire Journal International
WJK — Wiener Jahrbuch fuer Kunstgeschichte
WJKG — Wiener Jahrbuch fuer Kunstgeschichte
WJMDA — Western Journal of Medicine
WJR — Washington Journalism Review
WJS — Watchmaker, Jeweller, and Silversmith
WJSC — Western Journal of Speech Communication
WJSUD — World Journal of Surgery
WJ Surg — Western Journal of Surgery, Obstetrics, and Gynecology
W J Surgery — Western Journal of Surgery [*Portland*]
WJT — World, Journal, and Tribune
WJURDJ — World Journal of Urology
Wkb Krb — Weekberichten van de Kredietbank
Wkbl Fisc R — Weekblad voor Fiscaal Recht
Wkbl Ned B Gemambt — Weekblad voor de Nederlandse Bond van Gemeenteambtenaren
Wkg Girls Newsl — Working with Girls Newsletter
W Klin Wschr — Wiener Klinische Wochenschrift
W Kl Ph — Wochenschrift fuer Klassische Philologie
W Kl Ws — Wiener Klinische Wochenschrift
Wkly Cin Law Bul — Weekly Cincinnati Law Bulletin
Wkly Coal — Weekly Coal Production
Wkly Dig — New York Weekly Digest
Wkly Energy Rep — Weekly Energy Report
Wkly Epidemiol Rec — Weekly Epidemiological Record
Wkly Illus — Weekly Illustrated
Wkly Inf Bull — Weekly Information Bulletin
Wkly Law Bul — Weekly Law Bulletin
Wkly Law Gaz — Weekly Law Gazette
Wkly L Bul — Weekly Law Bulletin
Wkly L Gaz — Weekly Law Gazette
Wkly NC — Weekly Notes of Cases
Wkly Notes Cas — Weekly Notes of Cases
Wkly Notes Cas (PA) — Weekly Notes of Cases
Wkly Rec — Weekly Record
Wkly Register — Weekly Register
Wkly Rep — Weekly Reporter
WKMIA — Wakayama Igaku
Wk N — Weekly Notes of Cases
WKNDDH — Annual Report. Research Institute for Wakan-Yaku Toyama Medical and Pharmaceutical University
WKP — Wochenschrift fuer Klassische Philologie
WKPh — Wochenschrift fuer Klassische Philologie
Wks Engng — Works Engineering
Wks Engng Fact Serv — Works Engineering and Factory Services
Wks Mgmt — Works Management
Wk Study — Work Study
Wk Study Mgmt Serv — Work Study and Management Services [*Later, Management Services*]
WKUBA — Werkstatt und Betrieb
WKW — Working Woman
WKWSA — Wiener Klinische Wochenschrift. Supplementum (Austria)
WL — Wydawnictwo Literackie
WL — Wydawnictwo Lodzkie
WLA — Wissenschaftlicher Literaturanzeiger
W Law Bul — Weekly Law Bulletin
WLB — Weekly Law Bulletin
WLB — Wiener Library Bulletin
WLB — Wilson Library Bulletin
WLB — Wisconsin Library Bulletin
WLBu — Wilson Library Bulletin
WL Bull — Weekly Law Bulletin
WL Bull (Ohio) — Weekly Law Bulletin
Wld Aerospace Syst — World Aerospace System
Wld Aff — World Affairs
Wld Aff Jnl — World Affairs Journal
Wld Aff Q — World Affairs Quarterly
Wld Anim Rev — World Animal Review
Wld Archaeol — World Archaeology
Wld Archaeol Bull — World Archaeological Bulletin
Wld Archaeology — World Archaeology
Wld Cem — World Cement
Wld Cem Tech — World Cement Technology [*Later, World Cement*]
Wld Chr Ed — World Christian Education
Wld Conf Med Educ — World Conference on Medical Education

Wld Conf Psych — World Conference of Psychiatry
Wld Crops — World Crops
Wld Develop — World Development
Wld Dev Rpt — World Development Report
Wld Drink R — World Drinks Report - World Food Report
Wld Econ — World Economy
Wld En Out — World Energy Outlook
Wld Fd & Drk — World Food and Drink Report
Wld Fd Probl — World Food Problems
Wld Fishg — World Fishing
Wld Food Rt — World Food Report
Wld For Congr — World Forestry Congress. Proceedings
Wld For Congr Proc — World Forestry Congress. Proceedings
Wld Gas Rpt — World Gas Report
Wld Gold — World Mine Production of Gold
Wld Grain Tr Stat — World Grain Trade Statistics
Wld Hlth — World's Health
Wld Hlth Org Publ Hlth Pap — World Health Organization. Public Health Papers
Wld Hlth Org Techn Rep Ser — World Health Organization. Technical Report Series
Wld Hunger — World Hunger
Wld Lic Rev — World License Review
Wld Marxist Rev — World Marxist Review
Wld Marx R — World Marxist Review
Wld Med — World Medicine
Wld Med Ass Bull — World Medical Association. Bulletin
Wld Med J — World Medical Journal
Wld Ment Heal — World Mental Health
Wld Mil Ex — World Military Expenditures and Arms Transfers
Wld Mining — World Mining Equipment
Wld Min Reg — World Mines Register
Wld Money — World Money Outlook
Wld Orchid Conf — World Orchid Conference
Wld P & PDem — World Pulp and Paper Demand, Supply, and Trade
Wld Pap Tr Rev — World's Paper Trade Review
Wld People — World and People
Wld Plast — World Plastics
Wld Pol — World Politics. A Quarterly Journal of International Relations
Wld Polit — World Politics
Wld Pollen Spore Flora — World Pollen and Spore Flora
Wld Poult Sci J — World's Poultry Science Journal
Wld Pumps — World Pumps
Wld Qtly Energ Rev — World Quarterly Energy Review
WLDRA — Welder
Wld Raw Mat — World Demand for Raw Materials in 1985 and 2000
Wld Refrig Air Condit — World Refrigeration and Air Conditioning
Wld Rev — World Review
Wld Rev Pest Control — World Review of Pest Control
Wld Sci Rev — World Science Reviews
Wld Silver — World Production of Silver
Wld's Pap Trade Rev — World's Paper Trade Review
Wld Surv — World Survey
Wld Ten — World Tennis
Wld Tobacco — World Tobacco
Wld Today — World Today
Wld Trade — World Trade. Computer Age
Wld Trade Un Mov — World Trade Union Movement
Wld Trav — World Traveler
Wld Vet Abstr J — World Veterinary Abstracting Journal
Wld Wast — Management of World Waste
Wld Wide Abstr Gen Med — World-Wide Abstracts of General Medicine
Wld Work — World's Work
Wld Work Rep — World of Work Report
Wld Yrbk Educ — World Yearbook of Education
W LF — Women's Law Forum
WLF — Worklife
WLFMA — Welding and Metal Fabrication
WLG — Weekly Law Gazette
WLG — Wiener Linguistische Gazette
WL Gaz — Weekly Law Gazette (Reprint)
WL Gaz (Ohio) — Weekly Law Gazette (Ohio)
WLHPA — Wu Li Hsueh Pao
W Lit — World Literature Written in English
WLJ — Washburn Law Journal
WLJ — Western Law Journal
WLJ — Willamette Law Journal
WLJ — Wyoming Law Journal
WL Jour — Washburn Law Journal
WL Jour — Western Law Journal
WL Jour — Willamette Law Journal
WL Jour — Wyoming Law Journal
WLLR — Washington and Lee Law Review
WLM — Western Law Monthly
WLN — Wired Librarian's Newsletter
WLN — Writing Lab Newsletter
WLNED — Water Law Newsletter
WLNL — Wellness Newsletter
W Lond Med J — West London Medical Journal
WLP — Western Legal Publications Database
WLQ — Washington University. Law Quarterly
WLR — Washington Law Review
WLR — Wasser, Luft, und Betrieb. Zeitschrift fuer Umwelttechnik
WLR — Wisconsin Law Review
WLR — World Law Review
WLSBA — Wildlife Society. Bulletin

WLSH — Wochenblatt der Landesbauernschaft Schleswig-Holstein
WLSP — World List of Scientific Periodicals
WLT — Western Law Times
WLT — World Literature Today
WLub — Wydawnictwo Lubelskie
WLWE — World Literature Written in English
WM — Washington Monthly
WM — Wertpapier-Mitteilungen
WM — Westermanns Monatshefte
WM — Wissenschaftliche Mittheilungen aus Bosnien und der Herzegowina
WM — Works Management
WM — World Meetings
WM — World Mission
WM — World of Music
W Mail — Western Mail
W Mail Ann — Western Mail Annual
Wm and Mary L Rev — William and Mary Law Review
Wm & Mary Q — William and Mary Quarterly
Wm And Mary Quar — William and Mary College Quarterly Historical Magazine
Wm & Mary Rev VA L — William and Mary Review of Virginia Law
WMANT — Wissenschaftliche Monographien zum Alten und Neuen Testament
W Mass Bus — Western Massachusetts Business Journal
WMB — Women in Business
WMBH — Wissenschaftliche Mittheilungen aus Bosnien und der Herzegowina
WMCQ — William and Mary College. Quarterly
WMD — Water Mineral Development
W M Day Studies — Romance Studies Presented to William Morton Day
WMH — Wine Marketing Handbook
WMH — Wisconsin Magazine of History
WMHE — Women and Health
WML — Willamette Law Journal
Wm LJ — Willamette Law Journal
WMLR — William and Mary Law Review
WMLR — William Mitchell Law Review
Wm Mar Q — William and Mary Quarterly
Wm Mitchell L Rev — William Mitchell Law Review
WMMTA — World Minerals and Metals
WMN — Western Morning News
WMNI — Wildlife Management News (Iceland)
Wmn Lib — Women's Liberation
WMOBA — WMO [*World Meteorological Organization*] Bulletin
WMO Bull — WMO [*World Meteorological Organization*] Bulletin
W Monthly Mag — Western Monthly Magazine and Literary Journal
WMO Publ — WMO [*World Meteorological Organization*] Publication
WMO Rep Mar Sci Aff — World Meteorological Organization. Reports on Marine Science Affairs
WMO Spec Environ Rep — World Meteorological Organization. Special Environmental Report
WMO Tech Note — World Meteorological Organization. Technical Note
WMQ — William and Mary Quarterly
WMR — William and Mary Review of Virginia Law
WMR — World Marxist Review
WMSJ — William Morris Society. Journal
WMT — Auslandmerkte/Marches Etrangers
WMWG — Weichselland, Mitteilungen des Westpreussischen Geschichtsvereins
WMWOA — Wiener Medizinische Wochenschrift
WMY — Weird Mystery
WN — Calcutta Weekly Notes
WN — Wake Newsletter
WN — Wawatay News
WN — Weekblad voor het Notariaat
WN — Weekly Notes of English Law Reports
WN — Wiadomosci Numizmatyczne
WNA — Welcome to the North Atlantic
WNA — Wiadomosci Numizmatyczno-Archeologiczne
WNBGA — Weekblad voor de Nederlandse Bond van Gemeenteambtenaren
WNC — Weekly Notes of Cases
WN (Calc) — Calcutta Weekly Notes
WN Cas — Weekly Notes of Cases
WN Cas (PA) — Weekly Notes of Cases
WN Covers (NSW) — Weekly Notes Covers (New South Wales)
WNC (PA) — Weekly Notes of Cases
WN (Eng) — Weekly Notes of English Law Reports
W N Eng LR — Western New England Law Review
W New Eng L Rev — Western New England Law Review
WNID — Webster's New International Dictionary
WNJ — Whitman Numismatic Journal
Wn L — Wayne Law Review
Wn LR — Washington Law Review
Wn LR — Wayne Law Review
WN Misc — Weekly Notes, Miscellaneous
WNNR Spes Versl — WNNR [*Suid-Afrikaanse Wetenskaplike en Nywerheidnavorsingsraad*] SpesialeVerslag
WN (NSW) — Weekly Notes (New South Wales)
WNR — Weekblad voor Notaris-Ambt en Registratie
WNS — Technieuws Washington. Korte Berichten op Technisch Wetenschappelijk Gebied
WNT — Foreign Trade
Wn T — Washington Territory Reports
WNT — What's New in Travel
Wntr Sldr — Winter Soldier
WO — Welt des Orients
WO — World of Opera
WO — World Oil
WOB — World of Banking

WOC — Work and Occupations
WOC — World Coal
Wochbl Papierfabr — Wochenblatt fuer Papierfabrikation
Wochenbl Viehzucht — Wochenblatt der Viehzucht
Wochenschr Brau — Wochenschrift fuer Brauerei
Woch Klass Philol — Wochenschrift fuer Klassische Philologie
Woch Kl Phil — Wochenschrift fuer Klassische Philologie
Woch Kl Philol — Wochenschrift fuer Klassische Philologie
Woch Pap Fab — Wochenblatt fuer Papierfabrikation
Wochschr Architekten Ver Berlin — Wochenschrift des Architekten-Vereins zu Berlin
WOCOD — World Coal
WODCON — World Organization of Dredging Associations Proceedings of World Dredging Congress
WODED — World Development
WOE — World Economy
Woechentl Nachr Gel Sachen — Woechentliche Nachrichten von Gelehrten Sachen
Woelm Publ — Woelm Publication
Woert Sach — Woerter und Sachen
WOF — Worlds of Fantasy
WOHE — World Health
Wojsk Inst Chem Radiom Biul — Wojskowy Instytut Chemii i Radiometrii, Biuletyn
Wojsk Przegl Tech — Wojskowy Przeglad Techniczny
WOL — Weird and Occult Library
WOL — Worklife
Wolfen-Buetteler B — Wolfenbuetteler Beitraege
Wolfenbuetteler Forsch — Wolfenbuetteler Forschungen
Wolfenbuetteler Stud Aufklaerung — Wolfenbuetteler Studien zur Aufklaerung
Wolfenbuttel Barock Nachr — Wolfenbutteler Barock Nachrichten
Wolfenbuttel Beitr — Wolfenbutteler Beitraege
Wolfenbuttel Forsch — Wolfenbutteler Forschungen
Wolkenkratzer A J — Wolkenkratzer Art Journal
Wollen- Leinen-Ind — Wollen- und Leinen-Industrie
WoM — World of Music
WOMAA — Works Management
Woman Art J — Woman's Art Journal
Woman Cit — Woman Citizen
Woman Exec Bull — Woman Executive's Bulletin
Woman Home C — Woman's Home Companion
Womans A J — Woman's Art Journal
Womans City Club Bul Chicago — Woman's City Club Bulletin (Chicago)
Woman's H C — Woman's Home Companion
Woman's J — Woman's Journal
Womans Leader London — Woman's Leader and Common Cause (London)
Women — Women/Poems
Women and Hist — Women and History
Women and L — Women and Law
Women & Lit — Women and Literature
Women & Ther — Women and Therapy
Women Coach Clin — Women's Coaching Clinic
Women Hlth Mag — Women's Health Magazine
Women Law J — Women Lawyers Journal
Women Lawyers J — Women Lawyers Journal
Women Lit — Women and Literature
Women L Jour — Women Lawyers Journal
Women L Jour — Women's Law Journal
Women of Eur — Women of Europe
Women Peace Offic Assn Calif Yrbk — Women Peace Officers Association of California. Yearbook
Women Pol — Women and Politics
Women Rev — Women and Revolution
Women Rights L Rep — Women's Rights Law Reporter
Womens A Mag — Women's Art Magazine
Women's Bur Bull — Women's Bureau Bulletin
Women's LJ — Women's Law Journal
Women's Review — Women's Review of Books
Women's Rights L Rep — Women's Rights Law Reporter
Women's Rights L Reptr — Women's Rights Law Reporter
Women's Rights L Rptr — Women's Rights Law Reporter
Women's Rts L Rep Rutgers Univ — Women's Rights Law Reporter. Rutgers University
Women's Stud Assoc Conf Pap — Women's Studies Association. Conference Papers
Women's Studies — Women's Studies: An Interdisciplinary Journal
Womens Stud Interdiscip J — Women's Studies. An Interdisciplinary Journal
Womens Studs Newsl — Women's Studies Newsletter
Women Stud — Women's Studies: An Interdisciplinary Journal
Women Stud Abstr — Women Studies Abstracts
Women Stud Abstracts — Women Studies Abstracts
Women Stud Int Forum — Womens' Studies International Forum
Women Wear — Women's Wear Daily
Women Wkrs Bull — Women Workers Bulletin
WomHealth — Women and Health
Wom March — Women on the March
Womn Prss — Women's Press
Womn Rgts — Women's Rights Law Reporter
Womn Sprt — Womanspirit
WOMUA — World of Music
W Ont L Rev — Western Ontario Law Review
Wood & Wood Prod — Wood and Wood Products
Wood Brass Perc — Woodwind, Brass, and Percussion
Wood Fiber Sci J Soc Wood Sci Technol — Wood and Fiber Science. Journal. Society of Wood Science and Technology
Wood Ind — Wood Industry

Woodlds Res Index — Woodlands Research Index. Pulp and Paper Research Institute of Canada
Woodl Pap Pulp Pap Res Inst Can — Woodlands Papers. Pulp and Paper Research Institute of Canada
Woodl Res Note Union Camp Corp — Woodland Research Notes. Union Camp Corporation
Woodl Sect Index Canad Pulp Pap Ass — Woodlands Section Index. Canadian Pulp and Paper Association
Wood Mag — Woodwind Magazine
Wood Preserv — Wood Preserving
Wood Preserv (Chicago) — Wood Preserving (Chicago)
Wood Preserv N — Wood Preserving News
Wood Preserv News — Wood Preserving News
Wood Pres Rep For Prod Res Ind Developm Comm (Philippines) — Wood Preservation Report. Forest Products Research and Industries Development Commission College (Laguna, Philippines)
Wood Prod — Wood and Wood Products
Wood Res — Wood Research
Wood Sci — Wood Science
Wood Sci Te — Wood Science and Technology
Wood Sci Technol — Wood Science and Technology
Woods Hole Oceanogr Inst Annu Rep — Woods Hole Oceanographic Institution. Annual Report
Woods Hole Oceanogr Inst Annu Sea Grant Rep — Woods Hole Oceanographic Institution. Annual Sea Grant Report
Woods Hole Oceanogr Inst Collect Reprints — Woods Hole Oceanographic Institution. Collected Reprints
Woods Hole Oceanogr Inst Tech Rep — Woods Hole Oceanographic Institution. Technical Report
Wood South Afr — Wood Southern Africa
Wood Sthn Afr — Wood Southern Africa
Wood Tech — Wood Technic
Woodwind B — Woodwind, Brass, and Percussion
Woodwkg Ind — Woodworking Industry
Wood Wood Prod — Wood and Wood Products
Wood World — Woodwind World [*Later, Woodwind World - Brass and Percussion*]
Wood World-Brass — Woodwind World - Brass and Percussion
Woody Plant Biotechnol — Woody Plant Biotechnology
Woolh FC T — Transactions of the Woolhope Naturalists' Field Club
Woolhope Naturalists Field Club Trans — Woolhope Naturalists' Field Club Transactions
Wool Rec — Wool Record
Wool Rec — Wool Record and Textile World [*Later, Wool Record*]
Wool Rec Text World — Wool Record and Textile World
Wool Sci Rev — Wool Science Review
Wool Tech — Wool Technology and Sheep Breeding
Wool Tech & Sheep — Wool Technology and Sheep Breeding
Wool Tech & Sheep Breeding — Wool Technology and Sheep Breeding
Wool Technol — Wool Technology and Sheep Breeding
Wool Technol Sheep Breed — Wool Technology and Sheep Breeding
Wool Technol (Syd) — Wool Technology (Sydney)
Woolwld — Woolworld
Woolw P — Minutes of Proceedings of the Royal Artillery Institution (Woolwich)
Woo Sok Univ Med J — Woo Sok University. Medical Journal
Wo Peo — Work and People
WOPHA — Woman Physician
WOPOP — WOPOP: Working Papers on Photography
WOR — Wool Record and Textile World
WoR — World Review
Wor — Worldview
Worcester A Mus Annu — Worcester Art Museum Annual
Worcester A Mus Bull — Worcester Art Museum Bulletin
Worcester A Mus J — Worcester Art Museum Journal
Worcester Hist Soc Pub — Worcester Historical Society Publications
Worcester Med News — Worcester Medical News
Worcester Mus Ann — Worcester, Massachusetts. Worcester Art Museum. Annual
Worcester Museum News — News Bulletin and Calendar. Worchester Art Museum
Worcester Mus N Bul — Worcester, Massachusetts. Worcester Art Museum. News Bulletin and Calendar
Worc M — Worcester Magazine
Word and Inf Process — Word and Information Processing
Word Proc — Word Processing and Information Systems
Word Process and Inf Syst — Word Processing and Information Systems
Word Process Comput Inf Systems — Word Processing Computer Information Systems
Word Process Now — Word Processing Now
Word Process Syst — Word Processing Systems
Word Process World — Word Processing World
WordsC — Wordsworth Circle
Wordsworth — Wordsworth Circle
Word W — Word Watching
WORKD — Worklife
Work-Environ-Health — Work-Environment-Health
Working Papers — Working Papers for a New Society
Working Pap Ser Calif Agric Exp Stn Dep Agric Resour Econ — Working Paper Series. California Agricultural Experiment Station. Department of Agricultural and Resource Economics
Workmen's Comp L Rep CCH — Workmen's Compensation Law Reports. Commerce Clearing House
Workmen's Comp L Rev — Workmen's Compensation Law Review
Workm Insur Ser — Workman's Insurance Series
Work Pap Agric Econ — Working Papers in Agricultural Economics
Work Pap Aust Arid Zone Res Conf — Working Papers. Australian Arid Zone Research Conference

Work Pap Aust Cereal Pasture Plant Breed Conf — Working Papers. Australian Cereal and Pasture Plant Breeding Conference
Work Pap Bur Meteorol — Working Paper. Bureau of Meteorology
Work Papers — Working Papers Magazine
Work Pap Giannini Found Agric Econ Calif Agric Exp Stn — Working Paper. Giannini Foundation of Agricultural Economics. California Agricultural Experiment Station
Work Pap Lang Linguist — Working Papers in Language and Linguistics
Work Pap Ling (H) — Working Papers in Linguistics (Honolulu)
Work Pap New Soc — Working Papers for a New Society
Work Plant Maint — Work and Plant Maintenance
Work Prog — Work in Progress
Work Rel Abstr — Work Related Abstracts
Work Relat Abstr — Work Related Abstracts
Works and Plant Maint — Works and Plant Maintenance
Works Eng — Works Engineering
Works Eng Fact Serv — Works Engineering and Factory Services
Workshop Adv Methods Pharmacokinet Pharmacodyn Syst Anal — Workshop on Advanced Methods of Pharmacokinetic and Pharmacodynamic Systems Analysis
Workshop Comput Chem — Workshop Computers in Chemistry
Workshop Conf Hoechst — Workshop Conferences Hoechst
Workshop Enzymes Aquat Environ — Workshop on Enzymes in Aquatic Environments
Workshop Failure Anal Corros Eval Metallogr — Workshop on Failure Analysis, Corrosion Evaluation, and Metallography
Workshop High Temp Corros Adv Mater Prot Coat — Workshop on High Temperature Corrosion of Advanced Materials and Protective Coatings
Workshop Intense Hadron Facil Antiproton Phys — Workshop on Intense Hadron Facilities and Antiproton Physics
Workshop Interfaces New Mater — Workshop Interfaces in New Materials
Workshop Mater Sci Phys Non Conv Energy Sources — Workshop on Materials Science and Physics of Non-Conventional Energy Sources
Workshop Phase Sep Ordering — Workshop on Phase Separation with Ordering
Workshop Proc Int Workshop Act Matrix Liq Cryst Disp — Workshop Proceedings. International Workshop on Active Matrix Liquid Crystal Displays
Workshops Comput — Workshops in Computing
Workshop Ser Pharmacol Sect Nat Inst Ment Health — Workshop Series. Pharmacology Section. National Institute of Mental Health
Workshop Tungsten Other Adv Met ULSI Appl — Workshop on Tungsten and Other Advanced Metals for ULSI Applications
Works Inst Higher Nerv Act Acad Sci USSR Pathophysiol Ser — Works. Institute of Higher Nervous Activity. Academy of Sciences of the USSR. Pathophysiological Series
Works Inst Higher Nerv Act Acad Sci USSR Physiol Ser — Works. Institute of Higher Nervous Activity. Academy of Sciences of the USSR. Physiological Series
Works Inst Higher Nerv Act Pathophysiol Ser — Works. Institute of Higher Nervous Activity. Pathophysiological Series
Works Inst Higher Nerv Act Physiol Ser — Works. Institute of Higher Nervous Activity. Physiological Series
Works Pavlov Inst Physiol Acad Sci USSR — Works. Pavlov Institute of Physiology. Academy of Sciences of the USSR
Works Stud Water Res Inst Bratislava — Works and Studies. Water Research Institute Bratislava
Work Stud Abstr — Work Study and O and M Abstracts
Work Study and Manage Serv — Work Study and Management Services [*Later, Management Services*]
Work Vang — Workers Vanguard
Work Wom — Working Woman
World — National Geographic World
World — World Magazine
World A — World Archaeology
World Aff — World Affairs
World Affairs J — World Affairs. Journal
World Aff J — World Affairs
World Aff Q — World Affairs. Quarterly
World Ag — World Agriculture
World Agr — World Agriculture
World Agric — World Agriculture
World Agric Econ — World Agricultural Economics and Rural Sociology Abstracts
World Agri Econ & Rural Sociol Abstr — World Agricultural Economics and Rural Sociology Abstracts
World Alum Abstr — World Aluminum Abstracts
World Anim Rev — World Animal Review
World Anthropol — World Anthropology
World Archa — World Archaeology
World Archaeol — World Archaeology
World Archit — World Architecture
World Assn for Adult Ed B — World Association for Adult Education. Bulletin
World Bibl Social Security — World Bibliography of Social Security
World Bus W — World Business Weekly
World Cem — World Cement
World Cem Technol — World Cement Technology [*Later, World Cement*]
World Commod Rep Met Ed — World Commodity Report. Metals Edition
World Conf Earthquake Eng Proc — World Conference on Earthquake Engineering. Proceedings
World Congr In Vitro Fert Assisted Reprod — World Congress on In Vitro Fertilization and Assisted Reproduction
World Constr — World Construction
World Crops Prod Util Descr — World Crops Production Utilization Description
World Dev — World Development
World Devel — World Development
World Dist — World Distribution
World Dredging & Mar Const — World Dredging and Marine Construction

World Dredging Mar Constr — World Dredging and Marine Construction
World Econ — World Economy
World Eco S — World Economic Survey. Supplement
World Educ Rep — World Education Reports
World Energy Conf Trans — World Energy Conference. Transactions
World Farm — World Farming
World Fertil Surv Ctry Rep — World Fertility Survey. Country Reports
World Fertil Surv Sci Rep — World Fertility Survey. Scientific Reports
World Fert Surv — World Fertility Survey
World Fish Abstr — World Fisheries Abstracts
World For Ser Bull — World Forestry Series. Bulletin
World Health Organ Chron — World Health Organization. Chronicle
World Health Organ Tech Rep Ser — World Health Organization. Technical Report Series
World Health Stat Q — World Health Statistics. Quarterly
World Health Stat Rep — World Health Statistics. Report
World Highw — World Highways
World Hosp — World Hospitals
World Ir Nurs — World of Irish Nursing
World Jnl Trib — World Journal Tribune
World J Surg — World Journal of Surgery
World J Urol — World Journal of Urology
World Jus — World Justice
World List Pub Stds — Worldwide List of Published Standards
World Lit T — World Literature Today
World Lit Today — World Literature Today
World L Rev — World Law Review
World M — World of Music
World Marxist R — World Marxist Review
World Marx R — World Marxist Review
World Marx Rev — World Marxist Review
World Med — World Medicine
World Med Electron — World Medical Electronics
World Med Instrum — World Medical Instrumentation
World Med J — World Medical Journal
World Meet Outside US Can — World Meetings: Outside United States and Canada
World Meet Outs US Can — World Meetings: Outside United States and Canada
World Meet US Can — World Meetings: United States and Canada
World Metal Statis — World Metal Statistics
World Meteorol Organ Bull — World Meteorological Organization. Bulletin
World Meteorol Organ Publ — World Meteorological Organization. Publications
World Min — World Mining
World Min Equip — World Mining Equipment
World Miner Met — World Minerals and Metals
World Miner Stat — World Mineral Statistics
World Min US Ed — World Mining. United States Edition
World Mus — World of Music
World Neurol — World Neurology
World O — World Order
World Obstet Gynecol — World of Obstetrics and Gynecology
World Oil — World Oil Forecast. Review Issue
World Outl — World Outlook
World Pap — World Paper
World Patent Inf — World Patent Information
World Pet — World Petroleum
World Pet Cong Prepr — World Petroleum Congress. Preprints
World Pet Congr Proc — World Petroleum Congress. Proceedings
World Petrol — World Petroleum
World Pol — World Policy
World Pol — World Politics
World Poult — World's Poultry Science Journal
World Poultry Sci J — World's Poultry Science Journal
World Press R — World Press Review
World R — World Review
World Refrig — World Refrigeration
World Rep — World Report
World Resour — World Resources
World Res Ser — World Resources Series
World Rev — World Review
World Rev Anim Prod — World Review of Animal Production
World Rev Nutr Diet — World Review of Nutrition and Dietetics
World Rev Pest Contr — World Review of Pest Control
World Rev Pest Control — World Review of Pest Control
World R Pest Control — World Review of Pest Control
World's Butter Rev — World's Butter Review
World Sci Adv Ser Dyn Syst — World Scientific Advanced Series in Dynamical Systems
World Sci Lecture Notes Phys — World Scientific Lecture Notes in Physics
World Sci News — World Science News
World Sci Ser 20th Century Math — World Scientific Series in 20th Century Mathematics
World Sci Ser 20th Century Phys — World Scientific Series in 20th Century Physics
World Sci Ser Appl Anal — World Scientific Series in Applicable Analysis
World Sci Ser Comput Sci — World Scientific Series in Computer Science
World Sci Ser Contemp Chem Phys — World Scientific Series in Contemporary Chemical Physics
World Sci Ser Dir Condensed Matter Phys — World Scientific Series on Directions in Condensed Matter Physics
World Sci Ser Nonlinear Sci Ser A Monogr Treatises — World Scientific Series on Nonlinear Science. Series A. Monographs and Treatises
World Sci Ser Nonlinear Sci Ser B — World Scientific Series on Nonlinear Science. Series B. Special Theme Issues and Proceedings

World Sci Ser Nonlinear Sci Ser B Spec Theme Issues Proc — World Scientific Series on Nonlinear Science. Series B. Special Theme Issues and Proceedings
World Sci Ser Robot Intell Systems — World Scientific Series in Robotics and Intelligent Systems
World's Pap Trade Rev — World's Paper Trade Review
World's Poultry Cong Conf Papers Sect C — World's Poultry Congress. Conference Papers. Section C
World's Poultry Sci J — World's Poultry Science Journal
World's Poult Sci J — World's Poultry Science Journal
World Steel (Jpn) — World of Steel (Japan)
World Steel Metalwork Export Man — World Steel and Metalworking Export Manual
World Stud — World Studies Journal
World Surface Coat Abs — World Surface Coatings Abstracts
World Surf Coat — World Surface Coatings Abstracts
World Surf Coat Abstr — World Surface Coatings Abstracts
World Surv — World Survey
Worlds Wk — World's Work
World Text Abstr — World Textile Abstracts
World Textile Abs — World Textile Abstracts
World Textile Abstr — World Textile Abstracts
World Tr — World Trade
World Trade LJ — World Trade Law Journal
Worldwatch Pap — Worldwatch Paper
Worldwide Abstr — Worldwide Abstracts
Worldwide List Published Stand — Worldwide List of Published Standards
World-Wide MinAbs — World-Wide Mining Abstracts
Worldwide Nucl Power — Worldwide Nuclear Power
World Wide Web J Biol — World Wide Web Journal of Biology [*Electronic Publication*]
World Yr Bk Ed — World Yearbook of Education
Wormald J — Wormald Journal
Worm R — Wormwood Review
Worm Runner's Dig — Worm Runner's Digest
Wor Pol — World Politics
Wor R — World Review
WORSE9 — World Resources
Wort — Woerterbuch der Aegyptischen Sprache
Worth Star T — Fort Worth Star-Telegram
Wort U Wahrheit — Wort und Wahrheit
Wort Wahr — Wort und Wahrheit
WOS — Wonders of the Spaceways
WOT — Worlds of Tomorrow
WoTh — World Theatre
WOTHDJ — Women and Therapy
WOTRAC — Woods Hole Oceanographic Institution. Technical Report
Wound Repair Regen — Wound Repair and Regeneration
WOW — Welt des Orients (Wuppertal and Goettingen)
WOW — Wereld in Ontwikkeling. Veertiendaags Overzicht van Tijdschriftartikelen en Rapporten over Problemen van de Ontwikkelingsgebieden
WOW — World of Winners
Wow — Wort und Wahrheit
WoWa — Wort und Wahrheit
WOWBDG — Instytut Zootechniki w Polsce Wyniki Oceny Wartosci Hodowlanej Buhajow
WP — Waende Pompejis. Topographisches Verzeichnis der Bildmotive
WP — Waman Puma
WP — Washington Post
WP — Wiedza Powszechna
WP — Woodstock Papers
WP — Work in Progress
WP — World Petroleum
WP — World Politics
WPA — Journal of the Council of Writing Program Administrators
WPA — World Press Archives
W PA Hist Mag — Western Pennsylvania Historical Magazine
W Pakistan J Agr Res — West Pakistan Journal of Agricultural Research
W Papuan Issues — West Papuan Issues
WPBW — Washington Post Book World
WPCF — Water Pollution Control Federation. Journal
WPCF Highlights — Water Pollution Control Federation. Highlights
WPCFJ — Water Pollution Control Federation. Journal
WPC III — Third World Petroleum Congress. The Hague, 1951. Proceedings
WP DATA — World Petrochemicals
WPE — Work and People
WPEC — West Pakistan Engineering Congress
W Petro 2000 — World Petroleum Availability 1980-2000
WPF — Wirtschaftspruefung
WPFDM — Working Papers. Fondazione Dalle Molle
WPFJ — West Punjab Fruit Journal
WPHM — Western Pennsylvania Historical Magazine
WPHUJ — Working Papers. Hebrew University of Jerusalem
WPI — World Patents Index
WP/IS — Word Processing and Information Systems
WPL — Working Papers in Linguistics
WPLL — Washington (State). University. Publications in Language and Literature
WPLU — Working Papers. Lund University. Department of Linguistics
WPLUH — Working Papers in Linguistics (University of Hawaii)
WPN — World's Press News
WPNGL — Workpapers in Papua New Guinea Languages
WPNR — Weekblad voor Privaatrecht, Notariaat, en Registratie
WPOC — Water and Pollution Control
WPOCA — Water Pollution Control
W Pol Q — Western Political Quarterly

WPP — UCLA [*University of California at Los Angeles*] Working Papers in Phonetics
WPQ — Western Political Quarterly
WPR — Weekblad voor Privaatrecht, Notariaat, en Registratie
WPR — Weekly Pharmacy Reports: The Green Sheet
WPRCDZ — International Conference on Water Pollution Research. Proceedings
WPT — Paper. European Journal for the Pulp, Paper, and Board Industries
WPYEEJS — Working Papers in Yiddish and East European Jewish Studies
WPZ — Wiener Praehistorische Zeitschrift
WQ — Science Wonder Quarterly
WQ — Wilson Quarterly
WQ — Wind Quarterly
WQ — Wonder Stories Quarterly
WQ — Wool Quarterly
WR — Journal of Water Resources Planning and Management
WR — Sutherland's Weekly Report
WR — Washington Report. News and World Report Newsletter
WR — Weekly Record
WR — Weekly Reporter
WR — Weekly Reporter, Cape Provincial Division
WR — Weekly Review
WR — Welsh Review
WR — Western Review
WR — Westminster Review
WR — Wiseman Review
WR — Women's Review
WR — World Reporter
WRA — Water Resources Abstracts
WRA — Work Related Abstracts
WRABD — Wilhelm Roux' Archives of Developmental Biology
WRABDT — Roux's Archives of Developmental Biology
WRAMC Prog Notes — WRAMC [*Walter Reed Army Medical Center*] Progress Notes
WRAP — World Risk Analysis Package
WR Calc — Sutherland's Weekly Reporter, Calcutta
WRC Inf — WRC [*Water Research Centre*] Information
WRC Research Report — Water Resources Center. Research Report
WRD — Words
WRD — World's Fair
WRE — Tokyo Financial Review
W Reg R — Wetboek van Registratierechten
Wren Soc — Wren Society
WREP West Reg Ext Publ Coop Ext Serv — WREP. Western Region Extension Publication. Cooperative Extension Service
WRERA — Water Resources Research
W Res L Rev — Western Reserve Law Review
Wrest — Wrestling USA
W R Far East — Weekly Review of the Far East
WRH — Washington Report on the Hemisphere
WRI — Water-Resources Investigation
WRI Rep — WRI [*Wattle Research Institute*] Report
WRIS Technical Bulletin — Water Resources Information System. Technical Bulletin
Writ Am Hist — Writings on American History
Writ Cent S — Writers of the 21st Century. Series
Writ Ring — Writers' Ring
WRJ — Wallraf-Richartz-Jahrbuch
WRJCD9 — Water Pollution Research Journal of Canada
Wrk Paper — Working Papers for a New Society
Wrk Power — Workers Power
Wrk World — Workers' World
WRL — Western Reserve Law Review
WRL — Westminster Review (London)
W R LR — Women's Rights Law Reporter
WRLRAR — University of Wisconsin. Water Resources Center. Eutrophication Information Program. Literature Review
Wrocl Zap Num — Wroclawskie Zapiski Numizmatyczne
WROPA2 — University of Wisconsin. Water Resources Center. Eutrophication Information Program. Occasional Paper
W Roux A DB — Wilhelm Roux' Archives of Developmental Biology
WRP — United States News and World Report
WRp — World Reporter
WRRC — Women's Research and Resources Centre Newsletter
WRRC Report (Washington) — Water Resources Research Center. Report (Washington)
WRRC Spec Rep Univ MD — WRRC [*Water Resources Research Center*] Special Report. University of Maryland
WRRI Auburn Univ Bull — WRRI [*Water Resources Research Institute*]. Auburn University. Bulletin
WRU — Western Reserve University. Bulletin
WRZAA — Weltraumfahrt und Raketentechnik
Wrzb Jhrb — Wuerzburger Jahrbuecher fuer die Altertumswissenschaft
WS — Welt der Slaven
WS — Western Speech
WS — Wiener Studien
WS — Windspeaker
WS — Woerter und Sachen
WS — Women's Studies: An Interdisciplinary Journal
WS — Women's Studies International Forum
WS — Wonder Stories
WS — Word Study
WS — Wort und Sinn
WSA — Intereconomics. Monthly Review of International Trade and Development
WSA — Wolfenbuetteler Studien zur Aufklarung
WSA — Women Studies Abstracts

WSA — Wonder Story Annual
WSAH — World Smoking and Health
WS and H — World Smoking and Health
WSB — API [*American Petroleum Institute*] Weekly Statistical Bulletin
Wsb — Washburn Law Journal
WSBU — Wahlenbergia. Scripta Botanica Umensia
WSC — Ebareport. Weekly Special Survey of Turkish Business, Industrial Investment, and Contracts Markets
WSC — Wall Street Computer Review
WSC — Wen Shih Che
WSC — Western Snow Conference. Proceedings
WSC — World Survey of Climatology
WSCA — World Surface Coatings Abstracts
WSCF Books — World Student Christian Federation Books
WSCHP — Wen Shih Che Hsueh-Pao
Wschr Ges Hlkde — Wochenschrift fuer die Gesammte Heilkunde
WSCL — Wisconsin Studies in Contemporary Literature [*Later, Contemporary Literature*]
WSCPA — Western States Section. Combustion Institute. Paper
WSCS — Washington State College. Studies
WSD — Wirtschaftsdienst. Wirtschaftspolitische Monatsschrift
WSHPA8 — Acta Microbiologica Sinica
WSI — Women's Studies Index
WSIA J — WSIA [*Water Supply Improvement Association*] Journal
WSIA Journal — Water Supply Improvement Association. Journal
WSI Mitt — WSI [*Wirtschafts- und Sozialwissenschaftliches Institut*] Mitteilungen
WSJ — Wall Street Journal
WSJ — Wiener Slawistisches Jahrbuch
WSJ — WSFA [*Washington Science Fiction Association*] Journal
WSJ Europe — Wall Street Journal. European Edition
WSJHQ — Western States Jewish Historical Quarterly
WSJ NJ — Wall Street Journal 3 Star. Eastern (Princeton, NJ) Edition
W S Jour — Wallace Stevens Journal
WSK — Waste Age
WSL — University of Wisconsin Studies in Language and Literature
Ws L — Washington Law Review
WSL — Welt der Slaven
W Sl A — Wiener Slawistischer Almanach
WSlav — Welt der Slaven
WSLBA — Wasser, Luft, und Betrieb
WSLJb — Wiener Slawistisches Jahrbuch
WSLL — Wisconsin. University. Studies in Language and Literature
WSM — Walpole Society Magazine
WSM — World Solar Markets
WSMYA — Washington Monthly
WSN — Wallace Stevens Newsletter
WSNA Mini J — Washington State Nurses Association. Mini Journal
W Soc E J — Western Society of Engineers. Journal
Wsp — Wspolczesnosc
W Sport & P Act J — Women in Sport & Physical Activity Journal
W Sports — Women's Sports
WSQ — Wonder Stories Quarterly
WSR — Waterschapsbelangen
WSRB — Wall Street Review of Books
W St — Wiener Studien
WST — Wine and Spirit
WSt — Word Study
WSTED — Water Science and Technology
W St Parole & Prob Conf Proc — Western States Parole and Probation Conference. Proceedings
WSTS — World Semiconductor Trade Statistics
WSTSA — Wall Street Transcript
W Studien — Wiener Studien. Zeitschrift fuer Klassische Philologie
W St UL Rev — Western State University. Law Review
W Succ R — Wetboek van Successierechten
WSU/HB — Human Biology. Official Publication. Human Biology Council. Wayne State University. School of Medicine
W Sussex Hist — West Sussex History
WSW — Wirtschaftswissenschaft
WSWOA — Water and Sewage Works
WSWSA — Wasserwirtschaft-Wassertechnik
WSWTA — Wasserwirtschaft
WSZ — Vereniging Surinaams Bedrijfsleven. Weekbericht
WT — Weird Tales
WT — Wetenschappelijke Tijdingen
WT — Wieczory Teatralne
WT — World Tobacco
WT — World Today
WTA — World Tax Report
WTA — World Textile Abstracts
W Taksen — Wetboek van de met het Zegel Gelijkgestelde Taksen
WTD — World Today
WTF — Welcome to Finland
WTGR — Welcome to Greenland
W Th J — Westminster Theological Journal
WTHRA — Weather
WTHWA — Weatherwise
WTI — Welcome to Iceland
WTJ — Westminster Theological Journal
WTKK — Wen-Tzu Kai-Ko
WTM — Western Mail
WTN — Journal of World Trade Law
WTN — Wroclawskie Towarzystwo Naukowe
WTR — Weekly Transcript Reports
WTR — World Travel

W Trees — Western Trees, Parks, and Forests
WTS — Watersport. Maandblad voor de Zeilsport. Motorbootsport
WTT — Weird Terror Tales
WTTF — Welcome to the Faeroes
WTW — Materials Reclamation Weekly
WTW — Writers and Their Work
WTW — Wroclawskie Towarzystwo Naukowe
WT (Werkstattstech) Z Ind Fertigung — WT (Werkstattstechnik). Zeitschrift fuer Industrielle Fertigung
WTZ — Weird Tales
WTZIA — WT [*Werkstattstechnik*]. Zeitschrift fuer Industrielle Fertigung
Wt Z Ind Fe — Werkstattstechnik Zeitschrift fuer Industrielle Fertigung
WT Z Ind Fertigung — WT [*Werkstattstechnik*]. Zeitschrift fuer Industrielle Fertigung
WU — Weekly Underwriter
WUBOA — Wasser und Boden
WuD — Wort und Dienst. Jahrbuch der Theologischen Schule Bethel
Wuertb Jh — Jahreshefte des Vereins fuer Vaterlaendische Naturkunde in Wuerttemberg
Wuerttemb Aerztebl — Wuerttembergisches Aerzteblatt
Wuerttemberg Blaetter Km — Wuerttembergische Blaetter fuer Kirchenmusik
Wuerttembergisch Franken — Wuerttenbergisch-Franken. Jahrbuch des Historischen Vereins fuer Wuerttembergisches Franken
Wuerttemberg Jb Statistik & Landesknd — Wuerttembergische Jahrbuecher fuer Statistik und Landeskunde
Wuerttemberg Vjhft Landesgesch — Wuerttembergische Vierteljahreshefte fuer Landesgeschichte
Wuerttemb Wochenbl Landwirt — Wuerttembergisches Wochenblatt fuer Landwirtschaft
Wuertt Franken — Wuerttembergisch-Franken
Wuertt Jahrb F Statist U Landeskunde — Wuerttembergische Jahrbuecher fuer Statistik und Landeskunde
Wuertt Statist Landesamt Mitt — Wuerttembergisches Statistisches Landesamt. Mitteilungen
Wuerzb Bt I Arb — Arbeiten des Botanischen Instituts in Wuerzburg
Wuerzb J — Wuerzburger Jahrbuecher fuer die Altertumswissenschaft
Wuerzb Jahrb f d Alt — Wuerzburger Jahrbuecher fuer die Altertumswissenschaft
Wuerzb Jb Alt Wiss — Wuerzburger Jahrbuecher fuer die Altertumswissenschaft
Wuerzb Jb Ph Md Gs — Jahrbuecher der Philosophisch-Medicinischen Gesellschaft zu Wuerzburg
Wuerzb Nw Z — Wuerzburger Naturwissenschaftliche Zeitschrift. Herausgegeben von der Physikalisch-Medicinischen Gesellschaft
Wuerzb Ps Md Sb — Sitzungsberichte der Physikalisch-Medicinischen Gesellschaft zu Wuerzburg
Wuerzb Ps Md Vh — Verhandlungen der Physikalisch-Medicinischen Gesellschaft (Wuerzburg)
Wuerzburger Naturwiss Z — Wuerzburger Naturwissenschaftliche Zeitschrift
Wuerzburg Geogr Arb — Wuerzburger Geographische Arbeiten
Wuerzb Vh — Verhandlungen der Physikalisch-Medicinischen Gesellschaft (Wuerzburg)
Wuerz Jb — Wuerzburger Jahrbuecher fuer die Altertumswissenschaft
WuG — Wissenschaft und Gegenwart
WUGGAO — Contributions to Geology. University of Wyoming
Wuhan Univ J Nat Sci — Wuhan University Journal. Natural Sciences
WUKEE8 — Wuyi Science Journal
WuL — Wissen und Leben
W Underw — Weekly Underwriter
W Underw & Insur Press — Weekly Underwriter and the Insurance Press
WUNT — Wissenschaftliche Untersuchungen zum Neuen Testament
WUR — Wirtschaft und Recht. Zeitschrift fuer Wirtschaftspolitik und Wirtschaftsrecht mit Einschluss des Sozialrechtes und Arbeidsrechtes
Wurzburg Diozgeschbl — Wurzburger Diozesangeschichtsblaetter
Wurzburg Jb Altertwiss — Wuerzburger Jahrbuecher fuer die Altertumswissenschaft
WUS — Washington University. Studies
WUS — Wirtschaft und Statistik
WUS — Woerterbuch der Ugaritische Sprache
WuS — Woerter und Sachen. Zeitschrift fuer Indogermanische Sprachenwissenschaft
WUS — World University Service
WUSL — Wortkunst. Untersuchungen zur Sprach- und Literaturgeschichte
WUTS — Washington (State). University. Publications. Theses Series
WuW — Welt und Wort
W u W — Wirtschaft und Wettbewerb
WuWahr — Wort und Wahrheit
WuWe — Wissenschaft und Weltbild
WuWelt — Wissenschaft und Weltbild
Wuyi Sci J — Wuyi Science Journal
WV — Wiener Vorlegeblaetter fuer Archaeologische Uebungen
WV — World Vision
W Va — West Virginia Reports
WVA — West Vlaanderen Werkt
W Va Acad Sci Proc — West Virginia Academy of Sciences. Proceedings
W Va Acts — Acts of the Legislature of West Virginia
W Va Ag Dept — West Virginia. Department of Agriculture. Publications
W Va Ag Exp — West Virginia. Agricultural Experiment Station. Publications
W Va Agric Exp Stn Bull — West Virginia. Agricultural Experiment Station. Bulletin
W Va Agric Exp Stn Cir — West Virginia. Agricultural Experiment Station. Circular
W Va Agric Exp Stn Circ — West Virginia. Agricultural Experiment Station. Circular
W Va Agric Exp Stn Curr Rep — West Virginia. Agricultural Experiment Station. Current Report
W Va Agric Exp Stn Misc Publ — West Virginia. Agricultural Experiment Station. Miscellaneous Publication
W Va Agric For — West Virginia Agriculture and Forestry
W Va Agric For Exp Stn Bull — West Virginia. Agricultural and Forestry Experiment Station. Bulletin

W Va B Assn Proc — West Virginia Bar Association. Proceedings
W Va B Assn Rep — Western Virginia Bar Association. Report
W Va Coal Min Inst Proc — West Virginia Coal Mining Institute. Proceedings
W Va Code — West Virginia Code
W Va Crim Just Rev — West Virginia Criminal Justice Review
W Va Dent J — West Virginia Dental Journal
W Va Dep Mines Annu Rep — West Virginia. Department of Mines. Annual Report
W Va For Notes — West Virginia Forestry Notes
W Va For Notes W Va Univ Agric For Exp Stn — West Virginia Forestry Notes. West Virginia University. Agricultural and Forestry Experiment Station
W Va Geol Econ Surv Basic Data Rep — West Virginia. Geological and Economic Survey. Basic Data Report
W Va Geol Econ Surv Bull — West Virginia. Geological and Economic Survey. Bulletin
W Va Geol Econ Surv Circ Ser — West Virginia. Geological and Economic Survey. Circular Series
W Va Geol Econ Surv Cir Ser — West Virginia. Geological and Economic Survey. Circular Series
W Va Geol Econ Surv Coal Geol Bull — West Virginia. Geological and Economic Survey. Coal Geology Bulletin
W Va Geol Econ Surv Environ Geol Bull — West Virginia. Geological and Economic Survey. Environmental Geology Bulletin
W Va Geol Econ Surv Miner Resour Ser — West Virginia. Geological and Economic Survey. Mineral Resources Series
W Va Geol Econ Surv Newsl — West Virginia. Geological and Economic Survey. Newsletter
W Va Geol Econ Surv Rep Archeol Invest — West Virginia. Geological and Economic Survey. Report of Archeological Investigations
W Va Geol Econ Surv Rep Invest — West Virginia. Geological and Economic Survey. Report of Investigations
W Va Geol Econ Surv River Basin Bull — West Virginia. Geological and Economic Survey. River Basin Bulletin
W Va Geol Surv Rep — West Virginia. Geological Survey. Reports
W Va Geol Surv Rep Invest — West Virginia. Geological Survey. Report of Investigations
W Va G S — West Virginia. Geological Survey
WVaH — West Virginia History
W Va His — West Virginia History
W Va Hist — West Virginia History. A Quarterly Magazine
W Va Law Q — West Virginia Law Quarterly and the Bar
W Va Law R — West Virginia Law Review
W Va Lib — West Virginia Libraries
W Va Libr — West Virginia Libraries
W Va L Q — Western Virginia Law Quarterly
W Va LQ — West Virginia Law Quarterly
W Va LR — West Virginia Law Review
W Va L Rev — West Virginia Law Review
W Va Med J — West Virginia Medical Journal
W Va M J — West Virginia Medical Journal
WVARAY — West Virginia University. Agricultural Experiment Station. Current Report
W Var Sports — Women's Varsity Sports
W Va Univ Agric Exp Stn Curr Rep — West Virginia University. Agricultural Experiment Station. Current Report
W Va Univ Agric For Exp Stn Curr Rep — West Virginia University. Agricultural and Forestry Experiment Station. CurrentReport
W Va Univ Agri Exp Stn Bull — West Virginia University. Agricultural Experiment Station. Bulletin
W Va Univ Bull Proc Annu Appalachian Gas Meas Short Course — West Virginia University. Bulletin. Proceedings. Annual Appalachian Gas Measurement Short Course
W Va Univ Coal Res Bur Sch Mines Tech Rep — West Virginia University. Coal Research Bureau. School of Mines. Technical Report
W Va Univ Coal Res Bur Tech Rep — West Virginia University. Coal Research Bureau. Technical Report
W Va Univ Eng Sta Tech Bull — West Virginia University. Engineering Experiment Station. Technical Bulletin
W Va Univ Eng Exp Stn Bull — West Virginia University. Engineering Experiment Station. Bulletin
W Va Univ Eng Exp Stn Res Bull — West Virginia University. Engineering Experiment Station. Research Bulletin
W Va Univ Eng Exp Stn Tech Bull — West Virginia University. Engineering Experiment Station. Technical Bulletin
W Va Univ Rp Bd Reg — West Virginia University. Report of the Board of Regents
W Va U Phil — West Virginia University. Philological Papers
W v B Pr — Wetboek van Burgerlijk Procesrecht
W v B Rv — Wetboek van Burgerlijk Rechtsvordering
WVD — Wissenschaftliche Veroeffentlichungen des Deutschen Instituts fuer Laenderkunde
WVDO — Wissenschaftliche Veroeffentlichungen der Deutschen Orientgesellschaft
WVDOG — Wissenschaftliche Veroeffentlichungen der Deutschen Orient-Gesellschaft
WVF — West Virginia Folklore
W v F R — Weekblad voor Fiscaal Recht
WVH — West Virginia History
W v h N — Weekblad voor het Notariaat
WVHP — West Virginia Association for Health, Physical Education, Recreation, and Dance. Journal
W v h R — Weekblad van het Recht
W v K — Wetboek van Koophandel
W v K H — Wetboek voor het Koninkrijk Holland
WVL — West Virginia Law Review
WVLG — Wuerttembergische Vierteljahresschrift fuer Landesgeschichte
WVLQ — West Virginia Law Quarterly
WVLR — West Virginia Law Review

WVM — Wiener Voelkerkundliche Mitteilungen

WV Med J — West Virginia Medical Journal

W v M S — Wetboek van Militair Strafrecht

W v M Sr — Wetboek van Militair Strafrecht

W v NB — Weekblad voor de Nederlandse Bond van Gemeenteambtenaren

W v Pr N en R — Weekblad voor Privaatrecht, Notariaat, en Registratie

W v S — Wetboek van Strafrecht

W v Sr — Wetboek van Strafrecht

W v Str — Wetboek van Strafrecht

W v Sv — Wetboek van Strafvordering

WVUBPL — West Virginia University. Bulletin. Philological Studies

WV Univ Agric For Exp Stn Misc Publ — West Virginia University. Agriculture and Forestry Experiment Station. Miscellaneous Publication

WVUPP — West Virginia University. Philological Papers

WW — Australian Women's Weekly

WW — Journal of Waterway, Port, Coastal, and Ocean Engineering

WW — Window

WW — Wirkendes Wort

WW — Wissenschaft und Weisheit

WW — Woman's World

WW — Working Woman

WW — World's Work

Ww — Wroclaw

WW — Wyatt and Webb's Reports

WWA — World Water

WWAEA — Water and Wastes Engineering

WW & A'B — Wyatt, Webb, and A'Beckett's Victorian Reports

WW & A'B (E) — Wyatt, Webb, and A'Beckett's Reports (Equity)

WW & A'B (IE & M) — Wyatt, Webb, and A'Beckett's Reports (Insolvency, Ecclesiastical, and Matrimonial)

WW & A'B (M) — Wyatt, Webb, and A'Beckett's Reports (Mining)

WW & CB — Weekly Weather and Crop Bulletin

WWARA — Weltwirtschaftliches Archiv

WWATA — Water and Waste Treatment

W Ways — Word Ways

WWD — Weird World

WWD — Women's Wear Daily

WWe — Wissenschaft und Weisheit

WWENA — Water and Water Engineering

WWG — Who's Who in Germany

WWGN — Wildlife Working Group. Newsletter

WWI — Who's Who in Israel

WWJ — Who's Who in Japan

WWJOA — Water Well Journal

WWK — Continental Iron and Steel Trade Reports. Iron and Steel Trade Market Reports and Special Information

WWM — Ons Nuis Vakblad voor de Meubelhandel, Meubelmakerij, Meubelindustrie, Interieurarchitecteur, Behangerij, Stoffeerderij, en Detailhandel in Woningtextiel

WWM — Weekly Women's Magazine

WWM — Wide World Magazine

WWM — Working Woman

WWMS — Who's Who in Malaysia and Singapore

WWN — Walt Whitman Newsletter

W Work (Lond) — World's Work (London)

WWR — Walt Whitman Review

WWR — Washington Weekly Report

WWR — Western Weekly Reports

WWR (NS) — Western Weekly Reports, New Series

WWS — Western Writers Series

WWSCA — Wirtschaft und Wissenschaft

WWW — Wirtschaft und Wettbewerb. Zeitschrift fuer Kartellrecht, Wettbewerbsrecht, Marktorganisation

WX — Wawatay News Extra. Special Issues

WY — Wyoming Music Educator News-Letter

WYA — Writers for Young Adults. Biographies Master Index

Wyatt & W — Wyatt and Webb's Reports

Wyatt & Webb — Wyatt and Webb's Reports

Wyatt & W (Eq) — Wyatt and Webb's Reports (Equity)

Wyatt & W (IE & M) — Wyatt and Webb's Reports (Insolvency, Ecclesiastical, and Matrimonial)

Wyatt & W (IP & M) — Wyatt and Webb's Reports (Insolvency, Probate, and Matrimonial)

Wyatt W & A'B — Wyatt, Webb, and A'Beckett's Reports

Wyatt W & A'B (Eq) — Wyatt, Webb, and A'Beckett's Reports (Equity)

Wyatt W & A'B IE & M — Wyatt, Webb, and A'Beckett's Reports (Insolvency, Ecclesiastical, and Matrimonial)

Wyatt W & A'B IP & M — Wyatt, Webb, and A'Beckett's Victorian Insolvency, Probate, and Matrimonial Reports

Wyatt W & A'B Min — Wyatt, Webb, and A'Beckett's Reports (Mining)

Wychowanie M Szkole — Wychowanie Muzyczne w Szkole

Wy Commem Assoc Proc — Wyoming Commemorative Association. Proceedings

Wydz Mat Fiz Chem Uniw Poznan Ser Fiz — Wydzial Matematyki Fizyki i Chemii Uniwersytet Imeni Adama Mickiewicza w Poznaniu Seria Fizyaka

Wye Coll Dep Hop Res Annu Rep — Wye College. Department of Hop Research. Annual Report

WY Energy Ext Serv Update — Wyoming. Energy Extension Service. Update

Wy Hist And Geol Soc Proc — Wyoming Historical and Geological Society. Proceedings and Collections

Wykeham Eng Technol Ser — Wykeham Engineering and Technology Series

Wykeham Sci Ser — Wykeham Science Series

WY LJ — Wyoming Law Journal

Wyo — Wyoming Reports

Wyo Ag Exp — Wyoming. Agricultural Experiment Station. Publications

Wyo Agric Exp Stn Bull — Wyoming. Agricultural Experiment Station. Bulletin

Wyo Agric Exp Stn Cir — Wyoming. Agricultural Experiment Station. Circular

Wyo Agric Exp Stn Res J — Wyoming. Agricultural Experiment Station. Research Journal

Wyo Agric Exp Stn Sci Monogr — Wyoming. Agricultural Experiment Station. Science Monograph

Wyo Agric Ext Serv Bull — Wyoming. Agricultural Extension Service. Bulletin

Wyo Game Fish Comm Bull — Wyoming. Game and Fish Commission. Bulletin

Wyo Geol Assoc Earth Sci Bull — Wyoming Geological Association. Earth Science Bulletin

Wyo Geol Assoc Guideb Ann Field Conf — Wyoming Geological Association. Guidebook. Annual Field Conference

Wyo Geol Survey Bull Rept Inv — Wyoming. Geological Survey. Bulletin. Report of Investigations

Wyo Geol Surv Prelim Rep — Wyoming. Geological Survey. Preliminary Report

Wyo Geol Surv Rep Invest — Wyoming. Geological Survey. Report of Investigations

Wyo G Off B Wyo St G — Wyoming. Geologist's Office. Bulletin. Wyoming State Geologist

Wyo His Col — Wyoming State Historical Department. Proceedings and Collections

Wyo Issues — Wyoming Issues

Wyo Lib Roundup — Wyoming Library Roundup

Wyo L J — Wyoming Law Journal

Wyoming Agric Exp Sta Mimeogr Circ — Wyoming Agricultural College Agricultural Experiment Station. Mimeographed Circular

Wyoming Geol Survey Prelim Rept — Wyoming. Geological Survey. Preliminary Report

Wyoming Hist G Soc Pr Pub — Wyoming Historical and Geological Society. Proceedings and Collections. Publications

Wyo Nurse — Wyoming Nurse [*Formerly, Wyoming Nurses Newsletter*]

Wyo Nurses News — Wyoming Nurses Newsletter [*Later, Wyoming Nurse*]

Wyo Prog Rep — Wyoming Progress Report

Wyo Range Manage — Wyoming Range Management

W Yorks Gl S P — Proceedings of the Geological and Polytechnic Society of the West Riding of Yorkshire

W Yorks P Gl S — Proceedings of the Geological and Polytechnic Society of the West Riding of Yorkshire

Wyo Roundup — Wyoming Roundup

Wyo Sess Laws — Session Laws. Wyoming

Wyo Stat — Wyoming Statutes

Wyo St B Assn Proc — Wyoming State Bar Association. Proceedings

Wyo St G — Wyoming State Geologist

Wyo Univ Dep Geol Contrib Geol — Wyoming University. Department of Geology. Contributions to Geology

Wyo Univ Nat Resour Res Inst Bull — Wyoming University. Natural Resources Research Institute. Bulletin

Wyo Univ Nat Resour Res Inst Inf Cir — Wyoming University. Natural Resources Research Institute. Information Circular

Wyo Univ Natur Resour Inst Inform Circ — Wyoming University. Natural Resources Institute. Information Circular

Wyo Univ Sch Mines B — Wyoming University. School of Mines. Bulletin

Wyo Univ Water Resour Res Inst Water Resour Ser — Wyoming University. Water Resources Research Institute. Water Resources Series

Wyo Wild Life — Wyoming Wild Life

Wythe Cty Hist Rev — Wythe County Historical Review

WyTJ — Wesleyan Theological Journal

WYW — Weltwirtschaft

Wyz Szkol Ped Krakow Rocznik Nauk-Dydakt Prace Dydakt Mat — Wyzsza Szkola Pedagogiczna w Krakowie. Rocznik Naukowo-Dydaktyczny. Prace z Dydaktyki Matematyki

Wyz Szkol Ped Krakow Rocznik Nauk-Dydakt Prace Mat — Wyzsza Szkola Pedagogiczna w Krakowie. Rocznik Naukowo-Dydaktyczny. Prace Matematyczne

WZ — Westfaelische Zeitschrift

WZ — Wiedza i Zycie

WZ — Wissenschaft und Zeitgeist

WZ — Wort in der Zeit

WZ (Berlin) — Wissenschaftliche Zeitschrift. Humboldt-Universitaet (Berlin)

WzD — Wege zur Dichtung

W Zegel — Wetboek der Zegelrechten

WZEMAUG — Wissenschaftliche Zeitschrift. Ernst-Moritz-Arndt-Universitaet (Greifswald). Gesellschafts- und Sprachwissenschaftliche Reihe

WZE Wiss Z Elektrotech — WZE. Wissenschaftliche Zeitschrift der Elektrotechnik

WZFMA — Wissenschaftliche Zeitschrift. Friedrich-Schiller-Universitaet (Jena). Mathematisch-Naturwissenschaftliche Reihe

WZFSU — Wissenschaftliche Zeitschrift. Friedrich-Schiller-Universitaet (Jena). Gesellschafts- und Sprachwissenschaftliche Reihe

WZFSUJ — Wissenschaftliche Zeitschrift. Friedrich-Schiller-Universitaet (Jena). Gesellschafts- und Sprachwissenschaftliche Reihe

WZFSUJ GSR — Wissenschaftliche Zeitschrift. Friedrich-Schiller-Universitaet (Jena). Gesellschafts- und Sprachwissenschaftliche Reihe

WZGK — Westdeutsche Zeitschrift fuer Geschichte und Kunst

WZ (Griefswald) — Wissenschaftliche Zeitschrift. Ernst-Moritz-Arndt-Universitaet (Greifswald)

WZ (Halle) — Wissenschaftliche Zeitschrift. Martin-Luther-Universitaet (Halle-Wittenberg)

WZHB — Wissenschaftliche Zeitschrift der Humboldt-Universitaet zu Berlin

WZHMA — Wissenschaftliche Zeitschrift. Humboldt-Universitaet (Berlin). Mathematisch-Naturwissenschaftliche Reihe

WZHU — Wissenschaftliche Zeitschrift. Humboldt-Universitaet (Berlin). Gesellschafts- und Sprachwissenschaftliche Reihe

WZHUB — Wissenschaftliche Zeitschrift. Humboldt-Universitaet (Berlin). Gesellschafts- und Sprachwissenschaftliche Reihe

WZHW — Wissenschaftliche Zeitschrift der Martin-Luther-Universitaet. Halle-Wittenberg.Reihe Gesellschaft und Sprachwissenschaften

WZJ — Wissenschaftliche Zeitschrift. Friedrich-Schiller-Universitaet (Jena)

WZ (Jena) — Wissenschaftliche Zeitschrift. Friedrich-Schiller-Universitaet (Jena)

WZKM — Wiener Zeitschrift fuer die Kunde des Morgenlandes

WZKMU — Wissenschaftliche Zeitschrift. Karl-Marx-Universitaet

WZKMUL — Wissenschaftliche Zeitschrift. Karl-Marx-Universitaet (Leipzig). Gesellschafts- und Sprachwissenschaftliche Reihe

WZKS — Wiener Zeitschrift fuer die Kunde Suedasiens und Archiv fuer Indische Philosophie

WZKSO — Wiener Zeitschrift fuer die Kunde Sued- und Ostasiens und Archiv fuer Indische Philosophie

WZL — Wissenschaftliche Zeitschrift. Karl-Marx-Universitaet (Leipzig)

WZ (Leipzig) — Wissenschaftliche Zeitschrift. Karl-Marx-Universitaet (Leipzig)

W Z Leipzig Reihe GS — Wissenschaftliche Zeitschrift der Karl-Marx-Universitaet. Leipzig. Reihe Gesellschaft und Sprachwissenschaften

WZM — Wiener Zeitschrift fuer die Kunde des Morgenlandes

WZMLU — Wissenschaftliche Zeitschrift. Martin-Luther-Universitaet

WZMLUH — Wissenschaftliche Zeitschrift. Martin-Luther-Universitaet (Halle-Wittenberg). Gesellschafts- und Sprachwissenschaftliche Reihe

W Z Morg — Wiener Zeitschrift fuer die Kunde des Morgenlandes

WZMU — Wissenschaftliche Zeitschrift. Karl-Marx-Universitaet [*Leipzig*]. Gesellschafts- und Sprachwissenschaftliche Reihe

WZNDA — Wiener Zeitschrift fuer Nervenheilkunde und Deren Grenzgebiete

WZP — Wiener Zeitschrift fuer Philosophie, Psychologie, Paedagogik

WZPHP — Wissenschaftliche Zeitschrift. Paedagogische Hochschule (Potsdam). Gesellschafts- und Sprachwissenschaftliche Reihe

WZ Rostock — Wissenschaftliche Zeitschrift. Universitaet Rostock

WZsl — Wissenschaftliche Zeitschrift. Karl-Marx-Universitaet. Gesellschafts- und Sprachwissenschaftliche Reihe

WZTDA — Wissenschaftliche Zeitschrift. Technische Hochschule (Dresden)

WZTKA — Wissenschaftliche Zeitschrift. Technische Hochschule Karl-Marx-Stadt

WZUB — Wissenschaftliche Zeitschrift. Humboldt-Universitaet (Berlin). Gesellschafts- und Sprachwissenschaftliche Reihe

WZUG — Wissenschaftliche Zeitschrift. Ernst-Moritz-Arndt-Universitaet (Greifswald)

WZUH — Wissenschaftliche Zeitschrift. Martin-Luther-Universitaet (Halle-Wittenberg). Gesellschafts- und Sprachwissenschaftliche Reihe

WZUHW — Wissenschaftliche Zeitschrift. Martin-Luther-Universitaet (Halle-Wittenberg). Gesellschafts- und Sprachwissenschaftliche Reihe

WZUJ — Wissenschaftliche Zeitschrift. Friedrich-Schiller-Universitaet (Jena)

WZUL — Wissenschaftliche Zeitschrift. Karl-Marx-Universitaet (Leipzig)

WZUL — Wissenschaftliche Zeitschrift. Universitaet Leipzig. Gesellschafts- und Sprachwissenschaftliche Reihe

WZULeipzig — Wissenschaftliche Zeitschrift. Karl-Marx Universitaet. Gesellschafts- und Sprachwissenschaftliche Reihe (Leipzig)

WZUR — Wissenschaftliche Zeitschrift. Universitaet Rostock

WZUW — Wissenschaftliche Zeitschrift. Universitaet Wien

WZV — Wiener Zeitschrift fuer Volkskunde

X

Xa — Xanadu

XAARAY — US Department of Agriculture. Agricultural Research Service. ARS

XACIAH — US Department of Agriculture. Plant Inventory

XADMAY — US Air Force. Technical Documentary Report. SAM-TDR

XADRAF — US Army. Diamond Ordnance Fuze Laboratories. Technical Report

XALNA — Research Note FPL. Forest Products Laboratory

XBMIA — Report of Investigations. United States Bureau of Mines

XCRDA — Research and Development Report. United States Office of Coal Research

X Ctry Skier — X-Country Skier

XDIGA — US Geological Survey. Bulletin

XDQ — Revista Ximenez de Quesada

XEPPDW — US Environmental Protection Agency. Office of Pesticide Programs. Substitute Chemical Program. EPA-540

XF — Xudozestvennyj Fol'klor

XFWFA7 — US Fish and Wildlife Service. Fishery Bulletin

XFWLAP — US Fish and Wildlife Service. Wildlife Leaflet

XH — Xerogrammata Hochschulschriften

XIMIA — Information Circular. United States Bureau of Mines

Xi Psi Phi Q — Xi Psi Phi Quarterly

XIWSA — US Geological Survey. Water-Supply Paper

X J — X Journal

XL — Xudozestvennaja Literatura

XMOFA — Bureau of Mines. Open File Report

XMTPB — Technical Progress Report. United States Bureau of Mines

XNBSA — National Bureau of Standards. Special Publication

XNIPA — United States. Naval Institute. Proceedings

XNWRA — US News and World Report

XPARD6 — EPA [*Environmental Protection Agency*] Environmental Protection TechnologySeries

XPARD6 — US Environmental Protection Agency. Office of Research and Development. Research Reports. Ecological Research Series

X Q Rev — X. A Quarterly Review

XR — X: A Quarterly Review

X Rays Nat Sci Med Proc Symp — X-Rays in Natural Science and Medicine. Proceedings of a Symposium

X-Ray Spect — X-Ray Spectrometry

X-Ray Spectrom — X-Ray Spectrometry

XRRAAH — US Forest Service. Rocky Mountain Forest and Range Experiment Station. ResearchHighlights. Annual Report

XUS — Xavier University. Studies

XVII S — XVIIe Siecle

XXF — XXe Siecle Federaliste

XXs — XXe Siecle. Cahiers d'Art

Y

Y — Yellowjacket
Y — Ymer
Y — Yukon News
YA — Yeda-'am. Journal. Hebrew Folklore Society
YA — YIVO Annual
YaA — Yale Alumni Magazine
YAA — Yugoslav Survey
YAAR — Yacimientos Arqueologicos Espanoles
Yacht — Yachting
Yacht Boat Week — Yachting and Boating Weekly
YACN — Yukon Anniversaries Commission Newsletter
Yad Energ — Yadrena Energiya
Yadernaya Fiz — Akademiya Nauk SSSR. Yadernaya Fizika
Yad Fiz — Yadernaya Fizika
Yad Geofiz — Yadernaya Geofizika
Yad-Geofiz Issled Geofiz Sb — Yaderno-Geofizicheskie Issledovaniya, Geofizicheskii Sbornik
Ya Div Q — Yale Divinity Quarterly
Yad Konstanty — Yadernye Konstanty
Yad Magn Rezon — Yadernyi Magnitnyi Rezonans
Yad Magn Rezon Org Khim — Yadernyi Magnitnyi Rezonans v Organicheskoi Khimii
Yad Priborostr — Yadernoe Priborostroenie
Yad Vashem Stud Eur Jew Catastrophe Resist — Yad Vashem Studies on the European Jewish Catastrophe and Resistance
YAJ — Yeda-'am. Journal. Hebrew Folklore Society
YAJ — Yorkshire Archaeological Journal
YAKUA — Yakuzaigaku
YAKUA2 — Archives of Practical Pharmacy
Yakugaku Zasshi J Pharmaceut Soc Jap — Yakugaku Zasshi/Journal of the Pharmaceutical Society of Japan
Yale Art Gal Bul — Yale University. Art Gallery. Bulletin
Yale Associates Bul — Yale University. Associates in Fine Arts. Bulletin
Yale Bicen Pub Contr Miner — Yale Bicentennial Publications. Contributions to Mineralogy and Petrography
Yale Class Stud — Yale Classical Studies
Yale Class Studies — Yale Classical Studies Series
Yale ClSt — Yale Classical Studies
Yale Div Q — Yale Divinity Quarterly
Yale Forestry Bull — Yale University. School of Forestry. Bulletin
Yale French Stud — Yale French Studies
Yale Fr St — Yale French Studies
Yale Fr Stud — Yale French Studies
Yale Hist Pub Misc — Yale Historical Publications. Miscellaneous
Yale Ital S — Yale Italian Studies
Yale Ital Stud — Yale Italian Studies
Yale It Stud — Yale Italian Studies
Yale J Archit — Yale Journal of Architecture
Yale J Biol — Yale Journal of Biology and Medicine
Yale J Biol Med — Yale Journal of Biology and Medicine
Yale J Crit — Yale Journal of Criticism
Yale Jour Biol And Med — Yale Journal of Biology and Medicine
Yale J World Pub Ord — Yale Journal of World Public Order
Yale Law J — Yale Law Journal
Yale Law Jour — Yale Law Journal
Yale Lit Mag — Yale Literary Magazine
Yale L J — Yale Law Journal
Yale Math Monographs — Yale Mathematical Monographs
Yale R — Yale Review
Yale Rev — Yale Review
Yale Rev Law & Soc Act'n — Yale Review of Law and Social Action
Yale Rev of L and Soc Action — Yale Review of Law and Social Action
Yale Sci — Yale Scientific
Yale Scient Mag — Yale Scientific Magazine
Yale Sci Mag — Yale Scientific Magazine
Yale Sc Mo — Yale Scientific Monthly
Yale Stud World PO — Yale Studies in World Public Order
Yale Stud World Pub Ord — Yale Studies in World Public Order
Yale St Wld Pub Ord — Yale Studies in World Public Order
Yale U A G Bull — Yale University Art Gallery Bulletin
Yale U Lib Gaz — Yale University. Library. Gazette
Yale U Libr — Yale University. Library. Gazette
Yale Univ Art Gal Bull — Yale University. Art Gallery. Bulletin
Yale Univ B — Yale University. Art Gallery. Bulletin
Yale Univ Lib Gaz — Yale University. Library. Gazette

Yale Univ Peabody Mus Nat Hist Annu Rep — Yale University. Peabody Museum of Natural History. Annual Report
Yale Univ Peabody Mus Nat Hist Bull — Yale University. Peabody Museum of Natural History. Bulletin
Yale Univ Peabody Mus Nat History Bull — Yale University. Peabody Museum of Natural History. Bulletin
Yale Univ Sch For Bull — Yale University. School of Forestry. Bulletin
Yale Univ Sch For Environ Stud Bull — Yale University. School of Forestry and Environmental Studies. Bulletin
Yalkut Le Sivim Le Tekhnol U Le Minhal Shel Tekst — Yalkut Le-sivim, Le-Tekhnologyah U-le-minhal Shel Tekstil
Yalkut Le-Sivim Tekhnol U-Minhal Shel Tekst — Yalkut Le-sivim Tekhnologyah U-Minhal Shel Tekstil
Y Alm — Yurosholayimer Almanakh
Yamaguchi J Sci — Yamaguchi Journal of Science/Yamaguchi Daigaku Rigakkai Shi
Yamaguchi Med — Yamaguchi Medicine
YAPRA — Yadernoe Priborostroenie
Yard R — Yardbird Reader
Yarn Mark News — Yarn Market News
Yarosl Gos Univ Mezhvuz Temat Sb — Yaroslavskii Gosudarstvennyi Universitet. Mezhvuzovskii Tematicheskii Sbornik
Yawata Tech Rep — Yawata Technical Report
Yb — Yearbook of Comparative and General Literature
YB — Year Book of Reports of Cases
YB — Year Books
YB — YIVO Bleter
YB — Yorkshire Bulletin of Economic and Social Research
YB — Ysgrifau Beirniadol
Yb Agric Coop — Yearbook of Agricultural Cooperation
Yb Agric US Dep Agric — Yearbook of Agriculture. US Department of Agriculture
YB Air & Space L — Yearbook of Air and Space Law
Yb Amer Philos Soc — Yearbook of the American Philosophical Society
YB Ames — Year Book. Ames Foundation
Yb Ass Pacif Cst Geogr — Yearbook. Association of Pacific Coast Geographers
Yb Calif Avocado Soc — Yearbook. California Avocado Society
YBDRE3 — Year Book of Diagnostic Radiology
Yb Educ — Yearbook of Education
YB Eur Conv on Human Rights — Year Book. European Convention on Human Rights
YB Europ Conv HR — Yearbook. European Convention on Human Rights
Yb Gen Med — Yearbook of General Medicine
Yb Gen Surg — Yearbook of General Surgery
Yb Gloucester Beekprs Ass — Yearbook. Gloucestershire Bee-Keepers Association
YBHSEQ — Year Book of Hand Surgery
YB Hum Rts — Yearbook on Human Rights
YBICJ — Yearbook. International Court of Justice
YBICSU — Yearbook. International Council of Scientific Unions
Yb Ind Orthop Surg — Yearbook of Industrial and Orthopedic Surgery
Yb Ind Stat — Yearbook of Industrial Statistics
Yb Inter Amer M Research — Yearbook for Inter-American Musical Research
Yb Int Folk M Council — Yearbook. International Folk Music Council
Yb Int Folk Music Coun — Yearbook. International Folk Music Council
YB Int'l L Comm'n — Yearbook. International Law Commission
YB Int'l Org — Yearbook of International Organizations
YbLitgSt — Yearbook of Liturgical Studies
Yb Med — Yearbook of Medicine
Yb Med Ass Great Cy NY — Yearbook. Medical Association of the Greater City of New York
Yb Mus Fin Archit Helsinki — Yearbook of the Museum of Finnish Architecture (Helsinki)
Yb Neurol Psychiat Endocr — Yearbook of Neurology, Psychiatry, Endocrinology, and Neurosurgery
Yb N Mus Technol — Yearbook of the National Museum of Technology
Yb of Leg Stud — Year Book of Legal Studies
Yb of the Eur Conv on Human Rights — Yearbook. European Convention on Human Rights
Yb Ophthal — Yearbook of Ophthalmology
Yb Pediat — Yearbook of Pediatrics
Yb Phot — Yearbook of Photography
Yb Phys Anthrop — Yearbook of Physical Anthropolgoy
Yb Phys Med Rehabil — Yearbook of Physical Medicine and Rehabilitation
Yb Phys Soc — Yearbook. Physical Society
YBPS — Yearbook. British Pirandello Society
Yb R Hort Soc — Yearbook. Royal Horticulture Society

Yb R Vet Agric Coll — Yearbook. Royal Veterinary and Agricultural College
Yb Soc — Yearbook. Royal Society of London
Yb Soc Pol Britain — Yearbook of Social Policy in Britain
Yb Trad Music — Yearbook for Traditional Music
Yb US Dep Agric — Yearbook. United States Department of Agriculture
YBWA — Year Book of World Affairs
Yb Wld Aff — Yearbook of World Affairs
Yb World Aff — Yearbook of World Affairs
Yb Yorks Beekprs Ass — Yearbook. Yorkshire Beekeepers Association
YCC — Yearbook of Comparative Criticism
YCGL — Yearbook of Comparative and General Literature
YCHP — Yenching Journal of Chinese Studies
YCKKAK — Acta Gerontologica Japonica
YCLS — Yale Classical Studies
Y Cl St — Yale Classical Studies Series
Y Cl Stud — Yale Classical Studies
YCOMA — Yearbook. Coke Oven Managers' Association
YCS — Yale Classical Studies
YCS — Yearbook of Construction Statistics
YCS — Yorkshire Celtic Studies
YCSN — Yukon Conservation Society. Newsletter
Y C T — Young Cinema and Theatre
YCWCDP — Acta Botanica Yunnanica
YDKGA — Yamaguchi Daigaku Kogakubu Kenkyu Hokoku
YDNGAU — Bulletin. Faculty of Agriculture. Yamaguchi University
YDQ — Yale Divinity Quarterly
YDS — Yorkshire Dialect Society. Transactions
Yearb Agr Co-Op — Yearbook of Agricultural Co-Operation
Yearb Agric — Yearbook of Agriculture
Yearb Agric US Dep Agric — Yearbook of Agriculture. US Department of Agriculture
Yearb Agr USDA — Yearbook of Agriculture. US Department of Agriculture
Yearb Amer Phil Soc — Yearbook. American Philosophical Society
Yearb Am Iron Steel Inst — Yearbook. American Iron and Steel Institute
Yearb Am Pulp Pap Mil Supt Assoc — Yearbook. American Pulp and Paper Mill Superintendents Association
Yearb Anesth — Yearbook of Anesthesia
Yearb Bharat Krishak Samaj — Yearbook. Bharat Krishak Samaj
Yearb Bur Entomol Hangchow — Yearbook. Bureau of Entomology. Hangchow/Chekiang Sheng K'un Ch'ung Chu Nien K'an
Yearb Bur Miner Resour Geol Geophys — Yearbook. Bureau of Mineral Resources. Geology and Geophysics
Yearb Bur Miner Resour Geol Geo-Phys (Aus) — Yearbook. Bureau of Mineral Resources. Geology and Geophysics (Australia)
Yearb Calif Avocado Soc — Yearbook. California Avocado Society
Yearb Calif Macad Soc — Yearbook. California Macadamia Society
Yearb Can Soc Stud Educ — Yearbook. Canadian Society for the Study of Education
Yearb Carnegie Inst Wash — Yearbook. Carnegie Institute of Washington
Yearb Cent Res Inst Phys Hung — Yearbook. Central Research Institute for Physics. Hungarian Academy of Sciences
Yearb Child Lit Assoc — Yearbook. Children's Literature Association
Yearb Coke Oven Managers' Assoc — Yearbook. Coke Oven Managers' Association
Yearb Comp Gen Lit — Yearbook of Comparative and General Literature
Yearb Dermatol Syphilol — Yearbook of Dermatology and Syphilology
Yearb Drug Ther — Yearbook of Drug Therapy
Yearb Endocrinol — Yearbook of Endocrinology
Yearb Engl Stud — Yearbook of English Studies
Yearb Est Learned Soc Am — Yearbook. Estonian Learned Society in America
Yearb Fac Agr Univ Ankara — Yearbook. Faculty of Agriculture. University of Ankara
Yearb Gen Surg — Yearbook of General Surgery
Yearb High Educ — Yearbook of Higher Education
Yearb Inst Geochem Sib Div Acad Sci (USSR) — Yearbook. Institute of Geochemistry. Siberian Division. Academy of Sciences (USSR)
Yearb Leo Baeck Inst — Yearbook. Leo Baeck Institute
Yearb Med — Yearbook of Medicine
Yearb Nat Farmers' Ass — Yearbook. National Farmers' Association
Yearb Natl Inst Sci India — Yearbook. National Institute of Sciences of India
Yearb Ontario Rose Soc — Yearbook. Ontario Rose Society
Year Book Aust — Year Book Australia
Year Book Bibliogr Soc Chicago — Year Book. Bibliographical Society. Chicago. Bibliographical Society of America
Year Book Carnegie Inst Wash — Year Book. Carnegie Institution of Washington
Year Book Diagn Radiol — Year Book of Diagnostic Radiology
Yearbook East-Eur Econ — Yearbook of East-European Economics
Year Book Endocrinol — Year Book of Endocrinology
Year Book Hand Surg — Year Book of Hand Surgery
Year Book Indian Natl Sci Acad — Year Book. Indian National Science Academy
Year Book Indian Nat Sci Acad — Year Book. Indian National Science Academy
Year Book Natl Auricula Primula Soc North Sec — Year Book. National Auricula and Primula Society. Northern Section
Year Book Nucl Med — Year Book of Nuclear Medicine
Year Book Obstet Gynecol — Year Book of Obstetrics and Gynecology
Year Book Rhododendron Assoc — Year Book. Rhododendron Association
Yearb Pap Ind Manage Assoc — Yearbook. Paper Industry Management Association
Yearb Pathol Clin Pathol — Yearbook of Pathology and Clinical Pathology
Yearb Pediatr — Yearbook of Pediatrics
Yearb Pharm — Yearbook of Pharmacy
Yearb Phys Anthropol — Yearbook of Physical Anthropology
Yearb R Asiat Soc Bengal — Yearbook. Royal Asiatic Society of Bengal
Yearb Sci Future — Yearbook of Science and the Future
Yearb Wld Aff — Year Book of World Affairs

Year Endocrinol — Year in Endocrinology
Year Immunol — Year in Immunology
Year Metab — Year in Metabolism
Year's Work Eng Stud — Year's Work in English Studies
Yeast Genet Eng — Yeast Genetic Engineering
Yeats Eliot — Yeats Eliot Review
Yediot — Yediot Bahaqirat Eretz-Israel Weatiqoteha
YEE — Yale Economic Essays
YEIMEY — Year in Immunology
Yellow B R — Yellow Brick Road
Yellowstone-Bighorn Research Proj Contr — Yellowstone-Bighorn Research Project. Contribution
Yellowstone Libr and Mus Assoc Yellowstone Interpretive Ser — Yellowstone Library and Museum Association. Yellowstone Interpretive Series
Ye N Lett — Ye News Letter [*Washington, D.C.*]
YER — Yeats Eliot Review
YES — Yearbook of English Studies
Yessis Rev — Yessis Review of Soviet Physical Education and Sports
Yeung Nam Univ Inst Ind Technol Rep — Yeung Nam University. Institute of Industrial Technology. Report
Yezhegodnik Inst Istor Isk — Yezhegodnik Instituta Istorii Iskusstva
YF — Yiddishe Folk
Y Fr St — Yale French Studies
YFS — Yale French Studies
Ygg — Yggdrasill
YGKKA — Yuki Gosei Kagaku Kyokaishi
YGKSA — Yogyo Kyokai Shi
YGNR — Yukon Government News Release
YGS — Yale Germanic Studies
YHHPAL — Acta Pharmaceutica Sinica
YHMA — Yukon Historical and Museums Association. Newsletter
YHMAN — Yukon Historical and Museums Association. Newsletter
YHP — Yale Historical Publications
YHPM — Yale Historical Publications. Miscellany
YI — Yukon Indian News
YiA — Yivo Annual of Jewish Social Science
YICA — Yearbook on International Communist Affairs
YIFMC — Yearbook. International Folk Music Council
Yillik Arastirmalar Derg — Yillik Arastirmalar Dergisi
Yiptime — Yipster Times
YIS — Information Sheet. Yukon Territory. Bureau of Statistics
YIS — Yearbook of Italian Studies
Y It S — Yale Italian Studies
YIVO — YIVO Annual of Jewish Social Science
YJ — Youth Journal
YJCS — Yenching Journal of Chinese Studies
YJS — Yale Judaica Series
YK — Yiddishe Kultur
YKB — Yukon Bibliography
YKIGA — Yokohama Igaku
YKKKA — Yakugaku Kenkyu
YKKKA8 — Japanese Journal of Pharmacy and Chemistry
YKKZA — Yakugaku Zasshi
YKYRA — Yakubutsu Ryoho
YLG — Yale University. Library. Gazette
YLG News — Library Association. Youth Libraries Group News
YLJ — Yale Law Journal
YLM — Yale Literary Magazine
YLT — Yu-Yen-Hsueh Lun-Ts'ung
YM — Young Man
YM — Young Miss Magazine
YMJODW — Bulletin. Yamagata University. Medical Science
YMTM — Yikal Maya Than (Mexico)
YN — Yellowknifer
YN — Young Numismatist
YN — Youth and Nation
YNER — Yale Near Eastern Researches
YO — Yelmo
YOBGAD — Year Book of Obstetrics and Gynecology
Yoga Jnl — Yoga Journal
Yokogawa Tech Rep — Yokogawa Technical Report
Yokohama Math J — Yokohama Mathematical Journal
Yokohama Med Bull — Yokohama Medical Bulletin
Yokohama Med J — Yokohama Medical Journal
Yoko Iga — Yokohama Igaku
Yoko Med Bull — Yokohama Medical Bulletin
Yokufukai Geriatr J — Yokufukai Geriatric Journal
Yona Acta Med — Yonago Acta Medica
Yon Act Med — Yonago Acta Medica
Yonago Acta Med — Yonago Acta Medica
Yona Iga Zass — Yonago Igaku Zasshi
Yonsei Eng Rep — Yonsei Engineering Report
Yonsei Eng Rev — Yonsei Engineering Review
Yonsei J Med Sci — Yonsei Journal of Medical Science
Yonsei Med J — Yonsei Medical Journal
Yonsei Rep Trop Med — Yonsei Reports on Tropical Medicine
YOR — Bulletin of Economic Research
YorkCoHS — York County Historical Society. Papers
York Papers Ling — York Papers in Linguistics
York Paps in Linguistics — York Papers in Linguistics
York Pioneer And Hist Soc Rep — York Pioneer and Historical Society. Annual Report
Yorks Beekpr — Yorkshire Beekeeper
Yorks Bull Econ Soc Res — Yorkshire Bulletin of Economic and Social Research

Yorks Geol Soc Occas Publ — Yorkshire Geological Society. Occasional Publication
Yorks Gl S P — Proceedings of the Geological and Polytechnic Society of the West Riding of Yorkshire
Yorkshire A J — Yorkshire Archaeological Journal
Yorkshire Archaeol J — Yorkshire Archaeological Journal
Yorkshire Arch J — Yorkshire Archaeological Journal
Yorkshire Arch Journal — Yorkshire Archaeological Journal
Yorkshire Archt — Yorkshire Architect
Yorkshire Geol Soc Proc — Yorkshire Geological Society. Proceedings
Yorkshire G Polyt Soc Pr — Yorkshire Geological and Polytechnic Society. Proceedings
YOS — Yale Oriental Series
YoShlR — Yokohama Shiritsu Daigaku Ronso
YOSR — Yale Oriental Series
YOSR — Yale Oriental Series. Researches
Young Athl — Young Athlete
Young Child — Young Children
Young Cinema — Young Cinema and Theatre
Young Lib — Young Liberal
Your Comput — Your Computer
Your Mus Cue — Your Musical Cue
Your Okla Dent Assoc J — Your Oklahoma Dental Association Journal
Your Radiol — Your Radiologist
Youth Aid Bull — Youth Aid Bulletin
Youth and Soc — Youth and Society
Youth in Soc — Youth in Society
Youth Soc — Youth and Society
Youth Train News — Youth Training News
YOYUA — Yoyuen
YP — Yorkshire Post
YPA — Yearbook of Physical Anthropology (New York)
YPBRBML — Yale Papyri in the Beinecke Rare Book and Manuscript Library
YPD — Yellow Pages DataSystem
Yperm — Yperman. Bulletin de la Societe Belge d'Histoire de la Medecine
YPHJA — Yo-Up Hoeji
YPL — York Papers in Linguistics
YPLA — Your Public Lands. US Department of the Interior. Bureau of Land Mangement
YPMCM — Yearbook. Public Museum. City of Milwaukee
YPR — Yale Poetry Review
YQ — Youth Quarterly
YR — Yale Review
YR — Yukon Reports
Yrbk Agric — Yearbook of Agriculture. Using Our Natural Resources
Yrbk Austl — Yearbook Australia
Yr Bk (Charleston SC) — Year Book (Charleston, South Carolina)
Yrbk Comp & Gen Lit — Yearbook of Comparative and General Literature
Yrbk Compar & Gen Lit — Yearbook of Comparative and General Literature
Yrbk Educ — Yearbook of Education
Yrbk Sch Law — Yearbook of School Law
Yrbk Sp Educ — Yearbook of Special Education
Yrbk World Aff — Yearbook of World Affairs
YRNH — Yale Review (New Haven, Connecticut)
Y Rom St — Yale Romanic Studies
YRS — Yale Romanic Studies
YRS — Yearbook of Romanian Studies

YRTMA — Yonsei Reports on Tropical Medicine
YS — Yidishe Shprakh
YSCECP Reports — Yugoslav-Serbo-Croatian-English Contrastive Project. Reports
YSCECP Studies — Yugoslav-Serbo-Croatian-English Contrastive Project. Studies
YSE — Yale Studies in English
YSh — Yidishe Shprakh
YSHBDP — Bulletin. Vegetable and Ornamental Crops Research Station. Series B
YSKOD8 — Japanese Journal of Psychopharmacology
YT — Yale Theatre
YT — Yam (Tel Aviv)
YTELSA — Yearbook. Estonian Learned Society in America
YTM — Yearbook for Traditional Music
YU — Yukon News
Yu — Yunost'
Yuasa Tech Inf — Yuasa Technical Information
YUEN — Yukon Economic News
Yugo Exprt — Yugoslavia Export
Yugoslav L — Yugoslav Law
Yugosl Chem Pap — Yugoslav Chemical Papers
Yugosl Hop Symp Proc — Yugoslav Hop Symposium. Proceedings
Yugosl J Oper Res — Yugoslav Journal of Operations Research
Yugosl Law — Yugoslav Law
Yugosl Med Biochem — Yugoslav Medical Biochemistry
Yugosl Surv — Yugoslav Survey
Yugosl Zavod Geol Geofiz Istrazivanja Raspr — Yugoslavia Zavod za Geoloska i Geofizicka Istrazivanja. Rasprave
Yugosl Zavod Geol Geofiz Istrazivanja Vesn Geol — Yugoslavia Zavod za Geoloska i Geofizicka Istrazivanja. Vesnik. Geologija. Serija A
Yug Soc Soil Sci Publ — Yugoslav Society of Soil Science. Publication
Yug Surv — Yugoslav Survey
YUHPAA — Acta Horticulturalia
YU/IJCS — International Journal of Comparative Sociology. York University. Department of Sociology and Anthropology
YUIN — Yukon Indian News
Yuk Stat — Statutes of the Yukon Territory
YULG — Yale University. Library. Gazette
YUN — Yearbook of the United Nations
YUPA — Yale University Publications in Anthropology
YUTR — Yukon Teacher
YUUD — Yukon Update
YUWM — Yukon Water Management Bulletin. Westwater Research Centre
YVB — Yad Vashem Bulletin
Y Viewers — Young Viewers
YVN — Yad Vashem News
YVS — Yad Vashem Studies
YW — Yachting World
YW — Year's Work in Classical Studies
YW — Year's Work in English Studies
YW — Young Woman
YWA — Year's Work in Archaeology
YWC — Year's Work in Classical Studies
YWCS — Year's Work in Classical Studies
YWE — Year's Work in English Studies
YWES — Year's Work in English Studies
YWML — Year's Work in Modern Language Studies
YWMLS — Year's Work in Modern Language Studies
YYYC — Yu-Yen Yen-Chiu

Z

Z — Zagreb
Z — Zeitschrift fuer Romanische Philologie
Z — Zivot
Z — Zora
Z — Z Pola Walki
Z — Zven'ya
Z — Zwingliana
Z — Zycie
Z-A — Zaire-Afrique
ZA — Zeitschrift fuer Assyriologie und Verwandte Gebiete
ZA — Zeitschrift fuer Assyriologie und Vorderasiatische Archaeologie
ZA — Zeitschrift fuer Astrophysik
ZA — Zeitschrift fuer Deutsches Altertum und Deutsche Literatur
ZA — Zionist Archives
ZA — Ziva Antika
ZA — Zofinger Neujahrsblatt
ZA — Zoologischer Anzeiger
ZA — Zunz Archive. Jewish National and University Library
ZAA — Zeitschrift fuer Anglistik und Amerikanistik
Z Aachener Geschichtsver — Zeitschrift. Aachener Geschichtsverein
Z Aach Gesch Ver — Zeitschrift. Aachener Geschichtsverein
ZAAK — Zeitschrift fuer Aesthetik und Allgemeine Kunstwissenschaft
ZABIA — Zastita Bilja
Zaby Przyr Nieozyw — Zabytki Przyrody Nieozywionej Ziem Rzeczpospolitej Polskiej
Z Acclim — Zeitschrift fuer Acclimatisation
ZACFA — Fresenius' Zeitschrift fuer Analytische Chemie
ZA Ch — Zeitschrift fuer Angewandte Chemie
ZA Ch — Zeitschrift fuer Anorganische Chemie
ZA Ch — Zurnal Analiticeskoj Chimii
Zach Cor — Correspondance Astronomique, Geographique, Hydrographique et Statistique. Von Zach
Zach M Cor — Monatliche Correspondenz zur Befoerderung der Erd- und Himmels-Kunde. Von Zach
Z Acker Pflan — Zeitschrift fuer Acker-und-Pflanzenbau
Z Acker-Pflanzenb — Zeitschrift fuer Acker- und Pflanzenbau
Z Acker Pflanzenbau — Zeitschrift fuer Acker- und Pflanzenbau
Z Acker u Pflbau — Zeitschrift fuer Acker- und Pflanzenbau
ZACMA — Zeitschrift fuer Anorganische Chemie
Zad Rev — Zadarska Revija
ZADS — Zeitschrift. Allgemeiner Deutsche Sprachverein
ZAE — Zeitschrift fuer Allgemeine Erdkunde
ZAE — Zeitschrift fuer Angewandte Entomologie
ZAED Phys Daten — ZAED [Zentralstelle fuer Atomkernenergie-Dokumentation] Physik Daten
ZAeg — Zeitschrift fuer Aegyptische Sprache und Altertumskunde
ZAEG — Zeitschrift fuer Anatomie und Entwicklungsgeschichte
Z Aeg Spr — Zeitschrift fuer Aegyptische Sprache und Altertumskunde
Z Aegypt Sprache — Zeitschrift fuer Aegyptische Sprache und Altertumskunde
Z Aegypt Sprache Altertumskd — Zeitschrift fuer Aegyptische Sprache und Altertumskunde
ZAEKD — Zeszyty Naukowe. Akademia Ekonomiczna w Krakowie
Za Ekon Mater — Za Ekonomiyu Materialov
Za Ekon Topl — Za Ekonomiyu Topliva
Z Aerosol Forsch Ther — Zeitschrift fuer Aerosol Forschung und Therapie
Z Aerztl Fortbild — Zeitschrift fuer Aerztliche Fortbildung
Z Aerztl Fortbild (Jena) — Zeitschrift fuer Aerztliche Fortbildung (Jena)
Z Ae S — Zeitschrift fuer Aegyptische Sprache und Altertumskunde
Z Aes Allg Kunst — Zeitschrift fuer Aesthetik und Allgemeine Kunstwissenschaft
Z Aesth — Zeitschrift fuer Aesthetik und Allgemeine Kunstwissenschaft
ZAF — Zeitschrift fuer Aerztliche Fortbildung
ZAFBA — Zeitschrift fuer Aerztliche Fortbildung
ZAG — Zeitschrift des Aachener Geschichtsvereins
ZAG — Zeitschrift fuer Angewandte Geologie
Zagad Ekon Roln — Zagadnienia Ekonomiki Rolnej
Zagadn Ekon Roln — Zagadnienia Ekonomiki Rolnej
Zagadn Eksploatacji Masz — Zagadnienia Eksploatacji Maszyn
Zagadnienia Drgan Nieliniowych — Zagadnienia Drgan Nieliniowych
Zagadnienia Dyn Rozwoju Czlowieka Zesz Probl Kosmosu — Zagadnienie Dynamiki Rozwoju Czlowieka Zeszyty Problemowe Kosmosu
Zagad Tech Fal Ultradziek — Zagadnienia Techniki Fal Ultradzwiekowych
Zagazig J Pharm Sci — Zagazig Journal of Pharmaceutical Sciences
ZAGGD — Zeszyty Naukowe Akademii Gorniczo-Hutniczej Imienia Stanislawa Staszica. Gornictwo
Z Agrargesch Agrarsoziol — Zeitschrift fuer Agrargeschichte und Agrarsoziologie
Z Agrargesch u -Soziol — Zeitschrift fuer Agrargeschichte und Agrarsoziologie

Zagreber Studien — Zagreber Germanistische Studien
ZAGV — Zeitschrift. Aachener Geschichtsverein
Zahnaerztebl (Baden-Wuerttemb) — Zahnaerzteblatt (Baden-Wuerttemberg)
Zahnaerztl Gesundheitsdienst — Zahnaerztlicher Gesundheitsdienst
Zahnaerztl Mitt — Zahnaerztliche Mitteilungen
Zahnaerztl Prax — Zahnaerztliche Praxis
Zahnaerztl Praxisfuehr — Zahnaerztliche Praxisfuehrung
Zahnaerztl Rundsch — Zahnaerztliche Rundschau
Zahnaerztl Welt — Zahnaerztliche Welt
Zahnaerztl Welt Zahnaerztl Reform — Zahnaerztliche Welt und Zahnaerztliche Reform
Zahnaerztl Welt Zahnaerztl Rundsch — Zahnaerztliche Welt, Zahnaerztliche Rundschau
Zahnerh Kd — Zahnerhaltungskunde
Zahn Inf Die — Zahnaerztlicher Informationsdienst
Zahn-Mund-Kieferheilkd — Zahn-, Mund-, und Kieferheilkunde
Zahn- Mund- Kieferheilkd Zentralbl — Zahn-, Mund-, und Kieferheilkunde mit Zentralblatt
Zahn Prax — Zahnaerztliche Praxis
Zahn Rd — Zahnaerztliche Rundschau
Zahntechn — Zahntechnik
Zahntechn — Zahntechniker
Zahntechn Nachr — Zahntechnische Nachrichten
ZAICEL — Zeitschrift fuer Angewandte Ichthyologie
Zaire-Afr — Zaire-Afrique
ZAK — Zeitschrift fuer Aesthetik und Kunstwissenschaft
ZAK — Zeitschrift fuer Schweizerische Archaeologie und Kunstgeschichte
Zakhist Rosl — Zakhist Roslin
Za Khlopk Nezavisimost — Za Khlopkovuyu Nezavisimost
Zakhyst Rosl Resp Mizhvid Temat Nauk Zb — Zakhyst Roslyn Respublikans 'Kyi Mizhvidomchyi Tematychnyi Naukovyi Zbirnyk
Zakonomern Raspred Promesnykh Tsentrov Ionnykh Krist — Zakonomernosti Raspredeleniya Promesnykh Tsentrov v Ionnykh Kristallakh
Zakonomern Razmeshchenlya Polezn Iskop — Zakonomernosti Razmeshchenlya Poleznykh Iskopaemykh
Zakupki Sel'skokhoz Prod — Zakupki Sel'skokhozyaistvennykh Produktov
ZAL — Zeitschrift fuer Arabische Linguistik
Z Al Erdk — Zeitschrift fuer Allgemeine Erdkunde
Z Allgemeine Wissenschaftstheorie — Zeitschrift fuer Allgemeine Wissenschaftstheorie
Z Allgemeinmed — Zeitschrift fuer Allgemeinmedizin
Z Allg Med — Zeitschrift fuer Allgemeinmedizin der Landaerzt
Z Allg Mikr — Zeitschrift fuer Allgemeine Mikrobiologie
Z Allg Mikrobiol — Zeitschrift fuer Allgemeine Mikrobiologie. Morphologie, Physiologie, Genetik, und Oekologie der Mikrorganismen
Z Allg Oesterr Apoth Ver — Zeitschrift. Allgemeiner Oesterreichische Apotheker-Verein
Z Allg Physiol — Zeitschrift fuer Allgemeine Physiologie
Z Allg Wiss — Zeitschrift fuer Allgemeine Wissenschaftstheorie
Z Allg Wissenschaftstheor — Zeitschrift fuer Allgemeine Wissenschaftstheorie
Z Alternsforsch — Zeitschrift fuer Alternsforschung
Z Altt W — Zeitschrift fuer die Alttestamentliche Wissenschaft
Z Alt Wiss — Zeitschrift fuer die Alttestamentliche Wissenschaft
ZAM — Zeitschrift fuer Askese und Mystik
Zambezia Educ Suppl — Zambezia. The Education Supplement
Zambia Dep Game Fish Fish Res Bull — Zambia. Department of Game and Fisheries. Fisheries Research Bulletin
Zambia Dep Wildl Fish Natl Parks Annu Rep — Zambia. Department of Wildlife, Fisheries, and National Parks. Annual Report
Zambia Div For Res Annu Rep — Zambia. Division of Forest Research. Annual Report
Zambia Div For Res Res Pam — Zambia. Division of Forest Research. Research Pamphlet
Zambia For Res Bull — Zambia Forest Research Bulletin
Zambia Geogr Ass Mag — Zambia Geographical Association Magazine
Zambia Geogr Assoc Mag — Zambia Geographical Association. Magazine
Zambia Geol Surv Annu Rep — Zambia. Geological Survey. Annual Report
Zambia Geol Surv Dep Annu Rep — Zambia. Geological Survey. Department Annual Report
Zambia Geol Surv Dep Econ Rep — Zambia. Ministry of Lands and Mines. Geological Survey Department. Economic Report
Zambia Geol Surv Econ Rep — Zambia. Geological Survey. Economic Report
Zambia Geol Surv Rec — Zambia. Geological Survey. Records
Zambia Geol Surv Tech Rep — Zambia. Geological Survey. Technical Report
Zambia J Sci Technol — Zambia Journal of Science and Technology
Zambia Law J — Zambia Law Journal

Zambia Libr Assoc J — Zambia Library Association Journal
Zambia LJ — Zambia Law Journal
Zambia Minist Lands Nat Resour For Res Bull — Zambia. Ministry of Lands and Natural Resources. Forest Research Bulletin
Zambia Minist Rural Dev For Res Bull — Zambia. Ministry of Rural Development. Forest Research Bulletin
Zambia Mus J — Zambia Museums Journal
Zambia Nurse J — Zambia Nurse Journal
Zambia Rep Geol Surv — Zambia. Ministry of Lands and Mines. Report of the Geological Survey
ZA Mech — Zeitschrift fuer Angewandte Mechanik
ZAMM — Zeitschrift fuer Angewandte Mathematik und Mechanik
ZAMNA — ZFA (Zeitschrift fuer Allgemeinmedizin)
ZAMP — Zeitschrift fuer Angewandte Mathematik und Physik
Z Anal Anwendungen — Zeitschrift fuer Analysis und Ihre Anwendungen
Z Anal Chem — Fresenius' Zeitschrift fuer Analytische Chemie
Z Analit Chim — Zurnal Analiticeskoj Chimii
Z Analyt Chem — Zeitschrift fuer Analytische Chemie
Z Anat Entwicklungsgesch — Zeitschrift fuer Anatomie und Entwicklungsgeschichte
ZANCA — Zeitschrift fuer Analytische Chemie
Z An Ch — Zeitschrift fuer Anorganische Chemie
Z An Chim — Zurnal Analiticeskoj Chimii
ZANCO Ser A — ZANCO. Scientific Journal of Sulaimaniyah University. Series A. Pure and Applied Sciences
ZANCO Ser A Pure Appl Sci — ZANCO. Series A. Pure and Applied Sciences
Z & V — Zeiten und Voelker
ZANF — Zeitschrift fuer Assyriologie und Vorderasiatische Altertumskunde. Neue Folge
Z Ang & Amerik — Zeitschrift fuer Anglistik und Amerikanistik
Z Angew Baeder Klimaheilkd — Zeitschrift fuer Angewandte Baeder und Klimaheilkunde
Z Angew C — Zeitschrift fuer Angewandte Chemie
Z Angew Chem — Zeitschrift fuer Angewandte Chemie und Zentralblatt fuer Technische Chemie
Z Angew Entomol — Zeitschrift fuer Angewandte Entomologie
Z Angew Geol — Zeitschrift fuer Angewandte Geologie
Z Angew Ichthyol — Zeitschrift fuer Angewandte Ichthyologie
Z Angew Math Mech — Zeitschrift fuer Angewandte Mathematik und Mechanik
Z Angew Math Phys — Zeitschrift fuer Angewandte Mathematik und Physik
Z Angew Math und Mech — Zeitschrift fuer Angewandte Mathematik und Mechanik
Z Angew Met — Zeitschrift fuer Angewandte Meteorologie
Z Angew Mikrosk Klin Chem — Zeitschrift fuer Angewandte Mikroskopic und Klinische Chemie
Z Angew Mkr — Zeitschrift fuer Angewandte Mikroskopie
Z Angew Photogr Wiss Tech — Zeitschrift fuer Angewandte Photographie in Wissenschaft und Technik
Z Angew Phys — Zeitschrift fuer Angewandte Physik
Z Angew Psychol — Zeitschrift fuer Angewandte Psychologie und Psychologische Forschung
Z Angew Zool — Zeitschrift fuer Angewandte Zoologie
Z Ang Geol — Zeitschrift fuer Angewandte Geologie
Z Anglis Am — Zeitschrift fuer Anglistik und Amerikanistik
Z Ang Ma Me — Zeitschrift fuer Angewandte Mathematik und Mechanik
Z Ang Math — Zeitschrift fuer Angewandte Mathematik und Physik
Z Ang Math Mech — Zeitschrift fuer Angewandte Mathematik und Mechanik
Z Ang Math Phys — Zeitschrift fuer Angewandte Mathematik und Physik
Z Ang Ph — Zeitschrift fuer Angewandte Physik
Z Anorg A C — Zeitschrift fuer Anorganische und Allgemeine Chemie
Z Anorg Allg Chem — Zeitschrift fuer Anorganische und Allgemeine Chemie
Z Anorg C — Zeitschrift fuer Anorganische Chemie
Z Anorg Chem — Zeitschrift fuer Anorganische und Allgemeine Chemie
ZANPA — Zeitschrift fuer Experimentelle und Angewandte Psychologie
ZAnt — Ziva Antika
Zantedeschi A Fis — Annali di Fisica. Zantedeschi
Z Antimikrob Antineoplast Chemother — Zeitschrift fuer Antimikrobielle und Antineoplastische Chemotherapie
Zanzibar Protect Ann Rep Med Dept — Zanzibar Protectorate. Annual Report on the Medical Department
Z Ao Ch — Zeitschrift fuer Anorganische Chemie
ZA Oe R — Zeitschrift fuer Auslaendisches Oeffentliches Recht und Voelkerrecht
ZA Oe RV — Zeitschrift fuer Auslaendisches Oeffentliches Recht und Voelkerrecht
ZAO RV — Zeitschrift fuer Auslaendisches Oeffentliches Recht und Voelkerrecht
ZAOS — Zeitschrift fuer Afrikanische und Oceanische Sprachen
Za Ovladenie Tekh Kamenougol'n Promsti — Za Ovladenie Tekhnikoi v Kamenougol'noi Promyshlennosti
Zap Addz Pryr Nar Gasp — Zapiski Addzelu Pryrody i Narodnaj Gaspadarki
Zapadne Karpaty Ser Geol — Zapadne Karpaty. Seria Geologia
Zapadne Karpaty Ser Hydrogeol Inz Geol — Zapadne Karpaty. Seria. Hydrogeologia a Inzinierska Geologia
Zapadne Karpaty Ser Mineral Petrogr Geochem Metalogeneza — Zapadne Karpaty. Seria. Mineralogia, Petrografia, Geochemia, Metalogeneza
Zapadn Karpaty Ser Paleontol — Zapadne Karpaty. Seria Paleontologia
Zap Arm Otd Vses Mineral Ova — Zapiski Armyanskogo Otdeleniya Vsesoyuznogo Mineralogicheskogo Obshchestva
Zap Beloruss Gos Inst Sel'sk Lesn Khoz — Zapiski Belorusskogo Gosudarstvennogo Instituta Sel'skogo i Lesnogo Khozyaistva
Zap Centr Kavkazsk Otd Vsesojuzn Bot Obsc — Zapiski Central'no-Kavkazskogo Otdelenija Vsesojuznogo Botaniceskogo Obscestva
Zap Cukotsk Kraeved Muz — Zapiski Cukotskogo Kraevedceskogo Muzeja
Zap GO — Zapiski Geograficeskogo Obscestva
Zap Imp Akad Nauk — Zapiski Imperatorskago Akademii Nauk
Zap Imp Russk Geogr Obsc Obscej Geogr — Zapiski Imperatorskago Russkago Geograficeskogo Obscestva po Obscej Geografii

Zap Inst Jaz Lit Ist — Zapiski Gosudarstvennogo Instituta Jazyka, Literatury, i Istorii
Zap Inst Khim Akad Nauk Ukr RSR — Zapiski Institutu Khimii Akademiya Nauk Ukrains'koi RSR
Zapiski Odessa — Zapiski Odesskago Arkheologicheskago Obshchestva
Zapisnici Srp Geol Drus — Zapisnici Srpskog Geoloskog Drustva
Zap Kalm Nauc Issl Inst Jaz Lit Ist — Zapiski. Kalmyckij Naucno-Issledovatel'skij Institut Jazyka, Literatury, i Istorii
Zap Khar'k S-Kh Inst — Zapiski Khar'kovskogo Sel'skokhozyaistvennogo Instituta
Zap Kiiv Tov Prirodozn — Zapiski Kiivs'kogo Tovaristva Prirodoznavtsiv
Zap Kirg Otd Vses Mineral Ova — Zapiski Kirgizskogo Otdeleniya Vsesoyuznogo Mineralogicheskogo Obshchestva
Zap Komiteta Akklim — Zapiski Komiteta Akklimatizacija, Ucrezdennago pri Imperatorskom Moskovskom Obscestve Sel'skago Hozjajstva
Zap KORGO — Zapiski Kavkazskogo Otdela Russkogo Geograficeskogo Obscestva
Zap Leningrad Sel'skokhoz Inst — Zapiski Leningradskogo Sel'skokhozyaistvennogo Instituta
Zap Leningr Gorn Inst — Zapiski Leningradskogo Gornogo Instituta
Zap Leningr Sel'-Khoz Inst — Zapiski Leningradskogo Sel'skokhozyaistvennogo Instituta
Zap Leningr S-Kh Inst — Zapiski Leningradskogo Sel'skokhozyaistvennogo Instituta
Zap Nauchn Semin — Zapiski Nauchnykh Seminarov
Zap Nauchn Semin Leningr Otd Mat Inst Akad Nauk SSSR — Zapiski Nauchnykh Seminarov Leningradskoe Otdelenie Matematicheskii Institut Akademia Nauk SSSR
Zap Nauchn Sem Leningrad Otdel Mat Inst Steklov (LOMI) — Zapiski Nauchnykh Seminarov Leningradskogo Otdelenija Matematicheskogo Instituta Imeni V. A. Steklova Akademii Nauk SSSR (LOMI)
Zap Naucno Prikl Otd Tiflissk Bot Sada — Zapiski Naucno-Prikladnykh Otdelov Tiflisskago Botaniceskogo Sada. Tbilisi Botanikur Bagis Mecnierul-Bamogenebithi Ganqophilebatha Nacerebi/Scientific Papers. Applied Sections. Tiflis Botanical Garden
Zap Naucn Sem Leningrad Otdel Mat Inst Steklov — Zapiski Naucnyh Seminarov Leningradskogo Otdelenija Matematiceskogo Instituta Imeni V. A. Steklova Akademii Nauk SSSR
Zap Obsc Izuc Amursk Kraja Vladivostoksk Otd Priamursk Otd Ru — Zapiski Obscestva Izucenija Amurskogo Kraja Vladivostokskogo Otdelenija Priamurskogo Otdela Russkogo Geograficeskogo Obscestva
Zap Odess Ark Obshch — Zapiski Odesskoe Arkheologicheskoe Obshchestvo
ZAPPA — Zentralblatt fuer Allgemeine Pathologie und Pathologische Anatomie
Za Prog Proizvod — Za Progress Proizvodstva
Zap Rossijsk Akad Nauk — Zapiski Rossijskoj Akademii Nauk/Memoires de l'Academie des Sciences de Russie
Zap Ross Mineral Ova — Zapiski Rossiiskogo Mineralogicheskogo Obshchestva
Zap Semipalatinsk Pododtd Zapadno Sibirsk Otd Imp Russk Geogr — Zapiski Semipalatinskago Pododtdela Zapadno-Sibirskago Otdela Imperatorskago Russkago Geograficeskago Obscestva
Zap SKK Gor NII — Zapiski Severo-Kavkazskogo Kraevogo Gorskogo Naucno-Issledovatel'skogo Instituta
Zap Sredne Sibirsk Otd Gosud Russk Geogr Obsc — Zapiski Sredne-Sibirskogo Otdela Byvsego Krasnojarskogo Gosudarstvennogo Russkogo Geograficeskogo Obscestva/Memoirs. Middle-Siberian Section formerly Krasnojarsk-Section. State Russian Geographical Society
Zap Sverdl Otd Vses Bot Ova — Zapiski Sverdlovskogo Otdeleniya Vsesoyuznogo Botanicheskogo Obshchestva
Zap Sverdlov Otd Vsesoyuz Bot Obshch — Zapiski Sverdlovskogo Otdeleniya Vsesoyuznogo Botanicheskogo Obshchestva
Zap Tadzh Otd Vses Mineral Ova — Zapiski Tadzhikskogo Otdeleniya Vsesoyuznogo Mineralogicheskogo Obshchestva
Zap Tsentr Kavk Otd Vses Bot Ova — Zapiski Tsentral'no-Kavkazskogo Otdeleniya Vsesoyuznogo Botanicheskogo Obshchestva
Zap Ukr Otd Vses Mineral Ova — Zapiski Ukrainskogo Otdeleniya Vsesoyuznogo Mineralogicheskogo Obshchestva
Zap Uralsk Obsc Ljubit Estestv — Zapiski Ural'skago Obscestva Ljubitelej Estestvozanija/Bulletin de la Societe Ouralienne d'Amateurs des Sciences Naturelles
Zap Uzb Otd Vses Mineral Ova — Zapiski Uzbekistanskogo Otdeleniya Vsesoyuznogo Mineralogicheskogo Obshchestva
Zap Voronezh Sel'-Khoz Inst — Zapiski Voronezhskogo Sel'skokhozyaistvennogo Instituta
Zap Voronezh S-Kh Inst — Zapiski Voronezhskogo Sel'skokhozyaistvennogo Instituta
Zap Vost Sib Otd Vses Mineral Ova — Zapiski Vostochno-Sibirskogo Otdeleniya Vsesoyuznogo Mineralogicheskogo Obshchestva
Zap Vses Mineral Obshchest — Zapiski Vsesoyuznogo Mineralogicheskogo Obshchestva
Zap Vses Mineral O-Va — Zapiski Vsesoyuznogo Mineralogicheskogo Obshchestva
Zap Zabaik Fil Geogr Ova SSSR — Zapiski Zabaikal'skogo Filiala Geograficheskogo Obshchestva SSSR
Zap Zabaik Otd Vses Geogr O-Va — Zapiski Zabaikal'skogo Otdela Vsesoyuznogo Geograficheskogo Obshchestva
Zap Zapadno Sibirsk Otd Imp Russk Geogr Obsc — Zapiski Zapadno-Sibirskago Otdela Imperatorskago Russkago Geograficeskago Obscestva
Z Arbeitsgem Oesterr Entomol — Zeitschrift. Arbeitsgemeinschaft Oesterreichischer Entomologen
Z Arbeitswiss — Zeitschrift fuer Arbeitswissenschaft
Z Arbeitswiss N F — Zeitschrift fuer Arbeitswissenschaft. Neue Folge
Z Arch — Zeitschrift fuer Archaeologie
Z Archaeol — Zeitschrift fuer Archaeologie
Za Rekonstr Tekst Promsti — Za Rekonstruktsiyu Tekstil'noi Promyshlennosti
ZARSA — Zeszyty Naukowe. Akademia Rolnicza w Szczecinie
ZarSl — Zaranie Slaskie
Z Arztl Fortbild Jena — Zeitschrift fuer Arztliche Fortbildung (Jena)
ZAS — Zeitschrift fuer Aegyptische Sprache und Altertumskunde

ZAS — Zeitschrift fuer Afrikanische Sprachen
ZASA — Zeitschrift fuer Aegyptische Sprache und Altertumskunde
Zashch Korroz Khim Promsti — Zashchita ot Korrozii v Khimicheskoi Promyshlennosti
Zashch Met — Zashchita Metallov
Zashch Pokrytiya Met — Zashchitnye Pokrytiya na Metallakh
Zashch Rast (Kiev) — Zashchita Rastenii (Kiev)
Zashch Rast (Leningrad) — Zashchita Rastenii (Leningrad)
Zashch Rast (Mosc) — Zashchita Rastenii (Moscow)
Zashch Rast (Moscow) — Zashchita Rastenii (Moscow)
Zashch Rast Vred Bolez — Zashchita Rastenii ot Vreditelei i Boleznei
Zashch Rast Vred Bolezn — Zashchita Rastenii ot Vreditelei i Boleznei
Zashch Rast Vredit Bolez — Zashchita Rastenii ot Vreditelei i Boleznei
Zashch Truboprovodov Korroz — Zashchita Truboprovodov ot Korrozii
Z Asiat Studien — Zentralasiatische Studien
Za Soc Zemed — Za Socialisticke Zemedelstvi
Za Sots Sel'-Khoz Nauku — Za Sotsialisticheskuyu Sel'skokhozyaistvennuyu Nauku
Za Sots Sel'skokhoz Nauku Ser A — Za Sotsialisticheskuyu Sel'skokhozyaistvennuyu Nauku. Seriya A
ZASprache — Zeitschrift fuer Aegyptische Sprache und Altertumskunde
Z Assyr — Zeitschrift fuer Assyriologie
Zast Bilja — Zastita Bilja
Z Asthet Al — Zeitschrift fuer Asthetik und Allgemeine Kunstwissenschaft
ZastMat — Zastosowania Matematyki
Zast Mater — Zastita Materijala
Zastos Mat — Polska Akademia Nauk. Instytut Matematyczny. Zastosowania Matematyki
Zastosow Mat — Zastosowania Matematyki
Z Astrophys — Zeitschrift fuer Astrophysik
ZATB — Zeitschrift fuer die Alttestamentliche Wissenschaft. Beihefte
Za Tekh Prog (Baku) — Za Tekhnicheskii Progress (Baku)
Za Tekh Prog (Gorkly) — Za Tekhnicheskii Progress (Gorkly)
ZATPA — Za Tekhnicheskii Progress
Za Turf Ind — Za Turfyanuyu Industriyu
ZATW — Zeitschrift fuer die Alttestamentliche Wissenschaft
Z Augenheilkd — Zeitschrift fuer Augenheilkunde
Z Ausbau Entwicklungsl — Zeitschrift fuer den Ausbau der Entwicklungslehre
Z Auslaend Landwirtsch — Zeitschrift fuer Auslaendische Landwirtschaft
Z Auslaend Oeff Voelkerrecht — Zeitschrift fuer Auslaendisches Oeffentliches Recht und Voelkerrecht
Z Ausland Landwirt — Zeitschrift fuer Auslaendische Landwirtschaft
Z Ausl Oeff R — Zeitschrift fuer Auslaendisches Oeffentliches Recht und Voelkerrecht
Z Ausl Oeff Recht Voelkerrecht — Zeitschrift fuer Auslaendisches Oeffentliches Recht und Voelkerrecht
Z Ausl Oeff RVR — Zeitschrift fuer Auslaendisches Oeffentliches Recht und Voelkerrecht
ZAVA — Zeitschrift fuer Assyriologie und Vorderasiatische Archaeologie
Zav Lab — Zavodskaya Laboratoriya
Zavod Geol Geofiz Istraz Vesn Ser A — Zavod za Geoloska i Geofizicka Istrazivanja. Vesnik. Serija A. Geologija
Zavod Lab — Zavodskaya Laboratoriya
Zavod Lab Diagn Mater — Zavodskaya Laboratoriya, Diagnostika Materialov
ZAW — Zeitschrift fuer die Alttestamentliche Wissenschaft
ZAWEA — Zahnaerztliche Welt
Z Az — Zoologischer Anzeiger
ZB — Zeitschrift fuer Balkanologie
ZB — Zeitschrift fuer Betriebswirtschaft
ZB — Zeitschrift fuer Botanik
ZB — Zentralblatt fuer Bibliothekswesen
ZBA — Zeitschrift fuer Arbeitswissenschaft
ZBalk — Zeitschrift fuer Balkanologie
Z Balkanol — Zeitschrift fuer Balkanologie
Z Bauw — Zeitschrift fuer Bauwecon
Z Bayer Kg — Zeitschrift fuer Bayerische Kirchengeschichte
Z Bayer Kirchengesch — Zeitschrift fuer Bayerische Kirchengeschichte
Z Bayer Landesgesch — Zeitschrift fuer Bayerische Landesgeschichte
Z Bayer Ldg — Zeitschrift fuer Bayerische Landesgeschichte
Z Bayer Revisions Ver — Zeitschrift. Bayerischer Revisions Verein
Z Bay Land Gesch — Zeitschrift fuer Bayerische Landesgeschichte
ZBB — Zeitschrift fuer Bibliothekswesen und Bibliographie
ZBB — Zentralblatt fuer Bibliothekswesen
Zb Bioteh Fak Univ Edvarda Kardelja Ljublj Kmetijstvo — Zbornik Biotehniske Fakultete Univerze Edvarda Kardelja v Ljubljani. Kmetijstvo
Zb Bioteh Fak Univ Edvarda Kardelja Ljublj Vet — Zbornik Biotehniske Fakultete Univerze Edvarda Kardelja v Ljubljani Veterinarstvo
Zb Bioteh Fak Univ Ljubljani — Zbornik Biotehniske Fakultete Univerze v Ljubljani
Zb Bioteh Fak Univ Ljublj Kmetijstvo — Zbornik Biotehniske Fakultete Univerze v Ljubljani. Kmetijstvo
Zb Bioteh Fak Univ Ljublj Vet — Zbornik Biotehniske Fakultete Univerze v Ljubljani. Veterinarstvo
Zb Bioteh Fak Univ Ljublj Vet Supl — Zbornik Biotehniske Fakultete Univerze v Ljubljani. Veterinarstvo. Suplement
Zb Biotehn Fak Univ Ljublj — Zbornik Biotehniske Fakultete Univerze v Ljubljani
ZBBW — Zentralblatt fuer Bibliothekswesen
ZBCSA — Zentralblatt fuer Chirurgie. Supplement
ZBDLG — Zuercher Beitraege zur Deutschen Literatur und Geistesgeschichte
ZBDSS — Zuercher Beitraege zur Deutschen Sprach- und Stilgeschichte
Z Beamtenrecht — Zeitschrift fuer Beamtenrecht
Z Beih — Beihefte. Zeitschrift fuer Romanische Philologie
Z Beleuchtungswes Heizungs- Lueftungstech — Zeitschrift fuer Beleuchtungswesen Heizungs- und Lueftungstechnik
Z Berg Gesch V — Zeitschrift. Bergischer Geschichtsverein

Z Berg H Salw — Zeitschrift fuer das Berg-, Huetten-, und Salinenwesen in dem Preussischen Staate
Z Berg Huetten Salinenwes Dtsch Reich — Zeitschrift fuer das Berg-, Huetten-, und Salinenwesen im Deutschen Reich
Z Berg Huettenwes Huettenwes — Zeitschrift fuer Berg und Huettenwesen. Huettenwesen
Z Bergrecht — Zeitschrift fuer Bergrecht
Z Betriebsw — Zeitschrift fuer Betriebswirtschaft
Z Betriebswirtsch — Zeitschrift fuer Betriebswirtschaft
Z Bevoelkerungswiss — Zeitschrift fuer die Bevoelkerungswissenschaft
Z Bewasserungswirtsch — Zeitschrift fuer Bewasserungswirtschaft
ZBF — Zeitschrift fuer Betriebswirtschaftliche Forschung
ZBF — Zeitschrift fuer Buecherfreunde
Zb f Bibl — Zentralblatt fuer Bibliothekswesen
ZbFL — Zbornik za Filologiju i Lingvistiku
ZBG — Zeitschrift. Bergischer Geschichtsverein
Zb Geol Vied Zapadne Karpaty — Zbornik Geologicych Vied Zapadne Karpaty
ZBGR — Schweizerische Zeitschrift fuer Beurkundungs- und Grundbuchrecht
ZBGV — Zeitschrift. Bergischer Geschichtsverein
Z Bibliothekswes Bibliogr — Zeitschrift fuer Bibliothekswesen und Bibliographie
Z Bibliothekswesen und Bibl — Zeitschrift fuer Bibliothekswesen und Bibliographie
Z Bibliot u Bibliog — Zeitschrift fuer Bibliothekswesen und Bibliographie
Z Bibl und Bibliog — Zeitschrift fuer Bibliothekswesen und Bibliographie
Z Bienenforsch — Zeitschrift fuer Bienenforschung
Z Bild K — Zeitschrift fuer Bildende Kunst
Z Binnenfisch DDR — Zeitschrift fuer die Binnenfischerei der DDR
Zb Inst Khim Tekhnol Akad Nauk Ukr RSR — Zbirnik Institutu Khimichnoi Tekhnologii Akademiya Nauk Ukrains'koi RSR
Z Biochem — Zeitschrift fuer Biochemie
Z Biol — Zeitschrift fuer Biologie
Z Biol Tech Method — Zeitschrift fuer Biologische Technik und Methodik
Zbirka Izbran Poglav Fiz — Zbirka Izbranih Poglavij iz Fizike
Zbirka Izbran Poglav Mat — Zbirka Izbranih Poglavij iz Matematike
Zbirn Biol Fak — Zbirnyk Biologicnogo Fakul'tetu
Zbirn Prac Dniprovsk Biol Stanciji — Zbirnyk Prac' Dniprovs'koji Biologicnoji Stanciji. Travaux de la Station Biologique du Dniepre
ZbirP — Zbirnyk Prac' Naukovoji Sevcenkivs'koji Konferenciji
ZBJV — Zeitschrift. Bernischer Juristen-Verein
ZBK — Zeitschrift fuer Bildende Kunst
ZBK — Zeitschrift fuer Buchkunde
ZBKG — Zeitschrift fuer Bayerische Kirchengeschichte
ZBL — Zeitschrift fuer Bayerische Landesgeschichte
Z Bl — Zeitschrift fuer Biologie
Zbl — Zentralblatt fuer Mathematik und Ihre Grenzgebiete
Zbl Allg Path — Zentralblatt fuer Allgemeine Pathologie und Pathologische Anatomie
Zbl A Med — Zentralblatt fuer Arbeitsmedizin und Arbeitsschutz [Later, Zentralblatt fuer Arbeitsmedizin, Arbeitsschutz, und Prophylaxe]
Zbl Aughlkde — Centralblatt fuer Augenheilkunde
Zbl Bakt — Zentralblatt fuer Bakteriologie. International Journal of Medical Microbiology
Zbl Bakt A — Zentralblatt fuer Bakteriologie. Reihe A
Zbl Bakt B — Zentralblatt fuer Bakteriologie. Reihe B
Zbl Bibliothw — Centralblatt fuer Bibliothekwesen
Zbl DDR — Zentralblatt der Deutschen Demokratischen Republik
Zb Lek Fak (Kosice) — Zbornik Lekarskej Fakulty (Kosice)
Zb Lek Fak UPJS Kosice — Zbornik Lekarskej Fakulty UPJS Kosice
Zbl f Bibl — Zentralblatt fuer Bibliothekswesen
ZBLG — Zeitschrift fuer Bayerische Landesgeschichte
Zbl Ges Forstw — Centralblatt fuer das Gesamte Forstwesen
Zbl Hyg Umw — Zentralblatt fuer Hygiene und Umweltmedizin
Zbl Krkht Harnorg — Centralblatt fuer die Krankheiten der Harn- und Sexualorgane
Zbl Math — Zentralblatt fuer Mathematik und Ihre Grenzgebiete
Zbl Physiol — Centralblatt fuer Physiologie
Zbl Soz Vers — Zentralblatt fuer Sozialversicherung und Versorgung
Zbl Vet A — Zentralblatt fuer Veterinaermedizin. Reihe A
Zbl Vet B — Zentralblatt fuer Veterinaermedizin. Reihe B
Zb Meteorol Hidrol Rad — Zbornik Meteoroloskih i Hidroloskih Radova
Zb Nauk Pr Aspir Kiiv Inzh Budiv Inst — Zbirnik Naukovikh Prats Aspirantiv Kiivs'ki Inzhenerno-Budivel'nii Institut
Zb Nauk Pr Aspir Kyyiv Univ Pryr Nauky — Zbirnyk Naukovykh Prats' Aspirantiv Kyyivski Universytet Pryrodni Nauky
Zb Nauk Pr Bilotserk Dos Sel Statsiya — Zbirnyk Naukovykh Prats' Bilotserkiv'sta Doslidno-Selektsionna Statsiya
Zb Nauk Pr Khim Sil'sk Hospod Ukr Sil'skohospod Akad — Zbirnyk Naukovykh Prats' Khimicheskoho Sil'skoho Hospodarstva Ukrayinskoyi Sil'skohospodarskoyi Akademiyi
Zb Nauk Pr Kiiv Budiv Inst — Zbirnik Naukovikh Prats Kiivs'kii Budivel'nii Institut
Zb Nauk Pr L'viv Med Inst — Zbirnyk Naukovykh Prats' L'viv'kyi Medychni Instytut
Zb Nauk Pr Umans'kyi Sil'skohospod Inst — Zbirnyk Naukovykh Prats' Umans'kyi Sil'skohospodarskyi Instytut
Zb Nauk Rob Khark Derzh Med Inst — Zbirnik Naukovikh Robit Kharkivs'kogo Derzhavnogo Medichnogo Institutu
ZbNPAF — Zbirnyk Naukovych Prac' Aspirantiv z Filolohiji
Zbor Arheol Muz — Zbornik na Arheoloskiot Muzej
Zbor Muz Primenjene Umet — Zbornik Muzej Primenjene Umetnosti
Zbor Narod Muz Beogradu — Zbornik Narodnog Muzeja u Beogradu
Zborn Bioteh Fak Univ Ljublj Kmet — Zbornik Biotehniske Fakultete Univerze v Ljubljani. Kmetijstvo
Zborn Etnogr Inst Belgrade — Zbornik Radova. Etnografski Institut. Srpska Akademija Nauka i Umetnosti (Belgrade)
Zbornik Beograd — Zbornik Filozofskog Fakulteta. Beograd
Zbornik (Beograd) — Zbornik Narodnog Muzeja (Beograd)
Zbornik Ljubljana — Zbornik Filozofske Fakultete Ljubljana
Zbornik Nar Muz Beograd — Zbornik Narodnog Muzeja (Beograd)

Zbornik Rad (Beograd) — Zbornik Radova Vizantoloskog Instituta (Beograd)

Zbornik Rad Mat Inst (Beograd) — Zbornik Radova. Matematicki Institut (Beograd)

Zbornik Slov Nar Muz — Zbornik Slovenskeho Narodneho Muzea

Zborn Rad — Zbornik Radova

Zborn Rad Biol Inst Nar Republ Srbije — Zbornik Radova. Bioloski Institut N.R. Srbije. Recueil des Travaux. Institut Biologique

Zborn Rad Poljopriv Fak Univ Beogr — Zbornik Radova. Poljoprivrednog Fakulteta. Universitet u Beogradu

Zborn Slov Nar Moz Etnogr — Zbornik Slovenskeho Narodneho Mozea. Etnografia

Zborn Slov Nar Muz Prir Vedy — Zbornik Slovenskeho Narodneho Muzea Prirodne Vedy

Zbor Slov Muz — Zbornik Slovenskeho Narodneho Muzea

Zbor Slov Narod Muz — Zbornik Slovenskeho Narodneho Muzea

Z Bot — Zeitschrift fuer Botanik

ZBPHA — Zentralblatt fuer Bakteriologie, Parasitenkunde, Infektionskrankheiten, und Hygiene. Abteilung 1. Medizinisch-Hygienische Bakteriologie, Virusforschung, und Parasitologie. Originale

Zb Prac Chem Fak SVST (Bratislava) — Zbornik Prac Chemickotechnologickej Fakulty SVST (Bratislava)

Zb Prav Fak Zagrebu — Zbornik Pravnog Fakulteta u Zagrebu

Zb Pr Belarus Dzyarzh Med Inst — Zbornik Prats. Belaruski Dzyarzhauny Medychny Instytut

Zb Pr Chemickotechnol Fak SVST — Zbornik Prac Chemickotechnologickej Fakulty SVST

Zb Pr Chem-Technol Fak SVST — Zbornik Prac Chemickotechnologickej Fakulty SVST

Zb Pr Inst Teploenerg Akad Nauk Ukr RSR — Zbirnik Prats' Institut Teploenergetiki Akademiya Nauk Ukrains'koi RSR

Zb Prir Nauke Matica Srp — Zbornik za Prirodne Nauke Matica Srpska

Zb Pr Lek Fak Univ PJ Safarika Kosiciach — Zbornik Prac Lekarskej Fakulty Univerzity P. J. Safarika v Kosiciach

Zb Pr Nauk Inst Fiziol Kyyiv Univ — Zbirnyk Prats' Naukovodoslidnyts'koho Instytuta Fiziolohiyi Kyyivs'koho Universytetu

Zb Pr Naukovodosl Inst Fiziol Kyyiv Univ — Zbirnyk Prats' Naukovodoslidnyts'koho Instytuta Fiziolohiyi Kyyivs'koho Universytetu

Zb Pr Ukr Derzh Inst Nauk Prakt Vet — Zbirnik Prats' Ukrains'kii Derzhavnii Institut Naukovoi ta Praktichnoi Veterin arii

Zb Pr Ukr Inst Eksp Vet — Zbirnik Prats' Ukrains'kogo Institutu Eksperimental'noi Veterinarii

Zb Pr Ustavu Exp Farmakol SAV — Zbornik Prac Ustavu Experimentalnej Farmakologie SAV (Slovenska Akademia Vied)

Zb Pr Zool Muz Akad Nauk Ukr RSR — Zbirnyk Prats' Zoolohichnoho Muzeyu Akademiyi Nauk Ukrayinskoyi RSR

ZbR — Zbirnyk Robit Aspirantiv Romano-Germans'koji i Klazycnoji Filolohiji

Zb Rab Belarus Sel'Ska-Gaspad Inst — Zbornik Rabot Belaruskaga Sel'ska-Gaspadarchaga Instytuta

Zb Rad — Zbornik Radova Filozofskog Fakulteta u Nisu. Serija Matematika

Zb Rad Biol Inst (Beograd) — Zbornik Radova. Bioloski Institut (Beograd)

Zb Rad Biol Inst NR Srbye Beogr — Zbornik Radova. Bioloski Institut NR Srbye Beograd

Zb Rad Hrvat Geol Kongr — Zbornik Radova. Hrvatski Geoloski Kongres

Zb Rad Kragujevac — Zbornik Radova. Univerzitet Svetozar Markovic Kragujevac. Prirodno-Matematicki Fakultet

Zb Rad Math Inst Beograd NS — Beograd Matematicki Institut. Zbornik Radova. Nouvelle Serie

Zb Rad Mat Inst (Beograd) — Zbornik Radova. Nova Serija. Matematicki Institut (Beograd). Zbornik Radova. Nova Serija

Zb Rad Poljopr Fak Univ Beogradu — Zbornik Radova. Poljoprivrednog Fakulteta. Universitet u Beogradu

Zb Rad Poljopr Inst — Zbornik Radova. Poljoprivredni Institut

Zb Rad Poljopr Inst (Osijek) — Zbornik Radova. Poljoprivredni Institut (Osijek)

Zb Rad Poljopriv Fak Univ Beogradu — Zbornik Radova. Poljoprivrednog Fakulteta. Universitet u Beogradu

Zb Rad Prir Mat Fak — Zbornik Radova. Prirodno-Matematickog Fakulteta

Zb Rad Prir-Mat Fak Ser Fiz — Zbornik Radova. Prirodno-Matematickog Fakulteta. Serija za Fiziku

Zb Rad Prir-Mat Fak Univ Novom Sadu — Zbornik Radova. Prirodno-Matematickog Fakulteta Univerzitet u Novom Sadu

Zb Rad Prir Mat Fak Univ Nov Sadu Ser Hem — Zbornik Radova Prirodno-Matematickog Fakulteta. Univerzitet u Novom Sadu. Serija za Hemiju

Zb Rad Prirod Mat Fak Ser Mat — Zbornik Radova Prirodno-Matematichkog Fakulteta. Serija za Matematiku

Zb Rad Rud Geol Fak — Zbornik Radova. Rudarsko-Geoloskog Fakulteta

Zb Rad Srp Akad Nauka Geol Inst — Zbornik Radova. Srpska Akademija Nauka Geoloski Institut

Zb Rad Tekhnol Fak Novom Sadu — Zbornik Radova. Tekhnoloski Fakultet u Novom Sadu

Zb Rad Varazdin — Zbornik Radova. Sveuc. Zagrebu, Varazdin

Zb Rad Zavod Ratarstvo (Sarajevo) — Zbornik Radova. Zavod za Ratarstvo (Sarajevo)

Zbraslav Res Inst Land Reclam Improv Sci Monogr — Zbraslav Research Institute for Land Reclamation and Improvement. Scientific Monograph

ZbRFFZ — Zbornik Radova. Filozofskog Fakulteta. Svencilista u Zagrebu

ZbRL — Zbirnyk Robit Aspirantiv L'Vivskvj Derzavnyj Universitet

Zb Robit Aspir L'Viv Univ Pryr Nauk — Zbirnyk Robit Aspirantiv L'Vivs'kyi Universytet Pryrodnykh Nauk

ZBRS — Z's Briefs. CPSU [*Cooperative Park Studies Unit, University of Alaska*] Newsletter

ZbS — Zbornik za Slavistiku

ZBS — Zeitschrift. Deutscher Verein fuer Buchwesen und Schrifttum

ZbSAN — Zbornik Radova. Srpske Akademije Nauke

ZBSB — Zeitschriftenkatalog der Bayerischen Staatsbibliothek, Muenchen

Zb Slov Nar Muzea Muz Prir Vedy — Zbornik Slovenskeho Narodneho Muzea Prirodne Vedy

Zb Slov Nar Muz Prir Vedy — Zbornik Slovenskeho Narodneho Muzea Prirodne Vedy

Zb Ved Prac Lesn Fak Vys Sk Lesn Drev Zvolene — Zbornik Vedeckych Prac Lesnickej Fakulty Vysokej Skoly Lesnickej a Drevarskej vo Zvolene

Zb Ved Pr Drev Fak Tech Univ Zvolene — Zbornik Vedeckych Prac Drevarskej Fakulty Technickej Univerzity vo Zvolene

Zb Ved Pr Vys Sk Tech Kosiciach — Zbornik Vedeckych Prac. Vysokej Skoly Technickej v Kosiciach

ZBVL — Zuercher Beitraege zur Vergleichenden Literaturgeschichte

Zb Vojnomed Akad — Zbornik Vojnomedicinske Akademije

Zb Vychodoslovenskeho Muzea Ser AB Prir Vedy — Zbornik Vychodoslovenskeho Muzea. Seria AB. Prirodne Vedy

Zb Vysk Pr Vysk Ustav Zvaracskeho Bratislave — Zbornik Vyskumnych Prac Vyskumneho Ustavu Zvaracskeho v Bratislave

Zb Vyzk Pr Odboru Pap Celulozy — Zbornik Vyzkumnych Prac z Odboru Papiera a Celulozy

ZBW — Zeitschrift fuer Betriebswirtschaft

ZBW — Zentralblatt fuer Bibliothekswesen

Zb Zgodovino Naravoslovja Tek — Zbornik za Zgodovino Naravoslovja in Teknike

Z C — Zeitschrift fuer Chemie

ZC — Zuercher-Chronik

Z Cas — Zgodovinski Casopis

Z Chem — Zeitschrift fuer Chemie

Z Chem Apparatenkd — Zeitschrift fuer Chemische Apparatenkunde

Z Chemie (Lpz) — Zeitschrift fuer Chemie (Leipzig)

Z Chem Ind Kolloide — Zeitschrift fuer Chemie und Industrie der Kolloide

Z Chemother Verw Geb Teil 1 — Zeitschrift fuer Chemotherapie und Verwandte Gebiete. Teil 1. Originale

Z Chemother Verw Geb Teil 2 — Zeitschrift fuer Chemotherapie und Verwandte Gebiete. Teil 2. Referate

ZChK — Zeitschrift fuer Christliche Kunst

ZChrK — Zeitschrift fuer Christliche Kunst

Z C In — Zeitschrift fuer die Chemische Industrie

ZCK — Zeitschrift fuer Christliche Kunst

ZCP — Zeitschrift fuer Celtische Philologie

ZCP — Zeitschrift fuer Celtische Philologie und Volksforschung

ZCPh — Zeitschrift fuer Celtische Philologie

Zc Ph — Zeitschrift fuer Keltische Philologie und Volksforschung

ZCzest — Ziemia Czestochowska

ZD — Zeitschrift fuer Deutschkunde

ZD — Zielsprache Deutsch

ZD — Zuercher Denkmalpflege

ZDA — Zeitschrift fuer Deutsches Altertum und Deutsche Literatur

ZDADL — Zeitschrift fuer Deutsches Altertum und Deutsche Literatur

Z Dampfkessel Maschinenbetr — Zeitschrift fuer Dampfkessel und Maschinenbetrieb

Z Dampfkesselunters Versicher Ges — Zeitschrift. Dampfkesseluntersuchungs- und Versicherungs-Gesellschaft

ZDB — Zeitschriftendatenbank

ZDB — Zeitschrift fuer Deutsche Bildung

ZDE — Zentralstelle Dokumentation Elektrotechnik Database

ZDemogr — Zeitschrift fuer Demographie und Statistik der Juden

Z Desinfekt Gesundheitswes — Zeitschrift fuer Desinfektions- und Gesundheitswesen

Z Deut Alt — Zeitschrift fuer Deutsches Altertum und Deutsche Literatur

Z Deut Altertum Deut Llit — Zeitschrift fuer Deutsches Altertum und Deutsche Literatur

Z Deut Geol Ges — Zeitschrift. Deutsche Geologische Gesellschaft

Z Deut Morgenlaend Ges — Zeitschrift der Deutschen Morgenlaendischen Gesellschaft

Z Deut Phil — Zeitschrift fuer Deutsche Philologie

Z Deutsch Mykol Ges — Zeitschrift der Deutschen Mykologischen Gesellschaft

Z Deus Morgen G — Zeitschrift. Deutsche Morgenlaendische Gesellschaft

Z Deut Ver — Zeitschrift. Deutschen Verein fuer Kunstwissenschaft

ZDFALP — Z Dziejow Form Artystycznych Literaturze Polskiej

ZDG — Zeitschrift fuer Deutsche Geistesgeschichte

ZDG — Zeitschrift fuer Deutsche Geisteswissenschaft

ZDGG — Zeitschrift der Deutschen Geologischen Gesellschaft

ZDGG — Zeitschrift fuer Deutsche Geistesgeschichte

ZDK — Zeitschrift fuer Deutsche Kulturgeschichte

ZDK — Zeitschrift fuer Deutschkunde

ZDKAA — Zdravookhranenie Kazakhstana

ZDKP — Zeitschrift fuer Deutsche Kulturphilosophie

ZDL — Zeitschrift fuer Dialektologie und Linguistik

ZDM — Zeitschrift fuer Deutsche Mundarten

ZDM — Zentralblatt fuer Didaktik der Mathematik

ZDMG — Zeitschrift der Deutschen Morgenlaendischen Gesellschaft

ZDMG — Zeitschrift. Deutsche Morgenlaendische Gesellschaft

ZDMG Suppl — Zeitschrift der Deutschen Morgenlaendischen Gesellschaft. Supplement

ZD Musik — Zeitschriftendienst Musik

Zd Natkde Heilkde — Zeitschrift fuer Natur- und Heilkunde

Z Dnipr INO — Zapiski Dnipropetrovs'kogo Institutu Narodnoi Osviti

Zdorov'e Nauch Pop Gig Zhurnal — Zdorov'e Nauchno Populiarnyi Gigienicheskii Zhurnal

ZDP — Zeitschrift fuer Deutsche Philologie

ZDPh — Zeitschrift fuer Deutsche Philologie

ZDPV — Zeitschrift. Deutscher Palaestinaverein

Zdrav Aktual — Zdravotnicke Aktuality

Zdrav Delo — Zdravno Delo

Zdravookhr Beloruss — Zdravookhranenie Belorussii

Zdravookhr Belorussii — Zdravookhranenie Belorussii

Zdravookhr Kaz — Zdravookhranenie Kazakhstana

Zdravookhr Kirg — Zdravookhranenie Kirgizii

Zdravookhr Ross Fed — Zdravookhranenie Rossiiskoi Federatsii

Zdravookhr Sov Est Sb — Zdravookhranenie Sovetskoi Estonii Sbornik
Zdravookhr Tadzh — Zdravookhranenie Tadzhikistana
Zdravookhr Turkm — Zdravookhranenie Turkmenistana
Zdrav Prac — Zdravotnicka Pracovnice
Zdravst Vest — Zdravstveni Vestnik
Zdrav Techn Vzduchotech — Zdravotni Technika a Vzduchotechnika
Zdrav Tech Vzduchotech — Zdravotni Technika a Vzduchotechnika
Zdrav Vestn — Zdravstveni Vestnik
Zdrow Publiczne — Zdrowie Publiczne
ZdS — Zeitschrift der Savigny-Stiftung fuer Rechtsgeschichte
ZDS — Zeitschrift fuer Deutsche Sprache
ZDSJ — Zeitschrift fuer Demographie und Statistik der Juden
ZDStJ — Zeitschrift fuer Demographie und Statistik der Juden
Z Dt Geisteswiss — Zeitschrift fuer Deutsche Geisteswissenschaft
Z Dt Geol Ges — Zeitschrift. Deutsche Geologische Gesellschaft
Z Dt Geol Ges A Abh — Zeitschrift der Deutschen Geologischen Gesellschaft A. Abhandlungen
Z Dt Morgenl Ges — Zeitschrift der Deutschen Morgenlaendischen Gesellschaft
Z Dt Phil — Zeitschrift fuer Deutsche Philologie
Z Dtschen Morgenlaend Ges — Zeitschrift. Deutsche Morgenlaendische Gesellschaft
Z Dtsch Gemmol Ges — Zeitschrift der Deutschen Gemmologischen Gesellschaft (Idar-Oberstein)
Z Dtsch Geol Ges — Zeitschrift. Deutsche Geologische Gesellschaft
Z Dtschl Druckgewerbe — Zeitschrift fuer Deutschlands Drueckgewerbe
Z Dtsch Morgenl Ges — Zeitschrift. Deutsche Morganlaendische Gesellschaft
Z Dtsch Oel Fett Ind — Zeitschrift der Deutschen Oel- und Fett-Industrie
Z Dtsch Philol — Zeitschrift fuer Deutsche Philologie
Z Dt Spr — Zeitschrift fuer Deutsche Sprache
ZdV — Zeitschrift des Historischen Vereins fuer Steiermark
ZDV f Kw — Zeitschrift. Deutscher Verein fuer Kunstwissenschaft
ZDVGMS — Zeitschrift. Deutscher Verein fuer die Geschichte Maehrens und Schlesiens
ZDVK — Zeitschrift des Deutschen Vereins fuer Kunstwissenschaft
ZDV Kw — Zeitschrift. Deutscher Verein fuer Kunstwissenschaft
ZDW — Zeitschrift fuer Deutsche Wortforschung
ZDWDSU — Zeitschrift fuer Deutschwissenschaft und Deutschunterricht
ZDWF — Zeitschrift fuer Deutsche Wortforschung
Z d Z — Zeichen der Zeit
ZE — Zeitschrift fuer Ethnologie
ZEASA — Zeitschrift fuer Astrophysik
ZEB — Zeitschrift fuer Eingeborenen-Sprachen (Berlin)
ZEBED — Zeitschrift fuer Bergrecht
ZEBFA — Zhurnal Evolyutsionnoi Biokhimii i Fiziologii
ZEBLA — Zeitschrift fuer Biologie
ZECODK — Zeitschrift fuer Experimentelle Chirurgie. Transplantation und Kunstliche Organe
ZED — Zimbabwe Environment and Design
ZED — Zur Erkenntnis der Dichtung
ZEE — Zeitschrift fuer Evangelische Ethik
Z EEG-EMG — Zeitschrift fuer EEG-EMG
ZEELA — Zeitschrift fuer Elektrochemie
Zeew Gn N Vh — Nieuwe Verhandelingen van het Zeeuwsch Genootschap der Wetenschappen
Zeews Fruittelersbl — Zeeuws Fruittelersblad
ZEF — Zeitschrift fuer Erziehungswissenschaftliche Forschung
ZEH — Zeit. Wochenzeitung
Zei — Das Zeichen
Zeich Zeit — Zeichen der Zeit
ZEINA — Zeitschrift fuer Instrumentenkunde
Z Eisenbahnwes und Verkehrstech Glasers — Zeitschrift fuer Eisenbahnwesen und Verkehrstechnik. Glasers. Annalen
Z Eisenbahnwes Verkehrstech — Zeitschrift fuer Eisenbahnwesen und Verkehrstechnik. Glasers Annalen
Z Eisenbahnwes Verkehrstech Glasers Ann — Zeitschrift fuer Eisenbahnwesen und Verkehrstechnik. Glasers. Annalen
Z Eis Kaelte Ind — Zeitschrift fuer Eis-und Kaelte-Industrie
Zeiss Inf — Zeiss Information
Zeiss Inf Jena Rev — Zeiss Information with Jena Review
Zeiss Mitt — Zeiss Mitteilungen
Zeiss-Mitt Fortsch Tech Opt — Zeiss-Mitteilungen ueber Fortschritte der Technischen Optik
Zeiss-Mitt Fortsch Tech Optik — Zeiss-Mitteilungen ueber Fortschritte der Technischen Optik
Zeit — Zeitwende. Die Neue Furche
Zeit Angewandte Phot — Zeitschrift Angewandte Photographie
Zeit f Deutk — Zeitschrift fuer Deutschkunde
Zeit f Deut Phil — Zeitschrift fuer Deutsche Philologie
Zeit f Num — Zeitschrift fuer Numismatik
Zeit f Oest Gymn — Zeitschrift fuer die Deutsche-Oesterreichischen Gymnasien
Zeit f Rom Phil — Zeitschrift fuer Romanische Philologie
Zeit Fuer Celt Philol — Zeitschrift fuer Celtische Philologie
Zeit f Volk — Zeitschrift fuer Volkskunde
Zeitgemaesse Deponietech 4 Manuskriptsammelband Semin — Zeitgemaesse Deponietechnik 4. Manuskriptsammelband zum Seminar
Zeitgeschic — Zeitgeschichte
Zeit Physik — Zeitschrift fuer Physik
Zeits Ange Zoo — Zeitschrift fuer Angewandte Zoologie
Zeit Saug — Zeitschrift Saugetierkunde
Zeitsch D Bayer Statist Landesamts — Zeitschrift des Bayerischen Statistischen Landesamts
Zeitsch Des Bernischen Juristenvereins — Zeitschrift des Bernischen Juristenvereins
Zeitsch D Savigny Stift F Rechtsgesch — Zeitschrift der Savigny-Stiftung fuer Rechtsgeschichte

Zeitsch F Aerztl Fortbild — Zeitschrift fuer Aerztliche Fortbildung
Zeitsch F Ang Chem — Zeitschrift fuer Angewandte Chemie
Zeitsch F Ang Psychol — Zeitschrift fuer Angewandte Psychologie
Zeitsch F Geburtsh U Gynaek — Zeitschrift fuer Geburtshuelfe und Gynaekologie
Zeitsch F Gewerbe Hyg — Zeitschrift fuer Gewerbe-Hygiene, Unfall-Verhuetung und Arbeiter-Wohlfahrts-Einrichtungen
Zeitsch F Hyg U Infektionskr — Zeitschrift fuer Hygiene und Infektions-Krankheiten
Zeitsch F Indukt Abstammungs U Vererbungsl — Zeitschrift fuer Induktive Abstammungs- und Vererbungslehre
Zeitsch F Jued Wohlfartspfl — Zeitschrift fuer Juedische Wohlfahrtspflege
Zeitsch F Kinderforsch — Zeitschrift fuer Kinderforschung
Zeitsch F Kinderschutz — Zeitschrift fuer Kinderschutz, Familien-, und Berufsfuersorge
Zeitsch F Med Beamte — Zeitschrift fuer Medizinalbeamte
Zeitsch F Menschenk — Zeitschrift fuer Menschenkunde
Zeitsch F Ostrecht — Zeitschrift fuer Ostrecht
Zeitsch F Paedagog Psychol — Zeitschrift fuer Paedagogische Psychologie
Zeitsch F Psychis Hyg — Zeitschrift fuer Psychische Hygiene
Zeitsch F Psychoanal Paed — Zeitschrift fuer Psychoanalytische Paedagogik
Zeitsch F Psychol — Zeitschrift fuer Psychologie
Zeitsch F Rassenphysiol — Zeitschrift fuer Rassenphysiologie
Zeitsch F Rechtspfl In Bayern — Zeitschrift fuer Rechtspflege in Bayern
Zeitsch F Rel Psychol — Zeitschrift fuer Religionspsychologie
Zeitsch F Schulgesundhpflg — Zeitschrift fuer Schulgesundheitspflege und Soziale Hygiene
Zeitsch F Schweiz Recht — Zeitschrift fuer Schweizerisches Recht
Zeitsch F Sexualwissensch — Zeitschrift fuer Sexualwissenschaft und Sexualpolitik
Zeitsch F Tuberk — Zeitschrift fuer Tuberkulose
Zeitsch F Vergl Rechtswiss — Zeitschrift fuer Vergleichende Rechtswissenschaft
Zeitsch F Voelkerpsychol U Soz — Zeitschrift fuer Voelkerpsychologie und Soziologie
Zeitsch F Voelkerrecht — Zeitschrift fuer Voelkerrecht
Zeitschr Angew Geologie — Zeitschrift fuer Angewandte Geologie
Zeitschr Anorg u Allg Chemie — Zeitschrift fuer Anorganische und Allgemeine Chemie
Zeitschr Arch Mittelalter — Zeitschrift fuer Archaeologie des Mittelalters
Zeitschr Ethn — Zeitschrift fuer Ethnologie
Zeitschr f d Altert — Zeitschrift fuer die Altertumswissenschaft
Zeitschrf Pap u Epigr — Zeitschrift fuer Papyrologie und Epigraphik
Zeitschr f Vergleich Sprach — Zeitschrift fuer Vergleichende Sprachforschung auf dem Gebiete der Indogermanischen Sprachen
Zeitschr Geomorphologie — Zeitschrift fuer Geomorphologie
Zeitschr Geomorphologie Neue Folge — Zeitschrift fuer Geomorphologie. Neue Folge
Zeitschr Geophysik — Zeitschrift fuer Geophysik
Zeitschr Gletscherkunde u Glazialgeologie — Zeitschrift fuer Gletscherkunde und Glazialgeologie
Zeitschrift Aegypt — Zeitschrift fuer Aegyptische Sprache und Altertumskunde
Zeitschrlft f Roman Phllol — Zeitschrlft fuer Romanlsche Phllologie
Zeitschr Kristallographie — Zeitschrift fuer Kristallographie
Zeitschr Num Berlin — Zeitschrift fuer Numismatik (Berlin)
Zeitschr Physikal Chemie — Zeitschrift fuer Physikalische Chemie
Zeitschr Savigny Stift — Zeitschrift der Savigny-Stiftung fuer Rechtsgeschichte. Romanistische Abteilung
Zeitschr Savigny Stiftung — Zeitschrift der Savigny-Stiftung fuer Rechtsgeschichte. Romanistische Abteilung
Zeitschr Schweiz Arch Kunstgesch — Zeitschrift fuer Schweizerische Archaeologie und Kunstgeschichte
Zeits Ethnol — Zeitschrift fuer Ethnologie. Berliner Gesellschaft fuer Anthropologie, Ethnologie, und Urgeschichte
Zeits F Afrikan Sp — Zeitschrift fuer Afrikanische Sprachen
Zeits F Afrikan U Ocean Sp — Zeitschrift fuer Afrikanische und Oceanische Sprachen
Zeits f Assyr — Zeitschrift fuer Assyriologie und Vorderasiatische Archaeologie
Zeits F Eingeborenesp — Zeitschrift fuer Eingeborenensprachen
Zeits F Ethnol — Zeitschrift fuer Ethnologie
Zeits F Kinderheilk — Zeitschrift fuer Kinderheilkunde
Zeits F Kolonialsp — Zeitschrift fuer Kolonialsprachen
Zeits F Missionsk U Religionswis — Zeitschrift fuer Missionskunde und Religionswissenschaft
Zeits F Morphol U Anthropol — Zeitschrift fuer Morphologie und Anthropologie
Zeits F Politik — Zeitschrift fuer Politik
Zeits F Voelkerpsychol U Soziol — Zeitschrift fuer Voelkerpsychologie und Soziologie
Zeits Politik — Zeitschrift fuer Politik
Zeitw — Zeitwende
Zeitwahr — Zeitschrift fuer Wahrscheinlichkeitstheorie
ZEIZA — Zeitschrift fuer Elektrische Informations- und Energietechnik
ZEK — Zeitschrift fuer Evangelisches Kirchenrecht
ZEKIA — Zeitschrift fuer Kinderheilkunde
ZEKID8 — Zeitschrift fuer Kinderchirurgie
Z Eks Klin Med — Zurnal Eksperimental'noj i Kliniceskoj Mediciny
Z Eksper Teoret Fiz — Zurnal Eksperimental'noi i Teoreticeskoi Fiziki
ZELAD — Zeitschrift fuer Laermbekaempfung
Z El Ch — Zeitschrift fuer Elektrochemie und Angewandte Physikalische Chemie
Z Elek Informations- und Energietech — Zeitschrift fuer Elektrische Informations- und Energietechnik
Z Elektch — Zeitschrift fuer Elektrochemie
Z Elektr Inf & Energietech — Zeitschrift fuer Elektrische Informations- und Energietechnik
Z Elektr Inf Energietech — Zeitschrift fuer Elektrische Informations- und Energietechnik
Z Elektr Informationstech Energietech — Zeitschrift fuer Elektrische Informations- und Energietechnik

Z Elektr Inform Energietech — Zeitschrift fuer Elektrische Informations- und Energietechnik

Z Elektrochem — Zeitschrift fuer Elektrochemie

Z Elektrochem Angew Phy Chem — Zeitschrift fuer Elektrochemie und Angewandte Physikalische Chemie

Z Elektrotech — Zeitschrift fuer Elektrotechnik

Z Elekttech Elektch — Zeitschrift fuer Elektrotechnik und Elektrochemie

Zelezarski Zb — Zelezarski Zbornik

Zell Papier — Zellstoff und Papier

Zellstoffchem Abh — Zellstoffchemische Abhandlungen

Zellst Pap — Zellstoff und Papier

Zellst Pap (Berlin) — Zellstoff und Papier (Berlin)

Zellst Pap (Leipzig) — Zellstoff und Papier (Leipzig)

Zellwolle Dtsch Kunstseiden Ztg — Zellwolle und Deutsche Kunstseiden-Zeitung

ZELTB — Zeitschrift fuer Elektrotechnik

Z El Techn — Zeitschrift fuer Elektrotechnik

Zem Beton — Zement und Beton

Zemed Arch — Zemedelsky Archiv

Zemed Ekon — Zemedelska Ekonomika

Zemed Tech — Zemedelska Technika

Zemed Tech Cesk Akad Zemed Ustav Vedeckotech Inf Zemed — Zemedelska Technika. Ceskoslovenska Akademie Zemedelska Ustav Vedeckotechnickych Informaci Pro Zemedelstvi

Zemed Zahr — Zemedeistvi v Zahranici

Zemep Sb — Zemepisny Sbornik

Zemep Sborn — Zemepisny Sbornik

ZEMGA — Zeszyty Naukowe Akademii Gorniczo-Hutniczej. Elektryfikacja i Mechanizacja Gornictwa i Hutnictwa

ZEMHA — Zeitschrift fuer Erzbergbau und Metallhuettenwesen

ZEMIDI — Zentralblatt fuer Mikrobiologie

Zem-Kalk-Gips — Zement-Kalk-Gips

Zemled — Zemledelie

Zemled Mekh — Zemledel'cheskaya Mekhanika

Zemled Zhivotnovod Mold — Zemledelie i Zhivotnovodstvo Moldavii

Zemlerob Resp Mizhvid Temat Nauk Zb — Zemlerobstvo Respublikans'kyi Mizhvidomchyi Tematychnyi Naukovyi Zbirnyk

Zemleustroistvo Plan Sel'sk Naselennykh Punktov Geod — Zemleustroistvo. Planirovka Sel'skikh Naselennykh Punktov i Geodeziya

Zemlj Biljka — Zemljiste i Biljka

Zemlya Sib Dal'nevost — Zemlya Sibirskaya Dal'nevostochnaya

Zeml Zhivot Moldav — Zemledelie i Zhivotnovodstvo Moldavii

Zem ve Sk — Zemepis ve Skole

Z Energiewirtsch — Zeitschrift fuer Energiewirtschaft

ZeNo — Zeitschrift fuer Nationaloekonomie

Zentbl Bakt ParasitKde — Zentralblatt fuer Bakteriologie, Parasitenkunde, Infektionskrankheiten, und Hygiene

Zentbl Bakt ParasitKed Abt 1 or 2 — Zentralblatt fuer Bakteriologie, Parasitenkunde, Infektionskrankheiten, und Hygiene. Abteilung 1 or 2

Zentbl Biblioth — Zentralblatt fuer Bibliothekswesen

Zentbl Vet Med B — Zentralblatt fuer Veterinaermedizin. Reihe B

Zent Eur Giesserei Ztg — Zentral-Europaeische Giesserei-Zeitung

Zent Math — Zentralblatt fuer Mathematik und Ihre Grenzgebiete

Zentralb Bakteriol Parasitenkd Infektionskr — Zentralblatt fuer Bakteriologie, Parasitenkunde, und Infektionskrankheiten

Zentralbl Allg Pathol — Zentralblatt fuer Allgemeine Pathologie und Pathologische Anatomie

Zentralbl Allg Pathol Pathol Anat — Zentralblatt fuer Allgemeine Pathologie und Pathologische Anatomie

Zentralbl Arbeitsmed — Zentralblatt fuer Arbeitsmedizin und Arbeitsschutz [*Later, Zentralblatt fuer Arbeitsmedizin, Arbeitsschutz, und Prophylaxe*]

Zentralbl Arbeitsmed Arbeitsschutz — Zentralblatt fuer Arbeitsmedizin und Arbeitsschutz [*Later, Zentralblatt fuer Arbeitsmedizin, Arbeitsschutz, und Prophylaxe*]

Zentralbl Arbeitsmed Arbeitsschutz Prophyl — Zentralblatt fuer Arbeitsmedizin, Arbeitsschutz, und Prophylaxe

Zentralbl Arbeitsmed Arbeitsschutz Prophylaxe — Zentralblatt fuer Arbeitsmedizin, Arbeitsschutz, und Prophylaxe

Zentralbl Arbeitsmed Arbeitsschutz Prophyl Ergon — Zentralblatt fuer Arbeitsmedizin, Arbeitsschutz, Prophylaxe, und Ergonomie

Zentralbl Bakteriol — Zentralblatt fuer Bakteriologie

Zentralbl Bakteriol (B) — Zentralblatt fuer Bakteriologie, Parasitenkunde, Infektionskrankheiten, und Hygiene. Erste Abteilung. Originale Reihe B. Hygiene, Betriebshygiene, Praeventive Medizin

Zentralbl Bakteriol Mikrobiol Hyg 1 Abt Suppl — Zentralblatt fuer Bakteriologie, Mikrobiologie, und Hugiene. 1. Abteilung. Supplemente

Zentralbl Bakteriol Mikrobiol Hyg Abt 1 Orig A — Zentralblatt fuer Bakteriologie, Mikrobiologie, und Hygiene. Abteilung 1. Originale A. Medizinische Mikrobiologie, Infektionskrankheiten, und Parasitologie

Zentralbl Bakteriol Mikrobiol Hyg B — Zentralblatt fuer Bakteriologie, Mikrobiologie, und Hygiene. Serie B. Umwelthygiene, Krankenhaushygiene, Arbeitshygiene, Praeventive Medizin

Zentralbl Bakteriol Mikrobiol Hyg I Abt Orig A — Zentralblatt fuer Bakteriologie, Mikrobiologie, und Hygiene. I Abteilung. Originale A

Zentralbl Bakteriol Mikrobiol Hyg I Abt Orig C — Zentralblatt fuer Bakteriologie, Mikrobiologie, und Hygiene. I Abteilung. Originale C

Zentralbl Bakteriol Mikrobiol Hyg Ser A — Zentralblatt fuer Bakteriologie, Mikrobiologie, und Hygiene. Series A. Medical Microbiology, Infectious Diseases, Virology, Parasitology

Zentralbl Bakteriol Mikrobiol Hyg Ser B — Zentralblatt fuer Bakteriologie, Mikrobiologie, und Hygiene. Serie B.Umwelthygiene, Krankenhaushygiene, Arbeitshygiene, Praeventive Medizin

Zentralbl Bakteriol Naturwiss — Zentralblatt fuer Bakteriologie, Parasitenkunde, Infektionskrankheiten, und Hygiene. Zweite Naturwissenschaftliche Abteilung. Mikrobiologie der Landwirtschaft der Technologie und des Umweltschutzes

Zentralbl Bakteriol Orig A — Zentralblatt fuer Bakteriologie, Parasitenkunde, Infektionskrankheiten, und Hygiene. Erste Abteilung. Originale Reihe A. Medizinische Mikrobiologie und Parasitologie

Zentralbl Bakteriol (Orig B) — Zentralblatt fuer Bakteriologie, Parasitenkunde, Infektionskrankheiten, und Hygiene. Erste Abteilung. Originale Reihe B. Hygiene, Betriebshygiene, Praeventive Medizin

Zentralbl Bakteriol Parasitenkd Infektionskr Abt 1 — Zentralblatt fuer Bakteriologie, Parasitenkunde, und Infektionskrankheiten. Abteilung 1. Medizinische-Hygienische Bakteriologie Virusforschung und Tierische Parasitologie

Zentralbl Bakteriol Parasitenkd Infektionskrankheiten Hyg II — Zentralblatt fuer Bakteriologie, Parasitenkunde, Infektionskrankheiten, und Hygiene. Naturwissenschaftliche Abteilung

Zentralbl Bakteriol Parasitenkd Infektionskr Hyg Abt 1 Orig — Zentralblatt fuer Bakteriologie, Parasitenkunde, Infektionskrankheiten, und Hygiene. Abteilung 1 Originale

Zentralbl Bakteriol Parasitenkd Infektionskr Hyg Abt 1 Ref — Zentralblatt fuer Bakteriologie, Parasitenkunde, Infektionskrankheiten, und Hygiene. Abteilung 1. Medizinisch-Hygienische Bakteriologie, Virusforschung, und Parasitologie. Referate

Zentralbl Bakteriol Parasitenkd Infektionskr Hyg Abt 1 Suppl — Zentralblatt fuer Bakteriologie, Parasitenkunde, Infektionskrankheiten, und Hygiene. Abteilung 1. Supplementheft

Zentralbl Bakteriol Parasitenkd Infektionskr Hyg Abt 2 — Zentralblatt fuer Bakteriologie, Parasitenkunde, Infektionskrankheiten, und Hygiene. Abteilung 2. Allgemeine Landwirtschaftliche und Technische Mikrobiologie

Zentralbl Bakteriol Parasitenk Infektionskr Hyg — Zentralblatt fuer Bakteriologie, Parasitenkunde, Infektionskrankheiten, und Hygiene

Zentralbl Bauverwaltung — Zentralblatt der Bauverwaltung

Zentralbl Bibliothekswesen — Zentralblatt fuer Bibliothekswesen

Zentralbl Biochem Biophys — Zentralblatt fuer Biochemie und Biophysik

Zentralbl Biol Aerosol-Forsch — Zentralblatt fuer Biologische Aerosol-Forschung

Zentralbl Chir — Zentralblatt fuer Chirurgie

Zentralbl Chir Suppl — Zentralblatt fuer Chirurgie. Supplement

Zentralbl Didakt Math — ZDM. Zentralblatt fuer Didaktik der Mathematik

Zentralbl Exp Med — Zentralblatt der Experimentellen Medizin

Zentralbl F D Jurist Praxis — Zentralblatt fuer die Juristische Praxis

Zentralbl F Gynaek — Zentralblatt fuer Gynaekologie

Zentralbl F Handelsr — Zentralblatt fuer Handelsrecht

Zentralbl F Jugendrecht U Jugendwohlfahrt — Zentralblatt fuer Jugendrecht und Jugendwohlfahrt

Zentralbl F Psychotherap — Zentralblatt fuer Psychotherapie und Ihre Grenzgebiete Einschliessliche der Medizinischen Psychologie und Psychischen Hygiene

Zentralbl Geol Palaeontol Teil 1 — Zentralblatt fuer Geologie und Palaeontologie. Teil 1. Allgemeine, Angewandte, Regionale, und Historische Geologie

Zentralbl Geol Palaeontol Teil 2 — Zentralblatt fuer Geologie und Palaeontologie. Teil 2. Palaeontologie

Zentralbl Gesamte Forst Holzw — Zentralblatt fuer die Gesamte Forst- und Holzwirtschaft

Zentralbl Gesamte Forstwes — Zentralblatt fuer das Gesamte Forstwesen

Zentralbl Gesamte Hyg Einschluss Bakteriol Immunitaetsl — Zentralblatt fuer die Gesamte Hygiene mit Einschluss der Bakteriologie und Immunitaetslehre

Zentralbl Gesamte Hyg Ihre Grenzgeb — Zentralblatt fuer die Gesamte Hygiene und Ihre Grenzgebiete

Zentralbl Gesamte Physiol Pathol Stoffwechsels — Zentralblatt fuer die Gesamte Physiologie und Pathologie des Stoffwechsels

Zentralbl Gesamte Radiol — Zentralblatt fuer die Gesamte Radiologie

Zentralbl Gesamte Rechtsmed — Zentralblatt fuer die Gesamte Rechtsmedizin und Ihre Grenzgebiete

Zentralbl Gesamte Rechtsmed Grenzgeb — Zentralblatt fuer die Gesamte Rechtsmedizin und Ihre Grenzgebiete

Zentralbl Ges Hyg — Zentralblatt fuer die Gesamte Hygiene und Ihre Grenzgebiete

Zentralbl Gewerbehyg Unfallverhuet — Zentralblatt fuer Gewerbehygiene und Unfallverhuetung

Zentralbl Gynaekol — Zentralblatt fuer Gynaekologie

Zentralbl Huetten Walzwerke — Zentralblatt der Huetten- und Walzwerke

Zentralbl Hyg Umweltmed — Zentralblatt fuer Hygiene und Umweltmedizin

Zentralbl Industriebau — Zentralblatt fuer Industriebau

Zentralbl Inn Med — Zentralblatt fuer Innere Medizin

Zentralbl Math Ihre Grenzgeb — Zentralblatt fuer Mathematik Ihre Grenzgebiete

Zentralbl Mikrobiol — Zentralblatt fuer Mikrobiologie

Zentralbl Mineral Geol Palaeontol — Zentralblatt fuer Mineralogie, Geologie, und Palaeontologie

Zentralbl Mineral Geol Palaeontol Teil 1 — Zentralblatt fuer Mineralogie, Geologie, und Palaeontologie. Teil 1. Kristallographie und Mineralogie

Zentralbl Mineral Geol Palaeontol Teil 2 — Zentralblatt fuer Mineralogie, Geologie, und Palaeontologie. Teil 2. Gesteinskunde, Lagerstaettenkunde, Allgemeine, und Angewandte Geologie

Zentralbl Mineral Geol Palaeontol Teil 3 — Zentralblatt fuer Mineralogie, Geologie, und Palaeontologie. Teil 3. Historische und Regionale Geologie, Palaeontologie

Zentralbl Mineral Teil 1 — Zentralblatt fuer Mineralogie. Teil 1. Kristallographie und Mineralogie

Zentralbl Mineral Teil 2 — Zentralblatt fuer Mineralogie. Teil 2. Petrographie, Technische Mineralogie, Geochemie, und Lagerstaettenkunde

Zentralbl Mineral Teil 3 Hist Regionale Geol Palaeontol — Zentralblatt fuer Mineralogie, Geologie, und Palaeontologie. Teil 3. Historische und Regionale Geologie, Palaeontologie

Zentralbl Neurochir — Zentralblatt fuer Neurochirurgie

Zentralbl Papierind — Zentralblatt fuer die Papierindustrie

Zentralbl Pathol — Zentralblatt fuer Pathologie

Zentralbl Pharm — Zentralblatt fuer Pharmazie

Zentralbl Pharm Pharmakother Laboratoriumsdiagn — Zentralblatt fuer Pharmazie, Pharmakotherapie, und Laboratoriumsdiagnostik

Zentralbl Phlebol — Zentralblatt fuer Phlebologie

Zentralbl Physiol — Zentralblatt fuer Physiologie

Zentralbl Verkehrs-Med Verkehrs-Psychol Luft- Raumfahrt-Med — Zentralblatt fuer Verkehrs-Medizin, Verkehrs-Psychologie Luft-, und Raumfahrt-Medizin

Zentralbl Veterinaermed — Zentralblatt fuer Veterinaermedizin

Zentralbl Veterinaermed Beih — Zentralblatt fuer Veterinaermedizin. Beiheft

Zentralbl Veterinaermed Reihe A — Zentralblatt fuer Veterinaermedizin. Reihe A

Zentralbl Veterinaermed Reihe B — Zentralblatt fuer Veterinaermedizin. Reihe B

Zentralbl Veterinaermed Reihe C — Zentralblatt fuer Veterinaermedizin. Reihe C

Zentralbl Veterinarmed A — Zentralblatt fuer Veterinarmedizin. Reihe A

Zentralinst Festkoerperphys Werkstofforsch Wiss Ber — Zentralinstitut fuer Festkoerperphysik und Werkstofforschung. Wissenschaftliche Berichte

Zentralinst Kernforsch Rossendorf Dresden (Ber) — Zentralinstitut fuer Kernforschung Rossendorf bei Dresden (Bericht)

Zentralinst Versuchstierzucht Annu Rep — Zentralinstitut fuer Versuchstierzucht. Annual Report

Zentr Bibl — Zentralblatt fuer Bibliothekswesen

Zentr Org Ges Chir — Zentralorgan fuer die Gesamte Chirurgie und Ihre Grenzgebiete

Zent Umweltforsch Westfael Wilhelms Univ Vortr Stud — Zentrum fuer Umweltforschung der Westfaelischen Wilhelms-Universitaet. Vortraege und Studien

Z Entwick P — Zeitschrift fuer Entwicklungspsychologie und Paedagogische Psychologie

Zent Ztg Opt Mech — Zentral-Zeitung fuer Optik und Mechanik

ZEPAD — Zeitschrift fuer Parlamentsfragen

Zeph — Zephyrus. Seminario de Arqueologia y de la Seccion Arqueologica del Centro de Estudios Salmantinos

Z Erdkde — Zeitschrift fuer Erdkunde

Z Erdkde Unterr — Zeitschrift fuer den Erdkundeunterricht

Z Erdkundeunterricht — Zeitschrift fuer den Erdkundeunterricht

Z Erdk Unt — Zeitschrift fuer den Erdkundeunterricht

ZERED — Zeitschrift fuer Rechtspolitik

Z Erkr Atmungsorgane — Zeitschrift fuer Erkrankungen der Atmungsorgane

Z Ernaehrung — Zeitschrift fuer Ernaehrungswissenschaft

Z Ernaehrungsw — Zeitschrift fuer Ernaehrungswissenschaft

Z Ernaehrungswiss — Zeitschrift fuer Ernaehrungswissenschaft

Z Ernaehrungswiss Suppl — Zeitschrift fuer Ernaehrungswissenschaft. Supplementa

Z Ernaehr Wiss — Zeitschrift fuer Ernaehrungwissenschaft

Zernovoe Khoz — Zernovoe Khozyaistvo

Zernovye Maslichn Kul't — Zernovye i Maslichnye Kul'tury

Zero Popul Growth Natl Rep — Zero Population Growth. National Reporter

Zero Un — Zero Un Hebdo

Zero Un M — Zero Un Information Mensuel

Z Erzbergbau Metallhuettenwes — Zeitschrift fuer Erzbergbau und Metallhuettenwesen

ZES — Zeitschrift fuer Eingeborenen-Sprachen

ZESIA — Zeitschrift fuer Sinnephysiologie

ZE Spr — Zeitschrift fuer Eingeborenen-Sprachen

ZESTA — Zeitschrift fuer Schweisstechnik

Zesz Muz Etnogr Wrocl — Zeszyty Muzeum Etnograficznego Wroclawie

Zesz Nauk Akad Ekon — Zeszyty Naukowe Akademii Ekonomicznej w Katowicach

Zesz Nauk Akad Ekon Katowic — Zeszyty Naukowe Akademii Ekonomicznej w Katowicach

Zesz Nauk Akad Ekon Krakow — Zeszyty Naukowe Akademii Ekonomicznej w Krakowie

Zesz Nauk Akad Ekon Poznan — Zeszyty Naukowe Akademii Ekonomicznej w Poznaniu

Zesz Nauk Akad Ekon Poznaniu Ser 2 — Zeszyty Naukowe. Akademia Ekonomiczna w Poznaniu. Seria 2. Prace Habilitacyjne i Doktorskie

Zesz Nauk Akad Ekon Wroclaw — Zeszyty Naukowe Akademii Ekonomicznej w Wroclawiu

Zesz Nauk Akad Gorn Hutn (Cracow) Eletryf Mech Gorn Hutn — Zeszyty Naukowe Akademii Gorniczo-Hutniczej (Cracow). Elektryfikacja i Mechanizacja Gornictwa i Hutnictwa

Zesz Nauk Akad Gorn Hutn (Cracow) Geol — Zeszyty Naukowe Akademii Gorniczo-Hutniczej (Cracow). Geologia

Zesz Nauk Akad Gorn-Hutn (Cracow) Mat Fiz Chem — Zeszyty Naukowe Akademii Gorniczo-Hutniczej (Cracow). Matematyka, Fizyka, Chemia

Zesz Nauk Akad Gorn Hutn (Cracow) Metal Odlew — Zeszyty Naukowe Akademii Gorniczo-Hutniczej (Cracow). Metalurgia i Odlewnictwo

Zesz Nauk Akad Gorn-Hutn (Cracow) Rozpr — Zeszyty Naukowe Akademii Gorniczo-Hutniczej (Cracow). Rozprawy

Zesz Nauk Akad Gorn-Hutn Im Stanislawa Staszica Ceram — Zeszyty Naukowe Akademii Gorniczo-Hutniczej Imienia Stanislawa Staszica. Ceramica

Zesz Nauk Akad Gorn-Hutn Im Stanislawa Staszica Geol — Zeszyty Naukowe Akademii Gorniczo-Hutniczej Imienia Stanislawa Staszica. Geologia

Zesz Nauk Akad Gorn-Hutn Im Stanislawa Staszica Gorn — Zeszyty Naukowe Akademii Gorniczo-Hutniczej Imienia Stanislawa Staszica. Gornictwo

Zesz Nauk Akad Gorn-Hutn Im Stanislawa Staszica Mat Fiz Chem — Zeszyty Naukowe Akademii Gorniczo-Hutniczej Imienia Stanislawa Staszica. Matematyka, Fizyka, Chemia

Zesz Nauk Akad Gorn-Hutn Im Stanislawa Staszica Metal Odlew — Zeszyty Naukowe Akademii Gorniczo-Hutniczej Imienia Stanislawa Staszica. Metalurgia i Odlewnictwo

Zesz Nauk Akad Gorn-Hutn Im Stanislawa Staszica Ser Autom — Zeszyty Naukowe Akademii Gorniczo-Hutniczej Imienia Stanislawa Staszica. Seria Automatyka

Zesz Nauk Akad Gorn-Hutn Im Stanislawa Staszica Zesz Spec — Zeszyty Naukowe Akademii Gorniczo-Hutniczej Imienia Stanislawa Staszica. ZeszytSpecjalny

Zesz Nauk Akad Gorn-Hutn Im Staszica Gorn — Zeszyty Naukowe Akademii Gorniczo-Hutniczej Imienia Stanislawa Staszica. Gornictwo

Zesz Nauk Akad Gorn-Hutn Im Staszica Mat Fiz Chem — Zeszyty Naukowe Akademii Gorniczo-Hutniczej Imienia Stanislawa Staszica. Matematyka, Fizyka, Chemia

Zesz Nauk Akad Gorn-Hutn Im Staszica Zesz Spec — Zeszyty Naukowe Akademii Gorniczo-Hutniczej Imienia Stanislawa Staszica. ZeszytSpecjalny

Zesz Nauk Akad Gorn-Hutn (Krakow) Ceram — Zeszyty Naukowe Akademii Gorniczo-Hutniczej (Krakow). Ceramika

Zesz Nauk Akad Gorn-Hutn (Krakow) Elektryf Mech Gorn Hutn — Zeszyty Naukowe Akademii Gorniczo-Hutniczej (Krakow). Elektryfikacja i Mechanizacja Gornictwa i Hutnictwa

Zesz Nauk Akad Gorn-Hutn (Krakow) Geol — Zeszyty Naukowe Akademii Gorniczo-Hutniczej (Krakow). Geologia

Zesz Nauk Akad Gorn-Hutn (Krakow) Gorn — Zeszyty Naukowe Akademii Gorniczo-Hutniczej (Krakow). Gornictwo

Zesz Nauk Akad Gorn-Hutn Krakowie Rozpr — Zeszyty Naukowe Akademii Gorniczo-Hutniczej w Krakowie. Rozprawy

Zesz Nauk Akad Gorn-Hutn (Krakow) Mat Fiz Chem — Zeszyty Naukowe Akademii Gorniczo-Hutniczej (Krakow). Matematyka, Fizyka, Chemia

Zesz Nauk Akad Gorn-Hutn (Krakow) Metal Odlew — Zeszyty Naukowe Akademii Gorniczo-Hutniczej (Krakow). Metalurgia i Odlewnictwo

Zesz Nauk Akad Gorn-Hutn (Krakow) Ses Nauk — Zeszyty Naukowe Akademii Gorniczo-Hutniczej (Krakow). Sesja Naukowa

Zesz Nauk Akad Gorn-Hutn (Krakow) Sozologia Sozotechnika — Zeszyty Naukowe Akademii Gorniczo-Hutniczej (Krakow). Sozologia i Sozotechnika

Zesz Nauk Akad Gorn-Hutn (Krakow) Zesz Spec — Zeszyty Naukowe Akademii Gorniczo-Hutniczej (Krakow). Zeszyty Specjalny

Zesz Nauk Akad Gorn-Hutn Stanislawa Staszica Geol — Zeszyty Naukowe Akademii Gorniczo-Hutniczej Imienia Stanislawa Staszica. Geologia

Zesz Nauk Akad Gorn-Hutn Stanisl Staszica — Zeszyty Naukowe Akademii Gorniczo-Hutniczej Imienia Stanislawa Staszica. Metalurgia i Odlewnictwo

Zesz Nauk Akad Gorn-Hutn Stanisl Staszica Autom — Zeszyty Naukowe Akademii Gorniczo-Hutniczej Imienia Stanislawa Staszica. Automatyka

Zesz Nauk Akad Gorn-Hutn Stanisl Staszica Geol — Zeszyty Naukowe Akademii Gorniczo-Hutniczej Imienia Stanislawa Staszica. Geologia

Zesz Nauk Akad Gorn-Hutn Stanisl Staszica Mat Fiz Chem — Zeszyty Naukowe Akademii Gorniczo-Hutniczej Imienia Stanislawa Staszica. Matematyka, Fizyka, Chemia

Zesz Nauk Akad Roln Szczecinie — Zeszyty Naukowe. Akademia Rolnicza w Szczecinie

Zesz Nauk Akad Roln Szczecinie Ser Rybactwo Morsk — Zeszyty Naukowe Akademii Rolniczej w Szczecinie. Seria Rybactwo Morskie

Zesz Nauk Akad Roln Tech Olsztynie — Zeszyty Naukowe Akademii Rolniczo-Technicznej w Olsztynie

Zesz Nauk Akad Roln Tech Olsztynie Roln — Zeszyty Naukowe Akademii Rolniczo-Technicznej w Olsztynie. Rolnictwo

Zesz Nauk Akad Roln Tech Olsztynie Technol Zywn — Zeszyty Naukowe Akademii Rolniczo-Technicznej w Olsztynie. Technologia Zywnosci

Zesz Nauk Akad Roln Tech Olsztynie Zootech — Zeszyty Naukowe Akademii Rolniczo-Technicznej w Olsztynie. Zootechnika

Zesz Nauk Akad Roln Warszawie Melior Rolne — Zeszyty Naukowe Akademii Rolniczej w Warszawie. Melioracje Rolne

Zesz Nauk Akad Roln Warszawie Ogrod — Zeszyty Naukowe Akademii Rolniczej w Warszawie. Ogrodnictwo

Zesz Nauk Akad Roln Warszawie Technol Drewna — Zeszyty Naukowe Akademii Rolniczej w Warszawie. Technologia Drewna

Zesz Nauk Akad Roln Warszawie Technol Rolno Spozyw — Zeszyty Naukowe Akademii Rolniczej w Warszawie. Technologia Rolno-Spozyweza

Zesz Nauk Akad Roln Warszawie Zootech — Zeszyty Naukowe Akademii Rolniczej w Warszawie. Zootechnika

Zesz Nauk Akad Roln Wroclawiu Melior — Zeszyty Naukowe Akademii Rolniczej we Wroclawiu. Melioracja

Zesz Nauk Akad Roln Wroclawiu Roln — Zeszyty Naukowe Akademii Rolniczej we Wroclawiu. Rolnictwo

Zesz Nauk Akad Roln Wroclawiu Weter — Zeszyty Naukowe Akademii Rolniczej we Wroclawiu. Weterynaria

Zesz Nauk Akad Roln Wroclawiu Zootech — Zeszyty Naukowe Akademii Rolniczej we Wroclawiu. Zootechnika

Zesz Nauk Akad Roln Wrocl Wet — Zeszyty Naukowe Akademii Rolniczej we Wroclawiu. Weterynaria

Zesz Nauk Gorn — Zeszyty Naukowe Gornictwo

Zesz Nauk Inst Ciezkiej Synt Org Blachowni Slask — Zeszyty Naukowe Instytut Ciezkiej Syntezy Organicznej w Blachowni Slaskiej

Zesz Nauk Lesn Akad Roln Warsz — Zeszyty Naukowe. Lesnictwo-Akademia Rolnicza w Warszawie

Zesz Nauk Mat Fiz Chem — Zeszyty Naukowe. Matematyka, Fizyka, Chemia

Zesz Nauk Mechan Budownictwo Akad Roln-Tech Olsztyn — Zeszyty Naukowe. Mechanika i Budownictwo-Akademia Rolniczo-Techniczna w Olsztynie

Zesz Nauk Melior Rolne Akad Roln Warsz — Zeszyty Naukowe. Melioracje Rolne-Akademia Rolnicza w Warszawie

Zesz Nauk Ochr Wod Rybactwo Srodladowe — Zeszyty Naukowe. Ochrona Wod i Rybactwo Srodladowe

Zesz Nauk Politech Czestochow — Zeszyty Naukowe Politechniki Czestochowskiej

Zesz Nauk Politech Czestochow Metal — Zeszyty Naukowe Politechniki Czestochowskiej. Metalurgia

Zesz Nauk Politech Czestochow Nauki Tech Hutn — Zeszyty Naukowe Politechniki Czestochowskiej. Nauki Techniczne. Hutnictwo

Zesz Nauk Politech Gdansk Chem — Zeszyty Naukowe Politechniki Gdanskiej. Chemia

Zesz Nauk Politech Gdansk Elektr — Zeszyty Naukowe Politechniki Gdanskiej. Elektryka

Zesz Nauk Politech Gdansk Fiz — Zeszyty Naukowe Politechniki Gdanskiej. Fizyka

Zesz Nauk Politech Gdansk Mat — Zeszyty Naukowe Politechniki Gdanskiej. Matematyka

Zesz Nauk Politech Gdansk Mech — Zeszyty Naukowe Politechniki Gdanskiej. Mechanika

Zesz Nauk Politech Krakow Chem — Zeszyty Naukowe Politechniki Krakowskiej. Chemia

Zesz Nauk Politech Krakow Inz Technol Chem — Zeszyt Naukowe. Politechnika Krakowska, Inzynieria, i Technologia Chemiczna

Zesz Nauk Politech Krakow Mech — Zeszyty Naukowe Politechniki Krakowskiej. Mechanika

Zesz Nauk Politech Lod Budow — Zeszyty Naukowe Politechniki Lodzkiej. Budownictwo

Zesz Nauk Politech Lodz Chem — Zeszyty Naukowe Politechniki Lodzkiej. Chemia

Zesz Nauk Politech Lodz Chem Spozyw — Zeszyty Naukowe Politechniki Lodzkiej. Chemia Spozywcza

Zesz Nauk Politech Lodz Elek — Zeszyty Naukowe Politechniki Lodzkiej. Elektryka

Zesz Nauk Politech Lodz Elektr — Zeszyty Naukowe Politechniki Lodzkiej. Elektryka

Zesz Nauk Politech Lodz Fiz — Zeszyty Naukowe Politechnika Lodzka. Fizyka

Zesz Nauk Politech Lodz Inz Chem — Zeszyty Naukowe Politechniki Lodzkiej. Inzynieria Chemiczna

Zesz Nauk Politech Lodz Mech — Zeszyty Naukowe Politechniki Lodzkiej. Mechanika

Zesz Nauk Politech Lodz Wlok — Zeszyty Naukowe Politechniki Lodzkiej. Wlokiennictwo

Zesz Nauk Politech Poznan Chem Inz Chem — Zeszyty Naukowe Politechniki Poznanskiej. Chemia i Inzynieria Chemiczna

Zesz Nauk Politech Poznan Elektr — Zeszyty Naukowe Politechniki Poznanskiej. Elektryka

Zesz Nauk Politech Rzeszowskiej — Zeszyty Naukowe Politechniki Rzeszowskiej

Zesz Nauk Politech Slask — Zeszyty Naukowe Politechniki Slaskiej

Zesz Nauk Politech Slaska Energ — Zeszyty Naukowe Politechnika Slaska. Energetyka

Zesz Nauk Politech Slask Chem — Zeszyty Naukowe Politechniki Slaskiej. Chemia

Zesz Nauk Politech Slask Energ — Zeszyty Naukowe Politechniki Slaskiej. Energetyka

Zesz Nauk Politech Slask Gorn — Zeszyty Naukowe Politechniki Slaskiej. Gornictwo

Zesz Nauk Politech Slask Hutn — Zeszyty Naukowe Politechniki Slaskiej. Hutnictwo

Zesz Nauk Politech Slask Inz Sanit — Zeszyty Naukowe Politechniki Slaskiej. Inzynieria Sanitarna

Zesz Nauk Politech Slask Ser Elektr — Zeszyty Naukowe Politechniki Slaskiej. Seria Elektryka

Zesz Nauk Politech Slask Ser Mat-Fiz — Zeszyty Naukowe Politechniki Slaskiej. Seria Matematyka-Fizyka

Zesz Nauk Politech Swietokrz Probl Nauk Podst — Zeszyty Naukowe Politechniki Swietokrzyska. Problemy Nauk Podstawowych

Zesz Nauk Politech Szezecin Chem — Zeszyty Naukowe Politechniki Szezecinskiej. Chemia

Zesz Nauk Politech Szezecin Pr Monogr — Zeszyty Naukowe Politechniki Szezecinskiej. Prace Monografiezne

Zesz Nauk Politech Warsz Chem — Zeszyty Naukowe Politechniki Warszawskiej. Chemia

Zesz Nauk Politech Wroclaw Chem — Zeszyty Naukowe Politechniki Wroclawskiej. Chemia

Zesz Nauk Roln Akad Roln Warsz — Zeszyty Naukowe. Rolnictwo Akademia Rolnicza w Warszawie

Zesz Nauk Szk Gl Gospod Wiejsk Akad Roln Warszawie Ogrod — Zeszyty Naukowe Szkoly Glownej Gospodarstwa Wiejskiego. Akademii Rolniczej w Warszawie. Ogrodnictwo

Zesz Nauk Szk Gl Gospod Wiejsk Akad Roln Warszawie Wter — Zeszyty Naukowe Szkoly Glownej Gospodarstwa Wiejskiego. Akademii Rolniczej w Warszawie. Weterynaria

Zesz Nauk Szk Gl Gospod Wiejsk Akad Roln Warszawie Zootech — Zeszyty Naukowe Szkoly Glownej Gospodarstwa Wiejskiego. Akademii Rolniczej w Warszawie. Zootechnika

Zesz Nauk Szk Gl Gospod Wiejsk Akad Roln Warsz Ogrodn — Zeszyty Naukowe Szkoly Glownej Gospodarstwa Wiejskiego Akademii Rolniczej w Warszawie Ogrodnictwo

Zesz Nauk Szk Gl Gospod Wiejsk Warszawie Melior Rolne — Zeszyty Naukowe Szkoly Glownej Gospodarstwa Wiejskiego w Warszawie. Melioracje Rolne

Zesz Nauk Szk Gl Gospod Wiejsk Warszawie Ogrod — Zeszyty Naukowe Szkoly Glownej Gospodarstwa Wiejskiego w Warszawie. Ogrodnictwo

Zesz Nauk Szk Gl Gospod Wiejsk Warszawie Roln — Zeszyty Naukowe Szkoly Glownej Gospodarstwa Wiejskiego w Warszawie. Rolnictwo

Zesz Nauk Szk Gl Gospod Wiejsk Warszawie Technol Drewna — Zeszyty Naukowe Szkoly Glownej Gospodarstwa Wiejskiego w Warszawie. TechnologiaDrewna

Zesz Nauk Szk Gl Gospod Wiejsk Warszawie Zootech — Zeszyty Naukowe Szkoly Glownej Gospodarstwa Wiejskiego w Warszawie. Zootechnika

Zesz Nauk Szk Glo Gospod Wiejsk Warszawie Lesn — Zeszyty Naukowe Szkoly Glownej Gospodarstwa Wiejskiego w Warszawie. Lesnictwo

Zesz Nauk Szk Glow Gospod Wiejsk Warszawie — Zeszyty Naukowe Szkoly Glownej Gospodarstwa Wiejskiego w Warszawie

Zesz Nauk Szk Glown Plan Statystyki — Zeszyty Naukowe Szkoly Glownej Planowania i Statystyki

Zesz Nauk Szkol Gospod Wiejsk Warsz (Lesn) — Zeszyty Naukowe Szkola Glowna Gospodarstwa Wiejskiego w Warszawie (Lesnictwo)

Zesz Nauk Szkol Gospod Wiejsk Warsz Technol Drewna — Zeszyty Naukowe Szkola Glowna Gospodarstwa Wiejskiego w Warszawie. Technologia Drewna

Zesz Nauk Technol Drewna Akad Roln Warsz — Zeszyty Naukowe. Technologia Drewna-Akademia Rolnicza w Warszawie

Zesz Nauk Technol Zywn Akad Roln-Tech Olsztynie — Zeszyty Naukowe. Technologia Zywnosci-Akademia Rolniczo-Technicznej w Olsztynie

Zesz Nauk Tech Wyzsza Szk Inz Lublinie — Zeszyty Naukowo-Techniczny Wyzsza Szkola Inzynierska w Lublinie

ZeszNauKUL — Zeszyty Naukowe Katolickiego Uniwersytetu Lubelskiego

Zesz Nauk Uniw Jagiellon Acta Cosmol — Zeszyty Naukowe Uniwersytetu Jagiellonskiego. Acta Cosmologica

Zesz Nauk Uniw Jagiellon Pr Biol Mol — Zeszyty Naukowe Uniwersytetu Jagiellonskiego. Prace Biologii Molekularnej

Zesz Nauk Uniw Jagiellon Pr Chem — Zeszyty Naukowe Uniwersytetu Jagiellonskiego. Prace Chemiczne

Zesz Nauk Uniw Jagiellon Pr Etnogr — Zeszyty Naukowe Uniwersytetu Jagiellonskiego. Prace Etnograficzne

Zesz Nauk Uniw Jagiellon Pr Fiz — Zeszyty Naukowe Uniwersytetu Jagiellonskiego. Prace Fizyczne

Zesz Nauk Uniw Jagiellon Pr Zool — Zeszyty Naukowe Uniwersytetu Jagiellonskiego. Prace Zoologiczne

Zesz Nauk Uniw Jagiellon Ser Nauk Mat Przy — Zeszyty Naukowe Uniwersytetu Jagiellonskiego. Seria Nauk Matematyezno-Przyrodniczych. Matematyka, Fizyka, Chemia

Zesz Nauk Uniw Jagiellonsk Pr Bot — Zeszyty Naukowe Uniwersytetu Jagiellonskiego. Prace Botaniczne

Zesz Nauk Uniw Jagiellonsk Zool — Zeszyty Naukowe Uniwersytetu Jagiellonskiego. Prace Zoologiczne

Zesz Nauk Uniw Jagiellon Univ Iagellon Acta Chim — Zeszyty Naukowe Uniwersytetu Jagiellonskiego. Universitatis Iagellonicae Acta Chimica

Zesz Nauk Uniw Lodz — Zeszyty Naukowe Uniwersytetu Lodzkiego

Zesz Nauk Uniw Lodz Fiz — Zeszyty Naukowe Uniwersytetu Lodzkiego. Fizyka

Zesz Nauk Uniw Lodz Nauki Humanist-Spolecz — Zeszyty Naukowe Uniwersytetu Lodzkiego. Nauki Humanistyczno-Spoleczne

Zesz Nauk Uniw Lodz Nauki Mat Przyr — Zeszyty Naukowe Uniwersytetu Lodzkiego. Nauki Matematyczno-Przyrodnicze

Zesz Nauk Uniw Lodz Ser II — Zeszyty Naukowe Uniwersytetu Lodzkiego. Seria II. Nauki Matematyczno-Przyrodnicze

Zesz Nauk Uniw Lodz Ser III — Zeszyty Naukowe Uniwersytetu Lodzkiego. Seria III

Zesz Nauk Uniw Mikolja Kopernika Torun — Zeszyty Naukowe Uniwersytetu Imienia Mikolaja Kopernika w Toruniu

Zesz Nauk Uniw Opolskiego Chem — Zeszyty Naukowe Uniwersytetu Opolskiego. Chemia

Zesz Nauk Uniw Poznaniu Mat Fiz Chem — Zeszyty Naukowe Uniwersytetu Imienia Adama Mickiewicza w Poznaniu. Matematyka, Fizyka, Chemia

Zesz Nauk Uniw Slaski Katowicach Seke Chem — Zeszyty Naukowe Uniwersytet Slaski w Katowicach Sekeja Chemii

Zesz Nauk Weter Akad Roln Warsz — Zeszyty Naukowe. Weterynaria-Akademia Rolnicza w Warszawie

Zesz Nauk Wydz Mat Fiz Chem Uniw Gdanski Chem — Zeszyty Naukowe Wydzialu Matematyki, Fizyki, Chemii. Uniwersytet Gdanski. SeriaChemia

Zesz Nauk Wyzs Szk Ekon Poznaniu — Zeszyty Naukowe Wyzsej Szkoly Ekonomicznej w Poznaniu

Zesz Nauk Wyzs Szk Roln Krakowie — Zeszyty Naukowe Wyzszej Szkoly Rolniczej w Krakowie

Zesz Nauk Wyzs Szk Roln Krakowie Zootech — Zeszyty Naukowe Wyzszej Szkoly Rolniczej w Krakowie. Zootechnika

Zesz Nauk Wyzs Szk Roln Olsztynie — Zeszyty Naukowe Wyzszej Szkoly Rolniczej w Olsztynie

Zesz Nauk Wyzs Szk Roln Szczecinie — Zeszyty Naukowe Wyzsza Szkola Rolnicza w Szczecinie

Zesz Nauk Wyzs Szk Roln Wroclawiu — Zeszyty Naukowe Wyzszej Szkoly Rolniczej we Wroclawiu

Zesz Nauk Wyzs Szk Roln Wroclawiu Wet — Zeszyty Naukowe Wyzszej Szkoly Rolniczej we Wroclawiu. Weterynaria

Zesz Nauk Wyzssza Szk Ekon Poznaniu Ser 2 — Zeszyty Naukowe Wyzsza Szkola Ekonomiczna w Poznaniu. Seria 2. Prace Habilitacyjne i Doktorskie

Zesz Nauk Wyz Szkol Ekon — Zeszyty Naukowe Wyzszej Szkoly Ekonomicznej w Katowicach

Zesz Nauk Wyzsz Szk Inz Bialymstoku Mat Fiz Chem — Zeszyty Naukowe Wyzszej Szkoly Inzynierskiej w Bialymstoku Matematyka, Fizyka, Chemia

Zesz Nauk Wyzsz Szkoly Ekon Katowic — Zeszyty Naukowe Wyzszej Szkoly Ekonomicznej w Katowicach

Zesz Nauk Wyzsz Szkoly Ekon Poznan — Zeszyty Naukowe Wyzszej Szkoly Ekonomicznej w Poznaniu

Zesz Nauk Wyzsz Szk Pedagog Gdansku Mat Fiz Chem — Zeszyty Naukowe Wyzszej Szkoly Pedagogicznej w Gdansku. Matematyka, Fizyka, Chemia

Zesz Nauk Wyzsz Szk Pedagog Katowicach Sekc Fiz — Zeszyty Naukowe Wyzszej Szkoly Pedagogicznej w Katowicach. Sekcja Fizyki

Zesz Nauk Wyzsz Szk Roln Olsztynie — Zeszyty Naukowe Wyzszej Szkoly Rolniczej w Olsztynie

Zesz Nauk Wyzsz Szk Roln Szczecinie — Zeszyty Naukowe Wyzszej Szkoly Rolniczej w Szczecinie

Zesz Nauk Wyzsz Szk Roln Wroclawiu Melior — Zeszyty Naukowe Wyzszej Szkoly Rolniczej we Wroclawiu. Melioracja

Zesz Nauk Wyzsz Szk Roln Wroclawiu Roln — Zeszyty Naukowe Wyzszej Szkoly Rolniczej we Wroclawiu. Rolnictwo

Zesz Nauk Wyzsz Szk Roln Wroclawiu Weter — Zeszyty Naukowe Wyzszej Szkoly Rolniczej we Wroclawiu. Weterynaria

Zesz Nauk Wyzsz Szk Roln Wroclawiu Zootech — Zeszyty Naukowe Wyzszej Szkoly Rolniczej we Wroclawiu. Zootechnika

Zesz Nauk Wyzsz Szk Roln Wrocl Melior — Zeszyty Naukowe Wyzszej Szkoly Rolniczej we Wroclawiu. Melioracja

Zesz Nauk Wyzsz Szk Roln Wrocl Roln — Zeszyty Naukowe Wyzszej Szkoly Rolniczej we Wroclawiu. Rolnictwo

Zesz Nauk Zootech Akad Roln-Tech Olsztyn — Zeszyty Naukowe. Zootechnika-Akademia Rolniczo-Technicznej w Olsztynie

Zesz Nauk Zootech Akad Roln Warsz — Zeszyty Naukowe. Zootechnika-Akademia Rolnicza w Warszawie

Zesz NWSP — Zeszyty Naukowe Wyzsza Szkola Pedagogiczna w Katowicach

Zesz Probl Gorn — Zeszyty Problemowe Gornictwa
Zesz Probl Kosmosu — Zeszyty Problemowe Kosmosu
Zesz Probl Nauki Pol — Zeszyty Problemowe Nauki Polskiej
Zesz Probl Postep Nauk Roln — Zeszyty Problemowe Postepow Nauk Rolniczych
Zesz Probl Postepow Nauk Roln — Zeszyty Problemowe Postepow Nauk Rolniczych
Zesz Prob Postepow Nauk Roln — Zeszyty Problemowe Postepow Nauk Rolniczych
Zeszty Nauk Uniw Jagiellon Prace Mat — Zeszyty Naukowe Uniwersytetu Jagiellonskiego. Prace Matematyczne
Zesz Wrocl — Zeszyty Wroclawskie
Zeszyty Nauk Akad Gorn-Hutniczej Mat Fiz Chem — Zeszyty Naukowe Akademii Gorniczo-Hutniczej Imienia Stanislawa Staszica. Matematyka, Fizyka, Chemia
Zeszyty Nauk Geom — Zeszyty Naukowe Geometria
Zeszyty Nauk Politech Lodz Mat — Zeszyty Naukowe Politechniki Lodzkiej. Matematyka
Zeszyty Nauk Politech Rzeszowskiej Mat — Zeszyty Naukowe Politechniki Rzeszowskiej. Matematyka
Zeszyty Nauk Politech Rzeszowskiej Mat Fiz — Zeszyty Naukowe Politechniki Rzeszowskiej. Matematyka i Fizyka
Zeszyty Nauk Politech Slask Automat — Zeszyty Naukowe Politechniki Slaskiej. Automatyka
Zeszyty Nauk Politech Slask Mat-Fiz — Zeszyty Naukowe Politechniki Slaskiej. Seria Matematyka-Fizyka
Zeszyty Nauk Politech Szczecin — Zeszyty Naukowe Politechniki Szezecinskiej
Zeszyty Nauk Szkoly Glown Planowania i Statyst — Zeszyty Naukowe Szkoly Glownej Planowania i Statystyki
Zeszyty Nauk Uniw Jagiellon Prace Fiz — Zeszyty Naukowe Uniwersytetu Jagiellonskiego. Prace Fizyczne
Zeszyty Nauk Wyz Szkola Ped Powstancow Sl Opolu Mat — Zeszyty Naukowe Wyzsza Szkola Pedagogiczna im Powstancow Slaskich w Opolu. Matematyka
Zeszyty Nauk Wyz Szkoly Ped w Opolu Fiz — Zeszyty Naukowe Wyzszej Szkoly Pedagogicznej w Opolu. Fizyka
Zeszyty Nauk Wyz Szkoly Ped w Opolu Mat — Zeszyty Naukowe Wyzszej Szkoly Pedagogicznej w Opolu. Matematyka
Zetem — Zetemata. Monographien zur Klassischen Altertumswissenschaft
Zetetic Schol — Zetetic Scholar
ZETF — Zurnal Eksperimental'noi i Teoreticeskoi Fiziki
ZETFA — Zhurnal Eksperimentalnoi i Teoreticheskoi Fiziki
ZEthn — Zeitschrift fuer Ethnologie
Z Ethnl — Zeitschrift fuer Ethnologie
Z Ethnol — Zeitschrift fuer Ethnologie
Z Ethnolog — Zeitschrift fuer Ethnologie
ZETUA — Zeitschrift fuer Tuberkulose und Erkrankungen der Thoraxorgane
ZEUMD — Zeitschrift fuer Umweltpolitik
Zeumer's Q St — Zeumer's Quellen und Studien zur Verfassungsgeschichte des Deutschen Reichs in Mittelalter und Neuzeit
ZEURA — Zeitschrift fuer Urologie
ZEV A Eisenbahnwes Verkehrstech — ZEV. Zeitschrift fuer Eisenbahnwesen und Verkehrstecknik. Glasers Annalen
Z Evan Eth — Zeitschrift fuer Evangelische Ethik
Z Evang Kirchenrecht — Zeitschrift fuer Evangelisches Kirchenrecht
ZEVBA — Zeitschrift fuer Vererbungslehre
Z Ev Ethik — Zeitschrift fuer Evangelische Ethik
ZEV Glasers Ann — ZEV [*Zeitschrift fuer Eisenbahnwesen und Verkehrstechnik*] Glasers. Annalen
Z Ev K — Zeitschrift fuer Evangelisches Kirchenrecht
Z Ev Kr — Zeitschrift fuer Evangelisches Kirchenrecht
Z Exp Angew Psychol — Zeitschrift fuer Experimentelle und Angewandte Psychologie
Z Exp A Psy — Zeitschrift fuer Experimentelle und Angewandte Psychologie
Z Exp Chir — Zeitschrift fuer Experimentelle Chirurgie
Z Exp Chir Chir Forsch — Zeitschrift fuer Experimentelle Chirurgie und Chirurgische Forschung
Z Exp Chir Transplant Kuenstliche Organe — Zeitschrift fuer Experimentelle Chirurgie, Transplantation, und Kuenstliche Organe
Z Exper & Angew Psychol — Zeitschrift fuer Experimentelle und Angewandte Psychologie
Z Exp Pathol Ther — Zeitschrift fuer Experimentelle Pathologie und Therapie
Z Exp Psychol — Zeitschrift fuer Experimentelle Psychologie
ZF — Zentralblatt fuer das Gesamte Forstwesen
ZF — Zona Franca
Z f A — Zeitschrift fuer Agrargeschichte und Agrarsoziologie
Z f A — Zeitschrift fuer Anatomie und Entwicklungsgeschichte
ZfA — Zeitschrift fuer Archaeologie
Z f A — Zeitschrift fuer Astrophysik
ZFA (Dresden) — Zeitschrift fuer Alternsforschung (Dresden)
Z f Allg Med — Zeitschrift fuer Allgemeinmedizin
Z Farben Ind — Zeitschrift fuer Farben Industrie
Z Farben Text Chem — Zeitschrift fuer Farben- und Textil-Chemie
ZFA (Stuttgart) — Zeitschrift fuer Allgemeinmedizin (Stuttgart)
Z f Ausl Oeff Recht u Voelkerrecht — Zeitschrift fuer Auslaendisches Oeffentliches Recht und Voelkerrecht
ZfB — Zeitschrift fuer Buecherfreunde
ZfBK — Zeitschrift fuer Bayerische Kirchengeschichte
Z f BK — Zeitschrift fuer Bildende Kunst
ZfBL — Zeitschrift fuer Bayerische Landesgeschichte
ZfBw — Zentralblatt fuer Bibliothekswesen
ZfDA — Zeitschrift fuer Deutsches Altertum und Deutsche Literatur
Z f D Altert — Zeitschrift fuer Deutsches Altertum und Deutsche Literatur
Z f d AW — Zeitschrift fuer die Altertumswissenschaft
ZFDF — Zeitschrift fuer Freie Deutsche Forschung
ZFDG — Zeitschrift fuer Deutsche Geistesgeschichte
ZFDPh — Zeitschrift fuer Deutsche Philologie
Z f D Phil — Zeitschrift fuer Deutsche Philologie

ZfDSdJ — Zeitschrift fuer Demographie und Statistik der Juden
ZfE — Zeitschrift fuer Ethnologie
Z f Ethn — Zeitschrift fuer Ethnologie
ZFEU — Zeitschrift fuer Franzoesischen und Englischen Unterricht
ZFF — Zbornik Filozofske Fakultete Ljubljana
ZFFB — Zbornik Filozofskog Fakulteta (Belgrade)
ZfG — Zeitschrift fuer Geschichtswissenschaft
ZfgA — Zeitschrift fuer Geschichte und Altertumskunde Ermlands
ZFGV — Zeitschrift. Freiburger Geschichtsvereine
ZfHb — Zeitschrift fuer Hebraeische Bibliographie
ZFI-Mitt — ZFI [*Zentralinstitut fuer Isotopen- und Strahlenforschung*]-Mitteilungen
Z Fisch Hilfswiss — Zeitschrift fuer Fischerei und Deren Hilfswissenschaften
ZfK — Zeitschrift fuer Kunstgeschichte
ZfKg — Zeitschrift fuer Kunstgeschichte
Z f K Ph — Zeitschrift fuer Keltische Philologie und Volksforschung
ZFKPhil — Zbornik Filozofickej Fakulty Univerzity Komenskeho-Philologica
Z f Kulturaustausch — Zeitschrift fuer Kulturaustausch
ZFL — Zbornik za Filologiju i Lingvistiku
ZFL — Zeitschrift fuer Luftrecht- und Weltraumrechtsfragen
Z Fleisch Milchhyg — Zeitschrift fuer Fleisch- und Milchhygiene
Z Flugwiss — Zeitschrift fuer Flugwissenschaften
Z Flugwiss und Weltraumforsch — Zeitschrift fuer Flugwissenschaften und Weltraumforschung
Z Flugwiss Weltraumforsch — Zeitschrift fuer Flugwissenschaften und Weltraumforschung
ZFM — Zeitschrift fuer Musik
Zf Mus Theorie — Zeitschrift fuer Musiktheorie
ZfMw — Zeitschrift fuer Musikwissenschaft
ZfN — Zeitschrift fuer Numismatik
ZFNU — Zeitschrift fuer Neusprachlichen Unterricht
Z f Num — Zeitschrift fuer Numismatik
ZFO — ZFO. Zeitschrift fuer Fuehrung und Organisation
Z Forst Jagdwes — Zeitschrift fuer Forst- und Jagdwesen
ZfP — Dokumentation Zerstorungsfreie Pruefung
ZfP — Zeitschrift fuer Politik
Z f Pap Ep — Zeitschrift fuer Papyrologie und Epigraphik
ZfPhF — Zeitschrift fuer Philosophische Forschung
Z Franzoesische Spr Lit — Zeitschrift fuer Franzoesische Sprache und Literatur
Z Franz Spr — Zeitschrift fuer Franzoesische Sprache und Literatur
Z Franz Sprache Lit — Zeitschrift fuer Franzoesische Sprache und Literatur
Zf Rechtsgesch — Zeitschrift fuer Rechtsgeschichte
ZfRG — Zeitschrift fuer Religions- und Geistesgeschichte
ZfRP — Zeitschrift fuer Romanische Philologie
ZFRPH — Zeitschrift fuer Romanische Philologie
ZfRrSL — Zeitschrift fuer Franzoesische Sprache und Literatur
ZfRuGg — Zeitschrift fuer Religions- und Geistesgeschichte
ZfS — Zeitschrift fuer Franzoesische Sprache und Litteratur
ZfS — Zeitschrift fuer Semitistik und Verwandte Gebiete
ZfSchKg — Zeitschrift fuer Schweizerische Kirchengeschichte
Z f Schweiz Recht — Zeitschrift fuer Schweizerisches Recht/Revue de Droit Suisse/Revista di Diritto Svizzero
ZFSL — Zeitschrift fuer Franzoesische Sprache und Literatur
Zft Ethn — Zeitschrift fuer Ethnologie
Zft f Celt Phil — Zeitschrift fuer Celtische Philologie
Zft f D Alt — Zeitschrift fuer Deutsches Altertum und Deutsche Literatur
Zft f Fr Sp u Lit — Zeitschrift fuer Franzoesische Sprache und Literatur
Zft f Rom Phil — Zeitschrift fuer Romanische Philologie
Zft Num — Zeitschrift fuer Numismatik
Zft Rechtsg — Zeitschrift fuer Rechtsgeschichte
Z fuer Mission — Zeitschrift fuer Mission
Z fuer Missionswissenschaft und Religionswissenschaft — Zeitschrift fuer Missionswissenschaft und Religionswissenschaft
Z fur die Oest Gym — Zeitschrift fuer die Deutsche-Oesterreichischen Gymnasien
ZfV — Zeitschrift fuer Versicherungswesen
ZFV — Zeitschrift fuer Volkskunde
ZfW — Zeitschrift fuer Wuerttembergische Landesgeschichte
ZFYZD — Zhonghua Fangshe Yixue Yu Fanghu Zazhi
ZfZ — Zeitschrift fuer Assyriologie
ZG — Zeitschrift fuer Geomorphologie. Gebrueder Borntraeger
ZG — Zeitschrift fuer Geopolitik
ZG — Zeitschrift fuer Germanistik
ZG — Zeitschrift fuer Geschichtswissenschaft
Z Gaertn Bot — Zeitschrift fuer Gaertner, Botaniker, und Blumenfreunde
Z Gaerungsphysiol — Zeitschrift fuer Gaerungsphysiologie
ZGAKE — Zeitschrift fuer Geschichte und Altertumskunde der Ermlands
Z Gartenbau Vereins Koenigr Hannover — Zeitschrift des Gartenbau-Vereins fuer das Koenigreich Hannover
Z Gastroent — Zeitschrift fuer Gastroenterologie
Z Gastroenterol — Zeitschrift fuer Gastroenterologie
Z Gastroenterol Verh — Zeitschrift fuer Gastroenterologie. Verhandlungsband
ZGB — Zivilgesetzbuch
ZGdA — Zeitschrift fuer Geschichte der Architektur
ZGDJ — Zeitschrift zur Geschichte des Deutschen Judentums
ZGE — Zeitschrift der Gesellschaft fuer Erdkunde
ZGEB — Zeitschrift der Gesellschaft fuer Erdkunde zu Berlin
Z Geburtshilfe Gynaekol — Zeitschrift fuer Geburtshilfe und Gynaekologie [*Later, Zeitschrift fuer Geburtshilfe und Perinatologie*]
Z Geburtshilfe Neonatol — Zeitschrift fuer Geburtshilfe und Neonatologie
Z Geburtshilfe Perinatol — Zeitschrift fuer Geburtshilfe und Perinatologie
ZGEIA — Zhurnal Gigieny, Epidemiologii, Mikrobiologii, i Immunologii
ZGEMA — Zeitschrift fuer die Gesamte Experimentelle Medizin
Z Geol Wiss — Zeitschrift fuer Geologische Wissenschaften
Z Geomorph — Zeitschrift fuer Geomorphologie
Z Geomorphol — Zeitschrift fuer Geomorphologie
Z Geomorphol Suppl — Zeitschrift fuer Geomorphologie. Supplementband

Z Geophys — Zeitschrift fuer Geophysik
Z Geopolitik — Zeitschrift fuer Geopolitik
Z Ger Ling — Zeitschrift fuer Germanistische Linguistik
Z Gerontol — Zeitschrift fuer Gerontologie
Z Gerontol Geriatr — Zeitschrift fuer Gerontologie und Geriatrie
Z Gesamte Brauwes — Zeitschrift fuer das Gesamte Brauwesen
Z Gesamte Exp Med — Zeitschrift fuer die Gesamte Experimentelle Medizin
Z Gesamte Exp Med Einschl Exp Chir — Zeitschrift fuer die Gesamte Experimentelle Medizin. Einschliesslich Experimenteller Chirurgie
Z Gesamte Forstwes — Zeitschrift fuer das Gesamte Forstwesen
Z Gesamte Genossenschaftswes — Zeitschrift fuer das Gesamte Genossenschaftswesen
Z Gesamte Genossenschaftswesen — Zeitschrift fuer das Gesamte Genossenschaftswesen
Z Gesamte Getreide Muehlen Baeckereiwes — Zeitschrift fuer das Gesamte Getreide Muehlen- und Baeckereiwesen
Z Gesamte Getreidewes — Zeitschrift fuer das Gesamte Getreidewesen
Z Gesamte Giessereiprax — Zeitschrift fuer die Gesamte Giessereipraxis
Z Gesamte Hyg — Zeitschrift fuer die Gesamte Hygiene und Ihre Grenzgebiete
Z Gesamte Hyg Grenzgeb — Zeitschrift fuer die Gesamte Hygiene und Ihre Grenzgebiete
Z Gesamte Hyg Ihre Grenzgeb — Zeitschrift fuer die Gesamte Hygiene und Ihre Grenzgebiete
Z Gesamte Inn Med — Zeitschrift fuer die Gesamte Innere Medizin und Ihre Grenzgebiete
Z Gesamte Inn Med Grenzgeb — Zeitschrift fuer die Gesamte Innere Medizin und Ihre Grenzgebiete
Z Gesamte Inn Med Grenzgeb Klin Pathol Exp — Zeitschrift fuer die Gesamte Innere Medizin und Ihre Grenzgebiete. Klinik, Pathologie, Experiment
Z Gesamte Inn Med Ihre Grenzgeb — Zeitschrift fuer die Gesamte Innere Medizin und Ihre Grenzgebiete
Z Gesamte Inn Med Ihre Grenzgeb Suppl — Zeitschrift fuer die Gesamte Innere Medizin und Ihre Grenzgebiete. Supplementum
Z Gesamte Kaelte Ind — Zeitschrift fuer die Gesamte Kaelte-Industrie
Z Gesamte Kaelte Ind Beih Ser 1 — Zeitschrift fuer die Gesamte Kaelte-Industrie. Beihefte. Serie 1
Z Gesamte Kaelte Ind Beih Ser 2 — Zeitschrift fuer die Gesamte Kaelte-Industrie. Beihefte. Serie 2
Z Gesamte Kaelte-Ind Beih Ser 3 — Zeitschrift fuer die Gesamte Kaelte-Industrie. Beihefte. Serie 3
Z Gesamte Kreditwesen — Zeitschrift fuer das Gesamte Kreditwesen
Z Gesamte Muehlenwes — Zeitschrift fuer das Gesamte Muehlenwesen
Z Gesamte Naturwiss — Zeitschrift fuer die Gesamte Naturwissenschaft
Z Gesamte Nervenheilkd Psychother — Zeitschrift fuer die Gesamte Nervenheilkunde und Psychotherapie
Z Gesamte Neurol Psychiatr — Zeitschrift fuer die Gesamte Neurologie und Psychiatrie
Z Gesamte Phys Ther — Zeitschrift fuer die Gesamte Physikalische Therapie
Z Gesamte Schiess-Sprengstoffw — Zeitschrift fuer das Gesamte Schiess- und Sprengstoffwesen mit der Sonderabteilung Gasschutz
Z Gesamte Schiess Sprengstoffwes — Zeitschrift fuer das Gesamte Schiess- und Sprengstoffwesen
Z Gesamte Staatswiss — Zeitschrift fuer die Gesamte Staatswissenschaft
Z Gesamte Textilind — Zeitschrift fuer die Gesamte Textilindustrie
Z Gesamte Text-Ind — Zeitschrift fuer die Gesamte Textil-Industrie
Z Gesamte Versicherungswiss — Zeitschrift fuer die Gesamte Versicherungswissenschaft
Z Gesch Altertumskde Ermland — Zeitschrift fuer die Geschichte und Altertumskunde Ermlands
Z Gesch Arab Islam Wiss — Zeitschrift fuer Geschichte der Arabisch-Islamischen Wissenschaften
Z Gesch Erzieh u Unterr — Zeitschrift fuer Geschichte der Erziehung und des Unterrichts
Z Geschichtsw — Zeitschrift fuer Geschichtswissenschaft
ZGeschJud — Zeitschrift fuer die Geschichte der Juden
Z Gesch Landeskde Maehren — Zeitschrift fuer Geschichte und Landeskunde Maehrens
Z Gesch Naturwiss — Zeitschrift fuer Geschichte der Naturwissenschaften, Technik, und Medizin
Z Gesch Oberrhein — Zeitschrift fuer die Geschichte des Oberrheins
Z Gesch Oberrheins — Zeitschrift fuer die Geschichte des Oberrheins
Z Gesch Saar — Zeitschrift fuer die Geschichte der Saargegend
Z Gesch Sudetenl — Zeitschrift fuer Geschichte der Sudetenlaender
Z Geschv Muelheim — Zeitschrift des Geschichtsvereins. Muelheim an der Ruhr
Z Geschv (Muelheim) — Zeitschrift. Geschichtsverein Muelheim an der Ruhr (Muelheim, West Germany)
Z Gesch-Wiss — Zeitschrift fuer Geschichtswissenschaft
Z Ges Erdk Berl — Zeitschrift der Gesellschaft fuer Erdkunde zu Berlin
Z Ges Erdkde Berlin — Zeitschrift der Gesellschaft fuer Erdkunde zu Berlin
Z Ges Exp Med — Zeitschrift fuer die Gesamte Experimentelle Medizin
Z Ges Genossensch — Zeitschrift fuer das Gesamte Genossenschaftswesen
Z Ges Handelsrecht u Wirtsch Recht — Zeitschrift fuer das Gesamte Handelsrecht und Wirtschaftsrecht
Z Ges Inn Med — Zeitschrift fuer die Gesamte Innere Medizin und Ihre Grenzgebiete
Z Ges Kredit — Zeitschrift fuer das Gesamte Kreditwesen
Z Ges Schleswig-Holstein Gesch — Zeitschrift der Gesellschaft fuer Schleswig-Holsteinische Geschichte
Z Ges Staatswiss — Zeitschrift fuer die Gesamte Staatswissenschaft
Z Gesundheitstech Staedtehyg — Zeitschrift fuer Gesundheitstechnik und Staedtehygiene
ZGEU — Zeitschrift fuer Geschichte der Erziehung und des Unterrichts
ZGG — Zeitschrift fuer das Gesamte Genossenschaftswesen
ZGGJT — Zeitschrift. Gesellschaft fuer die Geschichte der Juden in der Tschechoslowakei

ZGGYA — Zeitschrift fuer Geburtshilfe und Gynaekologie [*Later, Zeitschrift fuer Geburtshilfe und Perinatologie*]
ZGJ — Zeitschrift fuer die Geschichte der Juden
ZGJD — Zeitschrift fuer die Geschichte der Juden in Deutschland
ZGJT — Zeitschrift. Gesellschaft fuer die Geschichte der Juden in der Tschechoslowakei
ZGL — Zeitschrift fuer Germanistische Linguistik
ZGLE — Zur Geschichte Lateinischer Eigennamen
ZGLEN — Zur Geschichte Lateinischer Eigennamen
Z Gletscherk Glazialgeol — Zeitschrift fuer Gletscherkunde und Glazialgeologie
ZGMFA — Zeszyty Naukowe Akademii Gorniczo-Hutniczej (Cracow). Matematyka, Fizyka, Chemia
ZGMPA — Zeitschrift fuer Geomorphologie
ZGO — Zeitschrift fuer die Geschichte des Oberrheins
Z Godschmiede Juwelerie Graveure — Zeitschrift fuer Goldschmiede Juwelerie und Graveure
ZGOR — Zeitschrift fuer die Geschichte des Oberrheins
ZGOrh — Zeitschrift fuer die Geschichte des Oberrheins
ZGS — Zeitschrift fuer die Gesamte Staatswissenschaft
ZGS — Zeitschrift fuer die Geschichte des Saargebiets
ZGSHG — Zeitschrift. Gesellschaft fuer Schleswig-Holsteinische Geschichte
ZGSSA — Zeitschrift fuer das Gesamte Schiess- und Sprengstoffwesen mit der Sonderabteilung Gasschutz
ZGW — Zeitschrift fuer Geschichtswissenschaft
ZGZAE6 — Chinese Journal of Orthopedics
Z Hals Nasen Ohrenheilkd — Zeitschrift fuer Hals Nasen- und Ohrenheilkunde
Zh Analit Khim — Zhurnal Analiticheskoi Khimii
Zh Anal Khim — Zhurnal Analiticheskoi Khimii
Z Haut-Geschlechtskr — Zeitschrift fuer Haut- und Geschlechtskrankheiten
Z Hautkr — Zeitschrift fuer Hautkrankheiten
ZHB — Zeitschrift fuer Hebraeische Bibliographie
Z Heeres U Uniformkde — Zeitschrift fuer Heeres- und Uniformkunde
Zh Ehksp Teor Fiz Pis'ma Red — Zhurnal Ehksperimental'noj i Teoreticheskoj Fiziki Pis'ma Redaktsiyu
Zh Ekol Khim — Zhurnal Ekologicheskoi Khimii
Zh Eksp and Teor Fiz Pis'ma v Red — Zhurnal Eksperimental'noi i Teoreticheskoi Fiziki. Pis'ma v Redaktsiyu
Zh Eksp Biol Med — Zhurnal Eksperimental'noi Biologii i Meditsiny
Zh Eksp i Teor Fiz — Zhurnal Eksperimentalnoi i Teoreticheskoi Fiziki
Zh Eksp Klin Med — Zhurnal Eksperimentalnoi i Klinicheskoi Meditsiny
Zh Eksp Teo — Zhurnal Eksperimentalnoi i Teoreticheskoi Fiziki
Zh Eksp Teor Fiz — Zhurnal Eksperimentalnoi i Teoreticheskoi Fiziki
Zh Eksp Teor Fiz Pis — Zhurnal Eksperimentalnoi i Teoreticheskoi Fiziki. Pis'ma
Zh Eksp Teor Fiz Pis'ma — Zhurnal Eksperimental'noi i Teoreticheskoi Fiziki. Pis'ma
Zheleznodorozhn Transp — Zhelezhodorozhnyi Transport
Zhelezn Splavy — Zheleznye Splavy
Zhelezobeton Konstr Chelyabinsk — Zhelezobetonnye Konstruktsii Chelyabinsk
Zh Evol Biokhim Fiziol — Zhurnal Evolyutsionnoi Biokhimii i Fiziologii
ZHF — Schmalenbachs Zeitschrift fuer Betriebswirtschaftliche Forschung
Zh Fiz Dosl — Zhurnal Fizichnikh Doslidzhen
Zh Fiz Khem Tsiklu Vseukr Akad Nauk — Zhurnal Fizichno-Khemichnogo Tsiklu Vseukrains'ka Akademiya Nauk
Zh Fiz Khim — Zhurnal Fizicheskoi Khimii
Zh Geofiz — Zhurnal Geofiziki
Zh Gig Epidemiol Mikrobiol Immunol — Zhurnal Gigieny, Epidemiologii, Mikrobiologii, i Immunologii
Zh Gorn Dela Metall Metall — Zhurnal Gornogo Dela i Metallurgii. Metallurgiya
Zhidkofazn Okislenie Nepredel'nykh Org Soedin — Zhidkofaznoe Okislenie Nepredel'nykh Organicheskikh Soedinenii
Zhilishchnoe Kommunal'n Khoz — Zhilishchnoe i Kommunal'noe Khozyaistvo
Z Hist Fors — Zeitschrift fuer Historische Forschung
Z Hist Ver Schwaben — Zeitschrift des Historischen Verein fuer Schwaben
Z Hist Waffen Und Kostuemkde — Zeitschrift fuer Historische Waffen- und Kostuemkunde
Zhivot Nauki — Zhivotnovudni Nauki
Zhivotnov'd Nauki — Zhivotnov'dni Nauki
Zhivotnovod — Zhivotnovodstvo
Zhivotnovod Vet — Zhivotnovodstvo i Veterinariya
Zhivotnovud — Zhivotnovodstvo
Zhivotnovud Nauki — Zhivotnovudni Nauki
ZHJID — Zhongguo Jiguang
Zh Khim Promsti — Zhurnal Khimicheskoi Promyshlennosti
Zh Khim Termodin Termokhim — Zhurnal Khimicheskoi Termodinamiki i Termokhimii
ZHKPA — Zhurnal Khimicheskoi Promyshlennosti
Zh Mikrob E — Zhurnal Mikrobiologii, Epidemiologii, i Immunobiologii
Zh Mikrobiol Epidemiol Immunobiol — Zhurnal Mikrobiologii, Epidemiologii, i Immunobiologii
Zh Mikrobiol Immunobiol — Zhurnal Mikrobiologii i Immunobiologii
Zh Nauchnoi i Prikl Fotogr i Kinematogr — Zhurnal Nauchnoi i Prikladnoi Fotografii i Kinematografii
Zh Nauchn Prikl Fotogr Kinematogr — Zhurnal Nauchnoi i Prikladnoi Fotografii i Kinematografii
Zh Nauch Prik Foto Kinematog — Zhurnal Nauchnoi i Prikladnoi Fotografii i Kinematografii
Zh Neorg Kh — Zhurnal Neorganicheskoi Khimii
Zh Neorg Khim — Zhurnal Neorganicheskoi Khimii
Zh Nevropatol Psikhiatr — Zhurnal Nevropatologii i Psikhiatrii Imeni S. S. Korsakova
Zh Nevropatol Psikhiatr Im S S Korsakova — Zhurnal Nevropatologii i Psikhiatrii Imeni S. S. Korsakova
ZHNID — Zhongguo Niangzao
Zh NP Fotog — Zhurnal Nauchnoi i Prikladnoi Fotografii i Kinematografii
Zh Obs Biol — Zhurnal Obshchei Biologii

Zh Obshch Biol — Zhurnal Obshchei Biologii
Zh Obshchei Khim — Zhurnal Obshchei Khimii
Zh Obshch Khim — Zhurnal Obshchei Khimii
Zh Obs Kh — Zhurnal Obshchei Khimii
Zh Opytn Agron — Zhurnal Opytnoi Agronomii
Zh Org Kh — Zhurnal Organicheskoi Khimii
Zh Org Khim — Zhurnal Organicheskoi Khimii
ZHPMA — Zentralblatt fuer Bakteriologie, Parasitenkunde, Infektionskrankheiten, und Hygiene. Erste Abteilung. Originale Reihe B. Hygiene, Betriebshygiene, Praeventive Medizin
ZHPMAT — Zentralblatt fuer Bakteriologie, Parasitenkunde, Infektionskrankheiten, und Hygiene. Erste Abteilung. Originale Reihe B. Hygiene, Betriebshygiene, Praeventive Medizin
Zh Priki Mekhan Tekh Fiz — Zhurnal Prikladnoi Mekhaniki i Tekhnicheskoi Fiziki
Zh Prikl Fiz — Zhurnal Prikladnoi Fiziki
Zh Prikl Khim — Zhurnal Prikladnoi Khimii
Zh Prikl Mekh Tekh Fiz — Zhurnal Prikladnoi Mekhaniki i Tekhnicheskoi Fiziki
Zh Prikl Spektrosk — Zhurnal Prikladnoi Spektroskopii
Zh Rezin Promsti — Zhurnal Rezinovoi Promyshlennosti
Zh Russ Fiz-Khim Ova — Zhurnal Russkago Fiziko-Khimicheskago Obshchestva
Zh Russ Fiz-Khim Ova Chast Fiz — Zhurnal Russkogo Fiziko-Khimicheskogo Obshchestva Chast Fizicheskaya
Zh Russ Fiz Khim Ova Chast Khim — Zhurnal Russkogo Fiziko-Khimicheskogo Ovshchestva Chast Khimicheskaya
Zh Russ Khim Ova — Zhurnal Russkago Khimicheskago Obshchestva
Zh Russ Khim Ova Fiz Ova — Zhurnal Russkago Khimicheskago Obshchestva i Fizicheskago Obshchestva
Zh Russ Metall Ova — Zhurnal Russkogo Metallurgicheskogo Obshchestva
Zh Sakh Promsti — Zhurnal Sakharnoi Promyshlennosti
Zh S'kh Nauk — Zhurnal po Sel'skokhozyaistvennym Naukam
Zh Strukt Khim — Zhurnal Strukturnoi Khimii
ZHT — Zeitschrift fuer Historische Theologie
Zh Tekh Fiz — Zhurnal Tekhnicheskoi Fiziki
ZHUCA — Zpravy Hornickeho Ustavu CSAV
Zhurnal Mikrobiol — Zhurnal Mikrobiologii
Zhur Nevropat I Psikhiat — Zhurnal Nevropatologii i Psikhiatrii
Zh Ushn Nos Gorl Bolezn — Zhurnal Ushnykh Nosovykh i Gorlovykh Boleznei
Zh Ushn Nosov Gorlov Bolez — Zhurnal Ushnykh Nosovykh i Gorlovykh Boleznei
Zhu Us Nos i Gorl Bol — Zhurnal Ushnykh Nosovykh i Gorlovykh Boleznei
ZHVNAS — Animal Science
ZHVNS — Zeitschrift. Historischer Verein fuer Niedersachsen
Zh Vopr Neirokhir — Zhurnal Voprosy Neirokhirurgii Imeni N. N. Burdenko
Zh Vopr Neirokhir Im N N Burdenko — Zhurnal Voprosy Neirokhirurgii Imeni N. N. Burdenko
ZHVS — Zeitschrift. Historischer Verein fuer Steiermark
Zh Vses Khi — Zhurnal Vsesoyuznogo Khimicheskogo Obshchestva Imeni D. I. Mendeleeva
Zh Vses Khim Obshch — Zhurnal Vsesoyuznogo Khimicheskogo Obshchestva
Zh Vses Khim Obshchest Mendeleeva — Zhurnal Vsesoiuznogo Khimicheskogo Obshchestva imeni D. I. Mendeleeva
Zh Vses Khim Ova — Zhurnal Vsesoyuznogo Khimicheskogo Obshchestva Imeni D. I. Mendeleeva
Zh Vses Khim Ova Im D I Mendeleeva — Zhurnal Vsesoyuznogo Khimicheskogo Obshchestva Imeni D. I. Mendeleeva
ZHVSt — Zeitschrift des Historischen Vereins fuer Steiermark
Zh Vychisl Mat i Mat Fiz — Zhurnal Vychislitel'noi Matematiki i Matematicheske Fiziki
Zh Vychisl Mat Mat Fiz — Zhurnal Vychislitel'noi Matematiki i Matematicheske Fiziki
Zh Vyssh Nerv Deyat — Zhurnal Vysshei Nervnoi Deyatel'nosti
Zh Vyssh Nervn Deyat Im I P Pavlova — Zhurnal Vysshei Nervnoi Deyatel'nosti Imeni I. P. Pavlova
Zh Vyss Ner — Zhurnal Vysshei Nervnoi Deyatel'nosti Imeni I. P. Pavlova
ZHW — Ziekenhuis
Z Hyg — Zeitschrift fuer Hygiene
Z Hyg — Zeltschrlft fuer Hyglene und Infectionskrankheiten
ZHYGA — Zeitschrift fuer die Gesamte Hygiene und Ihre Grenzgebiete
Z Hyg Infektionskr — Zeitschrift fuer Hygiene und Infektionskrankheiten
Z Hyg Infekt Kr — Zeitschrift fuer Hygiene und Infektionskrankheiten
Z Hyg InfektKrankh — Zeitschrift fuer Hygiene und Infektionskrankheiten
Z Hyg Zool Schaedlingsbekaempf — Zeitschrift fuer Hygienische Zoologie und Schaedlingsbekaempfung
Z I — Zeitschrift fuer Instrumentenbau
ZIALA — Zeitschrift fuer Immunitaets- und Allergieforschung
ZIAVA — Zeitschrift fuer Induktive Abstammungs- und Vererbungslehre
Zielspr Span — Zielsprache Spanisch
Zig Zag Forest — Zig-Zag Forestiere
ZII — Zeitschrift fuer Indologie und Iranistik
ZI Int — ZI [Ziegelindustrie] International
ZIK — Zbornik Istorije Knijizevnosti
ZiM — Ziemia i Morze
Zimbabwe Agric J — Zimbabwe Agricultural Journal
Zimbabwe Div Livest Pastures Annu Rep — Zimbabwe. Division of Livestock and Pastures. Annual Report
Zimbabwe Eng — Zimbabwe Engineer
Zimbabwe J Agric Res — Zimbabwe Journal of Agricultural Research
Zimbabwe J Econ — Zimbabwe Journal of Economics
Zimbabwe Rev — Zimbabwe Review
Zimbabwe Rhod Nurse — Zimbabwe Rhodesia Nurse
Zimbabwe Rhod Sci News — Zimbabwe-Rhodesia Science News
Zimbabwe Sci News — Zimbabwe Science News
Zimbabwe Vet J — Zimbabwe Veterinary Journal
Zimb Agric J — Zimbabwe Agricultural Journal
Zimb Eng — Zimbabwe Engineer
Zimb J Agric Res — Zimbabwe Journal of Agricultural Research

Zimb Law J — Zimbabwe Law Journal
Zimb Libr — Zimbabwe Librarian
Zimb Prehist — Zimbabwean Prehistory
Zimb Sci News — Zimbabwe Science News
ZIMG — Zeitschrift. Internationale Musik Gesellschaft
Z Immun -Allergie-Forsch — Zeitschrift fuer Immunitaets- und Allergieforschung
Z Immun Exp — Zeitschrift fuer Immunitaetsforschung. Experimentelle und Klinische Immunologie
Z ImmunForsch Exp Ther — Zeitschrift fuer Immunitaetsforschung und Experimentelle Therapie
Z Immunitaets-Allergieforsch — Zeitschrift fuer Immunitaets- und Allergieforschung
Z Immunitaetsforsch — Zeitschrift fuer Immunitaetsforschung
Z Immunitaetsforsch Allerg Klin Immunol — Zeitschrift fuer Immunitaetsforschung. Allergie und Klinische Immunologie
Z Immunitaetsforsch Exp Klin Immunol — Zeitschrift fuer Immunitaetsforschung. Experimentelle und Klinische Immunologie
Z Immunitaetsforsch Exp Klin Immunol Suppl — Zeitschrift fuer Immunitaetsforschung. Experimentelle und Klinische Immunologie. Supplemente
Z Immunitaetsforsch Exp Ther — Zeitschrift fuer Immunitaetsforschung und Experimentelle Therapie
Z Immunitaetsforsch Exp Ther 1 — Zeitschrift fuer Immunitaetsforschung und Experimentelle Therapie. 1. Originale
Z Immunitaetsforsch Exp Ther 1 Abt Orig — Zeitschrift fuer Immunitaetsforschung und Experimentelle Therapie. 1. AbteilungOriginale
Z Immunitaetsforsch Exp Ther 2 — Zeitschrift fuer Immunitaetsforschung und Experimentelle Therapie. 2. Referate
Z Immunitaetsforsch Immunobiol — Zeitschrift fuer Immunitaetsforschung. Immunobiology
Z Immunitaetsforsch Immunobiol Suppl — Zeitschrift fuer Immunitaetsforschung. Immunobiology. Supplemente
Z Immunitaetsforsch Suppl — Zeitschrift fuer Immunitaetsforschung. Supplemente
ZIMordASSR — Zapiski Naucno-Issledovatel'nogo Instituta pri Sovete Ministrov Mordovskoj ASSR
Zinat Raksti Rigas Politeh Inst — Zinatniskie Raksti. Rigas Politehniskais Instituts
Zinc Abstr — Zinc Abstracts
Zinc/Cadmium Res Dig — Zinc/Cadmium Research Digest
Zinc Res Dig — Zinc Research Digest
Z Indukt Abstammungs-Vererbungsl — Zeitschrift fuer Induktive Abstammungs- und Vererbungslehre
Z Indukt Abstamm u Vererblehre — Zeitschrift fuer Induktive Abstammungs- und Vererbungslehre
Zinn Verwend — Zinn und Seine Verwendung
Z Instk — Zeitschrift fuer Instrumentenkunde
Z Instrum — Zeitschrift fuer Instrumentenkunde
Z Instrumentenk — Zeitschrift fuer Instrumentenkunde
Z Instrumentenkd — Zeitschrift fuer Instrumentenkunde
Z Interne Revision — Zeitschrift Interne Revision
Z Int Inst Zuckerruebenforsch — Zeitschrift. Internationales Institut fuer Zuckerruebenforschung
Z Int Ver Bohring Bohrtech — Zeitschrift. Internationaler Verein der Bohringenieure und Bohrtechniker
Zionist Q — Zionist Quarterly
ZiP — Za i Przeciw
ZIP — ZIP Target Marketing
Ziraat Derg — Ziraat Dergisi
Ziraat Fak Derg Ege Univ — Ziraat Fakultesi Dergisi Ege Universitesi
Zisin J Seismol Soc Jpn — Zisin/Journal of the Seismological Society of Japan
Zisin Seismol Soc Jap J — Zisin/Seismological Society of Japan. Journal
ZIS Mitt — ZIS [Zentralinstitut fuer Schweisstechnik] Mitteilungen
ZIS Rep — ZIS (Zentralinstitut fuer Schweisstechnik der DDR) Report
ZIS (Zentralinst Schweisstech DDR) Mitt — ZIS (Zentralinstitut fuer Schweisstechnik der Deutschen Demokratischen Republik) Mitteilungen
ZIT — Zeitschrift Interne Revision
Ziv A — Archiv fuer die Zivilistische Praxis
Ziva — Ziva. Casopis pro Biologickou Praci
ZIVAN — Zapiski Instituta Vostokoveden'ia Akademii Nauk SSSR
Zivocisna Vyroba Cesk Akad Zemed Ustav Vedeckotech Inf Zemed — Zivocisna Vyroba-Ceskoslovenska Akademie Zemedelska. Ustav Vedeckotechnickych Informaci pro Zemedelstvi
Zivoc Vyroba — Zivocisna Vyroba
Zivotn Prostr — Zivotne Prostredie
ZIVP — Zivotne Prostredie
Ziv Pr — Archiv fuer die Zivilistische Praxis
Zl Ziegelind Int — Zl. Ziegelindustrie International
ZJ — Zeszyty Jezykoznawcze
ZJ — Zivi Jezici
Z Jagdwiss — Zeitschrift fuer Jagdwissenschaft
ZJARDK — Zimbabwe Journal of Agricultural Research
ZJKF — Zpravy Jednoty Klasickych Filologu
Z Journ — Zeitschrift fuer Journalistik
ZJS — Zoologische Jahrbuecher. Abteilungen fuer Systematik Oekologie, Geographie, und Biologie
ZJSTD — Zambia Journal of Science and Technology
ZK — Zeitschrift fuer Keilschriftforschung und Verwandte Gebiete
ZK — Zeitschrift fuer Kirchengeschichte
ZK — Zeitschrift fuer Kunstgeschichte
ZK — Zeitschrift fuer Kunstwissenschaft
ZKA — Zeitschrift fuer Kulturaustausch
ZKA — Zentralkatalog der Auslaendischen Literatur
Z Kardiol — Zeitschrift fuer Kardiologie
Z Kardiol Suppl — Zeitschrift fuer Kardiologie. Supplementum
Z Kath Theol — Zeitschrift fuer Katholische Theologie
ZK Ch — Zeitschrift fuer Kinderchirurgie und Grenzgebiete
Z Kde Deutschtum Ausl — Zeitschrift fuer die Kunde vom Deutschtum im Ausland

ZKG — Zeitschrift fuer Kirchengeschichte
ZKG — Zeitschrift fuer Kunstgeschichte
ZKG Int Ed B — ZKG International. Edition B
Z Kindch G — Zeitschrift fuer Kinderchirurgie und Grenzgebiete
Z Kinderchir — Zeitschrift fuer Kinderchirurgie
Z Kinderchir Grenzgeb — Zeitschrift fuer Kinderchirurgie und Grenzgebiete
Z Kinderheilkd — Zeitschrift fuer Kinderheilkunde
Z Kinder-Jugendpsychiatr — Zeitschrift fuer Kinder- und Jugendpsychiatrie
Z Kinder Jugendpsychiatr Psychother — Zeitschrift fuer Kinder- und Jugendpsychiatrie und Psychotherapie [Bern]
Z Kinderpsychiatr — Zeitschrift fuer Kinderpsychiatrie
Z Kind Jug — Zeitschrift fuer Kinder- und Jugendpsychiatrie
Z Kircheng — Zeitschrift fuer Kirchengeschichte
Z Kirchengesch — Zeitschrift fuer Kirchengeschichte
Z Kirch G — Zeitschrift fuer Kirchengeschichte
ZKJ — Zbornik za Knjizevnost i Jezik
ZKKOBW — Cancer Research and Clinical Oncology
ZKKODY — Gerontology Extension Lectures
ZKLCA — Zeitschrift fuer Klinische Chemie
Z Klin Chem — Zeitschrift fuer Klinische Chemie und Klinische Biochemie
Z Klin Chemie — Zeitschrift fuer Klinische Chemie
Z Klin Chem Klin Biochem — Zeitschrift fuer Klinische Chemie und Klinische Biochemie
Z Klin Med — Zeitschrift fuer Klinische Medizin
Z Klin Psychol Psychopathol Psychother — Zeitschrift fuer Klinische Psychologie, Psychopathologie, und Psychotherapie
Z Klin Psychol Psychother — Zeitschrift fuer Klinische Psychologie und Psychotherapie
Z Kl M — Zeitschrift fuer Klinische Medizin
ZKM — Zeitschrift fuer die Kunde des Morgenlandes
Z Koeln Zoo — Zeitschrift des Koelner Zoo
Z Kompr Fluess Gase Pressluft-Ind — Zeitschrift fuer Komprimierte und Fluessige Gase Sowie fuer die Pressluft-Industrie
ZK Ph — Zeitschrift fuer Keltische Philologie
ZKPVF — Zeitschrift fuer Keltische Philologie und Volksforschung
ZKR — Zeitschrift fuer das Gesamte Kreditwesen
ZKR — Zeitschrift fuer Kirchenrecht
Z Kr — Zeitschrift fuer Kristallographie, Kristallgeometrie, Kristallphysik, Kristallchemie
Z Kr — Zeitschrift fuer Krystallographie und Mineralogie
Z Krankenpfl — Zeitschrift fuer Krankenpflege
Z Krebsf Kl — Zeitschrift fuer Krebsforschung und Klinische Onkologie
Z Krebsforsch — Zeitschrift fuer Krebsforschung
Z Krebsforsch Klin Onkol — Zeitschrift fuer Krebsforschung und Klinische Onkologie
Z Kreislaufforsch — Zeitschrift fuer Kreislaufforschung
Z Kreisl Forsch — Zeitschrift fuer Kreislaufforschung
Z Kr F — Zeitschrift fuer Krebsforschung
Z Krist — Zeitschrift fuer Kristallographie, Kristallgeometrie, Kristallphysik, Kristallchemie
Z Kristall — Zeitschrift fuer Kristallographie, Kristallgeometrie, Kristallphysik, Kristallchemie
Z Kristallogr — Zeitschrift fuer Kristallographie
Z Kristallogr Kristallgeom Kristallphys Kristallchem — Zeitschrift fuer Kristallographie, Kristallgeometrie, Kristallphysik, Kristallchemie
Z Kristallogr Mineral — Zeitschrift fuer Kristallographie und Mineralogie
Z Kristallogr New Cryst Struct — Zeitschrift fuer Kristallographie. New Crystal Structures. International Journal for Structural, Physical, and Chemical Aspects of Crystalline Materials
ZKRU — Zeitschrift fuer Katholischen Religionsunterricht
Z Kryst Miner — Zeitschrift fuer Krystallographie und Mineralogie
ZKT — Zeitschrift fuer Katholische Theologie
ZKTh — Zeitschrift fuer Katholische Theologie
ZKUFAK — Journal of Rural Engineering and Development
ZKuG — Zeitschrift fuer Kunstgeschichte
Z Kult G — Zeitschrift fuer Kulturgeschichte
Z Kult-Tech Flurberein — Zeitschrift fuer Kulturtechnik und Flurbereinigung
Z Kulturaustausch — Zeitschrift fuer Kulturaustausch
Z Kulturtech — Zeitschrift fuer Kulturtechnik
Z Kulturtech Flurbereinig — Zeitschrift fuer Kulturtechnik und Flurbereinigung
Z Kulturtech Landentwicklung — Zeitschrift fuer Kulturtechnik und Landentwicklung
Z Kunst — Zeitschrift fuer Kunstgeschichte
ZKunstG — Zeitschrift fuer Kunstgeschichte
Z Kunstges — Zeitschrift fuer Kunstgeschichte
Z Kunstgesc — Zeitschrift fuer Kunstgeschichte
Z Kunstgesch — Zeitschrift fuer Kunstgeschichte
Z Kunst W — Zeitschrift des Deutschen Vereins fuer Kunstwissenschaft
Z Kunstwis — Zeitschrift fuer Kunstwissenschaft
ZKW — Zeitschrift fuer Kunstwissenschaft
ZKWL — Zeitschrift fuer Kirchliche Wissenschaft und Kirchliches Leben
ZL — Zavodskaja Laboratorija
ZL — Zoo Life
ZL — Zycie Literackie
Z Laboratoriumsdiagn — Zeitschrift fuer Laboratoriumsdiagnostik
Z Landeskult — Zeitschrift fuer Landeskultur
Z Landwirsch Versuchswes Dtsch Oesterr — Zeitschrift fuer das Landwirtschaftliche Versuchswesen im Deutsch-Oesterreich
Z Landwirtschaftswiss — Zeitschrift fuer Landwirtschaftswissenschaft
Z Landwirtsch Vers Untersuchungswes — Zeitschrift fuer Landwirtschaftliches Versuchs- und Untersuchungswesen
Z Landwirt Vers Untersuchungsw — Zeitschrift fuer Landwirtschaftliches Versuchs- und Untersuchungswesen
Z Landw Vereine Grossherzogth Hessen — Zeitschrift fuer die Landwirthschaftlichen Vereine des Grossherzogthums Hessen

Z Landw Ver u Unters Wes — Zeitschrift fuer Landwirtschaftliches Versuchs- und Untersuchungswesen
Z Lar Rhinol Otol — Zeitschrift fuer Laryngologie, Rhinologie, Otologie, und Ihre Grenzgebiete
Z Laryngol Rhinol Otol — Zeitschrift fuer Laryngologie, Rhinologie, Otologie, und Ihre Grenzgebiete
Z Laryngol Rhinol Otol Grenzgeb — Zeitschrift fuer Laryngologie, Rhinologie, Otologie, und Ihre Grenzgebiete
Z Laryngol Rhinol Otol Ihre Grenzgeb — Zeitschrift fuer Laryngologie, Rhinologie, Otologie, und Ihre Grenzgebiete
Z Lebensmit — Zeitschrift fuer Lebensmittel- Untersuchung und Forschung
Z Lebensmittel Untersuch Forsch — Zeitschrift fuer Lebensmittel- Untersuchung und Forschung
Z Lebensmittelunters u Forsch — Zeitschrift fuer Lebensmittel- Untersuchung und Forschung
Z Lebensmitt Untersuch — Zeitschrift fuer Lebensmittel- Untersuchung und Forschung
Z Lebensm-Technol-Verfahrenstech — Zeitschrift fuer Lebensmittel- Technologie und Verfahrenstechnik
Z Lebensm-Unters Forsch — Zeitschrift fuer Lebensmittel- Untersuchung und Forschung
Z Lebensm Unters Forsch A — Zeitschrift fuer Lebensmittel-Untersuchung und -Forschung A. Food Research and Technology
Z Leder Gerberei Chem — Zeitschrift fuer Leder- und Gerberei-Chemie
ZLGIA — Zapiski Leningradskogo Gornogo Instituta
ZLit — Zycie Literackie
Z Literaturwiss Linguist — Zeitschrift fuer Literaturwissenschaft und Linguistik
Z Lit Wiss — Zeitschrift fuer Literaturwissenschaft
ZLJ — Zambia Law Journal
ZLL — Zeitschrift fuer Literaturwissenschaft und Linguistik
ZLROA — Zeitschrift fuer Laryngologie, Rhinologie, Otologie
ZLSIA — Zapiski Leningradskogo Sel'skokhozyaistvennogo Instituta
ZLThK — Zeitschrift fuer die Gesamte Lutherische Theologie und Kirche
Z Luft-Weltraumrecht — Zeitschrift fuer Luft- und Weltraumrecht
ZLUMS — Zbornik za Likovne Umetnosti Matice Srpske
ZLW — Zeitschrift fuer Luftrecht und Weltraum-Rechtsfragen
Z Lymphol — Zeitschrift fuer Lymphologie
ZM — Zahnaerztliche Mitteilungen
ZM — Zeitschrift fuer Militaergeschichte
ZM — Zeitschrift fuer Missionskunde
ZM — Zeitschrift fuer Mundartforschung
ZM — Zeitschrift fuer Musik
ZM — Zycie i Mysl
ZMA — Zeitschrift fuer Morphologie und Anthropologie
Z Maehr Landesmus — Zeitschrift des Maehrischen Landesmuseums
ZM-AF — Zeitschrift fuer Mikroskopische-Anatomische Forschung
ZMaF — Zeitschrift fuer Mundartforschung
ZMag — Z Magazine
Z Markt Meinungs und Zukunftsforsch — Zeitschrift fuer Marktforschung, Meinungsforschung, und Zukunftsforschung
ZMAS — Zeitschrift fuer Morphologie und Anthropologie (Stuttgart)
Z Math Log — Zeitschrift fuer Mathematische Logik und Grundlagen der Mathematik
Z Math Logik Grundlagen Math — Zeitschrift fuer Mathematische Logik und Grundlagen der Mathematik
Z Math Logik Grundlag Math — Zeitschrift fuer Mathematische Logik und Grundlagen der Mathematik
Z Mat Phys — Zeitschrift fuer Mathematik und Physik
ZMBTA — Zement und Beton
Z Med Chem — Zeitschrift fuer Medizinische Chemie
Z Med Isotopenforsch Deren Grenzgeb — Zeitschrift fuer Medizinische Isotopenforschung und Deren Grenzgebiete
Z Med Lab Diagn — Zeitschrift fuer Medizinische Laboratoriumsdiagnostik
Z Med Laboratoriumsdiagn — Zeitschrift fuer Medizinische Laboratoriumsdiagnostik
Z Med Laboratoriumsdiagn Beil — Zeitschrift fuer Medizinische Laboratoriumsdiagnostik. Beilage
Z Med Labortech — Zeitschrift fuer Medizinische Labortechnik
Z Med Mikrobiol Immunol — Zeitschrift fuer Medizinische Mikrobiologie und Immunologie
Z Med Mikrosk — Zeitschrift fuer Medizinische Mikroskopie
Z Med Phys — Zeitschrift fuer Medizinische Physik
ZMEI — Zhurnal Mikrobiologii, Epidemiologii, i Immunobiologii
ZMEIA — Zhurnal Mikrobiologii, Epidemiologii, i Immunobiologii
Z Menschl Vererb-Konstitutionsl — Zeitschrift fuer Menschliche Vererbungs- und Konstitutionslehre
Z Menschl Vererbungs Konstitutionsl — Zeitschrift fuer Menschliche Vererbungs und Konstitutionslehre
Z Metallk — Zeitschrift fuer Metallkunde
Z Metallkd — Zeitschrift fuer Metallkunde
Z Metallkun — Zeitschrift fuer Metallkunde
Z Meteorol — Zeitschrift fuer Meteorologie
Z Met Schmuckwaren Fabr Verchrom — Zeitschrift fuer Metall- und Schmuckwaren. Fabrikation sowie Verchromung
ZMF — Zeitschrift fuer Mundartforschung
ZMFWA — Zeszyty Naukowe. Matematyka, Fizyka, Chemia
ZMG — Zentralblatt fuer Mathematik und Ihre Grenzgebiete
ZMGP — Zentralblatt fuer Mineralogie, Geologie, und Palaeontologie
ZMGPS — Zentralblatt fuer Mineralogie, Geologie, und Palaeontologie (Stuttgart)
ZMH — Zeitschrift. Museum Hildesheim
Z Mikrosk Anat Forsch — Zeitschrift fuer Mikroskopische-Anatomische Forschung
Z Mikrosk-Anat Forsch (Leipz) — Zeitschrift fuer Mikroskopische-Anatomische Forschung (Leipzig)
Z Militaergesch — Zeitschrift fuer Militaergeschichte
Z Militaermed — Zeitschrift fuer Militaermedizin

Z Miss — Zeitschrift fuer Missionswissenschaft und Religionswissenschaft

Z Missionswiss Religionswiss — Zeitschrift fuer Missionswissenschaft und Religionswissenschaft

Z Miss-u Relig Wiss — Zeitschrift fuer Missionswissenschaft und Religionswissenschaft

Z Miss W — Zeitschrift fuer Missionswissenschaft und Religionswissenschaft

ZMK — Zeitschrift fuer Missionskunde und Religionswissenschaft

ZMK — Zpravodaj Mistopisne Komise CSAV

ZMKBA6 — Zeszyty Naukowe Uniwersytetu Mikolaja Kopernika w Toruniu. Nauki Matematyczno-Przyrodniczne Biologia

ZML — Zoologische Mededeelingen Rijksmuseum van Natuurlijke Historie. Leiden

ZMM — Zeitschrift fuer Marktforschung, Meinungsforschung, und Zukunftsforschung

ZMMPAO — Zentralblatt fuer Bakteriologie, Parasitenkunde, Infektionskrankheiten, und Hygiene. Erste Abteilung. Originale Reihe A. Medizinische Mikrobiologie und Parasitologie

ZMNP — Zurnal Ministerstva Narodnogo Prosvescenija

Z Morph Anthrop — Zeitschrift fuer Morphologie und Anthropologie

Z Morph Okol Tiere — Zeitschrift fuer Morphologie und Oekologie der Tiere

Z Morphol Anthropol — Zeitschrift fuer Morphologie und Anthropologie

Z Morphol Oekol Tiere — Zeitschrift fuer Morphologie und Oekologie der Tiere

Z Morphologie und Anthrop — Zeitschrift fuer Morphologie und Anthropologie

Z Morphol Tiere — Zeitschrift fuer Morphologie der Tiere

Z Morph Tie — Zeitschrift fuer Morphologie der Tiere

ZMOTA — Zeitschrift fuer Morphologie und Oekologie der Tiere

ZMP — Zeitschrift fuer Musikpaedagogik

ZMP — Zurnal Moskovskoi Patriarkhii

ZMPHA — Zeitschrift fuer Mathematik und Physik

ZMR — Zeitschrift fuer Missionswissenschaft und Religionswissenschaft

ZMRW — Zeitschrift fuer Missionswissenschaft und Religionswissenschaft

ZMS — Zbornik Matice Srpske

Z Mth — Zeitschrift fuer Musiktheorie

ZMtheorie — Zeitschrift fuer Musiktheorie

Z Mth Ps — Zeitschrift fuer Mathematik und Physik

ZMVKA — Zeitschrift fuer Menschliche Vererbungs- und Konstitutionslehre

ZMW — Zeitschrift fuer Missionswissenschaft

Z Mw — Zeitschrift fuer Musikwissenschaft

Z Mykol — Zeitschrift fuer Mykologie

ZM Zahnaerztl Mitt A — ZM. Zahnaerztliche Mitteilungen. Ausgabe A

ZN — Zeitschrift fuer Namenforschung

ZN — Zeitschrift fuer Nationaloekonomie

ZN — Zeitschrift fuer Numismatik

ZN — Zeszyty Naukowe

Zn — Znamya

ZN — Zuger Neujahrsblatt

ZN — Zycie Nauki

ZNa — Zycie Nauki

ZNACD — Zeszyty Naukowe Akademii Gorniczo-Hutniczej Imienia Stanislawa Staszica. Matematyka, Fizyka, Chemia

ZNAGA — Zeszyty Naukowe Akademii Gorniczo-Hutniczej w Krakowie. Rozprawy

ZNAGB — Zeszyty Naukowe Akademii Gorniczo-Hutniczej (Krakow). Gornictwo

ZNAGD — Zeszyty Naukowe Akademii Gorniczo-Hutniczej Imienia Stanislawa Staszica. Geologia

ZNAGDF — Akademia Gorniczo-Hutnicza Imienia Stanislawa Staszica w Krakowie Zeszyty Naukowe Geologia

ZNAHD — Zeszyty Naukowe Akademii Gorniczo-Hutniczej Imienia Stanislawa Staszica. Elektryfikacja i Mechanizacja Gornictwa i Hutnictwa

Z Nahrungsm Unters Hyg Warenkd — Zeitschrift fuer Nahrungsmittel-Untersuchung Hygiene und Warenkunde

ZNAND — Zootecnica e Nutrizione Animale

Z Nat F — Zeitschrift fuer Naturforschung

Z Natforsch — Zeitschrift fuer Naturforschung

Z Natforsch A Phys Sci — Zeitschrift fuer Naturforschung. A. Physical Sciences

Z Nationalo — Zeitschrift fuer Nationaloekonomie

Z Nationaloekon — Zeitschrift fuer Nationaloekonomie

Z Nationaloekonom — Zeitschrift fuer Nationaloekonomie

Z Nat-Oekon — Zeitschrift fuer Nationaloekonomie

Z Nat Oekon — Zeitschrift fuer Nationaloekonomie/Journal of Economics

Z Naturf B — Zeitschrift fuer Naturforschung. Teil B

Z Naturf C — Zeitschrift fuer Naturforschung. Teil C. Biochemie, Biophysik, Biologie, Virologie

Z Naturfo A — Zeitschrift fuer Naturforschung. A

Z Naturfo B — Zeitschrift fuer Naturforschung. B

Z Naturfo C — Zeitschrift fuer Naturforschung. C

Z Naturforsch — Zeitschrift fuer Naturforschung

Z Naturforsch A — Zeitschrift fuer Naturforschung. Teil A. Astrophysik, Physik, und PhysikalischeChemie

Z Naturforsch A Phys Phys Chem — Zeitschrift fuer Naturforschung. Teil A. Physik, Physikalische Chemie, Kosmophysik

Z Naturforsch B — Zeitschrift fuer Naturforschung. Teil B

Z Naturforsch B Anorg Chem Org — Zeitschrift fuer Naturforschung. Teil B. Anorganische Chemie, Organische Chemie, Biophysik, Biologie

Z Naturforsch B Anorg Chem Org Chem — Zeitschrift fuer Naturforschung. Teil B. Anorganische Chemie, Organische Chemie

Z Naturforsch B Anorg Chem Org Chem Biochem Biophys Biol — Zeitschrift fuer Naturforschung. Teil B. Anorganische Chemie, Organische Chemie, Biochemie, Biophysik, Biologie

Z Naturforsch C — Zeitschrift fuer Naturforschung. Section C. Journal of Biosciences

Z Naturforsch C Biochem Biophys Biol Virol — Zeitschrift fuer Naturforschung. Teil C. Biochemie, Biophysik, Biologie, Virologie

Z Naturforsch C Biosci — Zeitschrift fuer Naturforschung. Teil C. Biosciences

Z Naturforsch Sect B — Zeitschrift fuer Naturforschung. Section B. Inorganic Chemistry, Organic Chemistry

Z Naturforsch Sect C Biosci — Zeitschrift fuer Naturforschung. Section C. Biosciences

Z Naturforsch Teil A — Zeitschrift fuer Naturforschung. Teil A

Z Naturforsch Teil B Anorg Chem Org Chem — Zeitschrift fuer Naturforschung. Teil B. Anorganische Chemie, Organische Chemie

Z Naturforsch Teil C — Zeitschrift fuer Naturforschung. Teil C. Biosciences

Z Naturforsch Teil C Biochem Biophys Biol Virol — Zeitschrift fuer Naturforschung. Teil C. Biochemie, Biophysik, Biologie, Virologie

Z Naturheilk — Zeitschrift fuer Naturheilkunde

Z Naturwiss-Med Grundlagenforsch — Zeitschrift fuer Naturwissenschaftlich-Medizinische Grundlagenforschung

ZNCAV — Zdenku Nejedlemu Ceskoslovenska Akademie Ved

ZN Ch — Zurnal Neorganiceskoj Chimii

Z Neorg Chim — Zurnal Neorganiceskoj Chimii

Z Neurol — Zeitschrift fuer Neurologie

Z Neutral — Zeitschrift Neutralitaet

Z Neut W — Zeitschrift fuer die Neutestamentliche Wissenschaft

Z Neut Wiss — Zeitschrift fuer die Neutestamentliche Wissenschaft und die Kunde der Aelteren Kirche

ZNF — Zeitschrift fuer Namenforschung

ZNG — Zeszyty Naukowe Wydzialu Humanistycznego, Wyzsza Szkola Pedagogiczna w Gdansku

ZNGGA — Zeszyty Naukowe Akademii Gorniczo-Hutniczej (Krakow). Geologia

ZNIO — Zaklad Narodowy Imeni Ossolinskich

ZNK — Zeszyty Naukowe, Sekcja Jezykoznawcza, Wyzsza Szkola Pedagogiczna w Katowicach

ZNKUL — Zeszyty Naukowe Katolickiego Uniwersytetu Lubelskiego

ZNLSA — Zeszyty Naukowe Politechniki Lodzkiej. Chemia Spozywcza

ZNM — Zbornik Narodnog Muzeja

ZNO — Zeitschrift fuer Nationaloekonomie

ZNPEA — Zeszyty Naukowe Politechniki Lodzkiej. Elektryka

ZNPED — Zeszyty Naukowe Politechniki Poznanskiej. Elektryka

ZNPIA — Zhurnal Nevropatologii i Psikhiatrii Imeni S. S. Korsakova

ZNPPD — Zeszyty Naukowe Politechniki Swietokrzyskiej. Seria P. Problemy Nauk Podstawowych

ZNS — Zeitschrift fuer Neuere Sprachen

ZNSCA — Zeszyty Naukowe Politechniki Slaskiej. Chemia

ZNSGA — Zeszyty Naukowe Politechniki Slaskiej. Gornictwo

ZNSL — Zeitschrift fuer Neufranzoesische Sprache und Literatur

ZNSPK — Zeszyty Naukowe Wyzszej Szkoly Pedagogicznej (Katowice)

ZNSPO — Zeszyty Naukowe Wyzszej Szkoly Pedagogicznej (Opole)

ZNSSA — Zeszyty Naukowe Akademii Gorniczo-Hutniczej (Krakow). Sozologia i Sozotechnika

ZNTFA — Zeitschrift fuer Naturforschung

ZNTHA — Zeszyty Naukowe Politechniki Czestochowskiej. Nauki Techniczne. Hutnictwo

Z Ntl W — Zeitschrift fuer die Neutestamentliche Wissenschaft

ZNTS — Zapysky Naukovoho Tovarystva Imeny Svecenka

ZNTSL — Zapysky Naukovoho Tovarystva Imeny Svecenka (Literature Series)

ZNTW — Zeitschrift fuer die Neutestamentliche Wissenschaft

ZNTZA — Zeszyty Naukowe Akademii Rolniczo-Technicznej w Olsztynie. Technologia Zywnosci

ZNU — Zeitschrift fuer Neusprachlichen Unterricht

ZNUFA — Zeszyty Naukowe Uniwersytetu Jagiellonskiego. Prace Fizyczne

ZNUG — Zeszyty Naukowe Uniwersytetu Gdanskiego

ZNUIA — Zeszyty Naukowe Uniwersytetu Imienia Adama Mickiewicza w Poznaniu. Matematyka, Fizyka, Chemia

ZNUJ — Zeszyty Naukowe Uniwersytetu Jagiellonskiego

ZNUL — Zeszyty Naukowe Uniwersytetu Lodzkiego

ZNULHist — Zeszyty Naukowe Uniwersytetu Lodzkiego. Nauki Humanistyczno-Spoleczne. Historia

ZNum — Zeitschrift fuer Numismatik

ZNUMD — Zeszyty Naukowe Uniwersytetu Jagiellonskiego. Prace Biologii Molekularnej

ZNUMK — Zeszyty Naukowe Uniwersytetu Mikolaja Kopernika

ZNUnWr — Zeszyty Naukowe Uniwersytetu Wroclawskiego

ZNUP — Zeszyty Naukowe Uniwersytetu Imienia Adama Mickiewicza w Poznaniu

ZNUPHSzt — Zeszyty Naukowe Uniwersytetu Imienia Adama Mickiewicza w Poznaniu. Historia Sztuki

ZNUT — Zeszyty Naukowe Uniwersytetu Mikolaja Kopernika w Toruniu. Nauki Humanistyczno-Spoleczne

ZNUW — Zeszyty Naukowe Uniwersytetu Wroclawskiego Imienia B. Bieruta

ZNUZA — Zeszyty Naukowe Uniwersytetu Jagiellonskiego. Prace Zoologiczne

Z Nw — Zeitschrift fuer die Gesammten Naturwissenschaften

ZNW — Zeitschrift fuer die Neutestamentliche Wissenschaft

ZNWB — Zeitschrift fuer die Neutestamentliche Wissenschaft (Berlin)

ZNWFA — Zeszyty Naukowe Wyzszej Szkoly Pedagogicznej w Katowicach. Sekcja Fizyki

ZNWKAK — Zeitschrift fuer die Neutestamentliche Wissenschaft und die Kunde der Aelteren Kirche

ZNWKU — Zeitschrift fuer die Neutestamentliche Wissenschaft und die Kunde des Urchristentums

ZNWSPK — Zeszyty Naukowe Wyzszej Szkoly Pedagogicznej (Katowice)

ZNWSPO — Zeszyty Naukowe Wyzszej Szkoly Pedagogicznej (Opole)

ZNWSPOp — Zeszyty Naukowe, Jezykoznawstwo, Wyzsza Szkola Pedagogiczna w Opolu

ZNZSA — Zeszyty Naukowe Akademii Gorniczo-Hutniczej (Cracow). Zeszyt Specjalny

ZO — Zeitschrift fuer Organisation

ZO — Zeitschrift fuer Ortsnamenforschung

ZO — Zeitschrift fuer Ostforschung

Zo A — Zoologischer Anzeiger

ZOAO — Zapiski Odesskago Arkheologicheskago Obshchestva

Z Oberschles Berg-Huettenmaenn Ver Kat — Zeitschrift des Oberschlesischen Berg- und Huettenmaennischen Vereins zu Katowiee

ZOBIDX — Zoo Biology

ZOBM — Zhurnal Obshchei Biologii (Moscow)

Zobozdrav Vestn — Zobozdravstveni Vestnik
Z Obsc Biol — Zurnal Obscej Biologii
Z Obsc Chim — Zurnal Obscej Chimii
ZOBW — Zeitschrift fuer Oesterreichisches Bibliothekswesen
Zod — Zodiaque
Z Oeff Chem — Zeitschrift fuer Oeffentliche Chemie
Z Oeff Gem Wirtsch Unterneh — Zeitschrift fuer Oeffentliche und Gemeinwirtschaftliche Unternehmen
Z Oeff Gem Wirtsch Unternehmen — Zeitschrift fuer Oeffentliche und Gemeinwirtschaftliche Unternehmen
Z Oeff Recht — Zeitschrift fuer Oeffentliches Recht
Z Oe G — Zeitschrift fuer die Deutsche-Oesterreichischen Gymnasien
ZOEG — Zeitschrift fuer die Oesterreichischen Gymnasien
ZOEG — Zeitschrift fuer Osteuropaeische Geschichte
Z Oe IAV — Zeitschrift des Oesterreichischen Ingenieur und Architekten Vereins
ZOEMS — Zeitschrift fuer die Oesterreichischen Mittelschulen
Z Oesterreich Ingen & Architekten Ver — Zeitschrift des Oesterreichischen Ingenieur-und-Architekten-Vereines
Z Oesterr Entomol Ver — Zeitschrift. Oesterreichischer Entomologe-Verein
Z Oesterr Ing Archit Ver — Zeitschrift des Oesterreichischen Ingenieur und Architekten Vereins
Z Oesterr Ver Gas Wasserfachmaennern — Zeitschrift. Oesterreichischer Verein von Gas- und Wasserfachmaennern
Z Oest G — Zeitschrift fuer die Deutsche-Oesterreichischen Gymnasien
ZOest G — Zeitschrift fuer die Oesterreichischen Gymnasien
ZOf — Zeitschrift fuer Ostforschung
Zof N — Zofinger Neujahrsblatt
ZOfo — Zeitschrift fuer Ostforschung
ZoG — Zeitschrift fuer die Deutsche-Oesterreichischen Gymnasien
ZOG — Zeitschrift fuer Osteuropaeische Geschichte
ZOGAAV — Zoologische Gaerten
Z Ohrh — Zeitschrift fuer Ohrenheilkunde
ZOLGA — Zoologica
Zolnierz Pol — Zolnierz Polski
Zolotaya Promst — Zolotaya Promyshlennost
ZON — Zeitschrift fuer Ortsnamenforschung
Zona Fran Caracas — Zona Franca (Caracas)
Zoning and Plan L Rep — Zoning and Planning Law Report
Zoo Biol — Zoo Biology
Zooiatr Rev Med Vet Prod Pecu — Zooiatria Revista de Medicina Veterinaria y Produccion Pecuaria
Zool Abh (Dres) — Zoologische Abhandlungen (Dresden)
Zool Afr — Zoologica Africana
Zool Ann — Zoologische Annalen
Zool Anz — Zoologischer Anzeiger
Zool Anzeiger — Zoologischer Anzeiger
Zool Anz (Leipzig) — Zoologischer Anzeiger (Leipzig)
Zool Anz Suppl — Zoologischer Anzeiger. Supplement
Zool B — Zoological Bulletin
Zool Beitr — Zoologische Beitraege
Zool Ber — Zoologischer Bericht
Zool Bidr Upps — Zoologiska Bidrag fran Uppsala
Zool Bidr Uppsala — Zoologiska Bidrag fran Uppsala
Zool Bijdr — Zoologische Bijdragen
Zool Biol Mar — Zoologia e Biologia Marinha
Zool Biol Mar (Sao Paulo) (Nova Ser) — Zoologia e Biologia Marinha (Sao Paulo) (Nova Serie)
Zool Entomol Listy — Zoologicke a Entomologicke Listy
Zool Gaert — Zoologische Gaerten
Zool Gart — Der Zoologische Garten
Zool Gart (Lpz) — Zoologische Gaerten (Leipzig)
Zool Inst Fac Sci Univ Tokyo Annu Rep — Zoological Institute. Faculty of Science. University of Tokyo. Annual Report
Zool Jahrb — Zoologische Jahrbuecher. Abteilung fuer Allgemeine Zoologie und Physiologie derTiere
Zool Jahrb Abt Allg Zool Physiol Tiere — Zoologische Jahrbuecher. Abteilung fuer Allgemeine Zoologie und Physiologie derTiere
Zool Jahrb Abt Anat Ontog Tiere — Zoologische Jahrbuecher. Abteilung fuer Anatomie und Ontogenie der Tiere
Zool Jahrb Abt Syst (Jena) — Zoologische Jahrbuecher. Abteilung fuer Systematik Oekologie und Geographie derTiere (Jena)
Zool Jahrb Abt Syst Oekol Geogr Tiere — Zoologische Jahrbuecher. Abteilung fuer Systematik Oekologie und Geographie derTiere
Zool Jb — Zoologische Jahrbuecher
Zool Jb Abt Allg Zool Physiol Tiere — Zoologische Jahrbuecher. Abteilung fuer Allgemeine Zoologie und Physiologie derTiere
Zool Jb Abt Syst Okol Geog Tiere — Zoologische Jahrbuecher. Abteilung fuer Systematik Oekologie und Geographie der Tiere
Zool Jhrb Abt Allg Zool Physiol Tiere — Zoologische Jahrbuecher. Abteilung fuer Allgemeine Zoologie und Physiologie derTiere
Zool J Linn — Zoological Journal. Linnean Society
Zool J Linnean Soc Lond — Zoological Journal. Linnean Society of London
Zool J Linn Soc — Zoological Journal. Linnean Society
Zool Listy — Zoologicke Listy
Zool Mag — Zoological Magazine
Zool Mag (Tokyo) — Zoological Magazine (Tokyo)
Zool Meded (Leiden) — Zoologische Mededelingen (Leiden)
Zool Meded Rijks Mus Nat Hist Leiden — Zoologische Mededelingen. Rijks Museum van Natuurlijke Historie te Leiden
Zool Muz Raksti Invertebrata — Zoologijas Muzeja Raksti. Invertebrata
Zoologica Pol — Zoologica Poloniae
Zoologica Scr — Zoologica Scripta
Zool Orient — Zoologica Orientalis
Zool Pol — Zoologica Poloniae

Zool Publ Victoria Univ Wellington — Zoology Publications. Victoria University of Wellington
Zool Rec — Zoological Record
Zool Res — Zoological Research
Zool Revy — Zoologisk Revy
Zool Sci — Zoological Science
Zool Sci (Tokyo) — Zoological Science (Tokyo)
Zool Scr — Zoologica Scripta
Zool Soc Egypt Bull — Zoological Society of Egypt. Bulletin
Zool Soc London Pr — Zoological Society of London. Proceedings
Zool Soc London Proc — Zoological Society of London. Proceedings
Zool Stud — Zoological Studies
Zool Verh — Zoologische Verhandelingen
Zool Verh (Leiden) — Zoologische Verhandelingen (Leiden)
Zool Verh Rijksmus Nat Hist (Leiden) — Zoologische Verhandelingen. Rijksmuseum van Natuurlijke Historie (Leiden)
Zool Z — Zoologicheskii Zhurnal
Zool Zentralbl — Zoologisches Zentralblatt
Zool Zh — Zoologicheskii Zhurnal
Zoonoses Res — Zoonoses Research
Zoophysiol Ecol — Zoophysiology and Ecology
Zoo Rec — Zoological Record
ZOOREO — Zoologica Orientalis
Zoo Rev Parque Zool Barc — Zoo. Revista del Parque Zoologico de Barcelona
Zootech Experiment Stn Res Bull — Zootechnical Experiment Station. Research Bulletin
Zootec Nutr Anim — Zootecnica e Nutrizione Animale
Zootec Vet — Zootecnica e Veterinaria
Zootec Vet Agric — Zootecnica. Veterinaria e Agricoltura
Zootec Vita — Zootecnia e Vita
Z Operations Res Ser A-B — Zeitschrift fuer Operations Research. Serie A. Serie B
Z Operat Res Ser A — Zeitschrift fuer Operations Research. Serie A. Theorie
Z Oper Res — Zeitschrift fuer Operations Research
Z Oper Res B — Zeitschrift fuer Operations Research. Serie B. Praxis
Z Oper Res Ser A — Zeitschrift fuer Operations Research. Serie A. Theorie
Z Oper Res Ser A-B — Zeitschrift fuer Operations Research. Serie A. Serie B
Z Oper Res Ser B — Zeitschrift fuer Operations Research. Serie B. Praxis
Z Oper Res Ser Praxis — Zeitschrift fuer Operations Research. Serie B. Praxis
Z Ophthalmol — Zeitschrift fuer die Ophthalmologie
ZOR — Zapiski Otdela Roukopisei
ZOR — Zeitschrfit fuer Oeffentliches Recht
ZOR — Zeitschrift fuer Operations Research
Z Organ — Zeitschrift fuer Organisation
ZOR Math Methods Oper Res — Zeitschrift fuer Operations Research. Mathematical Methods of Operations Research
ZORPB — Zeitschrift fuer Operations Research. Serie B. Praxis
Z Orthop — Zeitschrift fuer Orthopaedie und Ihre Grenzgebiete
Z Orthop Grenzgeb — Zeitschrift fuer Orthopaedie und Ihre Grenzgebiete
Z Orthop Ihre Grenzgeb — Zeitschrift fuer Orthopaedie und Ihre Grenzgebiete
ZOSC — Zoologica Scripta
Z Osteur Gesch — Zeitschrift fuer Osteuropaeische Geschichte
Z Osteur Recht — Zeitschrift fuer Osteuropaeisches Recht
Z Ostforsch — Zeitschrift fuer Ostforschung
Zost Gym — Zeitschrift fuer die Deutsche-Oesterreichischen Gymnasien
ZOVBW — Zeitschrift. Oesterreichischer Verein fuer Bibliothekswesen
ZP — Zeitschrift fuer Phonetik
ZP — Zeitschrift fuer Politik
ZPAAD — Zeitschrift fuer Physik. Sektion A. Atoms and Nuclei
ZPalV — Zeitschrift. Deutscher Palaestinaverein
Z Pap Pappe Zellul Holzst — Zeitschrift fuer Papier. Pappe, Zellulose, und Holzstoff
Z Papyrologie & Epig — Zeitschrift fuer Papyrologie und Epigraphik
Z Papyrologie Epigraphik — Zeitschrift fuer Papyrologie und Epigraphik
Z Parapsych — Zeitschrift fuer Parapsychologie und Grenzgebiete der Psychologie
Z Parasiten — Zeitschrift fuer Parasitenkunde
Z Parasitenkd — Zeitschrift fuer Parasitenkunde
Z ParasitKde — Zeitschrift fuer Parasitenkunde
Z Parlamentsfr — Zeitschrift fuer Parlamentsfragen
Z Parlamentsfragen — Zeitschrift fuer Parlamentsfragen
ZPAS — Zeitschrift fuer Phonetik und Allgemeine Sprachwissenschaft
ZPB — Zeitschrift fuer Parasitenkunde (Berlin)
ZPBBD — Zeitschrift fuer Physik. Sektion B. Condensed Matter and Quanta
ZPCAA — Zeitschrift fuer Physikalische Chemie. Abteilung A. Chemische Thermodynamik, Kinetik, Elektrochemie, Eigenschaftslehre
ZPCBA — Zeitschrift fuer Physikalische Chemie. Abteilung B. Chemie der Elementarprozesse, Aufbau der Materie
ZPCHA — Zeitschrift fuer Physiologische Chemie
ZPCLA — Zeitschrift fuer Physikalische Chemie (Leipzig)
ZPDBA — Zeitschrift fuer Pflanzenernaehrung, Duengung, und Bodenkunde
ZPE — Zeitschrift fuer Papyrologie und Epigraphik
ZPF — Zeitschrift fuer Philosophische Forschung
Z Pflan Bod — Zeitschrift fuer Pflanzenernaehrung Bodenkunde
Z Pflanzenernaehr Bodenkd — Zeitschrift fuer Pflanzenernaehrung und Bodenkunde
Z Pflanzenernaehr Dueng — Zeitschrift fuer Pflanzenernaehrung und Duengung
Z Pflanzenernaehr Dueng Bodenkd — Zeitschrift fuer Pflanzenernaehrung, Duengung, und Bodenkunde [Later, Zeitschrift fuer Pflanzenernaehrung und Bodenkunde]
Z Pflanzenernaehr Duengung Bodenk A Wiss Teil — Zeitschrift fuer Pflanzenernaehrung, Duengung, und Bodenkunde. A. Wissenschaftlicher Teil
Z Pflanzenernahr Dung Bodenkd — Zeitschrift fuer Pflanzenernaehrung, Duengung, und Bodenkunde
Z Pflanzenkr — Zeitschrift fuer Pflanzenkrankheiten
Z Pflanzenkr Gallenkd — Zeitschrift fuer Pflanzenkrankheiten und Gallenkunde

Z Pflanzenkr Pflanzenpathol Pflanzenschutz — Zeitschrift fuer Pflanzenkrankheiten, Pflanzenpathologie, und Pflanzenschutz

Z Pflanzenkr Pflanzenpathol Pflanzenschutz Sonderh — Zeitschrift fuer Pflanzenkrankheiten, Pflanzenpathologie, und Pflanzenschutz. Sonderheft

Z Pflanzenkr Pflanzenschutz — Zeitschrift fuer Pflanzenkrankheiten und Pflanzenschutz

Z Pflanzenp — Zeitschrift fuer Pflanzenphysiologie

Z Pflanzenphysiol — Zeitschrift fuer Pflanzenphysiologie

Z Pflanzenz — Zeitschrift fuer Pflanzenzuechtung

Z Pflanzenzuecht — Zeitschrift fuer Pflanzenzuechtung

Z PflErnahr Bodenk — Zeitschrift fuer Pflanzenernaehrung und Bodenkunde

Z PflErnahr Dung Bodenk — Zeitschrift fuer Pflanzenernaehrung, Duengung, und Bodenkunde [*Later, Zeitschrift fuer Pflanzenernaehrung und Bodenkunde*]

Z PflKrankh — Zeitschrift fuer Pflanzenkrankheiten, Pflanzenpathologie, und Pflanzenschutz

Z PflKrankh PflSchutz — Zeitschrift fuer Pflanzenkrankheiten und Pflanzenschutz

Z PflPhysiol — Zeitschrift fuer Pflanzenphysiologie

Z Pflzuecht — Zeitschrift fuer Pflanzenzuechtung

ZPFZ — Zbornik Pravnog Fakulteta u Zagreba

ZPh — Zeitschrift fuer Psychologie

ZPhF — Zeitschrift fuer Philosophische Forschung

Z Phil Forsch — Zeitschrift fuer Philosophische Forschung

Z Philos F — Zeitschrift fuer Philosophische Forschung

Z Philos Forsch — Zeitschrift fuer Philosophische Forschung

Z Ph Kr — Zeitschrift fuer Philosophie und Philosophische Kritik

ZPhon — Zeitschrift fuer Phonetik und Allgemeine Sprachwissenschaft

Z Phonetik Sprachwissenschaft und Kommunikationsforschung — Zeitschrift fuer Phonetik, Sprachwissenschaft, und Kommunikationsforschung

Z Phonetik Sprachwiss Komm Forsch — Zeitschrift fuer Phonetik, Sprachwissenschaft, und Kommunikationsforschung

Z Phon Sprachwiss Kommunikationsforsch — Zeitschrift fuer Phonetik, Sprachwissenschaft, und Kommunikationsforschung

Z Phys — Zeitschrift fuer Physik

Z Phys A — Zeitschrift fuer Physik. Sektion A. Atoms and Nuclei

Z Phys A At Nucl — Zeitschrift fuer Physik A. Atomic Nuclei

Z Phys A At Nuclei — Zeitschrift fuer Physik. A. Atomic Nuclei

Z Phys A Hadrons Nucl — Zeitschrift fuer Physik A. Hadrons and Nuclei

Z Phys A Hadrons Nuclei — Zeitschrift fuer Physik. A. Hadrons and Nuclei

Z Phys B — Zeitschrift fuer Physik. Sektion B. Condensed Matter and Quanta

Z Phys B Condens Mater — Zeitschrift fuer Physik. B. Condensed Matter

Z Phys C — Zeitschrift fuer Physik. Sektion C. Particles and Fields

Z Phys Chem — Zeitschrift fuer Physikalische Chemie

Z Phys Chem Abt A — Zeitschrift fuer Physikalische Chemie. Abteilung A. Chemische Thermodynamik, Kinetik, Elektrochemie, Eigenschaftslehre

Z Phys Chem Abt B — Zeitschrift fuer Physikalische Chemie. Abteilung B. Chemie der Elementarprozesse, Aufbau der Materie

Z Phys Chem Frankf Ausg Neue Folge — Zeitschrift fuer Physikalische Chemie. Frankfurter Ausgabe. Neue Folge

Z Phys Chem (Frankfurt/Main) — Zeitschrift fuer Physikalische Chemie (Frankfurt/Main)

Z Phys Chemie Stoechiom Verwandschaftsl — Zeitschrift fuer Physikalische Chemie, Stoechiometrie, und Verwandtschaftslehre

Z Phys Chem (Leipzig) — Zeitschrift fuer Physikalische Chemie (Leipzig)

Z Phys Chem Materialforsch — Zeitschrift fuer Physikalisch-Chemische Materialforschung

Z Phys Chem Munich — Zeitschrift fuer Physikalische Chemie (Munich)

Z Phys Chem Neue Folge — Zeitschrift fuer Physikalische Chemie. Neue Folge

Z Phys Chem Neue Fo (Wiesbaden) — Zeitschrift fuer Physikalische Chemie. Neue Folge (Wiesbaden)

Z Phys Chem (Wiesbaden) — Zeitschrift fuer Physikalische Chemie (Wiesbaden)

Z Phys Ch (F) — Zeitschrift fuer Physikalische Chemie (Frankfurt)

Z Phys Ch (L) — Zeitschrift fuer Physikalische Chemie (Leipzig)

Z Phys C Part Fields — Zeitschrift fuer Physik C. Particles and Fields

Z Phys D — Zeitschrift fuer Physik. D. Atoms, Molecules, and Clusters

Z Phys D At Mol Clusters — Zeitschrift fuer Physik D. Atoms, Molecules, and Clusters

Z Phys Diaet Ther — Zeitschrift fuer Physikalische und Diaetetische Therapie

ZPhys E A Hadrons Nucl — ZPhys-e. A. Hadrons and Nuclei [*electronic publication*]

ZPhys E B Condens Matter — ZPhys-e. B. Condensed Matter [*electronic publication*]

ZPhys E C Part Fields — ZPhys-e. C. Particles and Fields [*electronic publication*]

ZPhys E D At Mol Clusters — ZPhys-e. D. Atoms, Molecules, and Clusters [*electronic publication*]

Z Physik — Zeitschrift fuer Physik

Z Physiol Chem — Zeitschrift fuer Physiologische Chemie

Z Physiol Chem Hoppe-Seylers — Zeitschrift fuer Physiologische Chemie. Hoppe-Seylers

Z Physiother — Zeitschrift fuer Physiotherapie

Z Pilzkd — Zeitschrift fuer Pilzkunde

ZPJIAK — Zbirnyk Prat Jewrejskiej Istorychno-Arkheologichnoj Komisji

Z Plast Chir — Zeitschrift fuer Plastische Chirurgie

Z Pl C — Zeitschrift fuer Physiologische Chemie

ZPMPA — Zeitschrift fuer Psychotherapie und Medizinische Psychologie

Z Polit — Zeitschrift fuer Politik

Z Politik — Zeitschrift fuer Politik

Z Pol N F — Zeitschrift fuer Politik. Neue Folge

ZPPA — Zeitschrift fuer Wissenschaftliche Photographie, Photophysik, und Photochemie

ZPPK — Zeitschrift fuer Philosophie und Philosophische Kritik (Fichte's)

ZPPS — Zeitschrift fuer Pflanzenkrankheiten, Pflanzenpathologie, und Pflanzenschutz (Stuttgart)

Z Praeklin Geriatr — Zeitschrift fuer Praeklinische Geriatrie

Z Praeklin Klin Geriatr — Zeitschrift fuer Praeklinische und Klinische Geriatrie

Z Praeventivmed — Zeitschrift fuer Praeventivmedizin

Z Prakt Anaesth — Zeitschrift fuer Praktische Anaesthesie, Wiederbelebung, undIntensivtherapie

Z Prakt Baukst — Zeitschrift fuer Praktische Baukunst

Z Prakt Geol — Zeitschrift fuer Praktische Geologie

Zprava Cinnosti Masarykovy Akad Prace — Zprava o Cinnosti Masarykovy Akademie Prace

Z Praventivmed — Zeitschrift fuer Praeventivmedizin

Zprav List Kolektivu Pocumavsk Floristu — Zpravodajsky List Kolektivu Pocumavskych Floristu

Zpravy — Zpravy pro Cestinare

Zpravy Dendrol Sekce Ceskoslov Bot Spolecn — Zpravy Dendrologicke Sekce Ceskoslovenske Botanicke Spolecnosti

Zpravy JKF — Zpravy Jednoty Klasickych Filologu

Zpravy Krajskeho Vlastivedneho Muz Olomouc — Zpravy Krajskeho Vlastivedneho Muzea v Olomouci

Zpravy Krkonssk Nar Parku — Zpravy Krkonosskeho Narodniho Parku

Zpravy Okresn Mus V Trutnove — Zpravy Okresniho Musea v Trutnove

Zpravy Praha — Zpravy Ceskoslovenskeho Statniho Archeologickeho Ustavu. Praha

Zpravy Vlastiv Mus V Prostejove — Zpravy Vlastivedneho Musea v Prostejove

Zpravy Zemsk Vyzk Ustavu Hospod Pestovani Rostl V Brne — Zpravy Zemskeho Vyzkumneho Ustavu Hospodarskeho pro Pestovani Rostlin v Brne

Zpr Cesk Keram Sklarske Spol — Zpravy Ceskoslovenske Keramicke a Sklarske Spolecnosti

Zpr Csl Spol Antrop — Zpravy. Ceskoslovenska Spolecnost Antropologicka

Z Prikl Meh i Tehn Fiz — Zurnal Prikladnoi Mehaniki i Tehniceskoi Fiziki

ZprMK — Zpravodaj Mistopisne Komise CSAV

ZPs — Zeitschrift fuer Psychologie

Z Ps C — Zeitschrift fuer Physikalische Chemie, Stoechiometrie, und Verwandtschaftlehre

ZPSEA — Zeszyty Naukowe Politechnika Slaska. Energetyka

ZPSIA — Zeitschrift fuer Psychologie und Physiologie der Sinnesorgane

ZPSK — Zeitschrift fuer Phonetik, Sprachwissenschaft, und Kommunikationsforschung

ZPSMA — Zeitschrift fuer Psychosomatische Medizin [*Later, Zeitschrift fuer Psychosomatische Medizin und Psychoanalyse*]

ZPSS — Z Polskich Studiow Slawistycznych

Z Psych Hyg — Zeitschrift fuer Psychische Hygiene

Z Psychol — Zeitschrift fuer Psychologie

Z Psychol — Zeitschrift fuer Psychologie und Physiologie der Sinnesorgane

Z Psycholog — Zeitschrift fuer Psychologie

Z Psychol Physiol Sinnesorg — Zeitschrift fuer Psychologie und Physiologie der Sinnesorgane

Z Psychol Z Angew Psychol — Zeitschrift fuer Psychologie mit Zeitschrift fuer Angewandte Psychologie

Z Psychol Z Angew Psychol Charakterkd — Zeitschrift fuer Psychologie mit Zeitschrift fuer Angewandte Psychologie und Charakterkunde

Z Psychos M — Zeitschrift fuer Psychosomatische Medizin und Psychoanalyse

Z Psychosom Med — Zeitschrift fuer Psychosomatische Medizin [*Later, Zeitschrift fuer Psychosomatische Medizin und Psychoanalyse*]

Z Psychosom Med Psychoanal — Zeitschrift fuer Psychosomatische Medizin und Psychoanalyse

Z Psychother Med Psychol — Zeitschrift fuer Psychotherapie und Medizinische Psychologie

Z Psychot M — Zeitschrift fuer Psychotherapie und Medizinische Psychologie

ZPWCA — Zeszyty Naukowe Politechniki Wroclawskiej. Chemia

ZPYFA — Zeitschrift fuer Physikalische Chemie. Frankfurter Ausgabe. Neue Folge

ZR — Zadarska Revija

ZR — Zbornik Radova Vizantoloskog Instituta

ZR — Zeitschrift fuer Rechtsgeschichte

ZR — Zionist Record

ZR — Zionist Review

ZR — Zoological Record

ZRAO — Zapiski Imperatorskago Russkago Arkheologicheskago Obshchestva

Z Rassk — Zeitschrift fuer Rassenkunde

Z Rechtsmed — Zeitschrift fuer Rechtsmedizin

Z Rechtspolit — Zeitschrift fuer Rechtspolitik

Z Reich Geschmackstoffe — Zeitschrift fuer Reich- und Geschmackstoffe

Z Rel Geistesges — Zeitschrift fuer Religions- und Geistesgeschichte

Z Rel Gg — Zeitschrift fuer Religions- und Geistesgeschichte

Z Relig Geistesgesch — Zeitschrift fuer Religions- und Geistesgeschichte

Z Religions U Geistesgesch — Zeitschrift fuer Religions- und Geistesgeschichte

Z Relig- u Geistesgesch — Zeitschrift fuer Religions- und Geistesgeschichte

Z Reproduktionstech — Zeitschrift fuer Reproduktionstechnik

ZRG — Zeitschrift der Savigny-Stiftung fuer Rechtsgeschichte

ZRG — Zeitschrift fuer Rechtsgeschichte

ZRG — Zeitschrift fuer Religions- und Geistesgeschichte

ZRGA — Zeitschrift. Savigny-Stiftung fuer Rechtsgeschichte. Germanistische Abteilung

ZRGG — Zeitschrift fuer Religions- und Geistesgeschichte

ZRG (GA) — Zeitschrift. Savigny-Stiftung fuer Rechtsgeschichte. Germanistische Abteilung

ZRGGB — Zeitschrift fuer Religions- und Geistesgeschichte. Beihefte

ZRGGS — Zeitschrift fuer Religions- und Geistesgeschichte. Sonderhefte

ZRGR — Zeitschrift der Savigny-Stiftung fuer Rechtsgeschichte. Romanistische Abteilung

Z Rheinpreuss Landw Vereins — Zeitschrift des Rheinpreussischen Landwirthschaftlichen Vereins

Z Rhein Ver Dkmlpf & Heimatschutz — Zeitschrift des Rheinischen Vereins fuer Denkmalpflege und Heimatschutz

Z Rheumaforsch — Zeitschrift fuer Rheumaforschung

Z Rheumatol — Zeitschrift fuer Rheumatologie

Z Rheumatol Suppl — Zeitschrift fuer Rheumatologie. Supplement

ZRHMB — Zeitschrift fuer Rheumatologie

ZRI — Zeitschrift fuer die Religioesen Interessen des Judentums

ZRI — Zosen
ZRL — Zagadnienia Rodzajow Literackich
ZRNI — Zapiski Russkogo Naucnogo Instituta
ZRO — Zoological Record Online
Z Roman Ph — Zeitschrift fuer Romanische Philologie
Zroshuvane Zemlerob — Zroshuvane Zemlerobstvo
Zrosh Zemlerob — Zroshuvane Zemlerobstvo
ZRP — Zeitschrift fuer Romanische Philologie
ZRPBA — Zbornik Radova. Poljoprivrednog Fakulteta. Universitet u Beogradu
ZRPH — Zeitschrift fuer Romanische Philologie
ZRSAN — Zbornik Radova. Srpske Akademije Nauke
ZRSG — Zoological Record Search Guide
ZRSNDI — Zimbabwe Science News
ZRTLS — Zwolse Reeks van Taal- en Letterkundige Studies
ZRU — Zeitschrift fuer den Russisch-Unterricht
ZRVB — Zashchita Rastenii ot Vreditelei i Bolezni
ZRVI — Zbornik Radova Vizantoloskog Instituta
ZRZ — Zbornik Radova. Svenciliste u Zagrebu
ZS — Zeitschrift fuer die Gesamte Staatswissenschaft
ZS — Zeitschrift fuer Semitistik und Verwandte Gebiete
ZS — Zeitschrift fuer Slawistik
Z Saeugetierkd — Zeitschrift fuer Saeugetierkunde
ZSAK — Zeitschrift fuer Schweizerische Archaeologie und Kunstgeschichte
ZSAKG — Zeitschrift fuer Schweizerische Archaeologie und Kunstgeschichte
Zs Allg Erdk — Zeitschrift fuer Allgemeine Erdkunde
ZSANA — Zoologicheskii Sbornik. Zoologicheskii Institut. Akademiia Nauk Armianskoi SSR
Zs Anorg Chem — Zeitschrift fuer Anorganische Chemie
ZSav — Zeitschrift. Savigny-Stiftung fuer Rechtsgeschichte. Romanistische Abteilung
Z Savigny Stift Germanist Abt Kanonist Abt Romanist Abt — Zeitschrift der Savigny-Stiftung fuer Rechtsgeschichte. Germanistische Abteilung, Kanonistische Abteilung. Romanistische Abteilung
Z Savigny-Stift Rechtsgesch Kanon Abt — Zeitschrift. Savigny-Stiftung fuer Rechtsgeschichte. Kanonistische Abteilung
ZSavRG — Zeitschrift. Savigny-Stiftung fuer Rechtsgeschichte. Romanistische Abteilung
Z Sav RGRA — Zeitschrift der Savigny-Stiftung fuer Rechtsgeschichte. Romanistische Abteilung
Zs Bad Verwalt — Zeitschrift fuer Badische Verwaltung und Verwaltungsrechtspflege
Zs Berg- Huetten- u Salinen-Wesen — Zeitschrift fuer das Berg-, Huetten-, und Salinenwesen
ZS Ch — Zurnal Strukturnoj Chimii
Zschft f Ausl u Intl Privatr — Zeitschrift fuer Auslaendisches und Internationales Privatrecht
Zschft f Vergl Rechtswissenschaft — Zeitschrift fuer Vergleichende Rechtswissenschaft
Zschft Luft- u Weltr-Recht — Zeitschrift fuer Luftrecht- und Weltraumrechtsfragen
Zschft Rechtsvergl — Zeitschrift fuer Rechtsvergleichung
Zschft Savigny-Germ — Zeitschrift. Savigny-Stiftung fuer Rechtsgeschichte. Germanistische Abteilung
Zschft Savigny-Kanon — Zeitschrift. Savigny-Stiftung fuer Rechtsgeschichte. Kanonistische Abteilung
Zschft Savigny-Rom — Zeitschrift. Savigny-Stiftung fuer Rechtsgeschichte. Romanistische Abteilung
Z Sch G — Zeitschrift fuer Schweizerische Geschichte
Zschift f Ausl Offentl Recht — Zeitschrift fuer Auslaendisches Oeffentliches Recht und Voelkerrecht
Z Sch Kg — Zeitschrift fuer Schweizerische Kirchengeschichte
Z Schles Holst Gesch — Zeitschrift. Gesellschaft fuer Schleswig-Holsteinische Geschichte
Z Sch R — Zeitschrift fuer Schweizerisches Recht
Z Schw AKg — Zeitschrift fuer Schweizerische Archaeologie und Kunstgeschichte
Z Schw Alt — Zeitschrift fuer Schweizerische Archaeologie und Kunstgeschichte
Z Schw Arch — Zeitschrift fuer Schweizerische Archaeologie und Kunstgeschichte
Z Schweisstech — Zeitschrift fuer Schweisstechnik
Z Schweiz Altertknd — Zeitschrift fuer Schweizerische Altertumskunde
Z Schweiz Archaeol & Kstgesch — Zeitschrift fuer Schweizerische Archaeologie und Kunstgeschichte
Z Schweiz Archaeol Kunstgesch — Zeitschrift fuer Schweizerische Archaeologie und Kunstgeschichte
Z Schweiz Arch Kunstgesch — Zeitschrift fuer Schweizerische Archaeologie und Kunstgeschichte
Z Schweiz Gesch — Zeitschrift fuer Schweizerische Geschichte
Z Schweiz Kg — Zeitschrift fuer Schweizerische Archaeologie und Kunstgeschichte
ZSchwG — Zeitschrift fuer Schweizerische Geschichte
Z Schw KG — Zeitschrift fuer Schweizerische Kirchengeschichte
Zs d Deutschen Morgend Ges — Zeitschrift der Deutschen Morgenlaendischen Gesellschaft
ZSDG — Zeitschrift fuer Sudetendeutsche Geschichte
Zs D Morg Ges — Zeitschrift der Deutschen Morgenlaendischen Gesellschaft
Zs Dt Buergl R Frz Zivilr — Zeitschrift fuer Deutsches Buergerliches Recht und Franzoesisches Zivilrecht
ZSEM — Zeitschrift fuer Semitistik und Verwandte Gebiete
Z Semiotik — Zeitschrift fuer Semiotik
Z Sem VG — Zeitschrift fuer Semitistik und Verwandte Gebiete
Z Sev-Dvin OIMK — Zapiski Severo-Dvinskogo Obscestva Izucenija Mestnogo Kraja
ZSF — Zeitschrift fuer Sozialforschung
Zs f Rel Geist Gesch — Zeitschrift fuer Religions- und Geistesgeschichte
Zs Frw Gerichtsbkt Wuert — Zeitschrift fuer die Freiwillige Gerichtsbarkeit und die Gemeindeverwaltung inWuerttemberg
ZSG — Zeitschrift fuer Schweizerische Geschichte
Zs Ges Naturw — Zeitschrift fuer die Gesamten Naturwissenschaften

Zs Gletscherk — Zeitschrift fuer Gletscherkunde
ZSGRT — Zametki po Sistematike i Geografii Rastenii. Botanicheskii Institut (Tbilisi)
ZSHG — Zeitschrift der Gesellschaft fuer Schleswig-Holsteinische Geschichte
Zs Hist Ver Niedersachs — Zeitschrift des Historischen Vereins fuer Niedersachsen
Z Siebenburg Landesknd — Zeitschrift fuer Siebenburgische Landeskunde
Z Sinnephysiol — Zeitschrift fuer Sinnephysiologie
ZSISA — Zeszyty Naukowe Politechniki Slaskiej. Inzynieria Sanitarna
ZSK — Zeitschrift fuer Schweizerische Kirchengeschichte
ZSK — Ze Skarbca Kultury
ZSKG — Zeitschrift fuer Schweizerische Kirchengeschichte
ZSKHA — Zeitschrift fuer Kinderheilkunde. Referate
Z (Skopje) — Zbornik. Arheoloski Muzej na Makedonija (Skopje)
Zs Kryst — Zeitschrift fuer Krystallographie und Mineralogie
ZSL — Zeitschrift fuer Slawistik
Z Slav Ph — Zeitschrift fuer Slavische Philologie
Z Slav Phil — Zeitschrift fuer Slavische Philologie
Z Slav Philol — Zeitschrift fuer Slavische Philologie
Z Slawistik — Zeitschrift fuer Slawistik
ZSLPh — Zeitschrift fuer Slavische Philologie
Zs Math Phys — Zeitschrift fuer Mathematik und Physik [Leipzig]
Zs Miner (Leonhard) — Zeitschrift fuer Mineralogie (Leonhard)
ZSNED7 — Zimbabwe Science News
ZSNM — Zbornik Slovenskeho Narodneho Muzea
ZSNMAS — Acta Rerum Naturalium. Musei Nationalis Slovaci Bratislava
ZSNUA — Zeitschrift fuer Neurologie
Zs Oester Strafr — Zeitschrift fuer Oesterreichisches Strafrecht
ZSoF — Zeitschrift fuer Sozialforschung
ZSoW — Zeitschrift fuer Sozialwissenschaft
Z Soz — Zeitschrift fuer Sozialpsychologie
Z Soz — Zeitschrift fuer Soziologie
Z Sozforsch — Zeitschrift fuer Sozialforschung
Z Sozialpsy — Zeitschrift fuer Sozialpsychologie
Z Sozialreform — Zeitschrift fuer Sozialreform
Z Soziol — Zeitschrift fuer Soziologie
Z Soziolog — Zeitschrift fuer Soziologie
Z Soz Psych — Zeitschrift fuer Sozialpsychologie
Z Soz Psychol — Zeitschrift fuer Sozialpsychologie
Z Soz Ref — Zeitschrift fuer Sozialreform
Z Sozreform — Zeitschrift fuer Sozialreform
ZSP — Zeitschrift fuer Slavische Philologie
ZS Ph — Zeitschrift fuer Slavische Philologie
Z Spiritusind — Zeitschrift fuer Spiritusindustrie
Zs Popul Mitt Astron — Zeitschrift fuer Populaere Mitteilungen aus dem Gebiete der Astronomie und Verwandter Wissenschaften
Zs Prak G — Zeitschrift fuer Praktische Geologie
ZSR — Zeitschrift der Savigny-Stiftung fuer Rechtsgeschichte
ZSR — Zeitschrift fuer Schweizerisches Recht
ZSR — Zeitschrift fuer Sozialreform
Zs Rechtspflege Bayern — Zeitschrift fuer Rechtspflege in Bayern
ZSRG — Zeitschrift der Savigny-Stiftung fuer Rechtsgeschichte
ZSRK — Zeitschrift. Savigny-Stiftung fuer Rechtsgeschichte. Kanonistische Abteilung
ZSS — Zeitschrift der Savigny-Stiftung fuer Rechtsgeschichte
Zs Savignystiftg Rechtsgesch — Zeitschrift der Savigny-Stiftung fuer Rechtsgeschichte
ZSS f R — Zeitschrift der Savigny-Stiftung fuer Rechtsgeschichte
ZSSGerm — Zeitschrift. Savigny-Stiftung fuer Rechtsgeschichte. Germanistische Abteilung
ZSSKanon — Zeitschrift. Savigny-Stiftung fuer Rechtsgeschichte. Kanonistische Abteilung
ZSSR — Zeitschrift der Savigny-Stiftung fuer Rechtsgeschichte
ZSSR — Zeitschrift der Savigny-Stiftung fuer Rechtsgeschichte. Romanistische Abteilung
ZSSRGGerm — Zeitschrift. Savigny-Stiftung fuer Rechtsgeschichte. Germanistische Abteilung
ZSSRGKan — Zeitschrift. Savigny-Stiftung fuer Rechtsgeschichte. Kanonistische Abteilung
ZSSRGRom — Zeitschrift. Savigny-Stiftung fuer Rechtsgeschichte. Romanistische Abteilung
ZSSRom — Zeitschrift. Savigny-Stiftung fuer Rechtsgeschichte. Romanistische Abteilung
ZST — Zeitschrift fuer Systematische Theologie
Z Staatsw — Zeitschrift fuer die Gesamte Staatswissenschaft
ZSTh — Neue Zeitschrift fuer Systematische Theologie und Relgionsphilosophie
ZSTh — Zeitschrift fuer Systematische Theologie
Z Stomatol — Zeitschrift fuer Stomatologie
Z Str R — Schweizerische Zeitschrift fuer Strafrecht
Z Strukturn Him — Zurnal Strukturnoi Himii. Akademija Nauk SSR. Sibirskoe Otdelenie
Z Str W — Zeitschrift fuer die Gesamte Strafrechtswissenschaft
Z St W — Zeitschrift fuer die Gesamte Staatswissenschaft
Z St W — Zeitschrift fuer die Gesamte Strafrechtswissenschaft
Z Sudetendt Gesch — Zeitschrift fuer Sudetendeutsche Geschichte
ZSV — Schweizerische Zeitschrift fuer Volkswirtschaft und Statistik
Z Vglde Sprachforsch — Kuhns Zeitschrift fuer Vergleichende Sprachforschung
Zs Vulkan — Zeitschrift fuer Vulkanologie
Z Sw — Zeitschrift fuer die Gesamte Staatswissenschaft
ZSW — Zeitschrift fuer Sozialwissenschaft
ZSWODE — Zeszyty Naukowe Szkoly Glownej Gospodarstwa Wiejskiego. Akademii Rolniczej w Warszawie. Ogrodnictwo
ZSWRA — Zeszyty Naukowe Szkoly Glownej Gospodarstwa Wiejskiego w Warszawie. Rolnictwo
ZSysTh — Zeitschrift fuer Systematische Theologie
ZT — Zeitschrift fuer Tierpsychologie

ZT — Zuercher Taschenbuch
ZTB — Zuercher Taschenbuch
Z Tech Biol — Zeitschrift fuer Technische Biologie
Z Techn Fiz — Zurnal Techniceskoj Fiziki
Z Tech Phys — Zeitschrift fuer Technische Physik
Z Tech Ueberwach — Zeitschrift fuer die Technische Ueberwachung
Z Tech Univ (Berlin) — Zeitschrift. Technische Universitaet (Berlin)
Z Tech Univ (Hannover) — Zeitschrift. Technische Universitaet (Hannover)
ZTG — Zolltarifgesetz
Ztg 7 Produzentengal — Zeitungen der 7 Produzentengalerie
ZTGAK — Zeitschrift fuer Thueringische Geschichte und Altertumskunde
Ztg Elegante Welt — Zeitung fuer die Elegante Welt
Ztg Gesunde — Zeitung fuer Gesunde
Z Theol Kir — Zeitschrift fuer Theologie und Kirche
Z Th K — Zeitschrift fuer Theologie und Kirche
Z Th Kirche — Zeitschrift fuer Theologie und Kirche
Z Tierernaehr Futtermittelkd — Zeitschrift fuer Tierernaehrung und Futtermittelkunde
Z Tierphysiol — Zeitschrift fuer Tierphysiologie, Tierernaehrung, und Futtermittelkunde
Z Tierphysiol Tierernaehr Futtermittelk — Zeitschrift fuer Tierphysiologie, Tierernaehrung, und Futtermittelkunde
Z Tierphysiol Tiernaehr Futtermittelkd — Zeitschrift fuer Tierphysiologie, Tierernaehrung, und Futtermittelkunde
Z Tierpsychol — Zeitschrift fuer Tierpsychologie
Z Tierpsychol Beih — Zeitschrift fuer Tierpsychologie. Beihett
Z Tierz Zuechtungsbiol — Zeitschrift fuer Tierzuechtung und Zuechtungsbiologie
ZTK — Zeitschrift fuer Theologie und Kirche
ZTOS — Zydowskie Towarzystwo Ochrony Sierot
ZTOS — Zydowskie Towarzystwo Opieki Spolecznej
ZTP — Zeitschrift fuer Tropenmedizin und Parasitologie
ZTP — Zydowskie Towarzystwo Prezeciwgruzliczego
ZTPHA — Zeitschrift fuer Technische Physik
ZTPSA — Zeitschrift fuer Psychologie
Z Transp Psychol — Zeitschrift fuer Transpersonale Psychologie
Z Tropenmed Parasitol — Zeitschrift fuer Tropenmedizin und Parasitologie
Z Tropenwiss Tropenmed — Zeitschrift fuer Tropenwissenschaften und Tropenmedizin
Z Trop Med — Zeitschrift fuer Tropenmedizin und Parasitologie
Ztsch f Angew Psychol — Zeitschrift fuer Angewandte Psychologie und Psychologische Forschung
Ztsch f Angew Psychol Sammelforsch — Zeitschrift fuer Angewandte Psychologie und Psychologische Sammelforschung
Ztsch Gesch Erzieh u Unterr — Zeitschrift fuer Geschichte der Erziehung und des Unterrichts
Ztsch Mikr Fleischschau — Zeitschrift fuer Mikroskopische Fleischschau und Populaere Mikroskopie
Ztsch Militaeraerzte (Tokyo) — Zeitschrift fuer Militaeraerzte (Tokyo)
Ztschr Aerztli Fortbild — Zeitschrift fuer Aerztliche Fortbildung
Ztschr Augenh — Zeitschrift fuer Augenheilkunde
Ztschr Ethn — Zeitschrift fuer Ethnologie
Ztschr f Franz Spr u Litt — Zeitschrift fuer Franzoesische Sprache und Litteratur
Ztschr Fleisch u Milchhyg — Zeitschrift fuer Fleisch- und Milchhygiene
Ztschr f Roman Philol — Zeitschrift fuer Romanische Philologie
Ztschr Genossensch Tierversich — Zeitschrift fuer Genossenschaftlichen Tierversicherung
Ztschr Gewerbe Hyg — Zeitschrift fuer Gewerbe Hygiene
Ztschr Hyg — Zeitschrift fuer Hygiene
Ztschr Hyg u Infektionskr — Zeitschrift fuer Hygiene und Infektionskrankheiten
Ztschr Immunitaetsforsch u Exper Therap — Zeitschrift fuer Immunitaetsforschung und Experimentelle Therapie
Ztschr Infektionskr Haustiere — Zeitschrift fuer Infektionskrankheiten, Parasitaere Krankheiten, und Hygiene der Haustiere
Ztschr Klin Med (Berlin) — Zeitschrift fuer Klinische Medizin (Berlin)
Ztschr Krebsforsch — Zeitschrift fuer Krebsforschung
Ztschr Morphol u Oekol Tiere — Zeitschrift fuer Morphologie und Oekologie der Tiere
Ztschr Num — Zeitschrift fuer Numismatik
Ztschr Ophth — Zeitschrift fuer die Ophthalmologie
Ztschr Parasitenk (Berlin) — Zeitschrift fuer Parasitenkunde (Berlin)
Ztschr Parasitenk (Jena) — Zeitschrift fuer Parasitenkunde (Jena)
Ztschr Physiol Chem — Zeitschrift fuer Physiologische Chemie
Ztschr Sav Stift — Zeitschrift der Savigny-Stiftung fuer Rechtsgeschichte. Romanische Abteilung
Ztschr Tokio Med Gesellsch — Zeitschrift. Tokio Medizinischen Gesellschaft
Ztschr Vergleich Physiol — Zeitschrift fuer Vergleichende Physiologie
Ztschr Veterinaerk — Zeitschrift fuer Veterinaerkunde
Ztschr Wissensch Mikr — Zeitschrift fuer Wissenschaftliche Mikroskopie
Ztschr Wissensch Zool — Zeitschrift fuer Wissenschaftliche Zoologie
Z Tuberk — Zeitschrift fuer Tuberkulose
Z Tuberk Erkr Thoraxorgane — Zeitschrift fuer Tuberkulose und Erkrankungen der Thoraxorgane
Z Tuberkulose Erkr Thoraxorgane — Zeitschrift fuer Tuberkulose und Erkrankungen der Thoraxorgane
ZTUWA — Zeitschrift Technische Ueberwachung
ZTZ — Zeitschrift fuer Tierzuechtung und Zuechtungsbiologie
ZT Zue — Zeitschrift fuer Tierzuechtung und Zuechtungsbiologie
ZUBEAQ — Revue de Medecine des Accidents et des Maladies Professionnels
Zubolek Pregl — Zubolekarski Pregled
ZU Ch — Zeitschrift fuer Urologische Chirurgie
Zucker Beih — Zucker Beihefte
Zucker Frucht Gemueseverwert — Zucker- Frucht- und Gemueseverwertung
Zucker Sonderbeil — Zucker Sonderbeilage
Zucker Suesswaren Wirtsch — Zucker- und Suesswaren Wirtschaft

Zuck u SuesswarWirt — Zucker- und Suesswaren Wirtschaft
Zueger Neujbl — Zueger Neujahrsblatt
Zuercher Beitraege — Zuercher Beitraege zur Geschichtswissenschaft
Zuercher Beitraege — Zuercher Beitraege zur Rechtswissenschaft
Zuerch Taschenb — Zuercher Taschenbuch
Zuerich Illus — Zuercher Illustrierten
Zuer Mschr — Monatsschrift des Wissenschaftlichen Vereins in Zuerich
Zuer Mt — Mittheilungen der Naturforschenden Gesellschaft in Zuerich
Zuer N D Sch Gs — Neue Denkschriften der Allgemeinen Schweizerischen Gesellschaft fuer die Gesammten Naturwissenschaften (Neuchatel, Zuerich)
Zuer Ps Gs Jbr — Jahresbericht der Physikalischen Gesellschaft in Zuerich
Zuer Univ Geol Inst-Eidgenoss Tech Hochsch Geol Inst Mitt — Zuerich Universitaet. Geologisches Institut - Eidgenoessische Technische Hochschule. Geologisches Institut. Mitteilungen
Zuer Vjschr — Vierteljahrsschrift der Naturforschenden Gesellschaft in Zuerich
ZugerNjb — Zuger Neujahrsblatt
ZUJCA — Zeszyty Naukowe Uniwersytetu Jagiellonskiego. Prace Chemiczne
Zukuenftige Technol — Zukuenftige Technologien
ZUM — Zeitschrift fuer Urheber und Medienrecht
Z Umweltpolit — Zeitschrift fuer Umweltpolitik
ZUNBA — Zhurnal Ushnykh Nosovykh i Gorlovykh Boleznei
Z Unfallchir Versicherungsmed — Zeitschrift fuer Unfallchirurgie und Versicherungsmedizin
Z Unfallchir Versicherungsmed Berufskr — Zeitschrift fuer Unfallchirurgie, Versicherungsmedizin, und Berufskrankheiten
Z Unfallmed Berufskr — Zeitschrift fuer Unfallmedizin und Berufskrankheiten
Z Ungern — Zeitschrift von und fuer Ungern zur Befoerderung der Vaterlaendischen Geschichte, Erdkunde, und Literatur
Z Unter Lebensm — Zeitschrift fuer Untersuchung der Lebensmittel
Z Unternehmensgesch — Zeitschrift fuer Unternehmensgeschichte
Z Unternehmens U Ges Recht — Zeitschrift fuer Unternehmens- und Gesellschaftsrecht
Z Unters Lebensmittel — Zeitschrift fuer Untersuchung der Lebensmittel
Z Unters Nahr Genussm Gebrauchsgegenstaende — Zeitschrift fuer Untersuchung der Nahrungs- und Genussmittel Sowie der Gebrauchsgegenstaende
Z Unters Nahr-u Genussmittel — Zeitschrift fuer Untersuchung der Nahrungs- und Genussmittel
ZuP — Zellstoff und Papier
Zur Didak Phys Chem — Zur Didaktik der Physik und Chemie
Zurn Ekol Biocenol — Zurnal Ekologii i Biocenologii
Zurn Obsc Ljubit Komnatn Rast S Peterburge — Zurnaly Obscestva Ljubitelej Komnatnyj Rastenij i Akvariumov v S.-Peterburge
Zurn Russk Bot Obsc Akad Nauk — Zurnal Russkago Botaniceskago Obscestva pri Akademii Nauk. Journal de la Societe Botanique de Russie
Zurn Russk Fiz Him Obsc Imp S Peterburgsk Univ Cast Him — Zurnal Russkago Fiziko-Himiceskago Obscestva pri Imperatorskom S.-PeterburgskomUniversitete. Cast' Himiceskaja. Journal de la Societe Physico-Chemique Russe
Zurn Sadov — Zurnal Sadovodstva, Izdavaemyj Rossijskim Obscestvom Ljubitelej Sadovodstva v Moskve
Z Urol — Zeitschrift fuer Urologie
Z Urol Chir — Zeitschrift fuer Urologische Chirurgie
Z Urol Nephrol — Zeitschrift fuer Urologie und Nephrologie
ZV — Zeitschrift fuer Versicherung
ZV — Zeitschrift fuer Volkskunde
Zv — Zvezda
Zvaracsky Sb — Zvaracsky Sbornik
Z Verbraucherpol — Zeitschrift fuer Verbraucherpolitik
Z Verbraucherpolit — Zeitschrift fuer Verbraucherpolitik/Journal of Consumer Policy
Z Verbungsl — Zeitschrift fuer Vererbungslehre
Z Ver Dtsch Chem Teil A — Zeitschrift des Vereins Deutscher Chemiker. Teil A. Angewandte Chemie
Z Ver Dtsch Ing — Zeitschrift. Verein Deutscher Ingenieure
Z Ver Dtsch Zucker Ind — Zeitschrift. Verein der Deutschen Zucker-Industrie
Z Ver Dtsch Zucker Ind Allg Teil — Zeitschrift. Verein der Deutschen Zucker-Industrie. Allgemeiner Teil
Z Ver Dtsch Zucker Ind Tech Teil — Zeitschrift. Verein der Deutschen Zucker-Industrie. Technischer Teil
Z Vererbungsl — Zeitschrift fuer Vererbungslehre
Z Ver Gesch Berlins — Zeitschrift des Vereins fuer die Geschichte Berlins
Z Ver Gesch Bodensees — Zeitschrift des Vereins fuer die Geschichte Bodensees
Z Ver Gesch Mahrens & Schlesiens — Zeitschrift des Vereins fuer die Geschichte Mahrens und Schlesiens
Z Vergl Physiol — Zeitschrift fuer Vergleichende Physiologie
Z Vergl Rechtswiss — Zeitschrift fuer Vergleichende Rechtswissenschaft. Einschliesslich der Ethnologischen Rechtsforschung
Z Ver Hamburg Gesch — Zeitschrift des Vereins fuer Hamburgische Geschichte
Z Ver Hess Gesch & Landesknd — Zeitschrift des Vereins fuer Hessische Geschichte und Landeskunde
Z Ver Hess Gesch Landesk — Zeitschrift. Verein fuer Hessische Geschichte und Landeskunde
Z Ver Hessische Gesch — Zeitschrift. Verein fuer Hessische Geschichte und Landeskunde
Z Verkehrssicherheit — Zeitschrift fuer Verkehrssicherheit
Z Verkehrswiss — Zeitschrift fuer Verkehrswissenschaft
Z Ver Luebeck Gesch Altertumskde — Zeitschrift des Vereins fuer Luebeckische Geschichte und Altertumskunde
Z Ver Luebeck Gesch & Altertknd — Zeitschrift des Vereins fuer Luebeckische Geschichte und Altertumskunde
Z Vermessungswes — Zeitschrift fuer Vermessungswesen
Zverolek Obz — Zverolekarsky Obzor
Z Vers Kund — Zeitschrift fuer Versuchstierkunde
Z Versuchstierkd — Zeitschrift fuer Versuchstierkunde
ZVGAK — Zeitschrift fuer Vaterlaendische Geschichte und Altertumskunde

Z Vgl Physiol — Zeitschrift fuer Vergleichende Physiologie

Zvgl Spr — Zeitschrift fuer Vergleichende Sprachforschung auf dem Gebiete der Indogermanischen Sprachen

ZVGMS — Zeitschrift. Deutscher Verein fuer die Geschichte Maehrens und Schlesiens

ZVHFA — Zeitschrift fuer Vitamin-, Hormon-, und Fermentforschung

ZVHG — Zeitschrift. Verein fuer Hamburgische Geschichte

ZVHGL — Zeitschrift des Vereins fuer Hessische Geschichte und Landeskunde

ZVHGLK — Zeitschrift. Verein fuer Hessische Geschichte und Landeskunde

ZVI — Zbornik Radova Vizantoloskog Instituta

Z VitamForsch — Zeitschrift fuer Vitaminforschung

Z Vitam-Horm-Fermentforsch — Zeitschrift fuer Vitamin-, Hormon-, und Fermentforschung

Z Vitam-Horm- u Fermentforsch — Zeitschrift fuer Vitamin-, Hormon-, und Fermentforschung

Z Vitaminforsch — Zeitschrift fuer Vitaminforschung

ZVK — Zeitschrift fuer Volkskunde

ZVKOA — Zhurnal Vsesoyuznogo Khimicheskogo Obshchestva Imeni D. I. Mendeleeva

ZVKPS — Zeitschrift. Verein fuer Kirchengeschichte in der Provinz Sachsen und Anhalt

ZVL — Zeitschrift fuer Vergleichende Literaturgeschichte

ZVL — Zoologische Verhandelingen. Rijksmuseum van Natuurliche Historie (Leiden)

ZVLGA — Zeitschrift des Vereins fuer Luebeckische Geschichte und Altertumskunde

Z Vlksknd — Zeitschrift fuer Volkskunde

ZVNDA — Zhurnal Vysshei Nervnoi Deyatel'nosti Imeni I. P. Pavlova

ZVO — Zapiski Vostochnovo Otdeleniia

Z Volksernaehr — Zeitschrift fuer Volksernaehrung

Z Volkskde — Zeitschrift fuer Volkskunde

Z Volkskund — Zeitschrift fuer Volkskunde

Z Volkskunde — Zeitschrift fuer Volkskunde

ZVORAO — Zapiski Vostochnovo Otdeleniia Imperatorskovo Ruskavo Arkheologicheskavo Obshchestva

ZVR — Zeitschrift fuer Vergleichende Rechtswissenschaft

Z Vr D Zuckin — Zeitschrift des Vereins der Deutschen Zucker-Industrie

Z Vr Ruebenzuckin — Zeitschrift des Vereins fuer die Ruebenzucker-Industrie des Deutschen Reichs

ZVRW — Zeitschrift fuer Vergleichende Rechtswissenschaft

ZVS — Zeitschrift des Vereins fuer Volkskunde

ZVS — Zeitschrift fuer Vergleichende Sprachforschung

ZVS — Zeitschrift fuer Vergleichende Sprachforschung auf dem Gebiete der Indogermanischen Sprachen

ZVS — Zeitschrift fuer Voelkerpsychologie und Soziologie

ZVT — Zeitschrift fuer Verkehrswissenschaft

ZVT — Zvezda Vostoka (Tashkent)

ZVTGA — Zeitschrift. Verein fuer Thueringische Geschichte und Altertumskunde

ZVTGAK — Zeitschrift. Verein fuer Thueringische Geschichte und Altertumskunde

ZVV — Zeitschrift des Vereins fuer Volkskunde

ZVV — Zeitschrift. Verein fuer Volkskunde

ZvV — Zvezda Vostoka

Z Vycisl Mat i Mat Fiz — Zurnal Vycislitel'noi Matematiki i Matematiceskoi Fiziki

ZW — Zeitwende Monatsschrift

Z Wahrscheinlichkeitstheorie und Verw Gebiete — Zeitschrift fuer Wahrscheinlichkeitstheorie und Verwandte Gebiete

Z Wahrsch V — Zeitschrift fuer Wahrscheinlichkeitstheorie und Verwandte Gebiete

Z Wahrsch Verw Gebiete — Zeitschrift fuer Wahrscheinlichkeitstheorie und Verwandte Gebiete

Z Wasser Abwasser Forsch — Zeitschrift fuer Wasser- und Abwasserforschung

Z Wasserrecht — Zeitschrift fuer Wasserrecht

Z Wasser u Abwasserforsch — Zeitschrift fuer Wasser- und Abwasserforschung

Z Wasser Versorg Abwasserkunde — Zeitschrift fuer Wasser-Versorgung und Abwasserkunde

ZWBAA — Zeitschrift fuer Wissenschaftliche Biologie. Abteilung A

ZWEG — Zeitschrift der Wiener Entomologischen Gesellschaft

Z Weinbau Weinbereitung Ungarn Siebenbuergen — Zeitschrift fuer Weinbau und Weinbereitung in Ungarn und Siebenbuergen, fuer Weinbergbesitzer, Winzer, Landwirthe, und Weinhaendler

Z Weltforstwirtsch — Zeitschrift fuer Weltforstwirtschaft

Z Weltkongress — Zweiter Weltkongress der Musikbibliotheken

Z Werkstofftech — Zeitschrift fuer Werkstofftechnik

Z Werkstofftech J Mater Technol — Zeitschrift fuer Werkstofftechnik/Journal of Materials Technology

Z Westfalen — Zeitschrift Westfalen

Z Westpreuss Gesch Ver — Zeitschrift des Westpreussischen Geschichtsvereins

Z Westpreuss Geschver — Zeitschrift des Westpreussischen Geschichtsvereins

ZWF Z Wirtsch Fabrikbetr — ZWF Zeitschrift fuer Wirtschaftlichen Fabrikbetrieb

ZWF Z Wirtsch Fertigung — ZWF. Zeitschrift fuer Wirtschaftliche Fertigung

ZWG — Sudhoffs Archiv. Zeitschrift fuer Wissenschaftsgeschichte

ZWIBA — Zeitschrift fuer Wissenschaftliche Insektenbiologie

Zwick Vr Nt Jbr — Jahresbericht des Vereins fuer Naturkunde zu Zwickau

Z Wien Ent Ges — Zeitschrift. Wiener Entomologische Gesellschaft

Z Wien Entomol Ges — Zeitschrift. Wiener Entomologische Gesellschaft

Z Wien Entomol Ver — Zeitschrift. Wiener Entomologe-Verein

Zwierzeta Lab — Zwierzeta Laboratoryjne

Z Wirtschaftsgeog — Zeitschrift fuer Wirtschaftsgeographie

Z Wirtschaftsgeographie — Zeitschrift fuer Wirtschaftsgeographie

Z Wirtschaftsgruppe Zuckerind — Zeitschrift. Wirtschaftsgruppe Zuckerindustrie

Z Wirtschaftsgruppe Zuckerind Allg Teil — Zeitschrift. Wirtschaftsgruppe Zuckerindustrie. Allgemeiner Teil

Z Wirtschaftsgruppe Zuckerind Tech Teil — Zeitschrift. Wirtschaftsgruppe Zuckerindustrie. Technischer Teil

Z Wirtschaftspol — Zeitschrift fuer Wirtschaftspolitik

Z Wirtsch Fertigung — Zeitschrift fuer Wirtschaftliche Fertigung

Z Wirtsch Fertigung Autom — Zeitschrift fuer Wirtschaftliche Fertigung und Automatisierung

Z Wirtsch -u Soz -Wiss — Zeitschrift fuer Wirtschafts- und Sozialwissenschaften

Z Wirt- und Sozialwiss — Zeitschrift fuer Wirtschafts- und Sozialwissenschaften

Z Wiss Biol Abt A — Zeitschrift fuer Wissenschaftliche Biologie. Abteilung A

Z Wiss InsektBiol — Zeitschrift fuer Wissenschaftliche Insektenbiologie

Z Wiss Insektenbiol — Zeitschrift fuer Wissenschaftliche Insektenbiologie

Z Wiss Mikrosk — Zeitschrift fuer Wissenschaftliche Mikroskopie und fuer Mikroskopische Technik

Z Wiss Mikrosk Mikrosk Tech — Zeitschrift fuer Wissenschaftliche Mikroskopie und fuer Mikroskopische Technik

Z Wiss Phot — Zeitschrift fuer Wissenschaftliche Photographie, Photophysik, und Photochemie

Z Wiss Photogr Photophys Photchem — Zeitschrift fuer Wissenschaftliche Photographie, Photophysik, und Photochemie

Z Wiss Photogr Photophys Photochem — Zeitschrift fuer Wissenschaftliche Photographie, Photophysik, und Photochemie

Z Wiss Zool — Zeitschrift fuer Wissenschaftliche Zoologie

Z Wiss Zool Abt A — Zeitschrift fuer Wissenschaftliche Zoologie. Abteilung A

ZWL — Zeitschrift fuer Wuerttembergische Landesgeschichte

ZWLG — Zeitschrift fuer Wuerttembergische Landesgeschichte

ZWMIA — Zeitschrift fuer Wissenschaftliche Mikroskopie und fuer Mikroskopische Technik

ZWMZDP — Chinese Journal of Microbiology and Immunology

Zwolle Vooruitgang — Vooruitgang. Tijdschrift voor Wetenschap (Zwolle)

ZWP — Zeitschrift fuer Wissenschaftliche Photographie, Photophysik, und Photochemie

ZWPGV — Zeitschrift. Westpreussischer Geschichtsverein

ZWR — ZWR. Zahnaerztliche Welt, Zahnaerztliche Rundschau, Zahnaerztliche Reform

Z Ws Mkr — Zeitschrift fuer Wissenschaftliche Mikroskopie und fuer Mikroskopische Technik

ZWT — Zeitschrift fuer Wissenschaftliche Theologie

ZWTh — Zeitschrift fuer Wissenschaftliche Theologie

Z Wuerttemberg Landesgesch — Zeitschrift fuer Wuerttembergische Landesgeschichte

Zy — Zygon

Zycie Weteryn — Zycie Weterynaryjne

ZYDXDM — Journal. Zhejiang Medical University

Zymol Chem Colloidi — Zymologica e Chemica dei Colloidi

Zy Newsl — Zygon Newsletter

ZYWE — Zeszyty Wroclawskie

Zywienie Czlowieka Metab — Zywienie Czlowieka i Metabolizm

Zywn Technol Jakosc — Zywnosc, Technologia, Jakosc

ZZ — Zoologicheskii Zhurnal

ZZACA — Zeitschrift fuer Zellforschung und Mikroskopische Anatomie

Z Zelif Mikroskop Anat Abt B Chromosoma — Zeitschrift fuer Zellforschung und Mikroskopische Anatomie. Abteilung B. Chromosoma

Z Zellforsch Mikrosk Anat — Zeitschrift fuer Zellforschung und Mikroskopische Anatomie

Z Zellforsch Mikrosk Anat Abt Histochem — Zeitschrift fuer Zellforschung und Mikroskopische Anatomie. Abteilung Histochemie

Z Zool Syst Evolutionsforsch — Zeitschrift fuer Zoologische Systematik und Evolutionsforschung

ZzS — Zbornik za Slavistiku

ZZT — Zinruigaku Zassi (Tokyo)

Zztg Optik Mech — Centralzeitung fuer Optik und Mechanik

Z Zuckerind — Zeitschrift fuer die Zuckerindustrie

Z Zuckerind Boehm — Zeitschrift fuer die Zuckerindustrie in Boehmen

Z Zuckerind Boehm Machren — Zeitschrift fuer die Zuckerindustrie in Boehmen-Machren

Z Zuckerind Cech Repub — Zeitschrift fuer die Zuckerindustrie der Cechoslovakoschen Republik

Z Zuckin — Zeitschrift fuer Zuckerindustrie

Z Zuckin Boehm — Zeitschrift fuer Zuckerindustrie in Boehmen

Z Zuckind — Zeitschrift fuer die Zuckerindustrie

Z Zuecht A — Zeitschrift fuer Zuechtung. A

Z Zuecht B — Zeitschrift fuer Zuechtung. B